MATTHEW HENRY'S COMMENTARY on the WHOLE BIBLE

complete and unabridged
in one volume

MATTHEW HENRY'S COMMENTARY
on the WHOLE BIBLE

complete and unabridged
in one volume

WHEREIN EACH CHAPTER IS SUMMED UP IN ITS CONTENTS:
EACH PARAGRAPH REDUCED TO ITS PROPER HEADS,
THE SENSE GIVEN, AND LARGELY ILLUSTRATED WITH
PRACTICAL REMARKS AND OBSERVATIONS

GENESIS TO REVELATION

HENDRICKSON
PUBLISHERS

MATTHEW HENRY'S COMMENTARY ON THE WHOLE BIBLE
Complete and Unabridged in One Volume

Copyright © 1991 by Hendrickson Publishers, Inc.
ISBN: 0-943575-32-X

Fourth printing – January, 1995

Printed in the United States of America

CONTENTS

OLD TESTAMENT

NEW TESTAMENT

ORIGINAL PREFACE TO VOLUME ONE

Though it is most my concern, that I be able to give a good account to God and my own conscience, yet, perhaps, it will be expected that I give the world also some account of this bold undertaking; which I shall endeavour to do with all plainness, and as one who believes, that if men must be reckoned with in the great day, for every vain and idle word they speak, much more for every vain and idle line they write. And it may be of use, in the first place, to lay down those great and sacred principles which I go upon, and am governed by, in this endeavour to explain and improve these portions of holy writ; which endeavour I humbly offer to the service of those (and to those only I expect it will be acceptable) who agree with me in these six principles: —

I. That *religion is the one thing useful;* and to know, and love, and fear God our Maker, and in all the instances both of devout affection, and of good conversation, to *keep his commandments,* (Eccles. 12:13) is, without doubt, *the whole of man;* it is all in all to him. This the wisest of men, after a close and copious argument in his *Ecclesiastes,* lays down as the conclusion of his whole matter (the *Quod erat demonstrandum* of his whole discourse); and therefore I may be allowed to lay it down as a *postulatum,* and the foundation of this whole matter. It is necessary to mankind in general, that there should be religion in the world, absolutely necessary for the preservation of the honour of the human nature, and no less so for the preservation of the order of human societies. It is necessary to each of us in particular, that we be religious; we cannot otherwise answer the end of our creation, obtain the favour of our Creator, make ourselves easy now, or happy for ever. A man that is endued with the powers of reason, by which he is capable of knowing, serving, glorifying, and enjoying his Maker, and yet *lives without God in the world,* is certainly the most despicable and the most miserable animal under the sun.

II. That *divine revelation is necessary to true religion,* to the being and support of it. That faith without which *it is impossible to please God,* cannot come to any perfection by seeing the works of God, but it must come by *hearing the word of God,* Rom. 10:17. The rational soul, since it received that fatal shock by the fall, cannot have or maintain that just regard to the great author of its being, that observance of him, and expectation from him, which are both its duty and felicity, without some supernatural discovery made by himself of himself, and of his mind and will. Natural light, no doubt, is of excellent use, as far as it goes; but it is necessary that there be a divine revelation, to rectify its mistakes, and make up its deficiencies, to help us out where the light of nature leaves us quite at a loss, especially in the way and method of man's recovery from his lapsed state, and his restoration to his Maker's favour; which he cannot but be conscious to himself of the loss of, finding, by sad experience, his own present state to be sinful and miserable. Our own reason shows us the wound, but nothing short of a divine revelation can discover to us a remedy to be confided in. The case and character of those nations of the earth which had no other guide in their devotions than that of natural light, with some remains of the divine institution of sacrifices received by tradition from their fathers, plainly show how necessary divine revelation is to the subsistence of religion; for those that had not the word of God, soon lost God himself, became vain in their imaginations concerning him, and prodigiously vile and absurd in their worships and divinations. It is true, the Jews, who had the benefit of divine revelation, lapsed sometimes into idolatry, and admitted very gross corruptions; yet, with the help of the law and the prophets, they recovered and reformed: whereas the best and most admired philosophy of the heathen could never do any thing toward the cure of the vulgar idolatry, or so much as offered to remove any of those barbarous and ridiculous rites of their religion, which were the scandal and reproach of the human nature. Let men therefore pretend what they will, deists are, or will be, atheists; and those that, under colour of admiring the oracles of reason, set aside as useless the oracles of God, undermine the foundations of all religion, and do what they can to cut off all communication between man and his Maker, and to set that noble creature on a level with the beasts that perish.

III. That *divine revelation is not now to be found nor expected any where but in the scriptures of the Old and New Testament;* and there it is. It is true, there were religion and divine revelation before there was any written word; but to argue from thence, that the scriptures are not now necessary, it as absurd as it would be to argue that the world might do well enough without the sun, because in the creation the world had light three days before the sun was made. Divine revelations, when first given, were confirmed by visions, miracles, and prophecy; but they were to be transmitted to distant regions and future ages, with their proofs and evidences, by writing, the surest way of conveyance, and by which the knowledge of other memorable things is preserved and propagated. We have reason to think that even the ten commandments, though spoken with such solemnity at Mount Sinai, would have been, long before this, lost and forgotten, if they had been handed down by tradition only, and never had been put in writing: it is that which is written, that remains. The scripture indeed is not compiled as a methodical system or body of divinity, *secundum artem — according to the rules of art,* but several ways of writing, (histories, laws, prophecies, songs, epistles, and even proverbs,) at several times, and by several hands, as Infinite Wisdom saw fit. The end is effectually obtained; such things are plainly supposed and taken for granted, and such things are expressly revealed and made known, as, being all put together, sufficiently inform us of all the truths and laws of the holy religion we are to believe, and be governed by. That *all scripture is given by inspiration of God,* (2 Tim. 3:16) and that *holy men spake and wrote as they were moved by the Holy Ghost,* (2 Pt. 1:21) we are sure; but who dare pretend to describe that inspiration? None *knows the way of the Spirit,* nor how the thoughts were formed in the heart of him that was inspired, any more than we know the way of the soul into the body, or *how the bones are formed in the womb or her that is with child,* Eccles. 11:5. But we may be sure that the blessed Spirit did not only habitually prepare and qualify the penmen of scripture for that service, and put it into their hearts to write, but did likewise assist their understandings and memories in recording those things which they themselves had the knowledge of, and effectually secure them

from error and mistake; and what they could not know but by revelation, (as for instance, Gen. 1 and Jn. 1) the same blessed Spirit gave them clear and satisfactory information of. And no doubt, as far as was necessary to the end designed, they were directed by he Spirit, even in the language and expression; for there were *words which the Holy Ghost taught;* (1 Co. 2:13) and God saith to the prophet, *Thou shalt speak with my words,* Eze. 3:4. However, it is not material to us, who drew up the statute, nor what liberty he took in using his own words: when it is ratified, it is become the legislator's act, and binds the subject to observe the true intent and meaning of it. The scripture proves its divine authority and original both to the wise and to the unwise. Even to the unwise and least thinking part of mankind, it is abundantly proved by the many incontestable miracles wrought by Moses and the prophets, Christ and his apostles, for the confirmation of its truths and laws: it would be an intolerable reproach to eternal Truth, to suppose this divine seal affixed to a lie. Beside this, to the more wise and thinking, to the more considerate and contemplative it recommends itself by those innate excellences which are self-evident characteristics of its divine original. If we look carefully, we shall soon be aware of God's image and superscription upon it. A mind rightly disposed by a humble, sincere subjection to its Maker, will easily discover the image of God's wisdom in the awful depth of its mysteries; the image of his sovereignty in the commanding majesty of its style; the image of his unity in the wonderful harmony and symmetry of all its parts; the image of his holiness in the unspotted purity of its precepts; and the image of his goodness in the manifest tendency of the whole to the welfare and happiness of mankind in both worlds; in short, it is a work that fathers itself. And as atheists, so deists, notwithstanding their vain-glorious pretensions to reason, as if wisdom must die with them, run themselves upon the grossest and most dishonourable absurdities imaginable; for, if the scriptures be not the word of God, then there is no divine revelation now in the world, no discovery at all of God's mind concerning our duty and happiness: so that, let a man be ever so desirous and solicitous to do his Maker's will, he must, without remedy, perish in the ignorance of it, since there is no book but this that will undertake to tell him what it is, a consequence which can by no means be reconciled to the idea we have of the divine goodness. And (which is no less an absurdity), if the scriptures be not really a divine revelation, they are certainly as great a cheat as ever was put upon the world: but we have no reason to think them so; for bad men would never write so good a book, nor would Satan have so little subtlety as to help to cast out Satan; and good men would never do so wicked a thing as to counterfeit the broad seal of heaven and affix it to a patent of their own framing, though in itself ever so just. No, *there are not the words of him that hath a devil.*

IV. That the *scriptures of the Old and New Testament were purposely designed for our learning.* They might have been a divine revelation to those into whose hands they were first put, and yet we, at this distance, have been no way concerned in them; but it is certain that they were intended to be of universal and perpetual use and obligation to all persons, in all places and all ages, that have the knowledge of them, even unto us *upon whom the ends of the world have come.* See Rom. 15:4. Though we are not under the law as a covenant of innocency (for then, being guilty, we should unavoidable perish under its curse), yet it is not therefore an antiquated statute, but a standing declaration of the will of God concerning good and evil, sin and duty, and its claim to obedience is in as full force and virtue as ever: and *unto us is the gospel* of the ceremonial law *preached, as well as unto those* to whom it was first delivered, and much more plainly, Heb. 4:2. The histories of the Old Testament were written for our admonition and direction (1 Co. 10:11), and not barely for the information and entertainment of the curious. The prophets, though long since dead, prophesy again by their writings, *before peoples and nations* (Rev. 10:11), and Solomon's exhortation speaketh unto us as unto sons. The subject of the holy scripture is universal and perpetual, and therefore of common concern. It is intended, 1. To revive the universal and perpetual law of nature, the very remains of which (or ruins rather) in natural conscience, give us hints that we must look somewhere else for a fairer copy. 2. To reveal the universal and perpetual law of grace, which God's common beneficence to the children of men, such as puts them into a better state than that of devils, gives us some ground to expect. The divine authority likewise, which in this book commands our belief and obedience, is universal and perpetual, and knows no limits, either of time or place; it follows, therefore, that every nation and every age to which these sacred writings are transmitted are bound to receive them with the same veneration and pious regard that they commanded at their first entrance. Though God hath, in these last days, *spoken to us by his Son,* yet we are not therefore to think that what he spoke *at sundry times and in divers manners to the fathers* (Heb. 1:1) is of no use to us, or that the Old Testament is an almanac out of date; no, we are *built upon the foundation of the prophets,* as well as of *the apostles, Christ himself being the corner-stone* (Eph. 2:20), in whom both these sides of this blessed building meet and are united: they were those ancient records of the Jewish church which Christ and his apostles so oft referred to, so oft appealed to, and commanded us to search and to take heed to. The preachers of the gospel, like Jehoshaphat's judges, wherever they went, had this book of the law with them, and found it a great advantage to them to speak to those *that knew the law,* Rom. 7:1. That celebrated translation of the Old Testament in the Greek tongue by the Seventy, between 200 and 300 years before the birth of Christ, was to the nations a happy preparative for the entertainment of the gospel, by spreading the knowledge of the law; for as the New Testament expounds and completes the Old, and thereby makes it more serviceable to us now than it was to the Jewish church, so the Old Testament confirms and illustrates the New, and shows us Jesus Christ the same yesterday that he is to-day and will be for ever.

V. That *the holy scriptures were not only designed for our learning, but are the settled standing rule of our faith and practice,* by which we must be governed now and judged shortly: it is not only a book of general use (so the writings of good and wise men may be), but it is of sovereign and commanding authority, the statute-book of God's kingdom, which our oath of allegiance to him, as our supreme Lord, binds us to the observance of. *Whether we will hear or whether we will forbear,* we must be told that this is the oracle we are to consult and to be determined by, the touchstone we are to appeal to and try doctrines by, the rule we are to have an eye to, by which we must in every thing order our affections and conversations, and from which we must always take our measures. This is the *testimony,* this is the *law* which is bound up and sealed among the disciples, that word according to which if we do not speak, it is because *there is no light in us,* Isa. 8:16, 20. The making of the *light within* our rule, which by nature is darkness, and by grace is but a copy of, and conformable to, the written work, is setting the judge above the law; and the making of the traditions of the church rivals with the scriptures is no better: it is making the clock, which every one concerned puts backward or forward at pleasure, to correct the sun, that faithful measurer of time and days. These are absurdities which, being once granted, thousands follow, as we see by sad experience.

VI. That therefore *it is the duty of all Christians diligently to search the scriptures, and it is the office of ministers to guide and assist them therein.* How useful soever this book of books is in itself, it will be of no use to us if we do not acquaint ourselves with it, by reading it daily, and meditating upon it, that we may understand the mind of God in it, and may apply what we understand to ourselves for our direction, rebuke, and comfort, as there is occasion. It is the character of the holy and happy man that *his delight is in the law of the Lord;* and, as an evidence thereof, he converses with it as his constant companion, and advises with it as his most wise and trusty counsellor, for *in that law doth he meditate day and night,* Ps. 1:2. It concerns us to be ready in the scriptures, and to make ourselves so by constant reading and careful observation, and especially by earnest prayer to God for the promised gift of the Holy Ghost, whose office it is to *bring things to our remembrance* which Christ hath said to us (Jn. 14:26), that thus we may have some good word or other at hand for our use in our addresses to God and in our converse with men, in our resistance of Satan and in communing with our own hearts, and may be able, with the good householder, to bring out of this treasury *things new and old,* for the entertainment and edification both of ourselves and others. If any thing will *make a man of God perfect* in this world, will complete both a Christian and a minister, and *thoroughly furnish him for every good work,* it must be this. 2 Tim. 3:17. It concerns us also to be *mighty in the scriptures,* as Apollos was (Acts 18:24), that is, to be thoroughly acquainted with the true intent and meaning of them, that we may understand what we read, and may not misinterpret or misapply it, but by the conduct of the blessed Spirit may be *led into all truth* (Jn. 16:13), and may hold it fast *in faith and love,* and put every part of scripture to that use for which it was intended. The letter, either of law or gospel, profits little without the Spirit. The ministers of Christ are herein ministers to the Spirit for the good of the church; their business is to open and apply the scriptures; thence they must fetch their knowledge, thence their doctrines, devotions, directions, and admonitions, and thence their very language and expression. Expounding the scriptures was the most usual way of preaching in the first and purest ages of the church. What have the Levites to do but to teach Jacob the law (Deu. 33:10); not only to read it, but to *give the sense, and cause them to understand the reading?* Neh. 8:8. *How shall they do this except some man guide them?* Acts 8:31. As ministers would hardly be believed without Bibles to back them, so Bibles would hardly be understood without ministers to explain them; but if, having both, we perish in ignorance and unbelief, our blood will be upon our own head.

Being fully persuaded therefore of these things, I conclude that whatever help is offered to good Christians in searching the scriptures is real service done to the glory of God, and to the interests of his kingdom among men; and it is this that hath drawn me into this undertaking, which I have gone about in weakness, and in fear, and in much trembling (1 Co. 2:3), lest I should be found exercising myself in things to high for me, and so laudable an undertaking should suffer damage by an unskilful management. If any desire to know how so mean and obscure a person as I am, who in learning, judgment, felicity of expression, and all advantages for such a service, am *less than the least* of all my Master's servants, came to venture upon so great a work, I can give no other account of it than this: It has long been my practice, what little time I had to spare in my study from the constant preparations for the pulpit, to spend it in drawing up expositions upon some parts of the New Testament, not so much for my own use as purely for my entertainment, because I knew not now to employ my thoughts and time more to my satisfaction. *Trahit sua quemque voluptas — Every man that studies hath some beloved study, which is his delight above any other;* and this is mine. It is that learning which it was my happiness from a child to be trained up in, by my ever honoured father, whose memory must always be very dear and precious to me: he often reminded me that a good textuary is a good divine; and that I should read other books with this in my eye, that I might be the better able to understand and apply the scripture. While I was thus employing myself came out Mr. Burkitt's Exposition, of the Gospels first, and afterwards of the Act and the Epistles, which met with very good acceptance among serious people, and no doubt, by the blessing of God, will continue to do great service to the church. Soon after he had finished that work, it pleased God to call him to his rest, upon which I was urged, by some of my friends, and was myself inclined, to attempt the like upon the Old Testament, in the strength of the grace of Christ. This upon the *Pentateuch* is humbly offered as a specimen; if it find favour, and be found any way useful, it is my present purpose, in dependence upon divine aids, to go on, so long as God shall continue my life and health, and as my other work will permit. Many helps, I know, we have of this kind in our own language, which we have a great deal of reason to value, and to be very thankful to God for: but the scripture is a subject that can never be exhausted. *Semper habet aliquid relegentibus — However frequently we read it, we shall always meet with something new.* When David had amassed a vast treasure for the building of the temple, yet saith he to Solomon, *Thou mayest add thereto,* 1 Chr. 22:14. Such a treasure is scripture-knowledge; it is still capable of increase, till we all come to the perfect man. The scripture is a field or vineyard which finds work for variety of hands, and about which may be employed a great *diversity of gifts and operations,* but all from *the same Spirit* (1 Co. 12:4, 6) and for the glory of *the same Lord.* The learned in the languages and in ancient usages have been very serviceable to the church (the blessed occupant of this field), by their curious and elaborate searches into its various products, their anatomies of its plants, and the entertaining lectures they have read upon them. The philology of the critics has been of much more advantage to religion, and lent more light to sacred truth, than the philosophy of the school-

divines. The learned also in the arts of war have done great service in defending this garden of the Lord against the violent attacks of the powers of darkness, successfully pleading the cause of the sacred writings against the spiteful cavils of atheists, deists, and the profane scoffers of these latter days. Such as these stand in the posts of honour, and their praise is in all the churches: yet the labours of the vine-dressers and the husbandmen (2 Ki. 25:12), though they are the poor of the land who till this ground, and gather in the fruits of it, are no less necessary in their place, and beneficial to the household of God, that out of these precious fruits every one may have his *portion of meat in due season.* These are the labours to which, according to my ability, I have here set my hand. And as the plain and practical expositors would not, for a world, say of the learned critics, *There is no need of them;* so, it is hoped, those eyes and heads will not say to the hands and feet, *There is no need of you,* 1 Co. 12:21.

The learned have of late received very great advantage in their searches into this part of holy writ, and the books that follow (and still hope for more), by the excellent and most valuable labours of that great and good man bishop *Patrick,* whom, for vast reading, solid judgment, and a most happy application to these best of studies, even in his advanced years and honours, succeeding ages no doubt will rank among the first three of commentators, and bless God for him. Mr. *Pool's* English Annotations (which, having had so many impressions, we may suppose, have got into most hands) are of admirable use, especially for the explaining of scripture-phrases, opening the sense, referring to parallel scriptures, and the clearing of difficulties that occur. I have therefore all along been brief upon that which is there most largely discussed, and have industriously declined, as much as I could, what is to be found there; for I would not *actum agere — do what is done;* nor (if I may be allowed to borrow the apostle's words) *boast of things made ready to our hand,* 2 Co. 10:16. These and other annotations which are referred to the particular words and clauses they are designed to explain are most easy to be consulted upon occasion; but the exposition which (like this) is put into a continued discourse, digested under proper heads, is much more easy and ready to be read through for one's own or others' instruction. And, I think, the observing of the connection of each chapter (if there be occasion) with that which goes before, and the general scope of it, with the thread of the history or discourse, and the collecting of the several parts of it, to be seen at one view, will contribute very much to the understanding of it, and will give the mind abundant satisfaction in the general intention, though there may be here and there a difficult word or expression which the best critics cannot easily account for. This, therefore, I have here attempted. But we are concerned not only to understand what we read, but to improve it to some good purpose, and, in order thereunto, to be affected with it, and to receive the impressions of it. The word of God is designed to be not only a *light to our eyes,* the entertaining subject of our contemplation, but a *light to our feet* and a *lamp to our paths* (Ps. 119:105), to direct us in the way of our duty, and to prevent our turning aside into any by-way: we must therefore, in searching the scriptures, enquire, not only *What is this?* but, *What is this to us?* What use may we make of it? How may we accommodate it to some of the purposes of that divine and heavenly life which, by the grace of God, we are resolved to live? Enquiries of this kind I have here aimed to answer. When the stone is rolled from the well's mouth by a critical explication of the text, still there are those who would both drink themselves and water their flocks? but they complain that the *well is deep,* and *they have nothing to draw with;* how then shall they *come by this living water?* Some such may, perhaps, find a bucket here, or water drawn to their hands; and pleased enough shall I be with this office of the Gibeonites, to *draw water for the congregation of the Lord* out of these wells of salvation.

That which I aim at in the exposition is to give what I thought the genuine sense, and to make it as plain as I could to ordinary capacities, not troubling my readers with the different sentiments of expositors, which would have been to transcribe Mr. *Pool's* Latin Synopsis, where this is done abundantly to our satisfaction and advantage. As to the practical observations, I have not obliged myself to raise doctrines out of every verse or paragraph, but only have endeavoured to mix with the exposition such hints or remarks as I thought profitable *for doctrine, for reproof, for correction, for instruction in righteousness,* aiming in all to promote practical godliness, and carefully avoiding matters of doubtful disputation and strifes of words. It is only the prevalency of the power of religion in the hearts and lives of Christians that will redress our grievances, and turn our wilderness into a fruitful field. And since our Lord Jesus Christ is the true *treasure hidden in the field* of the Old Testament, and was the *Lamb slain from the foundation of the world,* I have been careful to observe what Moses wrote of him, to which he himself oft appealed. In the writings of the prophets we meet with more of the plain and express promises of the Messiah, and the grace of the gospel; but here, in the books of Moses, we find more of the types, both real and personal figures of him that was to come — shadows, of which the substance is Christ, Rom. 5:14. Those to whom *to live is Christ* will find in these that which is very instructive and affecting, and which will give great assistance to their faith, and love, and holy joy. This, in a particular manner, we search the scriptures for — to find what they testify of Christ and eternal life, Jn. 5:39. Nor is it any objection against the application of the ceremonial institutions to Christ and his grace that those to whom they were given could not discern this sense or use of them; but it is rather a reason why we should be very thankful that the veil which was upon their minds in the reading of the Old Testament is *done away in Christ,* 2 Co. 3:13, 14, 18. Though they then *could not stedfastly look to the end of that which is abolished,* it does not therefore follow but that we who are happily furnished with a key to these mysteries may in them, *as in a glass, behold the glory of the Lord Jesus.* And yet, perhaps, the pious Jews saw more of the gospel in their ritual than we think they did; they had at least a general expectation of *good things to come,* by faith in the promises made to the fathers, as we have of the happiness of heaven, though they could not of that world to come, any more than we can of this, form any distinct or certain idea. Our conceptions of the future state, perhaps, are as dark and confused, as short of the truth and as wide from it, as theirs then were of the kingdom of the Messiah: but God requires faith only according to the revelation he gives. They then were accountable for no more light than they had; and we now are accountable for that greater light which we have in the gospel, by the help of which we may find much more of Christ in the Old Testament than they could. If any think our observations sometimes take rise from that which to them seems too minute, let them remember that maxim of the Rabbin, *Non est in lege vel una litera à quâ non pendent magni montes —*

The law contains not a letter but what bears the weight of mountains. We are sure there is not an idle word in the Bible. I would desire the reader not only to read the text entire, before he reads the exposition, but, as the several verses are referred to in the exposition, to cast his eye upon them again, and then he will the better understand what he reads. And, if he have leisure, he will find it of use to him to turn to the scriptures which are sometimes only referred to for brevity's sake, comparing spiritual things with spiritual.

It is the declared purpose of the Eternal Mind, in all the operations both of providence and grace, to *magnify the law and to make it honourable* (Isa. 42:21), nay to *magnify his word above all his name* (Ps. 138:2), so that when we pray, *Father, glorify thy name,* we mean this, among other things, Father, magnify the holy Scriptures; and to that prayer, made in faith, we may be sure of that answer which was given to our blessed Saviour when he prayed it, with particular respect to the fulfilling of the scriptures in his own sufferings, *I have both glorified it, and I will glorify it yet again,* Jn. 12:28. To this great design I humbly desire to be some way serviceable, in the strength of that grace by which I am what I am, hoping that what may help to make the reading of the scripture more easy, pleasant, and profitable, will be graciously accepted by him that smiled on the widow's two mites cast into the treasury, as an intention to magnify it and make it honourable; and if I can but gain that point, in any measure, with some, I shall think my endeavours abundantly recompensed, however, by others, I and my performances may be vilified and made contemptible.

I have now nothing more to add than to recommend myself to the prayers of my friends, and them to the grace of the Lord Jesus; and so rest an unworthy dependent upon that grace, and, through that, an expectant of the *glory to be revealed.*

Chester, October 2, 1706 M.H.

ORIGINAL PREFACE TO VOLUME TWO

This second volume of methodized and practical expositions of the inspired writings ventures abroad with fear and trembling in the same plain and homely dress with the former on the Pentateuch. *Ornari res ipsa negat; contenta doceri — the subject requires no ornament; to have it apprehended is all.* But I trust, through grace, it proceeds from the same honest design to promote the knowledge of the scripture, in order to the reforming of men's hearts and lives. If I may but be instrumental to make my readers wise and good, wiser and better, more watchful against sin and more careful of their duty both to God and man, and, in order thereto, more in love with the word and law of God, I have all I desire, all I aim at. *May he that ministereth seed to the sower multiply the seed sown, by increasing the fruits of* our *righteousness,* 2 Co. 9:10. It is the history of the Jewish church and nation that fills this volume, from their first settlement in the promised land, after their 430 years' bondage in Egypt and their forty years' wandering in the wilderness, to their re-settlement there after their seventy years' captivity in Babylon — from Joshua to Nehemiah. The five books of Moses were taken up more with their laws, institutes, and charters; but all these books are purely historical, and in this way of writing a great deal of very valuable learning and wisdom has been conveyed from one generation to another. The chronology of this history, and the ascertaining of the times when the several events contained in it happened, would very much illustrate the history, and add to the brightness of it; it is therefore well worthy the search of the curious and ingenious, and they may find both pleasure and profit in perusing the labours of many learned men who have directed their studies that way. I confess I could willingly have entertained myself and reader, in this preface, with a calculation of the times through which this history passes; but I consider that such a babe in knowledge as I am could not pretend either to add to or correct what has been done by so many great writers, much less to decide the controversies that have been agitated among them. I had indeed some thoughts of consulting my worthy and ever-honoured friend Mr. Tallents of Shrewsbury, the learned author of the "View of Universal History," and of begging some advice and assistance from him in methodizing the contents of this history; but, in the very week in which I put my last hand to this part, it pleased God to put an end to his useful life (and useful it was to the last) and to call him to his rest, in the eighty-ninth year of his age: so that purpose was broken off, that thought of my heart. But that elaborate performance of his commonly called his "Chronological Tables" gives great light to this, as indeed to all other parts of history. And Dr. Lightfoot's "Chronology of the Old Testament," and Mr. Cradock's "History of the Old Testament Methodized," may also be of great use to such readers as I write for. As to the particular chronological difficulties which occur in the thread of this history, I have not been large upon them, because many times I could not satisfy myself, and how then could I satisfy my reader concerning them? I have not indeed met with any difficulties so great but that solutions might be given of them sufficient to silence the atheists and antiscripturists, and roll away from the sacred records all the reproach of contradiction and inconsistency with themselves; for, to do that, it is enough to show that the difference may be accommodated either this way or that, when at the same time one cannot satisfy one's self which way is the right. But it is well that these are things about which we may very safely and very comfortably be ignorant and unresolved. What concerns our salvation is plain enough, and we need not perplex ourselves about the niceties of chronology, genealogy, or chorography. At least my undertaking leads me not into those labyrinths. What is *profitable for doctrine, for reproof, for correction, and for instruction in righteousness,* is what I intend to observe, and I would endeavour to open what is dark and hard to be understood only in order to that. Every author must be taken in his way of writing; the sacred penman, as they have not left us formal systems, so they have not left us formal annals, but useful narratives of things proper for our direction in the way of duty, which some great judges of common writers have thought to be the most pleasant and profitable histories, and most likely to answer the end. The word of God *manifestis pascit, obscuris exercet* (Aug. in Joh. Tract. 45), as one of the ancients expresses it, that is, *it has enough in it that is easy to nourish the meanest to life eternal, yet enough that is difficult to try the industry and humility of the greatest.* There are several things which should recommend this part of sacred writ to our diligent and constant search.

I. That it is *history,* and therefore entertaining and very pleasant, edifying and very serviceable to the conduct of human life. It gratifies the inquisitive with the knowledge of that which the most intense speculation could not discover any other way. By a retirement into ourselves, and a serious contemplation of the objects we are surrounded with, close reasoning may advance many excellent truths without being beholden to any other. But for the knowledge of past events we are entirely indebted (and must be so) to the reports and records of others. A notion or hypothesis of man's own framing may gain him the reputation of a wit, but a history of man's own framing will lay him under the reproach of a cheat any further than as it respects that which he himself is an eye or ear-witness of. How much are we indebted then to the divine wisdom and goodness for these writings, which have made things so long since past as familiar to us as any of the occurrences of the age and place we live in! History is so edifying that parables and apologues have been invented to make up the deficiencies of it for our instruction concerning good and evil; and, whatever may be said of other history, we are sure that in this history there is no matter of fact recorded but what has its use and will help either to expound God's providence or guide man's prudence.

II. That it is *true* history, and what we may rely upon the credit of, and need not fear being deceived in. That which the heathens reckoned *tempus adēlon (which they knew nothing at all of)* and *tempus mythikon (the account of which was wholly fabulous)* is to us *tempus historikon, what we have a most authentic account of.* The Greeks were with them the most celebrated historians, and yet their successors in learning and dominion, the Romans, put them into no good name for their credibility, witness that of the poet: *Et quicquid Graecia mendax audet in historia — All that lying Greece has dared to record,* Juv. Sat. 10. But the history which we have before us is of undoubted certainty, and no cunningly devised fable. To be well assured of this is a great satisfaction, especially since we meet with so many things in it truly miraculous, and many more great and marvellous.

III. That it is *ancient* history, far more ancient than was ever pretended to come from any other hand. Homer the most ancient genuine heathen writer now entirely extant, is reckoned to have lived at the beginning of the Olympiads, near the time when it is computed that the city of Rome was founded by Romulus, which was but about the reign of Hezekiah king of Judah. And his writings pretend not to be historical, but poetical fiction all over: rhapsodies indeed they are, and the very Alcoran of paganism. The most ancient authentic historians now extant are Herodotus and Thucydides, who were contemporaries with the latest of our historians, Ezra and Nehemiah, and could not write with any certainty of events much before their own time. The obscurity, deficiency, and uncertainty of all ancient history, except that which we find in the scripture, is abundantly made out by the learned bishop Stillingfleet, in that most useful book, his *Origines Sacrae,* lib. i. Let the antiquity of this history not only recommend it to the curious, but recommend to us all that way of religion it directs us in, as the good old way, in which if we walk we *shall find rest for our souls,* Jer. 6:16.

IV. That it is *church* history, the history of the Jewish church, that sacred society, incorporated for religion, and the custody of the oracles and ordinances of God, by a charter under the broad seal of heaven, a covenant confirmed by miracles. Many great ant mighty nations there were at this time in the world, celebrated it is likely for wisdom, and learning, and valour, illustrious men and illustrious actions; yet the records of them are all lost, either in silence or fables, while that little inconsiderable people of the Jews that *dwelt alone,* and *was not reckoned among the nations* (Num. 23:9), makes so great a figure in the best known, most ancient, and most lasting of all histories; and no notice is taken in it of the affairs of other nations, except only as they fall in with the affairs of the Jews: *for the Lord's portion is his people; Jacob is the lot of his inheritance,* Deu. 32:8, 9. Such a concern has God for his church in every age, and so dear have its interests been to him. Let them therefore be so to us, that we may be *followers of him as dear children.*

V. That it is a *divine* history, given by inspiration of God, and a part of that blessed book which is to be the standing rule of our faith and practice. And we are not to think it a part of it which might have been spared, or which we may now pass over or cast a careless eye upon, as if it were indifferent whether we read it or no; but we are to read it as a sacred record, preserved for our benefit *on whom the ends of the world have come.* 1. This history is of great use for the understanding of some parts of the Old Testament. The account we have here of David's life and reign, and especially of his troubles, is a key to many of his Psalms; and much light is given to most of the prophecies by these histories. 2. Though we have not altogether so many types of Christ here as we had in the history and the law of Moses, yet even here we meet with many who were figures of him that was to come, such as Joshua, Samson, Solomon, Cyrus, but especially David, whose kingdom was typical of the kingdom of the Messiah and the covenant of royalty made with him, a dark representation of the covenant of redemption made with the eternal Word; nor know we how to call Christ the son of David unless we be acquainted with this history nor how to *receive* the declaration that John Baptist was the *Elias that was to come,* Mt. 11:14. 3. The state of the Jewish church which is here set before us was typical of the gospel church and the state of that in the days of the Messiah; and as the prophecies which related to it looked further to the latter days, so did the histories of it; and still *these things happened to them for ensamples,* 1 Co. 10:11. By the tenour of this history we are given to understand these three things concerning the church (for *the thing that hath been is that which shall be,* Eccl. 1:9): — (1.) That we are not to expect the perfect purity and unity of the church in this world, and therefore not to be stumbled, though we are grieved, at its corruptions, distempers, and divisions; we are not to think it strange concerning them, as though some strange thing happened, much less to think the worse of its laws and constitutions for the sake of them or to despair of its perpetuity. What wretched stains of idolatry, impiety, and immorality, appear on the Jewish church, and what a woeful breach was there between Judah and Ephraim! yet God took them (as I may say) with all their faults, and never wholly rejected them till they rejected the Messiah. *Israel hath not been forsaken, nor Judah, of their God, though their land was filled with sin against the Holy One of Israel,* Jer. 51:5. (2.) That we are not to expect the constant tranquillity and prosperity of the church. It was then often oppressed and afflicted from its youth, had its years of servitude as well as its days of triumph, was often obscured, diminished, impoverished, and brought low; and yet still God secured to himself a remnant, *a holy seed,* which was *the substance thereof,* Isa. 6:13. Let us not then be surprised to see the gospel church sometimes under hatches, and driven into the wilderness, and the gates of hell prevailing far against it. (3.) That yet we need not fear the utter extirpation of it. The gospel church is called the *Israel of God* (Gal. 6:16), and the *Jerusalem which is above* (Gal. 4:26), the *heavenly Jerusalem;* for as *Israel after the flesh,* and the *Jerusalem that then was,* by the wonderful care of the divine Providence, outrode all the storms with which they were tossed and threatened, and continued in being till they were made to resign all their honours to the gospel church, which they were the figures of, so shall that also, notwithstanding all its shocks, be preserved, till the mystery of God shall be finished, and the kingdom of grace shall have its perfection in the kingdom of glory. 4. This history is of great use to us for our direction in the way of our duty; it was written for our learning, that we may see the evil we should avoid and be armed against it, and the good we should do and be quickened to it. Though they are generally judges, and kings, and great men, whose lives are here written, yet in them even those of the meanest rank may see the deformity of sin and hate it, and the beauty of holiness and be in love with it; nay, the greater the person is the more evident are both these; for, if the great be good, it is their goodness that makes their greatness honourable; if bad, their greatness does but make their badness the more shameful. The failings even of good people are also recorded here for our admonition, that he who thinks he stands may take heed lest he fall, and that he who has fallen may not despair of forgiveness if he recover himself by repentance. 5. This history, as it shows what God requires of us, so it shows what we may expect from his providence, especially concerning states and kingdoms. By the dealings of God with the Jewish nation it appears that, as nations are, so they must expect to fare — that while princes and people serve the interests of God's kingdom among men he will secure and advance their interests, but that when they shake off his government, and rebel against him, they can look for no other than an inundation of judgments. It was so all along with Israel; while they kept close to God they prospered; when they forsook him every thing went cross. That great man archbishop Tillotson (*Vol. 1. Serm. 3.* on Prov. 14:34) suggests that though, as to particular persons, the providences of God are promiscuously administered in this world, because there is another world of rewards and punishments for them, yet it is not so with nations as such, but national virtues are ordinarily rewarded with temporal blessings and national sins punished with temporal judgments, because, as he says, public bodies and communities of men, as such, can be rewarded and punished only in this world, for in the next they will all be dissolved. So plainly are God's ways of disposing kingdoms laid before us in the glass of this history that I could wish Christian statesmen would think themselves as much concerned as preachers to acquaint themselves with it; they might fetch as good maxims of state and rules of policy from this as from the best of the Greek and Roman historians. We are blessed (as the Jews were) with a divine revelation, and make a national profession of religion and relation to God, and therefore are to look upon ourselves as in a peculiar manner under a divine regimen, so that the things which happened to them were designed for ensamples to us.

I cannot pretend to write for great ones. But if what is here done may be delightful to any in reading and helpful in understanding and improving this sacred history, and governing themselves by the dictates of it, let God have all the glory and let all the rivers return to the ocean whence they came. When I look back on what is done I see nothing to boast of, but a great deal to be ashamed of; and, when I look forward on what is to be done, I see nothing in myself to trust to for the doing of it. I have no sufficiency of my own; but *by the grace of God I am what I am,* and that grace will, I trust, be sufficient for me. *Surely in the Lord have I righteousness and strength.* That blessed *epichorēgia* which the apostle speaks of (Phil. 1:19), that continual supply or communication *of the Spirit of Jesus Christ,* is what we may in faith pray for, and depend upon, to furnish us for every good word and work. The pleasantness of the study has drawn me on to the writing of this, and the candour with which my friends have been pleased to receive my poor endeavours on the Pentateuch encourages me to publish it; it is done according to the best of my skill, not without some care and application of mind, in the same method and manner with that; I wish I could have done it in less compass, that it might have been more within reach of *the poor of the flock.* But then it would not have been so plain and full as I desire it may be for the benefit of the *lambs of the flock. Brevis esse laboro, obscurus fio — labouring to be concise I become obscure.* With a humble submission to the divine providence and its disposals, and a humble reliance on the divine grace and its guidance and operation, I purpose still to proceed, as I have time, in this work. Two volumes more will, if God permit, conclude the Old Testament; and then if my friends encourage me, and my God spare me and enable me for it, I intend to go on to the New Testament. For though *many have taken in hand to set forth in order a declaration of those* parts of scripture which are yet before us (Lu. 1:1), whose works *praise them in the gates* and are likely to outlive mine, yet while the subject is really so copious as it is and the manner of handling it may possibly be so various, and while one book comes into the hands of some and another into the hands of others, and all concur in the same design to advance the common interests of Christ's kingdom, the *common faith* once delivered to the saints, and the *common salvation* of precious souls (Tit. 1:4, Jude 3), I hope store of this kind will be thought no sore. I make bold to mention my purpose to proceed thus publicly in hopes I may have the advice of my friends in it, and their prayers for me that I may be made more *ready and mighty in the scriptures,* that understanding and utterance may be given to me, and that I may *obtain mercy of the Lord Jesus to be found* his *faithful* servant, who am less than the least of all that call him *Master.*

Chester, June 2, 1708. M.H.

ORIGINAL PREFACE TO VOLUME THREE

These five books of scripture which are contained in this third volume and which I have here endeavoured, according to the measure of the gift given to me, to explain and improve, for the use of those who desire to read them, not only with understanding, but to their edification — though they have the same divine origin, design, and authority, as those that went before, yet, upon some accounts, are of a very different nature from them, and from the rest of the sacred writings, such variety of methods has Infinite Wisdom seen fit to take in conveying the light of divine revelation to the children of men, that this heavenly food might have (as the Jews say of the manna) something in it agreeable to every palate and suited to every constitution. If every eye be not thus opened, every mouth will be stopped, and such as perish in their ignorance will be left without excuse. *We have piped unto you, and you have not danced, we have mourned unto you, and you have not lamented,* Mt. 11:17.

I. The books of scripture have hitherto been, for the most part, very plain and easy, narratives of matter of fact, which he that runs may read and understand, and which are milk for babes, such as they can receive and digest, and both entertain and nourish themselves with. The waters of the sanctuary have hitherto been but to the ankles or to the knees, such as a lamb might wade in, to drink of and wash in; but here we are advanced to a higher form in God's school, and have books put into our hands wherein are *many things dark and hard to be understood,* which we do not apprehend the meaning of so suddenly and so certainly as we could wish, the study of which requires a more close application of mind, a greater intenseness of thought, and the accomplishing of a diligent search, which yet the treasure hid in them, when it is found, will abundantly recompense. The waters of the sanctuary are here *to the loins,* and still as we go forward we shall find the waters still risen in the prophetical books, *waters to swim in* (Eze. 47:3–5), not fordable, nor otherwise to be passed over — depths in which an elephant will not find footing, *strong meat for strong men.* The same method is observable in the New Testament, where we find the plain history of Christ and his gospel placed first in the Evangelists and the Acts of the Apostles; then the mystery of both in the Epistles, which are more difficult to be understood; and, lastly, the prophesies of things to come in the apocalyptic visions. This method, so exactly observed in both the Testaments, directs us in what order to proceed both in studying the things of God ourselves and in teaching them to others; we must go in the order that the scripture does; and where can we expect to find a better method of divinity and a better method of preaching?

1. We must begin with those things that are most plain and easy, as, blessed be God, those things are which are most necessary to salvation and of the greatest use. We must lay our foundation firm, in a sound experimental knowledge of the principles of religion, and then the superstructure will be well reared and will stand firmly. It is not safe to launch out into the deep at first, nor to venture into points difficult and controverted until we have first thoroughly digested the elements of the oracles of God and turned them *in succum et sanguinem — into juice and blood.* Those that begin their Bible at the wrong end commonly use their knowledge of it in the wrong way. And, in training up others, we must be sure to ground them well at first in those truths of God which are plain, and in some measure level to their capacity, which we find they comprehend, and relish, and know how to make use of, and not amuse those that are weak with things above them, things of doubtful disputation, which they cannot apprehend any certainty of nor advantage by. Our Lord Jesus spoke the word to the people *as they were able to hear it* (Mk. 4:33) and had many things to say to his disciples which he did not say because as yet they *could not bear them,* Jn. 16:12, 13. And those whom St. Paul *could not speak to as unto spiritual* — though he blamed them for their backwardness, yet he accommodated himself to their weakness, and spoke to them *as unto babes in Christ,* 1 Co. 3:1, 2.

2. Yet we must not rest in these things. We must not be always children that have need of milk, but nourished up with that, and gaining strength, we must *go on to perfection* (Heb. 6:1), that having, *by reason of use, our spiritual senses exercised* (Heb. 5:14), we may come to full age, and put away childish things, and, *forgetting the things which are behind,* that is, so well remembering them (Phil. 3:13) that we need not be still poring over them as those that are ever learning the same lesson, we may reach forth to the things which are before. Though we must never think to learn above our Bible, as long as we are here in this world, yet we must still be getting forward in it. *You have dwelt long enough in this mountain;* now turn and take your journey onward in the wilderness towards Canaan. Our motto must be *Plus ultra — Onward.* And then shall we know if thus, by regular steps (Hos. 6:3), we *follow on to know the Lord* and what the mind of the Lord is.

II. The books of scripture have hitherto been mostly historical, but now the matter is of another nature; it is doctrinal and devotional, preaching and praying; and in this way of writing, as well as in the former, a great deal of excellent knowledge is conveyed, which serves very valuable purposes. It will be of good use to know not only what others did that went before us, and how they fared, but what their notions and sentiments were, what their thoughts and affections were, that we may, with the help of them, form our minds aright. Plutarch's Morals are reputed as a useful treasure in the commonwealth of learning as Plutarch's Lives, and the wise disquisitions and discourses of the philosophers as the records of the historians; nor is this divine philosophy (if I may so call it), which we have in these books, less needful, nor less serviceable, to the church, than the sacred history was. Blessed be God for both.

III. The Jews make these books to be given by a divine inspiration somewhat different from that both of Moses and the prophets. They divided the books of the Old Testament into the Law, the Prophets and the *ktwbym — Writings,* which Epiphanius emphatically translates *grapheia — things written,* and these books are more commonly called among the Greeks *Hag-*

iographa — Holy writings: the Jews attribute them to that distinct kind of inspiration which they call *rwh hqds — The Holy Spirit.* Moses they supposed to write by the Spirit in a way above all the other prophets, for *with him* God spoke *mouth to mouth, even apparently* (Num. 12:8) *knew him,* that is, conversed with him *face to face,* Deu. 34:10. He was made partaker of divine revelation (as Maimonides distinguishes, *De Fund. Legis, ch.* 7) *per vigiliam — while awake,* (See Mr. Smith's Discourses on Prophecy, *ch.* 11.) whereas God manifested himself to all the other prophets in a dream or vision: and he adds that Moses understood the words of prophecy without any perturbation or astonishment of mind, whereas the other prophets commonly fainted and were troubled. But the writers of the Hagiographa they suppose to be inspired in a degree somewhat below that of the other prophets, and to receive divine revelation, not as they did by dreams, and visions, and voices, but (as Maimonides describes it, *More Nevochim — part* 2 *c.* 45) they perceived some power to rise within them, and rest upon them, which urged and enabled them to write or speak far above their own natural ability, in psalms or hymns, or in history or in rules of good living, still enjoying the ordinary vigour and use of their senses. Let David himself describe it. *The Spirit of the Lord spoke by me, and his word was in my tongue; the God of Israel said, the Rock of Israel spoke to me,* 2 Sa. 23:2, 3. This gives such a magnificent account of the inspiration by which David wrote that I see not why it should be made inferior to that of the other prophets, for David is expressly called *a prophet,* Acts 2:29, 30. But, since our hand is in with the Jewish masters, let us see what books they account Hagiographa. These five that are now before us come, without dispute, into this rank of sacred writers, and the book of the Lamentations is not unfitly added to them. Indeed the Jews, when they would speak critically, reckon all those songs which we meet with in the Old Testament among the Hagiographa; for though they were penned by prophets, and under the direction of the Holy Ghost, yet, because they were not the proper result of a *visum propheticum — prophetic vision,* they were not strictly prophecy. As to the historical books, they distinguish (but I think it is a distinction without a difference); some of them they assign to the prophets, calling them the *prophetae priores — the former prophets,* namely, Joshua, Judges, and the two books of the Kings; but others they rank among the Hagiographa, as the book of Ruth (which yet is but an appendix to the book of Judges), the two books of Chronicles, with Ezra, Nehemiah, and the book of Esther, which last the rabbin have a great value for, and think it is to be had in equal esteem with the law of Moses itself, that it shall last as long as that lasts, and shall survive the writings of the Prophets. And, *lastly,* they reckon the book of Daniel among the Hagiographa, (Hil. Megil. c. 2, 11) for which no reason can be given, since he was not inferior to any of the prophets in the gift of prophecy; and therefore the learned Mr. Smith thinks that their placing him among the Hagiographical writers was fortuitous by mistake (Vid. Hottinger. Thesaur. *lib.* 2, *cap.* 1, 3). Mr. Smith, in his Discourse before quoted, though he supposes this kind of divine inspiration to be more "*pacate* and *serene* than that which was strictly called *prophecy,* not acting so much upon the imagination, but seating itself in the higher and purer faculties of the soul, yet shows that it manifested itself to be of a divine nature, not only as it always elevated pious souls into strains of devotion, or moved them strangely to dictate matters of true piety and goodness, but as it came in abruptly upon the minds of those holy men, and transported them from the temper of mind they were in before, so that they perceived themselves captivated by the power of some higher light than that which their own understanding commonly poured out upon them; and this, says he, was a kind of vital form to that light of divine and sanctified reason which they were perpetually possessed of and that constant frame of holiness and goodness which dwelt in their hallowed minds." We have reason to *glorify the God of Israel who gave such power unto men* and has here transmitted to us the blessed products of that power.

IV. The style and composition of these books are different from those that go before and those that follow. Our Saviour divides the books of the Old Testament into *the Law, the Prophets,* and *the Psalms* (Lu. 24:44), and thereby teaches us to distinguish those books that are poetical, or metrical, from the Law and the Prophets; and such are all these that are now before us, except Ecclesiastes, which yet, having something restrained in its style, may well enough be reckoned among them. They are books in verse, according to the ancient rules of versifying, though not according to the Greek and Latin *prosodies.* Some of the ancients call these five books *the second Pentateuch of the Old Testament* (Damascen. Orthod. Fid. 1.4, cap. 18.), five sacred volumes which are as the satellites to the five books of the law of Moses. *Gregory Nazianzen* (Vid. Suicer. Thesaur. in *stichēra — carm.* 33, p. 98) calls these *hai stichērai pente — the five metrical books;* first Job (so he reckons them up), then David, then the three of Solomon — Ecclesiastes, the Song, and Proverbs. *Amphilochius,* bishop at Iconium, in his iambic poem to *Seleucus,* reckons them up particularly, and calls them *stichēras pente Biblos — the five verse-books. Epiphanius (lib. de ponder. et mensur. p.* 533) *pente stichēreis — the five verse-books.* And *Cyril. Hierosol. Collect.* 4, *p.* 30 *(mihi — in my copy),* calls these five books *ta stichēra — books in verse.* Polychronius, in his prologue to Job, says that as *those that are without* call their tragedies and comedies *poiētika — poetics,* so, in sacred writ, those books which are composed in Hebrew metre (of which he reckons Job the first) we call *stichēra biblia — books in verse,* written *kata stichon — according to order.* What is written in metre, or rhythm, is so called from *metros — a measure,* and *arithmos — a number,* because regulated by certain measures, or numbers of syllables, which please the ear with their smoothness and cadency, and so insinuate the matter the more movingly and powerfully into the fancy. Sir William Temple, (Miscell, part 2.) in his essay upon poetry, thinks it is generally agreed to have been the first sort of writing that was used in the world, nay, that, in several nations, poetical compositions preceded the very invention or usage of letters. The Spaniards (he says) found in America many strains of poetry, and such as seemed to flow from a true poetic vein, before any letters were known in those regions. The same (says he) is probable of the Scythians and Grecians: the oracles of Apollo were delivered in verse. Homer and Hesiod wrote their poems (the very Alcoran of the pagan daemonology) many ages before the appearing of any of the Greek philosophers or historians; and long before them (if we may give credit to the antiquities of Greece), even before the days of David, Orpheus and Linus were celebrated poets and musicians in Greece; and at the same time Carmenta, the mother of Evander, who was the first that introduced letters among the natives of Greece, was so called *a carmine — from a song,* because she expressed herself in verse. And in such veneration was this way of writing among the ancients that their poets were called *vates — prophets,* and their muses were deified. But, which is more certain and considerable, the most ancient composition that we meet with in scripture was the song of Moses at the Red Sea (Ex. 15), which we find before the very first mention of writing, for that occurs not until Ex. 17:14, when God bade Moses write a memorial of the war with Amalek. The first, and indeed the true and general end of writing, is a help of memory; and poetry does in some measure answer that end, and even in the want of writing, much more with writing, helps to preserve the remembrance of ancient things. The book of *wars of the Lord* (Num. 21:14), and the book of Jasher (Jos. 10:13; 2 Sa. 1:18), seem to have been both written in poetic measures. Many sacred songs we meet with in the Old Testament, scattered both in the historical and prophetical books, penned on particular occasions, which, in the opinion of very competent judges, "have in them as true and noble strains of poetry and picture as are met with in any other language whatsoever, in spite of all disadvantages from translations into such different tongues and common prose, (Sir W. Temple, p. 329.) nay, are nobler examples of the true sublime style of poetry than any that can be found in the Pagan writers; the images are so strong, the thoughts so great, the expressions so divine, and the figures so admirably bold and moving, that the wonderful manner of these writers is quite inimitable." (Sir R. Blackmore's preface to Job.) It is fit that what is employed in the service of the sanctuary should be the best in its kind.

The books here put together are poetical. Job is an heroic poem, the book of Psalms a collection of divine odes or lyrics, Solomon's Song a pastoral and an epithalamium; they are poetical, and yet sacred and serious, grave and full of majesty. They have a poetic force and flame, with out poetic fury and fiction, and strangely command and move the affections, without corrupting the imagination or putting a cheat upon it; and, while they gratify the ear, they edify the mind and profit the more by pleasing. It is therefore much to be lamented that so powerful an art, which was at first consecrated to the honour of God, and has been so often employed in his service, should be debauched, as it has been, and is at this day, into the service of his enemies — that his corn, and wine, and oil should be prepared for Baal.

V. As the manner of the composition of these books is excellent, and very proper to engage the attention, move the affections, and fix them in the memory, so the matter is highly useful, and such as will be every way serviceable to us. They have in them the very sum and substance of religion, and what they contain is more fitted to our hand, and made ready for use, than any part of the Old Testament, upon which account, if we may be allowed to compare one star with another in the firmament of the scripture, these will be reckoned stars of the first magnitude. *All scripture is profitable* (and this part of it in a special manner) *for instruction* in doctrine, in devotion, and in the right ordering of the conversation. The book of Job directs us what we are to believe concerning God, the book of Psalms how we are to worship him, pay our homage to him, and maintain our communion with him, and then the book of the Proverbs shows very particularly how we are to govern ourselves *en pasē anastrophē — in every turn of human life;* thus shall the *man of God,* by a due attention to these lights, be *perfect, thoroughly furnished for every good work.* And these are placed according to their natural order, as well as according to the order of time; for very fitly are we first led into the knowledge of God, our judgments rightly formed concerning him, and our mistakes rectified, and then instructed how to worship him and to choose the things that please him. We have here much of natural religion, its principles, its precepts — much of God, his infinite perfections, his relations to man, and his government both of the world and of the church; here is much of Christ, who is the spring, and soul, and centre, of revealed religion, and whom both Job and David were eminent types of, and had clear and happy prospects of. We have here that which will be of use to enlighten our understandings, and to acquaint us more and more with the things of God, with the deep things of God — speculations to entertain the most contemplative, and discoveries to satisfy the most inquisitive and increase the knowledge of those that are most knowing. Here is that also which, with a divine light, will bring into the soul the heat and influence of a divine fire, will kindle and inflame pious and devout affections, on which wings we may soar upwards until we enter into the holiest. We may here be in the mount with God, to behold his beauty; and when we come down from that mount, if we retain (as we ought) the impressions of our devotion upon our spirits and make conscience of doing that good which the Lord our God here requires of us, our faces shall shine before all with whom we converse, who shall take occasion thence to *glorify our Father who is in heaven,* Mt. 5:16. Thus great, thus noble, thus truly excellent, is the subject, and thus capable of being improved, which gives me the more reason to be ashamed of the meanness of my performance, that the comment breathes so little of the life and spirit of the text. We often wonder at those that are not at all affected with the great things of God, and have no taste nor relish of them, because they know little of them; but perhaps we have more reason to wonder at ourselves, that conversing so frequently, so intimately, with them, we are not more affected with them, so as even to be wholly taken up with them, and in a continual transport of delight in the contemplation of them. We hope to be so shortly; in the mean time, though like the three disciples that were the witnesses of Christ's transfiguration upon the mount we are but dull and sleepy, yet we can say, *Master, it is good to be here;* here *let us make tabernacles,* Lu. 9:32, 33.

I have nothing here to boast of — nothing at all, but a great deal to be humbled for, that I have not come up to what I have aimed at in respect of fulness and exactness. In the review of the work, I find many defects, and those who are critical, perhaps, will meet with some mistakes in it; but I have done it with what care I could, and desire to be thankful to God who by his grace has carried me on in his work thus far: let that grace have all the glory (Phil. 2:13), which *works in us both to will and to do* whatever we will or do that is good or serves any good purpose. What is from God will, I trust, be to him, will be graciously accepted by him, *according to what a man has, and not according to what he had not,* and will be of some use to his church; and what is from myself (that is, all the defects and errors) will, I trust, be favourably passed by and pardoned. That prayer of *St. Austin* is mine, *Domine Deus, quaecunque dixi in his libris de tuo, agnoscant et tui; et quae de meo, et tu ignosce et tui — Lord God, whatever I have maintained in these books correspondent with what is contained in thine grant that thy people may approve as well as thyself; whatever is but the doctrine of my book forgive thou, and grant that thy people may forgive it also.* I must beg likewise to own, to the honour of our great Master, that I have found the work to be its own wages, and that the more we converse with the word of God the more it is to us as *the honey* and the *honeycomb,* Ps. 19:10. In gathering some gleaning of this harvest for others we may feast ourselves; and, when we are enabled by the grace of God to do so, we are best qualified to feed others. I was much pleased with a passage I lately met with of Erasmus, that great scholar and celebrated wit, in an epistle dedicatory before his book *De Ratione Concionandi,* where, as one weary of the world and the hurry of it, he expresses an earnest desire to spend the rest of his days in secret communion with Jesus Christ, encouraged by his gracious invitation to those who *labour and are heavy laden* to *come unto him for rest* (Mt. 11:28), and this alone is that which he thinks will yield him true satisfaction. I think his words worth transcribing, and such as deserve to be inserted among the testimonies of great men to serious godliness. *Neque quisquam facilè credat quàm miserè animus jamdudum affectet ab his laboribus in tranquillam otium secedere, quodque superest vitae (superest autem vix brevis palmus sive pugillus), solum cum eo solo colloqui, qui clamavit olim (nec hodiè mutat vocem suam), "Venite ad me, omnes qui laboratis et onerati estis, ego reficiam vos;" quandoquidem in tam turbulento, ne dicam furente, saeculo, in tot molestiis quas vel ipsa tempora publicè invehunt, vel privatim adfert oetas ac valetudo, nihil reperio in quo mens mea libentius conquiescat quàm in hoc arcano colloquio — No one will easily believe how anxiously, for a long time past, I have wished to retire from these labours into a scene of tranquility, and, during the remainder of life (dwindled, it is true, to the shortest span), to converse only with him who once cried (nor does he now retract), "Come unto me, all you that labour and are heavy laden, and I will refresh you," for in this turbulent, not to say furious, age, the many public sources of disquietude, connected with the infirmities of advancing age, leave no solace to my mind to be compared with this secret communion.* In the pleasing contemplation of the divine beauty and benignity we hope to spend a blessed eternity, and therefore in this work it is good t o spend as much as may be of our time.

One volume more, containing the prophetical books, will finish the Old Testament, if the Lord continue my life, and leisure, and ability of mind and body for this work. It is begun, and I find it will be larger than any of the other volumes, and longer in the doing; but, as God by his grace shall furnish me for it and assist me in it (without which grace I am nothing, less than nothing, worse than nothing), it shall be carried on with all convenient speed; and *sat citò, si sat benè — if with sufficient ability, it will be with sufficient speed.* I desire the prayers of my friends that God would *minister seed to the sower* and *bread to the eaters* (Isa. 55:10), that he would *multiply the seed sown* and *increase the fruits of our righteousness* (2 Co. 9:10), that so he who *sows and those who reap may rejoice together* (Jn. 4:36); and the great Lord of the harvest shall have the glory of all.

Chester, May 13, 1710 M.H.

ORIGINAL PREFACE TO VOLUME FOUR

Those books of scripture are all prophetical of which here, *in weakness, and in fear, and in much trembling,* we have endeavoured a methodical explication and a practical improvement. I call them *prophetical* because so they are for the main, though we have some histories (here and there brought in for the illustration of the prophecies) and a book of Lamentations. Our Saviour often puts *the Law and the Prophets* for all the Old Testament. The prophets, by waiving the ceremonial precepts, and not insisting on them, but only on the weightier matters of the law, plainly intimated the abolishing of that part of the law of Moses by the gospel; and by their many predictions of Christ, and the kingdom of his grace, they intimated the accomplishing the perfecting of that part of the law of Moses in the gospel. Thus the prophets were the *nexus — the connecting bond* between the law and the gospel, and are therefore fitly placed between them.

These books, being prophetical, are, as such, divine, and of heavenly origin and extraction. We have human laws, human histories, and human poems, as well as divine ones, but we can have no human prophecies. Wise and good men may make prudent conjectures concerning future events (*moral prognostications* we call them); but it is essential to true prophecy that it be of God. The learned Huetius (Demonstrat. Evang. *pag.* 15) lays this down for one of his axioms, *Omnis prophetica facultas à Deo est — The prophetic talent is entirely from God;* and he proves it to be the sense both of Jews and heathen that it is God's prerogative to foresee things to come, and that whoever had such a power had it from God. And therefore the Jews reckon all prophecy to be given by the highest degree of inspiration, except that which was peculiar to Moses. When our Saviour asked the chief priests whether John's baptism were from heaven or of men, they durst not say *Of men,* because the people counted him a prophet, and, if so, then not of men. The Hebrew name for a prophet is *nby' — a speaker, preacher,* or *orator, a messenger,* or *interpreter,* that delivers God's messages to the children of men, as a herald to proclaim war or an ambassador to treat of peace. But then it must be remembered that he was formerly called *r'h* or *ḥsh,* that is, *a seer* (1 Sa. 9:9); for prophets, with the eyes of their minds, first saw what they were to speak and then spoke what they had seen.

Prophecy, taken strictly, is the foretelling of things to come; and there were those to whom God gave this power, not only that it might be a sign for the confirming of the faith of the church concerning the doctrine preached when the things foretold should be fulfilled, but for warning, instruction, and comfort, in prospect of what they themselves might not live to see accomplished, but which should be fulfilled in its season: so predictions of things to come long after might be of present use.

The learned Dr. Grew (Cosmol. sacra, *lib.* 4, *cap.* 6) describes prophecy in this sense to be, "A declaration of the divine prescience, looking at any distance through a train of infinite causes, known and unknown to us, upon a sure and certain effect." Hence he infers, "That the being of prophecies supposes the non-being of contingents; for, though there are many things which seem to us to be contingents, yet, were they so indeed, there could have been no prophecy; and there can be no contingent seemingly so loose and independent but it is a link of some chain." And Huetius gives this reason why none but God can foretel things to come, Because every effect depends upon an infinite number of preceding causes, all which, in their order, must be known to him that foretels the effect, and therefore to God only, for he alone is omniscient. So Tully argues: *Qui teneat causas rerum futurarum, idem necesse est omnia teneat quae futura sint; quod facere nemo nisi Deus potest — He who knows the causes of future events must necessarily know the events themselves; this is the prerogative of God alone* (Cicero de Divin. *lib.* 1). And therefore we find that by *this* the God of Israel proves himself to be God, that by his prophets he foretold things to come, which came to pass according to the prediction, Isa. 46:9, 10. And by *this* he disproves the pretensions of the Pagan deities, that they could not show the *things that were to come to pass hereafter,* Isa. 41:23. Tertullian proves the divine authority of the scripture from the fulfilling of scripture-prophecies: *Idoneum, opinor, testimonium divinitatis, veritas divinationis — I conceive the accomplishment of prophecy to be a satisfactory attestation from God* (Apol. *cap.* 20). And, besides the foretelling of things to come, the discovering of things secret by revelation from God is a branch of prophecy, as Ahijah's discovering Jeroboam's wife in disguise, and Elisha's telling Gehazi what passed between him and Naaman. But (Du Pin, Hist. of the Canon. *lib.* 1, *cap.* 2) prophecy, in scripture language, is taken more largely for a declaration of such things to the children of men, either by word or writing, as God has revealed to those that speak or write it, by vision, dream, or inspiration, guiding their minds, their tongues, and pens, by his Holy Spirit, and giving them not only ability, but authority, to declare such things in his name, and to preface what they say with, *Thus saith the Lord.* In this sense it is said, The prophecy of scripture *came not in old time by the will of man,* as other pious moral discourses might, *but holy men spoke* and wrote *as they were moved by the Holy Ghost,* 2 Pt. 1:20, 21. The same Holy Spirit that moved upon the face of the waters to produce the world moved upon the minds of the prophets to produce the Bible.

Now I think it is worthy to be observed that all nations, having had some sense of God and religion, have likewise had a notion of prophets and prophecy, have had a veneration for them, and a desire and expectation of acquaintance and communion with the gods they worshipped in that way. Witness their oracles, their augurs, and the many arts of divination they had in use among them in all the ages ad all the countries of the world.

It is commonly urged as an argument against the atheists, to prove that there is a God, That all nations of the world acknowledged some god or other, some Being above them, to be worshipped and prayed to, to be trusted in and praised; the most ignorant and barbarous nations could not avoid the knowledge of it; the most learned and polite nations could not avoid the belief of it. And this is a sufficient proof of the general and unanimous consent of mankind to this truth, though far the greatest part of men made to themselves gods which yet were no gods. Now I think it may be urged with equal force against the Deists, for the proof of a divine revelation, that all nations of the world had, and had veneration for, that which they at least took to e a divine revelation, and could not live without it, though in this also they became *vain in their imaginations, and their foolish heart was darkened.* But, if there were not a true deity and a true prophecy, there would never have been pretended deities and counterfeit prophecies.

Lycurgus and Numa, those two great lawgivers of the Spartan and Roman commonwealths, brought their people to an observance of their laws by possessing them with a notion that they had them by divine revelation, and so making it a point of religion to observe them. And those that have been ever so little conversant with the Greek and Roman histories, as well as with the more ancient ones of Chaldea and Egypt cannot but remember what a profound deference their princes and great commanders, and not their unthinking commonalty only, paid to the oracles and prophets, and the prognostications of their soothsayers, which, in all cases of importance, were consulted with abundance of gravity and solemnity, and how often the resolutions of councils and the motions of mighty armies turned upon them, though they appeared ever so groundless and farfetched.

There is a full account given by that learned philosopher and physician Caspar Peucer (De Praecipuis Divinationum Generibus, *A.* 1591) of the many kinds of divination and prediction used among the Gentiles, by which they took on them to tell the fortune both of states and particular persons. They were all, he says, reduced by Plato to two heads: *Divinatio Mantikē,* which was a kind of inspiration, or was though to be so, the prophet or prophetess foretelling things to come by an internal *flatus* or fury; such was the oracle of Apollo at Delphos, and that of Jupiter Trophonius, which, with others like them, were famous for many ages, during the prevalency of the kingdom of darkness, but (as appears by some of the Pagan writers themselves) they were all silenced and struck dumb, when the gospel (that truly divine oracle) began to be preached to the nations. The other kind of divination was that which he calls *Oiōnistikē,* which was a prognostication by signs, according to rules of art, as by the flight of birds, the entrails of beasts, by stars or meteors, and abundance of ominous accidents, with which a foolish world was miserably imposed upon. A large account of this matter we have also in the late learned dissertations of Anton. Van Dale, to which I refer the reader (De *Verâ ac Falsâ Prophetiâ, A.* 1696). But nothing of this kind made a greater noise in the Gentile world than the oracles of the Sibyls and their prophecies. Their name signifies *a divine counsel: Sibyllae,* qu. *Siobulae, Sios,* in the Aeolic dialect, being put for *Theos.* Peucer says, "Almost every nation had its Sibyls, but those of Greece were most celebrated." They lived in several ages; the most ancient is said to be the *Sibylla Delphica,* who lived before the Trojan war, or about that time. The *Sibylla Erythrea* was the most noted; she lived about the time of Alexander the Great. But it the *Sibylla Cumana* of whom the story goes that she presented herself, and nine books of oracles, to Tarquinius Superbus, which she offered to sell him at so vast a rate that he refused to purchase them, upon which she burnt three, and, upon his second refusal, three more, but made him give the same rate for the remaining three, which were deposited with great care in the Capitol. But, those being afterwards burnt accidentally with the Capitol, a collection was made of other Sibylline oracles, and those are they which Virgil refers to in his fourth Eclogue

(Vid. Virg. Aeneid. *lib.* 6). All the oracles of the Sibyls that are extant were put together, and published, in Holland, not many years ago, by Seryatius Gallaeus, in Greek and Latin, with large and learned notes, together with all that could be met with of the metrical oracles that go under the names of Jupiter, Apollo, Serapis, and others, by Joannes Opsopaeus.

The oracles of the Sibyls were appealed to by many of the fathers for the confirmation of the Christian religion. Justin Martyr (Ad Graecos Cohortat. *juxta finem.*) appeals with a great deal of assurance, persuading the Greeks to give credit to that ancient Sibyl, whose works were extant all the world over; and to their testimony, and that of Hydaspis, he appeals concerning the general conflagration and the torments of hell. Clemens Alexandrinus (Apol. 2. *p.* mihi. 66. *l*) often quotes the Sibyls' verses with great respect; so does Lactantius (Quaest. et Respons. p. 436); St. Austin (Aug. de Div. Dei, *lib.* 18, *cap.* 23), *De Civitate Dei*, has the famous acrostic at large, said to be one of the oracles of the *Sibylla Erythrea*, the first letters of the verses making *Iēsous Christos Theou hyios Sōtēr — Jesus Christ the Son of God the Saviour.* Divers passages they produce out of those oracles which expressly foretel the coming of the Messiah, his being born of a virgin, his miracles, his sufferings, particularly his being buffeted, spit upon, crowned with thorns, having vinegar and gall given him to drink, etc. Whether these oracles were genuine and authentic or no has been much controverted among the learned. Baronius and the popish writers generally admit and applaud them, and build much upon them; so do some protestant writers; Isaac Vossius has written a great deal to support the reputation of them, and (as I find him quoted by Van Dale) will needs have it that they were formerly a part of the canon of scripture; and a learned prelate of our own nation, Bishop Montague, pleads largely, and with great assurance, for their authority, and is of opinion that some of them were divinely inspired. But many learned men look upon it to be a pious fraud, as they call it, concluding that those verses of the Sibyls which speak so very expressly of Christ and the future state were forged by some Christians and imposed upon the over-credulous. Huetius (Demonstrat. *p.* 748), though of the Romish church, condemns both the ancient and more modern compositions of the Sibyls, and refers his reader, for the proof of their vanity, to the learned Blondel. Van Dale and Gallaeus look upon them to be a forgery. And the truth is they speak so much more particularly and plainly concerning our Saviour and the future state than any of the prophets of the Old Testament do, that we must conclude St. Paul, who was the apostle of the Gentiles, guilty not only of a very great omission (that in all his preaching of the gospel to the Gentiles, and in all his epistles to the Gentile churches, he never so much as mentions the prophecies of the Sibyls, nor vouches their authority, as he does that of the Old-Testament prophets, in his preaching and writing to the Jews), but likewise of a very great mistake, in making it the particular advantage which the Jews had above the Gentiles that *to them were committed the oracles of God* (Rom. 3:1, 2), and that they were the children of the prophets, while he speaks of the Gentiles as sitting in darkness and being afar off. We cannot conceive that heathen women, and those actuated by daemons, should speak more clearly and fully of the Messiah than those holy men did who, we are sure, were moved by the Holy Ghost, nor that the Gentiles should be entrusted with larger and earlier discoveries of the great salvation than that people of whom, as concerning the flesh, Christ was to come. But enough, if not more than enough, of the pretenders to prophecy. It is a good remark which the learned Gallaeus makes upon the great veneration which the Romans had for the oracles of the Sibyls, for which he quotes Dionysius Halicarnassaeus, *Ouden oute Rōmaioi phylattousin, oute hosion ktēma oute hieron, hōs ta Sibylleia thesphata — The Romans preserve nothing with such sacred care, nor do they hold any thing in such high estimation, as the Sibylline oracles. Hi si pro vitreis suis thesauris adeò decertarunt, quid nos pro genuinis nostris, à Deo inspiratis? — If they had such a value for these counterfeits, how precious should the true treasure of the divine oracles be to us!* Of these we come next to speak.

Prophecy, we are sure, was of equal date with the church; for *faith comes,* not by thinking and seeing, as philosophy does, but by hearing, *by hearing the word of God,* Rom. 10:17. In the antediluvian period Adam received divine revelation in the promise of the Seed of the woman, and no doubt communicated it in the name of the Lord, to his seed, and was prophet, as well as priest, to his numerous family. Enoch was a prophet, and foretold perhaps the deluge, certainly the last judgment, that of the great day. *Behold the Lord comes,* Jude 14. When men began, as a church, to *call upon the name of the Lord* (Gen. 4:26), or to call themselves by his name, they were blessed with prophets, for the *prophecy came in old time* (2 Pt. 1:21); it is venerable for its antiquity. When God renewed his covenant of providence (and that a figure of the covenant of grace) with Noah and his sons, we soon after find Noah, as a prophet, foretelling, not only the servitude of Canaan, but God's enlarging Japhet by Christ, and his dwelling in the tents of Shem, Gen. 9:26, 27. And when, upon the general revolt of mankind to idolatry (as, in the former period, upon the apostasy of Cain), God distinguished a church for himself by the call of Abraham, and by his covenant with him and his seed, he conferred upon him and the other patriarchs the spirit of prophecy; for, when he reproved kings for their sakes, he said, *Touch not my anointed,* who have received that unction from the Holy One, and *do my prophets no harm,* Ps. 105:14, 15. And of Abraham he said expressly, *He is a prophet* (Gen. 20:7); and it was with a prophetic eye, as a seer, that *Abraham saw Christ's day* (Jn. 8:56), saw it as so great a distance, and yet with so great an assurance triumphed in it. And Stephen seems to speak of the first settling of a correspondence between him and God, by which he was established to be a prophet, when he says, *The God of glory appeared to him* (Acts 7:2), appeared in glory. Jacob, upon his death-bed, as a prophet, told his sons *what should befal them in the last days* (Gen. 49:1), and spoke very particularly concerning the Messiah.

Hitherto was the infancy of the church, and with it of prophecy; it was the dawning of that day; and that morning-light owed its rise to the Sun of righteousness, though he rose not till long after, but it shone more and more. During the bondage of Israel in Egypt, this, as other glories of the church, was eclipsed; but, as the church made a considerable and memorable advance in the deliverance of Israel out of Egypt and the forming of them into a people, so did the Spirit of prophecy in Moses, the illustrious instrument employed in that great service; and it was by that Spirit that he performed that service; so it is said, Hos. 12:13, *By a prophet the Lord brought Israel out of Egypt, and by a prophet was he preserved* through the wilderness to Canaan, that is, by Moses as a prophet. It appears, by what God said to Aaron, that there were then other prophets among them, to whom God made known himself and his will in dreams

and visions (Num. 12:6), but to Moses he spoke in a peculiar manner, *mouth to mouth, even apparently, and not in dark speeches,* Num. 12:8. Nay, such a plentiful effusion was there of the Spirit of prophecy at that time (because Moses was such a prophet as was to be a type of Christ the great prophet) that some of his Spirit was put upon seventy elders of Israel at once, and *they prophesied,* Num. 11:25. What they said was extraordinary, and not only under the direction of a prophetic inspiration, but under the constraint of a prophetic impulse, as appears by the case of Eldad and Meded.

When Moses, that great prophet, was laying down his office, he promised Israel that the *Lord God would raise them up a prophet of their brethren like unto him,* Deu. 18:15, 18. In these words, says the learned Bishop Stillingfleet (Orig. Sacr. *B.* 2, *c.* 4 — though, in their full and complete sense, they relate to Christ, and to him they are more than once applied in the New Testament), there is included a promise of an order of prophets, which should succeed Moses in the Jewish church, and be the *logia zōnta — the living oracles* among them (Acts 7:38), by which they might know the mind of God; for, in the next words, he lays down rules for the trial of prophets, whether what they said was of God or no, and it is observable that that promise comes in immediately upon an express prohibition of the Pagan rites of divination and the consulting of wizards and familiar spirits: "You shall not need to do that" (said Moses), "for, to your much better satisfaction, you shall have prophets divinely inspired, by whom you may know from God himself both what to do and what to expect." But as Jacob's dying prophecy concerning the sceptre in Judah, and the lawgiver between his feet, did not begin to be remarkably fulfilled till David's time, most of the Judges being of other tribes, so Moses's promise of a succession of prophets began not to receive its accomplishment till Samuel's time, a little before the other promise began to emerge and operate; and it was an introduction to the other, for it was by Samuel, as a prophet, that David was anointed king, which was an intimation that the prophetical office of our Redeemer should make way, both in the world and in the heart, for his kingly office; and therefore when he was asked, *Art thou a king?* (Jn. 18:37) he answered, not evasively, but very pertinently, *I came to bear witness to the truth,* and so to rule as a king purely by the power of truth.

During the government of the Judges there was a pouring out of the Spirit, but more as a Spirit of skill and courage for war than as a Spirit of prophecy. Deborah is indeed called *prophetess,* because of her extraordinary qualifications for judging Israel; but that is the only mention of prophecy, that I remember, in all the book of *Judges.* Extraordinary messages were sent by angels, as to Gideon and Manoah; and it is expressly said that before the word of the Lord came to Samuel (1 Sa. 3:1) it was *precious,* it was very scarce, there was *no open vision.* And it was therefore with more than ordinary solemnity that the word of the Lord came first to Samuel; and by degrees notice and assurance were given to all Israel *that Samuel was established to be a prophet of the Lord,* 1 Sa. 3:20. In Samuel's time, and by him, the schools of the prophets were erected, by which prophecy was dignified and provision made for a succession of prophets; for it should seem that in those colleges, hopeful young men were bred up in devotion, in a constant attendance upon the instruction the prophets gave from God, and under a strict discipline, as candidates, or probationers, for prophecy, who were called *the sons of the prophets;* and their religious exercises of prayer, conference, and psalmody especially, are called prophesyings; and their praefect, or president, is called *their father,* 1 Sa. 10:12. Out of these God ordinarily chose the prophets he sent; and yet not always: Amos was no prophet nor prophet's son (Amon 7:14), had not his education in the schools of the prophets, and yet was commissioned to go on God's errands, and, (which is observable) though he had not academical education himself, yet he seems to speak of it with great respect when he reckons it among the favours God had bestowed upon Israel that he *raised up of their sons for prophets and of their young men for Nazarites,* Amos 2:11.

It is worth noting that when the glory of the priesthood was eclipsed by the iniquity of the house of Eli, the desolations of Shiloh, and the obscurity of the ark, there was then a more plentiful effusion of the Spirit of prophecy than had been before; a standing ministry of another kind was thereby erected, and a succession of it kept up. And thus afterwards, in the kingdom of the ten tribes, where there was no legal priesthood at all, yet there were prophets and prophets; sons; in Ahab's time we meet with a hundred of them, whom Obadiah his by *fifty in a cave,* 1 Ki. 18:4. When the people of God, who desired to know his mind, were deprived of one way of instruction, God furnished them with another, and a less ceremonious one; for he left not himself without witness, nor them without a guide. And when they had no temple or altar that they could attend upon with any safety or satisfaction then had private meetings at the prophets' houses, to which the devout faithful worshippers of God resorted (as we find the good Shunamite did, 2 Ki. 4:23), and where they kept their new-moons and their sabbaths, comfortably, and to their edification.

David was himself a prophet; so St. Peter calls him (Acts 2:30); and, though we read not of God's speaking to him by dreams and visions, yet we are sure that *the Spirit of the Lord spoke by him, and his word was in his tongue* (2 Sa. 23:2), and he had those about him that were seers, that were his seers, as Gad and Iddo, that brought him messages from God, and wrote the history of his times. And now the productions of the Spirit of prophecy were translated into the service of the temple, not only in the model of the house which the Lord made David *understand in writing by his hand upon him* (1 Chr. 28:19), but in the worship performed there; for there we find Asaph, Heman, and Jeduthun, prophesying with harps and other musical instruments, according to the order of the king, not to foretel things to come, but to *give thanks* and to *praise the Lord* (1 Chr. 25:1–3); yet, in their psalms, they spoke much of Christ and his kingdom, and the glory to be revealed.

In the succeeding reigns, both of Judah and Israel, we frequently meet with prophets sent on particular errands to Rehoboam, Jeroboam, Asa, and other kings, who, it is probable, instructed the people in the things of God at other times, though it is not recorded. But, prophecy growing into contempt with many, God revived the honour of it, and put a new lustre upon it, in the power given to Elijah and Elisha to work miracles, and the great things that God did by them for the confirming of the people's faith in it, and the awakening of their regard to it, 2 Ki. 2:3, 4:1, 38; 5:22; 6:1. In their time, and by their agency, it should seem, the schools of the prophets were revived, and we find sons of the prophets, fellows of those sacred colleges, employed in carrying messages to the great men, as to Ahab (1 Ki. 20:35), and to Jehu, 2 Ki. 9:1.

Hitherto, the prophets of the Lord delivered their messages by word of mouth, only we read of one writing which came from Elijah the prophet to Jehoram king of Israel, 2 Chr. 21:12. The histories of those times which are left us were compiled by prophets, under a divine direction; and, when the Old Testament is divided into the law and the Prophets, the historical books are, for that reason, reckoned among the prophets. But, in the later times of the kingdoms of Judah and Israel, some of the prophets were divinely inspired to write their prophecies, or abstracts of them, and to leave them upon record, for the benefit of after-ages, that the children who should be born might praise the Lord for them, and, by comparing the event with the prediction, might have their faith confirmed. And, probably, those later prophets spoke more fully and plainly of the Messiah and his kingdom than their predecessors had done, and for that reason their prophecies were put in writing, not only for the encouragement of the pious Jews that looked for the consolation of Israel, but for the use of us Christians, upon whom the ends of the world have come, as David's psalms had been for the same reason, that the Old Testament and the New might mutually give light and lustre to each other. Many other faithful prophets there were at the same time, who spoke in God's name, who did not commit their prophecies to writing, but were of those whom God sent, rising up betimes and sending them, the contempt of whom, and of their messages, brought ruin without remedy upon that sottish people, that knew not the day of their visitation. In their captivity they had some prophets, some to *show them how long;* and though it was not by a prophet, like Moses, that they were brought out of Babylon, as they had been out of Egypt, but by Joshua the high priest first, and afterwards by Ezra the scribe, to show that God can do his work by ordinary means when he pleases, yet, soon after their return, the Spirit of prophecy was poured out plentifully, and continued (according to the Jews' computation) forty years in the second temple, but ceased in Malachi. Then (say the rabbin) *the Holy Spirit was taken from Israel,* and they had the benefit only of the *Bathkol — the daughter of a voice,* that is, a voice from heaven, which they look upon to be the lowest degree of divine revelation. Now herein they are witnesses against themselves for rejecting the true Messiah, for our Lord Jesus, and he only was spoken to by a voice from heaven at his baptism, his transfiguration, and his entrance on his sufferings.

In John the Baptist prophecy revived, and therefore in him the gospel is said to begin, when the church had had no prophets for above 300 years. We have not only the *vox populi — the voice of the people* to prove John a prophet, for all the people counted him so, but *vox Dei — the voice of God* too; for Christ calls him a prophet, Mt. 11:9, 10. He had an extraordinary commission from God to call people to repentance, was *filled with the Holy Ghost from his mother's womb,* and was *therefore* called the *prophet of the Highest,* because he *went before the face of the Lord, to prepare his way* (Lu. 1:15, 16); and though he did no miracle, nor gave any sign or wonder, yet this proved him a true prophet, *that all he said of Christ was true,* Jn. 10:41. Nay, and *this* proved him more than a prophet, than any of the other prophets, that whereas by other prophets Christ was discovered as at a great distance, by him he was discovered as already come, and he was enabled to say, *Behold the Lamb of God.* But after the ascension of our Lord Jesus there was a more plentiful effusion of the Spirit of prophecy than ever before; then was the promise fulfilled that God would *pour out his Spirit upon all flesh* (and not as hitherto upon the Jews only), and their *sons and their daughters should prophesy,* Acts 2:16, etc. The gift of tongues was one new product of the Spirit of prophecy, and given for a particular reason, that, the Jewish pale being taken down, all nations might be brought into the church. These and other gifts of prophecy, being for a sign, have long since ceased and laid aside, and we have no encouragement to expect the revival of them; but, on the contrary, are directed to call the scriptures the *more sure word of prophecy,* more sure than voices from heaven; and to them we are directed to *take heed,* to search them, and to hold them fast, 2 Pt. 1:19. All God's spiritual Israel know that they are established to be the *oracles of God* (1 Sa. 3:20), and if any add to, or take from, the book of that prophecy, they may read their doom in the close of it; God shall take blessings from them, and add curses to them, Rev. 22:18, 19).

Now concerning the prophets of the Old Testament, whose writings are before us, observe,

I. That they were all holy men. We are assured by the apostle that *the prophecy came in old time by holy men of God* (and *men of God* they were commonly called, because they were devoted to him), *who spoke as they were moved by the Holy Ghost.* They were men, *subject to like passions as we are* (so Elijah, one of the greatest of them, is said to have been, Jam. 5:17); but they were holy men, men that in the temper of their minds, and the tenour of their lives, were examples of serious piety. Though there were many pretenders, that, without warrant, said *Thus saith the Lord,* when he sent them not, and some that prophesied in Christ's name, but he never knew them, and they indeed were workers of iniquity (Mt. 7:22, 23), and though the cursing blaspheming lips of Balaam and Caiaphas, even when they actually designed mischief, were over-ruled to speak oracles, yet none were employed and commissioned to speak as prophets but those that had received the Spirit of grace and sanctification; for holiness becomes God's house. The Jewish doctors universally agree in this rule, That the Spirit of prophecy never rests upon any but a holy and wise man, and one whose passions are allayed (see Mr. Smith on Prophecy), or, as others express it, a humble man and a man of fortitude, that is, one that has power to keep his sensual animal part in due subjection to religion and right reason. And some of them (Gemara Schab. *c.* 2) give this rule, That the Spirit of prophecy does not reside where there are either, on the one hand, grief and melancholy, or, on the other hand, laughter and lightness of behaviour, and impertinent idle talk: and it is commonly observed by them, both from the musical instruments used in the schools of the prophets in Samuel's time and from the instance of Elisha's calling for a minstrel (2 Ki. 3:15), that the divine presence does not reside with sadness, but with cheerfulness, and Elisha, they say, had not yet recovered himself from the sorrow he conceived at parting with Elijah. They have also a tradition (but I know no ground for it) that all the while Jacob mourned for Joseph, the Shechinah, or Holy Spirit, withdrew from him. Yet I believe that when David intimates that by his sin in the matter of Uriah he had lost the right Spirit, and the free Spirit, Ps. 51:10, 12 (which therefore he begs might be renewed in him and restored to him), it was not because he was under grief, but because he was under guilt. And therefore, in order to the return of that right and free Spirit, he prays that God would create in him a clean heart.

II. That they had all a full assurance in themselves of their divine mission; and (though they could not always prevail to satisfy others) they were abundantly satisfied themselves that what they delivered as from God, and in his name, was indeed from him; and with the same assurance did the apostles speak of the word of life, as that which they had heard, and seen, and looked on, and which their hands had handled, 1 Jn. 1:1. Nathan spoke from himself when he encouraged David to build the temple, but afterwards knew he spoke from God when, in his name, he forbade him to do it. God had various ways of making known to his prophets the messages they were to deliver to his people; it should seem, ordinarily, to have been by the ministry of angels. In the Apocalypse Christ is expressly said to have *signified by his angel to his servant John,* Rev. 1:1. It was sometimes done in a vision when the prophet was awake, sometimes in a dream when the prophet was asleep, and sometimes by a secret but strong impression upon the mind of the prophet. But Maimonides has laid down, as a maxim, That all prophecy makes itself known to the prophet that it is prophecy indeed; that is, says another of the rabbin, By the vigour and liveliness of the perception whereby he apprehends the thing propounded (which Jeremiah intimates when he says, *The word of the Lord was as a fire in my bones,* Jer. 20:9), and therefore they always spoke with great assurance, knowing they should be justified, Isa. 1:7.

III. That in their prophesying, both in receiving their message from God and in delivering it to the people, they always kept possession of their own souls. Dan. 10:8. Though sometimes their bodily strength was overpowered by the abundance of the revelations, and their eyes were dazzled with the visionary light, as in the instances of Daniel and John (Rev. 1:17), yet still their understanding remained with them, and the free exercise of their reason. This is excellently well expressed by a learned writer of our own (Smith on Prophecy, p. 190): "The prophetical Spirit, seating itself in the rational powers as well as in the imagination, did never alienate the mind, but inform and enlighten it; and those that were actuated by it always maintained a clearness and consistency of reason, with strength and solidity of judgment. "For" (says he afterwards — Pag. 266) "God did not make use of idiots or fools to reveal his will by, but such whose intellects were entire and perfect; and he imprinted such a clear copy of his truth upon them as that it became their own sense, being digested fully into their understandings, so that they were able to deliver and represent it to others as truly as any can paint forth his own thoughts." God's messengers were speaking men, not speaking trumpets. The Fathers frequently took notice of this difference between the prophets of the Lord and the false prophets — that the pretenders to prophecy (who either were actuated by an evil spirit or were under the force of a heated imagination) underwent alienations of mind, and delivered what they had to say in the utmost agitation and disorder, as the Pythian prophetess, who delivered her infernal oracles with many antic gestures, tearing her hair and foaming at the mouth. And by this rule they condemned the Montanists, who pretended to prophecy, in the second century, that what they said was in a way of ecstasy, not like rational men, but like men in a frenzy. Chrysostom (in 1 Co. 12:1), having described the furious violent motions of the pretenders to prophecy, adds, *Ho de Prophētēs ouch houtōs — A true prophet does not do so. Sed mente sobriâ, et constanti animi staut, et intelligens quae profert, omnia pronunciat — He understands what he utters, and utters it soberly and calmly.* And Jerome, in his preface to his Commentaries upon Nahum, observes that it is called *the book of the vision of Nahum. Non enim loquitur en ekstasei,* sed est liber intelligentis omnia quae loquitur — For he speaks not in an ecstasy, but as one who understands every thing he says. And again (Prolog. in Habac.), *Non ut amens loquitur propheta, nec in morem insanientium foeminarum dat sine mente sonum — The prophet speaks not as an insane person, nor like women wrought into fury, does he utter sound without sense.*

IV. That they all aimed at one and the same thing, which was to bring people to repent of their sins and to return to God and to do their duty to him. This was the errand on which all God messengers were sent, to beat down sin, and to revive and advance serious piety. The burden of every son was, *Turn you now every one from his evil way; amend your ways and your doings, and execute judgment between a man and his neighbour,* Jer. 7:3, 5. See Zec. 7:8, 9; 8:16. The scope and design of all their prophecies were to enforce the precepts and sanctions of the law of Moses, the moral law, which is of universal and perpetual obligation. Here is nothing of the ceremonial institutes, of the carnal ordinances that were imposed only *till the times of reformation,* Heb. 9:10. Those were now waxing old and ready to vanish away; but they make it their business to press the great and *weighty matters of the law, judgment, mercy, and truth.*

V. That they all bore witness to Jesus Christ and had an eye to him. God raising up the *horn of salvation for us, in the house of his servant David,* was consonant to, and in pursuance of, what *he spoke by the mouth of his holy prophets who have been since the world began,* Lu. 1:69, 70. They prophesied of the grace that should come to us, and it was the Spirit of Christ in them, one and the same Spirit, that testified beforehand the *sufferings of Christ, and the glory that should follow,* 1 Pt. 1:10, 11. Christ was then made known, and yet comparatively hid, in the predictions of the prophets, as before in the types of the ceremonial law. And the learned Huetius (Demonstrat. Evang. p. 737) observes it as really admirable that so many persons, in different ages, should conspire with one consent, as it were, to foretel, some one particular and others another, concerning Christ, all which had, at length, their full accomplishment in him. *Ab ipsis mundi incunabulis, per quatuor annorum millia, uno ore venturum Christum praedixerunt viri complures, in ejusque ortu, vitâ, virtutibus, rebus gestis, morte, ac totâ denique Oikonomia* praemonstranda consenserunt — From the earliest period of time, for 4000 years, a great number of men have predicted the advent of Christ, and presented a harmonious statement of his birth, life, character, actions, and death, and of that economy which he came to establish.

VI. That these prophets were generally hated and abused in their several generations by those that lived with them. Stephen challenges his judges to produce an instance to the contrary: *Which of the prophets have not your fathers persecuted?* Yea, and, as it should seem, for this reason, because *they showed before of the coming of the Just One,* Acts 7:52. Some there were that trembled at the word of God in their mouths, but by the most they were ridiculed and despised, and (as ministers are now by profane people) made a jest of (Hos. 9:7); the prophet was the fool in the play. *Wherefore came this mad fellow unto thee?* (2 Ki. 9:11) said one of the captains concerning one of the sons of the prophets! The Gentiles never treated their false prophets so ill as the Jews did their true prophets, but, on the contrary, had them always in veneration. The Jews' mocking the messengers of the Lord, killing the prophets, and stoning those that were sent unto them, was as amazing unaccountable an instance of the enmity that is in the carnal mind against God as any that can be produced. And this makes their rejection of Christ's gospel the less strange, that the Spirit of prophecy, which, for many ages, was so much the glory of Israel, in every age met with so much opposition, and there were those that *always resisted the Holy Ghost* in the prophets, and *turned that glory into shame,* Acts 7:51. But this was it that was the measure-filling sin of Israel, that brought upon them both their first destruction by the Chaldeans and their final ruin by the Romans, 2 Chr. 36:16.

VII. That though men slighted these prophets, God owned them and put honour upon them. As they were men of God, his immediate servants and his messengers, so he always showed himself *the Lord God of the holy prophets* (Rev. 22:6), stood by them and strengthened them, and by his Spirit they were full of power; and those that slighted them, when they had lost them, were made to know, to their confusion, that *a prophet had been among them.* What was said of one of the primitive fathers of the prophets was true of them all, *The Lord was with them, and did let none of their words fall to the ground,* 1 Sa. 3:19. What they said by way of warning and encouragement, for the enforcing of their calls to repentance and reformation, was to be understood conditionally. When God spoke by them either, on the one hand, to build and to plant, or, on the other hand, to pluck up and pull down, the change of the people's way might produce a change of God's way (Jer. 18:7-10); such was Jonah's prophecy of Nineveh's ruin within forty days; or God might sometimes be better than his word in granting a reprieve. But what they said by way of prediction of a particular matter, and as a sign, did always come to pass exactly as it was foretold; yea, and the general predictions, sooner or later, took hold even of those that would fain have got clear of them (Zec. 1:6); for this is that which God glories in, that he *confirms the word of his servants* and *performs the counsel of his messengers,* Isa. 44:26.

In the opening these prophecies I have endeavoured to give the genuine sense of them, as far as I could reach it, by consulting the best expositors, considering the scope and coherence, and comparing spiritual things with spiritual, the spiritual things of the Old Testament with those of the New, and especially by prayer to God for the guidance and direction of the Spirit of truth. But, after all, thee are many things here *dark and hard to be understood,* concerning the certain meaning of which though I could not gain myself, much less expect to give my reader, full satisfaction, Yet I have not, with the *unlearned* and *unstable, wrested them* to the destruction of any, 2 Pt. 3:16. It is the prerogative of the *Lamb of God* to *take this book* and to *open all its seals.* I have likewise endeavoured to accommodate these prophecies to the use and service of those who desire to faith and holiness. And we shall find that whatever is *given by inspiration of God is profitable* (2 Tim. 3:16), though not all alike profitable, not all alike easy or improvable; but, when the mystery of God shall be finished, we shall see, what we are now bound to believe, that there is not one idle word in all the prophecies of this book. What God has said, as well as what he does, *we know not now, but we shall know hereafter.*

The pleasure I have had in studying and meditating upon those parts of these prophecies which are plain and practical, and especially those which are evangelical, has been an abundant balance to, and recompence for, the harder tasks we have met with in other parts that are more obscure. In many parts of this field the treasure must be dug for, as that in the mines; but in other parts the surface is covered with rich and precious products, with corn, and flocks, of which we may say, as was said of Noah, These same have comforted us greatly concerning our work and the toil of our hands, and have made it very pleasant and delightful; God grant it may be no less so to the readers!

And now let me desire the assistance of my friends, in setting up my Eben-Ezer here, in a thankful acknowledgment that hitherto the Lord has helped me. I desire to praise God that he has spared my life to finish the Old Testament, and has graciously given me some tokens of his presence with me in carrying this work, though the more I reflect upon myself the more unworthy I see myself of the honour of being thus employed, and the more need I see of Christ and his merit and grace. *Remember me, O my God! for good, and spare me according to the multitude of thy mercies.* The Lord forgive what is mine, and accept what is his own!

I purpose, if God continue my life and health, according to the measure of the grace given to me, and in a constant and entire dependence upon divine strength, to go through the New Testament in two volumes more. I intimated in my preface to the first volume that I had drawn up some expositions upon some parts of the New Testament; namely, The gospels of St. Matthew and St. John; but they are so large that, to make them bear some proportion to the rest, it is necessary that they be much contracted, so that I shall be obliged to write them all over again, and to make considerable alterations, and therefore I cannot expect they should be published but as these hitherto have been, if God permit, a volume every other year. I shall begin it now shortly, if the Lord will, and apply myself to it as closely as I can; and I earnestly desire the prayers of all that wish well to that undertaking that, if the Lord spare me to go on with it, I may be enabled to do it well, and so as that by it some may be led into the *riches of the full assurance of understanding in the mystery of God, even of the Father and of Christ,* Col. 2:2. And, if it shall please God to remove me by death before it be finished, I trust I shall be able to say not only, Welcome his blessed will, but, Welcome that blessed world, in which, though now we *know in part, and prophesy but in part, that knowledge which is perfect will come, and that which is partial will be done away* (1 Co. 13:8-10, 12), in which all our mistakes will be rectified, all our doubts resolved, all our deficiencies made up, all our endeavours in preaching, catechising, and expounding, superseded and rendered useless, and all our prayers swallowed up in everlasting praises, — in which prophecy, now so much admired, shall fail, and tongues shall cease, and the knowledge we have now shall vanish away, as the light of the morning-star does when the sun has risen, — in which we shall no longer see through a glass darkly, but face to face. In a believing, comfortable, well-grounded, expectation of that true and perfect light, I desire to continue, living and dying; in a humble and diligent preparation for it let me spend my time, and in the full enjoyment of it Oh that I may spend a glorious eternity!

July 18, 1712.   M.H.

ORIGINAL PREFACE TO VOLUME FIVE

The one half of our undertaking upon the New Testament (It may be proper to apprise the reader that the volume to which this preface was originally prefixed included the Acts of the Apostles, which in the present edition will commence the second volume, in order to secure a more equal division of the New Testament — the commentary on the remaining books being less extended than the author contemplated. — Ed.) is now, by the assistance of divine grace, finished, and presented to the reader, who, it is hoped, the Lord working with it, may hereby be somewhat helped in understanding and improving the sacred history of Christ and his apostles, and in making it, as it certainly is, the best exposition of our creed, in which these inspired writers are summed up, as is intimated by that evangelist who calls his gospel *A Declaration of those things which are most surely believed among us,* Lu. 1:1. And, as there is no part of scripture in the belief of which it concerns more to be established, so there is none with which the generality of Christians are more conversant, or which they speak of more frequently. It is therefore our duty, by constant pains in meditation and prayer, to come to an intimate acquaintance with the true intent and meaning of these narratives, what our concern is in them, and what we are to build upon them and draw from them; that we may not rest in such a knowledge of them as that which we had when in our childhood we were taught to read English out of the translation and Greek out of the originals of these books. We ought to know them as the physician does his dispensatory, the lawyer his books of reports, and the sailor his chart and compass; that is, to know how to make use of them in that to which we apply ourselves as our business in this world, which is to serve God here and enjoy him hereafter, and both in Christ the Mediator.

The great designs of the Christian institutes (of which these books are the fountains and foundations) were, to reduce the children of men to the fear and love of God, as the commanding active principle of their observance of him, and obedience to him, — to show them the way of their reconciliation to him and acceptance with him, and to bring them under obligations to Jesus Christ as Mediator, and thereby to engage them to all instances of devotion towards God and justice and charity towards all men, in conformity to the example of Christ, in obedience to his law, and in pursuance of his great intentions. What therefore I have endeavoured here has been with this view, to make these writings serviceable to the faith, holiness, and comfort of good Christians.

Now that these writings, thus made use of to serve these great and noble designs, may have their due influence upon us, it concerns us to be well established in our belief of their divine origin. And here we have to do with two sorts of people. Some embrace the Old Testament, but set that up in opposition to the New, pleading that, if that be right, this is wrong; and these are the Jews. Others, though they live in a Christian nation, and by baptism wear the Christian name, yet, under pretence of freedom of thought, despise Christianity, and consequently reject the New Testament, and therefore the Old of course. I confess it is strange that any now who receive the Old Testament should reject the New, since, besides all the particular proofs of the divine authority of the New Testament, there is such an admirable harmony between it and the Old. It agrees with the Old in all the main intentions of it, refers to it, builds upon it, shows the accomplishment of its types and prophecies, and thereby is the perfection and crown of it. Nay, if it be not true, the Old Testament must be false, and all the glorious promises which shine so brightly in it, and the performance of which was limited within certain periods of time, must be a great delusion, which we are sure they are not, and therefore must embrace the New Testament to support the reputation of the Old.

Those things in the Old Testament which the New Testament lays aside are the peculiarity of the Jewish nation and the observances of the ceremonial law, both which certainly were of divine appointment; and yet the New Testament does not at all clash with the Old; for,

1. They were always designed to be laid aside in the fulness of time. No other is to be expected than that the morning-star should disappear when the sun rises; and the latter parts of the Old Testament often speak of the laying aside of those things, and of the calling in of the Gentiles.

2. They were very honourable laid aside, and rather exchanged for that which was more noble and excellent, more divine and heavenly. The Jewish church was swallowed up in the Christian, the mosaic ritual in evangelical institutions. So that the New Testament is no more the undoing of the Old than the sending of a youth to the university is the undoing of his education in the grammar-school.

3. Providence soon determined this controversy (which is the only thing that seemed a controversy between the Old Testament and the New) by the destruction of Jerusalem, the desolations of the temple, the dissolution of the temple-service, and the total dispersion of all the remains of the Jewish nation, with a judicial defeat of all the attempts to incorporate it again, now for above 1600 years; and this according to the express predictions of Christ, a little before his death. And, as Christ would not have the doctrine of his being the Messiah much insisted on till the great conclusive proof of it was given by his resurrection from the dead, so the repeal of the ceremonial law, as to the Jews, was not much insisted on, but their keeping up the observation of it was connived at, till the great conclusive proof of its repeal was given by the destruction of Jerusalem, which made the observation of it for ever impracticable. And the manifest tokens of divine wrath which the Jews, considered as a people, even notwithstanding the prosperity of particular persons among them, continue under to this day, is a proof, not only of the truth of Christ's predictions concerning them, but that they lie under a greater guilt than that of idolatry (for which they lay under a desolation of 70 years), and this can be no other than crucifying Christ, and rejecting his gospel.

Thus evident it is that, in our expounding of the New Testament, we are not undoing what we did in expounding the Old; so far from it that we may appeal to the law and the prophets for the confirmation of the great truth which the gospels are written to prove — That our Lord Jesus is the Messiah promised to the fathers, who should come, and we are to look for no other. For though his appearing did not answer the expectation of the carnal Jews, who looked for a Messiah in external pomp and power, yet it exactly answered all the types, prophecies, and promises, of the Old Testament, which all had their accomplishment in him; and even his ignominious sufferings, which are the greatest stumbling-block to the Jews, were foretold concerning the Messiah; so that if he had not submitted to them we had failed in our proof; so fat it is from being weakened by them. Bishop Kidder's *Demonstration of the Christian's Messiah* has abundantly made out this truth, and answered the cavils (for such they are, rather than arguments) of the Jews against it, above any in our language.

But we live in an age when Christianity and the New Testament are more virulently and daringly attacked by some within their own bowels than by those upon their borders. Never were Moses and his writings so arraigned and ridiculed by any Jews, or Mahomet and his Alcoran by any Mussulmans, as Christ and his gospel by men that are baptized and called Christians; and this, not under colour of any other divine revelation, but in contempt and defiance of all divine revelation; and not by way of complaint that they meet with that which shocks their faith, and which, through their own weakness, they cannot get over, and therefore desire to be instructed in, and helped in the understanding of, and the reconciling of them to the truth which they have received, but by way of resolute opposition, as if they looked upon it as their enemy, and were resolved by all means possible to be the ruin of it, though they cannot say what evil it has done to the world or to them. If the pretence of it has transported many in the church of Rome into such corruptions of worship and cruelties of government as are indeed the scandal of human nature, yet, instead of being thereby prejudiced against pure Christianity, they should the rather appear more vigorously in defence of it, when they see so excellent an institution as this is in itself so basely abused and misrepresented. They pretend to a liberty of thought in their opposition to Christianity, and would be distinguished by the name of free-thinkers. I will not here go about to produce the arguments which, to all that are not wilfully ignorant and prejudiced against the truth, are sufficient to prove the divine origin and authority of the doctrine of Christ. The learned find much satisfaction in reading the apologies of the ancients for the Christian religion, when it was struggling with the polytheism and idolatry of the Gentiles. Justin Martyr and Tertullian, Lactantius and Minutius Felix, wrote admirable in defence of Christianity, when it was further sealed by the blood of the martyrs. But its patrons and advocates in the present day have another sort of enemies to deal with. The antiquity of the pagan theology, its universal prevalence, the edicts of princes, and the traditions and usages of the country, are not now objected to Christianity; but I know not what imaginary freedom of thought, and an unheard-of privilege of human nature, are assumed, not to be bound by any divine revelation whatsoever. Now it is easy to make out,

1. That those who would be thought thus to maintain a liberty of thinking as one of the privileges of human nature, and in defence of which they will take up arms against God himself, do not themselves think freely, nor give others leave to do so. In some of them a resolute indulgence of themselves in those vicious courses which they know the gospel if they admit it will make very uneasy to them, and a secret enmity to a holy heavenly mind and life, forbid them all free thought; for so strong a prejudice have their lusts and passions laid them under against the laws of Christ that they find themselves under a necessity of opposing the truths of Christ, upon which these laws are founded. *Perit judicium, quando res transit in affectum* — The judgment is overcome, when the decision is referred to the affections. Right or wrong, Christ's bonds must be broken, and his cords cast from them; and therefore, how evident soever the premises be, the conclusion must be denied, if it tend to fasten these bands and cords upon them; and where is the freedom of thought then? *While they promise themselves liberty, they themselves are the servants of corruption; for of whom a man is overcome of the same is he brought into bondage.* In others of them, a reigning pride and affectation of singularity, and a spirit of contradiction, those lusts of the mind, which are as impetuous and imperious as any of the lusts of the flesh and of the world, forbid a freedom of thinking, and enslave the soul in all its enquiries after religion. Those can no more think freely who resolve they will think by themselves than those can who resolve to think with their neighbours. Nor will they give others liberty to think freely; for it is not by reason and argument that they go about to convince us, but by jest and banter, and exposing Christianity and its serious professors to contempt. Now, considering how natural it is to most men to be jealous for their reputation, this is as great an imposition as can possibly be; and the unthinking are as much kept from free-thinking by the fear of being ridiculed in the club of those who set up for oracles in reason as by the fear of being cursed, excommunicated, and anathematized, by the counsel of those who set up for oracles in religion. And where is the free-thinking then?

2. That those who will allow themselves a true liberty of thinking, and will think seriously, cannot but embrace all Christ's sayings, as *faithful*, and well *worthy of all acceptation*. Let the corrupt bias of the carnal heart towards the world, and the flesh, and self (the most presumptuous idol of the three) be taken away, and let the doctrine of Christ be proposed first in its true colours, as Christ and his apostles have given it to us, and in its true light, with all its proper evidence, intrinsic and extrinsic; and then let the capable soul freely use its rational powers and faculties, and by the operation of the Spirit of grace, who alone works faith in all that believe, even the high thought, when once it becomes a free thought, freed from the bondage of sin and corruption, will, by a pleasing and happy power, be captivated, and brought into obedience to Christ; and, when he thus makes it free, it will be *free indeed*. Let any one who will give himself leave to think impartially, and be at the pains to think closely, read Mr. Baxter's *Reasons for the Christian Religion*, and he will find both that it goes to the bottom, and lays the foundation deep and firm, and also that it brings forth the top-stone in a believer's consent to God in Christ, to the satisfaction of any that are truly concerned about their souls and another world. The proofs of the truths of the gospel have been excellently well methodized, and enforced likewise, by bishop Stillingfleet, in his *Origines Sacrae;* by Grotius, in his book of the *Truth of the Christian Religion;* by Dr. Whitby, in his General Preface to his *Commentary on the New Testament;* and of late by Mr. Ditton, very argumentatively, in his discourse concerning

the Resurrection of Jesus Christ; and many others have herein done worthily. And I will not believe any man who rejects the New Testament and the Christian religion to have thought freely upon the subject, unless he has, with humility, seriousness, and prayer to God for direction, deliberately read these or the like books, which, it is certain, were written both with liberty and clearness of thought.

For my own part, if my thoughts were worth any one's notice, I do declare I have thought of this great concern with all the liberty that a reasonable soul can pretend to, or desire; and the result is that the more I think, and the more freely I think, the more fully I am satisfied that the Christian religion is the true religion, and that which, if I submit my soul sincerely to it, I may venture my soul confidently upon. For when I think freely,

1. I cannot but think that the God who made man a reasonable creature by his power has a right to rule him by his law, and to oblige him to keep his inferior faculties of appetite and passion, together with the capacities of thought and speech, in due subjection to the superior powers of reason and conscience. And, when I look into my own heart, I cannot but think that it was this which my Maker designed in the order and frame of my soul, and that herein he intended to support his own dominion in me.

2. I cannot but think that my happiness is bound up in the favour of God, and that his favour will, or will not, be towards me, according as I do, or do not, comply with the laws and ends of my creation, — that I am accountable to this God, and that from him my judgment proceeds, not only fr this world, but for my everlasting state.

3. I cannot but think that my nature is very unlike what the nature of man was as it came out of the Creator's hands, — that it is degenerated from its primitive purity and rectitude. I find in myself a natural aversion to my duty, and to spiritual and divine exercises, and a propensity to that which is evil, such an inclination towards the world and the flesh as amounts to a propensity to backslide from the living God.

4. I cannot but think that I am therefore, by nature, thrown out of the favour of God; for though I think he is a gracious and merciful God, yet I think he is also a just and holy God, and that I am become, by sin, both odious to his holiness and obnoxious to his justice. I should not think freely, but very partially, if I should think otherwise. I think I am guilty before God, have sinned, and come short of glorifying him, and of being glorified with him.

5. I cannot but think that, without some special discovery of God's will concerning me, and good-will to me, I cannot possibly recover his favour, be reconciled to him, or be so far restored to my primitive rectitude as to be capable of serving my Creator, and answering the ends of my creation, and becoming fit for another world; for the bounties of Providence to me, in common with the inferior creatures, cannot serve either as assurances that God is reconciled tome or means to reconcile me to God.

6. I cannot but think that the way of salvation, both from the guilt and from the power of sin, by Jesus Christ, and his mediation between God and man, as it is revealed by the New Testament, is admirable will fitted to all the exigencies of my case, to restore me both to the favour of God and to the government and enjoyment of myself. Here I see a proper method for the removing of the guilt of sin (that I may not die by the sentence of the law) by the all-sufficient merit and righteousness of the Son of God in our nature, and for the breaking of the power of sin (that I may not die by my own disease) by the all-sufficient influence and operation of the Spirit of God upon our nature. Every malady has herein its remedy, every grievance is hereby redressed, and in such a way as advances the honour of all the divine attributes and is suited and accommodated to human nature.

7. I cannot but think that what I find in myself of natural religion does evidently bear testimony to the Christian religion; for all that truth which is discovered to me by the light of nature is confirmed, and more clearly discovered, by the gospel; the very same thing which the light of nature gives me a confused sight of (like the sight of men as trees walking) the New Testament gives me a clear and distinct sight of. All that good which is pressed upon me by the law of nature is more fully discovered to me, and I find myself much more strongly bound to it by the gospel of Christ, the engagements it lays upon me to my duty, and the encouragements and assistances it gives me in my duty. And this is further confirming to me that there, just there, where natural light leaves me at a loss, and unsatisfied — tells me that hitherto it can carry me, but no further — the gospel takes me up, helps me out, and gives me all the satisfaction I can desire, and that is especially in the great business of the satisfying of God's justice for the sin of man. My own conscience asks, *Wherewith shall I come before the Lord, and bow myself before the most high God? Will he be pleased with thousands of rams?* But I am still at a loss; I cannot frame a righteousness from any thing I am, or have, in myself, or from any thing I can do for God or present to God, wherein I dare appear before him; but the gospel comes, and tells me that Jesus Christ had *made his soul an offering for sin*, and God has declared himself well-pleased with all believers in him; and this makes me easy.

8. I cannot but think that the proofs by which God has attested the truth of the gospel are the most proper that could be given in a case of this nature — that the power and authority of the Redeemer in the kingdom of grace should be exemplified to the world, not by the highest degree of the pomp and authority of the kings of the earth, as the Jews expected, but by the evidences of his dominion in the kingdom of nature, which is a much greater dignity and authority than any of the kings of the earth ever pretended to, and is no less than divine. And his miracles being generally wrought upon men, not only upon their bodies, as they were mostly when Christ was here upon earth, but, which is more, upon their minds, as they were mostly after the pouring out of the Spirit in the gift of tongues and other supernatural endowments, were the most proper confirmations possible of the truth of the gospel, which was designed for the making of men holy and happy.

9. I cannot but think that the methods taken for the propagation of this gospel, and the wonderful success of those methods, which are purely spiritual and heavenly, and destitute of all secular advantages and supports, plainly show that it was of God, for God was with it; and it could never have spread as it did, in the face of so much opposition, if it had not been accompanied with a power from on high. And the preservation of Christianity in the world to this day, notwithstanding the difficulties it has struggles with, is to me a standing miracle for the proof of it.

10. I cannot but think that the gospel of Christ has had some influence upon my soul, has

had such a command over me, and been such a comfort to me, as is a demonstration to myself, though it cannot be so to another, that it is of God. I have tasted in it *that the Lord is gracious;* and the most subtle disputant cannot convince one who has tasted honey that it is not sweet.

And now I appeal to him who knows the thoughts and intents of the heart that in all this I think freely (if it be possible for a man to know that he does so), and not under the power of any bias. Whether we have reason to think that those who, without any colour of reason, not only usurp, but monopolize, the character of free-thinkers, do so, let those judge who easily observe that they do not speak sincerely, but industriously dissemble their notions; and one instance I cannot but notice of their unfair dealing with their readers — that when, for the diminishing of the authority of the New Testament, they urge the various readings of the original, and quote an acknowledgment of Mr. Gregory of Christ-church, in his preface to his Works, *That no profane author whatsoever, etc.,* and yet suppress what immediately follows, as the sense of that learned man upon it, *That this is an invincible reason for the scriptures' part, etc.*

But while we are thus maintaining the divine origin and authority of the New Testament, as it has been received through all the ages of the church, we find our cause not only attacked by the enemies we speak of, but in effect betrayed by one who makes our New Testament almost double to what it really is, adding to the *Constitutions of the Apostles,* collected by *Clement,* together with the *Apostolical Canons,* and making those to be of equal authority with the writings of the evangelists, and preferable to the Epistles. By enlarging the lines of defence thus, without either cause or precedent, he gives great advantage to the invaders. Those *Constitutions of the Apostles* have many things in them very good, and may be of use, as other human compositions; but to pretend that they wee composed, as they profess to be, by the twelve apostles in concert at Jerusalem, *I Peter saying this, I Andrew saying that, etc.,* is the greatest imposition that can be practised upon the credulity of the simple.

1. It is certain there were a great many spurious writings which, in the early days of the church, went under the names of the apostles and apostolical men; so that it has always been complained of as impossible to find out any thing but the canon of scripture that could with any assurance be attributed to them. Baronius himself acknowledges it, *Cum apostolorum nomine tam facta quam dicta reperiantur esse supposititia; nec sic quid de illis à veris sincerisque spriptoribus narratum sit integrum et incorruptum remanserit, in desperationem planè quandam animum dejicunt posse unquam assequi quod verum certumque subsistat — Since so many of the acts and sayings ascribed to the apostles are found to be spurious, and even the narrations of faithful writers respecting them are not free from corruption, we must despair of ever being able to arrive at any absolute certainty about them.* — Ad An. Christ. 44, sect. 42, etc. There were Acts under the names of Andrew the apostle, Philip, Peter, Thomas; a Gospel under the names of Thaddeus, another of Barnabas, another of Bartholomew; a book concerning the infancy of our Saviour, another concerning his nativity, and many the like, which we all rejected as forgeries.

2. These *Constitutions* and *Canons,* among the rest, were condemned in the primitive church as apocryphal, and therefore justly rejected; because, though otherwise good, they pretended to be what really they were not, dictated by the twelve apostles themselves, as received from Christ. If Jesus Christ gave them such instructions, and they gave them in such a solemn manner to the church, as is pretended, it is unaccountable that there is not the least notice taken of any such thing done or designed in the *Gospels,* the *Acts,* or any of the *Epistles.*

Those who have judged the most favourable of these *Canons* and *Constitutions* have concluded that they were complied by some officious persons under the name of *Clement,* towards the end of the second century, above 150 years after Christ's ascension, out of the common practice of the churches; that is, that which the compilers were most acquainted with, or had respect for; when at the same time we have reason to think that the far greater number of Christian churches which by that time were planted had Constitutions of their own, which, if they had had the happiness to be transmitted to posterity, would have recommended themselves as well as these, or better. But, as the legislators of old put a reputation upon their laws by pretending to have received them from some deity or other, so church-governors studied to gain reputation to their sees by placing some apostolical man or other at the head of their catalogue of bishops (*see bishop Stillingfleet's Irenicum, p.* 302), and reputation to their Canons and Constitutions by fathering them upon the apostles. But how can it be imagined that the apostles should be all together at Jerusalem, to compose this book of *Canons* with so much solemnity, when we know that their commission was to go into all the world, and to preach the gospel to every creature? Accordingly, Eusebius tells us that Thomas went into Parthia, Andrew into Scythia, John into the lesser Asia; and we have reason to think that after their dispersion they never came together again, any more than the planters of the nations did after the Most High had separated the sons of Adam.

I think that any one who will compare these *Constitutions* with the writings which we are sure were given by inspiration of God will easily discern a vast difference in the style and spirit. *What is the chaff to the wheat?* "Where are ministers, in the style of the true apostles, called priests, high priests? Where do we find in the apostolical age, that age of suffering, of the placing of the bishop in his *throne?* Or of readers, singers, and porters, in the church?" (Edit. Joan. Clerici, p. 245.)

I fear the collector and compiler of those *Constitutions,* under the name of *Clement,* was conscious to himself of his honesty in it, in that he would not have them published before all, because of the mysteries contained in them; nor were they known or published till the middle of the fourth century, when the forgery could not be so well disproved. I cannot see any mysteries in them, that they should be concealed, if they had been genuine; but I am sure that Christ bids his apostles publish the mysteries of the kingdom of God upon the house-tops. And St. Paul, though there are mysteries in his epistles much more sublime than any of these *Constitutions,* charges that they should be read to all the holy brethren. Nay, these *Constitutions* are so wholly in a manner taken up either with moral precepts, or rules of practice in the church, that if they had been what they pretend they had been most fit to be published before all. And though the *Apocalypse* is so full of mysteries, yet a blessing is pronounced upon the readers and hearers of that prophecy. We must therefore conclude that, whenever they were written, by declining the light they owned themselves to be apocryphal, that is, hidden or concealed; that they durst not mingle themselves with what was given by divine inspiration; to allude to what is said of the ministers (Acts 5:13), *Of the rest durst no man join himself to* the apostles, *for the people magnified them.* So that even by their own confession they were not delivered to the churches with the other writings, when the New-Testament canon was solemnly sealed up with that dreadful sentence passed on those that *add unto these things.*

And as we have thus had attempts made of late upon the purity and sufficiency of our New Testament, by additions to it, so we have likewise had from another quarter a great contempt put upon it by the papal power. The occasion was this: — One Father Quesnel, a French papist, but a Jansenist, nearly thirty years ago, published *the New Testament* in French, in several small volumes, *with Moral Reflections* on every verse, to render the reading of it more profitable, and meditation upon it more easy. It was much esteemed in France, for the sake of the piety and devotion which appeared in it, and it had several impressions. The Jesuits were much disgusted, and solicited the pope for the condemnation of it, though the author of it was a papist, and many things in it countenanced popish superstition. After much struggling about it in the court of Rome a bull was at length obtained, at the request of the French king, from the present pope Clement 11 bearing date September 8, 1713, by which the said book, with what title or in what language soever it is printed, is prohibited and condemned; both the New Testament itself, because in many things varying from the vulgar Latin, and the Annotations, as containing divers propositions (above a hundred are enumerated) scandalous and pernicious, injurious to the church and its customs, impious, blasphemous, savouring of heresy. And the propositions are such as these — "That the grace of our Lord Jesus Christ is the effectual principle of all manner of good, is necessary for every good action; for without it nothing is done, nay nothing can be done" — "That it is a sovereign grace, and is an operation of the almighty hand of God" — "That, when God accompanies his word with the internal power of his grace, it operates in the soul the obedience which it demands" — "That faith is the first grace, and the fountain of all others" — "That it is in vain for us to call God our Father, if we do not cry to him with a spirit of love" — "That there is no God, nor religion, where there is no charity" — "That the catholic church comprehends the angels and all the elect and just men of the earth of all ages" — "That it had the Word incarnate for its head, and all the saints for its members" — "That it is profitable and necessary at all times, in all places, and for all sorts of persons, to know the holy Scriptures" — "That the holy obscurity of the word of God is no reason for the laity not reading it" — "That the Lord's day ought to be sanctified by reading books of piety, especially the holy scriptures" — And "that to forbid Christians from reading the scriptures is to prohibit the use of the light to the children of light." Many such positions as these, which the spirit of every good Christian cannot but relish as true and good, are condemned by the pope's bull as impious and blasphemous. And this bull, though strenuously opposed by a great number of the bishops in France, who were well affected to the notions of father Quesnel, was yet received and confirmed by the French king's letters patent, bearing date at Versailles, February 14, 1714, which forbid all manner of persons, upon pain of exemplary punishment, so much as to keep any of those books in their houses; and adjudge any that should hereafter write in defence of the propositions condemned by the pope as disturbers of the peace. It was registered the day following, February 15, by the Parliament of Paris, but with divers provisos and limitations.

By this is appears that popery is still the same thing that ever it was, an enemy to the knowledge of the scriptures, and to the honour of divine grace. What reason have we to bless God that we have liberty to read the scriptures, and have helps to understand and improve them, which we are concerned diligently to make a good use of, that we may not provoke God to give us up into the hands of those powers that would use us in like manner!

I am willing to hope that those to whom the reading of the *Exposition of the Old Testament* was pleasant will find this yet more pleasant; for this is that part of scripture which does most plainly testify of Christ, and in which that *gospel grace which appears unto all men, bringing salvation,* shines most clearly. This is the New-Testament milk for babes, the rest is strong meat for strong men. By these, therefore, let us be nourished and strengthened that we my be pressing on towards perfection; and that, having laid the foundation in the history of our blessed Saviour's life, death, and resurrection, and the first preaching of his gospel, we may build upon it by an acquaintance with the mysteries of godliness, to which we shall be further introduced in the Epistles.

I desire I may be read with a candid, and not a critical, eye. I pretend not to gratify the curious; the summit of my ambition is to assist those who are truly serious in searching the scriptures daily. I am sure the work is designed, and hope it is calculated, to promote piety towards God and charity towards our brethren, and that there is not only something in it which may edify, but nothing which may justly offend any good Christian.

If any receive spiritual benefit by my poor endeavours, it will be comfort to me, but let God have all the glory, and that free grace of his which has employed one that is utterly unworthy of such an honour, and enabled one thus far to go on in it who is utterly insufficient for such a service.

Having obtained help of God, I continue hitherto in it, and humbly depend upon the same good hand of my God to carry me on it that which remains, to gird my loins with needful strength and to make my way perfect; and for this I humbly desire the prayers of my friends. One volume more, I hope, will include what is yet to be done; and I will both go about it, and go on with it, as God shall enable me, withall convenient speed; but it is that part of the scripture which, of all others, requires the most care and pains in expounding it. But I trust that *as the day so shall the strength be.*

1721. M.H.

ORIGINAL PREFACE TO VOLUME SIX

After much expectation, and many enquiries, the last volume of the late reverend Mr. Henry's Exposition now appears in the world. The common disadvantages that attend posthumous productions will doubtless be discerned in this; but we hope, though there are diversities of gifts, there will be found to be the same spirit. Some of the relations and hearers of that excellent person have been at the pains of transcribing the notes they took in short-hand of this part of the holy scripture, when expounded by him in his family or in the congregation; they have furnished us with very good materials for the finishing of this great work, and we doubt not but that the ministers who have been concerned in it have made that use of those assistances which may entitle this composure to the honour of Mr. Henry's name; and, if so, they can very willingly conceal their own.

The New Testament may be very properly divided into two parts, the one *historical* the other *epistolary.* It is the exposition of the latter we now recommend, and shall offer some thoughts on the epistolary way of writing in general, and then proceed to observe the divine authority of these epistles, together with the style, matter, method, and design of them, leaving what might be said concerning the several inspired penmen to the prefaces appertaining to the particular epistles.

As to the epistolary way of writing, it may be sufficient to observe that it has usually three properties: — It may in some things be more *difficult* to be understood, but then it is very *profitable,* and very *pleasant;* these will be found to be the properties of these sacred letters. We shall meet with things not easy to be understood, especially in some parts of them, where we cannot so well discover the particular occasions on which they were written or the questions or matters of fact to which they refer; but this is abundantly compensated by the profit which will accrue to those that read them with due attention. They will find the strongest reasoning, the most moving expostulations, and warm and pressing exhortations, mixed with seasonable cautions and reproofs, which are all admirably fitted to impress the mind with suitable sentiments and affections. And how much solid pleasure and delight must this afford to persons of a serious and religious spirit, especially when they wisely and faithfully apply to themselves what they find to suit their case! Thus they will appear to be as truly written to them as if their names were superscribed on them. It is natural for us to be very much pleased in perusing a wise and kind letter, full of instruction and comfort, sent to us by an absent friend: how then should we prize this part of holy scripture, when we consider herein that our God and Saviour has written these letters *to us,* in which we have the great things of his law and gospel, the things that belong to our peace! By these means not only the holy apostles, *being dead, yet speak,* but the Lord of the prophets and apostles continues to speak and write to us; and while we read them with proper affections, and follow them with suitable petitions and thanksgivings, a blessed correspondence and intercourse will be kept up between heaven and us, while we are yet sojourners in the earth.

But it is the divine inspiration and authority of these epistles we are especially concerned to know; and it is of the last importance that in this our minds be fully established. And we have strong and clear evidence that these epistles were written by the apostles of our Lord Jesus, and that they (like the prophets of the Old Testament) spoke and wrote *as they were moved by the Holy Ghost.* These epistles have in all ages of the church been received by Christians as a part of those holy scriptures that are *given by inspiration of God, and are profitable for doctrine, for reproof, for correction, and for instruction in righteousness, and are able to make us wise to salvation through faith which is in Jesus Christ;* they are part of that perpetual universal rule of faith and life which contains doctrines and revelations we are bound to believe with a divine faith, as coming from the God of truth, and duties to be practised by us in obedience to the will of God, *acknowledging that the things written therein are the commandments of God,* 1 Co. 14:37. And, for the same reasons that lead us to acknowledge the other parts of the Bible to be the word of God, we must own these to be so too. If there is good reason (as indeed there is) to believe that the books of Moses were written by inspiration of God, there is the same reason to believe that the writings of the prophets were also from God, because the law and the prophets speak the same things, and such things as none but the Holy Ghost could teach; and, if we must with a divine faith believe the Old Testament to be a revelation from God, we cannot with any good reason question the divine authority of the New, when we consider how exactly the histories of the one agree with the prophecies of the other, and how the dark types and shadows of the law are illustrated and accomplished in the gospel. Nor can any person who pretends to believe the divine authority of the historical part of the New Testament, containing the Gospels and the Acts, with good reason question the equal authority of the epistolary part; for the subject-matter of all these epistles, as well as of the sermons of the apostles, is the *word of God* (Rom. 10:17; 1 Th. 2:13; Col. 1:25), and the *gospel of God* (Rom. 15:16; 2 Co. 11:7), and the *gospel of Christ,* 2 Co. 2:12. We *are built upon the foundation of the apostles and prophets, Jesus Christ himself being the chief corner-stone;* and, as Moses wrote of Christ, so did all the prophets, for the Spirit of Christ in them did testify of him. And the apostles confirmed what Christ himself began to teach, *God also bearing them witness with signs, and wonders, and divers miracles, and gifts of the Holy Ghost, according to his will,* Heb. 2:3, 4. The manifestation of God in the flesh, and the things *he began both to do and teach until the day in which he was taken up,* together with his sufferings unto death, and his resurrection (which things are declared to us, and are firmly to be believed, and strictly regarded by us), do give us an ample account of the way of life and salvation by Jesus Christ; but still it was the will of our blessed Lord that his apostles should not only publish his gospel to all the world, but also that, after his resurrection, they should declare some things more plainly concerning him than he thought fit to do while he was here on earth, for which end he promised to send his Holy Spirit *to teach them all things, to bring all things to their remembrance which he had spoken unto them,* Jn. 14:26. For he told them (Jn. 16:12, 13), *I have many things to say unto you, but you cannot bear them now; but when he, the Spirit of truth, is come, he shall lead you into all truth, and shall show you things to come.* Accordingly we find there was a wonderful effusion of the Holy Spirit upon the apostles (who in these epistles are called the *servants, ambassadors, and ministers* of Christ, *and stewards of the mysteries of God*), under whose infallible guidance they preached the gospel, and declared the whole counsel of God, and that with amazing courage and success, Satan every where falling down before them like lightning from heaven. That in preaching the gospel they were under the influence of the infallible Spirit is undeniable, from the miraculous gifts and powers they received for their work, particularly that gift of tongues so necessary for the publication of the gospel throughout the world to nations of different languages; nor must we omit that mighty power that accompanied the word preached, bringing multitudes to the obedience of faith, notwithstanding all opposition from earth and hell, and the potent lusts in the hearts of those who were *turned from idols to serve the living God, and to wait for his Son from heaven, whom he raised from the dead, even Jesus, that delivered us from the wrath to come.* Now that they were under the same mighty influence in writing these epistles as in preaching cannot be denied. Such infallible assistance seems to be as needful at least to direct their writing as their preaching, considering that these epistles were written to keep in memory those things that had been delivered by word of mouth (2 Pt. 1:15), and to rectify the mistakes that might arise about some expressions that had been used in preaching (2 Th. 2:2), and were to remain as a standing rule and record to which believers were to appeal, for defending the truth and discovering error, and a proper means to transmit the truths of the gospel to posterity, even to the end of time. Besides, the writers of these epistles have declared that what they wrote was from God: now they must know whether they had the special assistance of the divine Spirit or no, in their writing as well as preaching; and they in all things appear to have been men of such probity that they would not dare to say they had the Spirit of God when they had it not, or if they so much as doubted whether they had it or not; yea, they are careful, when they speak their own private opinion, or only under some common influence, to tell the world that not the *Lord,* but *they,* spoke those things, but that in the rest it was not they but the Lord, 1 Co. 7:10, 12, etc. And the apostle Paul makes the acknowledgment of this their inspiration to be a test to try those that pretended to be prophets or spiritual: *Let them* (says he) *acknowledge that the things I write unto you are the commandments of the Lord,* 1 Co. 14:37. And the apostle Peter gives this as the reason of his writing, that those he wrote to *might after his decease have those things always in remembrance* (2 Pt. 1:15), which afterwards he calls *the commandment of the apostles of the Lord* (*ch.* 3:1, 2), and so of the Lord himself. And the apostles John declareth (1 Jn. 4:6), *We are of God; he that knoweth God heareth us; he that is not of God heareth not us; by this we know the Spirit of truth, and the spirit of error.*

As to the style of these epistles, though it be necessary we should believe a divine influence superintending the several writers of them, yet it is not easy to explain the manner of it, nor to determine whether and in what particulars the words they wrote were dictated to them by the Holy Spirit, as mere *amanuenses,* or how far their own memories, and reasoning faculties, and other natural or acquired endowments, were employed under the inspection of the Spirit. We must believe that these holy men spoke and wrote *as they were moved by the Holy Ghost,* that he put them on and assisted them in this work. It is very probable that sometimes he not only suggested the very thoughts in their minds, but put words into their mouths, and always infallibly guided them into all truth, both when they expounded the scriptures of the Old Testament and when they gave rules for our faith and practice in the gospel church state. And yet perhaps it may be allowed, without any diminution to the authority of these epistles, that the penmen of them made some use of their own reasoning powers and different endowments in their manner of writing, as well as of their different sorts of chirography; and that by this we are to account for that difference of style which has been observed between the writings of Paul, who was brought up at the feet of Gamaliel, and those of Peter and John, who were fishermen. The like difference may be discerned between the style of the prophet Isaiah, who was educated in a court, and that of Amos, who was one of the herdsmen of Tekoa. However, the best way to understand these scriptures aright is not to criticise too nicely upon the words and phrases, but to attend carefully to the drift and design of these inspired writers in them.

The *subject-matter* of these epistles is entirely conformable to the rest of the scriptures. In them we find frequent reference to some passages of the Old Testament, and explanations of them: in the epistle to the Hebrews we have the best exposition of the Levitical law. Indeed the New Testament refers to, and in a manner builds upon, the Old, showing the accomplishment of all the ancient promises and prophecies concerning the Messiah, and explains all the antiquated types and *shadows of the good things that were then to come.* But, besides these references to the preceding part of holy writ, in some of these epistles there are contained prophecies, either wholly new or at least more largely and plainly revealed, as that in the *Revelation* concerning the rise, reign, and fall of antichrist, of which great apostasy we have some account in 2 Th. 2:3, 4, and in 1 Tim. 4:1–3. And in these epistles we have several of the great doctrines of the gospel more fully discussed than elsewhere, particularly the doctrine of original sin, of the sin that dwells in the regenerate, and of justification by the righteousness of Christ, of the abolishing of the Jewish rites and ceremonies, of the true nature and design of the seals of the new covenant, the obligations they bring us under, and their perpetual use in the Christian church.

The general method of these epistles is such as best serves the end or design of them, which is indeed the end of the whole scripture — practical godliness, out of a principle of divine love, a good conscience, and faith unfeigned. Accordingly most of the epistles begin with the great doctrines of the gospel, the articles of the Christian faith, which, when received, work by love, purify the conscience, and produce evangelical obedience; and, after these principles have been laid down, practical conclusions are drawn and urged from them. In taking this method there is a regard paid to the nature and faculties of the soul of man (where the understanding is to lead the way, the will, affections, and executive powers, to follow after), and to the nature of religion in general, which is a reasonable service. We are not to be determined by superstitious fancies, nor by blind passions, but by a sound judgment and good understanding in the mind and will of God. By this we are taught how necessary it is that faith and practice, truth and holiness, be joined together, that the performance of moral duties will never be acceptable to God, nor available to our own salvation, without the belief of the truth, since those who make shipwreck of the faith seldom maintain a good conscience, and the most solemn profession of the faith will never save those that *hold the truth in unrighteousness.*

The particular occasions upon which these epistles were written do not so evidently appear in them all as in some. The first to the Corinthians seems to have taken its rise from the unhappy divisions that so early rose in the churches of Christ, through the emulation of the ministers and personal affections of the people; but it does not confine itself to that subject. That to the Galatians seems directed chiefly against those judaizing teachers that went about to draw the Gentile converts away from the simplicity of the gospel in doctrine and worship. The epistle to the Hebrews is manifestly calculated to wean the converted Jews from those Mosaical rites and ceremonies for which they retained too great a fondness, and to reconcile them to the abolition of that economy. Those epistles that are directed to particular persons more evidently carry their design in them, which he that runs may read. But this is certain, none of these epistles are of private interpretation. Most of the psalms and of the prophecies of the Old Testament were penned or pronounced on particular occasions, and yet they are of standing and universal use, and very instructive even to us upon whom the ends of the world have come. And so are those epistles that seem to have been most limited in the rise and occasion of them. There will always be need enough to warn Christians against uncharitable divisions, against corrupting the faith and worship of the gospel; and, whenever the case is the same, these epistles are as certainly directed to such churches and persons as if they had been inscribed to them.

These general observations, we suppose, may be sufficient to introduce the reader into the book itself; let us now take a short view of the whole work, of which this posthumous piece is the conclusion. It is now about fourteen years since the first part of this exposition of the Bible was made public. In five years' time the Old Testament was finished in four volumes. The first volume of the New Testament was longer in hand; for though the ever-memorable author was always fully employed in the ordinary work of his ministry, yet those last years of his life, in which he drew up the exposition upon the historical part of the New Testament, were less at his own command than any other had been. His removal to Hackney, his almost continual preaching from day to day, his journeys to Chester, and the necessity of more frequent visits to his friends in and about London, together with a gradual sensible decay of health, will more than excuse the three years' time that passed before that was finished. And under such difficulties none but a man of his holy zeal, unwearied industry, and great sagacity, could have gone through such a service in that space of time. He lived not to see that volume published, though left by him ready for the press. The church of God was suddenly deprived of one of the most useful ministers of the age. We have been gathering up the fragments of those feasts with which he used to entertain his family and friends, in his delightful work of opening the scriptures. What remains is that we recommend the whole of this work to the acceptance and blessing of our God and Saviour, to whose honour and interest it was from the first directed and devoted. We need not be very solicitous about the acceptance it may meet with in the world: what has been before published has been received and read with great pleasure and advantage by the most serious experienced Christians in Great Britain and Ireland; and the many loud calls there have been for the publishing of this supplement, and reprinting the whole, leave us no room to doubt but that it will meet with a hearty welcome. Though it must be acknowledged that we live in an age which by feeding upon ashes and the wind, has very much lost the relish of every thing that is spiritual and evangelical, yet we persuade ourselves there will still be found many who, *by reason of use, have, their senses exercised to discern both good and evil.* Those that may think the expository notes too long, especially for family worship, may easily relieve themselves, either by reading a less part of the chapter at one time, or by abridging the annotations, and perusing the rest when they have more leisure; for, though it must be owned they are somewhat copious, yet we are persuaded that those who peruse them seriously will find nothing in them superfluous or impertinent; and, if any where some things in the comment do not seem to flow so naturally and necessarily from the text, we believe when they are well considered and compared it will appear they come under the analogy and general reason of the subject, and truly belong to it. If there be any that think this exposition of the Bible is too plain and familiar, that it wants the beauties of oratory and the strength of criticism, we only wish that they will read it over again with due attention, and we are pretty confident they will find the style natural, clear, and comprehensive; and we think they will hardly be able to produce one valuable criticism out of the most learned commentators but they will have it in this exposition, though couched in plain terms, and not brought in as of a critical nature. No man was more happy than Mr. Henry in that useful talent of making dark things plain, while too many, that value themselves upon their criticising faculty, affect rather to make plain things dark.

But we leave this great and good work to speak for itself, and doubt not but it will grow in its use and esteem, and will, through the blessing of God, help to revive and promote family religion and scriptural knowledge, and support the credit of scripture commentaries, though couched in human expressions. These have been always accounted the great treasures of the church, and when done with judgment, have been so far from lessening the authority of the Bible that they have greatly promoted its honour and usefulness.

The following are the ministers by whom the Exposition on the Epistolary writings, and the Revelation, was completed, as given by J. B. Williams, Esq., LL.D.,F.S.A., in his *Memoirs of the Life, Character, and Writings, of the Rev. Matthew Henry,* 8vo. p. 308.

Romans	Mr. [afterwards Dr.] John Evans
1 Corinthians	Mr. Simon Browne
2 Corinthians	Mr. Daniel Mayo
Galatians	Mr. Joshua Bayes
Ephesians	Mr. Samuel Rosewell
Philippians and Colossians	Mr. [afterwards Dr.] William Harris
1, 2 Thessalonians	Mr. Daniel Mayo
1, 2 Timothy	Mr. Benjamin Andrews Atkinson
Titus and Philemon	Mr. Jeremiah Smith
Hebrews	Mr. William Tong
James	Dr. S. Wright
1 Peter	Mr. Zec. Merrill
2 Peter	Mr. Joseph Hill
1, 2, and 3 John	Mr. John Reynolds, of Shrewsbury
Jude	Mr. John Billingsley
Revelations	Mr. William Tong

OLD TESTAMENT

GENESIS TO MALACHI

AN EXPOSITION, WITH PRACTICAL OBSERVATIONS, OF
THE FIRST BOOK OF MOSES, CALLED GENESIS

We have now before us the holy Bible, or *book*, for so *bible* signifies. We call it *the book*, by way of eminency; for it is incomparably the best book that ever was written, the book of books, shining like the sun in the firmament of learning, other valuable and useful books, like the moon and stars, borrowing their light from it. We call it the holy book, because it was written by holy men, and indited by the Holy Ghost; it is perfectly pure from all falsehood and corrupt intention; and the manifest tendency of it is to promote holiness among men. The great things of God's law and gospel are here *written* to us, that they might be reduced to a greater certainty, might spread further, remain longer, and be transmitted to distant places and ages more pure and entire than possibly they could be by report and tradition: and we shall have a great deal to answer for if these things which belong to our peace, being thus committed to us in black and white, be neglected by us as a strange and foreign thing, Hos. 8:12. The scriptures, or writings of the several inspired penmen, from Moses down to St. John, in which divine light, like that of the morning, shone gradually (the sacred canon being now completed), are all put together in this blessed Bible, which, thanks be to God, we have in our hands, and they make as perfect a day as we are to expect on this side of heaven. Every part was good, but all together very good. This is the *light that shines in a dark place* (2 Pt. 1:19), and a dark place indeed the world would be without the Bible.

We have before us that part of the Bible which we call the *Old Testament*, containing the acts and monuments of the church from the creation almost to the coming of Christ in the flesh, which was about four thousand years — the truths then revealed, the laws then enacted, the devotions then paid, the prophecies then given, and the events which concerned that distinguished body, so far as God saw fit to preserve to us the knowledge of them. This is called a *testament*, or *covenant* (*Diathēkē*), because it was a settled declaration of the *will* of God concerning man in a federal way, and had its force from the designed death of the great testator, *the Lamb slain from the foundation of the world*, Rev. 8:8. It is called the *Old Testament*, with relation to the *New*, which does not cancel and supersede it, but crown and perfect it, by the bringing in of that better hope which was typified and foretold in it; the Old Testament still remains glorious, though the New far exceeds in glory, 2 Co. 3:9.

We have before us that part of the Old Testament which we call the *Pentateuch*, or five books of Moses, that servant of the Lord who excelled all the other prophets, and typified the great prophet. In our Saviour's distribution of the books of the Old Testament into the *law*, the *prophets*, and the *psalms*, or *Hagiographa*, these are the *law*; for they contain not only the laws given to Israel, in the last four, but the laws given to Adam, to Noah, and to Abraham, in the first. These five books were, for aught we know, the first that ever were written; for we have not the least mention of any *writing* in all the book of Genesis, nor till God bade Moses write (Ex. 17:14); and some think Moses himself never learned to write till God set him his copy in the writing of the ten Commandments upon the tables of stone. However, we are sure these books are the most ancient writings now extant, and therefore best able to give us a satisfactory account of the most ancient things.

We have before us the first and longest of those five books, which we call *Genesis*, written, some think, when Moses was in Midian, for the instruction and comfort of his suffering brethren in Egypt: I rather think he wrote it in the wilderness, after he had been in the mount with God, where, probably, he received full and particular instructions for the writing of it. And, as he framed the tabernacle, so he did the more excellent and durable fabric of this book, exactly according to the pattern shown him in the mount, into which it is better to resolve the certainty of the things herein contained than into any tradition which possibly might be handed down from Adam to Methuselah, from him to Shem, from him to Abraham, and so to the family of Jacob. *Genesis* is a name borrowed from the Greek. It signifies the *original*, or *generation*: fitly is this book so called, for it is a history of originals — the creation of the world, the entrance of sin and death into it, the invention of arts, the rise of nations, and especially the planting of the church, and the state of it in its early days. It is also a history of generations — the generations of Adam, Noah, Abraham, etc., not endless, but useful genealogies. The beginning of the New Testament is called *Genesis* too (Mt. 1:1), *Biblos geneseōs*, the book of the *genesis*, or *generation*, of Jesus Christ. Blessed be God for that Book which shows us our remedy, as this opens our wound. Lord, upon our eyes, that we may see the wondrous things both of thy law and gospel!

CHAPTER 1

The foundation of all religion being laid in our relation to God as our Creator, it was fit that the book of divine revelations which was intended to be the guide, support, and rule, of religion in the world, should begin, as it does, with a plain and full account of the creation of the world — in answer to that first enquiry of a good conscience, "Where is God my Maker?" (Job 35:10). Concerning this the pagan philosophers wretchedly blundered, and became vain in their imaginations, some asserting the world's eternity and self-existence, others ascribing it to a fortuitous concourse of atoms: thus "the world by wisdom knew not God," but took a great deal of pains to lose him. The holy scripture therefore, designing by revealed religion to maintain and improve natural religion, to repair the decays of it and supply the defects of it, since the fall, for the reviving of the precepts of the law of nature, lays down, at first, this principle of the unclouded light of nature, That this world was, in the beginning of time, created by a Being of infinite wisdom and power, who was himself before all time and all worlds. The entrance into God's word gives this light, Ps. 119:130. The first verse of the Bible gives us a surer and better, a more satisfying and useful, knowledge of the origin of the universe, than all the volumes of the philosophers. The lively faith of humble Christians understands this matter better than the elevated fancy of the greatest wits, Heb. 11:3.

We have three things in this chapter: — I. A general idea given us of the work of creation (v. 1, 2). II. A particular account of the several days' work, registered, as in a journal, distinctly and in order. The creation of the light the first day (v. 3–5); of the firmament the second day (v. 6–8); of the sea, the earth, and its fruits, the third day (v. 9–13); of the lights of heaven the fourth day (v. 14–19); of the fish and fowl the fifth day (v. 20–23); of the beasts (v. 24, 25); of man (v. 26–28); and of food for both the sixth day (v. 29, 30). III. The review and approbation of the whole work (v. 31).

Verses 1–2

In these verses we have the work of creation in its epitome and in its embryo.

I. In its epitome, *v.* 1, where we find, to our comfort, the first article of our creed, that *God the Father Almighty is the Maker of heaven and earth*, and as such we believe in him.

1. Observe, in this verse, four things: —

(1.) The effect produced — *the heaven and the earth*, that is, the world, including the whole frame and furniture of the universe, the *world and all things therein*, Acts 17:24. The world is a great house, consisting of upper and lower stories, the structure stately and magnificent, uniform and convenient, and every room well and wisely furnished. It is the visible part of the creation that Moses here designs to account for; therefore he mentions not the creation of angels. But as the earth has not only its surface adorned with grass and flowers, but also its bowels en-

riched with metals and precious stones (which partake more of its solid nature and more valuable, though the creation of them is not mentioned here), so the heavens are not only beautified to our eye with glorious lamps which garnish its outside, of whose creation we here read, but they are within replenished with glorious beings, out of our sight, more celestial, and more surpassing them in worth and excellency than the gold or sapphires surpass the lilies of the field. In the visible world it is easy to observe, [1.] Great variety, several sorts of beings vastly differing in their nature and constitution from each other. *Lord, how manifold are thy works*, and all good! [2.] Great beauty. The azure sky and verdant earth are charming to the eye of the curious spectator, much more the ornaments of both. How transcendent then must the beauty of the Creator be! [3.] Great exactness and accuracy. To those that, with the help of microscopes, narrowly look into the works of nature, they appear far more fine than any of the works of art. [4.] Great power. It is not a lump of dead and inactive matter, but there is virtue, more or less, in every creature: the earth itself has a magnetic power. [5.] Great order, a mutual dependence of beings, an exact harmony of motions, and an admirable chain and connection of causes. [6.] Great mystery. There are phenomena in nature which cannot be solved, secrets which cannot be fathomed nor accounted for. But from what we see of heaven and earth we may easily enough infer the eternal power and Godhead of the great Creator, and may furnish ourselves with abundant matter for his praises. And let our make and place, as men, remind us of our duty as Christians, which is always to keep heaven in our eye and the earth under our feet.

(2.) The author and cause of this great work — GOD. The Hebrew word is *Elohim*, which bespeaks, [1.] The power of God the Creator. *El* signifies *the strong God*; and what less than almighty strength could bring all things out of nothing? [2.] The plurality of persons in the Godhead, Father, Son, and Holy Ghost. This plural name of God, in Hebrew, which speaks of him as many though he is one, was to the Gentiles perhaps a savour of death unto death, hardening them in their idolatry; but it is to us a savour of life unto life, confirming our faith in the doctrine of the Trinity, which, though but darkly intimated in the Old Tes-

tament, is clearly revealed in the New. The Son of God, the eternal Word and Wisdom of the Father, was with him when he made the world (Prov. 8:30), nay, we are often told that the world was made by him, and nothing made without him, Jn. 1:3, 10; Eph. 3:9; Col. 1:16; Heb. 1:2. O what high thoughts should this form in our minds of that great God whom we draw nigh to in religious worship, and that great Mediator in whose name we draw nigh!

(3.) The manner in which this work was effected: *God created it*, that is, made it out of nothing. There was not any pre-existent matter out of which the world was produced. The fish and fowl were indeed produced out of the waters and the beasts and man out of the earth; but that earth and those waters were made out of nothing. By the ordinary power of nature, it is impossible that any thing should be made out of nothing; no artificer can work, unless he has something to work on. But by the almighty power of God it is not only possible that something should be made of nothing (the God of nature is not subject to the laws of nature), but in the creation it is impossible it should be otherwise, for nothing is more injurious to the honour of the Eternal Mind than the supposition of eternal matter. Thus the excellency of the power is of God and all the glory is to him.

(4.) When this work was produced: *In the beginning*, that is, in the beginning of time, when that clock was first set a going: time began with the production of those beings that are measured by time. Before the beginning of time there was none but that Infinite Being that inhabits eternity. Should we ask why God made the world no sooner, we should but darken counsel by words without knowledge; for how could there be sooner or later in eternity? And he did make it in the beginning of time, according to his eternal counsels before all time. The Jewish Rabbies have a saying, that there were seven things which God created before the world, by which they only mean to express the excellency of these things: — The law, repentance, paradise, hell, the throne of glory, the house of the sanctuary, and the name of the Messiah. But to us it is enough to say, *In the beginning was the Word*, Jn. 1:1.

2. Let us learn hence, (1.) That atheism is folly, and atheists are the greatest fools in nature; for they see there is a world that could not make itself, and yet they will not

own there is a God that made it. Doubtless, they are without excuse, but the god of this world has blinded their minds. (2.) That God is sovereign Lord of all by an incontestable right. If he is the Creator, no doubt he is the owner and possessor of heaven and earth. (3.) That with God all things are possible, and therefore happy are the people that have him for their God, and whose help and hope stand in his name, Ps. 121:2; 124:8. (4.) That the God we serve is worthy of, and yet is exalted far above, all blessing and praise, Neh. 9:5, 6. If he made the world, he needs not our services, nor can be benefited by them (Acts 17:24, 25), and yet he justly requires them, and deserves our praise, Rev. 4:11. If all is of him, all must be to him.

II. Here is the work of creation in its embryo, *v.* 2, where we have an account of the first matter and the first mover.

1. A chaos was the first matter. It is here called the earth (though the earth, properly taken, was not made till the third day *v.* 10), because it did most resemble that which afterwards was called *earth,* mere earth, destitute of its ornaments, such a heavy unwieldy mass was it; it is also called *the deep,* both for its vastness and because the waters which were afterwards separated from the earth were now mixed with it. This immense mass of matter was it out of which all bodies, even the firmament and visible heavens themselves, were afterwards produced by the power of the Eternal Word. The Creator could have made his work perfect at first, but by this gradual proceeding he would show what is, ordinarily, the method of his providence and grace. Observe the description of this chaos. (1.) There was nothing in it desirable to be seen, for it was *without form and void. Toho* and *Bohu, confusion* and *emptiness;* so these words are rendered, Isa. 34:11. It was shapeless, it was useless, it was without inhabitants, without ornaments, the shadow or rough draught of things to come, *and not the image of the things,* Heb. 10:1. The earth is almost reduced to the same condition again by the sin of man, under which the creation groans. See Jer. 4:23, *I beheld the earth, and lo it was without form, and void.* To those who have their hearts in heaven this lower world, in comparison with that upper, still appears to be nothing but confusion and emptiness. There is no true beauty to be seen, no satisfying fulness to be enjoyed, in this earth, but in God only. (2.) If there had been any thing desirable to be seen, yet there was no light to see it by; for *darkness,* thick darkness, *was upon the face of the deep.* God did not create this darkness (as he is said to create the darkness of affliction, Isa. 45:7), for it was only the want of light, which yet could not be said to be wanted till something was made that might be seen by it; nor needs the want of it be much complained of, when there was nothing to be seen but confusion and emptiness. If the work of grace in the soul is a new creation, this chaos represents the state of an unregenerate graceless soul: *there* is disorder, confusion, and every evil work; it is empty of all good, for it is without God; it is dark, it is darkness itself. This is our condition by nature, till almighty grace effects a blessed change.

2. The Spirit of God was the first mover: He *moved upon the face of the waters.* When we consider the earth without form and void, methinks it is like the valley full of dead and dry bones. Can these live? Can this confused mass of matter be formed into a beautiful world? Yes, if a spirit of life from God enter into it, Eze. 37:9. Now there is hope concerning this thing; for the Spirit of God begins to work, and, if he work, who or what shall hinder? God is said to make the world by his Spirit, Ps. 33:6; Job 26:13; and by the same mighty worker the new creation is effected. He moved upon the face of the deep, as Elijah stretched himself upon the dead child, — as the *hen gathers her chickens under her wings,* and hovers over them, to warm and cherish them, Mt. 23:37, — as the eagle stirs up her nest, and *flutters* over her young (it is the same world that is here used), Deu. 32:11. Learn hence, That God is not only the author of all being, but the fountain of life and spring of motion. Dead matter would be for ever dead if he did not quicken it. And this makes it credible to us that God should raise the dead. That power which brought such a world as this out of confusion, emptiness, and darkness, at the beginning of time, can, at the end of time, bring our vile bodies out of the grave, though it is *a land of darkness as darkness itself, and without any order* (Job 10:22), and can make them glorious bodies.

Verses 3–5

We have here a further account of the first day's work, in which observe, 1. That the first of all visible beings which God created was light; not that by it he himself might see to work (for the darkness and light are both alike to him), but that by it we might see his works and his glory in them, and might work our works while it is day. The works of Satan and his servants are works of darkness; but he that doeth truth, and doeth good, cometh to the light, and coveteth it, *that his deeds may be made manifest,* Jn. 3:21. Light is the great beauty and blessing of the universe. Like the first-born, it does, of all visible beings, most resemble its great Parent in purity and power, brightness and beneficence; it is of great affinity with a spirit, and is next to it; though by it we see other things, and are sure that it is, yet we know not its nature, nor can describe what it is, or *by what way the light is parted,* Job 38:19, 24. By the sight of it let us be led to, and assisted in, the believing contemplation of him who is light, infinite and eternal light (1 Jn. 1:5), and the *Father of lights* (Jam. 1:17), and who dwells in inaccessible light, 1 Tim. 6:16. In the new creation, the first thing wrought in the soul is *light:* the blessed Spirit captives the will and affections by enlightening the understanding, so coming into the heart by the door, like the good shepherd whose own the sheep are, while sin and Satan, like thieves and robbers, climb up some other way. Those that by sin were darkness by grace become light in the world. 2. That the light was made by the word of God's power. He said, *Let there be light;* he willed and appointed it, and it was done immediately: *there was light,* such a copy as exactly answered the original idea in the Eternal Mind. O the power of the word of God! *He spoke, and it was done,* done really, effectually, and for perpetuity, not in show only, and to serve a present turn, for *he commanded, and it stood fast:* with him it was *dictum, factum — a word, and a world.* The world of God (that is, his will and the good pleasure of it) is quick and powerful. Christ is the Word, the essential eternal Word, and by him the light was produced, for *in him was light, and he is the true light, the light of the world,* Jn. 1:9; 9:5. The divine light which shines in sanctified souls is wrought by the power of God, the power of his word and of the Spirit of wisdom and revelation, opening the understanding, scattering the mists of ignorance and mistake, and giving the knowledge of the glory of God in the face of Christ, as at first, *God commanded the light to shine out of darkness,* 2 Co. 4:6. Darkness would have been perpetually upon the face of fallen man if the Son of God had not *come, and given us an understanding,* 1 Jn. 5:20. 3. That the light which God willed, when it was produced, he approved of: *God saw the light that it was good.* It was exactly as he designed it, and it was fit to answer the end for which he designed it. It was useful and profitable; the world, which now is a palace, would have been a dungeon without it. It was amiable and pleasant. *Truly the light is sweet* (Eccl. 11:7); *it rejoiceth the heart,* Prov. 15:30. What God commands he will approve and graciously accept; he will be well pleased with the work of his own hands. That is good indeed which is so in the sight of God, for he sees not as man sees. If the light is good, how good is he that is the fountain of light, from whom we receive it, and to whom we owe all praise for it and all the services we do by it! 4. That God *divided the light from the darkness,* so put them asunder as that they could never be joined together, or reconciled; for *what fellowship has light with darkness?* 2 Co. 6:14. And yet he divided time between them, the day for light and the night for darkness, in a constant and regular succession to each other. Though the darkness was now scattered by the light, yet it was not condemned to a perpetual banishment, but takes its turn with the light, and has its place, because it has its use; for, as the light of the morning befriends the business of the day, so the shadows of the evening befriend the repose of the night, and draw the curtains about us, that we may sleep the better. See Job 7:2. God has thus divided time between light and darkness, because he would daily remind us that this is a world of mixtures and changes. In heaven there is perfect and perpetual light, and no darkness at all; in hell, utter darkness, and no gleam of light. In that world between these two there is a great gulf fixed; but, in this world, they are counterchanged, and we pass daily from one to another, that we may learn to expect the like vicissitudes in the providence of God, peace and trouble, joy and sorrow, and may set the one over-against the other, accommodating ourselves to both as we do to the light and darkness, bidding both welcome, and making the best of both.

5. That God divided them from each other by distinguishing names: *He called the light day, and the darkness he called night.* He gave them names, as the Lord of both; for *the day is his, the night also is his,* Ps. 74:16. He is the Lord of time, and will be so, till day and night shall come to an end, and the stream of time be swallowed up in the ocean of eternity. Let us acknowledge God in the constant succession of day and night, and consecrate both to his honour, by working for him every day and resting in him every night, and meditating in his law day and night. 6. That this was the first day's work, and a good day's work it was. *The evening and the morning were the first day.* The darkness of the evening was before the light of the morning, that it might serve for a foil to it, to set it off, and make it shine the brighter. This was not only the first day of the world, but the first day of the week. I observe it to the honour of that day, because the new world began on the first day of the week likewise, in the resurrection of Christ, as the light of the world, early in the morning. In him the day-spring from on high has visited the world; and happy are we, for ever happy, if that *day-star arise in our hearts.*

Verses 6–8

We have here an account of the second day's work, the creation of the firmament, in which observe, 1. The command of God concerning it: *Let there be a firmament,* an *expansion,* so the Hebrew word signifies, like a sheet spread, or a curtain drawn out. This includes all that is visible above the earth, between it and the third heavens: the air, its higher, middle, and lower, regions — the celestial globe, and all the spheres and orbs of light above: it reaches as high as the place where the stars are fixed, for that is called here the *firmament of heaven* (*v.* 14, 15), and as low as the place where the birds fly, for that also is called the *firmament of heaven, v.* 20. When God had made the light, he appointed the air to be the receptacle and vehicle of its beams, and to be as a medium of communication between the invisible and the visible world; for, though between heaven and earth there is an inconceivable distance, yet there is not an impassable gulf, as there is between heaven and hell. This firmament is not a wall of partition, but a way of intercourse. See Job 26:7; 37:18; Ps. 104:3; Amos 9:6. 2. The creation of it. Lest it should seem as if God had only commanded it to be done, and some one else had done it, he adds, *And God made the firmament.* What God requires of us he himself works in us, or it is not done. He that commands faith, holiness, and love, creates them by the power of his grace going along with his word, that he may have all the praise. *Lord, give what thou commandest, and then command what thou pleasest.* The firmament is said to be *the work of God's fingers,* Ps. 8:3. Though the vastness of its extent declares it to be the work of his arm stretched out, yet the admirable fineness of its constitution shows that it is a curious piece of art, the work of his fingers. 3. The use and design of it — to *divide the waters from the waters,* that is, to distinguish between the waters that are wrapped up in the clouds and those that cover the sea, the waters in the air and those in the earth. See the difference between these two carefully observed, Deu. 11:10, 11, where Canaan is upon this account preferred to Egypt, that Egypt was moistened and made fruitful with the waters that are under the firmament, but Canaan with waters from above, out of the firmament, even the dew of heaven, which tarrieth not *for the sons of men,* Mic. 5:7. God has, in the firmament of his power, chambers, store-chambers, whence he *watereth the earth,* Ps. 14:13; 65:9, 10. He has also *treasures, or magazines, of snow and hail, which he hath reserved against the day of battle and war,* Job 38:22, 23. O what a great God is he who has thus provided for the comfort of all that serve him and the confusion of all that hate him! It is good having him our friend, and bad having him our enemy. 4. The naming of it: *He called the firmament heaven.* It is the visible heaven, the pavement of the holy city; above the firmament God is said to have his throne (Eze. 1:26), for he has prepared it in the heavens; the heavens therefore are said to rule, Dan. 4:26. *Is not God in the height of heaven?* Job 22:12. Yes, he is, and we should be led by the contemplation of the heavens that are in our eye to consider *our Father who is in heaven.* The height of the heavens should remind us of God's supremacy and the infinite distance there is between us and him; the brightness of the heavens and their purity should remind us of his glory, and majesty, and perfect holiness; the vastness of the heavens, their encompassing of the earth, and the influence they have upon it, should remind us of his immensity and universal providence.

Verses 9–13

The third day's work is related in these verses — the forming of the sea and the dry land, and the making of the earth fruitful. Hitherto the power of the Creator had been exerted and employed about the upper part of the visible word; the light of heaven was kindled, and the firmament of heaven fixed: but now he descends to this lower world, the earth, which was designed for the children of men, designed both for their habitation and for their maintenance; and here we have an account of the fitting of it for both, and building of their house and the spreading of their table. Observe,

I. How the earth was prepared to be a habitation for man, by the gathering of the waters together, and the making of the dry land to appear. Thus, instead of the confusion which there was (v. 2) when earth and water were mixed in one great mass, behold, now, there is order, by such a separation as rendered them both useful. God said, *Let it be so, and it was so;* no sooner said than done. 1. The waters which had covered the earth were ordered to retire, and to gather into one place, namely, those hollows which were fitted and appointed for their reception and rest. The waters, thus cleared, thus collected, and thus lodged, in their proper place, he called *seas.* Though they are many, in distant regions, and washing several shores, yet, either above ground or under ground, they have communication with each other, and so they are one, and the common receptacle of waters, into which all the rivers flow, Eccl. 1:7. Waters and seas often, in scripture, signify troubles and afflictions, Ps. 42:7; 69:2, 14, 15. God's own people are not exempted from these in this world; but it is their comfort that they are only waters under the heaven (there are none in heaven), and that they are all in the place that God has appointed them and within the bounds that he has set for them. How the waters were gathered together at first, and how they are still bound and limited by the same Almighty had that first confined them, are elegantly described, Ps. 14:6–9, and are there mentioned as matter of praise. *Those that go down to the sea in ships* ought to acknowledge daily the wisdom, power, and goodness, of the Creator, in making the great waters serviceable to man for trade and commerce; and *those that tarry at home* must own themselves indebted to him that keeps the sea with bars and doors in its decreed place, and stays its proud waves, Job 38:10, 11. 2. The dry land was made to appear, and emerge out of the waters, and was called *earth,* and *given to the children of men.* The earth, it seems, was in being before; but it was of no use, because it was under water. Thus many of God's gifts are received in vain, because they are buried; make them to appear, and they become serviceable. We who, to this day, enjoy the benefit of the dry land (though, since this, it was once deluged, and dried again) must own ourselves tenants to, and dependents upon, that God whose *hands formed the dry land,* Ps. 95:5; Jonah 1:9.

II. How the earth was furnished for the maintenance and support of man, v. 11, 12. Present provision was now made, by the immediate products of the upstart earth, which, in obedience to God's command, was no sooner made than it became fruitful, and brought forth grass for the cattle and herb for the service of man. Provision was likewise made for time to come, by the perpetuating of the several kinds of vegetables, which are numerous, various, and all curious, and every one *having its seed in itself after its kind,* that, during the continuance of man upon the earth, food might be fetched out of the earth for his use and benefit. *Lord, what is man, that he is thus visited and regarded* — that such care should be taken, and such provision made, for the support and preservation of those guilty and obnoxious lives which have been a thousand times forfeited! Observe here, 1. That not only the earth is the Lord's, but *the fulness thereof,* and he is the rightful owner and sovereign disposer, not only of it, but of all its furniture. The earth was *emptiness* (v. 2), but now, by a word's speaking, it has become full of God's riches, and his they are still — *his corn and his wine, his wool and his flax,* Hos. 2:9. Though the use of them is allowed to us, the property still remains in him, and to his service and honour they must be used. 2. That common providence is a continued creation, and in it *our Father worketh hitherto.* The earth still remains under the efficacy of this command, to bring forth grass, and herbs, and its annual prod-

ucts; and though, being according to the common course of nature, these are not standing miracles, yet they are standing instances of the unwearied power and unexhausted goodness of the world's great Maker and Master. 3. That though God, ordinarily, makes use of the agency of second causes, according to their nature, yet he neither needs them nor is tied to them; for, though the precious fruits of the earth are usually brought forth by the influences of the sun and moon (Deu. 33:14), yet here we find the earth bearing a great abundance of fruit, probable ripe fruit, before the sun and moon were made. 4. That it is good to provide things necessary before we have occasion to use them: before the beasts and man were made, here were grass and herbs prepared for them. God thus dealt wisely and graciously with man; let not man then be foolish and unwise for himself. 5. That God must have the glory of all the benefit we receive from the products of the earth, either for food or physic. It is he that *hears the heavens when they hear the earth,* Hos. 2:21, 22. And if we have, through grace, an interest in him who is the fountain, when the streams are dried up and the *fig-tree doth not blossom* we may rejoice in him.

Verses 14–19

This is the history of the fourth day's work, the creating of the sun, moon, and stars, which are here accounted for, not as they are in themselves and in their own nature, to satisfy the curious, but as they are in relation to this earth, to which they serve as lights; and this is enough to furnish us with matter for praise and thanksgiving. Holy Job mentions this as an instance of the glorious power of God, that *by the Spirit he hath garnished the heavens* (Job 26:13); and here we have an account of that garniture which is not only so much the beauty of the upper world, but so much the blessing of this lower; for though heaven is high, yet has it respect to this earth, and therefore should have respect from it. Of the creation of the lights of heaven we have an account,

I. In general, v. 14, 15, where we have 1. The command given concerning them: *Let there be lights in the firmament of heaven.* God had said, *Let there be light* (v. 3), and there was light; but this was, as it were, a chaos of light, scattered and confused: now it was collected and modelled, and made into several luminaries, and so rendered both more glorious and more serviceable. God is the God of order, and not of confusion; and, as he is light, so he is the Father and former of lights. Those lights were to be *in the firmament of heaven,* that vast expanse which encloses the earth, and is conspicuous to all; for *no man, when he has lighted a candle, puts it under a bushel, but on a candlestick* (Lu. 8:16), and a stately golden candlestick the firmament of heaven is, from which these candles give light *to all that are in the house.* The firmament itself is spoken of as having a brightness of its own (Dan. 12:3), but this was not sufficient to give light to the earth; and perhaps for this reason it is not expressly said of the second day's work, in which the firmament was made, that it was good, because, till it was adorned with these lights on the fourth day, it had not become serviceable to man. 2. The use they were intended to be of to this earth. (1.) They must be for the distinction of times, of day and night, summer and winter, which are interchanged by the motion of the sun, whose rising makes day, his setting night, his approach towards our tropic summer, his recess to the other winter: and thus, *under the sun,* there is *a season to every purpose,* Eccl. 3:1. (2.) They must be for the direction of actions. They are for signs of the change of weather, that the husbandman may order his affairs with discretion, foreseeing, by the face of the sky, when second causes have begun to work, whether it will be fair or foul, Mt. 16:2, 3. They do also *give light upon the earth,* that we may *walk* (Jn. 11:9), and *work* (Jn. 9:4), according as the duty of every day requires. The lights of heaven do not shine for themselves, nor for the world of spirits above, who need them not; but they shine for us, for our pleasure and advantage. Lord, what is man, that he should be thus regarded! Ps. 8:3, 4. How ungrateful and inexcusable are we, if, when God has set up these lights for us to work by, we sleep, or play, or trifle away the time of business, and neglect the great work we were sent into the world about! The lights of heaven are made to serve us, and they do it faithfully, and shine in their season, without fail: but we are set as lights in this world to serve God; and do we

in like manner answer the end of our creation? No, we do not, our light does not shine before God as his lights shine before us, Mt. 5:14. We burn our Master's candles, but do not mind our Master's work.

II. In particular, v. 16–18.

1. Observe, The lights of heaven are the sun, moon, and stars; and all these are the work of God's hands. (1.) The sun is the greatest light of all, more than a million times greater than the earth, and the most glorious and useful of all the lamps of heaven, a noble instance of the Creator's wisdom, power, and goodness, and an invaluable blessing to the creatures of this lower world. Let us learn from Ps. 19:1–6 how to give unto God the glory due unto his name, as the Maker of the sun. (2.) The moon is a less light, and yet is here reckoned one of the greater lights, because though, in regard to its magnitude and borrowed light, it is inferior to many of the stars, yet, by virtue of its office, as ruler of the night, and in respect of its usefulness to the earth, it is more excellent than they. Those are most valuable that are most serviceable; and those are the greater lights, not that have the best gifts, but that humbly and faithfully do the most good with them. *Whosoever will be great among you, let him be your minister,* Mt. 20:26. (3.) *He made the stars also,* which are here spoken of as they appear to vulgar eyes, without distinguishing between the planets and the fixed stars, or accounting for their number, nature, place, magnitude, motions, or influences; for the scriptures were written, not to gratify our curiosity and make us astronomers, but to lead us to God, and make us saints. Now these lights are said to *rule* (v. 16, 18); not that they have a supreme dominion, as God has, but they are deputy-governors, rulers under him. Here the less light, the moon, is said to rule *the night;* but in Ps. 136:9 the stars are mentioned as sharers in that government; *The moon and stars to rule by night.* No more is meant than that they *give light,* Jer. 31:35. The best and most honourable way of ruling is by giving light and doing good: those command respect that live a useful life, and so shine as lights.

2. Learn from all this, (1.) The sin and folly of that ancient idolatry, the worshipping of the sun, moon, and stars, which, some think, took rise, or countenance at least, from some broken traditions in the patriarchal age concerning the rule and dominion of the lights of heaven. But the account here given of them plainly shows that they are both God's creatures and man's servants; and therefore it is both a great affront to God and a great reproach to ourselves to make deities of them and give them divine honours. See Deu. 4:19. (2.) The duty and wisdom of daily worshipping that God who made all these things, and made them to be that to us which they are. The revolutions of the day and night oblige us to offer the solemn sacrifice of prayer and praise every morning and evening.

Verses 20–23

Each day, hitherto, has produced very noble and excellent beings, which we can never sufficiently admire; but we do not read of the creation of any living creature till the fifth day, of which these verses give us an account. The work of creation not only proceeded gradually from one thing to another, but rose and advanced gradually from that which was less excellent to that which was more so, teaching us to press towards perfection and endeavour that our last works may be our best works. It was on the fifth day that the fish and fowl were created, and both out of the waters. Though there is one kind of flesh of fishes, and another of birds, yet they were made together, and both out of the waters; for the power of the first Cause can produce very different effects from the same second causes. Observe, 1. The making of the fish and fowl, at first, v. 20, 21. God commanded them to be produced. He said, *Let the waters bring forth abundantly;* not as if the waters had any productive power of their own, but, "Let them be brought into being, the fish in the waters and the fowl out of them." This command he himself executed: *God created great whales,* etc. Insects, which perhaps are as various and as numerous as any species of animals, and their structure as curious, were part of this day's work, some of them being allied to the fish and others to the fowl. Mr. Boyle (I remember) says he admires the Creator's wisdom and power as much in an ant as in an elephant. Notice is here taken of the various sorts of fish and fowl, each after their kind, and of the great numbers of both that were produced, for the waters brought forth abundantly; and particular mention if made of great whales, the largest of fishes, whose bulk and strength, exceeding that of any other animal, are remarkable proofs of the power and greatness of the Creator. The express notice here taken of the whale, above all the rest, seems sufficient to determine what animal is meant by the Leviathan, Job 41:1. The curious formation of the bodies of animals, their different sizes, shapes, and natures, with the admirable powers of the sensitive life with which they are endued, when duly considered, serve, not only to silence and shame the objections of atheists and infidels, but to raise high thoughts and high praises of God in pious and devout souls, Ps. 104:25, etc. 2. The blessing of them, in order to their continuance. Life is a wasting thing. Its strength is not the strength of stones. It is a candle that will burn out, if it be not first blown out; and therefore the wise Creator not only made the individuals, but provided for the propagation of the several kinds; *God blessed them, saying, Be fruitful and multiply, v.* 22. God will bless his own works, and not forsake them; and *what he does shall be for a perpetuity,* Eccl. 3:14. The power of God's providence preserves all things, as at first his creating power produced them. Fruitfulness is the effect of God's blessing and must be ascribed to it; the multiplying of the fish and fowl, from year to year, is still the fruit of this blessing. Well, let us give to God the glory of the continuance of these creatures to this day for the benefit of man. See Job 12:7, 9. It is a pity that fishing and fowling, recreations innocent in themselves, should ever be abused to divert any from God and their duty, while they are capable of being improved to lead us to the contemplation of the wisdom, power, and goodness, of him that made all these things, and to engage us to stand in awe of him, as the fish and fowl do of us.

Verses 24–25

We have here the first part of the sixth day's work. The sea was, the day before, replenished with its fish, and the air with its fowl; and this day were made the beasts of the earth, the cattle, and the creeping things that pertain to the earth. Here, as before, 1. *The Lord gave the word;* he said, *Let the earth bring forth,* not as if the earth had any such prolific virtue as to produce these animals, or as if God resigned his creating power to it; but, "Let these creatures now come into being upon the earth, and out of it, in their respective kinds, conformable to the ideas of them in the divine counsels concerning their creation." 2. He also did the work; he made them all after their kind, not only of divers shapes, but of divers natures, manners, food, and fashions — some to be tame about the house, others to be wild in the fields — some living upon grass and herbs, others upon flesh — some harmless, and others ravenous — some bold, and others timorous — some for man's service, and not his sustenance, as the horse — others for his sustenance, and not his service, as the sheep — others for both, as the ox — and some for neither, as the wild beasts. In all this appears the manifold wisdom of the Creator.

Verses 26–28

We have here the second part of the sixth day's work, the creation of man, which we are, in a special manner, concerned to take notice of, that we may know ourselves. Observe,

I. That man was made last of all the creatures, that it might not be suspected that he had been, any way, a helper to God in the creation of the world: that question must be for ever humbling and mortifying to him, *Where wast thou,* or any of thy kind, *when I laid the foundations of the earth?* Job 38:4. Yet it was both an honour and a favour to him that he was made last: an honour, for the method of the creation was to advance from that which was less perfect to that which was more so; and a favour, for it was not fit he should be lodged in the palace designed for him till it was completely fitted up and furnished for his redemption. Man, as soon as he was made, had the whole visible creation before him, both to contemplate and to take the comfort of. Man was made the same day that the beasts were, because his body was made of the same earth with theirs; and, while he is in the body, he inhabits the same earth with them. God forbid that by indulging

the body and the desires of it we should make ourselves like the beasts that perish!

II. That man's creation was a more signal and immediate act of divine wisdom and power than that of the other creatures. The narrative of it is introduced with something of solemnity, and a manifest distinction from the rest. Hitherto, it had been said, "Let there be light," and "Let there be a firmament," and "Let the earth, or waters, bring forth" such a thing; but now the word of command is turned into a word of consultation, *"Let us make man,* for whose sake the rest of the creatures were made: this is a work we must take into our own hands." In the former he speaks as one having authority, in this as one having affection; for his *delights were with the sons of men,* Prov. 8:31. It should seem as if this were the work which he longed to be at; as if he had said, "Having at last settled the preliminaries, let us now apply ourselves to the business, *Let us make man.*" Man was to be a creature different from all that had been hitherto made. Flesh and spirit, heaven and earth, must be put together in him, and he must be allied to both worlds. And therefore God himself not only undertakes to make him, but is pleased so to express himself as if he called a council to consider of the making of him: *Let us make man.* The three persons of the Trinity, Father, Son, and Holy Ghost, consult about it and concur in it, because man, when he was made, was to be dedicated and devoted to Father, Son and Holy Ghost. Into that great name we are, with good reason, baptized, for to that great name we owe our being. Let him rule man who said, *Let us make man.*

III. That man was made in God's image and after his likeness, two words to express the same thing and making each other the more expressive; *image* and *likeness* denote the likest image, the nearest resemblance of any of the visible creatures. Man was not made in the likeness of any creature that went before him, but in the likeness of his Creator; yet still between God and man there is an infinite distance. Christ only is the *express image* of God's person, as the Son of his Father, having the same nature. It is only some of God's honour that is put upon man, who is God's image only as the shadow in the glass, or the king's impress upon the coin. God's image upon man consists in these three things: — 1. In his nature and constitution, not those of his body (for God has not a body), but those of his soul. This honour indeed God has put upon the body of man, that the Word was made flesh, the Son of God was clothed with a body like ours and will shortly clothe ours with a glory like that of his. And this we may safely say, That he by whom God made the worlds, not only the great world, but man the little world, formed the human body, at the first, according to the platform he designed for himself in the fulness of time. But it is the soul, the great soul, of man, that does especially bear God's image. The soul is a spirit, an intelligent immortal spirit, an influencing active spirit, herein resembling God, the Father of Spirits, and the soul of the world. *The spirit of man is the candle of the Lord.* The soul of man, considered in its three noble faculties, understanding, will, and active power, is perhaps the brightest clearest looking-glass in nature, wherein to see God. 2. In his place and authority: *Let us make man in our image, and let him have dominion.* As he has the government of the inferior creatures, he is, as it were, God's representative, or viceroy, upon earth; they are not capable of fearing and serving God, therefore God has appointed them to fear and serve man. Yet his government of himself by the freedom of his will has in it more of God's image than his government of the creatures. 3. In his purity and rectitude. God's image upon man consists in knowledge, righteousness, and true holiness, Eph. 4:24; Col. 3:10. He was upright, Eccl. 7:29. He had an habitual conformity of all his natural powers to the whole will of God. His understanding saw divine things clearly and truly, and there were no errors nor mistakes in his knowledge. His will complied readily and universally with the will of God, without reluctancy or resistance. His affections were all regular, and he had no inordinate appetites or passions. His thoughts were easily brought and fixed to the best subjects, and there was no vanity nor ungovernableness in them. All the inferior powers were subject to the dictates and directions of the superior, without any mutiny or rebellion. Thus holy, thus happy, were our first parents, in having the image of God upon them. And

this honour, put upon man at first, is a good reason why we should not speak ill one of another (Jam. 3:9), nor do ill one to another (Gen. 9:6), and a good reason why we should not debase ourselves to the service of sin, and why we should devote ourselves to God's service. But how art thou fallen, O son of the morning! How is this image of God upon man defaced! How small are the remains of it, and how great the ruins of it! The Lord renew it upon our souls by his sanctifying grace!

IV. That man was made male and female, and blessed with the blessing of fruitfulness and increase. God said, *Let us make man,* and immediately it follows, *So God created man;* he performed what he resolved. With us saying and doing are two things; but they are not so with God. He created him male and female, Adam and Eve — Adam first, out of earth, and Eve out of his side, *ch.* 2. It should seem that of the rest of the creatures God made many couples, but of man *did not he make one?* (Mal. 2:15), though he had the residue of the Spirit, whence Christ gathers an argument against divorce, Mt. 19:4, 5. Our first father, Adam, was confined to one wife; and, if he had put her away, there was no other for him to marry, which plainly intimated that the bond of marriage was not to be dissolved at pleasure. Angels were not made male and female, for they were not to propagate their kind (Lu. 20:34–36); but man was made so, that the nature might be propagated and the race continued. Fires and candles, the luminaries of this lower world, because they waste, and go out, have a power to light more; but it is not so with the lights of heaven: stars do not kindle stars. God made but one male and one female, that all the nations of men might know themselves to be made of one blood, descendants from one common stock, and might thereby be induced to love one another. God, having made them capable of transmitting the nature they had received, said to them, *Be fruitful, and multiply, and replenish the earth.* Here he gave them, 1. A large inheritance: *Replenish the earth;* it is this that is bestowed upon the children of men. They were made to *dwell upon the face of all the earth,* Acts 17:26. This is the place in which God has set man to be the servant of his providence in the government of the inferior creatures, and, as it were, the intelligence of this orb; to be the receiver of God's bounty, which other creatures live upon, but do not know it; to be likewise the collector of his praises in this lower world, and to pay them into the exchequer above (Ps. 145:10); and, lastly, to be a probationer for a better state. 2. A numerous lasting family, to enjoy this inheritance, pronouncing a blessing upon them, in virtue of which their posterity should extend to the utmost corners of the earth and continue to the utmost period of time. Fruitfulness and increase depend upon the blessing of God: Obed-edom had eight sons, *for God blessed him,* 1 Chr. 26:5. It is owing to this blessing, which God commanded at first, that the race of mankind is still in being, and that as *one generation passeth away another cometh.*

V. That God gave to man, when he had made him, a dominion over the inferior creatures, *over the fish of the sea and over the fowl of the air.* Though man provides for neither, he has power over both, much more *over every living thing that moveth upon the earth,* which are more under his care and within his reach. God designed hereby to put an honour upon man, that he might find himself the more strongly obliged to bring honour to his Maker. This dominion is very much diminished and lost by the fall; yet God's providence continues so much of it to the children of men as is necessary to the safety and support of their lives, and God's grace has given to the saints a new and better title to the creature than that which was forfeited by sin; for all is ours if we are Christ's, 1 Co. 3:22.

Verses 29–30

We have here the third part of the sixth day's work, which was not any new creation, but a gracious provision of food for all flesh, Ps. 136:25. He that made man and beast thus took care to preserve both, Ps. 36:6. Here is,

I. Food provided for man, *v.* 29. Herbs and fruits must be his meat, including corn and all the products of the earth; these were allowed him, but (it should seem) not flesh, till after the flood, *ch.* 9:3. And before the earth was deluged, much more before it was cursed for man's sake, its fruits, no doubt, were more pleasing to the taste and more strengthening and nourishing to the body than marrow and fatness, and all the portion of the king's meat, are now. See here, 1. That which should make us humble. As we were made out of the earth, so we are maintained out of it. Once indeed men did eat angels' food, bread from heaven; but they died (Jn. 6:49); it was to them but as food out of the earth, Ps. 104:14. There is meat that endures to everlasting life; the Lord evermore give us this. 2. That which should make us thankful. The Lord is for the body; from him we receive all the supports and comforts of this life, and to him we must give thanks. He gives us all things richly to enjoy, not only for necessity, but plenty, plenty, dainties, and varieties, for ornament and delight. How much are we indebted! How careful should we be, as we live upon God's bounty, to live to his glory! 3. That which should make us temperate and content with our lot. Though Adam had dominion given him over fish and fowl, yet God confined him, in his food, to herbs and fruits; and he never complained of it. Though afterwards he coveted forbidden fruit, for the sake of the wisdom and knowledge he promised himself from it, yet we never read that he coveted forbidden flesh. If God give us food for our lives, let us not, with murmuring Israel, ask food for our lusts, Ps. 78:18; see Dan. 1:15.

II. Food provided for the beasts, *v.* 30. *Doth God take care for oxen?* Yes, certainly, he provides food convenient for them, and not for oxen only, which were used in his sacrifices and man's service, but even the young lions and the young ravens are the care of his providence; they ask and have their meat from God. Let us give to God the glory of his bounty to the inferior creatures, that all are fed, as it were, at his table, every day. He is a great housekeeper, a very rich and bountiful one, that satisfies the desire of every living thing. Let this encourage God's people to cast their care upon him, and not to be solicitous respecting what they shall eat and what they shall drink. He that provided for Adam without his care, and still provides for all the creatures without their care, will not let those that trust him want any good thing, Mt. 6:26. He that feeds his birds will not starve his babes.

Verse 31

We have here the approbation and conclusion of the whole work of creation. As for God, his work is perfect; and if he begin he will also make an end, in providence and grace, as well as here in creation. Observe,

I. The review God took of his work: He *saw every thing that he had made.* So he does still; all the works of his hands are under his eye. He that made all sees all; he that made us sees us, Ps. 139:1–16. Omniscience cannot be separated from omnipotence. *Known unto God are all his works,* Acts 15:18. But this was the Eternal Mind's solemn reflection upon the copies of its own wisdom and the products of its own power. God has hereby set us an example of reviewing our works. Having given us a power of reflection, he expects we should use that power, see our way (Jer. 2:23), and think of it, Ps. 119:59. When we have finished a day's work, and are entering upon the rest of the night, we should commune with our own hearts about what we have been doing that day; so likewise when we have finished a week's work, and are entering upon the sabbath-rest, we should thus prepare to meet our God; and when we are finishing our life's work, and are entering upon our rest in the grave, that is a time to bring to remembrance, that we may die repenting, and so take leave of it.

II. The complacency God took in his work. When we come to review our works we find, to our shame, that much has been very bad; but, when God reviewed his, all was very good. He did not pronounce it good till he had seen it so, to teach us not to answer a matter before we hear it. The work of creation was a very good work. All that God made was well-made, and there was no flaw nor defect in it. 1. It was good. Good, for it is all agreeable to the mind of the Creator, just as he would have it to be; when the transcript came to be compared with the great original, it was found to be exact, no errata in it, not one misplaced stroke. Good, for it answers the end of its creation, and is fit for the purpose for which it was designed. Good, for it is serviceable to man, whom God had appointed lord of the visible creation. Good, for it is all for God's glory; there is that in the whole visible creation which is a demonstration of God's being and perfections, and which tends to beget, in the soul of man, a religious regard to him and veneration of him. 2. It was very good. Of each day's work (except the second) it was said that it was good, but now, it is very good. For, (1.) Now man was made, who was the chief of the ways of God, who was designed to be the visible image of the Creator's glory and the mouth of the creation in his praises. (2.) Now all was made; every part was good, but all together very good. The glory and goodness, the beauty and harmony, of God's works, both of providence and grace, as this of creation, will best appear when they are perfected. When the top-stone is brought forth we shall cry, *Grace, grace, unto it,* Zec. 4:7. Therefore judge nothing before the time.

III. The time when this work was concluded: *The evening and the morning were the sixth day;* so that in six days God made the world. We are not to think but that God could have made the world in an instant. He said that, *Let there be light, and there was light,* could have said, "Let there be a world," and there would have been a world, *in a moment, in the twinkling of an eye,* as at the resurrection, 1 Co. 15:52. But he did it in six days, that he might show himself a free-agent, doing his own work both in his own way and in his own time, — that his wisdom, power, and goodness, might appear to us, and be meditated upon by us, the more distinctly, — and that he might set us an example of working six days and resting the seventh; it is therefore made the reason of the fourth commandment. So much would the sabbath conduce to the keeping up of religion in the world that God had an eye to it in the timing of his creation. And now, as God reviewed his work, let us review our meditations upon it, and we shall find them very lame and defective, and our praises low and flat; let us therefore stir up ourselves, and all that is within us, to *worship him that made the heaven, earth, and sea, and the fountains of waters,* according to the tenour of the everlasting gospel, which is preached to every nation, Rev. 14:6, 7. All his works, in all places of his dominion, do bless him; and, therefore, *bless thou the Lord, O my soul!*

CHAPTER 2

This chapter is an appendix to the history of the creation, more particularly explaining and enlarging upon that part of the history which relates immediately to man, the favourite of this lower world. We have in it, I. The institution and sanctification of the sabbath, which was made for man, to further his holiness and comfort (*v.* 1–3). II. A more particular account of man's creation, as the centre and summary of the whole work (*v.* 1–7). III. A description of the garden of Eden, and the placing of man in it under the obligations of a law and covenant (*v.* 8–17). IV. The creation of the woman, her marriage to the man, and the institution of the ordinance of marriage (*v.* 18, etc.).

Verses 1–3

We have here, I. The settlement of the kingdom of nature, in God's resting from the work of creation, *v.* 1, 2. Here observe, 1. The creatures made both in heaven and earth are the *hosts* or *armies* of them, which denotes them to be numerous, but marshalled, disciplined, and under command. How great is the sum of them! And yet every one knows and keeps his place. God uses them as his hosts for the defence of his people and the destruction of his enemies; for he is the Lord of hosts, of all these hosts, Dan. 4:35. 2. The heavens and the earth are finished pieces, and so are all the creatures in them. So perfect is God's work that nothing can be added to it nor taken from it, Eccl. 3:14. God that began to build showed himself well able to finish. 3. After the end of the first six days God ceased from all works of creation. He has so ended his work as that though, in his providence, he worketh hitherto (Jn. 5:17), preserving and governing all the creatures, and particularly forming the spirit of man within him, yet he does not make any new species of creatures. In miracles, he has controlled and overruled nature, but never changed its settled course, nor repealed nor added to any of its establishments. 4. The eternal God, though infinitely happy in the enjoyment of himself, yet took a satisfaction in the work of his own hands. He did not rest, as one weary, but as one well-pleased with the instances of his own goodness and the manifestations of his own glory.

II. The commencement of the kingdom of grace, in the sanctification of the sabbath day, *v.* 3. He rested on that day, and took a complacency in his creatures, and then sanctified it, and appointed us, on that day, to rest and take a complacency in the Creator; and his rest is, in the fourth commandment, made a reason for ours, after six days' labour. Observe, 1. The solemn observance of one day in seven, as a day of holy rest and holy work, to God's honour, is the indispensable duty of all those to whom God has revealed his holy sabbaths. 2. The way of sabbath-sanctification is the good old way, Jer. 6:16. Sabbaths are as ancient as the world; and I see no reason to doubt that the sabbath, being now instituted in innocency, was religiously observed by the people of God throughout the patriarchal age. 3. The sabbath of the Lord is truly honourable, and we have reason to honour it — honour it for the sake of its antiquity, its great Author, the sanctification of the first sabbath by the holy God himself, and by our first parents in innocency, in obedience to him. 4. The sabbath day is a blessed day, for God blessed it, and that which he blesses is blessed indeed. God has put an honour upon it, has appointed us, on that day, to bless him, and has promised, on that day, to meet us and bless us. 5. The sabbath day is a holy day, for God has sanctified it. He has separated and distinguished it from the rest of the days of the week, and he has consecrated it and set it apart to himself and his own service and honour. Though it is commonly taken for granted that the Christian sabbath we observe, reckoning from the creation, is not the seventh but the first day of the week, yet being a seventh day, and we in it, celebrating the rest of God the Son, and the finishing of the work of our redemption, we may and ought to act faith upon this original institution of the sabbath day, and to commemorate the work of creation, to the honour of the great Creator, who is therefore worthy to receive, on that day, blessing, and honour, and praise, from all religious assemblies.

Verses 4–7

In these verses, I. Here is a name given to the Creator which we have not yet met with, and that is *Jehovah* — the LORD, in capital letters, which are constantly used in our English translation to intimate that in the original it is *Jehovah.* All along, in the first chapter, he was called *Elohim — a God of power;* but now *Jehovah Elohim — a God of power and perfection,* a finishing God. As we find him known by his name Jehovah when he appeared to perform what he had promised (Ex. 6:3), so now we have him known by that name, when he had perfected what he had begun. *Jehovah* is that great and incommunicable name of God which denotes his having his being of himself, and his giving being to all things; fitly therefore is he called by that name now that heaven and earth are finished.

II. Further notice taken of the production of plants and herbs, because they were made and appointed to be food for man, *v.* 5, 6. Here observe, 1. The earth did not bring forth its fruits of itself, by any innate virtue of its own but purely by the almighty power of God, which formed every plant and every herb before it grew in the earth. Thus grace in the soul, that plant of renown, grows not of itself in nature's soil, but is the work of God's own hands. 2. Rain also is the gift of God; it came not till *the Lord God caused it to rain.* If rain be wanted, it is God that withholds it; if rain come plentifully in its season, it is God that sends it; if it come in a distinguishing way, it is God that *causeth it to rain upon one city and not upon another,* Amos 4:7. 3. Though God, ordinarily, works by means, yet he is not tied to them, but when he pleases he can do his own work without them. As the plants were produced before the sun was made, so they were before there was either rain to water the earth or man to till it. Therefore though we must not tempt God in the neglect of means, yet we must trust God in the want of means. 4. Some way or other God will take care to water the plants that are of his own planting. Though as yet there was no rain, God made a mist equivalent to a shower, and with it *watered the whole face of the ground.* Thus he chose to fulfil his purpose by the weakest means, *that the excellency of the power might be of God.* Divine grace descends like a mist, or silent dew, and waters the church without noise, Deu. 32:2.

III. A more particular account of the creation of man, *v.* 7. Man is a little world, consisting of heaven and earth, soul and body. Now here we have an account of the origin of both and the putting of both together: let us seriously consider it, and say, to our Creator's praise, We are *fearfully and wonderfully made,* Ps. 139:14. Elihu, in the patriarchal age, refers to this history when he says (Job

33:6), *I also am formed out of the clay,* and (v. 4), *The breath of the Almighty hath given me life,* and (ch. 32:8), *There is a spirit in man.* Observe then,

1. The mean origin, and yet the curious structure, of the body of man. (1.) The matter was despicable. He was made *of the dust of the ground,* a very unlikely thing to make a man of; but the same infinite power that made the world of nothing made man, its master-piece, of next to nothing. He was made of the dust, the small dust, such as is upon the surface of the earth. Probably, not dry dust, but dust moistened with the mist that went up, v. 6. He was not made of gold-dust, powder of pearl, or diamond dust, but common dust, dust of the ground. Hence he is said to be of the earth, *choikos — dusty,* 1 Co. 15:47. And we also are of the earth, for we are his offspring, and of the same mould. So near an affinity is there between the earth and our earthly parents that our mother's womb, out of which we were born, is called *the earth* (Ps. 139:15), and the earth, in which we must be buried, is called our *mother's womb,* Job 1:21. Our foundation is in the earth, Job 4:19. Our fabric is earthly, and the fashioning of it like that of an earthen vessel, Job 10:9. Our food is out of the earth, Job 28:5. Our familiarity is with the earth, Job 17:14. Our fathers are in the earth, and our own final tendency is to it; and what have we then to be proud of? (2.) Yet the Maker was great, and the make fine. The Lord God, the great fountain of being and power, formed man. Of the other creatures it is said that they were *created* and *made;* but of man that he was *formed,* which denotes a gradual process in the work with great accuracy and exactness. To express the creation of this new thing, he takes a new word, a word (some think) borrowed from the potter's forming his vessel upon the wheel; for we are the clay, and God the potter, Isa. 64:8. The body of man is curiously wrought, Ps. 139:15, 16. *Materiam superabat opus — The workmanship exceeded the materials.* Let us present our bodies to God as living sacrifices (Rom. 12:1), as living temples (1 Co. 6:19), and then these vile bodies shall shortly be new-formed like Christ's glorious body, Phil. 3:21.

2. The high origin and the admirable serviceableness of the soul of man. (1.) It takes its rise from the breath of heaven, and is produced by it. It was not made of the earth, as the body was; it is a pity then that it should cleave to the earth, and mind earthly things. It came immediately from God; he gave it to be put into the body (Eccl. 12:7), as afterwards he gave the tables of stone of his own writing to be put into the ark, and the *urim* of his own framing to be put into the breast-plate. Hence God is not only the former but the Father of spirits. Let the soul which God has breathed into us breathe after him; and let it be for him, since it is from him. Into his hands let us commit our spirits, for from his hands we had them. (2.) It takes its lodging in a house of clay, and is the life and support of it. It is by it that man is a living soul, that is, a living man; for the soul is the man. The body would be a worthless, useless, loathsome carcase, if the soul did not animate it. To God that gave us these souls we must shortly give an account of them, how we have employed them, used them, proportioned them, and disposed of them; and if then it be found that we have lost them, though it were to gain the world, we shall be undone for ever. Since the extraction of the soul is so noble, and its nature and faculties are so excellent, let us not be of those fools that despise their own souls, by preferring their bodies before them, Prov. 15:32. When our Lord Jesus anointed the blind man's eyes with clay perhaps he intimated that it was he who at first formed man out of the clay; and when he *breathed on his disciples, saying, Receive you the Holy Ghost,* he intimated that it was he who at first breathed into man's nostrils the breath of life. He that made the soul is alone able to new-make it.

Verses 8–15

Man consisting of body and soul, a body made out of the earth and a rational immortal soul the breath of heaven, we have, in these verses, the provision that was made for the happiness of both; he that made him took care to make him happy, if he could but have kept himself so and known when he was well off. That part of man by which he is allied to the world of sense was made happy; for he was put in the paradise of God: that part by which he is allied to the world of spirits was well provided for; for he

was taken into covenant with God. Lord, what is man that he should be thus dignified — man that is a worm! Here we have,

I. A description of the garden of Eden, which was intended for the mansion and demesne of this great lord, the palace of this prince. The inspired penman, in this history, writing for the Jews first, and calculating his narratives for the infant state of the church, describes things by their outward sensible appearances, and leaves us, by further discoveries of the divine light, to be led into the understanding of the mysteries couched under them. Spiritual things were strong meat, which they could not yet bear; but he writes to them as unto carnal, 1 Co. 3:1. Therefore he does not so much insist upon the happiness of Adam's mind as upon that of his outward state. The Mosaic history, as well as the Mosaic law, has rather the patterns of heavenly things than the heavenly things themselves, Heb. 9:23. Observe,

1. The place appointed for Adam's residence was a garden; not an ivory house nor a palace overlaid with gold, but a garden, furnished and adorned by nature, not by art. What little reason have men to be proud of stately and magnificent buildings, when it was the happiness of man in innocency that he needed none! As clothes came in with sin, so did houses. The heaven was the roof of Adam's house, and never was any roof so curiously ceiled and painted. The earth was his floor, and never was any floor so richly inlaid. The shadow of the trees was his retirement; under them were his dining-rooms, his lodging-rooms, and never were any rooms so finely hung as these: Solomon's, in all their glory, were not arrayed like them. The better we can accommodate ourselves to plain things, and the less we indulge ourselves with those artificial delights which have been invented to gratify men's pride and luxury, the nearer we approach to a state of innocency. Nature is content with a little and that which is most natural, grace with less, but lust with nothing.

2. The contrivance and furniture of this garden were the immediate work of God's wisdom and power. The Lord God planted this garden, that is, he *had* planted it — upon the third day, when the fruits of the earth were made. We may well suppose to have been the most accomplished place for pleasure and delight that ever the sun saw, when the all-sufficient God himself designed it to be the present happiness of his beloved creature, man, in innocency, and a type and a figure of the happiness of the chosen remnant in glory. No delights can be agreeable nor satisfying to a soul but those that God himself has provided and appointed for it; no true paradise, but of God's planting. The light of our own fires, and the sparks of our own kindling, will soon leave us in the dark, Isa. 50:11. The whole earth was now a paradise compared with what it is since the fall and since the flood; the finest gardens in the world are a wilderness compared with what the whole face of the ground was before it was cursed for man's sake: yet that was not enough; God planted a garden for Adam. God's chosen ones shall have distinguishing favours shown them.

3. The situation of this garden was extremely sweet. It was in *Eden,* which signifies *delight* and *pleasure.* The place is here particularly pointed out by such marks and bounds as were sufficient, I suppose, when Moses wrote, to specify the place to those who knew that country; but now, it seems, the curious cannot satisfy themselves concerning it. Let it be our care to make sure a place in the heavenly paradise, and then we need not perplex ourselves with a search after the place of the earthly paradise. It is certain that, wherever it was, it had all desirable conveniences, and (which never any house nor garden on earth was) without any convenience. Beautiful for situation, the joy and the glory of the whole earth, was this garden: doubtless it was earth in its highest perfection.

4. The trees with which this garden was planted. (1.) It had all the best and choicest trees in common with the rest of the ground. It was beautiful and adorned with every tree that, for its height or breadth, its make or colour, its leaf or flower, was pleasant to the sight and charmed the eye; it was replenished and enriched with every tree that yielded fruit grateful to the taste and useful to the body, and so good for food. God, as a tender Father, consulted not only Adam's profit, but his pleasure; for there is a pleasure consistent with innocency, nay, there is a true and tran-

scendent pleasure in innocency. God delights in the prosperity of his servants, and would have them easy; it is owing to themselves if they be uneasy. When Providence puts us into an Eden of plenty and pleasure, we ought to *serve him with joyfulness and gladness of heart,* in the abundance of the good things he gives us. But, (2.) It had two extraordinary trees peculiar to itself; on earth there were not their like. [1.] There was the *tree of life in the midst of the garden,* which was not so much a memorandum to him of the fountain and author of his life, nor perhaps any natural means to preserve or prolong life; but it was chiefly intended to be a sign and seal to Adam, assuring him of the continuance of life and happiness, even to immortality and everlasting bliss, through the grace and favour of his Maker, upon condition of his perseverance in this state of innocency and obedience. Of this he might eat and live. Christ is now to us the tree of life (Rev. 2:7; 22:2), and the *bread of life,* Jn. 6:48, 53. [2.] There was the *tree of the knowledge of good and evil,* so called, not because it had any virtue in it to beget or increase useful knowledge (surely then it would not have been forbidden), but, *First,* Because there was an express positive revelation of the will of God concerning this tree, so that by it he might know moral good and evil. What is good? It is good not to eat of this tree. The distinction between all other moral good and evil was written in the heart of man by nature; but this, which resulted from a positive law, was written upon this tree. *Secondly,* Because, in the event, it proved to give Adam an experimental knowledge of good by the loss of it and of evil by the sense of it. As the covenant of grace has in it, not only *Believe and be saved,* but also, *Believe not and be damned* (Mk. 16:16), so the covenant of innocency had in it, not only "Do this and live," which was sealed and confirmed by the tree of life, but, "Fail and die," which Adam was assured of by this other tree: "Touch it at your peril;" so that, in these two trees, God set before him *good and evil, the blessing and the curse,* Deu. 30:19. These two trees were as two sacraments.

5. The rivers with which this garden was watered, v. 10–14. These four rivers (or one river branched into four streams) contributed much both to the pleasantness and the fruitfulness of this garden. The land of Sodom is said to be *well watered every where, as the garden of the Lord, ch.* 13:10. Observe, That which God plants he will take care to keep watered. The trees of righteousness are set by the rivers, Ps. 1:3. In the heavenly paradise there is a river infinitely surpassing these; for it is a river of the water of life, not coming out of Eden, as this, but proceeding out of the throne of God and of the Lamb (Rev. 22:1), a river that *makes glad the city of our God,* Ps. 46:4. Hiddekel and Euphrates are rivers of Babylon, which we read of elsewhere. By these the captive Jews sat down and *wept, when they remembered Sion* (Ps. 137:1); but methinks they had much more reason to weep (and so have we) at the remembrance of Eden. Adam's paradise was their prison; such wretched work has sin made. Of the land of Havilah it is said (v. 12), *The gold of that land is good,* and *there is bdellium and the onyx-stone:* surely this is mentioned that the wealth of which the land of Havilah boasted might be as foil to that which was the glory of the land of Eden. Havilah had gold, and spices, and precious stones; but Eden had that which was infinitely better, the tree of life, and communion with God. So we may say of the Africans and Indians: "They have the gold, but we have the gospel. The gold of their land is good, but the riches of ours are infinitely better."

II. The placing of man in this paradise of delight, v. 15, where observe,

1. How God put him in possession of it: *The Lord God took the man, and put him into the garden of Eden;* so v. 8, 15. Note here, (1.) Man was made *out* of paradise; for, after God had formed him, he put him into the garden: he was made of common clay, not of paradise-dust. He lived out of Eden before he lived in it, that he might see that all the comforts of his paradise-state were owing to God's free grace. He could not plead a tenant-right to the garden, for he was not born upon the premises, nor had any thing but what he received; all boasting was hereby for ever excluded. (2.) The same God that was the author of his being was the author of his bliss; the same hand that made him a living soul planted the tree of life for him, and settled him by it. He that made us is alone able to

make us happy; he that is the former of our bodies and the Father of our spirits, he, and none but he, can effectually provide for the felicity of both. (3.) It adds much to the comfort of any condition if we have plainly seen God going before us and putting us into it. If we have not forced providence, but followed it, and taken the hints of direction it has given us, we may hope to find a paradise where otherwise we could not have expected it. See Ps. 47:4.

2. How God appointed him business and employment. He put him there, not like Leviathan into the waters, to play therein, but to dress the garden and to keep it. Paradise itself was not a place of exemption from work. Note, here, (1.) We were none of us sent into the world to be idle. He that made us these souls and bodies has given us something to work with; and he that gave us this earth for our habitation has made us something to work on. If a high extraction, or a great estate, or a large dominion, or perfect innocency, or a genius for pure contemplation, or a small family, could have given a man a writ of ease, Adam would not have been set to work; but he that gave us being has given us business, to serve him and our generation, and to work out our salvation: if we do not mind our business, we are unworthy of our being and maintenance. (2.) Secular employments will vary well consist with a state of innocency and a life of communion with God. The sons and heirs of heaven, while they are here in this world, have something to do about this earth, which must have its share of their time and thoughts; and, if they do it with an eye to God, they are as truly serving him in it as when they are upon their knees. (3.) The husbandman's calling is an ancient and honourable calling; it was needful even in paradise. The garden of Eden, though it needed not to be weeded (for thorns and thistles were not yet a nuisance), yet must be dressed and kept. Nature, even in its primitive state, left room for the improvements of art and industry. It was a calling fit for a state of innocency, making provision for life, not for lust, and giving man an opportunity of admiring the Creator and acknowledging his providence: while his hands were about his trees, his heart might be with his God. (4.) There is a true pleasure in the business which God calls us to, and employs us in. Adam's work was so far from being an allay that it was an addition to the pleasures of paradise; he could not have been happy if he had been idle: it is still a law, He that will not work has no right to eat, 2 Th. 3:10; Prov. 27:23.

III. The command which God gave to man in innocency, and the covenant he then took him into. Hitherto we have seen God as man's powerful Creator and his bountiful Benefactor; now he appears as his Ruler and Lawgiver. God put him into the garden of Eden, not to live there as he might list, but to be under government. As we are not allowed to be idle in this world, and to do nothing, so we are not allowed to be wilful, and do what we please. When God had given man a dominion over the creatures, he would let him know that still he himself was under the government of his Creator.

Verses 16–17

Observe here, I. God's authority over man, as a creature that had reason and freedom of will. The Lord God commanded the man, who stood now as a public person, the father and representative of all mankind, to receive law, as he had lately received a nature, for himself and all his. God commanded all the creatures, according to their capacity; the settled course of nature is a law, Ps. 148:6; 104:9. The brute-creatures have their respective instincts; but man was made capable of performing reasonable service, and therefore received, not only the command of a Creator, but the command of a Prince and Master. Though Adam was a very great man, a very good man, and a very happy man, yet the Lord God commanded him; and the command was no disparagement to his greatness, no reproach to his goodness, nor any diminution at all to his happiness. Let us acknowledge God's right to rule us, and our own obligations to be ruled by him; and never allow any will of our own in contradiction to, or competition with, the holy will of God.

II. The particular act of this authority, in prescribing to him what he should do, and upon what terms he should stand with his Creator. Here is,

1. A confirmation of his present happiness to him, in that grant, *Of every tree in the garden thou mayest freely eat.* This was not only an allowance of liberty to him, in taking the delicious fruits of paradise, as a recompence for his care and pains in dressing and keeping it (1 Co. 9:7, 10), but it was, withal, an assurance of life to him, immortal life, upon his obedience. For the tree of life being put *in the midst of the garden* (*v.* 9), as the heart and soul of it, doubtless God had an eye to that especially in this grant; and therefore when, upon his revolt, this grant is recalled, no notice is taken of any tree of the garden as prohibited to him, except the tree of life (*ch.* 3:22), of which it is there said he might have eaten and *lived for ever,* that is, never died, nor ever lost his happiness. "Continue holy as thou art, in conformity to thy Creator's will, and thou shalt continue happy as thou art in the enjoyment of thy Creator's favour, either in this paradise or in a better." Thus, upon condition of perfect personal and perpetual obedience, Adam was sure of paradise to himself and his heirs for ever.

2. A trial of his obedience, upon pain of the forfeiture of all his happiness: *"But of the* other tree which stood very near the tree of life (for they are both said to be *in the midst of the garden),* and which was called the *tree of knowledge, in the day thou eatest thereof, thou shalt surely die;"* as if he had said, "Know, Adam, that thou art now upon thy good behaviour, thou art put into paradise upon trial; be observant, be obedient, and thou art made for ever; otherwise thou wilt be as miserable as now thou art happy." Here,

(1.) Adam is threatened with death in case of disobedience: *Dying thou shalt die,* denoting a sure and dreadful sentence, as, in the former part of this covenant, *eating thou shalt eat,* denotes a free and full grant. Observe [1.] Even Adam, in innocency, was awed with a threatening; fear is one of the handles of the soul, by which it is taken hold of and held. If he then needed this hedge, much more do we now. [2.] The penalty threatened is death: *Thou shalt die,* that is, "Thou shalt be debarred from the tree of life, and all the good that is signified by it, all the happiness thou hast, either in possession or prospect; and thou shalt become liable to death, and all the miseries that preface it and attend it." [3.] This was threatened as the immediate consequence of sin: *In the day thou eatest, thou shalt die,* that is, "Thou shalt become mortal and capable of dying; the grant of immortality shall be recalled, and that defence shall depart from thee. Thou shalt become obnoxious to death, like a condemned malefactor that is dead in the law" (only, because Adam was to be the root of mankind, he was reprieved); "nay, the harbingers and forerunners of death shall immediately seize thee, and thy life, thenceforward, shall be a dying life: and this, *surely;* it is a settled rule, *the soul that sinneth, it shall die.*"

(2.) Adam is tried with a positive law, not to eat of the fruit *of the tree of knowledge.* Now it was very proper to make trial of his obedience by such a command as this, [1.] Because the reason of it is fetched purely from the will of the Law-maker. Adam had in his nature an aversion to that which was evil in itself, and therefore he is tried in a thing which was evil only because it was forbidden; and, being in a small thing, it was the more fit to prove his obedience by. [2.] Because the restraint of it is laid upon the desires of the flesh and of the mind, which, in the corrupt nature of man, are the two great fountains of sin. This prohibition checked both his appetite towards sensitive delights and his ambitions of curious knowledge, that his body might be ruled by his soul and his soul by his God.

Thus easy, thus happy, was man in a state of innocency, having all that heart could wish to make him so. How good was God to him! How many favours did he load him with! How easy were the laws he gave him! How kind the covenant he made with him! Yet man, being in honour, understood not his own interest, but soon *became as the beasts that perish.*

Verses 18–20

Here we have, I. An instance of the Creator's care of man and his fatherly concern for his comfort, *v.* 18. Though God had let him know that he was a subject, by giving him a command, (*v.* 16, 17), yet here he lets him know also, for his encouragement in his obedience, that he was a friend, and a favourite, and one whose satisfaction he was tender of. Observe,

1. How God graciously pitied his solitude: *It is not good that man, this man, should be alone.* Though there was an upper world of angels and a lower world of brutes, and he between them, yet there being none of the same nature and rank of beings with himself, none that he could converse familiarly with, he might be truly said to be *alone.* Now he that made him knew both him and what was good for him, better than he did himself, and he said, "It is not good that he should continue thus alone." (1.) It is not for his comfort; for man is a sociable creature. It is a pleasure to him to exchange knowledge and affection with those of his own kind, to inform and to be informed, to love and to be beloved. What God here says of the first man Solomon says of all men (Eccl. 4:9, etc.), that *two are better than one,* and *woe to him that is alone.* If there were but one man in the world, what a melancholy man must he needs be! Perfect solitude would turn a paradise into a desert, and a palace into a dungeon. Those therefore are foolish who are selfish and would be place alone in the earth. (2.) It is not for the increase and continuance of his kind. God could have made a world of men at first, to replenish the earth, as he replenished heaven with a world of angels: but the place would have been too strait for the designed number of men to live together at once; therefore God saw fit to make up that number by a succession of generations, which, as God had formed man, must be from two, and those male and female; one will be ever one.

2. How God graciously resolved to provide society for him. The result of this reasoning concerning him was this kind resolution, *I will make a help-meet for him;* a help *like* him (so some read it), one of the same nature and the same rank of beings; a help *near* him (so others), one to cohabit with him, and to be always at hand; a help *before* him (so others), one that he should look upon with pleasure and delight. Note hence, (1.) In our best state in this world we have need of one another's help; for we are members one of another, and *the eye cannot say to the hand, I have no need of thee,* 1 Co. 12:21. We must therefore be glad to receive help from others, and give help to others, as there is occasion. (2.) It is God only who perfectly knows our wants, and is perfectly able to supply them all, Phil. 4:19. In him alone our help is, and from him are all our helpers. (3.) A suitable wife is a help-meet, and is from the Lord. The relation is then likely to be comfortable when meetness directs and determines the choice, and mutual helpfulness is the constant care and endeavour, 1 Co. 7:33, 34. (4.) Family-society, if it is agreeable, is a redress sufficient for the grievance of solitude. He that has a good God, a good heart, and a good wife, to converse with, and yet complains he wants conversation, would not have been easy and content in paradise; for Adam himself had no more: yet, even before Eve was created, we do not find that he complained of being alone, knowing that he *was not alone, for the Father was with him.* Those that are most satisfied in God and his favour are in the best way, and in the best frame, to receive the good things of this life, and shall be sure of them, as far as Infinite Wisdom sees good.

II. An instance of the creatures' subjection to man, and his dominion over them (*v.* 19, 20): *Every beast of the field and every fowl of the air God brought to Adam,* either by the ministry of angels, or by a special instinct, directing them to come to man as their master, teaching the ox betimes to know his owner. Thus God gave man livery and seisin of the fair estate he had granted him, and put him in possession of his dominion over the creatures. God brought them to him, that he might name them, and so might give, 1. A proof of his knowledge, as a creature endued with the faculties both of reason and speech, and so *taught more than the beasts of the earth and made wiser than the fowls of the heaven,* Job 35:11. And, 2. A proof of his power. It is an act of authority to impose names (Dan. 1:7), and of subjection to receive them. The inferior creatures did now, as it were, do homage to their prince at his inauguration, and swear fealty and allegiance to him. If Adam had continued faithful to his God, we may suppose the creatures themselves would so well have known and remembered the names Adam now gave them as to have come at his call, at any time, and answered to their names. God gave names to the day and night, to the firmament, to the earth, and to the sea; and he *calleth the stars by their names,* to show that he is the supreme Lord of these.

But he gave Adam leave to name the beasts and fowls, as their subordinate lord; for, having made him in his own image, he thus put some of his honour upon him.

III. An instance of the creatures' insufficiency to be a happiness for man: *But* (among them all) *for Adam there was not found a help meet for him.* Some make these to be the words of Adam himself; observing all the creatures come to him by couples to be named, he thus intimates his desire to his Maker: — "Lord, these have all helps meet for them; but what shall I do? Here is never a one for me." It is rather God's judgment upon the review. He brought them all together, to see if there were ever a suitable match for Adam in any of the numerous families of the inferior creatures; but there was none. Observe here, 1. The dignity and excellency of the human nature. On earth there was not its like, nor its peer to be found among all visible creatures; they were all looked over, but it could not be matched among them all. 2. The vanity of this world and the things of it; put them all together, and they will not make a help-meet for man. They will not suit the nature of his soul, nor supply its needs, nor satisfy its just desires, nor run parallel with its never-failing duration. God creates a new thing to be a help-meet for man — not so much the woman as the seed of the woman.

Verses 21–25

Here we have, I. The making of the woman, to be a help-meet for Adam. This was done upon the sixth day, as was also the placing of Adam in paradise, though it is here mentioned after an account of the seventh day's rest; but what was said in general (*ch.* 1:27), that God made man male and female, is more distinctly related here. Observe, 1. That Adam was first formed, then Eve (1 Tim. 2:13), and she was made of the man, and for the man (1 Co. 11:8, 9), all which are urged there as reasons for the humility, modesty, silence, and submissiveness, of that sex in general, and particularly the subjection and reverence which wives owe to their own husbands. Yet man being made last of the creatures, as the best and most excellent of all, Eve's being made after Adam, and out of him, puts an honour upon that sex, as the glory of the man, 1 Co. 11:7. If man is the head, she is the crown, a crown to her husband, the crown of the visible creation. The man was dust refined, but the woman was dust double-refined, one remove further from the earth. 2. That Adam slept while his wife was in making, that no room might be left to imagine that he had herein *directed the Spirit of the Lord, or been his counsellor,* Isa. 40:13. He had been made sensible of his want of a meet help; but, God having undertaken to provide him one, he does not afflict himself with any care about it, but lies down and sleeps sweetly, as one that had cast all his care on God, with a cheerful resignation of himself and all his affairs to his Maker's will and wisdom. Jehovah-jireh, let the Lord provide when and whom he pleases. If we graciously rest in God, God will graciously work for us and work all for good. 3. That *God caused a sleep to fall on Adam,* and made it a deep sleep, that so the opening of his side might be no grievance to him; while he knows no sin, God will take care he shall feel no pain. When God, by his providence, does that to his people which is grievous to flesh and blood, he not only consults their happiness in the issue, but by his grace he can so quiet and compose their spirits as to make them easy under the sharpest operations. 4. That the woman was *made of a rib out of the side of Adam;* not made out of his head to rule over him, nor out of his feet to be trampled upon by him, but out of his side to be equal with him, under his arm to be protected, and near his heart to be beloved. Adam lost a rib, and without any diminution to his strength or comeliness (for, doubtless, the flesh was closed without a scar); but in lieu thereof he had a help meet for him, which abundantly made up his loss: what God takes away from his people he will, one way or other, restore with advantage. In this (as in many other things) Adam was a figure of him that was to come; for out of the side of Christ, the second Adam, his spouse the church was formed, when he slept the sleep, the deep sleep, of death upon the cross, in order to which his side was opened, and there came out blood and water, blood to purchase his church and water to purify it to himself. See Eph. 5:25, 26.

II. The marriage of the woman to Adam. Marriage is honourable, but this surely was the most honourable marriage that ever was, in which God himself had all along an immediate hand. Marriages (they say) are made in heaven: we are sure this was, for the man, the woman, the match, were all God's own work; he, by his power, made them *both,* and now, by his ordinance, made them *one.* This was a marriage made in perfect innocency, and so was never any marriage since, 1. God, as *her* Father, brought the woman to the man, as his second self, and a help-meet for him. When he had made her, he did not leave her to her own disposal; no, she was his child, and she must not marry without his consent. Those are likely to settle to their comfort who by faith and prayer, and a humble dependence upon providence, put themselves under a divine conduct. That wife that is of God's making by special grace, and of God's bringing by special providence, is likely to prove a help-meet for a man. 2. From God, as *his* Father, Adam received her (*v.* 23): *"This is now bone of my bone.* Now I have what I wanted, and which all the creatures could not furnish me with, a help meet for me." God's gifts to us are to be received with a humble thankful acknowledgment of his wisdom in suiting them to us, and his favour in bestowing them on us. Probably it was revealed to Adam in a vision, when he was asleep, that this lovely creature, now presented to him, was a piece of himself, and was to be his companion and the wife of his covenant. Hence some have fetched an argument to prove that glorified saints in the heavenly paradise shall know one another. Further, in token of his acceptance of her, he gave her a name, not peculiar to her, but common to her sex: *She shall be called woman, Isha,* a *she-man,* differing from man in sex only, not in nature — made of man, and joined to man.

III. The institution of the ordinance of marriage, and the settling of the law of it, *v.* 24. The sabbath and marriage were two ordinances instituted in innocency, the former for the preservation of the church, the latter for the preservation of the world of mankind. It appears (by Mt. 19:4, 5) that it was God himself who said here, "A man must leave all his relations, to cleave to his wife;" but whether he spoke it by Moses, the penman, or by Adam (who spoke, *v.* 23), is uncertain. It should seem, they are the words of Adam, in God's name, laying down this law to all his posterity. 1. See here how great the virtue of a divine ordinance is; the bonds of it are stronger even than those of nature. To whom can we be more firmly bound than the fathers that begat us and the mothers that bore us? Yet the son must quit them, to be joined to his wife, and the daughter forget them, to cleave to her husband, Ps. 45:10, 11. 2. See how necessary it is that children should take their parents' consent along with them in their marriage, and how unjust those are to their parents, as well as undutiful, who marry without it; for they rob them of their right to them, and interest in them, and alienate it to another, fraudulently and unnaturally. 3. See what need there is both of prudence and prayer in the choice of this relation, which is so near and so lasting. That had need be well done which is to be done for life. 4. See how firm the bond of marriage is, not to be divided and weakened by having many wives (Mal. 2:15) nor to be broken or cut off by divorce, for any cause but fornication, or voluntary desertion. 5. See how dear the affection ought to be between husband and wife, such as there is to our own bodies, Eph. 5:28. These two are one flesh; let them then be one soul.

IV. An evidence of the purity and innocency of that state wherein our first parents were created, *v.* 25. They were both naked. They needed no clothes for defense against cold nor heat, for neither could be injurious to them. They needed none for ornament. Solomon in all his glory was not arrayed like one of these. Nay, they needed none for decency; they were naked, and had no reason to be ashamed. *They knew not what shame was,* so the Chaldee reads it. Blushing is now the colour of virtue, but it was not then the colour of innocency. Those that had no sin in their conscience might well have no shame in their faces, though they had no clothes to their backs.

CHAPTER 3

The story of this chapter is perhaps as sad a story (all things considered) as any we have in all the Bible. In the foregoing chapters we have had the pleasant view of the holiness and happiness of our first parents, the grace and favour of God, and the peace and beauty of the whole creation, all good, very good; but here the scene is altered. We have here an account of the sin and misery of our first parents, the wrath and curse of God against them, the peace of the creation disturbed, and its beauty stained and sullied, all bad, very bad. "How has the gold become dim, and the most fine gold changed!" O that our hearts were deeply affected with this record! For we are all nearly concerned in it; let it not be to us as a tale that is told. The general contents of this chapter we have (Rom. 5:12), "By one man sin entered into the world, and death by sin; and so death passed upon all men, for that all have sinned." More particularly, we have here, I. The innocent tempted (*v.* 1–5). II. The tempted transgressing (*v.* 6–8). III. The transgressors arraigned (*v.* 9, 10). IV. Upon their arraignment, convicted (*v.* 11–13). V. Upon their conviction, sentenced, (*v.* 14–19). VI. After sentence, reprieved (*v.* 20, 21). VII. Notwithstanding their reprieve, execution in part done (*v.* 22–24). And were it not for the gracious intimations here given of redemption by the promised seed, they, and all their degenerate guilty race, would have been left to endless despair.

Verses 1–5

We have here an account of the temptation with which Satan assaulted our first parents, to draw them into sin, and which proved fatal to them. Here observe,

I. The tempter, and that was the devil, in the shape and likeness of a serpent.

1. It is certain it was the devil that beguiled Eve. The devil and Satan is the old serpent (Rev. 12:9), a malignant spirit, by creation an angel of light and an immediate attendant upon God's throne, but by sin become an apostate from his first state and a rebel against God's crown and dignity. Multitudes of the angels fell; but this that attacked our first parents was surely the prince of the devils, the ring-leader in the rebellion: no sooner was he a sinner than he was a Satan, no sooner a traitor than a tempter, as one enraged against God and his glory and envious of man and his happiness. He knew he could not destroy man but by debauching him. Balaam could not curse Israel, but he could tempt Israel, Rev. 2:14. The game therefore which Satan had to play was to draw our first parents to sin, and so to separate between them and their God. Thus the devil was, from the beginning, a murderer, and the great mischief-maker. The whole race of mankind had here, as it were, but one neck, and at that Satan struck. The adversary and enemy is that wicked one.

2. It was the devil in the likeness of a serpent. Whether it was only the visible shape and appearance of a serpent (as some think those were of which we read, Ex. 7:12), or whether it was a real living serpent, actuated and possessed by the devil, is not certain: by God's permission it might be either. The devil chose to act his part in a serpent, (1.) Because it is a specious creature, has a spotted dappled skin, and then went erect. Perhaps it was a flying serpent, which seemed to come from on high as a messenger from the upper world, one of the seraphim; for the fiery serpents were flying, Isa. 14:29. Many a dangerous temptation comes to us in gay fine colours that are but skin-deep, and seems to come from above; for Satan can seem an angel of light. And, (2.) Because it is a subtle creature; this is here taken notice of. Many instances are given of the subtlety of the serpent, both to do mischief and to secure himself in it when it is done. We are directed to be wise as serpents. But this serpent, as actuated by the devil, was no doubt more subtle than any other; for the devil, though he has lost the sanctity, retains the sagacity of an angel, and is wise to do evil. He knew of more advantage by making use of the serpent than we are aware of. Observe, There is not any thing by which the devil serves himself and his own interest more than by unsanctified subtlety. What Eve thought of this serpent speaking to her we are not likely to tell, when I believe she herself did not know what to think of it. At first, perhaps, she supposed it might be a good angel, and yet, afterwards, she might suspect something amiss. It is remarkable that the Gentile idolaters did many of them worship the devil in the shape and form of a serpent, thereby avowing their adherence to that apostate spirit, and wearing his colours.

II. The person tempted was the woman, now alone, and at a distance from her husband, but near the forbidden tree. It was the devil's subtlety, 1. To assault the weaker vessel with his temptations. Though perfect in her kind, yet we may suppose her inferior to Adam in knowledge, and strength, and presence of mind. Some think Eve received the command, not immediately from God, but at second hand by her husband, and therefore might the more easily be persuaded to discredit it. 2. It was his policy to enter into discourse with her when she was alone.

Had she kept close to the side out of which she was lately taken, she would not have been so much exposed. There are many temptations, to which solitude gives great advantage; but the communion of saints contributes much tot heir strength and safety. 3. He took advantage by finding her near the forbidden tree, and probably gazing upon the fruit of it, only to satisfy her curiosity. Those that would not eat the forbidden fruit must not come near the forbidden tree. *Avoid it, pass not by it,* Prov. 4:15. 4. Satan tempted Eve, that by her he might tempt Adam; so he tempted Job by his wife, and Christ by Peter. It is his policy to send temptations by unsuspected hands, and theirs that have most interest in us and influence upon us.

III. The temptation itself, and the artificial management of it. We are often, in scripture, told of our danger by the temptations of Satan, hid *devices* (2 Co. 2:11), his *depths* (Rev. 2:24), his *wiles,* Eph. 6:11. The greatest instances we have of them are in his tempting of the two Adams, here, and Mt. 4. In this he prevailed, but in that he was baffled. What he spoke *to* them, of whom he had no hold by any corruption in them, he speaks *in* us by our own deceitful hearts and their carnal reasonings; this makes his assaults on us less discernible, but not less dangerous. That which the devil aimed at was to persuade Eve to cut forbidden fruit; and, to do this, he took the same method that he does still. He questioned whether it was a sin or no, *v.* 1. He denied that there was any danger in it, *v.* 4. He suggested much advantage by it, *v.* 5. And these are his common topics.

1. He questioned whether it was a sin or no to eat of this tree, and whether really the fruit of it was forbidden. Observe,

(1.) *He said to the woman, Yea, hath God said, You shall not eat?* The first word intimated something said before, introducing this, and with which it is connected, perhaps some discourse Eve had with herself, which Satan took hold of, and grafted this question upon. In the chain of thoughts one thing strangely brings in another, and perhaps something bad at last. Observe here, [1.] He does not discover his design at first, but puts a question which seemed innocent: "I hear a piece of news, pray is it true? has God forbidden you to eat of this tree?" Thus he would begin a discourse, and draw her into a parley. Those that would be safe have need to be suspicious, and shy of talking with the tempter. [2.] He quotes the command fallaciously, as if it were a prohibition, not only of that tree, but of all. God had said, *Of every tree you may eat, except one.* He, by aggravating the exception, endeavours to invalidate the concession: *Hath God said, You shall not eat of every tree?* The divine law cannot be reproached unless it be first misrepresented. [3.] He seems to speak it tauntingly, upbraiding the woman with her shyness of meddling with that tree; as if he had said, "You are so nice and cautious, and so very precise, because God has said, 'You shall not eat.'' The devil, as he is a liar, so he is a scoffer, from the beginning: and the scoffers of the last days are his children. [4.] That which he aimed at in the first onset was to take off her sense of the obligation of the command. "Surely you are mistaken, it cannot be that God should tie you out from this tree; he would not do so unreasonable a thing." See here, That it is the subtlety of Satan to blemish the reputation of the divine law as uncertain or unreasonable, and so to draw people to sin; and that it is therefore our wisdom to keep up a a firm belief of, and a high respect for, the command of God. Has God said, "You shall not lie, nor take his name in vain, nor be drunk," etc.? "Yes, I am sure he has, and it is well said, and by his grace I will abide by it, whatever the tempter suggests to the contrary."

(2.) In answer to this question the woman gives him a plain and full account of the law they were under, *v.* 2, 3. Here observe, [1.] It was her weakness to enter into discourse with the serpent. She might have perceived by his question that he had no good design, and should therefore have started back with a *Get thee behind me, Satan, thou art an offence to me.* But her curiosity, and perhaps her surprise, to hear a serpent speak, led her into further talk with him. Note, It is a dangerous thing to treat with a temptation, which ought at first to be rejected with disdain and abhorrence. The garrison that sounds a parley is not far from being surrendered. Those that would be kept from harm must keep out of harm's way. See Prov. 14:7; 19:27. [2.] It was her wisdom to take notice of the liberty God had granted them, in answer to his sly insinuation, as if God has put them into paradise only to tantalize them with the sight of fair but forbidden fruits. "Yea," says she, "we may eat of the fruit of the trees, thanks to our Maker, we have plenty and variety enough allowed us." Note, To prevent our being uneasy at the restraints of religion, it is good often to take a view of the liberties and comforts of it. [3.] It was an instance of her resolution that she adhered to the command, and faithfully repeated it, as of unquestionable certainty: *"God hath said,* I am confident he hath said it, You shall not eat of the fruit of this tree;" and that which she adds, *Neither shall you touch it,* seems to have been with a good intention, not (as some think) tacitly to reflect upon the command as too strict *(Touch not, taste not and handle not),* but to make a fence about it: "We must not eat, therefore we will not touch. It is forbidden in the highest degree, and the authority of the prohibition is sacred to us." [4.] She seems a little to waver about the threatening, and is not so particular and faithful in the repetition of that as of the precept. God has said, *In the day thou eatest thereof thou shalt surely die;* all she makes of that is, *Lest you die.* Note, Wavering faith and wavering resolutions give great advantage to the tempter.

2. He denies that there was any danger in it, insisting that, though it might be the transgressing of a precept, yet it would not be the incurring of a penalty: *You shall not surely die, v.* 4. "You shall not *dying die,"* so the word is, in direct contradiction to what God had said. Either, (1.) "It is not certain that you shall die," so some. "It is not so sure as you are made to believe it is." Thus Satan endeavours to shake that which he cannot overthrow, and invalidates the force of divine threatenings by questioning the certainty of them; and, when once it is supposed possible that there may be falsehood or fallacy in any word of God, a door is then opened to downright infidelity. Satan teaches men first to doubt and then to deny; he makes them sceptics first, and so by degrees makes them atheists. Or, (2.) "It is certain you shall not die," so others. He avers his contradiction with the same phrase of assurance that God had used in ratifying the threatening. He began to call the precept in question (*v.* 1), but, finding that the woman adhered to that, he quitted that battery, and made his second onset upon the threatening, where he perceived her to waver; for he is quick to spy all advantages, and to attack the wall where it is weakest: *You shall not surely die.* This was a lie, a downright lie; for, [1.] It was contrary to the word of God, which we are sure is true. See 1 Jn. 2:21, 27. It was such a lie as gave the lie to God himself. [2.] It was contrary to his own knowledge. When he told them there was no danger in disobedience and rebellion he said that which he knew, by woeful experience, to be false. He had broken the law of his creation, and had found, to his cost, that he could not prosper in it; and yet he tells our first parents they shall not die. He concealed his own misery, that he might draw them into the like: thus he still deceives sinners into their own ruin. He tells them that, though they sin, they shall not die; and gains credit rather than God, who tells them, *The wages of sin is death.* Note, Hope of impunity is a great support to all iniquity, and impenitency in it. *I shall have peace, though I walk in the imagination of my heart,* Deu. 29:19.

3. He promises them advantage by it, *v.* 5. Here he follows his blow, and it was a blow at the root, a fatal blow to the tree we are branches of. He not only would undertake that they should be no losers by it, thus binding himself to save them from harm; but (if they would be such fools as to venture upon the security of one that had himself become a bankrupt) he undertakes they shall be gainers by it, unspeakable gainers. He could not have persuaded them to run the hazard of ruining themselves if he had not suggested to them a great probability of bettering themselves.

(1.) He insinuates to them the great improvements they would make by eating of this fruit. And he suits the temptation to the pure state they were now in, proposing to them, not any carnal pleasures or gratifications, but intellectual delights and satisfactions. These were the baits with which he covered his hook. [1.] *"Your eyes shall be opened;* you shall have much more of the power and pleasure of contemplation than now you have; you shall fetch a larger compass in your intellectual views, and see further into things than now you do." He speaks as if now they were but dim-sighted, and short-sighted, in comparison of what they would be then. [2.] *"You shall be as gods,* as *Elohim,* mighty gods; not only omniscient, but omnipotent too;" or, "You shall be as God himself, equal to him, rivals with him; you shall be sovereigns and no longer subjects, self-sufficient and no longer dependent." A most absurd suggestion! As if it were possible for creatures of yesterday to be like their Creator that was from eternity. [3.] "You shall know *good and evil,* that is, every thing that is desirable to be known." To support this part of the temptation, he abuses the name given to this tree: it was intended to teach the practical knowledge of good and evil, that is, of duty and disobedience; and it would prove the experimental knowledge of good and evil, that is, of happiness and misery. In these senses, the name of the tree was a warning to them not to eat of it; but he perverts the sense of it, and wrests it to their destruction, as if this tree would give them a speculative notional knowledge of the natures, kinds, and originals, of good and evil. And, [4.] All this presently: *"In the day you eat thereof* you will find a sudden and immediate change for the better." Now in all these insinuations he aims to beget in them, *First,* Discontent with their present state, as if it were not so good as it might be, and should be. Note, No condition will of itself bring contentment, unless the mind be brought to it. Adam was not easy, no, not in paradise, nor the angels in their first state, Jude 6. *Secondly,* Ambition of preferment, as if they were fit to be gods. Satan had ruined himself by desiring to be like the Most High (Isa. 14:14), and therefore seeks to infect our first parents with the same desire, that he might ruin them too.

(2.) He insinuates to them that God had no good design upon them, in forbidding them this fruit: *"For God doth know* how much it will advance you; and therefore, in envy and ill-will to you, he hath forbidden it:" as if he durst not let them eat of that tree because then they would know their own strength, and would not continue in an inferior state, but be able to cope with him; or as if he grudged them the honour and happiness to which their eating of that tree would prefer them. Now, [1.] This was a great affront to God, and the highest indignity that could be done him, a reproach to his power, as if he feared his creatures, and much more a reproach to his goodness, as if he hated the work of his own hands and would not have those whom he has made to be made happy. Shall the best of men think it strange to be misrepresented and evil spoken of, when God himself is so? Satan, as he is the accuser of the brethren before God, so he accuses God before the brethren; thus he sows discord, and is the father of those that do so. [2.] It was a most dangerous snare to our first parents, as it tended to alienate their affections from God, and so to withdraw them from their allegiance to him. Thus still the devil draws people into his interest by suggesting to them hard thoughts of God, and false hopes of benefit and advantage by sin. Let us therefore, in opposition to him, always think well of God as the best good, and think ill of sin as the worst of evils: thus let us resist the devil, and he will flee from us.

Verses 6–8

Here we see what Eve's parley with the tempter ended in. Satan, at length, gains his point, and the strong-hold is taken by his wiles. God tried the obedience of our first parents by forbidding them the tree of knowledge, and Satan does, as it were, join issue with God, and in that very thing undertakes to seduce them into a transgression; and here we find how he prevailed, God permitting it for wise and holy ends.

I. We have here the inducements that moved them to transgress. The woman, being deceived by the tempter's artful management, was ringleader in the transgression, 1 Tim. 2:14. She was first in the fault; and it was the result of her consideration, or rather her inconsideration. 1. She saw no harm in this tree, more than in any of the rest. It was said of all the rest of the fruit-trees with which the garden of Eden was planted that they were *pleasant to the sight, and good for food, ch.* 2:9. Now, in her eye, this was like all the rest. It seemed as good for food as any of them, and she saw nothing in the colour of its fruit that threatened death or danger; it was as pleasant to the sight as any of them, and therefore, "What hurt could it do them? Why should this be forbidden them rather than any of the rest?" Note, When there is thought to be no more harm in forbidden fruit than in other fruit sin lies at the door, and Satan soon carries the day. Nay, perhaps it seemed to her to be better for food, more grateful to the taste, and more nourishing to the body, than any of the rest, and to her eye it was more pleasant than any. We are often betrayed into snares by an inordinate desire to have our senses gratified. Or, if it had nothing in it more inviting than the rest, yet it was the more coveted because it was prohibited. Whether it was so in her or not, we find that in us (that is, in our flesh, in our corrupt nature) there dwells a strange spirit of contradiction. *Nitimur in vetitum — We desire what is prohibited.* 2. She imagined more virtue in this tree than in any of the rest, that it was a tree not only not to be dreaded, but *to be desired to make one wise,* and therein excelling all the rest of the trees. This she *saw,* that is, she perceived and understood it by what the devil had said to her; and some think that she saw the serpent eat of that tree, and that he told her he thereby had gained the faculties of speech and reason, whence she inferred its power to make one wise, and was persuaded to think, "If it made a brute creature rational, why might it not make a rational creature divine?" See here how the desire of necessary knowledge, under the mistaken notion of wisdom, proves hurtful and destructive to many. Our first parents, who knew so much, did not know this — that they knew enough. Christ is a tree to be desired to make one wise, Col. 2:3; 1 Co. 1:30. Let us, by faith, feed upon him, that we may be wise to salvation. In the heavenly paradise, the tree of knowledge will not be a forbidden tree; for there we shall know as we are known. Let us therefore long to be there, and, in the mean time, not exercise ourselves in things too high or too deep for us, nor covet to be wise above what is written.

II. The steps of the transgression, not steps upward, but downward towards the pit — steps that take hold on hell. 1. She *saw.* She should have turned away her eyes from beholding vanity; but she enters into temptation, by looking with pleasure on the forbidden fruit. Observe, A great deal of sin comes in at the eyes. At these windows Satan throws in those fiery darts which pierce and poison the heart. The eye affects the heart with guilt as well as grief. Let us therefore, with holy Job, make a covenant with our eyes, not to look on that which we are in danger of lusting after, Prov. 23:31; Mt. 5:28. Let the fear of God be always to us for a covering of the eyes, *ch.* 20:16. 2. *She took.* It was her own act and deed. The devil did not take it, and put it into her mouth, whether she would or no; but she herself took it. Satan may tempt, but he cannot force; may persuade us to cast ourselves down, but he cannot cast us down, Mt. 4:6. Eve's taking was stealing, like Achan's taking the accursed thing, taking that to which she had no right. Surely she took it with a trembling hand. 3. She *did eat.* Perhaps she did not intend, when she looked, to take, nor, when she took, to eat; but this was the result. Note, The way of sin is downhill; a man cannot stop himself when he will. The beginning o it is as the breaking forth of water, to which it is hard to say, "Hitherto thou shalt come and no further." Therefore it is our wisdom to suppress the first emotions of sin, and to leave it off before it be meddled with. *Obsta principiis — Nip mischief in the bud.* 4. She *gave also to her husband with her.* It is probable that he was not with her when she was tempted (surely, if he had, he would have interposed to prevent the sin), but came to her when she had eaten, and was prevailed upon by her to eat likewise; for it is easier to learn that which is bad than to teach that which is good. She gave it to him, persuading him with the same arguments that the serpent had used with her, adding this to all the rest, that she herself had eaten of it, and found it so far from being deadly that it was extremely pleasant and grateful. *Stolen waters are sweet.* She gave it to him, under colour of kindness — she would not eat these delicious morsels alone; but really it was the greatest unkindness she could do him. Or perhaps she gave it to him that, if it should prove hurtful, he might share with her in the misery, which indeed looks strangely unkind, and yet may, without difficulty, be supposed to enter into the heart of one that had eaten forbidden fruit. Note, Those that have themselves done ill are commonly willing to draw in others to do the same. As was the devil, so was Eve, no sooner a sinner than a tempter. 5. *He did eat,* overcome by his wife's importunity. It is needless to ask, "What would have been the consequence if Eve only had transgressed?" The wisdom of God, we are sure, would have decided the difficulty, according to equity; but, alas! the case was not so; Adam also did eat. "And what great harm if he did?" say the corrupt and carnal reasonings of a vain mind. What harm! Why, this act involved disbelief of God's word, together with confidence in the devil's, discontent with his present state, pride in his own merits, and ambition of the honour which comes not from God, envy at God's perfections, and indulgence of the appetites of the body. In neglecting the tree of life of which he was allowed to eat, and eating of the tree of knowledge which was forbidden, he plainly showed a contempt of the favours God had bestowed on him, and a preference given to those God did not see fit for him. He would be both his own carver and his own master, would have what he pleased and do what he pleased: his sin was, in one word, *disobedience* (Rom. 5:19), disobedience to a plain, easy, and express command, which probably he knew to be a command of trial. He sinned against great knowledge, against many mercies, against light and love, the clearest light and the dearest love that ever sinner sinned against. He had no corrupt nature within him to betray him; but had a freedom of will, not enslaved, and was in his full strength, not weakened or impaired. He turned aside quickly. Some think he fell the very day on which he was made; but I see not how to reconcile this with God's pronouncing all *very good* in the close of the day. Others suppose he fell on the sabbath day: the better day the worse deed. However, it is certain that he kept his integrity but a very little while: being in honour, he continued not. But the greatest aggravation of his sin was that he involved all his posterity in sin and ruin by it. God having told him that his race should replenish the earth, surely he could not but know that he stood as a public person, and that his disobedience would be fatal to all his seed; and, if so, it was certainly both the greatest treachery and the greatest cruelty that ever was. The human nature being lodged entirely in our first parents, henceforward it could not but be transmitted from them under an attainder of guilt, a stain of dishonour, and an hereditary disease of sin and corruption. And can we say, then, that Adam's sin had but little harm in it?

III. The ultimate consequences of the transgression. Shame and fear seized the criminals, *ipso facto — in the fact itself;* these came into the world along with sin, and still attend it.

1. Shame seized them unseen, *v.* 7, where observe, (1.) The strong convictions they fell under, in their own bosoms: *The eyes of them both were opened.* It is not meant of the eyes of the body; these were open before, as appears by this, that the sin came in at them. Jonathan's eyes were enlightened by eating forbidden fruit (1 Sa. 14:27), that is, he was refreshed and revived by it; but theirs were not so. Nor is it meant of any advances made hereby in true knowledge; but the eyes of their consciences were opened, their hearts smote them for what they had done. Now, when it was too late, they saw the folly of eating forbidden fruit. They saw the happiness they had fallen from, and the misery they had fallen into. They saw a loving God provoked, his grace and favour forfeited, his likeness and image lost, dominion over the creatures gone. They saw their natures corrupted and depraved, and felt a disorder in their own spirits of which they had never before been conscious. They saw a law in their members warring against the law of their minds, and captivating them both to sin and wrath. They saw, as Balaam, when *his eyes were opened* (Num. 22:31), the angel of the Lord standing in the way, and his sword drawn in his hand; and perhaps they saw the serpent that had abused them insulting over them. The text tells us that they saw *that they were naked,* that is, [1.] That they were stripped, deprived of all the honours and joys of their paradise-state, and exposed to all the miseries that might justly be expected from an angry God. They were disarmed; their defence had departed from them. [2.] That they were shamed, for ever shamed, before God and angels. They saw themselves disrobed of all their ornaments and ensigns of honour, degraded from their dignity and disgraced in the highest degree, laid open to the contempt and reproach of heaven, and earth, and their own consciences. Now see here, *First,* What a dishonour and disquietment sin is; it makes mischief wherever it is admitted, sets men against themselves disturbs their peace, and destroys all their comforts. Sooner or later, it will have shame, either the shame of true repentance, which ends in glory, or that shame and everlasting contempt to which the wicked shall rise at the great day. Sin is a reproach to any people. *Secondly,* What deceiver Satan is. He told our first parents, when he tempted them, that their eyes should be opened; and so they were, but not as they understood it; they were opened to their shame and grief, not to their honour nor advantage. Therefore, when he speaks fair, believe him not. The most malicious mischievous liars often excuse themselves with this, that they only equivocate; but God will not so excuse them.

(2.) The sorry shift they made to palliate these convictions, and to arm themselves against them: *They sewed,* or platted, *fig-leaves together;* and to cover, at least, part of their shame from one another, they *made themselves aprons.* See here what is commonly the folly of those that have sinned. [1.] That they are more solicitous to save their credit before men than to obtain their pardon from God; they are backward to confess their sin, and very desirous to conceal it, as much as may be. *I have sinned, yet honour me.* [2.] That the excuses men make, to cover and extenuate their sins, are vain and frivolous. Like the aprons of fig-leaves, they make the matter never the better, but the worse; the shame, thus hidden, becomes the more shameful. Yet thus we are all apt to *cover our transgressions as Adam,* Job 31:33.

2. Fear seized them immediately upon their eating the forbidden fruit, *v.* 8. Observe here, (1.) What was the cause and occasion of their fear: They *heard the voice of the Lord God walking in the garden in the cool of the day.* It was the approach of the Judge that put them into a fright; and yet he came in such a manner as made it formidable only to guilty consciences. It is supposed that he came in a human shape, and that he who judged the world now was the same that shall judge the world at the last day, even *that man whom God has ordained.* He appeared to them now (it should seem) in no other similitude than that in which they had seen him when he put them into paradise; for he came to convince and humble them, not to amaze and terrify them. He came into the garden, not descending immediately from heaven in their view, as afterwards on mount Sinai (making either thick darkness his pavilion or the flaming fire his chariot), but he came into the garden, as one that was still willing to be familiar with them. He came walking, not running, not riding upon the wings of the wind, but walking deliberately, as one slow to anger, teaching us, when we are ever so much provoked, not to be hot nor hasty, but to speak and act considerately and not rashly. He came in the cool of the day, not in the night, when all fears are doubly fearful, nor in the heat of day, for he came not in the heat of his anger. *Fury is not in him,* Isa. 27:4. Nor did he come suddenly upon them; but they heard his voice at some distance, giving them notice of his coming, and probably it was a still small voice, like that in which he came to enquire after Elijah. Some think they heard him discoursing with himself concerning the sin of Adam, and the judgment now to be passed upon him, perhaps as he did concerning Israel, Hos. 11:8, 9. *How shall I give thee up?* Or, rather, they heard him calling for them, and coming towards them. (2.) What was the effect and evidence of their fear: *They hid themselves from the presence of the Lord God* — a sad change! Before they had sinned, if they had heard the voice of the Lord God coming towards them, they would have run to meet him, and with a humble joy welcomed his gracious visits. But, now that it was otherwise, God had become a terror to them, and then no marvel that they had become a terror to themselves, and were full of confusion. Their own consciences accused them, and set their sin before them in its proper colours. Their fig-leaves failed them, and would do them no service. God had come forth against them as an enemy, and the whole creation was at war with them; and as yet they knew not of any mediator between them and an angry God, so that nothing remained but a certain fearful looking for of judgment. In this fright they hid themselves among the bushes; having offended, they fled for the same. Knowing themselves guilty, they durst not stand a trial, but absconded, and fled

from justice. See here, [1.] The falsehood of the tempter, and the frauds and fallacies of his temptations. He promised them they should be safe, but now they cannot so much as think themselves so; he said they should not die, and yet now they are forced to fly or their lives; he promised them they should be advanced, but they see themselves abased — never did they seem so little as now; he promised them they should be knowing, but they see themselves at a loss, and know not so much as where to hide themselves; he promised them they should be as gods, great, and bold, and daring, but they are as criminals discovered, trembling, pale, and anxious to escape: they would not be subjects, and so they are prisoners. [2.] The folly of sinners, to think it either possible or desirable to hide themselves from God: can they conceal themselves from the Father of lights? Ps. 139:7, etc.; Jer. 23:24. Will they withdraw themselves from the fountain of life, who alone can give help and happiness? Jon. 2:8. [3.] The fear that attends sin. All that amazing fear of God's appearances, the accusations of conscience, the approaches of trouble, the assaults of inferior creatures, and the arrests of death, which is common among men, is the effect of sin. Adam and Eve, who were partners in the sin, were sharers in the shame and fear that attended it; and though hand joined in hand (hands so lately joined in marriage), yet could they not animate nor fortify one another: miserable comforters they had become to each other!

Verses 9–10

We have here the arraignment of these deserters before the righteous Judge of heaven and earth, who, though he is not tied to observe formalities, yet proceeds against them with all possible fairness, that he may be justified when he speaks. Observe here,

I. The startling question with which God pursued Adam and arrested him: *Where art thou?* Not as if God did not know where he was; but thus he would enter the process against him. "Come, where is this foolish man?" Some make it a bemoaning question: "Poor Adam, what has become of thee?" *"Alas for thee!"* (so some read it) *"How art thou fallen, Lucifer, son of the morning!* Thou that wast my friend and favourite, whom I had done so much for, and would have done so much more for; hast thou now forsaken me, and ruined thyself? Has it come to this?" It is rather an upbraiding question, in order to his conviction and humiliation: *Where art thou?* Not, In what *place?* but, In what *condition?* "Is this all thou hast gotten by eating forbidden fruit? Thou that wouldest vie with me, dost thou now fly from me?" Note, 1. Those who by sin have gone astray from God should seriously consider where they are; they are afar off from all good, in the midst of their enemies, in bondage to Satan, and in the high road to utter ruin. This enquiry after Adam may be looked upon as a gracious pursuit, in kindness to him, and in order to his recovery. If God had not called to him, to reclaim him, his condition would have been as desperate as that of fallen angels; this lost sheep would have wandered endlessly, if the good Shepherd had not sought after him, to bring him back, and, in order to that, reminded him where he was, where he should not be, and where he could not be either happy or easy. Note, 2. If sinners will but consider where they are, they will not rest till they return to God.

II. The trembling answer which Adam gave to this question: *I heard thy voice in the garden, and I was afraid, v.* 10. He does not own his guilt, and yet in effect confesses it by owning his shame and fear; but it is the common fault and folly of those that have done an ill thing, when they are questioned about it, to acknowledge no more than what is so manifest that they cannot deny it. Adam was afraid, because he was naked; not only unarmed, and therefore afraid to contend with God, but unclothed, and therefore afraid so much as to appear before him. We have reason to be afraid of approaching to God if we be not clothed and fenced with the righteousness of Christ, for nothing but this will be armour of proof and cover the shame of our nakedness. Let us therefore *put on the Lord Jesus Christ,* and then draw near with humble boldness.

Verses 11–13

We have here the offenders found guilty by their own confession, and yet endeavouring to excuse and extenuate their fault. They could not confess and justify what they had done, but they confess and palliate it. Observe,

I. How their confession was extorted from them. God put it to the man: *Who told thee that thou wast naked? v.* 11. "How camest thou to be sensible of thy nakedness as thy shame?" *Hast thou eaten of the forbidden tree?* Note, Though God knows all our sins, yet he will know them from us, and requires from us an ingenuous confession of them; not that he may be informed, but that we may be humbled. In this examination, God reminds him of the command he had given him: "I commanded thee not to eat of it, I thy Maker, I thy Master, I thy benefactor; I commanded thee to the contrary." Sin appears most plain and most sinful in the glass of the commandment, therefore God here sets it before Adam; and in it we should see our faces. The question put to the woman was, *What is this that thou hast done? v.* 13. "Wilt thou also own thy fault, and make confession of it? And wilt thou see what an evil thing it was?" Note, It concerns those who have eaten forbidden fruit themselves, and especially those who have enticed others to eat it likewise, seriously to consider what they have done. In eating forbidden fruit, we have offended a great and gracious God, broken a just and righteous law, violated a sacred and most solemn covenant, and wronged our own precious souls by forfeiting God's favour and exposing ourselves to his wrath and curse: in enticing others to eat of it, we do the devil's work, make ourselves guilty of other men's sins, and accessory to their ruin. *What is this that we have done?*

II. How their crime was extenuated by them in their confession. It was to no purpose to plead *not guilty.* The show of their countenances testified against them; therefore they become their own accusers: *"I did eat,"* says the man, "And so did I," says the woman; for when God judges he will overcome. But these do not look like penitent confessions; for instead of aggravating the sin, and taking shame to themselves, they excuse the sin, and lay the shame and blame on others. 1. Adam lays all the blame upon his wife. "She gave me of the tree, and pressed me to eat of it, which I did, only to oblige her" — a frivolous excuse. He ought to have taught her, not to have been taught by her; and it was no hard matter to determine which of the two he must be ruled by, his God or his wife. Learn, hence, never to be brought to sin by that which will not bring us off in the judgment; let not that bear us up in the commission which will not bear us out in the trial; let us therefore never be overcome by importunity to act against our consciences, nor ever displease God, to please the best friend we have in the world. But this is not the worst of it. He not only lays the blame upon his wife, but expresses it so as tacitly to reflect on God himself: "It is the woman whom thou gavest me, and gavest to be with me as my companion, my guide, and my acquaintance; she gave me of the tree, else I had not eaten of it." Thus he insinuates that God was accessory to his sin: he gave him the woman, and she gave him the fruit; so that he seemed to have it at but one remove from God's own hand. Note, There is a strange proneness in those that are tempted to say that they are tempted of God, as if our abusing God's gifts would excuse our violation of God's laws. God gives us riches, honours, and relations, that we may serve him cheerfully in the enjoyment of them; but, if we take occasion from them to sin against him, instead of blaming Providence for putting us into such a condition, we must blame ourselves for perverting the gracious designs of Providence therein. 2. Eve lays all the blame upon the serpent: *The serpent beguiled me.* Sin is a brat that nobody is willing to own, a sign that it is a scandalous thing. Those that are willing enough to take the pleasure and profit of sin are backward enough to take the blame and shame of it. "The serpent, that subtle creature of thy making, which thou didst permit to come into paradise to us, he beguiled me," or *made me to err;* for our sins are our errors. Learn hence, (1.) That Satan's temptations are all beguilings, his arguments are all fallacies, his allurements are all cheats; when he speaks fair, believe him not. Sin deceives us, and, by deceiving, cheats us. It is by the *deceitfulness of sin* that the heart is hardened. See Rom. 7:11; Heb. 3:13. (2.) That though Satan's subtlety drew us into sin, yet it will not justify us in sin: though he is the tempter, we are the sinners; and indeed it is our own lust that draws us aside and entices us, Jam. 1:14. Let it not therefore lessen our sorrow and humiliation for sin that we are beguiled into it; but rather let it increase our self-indignation that we should suffer ourselves to be beguiled by a known cheat and a sworn enemy. Well, this is all the prisoners at the bar have to say why sentence should not be passed and execution awarded, according to law; and this *all* is next to nothing, in some respects worse than nothing.

Verses 14–15

The prisoners being found guilty by their own confession, besides the personal and infallible knowledge of the Judge, and nothing material being offered in arrest of judgment, God immediately proceeds to pass sentence; and, in these verses, he begins (where the sin began) with the serpent. God did not examine the serpent, nor ask him what he had done nor why he did it; but immediately sentenced him, 1. Because he was already convicted of rebellion against God, and his malice and wickedness were notorious, not found by secret search, but openly avowed and declared as Sodom's. 2. Because he was to be for ever excluded from all hope of pardon; and why should any thing be said to convince and humble him who was to find no place for repentance? His wound was not searched, because it was not to be cured. Some think the condition of the fallen angels was not declared desperate and helpless, until now that they had seduced man into the rebellion.

I. The sentence passed upon the tempter may be considered as lighting upon the serpent, the brute-creature which Satan made use of which was, as the rest, made for the service of man, but was now abused to his hurt. Therefore, to testify a displeasure against sin, and a jealousy for the injured honour of Adam and Eve, God fastens a curse and reproach upon the serpent, and makes it to groan, being burdened. See Rom. 8:20. The devil's instruments must share in the devil's punishments. Thus the bodies of the wicked, though only instruments of unrighteousness, shall partake of everlasting torments with the soul, the principal agent. Even the ox that killed a man must be stoned, Ex. 21:28, 29. See here how God hates sin, and especially how much displeased he is with those who entice others into sin. It is a perpetual brand upon Jeroboam's name *that he made Israel to sin.* Now, 1. The serpent is here laid under the curse of God: *Thou art cursed above all cattle.* Even the creeping things, when God made them, were blessed of him (*ch.* 1:22), but sin turned the blessing into a curse. *The serpent was more subtle than any beast of the field* (*v.* 1), and here, *cursed above every beast of the field.* Unsanctified subtlety often proves a great curse to a man; and the more crafty men are to do evil the more mischief they do, and, consequently, they shall receive the greater damnation. Subtle tempters are the most accursed creatures under the sun. 2. He is here laid under man's reproach and enmity. (1.) He is to be for ever looked upon as a vile and despicable creature, and a proper object of scorn and contempt: *"Upon thy belly thou shalt go,* no longer upon feet, or half erect, but thou shalt crawl along, thy belly cleaving to the earth," an expression of a very abject miserable condition, Ps. 44:25; "and thou shalt not avoid eating dust with thy meat." His crime was that he tempted Eve to eat that which she should not; his punishment was that he was necessitated to eat that which he would not: *Dust thou shalt eat.* This denotes not only a base and despicable condition, but a mean and pitiful spirit; it is said of those whose courage has departed from them that they *lick the dust like a serpent,* Mic. 7:17. How sad it is that the serpent's curse should be the covetous worldling's choice, whose character it is that he *pants after the dust of the earth!* Amos 2:7. These choose their own delusions, and so shall their doom be. (2.) He is to be for ever looked upon as a venomous noxious creature, and a proper object of hatred and detestation: *I will put enmity between thee and the woman.* The inferior creatures being made for man, it was a curse upon any of them to be turned against man and man against them; and this is part of the serpent's curse. The serpent is hurtful to man, and often bruises his heel, because it can reach no higher; nay, notice is taken of his biting the horses' heels, *ch.* 49:17. But man is victorious over the serpent, and bruises his head, that is, gives him a mortal wound, aiming to destroy the whole generation of vipers. It is the effect of this curse upon the serpent that, though that creature is subtle and very dangerous, yet it prevails not (as it would if God gave it commission) to the destruction of mankind. This sentence pronounced upon the serpent is much fortified by that promise of God to his people, *Thou shalt tread upon the lion and the adder* (Ps. 91:13), and that of Christ to his disciples, *They shall take up serpents* (Mk. 16:18), witness Paul, who was unhurt by the viper that fastened upon his hand. Observe here, The serpent and the woman had just now been very familiar and friendly in discourse about the forbidden fruit, and a wonderful agreement there was between them; but here they are irreconcilably set at variance. Note, Sinful friendships justly end in mortal feuds: those that unite in wickedness will not unite long.

II. This sentence may be considered as levelled at the devil, who only made use of the serpent as his vehicle in this appearance, but was himself the principal agent. He that spoke through the serpent's mouth is here struck at through the serpent's side, and is principally intended in the sentence, which, like the pillar of cloud and fire, has a dark side towards the devil and a bright side towards our first parents and their seed. Great things are contained in these words.

1. A perpetual reproach is here fastened upon that great enemy both to God and man. Under the cover of the serpent, he is here sentenced to be, (1.) Degraded and accursed of God. It is supposed that the sin which turned angels into devils was pride, which is here justly punished by a great variety of mortifications couched under the mean circumstances of a serpent crawling on his belly and licking the dust. *How art thou fallen, O Lucifer!* He that would be above God, and would head a rebellion against him, is justly exposed here to contempt and lies to be trodden on; a man's pride will bring him low, and God will humble those that will not humble themselves. (2.) Detested and abhorred of all mankind. Even those that are really seduced into his interest yet profess a hatred and abhorrence of him; and all that are born of God make it their constant care to keep themselves, that this wicked one touch them not, 1 Jn. 5:18. He is here condemned to a state of war and irreconcilable enmity. (3.) Destroyed and ruined at last by *the great Redeemer*, signified by the breaking of his head. His subtle politics shall all be baffled, his usurped power shall be entirely crushed, and he shall be for ever a captive to the injured honour of divine sovereignty. By being told of this now he was tormented before the time.

2. A perpetual quarrel is here commenced between the kingdom of God and the kingdom of the devil among men; war is proclaimed between the seed of the woman and the seed of the serpent. That war in heaven between Michael and the dragon began now, Rev. 12:7. It is the fruit of this enmity, (1.) That there is a continual conflict between grace and corruption in the hearts of God's people. Satan, by their corruptions, assaults them, buffets them, sifts them, and seeks to devour them; they, by the exercise of their graces, resist him, wrestle with him, quench his fiery darts, force him to flee from them. Heaven and hell can never be reconciled, nor light and darkness; no more can Satan and a sanctified soul, for these are contrary the one to the other. (2.) That there is likewise a continual struggle between the wicked and the godly in this world. Those that love God account those their enemies that hate him, Ps. 139:21, 22. And all the rage and malice of persecutors against the people of God are the fruit of this enmity, which will continue while there is a godly man on this side heaven, and a wicked man on this side hell. *Marvel not therefore if the world hate you,* 1 Jn. 3:13.

3. A gracious promise is here made of Christ, as the deliverer of fallen man from the power of Satan. Though what was said was addressed to the serpent, yet it was said in the hearing of our first parents, who, doubtless, took the hints of grace here given them, and saw a door of hope opened to them, else the following sentence upon themselves would have overwhelmed them. Here was the dawning of the gospel day. No sooner was the wound given than the remedy was provided and revealed. Here, *in the head of the book,* as the word is (Heb. 10:7), in the beginning of the Bible, it is written of Christ, that he should *do the will of God.* By faith in this promise, we have reason to think, our first parents, and the patriarchs before the flood, were justified and saved and to this promise, and the benefit of it, instantly serving God day and night, they hoped

to come. Notice is here given them of three things concerning Christ: — (1.) His incarnation, that he should be *the seed of the woman,* the seed of *that* woman; therefore his genealogy (Lu. 3) goes so high as to show him to be the son of Adam, but God does the woman the honour to call him rather her seed, because she it was whom the devil had beguiled, and on whom Adam had laid the blame; herein God magnifies his grace, in that, though the woman was first in the transgression, yet she shall be saved *by* child-bearing (as some read it), that is, by the promised seed who shall descend from her, 1 Tim. 2:15. He was likewise to be the seed of a woman only, of a virgin, that he might not be tainted with the corruption of our nature; he was sent forth, *made of a woman* (Gal. 4:4), that this promise might be fulfilled. It is a great encouragement to sinners that their Saviour *is the seed of the woman, bone of our bone,* Heb. 2:11, 14. Man is therefore sinful and unclean, because he is *born of a woman* (Job 25:4), and therefore *his days are full of trouble,* Job 14:1. But the seed of the woman was made sin and a curse for us, so saving us from both. (2.) His sufferings and death, pointed at in Satan's *bruising his heel,* that is, his human nature. Satan tempted Christ in the wilderness, to draw him into sin; and some think it was Satan that terrified Christ in his agony, to drive him to despair. It was the devil that put it into the heart of Judas to betray Christ, of Peter to deny him, of the chief priests to prosecute him, of the false witnesses to accuse him, and of Pilate to condemn him, aiming in all this, by destroying the Saviour, to ruin the salvation; but, on the contrary, it was by death that Christ *destroyed him that had the power of death,* Heb. 2:14. Christ's heel was bruised when his feet were pierced and nailed to the cross, and Christ's sufferings are continued in the sufferings of the saints for his name. The devil tempts them, casts them into prison, persecutes and slays them, and so bruises the heel of Christ, who is afflicted in their afflictions. But, while the heel is bruised on earth, it is well that the head is safe in heaven. (3.) His victory over Satan thereby. Satan had now trampled upon the woman, and insulted over her; but the seed of the woman should be raised up in the fulness of time to avenge her quarrel, and to trample upon him, to spoil him, to lead him captive, and to *triumph over him,* Col. 2:15. *He shall bruise his head,* that is, he shall destroy all his politics and all his powers, and give a total overthrow to his kingdom and interest. Christ baffled Satan's temptations, rescued souls out of his hands, cast him out of the bodies of people, dispossessed the strong man armed, and divided his spoil: by his death, he gave a fatal and incurable blow to the devil's kingdom, a wound to the head of this beast, that can never be healed. As his gospel gets ground, *Satan falls* (Lu. 10:18) and is *bound,* Rev. 20:2. By his grace, he treads Satan under his people's feet (Rom. 16:20) and will shortly cast him into the lake of fire, Rev. 20:10. And the devil's perpetual overthrow will be the complete and everlasting joy and glory of the chosen remnant.

Verse 16

We have here the sentence passed upon the woman for her sin. Two things she is condemned to: a state of sorrow, and a state of subjection, proper punishments of a sin in which she had gratified her pleasure and her pride.

I. She is here put into a state of sorrow, one particular of which only is specified, that in bringing forth children; but it includes all those impressions of grief and fear which the mind of that tender sex is most apt to receive, and all the common calamities which they are liable to. Note, Sin brought sorrow into the world; it was this that made the world a vale of tears, brought showers of trouble upon our heads, and opened springs of sorrows in our hearts, and so deluged the world: had we known no guilt, we should have known no grief. The pains of child-bearing, which are great to a proverb, a scripture proverb, are the effect of sin; every pang and every groan of the travailing woman speak aloud the fatal consequences of sin: this comes of eating forbidden fruit. Observe, 1. The sorrows are here said to be multiplied, *greatly multiplied.* All the sorrows of this present time are so; many are the calamities which human life is liable to, of various kinds, and often repeated, the clouds returning after the rain, and no marvel that our sorrows are multiplied when our sins are: both are innumerable evils. The sorrows of child-bearing

are multiplied; for they include, not only the travailing throes, but the indispositions before (it is sorrow from the conception), and the nursing toils and vexations after; and after all, if the children prove wicked and foolish, they are, more than ever, the heaviness of her that bore them. Thus are the sorrows multiplied; as one grief is over, another succeeds in this world. 2. It is God that multiplies our sorrows: *I will do it.* God, as a righteous Judge, does it, which ought to silence us under all our sorrows; as many as they are, we have deserved them all, and more: nay, God, as a tender Father, does it for our necessary correction, that we may be humbled for sin, and weaned from the world by all our sorrows; and the good we get by them, with the comfort we have under them, will abundantly balance our sorrows, how greatly soever they are multiplied.

II. She is here put into a state of subjection. The whole sex, which by creation was equal with man, is, for sin, made inferior, and forbidden to *usurp authority,* 1 Tim. 2:11, 12. The wife particularly is hereby put under the dominion of her husband, and is not *sui juris — at her own disposal,* of which see an instance in that law, Num. 30:6–8, where the husband is empowered, if he please, to disannul the vows made by the wife. This sentence amounts only to that command, *Wives, be in subjection to your own husbands;* but the entrance of sin has made that duty a punishment, which otherwise it would not have been. If man had not sinned, he would always have ruled with wisdom and love; and, if the woman had not sinned, she would always have obeyed with humility and meekness; and then the dominion would have been no grievance: but our own sin and folly make our yoke heavy. If Eve had not eaten forbidden fruit herself, and tempted her husband to eat it, she would never have complained of her subjection; therefore it ought never to be complained of, though harsh; but sin must be complained of, that made it so. Those wives who not only despise and disobey their husbands, but domineer over them, do not consider that they not only violate a divine law, but thwart a divine sentence.

III. Observe here how mercy is mixed with wrath in this sentence. The woman shall have sorrow, but it shall be in bringing forth children, and the sorrow shall be *forgotten for joy that a child is born,* Jn. 16:21. She shall be subject, but it shall be to her own husband that loves her, not to a stranger, or an enemy: the sentence was not a curse, to bring her to ruin, but a chastisement, to bring her to repentance. It was well that enmity was not put between the man and the woman, as there was between the serpent and the woman.

Verses 17–19

We have here the sentence passed upon Adam, which is prefaced with a recital of his crime: *Because thou hast hearkened to the voice of thy wife,* v. 17. He excused the fault, by laying it on his wife: *She gave it me.* But God does not admit the excuse. She could but tempt him, she could not force him; though it was her fault to persuade him to eat, it was his fault to hearken to her. Thus men's frivolous pleas will, in the day of God's judgment, not only be overruled, but turned against them, and made the grounds of their sentence. *Out of thine own mouth will I judge thee.* Observe,

I. God put marks of his displeasure on Adam in three instances: —

1. His habitation is, by this sentence, cursed: *Cursed is the ground for thy sake;* and the effect of that curse is, *Thorns and thistles shall it bring forth unto thee.* It is here intimated that his habitation should be changed; he should no longer dwell in a distinguished, blessed, paradise, but should be removed to common ground, and that cursed. The ground, or earth, is here put for the whole visible creation, which, by the sin of man, is made subject to vanity, the several parts of it being not so serviceable to man's comfort and happiness as they were designed to be when they were made, and would have been if he had not sinned. God gave the earth to the children of men, designing it to be a comfortable dwelling to them. But sin has altered the property of it. It is now cursed for man's sin; that is, it is a dishonourable habitation, it bespeaks man mean, that his foundation is in the dust; it is a dry and barren habitation, its spontaneous productions are now weeds and briers, something nauseous or noxious; what good fruits

it produces must be extorted from it by the ingenuity and industry of man. Fruitfulness was its blessing, for man's service (*ch.* 1:11, 29), and now barrenness was its curse, for man's punishment. It is not what it was in the day it was created. Sin turned a fruitful land into barrenness; and man, having become as the wild ass's colt, has the wild ass's lot, *the wilderness for his habitation,* and the *barren land his dwelling,* Job 39:6; Ps. 68:6. Had not this curse been in part removed, for aught I know, the earth would have been for ever barren, and never produced any thing but thorns and thistles. The ground is *cursed,* that is, doomed to destruction at the end of time, when the earth, and *all the works that are therein, shall be burnt up* for the sin of man, the measure of whose iniquity will then be full, 2 Pt. 3:7, 10. But observe a mixture of mercy in this sentence. (1.) Adam himself is not cursed, as the serpent was (*v.* 14), but only the ground for his sake. God had blessings in him, even the holy seed: *Destroy it not, for that blessing is in it,* Isa. 65:8. And he had blessings in store for him; therefore he is not directly and immediately cursed, but, as it were, at second hand. (2.) He is yet above ground. The earth does not open and swallow him up; only it is not what it was: as he continues alive, notwithstanding his degeneracy from his primitive purity and rectitude, so the earth continues to be his habitation, notwithstanding its degeneracy from its primitive beauty and fruitfulness. (3.) This curse upon the earth, which cut off all expectations of a happiness in things below, might direct and quicken him to look for bliss and satisfaction only in things above.

2. His employments and enjoyments are all embittered to him.

(1.) His business shall henceforth become a toil to him, and he shall go on with it *in the sweat of his face, v.* 19. His business, before he sinned, was a constant pleasure to him, the garden was then dressed without any uneasy labour, and kept without any uneasy care; but now his labour shall be a weariness and shall waste his body; his care shall be a torment and shall afflict his mind. The curse upon the ground which made it barren, and produced thorns and thistles, made his employment about it much more difficult and toilsome. If Adam had not sinned, he had not sweated. Observe here, [1.] That labour is our duty, which we must faithfully perform; we are bound to work, not as creatures only, but as criminals; it is part of our sentence, which idleness daringly defies. [2.] That uneasiness and weariness with labour are our just punishment, which we must patiently submit to, and not complain of, since they are less than our iniquity deserves. Let not us, by inordinate care and labour, make our punishment heavier than God has made it; but rather study to lighten our burden, and wipe off our sweat, by eyeing Providence in all and expecting rest shortly.

(2.) His food shall henceforth become (in comparison with what it had been) unpleasant to him. [1.] The matter of his food is changed; he must now eat the herb of the field, and must no longer be feasted with the delicacies of the garden of Eden. Having by sin made himself like the beasts that perish, he is justly turned to be a fellow-commoner with them, and to *eat grass as oxen, till he know that the heavens do rule.* [2.] There is a change in the manner of his eating it: *In sorrow* (*v.* 17) and *in the sweat of his face* (*v.* 19) he must eat of it. Adam could not but eat in sorrow all the days of his life, remembering the forbidden fruit he had eaten, and the guilt and shame he had contracted by it. Observe, *First,* That human life is exposed to many miseries and calamities, which very much embitter the poor remains of its pleasures and delights. Some never eat with pleasure (Job 21:25), through sickness or melancholy; all, even the best, have cause to eat with sorrow for sin; and all, even the happiest in this world, have some allays to their joy: troops of diseases, disasters, and deaths, in various shapes, entered the world with sin, and still ravage it. *Secondly,* That the righteousness of God is to be acknowledged in all the sad consequences of sin. *Wherefore then should a living man complain?* Yet, in this part of the sentence, there is also a mixture of mercy. He shall sweat, but his toil shall make his rest the more welcome when he returns to his earth, as to his bed; he shall grieve, but he shall not starve; he shall have sorrow, but in that sorrow he shall eat bread, which shall strengthen his heart under his sorrows. He is not sentenced to eat dust as the serpent, only to eat the herb of the field.

3. His life also is but short. Considering how full of trouble his days are, it is in favour to him that they are few; yet death being dreadful to nature (yea, even though life be unpleasant) *that* concludes the sentence. "Thou shalt *return to the ground out of which thou wast taken;* thy body, that part of thee which was taken out of the ground, shall return to it again; for *dust thou art.*" This points either to the first original of his body; it was made *of the dust,* nay it was *made dust,* and was still so; so that there needed no more than to recall the grant of immortality, and to withdraw the power which was put forth to support it, and then he would, of course, *return to dust.* Or to the present corruption and degeneracy of his mind: *Dust thou art,* that is, "Thy precious soul is now lost and buried in the dust of the body and the mire of the flesh; it was made spiritual and heavenly, but it has become carnal and earthly." His doom is therefore read: *"To dust thou shalt return.* Thy body shall be forsaken by thy soul, and become itself a lump of dust; and then it shall be lodged in the grave, the proper place for it, and mingle itself with the dust of the earth," *our dust,* Ps. 104:29. *Earth to earth, dust to dust.* Observe here, (1.) That man is a mean frail creature, *little* as dust, the small dust of the balance — *light* as dust, altogether lighter than vanity — *weak* as dust, and of no consistency. Our strength is not the strength of stones; he that made us considers it, and *remembers that we are dust,* Ps. 103:14. Man is indeed the *chief part of the dust of the world* (Prov. 8:26), but still he is dust. (2.) That he is a mortal dying creature, and hastening to the grave. Dust may be raised, for a time, into a little cloud, and may seem considerable while it is held up by the wind that raised it; but, when the force of that is spent, it falls again, and returns to the earth out of which it was raised. Such a thing is man; a great man is but a great mass of dust, and must return to his earth. (3.) That sin brought death into the world. If Adam had not sinned, he would not have died, Rom. 5:12. God entrusted Adam with a spark of immortality, which he, by a patient continuance in well-doing, might have blown up into an everlasting flame; but he foolishly blew it out by wilful sin: and now death is *the wages of sin, and sin is the sting of death.*

II. We must not go off from this sentence upon our first parents, which we are all so nearly concerned in, and feel from, to this day, till we have considered two things: —

1. How fitly the sad consequences of sin upon the soul of Adam and his sinful race were represented and figured out by this sentence, and perhaps were more intended in it than we are aware of. Though that misery only is mentioned which affected the body, yet that was a pattern of spiritual miseries, the curse that entered into the soul. (1.) The pains of a woman in travail represent the terrors and pangs of a guilty conscience, awakened to a sense of sin; from the conception of lust, these sorrows are greatly multiplied, and, sooner or later, will come upon the sinner like pain upon a woman in travail, which cannot be avoided. (2.) The state of subjection to which the woman was reduced represents that loss of spiritual liberty and freedom of will which is the effect of sin. The dominion of sin in the soul is compared to that of a husband (Rom. 7:1–5), the sinner's desire is towards it, for he is fond of his slavery, and it rules over him. (3.) The curse of barrenness which was brought upon the earth, and its produce of briars and thorns, are a fit representation of the barrenness of a corrupt and sinful soul in that which is good and its fruitfulness in evil. It is all overgrown with thorns, and nettles cover the face of it; and therefore it is *nigh unto cursing,* Heb. 6:8. (4.) The toil and sweat bespeak the difficulty which, through the infirmity of the flesh, man labours under, in the service of God and the work of religion, so hard has it now become to *enter into the kingdom of heaven.* Blessed be God, it is not impossible. (5.) The embittering of his food to him bespeaks the soul's want of the comfort of God's favour, which is life, and the bread of life. (6.) The soul, like the body, returns to the dust of this world; its tendency is that way; it has an earthy taint, Jn. 3:31.

2. How admirably the satisfaction our Lord Jesus made by his death and sufferings answered to the sentence here passed upon our first parents. (1.) Did travailing pains come in with sin? We read of the *travail of Christ's soul* (Isa. 53:11); and the pains o death he was held by are called *ōdinai* (Acts 2:24), *the pains of a woman in travail.* (2.) Did subjection come in with sin? Christ was made under the law, Gal. 4:4. (3.) Did the curse come in with sin? Christ was made a curse for us, died a cursed death, Gal. 3:13. (4.) Did thorns come in with sin? He was crowned with thorns for us. (5.) Did sweat come in with sin? He for us did sweat as it were great drops of blood. (6.) Did sorrow come in with sin? He was a man of sorrows, his soul was, in his agony, exceedingly sorrowful. (7.) Did death come in with sin? He became obedient unto death. Thus is the plaster as wide as the wound. Blessed be God for Jesus Christ!

Verse 20

God having named the man, and called him *Adam,* which signifies *red earth,* Adam, in further token of dominion, named the woman, and called her *Eve,* that is, *life.* Adam bears the name of the dying body, Eve that of the living soul. The reason of the name is here given (some think, by Moses the historian, others, by Adam himself): *Because she was* (that is, was to be) *the mother of all living.* He had before called her *Ishah — woman,* as a wife; here he calls her *Evah — life,* as a mother. Now, 1. If this was done by divine direction, it was an instance of God's favour, and, like the new naming of Abraham and Sarah, it was a seal of the covenant, an assurance to them that, notwithstanding their sin and his displeasure against them for it, he had not reversed that blessing wherewith he had blessed them: *Be fruitful and multiply.* It was likewise a confirmation of the promise now made, that the seed of the woman, of this woman, should break the serpent's head. 2. If Adam did it of himself, it was an instance of his faith in the word of God. Doubtless it was not done, as some have suspected, in contempt or defiance of the curse, but rather in a humble confidence and dependence upon the blessing. (1.) The blessing of a reprieve, admiring the patience of God, that he should spare such sinners to be the parents of all living, and that he did not immediately shut up those fountains of the human life and nature, because they could send forth no other than polluted, poisoned, streams. (2.) The blessing of a Redeemer, and promised seed, to whom Adam had an eye, in calling his wife *Eve — life;* for he should be the life of all the living, and in him all the families of the earth should be blessed, in hope of which he thus triumphs.

Verse 21

We have here a further instance of God's care concerning our first parents, notwithstanding their sin. Though he corrects his disobedient children, and put them under the marks of his displeasure, yet he does not disinherit them, but, like a tender father, provides the herb of the field for their food and *coats of skins* for their clothing. Thus the father provided for the returning prodigal, Lu. 15:22, 23. If the Lord had been pleased to kill them, he would not have done this for them. Observe, 1. That clothes came in with sin. We should have had no occasion for them, either for defence or decency, if sin had not made us naked, to our shame. Little reason therefore we have to be proud of our clothes, which are but the badges of our poverty and infamy. 2. That when God made clothes for our first parents he made them warm and strong, but coarse and very plain: not robes of scarlet, but coats of skin. Their clothes were made, not of silk and satin, but plain skins; not trimmed, nor embroidered, none of the ornaments which the daughters of Sion afterwards invented, and prided themselves in. Let the poor, that are meanly clad, learn hence not to complain: having food and a covering, let them be content; they are as well done to as Adam and Eve were. And let the rich, that are finely clad, learn hence not to make the putting on of apparel their adorning, 1 Pt. 3:3. 3. That God is to be acknowledged with thankfulness, not only in giving us food, but in giving us clothes also, *ch.* 28:20. The wool and the flax are his, as well as *the corn and the wine,* Hos. 2:9. 4. These coats of skin had a significancy. The beasts whose skins they were must be slain, slain before their eyes, to show them what death is, and (as it is Eccl. 3:18) that they may see that they themselves were beasts, mortal and dying. It is supposed that they were slain, not for food, but for sacrifice, to typify the great sacrifice, which, in the latter end of the world, should be offered once for all. Thus the first thing that died was a sacrifice, or Christ in a figure, who is therefore said to be the *Lamb slain from the foundation of the world.* These sacrifices were divided between God and man, in token of reconciliation: the flesh was offered to God, a whole burnt-offering; the skins were given to man for clothing, signifying that, Jesus Christ having offered himself to God a sacrifice of a sweet-smelling savour, we are to clothe ourselves with his righteousness as with a garment, that the shame of our nakedness may not appear. Adam and Eve made for themselves aprons of fig-leaves, a covering too narrow for them to *wrap themselves in,* Isa. 28:20. Such are all the rags of our own righteousness. But God made them coats of skins; large, and strong, and durable, and fit for them; such is the righteousness of Christ. Therefore *put on the Lord Jesus Christ.*

Verses 22–24

Sentence being passed upon the offenders, we have here execution, in part, done upon them immediately. Observe here,

I. How they were justly disgraced and shamed before God and the holy angels, by the ironical upbraiding of them with the issue of their enterprise: *"Behold, the man has become as one of us, to know good and evil!* A goodly go he makes! Does he not? See what he has got, what preferments, what advantages, by eating forbidden fruit!" This was said to awaken and humble them, and to bring them to a sense of their sin and folly, and to repentance for it, that, seeing themselves thus wretchedly deceived by following the devil's counsel, they might henceforth pursue the happiness of God should offer in the way he should prescribe. God thus *fills their faces with shame, that they may seek his name,* Ps. 83:16. He puts them to this confusion, in order to their conversion. True penitents will thus upbraid themselves: "What fruit have I now by sin? Rom. 6:21. Have I gained what I foolishly promised myself in a sinful way? No, no, it never proved what it pretended to, but the contrary."

II. How they were justly discarded, and shut out of paradise, which was a part of the sentence implied in that, *Thou shalt eat the herb of the field.* Here we have,

1. The reason God gave why he shut man out of paradise; not only because he had put forth his hand, and taken of the tree of knowledge, which was his sin, but lest he should again put forth his hand, and take also of the tree of life (now forbidden him by the divine sentence, as before the tree of knowledge was forbidden by the law), and should dare to eat of that tree, and so profane a divine sacrament and defy a divine sentence, and yet flatter himself with a conceit that thereby he should live forever. Observe, (1.) There is a foolish proneness in those that have rendered themselves unworthy of the substance of Christian privileges to catch at the signs and shadows of them. Many that like not the terms of the covenant, yet, for their reputation's sake, are fond of the seals of it. (2.) It is not only justice, but kindness, to such, to be denied them; for, by usurping that to which they have no title, they affront God and make their sin the more heinous, and by building their hopes upon a wrong foundation they render their conversion the more difficult and their ruin the more deplorable.

2. The method God took, in giving him this bill of divorce, and expelling and excluding him from this garden of pleasure. He turned him out, and kept him out.

(1.) He turned him out, from the garden to the common. This is twice mentioned: *He sent him forth* (v. 23), and then *he drove him out,* v. 24. God bade him go out, told him that that was no place for him, he should no longer occupy and enjoy that garden; but he liked the place too well to be willing to part with it, and therefore God *drove him out,* made him go out, whether he would or no. This signified the exclusion of him, and all his guilty race, from that communion with God which was the bliss and glory of paradise. The tokens of God's favour to him and his delight in the sons of men, which he had in his innocent estate, were now suspended; the communications of his grace were withheld, and Adam became weak, and like other men, as Samson when the *Spirit of the Lord had departed from him.* His acquaintance with God was lessened and lost, and that correspondence which had been settled between man and his Maker was interrupted and broken off. He was driven out, as one unworthy of this

honour and incapable of this service. Thus he and all mankind, by the fall, forfeited and lost communion with God. But whither did he send him when he turned him out of Eden? He might justly have chased him out of the world (Job 18:18), but he only chased him out of the garden. He might justly have cast him down to hell, as he did the angels that sinned when he shut them out from the heavenly paradise, 2 Pt. 2:4. But man was only sent to till the ground out of which he was taken. He was sent to a place of toil, not to a place of torment. He was sent to the ground, not to the grave, — to the work-house, not to the dungeon, not to the prison-house, — to hold the plough, not to drag the chain. His tilling the ground would be recompensed by his eating of its fruits; and his converse with the earth whence he was taken was improvable to good purposes, to keep him humble, and to remind him of his latter end. Observe, then, that though our first parents were excluded from the privileges of their state of innocency, yet they were not abandoned to despair, God's thoughts of love designing them for a second state of probation upon new terms.

(2.) He kept him out, and forbade him all hopes of a re-entry; for he *placed at the east of the garden of Eden* a detachment of *cherubim,* God's hosts, armed with a dreadful and irresistible power, represented by flaming swords which turned every way, on that side the garden which lay next to the place whither Adam was sent, to keep the way that led to the tree of life, so that he could neither steal nor force an entry; for who can make a pass against an angel on his guard or gain a pass made good by such force? Now this intimated to Adam, [1.] That God was displeased with him. Though he had mercy in store for him, yet at present he was angry with him, was turned to be his enemy and fought against him, for here was a sword drawn (Num. 22:23); and he was to him a consuming fire, for it was a flaming sword. [2.] That the angels were at war with him; no peace with the heavenly hosts, while he was in rebellion against their Lord and ours. [3.] That the way to the tree of life was shut up, namely, that way which, at first, he was put into, the way of spotless innocency. It is not said that the cherubim were set to keep him and his for ever from the tree of life (thanks be to God, there is a paradise set before us, and a tree of life in the midst of it, which we rejoice in the hopes of); but they were set to keep that way of the tree of life which hitherto they had been in; that is, it was henceforward in vain for him and his to expect righteousness, life, and happiness, by virtue of the first covenant, for it was irreparably broken, and could never be pleaded, nor any benefit taken by it. The command of that covenant being broken, the curse of it is in full force; it leaves no room for repentance, but we are all undone if we be judged by that covenant. God revealed this to Adam, not to drive him to despair, but to oblige and quicken him to look for life and happiness in the promised seed, by whom the flaming sword is removed. God and his angels are reconciled to us, and a new and living way into the holiest is consecrated and laid open for us.

CHAPTER 4

In this chapter we have both the world and the church in a family, in a little family, in Adam's family, and a specimen given of the character and state of both in after-ages, nay, in all ages, to the end of time. As all mankind were represented in Adam, so that great distinction of mankind into saints and sinners, godly and wicked, the children of God and the children of the wicked one, was here represented in Cain and Abel, and an early instance is given of the enmity which was lately put between the seed of the woman and the seed of the serpent. We have here, I. The birth, names, and callings of Cain and Abel (v. 1, 2). II. Their religion, and different success in it (v. 3, 4 and part of v. 5). III. Cain's anger at God and the reproof of him for that anger (v. 5–7). IV. Cain's murder of his brother, and the process against him for that murder. The murder committed (v. 8). The proceedings against him. 1. His arraignment (v. 9, former part). 2. His plea (v. 9, latter part). 3. His conviction (v. 10). 4. The sentence passed upon him (v. 11, 12). 5. His complaint against the sentence (v. 13, 14). 6. The ratification of the sentence (v. 15). 7. The execution of the sentence (v. 15, 16). V. The family and posterity of Cain (v. 17–24). VI. The birth of another son and grandson of Adam (v. 25, 26).

Verses 1–2

Adam and Eve had many sons and daughters, ch. 5:4. But Cain and Abel seem to have been the two eldest. Some think they were twins, and, as Esau and Jacob, the elder hated and the younger loved. Though God had cast our first parents out of paradise, he did not write them child-

less; but, to show that he had other blessings in store for them, he preserved to them the benefit of that first blessing of increase. Though they were sinners, nay, though they felt the humiliation and sorrow of penitents, they did not write themselves comfortless, having the promise of a Saviour to support themselves with. We have here,

I. The names of their two sons. 1. *Cain* signifies *possession;* for Eve, when she bore him, said with joy, and thankfulness, and great expectation, *I have gotten a man from the* Lord. Observe, Children are God's gifts, and he must be acknowledged in the building up of our families. It doubles and sanctifies our comfort in them when we see them coming to us from the hand of God, who will not forsake the works and gifts of his own hand. Though Eve bore him with the sorrows that were the consequence of sin, yet she did not lose the sense of the mercy in her pains. Comforts, though alloyed, are more than we deserve; and therefore our complaints must not drown our thanksgivings. Many suppose that Eve had a conceit that this son was the promised seed, and that therefore she thus triumphed in him, as her words may be read, *I have gotten a man, the* Lord, God-man. If so, she was wretchedly mistaken, as Samuel, when he said, *Surely the* Lord's *anointed is before me,* 1 Sa. 16:6. When children are born, who can foresee what they will prove? He that was thought to be *a man, the* Lord, or at least a man from the Lord, and for his service as priest of the family, became an enemy to the Lord. The less we expect from creatures, the more tolerable will disappointments be. 2. *Abel* signifies *vanity.* When she thought she had obtained the promised seed in Cain, she was so taken up with that possession that another son was as vanity to her. To those who have an interest in Christ, and make him their all, other things are as nothing at all. It intimates likewise that the longer we live in this world the more we may see of the vanity of it. What, at first, we are fond of, as a possession, afterwards we see cause to be dead to, as a trifle. The name given to this son is put upon the whole race, Ps. 39:5. Every man is at his best estate *Abel — vanity.* Let us labour to see both ourselves and others so. *Childhood and youth are vanity.*

II. The employments of Cain and Abel. Observe, 1. They both had a calling. Though they were heirs apparent to the world, their birth noble and their possessions large, yet they were not brought up in idleness. God gave their father a calling, even in innocency, and he gave them one. Note, It is the will of God that we should every one of us have something to do in this world. Parents ought to bring up their children to business. "Give them a Bible and a calling (said good Mr. Dod), and God be with them." 2. Their employments were different, that they might trade and exchange with one another, as there was occasion. The members of the body politic have need one of another, and mutual love is helped by mutual commerce. 3. Their employments belonged to the husbandman's calling, their father's profession — a needful calling, for *the king himself is served of the field,* but a laborious calling, which required constant care and attendance. It is now looked upon as a mean calling; the *poor of the land* serve for *vinedressers and husbandmen,* Jer. 52:16. But the calling was far from being a dishonour to them; rather, they were an honour to it. 4. It should seem, by the order of the story, that Abel, though the younger brother, yet entered first into his calling, and probably his example drew in Cain. 5. Abel chose that employment which most befriended contemplation and devotion, for to these a pastoral life has been looked upon as being peculiarly favourable. Moses and David kept sheep, and in their solitudes conversed with God. Note, That calling or condition of life is best for us, and to be chosen by us, which is best for our souls, that which least exposes us to sin and gives us most opportunity of serving and enjoying God.

Verses 3–5

Here we have, I. The devotions of Cain and Abel. *In process of time,* when they had made some improvement in their respective callings (Heb. *At the end of days,* either at the end of the year, when they kept their feast of ingathering or perhaps an annual fast in remembrance of the fall, or at the end of the days of the week, the seventh day, which was the sabbath) — at some set time, Cain and Abel brought to Adam, as the priest of the family, each of them *an offering to the Lord,* for the doing of which we have reason to think there was a divine appointment given to Adam, as a token of God's favour to him and his thoughts of love towards him and his, notwithstanding their apostasy. God would thus try Adam's faith in the promise and his obedience to the remedial law; he would thus settle a correspondence again between heaven and earth, and give *shadows of good things to come.* Observe here, 1. That the religious worship of God is no novel invention, but an ancient institution. It is that which was *from the beginning* (1 Jn. 1:1); it is the *good old way,* Jer. 6:16. The city of our God is indeed that joyous city whose antiquity is of ancient days, Isa. 23:7. Truth got the start of error, and piety of profaneness. 2. That is a good thing for children to be well taught when they are young, and trained up betimes in religious services, that when they come to be capable of acting for themselves they may, of their own accord, *bring an offering to God.* In this *nurture of the Lord* parents must bring up their children, *ch.* 18:19; Eph. 6:4. 3. That we should every one of us honour God with what we have, according as he has prospered us. According as their employments and possessions were, so they brought their offering. See 1 Co. 16:1, 2. *Our merchandize and our hire,* whatever they are, must be *holiness to the Lord,* Isa. 23:18. He must have his dues of it in works of piety and charity, the support of religion and the relief of the poor. Thus we must now bring our offering with an upright heart; *and with such sacrifices God is well pleased.* 4. That hypocrites and evil doers may be found going as far as the best of God's people in the external services of religion. Cain brought an offering with Abel; nay, Cain's offering is mentioned first, as if he were the more forward of the two. A hypocrite may possibly hear as many sermons, say as many prayers, and give as much alms, as a good Christian, and yet, for want of sincerity, come short of acceptance with God. The Pharisee and the publican went to the temple to pray, Lu. 18:10.

II. The different success of their devotions. That which is to be aimed at in all acts of religion is God's acceptance: we speed well if we attain this, but in vain do we worship if we miss of it, 2 Co. 5:9. Perhaps, to a stander-by, the sacrifices of Cain and Abel would have seemed both alike good. Adam accepted them both, but God, *who sees not as man sees,* did not. God had *respect to Abel and to his offering,* and showed his acceptance of it, probably by fire from heaven; but to *Cain and his offering he had not respect.* We are sure there was a good reason for this difference; the Governor of the world, though an absolute sovereign, does not act arbitrarily in dispensing his smiles and frowns.

1. There was a difference in the characters of the persons offering. Cain was a wicked man, led a bad life, under the reigning power of the world and the flesh; and therefore his sacrifice was an *abomination to the Lord* (Prov. 15:8), *a vain oblation,* Isa. 1:13. God had no respect to Cain himself, and therefore no respect to his offering, as the manner of the expression intimates. But Abel was a righteous man; he is called *righteous Abel* (Mt. 23:35); his heart was upright and his life was pious; he was one of those whom God's countenance beholds (Ps. 11:7) and whose prayer is therefore his delight, Prov. 15:8. God had respect to him as a holy man, and therefore to his offering as a holy offering. The tree must be good, else the fruit cannot be pleasing to the heart-searching God.

2. There was a difference in the offerings they brought. It is expressly said (Heb. 11:4), Abel's was a *more excellent sacrifice* than Cain's: either (1.) In the nature of it. Cain's was only a sacrifice of acknowledgment offered to the Creator; the meat-offerings of the fruit of the ground were no more, and, for aught I know, they might be offered in innocency. But Abel brought a sacrifice of atonement, the blood whereof was shed in order to remission, thereby owning himself a sinner, deprecating God's wrath, and imploring his favour in a Mediator. Or, (2.) In the qualities of the offering. Cain brought *of the fruit of the ground,* any thing that came next to hand, what he had not occasion for himself or what was not marketable. But Abel was curious in the choice of his offering: not the lame, nor the lean, nor the refuse, but the *firstlings of the flock* — the best he had, *and the fat thereof* — the best of those best. Hence the Hebrew doctors give it for a general rule that every thing that is for the name of the good God must be the goodliest and best. It is fit that he who is the first and best should have the first and best of our time, strength, and service.

3. The great difference was this, that Abel offered in faith, and Cain did not. There was a difference in the principle upon which they went. Abel offered with an eye to God's will as his rule, and God's glory as his end, and in dependence upon the promise of a Redeemer; but Cain did what he did only for company's sake, or to save his credit, not in faith, and so it turned into sin to him. Abel was a penitent believer, like the publican that went away justified: Cain was unhumbled; his confidence was within himself; he was like the Pharisee who glorified himself, but was not so much as justified before God.

III. Cain's displeasure at the difference God made between his sacrifice and Abel's. Cain was very wroth, which presently appeared in his very looks, for his countenance fell, which bespeaks not so much his grief and discontent as his malice and rage. His sullen churlish countenance, and a down-look, betrayed his passionate resentments: he carried ill-nature in his face, and *the show of his countenance witnessed against him.* This anger bespeaks, 1. His enmity to God, and the indignation he had conceived against him for making such a difference between his offering and his brother's. He should have been angry at himself for his own infidelity and hypocrisy, by which he had forfeited God's acceptance; and his countenance should have fallen in repentance and holy shame, as the publican's, who *would not lift up so much as his eyes to heaven,* Lu. 18:13. But, instead of this, he flies out against God, as if he were partial and unfair in distributing his smiles and frowns, and as if he had done him a deal of wrong. Note, It is a certain sign of an unhumbled heart to quarrel with those rebukes which we have, by our own sin, brought upon ourselves. *The foolishness of man perverteth his way,* and then, to make bad worse, *his heart fretteth against the Lord,* Prov. 19:3. 2. His envy of his brother, who had the honour to be publicly owned. Though his brother had no thought of having any slur put upon him, nor did now insult over him to provoke him, yet he conceived a hatred of him as an enemy, or, which is equivalent, a rival. Note, (1.) It is common for those who have rendered themselves unworthy of God's favour by their presumptuous sins to have indignation against those who are dignified and distinguished by it. The Pharisees walked in this way of Cain, when they *neither entered into the kingdom of God themselves* nor *suffered those that were entering to go in,* Lu. 11:52. Their eye is evil, because their master's eye and the eye of their fellow-servants are good. (2.) Envy is a sin that commonly carries with it both its own discovery, in the paleness of the looks, and its own punishment, in the rottenness of the bones.

Verses 6–7

God is here reasoning with Cain, to convince him of the sin and folly of his anger and discontent, and to bring him into a good temper again, that further mischief might be prevented. It is an instance of God's patience and condescending goodness that he would deal thus tenderly with so bad a man, in so bad an affair. *He is not willing that any should perish, but that all should come to repentance.* Thus the father of the prodigal argued the case with the elder son (Lu. 15:28, etc.), and God with those Israelites who said, *The way of the Lord is not equal,* Eze. 18:25.

I. God puts Cain himself upon enquiring into the cause of his discontent, and considering whether it were indeed a just cause: *Why is thy countenance fallen?* Observe, 1. That God takes notice of all our sinful passions and discontents. There is not an angry look, an envious look, nor a fretful look, that escapes his observing eye. 2. That most of our sinful heats and disquietudes would soon vanish before a strict and impartial enquiry into the cause of them. *"Why am I wroth?* Is there a real cause, a just cause, a proportionable cause for it? Why am I so soon angry? Why so very angry, and so implacable?"

II. To reduce Cain to his right mind again, it is here made evident to him,

1. That he had no reason to be angry at God, for that he had proceeded according to the settled and invariable rules of government suited to a state of probation. He sets before men life and death, the blessing and the curse, and then *renders to them according to their works,* and differences them according as they difference themselves — so shall their doom be. The rules are just, and therefore his ways, according to those rules, must needs be equal, and he will be justified when he speaks.

(1.) God sets before Cain life and a blessing: *"If thou doest well, shalt thou not be accepted?* No doubt thou shalt, nay, thou knowest thou shalt;" either, [1.] "If thou hadst done well, as thy brother did, thou shouldst have been accepted, as he was." *God is no respecter of persons,* hates nothing that he had made, denies his favour to none but those who have forfeited it, and is an enemy to none but those who by sin have made him their enemy: so that if we come short of acceptance with him we must thank ourselves, the fault is wholly our own; if we had done our duty, we should not have missed of his mercy. This will justify God in the destruction of sinners, and will aggravate their ruin; there is not a damned sinner in hell, but, if he had done well, as he might have done, had been a glorious saint in heaven. Every mouth will shortly be stopped with this. Or, [2.] "If now thou do well, if thou repent of thy sin, reform thy heart and life, and bring thy sacrifice in a better manner, if thou not only do that which is good but do it well, thou shalt yet be accepted, thy sin shall be pardoned, thy comfort and honour restored, and all shall be well." See here the effect of a Mediator's interposal between God and man; we do not stand upon the footing of the first covenant, which left no room for repentance, but God had come upon new terms with us. Though we have offended, if we repent and return, we shall find mercy. See how early the gospel was preached, and the benefit of it here offered even to one of the chief of sinners.

(2.) He sets before him death and a curse: But *if not well,* that is, "Seeing thou didst not do well, didst not offer in faith and in a right manner, *sin lies at the door,"* that is, "sin was imputed to thee, and thou wast frowned upon and rejected as a sinner. So high a charge had not been laid at thy door, if thou hadst not brought it upon thyself, by not doing well." Or, as it is commonly taken, "If now thou wilt not do well, if thou persist in this wrath, and, instead of humbling thyself before God, harden thyself against him, *sin lies at the door,"* that is, [1.] Further sin. "Now that anger is in thy heart, murder is at the door." The way of sin is down-hill, and men go from bad to worse. Those who do not sacrifice well, but are careless and remiss in their devotion to God, expose themselves to the worst temptations; and perhaps the most scandalous sin lies at the door. Those who do not keep God's ordinances are in danger of committing all abominations, Lev. 18:30. Or, [2.] The punishment of sin. So near akin are sin and punishment that the same word in Hebrew signifies both. If sin be harboured in the house, the curse waits at the door, like a bailiff, ready to arrest the sinner whenever he looks out. It lies as if it slept, but it lies at the door where it will be soon awaked, and then it will appear that the damnation slumbered not. Sin will *find thee out,* Num. 32:23. Yet some choose to understand this also as an intimation of mercy. "If thou doest not well, *sin* (that is, *the sin-offering),* lies at the door, and thou mayest take the benefit of it." The same word signifies *sin* and *a sacrifice for sin.* "Though thou hast not done well, yet do not despair; the remedy is at hand; the propitiation is not far to seek; lay hold on it, and the iniquity of thy holy things shall be forgiven thee." Christ, the great sin-offering, is said to *stand at the door,* Rev. 3:20. And those well deserve to perish in their sins that will not go to the door for an interest in the sin-offering. All this considered, Cain had no reason to be angry at God, but at himself only.

2. That he had no reason to be angry at his brother: *"Unto thee shall be his desire,* he shall continue his respect to thee as an elder brother, and thou, as the first-born, shalt rule over him as much as ever." God's acceptance of Abel's offering did not transfer the birth-right to him (which Cain was jealous of), nor put upon him that excellency of dignity and of power which is said to belong to it, *ch.* 49:3. God did not so intend it; Abel did not so interpret it; there was no danger of its being improved to Cain's prejudice; why then should he be so much exasperated? Observe here, (1.) That the difference which God's grace makes does not alter the distinctions which God's providence makes, but preserves them, and obliges us to do the duty which results from them: believing servants must be obedient to

unbelieving masters. Dominion is not founded in grace, nor will religion warrant disloyalty or disrespect in any relation. (2.) That the jealousies which civil powers have sometimes conceived of the true worshippers of God as dangerous to their government, enemies to Caesar, and hurtful to kings and provinces (on which suspicion persecutors have grounded their rage against them) are very unjust and unreasonable. Whatever may be the case with some who call themselves Christians, it is certain that *Christians indeed* are the best subjects, and the quiet in the land; their desire is towards their governors, and these shall rule over them.

Verse 8

We have here the progress of Cain's anger, and the issue of it in Abel's murder, which may be considered two ways: —

I. As Cain's sin; and a scarlet, crimson, sin it was, a sin of the first magnitude, a sin against the light and law of nature, and which the consciences even of bad men have startled at. See in it, 1. The sad effects of sin's entrance into the world and into the hearts of men. See what a root of bitterness the corrupt nature is, which bears this gall and wormwood. Adam's eating forbidden fruit seemed but a little sin, but it opened the door to the greatest. 2. A fruit of the enmity which is in the seed of the serpent against the seed of the woman. As Abel leads the van in the *noble army of martyrs* (Mt. 23:35), so Cain stand in the front of the ignoble army of persecutors, Jude 11. So early did he that was after the flesh *persecute him that was after the Spirit; and so it is now,* more or less (Gal. 4:29), and so it will be till the war shall end in the eternal salvation of all the saints and the eternal perdition of all that hate them. 3. See also what comes of *envy, hatred, malice, and all uncharitableness;* if they be indulged and cherished in the soul, they are in danger of involving men in the horrid guilt of murder itself. Rash anger is heart-murder, Mt. 5:21, 22. Much more is malice so; he that hates his brother is already a murderer before God; and, if God leave him to himself, he wants nothing but an opportunity to render him a murderer before the world. Many were the aggravations of Cain's sin. (1.) It was his brother, his own brother, that he murdered, his own mother's son (Ps. 50:20), whom he ought to have loved, his younger brother, whom he ought to have protected. (2.) He was a good brother, one who had never done him any wrong, nor given him the least provocation in word or deed, but one whose desire had been always towards him, and who had been, in all instances, dutiful and respectful to him. (3.) He had fair warning given him, before, of this. God himself had told him what would come of it, yet he persisted in his barbarous design. (4.) It should seem that he covered it with a show of friendship and kindness: *He talked with Abel his brother,* freely and familiarly, lest Abel should suspect danger, and keep out of his reach. Thus Joab kissed Abner, and then killed him. Thus Absalom feasted his brother Amnon and then killed him. According to the Septuagint [a Greek version of the Old Testament, supposed to have been translated by seventy-two Jews, at the desire of Ptolemy Philadelphus, above 200 years before Christ], Cain said to Abel, *Let us go into the field;* if so, we are sure Abel did not understand it (according to the modern sense) as a challenge, else he would not have accepted it, but as a brotherly invitation to go together to their work. The Chaldee paraphrast adds that Cain, when they were in discourse in the field, maintained that there was no judgment to come, no future state, no rewards and punishments in the other world, and that when Abel spoke in defence of the truth Cain took that occasion to fall upon him. However, (5.) That which the scripture tells us was the reason why he slew him was a sufficient aggravation of the murder; it was *because his own works were evil and his brother's righteous,* so that herein he showed himself to be *of that wicked one* (1 Jn. 3:12), a *child of the devil,* as being *an enemy to all righteousness,* even in his own brother, and, in this, employed immediately by the destroyer. Nay, (6.) In killing his brother, he directly struck at God himself; for God's accepting Abel was the provocation pretended, and for this very reason he hated Abel, because God loved him. (7.) The murder of Abel was the more inhuman because there were now so few men in the world to replenish it. The life of a man is precious at any time; but it was in a special manner precious now, and could ill be spared.

II. As Abel's suffering. Death reigned ever since Adam sinned, but we read not of any taken captive by him till now; and now, 1. The first that dies is a saint, one that was accepted and beloved of God, to show that, though the promised seed was so far to destroy him that had the power of death as to save believers from its sting, yet still they should be exposed to its stroke. The first that went to the grave went to heaven. God would secure to himself the first-fruits, the first-born to the dead, that first opened the womb into another world. Let this take off the terror of death, that it was betimes the lot of God's chosen, which alters the property of it. Nay, 2. The first that dies is a martyr, and dies for his religion; and of such it may more truly be said than of soldiers that they die on the bed of honour. Abel's death has not only no curse in it, but it has a crown in it; so admirably well is the property of death altered that it is not only rendered innocent and offensive to those that die in Christ, but honourable and glorious to those that die for him. Let us not think it strange concerning the fiery trial, nor shrink if we be called to resist unto blood; for we know there is a crown of life for all that are faithful unto death.

Verses 9–12

We have here a full account of the trial and condemnation of the first murderer. Civil courts of judicature not being yet erected for this purpose, as they were afterwards (*ch.* 9:6), God himself sits Judge; for he is the God to whom vengeance belongs, and who will be sure to make inquisition for blood, especially the blood of saints. Observe,

I. The arraignment of Cain: *The Lord said unto Cain, Where is Abel thy brother?* Some think Cain was thus examined the next sabbath after the murder was committed, when *the sons of God came,* as usual, *to present themselves before the Lord,* in a religious assembly, and Abel was missing, whose place did not use to be empty; for the God of heaven takes notice who is present at and who is absent from public ordinances. Cain is asked, not only because there is just cause to suspect him, he having discovered a malice against Abel and having been last with him, but because God knew him to be guilty; yet he asks him, that he may draw from him a confession of his crime, for those who would be justified before God must accuse themselves, and the penitent will do so.

II. Cain's plea: he pleads *not guilty,* and adds rebellion to his sin. For, 1. He endeavours to cover a deliberate murder with a deliberate lie: *I know not.* He knew well enough what had become of Abel, and yet had the impudence to deny it. Thus, in Cain, the devil was both a murderer and a liar from the beginning. See how sinners' minds are blinded, and their hearts hardened by the deceitfulness of sin: those are strangely blind that think it possible to conceal their sins from a God that sees all, and those are strangely hard that think it desirable to conceal them from a God who pardons those only that confess. 2. He impudently charges his Judge with folly and injustice, in putting this question to him: *Am I my brother's keeper?* He should have humbled himself, and have said, *Am not I my brother's murderer?* But he flies in the face of God himself, as if he had asked him an impertinent question, to which he was no way obliged to give an answer: *"Am I my brother's keeper?* Surely he is old enough to take care of himself, nor did I ever take any charge of him." Some think he reflects on God and his providence, as if he had said, "Art not thou his keeper? If he be missing, on thee be the blame, and not on me, who never undertook to keep him." Note, A charitable concern for our brethren, as their keepers, is a great duty, which is strictly required of us, but is generally neglected by us. Those who are unconcerned in the affairs of their brethren, and take no care, when they have opportunity, to prevent their hurt in their bodies, goods, or good name, especially in their souls, do, in effect, speak Cain's language. See Lev. 19:17; Phil. 2:4.

III. The conviction of Cain, *v.* 10. God gave no direct answer to his question, but rejected his plea as false and frivolous: *"What hast thou done?* Thou makest a light matter of it; but hast thou considered what an evil thing it is, how deep the stain, how heavy the burden, of this guilt is? Thou thinkest to conceal it, but it is to no purpose, the evidence against thee is clear and incontestable: *The voice of thy brother's blood cries."* He speaks as if the blood itself were both witness and prosecutor, because God's own knowledge testified against him and God's own justice demanded satisfaction. Observe here, 1. Murder is a crying sin, none more so. Blood calls for blood, the blood of the murdered for the blood of the murderer; it cries in the dying words of Zechariah (2 Chr. 24:22), *The Lord look upon it and require it;* or in those of the souls under the altar (Rev. 6:10), *How long, Lord, holy, and true?* The patient sufferers cried for pardon *(Father, forgive them),* but their blood cries for vengeance. Though they hold their peace, their blood has a loud and constant cry, to which the ear of the righteous God is always open. 2. The blood is said to cry from the ground, the earth, which is said *to open her mouth to receive his brother's blood from his hand, v.* 11. The earth did, as it were, blush to see her own face stained with such blood, and therefore opened her mouth to hide that which she could no hinder. When the heaven revealed Cain's iniquity, the earth also rose up against him (Job 20:27), and groaned on being thus made *subject to vanity,* Rom. 8:20, 22. Cain, it is likely, buried the blood and the body, to conceal his crime; but "murder will out." He did not bury them so deep but the cry of them reached heaven. 3. In the original the word is plural, thy brother's *bloods,* not only his blood, but the blood of all those that might have descended from him; or the blood of all the seed of the woman, who should, in like manner, seal the truth with their blood. Christ puts all on one score (Mt. 23:35); or because account was kept of every drop of blood shed. How well is it for us that the blood of Christ speaks better things than that of Abel! Heb. 12:24. Abel's blood cried for vengeance, Christ's blood cries for pardon.

IV. The sentence passed upon Cain: *And now art thou cursed from the earth, v.* 11. Observe here,

1. He is cursed, separated to all evil, laid under the wrath of God, as it is revealed from heaven against all ungodliness and unrighteousness of men, Rom. 1:18. Who knows the extent and weight of a divine curse, how far it reaches, how deep it pierces? God's pronouncing a man cursed makes him so; for those whom he curses are cursed indeed. The curse for Adam's disobedience terminated on the ground: *Cursed is the ground for thy sake;* but that for Cain's rebellion fell immediately upon himself: *Thou art cursed;* for God had mercy in store for Adam, but none for Cain. We have all deserved this curse, and it is only in Christ that believers are saved from it and inherit the blessing, Gal. 3:10, 13.

2. He is cursed from the earth. Thence the cry came up to God, thence the curse came up to Cain. God could have taken vengeance by an immediate stroke from heaven, by the sword of an angel, or by a thunderbolt; but he chose to make the earth the avenger of blood, to continue him upon the earth, and not immediately to cut him off, and yet to make even this his curse. The earth is always near us, we cannot fly from it; so that, if this is made the executioner of divine wrath, our punishment is unavoidable: it is sin, that is, the punishment of sin, lying at the door. Cain found his punishment where he chose his portion and set his heart. Two things we expect from the earth, and by this curse both are denied to Cain and taken from him: *sustenance* and *settlement.* (1.) Sustenance out of the earth is here withheld from him. It is a curse upon him in his enjoyments, and particularly in his calling: *When thou tillest the ground, it shall not henceforth yield unto thee its strength.* Note, Every creature is to us what God makes it, a comfort or a cross, a blessing or a curse. If the earth yield not her strength to us, we must therein acknowledge God's righteousness; for we have not yielded our strength to him. The ground was cursed before to Adam, but it was now doubly cursed to Cain. That part of it which fell to his share, and of which he had the occupation, was made unfruitful and uncomfortable to him by the blood of Abel. Note, The wickedness of the wicked brings a curse upon all they do and all they have (Deu. 28:15, etc.), and this curse embitters all they have and disappoints them in all they do. (2.) Settlement on the earth is here denied him: *A fugitive and a vagabond shalt thou be in the earth.* By this he was condemned, [1.] To perpetual disgrace and reproach among men. It should be ever looked upon as a scandalous thing to harbour him, converse with him, or show him any countenance. And justly was a man that had divested himself of all humanity ab-

horred and abandoned by all mankind, and made infamous. [2.] To perpetual disquietude and horror in his own mind. His own guilty conscience should haunt him wherever he went, and make him *Magormissabib,* a *terror round about.* What rest can those find, what settlement, that carry their own disturbance with them in their bosoms wherever they go? Those must needs be fugitives that are thus tossed. There is not a more restless fugitive upon earth than he that is continually pursued by his own guilt, nor a viler vagabond than he that is at the beck of his own lusts.

This was the sentence passed upon Cain; and even in this there was mercy mixed, inasmuch as he was not immediately cut off, but had space given him to repent; for God is long-suffering to us-ward, not willing that any should perish.

Verses 13–15

We have here a further account of the proceedings against Cain.

I. Here is Cain's complaint of the sentence passed upon him, as hard and severe. Some make him to speak the language of despair, and read it, *My iniquity is greater than that it may be forgiven;* and so what he says is a reproach and affront to the mercy of God, which those only shall have the benefit of that hope in it. There is forgiveness with the God of pardons for the greatest sins and sinners; but those forfeit it who despair of it. Just now Cain made nothing of his sin, but now he is in the other extreme: Satan drives his vassals from presumption to despair. We cannot think too ill of sin, provided we do not think it unpardonable. But Cain seems rather to speak the language of indignation: *My punishment is greater than I can bear;* and so what he says is a reproach and affront to the justice of God, and a complaint, not of the greatness of his sin, but of the extremity of his punishment, as if this were disproportionable to his merits. Instead of justifying God in the sentence, he condemns him, not accepting the punishment of his iniquity, but quarrelling with it. Note, Impenitent unhumbled hearts are therefore not reclaimed by God's rebukes because they think themselves wronged by them; and it is an evidence of great hardness to be more concerned about our sufferings than about our sins. Pharaoh's care was concerning this death only, not this sin (Ex. 10:17); so was Cain's here. He is a living man, and yet complains of the punishment of his sin, Lam. 3:39. He thinks himself rigorously dealt with when really he is favourably treated; and he cries out of wrong when he has more reason to wonder that he is out of hell. Woe unto him that thus strives with his Maker, and enters into judgment with his Judge. Now, to justify this complaint, Cain descants upon the sentence. 1. He sees himself excluded by it from the favour of his God, and concludes that, being cursed, he is hidden from God's face, which is indeed the true nature of God's curse; damned sinners find it so, to whom it is said, *Depart from me you cursed.* Those are cursed indeed that are forever shut out from God's love and care and from all hopes of his grace. 2. He sees himself expelled from all the comforts of this life, and concludes that, being a fugitive, he is, in effect, *driven out this day from the face of the earth.* As good have no place on earth as not have a settled place. Better rest in the grave than not rest at all. 3. He sees himself excommunicated by it, and cut off from the church, and forbidden to attend on public ordinances. His hands being full of blood, he must *bring no more vain oblations,* Isa. 1:13, 15. Perhaps this he means when he complains that he is *driven out from the face of the earth;* for being shut out of the church, which none had yet deserted, he was *hidden from God's face,* being not admitted to come *with the sons of God to present himself before the Lord.* 4. He seen himself exposed by it to the hatred and ill-will of all mankind: *It shall come to pass that every one that finds me shall slay me.* Wherever he wanders, he goes in peril of his life, at least he thinks so; and, like a man in debt, thinks every one he meets a bailiff. There were none alive but his near relations; yet even of them he is justly afraid who had himself been so barbarous to his brother. Some read it, *Whatsoever* finds me shall slay me; not only, "Whosoever among men," but, "Whatsoever among all the creatures." Seeing himself thrown out of God's protection, he sees the whole creation armed against him. Note, Unpardoned guilt fills men with continual terrors, Prov. 28:1; Job 15:20, 21; Ps. 53:5. It is better to fear and not sin than to sin and then fear. Dr. Lightfoot thinks this word of Cain should be read as a wish: *Now, therefore, let it be that any that find me may kill me.* Being bitter in soul, he *longs for death, but it comes not* (Job 3:20–22), as those under spiritual torments do, Rev. 9:5, 6.

II. Here is God's confirmation of the sentence; for when he judges he will overcome, *v.* 15. Observe, 1. How Cain is protected in wrath by this declaration, notified, we may suppose, to all that little world which was then in being: *Whosoever slayeth Cain, vengeance shall be taken on him seven-fold,* because thereby the sentence he was under (that he should be a fugitive and a vagabond) would be defeated. Condemned prisoners are under the special protection of the law; those that are appointed sacrifices to public justice must not be sacrificed to private revenge. God having said in Cain's case, *Vengeance is mine, I will repay,* it would have been a daring usurpation for any man to take the sword out of God's hand, a contempt put upon an express declaration of God's mind, and therefore avenged seven-fold. Note, God has wise and holy ends in protecting and prolonging the lives even of very wicked men. God deals with some according to that prayer, *Slay them not, lest my people forget; scatter them by thy power,* Ps. 59:11. Had Cain been slain immediately, he would have been forgotten (Eccl. 8:10); but now he lives a more fearful and lasting monument of God's justice, hanged in chains, as it were. 2. How he is marked in wrath: *The Lord set a mark upon Cain,* to distinguish him from the rest of mankind and to notify that he was the man that murdered his brother, whom nobody must hurt, but every body must hoot at. God stigmatized him (as some malefactors are burnt in the cheek), and put upon him such a visible and indelible mark of infamy and disgrace as would make all wise people shun him, so that he could not be otherwise than a fugitive and a vagabond, and the off-scouring of all things.

Verses 16–18

We have here a further account of Cain, and what became of him after he was rejected of God.

I. He tamely submitted to that part of his sentence by which he was hidden from God's face; for (*v.* 16) *he went out from the presence of the Lord,* that is, he willingly renounced God and religion, and was content to forego its privileges, so that he might not be under its precepts. He forsook Adam's family and altar, and cast off all pretensions to the fear of God, and never came among good people, nor attended on God's ordinances, any more. Note, Hypocritical professors, that have dissembled and trifled with God Almighty, are justly left to themselves, to do something that is grossly scandalous, and so to throw off that form of godliness to which they have been a reproach, and under colour of which they have denied the power of it. Cain went out now from the presence of the Lord, and we never find that he came into it again, to his comfort. Hell is *destruction from the presence of the Lord,* 2 Th. 1:9. It is a perpetual banishment from the fountain of all good. This is the choice of sinners; and so shall their doom be, to their eternal confusion.

II. He endeavoured to confront that part of the sentence by which he was made a fugitive and a vagabond; for,

1. He chose his land. He went and *dwelt on the east of Eden,* somewhere distant from the place where Adam and his religious family resided, distinguishing himself and his accursed generation from the holy seed, his camp from the *camp of the saints and the beloved city,* Rev. 20:9. On the east of Eden, the cherubim were, with the flaming sword, *ch.* 3:24. There he chose his lot, as if to defy the terrors of the Lord. But his attempt to settle was in vain; for the land he dwelt in was to him *the land of Nod* (that is, of *shaking* or *trembling*), because of the continual restlessness and uneasiness of his own spirit. Note, Those that depart from God cannot find rest any where else. After Cain went out from the presence of the Lord, he never rested. Those that shut themselves out of heaven abandon themselves to a perpetual trembling. *"Return therefore to thy rest, O my soul,* to thy rest in God; else thou art for ever restless."

2. He built a city for a habitation, *v.* 17. *He was building a city,* so some read it, ever building it, but, a curse being upon him and the work of his hands, he could not finish it. Or, as we read it, he *built a city,* in token of a fixed separation from the church of God, to which he had no thoughts of ever returning. This city was to be the headquarters of the apostasy. Observe here, (1.) Cain's defiance of the divine sentence. God said he should be a *fugitive and a vagabond.* Had he repented and humbled himself, this curse might have been turned into a blessing, as that of the tribe of Levi was, that they should be *divided in Jacob and scattered in Israel;* but his impenitent unhumbled heart walking contrary to God, and resolving to fix in spite of heaven, that which might have been a blessing was turned into a curse. (2.) See what was Cain's choice, after he had forsaken God; he pitched upon a settlement in this world, as his rest for ever. Those who looked for the heavenly city chose, while on earth, to dwell in tabernacles; but Cain, as one that minded not *that* city, built himself one on earth. Those that are cursed of God are apt to seek their settlement and satisfaction here below, Ps. 17:14. (3.) See what method Cain took to defend himself against the terrors with which he was perpetually haunted. He undertook this building, to divert his thoughts from the consideration of his own misery, and to drown the clamours of a guilty conscience with the noise of axes and hammers. Thus many baffle their convictions by thrusting themselves into a hurry of worldly business. (4.) See how wicked people often get the start of God's people, and out-go them in outward prosperity. Cain and his cursed race dwell in a city, while Adam and his blessed family dwell in tents. We cannot judge of *love or hatred by all that is before us,* Eccl. 9:1, 2.

3. His family also was built up. Here is an account of his posterity, at least the heirs of his family, for seven generations. His son was *Enoch,* of the same name, but not of the same character, with that holy man that *walked with God, ch.* 5:22. Good men and bad may bear the same names: but God can distinguish between Judas Iscariot and Judas *not* Iscariot, Jn. 14:22. The names of more of his posterity are mentioned, and but just mentioned; not as those of the holy seed (*ch.* 5), where we have three verses concerning each, whereas here we have three or four in one verse. They are numbered in haste, as not valued or delighted in, in comparison with God's chosen.

Verses 19–22

We have here some particulars concerning Lamech, the seventh from Adam in the line of Cain. Observe,

I. His marrying two wives. It was one of the degenerate race of Cain who first transgressed that original law of marriage that two only should be one flesh. Hitherto one man had but one wife at a time; but Lamech took two. *From the beginning it was not so.* Mal. 2:15; Mt. 19:5. See here, 1. Those who desert God's church and ordinances lay themselves open to all manner of temptation. 2. When a bad custom is begun by bad men sometimes men of better characters are, through unwariness, drawn in to follow them. Jacob, David, and many others, who were otherwise good men, were afterwards ensnared in this sin which Lamech begun.

II. His happiness in his children, notwithstanding this. Though he sinned, in marrying two wives, yet he was blessed with children by both, and those such as lived to be famous in their generation, not for their piety, no mention is made of this (for aught that appears they were the heathen of that age), but for their ingenuity. They were not only themselves men of business, but men that were serviceable to the world, and eminent for the invention, or at least the improvement, of some useful arts. 1. Jabal was a famous shepherd; he delighted much in keeping cattle himself, and was so happy in devising methods of doing it to the best advantage, and instructing others in them, that the shepherds of those times, nay, the shepherds of after-times, called him *father;* or perhaps, his children after him being brought up to the same employment, the family was a family of shepherds. 2. Jubal was a famous musician, and particularly an organist, and the first that gave rules for the noble art or science of music. When Jabal had set them in a way to be rich, Jubal put them in a way to be merry. Those that spend their days in wealth will not be without the timbrel and harp, Job 21:12, 13. From his name, *Jubal,* probably the jubilee-trumpet was so called; for the best music was that which proclaimed liberty and redemption. Jabal was their Pan and Jubal their

Apollo. 3. Tubal Cain was a famous smith, who greatly improved the art of working in brass and iron, for the service both of war and husbandry. He was their Vulcan. See here, (1.) That worldly things are the only things that carnal wicked people set their hearts upon and are most ingenious and industrious about. So it was with this impious race of cursed Cain. Here were a father of shepherds and a father of musicians, but not a father of the faithful. Here was one to teach in brass and iron, but none to teach the good knowledge of the Lord. Here were devices how to be rich, and how to be mighty, and how to be merry, but nothing of God, nor of his fear and service, among them. Present things fill the heads of most people. (2.) That even those who are destitute of the knowledge and grace of God may be endued with many excellent and useful accomplishments, which may make them famous and serviceable in their generation. Common gifts are given to bad men, while God chooses to himself the foolish things of the world.

Verses 23–24

By this speech of Lamech, which is here recorded, and probably was much talked of in those times, he further appears to have been a wicked man, as Cain's accursed race generally were. Observe, 1. How haughtily and imperiously he speaks to his wives, as one that expected a mighty regard and observance: *Hear my voice, you wives of Lamech.* No marvel that he who had broken one law of marriage, by taking two wives, broke another, which obliged him to be kind and tender to those he had taken, and to give honour to the wife as to the weaker vessel. Those are not always the most careful to do their own duty that are highest in their demands of respect from others, and most frequent in calling upon their relations to know their place and do their duty. 2. How bloody and barbarous he was to all about him: *I have slain,* or (as it is in the margin) *I would slay a man in my wound, and a young man in my hurt.* He owns himself a man of a fierce and cruel disposition, that would lay about him without mercy, and kill all that stood in his way; be it a man, or a young man, nay, though he himself were in danger to be wounded and hurt in the conflict. Some think, because (*v.* 24) he compares himself with Cain, that he had murdered some of the holy seed, the true worshippers of God, and that he acknowledged this to be the wounding of his conscience and the hurt of his soul; and yet that, like Cain, he continued impenitent, trembling and yet unhumbled. Or his wives, knowing what manner of spirit he was of, how apt both to give and to resent provocation, were afraid lest somebody or other would be the death of him. "Never fear," says he, "I defy any man to set upon me; whosoever does, let me alone to make my part good with him; I will slay him, be he a man or a young man." Note, It is a common thing for fierce and bloody men to *glory in their shame* (Phil. 3:19), as if it were both their safety and their honour that they care not how many lives are sacrificed to their angry resentments, nor how much they are hated, provided they may be feared. *Oderint, dum metuant —Let them hate, provided they fear.* How impiously he presumes even upon God's protection in his wicked way, *v.* 24. He had heard that *Cain should be avenged sevenfold* (*v.* 15), that is, that if any man should dare to kill Cain he should be severely reckoned with and punished for so doing, though Cain deserved to die a thousand deaths for the murder of his brother, and hence he infers that if any one should kill him for the murders he had committed God would much more avenge his death. As if the special care God took to prolong and secure the life of Cain, for special reasons peculiar to his case (and indeed for his sorer punishment, as the beings of the damned are continued) were designed as a protection to all murderers. Thus Lamech perversely argues, "If God provided for the safety of Cain, much more for mine, who, though I have slain many, yet never slew my own brother, and upon no provocation, as he did." Note, The reprieve of some sinners, and the patience God exercises towards them, are often abused to the hardening of others in the like sinful ways, Eccl. 8:11. But, though justice strike some slowly, others cannot therefore be sure but that they may be taken away with a swift destruction. Or, if God should bear long with those who thus presume upon his forbearance, they do but hereby treasure up unto themselves *wrath against the day of wrath.*

Now this is all we have upon record in scripture concerning the family and posterity of cursed Cain, till we find them all cut off and perishing in the universal deluge.

Verses 25–26

This is the first mention of Adam in the story of this chapter. No question, the murder of Abel, and the impenitence and apostasy of Cain, were a very great grief to him and Eve, and the more because their own wickedness did now correct them and their backslidings did reprove them. Their folly had given sin and death entrance into the world; and now they smarted by it, being, by means thereof, deprived of *both their sons in one day, ch.* 27:45. When parents are grieved by their children's wickedness they should take occasion thence to lament that corruption of nature which was derived from them, and which is the root of bitterness. But here we have that which was a relief to our first parents in their affliction.

I. God gave them to see the re-building of their family, which was sorely shaken and weakened by that sad event. For, 1. They saw their seed, *another seed instead of Abel, v.* 25. Observe God's kindness and tenderness towards his people, in his providential dealings with them; when he takes away one comfort from them, he gives them another instead of it, which may prove a greater blessing to them than that was in which they thought their lives were bound up. This other seed was he in whom the church was to be built up and perpetuated, and he comes instead of Abel, for the succession of confessors is the revival of the martyrs and as it were the resurrection of God's slain witnesses. Thus we are *baptized for the dead* (1 Co. 15:29), that is, we are, by baptism, admitted into the church, for or instead of those who by death, especially by martyrdom, are removed out of it; and we fill up their room. Those who slay God's servants hope by this means to wear out the saints of the Most High; but they will be deceived. Christ shall still see his seed; God can out of stones raise up children for him, and make the blood of the martyrs the seed of the church, whose lands, we are sure, shall never be lost for want of heirs. This son, by a prophetic spirit, they called *Seth* (that is, *set, settled,* or *placed),* because, in his seed, mankind should continue to the end of time, and from him the Messiah should descend. While Cain, the head of the apostasy, is made a wanderer, Seth, from whom the true church was to come, is one fixed. In Christ and his church is the only true settlement. 2. They saw their seed's seed, *v.* 26. *To Seth was born a son called Enos,* that general name for all men, which bespeaks the weakness, frailty, and misery, of man's state. The best men are most sensible of these, both in themselves and their children. We are never so settled but we must remind ourselves that we are frail.

II. God gave them to see the reviving of religion in their family: *Then began men to call upon the name of the Lord, v.* 26. It is small comfort to a good man to see his children's children, if he do not, withal, see peace upon Israel, and those that come of him walking in the truth. Doubtless God's name was called upon before, but now, 1. The worshippers of God began to stir up themselves to do more in religion than they had done; perhaps not more than had been done at first, but more than had been done of late, since the defection of Cain. Now men began to worship God, not only in their closets and families, but in public and solemn assemblies. Or now there was so great a reformation in religion that it was, as it were, a new beginning of it. *Then* may refer, not to the birth of Enos, but to the whole foregoing story: *then,* when men saw in Cain and Lamech the sad effects of sin by the workings of natural conscience, — when they saw God's judgments upon sin and sinners, — *then* they were so much the more lively and resolute in religion. The worse others are the better we should be, and the more zealous. 2. The worshippers of God began to distinguish themselves. The margin reads it, *Then began men to be called by the name of the Lord,* or to call themselves by it. Now that Cain and those that had deserted religion had built a city, and begun to declare for impiety and irreligion, and called themselves the *sons of men,* those that adhered to God began to declare for him and his worship, and called themselves the *sons of God.* Now began the distinction between professors and profane, which has been kept up ever since, and will be while the world stands.

CHAPTER 5

This chapter is the only authentic history extant of the first age of the world from the creation to the flood, containing (according to the verity of the Hebrew text) 1656 years, as may easily be computed by the ages of the patriarchs, before they begat that son through whom the line went down to Noah. This is one of those which the apostle calls "endless genealogies" (1 Tim. 1:4), for Christ, who was the end of the Old Testament law, was also the end of the Old Testament genealogies; towards him they looked, and in him they centered. The genealogy here recorded in inserted briefly in the pedigree of our Saviour (Lu. 3:36–38), and is of great use to show that Christ was the "seed of the woman" that was promised. We have here an account, I. Concerning Adam (*v.* 1–5). II. Seth (*v.* 6–8). III. Enos (*v.* 9–11). Cainan (*v.* 12–14). V. Mahalaleel (*v.* 15–17). VI. Jared (*v.* 18–20). VII. Enoch (*v.* 21–24). VIII. Methuselah (*v.* 25–27). IX. Lamech and his son Noah (*v.* 28–32). All scripture, being given by inspiration of God, is profitable, though not all alike profitable.

Verses 1–5

The first words of the chapter are the title or argument of the whole chapter: it is *the book of the generations of Adam;* it is the list or catalogue of the posterity of Adam, not of all, but only of the *holy seed who were the substance thereof* (Isa. 6:13), and *of whom, as concerning the flesh, Christ came* (Rom. 9:5), the names, ages, and deaths, of those that were the successors of the first Adam in the custody of the promise, and the ancestors of the second Adam. The genealogy begins with Adam himself. Here is,

I. His creation, *v.* 1, 2, where we have a brief rehearsal of what was before at large related concerning the creation of man. This is what we have need frequently to hear of and carefully to acquaint ourselves with. Observe here, 1. That *God created man.* Man is not his own maker, therefore he must not be his own master; but the Author of his being must be the director of his motions and the centre of them. 2. That there was a day in which God created man. He was not from eternity, but of yesterday; he was not the first-born, but the junior of the creation. 3. That God made him in his own likeness, righteous and holy, and therefore, undoubtedly, happy. Man's nature resembled the divine nature more than that of any of the creatures of this lower world. 4. That God created them male and female (*v.* 2), for their mutual comfort as well as for the preservation and increase of their kind. Adam and Eve were both made immediately by the hand of God, both made in God's likeness; and therefore between the sexes there is not that great distance and inequality which some imagine. 5. That God blessed them. It is usual for parents to bless their children; so God, the common Father,, blessed his. But earthly parents can only beg a blessing; it is God's prerogative to command it. It refers chiefly to the blessing of increase, not excluding other blessings. 6. The he *called their name Adam. Adam* signifies *earth, red earth.* Now, (1.) God gave him this name. Adam had himself named the rest of the creatures, but he must not choose his own name, lest he should assume some glorious pompous title. But God gave him a name which would be a continual memorandum to him of the meanness of his original, and oblige him to *look unto the rock whence he was hewn and the hole of the pit whence he was digged,* Isa. 51:1. Those have little reason to be proud who are so near akin to dust. (2.) He gave this name both to the man and to the woman. Being at first one by nature, and afterwards one by marriage, it was fit they should both have the same name, in token of their union. The woman is *of the earth earthy* as well as the man.

II. The birth of his son *Seth, v.* 3. He was born in the hundred and thirtieth year of Adam's life; and probably the murder of Abel was not long before. Many other sons and daughters were born to Adam, besides Cain and Abel, before this; but no notice is taken of them, because an honourable mention must be made of his name only in whose loins Christ and the church were. But that which is most observable here concerning Seth is that Adam begat him *in his own likeness, after his image.* Adam was made in the image of God; but, when he was fallen and corrupt, he begat a son in his own image, sinful and defiled, frail, mortal, and miserable, like himself; not only a *man* like himself, consisting of body and soul, but a *sinner* like himself, guilty and obnoxious, degenerate and corrupt. Even the man after God's own heart owns himself *conceived and born in sin,* Ps. 51:5. This was Adam's own likeness, the reverse of that divine likeness in which Adam was made;

but, having lost it himself, he could not convey it to his seed. Note, Grace does not run in the blood, but corruption does. A sinner begets a sinner, but a saint does not beget a saint.

III. His age and death. He lived, in all, nine hundred and thirty years, and then he died, according to the sentence passed upon him, *To dust thou shalt return.* Though he did not die in the day he ate forbidden fruit, yet in that very day he became mortal. Then he began to die; his whole life afterwards was but a reprieve, a forfeited condemned life; nay, it was a wasting dying life: he was not only like a criminal sentenced, but as one already crucified, that dies slowly and be degrees.

Verses 6–20

We have here all that the Holy Ghost thought fit to leave upon record concerning five of the patriarchs before the flood, Seth, Enos, Cainan, Mahalaleel, and Jared. There is nothing observable concerning any of these particularly, though we have reason to think they were men of eminence, both for prudence and piety, in their day: but in general,

I. Observe how largely and expressly their generations are recorded. This matter, one would think, might have been delivered in fewer words; but it is certain that there is not one idle word in God's books, whatever there is in men's. It is thus plainly set down, 1. To make it easy and intelligible to the meanest capacity. When we are informed how old they were when they begat such a son, and how many years they lived afterwards, a very little skill in arithmetic will enable a man to tell how long they lived in all; yet the Holy Ghost sets down the sum total, for the sake of those that have not even so much skill as this. 2. To show the pleasure God takes in the names of his people. We found Cain's generation numbered in haste (*ch.* 4:18), but this account of the holy seed is enlarged upon, and given in words at length, and not in figures; we are told how long those lived that lived in God's fear, and when those died that died in his favour; but as for others it is no matter. *The memory of the just is blessed, but the name of the wicked shall rot.*

II. Their life is reckoned by days (*v.* 8): *All the days of Seth,* and so of the rest, which intimates the shortness of the life of man when it is at the longest, and the quick revolution of our times on earth. If they reckoned by days, surely we must reckon by hours, or rather make that our frequent prayer (Ps. 90:12), *Teach us to number our days.*

III. Concerning each of them, except Enoch, it is said, *and he died.* It is implied in the numbering of the years of their life that their life, when those years were numbered and finished, came to an end; and yet it is still repeated, *and he died,* to show that death passed upon all men without exception, and that it is good for us particularly to observe and improve the deaths of others for our own edification. Such a one was a strong healthful man, but he died; such a one was a great and rich man, but he died; such a one was a wise politic man, but he died; such a one was a very good man, perhaps a very useful man, but he died, etc.

IV. That which is especially observable is that they all lived very long; not one of them died till he had seen the revolution of almost eight hundred years, and some of them lived much longer, a great while for an immortal soul to be imprisoned in a house of clay. The present life surely was not to them such a burden as commonly it is now, else they would have been weary of it; nor was the future life so clearly revealed then as it is now under the gospel, else they would have been impatient to remove to it: long life to the pious patriarchs was a blessing and made them blessings. 1. Some natural causes may be assigned for their long life in those first ages of the world. It is very probable that the earth was more fruitful, that the productions of it were more strengthening, that the air was more healthful, and that the influences of the heavenly bodies were more benign, before the flood, than afterwards. Though man was driven out of paradise, yet the earth itself was then paradisiacal — a garden in comparison with its present wilderness-state: and some think that their great knowledge of the creatures, and of their usefulness both for food and medicine, together with their sobriety and temperance, contributed much to it; yet we do not find that those who were intemperate, as many were (Lu. 17:27),

were as short-lived as intemperate men generally are now. 2. It must chiefly be resolved into the power and providence of God. He prolonged their lives, both for the more speedy replenishing of the earth and for the more effectual preservation of the knowledge of God and religion, then, when there was no written word, but tradition was the channel of its conveyance. All the patriarchs here, except Noah, were born before Adam died; so that from him they might receive a full and satisfactory account of the creation, paradise, the fall, the promise, and those divine precepts which concerned religious worship and a religious life: and, if any mistake arose, they might have recourse to him while he lived, as to an oracle, for the rectifying of it, and after his death to Methuselah, and others, that had conversed with him: so great was the care of Almighty God to preserve in his church the knowledge of his will and the purity of his worship.

Verses 21–24

The accounts here run on for several generations without any thing remarkable, or any variation but of the names and numbers; but at length there comes in one that must not be passed over so, of whom special notice must be taken, and that is *Enoch,* the seventh from Adam: the rest, we may suppose, did virtuously, but he excelled them all, and was the brightest star of the patriarchal age. It is but little that is recorded concerning him; but this little is enough to make his name great, greater than the name of the other Enoch, who had a city called by his name. Here are two things concerning him: —

I. His gracious conversation in this world, which is twice spoken of: *Enoch walked with God after he begat Methuselah* (*v.* 22), and again, *Enoch walked with God, v.* 24. Observe,

1. The nature of his religion and the scope and tenour of his conversation: he *walked with God,* which denotes, (1.) True religion; what is godliness, but walking with God? The ungodly and profane are without God in the world, they walk contrary to him: but the godly walk with God, which presupposes reconciliation to God, for two cannot *walk together except they be agreed* (Amos 3:3), and includes all the parts and instances of a godly, righteous, and sober life. To walk with God is to set God always before us, and to act as those that are always under his eye. It is to live a life of communion with God both in ordinances and providences. It is to make God's word our rule and his glory our end in all our actions. It is to make it our constant care and endeavour in every thing to please God, and nothing to offend him. It is to comply with his will, to concur with his designs, and to be workers together with him. It is to be *followers of him as dear children.* (2.) Eminent religion. He was entirely dead to this world, and did not only walk after God, as all good men do, but he walked with God, as if he were in heaven already. He lived above the rate, not only of other men, but of other saints: not only good in bad times, but the best in good times. (3.) Activity in promoting religion among others. Executing the priest's office is called *walking before God,* 1 Sa. 2:30, 35, and see Zec. 3:7. Enoch, it should seem, was a priest of the most high God, and like Noah, who is likewise said to walk with God, he was a preacher of righteousness, and prophesied of Christ's second coming. Jude 14, *Behold, the Lord cometh with his holy myriads.* Now the Holy Spirit, instead of saying, Enoch *lived,* says, Enoch *walked with God;* for it is the life of a good man to walk with God. This was, [1.] The business of Enoch's life, his constant care and work; while others lived to themselves and the world, he lived to God. [2.] It was the joy and support of his life. Communion with God was to him better than life itself. *To me to live is Christ,* Phil. 1:21.

2. The date of his religion. It is said (*v.* 21), *he lived sixty-five years, and begat Methuselah;* but (*v.* 22) *he walked with God after he begat Methuselah,* which intimates that he did not begin to be eminent for piety till about that time; at first he walked but as other men. Great saints arrive at their eminence by degrees.

3. The continuance of his religion: he walked with God *three hundred years,* as long as he continued in this world. The hypocrite will not pray always; but the real saint that acts from a principle, and makes religion his choice, will persevere to the end, and walk with God while he lives, as one that hopes to live for ever with him, Ps. 104:33.

II. His glorious removal to a better world. As he did not live like the rest, so he did not die like the rest (*v.* 24): *He was not, for God took him;* that is, as it is explained (Heb. 11:5), *He was translated that he should not see death, and was not found, because God had translated him.* Observe,

1. When he was thus translated. (1.) What time of his life. It was when he had lived but three hundred and sixty-five years (a year of years), which, as men's ages went then, was in the midst of his days; for there was none of the patriarchs before the flood that did not more than double that age. But why did God take him so soon? Surely, because the world, which had now grown corrupt, was not worthy of him, or because he was so much above the world, and so weary of it, as to desire a speedy removal out of it, or because his work was done, and done the sooner for his minding it so closely. Note, God often takes those soonest whom he loves best, and the time they lose on earth is gained in heaven, to their unspeakable advantage. (2.) What time of the world. It was when all the patriarchs mentioned in this chapter were living, except Adam, who died fifty-seven years before, and Noah, who was born sixty-nine years after; those two had sensible confirmations to their faith other ways, but to all the rest, who were or might have been witnesses of Enoch's translation, it was a sensible encouragement to their faith and hope concerning a future state.

2. How his removal is expressed: *He was not, for God took him.* (1.) He was not any longer in this world; it was not the period of his being, but of his being here: he was *not found,* so the apostle explains it from the Septuagint; not found by his friends, who sought him as the sons of the prophets sought Elijah (2 Ki. 2:17); not found by his enemies, who, some think, were in quest of him, to put him to death in their rage against him for his eminent piety. It appears by his prophecy that there were then many ungodly sinners, who spoke hard speeches, and probably did hard things too, against God's people (Jude 15), but God hid Enoch from them, not under heaven, but in heaven. (2.) God took him body and soul to himself in the heavenly paradise, by the ministry of angels, as afterwards he took Elijah. He was changed, as those saints will be that shall be found alive at Christ's second coming. Whenever a good man dies God takes him, fetches him hence, and receives him to himself. The apostle adds concerning Enoch that, *before his translation, he had this testimony, that he pleased God,* and this was the good report he obtained. Note, [1.] Walking with God pleases God. [2.] We cannot walk with God so as to please him, but by faith. [3.] God himself will put an honour upon those that be faith walk with him so as to please him. He will own them now, and witness for them before angels and men at the great day. Those that have not this testimony before the translation, yet shall have it afterwards. [4.] Those whose conversation in the world is truly holy shall find their removal out of it truly happy. Enoch's translation was not only an evidence to faith of the reality of a future state, and of the possibility of the body's existing in glory in that state; but it was an encouragement to the hope of all that walk with God that they shall be for ever with him: signal piety shall be crowned with signal honours.

Verses 25–27

Concerning Methuselah observe, 1. The signification of his name, which some think was prophetical, his father Enoch being a prophet. *Methuselah* signifies, *he dies,* or *there is a dart,* or, *a sending forth,* namely, of the deluge, which came the very year that Methuselah died. If indeed his name was so intended and so explained, it was fair warning to a careless world, a long time before the judgment came. However, this is observable, that the longest liver that ever was carried death in his name, that he might be reminded of its coming surely, though it came slowly. 2. His age: he lived nine hundred and sixty-nine years, the longest we read of that ever any man lived on earth; and yet he died. The longest liver must die at last. Neither youth nor age will discharge from that war, for that is the end of all men: none can challenge life by long prescription, nor make that a plea against the arrests of death. It is commonly supposed that Methuselah died a little before the flood; the Jewish writers say, "seven days before," referring to *ch.* 7:10, and that he was taken away from the evil to come, which goes upon this presumption, which is generally received, that all the patriarchs mentioned in this chapter were holy good men. I am loth to offer any surmise to the contrary; and yet I see not that this can be any more inferred from their enrollment here among the ancestors of Christ than that all those kings of Judah were so whose names are recorded in his genealogy, many of whom, we are sure, were much otherwise: and, if this be questioned, it may be suggested as probable that Methuselah was himself drowned with the rest of the world; for it is certain that he died that year.

Verses 28–32

Here we have the first mention of Noah, of whom we shall read much in the following chapters. Observe,

I. His name, with the reason of it: *Noah* signifies *rest;* his parents gave him that name, with a prospect of his being a more than ordinary blessing to his generation: *This same shall comfort us concerning our work and toil of our hands, because of the ground which the Lord hath cursed.* Here is, 1. Lamech's complaint of the calamitous state of human life. By the entrance of sin, and the entail of the curse for sin, our condition has become very miserable: our whole life is spent in labour, and our time filled up with continual toil. God having cursed the ground, it is as much as some can do, with the utmost care and pains, to fetch a hard livelihood out of it. He speaks as one fatigued with the business of this life, and grudging that so many thoughts and precious minutes, which otherwise might have been much better employed, are unavoidably spent for the support of the body. 2. His comfortable hopes of some relief by the birth of this son: *This same shall comfort us,* which denotes not only the desire and expectation which parents generally have concerning their children (that, when they grow up, they will be comforts to them and helpers in their business, though they often prove otherwise), but an apprehension and prospect of something more. Very probably there were some prophecies that went before of him, as a person that should be wonderfully serviceable to his generation, which they so understood as to conclude that he was the promised seed, the Messiah that should come; and then it intimates that a covenant-interest in Christ as ours, and the believing expectation of his coming, furnish us with the best and surest comforts, both in reference to the wrath and curse of God which we have deserved and to the toils and troubles of this present time of which we are often complaining. "Is Christ ours? Is heaven ours? *This same shall comfort us.*"

II. His children, Shem, Ham, and Japheth. These Noah begat (the eldest of these) when he was 500 years old. It should seem that Japheth was the eldest (*ch.* 10:21), but Shem is put first because on him the covenant was entailed, as appears by *ch.* 9:26, where God is called the *Lord God of Shem.* To him, it is probable, the birth-right was given, and from him, it is certain, both Christ the head, and the church the body, were to descend. Therefore he is called *Shem,* which signifies a *name,* because in his posterity the name of God should always remain, till he should come out of his loins whose name is above every name; so that in putting Shem first Christ was, in effect, put first, who in all things must have the pre-eminence.

CHAPTER 6

The most remarkable thing we have upon record concerning the old world is the destruction of it by the universal deluge, the account of which commences in this chapter, wherein we have, I. The abounding iniquity of that wicked world (*v.* 1–5, 11, 12). II. The righteous God's just resentment of that abounding iniquity, and his holy resolution to punish it (*v.* 6, 7). III. The special favour of God to his servant Noah. 1. In the character given of him (*v.* 8–10) 2. In the communication of God's purpose to him (*v.* 13, 17). 3. In the directions he gave him to make an ark for his own safety (*v.* 14–16). 4. In the employing of him for the preservation of the rest of the creatures (*v.* 18–21). Lastly, Noah's obedience to the instructions given him (*v.* 22). And this concerning the old world is written for our admonition, upon whom the ends of the new would have come.

Verses 1–2

For the glory of God's justice, and for warning to a wicked world, before the history of the ruin of the old world, we have a full account of its degeneracy, its apostasy from God and rebellion against him. The destroying of it was an act, not of an absolute sovereignty, but of necessary justice, for the maintaining of the honour of God's government. Now here we have an account of two things which occasioned the wickedness of the old world: — 1. The increase of mankind: *Men began to multiply upon the face of the earth.* This was the effect of the blessing (*ch.* 1:28), and yet man's corruption so abused and perverted this blessing that it was turned into a curse. Thus sin takes occasion by the mercies of God to be the more exceedingly sinful. Prov. 29:16, *When the wicked are multiplied, transgression increaseth.* The more sinners the more sin; and the multitude of offenders emboldens men. Infectious diseases are most destructive in populous cities; and sin is a spreading leprosy. Thus in the New-Testament church, *when the number of the disciples was multiplied, there arose a murmuring* (Acts 6:1), and we read of a nation that was multiplied, not to the increase of their joy, Isa. 9:3. Numerous families need to be well-governed, lest they become wicked families. 2. Mixed marriages (*v.* 2): *The sons of God* (that is, the professors of religion, who were called by the name of the Lord, and called upon that name), *married the daughters of men,* that is, those that were profane, and strangers to God and godliness. The posterity of Seth did not keep by themselves, as they ought to have done, both for the preservation of their own purity and in detestation of the apostasy. They intermingled themselves with the excommunicated race of Cain: *They took them wives of all that they chose.* But what was amiss in these marriages? (1.) They chose only by the eye: *They saw that they were fair,* which was all they looked at. (2.) They followed the choice which their own corrupt affections made: they took *all that they chose,* without advice and consideration. But, (3.) That which proved of such bad consequence to them was that they *married strange wives, were unequally yoked with unbelievers,* 2 Co. 6:14. This was forbidden to Israel, Deu. 7:3, 4. It was the unhappy occasion of Solomon's apostasy (1 Ki. 11:1–4), and was of bad consequence to the Jews after their return out of Babylon, Ezra 9:1, 2. Note, Professors of religion, in marrying both themselves and their children, should make conscience of keeping within the bounds of profession. The bad will sooner debauch the good than the good reform the bad. Those that profess themselves the children of God must not marry without his consent, which they have not if they join in affinity with his enemies.

Verse 3

This comes in here as a token of God's displeasure at those who married strange wives; he threatens to withdraw from them his Spirit, whom they had grieved by such marriages, contrary to their convictions: fleshly lusts are often punished with spiritual judgments, the sorest of all judgments. Or as another occasion of the great wickedness of the old world; the Spirit of the Lord, being provoked by their resistance of his motions, ceased to strive with them, and then all religion was soon lost among them. This he warns them of before, that they might not further vex his Holy Spirit, but by their prayers might stay him with them. Observe in this verse,

I. God's resolution not always to strive with man by his Spirit. The Spirit then strove by Noah's preaching (1 Pt. 3:19, 20) and by inward checks, but it was in vain with the most of men; therefore, says God, *He shall not always strive.* Note, 1. The blessed Spirit strives with sinners, by the convictions and admonitions of conscience, to turn them from sin to God. 2. If the Spirit be resisted, quenched, and striven against, though he strive long, he will not strive always, Hos. 4:17. 3. Those are ripening apace for ruin whom the Spirit of grace has left off striving with.

II. The reason of this resolution: *For that he also is flesh,* that is, incurably corrupt, and carnal, and sensual, so that it is labour lost to strive with him. Can the Ethiopian change his skin? *He also,* that is, All, one as well as another, they have all sunk into the mire of flesh. Note, 1. It is the corrupt nature, and the inclination of the soul towards the flesh, that oppose the Spirit's strivings and render them ineffectual. 2. When a sinner has long adhered to that interest, and sided with the flesh against the Spirit, the Spirit justly withdraws his agency, and strives no more. None lose the Spirit's strivings but those that have first forfeited them.

III. A reprieve granted, notwithstanding: *Yet his days shall be one hundred and twenty years;* so long I will defer the judgment they deserve, and give them space to prevent it by their repentance and reformation. Justice said, *Cut them down;* but mercy interceded, *Lord, let them alone this year also;* and so far mercy prevailed, that a reprieve was obtained for six-score years. Note, The time of God's patience and forbearance towards provoking sinners is sometimes long, but always limited: reprieves are not pardons; though God bear a great while, he will not bear always.

Verses 4–5

We have here a further account of the corruption of the old world. When the *sons of God* had matched with the *daughters of men,* though it was very displeasing to God, yet he did not immediately cut them off, but waited to see what would be the issue of these marriages, and which side the children would take after; and it proved (as usually it does), that they took after the worst side. Here is,

I. The temptation they were under to oppress and do violence. They were *giants,* and they were *men of renown;* they became too hard for all about them, and carried all before them, 1. With their great bulk, as the sons of Anak, Num. 13:33. 2. With their great name, as the king of Assyria, Isa. 37:11. These made them the *terror of the mighty in the land of the living;* and, thus armed, they daringly insulted the rights of all their neighbours and trampled upon all that is just and sacred. Note, Those that have so much power over others as to be able to oppress them have seldom so much power over themselves as not to oppress; great might is a very great snare to many. This degenerate race slighted the honour their ancestors had obtained by virtue and religion, and made themselves a great name by that which was the perpetual ruin of their good name.

II. The charge exhibited and proved against them, *v.* 5. The evidence produced was incontestable. God saw it, and that was instead of a thousand witnesses. God sees all the wickedness that is among the children of men; it cannot be concealed from him now, and, if it be not repented of, it shall not be concealed by him shortly. Now what did God take notice of? 1. He observed that the streams of sin that flowed along in men's lives, and the breadth and depth of those streams: He *saw that the wickedness of man was great in the earth.* Observe the connection of this with what goes before: the oppressors were *mighty men and men of renown;* and, *then, God saw that the wickedness of man was great.* Note, The wickedness of a people is great indeed when the most notorious sinners are men of renown among them. Things are bad when bad men are not only honoured notwithstanding their wickedness, but honoured for their wickedness, and the vilest men exalted. Wickedness is then great when great men are wicked. Their wickedness was great, that is, abundance of sin was committed in all places, by all sorts of people; and such sin as was in its own nature most gross, and heinous, and provoking; it was committed daringly, and with a defiance of heaven, nor was any care taken by those that had power in their hands to restrain and punish it. This God saw. Note, All the sins of sinners are known to God the Judge. Those that are most conversant in the world, though they see much wickedness in it, yet they see but little of that which is; but God sees all, and judges aright concerning it, how great it is, nor can he be deceived in his judgment. 2. He observed the fountain of sin that was in men's hearts. Any one might see that *the wickedness of man was great,* for they declared their sin as Sodom; but God's eye went further: *He saw that every imagination of the thoughts of his heart was only evil continually* — a sad sight, and very offensive to God's holy eye! This was the bitter root, the corrupt spring: all the violence and oppression, all the luxury and wantonness, that were in the world, proceeded from the corruption of nature; lust conceived them, Jam. 1:15. See Mt. 15:19. (1.) The heart was naught; it was deceitful and desperately wicked. The principles were corrupt, and the habits and dispositions evil. (2.) The thoughts of the heart were so. Thought is sometimes taken for the settled judgment or opinion, and this was bribed, and biased, and misled; sometimes it signifies the workings of the fancy, and these were always either vain or vile, either weaving the spider's web or hatching the cockatrice's egg. (3.) The imagination of the thoughts of the heart was so, that is, their designs and devices were wicked. They did not do evil through mere carelessness, as those that walk at all adventures, not heeding what they do; but they did evil deliberately and designedly, contriving how to do mischief. It was bad indeed; for it was only evil, continually evil, and every imagination was so. There was no good to be fond among them, no, not at any time: the stream of sin was full, and strong, and constant; and God saw it; see Ps. 14:1–3.

Verses 6–7

Here is, I. God's resentment of man's wickedness. He did not see it as an unconcerned spectator, but as one injured and affronted by it; he saw it as a tender father sees the folly and stubbornness of a rebellious and disobedient child, which not only angers him, but grieves him, and makes him wish he had been written childless. The expressions here used are very strange: *It repented the Lord that he had made man upon the earth,* that he had made a creature of such noble powers and faculties, and had put him on this earth, which he built and furnished on purpose to be a convenient, comfortable, habitation for him; *and it grieved him at his heart.* These are expressions after the manner of men, and must be understood so as not to reflect upon the honour of God's immutability or felicity. 1. This language does not imply any passion or uneasiness in God (nothing can create disturbance to the Eternal Mind), but it expresses his just and holy displeasure against sin and sinners, against sin as odious to his holiness and against sinners as obnoxious to his justice. He is pressed by the sins of his creatures (Amos 2:13), wearied (Isa. 43:24), broken (Eze. 6:9), grieved (Ps. 95:10), and here *grieved to the heart,* as men are when they are wronged and abused by those they have ben very kind to, and therefore repent of their kindness, and wish they had never fostered that snake in their bosom which now hisses in their face and stings them to the heart. Does God thus hate sin? And shall we not hate it? Has our sin grieved him to the heart? And shall we not be grieved and pricked to the heart for it? O that this consideration may humble us and shame us, and that we may look on him whom we have thus grieved, and mourn! Zec. 12:10. 2. It does not imply any change of God's mind; for *he is in one mind, and who can turn him?* With him *there is not variableness.* But it expressed a change of his way. When God had made man upright, *he rested and was refreshed* (Ex. 31:17), and his way towards him was such as showed he was pleased with the work of his own hands; but, now that man had apostatized, he could not do otherwise than show himself displeased; so that the change was in man, not in God. God repented that he had made man; but we never find him repenting that he redeemed man (though that was a work of much greater expense), because special and effectual grace is given to secure the great ends of redemption; so that those *gifts and callings are without repentance,* Rom. 11:29.

II. God's resolution to destroy man for his wickedness, *v.* 7. Observe, 1. When God repented that he had made man, he resolved to destroy man. Thus those that truly repent of sin will resolve, in the strength of God's grace, to mortify sin and to destroy it, and so to undo what they have done amiss. We do but mock God in saying that we are sorry for our sin, and that it grieves us to the heart, if we continue to indulge it. In vain do we pretend a change of our mind if we do not evidence it by a change of our way. 2. He resolves to destroy man. The original word is very significant: *I will wipe off man from the earth* (so some), as dirt or filth is wiped off from a place which should be clean, and is thrown to the dunghill, the proper place for it. See 2 Ki. 21:13. Those that are the spots of the places they live in are justly wiped away by the judgments of God. *I will blot out man from the earth* (so others), as those lines which displease the author are blotted out a book, or as the name of a citizen is blotted out of the rolls of the freemen, when he is dead or disfranchised. 3. He speaks of man as his own creature even when he resolves upon his ruin: *Man whom I have created.* "Though I have created him, this shall not excuse him," Isa. 27:11. *He that made him will not save him;* he that is our Creator, if he be not our ruler, will be our destroyer. Or, "Because I have created him, and he has been so undutiful and ungrateful to his Creator, therefore I will destroy him:" those forfeit their lives that do not answer the end of their living. 4. Even the brute-creatures were to be involved in this destruction — *Beasts, and creeping things, and the fowls of the air.* These were made for man, and therefore must be destroyed with man; for it follows: *It repenteth me that I have made them;* for the end of their creation also was frustrated. They were made that man might serve and honour God with them; and therefore were destroyed because he had served his lusts with them, and made them subject to vanity. 5. God took up this resolution concerning man after his Spirit had been long striving with him in vain. None are ruined by the justice of God but those that hate to be reformed by the grace of God.

Verses 8–10

We have here Noah distinguished from the rest of the world, and a peculiar mark of honour put upon him. 1. When God was displeased with the rest of the world, he favoured Noah: *But Noah found grace in the eyes of the Lord, v.* 8. This vindicates God's justice in his displeasure against the world, and shows that he had strictly examined the character of every person in it before he pronounced it universally corrupt; for, there being one good man, he found him out, and smiled upon him. It also magnifies his grace towards Noah that he was made a vessel of God's mercy when all mankind besides had become the generation of his wrath: distinguishing favours bring under peculiarly strong obligations. Probably Noah did not find favour in the eyes of men; they hated and persecuted him, because both by his life and preaching he *condemned the world. But he found grace in the eyes of the Lord,* and this was honour and comfort enough. God made more account of Noah than of all the world besides, and this made him greater and more truly honourable than all the giants that were in those days, who became mighty men and men of renown. Let this be the summit of our ambition, to *find grace in the eyes of the Lord;* herein let us labour, that, present or absent, we may be accepted of him, 2 Co. 5:9. Those are highly favoured whom God favours. 2. When the rest of the world was corrupt and wicked, Noah kept his integrity: *These are the generations of Noah* (this is the account we have to give of him), *Noah was a just man, v.* 9. This character of Noah comes in here either, (1.) As the reason of God's favour to him; his singular piety qualified him for singular tokens of God's loving-kindness. Those that would find grace in the eyes of the Lord must be as Noah was and do as Noah did; God loves those that love him: or, (2.) As the effect of God's favour to him. It was God's good-will to him that produced this good work in him. He was a very good man, but he was no better than the grace of God made him, 1 Co. 15:10. Now observe his character. [1.] He *was a just man,* that is, justified before God by faith in the promised seed; for he was an *heir of the righteousness which is by faith,* Heb. 11:7. he was sanctified, and had right principles and dispositions implanted in him; and he was righteous in his conversation, one that made conscience of rendering to all their due, to God his due and to men theirs. Note, None but a downright honest man can find favour with God. That conversation which will be pleasing to God must be governed by *simplicity and godly sincerity,* not by *fleshly wisdom,* 2 Co. 1:12. God has sometimes chosen the foolish things of the world, but he never chose the knavish things of it. [2.] He was *perfect,* not with a sinless perfection, but a perfection of sincerity; and it is well for us that by virtue of the covenant of grace, upon the score of Christ's righteousness, sincerity is accepted as our gospel perfection. [3.] He *walked with God,* as Enoch had done before him. He was not only honest, but devout; he *walked,* that is, he acted with God, as one always under his eye. He lived a life of communion with God; it was his constant care to conform himself to the will of God, to please him, and to approve himself to him. Note, God looks down upon those with an eye of favour who sincerely look up to him with an eye of faith. But, [4.] That which crowns his character is that thus he was, and thus he did, *in his generation,* in that corrupt degenerate age in which his lot was cast. It is easy to be religious when religion is in fashion; but it is an evidence of strong faith and resolution to swim against a stream to heaven, and to appear for God when no one else appears for him: so Noah did, and it is upon record, to his immortal honour.

Verses 11–12

The wickedness of that generation is here again spoken of, either as a foil to Noah's piety — he was just and perfect, when all the earth was corrupt; or as a further justification of God's resolution to destroy the world, which he was now about to communicate to his servant Noah. 1. All kinds of sin was found among them, for it is said (*v.* 11) that the earth was, (1.) *Corrupt before God,* that is, in the matters of God's worship; either they had other gods before him, or they worshipped him by images, or they were corrupt and wicked in despite and contempt of God, daring him and defying him to his face. (2.) *The earth was also filled with violence* and injustice towards men. There was no order nor regular government; no man was safe in the possession of that which he had the most clear and incontestable right to, no, not the most innocent life; there was nothing but murders, rapes, and rapine. Note, Wickedness, as it is the shame of human nature, so it is the ruin of human society. Take away conscience and the fear of God, and men become beasts and devils to one another, like the fishes of the sea, where the greater devour the less. Sin fills the earth with violence, and so turns the world into a wilderness, into a cock-pit. 2. The proof and evidence of it were undeniable; for *God looked upon the earth,* and was himself an eye-witness of the corruption that was in it, of which before, *v.* 5. The righteous Judge in all his judgments proceeds upon the infallible certainty of his own omniscience, Ps. 33:13. 3. That which most aggravated the matter was the universal spreading of the contagion: *All flesh had corrupted his way.* It was not some particular nations or cities that were thus wicked but the whole world of mankind were so; there was none that did good, no, not one besides Noah. Note, When wickedness has become general and universal ruin is not far off; while there is a remnant of praying people in a nation, to empty the measure as it fills, judgments may be kept off a great while; but when all hands are at work to pull down the fences by sin, and none stand in the gap to make up the breach, what can be expected but an inundation of wrath?

Verses 13–21

Here it appears indeed that Noah *found grace in the eyes of the Lord.* God's favour to him was plainly intimated in what he said of him, *v.* 8–10, where his name is mentioned five times in five lines, when once might have served to make the sense clear, as if the Holy Ghost took a pleasure in perpetuating his memory; but it appears much more in what he says to him in these verses — the informations and instructions here given him.

I. God here makes Noah the *man of his counsel,* communicating to him his purpose to destroy this wicked world by water. As, afterwards, he told Abraham his resolution concerning Sodom (*ch.* 18:17, *Shall I hide from Abraham?*) so here "Shall I hide from Noah *the thing that I do,* seeing that he shall *become a great nation?*" Note, *The secret of the Lord is with those that fear him* (Ps. 25:14); it was with *his servants the prophets* (Amos 3:7), by a spirit of revelation, informing them particularly of his purposes; it is with all believers by a spirit of wisdom and faith, enabling them to understand and apply the general declarations of the written word, and the warnings there given. Now,

1. God told Noah, in general, that he would destroy the world (*v.* 13): *The end of all flesh has come before me; I will destroy them;* that is, the ruin of this wicked world is decreed and determined; *it has come,* that is, it will come surely, and come quickly. Noah, it is likely, in preaching to his neighbours, had warned them, in general, of the wrath of God that they would bring upon themselves by their wickedness, and now God seconds his endeavours by a particular denunciation of wrath, that Noah might try whether this would work upon them. Hence observe, (1.) That God *confirmeth the words of his messengers,* Isa. 44:26. (2.) That *to him that has,* and uses what he has for the good of others, *more shall be given,* more full instructions.

2. He told him, particularly, that he would destroy the world by a flood of waters: *And behold, I, even I, do bring a flood of waters upon the earth, v.* 17. God could have destroyed all mankind by the sword of an angel, a flaming sword turning every way, as he destroyed all the first-born of the Egyptians and the camp of the Assyrians; and then there needed no more than to set a mark upon Noah and his family for their preservation. But God chose to do it by a *flood of waters,* which should drown the world. The reasons, we may be sure, were wise and just, though to

us unknown. God has many arrows in his quiver, and he may use which he please: as he chooses the rod with which he will correct his children, so he chooses the sword with which he will cut off his enemies. Observe the manner of expression: *"I, even I, do bring a flood;* I that am infinite in power, and therefore *can* do it, infinite in justice, and therefore *will* do it." (1.) It intimates the certainty of the judgment: I, *even* I, will do it. That cannot but be done effectually which God himself undertakes the doing of. See Job 11:10. (2.) It intimates the tendency of it to God's glory and the honour of his justice. Thus he will be magnified and exalted in the earth, and all the world shall be made to know that he is the God *to whom vengeance belongs;* methinks the expression here is somewhat like that, Isa. 1:24, *Ah, I will ease me of mine adversaries.*

II. God here makes Noah the *man of his covenant,* another Hebrew periphrasis of a friend (*v.* 18): *But with thee will I establish my covenant.* 1. The covenant of providence, that the course of nature shall be continued to the end of time, notwithstanding the interruption which the flood would give to it. This promise was immediately made to Noah and his sons, *ch.* 9:8, etc. They were as trustees for all this part of the creation, and a great honour was thereby put upon him and his. 2. The covenant of grace, that God would be to him a God and that out of his seed God would take to himself a people. Note, (1.) When God makes a covenant, he establishes it, he makes it sure, he makes it good; his are everlasting covenants. (2.) The covenant of grace has in it the recompence of singular services, and the fountain and foundation of all distinguishing favours; we need desire no more, either to make up our losses for God or to make up a happiness for us in God, than to have his covenant established with us.

III. God here makes Noah a monument of sparing mercy, by putting him in a way to secure himself in the approaching deluge, that he might not perish with the rest of the world: *I will destroy them,* says God, *with the earth, v.* 13. "But *make thee an ark;* I will take care to preserve thee alive." Note, Singular piety shall be recompensed with distinguishing salvations, which are in a special manner obliging. This will add much to the honour and happiness of glorified saints, that they shall be saved when the greatest part of the world is left to perish. Now,

1. God directs Noah to *make an ark, v.* 14–15. This ark was like the hulk of a ship, fitted not to sail upon the waters (there was no occasion for that, when there should be no shore to sail to), but to float upon the waters, waiting for their fall. God could have secured Noah by the ministration of angels, without putting him to any care, or pains, or trouble, himself; but he chose to employ him in making that which was to be the means of his preservation, both for the trial of his faith and obedience and to teach us that none shall be saved by Christ but those only that *work out their salvation.* We cannot do it without God, and he will not without us. Both the providence of God, and the grace of God, own and crown the endeavours of the obedient and diligent. God gave him very particular instructions concerning this building, which could not but be admirably well fitted for the purpose when Infinite Wisdom itself was the architect. (1.) It must be made of *gopher-wood.* Noah, doubtless, knew what sort of wood that was, though we now do not, whether cedar, or cypress, or what other. (2.) He must make it three stories high within. (3.) He must divide it into cabins, with partitions, places fitted for the several sorts of creatures, so as to lose no room. (4.) Exact dimensions were given him, that he might make it proportionable, and might have room enough in it to answer the intention and no more. Note, Those that work for God must take their measures from him and carefully observe them. Note, further, It is fit that he who appoints us our habitation should fix the bounds and limits of it. (5.) He must *pitch it within and without* — without, to shed off the rain, and to prevent the water from soaking in — within, to take away the bad smell of the beasts when kept close. Observe, God does not bid him paint it, but pitch it. If God gives us habitations that are safe, and warm, and wholesome, we are bound to be thankful, though they are not magnificent or nice. (6.) He must make a little window towards the top, to let in light, and (some think) that through that window he might behold the desolations to be made in the earth. (7.) He must make a door in the side of it, by which to go in and out.

2. God promises Noah that he and his shall be preserved alive in the ark (*v.* 18): *Thou shalt come into the ark.* Note, What we do in obedience to God, we ourselves are likely to have the comfort and benefit of. *If thou be wise for thyself.* Nor was he himself only saved in the ark, but *his wife, and his sons, and his sons' wives.* Observe, (1.) The care of good parents; they are solicitous not only for their own salvation, but for the salvation of their families, and especially their children. (2.) The happiness of those children that have godly parents. Their parents' piety often procures them temporal salvation, as here; and it furthers them in the way to eternal salvation, if they improve the benefit of it.

IV. God here makes Noah a great blessing to the world, and herein makes him an eminent type of the Messiah, though not the Messiah himself, as his parents expected, *ch.* 5:29. 1. God made him a preacher to the men of that generation. As a watchman, he received the word from God's mouth, that he might give them warning, Eze. 3:17. Thus, *while the long-suffering of God waited,* by his Spirit in Noah, he *preached to* the old world, who, when Peter wrote, were *spirits in prison* (1 Pt. 3:18–20), and herein he was a type of Christ, who, in a land and age wherein all flesh had corrupted their way, went about preaching repentance and warning men of a deluge of wrath coming. 2. God made him a saviour to the inferior creatures, to keep the several kinds of them from perishing and being lost in the deluge, *v.* 19–21. This was a great honour put upon him, that not only in him the race of mankind should be kept up, and that from him should proceed a new world, the church, the soul of the world, and Messiah, the head of that church, but that he should be instrumental to preserve the inferior creatures, and so mankind should in him acquire a new title to them and their service. (1.) He was to provide shelter for them, that they might not be drowned. *Two of every sort, male and female,* he must take with him into the ark; and lest he should make any difficulty of gathering them together, and getting them in, God promises (*v.* 20) that they shall of their own accord come to him. He that makes the ox to know his owner and his crib then made him know his preserver and his ark. (2.) He was to provide sustenance for them, that they might not be starved, *v.* 21. He must victual his ship according to the number of his crew, that great family which he had now the charge of, and according to the time appointed for his confinement. Herein also he was a type of Christ, to whom it is owing that the world stands, by whom all things consist, and who preserves mankind from being totally cut off and ruined by sin; in him the holy seed is saved alive, and the creation rescued from the vanity under which it groans. Noah saved those whom he was to rule, so does Christ, Heb. 5:9.

Verse 22

Noah's care and diligence in building the ark may be considered, 1. As an effect of his faith in the word of God. God had told him he would shortly drown the world; he believed it, feared the threatened deluge, and, in that fear, prepared the ark. Note, We ought to mix faith with the revelation God has made of his wrath against all ungodliness and unrighteousness of men; the threatenings of the word are not false alarms. Much might have been objected against the credibility of this warning given to Noah. "Who could believe that the wise God, who made the world, should so soon unmake it again, that he who had drawn the waters off the dry land (*ch.* 1:9, 10) should cause them to cover it again? How would this be reconciled with the mercy of God, which is over all his works, especially that the innocent creatures should die for man's sin? Whence could water be had sufficient to deluge the world? And, if it must be so, why should notice be given of it to Noah only?" But Noah's faith triumphed over all these corrupt reasonings. 2. As an act of obedience to the command of God. Had he consulted with flesh and blood, many objections would have been raised against it. To rear a building, such a one as he never saw, so large, and of such exact dimensions, would put him upon a great deal of care, and labour, and expense. It would be a work of time; the vision was for a great while to come. His neighbours would ridicule him for his credulity, and he would be the song of the drunkards; his building would be called *Noah's folly.* If the worst came to the worst, as we say, each would fare as well as his neighbours. But these, and a thousand such objections, Noah by faith got over. His obedience was ready and resolute: *Thus did Noah,* willingly and cheerfully, without murmuring and disputing. God says, *Do this,* and he does it. It was also punctual and persevering: he did all exactly according to the instructions given him, and, having begun to build, did not leave off till he had finished it; so did he, and so must we do. 3. As an instance of wisdom for himself, thus to provide for his own safety. he feared the deluge, and therefore prepared the ark. Note, When God gives warning of approaching judgments, it is our wisdom and duty to provide accordingly. See Ex. 9:20, 21; Eze. 3:18. We must prepare to meet the Lord in his judgments on earth, flee to his name as a strong tower (Prov. 18:10), enter into our chambers (Isa. 26:20, 21), especially prepare to meet him at death and in the judgment of the great day, build upon Christ the Rock (Mt. 7:24), go into Christ the Ark. 4. As intended for warning to a careless world; and it was fair warning of the deluge coming. Every blow of his axes and hammers was a call to repentance, a call to them to prepare arks too. But, since by it he could not convince the world, by it he condemned the world, Heb. 11:7.

CHAPTER 7

In this chapter we have the performance of what was foretold in the foregoing chapter, both concerning the destruction of the old world and the salvation of Noah; for we may be sure that no word of God shall fall to the ground. There we left Noah busy about his ark, and full of care to get it finished in time, while the rest of his neighbours were laughing at him for his pains. Now here we see what was the end thereof, the end of his care and of their carelessness. And this famous period of the old world gives us some idea of the state of things when the world that now is shall be destroyed by fire, as that was by water. (See 2 Pt. 3:6, 7.) We have, in this chapter, I. God's gracious call to Noah to come into the ark (*v.* 1), and to bring the creatures that were to be preserved alive along with him (*v.* 2, 3), in consideration of the deluge at hand (*v.* 4). II. Noah's obedience to this heavenly vision (*v.* 5). When he was six hundred years old, he came with his family into the ark (*v.* 6, 7), and brought the creatures along with him (*v.* 8, 9), an account of which is repeated (*v.* 13–16), to which is added God's tender care to shut him in. III. The coming of the threatened deluge (*v.* 10); the causes of it (*v.* 11, 12); the prevalency of it (*v.* 17–20). IV. The dreadful desolations that were made by it in the death of every living creature upon earth, except those that were in the ark (*v.* 21–23). V. The continuance of it in full sea, before it began to ebb, one hundred and fifty days (*v.* 24).

Verses 1–4

Here is, I. A gracious invitation of Noah and his family into a place of safety, now that the flood of waters was coming, *v.* 1.

1. The call itself is very kind, like that of a tender father to his children, to come in doors, when he sees night or a storm coming: *Come thou, and all thy house,* that small family that thou hast, *into the ark.* Observe, (1.) Noah did not go into the ark till God bade him; though he knew it was designed for his place of refuge, yet he waited for a renewed command, and had it. It is very comfortable to follow the calls of Providence, and to see God going before us in every step we take. (2.) God does not bid him *go* into the ark, but *come* into it, implying that God would go with him, would lead him into it, accompany him in it, and in due time bring him safely out of it. Note, Wherever we are, it is very desirable to have the presence of God with us, for this is all in all to the comfort of every condition. It was this that made Noah's ark, which was a prison, to be to him not only a refuge, but a palace. (3.) Noah had taken a great deal of pains to build the ark, and now he was himself preserved alive in it. Note, What we do in obedience to the command of God, and in faith, we ourselves shall certainly have the comfort of, first or last. (4.) Not he only, but his house also, his wife and children, are called with him into the ark. Note, It is good to belong to the family of a godly man; it is safe and comfortable to dwell under such a shadow. One of Noah's sons was Ham, who proved afterwards a bad man, yet he was saved in the ark, which intimates, [1.] That wicked children often fare the better for the sake of their godly parents. [2.] That there is a mixture of bad with good in the best societies in earth, and we are not to think it strange. In Noah's family there was a Ham, and in Christ's family there was a Judas. There is no perfect purity on this side heaven. (5.) This call to Noah was a type of the call which the gospel gives to poor sinners. Christ is an ark already prepared, in whom alone we can be safe when death and judgment come. Now the burden of the song is, "Come, come;" the

word says, "Come;" ministers say, "Come;" the Spirit says, "Come, come into the ark."

2. The reason for this invitation is a very honourable testimony to Noah's integrity: *For thee have I seen righteous before me in this generation.* Observe, (1.) Those are righteous indeed that are righteous before God, that have not only the form of godliness by which they appear righteous before men, who may easily be imposed upon, but the power of it by which they approve themselves to God, who searches the heart, and cannot be deceived in men's characters. (2.) God takes notice of and is pleased with those that are righteous before him: *Thee have I seen.* In a world of wicked people God could see one righteous Noah; that single grain of wheat could not be lost, no, not in so great a heap of chaff. *The Lord knows those that are his.* (3.) God, that is a witness to, will shortly be a witness for, his people's integrity; he that sees it will proclaim it before angels and men, to their immortal honour. Those that obtain mercy to be righteous shall obtain witness that they are righteous. (4.) God is, in a special manner, pleased with those that are good in bad times and places. Noah was therefore illustriously righteous, because he was so in that wicked and adulterous generation. (5.) Those that keep themselves pure in times of common iniquity God will keep safe in times of common calamity; those that partake not with others in their sins shall not partake with them in their plagues; those that are better than others are, even in this life, safer than others, and it is better with them.

II. Here are necessary orders given concerning the brute-creatures that were to be preserved alive with Noah in the ark, *v.* 2, 3. They were not capable of receiving the warning and directions themselves, as man was, who herein is taught *more than the beasts of the earth, and made wiser than the fowls of heaven* — that he is endued with the power of foresight; therefore man is charged with the care of them: being under his dominion, they must be under his protection; and, though he could not secure every individual, yet he must carefully preserve every species, that no tribe, no, not the least considerable, might entirely perish out of the creation. Observe in this, 1. God's care for man, for his comfort and benefit. We do not find that Noah was solicitous of himself about this matter; but God consults our happiness more than we do ourselves. Though God saw that the old world was very provoking, and foresaw that the new one would be little better, yet he would preserve the brute creatures for man's use. *Doth God take care for oxen?* 1 Co. 9:9. Or was it not rather for man's sake that this care was taken? 2. Even the unclean beasts, which were least valuable and profitable, were preserved alive in the ark; for God's tender mercies are over all his works, and not over those only that are of most eminence and use. 3. Yet more of the clean were preserved than of the unclean. (1.) Because the clean were most for the service of man; and therefore, in favour to him, more of them were preserved and are still propagated. Thanks be to God, there are not herds of lions as there are of oxen, nor flocks of tigers as there are of sheep. (2.) Because the clean were for sacrifice to God; and therefore, in honour to him, more of them were preserved, three couple for breed, and the odd seventh for sacrifice, *ch.* 8:20. God gives us six for one in earthly things, as in the distribution of the days of the week, that in spiritual things we should be all for him. What is devoted to God's honour, and used in his service, is particularly blessed and increased.

III. Here is notice given of the now imminent approach of the flood: *Yet seven days, and I will cause it to rain, v.* 4. 1. "It shall be seven days *yet,* before I do it." After the hundred and twenty years had expired, God grants them a reprieve of seven days longer, both to show how slow he is to anger and that punishing work is his strange work, and also to give them some further space for repentance: but all in vain; these seven days were trifled away, after all the rest; they continued secure and sensual until the day that the flood came. 2. "It shall be *but* seven days." While Noah told them of the judgment at a distance, they were tempted to put off their repentance, because the vision was for a great while to come; but now he is ordered to tell them that it is at the door, that they have but one week more to turn them in, but one sabbath more to improve, to see if that will now, at last, awaken them to consider the things that belong to their peace, which otherwise will soon be hidden from their eyes. But it is common for those that have been careless of their souls during the years of their health, when they have looked upon death at a distance, to be as careless during the days, the seven days, of their sickness, when they see it approaching, their hearts being hardened by the deceitfulness of sin.

Verses 5–10

Here is Noah's ready obedience to the commands that God gave him. Observe, 1. He went into the ark, upon notice that the flood would come after seven days, though probably as yet there appeared no visible sign of its approach, no cloud arising that threatened it, nothing done towards it, but all continued serene and clear; for, as he prepared the ark by faith in the warning given that the flood would come, so he went into it by faith in this warning that it would come quickly, though he did not see that the second causes had yet begun to work. In every step he took, he walked by faith, and not by sense. During these seven days, it is likely, he was settling himself and his family in the ark, and distributing the creatures into their several apartments. This was the conclusion of that visible sermon which he had long been preaching to his careless neighbours, and which, one would think, might have awakened them; but, not obtaining that desired end, it left their blood upon their own heads. 2. He took all his family along with him, his wife, to be his companion and comfort (though it should seem that, after this, he had no children by her), his sons, and his sons' wives, that by them not only his family, but the world of mankind, might be built up. Observe, Though men were to be reduced to so small a number, and it would be very desirable to have the world speedily repeopled, yet Noah's sons were each of them to have but one wife, which strengthens the argument against having many wives; for from the beginning of this new world it was not so: as, at first, God made, so now he kept alive, but one woman for one man. See Mt. 19:4, 8. 3. The brute creatures readily went in with him. The same hand that at first brought them to Adam to be named now brought them to Noah to be preserved. The ox now knew his owner, and the ass his protector's crib, nay, even the wildest creatures flocked to it; but man had become more brutish than the brutes themselves, and did not know, did not consider, Isa. 1:3.

Verses 11–12

Here is, I. The date of this great event; this is carefully recorded, for the greater certainty of the story.

1. It was in the 600th year of Noah's life, which, by computation, appears to be 1656 years from the creation. The years of the old world are reckoned, not by the reigns of the giants, but the lives of the patriarchs; saints are of more account with God than princes. *The righteous shall be had in everlasting remembrance.* Noah was now a very old man, even as men's years went then. Note, (1.) The longer we live in this world the more we see of the miseries and calamities of it; it is therefore spoken of as the privilege of those that die young that their *eyes shall not see the evil* which is coming, 2 Ki. 22:20. (2.) Sometimes God exercises his old servants with extraordinary trials of obedience patience. The oldest of Christ's soldiers must not promise themselves a discharge from their warfare till death discharge them. Still they must gird on their harness, and not boast as though they had put it off. As the year of the deluge is recorded, so,

2. We are told that it was in the *second month, the seventeenth day of the month,* which is reckoned to be about the beginning of November; so that Noah had had a harvest just before, from which to victual his ark.

II. The second causes that concurred to this deluge. Observe,

1. In the self-same day that Noah was fixed in the ark, the inundation began. Note, (1.) Desolating judgments come not till God has provided for the security of his own people; see *ch.* 19:22, I can *do nothing till thou be come thither:* and we find (Rev. 7:3) that the winds are held till the servants of God are scaled. (2.) When good men are removed judgments are not far off; for they are *taken away from the evil to come,* Isa. 57:1. When they are called into the chambers, hidden in the grave, hidden in heaven, then God is *coming out of his place to punish,* Isa. 26:20, 21.

2. See what was done on that day, that fatal day to the world of the ungodly. (1.) *The fountains of the great deep were broken up.* Perhaps there needed no new creation of waters; what were already made to be, in the common course of providence, blessings to the earth, were now, by an extraordinary act of divine power, made the ruin of it. God has laid up the deep in storehouses (Ps. 33:7), and now he broke up those stores. As our bodies have in themselves those humours which, when God pleases, become the seeds and springs of mortal diseases, so the earth had in it bowels those waters which, at God's command, sprang up and flooded it. God had, in the creation, set *bars and doors* to the waters of *the sea,* that they *might not return to cover the earth* (Ps. 104:9; Job 38:9–11); and now he only removed those ancient land-marks, mounds, and fences, and the waters of the sea returned to cover the earth, as they had done at first, *ch.* 1:9. Note, All the creatures are ready to fight against sinful man, and any of them is able to be the instrument of his ruin, if God do but take off the restraints by which they are held in during the day of God's patience. (2.) *The windows of heaven were opened,* and *the waters which were above the firmament* were poured out upon the world; those treasures which God has *reserved against the time of trouble, the day of battle and war,* Job 38:22, 33. The rain, which ordinarily descends in drops, then came down in streams, or *spouts,* as they call them in the Indies, where clouds have been often known to *burst,* as they express it there, when the rain descends in a much more violent torrent than we have ever seen in the greatest shower. We read (Job 26:8) that *God binds up the waters in his thick clouds,* and the *cloud is not rent under them;* but now the bond was loosed, the cloud was rent, and such rains descended as were never known before nor since, in such abundance and of such continuance: the thick cloud was not, as ordinarily it is, wearied with waterings (Job 37:11), that is, soon spent and exhausted; but still the clouds returned after the rain, and the divine power brought in fresh recruits. It rained, without intermission or abatement, *forty days and forty nights* (*v.* 12), and that upon the whole earth at once, not, as sometimes, *upon one city and not upon another.* God made the world in six days, but he was forty days in destroying it; for he is slow to anger: but, though the destruction came slowly and gradually, yet it came effectually.

3. Now learn from this, (1.) That all the creatures are at God's disposal, and that he makes what use he pleases of them, whether *for correction, or for his land, or for mercy,* as Elihu speaks of the rain, Job 37:12, 12. (2.) That God often makes that which *should be for our welfare to become a trap,* Ps. 69:22. That which usually is a comfort and benefit to us becomes, when God pleases, a scourge and a plague to us. Nothing is more needful nor useful than water, both the springs of the earth and the showers of heaven; and yet now nothing was more hurtful, nothing more destructive: every creature is to us what God makes it. (3.) That it is impossible to escape the righteous judgments of God when they come against sinners with commission; for God can arm both heaven and earth against them; see Job 20:27. God can surround men with the messengers of his wrath, so that, if they look upwards, it is with horror and amazement, if they look to the earth, *behold, trouble and darkness,* Isa. 8:21, 11. Who then is able to stand before God, when he is angry? (4.) In this destruction of the old world by water God gave a specimen of the final destruction of the world that now is by fire. We find the apostle setting the one of these over against the other, 2 Pt. 3:6, 7. As there are waters under the earth, so Aetna, Vesuvius, and other volcanoes, proclaim to the world that there are subterraneous fires too; and fire often falls from heaven, many desolations are made by lightning; so that, when the time predetermined comes, between these two fires the earth and all the works therein shall be burnt up, as the flood was brought upon the old world out of the fountains of the great deep and through the windows of heaven.

Verses 13–16

Here is repeated what was related before of Noah's entrance into the ark, with his family and creatures that were marked for preservation. Now,

I. It is thus repeated for the honour of Noah, whose faith and obedience herein shone so brightly, by which he obtained a good report, and who herein appeared so great a favourite of Heaven and so great a blessing to this earth.

II. Notice is here taken of the beasts going in *each after his kind*, according to the phrase used in the history of the creation (*ch.* 1:21–25), to intimate that just as many kinds as were created at first were saved now, and no more; and that this preservation was as a new creation: a life remarkably protected is, as it were, a new life.

III. Though all enmities and hostilities between the creatures ceased for the present, and ravenous creatures were not only so mild and manageable as that the *wolf and the lamb lay down together*, but so strangely altered as that the *lion did eat straw like an ox* (Isa. 11:6, 7), yet, when this occasion was over, the restraint was taken off, and they were still of the same kind as ever; for the ark did not alter their constitution. Hypocrites in the church, that externally conform to the laws of that ark, may yet be unchanged, and then it will appear, one time or other, what kind they are after.

IV. It is added (and the circumstance deserves our notice), *The Lord shut him in, v.* 16. As Noah continued his obedience to God, so God continued his care of Noah: and here it appeared to be a very distinguishing care; for the shutting of this door set up a partition wall between him and all the world besides. God shut the door, 1. To secure him, and keep him safe in the ark. The door must be shut very *close*, lest the waters should break in and sink the ark, and very *fast*, lest any without should break it down. Thus God made up Noah, as he *makes up his jewels*, Mal. 3:17. 2. To exclude all others, and keep them for ever out. Hitherto the door of the ark stood open, and if any, even during the last seven days, had repented and believed, for aught I know they might have been welcomed into the ark; but now the door was shut, and they were cut off from all hopes of admittance: for God *shutteth, and none can open.*

V. There is much of our gospel duty and privilege to be seen in Noah's preservation in the ark. The apostle makes it a type of our baptism, that is, our Christianity, 1 Pt. 3:20,21. Observe then, 1. It is our great duty, in obedience to the gospel call, by a lively faith in Christ, to come into that way of salvation which God has provided for poor sinners. When Noah came into the ark, he quitted his own house and lands; so must we quit our own righteousness and our worldly possessions, whenever they come into competition with Christ. Noah must, for a while, submit to the confinements and inconveniences of the ark, in order to his preservation for a new world; so those that come into Christ to be saved by him must deny themselves, both in sufferings and services. 2. Those that come into the ark themselves should bring as many as they can in with them, by good instructions, by persuasions, and by a good example. *What knowest thou, O man, but thou mayest thus save his wife* (1 Co. 7:16), as Noah did his? There is room enough in Christ for all comers. 3. Those that by faith come into Christ, the ark, shall by the power of God be shut in, and kept as in a strong-hold *by the power of God*, 1 Pt. 1:5. God put Adam into paradise, but he did not shut him in, and so he threw himself out; but when he put Noah into the ark he shut him in, and so when he brings a soul to Christ he ensures its salvation: it is not in our own keeping, but in the Mediator's hand. 4. The door of mercy will shortly be shut against those that now make light of it. Now, *knock and it shall be opened;* but the time will come when it shall not, Lu. 13:25.

Verses 17–20

We are here told,

I. How long the flood was increasing — *forty days, v.* 17. The profane world, who believed not that it would come, probably when it came flattered themselves with hopes that it would soon abate and never come to extremity; but still it increased, it prevailed. Note, 1. When God judges he will overcome. If he begin, he will make an end; his way is perfect, both in judgment and mercy. 2. The gradual approaches and advances of God's judgments, which are designed to bring sinners to repentance, are often abused to the hardening of them in their presumption.

II. To what degree they increased: they rose so high that not only the low flat countries were deluged, but to make sure work, and that none might escape, the tops of the highest mountains were overflowed — *fifteen cubits*, that is, seven yards and a half; so that *in vain was salvation hoped for from hills or mountains*, Jer. 3:23. None of God's creatures are so high but his power can overtop them; and he will make them know that wherein they deal proudly he is above them. Perhaps the tops of the mountains were washed down by the strength of the waters, which helped much towards the prevailing of the waters above them; for it is said (Job 12:15), *He sends out the waters*, and they not only overflow, but overturn, the earth. Thus the refuge of lies was swept away, and the waters overflowed the hiding-place of those sinners (Isa. 28:17), and in vain they fly to them for safety, Rev. 6:16. Now the mountains departed, and the hills were removed, and nothing stood a man in stead but the *covenant of peace*, Isa. 54:10. There is no place on earth so high as to set men out of the reach of God's judgments, Jer. 49:16; Obad. 3:4. God's hand will *find out all his enemies*, Ps. 21:8. Observe how exactly they are fathomed *(fifteen cubits)*, not by Noah's plummet, but by his knowledge who *weighs the waters by measure*, Job 28:25.

III. What became of Noah's ark when the waters thus increased: *It was lifted up above the earth (v.* 17), and went upon the face of the waters, *v.* 18. When all other buildings were demolished by the waters, and buried under them, the ark alone subsisted. Observe, 1. The waters which broke down every thing else bore up the ark. That which to unbelievers is a savour of death unto death is to the faithful a savour of life unto life. 2. The more the waters increased the higher the ark was lifted up towards heaven. Thus sanctified afflictions are spiritual promotions; and as troubles abound consolations much more abound.

Verses 21–24

Here is, I. The general destruction of all flesh by the waters of the flood. *Come, and see the desolations which God makes in the earth* (Ps. 46:8), and how he lays heaps upon heaps. Never did death triumph, from its first entrance unto this day, as it did then. Come, and see Death upon his pale horse, and hell following with him, Rev. 6:7, 8.

1. All the cattle, fowl, and creeping things, died, except the few that were in the ark. Observe how this is repeated: *All flesh died, v.* 21. All in whose nostrils was the breath of life, of all that was on the dry land, *v.* 22. Every living substance, *v.* 23. And why so? Man only had done wickedly, and justly is God's hand against him; but *these sheep, what have they done?* I answer, (1.) We are sure God did them no wrong. He is the sovereign Lord of all life, for he is the sole fountain and author of it. He that made them as he pleased might unmake them when he pleased; and who shall say unto him, *What dost thou?* May he not do what he will with his own, which were created for his pleasure? (2.) God did admirably serve the purposes of his own glory by their destruction, as well as by their creation. Herein his holiness and justice were greatly magnified; by this it appears that he hates sin, and is highly displeased with sinners, when even the inferior creatures, because they are the servants of man and part of his possession, and because they have been abused to be the servants of sin, are destroyed with him. This makes the judgment the more remarkable, the more dreadful, and, consequently, the more expressive of God's wrath and vengeance. The destruction of the creatures was their deliverance from the bondage of corruption, which deliverance the whole creation now groans after, Rom. 8:21, 22. It was likewise an instance of God's wisdom. As the creatures were made for man when he was made, so they were multiplied for him when he was multiplied; and therefore, now that mankind was reduced to so small a number, it was fit that the beasts should proportionably be reduced, otherwise they would have had the dominion, and would have replenished the earth, and the remnant of mankind that was left would have been overpowered by them. See how God considered this in another case, Ex. 23:29, *Lest the beast of the field multiply against thee.*

2. All the men, women, and children, that were in the world (except that were in the ark) died. *Every man* (*v.* 21 and *v.* 23), and perhaps they were as many as are now upon the face of the earth, if not more. Now, (1.) We may easily imagine what terror and consternation seized on them when they saw themselves surrounded. Our Saviour tells us that till the very day that the flood came they were *eating and drinking* (Lu. 17:26, 27); they were drowned in security and sensuality before they were drowned in those waters, crying *Peace, peace*, to themselves, deaf and blind to all divine warnings. In this posture death surprised them, as 1 Sa. 30:16, 17. But O what an amazement were they in then! Now they see and feel that which they would not believe and fear, and are convinced of their folly when it is too late; now they find no place for repentance, though they seek it carefully with tears. (2.) We may suppose that they tried all ways and means possible for their preservation, but all in vain. Some climb to the tops of trees or mountains, and spin out their terrors there awhile. But the flood reaches them, at last, and they are forced to die with the more deliberation. Some, it is likely, cling to the ark, and now hope that this may be their safety which they had so long made their sport. Perhaps some get to the top of the ark, and hope to shift for themselves there; but either they perish there for want of food, or, by a speedier despatch, a dash of rain washes them off that deck. Others, it may be, hoped to prevail with Noah for admission into the ark, and pleaded old acquaintance, *Have we not eaten and drunk in thy presence? Hast thou not taught in our streets?* "Yes," might Noah say, "that I have, many a time, to little purpose. *I called but you refused; you set at nought all my counsel* (Prov. 1:24, 25), and now it is not in my power to help you: God has shut the door, and I cannot open it." Thus it will be at the great day. Neither climbing high in an outward profession, nor claiming relation to good people, will bring men to heaven, Mt. 7:22; 25:8, 9. Those that are not found in Christ, the ark, are certainly undone, undone for ever; salvation itself cannot save them. See Isa. 10:3. (3.) We may suppose that some of those that perished in the deluge had themselves assisted Noah, or were employed by him, in the building of the ark, and yet were not so wise as by repentance to secure themselves a place in it. Thus wicked ministers, though they may have been instrumental to help others to heaven, will themselves be thrust down to hell.

Let us now pause awhile and consider this tremendous judgment! Let our hearts meditate terror, the terror of this destruction. Let us see, and say, *It is a fearful thing to fall into the hands of the living God; who can stand before him when he is angry?* Let us see and say, *It is an evil thing, and a bitter, to depart from God.* The sin of sinners will, without repentance, be their ruin, first or last; if God be true, it will. *Though hand join in hand, yet the wicked shall not go unpunished.* The righteous God knows how to bring a flood upon the world of the ungodly, 2 Pt. 2:5. Eliphaz appeals to this story as a standing warning to a careless world (Job 22:15, 16), *Hast thou marked the old way, which wicked men have trodden, who were cut down out of time*, and sent into eternity, *whose foundation was overflown with the flood?*

II. The special preservation of Noah and his family: *Noah only remained alive, and those that were with him in the ark, v.* 23. Observe, 1. Noah lives. When all about him were monuments of justice, thousands falling on his right hand and ten thousands on his left, he was a monument of mercy. Only with his eyes might he *behold and see the reward of the wicked*, Ps. 91:7,8. *In the floods of great waters, they did not come nigh him*, Ps. 32:6. We have reason to think that, while the long-suffering of God waited, Noah not only preached to, but prayed for, that wicked world, and would have turned away the wrath; but his prayers return into his own bosom, and are answered only in his own escape, which is plainly referred to, Eze. 14:14, *Noah, Daniel, and Job, shall but deliver their own souls.* A mark of honour shall be set on intercessors. 2. He but lives. Noah remains alive, and this is all; he is, in effect, buried alive — cooped up in a close place, alarmed with the terrors of the descending rain, the increasing flood, and the shrieks and outcries of his perishing neighbours, his heart overwhelmed with melancholy thoughts of the desolations made. But he comforts himself with this, that he is in the way of duty and in the way of deliverance. And we are taught (Jer. 45:4, 5) that when desolating judgments are abroad we must not seek great nor pleasant things to ourselves, but reckon it an unspeakable favour if we have our lives given us for a prey.

CHAPTER 8

In the close of the foregoing chapter we left the world in ruins and the church in straits; but in this chapter we have the repair of the one and the enlargement of the other. Now the scene alters, and another face of things begins to be presented to us, and the brighter side of that cloud which there appeared so black and dark; for, though God contend long, he will not contend for ever, nor be always wrath. We have here, I. The earth made anew, by the recess of the waters, and the appearing of the dry land, now a second time, and both gradual. 1. The increase of the waters is stayed (*v.* 1, 2). 2. They begin sensibly to abate (*v.* 3). 3. After sixteen days' ebbing, the ark rests (*v.* 4). 4. After sixty days' ebbing, the tops of the mountains appeared above water (*v.* 5). 5. After forty days' ebbing, and twenty days before the mountains appeared, Noah began to send out his spies, a raven and a dove, to gain intelligence (*v.* 6–12). 6. Two months after the appearing of the tops of the mountains, the waters had gone, and the face of the earth was dry (*v.* 13), though not dried so as to be fit for man till almost two months after (*v.* 14). II. Man placed anew upon the earth, in which, 1. Noah's discharge and departure out of the ark (*v.* 15–19). 2. His sacrifice of praise, which he offered to God upon his enlargement (*v.* 20). 3. God's acceptance of his sacrifice, and the promise he made thereupon not to drown the world again (*v.* 21, 22). And thus, at length, mercy rejoices against judgment.

Verses 1–3

Here is, I. An act of God's grace: *God remembered Noah and every living thing.* This is an expression after the manner of men; for not any of his creatures (Lu. 12:6), much less any of his people, are forgotten of God, Isa. 49:15, 16. but, 1. The whole race of mankind, except Noah and his family, was now extinguished, and driven into the land of forgetfulness, to be remembered no more; so that God's remembering Noah was the return of his mercy to mankind, of whom he would not make a full end. It is a strange expression, Eze. 5:13, *When I have accomplished my fury in them, I will be comforted.* The demands of divine justice had been answered by the ruin of those sinners; he had eased him of his adversaries (Isa. 1:24), and now his spirit was quieted (Zec. 6:8), and *he remembered Noah and every living thing.* he remembered mercy in wrath (Hab. 3:2), remembered the days of old (Isa. 63:11), remembered the holy seed, and then remembered Noah. 2. Noah himself, though one that had found grace in the eyes of the Lord, yet seemed to be forgotten in the ark, and perhaps began to think himself so; for we do not find that God had told him how long he should be confined and when he should be released. Very good men have sometimes been ready to conclude themselves forgotten of God, especially when their afflictions have been unusually grievous and long. Perhaps Noah, though a great believer, yet when he found the flood continuing so long after it might reasonably be presumed to have done its work, was tempted to fear lest he that shut him in would keep him in, and began to expostulate. *How long wilt thou forget me?* But at length God returned in mercy to him, and this is expressed by remembering him. Note, Those that remember God shall certainly be remembered by him, how desolate and disconsolate soever their condition may be. He will appoint them a set time and remember them, Job 14:13. 3. With Noah, God remembered every living thing; for, though his delight is especially in the sons of men, yet he rejoices in all his works, and hates nothing that he has made. He takes special care, not only of his people's persons, but of their possessions — of them and all that belongs to them. He considered the cattle of Nineveh, Jon. 4:11.

II. An act of God's power over wind and water, both of which are at his beck, though neither of them is under man's control. Observe,

1. He commanded the wind, and said to that, *Go,* and it went, in order to the carrying off of the flood: *God made a wind to pass over the earth.* See here, (1.) What was God's remembrance of Noah: it was his relieving him. Note, Those whom God remembers he remembers effectually, for good; he remembers us to save us, that we may remember him to serve him. (2.) What a sovereign dominion God has over the winds. He has them in his fist (Prov. 30:4) and brings them out of his treasuries, Ps. 135:7. He sends them when, and whither, and for what purposes, he pleases. Even stormy winds fulfil his word, Ps. 148:8. It should seem, while the waters increased, there was no wind; for that would have added to the toss of the ark; but now God sent a wind, when it would not be so troublesome. Probably, it was a north wind, for that drives away rain. However, it was a drying wind, such a wind as God sent to divide the Red Sea before Israel, Ex. 14:21.

2. He remanded the waters, and said to them, *Come,* and they came. (1.) He took away the cause. He sealed up the springs of those waters, *the fountains of the great deep, and the windows of heaven.* Note, [1.] As God has a key to open, so he has a key to shut up again, and to stay the progress of judgments by stopping the causes of them: and the same hand that brings the desolation must bring the deliverance; to that hand therefore our eye must ever be. He that wounds is alone able to heal. See Job 12:14, 15. [2.] When afflictions have done the work for which they are sent, whether killing work or curing work, they shall be removed. God's word shall not return void, Isa. 55:10, 11. (2.) Then the effect ceased; not all at once, but by degrees: *The waters abated* (*v.* 1), returned from off the earth continually, Heb. they were *going and returning* (*v.* 3), which denotes a gradual departure. The heat of the sun exhaled much, and perhaps the subterraneous caverns soaked in more. Note, As the earth was not drowned in a day, so it was not dried in a day. In the creation, it was but one day's work to clear the earth from the waters that covered it, and to make it dry land; nay, it was but half a day's work, *ch.* 1:9, 10. But, the work of creation being finished, this work of providence was effected by the concurring influence of second causes, yet thus enforced by the almighty power of God. God usually works deliverance for his people gradually, that the day of small things may not be despised, nor the day of great things despaired of, Zec. 4:10. See Prov. 4:18.

Verses 4–5

Here we have the effects and evidences of the ebbing of the waters. 1. The ark rested. This was some satisfaction to Noah, to feel the house he was in upon firm ground, and no longer movable. It rested upon a mountain, whither it was directed, not by Noah's prudence (he did not steer it), but by the wise and gracious providence of God, that it might rest the sooner. Note, God has times and places of rest for his people after their tossings; and many a time he provides for their seasonable and comfortable settlement without their own contrivance and quite beyond their own foresight. The ark of the church, though sometimes tossed with tempests, and not comforted (Isa. 54:11), yet has its rests, Acts 9:31. 2. The tops of the mountains were seen, like little islands, appearing above the water. We must suppose that they were seen by Noah and his sons; for there were none besides to see them. It is probable that they had looked through the window of the ark every day, like the longing mariners, after a tedious voyage, to see if they could discover land, or as the prophet's servant (1 Ki. 18:43, 44), and at length they spy ground, and enter the day of the discovery in their journal. They felt ground above forty days before they saw it, according to Dr. Lightfoot's computation, whence he infers that, if the waters decreased proportionably, the ark drew eleven cubits in water.

Verses 6–12

We have here an account of the spies which Noah sent forth to bring him intelligence from abroad, a raven and a dove. Observe here,

I. That though God had told Noah particularly when the flood would come, even to a day (*ch.* 7:4), yet he did not give him a particular account by revelation at what times, and by what steps, it should *go away,* 1. Because the knowledge of the former was necessary to his preparing the ark, and settling himself in it; but the knowledge of the latter would serve only to gratify his curiosity, and the concealing of it from him would be the needful exercise of his faith and patience. And, 2. He could not foresee the flood, but by revelation; but he might, by ordinary means, discover the decrease of it, and therefore God was pleased to leave him to the use of them.

II. That though Noah by faith expected his enlargement, and by patience waited for it, yet he was inquisitive concerning it, as one that thought it long to be thus confined. Note, Desires of release out of trouble, earnest expectations of it, and enquiries concerning its advances towards us, will very well consist with the sincerity of faith and patience. *He that believes does not make haste* to run before God, but he does make haste to go forth to meet him, Isa. 28:16. Particularly, 1. Noah sent forth a raven through the window of the ark, which went forth, as the Hebrew phrase is, *going forth and returning,* that is, flying about, and feeding on the carcases that floated, but returning to the ark for rest; probably not in it, but upon it. This gave Noah little satisfaction; therefore, 2. He sent forth a dove, which returned the first time with no good news, but probably wet and dirty; but, the second time, she brought an olive-leaf in her bill, which appeared to be first plucked off, a plain indication that now the trees, the fruit-trees, began to appear above water. Note here, (1.) That Noah sent forth the dove the second time seven days after the first time, and the third time was after seven days too; and probably the first sending of her out was seven days after the sending forth of the raven. This intimates that it was done on the sabbath day, which, it should seem, Noah religiously observed in the ark. Having kept the sabbath in a solemn assembly of his little church, he then expected special blessings from heaven, and enquired concerning them. Having directed his prayer, he looked up, Ps. 5:3. (2.) The dove is an emblem of a gracious soul, which finding no rest for its foot, no solid peace or satisfaction in this world, this deluged defiling world, returns to Christ as to its ark, as to its Noah. The carnal heart, like the raven, takes up with the world, and feeds on the carrions it finds there; *but return thou to thy rest, O my soul,* to thy *Noah,* so the word is, Ps. 116:7. *O that I had wings like a dove,* to flee to him! Ps. 55:6. And as Noah put forth his hand, and took the dove, and pulled her in to him, into the ark, so Christ will graciously preserve, and help, and welcome, those that fly to him for rest. (3.) The olive-branch, which was an emblem of peace, was brought, not by the raven, a bird of prey, nor by a gay and proud peacock, but by a mild, patient, humble dove. It is a dove-like disposition that brings into the world earnests of rest and joy. (4.) Some make these things an allegory. The law was first sent forth like the raven, but brought no tidings of the assuaging of the waters of God's wrath, with which the world of mankind was deluged; therefore, in the fulness of time, God sent forth his gospel, as the dove, in the likeness of which the Holy Spirit descended, and this presents us with an olive-branch and brings in a better hope.

Verses 13–14

Here is, 1. The ground dry (*v.* 13), that is, all the water carried off it, which, upon the first day of the first month (a joyful new-year's-day it was), Noah was himself an eyewitness of. He *removed the covering of the ark,* not the whole covering, but so much as would suffice to give him a prospect of the earth about it; and a most comfortable prospect he had. For behold, behold and wonder, *the face of the ground was dry.* Note, (1.) It is a great mercy to see ground about us. Noah was much more sensible of it than we are; for mercies restored are much more affecting than mercies continued. (2.) The divine power which now renewed the face of the earth can renew the face of an afflicted troubled soul and of a distressed persecuted church. He can make dry ground to appear even where it seemed to have been lost and forgotten, Ps. 18:16. 2. The ground dried (*v.* 14), so as to be a fit habitation for Noah. Observe, Though Noah saw the ground dry the first day of the first month, yet God would not suffer him to go out of the ark till the twenty-seventh day of the second month. Perhaps Noah, being somewhat weary of his restraint, would have quitted the ark at first; but God, in kindness to him, ordered him to stay so much longer. Note, God consults our benefit rather than our desires; for he knows what is good for us better than we do for ourselves, and how long it is fit our restraints should continue and desired mercies should be delayed. We would go out of the ark before the ground is dried: and perhaps, if the door be shut, are ready to remove the covering, and to climb up some other way; but we should be satisfied that God's time of showing mercy is certainly the best time, when the mercy is ripe for us and we are ready for it.

Verses 15–19

Here is, I. Noah's dismission out of the ark, *v.* 15–17. Observe, 1. Noah did not stir till God bade him. As he had a command to go into the ark (*ch.* 7:1), so, how tedious soever his confinement there was, he would wait for a command to go out of it again. Note, We must in all our ways acknowledge God, and set him before us in all our removes. Those only go under God's protection that follow

God's direction and submit to his government. Those that steadily adhere to God's word as their rule, and are guided by his grace as their principle, and take hints from his providence to assist them in their application of general directions to particular cases, may in faith see him guiding their motions in their march through this wilderness. 2. Though God detained him long, yet at last he gave him his discharge; for *the vision is for an appointed time, and at the end it shall speak*, it shall speak truth (Hab. 2:3), it shall not lie. 3. God had said, *Come into the ark* which he says, not, *Come forth*, but, *Go forth*, which intimates that God, who went in with him, staid with him all the while, till he sent him out safely; for he has said, *I will not leave thee.* 4. Some observe that, when they were ordered into the ark, the men and the women were mentioned separately (*ch.* 6:18): *Thou, and thy sons, and thy wife, and thy sons' wives;* hence they infer that, during the time of mourning, they were apart, and their wives apart, Zec. 12:12. But now God did as it were new-marry them, sending out Noah and his wife together, and his sons and their wives together, that they might be fruitful and multiply. 5. Noah was ordered to bring the creatures out with him, that having taken the care of feeding them so long, and been at so much pains about them, he might have the honour of leading them forth by their armies, and receiving their homage.

II. Noah's departure when he had his dismission. As he would not go out without leave, so he would not, out of fear or humour, stay in when he had leave, but was in all points observant of the heavenly vision. Though he had been now a full year and ten days a prisoner in the ark, yet when he found himself preserved there, not only for a new life, but for a new world, he saw no reason to complain of his long confinement. Now observe, 1. Noah and his family came out alive, though one of them was a wicked Ham, whom, though he escaped the flood, God's justice could have taken away by some other stroke. But they are all alive. Note, When families have been long continued together, and no breaches made among them, it must be looked upon as a distinguishing favour, and attributed to the Lord's mercies. 2. Noah brought out all the creatures that went in with him, except the raven and the dove, which, probably, were ready to meet their mates at their coming out. Noah was able to give a very good account of his charge; for of all that were given to him he had lost none, but was faithful to him that appointed him, *pro hac vice — on this occasion,* high steward of his household.

Verses 20–22

Here is, I. Noah's thankful acknowledgment of God's favour to him, in completing the mercy of his deliverance, *v.* 20. 1. He *built an altar.* Hitherto he had done nothing without particular instructions and commands from God. He had a particular call into the ark, and another out of it; but, altars and sacrifices being already of divine institution for religious worship, he did not stay for a particular command thus to express his thankfulness. Those that have received mercy from God should be forward in returning thanks, and do it *not of constraint, but willingly.* God is pleased with free-will offerings, and praises that wait for him. Noah was now turned out into a cold and desolate world, where, one would have thought, his first care would have been to build a house for himself; but, behold, he begins with an altar for God: God, that is the first, must be first served; and he begins well that begins with God. 2. He offered a sacrifice upon his altar, *of every clean beast, and of every clean fowl* — one, the odd seventh that we read of, *ch.* 7:2, 3. Here observe, (1.) He offered only those that were clean; for it is not enough that we sacrifice, but we must sacrifice that which God appoints, according to the law of sacrifice, and not a corrupt thing. (2.) Though his stock of cattle was so small, and that rescued from ruin at so great an expense of care and pains, yet he did not grudge to give God his dues out of it. He might have said, "Have I but seven sheep to begin the world with, and must one of these seven be killed and burnt for sacrifice? Were it not better to defer it till we have greater plenty?" No, to prove the sincerity of his love and gratitude, he cheerfully gives the seventh to his God, as an acknowledgment that all was his, and owing to him. Serving God with our little is the way to make it more;

and we must never think that wasted with which God is honoured. (3.) See here the antiquity of religion: the first thing we find done in the new world was an act of worship, Jer. 6:16. We are now to express our thankfulness, not by burnt-offerings, but by the sacrifices of praise and the sacrifices of righteousness, by pious devotions and a pious conversation.

II. God's gracious acceptance of Noah's thankfulness. It was a settled rule in the patriarchal age: *If thou doest well, shalt thou not be accepted?* Noah was so. For,

1. God was well pleased with the performance, *v.* 21. He *smelt a sweet savour*, or, as it is in the Hebrew, *a savour of rest*, from it. As, when he had made the world at first on the seventh day, he rested and was refreshed, so, now that he had new-made it, in the sacrifice of the seventh he rested. He was well pleased with Noah's pious zeal, and these hopeful beginnings of the new world, as men are with fragrant and agreeable smells; though his offering was small it was according to his ability, and God accepted it. Having caused his anger to rest upon the world of sinners, he here caused his love to rest upon this little remnant of believers.

2. Hereupon, he took up a resolution never to drown the world again. Herein he had an eye, not so much to Noah's sacrifice as to Christ's sacrifice of himself, which was typified and represented by it, and which was indeed an *offering of a sweet-smelling savour,* Eph. *v.* 2. Good security is here given, and that which may be relied upon,

(1.) That this judgment should never be repeated. Noah might think, "To what purpose should the world be repaired, when, in all probability, for the wickedness of it, it will quickly be in like manner ruined again?" "No," says God, "it never shall." It was said (*ch.* 6:6), *It repented the Lord that he had made man;* now here he speaks as if it repented him that he had destroyed man: neither means a change of his mind, but both a change of his way. *It repented him concerning his servants,* Deu. 32:36. Two ways this resolve is expressed: — [1.] *I will not again curse the ground,* Heb. *I will not add to curse the ground any more.* God had cursed the ground upon the first entrance of sin (*ch.* 3:17), when he drowned it he added to that curse; but now he determines not to add to it any more. [2.] *Neither will I again smite any more every living thing;* that is, it was determined that whatever ruin God might bring upon particular persons, or families, or countries, he would never again destroy the whole world till the day shall come when time shall be no more. But the reason of this resolve is very surprising, for it seems the same in effect with the reason given for the destruction of the world: *Because the imagination of man's heart is evil from his youth, ch.* 6:5. But there is this difference — there it is said, *The imagination of man's heart is evil continually,* that is, "his actual transgressions continually cry against him;" here it is said, It is evil *from his youth or childhood.* It is bred in the bone; he brought it into the world with him; he was shapen and conceived in it. Now, one would think it should follow, "Therefore that guilty race shall be wholly extinguished, and *I will make a full end.*" No, "Therefore I will no more take this severe method; for," *First,* "He is rather to be pitied, for it is all the effect of sin dwelling in him; and it is but what might be expected from such a degenerate race: he is called a *transgressor from the womb,* and therefore it is not strange that he deals so very treacherously," Isa. 48:8. Thus God *remembers that he is flesh,* corrupt and sinful, Ps. 78:39. *Secondly,* "He will be utterly ruined; for, if he be dealt with according to his deserts, one flood must succeed another till all be destroyed." See here, 1. That outward judgments, though they may terrify and restrain men, yet cannot of themselves sanctify and renew them; the grace of God must work with those judgments. Man's nature was as sinful after the deluge as it had been before. 2. That God's goodness takes occasion from man's sinfulness to magnify itself the more; his reasons of mercy are all drawn from himself, not from any thing in us.

(2.) That the course of nature should never be discontinued (*v.* 22): "*While the earth remaineth,* and man upon it, there shall be *summer and winter* (not all winter as had been this last year), *day and night,*" not all night, as probably it was while the rain was descending. Here, [1.] It is plainly intimated that this earth is not to remain always; it, and all the works in it, must shortly be burnt up; and we look for *new heavens and a new earth,* when all these

things must be dissolved. But, [2.] As long as it does remain God's providence will carefully preserve the regular succession of times and seasons, and cause each to know its place. To this we owe it that the world stands, and the wheel of nature keeps it track. See here how changeable the times are and yet how unchangeable. *First,* The course of nature always changing. As it is with the times, so it is with the events of time, they are subject to vicissitudes — *day and night, summer and winter,* counterchanged. In heaven and hell it is not so, but on earth God *hath set the one over against the other. Secondly,* Yet never changed. It is constant in this inconstancy. These seasons have never ceased, nor shall cease, while the sun continued such a steady measurer of time and the moon such a *faithful witness in heaven.* This is *God's covenant of the day and of the night,* the stability of which is mentioned for the confirming of our faith in the covenant of grace, which is no less inviolable, Jer. 33:20, 21. We see God's promises to the creatures made good, and thence may infer that his promises to all believers shall be so.

CHAPTER 9

Both the world and the church were now again reduced to a family, the family of Noah, of the affairs of which this chapter gives us an account, of which we are the more concerned to take cognizance because from this family we are all descendants. Here is, I. The covenant of providence settled with Noah and his sons (*v.* 1–11). In this covenant, 1. God promises them to take care of their lives, so that, (1.) They should replenish the earth (*v.* 1, 7). (2.) They should be safe from the insults of the brute-creatures, which should stand in awe of them (*v.* 2). (3.) They should be allowed to eat flesh for the support of their lives; only they must not eat blood (*v.* 3, 4). (4.) The world should never be drowned again (*v.* 8–11). 2. God requires of them to take care of one another's lives, and of their own (*v.* 5, 6). II. The seal of that covenant, namely, the rainbow (*v.* 12–17). III. A particular passage of story concerning Noah and his sons, which occasioned some prophecies that related to after-times, 1. Noah's sin and shame (*v.* 20, 21). 2. Ham's impudence and impiety (*v.* 22). 3. The pious modesty of Shem and Japheth (*v.* 23). 4. The curse of Canaan, and the blessing of Shem and Japheth (*v.* 21–27). IV. The age and death of Noah (*v.* 28, 29).

Verses 1–7

We read, in the close of the foregoing chapter, the very kind things which God said in his heart, concerning the remnant of mankind which was now left to be the seed of a new world. Now here we have these kind things *spoken* to them. In general, *God blessed Noah and his sons* (*v.* 1), that is, he assured them of his good-will to them and his gracious intentions concerning them. This follows from what he said in his heart. Note, All God's promises of good flow from his purposes of love and the counsels of his own will. See Eph. 1:11, 3:11, and compare Jer. 29:11. *I know the thoughts that I think towards you.* We read (*ch.* 8:20) how *Noah blessed God,* by his altar and sacrifice. Now here we find God blessing Noah. Note, God will graciously bless (that is, do well for) those who sincerely bless (that is, speak well of) him. Those that are truly thankful for the mercies they have received take the readiest way to have them confirmed and continued to them.

Now here we have the *Magna Charta — the great charter* of this new kingdom of nature which was now to be erected, and incorporated, the former charter having been forfeited, and seized.

I. The grants of this charter are kind and gracious to men. Here is,

1. A grant of lands of vast extent, and a promise of a great increase of men to occupy and enjoy them,. The first blessing is here renewed: *Be fruitful, and multiply, and replenish the earth* (*v.* 1), and repeated (*v.* 7), for the race of mankind was, as it were, to begin again. Now, (1.) God sets the whole earth before them, tells them it is all their own, *while it remains,* to them and their heirs. Note, The earth God has given to the children of men, for a possession and habitation, Ps. 115:16. Though it is not a paradise, but a wilderness rather; yet it is better than we deserve. Blessed be God, it is not hell. (2.) He gives them a blessing, by the force and virtue of which mankind should be both multiplied and perpetuated upon earth, so that in a little time all the habitable parts of the earth should be more or less inhabited; and, though one generation should pass away, yet another generation should come, while the world stands, so that the stream of the human race should be supplied with a constant succession, and run parallel with the current of time, till both should be delivered up together into the ocean of eternity. Though death should still reign, and the Lord would still be known by his judgments,

yet the earth should never again be dispeopled as now it was, but still replenished, Acts 17:24–26.

2. A grant of power over the inferior creatures, *v.* 2. He grants, (1.) A title to them: *Into your hands they are delivered,* for your use and benefit. (2.) A dominion over them, without which the title would avail little: *The fear of you and the dread of you shall be upon every beast.* This revives a former grant (*ch.* 1:28), only with this difference, that man in innocence ruled by love, fallen man rules by fear. Now this grant remains in force, and thus far we have still the benefit of it, [1.] That those creatures which are any way useful to us are reclaimed, and we use them either for service or food, or both, as they are capable. The horse and ox patiently submit to the bridle and yoke, and the sheep is dumb both before the shearer and before the butcher; for the fear and dread of man are upon them. [2.] Those creatures that are any way hurtful to us are restrained, so that, though now and then man may be hurt by some of them, they do not combine together to rise up in rebellion against man, else God could by these destroy the world as effectually as he did by a deluge; it is one of God's sore judgments, Eze. 14:21. What is it that keeps wolves out of our towns, and lions out of our streets, and confines them to the wilderness, but this fear and dread? Nay, some have been tamed, Jas. 3:7.

3. A grant of maintenance and subsistence: *Every moving thing that liveth shall be meat for you, v.* 3. Hitherto, most think, man had been confined to feed only upon the products of the earth, fruits, herbs, and roots, and all sorts of corn and milk; so was the first grant, *ch.* 1:29. But the flood having perhaps washed away much of the virtue of the earth, and so rendered its fruits less pleasing and less nourishing, God now enlarged the grant, and allowed man to eat flesh, which perhaps man himself never thought of, till now that God directed him to it, nor had any more desire to than a sheep has to suck blood like a wolf. But now man is allowed to feed upon flesh, as freely and safely as upon the green herb. Now here see, (1.) That God is a good master, and provides, not only that we may live, but that we may live comfortably, in his service; not for necessity only, but for delight. (2.) That every *creature of God is good,* and nothing to be refused, 1 Tim. 4:4. Afterwards some meats that were proper enough for food were prohibited by the ceremonial law; but from the beginning, it seems, it was not so, and therefore is not so under the gospel.

II. The precepts and provisos of this character are no less kind and gracious, and instances of God's good-will to man. The Jewish doctors speak so often of the seven precepts of Noah, or of the sons of Noah, which they say were to be observed by all nations, that it may not be amiss to set them down. The first against the worship of idols. The second against blasphemy, and requiring to bless the name of God. The third against murder. The fourth against incest and all uncleanness. The fifth against theft and rapine. The sixth requiring the administration of justice. The seventh against eating of flesh with the life. These the Jews required the observance of from the *proselytes of the gate.* But the precepts here given all concern the life of man.

1. Man must not prejudice his own life by eating that food which is unwholesome and prejudicial to his health (*v.* 4): *"Flesh with the life thereof, which is the blood thereof* (that is, raw flesh), shall you not eat, as the beasts of prey do." It was necessary to add this limitation to the grant of liberty to eat flesh, lest, instead of nourishing their bodies by it, they should destroy them. God would hereby show, (1.) That though they were lords of the creatures, yet they were subjects to the Creator, and under the restraints of his law. That they must not be greedy and hasty in taking their food, but stay the preparing of it; not like Saul's soldiers (1 Sa. 14:32), nor *riotous eaters of flesh,* Prov. 23:20. (3.) That they must not be barbarous and cruel to the inferior creatures. They must be lords, but not tyrants; they might kill them for their profit, but not torment them for their pleasure, nor tear away the member of a creature while it was yet alive, and eat that. (4.) That during the continuance of the law of sacrifices, in which the blood made *atonement for the soul* (Lev. 17:11), signifying that the life of the sacrifice was accepted for the life of the sinner, blood must not be looked upon as a common thing, but must be *poured out before the Lord* (2 Sa. 23:16), either upon his altar or upon his earth. But, now that the great and true sacrifice has been offered, the obligation of the law ceases with the reason of it.

2. Man must not take away his own life: *Your blood of your lives will I require, v.* 5. Our lives are not so our own as that we may quit them at our own pleasure, but they are God's and we must resign them at his pleasure; if we in any way hasten our own deaths, we are accountable to God for it.

3. The beasts must not be suffered to hurt the life of man: *At the hand of every beast will I require it.* To show how tender God was of the life of man, though he had lately made such destruction of lives, he will have the beast put to death that kills a man. This was confirmed by the law of Moses (Ex. 21:28), and I think it would not be unsafe to observe it still. Thus God showed his hatred of the sin of murder, that men might hate it the more, and not only punish, but prevent it. And see Job 5:23.

4. Wilful murderers must be put to death. This is the sin which is here designed to be restrained by the terror of punishment (1.) God will punish murderers: *At the hand of every man's brother will I require the life of man,* that is, "I will avenge the blood of the murdered upon the murderer." 2 Chr. 24:22. When God requires the life of a man at the hand of him that took it away unjustly, the murderer cannot render that, and therefore must render his own in lieu of it, which is the only way left of making restitution. Note, The righteous God will certainly make inquisition for blood, though men cannot or do not. One time or other, in this world or in the next, he will both discover concealed murders, which are hidden from man's eye, and punish avowed and justified murders, which are too great for man's hand. (2.) The magistrate must punish murderers (*v.* 6): *Whoso sheddeth man's blood,* whether upon a sudden provocation or having premeditated it (for rash anger is heart-murder as well as malice prepense, Mt. 5:21, 22), *by man shall his blood be shed,* that is, by the magistrate, or whoever is appointed or allowed to be the avenger of blood. There are those who are ministers of God for this purpose, to be a protection to the innocent, by being a terror to the malicious and evildoers, and they must not *bear the sword in vain,* Rom. 13:4. Before the flood, as it should seem by the story of Cain, God took the punishment of murder into his own hands; but now he committed this judgment to men, to masters of families at first, and afterwards to the heads of countries, who ought to be faithful to the trust reposed in them. Note, Wilful murder ought always to be punished with death. It is a sin *which the Lord would not pardon* in a prince (2 Ki. 24:3, 4), and which therefore a prince should not pardon in a subject. To this law there is a reason annexed: *For in the image of God made he man* at first. Man is a creature dear to his Creator, and therefore ought to be so to us. God put honour upon him, let not us then put contempt upon him. Such remains of God's image are still even upon fallen man as that he who unjustly kills a man defaces the image of God and does dishonour to him. When God allowed men to kill their beasts, yet he forbade them to kill their slaves; for these are of a much more noble and excellent nature, not only God's creatures, but his image, Jam. 3:9. All men have something of the image of God upon them; but magistrates have, besides, the image of his power, and the saints the image of his holiness, and therefore those who shed the blood of princes or saints incur a double guilt.

Verses 8–11

Here is, I. The general establishment of God's covenant with this new world, and the extent of that covenant, *v.* 9, 10. Here observe, 1. That God is graciously pleased to deal with man in the way of a covenant, wherein God greatly magnifies his condescending favour, and greatly encourages man's duty and obedience, as a reasonable and gainful service. 2. That all God's covenants with man are of his own making: *I, behold, I.* It is thus expressed both to raise our admiration — "Behold, and wonder, that though God be high yet he has this respect to man," and to confirm our assurances of the validity of the covenant — "Behold and see, I make it; I that am faithful and able to make it good." 3. That God's covenants are established more firmly than the pillars of heaven or the foundations of the earth, and cannot be disannulled. 4. That God's covenants are made with the covenanters and with their seed; the promise is to them and their children. 5. That those may be taken into covenant with God, and receive the benefits of it, who yet are not capable of restipulating, or giving their own consent. For this covenant is made with *every living creature, every beast of the earth.*

II. The particular intention of this covenant. It was designed to secure the world from another deluge: *There shall not any more be a flood.* God had drowned the world once, and still it was as filthy and provoking as ever, and God foresaw the wickedness of it, and yet promised he would never drown it any more; for he deals not with us according to our sins. It is owing to God's goodness and faithfulness, not to any reformation of the world, that it has not often been deluged and that it is not deluged now. As the old world was ruined to be a monument of justice, so this world remains to this day, a monument of mercy, according to the oath of God, that the waters of Noah should no more return to cover the earth, Isa. 54:9. This promise of God keeps the sea and clouds in their decreed place, and *sets them gates and bars; hitherto they shall come,* Job 38:10, 11. If the sea should flow but for a few days, as it does twice every day for a few hours, what desolation would it make! And how destructive would the clouds be, if such showers as we have sometimes seen were continued long! But God, by flowing seas and sweeping rains, shows what he could do in wrath; and yet, by preserving the earth from being deluged between both, shows what he can do in mercy and will do in truth. Let us give him the glory of his mercy in promising and of his truth in performing. This promise does not hinder, 1. But that God may bring other wasting judgments upon mankind; for, though he has here bound himself not to use this arrow any more, yet he has other arrows in his quiver. 2. Nor but that he may destroy particular places and countries by the inundations of the sea or rivers. 3. Nor will the destruction of the world at the last day by fire be any breach of his promise. Sin which drowned the old world will burn this.

Verses 12–17

Articles of agreement among men are usually sealed, that the covenants may be the more solemn, and the performances of the covenants the more sure, to mutual satisfaction. God therefore, being *willing more abundantly to show to the heirs of promise the immutability of his councils,* has confirmed his covenant by a seal (Heb. 6:17), which makes the foundations we build on stand sure, 2 Tim. 2:19. The seal of this covenant of nature was natural enough; it was the *rainbow,* which, it is likely, was seen in the clouds before, when second causes concurred, but was never a seal of the covenant till now that it was made so by a divine institution. Now, concerning this seal of the covenant, observe, 1. This seal is affixed with repeated assurances of the truth of that promise of which it was designed to be the ratification: *I do set my bow in the cloud* (*v.* 23); it *shall be seen in the cloud* (*v.* 14), that the eye may affect the heart and confirm the faith; and it shall be *the token of the covenant* (*v.* 12, 13), *and I will remember my covenant, that the waters shall no more become a flood, v.* 15. Nay, as if the Eternal Mind needed a memorandum, *I will look upon it, that I may remember the everlasting covenant, v.* 16. Thus here is line upon line, that we might have sure and strong consolation who have laid hold of this hope. 2. The rainbow appears when the clouds are most disposed to wet, and returns after the rain; when we have most reason to fear the rain prevailing, then God shows this seal of the promise that it shall not prevail. Thus God obviates our fears with such encouragements as are both suitable and seasonable. 3. The thicker the cloud the brighter the bow in the cloud. Thus, as threatening afflictions abound, encouraging consolations much more abound, 2 Co. 1:5. 4. The rainbow appears when one part of the sky is clear, which intimates mercy remembered in the midst of wrath; and the clouds are hemmed as it were with the rainbow, that they may not overspread the heavens, for the bow is coloured rain or the edges of a cloud gilded. 5. The rainbow is the reflection of the beams of the sun, which intimates that all the glory and significancy of the seals of the covenant are derived from Christ the Sun of righteousness, who is also described with a *rainbow about his throne* (Rev. 4:3), and a *rainbow upon his head* (Rev. 10:1), which intimates, not only his majesty, but his mediatorship. 6. The rainbow has fiery colours in it, to signify that though God will not again drown the world, yet, when the mystery of God shall be finished, the world shall be consumed by fire. 7. A bow bespeaks terror, but this bow has neither string nor arrow, as the bow ordained against the persecutors has (Ps. 7:12, 13), and a bow alone will do little execution. It is a bow, but it is directed upwards, not towards the earth; for the seals of the covenant were intended to comfort, not to terrify. 8. As God looks upon the bow, that he may remember the covenant, so should we, that we also may be ever mindful of the covenant, with faith and thankfulness.

Verses 18–23

Here is, I. Noah's family and employment. The names of his sons are again mentioned (*v.* 18, 19) as those from whom the whole earth was overspread, by which it appears that Noah, after the flood, had no more children: all the world came from these three. Note, God, when he pleases, can make *a little one to become a thousand,* and greatly increase the latter end of those whose beginning was small. Such are the power and efficacy of a divine blessing. The business Noah applied himself to was that of *a husbandman,* Heb. *a man of the earth,* that is, a man dealing in the earth, that kept ground in his hand, and occupied it. We are all naturally men of the earth, made of it, living on it, and hastening to it: many are sinfully so, addicted to earthly things. Noah was by his calling led to trade in the fruits of the earth. He *began to be a husbandman,* that is, some time after his departure out of the ark, he returned to his old employment, from which he had been diverted by the building of the ark first, and probably afterwards by the building of a house on dry land for himself and family. For this good while he had been a carpenter, but now he began again to be a husbandman. Observe, Though Noah was a great man and a good man, an old man and a rich man, a man greatly favoured by heaven and honoured on earth, yet he would not live an idle life, nor think the husbandman's calling below him. Note, Though God by his providence may take us off from our callings for a time, yet when the occasion is over we ought with humility and industry to apply ourselves to them again, and, in the calling wherein we are called, faithfully to *abide with God,* 1 Co. 7:24.

II. Noah's sin and shame: *He planted a vineyard;* and, when he had gathered his vintage, probably he appointed a day of mirth and feasting in his family, and had his sons and their children with him, to rejoice with him in the increase of his house as well as in the increase of his vineyard; and we may suppose he prefaced his feast with a sacrifice to the honour of God. If this was omitted, it was just with God to leave him to himself, that he who did not begin with God might end with the beasts; but we charitably hope that it was not: and perhaps he appointed this feast with a design, at the close of it, to bless his sons, as *Isaac, ch.* 27:3, 4, *That I may eat, and that my soul may bless thee.* At this feast he *drank of the wine;* for who planteth a vineyard and *eateth not of the fruit of it?* But he drank too liberally, more than his head at this age would bear, for he was *drunk.* We have reason to think he was never drunk before nor after; observe how he came now to be overtaken in this fault. It was his sin, and a great sin, so much the worse for its being so soon after a great deliverance; but God left him to himself, as he did Hezekiah (2 Chr. 32:31), and has left this miscarriage of his upon record, to teach us, 1. That the fairest copy that ever mere man wrote since the fall had its blots and false strokes. It was said of Noah that he was *perfect in his generations* (*ch.* 6:9), but this shows that it is meant of sincerity, not a sinless perfection. 2. That sometimes those who, with watchfulness and resolution, have, by the grace of God, kept their integrity in the midst of temptation, have, through security, and carelessness, and neglect of the grace of God, been surprised into sin, when the hour of temptation has been over. Noah, who had kept sober in drunken company, is now drunk in sober company. *Let him that thinks he stands take heed.* 3. That we have need to be very careful, when we use God's good creatures plentifully, lest we use them to excess. Christ's disciples must take heed lest at any time *their hearts be overcharged,* Lu. 21:34. Now the consequence of Noah's sin was shame. He was *uncovered within his tent,* made naked to his shame, as Adam when he had eaten forbidden fruit. Yet Adam sought concealment; Noah is so destitute of thought and reason that he seeks no covering. This was a fruit of the vine that Noah did not think of. Observe here the great evil of the sin of drunkenness. (1.) It discovers men. What infirmities they have, they betray when they are drunk, and what secrets they are entrusted with are then easily got out of them. Drunken porters keep open gates. (2.) It disgraces men, and exposes them to contempt. As it shows them, so it shames them. Men say and do that when drunk which when they are sober they would blush at the thoughts of, Hab. 2:15, 16.

III. Ham's impudence and impiety: He *saw the nakedness of his father, and told his two brethren, v.* 22. To see it accidentally and involuntarily would not have been a crime; but, 1. He pleased himself with the sight, *as the Edomites looked upon the day of their brother* (Obad. 12), pleased, and insulting. Perhaps Ham had sometimes been himself drunk, and reproved for it by his good father, whom he was therefore pleased to see thus overcome. Note, It is common for those who walk in false ways themselves to rejoice at the false steps which they sometimes see others make. But charity rejoices not in iniquity, nor can true penitents that are sorry for their own sins rejoice in the sins of others. 2. *He told his two brethren without (in the street,* as the word is), in a scornful deriding manner, that his father might seem vile unto them. It is very wrong, (1.) To make a jest of sin (Prov. 14:9), and to be puffed up with that for which we should rather mourn, 1 Co. 5:2. And, (2.) To publish the faults of any, especially of parents, whom it is our duty to honour. Noah was not only a good man, but had been a good father to him; and this was a most base disingenuous requital to him for his tenderness. Ham is here called the *father of Canaan,* which intimates that he who was himself a father should have been more respectful to him that was his father.

IV. The pious care of Shem and Japheth to cover their poor father's shame, *v.* 23. They not only would not see it themselves, but provided that no one else might see it, herein setting us an example of charity with reference to other men's sin and shame; we must not only not say, *A confederacy,* with those that proclaim it, but we must be careful to conceal it, or at least to make the best of it, be doing as we would be done by. 1. There is a mantle of love to be thrown over the faults of all, 1 Pt. 4:8. 2. Besides this, there is a robe of reverence to be thrown over the faults of parents and other superiors.

Verses 24–27

Here, I. Noah comes to himself: He *awoke from his wine.* Sleep cured him, and, we may suppose, so cured him that he never relapsed into that sin afterwards. Those that sleep as Noah did should awake as he did, and not as that drunkard (Prov. 23:35) who says when he awakes, *I will seek it yet again.*

II. The spirit of prophecy comes upon him, and, like dying Jacob, he tells his sons what shall befal them, *ch.* 49:1.

1. He pronounces a curse on Canaan the son of Ham (*v.* 25), in whom Ham is himself cursed, either because this son of his was now more guilty than the rest, or because the posterity of this son was afterwards to be rooted out of their land, to make room for Israel. And Moses here records it for the animating of Israel in the wars of Canaan; though the Canaanites were a formidable people, yet they were of old an accursed people, and doomed to ruin. The particular curse is, *A servant of servants* (that is, the meanest and most despicable servant) *shall he be,* even *to his brethren.* Those who by birth were his equals shall by conquest be his lords. This certainly points at the victories obtained by Israel over the Canaanites, by which they were all either put to the sword or put under tribute (Jos. 9:23; Jdg. 1:28, 30, 33, 35), which happened not till about 800 years after this. Note, (1.) God often visits the iniquity of the fathers upon the children, especially when the children inherit the fathers' wicked dispositions, and imitate the fathers' wicked practices, and do nothing to cut off the entail of the curse. (2.) Disgrace is justly put upon those that put disgrace upon others, especially that dishonour and grieve their own parents. An undutiful child that mocks at his parents is *no more worthy to be called a son,* but deserves to be *made as a hired servant,* nay, as *a servant of servants,* among his brethren. (3.) Though divine curses operate slowly, yet, first or last, they will take effect. The Canaanites were under a curse of slavery, and yet, for a great while, had the dominion; for a family, a people, a person, may lie under the curse of God, and yet may long prosper in the world, till the measure of their iniquity, like that of the Canaanites, be full. Many are marked for ruin that are not yet ripe for ruin. Therefore, *Let not thy heart envy sinners.*

2. He entails a blessing upon Shem and Japheth.

(1.) He blesses Shem, or rather blesses God for him, yet so that it entitles him to the greatest honour and happiness imaginable, *v.* 26. Observe, [1.] He calls the Lord *the god of Shem;* and happy, thrice happy, *is that people whose God is the* LORD, Ps. 144:15. All blessings are included in this. This was the blessing conferred on Abraham and his seed; the God of heaven was *not ashamed to be called their God,* Heb. 11:16. Shem is sufficiently recompensed for his respect to his father by this, that the Lord himself puts this honour upon him, *to be his God,* which is a sufficient recompence for all our services and all our sufferings for his name. [2.] He gives to God the glory of that good work which Shem had done, and, instead of blessing and praising him that was the instrument, he blesses and praises God that was the author. Note, The glory of all that is at any time well done, by ourselves or others, must be humbly and thankfully transmitted to God, who works all our good works in us and for us. When we see men's good works we should glorify, not them, but *our Father,* Mt. 5:16. Thus David, in effect, blessed Abigail, when he *blessed God* that sent her (1 Sa. 25:32, 33), for it is an honour and a favour to be employed for God and used by him in doing good. [3.] He foresees and foretels that God's gracious dealings with Shem and his family would be such as would evidence to all the world that he was the God of Shem, on which behalf thanksgivings would by many be rendered to him: *Blessed be the Lord God of Shem.* [4.] It is intimated that the church should be built up and continued in the posterity of Shem; for of him came the Jews, who were, for a great while, the only professing people God had in the world. [5.] Some think reference is here had to Christ, who was the Lord God that, in his human nature, should descend from the loins of Shem; for of him, as concerning the flesh, Christ came. [6.] Canaan is particularly enslaved to him: *He shall be his servant.* Note, Those that have the Lord for their God shall have as much of the honour and power of this world as he sees good for them.

(2.) He blesses Japheth, and, in him, *the isles of the Gentiles,* which were peopled by his seed: *God shall enlarge Japheth, and he shall dwell in the tents of Shem, v.* 27. Now, [1.] Some make this to belong wholly to Japheth, and to denote either, *First,* His outward prosperity, that his seed should be so numerous and so victorious that they should be masters of the tents of Shem, which was fulfilled when the people of the Jews, the most eminent of Shem's race, were tributaries to the Grecians first and afterwards to the Romans, both of Japheth's seed. Note, Outward prosperity is no infallible mark of the true church: the tents of Shem are not always the tents of the conqueror. Or, *Secondly,* It denotes the conversion of the Gentiles, and the bringing of them into the church; and then we should read it, *God shall persuade Japheth* (for so the word signifies), and then, being so persuaded, *he shall dwell in the tents of Shem,* that is, Jews and Gentiles shall be united together in the gospel fold. After many of the Gentiles shall have been proselyted to the Jewish religion, both shall be one in Christ (Eph. 2:14, 15), and the Christian church, mostly made up of the Gentiles, shall succeed the Jews in the privileges of church-membership; the latter having first cast themselves out by their unbelief, the Gentiles shall dwell in their tents, Rom. 11:11, etc. Note, It is God only that can bring those again into the church who have separated themselves from it. It is the power of God that makes the gospel of Christ effectual to salvation, Rom. 1:16. And again, Souls are brought into the church, not by force, but by persuasion, Ps. 110:3. They are drawn by the cords of a man, and persuaded by reason to be religious. [2.] Others divide this between Japheth and Shem, Shem having not been directly blessed, *v.* 26. *First,* Japheth has the blessing of the earth beneath: *God shall enlarge Japheth,* enlarge his seed, enlarge his border. Japheth's prosperity peopled all Europe, a great part of Asia, and perhaps America. Note, God is to be acknowledged in all our enlargements. It is he that enlarges the coast and enlarges the heart. And again, many dwell in large tents that do not dwell in God's tents, as Japheth did. *Secondly,* Shem has the blessing of heaven above: *He shall* (that is, God shall) *dwell in the tents of Shem,* that is "From his loins *Christ shall come,* and in his seed the *church shall be continued.*" The birth-right was now to be divided between Shem and Japheth, Ham being utterly discarded. In the principality which they equally share Canaan shall be servant to both. The double portion is given to Japheth, whom God shall enlarge; but the priesthood is given to Shem, for *God shall dwell in the tents of Shem:* and certainly we are more happy if we have God dwelling in our tents than if we had there all the silver and gold in the world. It is better to dwell in tents with God than in palaces without him. In Salem, where is God's tabernacle, there is more satisfaction than in all the isles of the Gentiles. *Thirdly,* They both have dominion over Canaan: *Canaan shall be servant to them;* so some read it. When Japheth joins with Shem, Canaan falls before them both. When strangers become friends, enemies become servants.

Verses 28–29

Here see, 1. How God prolonged the life of Noah; he lived 950 years, twenty more than Adam and but nineteen less than Methuselah: this long life was a further reward of his signal piety, and a great blessing to the world, to which no doubt he continued a *preacher of righteousness,* with this advantage, that now all he preached to were his own children. 2. How God put a period to his life at last. Though he lived long, yet he died, having probably first seen many that descended from him dead before him. Noah lived to see two worlds, but, being an heir of the righteousness which is by faith, when he died he went to see a better than either.

CHAPTER 10

This chapter shows more particularly what was said in general (*ch.* 9:19), concerning the three sons of Noah, that "of them was the whole earth overspread;" and the fruit of that blessing (*ch.* 9:1, 7), "replenish the earth." Is is the only certain account extant of the origin of nations; and yet perhaps there is no nation but that of the Jews that can be confident from which of these seventy fountains (for so many there are here) it derives its streams. Through the want of early records, the mixtures of people, the revolutions of nations, and distance of time, the knowledge of the lineal descent of the present inhabitants of the earth is lost; nor were any genealogies preserved but those of the Jews, for the sake of the Messiah, only in this chapter we have a brief account, I. Of the posterity of Japheth (*v.* 2–5). II. The posterity of Ham (*v.* 6–20), and in this particular notice is taken of Nimrod (*v.* 8–10). III. The posterity of Shem (*v.* 21, etc.).

Verses 1–5

Moses begins with Japheth's family, either because he was the eldest, or because his family lay remotest from Israel and had least concern with them at the time when Moses wrote, and therefore he mentions that race very briefly, hastening to give an account of the posterity of Ham, who were Israel's enemies and of Shem, who were Israel's ancestors; for it is the church that the scripture is designed to be the history of, and of the nations of the world only as they were some way or other related to Israel and interested in the affairs of Israel. Observe, 1. Notice is taken that the sons of Noah had sons born to them after the flood, to repair and rebuild the world of mankind which the flood had ruined. He that had killed now makes alive. 2. The posterity of Japheth were allotted to the isles of the Gentiles (*v.* 5), which were solemnly, by lot, after a survey, divided among them, and probably this island of ours among the rest; all places beyond the sea from Judea are called *isles* (Jer. 25:22), and this directs us to understand that promise (Isa. 42:4), *the isles shall wait for his law,* of the conversion of the Gentiles to the faith of Christ.

Verses 6–14

That which is observable and improvable in these verses is the account here given of Nimrod, *v.* 8–10. He is here represented as a great man in his day: *He began to be a mighty one in the earth,* that is, whereas those that went before him were content to stand upon the same level with their neighbours, and though every man bore rule in his own house yet no man pretended any further, Nimrod's aspiring mind could not rest here; he was resolved to tower above his neighbours, not only to be eminent among them, but to lord it over them. The same spirit that actuated the giants before the flood (who became *mighty men, and men of renown, ch.* 6:4), now revived in him, so soon was that tremendous judgment which the pride and tyranny of those mighty men brought upon the world forgotten. Note, There are some in whom ambition and affectation of dominion seem to be bred in the bone; such there have been and will be, notwithstanding the wrath of God often revealed from heaven against them. Nothing on this side hell will humble and break the proud spirits of some men, in this like Lucifer, Isa. 14:14, 15. Now,

I. Nimrod was a great hunter; with this he began, and for this became famous to a proverb. Every great hunter is, in remembrance of him, called a *Nimrod.* 1. Some think he did good with his hunting, served his country by ridding it of the wild beasts which infested it, and so insinuated himself into the affections of his neighbours, and got to be their prince. Those that exercise authority either are, or at least would be called, *benefactors,* Lu. 22:25. 2. Others think that under pretence of hunting he gathered men under his command, in pursuit of another game he had to play, which was to make himself master of the country and to bring them into subjection. He was a *mighty hunter,* that is, he was a violent invader of his neighbours' rights and properties, and a persecutor of innocent men, carrying all before him, and endeavouring to make all his own by force and violence. He thought himself a mighty prince, but *before the Lord* (that is, in God's account) he was but a *mighty hunter.* Note, Great conquerors are but great hunters. Alexander and Caesar would not make such a figure in scripture-history as they do in common history; the former is represented in prophecy but as a he-goat pushing, Dan. 8:5. Nimrod was a mighty hunter *against* the Lord, so the Septuagint; that is, (1.) He set up idolatry, as Jeroboam did, for the confirming of his usurped dominion. That he might set up a new government, he set up a new religion upon the ruin of the primitive constitution of both. *Babel was the mother of harlots.* Or, (2.) He carried on his oppression and violence in defiance of God himself, daring Heaven with his impieties, as if he and his huntsmen could out-brave the Almighty, and were a match for the Lord of hosts and all his armies. *As if it were a small thing to weary men, he thinks to weary my God also,* Isa. 7:13.

II. Nimrod was a great ruler: *The beginning of his kingdom was Babel, v.* 10. Some way or other, by arts or arms, he got into power, either being chosen to it or forcing his way to it; and so laid the foundations of a monarchy, which was afterwards a head of gold, and the terror of the mighty, and bade fair to be universal. It does not appear that he had any right to rule by birth; but either his fitness for government recommended him, as some think, to an election, or by power and policy he advanced gradually, and perhaps insensibly, into the throne. See the antiquity of civil government, and particularly that form of it which lodges the sovereignty in a single person. If Nimrod and his neighbours began, other nations soon learned to incorporate under one head for their common safety and welfare, which, however it began, proved so great a blessing to the world that things were reckoned to go ill indeed when there *was no king in Israel.*

III. Nimrod was a great builder. Probably he was architect in the building of Babel, and there he began his kingdom; but, when his project to rule all the sons of Noah was baffled by the confusion of tongues, *out of that land he went forth into Assyria* (so the margin reads it, *v.* 11) *and built Nineveh, etc.,* that, having built these cities, he might command them and rule over them. Observe, in Nimrod, the nature of ambition. 1. It is boundless. Much would have more, and still cries, *Give, give.* 2. It is restless. Nimrod, when he had four cities under his command, could not be content till he had four more. 3. It is expensive. Nimrod will rather be at the charge of rearing cities than not have the honour of ruling them. The spirit of building is the common effect of a spirit of pride. 4. It is daring, and will stick at nothing. Nimrod's name signifies rebellion, which (if indeed he did abuse his power to the oppression of his neighbours) teaches us that tyrants to men are rebels to God, and their *rebellion is as the sin of witchcraft.*

Verses 15–20

Observe here, 1. The account of the posterity of Canaan, of the families and nations that descended from him, and of the land they possessed, is more particular than of any other in this chapter, because these were the nations that were to be subdued before Israel, and their land was in process of time to become the holy land, *Immanuel's land;* and this God had an eye to when, in the mean time, he cast the lot of that accursed devoted race in that spot of ground which he had selected for his own people; this Moses takes notice of, Deu. 32:8, *When the Most High divided to the nations their inheritance, he set the bounds of the people according to the number of the children of Israel.* 2. By this account it appears that the posterity of Canaan were numerous, and rich, and very pleasantly situated; and yet Canaan was under a curse, a divine curse, and not a curse causeless. Note, Those that are under the curse of God may yet perhaps thrive and prosper greatly in this world; for we cannot know love or hatred, the blessing or the curse, by what is before us, but by what is within us, Eccl. 9:1. The curse of God always works really and always terribly: but perhaps it is a secret curse, a curse to the soul, and does not work visibly, or a slow curse, and does not work immediately; but sinners are by it reserved for, and bound over to, a day of wrath. Canaan here has a better land than either Shem or Japheth, and yet they have a better lot, for they inherit the blessing.

Verses 21–32

Two things especially are observable in this account of the posterity of Shem: —

I. The description of Shem, *v.* 21. We have not only his name, *Shem,* which signifies *a name,* but two titles to distinguish him by: —

1. He was *the father of all the children of Eber.* Eber was his great grandson; but why should he be called the father of all *his* children, rather than of all Arphaxad's, or Salah's, etc.? Probably because Abraham and his seed, God's covenant-people, not only descended from Heber, but from him were called *Hebrews; ch.* 14:13, *Abram the Hebrew.* Paul looked upon it as his privilege that he was a *Hebrew of the Hebrews,* Phil. 3:5. Eber himself, we may suppose, was a man eminent for religion in a time of general apostasy, and a great example of piety to his family; and, the holy tongue being commonly called from him the *Hebrew,* it is probable that he retained it in his family, in the confusion of Babel, as a special token of God's favour to him; and from him the professors of religion were called *the children of Eber.* Now, when the inspired penman would give Shem an honourable title, he calls him *the father of the Hebrews.* Though when Moses wrote this, they were a poor despised people, bond-slaves in Egypt, yet, being God's people, it was an honour to a man to be akin to them. As Ham, though he had many sons, is disowned by being called *the father of Canaan,* on whose seed the *curse* was entailed (*ch.* 9:22), so Shem, though he had many sons, is dignified with the title of *the father of Eber,* on whose seed the blessing was entailed. Note, a family of saints is more truly honourable than a family of nobles, Shem's holy seed than Ham's royal seed, Jacob's twelve patriarchs than Ishmael's twelve princes, *ch.* 17:20. Goodness is true greatness.

2. He was *the brother of Japheth the elder,* by which it appears that, though Shem is commonly put first, he was not Noah's first-born, but Japheth was older. But why should this also be put as part of Shem's title and description, that he *was the brother of Japheth,* since it had been, in effect, said often before? And was he not as much brother to Ham? Probably this was intended to signify the union of the Gentiles with the Jews in the church. The sacred historian had mentioned it as Shem's honour that he was the father of the Hebrews; but, lest Japheth's seed should therefore be looked upon as for ever shut out from the church, he here reminds us that he *was the brother of Japheth,* not in birth only, but in blessing; for *Japheth was to dwell in the tents of Shem.* Note, (1.) Those are brethren in the best manner that are so by grace, and that meet in the covenant of God and in the communion of saints. (2.) God, in dispensing his grace, does not go by seniority, but the younger sometimes gets the start of the elder in coming into the church; *so the last shall be first and the first last.*

II. The reason of the name of Peleg (*v.* 25): Because *in his days* (that is, about the time of his birth, when his name was given him), *was the earth divided* among the children of men that were to inhabit it; either when Noah divided it by an orderly distribution of it, as Joshua divided the land of Canaan by lot, or when, upon their refusal to comply with that division, God, in justice, divided them by the confusion of tongues: whichsoever of these was the occasion, pious Heber saw cause to perpetuate the remembrance of it in the name of his son; and justly may our sons be called by the same name, for in our days, in another sense, is the earth, the church, most wretchedly divided.

CHAPTER 11

The old distinction between the sons of God and the sons of men (professors and profane) survived the flood, and now appeared again, when men began to multiply: according to this distinction we have, in this chapter, I. The dispersion of the sons of men at Babel (*v.* 1–9), where we have, 1. Their presumptuous provoking design, which was to build a city and a tower (*v.* 1–4). 2. The righteous judgment of God upon them in disappointing their design, by confounding their language, and so scattering them (*v.* 5–9). II. The pedigree of the sons of God down to Abraham (*v.* 10–26), with a general account of his family, and removal out of his native country (*v.* 27, etc.).

Verses 1–4

The close of the foregoing chapter tells us that *by* the sons of Noah, or *among* the sons of Noah, *the nations were divided in the earth after the flood,* that is, were distinguished into several tribes or colonies; and, the places having grown too strait for them, it was either appointed by Noah, or agreed upon among his sons, which way each several tribe or colony should steer its course, beginning with the countries that were next them, and designing to proceed further and further, and to remove to a greater distance from each other, as the increase of their several companies should require. Thus was the matter well settled, one hundred years after the flood, about the time of Peleg's birth; but the sons of men, it should seem, were loth to disperse into distant places; they thought the more the merrier and the safer, and therefore they contrived to keep together, and were *slack to go to possess the land which the Lord God of their fathers had given them* (Jos. 18:3), thinking themselves wiser than either God or Noah. Now here we have,

I. The advantages which befriended their design of keeping together, 1. They were all of *one language, v.* 1. If there were any different languages before the flood, yet Noah's only, which it is likely was the same with Adam's, was preserved through the flood, and continued after it. Now, while they all understood one another, they would be the more likely to love one another, and the more capable of helping one another, and the less inclinable to separate one from another. 2. They found a very convenient commodious place to settle in (*v.* 2), *a plain in the land of Shinar,* a spacious plain, able to *contain* them all, and a *fruitful* plain, able, according as their present numbers were, to support them all, though perhaps they had not considered what room there would be for them when their numbers should be increased. Note, Inviting accommodations, for the present, often prove too strong temptations to the neglect of both duty and interest, as it respects futurity.

II. The method they took to bind themselves to one another, and to settle together in one body. Instead of coveting to enlarge their borders by a peaceful departure under the divine protection, they contrived to fortify them, and, as those that were resolved to wage war with Heaven, they put themselves into a posture of defence. Their unanimous resolution is, *Let us build ourselves a city and a tower.* It is observable that the first builders of cities, both in the old world (*ch.* 4:17), and in the new world here, were not men of the best character and reputation: tents served God's subjects to dwell in; cities were first built by those that were rebels against him and revolters from him. Observe here,

1. How they excited and encouraged one another to set about this work. They said, *Go to, let us make brick* (*v.* 3), and again, (*v.* 4), *Go to, let us build ourselves a city;* by mutual excitements they made one another more daring and resolute. Note, Great things may be brought to pass when the undertakers are numerous and unanimous, and stir up one another. Let us learn to provoke one another to love and to good works, as sinners stir up and encourage one another to wicked works. See Ps. 122:1; Isa. 2:3, 5; Jer. 50:5.

2. What materials they used in their building. The country, being plain, yielded neither stone nor mortar, yet this did not discourage them from their undertaking, but they made brick to serve instead of stone, and slime or pitch instead of mortar. See here, (1.) What shift those will make that are resolute in their purposes: were we but zealously affected in a good thing, we should not stop our work so often as we do, under pretence that we want conveniences for carrying it on. (2.) What a difference there is between men's building and God's; when men build their Babel, brick and slime are their best materials; but, when God builds his Jerusalem, he lays even the *foundations of it with sapphires, and all its borders with pleasant stones,* Isa. 54:11, 12; Rev. 21:19.

3. For what ends they built. Some think they intended hereby to secure themselves against the waters of another flood. God had told them indeed that he would not again drown the world; but they would trust to a tower of their own making, rather than to a promise of God's making or an ark of his appointing. If, however, they had had this in their eye, they would have chosen to build their tower upon a mountain rather than upon a plain, but three things, it seems, they aimed at in building this tower: —

(1.) It seems designed for an affront to God himself; for they would build a tower *whose top might reach to heaven,* which bespeaks a defiance of God, or at least a rivalship with him. They would be *like the Most High,* or would come as near him as they could, not in holiness but in height. They forgot their place, and, scorning to creep on the earth, resolved to climb to heaven, not by the door or ladder, but some other way.

(2.) They hoped hereby to make themselves a name; they would do something to be talked of now, and to give posterity to know that there had been such men as they in the world. Rather than die and leave no memorandum behind them, they would leave this monument of their pride, and ambition, and folly. Note, [1.] Affectation of honour and a name among men commonly inspires with a strange ardour for great and difficult undertakings, and often betrays to that which is evil and offensive to God. [2.] It is just with God to bury those names in the dust which are raised by sin. These Babel-builders put themselves to a great deal of foolish expense to make themselves a name; but they could not gain even this point, for we do not find in any history the name of so much as one of these Babel-builders. Philo Judaeus says, They engraved every one his name upon a brick, *in perpetuam rei memoriam — as a perpetual memorial;* yet neither did this serve their purpose.

(3.) They did it to prevent their dispersion: *Lest we be scattered abroad upon the face of the earth.* "It was done" (says Josephus) "in disobedience to that command (*ch.* 9:1), *Replenish the earth.*" God orders them to disperse. "No," say they, "we will not, we will live and die together." In order hereunto, they engage themselves and one another in this vast undertaking. That they might unite in one glorious empire, they resolve to build this city and tower, to be the metropolis of their kingdom and the centre of their unity. It is probable that the band of ambitious Nimrod was in all this. He could not content himself with the command of a particular colony, but aimed at universal monarchy, in order to which, under pretence of uniting for their common safety, he contrives to keep them in one body, that, having them all under his eye, he might not fail to have them under his power. See the daring presumption of these sinners. Here is, [1.] A bold opposition to God: "You shall be scattered," says God. "But we will not," say they. *Woe unto him that thus strives with his maker.* [2.] A bold competition with God. It is God's prerogative to be universal monarch, Lord of all, and King of kings; the man that aims at it offers to step into the throne of God, who will not give his glory to another.

Verses 5–9

We have here the quashing of the project of the Babel-builders, and the turning of the counsel of those froward men headlong, that God's counsel might stand in spite of them. Here is,

I. The cognizance God took of the design that was on foot: *The Lord came down to see the city, v.* 5. It is an expression after the manner of men; he knew it as clearly and fully as men know that which they come to the place to view. Observe, 1. Before he gave judgment upon their cause, he enquired into it; for God is incontestably just and fair in all his proceedings against sin and sinners, and condemns none unheard. 2. It is spoken of an act of condescension in God to take notice even of this building, which the undertakers were so proud of ; for he humbles himself to behold the transactions, even the most considerable ones, of this lower world, Ps. 113:6. 3. It is said to be *the tower which the children of men built,* which intimates, (1.) Their weakness and frailty as men. It was a very foolish thing for the children of men, worms of the earth, to defy Heaven, and to provoke the Lord to jealousy. *Are they stronger than he?* (2.) Their sinfulness and obnoxiousness. They were the sons of *Adam,* so it is in the Hebrew; nay, of that Adam, that sinful disobedient Adam, whose children are by nature children of disobedience, children that are corrupters. (3.) Their distinction from the children of God, the professors of religion, from whom these daring builders had separated themselves, and built this tower to support and perpetuate the separation. Pious Eber is not found among this ungodly crew; for he and his are called the children of God, and therefore their souls come not into the secret, nor unite themselves to the assembly, of these children of men.

II. The counsels and resolves of the Eternal God concerning this matter; he did not come down merely as a spectator, but as a judge, as a prince, to *look upon these proud men, and abase them,* Job 40:11–14. Observe,

1. He suffered them to proceed a good way in their enterprise before he put a stop to it, that they might have space to repent, and, if they had so much consideration left, might be ashamed of it and weary of it themselves; and if not that their disappointment might be the more shameful, and every one that passed by might laugh at them, saying, *These men began to build, and were not able to finish,* that so the works of their hands, from which they promised themselves immortal honour, might turn to their perpetual reproach. Note, God has wise and holy ends in permitting the enemies of his glory to carry on their impious projects a great way, and to prosper long in their enterprises.

2. When they had, with much care and toil, made some considerable progress in their building, then God determined to break their measures and disperse them. Observe,

(1.) The righteousness of God, which appears in the considerations upon which he proceeded in this resolution, *v.* 6. Two things he considered: — [1.] Their oneness, as a reason why they must be scattered: *"Behold, the people are one, and they have all one language.* If they continue one, much of the earth will be left uninhabited; the power of their prince will soon be exorbitant; wickedness and profaneness will be insufferably rampant, for they will strengthen one another's hands in it; and, which is worst of all, there will be an overbalance to the church, and these children of men, if thus incorporated, will swallow up the little remnant of God's children." Therefore it is decreed that they must not be one. Note, Unity is a policy but it is not the infallible mark of a true church; yet, while the builders of Babel, though of different families, dispositions, and interests, were thus unanimous in opposing God, what a pity is it, and what a shame, that the builders of Sion, though united in one common head and Spirit, should be divided, as they are, in serving God! But marvel not at the matter. Christ came not to send peace. [2.] Their obstinacy: *Now nothing will be restrained from them;* and this is a reason why they must be crossed and thwarted in their design. God had tried, by his commands and admonitions, to bring them off from this project, but in vain; therefore he must take another course with them. See here, *First,* The sinfulness of sin, and the wilfulness of sinners; ever since Adam would not be restrained from the forbidden tree, his unsanctified seed have been impatient of restraint and ready to rebel against it. *Secondly,* See the necessity of God's judgments upon earth, to keep the world in some order and to tie the hands of those that will not be checked by law.

(2.) The wisdom and mercy of God in the methods that were taken for the defeating of this enterprise (*v.* 7): *Go to, let us go down, and there confound their language.* This was not spoken to the angels, as if God needed either their advice or their assistance, but God speaks it to himself, or the Father to the Son and Holy Ghost. They said, *Go to, let us make brick,* and *Go to, let us build a tower,* animating one another to the attempt; and now God says, *Go to, let us confound their language;* for, if men stir up themselves to sin, God will stir up himself to take vengeance, Isa. 59:17, 18. Now observe here, [1.] The mercy of God, in moderating the penalty, and not making it proportionable to the offence; for *he deals not with us according to our sins.* He does not say, *"Let us go down* now in thunder and lightning, and consume those rebels in a moment;" or, "Let the earth open, and swallow up them and their building, and let those go down quickly into hell who are climbing to heaven the wrong way." No; only, *"Let us go down,* and scatter them." They deserved death, but are only banished or transported; for the patience of God is very great towards a provoking world. Punishments are chiefly reserved for the future state. God's judgments on sinners in this life, compared with those which are reserved, are little more than restraints. [2.] The wisdom of God, in pitching upon an effectual expedient to stay proceedings, which was the confounding of their language, that they might not understand one another's speech, nor could they well join hands when their tongues were divided; so that this would be a very proper method both for taking them off from their building (for, if they could not understand one another, they could not help one another) and also for disposing them to scatter; for, when they could not understand one another, they could not take pleasure in one another. Note, God has various means, and effectual ones, to baffle and defeat the projects of proud men that set themselves against him, and particularly to divide them among themselves, either by dividing their spirits (Jdg. 9:23), or by dividing their tongues, as David prays, Ps. 55:9.

III. The execution of these counsels of God, to the blasting and defeating of the counsels of men, *v.* 8, 9. God made them know *whose word should stand, his or theirs,* as the expression is, Jer. 44:28. Notwithstanding their oneness and obstinacy, God was too hard for them, and wherein they dealt proudly he was above them; for *who ever hardened his heart against him and prospered?* Three things were done: —

1. Their language was confounded. God, who, when he made man, taught him to speak, and put words into his mouth fit to express the conceptions of his mind by, now caused these builders to forget their former language, and to speak and understand a new one, which yet was common to those of the same tribe or family, but not to others: those of one colony could converse together, but not with those of another. Now, (1.) This was a great miracle, and a proof of the power which God has upon the minds and tongues of men, which he turns as the rivers of water. (2.) This was a great judgment upon these builders; for, being thus deprived of the knowledge of the ancient and holy tongue, they had become incapable of communicating with the true church, in which it was retained, and probably it contributed much to their loss of the knowledge of the true God. (3.) We all suffer by it, to this day. In all the inconveniences we sustain by the diversity of languages, and all the pains and trouble we are at to learn the languages we have occasion for, we smart for the rebellion of our ancestors at Babel. Nay, and those unhappy controversies which are strifes of words, and arise from our misunderstanding one another's language, for aught I know are owing to this confusion of tongues. (4.) The project of some to frame a universal character, in order to a universal language, how desirable soever it may seem, is yet, I think, but a vain thing to attempt; for it is to strive against a divine sentence, by which the languages of the nations will be divided while the world stands. (5.) We may here lament the loss of the universal use of the Hebrew tongue, which from this time was the vulgar language of the Hebrews only, and continued so till the captivity in Babylon, where, even among them, it was exchanged for the Syriac. (6.) As the confounding of tongues divided the children of men and scattered them abroad, so the gift of tongues, bestowed upon the apostles (Acts 2), contributed greatly to the gathering together of the children of God, who were scattered abroad, and the uniting of them in Christ, that with one mind and one mouth they might glorify God, Rom. 15:6.

2. Their building was stopped: *They left off to build the city.* This was the effect of the confusion of their tongues; for it not only incapacitated them for helping one another, but probably struck such a damp upon their spirits that they could not proceed, since they saw, in this, the hand of the Lord gone out against them. Note, (1.) It is wisdom to leave off that which we see God fights against. (2.) God is ale to blast and bring to nought all the devices and designs of Babel-builders. He sits in heaven, and laughs at the counsels of the kings of the earth against him and his anointed; and will force them to confess that there is no wisdom nor counsel against the Lord, Prov. 21:30; Isa. 8:9, 10.

3. The builders were scattered abroad upon the face of the whole earth, *v.* 8, 9. They departed in companies, after their families, and after their tongues (*ch.* 10:5, 30, 31), to the several countries and places allotted to them in the division that had been made, which they knew before, but would not go to take possession of till now that they were forced to it. Observe here, (1.) The very thing which they feared came upon them. That dispersion which sought to evade by an act of rebellion they by this act brought upon themselves; for we are most likely to fall into that trouble which we seek to evade by indirect and sinful methods. (2.) It was God's work: *The Lord scattered them.* God's hand is to be acknowledged in all scattering providences; if the family be scattered, relations scattered, churches scattered, it is the Lord's doing. (3.) Though they were as firmly in league with one another as could be, yet the Lord scattered them; for no man can keep together what God will put asunder. (4.) Thus God justly took vengeance on them for their oneness in that presumptuous attempt to build their tower. Shameful dispersions are the just punishment of sinful unions. Simeon and Levi, who had been brethren in iniquity, were divided in Jacob, *ch.* 49:5,7; Ps. 83:3–13. (5.) They left behind them a perpetual memorandum of their reproach, in the name given to the place. It was called *Babel, confusion.* Those that aim at a great name commonly come off with a *bad* name. (6.) The children of men were now finally scattered, and never did, nor ever will, come all together again, till the great day, when the Son of man shall sit upon the throne of his glory, and all nations shall be gathered before him, Mt. 25:31, 32.

Verses 10–26

We have here a genealogy, not an endless genealogy, for here it ends in Abram, the friend of God, and leads further to Christ, the promised seed, who was the son of Abram, and from Abram the genealogy of Christ is reckoned (Mt. 1:1, etc.); so that put *ch.* 5, *ch.* 11, and Mt. 1, together, and you have such an entire genealogy of Jesus Christ as cannot be produced, for aught I know, concerning any person in the world, out of his line, and at such a distance from the fountain-head. And, laying these three genealogies together, we shall find that twice ten, and thrice fourteen, generations or descents, passed between the first and second Adam, making it clear concerning Christ that he was not only the Son of Abraham, but the Son of man, and the seed of woman. Observe here, 1. Nothing is left upon record concerning those of this line but their names and ages, the Holy Ghost seeming to hasten through them to the story of Abram. How little do we know of those that have gone before us in this world, even those that lived in the same places where we live, as we likewise know little of those that are our contemporaries in distant places! we have enough to do to mind the work of our own day, and let God alone to *require that which is past,* Eccl. 3:15. 2. There was an observable gradual decrease in the years of their lives. Shem reached to 600 years, which yet fell short of the age of the patriarchs before the flood; the next three came short of 500; the next three did not reach to 300; after them we read not of any that attained to 200, except Terah; and, not many ages after this, Moses reckoned seventy, or eighty, to be the utmost men ordinarily arrive at. When the earth began to be replenished, men's lives began to shorten; so that the decrease is to be imputed to the wise disposal of Providence, rather than to any decay of nature. For the elect's sake, men's days are shortened; and, being evil, it is well they are few, and *attain not to the years of the lives of our fathers, ch.* 47:9. 3. Eber, from whom the Hebrews were denominated, was the longest-lived of any that was born after the flood, which perhaps was the reward of his singular piety and strict adherence to the ways of God.

Verses 27–32

Here begins the story of Abram, whose name is famous, henceforward, in both Testaments. We have here,

I. His country: *Ur of the Chaldees.* This was the land of his nativity, an idolatrous country, where even the children of Eber themselves had degenerated. Note, Those who are, through grace, heirs of the land of promise, ought to remember what was the land of their nativity, what was their corrupt and sinful state by nature, the rock out of which they were hewn.

II. His relations, mentioned for his sake, and because of their interest in the following story. 1. His father was *Terah,* of whom it is said (Jos. 24:2) that he served other gods, on the other side of the flood, so early did idolatry gain footing in the world, and so hard is it even for those that have some good principles to swim against the stream. Though it is said (*v.* 26) that when Terah was seventy years old he begat Abram, Nahor, and Haran (which seems to tell us that Abram was the eldest son of Terah, and was born in his seventieth year), yet, by comparing *v.* 32, which makes Terah to die in his 205*th* year, with Acts 7:4 (where it is said that he was but seventy-five years old when he removed from Haran), it appears that he was born in the 130*th* year of Terah, and probably was his youngest son; for, in God's choices, the last are often first and the first last. We have, 2. Some account of his brethren. (1.) *Nahor,* out of whose family both Isaac and Jacob had their wives. (2.) *Haran,* the father of Lot, of whom it is here said (*v.* 28) *that he died before his father Terah.* Note, Children cannot be sure that they shall survive their parents; for death does not go by seniority, taking the eldest first. *The shadow of death is without any order,* Job 10:22. It is likewise said that he died *in Ur of the Chaldees,* before the happy removal of the family out of that idolatrous country. Note, It concerns us to hasten out of our natural state, lest death surprise us in it. 3. His wife was *Sarai,* who some think, was the same with Iscah, the daughter of Haran. Abram himself says of her that she was the daughter of his father, but not the daughter of his mother, *ch.* 20:12. She was ten years younger than Abram.

III. His departure out of Ur of the Chaldees, with his father Terah, his nephew Lot, and the rest of his family, in obedience to the call of God, of which we shall read more, *ch.* 12:1, etc. This chapter leaves them in Haran, or Charran, a place about mid-way between Ur and Canaan, where they dwelt till Terah's head was laid, probably because the old man was unable, through the infirmities of age, to proceed in his journey. Many reach to Charran, and yet fall short of Canaan; they are not far from the kingdom of God, and yet never come thither.

CHAPTER 12

The pedigree and family of Abram we had an account of in the foregoing chapter; here the Holy Ghost enters upon his story, and henceforward Abram and his seed are almost the only subject of the sacred history. In this chapter we have, I. God's call of Abram to the land of Canaan (*v.* 1–3). II. Abram's obedience to this call (*v.* 4, 5). III. His welcome to the land of Canaan (*v.* 6–9). IV. His journey to Egypt, with an account of what happened to him there. Abram's flight and fault (*v.* 10–13). Sarai's danger and deliverance (*v.* 14–20).

Verses 1–3

We have here the call by which Abram was removed out of the land of his nativity into the land of promise, which was designed both to try his faith and obedience and also to separate him and set him apart for God, and for special services and favours which were further designed. The circumstances of this call we may be somewhat helped to the knowledge of from Stephen's speech, Acts 7:2, where we are told, 1. That the God of glory appeared to him to give him this call, appeared in such displays of his glory as left Abram no room to doubt the divine authority of this call. God spoke to him afterwards in divers manners; but this first time, when the correspondence was to be settled, he appeared to him as *the God of glory,* and spoke to him. 2. That this call was given him in Mesopotamia, before he dwelt in Charran; therefore we rightly read it, *The Lord.* had *said unto Abram,* namely, in Ur of the Chaldees; and, in obedience to this call, as Stephen further relates the story (Acts 7:4), *he came out of the land of the Chaldeans, and dwelt in Charran, or Haran, about five years, and thence, when his father was dead,* by a fresh command, pursuant to the former, God removed him into the land of Canaan. some think that Haran was in Chaldea, and so was still a part of Abram's country, or that Abram, having staid there five years, began to call it his country, and to take root there, till God let him know this was not the place he was intended for. Note: If God loves us, and has mercy in store for us, he will not suffer us to take up our rest any where short of Canaan, but will graciously repeat his calls, till the good work begun be performed, and our souls repose in God only. In the call itself we have a precept and a promise.

I. A trying precept: *Get thee out of thy country, v.* 1. Now,

1. By this precept he was tried whether he loved his native soil and dearest friends, and whether he could willingly leave all, to go along with God. His country had become idolatrous, his kindred and his father's house were a constant temptation to him, and he could not continue with them without danger of being infected by them; therefore *Get thee out, lk-lk — Vade tibi, Get thee gone,* with all speed, *escape for thy life, look not behind thee, ch.* 19:17. Note, Those that are in a sinful state are concerned to make all possible haste out of it. *Get out for thyself* (so some read it), that is, for thy own good. Note, Those who leave their sins, and turn to God, will themselves be unspeakable gainers by the change, Prov. 9:12. This command which God gave to Abram is much the same with the gospel call by which all the spiritual seed of faithful Abram are brought into covenant with God. For, (1.) Natural affection must give way to divine grace. Our country is dear to us, our kindred dearer, and our father's house dearest of all; and yet they must all be hated (Lu. 14:26), that is, we must love them less than Christ, hate them in comparison with him, and, whenever any of these come in competition with him, they must be postponed, and the preference given to the will and honour of the Lord Jesus. (2.) Sin, and all the occasions of it, must be forsaken, and particularly bad company; we must abandon all the idols of iniquity which have been set up in our hearts, and get out of the way of temptation, plucking out even a right eye that leads us to sin (Mt. 5:29), willingly parting with that which is dearest to us, when we cannot keep it without hazard of our integrity. Those that resolve to keep the commandments of God must quit the society of evil doers, Ps. 119:115; Acts 2:40. (3.) The world, and all our enjoyments in it, must be looked upon with a holy indifference and contempt; we must no longer look upon it as our country, or home, but as our inn, and must accordingly sit loose to it and live above it, get out of it in affection.

2. By this precept he was tried whether he could trust God further than he saw him; for he must leave his own country, to go to a *land that God would show him.* He does not say, "It is a land that I will give thee," but merely, "a land that I will show thee." Nor does he tell him what land it was, nor what kind of land; but he must follow God with an implicit faith, and take God's word for it, in the general, though he had no particular securities given him that he should be no loser by leaving his country, to follow God. Note, Those that will deal with God must deal upon trust; we must quit the things that are seen for things that are not seen, and submit to the sufferings of this present time in hopes of a glory that is yet to be revealed (Rom. 8:18); for *it doth not yet appear what we shall be* (1 John iii. 2), any more than it did to Abram, when God called him to a land he would show him, so teaching him to live in a continual dependence upon his direction, and with his eye ever towards him.

II. Here is an encouraging promise, nay, it is a complication of promises, many, and exceedingly great and precious. Note, All God's precepts are attended with promises to the obedient. When he makes himself known also as a rewarder: if we obey the command, God will not fail to perform the promise. Here are six promises: —

1. *I will make of thee a great nation.* When God took him from his own people, he promised to make him the head of another; he cut him off from being the branch of a wild olive, to make him the root of a good olive. This promise was, (1.) A great relief to Abram's burden; for he had now no child. Note, God knows how to suit his favours to the wants and necessities of his children. He that has a plaster for every sore will provide one for that first which is most painful. (2.) A great trial to Abram's faith; for his wife had been long barren, so that, if he believe, it must be against hope, and his faith must build purely upon that power which *can out of stones raise up children unto Abraham,* and make them a great nation. Note, [1.] God makes nations: by him they are *born at once* (Isa. 66:8), and he speaks to build and plant them, Jer. 18:9. And, [2.] If a nation be made great in wealth and power, it is God that makes it great. [3.] God can raise great nations out of dry ground, and can make *a little one to be a thousand.*

2. *I will bless thee,* either particularly with the blessing of fruitfulness and increase, as he had blessed Adam and Noah, or, in general, *"I will bless thee* with all manner of blessings, both of the upper and the nether springs. Leave thy father's house, and I will give thee a father's blessing, better than that of they progenitors." Note, Obedient believers will be sure to inherit the blessing.

3. *I will make thy name great.* By deserting his country, he lost his name there. "Care not for that," says God, "but trust me, and I will make thee a greater name than ever thou couldst have had there." Having no child, he feared he should have no name; but God will make him a great nation, and so make him a great name. Note, (1.) God is the fountain of honour, and from him promotion comes, 1 Sa. 2:8. (2.) The name of obedient believers shall certainly be celebrated and made great. The best report is that which the elders obtained by faith, Heb. 11:2.

4. *Thou shalt be a blessing;* that is, (1.) "Thy happiness shall be a sample of happiness, so that those who would bless their friends shall only pray that God would make them like Abram;" as Ruth 4:11. Note, God's dealings with obedient believers are so kind and gracious that we need not desire for ourselves or our friends to be any better dealt with: to have God for our friend is blessedness enough. (2.) "Thy life shall be a blessing to the places where thou shalt sojourn." Note, Good men are the blessings of their country, and it is their unspeakable honour and happiness to be made so.

5. *I will bless those that bless thee and curse him that curseth thee.* This made it a kind of a league, offensive and defensive, between God and Abram. Abram heartily espoused God's cause, and here God promises to interest himself in his. (1.) He promises to be a friend to his friends, to take kindnesses shown to him as done to himself, and to recompense them accordingly. God will take care that none be losers, in the long run, by any service done for his people; even a cup of cold water shall be rewarded. (2.) He promises to appear against his enemies. There were those that hated and cursed even Abram himself; but, while their causeless curses could not hurt Abram, God's righteous curse would certainly overtake and ruin them, Num. 24:9. This is a good reason why we should bless those that curse us, because it is enough that God *will curse them,* Ps. 38:13–15.

6. *In thee shall all the families of the earth be blessed.* This was the promise that crowned all the rest; for it points at the Messiah, in whom *all the promises are yea and amen.* Note, (1.) Jesus Christ is the great blessing of the world, the greatest that ever the world was blessed with. He is a family blessing, by him salvation is brought to the house (Lu. 19:9); when we reckon up our family blessings, let us put Christ in the *imprimis — the first place,* as the blessing of blessings. But how are all the families of the earth blessed in Christ, when so many are strangers to him? *Answer,* [1.] All that are blessed are blessed in him, Acts 4:12 [2.] All that believe, of what family soever they shall be, shall be blessed in him. [3.] Some of all the families of the earth are blessed in him. [4.] There are some blessings which all the families of the earth are blessed with in Christ; for the gospel salvation is a *common salvation,* Jude 3. (2.) It is a great honour to be related to Christ; this made Abram's name great, that the Messiah was to descend from his loins, much more than that he should be the father of many nations. It was Abram's honour to be his father by nature; it will be ours to be his brethren by grace, Mt. 12:50.

Verses 4–5

Here is, I. Abraham's removal out of his country, out of Ur first and afterwards out of Haran, in compliance with the call of God: *So Abram departed;* he was not disobedient to the heavenly vision, but did as he was bidden, not conferring with flesh and blood, Gal. 1:15, 16. His obedience was speedy and without delay, submissive and without dispute; for he *went out, not knowing whither he went* (Heb. 11:8), but knowing whom he followed and under whose direction he went. Thus God *called him to his foot,* Isa. 41:2.

II. His age when he removed: he was *seventy-five years old,* an age when he should rather have had rest and settlement; but, if God will have him to begin the world again now in his old age, he will submit. Here is an instance of an old convert.

III. The company and cargo that he took with him.

1. He took his wife, and his nephew Lot, with him; not by force and against their wills, but by persuasion. Sarai, his wife, would be sure to go with him; God had joined them together, and nothing should put them asunder. If Abram leave all, to follow God, Sarai will leave all, to follow Abram, though neither of them knew whither. And it was a mercy to Abram to have such a companion in his travels, a help meet for him. Note, It is very comfortable when husband and wife agree to go together in the way to heaven. Lot also, his kinsman, was influenced by Abram's good example, who was perhaps his guardian after the death of his father, and he was willing to go along with him too. Note, Those that go to Canaan need not go alone, for, though few find the strait gate, blessed be God, some do; and it is our wisdom to go with those with whom God is (Zec. 8:23), wherever they go.

2. They took all their effects with them — *all their substance* and movable goods, *that they had gathered.* For, (1.) With themselves they would give up their all, to be at God's disposal, would keep back no part of the price, but venture all in one bottom, knowing it was a good bottom. (2.) They would furnish themselves with that which was requisite, both for the service of God and the supply of their family, in the country whither they were going. To have thrown away his substance, because God had promised to bless him, would have been to tempt God, not to trust him. (3.) They would not be under any temptation to return; therefore they leave not a hoof behind, lest that should make them *mindful of the country from which they came out.*

3. They took with them the *souls that they had gotten,* that is, (1.) The servants they had bought, which were part of their substance, but are called *souls,* to remind masters that their poor servants have souls, precious souls, which they ought to take care of and provide food convenient for. (2.) The proselytes they had made, and persuaded to attend the worship of the true God, and to go with them to Canaan: the souls which (as one of the rabbin expresses it) they had *gathered under the wings of the divine Majesty.* Note, Those who serve and follow God themselves should do all they can to bring others to serve and follow him too. These souls they are said to have *gained.* We must reckon ourselves true gainers if we can but win souls to Christ.

IV. Here is their happy arrival at their journey's end: *They went forth to go into the land of Canaan;* so they did before (*ch.* 11:31), and then took up short, but now they held on their way, and, by the good hand of their God upon them, to the land of Canaan they came, where by a fresh revelation they were told that this was the land God promised to show them. They were not discouraged by the difficulties they met with in their way, nor diverted by the delights they met with, but *pressed forward.* Note, 1. Those that set out for heaven must persevere to the end, still reaching forth to those things that are before. 2. That which we undertake in obedience to God's command, and a humble attendance upon his providence, will certainly succeed, and end with comfort at last.

Verses 6–9

One would have expected that Abram having had such an extraordinary call to Canaan some great event should have followed upon his arrival there, that he would have been introduced with all possible marks of honour and respect, and that the kings of Canaan should immediately have surrendered their crowns to him, and done him homage. But no; he comes not with observation, little notice is taken of him, for still God will have him to live by faith, and to look upon Canaan, even when he was in it, as a land of promise; therefore observe here,

I. How little comfort he had in the land he came to; for, 1. He had it not to himself: *The Canaanite was then in the land.* He found the country peopled and possessed by Canaanites, who were likely to be but bad neighbours and worse landlords; and, for aught that appears, he could not have ground to pitch his tent on but by their permission. Thus the accursed Canaanites seemed to be in better circumstances than blessed Abram. Note, The children of this world have commonly more of it than God's children. 2. He had not a settlement in it. He *passed through the land, v.* 6. He *removed to a mountain, v.* 8. He *journeyed, going on still, v.* 9. Observe here, (1.) Sometimes it is the lot of good men to be unsettled, and obliged often to remove their habitation. Holy David had his wanderings, his flittings, Ps. 56:8. (2.) Our removes in this world are often into various conditions. Abram sojourned, first in a plain (*v.* 6), then in a mountain, *v.* 8. God has set the one over-against the other. (3.) All good people must look upon themselves as strangers and sojourners in this world, and by faith sit loose to it as a strange country. So Abram did, Heb. 11:8–14. (4.) While we are here in this present state, we must be journeying, and going on still from strength to strength, as having not yet attained.

II. How much comfort he had in the God he followed; when he could have little satisfaction in converse with the Canaanites whom he found there, he had abundance of pleasure in communion with that God who brought him thither, and did not leave him. Communion with God is kept up by the word and by prayer, and by these, according to the methods of that dispensation, Abram's communion with God was kept up in the land of his pilgrimage.

1. God appeared to Abram, probably in a vision, and spoke to him good words and comfortable words: *Unto thy seed will I give this land.* Note, (1.) No place nor condition of life can shut us out from the comfort of God's gracious visits. Abram is a sojourner, unsettled among Canaanites; and yet here also he meets with him that lives and sees him. Enemies may part us and our tents, us and our altars, but not us and our God. Nay, (2.) With respect to those that faithfully follow God in a way of duty, though he lead them from their friends, he will himself make up that loss by his gracious appearances to them. (3.) God's promises are sure and satisfying to all those who conscientiously observe and obey his precepts; and those who, in compliance with God's call, leave or lose any thing that is dear to them, shall be sure of something else abundantly better in lieu of it. Abram had left the *land of his nativity:* "Well," says God, "I will give thee this land," Mt. 19:29. (4.) God reveals himself and his favours to his people by degrees; before he had promised to *show* him this land, now to *give* it to him: as grace is growing, so is comfort. (5.) It is comfortable to have land of God's giving, not by providence only, but by promise. (6.) Mercies to the children are mercies to the parents. "I will give it, not to thee, but to thy seed;" it is a grant in reversion to his seed, which yet, it should seem, Abram understood also as a grant to himself of a better land in reversion, of which this was a type; for he looked for a heavenly country, Heb. 11:16.

2. Abram attended on God in his instituted ordinances. He *built an altar unto the Lord who appeared to him, and called on the name of the Lord, v.* 7, 8. Now consider this, (1.) As done upon a special occasion. When God appeared to him, then and there he built an altar, with an eye to the God who appeared to him. Thus he returned God's visit, and kept up his correspondence with heaven, as one that resolved it should not fail on his side; thus he acknowledged, with thankfulness, God's kindness to him in making him that gracious visit and promise; and thus he testified his confidence in and dependence upon the word which God had spoken. Note, An active believer can heartily bless God for a promise the performance of which he does not yet see, and build an altar to the honour of God who appears to him, though he does not yet appear for him. (2.) As his constant practice, whithersoever he removed. As soon as Abram had got to Canaan, though he was but a stranger and sojourner there, yet he set up, and kept up, the worship of God in his family; and wherever he had a tent God had an altar, and that an altar sanctified by prayer. For he not only minded the ceremonial part of religion, the offering of sacrifice, but made conscience of the natural duty of seeking to his God, and calling on his name, that spiritual sacrifice with which God is well pleased. He preached concerning the name of the Lord, that is, he instructed his family and neighbours in the knowledge of the true God and his holy religion. The *souls he had gotten in Haran,* being discipled, must be further taught. Note, Those that would approve themselves the children of faithful Abram, and would inherit the blessing of Abram, must make conscience of keeping up the solemn worship of God, particularly in their families, according to the example of Abram. The way of family worship is a good old way, is no novel invention, but the ancient usage of all the saints. Abram was very rich and had a numerous family, was now unsettled and in the midst of enemies, and yet, wherever he pitched his tent, he built an altar. Wherever we go, let us not fail to take our religion along with us.

Verses 10–13

Here is, I. A famine in the land of Canaan, *a grievous famine.* That fruitful land was turned into barrenness, not only to punish the iniquity of the Canaanites who dwelt therein, but to exercise the faith of Abram who sojourned therein; and a very sore trial it was; it tried what he would think, 1. Of God that brought him thither, whether he would not be ready to say with his murmuring seed that he was brought forth to be *killed with hunger,* Ex. 16:3. Nothing short of a strong faith could keep up god thoughts of God under such a providence. 2. Of the land of promise, whether he would think the grant of it worth the accepting, and a valuable consideration for the relinquishing of his own country, when, for aught that now appeared, it was a land that *ate up the inhabitants.* Now he was tried whether he could preserve an unshaken confidence that the God who brought him to Canaan would maintain him there, and whether he could rejoice in him as the God of his salvation when the fig-tree did not blossom, Hab. 3:17, 18. Note, (1.) Strong faith is commonly exercised with divers temptations, that it may be *found to praise, and honour, and glory,* 1 Pt. 1:6, 7. (2.) It pleases God sometimes to try those with great afflictions who are but young beginners in religion. (3.) It is possible for a man to be in the way of duty, and in the way to happiness, and yet meet with great troubles and disappointments.

II. Abram's removal into Egypt, upon occasion of this famine. See how wisely God provides that there should be plenty in one place when there was scarcity in another, that, as members of the great body, we may not say to one another, *I have no need of you.* God's providence took care there should be a supply in Egypt, and Abram's prudence made use of the opportunity; for we tempt God, and do not trust him, if, in the time of distress, we use not the means he has graciously provided for our preservation: We must not expect needless miracles. But that which is especially observable here, to the praise of Abram, is that he did not offer to return, upon this occasion, to the country from which he came out, nor so much as towards it. The land of his nativity lay north-east from Canaan; and therefore, when he must, for a time, quit Canaan, he chooses to go to Egypt, which lay south-west, the contrary way, that he might not so much as seem to look back. See Heb. 11:15, 16. Further observe, When he went down into Egypt, it was to sojourn there, not to dwell there. Note, 1. Though Providence, for a time, may cast us into bad places, yet we ought to tarry there no longer than needs must; we may *sojourn* where we may not *settle.* 2. A good man, while he is on this side heaven, wherever he is, is but a sojourner.

III. A great fault which Abram was guilty of, in denying his wife, and pretending that she was his sister. The scripture is impartial in relating the misdeeds of the most celebrated saints, which are recorded, not for our imitation, but for our admonition, that he *who thinks he stands may take heed lest he fall.* 1. His fault was dissembling his relation to Sarai, equivocating concerning it, and teaching his wife, and probably all his attendants, to do so too. What he said was, in a sense, true (*ch.* 20:12), but with a purpose to deceive; he so concealed a further truth as in effect to deny it, and to expose thereby both his wife and the Egyptians to sin. 2. That which was at the bottom of it was a jealous timorous fancy he had that some of the Egyptians would be so charmed with the beauty of Sarai (Egypt producing few such beauties) that, if they should know he was her husband, they would find some way or other to take him off, that they might marry her. He presumes they would rather be guilty of murder than adultery, such a heinous crime was it then accounted and such a sacred regard was paid to the marriage bond; hence he infers, without any good reason, *They will kill me.* Note, The fear of man brings a snare, and many are driven to sin by the dread of death, Lu. 12:4, 5. The grace Abram was most eminent for was faith; and yet he thus fell through unbelief and distrust of the divine Providence, even *after God had appeared to him twice.* Alas! what will become of the willows, when the cedars are thus shaken?

Verses 14–20

Here is, I. The danger Sarai was in of having her chastity violated by the king of Egypt: and without doubt the peril of sin is the greatest peril we can be in. *Pharaoh's princes* (his pimps rather) *saw her, and,* observing what a comely woman she was, they *commended her before Pharaoh,* not for that which was really her praise — her virtue and modesty, her faith and piety (these were no excellencies in their eyes), but for her beauty, which they thought too good for the embraces of a subject. They recommended her to the king, and she was presently taken into Pharaoh's house, as Esther into the seraglio of Ahasuerus (Esth. 2:8), in order to her being taken into his bed. Now we must not look upon Sarai as standing fair for preferment, but as entering into temptation; and the occasions of it were her own beauty (which is a snare to many) and Abram's equivocation, which is a sin that commonly is an inlet to much sin. While Sarai was in this danger, Abram fared the better for her sake. Pharaoh gave him sheep, oxen, etc. (*v.* 16), to gain his consent, that he might the more readily prevail with her whom he supposed to be his sister. We cannot think that Abram expected this when he came down into Egypt, much less that he had an eye to it when he denied his wife; but God brought good out of evil. And thus the wealth of the sinner proves, in some way or other, to be laid up for the just.

II. The deliverance of Sarai from this danger. For if God did not deliver us, many a time, by prerogative, out of those straits and distresses which we bring ourselves into by our own sin and folly, and which therefore we could not expect any deliverance from by promise, we should soon be ruined, nay, we should have been ruined long before this. He deals not with us according to our deserts.

1. God chastised Pharaoh, and so prevented the progress of his sin. Note, Those are happy chastisements that hinder us in a sinful way, and effectually bring us to our duty, and particularly to the duty of restoring that which we have wrongfully taken and detained. Observe, Not Pharaoh only, but his house, was plagued, probably those princes especially that had commended Sarai to Pharaoh. Note, Partners in sin are justly made partners in the punishment. Those that serve others' lusts must expect to share in their plagues. We are not told particularly what these plagues were; but doubtless there was something in the plagues themselves, or some explication added to them, sufficient to convince them that it was for Sarai's sake that they were thus plagued.

2. Pharaoh reproved Abram, and then dismissed him with respect.

(1.) The reproof was calm, but very just: *What is this that thou hast done?* What an improper thing! How unbecoming a wise and good man! Note, If those that profess religion do that which is unfair and disingenuous, especially if they say that which borders upon a lie, they must expect to hear of it, and have reason to thank those that will tell them of it. We find a prophet of the Lord justly reproved and upbraided by a heathen ship-master, Jon. 1:6. Pharaoh reasons with him: *Why didst thou not tell me that she was thy wife?* intimating that, if he had known this, he would not have taken her into his house. Note, It is a fault too common among good people to entertain suspicions of others beyond what there is cause for. We have often found more of virtue, honour, and conscience, in some people than we thought they possessed; and it ought to be a pleasure to us to be thus disappointed, as Abram was here, who found Pharaoh to be a better man than he expected. Charity teaches us to hope the best.

(2.) The dismission was kind and very generous. He restored him his wife without offering any injury to her honour: *Behold thy wife, take her, v.* 19. Note, Those that would prevent sin must remove the temptation, or get out of the way of it. He also sent him away in peace, and was so far from any design to kill him, as he apprehended, that he took particular care of him. Note, We often perplex and ensnare ourselves with fears which soon appear to have been altogether groundless. We often fear where no fear is. We fear the *fury of the oppressor, as though he were ready to destroy,* when really there is no danger, Isa. 51:13. It would have been more for Abram's credit and comfort to have told the truth at first; for, after all, *honesty is the best policy.* Nay, it is said (*v.* 20), *Pharaoh commanded his men concerning him,* that is, [1.] He charged them not to injure him in any thing. Note, It is not enough for those in authority to do no hurt themselves, but they must restrain their servants, and those about them, from doing hurt. Or, [2.] He appointed them, when Abram was disposed to return home after the famine, to conduct him safely out of the country, as his convoy. Probably he was alarmed by the plagues (*v.* 17), and inferred from them that Abram was a particular favourite of Heaven, and therefore, through fear of their return, took special care he should receive no injury in his country. Note, God has often raised up friends for his people, by making men know that it is at their peril if they hurt them. It is a dangerous thing to offend Christ's little ones. Mt. 18:6. To this passage, among others, the Psalmist refers, Ps. 105:13–15, *He reproved kings for their sakes, saying Touch not my anointed.* Perhaps if Pharaoh had not *sent him away,* he would have been tempted to stay in Egypt and to forget the land of promise. Note, Sometimes God makes use of the enemies of his people to convince them, and remind them, that this world is not their rest, but that they must think of departing.

Lastly, Observe a resemblance between this deliverance of Abram out of Egypt and the deliverance of his seed thence: 430 years after Abram went into Egypt on occasion of a famine they went thither on occasion of a famine also; he was fetched out with great plagues on Pharaoh, so were they; as Abram was dismissed by Pharaoh, and enriched with the spoil of the Egyptians, so were they. For God's care of his people is the same *yesterday, to-day, and for ever.*

CHAPTER 13

In this chapter we have a further account concerning Abram. I. In general, of his condition and behaviour in the land of promise, which was now the land of his pilgrimage. 1. His removes (*v.* 1, 3, 4, 18). 2. His riches (*v.* 2). 3. His devotion (*v.* 4, 18). II. A particular account of a quarrel that happened between him and Lot. 1. The unhappy occasion of their strife (*v.* 5, 6). 2. The parties concerned in the strife, with the aggravation of it (*v.* 7). III. The making up of the quarrel, by the prudence of Abram (*v.* 8, 9). IV. Lot's departure from Abram to the plain of Sodom (*v.* 10–13). V. God's appearance to Abram, to confirm the promise of the land of Canaan to him (*v.* 14, etc.).

Verses 1–4

I. Here is Abram's return out of Egypt, *v.* 1. He came himself and brought all his with him back again to Canaan. Note, Though there may be occasion to go sometimes into places of temptation, yet we must hasten out of them as soon as possible. See Ruth 1:6.

II. His wealth: *He was very rich, v.* 2. He was very *heavy,* so the Hebrew word signifies; for *riches are a burden,* and those that *will be rich do but load themselves with thick clay,* Hab. 2:6. There is a burden of care in getting them, fear in keeping them, temptation in using them, guilt in abusing them, sorrow in losing them, and a burden of account, at last, to be given up concerning them. Great possessions do but make men heavy and unwieldy. Abram was not only rich in faith and good works, and in the promises, but he was *rich in cattle, and in silver and gold.* Note, 1. God, in his providence, sometimes makes good men rich men, and teaches them how to abound, as well as how to suffer want. 2. The riches of good men are the fruits of God's blessing. God has said to Abram, *I will bless thee;* and that blessing made him rich without sorrow, Prov. 10:22. 3. True piety will very well consist with great prosperity. Though it is hard for a rich man to get to heaven, yet it is not impossible, Mk. 10:23, 24. Abram was very rich and yet very religious. Nay, as piety is a friend to outward prosperity (1 Tim. 4:8), so outward prosperity, if well-managed, is an ornament to piety, and furnishes an opportunity of doing so much the more good.

III. His removal to Beth-el, *v.* 3, 4. Thither he went, not only because there he had formerly had his tent, and he was willing to go among his old acquaintance, but because there he had formerly had his altar: and, though the altar was gone (probably he himself having taken it down, when he left the place, lest it should be polluted by the idolatrous Canaanites), yet he *came to the place of the altar,* either to revive the remembrance of the sweet communion he had had with God in that place, or perhaps to pay the vows he had there made to God when he undertook his journey into Egypt. Long afterwards God sent Jacob to this same place on that errand (*ch.* 35:1), *Go up to Beth-el, where thou vowedst the vow.* We have need to be reminded, and should take all occasions to remind ourselves, of our solemn vows; and perhaps the place where they were made may help to bring them afresh to mind, and it may therefore do us good to visit it.

IV. His devotion there. His altar was gone, so that he could not offer sacrifice; but *he called on the name of the Lord,* as he had done, *ch.* 12:8. Note, 1. All God's people are praying people. You may as soon find a living man without breath as a living Christian without prayer. 2. Those that would approve themselves upright with their God must be constant and persevering in the services of religion. Abram did not leave his religion behind him in Egypt, as many do in their travels. 3. When we cannot do *what we would* we must make conscience of doing *what we can* in the acts of devotion. When we want an altar, let us not be wanting in prayer, but, wherever we are, call on the name of the Lord.

Verses 5–9

We have here an unhappy falling out between Abram and Lot, who had hitherto been inseparable companions (see *v.* 1, and *ch.* 12:4), but now parted.

I. The occasion of their quarrel was their riches. We read (*v.* 2) how rich Abram was; now here we are told (*v.* 5) that *Lot, who went with Abram,* was rich too; and therefore God blessed him with riches because he went with Abram. Note, 1. It is good being in good company, and going with those with whom God is, Zec. 8:23. 2. Those that are partners with God's people in their obedience and sufferings shall be sharers with them in their joys and comforts, Isa. 66:10. Now, they both being very rich, *the land was not able to bear them, that they might dwell* comfortably and peaceably together. So that their riches may be considered, (1.) As setting them at a distance one from another. Because the place was too strait for them, and they had not room for their stock, it was necessary they should live asunder. Note, Every comfort in this world has its cross attending it. Business is a comfort; but it has this inconvenience in it, that it allows us not the society of those we love, so often, nor so long, as we could wish. (2.) As setting them at variance one with another. Note, Riches are often an occasion of strife and contention among relations and neighbours. this is one of those *foolish and hurtful lusts which those that will be rich fall into,* 1 Tim. 6:9. Riches not only afford matter for contention, and are the things most commonly striven about, but they also stir up a spirit of contention, by making people proud and covetous. *Meum* and *tuum — Mine* and *thine,* are the great make-bates of the world. Poverty and travail, wants and wanderings, could not separate between Abram and Lot; but riches did. Friends are soon lost; but God is a friend from whose love neither the height of prosperity nor the depth of adversity shall separate us.

II. The immediate instruments of the quarrel were their servants. The strife began between *the herdsmen of Abram's cattle and the herdsmen of Lot's cattle, v.* 7. They strove, it is probable, which should have the better pasture or the better water; and both interested their masters in the quarrel. Note, Bad servants often make a great deal of mischief in families, by the pride and passion, their lying slandering, and tale-bearing. It is a very wicked thing for servants to do ill offices between relations and neighbours, and to sow discord; those that do so are the devil's agents and their masters' worst enemies.

III. The aggravation of the quarrel was that *the Canaanite and the Perizzite dwelt then in the land;* this made the quarrel, 1. Very dangerous. If Abram and Lot cannot agree to feed their flocks together, it is well if the common enemy do not come upon them and plunder them both. Note, The division of families and churches often proves the ruin of them. 2. Very scandalous. No doubt the eyes of all the neighbours were upon them, especially because of the singularity of their religion, and the extraordinary sanctity they professed; and notice would soon be taken of this quarrel, and improvement made of it, to their reproach, by the Canaanites and Perizzites. Note, The quarrels of professors are the reproach of profession, and give occasion, as much as any thing, to the enemies of the Lord to blaspheme.

IV. The making up of this quarrel was very happy. It is best to preserve the peace, that it be not broken; but the next best is, if differences do happen, with all speed to accommodate them, and quench the fire that has broken out. The motion for staying this strife was made by Abram, though he was the senior and superior relation, *v.* 8.

1. His petition for peace was very affectionate: *Let there be not strife, I pray thee.* Abram here shows himself to be a man, (1.) of a cool spirit, that had the command of his passion, and knew how to turn away wrath with a soft answer. Those that would keep the peace must never render railing for railing. (2.) Of a condescending spirit; he was willing to beseech even his inferior to be at peace, and made the first overture of reconciliation. Conquerors reckon it their glory to give peace by power; and it is no less so to give peace by the meekness of wisdom. Note, The people of God should always approve themselves a peaceable people; whatever others are for, they must be for peace.

2. His plea for peace was very cogent. (1.) "Let there be no strife *between me and thee.* Let the Canaanites and Perizzites contend about trifles; but let not thee and me fall out, who know better things, and look for a better country." Note, Professors of religion should, of all others, be careful to avoid contention. *You shall not be so,* Lu. 22:26. *We have no such custom,* 1 Co. 11:16. "Let there be no strife *between me and thee,* who have lived together and loved one another so long." Note, The remembrance of old friendships should quickly put an end to new quarrels which at any time happen. (2.) Let it be remembered that *we are brethren,* Heb. *we are men brethren;* a double argument. [1.] We are men; and, as men, we are mortal creatures — we may die to-morrow, and are concerned to be found in peace. We are rational creatures, and should be ruled by reason. We are men, and not brutes, men, and not children; we are sociable creatures, let us be so to the uttermost. [2.] We are brethren. Men of the same nature, of the same kindred and family, of the same religion, companions in obedience, companions in patience. Note, The consideration of our relation to each other, as brethren, should always prevail to moderate our passions, and either to prevent or put an end to our contentions. Brethren should love as brethren.

3. His proposal for peace was very fair. Many who profess to be for peace yet will do nothing towards it; but Abram hereby approved himself a real friend to peace that he proposed an unexceptionable expedient for the preserving of it: *Is not the whole land before thee? v.* 9. As if he had said, "Why should we quarrel for room, while there is room enough for us both?" (1.) He concludes that they must part, and is very desirous that they should part friends: *Separate thyself, I pray thee, from me.* What could be expressed more affectionately? He does not expel him, and force him away, but advises that he should separate himself. Nor does he charge him to depart, but humbly desires him to withdraw. Note, Those that have power to command, yet sometimes, for love's sake, and peace' sake, should rather beseech us, we may well afford to beseech one another, to *be reconciled,* 2 Co. 5:20. (2.) He offers him a sufficient share of the land they were in. Though God had promised Abram to give this land to his seed (*ch.* 12:7), and it does not appear that ever any such promise was made to Lot, which Abram might have insisted on, to the total exclusion of Lot, yet he allows him to come in partner with him, and tenders an equal share to one that had not an equal right, and will not make God's promise to patronise his quarrel, nor, under the protection of that, put any hardship on his kinsman. (3.) He give him his choice,

and offers to take up with his leavings: *If thou wilt take the left hand, I will go to the right.* There was all the reason in the world that Abram should choose first; yet he recedes from his right. Note, It is a noble conquest to be willing to yield for peace' sake; it is the conquest of ourselves, and our own pride and passion, Mt. 5:39, 40. It is not only the punctilios of honour, but even interest itself, that in many cases must be sacrificed to peace.

Verses 10–13

We have here the choice that Lot made when he parted from Abram. Upon this occasion, one would have expected, 1. That he should have expressed an unwillingness to part from Abram, and that, at least, he should have done it with reluctancy. 2. That he should have been so civil as to have remitted the choice back again to Abram. But we find not any instance of deference or respect to his uncle in the whole management. Abram having offered him the choice, without compliment he accepted it, and made his election. Passion and selfishness make men rude. Now, in the choice which Lot made, we may observe,

I. How much he had an eye to the goodness of the land. He *beheld all the plan of Jordan,* the flat country in which Sodom stood, that it was admirably *well watered every where* (and perhaps the strife had been about water, which made him particularly fond of that convenience), and so *Lot chose all that plain, v.* 10, 11. That valley, which was like the garden of Eden itself, now yielded him a most pleasant prospect. It was, in his eye, beautiful for situation, the joy of the whole earth; and therefore he doubted not but that it would yield him a comfortable settlement, and that in such a fruitful soil he should certainly thrive, and grow very rich: and this was all he looked at. But what came of it? Why, the next news we hear of him is that he is in the briars among them, he and his carried captive. While he lived among them, he vexed his righteous soul with their conversation, and never had a good day with them, till, at last, God fired the town over his head, and forced him to the mountain for safety who chose the plain for wealth and pleasure. Note, Sensual choices are sinful choices, and seldom speed well. Those who in choosing relations, callings, dwellings, or settlements are guided and governed by the lusts of the flesh, the lusts of the eye, or the pride of life, and consult not the interests of their souls and their religion, cannot expect God's presence with them, nor his blessing upon them, but are commonly disappointed even in that which they principally aimed at, and miss of that which they promised themselves satisfaction in. In all our choices this principle should overrule us, That that is best for us which is best for our souls.

II. How little he considered the wickedness of the inhabitants: *But the men of Sodom were wicked, v.* 13. Note, 1. Though all are sinners, yet some are greater sinners than others. The men of Sodom were sinners of the first magnitude, *sinners before the Lord,* that is, impudent daring sinners; they were so to a proverb. Hence we read of those that *declare their sin as Sodom, they hide it not,* Isa. 3:9. 2. That some sinners are the worse for living in a good land. So the Sodomites were: for this was the iniquity of Sodom, *pride, fulness of bread, and abundance of idleness;* and all these were supported by the great plenty their country afforded, Eze. 16:49. Thus *the prosperity of fools destroys them.* 3. That God often gives great plenty to great sinners. Filthy Sodomites dwell in a city, in a fruitful plain, while faithful Abram and his pious family dwell in tents upon the barren mountains. 4. When wickedness has come to the height, ruin is not far off. Abounding sins are sure presages of approaching judgments. Now Lot's coming to dwell among the Sodomites may be considered, (1.) As a great mercy to them, and a likely means of bringing them to repentance; for now they had a prophet among them and a preacher of righteousness, and, if they had hearkened to him, they might have been reformed, and the ruin prevented. Note, God sends preachers, before he sends destroyers; for he is not *willing that any should perish.* (2.) As a great affliction to Lot, who was not only grieved to see their wickedness (2 Pt. 2:7, 8), but was molested and persecuted by them, because he would not do as they did. Note, It has often been the vexatious lot of good men to live among wicked neighbours, to *sojourn in Mesech* (Ps. 120:5), and it cannot but be the more grievous, if, as Lot here, they have brought it upon themselves by an unadvised choice.

Verses 14–18

We have here an account of a gracious visit which God paid to Abram, to confirm the promise to him and his. Observe,

I. When it was that God renewed and ratified the promise: *After that Lot was separated from him,* that is, 1. After the quarrel was over; for those are best prepared for the visits of divine grace whose spirits are calm and sedate, and not ruffled with any passion. 2. After Abram's humble self-denying condescensions to Lot for the preserving of peace. It was then that God came to him with this token of his favour. Note, God will abundantly make up in spiritual peace what we lose for the preservation of neighbourly peace. When Abram had willingly offered Lot one-half of his right, God came, and confirmed the whole to him. 3. After he had lost the comfortable society of his kinsman, by whose departure his hands were weakened and his heart was saddened, then God came to him with these good words and comfortable words. Note, Communion with God may, at any time, serve to make up the want of conversation with our friends; when our relations are separated from us, yet God is not. 4. After Lot had chosen that pleasant fruitful vale, and had gone to take possession of it, lest Abram should be tempted to envy him and to repent that he had given him the choice, God comes to him, and assures him that what he had should remain to him and *his heirs for ever;* so that, though Lot perhaps had the better land, yet Abram had the better *title.* Lot had the paradise, such as it was, but Abram had the promise; and the event soon made it appear that, however it seemed now, Abram had really the better part. See Job 22:20. God owned Abram after his strife with Lot, as the churches owned Paul after his strife with Barnabas, Acts 15:39, 40.

II. The promises themselves with which God now comforted and enriched Abram. Two things he assures him of — a good land, and a numerous issue to enjoy it.

1. Here is the grant of a good land, a land famous above all lands, for it was to be the holy land, and Immanuel's land; this is the land here spoken of. (1.) God here shows Abram the land, as he had promised (*ch.* 12:1), and afterwards he showed it to Moses from the top of Pisgah. *Lot had lifted up his eyes and beheld the plain of Jordan* (*v.* 10), and he had gone to enjoy what he saw: "Come," says God to Abram, *"now lift thou up thy eyes, and look, and see thy own."* Note, That which God has to show us is infinitely better and more desirable than any thing that the world has to offer our view. The prospects of an eye of faith are much more rich and beautiful than those of an eye of sense. Those for whom the heavenly Canaan is designed in the other world have sometimes, by faith, a comfortable prospect of it in their present state; for we look at the *things that are not seen,* as real, though distant. (2.) He secures this land to him and his seed for ever (*v.* 15): *To thee will I give it;* and again (*v.* 17) *I will give it unto thee;* every repetition of the promise is a ratification of it. *To thee and thy seed,* not to Lot and his seed; they were not to have their inheritance in this land, and therefore Providence so ordered it that Lot should be separated from Abram first, and then the grant should be confirmed to him and his seed. Thus God often brings good out of evil, and makes men's sins and follies subservient to his own wise and holy counsels. *To thee and thy seed* — to thee to sojourn in as a stranger, to thy seed to dwell and rule in as proprietors. *To thee,* that is, *to thy seed.* The granting of it to him and his for ever intimates that it was typical of the heavenly Canaan, which is given to the spiritual seed of Abram for ever, Heb. 11:14. (3.) He gives him livery and seisin of it, though it was a reversion: *"Arise, walk through the land, v.* 17. Enter, and take possession, survey the parcels, and it will appear better than upon a distant prospect." Note, God is willing more abundantly to show to the heirs of promise the immutability of his covenant, and the inestimable worth of covenant blessings. *Go, walk about Sion,* Ps. 48:12.

2. Here is the promise of a numerous issue to replenish this good land, so that it should never be lost for want of heirs (*v.* 16): *I will make thy seed as the dust of the earth,* that is, "They shall increase incredibly, and, take them altogether, they shall be such a great multitude as no man can number." They were so in Solomon's time, 1 Ki. 4:20, *Judah and Israel were many as the sand which is by the sea in multitude.* This God here gives him the promise of. Note, The same God that provides the inheritance provides the heirs. He that has prepared the holy land prepares the holy seed; he that gives glory gives grace to make meet for glory.

Lastly, We are told what Abram did when God had thus confirmed the promise to him, *v.* 18. 1. He *removed his tent.* God bade him *walk through the land,* that is, "Do not think of fixing in it, but expect to be always unsettled, and walking through it to a better Canaan:" in compliance with God's will herein, *he removes his tent,* confirming himself to the condition of a pilgrim. 2. He *built there an altar,* in token of his thankfulness to God for the kind visit he had paid him. Note, When God meets us with gracious promises, he expects that we should attend him with our humble praises.

CHAPTER 14

We have four things in the story of this chapter. I. A war with the king of Sodom and his allies (*v.* 1–11). II. The captivity of Lot in that war (*v.* 12). III. Abram's rescue of Lot from that captivity, with the victory he obtained over the conquerors (*v.* 13–16). IV. Abram's return from the expedition (*v.* 17), with an account of what passed, 1. Between him and the king of Salem (*v.* 18–20). 2. Between him and the king of Sodom (*v.* 21–24). So that here we have that promise to Abram in part fulfilled, that God would make his name great.

Verses 1–12

We have here an account of the first war that ever we read of in scripture, which (though the wars of the nations make the greatest figure in history) we should not have had the history of if Abram and Lot had not been concerned in it. Now, concerning this war, we may observe,

I. The parties engaged in it. The invaders were four kings, two of them no less than kings of Shinar and Elam (that is, Chaldea and Persia), yet probably not the sovereign princes of those great kingdoms in their own persons, but either officers under them, or rather the heads and leaders of some colonies which came out of those great nations, and settled themselves near Sodom, but retained the names of the countries from which they had their origin. The invaded were the kings of five cities that lay near together in the plain of Jordan, namely, Sodom, Gomorrah, Admah, Zeboiim, and Zoar. Four of them are named, but not the fifth, the king of Zoar or Bela, either because he was much more mean and inconsiderable or because he was much more wicked and inglorious than the rest, and worthy to be forgotten.

II. The occasion of this war was the revolt of the five kings from under the government of Chedorlaomer. Twelve years they served him. Small joy they had of their fruitful land, while thus they were tributaries to a foreign power, and could not call what they had their own. Rich countries are a desirable prey, and idle luxurious countries are an easy prey, to growing greatness. The Sodomites were the posterity of Canaan whom Noah had pronounced a servant to Shem, from whom Elam descended; thus soon did that prophecy begin to e fulfilled. In the thirteenth year, beginning to be weary of their subjection, they rebelled, denied their tribute, and attempted to shake off the yoke and retrieve their ancient liberties. In the fourteenth year, after some pause and preparation, Chedorlaomer, in conjunction with his allies, set himself to chastise and reduce the rebels, and, since he could not have it otherwise, to fetch his tribute from them on the point of his sword. Note, Pride, covetousness, and ambition, are the lusts from which wars and fightings come. To these insatiable idols the blood of thousands has been sacrificed.

III. The progress and success of the war. The four kings laid the neighbouring countries waste and enriched themselves with the spoil of them (*v.* 5–7), upon the alarm of which it had been the wisdom of the king of Sodom to submit, and desire conditions of peace; for how could he grapple with an enemy thus flushed with victory? But he would rather venture the utmost extremity than yield, and it sped accordingly. *Quos Deus destruet eos dementat — Those whom God means to destroy he delivers up to infatuation.* 1. The forces of the king of Sodom and his allies were routed; and, it should seem, many of them perished in the slime-pits who had escaped the sword, *v.* 10.

In all places we are surrounded with deaths of various kinds, especially in the field of battle. 2. The cities were plundered, *v.* 11. All the goods of Sodom, and particularly their stores and provisions of victuals, were carried off by the conquerors. Note, When men abuse the gifts of a bountiful providence to gluttony and excess, it is just with God, and his usual way, by some judgment or other to strip them of that which they have so abused, Hos. 2:8, 9. 3. Lot was carried captive, *v.* 12. They took Lot among the rest, and his goods. Now Lot may here be considered, (1.) As sharing with his neighbours in this common calamity. Though he was himself a righteous man, and (which is here expressly noticed) Abram's brother's son, yet he was involved with the rest in all this trouble. Note, *All things come alike to all,* Eccl. 9:2. The best of men cannot promise themselves an exemption from the greatest troubles in this life; neither from our own piety nor our relation to those that are the favourites of heaven will be our security, when God's judgments are abroad. Note, further, Many an honest man fares the worse for his wicked neighbours. It is therefore our wisdom to separate ourselves, or at least to distinguish ourselves, from them (2 Co. 6:17), and so deliver ourselves, Rev. 18:4. (2.) As smarting for the foolish choice he made of a settlement here. This is plainly intimated when it is said, *They took Abram's brother's son, who dwelt in Sodom.* So near a relation of Abram should have been a companion and disciple of Abram, and should have abode by his tents; but, if he choose to dwell in Sodom, he must thank himself if he share in Sodom's calamities. Note, When we go out of the way of our duty we put ourselves from under God's protection, and cannot expect that the choices which are made by our lusts should issue to our comfort. Particular mention is made of their taking Lot's *goods,* those goods which had occasioned his contest with Abram and his separation from him. Note, It is just with God to deprive us of those enjoyments by which we have suffered ourselves to be deprived of our enjoyment of him.

Verses 13–16

We have here an account of the only military action we ever find Abram engaged in, and this he was prompted to, not by his avarice or ambition, but purely by a principle of charity; it was not to enrich himself, but to help his friend. Never was any military expedition undertaken, prosecuted, and finished, more honourably than this of Abram's. Here we have,

I. The tidings brought him of his kinsman's distress. Providence so ordered it that he now sojourned not far off, that he might be a very present help. 1. He is here called *Abram the Hebrew,* that is, the son and follower of Heber, in whose family the profession of the true religion was kept up in that degenerate age. Abram herein acted like a Hebrew — in a manner not unworthy of the name and character of a religious professor. 2. The tidings were brought by one that had escaped with his life for a prey. Probably he was a Sodomite, and as bad as the worst of them; yet knowing Abram's relation to Lot, and concern for him, he implores his help, and hopes to speed for Lot's sake. Note, The worst of men, in the day of their trouble, will be glad to claim acquaintance with those that are wise and good, and so get an interest in them. The rich man in hell called Abram *Father;* and the foolish virgins made court to the wise for a share of their oil.

II. The preparations he made for this expedition. The cause was plainly good, his call to engage in it was clear, and therefore, with all speed, he *armed his trained servants, born in his house,* to the number of *three hundred and eighteen* — a great family, but a small army, about as many as Gideon's that routed the Midianites, Jdg. 7:7. He drew out his *trained* servants, or his *catechised* servants, not only instructed in the art of war, which was then far short of the perfection which later and worse ages have improved it to, but instructed in the principles of religion; for Abram commanded his household to keep the way of the Lord. This shows that Abram was, 1. A great man, who had so many servants depending upon him, and employed by him, which was not only his strength and honour, but gave him a great opportunity of doing good, which is all that is truly valuable and desirable in great places and great estates. 2. A good man, who not only served God himself, but instructed all about him in the service of God. Note, Those that have great families have not only many bodies, but many souls besides their own, to take care of and provide for. Those that would be found the followers of Abram must see that their servants be catechised servants. 3. A wise man for, though he was a man of peace, yet he disciplined his servants for war, not knowing what occasion he might have, some time or other, so to employ them. Note, Though our holy religion teaches us to be for peace, yet it does not forbid us to provide for war.

III. His allies and confederates in this expedition. He prevailed with his neighbours, *Aner, Eshcol, and Mamre* (with whom he kept up a fair correspondence) to go along with him. It was his prudence thus to strengthen his own troops with their auxiliary forces; and probably they saw themselves concerned, in interest, to act, as they could, against this formidable power, lest their own turn should be next. Note, 1. It is our wisdom and duty to behave ourselves so respectfully and obligingly towards all men as that, whenever there is occasion, they may be willing and ready to do us a kindness. 2. Those who depend on God's help, yet, in times of distress, ought to make use of men's help, as Providence offers it; else they tempt God.

IV. His courage and conduct were very remarkable. 1. There was a great deal of bravery in the enterprise itself, considering the disadvantages he lay under. What could one family of husbandmen and shepherds do against the armies of four princes, who now came fresh from blood and victory? It was not a vanquished, but a victorious army, that he was to pursue; nor was he constrained by necessity to this daring attempt, but moved to it by generosity; so that, all things considered, it was, for aught I know, as great an instance of true courage as ever Alexander or Caesar was celebrated for. Note, Religion tends to make men, not cowardly, but truly valiant. The righteous is bold as a lion. The true Christian is the true hero. 2. There was a great deal of policy in the management of it. Abram was no stranger to the stratagems of war: He *divided himself,* as Gideon did his little army (Jdg. 7:16), that he might come upon the enemy from several quarters at once, and so make his few seem a great many; he made his attack by night, that he might surprise them. Note, Honest policy is a good friend both to our safety and to our usefulness. The serpent's head (provided it be nothing akin to the old serpent) may well become a good Christian's body, especially if it have a dove's eye in it, Mt. 10:16.

V. His success was very considerable, *v.* 15, 16. He defeated his enemies, and rescued his friends; and we do not find that he sustained any loss. Note, Those that venture in a good cause, with a good heart, are under the special protection of a good God, and have reason to hope for a good issue. Again, It is all one with the Lord *to save by many or by few,* 1 Sa. 14:6. Observe,

1. He rescued his kinsman; twice here he is called his *brother Lot.* The remembrance of the relation that was between them, both by nature and grace, made him forget the little quarrel that had been between them, in which Lot had by no means acted well towards Abram. Justly might Abram have upbraided Lot with his folly in quarrelling with him and removing from him, and have told him that he was well enough served, he might have known when he was well off; but, in the charitable breast of pious Abram, it is all forgiven and forgotten, and he takes this opportunity to give a real proof of the sincerity of his reconciliation. Note, (1.) We ought to be ready, whenever it is in the power of our hands, to succour and relieve those that are in distress, especially our relations and friends. *A brother is born for adversity,* Prov. 17:17. A friend in need is a friend indeed. (2.) Though others have been wanting in their duty to us, yet we must not therefore deny our duty to them. Some have said that they can more easily forgive their enemies than their friends; but we shall see ourselves obliged to forgive both if we consider, not only that our God, when we were enemies, reconciled us, but also that he *passeth by the transgression of the remnant of his heritage,* Mic. 7:18.

2. He rescued the rest of the captives, for Lot's sake, though they were strangers to him and such as he was under no obligation to at all; nay, though they were Sodomites, sinners before the Lord exceedingly, and though, probably, he might have recovered Lot alone by ransom, yet he brought back all the women, and the people, and their goods, *v.* 16. Note, As we have opportunity we must do good to all men. Our charity must be extensive, as opportunity offers itself. Wherever God gives life, we must not grudge the help we can give to support it. God does good to the just and unjust, and so must we, Mt. *v.* 45. This victory which Abram obtained over the kings the prophet seems to refer to, Isa. 41:2, *Who raised up the righteous man from the east, and made him rule over kings?* And some suggest that, as before he had a title to this land by grant, so now by conquest.

Verses 17–20

This paragraph begins with the mention of the respect which the king of Sodom paid to Abram at his return from the slaughter of the kings; but, before a particular account is given of this, the story of Melchizedek is briefly related, concerning whom observe,

I. Who he was. He was *king of Salem* and *priest of the most high God;* and other glorious things are said of him, Heb. 7:1, etc. 1. The rabbin, and most of our rabbinical writers, conclude that Melchizedek was Shem the son of Noah, who was king and priest to those that descended from him, according to the patriarchal model. But this is not at all probable; for why should his name be changed? And how came he to settle in Canaan? 2. Many Christian writers have thought that this was an appearance of the Son of God himself, our Lord Jesus, known to Abram, at this time, by this name, as afterwards, Hagar called him by another name, *ch.* 16:13. He appeared to him as a righteous king, owning a righteous cause, and giving peace. It is difficult to imagine that any mere man should be said to *be without father, without mother, and without descent, having neither beginning of days nor end of life,* Heb. 7:3. It is witnessed of Melchizedek that he liveth, and that he abideth a priest continually (*v.* 3, 8); nay (*v.* 13, 14), the apostle makes him of whom these things are spoken to be our Lord who sprang out of Judah. It is likewise difficult to think that any mere man should, at this time, be greater than Abram in the things of God, that Christ should be a priest after the order of any mere man, and that any human priesthood should so far excel that of Aaron as it is certain that Melchizedek's did. 3. The most commonly received opinion is that Melchizedek was a Canaanitish prince, that reigned in Salem, and kept up the true religion there; but, if so, why his name should occur here only in all the story of Abram, and why Abram should have altars of his own and not attend the altars of his neighbour Melchizedek who was greater than he, seem unaccountable. Mr. Gregory of Oxford tells us that the *Arabic Catena,* which he builds much upon the authority of, gives this account of Melchizedek, That he was the son of Heraclim, the son of Peleg, the son of Eber, and that his mother's name was Salathiel, the daughter of Gomer, the son of Japheth, the son of Noah.

II. What he did. 1. He *brought forth bread and wine,* for the refreshment of Abram and his soldiers, and in congratulation of their victory. This he did as a king, teaching us to do good and to communicate, and to be given to hospitality, according to our ability; and representing the spiritual provisions of strength and comfort which Christ has laid up for us in the covenant of grace for our refreshment, when we are wearied with our spiritual conflicts. 2. As priest of the most high God, he blessed Abram, which we may suppose a greater refreshment to Abram than his bread and wine were. Thus God, having raised up his Son Jesus, has sent him to bless us, as one having authority; and those whom he blesses are blessed indeed. Christ went to heaven when he was blessing his disciples (Lu. 24:51); for this is what he ever lives to do.

III. What he said, *v.* 19, 20. Two things were said by him: — 1. He blessed Abram from God: *Blessed be Abram, blessed of the most high God, v.* 19. Observe the titles he here gives to God, which are very glorious. (1.) *The most high God,* which bespeaks his absolute perfections in himself and his sovereign dominion over all the creatures; he is King of kings. Note, It will greatly help both our faith and our reverence in prayer to eye God as the most high God, and to call him so. (2.) *Possessor of heaven and earth,* that is, rightful owner, and sovereign Lord, of all the creatures, because he made them. This bespeaks him a great God, and greatly to be praised (Ps. 24:1), and those a happy people who have an interest in his favour and love. 2. He blessed God for Abram (*v.* 20): and *blessed be the most high God.* Note, (1.) In all our prayers, we must praise God, and join hallelujahs with all our hosannahs. These are the spiritual sacrifices we must offer up daily, and upon particular occasions. (2.) God, as the most high God, must have the glory of all our victories, Ex. 17:15;; 1 Sa. 7:10, 12; Jdg. 5:1, 2; 2 Chr. 20:21. In them he shows himself higher than our enemies (Ex. 18:11), and higher than we; for without him we could do nothing. (3.) We ought to give thanks for others' mercies as for our own, triumphing with those that triumph. (4.) Jesus Christ, our great high priest, is the Mediator both of our prayers and praises, and not only offers up ours, but his own for us. See Lu. 10:21.

IV. What was done to him: *Abram gave him tithes of all,* that is, of the spoils, Heb. 7:4. This may be looked upon, 1. As a gratuity presented to Melchizedek, by way of return for his tokens of respect. Note, Those that receive kindness should show kindness. Gratitude is one of nature's laws. 2. As an offering vowed and dedicated to the most high God, and therefore put into the hands of Melchizedek his priest. Note, (1.) When we have received some signal mercy from God, it is very fit that we should express our thankfulness by some special act of pious charity. God must always have his dues out of our substance, especially when, by any particular providence, he has either preserved or increased it to us. (2.) That the tenth of our increase is a very fit proportion to be set apart for the honour of God and the service of his sanctuary. (3.) That Jesus Christ, our great Melchizedek, is to have homage done him, and to be humbly acknowledged by every one of us as our king and priest; and not only the tithe of all, but all we have, must be surrendered and given up to him.

Verses 21–24

We have here an account of what passed between Abram and the king of Sodom, who succeeded him that fell in the battle (*v.* 10), and thought himself obliged to do this honour to Abram, in return for the good services he had done him. Here is,

I. The king of Sodom's grateful offer to Abram (*v.* 21): *Give me the soul, and take thou the substance;* so the Hebrew reads it. Here he fairly begs the persons, but as freely bestows the goods on Abram. Note, 1. Where a right is dubious and divided, it is wisdom to compound the matter by mutual concessions rather than to contend. The king of Sodom had an original right both to the persons and to the goods, and it would bear a debate whether Abram's acquired right by rescue would supersede his title and extinguish it; but, to prevent all quarrels, the king of Sodom makes this fair proposal. 2. Gratitude teaches us to recompense to the utmost of our power those that have undergone fatigues, run hazards, and been at expense for our service and benefit. *Who goes a warfare at his own charges?* 1 Co. 9:7. Soldiers purchase their pay dearer than any labourers, and are well worthy of it, because they expose their lives.

II. Abram's generous refusal of this offer. He not only resigned the persons to him, who, being delivered out of the hand of their enemies, ought to have served Abram, but he restored all the goods too. He would not take *from a thread to a shoe-latchet,* not the least thing that had ever belonged to the king of Sodom or any of his. Note, A lively faith enables a man to look upon the wealth of this world with a holy contempt, 1 Jn. 5:4. What are all the ornaments and delights of sense to one that has God and heaven ever in his eye? He resolves even to a thread and a shoe-latchet; for a tender conscience fears offending in a small matter. Now,

1. Abram ratifies this resolution with a solemn oath: *I have lifted up my hand to the Lord that I will not take any thing, v.* 22. Here observe, (1.) The titles he gives to God, *The most high God, the possessor of heaven and earth,* the same that Melchizedek had just now used, *v.* 19. Note, It is good to learn of others how to order our speech concerning God, and to imitate those who speak well in divine things. This improvement we are to make of the conversation of devout good men, we must learn to speak after them. (2.) The ceremony used in this oath: *I have lifted up my hand.* In religious swearing we appeal to God's knowledge of our truth and sincerity and imprecate his wrath if we swear falsely, and the *lifting up of the hand* is very significant and expressive of both. (3.) The matter of the oath, namely, that he would not take any reward from the king of Sodom, was lawful, but what he was not antecedently obliged to. [1.] Probably Abram vowed, before he went to the battle, that, if God would give him success, he would, for the glory of God and the credit of his profession, so far deny himself and his own right as to take nothing of the spoils to himself. Note, the vows we have made when we are in pursuit of a mercy must be carefully and conscientiously kept when we have obtained the mercy, though they were made against our interest. A citizen of Zion, if he has sworn, whether it be to God or man, though it prove to *his own hurt, yet he changeth not,* Ps. 15:4. Or, [2.] Perhaps Abram, now when he saw cause to refuse the offer made him, at the same time confirmed his refusal with this oath, to prevent further importunity. Note, *First,* There may be good reason sometimes why we should debar ourselves of that which is our undoubted right, as St. Paul, 1 Co. 8:13; 9:12. *Secondly,* That strong resolutions are of good use to put by the force of temptations.

2. He backs his refusal with a good reason: *Lest thou shouldest say, I have made Abram rich,* which would reflect reproach, (1.) Upon the promise and covenant of God, as if they would not have enriched Abram without the spoils of Sodom. And, (2.) Upon the piety and charity of Abram, as if all he had in his eye, when he undertook that hazardous expedition, was to enrich himself. Note, [1.] We must be very careful that we give no occasion to others to say things which they ought not. [2.] The people of God must, for their credit's sake, take heed of doing any thing that looks mean or mercenary, or that savours of covetousness and self-seeking. Probably Abram knew the king of Sodom to be a proud and scornful man, and one that would be apt to turn such a thing as this to his reproach afterwards, though most unreasonably. When we have to do with such men, we have need to act with particular caution.

3. He limits his refusal with a double proviso, *v.* 24. In making vows, we ought carefully to insert the necessary exceptions, that we may not afterwards say before the angel, *It was an error,* Eccl. 5:6. Abram here excepts, (1.) The food of his soldiers; they were worthy of their meat while they trod out the corn. This would give no colour to the king of Sodom to say that he had enriched Abram. (2.) The shares of his allies and confederates: *Let them take their portion.* Note, Those who are strict in restraining their own liberty yet ought not to impose those restraints upon the liberties of others, nor to judge of them accordingly. We must not make ourselves the standard to measure others by. A good man will deny himself that liberty which he will not deny another, contrary to the practice of the Pharisees, Mt. 23:4. There was not the same reason why Aner, Eshcol, and Mamre, should quit their right, that there was why Abram should. They did not make the profession that he made, nor were they, as he was, under the obligation of a vow. They had not the hopes that Abram had of a portion in the other world, and therefore, by all means, *let them take their portion* of this.

CHAPTER 15

In this chapter we have a solemn treaty between God and Abram concerning a covenant that was to be established between them. In the former chapter we had Abram in the field with Kings; here we find him in the mount with God; and, though there he looked great, yet, methinks, here he looks much greater: that honour have the great men of the world, but "this honour have all the saints." The covenant to be settled between God and Abram was a covenant of promises; accordingly, here is, I. A general assurance of God's kindness and good-will to Abram (*v.* 1). II. A particular declaration of the purposes of his love concerning him, in two things: — 1. That he would give him a numerous issue (*v.* 2–6). 2. That he would give him Canaan for an inheritance (*v.* 7–21). Either an estate without an heir, or an heir without an estate, would have been but a half comfort to Abram. But God ensures both to him; and that which made these two, the promised seed and the promised land, comforts indeed to this great believer was that they were both typical of those two invaluable blessings, Christ and heaven; and so we have reason to think, Abram eyed them.

Verse 1

Observe here, I. The time when God made this treaty with Abram: *After these things.* 1. After that famous act of generous charity which Abram had done, in rescuing his friends and neighbours out of distress, and that, *not for price nor reward.* After this, God made him this gracious visit. Note, Those that show favour to men shall find favour with God. 2. After that victory which he had obtained over four kings. Lest Abram should be too much elevated and pleased with that, God comes to him, to tell him he had better things in store for him. Note, A believing converse with Spiritual blessings is an excellent means to keep us from being too much taken up with temporal enjoyments. The gifts of common providence are not comparable to those of covenant love.

II. The manner in which God conversed with Abram: *The word of the Lord came unto Abram* (that is, God manifested himself and his will to Abram) *in a vision,* which supposes Abram awake, and some visible appearances of the Shechinah, or some sensible token of the presence of the divine glory. Note, The methods of divine revelation are adapted to our state in a world of sense.

III. The gracious assurance God gave him of his favour to him.

1. He called him by name — *Abram,* which was a great honour to him, and made his name great, and was also a great encouragement and assistance to his faith. Note, God's good word does us good when it is spoken by his Spirit to us in particular, and brought to our hearts. The word says, *Ho, every one* (Isa. 55:1), the Spirit says, *Ho, such a one.*

2. He cautioned him against being disquieted and confounded: *Fear not, Abram.* Abram might fear lest the four kings he had routed should rally again, and fall upon him to his ruin: "No," says God, *"Fear not.* Fear not their revenges, nor thy neighbour's envy; I will take care of thee." Note, (1.) Where there is great faith, yet there may be many fears, 2 Co. 7:5. (2.) God takes cognizance of his people's fears though ever so secret, and *knows their souls,* Ps. 31:7. (3.) It is the will of God that his people should not give way to prevailing fears, whatever happens. Let the sinners in Sion be afraid, but fear not, Abram.

3. He assured him of safety and happiness, that he should for ever be, (1.) As safe as God himself could keep him: *I am thy shield,* or, somewhat more emphatically, *I am a shield to thee,* present with thee, actually caring for thee. See 1 Chr. 17:24. Not only the God of Israel, but a God to Israel. Note, The consideration of this, that God himself is, and will be, a shield to his people to secure them from all destructive evils, a shield ready to them and a shield round about them, should be sufficient to silence all their perplexing tormenting fears. (2.) As happy as God himself could make him: I will be *thy exceedingly great reward;* not only thy rewarder, but thy reward. Abram had generously refused the rewards which the king of Sodom offered him, and here God comes, and tells him he shall be no loser by it. Note, [1.] The rewards of believing obedience and self-denial are exceedingly great, 1 Co. 2:9. [2.] God himself is the chosen and promised felicity of holy souls — chosen in this world, promised in a better. He is the *portion of their inheritance and their cup.*

Verses 2–6

We have here the assurance given to Abram of a numerous offspring which should descend from him, in which observe,

I. Abram's repeated complaint, *v.* 2, 3. This was that which gave occasion to this promise. The great affliction that sat heavy upon Abram was the want of a child; and the complaint of this he here *pours out before the Lord, and shows before him his trouble,* Ps. 142:2. Note, Though we must never complain of God, yet we have leave to complain to him, and to be large and particular in the statement of our grievances; and it is some ease to a burdened spirit to open its case to a faithful and compassionate friend: such a friend God is, whose ear is always open. Now his complaint is four-fold: — 1. That he had no child (*v.* 3): *Behold, to me thou hast given no seed;* not only no son, but *no seed;* if he had had a daughter, from her the promised Messiah might have come, who was to be the seed of the woman; but he had neither son nor daughter. He seems to lay an emphasis on that, *to me.* His neighbours were full of children, his servants had children born in his house. "But *to me,"* he complains, "thou hast given none;" and yet God had told him he should be a favourite above all. Note, Those that are written childless must see God writing them so. Again, God often withholds those temporal comforts from his own children which he gives plentifully to others that are strangers to him. 2. That he was never likely to have any, intimated in that *I go,* or *"I am going, childless,* going into years, going down the hill apace; nay, I am going out of the world, going the way of all the earth. *I die childless,"* so the Septuagint, "I leave the world, and leave no child behind me." 3. That his servants were for the present and were likely to be to him instead of sons. While he lived, *the steward of his house was Eliezer of Damascus;* to him he committed the care of his family and estate, who might be faithful, but only as a servant, not as a son. When he died, *one born in his house would be his heir,* and would bear rule over all that for which he had laboured, Eccl. 2:18, 19, 21. God had already told him that he would make of him *a great nation* (*ch.* 12:2), and his *seed as the dust of the earth* (*ch.* 13:16); but he had left him in doubt whether it should be his seed begotten or his seed adopted, by a son of his loins or only a son of his house. "Now, Lord," says Abram, "if it be only an adopted son it must be one of my servants, which will reflect disgrace upon the promised seed, that is to descend from him." Note, While promised mercies are delayed our unbelief and impatience are apt to conclude them denied. 4. That the want of a son was so great a trouble to him that it took away the comfort of all his enjoyments: *"Lord, what wilt thou give me?* All is nothing to me, if I have not a son." Now, If we suppose that Abram looked no further than a temporal comfort, this complaint was culpable. God had, by his providence, given him some good things, and more by his promise; and yet Abram makes no account of them, because he has not a son. It did very ill become the father of the faithful to say, *What wilt thou give me, seeing I go childless,* immediately after God had said, *I am thy shield, and thy exceedingly great reward.* Note, Those do not rightly value the advantages of their covenant-relation to God and interest in him who do not think them sufficient whatever. But, (2.) If we suppose that Abram, herein, had a eye to the promised seed, the importunity of his desire was very commendable: all was nothing to him, if he had not the earnest of that great blessing, and an assurance of his relation to the Messiah, of which God had already encouraged him to maintain the expectation. He has wealth, and victory, and honour; but, while he is kept in the dark about the main matter, it is all nothing to him. Note, Till we have some comfortable evidence of our interest in Christ and the new covenant, we should not rest satisfied with any thing else. "This, and the other, I have; but what will all this avail me, if I go Christless?" Yet thus far the complaint was culpable, that there was some diffidence of the promise at the bottom of it, and a weariness of waiting God's time. Note, True believers sometimes find it hard to reconcile God's promises and his providences, when they seem to disagree.

II. God's gracious answer to this complaint. To the first part of the complaint (*v.* 2) God gave no immediate answer, because there was something of fretfulness in it; but, when he renews his address somewhat more calmly (*v.* 3), God answered him graciously. Note, If we continue instant in prayer, and yet pray with a humble submission to the divine will, we shall not seek in vain. 1. God gave him an express promise of a son, *v.* 4. This that is born in thy house *shall not be thy heir,* as thou fearest, but one that shall *come forth out of thy own bowels shall be thy heir.* Note, (1.) God makes heirs; he says, "This shall not, and this shall;" and whatever men devise and design, in settling their estates, God's counsel shall stand. (2.) God is often better to us than our own fears, and gives the mercy we had long despaired of. 2. To affect him the more with this promise, he took him out, and showed him the stars (this vision being early in the morning, before day), and then tells him, *So shall thy seed be, v.* 5. (1.) So numerous; the stars seem innumerable to a common eye: Abram feared he should have no child at all, but God assured him that the descendants from his loins should be so many as not to be numbered. (2.) So illustrious, resembling the stars in splendour; for to *them pertained the glory,* Rom. 9:4. Abram's seed, according to his flesh, were like the dust of the earth (*ch.* 13:16), but his spiritual seed are like the stars of heaven, not only numerous, but glorious, and very precious.

III. Abram's firm belief of the promise God now made him, and God's favourable acceptance of his faith, *v.* 6. 1. He *believed in the Lord,* that is, he believed the truth of that promise which God had now made him, resting upon the irresistible power and the inviolable faithfulness of him that made it. *Hath he spoken, and shall he not make it good?* Note, Those who would have the comfort of the promises must mix faith with the promises. See how the apostle magnifies this faith of Abram, and makes it a standing example, Rom. 4:19–21. *He was not weak in faith; he staggered not at the promise;* he was *strong in faith; he was fully persuaded.* The Lord work such a faith in every one of us! Some think that his believing in the Lord respected, not only the Lord promising, but the Lord promised, the Lord Jesus, the Mediator of the new covenant. He *believed in him,* that is, received and embraced the divine revelation concerning him, and *rejoiced to see his day,* though at so great a distance, Jn. 8:56. 2. *God counted it to him for righteousness;* that is, upon the score of this he was accepted of God, and, as the rest of the patriarchs, by faith he *obtained witness that he was righteous,* Heb. 11:4. This is urged in the New Testament to prove that we are justified by faith without the works of the law (Rom. 4:3; Gal. 3:6); for Abram was so justified while he was yet uncircumcised. If Abram, that was so rich in good works was not justified by them, but by his faith, much less can we, that are so poor in them. This faith, which was imputed to Abram for righteousness, had lately struggled with unbelief (*v.* 2), and, coming off a conqueror, it was thus crowned, thus honoured. Note, A fiducial practical acceptance of, and dependence upon, God's promise of grace and glory, in and through Christ, is that which, according to the tenour of the new covenant, gives us a right to all the blessings contained in that promise. All believers are justified as Abram was, and it was his faith that was *counted to him for righteousness.*

Verses 7–11

We have here the assurance given to Abram of the land of Canaan for an inheritance.

I. God declares his purpose concerning it, *v.* 7. Observe here, Abram made no complaint in this matter, as he had done for the want of a child. Note, Those that are sure of an interest in the promised seed will see no reason to doubt of a title to the promised land. If Christ is ours, heaven is ours. Observe again, When he believed the former promise (*v.* 6) then God explained and ratified this to him. Note, To him that has (improves what he has) more shall be given. Three things God here reminds Abram of, for his encouragement concerning the promise of this good land: —

1. What God is in himself: *I am the Lord* Jehovah; and therefore, (1.) "I may give it to thee, for I am sovereign Lord of all, and have a right to dispose of the whole earth." (2.) "I can give it to thee, whatever opposition may be made, though by the sons of Anak." God never promises more than he is able to perform, as men often do. (3.) "I will make good my promise to thee." Jehovah is *not a man that he should lie.*

2. What he had done for Abram. He had brought him out of Ur of the Chaldees, *out of the fire of the Chaldees,* so some, that is, either from their idolatries (for the Chaldeans worshipped the fire), or from their persecutions. The Jewish writers have a tradition that Abram was cast into a fiery furnace for refusing to worship idols, and was miraculously delivered. It is rather a place of that name. Thence God brought him by an effectual call, brought him with a gracious violence, snatched him as a brand out of the burning. This was, (1.) A special mercy: "I brought thee, and left others, thousands, to perish there." *God called him alone,* Isa. 51:2. (2.) A spiritual mercy, a mercy to his soul, a deliverance from sin and its fatal consequences. If God save our souls, we shall want nothing that is good for us. (3.) A fresh mercy, lately bestowed, and therefore should be the more affecting, as that in the preface to the commandments, *I am the Lord that brought thee out of Egypt* lately. (4.) A foundation mercy, the beginning of mercy, peculiar mercy to Abram, and therefore a pledge and earnest of further mercy, Isa. 66:9. Observe how God speaks of it as that which he gloried in: *I am the Lord that brought thee out.* He glories in it as an act both of power and grace; compare Isa. 29:22, where he glories in it, long afterwards. *Thus saith the Lord who redeemed* Abraham, redeemed him from sin.

3. What he intended to do yet further for him: *"I brought thee* hither, on purpose *to give thee this land to inherit it,* not only to possess it, but to possess it as an inheritance, which is the sweetest and surest title." Note, (1.) The providence of God has secret but gracious designs in all its various dispensations towards good people; we cannot conceive the projects of Providence, till the event shows them in all their mercy and glory. (2.) The great thing God designs in all his dealings with his people is to bring them safely to heaven. They are *chosen to salvation* (2 Th. 2:13), *called to the kingdom* (1 Th. 2:12), *begotten to the inheritance* (1 Pt. 1:3, 4), and by all *made meet* for it, Col. 1:12, 13; 2 Co. 4:17.

II. Abram desires a sign: *Whereby shall I know that I shall inherit it? v.* 8. This did not proceed from distrust of God's power or promise, as that of Zacharias; but he desired this, 1. For the strengthening and confirming of his own faith; he believed (*v.* 6), but here he prays, *Lord, help me* against *my unbelief. Now* he believed, but he desired a sign to be treasured up against an hour of temptation, not knowing how his faith might, by some event or other, be shocked and tried. Note, We all need, and should desire, helps from heaven for the confirming of our faith, and should improve sacraments, which are instituted signs, for that purpose. See Jdg. 6:36–40; 2 Ki. 20:8–10; Isa. 7:11,12. 2. For the ratifying of the promise to his posterity, that they also might be brought to believe it. Note, Those that are satisfied themselves should desire that others also may be satisfied of the truth of God's promises. John sent his disciples to Christ, not so much for his own satisfaction as for theirs, Mt. 11:2, 3. Canaan was a type of heaven. Note, It is a very desirable thing to know that we shall inherit the heavenly Canaan, that is, to be confirmed in our belief of the truth of that happiness, and to have the evidences of our title to it more and more cleared up to us.

III. God directs Abram to make preparations for a sacrifice, intending by that to give him a sign, and Abram makes preparation accordingly (*v.* 9–11): *Take me a heifer,* etc. Perhaps Abram expected some extraordinary sign from heaven; but God gives him a sign upon a sacrifice. Note, Those that would receive the assurances of God's favour, and would have their faith confirmed, must attend instituted ordinances, and expect to meet with God in them. Observe, 1. God appointed that each of the beasts used for this service should be three years old, because then they were at their full growth and strength: God must be served with the best we have, for he is the best. 2. We do not read that God gave Abram particular directions how to manage these beasts and fowls, knowing that he was so well versed in the law and custom of sacrifices that he needed not any particular directions; or perhaps instructions were given him, which he carefully observed, thought they are not recorded: at least it was intimated to him that they must be prepared for the solemnity of ratifying a covenant; and he well knew the manner of preparing them. 3. Abram took as God appointed him, though as yet he knew not how these things should become a sign to him. This was not the first instance of Abram's implicit obedience. He divided the beasts in the midst, according to the ceremony used in confirming covenants, Jer. 34:18, 19, where it is said, They cut *the calf in twain, and passed between the parts.* 4. Abram, having prepared according to God's appointment, now set himself to wait for the sign God might give him by these, like the prophet upon his watch-tower, Hab. 2:1. While God's appearing to own his sacrifice was deferred, Abram continued waiting, and his expectations were raised by the delay; when *the fowls came down upon the carcasses* to prey upon them, as common and neglected things, *Abram drove them away* (*v.* 11), believing that the vision would, at the end, *speak, and not lie.* Note, A very watchful eye must be kept upon our spiritual sacrifices, that nothing be suffered to prey upon them and render them unfit for God's acceptance. When vain thoughts, like these fowls, come down upon our sacrifices, we must drive them away, and not suffer them to lodge within us, but *attend on God without distraction.*

Verses 12–16

We have here a full and particular discovery made to Abram of God's purposes concerning his seed. Observe,

I. The time when God came to him with this discovery: *When the sun was going down,* or *declining,* about the time of the *evening oblation,* 1 Ki. 18:36; Dan. 9:21. Early in the morning, before day, while the stars were yet to be seen, God had given him orders concerning the sacrifices (*v.* 5), and we may suppose it was, at least, his morning's work to prepare them and set them in order; when he had done this, he abode by them, praying and waiting till towards evening. Note, God often keeps his people long in expectation of the comforts he designs them, for the confirmation of their faith; but though the answers of prayer, and the performance of promises, come slowly, yet they come surely. *At evening time it shall be light.*

II. The preparatives for this discovery. 1. *A deep sleep fell upon Abram,* not a common sleep through weariness or carelessness, but a divine ecstasy, like that which the *Lord God caused to fall upon Adam* (*ch.* 2:21), that, being hereby wholly taken off from the view of things sensible, he might be wholly taken up with the contemplation of things spiritual. The doors of the body were locked up, that the soul might be private and retired, and might act the more freely and like itself. 2. With this sleep, *a horror of great darkness fell upon him.* How sudden a change! But just before we had him solacing himself in the comforts of God's covenant, and in communion with him; and here a *horror of great darkness* falls upon him. Note, The children of light do not always walk in the light, but sometimes clouds and darkness are round about them. This great darkness, which brought horror with it, was designed, (1.) To strike an awe upon the spirit of Abram, and to possess him with a holy reverence, that the familiarity to which God was pleased to admit him might not breed contempt. Note, Holy fear prepares the soul for holy joy; the spirit of bondage makes way for the spirit of adoption. God wounds first, and then heals; humbles first, and they lifts up, Isa. 6:5, 6, etc. (2.) To be a specimen of the methods of God's dealings with his seed. They must first be in the horror and darkness of Egyptian slavery, and then enter with joy into the good land; and therefore he must have the foretaste of their sufferings, before he had the foresight of their happiness. (3.) To be an indication of the nature of that covenant of peculiarity which God was now about to make with Abram. The Old-Testament dispensation, which was founded on that covenant, was a dispensation, [1.] Of darkness and obscurity, 2 Co. 3:13, 14. [2.] Of dread and horror, Heb. 12:18, etc.

III. The prediction itself. Several things are here foretold.

1. The suffering state of Abram's seed for a long time, *v.* 13. Let not Abram flatter himself with the hopes of nothing but honour and prosperity in his family; no, he must know, of a surety, that which he was loth to believe, that the promised seed should be a persecuted seed. Note, God sends the worst first; we must first suffer, and then reign. He also lets us know the worst before it comes, that when it comes it may not be a surprise to us, Jn. 16:4. Now we have here,

(1.) The particulars of their sufferings. [1.] They shall be strangers; so they were, first in Canaan (Ps. 105:12) and afterwards in Egypt; before they were lords of their own land they were strangers in a strange land. The inconveniences of an unsettled state make a happy settlement the more welcome. Thus the heirs of heaven are first strangers on earth, a land that is not theirs. [2.] They shall be servants; so they were to the Egyptians, Ex. 1:13. See how that which was the doom of the Canaanites (*ch.* 9:25) proves the distress of Abram's seed: they are made to serve, but with this difference, the Canaanites serve under a curse, the Hebrews under a blessing; and the *upright shall have dominion in the morning,* Ps. 49:14. [3.] They shall be sufferers. Those whom they serve shall afflict them; see Ex. 1:11. Note, Those that are blessed and beloved of God are often sorely afflicted by wicked men; and God foresees it, and takes cognizance of it.

(2.) The continuance of their sufferings — *four hundred years.* This persecution began with mocking, when Ishmael, the son of an Egyptian, persecuted Isaac, who was *born after the Spirit, ch.* 21:9; Gal. 4:29. It continued in loathing; for it was an abomination to the Egyptians to eat bread with the Hebrews, *ch.* 43:32; and it came at last to murder, the basest of murders, that of their new-born children; so that, more or less, it continued 400 years, though, in extremity, not so many. This was a long time, but a limited time.

2. The judgment of the enemies of Abram's seed: *That nation whom they shall serve,* even the Egyptians, *will I judge, v.* 14. This points at the plagues of Egypt, by which God not only constrained the Egyptians to release Israel, but punished them for all the hardships they had put upon them. Note, (1.) Though God may suffer persecutors and oppressors to trample upon his people a great while, yet he will certainly reckon with them at last; for his *day is coming,* Ps. 37:12, 13. (2.) The punishing of persecutors is the judging of them: it is a righteous thing with God, and a particular act of justice, to recompense tribulations to those that trouble his people. The judging of the church's enemies is God's work: *I will judge.* God can do it, for he is the Lord; he will do it, for he is his people's God, and he has said, *Vengeance is mine, I will repay.* To him therefore we must leave it, to be done in his way and time.

3. The deliverance of Abram's seed out of Egypt. That great event is here foretold: *Afterwards shall they come out with great substance.* It is here promised, (1.) That they should be enlarged: *Afterwards they shall come out;* that is, either after they have been afflicted 400 years, when the days of their servitude are fulfilled, or after the Egyptians are judged and plagued, then they may expect deliverance. Note, The destruction of oppressors is the redemption of the oppressed; they will not let God's people go till they are forced to it. (2.) That they should be enriched: *They shall come out with great substance;* this was fulfilled, Ex. 12:35, 36. God took care they should have, not only a good land to go to, but a good stock to carry with them.

4. Their happy settlement in Canaan, *v.* 16. They shall not only come out of Egypt, but *they shall come hither again,* hither to the land of Canaan, wherein thou now art. The discontinuance of their possession shall be no defeasance of their right: we must not reckon those comforts lost for ever that are intermitted for a time. The reason why they must not have the land of promise in possession till the fourth generation was because *the iniquity of the Amorites was not yet full.* Israel cannot be possessed of Canaan till the Amorites be dispossessed; and they are not yet ripe for ruin. The righteous God has determined that they shall not be cut off till they have persisted in sin so long, and arrived at such a pitch of wickedness, that there may appear some equitable proportion between their sin and their ruin; and therefore, till it come to that, the seed of Abram must be kept out of possession. Note, (1.) The measure of sin fills gradually. Those that continue impenitent in wicked ways are treasuring up unto themselves wrath. (2.) Some people's measure of sin fills slowly. The Sodomites, who were sinners before the Lord exceedingly, soon filled their measure; so did the Jews, who were, in profession, near to God. But the iniquity of the Amorites was long in the filling up. (3.) That this is the reason of the prosperity of wicked people; the measure of their sins is not yet full. The wicked *live, become old, and are mighty in power,* while God is *laying up their iniquity for their children,* Job 21:7, 19. See Mt. 23:32; Deu. 32:34.

5. Abram's peaceful quiet death and burial, before these things should come to pass, *v.* 15. As he should not live to see that good land in the possession of his family, but must die, as he lived, a stranger in it, so, to balance this, he should not live to see the troubles that should come upon his seed, much less to share in them. This is promised to Josiah, 2 Ki. 22:20. Note, Good men are sometimes greatly favoured by being *taken away from the evil to come,* Isa. 57:1. Let this satisfy Abram, that, for his part,

(1.) He shall *go to his fathers in peace.* Note, [1.] Even the friends and favourites of Heaven are not exempted from the stroke of death. Are we greater than our father Abram, who is dead? Jn. 8:53. [2.] Good men die willingly; they are not fetched, they are not forced, but they go; their soul is not required, as the rich fool's (Lu. 12:20), but cheerfully resigned: they would not live always. [3.] At death we go to our fathers, to all our fathers that have gone before us to the state of the dead (Job 21:32, 33), to our godly fathers that have gone before us to the state of the blessed, Heb. 12:23. The former thought helps to take off the terror of death, the latter puts comfort into it. [4.] Whenever a godly man dies, he dies in peace. If the way be piety, the end is peace, Ps. 37:37. Outward peace, to the last, is promised to Abram, peace and truth is his days, whatever should come afterwards (2 Ki. 20:19); peace with God, and everlasting peace, are sure to all the seed.

(2.) He shall be *buried in a good old age.* Perhaps mention is made of his burial here, where the land of Canaan is promised him, because a burying place was the first possession he had in it. He shall not only die in peace, but die in honour, die, and be buried decently; not only die in peace, but die in season, Job 5:26. Note, [1.] Old age is a blessing. It is promised in the firth commandment; it is pleasing to nature; and it affords a great opportunity for usefulness. [2.] Especially, if it be a good old age. Theirs may be called a good old age, *First,* That are old and healthful, not loaded with such distempers as make them weary of life. *Secondly,* That are old and holy, old disciples (Acts 21:16), whose hoary head is *found in the way of righteousness* (Prov. 16:31), old and useful, old and exemplary for godliness; theirs is indeed a good old age.

Verses 17–21

Here is, I. The covenant ratified (*v.* 17); the sign which Abram desired was given, at length, when the sun had gone down, so that it was dark; for that was a dark dispensation.

1. The *smoking furnace* signified the affliction of his seed in Egypt. They were there in the *iron furnace* (Deu. 4:20), the *furnace of affliction* (Isa. 48:10), labouring in the very fire. They were there in the smoke, their eyes darkened, that they could not see to the end of their troubles, and themselves at a loss to conceive what God would do with them. Clouds and darkness were round about them.

2. The *burning lamp* denotes comfort in this affliction; and this God showed to Abram, at the same time that he showed him the *smoking furnace.* (1.) Light denotes deliverance out of the furnace; their salvation was as *a lamp that burneth,* Isa. 62:1. When God came down to deliver them, he appeared in a bush that *burned, and was not consumed,* Ex. 3:2. (2.) The lamp denotes direction in the smoke. God's word was their lamp: this word to Abram was so, it was a light shining in a dark place. Perhaps this burning lamp prefigured the pillar of cloud and fire, which led them out of Egypt, in which God was. (3.) The burning lamp denotes the destruction of their enemies who kept them so long in the furnace. See Zec. 12:6. The same cloud that enlightened the Israelites troubled and burned the Egyptians.

3. The passing of these between the pieces was the confirming of the covenant God now made with him, that he might have strong consolation, being fully persuaded that what God promised he would certainly perform. It is probable that the furnace and lamp, which passed between the pieces, burnt and consumed them, and so completed the sacrifice, and testified God's acceptance of it, as of Gideon's (Jdg. 6:21), Manoah's (Jdg. 13:19, 20), and Solomon's, 2 Chr. 7:1. So it intimates, (1.) That God's covenants with man are made by sacrifice (Ps. l. 5.), by Christ, the great sacrifice: no agreement without atonement. (2.) God's acceptance of our spiritual sacrifices is a token for good and an earnest of further favours. See Jdg. 13:23. And by this we may know that he accepts our sacrifices if he kindle in our souls a holy fire of pious and devout affections in them.

II. The covenant repeated and explained: *In that same day,* that day never to be forgotten, *the Lord made a covenant with Abram,* that is, gave a promise to Abram, saying, *Unto thy seed have I given this land, v.* 18. Here is,

1. A rehearsal of the grant. He had said before, *To thy seed will I give this land, ch.* 12:7; 13:15. But here he says, *I have given it;* that is, (1.) I have given the promise of it, the charter is sealed and delivered, and cannot be disannulled. Note, God's promises are God's gifts, and are so to be accounted. (2.) The possession is as sure, in due time, as if it were now actually delivered to them. What God has promised is as sure as if it were already done; hence, it is said, *He that believes hath everlasting life* (Jn. 3:36), for he shall as surely go to heaven as if he were there already.

2. A recital of the particulars granted, such as is usual in the grants of lands. He specifies the boundaries of the land intended hereby to be granted, *v.* 18. And then, for the greater certainty, as is usual in such cases, he mentions in whose tenure and occupation these lands now were. Ten several nations, or tribes, are here spoken of (*v.* 19–21) that must be cast our, to make room for the *seed of Abram.* They were not possessed of all these countries when God brought them into Canaan. The bounds are fixed much narrower, Num. 34:2, 3, etc. But, (1.) In David's time, and Solomon's, their jurisdiction extended to the utmost of these limits, 2 Chr. 9:26. (2.) It was their own fault that they were not sooner and longer in possession of all these territories. They forfeited their right by their sins, and by their own sloth and cowardice kept themselves out

of possession. (3.) The land granted is here described in its utmost extent because it was to be a type of the heavenly inheritance, where there is room enough: in our father's house are many mansions. The present occupants are named, because their number, and strength, and long prescription, should be no hindrance to the accomplishment of this promise in its season, and to magnify God's love to Abram and his seed, in giving to that one nation the possessions of many nations, so precious were they in his sight, and so honourable, Isa. 43:4.

CHAPTER 16

Hagar is the person mostly concerned in the story of this chapter, an obscure Egyptian woman, whose name and story we never should have heard of if Providence had not brought her into the family of Abram. Probably she was one of those maid-servants whom the king of Egypt, among other gifts, bestowed upon Abram (*ch.* 14:16). Concerning her, we have four things in this chapter: — I. Her marriage to Abram her master (*v.* 1–3). II. Her misbehaviour towards Sarai her mistress (*v.* 4–6). III. Her discourse with an angel that met her in her flight (*v.* 7–14). IV. Her delivery of a son (*v.* 15, 16).

Verses 1–3

We have here the marriage of Abram to Hagar, who was his secondary wife. Herein, though some excuse may be made for him, he cannot be justified, for *from the beginning it was not so;* and, when it was so, it seems to have proceeded from an irregular desire to build up families for the speedier peopling of the world and the church. Certainly it must not be so now. Christ has reduced this matter to the first institution, and makes the marriage union to be between one man and one woman only. Now,

I. The maker of this match (would one think it?) was Sarai herself: she said to Abram, *I pray thee, go in unto my maid, v.* 2. Note, 1. It is the policy of Satan to tempt us by our nearest and dearest relations, or those friends that we have an opinion of and an affection for. The temptation is most dangerous when it is sent by a hand that is least suspected: it is our wisdom therefore to consider, not so much who speaks as what is spoken. 2. God's commands consult our comfort and honour much better than our own contrivances do. It would have been much more for Sarai's interest if Abram had kept to the rule of God's law instead of being guided by her foolish projects; but we often do ill for ourselves.

II. The inducement to it was Sarai's barrenness.

1. *Sarai bare Abram no children.* She was very fair (*ch.* 12:14), was a very agreeable, dutiful wife, and a sharer with him in his large possessions; and yet written childless. Note, (1.) God dispenses his gifts variously, loading us with benefits, but not overloading us: some cross or other is appointed to be an alloy to great enjoyments. (2.) The mercy of children is often given to the poor and denied to the rich, given to the wicked and denied to good people, though the rich have most to leave them and good people would take most care of their education. God does herein as it has pleased him.

2. She owned God's providence in this affliction: *The Lord hath restrained me from bearing.* Note, (1.) As, where children are, it is God that gives them (*ch.* 33:5), so where they are wanted it is he that withholds them, *ch.* 30:2. This evil is of the Lord. (2.) It becomes us to acknowledge this, that we may bear it, and improve it, as an affliction of his ordering for wise and holy ends.

3. She used this as an argument with Abram to marry his maid; and he was prevailed upon by this argument to do it. Note, (1.) When our hearts are too much set upon any creature-comfort, we are easily put upon the use of indirect methods for the obtaining of it. Inordinate desires commonly produce irregular endeavours. If our wishes be not kept in a submission to God's providence, our pursuits will scarcely be kept under the restraints of his precepts. (2.) It is for want of a firm dependence upon God's promise, and a patient waiting for God's time, that we go out of the way of our duty to catch at expected mercy. *He that believes does not make haste.*

4. Abram's compliance with Sarai's proposal, we have reason to think, was from an earnest desire of the promised seed, on whom the covenant should be entailed. God had told him that his heir should be a son of his body, but had not yet told him that it should be a son by Sarai; therefore he thought, "Why not by Hagar, since Sarai herself proposed it?" Note, (1.) Foul temptations may have very fair pretenses, and be coloured with that which is very plausible. (2.) Fleshly wisdom, as it anticipates God's time of mercy, so it puts us out of God's way. (3.) This would be happily prevented if we would ask counsel of God by the word and by prayer, before we attempt that which is important and suspicious. Herein Abram was wanting; he married without God's consent. *This persuasion came not of him that called him.*

Verses 4–6

We have here the immediate bad consequences of Abram's unhappy marriage to Hagar. A great deal of mischief it made quickly. When we do not well both sin and trouble lie at the door; and we may thank ourselves for the guilt and grief that follow us when we go out of the way of our duty. See it in this story.

I. Sarai is despised, and thereby provoked and put into a passion, *v.* 4. Hagar no sooner perceives herself with child by her master than she looks scornfully upon her mistress, upbraids her perhaps with her barrenness, insults over her, to make her to fret (as 1 Sa. 1:6), and boasts of the prospect she had of bringing an heir to Abram, to that good land, and to the promise. Now she thinks herself a better woman than Sarai, more favoured by Heaven, and likely to be better beloved by Abram; and therefore she will not submit as she has done. Note, 1. Mean and servile spirits, when favoured and advanced either by God or man, are apt to grow haughty and insolent, and to forget their place and origin. See Prov. 29:21; 30:21–23. It is a hard thing to bear honour aright. 2. We justly suffer by those whom we have sinfully indulged, and it is a righteous thing with God to make those instruments of our trouble whom we have made instruments of our sin, and to ensnare us in our own evil counsels: this stone will return upon him that rolleth it.

II. Abram is clamoured upon, and cannot be easy while Sarai is out of humour; she upbraids him vehemently, and very unjustly charges him with the injury (*v.* 5): *My wrong be upon thee,* with a most unreasonable jealousy suspecting that he countenanced Hagar's insolence; and, as one not willing to hear what Abram had to say for the rectifying of the mistake and the clearing of himself, she rashly appeals to God in the case: *The Lord judge between me and thee;* as if Abram had refused to right her. Thus does Sarai, in her passion, speak *as one of the foolish women speaketh.* Note, 1. It is an absurdity which passionate people are often guilty of to quarrel with others for that of which they themselves must bear the blame. Sarai could not but own that she had given her maid to Abram, and yet she cries out, *My wrong be upon thee,* when she should have said, *What a fool was I to do so!* That is never said wisely which pride and anger have the inditing of; when passion is upon the throne, reason is out of doors, and is neither heard nor spoken. 2. Those are not always in the right who are most loud and forward in appealing to God. Rash and bold imprecations are commonly evidences of guilt and a bad cause.

III. Hagar is afflicted, and driven from the house, *v.* 6. Observe, 1. Abram's meekness resigns the matter of the maid-servant to Sarai, whose proper province it was to rule that part of the family: *Thy maid is in thy hand.* Though she was his wife, he would not countenance nor protect her in any thing that was disrespectful to Sarai, for whom he still retained the same affection that ever he had. Note, Those who would keep up peace and love must return soft answers to hard accusations. Husbands and wives particularly should agree, and endeavour not to be both angry together. *Yielding pacifies great offenses.* See Prov. 15:1. 2. Sarai's passion will be revenged upon Hagar: *She dealt hardly with her,* not only confining her to her usual place and work as a servant, but probably making her to serve with rigour. Note, God takes notice of, and is displeased with, the hardships which harsh masters unreasonably put upon their servants. They ought to forbear threatening, with Job's thought, *Did not he that made me make him?* Job 31:15. 3. Hagar's pride cannot bear it, her high spirit having become impatient of rebuke: *She fled from her face.* She not only avoided her wrath for the present, as David did Saul's, but she totally deserted her service, and ran away from the house, forgetting, (1.) What wrong she hereby did to her mistress, whose servant she was, and to her master, whose wife she was. Note, Pride will hardly be restrained by *any* bonds of duty, no, not by *many.* (2.) That she herself had first given the provocation, by despising her mistress. Note, Those that suffer for their faults ought to bear their sufferings patiently, 1 Pt. 2:20.

Verses 7–9

Here is the first mention we have in scripture of an angel's appearance. Hagar was a type of the law, which was *given by the disposition of angels; but the world to come is not put in subjection to them,* Heb. 2:5. Observe,

I. How the angel arrested her in her flight, *v.* 7. It should seem, she was making towards her own country; for she was in the way to Shur, which lay towards Egypt. It were well if our afflictions would make us think of our home, the better country. But Hagar was now out of her place, and out of the way of her duty, and going further astray, when the angel found her. Note, 1. It is a great mercy to be stopped in a sinful way either by conscience or by Providence. 2. God suffers those that are out of the way to wander awhile, that when they see their folly, and what a loss they have brought themselves to, they may be the better disposed to return. Hagar was not stopped till she was in the wilderness, and had set down, weary enough, and glad of clear water to refresh herself with. God brings us into a wilderness, and there meets us, Hos. 2:14.

II. How he examined her, *v.* 8. Observe,

1. He called her *Hagar, Sarai's maid,* (1.) As a check to her pride. Though she was Abram's wife, and, as such, was obliged to return, yet he calls her *Sarai's maid,* to humble her. Note, Though civility teaches us to call others by their highest titles, yet humility and wisdom teach us to call ourselves by the lowest. (2.) As a rebuke to her flight. Sarai's maid ought to be in Sarai's tent, and not wandering in the wilderness and sauntering by a fountain of water. Note, It is good for us often to call to mind what our place and relation are. See Eccl. 10:4.

2. The questions the angel put to her were proper and very pertinent. (1.) *"Whence comest thou?* Consider that thou art running away both from the duty thou wast bound to and the privileges thou wast blessed with in Abram's tent." Note, It is a great advantage to live in a religious family, which those ought to consider who have that advantage, yet upon every slight inducement are forward to quit it. (2.) *"Whither wilt thou go?* Thou art running thyself into sin, in Egypt" (if she return to that people, she will return to their gods), "and into danger, in the wilderness," through which she must travel, Deu. 8:15. Note, Those who are forsaking God and their duty would do well to remember not only *whence they have fallen,* but *whither they are falling.* See Jer. 2:18, *What hast thou to do* (with Hagar) in the way of Egypt? Jn. 6:68.

3. Her answer was honest, and a fair confession: *I flee from the face of my mistress.* In this, (1.) She acknowledges her fault in fleeing from her mistress, and yet, (2.) Excuses it, that it was *from the face,* of displeasure, of her mistress. Note, Children and servants must be treated with mildness and gentleness, lest we provoke them to take any irregular courses and so become accessory to their sins, which will condemn us, though it will not justify them.

4. How he sent her back, with suitable and compassionate counsel: *"Return to thy mistress, and submit thyself under her hand, v.* 9. Go home, and humble thyself for what thou hast done amiss, and beg pardon, and resolve for the future to behave thyself better." He makes no question but she would be welcome, though it does not appear that Abram sent after her. Note, Those that have gone away from their place and duty, when they are convinced of their error, must hasten their return and reformation, how mortifying soever it may be.

Verses 10–14

We may suppose that the angel having given Hagar that good counsel (*v.* 9) to *return to her mistress* she immediately promised to do so, and was setting her face homeward; and then the angel went on to encourage her with an assurance of the mercy God had in store for her and her seed: for God will meet those with mercy that are returning to their duty. *I said, I will confess, and thou forgavest,* Ps. 32:5. Here is,

I. A prediction concerning her posterity given her for her comfort in her present distress. Notice is taken of her condition: *Behold, thou art with child;* and therefore this is not a fit place for thee to be in. Note, It is a great comfort to women with child to think that they are under the particular cognizance and care of the divine Providence. God graciously considers their case and suits supports to it. Now, 1. The angel assures her of a safe delivery, and that of a *son,* which Abram desired. This fright and ramble of hers might have destroyed her hope of an offspring; but God dealt not with her according to her folly: *Thou shalt bear a son.* She was saved in child-bearing, not only by providence, but by promise. 2. He names her child, which was an honour both to her and it: Call him *Ishmael, God will hear;* and the reason is, because the Lord has heard; he has, and therefore he will. Note, The experience we have had of God's seasonable kindness to us in distress would encourage us to hope for similar help in similar exigencies, Ps. 10:17. He has *heard thy affliction, v.* 11. Note, Even where there is little cry of devotion, the God of pity sometimes graciously hears the cry of affliction. Tears speak as well as prayers. This speaks comfort to the afflicted, that God not only sees what their afflictions are, but hears what they say. Note, further, Seasonable succours, in a day of affliction, ought always to be remembered with thankfulness to God. Such a time, in such a strait, *the Lord heard the voice of my affliction, and helped me.* See Deu. 26:7; Ps. 31:22. 3. He promises her a numerous offspring, (*v.* 10): *I will multiply thy seed exceedingly,* Heb. *multiplying, I will multiply it,* that is, multiply it in every age, so as to perpetuate it. It is supposed that the Turks at this day descend from Ishmael; and they are a great people. This was in pursuance of the promise made to Abram: *I will make thy seed as the dust of the earth, ch.* 13:16. Note, Many that are children of godly parents have, for their sakes, a very large share of outward common blessings, though, like Ishmael, they are not taken into covenant: many are multiplied that are not sanctified. 4. He gives a character of the child she should bear, which, however it may seem to us, perhaps was not very disagreeable to her (*v.* 12): *He will be a wild man; a wild ass of a man* (so the word is), rude, and bold, and fearing no man — untamed, untractable living at large, and impatient of service and restraint. Note, The children of the bondwoman, who are out of covenant with God, are, as they were born, like the wild ass's colt; it is grace that reclaims men, civilizes them, and makes them wise, and good for something. It is foretold, (1.) That he should live in strife, and in a state of war: *His hand against every man* — this is his *sin; and every man's hand against him* — this is his *punishment.* Note, Those that have turbulent spirits have commonly troublesome lives; those that are provoking, vexatious, and injurious to others, must expect to be repaid in their own coin. He that has his hand and tongue against every man shall have every man's hand and tongue against him, and he has no reason to complain of it. And yet, (2.) That he should live in safety, and hold his own against all the world: *He shall dwell in the presence of all his brethren;* though threatened and insulted by all his neighbours, yet he shall keep his ground, and for Abram's sake, more than his own, shall be able to make his part good with them. Accordingly we read (*ch.* 25:18), that he *died,* as he lived, *in the presence of all his brethren.* Note, Many that are much exposed by their own imprudence are yet strangely preserved by the divine Providence, so much better is God to them than they deserve, when they not only forfeit their lives by sin, but hazard them.

II. Hagar's pious reflection upon this gracious appearance of God to her, *v.* 13, 14. Observe in what she said,

1. Her awful adoration of God's omniscience and providence, with application of it to herself: *She called the name of the Lord that spoke unto her,* that is, thus she made confession of his name, this she said to his praise, *Thou God seest me:* this should be, with her, his name for ever, and this his memorial, by which she will know him and remember him while she lives, *Thou God seest me.* Note, (1.) The God with whom we have to do is a seeing God, and all-seeing God. *God is* (as the ancients express it) *all eye.* (2.) We ought to acknowledge this with application to ourselves. He that sees all sees me, as David (Ps. 139:1), *O Lord, thou hast searched me, and known me.* (3.) A believing regard to God, as a God that sees us, will be of great use to us in our returns to him. It is a proper word for a penitent: — [1.] "Thou seest my sin and folly." I have *sinned before thee,* says the prodigal; *in thy sight,* says David. [2.] "Thou seest my sorrow and affliction;" this Hagar especially refers to. When we have brought ourselves into distress by our own folly, yet God has not forsaken us. [3.] "Thou seest the sincerity and seriousness of my return and repentance. Thou seest my secret mournings for sin, and secret motions towards thee." [4.] "Thou seest me, if in any instance I depart from thee," Ps. 44:20, 21. This thought should always restrain us from sin and excite us to duty: *Thou God seest me.*

2. Her humble admiration of God's favour to her: *"Have I here also looked after him that seeth me?* Have I here *seen the back parts* of him that seeth me?" so it might be read, for the word is much the same with that, Ex. 33:23. She saw not *face to face,* but as *through a glass darkly,* 1 Co. 13:12. Probably she knew not who it was that talked with her, till he was departing (as Jdg. 6:21, 22; 13:21), and then she looked after him, with a reflection like that of the two disciples, Lu. 24:31, 32. Or, *Have I here seen him that sees me?* Note, (1.) The communion which holy souls have with God consists in their having an eye of faith towards him, as a God that has an eye of favour towards them. The intercourse is kept up by the eye. (2.) The privilege of our communion with God is to be looked upon with wonder and admiration, [1.] Considering what we are who are admitted to this favour. "Have I? I that am so mean, I that am so vile?" 2 Sa. 7:18. [2.] Considering the place where we are thus favoured — "*here* also? Not only in Abram's tent and at his altar, but *here* also, in this wilderness? Here, where I never expected it, where I was out of the way of my duty? *Lord, how is it?"* Jn. 14:22. Some make the answer to this question to be negative, and so look upon it as a penitent reflection; *"Have I here also,* in my distress and affliction, *looked after God?* No, I was a careless and unmindful of him as ever I used to be; and yet he has thus visited and regarded me:" for God often anticipates us with his favours, and is found of those that seek him not, Isa. 65:1.

III. The name which this gave to the place: *Beer-lahai-roi, The well of him that liveth and seeth me, v.* 14. It is probable that Hagar put this name upon it; and it was retained long after, *in perpetuam rei memoriam —a lasting memorial of this event.* This was a place where the God of glory manifested the special cognizance and care he took of a poor woman in distress. Note, 1. He that is all-seeing is ever-living; he lives and sees us. 2. Those that are graciously admitted into communion with God, and receive seasonable comforts from him, should tell others what he has done for their souls, that they also may be encouraged to seek him and trust in him. 3. God's gracious manifestations of himself to us are to be had in everlasting remembrance by us, and should never be forgotten.

Verses 15–16

It is here taken for granted, though not expressly recorded, that Hagar did as the angel commanded her, returning to here mistress and submitting herself; and then, in the fulness of time, she brought forth her son. Note, Those who obey divine precepts shall have the comfort of divine promises. This was the son of the bond-woman that was *born after the flesh* (Gal. 4:23), representing the unbelieving Jews, *v.* 25. Note, 1. Many who can call Abraham father are yet *born after the flesh,* Mt. 3:9. 2. The carnal seed in the church are sooner brought forth than the spiritual. It is an easier thing to persuade men to assume the form of godliness than to submit to the power of godliness.

CHAPTER 17

This chapter contains articles of agreement covenanted and concluded upon between the great Jehovah, the Father of mercies, on the one part, and pious Abram, the father of the faithful, on the other part. Abram is therefore called "the friend of God," not only because he was the man of his counsel, but because he was the man of his covenant; both these secrets were with him. Mention was made of this covenant (*ch.* 15:18), but here it is particularly drawn up, and put into the form of a covenant, that Abram might have strong consolation. Here are, I. The circumstances of the making of this covenant, the time and manner (*v.* 1), and the posture Abram was in (*v.* 3). II. The covenant itself. In the general scope of it (*v.* 1). And, afterwards, in the particular instances. 1. That he should be the father of many nations (*v.* 4, 6), and, in token of this, his name was changed (*v.* 5). 2. That God would be a God to him and his seed, and would give them the land of Canaan (*v.* 7, 8). And the seal of this part of the covenant was circumcision (*v.* 9–14). 3. That he should have a son by Sarai, and, in token thereof, her name was changed (*v.* 15, 16). This promise Abram received (*v.* 17). And his request for Ishmael (*v.* 18) was answered, abundantly to his satisfaction (*v.* 19–22). III. The circumcision of Abram and his family, according to God's appointment (*v.* 23, etc.).

Verses 1–3

Here is, I. The time when God made Abram this gracious visit: *When he was ninety-nine years old,* full thirteen years after the birth of Ishmael. 1. So long, it should seem, God's extraordinary appearances to Abram were intermitted; and all the communion he had with God was only in the usual was of ordinances and providences. Note, There are some special comforts which are not the daily bread, no, not of the best saints, but they are favoured with them now and then. On this side heaven they have convenient food, but not a continual feast. 2. So long the promise of Isaac was deferred. (1.) Perhaps to correct Abram's over-hasty marrying of Hagar. Note, The comforts we sinfully anticipate are justly delayed. (2.) That Abram and Sarai being so far stricken in age God's power, in this matter, might be the more magnified, and their faith the more tried. See Deu. 32:36; Jn. 11:6, 15. (3.) That a child so long waited for might be an *Isaac, a son indeed,* Isa. 54:1.

II. The way in which God made this covenant with him: *The Lord appeared to Abram,* in the *shechinah,* some visible display of God's immediate glorious presence with him. Note, God first makes himself known to us, and gives us a sight of him by faith, and then takes us into his covenant.

III. The posture Abram put himself into upon this occasion: *He fell on his face while God talked with him, v.* 3. 1. As one overcome by the brightness of the divine glory, and unable to bear the sight of it, though he had seen it several times before. Daniel and John did likewise, though they were also acquainted with the visions of the Almighty, Dan. 8:17; 10:9, 15; Rev. 1:17. Or, 2. As one ashamed of himself, and blushing to think of the honours done to one so unworthy. He looks upon himself with humility, and upon God with reverence, and, in token of both, *falls on his face,* putting himself into a posture of adoration. Note, (1.) God graciously condescends to talk with those whom he takes into covenant and communion with himself. He talks with them by his *word,* Prov. 6:22. He talks with them by his *Spirit,* Jn. 14:26. This honour have all his saints. (2.) Those that are admitted into fellowship with God are, and must be, very humble and very reverent in their approaches to him. If we say we have fellowship with him, and the familiarity breeds contempt, we deceive ourselves. (3.) Those that would receive comfort from God must set themselves to give glory to God and to worship at his footstool.

IV. The general scope and summary of the covenant laid down as the foundation on which all the rest was built; it is no other than the covenant of grace still made with all believers in Jesus Christ, *v.* 1. Observe here,

1. What we may expect to find God to us: *I am the Almighty God.* By this name he chose to make himself known to Abram rather than by his name *Jehovah,* Ex. 6:3. He used it to Jacob, *ch.* 28:3; 43:14; 48:3. It is the name of God that is mostly used throughout the book of Job, at least in the *discourses* of that book. After Moses, *Jehovah* is more frequently used, and this, *El-shaddai,* very rarely; it bespeaks the almighty power of God, either, (1.) As an avenger, from *sdh he laid waste,* so some; and they think God took this title from the destruction of the old world. This is countenanced by Isa. 13:6, and Joel 1:15. Or, (2.) As a benefactor *s* for *asr who,* and *dy sufficient.* He is a God that is enough; or, as our old English translation reads it here very significantly, *I am God all-sufficient.* Note, The God with whom we have to do is a God *that is enough.* [1.] He is enough in himself; he is self-sufficient; he has every thing, and he needs not any thing. [2.] He is enough to us, if we be in covenant with him: we have all in him, and we have enough in him, enough to satisfy our most enlarged desires, enough to supply the defect of every thing else, and to secure to us a happiness for our immortal souls. See Ps. 16:5, 6; 73:25.

2. What God requires that we should be to him. The covenant is mutual: *Walk before me, and be thou perfect,* that is, upright and sincere; for herein the covenant of grace is well-ordered that sincerity is our gospel perfection. Observe, (1.) That to be religious is to walk before God in our integrity; it is to set God always before us, and to think, and speak, and act, in every think, as those that

are always under his eye. It is to have a constant regard to his word as our rule and to his glory as our end in all our actions, and to be continually in his fear. It is to be *inward with him,* in all the duties of religious worship, for in them particularly we walk before God (1 Sa. 2:30), and to be *entire for him,* in all holy conversation. I know no religion but sincerity. (2.) That upright walking with God is the condition of our interest in his all-sufficiency. If we neglect him, or dissemble with him, we forfeit the benefit and comfort of our relation to him. (3.) A continual regard to God's all-sufficiency will have a great influence upon our upright walking with him.

Verses 4–6

The promise here is introduced with solemnity: *"As for me,"* says the great God, "behold, behold and admire it, behold and be assured of it, my covenant is with thee;" as before (*v.* 2), *I will make my covenant.* Note, The covenant of grace is a covenant of God's own making; this he glories in *(as for me),* and so may we. Now here,

I. It is promised to Abraham that he should be a *father of many nations;* that is, 1. That his seed after the flesh should be very numerous, both in Isaac and Ishmael, as well as in the sons of Keturah: something extraordinary is doubtless included in this promise, and we may suppose that the event answered to it, and that there have been, and are, more of the children of men descended from Abraham than from any one man at an equal distance with him from Noah, the common root. 2. That all believers in every age should be looked upon as his spiritual seed, and that he should be called, not only *the friend of God,* but *the father of the faithful.* In this sense the apostle directs us to understand this promise, Rom. 4:16, 17. He is the father of those in every nation that by faith enter into covenant with God, and (as the Jewish writers express it) *are gathered under the wings of the divine Majesty.*

II. In token of this his name was changed from *Abram, a high father,* to *Abraham, the father of a multitude.* This was, 1. To put an honour upon him. It is spoken of as the glory of the church that she shall be *called by a new name, which the mouth of the Lord shall name,* Isa. 62:2. Princes dignify their favourites by conferring new titles upon them; thus was Abraham dignified by him that is indeed the fountain of honour. All believers have a new name, Rev. 2:17. Some think it added to the honour of Abraham's new name that a letter of the name *Jehovah* was inserted into it, as it was a disgrace to Jeconiah to have the first syllable of his name cut off, because it was the same as the first syllable of the sacred name, Jer. 22:28. Believers are named from Christ, Eph. 3:15. 2. To encourage and confirm the faith of Abraham. While he was childless perhaps even his own name was sometimes an occasion of grief to him: why should he be called a high father who was not a father at all? But now that God had promised him a numerous issue, and had given him a name which signified so much, that name was his joy. Note, God calls things that are not as though they were. It is the apostle's observation upon this very thing, Rom. 4:17. He called Abraham *the father of a multitude* because he should prove to be so in due time, though as yet he had but one child.

Verses 7–14

Here is, I. The continuance of the covenant, intimated in three things: — 1. It is established; not to be altered nor revoked. It is fixed, it is ratified, it is made as firm as the divine power and truth can make it. 2. It is entailed; it is a covenant, not with Abraham only (then it would die with him), but with his seed after him, not only his seed after the flesh, but his spiritual seed. 3. It is everlasting in the evangelical sense and meaning of it. The covenant of grace is everlasting. It is from everlasting in the counsels of it, and to everlasting in the consequences of it; and the external administration of it is transmitted with the seal of it to the seed of believers, and the internal administration of it by the Spirit of Christ's seed in every age.

II. The contents of the covenant: it is a covenant of promises, exceedingly great and precious promises. Here are two which indeed are all-sufficient: — 1. That God would be their God, *v.* 7, 8. All the privileges of the covenant, all its joys and all its hopes, are summed up in this. A man needs desire no more than this to make him happy. What God is himself, that he will be to his people: his wisdom theirs, to guide and counsel them; his power theirs, to protect and support them; his goodness theirs, to supply and comfort them. What faithful worshippers can expect from the God they serve believers shall find in God as theirs. This is enough, yet not all. 2. That Canaan should be their everlasting possession, *v.* 8. God had before promised this land to Abraham and his seed, *ch.* 15:18. But here, where it is promised for an everlasting possession, surely it must be looked upon as a type of heaven's happiness, that everlasting rest which remains for the people of God, Heb. 4:9. This is that better country to which Abraham had an eye, and the grant of which was that which answered to the vast extent and compass of that promise, that God would be to them a God; so that, if God had not prepared and designed this, he would have been ashamed to be called their God, Heb. 11:16. As the land of Canaan was secured to the seed of Abraham according to the flesh, so heaven is secured to all his spiritual seed, by a covenant, and for a possession, truly everlasting. The offer of this eternal life is made in the word, and confirmed by the sacraments, to all that are under the external administration of the covenant; and the earnest of it is given to all believers, Eph. 1:14. Canaan is here said to be the land wherein Abraham was a stranger; and the heavenly Canaan is a land to which we are strangers, for it does not yet appear what we shall be.

III. The token of the covenant, and that is circumcision, for the sake of which the covenant is itself called the *covenant of circumcision,* Acts 7:8. It is here said to be the covenant which Abraham and his seed must keep, as a copy or counterpart, *v.* 9, 10. It is called a sign and seal (Rom. 4:11), for it was, 1. A confirmation to Abraham and his seed of those promises which were God's part of the covenant, assuring them that they should be fulfilled, that in due time Canaan would be theirs: and the continuance of this ordinance, after Canaan was theirs, intimates that these promises looked further to another Canaan, which they must still be in expectation of. See Heb. 4:8. 2. An obligation upon Abraham and his seed to that duty which was their port of the covenant; not only to the duty of accepting the covenant and consenting to it, and putting away the corruption of the flesh (which were more immediately and primarily signified by circumcision), but, in general, to the observance of all God's commands, as they should at any time hereafter be intimated and made known to them; for circumcision made men *debtors to do the whole law,* Gal. 5:3. Those who will have God to be to them a God must consent and resolve to be to him a people. Now, (1.) Circumcision was a bloody ordinance; for all things by the law were purged with blood, Heb. 9:22. See Ex. 24:8. But, the blood of Christ being shed, all bloody ordinances are now abolished; circumcision therefore gives way to baptism. (2.) It was peculiar to the males, though the women were also included in the covenant, for the man is the head of the woman. In our kingdom, the oath of allegiance is required only from men. Some think that the blood of the males only was shed in circumcision because respect was had in it to Jesus Christ and his blood. (3.) It was the flesh of the foreskin that was to be cut off, because it is by ordinary generation that sin is propagated, and with an eye to the promised seed, who was to come from the loins of Abraham. Christ having not yet offered himself to us, God would have man to enter into covenant by the offering of some part of his own body, and no part could be better spared. It is a secret part of the body; for the true circumcision is that of the heat: this honour God put upon an uncomely part, 1 Co. 12:23, 24. (4.) The ordinance was to be administered to children when they were eight days old, and not sooner, that they might gather some strength, to be able to undergo the pain of it, and that at least one sabbath might pass over them. (5.) The children of the strangers, of whom the master of the family was the true domestic owner, were to be circumcised (*v.* 12, 13), which looked favourable upon the Gentiles, who should in due time be brought into the family of Abraham, by faith. See Gal. 3:14. (6.) The religious observance of this institution was required under a very severe penalty, *v.* 14. The contempt of circumcision was a contempt of the covenant; if the parents did not circumcise their children, it was at their peril, as in the case of Moses, Ex. 4:24, 25. With respect to those that were not circumcised in their infancy, if, when they grew up, they did not themselves come under this ordinance, God would surely reckon with them. If they cut not off the flesh of their foreskin, God would cut them off from their people. It is a dangerous thing to make light of divine institutions, and to live in the neglect of them.

Verses 15–22

Here is, I. The promise made to Abraham of a son by *Sarai,* that son in whom the promise made to him should be fulfilled, that he should be the father of many nations; for *she also shall be a mother of nations, and kings of people shall be of her, v.* 16. Note, 1. God reveals the purposes of his good-will to his people by degrees. God had told Abraham long before that he should have a son, but never till now that he should have a son by *Sarai.* 2. The blessing of the Lord makes fruitful, and adds no sorrow with it, no such sorrow as was in Hagar's case. "I will bless her with the blessing of fruitfulness, and then thou shalt have a son of her." 3. Civil government and order are a great blessing to the church. It is promised, not only that *people,* but *kings of people,* should be of her; not a headless rout, but a well-modelled well-governed society.

II. The ratification of this promise was the change of *Sarai's* name into *Sarah* (*v.* 15), the same letter being added to her name that was to Abraham's, and for the same reasons. *Sarai* signifies *my princess,* as if her honour were confined to one family only. *Sarah* signifies *a princess* — namely, of *multitudes,* or signifying that from her should come the Messiah the prince, even the prince of the kings of the earth.

III. Abraham's joyful, thankful, entertainment of this gracious promise, *v.* 17. Upon this occasion he expressed, 1. Great humility: He *fell on his face.* Note, The more honours and favours God confers upon us the lower we should be in our own eyes, and the more reverent and submissive before God. 2. Great joy: He *laughed.* It was a laughter of delight, not of distrust. Note, Even the promises of a holy God, as well as his performances, are the joys of holy souls; there is the joy of faith as well as the joy of fruition. Now it was that Abraham rejoiced to see Christ's day. Now he saw it and was glad (Jn. 8:56); for, as he saw heaven in the promise of Canaan, so he saw Christ in the promise of Isaac. 3. Great admiration: *Shall a child be born to him that is a hundred years old?* He does not here speak of it as at all doubtful (for we are sure that *he staggered not at the promise,* Rom. 4:20), but as very wonderful and that which could not be effected but by the almighty power of God, and as very *kind,* and a favour which was the more affecting and obliging for this, that it was extremely surprising, Ps. 126:1, 2.

IV. Abraham's prayer for Ishmael: *O that Ishmael might live before thee! v.* 18. This he speaks, not as desiring that Ishmael might be preferred before the son he should have by Sarah; but, dreading lest he should be abandoned and forsaken of God, he puts up this petition on his behalf. Now that God is talking with him he thinks he has a very fair opportunity to speak a good word for Ishmael, and he will not let it slip. Note, 1. Though we ought not to prescribe to God, yet he gives us leave, in prayer, to be humbly free with him, and particular in making known our requests, Phil. 4:6. Whatever is the matter of our care and fear should be spread before God in prayer. 2. It is the duty of parents to pray for their children, for all their children, as Job, who offered burnt offerings according to the number of them all, Job 1:5. Abraham would not have it thought that, when God promised him a son by Sarah, which he so much desired, then his son by Hagar was forgotten; no, still he bears him upon his heart, and shows a concern for him. The prospect of further favours must not make us unmindful of former favours. 3. The great thing we should desire of God for our children is that they may live before him, that is, that they may be kept in covenant with him, and may have grace to walk before him in their uprightness. Spiritual blessings are the best blessings, and those for which we should be most earnest with God, both for ourselves and others. Those live well that live before God.

V. God's answer to his prayer; and it is an answer of peace. Abraham could not say that he sought God's face in vain.

1. Common blessings are secured to Ishmael (*v.* 20): *As for Ishmael,* whom thou art in so much care about, *I have*

heard thee; he shall find favour for thy sake; *I have blessed him,* that is, I have many blessings in store for him. (1.) His posterity shall be numerous: *I will multiply him exceedingly,* more than his neighbours. This is the fruit of the blessing, as that, *ch.* 1:28. (2.) They shall be considerable: *Twelve princes shall he beget.* We may charitably hope that spiritual blessings also were bestowed upon him, though the visible church was not brought out of his loins and the covenant was not lodged in his family. Note, Great plenty of outward good things is often given to those children of godly parents who are born after the flesh, for their parents' sake.

2. Covenant blessings are reserved for Isaac, and appropriated to him, *v.* 19, 21. If Abraham, in his prayer for Ishmael, meant that he would have the covenant made with him, and the promised seed to come from him, then God did not answer him in the letter, but in that which was equivalent, nay, which was every way better. (1.) God repeats to him the promise of a son by Sarah: *She shall bear thee a son indeed.* Note, Even true believers need to have God's promises doubled and repeated to them, that they may have strong consolation, Heb. 6:18. Again, Children of the promise are children indeed. (2.) He names that child — calls him *Isaac, laughter,* because Abraham rejoiced in spirit when this son was promised him. Note, If God's promises be our joy, his mercies promised shall in due time be our *exceeding* joy. Christ will be laughter to those that look for him; those that now rejoice in hope shall shortly rejoice in having that which they hope for: this is laughter that is not mad. (3.) He entails the covenant upon that child: *I will establish my covenant with him.* Note, God takes whom he pleases into covenant with himself, according to the good pleasure of his will. See Rom. 9:8, 18. Thus was the covenant settled between God and Abraham, with its several limitations and remainders, and then the conference ended: *God left off talking with him,* and the vision disappeared, *God went up from Abraham.* Note, Our communion with God here is broken and interrupted; in heaven it will be a continual and everlasting feast.

Verses 23–27

We have here Abraham's obedience to the law of circumcision. He himself and all his family were circumcised, so receiving the token of the covenant and distinguishing themselves from other families, that had no part nor lot in the matter. 1. It was an implicit obedience: He did *as God had said to him,* and did not ask why or wherefore. God's will was not only a law to him, but a reason; he did it because God told him. 2. It was a speedy obedience: *In the self-same day, v.* 23, 26. Sincere obedience is not dilatory, Ps. 119:60. While the command is yet sounding in our ears, and the sense of duty is fresh, it is good to apply ourselves to it immediately, lest we deceive ourselves by putting it off to a more convenient season. 3. It was a universal obedience: He did not circumcise his family and excuse himself, but set them an example; nor did he take the comfort of the seal of the covenant to himself only, but desired that all his might share with him in it. This is a good example to masters of families; they and their houses must serve the Lord. Though God's covenant was not established with Ishmael, yet he was circumcised; for children of believing parents, as such, have a right to the privileges of the visible church, and the seals of the covenant, whatever they may prove afterwards. Ishmael is blessed, and therefore circumcised. 4. Abraham did this though much might be objected against it. Though circumcision was painful, — though to grown men it was shameful, — though, while they were sore and unfit for action, their enemies might take advantage against them, as Simeon and Levi did against the Shechemites, — though Abraham was ninety-nine years old, and had been justified and accepted of God long since, — though so strange a thing done religiously might be turned to his reproach by the Canaanite and the Perizzite that dwelt then in the land, — yet God's command was sufficient to answer these and a thousand such objection: what God requires we must do, not *conferring with flesh and blood.*

CHAPTER 18

We have an account in this chapter of another interview between God and Abraham, probably within a few days after the former, as the reward of his cheerful obedience to the law of circumcision. Here is, I. The kind visit which God made him, and the kind entertainment which he gave to that visit (*v.* 1–8). II. The matters discoursed of between them. 1. The purposes of God's love concerning Sarah (*v.* 9–15). 2. The purposes of God's wrath concerning Sodom. (1.) The discovery God made to Abraham of his design to destroy Sodom (*v.* 16–22). (2.) The intercession Abraham made for Sodom (*v.* 23, etc.).

Verses 1–8

The appearance of God to Abraham seems to have had in it more of freedom and familiarity, and less of grandeur and majesty, than those we have hitherto read of; and therefore more resembles that great visit which, in the fullness of time, the Son of God was to make to the world, when the Word would be flesh, and appear as one of us. Observe here,

I. How Abraham expected strangers, and how richly his expectations were answered (*v.* 1): *He sat in the tent-door, in the heat of the day;* not so much to repose or divert himself as to seek an opportunity of doing good, by giving entertainment to strangers and travellers, there being perhaps no inns to accommodate them. Note, 1. We are likely to have the most comfort of those good works to which we are most free and forward. 2. God graciously visits those in whom he has first raised the expectation of him, and manifests himself to those that wait for him. When Abraham was thus sitting, he saw three men coming towards him. These three men were three spiritual heavenly beings, now assuming human bodies, that they might be visible to Abraham, and conversable with him. Some think that they were all created angels, others that one of them was the Son of God, the angel of the covenant, whom Abraham distinguished from the rest (*v.* 3), and who is called *Jehovah, v.* 13. The apostle improves this for the encouragement of hospitality, Heb. 13:2. Those that have been forward to entertain strangers have entertained angels, to their unspeakable honour and satisfaction. Where, upon a prudent and impartial judgment, we see no cause to suspect ill, charity teaches us to hope well and to show kindness accordingly. It is better to feed five drones, or wasps, than to starve one bee.

II. How Abraham entertained those strangers, and how kindly his entertainment was accepted. The Holy Ghost takes particular notice of the very free and affectionate welcome Abraham gave to the strangers. 1. He was very complaisant and respectful to them. Forgetting his age and gravity, he *ran to meet them* in the most obliging manner, and with all due courtesy *bowed himself towards the ground,* though as yet he knew nothing of them but that they appeared graceful respectable men. Note, Religion does not destroy, but improve, good manners, and teaches us to honour all men. Decent civility is a great ornament to piety. 2. He was very earnest and importunate for their stay, and took it as a great favour, *v.* 3, 4. Note, (1.) It becomes those whom God has blessed with plenty to be liberal and open-hearted in their entertainments, according to their ability, and (not in compliment, but cordially) to bid their friends welcome. We should take a pleasure in showing kindness to any; for both God and man love a cheerful giver. Who would *eat the bread of him that has an evil eye?* Prov. 23:6, 7. (2.) Those that would have communion with God must earnestly desire it and pray for it. God is a guest worth entertaining. 3. His entertainment, though it was very free, was yet plain and homely, and there was nothing in it of the gaiety and niceness of our times. His dining-room was an arbour under a tree; no rich table-linen, no side-board set with plate. His feast was a joint or two of veal, and some cakes baked on the hearth, and both hastily dressed up. Here were no dainties, no varieties, no forced-meats, no sweet-meats, but good, plain, wholesome food, though Abraham was very rich and his guests were very honourable. Note, We ought not to be curious in our diet. Let us be thankful for food convenient, though it be homely and common; and not be desirous of dainties, for they are deceitful meat to those that love them and set their hearts upon them. 4. He and his wife were both of them very attentive and busy, in accommodating their guests with the best they had. Sarah herself is cook and baker; Abraham runs to fetch the calf, brings out the milk and butter, and thinks it not below him to wait at table, that he might show how heartily welcome his guests were. Note, (1.) Those that have real merit need not take state upon them, nor are their prudent condescensions any disparagement to them. (2.) Hearty friendship will stoop to any thing but sin. Christ himself has taught us to wash one another's feet, in humble love. Those that thus abase themselves shall be exalted. Here Abraham's faith showed itself in good works; and so must ours, else it is dead, Jam. 2:21, 26. The father of the faithful was famous for charity, and generosity, and good housekeeping; and we must learn of him to *do good and to communicate.* Job did not eat his morsel alone, Job 31:17.

Verses 9–15

These heavenly guests (being sent to confirm the promise lately made to Abraham, that he should have a son by Sarah), while they are receiving Abraham's kind entertainment, they return his kindness. He receives angels, and has angels' rewards, a gracious message from heaven, Mt. 10:41.

I. Care is taken that Sarah should be within hearing. She must conceive by faith, and therefore the promise must be made to her, Heb. 11:11. It was the modest usage of that time that the women did not sit at meat with men, at least not with strangers, but confined themselves to their own apartments; therefore Sarah is here out of sight: but she must not be out of hearing. The angels enquire (*v.* 9), *Where is Sarah thy wife?* By naming her, they gave intimation enough to Abraham that, though they seemed strangers, yet they very well knew him and his family. By enquiring after her, they showed a friendly kind concern for the family and relations of one whom they found respectful to them. It is a piece of common civility, which ought to proceed from a principle of Christian love, and then it is sanctified. And, by speaking of her (she overhearing it), they drew her to listen to what was further to be said. *Where is Sarah thy wife?* say the angels. *"Behold in the tent,"* says Abraham. "Where should she be else? There she is in her place, as she uses to be, and is now within call." Note, 1. The daughters of Sarah must learn of her to be *chaste, keepers at home,* Tit. 2:5. There is nothing got by gadding. 2. Those are most likely to receive comfort from God and his promises that are in their place and in the way of their duty, Lu. 2:8.

II. The promise is then renewed and ratified, that she should have a son (*v.* 10): *"I will certainly return unto thee,* and visit thee next time with the performance, as now I do with the promise." God will return to those that bid him welcome, that entertain his visits: "I will return thy kindness, *Sarah thy wife shall have a son;"* it is repeated again, *v.* 14. Thus the promises of the Messiah were often repeated in the Old Testament, for the strengthening of the faith of God's people. We are slow of heart to believe, and therefore have need of line upon line to the same purport. This is that word of promise which the apostle quotes (Rom. 9:9) as that by the virtue of which Isaac was born. Note, 1. The same blessings which others have from common providence believers have from the promise, which makes them very sweet and very sure. 2. The spiritual seed of Abraham owe their life, and joy, and hope, and all, to the promise. They are born by the word of God, 1 Pt. 1:23.

III. Sarah thinks this too good news to be true, and therefore cannot as yet find in her heart to believe it: *Sarah laughed within herself, v.* 12. It was not a pleasing laughter of faith, like Abraham's (*ch.* 17:17), but it was a laughter of doubting and mistrust. Note, The same thing may be done from very different principles, of which God only, who knows the heart, can judge. The great objection which Sarah could not get over was her age: *"I am waxed old,* and past childbearing in the course of nature, especially having been hitherto barren, and (which magnifies the difficulty) *my lord is old also."* Observe here, 1. Sarah calls Abraham her *lord;* it was the only good word in this saying, and the Holy Ghost takes notice of it to her honour, and recommends it to the imitation of all Christian wives. 1 Pt. 3:6, *Sarah obeyed Abraham, calling him lord,* in token of respect and subjection. Thus must the wife reverence her husband, Eph. 5:33. And thus must we be apt to take notice of what is spoken decently and well, to the honour of those that speak it, though it may be mixed with that which is amiss, over which we should cast a mantle of love. 2. Human improbability often sets up in contradiction to the divine promise. The objections of sense are very apt to stumble and puzzle the weak faith even of true believers. It is hard to cleave to the first Cause, when second causes frown. 3. Even where there is true faith, yet there are often sore conflicts with unbelief, Sarah could say, *Lord, I believe* (Heb. 11:11), and yet must say, *Lord, help my unbelief.*

IV. The angel reproves the indecent expressions of her distrust, *v.* 13, 14. Observe, 1. Though Sarah was now most kindly and generously entertaining these angels, yet, when she did amiss, they reproved her for it, as Christ reproved Martha in her own house, Lu. 10:40, 41. If our friends be kind to us, we must not therefore be so unkind to them as to suffer sin upon them. 2. God gave this reproof to Sarah by Abraham her husband. To him he said, *Why did Sarah laugh?* perhaps because he had not told her of the promise which had been given him some time before to this purport, and which, if he had communicated it to her with its ratifications, would have prevented her from being so surprised now. Or Abraham was told of it that he might tell her of it. Mutual reproof, when there is occasion for it, is one of the duties of the conjugal relation. 3. The reproof itself is plain, and backed with a good reason: *Wherefore did Sarah laugh?* Note, It is good to enquire into the reason of our laughter, that it may not be the laughter of the fool, Eccl. 7:6. "Wherefore did I laugh?" Again, Our unbelief and distrust are a great offence to the God of heaven. He justly takes it ill to have the objections of sense set up in contradiction to his promise, as Lu. 1:18. 4. Here is a question asked which is enough to answer all the cavils of flesh and blood: *Is any thing too hard for the Lord?* (Heb. *too wonderful*), that is, (1.) Is any thing so secret as to escape his cognizance? No, not Sarah's laughing, though it was only *within herself.* Or, (2.) Is any thing so difficult as to exceed his power? No, not the giving of a child to Sarah in her old age.

V. Sarah foolishly endeavours to conceal her fault (*v.* 15): *She denied, saying, I did not laugh,* thinking nobody could contradict her: she told this lie, because *she was afraid;* but it was in vain to attempt concealing it from an all-seeing eye; she was told, to her shame, *Thou didst laugh.* Now, 1. There seems to be in Sarah a retraction of her distrust. Now she perceived, by laying circumstances together, that it was a divine promise which had been made concerning her, she renounced all doubting distrustful thoughts about it. But, 2. There was withal a sinful attempt to cover a sin with a lie. It is a shame to do amiss, but a greater shame to deny it; for thereby we add iniquity to our iniquity. Fear of a rebuke often betrays us into this snare. See Isa. 57:11, *Whom hast thou feared, that thou hast lied?* But we deceive ourselves if we think to impose upon God; he can and will bring truth to light, to our shame. *He that covers his sin cannot prosper,* for the day is coming which will discover it.

Verses 16–22

The messengers from heaven had now despatched one part of their business, which was an errand of grace to Abraham and Sarah, and which they delivered first; but now they have before them work of another nature. Sodom is to be destroyed, and they must do it, *ch.* 19:13. Note, As with the Lord there is mercy, so he is the God to whom vengeance belongs. Pursuant to their commission, we here find, 1. That *they looked towards Sodom* (*v.* 16); they set their faces against it in wrath, as God is said to look unto the host of the Egyptians, Ex. 14:24. Note, Though God has long seemed to connive at sinners, from which they have inferred that the Lord does not see, does not regard, yet, when the day of his wrath comes, he will look towards them. 2. That they *went towards Sodom* (*v.* 22), and accordingly we find two of them at Sodom, *ch.* 19:1. Whether the third was the Lord, before whom Abraham yet stood, and to whom he drew near (*v.* 23), as most think, or whether the third left them before they came to Sodom, and the Lord before whom Abraham stood was the *shechinah,* or that appearance of the divine glory which Abraham had formerly seen and conversed with, is uncertain. However, we have here,

I. The honour Abraham did to his guests: *He went with them to bring them on the way,* as one that was loth to part with such good company, and was desirous to pay his utmost respects to them. This is a piece of civility proper to be shown to our friends; but it must be done as the apostle directs (3 Jn. 6), *after a godly sort.*

II. The honour they did to him; for those that honour God he will honour. God communicated to Abraham his purpose to destroy Sodom, and not only so, but entered into a free conference with him about it. Having taken him, more closely than before, into covenant with himself (*ch.* 17), he here admits him into more intimate communion with himself than ever, as the man of his counsel. Observe here,

1. God's friendly thoughts concerning Abraham, *v.* 17–19, where we have his resolution to make known to Abraham his purpose concerning Sodom, with the reasons of it. If Abraham had not brought them on their way, perhaps he would not have been thus favoured; but he that loves to walk with wise men shall be wise, Prov. 13:20. See how God is pleased to argue with himself: *Shall I hide from Abraham* (or, as some read it, *Am I concealing from Abraham) that thing which I do?* "Can I go about such a thing, and not tell Abraham?" Thus does God, in his counsels, express himself, after the manner of men, with deliberation. But why must Abraham be of the cabinet-council? The Jews suggest that because God had granted the land of Canaan to Abraham and his seed therefore he would not destroy those cities which were a part of that land, without his knowledge and consent. But God here gives two other reasons: —

(1.) Abraham must know, for he is a friend and a favourite, and one that God has a particular kindness for and great things in store for. He is to become a great nation; and not only so, but in the Messiah, who is to come from his loins, *All nations of the earth shall be blessed.* Note, *The secret of the Lord is with those that fear him,* Ps. 25:14; Prov. 3:32. Those who by faith live a life of communion with God cannot but know more of his mind than other people, though not with a prophetical, yet with a prudential practical knowledge. They have a better insight than others into what is present (Hos. 14:9; Ps. 107:43), and a better foresight of what is to come, at least so much as suffices for their guidance and for their comfort.

(2.) Abraham must know, for he will teach his household: *I know Abraham* very well, that *he will command his children and his household after him, v.* 19. Consider this, [1.] As a very bright part of Abraham's character and example. He not only prayed with his family, but he taught them as a man of knowledge, nay, he commanded them as a man in authority, and was prophet and king, as well as priest, in his own house. Observe, *First,* God having made the covenant with him and his seed, and his household being circumcised pursuant to that, he was very careful to teach and rule them well. Those that expect family blessings must make conscience of family duty. If our children be the Lord's, they must be nursed for him; if they wear his livery, they must be trained up in his work. *Secondly,* Abraham took care not only of his children, but of his household; his servants were catechized servants. Masters of families should instruct and inspect the manners of all under their roof. The poorest servants have precious souls that must be looked after. *Thirdly,* Abraham made it his care and business to promote practical religion in his family. He did not fill their heads with matters of nice speculation, or doubtful disputation; but he taught them to keep *the way of the Lord, and to do judgment and justice,* that is, to be serious and devout in the worship of God and to be honest in their dealings with all men. *Fourthly,* Abraham, herein, had an eye to posterity, and was in care not only that his household with him, but that his household after him, should keep the way of the Lord, that religion might flourish in his family when he was in his grave. *Fifthly,* His doing this was the fulfilling of the conditions of the promises which God had made him. Those only can expect the benefit of the promises that make conscience of their duty. [2.] As the reason why God would make known to him his purpose concerning Sodom, because he was communicative of his knowledge, and improved it for the benefit of those that were under his charge. Note, To him that hath shall be given, Mt. 13:12; 25:29. Those that make a good use of their knowledge shall know more.

2. God's friendly talk with Abraham, in which he makes known to him purpose concerning Sodom, and allows him a liberty of application to him about the matter. (1.) He tells him of the evidence there was against Sodom: *The cry of Sodom is great, v.* 20. Note, Some sins, and the sins of some sinners, cry aloud to heaven for vengeance. The iniquity of Sodom was crying iniquity, that is, it was so very provoking that it even urged God to punish. (2.) The enquiry he would make upon this evidence: *I will go down now and see, v.* 21. Not as if there were any thing concerning which God is in doubt, or in the dark; but he is pleased thus to express himself after the manner of men, [1.] To show the incontestable equity of all his judicial proceedings. Men are apt to suggest that his way is not equal; but let them know that his judgments are the result of an eternal counsel, and are never rash or sudden resolves. He never punishes upon report, or common fame, or the information of others, but upon his own certain and infallible knowledge. [2.] To give example to magistrates, and those in authority, with the utmost care and diligence to enquire into the merits of a cause, before they give judgment upon it. [3.] Perhaps the decree is here spoken of as not yet peremptory, that room and encouragement might be given to Abraham to make intercession for them. Thus God looked if there were any to intercede, Isa. 59:16.

Verses 23–33

Communion with God is kept up by the word and by prayer. In the word God speaks to us; in prayer we speak to him. God had revealed to Abraham his purposes concerning Sodom; now from this Abraham takes occasion to speak to God on Sodom's behalf. Note, God's word then does us good when it furnishes us with matter for prayer and excites us to it. When God has spoken to us, we must consider what we have to say to him upon it. Observe,

I. The solemnity of Abraham's address to God on this occasion: *Abraham drew near, v.* 23. The expression intimates, 1. A holy concern: *He engaged his heart* to approach to God, Jer, 30:21. "Shall Sodom be destroyed, and I not speak one good word for it?" 2. A holy confidence: He drew near *with an assurance of faith,* drew near *as a prince,* Job 31:37. Note, When we address ourselves to the duty of prayer, we ought to remember that we are drawing near to God, that we may be filled with a reverence of him, Lev. 10:3.

II. The general scope of this prayer. It is the first solemn prayer we have upon record in the Bible; and it is a prayer for the sparing of Sodom. Abraham, no doubt, greatly abhorred the wickedness of the Sodomites; he would not have lived among them, as Lot did, if they would have given him the best estate in their country; and yet he prayed earnestly for them. Note, Though sin is to be hated, sinners are to be pitied and prayed for. God delights not in their death, nor should we desire, but deprecate, the woeful day. 1. He begins with a prayer that the righteous among them might be spared, and not involved in the common calamity, having an eye particularly to just Lot, whose disingenuous carriage towards him he had long since forgiven and forgotten, witness his friendly zeal to rescue him before by his sword and now by his prayers. 2. He improves this into a petition that all might be spared for the sake of the righteous that were among them, God himself countenancing this request, and in effect putting him upon it by his answer to his first address, *v.* 26. Note, We must pray, not only for ourselves, but for others also; for we are members of the same body, at least of the same body of mankind. *All we are brethren.*

III. The particular graces eminent in this prayer.

1. Here is great faith; and it is the prayer of faith that is the prevailing prayer. His faith pleads with God, orders the cause, and fills his mouth with arguments. He acts faith especially upon the righteousness of God, and is very confident.

(1.) That God will not *destroy the righteous with the wicked, v.* 23. No, *that be far from thee, v.* 25. We must never entertain any thought that derogates from the honour of God's righteousness. See Rom. 3:5, 6. Note, [1.] The righteous are mingled with the wicked in this world. Among the best there are, commonly, some bad, and among the worst some good: even in Sodom, one Lot. [2.] Though the righteous be among the wicked, yet the righteous God will not, certainly he will not, destroy the righteous with the wicked. Though in this world they may be involved in the same common calamities, yet in the great day a distinction with be made.

(2.) That the righteous shall not *be as the wicked, v.* 25. Though they may suffer with them, yet they do not suffer like them. Common calamities are quite another thing to the righteous than what they are to the wicked, Isa. 27:7.

(3.) That *the Judge of all the earth will do right;* undoubtedly he will, because he is the Judge of all the earth; it is the apostle's argument, Rom. 3:5, 6. Note, [1.] God is the Judge of all the earth; he gives charge to all, takes cognizance of all, and will pass sentence upon all. [2.] That God Almighty never did nor ever will do any wrong to any of the creatures, either by withholding that which is right or by exacting more than is right, Job 34:10, 11.

2. Here is great humility.

(1.) A deep sense of his own unworthiness (*v.* 27): *Behold now, I have taken upon me to speak unto the Lord, who am but dust and ashes;* and again, *v.* 31. He speaks as one amazed at his own boldness, and the liberty God graciously allowed him, considering God's greatness — he is *the Lord;* and his own meanness — *but dust and ashes.* Note, [1.] The greatest of men, the most considerable and deserving, are but dust and ashes, mean and vile before God, despicable, frail, and dying. [2.] Whenever we draw near to God, it becomes us reverently to acknowledge the vast distance that there is between us and God. He is the Lord of glory, we are worms of the earth. [3.] The access we have to the throne of grace, and the freedom of speech allowed us, are just matter of humble wonder, 2 Sa. 7:18.

(2.) An awful dread of God's displeasure: *O let not the Lord be angry* (*v.* 30), and again, *v.* 32. Note, [1.] The importunity which believers use in their addresses to God is such that, if they were dealing with a man like themselves, they could not but fear that he would be angry with them. But he with whom we have to do is *God and not man;* and, whoever he may seem, is not really *angry with the prayers of the upright* (Ps. 80:4), for they are *his delight* (Prov. 15:8), and he is pleased when he is wrestled with. [2.] That even when we receive special tokens of the divine favour we ought to be jealous over ourselves, lest we make ourselves obnoxious to the divine displeasure; and therefore we must bring the Mediator with us in the arms of our faith, to atone for *the iniquity of our holy things.*

3. Here is great charity. (1.) A charitable opinion of Sodom's character: as bad as it was, he thought there were several good people in it. It becomes us to hope the best of the worst places. Of the two it is better to err in that extreme. (2.) A charitable desire of Sodom's welfare: he used all his interest at the throne of grace for mercy for them. We never find him thus earnest in pleading with God for himself and his family, as here for Sodom.

4. Here are great boldness and believing confidence. (1.) He took the liberty to pitch upon a certain number of righteous ones which he supposed might be in Sodom. Suppose there be fifty, *v.* 24. (2.) He advanced upon God's concessions, again and again. As God granted much, he still begged more, with the hope of gaining his point. (3.) He brought the terms as low as he could for shame (having prevailed for mercy if there were but ten righteous ones in five cities), and perhaps so low that he concluded they would have been spared.

IV. The success of the prayer. He that thus wrestled prevailed wonderfully; as a prince he had power with God: it was but ask and have. 1. God's general good-will appears in this, that he consented to spare the wicked for the sake of the righteous. See how swift God is to show mercy; he even seeks a reason for it. See what great blessings good people are to any place, and how little those befriend themselves that hate and persecute them. 2. His particular favour to Abraham appeared in this, that he did not leave off granting till Abraham left off asking. Such is the power of prayer. Why then did Abraham leave off asking, when he had prevailed so far as to get the place spared it there were but ten righteous in it? Either, (1.) Because he owned that it deserved to be destroyed if there were not so many; *as the dresser of the vineyard,* who consented that the barren tree should be cut down if one year's trial more did not make it fruitful, Lu. 13:9. Or, (2.) Because God restrained his spirit from asking any further. When God has determined the ruin of a place, he forbids it to be prayed for, Jer. 7:16; 11:14; 14:11.

V. Here is the breaking up of the conference, *v.* 33. 1. *The Lord went his way.* The visions of God must not be constant in this world, where it is by faith only that we are to set God before us. God did not go away till Abraham had said all he had to say; for he is never weary of hearing prayer, Isa. 59:1. 2. *Abraham returned unto his*

place, not puffed up with the honour done him, nor by these extraordinary interviews taken off from the ordinary course of duty. He returned to his place to observe what that event would be; and it proved that his prayer was heard, and yet Sodom was not spared, because there were not ten righteous in it. We cannot expect too little from man nor too much from God.

CHAPTER 19

The contents of this chapter we have, 2 Pt. 2:6–8, where we find that "God, turning the cities of Sodom and Gomorrah into ashes, condemned them with an overthrow, and delivered just Lot." It is the history of Sodom's ruin, and Lot's rescue from that ruin. We read (*ch.* 18) of God's coming to take a view of the present state of Sodom, what its wickedness was, and what righteous persons there were in it: now here we have the result of that enquiry. I. It was found, upon trial, that Lot was very good (*v.* 1–3), and it did not appear that there was any more of the same character. II. It was found that the Sodomites were very wicked and vile (*v.* 4–11). III. Special care was therefore taken for the securing of Lot and his family, in a place of safety (*v.* 12–23). IV. Mercy having rejoiced therein, justice shows itself in the ruin of Sodom and the death of Lot's wife (*v.* 24–26), with a general repetition of the story (*v.* 27–29). V. A foul sin that Lot was guilty of, in committing incest with his two daughters (*v.* 30, etc.).

Verses 1–3

These angels, it is likely, were two of the three that had just before been with Abraham, the two created angels that were sent to execute God's purpose concerning Sodom. Observe here, 1. There was but one good man in Sodom, and these heavenly messengers soon found him out. Wherever we are, we should enquire out those of the place that live in the fear of God, and should choose to associate ourselves with them. Mt. 10:11, *Enquire who is worthy, and there abide.* Those of the same country, when they are in a foreign country, love to be together. 2. Lot sufficiently distinguished himself from the rest of his neighbours, at this time, which plainly set a mark upon him. He that did not act like the rest must not fare like the rest. (1.) Lot sat in the gate of Sodom at even. When the rest, it is likely, were tippling and drinking, he sat alone, waiting for an opportunity to do good. (2.) He was extremely respectful to men whose mien and aspect were sober and serious, though they did not come in state. He bowed himself to the ground, when he met them, as if, upon the first view, he discerned something divine in them. (3.) He was hospitable, and very free and generous in his invitations and entertainments. He courted these strangers to his house, and to the best accommodations he had, and gave them all the evidences that he could of his sincerity; for, [1.] When the angels, to try whether he was hearty in the invitation, declined the acceptance of it, at first (which is the common usage of modesty, and no reproach at all to truth and honesty), their refusal did not make him more importunate; for he *pressed upon them greatly* (*v.* 3), partly because he would be no means have them to expose themselves to the inconveniences and perils of lodging in the street of Sodom, and partly because he was desirous of their company and converse. He had not seen two such honest faces in Sodom this great while. Note, Those that live in bad places should know how to value the society of those that are wise and good, and earnestly desire it. [2.] When the angels accepted his invitation, he treated them nobly; he made a feast for them, and thought it well-bestowed on such guests. Note, Good people should be (with prudence) generous people.

Verses 4–11

Now it appeared, beyond contradiction, that the cry of Sodom was no louder than there was cause for. This night's work was enough to fill the measure. For we find here,

I. That they were all wicked, *v.* 4. Wickedness had become universal, and they were unanimous in any vile design. Here were old and young, and all from every quarter, engaged in this riot; the old were not past it, and the young had soon come up to it. Either they had no magistrates to keep the peace, and protect the peaceable, or their magistrates were themselves aiding and abetting. Note, When the disease of sin has become epidemical, it is fatal to any place, Isa. 1:5–7.

II. That they had arrived at the highest pitch of wickedness; they were *sinners before the Lord exceedingly* (*ch.* 13:13); for, 1. It was the most unnatural and abominable wickedness that they were now set upon, a sin that still

bears their name, and is called *Sodomy.* They were carried headlong by those vile affections (Rom. 1:26, 27), which are worse than brutish, and the eternal reproach of the human nature, and which cannot be thought of without horror by those that have the least spark of virtue and any remains of natural light and conscience. Note, Those that allow themselves in unnatural uncleanness are marked for the vengeance of eternal fire. See Jude 7. 2. They were not ashamed to own it, and to prosecute their design by force and arms. The practice would have been bad enough if it had been carried on by intrigue and wheedling; but they proclaimed war with virtue, and bade open defiance to it. Hence daring sinners are said to *declare their sin as Sodom,* Isa. 3:9. Note, Those that have become impudent in sin generally prove impenitent in sin; and it will be their ruin. Those have hard hearts indeed that sin with a high hand, Jer. 6:15. 3. When Lot interposed, with all the mildness imaginable, to check the rage and fury of their lust, they were most insolently rude and abusive to him. He ventured himself among them, *v.* 6. He spoke civilly to them, called them *brethren* (*v.* 7), and begged of them not to do so wickedly; and, being greatly disturbed at their vile attempt, he unadvisedly and unjustifiably offered to prostitute his two daughters to them, *v.* 8. It is true, of two evils we must choose the less; but of two sins we must choose neither, nor ever do evil that good may come of it. He reasoned with them, pleaded the laws of hospitality and the protection of his house which his guests were entitled to; but he might as well have offered reason to a roaring lion and a raging bear as to these head-strong sinners, who were governed only by lust and passion. Lot's arguing with them does but exasperate them; and, to complete their wickedness, and fill up the measure of it, they fall foul upon him. (1.) They ridicule him, charge him with the absurdity of pretending to be a magistrate, when he was not so much as a free-man of their city, *v.* 9. Note, It is common for a reprover to be unjustly upbraided as a usurper; and, while offering the kindness of a friend, to be charged with assuming the authority of a judge: as if a man might not speak reason without taking too much upon him. (2.) They threaten him, and lay violent hands upon him; and the good man is in danger of being pulled in pieces by this outrageous rabble. Note, [1.] Those that hate to be reformed hate those that reprove them, though with ever so much tenderness. Presumptuous sinners do by their consciences as the Sodomites did by Lot, baffle their checks, stifle their accusations, press hard upon them, till they have seared them and quite stopped their mouths, and so made themselves ripe for ruin. [2.] Abuses offered to God's messengers and to faithful reprovers soon fill the measure of a people's wickedness, and bring destruction without remedy. See Prov. 29:1, and 2 Chr. 36:16. If reproofs remedy not, there is no remedy. See 2 Chr. 25:16.

III. That nothing less than the power of an angel could save a good man out of their wicked hands. It was now past dispute what Sodom's character was and what course must be taken with it, and therefore the angels immediately give a specimen of what they further intended. 1. They rescue Lot, *v.* 10. Note, He that watereth shall be watered also himself. Lot was solicitous to protect them, and now they take effectual care for his safety, in return for his kindness. Note further, Angels are employed for the special preservation of those that expose themselves to danger by well-doing. The saints, at death, are pulled like Lot into a house of perfect safety, and the door shut for ever against those that pursue them. 2. They chastise the insolence of the Sodomites: *They smote them with blindness, v.* 11. This was designed, (1.) To put an end to their attempt, and disable them from pursuing it. Justly were those struck blind who had been deaf to reason. Violent persecutors are often infatuated so that they cannot push on their malicious designs against God's messengers, Job 5:14, 15. Yet these Sodomites, after they were struck blind, continued seeking the door, to break it down, till they were tired. No judgments will, of themselves, change the corrupt natures and purposes of wicked men. If their minds had not been blinded as well as their bodies, they would have said, as the magicians, *This is the finger of God,* and would have submitted. (2.) It was to be an earnest of their utter ruin, the next day. When God, in a way of righteous judgment, blinds men, their condition is already desperate, Rom. 11:8, 9.

Verses 12–14

We have here the preparation for Lot's deliverance.

I. Notice is given him of the approach of Sodom's ruin: *We will destroy this place, v.* 13. Note, The holy angels are ministers of God's wrath for the destruction of sinners, as well as of his mercy for the preservation and deliverance of his people. In this sense, the good angels become *evil angels,* Ps. 78:49.

II. He is directed to give notice to his friends and relations, that they, it they would, might be saved with him (*v.* 12): *"Hast thou here any besides,* that thou art concerned for? If thou hast, go tell them what is coming." Now this implies, 1. The command of a great duty, which was to do all he could for the salvation of those about him, to snatch them as brands out of the fire. Note, Those who through grace are themselves delivered out of a sinful state should do what they can for the deliverance of others, especially their relations. 2. The offer of great favour. They do not ask whether he knew any righteous ones in the city fit to be spared: no, they knew there were none; but they ask what relations he had there, that, whether righteous or unrighteous, they might be saved with him. Note, Bad people often fare the better in this world for the sake of their good relations. It is good being akin to a godly man.

III. He applies himself accordingly to his sons-in-law, *v.* 14. Observe, 1. The fair warning that Lot gave them: *Up, get you out of this place.* The manner of expression is startling and quickening. It was no time to trifle when the destruction was just at the door. They had not forty days to repent in, as the Ninevites had. Now or never they must make their escape. At midnight this cry was made. Such as this is our call to the unconverted, to turn and live. 2. The slight they put upon this warning: *He seemed to them as one that mocked.* They thought, perhaps, that the assault which the Sodomites had just now made upon his house had disturbed his head, and put him into such a fright that he knew not what he said; or they thought that he was not in earnest with them. Those who lived a merry life, and made a jest of everything, made a jest of this warning, and so they perished in the overthrow. Thus many who are warned of the misery and danger they are in by sin make a light matter of it, and think their ministers do but jest with them; such will perish with their blood upon their own heads.

Verses 15–23

Here is, I. The rescue of Lot out of Sodom. Thought there were not ten righteous men in Sodom, for whose sakes it might be spared, yet that one righteous man that was among them delivered his own soul, Eze. 14:14. Early in the morning his own guests, in kindness to him, turned him out of doors, and his family with him, *v.* 15. His daughters that were married perished with their unbelieving husbands; but those that continued with him were preserved with him. Observe,

1. With what a gracious violence Lot was brought out of Sodom, *v.* 16. It seems, though he did not make a jest of the warning given, as his sons-in-law did, yet he lingered, he trifled, he did not make so much haste as the case required. Thus many that are under some convictions about the misery of their spiritual state, and the necessity of a change, yet defer that needful work, and foolishly linger. Lot did so, and it might have been fatal to him it the angels had not *laid hold of his hand, and brought him forth,* and saved him with fear, Jude 23. Herein it is said, *The Lord was merciful to him;* otherwise he might justly have left him to perish, since he was so loth to depart. Note, (1.) The salvation of the most righteous men must be attributed to God's mercy, not to their own merit. We are saved by grace. (2.) God's power also must be acknowledged in the bringing of souls out of a sinful state. If God had not brought us forth, we had never come forth. (3.) If God had not been merciful to us, our lingering had been our ruin.

2. With what a gracious vehemence he was urged to make the best of his way, when he was *brought forth, v.* 17. (1.) He must still apprehend himself in danger of being consumed, and be quickened by the law of self-preservation to flee for his life. Note, A holy fear and trembling are found necessary to the working out of our salvation. (2.) He must therefore mind his business with the utmost care and diligence. He must not hanker after Sodom: *Look not behind thee.* He must not loiter by the way: *Stay not in the plain;* for it would all be made one dead sea. He must not take up short of the place of refuge appointed him: *Escape to the mountain.* Such as these are the commands given to those who through grace are delivered out of a sinful state. [1.] Return not to sin and Satan, for that is looking back to Sodom. [2.] Rest not in self and the world, for that is staying in the plain. And, [3.] Reach towards Christ and heaven, for that is escaping to the mountain, short of which we must not take up.

II. The fixing of a place of refuge for him. The mountain was first appointed for him to flee to, but, 1. He begged for a city of refuge, one of the five that lay together, called *Bela, ch.* 14:2, 18–20. It was Lot's weakness to think a city of his own choosing safer than the mountain of God's appointing. And he argued against himself when he pleaded, *Thou hast magnified thy mercy in saving my life, and I cannot escape to the mountain;* for could not he that plucked him out of Sodom, when he lingered, carry him safely to the mountain, though he began to tire? Could not he that saved him from greater evils save him from the less? He insists much in his petition upon the smallness of the place: *It is a little one, it is not?* therefore, it was to be hoped, not so bad as the rest. This gave a new name to the place; it was called *Zoar, a little one.* Intercessions for little ones are worthy to be remembered. 2. God granted him his request, though there was much infirmity in it, *v.* 21, 22. See what favour God showed to a true saint, though weak. (1.) Zoar was spared, to gratify him. Though his intercession for it was not, as Abraham's for Sodom, from a principle of generous charity, but merely from self-interest, yet God granted him his request, to show how much the fervent prayer of a righteous man avails. (2.) Sodom's ruin was suspended till he was safe: *I cannot do any thing till thou shalt have come thither.* Note, The very presence of good men in a place helps to keep off judgments. See what care God takes for the preservation of his people. The winds are held till God's servants are sealed, Rev. 7:3; Eze. 9:4.

III. It is taken notice of that the sun had risen when Lot entered into Zoar; for when a good man comes into a place he brings light along with him, or should do.

Verses 24–25

Then, when Lot had got safely into Zoar, then this ruin came; for good men are taken away from the evil to come. *Then,* when the sun had risen bright and clear, promising a fair day, then this storm arose, to show that it was not from natural causes. Concerning this destruction observe, 1. God was the immediate author of it. It was destruction from the Almighty: *The Lord rained — from the Lord* (*v.* 24), that is, God from himself, by his own immediate power, and not in the common course of nature. Or, God the Son from God the Father; for the Father has committed all judgment to the Son. Note, He that is the Saviour will be the destroyer of those that reject the salvation. 2. It was a strange punishment, Job 31:3. Never was the like before nor since. Hell was rained from heaven upon them. *Fire, and brimstone, and a horrible tempest, were the portion of their cup* (Ps. 11:6); not a flash of lightning, which is destructive enough when God gives it commission, but a shower of lightning. Brimstone was scattered upon their habitation (Job 18:15), and then the fire soon fastened upon them. God could have drowned them, as he did the old world; but he would show that he has many arrows in his quiver, fire as well as water. 3. It was a judgment that laid all waste: *It overthrew the cities,* and destroyed all the inhabitants of them, the plain, and all that grew upon the ground, *v.* 25. It was an utter ruin, and irreparable. That fruitful valley remains to this day a great lake, or dead sea; it is called *the Salt Sea,* Num. 34:12. Travellers say that it is about thirty miles long and ten miles broad; it has no living creature in it; it is not moved by the wind; the smell of it is offensive; things do not easily sink in it. The Greeks call it *Asphaltites,* from a sort of pitch which it casts up. Jordan falls into it, and is lost there. 4. It was a punishment that answered to their sin. Burning lusts against nature were justly punished with this preternatural burning. Those that went after strange flesh were destroyed by strange fire, Jude 7. They persecuted the angels with their rabble, and made Lot afraid; and now God persecuted them with his tempest, and made them afraid with his storm, Ps. 83:15. 5. It was designed for a standing revelation of the wrath of God against sin and sinners in all ages. It is, accordingly, often referred to in the scripture, and made a pattern of the ruin of Israel (Deu. 29:23), of Babylon (Isa. 13:19), of Edom (Jer. 49:18), of Moab and Ammon, Zep. 2:9. Nay, it was typical of *the vengeance of eternal fire* (Jude 7), and the ruin of all *that live ungodly* (2 Pt. 2:6), especially that despise the gospel, Mt. 10:15. It is in allusion to this destruction that the place of the damned is often represented by a lake that burns, as Sodom did, with fire and brimstone. Let us learn from it, (1.) The evil of sin, and the hurtful nature of it. Iniquity tends to ruin. (2.) The terrors of the Lord. See what a fearful thing it is to fall into the hands of the living God!

Verse 26

This also is written for our admonition. Our Saviour refers to it (Lu. 17:32), *Remember Lot's wife.* As by the example of Sodom the wicked are warned to turn from their wickedness, so by the example of Lot's wife the righteous are warned not to turn from their righteousness. See Eze. 3:18, 20. We have here,

I. The sin of Lot's wife: *She looked back from behind him.* This seemed a small thing, but we are sure, by the punishment of it, that it was a great sin, and exceedingly sinful. 1. She disobeyed an express command, and so sinned after the similitude of Adam's transgression, which ruined us all. 2. Unbelief was at the bottom of it; she questioned whether Sodom would be destroyed, and thought she might still have been safe in it. 3. She looked back upon her neighbours whom she had left behind with more concern than was fit, now that their day of grace was over, and divine justice was glorifying itself in their ruin. See Isa. 66:24. 4. Probably she hankered after her house and goods in Sodom, and was loth to leave them. Christ intimates this to be her sin (Lu. 17:31, 32); she too much regarded her *stuff.* 5. Her looking back evinced an inclination to go back; and therefore our Saviour uses it as a warning against apostasy from our Christian profession. We have all renounced the world and the flesh, and have set our faces heaven-ward; we are in the plain, upon our probation; and it is at our peril if we return into the interests we profess to have abandoned. Drawing back is to perdition, and looking back is towards it. *Let us therefore fear,* Heb. 4:1.

II. The punishment of Lot's wife for this sin. She was struck dead in the place; yet her body did not fall down, but stood fixed and erect like a pillar, or monument, not liable to waste nor decay, as human bodies exposed to the air are, but metamorphosed into a metallic substance which would last perpetually. Come, behold the goodness and severity of God (Rom. 11:22), towards Lot, who went forward, goodness; towards his wife, who looked back, severity. Though she was nearly related to a righteous man, though better than her neighbours, and though a monument of distinguishing mercy in her deliverance out of Sodom, yet God did not connive at her disobedience; for great privileges will not secure us from the wrath of God if we do not carefully and faithfully improve them. This pillar of salt should season us. Since it is such a dangerous thing to look back, let us always press forward, Phil. 3:13, 14.

Verses 27–29

Our communion with God consists in our gracious regard to him and his gracious regard to us; we have here therefore the communion that was between God and Abraham, in the event concerning Sodom, as before in the consultation concerning it, for communion with God is to be kept up in providences as well as in ordinances.

I. Here is Abraham's pious regard to God in this event, in two things: — 1. A careful expectation of the event, *v.* 27. *He got up early* to look towards Sodom; and, to intimate that his design herein was to see what became of his prayers, he went to the very place where he had stood before the Lord, and set himself there, as upon his watch tower, Hab. 2:1. Note, When we have prayed we must look after our prayers, and observe the success of them. We must direct our prayer as a letter, and then look up for an answer, direct our prayer as an arrow, and then look up to see whether it reach the mark, Ps. 5:3. Our enquiries after news must be in expectation of an answer to our prayers. 2. An awful observation of it: *He looked towards Sodom* (*v.* 28), not as Lot's wife did, tacitly reflecting upon the divine severity, but humbly adoring it and acquiescing in it. Thus the saints, when they see the smoke of Babylon's torment rising up for ever (like Sodom's here), will say again and again, *Alleluia,* Rev. 19:3. Those that have, in the day of grace, most earnestly interceded for sinners, will, in the day of judgment, be content to see them perish, and will glorify God in their destruction.

II. Here is God's favourable regard to Abraham, *v.* 29. As before when Abraham prayed for Ishmael, God heard him for Isaac, so now, when he prayed for Sodom, he heard him for Lot. *He remembered Abraham, and,* for his sake, *sent Lot out of the overthrow.* Note, 1. God will certainly give an answer of peace to the prayer of faith, in his own way and time; though, for a while, it seem to be forgotten, yet, sooner or later, it will appear to be remembered. 2. The relations and friends of godly people fare the better for their interest in God and intercessions with him; it was out of respect to Abraham that Lot was rescued: perhaps this word encouraged Moses long afterwards to pray (Ex. 32:13), *Lord, remember Abraham;* and see Isa. 63:11.

Verses 30–38

Here is, I. The great trouble and distress that Lot was brought into after his deliverance, *v.* 30. 1. He was frightened out of Zoar, durst not dwell there; probably because he was conscious to himself that it was a refuge of his own choosing and that herein he had foolishly prescribed to God, and therefore he could not but distrust his safety in it; or because he found it as wicked as Sodom, and therefore concluded it could not long survive it; or perhaps he observed the rise and increase of those waters which after the conflagration, perhaps from Jordan, began to overflow the plain, and which, mixing with the ruins, by degrees made the Dead Sea; in those waters he concluded Zoar must needs perish (though it had escaped the fire) because it stood upon the same flat. Note, Settlements and shelters of our own choosing, and in which we do not follow God, commonly prove uneasy to us. 2. He was forced to betake himself to the mountain, and to take up with a cave for his habitation there. Methinks it was strange that he did not return to Abraham, and put himself under his protection, to whom he had once and again owed his safety: but the truth is there are some good men that are not wise enough to know what is best for themselves. Observe, (1.) He was now glad to go to the mountain, the place which God had appointed for his shelter. Note, It is well if disappointment in our way drive us at last to God's way. (2.) He that, awhile ago, could not find room enough for himself and his stock in the whole land, but must jostle with Abraham, and get as far from him as he could, is now confined to a hole in a hill, where he has scarcely room to turn himself, and there he is solitary and trembling. Note, It is just with God to reduce those to poverty and restraint who have abused their liberty and plenty. See also in Lot what those bring themselves to, at last, that forsake the communion of saints for secular advantages; they will be beaten with their own rod.

II. The great sin that Lot and his daughters were guilty of, when they were in this desolate place. It is a sad story.

1. His daughters laid a very wicked plot to bring him to sin; and theirs was, doubtless, the greater guilt. They contrived, under pretence of cheering up the spirits of their father in his present condition, to make him drunk, and then to lie with him, *v.* 31, 32. (1.) Some think that their pretence was plausible. Their father had no sons, they had no husbands, nor knew they were to have any of the holy seed, or, if they had children by others, their father's name would not be preserved in them. Some think that they had the Messiah in their eye, who, they hoped, might descend form their father; for he came from Terah's elder son, who separated from the rest of Shem's posterity as well as Abraham, and was now signally delivered out of Sodom. Their mother, and the rest of the family, were gone; they might not marry with the cursed Canaanites; and therefore they supposed that the end they aimed at and the extremity they were brought to, would excuse the irregularity. Thus the learned Monsieur Allix. Note, Good intentions are often abused to patronize bad actions. But, (2.) Whatever their pretence was, it is certain that their project was very wicked and vile, and an impudent affront to the very light and law of nature. Note, [1.] The sight of God's most tremendous judgments upon sinners will not of itself, without the grace of God, restrain evil hearts from evil practices: one would wonder how the fire of lust could possibly kindle upon those, who had so lately been the eyewitnesses of Sodom's flames. [2.] Solitude has its temptations as well as company, and particularly to uncleanness. When Joseph was alone with his mistress he was in danger, *ch.* 39:11. Relations that dwell together, especially if solitary, have need carefully to watch even against the least evil thought of this kind, lest Satan get an advantage.

2. Lot himself, by his own folly and unwariness, was wretchedly overcome, and suffered himself so far to be imposed upon by his own children as, two nights together, to be drunk, and to commit incest, *v.* 33, etc. *Lord, what is man!* What are the best of men, when God leaves them to themselves! See here, (1.) The peril of security. Lot, who not only kept himself sober and chaste in Sodom, but was a constant mourner for the wickedness of the place and a witness against it, was yet, in the mountain, where he was alone, and as he thought quite out of the way of temptation, shamefully overtaken. Let him therefore that thinks he stands, stands high and stands firm, *take heed lest he fall.* No mountain, on this side the holy hill above, can set us out of the reach of Satan's fiery darts. (2.) The peril of drunkenness. It is not only a great sin itself, but it is the inlet of many sins; it may prove the inlet of the worst and mast unnatural sins, which may b a perpetual wound and dishonour. Excellently does Mr. Herbert describe it,

> He that is drunken may his mother kill
> Big with his sister —

A man may do that without reluctance, when he is drunk, which, when he is sober, he could not think of without horror. (3.) The peril of temptation from our dearest relations and friends, whom we love, and esteem, and expect kindness from. Lot, whose temperance and chastity were impregnable against the batteries of foreign force, was surprised into sin and shame by the base treachery of his own daughters: we must dread a snare wherever we are, and be always upon our guard.

3. In the close we have an account of the birth of the two sons, or grandsons (call them which you will), of Lot, Moab and Ammon, the fathers of two nations, neighbours to Israel, and which we often read of in the Old Testament; both together are called *the children of Lot,* Ps. 83:8. Note, Though prosperous births may attend incestuous conceptions, yet they are so far from justifying them that they rather perpetuate the reproach of them and entail infamy upon posterity; yet the tribe of Judah, of which our Lord sprang, descended from such a birth, and Ruth, a Moabitess, has a name in his genealogy, Mt. 1:3, 5.

Lastly, Observe that, after this, we never read any more of Lot, nor what became of him: no doubt he repented of his sin, and was pardoned; but from the silence of the scripture concerning him henceforward we may learn that drunkenness, as it makes men forgetful, so it makes them forgotten; and many a name, which otherwise might have been remembered with respect, is buried by it in contempt and oblivion.

CHAPTER 20

We are here returning to the story of Abraham; yet that part of it which is here recorded is not to his honour. The fairest marbles have their flaws, and, while there are spots in the sun, we must not expect any thing spotless under it. The scripture, it should be remarked, is impartial in relating the blemishes even of its most celebrated characters. We have here, I. Abraham's sin in denying his wife, and Abimelech's sin thereupon in taking her (*v.* 1, 2). II. God's discourse with Abimelech in a dream, upon this occasion, wherein he shows him his error (*v.* 3), accepts his plea (*v.* 4–6), and directs him to make restitution (*v.* 7). III. Abimelech's discourse with Abraham, wherein he chides him for the cheat he had put upon him (*v.* 8–10), and Abraham excuses it as well as he can (*v.* 11–13). IV. The good issue of the story, in which Abimelech restores Abraham his wife (*v.* 14–16), and Abraham, by prayer, prevails with God for the removal of the judgment Abimelech was under (*v.* 17, 18).

Verses 1–2

Here is, 1. Abraham's removal from Mamre, where he had lived nearly twenty years, into the country of the Philistines: *He sojourned in Gerar, v.* 1. We are not told upon what occasion he removed, whether terrified by the destruction of Sodom, or because the country round was for the present prejudiced by it, or, as some of the Jewish writers say, because he was grieved at Lot's incest with his daughters, and the reproach which the Canaanites cast upon him and his religion, for his kinsman's sake: doubtless there was some good cause for his removal. Note, In a world where we are strangers and pilgrims we cannot expect to be always in the same place. Again, Wherever we are, we must look upon ourselves but as sojourners. 2. His sin in denying his wife, as before (*ch.* 12:13), which was not only in itself such an equivocation as bordered upon a lie, and which, if admitted as lawful, would be the ruin of human converse and an inlet to all falsehood, but was also an exposing of the chastity and honour of his wife, of which he ought to have been the protector. But, besides this, it had here a two-fold aggravation: — (1.) He had been guilty of this same sin before, and had been reproved for it, and convinced of the folly of the suggestion which induced him to it; yet he returns to it. Note, It is possible that a good man may, not only fall into sin, but relapse into the same sin, through the surprise and strength of temptation and the infirmity of the flesh. Let backsliders repent then, but not despair, Jer. 3:22. (2.) Sarah, as it should seem, was now with child of the promised seed, or, at least, in expectation of being so quickly, according to the word of God; he ought therefore to have taken particular care of her now, as Jdg. 13:4. 3. The peril that Sarah was brought into by this means: *The king of Gerar sent, and took her* to his house, in order to the taking of her to his bed. Note, The sin of one often occasions the sin of others; he that breaks the hedge of God's commandments opens a gap to he knows not how many; the beginning of sin is as the letting forth of water.

Verses 3–7

It appears by this that God revealed himself by dreams (which evidenced themselves to be divine and supernatural) not only to his servants the prophets, but even to those who were out of the pale of the church and covenant; but then, usually, it was with some regard to God's own people as in Pharaoh's dream, to Joseph, in Nebuchadnezzar's, to Daniel, and here, in Abimelech's, to Abraham and Sarah, for he reproved this king for their sake, Ps. 105:14, 15.

I. God gives him notice of his danger (*v.* 3), his danger of *sin,* telling him that the woman is a man's wife, so that if he take her he will wrong her husband; his danger of death for this sin: *Thou art a dead man;* and God's saying so of a man makes him so. Note, Every wilful sinner ought to be told that he is a dead man, as the condemned malefactor, and the patient whose disease is mortal, are said to be so. If thou art a bad man, certainly thou art a dead man.

II. He pleads ignorance that Abraham and Sarah had agreed to impose upon him, and not to let him know that they were any more than brother and sister, *v.* 6. See what confidence a man may have towards God when his heart condemns him not, 1 Jn. 3:21. If our consciences witness to our integrity, and that, however we may have been cheated into a snare, we have not knowingly and wittingly sinned against God, it will be our rejoicing in the day of evil. He pleads with God as Abraham had done, *ch.* 18:23. *Wilt thou slay a righteous nation? v.* 4. Not such a nation as Sodom, which was indeed justly destroyed, but a nation which, in this matter, was innocent.

III. God gives a very full answer to what he had said.

1. He allows his plea, and admits that what he did he did in the integrity of his heart: *Yea, I know it, v.* 6. Note, It is matter of comfort to those that are honest that God knows their honesty, and will acknowledge it, though perhaps men that are prejudiced against them either cannot be convinced of it or will not own that they are.

2. He lets him know that he was kept from proceeding in the sin merely by the good hand of God upon him: *I withheld thee from sinning against me.* Abimelech was hereby kept from doing wrong, Abraham from suffering wrong, and Sarah from both. Note, (1.) There is a great deal of sin devised and designed that is never executed. As bad as things are in the world, they are not so bad as the devil and wicked men would have them. (2.) It is God that restrains men from doing the ill they would do. It is not from him that there is sin, but it is from him that there is not more sin, either by his influence upon men's minds, checking their inclination to sin, or by his providence, tak-

ing away the opportunity to sin. (3.) It is a great mercy to be hindered from committing sin; of this God must have the glory, whoever is the instrument, 1 Sa. 25:32, 33.

3. He charges him to make restitution: *Now therefore,* not that thou art better informed, *restore the man his wife, v.* 7. Note, Ignorance will excuse no longer than it continues. If we have entered upon a wrong course through ignorance this will not excuse our knowingly persisting in it, Lev. 5:3–5. The reasons why he must be just and kind to Abraham are, (1.) Because *he is a prophet,* near and dear to God, for whom God does in a particular manner concern himself. God highly resents the injuries done to his prophets, and takes them as done to himself. (2.) Being a prophet, *he shall pray for thee;* this is a prophet's reward, and a good reward it is. It is intimated that there was great efficacy in the prayers of a prophet, and that good men should be ready to help those with their prayers that stand in need of them, and should make, at least, this return for the kindnesses that are done them. Abraham was accessory to Abimelech's trouble, and therefore was obliged in justice to pray for him. (3.) It is at thy peril if thou do not restore her: *Know thou that thou shalt surely die.* Note, He that does wrong, whoever he is, prince or peasant, shall certainly receive for the wrong which he has done, unless he repent and make restitution, Col. 3:25. No injustice can be made passable with God, no, not by Caesar's image stamped upon it.

Verses 8–13

Abimelech, being thus warned of God in a dream, takes the warning, and, as one truly afraid of sin and its consequences, he rises early to obey the directions given him.

I. He has a caution for his servants, *v.* 8. Abraham himself could not be more careful than he was to command his household in this matter. Note, Those whom God has convinced of sin and danger ought to tell others what God has done for their souls, that they also may be awakened and brought to a like holy fear.

II. He has a chiding for Abraham. Observe,

1. The serious reproof which Abimelech gave to Abraham, *v.* 9, 10. His reasoning with Abraham upon this occasion was very strong, and yet very mild. Nothing could be said better; he does not reproach him, nor insult over him, does not say, "Is this your profession? I see, though you will not swear, you will lie. If these be prophets, I will beg to be freed from the sight of them:" but he fairly represents the injury Abraham had done him, and calmly signifies his resentment of it. (1.) He calls that sin which he now found he had been in danger of a great sin. Note, Even the light of nature teaches men that the sin of adultery is a very great sin: be it observed, to the shame of many who call themselves Christians, and yet make a light matter of it. (2.) He looks upon it that both himself and his kingdom would have been exposed to the wrath of God if he had been guilty of this sin, though ignorantly. Note, The sins of kings often prove the plagues of kingdoms; rulers should therefore, for their people's sake, dread sin. (3.) He charges Abraham with doing that which was not justifiable, in disowning his marriage. This he speaks of justly, and yet tenderly; he does not call him a liar and cheat, but tells him he had done *deeds that ought not to be done.* Note, Equivocation and dissimulation, however they may be palliated, are very bad things, and by no means to be admitted in any case. (4.) He takes it as a very great injury to himself and his family that Abraham had thus exposed them to sin: *"What have I offended thee?* If I had been thy worst enemy, thou couldst not have done me a worse turn, nor taken a more effectual course to be revenged on me." Note, We ought to reckon that those do us the greatest unkindness in the world that any way tempt us or expose us to sin, though they may pretend friendship, and offer that which is grateful enough to corrupt nature. (5.) He challenges him to assign a cause for his suspecting them as a dangerous people for an honest man to live among: *"What sawest thou, that thou hast done this thing? v.* 10. What reason hadst thou to think that if we had known her to be thy wife thou wouldst have been exposed to any danger by it?" Note, A suspicion of our goodness is justly reckoned a greater affront than a slight upon our greatness.

2. The poor excuse that Abraham made for himself. (1.) He pleaded the bad opinion he had of the place, *v.* 11. He thought within himself (though he could not give any good reason for his thinking so), *"Surely the fear of God is not in this place,* and then they will slay me." [1.] Little good is to be expected where no fear of God is. See Ps. 36:1. [2.] There are many places and persons that have more of the fear of God in them than we think they have: perhaps they are not called by our dividing name, they do not wear our badges, they do not tie themselves to that which we have an opinion of; and therefore we conclude they have not the fear of God in their hearts, which is very injurious both of Christ and Christians, and makes us obnoxious to God's judgment, Mt. 7:1. [3.] Uncharitableness and censoriousness are sins that are the cause of many other sins. When men have once persuaded themselves concerning such and such that they have not the fear of God, they think this will justify them in the most unjust and unchristian practices towards them. Men would not do ill if they did not first think ill.

(2.) He excused it from the guilt of a downright lie by making it out that, in a sense, she was his sister, *v.* 12. Some think she was own sister to Lot, who is called his *brother Lot* (*ch.* 14:16), though he was *his nephew;* so Sarah is called his *sister.* But those to whom he said, *She is my sister,* understood that she was so his sister as not to be capable of being his wife; so that it was an equivocation, with an intent to deceive.

(3.) He clears himself from the imputation of an affront designed to Abimelech in it by alleging that it had been his practice before, according to an agreement between him and his wife, when they first became sojourners (*v.* 13): *"When God caused me to wander from my father's house,* then we settled this matter." Note, [1.] God is to be acknowledged in all our wanderings. [2.] Those that travel abroad, and converse much with strangers, as they have need of the wisdom of the serpent, so it is requisite that that wisdom be ever tempered with the innocence of the dove. It may, for aught I know, be suggested that God denied to Abraham to punish them for this sinful compact if they will not own their marriage, why should God own it? But we may suppose that, after this reproof which Abimelech gave them, they agreed never to do so again, and then presently we read (*ch.* 21:1, 2) that *Sarah conceived.*

Verses 14–18

Here is, I. The kindness of a prince which Abimelech showed to Abraham. See how unjust Abraham's jealousies were. He fancied that if they knew that Sarah was his wife they would kill him; but, when they did know it, instead of killing him they were kind to him, frightened at least to be so by the divine rebukes they were under. 1. He gives him his royal licence to dwell where he pleased in his country, courting his stay because he gives him his royal gifts (*v.* 14), *sheep and oxen,* and (*v.* 16) *a thousand pieces of silver.* This he gave when he restored Sarah, either, [1.] By way of satisfaction for the wrong he had offered to do, in taking her to his house: when the Philistines restored the ark, being plagued for detaining it, they sent a present with it. The law appointed that when restitution was made something should be added to it, Lev. 6:5. Or, [2.] To engage Abraham's prayers for him; not as if prayers should be bought and sold, but we should endeavour to be kind to those of whose spiritual things we reap, 1 Co. 9:11. Note, It is our wisdom to get and keep an interest with those that have an interest in heaven, and to make those our friends who are the friends of God. [3.] He gives to Sarah good instruction, tells her that her husband (her *brother* he calls him, to upbraid her with calling him so) must be to her for *a covering of the eyes,* that is, she must look at no other, nor desire to be looked at by any other. Note, Yoke-fellows must be to each other for a covering of the eyes. The marriage-covenant is a covenant with the eyes, like Job's, *ch.* 31:1.

II. The kindness of a prophet which Abraham showed to Abimelech: he *prayed for him, v.* 17, 18. This honour God would put upon Abraham that, though Abimelech had restored Sarah, yet the judgment he was under should be removed upon the prayer of Abraham, and not before. Thus God healed Miriam, when Moses, whom she had most affronted, prayed for her (Num. 12:13), and was reconciled to Job's friends when Job, whom they had grieved, prayed for them (Job 42:8–10), and so did, as it were, give it under his hand that he was reconciled to them. Note, The prayers of good men may be a kindness to great men, and ought to be valued.

CHAPTER 21

In this chapter we have, I. Isaac, the child of promise born into Abraham's family (*v.* 1–8). II. Ishmael, the son of the bondwoman, cast out of it (*v.* 9–21). III. Abraham's league with his neighbour Abimelech (*v.* 22–32). IV. His devotion to his God (*v.* 33).

Verses 1–8

Long-looked-for comes at last. The vision concerning the promised seed is for an appointed time, and now, at the end, it speaks, and does not lie; few under the Old Testament were brought into the world with such expectation as Isaac was, not for the sake of any great person eminence at which he was to arrive, but because he was to be, in this very thin, a type of Christ, that seed which the holy God had so long promised and holy men so long expected. In this account of the first days of Isaac we may observe,

I. The fulfilling of God's promise in the conception and birth of Isaac, *v.* 1, 2. Note, God's providences look best and brightest when they are compared with his word, and when we observe how God, in them all, acts as he has said, as he has spoken. 1. Isaac was born according to the promise. The Lord visited Sarah in mercy, as he had said. Note, No word of God shall fall to the ground; for he is faithful that has promised, and God's faithfulness is the stay and support of his people's faith. He was born *at the set time of which God had spoken, v.* 2. Note, God is always punctual to his time; though his promised mercies come not at the time we set, they will certainly come at the time he sets, and that is the best time., 2. He was born by virtue of the promise: *Sarah by faith received strength to conceive* Heb. 11:11. God therefore by promise gave that strength. It was not by the power of common providence, but by the power of a special promise, that Isaac was born. A sentence of death was, as it were, passed upon the second causes: Abraham was old, and Sarah old, and both as good as dead; and then the word of God took place. Note, True believers, by virtue of God's promises, are enabled to do that which is above the power of human nature, for *by them they partake of a divine nature,* 2 Pt. 1:4.

II. Abraham's obedience to God's precept concerning Isaac.

1. He named him, as God commanded him, *v.* 3. God directed him to a name for a memorial, *Isaac, laughter;* and Abraham, whose office it was, gave him that name, though he might have designed him some other name of a more pompous signification. Note, It is fit that the luxuriancy of human invention should always yield to the sovereignty and plainness of divine institution; yet there was good reason for the name, for, (1.) When Abraham received the promise of him he laughed for joy, *ch.* 17:17. Note, When the sun of comfort has risen upon the soul it is good to remember how welcome the dawning of the day was, and with what exultation we embraced the promise. (2.) When Sarah received the promise she laughed with distrust and diffidence. Note, When God gives us the mercies we began to despair of we ought to remember with sorrow and shame our sinful distrusts of God's power and promise, when we were in pursuit of them. (3.) Isaac was himself, afterwards, laughed at by Ishmael (*v.* 9), and perhaps his name bade him expect it. Note, God's favourites are often the world's laughing-stocks. (4.) The promise which he was not only the son, but the heir of, was to be the joy of all the saints in all ages, and that which would fill their mouths with laughter.

2. He circumcised him, *v.* 4. The covenant being established with him, the seal of the covenant was administered to him; and though a bloody ordinance, and he a darling, yet it must not be omitted, no, nor deferred beyond the eighth day. God had kept time in performing the promise, and therefore Abraham must keep time in obeying the precept.

III. The impressions which this mercy made upon Sarah. 1. It filled her with joy (*v.* 6): *"God has made me to laugh;* he has given me both cause to rejoice and a heart to rejoice." Thus the mother of our Lord, Lu. 1:46, 47. Note, (1.) God bestows mercies upon his people to encourage their joy in his work and service; and, whatever is the matter of our joy, God must be acknowledged as the author of it, unless it be the *laughter of the fool.* (2.) When mercies have been long deferred they are the more welcome when they come. (3.) It adds to the comfort of any mercy to have our friends rejoice with us in it: *All that hear will laugh with me;* for laughing is catching. See Lu. 1:58. Others would rejoice in this instance of God's power and goodness, and be encouraged to trust in him. See Ps. 119:74.

2. It filled her with wonder, *v.* 7. Observe here, (1.) What it was she thought so wonderful: *That Sarah should give children suck,* that she should, not only bear a child, but be so strong and hearty at the age as to give it suck. Note, Mothers, if they be able, ought to be nurses to their own children. Sarah was a person of quality, was aged; nursing might be thought prejudicial of herself, or to the child, or to both; she had choice of nurses, no doubt, in her own family: and yet she would do her duty in this matter; and her daughters the good wives are while they thus *do well,* 1 Pt. 3:5, 6. See Lam. 4:3. (2.) How she expressed her wonder: *"Who would have said it?* The thing was so highly improbable, so near to impossible, that if any one but God had said it we could not have believed it." Note, God's favours to his covenant-people are such as surpass both their own and others' thoughts and expectations. Who could imagine that God should do so much for those that deserve so little, nay, for those that deserve so ill? See Eph. 3:20; 2 Sa. 7:18, 19. Who would have said that God should send his Son to die for us, his Spirit to sanctify us, his angels to attend us? Who would have said that such great sins should be pardoned, such mean services accepted, and such worthless worms taken into covenant and communion with the great and holy God?

IV. A short account of Isaac's infancy: *The child grew, v.* 8. Special notice is taken of this, though a thing of course, to intimate that the children of the promise are growing children. See Lu. 1:80; 2:40. Those that are born of God shall increase of God, Col. 2:19. He grew so as not always to need milk, but was able to bear strong meat, and then he was weaned. See Heb. 5:13, 14. And then it was that Abraham made a great feast for his friends and neighbours, in thankfulness to God for his mercy to him. He made this feast, not on the day that Isaac was born, that would have been too great a disturbance to Sarah; nor on the day that he was circumcised, that would have been too great a diversion from the ordinance; but on the day that he was weaned, because God's blessing upon the nursing of children, and the preservation of them throughout the perils of the infant age, are signal instances of the care and tenderness of the divine providence, which ought to be acknowledged, to its praise. See Ps. 22:9, 10; Hos. 11:1.

Verses 9–13

The casting out of Ishmael is here considered of, and resolved on.

I. Ishmael himself gave the occasion by some affronts he gave to Isaac his little brother, some think on the day that Abraham made the feast for joy that Isaac was safely weaned, which the Jews say was not till he was three years old, others say five. Sarah herself was an eye-witness of the abuse: she *saw the son of the Egyptian mocking* (*v.* 9), mocking Isaac, no doubt, for it is said, with reference to this (Gal. 4:29), that *he that was born after the flesh persecuted him that was born after the Spirit.* Ishmael is here called the *son of the Egyptian,* because, as some think, the 400 years' affliction of the seed of Abraham by the Egyptians began now, and was to be dated hence, *ch.* 15:13. She saw him *playing with Isaac,* so the Septuagint, and, in play, *mocking him.* Ishmael was fourteen years older than Isaac; and, when children are together, the elder should be careful and tender of the younger: but it argued a very base and sordid disposition in Ishmael to be abusive to a child that was no way a match for him. Note, 1. God takes notice of what children say and do in their play, and will reckon with them if they say or do amiss, though their parents do not. 2. Mocking is a great sin, and very provoking to God. 3. There is a rooted remaining enmity in the seed of the serpent against the seed of the woman. The children of promise must expect to be mocked. This is persecution, which those that will live godly must count upon. 4. None are rejected and cast out from God but those who have first deserved it. Ishmael is continued in Abraham's family till he becomes a disturbance, grief, and scandal to it.

II. Sarah made the motion: *Cast out this bond-woman, v.* 10. This seems to be spoken in some heat, yet it is quoted (Gal. 4:30) as if it had been spoken by a spirit of prophecy; and it is the sentence passed on all hypocrites and carnal people, though they have a place and a name in the visible church. All that are born after the flesh and not born again, that rest in the law and reject the gospel promise, shall certainly be cast out. It is made to point particularly at the rejection of the unbelieving Jews, who, though they were the seed of Abraham, yet, because they submitted not to the gospel covenant, were unchurched and disfranchised: and that which, above any thing, provoked God to cast them off was their mocking and persecuting the gospel church, God's Isaac, in its infancy, 1 Th. 2:16, Note, There are many who are familiarly conversant with the children of God in this world, and yet shall not partake with them in the inheritance of sons. Ishmael might be Isaac's play-fellow and school-fellow, yet not his fellow-heir.

III. Abraham was averse to it: *The thing was very grievous in Abraham's sight, v.* 11. 1. It grieved him that Ishmael had given such a provocation. Note, Children ought to consider that the more their parents love them the more they are grieved at their misconduct, and particularly at their quarrels among themselves. 2. It grieved him that Sarah insisted upon such a punishment. "Might it not suffice to correct him? would nothing less serve than to expel him?" Note, Even the needful extremities which must be used with wicked and incorrigible children are very grievous to tender parents, who cannot thus afflict willingly.

IV. God determined it, *v.* 12, 13. We may well suppose Abraham to be greatly agitated about this matter, loth to displease Sarah, and yet loth to expel Ishmael; in this difficulty God tells him what his will is, and then he is satisfied. Note, A good man desires no more in doubtful cases than to know his duty, and what God would have him do; and, when he is clear in this, he is, or should be, easy. To make Abraham so, God sets this matter before him in a true light, and shows him, 1. That the casting out of Ishmael was necessary to the establishment of Isaac in the rights and privileges of the covenant: *In Isaac shall thy seed be called.* Both Christ and the church must descend from Abraham through the loins of Isaac; this is the entail of the promise upon Isaac, and is quoted by the apostle (Rom. 9:7) to show that not all who come from Abraham's loins were the heirs of Abraham's covenant. Isaac, the promised son, must be the father of the promised seed; therefore, "Away with Ishmael, send him far enough, lest he corrupt the manners or attempt to invade the rights of Isaac." It will be his security to have his rival banished. The covenant seed of Abraham must be a peculiar people, a people by themselves, from the very first, distinguished, not mingled with those that were out of covenant; for this reason Ishmael must be separated. Abraham was *called alone,* and so must Isaac be. See Isa. 51:2. It is probable that Sarah little thought of this (Jn. 11:51), but God took what she said, and turned it into an oracle, as afterwards, *ch.* 27:10. 2. That the casting out of Ishmael should not be his ruin, *v.* 13. He shall be a *nation, because he is thy seed.* We are not sure that it was his eternal ruin. It is presumption to say that all those who are left out of the external dispensation from all his mercies: those may be saved who are not thus honoured. However, we are sure it was not his temporal ruin. Though he was chased out of the church, he was not *chased out of the world. I will make him a nation.* Note, (1.) Nations are of God's making: he founds them, he forms them, he fixes them. (2.) Many are full of the blessings of God's providence that are strangers to the blessings of his covenant. (3.) The children of this world often fare the better, as to outward things, for their relation to the children of God.

Verses 14–21

Here is, I. The casting out of the bond-woman, and her son from the family of Abraham, *v.* 14. Abraham's obedience to the divine command in this matter was speedy — *early in the morning,* we may suppose immediately after he had, in the night's visions, received orders to do this. It was also submissive; it was contrary to his judgment, at least to his own inclination, to do it; yet as soon as he perceives that it is the mind of God he makes no objections, but silently does as he is bidden, as one trained up to an implicit obedience. In sending them away without any attendants, on foot, and slenderly provided for, it is probable that he observed the directions given him. If Hagar and Ishmael had conducted themselves well in Abraham's family, they might have continued there; but they threw themselves out by their own pride and insolence, which were thus justly chastised. Note, By abusing our privileges we forfeit them. Those that know not when they are well off, in such a desirable place as Abraham's family, deserve to be cashiered, and to be made to know the worth of mercies by the want of them.

II. Their wandering in the wilderness, missing their way to the place Abraham designed them for a settlement.

1. They were reduced to great distress there. Their provisions were spent, and Ishmael was sick. He that used to be full fed in Abraham's house, where he waxed fat and kicked, now fainted and sunk, when he was brought to short allowance. Hagar is in tears, and sufficiently mortified. Now she wishes for the crumbs she had wasted and made light of at her master's table. Like one under the power of the spirit of bondage, she despairs of relief, counts upon nothing but *the death of the child* (*v.* 15, 16), though God had told her, before he was born, that he should live to be a man, a great man. We are apt to forget former promises, when present providences seem to contradict them; for we live by sense.

2. In this distress, God graciously appeared for their relief: he heard *the voice of the lad, v.* 17. We read not of a word he said; but his sighs, and groans, and calamitous state, cried aloud in the ears of mercy. An angel was sent to comfort Hagar, and it was not the first time that she had met with God's comforts in a wilderness; she had thankfully acknowledged the former kind visit which God made his in such a case (*ch.* 16:13), and therefore God now visited her again with seasonable succours. (1.) The angel assures her of the cognizance God took of her distress: *God has heard the voice of the lad where he is,* though he is in a wilderness (for, wherever we are, there is a way open heaven-ward); therefore *lift up the lad, and hold him in thy hand, v.* 18. Note, God's readiness to help us when we are in trouble must not slacken, but quicken, our endeavours to help ourselves. (2.) He repeats the promise concerning her son, that he should be *a great nation,* as a reason why she should bestir herself to help him. Note, It should engage our care and pains about children and young people to consider that we know not what God has designed them for, nor what great use Providence may make of them. (3.) He directs her to a present supply (*v.* 19): *He opened her eyes* (which were swollen and almost blinded with weeping), and then *she saw a well of water.* Note, Many that have reason enough to be comforted go mourning from day to day, because they do not see the reason they have for comfort. There is a well of water by them in the covenant of grace, but they are not aware of it; they have not the benefit of it, till the same God that opened their eyes to see their wound opens them to see their remedy, Jn. 16:6, 7. Now the apostle tells us that those things concerning Hagar and Ishmael are *allēgoroumena* (Gal. 4:24), they are to be allegorized; this then will serve to illustrate the folly, [1.] Of those who, like the unbelieving Jews, seek for righteousness by the law and the carnal ordinances of it, and not by the promise made in Christ, thereby running themselves into a wilderness of want and despair. Their comforts are soon exhausted, and if God save them not by his special prerogative, and by a miracle of mercy open their eyes and undeceive them, they are undone. [2.] Of those who seek for satisfaction and happiness in the world and the things of it. Those that forsake the comforts of the covenant and communion with God, and choose their portion in this earth, take up with a bottle of water, poor and slender provision, and that soon spent; they wander endlessly in pursuit of satisfaction, and, at length, sit down short of it.

III. The settlement of Ishmael, at last, in the wilderness of Paran (*v.* 20, 21), a wild place, fittest for a wild man; and such a one he was, *ch.* 16. 12. Those that are born after the flesh take up with the wilderness of this world, while the children of the promise aim at the heavenly Canaan, and cannot be at rest till they are there. Observe, 1. He had some tokens of God's presence: *God was with the lad;* his outward prosperity was owing to this. 2. By trade he was an archer, which intimates that craft was his excellency and sport his business: rejected Esau was a cunning hunter. 3. He matched among his mother's relations; she took him a wife out of Egypt: as great an archer as he was, he did not think he could take his aim well, in the business of marriage, if he proceeded without his mother's advice and consent.

Verses 22–32

We have here an account of the treaty between Abimelech and Abraham, in which appears the accomplishment of that promise (*ch.* 12:2) that God would *make his name great.* His friendship is valued, is courted, though a stranger, though a tenant at will to the Canaanites and Perizzites.

I. The league is proposed by Abimelech, and Phichol his prime-minister of state and general of his army.

1. The inducement to it was God's favour to Abraham (*v.* 22): *"God is with thee in all that thou doest,* and we cannot but take notice of it." Note, (1.) God in his providence sometimes shows his people such tokens for good that their neighbours cannot but take notice of it, Ps. 86:17. Their affairs do so visibly prosper, and they have such remarkable success in their undertakings, that a confession is extorted from all about them of God's presence with them. (2.) It is good being in favour with those that are in favour with God, and having an interest in those that have an interest in heaven, Zec. 8:23. *We will go with you, for we have heard that God is with you.* We do well for ourselves if we have fellowship with those that have fellowship with God, 1 Jn. 1:3.

2. The tenour of it was, in general, that there should be a firm and constant friendship between the two families, which should not upon any account be violated. This bond of friendship must be strengthened by the bond of an oath, in which the true God was appealed to, both as a witness of their sincerity and an avenger in case either side were treacherous, *v.* 23. Observe, (1.) He desires the entail of this league upon his posterity and the extension of it to his people. He would have his son, and his son's son, and his land likewise, to have the benefit of it. Good men should secure an alliance and communion with the favourites of Heaven, not for themselves only, but for theirs also. (2.) He reminds Abraham of the fair treatment he had found among them: *According to the kindness I have done unto thee.* As those that have received kindness must return it, so those that have shown kindness may expect it.

II. It is consented to by Abraham, with a particular clause inserted about a well. In Abraham's part of this transaction observe,

1. He was ready to enter into this league with Abimelech, finding him to be a man of honour and conscience, and that had the fear of God before his eyes: *I will swear, v.* 24. Note, (1.) Religion does not make men morose and unconversable; I am sure it ought not. We must not, under colour of shunning bad company, be sour to all company, and jealous of every body. (2.) An honest mind does not startle at giving assurances: if Abraham say that he will be true to Abimelech, he is not afraid to swear it; an oath is for confirmation.

2. He prudently settled the matter concerning a well, about which Abimelech's servants had quarrelled with him. Wells of water, it seems, were choice goods in that country: thanks be to God, that they are not so scarce in ours. (1.) Abraham mildly told Abimelech of it, *v.* 25. Note, If our brother trespass against us, we must, with the meekness of wisdom, tell him his fault, that the matter may be fairly accommodated and an end made of it, Mt. 18:15. (2.) He acquiesced in Abimelech's justification of himself in this matter: *I wot not who has done this thing, v.* 26. Many are suspected of injustice and unkindness that are perfectly innocent, and we ought to be glad when they clear themselves. The faults of servants must not be imputed to their masters, unless they know of them and justify them; and no more can be expected from an honest man than that he be ready to do right as soon as he knows that he has done wrong. (3.) He took care to have his title to the well cleared and confirmed, to prevent any disputes or quarrels for the future, *v.* 30. It is justice, as well as wisdom, to do thus, *in perptuam rei memoriam — that the circumstance may be perpetually remembered.*

3. He made a very handsome present to Abimelech, *v.* 27. It was not any thing curious or fine that he presented to him, but that which was valuable and useful — *sheep and oxen,* in gratitude for Abimelech's kindness to him, and in token of hearty friendship between them. The interchanging of kind offices is the improving of love: that which is mine is my friend's.

4. He ratified the covenant by an oath, and registered it by giving a new name to the place (*v.* 31), *Beer-sheba,* the *well of the oath,* in remembrance of the covenant they swore to, that they might be ever mindful of it; or *the well of seven,* in remembrance of the seven lambs given to Abimelech, as a consideration for his confirming Abraham's title to that well. Note, Bargains made must be remembered, that we may make them good, and may not break our word through oversight.

Verses 33–34

Observe, 1. Abraham, having got into a good neighbourhood, knew when he was well off, and continued a great while there. There he planted a grove for a shade to his tent, or perhaps an orchard of fruit-trees; and there, though we cannot say he settled, for God would have him, while he lived, to be a stranger and a pilgrim, yet he sojourned many days, as many as would consist with his character, as Abraham the *Hebrew,* or *passenger.* 2. There he made, not only a constant practice, but an open profession, of his religion: *There he called on the name of the Lord, the everlasting God,* probably in the grove he planted, which was his oratory or house of prayer. Christ prayed in a garden, on a mountain. (1.) Abraham kept up public worship, to which, probably, his neighbours resorted, that they might join with him. Note, Good men should not only retain their goodness wherever they go, but do all they can to propagate it, and make others good. (2.) In calling on the Lord, we must eye him as *the everlasting God, the God of the world,* so some. Though God had made himself known to Abraham as his God in particular, and in covenant with him, yet he forgets not to give glory to him as the Lord of all: *The everlasting God,* who was, before all worlds, and will be, when time and days shall be no more. See Isa. 40:28.

CHAPTER 22

We have here the famous story of Abraham's offering up his son Isaac, that is, his offering to offer him, which is justly looked upon as one of the wonders of the church. Here is, I. The strange command which God gave to Abraham concerning it (*v.* 1, 2). II. Abraham's strange obedience to this command (*v.* 3–10) III. The strange issue of this trial. 1. The sacrificing of Isaac was countermanded (*v.* 11, 12). 2. Another sacrifice was provided (*v.* 13, 14). 3. The covenant was renewed with Abraham hereupon (*v.* 15–19). Lastly, an account of some of Abraham's relations (*v.* 20, etc.)

Verses 1–2

Here is the trial of Abraham's faith, whether it continued so strong, so vigorous, so victorious, after a long settlement in communion with God, as it was at first, when by it he left his country: then it was made to appear that he loved God better than his father; now that he loved him better than his son. Observe here,

I. The time when Abraham was thus tried (*v.* 1): *After these things,* after all the other exercises he had had, all the hardships and difficulties he had gone through. Now, perhaps, he was beginning to think the storms had all blown over; but, after all, this encounter comes, which is sharper than any yet. Note, Many former trials will not supersede nor secure us from further trials; we have not yet put off the harness, 1 Ki. 20:11. See Ps. 30:6, 7.

II. The author of the trial: *God* tempted him, not to draw him to sin, so Satan tempts (if Abraham had sacrificed Isaac, he would not have sinned, his orders would have justified him, and borne him out), but to discover his graces, how strong they were, that they might be *found to praise, and honour, and glory,* 1 Pt. 1:7. Thus God tempted Job, that he might appear not only a good man, but a great man. *God did tempt Abraham;* he did *lift up Abraham,* so some read it; as a scholar that improves well is lifted up, when he is put into a higher form. Note, Strong faith is often exercised with strong trials and put upon hard services.

III. The trial itself. God appeared to him as he had formerly done, called him by name, *Abraham,* that name which had been given him in ratification of the promise. Abraham, like a good servant, readily answered, *"Here am I;* what says my Lord unto his servant?" Probably he expected some renewed promise like those, *ch.* 15:1, and 17:1. But, to his great amazement, that which God has to say to him is, in short, *Abraham, Go kill thy son;* and this command is given him in such aggravating language as makes the temptation abundantly more grievous. When God speaks, Abraham, no doubt, takes notice of every word, and listens attentively to it; and every word here is a sword in his bones: the trial is steeled with trying phrases. Is it any pleasure to the Almighty that he should afflict? No, it is not; yet, when Abraham's faith is to be tried, God seems to take pleasure in the aggravation of the trial, *v.* 2. Observe,

1. The person to be offered. (1.) *"Take thy son,* not thy bullocks and thy lambs;" how willingly would Abraham have parted with them by thousands to redeem Isaac! "No, *I will take no bullock out of thy house,* Ps. 50:9. I must have thy son: not thy servant, no, not the steward of thy house, that shall not serve the turn; I must have thy son." Jephthah, in pursuance of a vow, offered a daughter; but Abraham must offer his son, in whom the family was to be built up. "Lord, let it be an adopted son;" "No, (2.) *Thy only son;* thy only son by *Sarah."* Ishmael was lately cast out, to the grief of Abraham; and now Isaac only was left, and must he go too? Yes, (3.) "Take *Isaac,* him, by name, *thy laughter,* that *son indeed," ch.* 17:19. Not "Send for Ishmael back, and offer him;" no, it must be Isaac. "But, Lord, I love Isaac, he is to me as my own soul. Ishmael is not, and wilt thou take Isaac also? All this is against me:" Yea, (4.) That son *whom thou lovest.* It was a trial of Abraham's love to God, and therefore it must be in a beloved son, and that string must be touched most upon: in the Hebrew it is expressed more emphatically, and, I think, might very well be read thus: *Take now that son of thine, that only one of thine, whom thou lovest, that Isaac.* God's command must overrule all these considerations.

2. The place: *In the land of Moriah,* three days' journey off; so that he might have time to consider it, and, if he did it, must do it deliberately, that it might be a service the more reasonable and the more honourable.

3. The manner: *Offer him for a burnt-offering.* He must not only kill his son, but kill him as a sacrifice, kill him devoutly, kill him by rule, kill him with all that pomp and ceremony, with all that sedateness and composure of mind, with which he used to offer his burnt-offerings.

Verses 3–10

We have here Abraham's obedience to this severe command. *Being tried, he offered up Isaac,* Heb. 11:17. Observe,

I. The difficulties which he broke through in this act of obedience. Much might have been objected against it; as, 1. It seemed directly against an antecedent law of God, which forbids murder, under a severe penalty, *ch.* 9:5, 6. Now can the unchangeable God contradict himself? He that hates robbery for burnt-offering (Isa. 61:8) cannot delight in murder for it. 2. How would it consist with natural affection to his own son? It would be not only murder, but the worst of murders. Cannot Abraham be obedient but he must be unnatural? If God insist upon a human sacrifice, is there none but Isaac to be the offering, and none but Abraham to be the offerer? Must the father of the faithful be the monster of all fathers? 3. God gave him no reason for it. When Ishmael was to be cast out, a just cause was assigned, which satisfied Abraham; but here Isaac must die, and Abraham must kill him, and neither the one nor the other must know why or wherefore. If Isaac had been to die a martyr for the truth, or his life had been the ransom of some other life more precious, it would have been another matter; of if he had died as a criminal, a rebel against God or his parents, as in the case of the idolater (Deu. 13:8, 9), or the stubborn son (Deu. 21:18, 19), it might have passed as a sacrifice to justice. But the case is not so: he is dutiful, obedient, hopeful, son. "Lord, what profit is there in his blood?" 4. How would this consist with the promise? Was it not said that in *Isaac shall thy seed be called?* But what comes of that seed, if this pregnant bud be broken off so soon? 5. How should he ever look Sarah in the face again? With what face can he return to her and his family with the blood of Isaac sprinkled on his garments and staining all his raiment? *"Surely a bloody husband hast thou been to me"* would Sarah say (as Ex. 4:25, 26), and it would be likely to alienate her affections for ever both from him and from his God. 6. What would the

Egyptians say, and the Canaanites and the Perizzites who dwelt then in the land? It would be an eternal reproach to Abraham, and to his altars. "Welcome nature, if this be grace." These and many similar objection might have been made; but he was infallibly assured that it was indeed a command of God and not a delusion, and this was sufficient to answer them all. Note, God's commands must not be disputed, but obeyed; we must not consult with flesh and blood about them (Gal. 1:15, 16), but with a gracious obstinacy persist in our obedience to them.

II. The several steps of obedience, all which help to magnify it, and to show that he was guided by prudence, and governed by faith, in the whole transaction.

1. He rises early, *v.* 3. Probably the command was given in the visions of the night, and early the next morning he set himself about the execution of it — did not delay, did not demur, did not take time to deliberate; for the command was peremptory, and would not admit a debate. Note, Those that do the will of God heartily will do it speedily; while we delay, time is lost and the heart hardened.

2. He gets things ready for a sacrifice, and, as if he himself had been a Gibeonite, it should seem, with his own hands he cleaves the wood for the burnt-offering, that it might not be to seek when the sacrifice was to be offered. Spiritual sacrifices must thus be prepared for.

3. It is very probable that he said nothing about it to Sarah. This is a journey which she must know nothing of, lest she prevent it. There is so much in our own hearts to hinder our progress in duty that we have need, as much as may be, to keep out of the way of other hindrances.

4. He carefully looked about him, to discover the place appointed for this sacrifice, to which God had promised by some sign to direct him. Probably the direction was given by an appearance of the divine glory in the place, some pillar of fire reaching from heaven to earth, visible at a distance, and to which he pointed when he said (*v.* 5), "We will go yonder, where you see the light, and worship."

5. He left his servants at some distance off (*v.* 5), lest they should interpose, and create him some disturbance in his strange oblation; for Isaac was, no doubt, the darling of the whole family. Thus, when Christ was entering upon his agony in the garden, he took only three of his disciples with him, and left the rest at the garden door. Note, It is our wisdom and duty, when we are going to worship God, to lay aside all those thoughts and cares which may divert us from the service, leave them at the bottom of the hill, that we may attend on the Lord without distraction.

6. He obliged Isaac to carry the wood (both to try his obedience in a smaller matter first, and that he might typify Christ, who carried his own cross, Jn. 19:17), while he himself, though he knew what he did, with a steady and undaunted resolution carried the fatal knife and fire, *v.* 6. Note, Those that through grace are resolved upon the substance of any service or suffering for God must overlook the little circumstances which make it doubly difficult to flesh and blood.

7. Without any ruffle or disorder, he talks it over with Isaac, as if it had been but a common sacrifice that he was going to offer, *v.* 7, 8.

(1.) It was a very affecting question that Isaac asked him, as they were going together: *My father,* said Isaac; it was a melting word, which, one would think, would strike deeper into the breast of Abraham than his knife could into the breast of Isaac. He might have said, or thought, at least, "Call me not thy father who am now to be thy murderer; can a father be so barbarous, so perfectly lost to all the tenderness of a father?" Yet he keeps his temper, and keeps his countenance, to admiration; he calmly waits for his son's question, and this is it: *Behold the fire and the wood, but where is the lamb?* See how expert Isaac was in the law and custom of sacrifices. This it is to be well-catechised: this is, [1.] A trying question to Abraham. How could he endure to think that Isaac was himself the lamb? So it is, but Abraham, as yet, dares not tell him so. Where God knows the faith to be armour of proof, he will laugh at *the trial of the innocent,* Job 9:23. [2.] It is a teaching question to us all, that, when we are going to worship God, we should seriously consider whether we have every thing ready, especially the lamb for a burnt-offering. Behold, the fire is ready, the Spirit's assistance and God's acceptance; the wood is ready, the instituted ordinances designed to kindle our affections (which indeed, without the Spirit, are but like wood without fire, but the Spirit works by them); *all things are now ready,* but where is the lamb? Where is the heart? Is that ready to be offered up to God, to ascend to him as a burnt-offering?

(2.) It was a very prudent answer which Abraham gave him: *My son, God will provide himself a lamb.* This was the language, either, [1.] Of his obedience. "We must offer the lamb which God has appointed now to be offered;" thus giving him this general rule of submission to the divine will, to prepare him for the application of it to himself very quickly. Or, [2.] Of his faith. Whether he meant it so or not, this proved to be the meaning of it; a sacrifice was provided instead of Isaac. Thus, *First,* Christ, the great sacrifice of atonement, was of God's providing; when none in heaven or earth could have found a lamb for that burnt-offering, God himself found the ransom, Ps. 89:20. *Secondly,* All our sacrifices of acknowledgment are of God's providing too. It is he that prepares the heart, Ps. 10:17. The broken and contrite spirit is a sacrifice of God (Ps. 51:17), of his providing.

8. With the same resolution and composedness of mind, after many thoughts of heart, he applies himself to the completing of this sacrifice, *v.* 9, 10. He goes on with a holy wilfulness, after many a weary step, and with a heavy heart he arrives at length at the fatal place, builds the altar (an altar of earth, we may suppose, the saddest that ever he built, and he had built many a one), lays the wood in order for his Isaac's funeral pile, and now tells him the amazing news: "Isaac, thou art the lamb which God has provided." Isaac, for aught that appears, is as willing as Abraham; we do not find that he raised any objection against it, that he petitioned for his life, that he attempted to make his escape, much less that he struggled with his aged father, or made any resistance: Abraham does it, God will have it done, and Isaac has learnt to submit to both, Abraham no doubt comforting him with the same hopes with which he himself by faith was comforted. Yet it is necessary that a sacrifice be bound. The great sacrifice, which in the fullness of time was to be offered up, must be bound, and therefore so must Isaac. But with what heart could tender Abraham tie those guiltless hands, which perhaps had often been lifted up to ask his blessing, and stretched out to embrace him, and were now the more straitly bound with the cords of love and duty! However, it must be done. Having bound him, he lays him upon the altar, and his hand upon the head of his sacrifice; and now, we may suppose, with floods of tears, he gives, and takes, the final farewell of a parting kiss: perhaps he takes another for Sarah from her dying son. This being done, he resolutely forgets the bowels of a father, and puts on the awful gravity of a sacrificer. With a fixed heart, and an eye lifted up to heaven, he takes the knife, and stretches out his hand to give a fatal cut to Isaac's throat. Be astonished, O heavens! at this; and wonder, O earth! Here is an act of faith and obedience, which deserves to be a spectacle to God, angels, and men. Abraham's darling, Sarah's laughter, the church's hope, the heir of promise, lies ready to bleed and die by his own father's hand, who never shrinks at the doing of it. Now this obedience of Abraham in offering up Isaac is a lively representation, (1.) Of the love of God to us, in delivering up his only-begotten Son to suffer and die for us, as a sacrifice. It *pleased the Lord* himself to *bruise him.* See Isa. 53:10; Zec. 13:7. Abraham was obliged, both in duty and gratitude, to part with Isaac, and parted with him to a friend; but God was under no obligations to us, for we were enemies. (2.) Of our duty to God, in return for that love. We must tread in the steps of this faith of Abraham. God, by his word, calls us to part with all for Christ, — all our sins, though they have been as a right hand, or a right eye, or an Isaac — all those things that are competitors and rivals with Christ for the sovereignty of the heart (Lu. 14:26); and we must cheerfully let them all go. God, by his providence, which is truly the voice of God, calls us to part with an Isaac sometimes, and we must do it with a cheerful resignation and submission to his holy will, 1 Sa. 3:18.

Verses 11–14

Hitherto this story has been very melancholy, and seemed to hasten towards a most tragical period; but here the sky suddenly clears up, the sun breaks out, and a bright and pleasant scene opens. The same hand that had wounded and cast down here heals and lifts up; for, though he cause grief, he will have compassion. *The angel of the Lord,* that is, God himself, the eternal Word, the angel of the covenant, who was to be the great Redeemer and comforter, he interposed, and gave a happy issue to this trial.

I. Isaac is rescued, *v.* 11, 12. The command to offer him was intended only for trial, and it appearing, upon trial, that Abraham did indeed love God better than he loved Isaac, the end of the command was answered; and therefore the order is countermanded, without any reflection at all upon the unchangeableness of the divine counsels: *Lay not thy hand upon the lad.* Note, 1. Our creature-comforts are most likely to be continued to us when we are most likely to be continued to us when we are most willing to resign them up to God's will. 2. God's time to help and relieve his people is when they are brought to the greatest extremity. The more imminent the danger is, and the nearer to be put in execution, the more wonderful and the more welcome is the deliverance.

II. Abraham is not only approved, but applauded. He obtains an honourable testimony that he is righteous: *Now know I that thou fearest God.* God knew it before, but now Abraham had given a most memorable evidence of it. He needed do no more; what he had done was sufficient to prove the religious regard he had to God and his authority. Note, 1. When God, by his providence, hinders the performance of our sincere intentions in his services, he graciously accepts the will for the deed, and the honest endeavour, though it come short of finishing. 2. The best evidence of our fearing God is our being willing of serve and honour him with that which is dearest to us, and to part with all to him or for him.

III. Another sacrifice is provided instead of Isaac, *v.* 13. Now that the altar was built, and the wood laid in order, it was necessary that something should be offered. For, 1. God must be acknowledged with thankfulness for the deliverance of Isaac; and the sooner the better, when here is an altar ready. 2. Abraham's words must be made good: *God will provide himself a lamb.* God will not disappoint those expectations of his people which are of his own raising; but according to their faith it is to them. *Thou shalt decree a thing, and it shall be established.* 3. Reference must be had to the promised Messiah, the blessed seed. (1.) Christ was sacrificed in our stead, as this ram instead of Isaac, and his death was our discharge. *"Here am I* (said he,) *let these go their way."* (2.) Though that blessed seed was lately promised, and now typified by Isaac, yet the offering of him up should be suspended till the latter end of the world: and in the mean time the sacrifice of beasts should be accepted, as this ram was, as a pledge of that expiation which should one day be made by that great sacrifice. And it is observable that the temple, the place of sacrifice, was afterwards built upon this mount Moriah (2 Chr. 3:1); and mount Calvary, where Christ was crucified, was not far off.

IV. A new name is given to the place, to the honour of God, and for the encouragement of all believers, to the end of the world, cheerfully to trust in God in the way of obedience: *Jehovah-jireh, The Lord will provide* (*v.* 14), probably alluding to what he had said (*v.* 8), *God will provide himself a lamb.* I was not owing to any contrivance of Abraham, nor was it in answer to his prayer, though he was a distinguished intercessor; but it was purely the Lord's doing. Let it be recorded for the generations to come, 1. That *the Lord will see;* he will always have his eye upon his people in their straits and distresses, that he may come in with seasonable succour in the critical juncture. 2. That he will *be seen,* be seen *in the mount,* in the greatest perplexities of his people. He will not only manifest, but magnify, his wisdom, power, and goodness, in their deliverance. Where God sees and provides, he should be seen and praised. And, perhaps, it may refer to *God manifest in the flesh.*

Verses 15–19

Abraham's obedience was graciously accepted; but this was not all: here we have it recompensed, abundantly recompensed, before he stirred from the place; probably while the ram he had sacrificed was yet burning God sent him this gracious message, renewed and ratified his covenant with him. All covenants were made by sacrifice, so was this by the typical sacrifices of Isaac and the ram. Very high expressions of God's favour to Abraham are employed in this confirmation of the covenant with him, expressions exceeding any he had yet been blessed with. Note, Extraordinary services shall be crowned with extraordinary honours and comforts; and favours in the promise, though not yet performed, ought to be accounted real and valuable recompences. Observe, 1. God is pleased to make mention of Abraham's obedience as the consideration of the covenant; and he speaks of it with an encomium: *Because thou hast done this thing, and hast not withheld thy son, thine only son, v.* 16. He lays a strong emphasis on this, and (*v.* 18) praises it as an act of obedience: in it thou hast *obeyed my voice,* and to obey is better than sacrifice. Not that this was a proportionable consideration, but God graciously put this honour upon that by which Abraham had honoured him. 2. God now confirmed the promise with an oath. It was said and sealed before; but now it is sworn: *By myself have I sworn;* for he could swear by no greater, Heb. 6:13. Thus he interposed himself by an oath, as the apostle expresses it, Heb. 6:17. He did (to speak with reverence) even pawn his own life and being upon it *(As I live),* that by all those immutable things, in which it was impossible for God to lie, he and his might have strong consolation. Note, If we exercise faith, God will encourage it. Improve the promises, and God will ratify them. 3. The particular promise here renewed is that of a numerous offspring: *Multiplying, I will multiply thee, v.* 17. Note, Those that are willing to part with any thing for God shall have it made up to them with unspeakable advantage. Abraham has but one son, and is willing to part with that one, in obedience to God. "Well," said God, "thou shalt be recompensed with thousands and millions." What a figure does the seed of Abraham make in history! How numerous, how illustrious, were his known descendants, who, to this day, triumph in this, that they have Abraham to their father! Thus he received a thousand-fold in this life, Mt. 19:29. 4. The promise, doubtless, points at the Messiah, and the grace of the gospel. This is the oath sworn to our father Abraham, which Zacharias refers to, Lu. 1:73, etc. And so here is a promise, (1.) Of the great blessing of the Spirit: *In blessing, I will bless thee,* namely, with that best of blessings the Gift of the Holy Ghost; the promise of the Spirit was that blessing of Abraham which was to come upon the Gentiles through Jesus Christ, Gal. 3:14. (2.) Of the increase of the church that believers, his spiritual seed, should be numerous as the stars of heaven. (3.) Of spiritual victories: *Thy seed shall possess the gate of his enemies.* Believers, by their faith, overcome the world, and triumph over all the powers of darkness, and are more than conquerors. Probably Zacharias refers to this part of the oath (Lu. 1:74), *That we, being delivered out of the hand of our enemies, might serve him without fear.* But the crown of all is the last promise. (4.) Of the incarnation of Christ: *In thy see,* one particular person that shall descend from thee (for he speaks not of many, but of one, as the apostle observers, Gal. 3:16), *shall all the nations of the earth be blessed,* or shall *bless themselves,* as the phrase is, Isa. 65:16. In him all may be happy if they will, and all that belong to him shall be so, and shall think themselves so. Christ is the great blessing of the world. Abraham was ready to give up his son for a sacrifice to the honour of God, and, on that occasion, God promised to give his Son a sacrifice for the salvation of man.

Verses 20–24

This is recorded here, 1. To show that though Abraham saw his own family highly dignified with peculiar privileges, admitted into covenant, and blessed with the entail of the promise, yet he did not look with contempt and disdain upon his relations, but was glad to hear of the increase and prosperity of their families. 2. To make way for the following story of the marriage of Isaac to Rebekah, a daughter of this family.

CHAPTER 23

Here is, I. Abraham a mourner for the death of Sarah (*v.* 1, 2). II. Abraham a purchaser of a burying-place for Sarah. 1. The purchase humbly proposed by Abraham (*v.* 3, 4). 2. Fairly treated of, and agreed to, with a great deal of mutual civility and respect (*v.* 5–16). 3. The purchase-money paid (*v.* 16). 4. The premises conveyed and secured to Abraham (*v.* 17, 18, 20). 5. Sarah's funeral (*v.* 19).

Verses 1–2

We have here, 1. Sarah's age, *v.* 1. Almost forty years before, she had called herself old, *ch.* 18:12. Old people will die never the sooner, but may die the better, for reckoning themselves old. 2. Her death, *v.* 2. The longest liver must die at last. Abraham and Sarah had lived comfortably together many years; but death parts those whom nothing else could part. The special friends and favourites of Heaven are not exempted from the stroke of death. She died in the land of Canaan, where she had been above sixty years a sojourner. 3. Abraham's mourning for her; and he was a true mourner. He did not only perform the ceremonies of mourning according to the custom of those time, as the mourners that go about the streets, but he did sincerely lament the great loss he had of a good wife, and gave proof of the constancy of his affection to her to the last. Two words are used: he came both to *mourn* and to *weep.* His sorrow was not counterfeit, but real. He came to her tent, and sat down by the corpse, there to pay the tribute of his tears, that his eye might affect his heart, and that he might pay the greater respect to the memory of her that was gone. Note, It is not only lawful, but it is a duty, to lament the death of our near relations, both in compliance with the providence of God, who thus calls to weeping and mourning, and in honour to those to whom honour is due. Tears are a tribute due to our deceased friends. When a body is sown, it must be watered. But we must not sorrow as those that have no hope; for we have a good hope through grace both concerning them and concerning ourselves.

Verses 3–15

Here is, I. The humble request which Abraham made to his neighbours, the Hittites, for a burying-place among them, *v.* 3, 4. It was strange he had this to do now; but we are to impute it rather to God's providence than to his improvidence, as appears Acts 7:5, where it is said, *God gave him no inheritance in Canaan.* It were well if all those who take care to provide burying-places for their bodies after death were as careful to provide a resting-place for their souls. Observe here, 1. The convenient diversion which this affair gave, for the present, to Abraham's grief: He *stood up from before his dead.* Those that find themselves in danger of over-grieving for their dead relations, and are entering into that temptation, must take heed of poring upon their loss and sitting alone and melancholy. There must be a time of standing up from before their dead, and ceasing to mourn. For, thanks be to God, our happiness is not bound up in the life of any creature. Care of the funeral may, as here, be improved to divert grief for the death at first, when it is most in danger of tyrannizing. Weeping must not hinder sowing. 2. The argument he used with the children of Heth, which was this: *"I am a stranger and a sojourner with you,* therefore I am unprovided, and must become a humble suitor to you for a burying-place." This was one occasion which Abraham took to confess that he was a stranger and a pilgrim upon earth; he was not ashamed to own it thus publicly, Heb. 11:13. Note, The death of our relations should effectually remind us that we are not at home in this world. When they are gone, say, "We are going." 3. His uneasiness till this affair was settled, intimated in that word, *that I may bury my dead out of my sight.* Note, Death will make those unpleasant to our sight who while they lived were the desire of our eyes. The countenance that was fresh and lively becomes pale and ghastly, and fit to be removed into the land of darkness. While she was in his sight, it renewed his grief, which he would prevent.

II. The generous offer which the children of Heth made to him, *v.* 5, 6. They compliment him, 1. With a title of respect: *Thou art a prince of God among us,* so the word is; not only great, but good. He called himself a stranger and a sojourner; they call him a great prince; for those that humble themselves shall be exalted. God had promised to make Abraham's name great. 2. With a tender of the best of their burying-places. Note, Even the light of nature teaches us to be civil and respectful towards all, though they be strangers and sojourners. The noble generosity of these Canaanites shames and condemns the closeness, and selfishness, and ill-humour, of many that call themselves Israelites. Observe, These Canaanites would be glad to mingle their dust with Abraham's and to have their last end like his.

III. The particular proposal which Abraham made to them, *v.* 7–9. He returns them his thanks for their kind offer with all possible decency and respect; though a great man, an old man, and now a mourner, yet he stands up, and bows himself humbly before them, *v.* 7. Note, Religion teaches good manners; and those abuse it that place it in rudeness and clownishness. He then pitches upon the place he thinks most convenient, namely, the cave of Machpelah, which probably lay near him, and had not yet been used for a burying-place. The present owner was *Ephron.* Abraham cannot pretend to any interest in him, but he desires that they would improve theirs with him to get the purchase of that cave, and the field in which it was. Note, A moderate desire to obtain that which is convenient for us, by fair and honest means, is not such a coveting of that which is our neighbour's as is forbidden in the tenth commandment.

IV. The present which Ephron made to Abraham of his field: *The field give I thee, v.* 10, 11. Abraham thought he must be entreated to sell it; but, upon the first mention of it, without entreaty, Ephron freely gives it. Some men have more generosity than they are thought to have. Abraham, no doubt, had taken all occasions to oblige his neighbours, and do them any service that lay in his power; and now they return his kindness: for *he that watereth shall be watered also himself.* Note, If those that profess religion adorn their profession by eminent civility and serviceableness to all, they shall find it will rebound to their own comfort and advantage, as well as to the glory of God.

V. Abraham's modest and sincere refusal of Ephron's kind offer, *v.* 12, 13. Abundance of thanks he returns him for it (*v.* 12), makes his obeisance to him before the people of the land, that they might respect Ephron the more for the respect they saw Abraham give him (1 Sa. 15:30), but resolves to give him money for the field, even the full value of it. It was not in pride that Abraham refused the gift, or because he scorned to be beholden to Ephron; but, 1. In justice. Abraham was rich in silver and gold (*ch.* 13:2) and was able to pay for the field, and therefore would not take advantage of Ephron's generosity. Note, Honesty, as well as honour, forbids us to sponge upon our neighbours and to impose upon those that are free. Job reflected upon it with comfort, when he was poor, that he had not *eaten the fruits of his land without money,* Job 31:39. 2. In prudence. He would pay for it lest Ephron, when this good humour was over, should upbraid him with it, and say, *I have made Abraham rich* (*ch.* 14:23), or lest the next heir should question Abraham's title (because that grant was made without any consideration), and claim back the field. Thus David afterwards refused Araunah's offer, 2 Sa. 24:24. We know not what affronts we may hereafter receive from those that are now most kind and generous.

VI. The price of the land fixed by Ephron but not insisted on: *The land is worth four hundred shekels of silver* (about fifty pounds of our money), *but what is that between me and thee? v.* 14, 15. He would rather oblige his friend than have so much money in his pocket. Herein Ephron discovers, 1. A great contempt of worldly wealth. "What is that between me and thee? It is a small matter, not worth speaking of." Many a one would have said, "It is a deal of money; it will go far in a child's portion." But Ephron says, "What is that?" Note, It is an excellent thing for people to have low and mean thoughts of all the wealth of this world; it is that which is not, and in the abundance of which a man's life does not consist, Lu. 12:15. 2. Great courtesy, and obligingness to his friend and neighbour. Ephron was not jealous of Abraham as a resident foreigner, nor envious at him as a man likely to thrive and grow rich. He bore him no ill-will for his singularity in religion, but was much kinder to him than most people now-a-days are to their own brothers: *What is that between me and thee?* Note, No little thing should occasion demurs and differences between true friends. When we are tempted to be hot in resenting affronts, high in demanding our rights, or hard in denying a kindness, we should answer the temptation with this question: "What is that between me and my friend?"

Verses 16–20

We have here the conclusion of the treaty between

Abraham and Ephron about the burying-place. The bargain was publicly made before all the neighbours, *in the presence and audience of the sons of Heth, v.* 16, 17. Note, Prudence, as well as justice, directs us to be fair, and open, and above-board, in our dealings. Fraudulent contracts hate the light, and choose to be clandestine; but those that design honestly in their bargains care not who are witnesses to them. Our law countenances sales made in market-overt, and by deed enrolled. Observe, 1. Abraham, without fraud, covin, or further delay, pays the money, *v.* 16. He pays it readily, without hesitation, — pays it in full, without diminution, — and pays it by weight, current money with the merchant, without deceit. See how anciently money was used for the help of commerce; and see how honestly money should be paid where it is due. Observe, Though all the land of Canaan was Abraham's by promise, yet, the time of his possessing not having come, what he had now occasion for he bought and paid for. Note, Dominion is not founded in grace. The saints' title to an eternal inheritance does not entitle them to the possessions of this world, nor justify them in doing wrong. 2. Ephron honestly and fairly makes him a good title to the land, *v.* 17, 18, 20. The field, with all its appurtenances, is conveyed to Abraham and his heirs for ever, in open court, not by writing (it does not appear that writing was then used), but by such a public solemn declaration before witnesses as was sufficient to pass it. Note, As that which is bought must be honestly paid for, so that which is sold must be honestly paid for, so that which is sold must be honestly delivered and secured. 3. Abraham, thereupon, takes possession, and buries Sarah in the cave or vault (whether framed by nature or art is not certain) which was in the purchased field. It is probable that Abraham had buried servants out of his family since he came to Canaan, but the graves of the common people (2 Ki. 23:6) might suffice for them; now that Sarah was dead a peculiar place must be found for her remains. It is worth noting, (1.) That a burying-place was the first spot of ground Abraham possessed in Canaan. Note, When we are entering into the world it is good to think of our going out of it; for, as soon as we are born, we begin to die. (2.) That it was the only piece of land he ever possessed, though the country was all his own in reversion. Those that have least of this earth find a grave in it. Abraham provided, not cities, as Cain and Nimrod, but a sepulchre, [1.] To be a constant memorandum of death to himself and his posterity, that he and they might learn to die daily. This sepulchre is said to be *at the end of the field* (*v.* 9); for, whatever our possessions are, there is a sepulchre at the end of them. [2.] To be a token of his belief and expectation of the resurrection; for why should such care be taken of the body if it be thrown away for ever, and must not rise again? Abraham, in this, said plainly that he sought a better country, that is, a heavenly. Abraham is content to be still flitting, while he lives, but secures a place where, when he dies his flesh may rest in hope.

CHAPTER 24

Marriages and funerals are the changes of families, and the common news among the inhabitants of the villages. In the foregoing chapter we had Abraham burying his wife, here we have him marrying his son. These stories concerning his family, with their minute circumstances, are largely related, while the histories of the kingdoms of the world then in being, with their revolutions, are buried in silence; for the Lord knows those that are his. The subjoining of Isaac's marriage to Sarah's funeral (with a particular reference to it, *v.* 67) shows us that as "one generation passes away another generation comes;" and thus the entail both of the human nature, and of the covenant, is preserved. Here is, I. Abraham's care about the marrying of his son, and the charge he gave to his servant about it (*v.* 1–9). II. His servant's journey into Abraham's country, to seek a wife for his young master among his own relations (*v.* 10–14). III. The kind providence which brought him acquainted with Rebekah, whose father was Isaac's cousin-german (*v.* 15–28). IV. The treaty of marriage with her relations (*v.* 29–49). V. Their consent obtained (*v.* 50–60). VI. The happy meeting and marriage between Isaac and Rebekah (*v.* 61, etc.).

Verses 1–9

Three things we may observe here concerning Abraham: —

I. The care he took of a good son, to get him married, well married. It was high time to think of it now, for Isaac was about forty years old, and it had been customary with his ancestors to marry at thirty, or sooner, *ch.* 11:14, 18, 22, 24. Abraham believed the promise of the building up of his family, and therefore did not make haste; not more haste than good speed. Two considerations moved him to think of it now (*v.* 1): — 1. That he himself was likely to leave the world quickly, for he was *old, and well-stricken in age,* and it would be a satisfaction to him to see his son settled before he died; and, 2. That he had a good estate to leave behind him, for *the Lord had blessed him in all things;* and the blessing of the Lord makes rich. See how much religion and piety befriend outward prosperity. Now Abraham's pious care concerning his son was, (1.) That he should not marry a daughter of Canaan, but one of his kindred. He saw that the Canaanites were degenerating into great wickedness, and knew by revelation that they were designed for ruin, and therefore he would not marry his son among them, lest they should be either a snare to his soul, or at least a blot to his name. (2.) That yet he should not leave the land of Canaan, to go himself among his kindred, not even for the purpose of choosing a wife, lest he should be tempted to settle there. This caution is given *v.* 6, and repeated, *v.* 8. *"Bring not my son thither again,* whatever comes of it. Let him rather want a wife than expose himself to that temptation." Note, Parents in disposing of their children, should carefully consult the welfare of their souls, and their furtherance in the way to heaven. Those who through grace have escaped the corruption that is in the world through lust, and have brought up their children accordingly, should take heed of doing any thing by which they may be again entangled therein and overcome, 2 Pt. 2:20. Beware that you bring them not thither again, Heb. 11:15.

II. The charge he gave to a good servant, probably Eliezer of Damascus, one of whose conduct, fidelity, and affection to him and his family, he had had long experience. He trusted him with this great affair, and not Isaac himself, because he would not have Isaac go at all into that country, but marry there by proxy; and no proxy so fit as this *steward of his house.* This matter is settled between the master and the servant with a great deal of care and solemnity. 1. The servant must be bound by an oath to do his utmost to get a wife for Isaac from among his relations, *v.* 2–4. Abraham swears him to it, both for his own satisfaction and for the engagement of his servant to all possible care and diligence in this matter. Thus God swears his servants to their work, that, having sworn, they may perform it. Honour is here done to the eternal God; for he it is that is sworn by, to whom alone these appeals ought to be made. And some think honour is done to the covenant of circumcision by the ceremony here used of *putting his hand under his thigh.* Note, Swearing being an ordinance not peculiar to the church, but common to mankind, is to be performed by such signs as are the appointments and common usages of our country, for binding the person sworn. 2. He must be clear of this oath if, when he had done his utmost, he could not prevail. This proviso the servant prudently inserted (*v.* 5), putting the case that the woman would not follow him; and Abraham allowed the exception, *v.* 8. Note, Oaths are to be taken with great caution, and the matter sworn to should be rightly understood and limited, because it is a *snare to devour that which is holy, and, after vows, to make the enquiry* which should have been made before.

III. The confidence he put in a good God, who, he doubts not, will give his servant success in this undertaking, *v.* 7. He remembers that God had wonderfully brought him out of the land of his nativity, by the effectual call of his grace; and therefore doubts not but he will succeed him in his care not to bring his son thither again. He remembers also the promise God had made and confirmed to him that he would give Canaan to his seed, and thence infers that God would own him in his endeavours to match his son, not among those devoted nations, but to one that was fit to be the mother of such a seed. "Fear not therefore; he shall send his angel before thee to make thy way prosperous." Note, 1. Those that carefully keep in the way of duty, and govern themselves by the principles of their religion in their designs and undertakings, have good reason to expect prosperity and success in them. God will cause that to issue in our comfort in which we sincerely aim at his glory. 2. God's promises, and our own experiences, are sufficient to encourage our dependence upon God, and our expectations from him, in all the affairs of this life. 3. God's angels are ministering spirits, sent forth, not only for the protection, but for the guidance, of the heirs of promise, Heb. 1:14. *"He shall send his angel before thee,* and then thou wilt speed well."

Verses 10–28

Abraham's servant now begins to make a figure in this story; and, though he is not named, yet much is here recorded to his honour, and for an example to all servants, who shall be honoured if, by faithfully serving God and their masters, they adorn the doctrine of Christ (compare Prov. 27:18 with Titus 2:10); for there is no respect of persons with God, Col. 3:24, 25. A good servant that makes conscience of the duty of his place, and does it in the fear of God, though he make not a figure in the world nor have praise of men, yet shall be owned and accepted of God and have praise of him. Observe here,

I. How faithful Abraham's servant approved himself to his master. Having received his charge, he with all expedition set out on his journey, with an equipage suitable to the object of his negotiation (*v.* 10), *and he had all the goods of his master,* that is, a schedule or particular account of them, *in his hand,* to show to those with whom he was to treat; for, from first to last, he consulted his master's honour. Isaac being a type of Christ, some make this fetching of a wife for him to signify the espousing of the church by the agency of his servants the ministers. The church is the bride, the Lamb's wife, Rev. 21:9. Christ is the bridegroom, and ministers are the friends of the bridegroom (Jn. 3:29), whose work it is to persuade souls to consent to him, 2 Co. 11:2. The spouse of Christ must not be of the Canaanites, but of his own kindred, born again from above. Ministers, like Abraham's servant, must lay out themselves with the utmost wisdom and care to serve their master's interest herein.

II. How devoutly he acknowledged God in this affair, like one of that happy household which Abraham had *commanded to keep the way of the Lord,* etc., *ch.* 18:19. He arrived early in the evening (after many days' journeying) at the place of his destination, and reposed himself by a well of water, to consider how he might manage his business for the best. And,

1. He acknowledges God by a particular prayer (*v.* 12–14), wherein, (1.) He petitions for prosperity and good success in this affair: *Send me good speed, this day.* Note, We have leave to be particular in recommending our affairs to the conduct and care of the divine Providence. Those that would have good speed must pray for it. *This day, in this affair;* thus we must, in all our ways, acknowledge God, Prov. 3:6. And, if we thus look up to God in every undertaking which we are in care about, we shall have the comfort of having done our duty, whatever the issue be. (2.) He pleads God's covenant with his master Abraham: *O God of my master Abraham, show kindness to him.* Note, As the children of good parents, so the servants of good masters, have peculiar encouragement in the prayers they offer to God for prosperity and success. (3.) He proposes a sign (*v.* 14), not by it to limit God, nor with a design to proceed no further if he were not gratified in it; but it is a prayer, [1.] That God would provide a good wife for his young master, and this was a good prayer. He knew that *a prudent wife is from the Lord* (Prov. 19:14), and therefore that for this he will be enquired of. He desires that his master's wife might be humble and industrious woman, bred up to care and labour, and willing to put her hand to any work that was to be done; and that she might be of a courteous disposition, and charitable to strangers. When he came to seek a wife for his master, he did not go to the playhouse or the park, and pray that he might meet one there, but to *the well of water,* expecting to find one there well employed. [2.] That he would please to make his way, in this matter, plain and clear before him, by the concurrence of minute circumstances in his favour. Note, *First,* It is the comfort, as well as the belief, of a good man, that God's providence extends itself to the smallest occurrences and admirably serves its own purposes by them. Our times are in God's hand; not only events themselves, but the times of them. *Secondly,* It is our wisdom, in all our affairs, to follow Providence, and folly to force it. *Thirdly,* It is very desirable, and that which we may lawfully pray for, while in the general we set God's will before us as our rule, that he will, by hints of providence, direct us in the way of our duty, and give us indications what

his mind it. Thus he guides his people with his eye (Ps. 32:8), and leads them in a plain path, Ps. 27:11.

2. God owns him by a particular providence. He decreed the thing, and it was established to him, Job 22:28. According to his faith, so was it unto him. The answer to this prayer was, (1.) Speedy — *before he had made an end of speaking* (*v.* 15), as it is written (Isa. 65:24), *While they are yet speaking, I will hear.* Though we are backward to pray, God is forward to hear prayer. (2.) Satisfactory: the first that came to draw water was, and did, in every thing, according to his own heart. [1.] She was so well qualified that in all respects she answered the characters he wished for in the woman that was to be his master's wife, handsome and healthful, humble and industrious, very courteous and obliging to a stranger, and having all the marks of a good disposition. When she came to the well (*v.* 16), she went down and *filled her pitcher, and came up* to go home with it. She did not stand to gaze upon the strange man and his camels, but minded her business, and would not have been diverted from it but by an opportunity of doing good. She did not curiously nor confidently enter into discourse with him, but modestly answered him, with all the decorum that became her sex. What a degenerate age do we live in, in which appear all the instances of pride, luxury, and laziness, the reverse of Rebekah's character, whose daughters few are! Those instances of goodness which were then in honour are now in contempt. [2.] Providence so ordered it that she did that which exactly answered to his sign, and was wonderfully the counterpart of his proposal: she not only gave him drink, but, which was more than could have been expected, she offered her services to give his camels drink, which was the very sign he proposed. Note, *First,* God, in his providence, does sometimes wonderfully own the prayer of faith, and gratify the innocent desires of his praying people, even in little things, that he may show the extent of his care, and may encourage them at all times to seek to him and trust in him; yet we must take heed of being over-bold in prescribing to God, lest the event should weaken our faith rather than strengthen it. *Secondly,* It is good to take all opportunities of showing a humble, courteous, charitable, disposition, because, some time or other, it may turn more to our honour and benefit than we think of; some hereby have entertained angels, and Rebekah hereby, quite beyond her expectation at this time, was brought into the line of Christ and the covenant. *Thirdly,* There may be a great deal of obliging kindness in that which costs but little: our Saviour has promised a reward for a cup of cold water, Mt. 10:42. *Fourthly,* The concurrence of providences and their minute circumstances, for the furtherance of our success in any business, ought to be particularly observed, with wonder and thankfulness, to the glory of God: *The man wondered, v.* 21. We have been wanting to ourselves, both in duty and in comfort, by neglecting to observe Providence. [3.] Upon enquiry he found, to his great satisfaction, that she was a near relation to his master, and that the family she was of was considerable, and able to give him entertainment, *v.* 23–25. Note, Providence sometimes wonderfully directs those that by faith and prayer seek direction from heaven in the choice of suitable yoke-fellows: happy marriages those are likely to be that are made in the fear of God; and these, we are sure, are made in heaven.

3. He acknowledges God in a particular thanksgiving. He first paid his respects to Rebekah, in gratitude for her civility (*v.* 22), obliging her with such ornaments and attire as a maid, especially a bride, cannot forget (Jer. 2:32), which yet, we should think, ill suited the *pitcher of water;* but the ear-rings and bracelets she sometimes wore did not make her think herself above the labours of a virtuous woman (Prov. 31:13), who *works willingly with her hands;* nor the services of a child, who, while *under age, differs nothing from a servant,* Gal. 9:1. Having done this, he turns his wonder (*v.* 21) into worshipping: *Blessed be the Lord God of my master Abraham, v.* 26, 27. Observe here, (1.) He had prayed for good speed (*v.* 12), and now that he had sped well he gives thanks. Note, What we win by prayer we must wear with praise; for mercies in answer to prayer lay us under particular obligations. (2.) He had as yet but a comfortable prospect of mercy, and was not certain what the issue might prove; yet he gives thanks. Note, When God's favours are coming towards us we must meet them with our praises. (3.) He blesses God for success when he was negotiating for his master. Note, We should be thankful for our friend's mercies as for our own. (4.) He gives thanks that, being in the way, at a loss what course to steer, the Lord had led him. Note, In doubtful cases, it is very comfortable to see God leading us, as he led Israel in the wilderness by the pillar of cloud and fire. (5.) He thinks himself very happy, and owns God in it, that he was led to the *house of his master's brethren,* those of them that had come out of Ur of the Chaldees, though they had not come to Canaan, but remained in Haran. They were not idolaters, but worshippers of the true God, and inclinable to the religion of Abraham's family. Note, God is to be acknowledged in providing suitable yoke-fellows, especially such as are agreeable in religion. (6.) He acknowledges that God, herein, had not left his master *destitute of his mercy and truth.* God had promised to build up Abraham's family, yet it seemed destitute of the benefit of that promise; but now Providence is working towards the accomplishing of it. Note, [1.] God's faithful ones, how destitute soever they may be of worldly comforts, shall never be left destitute of God's mercy and truth; for God's mercy is an inexhaustible fountain, and his truth an inviolable foundation. [2.] It adds much to the comfort of any blessing to see in it the continuance of God's mercy and truth.

Verses 29–53

We have here the making up of the marriage between Isaac and Rebekah. It is related very largely and particularly, even to the minute circumstances, which, we should think, might have been spared, while other things of great moment and mystery (as the story of Melchizedek) are related in few words. Thus God conceals that which is curious from the wise and prudent, reveals to babes that which is common and level to their capacity (Mt. 11:25), and rules and *saves the world by the foolishness of preaching,* 1 Co. 1:21. Thus also we are directed to take notice of God's providence in the little common occurrences of human life, and in them also to exercise our own prudence and other graces; for the scripture was not intended for the use of philosophers and statesmen only, but to make us all wise and virtuous in the conduct of ourselves and families. Here is,

I. The very kind reception given to Abraham's servant by Rebekah's relations. Her brother Laban went to invite and conduct him in, but not till he saw the *ear-rings and the bracelets upon his sister's hands, v.* 30. "O," thinks Laban, "here is a man that there is something to be got by, a man that is rich and generous; we will be sure to bid him welcome!" We know so much of Laban's character, by the following story, as to think that he would not have been so free of his entertainment if he had not hoped to be well paid for it, as he was, *v.* 53. Note, *A man's gift maketh room for him* (Prov. 18:16), *which way soever it turneth, it prospereth,* Prov. 17:8. 1. The invitation was kind: *Come in, thou blessed of the Lord, v.* 31. They saw he was rich, and therefore pronounced him *blessed of the Lord;* or, perhaps, because they heard from Rebekah (*v.* 28) or the gracious words which proceeded out of his mouth, they concluded him a good man, and therefore *blessed of the Lord.* Note, Those that are blessed of God should be welcome to us. It is good owning those whom God owns. 2. The entertainment was kind, *v.* 32, 33. Both the house and stable were well furnished, and Abraham's servant was invited to the free use of both. Particular care was taken of the camels; for a *good man regardeth the life of his beast,* Prov. 12:10. If the ox knows his owner to serve him, the owner should know his ox to provide for him that which is fitting for him.

II. The full account which he gave them of his errand, and the court he made to them for their consent respecting Rebekah. Observe,

1. How intent he was upon his business; though he had come off a journey, and come to a good house, he would *not eat, till he had told his errand, v.* 33. Note, The doing of our work, and the fulfilling of our trusts, either for God or man, should be preferred by us before our necessary food: it was our Saviour's meat and drink, Jn. 4:34.

2. How ingenious he was in the management of it; he approved himself, in this matter, both a prudent man and a man of integrity, faithful to his master by whom he was trusted, and just to those with whom he now treated.

(1.) He gives a short account of the state of his master's family, *v.* 34–36. He was welcome before, but we may suppose him doubly welcome when he said, *I am Abraham's servant.* Abraham's name, no doubt, was well known among them and respected, and we might suppose them not altogether ignorant of his state, for Abraham knew theirs, *ch.* 22:20–24. Two things he suggests, to recommend his proposal: — [1.] That his master Abraham, through the blessing of God, had a very good estate; and, [2.] That he had settled it all upon Isaac, for whom he was now a suitor.

(2.) He tells them the charge his master had given him, to fetch a wife for his son from among his kindred, with the reason of it, *v.* 37, 38. Thus he insinuates a pleasing hint, that, though Abraham had removed to a country at so great a distance, yet he still retained the remembrance of his relations that he had left behind, and a respect for them. The highest degrees of divine affection must not divest us of natural affection. He likewise obviates an objection, That, if Isaac were deserving, he needed not send so far off for a wife: why did he not marry nearer home? "For a good reason," says he; "my master's son must not match with a Canaanite." He further recommends his proposal, [1.] From the faith his master had that it would succeed, *v.* 40. Abraham took encouragement from the testimony of his conscience that he *walked before God* in a regular course of holy living, and thence inferred that God would prosper him; probably he refers to that covenant which God had made with him (*ch.* 17:1), *I am God, all-sufficient, walk before me.* Therefore, says he *the God before whom I walk will send his angel.* Note, While we make conscience of our part of the covenant, we may take the comfort of God's part of it; and we should learn to apply general promises of particular cases, as there is occasion. [2.] From the care he himself had taken to preserve their liberty of giving or refusing their consent, as they should see cause, without incurring the guilt of perjury (*v.* 39–41), which showed him, in general, to be a cautious man, and particularly careful that their consent might not be forced, but be either free or not at all.

(3.) He relates to them the wonderful concurrence of providences, to countenance and further the proposal, plainly showing the finger of God in it. [1.] He tells them how he had prayed for direction by a sign, *v.* 42–44. Note, It is good dealing with those who be prayer take God along with them in their dealings. [2.] How God had answered his prayer in the very letter of it. Though he did but *speak in his heart* (v 45), which perhaps he mentions, lest it should be suspected that Rebekah had overheard his prayer and designedly humoured it. "No," says he, "I spoke *it in my heart,* so that none heard it but God, to whom thought are word, and from him the answer came," *v.* 46, 47. [3.] How he had immediately acknowledged God's goodness to him therein, *leading him,* as he here expresses it, *in the right way.* Note, God's way is always the *right way* (Ps. 107:7), and those are well led whom he leads.

(4.) He fairly refers the matter to their consideration, and waits their decision (*v.* 49): *"If you will deal kindly and truly with my master,* well and good: if you will be sincerely kind, you will accept the proposal, and I have what I came for; if not, do not hold me in suspense." Note, Those who deal fairly have reason to expect fair dealing.

(5.) They freely and cheerfully close with the proposal upon a very good principle (*v.* 50): *"The thing proceedeth from the Lord,* Providence smiles upon it, and we have nothing to say against it." They do not object distance of place, Abraham's forsaking them, or his having no land in possession, but person estate only: they do not question the truth of what this man said; but, [1.] They trust much to his integrity. It were well if honesty did so universally prevail among men that it might be as much an act of prudence as it is of good nature to take a man's word. [2.] They trust more to God's providence, and therefore by silence give consent, because it appears to be directed and disposed by Infinite Wisdom. Note, A marriage is then likely to be comfortable when it appears to proceed from the Lord.

(6.) Abraham's servant makes a thankful acknowledgment of the good success he had met with, [1.] To God: *He worshipped the Lord, v.* 52. Observe, *First,* As his good success went on, he went on to bless God. Those that *pray without ceasing* should *in every thing give thanks,* and own

God in every step of mercy. *Secondly,* God sent his angel before him, and so gave him success, *v.* 7, 40. But when he has the desired success, he worships God, not the angel. Whatever benefit we have by the ministration of angels, all the glory must be given to the Lord of the angels, Rev. 22:9. [2.] He pays his respects to the family also, and particularly to the bride, *v.* 53. He presented her, and her mother, and brother, with many precious things, both to give a real proof of his master's riches and generosity and in gratitude for their civility to him, and further to ingratiate himself with them.

Verses 54–61

Rebekah is here taking leave of her father's house; and 1. Abraham's servant presses for a dismission. Though he and his company were very welcome, and very cheerful there, yet he said, *Send me away* (*v.* 54), and again, *v.* 56. He knew his master would expect him home with some impatience; he had business to do at home which wanted him, and therefore, as one that preferred his work before his pleasure, he was for hastening home. Note, Lingering and loitering no way become a wise and good man; when we have despatched our business abroad we must not delay our return to our business at home, nor be longer from it than needs must; for as a bird that *wanders from her nest so is he that wanders from his place,* Prov. 27:8. 2. Rebekah's relations, from natural affection and according to the usual expression of kindness in that case, solicit for her stay some time among them, *v.* 55. They could not think of parting with her on a sudden, especially as she was about the remove so far off and it was not likely that they would ever see one another again: *Let her stay a few days, at least ten,* which makes it as reasonable a request as the reading in the margin seems to make it unreasonable, *a year,* or *at least ten months.* They had consented to the marriage, and yet were loth to part with her. Note, It is an instance of the vanity of this world that there is nothing in it so agreeable but it has its alloy. *Nulla est sincera voluptas — There is no unmingled pleasure.* They were pleased that they had matched a daughter of their family so well, and yet, when it came to the last, it was with great reluctance that they sent her away. 3. Rebekah herself determined the matter. To her they appealed, as it was fit they should (*v.* 57): *Call the damsel* (who had retired to her apartment with a modest silence) and *enquire at her mouth.* Note, As children ought not to marry without their parents' consent, so parents ought not to marry them without their own. Before the matter is resolved on, "Ask at the damsel's mouth;" she is a party principally concerned, and therefore ought to be principally consulted. Rebekah consented, not only to go, but to go immediately: *I will go, v.* 58. We may hope that the notice she had taken of the servant's piety and devotion gave her such an idea of the prevalence of religion and godliness in the family she was to go to made her desirous to hasten thither, and willing to forget her own people and her father's house, where religion had not so much the ascendant. 4. Hereupon she is sent away with Abraham's servant; not, we may suppose, the very next day after, but very quickly: her friends see that she has a good heart on it, and so they dismiss her, (1.) With suitable attendants — her *nurse* (*v.* 59), her *damsels, v.* 61. It seems, then, that when she went to the well for water it was not because she had not servants at command, but because she took a pleasure in works of humble industry. Now that she was going among strangers, it was fit she should take those with her with whom she was acquainted. Here is nothing said of her portion. Her personal merits were a portion in her, she needed none with her, nor did that ever come into the treaty of marriage. (2.) With hearty good wishes: *They blessed Rebekah, v.* 60. Note, When our relations are entering into a new condition, we ought by prayer to recommend them to the blessing and grace of God. Now that she was going to be a wife, they prayed that she might be a mother both of a numerous and of a victorious progeny. Perhaps Abraham's servant had told them of the promise God had lately made to his master, which it is likely, Abraham acquainted his household with, that God *would multiply his seed as the stars of heaven, and that they should possess the gate of their enemies* (*ch.* 22:17), to which promise they had an eye in this blessing, *Be thou the mother* of that seed.

Verses 62–67

Isaac and Rebekah are, at length, happily brought together. Observe,

I. Isaac was well employed when he met Rebekah: *He went out to meditate,* or pray, *in the field, at the even-tide, v.* 62, 63. Some think he expected the return of his servants about this time, and went out on purpose to meet them. But, it should seem, he went out on another errand, to take the advantage of a silent evening and a solitary field for meditation and prayer, those divine exercises by which we converse with God and our own hearts. Note, 1. Holy souls love retirement. It will do us good to be often left alone, walking alone and sitting alone; and, if we have the art of improving solitude, we shall find we are never less alone than when alone. 2. Meditation and prayer ought to be both our business and our delight when we are alone; while we have a God, a Christ, and a heaven, to acquaint ourselves with, and to secure our interest in, we need not want matter either for meditation or prayer, which, if they go together, will mutually befriend each other. 3. Our walks in the field are then truly pleasant when in them we apply ourselves to meditation and prayer. We there have a free and open prospect of the heavens above us and the earth around us, and the host and riches of both, by the view of which we should be led to the contemplation of the Maker and owner of all. 4. The exercises of devotion should be the refreshment and entertainment of the evening, to relieve us from the fatigue occasioned by the care and business of the day, and to prepare us for the repose and sleep of the night. 5. Merciful providences are then doubly comfortable when they find us well employed and in the way of our duty. Some think Isaac was now praying for good success in this affair that was depending, and meditating upon that which was proper to encourage his hope in God concerning it; and now, when he sets himself, as it were, upon his watch-tower, to see what God would answer him, as the prophet (Hab. 2:1), *he sees the camels coming.* Sometimes God sends in the mercy prayed for immediately, Acts 12:12.

II. Rebekah behaved herself very becomingly, when she met Isaac: understanding who he was, she *alighted off her camel* (*v.* 64), and*took a veil, and covered herself* (*v.* 65), in token of humility, modesty, and subjection. She did not reproach Isaac for not coming himself to fetch her, or, at least, to meet her a day's journey or two, did not complain of the tediousness of her journey, or the difficulty of leaving her relations, to come into a strange place; but, having seen Providence going before her in the affair, she accommodates herself with cheerfulness to her new relation. Those that by faith are espoused to Christ, and would be presented as chaste virgins to him, must, in conformity to his example, humble themselves, as Rebekah, who alighted when she saw Isaac on foot, and must put themselves into subjection to him who is their head (Eph. 5:24), as Rebekah, signifying it by the veil she put on, 1 Co. 11:10.

III. They were brought together (probably after some further acquaintance), to their mutual comfort, *v.* 67. Observe here, 1. What an affectionate son he was to his mother: it was about three years since her death, and yet he was not, till now, comforted concerning it; the wound which that affliction gave to his tender spirit bled so long, and was never healed till God brought him into this new relation. Thus crosses and comforts are balances to each other (Eccl. 7:14), and help to keep the scale even. 2. What an affectionate husband he was to his wife. Note, Those that have approved themselves well in one relation, it may be hoped, will do so in another: *She became his wife, and he loved her;* there was all the reason in the world why he should, for so *ought men to love their wives even an themselves.* The duty of the relation is then done, and the comfort of the relation is then enjoyed, when mutual love governs; for *there the Lord commands the blessing.*

CHAPTER 25

The sacred historian, in this chapter, I. Takes his leave of Abraham, with an account, 1. Of his children by another wife (*v.* 1–4). 2. Of his last will and testament (*v.* 5, 6). 3. Of his age, death, and burial (*v.* 7–10). II. He takes his leave of Ishmael, with a short account, 1. Of his children (*v.* 12–16). 2. Of his age and death (*v.* 17, 18). III. He enters upon the history of Isaac. 1. His prosperity (*v.* 11). 2. The conception and birth of his two sons, with the oracle of God concerning them (*v.* 19–26). 3. Their different characters (*v.* 27, 28). 4. Esau's selling his birthright to Jacob (*v.* 29–34).

Verses 1–10

Abraham lived, after the marriage of Isaac, thirty-five years, and all that is recorded concerning him during the time lies here in a very few verses. We hear no more of God's extraordinary appearances to him or trials of him; for all the days, even of the best and greatest saints, are not eminent days, some slide on silently, and neither come nor go with observation; such were these last days of Abraham. We have here,

I. An account of his children by Keturah, another wife whom he married after the death of Sarah. He had buried Sarah and married Isaac, the two dear companions of his life, and was now solitary. He wanted a nurse, his family wanted a governess, and it was not good for him to be thus alone. He therefore marries Keturah, probably the chief of his maid-servants, born in his house or bought with money. Marriage is not forbidden to old age. By her he had six sons, in whom the promise made to Abraham concerning the great increase of his posterity was in part fulfilled, which, it is likely, he had an eye to this marriage. The strength he received by the promise still remained in him, to show how much the virtue of the promise exceeds the power of nature.

II. The disposition which Abraham made of his estate, *v.* 5,6. After the birth of these sons, he set his house in order, with prudence and justice. 1. He made Isaac his heir, as he was bound to do, in justice to Sarah his first and principal wife, and to Rebekah who married Isaac upon the assurance of it, *ch.* 24:36. In this *all,* which he settled upon Isaac, are perhaps included the promise of the land of Canaan, and the entail of the covenant. Or, God having already made him the heir of the promise, Abraham therefore made him heir of his estate. Our affection and gifts should attend God's. 2. He gave portions to the rest of his children, both to Ishmael, though at first he was sent empty away, and to his sons by Keturah. It was justice to provide for them; parents that do not imitate him in this are worse than infidels. It was prudence to settle them in places distant from Isaac, that they might not pretend to divide the inheritance with him, nor be in any way a care or expense to him. Observe, He did this *while he yet lived,* lest it should not be done, or not so well done, afterwards. Note, In many cases it is wisdom for men to make their own hands their executors, and what they find to do to do it while they live, as far as they can. These *sons of the concubines* were sent into the country that lay east from Canaan, and their posterity were called *the children of the east,* famous for their numbers, Jdg. 6:5, 33. Their great increase was the fruit of the promise made to Abraham, that God would multiply his seed. God, in dispensing his blessings, does as Abraham did; common blessings he gives to the children of this world, as to the sons of the bondwoman, but covenant-blessings he reserves for the heirs of promise. All that he has is theirs, for they are his Isaacs, from whom the rest shall be for ever separated.

III. The age and death of Abraham, *v.* 7,8. He lived 175 years, just 100 years after he came to Canaan; so long he was a sojourner in a strange country. Though he lived long and lived well, though he did good and could ill be spared, yet he died at last. Observe how his death is here described. 1. He *gave up the ghost.* Hes life was not extorted from him, but he cheerfully resigned it; into the hands of the Father of spirits he committed his spirit. 2. He *died in a good old age, an old man;* so God had promised him. His death was his discharge from the burdens of his age: an old man would not *so* live always. It was also the crown of the glory of his old age. 3. He was *full of years,* or full of *life* (as it might be supplied), including all the conveniences and comforts of life. He did not live till the world was weary of him, but till he was weary of the world; he had had enough of it, and desired no more. *Vixi quantum satis est — I have lived long enough.* A good man, though he should not die old, dies full of days, satisfied with living here, and longing to live in a better place. 4. He *was gathered to his people.* His body was gathered to the congregation of the dead, and his soul to the congregation of the blessed. Note, Death gathers us to our people. Those that are our people while we live, whether the people of God or the children of this world, are the people to whom death will gather us.

IV. His burial, *v.* 9, 10. Here is nothing recorded of the pomp or ceremony of his funeral; only we are told, 1. Who buried him: *His sons Isaac and Ishmael.* It was the last office of respect they had to pay to their good father. Some distance there had formerly been between Isaac and Ishmael; but it seems either that Abraham had himself brought them together while he lived, or at least that his death reconciled them. 2. Where they buried him: in his own burying-place, which he had purchased, and in which he had buried Sarah. Note, Those that in life have been very dear to each other may not only innocently, but laudably, desire to be buried together, that in their deaths they may not be divided, and in token of their hopes of rising together.

Verses 11–18

Immediately after the account of Abraham's death, Moses begins the story of Isaac (*v.* 11), and tells us where he dwelt and how remarkably God blessed him. Note, The blessing of Abraham did not die with him, but survived to all the children of the promise. But he presently digresses from the story of Isaac, to give a short account of Ishmael, forasmuch as he also was a son of Abraham, and God had made some promises concerning him, which it was requisite we should know the accomplishment of. Observe here what is said, 1. Concerning his children. He had twelve sons, *twelve princes* they are called (*v.* 16), heads of families, which in process of time became nations, distinct tribes, numerous and very considerable. They peopled a very large continent, that lay between Egypt and Assyria, called *Arabia.* The names of his twelve sons are recorded. Midian and Kedar we often read of in scripture. And some very good expositors have taken notice of the signification of those three names which are put together (*v.* 14), as containing good advice to us all, *Mishma, Dumah,* and *Massa,* that is, *hear, keep silence,* and *bear;* we have them together in the same order, Jam. 1:19, *Be swift to hear, slow to speak, slow to wrath.* The posterity of Ishmael had not only tents in the fields, wherein they grew rich in times of peace; but they had towns and castles (*v.* 16), wherein they fortified themselves in time of war. Now the number and strength of this family were the fruit of the promise made to Hagar concerning Ishmael (*ch.* 16:10), and to Abraham, *ch.* 17:20 and 21:13. Note, Many that are strangers to the covenants of promise are yet blessed with outward prosperity for the sake of their godly ancestors. *Wealth and riches shall be in their house.* 2. Concerning himself. Here is an account of his age: He *lived* 137 *years* (*v.* 17) which is recorded to show the efficacy of Abraham's prayer for him (*ch.* 17:18), *O that Ishmael might live before thee!* Here is also an account of his death; he too *was gathered to his people;* but it is not said that he was *full of days,* though he lived to so great an age: he was not so weary of the world, nor so willing to leave it, as his good father was. Those words, *he fell in the presence of all his brethren,* whether they mean, as we take them, *he died,* or, as others, *his lot fell,* are designed to show the fulfilling of that word to Hagar (*ch.* 16:12), *He shall dwell in the presence of all his brethren,* that is, he shall flourish and be eminent among them, and shall hold his own to the last. Or he died with his friends about him, which is comfortable.

Verses 19–28

We have here an account of the birth of Jacob and Esau, the twin sons of Isaac and Rebekah: their entrance into the world was (which is not usual) one of the most considerable parts of their story; nor is much related concerning Isaac but what had reference to his father while he lived and to his sons afterwards. For Isaac seems not to have been a man of action, nor much tried, but to have spent his days in quietness and silence. Now concerning Jacob and Esau we are here told,

I. That they were prayed for. Their parents, after they had been long childless, obtained them by prayer, *v.* 20, 21. *Isaac was forty years old when he was married;* though he was an only son, and the person from whom the promised seed was to come, yet he made no haste to marry. He was sixty years old when his sons were born (*v.* 26), so that, after he was married, he had no child for twenty years. Note, Though the accomplishment of God's promise is always sure, yet it is often slow, and seems to be crossed and contradicted by Providence, that the faith of believers may be tried, their patience exercised, and mercies long waited for may be the more welcome when they come. While this mercy was delayed, Isaac did not approach to a handmaid's bed, as Abraham had done, and Jacob afterwards; for he loved Rebekah, *ch.* 26:67. But, 1. He prayed: he entreated the Lord for his wife. Though God had promised to multiply his family, he prayed for its increase; for God's promises must not supersede, but encourage, our prayers, and be improved as the ground of our faith. Though he had prayed for this mercy very often, and had continued his supplication many years, and it was not granted, yet he did not leave off praying for it; for men ought always to pray, and not to faint (Lu. 18:1), to pray without ceasing, and knock till the door be opened, He prayed *for* his wife; some read it *with* his wife. Note, Husbands and wives should pray together, which is intimated in the apostle's caution, that their *prayers be not hindered,* 1 Pt. 3:7. The Jews have a tradition that Isaac, at length, took his wife with him to mount Moriah, where God had promised that he would multiply Abraham's seed (*ch.* 22:17), and there, in his prayer with her and for her, pleaded the promise made in that very place. 2. God heard his prayer, and was entreated of him. Note, Children are the gift of God. Those that continue instant in prayer, as Isaac did, shall find, at last, that they did not *seek in vain,* Isa. 45:19.

II. That they were prophesied of before they were born, and great mysteries were wrapped up in the prophecies which went before of them, *v.* 22, 23. Long had Isaac prayed for a son; and now his wife is with child of two, to recompense him for his long waiting. Thus God often outdoes our prayers, and gives more than we are able to ask or think. Now Rebekah being with child of these two sons, observe here,

1. How she was perplexed in her mind concerning her present case: *The children struggled together within her.* The commotion she felt was altogether extraordinary and made her very uneasy. Whether she was apprehensive that the birth would be her death, or whether she was weary of the intestine tumult, or whether she suspected it to be an ill omen, it seems she was ready to wish that either she had not been with child or that she might die immediately, and not bring forth such a struggling brood: *If it be so,* or, *since it is so, Why am I thus?* Before, the want of children was her trouble, now, the struggle of the children is no loss so. Note, (1.) The comforts we are most desirous of are sometimes found to bring along with them more occasion of trouble and uneasiness that we thought of; vanity being written upon all things under the sun, God thus teaches us to read it. (2.) We are too apt to be discontented with our comforts, because of the uneasiness that attends them. We know not when we are pleased; we know neither how to want nor how to abound. This struggle between the kingdom of God and the kingdom of Satan, [1.] In the world. The seed of the woman and the seed of the serpent have been contending ever since the enmity was put between them (*ch.* 3:15), and this has occasioned a constant uneasiness among men. Christ himself came to *send fire on earth, and this division,* Lu. 12:49, 51. But let not this be offence to us. A holy war is better than the peace of the devil's palace. [2.] In the hearts of believers. No sooner is Christ formed in the soul than immediately there begins a conflict between the flesh and spirit, Gal. 5:17. The stream is not turned without a mighty struggle, which yet ought not to discourage us. It is better to have a conflict with sin than tamely to submit to it.

2. What course she took for her relief: *She went to enquire of the Lord.* Some think Melchizedek was now consulted as an oracle, or perhaps some *Urim* or *Teraphim* were now used to enquire of God by, as afterwards in the breast-plate of judgment. Note, The word and prayer, by both which we now enquire of the Lord, give great relief to those that are upon any account perplexed. It is a great relief to the mind to spread our case before the Lord, and ask counsel at his mouth. *Go into the sanctuary,* Ps. 73:17.

3. The information given her, upon her enquiry, which expounded the mystery: *Two nations are in thy womb,* *v.* 23. She was now pregnant, not only with two children, but two nations, which should not only in their manners and dispositions greatly differ from each other, but in their interests clash and contend with each other; and the issue of the contest should be that the elder should serve the younger, which was fulfilled in the subjection of the Edomites, for many ages, to the house of David, till they revolted, 2 Chr. 21:8. Observe here, (1.) God is a free agent in dispensing his grace; it is his prerogative to make a difference between those who have not as yet themselves done either good or evil. This the apostle infers hence, Rom. 9:12 (2.) In the struggle between grace and corruption in the soul, grace, the younger, shall certainly get the upper hand at last.

III. That when they were born there was a great difference between them, which served to confirm what had been foretold (*v.* 23), was presage of the accomplishment of it, and served greatly to illustrate the type.

1. There was a great difference in their bodies, *v.* 25. Esau, when he was born, was rough and hairy, as if he had been already a grown man, whence he had his name *Esau, made,* reared already. This was an indication of a very strong constitution, and gave cause to expect that he would be a very robust, daring, active man. But Jacob was smooth and tender as other children. Note, (1.) The difference of men's capacities, and consequently of their condition in the world, arises very much from the difference of their natural constitution; some are plainly designed by nature for activity and honour, others as manifestly marked for obscurity. This instance of the divine sovereignty in the kingdom of providence may perhaps help to reconcile us to the doctrine of the divine sovereignty in the kingdom of grace. (2.) It is God's usual way to choose the weak things of the world, and to pass by the mighty, 1 Co. 1:26, 27.

2. There was a manifest contest in their births. Esau, the stronger, came forth first; but Jacob's hand *took hold of his heel,* *v.* 26. This signified, (1.) Jacob's pursuit of the birthright and blessing; from the first, he reached forth to catch hold of it, and, if possible, to prevent his brother. (2.) His prevailing for it at last, that, in precess of time, he should undermine his brother, and gain his point. This passage is referred to (Hos. 12:8), and hence he had his name, *Jacob, a supplanter.*

3. They were very unlike in the temper of their minds, and the way of living they chose, *v.* 27. They soon appeared to be of very different dispositions. (1.) Esau was a man for this world. He was a man addicted to his sports, for he was a hunter; and a man who knew how to live by his wits, for he was a cunning hunter. Recreation was his business; he studied the art of it, and spent all his time in it. He never loved a book, nor cared for being within doors; but he was a man of the field, like Nimrod and Ishmael, all for the game, and never well but when he was upon the stretch in pursuit of it: in short, he set up for a gentleman and a soldier. (2.) Jacob was a man for the other world. He was not cut out for a statesman, nor did he affect to look great, but he was *a plain man, dwelling in tents,* an honest man that always meant well, and dealt fairly, that preferred the true delights of solitude and retirement to all the pretended pleasure of busy noisy sports: he dwelt in tents, [1.] As a shepherd. he was attached to that safe and silent employment of keeping sheep, to which also he bred up his children, *ch.* 46:34. Or, [2.] As a student. He frequented the tents of Melchizedek, or Heber, as some understand it, to be taught by them divine things. And this was that son of Isaac on whom the covenant was entailed.

4. Their interest in the affections of their parents was likewise different. They had but these two children, and, it seems, one was the father's darling and the other the mother's, *v.* 28. (1.) Isaac, though he was not a stirring man himself (for when he went into the fields he went to meditate and pray, not to hunt), yet loved to have his son active. Esau knew how to please him, and showed a great respect for him, by treating him often with venison, which gained him the affections of the good old man, and won upon him more than one would have thought. (2.) Rebekah was mindful of the oracle of God, which had given the preference to Jacob, and therefore she preferred him in her love. And, if it be lawful for parents to make a difference between their children upon any account, doubtless Rebekah was in the right, that loved him whom God loved.

Verses 29–34

We have here a bargain made between Jacob and Esau about the birthright, which was Esau's by providence but Jacob's by promise. It was a spiritual privilege, including the excellency of dignity and the excellency of power, as well as the double portion, *ch.* 49:3. It seemed to be such a birthright as had then the blessing annexed to it, and the entail of the promise. Now see,

I. Jacob's pious desire of the birthright, which yet he sought to obtain by indirect courses, not agreeable to his character as a plain man. It was not out of pride or ambition that he coveted the birthright, but with an eye to spiritual blessings, which he had got well acquainted with in his tents, while Esau had lost the scent of them in the field. For this he is to be commended, that he coveted earnestly the best gifts; yet in this he cannot be justified, that he took advantage of his brother's necessity to make him a very hard bargain (*v.* 31): *Sell me this day thy birthright.* Probably there had formerly been some communication between them about this matter, and then it was not so great a surprise upon Esau as here it seems to be; and, it may be, Esau had sometimes spoken slightly of the birthright and its appurtenances, which encouraged Jacob to make this proposal to him. And, if so, Jacob is, in some measure, excusable in what he did to gain his point. Note, Plain men that have their conversation in simplicity and godly sincerity, and without worldly wisdom, are often found wisest of all for their souls and eternity. Those are wise indeed that are wise for another world. Jacob's wisdom appeared in two things: — 1. He chose the fittest time, took the opportunity when it offered itself, and did not let it slip. 2. Having made the bargain, he made it sure, and got it confirmed by Esau's oath: *Swear to me this day, v.* 33. He took Esau when he was in the mind, and would not leave him a power of revocation. In a case of this nature, it is good to be sure.

II. Esau's profane contempt of the birthright, and the foolish sale he made of it. He is called *profane Esau* for it (Heb. 12:16), because *for one morsel of meat he sold his birthright,* as dear a morsel as ever was eaten since the forbidden fruit; and he lived to regret it when it was too late. Never was there such a foolish bargain as this which Esau now made; and yet he valued himself upon his policy, and had the reputation of a cunning man, and perhaps had often bantered his brother Jacob as a weak and simple man. Note, There are those that are penny-wise and pound-foolish, cunning hunters that can out-wit others and draw them into their snares, and yet are themselves imposed upon by Satan's wiles and led captive by him at his will. Again, God often chooses the foolish things of the world, by them to confound the wise. Plain Jacob makes a fool of cunning Esau. Observe the instances of Esau's folly.

1. His appetite was very strong, *v.* 29, 30. Poor Jacob had got some bread and pottage (*v.* 34) for his dinner, and was sitting down to it contentedly enough, without venison, when Esau came from hunting, hungry and weary, and perhaps had caught nothing. And now Jacob's pottage pleased his eye better than ever his game had done. Give me (says he) some of *that red, that red,* as it is in the original; it suited his own colour (*v.* 25), and, in reproach to him for this, he was ever afterwards called *Edom, red.* Nay, it should seem, he was so faint that he could not feed himself, nor had he a servant at hand to help him, but entreats his brother to feed him. Note, (1.) Those that addict themselves to sport *weary themselves for very vanity,* Hab. 2:13. They might do the most needful business, and gain the greatest advantages, with half the pains they take, and half the perils they run into, in pursuit of their foolish pleasures. (2.) Those that work with quietness are more constantly and comfortably provided for than those that hunt with noise: bread is not always to the wise, but those that trust in the Lord and do good verily they shall be fed, fed with daily bread; not as Esau, sometimes feasting and sometimes fainting. (3.) The gratifying of the sensual appetite is that which ruins thousands of precious souls: surely, if Esau was hungry and faint, he might have got a meal's meat cheaper than at the expense of his birthright; but he was unaccountably fond of the colour of this pottage, and could not deny himself the satisfaction of a mess of it, whatever it cost him. Never better can come of it, when men's *hearts walk after their eyes* (Job 31:7), and when they serve their own bellies: therefore look not thou upon the wine, or, as Esau, upon the pottage, when it is red, when it gives that colour in the cup, in the dish, which is most inviting, Prov. 23:31.

If we use ourselves to deny ourselves, we break the forces of most temptations.

2. His reasoning was very weak (*v.* 32): *Behold, I am at the point to die;* and, if he were, would nothing serve to keep him alive but this pottage? If the famine were now in the land (*ch.* 26:1), as Dr. Lightfoot conjectures, we cannot suppose Isaac so poor, or Rebekah so bad a housekeeper, but that he might have been supplied with food convenient, other ways, and might have saved his birthright: but his appetite has the mastery of him; he is in a longing condition, nothing will please him but this *red* this *red pottage,* and, to palliate his desire, he pretends he is at the point to die. If it had been so, was it not better for him to die in honour than to live in disgrace, to die under a blessing than to live under a curse? The birthright was typical of spiritual privileges, those of the church of the first-born. Esau was now tried how he would value them, and he shows himself sensible only of present grievances; may he but get relief against them, he cares not for his birthright. Better principled was Naboth, who would lose his life rather than sell his vineyard, because his part in the earthly Canaan signified is part in the heavenly, 1 Ki. 21:3. (1.) If we look on Esau's birthright as only a temporal advantage, what he said had something of truth in it, namely, that our worldly enjoyments, even those we are most fond of, will stand us in no stead in a dying hour (Ps. 49:6–8); they will not put by the stroke of death, nor ease the pangs nor remove the sting: yet Esau, who set up for a gentleman, should have had a greater and more noble spirit than to sell even such an honour so cheaply. (2.) But, being of a spiritual nature, his undervaluing it was the greatest profaneness imaginable. Note, It is egregious folly to part with our interest in God, and Christ, and heaven, for the riches, honours, and pleasures, of this world, as bad a bargain as his that sold a birthright for a dish of broth.

3. Repentance was hidden from his eyes (*v.* 34): *He did eat and drink,* pleased his palate, satisfied his cravings, congratulated himself on the good meal's meat he had had, and then carelessly rose up and went his way, without any serious reflections upon the bad bargain he had made, or any show of regret. Thus Esau despised his birthright; he used no means at all to get the bargain revoked, made no appeal to his father about it, nor proposed to his brother to compound the matter; but the bargain which his necessity had made (supposing it were so) his profaneness confirmed *ex post facto* — *after the deed;* and by his subsequent neglect and contempt he did, as it were, acknowledge a fine, and by justifying himself in what he had done he put the bargain past recall. Note, People are ruined, not so much by doing what is amiss, as by doing it and not repenting of it, doing it and standing to it.

CHAPTER 26

In this chapter we have, I. Isaac in adversity, by reason of a famine in the land, which, 1. Obliges him to change his quarters (*v.* 1). But, 2. God visits him with direction and comfort (*v.* 2–5). 3. He foolishly denies his wife, being in distress and is reproved for it by Abimelech (*v.* 6–11). II. Isaac in prosperity, by the blessing of God upon him (*v.* 12–14). And, 1. The Philistines were envious at him (*v.* 14–17). 2. He continued industrious in his business (*v.* 18–23). 3. God appeared to him, and encouraged him, and he devoutly acknowledged God (*v.* 24, 25). 4. The Philistines, at length, made court to him, and made a covenant with him (*v.* 26–33). 5. The disagreeable marriage of his son Esau was an alloy to the comfort of his prosperity (*v.* 34, 35).

Verses 1–5

Here, I. God tried Isaac by his providence. Isaac had been trained up in a believing dependence upon the divine grant of the land of Canaan to him and his heirs; yet now there is *a famine in the land, v.* 1. What shall he think of the promise when the promised land will not find him bread? Is such a grant worth accepting, upon such terms, and after so long a time? Yes, Isaac will still cleave to the covenant; and the less valuable Canaan in itself seems to be the better he is taught to value it, 1. As a token of God's everlasting kindness to him; and, 2. As a type of heaven's everlasting blessedness. Note, The intrinsic worth of God's promises cannot be lessened in a believer's eye by any cross providences.

II. He directed him under this trial by his word. Isaac finds himself straitened by the scarcity of provisions. Somewhere he must go for supply; it should seem, he set out for Egypt, whither his father went in the like strait, but

he takes Gerar in his way, full of thoughts, no doubt, which way he had best steer his course, till God graciously appeared to him, and determined him, abundantly to his satisfaction. 1. God bade him stay where he was, and *not go down into Egypt: Sojourn in this land, v.* 2, 3. There was a famine in Jacob's days, and God bade him *go down into Egypt* (*ch.* 46:3, 4), a famine in *Isaac's* days, and God bade him *not to go down,* a famine in Abraham's days, and God left him to his liberty, directing him neither way. This variety in the divine procedure (considering that Egypt was always a place of trial and exercise to God's people) some ground upon the different characters of these three patriarchs. Abraham was a man of very high attainments, and intimate communion with God; and to him all places and conditions were alike. Isaac was a very good man, but not cut out for hardship; therefore he is forbidden to go to Egypt. Jacob was inured to difficulties, strong and patient; and therefore he must go down into Egypt, that *the trial of his faith might be to praise, and honour, and glory.* Thus God proportions his people's trials to their strength. 2. He promised to be *with him, and bless him, v.* 3. As we may go any where with comfort when God's blessing goes with us, so we may stay any where contentedly if that blessing rest upon us. 3. He renewed the covenant with him, which had so often been made with Abraham, repeating and ratifying the promises of the land of Canaan, a numerous issue, and the Messiah, *v.* 3, 4. Note, Those that must live by faith have need often to review, and repeat to themselves, the promises they are to live upon, especially when they are called to any instance of suffering or self-denial. 4. He recommended to him the good example of his father's obedience, as that which had preserved the entail of the covenant in his family (*v.* 5): *"Abraham obeyed my voice;* do thou do so too, and the promise shall be sure to thee." Abraham's obedience is here celebrated, to his honour; for by it he obtained a good report both with God and men. A great variety of words is here used to express the divine will, to which Abraham was obedient *(my voice, my charge, my commandments, my statutes, and my laws),* which may intimate that Abraham's obedience was universal; he obeyed the original laws of nature, the revealed laws of divine worship, particularly that of circumcision, and all the extraordinary precepts God gave him, as that of quitting his country, and that (which some think is more especially referred to) of the offering up of his son, which Isaac himself had reason enough to remember. Note, Those only shall have the benefit and comfort of God's covenant with their godly parents that tread in the steps of their obedience.

Verses 6–11

Isaac had now laid aside all thoughts of going to Egypt, and, in obedience to the heavenly vision, sets up his staff in Gerar, the country in which he was born (*v.* 6), yet there he enters into temptation, the same temptation that his good father had been once and again surprised and overcome by, namely, to deny his wife, and to give out that she was his sister. Observe,

I. How he sinned, *v.* 7. Because his wife was handsome, he fancied the Philistines would find some way or other to take him off, that some of them might marry her; and therefore she must pass for his sister. It is an unaccountable thing that both these great and good men should be guilty of so strange a piece of dissimulation, by which they so much exposed both their own and their wives' reputation. But we see, 1. That very good men have sometimes been guilty of very great faults and follies. Let those therefore that stand take heed lest they fall, and those that have fallen not despair of being helped up again. 2. That there is an aptness in us to imitate even the weaknesses and infirmities of those we have a value for. We have need therefore to keep our foot, lest, while we aim to tread in the steps of good men, we sometimes tread in their by-steps.

II. How he was detected, and the cheat discovered, by the king himself. Abimelech (not the same that was in Abraham's days, *ch.* 20, for this was nearly 100 years after that, but this was the common name of the Philistine kings, as Caesar of the Roman emperors) saw Isaac more familiar and pleasant with Rebekah than he knew he would be with his sister (*v.* 8): he saw him sporting with her, or *laughing;* it is the same word with that from which Isaac has his name. He was *rejoicing with the wife of his youth,*

Prov. *v.* 18. It becomes those in that relation to be pleasant with one another, as those that are pleased with one another. Nowhere may a man more allow himself to be innocently merry than with his own wife and children. Abimelech charged him with the fraud (*v.* 9), showed him how frivolous his excuse was and what might have been the bad consequences of it (*v.* 10), and then, to convince him how groundless and unjust his jealousy of them was, took him and his family under his particular protection, forbidding any injury to be done to him or his wife upon pain of death, *v.* 11. Note, 1. A lying tongue is but for a moment. Truth is the daughter of time; and, in time, it will out. 2. One sin is often the inlet to many, and therefore the beginnings of sin ought to be avoided. 3. The sins of professors shame them before those that are without. 4. God can make those that are incensed against his people, though there may be some colour of cause for it, to know that it is at their peril if they do them any hurt. See Ps. 105:14, 15.

Verses 12–25

Here we have,

I. The tokens of God's good-will to Isaac. He *blessed him,* and prospered him, and made all that he had to thrive under his hands. 1. His corn multiplied strangely, *v.* 12. He had no land of his own, but took land of the Philistines, and sowed it; and (be it observed for the encouragement of poor tenants, that occupy other people's lands, and are honest and industrious) God blessed him with a great increase. He reaped *a hundred fold;* and there seems to be an emphasis laid upon the time: it was that *same year* when there was a famine in the land; while others scarcely reaped at all, he reaped thus plentifully. See Isa. 65:13, *My servants shall eat, but you shall be hungry,* Ps. 37:19, *In the days of famine they shall be satisfied.* 2. His cattle also increased, *v.* 14. And then, 3. He had *great store of servants,* whom he employed and maintained. Note, *As goods are increased those are increased that eat them,* Eccl. 5:11.

II. The tokens of the Philistines' ill-will to him. They *envied him, v.* 14. It is an instance, 1. Of the vanity of the world that the more men have of it the more they are envied, and exposed to censure and injury. *Who can stand before envy?* Prov. 27:4. See Eccl. 4:4. 2. Of the corruption of nature; for that is a bad principle indeed which makes men *grieve at the good of others,* as if it must needs be ill with me because it is well with my neighbor. (1.) They had already shown their ill-will to his family, by stopping up the wells which his father had digged, *v.* 15. This was spitefully done. Because they had not flocks of their own to water at these wells, they would not leave them for the use of others; so absurd a thing is malice. And it was perfidiously done, contrary to the covenant of friendship they had made with Abraham, *ch.* 21:31, 32. No bonds will hold ill-nature. (2.) They expelled him out of their country, *v.* 16, 17. The king of Gerar began to look upon him with a jealous eye. Isaac's house was like a court, and his riches and retinue eclipsed Abimelech's; and therefore he must go further off. They were weary of his neighborhood, because they saw that the Lord blessed him; whereas, for that reason, they should the rather have courted his stay, that they also might be blessed for his sake. Isaac does not insist upon the bargain he had made with them for the lands he held, nor upon his occupying and improving them, nor does he offer to contest with them by force, though he had become very great, but very peaceably departs thence further from the royal city, and perhaps to a part of the country less fruitful. Note, We should deny ourselves both in our rights and in our conveniences, rather than quarrel: a wise and a good man will rather retire into obscurity, like Isaac here into a valley, than sit high to be the butt of envy and ill-will.

III. His constancy and continuance in his business still. 1. He kept up his husbandry, and continued industrious to find wells of water, and to fit them for his use, *v.* 18, etc. Though he had grown very rich, yet he was as solicitous as ever about the state of his flocks, and still looked well to his herds; when men grow great, they must take heed of thinking themselves too big and too high for their business. Though he was driven from the conveniences he had had, and could not follow his husbandry with the same ease and advantage as before, yet he set himself to make the best of the country he had come into, which it is every man's prudence to do. Observe,

(1.) He opened the wells that his father had digged (*v.* 18), and out of respect to his father called them by the same names that he had given them. Note, In our searches after truth, that fountain of living water, it is good to make use of the discoveries of former ages, which have been clouded by the corruptions of later times. Enquire for the old way, the wells which our fathers digged, which the adversaries of truth have stopped up: *Ask thy elders, and they shall teach thee.*

(2.) His servants dug new wells, *v.* 19. Note, Though we must use the light of former ages, it does not therefore follow that we must rest in it, and make no advances. We must still be building upon their foundation, *running to and fro, that knowledge may be increased,* Dan. 12:4.

(3.) In digging his wells he met with much opposition, *v.* 20, 21. Those that open the fountains of truth must expect contradiction. The first two wells which they dug were called *Esek* and *Sitnah, contention* and *hatred.* See here, [1.] What is the nature of worldly things; they are makebates and occasions of strife. [2.] What is often the lot even of the most quiet and peaceable men in this world; those that avoid striving yet cannot avoid being striven with, Ps. 120:7. In this sense, Jeremiah was a *man of contention* (Jer. 15:10), and Christ himself, though he is the prince of peace. [3.] What a mercy it is to have plenty of water, to have it without striving for it. The more common this mercy is the more reason we have to be thankful for it.

(4.) At length he removed to a quiet settlement, cleaving to his peaceable principle, rather to fly than fight, and unwilling to dwell with those that hated peace, Ps. 120:6. He preferred quietness to victory. *He dug a well, and for this they strove not, v.* 22. Note, Those that follow peace, sooner or later, shall find peace; those that study to be quiet seldom fail of being so. How unlike was Isaac to his brother Ishmael, who, right or wrong, would hold what he had, against all the world! *ch.* 16:12. And which of these would we be found the followers of? This well they called *Rehoboth, enlargements,* room enough: in the two former wells we may see what the earth is, *straitness* and *strife;* men cannot thrive, for the throng of their neighbours. This well shows us what heaven is; it is *enlargement* and *peace,* room enough there, for there are many mansions.

2. He continued firm to his religion, and kept up his communion with God. (1.) God graciously appeared to him, *v.* 24. When the Philistines expelled him, forced him to remove from place to place, and gave him continual molestation, then God visited him, and gave him fresh assurances of his favour. Note, When men are found false and unkind, we may comfort ourselves that God is faithful and gracious; and his time to show himself so is when we are most disappointed in our expectations from men. When Isaac had come to Beer-sheba (*v.* 23) it is probable that it troubled him to think of his unsettled condition, and that he could not be suffered to stay long in a place; and, in the multitude of these thoughts within him, that same night that he came weary and uneasy to Beer-sheba God brought him his comforts to delight his soul. Probably he was apprehensive that the Philistines would not let him rest there: *Fear not,* says God to him, *I am with thee, and will bless thee.* Those may remove with comfort that are sure of God's presence with them wherever they go. (2.) He was not wanting in his returns of duty to God; for *there he built an altar, and called upon the name of the Lord, v.* 25. Note, [1.] Wherever we go, we must take our religion along with us. Probably Isaac's altars and his religious worship gave offence to the Philistines, and provoked them to be the more troublesome to him; yet he kept up his duty, whatever ill-will he might be exposed to by it. [2.] The comforts and encouragements God gives us by his word should excite and quicken us to every exercise of devotion by which God may be honoured and our intercourse with heaven maintained.

Verses 26–33

We have here the contests that had been between Isaac and the Philistines issuing in a happy peace and reconciliation.

I. Abimelech pays a friendly visit to Isaac, in token of the respect he had for him, *v.* 26. Note, *When a man's ways please the Lord he makes even his enemies to be at peace with him,* Prov. 16:7. King's hearts are in his hands, and when he pleases he can turn them to favour his people.

II. Isaac prudently and cautiously questions his sincerity in this visit, *v.* 27. Note, In settling friendships and correspondences, there is need of the wisdom of the serpent, as well as the innocence of the dove; nor is it any transgression of the law of meekness and love plainly to signify our strong perception of injuries received, and to stand upon our guard in dealing with those that have acted unfairly.

III. Abimelech professes his sincerity, in this address to Isaac, and earnestly courts his friendship, *v.* 28, 29. Some suggest that Abimelech pressed for this league with him because he feared lest Isaac, growing rich, should, some time or other, avenge himself upon them for the injuries he had received. However, he professes to do it rather from a principle of love. 1. He makes the best of their behaviour towards him. Isaac complained they had *hated him, and sent him away.* No, said Abimelech, *we sent thee away in peace.* They turned him off from the land he held of them; but they suffered him to take away his stock, and all his effects, with him. Note, The lessening of injuries is necessary to the preserving of friendship; for the aggravating of them exasperates and widens breaches. The unkindness done to us might have been worse. 2. He acknowledges the token of God's favour to him, and makes this the ground of their desire to be in league with him: *The Lord is with thee, and thou art the blessed of the Lord.* As if he had said, "Be persuaded to overlook and pass by the injuries offered thee; for God had abundantly made up to thee the damage thou receivedst." Note, Those whom God blesses and favours have reason enough to forgive those who hate them, since the worst enemy they have cannot do them any real hurt. Or, "For this reason we desire thy friendship, because *God is with thee.*" Note, It is good to be in covenant and communion with those who are in covenant and communion with God, 1 Jn. 1:3; present address to him was the result of mature deliberation: *We said, Let there be an oath between us.* Whatever some of his peevish envious subjects might mean otherwise, he and his prime-ministers of state, whom he had now brought with him, designed no other than a cordial friendship. Perhaps Abimelech had received, by tradition, the warning God gave to his predecessor not to hurt Abraham (*ch.* 20:7), and this made him stand in such awe of Isaac, who appeared to be as much the favourite of Heaven as Abraham was.

IV. Isaac entertains him and his company, and enters into a league of friendship with him, *v.* 30, 31. Here see how generous the good man was, 1. In giving: *He made them a feast,* and bade them welcome. (2.) In forgiving. He did not insist upon the unkindnesses they had done him, but freely entered into a covenant of friendship with them, and bound himself never to do them any injury. Note, Religion teaches us to be neighbourly, and, as much as in us lies, to *live peaceably with all men.*

V. Providence smiled upon what Isaac did; for the same day that he made this covenant with Abimelech his servants brought him the tidings of a well of water they had found, *v.* 32, 33. He did not insist upon the restitution of the wells which the Philistines had unjustly taken from him, lest this should break off the treaty, but sat down silent under the injury; and, to recompense him for this, immediately he is enriched with a new well, which, because it suited so well to the occurrence of the day, he called by an old name, *Beer-sheba, The well of the oath.*

Verses 34–35

Here is, 1. Esau's foolish marriage — foolish, some think, in marrying two wives together, for which perhaps he is called a *fornicator* (Heb. 12:16), or rather in marrying Canaanites, who were strangers to the blessing to Abraham, and subject to the curse of Noah, for which he is called *profane;* for hereby he intimated that he neither desired the blessing nor dreaded the curse of God. 2. The grief and trouble it created to his tender parents. (1.) It grieved them that he married without asking, or at least without taking, their advice and consent: see whose steps those children tread in who either contemn or contradict their parents in disposing of themselves. (2.) It grieved them that he married the daughters of Hittites, who had no religion among them; for Isaac remembered his father's care concerning him, that he should by no means marry a Canaanite. (3.) It should seem, the wives he married were provoking in their conduct towards Isaac and Rebekah; those children have little reason to expect the blessing of God who do that which is a grief of mind to their good parents.

CHAPTER 27

In this chapter we return to the typical story of the struggle between Esau and Jacob. Esau had profanely sold the birthright to Jacob; but Esau hopes he shall be never the poorer, nor Jacob the richer, for that bargain, while he preserves his interest in his father's affections, and so secures the blessing. Here therefore we find how he was justly punished for his contempt of the birthright (of which he foolishly deprived himself) with the loss of the blessing, of which Jacob fraudulently deprives him. Thus this story is explained, Heb. 12:16, 17, "Because he sold the birthright, when he would have inherited the blessing he was rejected." For those that make light of the name and profession of religion, and throw them away for a trifle, thereby forfeit the powers and privileges of it. We have here, I. Isaac's purpose to entail the blessing upon Esau (*v.* 1–5). II. Rebekah's plot to procure it for Jacob (*v.* 6–17). III. Jacob's successful management of the plot, and his obtaining the blessing (*v.* 18–29). IV. Esau's resentment of this, in which, 1. His great importunity with his father to obtain a blessing (*v.* 30–40). 2. His great enmity to his brother for defrauding him of the first blessing (*v.* 41, etc.).

Verses 1–5

Here is, I. Isaac's design to make his will, and to declare Esau his heir. The promise of the Messiah and the land of Canaan was a great trust, first committed to Abraham, inclusive and typical of spiritual and eternal blessings; this, by divine direction, he transmitted to Isaac. Isaac, being now old, and not knowing, or not understanding, or not duly considering, the divine oracle concerning his two sons, that the elder should serve the younger, resolves to entail all the honour and power that were wrapped up in the promise upon Esau his eldest son. In this he was governed more by natural affection, and the common method of settlements, than he ought to have been, if he know (as it is probable he did) the intimations God had given of his mind in this matter. Note, We are very apt to take our measures rather from our own reason than from divine revelation, and thereby often miss our way; we think the wise and learned, the mighty and noble, should inherit the promise; but God sees not as man sees. See 1 Sa. 16:6, 7.

II. The directions he gave to Esau, pursuant to this design. He calls him to him, *v.* 1. For Esau, though married, had not yet removed; and, though he had greatly grieved his parents by his marriage, yet they had not expelled him, but it seems were pretty well reconciled to him, and made the best of it. Note, Parents that are justly offended at their children yet must not be implacable towards them.

1. He tells him upon what considerations he resolved to do this now (*v.* 2): *"I am old,* and therefore must die shortly, yet *I know not the day of my death,* nor when I must die; I will therefore do that at this time which must be done some time." Note, (1.) Old people should be reminded by the growing infirmities of age to do quickly, and with all the little might they have, what their hand finds to do. See Jos. 13:1. (2.) The consideration of the uncertainty of the time of our departure out of the world (about which God has wisely kept us in the dark) should quicken us to do the work of the day in its day. The heart and the house should both be set, and kept, in order, because *at such an hour as we think not the son of man comes;* because we *know not the day of our death,* we are concerned to mind the business of life.

2. He bids him to get things ready for the solemnity of executing his last will and testament, by which he designed to make him his heir, *v.* 3, 4. Esau must go a hunting, and bring some venison, which his father will eat of, and then bless him. In this he designed, not so much the refreshment of his own spirits, that he might give the blessing in a lively manner, as it is commonly taken, but rather the receiving of a fresh instance of his son's filial duty and affection to him, before he bestowed this favour upon him. Perhaps Esau, since he had married, had brought his venison to his wives, and seldom to his father, as formerly (*ch.* 25:28), and therefore Isaac, before he would bless him, would have him show this piece of respect to him. Note, It is fit, if the *less be blessed of the greater,* that the greater should be served and honoured by the less He says, *That my soul may bless thee before I die.* Note, (1.) Prayer is the work of the soul, and not of the lips only; as the soul must be employed in blessing God (Ps. 103:1), so it must be in blessing ourselves and others: the blessing will not come to the heart if it do not come from the heart. (2.) The work of life must be done before we die, for it cannot be done afterwards (Eccl. 9:10); and it is very desirable, when we come to die, to have nothing else to do but to die. Isaac lived above forty years after this; let none therefore think that they shall die the sooner for making their wills and getting ready for death.

Verses 6–17

Rebekah is here contriving to procure for Jacob the blessing which was designed for Esau; and here,

I. The end was good, for she was directed in this intention by the oracle of God, by which she had been governed in dispensing her affections. God had said it should be so, that the elder should *serve the younger;* and therefore Rebekah resolves it shall be so, and cannot bear to see her husband designing to thwart the oracle of God. But,

II. The means were bad, and no way justifiable. If it was not a wrong to Esau to deprive him of the blessing (he himself having forfeited it by selling the birthright), yet it was a wrong to Isaac, taking advantage of his infirmity, to impose upon him; it was a wrong to Jacob too, whom she taught to deceive, by putting a lie into his mouth, or at least by putting one into his right hand. It would likewise expose him to endless scruples about the blessing, if he should obtain it thus fraudulently, whether it would stand him or his in any stead, especially if his father should revoke it, upon the discovery of the cheat, and plead, as he might, that it was nulled by an *error personae — a mistake of the person.* He himself also was aware of the danger, lest (*v.* 12), if he should miss of the blessing, as he might probably have done, he should bring upon himself his father's curse, which he dreaded above any thing; besides, he laid himself open to that divine curse which is pronounced upon him that *causeth the blind to wander out of the way,* Deu. 27:18. If Rebekah, when she heard Isaac promise the blessing to Esau, had gone, at his return from hunting, to Isaac, and, with humility and seriousness, put him in remembrance of that which God had said concerning their sons, — if she further had shown him how Esau had forfeited the blessing both by selling his birthright and by marrying strange wives, it is probable that Isaac would have been prevailed upon knowingly and wittingly to confer the blessing upon Jacob, and needed not thus to have been cheated into it. This would have been honourable and laudable, and would have looked well in the history; but God left her to herself, to take this indirect course, that he might have the glory of bringing good out of evil, and of serving his own purposes by the sins and follies of men, and that we might have the satisfaction of knowing that, though there is so much wickedness and deceit in the world, God governs it according to his will, to his own praise. See Job 12:16, *With him are strength and wisdom, the deceived and the deceiver are his.* Isaac had lost the sense of seeing, which, in this case, could not have been imposed upon, Providence having so admirably well ordered the difference of features that no two faces are exactly alike: conversation and commerce could scarcely be maintained if there were not such a variety. Therefore she endeavours to deceive, 1. His sense of tasting, by dressing some choice pieces of kid, seasoning them, serving them up, so as to make him believe they were venison: this it was no hard matter to do. See the folly of those that are nice and curious in their appetite, and take a pride in humouring it. It is easy to impose upon them with that which they pretend to despise and dislike, so little perhaps does it differ from that to which they give a decided preference. Solomon tells us that dainties are *deceitful meat;* for it is possible for us to be deceived by them in more ways than one, Prov. 23:32. 2. His sense of feeling and smelling. She put Esau's clothes upon Jacob, his best clothes, which, it might be supposed, Esau would put on, in token of joy and respect to his father, when he was to receive the blessing. Isaac knew these, by the stuff, shape, and smell, to be Esau's. If we would obtain a blessing from our heavenly Father, we must come for it in the garments of our elder brother, clothed with his righteousness, who is the first-born among many brethren. Lest the smoothness and softness of Jacob's hands and neck should betray him, she covered them, and probably part of his face, with the skins of the kids that were newly killed, *v.* 16. Esau was rough indeed when nothing less than these would serve to make Jacob like him.. Those that affect to seem rough and rugged in their carriage put the beast upon the man, and really shame themselves, by thus disguising themselves. And, *lastly,* it was a very rash word which Rebekah spoke, when Jacob objected the danger of a curse: *Upon me be thy curse, my son, v.* 13. Christ indeed, who is mighty to save, because mighty to bear, has said, *Upon me be the curse, only obey my voice;* he has borne the burden of the curse, the curse of the law, for all those that will take upon them the yoke of the command, the command of the gospel. But it is too daring for any creature to say, *Upon me be the curse,* unless it be that curse causeless which we are sure *shall not come,* Prov. 26:2.

Verses 18–29

Observe here, I. The art and assurance with which Jacob managed this intrigue. Who would have thought that this plain man could have played his part so well in a design of this nature? His mother having put him in the way of it, and encouraged him in it, he dexterously applied himself to those methods which he had never accustomed himself to, but had always conceived an abhorrence of. Note, Lying is soon learnt. The psalmist speaks of those who, *as soon as they are born, speak lies,* Ps. 58:3; Jer. 9:5. I wonder how honest Jacob could so readily turn his tongue to say (*v.* 19), *I am Esau thy first-born;* nor do I see how the endeavour of some to bring him off with that equivocation, *I am made thy first-born,* namely by purchase, does him any service; for when his father asked him (*v.* 24), *Art thou my very son Esau?* he said, *I am.* How could he say, *I have done as thou badest me,* when he had received no command from his father, but was doing as his mother bade him? How could he say, *Eat of my venison,* when he knew it came, not from the field, but from the fold? But especially I wonder how he could have the assurance to father it upon God, and to use his name in the cheat (*v.* 20): *The Lord thy God brought it to me.* Is this Jacob? Is this Israel indeed, without guile? It is certainly written, not for our imitation, but for our admonition. *Let him that thinks he stands take heed lest he fall.* Good men have sometimes failed in the exercise of those graces for which they have been most eminent.

II. The success of this management. Jacob with some difficulty gained his point, and obtained the blessing.

1. Isaac was at first dissatisfied, and would have discovered the fraud if he could have trusted his own ears; for *the voice was Jacob's voice, v.* 22. Providence has ordered a strange variety of voices as well as faces, which is also of use to prevent our being imposed upon; and the voice is a thing not easily disguised nor counterfeited. This may be alluded to to illustrate the character of a hypocrite. His voice is Jacob's voice, but his hands are Esau's. He speaks the language of a saint, but does the works of a sinner; but the judgement will be, as here, by the hands.

2. At length he yielded to the power of the cheat, *because the hands were hairy* (*v.* 23), not considering how easy it was to counterfeit that circumstance; and now Jacob carries it on dexterously, sets his venison before his father, and waits at table very officiously, till dinner is done, and the blessing comes to be pronounced in the close of this solemn feast. That which in some small degree extenuates the crime of Rebekah and Jacob is that the fraud was intended, not so much to hasten the fulfilling, as to prevent the thwarting, of the oracle of God: the blessing was just going to be put upon the wrong head, and they thought it was time to bestir themselves. Now let us see how Isaac gave Jacob his blessing, *v.* 26–29. (1.) He embraced him, in token of a particular affection to him. Those that are blessed of God are kissed with the kisses of his mouth, and they do, by love and loyalty, *kiss the Son,* Ps. 2:12. (2.) He praised him. *He smelt the smell of his raiment, and said, See, the smell of my son is as the smell of a field which the Lord hath blessed,* that is, like that of the most fragrant flowers and spices. It appeared that God had blessed him, and therefore Isaac would bless him. (3.) He prayed for him, and therein prophesied concerning him. It is the duty of parents to pray for their children, and to bless them in the name of the Lord. And thus, as well as by their baptism, to do what they can to preserve and perpetuate the entail of the covenant in their families. But this was an extraordinary blessing; and Providence so ordered it that Isaac should bestow it upon Jacob ignorantly and

by mistake, that it might appear he was beholden to God for it, and not to Isaac. Three things Jacob is here blessed with: — [1.] Plenty (v. 28), heaven and earth concurring to make him rich. [2.] Power (v. 29), particularly dominion over his brethren, namely, Esau and his posterity. [3.] Prevalency with God, and a great interest in Heaven: *"Cursed by every one that curseth thee and blessed be he that blesseth thee.* Let God be a friend to all thy friends, and an enemy to all they enemies." More is certainly comprised in this blessing than appears *prima facie — at first sight.* It must amount to an entail of the promise of the Messiah, and of the church; this was, in the patriarchal dialect, *the blessing:* something spiritual, doubtless, is included in it. *First,* That from him should come the Messiah, who should have a sovereign dominion on earth. It was that top-branch of his family which people should serve and nations bow down to. See Num. 24:19, *Out of Jacob shall come he that shall have dominion,* the star and *sceptre, v.* 17. Jacob's dominion over Esau was to be only typical of this, *ch.* 49:10. *Secondly,* That from him should come the church, which should be particularly owned and favoured by Heaven. It was part of the blessing of Abraham, when he was first called to be the father of the faithful (*ch.* 12:3), *I will bless those that bless thee;* therefore, when Isaac afterwards confirmed the blessing to Jacob, he called it *the blessing of Abraham, ch.* 28:4. Balaam explains this too, Num. 24:9. Note, It is the best and most desirable blessing to stand in relation to Christ and his church, and to be interested in Christ's power and the church's favours.

Verses 30–40

Here is, I. The covenant-blessing denied to Esau. He that made so light of the birthright *would now have inherited the blessing, but he was rejected, and found no place of repentance* in his father, *though he sought it carefully with tears,* Heb. 12:17. Observe, 1. How carefully he sought it. He prepared the savoury meat, as his father had directed him, and then begged the blessing which his father had encouraged him to expect, *v.* 31. When he understood that Jacob had obtained it surreptitiously, he *cried with a great and exceedingly bitter cry, v.* 34. No man could have laid the disappointment more to heart than he did; he made his father's tent to ring with his grief, and again (*v.* 38) *lifted up his voice and wept.* Note, The day is coming when those that now make light of the blessings of the covenant, and sell their title to them for a thing of nought, will in vain be importunate for them. Those that will not so much as ask and seek now will knock shortly, and cry, *Lord, Lord.* Slighters of Christ will then be humble suitors to him. 2. How he was rejected. Isaac, when first made sensible of the imposition that had been practised on him, *trembled exceedingly, v.* 33. Those that follow the choice of their own affections, rather than the dictates of the divine will, involve themselves in such perplexities as these. But he soon recovers himself, and ratifies the blessing he had given to Jacob: *I have blessed him, and he shall be blessed;* he might, upon very plausible grounds, have recalled it, but now, at last, he is sensible that he was in an error when he designed it for Esau. Either himself recollecting the divine oracle, or rather having found himself more than ordinarily filled with the Holy Ghost when he gave the blessing to Jacob, he perceived that God did, as it were, say Amen to it. Now, (1.) Jacob was hereby confirmed in his possession of the blessing, and abundantly satisfied of the validity of it, though he obtained it fraudulently; hence too he had reason to hope that God graciously overlooked and pardoned his misconduct. (2.) Isaac hereby acquiesced in the will of God, though it contradicted his own expectations and affection. He had a mind to give Esau the blessing, but, when he perceived the will of God was otherwise, he submitted; and this he did *by faith* (Heb. 11:20), as Abraham before him, when he had solicited for Ishmael. May not God do what he will with his own? (3.) Esau hereby was cut off from the expectation of that special blessing which he thought to have preserved to himself when he sold his birthright. We, by this instance, are taught, [1.] That *it is not of him that willeth, nor of him that runneth, but of God that showeth mercy,* Rom. 9:16. The apostle seems to allude to this story. Esau had a good will to the blessing, and ran for it; but God that showed mercy designed it for Jacob, *that the purpose of God according to election might stand, v.* 11. The Jews,

like Esau, hunted *after the law of righteousness (v.* 31), yet missed of the blessing of righteousness, *because they sought it by the works of the law (v.* 32); while the Gentiles, who, like Jacob, sought it by faith in the oracle of God, obtained it by force, with that violence which the kingdom of heaven suffers. See Mt. 11:12. [2.] That those who undervalue their spiritual birthright, and can afford to sell it for a morsel of meat, forfeit spiritual blessings, and it is just with God to deny them those favours they were careless of. Those that will part with their wisdom and grace, with their faith and a good conscience, for the honours, wealth, or pleasures, of this world, however they may pretend a zeal for the blessing, have already judged themselves unworthy of it, and so shall their doom be. [3.] That those who lift up hands in wrath lift them up in vain. Esau, instead of repenting of his own folly, reproached his brother, unjustly charged him with taking away the birthright which he had fairly sold to him (*v.* 36), and conceived malice against him for what he had now done, *v.* 41. Those are not likely to speed in prayer who turn those resentments upon their brethren which they should turn upon themselves, and lay the blame of their miscarriages upon others, when they should take shame to themselves. [4.] That those who seek not till it is too late will be rejected. This was the ruin of Esau, he did not come in time. As there is an accepted time, a time when God will be found, so there is a time when he will not answer those that call upon him, because they neglected the appointed season. See Prov. 1:28. The time of God's patience and our probation will not last always; the day of grace will come to an end, and the door will be shut. Then many that now despise the blessing will seek it carefully; for then they will know how to value it, and will see themselves undone, for ever undone, without it, but to no purpose, Lu. 13:25–27. O that we would therefore, in this our day, *know the things that belong to our peace!*

II. Here is a common blessing bestowed upon Esau.
1. This he desired: *Bless me also, v.* 34. *Hast thou not reserved a blessing for me? v.* 36. Note, (1.) The worst of men know how to wish well to themselves; and even those who profanely sell their birthright seem piously to desire the blessing. Faint desires of happiness, without a right choice of the end and a right use of the means, deceive many into their own ruin. Multitudes go to hell with their mouths full of good wishes. The desire of the slothful and unbelieving kills them. Many will seek to enter in, as Esau, who shall not be able, because they do not strive, Lu. 13:24. (2.) It is the folly of most men that they are willing to take up with any good (Ps. 4:6), as Esau here, who desired but a second-rate blessing, a blessing separated from the birthright. Profane hearts think any blessing as good as that from God's oracle: *Hast thou but one?* As if he had said, "I will take up with any: though I have not the blessing of the church, yet let me have some blessing."
2. This he had; and let him make his best of it, *v.* 39, 40.
(1.) It was a good thing, and better than he deserved. It was promised him, [1.] That he should have a competent livelihood — *the fatness of the earth, and the dew of heaven.* Note, Those that come short of the blessings of the covenant may yet have a very good share of outward blessings. God gives good ground and good weather to many that reject his covenant, and have no part nor lot in it. [2.] That by degrees he should recover his liberty. If Jacob must rule (*v.* 29), Esau must serve; but he has this to comfort him, he shall *live by his sword.* He shall serve, but he shall not starve; and, at length, after much skirmishing, he shall break the yoke of bondage, and wear marks of freedom. This was fulfilled (2 Ki. 8:20, 22) when the Edomites revolted.
(2.) Yet it was far short of Jacob's blessing. For him God had reserved some better thing. [1.] In Jacob's blessing *the dew of heaven* is put first, as that which he most valued, and desired, and depended upon; in Esau's *the fatness of the earth* is put first, for it was this that he had the first and principal regard to. [2.] Esau has these, but Jacob has them from God's hand: *God give thee the dew of heaven, v.* 28. It was enough to Esau to have the possession; but Jacob desired it by promise, and to have it from covenant-love. [3.] Jacob shall have dominion over his brethren: hence the Israelites often ruled over the Edomites. Esau shall have dominion, that is, he shall gain some power and interest, but shall never have dominion over his brother:

we never find that the Jews were sold into the hands of the Edomites, or that they oppressed them. But the great difference in that there is nothing in Esau's blessing that points at Christ, nothing that brings him or his into the church and covenant of God, without which the fatness of the earth, and the plunder of the field, will stand him in little stead. Thus Isaac by faith blessed them both according as their lot should be. Some observe that Jacob was blessed with a *kiss* (*v.* 27), so was not Esau.

Verses 41–46

Here is, I. The malice Esau bore to Jacob upon account of the blessing which he had obtained, *v.* 41. Thus he went in the way of Cain, who slew his brother because he had gained that acceptance with God of which he had rendered himself unworthy. Esau's hatred of Jacob was, 1. A causeless hatred. He hated him for no other reason but because his father blessed him and God loved him. Note, The happiness of saints is the envy of sinners. Whom Heaven blesses, hell curses. 2. It was a cruel hatred. Nothing less would satisfy him than to slay his brother. It is the blood of the saints that persecutors thirst after: *I will slay my brother.* How could he say that word without horror? How could he call him *brother,* and yet vow his death? Note, The rage of persecutors will not be tied up by any bonds, no, not the strongest and most sacred. 3. It was a politic hatred. He expected his father would soon die, and then titles must be tried and interests contested between the brothers, which would give him a fair opportunity for revenge. He thinks it not enough to *live by his sword himself* (*v.* 40), unless his brother die by it. He is loth to grieve his father while he lives, and therefore puts off the intended murder till his death, not caring how much he then grieved his surviving mother. Note, (1.) Those are bad children to whom their good parents are a burden, and who, upon any account, long for the days of mourning for them. (2.) Bad men are long held in by external restraints from doing the mischief they would do, and so their wicked purposes come to nought. (3.) Those who think to defeat God's purposes will undoubtedly be disappointed themselves. Esau aimed to prevent Jacob, or his seed, from having the dominion, by taking away his life before he was married; but who can disannul what God has spoken? Men may fret at God's counsels, but cannot change them.

II. The method Rebekah took to prevent the mischief.
1. She gave Jacob warning of his danger, and advised him to withdraw for a while, and shift for his own safety. She tells him what she heard of Esau's design, that he comforted himself with the hope of an opportunity to kill his brother, *v.* 42. Would one think that such a bloody barbarous thought as this could be a comfort to a man? If Esau could have kept his design to himself his mother would not have suspected it; but men's impudence in sin is often their infatuation; and they cannot accomplish their wickedness because their rage is too violent to be concealed, and a bird of the air carries the voice. Observe here, (1.) What Rebekah feared — lest she *should be deprived of them both in one day* (*v.* 45), deprived, not only of the murdered, but of the murderer, who either by the magistrate, or by the immediate hand of God, would by sacrificed to justice, which she herself must acquiesce in, and not obstruct: or, if not so, yet thenceforward she would be deprived of all joy and comfort in him. Those that are lost to virtue are in a manner lost to all their friends. With what pleasure can a child be looked upon that can be looked upon as no other than a child of the devil? (2.) What Rebekah hoped — that, if Jacob for a while kept out of sight, the affront which his brother resented so fiercely would by degrees go out of mind. The strength of passions is weakened and taken off by the distances both of time and place. She promised herself that his brother's anger would turn away. Note, Yielding pacifies great offences; and even those that have a good cause, and God on their side, must yet use this with other prudent expedients for their own preservation.

2. She impressed Isaac with an apprehension of the necessity of Jacob's going among her relations upon another account, which was to take a wife, *v.* 46. She would not tell him of Esau's wicked design against the life of Jacob, lest it should trouble him; but prudently took another way to gain her point. Isaac saw as uneasy as he was to Esau's being unequally yoked with Hittites; and therefore, with

a very good colour of reason, she moves to have Jacob married to one that was better principled. Note, One miscarriage should serve as a warning to prevent another; those are careless indeed that stumble twice at the same stone. Yet Rebekah seems to have expressed herself somewhat too warmly in the matter, when she said, *What good will my life do me if Jacob marry a Canaanite?* Thanks be to God, all our comfort is not lodged in one hand; we may do the work of life, and enjoy the comforts of life, though every thing do not fall out to our mind, and though our relations be not in all respects agreeable to us. Perhaps Rebekah spoke with this concern because she saw it necessary, for the quickening of Isaac, to give speedy orders in this matter. Observe, Though Jacob was himself very towardly, and well fixed in his religion, yet he had need to be put out of the way of temptation. Even he was in danger both of following the bad example of his brother and of being drawn into a snare by it. We must not presume too far upon the wisdom and resolution, no, not of those children that are most hopeful and promising; but care must be taken to keep them out of harm's way.

CHAPTER 28

We have here, I. Jacob parting with his parents, to go to Padanaram; the charge his father gave him (*v.* 1, 2), the blessing he sent him away with (*v.* 3, 4), his obedience to the orders given him (*v.* 5, 10), and the influence this had upon Esau (*v.* 6–9). II. Jacob meeting with God, and his communion with him by the way. And there, 1. his vision of the ladder (*v.* 11, 12). 2. The gracious promises God made him (*v.* 13–15). 3. The impression this made upon him (*v.* 16–19). 4. The vow he made to God, upon this occasion (*v.* 20, etc.).

Verses 1–5

Jacob had no sooner obtained the blessing than immediately he was forced to flee from his country; and, as it if were not enough that he was a stranger and sojourner there, he must go to be more so, and no better than an exile, in another country. Now *Jacob fled into Syria,* Hos. 12:12. He was blessed with plenty of corn and wine, and yet he went away poor, was blessed with government, and yet went out to service, a hard service. This was, 1. Perhaps to correct him for his dealing fraudulently with his father. The blessing shall be confirmed to him, and yet he shall smart for the indirect course he took to obtain it. While there is such an alloy as there is of sin in our duties, we must expect an alloy of trouble in our comforts. However, 2. It was to teach us that those who inherit the blessing must expect persecution; those who have peace in Christ shall have tribulation in the world, Jn. 16:33. Being told of his before, we must not think it strange, and, being assured of a recompence hereafter, we must not think it hard. We may observe, likewise, that God's providences often seem to contradict his promises, and to go cross to them; and yet, when the mystery of God shall be finished, we shall see that all was for the best, and that cross providences did but render the promises and the accomplishment of them the more illustrious. Now Jacob is here dismissed by his father,

I. With a solemn charge: *He blessed him, and charged him, v.* 1, 2. Note, Those that have the blessing must keep the charge annexed to it, and not think to separate what God has joined. The charge is like that in 2 Co. 6:14, *Be not unequally yoked with unbelievers;* and all that inherit the promises of the remission of sins, and the gift of the Holy Ghost, must keep this charge, which follows those promises, *Save yourselves from this untoward generation,* Acts 2:38–40. Those that are entitled to peculiar favours must be a peculiar people. If Jacob be an heir of promise, he must *not take a wife of the daughters of Canaan;* those that profess religion should not marry those that are irreligious.

II. With a solemn blessing, *v.* 3, 4. He had before blessed him unwittingly; now he does it designedly, for the greater encouragement of Jacob in that melancholy condition to which he was now removing. This blessing is more express and full than the former; it is an entail of the blessing of Abraham, that blessing which was poured on the head of Abraham like the anointing oil, thence to run down to his chosen seed, as the skirts of his garments. It is a gospel blessing, the blessing of church-privileges, that is the blessing of Abraham, which upon the Gentiles through faith, Gal. 3:14. It is a blessing from God Almighty, by which name God appeared to the patriarchs, Ex. 6:3. Those are blessed indeed whom God Almighty blesses; for he commands and effects the blessing. Two great promises Abraham was blessed with, and Isaac here entails them both upon Jacob.

1. The promise of heirs: *God make thee fruitful, and multiply thee, v.* 3. (1.) Through his loins should descend from Abraham that people who should be numerous as the stars of heaven, and the sand of the sea, and who should increase more than the rest of the nations, so as to be *an assembly of people,* as the margin reads it. And never was such a multitude of people so often gathered into one assembly as the tribes of Israel were in the wilderness, and afterwards. (2.) Through his loins should descend from Abraham that person in whom all the families of the earth should be blessed, and to whom the gathering of the people should be. Jacob had in him a multitude of people indeed, for all things in heaven and earth are united in Christ (Eph. 1:10), all centre in him, that corn of wheat, which falling to the ground, produced much fruit, Jn. 12:24.

2. The promise of an inheritance for those heirs: *That thou mayest inherit the land of thy sojournings, v.* 4. Canaan was hereby entailed upon the seed of Jacob, exclusive of the seed of Esau. Isaac was now sending Jacob away into a distant country, to settle there for some time; and, lest this should look like disinheriting him, he here confirms the settlement of it upon him, that he might be assured that the discontinuance of his possession should be no defeasance of his right. Observe, He is here told that he should inherit the land wherein he sojourned. Those that are sojourners now shall be heirs for ever: and, even now, those do most inherit the earth (though they do not inherit most of it) that are most like strangers in it. Those have the best enjoyment of present things that sit most loose to them. This promise looks as high as heaven, of which Canaan was a type. This was the better country, which Jacob, with the other patriarchs, had in his eye, when he confessed himself a stranger and pilgrim upon the earth, Heb. 11:13.

Jacob, having taken leave of his father, was hastened away with all speed, lest his brother should find an opportunity to do him a mischief, and away he went to Padanaram, *v.* 5. How unlike was his taking a wife thence to his father's! Isaac had servants and camels sent to fetch his; Jacob must go himself, go alone, and go afoot, to fetch his: he must go too in a fright from his father's house, not knowing when he might return. Note, If God, in his providence, disable us, we must be content, though we cannot keep up the state and grandeur of our ancestors. We should be more in care to maintain their piety than to maintain their dignity, and to be as good as they were than to be as great. Rebekah is here called *Jacob's and Esau's mother.* Jacob is named first, not only because he had always been his mother's darling, but because he was now make his father's heir, and Esau was, in this sense, set aside. Note, The time will come when piety will have precedency, whatever it has now.

Verses 6–9

This passage concerning Esau comes in in the midst of Jacob's story, either, 1. To show the influence of a good example. Esau, though the greater man, now begins to think Jacob the better man, and disdains not to take him for his pattern in this particular instance of marrying with a daughter of Abraham. The elder children should give to the younger an example of tractableness and obedience; it is bad if they do not: but it is some alleviation if they take the example of it from them, as Esau here did from Jacob. Or, 2. To show the folly of an after-wit. Esau did well, but he did it when it was too late, He *saw that the daughters of Canaan pleased not his father,* and he might have seen that long ago if he had consulted his father's judgment as much as he did his palate. And how did he now mend the matter? Why, truly, so as to make bad worse. (1.) He married a daughter of Ishmael, the son of the bond-woman, who was cast out, and was not to inherit with Isaac and his seed, thus joining with a family which God had rejected, and seeking to strengthen his own pretensions by the aid of another pretender. (2.) He took a third wife, while, for aught that appears, his other two were neither dead nor divorced. (3.) He did it only to please his father, not to please God. Now that Jacob was sent into a far country Esau would be all in all at home, and he hoped so to humour his father as to prevail with him to make a new will, and entail the promise upon him, revoking the settlement lately made upon Jacob. And thus, [1.] He was wise when it was too late, like Israel that would venture when the decree had gone forth against them (Num. 14:40), and the foolish virgins, Mt. 25:11. [2.] He rested in a partial reformation, and thought, by pleasing his parents in one thing, to atone for all his other miscarriages. It is not said that when he saw how obedient Jacob was, and how willing to please his parents, he repented of his malicious design against him: no, it appeared afterwards that he persisted in that, and retained his malice. Note, Carnal hearts are apt to think themselves as good as they should be, because perhaps, in some one particular instance, they are not so bad as they have been. Thus Micah retains his idols, but thinks himself happy in having a Levite to be his priest, Jdg. 17:13.

Verses 10–15

We have here Jacob upon his journey towards Syria, in a very desolate condition, like one that was sent to seek his fortune; but we find that, though he was alone, yet he was not alone, for *the Father was with him,* Jn. 16:32. If what is here recorded happened (as it should seem it did) the first night, he had made a long day's journey from Beersheba to Bethel, above forty miles. Providence brought him to a convenient place, probably shaded with trees, to rest himself in that night; and there he had,

I. A hard lodging (*v.* 11), the *stones for his pillows,* and the heavens for his canopy and curtains. As the usage then was, perhaps this was not so bad as it seems how to us; but we should think, 1. He lay very cold, the cold ground for his bed, and, which one would suppose made the matter worse, a cold stone for his pillow, and in the cold air. 2. Very uneasy. If his bones were sore with his day's journey, his night's rest would but make them sorer. 3. Very much exposed. He forgot that he was fleeing for his life; or had his brother, in his rage, pursued, or sent a murderer after him, here he lay ready to be sacrificed, and destitute of shelter and defence. We cannot think it was by reason of his poverty that he was so ill accommodated, but, (1.) It was owing to the plainness and simplicity of those times, when men did not take so much state, and consult their ease so much, as in these later times of softness and effeminacy. (2.) Jacob had been particularly used to hardships, as a plain man dwelling in tents; and, designing now to go to service, he was the more willing to inure himself to them; and, as it proved, it was well, *ch.* 31:40. (3.) His comfort in the divine blessing, and his confidence in the divine protection, made him easy, even when he lay thus exposed; being sure that his God made him to dwell in safety, he could lie down and sleep upon a stone.

II. In his hard lodging he had a pleasant dream. Any Israelite indeed would be willing to take up with Jacob's pillow, provided he might but have Jacob's dream. Then, and there, he *heard the words of God, and saw the visions of the Almighty.* It was the best night's sleep he ever had in his life. Note, God's time to visit his people with his comforts is when they are most destitute of other comforts, and other comforters; when afflictions in the way of duty (as these were) do abound, then shall consolations so much the more abound. Now observe here,

1. The encouraging vision Jacob saw, *v.* 12. He saw a ladder which reached from earth to heaven, the angels ascending and descending upon it, and God himself at the head of it. Now this represents the two things that are very comfortable to good people at all times, and in all conditions: — (1.) The providence of God, by which there is a constant correspondence kept up between heaven and earth. The counsels of heaven are executed on earth, and the actions and affairs of this earth are all known in heaven are executed on earth, and the actions and affairs of this earth are all known in heaven and judged there. Providence does its work gradually, and by steps. Angels are employed as ministering spirits, to serve all the purposes and designs of Providence, and the wisdom of God is at the upper end of the ladder, directing all the motions of second causes to the glory of the first Cause. The angels are active spirits, continually ascending and descending; they rest not, day nor night, from service, according to the posts assigned them. They ascend, to give account of what

they have done, and to receive orders; and then descend, to execute the orders they have received. Thus we should always abound in the work of the Lord, that we may do it as the angels do it, Ps. 103:20, 21. This vision gave very seasonable comfort to Jacob, letting him know that he had both a good guide and a good guard, in his going out and coming in, — that, though he was made to wander from his father's house, yet still he was the care of a kind Providence, and the charge of the holy angels. This is comfort enough, though we should not admit the notion which some have, that the tutelar angels of Canaan were ascending, having guarded Jacob out of their land, and the angels of Syria descending to take him into their custody. Jacob was now the type and representative of the whole church, with the guardianship of which the angels are entrusted. (2.) The mediation of Christ. He is this ladder, the foot on earth in his human nature, the top in heaven in his divine nature: or the former in his humiliation, the latter in his exaltation. All the intercourse between heaven and earth, since the fall, is by this ladder. Christ is the way; all God's favours come to us, and all our services go to him, by Christ. If God dwell with us, and we with him, it is by Christ. We have no way of getting to heaven, but by this ladder; if we climb up any other way we are thieves and robbers. To this vision our Saviour alludes when he speaks of the angels of God *ascending and descending upon the son of man* (Jn. 1:51); for the kind offices the angels do us, and the benefits we receive by their ministration, are all owing to Christ, who has reconciled things on earth and things in heaven (Col. 1:20), and made them all meet in himself, Eph. 1:10.

2. The encouraging words Jacob heard. God now brought him into the wilderness, and spoke comfortably to him, spoke from the head of the ladder; for all the glad tidings we receive from heaven come through Jesus Christ.

(1.) The former promises made to his father were repeated and ratified to him, *v.* 13, 14. In general, God intimated to him that he would be the same to him that he had been to Abraham and Isaac. Those that tread in the steps of their godly parents are interested in their covenant and entitled to their privileges. Particularly, [1.] The land of Canaan is settled upon him, *the land whereon thou liest;* as if by his lying so contentedly upon the bare ground he had taken livery and seisin of the whole land. [2.] It is promised him that his posterity should multiply exceedingly as the dust of the earth — that, though he seemed now to be plucked off as a withered branch, yet he should become a flourishing tree, that should send out his boughs unto the sea. These were the blessings with which his father had blessed him (*v.* 3, 4), and God here said Amen to them, that he might have strong consolation. [3.] It is added that the Messiah should come from his loins, in whom all the families of the earth should be blessed. Christ is the great blessing of the world. All that are blessed, whatever family they are of, are blessed in him, and none of any family are excluded from blessedness in him, but those that exclude themselves.

(2.) Fresh promises were made him, accommodated to his present condition, *v.* 15. [1.] Jacob was apprehensive of danger from his brother Esau; but God promises to keep him. Note, Those are safe whom god protects, whoever pursues them. [2.] He had now a long journey before him, had to travel alone, in an unknown road, to an unknown country; but, *behold, I am with thee,* says God. Note, Wherever we are, we are safe, and may be easy, if we have God's favourable presence with us. [3.] He knew not, but God foresaw, what hardships he should meet with in his uncle's service, and therefore promises to preserve him in all places. Note, God knows how to give his people graces and comforts accommodated to the events that shall be, as well as to those that are. [4.] He was now going as an exile into a place far distant, but God promises him to bring him back again to this land. Note, He that preserves his people's going out will also take care of their coming in, Ps. 121:8. [5.] He seemed to be forsaken of all his friends, but God here gives him this assurance, *I will not leave thee.* Note, Whom God loves he never leaves. This promise is sure to all the seed, Heb. 13:5. [6.] Providences seemed to contradict the promises; he is therefore assured of the performance of them in their season: All shall *be done that I have spoken to thee of.* Note, Saying and doing are not two things with God, whatever they are with us.

Verses 16–22

God manifested himself and his favour to Jacob when he was asleep and purely passive; for the spirit, like the wind, blows when and where he listeth, and God's grace, like the dew, tarrieth not for the sons of men, Mic. *v.* 7. But Jacob applied himself to the improvement of the visit God had made him when he was awake; and we may well think he awaked, as the prophet did (Jer. 31:26), and behold his sleep was sweet to him. Here is much of Jacob's devotion on this occasion.

I. He expressed a great surprise at the tokens he had of God's special presence with him in that place: *Surely the Lord is in this place and I knew it not, v.* 16. Note, 1. God's manifestations of himself to his people carry their own evidence along with them. God can give undeniable demonstrations of his presence, such as give abundant satisfaction to the souls of the faithful that God is with them of a truth, satisfaction not communicable to others, but convincing to themselves. 2. We sometimes meet with God where we little thought of meeting with him. He is where we did not think he had been, is found where we asked not for him. No place excludes divine visits (*ch.* 16:13, *here also*); wherever we are, in the city or in the desert, in the house or in the field, in the shop or in the street, we may keep up our intercourse with Heaven if it be not our own fault.

II. It struck an awe upon him (*v.* 17): *He was afraid;* so far was he from being puffed up, and exalted above measure, with the abundance of the revelations (2 Co. 12:7), that he was afraid. Note, The more we see of God the more cause we see for holy trembling and blushing before him. Those to whom God is pleased to manifest himself are thereby laid, and kept, very low in their own eyes, and see cause to fear even the Lord and his goodness, Hos. 3:5. He said, *How dreadful is this place!* that is, "The appearance of God in this place is never to be thought of, but with a holy awe and reverence. I shall have a respect for this place, and remember it by this token, as long as I live:" not that he thought the place itself any nearer the divine visions than other places; but what he saw there at this time was, as it were, *the house of God,* the residence of the divine Majesty, and *the gate of heaven,* that is, the general rendezvous of the inhabitants of the upper world, as the meetings of a city were in their gates; or the angels ascending and descending were like travellers passing and re-passing through the gates of a city. Note, 1. God is in a special manner present where his grace is revealed and where his covenants are published and sealed, as of old by the ministry of angels, so now by instituted ordinances, Mt. 28:20. 2. Where God meets us with his special presence we ought to meet him with the most humble reverence, remembering his justice and holiness, and our own meanness and vileness.

III. He took care to preserve the memorial of it two ways: 1. He set up the stone for a pillar (*v.* 18); not as if he thought the visions of his head were any way owing to the stone on which it lay, but thus he would mark the place against he came back, and erect a lasting monument of God's favour to him, and because he had not time now to build an altar here, as Abraham did in the places where God appeared to him, *ch.* 12:7. He therefore *poured oil on the top of this stone,* which probably was the ceremony then used in dedicating their altars, as an earnest of his building an altar when he should have conveniences for it, as afterwards he did, in gratitude to God for this vision, *ch.* 35:7. Note, Grants of mercy call for returns of duty, and the sweet communion we have with God ought ever to be remembered. 2. He gave a new name to the place, *v.* 19. It had been called *Luz, an almond-tree;* but he will have it henceforward called *Beth-el, the house of God.* This gracious appearance of God to him put a greater honour upon it, and made it more remarkable, than all the almond-trees that flourished there. This is that Beth-el where, long after, it is said, *God found Jacob, and there* (in what he said to him) *he spoke with us,* Hos. 12:4. In process of time, this *Beth-el, the house of God,* became *Beth-aven, a house of vanity* and iniquity, when Jeroboam set up one of his calves there.

IV. He made a solemn vow upon this occasion, *v.* 20–22. By religious vows we give glory to God, own our dependence upon him, and lay a bond upon our own souls to engage and quicken our obedience to him. Jacob was now in fear and distress; and it is seasonable to make vows in times of trouble, or when we are in pursuit of any special mercy, Jon. 1:16; Ps. 66:13, 14; 1 Sa. 1:11; Num. 21:1–3. Jacob had now had a gracious visit from heaven. God had renewed his covenant with him, and the covenant is mutual. When God ratifies his promises to us, it is proper for us to repeat our promises to him. Now in this vow observe, 1. Jacob's faith. God had said (*v.* 15), *I am with thee, and will keep thee.* Jacob takes hold of this, and infers, *"Seeing God will be with me, and will keep me,* as he hath said, and (which is implied in that promise) will provide comfortably for me, — and seeing he has promised to *bring me again to this land,* that is, *to the house of my father,* whom I hope to find alive at my return *in peace"* (so unlike was he to Esau who longed for the days of mourning for his father), — "I depend upon it." Note, God's promises are to be the guide and measure of our desires and expectations. 2. Jacob's modesty and great moderation in his desires. He will cheerfully content himself with bread to eat, and raiment to put on; and, though God's promise had now made him heir to a very great estate, yet he indents not for soft clothing and dainty meat. Agur's wish is his, *Feed me with food convenient for me;* and see 1 Tim. 6:8. Nature is content with a little, and grace with less. Those that have most have, in effect, no more for themselves than food and raiment; of the overplus they have only either the keeping or the giving, not the enjoyment: if God give us more, we are bound to be thankful, and to use it for him; if he give us but this, we are bound to be content, and cheerfully to enjoy him in it. 3. Jacob's piety, and his regard to God, which appear here, (1.) In what he desired, that God would be with him and keep him. Note, We need desire no more to make us easy and happy, wherever we are, than to have God's presence with us and to be under his protection. It is comfortable, in a journey, to have a guide in an unknown way, a guard in a dangerous way, to be well carried, well provided for, and to have good company in any way; and those that have God with them have all this in the best manner. (2.) In what he designed. His resolution is, [1.] In general, to cleave to the Lord, as his God in covenant: *Then shall the Lord be my God.* Not as if he would disown him and cast him off if he should want food and raiment; no, though he slay us, we must cleave to him; but "then I will rejoice in him as my God; then I will more strongly engage myself to abide with him." Note, Every mercy we receive from God should be improved as an additional obligation upon us to walk closely with him as our God. [2.] In particular, that he would perform some special acts of devotion, in token of his gratitude. *First,* "This pillar shall keep possession here till I come back in peace, and then it shall be God's house," that is, "an altar shall be erected here to the honour of God." *Secondly,* "The house of god shall not be unfurnished, nor his altar without a sacrifice: *Of all that thou shalt give me I will surely give the tenth unto thee,* to be spent either upon God's altars or upon his poor," both which are his receivers in the world. Probably it was according to some general instructions received from heaven that Abraham and Jacob offered the tenth of their acquisitions to God. Note, 1. God must be honoured with our estates, and must have his dues out of them. When we receive more than ordinary mercy from God we should study to give some signal instances of gratitude to him. 2. The tenth is a very fit proportion to be devoted to God and employed for him, though, as circumstances vary, it may be more or less, as God prospers us, 1 Co. 16:2; 2 Co. 9:7.

CHAPTER 29

This chapter gives us an account of God's providences concerning Jacob, pursuant to the promises made to him in the foregoing chapter. I. How he was brought in safety to his journey's end, and directed to his relations there, who bade him welcome (*v.* 1–14). II. How he was comfortably disposed of in marriage (*v.* 15–30). III. How his family was built up in the birth of four sons (*v.* 31–35). The affairs of princes and mighty nations that were then in being are not recorded in the book of God, but are left to be buried in oblivion; while these small domestic concerns of holy Jacob are particularly recorded with their minute circumstances, that they may be in everlasting remembrance. For "the memory of the just is blessed."

Verses 1–8

All the stages Israel's march to Canaan are distinctly noticed, but no particular journal is kept of Jacob's expedition further than Beth-el; no, he had no more such happy nights as he had at Beth-el, no more such visions of the Almighty. That was intended for a feast; he must not expect it to be his daily bread. But, 1. We are here told how cheerfully he proceeded in his journey after the sweet communion he had with God at Beth-el: *Then Jacob lifted up his feet;* so the margin reads it, *v.* 1. Then he went on with cheerfulness and alacrity, not burdened with his cares, nor cramped with his fears, being assured of God's gracious presence with him. Note, After the visions we have had of God, and the vows we have made to him in solemn ordinances, we should run the way of his commandments with enlarged hearts, Heb. 12:1. 2. How happily he arrived at his journey's end. Providence brought him to the very field where his uncle's flocks were to be watered, and there he met with Rachel, who was to be his wife. Observe, (1.) The divine Providence is to be acknowledged in all the little circumstances which concur to make a journey, or other undertaking, comfortable and successful. If, when we are at a loss, we meet seasonably with those that can direct us — if we meet with a disaster, and those are at hand that will help us — we must not say that it was by chance, nor that fortune therein favoured us, but that it was by Providence, and that God therein favoured us. Our ways are ways of pleasantness, if we continually acknowledge God in them. (2.) Those that have flocks must look well to them, and be diligent to know their state, Prov. 27:23. What is here said of the constant care of the shepherds concerning their sheep (*v.* 2, 3, 7, 8) may serve to illustrate the tender concern which our Lord Jesus, the great Shepherd of the sheep, has for his flock, the church; for he is the good Shepherd, that knows his sheep, and is known of them, Jn. 10:14. The stone at the well's mouth, which is so often mentioned here, was either to secure their property in it (for water was scarce, it was not there *usus communis aquarum — for every one's use*), or it was to save the well from receiving damage from the heat of the sun, or from any spiteful hand, or to prevent the lambs of the flock from being drowned in it. (3.) Separate interests should not take us from joint and mutual help; when all the shepherds came together with their flocks, then, like loving neighbours, at watering-time, they watered their flocks together. (4.) It becomes us to speak civilly and respectfully to strangers. Though Jacob was no courtier, but a plain man, dwelling in tents, and a stranger to compliment, yet he addresses himself very obligingly to the people he met with, and calls them his *brethren, v.* 4. The law of kindness in the tongue has a commanding power, Prov. 31:26. Some think he calls them brethren because they were of the same trade, shepherds like him. Though he was now upon his preferment, he was not ashamed of his occupation. (5.) Those that show respect have usually respect shown to them. As Jacob was civil to these strangers, so he found them civil to him. When he undertook to teach them how to despatch their business (*v.* 7), they did not bid him meddle with his own concerns and let them alone; but, though he was a stranger, they gave him the reason of their delay, *v.* 8. Those that are neighbourly and friendly shall have neighbourly and friendly usage.

Verses 9–14

Here we see, 1. Rachel's humility and industry: *She kept her father's sheep* (*v.* 9), that is, she took the care of them, having servants under her that were employed about them. Rachel's name signifies *a sheep.* Note, Honest useful labour is that which nobody needs be ashamed of, nor ought it to be a hindrance to any one's preferment. 2. Jacob's tenderness and affection. When he understood that this was his kinswoman (probably he had heard of her name before), knowing what his errand was into that country, we may suppose it struck his mind immediately that his must be his wife. Being already smitten with her ingenuous comely face (though it was probably sun-burnt, and she was in the homely dress of a shepherdess), he is wonderfully officious, and anxious to serve her (*v.* 10), and addresses himself to her with tears of joy and kisses of love, *v.* 11. She runs with all haste to tell her father; for she will by no means entertain her kinsman's address without her father's knowledge and approbation, *v.* 12. These mutual respects, at their first interview, were good presages of their being a happy couple. 3. Providence made that which seemed contingent and fortuitous to give speedy satisfaction to Jacob's mind, as soon as ever he came to the place which he was bound for. Abraham's servant, when he came upon a similar errand, met with similar encouragement. Thus God guides his people with his eye, Ps. 32:8. It is a groundless conceit which some of the Jewish writers have, that Jacob, when he kissed Rachel, wept because he had been set upon in his journey by Eliphaz the eldest son of Esau, at the command of his father, and robbed of all his money and jewels, which his mother had given him when she sent him away. It was plain that it was his passion for Rachel, and the surprise of this happy meeting, that drew these tears from his eyes. 4. Laban, though none of the best-humoured men, bade him welcome, was satisfied in the account he gave of himself, and of the reason of his coming in such poor circumstances. While we avoid the extreme, on the one hand, of being foolishly credulous, we must take heed of falling into the other extreme, of being uncharitably jealous and suspicious. Laban owned him for his kinsman: *Thou art my bone and my flesh, v.* 14. Note, Those are hard-hearted indeed that are unkind to their relations, and that *hide themselves from their own flesh,* Isa. 58:7.

Verses 15–30

Here is, I. The fair contract made between Laban and Jacob, during the month that Jacob spent there as a guest, *v.* 14. It seems he was not idle, nor did he spend his time in sport and pastime; but like a man of business, though he had no stock of his own, he applied himself to serve his uncle, as he had begun (*v.* 10) when he *watered his flock.* Note, Wherever we are, it is good to be employing ourselves in some useful business, which will turn to a good account to ourselves or others. Laban, it seems, was so taken with Jacob's ingenuity and industry about his flocks that he was desirous he should continue with him, and very fairly reasons thus: *"Because thou art my brother, shouldst thou therefore serve me for nought? v.* 15. No, what reason for that?" If Jacob be so respectful to his uncle as to give him his service without demanding any consideration for it, yet Laban will not be so unjust to his nephew as to take advantage either of his necessity or of his good-nature. Note, Inferior relations must not be imposed upon; if it be their duty to serve us, it is our duty to reward them. Now Jacob had a fair opportunity to make known to Laban the affection he had for his daughter Rachel; and, having no worldly goods in his hand with which to endow her, he promises him seven years' service, upon condition that, at the end of the seven years, he would bestow her upon him for his wife. It appears by computation that Jacob was now seventy-seven years old when he bound himself apprentice for a wife, *and for a wife he kept sheep,* Hos. 12:12. His posterity are there reminded of it long afterwards, as an instance of the meanness of their origin: probably Rachel was young, and scarcely marriageable, when Jacob first came, which made him the more willing to stay for her till his seven years' service had expired.

II. Jacob's honest performance of his part of the bargain, *v.* 20. He served seven years for Rachel. If Rachel still continued to keep her father's sheep (as she did, *v.* 9), his innocent and religious conversation with her, while they kept the flocks, could not but increase their mutual acquaintance and affection (Solomon's song of love is a pastoral); if she now left it off, his easing her of that care was very obliging. Jacob honestly served out his seven years, and did not forfeit his indentures, though he was old; nay, he served them cheerfully: *They seemed to him but a few days, for the love he had to her,* as if it were more his desire to earn her than to have her. Note, Love makes long and hard services short and easy; hence we read of *the labour of love,* Heb. 6:10. If we know how to value the happiness of heaven, the sufferings of this present time will be as nothing to us in comparison of it. An age of work will be but as a few days to those that love God and long for Christ's appearing.

III. The base cheat which Laban put upon him when he was out of his time: he put Leah into his arms instead of Rachel, *v.* 23. This was Laban's sin; he wronged both Jacob and Rachel, whose affections, doubtless, were engaged to each other, and, if (as some say) Leah was herein no better than an adulteress, it was no small wrong to her too. But it was Jacob's affliction, a damp to the mirth of the marriage-feast, when in the morning behold it was Leah, *v.* 25. It is easy to observe here how Jacob was paid in his own coin. He had cheated his own father when he pretended to be Esau, and now his father-in-law cheated him. Herein, how unrighteous soever Laban was, the Lord was righteous; as Judges 1:7. Even the righteous, if they take a false step, are sometimes thus recompensed on the earth. Many that are not, like Jacob, disappointed in the person, soon find themselves, as much to their grief, disappointed in the character. The choice of that relation therefore, on both sides, ought to be made with good advice and consideration, that, if there should be a disappointment, it may not be aggravated by a consciousness of mismanagement.

IV. The excuse and atonement Laban made for the cheat. 1. The excuse was frivolous: *It must not be so done in our country, v.* 26. We have reason to think there was no such custom of his country as he pretends; only he banters Jacob with it, and laughs at his mistake. Note, Those that can do wickedly and then think to turn it off with a jest, though they may deceive themselves and others, will find at last that God is not mocked. But if there had been such a custom, and he had resolved to observe it, he should have told Jacob so when he undertook to serve him for his younger daughter. Note, As saith the proverb of the ancients, *Wickedness proceeds from the wicked,* 1 Sa. 24:13. Those that deal with treacherous men must expect to be dealt treacherously with 2. His compounding the matter did but make bad worse: *We will give thee this also, v.* 27. Hereby he drew Jacob into the sin, and snare, and disquiet, of multiplying wives, which remains a blot in his escutcheon, and will be so to the end of the world. Honest Jacob did not design it, but to have kept as true to Rachel as his father had done to Rebekah. He that had lived without a wife to the eighty-fourth year of his age could then have been very well content with one; but Laban, to dispose of his two daughters without portions, and to get seven years' service more out of Jacob, thus imposes upon him, and draws him into such a strait by his fraud, that (the matter not being yet settled, as it was afterwards by the divine law, Lev. 18:18, and more fully since by our Saviour, Mt. 19:5) he had some colourable reasons for marrying them both. He could not refuse Rachel, for he had espoused her; still less could he refuse Leah, for he had married her; and therefore Jacob must *be content, and take two talents,* 2 Kings *v.* 23. Note, One sin is commonly the inlet of another. Those that go in by one door of wickedness seldom find their way out but by another. The polygamy of the patriarchs was, in some measure, excusable in them, because, though there was a reason against it as ancient as Adam's marriage (Mal. 2:15), yet there was no express command against it; it was in them a sin of ignorance. It was not he product of any sinful lust, but for the building up of the church, which was the good that Providence brought out of it; but it will by no means justify the like practice now, when God's will is plainly made known, that one man and one woman only must be joined together, 1 Co. 7:2. The having of many wives suits well enough with the carnal sensual spirit of the Mahomedan imposture, which allows it; but we have not so learned Christ. Dr. Lightfoot makes Leah and Rachel to be figures of the two churches, the Jews under the law and the Gentiles under the gospel: the younger the more beautiful, and more in the thoughts of Christ when he came in the form of a servant; but he other, like Leah, first embraced: yet in this the allegory does not hold, that the Gentiles, the younger, were more fruitful, Gal. 4:27.

Verses 31–35

We have here the birth of four of Jacob's sons, all by Leah. Observe, 1. That Leah, who was less beloved, was blessed with children, when Rachel was denied that blessing, *v.* 31. See how Providence, in dispensing its gifts, observes a proportion, to keep the balance even, setting crosses and comforts one over-against another, that none may be either too much elevated or too much depressed. Rachel wants children, but she is blessed with her husband's love; Leah wants that, but she is fruitful. Thus it was between Elkana's two wives (1 Sa. 1:5); for the Lord is wise and righteous. *When the Lord saw that Leah was hated,* that is, loved less than Rachel, in which sense it is required that we hate father and mother, in comparison with Christ (Lu. 14:26), then the Lord granted her a child, which was a rebuke to Jacob, for making so great a difference between those that he was equally related to, — a check to Rachel, who perhaps insulted over her sister upon that account, — and a comfort to Leah, that she might not be overwhelmed with the contempt put upon her: thus *God giveth abundant honour to that which lacked,* 1 Co. 12:24. 2. The names she gave her children were expressive of her respectful regards both to God and to her husband. (1.) She appears very ambitious of her husband's love: she reckoned the want of it her affliction (*v.* 32); not upbraiding him with it as his fault, nor reproaching him for it, and so making herself uneasy to him, but laying it to heart as her grief, which yet she had reason to bear with the more patience because she herself was consenting to the fraud by which she became his wife; and we may well bear that trouble with patience which we bring upon ourselves by our own sin and folly. She promised herself that the children she bore him would gain her the interest she desired in his affections. She called her first-born *Reuben (see a son),* with this pleasant thought, *Now will my husband love me;* and her third son *Levi (joined),* with this expectation, *Now will my husband by joined unto me, v.* 34. Mutual affection is both the duty and comfort of that relation; and yoke-fellows should study to recommend themselves to each other, 1 Co. 7:33, 34. (2.) She thankfully acknowledges the kind providence of God in it: *The Lord hath looked upon my affliction, v.* 32. *"The Lord hath heard,* that is, taken notice of it, *that I was hated* (for our afflictions, as they are before God's eyes, so they have a cry in his ears), *he has therefore given me this son."* Note, Whatever we have that contributes either to our support and comfort under our afflictions or to our deliverance from them, God must be owned in it, especially his pity and tender mercy. Her fourth she called *Judah (praise),* saying, *Now will I praise the Lord, v.* 35. And this was he of whom, as concerning the flesh, Christ came. Note, [1.] Whatever is the matter of our rejoicing ought to be the matter of our thanksgiving. Fresh favours should quicken us to praise God for former favours. *Now will I praise the Lord* more and better than I have done. [2.] All our praises must centre in Christ, both as the matter of them and as the Mediator of them. He descended from him whose name was praise, for he is our praise. Is Christ formed in my heart? *Now will I praise the Lord.*

CHAPTER 30

In this chapter we have an account of the increase, I. Of Jacob's family. Eight children more we find registered in this chapter; Dan and Naphtali by Bilhah, Rachel's maid (*v.* 1–8). Gad and Asher by Zilpah, Leah's maid (*v.* 9–13). Issachar, Zebulun, and Dinah, by Leah (*v.* 14–21). And, last of all, Joseph, by Rachel (*v.* 22–24). II. Of Jacob's estate. He makes a new bargain with Laban (*v.* 25–34). And in the six years' further service he did to Laban God wonderfully blessed him, so that his stock of cattle became very considerable (*v.* 35–43). Herein was fulfilled the blessing with which Isaac dismissed him (*ch.* 28:3), "God make thee fruitful, and multiply thee." Even these small matters concerning Jacob's house and field, though they seem inconsiderable, are improvable for our learning. For the scriptures were written, not for princes and statesmen, to instruct them in politics; but for all people, even the meanest, to direct them in their families and callings: yet some things are here recorded concerning Jacob, not for imitation, but for admonition.

Verses 1–13

We have here the bad consequences of that strange marriage which Jacob made with the two sisters. Here is,

I. An unhappy disagreement between him and Rachel (*v.* 1, 2), occasioned, not so much by her own barrenness as by her sister's fruitfulness. Rebekah, the only wife of Isaac, was long childless, and yet we find no uneasiness between her and Isaac; but here, because Leah bears children, Rachel cannot live peaceably with Jacob.

1. Rachel frets. She *envied her sister, v.* 1. Envy is grieving at the good of another, than which no sin is more offensive to God, nor more injurious to our neighbour and ourselves. She considered not that it was God that made the difference, and that though, in this single instance her sister was preferred before her, yet in other things she had the advantage. Let us carefully watch against all the risings and workings of this passion in our minds. Let not our eye be evil towards any of our fellow-servants because our master's is good. But this was not all; she said to Jacob, *Give me children, or else I die.* Note, We are very apt to err in our desires of temporal mercies, as Rachel here. (1.) One child would not content her; but, because Leah

has more than one, she must have more too: *Give me children.* (2.) Her heart is inordinately set upon it, and, if she have not what she would have, she will throw away her life, and all the comforts of it. "Give them to me, or *else I die,"* that is, "I shall fret myself to death; the want of this satisfaction will shorten my days." Some think she threatens Jacob to lay violent hands upon herself, if she could not obtain this mercy. (3.) She did not apply to God by prayer, but to Jacob only, forgetting that *children are a heritage of the Lord,* Ps. 127:3. We wrong both God and ourselves when our eye is more to men, the instruments of our crosses and comforts, than to God the author. Observe a difference between Rachel's asking for this mercy and Hannah's, 1 Sa. 1:10, etc. Rachel envied; Hannah wept. Rachel must have children, and she died of the second; Hannah prayed for one child, and she had four more. Rachel is importunate and peremptory; Hannah is submissive and devout. *If thou wilt give me a child, I will give him to the Lord.* Let Hannah be imitated, and not Rachel; and let our desires be always under the direction and control of reason and religion.

2. Jacob chides, and most justly. He loved Rachel, and therefore reproved her for what she said amiss, *v.* 2. Note, Faithful reproofs and products and instances of true affection, Ps. 141:5; Prov. 27:5, 6. Job reproved his wife when she spoke the language of the foolish women, Job 2:10. See 1 Co. 7:16. He was angry, not at the person, but at the sin; he expressed himself so as to show this displeasure. Note, sometimes it is requisite that a reproof should be given warm, like a medical potion; not too hot, lest it scald the patient; yet not cold, lest it prove ineffectual. It was a very grave and pious reply which Jacob gave to Rachel's peevish demand: *Am I in God's stead?* The Chaldee paraphrases it well, *Dost thou ask sons of me? Oughtest thou not to ask them from before the Lord?* The Arabic reads it, *"Am I above God? can I give thee that which God denies thee?"* This was said like a plain man. Observe, (1.) He acknowledges the hand of God in the affliction which he was a sharer with her in: He *hath withheld the fruit of the womb.* Note, Whatever we want, it is God that withholds it, a sovereign Lord, most wise, holy, and just, that may do what he will with his own, and is debtor to no man, that never did, nor ever can do, any wrong to any of his creatures. The keys of the clouds, of the heart, of the grave, and of the womb, are four keys which God had in his hand, and which (the rabbin say) he entrusts neither with angels nor seraphim. See Rev. 3:7. Job 11:10; 12:14. (2.) He acknowledges his own inability to alter what God had appointed: *"Am I in God's stead?* What! dost thou make a god of me?" *Deos qui rogat ille facit — He to whom we offer supplications is to us a god.* Note, [1.] There is no creature that is, or can be, to us, in God's stead. God may be to us instead of any creature, as the sun instead of the moon and stars; but the moon and all the stars will not be to us instead of the sun. No creature's wisdom, power, and love, will be to us instead of God's. [2.] It is therefore our sin and folly to place any creature in God's stead, and to place that confidence in any creature which is to be placed in God only.

II. An unhappy agreement between him and the two handmaids.

1. At the persuasion of Rachel, he took Bilhah her handmaid to wife, that, according to the usage of those times, his children by her might be adopted and owned as her mistress's children, *v.* 3, etc. She would rather have children by reputation than none at all, children that she might fancy to be her own, and call her own, though they were not so. One would think her own sister's children were nearer akin to her than her maid's, and she might with more satisfaction have made them her own if she had so pleased; but (so natural is it for us all to be fond of power) children that she had a right to rule were more desirable to her than children that she had more reason to love; and, as an early instance of her dominion over the children born in her apartment, she takes a pleasure in giving them names that carry in them nothing but marks of emulation with her sister, as if she had overcome her, (1.) At law. She calls the first son of her handmaid *Dan (judgement),* saying, *"God hath judged me"* (*v.* 6), that is, "given sentence in my favour." (2.) In battle. she calls the next *Naphtali (wrestlings),* saying, *I have wrestled with my sister, and have prevailed* (*v.* 8); as if all Jacob's sons must be born men of

contention. See what roots of bitterness envy and strife are, and what mischief they make among relations.

2. At the persuasion of Leah, he took Zilpah her handmaid to wife also, *v.* 9. Rachel had done that absurd and preposterous thing of giving her maid to her husband, in emulation with Leah; and now Leah (because she missed one year in bearing children) does the same, to be even with her, or rather to keep before her. See the power of jealousy and rivalship, and admire the wisdom of the divine appointment, which unites one man and one woman only; for *God hath called us to peace* and purity, 1 Co. 7:15. Two sons Zilpah bore to Jacob, whom Leah looked upon herself as entitled to, in token of which she called one *Gad* (*v.* 11), promising herself a little *troop* of children; and children are the militia of a family, they fill the quiver, Ps. 127:4, 5. The other she called *Asher (happy),* thinking herself happy in him, and promising herself that her neighbours would think so too: *The daughters will call me blessed, v.* 13. Note, It is an instance of the vanity of the world, and the foolishness bound up in our hearts, that most people value themselves and govern themselves more by reputation than either by reason or religion; they think themselves blessed if the daughters do but call them so. There was much amiss in the contest and competition between these two sisters, yet God brought good out of this evil; for, the time being now at hand when the seed of Abraham must begin to increase and multiply, thus Jacob's family was replenished with twelve sons, heads of the thousands of Israel, from whom the celebrated twelve tribes descended and were named.

Verses 14–24

Here is, I. Leah fruitful again, after she had, for some time, left off bearing. Jacob, it should seem, associated more with Rachel than with Leah. The law of Moses supposes it a common case that, if a man had two wives, one would be beloved and the other hated, Deu. 21:15. But at length Rachel's strong passions betrayed her into a bargain with Leah that Jacob should return to her apartment. Reuben, a little lad, five or six years old, playing in the field, found *mandrakes, dudaim.* It is uncertain what they were, the critics are not agreed about them; we are sure they were some rarities, either fruits or flowers that were very pleasant to the smell, Cant. 7:13. Note, The God of nature has provided, not only for our necessities, but for our delights; there are products of the earth in the exposed fields, as well as in the planted protected gardens, that are very valuable and useful. How plentifully is nature's house furnished and her table spread! Her precious fruits offer themselves to be gathered by the hands of little children. It is a laudable custom of the devout Jews, when they find pleasure, suppose in eating an apple, to lift their hearts, and say, "Blessed be he that made this fruit pleasant!" Or, in smelling a flower, "Blessed be he that made this flower sweet." Some think these mandrakes were jessamine flowers. Whatever they were, Rachel could not see them in Leah's hands, where the child had placed them, but she must covet them. She cannot bear the want of these pretty flowers, but will purchase them at any rate. Note, There may be great sin and folly in the inordinate desire of a small thing. Leah takes this advantage (as Jacob had of Esau's coveting his red pottage) to obtain that which was justly due to her, but to which Rachel would not otherwise have consented. Note, Strong passions often thwart one another, and those cannot but be continually uneasy that are hurried on by them. Leah is overjoyed that she shall have her husband's company again, that her family might yet further be built up, which is the blessing she desires and devoutly prays for, as is intimated, *v.* 17, where it is said, *God hearkened unto Leah.* The learned bishop Patrick very well suggests here that the true reason of this contest between Jacob's wives for his company, and their giving him their maids to be his wives, was the earnest desire they had to fulfil the promise made to Abraham (and now lately renewed to Jacob), that his seed should be as the stars of heaven for multitude, and that in one seed of his, the Messiah, all the nations of the earth should be blessed. And he thinks it would have been below the dignity of this sacred history to take such particular notice of these things if there had not been some such great consideration in them. Leah was now blessed with two sons; the first she called *Issachar (a hire),* reckoning herself well repaid for her mandrakes, nay (which is a strange construction of the providence) rewarded for giving her maid to her husband. Note, We abuse God's mercy when we reckon that his favours countenance and patronize our follies. The other she called *Zebulun (dwelling),* owning God's bounty to her: *God has endowed me with a good dowry, v.* 20. Jacob had not endowed her when he married her, nor had he wherewithal in possession; but she reckons a family of children not a bill of charges, but a good dowry, Ps. 113:9. She promises herself more of her husband's company now that she had borne him six sons, and that, in love to his children at least, he would often visit her lodgings. Mention is made (*v.* 21) of the birth of a daughter, *Dinah,* because of the following story concerning her, *ch.* 34. Perhaps Jacob had other daughters, though their names are not registered.

II. Rachel fruitful at last (*v.* 22): *God remembered Rachel,* whom he seemed to have forgotten, and *hearkened to her* whose prayers had been long denied; and then she bore a son. Note, As God justly denies the mercy we have been inordinately desirous of, so sometimes he graciously grants, at length, that which we have long waited for. He corrects our folly, and yet considers our frame, and does not contend for ever. Rachel called her son *Joseph,* which in Hebrew is akin to two words of a contrary signification, *Asaph (abstulit), He has taken away my reproach,* as if the greatest mercy she had in this son was that she had saved her credit; and *Jasaph (addidit), The Lord shall add to me another son,* which may be looked upon either as the language of her inordinate desire (she scarcely knows how to be thankful for one unless she may be sure of another), or of her faith — she takes this mercy as an earnest of further mercy. "Has God given me his grace? I may call it Joseph, and say, He shall add more grace! Has he given me his joy? I may call it Joseph, and say, He will give me more joy. Has he begun, and shall he not make an end?"

Verses 25–36

We have here,

I. Jacob's thoughts of home. He faithfully served his time out with Laban, even his second apprenticeship, though he was an old man, had a large family to provide for, and it was high time for him to set up for himself. Though Laban's service was hard, and he had cheated him in the first bargain he had made, yet Jacob honestly performs his engagements. Note, A good man, though he swear to his own hurt, will not change. And though others have deceived us this will not justify us in deceiving them. Our rule is to do as we *would be* done by, not as we *are* done by. Jacob's term having expired, he begs leave to be gone, *v.* 25. Observe, 1. He retained his affection for the land of Canaan, not only because it was the land of his nativity, and his father and mother were there, whom he longed to see, but because it was the land of promise; and, in token of his dependence upon the promise of it, though he sojourn in Haran he can by no means think of settling there. Thus should we be affected towards our heavenly country, looking upon ourselves as strangers here, viewing the heavenly country as our home, and longing to be there, as soon as the days of our service upon earth are numbered and finished. We must not think of taking root here, for this is not our place and country, Heb. 13:14. 2. He was desirous to go to Canaan, though he had a great family to take with him, and no provision yet made for them. He had got wives and children with Laban, but nothing else; yet he does not solicit Laban to give him either a portion with his wives or the maintenance of some of his children. No, all his request is, *Give me my wives and my children, and send me away, v.* 25, 26. Note, Those that trust in God, in his providence and promise, though they have great families and small incomes, can cheerfully hope that he who sends mouths will send meat. He who feeds the brood of the ravens will not starve the seed of the righteous.

II. Laban's desire of his stay, *v.* 27. In love to himself, not to Jacob or to his wives or children, Laban endeavours to persuade him to continue his chief shepherd, entreating him, by the regard he bore him, not to leave him: *If I have found favour in thy eyes, tarry.* Note, Churlish selfish men know how to give good words when it is to serve their own ends. Laban found that his stock had wonderfully increased with Jacob's good management, and he owns it, with very good expressions of respect both to God and Jacob: *I have learned by experience that the Lord has blessed me for thy sake.* Observe, 1. Laban's learning: *I have learned by experience.* Note, There is many a profitable good lesson to be learned by experience. We are very unapt scholars if we have not learned by experience the evil of sin, the treachery of our own hearts, the vanity of the world, the goodness of God, the gains of godliness, and the like. 2. Laban's lesson. He owns, (1.) That his prosperity was owing to God's blessing: *The Lord has blessed me.* Note, worldly men, who choose their portion in this life, are often blessed with an abundance of this world's goods. Common blessings are given plentifully to many that have no title to covenant-blessings. (3.) That Jacob's piety had brought that blessing upon him: *The Lord has blessed me,* not for my own sake (let not such a man as Laban, that lives without God in the world, *think that he shall receive any thing of the Lord,* Jam. 1:7), but *for thy sake.* Note, [1.] Good men are blessings to the places where they live, even where they live meanly and obscurely, as Jacob in the field, and Joseph in the prison, *ch.* 39:23. [2.] God often blesses bad men with outward mercies for the sake of their godly relations, though it is seldom that they have either the wit to see it or the grace to own it, as Laban did here.

III. The new bargain they came upon. Laban's craft and covetousness took advantage of Jacob's plainness, honesty, and good-nature; and, perceiving that Jacob began to be won upon by his fair speeches, instead of making him a generous offer and bidding high, as he ought to have done, all things considered, he puts it upon him to make his demands (*v.* 28): *Appoint me thy wages,* knowing he would be very modest in them, and would ask less than he could for shame offer. Jacob accordingly makes a proposal to him, in which,

1. He shows what reason he had to insist upon so much, considering, (1.) That Laban was bound in gratitude to do well for him, because he had served him not only faithfully, but very successfully, *v.* 30. Yet here observe how he speaks, like himself, very modestly. Laban had said, *The Lord has blessed me for thy sake;* Jacob will not say so, but, *The Lord has blessed thee since my coming.* Note, Humble saints take more pleasure in doing good than in hearing of it again. (2.) That he himself was bound in duty to take care of his own family: *Now, when shall I provide for my own house also?* Note, Faith and charity, though they are excellent things, must not take us off from making necessary provisions for our own support, and the support of our families. We must, like Jacob, *trust in the Lord and do good,* and yet we must, like him, provide for our own houses also; he that does not the latter *is worse than an infidel,* 1 Tim. 5:8.

2. He is willing to refer himself to the providence of God, which, he knew, extends itself to the smallest things, even the colour of the cattle; and he will be content to have for his wages the sheep and goats of such and such a colour, speckled, spotted, and brown, which should hereafter be brought forth, *v.* 32, 33. This, he thinks, will be a most effectual way both to prevent Laban's cheating him and to secure himself from being suspected of cheating Laban. Some think he chose this colour because in Canaan it was generally most desired and delighted in; their shepherds in Canaan are called *Nekohim* (Amos 1:1), the word here used for *speckled;* and Laban was willing to consent to this bargain because he thought if the few he has that were now speckled and spotted were separated from the rest, which by agreement was to be done immediately, the body of the flock which Jacob was to tend, being of one colour, either all black or all white, would produce few or none of mixed colours, and so he should have Jacob's service for nothing, or next to nothing. According to this bargain, those few that were party-coloured were separated, and put into the hands of Laban's sons, and sent three days' journey off; so great was Laban's jealously lest any of them should mix with the rest of the flock, to the advantage of Jacob. And now a fine bargain Jacob has made for himself! Is this his providing for his own house, to put it upon such an uncertainty? If these cattle bring forth, as usually cattle do, young ones of the same colour with themselves, he must still serve for nothing, and be a drudge and a beggar all the days of his life; but he knows whom he has trusted, and the event showed, (1.) That he took the best way that could be taken with Laban, who otherwise would certainly have been too hard for him. And, (2.) That it was not in vain to rely upon the divine providence, which owns and blesses honest humble diligence. Those that find men whom they deal with unjust and unkind shall not find God so, but, some way or other, he will recompense the injured, and be a good pay-master to those that commit their cause to him.

Verses 37–43

Here is Jacob's honest policy to make his bargain more advantageous to himself than it was likely to be. If he had not taken some course to help himself, it would have been a bad bargain indeed, which he knew Laban would never consider, or rather would be well pleased to see him a loser by, so little did Laban consult any one's interest but his own. Now Jacob's contrivances were, 1. To set peeled sticks before the cattle where they were watered, that, looking much at those unusual party-coloured sticks, by the power of imagination they might bring forth young ones in like manner party-coloured, *v.* 37–39. Probably this custom was commonly used by the shepherds of Canaan, who coveted to have their cattle of this motley colour. Note, It becomes a man to be master of his trade, whatever it is, and to be not only industrious, but ingenious in it, and to be versed in all its lawful arts and mysteries; for what is a man but his trade? There is a discretion which God teaches the husbandman (as plain a trade as that is), and which he ought to learn, Isa. 28:26. 2. When he began to have a stock of ringstraked and brown, he contrived to set them first, and to put the faces of the rest towards them, with the same design as in the former contrivance; but would not let his own, that were of one colour, *v.* 40. Strong impressions, it seems, are made by the eye, with which therefore we have need to make a covenant. 3. When he found that his project succeeded, through the special blessing of God upon it, he contrived, by using it only with the stronger cattle, to secure to himself those that were most valuable, leaving the feebler to Laban, *v.* 41, 42. Thus *Jacob increased exceedingly* (*v.* 43), and grew very rich in a little time. This success of his policy, it is true, was not sufficient to justify it, if there had been any thing fraudulent or unjust in it, which we are sure there was not, for he did it by divine direction (*ch.* 31:12); nor was there any thing in the thing itself but the honest improvement of a fair bargain, which the divine providence wonderfully prospered, both in justice to Jacob whom Laban had wronged and dealt hardly with and in pursuance of the particular promises made to him of the tokens of the divine favour. Note, Those who, while their beginning is small, are humble and honest, contented and industrious, are in a likely way to see their latter end greatly increasing. He that is faithful in a little shall be entrusted with more. He that is faithful in that which is another man's shall be entrusted with something of his own. Jacob, who had been a just servant, became a rich master.

CHAPTER 31

Jacob was a very honest good man, a man of great devotion and integrity, yet he had more trouble and vexation than any of the patriarchs. He left his father's house in a fright, went to his uncle's in distress, very hard usage he met with there, and now is going back surrounded with fears. Here is, I. His resolution to return (*v.* 1–16). II. His clandestine departure, (*v.* 17–21). III. Laban's pursuit of him in displeasure (*v.* 22–25). IV. The hot words that passed between them (*v.* 26–42). V. There amicable agreement at last (*v.* 43, etc.).

Verses 1–16

Jacob is here taking up a resolution immediately to quit his uncle's service, to take what he had and go back to Canaan. This resolution he took up upon a just provocation, by divine direction, and with the advice and consent of his wives.

I. Upon a just provocation; for Laban and his sons had become very cross and ill-natured towards him, so that he could not stay among them with safety or satisfaction.

1. Laban's sons showed their ill-will in what they said, *v.* 1. It should seem they said it in Jacob's hearing, with a design to vex him. The last chapter began with Rachel's envying Leah; this begins with Laban's sons envying Jacob. Observe, (1.) How greatly they magnify Jacob's prosperity: *He has gotten all this glory.* And what was this glory that they made so much ado about? It was a parcel of brown sheep and speckled goats (and perhaps the fine

colours made them seem more glorious), and some camels and asses, and such like trading; and this was *all this glory.* Note, Riches are glorious things in the eyes of carnal people, while to all those that are conversant with heavenly things they have no glory in comparison with the glory which excelleth. Men's over-valuing worldly wealth is that fundamental error which is the root of covetousness, envy, and all evil. (2.) How basely they reflect upon Jacob's fidelity, as if what he had he had not gotten honestly: *Jacob has taken away all that was our father's.* Not all, surely. What had become of those cattle which were committed to the custody of Laban's sons, and sent *three days' journey* off? *ch.* 30:35, 36. They mean all that was committed to him; but, speaking invidiously, they express themselves thus generally. Note, [1.] Those that are ever so careful to keep a good conscience cannot always be sure of a good name. [2.] This is one of the vanities and vexations which attend outward prosperity, that it makes a man to be envied of his neighbors (Eccl. 4:4), and *who can stand before envy?* Prov. 27:4. Whom Heaven blesses hell curses, and all its children on earth.

2. Laban himself said little, but his countenance was not towards Jacob as it used to be; and Jacob could not but take notice of it, *v.* 2, 5. He was but a churl at the best, but now he was more churlish than formerly. Note, Envy is a sin that often appears in the countenance; hence we read of an *evil eye,* Prov. 23:6. Sour looks may do a great deal towards the ruin of peace and love in a family, and the making of those uneasy of whose comfort we ought to be tender. Laban's angry countenance lost him the greatest blessing his family ever had, and justly.

II. By divine direction and under the convoy of a promise: *The Lord said unto Jacob, Return, and I will be with thee, v.* 3. Though Jacob had met with very hard usage here, yet he would not quit his place till God bade him. He came thither by orders from Heaven, and there he would stay till he was ordered back. Note, It is our duty to set ourselves, and it will be our comfort to see ourselves, under God's guidance, both in our going out and in our coming in. The direction he had from Heaven is more fully related in the account he gives of it to his wives (*v.* 10-13), where he tells them of a dream he had about the cattle, and the wonderful increase of those of his colour; and how the angel of God, in that dream (for I suppose the dream spoken of *v.* 10 and that *v.* 11 to be the same), took notice of the workings of his fancy in his sleep, and instructed him, so that it was not by chance, or by his own policy, that he obtained that great advantage; but, 1. by the providence of God, who had taken notice of the hardships Laban had put upon him, and took this way to recompense him: *"For I have seen all the Laban doeth unto thee,* and herein I have an eye to that." Note, There is more of equity in the distributions of the divine providence than we are aware of, and by them the injured are recompensed really, though perhaps insensibly. Nor was it only by the justice of providence that Jacob was thus enriched, but, 2. In performance of the promise intimated in what is said *v.* 13, *I am the God of Beth-el,* This was the place where the covenant was renewed with him. Note, Worldly prosperity and success are doubly sweet and comfortable when we see them flowing, not from common providence, but from covenant-love, *to perform the mercy promised —* when we have them from God as *the God of Beth-el,* from those promises of the life which now is that belong to godliness. Jacob, even when he had this hopeful prospect of growing rich with Laban, must think of returning. When the world begins to smile upon us we must remember it is not our home. *Now arise* (*v.* 13) *and return,* (1.) To thy devotions in Canaan, the solemnities of which had perhaps been much intermitted while he was with Laban. The times of this servitude God had winked at; but now, "Return to the place where thou anointedst the pillar and vowedst the vow. Now that thou beginnest to grow rich it is time to think of an altar and sacrifices again." (2.) To thy comforts in Canaan: *Return to the land of thy kindred.* He was here among his near kindred; but those only he must look upon as his kindred in the best sense, the kindred he must live and die with, to whom pertained the covenant. Note, The heirs of Canaan must never reckon themselves at home till they come thither, however they may seem to take root here.

III. With the knowledge and consent of his wives. Observe,

1. He sent for Rachel and Leah to him to the field (*v.* 4), that he might confer with them more privately, or because one would not come to the other's apartment and he would willingly talk with them together, or because he had work to do in the field which he would not leave. Note, Husbands that love their wives will communicate their purposes and intentions to them. Where there is a mutual affection there will be a mutual confidence. And the prudence of the wife should engage the heart of her husband to trust in her, Prov. 31:11. Jacob told his wives, (1.) How faithfully he had served their father, *v.* 6. Note, If others do not do their duty to us, yet we shall have the comfort of having done ours to them. (2.) How unfaithfully their father had dealt with him *v.* 7. He would never keep to any bargain that he made with him, but, after the first year, still as he saw Providence favour Jacob with the colour agreed on, every half year of the remaining five he changed it for some other colour, which made it ten times; as if he thought not only to deceive Jacob, but the divine Providence, which manifestly smiled upon him. Note, Those that deal honestly are not always honestly dealt with. (3.) How God had owned him notwithstanding. He had protected him from Laban's ill-will: *God suffered him not to hurt me.* Note, Those that keep close to God shall be kept safely by him. He had also provided plentifully for him, notwithstanding Laban's design to ruin him: *God has taken away the cattle of your father, and given them to me, v.* 9. Thus the righteous God paid Jacob for his hard service out of Laban's estate; as afterwards he paid the seed of Jacob for their serving the Egyptians, with their spoils. Note, God is not unrighteous to forget his people's work and labour of love, though men be so, Heb. 6:10. Providence has ways of making those honest in the event that are not so in their design. Note, further, *The wealth of the sinner is laid up for the just,* Prov. 13:22. (4.) He told them of the command God had given him, in a dream, to return to his own country (*v.* 13), that they might not suspect his resolution to arise from inconstancy, or any disaffection to their country or family, but might see it to proceed from a principle of obedience to his God, and dependence on him.

2. His wives cheerfully consented to his resolution. They also brought forward their grievances, complaining that their father had been not only unkind, but unjust, to them (*v.* 14-16), that he looked upon them as strangers, and was without natural affection towards them; and, whereas Jacob had looked upon the wealth which God had transferred from Laban to him as his wages, they looked upon it as their portions; so that, both ways, God forced Laban to pay his debts, both to his servant and to his daughters. So then it seemed, (1.) They were weary of their own people and their father's house, and could easily forget them. Note, This good use we should make of the unkind usage we meet with from the world, we should sit the more loose to it, and be willing to leave it and desirous to be at home. (2.) They were willing to go along with their husband, and put themselves with him under the divine direction: *Whatsoever God hath said unto thee do.* Note, Those wives that ar their husband's meet helps will never be their hindrances in doing that to which God calls them.

Verses 17–24

Here is, I. Jacob's flight from Laban. We may suppose he had been long considering of it, and casting about in his mind respecting it; but when now, at last, God had given him positive orders to go, he made no delay, nor was he disobedient to the heavenly vision. The first opportunity that offered itself he laid hold of, when Laban was shearing his sheep (*v.* 19), that part of his flock which was in the hands of his sons three days' journey off. Now, 1. It is certain that it was lawful for Jacob to leave his service suddenly, without giving a quarter's warning. It was not only justified by the particular instructions God gave him, but warranted by the fundamental law of self-preservation, which directs us, when we are in danger, to shift for our own safety, as far as we can do it without wronging our consciences. 2. It was his prudence to steal away unawares to Laban, lest, if Laban had known, he should have hindered him or plundered him. 3. It was honestly done to take no more than his own with him, the *cattle of his getting,*

v. 18. He took what Providence gave him, and was content with that, and would not take the repair of his damages into his own hands. Yet Rachel was not so honest as her husband; she *stole her father's images* (*v.* 19) and carried them away with her. The Hebrew calls them *teraphim.* Some think they were only little representations of the ancestors of the family, in statues or pictures, which Rachel had a particular fondness for, and was desirous to have with her, now that she was going into another country. It should rather seem that they were images for a religious use, *penates, household-gods,* either worshipped or consulted as oracles; and we are willing to hope (with bishop Patrick) that she took them away not out of covetousness of the rich metal they were made of, much less for her own use, or out of any superstitious fear lest Laban, by consulting his *teraphim,* might know which way they had gone (Jacob, no doubt, dwelt with his wives as a man of knowledge, and they were better taught than so), but out of a design hereby to convince her father of the folly of his regard to those as gods which could not secure themselves, Isa. 46:1, 2.

II. Laban's pursuit of Jacob. Tidings were brought him, on the third day, that Jacob had fled; he immediately raises the whole clan, takes his brethren, that is, the relations of his family, that were all in his interests, and pursues Jacob (as Pharaoh and his Egyptians afterwards pursued the seed of Jacob), to bring him back into bondage again, or with design to strip him of what he had. Seven days' journey he marched in pursuit of him, *v.* 23. He would not have taken half the pains to have visited his best friends. But the truth is bad men will do more to serve their sinful passions than good men will to serve their just affections, and are more vehement in their anger than in their love. Well, at length Laban, overtook him, and the very night before he came up with him God interposed in the quarrel, rebuked Laban and sheltered Jacob, charging Laban not to *speak unto him either good or bad* (*v.* 24), that is, to say nothing against his going on with his journey, for that it proceeded from the Lord. The same Hebraism we have, *ch.* 24:50. Laban, during his seven day's march, had been full of rage against Jacob, and was now full of hopes that his lust should be satisfied upon him (Ex. 15:9); but God comes to him, and with one word ties his hands, though he does not turn his heart. Note, 1. In a dream, and in slumberings upon the bed, God has ways of opening the *ears of men, and sealing their instruction,* Job 33:15, 16. Thus he admonishes men by their consciences, in secret whispers, which the man of wisdom will hear and heed. 2. The safety of good men is very much owing to the hold God has of the consciences of bad men and the access he has to them. 3. God sometimes appears wonderfully for the deliverance of his people when they are upon the very brink of ruin. The Jews were saved from Haman's plot when the king's decree drew hear to be put in execution, Esth. 9:1.

Verses 25–35

We have here the reasoning, not to say the rallying, that took place between Laban and Jacob at their meeting, in that mountain which was afterwards called *Gilead, v.* 25. Here is,

I. The high charge which Laban exhibited against him. He accuses him,

1. As a renegade that had unjustly deserted his service. To represent Jacob as a criminal, he will have it thought that he intended kindness to his daughters (*v.* 27, 28), that he would have dismissed them with all the marks of love and honour that could be, that he would have made a solemn business of it, would have kissed his little grandchildren (and that was all he would have given them), and, according to the foolish custom of the country, would have sent them away *with mirth, and with songs, with tabret, and with harp:* not as Rebekah was sent away out of the same family, above 120 years before, with prayers and blessings (*ch.* 24:60), but with sport and merriment, which was a sign that religion had very much decayed in the family, and that they had lost their seriousness. However, he pretends they would have been treated with respect at parting. Note, It is common for bad men, when they are disappointed in their malicious projects, to pretend that they designed nothing but what was kind and fair. When they cannot do the mischief they intended, they are loth it

should be thought that they ever did intend it. When they have not done what they should have done they come off with this excuse, that they would have done it. Men may thus be deceived, but God cannot. He likewise suggests that Jacob had some bad design in stealing away thus (v. 26), that he took his wives away as captives. Note, Those that mean ill themselves are most apt to put the worst construction upon what others do innocently. The insinuating and the aggravating of faults are the artifices of a designing malice, and those must be represented (though never so unjustly) as intending ill against whom ill is intended. Upon the whole matter, (1.) He boasts of his own power (v. 29): *It is in the power of my hand to do you hurt.* He supposes that he had both right on his side (*a good action*, as we say, against Jacob) and *strength* on his side, either to avenge the wrong or recover the right. Note, Bad people commonly value themselves much upon their power to do hurt, whereas a power to do good is much more valuable. Those that will do nothing to make themselves amiable love to be thought formidable. And yet, (2.) He owns himself under the check and restraint of God's power; and, though it redounds much to the credit and comfort of Jacob, he cannot avoid telling him the caution God had given him the night before in a dream, *Speak not to Jacob good nor bad.* Note, As God has all wicked instruments in a chain, so when he pleases he can make them sensible of it, and force them to own it to his praise, as protector of the good, as Balaam did. Or we may look upon this as an instance of some conscientious regard felt by Laban for God's express prohibitions. As bad as he was he durst not injure one whom he saw to be the particular care of Heaven. Note, A great deal of mischief would be prevented if men would but attend to the caveats which their own consciences give them in slumberings upon the bed, and regard the voice of God in them.

2. As a thief, v. 30. Rather than own that he had given him any colour of provocation to depart, he is willing to impute it to a foolish fondness for his father's house, which made him that he would needs begone; but then (says he) *wherefore hast thou stolen my gods?* Foolish man! to call those his gods that could be stolen! Could he expect protection from those that could neither resist nor discover their invaders? Happy are those who have the Lord for their God, for they have a God that they cannot be robbed of. Enemies may steal our goods, but not our God. Here Laban lays to Jacob's charge things that he knew not, the common distress of oppressed innocency.

II. Jacob's apology for himself. Those that commit their cause to God, yet are not forbidden to plead it themselves with meekness and fear. 1. As to the charge of stealing away his own wives he clears himself by giving the true reason why he went away unknown to Laban, v. 31. He feared lest Laban would by force take away his daughters, and so oblige him, by the bond of his affection to his wives, to continue in his service. Note, Those that are unjust in the least, it may be suspected, will be unjust also in much, Lu. 16:10. If Laban deceive Jacob in his wages, it is likely he will make no conscience of robbing him of his wives, and putting those asunder whom God has joined together. What may not be feared from men that have no principle of honesty? 2. As to the charge of stealing Laban's gods he pleads not guilty, v. 32. He not only did not take them himself (he was not so fond of them), but he did not know that they were taken. Yet perhaps he spoke too hastily and inconsiderately when he said, "Whoever had taken them, *let him not live;*" upon this he might reflect with some bitterness when, not long after, Rachel who had taken them died suddenly in travail. How just soever we think ourselves to be, it is best to forbear imprecations, lest they fall heavier than we imagine.

III. The diligent search Laban made for his gods (v. 33–35), partly out of hatred to Jacob, whom he would gladly have an occasion to quarrel with, partly out of love to his idols, which he was loth to part with. We do not find that he searched Jacob's flocks for stolen cattle; but he searched his furniture for stolen gods. He was of Micah's mind, *You have taken away my gods, and what have I more?* Jdg. 18:24. Were the worshippers of false gods so set upon their idols? did they thus walk in the name of their gods? and shall not we be as solicitous in our enquires after the true God? When he has justly departed from us, how carefully should we ask, *Where is God my Maker? O that I knew*

where I might find him! Job 23:3. Laban, after all his searches, missed of finding his gods, and was baffled in his enquiry with a sham; but our God will not only by found of those that seek him, but they shall find him their bountiful rewarder.

Verses 36–42

See in these verses,

I. The power of provocation. Jacob's natural temper was mild and calm, and grace had improved it; he was a smooth man, and a plain man; and yet Laban's unreasonable carriage towards him put him into a heat that transported him into a heat that transported him into some vehemence, v. 36, 37. His chiding with Laban, though it may admit of some excuse, was not justifiable, nor is it written for our imitation. Grievous words stir up anger, and commonly do but make bad worse. It is a very great affront to one that bears an honest mind to be charged with dishonesty, and yet even this we must learn to bear with patience, committing our cause to God.

II. The comfort of a good conscience. This was Jacob's rejoicing, that when Laban accused him his own conscience acquitted him, and witnessed for him that he had been in all things willing and careful to live honestly, Heb. 13:18. Note, Those that in any employment have dealt faithfully, if they cannot obtain the credit of it with men, yet shall have the comfort of it in their own bosoms.

III. The character of a good servant, and particularly of a faithful shepherd. Jacob had approved himself such a one, v. 38–40. 1. He was very careful, so that, through his oversight or neglect, the ewes did not cast their young. His piety also procured a blessing upon his master's effects that were under his hands. Note, Servants should take no less care of what they are entrusted with for their masters than if they were entitled to it as their own. 2. He was very honest, and took none of that for his own eating which was not allowed him. He contented himself with mean fare, and coveted not to feast upon the rams of the flock. Note, Servants must not be dainty in their food, nor covet what is forbidden them, but in that, and other instances, show all good fidelity. 3. He was very laborious, v. 40. He stuck to his business, all weathers; and bore both heat and cold with invincible patience. Note, Men of business, that intend to make something of it, must resolve to endure hardness. Jacob is here an example to ministers; they also are shepherds, of whom it is required that hey be true to their trust and willing to take pains.

IV. The character of a hard master. Laban had been such a one to Jacob. Those are bad masters, 1. Who exact from their servants that which is unjust, by obliging them to make good that which is not damaged by any default of theirs. This Laban did, v. 39. Nay, if there has been a neglect, yet it is unjust to punish above the proportion of the fault. That may be an inconsiderable damage to the master which would go near to ruin a poor servant. 2. Those also are bad masters who deny to their servants that which is just and equal. This Laban did, v. 41. It was unreasonable for him to make Jacob serve fro his daughters, when he had in reversion so great an estate secured to him by the promise of God himself; as it was also to give him his daughters without portions, when it was in the power of his hands to do well for them. Thus he robbed the poor because he was poor, as he did also by changing his wages.

V. The care of providence for the protection of injured innocence, v. 42. God took cognizance of the wrong done to Jacob, and repaid him whom Laban would otherwise have sent empty away, and rebuked Laban, who otherwise would have swallowed him up. Note, God is the patron of the oppressed; and those who are wronged and yet not ruined, cast down and yet not destroyed, must acknowledge him in their preservation and give him the glory of it. Observe, 1. Jacob speaks of god as the God of his father, intimating that he thought himself unworthy to be thus regarded, but was beloved for the father's sake. 2. He calls him the God of Abraham, and the fear of Isaac; for Abraham was dead, and had gone to that world where perfect love casts out fear; but Isaac was yet alive, sanctifying the Lord in his heart, as his fear and his dread

Verses 43–55

We have here the compromising of the matter between Laban and Jacob. Laban had nothing to say in reply to

Jacob's remonstrance: he could neither justify himself nor condemn Jacob, but was convicted by his own conscience of the wrong he had done him; and therefore desires to hear no more of the matter He is not willing to own himself in a fault, nor to ask Jacob's forgiveness, and make him satisfaction, as he ought to have done. But,

I. He turns it off with a profession of kindness for Jacob's wives and children (v. 43): *These daughters are my daughters.* When he cannot excuse what he has done, he does, in effect, own what he should have done; he should have treated them as his own, but he had counted them as strangers, v. 15. Note, It si common for those who are without natural affection to pretend much to it when it will serve a turn. Or perhaps Laban said this in a vain-glorious say, as one that loved to talk big, and use great swelling words of vanity: "All that thou seest is mine." It was not so, it was all Jacob's, and he had paid dearly for it; yet Jacob let him have his saying, perceiving him coming into a better humour. Note, Property lies near the hearts of worldly people. They love to boast of it, "This is mine, and the other is mine," as Nabal, 1 Sa. 25:11, *my bread and my water.*

II. He proposes a covenant of friendship between them, to which Jacob readily agrees, without insisting upon Laban's submission, much less his restitution. Note, When quarrels happen, we should be willing to be friends again upon any terms: peace and love are such valuable jewels that we can scarcely buy them too dearly. Better sit down losers than go on in strife. Now observe here,

1. The substance of this covenant. Jacob left it wholly to Laban to settle it. The tenour of it was, (1.) That Jacob should be a good husband to his wives, that he should not afflict them, nor marry other wives besides them, v. 50. Jacob had never given him any cause to suspect that he would be any other than a kind husband; yet, as if he had, he was willing to come under this engagement. Though Laban had afflicted them himself, yet he will bind Jacob that he shall not afflict them. Note, Those that are injurious themselves are commonly most jealous of others, and those that do not do their own duty are most peremptory in demanding duty from others. (2.) That he should never be a bad neighbour to Laban, v. 52. It was agreed that no act of hostility should ever pass between them, that Jacob should forgive and forget all the wrongs he had received and not remember them against Laban or his family in after-times. Note, We may resent an injury which yet we may not revenge.

2. The ceremony of this covenant. It was made and ratified with great solemnity, according to the usages of those times. (1.) A pillar was erected (v. 45), and a heap of stones raised (v. 46), to perpetuate the memory or the ting, the way of recording agreements by writing being then either not known or not used. (2.) A sacrifice was offered (v. 54), a sacrifice of peace-offerings. Note, Our peace with God is that which puts true comfort into our peace with our friends. If parties contend, the reconciliation of both to him will facilitate their reconciliation one to another. (3.) They did eat bread together (v. 46), jointly partaking of the feast upon the sacrifice, v. 54. This was in token of a hearty reconciliation. Covenants of friendship were anciently ratified by the parties eating and drinking together. It was in the nature of a love-feast. (4.) They solemnly appealed to God concerning their sincerity herein, [1.] As a witness (v. 49): *The Lord watch between me and thee,* that is, "The Lord take cognizance of every thing that shall be done on either side in violation of this league. When we are out of one another's sight, let his be a restraint upon us, that wherever we are we are under God's eye." This appeal is convertible into a prayer. Friends at a distance from each other may take the comfort of this, that when they cannot know or succour one another God watches between them, and has his eye on them both. [2.] As a Judge, v. 53. *The God of Abraham* (from whom Jacob descended), *and the God of Nahor* (from whom Laban descended), *the God of their father* (the common ancestor, form whom they both descended), *judge betwixt us.* God's relation to them is thus expressed to intimate that they worshipped one and the same God, upon which consideration there ought to be no enmity between them. Note, Those that have one God should have one heart: those that agree in religion should strive to agree in every thing else. God is Judge between contending parties, and he will judge righteous-

ly; whoever does wrong, it is at his peril. (5.) They gave a new name to the place, *v.* 47, 48. Laban called it in Syriac, and Jacob in Hebrew, *the heap of witness;* and (*v.* 49) it was called *Mizpah, a watch-tower.* Posterity being included in the league, care was taken that thus the memory of it should be preserved. These names are applicable to the seals of the gospel covenant, which are witnesses to us if we be faithful, but witnesses to us if we be faithful, but witnesses against us if we be false. The name Jacob gave this heap *(Galeed)* stuck by it, not the name Laban gave it. In all this rencounter, Laban was noisy and full of words, affecting to say much; Jacob was silent, and said little. When Laban appealed to God under many titles, Jacob only *swore by the fear of his father Isaac,* that is, the God whom his father Isaac feared, who had never served other gods, as Abraham and Nahor had done. Two words of Jacob's were more memorable than all Laban's speeches and vain repetitions: *for the words of wise men are heard in quiet, more than the cry of him that ruleth among fools,* Eccl. 9:17.

Lastly, After all this angry parley, they part friends, *v.* 55. Laban very affectionately *kissed his sons and his daughters, and blessed them,* and then went back in peace. Note, God is often better to us than our fears, and strangely overrules the spirits of men in our favour, beyond what we could have expected; for it is not in vain to trust in him.

CHAPTER 32

We have here Jacob still upon his journey towards Canaan. Never did so many memorable things occur in any march as in this of Jacob's little family. By the way he meets, I. With good tidings from his God (*v.* 1, 2). II. With bad tidings from his brother, to whom he sent a message to notify his return (*v.* 3–6). In his distress, 1. He divides his company (*v.* 7, 8). 2. He makes his prayer to God (*v.* 9–12). 3. He sends a present to his brother (*v.* 13–23). 4. He wrestles with the angel (*v.* 24–32).

Verses 1–2

Jacob, having got clear of Laban, pursues his journey homewards towards Canaan: when God has helped us through difficulties we should go on our way heaven-ward with so much the more cheerfulness and resolution. Now, 1. Here is Jacob's convoy in his journey (*v.* 1): *The angels of God met him,* in a visible appearance, whether in a vision by da or in a dream by night, as when he saw them upon the ladder (*ch.* 28:12), is uncertain. Note, Those that keep in a good way have always a good guard; angels themselves are ministering spirits for their safety, Heb. 1:14. Where Jacob pitched his tents, they pitched theirs about him, Ps. 34:7. They met him, to bid him welcome to Canaan again; a more honourable reception this was than ever any prince had, that was met by the magistrates of a city in their formalities. They met him to congratulate him on his arrival, as well as on his escape from Laban; for they have pleasure in the prosperity of God's servants. They had invisibly attended him all along, but now they appeared to him, because he had greater dangers before him than those he had hitherto encountered. Note, When God designs his people for extraordinary trials, he prepares them by extraordinary comforts. We should think it had been more seasonable for these angels to have appeared to him amidst the perplexity and agitation occasioned first by Laban, and afterwards by Esau, than in this calm and quiet interval, when he saw not himself in any imminent peril; but God will have us, when we are in peace, to provide for trouble, and, when trouble comes, to live upon former observations and experiences; for *we walk by faith, not by sight.* God's people, at death, are returning to Canaan, to their Father's house; and then the angels of God will meet them, to congratulate them on the happy finishing of their servitude, and to carry them to their rest. 2. The comfortable notice he took of this convoy, *v.* 2. *This is God's host,* and therefore, (1.) It is a powerful host; very great is he that is thus attended, and very safe that is thus guarded. (2.) God must have the praise of this protection: "This I may thank God for, for it is his host." A good man may with an eye of faith see the same that Jacob saw with his bodily eyes, by believing that promise (Ps. 91:11), *He shall give his angels charge over thee.* What need have we to dispute whether every particular saint has a guardian angel, when we are sure he has a guard of angels about him? To preserve the remembrance of this favour, Jacob gave a name to the place from it, *Mahanaim, two hosts,* or *two camps.* That is, say some of the rabbin, one host of the guardian angels of Mesopotamia, who conducted Jacob thence, and delivered him safely to the other host of the angels of Canaan, who met him upon the borders where he now was. Rather, they appeared to him in two hosts, one on either side, or one in the front and the other in the rear, to protect him from Laban behind and Esau before, that they might be a complete guard. Thus he is *compassed* with God's favour. Perhaps in allusion to this the church is called *Mahanaim, two armies,* Cant. 6:13. Here were Jacob's family, which made one army, representing the church militant and itinerant on earth; and the angels, another army, representing the church triumphant and at rest in heaven.

Verses 3–8

Now that Jacob was re-entering Canaan God, by the vision of angels, reminded him of the friends he had when he left it, and thence he takes occasion to remind himself of the enemies he had, particularly Esau. It is probable that Rebekah had sent him word of Esau's settlement in Seir, and of the continuance of his enmity to him. What shall poor Jacob do? He longs to see his father, and yet he dreads to see his brother. He rejoices to see Canaan again, and yet cannot but rejoice with trembling because of Esau.

I. He sends a very kind and humble message to Esau. It does not appear that his way lay through Esau's country, or that he needed to ask his leave for a passage; but his way lay near it, and he would not go by him without paying him the respect due to a brother, a twin-brother, an only brother, an elder brother, a brother offended. Note, 1. Though our relations fail in their duty to us, yet we must make conscience of doing our duty to them. 2. It is a piece of friendship and brotherly love to acquaint our friends with our condition, and enquire into theirs. Acts of civility may help to slay enmities. Jacob's message to him is very obliging, *v.* 4, 5. (1.) He calls Esau his lord, himself his servant, to intimate that he did not insist upon the prerogatives of the birthright and blessing he had obtained for himself, but left it to God to fulfil his own purpose in his seed. Note, *Yielding pacifies great offences,* Eccl. 10:4. We must not refuse to speak in a respectful an submissive manner to those that are ever so unjustly exasperated against it (2.) He gives him a short account of himself, that he was not a fugitive and a vagabond, but, though long absent, had had a certain dwelling-place, with his own relations: *I have sojourned with Laban, and staid there till now;* and that he was not a beggar, nor did he come home, as the prodigal son, destitute of necessaries and likely to be a charge to his relations; no, *I have oxen and asses.* This he knew would (if any thing) recommend him to Esau's good opinion. And, (3.) He courts his favour: *I have sent, that I might find grace in thy sight.* Note, It is no disparagement to those that have the better cause to become petitioners for reconciliation, and to sue for peace as well as right.

II. He receives a very formidable account of Esau's warlike preparations against him (*v.* 6), not a word, but a blow, a very coarse return to his kind message, and a sorry welcome home to a poor brother: *He comes to meet thee, and four hundred men with him.* He is now weary of waiting for the days of mourning for this good father, and even before they come he resolves to slay his brother. 1. He remembers the old quarrel, and will now be avenged on him for the birthright and blessing, and, if possible, defeat Jacob's expectations from both. Note, malice harboured will last long, and find an occasion to break out with violence a great while after the provocations given. Angry men have good memories. 2. He envies Jacob what little estate he had, and, though he himself was now possessed of a much better, yet nothing will serve him but to feed his eyes upon Jacob's ruin, and fill his fields with Jacob's spoils. Perhaps the account Jacob sent him of his wealth did but provoke him the more. 3. He concludes it easy to destroy him, now that he was upon the road, a poor weary traveller, unfixed, and (as he thinks) unguarded. Those that have the serpent's poison have commonly the serpent's policy, to take the first and fairest opportunity that offers itself for revenge. 4. He resolves to do it suddenly, and before Jacob had come to his father, lest he should interpose and mediate between them. Esau was one of those that hated peace; when Jacob speaks, speaks peaceably, *he* is for war, Ps. 120:6, 7. Out he marches, spurred on with rage, and intent on blood and murders; four hundred men he had with him, probably such as used to hunt with him, armed, no doubt, rough and cruel like their leader, ready to execute the word of command though ever so barbarous, and now breathing nothing but threatenings and slaughter. The tenth part of these were enough to cut off poor Jacob, and his guiltless helpless family, root and branch. No marvel therefore that it follows (*v.* 7), *then Jacob was greatly afraid and distressed,* perhaps the more so from having scarcely recovered the fright Laban had put him in. Note, Many are the troubles of the righteous in this world, and sometimes the end of one is but the beginning of another. The clouds return after the rain. Jacob, though a man of great faith, yet was now greatly afraid. Note, A lively apprehension of danger, and a quickening fear arising from it, may very well consist with a humble confidence in God's power and promise. Christ himself, in his agony, was sorely amazed.

III. He puts himself into the best posture of defence that his present circumstances will admit. It was absurd to think of making resistance, all his contrivance is to make an escape, *v.* 7, 8. He thinks it prudent not to venture all in one bottom, and therefore divides what he had into two companies, that, if one were smitten, the other might escape. Like a tender careful master of a family, he is more solicitous for their safety than for his own. He divided his company, not as Abraham (*ch.* 14:15), for fight, but for flight.

Verses 9–12

Our rule is to call upon God in the time of trouble; we have here an example to this rule, and the success encourages us to follow this example. It was now a time of Jacob's trouble, but he shall be saved out of it; and here we have him praying for that salvation, Jer. 30:7. In his distress he sought the Lord, and he heard him. Note, Times of fear should be times of prayer; whatever frightens us should drive us to our knees, to our God. Jacob had lately seen his guard of angels, but, in this distress, he applied to God, not to them; he knew they were his fellow-servants, Rev. 22:9. Nor did he consult Laban's *teraphim;* it was enough for him that he had a God to go to. To him he addresses himself with all possible solemnity, so running for safety into the name of the Lord, *as a strong tower,* Prov. 18:10. This prayer is the more remarkable because it won him the honour of being an *Israel, a prince with God,* and the father of the praying remnant, who are hence called *the seed of Jacob,* to whom he never said, *Seek you me in vain.* Now it is worth while to enquire what there was extraordinary in this prayer, that it should gain the petitioner all this honour.

I. The request itself is one, and very express: *Deliver me from the hand of my brother, v.* 11. Though there was no human probability on his side, yet he believed the power of God could rescue him as a lamb out of the bloody jaws of the loin. Note, 1. We have leave to be particular in our addresses to God, to mention the particular straits and difficulties we are in; for the God with whom we have to do is one we may be free with: *we have liberty of speech* (*parrēsia*) at the throne of grace. 2. When our brethren aim to be our destroyers, it is our comfort that we have a Father to whom we may apply as our deliverer.

II. The pleas are many, and very powerful; never was cause better ordered, Job 23:4. He offers up his request with great faith, fervency, and humility. How earnestly does he beg! *Deliver me, I pray thee, v.* 11. His fear made him importunate. With what holy logic does he argue! With what divine eloquence does he plead! Here is a noble copy to write after.

1. He addresses himself to God as the God of his fathers, *v.* 9. Such was the humble self-denying sense he had of his own unworthiness that he did not call God his own God, but a God in covenant with his ancestors: *O God of my father Abraham, and God of my father Isaac;* and this he could the better plead because the covenant, by divine designation, was entailed upon him. Note, God's covenant with our fathers may be a comfort to us when were are in distress. It has often been so to the Lord's people, Ps. 22:4, 5. Being born in God's house, we are taken under his special protection.

2. He produces his warrant: *Thou saidst unto me, Return unto thy country.* He did not rashly leave his place

with Laban, nor undertake this journey out of a fickle humour, or a foolish fondness for his native country, but in obedience to God's command. Note, (1.) We may be in the way of our duty, and yet may meet with trouble and distress in that way. As prosperity will not prove us in the right, so cross events will not prove us in the wrong; we may be going whither God calls us, and yet may think our way hedged up with thorns. (2.) We may comfortably trust God with our safety, while we carefully keep to our duty. If God be our guide, he will be our guard.

3. He humbly acknowledges his own unworthiness to receive any favour from God (*v.* 10): *I am not worthy;* it is an unusual plea. Some would think he should have pleaded that what was now in danger was his own, against all the world, and that he had earned it dear enough; no, he pleads, *Lord, I am not worthy of it.* Note, Self-denial and self-abasement well become us in all our addresses to the throne of grace. Christ never commended any of his petitioners so much as him who said, *Lord, I am not worthy* (Mt. 8:8), and her who said, *Truth, Lord, yet the dogs eat of the crumbs which fall from their master's table,* Mt. 15:27. Now observe here, (1.) How magnificently and honourably he speaks of the mercies of God to him. We have here, *mercies,* in the plural number, and inexhaustible spring, and innumerable streams; *mercies and truth,* that is, past mercies given according to the promise, and further mercies secured by the promise. Note, What is laid up in God's truth, as well as what is laid out in God's mercies, is the matter both of the comforts and the praises of active believers. Nay, observe, it is *all* the mercies, and *all* the truth; the manner of expression is copious, and intimates that his heart was full of God's goodness. (2.) How meanly and humbly he speaks of himself, disclaiming all thought of his own merit: *"I am not worthy of the least of all thy mercies,* much less am I worthy of so great a favour as this I am now suing for." Jacob was a considerable man, and, upon many accounts, very deserving, and, in treating with Laban, had justly insisted on his merits, but not before God. *I am less than all thy mercies;* so the word is. Note, The best and greatest of men are utterly unworthy of the least favour from God, and just be ready to own it upon all occasions. It was the excellent Mr. Herbert's motto, *Less than the least of all God's mercies.* Those are best prepared for the greatest mercies that see themselves unworthy of the least.

4. He thankfully owns God's goodness to him in his banishment, and how much it had outdone his expectations: *"With my staff I passed over this Jordan,* poor and desolate, like a forlorn and despised pilgrim;" he had no guides, no companions, no attendants, no conveniences for travel, but his staff only, nothing else to stay himself upon; *"and now I have become two bands,* now I am surrounded with a numerous and comfortable retinue of children and servants:" though it was his distress that had now obliged him to divide his family into two bands, yet he makes use of that for the magnifying of the mercy of his increase. Note, (1.) The increase of our families is then comfortable indeed to us when we see God's mercies, and his truth, in it. (2.) Those whose latter end greatly increases ought, with humility and thankfulness, to remember how small their beginning was. Jacob pleads, "Lord, thou didst keep me when I went out with only my staff, and had but one life to lose; wilt thou not keep me now that so many are embarked with me?"

5. He urges the extremity of the peril he was in: *Lord, deliver me from Esau, for I fear him, v.* 11. The people of God have not been shy of telling God their fears; for they know he takes cognizance of them, and considers them. The fear that quickens prayer is itself pleadable. It was not a robber, but a murderer, that he was afraid of; nor was it his own life only that lay at stake, but the mothers' and the children's, that had left their native soil to go along with him. Note, Natural affection may furnish us with allowable acceptable pleas in prayer.

6. He insists especially upon the promise God had made him (*v.* 9): *Thou saidst, I will deal well with thee,* and again, in the close (*v.* 12): *Thou saidst, I will surely do thee good.* Note, (1.) The best we can say to God in prayer is what he has said to us. God's promises, as they are the surest guide of our desires in prayer, and furnish us with the best petitions, so they are the firmest ground of our hopes, and furnish us with the best pleas. "Lord, thou saidst thus and thus; and wilt thou not be as good as thy word, the word upon which thou had *caused me to hope?"* Ps. 119:49. (2.) The most general promises are applicable to particular cases. "Thou saidst, *I will do thee good;* Lord, do me good in this matter." He pleads also a particular promise, that of *the multiplying of hes seed.* "Lord, what will become of that promise, if they be all cut off?" Note, [1.] There are promises to the families of good people, which are improvable in prayer for family-mercies, ordinary and extraordinary, *ch.* 17:7; Ps. 112:2; 102:28. [2.] The world's threatenings should drive us to God's promises.

Verses 13–23

Jacob, having piously made God his friend by a prayer, is here prudently endeavouring to make Esau his friend by a present. He had prayed to God to deliver him from the had of Esau, for he feared him; but neither did his fear sink into such a despair as dispirits for the use of means, nor did his prayer make him presume upon God's mercy, without the use of means. Note, When we have prayed to God for any mercy, we must second our prayers with our endeavours; else, instead of trusting god, we tempt him; we must so depend upon God's providence as to make use of our own prudence. "Help thyself, and God will help thee;" God answers our prayers by teaching us to order our affairs with discretion. To pacify Esau,

I. Jacob sent him a very noble present, not of jewels or fine garments (he had them not), but of cattle, to the number of 580 in all, *v.* 13–15. Now, 1. It was an evidence of the great increase with which God had blessed Jacob that he could spare such a number of cattle out of his stock. 2. It was an evidence of his wisdom that he would willingly part with some, to secure the rest; some men's covetousness loses them more than ever it gained them, and, by grudging a little damage; *skin for skin, and all that a man has,* if he be a wise man, *he will give for his life.* 3. It was a present that he thought would be acceptable to Esau, who had traded so much in hunting wild beasts that perhaps he was but ill furnished with tame cattle with which to stock his new conquests. And we may suppose that the mixed colours of Jacob's cattle, ring-straked, speckled, and spotted, would please Esau's fancy. 4. He promised himself that by this present he should gain Esau's favour; for a gift commonly *prospers, which way soever it turns* (Prov. 17:8), *and makes room for a man* (Prov. 18:16); nay, *it pacifies anger and strong wrath,* Prov. 21:14. Note, [1.] We must not despair of reconciling ourselves even to those that have been most exasperated against us; we ought not to judge men unappeasable, till we have tried to appease them. [2.] Peace and love, though purchased dearly, will prove a good bargain to the purchaser. Many a morose ill-natured man would have said, in Jacob's case, "Esau has vowed my death without cause, and he shall never be a farthing the better for me; I will see him far enough before I will send him a present:" but Jacob forgives and forgets.

II. He sent him a very humble message, which he ordered his servants to deliver in the best manner, *v.* 17, 18. They must call Esau their *lord,* and Jacob his *servant;* they must tell him the cattle they had was a small present which Jacob had sent him, as a specimen of his acquisitions while he was abroad. The cattle he sent were to be disposed of in several droves, and the servants that attended each drove were to deliver the same message, that the present might appear the more valuable, and his submission, so often repeated, might be the more likely to influence Esau. They must especially take care to tell him that Jacob was coming after (*v.* 18–20), that he might not suspect he had fled through fear. Note, A friendly confidence in men's goodness may help to prevent the mischief designed us by their badness: if Jacob will seem not to be afraid of Esau, Esau, it may be hoped, will not be a terror to Jacob.

Verses 24–32

We have here the remarkable story of Jacob's wrestling with the angel and prevailing, which is referred to, Hos. 12:4. Very early in the morning, a great while before day, Jacob had helped his wives and his children over the river, and he desired to be private, and was left alone, that he might again more fully spread his cares and fears before God in prayer. Note, We ought to continue instant in prayer, always to pray and not to faint: frequency and importunity in prayer prepare us for mercy. While Jacob was earnest in prayer, *stirring up himself to take hold on God,* an angel takes hold on him. Some think this was a created angel, the *angel of his presence* (Isa. 63:9), one of those that *always behold the face of our Father* and attend on the *shechinah,* or the divine Majesty, which probably Jacob had also in view. Others think it was Michael our prince, the eternal Word, the angel of the covenant, who is indeed the Lord of the angels, who often appeared in a human shape before he assumed the human nature for a perpetuity; whichsoever it was, we are sure *God's name was in him,* Ex. 23:21. Observe,

I. How Jacob and this angel engaged, *v.* 24. It was a single combat, hand to hand; they had neither of them any seconds. Jacob was now full of care and fear about the interview he expected, next day, with his brother, and, to aggravate the trial, God himself seemed to come forth against him as an enemy, to oppose his entrance into the land of promise, and to dispute the pass with him, not suffering him to follow his wives and children whom he had sent before. Note, Strong believers must expect divers temptations, and strong ones. We are told by the prophet (Hos. 12:4) how *Jacob wrestled:* he *wept, and made supplication;* prayers and tears were his weapons. It was not only a corporal, but a spiritual, wrestling, by the vigorous actings of faith and holy desire; and thus all the spiritual seed of Jacob, that pray in praying, still wrestle with God.

II. What was the success of the engagement. 1. Jacob kept his ground; though the struggle continued long, the angel, *prevailed not against him* (*v.* 25), that is, this discouragement did not shake his faith, nor silence his prayer. It was not in his own strength that he wrestled, nor by his own strength that he prevailed, but in and by strength derived from Heaven. That of Job illustrates this (Job 23:6), *Will he plead against me with his great power?* No (had the angel done so, Jacob had been crushed), *but he will put strength in me;* and by that *strength Jacob had power over the angel,* Hos. 12:4. Note, We cannot prevail with God but in his own strength. It is his Spirit that intercedes in us, and *helps our infirmities,* Rom. 8:26. 2. The angel put out Jacob's thigh, to show him what he could do, and that it was God he was wrestling with, for no man could disjoint his thigh with a touch. Some think that Jacob felt little or no pain from this hurt; it is probable that he did not, for he did not so much as halt till the struggle was over (*v.* 31), and, if so, this was an evidence of a divine touch indeed, which wounded and healed at the same time. Jacob prevailed, and yet had his thigh put out. Note, Wrestling believers may obtain glorious victories, and yet come off with broken bones; for *when they are weak then are they strong,* weak in themselves, but strong in Christ, 2 Co. 12:10. Our honours and comforts in this world have their alloys. 3. The angel, by an admirable condescension, mildly requests Jacob to let him go (*v.* 26), as God said to Moses (Ex. 32:10), *Let me alone.* Could not a mighty angel get clear of Jacob's grapples? He could; but thus he would put an honour on Jacob's faith and prayer, and further try his constancy. *The king is held in the galleries* (Cant. 7:5); *I held him* (says the spouse) *and would not let him go,* Cant. 3:4. The reason the angel gives why he would be gone is *because the day breaks,* and therefore he would not any longer detain Jacob, who had business to do, a journey to go, a family to look after, which, especially in this critical juncture, called for his attendance. Note, Every thing is beautiful in its season; even the business of religion, and the comforts of communion with God, must sometimes give way to the necessary affairs of this life: God *will have mercy, and not sacrifice.* 4. Jacob persists in his holy importunity: *I will not let thee go, except thou bless me;* whatever becomes of his family and journey, he resolves to make the best he can of this opportunity, and not to lose the advantage of his victory: he does not mean to wrestle all night for nothing, but humbly resolves he will have a blessing, and rather shall all his bones be put out of joint than he will go away without one. The credit of a conquest will do him no good without the comfort of a blessing. In begging this blessing he owns his inferiority, though he seemed to have the upper hand in the struggle; for *the less is blessed of the better.* Note, Those that would have the blessing of Christ must be in good earnest, and be importunate for it, as those that resolve to have no denial. It is the fervent prayer that is the effectual prayer. 5. The angel puts a perpetual mark of honour upon him, by changing his name (v. 27, 28): "Thou art a brave combatant" (says the angel), "a man of heroic resolution; what is thy name?" "Jacob," says he, a *supplanter;* so *Jacob* signifies: "Well," says the angel, "be thou never so called any more; henceforth thou shalt be celebrated, not for craft and artful management, but for true valour; thou shalt be called *Israel, a prince with God,* a name greater than those of the great men of the earth." He is a prince indeed that is a prince with God, and those are truly honourable that are mighty in prayer, Israels, Israelites indeed. Jacob is here knighted in the field, as it were, and has a title of honour given him by him that is the fountain of honour, which will remain, to his praise, to the end of time. Yet this was not all; having power with God, he shall have power with men too. Having prevailed for a blessing from heaven, he shall, no doubt, prevail for Esau's favour. Note, Whatever enemies we have, if we can but make God our friend, we are well off; those that by faith have power on earth as they have occasion for. 6. He dismisses him with a blessing, v. 29. Jacob desired to know the angel's name, that he might, according to his capacity, do him honour, Jdg. 13:17. But that request was denied, that he might not be too proud of his conquest, nor think he had the angel at such an advantage as to oblige him to what he pleased. No, *"Wherefore dost thou ask after my name?* What good will it do thee to know that?" The discovery of that was reserved for his death-bed, upon which he was taught to call him *Shiloh.* But, instead of telling him his name, he gave him his blessing, which was the thing he wrestled for: *He blessed him there,* repeated and ratified the blessing formerly given him. Note, Spiritual blessings, which secure our felicity, are better and much more desirable than fine notions which satisfy our curiosity. An interest in the angel's blessing is better than an acquaintance with his name. The tree of life is better than the tree of knowledge. Thus Jacob carried his point; a blessing he wrestled for, and a blessing he had; nor did ever any of his praying seed seek in vain. See how wonderfully God condescends to countenance and crown importunate prayer: those that resolve, though God slay them, yet to trust in him, will, at length, be more than conquerors. 7. Jacob gives a new name to the place; he calls it *Peniel, the face of God* (v. 30), because there he had seen the appearance of God, and obtained the favour of God. Observe, The name he gives to the place preserves and perpetuates, not the honour of his valour or victory, but only the honour of God's free grace. He does not say, "In this place I wrestled with God, and prevailed;" but, "In this place I saw God face to face, and my life was preserved;" not, "It was my praise that I came off a conqueror, but it was God's mercy that I escaped with my life." Note, It becomes those whom God honours to take shame to themselves, and to admire the condescensions of his grace to them. Thus David did, after God had sent him a gracious message (2 Sa. 7:18), *Who am I, O Lord God?* 8. The memorandum Jacob carried of this in his bones: *He halted on his thigh* (v. 31); some think he continued to do so to his dying-day; and, if he did, he had no reason to complain, for the honour and comfort he obtained by this struggle were abundantly sufficient to countervail the damage, though he went limping to his grave. He had no reason to look upon it as his reproach thus *to bear in his body the marks of the Lord Jesus* (Gal. 6:17); yet it might serve, like Paul's thorn in the flesh, to keep him from being lifted up with the abundance of the revelations. Notice is taken of the sun's rising upon him when he passed over *Penuel;* for it is sunrise with that soul that has communion with God. The inspired penman mentions a traditional custom which the seed of Jacob had, in remembrance of this, never to eat of that sinew, or muscle, in any beast, by which the hip-bone is fixed in its cup: thus they preserved the memorial of this story, and gave occasion to their children to enquire concerning it; they also did honour to the memory of Jacob. And this use we may still make of it, to acknowledge the mercy of God, and our obligations to Jesus Christ, that we may now keep up our communion with God, in faith, hope, and love, without peril either of life or limb.

CHAPTER 33

We read, in the former chapter, how Jacob had power with God, and prevailed; here we find what power he had with men too, and how his broth-

er Esau was mollified, and, on a sudden, reconciled to him; for so it is written, Prov. 16:7, "When a man's ways please the Lord, he maketh even his enemies to be at peace with him." Here is, I. A very friendly meeting between Jacob and Esau (v. 1–4). II. Their conference at their meeting, in which they vie with each other in civil and kind expressions. Their discourse is 1. About Jacob's family (v. 5–7). 2. About the present he had sent (v. 8–11). 3. About the progress of their journey (v. 12–15). III. Jacob's settlement in Canaan, his house, ground, and altar (v. 16–20).

Verses 1–4

Here, I. Jacob discovered Esau's approach, v. 1. Some think that his lifting up his eyes denotes his cheerfulness and confidence, in opposition to a dejected countenance; having by prayer committed his case to God, he went on his way, *and his countenance was no more sad,* 1 Sa. 1:18. Note, Those that have cast their care upon God may look before them with satisfaction and composure of mind, cheerfully expecting the issue, whatever it may be; come what will, nothing can come amiss to him whose heart is fixed, trusting in God. Jacob sets himself upon his watchtower to see what answer God will give to his prayers, Hab. 2:1.

II. He put his family into the best order he could to receive him, whether he should come as a friend or as an enemy, consulting their decency if he came as a friend and their safety if he came as an enemy, v. 1, 2. Observe what a different figure these two brothers made. Esau is attended with a guard of 400 men, and looks big; Jacob is followed by a cumbersome train of women and children that are his care, and he looks tender and solicitous for their safety; and yet Jacob had the birthright, and was to have the dominion, and was every way the better man. Note, It is no disparagement to very great and good men to give a personal attendance to their families, and to their family affairs. Jacob, at the head of his household, set a better example than Esau at the head of his regiment.

III. At their meeting, the expressions of kindness were interchanged in the best manner that could be between them.

1. Jacob bowed to Esau, v. 3. Though he feared Esau as an enemy, yet he did obeisance to him as an elder brother, knowing and remembering perhaps that when Abel was preferred in God's acceptance before his elder brother Cain, yet God undertook for him to Cain that he should not be wanting in the duty and respect owing by a younger brother. *Unto thee shall be his desire, and thou shalt rule over him,* ch. 4:7. Note, (1.) The way to recover peace where it has been broken is to do our duty, and pay our respects, upon all occasions, as if it had never been broken. It is the remembering and repeating of matters that separates friends and perpetuates the separation. (2.) A humble submissive carriage goes a great way towards the turning away of wrath. Many preserve themselves by humbling themselves: the bullet flies over him that stoops.

2. Esau embraced Jacob (v. 4): *He ran to meet him,* not in passion, but in love; and, as one heartily reconciled to him, he received him with all the endearments imaginable, *embraced him, fell on his neck, and kissed him.* Some think that when Esau came out to meet Jacob it was with no bad design, but that he brought his 400 men only for state, that he might pay so much the greater respect to his returning brother. It is certain that Jacob understood the report of his messengers otherwise, ch. 32:5, 6. Jacob was a man of prudence and fortitude, and we cannot suppose him to admit of a groundless fear to such a degree as he did this, nor that the Spirit of God would stir him up to pray such a prayer as he did for deliverance from a merely imaginary danger: and, if there was not some wonderful change wrought upon the spirit of Esau at this time, I see not how wrestling Jacob could be said to obtain such power with men as to denominate him a *prince.* Note, (1.) God had the hearts of all men in his hands, and can turn them when and how he pleases, by a secret, silent, but resistless power. He can, of a sudden, convert enemies into friends, as he did two Sauls, one by restraining grace (1 Sa. 26:21, 25), the other by renewing grace, Acts 9:21, 22. (2.) It is not in vain to trust in God, and to call upon him in the day of trouble; those that do so often find the issue much better than they expected.

3. They both wept. Jacob wept for joy, to be thus kindly received by his brother whom he had feared; and Esau perhaps wept for grief and shame, to think of the bad design he had conceived against his brother, which he found

himself strangely and unaccountably prevented from executing.

Verses 5–15

We have here the discourse between the two brothers at their meeting, which is very free and friendly, without the least intimation of the old quarrel. It was the best way to say nothing of it. They converse,

I. About Jacob's retinue, v. 5–7. Eleven or twelve little ones, the eldest of them no fourteen years old, followed Jacob closely: *Who are these?* says Esau. Jacob had sent him an account of the increase of his estate (ch. 32:5), but made no mention of his children; perhaps because he would not expose them to his rage if he should meet him as an enemy, or would please him with the unexpected sight if he should meet him as a friend: Esau therefore had reason to ask, *Who are those with thee?* to which common question Jacob returns a serious answer, such as became his character: They are *the children which God hath graciously given thy servant.* It had been a sufficient answer to the question, and fit enough to be given to profane Esau, if he had only said, "They are my children;" but then Jacob would not have spoken like himself, like a man whose eyes were ever towards the Lord. Note, It becomes us not only to do common actions, but to speak of them, *after a godly sort,* 3 Jn. 6. Jacob speaks of his children, 1. As God's gifts; they are a *heritage of the Lord,* Ps. 128:3; 112:9; 107:41. 2. As choice gifts; he hath graciously given them. Though they were many, and now much his care, and as yet but slenderly provided for, yet he accounts them great blessings. His wives and children, hereupon, come up in order, and pay their duty to Esau, as he had done before them (v. 6, 7); for it becomes the family to show respect to those to whom the master of the family shows respect.

II. About the present he had sent him.

1. Esau modestly refused it because he had enough, and did not need it, v. 9. Note, Those who wish to be considered men of honour will not *seem* to be mercenary in their friendship: whatever influence Jacob's present had upon Esau to pacify him, he would not have it thought that it had any, and therefore he refused it. His reason is *I have enough,* I have *much* (so the word is), so much that he was not willing to take any thing that was his brother's. Note, (1.) Many that come short of spiritual blessings, and are out of covenant, yet have much of this world's wealth. Esau had what was promised him, the fatness of the earth and a livelihood by his sword. (2.) It is a good thing for those that have much to know that they have enough, though they have not so much as some others have. Even Esau can say, *I have enough.* (3.) Those that are content with what they have must show it by not coveting what others have. Esau, for his part, needs it not, either to supply him, for he was rich, or to pacify him, for he was reconciled: we should take heed lest at any time our covetousness impose upon the courtesy of others, and meanly take advantage of their generosity.

2. Jacob affectionately urges him to accept it, and prevails, v. 10, 11. Jacob sent it, through fear (ch. 32:20), but, the fear being over, he now importunes his acceptance of it for love, to show that he desired his brother's friendship, and did not merely dread his wrath; two things he urges: — (1.) The satisfaction he had in his brother's favour, of which he thought himself bound to make this thankful acknowledgment. It is a very high compliment that he passes upon him: *I have seen thy face, as though I had seen the face of God,* that is, "I have seen thee reconciled to me, and at peace with me, as I desire to see God reconciled." Or the meaning is that Jacob saw God's favour to him in Esau's: it was a token for good to him that God had accepted his prayers. Note, Creature-comforts are comforts indeed to us when they are granted as answers to prayer, and are tokens of our acceptance with God. Again, It is matter of great joy to those that are of a peaceable and affectionate disposition to recover the friendship of those relations with whom they have been at variance. (2.) The competency he had of this world's goods: *God has dealt graciously with me.* Note, If what we have in this world increase under our hands, we must take notice of it with thankfulness, to the glory of God, and own that therein he has dealt graciously with us, better than we deserve. It is he that gives *power to get wealth,* Deu. 8:18. He adds,

"And *I have enough;* I have *all,*" so the word is. Esau's enough was much, but Jacob's enough was all. Note, a godly man, though he have but little in the world, yet may truly say, "I have all," [1.] Because he has the God of all, and has all in him; all is yours if you be Christ's, 1 Co. 3:22. [2.] Because he has the comfort of all. *I have all, and abound,* Phil. 4:18. He that thinks he has all is sure he has enough. He has all in prospect; he will have all shortly, when he comes to heaven: upon this principle Jacob urged Esau, and he took his present. Note, It is an excellent thing when men's religion makes them generous, free-hearted, and open-handed, scorning to do a thing that is paltry and sneaking.

III. About the progress of their journey. 1. Esau offers himself to be his guide and companion, in token of sincere reconciliation, *v.* 12. We never find that Jacob and Esau were so sociable with one another, and so affectionate, as they were now. Note, As for God his work is perfect. He made Esau, not only not an enemy, but a friend. This bone that had been broken, being well set, became stronger than ever. Esau has become fond of Jacob's company, courts him to Mount Seir: let us never despair of any, nor distrust God in whose hand all hearts are. Yet Jacob saw cause modestly to refuse this offer (*v.* 13, 14), wherein he shows a tender concern for his own family and flocks, like a good shepherd and a good father. He must consider the children, and the flocks, with young, and not lead the one, nor drive the other, too fast. This prudence and tenderness of Jacob ought to be imitated by those that have the care and charge of young people in the things of God. They must not be over-driven, at first, by heavy tasks in religious services, but led, as they can bear, having their work made as easy to them as possible. Christ, the good Shepherd, does so, Isa. 40:11. Now Jacob will not desire Esau to slacken his pace, nor force his family to quicken theirs, nor leave them, to keep company with his brother, as many would have done, that love any society better than their own house; but he desires Esau to march before, and promises to follow him leisurely, as he could get forward. Note, It is an unreasonable thing to tie others to our rate; we may come with comfort, at last, to the same journey's end, though we do not journey together, either in the same path or with the same pace. There may be those with whom we cannot fall in and yet with whom we need not fall out by the way. Jacob intimates to him that it was his present design to come to him to Mount Seir; and we may presume he did so, after he had settled his family and concerns elsewhere, though that visit is not recorded. Note, When we have happily recovered peace with our friends we must take care to cultivate it, and not to be behindhand with them in civilities. 2. Esau offers some of his men to be his guard and convoy, *v.* 15. He saw Jacob but poorly attended, no servants but his husbandmen and shepherds, no pages or footmen; and therefore, thinking he was as desirous as himself (if he could afford it) to take state upon him, and look great, he would needs lend him some of his retinue, to attend upon him, that he might appear like Esau's brother; but Jacob humbly refuses his offer, only desiring he would not take it amiss that he did not accept it: *What needeth it?* (1.) Jacob is humble, and needs it not for state; he desires not to make a fair show in the flesh, by encumbering himself with a needless retinue. Note, It is the vanity of pomp and grandeur that they are attended with a great deal of which it may be said, *What needeth it?* (2.) Jacob is under the divine protection, and needs it not for safety. Note, Those are sufficiently guarded that have God for their guard and are under a convoy of his hosts, as Jacob was. Those need not be beholden to an arm of flesh that have God for their arm every morning. Jacob adds, "Only *let me find grace in the sight of my lord;* having thy favour, I have all I need, all I desire from thee." If Jacob thus valued the good-will of a brother, much more reason have we to reckon that we have enough if we have the good-will of our God.

Verses 16–20

Here, 1. Jacob comes to Succoth. Having in a friendly manner parted with Esau, who had gone to his own country (*v.* 16), he comes to a place where, it should seem, he rested for some time, set up booths for his cattle, and other conveniences for himself and family. The place was afterwards known by the name of Succoth, a city in the tribe

of Gad, on the other side Jordan (it signifies booths), that when his posterity afterwards dwelt in houses of stone, they might remember that *the Syrian ready to perish* was their father, who was glad of booths (Deu. 26:5); such was the rock whence they were hewn. 2. He comes to Shechem; we read it, to *Shalem, a city of Shechem;* the critics generally incline to read it appellatively: *he came safely, or in peace, to the city of Shechem.* After a perilous journey, in which he had met with many difficulties, he came safely, at last, into Canaan. Note, Diseases and dangers should teach us how to value health and safety, and should help to enlarge our hearts in thankfulness, when our going out and coming in have been signally preserved. Here, (1.) He buys a field, *v.* 19. Though the land of Canaan was his by promise, yet, the time for taking possession not having yet come, he is content to pay for his own, to prevent disputes with the present occupants. Note, Dominion is not founded in grace. Those that have heaven on free-cost must not expect to have earth so. (2.) He builds an altar, *v.* 20. [1.] In thankfulness to God, for the good hand of his providence over him. He did not content himself with verbal acknowledgments of God's favour to him, but made real ones: [2.] That he might keep up religion, and the worship of God, in his family. Note, Where we have a tent God must have an altar, where we have a house he must have a church in it. He dedicated this altar, where we have a house he must have a church in it. He dedicated this altar to the honour of *El-elohe-Israel — God, the God of Israel,* to the honour of God, in general, the only living and true God, the best of beings and first of causes; and to the honour of the God of Israel, as a God in covenant with him. Note, In our worship of God we must be guided and governed by the joint-discoveries both of natural and revealed religion. God had lately called him by the name of *Israel,* and now he calls God *the God of Israel;* though he is styled *a prince with God,* God shall still be a prince with him, his Lord and his God. Note, Our honours then become honours indeed to us when they are consecrated to God's honour; Israel's God is Israel's glory.

CHAPTER 34

At this chapter begins the story of Jacob's afflictions in his children, which were very great, and are recorded to show, 1. The vanity of this world. That which is dearest to us may prove our greatest vexation, and we may meet with the greatest crosses in those things of which we said, "This same shall comfort us." 2. The common griefs of good people. Jacob's children were circumcised, were well taught, and prayed for, and had very good examples set them; yet some of them proved very untoward. "The race is not to the swift, nor the battle to the strong." Grace does not run in the blood, and yet the interrupting of the entail of grace does not cut off the entail of profession and visible church-privileges: nay, Jacob's sons, though they were his grief in some things, yet were all taken into covenant with God. In this chapter we have, I. Dinah debauched (*v.* 1–5). II. A treaty of marriage between her and Shechem who had defiled her (*v.* 6–19). III. The circumcision of the Shechemites, pursuant to that treaty (*v.* 20–24). IV. The perfidious and bloody revenge which Simeon and Levi took upon them (*v.* 25–31).

Verses 1–5

Dinah was, for aught that appears, Jacob's only daughter, and we may suppose her therefore the mother's fondling and the darling of the family, and yet she proves neither a joy nor a credit to them; for those children seldom prove either the best or the happiest that are most indulged. She is reckoned now but fifteen or sixteen years of age when she here occasioned so much mischief. Observe, 1. Her vain curiosity, which exposed her. She went out, perhaps unknown to her father, but by the connivance of her mother, *to see the daughters of the land* (*v.* 1); probably it was at a ball, or on some public day. Being an only daughter, she thought herself solitary at home, having none of her own age and sex to converse with; and therefore she must needs go abroad to divert herself, to keep off melancholy, and to accomplish herself by conversation better than she could in her father's tents. Note, It is a very good thing for children to love home; it is parents' wisdom to make it easy to them, and children's duty then to be easy in it. Her pretence was *to see the daughters of the land,* to see how they dressed, and how they danced, and what was fashionable among them. She went to *see,* yet that was not all, she went to be *seen* too; she went to see the daughters of the land, but, it may be, with some thoughts of the sons of the land too. I doubt she went to get an acquaintance with those Canaanites, and to learn their way. Note, The pride and vanity of young people be-

tray them into many snares. 2. The loss of her honour by this means (*v.* 2): *Shechem, the prince of the country,* but a slave to his own lusts, took her, and lay with her, it should seem, not so much by force as by surprise. Note, Great men think they may do any thing; and what more mischievous than untaught and ungoverned youth? See what came of Dinah's gadding: young women must learn to be *chaste, keepers at home;* these properties are put together, Tit. 2:5, for those that are not keepers at home expose their chastity. Dinah went abroad to look about her; but, if she had looked about her as she ought, she would not have fallen into this snare. Note, The beginning of sin is as the letting forth of water. How great a matter does a little fire kindle! We should therefore carefully avoid all occasions of sin and approaches to it. 3. The court Shechem made to her, after he had defiled her. This was fair and commendable, and made the best of what was bad; he loved her (not as Amnon, 2 Sa. 13:15), and he engaged his father to make a match for him with her, *v.* 4. 4. The tidings brought to poor Jacob, *v.* 5. As soon as his children grew up they began to be a grief to him. Let not godly parents, that are lamenting the miscarriages of their children, think their case singular or unprecedented. The good man *held his peace,* as one astonished, that knows not what to say: or he said nothing, for fear of saying amiss, as David (Ps. 39:1, 2); he smothered his resentments, lest, if he had suffered them to break out, they should have transported him into any decencies. Or, it should seem, he had left the management of his affairs very much (too much I doubt) to his sons, and he would do nothing without them: or, at least, he knew they would make him uneasy if he did, they having shown themselves, of late, upon all occasions, bold, forward, and assuming. Note, Things never go well when the authority of a parent runs low in a family. Let every man *bear rule in his own house, and have his children in subjection with all gravity.*

Verses 6–17

Jacob's sons, when they heard of the injury done to Dinah, showed a very great resentment of it, influenced perhaps rather by jealousy for the honour of their family than by a sense of virtue. Many are concerned at the shamefulness of sin that never lay to heart the sinfulness of it. It is here called *folly in Israel* (*v.* 7), according to the language of after-times; for Israel was not yet a people, but a family only. Note, 1. Uncleanness is folly; for it sacrifices the favour of God, peace of conscience, and all the soul can pretend to that is sacred and honourable, to a base and brutish lust. 2. This folly is most shameful in *Israel,* in a family of Israel, where God is known and worshipped, as he was in Jacob's tents, by the name of *the God of Israel.* Folly in Israel is scandalous indeed. 3. It is a good thing to have sin stamped with a bad name: uncleanness is here proverbially called *folly in Israel,* 2 Sa. 13:12. Dinah is here called *Jacob's daughter,* for warning to all the daughters of Israel, that they betray not themselves to this folly.

Hamor came to treat with Jacob himself, but he turns him over to his sons; and here we have a particular account of the treaty, in which, it is a shame to say, the Canaanites were more honest than the Israelites.

I. Hamor and Shechem fairly propose this match, in order to a coalition in trade. Shechem is deeply in love with Dinah; he will have her upon any terms, *v.* 11, 12. His father not only consents, but solicits for him, and gravely insists upon the advantages that would follow from the union of the families, *v.* 9, 10. He shows no jealousy of Jacob, though he was a stranger, but rather an earnest desire to settle a correspondence with him and his family, making him that generous offer, *The land shall be before you, trade you therein.*

II. Jacob's sons basely pretend to insist upon a coalition in religion, when really they designed nothing less. If Jacob had taken the management of this affair into his own hands, it is probable that he and Hamor would soon have concluded it; but Jacob's sons meditate only revenge, and a strange project they have for the compassing of it — the Shechemites must be circumcised; not to make them holy (they never intended that), but to make them sore, that they might become an easier prey to their sword. 1. The pretence was specious. "It is the honour of Jacob's family that they carry about with them the token of God's covenant with them; and it will be a reproach to those that are thus dignified and distinguished to enter into such a strict alliance with those that are *uncircumcised* (*v.* 14); and therefore, *if you will be circumcised, then we will become one people with you,"* *v.* 15, 16. Had they been sincere herein their proposal of these terms would have had in it something commendable; for Israelites should not intermarry with Canaanites, professors with profane; it is a great sin, or at least the cause and inlet of a great deal, and has often been of pernicious consequence. The interest we have in any persons, and the hold we have of them, should be wisely improved by us, to bring them to the love and practice of religion *(He that winneth souls is wise);* but then we must not, like Jacob's sons, think it enough to persuade them to submit to the external rites of religion, but must endeavour to convince them of its reasonableness, and to bring them acquainted with the power of it. 2. The intention was malicious, as appears by the sequel of the story; all they aimed at was to prepare them for the day of slaughter. Note, Bloody designs have often been covered, and carried on, with a pretence of religion; thus they have been accomplished most plausibly and most securely: but this dissembled piety is, doubtless, double iniquity. Religion is never more injured, nor are God's sacraments more profaned, than when they are thus used for a cloak of maliciousness. Nay, if Jacob's sons had not had this bloody design, I do not see how they could justify their offering the sacred sign of circumcision, the seal of God's covenant, to these devoted Canaanites, who had no part nor lot in the matter. Those had no right to the seal that had no right to the promise. *It is not meet to take the children's bread, and cast it to dogs:* but Jacob's sons valued not this, while they could make it serve their turn.

Verses 18–24

Here, 1. Hamor and Shechem gave consent themselves to be circumcised, *v.* 18, 19. To this perhaps they were moved, not only by the strong desire they had to bring about this match, but by what they might have heard of the sacred and honourable intentions of this sign, in the family of Abraham, which, it is probable, they had some confused notions of, and of the promises confirmed by it, which made them the more desirous to incorporate with the family of Jacob, Zec. 8:23. Note, Many who know little of religion, yet know so much of it as makes them willing to join themselves with those that are religious. Again, If a man would take upon him a form of religion to gain a good wife, much more should we embrace the power of it to gain the favour of a good God, even circumcise our hearts to love him, and, as Shechem here, *not defer to do the thing.* 2. They gained the consent of the men of their city, Jacob's sons requiring that they also should be circumcised. (1.) They themselves had great influences upon them by their command and example. Note, Religion would greatly prevail if those in authority, who, like Shechem, are more honourable than their neighbours, would appear forward and zealous for it. (2.) They urged an argument which was very cogent (*v.* 23), *Shall not their cattle and their substance be ours?* They observed that Jacob's sons were industrious thriving people, and promised themselves and their neighbours advantage by an alliance with them; it would improve ground and trade, and bring money into their country. Now, [1.] It was bad enough to marry upon this principle: yet we see covetousness the greatest matchmaker in the world, and nothing designed so much, with many, as the laying of house to house, and field to field, without regard had to any other consideration. [2.] It was worse to be circumcised upon this principle. The Shechemites will embrace the religion of Jacob's family only in hopes of interesting themselves thereby in the riches of that family. Thus there are many with whom gain is godliness, and who are more governed and influenced by their secular interest than by any principle of their religion.

Verses 25–31

Here, we have Simeon and Levi, two of Jacob's sons, young men not much above twenty years old, cutting the throats of the Shechemites, and thereby breaking the heart of their good father.

I. Here is the barbarous murder of the Shechemites. Jacob himself was used to the sheep-hook, but his sons had got swords by their sides, as if they had been the seed of Esau, who was to live by his sword; we have them here,

1. Slaying the inhabitants of Shechem — *all the males,* Hamor and Shechem particularly, with whom they had been treating in a friendly manner but the other day, yet with a design upon their lives. Some think that all Jacob's sons, when they wheedled the Shechemites to be circumcised, designed to take advantage of their soreness, and to rescue Dinah from among them; but that Simeon and Levi, not content with that, would themselves avenge the injury — and they did it with a witness. Now, (1.) It cannot be denied but that God was righteous in it. Had the Shechemites been circumcised in obedience to any command of God, their circumcision would have been their protection; but when they submitted to that sacred rite only to serve a turn, to please their prince and to enrich themselves, it was just with God to bring this upon them. Note, As nothing secures us better than true religion, so nothing exposes us more than religion only pretended to. (2.) But Simeon and Levi were most unrighteous. [1.] It was true that Shechem had *wrought folly against Israel,* in defiling Dinah; but it ought to have been considered how far Dinah herself had been accessory to it. Had Shechem abused her in her own mother's tent, it would have been another matter; but she went upon his ground, and perhaps by her indecent carriage had struck the spark which began the fire: when we are severe upon the sinner we ought to consider who was the tempter. [2.] It was true that Shechem had done ill; but he was endeavouring to atone for it, and was as honest and honourable, *ex post facto — after the deed,* as the case would admit: it was not the case of the Levite's concubine that was abused to death; nor does he justify what he has done, but courts a reconciliation upon any terms. [3.] It was true that Shechem had done ill; but what was that to all the Shechemites? Does one man sin, and will they be wroth with all the town? Must the innocent fall with the guilty? This was barbarous indeed. [4.] But that which above all aggravated the cruelty was the most perfidious treachery that was in it. The Shechemites had submitted to their conditions, and had done that upon which they had promised to become one people with them (*v.* 16); yet they act as sworn enemies to those to whom they had lately become sworn friends, making as light of their covenant as they did of the laws of humanity. And are these the sons of Israel? *Cursed be their anger, for it was fierce.* [5.] This also added to the crime, that they made a holy ordinance of God subservient to their wicked design, so making that odious; as if it were not enough for them to shame themselves and their family, they bring a reproach upon that honourable badge of their religion; justly would it be called a bloody ordinance.

2. Seizing the prey of Shechem, and plundering the town. They rescued Dinah (*v.* 26), and, if that was all they came for, they might have done that without blood, as appears by their own showing (*v.* 17); but they aimed at the spoil; and, though Simeon and Levi only were the murderers, yet it is intimated that others of the sons of Jacob *came upon the slain and spoiled the city* (*v.* 27), and so became accessory to the murder. In them it was manifest injustice; yet here we may observe the righteousness of God. The Shechemites were willing to gratify the sons of Jacob by submitting to the penance of circumcision, upon this principle, *Shall not their cattle and their substance be ours?* (*v.* 23), and see what was the issue; instead of making themselves masters of the wealth of Jacob's family, Jacob's family become masters of their wealth. Note, Those who unjustly grasp at that which is another's justly lose that which is their own.

II. Here is Jacob's resentment of this bloody deed of Simeon and Levi, *v.* 30. Two things he bitterly complains of: — 1. The reproach they had brought upon him thereby: *You have troubled me,* put me into a disorder, for you have made me *to stink among the inhabitants of the land,* that is, "You have rendered me and my family odious among them. What will they say of us and our religion? We shall be looked upon as the most perfidious barbarous people in the world." Note, The gross misconduct of wicked children is the grief and shame of their godly parents. Children should be the joy of their parents; but wicked children are their trouble, sadden their hearts, break their spirits, and make them go mourning from day to day. Children should be an ornament to their parents; but wicked children are their reproach, and are as dead flies in the pot of ointment: but let such children know that, if they repent not, the grief they have caused to their parents, and the damage religion has sustained in its reputation through them, will come into the account and be reckoned for. 2. The ruin they had exposed him to. What could be expected, but that the Canaanites, who were numerous and formidable, would confederate against him, and he and his little family would become an easy prey to them? *I shall be destroyed, I and my house.* If all the Shechemites must be destroyed for the offence of one, why not all the Israelites for the offence of two? Jacob knew indeed that God had promised to preserve and perpetuate his house; but he might justly fear that these vile practices of his children would amount to a forfeiture, and cut off the entail. Note, When sin is in the house, there is reason to fear ruin at the door. The tender parents foresee those bad consequences of sin which the wicked children have no dread of. One would think this should have made them to relent, and they should have humbled themselves to their good father, and begged his pardon; but, instead of this, they justify themselves, and give him this insolent reply, *Should he deal with our sister as with a harlot?* No, he should not; but, if he do, must they be their own avengers? Will nothing less than so many lives, and the ruin of a whole city, serve to atone for an abuse done to one foolish girl? By their question they tacitly reflect upon their father, as if he would have been content to let them deal with his daughter as with a harlot. Note, It is common for those who run into one extreme to reproach and censure those who keep the mean as if they ran into the other. Those who condemn the rigour of revenge shall be misrepresented, as if they countenanced and justified the offence.

CHAPTER 35

In this chapter we have three communions and three funerals. I. Three communions between God and Jacob. 1. God ordered Jacob to Beth-el; and, in obedience to that order, he purged his house of idols, and prepared for that journey (*v.* 1–5). 2. Jacob built an altar at Beth-el, to the honour of God that had appeared to him, and in performance of his vow (*v.* 6, 7). 3. God appeared to him again, and confirmed the change of his name and covenant with him (*v.* 9–13), of which appearance Jacob made a grateful acknowledgment (*v.* 14, 15). II. Three funerals. 1. Deborah's (*v.* 8). 2. Rachel's (*v.* 16–20). 3. Isaac's (*v.* 27–29). Here is also Rueben's incest (*v.* 22), and an account of Jacob's sons (*v.* 23–26).

Verses 1–5

Here, I. God reminds Jacob of his vow at Beth-el, and sends him thither to perform it, v 1. Jacob had said in the day of his distress, *If I come again in peace, this stone shall be God's house, ch.* 28:22. God had performed his part of the bargain, and had given Jacob more than bread to eat and raiment to put on — he had got an estate, and had become two bands; but, it should seem, he had forgotten his vow, or at least had too long deferred the performance of it. Seven or eight years it was now since he came to Canaan; he had purchased ground there, and had built an altar in remembrance of God's last appearance to him when he called him *Israel* (*ch.* 33:19, 20); but still Beth-el is forgotten. Note, Time is apt to wear out the sense of mercies and the impressions made upon us by them; it should not be so, but so it is. God had exercised Jacob with a very sore affliction in his family (*ch.* 34), to see if this would bring his vow to his remembrance, and put him upon the performance of it, but it had not this effect; therefore God comes himself and puts him in mind of it: *Arise, go to Beth-el.* Note, 1. As many as God loves he will remind of neglected duties, one way or other, by conscience or by providences. 2. When we have vowed a vow to God, it is best not to defer the payment of it (Eccles. 5:4), yet better late than never. God bade him go to Beth-el and dwell there, that is, not only go himself, but take his family with him, that they might join with him in his devotions. Note, In Beth-el, the house of God, we should desire to dwell, Ps. 27:4. That should be our home, not our inn. God reminds him not expressly of his vow, but of the occasion of it: *When thou fleddest from the face of Esau.* Note, The remembrance of former afflictions should bring to mind the workings of our souls under them, Ps. 66:13, 14.

II. Jacob commands his household to prepare for this solemnity; not only for the journey and remove, but for the religious services that were to be performed, *v.* 2, 3.

Note, 1. Before solemn ordinances, there must be solemn preparation. *Wash you, make you clean,* and then *come, and let us reason together,* Isa. 1:16–18. 2. Masters of families should use their authority for the promoting of religion in their families. Not only we, but our houses also, should serve the Lord, Jos. 24:15. Observe the commands he gives his household, like Abraham, *ch.* 18:19. (1.) They must *put away the strange gods.* Strange gods in Jacob's family! Strange things indeed! Could such a family, that was taught the good knowledge of the Lord, admit them? Could such a master, to whom God had appeared twice, and oftener, connive at them? Doubtless this was his infirmity. Note, Those that are good themselves cannot always have those about them so good as they should be. In those families where there is a face of religion, and an altar to God, yet many times there is much amiss, and more strange gods than one would suspect. In Jacob's family, Rachel had her *teraphim,* which, it is to be feared, she secretly made some superstitious use of. The captives of Shechem brought their gods along with them, and perhaps Jacob's sons took some with the plunder. However they came by them, now they must *put them away.* (2.) They must be clean, and *change their garments;* they must observe a due decorum, and make the best appearance they could. Simeon and Levi had their hands full of blood, it concerned them particularly to wash, and to put off their garments that were so stained. These were but ceremonies, signifying the purification and change of the heart. What are clean clothes, and new clothes, without a clean heart, and a new heart? Dr. Lightfoot, by their *being clean,* or *washing* themselves, understands Jacob's admission of the proselytes of Shechem and Syria into his religion by baptism, because circumcision had become odious. 3. They must go with him to Bethel, *v.* 3. Note, Masters of families, when they go up to the house of God, should bring their families with them.

III. His family surrendered all they had that was idolatrous or superstitious, *v.* 4. Perhaps, if Jacob had called for them sooner, they would sooner have parted with them, being convicted by their own consciences of the vanity of them. Note, Sometimes attempts for reformation succeed better than one could have expected, and people are not so obstinate against them as we feared. Jacob's servants, and even the retainers of his family, gave him all the strange gods, and the ear-rings they wore, either as charms or to the honour of their gods; they parted with all. Note, Reformation is not sincere if it be not universal. We hope they parted with them cheerfully, and without reluctance, as Ephraim did, when he said, *What have I to do any more with idols?* (Hos. 14:8), or that people that said to their idols, *Get you hence,* Isa. 30:22. Jacob took care to bury their images, we may suppose in some place unknown to them, that they might not afterwards find them and return to them. Note, We must be wholly separated from our sins, as we are from those that are dead and buried out of our sight, cast them *to the moles and the bats,* Isa. 2:20.

IV. He removes without molestation from Shechem to Bethel, *v.* 5. *The terror of God was upon the cities.* Though the Canaanites were much exasperated against the sons of Jacob for their barbarous usage of the Shechemites, yet they were so restrained by a divine power that they could not take this fair opportunity, which now offered itself, when they were upon their march, to avenge their neighbours' quarrel. Note, The way of duty is the way of safety. While there was sin in Jacob's house, he was afraid of his neighbours; but now that the strange gods were put away, and they were all going together to Bethel, his neighbours were afraid of him. When we are about God's work, we are under special protection. God is with us, while we are with him; and, if he be for us, who can be against us? See Ex. 34:24, *No man shall desire thy land, when thou goest up to appear before the Lord.* God governs the world more by secret terrors on men's minds than we are aware of.

Verses 6–15

Jacob and his retinue having safely arrived at Bethel, we are here told what passed there.

I. There he built an altar (*v.* 7), and no doubt offered sacrifice upon it, perhaps the tenth of his cattle, according to his vow, *I will give the tenth unto thee.* With these sacrifices he joined praises for former mercies, particularly that which the sight of the place brought afresh to his remembrance; and he added prayers for the continuance of God's favour to him and his family. And he called the place (that is, *the altar) El-beth-el, the God of Bethel.* As, when he made a thankful acknowledgment of the honour God had lately done him in calling him *Israel,* he worshipped God by the name of *El-elohe Israel;* so, now that he was making a grateful recognition of God's former favour to him at Bethel, he worships God by the name of *El-beth-el, the God of Bethel,* because there God appeared to him. Note, The comfort which the saints have in holy ordinances is not so much from *Bethel, the house of God,* as from *El-beth-el, the God of the house.* The ordinances are but empty things if we do not meet with God in them.

II. There he buried Deborah, Rebekah's nurse, *v.* 8. We have reason to think that Jacob, after he came to Canaan, while his family dwelt near Shechem, went himself (it is likely, often) to visit his father Isaac at Hebron. Rebekah probably was dead, but her old nurse (of whom mention is made *ch.* 24:59) survived her, and Jacob took her to his family, to be a companion to his wives, her country-women, and an instructor to his children; while they were at Beth-el, she died, and died lamented, so much lamented that the oak under which she was buried was called *Allon-bachuth, the oak of weeping.* Note, 1. Old servants in a family, that have in their time been faithful and useful, ought to be respected. Honour was done to this nurse, at her death, by Jacob's family, though she was not related to them, and though she was aged. Former services, in such a case, must be remembered. 2. We do not know where death may meet us; perhaps at Beth-el, the house of God. Therefore let us be always ready. 3. Family-afflictions may come even when family-reformation and religion are on foot. Therefore rejoice with trembling.

III. There God appeared to him (*v.* 9), to own his altar, to answer to the name by which he had called him, *The God of Bethel* (*v.* 7), and to comfort him under his affliction, *v.* 8. Note, God will appear to those in a way of grace that attend on him in a way of duty. Here, 1. He confirmed the change of his name, *v.* 10. It was done before by the angel that wrestled with him (*ch.* 32:28), and here it was ratified by the divine Majesty, or *Shechinah,* that appeared to him. There it was to encourage him against the fear of Esau, here against the fear of the Canaanites. Who can be too hard for Israel, a prince with God? It is below those who are thus dignified to droop and despond. 2. He renewed and ratified the covenant with him, by the name *El-shaddai. I am God Almighty, God all-sufficient* (*v.* 11), able to make good the promise in due time, and to support thee and provide for thee in the mean time. Two things are promised him which we have met with often before: — (1.) That he should be the father of a great nation, great in honour and power — *a company of nations shall be of thee* (every tribe of Israel was a nation, and all the twelve a company of nations), great in honour and power — *kings shall come out of thy loins.* (2.) That he should be the master of a good land (*v.* 12), described by the grantees, Abraham and Isaac, to whom it was promised, not by the occupants, the Canaanites in whose possession it now was. The land that was given to Abraham and Isaac is here entailed on Jacob and his seed. He shall not have children without an estate, which is often the case of the poor, nor an estate without children, which is often the grief of the rich; but both. These two promises had a spiritual signification, of which we may suppose Jacob himself had some notion, though not so clear and distinct as we now have; for, without doubt, Christ is the promised seed, and heaven is the promised land; the former is the foundation, and the latter the top-stone, of all God's favours. 3. He then went up from him, or *from over him,* in some visible display of glory, which had hovered over him while he talked with him, *v.* 13. Note, The sweetest communions the saints have with God in this world are short and transient, and soon have an end. Our vision of God in heaven will be everlasting; there we shall be ever with the Lord; it is not so here.

IV. There Jacob erected a memorial of this, *v.* 14. 1. He set up a pillar. When he was going to Padan-aram, he set up for a pillar that stone on which he had laid his head. This was agreeable enough to his low condition and his hasty flight; but now he took time to erect one more stately, more distinguishable and durable, probably placing that stone in it. In token of his intending it for a sacred memorial of his communion with God, he poured oil and the other ingredients of a drink-offering upon it. His vow was, *This stone shall be God's house,* that is, shall be set up for his honour, as houses to the praise of their builders; and here he performs it, transferring it to God by anointing it. 2. He confirmed the name he had formerly given to the place (*v.* 15), *Beth-el, the house of God.* Yet this very place afterwards lost the honour of its name, and became *Beth-aven, a house of iniquity;* for here it was that Jeroboam set up one of his calves. It is impossible for the best man to entail upon a place so much as the profession and form of religion.

Verses 16–20

We have here the story of the death of Rachel, the beloved wife of Jacob. 1. She fell in travail by the way, not able to reach to Bethlehem, the next town, though they were near it; so suddenly does pain sometimes come upon a woman in travail, which she cannot escape, or put off. We may suppose Jacob had soon a tent up, convenient enough for her reception. 2. Her pains were violent. She had hard labour, harder than usual: this was the effect of sin, *ch.* 3:16. Note, Human life begins with sorrow, and the roses of its joy are surrounded with thorns. 3. The midwife encouraged her, *v.* 17. No doubt she had her midwife with her, ready at hand, yet that would not secure her. Rachel had said, when she bore Joseph, *God shall add another son,* which now the midwife remembers, and tells her her words were made good. Yet this did not avail to keep up her spirits; unless God command away fear, no one else can. He only says as one having authority, *Fear not.* We are apt, in extreme perils, to comfort ourselves and our friends with the hopes of a temporal deliverance, in which we may be disappointed; we had better found our comforts on that which cannot fail us, the hope of eternal life. 4. Her travail was to the life of the child, but to her own death. Note, Though the pains and perils of childbearing were introduced by sin, yet they have sometimes been fatal to very holy women, who, though not saved in childbearing, are saved through it with an everlasting salvation. Rachel had passionately said, *Give me children, or else I die;* and now that she had children (for this was her second) she died. Her dying is here called *the departing of her soul.* Note, The death of the body is but the departure of the soul to the world of spirits. 5. Her dying lips called her new-born son *Ben-oni, The son of my sorrow.* And many a son, not born in such hard labour, yet proves the son of his parent's sorrow, and the heaviness of her that bore him. Children are enough the sorrow of their poor mothers in the breeding, bearing, and nursing of them; they should therefore, when they grow up, study to be their joy, and so, if possible, to make them some amends. But Jacob, because he would not renew the sorrowful remembrance of the mother's death every time he called his son by his name, changed his name, and called him *Benjamin, The son of my right hand;* that is, "very dear to me, set on my right hand for a blessing, the support of my age, like the staff in my right hand." 6. Jacob buried her near the place where she died. As she died in child-bed, it was convenient to bury her quickly; and therefore he did not bring her to the burying-place of his family. If the soul be at rest after death, it matters little where the body lies. In the place where the tree falls, there let it be. No mention is made of the mourning that was at her death, because that might easily be taken for granted. Jacob, no doubt, was a true mourner. Note, Great afflictions sometimes befal us immediately after great comforts. Lest Jacob should be lifted up with the visions of the Almighty with which he was honoured, this was sent as a thorn in the flesh to humble him. Those that enjoy the favours peculiar to the children of God must yet expect the troubles that are common to the children of men. Deborah, who, had she lived, would have been a comfort to Rachel in her extremity, died but a little before. Note, When death comes into a family, it often strikes double. God by it speaks once, yea, twice. The Jewish writers say, "The death of Deborah and Rachel was to expiate the murder of the Shechemites, occasioned by Dinah, a daughter of the family." 7. Jacob set up a pillar upon her grave, so that it was known, long after, to be Rachel's sepulchre (1 Sa. 10:2), and Providence so ordered it that this place afterwards fell in the lot of Benjamin. Jacob set up a pillar in remembrance of his joys (*v.* 14), and here he sets up one in remembrance of his sorrows; for, as it may be of use to ourselves to keep both in mind, so it may be of use to others to transmit the memorials of both: the church, long afterwards, owned that what God said to Jacob at Bethel, both by his word and by his rod, he intended for their instruction (Hos. 12:4), *There he spoke with us.*

Verses 21–29

Here is, 1. Jacob's removal, *v.* 21. He also, as his fathers, sojourned in the land of promise as in a strange country, and was not long in a place. Immediately after the story of Rachel's death he is here called *Israel* (*v.* 21, 22), and not often so afterwards: the Jews say, "The historian does him this honour here because he bore that affliction with such admirable patience and submission to Providence." Note, Those are Israel's indeed, princes with God, that support the government of their own passions. He that has this rule over his own spirit is better than the mighty. Israel, a prince with God, yet dwells in tents; the city is reserved for him in the other world. 2. The sin of Reuben. A piece of abominable wickedness it was that he was guilty of (*v.* 22), that very sin which the apostle says (1 Cor 5:1) is not so much as named among the Gentiles, *that one should have his father's wife.* It is said to have been *when Israel dwelt in that land;* as if he were then absent from his family, which might be the unhappy occasion of these disorders. Though perhaps Bilhah was the greater criminal, and it is probable was abandoned by Jacob for it, yet Reuben's crime was so provoking that, for it, he lost his birthright and blessing, *ch.* 49:4. The first-born is not always the best, nor the most promising. This was Reuben's sin, but it was Jacob's affliction; and what a sore affliction it was is intimated in a little compass, *and Israel heard it.* No more is said — that is enough; he heard it with the utmost grief and shame, horror and displeasure. Reuben thought to conceal it, that his father should never hear of it; but those that promise themselves secresy in sin are generally disappointed; a bird of the air carries the voice. 3. A complete list of the sons of Jacob, now that Benjamin the youngest was born. This is the first time we have the names of these heads of the twelve tribes together; afterwards we find them very often spoken of and enumerated, even to the end of the Bible, Rev. 7:4; 21:12. 4. The visit which Jacob made to his father Isaac at Hebron. We may suppose he had visited him before since his return, for he *sorely longed after his father's house;* but never, till now, brought his family to settle with him, or near him, *v.* 27. Probably he did this now upon the death of Rebekah, by which Isaac was left solitary, and not disposed to marry again. 5. The age and death of Isaac are here recorded, though it appears, by computation, that he died not till many years after Joseph was sold into Egypt, and much about the time that he was preferred there. Isaac, a mild quiet man, lived the longest of all the patriarchs, for he was 180 years old; Abraham was but 175. Isaac lived about forty years after he had made his will, *ch.* 27:2. We shall not die an hour the sooner, but abundantly the better, for our timely setting our heart and house in order. Particular notice is taken of the amicable agreement of Esau and Jacob, in solemnizing their father's funeral (*v.* 29), to show how wonderfully God had changed Esau's mind since he vowed his brother's murder immediately after his father's death, *ch.* 27:41. Note, God has many ways of preventing bad men from doing the mischief they intended; he can either tie their hands or turn their hearts.

CHAPTER 36

In this chapter we have an account of the posterity of Esau, who, from him, were called Edomites, that Esau who sold his birthright, and lost his blessing, and was not loved of God as Jacob was. Here is a brief register kept of his family for some generations. 1. Because he was the son of Isaac, for whose sake this honour is put upon him. 2. Because the Edomites were neighbours to Israel, and their genealogy would be of use to give light to the following stories of what passed between them. 3. It is to show the performance of the promise to Abraham, that he should be "the father of many nations," and of that answer which Rebekah had from the oracle she consulted, "Two nations are in thy womb," and of the blessing of Isaac, "Thy dwelling shall be the fatness of the earth." We have here, I. Esau's wives (*v.* 1–5). II. His remove to mount Seir (*v.* 6–8). III. The names of his sons (*v.* 9–14). IV. The dukes who descended of his sons (*v.* 15–19). V. The dukes of the Horites (*v.* 20–30). VI. The kings and dukes of Edom (*v.* 31–43). Little more is recorded than their names, because the history of those that were out of the church (though perhaps it might have been serviceable in politics) would have been of little use in divinity. It is in the church that the memorable instances are found of special grace, and special providence; for that is the enclosure, the rest is common. This chapter is abridged, 1 Chr. 1:35, etc.

Verses 1–8

Observe here, 1. Concerning Esau himself, *v.* 1. He is called *Edom* (and again, *v.* 8), that name by which was perpetuated the remembrance of the foolish bargain he made, when he sold his birthright for *that red, that red pottage.* The very mention of that name is enough to intimate the reason why his family is turned off with such a short account. Note, If men do a wrong thing they must thank themselves, when it is, long afterwards, remembered against them to their reproach. 2. Concerning his wives, and the children they bore him in the land of Canaan. He had three wives, and, by them all, but five sons: many a one has more by one wife. God in his providence often disappoints those who take indirect courses to build up a family; yet here the promise prevailed, and Esau's family was built up. 3. Concerning his removal to mount Seir, which was the country God had given him for a possession, when he reserved Canaan for the seed of Jacob. God owns it, long afterwards: *I gave to Esau mount Seir* (Deu. 2:5; Jos. 24:4), which was the reason why the Edomites must not be disturbed in their possession. Those that have not a right by promise, such as Jacob had, to Canaan, may have a very good title by providence to their estates, such as Esau had to mount Seir. Esau had begun to settle among his wives' relations, in Seir, before Jacob came from Padan-aram, *ch.* 32:3. Isaac, it is likely, had sent him thither (as Abraham in his life-time had sent the sons of the concubines from Isaac his son into the east country, *ch.* 25:6), that Jacob might have the clearer way made for him to the possession of the promised land. During the life of Isaac, however, Esau had probably still some effects remaining in Canaan; but, after his death, he wholly withdrew to mount Seir, took with him what came to his share of his father's personal estate, and left Canaan to Jacob, not only because he had the promise of it, but because Esau perceived that if they should continue to thrive as they had begun there would not be room for both. *Thus dwelt Esau in Mount Seir, v.* 8. Note, Whatever opposition may be made, God's word will be accomplished, and even those that have opposed it will see themselves, some time or other, under a necessity of yielding to it, and acquiescing in it. Esau had struggled for Canaan, but now he tamely retires to mount Seir; for God's counsels shall certainly stand, concerning the times before appointed, and the bounds of our habitation.

Verses 9–19

Observe here, 1. That only the names of Esau's sons and grandsons are recorded, only their names, not their history; for it is the church that Moses preserves the records of, not the record of those that are without. Those elders that lived by faith alone obtained a good report. It is Sion that produces men of renown, not Seir, Ps. 87:5. Nor does the genealogy go any further than the third and fourth generation; the very names of all after are buried in oblivion. It is only the pedigree of the Israelites, who were to be the heirs of Canaan, and of whom were to come the promised seed, and the holy seed, that is drawn out to any length, as far as there was occasion for it, even of all the tribes till Canaan was divided among them, and of the royal line till Christ came. 2. That these sons and grandsons of Esau are called *dukes, v.* 15–19. Probably they were military commanders, dukes, or captains, that had soldiers under them; for Esau and his family lived *by the sword, ch.* 27:40. Note, Titles of honour have been more ancient out of the church than in it. Esau's sons were dukes when Jacob's sons were but plain shepherds, *ch.* 47:3. This is not a reason why such titles should not be used among Christians; but it is a reason why men should not overvalue themselves, or others, for the sake of them. There is an honour that comes from God, and a name in his house that is infinitely more valuable. Edomites may be dukes with men, but Israelites indeed are made to our God kings and priests. 3. We may suppose those dukes had numerous families of children and servants that were their dukedoms. God promised to multiply Jacob, and to enrich him; yet Esau increases, and is enriched first. Note, It is no new thing for the men of this world to be full of children, and to have their bellies too *filled with hidden treasures,* Ps. 17:14. God's promise to Jacob began to work late, but the effect of it remained longer, and it had its complete accomplishment in the spiritual Israel.

Verses 20–30

In the midst of this genealogy of the Edomites here is inserted the genealogy of the Horites, those Canaanites, or Hittites (compare *ch.* 26:34), that were the natives of Mount Seir. Mention is made of them, *ch.* 14:6, and of their interest in Mount Seir, before the Edomites took possession of it, Deu. 2:12, 22. This comes in here, not only to give light to the story, but to be a standing reflection upon the Edomites for intermarrying with them, by which, it is probable, they learned their way, and corrupted themselves. Esau having sold his birthright, and lost his blessing, and entered into alliance with the Hittites, his posterity and the sons of Seir are here reckoned together. Note, Those that treacherously desert God's church are justly numbered with those that were never in it; apostate Edomites stand on the same ground with accursed Horites. Particular notice is taken of one Anah who fed the asses of Zibeon his father (*v.* 24), and yet is called *duke Anah, v.* 29. Note, Those that expect to rise high should begin low. An honourable descent should not keep men from an honest employment, nor a mean employment hinder any man's preferment. This Anah was not only industrious in his business, but ingenious too, and successful; for he found *mules,* or (as some read it) *waters, hot-baths,* in the wilderness. Those that are diligent in their business sometimes find more advantages than they expected.

Verses 31–43

By degrees, it seems, the Edomites wormed out the Horites, obtained full possession of the country, and had a government of their own. 1. They were ruled by kings, who governed the whole country, and seem to have come to the throne by election, and not by lineal descent; so bishop Patrick observes. These kings reigned in *Edom before there reigned any king over the children of Israel,* that is, before Moses's time, for *he was king in Jeshurun, v.* 3. God had lately promised *Jacob that kings should come out of his loins* (*ch.* 35:11), yet Esau's blood becomes royal long before any of Jacob's did. Note, In external prosperity and honour, the children of the covenant are often cast behind, and those that are out of covenant get the start. The triumphing of the wicked may be quick, but it is short; soon ripe, and as soon rotten: but the products of the promise, though they are slow, are sure and lasting; *at the end it shall speak, and not lie.* We may suppose it was a great trial to the faith of God's Israel to hear of the pomp and power of the kings of Edom, while they were bond-slaves in Egypt; but those that look for great things from God must be content to wait for them; God's time is the best time. 2. They were afterwards governed by dukes, again here named, who, I suppose, ruled all at the same time in several places in the country. Either they set up this form of government in conformity to the Horites, who had used it (*v.* 29), or God's providence reduced them to it, as some conjecture, to correct them for their unkindness to Israel, in refusing them a passage though their country, Num. 20:18. Note, When power is abused, it is just with God to weaken it, by turning it into divers channels. *For the transgression of a land, many are the princes thereof.* Sin brought Edom from kings to dukes, from crowns to coronets. We read of the dukes of Edom (Ex. 15:15), yet, long afterwards, of their kings again. 3. Mount Seir is called *the land of their possession, v.* 43. While the Israelites dwelt in the house of bondage, and their Canaan was only the land of promise, the Edomites dwelt in their own habitations, and Seir was in their possession. Note, The children of this world have their all in hand, and nothing in hope (Lu. 16:25); while the children of God have their all in hope, and next to nothing in hand. But, all things considered, it is better to have Canaan in promise than mount Seir in possession.

CHAPTER 37

At this chapter begins the story of Joseph, who, in every subsequent chapter but one to the end of this book, makes the greatest figure. He was Jacob's eldest son by his beloved wife Rachel, born, as many eminent men were, of a mother that had been long barren. His story is so remarkably divided between his humiliation and his exaltation that we cannot avoid seeing something of Christ in it, who was first humbled and then exalted, and, in many instances, so as to answer the type of Joseph. It also shows the lot of Christians, who must through many tribulations enter into the kingdom. In this chapter we have, I. The malice his brethren bore against him. They hated him, 1. Because he informed his father of their wickedness (*v.* 1, 2). 2. Because his father loved him (*v.* 3, 4). 3. Because he dreamed of his dominion over them (*v.* 5–11). II. The mischiefs his brethren designed and did to him. 1. The kind visit he made them gave an opportunity (*v.* 12–17). 2. They designed to slay him, but determined to starve him (*v.* 18–24). 3. They changed their purpose, and sold him for a slave (*v.* 25–28). 4. They made their father believe that he was torn in pieces (*v.* 29–35). 5. He was sold into Egypt to Potiphar (*v.* 36). And all this was working together for good.

Verses 1–4

Moses has no more to say of the Edomites, unless as they happen to fall in Israel's way; but now applies himself closely to the story of Jacob's family: *These are the generations of Jacob.* His is not a bare barren genealogy as that of Esau (*ch.* 36:1), but a memorable useful history. Here is, 1. Jacob a sojourner with his father Isaac, who has yet living, *v.* 1. We shall never be at home, till we come to heaven. 2. Joseph, a shepherd, *feeding the flock with his brethren, v.* 2. Though he was his father's darling, yet he was not brought up in idleness or delicacy. Those do not truly love their children that do not inure them to business, and labour, and mortification. The fondling of children is with good reason commonly called the spoiling of them. Those that are trained up to do nothing are likely to be good for nothing. 3. Joseph beloved by his father (*v.* 3), partly for his dear mother's sake that was dead, and partly for his own sake, because he was the greatest comfort of his old age; probably he waited on him, and was more observant of him than the rest of his sons; he was the *son of the ancient* so some; that is, when he was a child, he was as grave and discreet as if he had been an old man, a child, but not childish. Jacob proclaimed his affection to him by dressing him finer than the rest of his children: He *made him a coat of divers colours,* which probably was significant of further honors intended him. Note, Though those children are happy that have that in them which justly recommends them to their parents' particular love, yet it is the prudence of parents not to make a difference between one child and another, unless there be a great and manifest cause given for it by the children's dutifulness or undutifulness; paternal government must be impartial, and managed with a steady hand. 4. Joseph hated by his brethren, (1.) Because his father loved him; when parents make a difference, children soon take notice of it, and it often occasions feuds and quarrels in families. (2.) Because he *brought to his father their evil report.* Jacob's sons did that, when they were from under his eye, which they durst not have done if they had been at home with him; but Joseph gave his father an account of their bad carriage, that he might reprove and restrain them; not as a malicious talebearer, to sow discord, but as a faithful brother, who, when he durst not admonish them himself, represented their faults to one that had authority to admonish them. Note, [1.] It is common for friendly monitors to be looked upon as enemies. Those that hate to be reformed hate those that would reform them, Prov. 9:8. [2.] It is common for those that are beloved of God to be hated by the world; whom Heaven blesses, hell curses. To those to whom God speaks comfortably wicked men will not speak peaceably. It is said here of Joseph, *the lad was with the sons of Bilhah;* some read it, and he was *servant to them,* they made him their drudge.

Verses 5–11

Here, I. Joseph relates the prophetical dreams he had, *v.* 6, 7, 9, 10. Though he was now very young (about seventeen years old), yet he was pious and devout, and well-inclined, and this fitted him for God's gracious discoveries of himself to him. Joseph had a great deal of trouble before him, and therefore God gave him betimes this prospect of his advancement, to support and comfort him under the long and grievous troubles with which he was to be exercised. Thus Christ had a *joy set before him,* and so have Christians. Note, God has ways of preparing his people beforehand for the trials which they cannot foresee, but which he has an eye to in the comforts with which he furnishes them. His dreams were, 1. That his brethren's sheaves all bowed to his, intimating upon what occasion they should be brought to do homage to him, namely, in seeking to him for corn; their empty sheaves should bow to his full one. 2. That the sun, and moon, and eleven stars, did obeisance to him, *v.* 9. Joseph was more of a prophet than a politician, else he would have kept this to himself, when he could not but know that his brethren did already hate him and that this would but the more exasperate them. But, if he told it in his simplicity, yet God directed it for the mortification of his brethren. Observe, Joseph dreamed of his preferment, but he did not dream of his imprisonment. Thus many young people, when they are setting out in the world, think of nothing but prosperity and pleasure, and never dream of trouble.

II. His brethren take it very ill, and are more and more enraged against him (*v.* 8): *Shalt thou indeed reign over us?* See here, 1. How truly they interpreted his dream, that he should reign over them. Those become the expositors of his dream who were enemies to the accomplishment of it, as in Gideon's story (Jdg. 7:13, 14); they perceived that he spoke of them, Mt. 21:45. The event exactly answered to this interpretation, *ch.* 42:6, etc. 2. How scornfully they resented it: *"Shalt thou,* who are but one, *reign over us,* who are many? Thou, who are the youngest, over us who are older?" Note, The reign and dominion of Jesus Christ, our Joseph, have been, and are, despised and striven against by a carnal and unbelieving world, who cannot endure to think that this man should reign over them. The dominion also of the upright, in the morning of the resurrection, is thought of with the utmost disdain.

III. His father gives him a gentle rebuke for it, yet observes the saying, *v.* 10, 11. Probably he checked him for it, to lessen the offence which his brethren would be apt to take at it; yet he took notice of it more than he seemed to do: he insinuated that it was but an idle dream, because his mother was brought in, who had been dead some time since; whereas *the sun, moon, and eleven stars,* signify no more than the whole family that should have a dependence upon him, and be glad to be beholden to him. Note, The faith of God's people in God's promises is often sorely shaken by their misunderstanding the promises and then suggesting the improbabilities that attend the performance; but God is doing his own work, and will do it, whether we understand him aright or no. Jacob, like Mary (Lu. 2:51), kept these things in his heart, and no doubt remembered them long afterwards, when the event answered to the prediction.

Verses 12–22

Here is, I. The kind visit which Joseph, in obedience to his father's command, made to his brethren, who were feeding the flock at Shechem, many miles off. Some suggest that they went thither on purpose, expecting that Joseph would be sent to see them, and that then they should have an opportunity to do him a mischief. However, Joseph and his father had both of them more of the innocence of the dove than of the wisdom of the serpent, else he had never come thus into the hands of those that hated him: but God designed it all for good. See in Joseph an instance, 1. Of dutifulness to his father. Though he was his father's darling, yet he was made, and was willing to be, his father's servant. How readily does he wait his father's orders! *Here I am, v.* 13. Note, Those children that are best beloved by their parents should be most obedient to their parents; and then their love is well-bestowed and well-returned. 2. Of kindness to his brethren. Though he knew they hated him and envied him, yet he made no objections against his father's commands, either from the distance of the place or the danger of the journey, but cheerfully embraced the opportunity of showing his respect to his brethren. Note, It is a very good lesson, though it is learnt with difficulty and rarely practised, *to love those that hate us;* if our relations do not their duty to us, yet we must not be wanting in our duty to them. This is thankworthy. Joseph was sent by his father to Shechem, to see whether his brethren were well there, and whether the country had not risen upon them and destroyed them, in revenge of their barbarous murder of the Shechemites some years before. But Joseph, not finding them there, went to Dothan, which showed that he undertook this journey, not only in obedience to his father (for then he might have returned when he missed them at Shechem, having done what his father told him), but out of love to his brethren, and therefore he sought diligently till he found them. Thus, let brotherly love continue, and let us give proofs of it.

II. The bloody and malicious plot of his brethren against him, who rendered good for evil, and, for his love, were his adversaries. Observe, 1. How deliberate they were in the contrivance of this mischief: when they *saw him afar off, they conspired against him, v.* 18. It was not in a heat, or upon a sudden provocation, that they thought to slay him, but from malice prepense, and in cold blood. Note, Whosoever hateth his brother is a murderer; for he will be one if he have an opportunity, 1 Jn. 3:15. Malice is a most mischievous thing, and is in danger of making bloody work where it is harboured and indulged. The more there is of a project and contrivance in a sin the worse it is; it is bad to do evil, but worse to devise it. 2. How cruel they were in their design; nothing less than his blood would satisfy them: *Come, and let us slay him, v.* 20. Note, The old enmity hunts for the precious life. It is the *blood-thirsty* that *hate the upright* (Prov. 29:10), and it is the blood of the saints that the harlot is drunk with. 3. How scornfully they reproached him for his dreams (*v.* 19): *This dreamer cometh;* and (*v.* 20), *We shall see what will become of his dreams.* This shows what it was that fretted and enraged them. They could not endure to think of doing homage to him; this was what they were plotting to prevent by the murder of him. Note, Men that fret and rage at God's counsels are impiously aiming to defeat them; but they imagine a vain thing, Ps. 2:1–3. God's counsels will stand. 4. How they agreed to keep one another's counsel, and to cover the murder with a lie: *We will say, Some evil beast hath devoured him;* whereas in thus consulting to devour him they proved themselves worse than the most evil beasts; for evil beasts prey not on those of their own kind, but they were tearing a piece of themselves.

III. Reuben's project to deliver him, *v.* 21, 22. Note, God can raise up friends for his people, even among their enemies; for he has all hearts in his hands. Reuben, of all the brothers, had most reason to be jealous of Joseph, for he was the first-born, and so entitled to those distinguishing favours which Jacob was conferring on Joseph; yet he proves his best friend. Reuben's temper seems to have been soft and effeminate, which had betrayed him to the sin of uncleanness; while the temper of the next two brothers, Simeon and Levi, was fierce, which betrayed them to the sin of murder, a sin which Reuben startled at the thought of. Note, Our natural constitution should be guarded against those sins to which it is most inclinable, and improved (as Reuben's here) against those sins to which it is most averse. Reuben made a proposal which they thought would effectually answer their intention of destroying Joseph, and yet which he designed should answer his intention of rescuing Joseph out of their hands and restoring him to his father, probably hoping thereby to recover his father's favour, which he had lately lost; but God overruled all to serve his own purpose of making Joseph an instrument to save much people alive. Joseph was here a type of Christ. Though he was the beloved Son of his Father, and hated by a wicked world, yet the Father sent him out of his bosom to visit us in great humility and love. He came from heaven to earth, to seek and save us; yet then malicious plots were laid against him. He came to his own, and his own not only received him not, but consulted against him: *This is the heir, come let us kill him; Crucify him, crucify him.* This he submitted to, in pursuance of his design to redeem and save us.

Verses 23–30

We have here the execution of their plot against Joseph. 1. They stripped him, each striving to seize the envied coat of many colours, *v.* 23. Thus, in imagination, they degraded him from the birthright, of which perhaps this was the badge, grieving him, affronting their father, and making themselves sport, while they insulted over him. "Now, Joseph, where is the fine coat?" Thus our Lord Jesus was stripped of his seamless coat, and thus his suffering saints have first been industriously divested of their privileges and honours, and then made the off-scouring of all things. 2. They went about to starve him, throwing him into a dry pit, to perish there with hunger and cold, so cruel were their tender mercies, *v.* 24. Note, Where envy reigns pity is banished, and humanity itself is forgotten,

Prov. 27:4. So full of deadly poison is malice that the more barbarous any thing is the more grateful it is. Now Joseph begged for his life, in *the anguish of his soul* (*ch.* 42:21), entreated, by all imaginable endearments, that they would be content with his coat and spare his life. He pleads innocence, relation, affection, submission; he weeps and makes supplication, but all in vain. Reuben alone relents and intercedes for him, *ch.* 42:22. But he cannot prevail to save Joseph from the horrible pit, in which they resolve he shall die by degrees, and be buried alive. Is this he to whom his brethren must do homage? Note, God's providences often seem to contradict his purposes, even then they are serving them, and working at a distance towards the accomplishment of them. 3. They slighted him when he was in distress, and were not grieved for the affliction of Joseph; for when he was pining away in the pit, bemoaning his own misery, and with a languishing cry calling to them for pity, *they sat down to eat bread, v.* 25. (1.) They felt no remorse of conscience for the sin; if they had, it would have spoiled their appetite for their meat, and the relish of it. Note, A great force put upon conscience commonly stupefies it, and for the time deprives it both of sense and speech. Daring sinners are secure ones. But the consciences of Joseph's brethren, though asleep now, were roused long afterwards, *ch.* 42:21. (2.) They were now pleased to think how they were freed from the fear of their brother's dominion over them, and that, on the contrary, they had turned the wheel upon him. They made merry over him, as the persecutors over the two witnesses that had tormented them, Rev. 11:10. Note, Those that oppose God's counsels may possibly prevail so far as to think they have gained their point, and yet be deceived. 4. They sold him. A caravan of merchants very opportunely passed by (Providence so ordering it), and Judah made the motion that they should sell Joseph to them, to be carried far enough off into Egypt, where, in all probability, he would be lost, and never heard of more. (1.) Judah proposed it in compassion to Joseph (*v.* 26): *"What profit is it if we slay our brother?* it will be less guilt, and more gain, to sell him." Note, When we are tempted to sin, we should consider the unprofitableness of it. It is what there is nothing to be got by. (2.) They acquiesced in it, because they thought that if he were sold for a slave he would never be a lord, if sold into Egypt he would never be their lord; yet all this was working towards it. Note, The wrath of man shall praise God, and the remainder of wrath he will restrain, Ps. 76:10. Joseph's brethren were wonderfully restrained from murdering him, and their selling him was as wonderfully turned to God's praise. As Joseph was sold by the contrivance of Judah for twenty pieces of silver, so was our Lord Jesus for thirty, and by one of the same name too, *Judas.* Reuben (it seems) had gone away from his brethren, when they sold Joseph, intending to come round some other way to the pit, and to help Joseph out of it, and return him safely to his father. This was a kind project, but, if it had taken effect, what had become of God's purpose concerning his preferment in Egypt? Note, There are many devices in man's heart, many devices of the enemies of God's people to destroy them and of their friends to help them, which perhaps are both disappointed, as these were; but the counsel of the Lord, that shall stand. Reuben thought himself undone, because the child was sold: *I, whither shall I go? v.* 30. He being the eldest, his father would expect from him an accounts of Joseph; but, as it proved, they would all have been undone if he had not been sold.

Verses 31–36

I. Joseph would soon be missed, great enquiry would be made for him, and therefore his brethren have a further design, to make the world believe that Joseph was torn in pieces by a wild beast; and this they did, 1. To clear themselves, that they might not be suspected to have done him any mischief. Note, We have all learned of Adam to cover our transgression, Job 31:33. When the devil has taught men to commit one sin, he then teaches them to conceal it with another, theft and murder with lying and perjury; but he that covers his sin shall not prosper long. Joseph's brethren kept their own and one another's counsel for some time, but their villany came to light at last, and it is here published to the world, and the remembrance of it transmitted to every age. 2. To grieve their good father. It seems designed by them on purpose to be revenged upon him for his distinguishing love of Joseph. It was contrived on purpose to create the utmost vexation to him. They sent him Joseph's coat of many colours, with one colour more than it had had, a bloody colour, *v.* 32. They pretended they had found it in the fields, and Jacob himself must be scornfully asked, *Is this thy son's coat?* Now the badge of his honour is the discovery of his fate; and it is rashly inferred from the bloody coat that *Joseph, without doubt, is rent in pieces.* Love is always apt to fear the worst concerning the person beloved; there is a love that casteth out fear, but that is a perfect love. Now let those that know the heart of a parent suppose the agonies of poor Jacob, and put their souls into his soul's stead. How strongly does he represent to himself the direful idea of Joseph's misery! Sleeping or waking, he imagines he sees the wild beast setting upon Joseph, thinks he hears his piteous shrieks when the lion roared against him, makes himself tremble and grow chill, many a time, when he fancies how the beast sucked his blood, tore him limb from limb, and left no remains of him, but the coat of many colours, to carry the tidings. And no doubt it added no little to the grief that he had exposed him, by sending him, and sending him all alone, on this dangerous journey, which proved so fatal to him. This cuts him to the heart, and he is ready to look upon himself as an accessory to the death of his son. Now, (1.) Endeavours were used to comfort him. His sons basely pretended to do it (*v.* 35); but miserable hypocritical comforters were they all. Had they really desired to comfort him, they might easily have done it, by telling him the truth, "Joseph is alive, he is indeed sold into Egypt, but it will be an easy thing to send thither and ransom him." This would have *loosened his sackcloth, and girded him with gladness* presently. I wonder their countenances did not betray their guilt, and with what face they could pretend to condole with Jacob on the death of Joseph, when they knew he was alive. Note, The heart is strangely hardened by the deceitfulness of sin. But, (2.) It was all in vain: *Jacob refused to be comforted, v.* 35. He was an obstinate mourner, resolved to go down to the grave mourning. It was not a sudden transport of passion, like that of David, *Would God I had died for thee, my son, my son!* But, like Job, he hardened himself in sorrow. Note, [1.] Great affection to any creature does not prepare for so much the greater affliction, when it is either removed from us or embittered to us. Inordinate love commonly ends in immoderate grief; as much as the sway of the pendulum throws one way, so much it will throw the other way. [2.] Those consult neither the comfort of their souls nor the credit of their religion that are determined in their sorrow upon any occasion whatsoever. We must never say, "We will go to our grave mourning," because we know not what joyful days Providence may yet reserve for us, and it is our wisdom and duty to accommodate ourselves to Providence. [3.] We often perplex ourselves with imaginary troubles. We fancy things worse than they are, and then afflict ourselves more than we need. Sometimes there needs no more to comfort us than to undeceive us: it is good to hope the best.

II. The Ishmaelites and Midianites having bought Joseph only to make their market of him, here we have him sold again (with gain enough to the merchants, no doubt) to Potiphar, *v.* 36. Jacob was lamenting the loss of his life; had he known all he would have lamented, though not so passionately, the loss of liberty. Shall Jacob's freeborn son exchange the best robe of his family for the livery of an Egyptian lord, and all the marks of servitude? How soon was the land of Egypt made a house of bondage to the seed of Jacob! Note, It is the wisdom of parents not to bring up their children too delicately, because they know not to what hardships and mortifications Providence may reduce them before they die. Jacob little thought that ever his beloved Joseph would be thus bought and sold for a servant.

CHAPTER 38

This chapter gives us an account of Judah and his family, and such an account it is that one would wonder that, of all Jacob's sons, our Lord should spring out of Judah, Heb. 7:14. If we were to form a character of him by this story, we should not say, "Judah, thou art he whom thy brethren shall praise," *ch.* 49:8. But God will show that his choice is of grace and not of merit, and that Christ came into the world to save sinners, even the chief, and is not ashamed, upon their repentance, to be allied to them, also that the worth and worthiness of Jesus Christ are personal, of himself, and not derived from his ancestors. Humbling himself to be "made in the likeness of sinful flesh," he was pleased to descend from some that were infamous. How little reason had the Jews, who were so called from this Judah, to boast, as they did, that they were not born of fornication! Jn. 8:41. We have, in this chapter, I. Judah's marriage and issue, and the untimely death of his two eldest sons (*v.* 1–11). II. Judah's incest with his daughter-in-law Tamar, without his knowing it (*v.* 12–23). III. His confusion, when it was discovered (*v.* 24–26). IV. The birth of his twin sons, in whom his family was built up (*v.* 27, etc.).

Verses 1–11

Here is, 1. Judah's foolish friendship with a Canaanite-man. He went down from his brethren, and withdrew for a time from their society and his father's family, and got to be intimately acquainted with one Hirah, an Adullamite, *v.* 1. It is computed that he was now not much above fifteen or sixteen years of age, an easy prey to the tempter. Note, When young people that have been well educated begin to change their company, they will soon change their manners, and lose their good education. Those that go down from their brethren, that despise and forsake the society of the seed of Israel, and pick up Canaanites for their companions, are going down the hill apace. It is of great consequence to young people to choose proper associates; for these they will imitate, study to recommend themselves to, and, by their opinion of them, value themselves: an error in this choice is often fatal. 2. His foolish marriage with a Canaanite-woman, a match made, not by his father, who, it should seem, was not consulted, but by his new friend Hirah, *v.* 2. Many have been drawn into marriages scandalous and pernicious to themselves and their families by keeping bad company, and growing familiar with bad people: one wicked league entangles men in another. Let young people be admonished by this to take their good parents for their best friends, and to be advised by them, and not by flatterers, who wheedle them, to make a prey of them. 3. His children by this Canaanite, and his disposal of them. Three sons he had by her, Er, Onan, and Shelah. It is probable that she embraced the worship of the God of Israel, at least in profession, but, for aught that appears, there was little of the fear of God in the family. Judah married too young, and very rashly; he also married his sons too young, when they had neither wit nor grace to govern themselves, and the consequences were very bad. (1.) His first-born, *Er,* was notoriously wicked; he was so *in the sight of the Lord,* that is, in defiance of God and his law; or, if perhaps he was not wicked in the sight of God, to whom all men's wickedness is open; and what came of it? Why, God cut him off presently (*v.* 7): *The Lord slew him.* Note, Sometimes God makes quick work with sinners, and takes them away in his wrath, when they are but just setting out in a wicked course of life. (2.) The next son, *Onan,* was, according to the ancient usage, married to the widow, to preserve the name of his deceased brother that died childless. Though God had taken away his life for his wickedness, yet they were solicitous to preserve his memory; and their disappointment therein, through Onan's sin, was a further punishment of his wickedness. The custom of marrying the brother's widow was afterwards made one of the laws of Moses, Deu. 25:5. Onan, though he consented to marry the widow, yet, to the great abuse of his own body, of the wife that he had married, and of the memory of his brother that was gone, he refused to raise up seed unto his brother, as he was in duty bound. This was so much the worse because the Messiah was to descend from Judah, and, had he not been guilty of this wickedness, he might have had the honour of being one of his ancestors. Note, Those sins that dishonour the body and defile it are very displeasing to God and evidences of vile affections. (3.) *Shelah,* the third son, was reserved for the widow (*v.* 11), yet with a design that he should not marry so young as his brothers had done, *lest he die also.* Some think that Judah never intended to marry Shelah to Tamar, but unjustly suspected her to have been the death of her two former husbands (whereas it was their own wickedness that slew them), and then sent her to her father's house, with a charge to remain a widow. If so, it was an inexcusable piece of prevarication that he was guilty of. However, Tamar acquiesced for the present, and waited the issue.

Verses 12–23

It is a very ill-favoured story that is here told concerning Judah; one would not have expected such folly in Israel. Judah had buried his wife; and widowers have need to stand upon their guard with the utmost caution and resolution against all fleshly lusts. He was unjust to his daughter-in-law, either through negligence or design, in not giving her his surviving son, and this exposed her to temptation.

I. Tamar wickedly prostituted herself as a harlot to Judah, that, if the son might not, the father might raise up seed to the deceased. Some excuse this by suggesting that, though she was a Canaanite, yet she had embraced the true religion, and believed the promise made to Abraham and his seed, particularly that of the Messiah, who was to descend from the loins of Judah, and that she was therefore thus earnestly desirous to have a child by one of that family that she might have the honour, or at least stand fair for the honour, of being the mother of the Messiah. And, if this was indeed her desire, it had its success; she is one of the four women particularly named in the genealogy of Christ, Mt. 1:3. Her sinful practice was pardoned, and her good intention was accepted, which magnifies the grace of God, but can by no means be admitted to justify or encourage the like. Bishop Patrick thinks it probable that she hoped Shelah, who was by right her husband, might have come along with his father, and that he might have been allured to her embraces. There was a great deal of plot and contrivance in Tamar's sin. 1. She took an opportunity for it, when Judah had a time of mirth and feasting with his sheep-shearers. Note, Time of jollity often prove times of temptation, particularly to the sin of uncleanness; when men are fed to the full, the reins are apt to be let loose. 2. She exposed herself as a harlot *in an open place, v.* 14. Those that are, and would be, chaste, must be *keepers at home,* Tit. 2:5. It should seem, it was the custom of harlots, in those times, to cover their faces, that, though they were not ashamed, yet they might seem to be so. The sin of uncleanness did not then go so barefaced as it does now.

II. Judah was taken in the snare, and though it was ignorantly that he was guilty of incest with his daughter-in-law (not knowing who she was), yet he was willfully guilty of fornication: whoever she was, he knew she was not his wife, and therefore not to be touched. Nor was his sin capable, in the least, of such a charitable excuse as some make for Tamar, that though the action was bad the intention possibly might be good. Observe, 1. Judah's sin began in the eye (*v.* 15): *He saw her.* Note, Those have eyes, and hearts too, full of adultery (as it is 2 Pt. 2:14), that catch at every bait that presents itself to them and are as tinder to every spark. We have need to make a covenant with our eyes, and to turn them from beholding vanity, lest the eye infect the heart. 2. It added to the scandal that the hire of a harlot (than which nothing is more infamous) was demanded, offered, and accepted — *a kid from the flock,* a goodly price at which her chastity and honour were valued! Nay, had the consideration been thousands of rams, and ten thousand rivers of oil, it had not been a valuable consideration. The favour of God, the purity of the soul, the peace of conscience, and the hope of heaven, are too precious to be exposed to sale at any such rates; the Topaz of Ethiopia cannot equal them: what are those profited that lose their souls to gain the world? 3. It turned to the reproach of Judah that he left his jewels in pawn for a kid. Note, Fleshly lusts are not only brutish, but sottish, and ruining to men's secular interests. It is plain that whoredom, as well as wine, and new wine, takes away the heart first, else it would never take away the signet and the bracelets.

III. He lost his jewels by the bargain; he sent the kid, according to this promise, to redeem his pawn, but the supposed harlot could not be found. He sent it by his friend (who was indeed his *back-friend,* because he was aiding and abetting in his evil deeds) the Adullamite, who came back without the pledge. It is a good account (if it be but true) of any place which they here gave, *there is no harlot in this place;* for such sinners are the scandals and plagues of any place. Judah sits down content to lose his signet and his bracelets, and forbids his friend to make any further enquiry after them, giving this reason, *lest we be shamed, v.* 23. Either, 1. Lest his sin should come to be known publicly, and be talked of. Fornication and uncleanness have ever been looked upon as scandalous things and the reproach and shame of those that are convicted of them. Nothing will make those blush that are not ashamed of these. 2. Lest he should be laughed at as a fool for trusting a strumpet with his signet and his bracelets. He expresses no concern about the sin, to get that pardoned, only about the shame, to prevent that. Note, There are many who are more solicitous to preserve their reputation with men than to secure the favour of God and a good conscience; *lest we be shamed* goes further with them than *lest we be damned.*

Verses 24–30

Here is, I. Judah's rigour against Tamar, when he heard she was an adulteress. She was, in the eye of the law, Shelah's wife, and therefore her being with child by another was looked upon as an injury and reproach to Judah's family: *Bring her forth therefore,* says Judah, the master of the family, and *let her be burnt;* not burnt to death, but burnt in the cheek or forehead, stigmatized for a harlot. This seems probable, *v.* 24. Note, it is a common thing for men to be severe against those very sins in others in which yet they allow themselves; and so, in judging others, they condemn themselves, Rom. 2:1; 14:22. If he designed that she should be burnt to death, perhaps, under pretence of zeal against the sin, he was contriving how to get rid of his daughter-in-law, being loath to marry Shelah to her. Note, It is a common thing, but a very bad thing, to cover malice against men's persons with a show of zeal against their vices.

II. Judah's shame, when it was made to appear that he was the adulterer. She produced *the ring and the bracelets* in court, which justified the fathering of the child upon Judah, *v.* 25, 26. Note, The wickedness that has been most secretly committed, and most industriously concealed, yet sometimes is strangely brought to light, to the shame and confusion of those who have said, *No eye sees.* A bird of the air may carry the voice; however, there is a destroying day coming, when all will be laid open. Some of the Jewish writers observe that as Judah had said to his father, *See, is this thy son's coat?* (*ch.* 37:32) so it was now said to him, "See, are these thy signet and bracelets?" Judah, being convicted by his own conscience, 1. Confesses his sin: *She has been more righteous than I.* He owns that a perpetual mark of infamy should be fastened rather upon him, who had been so much accessory to it. Note, Those offenders ought to be treated with the greatest tenderness to whom we have any way given occasion of offending. If servants purloin, and their masters, by withholding from them what is due, tempt them to it, they ought to forgive them. 2. He never returned to it again: *He knew her again no more.* Note, Those do not truly repent of their sins that do not forsake them.

III. The building up of Judah's family hereby, notwithstanding, in the birth of Pharez and Zarah, from whom descended the most considerable families of the illustrious tribe of Judah. It should seem, the birth was hard to the mother, by which she was corrected for her sin. The children also, like Jacob and Esau, struggled for the birthright, and Pharez obtained it, who is ever named first, and from him Christ descended. He had his name from his breaking forth before his brother: *This breach be upon thee,* which is applicable to those that sow discord, and create distance, between brethren. The Jews, as Zarah, bade fair for the birthright, and were marked with a scarlet thread, as those that came out first; but the Gentiles, like Pharez, as a son of violence, got the start of them, by that violence which the kingdom of heaven suffers, and attained to the righteousness of which the Jews came short. Yet, when the fulness of time is come, all Israel shall be saved. Both these sons are named in the genealogy of our Saviour (Mt. 1:3), to perpetuate the story, as an instance of the humiliation of our Lord Jesus. Some observe that the four eldest sons of Jacob fell under very foul guilt, Reuben and Judah under the guilt of incest, Simeon and Levi under that of murder; yet they were patriarchs, and from Levi descended the priests, from Judah the kings and Messiah. Thus they became examples of repentance, and monuments of pardoning mercy.

CHAPTER 39

At this chapter we return to the story of Joseph. We have him here, I. A servant, a slave in Potiphar's house (*v.* 1), and yet there greatly honoured and favoured, 1. By the providence of God, which made him, in effect, a master (*v.* 2–6). 2. By the grace of God, which made him more than a conqueror over a strong temptation to uncleanness (*v.* 7–12). II. We have him here a sufferer, falsely accused (*v.* 13–18), imprisoned (*v.* 19, 20), and yet his imprisonment made both honourable and comfortable by the tokens of God's special presence with him (*v.* 21–23). And herein Joseph was a type of Christ, "who took upon him the form of a servant," and yet then did that which made it evident that "God was with him," who was tempted by Satan, but overcame the temptation, who was falsely accused and bound, and yet had all things committed to his hand.

Verses 1–6

Here is, I. Joseph bought (*v.* 1), and he that bought him, whatever he gave for him, had a good bargain of him; it was better than the merchandise of silver. The Jews have a proverb, "If the world did not know the worth of good men, they would hedge them about with pearls." He was sold to an officer of Pharaoh, with whom he might get acquainted with public persons and public business, and so be fitted for the preferment for which he was designed. Note, 1. What God intends men for he will be sure, some way or other, to qualify them for. 2. Providence is to be acknowledged in the disposal even of poor servants and in their settlements, and therein may perhaps be working towards something great and important.

II. Joseph blessed, wonderfully blessed, even in the house of his servitude.

1. God prospered him, *v.* 2,3. Perhaps the affairs of Potiphar's family had remarkably gone backward before; but, upon Joseph's coming into it, a discernible turn was given to them, and the face and posture of them altered on a sudden. Though, at first, we may suppose that his hand was put to the meanest services, even in those appeared his ingenuity and industry; a particular blessing of Heaven attended him, which, as he rose in his employment, became more and more discernible. Note, (1.) Those that have wisdom and grace have that which cannot be taken away from them, whatever else they are robbed of. Joseph's brethren had stripped him of his coat of many colours, but they could not strip him of his virtue and prudence. (2.) Those that can separate us from all our friends, yet cannot deprive us of the gracious presence of our God. When Joseph had none of all his relations with him, he had his God with him, even in the house of the Egyptian. Joseph was separated from his brethren, but not from his God; banished from his father's house, but *the Lord was with him,* and this comforted him. (3.) It is God's presence with us that makes all we do prosperous. Those that would prosper must therefore make God their friend; and those that do prosper must therefore give God the praise.

2. His master preferred him, by degrees made him steward of his household, *v.* 4. Note, (1.) Industry and honesty are the surest and safest way both of rising and thriving: *Seest thou a man* prudent, and faithful, and *diligent in his business? He shall stand before kings* at length, and not always *before mean men.* (2.) It is the wisdom of those that are in any sort of authority to countenance and employ those with whom it appears that the presence of God is, Ps. 101:6. Potiphar knew what he did when he put all into the hands of Joseph; for he knew it would prosper better there than in his own hand. (3.) He that is faithful in a few things stand fair for being made ruler over many things, Mt. 25:21. Christ goes by this rule with his servants. (4.) It is a great ease to a master to have those employed under him that are trusty. Potiphar was so well satisfied with Joseph's conduct that *he knew not aught he had, save the bread which he did eat, v.* 6. The servant had all the care and trouble of the estate; the master had only the enjoyment of it: an example not to be imitated by any master, unless he could be sure that he had one in all respects like Joseph for a servant.

3. God favoured his master for his sake (*v.* 5): *He blessed the Egyptian's house,* though he was an Egyptian, a stranger to the true God, *for Joseph's sake;* and he himself, like Laban, soon learned it by experience, *ch.* 30:27. Note, (1.) Good men are the blessings of the places where they live; even good servants may be so, though mean, and lightly esteemed. (2.) The prosperity of the wicked is, one way or other, for the sake of the godly. Here was a wicked family blessed for the sake of one good servant in it.

Verses 7–12

Here is, I. A most shameful instance of impudence and immodesty in Joseph's mistress, the shame and scandal of her sex, perfectly lost to all virtue and honour, and not to be mentioned, nor thought of, without the utmost indignation. It was well that she was an Egyptian; for we must have shared in the confusion if such folly had been found in Israel. Observe,

I. Her sin began in the eye: She *cast her eyes upon Joseph* (*v.* 7), who *was a goodly person, and well-favoured, v.* 6. Note, (1.) Remarkable beauty, either of men or women, often proves a dangerous snare both to themselves and others, which forbids pride in it and commands constant watchfulness against the temptation that attends it; favour is deceitful — deceiving. (2.) We have great need to make a covenant with our eyes (Job 31:1), lest the eye infect the heart. Joseph's mistress had a husband that ought to have been to her for a covering of the eyes from all others, *ch.* 20:16.

2. She was daring and shameless in the sin. With an impudent face, and a harlot's forehead, she said, *Lie with me,* having already, by her wanton looks and unchaste desires, committed adultery with him in her heart. Note, Where the unclean spirit gets possession and dominion in a soul, it is as with the possessed of the devils (Lu. 8:27, 29), the clothes of modesty are thrown off and the bands and fetters of shame are broken in pieces. When lust has got head, it will stick at nothing, blush at nothing; decency, and reputation, and conscience, are all sacrificed to that Baal-peor. 3. She was urgent and violent in the temptation. Often she had been denied with the strongest reasons, and yet as often renewed her vile solicitations. She *spoke to him day by day, v.* 10. Now this was, (1.) Great wickedness in her, and showed her heart fully set to do evil. (2.) A great temptation to Joseph. The hand of Satan, no doubt, was in it, who, when he found he could not overcome him with troubles and the frowns of the world (for in them he still held fast his integrity), assaulted him with soft and charming pleasures, which have ruined more than the former, and have slain their ten-thousands.

II. Here is a most illustrious instance of virtue and resolved chastity in Joseph, who, by the grace of God, was enabled to resist and overcome this temptation; and, all things considered, his escape was, for aught I know, as great an instance of the divine power as the deliverance of the three children out of the fiery furnace.

1. The temptation he was assaulted with was very strong. Never was a more violent onset made upon the fort of chastity than this recorded here. (1.) The sin he was tempted to was uncleanness, which considering his youth, his beauty, his single state, and his plentiful living at the table of a ruler, was a sin which, one would think, might most easily beset him and betray him. (2.) The tempter was his mistress, a person of quality, whom it was his place to obey and his interest to oblige, whose favour would contribute more than any thing to his preferment, and by whose means he might arrive at the highest honours of the court. On the other hand, it was at his utmost peril if he slighted her, and made her his enemy. (3.) Opportunity makes a thief, makes an adulterer, and that favoured the temptation. The tempter was in the house with him; his business led him to be, without any suspicion, where she was; none of the family were within (*v.* 11); there appeared no danger of its being ever discovered, or, if it should be suspected, his mistress would protect him. (4.) To all this was added importunity, frequent constant importunity, to such a degree that, at last, she laid violent hands on him.

2. His resistance of the temptation was very brave, and the victory truly honourable. The almighty grace of God enabled him to overcome this assault of the enemy,

(1.) By strength of reason; and wherever right reason may be heard, religion no doubt will carry the day. He argues from the respect he owed both to God and his master, *v.* 8, 9. [1.] He would not wrong his master, nor do such an irreparable injury to his honour. He considers, and urges, how kind his master had been to him, what a confidence he had reposed in him, in how many instances he had befriended him, for which he abhorred the thought of making such an ungrateful return. Note, We are bound in honour, as well as justice and gratitude, not in any thing to injure those that have a good opinion of us and place a trust in us, how secretly soever it may be done. See how he argues (*v.* 9): *"There is none greater in this house than I,* therefore I will not do it." Note, Those that are great, instead of being proud of their greatness, should use it as an argument against sin. "Is none greater than I? Then I will scorn to do a wicked thing; it is below me to serve a base lust; I will not disparage myself so much." [2.] He would not offend his God. This is the chief argument with which he strengthens his aversion to the sin. *How can I do this?* not only, How shall I? or, How dare I? but, *How can I? Id possumus, quod jure possumus — We can do that which we can do lawfully.* It is good to shut out sin with the strongest bar, even that of an impossibility. He that is born of God cannot sin, 1 Jn. 3:9. Three arguments Joseph urges upon himself. *First,* He considers who he was that was tempted. *"I;* others may perhaps take their liberty, but *I* cannot. *I* that am an Israelite in covenant with God, that profess religion, and relation to him: it is next to impossible for me to do so." *Secondly,* What the sin was to which he was tempted: *This great wickedness.* Others might look upon it as a small matter, a peccadillo, a trick of youth; but Joseph had another idea of it. In general, when at any time we are tempted to sin, we must consider the great wickedness there is in it, let sin appear sin (Rom. 7:13), call it by its own name, and never go about to lessen it. Particularly let the sin of uncleanness always be looked upon as great wickedness, as an exceedingly sinful sin, that wars against the soul as much as any other. *Thirdly,* Against whom he was tempted to sin — *against God;* not only, "How shall I do it, and sin against my master, my mistress, myself, my own body and soul; but against God?" Note, Gracious souls look upon this as the worst thing in sin that it is against God, against his nature and his dominion, against his love and his design. Those that love God do for this reason hate sin.

(2.) By stedfastness of resolution. The grace of God enabled him to overcome the temptation by avoiding the tempter. [1.] He *hearkened not to her,* so much as to be with her, *v.* 10. Note, Those that would be kept from harm must keep themselves out of harm's way. *Avoid it, pass not by it.* Nay, [2.] When she laid hold of him, he *left his garment in her hand, v.* 12. He would not stay so much as to parley with the temptation, but flew out from it with the utmost abhorrence; he left his garment, as one escaping for his life. Note, It is better to lose a good coat than a good conscience.

Verses 13–18

Joseph's mistress, having tried in vain to make him a criminal, now endeavours to represent him as one; so to be revenged on him for his virtue. Now was her love turned into the utmost rage and malice, and she pretends she cannot endure the sight of him whom awhile ago she could not endure out of her sight. Chaste and holy love will continue, though slighted; but sinful love, like Amnon's to Tamar, is easily changed into sinful hatred. 1. She accused him to his fellow servants (*v.* 13–15) and gave him a bad name among them. Probably they envied him his interest in their master's favour, and his authority in the house; and perhaps found themselves aggrieved sometimes by his fidelity, which prevented their purloining; and therefore they were glad to hear any thing that might tend to his disgrace, and, if there was room for it, incensed their mistress yet more against him. Observe, When she speaks of her husband, she does not call him her husband, or her lord, but only *he;* for she had forgotten the covenant of her God, that was between them. Thus the adulteress (Prov. 7:19) calls her husband *the good man.* Note, Innocence itself cannot secure a man's reputation. Not every one that keeps a good conscience can keep a good name. 2. She accused him to his master, who had power in his hand to punish him, which his fellow servants had not, *v.* 17, 18. Observe, (1.) What an improbable story she tells, producing his garment as an evidence that he had offered violence to her, which was a plain indication that she had offered violence to him. Note, Those that have broken the bonds of modesty will never be held by the bonds of truth. No marvel that she who had impudence enough to say, *Lie with me,* had front enough to say, "He would have lien with me." Had the lie been told to conceal her own crime it would have been bad enough, yet, in some degree, excusable; but it was told to be revenged upon his virtue, a most malicious lie. And yet, (2.) She manages it so as to incense her husband against him, reflecting upon him for bringing this Hebrew servant among them, perhaps at first against her mind, because he was a Hebrew. Note, It is no new thing for the best of men to be falsely accused of the worst of crimes by those who themselves are the worst of criminals. As this matter was represented, one would have thought chaste Joseph a very bad man and his wanton mistress a virtuous woman; it is well that there is a day of discovery coming, in which all shall appear in their true characters. This was not the first time that Joseph's coat was made use of as a false witness concerning him; his father had been deceived by it before, now his master.

Verses 19–23

Here is, 1. Joseph wronged by his master. He believed the accusation, and either Joseph durst not make his defence by telling the truth, as it would reflect too much upon his mistress, or his master would not hear it, or would not believe it, and there is no remedy, he is condemned to perpetual imprisonment, *v.* 19, 20. God restrained his wrath, else he had put him to death; and that wrath which imprisoned him God made to turn to his praise, in order to which Providence so disposed that he should be shut up among the king's prisoners, the state-prisoners. Potiphar, it is likely, chose that prison because it was the worst; for there the iron entered into the soul (Ps. 105:18), but God designed to pave the way to his enlargement. He was committed to the king's prison, that he might thence be preferred to the king's person. Note, Many an action of false imprisonment will, in the great day, be found to lie against the enemies and persecutors of God's people. Our Lord Jesus, like Joseph here, was bound, and numbered with the transgressors. 2. Joseph owned and righted by his God, who is, and will be, the just and powerful patron of oppressed innocence. Joseph was at a distance from all his friends and relations, had not them with him to comfort him, or to minister to him, or to mediate for him; but *the Lord was with Joseph, and showed him mercy, v.* 21. Note, (1.) God despises not his prisoners, Ps. 69:33. No gates nor bars can shut out his gracious presence from his people; for he has promised that he will never leave them. (2.) Those that have a good conscience in a prison have a good God there. Integrity and uprightness qualify us for the divine favour, wherever we are. Joseph is not long a prisoner before he becomes a little ruler even in the prison, which is to be attributed, under God, [1.] To the keeper's favour. God *gave him favour in the sight of the keeper of the prison.* Note, God can raise up friends for his people even where they little expect to find them, and can *make them to be pitied* even of those that carry them captive, Ps. 106:46. [2.] To Joseph's fitness for business. The keeper saw that God was with him, and that every thing prospered under his hand; and therefore entrusted him with the management of the affairs of the prison, *v.* 22, 23. Note, Wisdom and virtue will shine in the narrowest spheres. A good man will do good wherever he is, and will be a blessing even in bonds and banishment; for the Spirit of the Lord is not bound nor banished, witness St. Paul, Phil. 1:12, 13.

CHAPTER 40

In this chapter things are working, though slowly, towards Joseph's advancement. I. Two of Pharaoh's servants are committed to prison, and there to Joseph's care, and so become witnesses of his extraordinary conduct (*v.* 1–4). II. They dreamed each of them a dream, which Joseph interpreted (*v.* 5–19), and the event verified the interpretation (*v.* 20–22), and so they became witnesses of his extraordinary skill. III. Joseph recommends his case to one of them, whose preferment he foresaw (*v.* 14, 15), but in vain (*v.* 23).

Verses 1–4

We should not have had this story of Pharaoh's butler and baker recorded in scripture if it had not been serviceable to Joseph's preferment. The world stands for the sake of the church, and is governed for its good. Observe, 1. Two of the great officers of Pharaoh's court, having offended the king, are committed to prison. Note, High places are slippery places; nothing more uncertain than the favour of princes. Those that make God's favour their happiness, and his service their business, will find him a better Master than Pharaoh was, and not so extreme to mark what they do amiss. Many conjectures there are concerning the offence of these servants of Pharaoh; some make it no less than an attempt to take away his life, others no more than the casual lighting of a fly into his cup and a little sand into his bread. Whatever it was, Providence by this means brought them into the prison where Joseph was. 2. The *captain of the guard* himself, who was Potiphar, charged Joseph with them (*v.* 4), which intimates that he began now to be reconciled to him, and perhaps to be convinced of his innocence, though he durst not release him for fear of disobliging his wife. John Baptist must lose his head, to please Herodias.

Verses 5–19

Observe, I. The special providence of God, which filled the heads of these two prisoners with unusual dreams, such as made extraordinary impressions upon them, and carried with them evidences of a divine origin, both in one night. Note, God has immediate access to the spirits of men, which he can make serviceable to his own purposes whenever he pleases, quite beyond the intention of those concerned. To him all hearts are open, and anciently he spoke not only to his own people, but to others, in dreams, Job 33:15. Things to come were thus foretold, but very obscurely.

II. The impression which was made upon these prisoners by their dreams (*v.* 6): *They were sad.* It was not the prison that made them sad (they were pretty well used to that, and perhaps lived jovially there), but the dream. Note, God has more ways than one to sadden the spirits of those that are to be made sad. Those sinners that are hardy enough under outward troubles, and will not yield to them, yet God can find out a way to punish; he can take off their wheels, by wounding their spirits, and laying loads upon them.

III. Joseph's great tenderness and compassion towards them. He enquired with concern, *Wherefore look you so sadly to-day? v.* 7. Joseph was their keeper, and in that office he was mild. Note, It becomes us to take cognizance of the sorrows even of those that are under our check. Joseph was their companion in tribulation, he was now a prisoner with them, and had been a dreamer too. Note, Communion in sufferings helps to work compassion towards those that do suffer. Let us learn hence, 1. To concern ourselves in the sorrows and troubles of others, and to enquire into the reason of the sadness of our brethren's countenances; we should be often considering the tears of the oppressed, Eccl. 4:1. It is some relief to those that are in trouble to be taken notice of. 2. To enquire into the causes of our own sorrow, "Wherefore do I look so sadly? Is there a reason? Is it a good reason? Is there not a reason for comfort sufficient to balance it, whatever it is? *Why art thou cast down, O my soul?*"

IV. The dreams themselves, and the interpretation of them. That which troubled these prisoners was that being confined they could not have recourse to the diviners of Egypt who pretended to interpret dreams: *There is no interpreter* here in the prison, *v.* 8. Note, There are interpreters which those that are in prison and sorrow should wish to have with them, to instruct them in the meaning and design of Providence (Elihu alludes to such, when he says, If *there be an interpreter, one among a thousand, to show unto man his uprightness,* Job 33:23, 24), interpreters to guide their consciences, not to satisfy their curiosity. Joseph hereupon directed them which way to look: *Do not interpretations belong to God?* He means the God whom he worshipped, to the knowledge of whom he endeavours hereby to lead them. Note, It is God's prerogative to foretel things to come, Isa. 46:10. He must therefore have the praise of all the gifts of foresight which men have, ordinary or extraordinary. Joseph premises a caveat against his own praise, and is careful to transmit the glory to God, as Daniel, *ch.* 2:30. Joseph suggests, "If interpretations belong to God, he is a free agent, and may communicate the power to whom he pleases, and therefore tell me your dreams." Now, 1. The chief butler's dream was a happy presage of his enlargement, and re-advancement, within three days; and so Joseph explained it to him, *v.* 12, 13. Probably it had been usual with him to press the full-ripe grapes immediately into Pharaoh's cup, the simplicity of that age not being acquainted with the modern arts of making the wine fine. Observe, Joseph foretold the chief butler's deliverance, but he did not foresee his own. He had long before dreamt of his own honour, and the obeisance which his brethren should do to him, with the remembrance of which he must now support himself, without any new or fresh discoveries. The visions that are for the comfort of God's saints are for a great while to come, and relate to things that are very far off, while the foresights of others, like this recorded there, look but three days before them. 2. The chief baker's dream portended his ignominious death, *v.* 18, 19. The happy interpretation of the other's dream encouraged him to relate his. Thus hypocrites, when they hear good things promised to good Christians, would put in for a share, though they have no part nor lot in the matter. It was not Joseph's fault that he brought him no better tidings. Ministers are but interpreters, they cannot make the thing otherwise than it is; if therefore they deal faithfully, and their message prove unpleasing, it is not their fault. Bad dreams cannot expect a good interpretation.

V. The improvement Joseph made of this opportunity to get a friend at court, *v.* 14, 15. He modestly bespoke the favour of the chief butler, whose preferment he foretold: *But think of me when it shall be well with thee.* Though the respect paid to Joseph made the prison as easy to him as a prison could be, yet none can blame him for being desirous of liberty. See here, 1. What a modest representation he makes of his own case, *v.* 15. He does not reflect upon his brethren that sold him; he only says, *I was stolen out of the land of the Hebrews,* that is, unjustly sent thence, no matter where the fault was. Nor does he reflect on the wrong done him in this imprisonment by his mistress that was his prosecutrix, and his master that was his judge; but mildly avers his own innocence: *Here have I done nothing that they should put me into the dungeon.* Note, When we are called to vindicate ourselves we should carefully avoid, as much as may be, speaking ill of others. Let us be content to prove ourselves innocent, and not be fond of upbraiding others with their guilt. 2. What a modest request he makes to the chief butler: "Only, *think of me.* Pray do me a kindness, if it lie in your way." And his particular petition is, *Bring me out of this house.* He does not say, "Bring me into Pharaoh's house, get me a place at court." No, he begs for enlargement, not preferment. Note, Providence sometimes designs the greatest honours for those that least covet or expect them.

Verses 20–23

Here is, 1. The verifying of Joseph's interpretation of the dreams, on the very day prefixed. The chief butler and baker were both advanced, one to his office, the other to the gallows, and both at the three days' end. Note, Very great changes, both for the better and for the worse, often happen in a very little time, so sudden are the revolutions of the wheel of nature. The occasion of giving judgement severally upon their case was the solemnizing of Pharaoh's birth-day, on which, all his servants being obliged by custom to attend him, these two came to be enquired after, and the cause of their commitment looked into. The solemnizing of the birth-day of princes has been an ancient piece of respect done them; and if it be not abused, as Jeroboam's was (Hos. 7:5), and Herod's (Mk. 6:21), is a usage innocent enough: and we may all profitably take notice of our birth-days, with thankfulness for the mercies of our birth, sorrow for the sinfulness of it, and an expectation of the day of our death as better than the day of our birth. On Pharaoh's birth-day he lifted up the head of these two prisoners, that is, arraigned and tried them (when Naboth was tried he was *set on high* among the people, 1 Ki. 21:9), and *he restored the chief butler,* and *hanged the chief baker.* If the butler was innocent and the baker guilty, we must own the equity of Providence in clearing up the innocency of the innocent, and making the sin of the guilty to find him out. If both were either equally innocent or equally guilty, it is an instance of the arbitrariness of such great princes as pride themselves in that power which Nebuchadnezzar set up for (Dan. 5:19, *whom he would he slew, and whom he would he kept alive*), forgetting that there is a higher than they, to whom they are accountable. 2. The disappointing of Joseph's expectation from the chief butler: He *remembered not Joseph, but forgot him, v.* 23. (1.) See here an instance of base ingratitude; Joseph had deserved well at his hands, had ministered to him, sympathized with him, helped him to a favourable interpretation of his dream, had recommended himself to him as an extraordinary person upon all accounts; and yet he forgot him. We must not think it strange if in this world we have hatred shown us for our love, and slights for our respects. (2.) See how apt those that are themselves at ease are to forget others in distress. Perhaps it is in allusion to this story that the prophet speaks of those that *drink wine in bowls, and are not grieved for the affliction of Joseph,* Amos 6:6. Let us learn hence to cease from man. Joseph perhaps depended too much upon his interest in the chief butler, and promised himself too much from him; he learned by his disappointment to trust in God only. We cannot expect too little from man nor too much from God.

Some observe the resemblance between Joseph and Christ in this story. Joseph's fellow-sufferers were like the two thieves that were crucified with Christ — the one saved, the other condemned. (It is Dr. Lightfoot's remark, from Mr. Broughton.) One of these, when Joseph said to him, *Remember me when it shall be well with thee,* forget him; but one of those, when he said to Christ, *Remember me when thou comest into thy kingdom,* was not forgotten. We justly blame the chief butler's ingratitude to Joseph, yet we conduct ourselves much more disingenuously towards the Lord Jesus. Joseph had but foretold the chief butler's enlargement, but Christ wrought out ours, mediated with the King of kings for us; yet we forget him, though often reminded of him, though we have promised never to forget him: thus ill do we requite him, like foolish people and unwise.

CHAPTER 41

Two things Providence is here bringing about: — I. The advancement of Joseph. II. The maintenance of Jacob and his family in a time of famine; for the eyes of the Lord run to and fro through the earth, and direct the affairs of the children of men for the benefit of those few whose hearts are upright with him. In order to these, we have here, 1. Pharaoh's dreams (*v.* 1–8). 2. The recommendation of Joseph to him for an interpreter (*v.* 9–13). 3. The interpretation of the dreams, and the prediction of seven years of plenty and seven years of famine in Egypt, with the prudent advice given to Pharaoh thereupon (*v.* 14–36). 4. The preferment of Joseph to a place of the highest power and trust in Egypt (*v.* 37–45). 5. The accomplishment of Joseph's prediction, and his fidelity to his trust (*v.* 46, etc.).

Verses 1–8

Observe, 1. The delay of Joseph's enlargement. It was not till *the end of two full years* (*v.* 1); so long he waited after he had entrusted the chief butler with his case and began to have some prospect of relief. Note, We have need of patience, not only bearing, but waiting, patience. Joseph lay in prison until the time that his word came, Ps. 105:19. There is a time set for the deliverance of God's people; that time will come, though it seem to tarry; and, when it comes, it will appear to have been the best time, and therefore we ought to wait for it (Hab. 2:3), and not think two full years too long to continue waiting. 2. The means of Joseph's enlargement, which were Pharaoh's dreams, here related. If we were to look upon them as ordinary dreams, we might observe from them the follies and absurdities of a roving working fancy, how it represents to itself tame cows as beasts of prey (nay, more ravenous than any, eating up those of their own kind), and ears of corn as devouring one another. Surely in the multitude of dreams, nay, even in one dream, there are divers vanities, Eccl. 5:7. Now that God no longer speaks to us in that way, I think it is no matter how little we either heed them or tell them. Foolish dreams related can make no better than foolish talk. But these dreams which Pharaoh dreamed carried their own evidence with them that they were sent of God; and therefore, when he awoke, his spirit was troubled, *v.* 8. It cannot but put us into a concern to receive any extraordinary message from heaven, because we are conscious to ourselves that we have no reason to expect any good tidings thence. His magicians were puzzled, the rules of their art failed them: these dreams of Pharaoh, it seems, did not fall within the compass of them, so that they could not offer at the interpretation of them. This was to make Joseph's performance by the Spirit of God the more admirable. Human reason, prudence, and foresight, must be nonplussed, that divine revelation may appear the more glorious in the contrivance of our redemption, 1 Cor. 2:13, 14. Compare with this story, Dan. 2:27; 4:7; 5:8. Joseph's own dreams were the occasion of his troubles, and now Pharaoh's dreams were the occasion of his enlargement.

Verses 9–16

Here is, 1. The recommending of Joseph to Pharaoh for an interpreter. The chief butler did it more in compliment to Pharaoh, to oblige him, than in gratitude to Joseph, or in compassion for his case. He makes a fair confession (*v.* 9): *"I remember my faults this day,* in forgetting Joseph." Note, It is best to remember our duty, and to do it in its time; but, if we have neglected that, it is next best to remember our faults, and repent of them, and do our duty at last; better late than never. Some think he means his faults against Pharaoh, for which he was imprisoned; and then he would insinuate that, though Pharaoh had forgiven him, he had not forgiven himself. The story he had to tell was, in short, That there was an obscure young man in the king's prison, who had very properly interpreted his dream, and the chief baker's (the event corresponding in each with the interpretation), and that he would recommend him to the king his master for an interpreter. Note, God's time for the enlargement of his people will appear at last to be the fittest time. If the chief butler had at first used his interest for Joseph's enlargement, and had obtained it, it is probable that upon his release he would have gone back to *the land of the Hebrews* again, which he spoke of so feelingly (*ch.* 40:15), and then he would neither have been so blessed himself, nor such a blessing to his family, as afterwards he proved. But staying two years longer, and coming out now upon this occasion, at last, to interpret the king's dreams, way was made for his very great preferment. Those that patiently wait for God shall be paid for their waiting, not only principal but interest, Lam. 3:26. 2. The introducing of Joseph to Pharaoh. The king's business requires haste. Joseph is sent for out of the dungeon with all speed; Pharaoh's order discharged him both from his imprisonment and from his servitude, and made him a candidate for some of the highest trusts at court. The king can scarcely allow him time, but that decency required it, to shave himself, and to change his raiment, *v.* 14. It is done with all possible expedition, and Joseph is brought in, perhaps almost as much surprised as Peter was, Acts 12:9. So suddenly is his captivity brought back that he is as one that dreams, Ps. 126:1. Pharaoh immediately, without enquiring who or whence he was, tells him his business, that he expected he should interpret his dream, *v.* 15. To which, Joseph makes him a very modest decent reply, (*v.* 16), in which, (1.) He gives honour to God. "It is not in me, God must give it." Note, Great gifts appear most graceful and illustrious when those that have them use them humbly, and take not the praise of them to themselves, but give it to God. To such God gives more grace. (2.) He shows respect to Pharaoh, and hearty good-will to him and his government, in supposing that the interpretation would be an answer of peace. Note, Those that consult God's oracles may expect an answer of peace. If Joseph be made the interpreter, hope the best.

Verses 17–32

Here, I. Pharaoh relates his dream. He dreamt that he stood upon the bank of the river Nile, and saw the kine, both the fat ones and the lean ones, come out of the river. For the kingdom of Egypt had no rain, as appears, Zec. 14:18, but the plenty of the year depended upon the overflowing of the river, and it was about one certain time of the year that it overflowed. If it rose to fifteen or sixteen cubits, there was plenty; if to twelve or thirteen only, or under, there was scarcity. See how many ways Providence has of dispensing its gifts; yet, whatever the second causes are, our dependence is still the same upon the first Cause, who makes every creature that to us that it is, be it rain or river.

II. Joseph interprets his dream, and tells him that it signified seven years of plenty now immediately to ensue, which should be succeeded by as many years of famine. Observe, 1. The two dreams signified the same thing, but the repetition was to denote the certainty, the nearness, and the importance, of the event, *v.* 32. Thus God has often shown *the immutability of his counsel by two immutable things,* Heb. 6:17, 18. The covenant is sealed with two sacraments; and in the one of them there are both bread and wine, wherein the dream is one, and yet it is doubled, for the thing is certain. 2. Yet the two dreams had a distinct reference to the two things wherein we most experience plenty and scarcity, namely, grass and corn. The plenty and scarcity of grass for the cattle were signified by the fat kine and the lean ones; the plenty and scarcity of herb for the service of man by the full ears and the thin ones. 3. See what changes the comforts of this life are subject to. After great plenty may come great scarcity; how strong soever we may think our mountain stands, if God speak the word, it will soon be moved. We cannot be sure that *to-morrow shall be as this day,* next year as this, and *much more abundant,* Isa. 56:12. We must learn how to want, as well as how to abound. 4. See the goodness of God in sending the seven years of plenty before those of famine, that provision might be made accordingly. Thus he *sets the one over-against the other,* Eccl. 7:14. With what wonderful wisdom has Providence, that great housekeeper, ordered the affairs of this numerous family from the beginning hitherto! Great variety of seasons there have been, and the product of the earth is sometimes more and sometimes less; yet, take one time with another, what was miraculous concerning the manna is ordinarily verified in the common course of Providence, *He that gathers much has nothing over, and he that gathers little has no lack,* Ex. 16:18. 5. See the perishing nature of our worldly enjoyments. The great increase of the years of plenty was quite lost and swallowed up in the years of famine; and the overplus of it, which seemed very much, yet did but just serve to keep men alive, *v.* 29–31. *Meat for the belly, and the belly for meats, but God shall destroy both it and them,* 1 Co. 6:13. There is bread which *endures to everlasting life,* which shall not be forgotten, and which it is worth while to labour for, Jn. 6:27. Those that make the things of this world their good things will find but little pleasure in remembering that they have received them, Lu. 16:25. 6. Observe, God revealed this beforehand to Pharaoh, who, as king of Egypt, was to be the father of his country, and to make prudent provision for them. Magistrates are called *shepherds,* whose care it must be, not only to rule, but to feed.

Verses 33–45

Here is, I. The good advice that Joseph gave to Pharaoh, which was, 1. That in the years of plenty he should lay up for the years of famine, buy up corn when it was cheap, that he might both enrich himself and supply the country when it would be dear and scarce. Note, Fair warning should always be followed with good counsel. Therefore the prudent man foresees the evil, that he may hide himself. God has in his word told us of a day of trial and exigence before us, when we shall need all the grace we can get, and all little enough, "Now, therefore, provide accordingly." Note, further, Times of gathering must be diligently improved, because there will come a time of spending. Let us go to the ant, and learn of her this wisdom, Prov. 6:6–8. 2. Because that which is everybody's work commonly proves nobody's work, he advises Pharaoh to appoint officers who should make it their business, and to select some one person to preside in the affair, *v.* 33. Probably, if Joseph had not advised this, it would not have been done; Pharaoh's counsellors could no more improve the dream than his magicians interpret it; therefore it is said of him (Ps. 105:22) that he *taught the senators wisdom.* Hence we may justly infer with Solomon (Eccl. 4:13), *Better is a poor and a wise child than an old and foolish king.*

II. The great honour that Pharaoh did to Joseph. 1. He gave him an honourable testimony: He is *a man in whom the Spirit of God is;* and this puts a great excellency upon any man; such men ought to be valued, *v.* 38. He is a nonsuch for prudence: *There is none so discreet and wise as thou art, v.* 39. Now he is abundantly recompensed for the disgrace that had been done him; and his righteousness is as the morning light, Ps. 37:6. 2. He put him into an honourable office; not only employed him to buy up corn, but made him prime-minister of state, comptroller of the household — *Thou shalt be over my house,* chief justice of the kingdom — *according to thy word shall all my people be ruled,* or *armed,* as some read it, and then it bespeaks him general of the forces. Him commission was very ample: *I have set thee over all the land of Egypt* (*v.* 41); *without thee shall no man life up his hand or foot* (*v.* 44); all the affairs of the kingdom must pass through his hand. Nay (*v.* 40), *only in the throne will I be greater than thou.* Note, It is the wisdom of princes to prefer those, and the happiness of people to have those preferred, to places of power and trust, in whom the Spirit of God is. It is probable that there were those about the court who opposed Joseph's preferment, which occasioned Pharaoh so often to repeat the grant, and with that solemn sanction (*v.* 44), *I am Pharaoh.* When the proposal was made that there should be a corn-master-general nominated, it is said (*v.* 37), *Pharaoh's servants were all pleased* with the proposal, each hoping for the place; but when Pharaoh said to them, "Joseph shall be the man," we do not read that they made him any answer, being uneasy at it, and acquiescing only because they could not help it. Joseph had enemies, no doubt, archers that shot at him, and hated him (*ch.* 49:23), as Daniel, *ch.* 6:4. 3. He put upon him all the marks of honour imaginable, to recommend him to the esteem and respect of the people as the king's favourite, and one whom he delighted to honour. (1.) He gave him his own ring, as a ratification of his commission, and in token of peculiar favour; or it was like delivering him the great seal. (2.) He put fine clothes upon him, instead of his prison garments. For those that are in kings' palaces must wear soft clothing; he that, in the morning, was dragging his fetters of iron, before night was adorned with a chain of gold. (3.) He made him *ride in the second chariot* to his own, and ordered all to do homage to him: *"Bow the knee,* as to Pharaoh himself." (4.) He gave him a new name, to show his authority over him, and yet such a name as bespoke the value he had for him, *Zaphnathpaaneah — A revealer of secrets.* (5.) He married him honourably to a prince's daughter. Where God had been liberal in giving wisdom and other merits, Pharaoh was not sparing in conferring honours. Now this preferment of Joseph was, [1.] An abundant recompense for his innocent and patient suffering, a lasting instance of the equity and goodness of Providence, and an encouragement to all good people to trust in a good God. [2.] It was typical of the exaltation of Christ, that great *revealer of secrets* (Jn. 1:18), or, as some translate Joseph's new name, the *Saviour of the world.* The brightest glories of the upper world are put upon him, the highest trust is lodged in his hand, and all power is given to him both in heaven and earth. He is gatherer, keeper, and disposer, of all the stores of divine grace, and chief ruler of the kingdom of God among men. The work of minsters is to cry before him, *"Bow the knee; kiss the Son."*

Verses 46–57

Observe here, I. The building of Joseph's family in the birth of two sons, Manasseh and Ephraim, *v.* 50–52. In the names he gave them, he owned the divine Providence giving this happy turn to his affairs, 1. He was made to forget his misery, Job 11:16. We should bear our afflictions when they are present as those that know not but Providence may so outweigh them by after-comforts as that we may even forget them when they are past. But could he be so unnatural as to *forget all his father's house?* He means the unkindness he received from his brethren, or perhaps the wealth and honour he expected from his father, with the birthright. The robes he now wore made him forget the coat of divers colours which he wore in his father's house. 2. He was made *fruitful in the land of his affliction.* It had been the land of his affliction, and in some sense it was still so, for it was not Canaan, the land of promise. His distance from his father was still his affliction. Note, Light is sometimes sown for the righteous in a barren and unlikely soil; and yet if God sow it, and water it, it will come up again. The afflictions of the saints promote their fruitfulness. *Ephraim* signifies *fruitfulness,* and *Manasseh forgetfulness,* for these two often go together; when Jeshurun waxed fat, he forgot God his Maker.

II. The accomplishment of Joseph's predictions. Pharaoh had great confidence in the truth of them, perhaps finding in his own mind, beyond what another person could, an exact correspondence between them and his dreams, as between the key and the lock; and the event showed that he was not deceived. The seven plenteous years came (*v.* 47), and, at length, they were ended, *v.* 53. Note, We ought to foresee the approaching period of the days both of our prosperity and of our opportunity, and therefore must not be secure in the enjoyment of our prosperity nor slothful in the improvement of our opportunity; years of plenty will end, therefore, Whatever thy hand finds to do do it; and gather in gathering time. *The morning cometh and also the night* (Isa. 21:12), the plenty and also the famine. *The seven years of dearth began to come, v. 54.* See what changes of condition we are liable to in this world, and what need we have to be joyful in a day of prosperity and in a day of adversity to consider, Eccl. 7:14. This famine, it seems, was not only in Egypt, but in other lands, in *all lands,* that is, all the neighbouring countries; *fruitful lands* are soon *turned into barrenness for the iniquity of those that dwell therein,* Ps. 107:34. It is here said that *in the land of Egypt there was bread,* meaning probably, not only that which Joseph had bought up for the king, but that which private persons, by his example, and upon the public notice of this prediction, as well as by the rules of common prudence, had laid up.

III. The performance of Joseph's trust. He was found faithful to it, as a steward ought to be. 1. He was diligent in laying up, while the plenty lasted, *v.* 48, 49. He that thus gathers is a wise son. 2. He was prudent and careful in giving out, when the famine came, and kept the markets low by furnishing them at reasonable rates out of his stores. The people in distress cried to Pharaoh, as that woman to the king of Israel (2 Ki. 6:26), *Help, my lord, O king:* he sent them to his treasurer, *Go to Joseph.* Thus God in the gospel directs those that apply to him for mercy and grace to *go to the Lord Jesus,* in whom all fulness dwells; and, *What he saith to you, do.* Joseph, no doubt, with wisdom and justice fixed the price of the corn he sold, so that Pharaoh, whose money had bought it up, might have a reasonable profit, and yet the country might not be oppressed, nor advantage taken of their prevailing necessity; while he that withholdest corn when it is dear, in hopes it will yet grow dearer, though people perish for want of it, has many a curse for so doing (and it is not a curse causeless), *blessings shall be upon the head of him that* thus *selleth it,* Prov. 11:26. And let the price be determined by that golden rule of justice, to do as we would be done by.

CHAPTER 42

We had, in the foregoing chapter, the fulfilling of the dreams which Joseph had interpreted: in this and the following chapters we have the fulfilling of the dreams which Joseph himself had dreamed, that his father's family should do homage to him. The story is very largely and particularly related of what passed between Joseph and his brethren, not only because it is an entertaining story, and probably was much talked of, both among the Israelites and among the Egyptians, but because it is very instructive, and it gave occasion for the removal of Jacob's family into Egypt, on which so many great events afterwards depended. We have, in this chapter, I. The humble application of Jacob's sons to Joseph to buy corn (*v.* 1–6). II. The fright Joseph put them into, for their trial (*v.* 7–20). III. The conviction they were now under of their sin concerning Joseph long before (*v.* 21–24). IV. Their return to Canaan with corn, and the great distress their good father was in upon hearing the account of their expedition (*v.* 25, etc.).

Verses 1–6

Though Jacob's sons were all married, and had families of their own, yet, it should seem, they were still incorporated in one society, under the conduct and presidency of their father Jacob. We have here,

I. The orders he gave them to go and buy corn in Egypt, *v.* 1, 2. Observe, 1. The famine was grievous in the land of Canaan. It is observable that all the three patriarchs, to whom Canaan was the land of promise, met with famine in that land, which was not only to try their faith, whether they could trust God though he should slay them, though he should starve them, but to teach them to seek the better country, that is, the heavenly, Heb. 11:14–16. We have need of something to wean us from this world, and make us long for a better. 2. Still, when there was famine in Canaan, there was corn in Egypt. Thus Providence orders it, that one place should be a succour and supply to another; for we are all brethren. The Egyptians, the seed of accursed Ham, have plenty, when God's blessed Israel want: Thus God, in dispensing common favours, often crosses hands. Yet observe, The plenty Egypt now had was owing, under God, to Joseph's prudence and care: if his brethren had not sold him into Egypt, but respected him according to his merits, who knows but he might have done the same thing for Jacob's family which now he had done for Pharaoh, and the Egyptians might then have come to them to buy corn? but those who drive away from among them wise and good men know not what they do. 3. *Jacob saw that there was corn in Egypt;* he saw the corn that his neighbours had bought there and brought home. It is a spur to exertion to see where supplies are to be had, and to see others supplied. Shall others get food for their

souls, and shall we starve while it is to be had? 4. He reproved his sons for delaying to provide corn for their families. *Why do you look one upon another?* Note, When we are in trouble and want, it is folly for us to stand looking upon one another, that is, to stand desponding and despairing, as if there were no hope, no help, — to stand disputing either which shall have the honour of going first or which shall have the safety of coming last, — to stand deliberating and debating what we shall do, and doing nothing, — to stand dreaming under a spirit of slumber, as if we had nothing to do, and to stand delaying, as if we had time at command. Let it never be said, "We left that to be done to-morrow which we could a well have done to-day." 5. He quickened them to go to Egypt: *Get you down thither.* Masters of families must not only pray for daily bread for their families, and food convenient, but must lay out themselves with care and industry to provide it.

II. Their obedience to these orders, *v.* 3. They *went down to buy corn;* they did not send their servants, but very prudently went themselves, to lay out their own money. Let none think themselves too great nor too good to take pains. Masters of families should see with their own eyes, and take heed of leaving too much to servants. Only Benjamin went not with them, for he was his father's darling. To Egypt they came, among others, and, having a considerable cargo of corn to buy, they were brought before Joseph himself, who probably expected they would come; and, according to the laws of courtesy, *they bowed down themselves before him, v.* 6. Now their empty sheaves did obeisance to his full one. Compare this with Isa. 60:14 and Rev. 3:9.

Verses 7–20

We may well wonder that Joseph, during the twenty years that he had now been in Egypt, especially during the last seven years that he had been in power there, never sent to his father to acquaint him with his circumstances; nay, it is strange that he who so often *went throughout all the land of Egypt* (ch. 41:45, 46) never made an excursion to Canaan, to visit his aged father, when he was in the borders of Egypt, that lay next to Canaan. Perhaps it would not have been above three or four days' journey for him in his chariot. It is a probable conjecture that his whole management of himself in this affair was by special direction from Heaven, that the purpose of God concerning Jacob and his family might be accomplished. When Joseph's brethren came, he knew them by many a satisfactory token, but they knew not him, little thinking to find him there, *v.* 8. He *remembered the dreams* (*v.* 9), but they had forgotten them. The laying up of God's oracles in our hearts will be of excellent use to us in all our conduct. Joseph had an eye to his dreams, which he knew to be divine, in his carriage towards his brethren, and aimed at the accomplishment of them and the bringing of his brethren to repentance for their former sins; and both these points were gained.

I. He showed himself very rigorous and harsh with them. The very manner of his speaking, considering the post he was in, was enough to frighten them; for *he spoke roughly to them, v.* 7. He charged them with bad designs against the government (*v.* 9), treated them as dangerous persons, saying, *You are spies,* and protesting *by the life of Pharaoh* that they were so, *v.* 16. Some make this an oath, others make it no more than a vehement asseveration, like that, *as thy soul liveth;* however it was more than yea, yea, and nay, nay, and therefore came of evil. Note, Bad words are soon learned by converse with those that use them, but not so soon unlearned. Joseph, by being much at court, got the courtier's oath, *By the life of Pharaoh,* perhaps designing hereby to confirm his brethren in their belief that he was an Egyptian, and not an Israelite. They knew this was not the language of a son of Abraham. When Peter would prove himself no disciple of Christ, he cursed and swore. Now why was Joseph thus hard upon his brethren? We may be sure it was not from a spirit of revenge, that he might now trample upon those who had formerly trampled upon him; he was not a man of that temper. But, 1. It was to enrich his own dreams, and complete the accomplishment of them. 2. It was to bring them to repentance. 3. It was to get out of them an account of the state of their family, which he longed to know: they

would have discovered him if he had asked as a friend, therefore he asks as a judge. Not seeing his brother Benjamin with them, perhaps he began to suspect that they had made away with him too, and therefore gives them occasion to speak of their father and brother. Note, God in his providence sometimes seems harsh with those he loves, and speaks roughly to those for whom yet he has great mercy in store.

II. They, hereupon, were very submissive. They spoke to him with all the respect imaginable: *Nay, my lord (v.* 10) — a great change since they said, *Behold, this dreamer comes.* They very modestly deny the charge: *We are no spies.* They tell him their business, that they came to buy food, a justifiable errand, and the same that many strangers came to Egypt upon at this time. They undertake to give a particular account of themselves and their family (*v.* 13), and this was what they wanted.

III. He clapped them all up in prison for three days, *v.* 17. Thus God deals with the souls he designs for special comfort and honour; he first humbles them, and terrifies them, and brings them under a spirit of bondage, and then binds up their wounds by the Spirit of adoption.

IV. He concluded with them, at last, that one of them should be left as a hostage, and the rest should go home and fetch Benjamin. It was a very encouraging word he said to them (*v.* 18): *I fear God;* as if he had said, "You may assure yourselves I will do you no wrong; I dare not, for I know that, high as I am, there is one higher than I." Note, With those that fear God we have reason to expect fair dealing. The fear of God will be a check upon those that are in power, to restrain them from abusing their power to oppression and tyranny. Those that have no one else to stand in awe of ought to stand in awe of their own consciences. See Neh. 5:15, *So did not I, because of the fear of God.*

Verses 21–28

Here is, I. The penitent reflection Joseph's brethren made upon the wrong they had formerly done to him, *v.* 21. They talked the matter over in the Hebrew tongue, not suspecting that Joseph, whom they took for a native of Egypt, understood them, much less that he was the person they spoke of.

1. They remembered with regret the barbarous cruelty wherewith they persecuted him: *We are verily guilty concerning our brother.* We do not read that they said this during their three days' imprisonment; but now, when the matter had come to some issue and they saw themselves still embarrassed, now they began to relent. Perhaps Joseph's mention of *the fear of God* (*v.* 18) put them upon consideration and extorted this reflection. Now see here, (1.) The office of conscience; it is a remembrancer, to bring to mind things long since said and done, to show us wherein we have erred, though it was long ago, as the reflection here mentioned was above twenty years after the sin was committed. As time will not wear out the guilt of sin, so it will not blot out the records of conscience; when the guilt of this sin of Joseph's brethren was fresh they made light of it, and sat down to eat bread; but now, long afterwards, their consciences reminded them of it. (2.) The benefit of affliction; they often prove the happy and effectual means of awakening conscience, and bringing sin to our remembrance, Job 13:26. (3.) The evil of guilt concerning our brethren; of all their sins, it was this that conscience now reproached them for. Whenever we think we have wrong done us, we ought to remember the wrong we have done to others, Eccl. 7:21, 22.

2. Reuben alone remembered, with comfort, that he had been an advocate for his brother, and had done what he could to prevent the mischief they did him (*v.* 22): *Spoke I not unto you, saying, Do not sin against the child?* Note, (1.) It is an aggravation of any sin that it was committed against admonitions. (2.) When we come to share with others in their calamities, it will be a comfort to us if we have the testimony of our consciences for us that we did not share with them in their iniquities, but, in our places, witnessed against them. This shall be our rejoicing in the day of evil, and shall take out the sting.

II. Joseph's tenderness towards them upon this occasion. He retired from them to weep, *v.* 24. Though his reason directed that he should still carry himself as a stranger to them, because they were not as yet humbled enough, yet natural affection could not but work, for he was a man of a tender spirit. This represents the tender mercies of our God towards repenting sinners. See Jer. 31:20, *Since I spoke against him I do earnestly remember him still.* See Jdg. 10:16.

III. The imprisonment of Simeon, *v.* 24. He chose him for the hostage probably because he remembered him to have been his most bitter enemy, or because he observed him now to be least humbled and concerned; he bound him *before their eyes* to affect them all; or perhaps it is intimated that, though he bound him with some severity before them, yet afterwards, when they were gone, he took off his bonds.

IV. The dismission of the rest of them. They came for corn, and corn they had; and not only so, but every man had his money restored in his sack's mouth. Thus Christ, our Joseph, gives out supplies without money and without price. Therefore the poor are invited to buy, Rev. 3:17, 18. This put them into great consternation (*v.* 28): *Their heart failed them, and they were afraid, saying one to another, What is this that God hath done to us?*

1. It was really a merciful event; for I hope they had no wrong done to them when they had their money given them back, but a kindness; yet they were thus terrified by it. Note, (1.) Guilty consciences are apt to take good providences in a bad sense, and to put wrong constructions even upon those things that make for them. They flee when none pursues. (2.) Wealth sometimes brings as much care along with it as want does, and more too. If they had been robbed of their money, they could not have been worse frightened than they were now when they found their money in their sacks. Thus he whose ground brought forth plentifully said, *What shall I do?* Lu. 12:17.

2. Yet in their circumstances it was very amazing. They knew that the Egyptians abhorred a Hebrew (ch 43:32), and therefore, since they could not expect to receive any kindness from them, they concluded that this was done with a design to pick a quarrel with them, and the rather because the man, the lord of the land, had charged them as spies. Their own consciences also were awake, and their sins set in order before them; and this put them into confusion. Note, (1.) When men's spirits are sinking every thing helps to sink them. (2.) When the events of Providence concerning us are surprising it is good to enquire what it is that God has done and is doing with us, and to consider the operation of his hands.

Verses 29–38

Here is, 1. The report which Jacob's sons made to their father of the great distress they had been in in Egypt; how they had been suspected, and threatened, and obliged to leave Simeon a prisoner there, till they should bring Benjamin with them thither. Who would have thought of this when they left home? When we go abroad we should consider how many sad accidents, that we little think of, may befall us before we return home. *We know not what a day may bring forth;* we ought therefore to be always ready for the worst. 2. The deep impression this made upon the good man. The very bundles of money which Joseph returned, in kindness to his father, frightened him (*v.* 35); for he concluded it was done with some mischievous design, or perhaps suspected his own sons to have committed some offence, and so to have run themselves into a *praemunire — a penalty,* which is intimated in what he says (*v.* 36): *Me have you bereaved.* He seems to lay the fault upon them; knowing their characters, he feared they had provoked the Egyptians, and perhaps forcibly, or fraudulently, brought home their money. Jacob is here much out of temper. (1.) He has very melancholy apprehensions concerning the present state of his family: *Joseph is not, and Simeon is not;* whereas Joseph was in honour and Simeon in the way to it. Note, We often perplex ourselves with our own mistakes, even in matters of fact. True griefs may arise from false intelligence and suppositions, 2 Sa. 13:31. Jacob gives up Joseph for gone, and Simeon and Benjamin as being in danger; and he concludes, *All these things are against me.* It proved otherwise, that all these were for him, were working together for his good and the good of his family: yet here he thinks them all against him. Note, Through our ignorance and mistake, and the weakness of our faith, we often apprehend that to be against us which is really for us. We are afflicted in body, estate, name, and relations; and we think all these things are against us, whereas these are really working for us the weight of glory. (2.) He is at present resolved that Benjamin shall not go down. Reuben will undertake to bring him back in safety (*v.* 37), not so much as putting in, *If the Lord will,* nor expecting the common disasters of travellers; but he foolishly bids Jacob slay his two sons (which, it is likely, he was very proud of) if he brought him not back; as if the death of two grandsons could satisfy Jacob for the death of a son. No, Jacob's present thoughts are, *My son shall not go down with you.* He plainly intimates a distrust of them, remembering that he never saw Joseph since he had been with them; therefore, "Benjamin shall not go with you, by the way in which you go, for *you will bring down my gray hairs with sorrow to the grave.*" Note, It is bad with a family when children conduct themselves so ill that their parents know not how to trust them.

CHAPTER 43

Here the story of Joseph's brethren is carried on, and very particularly related I. Their melancholy parting with their father Jacob in Canaan (*v.* 1–14). II. Their pleasant meeting with Joseph in Egypt (*v.* 15, etc.). For on this occasion nothing occurs there but what is agreeable and pleasant.

Verses 1–10

Here, 1. Jacob urges his sons to go and buy more corn in Egypt, *v.* 1, 2. The famine continued; and the corn they had bought was all spent, for it is meat that perisheth. Jacob, as a good master of a family, is in care to provide for those of his own house food convenient; and shall not God provide for his children, for *the household of faith?* Jacob bids them go again and buy a *little* food; now, in time of scarcity, a little must suffice, for nature is content with a little. 2. Judah urges him to consent that Benjamin should go down with them, how much soever it went against his feelings and previous determination. Note, It is not at all inconsistent with the honour and duty which children owe their parents humbly and modestly to advise them, and, as occasion is, to reason with them. *Plead with your mother, plead,* Hos. 2:2. (1.) He insists upon the absolute necessity they were under of bringing Benjamin with them, of which he, who was a witness to all that had passed in Egypt, was a more competent judge than Jacob could be. Joseph's protestation (*v.* 3) may be alluded to to show upon what terms we must draw nigh to God; unless we bring Christ along with us in the arms of our faith, we cannot see the face of God with comfort. (2.) He engages to take all possible care of him, and to do his utmost for his safety, *v.* 8, 9. Judah's conscience had lately smitten him for what he had done a great while ago against Joseph (*ch.* 42:21); and, as an evidence of the truth of his repentance, he is ready to undertake, as far as a man could do it, for Benjamin's security. He will not only not wrong him, but will do all he can to protect him. This is restitution, as far as the case will admit; when he knew not how he could restore Joseph, he would make some amends for the irreparable injury he had done him by doubling his care concerning Benjamin.

Verses 11–14

Observe here, I. Jacob's persuasibleness. He would be ruled by reason, though they were his inferiors that urged it. He saw the necessity of the case; and, since there was no remedy, he consented to yield to the necessity (*v.* 11): *"If it must be so now, take your brother.* If no corn can be had but upon those terms, we may as well expose him to the perils of the journey as suffer ourselves and families, and Benjamin amongst the rest, to perish for want of bread." *Skin for skin, and all that a man has,* even a Benjamin, the dearest of all, *will he give for his life.* No death so dreadful as that by famine, Lam. 4:9. Jacob had said (*ch.* 42:38), *My son shall not go down;* but now he is over-persuaded to consent. Note, It is no fault, but our wisdom and duty, to alter our purposes and resolutions when there is a good reason for our so doing. Constancy is a virtue, but obstinacy is not. It is God's prerogative not to repent, and to make unchangeable resolves.

II. Jacob's prudence and justice, which appeared in three things: — 1. He sent back the money which they had found in the sacks' mouths, with this discreet construction of it, *Peradventure it was an oversight.* Note, Honesty obliges us to make restitution, not only of that which comes to us by our own fault, but of that which comes to us by the mistakes of others. Though we get it by oversight, if we keep it when the oversight is discovered, it is kept by deceit. In the stating of accounts, errors must be excepted, even those that make for us as well as those that make against us. Jacob's words furnish us with a favourable construction to put upon that which we are tempted to resent as an injury and affront; pass it by, and say, *Peradventure it was an oversight.* 2. He sent double money, as much again as they took the time before, upon supposition that the price of corn might have risen, — or to show a generous spirit, that they might be the more likely to find generous treatment with *the man, the lord of the land.* 3. He sent a present of such things as the land afforded, and as were scarce in Egypt — *balm and honey, etc.* (*v.* 11), the commodities that Canaan exported, *ch.* 37:25. Note, (1.) Providence dispenses its gifts variously. Some countries produce one commodity, others another, that commerce may be preserved. (2.) Honey and spice will never make up the want of bread-corn. The famine was sore in Canaan, and yet they had balm and myrrh, etc. We may live well enough upon plain food without dainties; but we cannot live upon dainties without plain food. Let us thank God that that which is most needful and useful is generally most cheap and common. (3.) A *gift in secret pacifies wrath,* Prov. 21:14. Jacob's sons were unjustly accused as spies, yet Jacob was willing to be at the expense of a present, to pacify the accuser. Sometimes we must not think it too much to buy peace even where we may justly demand it, and insist upon it as our right.

III. Jacob's piety appearing in his prayer: *God Almighty give you mercy before the man! v.* 14. Jacob had formerly turned an angry brother into a kind one with a present and a prayer; and here he betakes himself to the same tried method, and it sped well. Note, Those that would find mercy with men must seek it of God, who has all hearts in his hands, and turns them as he pleases.

IV. Jacob's patience. He concludes all with this: *"If I be bereaved of my children, I am bereaved;* If I must part with them thus one after another, I must acquiesce, and say, *The will of the Lord be done."* Note, It is our wisdom to reconcile ourselves to the sorest afflictions, and make the best of them; for there is nothing got by striving with our Maker, 2 Sa. 15:25, 26.

Verses 15–25

Jacob's sons, having got leave to take Benjamin with them, were observant of the orders their father had given them, and went down the second time into Egypt to buy corn. If we should ever know what a famine of the word means, let us not think it much to travel as far for spiritual food as they did for corporal food. Now here we have an account of what passed between them and Joseph's steward, who, some conjecture, was in the secret, and knew them to be Joseph's brethren, and helped to humour the thing; I rather think not, because no man was permitted to be present when Joseph afterwards made himself known to them, *ch.* 45:1. Observe, 1. Joseph's steward has orders from his master (who was busy selling corn, and receiving money) to take them to his house, and make ready for their entertainment. Though Joseph saw Benjamin there, he would not leave his work at working-time, nor trust another with it. Note, Business must take place of civility in its season. Our needful employments must not be neglected, no, not to pay respect to our friends. 2. Even this frightened them: *They were afraid, because they were brought into Joseph's house, v.* 18. The just challenges of their own consciences, and Joseph's violent suspicions of them, forbade them to expect any favour, and suggested to them that this was done with a bad design upon them. Note, Those that are guilty and timorous are apt to make the worst of every thing. Now they thought they should be reckoned with about the money in the sacks' mouths, and should be charged as cheats, and men not fit to be dealt with, who had taken advantage of the hurry of the market to carry off their corn unpaid for. They therefore laid the case before the steward, that he, being apprized of it, might stand between them and danger; and, as a substantial proof of their honesty, before they were charged with taking back their money they produced it. Note, Integrity and uprightness will preserve us, and will clear themselves as the light of the morning. 3. The steward encouraged them (*v.* 23): *Peace be to you, fear not;* though he knew not what his master drove at, yet he was aware these were men whom he meant no harm to, while he thus amused them; and therefore he directs them to look at the divine Providence in the return of their money: *Your God, and the God of your father, has given you treasure in your sacks.* Observe, (1.) Hereby he shows that he had no suspicion at all of dishonesty in them: for of what we get by deceit we cannot say, "God gives it to us." (2.) Hereby he silences their further enquiry about it. "Ask not how it came thither; Providence brought it to you, and let that satisfy you." (3.) It appears by what he said that, by his good master's instructions, he was brought to the knowledge of the true God, the God of the Hebrews. It may justly be expected that those who are servants in religious families should take all fit occasions to speak of God and his providence with reverence and seriousness. (4.) He directs them to look up to God, and acknowledge his providence in the good bargain they had. We must own ourselves indebted to God, as *our God and the God of our fathers* (a God in covenant with us and them) for all our successes and advantages, and the kindnesses of our friends; for every creature is that to us, and no more, which God makes it to be. The steward encouraged them, not only in words but in deeds; for he made very much of them till his master came, *v.* 24.

Verses 26–34

Here is, I. The great respect that Joseph's brethren paid to him. When they brought him the present, *they bowed themselves before him* (*v.* 26); and again, when they gave him an account of their father's health, *they made obeisance,* and called him, *Thy servant our father, v.* 28. Thus were Joseph's dreams fulfilled more and more: and even the father, by the sons, *bowed before him,* according to the dream, *ch.* 37:10. Probably Jacob had directed them, if they had occasion to speak of him to *the man, the lord of the land,* to call him *his servant.*

II. The great kindness that Joseph showed to them, while they little thought it was a brotherly kindness. Here is,

1. His kind enquiry concerning Jacob: *Is he yet alive?* — a very fit question to be asked concerning any, especially concerning old people; for we are dying daily: it is strange that we are *yet alive.* Jacob had said many years before, *I will go to the grave to my son;* but *he is yet alive:* we must not die when we will.

2. The kind notice he took of Benjamin, his own brother. (1.) He put up a prayer for him: *God be gracious unto thee, my son, v.* 29. Joseph's favour, though he was the lord of the land, would do him little good, unless God were gracious to him. Many seek the ruler's favour, but Joseph directs him to seek the favour of the ruler of rulers. (2.) He shed some tears for him, *v.* 30. His natural affection to his brother, his joy to see him, his concern at seeing him and the rest of them in distress for bread, and the remembrance of his own griefs since he last saw him, produced a great agitation in him, which perhaps was the more uneasy because he endeavoured to stifle and suppress it; but he was forced to retire into his closet, there to give vent to his feeling by tears. Note, [1.] Tears of tenderness and affection are no disparagement at all, even to great and wise men. [2.] Gracious weepers should not proclaim their tears. *My soul shall weep in secret,* says the prophet, Jer. 13:17. *Peter went out and wept bitterly.* See Mt. 26:75.

3. His kind entertainment of them all. When his weeping had subsided so that he could refrain himself, he sat down to dinner with them, treated them nobly, and yet contrived every thing to amuse them.

(1.) He ordered three tables to be spread, one for his brethren, another for the Egyptians that dined with him (for so different were their customs that they did not care to eat together), another for himself, who durst not own himself a Hebrew, and yet would not sit with the Egyptians. See here an instance, [1.] Of hospitality and good house-keeping, which are very commendable, according as the ability is. [2.] Of compliance with people's humours, even whimsical ones, as bishop Patrick calls this of the Egyptians not eating with the Hebrews. Though Joseph was the lord of the land, and orders were given that all people should obey him, yet he would not force the Egyptians to eat with the Hebrews, against their minds, but let them enjoy their humours. Spirits truly generous hate to impose. [3.] Of the early distance between Jews and Gentiles; one table would not hold them.

(2.) He placed his brethren according to their seniority (*v.* 33), as if he *could certainly divine.* Some think they placed themselves so, according to their custom; but, if so, I see not why such particular notice is taken of it, especially as a thing they marvelled at.

(3.) He gave them a very plentiful entertainment, sent messes to them from his own table, *v.* 34. This was the more generous in him, and the more obliging to them, because of the present scarcity of provisions. In a day of famine, it is enough to be fed; but here they were feasted. Perhaps they had not had such a good dinner for many months. It is said, *They drank and were merry;* their cares and fears were now over, and they ate their bread with joy, concluding they were now upon good terms with the man, the lord of the land. If God accept our works, *our present,* we have reason to be cheerful. Yet when we sit, as they here did, to eat with a ruler, we should consider what is before us, and not indulge our appetite, nor be desirous of dainties, Prov. 23:1–3. Joseph gave them to understand that Benjamin was his favourite; for his mess was *five times as much as any of theirs,* not as if he would have him eat so much more than the rest, for then he must eat more than would do him good (and it is no act of friendship, but rather an injury and unkindness, to press any either to eat or drink to excess), but thus he would testify his particular respect for him, that he might try whether his brethren would envy Benjamin his larger messes, as formerly they had envied himself his finer coat. And it must be our rule, in such cases, to be content with what we have, and not to grieve at what others have.

CHAPTER 44

Joseph, having entertained his brethren, dismissed them; but here we have them brought back in a greater fright than any they had been in yet. Observe, I. What method he took both to humble them further and also to try their affection to his brother Benjamin, by which he would be able to judge of the sincerity of their repentance for what they had done against himself, of which he was desirous to be satisfied before he manifested his reconciliation to them. This he contrived to do by bringing Benjamin into distress (*v.* 1–17). II. The good success of the experiment; he found them all heartily concerned, and Judah particularly, both for the safety of Benjamin and for the comfort of their aged father (*v.* 18, etc.).

Verses 1–17

Joseph heaps further kindnesses upon his brethren, fills their sacks, returns their money, and sends them away full of gladness; but he also exercises them with further trials. Our God thus humbles those whom he loves and loads with benefits. Joseph ordered his steward to put a fine silver cup which he had (and which, it is likely, was used at his table when they dined with him) into Benjamin's sack's mouth, that it might seem as if he had stolen it from the table, and put it here himself, after his corn was delivered to him. If Benjamin had stolen it, it had been the basest piece of dishonesty and ingratitude that could be and if Joseph, by ordering it to be there, had designed really to take advantage against him, it had been in him most horrid cruelty and oppression; but it proved, in the issue, that there was no harm done, nor any designed, on either side. Observe,

I. How the pretended criminals were pursued and arrested, on suspicion of having stolen a silver cup. The steward charged them with ingratitude — rewarding evil for good; and with folly, in taking away a cup of daily use, and which therefore would soon be missed, and diligent search made for it; for so it may be read: *Is not this it in which my lord drinketh* (as having a particular fondness for it), *and for which he would search thoroughly? v.* 5. Or, "By which, leaving it carelessly at your table, he would make trial whether you were honest men or no."

II. How they pleaded for themselves. They solemnly protested their innocence, and detestation of so base a thing (*v.* 7), urged it as an instance of their honesty that they had brought their money back (*v.* 8), and offered to submit to the severest punishment if they should be found guilty, *v.* 9, 10.

III. How the theft was fastened upon Benjamin. In his sack the cup was found to whom Joseph had been particularly kind. Benjamin, no doubt, was ready to deny, upon oath, the taking of the cup, and we may suppose him as little liable to suspicion as any of them; but it is in vain to confront such notorious evidence: the cup is found in his custody; they dare not arraign Joseph's justice, nor so much as suggest that perhaps he that had put their money in their sacks' mouths had put the cup there; but they throw themselves upon Joseph's mercy. And,

IV. Here is their humble submission, *v.* 16. 1. They acknowledge the righteousness of God: *God hath found out the iniquity of thy servants,* perhaps referring to the injury they had formerly done to Joseph, for which they thought God was now reckoning with them. Note, Even in those afflictions wherein we apprehend ourselves wronged by men yet we must own that God is righteous, and finds out our iniquity. 2. They surrender themselves prisoners to Joseph: *We are my lord's servants.* Now Joseph's dreams were accomplished to the utmost. Their bowing so often, and doing homage, might be looked upon but as a compliment, and no more than what other strangers did; but the construction they themselves, in their pride, had put upon his dreams was, *Shalt though have dominion over us?* (*ch.* 37:8), and in this sense it is now at length fulfilled,; they own themselves his vassals. Since they did invidiously so understand it, so it shall be fulfilled in them.

V. Joseph, with an air of justice, gives sentence that Benjamin only should be kept in bondage, and the rest should be dismissed; for why should any suffer but the guilty? Perhaps Joseph intended hereby to try Benjamin's temper, whether he could bear such a hardship as this with the calmness and composure of mind that became a wise and good man: in short, whether he was indeed his own brother, in *spirit* as well as *blood;* for Joseph himself had been falsely accused, and had suffered hard things in consequence, and yet kept possession of his own soul. However, it is plain he intended hereby to try the affection of his brethren to Benjamin and to their father. If they had gone away contentedly, and left Benjamin in bonds, no doubt Joseph would soon have released and promoted him, and sent notice to Jacob, and would have left the rest of his brethren justly to suffer for their hard-heartedness; but they proved to be better to Benjamin than he feared. Note, We cannot judge what men are by what they have been formerly, nor what they will do by what they have done: age and experience may make men wiser and better. Those that had sold Joseph would not now abandon Benjamin. The worst may mend in time.

Verses 18–34

We have here a most ingenious and pathetic speech which Judah made to Joseph on Benjamin's behalf, to obtain his discharge from the sentence passed upon him. Perhaps Judah was a better friend to Benjamin than the rest were, and more solicitous to bring him off; or he thought himself under greater obligations to attempt it than the rest, because he had passed his word to his father for his safe return; or the rest chose him for their spokesman, because he was a man of better sense, and better spirit, and had a greater command of language than any of them. His address, as it is here recorded, is so very natural and so expressive of his present feelings that we cannot but suppose Moses, who wrote it so long after, to have written it under the special direction of him that made man's mouth.

I. A great deal of unaffected art, and unstudied unforced rhetoric, there is in this speech. 1. He addresses himself to Joseph with a great deal of respect and deference, calls him his *lord,* himself and his brethren his *servants,* begs his patient hearing, and ascribes sovereign authority to him: *"Thou art even as Pharaoh,* one whose favour we desire and whose wrath we dread as we do Pharaoh's." Religion does not destroy good manners, and it is prudence to speak respectfully to those at whose mercy we lie: titles of honour to those that are entitled to them are not flattering titles. 2. He represented Benjamin as one well worthy of his compassionate consideration (*v.* 20); he was *a little one,* compared with the rest of them; the youngest, not acquainted with the world, nor ever inured to hardship, having always been brought up tenderly with his father. It made the case the more pitiable that he alone was left of his mother, and his brother was dead, namely, *Joseph.* Little did Judah think what a tender point he touched upon now. Judah knew that Joseph was sold, and therefore had reason enough to think that he was alive; at least he could not be sure that he was dead: but they had made their father believe he was dead; and now they had told that lie so long that they had forgotten the truth, and begun to believe the lie themselves. 3. He urged it very closely that Joseph had himself constrained them to bring Benjamin with them, had expressed a desire to see him (*v.* 21), and had forbidden them his presence unless they brought Benjamin with them (*v.* 23, 26), all which intimated that he designed him some kindness; and must he be brought with so much difficulty to the preferment of a perpetual slavery? Was he not brought to Egypt, in obedience, purely in obedience, to the command of Joseph? and would he not show him some mercy? Some observe that Jacob's sons, in reasoning with their father, had said, *We will not go down unless Benjamin go with us* (*ch.* 43:5); but that when Judah comes to relate the story he expresses it more decently: "*We cannot go down* with any expectation to speed well." Indecent words spoken in haste to our superiors should be recalled and amended. 4. The great argument he insisted upon was the insupportable grief it would be to his aged father if Benjamin should be left behind in servitude: *His father loveth him, v.* 20. This they had pleaded against Joseph's insisting on his coming down (*v.* 22): "*If he should leave his father, his father would die;* much more if now he be left behind, never more to return to him." This the old man, of whom they spoke, had pleaded against his going down: *If mischief befal him, you shall bring down my gray hairs,* that crown of glory, *with sorrow to the grave, v.* 29. This therefore Judah presses with a great deal of earnestness: *"His life is bound up in the lad's life* (*v.* 30); when he sees that the lad is not with us, he will faint away, and die immediately (*v.* 31), or will abandon himself to such a degree of sorrow as will, in a few days, make an end of him." And, *lastly,* Judah pleads that, for his part, he could not bear to see this: *Let me not see the evil that shall come on my father, v.* 34. Note, It is the duty of children to be very tender of their parents' comfort, and to be afraid of every thing that may be an occasion of grief to them. Thus the love that descended first must again ascend, and something must be done towards a recompense for their care. 5. Judah, in honour to the justice of Joseph's sentence, and to show his sincerity in this plea, offers himself to become a bondsman instead of Benjamin, *v.* 33. Thus the law would be satisfied; Joseph would be no loser (for we may suppose Judah a more able-bodied man than Benjamin, and fitter for service); and Jacob would better bear the loss of him than of Benjamin. Now, so far was he from grieving at his father's particular fondness for Benjamin, that he was himself willing to be a bondman to indulge it.

Now, had Joseph been, as Judah supposed him, an utter stranger to the family, yet even common humanity could not but be wrought upon by such powerful reasonings as these; for nothing could be said more moving, more tender; it was enough to melt a heart of stone. But to Joseph, who was nearer akin to Benjamin than Judah himself was, and who, at this time, felt a greater affection both for him and his aged father than Judah did, nothing could be more pleasingly nor more happily said. Neither Jacob nor Benjamin needed an intercessor with Joseph; for he himself loved them.

II. Upon the whole matter let us take notice, 1. How prudently Judah suppressed all mention of the crime that was charged upon Benjamin. Had he said any thing by way of acknowledgment of it, he would have reflected on Benjamin's honesty, and seemed too forward to suspect that; had he said any thing by way of denial of it, he would have reflected on Joseph's justice, and the sentence he had passed: therefore he wholly waives that head, and appeals to Joseph's pity. Compare with this that of Job, in humbling himself before God (Job 9:15), *Though I were righteous, yet would I not answer;* I would not argue, but petition; *I would make supplication to my Judge.* 2. What good reason dying Jacob had to say, *Judah, thou art he whom they brethren shall praise* (*ch.* 49:8), for he excelled them all in boldness, wisdom, eloquence, and especially tenderness for their father and family. 3. Judah's faithful adherence to Benjamin, now in his distress, was recompensed long after by the constant adherence of the tribe of Benjamin to the tribe of Judah, when all the other ten tribes deserted it. 4. How fitly does the apostle, when he is discoursing of the mediation of Christ, observe, that *our Lord sprang out of Judah* (Heb. 7:14); for, like his father Judah, he not only *made intercession for the transgressors,* but he became a surety for them, as it follows there (*v.* 22), testifying therein a very tender concern both for his father and for his brethren.

CHAPTER 45

It is a pity that this chapter and the foregoing should be parted, and read asunder. There we had Judah's intercession for Benjamin, with which, we may suppose, the rest of his brethren signified their concurrence; Joseph let him go on without interruption, heard all he had to say, and then answered it all in one word, "I am Joseph." Now he found his brethren humbled for their sins, mindful of himself (for Judah had mentioned him twice in his speech), respectful to their father, and very tender of their brother Benjamin; now they were ripe for the comfort he designed them, by making himself known to them, the story of which we have in this chapter. It was to Joseph's brethren as clear shining after rain, nay, it was to them as life from the dead. Here is, I. Joseph's discovery of himself to his brethren, and his discourse with them upon that occasion (*v.* 1–15). II. The orders Pharaoh, hereupon, gave to fetch Jacob and his family down to Egypt, and Joseph's despatch of his brethren, accordingly, back to his father with those orders (*v.* 16–24). III. The joyful tidings of this brought to Jacob (*v.* 25, etc.).

Verses 1–15

Judah and his brethren were waiting for an answer, and could not but be amazed to discover, instead of the gravity of a judge, the natural affection of a father or brother.

I. Joseph ordered all his attendants to withdraw, *v.* 1. The private conversations of friends are the most free. When Joseph would put on love he puts off state, and it was not fit his servants should be witnesses of this. Thus Christ graciously manifests himself and his loving-kindness to his people, out of the sight and hearing of the world.

II. Tears were the preface or introduction to his discourse, *v.* 2. He had dammed up this stream a great while, and with much ado: but now it swelled so high that he could no longer contain, but *he wept aloud,* so that those whom he had forbidden to see him could not but hear him. These were tears of tenderness and strong affection, and with these he threw off that austerity with which he had hitherto carried himself towards his brethren; for he could bear it no longer. This represents the divine compassion towards returning penitents, as much as that of the father of the prodigal, Lu. 15:20; Hos. 14:8, 9.

III. He very abruptly (as one uneasy till it was out) tells them who he was: *I am Joseph.* They knew him only by his Egyptian name, *Zaphnath-paaneah,* his Hebrew name being lost and forgotten in Egypt; but now he teaches them to call him by that: *I am Joseph;* nay, that they might not suspect it was another of the same name, he explains himself (*v.* 4): *I am Joseph, your brother.* This would both humble them yet more for their sin in selling him, and would encourage them to hope for kind treatment. Thus when Christ would convince Paul he said, *I am Jesus;* and when he would comfort his disciples he said, *It is I, be not afraid.* This word, at first, startled Joseph's brethren; they started back through fear, or at least stood still astonished; but Joseph called kindly and familiarly to them: *Come near, I pray you.* Thus when Christ manifests himself to his people he encourages them to draw near to him with a true heart. Perhaps, being about to speak of their selling him, he would not speak aloud, lest the Egyptians should overhear, and it should make the Hebrews to be yet more an abomination to them; therefore he would have them come near, that he might whisper with them, which, now that the tide of his passion was a little over, he was able to do, whereas at first he could not but cry out.

IV. He endeavours to assuage their grief for the injuries they had done him, by showing them that whatever they designed God meant it for good, and had brought much good out of it (*v.* 5): *Be not grieved, nor angry with yourselves.* Sinners must grieve, and be angry with themselves, for their sins; yea, though God by his power brings good out of them, for no thanks are due to the sinner for this: but true penitents should be greatly affected when they see God thus bringing good out of evil, *meat out of the eater.* Though we must not with this consideration extenuate our own sins and so take off the edge of our repentance, yet it may be well thus to extenuate the sins of others and so take off the edge of our angry resentments. Thus Joseph does here; his brethren needed not to fear that he would avenge upon them an injury which God's providence had made to turn so much to his advantage and that of his family. Now he tells them how long the famine was likely to last — *five years;* yet (*v.* 6) what a capacity he was in of being kind to his relations and friends, which is the greatest satisfaction that wealth and power can give to a good man, *v.* 8. See what a favourable colour he puts upon the injury they had done him: *God sent me before you, v.* 5, 7. Note, 1. God's Israel is the particular care of God's providence. Joseph reckoned that his advancement was not so much designed to save a whole kingdom of Egyptians as to preserve a small family of Israelites: *for the Lord's portion is his people;* whatever becomes of theirs, they shall be secured. 2. Providence looks a great way forward, and has a long reach. Even long before the years of plenty, Providence was preparing for the supply of Jacob's house in the years of famine. The psalmist praises God for this (Ps. 105:17): *He sent a man before them, even Joseph.* God sees his work from the beginning to the end, but we do not, Eccl. 3:11. How admirable are the projects of providence! How remote its tendencies! What wheels are there within wheels, and yet all directed by the eyes in the wheels, and the spirit of the living creature! Let us therefore judge nothing before the time. 3. God often works by contraries. The envy and contention of brethren threaten the ruin of families, yet, in this instance, they prove the occasion of preserving Jacob's family. Joseph could never have been *the shepherd and stone of Israel* if his brethren had not shot at him, and hated him; even those that had wickedly sold Joseph into Egypt yet themselves reaped the benefit of the good God brought out of it; as those that put Christ to death were many of them saved by his death. 4. God must have all the glory of the seasonable preservations of his people, by what way soever they are effected. *It was not you that sent me hither, but God, v.* 8. As, on the one hand, they must not fret at it, because it ended so well, so on the other hand they must not be proud of it, because it was God's doing, and not theirs. They designed, by selling him into Egypt, to defeat his dreams, but God thereby designed to accomplish them. Isa. 10:7, *Howbeit he meaneth not so.*

V. He promises to take care of his father and all the family during the rest of the years of famine. 1. He desires that his father may speedily be made glad with the tidings of his life and dignity. His brethren must hasten to Canaan, and must inform Jacob that his son Joseph was *lord of all Egypt;* (*v.* 9): they must tell him of all his glory there, *v.* 13. He knew it would be a refreshing oil to his hoary head and a sovereign cordial to his spirits. If any thing would make him young again, this would. He desires them to give themselves, and take with them to their father, all possible satisfaction of the truth of these surprising tidings: *Your eyes see that it is my mouth, v.* 12. If they would recollect themselves, they might remember something of his features, speech, etc., and be satisfied. 2. He is very earnest that his father and all his family should come to him to Egypt: *Come down unto me, tarry not, v.* 9. He allots his dwelling in Goshen, that part of Egypt which lay towards Canaan, that they might be mindful of the country from which they were to come out, *v.* 10. He promises to provide for him: *I will nourish thee, v.* 11. Note, It is the duty of children, if the necessity of their parents do at any time require it, to support and supply them to the utmost of their ability; and *Corban* will never excuse them, Mk. 7:11. This is showing piety at home, 1 Tim. 5:4. Our Lord Jesus being, like Joseph, exalted to the highest honours and powers of the upper world, it is his will that all that are his should be with him where he is, Jn. 17:24. This is his commandment, that we be with him now in faith and hope, and a heavenly conversation; and this is his promise, that we shall be for ever with him.

VI. Endearments were interchanged between him and his brethren. He began with the youngest, his own brother Benjamin, who was but about a year old when Joseph was separated from his brethren; they wept on each other's neck (*v.* 14), perhaps to think of their mother Rachel, who died in travail of Benjamin. Rachel, in her husband, Jacob, had been lately weeping for her children, because, in his apprehension, they were not — Joseph gone, and Benjamin going; and now they were weeping for her, because she was not. After he had embraced Benjamin, he, in like manner, caressed them all (*v.* 15); and then *his brethren talked with him* freely and familiarly of all the affairs of their father's house. After the tokens of true reconciliation follow the instances of a sweet communion.

Verses 16–24

Here is, 1. The kindness of Pharaoh to Joseph, and to his relations for his sake: he bade his brethren welcome (v. 16), though it was a time of scarcity, and they were likely to be a charge to him. Nay, because it pleased Pharaoh, it pleased his servants too, at least they pretended to be pleased because Pharaoh was. He engaged Joseph to send for his father down to Egypt, and promised to furnish them with all conveniences both for his removal thither and his settlement there. If the good of all the land of Egypt (as it was not better stocked than any other land, thanks to Joseph, under God) would suffice him, he was welcome to it all, it was all his own, even *the fat of the land* (v. 18), so that they need not *regard their stuff*, v. 20. What they had in Canaan he reckoned but stuff, in comparison with what he had for them in Egypt; and therefore if they should be constrained to leave some of that behind them, let them not be discontented; Egypt would afford them enough to make up the losses of their removal. Thus those for whom Christ intends shares in his heavenly glory ought not to regard the stuff of this world: The best of its enjoyments are but stuff, but lumber; we cannot make sure of it while we are here, much less can we carry it away with us; let us not therefore be solicitous about it, nor set our eyes or hearts upon it. There are better things reserved for us in that blessed land whither our Joseph has gone to prepare a place.

II. The kindness of Joseph to his father and brethren. Pharaoh was respectful to Joseph, in gratitude, because he had been an instrument of much good to him and his kingdom, not only preserving it from the common calamity, but helping to make it considerable among the nations; for all their neighbours would say, "Surely the Egyptians are a wise and an understanding people, that are so well stocked in a time of scarcity." For this reason Pharaoh never thought any thing too much that he could do for Joseph. Note, There is a gratitude owing even to inferiors; and when any have shown us kindness we should study to requite it, not only to them, but to their relations. And Joseph likewise was respectful to his father and brethren in duty, because they were his near relations, though his brethren had been his enemies, and his father long a stranger. 1. He furnished them for necessity, v. 21. He gave them wagons and provisions for the way, both going and coming; for we never find that Jacob was very rich, and, at this time, when the famine prevailed, we may suppose he was rather poor. 2. He furnished them for ornament and delight. To his brethren he gave two suits a piece of good clothes, to Benjamin five suits, and money besides in his pocket, v. 22. To his father he sent a very handsome present of the varieties of Egypt, v. 23. Note, Those that are wealthy should be generous, and devise liberal things; what is an abundance good for, but to do good with it? 3. He dismissed them with a seasonable caution: *See that you fall not out by the way*, v. 24. He knew they were but too apt to be quarrelsome; and what had lately passed, which revived the remembrance of what they had done formerly against their brother, might give them occasion to quarrel. Joseph had observed them to contend about it, *ch.* 42:22. To one they would say, "It was you that first upbraided him with his dreams;" to another, "It was you that stripped him of his fine coat;" to another, "It was you that threw him into the pit," etc. Now Joseph, having forgiven them all, lays this obligation upon them, not to upbraid one another. This charge our Lord Jesus has given to us, *that we love one another*, that we live in peace, that whatever occurs, or whatever former occurrences are remembered, we fall not out. For, (1.) We are brethren, we have all one Father. (2.) We are his brethren, and we shame our relation to him *who is our peace*, if we fall out. (3.) We are guilty, *verily guilty*, and, instead of quarrelling with one another, have a great deal of reason to fall out with ourselves. (4.) We are, or hope to be, forgiven of God whom we have all offended, and therefore should be ready to forgive one another. (5.) We are *by the way*, a way that lies through the land of Egypt, where we have many eyes upon us, that seek occasion and advantage against us, a way that leads to Canaan, where we hope to be for ever in perfect peace.

Verses 25–28

We have here the good news brought to Jacob. 1. The

relation of it, at first, sunk his spirits. When, without any preamble, his sons came in, crying, *Joseph is yet alive*, each striving which should first proclaim it, perhaps he thought they bantered him, and the affront grieved him; or the very mention of Joseph's name revived his sorrow, so that his heart fainted, v. 26. It was a good while before he came to himself. He was in such care and fear about the rest of them that at this time it would have been joy enough to him to hear that Simeon was released, and that Benjamin had come safely home (for he had been ready to despair concerning both these); but to hear that *Joseph is alive* is too good news to be true; he faints, for he believes it not. Note, We faint, because we do not believe; David himself had fainted if he had not believed, Ps. 27:13. 2. The confirmation of it, by degrees, revived his spirit. Jacob had easily believed his sons formerly when they told him, *Joseph is dead;* but he can hardly believe them now that they tell him, *Joseph is alive*. Weak and tender spirits are influenced more by fear than hope, and are more apt to receive impressions that are discouraging than those that are encouraging. But at length Jacob is convinced of the truth of the story, especially when he sees the wagons which were sent to carry him (for seeing is believing), then his *spirit revived*. Death is as the wagons which are sent to fetch us to Christ: the very sight of it approaching should revive us. Now Jacob is called Israel (v. 28), for he begins to recover his wonted vigour. (1.) It pleases him to think that Joseph is alive. He says nothing of Joseph's glory, of which they told him; it was enough to him that Joseph was alive. Note, Those that would be content with less degrees of comfort are best prepared for greater. (2.) It pleases him to think of going to see him. Though he was old, and the journey long, yet he would go to see Joseph, because Joseph's business would not permit him to come to see him. Observe, He says, *"I will go and see him,"* not, "I will go and live with him;" Jacob was old, and did not expect to live long; "But I will go and see him *before I die*, and then let me depart in peace; let my eyes be refreshed with this sight before they are closed, and then it is *enough*, I need no more to make me happy in this world." Note, It is good for us all to make death familiar to us, and to speak of it as near, that we may think how little we have to do before we die, that we may do it with all our might, and may enjoy our comforts as those that must quickly die, and leave them.

CHAPTER 46

Jacob is here removing to Egypt in his old age, forced thither by a famine, and invited thither by a son. Here, I. God sends him thither (v. 1–4). II. All his family goes with him (v. 5–27). III. Joseph bids him welcome (v. 28–34).

Verses 1–4

The divine precept is, *In all thy ways acknowledge God;* and the promise annexed to it is, *He shall direct thy paths*. Jacob has here a very great concern before him, not only a journey, but a removal, to settle in another country, a change which was very surprising to him (for he never had any other thoughts than to live and die in Canaan), and which would be of great consequence to his family for a long time to come. Now here we are told,

I. How he acknowledged God in this way. He *came to Beersheba*, from Hebron, where he now dwelt; and there *he offered sacrifices to the God of his father Isaac*, v. 1. He chose that place, in remembrance of the communion which his father and grandfather had with God in that place. Abraham called on God there (*ch.* 21:33), so did Isaac (*ch.* 26:25), and therefore Jacob made it the place of his devotion, the rather because it lay in his way. In his devotion, 1. He had an eye to God as the God of his father Isaac, that is, a God in covenant with him; for by Isaac the covenant was entailed upon him. God had forbidden Isaac to go down to Egypt when there was a famine in Canaan (*ch.* 26:2), which perhaps Jacob calls to mind when he consults God as the God of his father Isaac, with this thought, "Lord, though I am very desirous to see Joseph, yet if thou forbid me to go down to Egypt, as thou didst my father Isaac, I will submit, and very contentedly stay where I am." 2. He *offered sacrifices*, extraordinary sacrifices, besides those at his stated times; these sacrifices were offered, (1.) By way of thanksgiving for the late blessed change of the face of his family, for the good news he had received concerning Joseph, and for the hopes he

had of seeing him. Note, We should give God thanks for the beginnings of mercy, though they are not yet perfected; and this is a decent way of begging further mercy. (2.) By way of petition for the presence of God with him in his intended journey; he desired by these sacrifices to make his peace with God, to obtain the forgiveness of sin, that he might take no guilt along with him in this journey, for that is a bad companion. By Christ, the great sacrifice, we must reconcile ourselves to God, and offer up our requests to him. (3.) By way of consultation. The heathen consulted their oracles by sacrifice. Jacob would not go till he had asked God's leave: "Shall I go down to Egypt, or back to Hebron?" Such must be our enquiries in doubtful cases; and, though we cannot expect immediate answers from heaven, yet, if we diligently attend to the directions of the word, conscience, and providence, we shall find it is not in vain to ask counsel of God.

II. How God directed his paths: *In the visions of the night* (probably the very next night after he had offered his sacrifices, as 2 Chr. 1:7) *God spoke unto him, v.* 2. Note, Those who desire to keep up communion with God shall find that it never fails on his side. If we speak to him as we ought, he will not fail to speak to us. God called him by name, by his old name, *Jacob, Jacob*, to remind him of his low estate; his present fears did scarcely become an Israel. Jacob, like one well acquainted with the visions of the Almighty, and ready to obey them, answers, *"Here I am,"* ready to receive orders:" and what has God to say to him?

1. He renews the covenant with him: *I am God, the God of thy father* (v. 3); that is, "I am what thou ownest me to be: thou shalt find me a God, a divine wisdom and power engaged for thee; and thou shalt find me the God of thy father, true to the covenant made with him."

2. He encourages him to make this removal of his family: *Fear not to go down into Egypt*. It seems, though Jacob, upon the first intelligence of Joseph's life and glory in Egypt, resolved, without any hesitation, *I will go and see him;* yet, upon second thoughts, he saw some difficulties in it, which he knew not well how to get over. Note, Even those changes that seem to have in them the greatest joys and hopes, yet have an alloy of cares and fears, *Nulla est sincera voluptas — There is no unmingled pleasure*. We must always rejoice with trembling. Jacob had many careful thoughts about this journey, which God took notice of. (1.) He was old, 130 years old; and it is mentioned as one of the infirmities of old people that they are *afraid of that which is high, and fears are in the way*, Eccl. 12:5. It was a long journey, and Jacob was unfit for travel, and perhaps remembered that his beloved Rachel died in a journey. (2.) He feared lest his sons should be tainted with the idolatry of Egypt, and forget the God of their fathers, or enamoured with the pleasures of Egypt, and forget the land of promise. (3.) Probably he thought of what God had said to Abraham concerning the bondage and affliction of his seed (*ch.* 15:13), and was apprehensive that his removal to Egypt would issue in that. Present satisfactions should not take us off from the consideration and prospect of future inconveniences, which possibly may arise from what now appears most promising. (4.) He could not think of laying his bones in Egypt. But, whatever his discouragements were, this was enough to answer them all, *Fear not to go down into Egypt*.

3. He promises him comfort in the removal. (1.) That he should multiply in Egypt: "*I will there*, where thou fearest that thy family will sink and be lost, *make it a great nation*. That is the place Infinite Wisdom has chosen for the accomplishment of that promise." (2.) That he should have God's presence with him: *I will go down with thee into Egypt*. Note, Those that go whither God sends them shall certainly have God with them, and that is enough to secure them wherever they are and to silence their fears; we may safely venture even into Egypt if God go down with us. (3.) That neither he nor his should be lost in Egypt: *I will surely bring thee up again*. Though Jacob died in Egypt, yet this promise was fulfilled, [1.] In the bringing up of his body, to be buried in Canaan, about which, it appears, he was very solicitous, *ch.* 49:29, 32. [2.] In the bringing up of his seed to be settled in Canaan. Whatever low or darksome valley we are called into at any time, we may be confident, if God go down with us into it, that he will surely bring us up again. If he go with us down to death, he will surely bring us up again to glory. (4.) That

living and dying, his beloved Joseph should be a comfort to him: *Joseph shall put his hand upon thine eyes.* This is a promise that Joseph should live as long as he lived, that he should be with him at his death, and close his eyes with all possible tenderness and respect, as the dearest relations used to do. Probably Jacob, in the multitude of this thought within him, had been wishing that Joseph might do this last office of love for him: *Ille meos oculos comprimat — Let him close my eyes;* and God thus answered him in the letter of his desire. Thus God sometimes gratifies the innocent wishes of his people, and makes not only their death happy, but the very circumstances of it agreeable.

Verses 5–27

Old Jacob is here flitting. Little did he think of ever leaving Canaan; he expected, no doubt, *to die in his nest,* and to leave his seed in actual possession of the promised land: but Providence orders it otherwise. Note, Those that think themselves well settled may yet be unsettled in a little time. Even old people, who think of no other removal than that to the grave (which Jacob had much upon his heart, *ch.* 37:35; 42:38), sometimes live to see great changes in their family. It is good to be ready, not only for the grave, but for whatever may happen betwixt us and the grave. Observe, 1. How Jacob was conveyed; not in a chariot, though chariots were then used, but in a wagon, *v.* 5. Jacob had the character of a plain man, who did not affect any thing stately or magnificent; his son rode in a chariot (*ch.* 41:43), but a wagon would serve him. 2. The removal of what he had with him. (1.) His effects (*v.* 6), *cattle and goods;* these he took with him that he might not wholly be beholden to Pharaoh for a livelihood, and that it might not afterwards be said of them, "that they came beggars to Egypt." (2.) His family, *all his seed, v.* 7. It is probable that they had continued to live together in common with their father; and therefore when he went they all went, which perhaps they were the more willing to do, because, though they had heard that the land of Canaan was promised them, yet, to this day, they had none of it in possession. We have here a particular account of the names of Jacob's family, *his sons' sons,* most of whom are afterwards mentioned as heads of houses in the several tribes. See Num. 26:5, etc. Bishop Patrick observes that Issachar called his eldest son *Tola,* which signifies a *worm,* probably because when he was born he was a very little weak child, a worm, and no man, not likely to live; and yet there sprang from him a very numerous offspring, 1 Chr. 7:2. Note, Living and dying do not go by probability. The whole number that went down into Egypt was sixty-six (*v.* 26), to which add Joseph and his two sons, who were there before, and Jacob himself, the head of the family, and you have the number of seventy, *v.* 27. The Septuagint makes them seventy-five, and Stephen follows them (Acts 7:14), the reason of which we leave to the conjecture of the critics; but let us observe, [1.] Masters of families ought to take care of all under their charge, and to provide for those of their own house food convenient both for body and soul. When Jacob himself removed to a land of plenty, he would not leave any of his children behind him to starve in a barren land. [2.] Though the accomplishment of promises is always sure, yet it is often slow. It was now 215 years since God had promised Abraham to make of him a great nation (*ch.* 12:2); and yet that branch of his seed on which the promise was entailed had increased only to seventy, of which this particular account is kept, that the power of God in multiplying these seventy to so vast a multitude, even in Egypt, may appear the more illustrious. When God pleases, *a little one shall become a thousand,* Isa. 60:22.

Verses 28–34

We have here, I. The joyful meeting between Jacob and his son Joseph, in which observe,

1. Jacob's prudence in sending Judah before him to Joseph, to give him notice of his arrival in Goshen. This was a piece of respect owing to the government, under the protection of which these strangers had come to put themselves, *v.* 28. We should be very careful not to give offence to any, especially not to the higher powers.

2. Joseph's filial respect to him. He went in his chariot to met him, and, in the interview, showed, (1.) How much he honoured him: *He presented himself unto him.* Note, It is the duty of children to reverence their parents, yea, though Providence, as to outward condition, has advanced them above their parents. (2.) How much he loved him. Time did not wear out the sense of his obligations, but his tears which he shed abundantly upon his father's neck, for joy to see him, were real indications of the sincere and strong affection he had for him. See how near sorrow and joy are to each other in this world, when tears serve for the expression of both. In the other world weeping will be restrained to sorrow only; in heaven there is perfect joy, but no tears of joy: all tears, even those, shall there be wiped away, because the joys there are, as no joys are here, without any alloy. When Joseph embraced Benjamin he *wept upon his neck,* but when he embraced his father he *wept upon his neck a good while;* his brother Benjamin was dear, but his father Jacob must be dearer.

3. Jacob's great satisfaction in this meeting: *Now let me die, v.* 30. Not but that it was further desirable to live with Joseph, and to see his honour and usefulness; but he had so much pleasure and satisfaction in this first meeting that he thought it too much to desire or expect any more in this world, where our comforts must always be imperfect. Jacob wished to die immediately, and lived seventeen years longer, which, as our lives go now, is a considerable part of a man's age. Note, Death will not always come just when we call for it, whether in a passion of sorrow or in a passion of joy. Our times are in God's hand, and not in our own; we must die just when God pleases, and not either just when we are surfeited with the pleasures of life or just when we are overwhelmed with its griefs.

II. Joseph's prudent care concerning his brethren's settlement. It was justice to Pharaoh to let him know that such a colony had come to settle in his dominions. Note, If others repose a confidence in us, we must not be so base and disingenuous as to abuse it by imposing upon them. If Jacob and his family should come to be a charge to the Egyptians, yet it should never be said that they came among them clandestinely and by stealth. Thus Joseph took care to pay his respects to Pharaoh, *v.* 31. But how shall he dispose of his brethren? Time was when they were contriving to get rid of him; now he is contriving to settle them to their satisfaction and advantage: This is rendering good for evil. Now, 1. He would have them to live by themselves, separate as much as might be from the Egyptians, *in the land of Goshen,* which lay nearest to Canaan, and which perhaps was more thinly peopled by the Egyptians, and well furnished with pastures for cattle. He desired they might live separately, that they might be in the less danger both of being infected by the vices of the Egyptians and of being insulted by the malice of the Egyptians. Shepherds, it seems, *were an abomination to the Egyptians,* that is, they looked upon them with contempt, and scorned to converse with them; and he would not send for his brethren to Egypt to be tramped upon. And yet, 2. He would have them to continue shepherds, and not to be ashamed to own that as their occupation before Pharaoh. He could have employed them under himself in the corn-trade, or perhaps, by his interest in the king, might have procured places for them at court or in the army, and some of them, at least, were deserving enough; but such preferments would have exposed them to the envy of the Egyptians, and would have tempted them to forget Canaan and the promise made unto their fathers; therefore he contrives to continue them in their old employment. Note, (1.) An honest calling is no disparagement, nor ought we to account it so either in ourselves or in our relations, but rather reckon it a shame to be idle, or to have nothing to do. (2.) It is generally best for people to abide in the callings that they have been bred to, and used to, 1. Cor. 7:24. Whatever employment or condition God, in his providence, has allotted for us, let us accommodate ourselves to it, and satisfy ourselves with it, and *not mind high things.* It is better to be the credit of a mean post than the shame of a high one.

CHAPTER 47

In this chapter we have instances, I. Of Joseph's kindness and affection to his relations, presenting his brethren first and then his father to Pharaoh (*v.* 1–10), settling them in Goshen, and providing for them there (*v.* 11, 12), and paying his respects to his father when he sent for him (*v.* 27–31). II. Of Joseph's justice between prince and people in a very critical affair, selling Pharaoh's corn to his subjects with reasonable profits to Pharaoh, and yet without any wrong to them (*v.* 13, etc.). Thus he approved himself wise and good, both in his private and in his public capacity.

Verses 1–12

Here is, I. The respect which Joseph, as a subject, showed to his prince. Though he was his favourite, and prime-minister of state, and had had particular orders from him to send for his father down to Egypt, yet he would not suffer him to settle till he had given notice of it to Pharaoh, *v.* 1. Christ, our Joseph, disposes of his followers in his kingdom as it is prepared of his Father, saying, *It is not mine to give,* Mt. 20:23.

II. The respect which Joseph, as a brother, showed to his brethren, notwithstanding all the unkindness he had formerly received from them.

1. Though he was a great man, and they were comparatively mean and despicable, especially in Egypt, yet he owned them. Let those that are rich and great in the world learn hence not to overlook nor despise their poor relations. Every branch of the tree is not a top branch; but, because it is a lower branch, is it therefore not of the tree? Our Lord Jesus, like Joseph here, is not *ashamed to call us brethren.*

2. They being strangers and no courtiers, he introduced some of them to Pharaoh, *to kiss his hand,* as we say, intending thereby to put an honour upon them among the Egyptians. Thus Christ presents his brethren in the court of heaven, and improves his interest for them, though in themselves unworthy and *an abomination to the Egyptians.* Being presented to Pharaoh, according to the instructions which Joseph had given them, they tell him, (1.) What was their business — that they were shepherds, *v.* 3. Pharaoh asked them (and Joseph knew it would be one of his first questions, *ch.* 46:33), *What is your occupation?* He takes it for granted they had something to do, else Egypt should be no place for them, no harbour for idle vagrants. If they would not work, they should not eat of his bread in this time of scarcity. Note, All that have a place in the world should have an employment in it according to their capacity, some occupation or other, mental or manual. Those that need not work for their bread must yet have something to do, to keep them from idleness. Again, Magistrates should enquire into the occupation of their subjects, as those that have the care of the public welfare; for idle people are as drones in the hive, unprofitable burdens of the commonwealth. (2.) What was their business in Egypt — to sojourn in the land (*v.* 4), not to settle there for ever, only to sojourn there for a time, while the famine so prevailed in Canaan, which lay high, that it was not habitable for shepherds, the grass being burnt up much more than in Egypt, which lay low, and where the corn chiefly failed, while there was tolerably good pasture.

3. He obtained for them a grant of a settlement in the land of Goshen, *v.* 5, 6. This was an instance of Pharaoh's gratitude to Joseph; because he had been such a blessing to him and his kingdom, he would be kind to his relations, purely for his sake. He offered them preferment as shepherds over his cattle, provided they were men of activity; for it is the man who is diligent in his business that shall stand before kings. And, whatever our profession or employment is, we should aim to be excellent in it, and to prove ourselves ingenious and industrious.

III. The respect Joseph, as a son, showed to his father.

1. He presented him to Pharaoh, *v.* 7. And here,

(1.) Pharaoh asks Jacob a common question: *How old art thou? v.* 8. A question usually put to old men, for it is natural to us to admire old age and to reverence it (Lev. 19:32), as it is very unnatural and unbecoming to despise it, Isa. 3:5. Jacob's countenance, no doubt, showed him to be very old, for he had been a man of labour and sorrow; in Egypt people were not so long-lived as in Canaan, and therefore Pharaoh looks upon Jacob with wonder; he was as a show in his court. When we are reflecting upon ourselves, this should come into the account, "How old are we?"

(2.) Jacob gives Pharaoh an uncommon answer, *v.* 9. He speaks as becomes a patriarch, with an air of seriousness, for the instruction of Pharaoh. Though our speech be not always of grace, yet it must thus be always with grace. Observe here, [1.] He calls his life *a pilgrimage,* looking upon himself as a stranger in this world, and a traveller towards another world: this earth his inn, not his home. To this the apostle refers (Heb. 11:13), *They confessed that they were strangers and pilgrims.* He not only reckoned himself a pilgrim now that he was in Egypt, a strange country in which he never was before; but his life, even in the land of his nativity, was a pilgrimage, and those who so reckon it can the better bear the inconvenience of banishment from their native soil; they are but pilgrims still, and so they were always. [2.] He reckons his life by *days;* for, even so, it is soon reckoned, and we are not sure of the continuance of it for a day to an end, but may be turned out of this tabernacle at less than an hour's warning. Let us therefore number our days (Ps. 90:12), and measure them, Ps. 39:4. [3.] The character he gives of them is, *First,* That they were few. Though he had now lived 130 years, they seemed to him but a few days, in comparison with the days of eternity, the eternal God, and the eternal state, in which a thousand years (longer than ever any man lived) are but as one day. *Secondly,* That they were evil. This is true concerning man in general, *he is of few days, and full of trouble* (Job 14:1); and, since his days are evil, it is well they are few. Jacob's life, particularly, had been made up of evil days; and the pleasantest days of his life were yet before him. *Thirdly,* That they were short of the days of his fathers, not so many, not so pleasant, as their days. Old age came sooner upon him than it had done upon some of his ancestors. As the young man should not be proud of his strength or beauty, so the old man should not be proud of his age, and the crown of his hoary hairs, though others justly reverence it; for those who are accounted very old attain not to the years of the patriarchs. The hoary head is a crown of glory only when it is found in the way of righteousness.

(3.) Jacob both addresses himself to Pharaoh and takes leave of him with a blessing (*v.* 7): *Jacob blessed Pharaoh,* and again, *v.* 10, which was not only an act of civility (he paid him respect and returned him thanks for his kindness), but an act of piety — he prayed for him, as one having the authority of a prophet and a patriarch. Though in worldly wealth Pharaoh was the greater, yet, in interest with God, Jacob was the greater; he was God's anointed, Ps. 105:15. And a patriarch's blessing was not a thing to be despised, no, not by a potent prince. Darius valued the prayers of the church for himself and for his sons, Ezra 6:10. Pharaoh kindly received Jacob, and, whether in the name of a prophet or no, thus he had a prophet's reward, which sufficiently recompensed him, not only for his courteous converse with him, but for all the other kindnesses he showed to him and his.

2. He provided well for him and his, *placed him in Goshen* (*v.* 11), *nourished him* and all his with food convenient for them, *v.* 12. This bespeaks, not only Joseph a good man, who took this tender care of his poor relations, but God a good God, who raised him up for this purpose, and put him into a capacity of doing it, as Esther came to the kingdom for such a time as this. What God here did for Jacob he has, in effect, promised to do for all his, that serve him and trust in him. Ps. 37:19, *In the days of famine they shall be satisfied.*

Verses 13–26

Care being taken of Jacob and his family, the preservation of which was especially designed by Providence in Joseph's advancement, an account is now given of the saving of the kingdom of Egypt too from ruin; for God is King of nations as well as King of saints, and provideth food for all flesh. Joseph now returns to the management of that great trust which Pharaoh had lodged in his hand. It would have been pleasing enough to him to have gone and lived with his father and brethren in Goshen; but his employment would not permit it. When he had seen his father, and seen him well settled, he applied himself as closely as ever to the execution of his office. Note, Even natural affection must give way to necessary business. Parents and children must be content to be absent one from another, when it is necessary, on either side, for the service of God or their generation. In Joseph's transactions with the Egyptians observe,

I. The great extremity that Egypt, and the parts adjacent, were reduced to by the famine. There was no bread, and they *fainted* (*v.* 13), they were ready to die, *v.* 15, 19. 1. See here what a dependence we have upon God's prov-

idence. If its usual favours are suspended but for a while, we die, we perish, we all perish. All our wealth would not keep us from starving if the rain of heaven were but withheld for two or three years. See how much we lie at God's mercy, and let us keep ourselves always in his love. 2. See how much we smart by our own improvidence. If all the Egyptians had done for themselves in the seven years of plenty as Joseph did for Pharaoh, they had not been now in these straits; but they regarded not the warning they had of the years of famine, concluding that to-morrow shall be as this day, next year as this, and much more abundant. Note, Because man knows not his time (his time of gathering when he has it) therefore his misery is great upon him when the spending time comes, Eccl. 8:6, 7. 3. See how early God put a difference between the Egyptians and the Israelites, as afterwards in the plagues, Ex. 8:22; 9:4, 26; 10:23. Jacob and his family, though strangers, were plentifully fed on free cost, while the Egyptians were dying for want. See Isa. 65:13, *My servants shall eat, but you shall be hungry. Happy art thou, O Israel.* Whoever wants, God's children shall not, Ps. 34:10.

II. The price they had come up to, for their supply, in this exigency. 1. They parted with all their money which they had hoarded up, *v.* 14. Silver and gold would not feed them, they must have corn. All the money of the kingdom was by this means brought into the exchequer. 2. When the money failed, they parted with all their cattle, those for labour, as the horses and asses, and those for food, as the flocks and the herds, *v.* 17. By this it should seem that we may better live upon bread without flesh than upon flesh without bread. We may suppose they parted the more easily with their cattle because they had little or no grass for them; and now Pharaoh saw in reality what he had before seen in vision, nothing but lean kine. 3. When they had sold their stocks off their land, it was easy to persuade themselves (rather than starve) to sell their land too; for what good would that do them, when they had neither corn to sow it nor cattle to eat of it? They therefore sold that next, for a further supply of corn. 4. When their land was sold, so that they had nothing to live on, they must of course sell themselves, that they might live purely upon their labour, and hold their lands by the base tenure of villenage, at the courtesy of the crown. Note, *Skin for skin, and all that a man hath,* even liberty and property (those darling twins), *will he give for his life;* for life is sweet. There are few (though perhaps there are some) who would even dare to die rather than live in slavery, and dependence on an arbitrary power. And perhaps there are those who, in that case, could die by the sword, in a heat, who yet could not deliberately die by famine, which is much worse, Lam. 4:9. Now it was a great mercy to the Egyptians that, in this distress, they could have corn at any rate; if they had all died for hunger, their lands perhaps would have escheated to the crown of course, for want of heirs; they therefore resolved to make the best of bad.

III. The method which Joseph took to accommodate the matter between prince and people, so that the prince might have his just advantage, and yet the people not be quite ruined. 1. For their lands, he needed not come to any bargain with them while the years of famine lasted; but when these were over (for God will not contend for ever, nor will he be always wroth) he came to an agreement, which it seems both sides were pleased with, that the people should occupy and enjoy the lands, as he thought fit to assign them, and should have seed to sow them with out of the king's stores, for their own proper use and behoof, yielding and paying only a fifth part of the yearly profits as a chief rent to the crown. This became a standing law, *v.* 26. And it was a very good bargain to have food for their lands, when otherwise they and theirs must have starved, and then to have their lands again upon such easy terms. Note, Those ministers of state are worthy of double honour, both for wisdom and integrity, that keep the balance even between prince and people, so that liberty and property may not intrench upon prerogative, nor the prerogative bear hard upon liberty and property: in the multitude of such counsellors there is safety. If afterwards the Egyptians thought it hard to pay so great a duty to the king out of their lands, they must remember, not only how just, but how kind, the first imposing of it was. They might thankfully pay a fifth where all was due. It is observable how faithful Joseph was to

him that appointed him. He did not put the money into his own pocket, nor entail the lands upon his own family; but converted both entirely to Pharaoh's use; and therefore we do not find that his posterity went out of Egypt any richer than the rest of their poor brethren. Those in public trusts, if they raise great estates, must take heed that it be not at the expense of a good conscience, which is much more valuable. 2. For their persons, he removed them to cities, *v.* 21. He transplanted them, to show Pharaoh's sovereign power over them, and that they might, in time, forget their titles to their lands, and be the more easily reconciled to their new condition of servitude. The Jewish writers say, "He removed them thus from their former habitations because they reproached his brethren as strangers, to silence which reproach they were all made, in effect, strangers." See what changes a little time may make with a people, and how soon God can empty those from vessel to vessel who had settled upon their lees. How hard soever this seems to have been upon them, they themselves were at this time sensible of it as a very great kindness, and were thankful they were not worse used: *Thou hast saved our lives, v.* 25. Note, There is good reason that the Saviour of our lives should be the Master of our lives. "Thou hast saved us; do what thou wilt with us."

IV. The reservation he made in favour of the priests. They were maintained on free cost, so that they needed not to sell their lands, *v.* 22. *All people will thus walk in the name of their God;* they will be kind to those that attend the public service of their God, and that minister to them in holy things; and we should, in like manner, honour our God, by esteeming his ministers highly in love for their work's sake.

Verses 27–31

Observe, 1. The comfort Jacob lived in (*v.* 27, 28); while the Egyptians were impoverished in their own land, Jacob was replenished in a strange land. He lived seventeen years after he came into Egypt, far beyond his own expectation. Seventeen years he had nourished Joseph (for so old he was when he was sold from him, *ch.* 37:2), and now, by way of requital, seventeen years Joseph nourished him. Observe how kindly Providence ordered Jacob's affairs, that when he was old, and least able to bear care or fatigue, he had least occasion for it, being well provided for by his son without his own forecast. Thus God considers the frame of his people. 2. The care Jacob died in. At last *the time drew nigh that Israel must die, v.* 29. Israel, a prince with God, that had power over the angel and prevailed, yet must yield to death. There is no remedy, he *must* die: it is appointed for all men, therefore for him; and there is no discharge in that war. Joseph supplied him with bread, that he might not die by famine; but this did not secure him from dying by age or sickness. He died by degrees; his candle was not blown out, but gradually burnt down to the socket, so that he saw, at some distance, the time drawing nigh. Note, It is an improvable advantage to see the approach of death before we feel its arrests, that we may be quickened to do what our hand finds to do with all our might: however, it is not far from any of us. Now Jacob's care, as he saw the day approaching, was about his burial, not the pomp of it (he was no way solicitous about that), but the place of it. (1.) He would be buried in Canaan. This he resolved on, not from mere humour, because Canaan was the land of his nativity, but in faith, because it was the land of promise (which he desired thus, as it were, to keep possession of, till the time should come when his posterity should be masters of it), and because it was a type of heaven, that better country which he that said these things declared plainly that he was in expectation of, Heb. 11:14. He aimed at a good land, which would be his rest and bliss on the other side death. (2.) He would have Joseph sworn to bring him thither to be buried (*v.* 29, 31), that Joseph, being under such a solemn obligation to do it, might have that to answer to the objections which otherwise might have been made against it, and for the greater satisfaction of Jacob now in his dying minutes. Nothing will better help to make a death-bed easy than the certain prospect of a rest in Canaan after death. (3.) When this was done *Israel bowed himself upon the bed's head,* yielding himself, as it were, to the stroke of death ("Now let it come, and it shall be welcome"), or worshipping God, as it is explained, Heb. 11:21, giving

God thanks for all his favours, and particularly for this, that Joseph was ready, not only to put his hand upon his eyes to close them, but under his thigh to give him the satisfaction he desired concerning his burial. Thus those that go down to the dust should, with humble thankfulness, bow before God, the God of their mercies, Ps. 22:29.

CHAPTER 48

The time drawing nigh that Israel must die, having, in the former chapter, given order about his burial, in this he takes leave of his grand-children by Joseph, and in the next of all his children. Thus Jacob's dying words are recorded, because he then spoke by a spirit of prophecy; Abraham's and Isaac's are not. God's gifts and graces shine forth much more in some saints than in others upon their death-beds. The Spirit, like the wind, blows where it listeth. In this chapter, I. Joseph, hearing of his father's sickness, goes to visit him, and takes his two sons with him (*v.* 1, 2). II. Jacob solemnly adopts his two sons, and takes them for his own (*v.* 3–7). III. He blesses them (*v.* 8–16). IV. He explains and justifies the crossing of his hands in blessing them (*v.* 17–20). V. He leaves a particular legacy to Joseph (*v.* 21, 22).

Verses 1–7

Here, I. Joseph, upon notice of his father's illness, goes to see him; though a man of honour and business, yet he will not fail to show this due respect to his aged father, *v.* 1. Visiting the sick, to whom we lie under obligations, or may have opportunity of doing good, either for body or soul, is our duty. The sick bed is a proper place both for giving comfort and counsel to others and receiving instruction ourselves. Joseph took his two sons with him, that they might receive their dying grandfather's blessing, and that what they might see in him, and hear from him, might make an abiding impression upon them. Note, 1. It is good to acquaint young people that are coming into the world with the aged servants of God that are going out of it, whose dying testimony to the goodness of God, and the pleasantness of wisdom's ways, may be a great encouragement to the rising generation. Manasseh and Ephraim (I dare say) would never forget what passed at this time. 2. Pious parents are desirous of a blessing, not only for themselves, but for their children. "O that they may live before God!" Joseph had been, above all his brethren, kind to his father, and therefore had reason to expect particular favour from him.

II. Jacob, upon notice of his son's visit, prepared himself as well as he could to entertain him, *v.* 2. He did what he could to rouse his spirits, and to stir up the gift that was in him; what little was lift of bodily strength he put forth to the utmost, and *sat upon the bed.* Note, It is very good for sick and aged people to be as lively and cheerful as they can, that they may not faint in the day of adversity. *Strengthen thyself,* as Jacob here, and God will strengthen thee; hearten thyself and help thyself, and God will help and hearten thee. Let the spirit sustain the infirmity.

III. In recompence to Joseph for all his attentions to him, he adopted his two sons. In this charter of adoption there is, 1. A particular recital of God's promise to him, to which this had reference: *"God blessed me* (*v.* 3), and let that blessing be entailed upon them." God had promised him two things, a numerous issue, and Canaan for an inheritance (*v.* 4); and Joseph's sons, pursuant hereunto, should each of them multiply into a tribe, and each of them have a distinct lot in Canaan, equal with Jacob's own sons. See how he blessed them by faith in that which God had said to him, Heb. 11:21. Note, In all our prayers, both for ourselves and for our children, we ought to have a particular eye to, and remembrance of, God's promises to us. 2. An express reception of Joseph's sons into his family: *"Thy sons are mine* (*v.* 5), not only my grandchildren, but as my own children." Though they were born in Egypt, and their father was then separated from his brethren, which might seem to have cut them off from the heritage of the Lord, yet Jacob takes them in, and owns them for visible church members. He explains this at *v.* 16, *Let my name be named upon them, and the name of my fathers;* as if he had said, "Let them not succeed their father in his power and grandeur here in Egypt, but let them succeed me in the inheritance of the promise made to Abraham," which Jacob looked upon as much more valuable and honourable, and would have them to prize and covet accordingly. Thus the aged dying patriarch teaches these young persons, now that they were of age (being about twenty-one years old), not to look upon Egypt as their home, nor to incorporate themselves with the Egyptians, but to take their lot with the people of God, as Moses afterwards in the like temptation, Heb. 11:24–26. And because it would be a piece of self-denial in them, who stood so fair for preferment in Egypt, to adhere to the despised Hebrews, to encourage them he constitutes each of them the head of a tribe. Note, Those are worthy of double honour who, through God's grace, break through the temptations of worldly wealth and preferment, to embrace religion in disgrace and poverty. Jacob will have Ephraim and Manasseh to believe that it is better to be low and in the church than high and out of it, to be called by the name of poor Jacob than to be called by the name of rich Joseph. 3. A proviso inserted concerning the children he might afterwards have; they should not be accounted heads of tribes, as Ephraim and Manasseh were, but should fall in with either the one or the other of their brethren, *v.* 6. It does not appear that Joseph had any more children; however, it was Jacob's prudence to give this direction, for the preventing of contest and mismanagement. Note, In making settlements, it is good to take advice, and to provide for what may happen, while we cannot foresee what will happen. Our prudence must attend God's providence. 4. Mention is made of the death and burial of Rachel, Joseph's mother, and Jacob's best beloved wife (*v.* 7), referring to that story, *ch.* 35:19. Note, (1.) When we come to die ourselves, it is good to call to mind the death of our dear relations and friends, that have gone before us, to make death and the grave the more familiar to us. See Num. 27:13. Those that were to us as our own souls are dead and buried; and shall we think it much to follow them in the same path? (2.) The removal of dear relations from us is an affliction the remembrance of which cannot but abide with us a great while. Strong affections in the enjoyment cause long afflictions in the loss.

Verses 8–22

Here is, I. The blessing with which Jacob blessed the two sons of Joseph, which is the more remarkable because the apostle makes such particular mention of it (Heb. 11:21), while he says nothing of the blessing which Jacob pronounced on the rest of his sons, though that also was done in faith. Observe here,

1. Jacob was blind for age, *v.* 10. It is one of the common infirmities of old age. *Those that look out at the windows are darkened,* Eccl. 12:3. It is folly to *walk in the sight of our eyes,* and to suffer our hearts to go after them, while we know death will shortly close them, and we do not know but some accident between us and death may darken them. Jacob, like his father before him, when he was old, was dim-sighted. Note, (1.) Those that have the honour of age must therewith be content to take the burden of it. (2.) The eye of faith may be very clear even when the eye of the body is very much clouded.

2. Jacob was very fond of Joseph's sons: *He kissed them and embraced them, v.* 10. It is common for old people to have a very particular affection for their grand-children, perhaps more than they had for their own children when they were little, which Solomon gives a reason for (Prov. 17:6), *Children's children are the crown of old men.* With what satisfaction does Jacob say here (*v.* 11), *I had not thought to see thy face* (having many years given him up for lost), *and, lo, God has shown me also thy seed!* See here, (1.) How these two good men own God in their comforts. Joseph says (*v.* 9), *They are my sons whom God has given me,* and, to magnify the favour, he adds, *"In this place* of my banishment, slavery, and imprisonment." Jacob says here, *God has shown me thy seed.* Our comforts are then doubly sweet to us when we see them coming from God's hand. (2.) How often God, in his merciful providences, outdoes our expectations, and thus greatly magnifies his favours. He not only prevents our fears, but exceeds our hopes. We may apply this to the promise which is made to us and to our children. We could not have thought that we should have been taken into covenant with God ourselves, considering how guilty and corrupt we are; and yet, lo, he has shown us our seed also in covenant with him.

3. Before he entails his blessing, he recounts his experiences of God's goodness to him. He had spoken (*v.* 3) of God's appearing to him. The particular visits of his grace, and the special communion we have sometimes had with him, ought never to be forgotten. But (*v.* 15, 16) he mentions the constant care which the divine Providence had taken of him all his days. (1.) He had *fed him all his life long unto this day, v.* 15. Note, As long as we have lived in this world we have had continual experience of God's goodness to us, in providing for the support of our natural life. Our bodies have called for daily food, and no little has gone to feed us, yet we have never wanted food convenient. He that has fed us *all our life long* surely will not fail us at last. (2.) He had by his angel *redeemed him from all evil, v.* 16. A great deal of hardship he had known in his time, but God had graciously kept him from the evil of his troubles. Now that he was dying he looked upon himself as *redeemed from all evil,* and bidding an everlasting farewell to sin and sorrow. Christ, the Angel of the covenant, is he that redeems us from all evil, 2 Tim. 4:18. Note, [1.] It becomes the servants of God, when they are old and dying, to witness for our God that they have found him gracious. [2.] Our experiences of God's goodness to us are improvable, both for the encouragement of others to serve God, and for encouragement to us in blessing them and praying for them.

4. When he confers the blessing and name of Abraham and Isaac upon them he recommends the pattern and example of Abraham and Isaac to them. *v.* 15. He calls God the *God before whom his fathers Abraham and Isaac walked,* that is, in whom they believed, whom they observed and obeyed, and with whom they kept up communion in instituted ordinances, according to the condition of the covenant. *Walk before me, ch.* 17:1. Note, (1.) Those that would inherit the blessing of their godly ancestors, and have the benefit of God's covenant with them, must tread in the steps of their piety. (2.) It should recommend religion and the service of God to us that God was the God of our fathers, and that they had satisfaction in walking before him.

5. In blessing them, he *crossed hands.* Joseph placed them so as that Jacob's right hand should be put on the head of Manasseh the elder, *v.* 12, 13. But Jacob would put it on the head of Ephraim the younger, *v.* 14. This displeased Joseph, who was willing to support the reputation of his first-born, and would therefore have removed his father's hands, *v.* 17, 18. But Jacob gave him to understand that he know what he did, and that he did it not by mistake, nor in a humour, nor from a partial affection to one more than the other, but from a spirit of prophecy, and in compliance with the divine counsels. Manasseh should be great, but truly Ephraim should be greater. When the tribes were mustered in the wilderness, Ephraim was more numerous than Manasseh, and had the standard of that squadron (Num. 1:32, 33, 35; 2:18, 20), and is named first, Ps. 80:2. Joshua was of that tribe, so was Jeroboam. The tribe of Manasseh was divided, one half on one side Jordan, the other half on the other side, which made it the less powerful and considerable. In the foresight of this, *Jacob crossed hands.* Note. (1.) God, in bestowing his blessings upon his people, gives more to some than to others, more gifts, graces, and comforts, and more of the good things of this life. (2.) He often gives most to those that are least likely. He chooses the weak things of the world; raises the poor out of the dust. Grace observes not the order of nature, nor does God prefer those whom we think fittest to be preferred, but as it pleases him. It is observable how often God, by the distinguishing favours of his covenant, advanced the younger above the elder, Abel above Cain, Shem above Japheth, Abraham above Nahor and Haran, Isaac above Ishmael, Jacob above Esau; Judah and Joseph were preferred before Reuben, Moses before Aaron, David and Solomon before their elder brethren. See 1 Sa. 16:7. He tied the Jews to observe the birthright (Deu. 21:17), but he never tied himself to observe it. Some make this typical of the preference given to the Gentiles above the Jews; the Gentile converts were much more numerous than those of the Jews. See Gal. 4:27. Thus free grace becomes more illustrious.

II. The particular tokens of his favour to Joseph. 1. He left with him the promise of their return out of Egypt, as a sacred trust: *I die, but God shall be with you, and bring you again, v.* 21. Accordingly, Joseph, when he died, left it with his brethren, *ch.* 50:24. This assurance was given them, and carefully preserved among them, that they might neither love Egypt too much when it favoured them, nor fear it too much when it frowned upon them. These words of Jacob furnish us with comfort in reference to the death of our friends: *They die;* but God shall be with us, and his gracious presence is sufficient to make up the loss: they leave us, but he will never fail us. Further, He will bring us to the land of our fathers, the heavenly Canaan, whither our godly fathers have gone before us. If God be with us while we stay behind in this world, and will receive us shortly to be with those that have gone before to a better world, we ought not to sorrow as those that have no hope. 2. He bestowed one portion upon him above his brethren, *v.* 22. The lands bequeathed are described to be those which he *took out of the hand of the Amorite with his sword, and with his bow.* He purchased them first (Jos. 24:32), and, it seems, was afterwards disseized of them by the Amorites, but retook them by the sword, repelling force by force, and recovering his right by violence when he could not otherwise recover it. These lands he settled upon Joseph; mention is made of this grant, Jn. 4:5. Pursuant to it, this parcel of ground was given to the tribe of Ephraim as their right, and the lot was never cast upon it; and in it Joseph's bones were buried, which perhaps Jacob had an eye to as much as to any thing in this settlement. Note, It may sometimes be both just and prudent to give some children portions above the rest; but a grave is that which we can most count upon as our own in this earth.

CHAPTER 49

This chapter is a prophecy; the likest to it we have yet met with was that of Noah, *ch.* 9:25, etc. Jacob is here upon his death-bed, making his will. He put it off till now, because dying men's words are apt to make deep impressions, and to be remembered long: what he said here, he could not say when he would, but as the Spirit gave him utterance, who chose this time, that divine strength might be perfected in his weakness. The twelve sons of Jacob were, in their day, men of renown, but the twelve tribes of Israel, which descended and were denominated from them, were much more renowned; we find their names upon the gates of the New Jerusalem, Rev. 21:12. In the prospect of this their dying father says something remarkable of each son, or of the tribe that bore his name. Here is, I. The preface (*v.* 1, 2). II. Th prediction concerning each tribe (*v.* 3–28). III. The charge repeated concerning his burial (*v.* 29–32). IV. His death (*v.* 33).

Verses 1–4

Here is, I. The preface to the prophecy, in which, 1. The congregation is called together (*v.* 2): *Gather yourselves together;* let them all be sent for from their several employments, to see their father die, and to hear his dying words. It was a comfort to Jacob, now that he was dying, to see all his children about him, and none missing, though he had sometimes thought himself bereaved. It was of use to them to attend him in his last moments, that they might learn of him how to die, as well as how to live: what he said to each he said in the hearing of all the rest; for we may profit by the reproofs, counsels, and comforts, that are principally intended for others. His calling upon them once and again to gather together intimated both a precept to them to unite in love, (to keep together, not to mingle with the Egyptians, not to forsake the assembling of themselves together,) and a prediction that they should not be separated from each other, as Abraham's sons and Isaac's were, but should be incorporated, and all make one people. 2. A general idea is given of the intended discourse (*v.* 1): *That I may tell you that which shall befal you* (not your persons, but your posterity) *in the latter days;* this prediction would be of use to those that came after them, for the confirming of their faith and the guiding of their way, on their return to Canaan, and their settlement there. We cannot tell our children what shall befal them or their families in this world; but we can tell them, from the word of God, what will befal them in the last day of all, according as they conduct themselves in this world. 3. Attention is demanded (*v.* 2): *"Hearken to Israel your father;* let Israel, that has prevailed with God, prevail with you." Note, Children must diligently hearken to what their godly parents say, particularly when they are dying. *Hear, you children, the instruction of a father,* which carries with it both authority and affection, Prov. 4:1.

II. The prophecy concerning Reuben. He begins with him (*v.* 3, 4), for he was the firstborn; but by committing uncleanness with his father's wife, to the great reproach of the family to which he ought to have been an ornament, he forfeited the prerogatives of the birthright; and his dying father here solemnly degrades him, though he does not disown nor disinherit him: he shall have all the

privileges of a son, but not of a firstborn. We have reason to think Reuben had repented of his sin, and it was pardoned; yet it was a necessary piece of justice, in detestation of the villany, and for warning to others, to put this mark of disgrace upon him. Now according to the method of degrading, 1. Jacob here puts upon him the ornaments of the birthright (*v.* 3), that he and all his brethren might see what he had forfeited, and, in that, might see the evil of the sin: as the firstborn, he was his father's joy, almost his pride, being *the beginning of his strength.* How welcome he was to his parents his name bespeaks, *Reuben, See a son.* To him belonged the excellency of dignity above his brethren, and some power over them. Christ Jesus is the firstborn among many brethren, and to him, of right, belong the most excellent power and dignity: his church also, through him, is a church of firstborn. 2. He then strips him of these ornaments (*v.* 4), lifts him up, that he may cast him down, by that one word, *"Thou shalt not excel;* a being thou shalt have as a tribe, but not an excellency." No judge, prophet, nor prince, is found of that tribe, nor any person of renown except Dathan and Abiram, who were noted for their impious rebellion against Moses. That tribe, as not aiming to excel, meanly chose a settlement on the other side Jordan. Reuben himself seems to have lost all that influence upon his brethren to which his birthright entitled him; for *when he spoke unto them they would not hear, ch.* 42:22. Those that have not understanding and spirit to support the honours and privileges of their birth will soon lose them, and retain only the name of them. The character fastened upon Reuben, for which he is laid under this mark of infamy, is that he was *unstable as water.* (1.) His virtue was unstable; he had not the government of himself and his own appetites: sometimes he would be very regular and orderly, but at other times he deviated into the wildest courses. Note, Instability is the ruin of men's excellency. Men do not thrive because they do not fix. (2.) His honour consequently was unstable; it departed from him, vanished into smoke, and became as water spilt upon the ground. Note, Those that throw away their virtue must not expect to save their reputation. Jacob charges him particularly with the sin for which he was thus disgraced: *Thou went est up to thy father's bed.* It was forty years ago that he had been guilty of this sin, yet now it is remembered against him. Note, As time will not of itself wear off the guilt of any sin from the conscience, so there are some sins whose stains it will not wipe off from the good name, especially seventh-commandment sins. Reuben's sin left an indelible mark of infamy upon his family, a dishonour that was a wound not to be healed without a scar, Prov. 6:32, 33. Let us never do evil, and then we need not fear being told of it.

Verses 5–7

These were next in age to Reuben, and they also had been a grief and shame to Jacob, when they treacherously and barbarously destroyed the Shechemites, which he here remembers against them. Children should be afraid of incurring their parents' just displeasure, lest they fare the worse for it long afterwards, and, when they would inherit the blessing, be rejected. Observe, 1. The character of Simeon and Levi: they were brethren in disposition; but, unlike their father, they were passionate and revengeful, fierce and uncontrollable; their swords, which should have been only weapons of defence, were (as the margin reads it, *v.* 5) *weapons of violence,* to do wrong to others, not to save themselves from wrong. Note, It is no new thing for the temper of children to differ very much from that of their parents. We need not think this strange: it was so in Jacob's family. It is not in the power of parents, no, not by education, to form the dispositions of their children; Jacob bred his sons to every thing that was mild and quiet, and yet they proved to be thus furious. 2. A proof of this is the murder of the Shechemites, which Jacob deeply resented at the time (*ch.* 34:30) and still continued to resent. They slew a man, Shechem himself, and many others; and, to effect that, they digged down a wall, broke the houses, to plunder them, and murder the inhabitants. Note, The best governors cannot always restrain those under their charge from committing the worst villanies. And when two in a family are mischievous they commonly make one another so much the worse, and it were wisdom to part them. Simeon and Levi, it is probable, were most active in the

wrong done to Joseph, to which some think Jacob has here some reference; for in their anger they would have slain *that man.* Observe what a mischievous thing self-will is in young people: Simeon and Levi would not be advised by their aged and experienced father; no, they would be governed by their own passion rather than by his prudence. Young people would better consult their own interests if they would less indulge their own will. 3. Jacob's protestation against this barbarous act of theirs: *O my soul, come not thou into their secret.* Hereby he professes not only his abhorrence of such practices in general, but his innocence particularly in that matter. Perhaps he had been suspected as, under-hand, aiding and abetting; he therefore thus solemnly expresses his detestation of the fact, that he might not die under that suspicion. Note, Our soul is our honour; by its powers and faculties we are distinguished from, and dignified above, the beasts that perish. Note, further, We ought, from our hearts, to detest and abhor all society and confederacy with bloody and mischievous men. We must not be ambitious of coming into their secret, or knowing the depths of Satan. 4. His abhorrence of those brutish lusts that led them to this wickedness: *Cursed be their anger.* He does not curse their persons, but their lusts. Note, (1.) Anger is the cause and original of a great deal of sin, and exposes us to the curse of God, and his judgment, Mt. 5:22. (2.) We ought always, in the expressions of our zeal, carefully to distinguish between the sinner and the sin, so as not to love nor bless the sin for the sake of the person, nor to hate nor curse the person for the sake of the sin. 5. A token of displeasure which he foretels their posterity should lie under for this: *I will divide them.* The Levites were scattered throughout all the tribes, and Simeon's lot lay not together, and was so strait that many of the tribe were forced to disperse themselves in quest of settlements and subsistence. This curse was afterwards turned into a blessing to the Levites; but the Simeonites, for Zimri's sin (Num. 25:14), had it bound on. Note, Shameful dispersions are the just punishment of sinful unions and confederacies.

Verses 8–12

Glorious things are here said of Judah. The mention of the crimes of the three elder of his sons had not so put the dying patriarch out of humour but that he had a blessing ready for Judah, to whom blessings belonged. Judah's name signifies *praise,* in allusion to which he says, *Thou art he whom thy brethren shall praise, v.* 8. God was praised for him (*ch.* 29:35), praised by him, and praised in him; and therefore his brethren shall praise him. Note, Those that are to God for a praise shall be the praise of their brethren. It is prophesied that, 1. The tribe of Judah should be victorious and successful in war: *Thy hand shall be in the neck of thy enemies.* This was fulfilled in David, Ps. 18:40. 2. It should be superior to the rest of the tribes; not only in itself more numerous and illustrious, but having a dominion over them: *Thy father's children shall bow down before thee.* Judah was the *lawgiver,* Ps. 60:7. That tribe led the van through the wilderness, and in the conquest of Canaan, Jdg. 1:2. The prerogatives of the birthright which Reuben had forfeited, the excellence of dignity and power, were thus conferred upon Judah. Observe, "Thy brethren shall bow down before thee, and yet shall praise thee, reckoning themselves happy in having so wise and bold a commander." Note, Honour and power are then a blessing to those that have them when they are not grudged and envied, but praised and applauded, and cheerfully submitted to. 3. It should be a strong and courageous tribe, and so qualified for command and conquest: *Judah is a lion's whelp, v.* 9. The lion is the king of beasts, the terror of the forest when he roars; when he seizes his prey, none can resist him; when he goes up from the prey, none dare pursue him to revenge it. By this it is foretold that the tribe of Judah should become very formidable, and should not only obtain great victories, but should peaceably and quietly enjoy what was obtained by those victories — that they should make war, not for the sake of war, but for the sake of peace. Judah is compared, not to a lion *rampant,* always tearing, always raging, always ranging; but to a lion *couchant,* enjoying the satisfaction of his power and success, without creating vexation to others: this is to be truly great. 4. It should be the royal tribe, and the tribe from which Messiah the Prince should come: *The sceptre shall not depart from Judah, till Shiloh come, v.* 10. Jacob here foresees and foretels, (1.) That the sceptre should come into the tribe of Judah, which was fulfilled in David, on whose family the crown was entailed. (2.) That Shiloh should be of this tribe — his seed, that promised seed, in whom the earth should be blessed: *that peaceable and prosperous one,* or *the Saviour,* so others translate it, he shall come of Judah. Thus dying Jacob, at a great distance, saw Christ's day, and it was his comfort and support on his death-bed. (3.) That after the coming of the sceptre into the tribe of Judah it should continue in that tribe, at least a government of their own, till the coming of the Messiah, in whom, as the king of the church, and the great high priest, it was fit that both the priesthood and the royalty should determine. Till the captivity, all along from David's time, the sceptre was in Judah, and subsequently the governors of Judea were of that tribe, or of the Levites that adhered to it (which was equivalent), till Judea became a province of the Roman empire, just at the time of our Saviour's birth, and was at that time taxed as one of the provinces, Lu. 2:1. And at the time of his death the Jews expressly owned, *We have no king but Caesar.* Hence it is undeniably inferred against the Jews that our Lord Jesus is he that should come, and that we are to look for no other; for he came exactly at the time appointed. Many excellent pens have been admirable well employed in explaining and illustrating this famous prophecy of Christ. 5. It should be a very fruitful tribe, especially that it should abound with milk for babes, and wine to make glad the heart of strong men (*v.* 11,12) — vines so common in the hedge-rows and so strong that they should tie their asses to them, and so fruitful that they should load their asses from them — wine as plentiful as water, so that the men of that tribe should be very healthful and lively, their eyes brisk and sparkling, their teeth white. Much of what is here said concerning Judah is to be applied to our Lord Jesus. (1.) He is the ruler of all his father's children, and the conqueror of all his father's enemies; and he it is that is the praise of all the saints. (2.) He is *the lion of the tribe of Judah,* as he is called with reference to this prophecy (Rev. 5:5), who, having spoiled principalities and powers, went up a conqueror, and couched so as none can stir him up, when he sat down on the right hand of the Father. (3.) To him belongs the sceptre; he is the *lawgiver,* and *to him shall the gathering of the people be,* as the desire of all nations (Hag. 2:7), who, being lifted up from the earth, should draw all men unto him (Jn. 12:32), and in whom the children of God that are scattered abroad should meet as the centre of their unity, Jn. 11:52. (4.) In him there is plenty of all that which is nourishing and refreshing to the soul, and which maintains and cheers the divine life in it; in him we may have wine and milk, the riches of Judah's tribe, without money and without price, Isa. 55:1.

Verses 13–21

Here we have Jacob's prophecy concerning six of his sons.

I. Concerning Zebulun (*v.* 13), that his posterity should have their lot upon the seacoast, and should be merchants, and mariners, and traders at sea. This was fulfilled when, two or three hundred years after, the land of Canaan was divided by lot, and the *border of Zebulun went up towards the sea,* Jos. 19:11. Had they chosen their lot themselves, or Joshua appointed it, we might have supposed it done with design to make Jacob's words good; but, being done by lot, it appears that it was divinely disposed, and Jacob divinely inspired. Note, The lot of God's providence exactly agrees with the plan of God's counsel, like a true copy with the original. If prophecy says, *Zebulun shall be a haven of ships,* Providence will so plant him. Note, 1. God appoints the bounds of our habitation. 2. It is our wisdom and duty to accommodate ourselves to our lot and to improve it. If Zebulun dwell at the haven of the sea, let him be for a haven of ships.

II. Concerning Issachar, *v.* 14, 15. 1. That the men of that tribe should be strong and industrious, fit for labour and inclined to labour, particularly the toil of husbandry, like the ass, that patiently carries his burden, and, by using himself to it, makes it the easier. Issachar submitted to two burdens, tillage and tribute. It was a tribe that took pains, and, thriving thereby, was called upon for rents and taxes. 2. That they should be encouraged in their labour by the goodness of the land that should fall to their lot. (1.) *He saw that rest* at home *was good.* Note, The labour of the husbandman is really rest, in comparison with that of soldiers and seamen, whose hurries and perils are such that those who tarry at home in the most constant service have no reason to envy them. (2.) *He saw that the land was pleasant,* yielding not only pleasant prospects to charm the eye of the curious, but pleasant fruits to recompense his toils. Many are the pleasures of a country life, abundantly sufficient to balance the inconveniences of it, if we can but persuade ourselves to think so, Issachar, in prospect of advantage, *bowed his shoulders to bear:* let us, with an eye of faith, see the heavenly rest to be good, and that land of promise to be pleasant; and this will make our present services easy, and encourage us to bow our shoulder to them.

III. Concerning Dan, *v.* 16, 17. What is said concerning Dan has reference either, 1. To that tribe in general, that though Dan was one of the sons of the concubines yet he should be a tribe governed by judges of his own as well as other tribes, and should, by art, and policy, and surprise, gain advantages against his enemies, like a serpent suddenly biting the heel of the traveller. Note, In God's spiritual Israel there is no distinction made of *bond or free,* Col. 3:11. Dan shall be incorporated by as good a charter as any of the other tribes. Note, also, Some, like Dan, may excel in the subtlety of the serpent, as others, like Judah, in the courage of the lion; and both may do good service to the cause of God against the Canaanites. Or it may refer, 2. To Samson, who was of that tribe, and judged Israel, that is, delivered them out of the hands of the Philistines, not as the other judges, by fighting them in the field, but by the vexations and annoyances he gave them underhand: when he pulled the house down under the Philistines that were upon the roof of it, he made the horse throw his rider.

Thus was Jacob going on with his discourse; but now, being almost spent with speaking, and ready to faint and die away, he relieves himself with those words which come in as a parenthesis (*v.* 18), *I have waited for thy salvation, O Lord!* as those that are fainting are helped by taking a spoonful of a cordial, or smelling at a bottle of spirits; or, if he must break off here, and his breath will not serve him to finish what he intended, with these words he pours out his soul into the bosom of his God, and even breathes it out. Note, The pious ejaculations of a warm and lively devotion, though sometimes they may be incoherent, are not therefore to be censured as impertinent; that may be uttered affectionately which does not come in methodically. It is no absurdity, when we are speaking to men, to lift up our hearts to God. The salvation he waited for was *Christ,* the promised seed, whom he had spoken of, *v.* 10. Now that he was going to be gathered to his people, he breathes after him to whom the gathering of the people shall be. The salvation he waited for was also *heaven,* the better country, which he declared plainly that he sought (Heb. 11:13, 14), and continued seeking, now that he was in Egypt. Now that he is going to enjoy the salvation he comforts himself with this, that he had waited for the salvation. Note, It is the character of a living saint that he waits for the salvation of the Lord. Christ, as our way to heaven, is to be waited on: and heaven, as our rest in Christ, is to be waited for. Again, It is the comfort of a dying saint thus to have waited for the salvation of the Lord; for then he shall have what he has been waiting for: long-looked-for will come.

IV. Concerning Gad, *v.* 19. He alludes to his name, which signifies a *troop,* foresees the character of that tribe, that it should be a warlike tribe, and so we find (1 Chr. 12:8); the *Gadites were men of war fit for the battle.* He foresees that the situation of that tribe on the other side Jordan would expose it to the incursions of its neighbours, the Moabites and Ammonites; and, that they might not be proud of their strength and valour, he foretels that the troops of their enemies should, in many skirmishes, overcome them; yet, that they might not be discouraged by their defeats, he assures them that they should *overcome at the last,* which was fulfilled when, in Saul's time and David's, the Moabites and Ammonites were wholly subdued: see 1 Chr. 5:18, etc. Note, The cause of God and his people, though it may seem for a time to be baffled and run down, will yet be victorious at last. *Vincimur in praelio, sed non in bello — We are foiled in a battle, but not in a campaign.* Grace in the soul is often foiled in its conflicts, troops of corruption overcome it, but the cause is God's, and grace will in the issue come off conqueror, yea, *more than conqueror,* Rom. 8:37.

V. Concerning Asher (*v.* 20), that it should be a very rich tribe, replenished not only with bread for necessity, but with fatness, with *dainties, royal dainties* (for the king himself is *served of the field,* Eccl. 5:9), and these exported out of Asher to other tribes, perhaps to other lands. Note, The God of nature has provided for us not only necessaries but dainties, that we might call him a bountiful benefactor; yet, whereas all places are competently furnished with necessaries, only some places afford dainties. Corn is more common than spices. Were the supports of luxury as universal as the supports of life, the world would be worse than it is, and that it needs not be.

VI. Concerning Naphtali (*v.* 21), a tribe that carries struggles in its name; it signifies *wrestling,* and the blessing entailed upon it signifies prevailing; it is *a hind let loose.* Though we find not this prediction so fully answered in the event as some of the rest, yet, no doubt, it proved true that those of this tribe were, 1. As the loving hind (for that is her epithet, Prov. 5:19), friendly and obliging to one another and to other tribes; their converse remarkably kind and endearing. 2. As the loosened hind, zealous for their liberty. 3. As the swift hind (Ps. 18:33), quick in despatch of business; and perhaps, 4. As the trembling, timorous in times of public danger. It is rare that those that are most amiable to their friends are most formidable to their enemies. 5. That they should be affable and courteous, their language refined, and they complaisant, *giving goodly words.* Note, Among God's Israel there is to be found a great variety of dispositions, contrary to each other, yet all contributing to the beauty and strength of the body, Judah like a lion, Issachar like an ass, Dan like a serpent, Naphtali like a hind. Let not those of different tempers and gifts censure one another, nor envy one another, any more than those of different statures and complexions.

Verses 22–27

He closes with the blessings of his best beloved sons, Joseph and Benjamin; with these he will breathe his last.

I. The blessing of Joseph, which is very large and full. He is compared (*v.* 22) to *a fruitful bouth,* or young tree; for God had made him fruitful in the land of his affliction; he owned it. *ch.* 41:52. His two sons were as branches of a vine, or other spreading plant, *running over the wall.* Note, God can make those fruitful, great comforts to themselves and others, who have been looked upon as dry and withered. More is recorded in the history concerning Joseph than concerning any other of Jacob's sons; and therefore what Jacob says of him is historical as well as prophetical. Observe,

1. The providences of God concerning Joseph, *v.* 23, 24. These are mentioned to the glory of God, and for the encouragement of Jacob's faith and hope, that God had blessings in store for his seed. Here observe (1.) Joseph's straits and troubles, *v.* 23. Though he now lived at ease and in honour, Jacob reminds him of the difficulties he had formerly waded through. He had had many enemies, here called *archers,* being skilful to do mischief, masters of their art of persecution. They hated him: there persecution begins. They shot their poisonous darts at him, and thus they sorely grieved him. His brethren, in his father's house, were very spiteful towards him, mocked him, stripped him, threatened him, sold him, thought they had been the death of him. His mistress, in the house of Potiphar, sorely grieved him, and shot at him, when she impudently assaulted his chastity (temptations are fiery darts, thorns in the flesh, sorely grievous to gracious souls); when she prevailed not in this, she hated him, and shot at him by her false accusations, arrows against which there is little fence but the hold God has in the consciences of the worst of men. Doubtless he had enemies in the court of Pharaoh, that envied his preferment, and sought to undermine him. (2.) Joseph's strength and support under all these troubles (*v.* 24): *His bow abode in strength,* that is, his faith did not fail, but he kept his ground, and came off a conqueror. The *arms of his hands were made strong,* that is, his other graces did their part, his wisdom, courage, and patience, which are better than weapons of war. In short, he main-

tained both his integrity and his comfort through all his trials; he bore all his burdens with an invincible resolution, and did not sink under them, nor do any thing unbecoming him. (3.) The spring and fountain of this strength; it was *by the hands of the mighty God,* who was therefore able to strengthen him, and *the God of Jacob,* a God in covenant with him, and therefore engaged to help him. All our strength for the resisting of temptations, and the bearing of afflictions, comes from God: his grace is sufficient, and his strength is perfected in our weakness. (4.) The state of honour and usefulness to which he was subsequently advanced: *Thence* (from this strange method of providence) he became the *shepherd and stone,* the feeder and supporter, *of* God's *Israel,* Jacob and his family. Herein Joseph was a type, [1.] Of Christ; he was shot at and hated, but borne up under his sufferings (Isa. 50:7–9), and was afterwards advanced to be *the shepherd and stone.* [2.] Of the church in general, and particular believers; hell shoots its arrows against the saints, but Heaven protects and strengthens them, and will crown them.

2. The promises of God to Joseph. See how these are connected with the former: *Even by the God of thy father Jacob, who shall help thee, v.* 25. Note, Our experiences of God's power and goodness in strengthening us hitherto are our encouragements still to hope for help from him; he that has helped us will help: we may build much upon our *Eben-ezers.* See what Joseph may expect from *the Almighty,* even *the God of his father.* (1.) He shall help thee in difficulties and dangers which may yet be before thee, help thy seed in their wars. Joshua came from him, who commanded in chief in the wars of Canaan. (2.) He shall bless thee; and he only blesses indeed. Jacob prays for a blessing upon Joseph, but the God of Jacob commands the blessing. Observe the blessings conferred on Joseph. [1.] Various and abundant blessings: *Blessings of heaven above* (rain in its season, and fair weather in its season, and the benign influences of the heavenly bodies); *blessings of the deep that lieth under* this earth, which, compared with the upper world, is but a great deep, with subterraneous mines and springs. Spiritual blessings are blessings of heaven above, which we ought to desire and seek for in the first place, and to which we must give the preference; while temporal blessings, those of this earth, must lie under in our account and esteem. *Blessings of the womb and the breasts* are given when children are safely born and comfortably nursed. In the word of God, by which we are born again, and nourished up (1 Pt. 1:23; 2:2), there are to the new man blessings both of the womb and the breasts. [2.] Eminent and transcendent blessings, which *prevail above the blessings of my progenitors, v.* 26. His father Isaac had but one blessing, and, when he had given that to Jacob, he was at a loss for a blessing to bestow upon Esau; but Jacob had a blessing for each of his twelve sons, and now, at the latter end, a copious one for Joseph. The great blessing entailed upon that family was increase, which did not so immediately and so signally follow the blessings which Abraham and Isaac gave to their sons as it followed the blessing which Jacob gave to his; for, soon after his death, they multiplied exceedingly. [3.] Durable and extensive blessings: *Unto the utmost bounds of the everlasting hills,* including all the productions of the most fruitful hills, and lasting as long as they last, Isa. 54:10. Note, the blessings of the everlasting God include the riches of the everlasting hills, and much more. Well, of these blessings it is here said, *They shall be,* so it is a promise, or, *Let them be,* so it is a prayer, *on the head of Joseph,* to which let them be as a crown to adorn it and a helmet to protect it. Joseph *was separated from his brethren* (so we read it) for a time; yet, as others read it, *he was a Nazarite among his brethren,* better and more excellent than they. Note, It is no new thing for the best men to meet with the worst usage, for Nazarites among their brethren to be cast out and separated from their brethren; but the blessing of God will make it up to them.

II. The blessing of Benjamin (*v.* 27): He *shall raven as a wolf;* it is plain by this that Jacob was guided in what he said by a spirit of prophecy, and not by natural affection; else he would have spoken with more tenderness of his beloved son Benjamin, concerning whom he only foresees and foretels this, that his posterity should be a warlike tribe, strong and daring, and that they should enrich themselves with the spoils of their enemies — that they should be active and busy in the world, and a tribe as much feared by their neighbours as any other: *In the morning, he shall devour the prey,* which he seized and divided over night. Or, in the first times of Israel, they shall be noted for activity, though many of them left-handed, Jdg. 3:15; 20:16. Ehud the second judge, and Saul the first king, were of this tribe; and so also in the last times Esther and Mordecai, by whom the enemies of the Jews were destroyed, were of this tribe. The Benjamites ravened like wolves when they desperately espoused the cause of the men of Gibeah, those men of Belial, Jdg. 20:14. Blessed Paul was of this tribe (Rom. 11:1; Phil. 3:5); and he did, in the morning of his day, devour the prey as a persecutor, but, in the evening, divided the spoil as a preacher. Note, God can serve his own purposes by the different tempers of men; *the deceived and the deceiver are his.*

Verses 28–33

Here is, I. The summing up of the blessings of Jacob's sons, *v.* 28. Though Reuben, Simeon, and Levi were put under the marks of their father's displeasure, yet he is said to *bless them every one according to his blessing;* for none of them were rejected as Esau was. Note, Whatever rebukes of God's word or providence we are under at any time, yet, as long as we have an interest in God's covenant, a place and a name among his people, and good hopes of a share in the heavenly Canaan, we must account ourselves blessed.

II. The solemn charge Jacob gave them concerning his burial, which is a repetition of what he had before given to Joseph. See how he speaks of death, now that he is dying: *I am to be gathered unto my people, v.* 29. Note, It is good to represent death to ourselves under the most desirable images, that the terror of it may be taken off. Though it separates us from our children and our people in this world, it gathers us to our fathers and to our people in the other world. Perhaps Jacob uses this expression concerning death as a reason why his sons should bury him in Canaan; for, says he, *"I am to be gathered unto my people,* my soul must go to *the spirits of just men made perfect:* and therefore bury me with my fathers, Abraham and Isaac, and their wives," *v.* 31. Observe, 1. His heart was very much upon it, not so much from a natural affection to his native soil as from a principle of faith in the promise of God, that Canaan should be the inheritance of his seed in due time. Thus he would keep up in his sons a remembrance of the promised land, and not only would have their acquaintance with it renewed by a journey thither on that occasion, but their desire towards it and their expectation of it preserved. 2. He is very particular in describing the place both by the situation of it and by the purchase Abraham had made of it for a burying-place, *v.* 30, 32. He was afraid lest his sons, after seventeen years' sojourning in Egypt, had forgotten Canaan, and even the burying-place of their ancestors there, or lest the Canaanites should dispute his title to it; and therefore he specifies it thus largely, and the purchase of it, even when he lies a-dying, not only to prevent mistakes, but to show how mindful he was of that country. Note, It is, and should be, a great pleasure to dying saints to fix their thoughts upon the heavenly Canaan, and the rest they hope for there after death.

III. The death of Jacob, *v.* 33. When he had finished both his blessing and his charge (both which are included in the commanding of his sons), and so had finished his testimony, he addressed himself to his dying work. 1. He put himself into a posture for dying; having before seated himself upon the bed-side, to bless his sons (the spirit of prophecy bringing fresh oil to his expiring lamp, Dan. 10:19), when that work was done, *he gathered up his feet into the bed,* that he might lie along, not only as one patiently submitting to the stroke, but as one cheerfully composing himself to rest, now that he was weary. *I will lay me down, and sleep.* 2. He freely resigned his spirit into the hand of God, the Father of spirits: *He yielded up the ghost.* 3. His separated soul went to the assembly of the souls of the faithful, which, after they are delivered from the burden of the flesh, are in joy and felicity: he was *gathered to his people.* Note, If God's people be our people, death will gather us to them.

CHAPTER 50

Here is, I. The preparation for Jacob's funeral (*v.* 1–6). II. The funeral itself (*v.* 7–14). III. The settling of a good understanding between Joseph and his brethren after the death of Jacob (*v.* 15–21). IV. The age and death of Joseph (*v.* 22–26). Thus the book of Genesis, which began with the origin of light and life, ends with nothing but death and darkness; so sad a change has sin made.

Verses 1–6

Joseph is here paying his last respects to his deceased father. 1. With tears and kisses, and all the tender expressions of a filial affection, he takes leave of the deserted body, *v.* 1. Though Jacob was old and decrepit, and must needs die in the course of nature — though he was poor comparatively, and a constant charge to his son Joseph, yet such an affection he had for a loving father, and so sensible was he of the loss of a prudent, pious, praying father, that he could not part with him without floods of tears. Note, As it is an honour to die lamented, so it is the duty of survivors to lament the death of those who have been useful in their day, though for some time they may have survived their usefulness. The departed soul is out of the reach of our tears and kisses, but with them it is proper to show our respect to the poor body, of which we look for a glorious and joyful resurrection. Thus Joseph showed his faith in God, and love to his father, by kissing his pale and cold lips, and so giving an affectionate farewell. Probably the rest of Jacob's sons did the same, much moved, no doubt, with his dying words. 2. He ordered the body to be embalmed (*v.* 2), not only because he died in Egypt, and that was the manner of the Egyptians, but because he was to be carried to Canaan, which would be a work of time, and therefore it was necessary the body should be preserved as well as it might be from putrefaction. See how vile our bodies are, when the soul has forsaken them; without a great deal of art, and pains, and care, they will, in a very little time, become noisome. If the body have been dead four days, by that time it is offensive. 3. He observed the ceremony of solemn mourning for him, *v.* 3. Forty days were taken up in embalming the body, which the Egyptians (they say) had an art of doing so curiously as to preserve the very features of the face unchanged; all this time, and thirty days more, seventy in all, they either confined themselves and sat solitary, or, when they went out, appeared in the habit of close mourners, according to the decent custom of the country. Even the Egyptians, many of them, out of the great respect they had for Joseph (whose good offices done for the king and country were now fresh in remembrance), put themselves into mourning for his father: as with us, when the court goes into mourning, those of the best quality do so too. About ten weeks was the court of Egypt in mourning for Jacob. Note, What they did in state, we should do in sincerity, *weep with those that weep,* and mourn with those that mourn, as being ourselves also in the body. 4. He asked and obtained leave of Pharaoh to go to Canaan, thither to attend the funeral of his father, *v.* 4–6. (1.) It was a piece of necessary respect to Pharaoh that he would not go without leave; for we may suppose that, though his charge about the corn was long since over, yet he continued a prime-minister of state, and therefore would not be so long absent from his business without licence. (2.) He observed a decorum, in employing some of the royal family, or some of the officers of the household, to intercede for this licence, either because it was not proper for him in the days of his mourning to come into the presence-chamber, or because he would not presume too much upon his own interest. Note, Modesty is a great ornament to dignity. (3.) He pleaded the obligation his father had laid upon him, by an oath, to bury him in Canaan, *v.* 5. It was not from pride or humour, but from his regard to an indispensable duty, that he desired it. All nations reckon that oaths must be performed, and the will of the dead must be observed. (4.) He promised to return: *I will come again.* When we return to our own houses from burying the bodies of our relations, we say, "We have left them behind;" but, if their souls have gone to our heavenly Father's house, we may say with more reason, "They have left us behind." (5.) He obtained leave (*v.* 6): *Go and bury thy father.* Pharaoh was willing his business should stand still so long; but the service of Christ is more needful, and therefore he would not allow one that had work to do for him to go first and bury his father; no, *Let the dead bury their dead,* Mt. 8:22.

Verses 7–14

We have here an account of Jacob's funeral. Of the funerals of the kings of Judah, usually, no more is said than this, *They were buried with their fathers in the city of David:* but the funeral of the patriarch Jacob is more largely and fully described, to show how much better God was to him than he expected (he had spoken more than once of dying for grief, and going to the grave bereaved of his children, but, behold, he dies in honour, and is followed to the grave by all his children), and also because his orders concerning his burial were given and observed in faith, and in expectation both of the earthly and of the heavenly Canaan. Now, 1. It was a stately funeral. He was attended to the grave, not only by his own family, but by the courtiers, and all the great men of the kingdom, who, in token of their gratitude to Joseph, showed this respect to his father for his sake, and did him honour at his death. Though the Egyptians had had an antipathy to the Hebrews, and had looked upon them with disdain (*ch.* 43:32), yet now, that they were better acquainted with them, they began to have a respect for them. Good old Jacob had conducted himself so well among them as to gain universal esteem. Note, Professors of religion should endeavour, by wisdom and love, to remove the prejudices which many may have conceived against them because they do not know them. There went abundance of chariots and horsemen, not only to attend them a little way, but to go through with them. Note, The decent solemnities of funerals, according to a man's situation, are very commendable; and we must not say of them, *To what purpose is this waste?* See Acts 8:2; Lu. 7:12. 2. It was a sorrowful funeral (*v.* 10, 11); standers-by took notice of it as a grievous mourning. Note, The death of good men is a great loss to any place, and ought to be greatly lamented. Stephen dies a martyr, and yet devout men make great lamentations for him. The solemn mourning for Jacob gave a name to the place, *Abel-Mizraim, the mourning of the Egyptians,* which served for a testimony against the next generation of the Egyptians, who oppressed the posterity of this Jacob to whom their ancestors showed such respect.

Verses 15–21

We have here the settling of a good correspondence between Joseph and his brethren, now that their father was dead. Joseph was at court, in the royal city; his brethren were in Goshen, remote in the country; yet the keeping up of a good understanding, and a good affection, between them, would be both his honour and their interest. Note, When Providence has removed the parents by death, the best methods ought to be taken, not only for the preventing of quarrels among the children (which often happen about the dividing of the estate), but for the preserving of acquaintance and love, that unity may continue even when that centre of unity is taken away.

I. Joseph's brethren humbly make their court to him for his favour. 1. They began to be jealous of Joseph, not that he had given them any cause to be so, but the consciousness of guilt, and of their own inability in such a case to forgive and forget, made them suspicious of the sincerity and constancy of Joseph's favour (*v.* 15): *Joseph will peradventure hate us.* While their father lived, they thought themselves safe under his shadow; but now that he was dead they feared the worst from Joseph. Note, A guilty conscience exposes men to continual frights, even where no fear is, and makes them suspicious of every body, as Cain, *ch.* 4:14. Those that would be fearless must keep themselves guiltless. If our heart reproach us not, then have we confidence both towards God and man. 2. They humbled themselves before him, confessed their fault, and begged his pardon. They did it by proxy (*v.* 17); they did it in person, *v.* 18. Now that the sun and moon had set, the eleven stars did homage to Joseph, for the further accomplishment of his dream. They speak of their former offence with fresh regret: *Forgive the trespass.* They throw themselves at Joseph's feet, and refer themselves to his mercy: *We are thy servants.* Thus we must bewail the sins we committed long ago, even those which we hope through grace are forgiven; and, when we pray to God for pardon, we must promise to be his servants. 3. They pleaded their relation to Jacob and to Jacob's God. (1.) To Jacob, urging that he directed them to make this submission, rather because he questioned whether they would do their duty in humbling themselves than because he questioned whether Joseph would do his duty in forgiving them; nor could he reasonably expect Joseph's kindness to them unless they thus qualified themselves for it (*v.* 16): *Thy father did command.* Thus, in humbling ourselves to Christ by faith and repentance, we may plead that it is the command of his Father, and our Father, that we do so. (2.) To Jacob's God. They plead (*v.* 17), *We* are the*servants of the God of thy father;* not only children of the same Jacob, but worshippers of the same Jehovah. Note, Though we must be ready to forgive all that are any way injurious to us, yet we must especially take heed of bearing malice towards any that are the servants of the God of our father: such we should always treat with a peculiar tenderness; for we and they have the same Master.

II. Joseph, with a great deal of compassion, confirms his reconciliation and affection to them; his compassion appears, *v.* 17. *He wept when they spoke to him.* These were tears of sorrow for their suspicion of him, and tears of tenderness upon their submission. In his reply, 1. He directs them to look up to God in their repentance (*v.* 19): *Am I in the place of God?* He, in his great humility, thought they showed him too much respect, as if all their happiness were bound up in his favour, and said to them, in effect, as Peter to Cornelius, *"Stand up, I myself also am a man.* Make your peace with God, and then you will find it an easy matter to make your peace with me." Note, When we ask forgiveness of those whom we have offended we must take heed of putting them in the place of God, by dreading their wrath and soliciting their favour more than God's. "Am I in the place of God, to whom alone vengeance belongs? No, I will leave you to his mercy." Those that avenge themselves step into the place of God, Rom. 12:19. 2. He extenuates their fault, from the consideration of the great good which God wonderfully brought out of it, which, though it should not make them the less sorry for their sin, yet might make him the more willing to forgive it (*v.* 20): *You thought evil* (to disappoint the dreams), *but God meant it unto good,* in order to the fulfilling of the dreams, and the making of Joseph a greater blessing to his family than otherwise he could have been. Note, When God makes use of men's agency for the performance of his counsels, it is common for him to mean one thing and them another, even the quite contrary, but God's counsel shall stand. See Isa. 10:7. Again, God often brings good out of evil, and promotes the designs of his providence even by the sins of men; not that he is the author of sin, far be it from us to think so; but his infinite wisdom so overrules events, and directs the chain of them, that, in the issue, that ends in his praise which in its own nature had a direct tendency to his dishonour; as the putting of Christ to death, Acts 2:23. This does not make sin the less sinful, nor sinners the less punishable, but it redounds greatly to the glory of God's wisdom. 3. He assures them of the continuance of his kindness to them: *Fear not; I will nourish you, v.* 21. See what an excellent spirit Joseph was of, and learn of him to render good for evil. He did not tell them they were upon their good behaviour, and he would be kind to them if he saw they conducted themselves well; no, he would not thus hold them in suspense, nor seem jealous of them, though they had been suspicious of him: *He comforted them,* and, to banish all their fears, *he spoke kindly to them.* Note, Broken spirits must be bound up and encouraged. Those we love and forgive we must not only do well for but speak kindly to.

Verses 22–26

Here is, I. The prolonging of Joseph's life in Egypt: he lived to be *a hundred and ten years old, v.* 22. Having honoured his father, his days were long in the land which, for the present, God had given him; and it was a great mercy to his relations that God continued him so long, a support and comfort to them.

II. The building up of Joseph's family: he lived to see his great-grand-children by both his sons (*v.* 23), and probably he saw his two sons solemnly owned as heads of distinct tribes, equal to any of his brethren. It contributes much to the comfort of aged parents if they see their posterity in a flourishing condition, especially if with it they see peace upon Israel, Ps. 128:6.

III. The last will and testament of Joseph published in the presence of his brethren, when he saw his death approaching. Those that were properly his brethren perhaps were some of them dead before him, as several of them were older than he; but to those of them who yet survived, and to the sons of those who were gone, who stood up in their fathers' stead, he said this. 1. He comforted them with the assurance of their return to Canaan in due time: *I die, but God will surely visit you, v.* 24. To this purport Jacob had spoken to him, *ch.* 48:21. Thus must we comfort others with the same comforts with which we ourselves have been comforted of God, and encourage them to rest on those promises which have been our support. Joseph was, under God, both the protector and the benefactor of his brethren; and what would become of them now that he was dying? Why, let this be their comfort, *God will surely visit you.* Note, God's gracious visits will serve to make up the loss of our best friends. They die; but we may live, and live comfortably, if we have the favour and presence of God with us. He bids them be confident: *God will bring you out of this land,* and therefore, (1.) They must not hope to settle there, nor look upon it as their rest for ever; they must set their hearts upon the land of promise, and call that their home. (2.) They must not fear sinking, and being ruined there; probably he foresaw the ill usage they would meet with there after his death, and therefore gives them this word of encouragement: *"God will bring you* in triumph *out of this land* at last." Herein he has an eye to the promise, *ch.* 15:13, 14, and, in God's name, assures them of the performance of it. 2. For a confession of his own faith, and a confirmation of theirs, he charges them to keep him unburied till that day, that glorious day, should come, when they should be settled in the land of promise, *v.* 25. He makes them promise him with an oath that they would bury him in Canaan. In Egypt they buried their great men very honourably and with abundance of pomp; but Joseph prefers a significant burial in Canaan, and that deferred too almost 200 years, before a magnificent one in Egypt. Thus Joseph, by faith in the doctrine of the resurrection and the promise of Canaan, gave *commandment concerning his bones,* Heb. 11:22. He dies in Egypt; but lays his bones at stake that God will surely visit Israel, and bring them to Canaan.

IV. The death of Joseph, and the reservation of his body for a burial in Canaan, *v.* 26. He was *put in a coffin in Egypt,* but not buried till his children had received their inheritance in Canaan, Jos. 24:32. Note, 1. If the separate soul, at death, do but return to its rest with God, the matter is not great though the deserted body find not at all, or not quickly, its rest in the grave. 2. Yet care ought to be taken of the dead bodies of the saints, in the belief of their resurrection; for there is a covenant with the dust, which shall be remembered, and a commandment is given concerning the bones.

AN EXPOSITION, WITH PRACTICAL OBSERVATIONS, OF

THE SECOND BOOK OF MOSES, CALLED EXODUS

Moses (the *servant of the Lord* in writing for him as well as in acting for him — with the pen of God as well as with the rod of God in his hand) having, in the first book of his history, preserved and transmitted the records of the church, while it existed in private families, comes, in this second book, to give us an account of its growth into a great nation; and, as the former furnishes us with the best economics, so this with the best politics. The beginning of the former book shows us how God formed the world for himself; the beginning of this shows us how he formed Israel for himself, and both show forth his praise, Isa. 43:21. There we have the creation of the world in history, here the redemption of the world in type. The Greek translators called this book *Exodus* (which signifies a *departure* or *going out*) because it begins with the story of the going out of the children of Israel from Egypt. Some allude to the names of this and the foregoing book, and observe that immediately after *Genesis,* which signifies the *beginning* or *original,* follows *Exodus,* which signifies *a departure;* for a time to be born is immediately succeeded by a time to die. No sooner have we made our entrance into the world than we must think of making our exit, and going out of the world. When we begin to live we begin to die. The forming of Israel into a people was a new creation. As the earth was, in the beginning, first fetched from under water, and then beautified and replenished, so Israel was first by an almighty power made to emerge out of Egyptian slavery, and then enriched with God's law and tabernacle. This book gives us, I. The accomplishment of the promises made before to Abraham (*ch.* 1–19), and then, II. The establishment of the ordinances which were afterwards observed by Israel (*ch.* 20–40). Moses, in this book, begins, like Caesar, to write his own Commentaries; nay, a greater, a far greater, than Caesar is here. But henceforward the penman is himself the hero, and gives us the history of those things of which he was himself an eye and ear-witness, *et quorum pars magna fuit — and in which he bore a conspicuous part.* There are more types of Christ in this book than perhaps in any other book of the Old Testament; for Moses wrote of him, Jn. 5:46. The way of man's reconciliation to God, and coming into covenant and communion with him by a Mediator, is here variously represented; and it is of great use to us for the illustration of the New Testament, now that we have that to assist us in the explication of the Old.

CHAPTER 1

We have here, I. God's kindness to Israel, in multiplying them exceedingly (*v.* 1–7). II. The Egyptians' wickedness to them, 1. Oppressing and enslaving them (*v.* 8–14). 2. Murdering their children (*v.* 15–22). Thus whom the court of heaven blessed the country of Egypt cursed, and for that reason.

Verses 1–7

In these verses we have, 1. A recital of the names of the *twelve patriarchs,* as they are called, Acts 7:8. Their names are often repeated in scripture, that they may not sound uncouth to us, as other hard names, but that, by their occurring so frequently, they may become familiar to us; and to show how precious God's spiritual Israel are to him, and how much he delights in them. The account which was kept of the number of Jacob's family, when they went down into Egypt; they were in all *seventy souls* (*v.* 5). according to the computation we had, Gen. 46:27. This was just the number of the nations by which the earth was peopled, according to the account given, Gen. 10. *For when the Most High separated the sons of Adam, he set the bounds of the people according to the number of the children of Israel,* as Moses observes, Deu. 32:8. Notice is here taken of this that their increase in Egypt might appear the more wonderful. Note, It is good for those whose latter end greatly increases often to remember how small their beginning was, Job 8:7. 3. The death of Joseph, *v.* 6. *All that generation* by degrees wore off. Perhaps all Jacob's sons died much about the same time; for there was not more than seven years' difference in age between the eldest and the youngest of them, except Benjamin; and, when death comes into a family, sometimes it makes a full end in a little time. When Joseph, the stay of the family, died, the rest went off apace. Note, We must look upon ourselves and our brethren, and all we converse with, as dying and hastening out of the world. This generation passeth away, as that did which went before. 4. The strange increase of Israel in Egypt, *v.* 7. Here are four words used to express it: They *were fruitful,* and *increased abundantly,* like fishes or insects, so that they *multiplied;* and, being generally healthful and strong, they *waxed exceedingly mighty,* so that they began almost to outnumber the natives, for the land was in all places filled with them, at least Goshen, their own allotment. Observe, (1.) Though, no doubt, they increased considerably before, yet, it should seem, it was not till after the death of Joseph that it began to be taken notice of as extraordinary. Thus, when they lost the benefit of his protection, God made their numbers their defence, and they became better able than they had been to shift for themselves. If God continue our friends and relations to us while we most need them, and remove them when they can be better spared, let us own that he is wise, and not complain that he is hard upon us. After the death of Christ, our Joseph, his gospel Israel began most remarkably to increase: and his death had an influence upon it; it was like the sowing of a corn of wheat, which, if it die, bringeth forth much fruit, Jn. 12:24. (2.) This wonderful increase was the fulfillment of the promise long before made unto the fathers. From the call of Abraham, when God first told him he would make of him a great nation, to the deliverance of his seed out of Egypt, it was 430 years, during the first 215 of which they were increased but to seventy, but, in the latter half, those seventy multiplied to 600,000 fighting men. Note, [1.] Sometimes God's providences may seem for a great while to thwart his promises, and to go counter to them, that his people's faith may be tried, and his own power the more magnified. [2.] Though the performance of God's promises is sometimes slow, yet it is always sure; *at the end it shall speak, and not lie,* Hab. 2:3.

Verses 8–14

The land of Egypt here, at length, becomes to Israel a house of bondage, though hitherto it had been a happy shelter and settlement for them. Note, The place of our satisfaction may soon become the place of our affliction, and that may prove the greatest cross to us of which we said, *This same shall comfort us.* Those may prove our sworn enemies whose parents were our faithful friends; nay, the same persons that loved us may possibly turn to hate us: therefore cease from man, and say not concerning any place on this side heaven, *This is my rest for ever.* Observe here,

I. The obligations they lay under to Israel upon Joseph's account were forgotten: *There arose a new king,* after several successions in Joseph's time, *who knew not Joseph, v.* 8. All that knew him loved him, and were kind to his relations for his sake; but when he was dead he was soon forgotten, and the remembrance of the good offices he had done was either not retained or not regarded, nor had it any influence upon their councils. Note, the best and the most useful and acceptable services done to men are seldom remembered, so as to be recompensed to those that did them, in the notice taken either of their memory, or of their posterity, after their death, Eccl. 9:5, 15. Therefore our great care should be to serve God, and please him, who is not unrighteous, whatever men are, to forget our work and labour of love, Heb. 6:10. If we work for men only, our works, at furthest, will die with us; if for God, they will follow us, Rev. 14:13. This king of Egypt knew not Joseph; and after him arose one that had the impudence to say, *I know not the Lord, ch.* 5:2. Note, Those that are unmindful of their other benefactors, it is to be feared, will forget the supreme benefactor, 1 Jn. 4:20.

II. Reasons of state were suggested for their dealing hardly with Israel, *v.* 9, 10. 1. They are represented as more and mightier than the Egyptians; certainly they were not so, but the king of Egypt, when he resolved to oppress them, would have them thought so, and looked on as a formidable body. 2. Hence it is inferred that if care were not taken to keep them under they would become dangerous to the government, and in time of war would side with their enemies and revolt from their allegiance to the crown of Egypt. Note, It has been the policy of persecutors to represent God's Israel as a dangerous people, *hurtful to kings and provinces,* not fit to be trusted, nay, not fit to be tolerated, that they may have some pretence for the barbarous treatment they design them, Ezra 4:12, etc.; Esth. 3:8. Observe, The thing they feared was lest they should *get them up out of the land,* probably having heard them speak of the promise made to their fathers that they should settle in Canaan. Note, The policies of the church's enemies aim to defeat the promises of the church's God, but in vain; God's counsels shall stand. 3. It is therefore proposed that a course be taken to prevent their increase: *Come on, let us deal wisely with them, lest they multiply.* Note, (1.) The growth of Israel is the grief of Egypt, and that against which the powers and policies of hell are levelled. (2.) When men deal wickedly, it is common for them to imagine that they deal wisely; but the folly of sin will, at last, be manifested before all men.

III. The method they took to suppress them, and check their growth, *v.* 11, 13, 14. The Israelites behaved themselves so peaceably and inoffensively that they could not find any occasion of making war upon them, and weakening them by that means: and therefore, 1. They took care to keep them poor, by charging them with heavy taxes, which, some think, is included in the *burdens* with which they afflicted them. 2. By this means they took an effectual course to make them slaves. The Israelites, it should seem, were much more industrious laborious people than the Egyptians, and therefore Pharaoh took care to find them work, both in building (they built him *treasure-cities*), and in husbandry, even *all manner of service in the field:* and this was exacted from them with the utmost rigour and severity. Here are many expressions used, to affect us with the condition of God's people. They had *taskmasters* set over them, who were directed, not only to burden them, but, as much as might be, *to afflict them with their burdens,* and contrive how to make them grievous. They not only made them serve, which was sufficient for Pharaoh's profit, but they made them *serve with rigour,* so that their lives became bitter to them, intending hereby, (1.) To break their spirits, and rob them of every thing in them that was ingenuous and generous. (2.) To ruin their health and shorten their days, and so diminish their numbers. (3.) To discourage them from marrying, since their children would be born to slavery. (4.) To oblige them to desert the Hebrews, and incorporate themselves with the Egyptians. Thus he hoped to cut off the name of Israel, that it might be no more in remembrance. And it is to be feared that the oppression they were under had this bad effect upon them, that it brought over many of them to join with the Egyptians in their idolatrous worship; for we read (Jos. 24:14) that they served other gods in Egypt; and, though it is not mentioned here in this history, yet we find (Eze. 20:8) that God had threatened to destroy them for it, even while they were in the land of Egypt: however, they were kept a distinct body, unmingled with the Egyptians, and by their other customs separated from them, which was *the Lord's doing, and marvellous.*

IV. The wonderful increase of the Israelites, notwithstanding the oppressions they groaned under (*v.* 12): *The more they afflicted them the more they multiplied,* sorely to the grief and vexation of the Egyptians. Note, 1. Times of affliction have often been the church's growing times, *Sub pondere crescit — Being pressed, it grows.* Christianity spread most when it was persecuted: the blood of the martyrs was the seed of the church. 2. Those that take counsel against the Lord and his Israel do but imagine a vain thing (Ps. 2:1), and create so much the greater vexation to themselves: hell and earth cannot diminish those whom Heaven will increase.

Verses 15–22

The Egyptians' indignation at Israel's increase, notwithstanding the many hardships they put upon them, drove them at length to the most barbarous and inhuman methods of suppressing them, by the murder of their children. It was strange that they did not rather pick quarrels with the grown men, against whom they might perhaps find some occasion: to be thus bloody towards the infants, whom all must own to be innocents, was a sin which they had to cloak for. Note, 1. There is more cruelty in the corrupt heart of man than one would imagine, Rom. 3:15, 16. The enmity that is in the seed of the serpent against the seed of the woman divests men of humanity itself, and makes them forget all pity. One would not think it possible that ever men should be so barbarous and bloodthirsty as the persecutors of God's people have been, Rev. 17:6. 2. Even confessed innocence is no defence against the old enmity. What blood so guiltless as that of a child new-born? Yet that is prodigally shed like water, and sucked with delight like milk or honey. Pharaoh and Herod sufficiently proved themselves agents for that *great red dragon, who stood to devour the man-child as soon as it was born,* Rev. 12:3, 4. Pilate delivered Christ to be crucified, after he had confessed that he found no fault in him. It is well for us that, though man can kill the body, this is all he can do. Two bloody edicts are here signed for the destruction of all the male children that were born to the Hebrews.

I. The midwives were commanded to murder them. Observe, 1. The orders given them, *v.* 15, 16. It added much to the barbarity of the intended executions that the *midwives* were appointed to be the executioners; for it was to make them, not only bloody, but perfidious, and to oblige them to betray a trust, and to destroy those whom they undertook to save and help. Could he think that their sex would admit such cruelty, and their employment such base treachery? Note, Those who are themselves barbarous think to find, or make, others as barbarous. Pharaoh's project was secretly to engage the midwives to stifle the men-children as soon as they were born, and then to lay it upon the difficulty of the birth, or some mischance common in that case, Job 3:11. The two midwives he tampered with in order hereunto are here named; and perhaps, at this time, which was above eighty years before their going out of Egypt, those two might suffice for all the Hebrew women, at least so many of them as lay near the court, as it is plain by *ch.* 2:5, 6, many of them did, and of them he was most jealous. They are called *Hebrew midwives,* probably not because they were themselves Hebrews (for surely Pharaoh could never expect they should be so barbarous to those of their own nation), but because they were generally made use of by the Hebrews; and, being Egyptians, he hoped to prevail with them. 2. Their pious disobedience to this impious command, *v.* 17. *They feared God,* regarded his law, and dreaded his wrath more than Pharaoh's and therefore saved the men-children alive. Note, If men's commands be any way contrary to the commands of God, we must obey God and not man, Acts 4:19; *v.* 29. No power on earth can warrant us, much less oblige us, to sin against God, our chief Lord. Again, Where the fear of God rules in the heart, it will preserve it from the snare which the inordinate fear of man brings. 3. Their justifying themselves in this disobedience, when they were charged with it as a crime, *v.* 18. They gave a reason for it, which, it seems, God's gracious promise furnished them with — that they came too late to do it, for generally the children were born before they came, *v.* 19. I see no reason we have to doubt the truth of this; it is plain that the Hebrews were now under an extraordinary blessing of increase, which may well be supposed to have this effect, that the women had very quick and easy labour, and, the mothers and children being both lively, they seldom needed the help of midwives: this these midwives took notice of, and, concluding it to the finger of God, were thereby emboldened to disobey the king, in favour of those whom Heaven thus favoured, and with this justified themselves before Pharaoh, when he called them to an account for it. Some of the ancient Jews expound it thus, *Ere the midwife comes to them they pray to their Father in heaven, and he answereth them, and they do bring forth.* Note, God is a readier helper to his people in distress than any other helpers are, and often anticipates them with the blessings of his goodness; such deliverances lay them under peculiarly strong obligations. 4. The recompence God gave them for their tenderness towards his people: *He dealt well with them, v.* 20. Note, God will be behind-hand with none for any kindness done to his people, taking it as done to himself. In particular, *he made them houses* (*v.* 21), built them up into families, blessed their children, and prospered them in all they did. Note, The services done for God's Israel are often repaid in kind. The midwives kept up the Israelites' houses, and, in recompence for it, *God made them houses.* Observe, The recompence has relation to the principle upon which they went: *Because they feared God, he made them houses.* Note, Religion and piety are good friends to outward prosperity: the fear of God in a house will help to build it up and establish it. Dr. Lightfoot's notion of it is, That, for their piety, they were married to Israelites, and Hebrew families were built up by them.

II. When this project did not take effect, Pharaoh gave public orders to all his people to drown all the male children of the Hebrews, *v.* 22. We may suppose it was made highly penal for any to know of the birth of a son to an Israelite, and not to give information to those who were appointed to throw him into the river. Note, The enemies of the church have been restless in their endeavours to *wear out the saints of the Most High,* Dan. 7:25. But *he that sits in heaven shall laugh at them.* See Ps. 2:4.

CHAPTER 2

This chapter begins the story of Moses, that man of renown, famed for his intimate acquaintance with Heaven and his eminent usefulness on earth, and the most remarkable type of Christ, as a prophet, saviour, lawgiver, and mediator, in all the Old Testament. The Jews have a book among them of the life of Moses, which tells a great many stories concerning him, which we have reason to think are mere fictions; what he has recorded concerning himself is what we may rely upon, for we know that his record is true; and it is what we may be satisfied with, for it is what Infinite Wisdom thought fit to preserve and transmit to us. In this chapter we have, I. The perils of his birth and infancy (*v.* 1–4). II. His preservation through those perils, and the preferment of his childhood and youth (*v.* 5–10). III. The pious choice of his riper years, which was to own the people of God. 1. He offered them his service at present, if they would accept it (*v.* 11–14). 2. He retired, that he might reserve himself for further service hereafter (*v.* 15–22). IV. The dawning of the day of Israel's deliverance (*v.* 23, etc.).

Verses 1–4

Moses was a Levite, both by father and mother. Jacob left Levi under marks of disgrace (Gen. 49:5); and yet, soon after, Moses appears a descendant from him, that he might typify Christ, who came in the likeness of sinful flesh and was made a curse for us. This tribe began to be distinguished from the rest by the birth of Moses, as afterwards it became remarkable in many other instances. Observe, concerning this newborn infant,

I. How he was hidden. It seems to have been just at the time of his birth that the cruel law was made for the murder of all the male children of the Hebrews; and many, no doubt, perished by the execution of it. The parents of Moses had Miriam and Aaron, both older than he, born to them before this edict came out, and had nursed them without that peril: but those that begin the world in peace know not what troubles they may meet with before they have got through it. Probably the mother of Moses was full of anxiety in the expectation of his birth, now that this edict was in force, and was ready to say, *Blessed are the barren that never bore,* Lu. 23:29. Better so than bring forth children to the murderer, Hos. 9:13. Yet this child proves the glory of his father's house. Thus that which is most our fear often proves, in the issue, most our joy. Observe the beauty of providence: just at the time when Pharaoh's cruelty rose to this height the deliverer was born, though he did not appear for many years after. Note, When men are projecting the church's ruin God is preparing for its salvation. Moses, who was afterwards to bring Israel out of this house of bondage, was himself in danger of falling a sacrifice to the fury of the oppressor, God so ordering it that, being afterwards told of this, he might be the more animated with a holy zeal for the deliverance of his brethren out of the hands of such bloody men. 1. His parents observed him to be a *goodly child,* more than ordinarily beautiful; he was *fair to God,* Acts 7:20. They fancied he had a lustre in his countenance that was something more than human, and was a specimen of the shining of his face afterwards, Ex. 34:29. Note, God sometimes gives early earnests of his gifts, and manifests himself betimes in those for whom and by whom he designs to do great things. Thus he put an early strength into Samson (Judge 13:24, 25), an early forwardness into Samuel (1 Sa. 2:18), wrought an early deliverance for David (1 Sa. 17:37), and began betimes with Timothy, 1 Tim. 3:15. 2. Therefore they were the more solicitous for his preservation, because they looked upon this as an indication of some kind purpose of God concerning him, and a happy omen of something great. Note, A lively active faith can take encouragement from the least intimation of the divine favour; a merciful hint of Providence will encourage those whose spirits make diligent search, *Three months* they hid him in some private apartment of their own house, though probably with the hazard of their own lives, had he been discovered. Herein Moses was a type of Christ, who, in his infancy, was forced to abscond, and in Egypt too (Mt. 2:13), and was wonderfully preserved, when many innocents were butchered. It is said (Heb. 11:23) that the parents of Moses *hid him by faith;* some think they had a special revelation to them that the deliverer should spring from their loins; however they had the general promise of Israel's preservation, which they acted faith upon, and in that faith hid their child, not being afraid of the penalty annexed to the king's commandment. Note, Faith in God's promise is so far from superseding that it rather excites and quickens to the use of lawful means for the obtaining of mercy. Duty is ours, events are God's. Again, Faith in God will set us above the ensnaring fear of man.

II. How he was exposed. At three months' end, probably when the searchers came about to look for concealed children, so that they could not hide him any longer (their faith perhaps beginning now to fail), they put him in an ark of bulrushes by the *river's brink* (*v.* 3), and set his little sister at some distance to watch what would become of him, and into whose hands he would fall, *v.* 4. God put it into their hearts to do this, to bring about his own purposes, that Moses might by this means be brought into the hands of Pharaoh's daughter, and that by his deliverance from this imminent danger a specimen might be given of the deliverance of God's church, which now lay thus exposed. Note, 1. God takes special care of the outcasts of Israel (Ps. 147:2); they are *his* outcasts, Isa. 16:4. Moses seemed quite abandoned by his friends; his own mother durst not own him: but now the Lord took him up and protected him, Ps. 27:10. 2. In times of extreme difficulty it is good to venture upon the providence of God. Thus to have exposed their child while they might have preserved it, would have been to tempt Providence; but, when they could not, it was to trust to Providence. "Nothing venture, nothing win." *If I perish, I perish.*

Verses 5–10

Here is, I. Moses saved from perishing. Come see the place where that great man lay when he was a little child; he lay in a bulrush-basket by the river's side. Had he been left to lie there, he must have perished in a little time with hunger, if he had not been sooner washed into the river or devoured by a crocodile. Had he fallen into any other hands than those he did fall into, either they would not, or durst not, have done otherwise than have thrown him straightway into the river; but Providence brings no less a person thither than Pharaoh's daughter, just at that juncture, guides her to the place where this poor forlorn infant lay, and inclines her heart to pity it, which she dares do when none else durst. Never did poor child cry so seasonably, so happily, as this did: *The babe wept,* which moved the compassion of the princess, as no doubt his beauty did, *v.* 5, 6. Note, 1. Those are hard-hearted indeed that have not a tender compassion for helpless infancy. How pathetically does God represent his compassion for the Israelites in general considered in this pitiable state! Eze. 16:5, 6. 2. It is very commendable in persons of quality to take cognizance of the distresses of the meanest, and to be helpful and charitable to them. 3. God's care of us in our infancy ought to be often made mention of by us to his praise. Though we were not thus exposed (that we were not was God's mercy) yet many were the perils we were surrounded with in our infancy, out of which the Lord delivered us, Ps. 22:9, 10. 4. God often raises up friends for his people even among their enemies. Pharaoh cruelly seeks Israel's destruction, but his own daughter charitably compassionates a Hebrew child, and not only so, but, beyond her intention, preserves Israel's deliverer. *O Lord, how wonderful are thy counsels!*

II. Moses well provided with a good nurse, no worse than his own dear mother, *v.* 7–9. Pharaoh's daughter thinks it convenient that he should have a Hebrew nurse (pity that so fair a child should be suckled by a sable Moor), and the sister of Moses, with art and good management, introduces the mother into the place of a nurse, to the great advantage of the child; for mothers are the best nurses, and those who receive the blessings of the breasts with those of the womb are not just if they give them not to those for whose sake they received them: it was also an unspeakable satisfaction to the mother, who received her son as life from the dead, and now could enjoy him without fear. The transport of her joy, upon this happy turn, we may suppose sufficient to betray her to be the true mother (had there been any suspicion of it) to a less discerning eye than that of Solomon, 1 Ki. 3:27.

III. Moses preferred to be the son of Pharaoh's daughter (*v.* 10), his parents herein perhaps not only yielding to necessity, having nursed him *for her,* but too much pleased with the honour thereby done to their son; for the smiles of the world are stronger temptations than its frowns, and more difficult to resist. The tradition of the Jews is that Pharaoh's daughter had no child of her own, and that she was the only child of her father, so that when he was adopted for her son he stood fair for the crown: however it is certain he stood fair for the best preferments of the court in due time, and in the mean time had the advantage of the best education and improvements of the court, with the help of which, having a great genius, he became master of all the lawful learning of the Egyptians, Acts 7:22. Note, 1. Providence pleases itself sometimes in raising the poor out of the dust, to set them among princes, Ps. 113:7, 8. Many who, by their birth, seem marked for obscurity and poverty, by surprising events of Providence are brought to sit at the upper end of the world, to make men know that *the heavens do rule.* 2. Those whom God designs for great services he find out ways to qualify and prepare beforehand. Moses, by having his education in a court, is the fitter to be a prince and *king in Jeshurun;* by having his education in a learned court (for such the Egyptian then was) is the fitter to be an historian; and by having his education in the court of Egypt is the fitter to be employed, in the name of God, as an ambassador to that court.

IV. Moses named. The Jews tell us that his father, at his circumcision, called him *Joachim,* but Pharaoh's daughter called him *Moses, Drawn out of the water,* so it signifies in the Egyptian language. The calling of the Jewish lawgiver by an Egyptian name is a happy omen to the Gentile world, and gives hopes of that day when it shall be said, *Blessed be Egypt my people,* Isa. 19:25. And his tuition at court was an earnest of the performance of that promise, Isa. 49:23, *Kings shall be thy nursing fathers, and queens thy nursing mothers.*

Verses 11–15

Moses had now passed the first forty years of his life in the court of Pharaoh, preparing himself for business; and now it was time for him to enter upon action, and,

I. He boldly owns and espouses the cause of God's people: *When Moses was grown he went out unto his brethren, and looked on their burdens, v.* 11. The best exposition of these words we have from an inspired pen, Heb. 11:24–26, where we are told that by this he expressed, 1. His holy contempt of the honours and pleasures of the Egyptian court; he *refused to be called the son of Pharaoh's daughter,* for *he went out.* The temptation was indeed very strong. He had a fair opportunity (as we say) to make his fortune, and to have been serviceable to Israel too, with his interest at court. He was obliged, in gratitude as well as interest, to Pharaoh's daughter, and yet he obtained a glorious victory by faith over his temptation. He reckoned it much more his honour and advantage to be a son of Abraham than to be the son of Pharaoh's daughter. 2. His tender concern for his poor brethren in bondage, with whom (though he might easily have avoided it) he *chose to suffer affliction;* he looked on their burdens as one that not only pitied them, but was resolved to venture with them, and, if occasion were, to venture for them.

II. He gives a specimen of the great things he was afterwards to do for God and his Israel in two little instances, related particularly by Stephen (Acts 7:23, etc.) with design to show how their fathers had *always resisted the Holy Ghost* (*v.* 51), even in Moses himself, when he first appeared as their deliverer, wilfully shutting their eyes against this day-break of their enlargement. He found himself, no doubt, under a divine direction and impulse in what he did, and that he was in an extraordinary manner called of God to do it. Now observe,

1. Moses was afterwards to be employed in plaguing the Egyptians for the wrongs they had done to God's Israel; and, as a specimen of that, he killed the Egyptian who smote the Hebrew (*v.* 11, 12); probably it was one of the Egyptian taskmasters, whom he found abusing his Hebrew slave, a relation (as some think) of Moses, a man of the same tribe. It was by special warrant from Heaven (which makes not a precedent in ordinary cases) that Moses slew the Egyptian, and rescued his oppressed brother. The Jew's tradition is that he did not slay him with any weapon, but, as Peter slew Ananias and Sapphira, with the word of his mouth. His *hiding him in the sand* signified that hereafter Pharaoh and all his Egyptians should, under the control of the rod of Moses, be buried in the sand of the Red Sea. His taking care to execute this justice privately, when no man saw, was a piece of needful prudence and caution, it being but an assay; and perhaps his faith was as yet weak, and what he did was with some hesitation. Those who come to be of great faith, yet began with a little, and at first spoke tremblingly.

2. Moses was afterwards to be employed in governing Israel, and as a specimen of this, we have him here trying to end a controversy between two Hebrews, in which he is forced (as he did afterwards for forty years) to suffer their manners. Observe here,

(1.) The unhappy quarrel which Moses observed between two Hebrews, *v.* 13. It does not appear what was the occasion; but, whatever it was, it was certainly very unseasonable for Hebrews to strive with one another when they were all oppressed and ruled with rigour by the Egyptians. Had they not beating enough from the Egyptians, but they must beat one another? Note, [1.] Even sufferings in common do not always unite God's professing people to one another, so much as one might reasonably expect. [2.] When God raises up instruments of salvation for the church they will find enough to do, not only with oppressing Egyptians, to restrain them, but with quarrelsome Israelites, to reconcile them.

(2.) The way he took of dealing with them; he marked him that caused the division, that did the wrong, and mildly reasoned with him: *Wherefore smitest thou thy fellow?* The injurious Egyptian was killed, the injurious Hebrew was only reprimanded; for what the former did was from a rooted malice, what the latter did we may suppose was only upon a sudden provocation. The wise God makes, and, according to his example, all wise governors make, a difference between one offender and another, according to the several qualities of the same offence. Moses endeavoured to make them friends, a good office; thus we find Christ often reproving his disciples' strifes (Lu. 9:46, etc.; 22:24, etc.), for he was a prophet like unto Moses, a healing prophet, a peacemaker, who visited his brethren with a design to slay all enmities. The reproof Moses gave on this occasion may still be of use, *Wherefore smitest thou thy fellow?* Note, Smiting our fellows is bad in any, especially in Hebrews, smiting with tongue or hand, either in a way of persecution or in a way of strife and contention. Consider the person thou smitest; it is thy fellow, thy fellow-creature, thy fellow-christian, it is thy fellow-servant, thy fellow-sufferer. Consider the cause, *Wherefore smitest?* Perhaps it is for no cause at all, or no just cause, or none worth speaking of.

(3.) The ill success of his attempt (*v.* 14): *He said, Who made thee a prince?* He that did the wrong thus quarrelled with Moses; the injured party, it should seem, was inclinable enough to peace, but the wrong-doer was thus touchy. Note, It is a sign of guilt to be impatient of reproof; and it is often easier to persuade the injured to bear the trouble of taking wrong than the injurious to bear the conviction of having *done wrong.* 1 Co. 6:7, 8. It was a very wise and mild reproof which Moses gave to this quarrelsome Hebrew, but he could not bear it, he kicked against the pricks (Act 9:5), and crossed questions with his reprover. [1.] He challenges his authority: *Who made thee a prince?* A man needs no great authority for the giving of a friendly reproof, it is an act of kindness; yet this man needs will interpret it an act of dominion, and represents his reprover as imperious and assuming. Thus when people dislike good discourse, or a seasonable admonition, they will call it *preaching,* as if a man could not speak a work for God and against sin but he took too much upon him. Yet Moses was indeed a prince and a judge, and knew it, and thought the Hebrews would have understood it, and struck in with him; but they stood in their own light, and *thrust him away,* Acts 7:25, 27. [2.] He upbraids him with what he had done in killing the Egyptian: *Intendest thou to kill me?* See what base constructions malice puts upon the best words and actions. Moses, for reproving him is immediately charged with a design to kill him. An attempt upon his sin was interpreted an attempt upon his life; and his having killed the Egyptian was thought sufficient to justify the suspicion; as if Moses made no difference between an Egyptian and a Hebrew. If Moses, to right an injured Hebrew, had put his life in his hand, and slain an Egyptian, he ought therefore to have submitted to him, not only as a friend to the Hebrews, but as a friend that had more than ordinary power and zeal. But he throws that in his teeth as a crime which was bravely done, and was intended as a specimen of the promised deliverance; if the Hebrews had taken the hint, and come in to Moses as their head and captain, it is probable that they would have been delivered now; but, despising their deliverer, their deliverance was justly deferred, and their bondage prolonged forty years, as afterwards their despising Canaan kept them out of it forty years more. *I would, and you would not.* Note, Men know not what they do, nor what enemies they are to their own interest, when they resist and despise faithful reproofs and reprovers. When the Hebrews strove with Moses, God sent him away into Midian, and they never heard of him for forty years; thus the things that belonged to their peace were hidden from their eyes, because they knew not the day of their visitation. As to Moses, we may look on it as a great damp and discouragement to him. He was now *choosing to suffer affliction with the people of God,* and embracing *the reproach of Christ;* and now, at his first setting out, to meet with this affliction and reproach from them was a very sore trial of his resolution. He might have said, "If this be the spirit of the Hebrews, I will go to court again, and be the son of Pharaoh's daughter." Note, *First,* We must take heed of being prejudiced against the ways and people of God by the follies and peevishness of some particular persons that profess religion. *Secondly,* It is no new thing for the church's best friends to meet with a great deal of opposition and discouragement in their healing, saving attempts, even from their own mother's children; Christ himself was set at nought by the builders, and is still rejected by those he would save.

(4.) The flight of Moses to Midian, in consequence. The affront given him thus far proved a kindness to him; it gave him to understand that his killing the Egyptian was discovered, and so he had time to make his escape, otherwise the wrath of Pharaoh might have surprised him and taken him off. Note, God can overrule even the strife of tongues, so as, one way or other, to bring good to his people out of it. Information was brought to Pharaoh (and it is well if it was not brought by the Hebrew himself whom Moses reproved) of his killing the Egyptian; warrants are presently out for the apprehending of Moses, which obliged him to shift for his own safety, by flying into the land of Midian, *v.* 15. [1.] Moses did this out of a prudent care of his own life. If this be his forsaking of Egypt which the apostle refers to as done by faith (Heb. 11:27), it teaches us that when we are at any time in trouble and danger for doing our duty the grace of faith will be of good use to us in taking proper methods for our own preservation. Yet there it is said, *He feared not the wrath of the king;* here it is said he *feared, v.* 14. He did not fear with a fear of diffidence and amazement, which weakens and has torment, but with a fear of diligence, which quickened him to take that way which Providence opened to him for his own preservation. [2.] God ordered it for wise and holy ends. Things were not yet ripe for Israel's deliverance: the measure of Egypt's iniquity was not yet full; the Hebrews were not sufficiently humbled, nor were they yet increased to such a multitude as God designed; Moses is to be further fitted for the service, and therefore is directed to withdraw for the present, till the time to favour Israel, even the set time, should come. God guided Moses to Midian because the Midianites were of the seed of Abraham, and retained the worship of the true God among them, so that he might have not only a safe but a comfortable settlement among them. And through this country he was afterwards to lead Israel, with which (that he might do it the better) he now had opportunity of making himself acquainted. Hither he came, and sat down by a well, tired and thoughtful, at a loss, and waiting to see which way Providence would direct him. It was a great change with him, since he was but the other day at ease in Pharaoh's court: thus God tried his faith, and it was found to praise and honour.

Verses 16–22

Moses here gains a settlement in Midian, just as his father Jacob had gained one in Syria, Gen. 29:2, etc. And both these instances should encourage us to trust Providence, and to follow it. Events that seem inconsiderable, and purely accidental, afterwards appear to have been designed by the wisdom of God for very good purposes, and of great consequence to his people. A casual transient occurrence has sometimes occasioned the greatest and happiest turns of a man's life. Observe,

I. Concerning the seven daughters of Reuel the priest or prince of Midian. 1. They were humble, and very industrious, according as the employment of the country was: they *drew water for their father's flock, v.* 16. If their father was a prince, it teaches us that even those who are honourably born, and are of quality and distinction in their country, should yet apply themselves to some useful business, and what their hand finds to do do it with all their might. Idleness can be no one's honour. If their father was a priest, it teaches us that ministers' children should, in a special manner, be examples of humility and industry. 2. They were modest, and would not ask this strange Egyptian to come home with them (though handsome and a great courtier), till their father sent for him. Modesty is the ornament of woman.

II. Concerning Moses. He was taken for an Egyptian (v. 19); and strangers must be content to be the subjects of mistake; but it is observable, 1. How ready he was to help Reuel's daughters to water their flocks. Though bred in learning and at court, yet he knew how to turn his hand to such an office as this when there was occasion; nor had he learned of the Egyptians to despise shepherds. Note, Those that have had a liberal education yet should not be strangers to servile work, because they know not what necessity Providence may put them in of working for themselves, or what opportunity Providence may give them of being serviceable to others. These young women, it seems, met with some opposition in their employment, more than they and their servants could conquer; the shepherds of some neighbouring prince, as some think, or some idle fellows that called themselves shepherds, *drove away their flocks;* but Moses, though melancholy and in distress, *stood up and helped them,* not only to get clear of the shepherds, but, when that was done, to water the flocks. This he did, not only in complaisance to the daughters of Reuel (though that also did very well become him), but because, wherever he was, as occasion offered itself, (1.) He loved to be doing justice, and appearing in the defence of such as he saw injured, which every man ought to do as far as it is in the power of his hand to do it. (2.) He loved to be doing good. Wherever the Providence of God casts us we should desire and endeavour to be useful; and, when we cannot do the good we would, we must be ready to do the good we can. And he that is faithful in a little shall be entrusted with more. 2. How well he was paid for his serviceableness. When the young women acquainted their father with the kindnesses they had received from this stranger, he sent to invite him to his house, and made much of him, v. 20. Thus God will recompense the kindnesses which are at any time shown to his children; they shall in no wise lose their reward. Moses soon recommended himself to the esteem and good affection of this prince of Midian, who took him into his house, and, in process of time, married one of his daughters to him (v. 21), by whom he had a son, whom he called *Gershom, a stranger there* (v. 22), that if ever God should give him a home of his own he might keep in remembrance the land in which he had been a stranger. Now this settlement of Moses in Midian was de-

signed by Providence, (1.) To shelter him for the present. God will find hiding-places for his people in the day of their distress; nay, he will himself be to them a little sanctuary, and will secure them, either under heaven or in heaven. But, (2.) It was also designed to prepare him for the great services he was further designed for. His manner of life in Midian, where he kept the flock of his father-in-law (having none of his own to keep), would be of use to him, [1.] To inure him to hardship and poverty, that he might learn how to want as well as how to abound. Those whom God intends to exalt he first humbles. [2.] To inure him to contemplation and devotion. Egypt accomplished him as a scholar, a gentleman, a statesman, a soldier, all which accomplishments would be afterwards of use to him; but yet he lacked one thing, in which the court of Egypt could not befriend him. He that was to do all by divine revelation must know, by a long experience, what it was to live a life of communion with God; and in this he would be greatly furthered by the solitude and retirement of a shepherd's life in Midian. By the former he was prepared to rule in Jeshurun, but by the latter he was prepared to converse with God in Mount Horeb, near which mount he had spent much of his time. Those that know what it is to be alone with God in holy exercises are acquainted with better delights than ever Moses tasted in the court of Pharaoh.

Verses 23–25

Here is, 1. The continuance of the Israelites' bondage in Egypt, v. 23. Probably the murdering of their infants did not continue; this part of their affliction attended only the period immediately connected with the birth of Moses, and served to signalize it. The Egyptians now were content with their increase, finding that Egypt was enriched by their labour; so that they might have them for slaves, they cared not how many they were. On this therefore they were intent, to keep them all at work, and make the best hand they could of their labour. When one Pharaoh died, another rose up in his place that was governed by the same maxims, and was as cruel to Israel as his predecessors. If there was sometimes a little relaxation, yet it presently revived again with as much rigour as ever; and probably, as the more Israel were oppressed the more they multiplied, so the more they multiplied the more they were oppressed. Note, Sometimes God suffers the rod of the wicked to lie very long and very heavily on the lot of the righteous. If Moses, in Midian, at any time began to think how much better his condition might have been had he staid among the courtiers, he must of himself think this also, how much worse it would have been if he had had his lot with brethren: it was a great degradation to him to be keeping sheep in Midian, but better so than making brick in Egypt. The consideration of our brethren's afflictions would help to reconcile us to our own. 2. The preface to their deliverance at last. (1.) *They cried, v.* 23. Now, at last, they began to think of God under their troubles, and to return to him from the idols they had served, Eze. 20:8. Hitherto they had fretted at the instruments of their trouble, but God was not in all their thoughts. Thus *hypocrites in heart heap up wrath; they cry not when he binds them,* Job 36:13. But before God unbound them he put it into their hearts to cry unto him, as it is explained, Num. 20:16. Note, It is a good sign that God is coming towards us with deliverance when he inclines and enables us to cry to him for it. (2.) *God heard, v.* 24, 25. The name of God is here emphatically prefixed to four different expressions of a kind intention towards them. [1.] *God heard their groaning;* that is, he made it to appear that he took notice of their complaints. The groans of the oppressed cry aloud in the ears of the righteous God, to whom vengeance belongs, especially the groans of God's spiritual Israel; he knows the burdens they groan under and the blessings they groan after, and that the blessed Spirit, by these groanings, makes intercession in them. [2.] *God remembered his covenant,* which he seemed to have forgotten, but of which he is ever mindful. This God had an eye to, and not to any merit of theirs, in what he did for them. See Lev. 26:42. (3.) *God looked upon the children of Israel.* Moses looked upon them and pitied them (v. 11); but now God looked upon them and helped them. (4.) *God had a respect unto them,* a favourable respect to them as his own. The frequent repetition of the name of God here intimates that now we are to expect something great, *Opus Deo dignum — A work worthy of God.* His eyes, which run to and fro through the earth, are now fixed upon Israel, to show himself strong, to show himself a God in their behalf.

CHAPTER 3

As prophecy had ceased for many ages before the coming of Christ, that the revival and perfection of it in that great prophet might be the more remarkable, so vision had ceased (for aught that appears) among the patriarchs for some ages before the coming of Moses, that God's appearances to him for Israel's salvation might be the more welcome; and in this chapter we have God's first appearance to him in the bush and the conference between God and Moses in that vision. Here is, I. The discovery God was pleased to make of his glory to Moses at the bush, to which Moses was forbidden to approach too near (v. 1–5). II. A general declaration of God's grace and good-will to his people, who were beloved for their fathers' sakes (v. 6). III. A particular notification of God's purpose concerning the deliverance of Israel out of Egypt. 1. He assures Moses it should now be done (v. 7–9). 2. He gives him a commission to act in it as his ambassador both to Pharaoh (v. 10) and to Israel (v. 16). 3. He answers the objection Moses made of his own unworthiness (v. 11, 12). 4. He gives him full instructions what to say both to Pharaoh and to Israel (v. 13–18). 5. He tells him beforehand what the issue would be (v. 19, etc.).

Verses 1–6

The years of the life of Moses are remarkably divided into three forties: the first forty he spent as a prince in Pharaoh's court, the second a shepherd in Midian, the third a king in Jeshurun; so changeable is the life of men, especially the life of good men. He had now finished his second forty, when he received his commission to bring Israel out of Egypt. Note, Sometimes it is long before God calls his servants out of that work which of old he designed them for, and has been graciously preparing them for. Moses was born to be Israel's deliverer, and yet not a word is said of it to him till he is eighty years of age. Now observe,

I. How this appearance of God to him found him employed. He was keeping the flock (tending sheep) near mount Horeb, v. 1. This was a poor employment for a man of his parts and education, yet he rests satisfied with it, and thus learns meekness and contentment to a high degree, for which he is more celebrated in sacred writ than for all his other learning. Note, 1. In the calling to which we are called we should abide, and not be given to change. 2. Even those that are qualified for great employments and services must not think it strange if they be confined to obscurity; it was the lot of Moses before them, who foresaw nothing to the contrary but that he should die, as he had lived a great while, a poor despicable shepherd. Let those that think themselves buried alive be content to shine like lamps in their sepulchres, and wait till God's time come for setting them on a candlestick. Thus employed Moses was, when he was honoured with this vision. Note, (1.) God will encourage industry. The shepherds were keeping their flocks when they received the tidings of our Saviour's birth, Lu. 2:8. Satan loves to find us idle; God is well pleased when he find us employed. (2.) Retirement is a good friend to our communion with God. When we are alone, the Father is with us. Moses saw more of God in a desert than ever he had seen in Pharaoh's court.

II. What the appearance was. To his great surprise he saw a bush burning, when he perceived no fire either from earth or heaven to kindle it, and, which was more strange, it did not consume, v. 2. It was an angel of the Lord that appeared to him; some think, a created angel, who speaks in the language of him that sent him; others, the second person, the angel of the covenant, who is himself Jehovah. It was an extraordinary manifestation of the divine presence and glory; what was visible was produced by the ministry of an angel, but he heard God in it speaking to him. 1. He saw a flame of fire; *for our God is a consuming fire.* When Israel's deliverance out of Egypt was promised to Abraham, he saw a burning lamp, which signified the light of joy which that deliverance should cause (Gen. 15:17); but now it shines brighter, as a flame of fire, for God in that deliverance brought terror and destruction to his enemies, light and heat to his people, and displayed his glory before all. See Isa. 10:17. 2. This fire was not in a tall and stately cedar, but in a bush, *a thorny bush, so* the word signifies; for God chooses the weak and despised things of the world (such as Moses, now a poor shepherd), with them to confound the wise; he delights to beautify and crown the humble. 3. *The bush burned,* and yet *was not consumed,* an emblem of the church now in bondage in Egypt, burning in the brick-kilns, yet not consumed; perplexed, but not in despair; cast down, but not destroyed.

III. The curiosity Moses had to enquire into this extraordinary sight: *I will turn aside and see, v.* 3. He speaks as one inquisitive and bold in his enquiry; whatever it was, he would, if possible, know the meaning of it. Note, Things revealed belong to us, and we ought diligently to enquire into them.

IV. The invitation he had to draw near, yet with a caution not to come too near, nor rashly.

1. God gave him a gracious call, to which he returned a ready answer, *v.* 4. When God saw that he took notice of the burning bush, and turned aside to see it, and left his business to attend it, then God called to him. If he had carelessly neglected it as an *ignis fatuus — a deceiving meteor,* a thing not worth taking notice of, it is probable that God would have departed, and said nothing to him; but, when he turned aside, God called to him. Note, Those that would have communion with God must attend upon him, and approach to him, in those ordinances wherein he is pleased to manifest himself, and his power and glory, though it be in a bush; they must come to the treasure, though in an earthen vessel. Those that seek God diligently shall find him, and find him their bountiful rewarder. *Draw nigh to God, and he will draw nigh to you.* God called him by name, *Moses, Moses.* This which he heard could not but surprise him much more than what he saw. The word of the Lord always went along with the glory of the Lord, for every divine vision was designed for divine revelation, Job 4:16, etc.; 32:14–15. Divine calls are then effectual, (1.) When the Spirit of God makes them particular, and calls us by name. The word calls, *Ho, every one!* The Spirit, by the application of that, calls, *Ho, such a one! I know thee by name,* Ex. 33:12. (2.) When we return an obedient answer to them, as Moses here, "*Here am I, what saith my Lord unto his servant? Here am I,* not only to hear what is said, but to do what I am bidden."

2. God gave him a needful caution against rashness and irreverence in his approach, (1.) He must keep his distance; draw near, but not too near; so near as to hear, but not so near as to pry. His conscience must be satisfied, but not his curiosity; and care must be taken that familiarity do not breed contempt. Note, In all our approaches to God, we ought to be deeply affected with the infinite distance there is between us and God, Eccl. 5:2. Or this may be taken as proper to the Old-Testament dispensation, which was a dispensation of darkness, bondage, and terror, from which the gospel happily frees us, giving us boldness to enter into the holiest, and inviting us to draw near. (2.) He must express his reverence, and his readiness to obey: *Put off thy shoes from off thy feet,* as a servant. Putting off the shoe was then what putting off the hat is now, a token of respect and submission. "The ground, for the present, is *holy ground,* made so by this special manifestation of the divine presence, during the continuance of which it must retain this character; therefore tread not on that ground with soiled shoes." *Keep thy foot,* Eccl. 5:1. Note, We ought to approach to God with a solemn pause and preparation; and, though bodily exercise alone profits little, yet we ought to glorify God with our bodies, and to express our inward reverence by a grave and reverent behaviour in the worship of God, carefully avoiding everything that looks light, and rude, and unbecoming the awfulness of the service.

V. The solemn declaration God made of his name, by which he would be known to Moses: *I am the God of thy father, v.* 6. 1. He lets him know that it is God who speaks to him, to engage his reverence and attention, his faith and obedience; for this is enough to command all these: *I am the Lord.* Let us always hear the word *as the word of God,* 1 Th. 2:13. 2. He will be known as the God of his father, his pious father Amram, and the God of Abraham, Isaac, and Jacob, his ancestors, and the ancestors of all Israel, for whom God was now about to appear. By this God designed, (1.) To instruct Moses in the knowledge of another world, and to strengthen his belief of a future state. Thus it is interpreted by our Lord Jesus, the best expositor of scripture, who from this proves that the dead are raised, against the Sadducees. *Moses,* says he, *showed it at the bush* (Lu. 20:37), that is, God there showed it to him, and in him to us, Mt. 22:31, etc. Abraham was dead, and yet God is the God of Abraham; therefore Abraham's soul

lives, to which God stands in relation; and, to make his soul completely happy, his body must live again in due time. This promise made unto the fathers, that God would be their God, must include a future happiness; for he never did anything for them in this world sufficient to answer to the vast extent and compass of that great word, but, having prepared for them a city, he is not ashamed to be called their God, Heb. 11:16; and see Acts 26:6, 7; 24:15. (2.) To assure Moses of the fulfillment of all those particular promises made to the fathers. He may confidently expect this, for by these words it appears that God remembered his covenant, *ch.* 2:24. Note, [1.] God's covenant-relation to us as our God is the best support in the worst of times, and a great encouragement to our faith in particular promises. [2.] When we are conscious to ourselves of our own great unworthiness we may take comfort from God's relation to our fathers, 2 Chr. 20:6.

VI. The solemn impression this made upon Moses: He *hid his face,* as one both ashamed and afraid to look upon God. Now that he knew it was a divine light his eyes were dazzled with it; he was not afraid of a burning bush till he perceived that God was in it. Yea, though God called himself *the God of his father,* and a God in covenant with him, yet he was afraid. Note, 1. The more we see of God the more cause we shall see to worship him with reverence and godly fear. 2. Even the manifestations of God's grace and covenant-love should increase our humble reverence of him.

Verses 7–10

Now that Moses had put off his shoes (for, no doubt, he observed the orders given him, *v.* 5), and covered his face, God enters upon the particular business that was now to be concerted, which was the bringing of Israel out of Egypt. Now, after forty years of Israel's bondage and Moses's banishment, when we may suppose both he and they began to despair, they of being delivered and he of delivering them, at length, the time has come, even the year of the redeemed. Note, God often comes for the salvation of his people when they have done looking for him. *Shall he find faith?* Lu. 18:8.

Here is, I. The notice God takes of the afflictions of Israel (*v.* 7, 9): *Seeing I have seen,* not only, *I have surely seen,* but I have strictly observed and considered the matter. Three things God took cognizance of: — 1. *Their sorrows, v.* 7. It is likely they were not permitted to make a remonstrance of their grievances to Pharaoh, nor to seek relief against their task-masters in any of his courts, nor scarcely durst complain to one another; but God observed their tears. Note, Even the secret sorrows of God's people are known to him. 2. Their cry: *I have heard their cry* (*v.* 7), *it has come unto me, v.* 9. Note, God is not deaf to the cries of his afflicted people. 3. The tyranny of their persecutors: *I have seen the oppression, v.* 9. Note, As the poorest of the oppressed are not below God's cognizance, so the highest and greatest of their oppressors are not above his check, but he will surely visit for these things.

II. The promise God makes of their speedy deliverance and enlargement: *I have come down to deliver them, v.* 8. 1. It denotes his resolution to deliver them, and that his heart was upon it, so that it should be done speedily and effectually, and by methods out of the common road of providence: when God does something very extraordinary he is said to *come down* to do it, as Isa. 64:1. 2. This deliverance was typical of our redemption by Christ, in which the eternal Word did indeed come down from heaven to deliver us: it was his errand into the world. He promises also their happy settlement in the land of Canaan, that they should exchange bondage for liberty, poverty for plenty, labour for rest, and the precarious condition of tenants at will for the ease and honour of lords proprietors. Note, Whom God by his grace delivers out of a spiritual Egypt he will bring to a heavenly Canaan.

III. The commission he gives to Moses in order hereunto, *v.* 10. He is not only sent as a prophet to Israel, to assure them that they should speedily be delivered (even that would have been a great favour), but he is sent as an ambassador to Pharaoh, to treat with him, or rather as a herald at arms, to demand their discharge, and to denounce war in case of refusal; and he is sent as a prince to Israel, to conduct and command them. Thus is he taken from *following the ewes great with young,* to a pastoral

office much more noble, as David, Ps. 78:71. Note, God is the fountain of power, and the powers that be are ordained of him as he pleases. The same hand that now fetched a shepherd out of a desert, to be the planter of a Jewish church, afterwards fetched fishermen from their ships, to be the planters of the Christian church, *That the excellency of the power might be of God.*

Verses 11–15

God, having spoken to Moses, allows him also a liberty of speech, which he here improves; and,

I. He objects his own insufficiency for the service he was called to (*v.* 11): *Who am I?* He thinks himself unworthy of the honour, and not *par negotio — equal to the task.* He thinks he wants courage, and therefore cannot go to Pharaoh, to make a demand which might cost the demandant his head: he thinks he wants skill, and therefore cannot bring forth the children of Israel out of Egypt; they are unarmed, undisciplined, quite dispirited, utterly unable to help themselves; it is morally impossible to bring them out. 1. Moses was incomparably the fittest of any man living for this work, eminent for learning, wisdom, experience, valour, faith, holiness; and yet he says, *Who am I?* Note, The more fit any person is for service commonly the less opinion he has of himself: see Judge. 9:8, etc. 2. The difficulties of the work were indeed very great, enough to startle the courage and stagger the faith of Moses himself. Note, Even wise and faithful instruments may be much discouraged at the difficulties that lie in the way of the church's salvation. 3. Moses had formerly been very courageous when he slew the Egyptian, but now his heart failed him; for good men are not always alike bold and zealous. 4. Yet Moses is the man that does it at last; for God gives grace to the lowly. Modest beginnings are very good presages.

II. God answers this objection, *v.* 12. 1. He promises him his presence: *Certainly I will be with thee,* and that is enough. Note, Those that are weak in themselves may yet do wonders, being strong in the Lord and in the power of his might; and those that are most diffident of themselves may be most confident in God. God's presence puts an honour upon the worthless, wisdom and strength into the weak and foolish, makes the greatest difficulties dwindle to nothing, and is enough to answer all objections. 2. He assures him of success, and that the Israelites should serve God upon this mountain. Note, (1.) Those deliverances are most valuable which open to us a door of liberty to serve God. (2.) If God gives us opportunity and a heart to serve him, it is a happy and encouraging earnest of further favours designed us.

III. He begs instructions for the executing of his commission, and has them, thoroughly to furnish him. He desires to know by what name God would at this time make himself known, *v.* 13.

1. He supposes the children of Israel would ask him, *What is his name?* This they would ask either, (1.) To perplex Moses: he foresaw difficulty, not only in dealing with Pharaoh, to make him willing to part with them, but in dealing with them, to make them willing to remove. They would be scrupulous and apt to cavil, would bid him produce his commission, and probably this would be the trial: "Does he know the name of God? Has he the watch-word?" Once he was asked, *Who made thee a judge?* Then he had not his answer ready, and he would not be nonplussed so again, but would be able to tell in whose name he came. Or, (2.) For their own information. It is to be feared that they had grown very ignorant in Egypt, by reason of their hard bondage, want of teachers, and loss of the sabbath, so that they needed to be told the first principles of the oracles of God. Or this question, *What is his name?* amounted to an enquiry into the nature of the dispensation they were now to expect: "How will God in it be known to us, and what may we depend upon from him?"

2. He desires instructions what answer to give them: "*What shall I say to them?* What name shall I vouch to them for the proof of my authority? I must have something great and extraordinary to say to them; what must it be? If I must go, let me have full instructions, that I may not run in vain." Note, (1.) It highly concerns those who speak to people in the name of God to be well prepared beforehand. (2.) Those who would know what to say must go to God, to the word of his grace and to the throne of

his grace, for instructions, Eze. 2:7; 3:4, 10, 17. (3.) Whenever we have any thing to do with God, it is desirable to know, and our duty to consider, what is his name.

IV. God readily gives him full instructions in this matter. Two names God would now be known by: —

1. A name that denotes what he is in himself (*v.* 14): *I am that I am.* This explains his name *Jehovah,* and signifies, (1.) That he is self-existent; he has his being of himself, and has no dependence upon any other: the greatest and best man in the world must say, By the grace of God *I am what I am;* but God says absolutely — and it is more than any creature, man or angel, can say — *I am that I am.* Being self-existent, he cannot but be self-sufficient, and therefore all-sufficient, and the inexhaustible fountain of being and bliss. (2.) That he is eternal and unchangeable, and always the same, yesterday, to-day, and for ever; he will be what he will be and what he is; see Rev. 1:8. (3.) That we cannot by searching find him out. This is such a name as checks all bold and curious enquiries concerning God, and in effect says, *Ask not after my name, seeing it is secret,* Jdg. 13:18; Prov. 30:4. Do we ask what is God? Let it suffice us to know that he is what he is, what he ever was, and ever will be. *How little a portion is heard of him!* Job 26:14. (4.) That he is faithful and true to all his promises, unchangeable in his word as well as in his nature, and not a man that he should lie. Let Israel know this, *I AM hath sent me unto you.*

2. A name that denotes what he is to his people. Lest that name *I AM* should amuse and puzzle them, he is further directed to make use of another name of God more familiar and intelligible: *The Lord God of your fathers hath sent me unto you* (*v.* 15): Thus God had made himself know to him (*v.* 6), and thus he must make him known to them, (1.) That he might revive among them the religion of their fathers, which, it is to be feared, was much decayed and almost lost. This was necessary to prepare them for deliverance, Ps. 80:19. (2.) That he might raise their expectations of the speedy performance of the promises made unto their fathers. Abraham, Isaac, and Jacob, are particularly named, because with Abraham the covenant was first made, and with Isaac and Jacob often expressly renewed; and these three were distinguished from their brethren, and chosen to be the trustees of the covenant, when their brethren were rejected. God will have this to be his name for ever, and it has been, is, and will be, his name, by which his worshippers know him, and distinguish him from all false gods; see 1 Ki. 18:36. Note, God's covenant-relation to his people is what he will be ever mindful of, what he glories in, and what he will have us never forget, but give him the glory of: if he will have this to be his memorial unto all generations, we have all the reason in the world to make it so with us, for it is a precious memorial.

Verses 16–22

Moses is here more particularly instructed in his work, and informed beforehand of his success. 1. He must deal with the elders of Israel, and raise their expectation of a speedy removal to Canaan, *v.* 16, 17. He must repeat to them what God had said to him, as a faithful ambassador. Note, That which ministers have received of the Lord they must deliver to his people, and keep back nothing that is profitable. Lay an emphasis on that, *v.* 17: *"I have said, I will bring you up;* that is enough to satisfy them, *I have said it:"* hath he spoken, and will he not make it good? With us saying and doing are two things, but they are not so with God, for he is in one mind and who can turn him? "I have said it, and all the world cannot gainsay it. My counsel shall stand." His success with the elders of Israel would be good; so he is told (*v.* 18): *They shall hearken to thy voice,* and not thrust thee away as they did forty years ago. He who, by his grace, inclines the heart, and opens the ear, could say beforehand, *They shall hearken to thy voice,* having determined to make them willing in this day of power. 2. He must deal with the king of Egypt (*v.* 18), he and the elders of Israel, and in this they must not begin with a demand, but with a humble petition; that gentle and submissive method must be first tried, even with one who, it was certain, would not be wrought upon by it: *We beseech thee, let us go.* Moreover, they must only beg leave of Pharaoh to go as far as Mount Sinai to worship God, and say nothing to him of going quite away to Canaan; the latter would have been immediately rejected, but the former was a very modest and reasonable request, and his denying it was utterly inexcusable and justified them in the total deserting of his kingdom. If he would not give them leave to go and sacrifice at Sinai, justly did they go without leave to settle in Canaan. Note, The calls and commands which God sends to sinners are so highly reasonable in themselves, and delivered to them in such a gentle winning way, that the mouth of the disobedient must needs be for ever stopped. As to his success with Pharaoh, Moses is here told, (1.) That petitions, and persuasions, and humble remonstrances, would not prevail with him, no, nor a mighty hand stretched out in signs and wonders: *I am sure he will not let you go, v.* 19. Note, God sends his messengers to those whose hardness and obstinacy he certainly knows and foresees, that it may appear he would have them turn and live. (2.) That plagues should compel him to it: *I will smite Egypt,* and then he will *let you go, v.* 20. Note, Those will certainly be broken by the power of God's hand that will not bow to the power of his word; we may be sure that *when God judges he will overcome.* (3.) That his people should be more kind to them, and furnish them at their departure with abundance of plate and jewels, to their great enriching: *I will give this people favour in the sight of the Egyptians, v.* 21, 22. Note, [1.] God sometimes makes the enemies of his people, not only to be at peace with them, but to be kind to them. [2.] God has many ways of balancing accounts between the injured and the injurious, of righting the oppressed, and compelling those that have done wrong to make restitution; for he sits in the throne judging right.

CHAPTER 4

This chapter, I. Continues and concludes God's discourse with Moses at the bush concerning this great affair of bringing Israel out of Egypt. 1. Moses objects the people's unbelief (*v.* 1), and God answers that objection by giving him a power to work miracles, (1.) To turn his rod into a serpent, and then into a rod again (*v.* 2–5). (2.) To make his hand leprous, and then whole again (*v.* 6–8). (3.) To turn the water into blood (*v.* 9). 2. Moses objects his own slowness of speech (*v.* 10), and begs to be excused (*v.* 13); but God answers this objection, (1.) By promising him his presence (*v.* 11, 12). (2.) By joining Aaron in commission with him (*v.* 14–16). (3.) By putting an honour upon the very staff in his hand (*v.* 17). II. It begins Moses's execution of his commission. 1. He obtains leave of his father-in-law to return into Egypt (*v.* 18). 2. He receives further instructions and encouragements from God (*v.* 19, 21–23). 3. He hastens his departure, and takes his family with him (*v.* 20). 4. He meets with some difficulty in the way about the circumcising of his son (*v.* 24–26). 5. He has the satisfaction of meeting his brother Aaron (*v.* 27, 28). 6. He produces his commission before the elders of Israel, to their great joy (*v.* 29–31). And thus the wheels were set a going towards that great deliverance.

Verses 1–9

It was a very great honour that Moses was called to when God commissioned him to bring Israel out of Egypt; yet he is with difficulty persuaded to accept the commission, and does it at last with great reluctance, which we should rather impute to a humble diffidence of himself and his own sufficiency than to any unbelieving distrust of God and his word and power. Note, Those whom God designs for preferment he clothes with humility; the most fit for service are the least forward.

I. Moses objects that in all probability the people would not *hearken to his voice* (*v.* 1), that is, they would not take his bare word, unless he showed them some sign, which he had not been yet instructed to do. This objection cannot be justified, because it contradicts what God had said (*ch.* 3:18), *They shall hearken to thy voice.* If God says, *They will,* does it become Moses to say, *They will not?* Surely he means, "Perhaps they will not at first, or some of them will not." If there should be some gainsayers among them who would question his commission, how should he deal with them? And what course should he take to convince them? He remembered how they had once rejected him, and feared it would be so again. Note, 1. Present discouragements often arise from former disappointments. 2. Wise and good men have sometimes a worse opinion of people than they deserve. Moses sad (*v.* 1), *They will not believe me;* and yet he was happily mistaken, for it is said (*v.* 31), *The people believed;* but then the signs which God appointed in answer to this objection were first wrought in their sight.

II. God empowers him to work miracles, directs him to three particularly, two of which were now immediately wrought for his own satisfaction. Note, True miracles are the most convincing external proofs of a divine mission attested by them. Therefore our Saviour often appealed to his works (as Jn. 5:36), and Nicodemus owns himself convinced by them, Jn. 3:2. And here Moses, having a special commission given him as a judge and lawgiver to Israel, has this seal affixed to his commission, and comes supported by these credentials.

1. The rod in his hand is made the subject of a miracle, a double miracle: it is but thrown out of his hand and it becomes a serpent; he resumes it and it becomes a rod again, *v.* 2–4. Now, (1.) Here was a divine power manifested in the change itself, that a dry stick should be turned into a living serpent, a lively one, so formidable a one that Moses himself, on whom, it should seem, it turned in some threatening manner, *fled from before it,* though we may suppose, in that desert, serpents were no strange things to him; but what was produced miraculously was always the best and strongest of the kind, as the water turned to wine: and, then, that this living serpent should be turned into a dry stick again, this was the Lord's doing. (2.) Here was an honour put upon Moses, that this change was wrought upon his throwing it down and taking it up, without any spell, or charm, or incantation: his being empowered thus to act under God, out of the common course of nature and providence, was a demonstration of his authority, under God, to settle a new dispensation of the kingdom of grace. We cannot imagine that the God of truth would delegate such a power as this to an impostor. (3.) There was a significancy in the miracle itself. Pharaoh had turned the rod of Israel into a serpent, representing them as dangerous (*ch.* 1:10), causing their belly to cleave to the dust, and seeking their ruin; but now they should be turned into a rod again: or, thus Pharaoh had turned the rod of government into the serpent of oppression, from which Moses had himself fled into Midian; but by the agency of Moses the scene was altered again. (4.) There was a direct tendency in it to convince the children of Israel that Moses was indeed sent of God to do what he did, *v.* 5. Miracles were for signs to those that believed not, 1 Co. 14:22.

2. His hand itself is next made the subject of a miracle. He puts it once into his bosom, and takes it out leprous; he puts it again into the same place, and takes it out well, *v.* 6, 7. This signified, (1.) That Moses, by the power of God, should bring sore diseases upon Egypt, and that, at his prayer, they should be removed. (2.) That whereas the Israelites in Egypt had become leprous, polluted by sin, and almost consumed by oppression (a leper is *as one dead,* Num. 12:12), by being taken into the bosom of Moses they should be cleansed and cured, and have all their grievances redressed. (3.) That Moses was not to work miracles by his own power, nor for his own praise, but by the power of God and for his glory; the leprous hand of Moses does for ever exclude boasting. Now it was supposed that, if the former sign did not convince, this latter would. Note, God is willing more abundantly to show the truth of his word, and is not sparing in his proofs; the multitude and variety of the miracles corroborate the evidence.

3. He is directed, when he shall come to Egypt, to turn some of the water of the river into blood, *v.* 9. This was done, at first, as a sign, but, not gaining due credit with Pharaoh, the whole river was afterwards turned into blood, and then it became a plague. He is ordered to work this miracle in case they would not be convinced by the other two. Note, Unbelief shall be left inexcusable, and convicted of a wilful obstinacy. As to the people of Israel, God had said (*ch.* 3:18), *They shall hearken;* yet he appoints these miracles to be wrought for their conviction, for he that has ordained the end has ordained the means.

Verses 10–17

Moses still continues backward to the service for which God had designed him, even to a fault; for now we can no longer impute it to his humility and modesty, but must own that here was too much of cowardice, slothfulness, and unbelief in it. Observe here,

I. How Moses endeavours to excuse himself from the work.

1. He pleads that he was no good spokesman: *O my Lord! I am not eloquent, v.* 10. He was a great philosopher, statesman, and divine, and yet no orator; a man of a clear head, great thought, and solid judgment, but had not a voluble tongue, or ready utterance, and therefore he thought himself unfit to speak before great men about great

affairs, and in danger of being run down by the Egyptians. Observe, (1.) We must not judge of men by the readiness and fluency of their discourse. Moses was *mighty in word* (Acts 7:22), and yet not eloquent: what he said was strong and nervous, and to the purpose, and distilled as the dew (Deu. 32:2), though he did not deliver himself with that readiness, ease, and elegance, that some do, who have not the tenth part of his sense. St. Paul's speech was contemptible, 2 Co. 10:10. A great deal of wisdom and true worth is concealed by a slow tongue. (2.) God is pleased sometimes to make choice of those as his messengers who have fewest of the advantages of art or nature, that his grace in them may appear the more glorious. Christ's disciples were no orators, till the Spirit made them such.

2. When this plea was overruled, and all his excuses were answered, he begged that God would send somebody else on this errand and leave him to keep sheep in Midian (*v.* 13): "Send by any hand but mine; thou canst certainly find one much more fit." Note, An unwilling mind will take up with a sorry excuse rather than none, and is willing to devolve those services upon others that have any thing of difficulty or danger in them.

II. How God condescends to answer all his excuses. Though *the anger of the Lord was kindled against him* (*v.* 14), yet he continued to reason with him, till he had overcome him. Note, Even self-diffidence, when it grows into an extreme — when it either hinders us from duty or clogs us in duty, or when it discourages our dependence upon the grace of God — is very displeasing to him. God justly resents our backwardness to serve him, and has reason to take it ill; for he is such a benefactor as is beforehand with us, and such a rewarder as will not be behindhand with us. Note further, God is justly displeased with those whom yet he does not reject: he vouchsafes to reason the case even with his froward children, and overcomes them, as he did Moses here, with grace and kindness.

1. To balance the weakness of Moses, he here reminds him of his own power, *v.* 11. (1.) His power in that concerning which Moses made the objection: *Who has made man's mouth? Have not I the Lord?* Moses knew that God made man, but he must be reminded now that God made man's mouth. An eye to God as Creator would help us over a great many of the difficulties which lie in the way of our duty, Ps. 124:8. God, as the author of nature, has given us the power and faculty of speaking; and from him, as the fountain of gifts and graces, comes the faculty of speaking well, the *mouth and wisdom* (Lu. 21:15), the *tongue of the learned* (Isa. 50:4); he *pours grace into the lips*, Ps. 45:2. (2.) His power in general over the other faculties. Who but God *makes the dumb and the deaf, the seeing and the blind?* [1.] The perfections of our faculties are his work, he makes the *seeing;* he formed the eye (Ps. 94:9); he opens the understanding, the eye of the mind, Lu. 24:45. [2.] Their imperfections are from him too; he make the *dumb*, and *deaf*, and blind. Is there any evil of this kind, and the Lord has not done it? No doubt he has, and always in wisdom and righteousness, and for his own glory, Jn. 9:3. Pharaoh and the Egyptians were made deaf and blind spiritually, as Isa. 6:9, 10. But God knew how to manage them, and get himself honour upon them.

2. To encourage him in this great undertaking, he repeats the promise of his presence, not only in general, *I will be with thee* (ch. 3:12), but in particular, *"I will be with thy mouth*, so that the imperfection in thy speech shall be no prejudice to thy message." It does not appear that God did immediately remove the infirmity, whatever it was; but he did that which was equivalent, he taught him what to say, and then let the matter recommend itself: if others spoke more gracefully, none spoke more powerfully. Note, Those whom God employs to speak for him ought to depend upon him for instructions, and *it shall be given them what they shall speak*, Mt. 10:19.

3. He joins Aaron in commission with him. He promises that Aaron shall meet him opportunely, and that he will be glad to see him, they having not seen one another (it is likely) for many years, *v.* 14. He directs him to make use of Aaron as his spokesman, *v.* 16. God might have laid Moses wholly aside, for his backwardness to be employed; but he considered his frame, and ordered him an assistant. Observe, (1.) Two are better than one, Eccl. 4:9. God will have his two witnesses (Rev. 11:3), that out of their mouths every word may be established. (2.) Aaron was the

brother of Moses, divine wisdom so ordering it, that their natural affection one to another might strengthen their union in the joint execution of their commission. Christ sent his disciples two and two, and some of the couples were brothers. (3.) Aaron was the elder brother, and yet he was willing to be employed under Moses in this affair, because God would have it so. (4.) Aaron could speak well, and yet was far inferior to Moses in wisdom. God dispenses his gifts variously to the children of men, that we may see our need one of another, and each may contribute something to the good of the body, 1 Co. 12:21. The tongue of Aaron, with the head and heart of Moses, would make one completely fit for this embassy. (5.) God promises, *I will be with thy mouth, and with his mouth.* Even Aaron, that could speak well, yet could not speak to purpose unless God was with his mouth; without the constant aids of divine grace the best gifts will fail.

4. He bids him take the rod with him in his hand (*v.* 17), to intimate that he must bring about his undertaking rather by acting than by speaking; the signs he should work with this rod might abundantly supply the want of eloquence; one miracle would do him better service than all the rhetoric in the world. *Take this rod*, the rod he carried as a shepherd, that he might not be ashamed of that mean condition out of which God called him. This rod must be his staff of authority, and must be to him instead both of sword and sceptre.

Verses 18–23

Here, I. Moses obtains leave of his father-in-law to return into Egypt, *v.* 18. His father-in-law had been kind to him when he was a stranger, and therefore he would not be so uncivil as to leave his family, nor so unjust as to leave his service, without giving him notice. Note, The honour of being admitted into communion with God, and of being employed for him, does not exempt us from the duties of our relations and callings in this world. Moses said nothing to his father-in-law (for aught that appears) of the glorious manifestation of God to him; such favours we are to be thankful for to God, but not to boast of before men.

II. He receives from God further encouragements and directions in his work. After God had appeared to him in the bush to settle a correspondence, it should seem, he often spoke to him, as there was occasion, with less overwhelming solemnity. And, 1. He assures Moses that the coasts were clear. Whatever new enemies he might make by his undertaking, his old enemies were *all dead, all that sought his life, v.* 19. Perhaps some secret fear of falling into their hands was at the bottom of Moses's backwardness to go to Egypt, though he was not willing to own it, but pleaded unworthiness, insufficiency, want of elocution, etc. Note, God knows all the temptations his people lie under, and how to arm them against their secret fears, Ps. 142:3. 2. He orders him to do the miracles, not only before the elders of Israel, but before Pharaoh, *v.* 21. There were some alive perhaps in the court of Pharaoh who remembered Moses when he was the son of Pharaoh's daughter, and had many a time called him a fool for deserting the honours of that relation; but he is now sent back to court, clad with greater powers than Pharaoh's daughter could have advanced him to, so that it might appear he was no loser by his choice: this wonder-working rod did more adorn the hand of Moses than the sceptre of Egypt could have done. Note, Those that look with contempt upon worldly honours shall be recompensed with the honour that cometh from God, which is the true honour. 3. That Pharaoh's obstinacy might be no surprise nor discouragement to him, God tells him before that he would *harden his heart*. Pharaoh had hardened his own heart against the groans and cries of the oppressed Israelites, and shut up the bowels of his compassion from them; and now God, in a way of righteous judgment, hardens his heart against the conviction of the miracles, and the terror of the plagues. Note, Ministers must expect with many to labour in vain: we must not think it strange if we meet with those who will not be wrought upon by the strongest arguments and fairest reasonings; yet our judgment is with the Lord. 4. Words are put into his mouth with which to address Pharaoh, *v.* 22, 23. God had promised him (*v.* 12), *I will teach thee what thou shalt say;* and here he does teach him. (1.) He must deliver his message in the name of the great Jehovah: *Thus saith the Lord;* this is the first time *that* pref-

ace is used by any man which afterwards is used so frequently by all the prophets: whether Pharaoh will hear, or whether he will forbear, Moses must tell him, *Thus saith the Lord.* (2.) He must let Pharaoh know Israel's relation to God, and God's concern for Israel. *Is Israel a servant? is he a home-born slave?* Jer. 2:14. "No, *Israel is my son, my firstborn, precious in my sight, honourable,* and dear to me, not to be thus insulted and abused." (3.) He must demand a discharge for them: *"Let my son go;* not only my servant whom thou hast no right to detain, but my son whose liberty and honour I am very jealous for. It is my son, my son that serves me, and therefore must be spared, must be pleaded for," Mal. 3:17. (4.) He must threaten Pharaoh with the death of the first-born of Egypt, in case of a refusal: *I will slay thy son, even thy firstborn.* As men deal with God's people, let them expect to be themselves dealt with; with the froward he will wrestle.

III. Moses addresses himself to this expedition. When God had assured him (*v.* 19) that the men were dead who sought his life, immediately it follows (*v.* 20), he took his *wife, and his sons,* and set out for Egypt. Note, Though corruption may object much against the services God calls us to, yet grace will get the upper hand, and will be obedient to the heavenly vision.

Verses 24–31

Moses is here going to Egypt, and we are told,

I. How God met him in anger, *v.* 24–26. This is a very difficult passage of story; much has been written, and excellently written, to make it intelligible; we will try to make it improving. Here is,

1. The sin of Moses, which was neglecting to circumcise his son. This was probably the effect of his being unequally yoked with a Midianite, who was too indulgent of her child, while Moses was too indulgent of her. Note, (1.) We have need to watch carefully over our own hearts, lest fondness for any relation prevail above our love to God, and take us off from our duty to him. It is charged upon Eli that he *honoured his sons more than God* (1 Sa. 2:29); and see Mt. 10:37. (2.) Even good men are apt to cool in their zeal for God and duty when they have long been deprived of the society of the faithful: solitude has its advantages, but they seldom counterbalance the loss of Christian communion.

2. God's displeasure against him. He met him, and, probably by a sword in an angel's hand, sought to kill him. This was a great change; very lately God was conversing with him, and lodging a trust in him, as a friend; and now he is coming forth against him as an enemy. Note, (1.) Omissions are sins, and must come into judgment, and particularly the contempt and neglect of the seals of the covenant; for it is a sign that we undervalue the promises of the covenant, and are displeased with the conditions of it. He that has made a bargain, and is not willing to seal and ratify it, one may justly suspect, neither likes it nor designs to stand to it. (2.) God takes notice of, and is much displeased with, the sins of his own people. If they neglect their duty, let them expect to hear of it by their consciences, and perhaps to feel from it by cross providences: for this cause many are sick and weak, as some think Moses was here.

3. The speedy performance of the duty for the neglect of which God had now a controversy with him. His son must be circumcised; Moses is unable to circumcise him; therefore, in this case of necessity, Zipporah does it, whether with passionate words (expressing her dislike of the ordinance itself, or at least the administration of it to so young a child, and in a journey), as to me it seems, or with proper words — solemnly expressing the espousal of the child to God by the covenant of circumcision (as some read it) or her thankfulness to God for sparing her husband, giving him a new life, and thereby giving her, as it were, a new marriage to him, upon her circumcising her son (as others read it) — I cannot determine: but we learn, (1.) That when God discovers to us what is amiss in our lives we must give all diligence to amend it speedily, and particularly return to the duties we have neglected. (2.) The putting away of our sins is indispensably necessary to the removal of God's judgements. This is the voice of every rod, it calls to us to return to him that smites us.

4. The release of Moses thereupon: *So he let him go;* the distemper went off, the destroying angel withdrew, and

all was well: only Zipporah cannot forget the fright she was in, but will unreasonably call Moses *a bloody husband*, because he obliged her to circumcise the child; and, upon this occasion (it is probable), he sent them back to his father-in-law, that they might not create him any further uneasiness. Note, (1.) When we return to God in a way of duty he will return to us in a way of mercy; take away the cause, and the effect will cease. (2.) We must resolve to bear it patiently, if our zeal for God and his institutions be misinterpreted and discouraged by some that should understand themselves, and us, and their duty, better, as David's zeal was misinterpreted by Michal; but if this be to be vile, if this be to be bloody, we must be yet more so. (3.) When we have any special service to do for God we should remove as far from us as we can that which is likely to be our hindrance. *Let the dead bury their dead, but follow thou me.*

II. How Aaron met him in love, *v.* 27, 28. 1. God sent Aaron to meet him, and directed him where to find him, in the wilderness that lay towards Midian. Note, The providence of God is to be acknowledged in the comfortable meeting of relations and friends. 2. Aaron made so much haste, in obedience to his God, and in love to his brother, that he met him *in the mount of God*, the place where God had met with him. 3. They embraced one another with mutual endearments. The more they saw of God's immediate direction in bringing them together the more pleasant their interview was: they *kissed*, not only in token of brotherly affection, and in remembrance of ancient acquaintance, but as a pledge of their hearty concurrence in the work to which they were jointly called. 4. Moses informed his brother of the commission he had received, with all the instructions and credentials affixed to it. *v.* 28. Note, What we know of God we should communicate for the benefit of others; and those that are fellow-servants to God in the same work should use a mutual freedom, and endeavour rightly and fully to understand one another.

III. How the elders of Israel met him in faith and obedience. When Moses and Aaron first opened their commission in Egypt, said what they were ordered to say, and, to confirm it, did what they were ordered to do, they met with a better reception than they promised themselves, *v.* 29-31. 1. The Israelites gave credit to them: *The people believed*, as God had foretold (*ch.* 3:18), knowing that no man could do those works that they did, unless God were with him. They gave glory to God: *They bowed their heads and worshipped*, therein expressing not only their humble thankfulness to God, who had raised them up and sent them a deliverer, but also their cheerful readiness to observe orders, and pursue the methods of their deliverance.

CHAPTER 5

Moses and Aaron are here dealing with Pharaoh, to get leave of him to go and worship in the wilderness. I. They demand leave in the name of God (*v.* 1), and he answers their demand with a defiance of God (*v.* 2). II. They beg leave in the name of Israel (*v.* 3), and he answers their request with further orders to oppress Israel (*v.* 4-9). These cruel orders were, 1. Executed by the task-masters (*v.* 10-14). 2. Complained of to Pharaoh, but in vain (*v.* 15-19). 3. Complained of by the people to Moses (*v.* 20, 21), and by him to God (*v.* 22, 23).

Verses 1-2

Moses and Aaron, having delivered their message to the elders of Israel, with whom they found good acceptance, are now to deal with Pharaoh, to whom they come in peril of their lives — Moses particularly, who perhaps was out-lawed for killing the Egyptian forty years before, so that if any of the old courtiers should happen to remember that against him now it might cost him his head. Their message itself was displeasing, and touch Pharaoh both in his honour and in his profit, two tender points; yet these faithful ambassadors boldly deliver it, whether he will hear or whether he will forbear.

I. Their demand is piously bold: *Thus saith the Lord God of Israel, Let my people go, v.* 1. Moses, in treating with the elders of Israel, is directed to call God *the God of their fathers;* but, in treating with Pharaoh, they call him *the God of Israel*, and it is the first time we find him called so in scripture: he is called *the God of Israel*, the *person* (Gen. 33:20); but here it is Israel, the *people*. They are just beginning to be formed into a people when God is called their God. Moses, it is likely, was directed to call him so,

at least it might be inferred from *ch.* 9:22, *Israel is my son.* In this great name they deliver their message: *Let my people go.* 1. They were God's people, and therefore Pharaoh ought not to detain them in bondage. Note, God will own his own people, though ever so poor and despicable, and will find a time to plead their cause. "The Israelites are slaves in Egypt, but they are my people," says God, "and I will not suffer them to be always trampled upon." See Isa. 52:4, 5. 2. He expected services and sacrifices from them, and therefore they must have leave to go where they could freely exercise their religion, without giving offence to, or receiving offence from, the Egyptians. Note, God delivers his people out of the hand of their enemies, that they may serve him, and serve him cheerfully, that they may hold a feast to him, which they may do, while they have his favour and presence, even in a wilderness, a dry and barren land.

II. Pharaoh's answer is impiously bold: *Who is the Lord, that I should obey his voice? v.* 2. Being summoned to surrender, he thus hangs out the flag of defiance, hectors Moses and the God that sends him, and peremptorily refuses to let Israel go; he will not treat about it, nor so much as bear the mention of it. Observe, 1. How scornfully he speaks of the God of Israel: *"Who is Jehovah?* I neither know him nor care for him, neither value him nor fear him:" it is a hard name that he never heard of before, but he resolves it shall be no bug-bear to him. Israel was now a despised oppressed people, looked on as the tail of the nation, and, by the character they bore, Pharaoh makes his estimate of their God, and concludes that he made no better a figure among the gods than his people did among the nations. Note, Hardened persecutors are more malicious against God himself than they are against his people. See Isa. 37:23. Again, Ignorance and contempt of God are at the bottom of all the wickedness that is in the world. Men know not the Lord, or have very low and mean thoughts of him, and therefore they obey not his voice, nor will let any thing go for him. 2. How proudly he speaks of himself: *"That I should obey his voice;* I, the king of Egypt, a great people, obey the God of Israel, a poor enslaved people? Shall I, that rule the Israel of God, obey the God of Israel? No, it is below me; I scorn to answer his summons." Note, Those are the children of pride that are the *children of disobedience*, Job 41:34; Eph. 5:6. Proud men think themselves too good to stoop even to God himself, and would not be under control, Jer. 43:2. Here is the core of the controversy: God must rule, but man will not be ruled. "I will have my will done," says God: "But I will do my own will," says the sinner. 3. How resolutely he denies the demand: *Neither will I let Israel go.* Note, Of all sinners none are so obstinate, nor so hardly persuaded to leave their sin, as persecutors are.

Verses 3-9

Finding that Pharaoh had no veneration at all for God, Moses and Aaron next try whether he had any compassion for Israel, and become humble suitors to him for leave to go and sacrifice, but in vain.

I. Their request is very humble and modest, *v.* 3. They make no complaint of the rigour they were ruled with. They plead that the journey they designed was not a project formed among themselves, but that their God had met with them, and called them to it. They beg with all submission: *We pray thee.* The poor useth entreaties; though God may summon princes that oppress, it becomes us to beseech and make supplication to them. What they ask is very reasonable, only for a short vacation, while they went three days' journey into the desert, and that on a good errand, and unexceptionable: *"We will sacrifice unto the Lord our God*, as other people do to theirs;" and, *lastly*, they give a very good reason, "Lest, if we quite cast off his worship, he fall upon us with one judgment or other, and then Pharaoh will lose his vassals."

II. Pharaoh's denial of their request is very barbarous and unreasonable, *v.* 4-9.

1. His suggestions were very unreasonable. (1.) That the people were idle, and that therefore they talked of going to sacrifice. The cities they built for Pharaoh, and the other fruit of their labours, were witnesses for them that they were not idle; yet he thus basely misrepresents them, that he might have a pretence to increase their burdens. (2.) That Moses and Aaron made them idle with vain words,

v. 9. God's words are here called vain words; and those that called them to the best and most needful business are accused of making them idle. Note, The malice of Satan has often represented the service and worship of God as fit employment for those only that have nothing else to do, and the business only of the idle; whereas indeed it is the indispensable duty of those that are most busy in the world.

2. His resolutions hereupon were most barbarous. (1.) Moses and Aaron themselves must get to *their burdens* (*v.* 4); they are Israelites, and, however God had distinguished them from the rest, Pharaoh makes no difference: they must share in the common slavery of their nation. Persecutors have always taken a particular pleasure in putting contempt and hardship upon the ministers of the churches. (2.) The usual tale of bricks must be exacted, without the usual allowance of straw to mix with the clay, or to burn the bricks with, that thus more work might be laid upon the men, which if they performed, they would be broken with labour; and, if not, they would be exposed to punishment.

Verses 10-14

Pharaoh's orders are here put in execution; straw is denied, and yet the work not diminished. 1. The Egyptian task-masters were very severe. Pharaoh having decreed unrighteous decrees, the task-masters were ready to write the grievousness that he had prescribed, Isa. 10:1. Cruel princes will never want cruel instruments to be employed under them, who will justify them in that which is most unreasonable. These task-masters insisted upon the daily tasks, as when there was straw, *v.* 13. See what need we have to pray that *we may be delivered from unreasonable and wicked men*, 2 Th. 3:2. The enmity of the serpent's seed against the seed of the woman is such as breaks through all the laws of reason, honour, humanity, and common justice. 2. The people hereby were dispersed throughout all the land of Egypt, to gather stubble, *v.* 12. By this means Pharaoh's unjust and barbarous usage of them came to be known to all the kingdom, and perhaps caused them to be pitied by their neighbours, and made Pharaoh's government less acceptable even to his own subjects: goodwill is never got by persecution. 3. The Israelite-officers were used with particular harshness, *v.* 14. Those that were the fathers of the houses of Israel paid dearly for their honour; for from them immediately the service was exacted, and they were beaten when it was not performed. See here, (1.) What a miserable thing slavery is, and what reason we have to be thankful to God that we are a free people, and not oppressed. Liberty and property are valuable jewels in the eyes of those whose services and possessions lie at the mercy of an arbitrary power. (2.) What disappointments we often meet with after the raising of our expectations. The Israelites were now lately encouraged to hope for enlargement, but behold greater distresses. This teaches us always to rejoice with trembling. (3.) What strange steps God sometimes takes in delivering his people; he often brings them to the utmost straits when he is just ready to appear for them. The lowest ebbs go before the highest tides; and very cloudy mornings commonly introduce the fairest days, Deu. 32:36. God's time to help is when things are at the worst; and Providence verifies the paradox, *The worse the better.*

Verses 15-23

It was a great strait that the head-workmen were in, when they must either abuse those that were under them or be abused by those that were over them; yet, it should seem, rather than they would tyrannize, they would be tyrannized over; and they were so. In this evil case (*v.* 19), observe,

I. How justly they complained to Pharaoh: They *came and cried unto Pharaoh, v.* 15. Whither should they go with a remonstrance of their grievances but to the supreme power, which is ordained for the protection of the injured? As bad as Pharaoh was his oppressed subjects had liberty to complain to him; there was no law against petitioning: it was a very modest, but moving, representation that they made of their condition (*v.* 16): *Thy servants are beaten* (severely enough, no doubt, when things were in such a ferment), and yet *the fault is in thy own people*, the task-masters, who deny us what is necessary for carrying on our work. Note, It is common for those to be most rigorous in blaming others who are most blameworthy themselves. But what did they get by this complaint? It did but make bad worse. 1. Pharaoh taunted them (*v.* 17); when they were almost killed with working, he told them they were idle: they underwent the fatigue of industry, and yet lay under the imputation of slothfulness, while nothing appeared to ground the charge upon but this, that they said, *Let us go and do sacrifice.* Note, It is common for the best actions to be mentioned under the worst names; holy diligence in the best business is censured by many as a culpable carelessness in the business of the world. It is well for us that men are not to be our judges, but a God who knows what the principles are on which we act. Those that are diligent in doing sacrifice to the Lord will, with God, escape the doom of the slothful servant, though, with men, they do not. 2. He bound on their burdens: *Go now and work. v.* 18. Note, Wickedness proceedeth from the wicked; what can be expected from unrighteous men but more unrighteousness?

II. How unjustly they complained of Moses and Aaron: *The Lord look upon you, and judge, v.* 21. This was not fair. Moses and Aaron had given sufficient evidence of their hearty good-will to the liberties of Israel; and yet, because things succeed not immediately as they hoped, they are reproached as accessaries to their slavery. They should have humbled themselves before God, and taken to themselves the shame of their sin, which turned away good things from them; but, instead of this, they fly in the face of their best friends, and quarrel with the instruments of their deliverance, because of some little difficulties and obstructions they met with in effecting it. Note, Those that are called out to public service for God and their generation must expect to be tried, not only by the malicious threats of proud enemies, but by the unjust and unkind censures of unthinking friends, who judge only by outward appearance and look but a little way before them. Now what did Moses do in this strait? It grieved him to the heart that the event did not answer, but rather contradict, his expectation; and their upbraidings were very cutting, and like a sword in his bones; but, 1. He returned to the Lord (*v.* 22), to acquaint him with it, and to represent the case to him: he knew that what he had said and done was by divine direction; and therefore what blame is laid upon him for it he considers as reflecting upon God, and, like Hezekiah, spreads it before him as interested in the cause, and appeals to him. Compare this with Jer. 20:7–9. Note, When we find ourselves, at any time, perplexed and embarrassed in the way of our duty, we ought to have recourse to God, and lay open our case before him by faithful and fervent prayer. If we retreat, let us retreat to him, and no further. 2. He expostulated with him, *v.* 22, 23. He knew not how to reconcile the providence with the promise and the commission which he had received. "Is this God's coming down to deliver Israel? Must I, who hoped to be a blessing to them, become a scourge to them? By this attempt to get them out of the pit, they are but sunk the deeper into it." Now he asks, (1.) *Wherefore hast thou so evil entreated this people?* Note, Even when God is coming towards his people in ways of mercy, he sometimes takes such methods as that they may think themselves but ill treated. The instruments of deliverance, when they aim to help, are found to hinder, and that becomes a trap which, it was hoped, would have been for their welfare, God suffering it to be so that we may learn to cease from man, and may come off from a dependence upon second causes. Note, further, When the people of God think themselves ill treated, they should go to God by prayer, and plead with him, and that is the way to have better treatment in God's good time. (2.) *Why is it thou hast sent me?* Thus, [1.] He complains of his ill success: "Pharaoh has done evil to this people, and not one step seems to be taken towards their deliverance." Note, It cannot but sit very heavily upon the spirits of those whom God employs for him to see that their labour does no good, and much more to see that it does hurt eventually, though not designedly. It is uncomfortable to a good minister to perceive that his endeavours for men's conviction and conversion do but exasperate their corruptions, confirm their prejudices, harden their hearts, and seal them up under unbelief. This makes them go in the bitterness of their souls, as the prophet, Eze. 3:14. Or, [2.] He enquires what was further to be done: *Why hast thou sent me?* that is, "What other method shall I take in pursuance of my commission?" Note, Disappointments in our work must not drive us from our God, but still we must consider why we are sent.

CHAPTER 6

Much ado there was to bring Moses to his work, and when the ice was broken, some difficulty having occurred in carrying it on, there was no less ado to put him forward in it. Witness this chapter, in which, I. God satisfies Moses himself in an answer to his complaints in the close of the foregoing chapter (*v.* 1). II. He gives him fuller instructions than had yet been given him what to say to the children of Israel, for their satisfaction (*v.* 2–8), but to little purpose (*v.* 9). III. He sends him again to Pharaoh (*v.* 10, 11). But Moses objects against that (*v.* 12), upon which a very strict charge is given to him and his brother to execute their commission with vigour (*v.* 13). IV. Here is an abstract of the genealogy of the tribes of Reuben and Simeon, to introduce that of Levi, that the pedigree of Moses and Aaron might be cleared (*v.* 14–25), and then the chapter concludes with a repetition of so much of the preceding story as was necessary to make way for the following chapter.

Verses 1–9

Here, I. God silences Moses's complaints with the assurance of success in this negotiation, repeating the promise made him in *ch.* 3:20, *After that, he will let you go.* When Moses was at his wit's end, wishing he had staid in Midian, rather than have come to Egypt to make bad worse — when he was quite at a loss what to do — *Then the Lord said unto Moses,* for the quieting of his mind, *"Now shalt thou see what I will do to Pharaoh* (*v.* 1); now that the affair has come to a crisis, things are as bad as they can be, Pharaoh is in the height of pride and Israel in the depth of misery, now is my time to appear." See Ps. 12:5, *Now will I arise.* Note, Man's extremity is God's opportunity of helping and saving. Moses had been expecting what God would do; but now he shall see what he will do, shall see his day at length, Job 24:1. Moses had been trying what he could do, and could effect nothing. "Well," says God, "now thou shalt see what *I* will do; let me alone to deal with this proud man," Job 40:12, 13. Note, Then the deliverance of God's church will be accomplished, when God takes the work into his own hands. *With a strong hand,* that is, being forced to it by a strong hand, *he shall let them go.* Note, As some are brought to their duty by the strong hand of God's grace, who are made willing in the day of his power, so others by the strong hand of his justice, breaking those that would not bend.

II. He gives him further instructions, that both he and the people of Israel might be encouraged to hope for a glorious issue of this affair. Take comfort,

1. From God's name, Jehovah, *v.* 2, 3. He begins with this, *I am Jehovah,* the same with, *I am that I am,* the fountain of being, and blessedness, and infinite perfection. The patriarchs knew this name, but they did not know him in this matter by that which this name signifies. God would now be known by his name *Jehovah,* that is, (1.) A God performing what he had promised, and so inspiring confidence in his promises. (2.) A God perfecting what he had begun, and finishing his own work. In the history of the creation, God is never called Jehovah till the heavens and the earth were finished, Gen. 2:4. When the salvation of the saints is completed in eternal life, then he will be known by his name Jehovah (Rev. 22:13); in the mean time they shall find him, for their strength and support, *El-shaddai, a God all-sufficient,* a God that is enough and will be so, Mic. 7:20.

2. From his covenant: *I have established my covenant, v.* 4. Note, The covenants God makes he establishes; they are made as firm as the power and truth of God can make them. We may venture our all upon this bottom.

3. From his compassions (*v.* 5): *I have heard the groaning of the children of Israel;* he means their groaning on occasion of the late hardships put upon them. Note, God take notice of the increase of his people's calamities, and observes how their enemies grow upon them.

4. From his present resolutions, *v.* 6–8. Here is line upon line, to assure them that they should be brought triumphantly out of Egypt (*v.* 6), and should be put in possession of the land of Canaan (*v.* 8): *I will bring you out. I will rid you. I will redeem you. I will bring you into the land of Canaan,* and *I will give it to you.* Let man take the shame of his unbelief, which needs such repetitions; and let God have the glory of his condescending grace, which gives us such repeated assurances for our satisfaction.

5. From his gracious intentions in all these, which were great, and worthy of him, *v.* 7. (1.) He intended their happiness: *I will take you to me for a people,* a peculiar people, and *I will be to you a God;* more than this we need not ask, we cannot have, to make us happy. (2.) He intended his own glory: *You shall know that I am the Lord.* God will attain his own ends, nor shall we come short of them if we make them our chief end too. Now, one would think, these good words, and comfortable words, should have revived the drooping Israelites, and cause them to forget their misery; but, on the contrary, their miseries made them regardless of God's promises (*v.* 9): *They harkened not unto Moses for anguish of spirit.* That is, [1.] They were so taken up with their troubles that they did not heed him. [2.] They were so cast down with their late disappointment that they did not believe him. [3.] They had such a dread of Pharaoh's power and wrath that they durst not themselves move in the least towards their deliverance. Note, *First,* Disconsolate spirits often put from them the comforts they are entitled to, and stand in their own light. See Isa. 28:12. *Secondly,* Strong passions oppose strong consolations. By indulging ourselves in discontent and fretfulness, we deprive ourselves of the comfort we might have both from God's word and from his providence, and must thank ourselves if we go comfortless.

Verses 10–13

Here, I. God sends Moses the second time to Pharaoh (*v.* 11) upon the same errand as before, to command him, at his peril, that he *let the children of Israel go.* Note, God repeats his precepts before he begins his punishments. Those that have often been called in vain to leave their sins must yet be called again and again, whether they will hear or whether they will forbear, Eze. 3:11. God is said to *hew* sinners by his prophets (Hos. 6:5), which denotes the repetition of the strokes. *How often would I have gathered you?*

II. Moses makes objections, as one discouraged, and willing to give up the cause, *v.* 12. He pleads, 1. The unlikelihood of Pharaoh's hearing: *"Behold the children of Israel have not hearkened unto me;* they give no heed, no credit, to what I have said; how then can I expect that Pharaoh should hear me? If the anguish of their spirit makes them deaf to that which would compose and comfort them, much more will the anger of his spirit, his pride and insolence, make him deaf to that which will but exasperate and provoke him." If God's professing people hear not his messengers, how can it be thought that his professed enemy should? Note, The frowardness and untractableness of those that are called Christians greatly discourage ministers, and make them ready to despair of success in dealing with those that are atheistical and profane. We would be instrumental to unite Israelites, to refine and purify them, to comfort and pacify them; but, if they hearken not to us, how shall we prevail with those in whom we cannot pretend to such an interest? But with God all things are possible. 2. He pleads the unreadiness and infirmity of his own speaking: *I am of uncircumcised lips;* it is repeated, *v.* 30. He was conscious to himself that he had not the gift of utterance, had no command of language; his talent did not lie that way. To this objection God had given a sufficient answer before, and therefore he ought not to have insisted upon it, for the sufficiency of grace can supply the defects of nature at any time. Note, Though our infirmities ought to humble us, yet they ought not to discourage us from doing our best in any service we have to do for God. His strength is made perfect in our weakness.

III. God again joins Aaron in commission with Moses, and puts an end to the dispute by interposing his own authority, and giving them both a solemn charge, upon their allegiance to their great Lord, to execute it with all possible expedition and fidelity. When Moses repeats his baffled arguments, he shall be argued with no longer, but God gives him a charge, and Aaron with him, both to the children of Israel and to Pharaoh, *v.* 13. Note, God's authority is sufficient to answer all objections, and binds us to obedience, without murmuring or disputing, Phil. 2:14. Moses himself has need to be charged, and so has Timothy, 1 Tim. 6:13; 2 Tim. 4:1.

Verses 14–30

I. We have here a genealogy, not an endless one, such

as the apostle condemns (1 Tim. 1:4), for it ends in those two great patriots Moses and Aaron, and comes in here to show that they were Israelites, bone of their bone and flesh of their flesh whom they were sent to deliver, raised up unto them of their brethren, as Christ also should be, who was to be the prophet and priest, the Redeemer and lawgiver, of the people of Israel, and whose genealogy also, like this, was to be carefully preserved. The heads of the houses of three of the tribes are here named, agreeing with the accounts we had, Gen. 46. Dr. Lightfoot thinks that Reuben, Simeon, and Levi, are thus dignified here by themselves for this reason, because they were left under marks of infamy by their dying father, Reuben for his incest and Simeon and Levi for their murder of the Shechemites; and therefore Moses would put this particular honour upon them, to magnify God's mercy in their repentance and remission, as a pattern to those that should afterwards believe: the two former seem rather to be mentioned only for the sake of a third, which was Levi, from whom Moses and Aaron descended, and all the priests of the Jewish church. Thus was the tribe of Levi distinguished betimes. Observe here, 1. That Kohath, from whom Moses and Aaron, and all the priests, derived their pedigree, was a younger son of Levi, *v.* 16. Note, The grants of God's favours do not go by seniority of age and priority of birth, but the divine sovereignty often prefers the younger before the elder, so crossing hands. 2. That the ages of Levi, Kohath, and Amram, the father, grandfather, and great grandfather, of Moses, are here recorded; they all lived to a great age, Levi to 137, Kohath to 133, and Amram to 137. Moses himself came much short of them, and fixed seventy or eighty for the ordinary stretch of human life (Ps. 90:10); for now that God's Israel was multiplied and had become a great nation, and divine revelation was by the hand of Moses committed to writing and no longer trusted to tradition, the two great reasons for the long lives of the patriarchs had ceased, and therefore henceforward fewer years must serve men. 3. That Aaron married Elisheba (the same name with that of the wife of Zecharias, Elizabeth, as Miriam is the same with Mary), daughter of Amminadab, one of the chief of the fathers of the tribe of Judah; for the tribes of Levi and Judah often intermarried, *v.* 23. 4. It must not be omitted that Moses has recorded the marriage of his father Amram with Jochebed his own aunt (*v.* 20); and it appears by Num. 26:59 that it must be taken strictly for his father's own sister, at least by the half blood. This marriage was afterwards forbidden as incestuous (Lev. 18:12), which might be looked upon as a blot upon his family, though before that law; yet Moses does not conceal it, for he sought not his own praise, but wrote with a sincere regard to truth, whether it smiled or frowned upon him. 5. He concludes it with a particular mark of honour on the persons he is writing of, though he himself was one of them, *v.* 26, 27. These are *that Moses and Aaron* whom God pitched upon to be his plenipotentiaries in this treaty. These were those to whom *God spoke* (*v.* 26), and who *spoke to Pharaoh* on Israel's behalf, *v.* 27. Note, Communion with God and serviceableness to his church are things that, above any other, put true honour upon men. Those are great indeed with whom God converses and whom he employs on his service. Such were that Moses and Aaron; and something of this honour have all his saints, who are made to our God kings and priests.

II. In the close of the chapter Moses returns to his narrative, from which he had broken off somewhat abruptly (*v.* 13), and repeats, 1. The charge God had given him to deliver his message to Pharaoh (*v.* 29): *Speak all that I say unto thee,* as a faithful ambassador. Note, Those that go on God's errand must not shun to declare *the whole counsel of God.* 2. His objection against it, *v.* 30. Note, Those that have at any time spoken unadvisedly with their lips ought often to reflect upon it with regret, as Moses seems to do here.

CHAPTER 7

In this chapter, I. The dispute between God and Moses finishes, and Moses applies himself to the execution of his commission, in obedience to God's command (*v.* 1–7). II. The dispute between Moses and Pharaoh begins, and a famous trial of skill it was. Moses, in God's name, demands Israel's release; Pharaoh denies it. The contest is between the power of the great God and the power of a proud prince; and it will be found, in the issue, that when God judgeth he will overcome. 1. Moses confirms the demand he had made to Pharaoh, by a miracle, turning his rod into a serpent; but Pharaoh hardens his heart against this conviction (*v.* 8–13). 2. He chastises his disobedience by a plague, the first of the ten, turning the waters into blood; but Pharaoh hardens his heart against this correction, *v.* 14, etc.).

Verses 1–7

Here, I. God encourages Moses to go to Pharaoh, and at last silences all his discouragements. 1. He clothes him with great power and authority (*v.* 1): *I have made thee a god to Pharaoh;* that is, my representative in this affair, as magistrates are called *gods,* because they are God's vicegerents. He was authorized to speak and act in God's name and stead, and, under the divine direction, was endued with a divine power to do that which is above the ordinary power of nature, and invested with a divine authority to demand obedience from a sovereign prince and punish disobedience. Moses was a god, but he was only a *made* god, not essentially one by nature; he was no god but by commission. He was a god, but he was a god only to Pharaoh; the living and true God is a God to all the world. It is an instance of God's condescension, and an evidence that his thoughts towards us are thoughts of peace, that when he treats with men he treats by men, whose terror shall not make us afraid. 2. He again nominates him an assistant, his brother Aaron, who was not a man of uncircumcised lips, but a notable spokesman: "He shall be *thy prophet,*" that is, "he shall speak from thee to Pharaoh, as prophets do from God to the children of men. Thou shalt, as a god, inflict and remove the plagues, and Aaron, as a prophet, shall denounce them, and threaten Pharaoh with them." 3. He tells him the worst of it, that Pharaoh would not hearken to him, and yet the work should be done at last, Israel should be delivered and God therein would be glorified, *v.* 4, 5. The Egyptians, who would not know the Lord, should be made to know him. Note, It is, and ought to be, satisfaction enough to God's messengers that, whatever contradiction and opposition may be given them, thus far they shall gain their point, that God will be glorified in the success of their embassy, and all his chosen Israel will be saved, and then they have no reason to say that they have laboured in vain. See here, (1.) How God glorifies himself; he makes people know that he is Jehovah. Israel is made to know it by the performance of his promises to them (*ch.* 6:3), and the Egyptians are made to know it by the pouring out of his wrath upon them. Thus God's name is exalted both in those that are saved and in those that perish. (2.) What method he takes to do this: he humbles the proud, and exalts the poor, Lu. 1:51, 52. If God stretch out his hand to sinners in vain, he will at last stretch out his hand upon them; and who can bear the weight of it?

II. Moses and Aaron apply themselves to their work without further objection: *They did as the Lord commanded them, v.* 6. Their obedience, all things considered, was well worthy to be celebrated, as it is by the Psalmist (ps. 105:28), *They rebelled not against his word,* namely, Moses and Aaron, whom he mentions, *v.* 26. Thus Jonah, though at first he was very averse, at length went to Nineveh. Notice is taken of the age of Moses and Aaron when they undertook this glorious service. Aaron the elder (and yet the inferior in office) was eighty-three, Moses was eighty; both of them men of great gravity and experience, whose age was venerable, and whose years might teach wisdom, *v.* 7. Joseph, who was to be only a servant to Pharaoh, was preferred at thirty years old; but Moses, who was to be a god to Pharaoh, was not so dignified until he was eighty years old. It was fit that he should long wait for such an honour, and be long in preparing for such a service.

Verses 8–13

The first time that Moses made his application to Pharaoh, he produced his instructions only; now he is directed to produce his credentials, and does accordingly. 1. It is taken for granted that Pharaoh would challenge these demandants to work a miracle, that, by a performance evidently above the power of nature, they might prove their commission from the God of nature. Pharaoh will say, *Show a miracle;* not with any desire to be convinced, but with the hope that none will be wrought, and then he would have some colour for his infidelity. 2. Orders are therefore given to turn the rod into a serpent, according to the instructions, *ch.* 4:3. The same rod that was to give the signal of the other miracles is now itself the subject of a miracle, to put a reputation upon it. Aaron cast his rod to the ground, and instantly it became a serpent, *v.* 10. This was proper, not only to affect Pharaoh with wonder, but to strike a terror upon him. Serpents are hurtful dreadful animals; the very sight of one, thus miraculously produced, might have softened his heart into a fear of that God by whose power it was produced. This first miracle, though it was not a plague, yet amounted to the threatening of a plague. If it made not Pharaoh feel, it made him fear; and this is God's method of dealing with sinners — he comes upon them gradually. 3. This miracle, though too plain to be denied, is enervated, and the conviction of it taken off, by the magicians' imitation of it, *v.* 11, 12. Moses had been originally instructed in the learning of the Egyptians, and was suspected to have improved himself in magical arts in his long retirement; the magicians are therefore sent for, to vie with him. And some think those of that profession had a particular spite against the Hebrews ever since Joseph put them all to shame, by interpreting a dream which they could make nothing of, in remembrance of which slur put on their predecessors these magicians withstood Moses, as it is explained, 2 Tim. 3:8. Their rods became serpents, real serpents; some think, by the power of God, beyond their intention or expectation, for the hardening of Pharaoh's heart; others think, by the power of evil angels, artfully substituting serpents in the room of the rods, God permitting the delusion to be wrought for wise and holy ends, that those might believe a lie who received not the truth: and herein the Lord was righteous. Yet this might have helped to frighten Pharaoh into a compliance with the demands of Moses, that he might be freed from these dreadful unaccountable phenomena, with which he saw himself on all sides surrounded. But to the seed of the serpent these serpents were no amazement. Note, God suffers the lying spirit to do strange things, that the faith of some may be tried and manifested (Deu. 13:3; 1 Co. 11:19), that the infidelity of others may be confirmed, and that he who is filthy may be filthy still, 2 Co. 4:4. 4. Yet, in this contest, Moses plainly gains the victory. The serpent which Aaron's rod was turned into swallowed up the others, which was sufficient to have convinced Pharaoh on which side the right lay. Note, Great is the truth, and will prevail. The cause of God will undoubtedly triumph at last over all competition and contradiction, and will reign alone, Dan. 2:44. But Pharaoh was not wrought upon by this. The magicians having produced serpents, he had this to say, that the case between them and Moses was disputable; and the very appearance of an opposition to truth, and the least head made against it, serve those for a justification of their infidelity who are prejudiced against the light and love of it.

Verses 14–25

Here is the first of the ten plagues, the turning of the water into blood, which was, 1. A dreadful plague, and very grievous. The very sight of such vast rolling streams of blood, pure blood no doubt, florid and high-colored, could not but strike a horror upon people: much more afflictive were the consequences of it. Nothing more common than water: so wisely has Providence ordered it, and so kindly, that that which is so needful and serviceable to the comfort of human life should be cheap, and almost every where to be had; but now the Egyptians must either drink blood, or die for thirst. Fish was much of their food (Num. 11:5), but the changing of the waters was the death of the fish; it was a pestilence in that element (*v.* 21): *The fish died.* In the general deluge they escaped, because perhaps they had not then contributed so much to the luxury of man as they have since; but in this particular judgment they perished (Ps. 105:29): *He slew their fish;* and when another destruction of Egypt, long afterwards, is threatened, the disappointment of those that make sluices and ponds for fish is particularly noticed, Isa. 19:10. Egypt was a pleasant land, but the noisome stench of dead fish and blood, which by degrees would grow putrid, now rendered it very unpleasant. 2. It was a righteous plague, and justly inflicted upon the Egyptians. For, (1.) Nilus, the river of Egypt, was their idol; they and their land derived so much benefit from it that they served and worshipped it more than the Creator. The true fountain of the Nile being unknown to them, they paid all their devotions to its streams: here therefore God punished them, and turned that into blood which they had turned into a god. Note, That creature which we idolize God justly removes from us, or embitters to us. He makes that a scourge to us which we make a competitor with him. (2.) They had stained the river with the blood of the Hebrews' children, and now God made that river all bloody. Thus he gave them blood to drink, for they were worthy, Rev. 16:6. Note, Never any thirsted after blood, but, sooner or later, they had enough of it. 3. It was a significant plague. Egypt had a great dependence upon their river (Zec. 14:18), so that in smiting the river they were warned of the destruction of all the productions of their country, till it came at last to their first-born; and this red river proved a direful omen of the ruin of Pharaoh and all his forces in the Red Sea. This plague of Egypt is alluded to in the prediction of the ruin of the enemies of the New-Testament church, Rev. 16:3, 4. But there the sea, as well as the rivers and fountains of water, is turned into blood; for spiritual judgments reach further, and strike deeper, than temporal judgments do. And, *lastly,* let me observe in general concerning this plague that one of the first miracles Moses wrought was turning water into blood, but one of the first miracles our Lord Jesus wrought was turning water into wine; for the law was given by Moses, and it was a dispensation of death and terror; but grace and truth, which, like wine, make glad the heart, came by Jesus Christ. Observe,

I. Moses is directed to give Pharaoh warning of this plague. "Pharaoh's heart is hardened (*v.* 14), therefore go and try what this will do to soften it," *v.* 15. Moses perhaps may not be admitted into Pharaoh's presence-chamber, or the room of state where he used to give audience to ambassadors; and therefore he is directed to meet him by the river's brink, whither God foresaw he would come in the morning, either for the pleasure of a morning's walk or to pay his morning devotions to the river: for thus all people will walk, every one in the name of his god; they will not fail to worship their god every morning. There Moses must be ready to give him a new summons to surrender, and, in case of a refusal, to tell him of the judgment that was coming upon that very river on the banks of which they were now standing. Notice is thus given him of it beforehand, that they might have no colour to say it was a chance, or to attribute it to any other cause, but that it might appear to be done by the power of the God of the Hebrews, and as a punishment upon him for his obstinacy. Moses is expressly ordered to take the rod with him, that Pharaoh might be alarmed at the sight of that rod which had so lately triumphed over the rods of the magicians. Now learn hence, 1. That the judgments of God are all known to himself beforehand. He knows what he will do in wrath as well as in mercy. Every consumption is a consumption determined, Isa. 10:23. 2. That men cannot escape the alarms of God's wrath, because they cannot go out of the hearing of their own consciences: he that made their hearts can make his sword to approach them. 3. That God warns before he wounds; for he is *long-suffering, not willing that any should perish, but that all should come to repentance.*

II. Aaron (who carried the mace) is directed to summon the plague by smiting the river with his rod, *v.* 19, 20. It was done in the sight of Pharaoh and his attendants; for God's true miracles were not performed, as Satan's lying wonders were, by those that peeped and muttered: truth seeks no corners. An amazing change was immediately wrought; all the waters, not only in the rivers but in all their ponds, were turned into blood. 1. See here the almighty power of God. Every creature is that to us which he makes it to be, water or blood. 2. See the mutability of all things under the sun, and what changes we may meet with in them. That which is water to-day may be blood to-morrow; what is always vain may soon become vexatious. A river, at the best, is transient; but divine justice can quickly make it malignant. 3. See what mischievous work sin makes. if the things that have been our comforts prove our crosses, we must thank ourselves: it is sin that turns our waters into blood.

III. Pharaoh endeavours to confront the miracle, because he resolves not to humble himself under the plague. He sends for the magicians, and, by God's permission, they ape the miracle with their enchantments (*v.* 22), and this serves Pharaoh for an excuse not to set his heart to this also (*v.* 23), and a pitiful excuse it was. Could they have turned the river of blood into water again, this would have been something to the purpose; then they would have proved their power, and Pharaoh would have been obliged to them as his benefactors. But for them, when there was such scarcity of water, to turn more of it into blood, only to show their art, plainly intimates that the design of the devil is only to delude his devotees and amuse them, not to do them any real kindness, but to keep them from doing a real kindness to themselves by repenting and returning to their God.

IV. The Egyptians, in the mean time, are seeking for relief against the plague, digging round about the river for water to drink, *v.* 24. Probably they found some, with much ado, God remembering mercy in the midst of wrath; for he is full of compassion, and would not let the subjects smart too much for the obstinacy of their prince.

V. The plague continued seven days (*v.* 25), and, in all that time, Pharaoh's proud heart would not let him so much as desire Moses to intercede for the removal of it. Thus the hypocrites in heart heap up wrath; *they cry not when he binds them* (Job 36:13); and then no wonder that his anger is not turned away, but his hand is stretched out still.

CHAPTER 8

Three more of the plagues of Egypt are related in this chapter, I. That of the frogs, which is, 1. Threatened (*v.* 1–4). 2. Inflicted (*v.* 5, 6). 3. Mimicked by the magicians (*v.* 7). 4. Removed, at the humble request of Pharaoh (*v.* 8–14), who yet hardens his heart, and, notwithstanding his promise while the plague was upon him (*v.* 8), refuses to let Israel go (*v.* 15). II. The plague of lice (*v.* 16, 17), by which, 1. The magicians were baffled (*v.* 18, 19), and yet, 2. Pharaoh was hardened (*v.* 19). III. That of flies. 1. Pharaoh is warned of it before (*v.* 20, 21), and told that the land of Goshen should be exempt from this plague (*v.* 22, 23). 2. The plague is brought (*v.* 24). 3. Pharaoh treats with Moses about the release of Israel, and humbles himself (*v.* 25–29). 4. The plague is thereupon removed (*v.* 31), and Pharaoh's heart hardened (*v.* 32).

Verses 1–15

Pharaoh is here first threatened and then plagued with frogs, as afterwards, in this chapter, with lice and flies, little despicable inconsiderable animals, and yet by their vast numbers rendered sore plagues to the Egyptians. God could have plagued them with lions, or bears, or wolves, or with vultures or other birds of prey; but he chose to do it by these contemptible instruments. 1. That he might magnify his own power. He is Lord of the hosts of the whole creation, has them all at his beck, and makes what use he pleases of them. Some have thought that the power of God is shown as much in the making of an ant as in the making of an elephant; so is his providence in serving his own purposes by the least creatures as effectually as by the strongest, that the excellency of the power, in judgment as well as mercy, may be of God, and not of the creature. See what reason we have to stand in awe of this God, who, when he pleases, can arm the smallest parts of the creation against us. If God be our enemy, all the creatures are at war with us. 2. That he might humble Pharaoh's pride, and chastise his insolence. What a mortification must it needs be to this haughty monarch to see himself brought to his knees, and forced to submit, by such despicable means! Every child is, ordinarily, able to deal with those invaders, and can triumph over them; yet now so numerous were their troops, and so vigorous their assaults, that Pharaoh, with all his chariots and horsemen, could make no head against them. Thus he *poureth contempt upon princes* that offer contempt to him and his sovereignty, and makes those who will not own him above them to know that, when he pleases, he can make the meanest creature to insult them and trample upon them. As to the plague of frogs we may observe,

I. How it was threatened. Moses, no doubt, attended the divine Majesty daily for fresh instructions, and (perhaps while the river was yet blood) he is here directed to give notice to Pharaoh of another judgment coming upon him, in case he continue obstinate: *If thou refuse to let them go,* it is at thy peril, *v.* 1, 2. Note, God does not punish men for sin unless they persist in it. *If he turn not, he will whet his sword* (Ps. 7:12), which implies favour *if he turn.* So here, *If thou refuse, I will smite thy borders,* intimating that if Pharaoh complied the controversy should immediately be dropped. The plague threatened, in case of refusal, was formidably extensive. Frogs were to make such an inroad upon them as should make them uneasy in their houses, in their beds, and at their tables; they should not be able to eat, nor drink, nor sleep in quietness, but, wherever they were, should be infested by them, *v.* 3, 4. Note, 1. God's curse upon a man will pursue him wherever he goes, and lie heavily upon him whatever he does. See Deu. 28:16, etc. 2. There is no avoiding divine judgments when they invade with commission.

II. How it was inflicted. Pharaoh not regarding the alarm, nor being at all inclined to yield to the summons, Aaron is ordered to draw out the forces, and with his outstretched arm and rod to give the signal of battle. *Dictum factum — No sooner said then done;* the host is mustered, and, under the direction and command of an invisible power, shoals of frogs invade the land, and the Egyptians, with all their art and all their might, cannot check their progress, nor so much as give them a diversion. Compare this with that prophecy of an army of locusts and caterpillars, Joel 2:2, etc.; and see Isa. 34:16, 17. Frogs came up, at the divine call, and *covered the land.* Note, God has many ways of disquieting those that live at ease.

III. How the magicians were permitted to imitate it, *v.* 7. They also brought up frogs, but could not remove those that God sent. The unclean spirits which came *out of the mouth of the dragon* are said to be like frogs, which go forth to the kings of the earth, to deceive them (Rev. 16:13), which probably alludes to these frogs, for it follows the account of the turning of the waters into blood. The dragon, like the magicians, intended by them to deceive, but God intended by them to destroy those that would be deceived.

IV. How Pharaoh relented under this plague: it was the first time he did so, *v.* 8. He begs of Moses to intercede for the removal of the frogs, and promises fair that he will let the people go. He that a little while ago had spoken with the utmost disdain both of God and Moses is now glad to be beholden to the mercy of God and the prayers of Moses. Note, Those that bid defiance to God and prayer in a day of extremity will, first or last, be made to see their need of both, and will cry, *Lord, Lord,* Mt. 7:22. Those that have bantered prayer have been brought to beg it, as the rich man that had scorned Lazarus courted him for a drop of water.

V. How Moses fixes the time with Pharaoh, and then prevails with God by prayer for the removal of the frogs. Moses, to show that his performances had no dependence upon the conjunctions or oppositions of the planets, or the luckiness of any one hour more than another, bids Pharaoh name his time. *Nellum occurrit tempus regi — No time fixed on by the king shall be objected to, v.* 9. *Have thou this honour over me,* tell me *against when I shall entreat for thee.* This was designed for Pharaoh's conviction, that, if his eyes were not opened by the plague, they might by the removal of it. So various are the methods God takes to bring men to repentance. Pharaoh sets the time for *tomorrow, v.* 10. And why not immediately? Was he so fond of his guests that he would have them stay another night with him? No, but probably he hoped that they would go away of themselves, and then he should get clear of the plague without being obliged either to God or Moses. However, Moses joins issue with him upon it: *"Be it according to thy word,* it shall be done just when thou wouldst have it done, *that thou mayest know that,* whatever the magicians pretend to, *there is none like unto the Lord our God.* None has such a command as he has over all the creatures, nor is any one so ready to forgive those that humble themselves before him." Note, The great design both of judgments and mercies is to convince us that there is none like the Lord our God, none so wise, so mighty, so good, no enemy so formidable, no friend so desirable, so valuable. Moses, hereupon, applies to God, prays earnestly to him, to remand the frogs, *v.* 12. Note, We must pray for our enemies and persecutors, even the worst as Christ did. In answer to the prayer of Moses, the frogs that came up one day perished the next, or the next but one. They all died (*v.* 13), and, that it might appear that they were real frogs, their dead bodies were left to be raked together in heaps, so that the smell of them became offensive, *v.* 14. Note, The great Sovereign of the world makes what use he pleases of the lives and deaths of his creatures; and he that gives a being, to serve one purpose, may, without wrong to his justice, call for it again immediately, to serve another purpose.

VI. What was the issue of this plague (*v.* 15): *When Pharaoh saw there was a respite,* without considering either what he had lately felt or what he had reason to fear, he hardened his heart. Note, 1. Till the heart is renewed by the grace of God, the impressions made by the force of affliction do not abide; the convictions wear off, and the promises that were extorted are forgotten. Till the disposition of the air is changed, what thaws in the sun will freeze again in the shade. 2. God's patience is shamefully abused by impenitent sinners. The respite he gives them, to lead them to repentance, they are hardened by; and while he graciously allows them a truce, in order to the making of their peace, they take that opportunity to rally again the baffled forces of an obstinate infidelity. See Eccl. 8:11; Ps. 78:34, etc.

Verses 16–19

Here is a short account of the plague of lice. It does not appear that any warning was given of it before. Pharaoh's abuse of the respite granted to him might have been a sufficient warning to him to expect another plague: for if the removal of an affliction harden us, and so we lose the benefit of it, we may conclude it goes away with a purpose to return or to make room for a worse. Observe,

I. How this plague of lice was inflicted on the Egyptians, *v.* 16, 17. The frogs were produced out of the waters, but these live out of *the dust of the earth;* for out of any part of the creation God can fetch a scourge, with which to correct those that rebel against him. He has many arrows in his quiver. Even the dust of the earth obeys him. *"Fear not then, thou worm Jacob,* for God can use thee as a threshing instrument, if he please," Isa. 41:14, 15. These lice, no doubt, were extremely vexatious, as well as scandalous, to the Egyptians. Though they had respite, they had respite but awhile, Rev. 11:14. The second woe was past, but behold the third woe came very quickly.

II. How the magicians were baffled by it, *v.* 18. They attempted to imitate it, but they could not. When they failed in this, it should seem they attempted to remove it; for it follows, *So there were lice upon man and beast,* in spite of them. This forced them to confess themselves overpowered: *This is the finger of God,* v. 19; that is, "This check and restraint put upon us must needs be from a divine power." Note, 1. God has the devil in a chain, and limits him both as a deceiver and as a destroyer; *hitherto he shall come, but no further.* The devil's agents when God permitted them, could do great things; but when he laid an embargo upon them, though but with his finger, they could do nothing. The magicians' inability, in this less instance, showed whence they had their ability in the former instances which seemed greater, and that they had no power against Moses but what was given them from above. 2. Sooner or later God will extort, even from his enemies, an acknowledgment of his own sovereignty and overruling power. It is certain they must all (as we say) knock under at last, as Julian the apostate did, when his dying lips confessed, *Thou hast overcome me, O thou Galilean!* God will not only be too hard for all opposers, but will force them to own it.

III. How Pharaoh, notwithstanding this, was made more and more obstinate (*v.* 19); even those that had deceived him now said enough to undeceive him, and yet he grew more and more obstinate. Even the miracles and the judgments were to him a savour of death unto death. Note, Those that are not made better by God's word and providences are commonly made worse by them.

Verses 20–32

Here is the story of the plague of flies, in which we are told,

I. How it was threatened, like that of frogs, before it was inflicted. Moses is directed (*v.* 20) to rise early in the morning, to meet Pharaoh when he came forth to the water, and there to repeat his demands. Note, 1. Those that would bring great things to pass for God and their generation must rise early, and redeem time in the morning. Pharaoh was early up at his superstitious devotions to the river; and shall we be for more sleep and more slumber when any service is to be done which would pass well in our account in the great day? 2. Those that would approve themselves God's faithful servants must not be afraid of the face of man. Moses must *stand before Pharaoh,* proud as he was, and tell him that which was in the highest degree humbling, must challenge him (if he refused to re-

lease his captives) to engage with any army of flies, which would obey God's orders of Pharaoh would not. See a similar threatening, Isa. 7:18, *The Lord will hiss* (or whistle) *for the fly and the bee,* to come and serve his purposes.

II. How the Egyptians and the Hebrews were to be remarkably distinguished in this plague, *v.* 22, 23. It is probable that this distinction had not been so manifest and observable in any of the foregoing plagues as it was to be in this. Thus, as the plague of lice was made more convincing than any before it, by its running the magicians aground, so was this, by the distinction made between the Egyptians and the Hebrews. Pharaoh must be made to know that *God is the Lord in the midst of the earth;* and by this it will be known beyond dispute. 1. Swarms of flies, which seem to us to fly at random, shall be manifestly under the conduct of an intelligent mind, while they are above the direction of any man. "Hither they shall go," says Moses, "and thither they shall not come;" and the performance is punctually according to this appointment, and both, compared, amount to a demonstration that he that said it and he that did it was the same, even a Being of infinite power and wisdom. 2. The servants and worshippers of the great Jehovah shall be preserved from sharing in the common calamities of the place they live in, so that the plague which annoys all their neighbours shall not approach them; and this shall be an incontestable proof that God is *the Lord in the midst of the earth.* Put both these together, and it appears that *the eyes of the Lord run to and fro through the earth,* and through the air too, to direct that which to us seems most casual, to serve some great designed end, that he may *show himself strong on the behalf of those whose hearts are upright with him,* 2 Chr. 16:9. Observe how it is repeated: *I will put a division between my people and thy people v.* 23. Note, The Lord knows those that are his, and will make it appear, perhaps in this world, certainly in the other, that he has set them apart for himself. A day will come when you shall *return and discern between the righteous and the wicked* (Mal. 3:18), *the sheep and the goats* (Mt. 25:32; Eze. 34:17), though now intermixed.

III. How it was inflicted, the day after it was threatened: *There came a grievous swarm of flies* (*v.* 24), flies of divers sorts, and such as devoured them, Ps. 78:45. The prince of the power of the air has gloried in being *Beelzebub — the god of flies;* but here it is proved that even in *that* he is a pretender and a usurper, for even with swarms of flies God fights against his kingdom and prevails.

IV. How Pharaoh, upon this attack, sounded a parley, and entered into a treaty with Moses and Aaron about a surrender of his captives: but observe with what reluctance he yields.

1. He is content they should sacrifice to their God, provided they would do it in the land of Egypt, *v.* 25. Note, God can extort a toleration of his worship, even from those that are really enemies to it. Pharaoh, under the smart of the rod, is content they should do sacrifice, and will allow liberty of conscience to God's Israel, even in his own land. But Moses will not accept his concession; he cannot do it, *v.* 26. It would be an abomination to God should they offer the Egyptian sacrifices, and an abomination to the Egyptians should they offer to God their own sacrifices, as they ought; so that they could not sacrifice in the land without incurring the displeasure either of their God or of their task-masters; therefore he insists: *We will go three days' journey into the wilderness, v.* 27. Note, Those that would offer an acceptable sacrifice to God must, (1.) Separate themselves from the wicked and profane; for we cannot have fellowship both with the Father of lights and with the works of darkness, both with Christ and with Belial, 2 Co. 6:14, etc.; Ps. 26:4, 6. (2.) They must retire from the distractions of the world, and get as far as may be from the noise of it. Israel cannot keep the feast of the Lord either among the brick-kilns or among the flesh-pots of Egypt; no, *We will go into the wilderness,* Hos. 2:14; Cant. 7:11. (3.) They must observe the divine appointment: "We will sacrifice as God shall command us, and not otherwise." Though they were in the utmost degree of slavery to Pharaoh, yet in the worship of God, they must observe his commands and not Pharaoh's.

2. When this proposal is rejected, he consents for them to go into the wilderness, provided they do not go *very far away,* not so far but that he might fetch them back

again, *v.* 28. It is probable he had heard of their design upon Canaan, and suspected that if once they left Egypt they would never come back again; and therefore, when he is forced to consent that they shall go (the swarms of flies buzzing the necessity in his ears), yet he is not willing that they should go out of his reach. Thus some sinners who, in a pang of conviction, part with their sins, yet are loth they should go very far away; for, when the fright is over, they will return to them again. We observe here a struggle between Pharaoh's convictions and his corruptions; his convictions said, "Let them go;" his corruptions said, "Yet not very far away:" but he sided with his corruptions against his convictions, and this was his ruin. This proposal Moses so far accepted as that he promised the removal of this plague upon it, *v.* 29 See here, (1.) How ready God is to accept sinners' submissions. Pharaoh does but say, *Entreat for me* (though it is with regret that he humbles so far), and Moses promises immediately, *I will entreat the Lord for thee,* that Pharaoh might see what the design of the plague was, not to bring him to ruin, but to bring him to repentance. With what pleasure did God say (1 Ki. 21:29), *Seest thou how Ahab humbles himself?* (2.) What need we have to be admonished that we be sincere in our submission: *But let not Pharaoh deal deceitfully any more.* Those that deal deceitfully are justly suspected, and must be cautioned not to return again to folly, after God has once more spoken peace. *Be not deceived, God is not mocked;* if we think to put a cheat upon God by a counterfeit repentance, and a fraudulent surrender of ourselves to him, we shall prove, in the end, to have put a fatal cheat upon our own souls.

Lastly, The issue of all was that God graciously removed the plague (*v.* 30, 31), but Pharaoh perfidiously returned to his hardness, and *would not let the people go, v.* 32. His pride would not let him part with such a flower of his crown as his dominion over Israel was, nor his covetousness with such a branch of his revenue as their labours were. Note, Reigning lusts break through the strongest bounds, and make men impudently presumptuous and scandalously perfidious. Let not sin therefore reign; for, if it do, it will betray and hurry us to the grossest absurdities.

CHAPTER 9

In this chapter we have an account of three more of the plagues of Egypt. I. Murrain among the cattle, which was fatal to them (*v.* 1–7). II. Boils upon man and beast (*v.* 8–12). III. Hail, with thunder and lightning. 1. Warning is given of this plague (*v.* 13–21). 2. It is inflicted, to their great terror (*v.* 22–26). 3. Pharaoh, in a fright, renews his treaty with Moses, but instantly breaks his word (*v.* 27, etc.).

Verses 1–7

Here is, I. Warning given of another plague, namely, the murrain of beasts. When Pharaoh's heart was hardened, after he had seemed to relent under the former plague, then Moses is sent to tell him there is another coming, to try what that would do towards reviving the impressions of the former plagues. Thus is the wrath of God revealed from heaven, both in his word and in his works, *against all ungodliness and unrighteousness of men.* 1. Moses puts Pharaoh in a very fair way to prevent it: *Let my people go, v.* 1. This was still the demand. God will have Israel released; Pharaoh opposes it, and the trial is, *whose word shall stand.* See how jealous God is for his people. When *the year of his redeemed has come,* he will *give Egypt for their ransom;* that kingdom shall be ruined, rather than Israel shall not be delivered. See how reasonable God's demands are. Whatever he calls for, it is but *his own:* They are my people, therefore let them go. 2. He describes the plague that should come, if he refused, *v.* 2, 3. *The hand of the Lord* immediately, without the stretching out of Aaron's hand, *is upon the cattle,* many of which, some of all kinds, should die by a sort of pestilence. This was greatly to the loss of the owners: they had made Israel poor, and now God would make them poor. Note, The hand of God is to be acknowledged even in the sickness and death of cattle, or other damage sustained in them; for a *sparrow falls not to the ground without our Father.* 3. As an evidence of the special hand of God in it, and of his particular favour to his own people, he foretels that none of their cattle should die, though they breathed in the same air and drank of the same water with the Egyptians' cattle: *The Lord shall sever, v.* 4. Note, When God's judgments are abroad, though they may fall both on the righteous and the wicked, yet God makes such a distinction that they are not the same to the one that they are to the other. See Isa. 27:7. The providence of God is to be acknowledged with thankfulness in the life of the cattle, for he preserveth man and beast, Ps. 36:6. 4. To make the warning the more remarkable, the time is fixed (*v.* 5): *To-morrow* it shall be done. We know not what any day will bring forth, and therefore we cannot say what we will do to-morrow, but it is not so with God.

II. The plague itself inflicted. The cattle died, *v.* 6. Note, The creature is made subject to vanity by the sin of man, being liable, according to its capacity, both to serve his wickedness and to share in his punishment, as in the universal deluge. Rom. 8:20, 22. Pharaoh and the Egyptians sinned; but the *sheep, what had they done?* Yet they are plagued. See Jer. 12:4, For the *wickedness of the land, the beasts are consumed.* The Egyptians afterwards, and (some think) now, worshipped their cattle; it was among them that the Israelites learned to make a god of a calf: in this therefore the plague here spoken of meets with them. Note, What we make an idol of it is just with God to remove from us, or embitter to us. See Isa. 19:1.

III. The distinction put between the cattle of the Egyptians and the Israelites' cattle, according to the word of God: Not *one of the cattle of the Israelites died, v.* 6, 7. Does God take care of oxen? Yes, he does; his providence extends itself to the meanest of his creatures. But it is written also for our sakes, that, trusting in God, and making him our refuge, we may not be *afraid of the pestilence that walketh in darkness,* no, not though *thousands fall at our side,* Ps. 91:6, 7. Pharaoh sent to see if the cattle of the Israelites were infected, not to satisfy his conscience, but only to gratify his curiosity, or with design, by way of reprisal, to repair his own losses out of their stocks; and, having no good design in the enquiry, the report brought to him made no impression upon him, but, on the contrary, his heart was hardened. Note, To those that are wilfully blind, even those methods of conviction which are ordained to life prove a savour of death unto death.

Verses 8–12

Observe here, concerning the plague of boils and blains,

I. When they were not wrought upon by the death of their cattle, God sent a plague that seized their own bodies, and touched them to the quick. If less judgments do not do their work, God will send greater. Let us therefore humble ourselves under the mighty hand of God, and go forth to meet him in the way of his judgments, that his anger may be turned away from us.

II. The signal by which this plague was summoned was the sprinkling of warm ashes from the *furnace, towards heaven* (*v.* 8, 10), which was to signify the heating of the air with such an infection as should produce in the bodies of the Egyptians sore boils, which would be both noisome and painful. Immediately upon the scattering of the ashes, a scalding dew came down out of the air, which blistered wherever it fell. Note, Sometimes God shows men their sin in their punishment; they had oppressed Israel in the furnaces, and now the ashes of the furnace are made as much a terror to them as ever their task-masters had been to the Israelites.

III. The plague itself was very grievous — a common eruption would be so, especially to the nice and delicate, but these eruptions were inflammations, like Job's. This is afterwards called the *botch of Egypt* (Deu. 28:27), as if it were some new disease, never heard of before, and known ever after by that name, Note, Sores in the body are to be looked upon as the punishments of sin, and to be hearkened to as calls to repentance.

IV. The magicians themselves were struck with these boils, *v.* 11. 1. Thus they were punished, (1.) For helping to harden Pharaoh's heart, as Elymas for seeking to ;*pervert the right ways of the Lord;* God will severely reckon with those that strengthen the hands of the wicked in their wickedness. (2.) For pretending to imitate the former plagues, and making themselves and Pharaoh sport with them. Those that would produce lice shall, against their wills, produce boils. Note, It is ill jesting with God's judgments, and more dangerous than playing with fire. *Be you not mockers, lest your bands be made strong.* 2. Thus they were shamed in the presence of their admirers. How weak were their enchantments, which could not so much as secure themselves! The devil can give no protection to those that are in confederacy with him. 3. Thus they were driven from the field. Their power was restrained before (*ch.* 8:18), but they continued to confront Moses, and confirm Pharaoh in his unbelief, till now, at length, they were forced to retreat, and could not stand before Moses, to which the apostle refers (2 Tim. 3:9) when he says that their *folly was made manifest unto all men.*

V. Pharaoh continued obstinate, for now *the Lord hardened* his heart, *v.* 12. Before, he had hardened his own heart, and resisted the grace of God; and now God justly gave him up to his own heart's lusts, to a reprobate mind, and strong delusions, permitting Satan to blind and harden him, and ordering every thing, henceforward, so as to make him more and more obstinate. Note, Wilful hardness is commonly punished with judicial hardness. If men shut their eyes against the light, it is just with God to close their eyes. Let us dread this as the sorest judgment a man can be under on this side hell.

Verses 13–21

Here is, I. A general declaration of the wrath of God against Pharaoh for his obstinacy. Though God has hardened his heart (*v.* 12), yet Moses must repeat his applications to him; God suspends his grace and yet demands obedience, to punish him for requiring bricks of the children of Israel when he denied them straw. God would likewise show forth a pattern of long-suffering, and how he waits to be gracious to a *rebellious and gainsaying people* Six times the demand had been made in vain, yet Moses must make it the seventh time: *Let my people go, v.* 13. A most dreadful message Moses is here ordered to deliver to him, whether he will hear or whether he will forbear. 1. He must tell him that he is marked for ruin, that he now stands as the butt at which God would shoot all the arrows of his wrath, *v.* 14, 15. "Now I will send *all my plagues."* Now that no place is found for repentance in Pharaoh, nothing can prevent his utter destruction, for that only would have prevented it. Now that God begins to *harden his heart,* his case is desperate. "I will send my plagues *upon thy heart,* not only temporal plagues upon thy body, but spiritual plagues upon thy soul." Note, God can send plagues upon thy soul." Note, God can send plagues upon the heart, either by making it senseless or by making it hopeless — and these are the worst plagues. Pharaoh must now expect no respite, no cessation of arms, but to be followed with plague upon plague, till he is utterly consumed. Note, When God judges he will overcome; none ever hardened his heart against him and prospered. 2. He must tell him that he is to remain in history a standing monument of the justice and power of God's wrath (*v.* 16): *"For this cause have I raised thee up* to the throne at this time, and made thee to stand the shock of the plagues hitherto, to *show in thee my power."* Providence ordered it so that Moses should have a man of such a fierce and stubborn spirit as he was to deal with; and every thing was so managed in this transaction as to make it a most signal and memorable instance of the power God has to humble and bring down the proudest of his enemies. Every thing concurred to signalize this, that God's name (that is, his incontestable sovereignty, his irresistible power, and his inflexible justice) might be declared throughout all the earth, not only to all places, but through all ages while the earth remains. Note, God sometimes raises up very bad men to honour and power, spares them long, and suffers them to grow insufferably insolent, that he may be so much the more glorified in their destruction at last. See how the neighbouring nations, at that time, improved the ruin of Pharaoh to the glory of God. Jethro said upon it, *Now know I that the Lord is greater than all gods,* 18:11. The apostle illustrates the doctrine of God's sovereignty with this instance, Rom. 9:17. To justify God in these resolutions, Moses is directed to ask him (*v.* 17), *As yet exaltest thou thyself against my people?* Pharaoh was a great king; God's people were poor shepherds at the best, and now poor slaves; and yet Pharaoh shall be ruined if he exalt himself against them, for it is considered as exalting himself against God. This was not the first time that God reproved kings for their sakes, and let them know that he would not suffer his people to be trampled upon and insulted, no, not by the most powerful of them.

II. A particular prediction of the plague of hail (*v.* 18), and a gracious advice to Pharaoh and his people to send for their servants and cattle out of the field, that they might be sheltered from the hail, *v.* 19. Note, When God's justice threatens ruin his mercy, at the same time, shows us a way of escape from it, so unwilling is he that any should perish. See here what care God took, not only to distinguish between Egyptians and Israelites, but between some Egyptians and others. If Pharaoh will not yield, and so prevent the judgment itself, yet an opportunity is given to those that have any dread of God and his word to save themselves from sharing in the judgment. Note, Those that will take warning may take shelter; and those that will not may thank themselves if they fall by the overflowing scourge, and the hail which will *sweep away the refuge of lies,* Isa. 28:17. See the different effect of this warning. 1. *Some believed the things that were spoken,* and they feared, and housed their servants and cattle (*v.* 20), like Noah (Heb. 11:7), and it was their wisdom. Even among the servants of Pharaoh there were some that trembled at God's word; and shall not the sons of Israel dread it? But, 2. Others believed not: though, whatever plague Moses had hitherto foretold, the event exactly answered to the prediction; and though, if they had had any reason to question this, it would have been no great damage to them to have kept their cattle in the house for one day, and so, supposing it a doubtful case, to have chosen the surer side; yet they were so foolhardy as in defiance to the truth of Moses, and the power of God (of both which they had already had experience enough, to their cost), to leave their cattle in the field, Pharaoh himself, it is probable, giving them an example of the presumption, *v.* 21. Note, Obstinate infidelity, which is deaf to the fairest warnings and the wisest counsels, leaves the blood of those that perish upon their own heads.

Verses 22–35

The threatened plague of hail is here summoned by the powerful hand and rod of Moses (*v.* 22, 23), and it obeys the summons, or rather the divine command; for *fire and hail fulfil God's word,* Ps. 148:8. And here we are told,

I. What desolations it made upon the earth. The thunder, and fire from heaven (or lightning), made it both the more dreadful and the more destroying, *v.* 23, 24. Note, God makes the clouds, not only his store-houses whence he drops fatness on his people, but his magazines whence, when he pleases, he can draw out a most formidable train of artillery, with which to destroy his enemies. He himself speaks of the *treasures of hail which he hath reserved against the day of battle and war,* Job 38:22, 23. Woeful havoc this hail made in the land of Egypt. It killed both men and cattle, and battered down, not only the herbs, but the trees, *v.* 25. The corn that was above ground was destroyed, and that only preserved which as yet had not come up, *v.* 31, 32. Note, God has many ways of *taking away the corn in the season thereof* (Hos. 2:9), either by a secret blasting, or a noisy hail. In this plague the *hot thunderbolts,* as well as the hail, are said to destroy *their flocks,* Ps. 78:47, 48; and see Ps. 105:32, 33. Perhaps David alludes to this when, describing God's glorious appearances for the discomfiture of his enemies, he speaks of the hailstones and coals of fire he threw among them, Ps. 18:12, 13. And there is a plan reference to it on the pouring out of the seventh vial, Rev. 16:21. Notice is here taken (*v.* 26) of the land of Goshen's being preserved from receiving any damage by this plague. God has the directing of the pregnant clouds, and causes it to rain or hail on one city and not on another, either in mercy or in judgment.

II. What a consternation it put Pharaoh in. See what effect it had upon him, 1. He humbled himself to Moses in the language of a penitent, *v.* 27, 28. No man could have spoken better. He owns himself on the wrong side in his contest with the God of the Hebrews: *"I have sinned* in standing it out so long." He owns the equity of God's proceedings against him: *The Lord is righteous,* and must be justified when he speaks, though he speak in thunder and lightning. He condemns himself and his land: *"I and my people are wicked,* and deserve what is brought upon us." He begs the prayers of Moses: *"Entreat the Lord* for me, that this direful plague may be removed." And, *lastly,* he promises to yield up his prisoners: *I will let you go.* What could one desire more? And yet his heart was hardened all this while. Note, The terror of the rod often extorts penitent acknowledgments from those who have no penitent affections; under the surprise and smart of affliction, they start up, and say that which is pertinent enough, not because they are deeply affected, but because they know that they should be and that *it is meet to be said.* 2. Moses, hereupon, becomes an intercessor for him with God. Though he had all the reason in the world to think that he would immediately repent of his repentance, and told him so (*v.* 30), yet he promises to be this friend in the court of heaven. Note, Even those whom we have little hopes of, yet we should continue to pray for, and to admonish, 1 Sa. 12:23. Observe, (1.) The place Moses chose for his intercession. He went *out of the city* (*v.* 33), not only for privacy in his communion with God, but to show that he durst venture abroad into the field, notwithstanding the hail and lightning which kept Pharaoh and his servants withindoors, knowing that every hail-stone had its direction from his God, who meant him no hurt. Note, Peace with God makes men thunderproof, for thunder is the voice of their Father. (2.) The gesture: He *spread abroad his hands unto the Lord* — an outward expression of earnest desire and humble expectation. Those that come to God for mercy must stand ready to receive it. (3.) The end Moses aimed at in interceding for him: *That thou mayest know,* and be convinced, *that the earth is the Lord's* (*v.* 29), that is, that God has a sovereign dominion over all the creatures, that they all are ruled by him, and therefore that thou oughtest to be so. See what various methods God uses to bring men to their proper senses. Judgments are sent, judgments removed, and all for the same end, to make men know that he Lord reigns. (4.) The success of it. [1.] He prevailed with God, *v.* 33. But, [2.] He could not prevail with Pharaoh: *He sinned yet more, and hardened his heart, v.* 34, 35. The prayer of Moses opened and shut heaven, like Elias's (Jam. 5:17, 18), and such is the power of God's two witnesses (Rev. 11:6); yet neither Moses nor Elias, nor those two witnesses, could subdue the hard hearts of men. Pharaoh was frightened into a compliance by the judgment, but, when it was over, his convictions vanished, and his fair promises were forgotten. Note, Little credit is to be given to confessions upon the rack. Note also, Those that are not bettered by judgments and mercies are commonly made worse.

CHAPTER 10

The eighth and ninth of the plagues of Egypt, that of locusts and that of darkness, are recorded in this chapter. I. Concerning the plague of locusts, 1. God instructs Moses in the meaning of these amazing dispensations of his providence (*v.* 1, 2). 2. He threatens the locusts (*v.* 3–6). 3. Pharaoh, at the persuasion of his servants, is willing to treat again with Moses (*v.* 7–9), but they cannot agree (*v.* 10, 11). 4. The locusts come (*v.* 12-15). 5. Pharaoh cries Peccavi — I have offended (*v.* 16, 17), whereupon Moses prays for the removal of the plague, and it is done; but Pharaoh's heart is still hardened (*v.* 18–20). II. Concerning the plague of darkness, 1. It is inflicted (*v.* 21–23). 2. Pharaoh again treats with Moses about a surrender, but the treaty breaks off in a heat (*v.* 26, etc.).

Verses 1–11

Here, I. Moses is instructed. We may well suppose that he, for his part, was much astonished both at Pharaoh's obstinacy and at God's severity, and could not but be compassionately concerned for the desolations of Egypt, and at a loss to conceive what this contest would come to at last. Now here God tells him what he designed, not only Israel's release, but the magnifying of his own name: *That thou mayest tell* in thy writings, which shall continue to the world's end, *what I have wrought in Egypt,* v. 1, 2. The ten plagues of Egypt must be inflicted, that they may be recorded for the generations to come as undeniable proofs, 1. Of God's overruling power in the kingdom of nature, his dominion over all the creatures, and his authority to use them either as servants to his justice or sufferers by it, according to the counsel of his will. 2. Of God's victorious power over the kingdom of Satan, to restrain the malice and chastise the insolence of his and his church's enemies. These plagues are standing monuments of the greatness of God, the happiness of the church, and the sinfulness of sin, and standing monitors to the children of men in all ages not to *provoke the Lord to jealousy* nor to *strive with their Maker.* The benefit of these instructions to the world sufficiently balances the expense.

II. Pharaoh is reproved (*v.* 3): *Thus saith the Lord God of the poor,* despised, persecuted, Hebrews, *How long wilt thou refuse to humble thyself before me?* Note, It is justly

expected from the greatest of men that they humble themselves before the great God, and it is at their peril if they refuse to do it. This has more than once been God's quarrel with princes. Belshazzar did not humble his heart, Dan. 5:22. Zedekiah humbled not himself before Jeremiah, 2 Chr. 36:12. Those that will not humble themselves God will humble. Pharaoh had sometimes pretended to humble himself, but no account was made of it, because he was neither sincere nor constant in it.

III. The plague of locusts is threatened, *v.* 4–6. The hail had broken down the fruits of the earth, but these locusts should come and devour them: and not only so, but they should fill their houses, whereas the former inroads of these insects had been confined to their lands. This should be much worse than all the calamities of that king which had ever been known. Moses, when he had delivered his message, not expecting any better answer than he had formerly, *turned himself and went out from* Pharaoh, *v.* 6. Thus Christ appointed his disciples to depart from those who would not receive them, and to *shake off the dust of their feet for a testimony against them;* and ruin is not far off from those who are thus justly abandoned by the Lord's messengers, 1 Sa. 15:27, etc.

IV. Pharaoh's attendants, his ministers of state, or privy-counsellors, interpose, to persuade him to come to some terms with Moses, *v.* 7. They, as in duty bound, represent to him the deplorable condition of the kingdom *(Egypt is destroyed),* and advise him by all means to release his prisoners *(Let the men go);* for Moses, they found, would be a snare to them till it was done, and it were better to consent at first than to be compelled at last. The Israelites had become a burdensome stone to the Egyptians, and now, at length, the princes of Egypt were willing to be rid of them, Zec. 12:3. Note, It is a thing to be regretted (and prevented, if possible) that a whole nation should be ruined for the pride and obstinacy of its princes, *Salus populi suprema lex — To consult the welfare of the people is the first of laws.*

V. A new treaty is, hereupon, set on foot between Pharaoh and Moses, in which Pharaoh consents for the Israelites to go into the wilderness to do sacrifice; but the matter in dispute was who should go, *v.* 8. 1. Moses insists that they should take their whole families, and all their effects, along with them, *v.* 9. note, Those that serve God must serve him with all they have. Moses pleads, "We must hold a feast, therefore we must have our families to feast with, and our flocks and herds to feast upon, to the honour of God." 2. Pharaoh will by no means grant this: he will allow the men to go, pretending that this was all they desired, though this matter was never yet mentioned in any of the former treaties; but, for the *little ones,* he resolves to keep them as hostages, to oblige them to return, *v.* 10, 11. In a great passion he curses them, and threatens that, if they offer to remove their little ones, they will do it at their peril. Note, Satan does all he can to hinder those that serve God themselves from bringing their children in to serve him. He is a sworn enemy to early piety, knowing how destructive it is to the interests of his kingdom; whatever would hinder us from engaging our children to the utmost in God's service, we have reason to suspect the hand of Satan in it. 3. The treaty, hereupon, breaks off abruptly; those that before went out from Pharaoh's presence (*v.* 6) were now driven out. Those will quickly hear their doom that cannot bear to hear their duty. See 2 Chr. 25:16. *Quos Deus destruet eos dementat — Whom God intends to destroy he delivers up to infatuation.* Never was man so infatuated to his own ruin as Pharaoh was.

Verses 12–20

Here is, I. The invasion of the land by the locusts — *God's great army,* Joel 2:11. God bids *Moses stretch out his hand* (*v.* 12), to beckon them, as it wee (for they came at a call), and he *stretched forth his rod, v.* 13. Compare *ch.* 9:22 23. Moses ascribes it to the stretching out, not of his own hand, but the *rod of God,* the instituted sign of God's presence with him. The locusts obey the summons, and fly upon the wings of the wind, the east wind, and *caterpillars without number,* as we are told, Ps. 105:34, 35. A formidable army of horse and foot might more easily have been resisted than this host of insects. Who then is able to stand before the great God?

II. The desolations they made in it (*v.* 15): They *cov-*

ered the face of the earth, and *ate up the fruit* of it. The earth God has *given to the children of men;* yet, when God pleases, he can disturb their possession and send locusts and caterpillars to force them out. Herbs grow *for the service of man;* yet, when God pleases, those contemptible insects shall not only be fellow-commoners with him, but shall plunder him, and eat the bread out of his mouth. Let our labour be, not for the habitation and meat which thus lie exposed, but for those which *endure to eternal life,* which cannot be thus invaded, nor thus corrupted.

III. Pharaoh's admission, hereupon, *v.* 16, 17. He had driven Moses and Aaron from him (*v.* 11), telling them (it is likely) he would have no more to do with them. But now he calls for them again in all haste, and makes court to them with as much respect as before he had dismissed them with disdain. Note, The day will come when those who set at nought their counsellors, and despise all their reproofs, will be glad to make an interest in them and engage them to intercede on their behalf. The foolish virgins court the wise to *give them of their oil;* and see Ps. 141:6. 1. Pharaoh confesses his fault: *I have sinned against the Lord your God, and against you.* He now sees his own folly in the slights and affronts he had put on God and his ambassadors, and *seems* at least, to repent of it. When God convinces men of sin, and humbles them for it, their contempt of God's ministers, and the word of the Lord in their mouths, will certainly come into the account, and lie heavily upon their consciences. Some think that when Pharaoh said, "The LORD *your* God," he did in effect say, "The LORD shall not be *my* God." Many treat with God as a potent enemy, whom they are willing not to be at war with, but care not for treating with him as their rightful prince, to whom they are willing to submit with loyal affection. True penitents lament sin as committed against God, even their own God, to whom they stand obliged. 2. He begs pardon, not of God, as penitents ought, but of Moses, which was more excusable in him, because, by a special commission, Moses was made a *god to Pharaoh,* and *whosesoever sins he remitted* they were forgiven; when he prays, *Forgive this once,* he, in effect, promises not to offend in like manner any more, yet seems loth to express that promise, nor does he say any thing particularly of letting the people go. Note, Counterfeit repentance commonly cheats men with general promises and is loth to covenant against particular sins. 3. He entreats Moses and Aaron to pray for him. There are those who, in distress, implore the help of other persons' prayers, but have no mind to pray for themselves, showing thereby that they have no true love to God, nor any delight in communion with him. Pharaoh desires their prayers *that this death* only might be taken away, not *this sin:* he deprecates the plague of locusts, not the plague of a hard heart, which yet was much the more dangerous.

IV. The removal of the judgment, upon the prayer of Moses, *v.* 18, 19. This was, 1. As great an instance of the power of God as the judgment itself. An east wind brought the locusts, and now a west wind carried them off. Note, Whatever point of the compass the wind is in, it is fulfilling God's word, and turns about by his counsel. The *wind bloweth where it listeth,* as it respects any control of ours; not so as it respects the control of God: he *directeth it under the whole heaven.* 2. It was as great a proof of the authority of Moses, and as firm a ratification of his commission and his interest in that God who both *makes peace* and *creates evil,* Isa. 45:7. Nay, hereby he not only commanded the respect, but recommended himself to the good affections of the Egyptians, inasmuch as, while the judgment came in obedience to his summons, the removal of it was in answer to his prayers. He never desired the woeful day, though he threatened it. His commission indeed ran against Egypt, but his intercession was for it, which was a good reason why they should love him, though they feared him. 3. It was also as strong an argument for their repentance as the judgment itself; for by this it appeared that God is ready to forgive, and swift to show mercy. If he turn away a particular judgment, as he did often from Pharaoh, or defer it, as in Ahab's case, upon the profession of repentance and the outward tokens of humiliation, what will he do if we be sincere, and how welcome will true penitents be to him! O that this goodness of God might lead us to repentance!

V. Pharaoh's return to his impious resolution again not

to let the people go (*v.* 20), through the righteous hand of God upon him, hardening his heart, and confirming him in his obstinacy. Note, Those that have often baffled their convictions, and stood it out against them, forfeit the benefit of them, and are justly given up to those lusts of their own hearts which (how strong soever their convictions) prove too strong for them.

Verses 21–29

Here is, I. The plague of darkness brought upon Egypt, and a most dreadful plague it was, and therefore is put first of the ten in Ps. 105:28, though it was one of the last; and in the destruction of the spiritual Egypt it is produced by the fifth vial, which is poured out upon the *seat of the beast,* Rev. 16:10. *His kingdom was full of darkness.* Observe particularly concerning this plague, 1. That it was a total darkness. We have reason to think, not only that the lights of heaven were clouded, but that all their fires and candles were put out by the damps or clammy vapours which were the cause of this darkness; for it is said (*v.* 23), They *saw not one another.* It is threatened to the wicked (Job 18:5, 6) that the *spark of his fire shall not shine* (even *the sparks of his own kindling,* as they are called, Isa. 50:11), and that the *light shall be dark in his tabernacle.* Hell is *utter darkness.* The light of *a candle shall shine no more at all in thee,* Rev. 18:23. 2. That it was darkness which *might be felt* (*v.* 21), felt in its *causes* by their fingers' ends (so thick were the fogs), felt in its *effects,* some think, by their eyes, which were pricked with pain, and made the more sore by their rubbing them. Great pain is spoken of as the effect of that darkness, Rev. 16:10, which alludes to this. 3. No doubt it astonished and terrified them. The cloud of locusts, which had *darkened the land* (*v.* 15), was nothing to this. The tradition of the Jews is that in this darkness they were terrified by the apparitions of evil spirits, or rather by dreadful sounds and murmurs which they made, or (which is no less frightful) by the horrors of their own consciences; and this is the plague which some think is intended (for, otherwise, it is not mentioned at all there) Ps. 78:49, *He poured upon them the fierceness of his anger, by sending evil angels among them;* for to those to whom the devil has been a deceiver he will, at length, be a terror. 4. It continued three days, *six nights* (says bishop Hall) *in one;* so long they were imprisoned by those chains of darkness, and the most lightsome palaces were perfect dungeons. No *man rose from his place, v.* 23. They were all confined to their houses; and such a terror seized them that few of them had the courage to go from the chair to the bed, or from the bed to the chair. Thus were they *silent in darkness,* 1 Sa. 2:9. Now Pharaoh had time to consider, if he would have improved it. Spiritual darkness is spiritual bondage; while Satan blinds men's eyes that they see not, he binds them hands and feet that they work not for God, nor move towards heaven. They *sit in darkness.* 5. It was a righteous thing with God thus to punish them. Pharaoh and his people had rebelled against the light of God's word, which Moses spoke to them; justly therefore are they punished with darkness, for they loved it and chose it rather. The blindness of their minds brings upon them this darkness of the air. Never was mind so blinded as Pharaoh's, never was air so darkened as Egypt's. The Egyptians by their cruelty would have extinguished the lamp of Israel, and quenched their coal; justly therefore does God put out their lights. Compare it with the punishment of the Sodomites, Gen. 19:11. Let us dread the consequences of sin; if three days' darkness was so dreadful, what will everlasting darkness be? 6. The children of Israel, at the same time, had *light in their dwellings* (*v.* 23), not only in the land of Goshen, where most of them dwelt, but in the habitations of those who were dispersed among the Egyptians: for that some of them were thus dispersed appears from the distinction afterwards appointed to be put on their door-posts, *ch.* 12:7. This is an instance, (1.) Of the power of God above the ordinary power of nature. We must not think that we share in common mercies as a matter of course, and therefore that we owe no thanks to God for them; he could distinguish, and withhold that from us which he grants to other. He does indeed ordinarily make his sun to shine on the just and unjust; but he could make a difference, and we must own ourselves indebted to his mercy that he does not. (2.) Of the particular favour he bears to his people: they *walk in the light* when others *wander* endlessly *in thick darkness;* wherever there is an Israelite indeed, though in this dark world, there is light, there is a *child of light,* one for whom *light is sown,* and whom the *day-spring from on high visits.* When God made this difference between the Israelites and the Egyptians, who would not have preferred the poorest cottage of an Israelite to the finest palace of an Egyptian? There is still a real difference, though not so discernible a one, between the house of the wicked, which is under a curse, and the habitation of the just, which is blessed, Prov. 3:33. We should believe in that difference, and govern ourselves accordingly. Upon Ps. 105:28, *He sent darkness and made it dark, and they rebelled not against his word,* some ground a conjecture that, during these three days of darkness, the Israelites were circumcised, in order to their celebrating the passover which was now approaching, and that the command which authorized this was the word against which they rebelled not; for their circumcision, when they entered Canaan, is spoken of as a second general circumcision, Jos. 5:2. During these three days of darkness to the Egyptians, if God had so pleased, the Israelites, by the light which they had, might have made their escape, and without asking leave of Pharaoh; but God would bring them out *with a high hand,* and not by stealth, nor in haste, Isa. 52:12.

II. Here is the impression made upon Pharaoh by this plague, much like that of the foregoing plagues. 1. It awakened him so far that he renewed the treaty with Moses and Aaron, and now, at length, consented that they should take their little ones with them, only he would have their cattle left in pawn, *v.* 24. It is common for sinners thus to bargain with God Almighty. Some sins they will leave, but not all; they will leave their sins for a time, but they will not bid them a final farewell; they will allow him some share in their hearts, but the world and the flesh must share with him: thus they mock God, but they deceive themselves. Moses resolves not to abate in his terms: *Our cattle shall go with us, v.* 26. Note, The terms of reconciliation are so fixed that though men dispute them ever so long they cannot possibly alter them, nor bring them lower. We must come up to the demands of God's will, for we cannot expect he should condescend to the provisos of our lusts. God's messengers must always be bound up by that rule (Jer. 15:19), *Let them return unto thee, but return not thou unto them.* Moses gives a very good reason why they must take their cattle with them; they must go to do sacrifice, and therefore they must take wherewithal. What numbers and kinds of sacrifices would be required they did not yet know, and therefore they must take all they had. Note, With ourselves, and our children, we must devote all our worldly possessions to the service of God, because we know not what use God will make of what we have, nor in what way we may be called upon to honour God with it. 2. Yet it exasperated him so far that, when he might not make his own terms, he broke off the conference abruptly, and took up a resolution to treat no more. Wrath now came upon him to the utmost, and he became outrageous beyond all bounds, *v.* 28. Moses is dismissed in anger, forbidden the court upon pain of death, forbidden so much as to meet Pharaoh any more, as he had been used to do, by the river's side: *In that day thou seest my face, thou shalt die.* Prodigious madness! Had he not found that Moses could plague him without seeing his face? Or had he forgotten how often he had sent for Moses as his physician to heal him and ease him of his plagues? and must he now be bidden to come near him no more? Impotent malice! To threaten him with death who was armed with such a power, and at whose mercy he had so often laid himself. What will not hardness of heart and contempt of God's word and commandments bring men to? Moses takes him at his word (*v.* 29): *I will see thy face no more,* that is, "after this time;" for this conference did not break off till *ch.* 11:8, when Moses went out *in a great anger,* and told Pharaoh how soon he would change his mind, and his proud spirit would come down, which was fulfilled (*ch.* 12:31), when Pharaoh became a humble supplicant to Moses to depart. So that, after this interview, Moses came no more, till he was sent for. Note, When men drive God's word from them he justly permits their delusions, and answers them according to the multitude of their idols. When the Gadarenes desired Christ to depart, he presently left them.

CHAPTER 11

Pharaoh had told Moses to get out of his presence (*ch.* 10:28), and Moses had promised this should be the last time he would trouble him, yet he resolves to say out what he had to say, before he left him; accordingly, we have in this chapter, I. The instructions God had given to Moses, which he was now to pursue (*v.* 1, 2), together with the interest Israel and Moses had in the esteem of the Egyptians (*v.* 3). II. The last message Moses delivered to Pharaoh, concerning the death of the firstborn (*v.* 4–8). III. A repetition of the prediction of Pharaoh's hardening his heart (*v.* 9), and the event answering to it (*v.* 10).

Verses 1–3

Here is, I. The high favour Moses and Israel were in with God. 1. Moses was a favourite of Heaven, for God will not hide from him the thing he will do. God not only makes him his messenger to deliver his errands, but communicates to him his purpose (as the man of his counsel) that he would bring one plague more, and but one, upon Pharaoh, by which he would complete the deliverance of Israel, *v.* 1. Moses longed to see an end of this dreadful work, to see Egypt no more plagued and Israel no more oppressed: "Well," says God, "now it is near an end; the warfare shall shortly be accomplished, the point gained; Pharaoh shall be forced to own himself conquered, and to give up the cause." After all the rest of the plagues, God says, *I will bring one more.* Thus, after all the judgments executed upon sinners in this world, still there is one more reserved to be brought on them in the other world, which will completely humble those whom nothing else would humble. 2. The Israelites were favourites of Heaven; for God himself espouses their injured cause, and takes care to see them paid for all their pains in serving the Egyptians. This was the last day of their servitude; they were about to go away, and their masters, who had abused them in their work, would not have defrauded them of their wages, and have sent them away empty; while the poor Israelites were so fond of liberty that they would be satisfied with that, without pay, and would rejoice to get that upon any terms: but he that *executeth righteousness and judgment for the oppressed* provided that the labourers should not lose their hire, and ordered them to demand it now at their departure (*v.* 2), *in jewels of silver and jewels of gold,* to prepare for which God, by the plagues, had now made the Egyptians as willing to part with them upon any terms as, before, the Egyptians, by their severities, had made them willing to go upon any terms. Though the patient Israelites were content to lose their wages, yet God would not let them go without them. Note, One way or other, God will give redress to the injured, who in a humble silence commit their cause to him; and he will see to it that none be losers at last by their patient suffering any more than by their services.

II. The high favour Moses and Israel were in with the Egyptians, *v.* 3. 1. Even the people that has been hated and despised now came to be respected; the wonders wrought on their behalf put an honour upon them and made them considerable. How great do they become for whom God thus fights! Thus *the Lord gave them favour* in the sight of the Egyptians, by making it appear how much he favoured them: he also changed the spirit of the Egyptians towards them, and made them to be pitied of their oppressors, Ps. 106:46. 2. *The man Moses was very great.* How could it be otherwise when they saw what power he was clothed with, and what wonders were wrought by his hand? Thus the apostles, though otherwise despicable men, came to be magnified, Acts 5:13. Those that honour God he will honour; and with respect to those that approve themselves faithful to him, how meanly soever they may pass through this world, there is a day coming when they will look great, very great, in the eyes of all the world, even theirs who now look upon them with the utmost contempt. Observe, Though Pharaoh hated Moses, there were those of Pharaoh's servants that respected him. Thus in Caesar's household, even Nero's, there were some that had an esteem for blessed Paul, Phil. 1:13.

Verses 4–10

Warning is here given to Pharaoh of the last and conquering plague which was now to be inflicted. This was the *death of all the first-born in* Egypt at once, which had been first threatened (*ch.* 4:23, *I will slay thy son, thy first-*

born), but is last executed; less judgments were tried, which, if they had done the work would have prevented this. See how slow God is to wrath, and how willing to be met with in the way of his judgments, and to have his anger turned away, and particularly how precious the lives of men are in his eyes: if the death of their cattle had humbled and reformed them, their children would have been spared; but, if men will not improve the gradual advances of divine judgments, they must thank themselves if they find, in the issue, that the worst was reserved for the last. 1. The plague itself is here particularly foretold, *v.* 4–6. The time is fixed — about midnight, the very next midnight, the dead time of the night; when they were all asleep, all their first-born should sleep the sleep of death, not silently and insensibly, so as not to be discovered till morning, but so as to rouse the families at midnight to stand by and see them die. The extent of this plague is described, *v.* 5. The prince that was to succeed in the throne was not too high to be reached by it, nor were the slaves at the mill too low to be taken notice of. Moses and Aaron were not ordered to summon this plague; no *I will go out, saith the Lord, v.* 4. *It is a fearful thing to fall into the hands of the living God;* what is hell but this? 2. The special protection which the children of Israel should be under, and the manifest difference that should be put between them and the Egyptians. While angels drew their swords against the Egyptians, there should not so much as a dog bark at any of the children of Israel, *v.* 7. An earnest was hereby given of the difference which shall be put in the great day between God's people and his enemies: did men know what a difference God puts, and will put to eternity, between those that serve him and those that serve him not, religion would not seem to them such an indifferent thing as they make it, nor would they act in it with so much indifference as they do. 3. The humble submission which Pharaoh's servants should make to Moses, and how submissively they should request him to go (*v.* 8): *They shall come down, and bow themselves.* Note, The proud enemies of God and his Israel shall be made to fall under at last (Rev. 3:9), and shall be found liars to them, Deu. 33:29. When Moses had thus delivered his message, it is said, *He went out from Pharaoh in a great anger,* though he was the meekest of all the men of the earth. Probably he expected that the very threatening of the death of the first-born would have induced Pharaoh to comply, especially as Pharaoh had complied so far already, and had seen how exactly all Moses's predictions hitherto were fulfilled. But it had not that effect; his proud heart would not yield, no, not to save all the firstborn of his kingdom: no marvel that men are not deterred from vicious courses by the prospects given them of eternal misery in the other world, when the imminent peril they run of the loss of all that is dear to them in this world will not frighten them. Moses, hereupon, was provoked to a holy indignation, being grieved (as our Saviour afterwards) for the *hardness of his heart,* Mk. 3:5. Note, It is a great vexation to the spirits of good ministers to see people deaf to all the fair warnings given them, and running headlong upon ruin, notwithstanding all the kind methods taken to prevent it. Thus Ezekiel went in *the bitterness of his spirit* (Eze. 3:14), because God had told him that the house of Israel would not hearken to him, *v.* 7. To be angry at nothing but sin is the way not to sin in anger. Moses, having thus adverted to the disturbance which Pharaoh's obstinacy gave him, (1.) Reflects upon the previous notice God had given him of this (*v.* 9): *The Lord said unto Moses, Pharaoh shall not hearken to you.* The scripture has foretold the incredulity of those who should hear the gospel, that it might not be a surprise nor stumbling-block to us, Jn. 12:37, 38; Rom. 10:16. Let us think never the worse of the gospel of Christ for the slights men generally put upon it, for we were told before what cold entertainment it would meet with. (2.) He recapitulates all he had said before to this purport (*v.* 10), that Moses did all these wonders, as they are here related, before Pharaoh (he himself was an eye-witness of them), and yet he could not prevail, which was a certain sign that God himself had, in a way of righteous judgment, hardened his heart. Thus the Jews' rejection of the gospel of Christ was so gross an absurdity that it might easily be inferred from it that *God had given them the spirit of slumber,* Rom. 11:8.

CHAPTER 12

This chapter gives an account of one of the most memorable ordinances, and one of the most memorable providences, of all that are recorded in the Old Testament. I. Not one of all the ordinances of the Jewish church was more eminent than that of the passover, nor is any one more frequently mentioned in the New Testament; and we have here an account of the institution to it. The ordinance consisted of three parts: — 1. The killing and eating of the paschal lamb (*v.* 1–6, 8–11). 2. The sprinkling of the blood upon the door-posts, spoken of as a distinct thing (Heb. 11:28), and peculiar to this first passover (*v.* 7), with the reason for it (*v.* 13). 3. The feast of unleavened bread for seven days following; this points rather at what was to be done afterwards, in the observance of this ordinance (*v.* 14–20). This institution is communicated to the people, and they are instructed in the observance, (1.) Of this first passover (*v.* 21–23). (2.) Of the after passovers (*v.* 24–27). And the Israelites' obedience to these orders (*v.* 28). II. Not one of all the providences of God concerning the Jewish church was more illustrious, or is more frequently mentioned, than the deliverance of the children of Israel out of Egypt. 1. The firstborn of the Egyptians are slain (*v.* 29, 30). 2. Orders are given immediately for their discharge (*v.* 31–33). 3. They begin their march. (1.) Loaded with their own effects (*v.* 34). (2.) Enriched with the spoils of Egypt (*v.* 35, 36). (3.) Attended with a mixed multitude (*v.* 37, 38). (4.) Put to their shifts for present supply (*v.* 39). The event is dated (*v.* 40–42). Lastly, A recapitulation in the close, [1.] Of this memorable ordinance, with some additions (*v.* 43–49). [2.] Of this memorable providence (*v.* 50, 51).

Verses 1–20

Moses and Aaron here *receive of the Lord* what they were afterwards to *deliver to the people* concerning the ordinance of the passover, to which is prefixed an order for a new style to be observed in their months (*v.* 1, 2): *This shall be to you the beginning of months.* They had hitherto begun their year from the middle of September, but henceforward they were to begin it from the middle of March, at least in all their ecclesiastical computations. Note, It is good to begin the day, and begin the year, and especially to begin our lives, with God. This new calculation began the year with the spring, which *reneweth the face of the earth,* and was used as a figure of the coming of Christ, Cant. 2:11, 12. We may suppose that, while Moses was bringing the ten plagues upon the Egyptians, he was directing the Israelites to prepare for their departure at an hour's warning. Probably he had be degrees brought them near together from their dispersions, for their are here called *the congregation of Israel* (*v.* 3), and to them as a congregation orders are here sent. Their amazement and hurry, it is easy to suppose, were great; yet now they must apply themselves to the observance of a sacred rite, to the honour of God. Note, When our heads are fullest of care, and our hands of business, yet we must not forget our religion, nor suffer ourselves to be indisposed for acts of devotion.

I. God appointed that on the night wherein they were to go out of Egypt they should, in each of their families, *kill a lamb,* or that two or three families, if they were small, should join for a lamb. The lamb was to be got ready four days before and that afternoon they were to *kill it* (*v.* 6) as a sacrifice; not strictly, for it was not offered *upon the altar,* but as a religious ceremony, acknowledging God's goodness to them, not only in preserving them from, but in delivering them by, the plagues inflicted on the Egyptians. See the antiquity of family-religion; and see the convenience of the joining of small families together for religious worship, that it may be made the more solemn.

II. The lamb so slain they were to eat, roasted (we may suppose, in its several quarters), with unleavened bread and bitter herbs, because they were to eat it *in haste* (*v.* 11), and to leave none of it until the morning; for God would have them to depend upon him for their daily bread, and not to take thought for the morrow. He that led them would feed them.

III. Before they ate the flesh of the lamb, they were to sprinkle the blood upon the doorposts, *v.* 7. By this their houses were to be distinguished from the houses of the Egyptians, and so their first-born secured from the sword of the destroying angel, *v.* 12, 13. Dreadful work was to be made this night in Egypt; all the first-born both of man and beast were to be slain, and judgment executed upon the gods of Egypt. Moses does not mention the fulfillment, in this chapter, yet he speaks of it Num. 33:4. It is very probable that the idols which the Egyptians worshipped were destroyed, those of metal melted, those of wood consumed, and those of stone broken to pieces, whence Jethro infers (*ch.* 18:11), *The Lord is greater than all gods.* The same angel that destroyed their first-born demolished their idols, which were no less dear to them. For the protection of Israel from this plague they were ordered to sprinkle the blood of the lamb upon the door-posts, their doing which would be accepted as an instance of their faith in the divine warnings and their obedience to the divine precepts. Note, 1. If in times of common calamity God will secure his own people, and set a mark upon them; they shall be hidden either in heaven or under heaven, preserved either from the stroke of judgments or at least from the sting of them. 2. The blood of sprinkling is the saint's security in times of common calamity; it is this that marks them for God, pacifies conscience, and gives them boldness of access to the throne of grace, and so becomes a wall of protection round them and a wall of partition between them and the children of this world.

IV. This was to be annually observed as a feast of the Lord in their generations, to which the *feast of unleavened bread* was annexed, during which, for seven days, they were to eat no bread but what was unleavened, in remembrance of their being confined to such bread, of necessity, for many days after they came out of Egypt, *v.* 14–20. The appointment is inculcated for their better direction, and that they might not mistake concerning it, and to awaken those who perhaps in Egypt had grown generally very stupid and careless in the matters of religion to a diligent observance of the institution. Now, without doubt, there was much of the gospel in this ordinance; it is often referred to in the New Testament, and, in it, to us is *the gospel preached,* and *not to them only,* who *could not stedfastly look to the end of these things,* Heb. 4:2; 2 Co. 3:13.

1. The paschal lamb was typical. Christ is *our Passover,* 1 Co. 5:7. (1.) It was to be a *lamb;* and Christ is *the Lamb of God* (Jn. 1:29), often in the Revelation called the *Lamb,* meek and innocent as a lamb, dumb before the shearers, before the butchers. (2.) It was to be a *male of the first year* (*v.* 5), in its prime; Christ offered up himself in the midst of his days, not in infancy with the babes of Bethlehem. It denotes the strength and sufficiency of the Lord Jesus, on whom our help was laid. (3.) It was to be *without blemish* (*v.* 5), denoting the purity of the Lord Jesus, a Lamb *without spot,* 1 Pt. 1:19. The judge that condemned him (as if his trial were only like the scrutiny that was made concerning the sacrifices, whether they were without blemish or no) pronounced him innocent. (4.) It was to be set apart four days before (*v.* 3, 6), denoting the designation of the Lord Jesus to be a Saviour, both in the purpose and in the promise. It is very observable that as Christ was crucified at the passover, so he solemnly entered into Jerusalem four days before, the very day that the paschal lamb was set apart. (5.) It was to be *slain,* and *roasted with fire* (*v.* 6–9), denoting the exquisite sufferings of the Lord Jesus, even unto death, the death of the cross. The wrath of God is as fire, and Christ was made a curse for us. (6.) It was to be killed by the whole congregation between the two evenings, that is, between three o'clock and six. Christ suffered in the *end of the world* (Heb. 9:26), by the hand of the Jews, the whole multitude of them (Lu. 23:18), and for the good of all his spiritual Israel. (7.) Not *a bone of it must be broken* (*v.* 46), which is expressly said to be fulfilled in Christ (Jn. 19:33, 36), denoting the unbroken strength of the Lord Jesus.

2. The sprinkling of the blood was typical. (1.) It was not enough that the blood of the lamb was shed, but it must be sprinkled, denoting the application of the merits of Christ's death to our souls; we must *receive the atonement,* Rom. 5:11. (2.) It was to be sprinkled with *a bunch of hyssop* (*v.* 22) *dipped in the basin.* The everlasting covenant, like the basin, in the conservatory of this blood, the benefits and privileges purchased by it are laid up for us there; faith is the bunch of hyssop by which we apply the promises to ourselves and the benefits of the blood of Christ laid up in them. (3.) It was to be sprinkled upon the *door-posts,* denoting the open profession we are to make of faith in Christ, and obedience to him, as those that are not ashamed to own our dependence upon him. The mark of the beast may be received on the forehead or in the right hand, but the seal of the *Lamb* is always *in the forehead,* Rev. 7:3. There is a back-way to hell, but no backway to heaven; no, the only way to this is a high-way, Isa. 35:8. (4.) It was to be sprinkled upon the *lintel* and the *side-posts,* but not upon the *threshold* (*v.* 7), which cautions us

to take heed of trampling under foot the blood of the covenant, Heb. 10:29. It is precious blood, and must be precious to us. (5.) The blood, thus sprinkled, was a means of the preservation of the Israelites from the destroying angel, who had nothing to do where the blood was. If the blood of Christ be sprinkled upon our consciences, it will be our protection from the wrath of God, the curse of the law, and the damnation of hell, Rom. 8:1.

3. The solemnly eating of the lamb was typical of our gospel-duty to Christ. (1.) The paschal lamb was killed, not to be looked upon only, but to be fed upon; so we must by faith make Christ ours, as we do that which we eat, and we must receive spiritual strength and nourishment from him, as from our food, and have delight and satisfaction in him, as we have in eating and drinking when we are hungry or thirsty: see Jn. 6:53–55. (2.) It was to be all eaten; those that by faith feed upon Christ must feed upon a whole Christ; they must take Christ and his yoke, Christ and his cross, as well as Christ and his crown. *Is Christ divided?* Those hat gather much of Christ will have nothing over. (3.) It was to be eaten immediately, not deferred till morning, *v.* 10. *To-day* Christ is offered, and is to be accepted while it is called to-day, before we sleep the sleep of death. (4.) It was to be eaten *with bitter herbs* (*v.* 8), in remembrance of the bitterness of their bondage in Egypt. We must feed upon Christ with sorrow and brokenness of heart, in remembrance of sin; this will give an admirable relish to the paschal lamb. Christ will be sweet to us if sin be bitter. (5.) It was to be eaten in a departing posture (*v.* 11); when we feed upon Christ by faith we must absolutely forsake the rule and dominion of sin, shake off Pharaoh's yoke; and we must sit loose to the world, and every thing in it, forsake all for Christ, and reckon it no bad bargain, Heb. 13:13, 14.

4. The feast of unleavened bread was typical of the Christian life, 1 Co. 5:7, 8. Having received Christ Jesus the Lord, (1.) We must keep a feast in holy joy, continually delighting ourselves in Christ Jesus; no *manner of work must be done* (*v.* 16), no care admitted or indulged, inconsistent with, or prejudicial to, this holy joy: if true believers have not a continual feast, it is their own fault. (2.) It must be a feast of unleavened bread, kept in charity, without the leaven of malice, and in sincerity, without the leaven of hypocrisy. The law was very strict as to the passover, and the Jews were so in their usages, that no leaven should be *found in their houses, v.* 19. All the old leaven of sin must be put far from us, with the utmost caution and abhorrence, if we would keep the feast of a holy life to the honour of Christ. (3.) It was by an *ordinance for ever* (*v.* 17); as long as we live, we must continue feeding upon Christ and rejoicing in him, always making thankful mention of the great things he has done for us.

Verses 21–28

I. Moses is here, as a faithful steward in God's house, teaching the children of Israel to *observe all things which God had commanded him;* and no doubt he gave the instructions as largely as he received them, though they are not so largely recorded. It is here added,

1. That this night, when the first-born were to be destroyed, no Israelite must *stir out of doors till morning,* that is, till towards morning, when they would be called to march out of Egypt, *v.* 22. Not but that the destroying angel could have known an Israelite from an Egyptian in the street; but God would intimate to them that their safety was owing to the *blood of sprinkling;* if they put themselves from under the protection of that, it was at their peril. Those whom God has marked for himself must not mingle with evil doers: see Isa. 26:20, 21. They must not go out of the doors, lest they should straggle and be out of the way when they should be summoned to depart: they must stay within, to *wait for the salvation of the Lord,* and it is good to do so.

2. That hereafter they should carefully teach their children the meaning of this service, *v.* 26, 27. Observe,

(1.) The question which the children would ask concerning this solemnity (which they would soon take notice of in the family): *"What mean you by this service?* What is he meaning of all this care and exactness about eating this lamb, and this unleavened bread, more than about common food? Why such a difference between this meal and other meals?" Note, [1.] It is a good thing to see children inquisitive about the things of God; it is to be hoped that those who are careful to ask for the way will find it. Christ himself, when a child, *heard and asked questions,* Lu. 2:46. [2.] It concerns us all rightly to understand the meaning of those holy ordinances wherein we worship God, what is the nature and what the end of them, what is signified and what intended, what is the duty expected from us in them and what are the advantages to be expected by us. Every ordinance has a meaning; some ordinances, as sacraments, have not their meaning so plain and obvious as others have; therefore we are concerned to search, that we may not offer *the blind for sacrifice,* but may do a reasonable service. If either we are ignorant of, or mistake about, the meaning of holy ordinances, we can neither please God nor profit ourselves.

(2.) The answer which the parents were to return to this question (*v.* 27): *You shall say, It is the sacrifice of the Lord's passover,* that is, "By the killing and sacrificing of this lamb, we keep in remembrance the work of wonder and grace which God did for our fathers, when," [1.] "To make way for our deliverance out of bondage, he slew the firstborn of the Egyptians, so compelling them to sign our discharge;" and, [2.] "Though there were *with us, even with us, sins against the Lord our God,* for which the destroying angel, when he was abroad doing execution, might justly have destroyed our first-born too, yet God graciously appointed and accepted the family-sacrifice of a lamb, instead of the first-born, as, of old, the ram instead of Isaac, and in every house where the lamb was slain the first-born were saved." The repetition of this solemnity in the return of every year was designed, *First,* To look backward as a memorial, that in it they might remember what great things God had done for them and their fathers. The word *pesach* signifies a *leap,* or *transition;* it is a passing over; for the destroying angel passed over the houses of the Israelites, and did not destroy their first-born. When God brings utter ruin upon his people he says, *I will not pass by them any more* (Amos 7:8; 8:2), intimating how often he had passed by them, as now when the destroying angel passed over their houses. Note, 1. Distinguishing mercies lay under peculiar obligations. When *a thousand fall at our side, and ten thousand at our right hand,* and yet we are preserved, and have our lives given us for a prey, this should greatly affect us, Ps. 91:7. In war or pestilence, if the arrow of death have passed by us, passed over us, hit the next to us and just missed us, we must not say it was by chance that we were preserved but by the special providence of our God. 2. Old mercies to ourselves, or to our fathers, must not be forgotten, but be had in everlasting remembrance, that God may be praised, our faith in him encouraged, and our hearts enlarged in his service. *Secondly,* It was designed to look forward as an earnest of the great sacrifice of the Lamb of God in the fulness of time, instead of us and our first-born. We were obnoxious to the sword of the destroying angel, but *Christ our passover was sacrificed for us,* his death was our life, and thus he was the *Lamb slain from the foundation of the world,* from the foundation of the Jewish church: Moses kept the passover by faith in Christ, for Christ was *the end of the law for righteousness.*

II. The people received these instructions with reverence and ready obedience. 1. They *bowed the head and worshipped* (*v.* 27): they hereby signified their submission to this institution as a law, and their thankfulness for it as a favour and privilege. Note, When God gives law to us, we must give honour to him; when he speaks, we must *bow our heads and worship.* 2. They *went away and did* as they were commanded, *v.* 23. Here was none of that discontent and murmuring among them which we read of, *ch. v.* 20, 21. The plagues of Egypt had done them good, and raised their expectations of a glorious deliverance, which before they despaired of; and now they went forth to meet it in the way appointed. Note, The perfecting of God's mercies to us must be waited for in a humble observance of his institutions.

Verses 29–36

Here we have, I. The Egyptians' sons, even their first-born, slain, *v.* 29, 30. If Pharaoh would have taken the warning which was given him of this plague, and would thereupon have released Israel, what a great many dear and valuable lives might have been preserved! But see what obstinate infidelity brings upon men. Observe, 1. The time when this blow was given: It was *at midnight,* which added to the terror of it. The three preceding nights were made dreadful by the additional plague of darkness, which might be felt, and doubtless disturbed their repose; and now, when they hoped for one quiet night's rest, at midnight was the alarm given. When the destroying angel drew his sword against Jerusalem, it was in the day-time (2 Sa. 24:15), which made it the less frightful; but the destruction of Egypt was by a *pestilence walking in darkness,* Ps. 91:6. Shortly there will be an alarming cry at midnight, *Behold, the bridegroom cometh.* 2. On whom the plague fastened — on *their first-born,* the joy and hope of their respective families. They had slain the Hebrews' children, and now God slew theirs. Thus he visits the iniquity of the fathers upon the children; and he is *not unrighteous who taketh vengeance.* 3. How far it reached — from the throne to the dungeon. Prince and peasant stand upon the same level before God's judgments, for there is no respect of persons with him; see Job 34:29, 20. Now the *slain of the Lord were many; multitudes, multitudes,* fall in this *valley of decision,* when the controversy between God and Pharaoh was to be determined. 4. What an outcry was made upon it: *There was a great cry in Egypt,* universal lamentation for their *only* son (with many), and with all for their *first-born.* If any be suddenly taken ill in the night, we are wont to call up neighbours; but the Egyptians could have no help, no comfort, from their neighbours, all being involved in the same calamity. Let us learn hence, (1.) To tremble before God, and to be *afraid of his judgments,* Ps. 119:120. Who is able to stand before him, or dares resist him? (2.) To be thankful to God for the daily preservation of ourselves and our families: lying so much exposed, we have reason to say, "It is of the Lord's mercies that we are not consumed."

II. God's sons, even his first-born, released; this judgment conquered Pharaoh, and obliged him to *surrender at discretion,* without capitulating. Men had better come up to God's terms at first, for he will never come down to theirs, let them object as long as they will. Now Pharaoh's pride is abased, and he yields to all that Moses had insisted on: *Serve the Lord as you have said* (*v.* 31), and *take your flocks as you have said, v.* 32. Note, God's word will stand, and we shall get nothing by disputing it, or delaying to submit to it. Hitherto the Israelites were not permitted to depart, but now things had come to the last extremity, in consequence of which, 1. They are commanded to depart: *Rise up, and get you forth, v.* 31. Pharaoh had told Moses he should *see his face no more;* but now he sent for him. Those will seek God early in their distress who before had set him at defiance. Such a fright he was now in that he gave orders by night for their discharge, fearing lest, if he delayed any longer, he himself should fall next; and that he sent them out, not as men hated (as the pagan historians have represented this matter), but as men feared, is plainly discovered by his humble request to them (*v.* 32): *"Bless me also;* let me have your prayers, that I may not be plagued for what is past, when you are gone." Note, Those that are enemies to God's church are enemies to themselves, and, sooner or later, they will be made to see it. 2. They are hired to depart by the Egyptians; they cried out (*v.* 33), *We be all dead men.* Note, When death comes into our houses, it is seasonable for us to think of our own mortality. Are our relations dead? It is easy to infer thence that we are dying, and, in effect, already dead men. Upon this consideration they were urgent with the Israelites to be gone, which gave great advantage to the Israelites in borrowing their jewels, *v.* 35, 36. When the Egyptians urged them to be gone, it was easy for the to say that the Egyptians had kept them poor, that they could not undertake such a journey with empty purses, but, that, if they would give them wherewithal to bear their charges, they would be gone. And this the divine Providence designed in suffering things to come to this extremity, that they, becoming formidable to the Egyptians, might have what they would, for asking; the Lord also, by the influence he has on the minds of people, inclined the hearts of the Egyptians to furnish them with what they desired, they probably intending thereby to *make atonement,* that the plagues might be stayed, as the Philistines, when they returned the ark, sent a present with it for a trespass-offering, having an eye to this precedent

1 Sa. 6:3, 6. The Israelites might receive and keep what they thus borrowed, or rather required, of the Egyptians, (1.) As justly as servants receive wages from their masters for work done, and sue for it if it be detained. (2.) As justly as conquerors take the spoils of their enemies whom they have subdued; Pharaoh was in rebellion against the *God of the Hebrews,* by which all that he had was forfeited. (3.) As justly as subjects receive the estates granted to them by their prince. God is the sovereign proprietor of the earth, and the fulness thereof; and, if he take from one and give to another, who may say unto him, *What doest thou?* It was by God's special order and appointment that the Israelites did what they did, which was sufficient to justify them, and bear them out; but what they did will by no means authorize others (who cannot pretend to any such warrant) to do the same. Let us remember, [1.] That the King of kings can do no wrong. [2.] That he will do right to those whom men injure, Ps. 146:7. Hence it is that the *wealth of the sinner* often proves to be *laid up for the just,* Prov. 13:22; Job 27:16, 17.

Verses 37–42

Here is the departure of the children of Israel out of Egypt; having obtained their dismission, they set forward without delay, and did not defer to a more convenient season. Pharaoh was now in a good mind; but they had reason to think he would not long continue so, and therefore it was no time to linger. We have here an account, 1. Of their number, about 600,000 men (*v.* 37), besides women and children, which I think, we cannot suppose to make less than 1,200,000 more. What a vast increase was this, to arise from seventy souls in little more than 200 years' time! See the power and efficacy of that blessing, when God commands it, *Be fruitful and multiply.* This was typical of the multitudes that were brought into the gospel church when it was first founded; *so mightily grew the word of God, and prevailed.* 2. Of their retinue (*v.* 38): *A mixed multitude went up with them,* hangers on to that great family, some perhaps willing to leave their country, because it was laid waste by the plagues, and to seek their fortune, as we say, with the Israelites; others went out of curiosity, to see the solemnities of Israel's sacrifice to their God, which had been so much talked of, and expecting to see some glorious appearances of their God to them in the wilderness, having seen such glorious appearances of their God for them in the field of Zoan, Ps. 78:12. Probably the greatest part of this mixed multitude were but a rude unthinking mob, that followed the crowd they knew not why; we afterwards find that they proved a snare to them (Num. 11:4), and it is probable that when, soon afterwards, they understood that the children of Israel were to continue forty years in the wilderness, they quitted them, and returned to Egypt. Note, There were always those among the Israelites that were not Israelites, and there are still hypocrites in the church, who make a deal of mischief, but will be shaken off at last. 3. Of their effects. They had with them *flocks and herds,* even *very much cattle.* This is taken notice of because it was long before Pharaoh would give them leave to remove their effects, which were chiefly cattle, Gen. 46:32. 4. Of the provision made for the camp, which was very poor and slender. They brought some dough with them out of Egypt in their knapsacks, *v.* 34. They had prepared to bake, the next day, in order to their removal, understanding it was very near; but, being hastened away sooner than they thought of, by some hours, they took the dough as it was, unleavened; when they came to Succoth, their first stage, they baked unleavened cakes, and, though these were of course insipid, yet the liberty they were brought into made this the most joyful meal they had ever eaten in their lives. Note, The servants of God must not be slaves to their appetites, nor solicitous to wind up all the delights of sense to their highest pitch. We should be willing to take up with dry bread, nay, with unleavened bread, rather than neglect or delay any service we have to do for God, as those whose meat and drink it is to do his will. 5. Of the date of this great event: it was just 430 years from the promise made to Abraham (as the apostle explains it, Gal. 3:17) at his first coming into Canaan, during all which time *the children of Israel,* that is, [illegible] Hebrews, the distinguished chosen seed, were sojourn[illegible] a land that was not theirs, either Canaan or Egypt. [illegible] the promise God made to Abraham of a settlement lay dormant and unfulfilled, but now, at length, it revived, and things began to work towards the accomplishment of it. The first day of the march of Abraham's seed towards Canaan was just 430 years (it should seem to a day) from the promise made to Abraham, Gen. 12:2, *I will make of thee a great nation.* See how punctual God is to his time; though his promises be not performed quickly, they will be accomplished in their season. 6. Of the memorableness of it: *It is a night to be much observed, v.* 42. (1.) The providences of that first night were very observable; memorable was the destruction of the Egyptians, and the deliverance of the Israelites by it; God herein made himself taken notice of. (2.) The ordinances of that night, in the annual return of it, were to be carefully observed: *This is that night of the Lord,* that remarkable night, to be celebrated in all generations. Note, The great things God does for his people are not to be a nine days' wonder, as we say, but the remembrance of them is to be perpetuated throughout all ages, especially the work of our redemption by Christ. This first passover-night was a night of the Lord *much to be observed;* but the last passover-night, in which Christ was betrayed (and in which the passover, with the rest of the ceremonial institutions, was superseded and abolished), was a night of the Lord *much more to be observed,* when a yoke heavier than that of Egypt was broken from off our necks, and a land better than that of Canaan set before us. That was a temporal deliverance to be celebrated *in their generation;* this is an eternal redemption to be celebrated in the praises of glorious saints, *world without end.*

Verses 43–51

Some further precepts are here given concerning the passover, as it should be observed in times to come.

I. *All the congregation of Israel must keep it, v.* 47. All that share in God's mercies should join in thankful praises for them. Though it was observed in families apart, yet it is looked upon as the act of the whole congregation; for the smaller communities constituted the greater. The New-Testament passover, the Lord's supper, ought not to be neglected by any who are capable of celebrating it. He is unworthy the name of an Israelite that can contentedly neglect the commemoration of so great a deliverance. 1. No stranger that was uncircumcised might be admitted to eat of it, *v.* 43, 45, 48. None might sit at the table but those that came in by the door; nor may any now approach to the improving ordinance of the Lord's supper who have not first submitted to the initiating ordinance of baptism. We must be born again by the word ere we can be nourished by it. Nor shall any partake of the benefit of Christ's sacrifice, or feast upon it, who are not first circumcised in heart, Col. 2:11. 2. Any stranger that was circumcised might be welcome to eat of the passover, even *servants, v.* 44. If, by circumcision, they would make themselves debtors to the law in its burdens, they were welcome to share in the joy of its solemn feasts, and not otherwise. Only it is intimated (*v.* 48) that those who were masters of families must not only be circumcised themselves, but have all their males circumcised too. If in sincerity, and with that zeal which the thing required and deserves, we give up ourselves to God, we shall, with ourselves, give up all we have to him, and do our utmost that all ours may be his too. Here is an early indication of favour to the poor Gentiles, that the stranger, if circumcised, stands upon the same level with the home-born Israelite. *One law* for both, *v.* 49. This was a mortification to the Jews, and taught them that it was their dedication to God, not their descent from Abraham, that entitled them to their privileges. A sincere proselyte was as welcome to the passover as a native Israelite, Isa. 56:6, 7.

II. *In one house shall it be eaten* (*v.* 46), for good-fellowship sake, that they might rejoice together, and edify one another in the eating of it. None of it must be carried to another place, nor left to another time; for God would not have them so taken up with care about their departure as to be indisposed to take the comfort of it, but to leave Egypt, and enter upon a wilderness, with cheerfulness, and, in token of that, to eat a good hearty meal. The papists' carrying their consecrated host from house to house is not only superstitious in itself, but contrary to this typical law of the passover, which directed that no part of the lamb should be carried abroad.

The chapter concludes with a repetition of the whole matter, that the children of Israel did as they were bidden, and God did for them as he promised (*v.* 50, 51); for he will certainly be the author of salvation to those that obey him.

CHAPTER 13

In this chapter we have, I. The commands God gave to Israel, 1. To sanctify all their firstborn to him (*v.* 1, 2). 2. To be sure to remember their deliverance out of Egypt (*v.* 3, 4), and, in remembrance of it, to keep the feast of unleavened bread (*v.* 5–7). 3. To transmit the knowledge of it with all possible care to their children (*v.* 8–10). 4. To set apart unto God the firstlings of their cattle (*v.* 11–13), and to explain that also to their children (*v.* 14–16). II. The care God took of Israel, when he had brought them out of Egypt. I. Choosing their way for them (*v.* 17, 18). 2. Guiding them in the way (*v.* 20–22). And III. Their care of Joseph's bones (*v.* 19).

Verses 1–10

Care is here taken to perpetuate the remembrance,

I. Of the preservation of Israel's firstborn, when the firstborn of the Egyptians were slain. In memory of that distinguishing favour, and in gratitude for it, the firstborn, in all ages, were to be consecrated to God, as his peculiars (*v.* 2), and to be redeemed, *v.* 13. God, who by the right of creation is proprietor and sovereign of all the creatures, here lays claim in particular to the firstborn of the Israelites, by right of protection: *Sanctify to me all the firstborn.* The parents were not to look upon themselves as interested in their firstborn, till they had first solemnly presented them to God, recognized his title to them, and received them back, at a certain rate, from him again. Note, 1. That which is by special distinguishing mercy spared to us should be in a peculiar manner dedicated to God's honour; at least some grateful acknowledgment, in works of piety and charity, should be made, when our lives, or the lives of our children, have been given us for a prey. 2. God, who is the first and best, should have the first and best, and to him we should resign that which is most dear to us, and most valuable. The firstborn were the joy and hope of their families. Therefore *they shall be mine,* says God. By this is will appear that we love God best (as we ought) if we are willing to part with that to him which we love best in this world. 3. It is the *church of the firstborn* that is sanctified to God, Heb. 12:23. Christ it the *firstborn among many brethren* (Rom. 8:29), and, by virtue of their union with him, all that are born again, and born from above, are accounted as firstborn. There is an *excellency of dignity and power* belonging to them; and, *if children, then heirs.*

II. The remembrance of their coming out of Egypt must also be perpetuated: *"Remember this day, v.* 3. Remember it by a good token, as the most remarkable day of your lives, the birthday of your nation, or the day of its coming of age, to be no longer under the rod." Thus the day of Christ's resurrection is to be remembered, for in it we were raised up with Christ out of death's *house of bondage.* The scripture tells us not expressly what day of the *year* Christ rose (as Moses told the Israelites what day of the year they were brought out of Egypt, that they might remember it yearly), but very particularly what day of the *week* it was, plainly intimating that, as the more valuable deliverance, and of greater importance, it should be remembered *weekly.* Remember it, for *by strength of hand the Lord brought you out.* Note, The more of God and his power appears in any deliverance, the more memorable it is. Now, that it might be remembered,

1. They must be sure to *keep the feast of unleavened bread, v.* 5–7. It was not enough that they remembered it, but they must celebrate the memorial of it in that way which God had appointed, and use the instituted means of preserving the remembrance of it. So, under the gospel, we must not only remember Christ, but *do this in remembrance* of him. Observe, How strict the prohibition of leaven is (*v.* 7); not only no leaven must be eaten, but none must be seen, no, not in all their quarters. Accordingly, the Jews' usage was, before the feast of the passover, to cast all the leavened bread out of their houses: they burnt it, or buried it, or broke it small and scattered it in the wind; they searched diligently with lighted candles in all the corners of their houses, lest any leaven should remain. The care and strictness enjoined in this matter were designed, (1.) To make the feast the more solemn, and consequently the more taken notice of by their chil-

dren, who would ask, "Why is so much ado made?" (2.) To teach us how solicitous we should be to put away from us all sin, 1 Co. 5:7.

2. They must instruct their children in the meaning of it, and relate to them the story of their deliverance out of Egypt, *v.* 8. Note, (1.) Care must be taken betimes to instruct children in the knowledge of God. Here is an ancient law for catechising. (2.) It is particularly of great use to acquaint children betimes with the stories of the scripture, and to make them familiar to them. (3.) It is a debt we owe to the honour of God, and to the benefit of our children's souls, to tell them of the great works God has done for his church, both those which we have seen with our eyes done in our day and which we have heard with our ears and our fathers have told us: *Thou shalt show thy son in that day* (the day of the feast) these things. When they were celebrating the ordinance, they must explain it. *Every thing is beautiful in its season.* The passover is appointed *for a sign, and for a memorial,* that *the Lord's law may be in thy mouth.* Note, We must retain the remembrance of God's works, that we may remain under the influence of God's law. And those that have God's law in their heart should have it in their mouth, and be often speaking of it, the more to affect themselves and to instruct others.

Verses 11–16

Here we have,

I. Further directions concerning the dedicating of their firstborn to God. 1. The firstlings of their cattle were to be dedicated to God, as part of their possessions. Those of clean beasts — calves, lambs, and kids — if males, were to be sacrificed, Ex. 22:30; Num. 18:17, 18. Those of unclean beasts, as colts, were to be redeemed with a lamb, or knocked on the head. For whatsoever is unclean (as we all are by nature), if it be not redeemed, will be destroyed, *v.* 11, 13. 2. The firstborn of their children were to be redeemed, and by no means sacrificed, as the Gentiles sacrificed their children to Moloch. The price of the redemption of the firstborn was fixed by the law (Num. 18:16) at *five sheckles.* We were all obnoxious to the wrath and curse of God; by the blood of Christ we are redeemed, that we may be joined to the *church of the firstborn.* They were to redeem their children, as well as the firstlings of the unclean beasts, for our children are by nature polluted. *Who can bring a clean thing out of an unclean?*

II. Further directions concerning the catechising of their children, and all those of the rising generation, from time to time, in this matter. It is supposed that, when they saw all the firstlings thus devoted, they would ask the meaning of it, and their parents and teachers must tell them (*v.* 14–16) that God's special propriety in their firstborn, and all their firstlings, was founded in his special preservation of them from the sword of the destroying angel. Being thus delivered, they must serve him. Note, 1. Children should be directed and encouraged to ask their parents questions concerning the things of God, a practice which would be perhaps of all others the most profitable way of catechising; and parents must furnish themselves with useful knowledge, that they may be ready always to give an answer to their enquiries. If ever the *knowledge of God cover the earth,* as the waters do the sea, the fountains of family-instruction must first be broken up. 2. We should all be able to show cause for what we do in religion. As sacraments are sanctified by the word, so they must be explained and understood by it. God's service is reasonable, and it is then acceptable when we perform it intelligently, knowing what we do and why we do it. 3. It must be observed how often it is said in this chapter that *by strength of hand* (*v.* 3, 14, 16), *with a strong hand* (*v.* 9), the Lord brought them out of Egypt. The more opposition is given to the accomplishment of God's purposes the more is his power magnified therein. It is a strong hand that conquers hard hearts. Sometimes God is said to work deliverance *not by might nor power* (Zec. 4:6), not by such visible displays of his power as that recorded here. 4. Their posterity that should be born in Canaan are directed to say, *The Lord brought us out of Egypt, v.* 14, 16. Mercies to our fathers are mercies to us; we reap the benefit of them, and therefore must keep up a grateful remembrance of them. We stand upon the bottom of former deliverances, and were in the loins of our ancestors when they were delivered. Much more reason have we to say that in the death and resurrection of Jesus Christ we were redeemed.

Verses 17–22

Here is, I. The choice God made of their way, *v.* 17, 18. He was their guide. Moses gave them direction but as he received it from the Lord. Note, The way of man is not in himself, Jer. 10:23. He may *devise his way,* and design it; but, after all, it is God that *directs his steps,* Prov. 16:9. Man proposes, but God disposes, and in his disposal we must acquiesce, and set ourselves to follow providence. There were two ways from Egypt to Canaan. One was a short cut from the north of Egypt to the south of Canaan, perhaps about four or five days' journey; the other was much further about, through the wilderness, and that was the way in which God chose to lead his people Israel, *v.* 18. 1. There were many reasons why God led them *through the way of the wilderness of the Red Sea.* The Egyptians were to be drowned in the Red Sea. The Israelites were to be humbled and proved in the wilderness, Deu. 8:2. God had given it to Moses for a sign (*ch.* 3:12), *You shall serve God in this mountain.* They had again and again told Pharaoh that they must go *three days' journey into the wilderness to do sacrifice,* and therefore it was requisite that they should bend their march that way, else they would justly have been exclaimed against as notorious dissemblers. Before they entered the lists with their enemies, matters must be settled between them and their God, laws must be given, ordinances instituted, covenants sealed, and the original contract ratified, for the doing of which it was necessary that they should retire into the solitudes of a wilderness, the only closet for such a crowd; the high road would be no proper place for these transactions. It is said (Deu. 32:10), *He led them about,* some hundreds of miles about, and yet (Ps. 107:7), *He led them forth by the right way.* God's way is the right way, though it seem *about.* If we think he leads not his people the nearest way, yet we may be sure he leads them the best way, and so it will appear when we come to our journey's end. *Judge nothing before the time.* 2. There was one reason why God did not lead them the nearest way, which would have brought them after a few days' march to *the land of the Philistines* (for it was that part of Canaan that lay next to Egypt), namely, because they were not as yet fit for war, much less for war with the Philistines, *v.* 17. Their spirits were broken with slavery; it was not easy for them to turn their hands of a sudden from the trowel to the sword. The Philistines were formidable enemies, too fierce to be encountered by raw recruits; it was more suitable that they should begin with the Amalekites, and be prepared for the wars of Canaan by experiencing the difficulties of the wilderness. Note, God proportions his people's trials to their strength, and will *not suffer them to be tempted above what they are able,* 1 Co. 10:13. That promise, if compared with the foregoing verses, will seem to refer to this event, as an instance of it. *God knows our frame,* and considers our weakness and faintheartedness, and by less trials will prepare us for greater. God is said to bring Israel out of Egypt as the eagle *brings up her young ones* (Deu. 32:11), teaching them by degrees to fly. Orders being thus given which way they should go, we are told, (1.) That they went up themselves, not as a confused rout, but in good order, rank and file: they *went up harnessed, v.* 18. They went up by *five in a rank* (so some), in *five squadrons,* so others. They marched like an army with banners, which added much to their strength and honour. (2.) That they took the *bones of Joseph* along with them (*v.* 19), and probably the bones of the rest of Jacob's sons, unless (as some think) they had been privately carried to Canaan (Acts 7:16), severally as they died. Joseph had particularly appointed that his bones should be carried up when God should visit the (Gen. 50:25, 26), so that their carrying up his bones was not only a performance of the oath their fathers had sworn to Joseph, but an acknowledgment of the performance of God's promise to them by Joseph that he would visit them and bring them out of the land of Egypt, and an encouragement to their faith and hope that he would fulfil the other part of the promise, which was to bring them to Canaan, in expectation of which they carried these bones with them while they wandered in the desert. They might think, "Joseph's bones must rest at last, and then we shall." Moses is said to take these bones with him. Moses was now a very great man; so had Joseph been in his day, yet he was now but a box full of dry bones; this was all that remained of him in this world, which might serve for a monitor to Moses to remember his mortality. *I have said, You are gods;* it was said so to Moses expressly (*ch.* 7:1); *but you shall die like men.*

II. Here is the guidance they were blessed with in the way: *The Lord went before them in a pillar, v.* 21, 22. In the first two stages it was enough that God directed Moses whither to march: he knew the country and the road well enough; but now that they had come *to the edge of the wilderness* (*v.* 20) they would have occasion for a guide; and a very good guide they had, one that was infinitely wise, kind, and faithful: *The Lord went before them,* the *shechinah* (or appearance of the divine Majesty, which was typical of Christ) or a previous manifestation of the eternal Word, which, in the fulness of time, was to be *made flesh,* and *dwell among us.* Christ was with the church in the wilderness, 1 Co. 10:9. Now *their King passed before them, even the Lord on the head of them,* Mic. 2:13. Note, Those whom God brings into a wilderness he will not leave nor lose there, but will take care to lead them through it; we may well think it was a very great satisfaction to Moses and the pious Israelites to be sure that they were under divine guidance. Those needed not to fear missing their way who were thus led, nor being lost who were thus directed; those needed not to fear being benighted who were thus illuminated, nor being robbed who were thus protected. Those who make the glory of God their end, and the word of God their rule, the Spirit of God the guide of their affections, and the providence of God the guide of their affairs, may be confident that *the Lord goes before them,* as truly as he went before Israel in the wilderness, though not so sensibly; we must live by faith. 1. They had sensible evidences of God's going before them. They all saw an appearance from heaven of a pillar, which in the bright day appeared cloudy, and in the dark night appeared fiery. We commonly see that that which is a flame in the night is a smoke in the day; so was this. God gave them this ocular demonstration of his presence, in compassion to the infirmity of their faith, and in compliance with that infant state of the church, which needed to be thus lisped to in their own language; but blessed are *those that have not seen and yet have believed* God's gracious presence with them, according to his promise. 2. They had sensible effects of God's going before them in this pillar. For, (1.) It led the way in that vast howling wilderness, in which there was no road, no track, no way-mark, of which they had no maps, through which they had no guides. When they marched, this pillar went before them, at the rate that they could follow, and appointed the place of their encampment, as Infinite Wisdom saw fit, which both eased them from care, and secured them from danger, both in moving and in resting. (2.) It sheltered them by day from the heat, which, at some times of the year, was extreme. (3.) It gave them light by night when they had occasion for it, and at all times made their camp pleasant and the wilderness they were in less frightful.

III. These were constant standing miracles (*v.* 22): He *took not away the pillar of cloud;* no, not when they seemed to have less occasion for it, travelling through inhabited countries, no, not when they murmured and were provoking; it never left them, till it brought them to the borders of Canaan. It was a cloud which the wind could not scatter. This favour is acknowledged with thankfulness long afterwards, Neh. 9:19; Ps. 78:14. There was something spiritual in this pillar of cloud and fire. 1. The children of Israel were baptized unto Moses in this cloud, which, some think, distilled dew upon them, 1 Co. 10:2. By coming under this cloud, they signified their putting themselves under the divine guidance and command by the ministry of Moses. Protection draws allegiance; this cloud was the badge of God's protection, and so became the bond of their allegiance. Thus they were initiated, and admitted under that government, now when they were entering upon the wilderness. 2. Some make this cloud a type f Christ. The cloud of his human nature was a veil to the light and fire of his divine nature; we find him (Rev. 10:1) *clothed with a cloud, and his feet as pillars of fire.* Christ is our way, the light of our way and the guide of it. 3. It signified the special guidance and protection which the church of Christ is under in this world. God himself is the keeper of Israel, and he *neither slumbers nor sleeps,* Ps. 121:4; Isa. 27:3. There is a defence created, not only on Sion's assemblies, but on every dwelling-place in Sion. See Isa. 4:5, 6. Nay, every Israelite indeed is hidden under the shadow of God's wings (Ps. 17:8); angels, whose ministry was made use of in this cloud, are employed for their good, and pitch their tents about them. *Happy art thou, O Israel! who is like unto thee, O people?*

CHAPTER 14

The departure of the children of Israel out of Egypt (which was indeed the birth of the Jewish church) is made yet more memorable by further works of wonder, which were wrought immediately upon it. Witness the records of this chapter, the contents whereof, together with a key to it, we have, Heb. 11:29. "They passed through the Red Sea as by dry land, which the Egyptians assaying to do were drowned;" and this they did by faith, which intimates that there was something typical and spiritual in it. Here is, I. The extreme distress and danger that Israel was in at the Red Sea. 1. Notice was given of it to Moses before (*v.* 1–4). 2. The cause of it was Pharaoh's violent pursuit of them (*v.* 5–9). 3. Israel was in a great consternation upon it (*v.* 10–12). 4. Moses endeavours to encourage them (*v.* 13, 14). II. The wonderful deliverance that God wrought for them out of this distress. 1. Moses is instructed concerning it (*v.* 15–18). 2. Lines that could not be forced are set between the camp of Israel and Pharaoh's camp (*v.* 19, 20). 3. By the divine power the Red Sea is divided (*v.* 31), and is made, (1.) A lane to the Israelites, who marched safely through it (*v.* 22, 29). But, (2.) To the Egyptians it was made, [1.] An ambush into which they were drawn (*v.* 23–25). And, [2.] A grave in which they were all buried (*v.* 26–28). III. The impressions this made upon the Israelites (*v.* 30, 31).

Verses 1–9

We have here,

I. Instructions given to Moses concerning Israel's motions and encampments, which were so very surprising that if Moses had not express orders about them before they would scarcely have been persuaded to follow the pillar of cloud and fire. That therefore there might be no scruple nor dissatisfaction about it, Moses is told before, 1. Whither they must go, *v.* 1, 2. They had got to the edge of the wilderness (*ch.* 13:20), and a stage or two more would have brought them to Horeb, the place appointed for their serving God; but, instead of going forward, they are ordered to turn short off, on the right hand from Canaan, and to march towards the Red Sea. Where they were, at Etham, there was no sea in their way to obstruct their passage: but God himself orders them into straits, which might give them an assurance that when his purposes were served he would without fail bring them out of those straits. Note, God sometimes raises difficulties in the way of the salvation of his people, that he may have the glory of subduing them, and helping his people over them. 2. What God designed in these strange orders. Moses would have yielded an implicit obedience, though God had given him no reason; but shall he hide from Moses the thing that he does? No, Moses shall know, (1.) That Pharaoh has a design to ruin Israel, *v.* 3. (2.) That therefore God has a design to ruin Pharaoh, and he takes this way to effect it, *v.* 4. Pharaoh's sagacity would conclude that Israel was entangled in the wilderness and so would become an easy prey to him; and, that he might be the more apt to think so, God orders them into yet greater entanglements; also, by turning them so much out of their road, he amazes him yet more, and gives him further occasion to suppose that they were in a state of embarrassment and danger. And thus (says God) *I will be honoured upon Pharaoh.* Note, [1.] All men being made for the honour of their Maker, those whom he is not honoured by he will be honoured upon. [2.] What seems to tend to the church's ruin is often overruled to the ruin of the church's enemies, whose pride and malice are fed by Providence, that they may be ripened for destruction.

II. Pharaoh's pursuit of Israel, in which, while he gratifies his own malice and revenge, he is furthering the accomplishment of God's counsels concerning him. *It was told him that the people fled, v.* 5. Such a fright was he in, when he gave them leave to go, that when the fright was a little over he either forgot, or would not own, that they departed with his consent, and therefore was willing that it should be represented to him as a revolt from their allegiance. Thus what may easily be justified is easily condemned, by putting false colours upon it. Now, hereupon,

1. He reflects upon it with regret that he had connived their departure. He and his servants, though it was with greatest reason in the world that they had let Israel go, were now angry with themselves for it: *Why have we done thus?* (1.) It vexed them that Israel had their liberty, that they had lost the profit of their labours, and the pleasure of chastising them. It is meat and drink to proud persecutors to trample upon the saints of the Most High, and say to their souls, *Bow down, that we may go over;* and therefore it vexes them to have their hands tied. Note, The liberty of God's people is a heavy grievance to their enemies, Esth. 5:12, 13; Acts 5:17, 33. (2.) It aggravated the vexation that they themselves had consented to it, thinking now that they might have hindered it, and that they needed not to have yielded, though they had stood it out to the last extremity. Thus God makes men's envy and rage against his people a torment to themselves, Ps. 112:10. It was well done to let Israel go, and what they would have reflected on with comfort if they had done it from an honest principle; but doing it by constraint, they called themselves a thousand fools for doing it, and passionately wished it undone again. Note, It is very common, but very absurd and criminal, for people to repent of their good deeds; their justice and charity, and even their repentance, are repented of. See an instance somewhat like this, Jer. 34:10, 11.

2. He resolves, if possible, either to reduce them or to be revenged on them; in order to this, he levies an army, musters all his force of chariots and horsemen, *v.* 17, 18 (for, it should seem, he took no foot with him, because the king's business required haste), and thus he doubts not but he shall re-enslave them, *v.* 6, 7. It is easy to imagine what a rage Pharaoh was now in, roaring like a lion disappointed of his prey, how his proud heart aggravated the affront, swelled with indignation, scorned to be baffled, longed to be revenged: and now all the plagues are as if they had never been. He has quite forgotten the sorrowful funerals of his firstborn, and can think of nothing but making Israel feel his resentments; now he thinks he can be too hard for God himself; for, otherwise, could he have hoped to conquer a people so dear to him? God gave him up to these passions of his own heart, and so hardened it. It is said (*v.* 8), The children of Israel went out with *a high hand,* that is, with a great deal of courage and bravery, triumphing in their release, and resolved to break through the difficulties that lay in their way. *But the Egyptians (v.* 9) pursued after them. Note, Those that in good earnest set their faces heaven-ward, and will live godly in Christ Jesus, must expect to be set upon by Satan's temptations and terrors. He will not tamely part with any out of his service, nor go out without raging, Mk. 9:26.

Verses 10–14

We have here, I. The fright that the children of Israel were in when they perceived that Pharaoh pursued them, *v.* 10. They knew very well the strength and rage of the enemy, and their own weakness; numerous indeed they were, but all on foot, unarmed, undisciplined, disquieted by long servitude, and (which was worst of all) now penned up by the situation of their camp, so that they could not make their escape. On the one hand was Pi-hahiroth, a range of craggy rocks impassable; on the other hand were Migdol and Baalzephon, which, some think were forts and garrisons upon the frontiers of Egypt; before them was the sea; behind them were the Egyptians: so that there was no way open for them but upwards, and thence their deliverance came. Note, We may be in the way of our duty, following God and hastening towards heaven, and yet may be in great straits, *troubled on every side,* 2 Co. 4:8. In this distress, no marvel that the children of Israel were sorely afraid; their father Jacob was so in a like case (Gen. 32:7); when without are fightings, it cannot be otherwise but that within are fears: what therefore was the fruit of this fear? According as that was, the fear was good or evil. 1. Some of them cried out unto the Lord; their fear set them a praying, and that was a good effect of it. God brings us into straits that he may bring us to our knees. 2. Others of them cried out against Moses; their fear set them a murmuring, *v.* 11, 12. They give up themselves for lost; and as if God's arm were shortened all of a sudden, and he were not as able to work miracles to-day as he was yesterday, they despair of deliverance, and can count upon nothing but *dying in the wilderness.* How inexcusable was their distrust! Did they not see themselves under the guidance and protection of a pillar from heaven? And can almighty power fail them, or infinite goodness be false to them? Yet this was not the worst; they quarrel with Moses for bringing them out of Egypt, and, in quarrelling with him, fly in the face of God himself, and provoke him to wrath whose favour was now the only succour they had to flee to. As the Egyptians were angry with themselves for the best deed they ever did, so the Israelites were angry with God for the greatest kindness that was ever done them; so gross are the absurdities of unbelief. They here express, (1.) A sordid contempt of liberty, preferring servitude before it, only because it was attended with some difficulties. A generous spirit would have said, "If the worst come to the worst," as we say, "It is better to die in the field of honour than to live in the chains of slavery;" nay, under God's conduct, they could not miscarry, and therefore they might say, "Better live God's freemen in the open air of a wilderness than the Egyptians' bondmen in the smoke of the brick-kilns." But because, for the present, they are a little embarrassed, they are angry that they were not left buried alive in their house of bondage. (2.) Base ingratitude to Moses, who had been the faithful instrument of their deliverance. They condemn him, as if he had dealt hardly and unkindly with them, whereas it was evident, beyond dispute, that whatever he did, and however it issued, it was by direction from their God, and with design for their good. What they had said in a former ferment (when they hearkened not to Moses for anguish of spirit), they repeat and justify in this: *We said in Egypt, Let us alone;* and it was ill-said, yet more excusable, because then they had not had so much experience as they had now of God's wonderful appearances in their favour. But they had as soon forgotten the miracles of mercy as the Egyptians had forgotten the miracles of wrath; and they, as well as the Egyptians, hardened their hearts, at last, to their own ruin; as Egypt after ten plagues, so Israel after ten provocations, of which this was the first (Num. 14:22), were sentenced to die in the wilderness.

II. The seasonable encouragement that Moses gave them in this distress, *v.* 13, 14. He answered not these fools according to their folly. God bore with the provocation they gave to him, and did not (as he might justly have done) chose their delusions, and bring their fears upon them; and therefore Moses might well afford to pass by the affront they put upon him. Instead of chiding them, he comforts them, and with an admirable presence and composure of mind, not disheartened either by the threatenings of Egypt or the tremblings of Israel, stills their murmuring, with the assurance of a speedy and complete deliverance: *Fear you not.* Note, It is our duty and interest, when we cannot get out of our troubles, yet to get above our fears, so that they may only serve to quicken our prayers and endeavours, but may not prevail to silence our faith and hope. 1. He assures them that God would deliver them, that he would undertake their deliverance, and that he would effect it in the utter ruin of their pursuers: *The Lord shall fight for you.* This Moses was confident of himself, and would have them to be so, though as yet he knew not how or which way it would be brought to pass. God had assured him that Pharaoh and his host should be ruined, and he comforts them with the same comforts wherewith he had been comforted. 2. He directs them to leave it to God, in a silent expectation of the event: "*Stand still,* and think not to save yourselves either by fighting or flying; wait God's orders, and observe them; be not contriving what course to take, but follow your leader; wait God's appearances, and take notice of them, that you may see how foolish you are to distrust them. Compose yourselves, by an entire confidence in God, into a peaceful prospect of the great salvation God is now about to work for you. Hold your peace; you need not so much as give a shout against the enemy, as Jos. 6:16. The work shall be done without any concurrence of yours." Note, (1.) If God himself bring his people into straits, he will himself discover a way to bring them out again. (2.) In times of great difficulty and great expectation, it is our wisdom to keep our spirits calm, quiet, and sedate; for then we are in the best frame both to do our own work and to *consider the work of God. Your strength is to sit still* (Isa. 30:7), *for the Egyptians shall help in vain,* and threaten to hurt in vain.

Verses 15–20

We have here,

I. Direction given to Israel's leader.

1. What he must do himself. He must, for the present, leave off praying, and apply himself to his business (*v.* 15): *Wherefore cryest thou unto me?* Moses, though he was assured of a good issue to the present distress, yet did not neglect prayer. We read not of one word he said in prayer, but he lifted up to God his heart, the language of which God well understood and took notice of. Moses's silent prayers of faith prevailed more with God than Israel's loud outcries of fear, *v.* 10. Note, (1.) Praying, if of the right kind, is *crying to God,* which denotes it to be the language both of a natural and of an importunate desire. (2.) To quicken his diligence. Moses had something else to do besides praying; he was to command the hosts of Israel, and it was now requisite that he should be at his post. *Every thing is beautiful in its season.*

2. What he must order Israel to do. *Speak to them, that they go forward.* Some think that Moses had prayed, not so much for their deliverance (he was assured of that) as for the pardon of heir murmurings, and that God's ordering them to go forward was an intimation of the pardon. There is no going forward with any comfort but in the sense of our reconciliation to God. Moses had bidden them stand still, and expect orders from God; and now orders are given. They thought they must have been directed either to the right hand or to the left. "No," says God, "speak to them to go forward, directly to the sea-side;" as if there had lain a fleet of transport-ships ready for them to embark in. Note, When we are in the way of our duty, though we met with difficulties, we must go forward, and not stand in mute astonishment; we must mind present work and then leave the even to God, use means and trust him with the issue.

3. What he might expect God to do. Let the children of Israel go as far as they can upon dry ground, and then God will divide the sea, and open a passage for them through it, *v.* 16–18. God designs, not only to deliver the Israelites, but to destroy the Egyptians; and the plan of his counsels is accordingly. (1.) He will show favour to Israel; the waters shall be divided for them to pass through, *v.* 16. The same power could have congealed the waters for them to pass over; but Infinite Wisdom chose rather to divide the waters for them to pass through; for that way of salvation is always pitched upon which is most humbling. Thus it is said, with reference to this (Isa. 63:13, 14), *He led them through the deep, as a beast goes down into the valley,* and thus *made himself a glorious name.* (2.) He will get him honour upon Pharaoh. If the due rent of honour be not paid to the great landlord, by and from whom we have and hold our beings and comforts, he will distrain for it, and recover it. God will be a loser by no man. In order to this, it is threatened: *I, behold I, will harden Pharaoh's heart, v.* 17. The manner of expression is observable: *I, behold I, will do it.* "I, that may do it;" so it is the language of his sovereignty. We may not contribute to the hardening of any man's heart, nor withhold any thing that we can do towards the softening of it; but God's grace is his own, *he hath mercy on whom he will have mercy, and whom he will be hardeneth.* "I, that can do it;" so it is the language of his power; none but the Almighty can make the heart soft (Job 23:16), nor can any other being make it hard. "I, that will do it;" for it is the language of his justice; it is a righteous thing with God to put those under the impressions of his wrath who have long resisted the influences of his grace. It is spoken in a way of triumph over this obstinate and presumptuous rebel: *"I even I,* will take an effectual course to humble him; he shall break that would not bend." It is an expression like that (Isa. 1:24), *Ah, I will ease me of my adversaries.*

II. A guard set upon Israel's camp where it now lay most exposed, which was *in the rear, v.* 19, 20. *The angel of God,* whose ministry was made use of in the pillar of cloud and fire, went from *before the camp of Israel,* where they did not now need a guide (there was no danger of missing their way through the sea, nor needed they any other word of command than to go forward), and it came behind them, where now they needed a guard (the Egyptians being just ready to seize the hindmost of them), and so was a wall of partition between them. There it was of use to the Israelites, not only to protect them, but to light them through the sea, and, at the same time, it confounded the Egyptians, so that they lost sight of their prey just when they were ready to lay hands on it. The word and providence of God have a black and dark side towards sin and sinners, but a bright and pleasant side towards those that are Israelites indeed. That which is a savour of life unto life to some is a savour of death unto death to others. This was not the first time that he who in the beginning divided between light and darkness (Gen. 1:4), and still forms both (Isa. 45:7), had, at the same time, allotted darkness to the Egyptians and light to the Israelites, a specimen of the endless distinction which will be made between the inheritance of the saints in light and that utter darkness which for ever will be the portion of hypocrites. God will separate between the precious and the vile.

Verses 21–31

We have here the history of that work of wonder which is so often mentioned both in the Old and New Testament, the dividing of the Red Sea before the children of Israel. It was the terror of the Canaanites (Jos. 2:9, 10), the praise and triumph of the Israelites, Ps. 114:3; 106:9; 136:13, 14. It was a type of baptism, 1 Co. 10:1, 2. Israel's passage through it was typical of the conversion of souls (Isa. 11:15), and the Egyptians' perdition in it was typical of the final ruin of all impenitent sinners, Rev. 20:14. Here we have,

I. An instance of God's almighty power in the kingdom of nature, in dividing the sea, and opening a passage through the waters. It was a bay, or gulf, or arm of the sea, two or three leagues over, which was divided, *v.* 21. The instituted sign made use of was Moses's stretching out his hand over it, to signify that it was done in answer to his prayer, for the confirmation of his mission, and in favour to the people whom he led. The natural sign was a strong east wind, signifying that it was done by the power of God, whom the winds and the seas obey. If there be any passage in the book of Job which has reference to the miracles wrought for Israel's deliverance out of Egypt, it is that in Job 26:12, *He divideth the sea with his power, and by his understanding he smileth through Rahab* (so the word is), that is, Egypt. Note, God can bring his people through the greatest difficulties, and force a way where he does not find it. The God of nature has not tied himself to its laws, but, when he pleases, dispenses with them, and then the fire does not burn, nor the water flow.

II. An instance of his wonderful favour to his Israel. They went through the sea to the opposite shore, for I cannot suppose, with some, that they fetched a compass, and came out again on the same side, *v.* 22. They *walked upon dry land in the midst of the sea, v.* 29. And the pillar of cloud, *that glory of the Lord,* being their *rearward* (Isa. 58:8), that the Egyptians might not charge them in the flank, the *waters were a wall to them* (it is twice mentioned) *on their right hand and on their left.* Moses and Aaron, it is probable, ventured first into this untrodden path, and then all Israel after them; and this march through the paths of the great waters would make their march afterwards, through the wilderness, less formidable. Those who had followed God through the sea needed not to fear following him whithersoever he led them. This march through the sea was in the night, and not a moon-shiny night, for it was seven days after the full moon, so that they had no light but what they had from the pillar of cloud and fire. This made it the more awful; but where God leads us he will light us; while we follow his conduct, we shall not want his comforts.

This was done, and recorded, in order to encourage God's people in all ages to trust in him in the greatest straits. What cannot he do who did this? What will not he do for those hat fear and love him who did this for these murmuring unbelieving Israelis, who yet were *beloved for their fathers' sake,* and for the sake of a remnant among them? We find the saints, long afterwards, making themselves sharers in the triumphs of this march (Ps. 66:6): *They went through the flood on foot; there did we rejoice in him:* and see how this work of wonder is improved, Ps. 77:11, 16, 19.

III. An instance of his just and righteous wrath upon his and his people's enemies, the Egyptians. Observe here, 1. How they were infatuated. In the heat of their pursuit, they went after the Israelites *into the midst of the sea, v.* 23. "Why," thought they, "may not we venture where Israel did?" Once or twice the magicians of Egypt had done what Moses did, with their enchantments; Pharaoh remembered this, but forgot how they were nonplussed at last. They were more advantageously provided with chariots and horses, while the Israelites were on foot. Pharaoh had said, *I know not the Lord;* and by this it appeared he did not, else he would not have ventured thus. None so bold as those that are blind. Rage against Israel made them thus daring and inconsiderate: they had long hardened their own hearts; and now God hardened them to their ruin, and hid from their eyes the things that belonged to their peace and safety. *Surely in vain is the net spread in the sight of any bird* (Prov. 1:17); yet so blind where the Egyptians that they *hastened to the snare,* Prov. 7:23. Note, The ruin of sinners is brought on by their own presumption, which hurries them headlong into the pit. They are self-destroyers. 2. How they were troubled and perplexed, *v.* 24, 25. For some hours they marched through the divided waters as safely and triumphantly as Israel did, not doubting but, that, in a little time, they should gain their point. But, *in the morning watch, the Lord looked upon the host of the Egyptians, and troubled them.* Something or other they saw or heard from the pillar of cloud and fire which put them into great consternation, and gave them an apprehension of their ruin before it was brought upon them. Now it appeared that the *triumphing of the wicked is short,* and that God has ways to frighten sinners into despair, before he plunges them into destruction. *He cuts off the spirit of princes, and is terrible to the kings of the earth.* (1.) They had hectored and boasted as if the day were their own; but now they were troubled and dismayed, struck with a panic-fear. (2.) They had driven furiously; but now they drove heavily, and found themselves plugged and embarrassed at every step; the way grew deep, their hearts grew sad, their wheels dropped off, and the axle-trees failed. Thus can God check the violence of those that are in pursuit of his people. (3.) They had been flying upon the back of Israel, as the hawk upon the trembling dove; but now they cried, *Let us flee from the face of Israel,* which had become to them *like a torch of fire in a sheaf,* Zec. 12:6. Israel has now, all of a sudden, become as much a terror to them as they had been to Israel. They might have let Israel alone and would not; now they would flee from the face of Israel and cannot. Men will not be convinced, till it is too late, that those who meddle with God's people meddle to their own hurt; when the Lord shall come with ten thousands of his saints, to execute judgment, the mighty men will in vain seek to shelter themselves under rocks and mountains *from the face of Israel* and Israel's King, Rev. 6:15. Compare with this story, Job 27:20, etc. 3. How they were all drowned. As soon as ever the children of Israel had got safely to the shore, Moses was ordered to *stretch out his hand over the sea,* and thereby give a signal to the waters to close again, as before, upon he word of command, they had *opened to the right and the left, v.* 29. He did so, and immediately the waters returned to their place, and overwhelmed all the host of the Egyptians, *v.* 27, 28. Pharaoh and his servants, who had hardened one another in sin, now fell together, and not one escaped. An ancient tradition says that Pharaoh's magicians, Jannes and Jambres, perished with the rest, as Balaam with the Midianites whom he had seduced, Num. 31:8. And now, (1.) God avenged upon the Egyptians the blood of the firstborn whom they had drowned: and the principal is repaid with interest, it is recompensed double, full-grown Egyptians for newborn Israelites; thus the Lord is righteous, and precious is his people's blood in his sight, Ps. 72:14. (2.) God reckoned with Pharaoh for all his proud and insolent conduct towards Moses his ambassador. Mocking the messengers of the Lord, and playing the fool with them, bring ruin without remedy. Now God *got him honour upon Pharaoh,* looking upon that proud man, and abasing him, Job. 40:12. Come and see the desolations he made, and write it, not in water, but with an iron pen in the rock for ever. Here lies that bloody tyrant who bade defiance to his Maker, to his demands, threatenings, and judgments; a rebel to God, and a slave to his own barbarous passions; perfectly lost to humanity, virtue, and all true honour; here he lies, buried in the deep, a perpetual monument of divine justice. Here he went down to the pit, though he was the terror of the mighty in the land of the living. This is Pharaoh and all his multitude, Eze. 31:18.

IV. Here is the notice which the Israelites took of this

wonderful work which God wrought for them, and the good impressions which it made upon them for the present.

1. They saw the Egyptians dead upon the sands, *v.* 30. Providence so ordered it that the next tide threw up the dead bodies, (1.) For the greater disgrace of the Egyptians. Now the beasts and birds of prey were called to *eat the flesh of the captains and mighty men,* Rev. 19:17, 18. The Egyptians were very nice and curious in embalming and preserving the bodies of their great men, but here the utmost contempt is poured upon all the grandees of Egypt; see how they lie, heaps upon heaps, as dung upon the face of the earth. (2.) For the greater triumph of the Israelites, and to affect them the more with their deliverance; for the eye affects the heart. See Isa. 66:24, *They shall go forth, and look upon the carcases of the men that have transgressed against me.* Probably they stripped the slain and, having borrowed jewels of their neighbours before, which (the Egyptians having by this hostile pursuit of them broken their faith with them) henceforward they were not under any obligation to restore, they now got arms from them, which, some think, they were not before provided with. Thus, when God broke the heads of Leviathan in pieces, *he gave him to be meat to the people inhabiting the wilderness,* Ps. 74:14.

2. The sight of this great work greatly affected them, and now they *feared the Lord, and believed the Lord, and his servant Moses, v.* 31. Now they were ashamed of their distrusts and murmurings, and, in the good mind they were in, they would never again despair of help from Heaven, no, not in the greatest straits; they would never again quarrel with Moses, nor talk of returning to Egypt. They were now baptized unto Moses in the sea, 1 Co. 10:2. This great work which God wrought for them by the ministry of Moses bound them effectually to follow his directions, under God. This confirmed their faith in the promises that were yet to be fulfilled; and, being brought thus triumphantly out of Egypt, they did not doubt that they should be in Canaan shortly, having such a God to trust to, and such a mediator between them and him. O that there had been such a heart in them as now there seemed to be! Sensible mercies, when they are fresh, make sensible impressions; but with many these impressions soon wear off: while they see God's works, and feel the benefit of them, they fear him and trust in him; but they soon forget his works, and then they slight him. How well were it for us if we were always in as good a frame as we are in sometimes!

CHAPTER 15

In this chapter, I. Israel looks back upon Egypt with a song of praise for their deliverance. Here is, 1. The song itself (*v.* 1–19). 2. The solemn singing of it (*v.* 20, 21). II. Israel marches forward in the wilderness (*v.* 22), and there, 1. Their discontent at the waters of Marah (*v.* 23, 24), and the relief granted them (*v.* 25, 26). 2. Their satisfaction in the waters of Elim (*v.* 27).

Verses 1–21

Having read how that complete victory of Israel over the Egyptians was obtained, here we are told how it was celebrated; those that were to hold their peace while the deliverance was in working (*ch.* 14:14) must not hold their peace now that it was wrought; the less they had to do then the more they had to do now. If God accomplishes deliverance by his own immediate power, it redounds so much the more to his glory. Moses, no doubt by divine inspiration, indited this song, and delivered it to the children of Israel, to be sung before they stirred from the place where they saw the Egyptians dead upon the shore. Observe, 1. They expressed their joy in God, and thankfulness to him, by singing; it is almost natural to us thus to give vent to our joy and the exultations of our spirit. By this instance it appears that the singing of psalms, as an act of religious worship, was used in the church of Christ before the giving of the ceremonial law, and therefore was no part of it, nor abolished with it. Singing is as much the language of holy joy as praying is of holy desire. 2. Moses, who had gone before them through the sea, goes before them in the song, and composes it for them. Note, Those that are active in public services should not be neuters in public praises. 3. When the mercy was fresh, and they were much affected with it, then they sang this song. Note, When we have received special mercy from God, we ought to be quick and speedy in our returns of praise to him, before time and the deceitfulness of our own hearts efface the good impressions that have been made. David sang his triumphant song in the day that the Lord delivered him, 2 Sa. 22:1. *Bis dat qui cito dat — He gives twice who gives quickly.* 4. When they *believed the Lord* (*ch.* 14:31) then they sang this song: it was a song of faith; this connection is observed (Ps. 106:12): *Then believed they his words, they sang his praise.* If with the heart man believes, thus confession must be made. Here is,

I. The song itself; and,

1. We may observe respecting this song, that it is, (1.) An ancient song, the most ancient that we know of. (2.) A most admirable composition, the style lofty and magnificent, the images lively and proper, and the whole very moving. (3.) It is a holy song, consecrated to the honour of God, and intended to exalt his name and celebrate his praise, and his only, not in the least to magnify any man: holiness to the Lord is engraven in it, and to him they made melody in the singing of it. (4.) It is a typical song. The triumphs of the gospel church, in the downfall of its enemies, are expressed in the song of Moses and the song of the Lamb put together, which are said to be sung upon a sea of glass, as this was upon the Red Sea, Rev. 15:2, 3.

2. Let us observe what Moses chiefly aims at in this song.

(1.) He gives glory to God, and triumphs in him; this is first in his intention (*v.* 1): *I will sing unto the Lord.* Note, All our joy must terminate in God, and all our praises be offered up to him, the Father of lights and Father of mercies, *for he hath triumphed.* Note, All that love God triumph in his triumphs; what is his honour should be our joy. Israel rejoiced in God, [1.] As their own God, and therefore their *strength, song,* and *salvation, v.* 2. Happy therefore the people whose God is the Lord; they need no more to make them happy. They have work to do, temptations to grapple with, and afflictions to bear, and are weak in themselves; but he strengthens them: his grace is their strength. They are often in sorrow, upon many accounts, but in him they have comfort, he is *their song;* sin, and death, and hell, threaten them, but he is, and will be, *their salvation:* See Isa. 12:2. [2.] *As their fathers' God.* This they take notice of, because, being conscious to themselves of their own unworthiness and provocations, they had reason to think that what God had now done for them was for their *fathers' sake,* Deu. 4:37. Note, The children of the covenant ought to improve their fathers' relation to God as their God for comfort, for caution, and for quickening. [3.] As a God of infinite power (*v.* 3): *The Lord is a man of war,* that is, well able to deal with all those that strive with their Maker, and will certainly be too hard for them. [4.] As a God of matchless and incomparable perfection, *v.* 11. This is expressed, *First,* More generally: *Who is like unto thee, O Lord, among the gods!* This is pure praise, and a high expression of humble adoration. — It is a challenge to all other gods to compare with him: "Let them stand forth, and pretend their utmost; none of them dare make the comparison." Egypt was notorious for the multitude of its gods, but the *God of the Hebrews* was too hard for them and baffled them all, Num. 38:4; Deu. 32:23–39. The princes and potentates of the world are called *gods,* but they are feeble and mortal, none of them all comparable to Jehovah, the almighty and eternal God. — It is confession of his infinite perfection, as transcendent and unparalleled. Note, God is to be worshipped and adored as a being of such infinite perfection that there is none like him, nor any to be compared with him, as one that in all things has and must have the pre-eminence, Ps. 89:6. *Secondly,* More particularly, 1. *He is glorious in holiness;* his holiness is his glory. It is that attribute which angels adore, Isa. 6:3. His holiness appeared in the destruction of Pharaoh, his hatred of sin, and his wrath against obstinate sinners. It appeared in the deliverance of Israel, his delight in the holy seed, and his faithfulness to his own promise. God is *rich in mercy* — this is his treasure, *glorious in holiness* — this is his honour. Let us always give thanks at the remembrance of his holiness. 2. *He is fearful in praises.* That which is the matter of our praise, though it is joyful to the servants of God, is dreadful and very terrible to his enemies, Ps. 66:1–3. Or it directs us in the manner of our praising God; we should praise him with a humble holy awe, and *serve the Lord with fear.* Even our spiritual joy and triumph must be balanced with a religious fear. 3. He is *doing wonders,* wondrous to all, being above the power and out of the common course of nature; especially wondrous to us, in whose favour they are wrought, who are so unworthy that we had little reason to expect them. They were wonders of power and wonders of grace; in both God was to be humbly adored.

(2.) He describes the deliverance they were now triumphing in, because the song was intended, not only to express and excite their thankfulness for the present, but to preserve and perpetuate the remembrance of this work of wonder to after-ages. Two things were to be taken notice of: —

[1.] The destruction of the enemy; the waters were divided, *v.* 8. *The floods stood upright as a heap.* Pharaoh and all his hosts were buried in the waters. *The horse and his rider* could not escape (*v.* 1), the *chariots,* and the *chosen captains* (*v.* 4); they themselves went into the sea, and they were overwhelmed, *v.* 19. *The depths, the sea, covered them,* and the proud waters went over the proud sinners; they *sank like a stone, like lead* (*v.* 5, 10), under the weight of their own guilt and God's wrath. Their sin had made them hard like a stone, and now they justly sink like a stone. Nay, *the earth itself swallowed them* (*v.* 12); their dead bodies sank into the sands upon which they were thrown up, which sucked them in. Those whom the Creator fights against the whole creation is at war with. All this was the Lord's doing, and his only. It was an act of his power: *Thy right hand, O Lord,* not ours, *has dashed in pieces the enemy, v.* 6. It was with *the blast of thy nostrils* (*v.* 8), and *thy wind* (*v.* 10), and the *stretching out of thy right hand, v.* 12. It was an instance of his transcendent power — in *the greatness of thy excellency;* and it was the execution of his justice: *Thou sentest forth thy wrath, v.* 7. This destruction of the Egyptians was made the more remarkable by their pride and insolence, and their strange assurance of success: *The enemy said, I will pursue, v.* 9. Here is, *First,* Great confidence. When they pursue, they do not question but they shall overtake; and, when they overtake, they do not question but they shall overcome, and obtain so decisive a victory as to *divide the spoil.* Note, It is common for men to be most elevated with the hope of success when they are upon the brink of ruin, which makes their ruin so much the sorer. See Isa. 37:24, 25. *Secondly,* Great cruelty — nothing but killing, and slaying, and destroying, and this will satisfy his lust; and a barbarous lust that is which so much blood must be the satisfaction of. Note, It is a cruel hatred with which the church is hated; its enemies are bloody men. This is taken notice of here to show, 1. That God resists the proud, and delights to humble those who lift up themselves; he that says, "I will, and I will, whether God will or no," shall be made to know that wherein he deals proudly God is above him. 2. That those who thirst for blood shall have enough of it. Those who love to be destroying shall be destroyed; for we know who has said, *Vengeance is mine, I will repay.*

[2.] The protection and guidance of Israel (*v.* 13): *Thou in thy mercy hast led forth the people,* led them forth out of the bondage Egypt, led them forth out of the perils of the Red Sea, *v.* 19. *But the children of Israel went on dry land.* Note, The destruction of the wicked serves for a foil to set off the salvation of Israel, and to make it the more illustrious, Isa. 45:13–15.

(3.) He sets himself to improve this wonderful appearance of God for them. [1.] In order to quicken them to serve God: in consideration of this, *I will prepare him habitation, v.* 2. God having preserved them, and prepared a covert for them under which they had been safe and easy, they resolve to spare no cost nor pains for the erecting of a tabernacle to his honour, and there they will exalt him, and mention, to his praise, the honour he had got upon Pharaoh. God had now exalted them, making them great and high, and therefore they will exalt him, by speaking of his infinite height and grandeur. Note, Our constant endeavour should be, by praising his name and serving his interests, to exalt God; and it is an advancement to us to be so employed. [2.] In order to encourage them to trust in God. So confident is this Psalmist of the happy issue of the salvation which was so gloriously begun that he looks upon it as in effect finished already: *"Thou hast guided them to thy holy habitation, v.* 13. Thou hast thus put them into the way to it, and wilt in due time bring them to the end of that way," for God's work is perfect; or, *"Thou hast guided them* to attend thy holy habitation in heaven with their praises." Note, Those whom God takes under his direction he will guide to his holy habitation in faith now, and in fruition shortly. Two ways this great deliverance was encouraging: — *First,* It was such an instance of God's power as would terrify their enemies, and quite dishearten them, *v.* 14–16. The very report of the overthrow of the Egyptians would be more than half the over throw of all their other enemies; it would sink their spirits, which would go far towards the sinking of their powers and interests; he Philistines, Moabites, Edomites, and Canaanites (with each of which nations Israel was to grapple), would be alarmed by it, would be quite dispirited, and would conclude it was in vain to fight against Israel, when a God of such power fought for them. It had this effect; the Edomites were afraid of them (Deu. 2:4), so were the Moabites (Num. 22:3), and the Canaanites, Jos. 2:9, 10; *v.* 1. Thus God sent his fear before them (*ch.* 23:27), and cut off the spirit of princes. *Secondly,* It was such a beginning of God's favour to them as gave them an earnest of he perfection of his kindness. This was but in order to something further: *Thou shalt bring them in, v.* 17. If he thus *bring them out of Egypt,* notwithstanding their unworthiness, and the difficulties that lay in the way of their escape, doubtless he will bring them into Canaan; for has he begun (*so* begun), and will he not make an end? Note, Our experiences of God's power and favour should be improved for the support of our expectations. "Thou *hast,* therefore, not only thou *canst,* but we trust thou *wilt,*" is good arguing. *Thou wilt plant them in the place which thou has made for thee to dwell in.* Note, It is good dwelling where God dwells, in his church on earth (Ps. 27:4), in his church in heaven, Jn. 17:24. Where he says, "This is my rest for ever," we should say, "Let it be ours." *Lastly,* The great ground of the encouragement which they draw from this work of wonder is, *The Lord shall reign for ever and ever, v.* 18. They had now seen an end of Pharaoh's reign; but time itself shall not put a period to Jehovah's reign, which, like himself, is eternal, and not subject to change. Note, It is the unspeakable comfort of all God's faithful subjects, not only that he does reign universally and with an incontestable sovereignty, but that he will reign eternally, and there shall be no end of his dominion.

II. The solemn singing of this song, *v.* 20, 21. Miriam (or Mary, it is the same name) presided in an assembly of the women, who (according to the softness of their sex, and the common usage of those times for expressing joy, with timbrels and dances) sang this song. Moses led the psalm, and gave it out for the men, and then Miriam for the women. Famous victories were wont to be applauded by the daughters of Israel (1 Sa. 18:6, 7); so was this. When God brought Israel out of Egypt, it is said (Micah 6:4), *He sent before them Moses, Aaron, and Miriam,* though we read not of any thing memorable that Miriam did but this. But those are to be reckoned great blessings to a people who assist them, and go before them, in praising God.

Verses 22–27

It should seem, it was with some difficulty that Moses prevailed with Israel to leave that triumphant shore on which they sang the foregoing song. They were so taken up with the sight, or with the song, or with the spoiling of the dead bodies, that they cared not to go forward, but Moses with much ado brought them from the Red Sea into a wilderness. The pleasures of our way to Canaan must not retard our progress, but quicken it, though we have a wilderness before us. Now here we are told,

I. That in the wilderness of Shur they had no water, *v.* 22. This was a sore trial to the young travellers, and a diminution to their joy; thus God would train them up to difficulties. David, in a dry and thirsty land where no water is, reaches forth towards God, Ps. 63:1.

II. That at Marah they had water, but it was bitter, so that though they had been three days without water they could not drink it, because it was extremely unpleasant to the taste or was likely to be prejudicial to their health, or was so brackish that it rather increased their thirst than quenched it, *v.* 23. Note, God can embitter that to us from which we promise ourselves most satisfaction, and often does so in the wilderness of this world, that our wants and disappointments in the creature may drive us to the Creator, in whose favour alone true comfort is to be had. Now in this distress, 1. The people fretted and quarrelled with Moses, as if he had done ill by them. *What shall we drink?* is all their clamour, *v.* 24. Note, The greatest joys and hopes are soon turned into the greatest griefs and fears with those that live by sense only, and not by faith. 2. Moses prayed: *He cried unto the Lord, v.* 25. The complaints which they brought to him he brought to God, on whom, notwithstanding his elevation, Moses owned a constant dependence. Note, It is the greatest relief of the cares of magistrates and ministers, when those under their charge make them uneasy, that they may have recourse to God by prayer: he is the guide of the church's guides and to him, as the Chief Shepherd, the under-shepherds must upon all occasions apply. 3. God provided graciously for them. He directed Moses to a tree, which he cast into the waters, in consequence of which, all of a sudden, they were made sweet. Some think this wood had a peculiar virtue in it for this purpose, because it is said, *God showed him the tree.* God is to be acknowledged, not only in the creating of things useful for man, but in discovering their usefulness. Or perhaps this was only a sign, and not at all a means, of the cure, any more than the brazen serpent, or Elisha's casting one cruse full of salt into the waters of Jericho. Some make this tree typical of the cross of Christ, which sweetens the bitter waters of affliction to all the faithful, and enables them to rejoice in tribulation. The Jews' tradition is that the wood of this tree was itself bitter, yet it sweetened the waters of Marah; the bitterness of Christ's sufferings and death alters the property of ours. 4. Upon this occasion, God came upon terms with them, and plainly told them, now that they had got clear of the Egyptians, and had entered into the wilderness, that they were upon their good behaviour, and that according as they carried themselves so it would be well or ill with them: *There he made a statute and an ordinance,* and settled matters with them. *There he proved them,* that is, there he put them upon the trial, admitted them as probationers for his favour. In short, he tells them, *v.* 26, (1.) What he expected from them, and that was, in one word, obedience. They must diligently *hearken to his voice, and give ear to his commandments,* that they might know their duty, and not transgress through ignorance; and they must take care in every thing to do that which was right in God's sight, and to *keep all his statutes.* They must not think, now that they were delivered from their bondage in Egypt, that they had no lord over them, but were their own masters; no, therefore they must look upon themselves as God's servants, because he had *loosed their bonds,* Ps. 116:16; Lu. 1:74, 75. (2.) What they might then expect from him: *I will put none of these diseases upon thee,* that is, "I will not bring upon thee any of the plagues of Egypt." This intimates that, if they were rebellious and disobedient, the very plagues which they had seen inflicted upon their enemies should be brought upon them; so it is threatened, Deu. 28:60. God's judgments upon Egypt, as they were mercies to Israel, opening the way to their deliverance, so they were warnings to Israel, and designed to awe them into obedience. Let not the Israelites think, because God had thus highly honoured them in the great things he had done for them, and had proclaimed them to all the world his favourites, that therefore he would connive at their sins and let them do as they would. No, God is no respecter of persons; a rebellious Israelite shall fare no better than a rebellious Egyptian; and so they found, to their cost, before the got to Canaan. "But, if thou wilt be obedient, thou shalt be safe and happy;" the threatening is implied only, but the promise is expressed: *"I am the Lord that healeth thee,* and will take care of thy comfort wherever thou goest." Note, God is the great physician. If we be kept well, it is he that keeps us; if we be made well, it is he that restores us; he is our life, and the length of our days.

III. That at Elim they had good water, and enough of it, *v.* 27. Though God may, for a time, order his people to encamp by the waters of Marah, yet that shall not always be their lot. See how changeable our condition is in this world, from better to worse, from worse to better. Let us therefore learn both how to be abased and how to abound, to rejoice as though we rejoiced not when we are full, and to weep as though we wept not when we are emptied. Here were twelve wells for their supply, one for every tribe, that they might not strive for water, as their fathers had sometimes done; and, for their pleasure, there were seventy palm-trees, under the shadow of which their great men might repose themselves. Note, God can find places of refreshment for his people even in the wilderness of this world, wells in the valley of Baca, lest they should faint in their mind with perpetual fatigue: yet, whatever our delights may be in the land of our pilgrimage, we must remember that we do but encamp by them for a time, that here we have no continuing city.

CHAPTER 16

This chapter gives us an account of the victualling of the camp of Israel. I. Their complaint for want of bread (*v.* 1–3). II. The notice God gave them beforehand of the provision he intended to make for them (*v.* 4–12). III. The sending of the manna (*v.* 13–15). IV. The laws and orders concerning the manna. 1. That they should gather it daily for their daily bread (*v.* 16–21). 2. That they should gather a double portion on the sixth day (*v.* 22–26). 3. That they should expect none on the seventh day (*v.* 27–31). 4. That they should preserve a pot of it for a memorial (*v.* 32, etc.).

Verses 1–12

The host of Israel, it seems, took along with them out of Egypt, when they came thence on the fifteenth day of the first month, a month's provisions, which, by the fifteenth day of the second month, was all spent; and here we have,

I. Their discontent and murmuring upon that occasion, *v.* 2, 3. The whole congregation, the greatest part of them, joined in this mutiny; it was not immediately against God that they murmured, but (which was equivalent) against Moses and Aaron, God's vicegerents among them. 1. They count upon being killed in the wilderness — nothing less, at the first appearance of disaster. If the Lord had been pleased to kill them, he could easily have done that in the Red Sea; but then he preserved them, and now could as easily provide for them. It argues great distrust of God, and of his power and goodness, in every distress and appearance of danger to despair of life, and to talk of nothing but being speedily killed. 2. They invidiously charge Moses with a design to starve them when he brought them out of Egypt; whereas what he had done was both by order from God and with a design to promote their welfare. Note, It is no new thing for the greatest kindnesses to be misinterpreted and basely represented as the greatest injuries. The worst colours are sometimes put upon the best actions. Nay, 3. They so far undervalue their deliverance that they wish they had died in Egypt, nay, and died by the hand of the Lord too, that is, by some of the plagues which cut off the Egyptians, as if it were not the hand of the Lord, but of Moses only, that brought them into this hungry wilderness. It is common for people to say of that pain, or sickness, or sore, of which they see not the second causes, "It is what pleases God," as if that were not so likewise which comes by the hand of man, or some visible accident. Prodigious madness! They would rather die by the fleshpots of Egypt, where they found themselves with provision, than live under the guidance of the heavenly pillar in a wilderness and be provided for by the hand of God! they pronounce it better to have fallen in the destruction of God's enemies than to bear the fatherly discipline of his children! We cannot suppose that they had any great plenty in Egypt, how largely soever they now talk of the flesh-pots; nor could they fear dying for want in the wilderness, while they had their flocks and herds with them. But discontent magnifies what is past, and vilifies what is present, without regard to truth or reason. None talk more absurdly than murmurers. Their impatience, ingratitude, and distrust of God, were so much the worse in that they had lately received such miraculous favours, and convincing proofs both that God could help them in the greatest exigencies and that really he had mercy in store for them. See how *soon they forgot his works, and provoked him at the sea, even at the Red Sea,* Ps. 106:7–13. Note, Experiences of God's mercies greatly aggravate our distrusts and murmurings.

II. The care God graciously took for their supply. Justly he might have said, "I will rain fire and brimstone upon these murmurers, and consume them;" but, quite contrary, he promises to rain bread upon them. Observe,

1. How God makes known to Moses his kind intentions, that he might not be uneasy at their murmurings, nor be tempted to wish he had let them alone in Egypt. (1.) He takes notice of the people's complaints: *I have heard the murmurings of the children of Israel, v.* 12. As a God of pity, he took cognizance of their necessity, which was the

occasion of their murmuring; as a just and holy God, he took cognizance of their base and unworthy reflections upon his servant Moses, and was much displeased with them. Note, When we begin to fret and be uneasy, we ought to consider that God hears all our murmurings, though silent, and only the murmurings of the heart. Princes, parents, masters, do not hear all the murmurs of their inferiors against them, and it is well they do not, for perhaps they could not bear it; but God hears, and yet bears. We must not think, because God does not immediately take vengeance on men for their sins, that therefore he does not take notice of them; no, he hears the murmurings of Israel, and is grieved with this generation, and yet continues his care of them, as the tender parent of the froward child. (2.) He promises them a speedy, sufficient, and constant supply, *v.* 4. Man being made out of the earth, his Maker has wisely ordered him food out of the earth, Ps. 104:14. But the people of Israel, typifying the church of the first-born that are written in heaven, and born from above, and being themselves immediately under the direction and government of heaven, receiving their charters, laws, and commissions, from heaven, from heaven also received their food: their law being given by the disposition of angels, they did also eat angels' food. See what God designed in making this provision for them: *That I may prove them, whether they will walk in my law or no.* [1.] Thus he tried whether they would trust him, and walk in the law of faith or no, whether they could live from hand to mouth, and (though now uneasy because their provisions were spent) could rest satisfied with the bread of the day in its day, and depend upon God for fresh supplies to-morrow. [2.] Thus he tried whether they would serve him, and be always faithful to so good a Master, that provided so well for his servants; and hereby he made it appear to all the world, in the issue, what an ungrateful people they were, whom nothing could affect with a sense of obligation. Let *favour be shown* to them, yet *will they not learn righteousness,* Isa. 26:10.

2. How Moses made known these intentions to Israel, as God ordered him. Here Aaron was his prophet, as he had been to Pharaoh. Moses directed Aaron what to *speak to the congregation of Israel* (*v.* 9); and some think that, while Aaron was giving a public summons to the congregation to *come near before the Lord,* Moses retired to pray, and that the appearance of the glory of the Lord (*v.* 10) was in answer to his prayer. They are called to come near, as Isa. 1:18, *Come, and let us reason together.* Note, God condescends to give even murmurers a fair hearing; and shall we then despise the cause of our inferiors when they contend with us? Job 31:13. (1.) He convinces them of the evil of their murmurings. They thought they reflected only upon Moses and Aaron, but here they are told that God was struck at through their sides. This is much insisted on (*v.* 7, 8): "*Your murmurings are not against us,* then we would have been silent, but *against the Lord;* it was he that led you into these straits, and not we." Note, When we murmur against those who are instruments of any uneasiness to us, whether justly or unjustly, we should do well to consider how much we reflect upon God by it; men are but God's hand. Those that quarrel with the reproofs and convictions of the word, and are angry with their ministers when they are touched in a tender part, know not what they do, for therein they strive with their Maker. Let this for ever stop the mouth of murmuring, that it is daring impiety to murmur at God, because he is God; and gross absurdity to murmur at men, because they are but men. (2.) He assures them of the supply of their wants, that since they had harped upon the flesh-pots so much they should for once have flesh in abundance that evening, and bread the next morning, and so on every day thenceforward, *v.* 8, 12. Many there are of whom we say that they are better fed than taught; but the Israelites were thus fed, that they might be taught. *He led him about, he instructed him* (Deu. 32:10); and, as to this instance, see Deu. 8:3, *He fed thee with manna, that thou mightest know that man doth not live by bread only.* And, besides this, here are two things mentioned, which he intended to teach them by sending them manna: — [1.] *By this you shall know that the Lord* [illegible]*ath brought you out from the land of Egypt, v.* 6. That [illegible] were brought out of Egypt was plain enough; but so [illegible]ely sottish and short-sighted were they that they said [illegible] Moses that brought them out, *v.* 3. Now God sent them manna, to prove that it was no less than infinite power and goodness that brought them out, and this could perfect what was begun. If Moses only had brought them out of Egypt, he could not thus have fed them; they must therefore own that that was the Lord's doing, because this was so, and both were marvellous in their eyes; yet, long afterwards, they needed to be told that *Moses gave them not this bread from heaven,* Jn. 6:32. [2.] *By this you shall know that I am the Lord your God, v.* 12. This gave proof of his power as the Lord, and his particular favour to them as their God. When God plagued the Egyptians, it was to make them know that he was the Lord; when he provided for the Israelites, it was to make them know that he was their God.

3. How God himself manifested his glory, to still the murmurings of the people, and to put a reputation upon Moses and Aaron, *v.* 10. While Aaron was speaking, *the glory of the Lord appeared in the cloud.* The cloud itself, one would think, was enough both to strike an awe upon them and to give encouragement to them; yet, in a few days, it had grown so familiar to them that it made no impression upon them, unless it shone with an unusual brightness. Note, What God's ministers say to us is then likely to do us good when the glory of God shines in with it upon our souls.

Verses 13–21

Now they begin to be provided for by the immediate hand of God.

I. He makes them a feast, at night, of delicate fowl, *feathered fowl* (Ps. 78:27), therefore not *locusts,* as some think; quails, or pheasants, or some wild fowl, came up, and covered the camp, so tame that they might take up as many of them as they pleased. Note, God gives us of the good things of this life, not only for necessity, but for delight, that we may not only serve him, but serve him cheerfully.

II. Next morning he rained manna upon them, which was to be continued to them for their daily bread. 1. That which was provided for them was manna, which descended from the clouds, so that, in some sense, they might be said to live upon the air. It came down in dew that melted, and yet was itself of such a consistency as to serve for nourishing strengthening food, without any thing else. They called it *manna, manhu,* "What is this?" Either, "What a poor thing this is!" despising it: or, "What a strange thing this is!" admiring it: or, "It is a portion, no matter what it is; it is that which our God has allotted us, and we will take it and be thankful," *v.* 14, 15. It was pleasant food; the Jews say that it was palatable to all, however varied their tastes. It was wholesome food, light of digestion, and very necessary (Dr. Grew says) to cleanse them from disorders with which he thinks it probable that they were, in the time of their bondage, more or less infected, which disorders a luxurious diet would have made contagious. By this spare and plain diet we are all taught a lesson of temperance, and forbidden to desire dainties and varieties. 2. They were to gather it every morning (*v.* 21), *the portion of a day in his day, v.* 4. Thus they must live upon daily providence, as the fowls of the air, of which it is said, *That which thou givest them they gather* (Ps. 104:28); not to-day for to-morrow: *let the morrow take thought for the things of itself.* To this daily raining and gathering of manna our Saviour seems to allude when he teaches us to pray, *Give us this day our daily bread.* We are hereby taught, (1.) Prudence and diligence in providing food convenient for ourselves and our household. What God graciously gives we must industriously gather; with quietness working, and eating our own bread, not the bread either of idleness or deceit. God's bounty leaves room for man's duty; it did so even when manna was rained: they must not eat till they have gathered. (2.) Contentment and satisfaction with a sufficiency. They must gather, *every man according to his eating;* enough is as good as a feast, and more than enough is as bad as a surfeit. Those that have most have, for themselves, but food, and raiment, and mirth; and those that have least generally have these: so that *he who gathers much has nothing over, and he who gathers little has no lack.* There is not so great a disproportion between one and another in the comforts and enjoyments of the things of this life as there is in the property and possession of the things themselves. (3.) Dependence upon Providence: *Let no man leave till morning* (*v.* 19), but let them learn to go to bed and sleep quietly, though they have not a bit of bread in their tent, nor in all their camp, trusting that God, with the following day, will bring them their daily bread." It was surer and safer in God's store-house than in their own, and would thence come to them sweeter and fresher. Read with this, Mt. 6:25, *Take no thought for your life,* etc. See here the folly of hoarding. The manna that was laid up by some (who thought themselves wiser and better managers than their neighbours, and who would provide in case it should fail next day), putrefied, and bred worms, and became good for nothing. Note, That proves to be most wasted which is covetously and distrustfully spared. Those riches are corrupted, James 5:2, 3. Let us set ourselves to think, [1.] Of that great power of God which fed Israel in the wilderness, and made miracles their daily bread. What cannot this God do, who prepared a table in the wilderness, and furnished it richly even for those who questioned whether he could or no? Ps. 78:19, 20. Never was there such a market of provisions as this, where so many hundred thousand men were daily furnished, without money and without price. Never was there such an open house kept as God kept in the wilderness for forty years together, nor such free and plentiful entertainment given. The feast which Ahasuerus made, to show the *riches of his kingdom,* and the *honour of his majesty,* was nothing to this, Est. 1:4. It is said (*v.* 21), *When the sun waxed hot, it melted;* as if what was left were drawn up by the heat of the sun into the air to be the seed of the next day's harvest, and so from day to day. [2.] Of that constant providence of God which *gives food to all flesh, for his mercy endures for ever,* Ps. 136:25. He is a great house-keeper that provides for all the creatures. The same wisdom, power, and goodness that now brought food daily out of the clouds, are employed in the constant course of nature, bringing food yearly out of the earth, and giving us all things richly to enjoy.

Verses 22–31

We have here, 1. A plain intimation of the observing of a *seventh day sabbath,* not only before the giving of the law upon Mount Sinai, but before the bringing of Israel out of Egypt, and therefore, *from the beginning,* Gen. 2:3. If the sabbath had now been first instituted, how could Moses have understood what God said to him (*v.* 5), concerning a double portion to be gathered on the sixth day, without making any express mention of the sabbath? And how could the people so readily take the hint (*v.* 22), even to the surprise of the rulers, before Moses had declared that it was done with a regard to the sabbath, if they had not had some knowledge of the sabbath before? The setting apart of one day in seven for holy work, and, in order to that, for holy rest, was a divine appointment ever since God created man upon the earth, and the most ancient of positive laws. The way of sabbath-sanctification is the good old way. 2. The double provision which God made for the Israelites, and which they were to make for themselves, on the sixth day: God gave them *on the sixth day the bread of two days, v.* 29. Appointing them to rest on the seventh day, he took care that they should be no losers by it; and none ever will be losers by serving God. On that day they were to fetch in enough for two days, and to prepare it, *v.* 23. The law was very strict, that they must bake and seeth, the day before, and not on the sabbath day. This does not now make it unlawful for us to dress meat on the Lord's day, but directs us to contrive our family affairs so that they may hinder us as little as possible in the work of the sabbath. Works of necessity, no doubt, are to be done on that day; but it is desirable to have as little as may be to do of things necessary to the life that now is, that we may apply ourselves the more closely to the one thing needful. That which they kept of for their food on the sabbath day did not putrefy, *v.* 24. When they kept it in opposition to a command (*v.* 20) it stank; when they kept it in obedience to a command it was sweet and good; for every thing is sanctified by the *word of God and prayer.* 3. The intermission of the manna on the seventh day. God did not send it then, and therefore they must not expect it, nor go out to gather, *v.* 25, 26. This showed that it was not produced by natural causes, and that it was designed for a confirmation of the divine authority of the law which was to be given by Moses.

Thus God took an effectual course to make them *remember the sabbath day;* they could not forget it, nor the day of preparation for it. Some, it seems, went out on the seventh day, expecting to find manna (*v.* 27); but they found none, for those that will find must seek in the appointed time: seek the Lord *while he may be found.* God, upon this occasion, said to Moses, *How long refuse you to keep my commandments? v.* 28. Why did he say this to Moses? He was not disobedient. No, but he was the ruler of a disobedient people, and God charges it upon him that he might the more warmly charge it upon them, and might take care that their disobedience should not be through any neglect or default of his. It was for going out to seek for manna on he seventh day that they were thus reproved. Note, (1.) Disobedience, even in a small matter, is very provoking. (2.) God is jealous for the honour of his sabbaths. If walking out on the sabbath to seek for food was thus reproved, walking out on that day purely to find our own pleasure cannot be justified.

Verses 32–36

God having provided manna to be his people's food in the wilderness, and to be to them a continual feast, we are here told, 1. How the memory of it was preserved. An omer of this manna was laid up in *a golden pot,* as we are told (Heb. 9:4), and kept *before the testimony,* or the ark, when it was afterwards made, *v.* 32–34. The preservation of this manna from waste and corruption was a standing miracle, and therefore the more proper memorial of this miraculous food. "Posterity shall *see the bread,*" says God, *"wherewith I have fed you in the wilderness,"* see what sort of food it was, and how much each man's daily proportion of it was, that it may appear they were neither kept to hard fare nor to short allowance, and then judge between God and Israel, whether they had any cause given them to murmur and find fault with their provisions, and whether they and their seed after them had not a great deal of reason gratefully to won God's goodness to them. Note, Eaten bread must not be forgotten. God's miracles and mercies are to be had in everlasting remembrance, for our encouragement to trust in him at all times. 2. How the mercy of it was continued as long as they had occasion for it. The manna never ceased till they came to the borders of Canaan, where there was bread enough and to spare, *v.* 35. See how constant the care of Providence is; seedtime and harvest fail not, while the earth remains. Israel was very provoking in the wilderness, yet the manna never failed them: thus still God causes his rain to fall on the just and unjust. The manna is called *spiritual meat* (1 Co. 10:3), because it was typical of spiritual blessings in heavenly things. Christ himself is the true manna, the bread of life, of which this was a figure, Jn. 6:49–51. The word of God is the manna by which our souls are nourished, Mt. 4:4. The comforts of the Spirit are hidden manna, Rev. 2:17. These come from heaven, as the manna did, and are the support and comfort of the divine life in the soul, while we are in the wilderness of this world. It is food for *Israelites,* for those only that follow the pillar of cloud and fire. It is to be *gathered;* Christ in the word is to be applied to the soul, and the means of grace are to be used. We must every one of us gather for ourselves, and gather in the morning of our opportunities, which if we let slip, it may be too late to gather. The manna they gathered must not be hoarded up, but eaten; those that have received Christ must by faith live upon him, and not receive his grace in vain. There was manna enough for all, enough for each, and none had too much; so in Christ there is a complete sufficiency, and no superfluity. But those that did eat manna hungered again, died at last, and with many of them God was not well-pleased; whereas those that feed on Christ by faith shall never hunger, and shall die no more, and with them God will be for ever well pleased. The Lord evermore give us this bread!

CHAPTER 17

Two passages of story are recorded in this chapter, I. The watering of the host of Israel. 1. In the wilderness they wanted water (*v.* 1). 2. In their want they chided Moses (*v.* 2, 3). 3. Moses cried to God (*v.* 4). 4. God ordered him to smite the rock, and fetch water out of that; Moses did so (*v.* 5, 6). 5. The place named from it (*v.* 7). II. The defeating of the host of Amalek. 1. The victory obtained by the prayer of Moses (*v.* 8–12). 2. By the sword of Joshua (*v.* 13). 3. A record kept of it (*v.* 14, 16). And these things which happened to them are written for our instruction in our spiritual journey and warfare.

Verses 1–7

Here is, I. The strait that the children of Israel were in for want of water; once before the were in the like distress, and now, a second time, *v.* 1. They journeyed *according to the commandment of the Lord,* led by the pillar of cloud and fire, and yet they came to a place where there was no water for them to drink. Note, We may be in the way of our duty, and yet may meet with troubles, which Providence brings us into for the trial of our faith, and that God may be glorified in our relief.

II. Their discontent and distrust in this strait. It is said (*v.* 3), They *thirsted there for water.* If they had no water to drink, they must needs thirst; but this intimates, not only that they wanted water and felt the inconvenience of that want, but that their passion sharpened their appetites and they were violent and impatient in their desire; their thirst made them outrageous. Natural desires, and those that are most craving, have need to be kept under the check and control of religion and reason. See what was the language of this inordinate desire. 1. They challenged Moses to supply them (*v.* 2): *Give us water, that we may drink,* demanding it as a debt, and strongly suspecting that he was not able to discharge it. Because they were supplied with bread, they insist upon it that they must be supplied with water too; and indeed to those that by faith and prayer live a life of dependence upon God one favour is an earnest of another, and may be humbly pleaded; but the unthankful and unbelieving have reason to think that the abuse of former favours is the forfeiture of further favours: *Let not them think that they shall receive any thing* (James 1:7), yet they are ready to demand every thing. 2. They quarrelled with him for bringing them out of Egypt, as if, instead of delivering them, he designed to murder them, than which nothing could be more base and invidious, *v.* 3. Many that have not only designed well, but done well, for their generation, have had their best services thus misconstrued, and their patience thereby tried, by unthinking unthankful people. To such a degree their malice against Moses rose that they were *almost ready to stone him, v.* 4. *Many good works he had shown them;* and for which of these would they stone him? Jn. 10:32. Ungoverned passions, provoked by the crossing of unbridled appetites, sometimes make men guilty of the greatest absurdities, and act like madmen, that cast firebrands, arrows, and death, among their best friends. 3. They began to question whether God were with them or not: They *tempted the Lord, saying, "Is the Lord among us or not? v.* 7. Is Jehovah among us by that name by which he made himself known to us in Egypt?" They question his essential presence — whether there was a God or not; his common providence — whether that God governed the world; and his special promise — whether he would be as good as his word to them. This is called their *tempting God,* which signifies, not only a distrust of God in general, but a distrust of him after they had received such proofs of his power and goodness, for the confirmation of his promise. They do, in effect, suppose that Moses was an impostor, Aaron a deceiver, the pillar of cloud and fire a mere sham and illusion, which imposed upon their senses, that long series of miracles which had rescued them, served them, and fed them, a chain of cheats, and the promise of Canaan a banter upon them; it was all so, if *the Lord was not among them.* Note, It is a great provocation to God for us to question his presence, providence, or promise, especially for his Israel to do it, who are so peculiarly bound to trust him.

III. The course that Moses took, when he was thus set upon, and insulted. 1. He reproved the murmurers (*v.* 2): *Why chide you with me?* Observe how mildly he answered them; it was well that he was a man of extraordinary meekness, else their tumultuous conduct would have made him lose the possession of himself: it is folly to answer passion with passion, for that makes bad worse; but *soft answers turn away wrath.* He showed them whom their murmurings reflected upon, and that the reproaches they cast on him fell on God himself: *You tempt the Lord;* that is, "By distrusting his power, you try his patience, and so provoke his wrath." 2. He made his complaint to God (*v.* 4): *Moses cried unto the Lord.* This servant came, and showed his Lord all these things, Lu. 14:21. When men unjustly censure us and quarrel with us, it will be a great relief to us to go to God, and by prayer lay the case before him and leave it with him: if men will not hear us, God will; if their bad conduct towards us ruffle our spirits, God's consolations will compose them. Moses begs of God to direct him what he should do, for he was utterly at a loss; he could not of himself either supply their want or pacify their tumult; God only could do it. He pleads his own peril: *"They are almost ready to stone me;* Lord, if thou hast any regard to the life of thy poor servant, interpose now."

IV. God's gracious appearance for their relief, *v.* 5, 6. He orders Moses to go on before the people, and venture himself in his post, though they spoke of stoning him. He must take his rod with him, not (as God might justly have ordered) to summon some plague or other to chastise them for their distrust and murmuring, but to fetch water for their supply. O the wonderful patience and forbearance of God towards provoking sinners! He loads those with benefits that make him to serve with their sins, maintains those that are at war with him, and reaches out the hand of his bounty to those that lift up the heel against him. Thus he teaches us, if our enemy hunger, to feed him, and if he thirst, as Israel did now, *to give him drink,* Rom. 12:20; Mt. 5:44, 45. Will he fail those that trust him, when he was so liberal even to those that tempted him? If God had only shown Moses a fountain of water in the wilderness, as he did Hagar not far hence (Gen. 21:19), that would have been a great favour; but that he might show his power as well as his pity, and make it a miracle of mercy, he gave them water out of a rock. He directed Moses whither to go, and appointed him to take some of the elders of Israel with him, to be witnesses of what was done, that they might themselves be satisfied, and might satisfy others, of the certainty of God's presence with them. He promised to meet him there in the cloud of glory (to encourage him), and ordered him to smite the rock; Moses obeyed, and immediately water came out of the rock in great abundance, which ran throughout the camp in streams and rivers (Ps. 78:15, 16), and followed them wherever they went in that wilderness: it is called *a fountain of waters,* Ps. 114:8. God showed the care he took of his people in giving them water when they wanted it; he showed his power in fetching the water out of a rock; and he put an honour upon Moses in appointing the water to flow out upon his smiting the rock. This fair water, that came out of the rock, is called *honey and oil* (Deu. 32:13), because the people's thirst made it doubly pleasant; coming when they were in extreme want, it was like honey and oil to them. It is probable that the people digged canals for the conveyance of it, and pools for the reception of it, in like manner as, long afterwards, passing through the valley of Baca, they made it a well, Ps. 84:6; Num. 21:18. Let this direct us to live in a dependence, 1. Upon God's providence, even in the greatest straits and difficulties. God can open fountains for our supply where we least expect them, *waters in the wilderness* (Isa. 43:20), because he makes a *way in the wilderness, v.* 19. Those who, in this wilderness, keep to God's way, may trust him to provide for them. While we follow the pillar of cloud and fire, surely goodness and mercy shall follow us, like the water out of the rock. 2. Upon Christ's grace: *That rock was Christ,* 1 Co. 10:4. The graces and comforts of the Spirit are compared to *rivers of living water,* Jn. 7:38, 39; 4:14. These flow from Christ, who is the rock smitten by the law of Moses, for he was made under the law. Nothing will supply the needs, and satisfy the desires, of a soul, but water out of this rock, this fountain opened. The pleasures of sense are puddle-water; spiritual delights are rock-water, so pure, so clear, so refreshing — rivers of pleasure.

V. A new name was, upon this occasion, given to the place, preserving the remembrance, not of the mercy of their supply (the water that followed them was sufficient to do that), but of the sin of their murmuring — *Massah, temptation,* because they tempted God; *Meribah, strife,* because they chid with Moses, *v.* 7. There was thus a remembrance kept of sin, both for the disgrace of the sinners themselves (sin leaves a blot upon the name) and for warning to their seed to take heed of sinning after the similitude of their transgression.

Verses 8–16

We have here the story of the war with Amalek, which, we may suppose, was the first that was recorded in the *book of the wars of the Lord,* Num. 21:14. Amalek was the first of the nations that Israel fought with, Num. 24:20. Observe,

I. Amalek's attempt: They *came out, and fought with Israel, v.* 8. The Amalekites were the posterity of Esau, who hated Jacob because of the birthright and blessing, and this was an effort of the hereditary enmity, a malice that ran in the blood, and perhaps was now exasperated by the working of the promise towards an accomplishment. Consider this, 1. As Israel's affliction. They had been quarrelling with Moses (*v.* 2), and now God sends Amalekites to quarrel with them; wars abroad are the just punishment of strifes and discontents at home. 2. As Amalek's sin; so it is reckoned, Deu. 25:17, 18. They did not boldly front them as a generous enemy, but without any provocation given by Israel, or challenge given to them, basely fell upon their rear, and smote those that were faint and feeble and could neither make resistance nor escape. Herein they bade defiance to that power which had so lately ruined the Egyptians; but in vain did they attack a camp guarded and victualled by miracles: verily they knew not what they did.

II. Israel's engagement with Amalek, in their own necessary defence against the aggressors. Observe,

1. The post assigned to Joshua, of whom this is the first mention: he is nominated commander-in-chief in this expedition, that he might be trained up to the services he was designed for after the death of Moses, and be a *man of war from his youth.* He is ordered to draw out a detachment of choice men from the thousands of Israel and to drive back the Amalekites, *v.* 9. When the Egyptians pursued them Israel must stand still and see what God would do; but now it was required that they should bestir themselves. Note, God is to be trusted in the use of means.

2. The post assumed by Moses: *I will stand on the top of the hill with the rod of God in my hand, v.* 9. See how God qualifies his people for, and calls them to, various services for the good of his church: Joshua fights, Moses prays, and both minister to Israel. Moses went up to the top of the hill, and placed himself, probably, so as to be seen by Israel; there he held up *the rod of God in his hand,* that wonder-working rod which had summoned the plagues of Egypt, and under which Israel had passed out of the house of bondage. This rod Moses held up to Israel, to animate them; the rod was held up as the banner to encourage the soldiers, who might look up, and say, "Yonder is the rod, and yonder the hand that used it, when such glorious things were wrought for us." Note, It tends much to the encouragement of faith to reflect upon the great things God has done for us, and review the monuments of his favours. Moses also held up this rod to God, by way of appeal to him: "Is not the battle the Lord's? Is not he able to help, and engaged to help? Witness this rod, the voice of which, thus held up, is (Isa. 51:9, 10), *Put on strength, O arm of the Lord; art not thou it that hath cut Rahab?"* Moses was not only a standard-bearer, but an intercessor, pleading with God for success and victory. Note, When the host goes forth against the enemy earnest prayers should be made to the God of hosts for his presence with them. It is here the praying legion that proves the thundering legion. There, in Salem, in Sion where prayers were made, there the victory was won, *there broke the arrows of the bow,* Ps. 76:2, 3. Observe, (1.) How Moses was tired (*v.* 12): *His hands were heavy.* The strongest arm will fail with being long extended; it is God only whose hand is *stretched out still.* We do not find that Joshua's hands were heavy in fighting, but Moses's hands were heavy in praying. The more spiritual any service is the more apt we are to fail and flag in it. Praying work, if done with due intenseness of mind and vigour of affection, will be found hard work, and, though *the spirit be willing, the flesh will be weak.* Our great Intercessor in heaven faints not, nor is he weary, though he attends continually to this very thing. (2.) What influence the rod of Moses had upon the battle (*v.* 11): *When Moses held up his hand* in prayer (so the Chaldee explains it) *Israel prevailed,* but, *when he let down his hand* from prayer, *Amalek prevailed.* To convince Israel that the hand of Moses (with whom they had just now been chiding) contributed more to their safety than their own hands, his rod than their sword, the success rises and falls as Moses lifts up or lets down his hands. It seems, the scale wavered for some time, before it turned on Israel's side. Even the best cause must expect disappointments as an alloy to its successes; though the battle be the Lord's, Amalek may prevail for a time. The reason was, Moses let down his hands. Note, The church's cause is, commonly, more or less successful according as the church's friends are more or less strong in faith and fervent in prayer. (3.) The care that was taken for the support of Moses. When he could not stand any longer he sat down, not in a chair of state, but upon a stone (*v.* 12); when he could not hold up his hands, he would have them held up. Moses, the man of God, is glad of the assistance of Aaron his brother, and Hur, who, some think, was his brother-in-law, the husband of Miriam. We should not be shy either of asking help from others or giving help to others, for we are members one of another. Moses's hands, thus stayed, were *steady till the going down of the sun;* and, though it was with much ado that he held out, yet his willing mind was accepted. No doubt it was a great encouragement to the people to see Joshua before them in the field of battle and Moses above them upon the top of the hill: Christ is both to us — our Joshua, the captain of our salvation who fights our battles, and our Moses, who, in the upper world, ever lives making intercession, that our faith fail not.

III. The defeat of Amalek. Victory had hovered awhile between the camps; sometimes Israel prevailed and sometimes Amalek, but Israel carried the day, *v.* 13. Though Joshua fought with great disadvantages — his soldiers undisciplined, ill-armed, long inured to servitude, and apt to murmur; yet by them God wrought a great salvation, and made Amalek pay dearly for his insolence. Note, Weapons formed against God's Israel cannot prosper long, and shall be broken at last. The cause of God and his Israel will be victorious. Though God gave the victory, yet it is said, *Joshua discomfited Amalek,* because Joshua was a type of Christ, and of the same name, and in him it is that we are more than conquerors. It was his arm alone that spoiled principalities and powers, and routed all their force.

IV. The trophies of this victory set up. 1. Moses took care that God should have the glory of it (*v.* 15); instead of setting up a triumphal arch, to the honour of Joshua (though it had been a laudable policy to put marks of honour upon him), he builds an altar to the honour of God, and we may suppose it was not an altar without sacrifice; but that which is most carefully recorded is the inscription upon the altar, *Jehovah-nissi — The Lord is my banner,* which probably refers to the lifting up of the rod of God as a banner in this action. The presence and power of Jehovah were the banner under which they enlisted, by which they were animated and kept together, and therefore which they erected in the day of their triumph. In the name of our God we must always lift up our banners, Ps. 20:5. It is fit that he who does all the work should have all the praise. 2. God took care that posterity should have the comfort and benefit of it: *"Write this for a memorial,* not in loose papers, but in a book, *write it,* and then *rehearse it in the ears of Joshua,* let him be entrusted with this memorial, to transmit it to the generations to come." Moses must now begin to keep a diary or journal of occurrences; it is the first mention of writing that we find in scripture, and perhaps the command was not given till after the writing of the law upon the tables of stone: "Write it *in perpetuam rei memoriam — that the event may be had in perpetual remembrance;* that which is written remains." (1.) "Write what has been done, what Amalek has done against Israel; write in gall their bitter hatred, write in blood their cruel attempts, let them never be forgotten, nor yet what God has done for Israel in saving them from Amalek. Let ages to come know that God fights for his people, and *he that touches them touches the apple of his eye."* (2.) Write what shall be done. [1.] That in process of time Amalek shall be totally ruined and rooted out (*v.* 14), that he shall be remembered only in history." Amalek would have cut off the name of Israel, that it might be no more in remembrance (Ps. 83:4, 7); and therefore God not only disappoints him in this, but cuts off his name. "Write it for the encouragement of Israel, whenever the Amalekites are an annoyance to them, that Israel will at last undoubtedly triumph in the fall of Amalek." This sentence was executed in part by Saul (1 Sa. 15), and completely by David (*ch.* 30; 2 Sa. 1:1; 8:12); after his time we never read so much as of the name of Amalek. [2.] This is the mean time God would have a continual controversy with him (*v.* 16): *Because his hand is upon the throne of the Lord,* that is, against the camp of Israel in which the Lord ruled, which was the *place of his sanctuary,* and is therefore called a *glorious high throne from the beginning* (Jer. 17:12); therefore the Lord will have *war with Amalek from generation to generation.* This was written for direction to Israel never to make any league with the Amalekites, but to look upon them as irreconcilable enemies, doomed to ruin. Amalek's destruction was typical of the destruction of all the enemies of Christ and his kingdom. Whoever *make war with the Lamb, the Lamb will overcome them.*

CHAPTER 18

This chapter is concerning Moses himself, and the affairs of his own family. I. Jethro his father-in-law brings to him his wife and children (*v.* 1–6). II. Moses entertains his father-in-law with great respect (*v.* 7), with good discourse (*v.* 8–11), with a sacrifice and a feast (*v.* 12). III. Jethro advises him about the management of his business as a judge in Israel, to take inferior judges in to his assistance (*v.* 13–23), and Moses, after some time, takes his counsel (*v.* 24–26), and so they part (*v.* 27).

Verses 1–6

This incident may very well be allowed to have happened as it is placed here, before the giving of the law, and not, as some place it, in connection with what is recorded, Num. 10:11, 29, etc. Sacrifices were offered before; in these mentioned here (*v.* 12) it is observable that *Jethro* is said to take them, not *Aaron.* And as to Jethro's advising Moses to constitute judges under him, though it is intimate (*v.* 13) that the occasion of his giving that advice was *on the morrow,* yet it does not follow but that Moses's settlement of that affair might be some time after, when the law was given, as it is placed, Deu. 1:9. It is plain that Jethro himself would not have him make this alteration in the government till he had received instructions from God about it (*v.* 23), which he did not till some time after. Jethro comes,

I. To congratulate the happiness of Israel, and particularly the honour of Moses his son-in-law; and now Jethro thinks himself well paid for all the kindness he had shown to Moses in his distress, and his daughter better matched than he could have expected. Jethro could not but hear what all the country rang of, the glorious appearances of God for his people Israel (*v.* 1); and he comes to enquire, and inform himself more fully thereof (see Ps. 111:2), and to rejoice with them as one that had a true respect both for them and for their God. Though he, as a Midianite, was not to share with them in the promised land, yet he shared with them in the joy of their deliverance. We may thus make the comforts of others our own, by taking pleasure, as God does, in the *prosperity of the righteous.*

II. To bring Moses's wife and children to him. It seems, he had sent them back, probably from the inn where his wife's aversion to the circumcision of her son had like to have cost him his life (*ch.* 4:25); fearing lest they should prove a further hindrance, he sent them home to his father-in-law. He foresaw what discouragements he was likely to meet with in the court of Pharaoh, and therefore would not take any with him in his own family. He was of that tribe that said to his father, *I have not known him,* when service was to be done for God, Deu. 33:9. Thus Christ's disciples, when they were to go upon an expedition not much unlike that of Moses, were to forsake *wife and children,* Mt. 19:29. But though there might be reason for the separation that was between Moses and his wife for a time, yet they must come together again, as soon as ever they could with any convenience. It is the law of the relation. *You husbands, dwell with your wives,* 1 Pt. 3:7. Jethro, we may suppose, was glad of his daughter's company, and fond of her children, yet he would not keep her from her husband, nor them from their father, *v.* 5, 6. Moses must have his family with him, that while he ruled the church of God he might set a good example of prudence in family-government, 1 Tim. 3:5. Moses had now a great deal both of honour and care put upon him, and it was fit that his wife should be with him to share with him in both. Notice is taken of the significant names of his two sons. 1. The eldest was called *Gershom* (*v.* 3), *a stranger,* Moses designing thereby, not only a memorial of his own condition, but a memorandum to his son of his condition also: for we are all strangers upon earth, as all our fathers were. Moses had a great uncle almost of the same name, *Gershon, a stranger;* for though he was born in Canaan (Gen. 46:11), yet even there the patriarchs confessed themselves strangers. 2. The other he called *Eliezer* (v. 4), *My God a help,* as we translate it; it looks back to his deliverance from Pharaoh, when he made his escape, after the slaying of the Egyptian; but, if this was (as some think) the son that was circumcised at the inn as he was going, I would rather translate it so as to look forward, which the original will bear, *The Lord is my help, and will deliver me* from the sword of Pharaoh, which he had reason to expect would be drawn against him when he was going to fetch Israel out of bondage. Note, When we are undertaking any difficult service for God and our generation, it is good for us to encourage ourselves in God as our help: he that has delivered does and will deliver.

Verses 7–12

Observe here, I. The kind greeting that took place between Moses and his father-in-law, v. 7. Though Moses was a prophet of the Lord, a great prophet, and king in Jeshurun, yet he showed a very humble respect to his father-in-law. However God in his providence is pleased to advance us, we must make conscience of giving honour to whom honour is due, and never look with disdain upon our poor relations. Those that stand high in the favour of God are not thereby discharged from the duty they owe to men, nor will that justify them in a stately haughty carriage. Moses went out to meet Jethro, did *homage to him, and kissed him.* Religion does not destroy good manners. *They asked each other of their welfare.* Even the kind How-do-you-do's that pass between them are taken notice of, as the expressions and improvements of mutual love and friendship.

II. The narrative that Moses gave his father-in-law of the great things God had done for Israel, v. 8. This was one thing Jethro came for, to know more fully and particularly what he had heard the general report of. Note, Conversation concerning *God's wondrous works* is profitable conversation; it is *good, and to the use of edifying,* Ps. 105:2. Compare Ps. 145:11, 12. Asking and telling news, and discoursing of it, are not only an allowable entertainment of conversation, but are capable of being tuned to a very good account, by taking notice of God's providence, and the operations and tendencies of that providence, in all occurrences.

III. The impressions this narrative made upon Jethro. 1. He congratulated God's Israel: *Jethro rejoiced,* v. 9. He not only rejoiced in the honour done to his son-in-law, but in *all the goodness done to Israel,* v. 9. Note, Public blessings are the joy of public spirits. While the Israelites were themselves murmuring, notwithstanding all God's goodness to them, here was a Midianite rejoicing. This was not the only time that the faith of the Gentiles shamed the unbelief of the Jews; see Mt. 8:10. Standers-by were more affected with the favours God had shown to Israel than those were that received them. 2. He gave the glory to Israel's God (v. 10): *"Blessed be Jehovah"* (for by that name he is now known), *"who hath delivered you,* Moses and Aaron, *out of the hand of Pharaoh,* so that though he designed your death he could not effect it, and by your ministry has *delivered the people."* Note, Whatever we have the joy of God must have the praise of. 3. His faith was hereby confirmed, and he took this occasion to make a solemn profession of it: *Now know I that Jehovah is greater than all gods,* v. 11. Observe, (1.) The matter of his faith: that the God of Israel is greater than all pretenders, all false and counterfeit-deities, that usurp divine honours; he silences them, subdues them, and is too hard for them all, and therefore is himself the only *living and true God.* He is also higher than all princes and potentates (who are called gods), and has both an incontestable authority over them and an irresistible power to control and over-rule them; he manages them all as he pleases, and gets honour upon them, how great soever they are. (2.) The confirmation and improvement of his faith: *Now know I;* he knew it before, but now he knew it better; his faith great up to a full assurance, upon this fresh evidence. Those obstinately shut their eyes against the clearest light who do not know that *the Lord is greater than all gods.* (3.) The

ground and reason upon which he built it: *For wherein they dealt proudly,* the magicians, and the idols which the Egyptians worshipped, or Pharaoh and his grandees (they both opposed God and set up in competition with him), *he was above them.* The magicians were baffled, the idols shaken, Pharaoh humbled, his powers broken, and, in spite of all their confederacies, God's Israel was rescued out of their hands. Note, Sooner or later, God will show himself above those that by their proud dealings contest with him. He that *exalts himself* against God *shall be abased.*

IV. The expressions of their joy and thankfulness. They had communion with each other both in a feast and in a sacrifice, v. 12. Jethro, being hearty in Israel's interests, was cheerfully admitted though a Midianite, into fellowship with Moses and the elders of Israel, *forasmuch as he also was a son of Abraham,* though of a younger house. 1. They joined in a sacrifice of thanksgiving: *Jethro took burnt offerings for God,* and probably offered them himself, for he was a priest in Midian, and a worshipper of the true God, and the priesthood was not yet settled in Israel. Note, Mutual friendship is sanctified by joint-worship. It is a very good thing for relations and friends, when they come together, to join in the spiritual sacrifice of prayer and praise, as those that meet in Christ the centre of unity. 2. They joined in a feast of rejoicing, a feast upon the sacrifice. Moses, upon this occasion, invited his relations and friends to an entertainment in his own tent, a laudable usage among friends, and which Christ himself, not only warranted, but recommended, by his acceptance of such invitations. This was a temperate feast: *They did eat bread;* this bread, we may suppose, was manna. Jethro must see and taste that bread from heaven, and, though a Gentile, is as welcome to it as any Israelite; the Gentiles still are so to Christ the bread of life. It was a feast kept after a godly sort: *They did eat bread before God,* soberly, thankfully, in the fear of God; and their table-talk was such as became saints. Thus we must eat and drink to the glory of God, behaving ourselves at our tables as those who believe that God's eye is upon us.

Verses 13–27

Here is, I. The great zeal and industry of Moses as a magistrate.

1. Having been employed to redeem Israel out of the house of bondage, herein he is a further type of Christ, that he is employed as a lawgiver and a judge among them. (1.) He was to answer enquiries, to acquaint them with the will of God in doubtful cases, and to explain the laws of God that were already given them, concerning the sabbath, the man, etc., beside the laws of nature, relating both to piety and equity, v. 15. *They came to enquire of God;* and happy it was for them that they had such an oracle to consult: we are ready to wish, many a time, that we had some such certain way of knowing God's mind when we are at a loss what to do. Moses was faithful both to him that appointed him and to those that consulted him, and made them *know the statutes of God and his laws,* v. 16. His business was, not to make laws, but to make known God's laws; his place was but that of a servant. (2.) He was to decide controversies, and determine matters in variance, judging between a man and his fellow, v. 16. And, if the people were as quarrelsome one with another as they were with God, no doubt he had a great many causes brought before him, and the more because their trials put them to no expense, nor was the law costly to them. When a quarrel happened in Egypt, and Moses would have reconciled the contenders, they asked, *Who made thee a prince and a judge?* But now it was past dispute that God had made him one; and they humbly attend him whom they had then proudly rejected.

2. Such was the business Moses was called to, and it appears that he did it, (1.) With great consideration, which, some think, is intimated in his posture: he *sat* to judge (v. 13), composed and sedate. (2.) With great condescension to the people, who stood *by him,* v. 14. He was very easy of access; the meanest Israelite was welcome himself to bring his cause before him. (3.) With great constancy and closeness of application. [1.] Though Jethro, his father-in-law, was with him, which might have given him a good pretence for a vacation (he might have adjourned the court for that day, or at least have shortened it), yet he sat, even the next day after his coming, *from morning till evening.*

Note, Necessary business must always take place of ceremonious attentions. It is too great a compliment to our friends to prefer the enjoyment of their company before our duty to God, which ought to be done, while yet the other is not left undone. [2.] Though Moses was advanced to great honour, yet he did not therefore take his case and throw upon others the burden of care and business; no, he thought his preferment, instead of discharging him from service, made it more obligatory upon him. Those think of themselves above what is meet who think it below them to do good. It is the honour even of angels themselves to be serviceable. [3.] Though the people had been provoking to him, and were ready to stone him (ch. 17:4), yet still he made himself the servant of all. Note, Though others fail in their duty to us, yet we must not therefore neglect ours to them. [4.] Though he was an old man, yet he kept to his business from morning to night, and made it his meat and drink to do it. God had given him great strength both of body and mind, which enabled him to go through a great deal of work with ease and pleasure; and, for the encouragement of others to spend and be spent in the service of God, it proved that after all his labours his natural force was not diminished. Those that wait on the Lord and his service shall renew their strength.

II. The great prudence and consideration of Jethro as a friend.

1. He disliked the method that Moses took, and was so free with him as to tell him so, v. 14, 17, 18. He thought it was too much business for Moses to undertake alone, that it would be a prejudice to his health and too great a fatigue to him, and also that it would make the administration of justice tiresome to the people; and therefore he tells him plainly, *It is not good.* Note, There may be overdoing even in well-doing, and therefore our zeal must always be governed by discretion, that our good may not be evil spoken of. Wisdom is profitable to direct, that we may neither content ourselves with less than our duty nor over-task ourselves with that which is beyond our strength.

2. He advised him to such a model of government as would better answer the intention, which was, (1.) That he should reserve to himself all applications to God (v. 19): *Be thou for them to God-ward;* that was an honour in which it was not fit any other should share with him, Num. 12:6–8. Also whatever concerned the whole congregation in general must pass through his hand, v. 20. But, (2.) That he should appoint judges in the several tribes and families, who should try causes between man and man, and determine them, which would be done with less noise, and more despatch, than in the general assembly wherein Moses himself presided. Thus they must be governed as a nation by a king as supreme, and inferior magistrates sent and commissioned by him, 1 Pt. 2:13, 14. Thus many hands would make light work, causes would be sooner heard, and the people eased by having justice thus brought to their tent-doors. Yet, (3.) An appeal might lie, if there were just cause for it, from these inferior courts to Moses himself; at least if the judges were themselves at a loss: *Every great matter they shall bring unto thee,* v. 22. Thus that great man would be the more serviceable by being employed only in great matters. Note, Those whose gifts and stations are most eminent may yet be greatly furthered in their work by the assistance of those that are every way their inferiors, whom therefore they should not despise. The head has need of the hands and feet, 1 Co. 12:21. Great men should not only study to be useful themselves, but contrive how to make others useful, according as their capacity is. Such is Jethro's advice, by which it appears that though Moses excelled him in prophecy he excelled Moses in politics; yet,

3. He adds two qualifications to his counsel: — (1.) That great care should be taken in the choice of the persons who should be admitted into this trust (v. 21); they must be *able men,* etc. It was requisite that they should be men of the very best character, [1.] For judgment and resolution — *able men,* men of good sense, that understood business, and bold men, that would not be daunted by frowns or clamours. Clear heads and stout hearts make good judges. [2.] For piety and religion — *such as fear God,* as believe there is a God above them, whose eye is upon them, to whom they are accountable, and of whose judgment they stand in awe. Conscientious men, that dare not do a base thing, though they could do it ever so secretly

and securely. The fear of God is that principle which will best fortify a man against all temptations to injustice, Neh. 5:15; Gen. 42:18. [3.] For integrity and honesty — *men of truth,* whose word one may take, and whose fidelity one may rely upon, who would not for a world tell a lie, betray a trust, or act an insidious part. [4.] For noble and generous contempt of worldly wealth — *hating covetousness,* not only not seeking bribes nor aiming to enrich themselves, but abhorring the thought of it; he is fit to be a magistrate, and he alone, who *despiseth the gain of oppressions, and shaketh his hands from the holding of bribes,* Isa. 33:15. (2.) That he should attend God's direction in the case (*v.* 23): *If thou shalt do this thing, and God command thee so.* Jethro knew that Moses had a better counsellor than he was, and to his counsel he refers him. Note, Advice must be given with a humble submission to the word and providence of God, which must always overrule.

Now Moses did not despise this advice because it came from one not acquainted, as he was, with the words of God and the visions of the Almighty; but he *hearkened to the voice of his father-in-law, v.* 24. When he came to consider the thing, he saw the reasonableness of what his father-in-law proposed and resolved to put it in practice, which he did soon afterwards, when he had received directions from God in the matter. Note, Those are not so wise as they would be thought to be who think themselves too wise to be counselled; for *a wise man* (one who is truly so) *will hear, and will increase learning,* and not slight good counsel, though given by an inferior. Moses did not leave the election of the magistrates to the people, who had already done enough to prove themselves unfit for such a trust; but he chose them, and appointed them, some for greater, others for less division, the less probably subordinate to the greater. We have reason to value government as a very great mercy, and to thank God for laws and magistrates, so that we are not like *the fishes of the sea, where the greater devour the less.*

III. Jethro's return to his own land, *v.* 27. No doubt he took home with him the improvements he had made in the knowledge of God, and communicated them to his neighbours for their instruction. It is supposed that the Kenites (mentioned in 1 Sa. 15:6) were the posterity of Jethro (compare Jdg. 1:16), and they are there taken under special protection, for the kindness their ancestor here showed to Israel. The good-will shown to God's people, even in the smallest instances, shall in no wise lose its reward, but shall be recompensed, at furthest, in the resurrection.

CHAPTER 19

This chapter introduces the solemnity of the giving of the law upon mount Sinai, which was one of the most striking appearances of the divine glory that ever was in this lower world. We have here, I. The circumstances of time and place (*v.* 1, 2). II. The covenant between God and Israel settled in general. The gracious proposal God made to them (*v.* 3–6), and their consent to the proposal (*v.* 7, 8). III. Notice given three days before of God's design to give the law out of a thick cloud (*v.* 9). Orders given to prepare the people to receive the law (*v.* 10–13), and care taken to execute those orders (*v.* 14, 15). IV. A terrible appearance of God's glory upon mount Sinai (*v.* 16–20). V. Silence proclaimed, and strict charges given to the people to observe decorum while God spoke to them (*v.* 21, etc.).

Verses 1–8

Here is, I. The date of that great charter by which Israel was incorporated. 1. The time when it bears date (*v.* 1) — *in the third month* after they came out of Egypt. It is computed that the law was given just fifty days after their coming out of Egypt, in remembrance of which the feast of Pentecost was observed the fiftieth day after the passover, and in compliance with which the Spirit was poured out upon the apostles at the feast of pentecost, fifty days after the death of Christ. In Egypt they had spoken of a three days' journey into the wilderness to the place of their sacrifice (*ch.* 5:3), but it proved to be almost a two months' journey; so often are we out in the calculation of times, and things prove longer in the doing than we expected. 2. The place whence it bears date — from *mount Sinai,* a place which nature, not art, had made eminent and conspicuous, for it was the highest in all that range of mountains. Thus God put contempt upon cities, and palaces, and magnificent structures, setting up his pavilion on the top of a high mountain, in a waste and barren desert, there to carry on this treaty. It is called *Sinai,* from the multitude of thorny bushes that overspread it.

II. The charter itself. Moses was called up the mountain (on the top of which God had pitched his tent, and at the foot of which Israel had pitched theirs), and was employed as the mediator, or rather no more than the messenger of the covenant: *Thus shalt thou say to the house of Jacob, and tell the children of Israel, v.* 3. Here the learned bishop Patrick observes that the people are called by the names both of *Jacob* and *Israel,* to remind them that those who had lately been as low as Jacob when he went to Padan-aram had now grown as great as God made him when he came thence (justly enriched with the spoils of him that had oppressed him) and was called *Israel.* Now observe, 1. That the maker, and first mover, of the covenant, is God himself. Nothing was said nor done by this stupid unthinking people themselves towards this settlement; no motion made, no petition put up for God's favour, but this blessed charter was granted *ex mero motu — purely out of God's own good-will.* Note, In all our dealings with God, free grace anticipates us with the blessings of goodness, and all our comfort is owing, not to our knowing God, but rather to our being *known of him,* Gal. 4:9. *We love him,* visit him, and covenant with him, *because he first loved us,* visited us, and covenanted with us. God is the Alpha, and therefore must be the Omega. 2. That the matter of the covenant is not only just and unexceptionable, and such as puts no hardship upon them, but kind and gracious, and such as gives them the greatest privileges and advantages imaginable. (1.) He reminds them of what he had done for them, *v.* 4. He had righted them, and avenged them upon their persecutors and oppressors: "*You have seen what I did unto the Egyptians,* how many lives were sacrificed to Israel's honour and interests:" He had given them unparalleled instances of his favour to them, and his care of them: *I bore you on eagles' wings,* a high expression of the wonderful tenderness God had shown for them. It is explained, Deu. 32:11, 12. It denotes great speed. God not only came upon the wing for their deliverance (when the set time was come, he rode on a cherub, and did fly), but he hastened them out, as it were, upon the wing. He did it also with great ease, with the strength as well as with the swiftness of an eagle: those that faint not, nor are weary, are said to *mount up with wings as eagles,* Isa. 40:31. Especially, it denotes God's particular care of them and affection to them. Even Egypt, that iron furnace, was the nest in which these young ones were hatched, where they were first formed as the embryo of a nation; when, by the increase of their numbers, they grew to some maturity, they were carried out of that nest. Other birds carry their young in their talons, but the eagle (they say) upon her wings, so that even those archers who shoot flying cannot hurt the young ones, unless they first shoot through the old one. Thus, in the Red Sea, the pillar of cloud and fire, the token of God's presence, interposed itself between the Israelites and their pursuers (lines of defence which could not be forced, a wall which could not be penetrated): yet this was not all; their way so paved, so guarded, was glorious, but their end much more so: *I brought you unto myself.* They were brought not only into a state of liberty and honour, but into covenant and communion with God. This, this was the glory of their deliverance, as it is of ours by Christ, that he died, *the just for the unjust, that he might bring us to God.* This God aims at in all the gracious methods of his providence and grace, to bring us back to himself, from whom we have revolted, and to bring us home to himself, in whom alone we can be happy. He appeals to themselves, and their own observation and experience, for the truth of what is here insisted on: *You have seen what I did;* so that they could not disbelieve God, unless they would first disbelieve their own eyes. They saw how all that was done was purely the Lord's doing. It was not they that reached towards God, but it was he that brought them to himself. Some have well observed that the *Old-Testament church* is said to be borne upon eagles' wings, denoting the power of that dispensation, which was carried on with *a high hand an outstretched arm;* but the *New-Testament church* is said to be gathered by the Lord Jesus, *as a hen gathers her chickens under her wings* (Mt. 23:37), denoting the grace and compassion of that dispensation, and the admirable condescension and humiliation of the Redeemer. (2.) He tells them plainly what he expected and required from them in one word, obedience (*v.* 5), that they should *obey his voice indeed and keep his covenant.* Being thus saved by him, that which he insisted upon was that they should be ruled by him. The reasonableness of this demand is, long after, pleaded with them, that *in the day he brought them out of the land of Egypt* this was the condition of the covenant, *Obey my voice* (Jer. 7:23); and this he is said to protest earnestly to them, Jer. 11:4, 7. Only obey *indeed,* not in profession and promise only, not in pretence, but in sincerity. God had shown them real favours, and therefore required real obedience. (3.) He assures them of the honour he would put upon them, and the kindness he would show them, in case they did thus keep his covenant (*v.* 5, 6): *Then you shall be a peculiar treasure to me.* He does not specify any one particular favour, as giving them the land of Canaan, or the like, but expresses it in that which was inclusive of all happiness, that he would be to them a God in covenant, and they should be to him a people. [1.] God here asserts his sovereignty over, and propriety in, the whole visible creation: *All the earth is mine.* Therefore he needed them not; he that had so vast a dominion was great enough, and happy enough, without concerning himself for so small a demesne as Israel was. All nations on the earth being his, he might choose which he pleased for his peculiar, and act in a way of sovereignty. [2.] He appropriates Israel to himself, *First,* As a people dear unto him. *You shall be a peculiar treasure;* not that God was enriched by them, as a man is by his treasure, but he was pleased to value and esteem them as a man does his treasure; they were *precious in his sight and honourable* (Isa. 43:4); he *set his love upon them* (Deu. 7:7), took them under his special care and protection, as a treasure that is kept under lock and key. He looked upon the rest of the world but as trash and lumber in comparison with them. By giving them divine revelation, instituted ordinances, and promises inclusive of eternal life, by sending his prophets among them, and pouring out his Spirit upon them, he distinguished them from, and dignified them above, all people. And this honour have all the saints; they are unto God a *peculiar people* (Tit. 2:14), his when he *makes up his jewels. Secondly,* As a people devoted to him, to his honour and service (*v.* 6), a *kingdom of priests,* a *holy nation.* All the Israelites, if compared with other people, were priests unto God, so near were they to him (Ps. 148:14), so much employed in his immediate service, and such intimate communion they had with him. When they were first made a free people it was that they might *sacrifice to the Lord their God,* as *priests;* they were under God's immediate government, and the tendency of the laws given them was to distinguish them from others, and engage them for God as a holy nation. Thus all believers are, through Christ, made to our God kings and priests (Rev. 1:6), *a chosen generation, a royal priesthood,* 1 Pt. 2:9.

III. Israel's acceptance of this charter, and consent to the conditions of it. 1. Moses faithfully delivered God's message to them (*v.* 7): He *laid before their faces all those words;* he not only explained to them what God had given him in charge, but he put it to their choice whether they would accept these promises upon these terms or no. His laying it to their faces denotes his laying it to their consciences. 2. They readily agreed to the covenant proposed. They would oblige themselves to obey the voice of God, and take it as a great favour to be made a kingdom of priests to him. They answered together as one man, *nemine contradicente — without a dissentient voice* (*v.* 8): *All that the Lord hath spoken we will do.* Thus they strike the bargain, accepting the Lord to be to them a God, and giving up themselves to be to him a people. O that there had been such a heart in them! 3. Moses, as a mediator, returned the words of the people to God, *v.* 8. Thus Christ, the Mediator between us and God, as a prophet reveals God's will to us, his precepts and promises, and then as a priest offers up to God our spiritual sacrifices, not only of prayer and praise, but of devout affections and pious resolutions, the work of his own Spirit in us. Thus he is that blessed *days-man who lays his hand upon us both.*

Verses 9–15

Here, I. God intimates to Moses his purpose of coming down upon mount Sinai, in some visible appearance of his glory, in *a thick cloud* (*v.* 9); for he said that he would *dwell in the thick darkness* (2 Chr. 6:1), and make this his pavilion (Ps. 18:11), *holding back the face of his throne* when he set it upon *mount Sinai, and spreading a cloud upon it,* Job 26:9. This thick cloud was to prohibit curious enquiries into things secret, and to command an awful adoration of that which was revealed. God would come down *in the sight of all the people* (*v.* 11); though they should see no manner of similitude, yet they should see so much as would convince them that God was among them of a truth. And so high was the top of mount Sinai that it is supposed that not only the camp of Israel, but even the countries about, might discern some extraordinary appearance of glory upon it, which would strike a terror upon them. It seems also to have been particularly intended to put an honour upon Moses: *That they may hear when I speak with thee, and believe thee for ever, v.* 9. Thus the correspondence was to be first settled by a sensible appearance of the divine glory, which was afterwards to be carried on more silently by the ministry of Moses. In like manner, the Holy Ghost descended visibly upon Christ at his baptism, and all that were present heard God speak to him (Mt. 3:17), that afterwards, without the repetition of such visible tokens, they might believe him. So likewise the Spirit descended in cloven tongues upon the apostles (Acts 2:3), that they might be believed. Observe, When the people had declared themselves willing to obey the voice of God, then God promised they should hear his voice; for, if any man be resolved to *do his will, he shall know it,* Jn. 7:17.

II. He orders Moses to make preparation for this great solemnity, giving him two days' time for it.

1. He must *sanctify the people* (*v.* 10), as Job, before this, sent and *sanctified his sons,* Job 1:5. He must raise their expectation by giving them notice what God would do, and assist their preparation by directing them what they must do. *"Sanctify them,"* that is, "Call them off from their worldly business, and call them to religious exercises, meditation and prayer, that they may receive the law from God's mouth with reverence and devotion. *Let them be ready," v.* 11. Note, When we are to attend upon God in solemn ordinances it concerns us to sanctify ourselves, and to get ready beforehand. Wandering thoughts must be gathered in, impure affections abandoned, disquieting passions suppressed, nay, and all cares about secular business, for the present, dismissed and laid by, that our hearts may be *engaged to approach unto God.* Two things particularly prescribed as signs and instances of their preparation: — (1.) In token of their cleansing themselves from all sinful pollutions, that they might be holy to God, they must *wash their clothes* (*v.* 10), and they did so (*v.* 14); not that God regards our clothes; but while they were washing their clothes he would have them think of washing their souls by repentance from the sins they had contracted in Egypt and since their deliverance. It becomes us to appear in clean clothes when we wait upon great men; so clean hearts are required in our attendance on the great God, who sees them as plainly as men see our clothes. This is absolutely necessary to our acceptably worshipping God. See Ps. 26:6; Isa. 1:16–18; Heb. 10:22. (2.) In token of their devoting themselves entirely to religious exercises, upon this occasion, they must abstain even from lawful enjoyments during these three days, and not *come at their wives, v.* 15. See 1 Co. 7:5.

2. He must *set bounds about the mountain, v.* 12, 13. Probably he drew a line, or ditch, round at the foot of the hill, which none were to pass upon pain of death. This was to intimate, (1.) That humble awful reverence which ought to possess the minds of all those that worship God. We are mean creatures before a great Creator, vile sinners before a holy righteous Judge; and therefore a godly fear and shame well become us, Heb. 12:28; Ps. 2:11. (2.) The distance at which worshippers were kept, under that dispensation, which we ought to take notice of, that we may the more value our privilege under the gospel, having *boldness to enter into the holiest by the blood of Jesus,* Heb. 10:19.

3. He must order the people to attend upon the summons that should be given (*v.* 13): *"When the trumpet soundeth long* then let them take their places at the foot of the mount, and so sit down at God's feet," as it is explained, Deu. 33:3. Never was so great a congregation called together, and preached to, at once, as this was here. No one man's voice could have reached so many, but the voice of God did.

Verses 16–25

Now, at length, comes that memorable day, that terrible day of the Lord, that day of judgment, in which *Israel heard the voice of the Lord God* speaking to them *out of the midst of the fire, and lived,* Deu. 4:33. Never was there such a sermon preached, before nor since, as this which was here preached to the church in the wilderness. For,

I. The preacher was God himself (*v.* 18): *The Lord descended in fire,* and (*v.* 20), *The Lord came down upon mount Sinai.* The *shechinah,* or glory of the Lord, appeared in the sight of all the people; he *shone forth from mount Paran with ten thousands of his saints* (Deu. 33:2), that is, attended, as the divine Majesty always is, by a multitude of the holy angels, who were both to grace the solemnity and to assist at it. Hence the law is said to be given *by the disposition of angels,* Acts 7:53.

II. The pulpit (or throne rather) was mount Sinai, hung with a *thick cloud* (*v.* 16), covered with *smoke* (*v.* 18), and made to *quake* greatly. Now it was that the earth *trembled at the presence of the Lord,* and the *mountains skipped like rams* (Ps. 114:4, 7), that Sinai itself, though rough and rocky, *melted from before the Lord God of Israel,* Jdg. 5:5. Now it was that the *mountains saw him, and trembled* (Hab. 3:10), and were witnesses against a hard-hearted unmoved people, whom nothing would influence.

III. The congregation was called together by the *sound of a trumpet, exceedingly loud* (*v.* 16), and *waxing louder and louder, v.* 19. This was done by the ministry of the angels, and we read of trumpets sounded by angels, Rev. 8:6. It was the *sound of the trumpet that made all the people tremble,* as those who knew their own guilt, and who had reason to expect that the sound of this trumpet was to them the *alarm of war.*

IV. Moses brought the hearers to the place of meeting, *v.* 17. He that had led them out of the bondage of Egypt now led them to receive the law from God's mouth. Public persons are indeed public blessings when they lay out themselves in their places to promote the public worship of God. Moses, at the head of an assembly worshipping God, was as truly great as Moses at the head of an army in the field.

V. The introductions to the service were *thunders and lightnings, v.* 16. These were designed to strike an awe upon the people, and to raise and engage their attention. Were they asleep? The thunders would awaken them. Were they looking another way? The lightnings would engage them to turn their faces towards him that spoke to them. Thunder and lightning have natural causes, but the scripture directs us in a particular manner to take notice of the power of God, and his terror, in them. Thunder is the voice of God, and lightning the fire of God, proper to engage the senses of sight and hearing, those senses by which we receive so much of our information.

VI. Moses is God's minister, who is spoken to, to command silence, and keep the congregation in order: *Moses spoke, v.* 19. Some think it was now that he said, *I exceedingly fear and quake* (Heb. 12:21); but God stilled his fear by his distinguishing favour to him, in calling him up to the top of the mount (*v.* 20), by which also he tried his faith and courage. No sooner had Moses got up a little way towards the top of the mount than he was sent down again to keep the people from *breaking through to gaze, v.* 21. Even the priests or princes, the heads of the houses of their fathers, who officiated for their respective families, and therefore are said to *come near to the Lord* at other times, must now keep their distance, and conduct themselves with a great deal of caution. Moses pleads that they needed not to have any further orders given them, effectual care being taken already to prevent any intrusions, *v.* 23. But God, who knew their wilfulness and presumption, and what was now in the hearts of some of them, hastens him down with this in charge, that neither the priests nor the people should offer to force the lines that were set, to *come up unto the Lord,* but Moses and Aaron on, the men whom God delighted to honour. Observe, 1. What it was that God forbade them — breaking through to gaze; enough was provided to awaken their consciences, but they were not allowed to gratify their vain curiosity. They might see, but not gaze. Some of them, probably, were desirous to see some similitude, that they might know how to make an image of God, which he took care to prevent, for they *saw no manner of similitude,* Deu. 4:5. Note, In divine things we must not covet to know more than God would have us know; and he has allowed us as much as is good for us. A desire of forbidden knowledge was the ruin of our first parents. Those that would be wise above what is written, and intrude into those things which they have not seen, need this admonition, that they *break not through to gaze.* 2. Under what penalty it was forbidden: *Lest the Lord break forth upon them* (*v.* 22–24), and *many of them perish.* Note, (1.) The restraints and warnings of the divine law are all intended for our good, and to keep us out of that danger into which we should otherwise, by our own folly, run ourselves. (2.) It is at our peril if we break the bounds that God has set us, and intrude upon that which he has not allowed us; the Bethshemites and Uzzah paid dearly for their presumption. And, even when we are called to approach God, we must remember that he is in heaven and we upon earth, and therefore it behoves us to exercise reverence and godly fear.

CHAPTER 20

All things being prepared for the solemn promulgation of the divine law, we have, in this chapter, I. The ten commandments, as God himself spoke them upon mount Sinai (*v.* 1–17), as remarkable a portion of scripture as any in the Old Testament. II. The impressions made upon the people thereby (*v.* 18–21). III. Some particular instructions which God gave privately to Moses, to be by him communicated to the people, relating to his worship (*v.* 22, etc.).

Verses 1–11

Here is, I. The preface of the law-writer, Moses: *God spoke all these words, v.* 1. The law of the ten commandments is, 1. A law of God's making. They are enjoined by the infinite eternal Majesty of heaven and earth. And *where the word of the King* of kings *is surely there is power.* 2. It is a law of his own speaking. God has many ways of speaking to the children of men (Job 33:14); *once, yea twice* — by his Spirit, by conscience, by providences, by his voice, all which we ought carefully to attend to; but he never spoke, at any time, upon any occasion, as he spoke the ten commandments, which therefore we ought to hear with the *more earnest heed.* They were not only spoken audibly (so he owned the Redeemer by a voice from heaven, Mt. 3:17), but with a great deal of dreadful pomp. This law God had given to man before (it was written in his heart by nature); but sin had so defaced that writing that it was necessary, in this manner, to revive the knowledge of it.

II. The preface of the Law-maker: *I am the Lord thy God, v.* 2. Herein, 1. God asserts his own authority to enact this law in general: "I am the Lord who command thee all that follows." 2. He proposes himself as the sole object of that religious worship which is enjoined in the first four of the commandments. They are here bound to obedience by a threefold cord, which, one would think, could not *easily be broken.* (1.) Because God *is the Lord* — Jehovah, self-existent, independent, eternal, and the fountain of all being and power; therefore he has an incontestable right to command us. He that gives being may give law; and therefore he is able to bear us out in our obedience, to reward it, and to punish our disobedience. (2.) He was their God, a God in covenant with them, their God by their own consent; and, if they would not keep his commandments, who would? He had laid himself under obligations to them by promise, and therefore might justly lay his obligations on them by precept. Though that covenant of peculiarity is now no more, yet there is another, by virtue of which all that are baptized are taken into relation to him as their God, and are therefore unjust, unfaithful, and very ungrateful, if they obey him not. (3.) He had *brought them out of the land of Egypt;* therefore they were bound in gratitude to obey him, because he had done them so great a kindness, had brought them out of a grievous slavery into a glorious liberty. They themselves had been eyewitnesses of the great things God had done in order to their deliverance, and could not but have observed that every circumstance of it heightened their obligation. They were now enjoying the blessed fruits of their deliverance, and in expectation of a speedy settlement in Canaan; and could they think any thing too much to do for him that had done so much for them? Nay, by redeeming them, he acquired a further right to rule them; they owed their service to him to whom they owed their freedom, and whose they were by purchase. And thus Christ, having rescued us out of the bondage of sin, is entitled to the best service we can do him, Lu. 1:74. Having loosed our bonds, he has bound us to obey him, Ps. 116:16.

III. The law itself. The first four of the ten commandments, which concern our duty to God (commonly called *the first table*), we have in these verses. It was fit that those should be put first, because man had a Maker to love before he had a neighbour to love; and justice and charity are acceptable acts of obedience to God only when they flow from the principles of piety. It cannot be expected that he should be true to his brother who is false to his God. Now our duty to God is, in one word, to worship him, that is, to give to him the glory due to his name, the inward worship of our affections, the outward worship of solemn address and attendance. This is spoken of as the sum and substance of the everlasting gospel. Rev. 14:7, *Worship God*.

1. The first commandment concerns the object of our worship, Jehovah, and him only (*v*. 3): *Thou shalt have no other gods before me*. The Egyptians, and other neighbouring nations, had many gods, the creatures of their own fancy, strange gods, *new gods;* this law was prefixed because of that transgression, and, Jehovah being the God of Israel, they must entirely cleave to him, and not be for any other, either of their own invention or borrowed from their neighbours. This was the sin they were most in danger of now that the world was so overspread with polytheism, which yet could not be rooted out effectually but by the gospel of Christ. The sin against this commandment which *we* are most in danger of is giving the glory and honour to any creature which are due to God only. Pride makes a god of self, covetousness makes a god of money, sensuality makes a god of the belly; whatever is esteemed or loved, feared or served, delighted in or depended on, more than God, that (whatever it is) we do in effect make a god of. This prohibition includes a precept which is the foundation of the whole law, that we take the Lord for our God, acknowledge that he is God, accept him for ours, adore him with admiration and humble reverence, and set our affections entirely upon him. In the last words, *before me*, it is intimated, (1.) That we cannot have any other God but he will certainly know it. There is none besides him but what is before him. Idolaters covet secresy; but *shall not God search this out?* (2.) That it is very provoking to him; it is a sin that dares him to his face, which he cannot, which he will not, overlook, nor connive at. See Ps. 44:20, 21.

2. The second commandment concerns the ordinances of worship, or the way in which God will be worshipped, which it is fit that he himself should have the appointing of. Here is,

(1.) The prohibition: we are here forbidden to worship even the true God by images, *v.* 4, 5. [1.] The Jews (at least after the captivity) thought themselves forbidden by this commandment to make any image or picture whatsoever. Hence the very images which the Roman armies had in their ensigns are called *an abomination* to them (Mt. 24:15), especially when they were set up *in the holy place*. It is certain that it forbids making any image of God (for *to whom can we liken him?* Isa. 40:18, 15), or the image of any creature for a religious use. It is called the changing of the truth of God into a lie (Rom. 1:25), for an image is a teacher of lies; it insinuates to us that God has a body, whereas he is an infinite spirit, Hab. 2:18. It also forbids us to make images of God in our fancies, as if he were a man as we are. Our religious worship must be governed by the power of faith, not by the power of imagination. They must not make such images or pictures as the heathen worshipped, lest they also should be tempted to worship them. Those who would be kept from sin must keep themselves from the occasions of it. [2.] They must not *bow down to them* occasionally, that is, show any sign of respect or honour to them, much less serve them constantly, by sacrifice or incense, or any other act of religious worship. When they paid their devotion to the true God, they must not have any image before them, for the directing, exciting, or assisting of their devotion. Though the worship was designed to terminate in God, it would not please him if it came to him through an image. The best and most ancient lawgivers among the heathen forbade the setting up of images in their temples. This practice was forbidden in Rome by Numa, a pagan prince; yet commanded in

Rome by the pope, a Christian bishop, but, in this, antichristian. The use of images in the church of Rome, at this day, is so plainly contrary to the letter of this command, and so impossible to be reconciled to it, that in all their catechisms and books of devotion, which they put into the hands of the people, they leave out this commandment, joining the reason of it to the first; and so the third commandment they call the second, the fourth the third, etc.; only, to make up the number ten, they divide the tenth into two. Thus have they committed two great evils, in which they persist, and from which they hate to be reformed; they take away from God's word, and add to his worship.

(2.) The reasons to enforce this prohibition (*v*. 5, 6), which are, [1.] God's jealousy in the matters of his worship: "*I am the Lord* Jehovah, and *thy God, am a jealous God,* especially in things of this nature." This intimates the care he has of his own institutions, his hatred of idolatry and all false worship, his displeasure against idolaters, and that he resents every thing in his worship that looks like, or leads to, idolatry. Jealousy is quicksighted. Idolatry being spiritual adultery, as it is very often represented in scripture, the displeasure of God against it is fitly called *jealousy*. If God is jealous herein, we should be so, afraid of offering any worship to God otherwise than as he has appointed in his word. [2.] The punishment of idolaters. God looks upon them as haters of him, though they perhaps pretend love to him; he will *visit their iniquity,* that is, he will very severely punish it, not only as a breach of his law, but as an affront to his majesty, a violation of the covenant, and a blow at the root of all religion. He will *visit it upon the children,* that is, this being a sin for which churches shall be unchurched and a bill of divorce given them, the children shall be cast out of covenant and communion together with the parents, as with the parents the children were at first taken in. Or he will bring such judgments upon a people as shall be the total ruin of families. If idolaters live to be old, so as to see their children of the third or fourth generation, it shall be the vexation of their eyes, and the breaking of their hearts, to see them fall by the sword, carried captive, and enslaved. Nor is it an unrighteous thing with God (if the parents died in their iniquity, and the children tread in their steps, and keep up false worships, because they received them by tradition from their fathers), when the measure is full, and God comes by his judgments to reckon with them, to bring into the account the idolatries their fathers were guilty of. Though he bear long with an idolatrous people, he will not bear always, but by the fourth generation, at furthest, he will begin to visit. Children are dear to their parents; therefore, to deter men from idolatry, and to show how much God is displeased with it, not only a brand of infamy is by it entailed upon families, but the judgments of God may for it be executed upon the poor children when the parents are dead and gone. [3.] The favour God would show to his faithful worshippers: *Keeping mercy for thousands* of persons, thousands of generations *of those that love me, and keep my commandments*. This intimates that the second commandment, though, in the letter of it, it is only a prohibition of false worships, yet includes a precept of worshipping God in all those ordinances which he has instituted. As the first commandment requires the inward worship of love, desire, joy, hope, and admiration, so the second requires the outward worship of prayer and praise, and solemn attendance on God's word. Note, *First,* Those that truly love God will make it their constant care and endeavour to keep his commandments, particularly those that relate to his worship. Those that love God, and keep those commandments, shall receive grace to keep his other commandments. Gospel worship will have a good influence upon all manner of gospel obedience. *Secondly,* God has mercy in store for such. Even they need mercy, and cannot plead merit; and mercy they shall find with God, merciful protection in their obedience and a merciful recompence of it. *Thirdly,* This mercy shall extend to thousands, much further than the wrath threatened to those that hate him, for that reaches but to the third or fourth generation. The streams of mercy run now as full, as free, and as fresh, as ever.

3. The third commandment concerns the manner of our worship, that it be done with all possible reverence and seriousness, *v.* 7. We have here,

(1.) A strict prohibition: *Thou shalt not take the name of the Lord thy God in vain*. It is supposed that, having taken Jehovah for their God, they would make mention of his name (for thus *all people will walk every one in the name of his god*); this command gives a needful caution not to mention it in vain, and it is still as needful as ever. We take God's name in vain, [1.] By hypocrisy, making a profession of God's name, but not living up to that profession. Those that name the name of Christ, but do not depart from iniquity, as that name binds them to do, name it in vain; their worship is vain (Mt. 15:7–9), their oblations are vain (Isa. 1:11, 13), their religion is vain, Jam. 1:26. [2.] By covenant-breaking; if we make promises to God, binding our souls with those bonds to that which is good, and yet perform not to the Lord our vows, we take his name in vain (Mt. 5:33), it is folly, and God *has no pleasure in fools* (Eccl. 5:4), nor will he be *mocked,* Gal. 6:7. [3.] By rash swearing, mentioning the name of God, or any of his attributes, in the form of an oath, without any just occasion for it, or due application of mind to it, but as a byword, to no purpose at all, or to no good purpose. [4.] By false swearing, which, some think, is chiefly intended in the letter of the commandment; so it was expounded by those of old time. *Thou shalt not forswear thyself,* Mt. 5:33. One part of the religious regard the Jews were taught to pay to their God was to *swear by his name,* Deu. 10:20. But they affronted him, instead of doing him honour, if they called him to be witness to a lie. [5.] By using the name of God lightly and carelessly, and without any regard to its awful significancy. The profanation of the forms of devotion is forbidden, as well as the profanation of the forms of swearing; as also the profanation of any of those things whereby God makes himself known, his word, or any of his institutions; when they are either turned into charms and spells, or into jest and sport, the name of God is taken in vain.

(2.) A severe penalty: *The Lord will not hold him guiltless;* magistrates, who punish other offences, may not think themselves concerned to take notice of this, because it does not immediately offer injury either to private property or the public peace; but God, who is jealous for his honour, will not thus connive at it. The sinner may perhaps hold himself guiltless, and think there is no harm in it, and that God will never call him to an account for it. To obviate this suggestion, the threatening is thus expressed, God will *not hold him guiltless,* as he hopes he will; but more is implied, namely, that God will himself be the avenger of those that take his name in vain, and they will find it a fearful thing to fall into the hands of the living God.

4. The fourth commandment concerns the time of worship. God is to be served and honoured daily, but one day in seven is to be particularly dedicated to his honour and spent in his service. Here is,

(1.) The command itself (*v.* 8): *Remember the sabbath day to keep it holy;* and (*v.* 10), *In it thou shalt do no manner of work*. It is taken for granted that the sabbath was instituted before; we read of God's blessing and sanctifying a seventh day from the beginning (Gen. 2:3), so that this was not the enacting of a new law, but the reviving of an old law. [1.] They are told what is the day they must religiously observe — *a seventh, after six days' labour;* whether this was the seventh by computation from the first seventh, or from the day of their coming out of Egypt, or both, is not certain: now the precise day was notified to them (*ch*. 16:23), and from this they were to observe the seventh. [2.] How it must be observed. *First,* As a day of rest; they were to do no manner of work on this day in their callings or worldly business. *Secondly,* As a holy day, set apart to the honour of the holy God, and to be spent in holy exercises. God, by blessing it, had made it holy; they, by solemnly blessing him, must keep it holy, and not alienate it to any other purpose than that for which the difference between it and other days was instituted. [3.] Who must observe it: *Thou, and thy son, and thy daughter;* the wife is not mentioned, because she is supposed to be one with the husband and present with him, and, if he sanctify the sabbath, it is taken for granted that she will join with him; but the rest of the family are specified. Children and servants must keep the sabbath, according to their age and capacity: in this, as in other instances of religion, it is expected that masters of families should take care, not only to serve the Lord themselves, but that their houses also should serve him, at least that it may not be through their neglect if they do not, Jos. 24:15. Even the proselyted strangers must observe a difference between this day and other days, which, if it laid some restraint upon them then, yet proved a happy indication of God's gracious purpose, in process of time, to bring the Gentiles into the church, that they might share in the benefit of sabbaths. Compare Isa. 56:6, 7. God takes notice of what we do, particularly what we do on sabbath days, though we should be where we are strangers. [4.] A particular memorandum put upon this duty: *Remember it.* It is intimated that the sabbath was instituted and observed before; but in their bondage in Egypt they had lost their computation, or were restrained by their task-masters, or, through a great degeneracy and indifference in religion, they had let fall the observance of it, and therefore it was requisite they should be reminded of it. Note, Neglected duties remain duties still, notwithstanding our neglect. It also intimates that we are both apt to forget it and concerned to remember it. Some think it denotes the preparation we are to make for the sabbath; we must think of it before it comes, that, when it does come, we may keep it holy, and do the duty of it.

(2.) The reasons of this command. [1.] We have time enough for ourselves in those six days, on the seventh day let us serve God; and time enough to tire ourselves, on the seventh it will be a kindness to us to be obliged to rest. [2.] This is God's day: it is the *sabbath of the Lord thy God,* not only instituted by him, but consecrated to him. It is sacrilege to alienate it; the sanctification of it is a debt. [3.] It is designed for a memorial of the creation of the world, and therefore to be observed to the glory of the Creator, as an engagement upon ourselves to serve him and an encouragement to us to trust in him who made heaven and earth. By the sanctification of the sabbath, the Jews declared that they worshipped the God that made the world, and so distinguished themselves from all other nations, who worshipped gods which they themselves made. [4.] God has given us an example of rest, after six days' work: he *rested the seventh day,* took a complacency in himself, and *rejoiced in the work of his hand,* to teach us, on that day, to take a complacency in him, and to give him the glory of his works, Ps. 92:4. The sabbath began in the finishing of the work of creation, so will the everlasting sabbath in the finishing of the work of providence and redemption; and we observe the weekly sabbath in expectation of that, as well as in remembrance of the former, in both conforming ourselves to him we worship. [5.] He has himself *blessed the sabbath day and sanctified it.* He has put an honour upon it by setting it apart for himself; it is the holy of the Lord and honourable: and he has put blessings into it, which he has encouraged us to expect from him in the religious observance of that day. It is *the day which the Lord hath made,* let not us do what we can to unmake it. He has blessed, honoured, and sanctified it, let not us profane it, dishonour it, and level that with common time which God's blessing has thus dignified and distinguished.

Verses 12–17

We have here the laws of the second table, as they are commonly called, the last six of the ten commandments, comprehending our duty to ourselves and to one another, and constituting a comment upon the second great commandment, *Thou shalt love thy neighbour as thyself.* As religion towards God is an essential branch of universal righteousness, so righteousness towards men is an essential branch of true religion. Godliness and honesty must go together.

I. The fifth commandment concerns the duties we owe to our relations; those of children to their parents are alone specified: *Honour thy father and thy mother,* which includes, 1. A decent respect to their persons, an inward esteem of them outwardly expressed upon all occasions in our conduct towards them. *Fear them* (Lev. 19:3), *give them reverence,* Heb. 12:9. The contrary to this is mocking at them and despising them, Prov. 30:17. 2. Obedience to their lawful commands; so it is expounded (Eph. 6:1–3): *"Children, obey your parents,* come when they call you, go where they send you, do what they bid you, refrain from what they forbid you; and this, as children, cheerfully, and from a principle of love." Though you have said, "We will not," yet afterwards repent and obey, Mt. 21:29. 3. Submission to their rebukes, instructions, and corrections; not only to the good and gentle, but also to the froward, out of conscience towards God. 4. Disposing of themselves with the advice, direction, and consent, of parents, not alienating their property, but with their approbation. 5. Endeavouring, in every thing, to be the comfort of their parents, and to make their old age easy to them, maintaining them if they stand in need of support, which our Saviour makes to be particularly intended in this commandment, Mt. 15:4– 6. The reason annexed to this commandment is a promise: *That thy days may be long in the land which the Lord thy God giveth thee.* Having mentioned, in the preface to the commandments, has bringing them out of Egypt as a reason for their obedience, he here, in the beginning of the second table, mentions his bringing them into Canaan, as another reason; that good land they must have upon their thoughts and in their eye, now that they were in the wilderness. They must also remember, when they came to that land, that they were upon their good behaviour, and that, if they did not conduct themselves well, their days should be shortened in that land, both the days of particular persons who should be cut off from it, and the days of their nation which should be removed out of it. But here a long life in that good land is promised particularly to obedient children. Those that do their duty to their parents are most likely to have the comfort of that which their parents gather for them and leave to them; those that support their parents shall find that God, the common Father, will support them. This promise is expounded (Eph. 6:3), *That it may be well with thee, and thou mayest live long on the earth.* Those who, in conscience towards God, keep this and the rest of God's commandments, may be sure that it shall be well with them, and that they shall live as long on earth as Infinite Wisdom sees good for them, and that what they may seem to be cut short of on earth shall be abundantly made up in eternal life, the heavenly Canaan which God will give them.

II. The sixth commandment concerns our own and our neighbour's life (*v.* 13): *"Thou shalt not kill;* thou shalt not do any thing hurtful or injurious to the health, ease, and life, of thy own body, or any other person's unjustly." This is one of the laws of nature, and was strongly enforced by the precepts given to Noah and his sons, Gen. 9:5, 6. It does not forbid killing in lawful war, or in our own necessary defence, nor the magistrate's putting offenders to death, for those things tend to the preserving of life; but it forbids all malice and hatred to the person of any (for *he that hateth his brother is a murderer*), and all personal revenge arising therefrom; also all rash anger upon sudden provocations, and hurt said or done, or aimed to be done, in passion: of this our Saviour expounds this commandment, Mt. 5:22. And, as that which is worst of all, it forbids persecution, laying wait for the blood of the innocent and excellent ones of the earth.

III. The seventh commandment concerns our own and our neighbour's chastity: *Thou shalt not commit adultery, v.* 14. This is put before the sixth by our Saviour (Mk. 10:19): *Do not commit adultery, do not kill;* for our chastity should be as dear to us as our lives, and we should be as much afraid of that which defiles the body as of that which destroys it. This commandment forbids all acts of uncleanness, with all those fleshly lusts which produce those acts and war against the soul, and all those practices which cherish and excite those fleshly lusts, as looking, in order to lust, which, Christ tells us, is forbidden in this commandment, Mt. 5:28.

IV. The eighth commandment concerns our own and our neighbour's wealth, estate, and goods: *Thou shalt not steal, v.* 15. Though God had lately allowed and appointed them to spoil the Egyptians in a way of just reprisal, yet he did not intend that it should be drawn into a precedent and that they should be allowed thus to spoil one another. This command forbids us to rob ourselves of what we have by sinful spending, or of the use and comfort of it by sinful sparing, and to rob others by removing the ancient landmarks, invading our neighbour's rights, taking his goods from his person, or house, or field, forcibly or clandestinely, over-reaching in bargains, nor restoring what is borrowed or found, withholding just debts, rents, or wages, and (which is worst of all) to rob the public in the coin or revenue, or that which is dedicated to the service of religion.

V. The ninth commandment concerns our own and our neighbour's good name: *Thou shalt not bear false witness, v.* 16. This forbids, 1. Speaking falsely in any matter, lying, equivocating, and any way devising and designing to deceive our neighbour. 2. Speaking unjustly against our neighbour, to the prejudice of his reputation; and (which involves the guilty of both), 3. Bearing false witness against him, laying to his charge things that he knows not, either judicially, upon oath (by which the third commandment, and the sixth of eighth, as well as this, are broken), or extrajudicially, in common converse, slandering, backbiting, tale-bearing, aggravating what is done amiss and making it worse than it is, and any way endeavouring to raise our own reputation upon the ruin of our neighbour's.

VI. The tenth commandment strikes at the root: *Thou shalt not covet, v.* 17. The foregoing commands implicitly forbid all desire of doing that which will be an injury to our neighbour; this forbids all inordinate desire of having that which will be a gratification to ourselves. "O that such a man's house were mine! Such a man's wife mine! Such a man's estate mine!" This is certainly the language of discontent at our own lot, and envy at our neighbour's; and these are the sins principally forbidden here. St. Paul, when the grace of God caused the scales to fall from his eyes, perceived that this law, *Thou shalt not covet,* forbade all those irregular appetites and desires which are the first-born of the corrupt nature, the first risings of the sin that dwelleth in us, and the beginnings of all the sin that is committed by us: this is that lust which, he says, he had not known the evil of, if this commandment, when it came to his conscience in the power of it, had not shown it to him, Rom. 7:7. God give us all to see our face in the glass of this law, and to lay our hearts under the government of it!

Verses 18–21

I. The extraordinary terror with which the law was given. Never was any thing delivered with such awful pomp; every word was accented, and every sentence paused, with thunder and lightning, much louder and brighter, no doubt, than ordinary. And why was the law given in this dreadful manner, and with all this tremendous ceremony? 1. It was designed (once for all) to give a sensible discovery of the glorious majesty of God, for the assistance of our faith concerning it, that, *knowing the terror of the Lord,* we may be persuaded to live in his fear. 2. It was a specimen of the terrors of the general judgment, in which sinners will be called to an account for the breach of this law: the archangel's trumpet will then sound an alarm, to give notice of the Judge's coming, and a *fire shall devour before him.* 3. It was an indication of the terror of those convictions which the law brings into conscience, to prepare the soul for the comforts of the gospel. Thus was the law given by Moses in such a way as might startle, affright, and humble men, that the *grace and truth which came by Jesus Christ* might be the more welcome. The apostle largely describes this instance of the terror of that dispensation, as a foil to set off our privileges, as Christians, in the light, liberty, and joy, of the New-Testament dispensation, Heb. 12:18, etc.

II. The impression which this made, for the present, upon the people; they must have had stupid hearts indeed, if this had not affected them. 1. *They removed, and stood afar off, v.* 18. Before God began to speak, they were thrusting forward to gaze (*ch.* 19:21); but now they were effectually cured of their presumption, and taught to keep their distance. 2. *They entreated that the word should not be so spoken to them any more* (Heb. 12:19), but begged that God would speak to them by Moses, *v.* 19. Hereby they obliged themselves to acquiesce in the mediation of Moses, they themselves nominating him as a fit person to deal between them and God, and promising to hearken to him as to God's messenger; hereby also they teach us to acquiesce in that method which Infinite Wisdom takes, of speaking to us by men like ourselves, whose *terror shall not make us afraid, nor their hand be heavy upon us.* Once God tried the expedient of speaking to the children of men immediately, but it was found that they could not bear it; it rather drove men from God than brought them to him, and, as it proved in the issue, though it terrified them, it did not deter them from idolatry, for soon after this they worshipped the golden calf. Let us therefore rest satisfied with the instructions given us by the scriptures and the ministry; for, if we believe not them, neither should we be persuaded though God should speak to us in thunder and lightning, as he did from Mount Sinai: here that matter was determined.

III. The encouragement Moses gave them, by explaining the design of God in his terror (*v.* 20): *Fear not,* that is, "Think not that the thunder and fire are designed to consume you," which was the thing they feared (*v.* 19, *lest we die*); thunder and lightning constituted one of the plagues of Egypt, but Moses would not have them think they were sent to them on the same errand on which they were sent to the Egyptians: no, they were intended, 1. To prove them, to try how they would like dealing with God immediately, without a mediator, and so to convince them how admirably well God had chosen for them, in putting Moses into that office. Ever since Adam fled, upon hearing God's voice in the garden, sinful man could not bear either to speak to God or hear from him immediately. 2. To keep them to their duty, and prevent their sinning against God. He encourages them, saying, *Fear not,* and yet tells them that God thus spoke to them, *that his fear might be before their face.* We must not fear with amazement — with that fear which has torment, which only works upon the fancy for the present, sets us a trembling, genders to bondage, betrays us to Satan, and alienates us from God; but we must always have in our minds a reverence of God's majesty, a dread of his displeasure, and an obedient regard to his sovereign authority over us: this fear will quicken us to our duty and make us circumspect in our walking. Thus *stand in awe, and sin not,* Ps. 4:4.

IV. The progress of their communion with God by the mediation of Moses, *v.* 21. While the people continued to stand afar off, conscious of guilt and afraid of God's wrath, *Moses drew near unto the thick darkness;* he *was made to draw near,* so the word is: Moses, of himself, durst not have ventured into the thick darkness, if God had not called him, and encouraged him, and, as some of the rabbies suppose, sent an angel to take him by the hand, and lead him up. Thus it is said of the great Mediator, *I will cause him to draw near* (Jer. 30:21), and by him it is that we also are introduced, Eph. 3:12.

Verses 22–26

Moses having gone into *the thick darkness, where God was,* God there spoke in his hearing only, privately and without terror, all that follows hence to the end of *ch.* 23, which is mostly an exposition of the ten commandments; and he was to transmit it by word of mouth first, and afterwards in writing, to the people. The laws in these verses related to God's worship.

I. They are here forbidden to make images for worship (*v.* 22, 23): *You have seen that I have talked with you from heaven* (such was his wonderful condescension, much more than for some mighty prince to talk familiarly with a company of poor beggars); now *you shall not make gods of silver.*

1. This repetition of the second commandment comes in here, either (1.) As pointing to that which God had chiefly in view in giving them this law in this manner, that is, their peculiar addictedness to idolatry, and the peculiar sinfulness of that crime. Ten commandments God had given them, but Moses is ordered to inculcate upon them especially the first two. They must not forget any of them, but they must be sure to remember those. Or, (2.) As pointing to that which might properly be inferred from God's speaking to them as he had done. He had given them sufficient demonstration of his presence among them; they needed not to make images of him, as if he were absent. Besides, they had only seen that he talked with them; they had seen no manner of similitude, so that they could not make any image of God; and his manifesting himself to them only by a voice plainly showed them that they must not make any such image, but keep up their communion with God by his word, and not otherwise.

2. Two arguments are here hinted against image-worship — (1.) That thereby they would affront God, intimated in that, *You shall not make with me gods.* Though they pretended to worship them but as representations of God, yet really they made them rivals with God, which

he would not endure. (2.) That thereby they would abuse themselves, intimated in that, *"You shall not make unto you gods;* while you think by them to assist your devotion, you will really corrupt it, and put a cheat upon yourselves." At first, it should seem, they made their images for worship of gold and silver, pretending, by the richness of those metals, to honour God, and, by the brightness of them, to affect themselves with his glory; but, even in these, they *changed the truth of God into a lie,* and so, by degrees, were justly given up to such strong delusions as to worship images of wood or stone.

II. They are here directed in making altars for worship: it is meant of occasional altars, such as they reared now in the wilderness, before the tabernacle was erected, and afterwards upon special emergencies, for present use, such as Gideon built (Jdg. 6:24), Manoah (Jdg. 13:19), Samuel (1 Sa. 7:17), and many others. We may suppose, now that the people of Israel were, with this glorious discovery which God had made of himself to them, that many of them would incline, in this pang of devotion, to offer sacrifice to God; and, it being necessary to a sacrifice that there be an alter, they are here appointed,

1. To make their altars very plain, either of *earth* or of *unhewn stone, v.* 24, 25. That they might not be tempted to think of a graven image, they must not so much as hew into shape the stones that they made their altars of, but pile them up as they were, in the rough. This rule being prescribed before the establishment of the ceremonial law, which appointed altars much more costly, intimates that, after the period of that law, plainness should be accepted as the best ornament of the external services of religion, and that gospel-worship should not be performed with external pomp and gaiety. The beauty of holiness needs no paint, nor do those do any service to the spouse of Christ that dress her in the attire of a harlot, as the church of Rome does: an *altar of earth* does best.

2. To make their altars very low (*v.* 26), so that they might not go up by steps to them. That the higher the altar was, and the nearer heaven, the more acceptable the sacrifice was, was a foolish fancy of the heathen, who therefore chose high places; in opposition to this, and to show that it is the elevation of the heart, not of the sacrifice, that God looks at, they were here ordered to make their altars low. We may suppose that the altars they reared in the wilderness, and other occasional altars, were designed only for the sacrifice of one beast at a time; but the altar in Solomon's temple, which was to be made much longer and broader, that it might contain many sacrifices at once, was made ten cubits high, that the height might bear a decent proportion to the length and breadth; and to that it was requisite they should go up by steps, which yet, no doubt, were so contrived as to prevent the inconvenience here spoken of, the *discovering of their nakedness* thereon.

III. They are here assured of God's gracious acceptance of their devotions, wherever they were paid according to his will (*v.* 24): *In all places where I record my name,* or where my name is recorded (that is, where I am worshipped in sincerity), *I will come unto thee, and I will bless thee.* Afterwards, God chose one particular place wherein to record his name: but that being taken away now under the gospel, when men are encouraged to pray every where, this promise revives in its full extent, that, wherever God's people meet in his name to worship him, he will be *in the midst of them,* he will honour them with his presence, and reward them with the gifts of his grace; there he will come unto them, and will bless them, and more than this we need not desire for the beautifying of our solemn assemblies.

CHAPTER 21

The laws recorded in this chapter relate to the fifth and sixth commandments; and though they are not accommodated to our constitution, especially in point of servitude, nor are the penalties annexed binding on us, yet they are of great use for the explanation of the moral law, and the rules of natural justice. Here are several enlargements, I. Upon the fifth commandment, which concerns particular relations. 1. The duty of masters towards their servants, their men-servants (*v.* 2–6), and the maidservants (*v.* 7–11). 2. The punishment of disobedient children that strike their parents (*v.* 15), or curse them (*v.* 17). II. Upon the sixth commandment, which forbids all violence offered to the person of a man. Here is, 1. Concerning murder (*v.* 12–14). 2. Man-stealing (*v.* 16). 3. Assault and battery (*v.* 18, 19). 4. Correcting a servant (*v.* 20, 21). 5. Hurting a woman with child (*v.* 22, 23). 6. The law of retaliation (*v.* 24, 25). 7. Maiming a servant (*v.* 26, 27). 8. An ox goring (*v.* 28–32). 9. Damage by opening a pit (*v.* 33, 34). 10. Cattle fighting (*v.* 35, 36).

Verses 1–11

The first verse is the general title of the laws contained in this and the two following chapters, some of them relating to the religious worship of God, but most of them relating to matters between man and man. Their government being purely a Theocracy, that which in other states is to be settled by human prudence was directed among them by a divine appointment, so that the constitution of their government was peculiarly adapted to make them happy. These laws are called *judgments,* because they are framed in infinite wisdom and equity, and because their magistrates were to give judgment according to the people. In the doubtful cases that had hitherto occurred, Moses had particularly enquired of God for them, as appeared, *ch.* 18:15; but now God gave him statutes in general by which to determine particular cases, which likewise he must apply to other like cases that might happen, which, falling under the same reason, fell under the same rule. He begins with the laws concerning servants, commanding mercy and moderation towards them. The Israelites had lately been servants themselves; and now that they had become, not only their own masters, but masters of servants too, lest they should abuse their servants, as they themselves had been abused and ruled with rigour by the Egyptian task-masters, provision was made by these laws for the mild and gentle usage of servants. Note, If those who have had power over us have been injurious to us this will not in the least excuse us if we be in like manner injurious to those who are under our power, but will rather aggravate our crime, because, in that case, we may the more easily put our souls into their soul's stead. Here is,

I. A law concerning men-servants, sold, either by themselves or their parents, through poverty, or by the judges, for their crimes; even those of the latter sort (if Hebrews) were to continue in slavery but seven years at the most, in which time it was taken for granted that they would sufficiently have smarted for their folly or offence. At the seven years' end the servant should either go out free (*v.* 2, 3), or his servitude should thenceforward be his choice, *v.* 5, 6. If he had a wife given him by his master, and children, he might either leave them and go out free himself, or, if he had such a kindness for them that he would rather tarry with them in bondage than go out at liberty without them, he was to have his ear bored through to the doorpost and serve till the death of his master, or the year of jubilee.

1. By this law God taught, (1.) The Hebrew servants generosity, and a noble love of liberty, for they were the Lord's freemen; a mark of disgrace must be put upon him who refused liberty when he might have it, though he refused it upon considerations otherwise laudable enough. Thus Christians, being *bought with a price, and called unto liberty,* must not be the servants of men, nor of the lusts of men, 1 Co. 7:23. There is a free and princely spirit that much helps to uphold a Christian, Ps. 51:12. He likewise taught, (2.) The Hebrew masters not to trample upon their poor servants, knowing, not only that they had been by birth upon a level with them, but that, in a few years, they would be so again. Thus Christian masters must look with respect on believing servants, Phlm. 16.

2. This law will be further useful to us, (1.) To illustrate the right God has to the children of believing parents, as such, and the place they have in his church. They are by baptism enrolled among his servants, because they are *born in his house,* for they are therefore *born unto him,* Eze. 16:20. David owns himself God's servant, as he was *the son of his handmaid* (Ps. 116:16), and therefore entitled to protection, Ps. 86:16. (2.) To explain the obligation which the great Redeemer laid upon himself to prosecute the work of our salvation, for he says (Ps. 40:6), *My ears hast thou opened,* which seems to allude to this law. He loved his Father, and his captive spouse, and the children that were given him, and would not go out free from his undertaking, but engaged to serve in it for ever, Isa. 42:1, 4. Much more reason have we thus to engage ourselves to serve God for ever; we have all the reason in the world to love our Master and his work, and to have our ears bored to his door-posts, as those who desire not to go out free from his service, but to be found more and more free to it, and in it, Ps. 84:10.

Concerning maid-servants, whom their parents, through extreme poverty, had sold, when they were very young, to such as they hoped would marry them when they grew up; if they did not, yet they must not sell them to strangers, but rather study how to make them amends for the disappointment; if they did, they must maintain them handsomely, v. 7–11. Thus did God provide for the comfort and reputation of the daughters of Israel, and has taught husbands to *give honour to their wives* (be their extraction ever so mean) as to the *weaker vessels*, 1 Pt. 3:7.

Verses 12–21

Here is, I. A law concerning murder. He had lately said, *Thou shalt not kill;* here he provides, 1. For the punishing of wilful murder (v. 12): *He that smiteth a man,* whether upon a sudden passion or in malice prepense, *so that he die,* the government must take care that the murderer be *put to death,* according to that ancient law (Gen. 9:6), *Whoso sheddeth man's blood, by man shall his blood be shed.* God, who by his providence gives and maintains life, thus by his law protects it; so that mercy shown to a wilful murderer is real cruelty to all mankind besides: such a one, God here says, shall be taken even *from his altar* (v. 14), to which he might flee for protection; and, if God will not shelter him, let him *flee to the pit, and let no man stay him.* 2. For the relief of such as killed by accident, *per infortunium* — *by misfortune,* or *chance-medley,* as our law expresses it, when a man, in doing a lawful act, without intent of hurt to any, happens to kill another, or, as it is here described, *God delivers him into his hand;* for nothing comes to pass by chance; what seems to us purely casual is ordered by the divine Providence, for wise and holy ends secret to us. In this case God provided cities of refuge for the protection of those whose infelicity it was, but not their fault, to occasion the death of another, v. 13. With us, who know no avengers of blood but the magistrates, the law itself is a sufficient sanctuary for those whose minds are innocent, though their hands are guilty, and there needs no other.

II. Concerning rebellious children. It is here made a capital crime, to be punished with death, for children either, 1. To strike their parents (v. 15) so as either to draw blood or to make the place struck black and blue. Or, 2. To curse their parents (v. 17), if they profaned any name of God in doing it, as the rabbies say. Note, The undutiful behaviour of children towards their parents is a very great provocation to God our common Father; and, if men do not punish it, he will. Those are perfectly lost to all virtue, and abandoned to all wickedness, that have broken through the bonds of filial reverence and duty to such a degree as in word or action to abuse their own parents. What yoke will those bear that have shaken off this? Let children take heed of entertaining in their minds any such thought or passions towards their parents as savour of undutifulness and contempt; for the righteous God searches the heart.

III. Here is a law against man-stealing (v. 16): *He that steals a man* (that is, a person, man, woman, or child), with design to sell him to the Gentiles (for no Israelite would buy him), was adjudged to death by this statute, which is ratified by the apostle (1 Tim. 1:10), where *men-stealers* are reckoned among those wicked ones against whom laws must be made by Christian princes.

IV. Care is here taken that satisfaction be made for hurt done to a person, though death do not ensue, v. 18, 19. He that did the hurt must be accountable for damages, and pay, not only for the cure, but for the loss of time, to which the Jews add that he must likewise give some recompence both for the pain and for the blemish, if there were any.

V. Direction is given what should be done if a servant died by his master's correction. This servant must not be an Israelite, but a Gentile slave, as the negroes to our planters; and it is supposed that he smite him with a rod, and not with any thing that was likely to give a mortal wound; yet, if he died under his hand, he should be punished for his cruelty, at the discretion of the judges, upon consideration of circumstances, v. 20. But, if he continued a day or two after the correction given, the master was supposed to suffer enough by losing his servant, v. 21. Our law makes the death of a servant, by his master's reasonable beating of him, but *chance-medley.* Yet let all masters take heed of tyrannizing over their servants; the gospel teaches them even to forbear and moderate threatenings (Eph. 6:9), con-

sidering with holy Job, *What shall I do, when God riseth up?* Job 31:13–15.

Verses 22–36

Observe here,

I. The particular care which the law took of women with child, that no hurt should be done them which might occasion their mis-carrying. The law of nature obliges us to be very tender in that case, lest the tree and fruit be destroyed together, v. 22, 23. Women with child, who are thus taken under the special protection of the law of God, if they live in his fear, may still believe themselves under the special protection of the providence of God, and hope that they shall be saved in child-bearing. On this occasion comes in that general law of retaliation which our Saviour refers to, Mt. 5:38, *An eye for an eye.* Now, 1. The execution of this law is not hereby put into the hands of private persons, as if every man might avenge himself, which would introduce universal confusion, and make men like the fishes of the sea. The tradition of the elders seems to have put this corrupt gloss upon it, in opposition to which our Saviour commands us to forgive injuries, and not to meditate revenge, Mt. 5:39. 2. God often executes it in the course of his providence, making the punishment, in many cases, to answer to the sin, as Jdg. 1:7; Isa. 33:1; Hab. 2:13; Mt. 26:52. 3. Magistrates ought to have an eye to this rule in punishing offenders, and doing right to those that are injured. Consideration must be had of the nature, quality, and degree of the wrong done, that reparation may be made to the party injured, and others deterred from doing the like; either *an eye* shall go *for an eye,* or the forfeited eye shall be redeemed by a sum of money. Note, He that does wrong must expect one way or other to receive *according to the wrong he has done,* Col. 3:25. God sometimes brings men's violent dealings upon their own heads (Ps. 7:16); and magistrates are in this the ministers of the justice, that they are *avengers* (Rom. 13:4), and they shall not bear the sword in vain.

II. The care God took of servants. If their masters maimed them, though it was only striking out a tooth, that should be their discharge, v. 26, 27. This was intended, 1. To prevent their being abused; masters would be careful not to offer them any violence, lest they should lose their service. 2. To comfort them if they were abused; the loss of a limb should be the gaining of their liberty, which would do something towards balancing both the pain and disgrace they underwent. Nay,

III. *Does God take care for oxen?* Yes, it appears by the following laws in this chapter that he does, *for our sakes,* 1 Co. 9:9, 10. The Israelites are here directed what to do,

1. In case of hurt done by oxen, or any other brutecreature; for the law, doubtless, was designed to extend to all parallel cases. (1.) As an instance of God's care of the life of man (though forfeited a thousand times into the hands of divine justice), and in token of his detestation of the sin of murder. If an ox killed any man, woman, or child, the ox was to be *stoned* (v. 28); and, because the greatest honour of the inferior creatures is to be serviceable to man, the criminal is denied that honour: his *flesh shall not be eaten.* Thus God would keep up in the minds of his people a rooted abhorrence of the sin of murder and every thing that was barbarous. (2.) To make men careful that none of their cattle might do hurt, but that, by all means possible, mischief might be prevented. If the owner of the beast knew that he was mischievous, he must answer for the hurt done, and, according as the circumstances of the case proved him to be more or less accessory, he must either be *put to death* or ransom his life with a sum of money, v. 29–32. Some of our ancient books make this felony, by the common law of England, and give this reason, "The owner, by suffering his beast to go at liberty when he knew it to be mischievous, shows that he was very willing that hurt should be done." Note, It is not enough for us not to do mischief ourselves, but we must take care that no mischief be done by those whom it is in our power to restrain, whether man or beast.

2. In case of hurt done to oxen, or other cattle. (1.) If they fall into a pit, and perish there, he that opened the pit must make good the loss, v. 33, 34. Note, We must take heed not only of doing that which will be hurtful, but of doing that which may be so. It is not enough not to design and devise mischief, but we must contrive to prevent mis-

chief, else we become accessory to our neighbours' damage. Mischief done in malice is the great transgression; but mischief done through negligence, and for want of due care and consideration, is not without fault, but ought to be reflected upon with great regret, according as the degree of the mischief is: especially we must be careful that we do nothing to make ourselves accessory to the sins of others, by laying an occasion of offence in our brother's way, Rom. 14:13. (2.) If cattle fight, and one kill another, the owners shall equally share in the loss, v. 35. Only if the beast that had done the harm was known to the owner to have been mischievous he shall answer for the damage, because he ought either to have killed him or kept him up, v. 36. The determinations of these cases carry with them the evidence of their own equity, and give such rules of justice as were then, and are still, in use, for the decision of similar controversies that arise between man and man. But I conjecture that these cases might be specified, rather than others (though some of them seem minute), because they were then cases in fact actually depending before Moses; for in the wilderness where they lay closely encamped, and had their flocks and herds among them, such mischiefs as these last mentioned were likely enough to occur. That which we are taught by these laws is that we should be very careful to do no wrong, either directly or indirectly; and that, if we have done wrong, we must be very willing to make satisfaction, and desirous that nobody may lose by us.

CHAPTER 22

The laws of this chapter relate, I. To the eighth commandment, concerning theft (v. 1–4), trespass by cattle (v. 5), damage by fire (v. 6), trusts (v. 7–13), borrowing cattle (v. 14, 15), or money (v. 25–27). II. To the seventh commandment. Against fornication (v. 16, 17), bestiality (v. 19). III. To the first table, forbidding witchcraft (v. 18), idolatry (v. 20). Commanding to offer the firstfruits (v. 29, 30). IV. To the poor (v. 21–24). V. To the civil government (v. 28). VI. To the peculiarity of the Jewish nation (v. 31).

Verses 1–6

Here are the laws,

I. Concerning theft, which are these: — 1. If a man steal any cattle (in which the wealth of those times chiefly consisted), and they be found in his custody, he must restore double, v. 4. Thus he must both satisfy for the wrong and suffer for the crime. But it was afterwards provided that if the thief were touched in conscience, and voluntarily confessed it, before it was discovered or enquired into by any other, then he should only make restitution of what he had stolen, and add to it a fifth part, Lev. 6:4, 5. 2. If he had killed or sold the sheep or ox he had stolen, and thereby persisted in his crime, he must restore *five oxen for an ox, and four sheep for a sheep* (v. 1), more for an ox than for a sheep because the owner, besides all the other profit, lost the daily labour of his ox. This law teaches us that fraud and injustice, so far from enriching men, will impoverish them: if we unjustly get and keep that which is another's, it will not only waste itself, but it will consume that which is our own. 3. If he was not able to make restitution, he must be sold for a slave, v. 3. The court of judgment was to do it, and it is probable that the person robbed had the money. Thus with us, in some cases, felons are transported into plantations where alone Englishmen know what slavery is. 4. If a thief broke a house in the night, and was killed in the doing of it, his blood was upon his own head, and should not be required at the hand of him that shed it, v. 2. As he that does an unlawful act bears the blame of the mischief that follows to others, so likewise of that which follows to himself. A man's house is his castle, and God's law, as well as man's, sets a guard upon it; he that assaults it does so at his peril. Yet, if it was in the day-time that the thief was killed, he that killed him must be accountable for it (v. 3), unless it was in the necessary defence of his own life. Note, We ought to be tender of the lives even of bad men; the magistrate must afford us redress, and we must not avenge ourselves.

II. Concerning trespass, v. 5. He that wilfully put his cattle into his neighbour's field must make restitution of the best of his own. Our law makes a much greater difference between this and other thefts than the law of Moses did. The Jews hence observed it as a general rule that restitution must always be made of the best, and that no man should keep any cattle that were likely to trespass upon his neighbours or do them any damage. We should be more careful not to do wrong than not to suffer wrong, because to suffer wrong is only an affliction, but to do wrong is a sin, and sin is always worse than affliction.

III. Concerning damage done by fire, *v.* 6. He that designed only the burning of thorns might become accessory to the burning of corn, and should not be held guiltless. Men of hot and eager spirits should take heed, lest, while they pretend only to pluck up the tares, they root out the wheat also. If the fire did mischief, he that kindled it must answer for it, though it could not be proved that he designed the mischief. Men must suffer for their carelessness, as well as for their malice. We must take heed of beginning strife; for, though it seem but little, we know not how great a matter it may kindle, the blame of which we must bear, if, with the madman, we cast fire-brands, arrows, and death, and pretend we mean no harm. It will make us very careful of ourselves, if we consider that we are accountable, not only for the hurt we do, but for the hurt we occasion through inadvertency.

Verses 7–15

These laws are,

I. Concerning trusts, *v.* 7–13. If a man deliver goods, suppose to a carrier to be conveyed, or to a warehouse-keeper to be preserved, or cattle to a farmer to be fed, upon a valuable consideration, and if a special confidence be reposed in the person they are lodged with, in case these goods be stolen or lost, perish or be damaged, if it appear that it was not by any fault of the trustee, the owner must stand to the loss, otherwise he that has been false to this trust must be compelled to make satisfaction. The trustee must aver his innocence upon oath before the judges, if the case was such as afforded no other proof, and they were to determine the matter according as it appeared. This teaches us, 1. That we ought to be very careful of every thing we are entrusted with, as careful of it, though it be another's, as if it were our own. It is unjust and base, and that which all the world cries shame on, to betray a trust. 2. That there is such a general failing of truth and justice upon earth as gives too much occasion to suspect men's honesty whenever it is their interest to be dishonest. 3. That *an oath for confirmation is an end of strife*, Heb. 6:16. It is called an *oath for the Lord* (*v.* 11), because to him the appeal is made, not only as to a witness of truth, but as to an avenger of wrong and falsehood. Those that had offered injury to their neighbour by doing any unjust thing, yet, it might be hoped, had not so far debauched their consciences as to profane an oath of the Lord, and call the God of truth to be witness to a lie: perjury is a sin which natural conscience startles at as much as any other. The religion of an oath is very ancient, and a plain indication of the universal belief of a God, and a providence, and a judgment to come. 4. That magistracy is an ordinance of God, designed, among other intentions, to assist men both in discovering rights disputed and recovering rights denied; and great respect ought to be paid to the determination of the judges. 5. That there is no reason why a man should suffer for that which he could not help: masters should consider this, in dealing with their servants, and not rebuke that as a fault which was a mischance, and which they themselves, had they been in their servants' places, could not have prevented.

II. Concerning loans, *v.* 14, 15. If a man (suppose) lent his team to his neighbour, if the owner was with it, or was to receive profit for the loan of it, whatever harm befel the cattle the owner must stand to the loss of: but if the owner was so kind to the borrower as to lend it to him gratis, and put such a confidence in him as to trust it from under his own eye, then, if any harm happened, the borrower must make it good. Let us learn hence to be very careful not to abuse any thing that is lent us; it is not only unjust, but base and disingenuous, inasmuch as it is rendering evil for good; we should much rather choose to lose ourselves than that any should sustain loss by their kindness to us. *Alas, master! for it was borrowed*, 2 Ki. 6:5.

Verses 16–24

Here is, I. A law that he who debauched a young woman should be obliged to marry her, *v.* 16, 17. If she was betrothed to another, it was death to debauch her (Deu. 22:23, 24); but the law here mentioned respects her as single. But, if the father refused her to him, he was to

give satisfaction in money for the injury and disgrace he had done her. This law puts an honour upon marriage and shows likewise how improper a thing it is that children should marry without their parents' consent: even here, where the divine law appointed the marriage, both as a punishment to him that had done wrong and a recompence to her that had suffered wrong, yet there was an express reservation for the father's power; if he denied his consent, it must be no marriage.

II. A law which makes witchcraft a capital crime, *v.* 18. Witchcraft not only gives that honour to the devil which is due to God alone, but bids defiance to the divine Providence, wages war with God's government, and puts his work into the devil's hand, expecting him to do good and evil, and so making him indeed *the god of this world;* justly therefore was it punished with death, especially among a people that were blessed with a divine revelation, and cared for by divine Providence above any people under the sun. By our law, consulting, covenanting with, invocating, or employing, any evil spirit, to any intent whatsoever, and exercising any enchantment, charm, or sorcery, whereby hurt shall be done to any person whatsoever, is made felony, without benefit of clergy; also pretending to tell where goods lost or stolen may be found, or the like, is an iniquity punishable by the judge, and the second offence with death. The justice of our law herein is supported by the law of God recorded here.

III. Unnatural abominations are here made capital; such beasts in the shape of men as are guilty of them are unfit to live (*v.* 19): *Whosoever lies with a beast shall die.*

IV. Idolatry is also made capital, *v.* 20. God having declared himself jealous in this matter, the civil powers must be jealous in it too, and utterly destroy those persons, families, and places of Israel, that worshipped any god, save the Lord: this law might have prevented the woeful apostasies of the Jewish nation in after times, if those that should have executed it had not been ringleaders in the breach of it.

V. A caution against oppression. Because those who were empowered to punish other crimes were themselves most in danger of this, God takes the punishing of it into his own hands.

1. Strangers must not be abused (*v.* 21), not wronged in judgment by the magistrates, not imposed upon in contracts, nor must any advantage be taken of their ignorance or necessity; no, nor must they be taunted, trampled upon, treated with contempt, or upbraided with being strangers; for all these were vexations, and would discourage strangers from coming to live among them, or would strengthen their prejudices against their religion, to which, by all kind and gentle methods, they should endeavour to proselyte them. The reason given why they should be kind to strangers is, "*You were strangers in Egypt*, and knew what it was to be vexed and oppressed there," Note, (1.) Humanity is one of the laws of religion, and obliges us particularly to be tender of those that lie most under disadvantages and discouragements, and to extend our compassionate concern to strangers, and those to whom we are not under the obligations of alliance or acquaintance. Those that are strangers to us are known to God, and he preserves them, Ps. 146:9. (2.) Those that profess religion should study to oblige strangers, that they may thereby recommend religion to their good opinion, and take heed of doing any thing that may tempt them to think ill of it or its professors, 1 Pt. 2:12. (3.) Those that have themselves been in poverty and distress, if Providence enrich and enlarge them, ought to show a particular tenderness towards those that are now in such circumstances as they were in formerly, doing now by them as they then wished to be done by.

2. Widows and fatherless must not be abused (*v.* 22): *You shall not afflict them*, that is, "You shall comfort and assist them, and be ready upon all occasions to show them kindness." In making just demands from them, their condition must be considered, who have lost those that should deal for them, and protect them; they are supposed to be unversed in business, destitute of advice, timorous, and of a tender spirit, and therefore must be treated with kindness and compassion; no advantage must be taken against them, nor any hardship put upon them, from which a husband or a father would have sheltered them. For, (1.) God takes particular cognizance of their case, *v.* 23. Having no

one else to complain and appeal to, they will *cry unto God*, and he will be sure *to hear them;* for his law and his providence are guardians to the widows and fatherless, and if men do not pity them, and will not hear them, he will. Note, It is a great comfort to those who are injured and oppressed by men that they have a God to go to who will do more than *give them the hearing;* and it ought to be a terror to those who are oppressive that they have the cry of the poor against them, which God will hear. Nay, (2.) He will severely reckon with those that do oppress them. Though they escape punishments from men, God's righteous judgments will pursue and overtake them, *v.* 24. Men that have a sense of justice and honour will espouse the injured cause of the weak and helpless; and shall not the righteous God do it? Observe the equity of the sentence here passed upon those that oppress the widows and fatherless: their wives shall become widows, and their children fatherless; and the Lord is known by these judgments, which he sometimes executes still.

Verses 25–31

Here is, I. A law against extortion in lending. 1. They must not receive use for money from any that borrowed for necessity (*v.* 25), as in that case, Neh. 5:5, 7. And such provision the law made for the preservation of estates to their families by the year of jubilee that a people who had little concern in trade could not be supposed to borrow money but for necessity, and therefore it is generally forbidden among themselves; but to a stranger, whom yet they might not oppress, they were allowed to lend upon usury: this law, therefore, in the strictness of it, seems to have been peculiar to the Jewish state; but, in the equity of it, it obliges us to show mercy to those of whom we might take advantage, and to be content to share, in loss as well as profit, with those we lend to, if Providence cross them; and, upon this condition, it seems as lawful to receive interest for my money, which another takes pains with and improves, but runs the hazard of, in trade, as it is to receive rent for my land, which another takes pains with and improves, but runs the hazard of, in husbandry. 2. They must not take a poor man's bed-clothes in pawn; but, if they did, must restore them by bed-time, *v.* 26, 27. Those who lie soft and warm themselves should consider the hard and cold lodgings of many poor people, and not do any thing to make bad worse, or to add affliction to the afflicted.

II. A law against the contempt of authority (*v.* 28): *Thou shalt not revile the gods*, that is, the *judges* and *magistrates*, for their executing these laws; they must do their duty, whoever suffer by it. Magistrates ought not to fear the reproach of men, nor their revilings, but to despise them as long as they keep a good conscience; but those that do revile them for their being a terror to evil works and workers reflect upon God himself, and will have a great deal to answer for another day. We find those under a black character, and a heavy doom, that *despise dominion, and speak evil of dignities*, Jude 8. Princes and magistrates are our fathers, whom the fifth commandment obliges us to honour and forbids us to revile. St. Paul applies this law to himself, and owns that he ought not to *speak evil of the ruler of his people;* no, not though the ruler was then his most unrighteous persecutor, Acts 23:5; see Eccl. 10:20.

III. A law concerning the offering of their first-fruits to God, *v.* 29, 30. It was appointed before (*ch.* 13), and it is here repeated: *The firstborn of thy sons shalt thou give unto me;* and much more reason have we to give ourselves, and all we have, to God, who *spared not his own Son, but delivered him up for us all.* The first ripe of their corn they must not delay to offer. There is danger, if we delay our duty, lest we wholly omit it; and by slipping the first opportunity, in expectation of another, we suffer Satan to cheat us of all our time. Let not young people delay to offer to God the first-fruits of their time and strength, lest their delays come, at last, to be denials, through the deceitfulness of sin, and the more convenient season they promise themselves never arrive. Yet it is provided that the firstlings of their cattle should not be dedicated to God till they were past seven days old, for then they began to be good for something. Note, God is the first and best, and therefore must have the first and best.

IV. A distinction put between the Jews and all other people: *You shall be holy men unto me;* and one mark of that honourable distinction is appointed in their diet, which was, that they should not *eat any flesh that was torn of beasts* (v. 31), not only because it was unwholesome, but because it was paltry, and base, and covetous, and a thing below those who were holy men unto God, to eat the leavings of the beasts of prey. We that are sanctified to God must not be curious in our diet; but we must be conscientious, not feeding ourselves without fear, but eating and drinking by rule, the rule of sobriety, to the glory of God.

CHAPTER 23

This chapter continues and concludes the acts that passed in the first session (if I may so call it) upon mount Sinai. Here are, I. Some laws of universal obligation, relating especially to the ninth commandment, against bearing false witness (v. 1), and giving false judgment (v. 2, 3, 6–8). Also a law of doing good to our enemies (v. 4, 5), and not oppressing strangers (v. 9). II. Some laws peculiar to the Jews. The sabbatical year (v. 10, 11), the three annual feasts (v. 14–17), with some laws pertaining thereto. III. Gracious promises of the completing of the mercy God had begun for them, upon condition of their obedience. That God would conduct them through the wilderness (v. 20–24), that he would prosper all they had (v. 25, 26), that he would put them in possession of Canaan (v. 27–31). But they must not mingle themselves with the nations (v. 32, 33).

Verses 1–9

Here are, I. Cautions concerning judicial proceedings; it was not enough that they had good laws, better than ever any nation had, but care must be taken for the due administration of justice according to those laws.

1. The witnesses are here cautioned that they neither occasion an innocent man to be indicted, by raising a false report of him and setting common fame against him, nor assist in the prosecution of an innocent man, or one whom they do not know to be guilty, by *putting their hand* in swearing as witnesses against him, v. 1. Bearing false witness against a man, in a matter that touches his life, has in it all the guilty of lying, perjury, malice, theft, murder, with the additional stains of colouring all with a pretence of justice and involving many others in the same guilt. There is scarcely any one act of wickedness that a man can possibly be guilty of which has in it a greater complication of villanies than this has. Yet the former part of this caution is to be extended, not only to judicial proceedings, but to common conversation; so that slandering and backbiting are a special of falsewitness-bearing. A man's reputation lies as much at the mercy of every company as his estate or life does at the mercy of a judge or jury; so that he who raises, or knowingly spreads, a false report against his neighbour, especially if the report be made to wise and good men whose esteem one would desire to enjoy, sins as much against the laws of truth, justice, and charity, as a false witness does — with this further mischief, that he leaves it not in the power of the person injured to obtain redress. That which we translate, Thou shalt not *raise*, the margin reads, Thou shalt not *receive* a false report; for sometimes the receiver, in this case, is as bad as the thief; and a backbiting tongue would not do so much mischief as it does if it were not countenanced. Sometimes we cannot avoid hearing a false report, but we must not receive it, that is, we must not hear it with pleasure and delight as those that rejoice in iniquity, nor give credit to it as long as there remains any cause to question the truth of it. This is charity to our neighbour's good name, and doing as we would be done by.

2. The judges are here cautioned not to pervert judgment. (1.) They must not be overruled, either by might or multitude, to go against their consciences in giving judgment, v. 2. With the Jews causes were tried by a bench of justices, and judgment given according to the majority of votes, in which cause every particular justice must go according to truth, as it appeared to him upon the strictest and most impartial enquiry, though the multitude of the people, and their outcries, or, the sentence of the *rabbim* (we translate it *many*), the more ancient and honourable of the justices, went the other way. Therefore (as with us), among the Jews, the junior upon the bench voted first, that he might not be swayed nor overruled by the authority of the senior. Judges must not respect the persons either of the parties or of their fellow-judges. The former part of this verse also gives a general rule for all, as well as judges, not *to follow a multitude to do evil*. General usage will never excuse us in a bad practice; nor is the broad way ever the better or safer for its being tracked and crowded. We must enquire what we ought to do, not

what the majority do; because we must be judged by our Master, not by our fellow-servants, and it is too great a compliment to be willing to go to hell for company. (2.) They must not pervert judgment, no, not in favour of a poor man, v. 3. Right must in all cases take place and wrong must be punished, and justice never biassed nor injury connived at under pretence of charity and compassion. If a poor man be a bad man, and do a bad thing, it is foolish pity to let him fare the better for his poverty, Deu. 1:16, 17. (3.) Neither must they pervert judgment in prejudice to a poor man, nor suffer him to be wronged because he had not wherewithal to right himself; in such cases the judges themselves must become advocates for the poor, as far as their cause was good and honest (v. 6): *"Thou shalt not wrest the judgment of the poor;* remember they are thy poor, bone of thy bone, thy poor neighbours, thy poor brethren; let them not therefore fare the worse for being poor."* (4.) They must dread the thoughts of assisting or abetting a bad cause (v. 7): *"Keep thyself far from a false matter;* do not only keep thyself free from it, nor think it enough to say thou art unconcerned in it, but keep far from it, dread it as a dangerous snare. The innocent and righteous thou wouldest not, for all the world, slay with thy own hands; keep far therefore from a false matter, for thou knowest not but it may end in that, and the righteous God will not leave such wickedness unpunished: *I will not justify the wicked,"* that is, "I will condemn him that unjustly condemns others." Judges themselves are accountable to the great judge. (5.) They must not take bribes, v. 8. They must not only not be swayed by a gift to give an unjust judgment, to condemn the innocent, or acquit the guilty, or adjudge a man's right from him, but they must not so much as take a gift, lest it should have a bad influence upon them, and overrule them, contrary to their intentions; for it has a strange tendency to blind those that otherwise would do well. (6.) They must not oppress a stranger, v. 9. Though aliens might not inherit lands among them, yet they must have justice done them, must peaceably enjoy their own, and be redressed if they were wronged, though they were strangers to the commonwealth of Israel. It is an instance of the equity and goodness of our law, that, if an alien be tried for any crime except treason, the one half of his jury, if he desire it, shall be foreigners; they call it a trial *per mediatatem linguae,* a kind provision that strangers may not be oppressed. The reason here given is the same with that in *ch.* 22:21, You were strangers, which is here elegantly enforced, You know the heart of a stranger; you know something of the griefs and fears of a stranger by sad experience, and therefore, being delivered, can the more easily put your souls into their souls' stead.

II. Commands concerning neighbourly kindnesses. We must be ready to do all good offices, as there is occasion, for any body, yea even for those that have done us ill offices, v. 4, 5. The command of loving our enemies, and doing good to those that hate us, is not only a *new,* but an *old* commandment, Prov. 25:21, 22. Infer hence, 1. If we must do this kindness for an enemy, much more for a friend, though an enemy only is mentioned, because it is supposed that a man would not be unneighbourly to any unless such as he had a particular spleen against. 2. If it be wrong not to prevent our enemy's loss and damage, how much worse is it to occasion harm and loss to him, or any thing he has. 3. If we must bring back our neighbours' cattle when they go astray, much more must we endeavour, by prudent admonitions and instructions, to bring back our neighbours themselves, when they go astray in any sinful path, see Jam. 5:19, 20. And, if we must endeavour to help up a fallen ass, much more should we endeavour, by comforts and encouragements, to help up a sinking spirit, *saying to those that are of a fearful heart,* Be strong. We must seek the relief and welfare of others as our own, Phil. 2:4. *If thou sayest, Behold, we know it not, doth not he that pondereth the heart consider it?* See Prov. 24:11, 12.

Verses 10–19

Here is, I. The institution of the sabbatical year, v. 10, 11. Every seventh year the land was to rest; they must not plough nor sow it at the beginning of the year, and then they could not expect any great harvest at the end of the year: but what the earth did produce of itself should be eaten from hand to mouth, and not laid up. Now this was

designed, 1. To show what a plentiful land that was into which God was bringing them — that so numerous a people could have rich maintenance out of the produce of so small a country, without foreign trade, and yet could spare the increase of every seventh year. 2. To remind them of their dependence upon God their great landlord, and their obligation to use the fruit of their land as he should direct. Thus he would try their obedience in a matter that nearly touched their interest. Afterwards we find that their disobedience to this command was a forfeiture of the promises, 2 Chr. 36:21. 3. To teach them a confidence in the divine Providence, while they did their duty — that, as the sixth day's manna served for two day's meat, so the sixth year's increase should serve for two years' subsistence. Thus they must learn not to *take thought for their life,* Mt. 6:25. If we are prudent and diligent in our affairs, we may trust Providence to furnish us with the bread of the day in its day.

II. The repetition of the law of the fourth commandment concerning the weekly sabbath, v. 12. Even in the year of rest they must not think that the sabbath day was laid in common with the other days, but, even that year, it must be religiously observed; yet thus some have endeavoured to take away the observance of the sabbath, by pretending that every day must be a sabbath day.

III. All manner of respect to the gods of the heathen is here strictly forbidden, v. 13. A general caution is prefixed to this, which has reference to all these precepts: *In all things that I have said unto you, be circumspect.* We are in danger of missing our way on the right hand and on the left, and it is at our peril if we do; therefore we have need to look about us. A man may ruin himself through mere carelessness, but he cannot save himself without great care and circumspection: particularly, since idolatry was a sin which they were much addicted to, and would be greatly tempted to, they must endeavour to blot out the remembrance of the gods of the heathen, and must disuse and forget all their superstitious forms of speech, and never mention them but with detestation. In Christian schools and academies (for it is in vain to think of reforming the play-houses), it were to be wished that the names and stories of the heathen deities, or demons rather, were not so commonly and familiarly used as they are, even with intimations of respect, and sometimes with forms of invocation. Surely we have *not so learned Christ.*

IV. Their solemn religious attendance on God in the place which he should choose is here strictly required, v. 14–17. 1. Thrice a year all their males must come together in a holy convocation, that they might the better know and love one another, and keep up their communion as a dignified and peculiar people. 2. They must come together *before the Lord* (v. 17) to present themselves before him, looking towards the place where his honour dwelt, and to pay their homage to him as their great Lord, from and under whom they held all their enjoyments. 3. They must feast together before the Lord, eating and drinking together, in token of their joy in God and their grateful sense of his goodness to them; for *a feast is made for laughter,* Eccl. 10:19. O what a good Master do we serve, who has made it our duty to *rejoice before him,* who feasts his servants when they are in waiting! Never let religion be called a melancholy thing, when its solemn services are solemn feasts. 4. They must not *appear before God empty,* v. 15. Some free-will offering or other they must bring, in token of their respect and gratitude to their great benefactor; and, as they were not allowed to come empty-handed, so we must not come to worship God empty-hearted; our souls must be filled with grace, with pious and devout affections, holy desires towards him, and dedications of ourselves to him, for *with such sacrifices God is well-pleased.* 5. The passover, pentecost, and feast of tabernacles, in spring, summer, and autumn, were the three times appointed for their attendance: not in winter, because travelling was then uncomfortable; not in the midst of their harvest, because then they were otherwise employed; so that they had no reason to say that he *made them to serve with an offering,* or *wearied them with incense.*

V. Some particular directions are here given about the three feasts, though not so fully as afterwards. 1. As to the passover, it was not to be offered with leavened bread, for at that feast all leaven was to be cast out, nor was the fat of it to remain until the morning, lest it should become offensive, *v.* 18. 2. At the feast of pentecost, when they were to begin their harvest, they must bring *the first of their first-fruits* to God, by the pious presenting of which the whole harvest was sanctified, *v.* 19. 3. At the feast of *ingathering,* as it is called (*v.* 16), they must give God thanks for the harvest-mercies they had received, and must depend upon him for the next harvest, and must not think to receive benefit by that superstitious usage of some of the Gentiles, who, it is said, at the end of their harvest, *seethed a kid in its dam's milk,* and sprinkled that milk-pottage, in a magical way, upon their gardens and fields, to make them more fruitful next year. But Israel must abhor such foolish customs.

Verses 20–33

Three gracious promises are here made to Israel, to engage them to their duty and encourage them in it; and each of the promises has some needful precepts and cautions joined to it.

I. It is here promised that they should be guided and kept in their way through the wilderness to the land of promise: *Behold, I send an angel before thee* (*v.* 20), *my angel* (*v.* 23), a created angel, say some, a minister of God's providence, employed in conducting and protecting the camp of Israel; that it might appear that God took a particular care of them, he appointed one of his chief servants to make it his business to attend them, and see that they wanted for nothing. Others suppose it to be the Son of God, the angel of the covenant; for the Israelites in the wilderness are said to *tempt Christ;* and we may as well suppose him God's messenger, and the church's Redeemer, before his incarnation, as *the Lamb slain from the foundation of the world.* And we may the rather think he was pleased to undertake the deliverance and guidance of Israel because they were typical of his great undertaking. It is promised that this blessed angel should *keep them in the way,* though it lay through a wilderness first, and afterwards through their enemies' country; thus God's spiritual Israel shall be kept through the wilderness of this earth, and from the insults of the gates of hell. It is also promised that he should bring them into the place which God had not only designed but prepared for them: and thus Christ has prepared a place for his followers, and will preserve them to it, for he is faithful to him that appointed him. The precept joined with this promise is that they be observant of, and obedient to, this angel whom God would send before them (*v.* 21): *"Beware of him, and obey his voice* in every thing; *provoke him not* in any thing, for it is at your peril if you do, he will *visit your iniquity."* Note, 1. Christ is the author of salvation to those only that obey him. The word of command is *Hear you him,* Mt. 17:5. *Observe what he hath commanded,* Mt. 28:20. 2. Our necessary dependence upon the divine power and goodness should awe us into obedience. We do well to take heed of provoking our protector and benefactor, because if our defence depart from us, and the streams of his goodness be cut off, we are undone. Therefore, *"Beware of him,* and carry it towards him with all possible reverence and caution. Fear the *Lord, and his goodness."* 3. Christ will be faithful to those who are faithful to him, and will espouse their cause who adhere to his: *I will be an adversary to thine adversaries, v.* 22. The league shall be offensive and defensive, like that with Abraham, *I will bless him that blesseth thee, and curse him that curseth thee.* Thus is God pleased to twist his interests and friendships with his people's.

II. It is promised that they should have a comfortable settlement in the land of Canaan, which they hoped now (though it proved otherwise) within a few months to be in the possession of, *v.* 24–26. Observe, 1. How reasonable the conditions of this promise are — only that they should serve their own God, who was indeed the only true God, and not the gods of the nations, which were no gods at all, and which they had no reason at all to have any respect for. They must not only not worship their gods, but they must utterly overthrow them, in token of their great abhorrence of idolatry, their resolution never to worship idols themselves, and their care to prevent any other from worshipping them; as the converted conjurors *burnt their books,* Acts 19:19. 2. How rich the particulars of this promise are. (1.) The comfort of their food. He shall *bless thy bread and thy water;* and God's blessing will make bread and water more refreshing and nourishing than a feast of fat things and wines on the lees without that blessing. (2.) The continuance of their health: *"I will take sickness away,* either prevent it or remove it. Thy land shall not be visited with epidemical diseases, which are very dreadful, and sometimes have laid countries waste." (3.) The increase of their wealth. Their cattle should not be barren, nor cast their young, which is mentioned as an instance of prosperity, Job 21:10. (4.) The prolonging of their lives to old age: *"The number of thy days I will fulfil,* and they shall not be cut off in the midst by untimely deaths." Thus hath godliness the *promise of the life that now is.*

III. It is promised that they should conquer and subdue their enemies, the present occupants of the land of Canaan, who must be driven out to make room for them. This God would do, 1. Effectually by his power (*v.* 17, 18); not so much by the sword and bow of Israel as by the terrors which he would strike into the Canaanites. Though they were so obstinate as not to be willing to submit to Israel, resign their country, and retire elsewhere, which they might have done, yet they were so dispirited that they were not able to stand before them. This completed their ruin; such power had the devil in them that they would resist, but such power had God over them that they could not. *I will send my fear before thee;* and those that fear will soon flee. Hosts of hornets made way for the hosts of Israel; such mean creatures can God make use of for the chastising of his people's enemies, as in the plagues of Egypt. When God pleases, hornets can drive out Canaanites, as well as lions could, Jos. 24:12. 2. He would do it gradually, in wisdom (*v.* 29, 30), not all at once, but by little and little. As the Canaanites had kept possession till Israel had grown into a people, so there should still be some remains of them till Israel should grow so numerous as to replenish the whole. Note, The wisdom of God is to be observed in the gradual advances of the church's interests. It is in real kindness to the church that its enemies are subdued by little and little; for thus we are kept upon our guard, and in a continual dependence upon God. Corruptions are thus driven out of the hearts of God's people; not all at once, but by little and little; the old man is crucified, and therefore dies slowly. God, in his providence, often delays mercies, because we are not ready for them. Canaan has room enough to receive Israel, but Israel is not numerous enough to occupy Canaan. We are not straitened in God; if we are straitened, it is in ourselves. The land of Canaan is promised them (*v.* 31) in its utmost extent, which yet they were not possessed of till the days of David; and by their sins they soon lost possession. The precept annexed to this promise is that they should not make any friendship, nor have any familiarity, with idolaters, *v.* 32, 33. Idolaters must not so much as sojourn in their land, unless they renounced their idolatry. Thus they must avoid the reproach of intimacy with the worshippers of false gods and the danger of being drawn to worship with them. By familiar converse with idolaters, their dread and detestation of the sin would wear off; they would think it no harm, in compliment to their friends, to pay some respect to their gods, and so by degrees would be drawn into the fatal snare. Note, Those that would be kept from bad courses must keep from bad company; it is dangerous living in a bad neighbourhood; others' sins will be our snares, if we look not well to ourselves. We must always look upon our greatest danger to be from those that would cause us to sin against God. Whatever friendship is pretended, that is really our worst enemy that draws us from our duty.

CHAPTER 24

Moses, as mediator between God and Israel, having received divers laws and ordinances from God privately in the three foregoing chapters, in this chapter, I. Comes down to the people, acquaints them with the laws he had received, and takes their consent to those laws (*v.* 3), writes the laws, and reads them to the people, who repeat their consent (*v.* 4–7), and then by sacrifice, and the sprinkling of blood, ratifies the covenant between them and God (*v.* 5, 6, 8). II. He returns to God again, to receive further directions. When he was dismissed from his former attendance, he was ordered to attend again (*v.* 1, 2). He did so with seventy of the elders, to whom God made a discovery of his glory (*v.* 9–11). Moses is ordered up into the mount (*v.* 12, 13); the rest are ordered down to the people (*v.* 14). The cloud of glory is seen by all the people on the top of mount Sinai (*v.* 15–17), and Moses is therewith God forty days and forty nights (*v.* 18).

Verses 1–8

The first two verses record the appointment of a second session upon mount Sinai, for the making of laws, when an end was put to the first. When a communion is begun between God and us, it shall never fail on his side, if it do not first fail on ours. Moses is directed to bring Aaron and his sons, and the seventy elders of Israel, that they might be witnesses of the glory of God, and that communion with him to which Moses was admitted; and that their testimony might confirm the people's faith. In this approach, 1. They must all be very reverent: *Worship you afar off, v.* 1. Before they came near, they must worship. Thus we must enter into God's gates with humble and solemn adorations, draw near as those that know our distance, and admire the condescensions of God's grace in admitting us to draw near. Are great princes approached with the profound reverences of the body? And shall not the soul that draws near to God be bowed before him? 2. They must none of them come so near as Moses, *v.* 2. They must come up to the Lord (and those that would approach to God must *ascend*), but Moses alone must come near, being therein a type of Christ, who, as the high priest, entered alone into the most holy place.

In the following verses, we have the solemn covenant made between God and Israel, and the exchanging of the ratifications; and a very solemn transaction it was, typifying the covenant of grace between God and believers through Christ.

I. Moses told the people the words of the Lord, *v.* 3. He did not lead them blindfold into the covenant, nor teach them a devotion that was the daughter of ignorance; but laid before them all the precepts, general and particular, in the foregoing chapters; and fairly put it to them whether they were willing to submit to these laws or no.

II. The people unanimously consented to the terms proposed, without reservation or exception: *All the words which the Lord hath said will we do.* They had before consented in general to be under God's government (*ch.* 19:8); here they consent in particular to these laws now given. *O that there had been such a heart in them!* How well were it if people would but be always in the same good mind that sometimes they seem to be in! Many consent to the law, and yet do not live up to it; they have nothing to except against it, and yet will not persuade themselves to be ruled by it.

This is the tenour of the covenant, That, if they would observe the foregoing precepts, God would perform the foregoing promises. "Obey, and be happy." Here is the bargain made. Observe,

1. How it was engrossed in the book of the covenant: *Moses wrote the words of the Lord* (*v.* 4), that there might be no mistake; probably he had written them as God dictated them on the mount. As soon as ever God had separated to himself a peculiar people in the world, he governed them by a written word, as he has done ever since, and will do while the world stands and the church in it. Moses, having engrossed the articles of agreement concluded upon between God and Israel, *read them in the audience of the people* (*v.* 7), that they might be perfectly apprised of the thing, and might try whether their second thoughts were the same with their first, upon the whole matter. And we may suppose they were so; for their words (*v.* 7) are the same with what they were (*v.* 3), but something stronger: *All that the Lord hath said* (be it good, or be it evil, to flesh and blood, Jer. 42:6) *we will do;* so they had said before, but now they add, *"And will be obedient;* not only we will do what has been commanded, but in every thing which shall further be ordained *we will be obedient."* Bravely resolved! if they had but stuck to their resolution. See here that God's covenants and commands are so incontestably equitable in themselves, and so highly advantageous to us, that the more we think of them, and the more plainly and fully they are set before us, the more reason we shall see to comply with them.

2. How it was sealed by the blood of the covenant, that Israel might receive strong consolations from the ratifying of God's promises to them, and might lie under strong obligations from the ratifying of their promises to God. Thus has Infinite Wisdom devised means that we may be confirmed both in our faith and in our obedience, may be both encouraged in our duty and engaged to it. The covenant must be made by sacrifice (Ps. 50:5), because, since man

has sinned, and forfeited his Creator's favour, there can be no fellowship by covenant till there be first friendship and atonement by sacrifice.

(1.) In preparation therefore for the parties interchangeably putting their seals to this covenant, [1.] Moses builds an altar, to the honour of God, which was principally intended in all the altars that were built, and which was the first thing to be looked at in the covenant they were now to seal. No addition to the perfections of the divine nature can be made by any of God's dealings with the children of men, but in them his perfections are manifested and magnified, and his honour is shown forth; therefore he will not be represented by an altar, to signify that all he expected from them was that they should do him honour, and that, being his people, they should be to him for a name and a praise. [2.] He erects twelve pillars, according to the number of the tribes. These were to represent the people, the other party to the covenant; and we may suppose that they were set up against the altar, and that Moses, as mediator, passed to and fro between them. Probably each tribe set up and knew its own pillar, and their elders stood by it. [3.] He appointed sacrifices to be offered upon the altar (*v.* 5), burnt-offerings and peace-offerings, which yet were designed to be expiatory. We are not concerned to enquire who these young men were that were employed in offering these sacrifices; for Moses was himself the priest, and what they did was purely as his servants, by his order and appointment. No doubt they were men who by their bodily strength were qualified for the service, and by their station among the people were fittest for the honour.

(2.) Preparation being thus made, the ratifications were very solemnly exchanged. [1.] The blood of the sacrifice which the people offered was (part of it) sprinkled upon the altar (*v.* 6), which signifies the people's dedicating themselves, their lives, and beings, to God, and to his honour. In the blood (which is the life) of the dead sacrifices all the Israelites were presented unto God as living sacrifices, Rom. 12:1. [2.] The blood of the sacrifice which God had owned and accepted was (the remainder of it) sprinkled either upon the people themselves (*v.* 8) or upon the pillars that represented them, which signified God's graciously conferring his favour upon them and all the fruits of that favour, and his giving them all the gifts they could expect or desire from a God reconciled to them and in covenant with them by sacrifice. This part of the ceremony was thus explained: "*Behold the blood of the covenant;* see here how God has sealed to you to be a people; his promises to you, and yours to him, are both *yea and amen.*" Thus our Lord Jesus, the Mediator of the new covenant (of whom Moses was a type), having offered up himself a sacrifice upon the cross, that his blood might be indeed the blood of the covenant, sprinkled it upon the altar in his intercession (Heb. 9:12), and sprinkles it upon his church by his word and ordinances and the influences and operations of the Spirit of promise, by whom we are sealed. He himself seemed to allude to this solemnity when, in the institution of the Lord's supper, he said, *This cup is the New Testament* (or covenant) *in my blood.* Compare with this, Heb. 9:19, 20.

Verses 9–11

The people having, besides their submission to the ceremony of the sprinkling of blood, declared their well-pleasedness in their God and his law, again and again, God here gives to their representatives some special tokens of his favour to them (for God meets him that rejoices and works righteousness), and admits them nearer to him than they could have expected. Thus, in the New-Testament church, we find the *four living creatures,* and the *four and twenty elders,* honoured with places round the throne, being *redeemed unto God* by the *blood of the Lamb* which is *in the midst of the throne,* Rev. 4:4, 6; 5:8, 9. Observe, 1. They saw the God of Israel (*v.* 10), that is, they had some glimpse of his glory, in light and fire, though they saw *no manner of similitude,* and his being *no man hath seen nor can see,* 1 Tim. 6:16. They saw the place where the God of Israel stood (so the Septuagint), something that came near a similitude, but was not; whatever they saw, it was certainly something of which no image nor picture could be made, and yet enough to satisfy them that God was with them of a truth. Nothing is described but that which was under his feet; for our conceptions of God are all below him, and fall infinitely short of being adequate. They saw not so much as God's feet; but at the bottom of the brightness, and as the footstool or pedestal of it, they saw a most rich and splendid pavement, such as they never saw before nor after, as it had been of sapphires, azure or sky-coloured. The heavens themselves are the pavement of God's palace, and his throne is above the firmament. See how much better wisdom is than the precious onyx or the sapphires, for wisdom was from eternity God's delight (Prov. 8:30), and lay in his bosom, but the sapphires are the pavement under his feet; there let us put all the wealth of this world, and not in our hearts. 2. *Upon the nobles* (or elders) *of Israel, he laid not his hand, v.* 11. Though they were men, the dazzling splendour of his glory did not overwhelm them; but it was so moderated (Job 26:9), and they were so strengthened (Dan. 10:19), that they were able to bear it. Nay, though they were sinful men, and obnoxious to God's justice, yet he did not lay his punishing avenging hand upon them, as they feared he would. When we consider what a consuming fire God is, and what stubble we are before him, we shall have reason to say, in all our approaches to him, *It is of the Lord's mercies that we are not consumed.* 3. *They saw God, and did eat and drink.* They had not only their lives preserved, but their vigour, courage, and comfort; it cast no damp upon their joy, but rather increased and elevated it. They *feasted upon the sacrifice,* before God, in token of their cheerful consent to the covenant now made, their grateful acceptance of the benefits of it, and their communion with God, in pursuance of that covenant. Thus believers *eat and drink with Christ at his table,* Lu. 22:30. Blessed are those that shall eat bread in the kingdom of our Father, and drink of the wine new there.

Verses 12–18

The public ceremony of sealing the covenant being over, Moses is called up to receive further instructions, which we have in the following chapters.

I. He is called up into the mount, and there he remains six days at some distance. Orders are given him (*v.* 12): *Come up to the mount, and be there,* that is, "Expect to continue there for some considerable time." Those that would have communion with God must not only come to ordinances, but they must abide by them. Blessed are those that dwell in his house, not that merely call there. "Come up, and *I will give thee a law, that thou mayest teach them.*" Moses taught them nothing but what he had received from the Lord, and he received nothing from the Lord but what he taught them; for he was faithful both to God and Israel, and did neither add nor diminish, but kept close to his instructions. Having received these orders, 1. He appointed Aaron and Hur to be as lords-justices in his absence, to keep the peace and good order in the congregation, *v.* 14. The care of his government he would leave behind him when he went up into the mount, that he might not have that to distract his mind; and yet he would not leave the people as sheep having no shepherd, no, not for a few days. Good princes find their government a constant care, and their people find it a constant blessing. 2. He took Joshua up with him into the mount, *v.* 13. Joshua was his minister, and it would be a satisfaction to him to have him with him as a companion, during the six days that he tarried in the mount, before God called to him. Joshua was to be his successor, and therefore thus he was honoured before the people, above the rest of the elders, that they might afterwards the more readily take him for their governor; and thus he was prepared for service, by being trained up in communion with God. Joshua was a type of Christ, and (as the learned bishop Pearson well observes) Moses takes him with him into the mount, because without Jesus, in whom are hid all the treasures of wisdom and knowledge, there is no looking into the secrets of heaven, nor approaching the glorious presence of God. 3. A cloud covered the mount six days, a visible token of God's special presence there, for he so shows himself to us as at the same time to conceal himself from us. He lets us know so much as to assure us of his presence, power, and grace, but intimates to us that we cannot find him out to perfection. During these six days Moses staid waiting upon the mountain for a call into the presence-chamber, *v.* 15, 16. God thus tried the patience of Moses, and his obedience to that command (*v.* 12), *Be there.* If Moses had been tired before the seventh day (as Saul, 1 Sa. 13:8, 9), and had said, *What should I wait for the Lord any longer?* he would have lost the honour of entering into the cloud; but communion with God is worth waiting for. And it is fit we should address ourselves to solemn ordinances with a solemn pause, taking time to compose ourselves, Ps. 108:1.

II. He is called up into a cloud on the seventh day, probably on the sabbath day, *v.* 16. Now, 1. The thick cloud opened in the sight of all Israel, and the glory of the Lord broke forth *like devouring fire, v.* 17. God, even our God, is a consuming fire, and so he was pleased to manifest himself in the giving of the law, that, knowing the terrors of the Lord, we may be persuaded to obey, and may by them be prepared for the comforts of the gospel, and that the *grace and truth* which come by Jesus Christ may be the more acceptable. 2. The entrance of Moses into the cloud was very wonderful: *Moses went into the midst of the cloud, v.* 18. It was an extraordinary presence of mind which the grace of God furnished him with by his six day's' preparation, else he durst not have ventured into the cloud, especially when it broke out in devouring fire. Moses was sure that he who called him would protect him; and even those glorious attributes of God which are most terrible to the wicked the saints with a humble reverence rejoice in. He that walks righteously, and speaks uprightly, is able to *dwell even with this devouring fire,* as we are told, Isa. 33:14, 15. There are persons and works that will abide the fire, 1 Co. 3:12, etc., and some that will have confidence before God. 3. His continuance in the cloud was no less wonderful; he was there *forty days and forty nights.* It should seem, the six days (*v.* 16) were not part of the forty; for, during those six days, Moses was with Joshua, who did eat of the manna, and drink of the brook, mentioned, Deu. 9:21, and while they were together it is probable that Moses did eat and drink with him; but when Moses was called *into the midst of the cloud* he left Joshua without, who continued to eat and drink daily while he waited for Moses's return, but thenceforward Moses fasted. Doubtless God could have said what he had now to say to Moses in one day, but, for the greater solemnity of the thing, he kept him with him in the mount *forty days and forty nights.* We are hereby taught to spend much time in communion with God, and to think that time best spent which is so spent. Those that would get the knowledge of God's will must meditate *thereon day and night.*

CHAPTER 25

At this chapter begins an account of the orders and instructions God gave to Moses upon the mount for the erecting and furnishing of a tabernacle to the honour of God. We have here, I. Orders given for a collection to be made among the people for this purpose (*v.* 1–9). II. Particular instructions, 1. Concerning the ark of the covenant (*v.* 10–22). 2. The table of showbread (*v.* 23–30). 3. The golden candlestick (*v.* 31, etc.).

Verses 1–9

We may suppose that when Moses went into the midst of the cloud, and abode there so long, where the holy angels attended the *shechinah,* or divine Majesty, he saw and heard very glorious things relating to the upper world, but they were things which it was not lawful nor possible to utter; and therefore, in the records he kept of the transactions there, he says nothing to satisfy the curiosity of those who would intrude into the things which they have not seen, but writes that only which he was to speak to the children of Israel. For the scripture is designed to direct us in our duty, not to fill our heads with speculations, nor to please our fancies.

In these verses God tells Moses his intention in general, that the children of Israel should build him a sanctuary, for he designed to *dwell among them* (*v.* 8); and some think that, though there were altars and groves used for religious worship before this, yet there never was any house, or temple, built for sacred uses in any nation before this tabernacle was erected by Moses, and that all the temples which were afterwards so much celebrated among the heathen took rise from this and pattern by it. God had chosen the people of Israel to be a peculiar people to himself (above all people), among whom divine revelation, and a religion according to it, should be lodged and established: he himself would be their King. As their King, he had already given them laws for the government of themselves, and their dealings one with another, with some general rules for religious worship, according to the light of reason and the law of nature, in the ten commandments and the following comments upon them. But this was not thought sufficient to distinguish them from other nations, or to answer to the extent of that covenant which God would make with them to be *their God;* and therefore,

I. He orders a royal palace to be set up among them for himself, here called a *sanctuary*, or *holy place*, or *habitation*, of which it is said (Jer. 17:12), *A glorious high throne from the beginning is the place of our sanctuary.* This sanctuary is to be considered,

1. As ceremonial, consonant to the to the other institutions of that dispensation, which consisted in carnal ordinances (Heb. 9:10); hence it is called a *worldly sanctuary*, Heb. 9:1. God in it kept his court, as Israel's King. (1.) There he manifested his presence among them, and it was intended for a sign or token of his presence, that, while they had that in the midst of them, they might never again ask, *Is the Lord among us or not?* And, because in the wilderness they dwelt in tents, even this royal palace was ordered to be a tabernacle too, that it might move with them, and might be an instance of the condescension of the divine favour. (2.) There he ordered his subjects to attend him with their homage and tribute. Thither they must come to consult his oracles, thither they must bring their sacrifices, and there all Israel must meet, to pay their joint respects to the God of Israel.

2. As typical; the holy places made with hands were the *figures of the true*, Heb. 9:24. The gospel church is the true *tabernacle, which the Lord hath pitched, and not man,* Heb. 8:2. The body of Christ, in and by which he made atonement, was the *greater and more perfect tabernacle*, Heb. 9:11. *The Word was made flesh, and dwelt among us,* as in a tabernacle.

II. When Moses was to erect this palace, it was requisite that he should first be instructed where he must have the materials, and where he must have the model; for he could neither contrive it by his own ingenuity nor build it at his own charge; he is therefore directed here concerning both.

1. The people must furnish him with the materials, not by a tax imposed upon them, but by a voluntary contribution. This is the first thing concerning which orders are here given.

(1.) *Speak unto the children of Israel that they bring me an offering;* and there was all the reason in the world that they should, for (v. 1), [1.] It was God himself that had not only enlarged them, but enriched them with the spoils of the Egyptians. He had instructed them to borrow, and he had inclined the Egyptians to lend, so that from him they had their wealth, and therefore it was fit they should devote it to him and use it for him, and thus make a grateful acknowledgement of the favours they had received. Note, *First*, The best use we can make of our worldly wealth is to honour God with it in works of piety and charity. *Secondly*, When we have been blessed with some remarkable success in our affairs, and have had, as we say, a good turn, it may be justly expected that we should do something more than ordinary for the glory of God, consecrating our gain, in some reasonable proportion of it, to the Lord of the whole earth, Mic. 4:13. [2.] The sanctuary that was to be built was intended for their benefit and comfort, and therefore they must be at the expense of it. They had been unworthy of the privilege if they had grudged at the charge. They might well afford to offer liberally for the honour of God, while they lived at free quarters, having food for themselves and their families rained upon them daily from heaven. We also must own that we have our all from God's bounty, and therefore ought to use all for his glory. Since we live upon him, we must live to him.

(2.) This offering must be given willingly, and with the heart, that is, [1.] It was not prescribed to them what or how much they must give, but it was left to their generosity, that they might show their good-will to the house of God and the offices thereof, and might do it with a holy emulation, the zeal of a few *provoking many*, 2 Co. 9:2. We should ask, not only, "What must we do?" but, "What may we do for God?" [2.] Whatever they gave, they must give it cheerfully, not grudgingly and with reluctance, for *God loves a cheerful giver,* 2 Co. 9:7. What is laid out in the service of God we must reckon well bestowed.

(3.) The particulars are here mentioned which they must

offer (v. 3–7), all of them things that there would be occasion for in the tabernacle, or the service of it. Some observe that here was gold, silver, and brass, provided, but no iron; that is the military metal, and this was to be a house of peace. Every thing that was provided was very rich and fine, and the best of the sort; for God, who is the best, should have the best.

2. God himself would furnish him with the model: *According to all that I show thee, v.* 9. God showed him an exact plan of it, in miniature, which he must conform to in all points. Thus Ezekiel saw in vision the form of the house and the fashion thereof, Eze. 43:11. Note, Whatsoever is done in God's service must be done by his direction, and not otherwise. Yet God did not only show him the model, but gave him also particular directions how to frame the tabernacle according to that model, in all the parts of it, which he goes over distinctly in this and the following chapters. When Moses, in the beginning of Genesis, was to describe the creation of the world, though it is such a stately and curious fabric and made up of such a variety and vast number of particulars, yet he gave a very short and general account of it, and nothing compared with what the wisdom of this world would have desired and expected from one that wrote by divine revelation; but, when he comes to describe the tabernacle, he does it with the greatest niceness and accuracy imaginable. He that gave us no account of the lines and circles of the globe, the diameter of the earth, or the height and magnitude of the stars, has told us particularly the measure of every board and curtain of the tabernacle; for God's church and instituted religion are more precious to him and more considerable than all the rest of the world. And the scriptures were written, not to describe to us the works of nature, a general view of which is sufficient to lead us to the knowledge and service of the Creator, but to acquaint us with the methods of grace, and those things which are purely matters of divine revelation. The blessedness of the future state is more fully represented under the notion of a new Jerusalem than under the notion of new heavens and a new earth.

Verses 10–22

The first thing which is here ordered to be made is the ark with its appurtenances, the furniture of the most holy place, and the special token of God's presence, for which the tabernacle was erected to be the receptacle.

I. The ark itself was a chest, or coffer, in which the two tables of the law, written with the finger of God, were to be honourably deposited, and carefully kept. The dimensions of it are exactly ordered; if the Jewish cubit was, as some learned men compute, three inches longer than our half-yard (twenty-one inches in all), this chest or cabinet was about fifty-two inches long, thirty-one broad, and thirty-one deep. It was overlaid within and without with thin plates of gold. It had a crown, or cornice, of gold, round it, with rings and staves to carry it with; and in it he must put the testimony, *v.* 10–16. The tables of the law are called the *testimony* because God did in them testify his will: his giving them that law was in token of his favour to them; and their acceptance of it was in token of their subjection and obedience to him. This law was a testimony to them, to direct them in their duty, and would be a testimony against them if they transgressed. The ark is called the *ark of the testimony* (ch. 30:6), and the tabernacle the *tabernacle of the testimony* (Num. 10:11) or witness, Acts 7:44. The gospel of Christ is also called a testimony or witness, Mt. 24:14. It is observable, 1. That the tables of the law were carefully preserved in the ark for the purpose, to teach us to make much of the word of God, and to hide it in our hearts, in our innermost thoughts, as the ark was placed in the holy of holies. It intimates likewise the care which divine Providence ever did, and ever will, take to preserve the records of divine revelation in the church, so that even in the latter days there shall be seen in his temple the *ark of his testament*. See Rev. 11:19. 2. That this ark was the chief token of God's presence, which teaches us that the first and great evidence and assurance of God's favour is the putting of his law in the heart. God dwells where that rules, Heb. 8:10. 3. That provision was made for the carrying of this ark about with them in all their removals, which intimates to us that, wherever we go, we should take our religion along

with us, always bearing about with us the love of the Lord Jesus, and his law.

II. The mercy-seat was the covering of the ark or chest, made of solid gold, exactly to fit the dimensions of the ark, *v.* 17, 21. This *propitiatory covering*, as it might well be translated, was a type of Christ, the great propitiation, whose satisfaction fully answers the demands of the law, covers our transgressions, and comes between us and the curse we deserve. Thus he is the *end of the law for righteousness.*

III. The cherubim of gold were fixed to the mercy-seat, and of a piece with it, and spread their wings over it, *v.* 18. It is supposed that these cherubim were designed to represent the holy angels, who always attended the *shechinah*, or divine Majesty, particularly at the giving of the law; not by any effigies of an angel, but some emblem of the angelical nature, probably some one of those four faces spoken of, Eze. 1:10. Whatever the faces were, they looked one towards another, and both downward towards the ark, while their wings were stretched out so as to touch one another. The apostle calls them *cherubim of glory shadowing the mercy-seat,* Heb. 9:5. It denotes their attendance upon the Redeemer, to whom they were ministering spirits, their readiness to do his will, their special presence in the assemblies of saints (Ps. 68:17; 1 Co. 11:10), and their desire to look into the mysteries of the gospel which they diligently contemplate, 1 Pt. 1:12. God is said to dwell, or sit, *between the cherubim*, on the mercy-seat (Ps. 80:1), and thence he here promises, for the future, to meet with Moses, and to *commune with him, v.* 22. There he would give law, and there he would give audience, as a prince on his throne; and thus he manifests himself willing to be reconciled to us, and keep up communion with us, in and by the mediation of Christ. In allusion to this mercy-seat, we are said to come boldly to *the throne of grace* (Heb. 4:16); for we *are not under the law*, which is covered, *but under grace*, which is displayed; its wings are stretched out, and we are invited to come under the shadow of them, Ruth 2:12.

Verses 23–30

Here is, 1. A table ordered to be made of wood overlaid with gold, which was to stand, not in the holy of holies (nothing was in that but the ark with its appurtenances), but in the outer part of the tabernacle, called the *sanctuary*, or *holy place*, Heb. 9:2, 23, etc. There must also be the usual furniture of the sideboard, dishes and spoons, etc., and all *of gold, v.* 29. 2. This table was to be always spread, and furnished with the show-bread (v. 30), or *bread of faces*, twelve loaves, one for each tribe, set in two rows, six in a row; see the law concerning them, Lev. 24:5, etc. The tabernacle being God's house, in which he was pleased to say that he would dwell among them, he would show that he kept a good house. In the royal palace it was fit that there should be a royal table. Some make the twelve loaves to represent the twelve tribes, set before God as his people and *the corn of his floor,* as they are called, Isa. 21:10. As the ark signified God's being present with them, so the twelve loaves signified their being presented to God. This bread was designed to be, (1.) A thankful acknowledgement of God's goodness to them, in giving them their daily bread, manna in the wilderness, where he prepared a table for them, and, in Canaan, the corn of the land. Hereby they owned their dependence upon Providence, not only for the corn in the field, which they gave thanks for in offering the sheaf of first-fruits, but for the bread in their houses, that, when it was brought home, God did not *blow upon it*, Hag. 1:9. Christ has taught us to pray every day for the bread of the day. (2.) A token of their communion with God. This bread on God's table being made of the same corn with the bread on their own tables, God and Israel did, as it were, eat together, as a pledge of friendship and fellowship; he supped with them, and they with him. (3.) A type of the spiritual provision which is made in the church, by the gospel of Christ, for all that are made priests to our God. *In our Father's house there is bread enough and to spare*, a loaf for every tribe. All that attend in God's house shall be abundantly satisfied with the goodness of it, Ps. 36:8. Divine consolations are the continual feast of holy souls, notwithstanding there are those to whom *the table of the Lord*, and the *meat thereof* (because it is plain bread), are *contemptible*, Mal. 1:12. Christ has a table in his kingdom, at which all his saints shall for every eat and drink with him, Lu. 22:30.

Verses 31–40

I. The next thing ordered to be made for the furnishing of God's palace was a rich stately candlestick, all of pure gold, not hollow, but solid. The particular directions here given concerning it show, 1. That it was very magnificent, and a great ornament to the place; it had many branches drawn from the main shaft, which had not only their bowls (to put the oil and the kindled wick in) for necessity, but knops and flowers for ornament. 2. That it was very convenient, and admirably contrived both to scatter the light and to keep the tabernacle clean from smoke and snuffs. 3. That it was very significant. The tabernacle had no windows by which to let in the light of the day, all its light was candle-light, which intimates the comparative darkness of that dispensation, while the Sun or righteousness had not as yet risen, nor had the day-star from on high yet visited his church. Yet God left not himself without witness, nor them without instruction; the commandment was a lamp, and the law a light, and the prophets were branches from that lamp, which gave light in their several ages to the Old-Testament church. The church is still dark, as the tabernacle was, in comparison with what it will be in heaven; but the word of God is the candlestick, *a light shining in a dark place* (2 Pt. 1:19), and a dark place indeed the world would be without it. The Spirit of God, in his various gifts and graces, is compared to the *seven lamps* which *burn before the throne,* Rev. 4:5. The churches are golden candlesticks, the lights of the world, *holding forth the word of life* as the candlestick does the light, Phil. 2:15, 16. Ministers are to light the lamps, and snuff them (*v.* 37), by opening the scriptures. The treasure of this light is now put into *earthen vessels,* 2 Co. 4:6, 7. The branches of the candlestick spread every way, to denote the diffusing of the light of the gospel into all parts by the Christian ministry, Mt. 5:14, 15. There is a *diversity of gifts,* but the same Spirit gives to each to profit withal.

II. There is in the midst of these instructions an express caution given to Moses, to take heed of varying from his model: *Make them after the pattern shown thee, v.* 40. Nothing was left to his own invention, or the fancy of the workmen, or the people's humour; but the will of God must be religiously observed in every particular. Thus, 1. All God's providences are exactly according to his counsels, and the copy never varies from the original. Infinite Wisdom never changes its measures; whatever is purposed shall undoubtedly be performed. 2. All his ordinances must be administered according to his institutions. Christ's instruction to his disciples (Mt. 28:20) is similar to this: *Observe all things whatsoever I have commanded you.*

CHAPTER 26

Moses here receives instructions, I. Concerning the inner curtains of the tent or tabernacle, and the coupling of those curtains (*v.* 1–6). II. Concerning the outer curtains which were of goats' hair, to strengthen the former (*v.* 7–13). III. Concerning the case or cover which was to secure it from the weather (*v.* 14). IV. Concerning the boards which were to be reared up to support the curtains, with their bars and sockets (*v.* 15–30). V. The partition between the holy place and the most holy (*v.* 31–35). VI. The veil for the door (*v.* 36, 37). These particulars, thus largely recorded, seem of little use to us now; yet, having been of great use to Moses and Israel, and God having thought fit to preserve down to us the remembrance of them, we ought not to overlook them. Even the antiquity renders this account venerable.

Verses 1–6

I. The house must be a *tabernacle* or *tent,* such as soldiers now use in the camp, which was both a mean dwelling and a movable one; and yet the ark of God had not better, till Solomon built the temple 480 years after this, 1 Ki. 6:1. God manifested his presence among them thus in a tabernacle, 1. In compliance with their present condition in the wilderness, that they might have him with them wherever they went. Note, God suits the tokens of his favour, and the gifts of his grace, to his people's wants and necessities, according as they are, accommodating his mercy to their state, prosperous or adverse, settled or unsettled. *When thou passest through the waters, I will be with thee,* Isa. 43:2. 2. That it might represent the state of God's church in this world, it is a *tabernacle-state,* Ps. 15:1. *We have here no continuing city;* being strangers in this world, and travellers towards a better, we shall never

be fixed till we come to heaven. Church-privileges are movable goods, from one place to another; the gospel is not tied to any place; the candlestick is in a tent, and may easily be taken away, Rev. 2:5. If we make much of the tabernacle, and improve the privilege of it, wherever we go it will accompany us; but, if we neglect and disgrace it, wherever we stay it will forsake us. *What hath my beloved to do in my house?* Jer. 11:15.

II. The curtains of the tabernacle must correspond to a divine pattern. 1. They were to be very rich, the best of the kind, *fine twined linen;* and colours very pleasing, *blue,* and *purple,* and *scarlet.* 2. They were to be embroidered with cherubim (*v.* 1), to intimate that the angels of God pitch their tents round about the church, Ps. 34:7. As there were cherubim over the mercy-seat, so there were round the tabernacle; for we find the angels compassing, not only the throne, but the elders; see Rev. 5:11. 3. There were to be two hangings, five breadths in each, sewed together, and the two hangings coupled together with golden clasps, or tacks, so that it might be all one tabernacle, *v.* 6. Thus the churches of Christ and the saints, though they are many, are yet one, being *fitly joined together* in holy love, and by the *unity of the Spirit,* so growing into one *holy temple* in *the Lord,* Eph. 2:21, 22; 4:16. This tabernacle was very strait and narrow; but, at the preaching of the gospel, the church is bidden to *enlarge the place of her tent,* and to *stretch forth her curtains,* Isa. 54:2.

Verses 7–14

Moses is here ordered to make a double covering for the tabernacle, that it might not rain in, and that the beauty of those fine curtains might not be damaged. 1. There was to be a covering of hair camlet curtains, which were somewhat larger every way than the inner curtains, because they were to enclose them, and probably were stretched out at some little distance from them, *v.* 7, etc. These were coupled together with brass clasps. The stuff being less valuable, the tacks were so; but the brass tacks would answer the intention as effectually as the golden ones. The bonds of unity may be as strong between curtains of goats' hair as between those of purple and scarlet. 2. Over this there was to be another covering, and that a double one (*v.* 14), one of *rams' skins dyed red,* probably dressed with the wool on; another of *badgers' skins,* so we translate it, but it should rather seem to have been some strong sort of leather (but very fine), for we read of the best sort of shoes being made of it, Eze. 16:10. Now observe here, (1.) That the outside of the tabernacle was coarse and rough, the beauty of it was in the inner curtains. Those in whom God dwells must labour to be better than they seem to be. Hypocrites put the best side outwards, like *whited sepulchres;* but *the king's daughter is all glorious within* (Ps. 45:13); in the eye of the world black as the tents of Kedar, but, in the eye of God, comely as the curtains of Solomon, Cant. 1:5. Let our adorning be that of the hidden man of the heart, which God values, 1 Pt. 3:4. (2.) That where God places his glory he will create a defence upon it; even upon the habitations of the righteous there shall be a covert, Isa. 6:5, 6. The protection of Providence shall always be upon the beauty of holiness. God's tent will be a pavilion, Ps. 27:5.

Verses 15–30

Very particular directions are here given about the boards of the tabernacle, which were to bear up the curtains, as the stakes of a tent which had need to be strong, Isa. 54:2. These boards had tenons which fell into the mortises that were made for them in silver bases. God took care to have every thing strong, as well as fine, in his tabernacle. Curtains without boards would have been shaken by every wind; but *it is a good thing* to have the *heart established with grace,* which is as the boards to support the curtains of profession, which otherwise will not hold out long. The boards were coupled together with gold rings at top and bottom (*v.* 24), and kept firm with bars that ran through golden staples in every board (*v.* 26), and the boards and bars were all richly gilded, *v.* 29. Thus every thing in the tabernacle was very splendid, agreeable to that infant state of the church, when such things were proper enough to please children, to possess the minds of the worshippers with a reverence of the divine glory, and to affect them with the greatness of that prince who said, *Here*

will I dwell; in allusion to this the new Jerusalem is said to be of *pure gold,* Rev. 21:18. But the builders of the gospel church said, *Silver and gold have we none;* and yet the glory of their building far exceeded that of the tabernacle, 2 Co. 3:10, 11. *How much better is wisdom than gold!* No orders are given here about the floor of the tabernacle; probably that also was boarded; for we cannot think that within all these fine curtains they trod upon the cold or wet ground; if it was so left, it may remind us of *ch.* 20:24, *An altar of earth shalt thou make unto me.*

Verses 31–37

Two veils are here ordered to be made, 1. One for a partition between the holy place and the most holy, which not only forbade any to enter, but forbade them so much as to look into the holiest of all, *v.* 31, 33. Under that dispensation, divine grace was veiled, but now we behold it with open face, 2 Co. 3:18. The apostle tells us (Heb. 9:8, 9) what was the meaning of this veil; it intimated that the ceremonial law *could not make the comers thereunto perfect,* nor would the observance of it bring men to heaven; the *way into the holiest of all was not made manifest while the first tabernacle was standing;* life and immortality lay concealed till they were *brought to light by the gospel,* which was therefore signified by the rending of this veil at the death of Christ, Mt. 27:51. We have not *boldness to enter into the holiest,* in all acts of devotion, *by the blood of Jesus,* yet such as obliges us to a holy reverence and a humble sense of our distance. 2. Another veil was for the outer door of the tabernacle, *v.* 36, 37. Through this first veil the priests went in every day to minister in the holy place, but not the people, Heb. 9:6. This veil, which was all the defence the tabernacle had against thieves and robbers, might easily be broken through, for it could be neither locked nor barred, and the abundance of wealth in the tabernacle, one would think, might be a temptation; but by leaving it thus exposed, (1.) The priests and Levites would be so much the more obliged to keep a strict watch upon it, and, (2.) God would show his care of his church on earth, though it is weak and defenceless, and continually exposed. A curtain shall be (if God please to make it so) as strong a defence to his house as gates of brass and bars of iron.

CHAPTER 27

In this chapter directions are given, I. Concerning the brazen altar for burnt-offerings (*v.* 1–8). II. Concerning the court of the tabernacle, with the hangings of it (*v.* 9–19). III. Concerning oil for the lamp (*v.* 20, 21).

Verses 1–8

As God intended in the tabernacle to manifest his presence among his people, so there they were to pay their devotions to him, not in the tabernacle itself (into that only the priests entered as God's domestic servants), but in the court before the tabernacle, where, as common subjects, they attended. There an altar was ordered to be set up, to which they must bring their sacrifices, and on which their priests must offer them to God: and this altar was to sanctify their gifts. Here they were to present their services to God, as from the mercy-seat he gave his oracles to them; and thus a communion was settled between God and Israel. Moses is here directed about, 1. The dimensions of it; it was square, *v.* 1. 2. The horns of it (*v.* 2), which were for ornament and for use; the sacrifices were *bound with cords to the horns of the altar,* and to them malefactors fled for refuge. 3. The materials; it was of wood overlaid with brass, *v.* 1, 2. 4. The appurtenances of it (*v.* 3), which were all of brass. 5. The grate, which was let into the hollow of the altar, about the middle of it, in which the fire was kept, and the sacrifice burnt; it was made of network like a sieve, and hung hollow, that the fire might burn the better, and that the ashes might fall through into the hollow of the altar, *v.* 4, 5. 6. The staves with which it must be carried, *v.* 6, 7. And, *lastly,* he is referred to the pattern shown him, *v.* 8.

Now this brazen altar was a type of Christ dying to make atonement for our sins: the wood would have been consumed by the fire from heaven if it had not been secured by the brass; nor could the human nature of Christ have borne the wrath of God if it had not been supported by a divine power. Christ sanctified himself for his church, as their altar (Jn. 17:19), and by his mediation sanctifies the daily services of his people, who have also *a right to eat of this altar* (Heb. 13:10), for they serve at it as spiritual priests. To the horns of this altar poor sinners fly for refuge when justice pursues them, and they are safe in virtue of the sacrifice there offered.

Verses 9–19

Before the tabernacle there was to be a court or yard, enclosed with hangings of the finest linen that was used for tents. This court, according to the common computation of cubits, was fifty yards long, and twenty-five broad. Pillars were set up at convenient distances, in sockets of brass, the pillars filleted with silver, and silver tenter-hooks in them, on which the linen hangings were fastened: the hanging which served for the gate was finer than the rest, *v.* 16. This court was a type of the church, enclosed and distinguished from the rest of the world, the enclosure supported by pillars, denoting the stability of the church, hung with the clean linen, which is said to be the *righteousness of saints*, Rev. 19:8. These were the courts David longed for and coveted to reside in (Ps. 84:2, 10), and into which the people of God entered with praise and thanksgiving (Ps. 100:4); yet this court would contain but a few worshippers. Thanks be to God, now, under the gospel, the enclosure is taken down. God's will is that men *pray every where;* and there is room for all that in every place call on the name of Jesus Christ.

Verses 20–21

We read of the candlestick in the twenty-fifth chapter; here is an order given for the keeping of the lamps constantly burning in it, else it was useless; in every candlestick there should be a burning and shining light; candlesticks without candles are as *wells without water* or as *clouds without rain.* Now, 1. The people were to provide the oil; from them the Lord's ministers must have their maintenance. Or, rather, the pure oil signified the gifts and graces of the Spirit, which are communicated to all believers from Christ the good olive, of whose fulness we receive (Zec. 4:11, 12), and without which our light cannot shine before men. 2. The priests were to light the lamps, and to tend them; it was part of their daily service to *cause the lamp to burn always,* night and day; thus it is the work of ministers, by the preaching and expounding of the scriptures (which are as a lamp), to enlighten the church, God's tabernacle upon the earth, and to direct the spiritual priests in his service. This is to be *a statute for ever,* that the lamps of the word be lighted as duly as the incense of prayer and praise is offered.

CHAPTER 28

Orders being given for the fitting up of the place of worship, in this and the following chapter care is taken about the priests that were to minister in this holy place, as the menial servants of the God of Israel. He hired servants, as a token of his purpose to reside among them. In this chapter, I. He pitches upon the persons who should be his servants (*v.* 1). II. He appoints their livery; their work was holy, and so must their garments be, and unanswerable to the glory of the house which was now to be erected (*v.* 2–5). 1. He appoints the garments of his head-servant, the high priest, which were very rich. (1.) An ephod and girdle, (*v.* 6–14). (2.) A breast-plate of judgment (*v.* 15–29), in which must be put the urim and thummim (*v.* 30). (3.) The robe of the ephod (*v.* 31–35). (4.) The mitre (*v.* 36–39). 2. The garments of the inferior priests (*v.* 40–43). And these also were shadows of good things to come.

Verses 1–5

We have here,

I. The priests nominated: *Aaron and his sons, v.* 1. Hitherto every master of a family was priest to his own family, and offered, as he saw cause, upon altars of earth; but now that the families of Israel began to be incorporated into a nation, and a *tabernacle of the congregation* was to be erected, as a visible centre of their unity, it was requisite there should be a public priesthood instituted. Moses, who had hitherto officiated, and is therefore reckoned among the *priests of the Lord* (Ps. 99:6), had enough to do as their prophet to consult the oracle for them, and as their prince to judge among them; nor was he desirous to engross all the honours to himself, or to entail that of the priesthood, which alone was hereditary, upon his own family, but was very well pleased to see his brother Aaron invested in this office, and his sons after him, while (how great soever he was) his sons after him would be but common Levites. It is an instance of the humility of that great man, and an

evidence of his sincere regard for the glory of God, that he had so little regard to the preferment of his own family. Aaron, who had humbly served as a prophet to his younger brother Moses, and did not decline the office (*ch.* 7:1), is now advanced to be a priest, a high priest to God; for he will exalt those that abase themselves. Nor could any man have *taken this honour to himself,* but he that was *called of God to it,* Heb. 5:4. God had said of Israel in general that they should be to him a *kingdom of priests, ch.* 19:6. But because it was requisite that those who ministered at the altar should give themselves wholly to the service, and because that which is every body's work will soon come to be nobody's work, God here chose from among them one to be a family of priests, the father and his four sons; and from Aaron's loins descended all the priests of the Jewish church, of whom we read so often, both in the Old Testament and in the New. A blessed thing it is when real holiness goes, as the ceremonial holiness did, by succession in a family.

II. The priests' garments appointed, *for glory and beauty, v.* 2. Some of the richest materials were to be provided (*v.* 5), and the best artists employed in the making of them, whose skill God, by a *special gift* for this purpose, would improve to a very high degree, *v.* 3. Note, Eminence, even in common arts, is a gift of God, it comes from him, and, as there is occasion, it ought to be used for him. He that teaches the husbandman discretion teaches the tradesman also; both therefore ought to honour God with their gain. Human learning ought particularly to be consecrated to the service of the priesthood, and employed for the adorning of those that minister about holy things. The garments appointed were, 1. Four, which both the high priest and the inferior priests wore, namely, the linen breeches, the linen coat, the linen girdle which fastened it to them, and the bonnet or turban; that which the high priest wore is called *a mitre.* 2. Four more, which were peculiar to the high priest, namely, the ephod, with the curious girdle of it, the breast-plate of judgment, the long robe with the bells and pomegranates at the bottom of it, and the golden plate on his forehead. These glorious garments were appointed, (1.) That the priests themselves might be reminded of the dignity of their office, and might behave themselves with due decorum. (2.) That the people might thereby be possessed with a holy reverence of that God whose ministers appeared in such grandeur. (3.) That the priests might be types of Christ, who should offer himself without spot to God, and of all Christians, who have the beauty of holiness put upon them, in which they are consecrated to God. Our adorning, now under the gospel, both that of ministers and Christians, is not to be of gold, and pearl, and costly array, but the *garments of salvation, and the robe of righteousness,* Isa. 61:10; Ps. 132:9, 16. As the filthy garments wherewith Joshua the high priest was clothed signified the iniquity which cleaved to his priesthood, from which care was taken that it should be purged (Zec. 3:3, 4.), so those *holy garments* signified the perfect purity that there is in the priesthood of Christ; he is holy, harmless, and undefiled.

Verses 6–14

Directions are here given concerning the ephod, which was the outmost garment of the high priest. *Linen* ephods were worn by the inferior priests, 1 Sa. 22:18. Samuel wore one when he was a child (1 Sa. 2:18), and David when he danced before the ark (2 Sa. 6:14); but this which the high priest only wore was called a *golden ephod,* because there was a great deal of gold woven into it. It was a short coat without sleeves, buttoned closely to him, with a curious girdle of the same stuff (*v.* 6–8); the shoulder-pieces were buttoned together with two precious stones set in gold, one on each shoulder, on which were engraven the names of the *children of Israel, v.* 9–12. In allusion to this, 1. Christ our high priest appeared to John *girt about the breast with a golden girdle,* such as was the curious girdle of the ephod, Rev. 1:13. Righteousness is the girdle of his loins (Isa. 11:6), and should be of ours, Eph. 6:14. He is girt with strength for the work of our salvation, and is ready for it. 2. The government is said to be *upon his shoulders* (Isa. 9:6), as Aaron had the names of all Israel upon his shoulders in precious stone. He presents to himself and to his Father *a glorious church,* Eph. 5:27. He has power to support them, interest to recommend them, and it is in him that

they are remembered with honour and favour. He bears them before the Lord *for a memorial* (*v.* 12), in token of his *appearing before God* as the representative of all Israel and an advocate for them.

Verses 15–30

The most considerable of the ornaments of the high priest was this breast-plate, a rich piece of cloth, curiously wrought with gold and purple, etc., two spans long and a span broad, so that, being doubled, it was a span square, *v.* 16. This was fastened to the ephod with wreathen chains of gold (*v.* 13, 14, 22, etc.) both at top and bottom, so that *the breast-plate might not be loosed from the ephod, v.* 28. The ephod was the garment of service; the breast-plate of judgment was an emblem of honour: these two must by no means be separated. If any man will *minister unto the Lord,* and *do his will,* he shall *know his doctrine.* In this breast-plate,

I. The tribes of Israel were recommended to God's favour in twelve precious stones, *v.* 17–21, 19. Some question whether Levi had a precious stone with his name or no. If not, Ephraim and Manasseh were reckoned distinct, as Jacob had said they should be, and the high priest himself, being head of the tribe of Levi, sufficiently represented that tribe. If there was a stone for Levi, as is intimated by this, that they were *engraven according to their birth* (*v.* 10), Ephraim and Manasseh were one in Joseph. Aaron was to bear their names for a *memorial before the Lord continually,* being *ordained for men,* to represent them in things pertaining to God, herein typifying our great high priest, who always appears in the presence of God for us. 1. Though the people were forbidden to come near, and obliged to keep their distance, yet by the high priest, who had their names on his breast-plate, they entered into the holiest; so believers, even while they are here on this earth, not only *enter into the holiest,* but by faith are made to *sit with Christ in heavenly places,* Eph. 2:6. 2. The name of each tribe was engraven in a precious stone, to signify how precious, in God's sight, believers are, and how honourable, Isa. 43:4. They shall be his in the day he *makes up his jewels,* Mal. 3:17. How small and poor soever the tribe was, it was a precious stone in the breast-plate of the high priest; thus are all the saints dear to Christ, and his delight is in them as the excellent ones of the earth, however men may esteem them as *earthen pitchers,* Lam. 4:2. 3. The high priest had the names of the tribes both on his shoulders and on his breast, intimating both the power and the love with which our Lord Jesus intercedes for those that are his. He not only bears them up *upon his heart,* as the expression here is (*v.* 29), *carries them in his bosom* (Isa. 40:11), with the most tender affection. How near should Christ's name be to our hearts, since he is pleased to lay our names so near his! and what a comfort it is to us, in all our addresses to God, that the great high priest of our profession has the names of all his Israel upon his breast before the Lord *for a memorial,* presenting them to God as the people of his choice, who were to be made *accepted in the beloved!* Let not any good Christians fear that God has forgotten them, nor question his being mindful of them upon all occasions, when they are not only engraven upon the *palms of his hands* (Isa. 49:16), but engraven upon the heart of the great intercessor. See Cant. 8:6.

II. The urim and thummim, by which the will of God was made known in doubtful cases, were put in this breast-plate, which is therefore called the *breast-plate of judgment, v.* 30. *Urim* and *thummim* signify *light* and *integrity;* many conjectures there are among the learned what they were; we have no reason to think they were any thing that Moses was to make more than what was before ordered, so that either God made them himself, and gave them to Moses, for him to put into the breast-plate, when other things were prepared (Lev. 8:8), or no more is meant than a declaration of the further use of what was already ordered to be made. I think the words may be read thus, *And thou shalt give,* or *add,* or *deliver, to the breast-plate of judgment, the illuminations and perfections, and they shall be upon the heart of Aaron;* that is, "He shall be endued with a power of knowing and making known the mind of God in all difficult doubtful cases, relating either to the civil or ecclesiastical state of the nation." Their government was a theocracy: God was their King, the high priest was, under God, their ruler, the urim and thummim were his cabinet-council; probably Moses wrote upon the breast-plate, or wove into it, these words, *Urim* and *Thummim*, to signify that the high priest, having on him this breast-plate, and asking counsel of God in any emergency relating to the public, should be directed to take those measures, and give that advice, which God would own. If he was standing before the ark (but without the veil) probably he received instructions from off the mercy-seat, as Moses did (*ch.* 25:22); thus, it should seem, Phinehas did, Jdg. 20:27, 28. If he was at a distance from the ark, as Abiathar was when he enquired of the Lord for David (1 Sa. 23:6, etc.), then the answer was given either by a voice from heaven or rather by an impulse upon the mind of the high priest, which last is perhaps intimated in that expression, *He shall bear the judgment of the children of Israel upon his heart.* This oracle was of great use to Israel; Joshua consulted it (Num. 27:21), and, it is likely, the judges after him. It was lost in the captivity, and never regained after, though, it should seem, it was expected, Ezra 2:63. But it was a shadow of good things to come, and the substance is Christ. He is our oracle; by him God in these last days makes known himself and his mind to us, Heb. 1:2; Jn. 1:18. Divine revelation centres in him, and comes to us through him; he is the light, the true light, the faithful witness, the truth itself, and from him we receive the Spirit of truth, who leads into all truth. The joining of the breast-plate to the ephod denotes that his prophetical office was founded in his priesthood; and it was by the merit of his death that he purchased this honour for himself and this favour for us. It was the *Lamb that had been slain* that was worthy to *take the book* and to *open the seals*, Rev. 5:9.

Verses 31–39

Here is, 1. Direction given concerning *the robe of the ephod, v.* 31–35. This was next under the ephod, and reached down to the knees, was without sleeves, and was put on over their head, having holes on the sides to put the arms through, or, as Maimonides describes it, was not sewed together on the sides at all. The hole on the top, through which the head was put, was carefully bound about, that it might not tear in the putting on. In religious worship, care must be taken to prevent every thing that may distract the minds of the worshippers, or render the service despicable. Round the skirts of the robe were hung golden bells, and the representations of pomegranates made of yarn of divers colours. The pomegranates added to the beauty of the robe, and the sound of the bells gave notice to the people in the outer court when he went into the holy place to burn incense, that they might then apply themselves to their devotions at the same time (Lu. 1:10), in token of their concurrence with him in his offering, and their hopes of the ascent of their prayers to God in virtue of the incense he offered. Aaron must come near to minister in the garments that were appointed him, *that he die not.* It is at his peril if he attend otherwise than according to the institution. This intimates that we must serve the Lord *with fear and holy trembling,* as those that know we deserve to die, and are in danger of making some fatal mistake. Some make the bells of the holy robe to typify the sound of the gospel of Christ in the world, giving notice of his entrance within the veil for us. *Blessed are those that hear this joyful sound,* Ps. 89:15. The adding of the pomegranates, which are a fragrant fruit, denotes the sweet savour of the gospel, as well as the joyful sound of it, for it is a *savour of life unto life.* The church is called an *orchard of pomegranates.* 2. Concerning the golden plate fixed upon Aaron's forehead, on which must be engraven, *Holiness to the Lord (v.* 36, 37), or *The holiness of Jehovah.* Aaron must hereby be reminded that God is holy, and that his priests must be holy. *Holiness becomes his house* and household. The high priest must be sequestered from all pollution, and consecrated to God and to his service and honour, and so must all his ministrations be. All that attend in God's house must have *Holiness to the Lord* engraven upon their foreheads, that is, they must be holy, devoted to the Lord, and designing his glory in all they do. This must appear in their forehead, in an open profession of their relation to God, as those that are not ashamed to own it, and in a conversation in the world

answerable to it. It must likewise be engraven like the engravings of a signet, so deep, so durable, not painted to be washed off, but sincere and lasting; such must our *holiness to the Lord* be. Aaron must have this upon his forehead, that he may *bear the iniquity of the holy things (v.* 38), and that *they may be accepted before the Lord.* Herein he was a type of Christ, the great Mediator between God and man, through whom it is that we have to do with God. (1.) Through him what is amiss in our services is pardoned. The divine law is strict; in many things we come short of our duty, so that we cannot but be conscious to ourselves of much iniquity cleaving even to our holy things; when we would do good evil is present; even this would be our ruin if God should enter into judgment with us. But Christ, our high priest, bears this iniquity, bears it for us so as to bear it from us, and through him it is forgiven to us and not laid to our charge. (2.) Through him what is good is accepted; our persons, our performances, are pleasing to God upon the account of Christ's intercession, and not otherwise, 1 Pt. 2:5. His being *holiness to the Lord* recommends all those to the divine favour that are interested in his righteousness, and clothed with his Spirit; and therefore he has said it was for our sakes that he *sanctified himself,* Jn. 17:19. Having *such a high priest,* we come *boldly to the throne of grace,* Heb. 4:14–16. 3. The rest of the garments are but named (*v.* 39), because there was nothing extraordinary in them. The embroidered coat of fine linen was the innermost of the priestly garments; it reached to the feet, and the sleeves to the wrists, and was bound to the body with a girdle or sash of needle-work. The mitre, or diadem, was of linen, such as kings anciently wore in the east, typifying the kingly office of Christ. He is a *priest upon a throne* (Zec. 6:13), a priest with a crown. These two God has joined, and we must not think to separate them.

Verses 40–43

We have here, 1. Particular orders about the vestments of the inferior priests. They were to have coats, and girdles, and bonnets, of the same materials with those of the high priest; but there was a difference in shape between their bonnets and his mitre. Theirs, as his, were to be *for glory and beauty (v.* 40), that they might look great in their ministration: yet all this glory was nothing compared with the glory of grace, this beauty nothing to the beauty of holiness, of which these holy garments were typical. They are particularly ordered, in their ministration, to wear *linen breeches, v.* 42. This teaches us modesty and decency of garb and gesture at all times, especially in public worship, in which a veil is becoming, 1 Co. 11:5, 6, 10. It also intimates what need our souls have of a covering, when we come before God, that the *shame of their nakedness may not appear.* 2. A general rule concerning the garments both of the high priest and of the inferior priests, that they were to be put upon them, at first, when they were consecrated, in token of their being invested in the office (*v.* 41), and then they were to wear them in all their ministrations, but not at other times (*v.* 43), and this at their peril, lest they *bear iniquity and die.* Those who are guilty of omissions in duty, as well as omissions of duty, shall *bear their iniquity.* If the priests perform the instituted service, and do not do it in the appointed garments, it is (say the Jewish doctors) as if a stranger did it, and the *stranger that comes nigh shall be put to death.* Nor will God connive at the presumptions and irreverences even of those whom he causes to draw most near to him; if Aaron himself put a slight upon the divine institution, he shall bear iniquity, and die. To us these garments typify, (1.) The *righteousness of Christ;* if we appear not before God in this, we shall *bear iniquity and die.* What have we to do at the wedding-feast without a wedding-garment, or at God's altar without the array of his priests? Mt. 22:12, 13. (2.) The *armour of God* prescribed Eph. 6:13. If we venture without that armour, our spiritual enemies will be the death of our souls, and we shall bear the iniquity, our blood will be upon our own heads. Blessed is he therefore that watcheth, and keepeth his garments, Rev. 16:15. 3. This is said to be a *statute for ever,* that is, it is to continue as long as the priesthood continues. But it is to have its perpetuity in the substance of which these things were the shadows.

CHAPTER 29

Particular orders are given in this chapter, I. Concerning the consecration of the priests, and the sanctification of the altar (*v.* 1–37). II. Concerning the daily sacrifice (*v.* 38–41). To which gracious promises are annexed that God would own and bless them in all their services (*v.* 42, etc.).

Verses 1–37

Here is, I. The law concerning the consecration of Aaron and his sons to the priest's office, which was to be done with a great deal of ceremony and solemnity, that they themselves might be duly affected with the greatness of the work to which they were called, and that the people also might learn to magnify the office and none might dare to invade it.

1. The ceremonies wherewith it was to be done were very fully and particularly appointed, because nothing of this kind had been done before, and because it was to be a statute for ever that the high priest should be thus inaugurated. Now,

(1.) The work to be done was the consecrating of the persons whom God had chosen to be priests, by which they devoted and gave up themselves to the service of God and God declared his acceptance of them; and the people were made to know that they *glorified not themselves* to be made priests, but were *called of God,* Heb. 5:4, 5. They were thus distinguished from common men, sequestered from common services, and set apart for God and an immediate attendance on him. Note, All that are to be employed for God are to be sanctified to him. The person must first be accepted, and then the performance. The Hebrew phrase for consecrating *is filling the hand (v.* 9): *Thou shalt fill the hand of Aaron and his sons,* and the *ram of consecration* is the *ram of fillings, v.* 22, 26. The consecrating of them was the perfecting of them; Christ is said to be *perfect* or *consecrated for evermore,* Heb. 7:28. Probably the phrase here is borrowed from the putting of the sacrifice into their hand, to be waved before the Lord, *v.* 24. But it intimates, [1.] That ministers have their hands full; they have no time to trifle, so great, so copious, so constant is their work. [2.] That they must have their hands filled. Of necessity *they must have something to offer,* and they cannot find it in themselves, it must be given them from above. They cannot fill the people's hearts unless God fill their hands; to him therefore they must go, and *receive from his fulness.*

(2.) The person to do it was Moses, by God's appointment. Though he was *ordained for men,* yet the people were not to consecrate him; Moses the *servant of the Lord,* and his agent herein, must do it. By God's special appointment he now did the priest's work, and therefore that which was the priest's part of the sacrifice was here ordered to be his, *v.* 26.

(3.) The place was at the *door of the tabernacle of meeting, v.* 4. God was pleased to dwell in the tabernacle, the people attending in the courts, so that the door between the court and the tabernacle was the fittest place for those to be consecrated in who were to mediate between God and man, and to stand between both, and *lay their hands* (as it were) *upon both.* They were consecrated at the door, for they were to be door-keepers.

(4.) It was done with many ceremonies.

[1.] They were to be washed (*v.* 4), signifying that those must be clean who *bear the vessels of the Lord,* Isa. 52:11. Those that would *perfect holiness* must *cleanse themselves from all filthiness of flesh and spirit,* 2 Co. 7:1; Isa. 1:16–18. They were now washed all over; but afterwards, when they went in to minister, they washed only their hands and feet (*ch.* 30:19); for *he that is washed needs* no more, Jn. 13:10.

[2.] They were to be clothed with the holy garments (*v.* 5, 6, 8, 9), to signify that it was not sufficient for them to put away the pollutions of sin, but they must put on the graces of the Spirit, be *clothed with righteousness,* Ps. 132:9. They must be girded, as men prepared and strengthened for their work; and they must be robed and crowned, as men that counted their work and office their true honour.

[3.] The high priest was to be anointed with the *holy anointing oil (v.* 7), that the church might be filled and delighted with the sweet savour of his administrations (for *ointment and perfume rejoice the heart*), and in token of the pouring out of the Spirit upon him, to qualify him for his work. Brotherly love is compared to this oil with which

Aaron was anointed, Ps. 133:2. The inferior priests are said to be anointed (ch. 30:30), not on their heads, as the high priest (Lev. 21:10), the oil was only mingled with the blood that was sprinkled upon their garments.

[4.] Sacrifices were to be offered for them. The covenant of priesthood, as all other covenants, must be made by sacrifice.

First, There must be a sin-offering, to make atonement for them, v. 10–14. The law made those priests that had infirmity, and therefore they must first offer for their own sin, before they could make atonement *for the people,* Heb. 7:27, 28. They were to put their hand on the head of their sacrifice (v. 10), confessing that they deserved to die for their own sin, and desiring that the killing of the beast might expiate their guilt, and be accepted as a vicarious satisfaction. It was used as other sin-offerings were; only, whereas the flesh of other sin-offerings was eaten by the priests (Lev. 10:18), in token of the priest's taking away the sin of the people, this was appointed to be all burnt without the camp (v. 14), to signify the imperfection of the legal dispensation (as the learned bishop Patrick notes); for the sins of the priests themselves could not be taken away by those sacrifices, but they must expect a better high priest and a better sacrifice.

Secondly, There must be a burnt-offering, a ram wholly burnt, to the honour of God, in token of the dedication of themselves wholly to God and to his service, as living sacrifices, kindled with the fire and ascending in the flame of holy love, v. 15–18. The sin-offering must first be offered and then the burnt-offering; for, till guilt be removed, no acceptable service can be performed, Isa. 6:7.

Thirdly, There must be a peace-offering; it is called *the ram of consecration,* because there was more in this peculiar to the occasion than in the other two. In the burnt-offering God had the glory of their priesthood, in this they had the comfort of it; and, in token of a mutual covenant between God and them, 1. The blood of the sacrifice was divided between God and them (v. 20, 21); part of the blood was *sprinkled upon the altar round about,* and part put upon them, upon their bodies (v. 20), and upon their garments, v. 21. Thus the benefit of the expiation made by the sacrifice was applied and assured to them, and their whole selves from head to foot sanctified to the service of God. The blood was put upon the extreme parts of the body, to signify that it was all, as it were, enclosed and taken in for God, the tip of the ear and the great toe not excepted. We reckon that the blood and oil sprinkled upon garments spot and stain them; yet the holy oil, and the blood of the sacrifice, sprinkled upon their garments, must be looked upon as the greatest adorning imaginable to them, for they signified the blood of Christ, and the graces of the Spirit, which constitute and complete the beauty of holiness, and recommend us to God; we read of robes *made white with the blood of the Lamb.* 2. The *flesh of the sacrifice,* with the meat-offering annexed to it, was likewise divided between God and them, that (to speak with reverence) God and they might feast together, in token of friendship and fellowship. (1.) Part of it was to be first waved before the Lord, and then burnt upon the altar; part of the *flesh* (v. 22), part of the *bread,* for bread and flesh must go together (v. 23); these were first put into the hands of Aaron to be waved to and fro, in token of their being offered to God (who, though unseen, yet compasses us round on every side), and then they were to be burnt upon the altar (v. 24, 25), for the altar was to devour God's part of the sacrifice. Thus God admitted Aaron and his sons to be his servants, and wait at his table, taking the mat of his altar from their hands. Here, in a parenthesis, as it were, comes in the law concerning the priests' part of the peace-offerings afterwards, the breast and shoulder, which were now divided; Moses had the breast, and the shoulder was burnt on the altar with God's part, v. 26–28. (2.) The other part, both of the flesh of the ram and of the bread, Aaron and his sons were to eat at the door of the tabernacle (v. 31–33), to signify that he called them not only *servants* but *friends,* Jn. 15:15. He *supped with them,* and *they with him.* Their eating of the things wherewith *the atonement was made* signified their *receiving the atonement,* as the expression is (Rom. 5:11), their thankful acceptance of the benefit of it, and their joyful communion with God thereupon, which was the true intent and meaning of a feast upon a sacrifice. If any of it was left, it must be burnt, that

it might not be in any danger of putrefying, and to show that it was an extraordinary peace-offering.

2. The time that was to be spent in this consecration: *Seven days shalt thou consecrate them,* v. 35. Though all the ceremonies were performed on the first day, yet, (1.) They were not to look upon their consecration as completed till the seven days' end, which put a solemnity upon their admission, and a distance between this and their former state, and obliged them to enter upon their work with a pause, giving them time to consider the weight and seriousness of it. This was to be observed in after-ages, v. 30. He that was to succeed Aaron in the high-priesthood must put on the holy garments seven days together, in token of a deliberate and gradual advance into his office, and that one sabbath might pass over him in his consecration. (2.) Every day of the seven, in this first consecration, a bullock was to be offered for a sin-offering (v. 36), which was to intimate to them, [1.] That it was of very great concern to them to get their sins pardoned, and that though atonement was made, and they had the comfort of it, yet they must still keep up a penitent sense of sin and often repeat the confession of it. [2.] That those sacrifices which were thus offered day by day to make atonement could not make the *comers thereunto perfect,* for then they would have ceased to be offered, as the apostle argues, Heb. 10:1, 2. They must therefore expect the *bringing in of a better hope.*

3. This consecration of the priests was a *shadow of good things to come.* (1.) Our Lord Jesus is the great high-priest of our profession, called of God to be so, consecrated for evermore, anointed with the Spirit above his fellows (whence he is called *Messiah,* the *Christ*), clothed with the holy garments, even with glory and beauty, sanctified by his own blood, not that of bullocks and rams (Heb. 9:12), *made perfect,* or consecrated, *through sufferings,* Heb. 2:10. Thus in him this was a perpetual statute, v. 9. (2.) All believers are spiritual priests, to offer spiritual sacrifices (1 Pt. 2:5), washed in the blood of Christ, and so *made to our God priests,* Rev. 1:5, 6. They also are clothed with the beauty of holiness, and have received the anointing, 1 Jn. 2:27. Their hands are filled with work, to which they must continually attend; and it is through Christ, the great sacrifice, that they are dedicated to this service. His blood *sprinkled upon the conscience purges it from dead works, that they may,* as priests, *serve the living God.* The Spirit of God (as Ainsworth notes) is called the *finger of God* (Lu. 11:20, compared with Mt. 12:28), and by him the merit of Christ is effectually applied to our souls, as here Moses with his finger was to put the blood upon Aaron. It is likewise intimated that gospel ministers are to be solemnly set apart to the work of the ministry with great deliberation and seriousness both in the ordainers and in the ordained, as those that are to be employed in a great work and entrusted with a great charge.

II. The consecration of the altar, which seems to have been coincident with that of the priests, and the sin-offerings which were offered every day for seven days together had reference to the altar as well as the priests, v. 36, 37. An *atonement* was *made for the altar.* Though that was not a subject capable of sin, nor, having never yet been used, could it be said to be polluted with the sins of the people, yet, since the fall, there can be no sanctification to God but there must first be *an atonement for sin,* which renders us both unworthy and unfit to be employed for God. The altar was also *sanctified,* not only set apart itself to a sacred use, but made so holy as to *sanctify the gifts* that were offered upon it, Mt. 23:19. Christ is our altar; for our sakes he sanctified himself, that we and our performances might be sanctified and recommended to God, Jn. 17:19.

Verses 38–46

In this paragraph we have,

I. The daily service appointed. A lamb was to be offered upon the altar every morning, and a lamb every evening, each with a meat-offering, both made by fire, as a *continual burnt-offering throughout their generations,* v. 38–41. Whether there were any other sacrifices to be offered or not, these were sure to be offered, at the public charge, for the benefit and comfort of all Israel, to make atonement for their daily sins, and to be an acknowledgement to God of their daily mercies. This was that which

the duty of every day required. The taking away of this daily sacrifice by Antiochus, for so many evenings and mornings, was that great calamity of the church which was foretold, Dan. 8:11. Note, 1. This typified the continual intercession which Christ ever lives to make, in virtue of his satisfaction, for the continual sanctification of his church: though he offered himself *once for all,* yet that one offering thus becomes a continual offering. 2. This teaches us to offer up to God the spiritual sacrifices of prayer and praise every day, morning and evening, in humble acknowledgement of our dependence upon him and our obligations to him. Our daily devotions must be looked upon as the most needful of our daily works and the most pleasant of our daily comforts. Whatever business we have, this must never be omitted, either morning or evening; prayer-time must be kept up as duly as meat-time. The daily sacrifices were as the daily meals in God's house, and therefore they were always attended with bread and wine. Those starve their own souls that keep not up a constant attendance on the throne of grace.

II. Great and precious promises made of God's favour to Israel, and the tokens of his special presence with them, while they thus kept up his institutions among them. He speaks as one well pleased with the appointment of the daily sacrifice; for, before he proceeds to the other appointments that follow, he interposes these promises. It is constancy in religion that brings in the comfort of it. He promises, 1. That he would keep up communion with them; that he would not only meet Moses, and speak to him, but that he would *meet the children of Israel,* (v. 43), to accept the daily sacrifices offered up on their behalf. Note, God will not fail to give those the meeting who diligently and conscientiously attend upon him in the ordinances of his own appointment. 2. That he would own his own institutions, the tabernacle, the altar, the priesthood (v. 43, 44); he would take possession of that which was consecrated to him. Note, What is sanctified to the glory of God shall be sanctified by his glory. If we do our part, God will do his, and will mark and fit that for himself which is in sincerity given up to him. 3. That he would reside among them as God in covenant with them, and would give them sure and comfortable tokens of his peculiar favour to them, and his special presence with them (v. 45, 45): *I will dwell among the children of Israel.* Note, Where God sets up the tabernacle of his ordinances he will himself dwell. *Lo, I am with you always,* Mt. 28:20. Those that abide in God's house shall have God to abide with them. *I will be their God, and they shall know* that I am so. Note, Those are truly happy that have a covenant-interest in God as theirs and the comfortable evidence of that interest. If we have this, we have enough, and need no more to make us happy.

CHAPTER 30

Moses is, in this chapter, further instructed, I. Concerning the altar of incense (v. 1–10). II. Concerning the ransom-money which the Israelites were to pay, when they were numbered (v. 11–16). III. Concerning the laver of brass, which was set for the priests to wash in (v. 17–21). IV. Concerning the making up of the anointing oil, and the use of it (v. 22–33). V. Concerning the incense and perfume which were to be burned on the golden altar (v. 34, etc.).

Verses 1–10

I. The orders given concerning the altar of incense are, 1. That it was to be made of wood, and covered with gold, pure gold, about a yard high and half a yard square, with horns at the corners, a golden cornice round it, with rings and staves of gold, for the convenience of carrying it, v. 1–5. It does not appear that there was any grate to this altar for the ashes to fall into, that they might be taken away; but, when they burnt incense, a golden censer was brought with coals in it, and placed upon the altar, and in that censer the incense was burnt, and with it all the coals were taken away, so that no coals nor ashes fell upon the altar. The measure of the altar of incense in Ezekiel's temple is double to what it is here (Eze. 41:22), and it is there called *an altar of wood,* and there is no mention of gold, to signify that the incense, in gospel times, should be spiritual, the worship plain, and the service of God enlarged, for *in every place incense should be offered,* Mal. 1:11. 2. That it was to be placed before the veil, on the outside of that partition, but before the mercy-seat, which was within the veil, v. 6. For though he that ministered at the altar could not see the mercy-seat, the veil interposing, yet he must look towards it, and direct his incense that way, to teach us that though we cannot with our bodily eyes see the throne of grace, that blessed mercy-seat (for it is such a throne of glory that God, in compassion to us, holds back the face of it, and spreads a cloud upon it), yet we must in prayer by faith set ourselves before it, direct our prayer, and look up. 3. That Aaron was to burn sweet incense upon this altar, every morning and every evening, about half a pound at a time, which was intended, not only to take away the ill smell of the flesh that was burnt daily on the brazen altar, but for the honour of God, and to show the acceptableness of his people's services to him, and the pleasure which they should take in ministering to him, *v.* 7, 8. As by the offerings on the brazen altar satisfaction was made for what had been done displeasing to God, so, by the offering on this, what they did well was, as it were, recommended to the divine acceptance; for our two great concerns with God are to be acquitted from guilt and accepted as righteous in his sight. 4. That nothing was to be offered upon it but incense, nor any incense but that which was appointed, *v.* 9. God will have his own service done according to his own appointment, and not otherwise. 5. That this altar should be purified with the blood of the sin-offering put upon the *horns of it,* every year, upon *the day of atonement, v.* 10. See Lev. 16:18, 19. The high priest was to take this in his way, as he came out from the holy of holies. This was to intimate to them that the sins of the priests who ministered at this altar, and of the people for whom they ministered, put a ceremonial impurity upon it, from which it must be cleansed by the blood of atonement.

II. This incense-altar typified, 1. The mediation of Christ. The brazen altar in the court was a type of Christ dying on earth; the golden altar in the sanctuary was a type of Christ interceding in heaven, in virtue of his satisfaction. This altar was before the mercy-seat; for Christ always appears in the presence of God for us; he is our *advocate with the father* (1 Jn. 2:1), and his intercession is unto God of a sweet-smelling savour. This altar had a crown fixed to it; for Christ intercedes as king. *Father, I will,* Jn. 17:24. 2. The devotions of the saints, whose prayers are said to be set forth before God as incense, Ps. 141:2. As the smoke of the incense ascended, so much our desires towards God rise in prayer, being kindled with the fire of holy love and other pious affections. When the priest was burning incense the people were praying (Lu. 1:10), to signify that prayer is the true incense. This incense was offered daily, it was a perpetual incense (*v.* 8); for we must pray always, that is, we must keep up stated times for prayer every day, morning and evening, at least, and never omit it, but thus pray without ceasing. The lamps were dressed or lighted at the same time that the incense was burnt, to teach us that the reading of the scriptures (which are our light and lamp) is a part of our daily work, and should ordinarily accompany our prayers and praises. When we speak to God we must hear what God says to us, and thus the communion is complete. The devotions of sanctified souls are well-pleasing to God, of a sweet-smelling savour; the prayers of saints are compared to sweet odours (Rev. 5:8), but it is the incense which Christ adds to them that makes them acceptable (Rev. 8:3), and his blood that atones for the guilt which cleaves to our best services. And, if the heart and life be not holy, even *incense is an abomination* (Isa. 1:13), and he that offers it is *as if he blessed an idol,* Isa. 66:3.

Verses 11–16

Some observe that the repetition of those words, *The Lord spoke unto Moses,* here and afterwards (*v.* 17, 22, 34), intimates that God did not deliver these precepts to Moses in the mount, in a continued discourse, but with many intermissions, giving him time either to write what was said to him or at least to charge his memory with it. Christ gave instructions to his disciples as they were able to hear them. Moses is here ordered to levy money upon the people by way of poll, so much a head, for the service of the tabernacle. This he must do when he numbered the people. Some think that it refers only to the first numbering of them, now when the tabernacle was set up; and that this tax was to make up what was deficient in the voluntary contributions for the finishing of the work, or rather for the beginning of the service in the tabernacle. Oth-

ers think that it was afterwards repeated upon any emergency and always when the people were numbered, and that David offended in not demanding it when he numbered the people. But many of the Jewish writers, and others from them, are of opinion that it was to be an annual tribute, only it was begun when Moses first numbered the people. This was that tribute-money which Christ paid, for fear of offending his adversaries (Mt. 17:27), when yet he showed good reason why he should have been excused. Men were appointed in every city to receive this payment yearly. Now, 1. The tribute to be paid was *half a shekel,* about fifteen pence of our money. The rich were not to give more, nor the poor less (*v.* 15), to intimate that the souls of the rich and poor are alike precious, and that God is *no respecter of persons,* Acts 10:34; Job 34:19. In other offerings men were to give according to their ability; but this, which was the *ransom of the soul,* must be alike for all; for the rich have as much need of Christ as the poor, and the poor are as welcome to him as the rich. They both alike contributed to the maintenance of the temple-service, because both were to have a like interest in it and benefit by it. In Christ and his ordinances *rich and poor meet together; the Lord is the Maker,* the Lord Christ is the Redeemer of them both, Prov. 22:2. The Jews say, "If a man refused to pay this tribute, he was not comprehended in the expiation." 2. this tribute was to be paid as a *ransom of the soul, that there might be no plague among them.* Hereby they acknowledged that they received their lives from God, that they had forfeited their lives to him, and that they depended upon his power and patience for the continuance of them; and thus they did homage to the God of their lives, and deprecated those plagues which their sins had deserved. 3. This money that was raised was to be employed in the service of the tabernacle (*v.* 16); with it they bought sacrifices, flour, incense, wine, oil, fuel, salt, priests' garments, and all other things which the whole congregation was interested in. Note, Those that have the benefit of God's tabernacle among them must be willing to defray the expenses of it, and not grudge the necessary charges of God's public worship. Thus we must honour the Lord with our substance, and reckon that best laid out which is laid out in the service of God. Money indeed cannot make an *atonement for the soul,* but it may be used for the honour of him who has made the atonement, and for the maintenance of the gospel by which the atonement is applied.

Verses 17–21

Orders are here given, 1. For the making of a laver, or font, of brass, a large vessel, that would contain a good quantity of water, which was to be set near the door of the tabernacle, *v.* 18. The foot of brass, it is supposed, was so contrived as to receive the water, which was let into it out of the laver by spouts or cocks. They then had a laver for the priests only to wash in, but to us now there is a fountain open for Judah and Jerusalem to wash in (Zec. 13:1), an inexhaustible *fountain of living water,* so that it is our own fault if we remain in our pollution. 2. For the using of this laver. Aaron and his sons must wash their hands and feet at this laver every time they went in to minister, every morning, at least, *v.* 19–21. For this purpose clean water was put into the laver fresh every day. Though they washed themselves ever so clean at their own houses, that would not serve; they must wash at the laver, because that was appointed for washing, 2 Ki. 5:12–14. This was designed, (1.) To teach them purity in all their ministrations, and to possess them with a reverence of God's holiness and a dread of the pollutions of sin. They must not only wash and be made clean when they were first consecrated, but they must wash and be kept clean whenever they went in to minister. He only shall *stand in God's holy place* that has *clean hands and a pure heart,* Ps. 24:3, 4. And, (2.) It was to teach us, who are daily to attend upon God, daily to renew our repentance for sin and our believing application of the blood of Christ to our souls for remission; for in many things we daily offend and contract pollution, Jn. 13:8, 10; Jam. 3:2. This is the preparation we are to make for solemn ordinances. *Cleanse your hands and purify your hearts,* and then *draw nigh to God,* Jam. 4:8. To this law David alludes in Ps. 26:6, *I will wash my hands in innocency, so will I compass thine altar, O Lord.*

Verses 22–38

Directions are here given for the composition of the holy anointing oil and the incense that were to be used in the service of the tabernacle; with these God was to be honoured, and therefore he would appoint the making of them; for nothing comes *to* God but what comes *from* him. 1. The holy anointing oil is here ordered to be made up the ingredients, and their quantities, are prescribed, *v.* 23–25. Interpreters are not agreed concerning them; we are sure, in general, they were the best and fittest for the purpose; they must needs be so when the divine wisdom appointed them for the divine honour. It was to be compounded *secundum artem — after the art of the apothecary* (*v.* 25); the spices, which were in all nearly half a hundred weight, were to be infused in the oil, which was to be about five or six quarts, and then strained out, leaving an admirable sweet smell in the oil. With this oil God's tent and all the furniture of it were to be anointed; it was to be used also in the consecration of the priests, *v.* 26–30. It was to be continued *throughout their generations, v.* 31. The tradition of the Jews is that this very oil which was prepared by Moses himself lasted till near the captivity. But bishop Patrick shows the great improbability of the tradition, and supposes that it was repeated according to the prescription here, for Solomon was anointed with it (2 Ki. 1:39), and some other of the kings; and all the high priests with such a quantity of it that it ran down to the skirts of the garments; and we read of the making up of this ointment (1 Chr. 9:30): yet all agree that in the second temple there was none of this holy oil, which he supposes was owing to a notion they had that it was not lawful to make it up, Providence overruling that want as a presage of the better unction of the Holy Ghost in gospel times, the variety of whose gifts was typified by these several sweet ingredients. To show the excellency of holiness, there was that in the tabernacle which was in the highest degree grateful both to the sight and to the smell. Christ's name is said to be as *ointment poured forth* (Cant. 1:3), and the good name of Christians better than *precious ointment,* Eccl. 7:1. 2. The incense which was burned upon the golden altar was prepared of sweet spices likewise, though not so rare and rich as those of which the anointing oil was compounded, *v.* 34, 35. This was prepared once a year (the Jews say), a pound for each day of the year, and three pounds over for the day of atonement. When it was used, it was to be beaten very small: thus it pleased the Lord to bruise the Redeemer when he offered himself for a sacrifice of a sweet-smelling savour. 3. Concerning both these preparations the same law is here given (*v.* 32, 33, 37, 38), that the like should not be made for any common use. Thus God would preserve in the people's minds a reverence for his own institutions, and teach us not to profane nor abuse any thing whereby God makes himself known, as those did who invented to themselves (for their common entertainments) instruments of music like David, Amos 6:5. It is a great affront to God to jest with sacred things, particularly to make sport with the word and ordinances of God, or to treat them with lightness, Mt. 22:5. That which is God's peculiar must not be used as a common thing.

CHAPTER 31

God is here drawing towards a conclusion of what he had to say to Moses upon the mount, where he had now been with him forty days and forty nights; and yet no more is recorded of what was said to him in all that time than what we have read in the six chapters foregoing. In this, I. He appoints what workmen should be employed in the building and furnishing of the tabernacle (*v.* 1–11). II. He repeats the law of the sabbath, and the religious observance of it (*v.* 12–17). III. He delivers to him the two tables of the testimony at parting (*v.* 18).

Verses 1–11

A great deal of fine work God had ordered to be done about the tabernacle; the materials the people were to provide, but who must put them into form? Moses himself was learned in all the learning of the Egyptians, nay, he was well acquainted with the words of God, and the visions of the Almighty; but he knew not how to engrave or embroider. We may suppose that there were some very ingenious men among the Israelites; but, having lived all their days in bondage in Egypt, we cannot think they were any of them instructed in these curious arts. They knew how to make brick and work in clay, but to work in gold and in cutting diamonds was what they had never been brought up to. How should the work be done with the neatness and exactness that were required when they had no goldsmiths or jewellers but what must be made out of masons and bricklayers? We may suppose that there were a sufficient number who would gladly be employed, and would do their best; but it would be hard to find out a proper person to preside in this work. *Who was sufficient for these things?* But God takes care of this matter also.

I. He nominates the persons that were to be employed, that there might be no contest about the preferment, nor envy at those that were preferred, God himself having made the choice. 1. Bezaleel was to be the architect, or master workman, *v.* 2. He was of the tribe of Judah, a tribe that God delighted to honour; the grandson of Hur, probably that Hur who had helped to hold up Moses's hands (*ch.* 17), and was at this time in commission with Aaron for the government of the people in the absence of Moses (*ch.* 24:14); out of that family which was of note in Israel was the workman chosen, and it added no little honour to the family that a branch of it was employed, though but as a mechanic, or handicraft tradesman, for the service of the tabernacle. The Jews' tradition is that Hur was the husband of Miriam; and, if so, it was requisite that God should appoint him to this service, lest, if Moses himself had done it, he should be thought partial to his own kindred, his brother Aaron also being advanced to the priesthood. God will put honour upon Moses's relations, and yet will make it to appear that he takes not the honour to himself or his own family, but that it is purely the Lord's doing. 2. Aholiab, of the tribe of Dan, is appointed next to Bezaleel, and partner with him, *v.* 6. Two are better than one. Christ sent forth his disciples who were to rear the gospel tabernacle, two and two, and we read of his two witnesses. Aholiab was of the tribe of Dan, which was one of the less honourable tribes, that the tribes of Judah and Levi might not be lifted up, as if they were to engross all the preferments; to prevent a schism in the body, God gives honour to *that part which lacked,* 1 Co. 12:24. *The head cannot say to the foot, I have no need of thee.* Hiram, who was the head workman in the building of Solomon's temple, was also of the tribe of Dan, 2 Chr. 2:14. 3. There were others that were employed by and under these in the several operations about the tabernacle, *v.* 6. Note, When God has work to do he will never want instruments to do it with, for all hearts and heads too are under his eye, and in his hand; and those may cheerfully go about any service for God, and go on in it, who have reason to think that, one way or other, he has called them to it; for whom he calls he will own and bear out.

II. He qualifies these persons for the service (*v.* 3): *I have filled him with the Spirit of God;* and (*v.* 6) *in the hearts of all that are wise-hearted I have put wisdom.* Note, 1. Skill in common arts and employments is the gift of God; from him are derived both the faculty and the improvement of the faculty. It is he that puts even this *wisdom into the inward parts,* Job 38:36. He teaches the husbandman discretion (Isa. 28:26), and the tradesman too; and he must have the praise of it. 2. God dispenses his gifts variously, one gift to one, another to another, and all for the good of the whole body, both of mankind and of the church. Moses was fittest of all to govern Israel, but Bezaleel was fitter than he to build the tabernacle. The common benefit is very much supported by the variety of men's faculties and inclinations; the genius of some leads them to be serviceable one way, of others another way, and *all these worketh that one and the self-same Spirit,* 1 Co. 12:11. This forbids pride, envy, contempt, and carnal emulation, and strengthens the bond of mutual love. 3. Those whom God calls to any service he will either find, or make, fit for it. If God give the commission, he will in some measure give the qualifications, according as the service is. The work, that was to be done here was to make the tabernacle and the utensils of it, which are here particularly reckoned up, *v.* 7, etc. And for this the persons employed were enabled to *work in gold, and silver, and brass.* When Christ sent his apostles to rear the gospel tabernacle, he poured out his Spirit upon them, to enable them to speak with tongues the wonderful works of God; not to work upon metal, but to work upon men; so much more excellent were the gifts, as the tabernacle to be pitched was a *greater and more perfect tabernacle,* as the apostle calls it, Heb. 9:11.

Verses 12–18

Here is, I. A strict command for the sanctification of the sabbath day, *v.* 13–17. The law of the sabbath had been given them before any other law, by way of preparation (*ch.* 16:23); it had been inserted in the body of the moral law, in the fourth commandment; it had been annexed to the judicial law (*ch.* 23:12); and here it is added to the first part of the ceremonial law, because the observance of the sabbath is indeed the hem and hedge of the whole law; where no conscience is made of that, farewell both godliness and honesty; for, in the moral law, it stands in the midst between the two tables. Some suggest that it comes in here upon another account. Orders were now given that a tabernacle should be set up and furnished for the service of God with all possible expedition; but lest they should think that the nature of the work, and the haste that was required, would justify them in working at it on sabbath days, that they might get it done the sooner, this caution is seasonably inserted, *Verily,* or *nevertheless, my sabbaths you shall keep.* Though they must hasten the work, yet they must not make more haste than good speed; they must not break the law of the sabbath in their haste: even tabernacle-work must give way to the sabbath-rest; so jealous is God for the honour of his sabbaths. Observe what is here said concerning the sabbath day.

1. The nature, meaning, and intention, of the sabbath, by the declaration of which God puts an honour upon it, and teaches us to value it. Divers things are here said of the sabbath. (1.) *It is a sign between me and you* (*v.* 13), and again, *v.* 17. The institution of the sabbath was a great instance of God's favour to them, and a sign that he had distinguished them from all other people; and their religious observance of the sabbath was a great instance of their duty and obedience to him. God, by sanctifying this day among them, let them know that he sanctified them, and set them apart for himself and his service; otherwise he would not have revealed to them his holy sabbaths, to be the support of religion among them. Or it may refer to the law concerning the sabbath, *Keep my sabbaths, that you may know that I the Lord do sanctify you.* Note, If God by his grace incline our hearts to keep the law of the fourth commandment, it will be an evidence of a good work wrought in us by his Spirit. If we sanctify God's day, it is a sign between him and us that he has sanctified our hearts: hence it is the character of the blessed man that he *keepeth the sabbath from polluting it,* Isa. 56:2. The Jews, by observing one day in seven, after six days' labour, testified and declared that they worshipped the God who made the world in six days, and rested the seventh; and so distinguished themselves from other nations, who, having first lost the sabbath, which was instituted to be a memorial of the creation, by degrees lost the knowledge of the Creator, and gave that honour to the creature which was due to him alone. (2.) *It is holy unto you* (*v.* 14), that is, "It is designed for your benefit as well as for God's honour;" *the sabbath was made for man.* Or, "It shall be accounted holy by you, and shall so be observed, and you shall look upon it a sacrilege to profane it." (3.) It is the *sabbath of rest, holy to the Lord, v.* 15. It is separated from common use, and designed for the honour and service of God, and by the observance of it we are taught to rest from worldly pursuits and the service of the flesh, and to devote ourselves, and all we are, have, and can do, to God's glory. (4.) It was to be observed *throughout their generations,* in every age, *for a perpetual covenant. v.* 16. This was to be one of the most lasting tokens of that covenant which was between God and Israel.

2. The law of the sabbath. They must keep it (*v.* 13, 14, 16), keep it as a treasure, as a trust, observe it and preserve it, keep it from polluting it, keep it up as a sign between God and them, keep it and never part with it. The Gentiles had anniversary-feasts, to the honour of their gods; but it was peculiar to the Jews to have a weekly festival; this therefore they must carefully observe.

3. The reason of the sabbath; for God's laws are not only backed with the highest authority, but supported with the best reason. God's own example is the great reason, *v.* 17. As the work of creation is worthy to be thus commemorated, so the great Creator is worthy to be thus imitated, by a holy rest, the seventh day, after six days' labour, especially since we hope, in further conformity to the same example, shortly to rest with him from all our labours.

4. The penalty to be inflicted for the breach of this law: "Every one that *defileth the sabbath,* by doing *any work therein* but works of piety and mercy, *shall be cut off from among his people* (*v.* 14); *he shall surely be put to death. v.* 15. The magistrate must cut him off the sword of justice if the crime can be proved; if it cannot, or if the magistrate be remiss, and do not do his duty, God will take the work into his own hands, and cut him off by a stroke from heaven, and his family shall be rooted out of Israel." Note, The contempt and profanation of the sabbath day is an iniquity to be punished by the judges; and, if men do not punish it, God will, here or hereafter, unless it be repented of.

II. The delivering of the two tables of testimony to Moses. God had promised him these tables when he called him up into the mount (*ch.* 24:12), and now, when he was sending him down, he delivered them to him, to be carefully and honourably deposited in the ark, *v.* 18. 1. The ten commandments which God had spoken upon mount Sinai in the hearing of all the people were now written, *in perpetuam rei memoriam — for a perpetual memorial,* because that which is written remains. 2. They were written in *tables of stone,* prepared, not by Moses, as it should seem (for it is intimated, *ch.* 24:12, that he found them ready written when he went up to the mount), but, as some think, by the ministry of angels. The law was written in *tables of stone,* to denote the perpetual duration of it (what can be supposed to last longer than that which is written in stone, and laid up?), to denote likewise the hardness of our hearts; one might more easily write in stone than write any thing that is good in our corrupt and sinful hearts. 3. They were written *with the finger of God,* that is, by his will and power immediately, without the use of any instrument. It is God only that can write his law in the heart; he *gives a heart of flesh,* and then, by his Spirit, which is the *finger of God,* he writes his will in the *fleshly tables of the heart,* 2 Co. 3:3. 4. They were written in two tables, being designed to direct us in our duty both towards God and towards man. 5. They are called *tables of testimony,* because this written law testified both the will of God concerning them and his good-will towards them, and would be a testimony against them if they were disobedient. 6. They were delivered to Moses, probably with a charge, before he laid them up in the ark, to show them publicly, that they might be *seen and read of all men,* and so what they had heard with the hearing of the ear might now be brought to their remembrance. Thus *the law was given by Moses, but grace and truth came by Jesus Christ.*

CHAPTER 32

It is a very lamentable interruption which the story of this chapter gives to the record of the establishment of the church, and of religion among the Jews. Things went on admirably well towards that happy settlement: God had shown himself very favourable, and the people also had seemed to be pretty tractable. Moses had now almost completed his forty days upon the mount, and, we may suppose, was pleasing himself with the thoughts of the very joyful welcome he should have to the camp of Israel at his return, and the speedy setting up of the tabernacle among them. But, behold, the measures are broken, the sin of Israel turns away those good things from them, and puts a stop to the current of God's favours; the sin that did the mischief (would you think it?) was worshipping a golden calf. The marriage was ready to be solemnized between God and Israel, but Israel plays the harlot, and so the match is broken, and it will be no easy matter to piece it again. Here is, I. The sin of Israel, and of Aaron particularly, in making the golden calf for a god (*v.* 1–4), and worshipping it (*v.* 5, 6). II. The notice which God gave of this to Moses, who was now in the mount with him (*v.* 7, 8), and the sentence of his wrath against them (*v.* 9, 10). III. The intercession which Moses immediately made for them in the mount (*v.* 11–13), and the prevalency of that intercession (*v.* 14). IV. His coming down from the mount, when he became an eye-witness of their idolatry (*v.* 15–19), in abhorrence of which, and as an expression of just indignation, he broke the tables (*v.* 19), and burnt the golden calf (*v.* 20). V. The examination of Aaron about it (*v.* 21–24). VI. Execution done upon the ring-leaders in the idolatry (*v.* 25–29). VII. The further intercession Moses made for them, to turn away the wrath of God from them (*v.* 30–32), and a reprieve granted thereupon, reserving them for a further reckoning (*v.* 33, etc.).

Verses 1–6

While Moses was in the mount, receiving the law from God, the people had time to meditate upon what had been delivered, and prepare themselves for what was further to be revealed, and forty days was little enough for that work; but, instead of that, there were those among them that were contriving how to break the laws they had already received, and to anticipate those which they were in expectation of. On the thirty-ninth day of the forty, the plot broke out of rebellion against the Lord. Here is,

I. A tumultuous address which the people made to Aaron, who was entrusted with the government in the absence of Moses: *Up, make us gods, which shall go before us, v.* 1.

1. See the ill effect of Moses's absence from them; if he had not had God's call both to go and stay, he would not have been altogether free from blame. Those that have the charge of others, as magistrates, ministers, and masters of families, ought not, without just cause, to absent themselves from their charge, *lest Satan get advantage* thereby.

2. See the fury and violence of a multitude when they are influenced and corrupted by such as lie in wait to deceive. Some few, it is likely, were at first possessed with this humour, while many, who would never have thought of it if they had not put it into their hearts, were brought to follow their pernicious ways; and presently such a multitude were carried down the stream that the few who abhorred the proposal durst not so much as enter their protestation against it. *Behold how great a matter a little fire kindles!* Now what was the matter with this giddy multitude?

(1.) They were weary of waiting for the promised land. They thought themselves detained too long at mount Sinai; though there they lay very safe and very easy, well fed and well taught, yet they were impatient to be going forward. They had a God that staid with them, and manifested his presence with them by the cloud; but this would not serve. They must have a god to go before them; they are for hastening to the land *flowing with milk and honey,* and cannot stay to take their religion along with them. Note, Those that would anticipate God's counsels are commonly precipitate in their own. We must first wait for God's law before we catch at his promises. He that believeth doth not make haste, not more haste than good speed.

(2.) They were weary of waiting for the return of Moses. When he went up into the mount, he had not told them (for God had not told him) how long he must stay; and therefore, when he had outstayed their time, though they were every way well provided for in his absence, some bad people advanced I know not what surmises concerning his delay: *As for this Moses, the man that brought us up out of Egypt, we wot not what has become of him.* Observe, [1.] How slightly they speak of his person — *this Moses.* Thus ungrateful are they to Moses, who had shown such a tender concern for them, and thus do they walk contrary to God. While God delights to put honour upon him, they delight to put contempt upon him, and this to the face of Aaron his brother, and now his viceroy. Note, The greatest merits cannot secure men from the greatest indignities and affronts in this ungrateful world. [2.] How suspiciously they speak of his delay: *We wot not what has become of him.* They thought he was either consumed by the devouring fire or starved for want to food, as if that God who kept and fed them, who were so unworthy, would not take care for the protection and supply of Moses his favourite. Some of them, who were willing to think well of Moses, perhaps suggested that he was translated to heaven like Enoch; while others that cared not how ill they thought of him insinuated that he had deserted his undertaking, as unable to go on with it, and had returned to his father-in-law to keep his flock. All these suggestions were perfectly groundless and absurd, nothing could be more so; it was easy to tell *what had become of him:* he was seen to go into the cloud, and the cloud he went into was still seen by all Israel upon the top of the mount; they had all the reason in the world to conclude that he was safe there; if the Lord had been pleased to kill him, he would not have shown him such favours as these. If he tarried long, it was because God had a great deal to say to him, for their good; he resided upon the mount as the ambassador, and he would certainly return as soon as he had finished the business he went upon; and yet they make this the colour for their wicked proposal: *We wot not what has become of him.* Note, *First,* Those that are resolved to think ill, when they have ever so much reason to think well, commonly pretend that they know not what to think. *Secondly,* Misinterpretations of our Redeemer's delays are the occasion of a great deal of wickedness. Our Lord Jesus has gone up into the mount of glory, where he is appearing in the presence of Gold for us, but out of our sight; the heavens must contain him, must conceal him, that we may live by faith. There he has been long; there he is yet. Hence unbelievers suggest that they know not what has become of him; and ask, *Where is the promise of his coming?* (2 Pt. 3:4), as if, because he has not come yet, he would never come. The wicked servant emboldens himself in his impieties with this consideration, *My Lord delays his coming. Thirdly,* Weariness in waiting betrays us to a great many temptations. This began Saul's ruin; he staid for Samuel to the last hour of the time appointed, but had not patience to stay that hour (1 Sa. 13:8, etc.); so Israel here, if they could but have staid one day longer, would have seen what had become of Moses. *The Lord is a God of judgment,* and must be waited for till he comes waited for though he tarry; and then we shall not lose our labour, for he that shall come will come, and will not tarry.

(3.) They were weary of waiting for a divine institution of religious worship among them for that was the thing they were now in expectation of. They were told that they must *serve God in this mountain,* and fond enough they would be of the pomp and ceremony of it; but, because that was not appointed them so soon as they wished, they would set their own wits on work to devise signs of God's presence with them, and would glory in them, and have a worship of their own invention, probably such as they had seen among the Egyptians; for Stephen says that when they said unto Aaron, *Make us gods,* they did, in heart, *turn back into Egypt,* Acts 7:39, 40. This was a very strange motion, *Up, make us gods.* If they knew not what had become of Moses, and thought him lost, it would have been decent for them to have appointed a solemn mourning for him for certain days; but see how soon so great a benefactor is forgotten. If they had said, "Moses is lost, make us a governor," there would have been some sense in it, though a great deal of ingratitude to the memory of Moses, and contempt of Aaron and Hur who were left lords-justices in his absence; but to say, *Moses is lost, make us a god,* was the greatest absurdity imaginable. Was Moses their god? Had he ever pretended to be so? Whatever had become of Moses, was it not evident, beyond contradiction that God was still with them? And had they any room to question his leading their camp who victualled it so well every day? Could they have any other god that would provide so well for them as he had done, nay as he now did? And yet, *Make us gods, which shall go before us! Gods!* How many would they have? Is not one sufficient? *Make us gods!* and what good would gods of their own making do them? They must have such gods to go before them as could not go themselves further than they were carried. So wretchedly besotted and intoxicated are idolaters: they are *mad upon their idols,* Jer. 50:38.

II. Here is the demand which Aaron makes of their jewels thereupon: *Bring me your golden ear-rings, v.* 2. We do not find that he said one word to discountenance their proposal; he did not reprove their insolence, did not reason with them to convince them of the sin and folly of it, but seemed to approve the motion, and showed himself not unwilling to humour them in it. One would hope he designed, at first, only to make a jest of it, and, by setting up a ridiculous image among them, to expose the motion, and show them the folly of it. But, if so, it proved ill jesting with sin: it is of dangerous consequence for the unwary fly to play about the candle. Some charitably suppose that when Aaron told them to break off their ear-rings, and bring them to him, he did it with design to crush the proposal, believing that though their covetousness would have let them *lavish gold out of the bag* to make an idol of (Isa. 46:6), yet their pride would not have suffered them to part with the golden ear-rings. But it is not safe to try how far men's sinful lusts will carry them in a sinful way, and what expense they will be at; it proved here a dangerous experiment.

III. Here is the making of the golden calf, *v.* 3, 4. 1. The people brought in their ear-rings to Aaron, whose demand of them, instead of discouraging the motion, perhaps did rather gratify their superstition, and beget in them a fancy that the gold taken from their ears would be the most acceptable, and would make the most valuable god. Let their readiness to part with their rings to make an idol of shame us out of our niggardliness in the service of the true God. Did they not draw back from the charge of their idolatry? And shall we grudge the expenses of our religion, or starve so good a cause? 2. Aaron melted down their rings, and, having a mould prepared for the purpose, poured the melted gold into it, and then produced it in the shape of an ox or calf, giving it some finishing strokes with a graving tool. Some think that Aaron chose this figure, for a sign or token of the divine presence, because he thought the head and horns of an ox a proper emblem of the divine power, and yet, being so plain and common a thing, he hoped the people would not be so sottish as to worship it. But it is probable that they had learnt of the Egyptians thus to represent the Deity, for it is said (Eze. 20:8), *They did not forsake the idols of Egypt,* and (*ch.* 23:8), *Neither left she her whoredoms brought from Egypt. Thus they changed their glory into the similitude of an ox* (Ps. 106:20), and proclaimed their own folly, beyond that of other idolaters, who worshipped the host of heaven.

IV. Having made the calf in Horeb, they *worshipped the graven image,* Ps. 106:19. Aaron, seeing the people fond of their calf, was willing yet further to humour them, and he built an altar before it, and proclaimed a feast to the honour of it (*v.* 5), a feast of dedication. Yet he calls it *a feast to Jehovah;* for, brutish as they were, they did not imagine that this image was itself a god, nor did they design to terminate their adoration in the image, but they made it for a representation of the true God, whom they intended to worship in and through this image; and yet this did not excuse them from gross idolatry, any more than it will excuse the papists, whose plea it is that they do not worship the image, but God by the image, so making themselves just such idolaters as the worshippers of the golden calf, whose feast was a feast to Jehovah, and proclaimed to be so, that the most ignorant and unthinking might not mistake it. The people are forward enough to celebrate this feast (*v.* 6): *They rose up early on the morrow,* to show how well pleased they were with the solemnity, and, according to the ancient rites of worship, they offered sacrifice to this new-made deity, and then feasted upon the sacrifice; thus having, at the expense of their ear-rings, made their god, they endeavour, at the expense of their beasts, to make this god propitious. Had they offered these sacrifices immediately to Jehovah, without the intervention of an image, they might (for aught I know) have been accepted (*ch.* 20:24); but having set up an image before them as a symbol of God's presence, and so changed the truth of God into a lie, these sacrifices were an abomination, nothing could be more so. When the idolatry of theirs is spoken of in the New Testament the account of their feast upon the sacrifice is quoted and referred to (1 Co. 10:7): *They sat down to eat and drink* of the remainder of what was sacrificed, and then *rose up to play,* to play the fool, to play the wanton. Like god, like worship. They would not have made a calf their god if they had not first made their belly their god; but, when the god was a jest, no marvel that the service was sport. Being *vain in their imaginations,* they became vain in their worship, so great was this vanity. Now, 1. It was strange that any of the people, especially so great a number of them, should do such a thing. Had they not, but the other day, in this very place, heard the voice of the Lord God speaking to them out of the midst of the fire, *Thou shalt not make to thyself any graven image?* Had they not heard the thunder, seen the lightnings, and felt the earthquake, with the dreadful pomp of which this law was given? Had they not been particularly cautioned not to make *gods of gold? ch.* 20:23. Nay, had they not themselves solemnly entered into covenant with God, and promised that all that which he had said unto them they *would do, and would be obedient? ch.* 24:7. And yet, before they stirred from the place where this covenant had been solemnly ratified, and before the cloud was removed from the top of mount Sinai, thus to break an express command, in defiance of an express threatening that this *iniquity should be visited upon them and their children* — what shall be think of it? It is a plain indication that the law was no more able to sanctify than it was to justify; by it is the knowledge of sin, but not the cure of it. This is intimated in the emphasis laid upon the place where this sin was committed (Ps. 106:19). *They made a calf in Horeb,* the very place where the law was given. It was otherwise with those that received the gospel; they immediately *turned from idols;* 1 Th. 1:9. 2. It was especially strange that Aaron should be so deeply implicated in this sin, that he should make the calf, and proclaim the feast! Is this Aaron, the saint of the Lord, the brother of Moses his prophet, that could *speak so well.* (*ch.* 4:14), and yet speaks not one word against this idolatry? Is this he that had not only seen, but had been employed in summoning, the plagues of Egypt, and the judgments, executed upon the gods of the Egyptians? What! and yet himself copying out the abandoned idolatries of Egypt? With what face could they say, *These are thy gods that brought thee out of Egypt,* when they thus bring the idolatry of Egypt (the worst thing there) along with them? Is this Aaron, who had been with Moses in the mount (*ch.* 19:24; 24:9), and knew that there was no manner of similitude seen there, by which they might make an image? Is this Aaron who was entrusted with the care of the people in the absence of Moses? Is he aiding and abetting in this rebellion against the Lord? How was it possible that he should ever do so sinful a thing? Either he was strangely surprised into it, and did it when he was half asleep, or he was frightened into it by the outrages of the rabble. The Jews have a tradition that his colleague Hur opposing it the people fell upon him and stoned him (and therefore we never read of him after) and that this frightened Aaron into a compliance. And God left him to himself, [1.] To teach us what the best of men are when they are so left, that we may *cease from man,* and that he who *thinks he stands may take heed lest he fall.* [2.] Aaron was, at this time, destined by the divine appointment to the great office of the priesthood; though he knew it not, Moses in the mount did. Now, lest he should be *lifted up, above measure,* with the honours that were to be put upon him, a messenger of Satan was suffered to prevail over him, that the remembrance thereof might keep him humble all his days. He who had once shamed himself so far as to build an altar to a golden calf must own himself altogether unworthy of the honour of attending at the altar of God, and purely indebted to free grace for it. Thus pride and boasting were for ever silenced, and a good effect brought out of a bad cause. By this likewise it was shown that *the law made those priests who had infirmity, and needed first to offer for their own sins.*

Verses 7–14

Here, I. God acquaints Moses with what was doing in the camp while he was absent, *v.* 7, 8. He could have told him sooner, as soon as the first step was taken towards it, and have hastened him down to prevent it; but he suffered it to come to this height, for wise and holy ends, and then sent him down to punish it. Note, It is no reproach to the holiness of God that he suffers sin to be committed, since he knows, not only how to restrain it when he pleases, but how to make it serviceable to the designs of his own glory. Observe what God here says to Moses concerning this sin. 1. That they had *corrupted themselves.* Sin is the corruption or depravation of the sinner, and it is a self-corruption; *every man is tempted when he is drawn aside of his own lust.* 2. That they had *turned aside out of the way.* Sin is a deviation from the way of our duty into a by-path. When they promised to do all that God should command them, they set out as fair as could be; but now they missed their way, and turned aside. 3. That they had turned aside quickly, quickly after the law was given them and they had promised to obey it, quickly after God had done such great things for them and declared his kind intentions to do greater. *They soon forgot his works.* To fall into sin quickly after we have renewed our covenants with God, or received special mercy from him, is very provoking. 4. He tells him particularly what they had done: *They have made a calf, and worshipped it.* Note, Those sins which are concealed from our governors are naked and open before God. He sees that which they cannot discover, nor is any of the wickedness in the world hidden from him. We could not bear to see the thousandth part of that provocation which God sees every day and yet keeps silence. 5. He seems to disown them, in saying to Moses, They are *thy people whom thou broughtest up out of the land of Egypt;* as if he had said, "I will not own any relation to them, or concern for them; let it never be said that they are my people, or that I brought them out of Egypt." Note, Those that corrupt themselves not only

shame themselves, but even make God himself ashamed of them and of his kindness to them. 6. He sends him down to them with all speed: *Go, get thee down.* He must break off even his communion with God to go and do his duty as a magistrate among the people; so must Joshua, *ch.* 7:10. Every thing is beautiful in its season.

II. He expresses his displeasure against Israel for this sin, and the determination of his justice to cut them off, *v.* 9, 10. 1. He gives this people their true character: *"It is a stiff-necked people,* unapt to come under the yoke of the divine law, and governed as it were by a spirit of contradiction, averse to all good and prone to evil, obstinate against the methods employed for their cure." Note, The righteous God sees, not only what we do, but what we are, not only the actions of our lives, but the dispositions of our spirits, and has an eye to them in all his proceedings. 2. He declares what was their just desert — that his wrath should *wax hot against them,* so as to consume them at once, and *blot out their name from under heaven* (Deu. 9:14); not only cast them out of covenant, but chase them out of the world. Note, Sin exposes us to the wrath of God; and that wrath, if it be not allayed by divine mercy, will burn us up as stubble. It were just with God to let the law have its course against sinners, and to cut them off immediately in the very act of sin; and, if he should do so, it would be neither loss nor dishonour to him. 3. He holds out inducements to Moses not to intercede for them: *Therefore, let me alone.* What did Moses, or what could he do, to hinder God from consuming them? When God resolves to abandon a people, and the decree of ruin has gone forth, no intercession can prevent it, Eze. 14:14; Jer. 15:1. But God would thus express the greatness of his just displeasure against them, after the manner of men, who would have none to intercede for those they resolve to be severe with. Thus also he would put an honour upon prayer, intimating that nothing but the intercession of Moses could save them from ruin, that he might be a type of Christ, by whose mediation alone God would *reconcile the world unto himself.* That the intercession of Moses might appear the more illustrious, God fairly offers him that, if he would not interpose in this matter, he would *make of him a great nation,* that either, in process of time, he would raise up a people out of his loins, or that he would immediately, by some means or other, bring another great nation under his government and conduct, so that he should be no loser by their ruin. Had Moses been of a narrow selfish spirit, he would have closed with this offer; but he prefers the salvation of Israel before the advancement of his own family. Here was a man fit to be a governor.

III. Moses earnestly intercedes with God on their behalf (*v.* 11–13): he besought the Lord his God. If God would not be called *the God of Israel,* yet he hoped he might address him as *his own God.* What interest we have at the throne of grace we should improve for the church of God, and for our friends. Now Moses is standing in the gap to turn away the wrath of God, Ps. 106:23. He wisely took the hint which God gave him when he said, *Let me alone,* which, though it seemed to forbid his interceding, did really encourage it, by showing what power the prayer of faith has with God. In such a case, God *wonders if there be no intercessor,* Isa. 59:16. Observe, 1. His prayer (*v.* 12): *Turn from thy fierce wrath;* not as if he thought God was not justly angry, but he begs that he would not be so greatly angry as to consume them. "Let mercy rejoice against judgment; *repent of this evil;* change the sentence of destruction into that of correction." 2. His pleas. He fills his mouth with arguments, not to move God, but to express his own faith and to excite his own fervency in prayer. He urges, (1.) God's interest in them, the great things he had already done for them, and the vast expense of favours and miracles he had been at upon them, *v.* 11. God had said to Moses (*v.* 7), They are *thy people, whom thou broughtest up out of Egypt;* but Moses humbly turns them back upon God again: "They are *thy people,* thou art their Lord and owner; I am but their servant. *Thou broughtest them forth out of Egypt;* I was but the instrument in thy hand; that was done in order to their deliverance which thou only couldest do." Though their being his people was a reason why he should be angry with them for setting up another god, yet it was a reason why he should not be so angry with them as to consume them. Nothing is more natural than for a father to correct his son, but nothing more un-

natural than for a father to slay his son. And as the relation is a good plea ("they are *thy people*"), so is the experience they had had of his kindness to them: "Thou *broughtest them out of Egypt,* though they were unworthy, and had there served the gods of the Egyptians, Jos. 24:15. If thou didst that for them, notwithstanding their sins in Egypt, wilt thou undo it for their sins of the same nature in the wilderness?" (2.) He pleads the concern of God's glory (*v.* 12): *Wherefore should the Egyptians say, For mischief did he bring them out?* Israel is dear to Moses as his kindred, as his charge; but it is the glory of God that he is most concerned for; this lies nearer his heart than any thing else. If Israel could perish without any reproach to God's name, Moses could persuade himself to sit down contented; but he cannot bear to hear God reflected on, and therefore this he insists upon, *Lord, what will the Egyptians say?* Their eyes, and the eyes of all the neighbouring nations, were now upon Israel; from the wondrous beginnings of that people, they raised their expectations of something great in their latter end; but, if a people so strangely saved should be suddenly ruined, what would the world say of it, especially the Egyptians, who have such an implacable hatred both to Israel and to the God of Israel? They would say, "God was either weak, and could not, or fickle, and would not, complete the salvation he began; he brought them forth to that mountain, not to sacrifice (as was pretended), but to be sacrificed." They will not consider the provocation given by Israel, to justify the proceeding, but will think it cause enough for triumph that God and his people could not agree, but that their God had done that which they (the Egyptians) wished to see done. Note, The glorifying of God's name, as it ought to be our first petition (it is so in the Lord's prayer), so it ought to be our great plea, Ps. 79:9 *Do not disgrace the throne of thy glory,* Jer. 14:21; and see Jer. 33:8, 9. And, if we would with comfort plead this with God as a reason why he should not destroy us, we ought to plead it with ourselves as a reason why we should not offend him: *What will the Egyptians say?* We ought always to be careful that the name of God and his doctrine be not blasphemed through us. (3.) He pleads God's promise to the patriarchs that he would multiply their seed, and give them the land of Canaan for an inheritance, and this promise confirmed by an oath, an oath by himself, since he could swear by no greater, *v.* 13. God's promises are to be our pleas in prayer; for what he has promised he is able to perform, and the honour of this truth is engaged for the performance of it. "Lord, if Israel be cut off, what will become of the promise? Shall their unbelief make that of no effect? God forbid." Thus we must take our encouragement in prayer from God only.

IV. God graciously abated the rigour of the sentence, and *repented of the evil he thought to do* (*v.* 14); though he designed to punish them, yet he would not ruin them. See here, 1. The power of prayer; God suffers himself to be prevailed with by the humble believing importunity of intercessors. 2. The compassion of God towards poor sinners, and how ready he is to forgive. Thus he has given other proofs besides his own oath that he has no pleasure in the death of those that die; for he not only pardons upon the repentance of sinners, but spares and reprieves upon the intercession of others for them.

Verses 15–20

Here is, I. The favour of God to Moses, in trusting him with the two tables of the testimony, which, though of common stone, were far more valuable than all the precious stones that adorned the breast-plate of Aaron. The topaz of Ethiopia could not equal them, *v.* 15, 16. God himself, without the ministry either of man or angel (for aught that appears), wrote the ten commandments on these tables, *on both their sides,* some on one table and some on the other, so that they were folded together like a book, to be deposited in the ark.

II. The familiarity between Moses and Joshua. While Moses was in the cloud, as in the presence-chamber, Joshua continued as near as he might, in the anti-chamber (as it were), waiting till Moses came out, that he might be ready to attend him; and though he was all alone for forty days (fed, it is likely, with manna), yet he was not weary of waiting, as the people were, but when Moses came down he came with him, and not till then. And here we are told what constructions they put upon the noise that they heard in the camp, *v.* 17, 18. Though Moses had been so long in immediate converse with God, yet he did not disdain to talk freely with his servant Joshua. Those whom God advances he preserves from being puffed up. Nor did he disdain to talk of the affairs of the camp. Blessed Paul was not the less mindful of the church on earth for having been in the third heavens, where he heard unspeakable words. Joshua, who was a military man, and had the command of the train-bands, feared there was *a noise of war in the camp,* and then he would be missed; but Moses, having received notice of it from God, better distinguished the sound, and was aware that it was *the voice of those that sing.* It does not however appear that he told Joshua what he knew of the occasion of their singing; for we should not be forward to proclaim men's faults: they will be known too soon.

III. The great and just displeasure of Moses against Israel, for their idolatry. Knowing what to expect, he was presently aware of the golden calf, and the sport the people made with it. He saw how merry they could be in his absence, how soon he was forgotten among them, and what little thought they had of him and his return. He might justly take this ill, as an affront to himself, but this was the least part of the grievance; he resented it as an offence to God, and the scandal of his people. See what a change it is to come down from the mount of communion with God to converse with a world that *lies in wickedness.* In God we see nothing but what is pure and pleasant, in the world nothing but pollution and provocation. Moses was the meekest man on the earth, and yet when he saw *the calf, and the dancing,* his *anger waxed hot.* Note, It is no breach of the law of meekness to show our displeasure at the wickedness of the wicked. Those are *angry and sin not* that are angry at sin only, not as against themselves, but as against God. Ephesus is famous for patience, and yet *cannot bear those that are evil,* Rev. 2:2. It becomes us to be cool in our own cause, but warm in God's. Moses showed himself very angry, both by breaking the tables and burning the calf, that he might, by these expressions of strong indignation, awaken the people to a sense of the greatness of the sin they had been guilty of, which they would have been ready to make light of if he had not thus shown his resentment, as one in earnest for their conviction. 1. To convince them that they had forfeited and lost the favour of God, *he broke the tables, v.* 19. Though God knew of their sin, before Moses came down, yet he did not order him to leave the tables behind him, but gave them to him to take down in his hand, that the people might see how forward God was to take them into covenant with himself, and that nothing but their own sin prevented it; yet he put in into his heart, when the iniquity of Ephraim was discovered (as the expression is, Hos. 7:1), to break the tables before their eyes (as it is Deu. 9:17), that the sight of it might the more affect them, and fill them with confusion, when they saw what blessings they had lost. Thus, they being guilty of so notorious an infraction of the treaty now on foot, the writings were torn, even when they lay ready to be sealed. Note, The greatest sign of God's displeasure against any person or people is his taking his law from them. The breaking of the tables is the breaking of the *staff of beauty and band* (Zec. 11:10, 14); it leaves a people unchurched and undone. Some think that Moses sinned in breaking the tables, and observe that, when men are angry, they are in danger of breaking all God's commandments; but it rather seems to be an act of justice than of passion, and we do not find that he himself speaks of it afterwards (Deu. 9:17) with any regret. 2. To convince them that they had betaken themselves to a God that could not help them, he *burnt the calf* (*v.* 20), melted it down, and then filed it to dust; and, that the powder to which it was reduced might be taken notice of throughout the camp, he strewed it upon that water of which they all drank. That it might appear that *an idol is nothing in the world* (1 Co. 8:4); he reduced this to atoms, that it might be as near nothing as could be. To show that false gods cannot help their worshippers, he here showed that this could not save itself, Isa. 46:1, 2. And to teach us that all the relics of idolatry ought to be abolished, and that the names of Baalim should be taken away, the very dust to which it was ground was scattered. Filings of gold are precious (we say), and therefore are carefully gathered up; but the filings of the golden calf were odious, and must be scattered with detestation. Thus the idols of silver and gold must be cast to the moles and the bats (Isa. 2:20; 30:22), and Ephraim shall say, *What have I to do any more with idols?* His mixing this powder with their drink signified to them that the curse they had thereby brought upon themselves would mingle itself with all their enjoyments, and embitter them; it would enter into their bowels like water, and like oil into their bones. *The backslider in heart shall be filled with his own ways;* he shall drink as he brews. These were indeed waters of Marah.

Verses 21–29

Moses, having shown his just indignation against the sin of Israel by breaking the tables and burning the calf, now proceeds to reckon with the sinners and to call them to an account, herein acting as the representative of God, who is not only a holy God, and hates sin, but a just God, and is engaged in honour to punish it, Isa. 59:18. Now,

I. He begins with Aaron, as God began with Adam, because he was the principal person, though not first in the transgression, but drawn into it. Observe here,

1. The just reproof Moses gives him, *v.* 21. He does not order him to be cut-off, as those (*v.* 27) that had been the ring-leaders in the sin. Note, A great deal of difference will be made between those that presumptuously rush into sin and those that through infirmity are surprised into it, between those that overtake the fault that flees from them and those that are overtaken in the fault they flee from. See Gal. 6:1. Not but that Aaron deserved to be cut off for this sin, and would have been so if Moses had not interceded particularly for him, as appears Deu. 9:20. And having prevailed with God for him, to save him from ruin, he here expostulates with him, to bring him to repentance. He puts Aaron upon considering, (1.) What he had done to this people: *Thou hast brought so great a sin upon them.* The sin of idolatry is a great sin, so great a sin that the evil of it cannot be expressed; the people, as the first movers, might be said to bring the sin upon Aaron; but he being a magistrate, who should have suppressed it, and yet aiding and abetting it, might truly be said to bring it upon them, because he hardened their hearts and strengthened their hands in it. It is a shocking thing for governors to humour people in their sins, and give countenance to that to which they should be a terror. Observe, in general, Those who bring sin upon others, either by drawing them into it or encouraging them in it, do more mischief than they are aware of; we really hate those whom we either bring or suffer sin upon, Lev. 19:17. Those that share in sin help to break their partners, and really ruin one another. (2.) What moved him to it: *What did this people unto thee?* He takes it for granted that it must needs be something more than ordinary that prevailed with Aaron to do such a thing, thus insinuating an excuse for him, because he knew that his heart was upright: "*What did they?* Did they accost thee fairly, and wheedle thee into it; and durst thou displease thy God, to please the people? Did they overcome thee by importunity; and hadst thou so little resolution left as to yield to the stream of a popular clamour? Did they threaten to stone thee; and couldest not thou have opposed God's threatenings to theirs, and frightened them worse than they could frighten thee?" Note, We must never be drawn into sin by any thing that man can say or do to us, for it will not justify us to say that we were so drawn in. Men can but tempt us to sin; they cannot force us. Men can but frighten us; if we do not comply, they cannot hurt us.

2. The frivolous excuse Aaron makes for himself. We will hope that he testified his repentance for the sin afterwards better than he did now; for what he says here has little in it of the language of a penitent. If a just man fall, he shall rise again, but perhaps not quickly. (1.) He deprecates the anger of Moses only, whereas he should have deprecated God's anger in the first place: *Let not the anger of my Lord wax hot, v.* 22. (2.) He lays all the fault upon the people: *They are set on mischief, and they said, Make us gods.* It is natural to us to endeavour thus to transfer our guilt; we have it in our kind, Adam and Eve did so; sin is a brat that nobody is willing to own. Aaron was now the chief magistrate and had power over the people, and yet pleads that the people overpowered him; he that had authority to restrain them, yet had so little resolution as to yield to them. (3.) It is well if he did not intend a reflection upon Moses, as accessory to the sin, by staying so long on the mount, in repeating, without need, that invidious surmise of the people, *As for this Moses, we know not what has become of him, v.* 23. (4.) He extenuates and conceals his own share in the sin, as if he had only bidden them *break off their gold* that they had about them, intending to make a hasty assay for the present, and to try what he could make of the gold that was next hand: and childishly insinuates that when he cast the gold into the fire it came out, either by accident or by the magic art of some of the mixed multitude (as the Jewish writers dream), in this shape; but not a word of his graving and fashioning it, *v.* 24. But Moses relates to all ages what he did (*v.* 4), though he himself here would not own it. Note, *He that covers his sin shall not prosper,* for sooner or later it will be discovered. Well, this was all Aaron had to say for himself; and he had better have said nothing, for his defence did but aggravate his offence; and yet he is not only spared, but preferred; as sin did abound, grace did much more abound.

II. The people are next to be judged for this sin. The approach of Moses soon spoiled their sport and turned their dancing into trembling. Those that hectored Aaron into a compliance with them in their sin durst not look Moses in the face, nor make the least opposition to the severity which he thought fit to use both against the idol and against the idolaters. Note, It is not impossible to make those sins which were committed with daring presumption appear contemptible, when the insolent perpetrators of them slink away overwhelmed in their own confusion. *The king that sits upon the throne of judgment scatters away all evil with his eyes.* Observe two things: —

1. How they were exposed to shame by their sin: *The people were naked* (*v.* 25), not so much because they had some of them lost their ear-rings (that was inconsiderable), but because they had lost their integrity, and lay under the reproach of ingratitude to their best benefactor, and a treacherous revolt from their rightful Lord. It was a shame to them, and a perpetual blot, that they *changed their glory into the similitude of an ox.* Other nations boasted that they were true to their false gods; well may Israel blush for being false to the true God. Thus were they *made naked,* stripped of their ornaments, and exposed to contempt; stripped of their armour, and liable to insults. Thus our first parents, when they had sinned, became *naked, to their shame.* Note, Those that do dishonour to God really bring the greatest dishonour upon themselves: so Israel here did, and Moses was concerned to see it, though they themselves were not; he *saw that they were naked.*

2. The course that Moses took to roll away this reproach, not by concealing the sin, or putting any false colour upon it, but by punishing it, and so bearing a public testimony against it. Whenever it should be case in their teeth that they had *made a calf in Horeb,* they might have this to say, in answer to those that reproached them, that though it was true there were those that did so, yet justice was executed upon them. The government disallowed the sin, and suffered not the sinners to go unpunished. They did so, but they paid dearly for it. Thus (said God) thou shalt *put the evil away,* Deu. 13:5. Observe here,

(1.) By whom vengeance was taken — by the children of Levi (*v.* 26, 28); not by the immediate hand of God himself, as on Nadab and Abihu, but by the sword of man, to teach them that idolatry was an *iniquity to be punished by the judge,* being a *denial of the God that is above,* Job 31:28; Deu. 13:9. It was to be done by the sword of their own brethren, that the execution of justice might redound more to the honour of the nation. And, if they must fall now into the hands of man, better so than flee before their enemies. The innocent must be culled out to be the executioners of the guilty, that it might be the more effectual warning to themselves, that they did not the like another time; and the putting of them upon such an unpleasant service, and so much against the grain as this must needs be, to kill their next neighbours, was a punishment to them too for not appearing sooner to prevent the sin, and make head against it. The Levites particularly were employed in doing this execution; for, it should seem, there were more of them than of any other tribe that had kept themselves free from the contagion, which was the more laudable because Aaron, the head of their tribe, was so deeply concerned in it. Now here we are told, [1.] How the Levites were called out to this service: *Moses stood in the gate of the camp,* the place of judgment; there he *displayed a banner,* as it were, because of the truth, to enlist soldiers for God. He proclaimed, *Who is on the Lord's side?* The idolaters had set up the golden calf for their standard, and now Moses set up his, in opposition to them. Now *Moses clad himself with zeal* as with a robe, and summoned all those to appear forthwith that were on God's side, against the golden calf. He does not proclaim, as Jehu, *"Who is on my side* (2 Ki. 9:32), to avenge the indignity done to me?" but, *Who is on the Lord's side?* It was God's cause that he espoused *against the evil-doers,* Ps. 94:16. Note, *First,* There are two great interests on foot in the world, with the one or the other of which all the children of men are siding. The interest of sin and wickedness is the devil's interest, and all wicked people side with that interest; the interest of truth and holiness is God's interest, with which all godly people side; and it is a case that will not admit a neutrality. *Secondly,* It concerns us all to enquire whether we are on the Lord's side or not. *Thirdly,* Those who are on his side are comparatively but few, and sometimes seem fewer than really they are. *Fourthly,* God does sometimes call out those that are on his side to appear for him, as witnesses, as soldiers, as intercessors. [2.] How they were commissioned for this service (*v.* 27): *Slay every man his brother,* that is, "Slay all those that you know to have been active for the making and worshipping of the golden calf, though they were your own nearest relations, or dearest friends." The crime was committed publicly, the Levites saw who of their acquaintance were concerned in it, and therefore needed no other direction than their own knowledge whom to slay. And probably the greatest part of those that were guilty were known, and known to be so, by some or other of the Levites who were employed in the execution. Yet, it should seem, they were to slay those only whom they found *abroad in the streets* of the camp; for it might be hoped that those who had retired into their tents were ashamed of what they had done, and were upon their knees, repenting. Those are marked for ruin who persist in sin, and are not ashamed of the abominations they have committed, Jer. 8:12. But how durst the Levites encounter so great a body, who probably were much enraged by the burning of their calf? It is easy to account for this; a sense of guilt disheartened the delinquents, and a divine commission animated the executioners. And one thing that put life into them was that Moses had said, *Consecrate yourselves to day to the Lord, that he may bestow a blessing upon you,* thereby intimating to them that they now stood fair for preferment and that, if they would but signalize themselves upon this occasion, it would be construed into such a consecration of themselves to God, and to his service, as would put upon their tribe a perpetual honour. Those that consecrate themselves to the Lord he will set apart for himself. Those that do the duty shall have the dignity; and, if we do signal services for God, he will bestow especial blessings upon us. There was a blessing designed for the tribe of Levi; now says Moses, *"Consecrate yourselves to the Lord,* that you may qualify yourselves to receive the blessing." The Levites were to assist in the offering of sacrifice to God; and now they must begin with the offering of these sacrifices to the honour of divine justice. Those that are to minister about holy things must be not only sincere and serious, but warm and zealous, bold and courageous, for God and godliness. Thus all Christians, but especially ministers, must *forsake father and mother,* and prefer the service of Christ and his interest far before their nearest and dearest relations; for if we love our relations better than Christ we are not *worthy of him.* See how this zeal of the Levites is applauded, Deu. 33:9.

(2.) On whom vengeance is taken: *There fell of the people that day about 3000 men, v.* 28. Probably these were but few, in comparison with the many that were guilty; but these were the men that headed the rebellion, and were therefore picked out, to be made examples of, for terror to all others. Those that in the morning were shouting and dancing before night were dying in their own blood; such a sudden change do the judgments of God sometimes make with sinners that are secure and jovial in their sin, as with Belshazzar by the handwriting upon the wall. This is written for warning to us. 1 Co. 10:7, *Neither be you idolaters, as were some of them.*

Verses 30–35

Moses, having executed justice upon the principal offenders, is here dealing both with the people and with God.

I. With the people, to bring them to repentance, *v.* 30.

1. When some were slain, lest the rest should imagine that, because they were exempt from the capital punishment, they were therefore looked upon as free from guilt, Moses here tells the survivors, *You have sinned a great sin,* and therefore, though you have escaped this time, *except you repent, you shall all likewise perish.* That they might not think lightly of the sin itself, he calls it *a great sin;* and that they might not think themselves innocent, because perhaps they were not all so deeply guilty as some of those that were put to death, he tells them all, *You have sinned a great sin.* The work of ministers is to show people their sins, and the greatness of their sins. *"You have sinned,* and therefore you are undone if your sins be not pardoned, for ever undone without a Saviour. It is a great sin, and therefore calls for great sorrow, for it puts you in great danger." To affect them with the greatness of their sin he intimates to them what a difficult thing it would be to make up the quarrel which God had with them for it. (1.) It would not be done, unless he himself *went up unto the Lord* on purpose, and gave as long and as solemn attendance as he had done for the receiving of the law. And yet, (2.) Even so it was but a peradventure that he should make atonement for them; the case was extremely hazardous. This should convince us of the great evil there is in sin, that he who undertook to make atonement found it no easy thing to do it; he must *go up to the Lord* with his own blood to *make atonement.* The malignity of sin appears in the price of pardons.

2. Yet it was some encouragement to the people (when they were told that they had *sinned a great sin*) to hear that Moses, who had so great an interest in heaven and so true an affection for them, would *go up unto the Lord to make atonement* for them. Consolation should go along with conviction: first wound, and then heal; first show people the greatness of their sin, and then make known to them the atonement, and give them hopes of mercy. *Moses will go up unto the Lord,* though it be but a *peradventure* that he should make atonement. Christ, the great Mediator, went upon greater certainty than this, for he had lain in the bosom of the Father, and perfectly knew all his counsels. But to us poor supplicants it is encouragement enough in prayer for particular mercies that *peradventure* we may obtain them, though we have not an absolute promise. Zep. 2:3, *It may be, you shall be hid.* In our prayers for others, we should be humbly earnest with God, though it is but a *peradventure that God will give them repentance,* 2 Tim. 2:25.

II. He intercedes with God for mercy. Observe,

1. How pathetic his address was. *Moses returned unto the Lord,* not to receive further instructions about the tabernacle: there were no more conferences now about that matter. Thus men's sins and follies make work for their friends and ministers, unpleasant work, many times, and give great interruptions to that work which they delight in. Moses in this address expresses, (1.) His great detestation of the people's sin, *v.* 31. He speaks as one overwhelmed with the horror of it: *Oh! this people have sinned a great sin.* God had first told him of it (*v.* 7), and now he tells God of it, by way of lamentation. He does not call them God's people, he knew they were unworthy to be called so; but this people, this treacherous ungrateful people, they have made for themselves gods of gold. It is a great sin indeed to make gold our god, as those do that make it their hope, and set their heart on it. He does not go about to excuse or extenuate the sin; but what he had said to them by way of conviction he says to God by way of confession: *They have sinned a great sin;* he came not to make apologies, but to make atonement. "Lord, pardon the sin, *for it is great,"* Ps. 25:11. (2.) His great desire of the people's welfare (*v.* 32): *Yet now* it is not too great a sin for infinite mercy to pardon, and therefore *if thou wilt forgive their sin.* What then Moses? It is an abrupt expression, *"If thou wilt,* I desire no more; *if thou wilt,* thou wilt be praised, I shall be pleased, and abundantly recompensed for my intercession." It is an expression like that of the dresser of the vineyard (Lu. 13:9), *If it bear fruit;* or, *If thou wilt forgive,* is as much as, "O that thou wouldest forgive!" as Lu. 19:42, *If thou hadst known* is, *O that thou hadst known.* "But *if not,* if the decree has gone forth, and there is no remedy, but they must be ruined; if this punishment which has already been inflicted on many is not sufficient (2 Co. 2:6), but they must all be cut off, *blot me, I pray thee, out of the book which thou hast written;"* that is, "If they must be cut off, let me be cut off with them, and cut short of Canaan; if all Israel must perish, I am content to perish with them; let not the land of promise be mine by survivorship." This expression may be illustrated from Eze. 13:9, where this is threatened against the false prophets, *They shall not be written in the writing of the house of Israel, neither shall they enter into the land of Israel.* God had told Moses that, if he would not interpose he would make of him a *great nation, v.* 10. "No," says Moses, "I am so far from desiring to see my name and family built up on the ruins of Israel, that I will choose rather to sink with them. If I cannot prevent their destruction, let me not see it (Num. 11:15); let me not be *written among the living* (Isa. 4:3), nor among those that are marked for preservation; even let me die in the last ditch." Thus he expresses his tender affection for the people, and is a type of the good Shepherd, that *lays down his life for the sheep* (Jn. 10:11), who was to be *cut off from the land of the living for the transgression of my people,* Isa. 53:8; Dan. 9:26. He is also an example of public-spiritedness to all, especially to those in public stations. All private interests must be made subordinate to the good and welfare of communities. It is no great matter what becomes of us and our families in this world, so that it go well with the church of God, and there be peace upon Israel. Moses thus importunes for a pardon, and wrestles with God, not prescribing to him ("If thou wilt not forgive, thou art either unjust or unkind"); no, he is far from that; but, "If not, let me die with the Israelites, and the will of the Lord be done."

2. Observe how prevalent his address was. God would not take him at his word; no, he will not blot any out of his book but those that by their wilful disobedience have forfeited the honour of being enrolled in it (*v.* 33); the soul that sins shall die, and not the innocent for the guilty. This was also an intimation of mercy to the people, that they should not all be destroyed in a body, but those only that had a hand in the sin. Thus Moses gets ground by degrees. God would not at first give him full assurances of his being reconciled to them, lest, if the comfort of a pardon were too easily obtained, they should be emboldened to do the like again, and should not be made sensible enough of the evil of the sin. Comforts are suspended that convictions may be the deeper impressed: also God would hereby exercise the faith and zeal of Moses, their great intercessor. Further, in answer to the address of Moses, (1.) God promises, notwithstanding this, to go on with his kind intention of giving them the land of Canaan, the land he had *spoken to them of, v.* 34. Therefore he sends Moses back to them to lead them, though they were unworthy of him, and promises that his angel should go before them, some created angel that was employed in the common services of the kingdom of providence, which intimated that they were not to expect any thing for the future to be done for them out of the common road of providence, not any thing extraordinary. Moses afterwards obtained a promise of God's special presence with them (*ch.* 33:14, 17); but at present this was all he could prevail for. (2.) Yet he threatens to remember this sin against them when hereafter he should see cause to punish them for other sins: *"When I visit, I will visit* for this among the rest. Next time I take the rod in hand, they shall have one stripe the more for this." The Jews have a saying, grounded on this, that henceforward no judgment fell upon Israel but there was in it an ounce of the powder of the golden calf. I see no ground in scripture for the opinion some are of, that God would not have burdened them with such a multitude of sacrifices and other ceremonial institutions if they had not provoked him by worshipping the golden calf. On the contrary, Stephen says that when they *made a calf, and offered sacrifice to the idol, God turned, and gave them up to worship the host of heaven* (Acts 7:41, 42); so that the strange addictedness of that people to the sin of idolatry was a just judgment upon them for making and worshipping the golden calf, and a judgment they were never quite

freed from till the captivity of Babylon. See Rom. 1:23–25. Note, Many that are not immediately cut off in their sins are reserved for a further day of reckoning: vengeance is slow, but sure. For the present, *the Lord plagued the people* (*v.* 35), probably by the pestilence, or some other infectious disease, which was a messenger of God's wrath, and an earnest of worse. Aaron made the calf, and yet it is said the people made it, because they worshipped it. *Deos qui rogat, ille facit — He who asks for gods makes them.* Aaron was not plagued, but the people; for his was a sin of infirmity, theirs a presumptuous sin, between which there is a great difference, not always discernable to us, but evident to God, whose judgment therefore, we are sure, is according to truth. Thus Moses prevailed for a reprieve and a mitigation of the punishment, but could not wholly turn away the wrath of God. This (some think) bespeaks the inability of the law of Moses to reconcile men to God and to perfect our peace with him, which was reserved for Christ to do, in whom alone it is that God so pardons sin as to *remember it no more.*

CHAPTER 33

In this chapter we have a further account of the mediation of Moses between God and Israel, for the making up of the breach that sin had made between them. I. He brings a very humbling message from God to them (*v.* 1–3, 5), which has a good effect upon them, and helps to prepare them for mercy (*v.* 4, 6). II. He settles a correspondence between God and them, and both God and the people signify their approbation of that correspondence, God by descending in a cloudy pillar, and the people by worshipping at the tent doors (*v.* 7–11). III. He is earnest with God in prayer, and prevails, 1. For a promise of his presence with the people (*v.* 12–17). 2. For a sight of his glory for himself (*v.* 18, etc.).

Verses 1–6

Here is, I. The message which God sent by Moses to the children of Israel, signifying the continuance of the displeasure against them, and the bad terms they yet stood upon with God. This he must let them know for their further mortification. 1. He applies to them a mortifying name, by giving them their just character — *a stiff-necked people, v.* 3, 5. "Go," says God to Moses, "go and tell them that they are so." He that knows them better than they know themselves says so of them. God would have brought them under the yoke of his law, and into the bond of his covenant, but their necks were too stiff to bow to them. God would have cured them of their corrupt and crooked dispositions, and have set them straight; but they were wilful and obstinate, and hated to be reformed, and would not have God to reign over them. Note, God judges of men by the temper of their minds. We know what man does; God knows what he is: we know what proceeds from man; God knows what is in man, and nothing is more displeasing to him than stiff-neckedness, as nothing in children is more offensive to their parents and teachers than stubbornness. 2. He tells them what they deserved, that he should *come into the midst of them in a moment, and consume them, v.* 5. Had he dealt with them according to their sins, he had taken them away with a swift destruction. Note, Those whom God pardons must be made to know what their sin deserved, and how miserable they would have been if they had been unpardoned, that God's mercy may be the more magnified. 3. He bids them *depart and go up hence* to the land of Canaan, *v.* 1. This mount Sinai, where they now were, was the place appointed for the setting up of God's tabernacle and solemn worship among them; this was not yet done, so that in bidding them depart hence God intimates that it should not be done — "Let them go forward as they are;" and so it was very expressive of God's displeasure. 4. He turns them over to Moses, as the people whom he had brought up out of the land of Egypt, and leaves it to him to lead them to Canaan. 5. Though he promises to make good his covenant with Abraham, in giving them Canaan, yet he denies them the extraordinary tokens of his presence, such as they had hitherto been blessed with, and leaves them under the common conduct of Moses their prince, and the common convoy of a guardian angel: *"I will send an angel before thee,* for thy protector, otherwise the evil angels would soon destroy thee; but *I will not go up in the midst of thee, lest I consume thee"* (*v.* 2, 3); not as if an angel would be more patient and compassionate than God, but their affronts given to an angel would not be so provoking as those given to the *shechinah,* or divine Majesty itself. Note, The greater the privileges we enjoy the greater is our danger if we do not improve them and live up to them. 6. He speaks as one that was at a loss what course to take with them. Justice said, "Cut them off, and consume them." Mercy said, *"How shall I give thee up, Ephraim?"* Hos. 11:8. Well, says God, *put off thy ornaments, that I may know what to do with thee;* that is, "Put thyself into the posture of a penitent, that the dispute may be determined in thy favour, and mercy may rejoice against judgment," *v.* 5. Note, Calls to repentance are plain indications of mercy designed. If the Lord were pleased to kill us, justice knows what to do with a stiff-necked people: but God has no pleasure in the death of those that die; let them return and repent, and then mercy, which otherwise is at a loss, knows what to do.

II. The people's melancholy reception of this message; it was evil tidings to them to hear that they should not have God's special presence with them, and therefore, 1. *They mourned* (*v.* 4), mourned for their sin which had provoked God to withdraw from them, and mourned for this as the sorest punishment of their sin. When 3000 of them were at one time laid dead upon the spot by the Levites' sword, we do not find that they mourned for this (hoping that it would help to expiate the guilt); but when God denied them his favourable presence then they mourned and were in bitterness. Note, Of all the bitter fruits and consequences of sin, that which true penitents most lament, and dread most, is God's departure from them. God had promised that, notwithstanding their sin, he would give them the *land flowing with milk and honey.* but they could have small joy of that if they had not God's presence with them. Canaan itself would be no pleasant land without that; therefore, if they want that, they mourn. 2. In token of great shame and humiliation, those that were undressed did *not put on their ornaments* (*v.* 4), and those that were dressed *stripped themselves of their ornaments, by the mount;* or, as some read it, *at a distance from the mount* (*v.* 6), standing afar off like the publican, Lu. 18:13. God bade them *lay aside their ornaments* (*v.* 5), and they did so, both to show, in general, their deep mourning, and, in particular, to take a holy revenge upon themselves for giving their ear-rings to make the golden calf of. Those that would part with their ornaments for the maintenance of their sin could do no less than lay aside their ornaments in token of their sorrow and shame for it. When the *Lord God calls to weeping and mourning* we must comply with the call, and not only fast from pleasant bread (Dan. 10:3), but lay aside our ornaments; even those that are decent enough at other times are unseasonably worn on days of humiliation or in times of public calamity, Isa. 3:18.

Verses 7–11

Here is, I. One mark of displeasure put upon them for their further humiliation: *Moses took the tabernacle,* not his own tent for his family, but the tent wherein he gave audience, heard causes, and enquired of God, the *guildhall* (as it were) of their camp, and *pitched it without, afar off from the camp* (*v.* 7), to signify to them that they had rendered themselves unworthy of it, and that, unless peace was made, it would return to them no more. God would thus let them know that he was at variance with them: *The Lord is far from the wicked.* Thus the glory of the Lord departed from the temple when it was polluted with sin, Eze. 10:4, 11:23. Note, It is a sign that God is angry when he removes his tabernacle, for his ordinances are fruits of his favour and tokens of his presence; while we have them with us we have him with us. Perhaps this tabernacle was a plan, or model rather, of the tabernacle that was afterwards to be erected, a hasty draught from the pattern shown him in the mount, designed for direction to the workmen, and used, in the mean time, as a tabernacle of meeting between God and Moses about public affairs. This was set up at a distance, to affect the people with the loss of that glorious structure which, if they had not forsaken their own mercies for lying vanities, was to have been set up in the midst of them. Let them see what they had forfeited.

II. Many encouragements give them, notwithstanding, to hope that God would yet be reconciled to them.

1. Though the tabernacle was removed, yet every one that was disposed to seek the Lord was welcome to follow it, *v.* 7. Private persons, as well as Moses, were invited and encouraged to apply to God, as intercessors upon this occasion. A place was appointed for them to go to *without the camp,* to solicit God's return to them. Thus when Ezra (a second Moses) interceded for Israel there were assembled to him many that *trembled at God's word,* Ezra 9:4. When God designs mercy, he stirs up prayer. *He will be* sought unto (Eze. 36:37); and, thanks be to his name, he may be sought unto, and will not reject the intercession of the poorest. Every Israelite that sought the Lord was welcome to this tabernacle, as well as Moses *the man of God.*

2. Moses undertook to mediate between God and Israel. He *went out to the tabernacle,* the place of treaty, probably pitched between them and the mount (*v.* 8), and he *entered into the tabernacle, v.* 9. That cause could not but speed well which had so good a manager; when their judge (under God) becomes their advocate, and he who was appointed to be their law-giver is an intercessor for them, there is *hope in Israel concerning this thing.*

3. The people seemed to be in a very good mind and well disposed towards a reconciliation. (1.) When Moses went out to go to the tabernacle, the people *looked after him* (*v.* 8), in token of their respect to him whom before they had slighted, and their entire dependence upon his mediation. By this it appeared that they were very solicitous about this matter, desirous to be at peace with God and concerned to know what would be the issue. Thus the disciples looked after our Lord Jesus, when he ascended on high to enter into the holy place not made with hands, till a *cloud received him out of their sight,* as Moses here. And we must with an eye of faith follow him likewise thither, where he is appearing in the presence of God for us; then shall we have the benefit of his mediation. (2.) When they saw the cloudy pillar, that symbol of God's presence, give Moses the meeting, they all *worshipped, every man at his tent door, v.* 10. Thereby they signified, [1.] Their humble adoration of the divine Majesty, which they will ever worship, and not gods of gold any more. [2.] Their joyful thankfulness to God that he was pleased to show them this token for good, and give them hopes of a reconciliation; for, if he had been pleased to kill them, he would not have shown them such things as these, would not have raised them up such a mediator, nor given him such countenance. [3.] Their hearty concurrence with Moses as their advocate in every thing he should promise for them, and their expectation of a comfortable and happy issue of this treaty. Thus must we worship God in our tents with an eye to Christ as the Mediator. Their worshipping in their tent doors declared plainly that they were not ashamed publicly to own their respect to God and Moses, as they had publicly worshipped the calf.

4. God was, in Moses, reconciling Israel to himself, and manifested himself very willing to be at peace. (1.) God met Moses at the place of treaty, *v.* 9. The cloudy pillar, which had withdrawn itself from the camp when it was polluted with idolatry, now returned to this tabernacle at some distance, coming back gradually. If our hearts go forth towards God to meet him he will graciously come down to meet us. (2.) God *talked with Moses* (*v.* 9), *spoke to him face to face, as a man speaks to his friend* (*v.* 11), which intimates that God revealed himself to Moses, not only with greater clearness and evidence of divine light than to any other of the prophets, but also with greater expressions of particular kindness and grace. He spoke, not as a prince to a subject, but as a *man to his friend,* whom he loves, and with whom he takes sweet counsel. This was great encouragement to Israel, to see their advocate so great a favourite; and, that they might be encouraged by it, *Moses turned again into the camp,* to tell the people what hopes he had of bringing this business to a good issue, and that they might not despair if he should be long absent. But, because he intended speedily to return to the tabernacle of the congregation, he left Joshua there, for it was not fit that the place should be empty, so long as the cloud of glory *stood at the door* (*v.* 9); but, if God had any thing to say out of that cloud while Moses was absent, Joshua was there, ready to hear it.

Verses 12–23

Moses, having returned to the door of the tabernacle, becomes a humble and importunate supplicant there for two very great favours, and as a prince he has power with

God, and prevails for both: herein he was a type of Christ the great intercessor, *whom the Father heareth always.*

I. He is very earnest with God for a grant of his presence with Israel in the rest of their march to Canaan, notwithstanding their provocations. The people had by their sin deserved the wrath of God, and for the turning away of that Moses had already prevailed, *ch.* 32:14. But they had likewise forfeited God's favourable presence, and all the benefit and comfort of that, and this Moses is here begging for the return of. Thus, by the intercession of Christ, we obtain not only the removal of the curse, but an assurance of the blessing; we are not only saved from ruin, but become entitled to everlasting happiness. Observe how admirably Moses orders this cause before God, and *fills his mouth with arguments.* What a value he expresses for God's favour, what a concern for God's glory and the welfare of Israel. How he pleads, and how he speeds.

1. How he pleads. (1.) He insists upon the commission God had given him to *bring up this people, v.* 12. This he begins with: "Lord, it is thou thyself that employest me; and wilt thou not own me? I am in the way of my duty; and shall I not have thy presence with me in that way?" Whom God calls out to any service he will be sure to furnish with necessary assistances. "Now, Lord, thou hast ordered me a great work, and yet left me at a loss how to go about it, and to through with it." Note, Those that sincerely design and endeavour to do their duty may in faith beg of God direction and strength for the doing of it. (2.) He improves the interest he himself had with God, and pleads God's gracious expressions of kindness to him: *Thou hast said, I know thee by name,* as a particular friend and confidant, *and thou hast also found grace in my sight,* above any other. *Now, therefore,* says Moses, if it be indeed so, that *I have found grace in thy sight, show me the way, v.* 13. What favour God had expressed to the people they had forfeited the benefit of, there was no insisting upon that; and therefore Moses lays the stress of his plea upon what God had said to him, which, though he owns himself unworthy of, yet he hopes he has not thrown himself out of the benefit of. By this therefore he takes hold on God: "Lord, if ever thou wilt do any thing for me, do this for the people." Thus our Lord Jesus, in his intercession, presents himself to the Father, as one in whom he is always well pleased, and so obtains mercy for us with whom he is justly displeased; and we are *accepted in the beloved.* Thus also men of public spirit love to improve their interest both with God and man for the public good. Observe what it is he is thus earnest for: *Show me thy way,* that I may know that *I find grace in thy sight.* Note, Divine direction is one of the best evidences of divine favour. By this we may know that we *find grace in God's sight,* if we find grace in our hearts to guide and quicken us in the way of our duty. God's good work in us is the surest discovery of his good-will towards us. (3.) He insinuates that the people also, though most unworthy, yet were in some relation to God: *"Consider that this nation is thy people,* a people that thou hast done great things for, redeemed to thyself, and taken into covenant with thyself; Lord, they are thy own, do not leave them." The offended father considers this, "My child is foolish and froward, but he is my child, and I cannot abandon him." (4.) He expresses the great value he had for the presence of God. When God said, *My presence shall go with thee,* he caught at that word, as that which he could not live and move without: *"If thy presence go not with me, carry us not up hence," v.* 15. He speaks as one that dreaded the thought of going forward without God's presence, knowing that their marches could not be safe, nor their encampments easy, if they had not God with them. "Better lie down and die here in the wilderness than go forward to Canaan without God's presence." Note, Those who know how to value God's favours are best prepared to receive them. Observe how earnest Moses is in this matter; he begs as one that would take no denial. "Here we will stay till we obtain thy favour; like Jacob, *I will not let thee go except thou bless me."* And observe how he advances upon God's concessions; the kind intimations given him make him yet more importunate. Thus God's gracious promises, and the advances of mercy towards us, should not only encourage our faith, but excite our fervency in prayer. (5.) He concludes with an argument taken from God's glory (*v.* 16): *"Wherein shall it be known* to the nations that have their eyes upon us that *I and thy people* (with whom my interests are all blended) *have found grace in thy sight,* distinguishing favour, so as to be *separated from all people on earth?* How will it appear that we are indeed thus honoured? *Is it not in that thou goest with us?* Nothing short of this can answer these characters. Let it never be said that we are a peculiar people, and highly favoured, for we stand but upon a level with the rest of our neighbours unless thou go with us; sending an angel with us will not serve." He lays a stress upon the place — *"here* in this wilderness, whither thou hast led us, and where we shall be certainly lost if thou leave us." Note, God's special presence with us in this wilderness, by his Spirit and grace, to direct, defend, and comfort us, is the surest pledge of his special love to us and will redound to his glory as well as our benefit.

2. Observe how he speeds. He obtained an assurance of God's favour, (1.) To himself (*v.* 14): *"I will give thee rest,* I will take care to make thee easy in this matter; however it be, thou shalt have satisfaction." Moses never entered Canaan, and yet God made good his word that he would give him rest, Dan. 12:13. (2.) To the people for his sake. Moses was not content with that answer which bespoke favour to himself only, he must gain a promise, an express promise, for the people too, or he is not at rest; gracious generous souls think it not enough to get to heaven themselves, but would have all their friends go thither too. And in this also Moses prevailed: *I will do this thing also that thou hast spoken, v.* 17. Moses is not checked as an unreasonable beggar, whom no saying would serve, but he is encouraged. God grants as long as he asks, *gives liberally,* and *does not upbraid* him. See the power of prayer, and be quickened hereby to ask, and seek, and knock, and to *continue instant in prayer, to pray always and not to faint.* See the riches of God's goodness. When he has done much, yet he is willing to do more: *I will do this also* — above *what we are able to ask or think.* See, in type, the prevalency of Christ's intercession, which he ever lives to make for all those that come to God by him, and the ground of that prevalency. It is purely his own merit, not any thing in those for whom he intercedes; it is because *thou hast found grace in my sight.* And now the matter is settled, God is perfectly reconciled to them, his presence in the pillar of cloud returns to them and shall continue with them; all is well again, and henceforth we hear no more of the golden calf. *Lord, who is a God like unto thee, pardoning iniquity?*

II. Having gained this point, he next begs *a sight of God's glory,* and is heard in this matter also. Observe,

1. The humble request Moses makes: *I beseech thee, show me thy glory, v.* 18. Moses had lately been in the mount with God, had continued there a great while, and had enjoyed as intimate a communion with God as ever any man had on this side heaven; and yet he is still desiring a further acquaintance. All that are effectually called to the knowledge of God and fellowship with him, though they desire nothing more than God, are nevertheless still coveting more and more of him, till they come to see as they are seen. Moses had wonderfully prevailed with God for one favour after another, and the success of his prayers emboldened him to go on still to seek God; the more he had the more he asked: when we are in a good frame at the throne of grace, we should endeavour to preserve and improve it, and strike while the iron is hot: *"Show me thy glory; make me to see* it" (so the word is); "make it some way or other visible, and enable me to bear the sight of it." Not that he was so ignorant as to think God's essence could be seen with bodily eyes; but, having hitherto only heard a voice out of a pillar of cloud or fire, he desired to see some representation of the divine glory, such as God saw fit to gratify him with. It was not fit that the people should see any similitude when the Lord spoke unto them, *lest they should corrupt themselves;* but he hoped that there was not that danger in his seeing some similitude. Something it was more than he had yet seen that Moses desired. If it was purely for the assisting of his faith and devotion, the desire was commendable; but perhaps there was in it a mixture of human infirmity. God will have us walk by faith, not by sight, in this world; and *faith comes by hearing.* Some think that Moses desired a sight of God's glory as a token of his reconciliation, and an earnest of that presence which he had promised them; but he knew not what he asked.

2. The gracious reply God made to this request. (1.) He denied that which was not fit to be granted, and which Moses could not bear: *Thou canst not see my face, v.* 20. A full discovery of the glory of God would quite overpower the faculties of any mortal man in this present state, and overwhelm him, even Moses himself. Man is mean and unworthy of it, weak and could not bear it, guilty and could not but dread it. It is in compassion to our infirmity that God *holdeth back the face of his throne, and spreadeth a cloud upon it,* Job 26:9. God has said that *here* (that is, in this world) his *face shall not be seen* (*v.* 23); that is an honour reserved for the future state, to be the eternal bliss of holy souls: should men in this state know what it is, they would not be content to live short of it. There is a knowledge and enjoyment of God which must be waited for in another world, when we shall *see him as he is,* 1 Jn. 3:2. In the mean time let us adore the height of what we do know of God, and the depth of what we do not. Long before this, Jacob had spoken of it with wonder that he had *seen God face to face,* and yet *his life was preserved,* Gen. 32:30. Sinful man dreads the sight of God his Judge; but holy souls, being *by the Spirit of the Lord changed into the same image, behold with open face the glory of the Lord.* 2 Co. 3:18. (2.) He granted that which would be abundantly satisfying. [1.] He should hear what would please him (*v.* 19): *I will make all my goodness pass before thee.* He had given him wonderful instances of his goodness in being reconciled to Israel: but that was only goodness in the stream; he would show him goodness in the spring — *all his goodness.* This was a sufficient answer to his request. "Show me thy glory," says Moses. "I will show thee my goodness," says God. Note, God's goodness is his glory; and he will have us to know him by the glory of his mercy more than by the glory of his majesty; for we must fear even *the Lord and his goodness,* Hos. 3:5. That especially which is the glory of God's goodness is the sovereignty of it, that he will be *gracious to whom he will be gracious,* that, as an absolute proprietor, he makes what difference he pleases in bestowing his gifts, and is not debtor to any, nor accountable to any *(may he not do what he will with his own?);* also that all his reasons of mercy are fetched from within himself, not from any merit in his creatures: as he has mercy on whom he will, so, because he will. *Even so, Father, because it seemed good in thy sight.* It is never said, "I will be angry at whom I will be angry," for his wrath is always just and holy; but *I will show mercy on whom I will show mercy,* for his grace is always free. He never damns by prerogative, but by prerogative he saves. The apostle quotes this (Rom. 9:15) in answer to those who charged God with unrighteousness in giving that grace freely to some which he withholds justly from others. [2.] He should see what he could bear, and what would suffice him. The matter is concerted so as that Moses might be safe and yet satisfied. *First,* Save in a *cleft of the rock, v.* 21, 22. In this he was to be sheltered from the dazzling light and devouring fire of God's glory. This was the rock in Horeb out of which water was brought, of which it is said, *That rock was Christ,* 1 Co. 10:4. It is in the clefts of this rock that we are secured from the wrath of God, which otherwise would consume us; God himself will protect those that are thus hid. And it is only through Christ that we have *the knowledge of the glory of God.* None can see his glory to their comfort but those who stand upon this rock, and take shelter in it. *Secondly,* He was satisfied with a sight of his back-parts, *v.* 23. He should see more of God than any ever saw on earth, but not so much as those see who are in heaven. The face, in man, is the seat of majesty, and men are known by their faces; in them we take a full view of men. That sight of God Moses might not have, but such a sight as we have of a man who has gone past us, so that we only see his back, and have (as we say) a blush of him. We cannot be said to look at God, but rather to look after him (Gen. 16:13); for we see *through a glass darkly.* When we see what God has done in his works, observe the goings of our God, our King, we see (as it were) his back-parts. The best thus *know but in part,* and we cannot order our speech concerning God, by reason of darkness, any more than we can describe a man whose face we never saw. Now Moses was allowed to see only the back-parts; but long afterwards, when he was a witness

to Christ's transfiguration, he saw *his face shine as the sun.* If we faithfully improve the discoveries God gives us of himself while we are here, a brighter and more glorious scene will shortly be opened to us; for *to him that hath shall be given.*

CHAPTER 34

God having in the foregoing chapter intimated to Moses his reconciliation to Israel, here gives proofs of it, proceeding to settle his covenant and communion with them. Four instances of the return of his favour we have in this chapter: — I. The orders he gives to Moses to come up to the mount, the next morning, and bring two tables of stone with him (*v.* 1–4). II. His meeting him there, and the proclamation of his name (*v.* 5–9). III. The instructions he gave him there, and his converse with him for forty days together, without intermission (*v.* 10–28). IV. The honour he put upon him when he sent him down with his face shining (*v.* 29–35). In all this God dealt with Moses as a public person, and mediator between him and Israel, and a type of the great Mediator.

Verses 1–4

The treaty that was on foot between God and Israel being broken off abruptly, by their worshipping the golden calf, when peace was made all must be begun anew, not where they left off, but from the beginning. Thus backsliders must *repent, and do their first works,* Rev. 2:5.

I. Moses must prepare for the renewing of the tables, *v.* 1. Before, God himself provided the tables, and wrote on them; now, Moses mus *hew out the tables,* and God would only write upon them. Thus, in the first writing of the law upon the heart of man in innocency, both the tables and the writing were the work of God; but when those were broken and defaced by sin, and the divine law was to be preserved in the scriptures, God therein made use of the ministry of man, and Moses first. But the prophets and apostles did only hew the tables, as it were; the writing was God's still, for *all scripture is given by inspiration of God.* Observe, When God was reconciled to them, he ordered the tables to be renewed, and wrote his law in them, which plainly intimates to us, 1. That even under the gospel of peace and reconciliation by Christ (of which the intercession of Moses was typical) the moral law should continue to bind believers. Though Christ has redeemed us from the curse of the law, yet not from the command of it, but still we are *under the law to Christ;* when our Saviour, in his sermon on the mount, expounded the moral law, and vindicated it from the corrupt glosses with which the scribes and Pharisees had broken it (Mt. *v.* 19), he did in effect renew the tables, and make them like the first, that is, reduce the law to its primitive sense and intention. 2. That the best evidence of the pardon of sin and peace with God is the writing of the law in the heart. The first token God gave of his reconciliation to Israel was the renewing of the tables of the law; thus the first article of the new covenant is, *I will write my law in their heart* (Heb. 8:10), and it follows (*v.* 12), *for I will be merciful to their unrighteousness.* 3. That, if we would have God to write the law in our hearts, we must prepare our hearts for the reception of it. The heart of stone must be hewn by conviction and humiliation for sin (Hos. 6:5), the *superfluity of naughtiness* must be taken off (James 1:21), the heart made smooth, and laboured with, that the word may have a place in it. Moses did accordingly hew out the *tables of stone,* or slate, for they were so slight and thin that Moses carried them both in his hand; and, for their dimensions, they must have been somewhat less, and perhaps not much, than the ark in which they were deposited, which was a yard and quarter long, and three quarters broad. It should seem there was nothing particularly curious in the framing of them, for there was no great time taken; Moses had them ready presently, to take up with him, next morning. They were to receive their beauty, not from the art of man, but from the finger of God.

II. Moses must attend again on the top of mount Sinai, and present himself to God there, *v.* 2. Though the absence of Moses, and his continuance so long on the mount, had lately occasioned their making the golden calf, yet God did not therefore alter his measures, but he shall come up and tarry as long as he had done, to try whether they had learned to wait. To strike an awe upon the people, they are directed to keep their distance, none must come up with him, *v.* 3. They had said (*ch.* 32:1), *We know not what has become of him,* and God will not let them know. Moses, accordingly, *rose up early* (*v.* 4) to go to the place appointed, to show how forward he was to present himself before God and loth to lose time. It is good to be early at our devotions. The morning is perhaps as good a friend to the graces as it is to the muses.

Verses 5–9

No sooner had Moses got to the top of the mount than God gave him the meeting (*v.* 5): *The Lord descended,* by some sensible token of his presence, and manifestation of his glory. His descending bespeaks his condescension; he humbles himself to take cognizance of those that humble themselves to walk with him. Ps. 113:6, *Lord, what is man, that he should be thus visited?* He descended *in the cloud,* probably that pillar of cloud which had hitherto gone before Israel, and had the day before met Moses at the door of the tabernacle. This cloud was to strike an awe upon Moses, that the familiarity he was admitted to might not breed contempt. The disciples *feared, when they entered the cloud.* His making a cloud his pavilion intimated that, though he made known much of himself, yet there was much more concealed. Now observe,

I. How God proclaimed his name (*v.* 6, 7): he did it *in transitu — as he passed by him.* Fixed views of God are reserved for the future state; the best we have in this world are transient. God now was performing what he had promised Moses, the day before, that his glory should pass by, *ch.* 33:22. He *proclaimed the name of the Lord,* by which he would make himself known. He had made himself known to Moses in the glory of his self-existence and self-sufficiency when he proclaimed that name, *I am that I am;* now he makes himself known in the glory of his grace, and goodness, and all-sufficiency to us. Now that God is about to publish a second edition of the law he prefaces it with this proclamation; for it is God's grace or goodness that gives the law, especially the remedial law. The pardon of Israel's sin in worshipping the calf was now to pass the seals; and God, by this declaration, would let them know that he pardoned *ex mero motu — merely out of his own good pleasure,* not for their merits' sake, but from his own inclination to forgive. The proclaiming of it denotes the universal extent of God's mercy. He is not only good to Israel, but good to all; let all take notice of it. He that hath an ear, let him hear, and know, and believe,

1. That the God with whom we have to do is a great God. He is Jehovah, the Lord, who has his being of himself, and is the fountain of all being, *Jehovah-El, the Lord, the strong God,* a God of almighty power himself, and the original of all power This is prefixed before the display of his mercy, to teach us to think and to speak even of God's grace and goodness with great seriousness and a holy awe, and to encourage us to depend upon these mercies; they are not the mercies of a man, that is frail and feeble, false and fickle, but the mercies of the Lord, the Lord God; therefore sure mercies, and sovereign mercies, mercies that may be trusted, but not tempted.

2. That he is a good God. His greatness and goodness illustrate and set off each other. That the terror of his greatness may not make us afraid, we are told how good he is; and, that we may not presume upon his goodness, we are told how great he is. Many words are here heaped up, to acquaint us with, and convince us of, God's goodness, and to show how much his goodness is both his glory and his delight, yet without any tautology. (1.) He is *merciful.* This bespeaks his tender compassion, like that of a father to his children. This is put first, because it is the first wheel in all the instances of God's good-will to fallen man, whose misery makes him an object of pity, Jdg. 10:16; Isa. 63:9. Let us not then have either hard thoughts of God or hard hearts towards our brethren. (2.) He is *gracious.* This bespeaks both freeness and kindness; it intimates not only that he has a compassion to his creatures, but a complacency in them and in doing good to them, and this of his own good-will, and not for the sake of any thing in them. His mercy is grace, free grace; this teaches us to be not only pitiful, but courteous, 1 Pt. 3:8. (3.) He is *long-suffering.* This is a branch of God's goodness which the wickedness of sinners gives occasion for; that of Israel had done so: they had tried his patience, and experienced it. He is long-suffering, that is, he is slow to anger, and delays the execution of his justice; he waits to be gracious, and lengthens out the offers of his mercy. (4.) He is *abundant in goodness and truth.* This bespeaks plentiful goodness, goodness abounding above our deserts, above our conception and expression. The springs of mercy are always full, the streams of mercy always flowing; there is mercy enough in God, enough for all, enough for each, enough for ever. It bespeaks promised goodness, goodness and truth put together, goodness engaged by promise, and his faithfulness pledged for the security of it. He not only does good, but by his promise he raises our expectation of it, and even binds himself to show mercy. (5.) He keepeth *mercy for thousands.* This denotes, [1.] Mercy extended to thousands of persons. When he gives to some, still he keeps for others, and is never exhausted; he has mercy enough for all the thousands of Israel, when they shall *multiply as the sand.* [2.] Mercy entailed upon thousands of generations, even those upon whom the ends of the world have come; nay, the line of it is drawn parallel with that of eternity itself. (6.) He *forgiveth iniquity, transgression, and sin.* Pardoning mercy is specified, because in this divine grace is most magnified, and because in this divine grace is most magnified, and because it is this which opens the door to all other gifts of his divine grace, and because of this he had lately given a very pregnant proof. He forgives offences of all sorts — *iniquity, transgression, and sin,* multiplies his pardons; and with him is *plenteous redemption.*

3. That he is a just and holy God. For, (1.) *He will by no means clear the guilty.* Some read it so as to express a mitigation of wrath, even when he does punish: *When he empties, he will not make quite desolate;* that is, "He does not proceed to the greatest extremity, till there be no remedy." As we read it, we must expound it that he will by no means connive at the guilty, as if he took no notice of their sin. Or, he will not clear the impenitently guilty, that go on still in their trespasses: he will not clear the guilty without some satisfaction to his justice, and necessary vindications of the honour of his government. (2.) *He visits the iniquity of the fathers upon the children.* He may justly do it, for all souls are his, and there is a malignity in sin that taints the blood. He sometimes will do it, especially for the punishment of idolaters. Thus he shows his hatred to sin, and displeasure against it; yet he *keepeth not his anger for ever,* but visits to the third and fourth generation only, while he *keepeth his mercy for thousands.* Well, this is God's name for ever, and this is his memorial unto all generations.

II. How Moses received this declaration which God made of himself, and of his grace and mercy. It should seem as if Moses accepted this as a sufficient answer to his request that God would *show him his glory;* for we read not that he went into the cleft of the rock, whence to gain a sight of God's back parts. Perhaps this satisfied him, and he desired no more; as we read not that Thomas did *thrust his hand into Christ's side,* though Christ invited him to do it. God having thus proclaimed his name, Moses says, "It is enough, I expect no more till I come to heaven;" at least he did not think fit to relate what he saw. Now we are here told,

1. What impression it made upon him: *Moses made haste, and bowed his head, v.* 8. Thus he expressed, (1.) His humble reverence and adoration of God's glory, giving him *the honour due to that name* he had thus proclaimed. Even the goodness of God must be looked upon by us with a profound veneration and holy awe. (2.) His joy in this discovery which God had made of himself, and his thankfulness for it. We have reason gratefully to acknowledge God's goodness to us, not only in the real instances of it, but in the declarations he has made of it by his word; not only that he is, and will be, gracious to us, but that he is pleased to let us know it. (3.) His holy submission to the will of God, made known in this declaration, subscribing to his justice as well as mercy, and putting himself and his people Israel under the government and direction of such a God as Jehovah had now proclaimed himself to be. Let this God be our God for ever and ever.

2. What improvement he made of it. He immediately grounded a prayer upon it (*v.* 9); and a more earnest affectionate prayer it is, (1.) For the presence of God with his people Israel in the wilderness: *"I pray thee, go among us,* for thy presence is all in all to our safety and success." (2.) For pardon of sin: *"O pardon our iniquity and our sin,* else we cannot expect thee to go among us." And, (3.) For the privileges of a peculiar people: "Take us for *thy inheritance,* which thou wilt have a particular eye to, and

concern for, and delight in." These things God had already promised, and given Moses assurances of, and yet he prays for them, not as doubting the sincerity of God's grants, but as one solicitous for the ratification of them. God's promises are intended, not to supersede, but to direct and encourage, prayer. Those who have some good hopes, through grace, that their sins are pardoned, must yet continue to pray for pardon, for the renewing of their pardon, and the clearing of it more and more to their souls. The more we see of God's goodness the more ashamed we should be of our own sins, and the more earnest for an interest in it. God had said, in the close of the proclamation, that he would *visit the iniquity upon the children;* and Moses here deprecates that. "Lord, do not only pardon it to them, but to their children, and let our covenant-relation to thee be entailed upon our posterity, as an inheritance." Thus Moses, like a man of a truly public spirit, intercedes even for the children that should be born. But it is a strange plea he urges: *For it is a stiff-necked people.* God had given this as a reason why he would not go along with them, ch. 33:3. "Yea," says Moses, "the rather go along with us; for the worse they are the more need they have of thy presence and grace to make them better." Moses sees them so stiff-necked that, for his part, he has neither patience nor power enough to deal with them. "Therefore, Lord, do thou go among us, else they will never be kept in awe. Thou wilt spare, and bear with them, for thou art *God, and not man,*" Hos. 11:9.

Verses 10–17

Reconciliation being made, a covenant of friendship is here settled between God and Israel. The traitors are not only pardoned, but preferred and made favourites again. Well may the assurances of this be ushered in with a *behold,* a word commanding attention and admiration: *Behold, I make a covenant.* When the covenant was broken, it was Israel that broke it; now that it comes to be renewed, it is God that makes it. If there be quarrels, we must bear all the blame; if there be peace, God must have all the glory. Here is,

I. God's part of this covenant, what he would do for them, *v.* 10, 11. 1. In general: *Before all thy people, I will do marvels.* Note, Covenant-blessings are marvellous things (Ps. 98:1), marvels in the kingdom of grace; those mentioned here were marvels in the kingdom of nature, the drying up of Jordan, the standing still of the sun, etc. Marvels indeed, for they were without precedent, *such as have not been done in all the earth.* They were the joy of Israel, and the confirmation of their faith: *Thy people shall see,* and own *the work of the Lord.* And they were the terror of their enemies: *It is a terrible thing that I will do.* Nay, even God's own people should see them with astonishment. 2. In particular: *I drive out before thee the Amorite.* God, as King of nations, plucks up some, to plant others, as it pleases him; as King of saints, he made room for the vine he brought out of Egypt, Ps. 80:8, 9. Kingdoms are sacrificed to Israel's interests, Isa. 43:3, 4.

II. Their part of the covenant: *Observe that which I command thee.* We cannot expect the benefit of the promises unless we make conscience of the precepts.

1. The two great precepts are, (1.) *Thou shalt worship no other gods* (*v.* 14), not give divine honour to any creature, or any name whatsoever, the creature of fancy. A good reason is annexed. It is at thy peril if thou do: *For the Lord, whose name is Jealous, is a jealous God,* as tender in the matters of his worship as the husband is of the honour of the marriage-bed. Jealousy is called the *rage of a man* (Prov. 6:34), but it is *God's holy and just displeasure.* Those cannot worship God aright who do not worship him alone. (2.) *"Thou shalt make thee no molten god* (*v.* 17); thou shalt not worship the true God by images." This was the sin they had lately fallen into, which therefore they are particularly cautioned against.

2. Fences are here erected about these two precepts by two others: (1.) That they might not be tempted to worship other gods, they must not join in affinity or friendship with those that did (*v.* 12): "*Take heed to thyself,* for thou art upon thy good behaviour. It is a sin that thou art prone to and that will easily beset thee, and therefore be very cautious, and carefully abstain from all appearances of it and advances towards it. *Make no covenant with the inhabitants of the land."* If God, in kindness to them, drove

out the Canaanites, they ought, in duty to God, not to harbour them. What could be insisted on more reasonable than this? If God make war with the Canaanites, let not Israel make peace with them. If God take care that the Canaanites be not their lords, let them take care that they be not their snares. It was for their civil interest to complete the conquest of the land; so much does God consult our benefit in the laws he gives us. They must particularly take heed of intermarrying with them, *v.* 15, 16. If they espoused their children, they would be in danger of espousing their gods; such is the corruption of nature that the bad are much more likely to debauch the good than the good to reform the bad. The way of sin is downhill: those that are in league with idolaters will come by degrees to be in love with idolatry; and those that are prevailed upon to eat of the idolatrous sacrifice will come at length to offer it. *Obsta principiis — Nip the mischief in the bud.* (2.) That they might not be tempted to make molten gods, they must utterly destroy those they found and all that belong to them, the altars and groves (*v.* 13), lest, if these were left standing, they should be brought, in process of time, either to use them or to take pattern by them, or to abate in their detestation and dread of idolatry. The relics of idolatry ought to be abolished as affronts to the holy God and a great reproach to human nature. Let it never be said that men who pretend to reason were ever guilty of such absurdities as to make gods of their own and worship them.

Verses 18–27

Here is a repetition of several appointments made before, especially relating to their solemn feasts. When they had made the calf, they proclaimed a feast in honour of it; now, that they might never do so again, they are here charged with the observance of the feasts which God had instituted. Note, Men need not be drawn from their religion by the temptation of mirth, for we serve a Master that has abundantly provided for the joy of his servants: serious godliness is a continual feast, and joy in God always.

I. Once a week they must rest (*v.* 21), *even in earing time, and in harvest,* the most busy times of the year. All worldly business must give way to that holy rest; harvest-work will prosper the better for the religious observance of the sabbath-day in harvest-time. Hereby we must show that we prefer our communion with God, and our duty to him, before either the business or the joy of harvest.

II. Thrice a year they must feast (*v.* 23); they must then appear *before the Lord, God, the God of Israel.* In all our religious approaches to God, we must eye him as the Lord God, infinitely blessed, great, and glorious, that we may worship him with reverence and godly fear, as the God of Israel, a God in covenant with us, that we may be encouraged to trust in him, and to serve him cheerfully. We always are before God; but, in holy duties, we present ourselves before him, as servants to receive commands, as petitioners to sue for favours, and we have reason to do both with joy. But it might be suggested that, when all the males from every part of the country had gone up to worship in the place that God should choose, the country would be left exposed to the insults of their neighbours; and what would become of the poor women and children, and sick and aged, that were left at home? Trust God with them (*v.* 24): *Neither shall any man desire thy land;* not only they shall not invade it, but they shall not so much as think of invading it. Note, 1. All hearts are in God's hands, and under his check; he can lay a restraint, not only upon men's actions, but upon their desires. Canaan was a desirable land, and the neighbouring nations were greedy enough; and yet God says, "They shall not desire it." Let us check all sinful desires in our own hearts against God and his glory, and then trust him to check all sinful desires in the hearts of others against us and our interest. 2. The way of duty is the way of safety. If we serve God, he will preserve us; and those that venture for him shall never lose by him. While we are employed in God's work, and are attending upon him, we are taken under special protection, as noblemen and members of parliament are privileged from arrests.

III. The three feasts are here mentioned, with their appendages. 1. The passover, and the feast of unleavened bread, in remembrance of their deliverance out of Egypt; and to this is annexed the law of the redemption of the first-born, *v.* 18–20. This feast was instituted, ch. 12:13, and

urged again, *ch.* 23:15. 2. The feast of weeks, that is, that of pentecost, seven weeks after the passover; and to this is annexed the law of the first-fruits. 3. The feast of ingathering at the year's end, which was the feast of tabernacles (*v.* 22): of these also he had spoken before, *ch.* 23:16. As to those laws repeated here (*v.* 25, 26), that against leaven relates to the passover, that of the first-fruits to the feast of pentecost, and therefore that against seething the kid in his mother's milk in all probability relates to the feast of in-gathering, at which God would not have them use that superstitious ceremony, which probably they had seen the Egyptians, or some other of the neighbouring nations, bless their harvests with.

IV. With these laws, here repeated, it is probable all that was said to him when he was before upon the mount was repeated likewise, and the model of the tabernacle shown him again, lest the ruffle and discomposure, which the golden calf had put him into should have bereaved him of the ideas he had in mind of what he had seen and heard; also in token of a complete reconciliation, and to show that *not one jot or tittle of the law should pass away,* but that all should be carefully preserved by the great Mediator, who came not to destroy, but to fulfil, Mt. *v.* 17, 18. And in the close, 1. Moses is ordered to write these words (*v.* 27), that the people might be the better acquainted with them by a frequent perusal, and that they might be transmitted to the generations to come. We can never be enough thankful to God for the written word. 2. He is told that according to the tenour of these words God would make a covenant with Moses and Israel; not with Israel immediately, but with them in Moses a mediator. Thus the covenant of grace is made with believers through Christ, who is *given for a covenant to the people,* Isa. 49:8. And, as here the covenant was made according to the tenour of the command, so it is still; for we are by baptism brought into covenant, that we may be *taught to observe all things whatsoever Christ has commanded us,* Mt. 28:19, 20.

Verses 28–35

Here is, I. The continuance of Moses in the mount, where he was miraculously sustained, *v.* 28. He was there in very intimate communion with God, without interruption, forty days and forty nights, and did not think it long. When we are weary of an hour or two spent in attendance upon God and adoration of him, we should think how many days and nights Moses spent with him, and of the eternal day we hope to spend in praising him. During all this time Moses did neither eat nor drink. Though he had before been kept so long fasting, yet he did not, this second time, take up so many days' provision along with him, but believed that *man lives not by bread alone,* and encouraged himself with the experience he had of the truth of it. So long he continued without meat and drink (and probably without sleep too), for, 1. The power of God supported him, that he did not need it. He who made the body can nourish it without ordinary means, which he uses, but is not tied to. *The life is more than meat.* 2. His communion with God entertained him, so that he did not desire it. He had meat to eat which the world knew not of, for it was his meat and drink to hear the word of God and pray. The abundant satisfaction his soul had in the word of God and the visions of the Almighty made him forget the body and the pleasures of it. When God would treat his favourite Moses, it was not with meat and drink, but with his light, law, and love, with the knowledge of himself and his will; then man did indeed eat angels' food. See what we should value as the truest pleasure. *The kingdom of God is not meat and drink,* neither the abundance nor delicacy of food, but *righteousness and peace and joy in the Holy Ghost.* As Moses, so Elijah and Christ, fasted forty days and forty nights. The more dead we are to the delights of sense the better prepared we are for the pleasures of heaven.

II. The coming down of Moses from the mount, greatly enriched and miraculously adorned.

1. He came down enriched with the best treasure; for he brought in his hands the two tables of the law, written with the finger of God, 5:28, 29. It is a great favour to have the law given us; this favour was shown to Israel, Ps. 147:19, 20. It is a great honour to be employed in delivering God's law to others; this honour was done to Moses.

2. He came down adorned with the best beauty; for

the *skin of his face shone, v.* 29. This time of his being in the mount he heard only what he had heard before, but he saw more of the glory of God, which having with open face beheld, he was in some measure *changed into the same image from glory to glory,* 2 Co. 3:18. The last time he came down from the mount with the glory of a magistrate, to frown upon and chastise Israel's idolatry; now with the glory of an angel, with tidings of peace and reconciliation. Then he came with a rod, now with the spirit of meekness. Now,

(1.) This may be looked upon, [1.] As a great honour done to Moses, that the people might never again question his mission nor think nor speak lightly of him. He carried his credentials in his very countenance, which, some think, retained, as long as he lived, some remainders of this glory, which perhaps contributed to the vigour of his old age; that eye could not wax dim which had seen God, nor that face become wrinkled which had shone with his glory. The Israelites could not look him in the face but they must there read his commission. Thus it was done to the man whom the King of kings did delight to honour. Yet, after this, they murmured against him; for the most sensible proofs will not of themselves conquer an obstinate infidelity. The shining of Moses's face was a great honour to him; yet that was no glory, in comparison with the glory which excelled. We read of our Lord Jesus, not only that *his face shone* as the sun, but his whole body also, for his *raiment was white and glistering,* Lu. 9:29. But, when he came down from the mount, he quite laid aside that glory, it being his will that we should *walk by faith, not by sight.* [2.] It was also a great favour to the people, and an encouragement to them, that God put this glory upon him, who was their intercessor, thereby giving them assurance that he was accepted, and they through him. Thus the advancement of Christ, our advocate with the Father, is the great support of our faith. [3.] It was the effect of his sight of God. Communion with God, *First,* Makes the face to shine in true honour. Serious godliness puts a lustre upon a man's countenance, such as commands esteem and affection. *Secondly,* It should make the face to shine in universal holiness. When we have been in the mount with God, we should let our *light shine before men,* in humility, meekness, and all the instances of a heavenly conversation; thus must the *beauty of the Lord our God be upon us,* even the *beauty of holiness,* that all we converse with may *take knowledge of us that we have been with Jesus,* Acts 4:13.

(2.) Concerning the shining of Moses's face observe here, [1.] Moses was not aware of it himself: *He wist not that the skin of his face shone, v.* 29. Thus, *First,* It is the infelicity of some that, though their faces shine in true grace, yet they do not know it, to take the comfort of it. Their friends see much of God in them, but they themselves are ready to think they have no grace. *Secondly,* It is the humility of others that, though their faces shine in eminent gifts and usefulness, yet they do not know it, to be puffed up with it. Whatever beauty God puts upon us, we should still be filled with a humble sense of our own unworthiness, and manifold infirmities, as will make us even overlook and forget that which makes our faces shine. [2.] Aaron and the children of Israel saw it, and *were afraid, v.* 30. The truth of it was attested by a multitude of witnesses, who were also conscious of the terror of it. It not only dazzled their eyes, but struck such an awe upon them as obliged them to retire. Probably they doubted whether it were a token of God's favour or of his displeasure; and, though it seemed most likely to be a good omen, yet, being conscious of guilt, they feared the worst, especially remembering the posture Moses found them in when he came last down from the mount. Holiness will command reverence; but the sense of sin makes men afraid of their friends, and even of that which really is a favour to them. [3.] Moses put a *veil upon his face,* when he perceived that it shone, *v.* 33, 35. *First,* This teaches us all a lesson of modesty and humility. We must be content to have our excellences obscured, and a veil drawn over them, not coveting to *make a fair show in the flesh.* Those that are truly desirous to be owned and accepted of God will likewise desire not to be taken notice of nor applauded by men. *Qui bene latuit, bene vixit — There is a laudable concealment. Secondly,* It teaches ministers to accommodate themselves to the capacities of people, and to preach to them as they are able to bear it. Let all that art and all that learning be veiled which tend to amusement rather than edification, and let the strong condescend to the infirmities of the weak. *Thirdly,* This veil signified the darkness of that dispensation. The ceremonial institutions had in them much of Christ, much of the grace of the gospel, but a veil was drawn over it, so that the children of Israel could not distinctly and *stedfastly see those good things to come which the law had the shadow of.* It was beauty veiled, gold in the mine, a pearl in the shell; but, thanks be to God, by the gospel life and immortality are brought to light, the veil is taken away from off the Old Testament; yet still it remains upon the hearts of those who shut their eyes against the light. Thus the apostle expounds this passage, 2 Co. 3:13–15. [4.] When Moses *went in before the Lord,* to speak with him in the tabernacle of meeting, he *put off the veil, v.* 34. Then there was no occasion for it, and, before God, every man does and must appear unveiled; for *all things are naked and open before the eyes of him with whom we have to do,* and it is folly for us to think of concealing or disguising any thing. Every veil must be thrown aside when we come to present ourselves unto the Lord. This signified also, as it is explained (2 Co. 3:16), that when a soul turns to the Lord the veil shall be taken away, and with open face it may behold his glory. And when we shall come before the Lord in heaven, to be there for ever speaking with him, the veil shall not only be taken off from the divine glory, but from our hearts and eyes, that we may see as we are seen, and know as we are known.

CHAPTER 35

What should have been said and done upon Moses' coming down the first time from the mount, if the golden calf had not broken the measures and put all into disorder, now at last, when with great difficulty reconciliation was made, begins to be said and done; and that great affair of the setting up of God's worship is put into its former channel again, and goes on now without interruption. I. Moses gives Israel those instructions, received from God, which required immediate observance. 1. Concerning the sabbath (*v.* 1–3). 2. Concerning the contribution that was to be made for the erecting of the tabernacle (*v.* 4–9). 3. Concerning the framing of the tabernacle and the utensils of it (*v.* 10–19). II. The people bring in their contributions (*v.* 20–29). III. The head-workmen are nominated (*v.* 30, etc.).

Verses 1–19

It was said in general (*ch.* 34:32), *Moses gave them in commandment all that the Lord has spoken with him.* But, the erecting and furnishing of the tabernacle being the work to which they were now immediately to apply themselves, there is particular mention of the orders given concerning it.

I. All the congregation is summoned to attend (*v.* 1); that is, the heads and rulers of the congregation, the representatives of the several tribes, who must receive instructions from Moses as he had received them from the Lord, and must communicate them to the people. Thus John, being commanded to write to the seven churches what had been revealed to him, writes it to the angels, or ministers, of the churches.

II. Moses gave them in charge all that (and that only) which God had commanded him; thus he approved himself faithful both to God and Israel, between whom he was a messenger or mediator. If he had added, altered, or diminished, he would have been false to both. But, both sides having reposed a trust in him, he was true to the trust; yet he was faithful as a servant only, but *Christ as a Son,* Heb. 3:5, 6.

III. He begins with the law of the sabbath, because that was much insisted on in the instructions he had received (*v.* 21, 3): *Six days shall work be done,* work for the tabernacle, the work of the day that was now to be done in its day; and they had little else to do here in the wilderness, where they had neither husbandry nor merchandise, neither food to get nor clothes to make: *but on the seventh day* you must not strike a stroke, no, not at the tabernacle-work; the honour of the sabbath was above that of the sanctuary, more ancient and more lasting; that must be to you a holy day, devoted to God, and not be spent in common business. It is a sabbath of rest. It is a *sabbath of sabbaths* (so some read it), more honourable and excellent than any of the other feasts, and should survive them all. A *sabbath of sabbatism,* so others read it, being typical of that sabbatism or rest, both spiritual and eternal, which *remains for the people of God,* Heb. 4:9. It is a sabbath of rest, that is, in which a rest from all worldly labour must be very carefully and strictly observed. It is a sabbath and a little sabbath, so some of the Jews would have it read; not only observing the whole day as a sabbath, but an hour before the beginning of it, and an hour after the ending of it, which they throw in over and above out of their own time, and call *a little sabbath,* to show how glad they are of the approach of the sabbath and how loth to part with it. It is a sabbath of rest, but it is rest to the Lord, to whose honour it must be devoted. A penalty is here annexed to the breach of it: *Whosoever doeth work therein shall be put to death.* Also a particular prohibition of kindling fires on the sabbath day for any servile work, as smith's work, or plumbers, etc.

IV. He orders preparation to be made for the setting up of the tabernacle. Two things were to be done: —

1. All that were able must contribute: *Take you from among you an offering, v.* 5. The tabernacle was to be dedicated to the honour of God, and used in his service; and therefore what was brought for the setting up and furnishing of that was *an offering to the Lord.* Our goodness extends not to God, but what is laid out for the support of his kingdom and interest among men he is pleased to accept as an offering to himself; and he requires such acknowledgements of our receiving our all from him and such instances of our dedicating our all to him. The rule is, *Whosoever is of a willing heart let him bring.* It was not to be a tax imposed upon them, but a benevolence or voluntary contribution, to intimate to us, (1.) That God has not made our yoke heavy. He is a prince that does not burden his subjects with taxes, nor *make them to serve with an offering,* but *draws with the cords of a man,* and leaves it to ourselves to *judge what is right;* his is a government that there is no cause to complain of, for he does not rule with rigour. (2.) That God loves a cheerful giver, and is best pleased with the free-will offering. Those services are acceptable to him that come from the willing heart of a willing people, Ps. 110:3.

2. All that were skilful must work: *Every wise-hearted among you shall come, and make, v.* 10. See how God dispenses his gifts variously; and, *as every man hath received the gift, so he must minister,* 1 Pt. 4:10. Those that were rich must bring in materials to work on; those that were ingenious must serve the tabernacle with their ingenuity; as they needed one another, so the tabernacle needed them both, 1 Co. 12:7–21. The work was likely to go on when some helped with their purses, others with their hands, and both with a willing heart. Moses, as he had told them what must be given (*v.* 5–9), so he gives them the general heads of what must be made (*v.* 11–19), that, seeing how much work was before them, they might apply themselves to it the more vigorously, and every hand might be busy; and it gave them such an idea of the fabric designed that they could not but long to see it finished.

Verses 20–29

Moses having made known to them the will of God, they went home and immediately put in practice what they had heard, *v.* 20. O that every congregation would thus depart from the hearing of the word of God, with a full resolution to be *doers of the same!* Observe here,

I. The offerings that were brought for the service of the tabernacle (*v.* 21, etc.), concerning which many things may be noted. 1. It is intimated that they brought their offerings immediately; they departed to their tents immediately to fetch their offering, and did not desire time to consider of it, lest their zeal should be cooled by delays. What duty God convinces us of, and calls us to, we should set about speedily. No season will be more convenient than the present season. 2. It is said that *their spirits made them willing (v.* 21), and their hearts, *v.* 29. What they did they did cheerfully, and from a good principle. They were willing, and it was not any external inducement that made them so, but their spirits. It was from a principle of love to God and his service, a desire of his presence with them in his ordinances, gratitude for the great things he had done for them, faith in his promise of what he would further do (or, at least, from the present consideration of these things), that they were willing to offer. What we give and do for God is then acceptable when it comes from a good principle in the heart and spirit. 3. When it is said that as many as were willing-hearted brought their offerings (*v.* 22), it should seem as if there were some who were not, who loved their gold better than their God, and would not part with it, no, not for the service of the tabernacle. Such there are, who will be called Israelites, and yet will not be moved by the equity of the thing, God's expectations from them, and the good examples of those about them, to part with any thing for the interests of God's kingdom: they are for the true religion, provided it be cheap and will cost them nothing. 4. The offerings were of divers kinds, according as they had; those that had gold and precious stones brought them, not thinking any thing too good and too rich to part with for the honour of God. Those that had not precious stones to bring brought goats' hair, and rams' skins. If we cannot do as much as others for God, we must not therefore sit still and do nothing: if the meaner offerings which are according to our ability gain us not such a reputation among men, yet they shall not fail of acceptance with God, who requires *according to what a man hath, and not according to what he hath not,* 2 Co. 8:12; 2 Ki. 5:23. Two mites from a pauper were more pleasing than so many talents from a Dives. God has an eye to the heart of the giver more than to the value of the gift. 5. Many of the things they offered were their ornaments, bracelets and rings, and tablets or lockets (*v.* 22); and even the women parted with these. *Can a maid forget her ornaments?* Thus far they forgot them that they preferred the beautifying of the sanctuary before their own adorning. Let this teach us, in general, to part with that for God, when he calls for it, which is very dear to us, which we value, and value ourselves by; and particularly to lay aside our ornaments, and deny ourselves in them, when either they occasion offence to others or feed our own pride. If we think those gospel rules concerning our clothing too strict (1 Tim. 2:9, 10; 1 Pt. 3:3, 4), I fear we should scarcely have done as these Israelites did. If they thought their ornaments well bestowed upon the tabernacle, shall not we think the want of ornaments well made up by the graces of the Spirit? Prov. 1:9. 6. These rich things that they offered, we may suppose, were mostly the spoils of the Egyptians; for the Israelites in Egypt were kept poor, till they borrowed at parting. And we may suppose the rulers had better things (*v.* 27), because, having more influence among the Egyptians, they borrowed larger sums. Who would have thought that ever the wealth of Egypt should have been so well employed? but thus God has often made *the earth to help the woman,* Rev. 12:16. It was by a special providence and promise of God that the Israelites got all that spoil, and therefore it was highly fit that they should devote a part of it to the service of that God to whom they owed it all. Let every man give *according as God hath prospered him,* 1 Co. 16:2. Extraordinary successes should be acknowledged by extraordinary offerings. Apply it to human learning, arts and sciences, which are borrowed, as it were, from the Egyptians. Those that are enriched with these must devote them to the service of God and his tabernacle: they may be used as helps to understand the scriptures, as ornaments or handmaids to divinity. But then great care must be taken that Egypt's gods mingle not with Egypt's gold. Moses, though learned in all the learning of the Egyptians, did not therefore pretend, in the least instance, to correct the pattern shown him in the mount. The furnishing of the tabernacle with the riches of Egypt was perhaps a good omen to the Gentiles, who, in the fulness of time, should be brought into the gospel tabernacle, and their silver and their gold with them (Isa. 60:9), and it should be said, *Blessed be Egypt my people,* Isa. 19:25. 7. We may suppose that the remembrance of the offerings made for the golden calf made them the more forward in these offerings. Those that had then parted with their ear-rings would not testify their repentance by giving the rest of their jewels to the service of God: godly sorrow worketh such a revenge, 2 Co. 7:11. And those that had kept themselves pure from that idolatry yet argued with themselves, "Were they so forward in contributing to an idol, and shall we be backward or sneaking in our offerings to the Lord?" Thus some good was brought even out of that evil.

II. The work that was done for the service of the tabernacle (*v.* 25): *The women did spin with their hands.* Some spun fine work, of blue and purple; others coarse work, of goats' hair, and yet theirs also is said to be done in wisdom, *v.* 26. As it is not only rich gifts, so it is not only fine work that God accepts. Notice is here taken of the good women's work for God, as well as of Bezaleel's and Aholiab's. The meanest hand for the honour of God, shall have an honourable recompence. Mary's anointing of Christ's head shall be told for a memorial (Mt. 26:13); and a record is kept of the women that laboured in the gospel tabernacle (Phil. 4:3), and were helpers to Paul in Christ Jesus, Rom. 16:3. It is part of the character of the virtuous woman that she layeth *her hands to the spindle,* Prov. 31:19. This employment was here turned to a pious use, as it may be still (though we have no hangings to make for the tabernacle) by the imitation of the charity of Dorcas, who made coats and garments for poor widows, Acts 9:39. Even those that are not in a capacity to give in charity may yet work in charity; and thus the poor may relieve the poor, and those that have nothing but their limbs and senses may be very charitable in the labour of love.

Verses 30–35

Here is the divine appointment of the master-workmen, that there might be no strife for the office, and that all who were employed in the work might take direction from, and give account to, these general inspectors; for God is the God of order and not of confusion. Observe, 1. Those whom God called by name to this service he *filled with the Spirit of God,* to qualify them for it, *v.* 30, 31. Skill in secular employments is God's gift, and comes from above, Jam. 1:17. From him the faculty is, and the improvement of it. To his honour therefore all knowledge must be devoted, and we must study how to serve him with it. The work was extraordinary which Bezaleel was designed for, and therefore he was qualified in an extraordinary manner for it; thus when the apostles were appointed to be master-builders in setting up the gospel tabernacle they were *filled with the Spirit of God in wisdom and understanding.* 2. The were appointed, not only to devise, but to work (*v.* 32), *to work all manner of work, v.* 35. Those of eminent gifts, that are capable of directing others, must not thing that these will excuse them in idleness. Many are ingenious enough in cutting out work for other people, and can tell what this man and that man should do, but the burdens they ind on others they themselves *will not touch with one of their fingers.* These will fall under the character of slothful servants. 3. They were not only to devise and work themselves, but they were to teach others, *v.* 34. Not only had Bezaleel power to command, but he was to take pains to instruct. Those that rule should teach; and those to whom God had given knowledge should be willing to communicate it for the benefit of others, not coveting to monopolize it.

CHAPTER 36

In this chapter, I. The work of the tabernacle is begun (*v.* 1–4). II. A stop is put to the people's contributions (*v.* 5–7). III. A particular account is given of the making of the tabernacle itself; the fine curtains of it (*v.* 8–13). The coarse ones (*v.* 14–19). The boards (*v.* 20–30). The bars (*v.* 31–34). The partition veil (*v.* 35, 36). And the hanging for the door (*v.* 37, etc.).

Verses 1–7

I. The workmen set in without delay. Then they wrought, *v.* 1. When God had qualified them for the work, then they applied themselves to it. Note, The talents we are entrusted with must not be laid up, but laid out; not hid in a napkin, but traded with. What have we all our gifts for, but to do good with them? They began when Moses called them, *v.* 2. Even those whom God has qualified for, and inclined to, the service of the tabernacle, yet must wait for a regular call to it, either extraordinary, as that of prophets and apostles, or ordinary, as that of pastors and teachers. And observe who they were that Moses called: Those *in whose heart God had put wisdom* for this purpose, beyond their natural capacity, and *whose heart stirred them up to come to the work* in good earnest. Note, Those are to be called to the building of the gospel tabernacle whom God has by his grace made in some measure fit for the work and free to engage in it. Ability and willingness (with resolution) are the two things to be regarded in the call of ministers. Has God given them not only knowledge, but wisdom? (for those that would win souls must be wise, and have their hearts stirred up to come to the work, and not to the honour only; to do it, and not to talk of it only), let them come to it with full purpose of heart to go through with it. The materials which the people had contributed were delivered by Moses to the workmen, *v.* 3. They could not create a tabernacle, that is, make it out of nothing, nor work, unless they had something to work upon; the people therefore brought the materials and Moses put them into their hands. Precious souls are the materials of the gospel tabernacle; they are *built up a spiritual house,* 1 Pt. 2:5. To this end they are to offer themselves a free-will offering to the Lord, for his service (Rom. 15:16), and they are then committed to the care of his ministers, as builders, to be framed and wrought upon by their edification and increase in holiness, till they all come, like the curtains of the tabernacle, *in the unity of the faith, to be a holy temple,* Eph. 2:21, 22; 4:12, 13.

II. The contributions restrained. The people continued to bring *free offerings every morning, v.* 3. Note, We should always make it our morning's work to bring our offerings unto the Lord; even the spiritual offerings of prayer and praise, and a broken heart surrendered entirely to God. This is that which the duty of every day requires. God's compassions are new every morning, and so must our duty to him be. Probably there were some that were backward at first to bring their offering, but their neighbours' forwardness stirred them up and shamed them. The zeal of some provoked many. There are those who will be content to follow who yet do not care for leading in a good work. It is best to be forward, but better late than never. Or perhaps some who had offered at first, having pleasure in reflecting upon it, offered more; so far were they from grudging what they had contributed, that they doubled their contribution. Thus, in charity, *give a portion to seven, and also to eight;* having given much, give more. Now observe, 1. The honesty of the workmen. When they had cut out their work, and found how their stuff held out, and that the people were still forward to bring in more, they went in a body to Moses to tell him that there needed no more contributions, *v.* 4, 5. Had they sought their own things, they had now a fair opportunity of enriching themselves by the people's gifts; for they might have made up their work, and converted the overplus to their own use, as perquisites of their place. But they were men of integrity, that scorned to do so mean a thing as to sponge upon the people, and enrich themselves with that which was offered to the Lord. Those are the greatest cheats that cheat the public. If to murder many is worse than to murder one, by the same rule to defraud communities, and to rob the church or state, is a much greater crime than to pick the pocket of a single person. But these workmen were not only ready to account for all they received, but were not willing to receive more than they had occasion for, lest they should come either into the temptation or under the suspicion of taking it to themselves. These were men that knew when they had enough. 2. The liberality of the people. Though they saw what an abundance was contributed, yet they continued to offer, till they were forbidden by proclamation, *v.* 6, 7. A rare instance! Most need a spur to quicken their charity; few need a bridle to check it, yet these did. Had Moses aimed to enrich himself, he might have suffered them still to bring in their offerings; and when the work was finished might have taken the remainder to himself: but he also preferred the public before his own private interest, and was therein a good example to all in public trusts. It is said (*v.* 6), *The people were restrained from bringing;* they looked upon it as a restraint upon them not to be allowed to do more for the tabernacle; such was the zeal of those people, who gave *to their power, yea, and beyond their power, praying* the collectors *with much entreaty to receive the gift,* 2 Co. 8:3, 4. These were the fruits of a first love; in these last-days charity has grown too cold for us to expect such things from it.

Verses 8–13

The first work they set about was the framing of the house, which must be done before the furniture of it was prepared. This house was not made of timber or stone, but of curtains curiously embroidered and coupled together. This served to typify the state of the church in this world, the palace of God's kingdom among men. 1. Though it is upon the earth, yet its foundation is not in the earth, as that of a house is; no, Christ's kingdom is not of this world, nor founded in it. 2. It is mean and mutable, and in a militant state; shepherds dwelt in tents, and God is the Shepherd of Israel; soldiers dwelt in tents, and the Lord is a man of war, and his church marches through an enemy's country, and must fight its way. The kings of the earth enclose themselves in cedar (Jer. 22:15), but the ark of God was lodged in curtains only. 3. Yet there is a beauty in holiness; the curtains were embroidered, so is the church adorned with the gifts and graces of the Spirit, that *raiment of needle-work,* Ps. 45:14. 4. The several societies of believers are united in one, and, as here, all *become one tabernacle; for there is one Lord, one faith, and one baptism.*

Verses 14–34

Here, 1. The shelter and special protection that the church is under are signified by the curtains of hair-cloth, which were spread over the tabernacle, and the covering of rams' skins and badgers' skins over them, *v.* 14–19. God has provided for his people a *shadow from the heat, and a covert from storm and rain,* Isa. 4:6. They are armed against all weathers; the sun and the moon shall not smite them: and they are protected from the storms of divine wrath, that hail which will *sweep away the refuge of lies,* Isa. 28:17. Those that dwell in God's house shall find, be the tempest ever so violent, or the dropping ever so continual, it does not rain in. 2. The strength and stability of the church, though it is but a tabernacle, are signified by the boards and bars with which the curtains were borne up, *v.* 20–34. The boards were coupled together and joined by the bars which shot through them; for the union of the church, and the hearty agreement of those that are its stays and supporters, contribute abundantly to its strength and establishment.

Verses 35–38

In the building of a house there is a great deal of work about the doors and partitions. In the tabernacle these were answerable to the rest of the fabric; there were curtains for doors, and veils for partitions. 1. There was a veil made for a partition between the holy place, and the most holy, *v.* 35, 36. This signified the darkness and distance of that dispensation, compared with the New Testament, which shows us the glory of God more clearly and invites us to draw near to it; and the darkness and distance of our present state, in comparison with heaven, where we shall be *ever with the Lord* and *see him as he is.* 2. There was a veil made for the door of the tabernacle, *v.* 37, 38. At this door the people assembled, though forbidden to enter; for, while we are in this present state, we must get as near to God as we can.

CHAPTER 37

Bezaleel and his workmen are still busy, making I. The ark with the mercy-seat and the cherubim (*v.* 1–9). II. The table with its vessels (*v.* 10–16). III. The candlestick with its appurtenances (*v.* 17–24). IV. The golden altar for incense (*v.* 25–28). V. The holy oil and incense (*v.* 29). The particular appointment concerning each of which we had before the 25th and 30th chapters.

Verses 1–9

I. It may be thought strange that Moses, when he had recorded so fully the instructions given him upon the mount for the making of all these things, should here record as particularly the making of them, when it might have sufficed only to have said, in a few words, that each of these things was made exactly according to the directions before recited. We are sure that Moses, when he wrote by divine inspiration, used no vain repetitions; there are no idle words in scripture. Why then are so many chapters taken up with this narrative, which we are tempted to think needless and tedious? But we must consider, 1. That Moses wrote primarily for the people of Israel, to whom it would be of great use to read and hear often of these divine and sacred treasures with which they were entrusted. These several ornaments wherewith the tabernacle was furnished they were not admitted to see, but the priests only, and therefore it was requisite that they should be thus largely described particularly to them. That which they ought to read again (lest they should fail of doing it) is written again and again: thus many of the same passages of the history of Christ are in the New Testament related by two or three, and some by four of the evangelists, for the same reason. The great things of God's law and gospel we need to have inculcated upon us again and again. To write the same (says St. Paul) to me *is not grievous, but for you it is safe,* Phil. 3:1. 2. Moses would thus show the great care which he and his workmen took to make every thing exactly according to the pattern shown him in the mount. Having before given us the original, he here givers us the copy, that we may compare them, and observe how exactly they agree. Thus he appeals to every reader concerning his fidelity to him that appointed him, in all his house, and in all the particulars of it, Heb. 3:5. And thus he teaches us to have respect to all God's commandments, even to every iota and tittle of them. 3. It is intimated hereby that God takes delight in the sincere obedience of his people, and keeps an exact account of it, which shall be produced to their honour in the resurrection of the just. None can be so punctual in their duty, but God will be as punctual in his notices of it. He is *not unrighteous to forget the work and labour of love,* in any instance of it, Heb. 6:10. 4. The spiritual riches and beauties of the gospel tabernacle are hereby recommended to our frequent and serious consideration. Go walk about this Zion, view it and review it: the more you contemplate the glories of the church, the more you will admire them and be in love with them. The charter of its privileges, and the account of its constitution, will very well bear a second reading.

II. In these verses we have an account of the making of the ark, with its glorious and most significant appurtenances, the mercy-seat and the cherubim. Consider these three together, and they represent the glory of a holy god, the sincerity of a holy heart, and the communion that is between them, in and by a Mediator. 1. It is the glory of a holy god that he dwells between the cherubim; that is, is continually attended and adored by the blessed angels, whose swiftness was signified by their faces being one towards another. 2. It is the character of an upright heart that, like the ark of the testimony, it has the law of God hid and kept in it. 3. By Jesus Christ, the great propitiation, there is reconciliation made, and a communion settled, between us and God: he interposes between us and God's displeasure; and not only so, but through him we become entitled to God's favour. If he write his law in our heart, he will be to us a God and we shall be to him a people. From the mercy-seat he will teach us, there he will accept us, and show himself merciful to our unrighteousness; and under the shadow of his wings we shall be safe and easy.

Verses 10–24

Here is, 1. The making of the table on which the show-bread was to be continually placed. God is a good householder, that always keeps a plentiful table. Is the world his tabernacle? His providence in it spreads a table for all the creatures: he *provides food for all flesh.* Is the church his tabernacle? His grace in it spreads a table for all believers, furnished with the bread of life. But observe how much the dispensation of the gospel exceeds that of the law. Though here was a table furnished, it was only with *show-bread,* bread to be looked upon, not to be fed upon, while it was on this table, and afterwards only by the priests; but to the table which Christ has spread in the new covenant all real Christians are invited guests; and to them it is said, *Eat, O friends, come eat of my bread.* What the law gave but a sight of at a distance, the gospel gives the enjoyment of, and a hearty welcome to. 2. The making of the candlestick, which was not of wood overlaid with gold, but all beaten work of pure gold only, *v.* 17, 22. This signified that light of divine revelation with which God's church upon earth (which is his tabernacle among men) has always been enlightened, being always supplied with fresh oil from Christ the good Olive, Zec. 4:2, 3. God's manifestations of himself in this world are but candle-light compared with the daylight of the future state. The Bible is a golden candlestick; it is of pure gold, Ps. 19:10. From it light is diffused to every part of God's tabernacle, that by it his spiritual priests may see to minister unto the Lord, and to do the service of his sanctuary. This candlestick has not only its bowls for necessary use, but its knops and flowers for ornament; there are many things which God saw fit to beautify his word with which we can no more give a reason for than for these knops and flowers, and yet we are sure that they were added for a good purpose. Let us bless God for this candlestick, have an eye to it continually, and dread the removal of it out of its place.

Verses 25–29

Here is, 1. The making of the golden altar, on which incense was to be burnt daily, which signified both the prayers of saints and the intercession of Christ, to which are owing the acceptableness and success of those prayers. The rings and staves, and all the appurtenances of this altar, were overlaid with gold, as all the vessels of the table and candlestick were of gold, for these were used in the holy place. God is the best, and we must serve him with the best we have; but the best we can serve him with in his courts on earth is but as brass, compared with the gold, the sinless and spotless perfection, with which his saints shall serve him in his holy place above. 2. The preparing of the incense which was to be burnt upon this altar, and with it the holy anointing oil (*v.* 29), according to the dispensatory, *ch.* 30:22, etc. God taught Bezaleel this art also; so that though he was not before acquainted with it yet he made up these things according to the work of the apothecary, as dexterously and exactly as if he had been bred up to the trade. Where God gives wisdom and grace, it will make the man of God *perfect, thoroughly furnished to every good work.*

CHAPTER 38

Here is an account, I. Of the making of the brazen altar (*v.* 1–7), and the laver (*v.* 8). II. The preparing of the hangings for the enclosing of the court in which the tabernacle was to stand (*v.* 9–20). III. A summary of the gold, silver, and brass, that was contributed to, and used in, the preparing of the tabernacle (*v.* 21, etc.).

Verses 1–8

Bezaleel having finished the gold-work, which, though the richest, yet was ordered to lie most out of sight, in the tabernacle itself, here goes on to prepare the court, which lay open to the view of all. Two things the court was furnished with, and both made of brass: —

I. An altar of burnt-offering, *v.* 1–7. On this all their sacrifices were offered, and it was this which, being sanctified itself for this purpose by the divine appointment, sanctified the gift that was in faith offered on it. Christ was himself the altar to his own sacrifice of atonement, and so he is to all our sacrifices of acknowledgment. We must have an eye to him in offering them, as God has in accepting them.

II. A laver, to hold water for the priests to wash in when they went in to minister, *v.* 8. This signified the provision that is made in the gospel of Christ for the cleansing of our souls from the moral pollution of sin by the merit and grace of Christ, that we may be fit to serve the holy God in holy duties. This is here said to be made of the *looking-glasses* (or mirrors) of the women that assembled at the door of the tabernacle.

1. It should seem these women were eminent and exemplary for devotion, attending more frequently and seriously at the place of public worship than others did; and notice is here taken of it to their honour. Anna was such a one long afterwards, who *departed not from the temple, but served God with fastings and prayers night and day,* Lu. 2:37. It seems in every age of the church there have been some who have thus distinguished themselves by their serious zealous piety, and they have thereby distinguished themselves; for devout women are really honourable women (Acts 13:50), and not the less so for their being called, by the scoffers of the latter days, *silly women.* Probably these women were such as showed their zeal upon this occasion, by assisting in the work that was now going on for the service of the tabernacle. They assembled by *troops,* so the word is; a blessed sight, to see so many, and those so zealous and so unanimous, in this good work.

2. These women parted with their mirrors (which were of the finest brass, burnished for that purpose) for the use of the tabernacle. Those women that admire their own beauty, are in love with their own shadow, and make the putting on of apparel their chief adorning by which they value and recommend themselves, can but ill spare their *looking-glasses;* yet these women offered *them* to God, either, (1.) In token of their repentance for the former abuse of them, to the support of their pride and vanity; now that they were convinced of their folly, and had devoted themselves to the service of God at the door of the tabernacle, they thus threw away that which, though lawful and useful in itself, yet had been an occasion of sin to them. Thus Mary Magdalene, who had been a sinner, when she became a penitent wiped Christ's feet with her hair. Or, (2.)

In token of their great zeal for the work of the tabernacle; rather than the workmen should want brass, or not have of the best, they would part with their mirrors, though they could not do well without them. God's service and glory must always be preferred by us before any satisfactions or accommodations of our own. Let us never complain of the want of that which we may honour God by parting with.

3. These mirrors were used for the making of the laver. Either they were artfully joined together, or else molten down and cast anew; but it is probable that the laver was so brightly burnished that the sides of it still served for mirrors, that the priests, when they came to wash, might there see their faces, and so discover the spots, to wash them clean. Note, In the washing of repentance, there is need of the looking-glass of self-examination. The word of God is a glass, in which we may see our own faces (see Jam. 1:23); and with it we must compare our own hearts and lives, that, finding out our blemishes, we may wash with particular sorrow, and application of the blood of Christ to our souls. Usually the more particular we are in the confession of sin the more comfort we have in the sense of the pardon.

Verses 9–20

The walls of the court, or church-yard, were like the rest curtains or hangings, made according to the appointment, *ch.* 27:9, etc. This represented the state of the Old-Testament church: it was a garden enclosed; the worshippers were then confined to a little compass. But the enclosure being of curtains only intimated that the confinement of the church in one particular nation was not to be perpetual. The dispensation itself was a tabernacle-dispensation, movable and mutable, and in due time to be taken down and folded up, when the place of the tent should be enlarged and its cords lengthened, to make room for the Gentile world, as is foretold, Isa. 54:2, 3. The church here on earth is but the court of God's house, and happy they that tread these courts and flourish in them; but through these courts we are passing to the holy place above. *Blessed are those that dwell in that house* of God: they well be *still praising him.* The enclosing of a court before the tabernacle teaches us a gradual approach to God. The priests that ministered must pass through the holy court, before they entered the holy house. Thus before solemn ordinances there ought to be the separated and enclosed court of a solemn preparation, in which we must wash our hands, and so draw near with a true heart.

Verses 21–31

Here we have a breviat of the account which, by Moses's appointment, the Levites took and kept of the gold, silver, and brass, that was brought in for the tabernacle's use, and how it was employed. Ithamar the son of Aaron was appointed to draw up this account, and was thus by less services trained up and fitted for greater, *v.* 21. Bezaleel and Aholiab must bring in the account (*v.* 22, 23), and Ithamar must audit it, and give it in to Moses. And it was thus: — 1. All the gold was a free-will offering; every man brought as he could and would, and it amounted to twenty-nine talents, and 730 shekels over, which some compute to be about 150,000*l.* worth of gold, according to the present value of it. Of this were made all the golden furniture and vessels. 2. The silver was levied by way of tax; every man was assessed half a shekel, a kind of poll-money, which amounted in the whole to 100 talents, and 1775 shekels over, *v.* 25, 26. Of this they made the sockets into which the boards of the tabernacle were let, and on which they rested; so that they were as the foundation of the tabernacle, *v.* 27. The silver amounted to about 34,000*l.* of our money. The raising of the gold by voluntary contribution, and of the silver by way of tribute, shows that either way may be taken for the defraying of public expenses, provided that nothing be done with partiality. 3. The brass, though less valuable, was of use not only for the brazen altar, but for the sockets of the court, which probably in other tents were of wood: but it is promised (Isa. 60:17), *For wood I will bring brass.* See how liberal the people were and how faithful the workmen were, in both which respects their good example ought to be followed.

CHAPTER 39

This chapter gives us an account of the finishing of the work of the tabernacle. I. The last things prepared were the holy garments. The ephod and its curious girdle (*v.* 1–5). The onyx-stones for the shoulders (*v.* 6, 7). The breastplate with the precious stones in it (*v.* 8–21). The robe of the ephod (*v.* 22–26). The coats, bonnets, and breeches, for the inferior priests (*v.* 27–29). And the plate of the holy crown (*v.* 30, 31). II. A summary account of the whole work, as it was presented to Moses when it was all finished (*v.* 32, etc.).

Verses 1–31

In this account of the making of the priests' garments, according to the instructions given (*ch.* 28), we may observe, 1. That the priests' garments are called here *clothes of service, v.* 1. Note, Those that wear robes of honour must look upon them as clothes of service; for from those upon whom honour is put service is expected. It is said of those that are arrayed in white robes that they *are before the throne of God, and serve him day and night in his temple,* Rev. 7:13, 15. Holy garments were not made for men to sleep in, or to strut in, but to do service in; and then they are indeed for glory and beauty. The Son of man himself *came not to be ministered unto, but to minister.* 2. That all the six paragraphs here, which give a distinct account of the making of these holy garments, conclude with those words, *as the Lord commanded Moses, v.* 5, 7, 21, 26, 29, 31. The like is not in any of the foregoing accounts, as if in these, more than any other of the appurtenances of the tabernacle, they had a particular regard to the divine appointment, both for warrant and for direction. It is an intimation to all the Lord's ministers to make the word of God their rule in all their ministrations, and to act in observance of and obedience to the command of God. 3. That these garments, in conformity to the rest of the furniture of the tabernacle, were very rich and splendid; the church in its infancy was thus taught, thus pleased, with the rudiments of this world; but now under the gospel, which is the ministration of the Spirit, to affect and impose such pompous habits as the church of Rome does, under pretence of decency and instruction, is to betray *the liberty wherewith Christ has made us free,* and to entangle the church again in the bondage of those carnal ordinances which were imposed only till the time of reformation. 4. That they were all shadows of good things to come, but the substance is Christ, and the grace of the gospel; when therefore the substance has come, it is a jest to be fond of the shadow. (1.) Christ is our great high-priest; when he undertook the work of our redemption, he put on the clothes of service — he arrayed himself with the gifts and graces of the Spirit, which he received not by measure — girded himself with the curious girdle of resolution, to go through with his undertaking — charged himself with the curious girdle of resolution, to go through with his undertaking — charged himself with all God's spiritual Israel, bore them on his shoulders, carried them in his bosom, laid them near his heart, engraved them on the palms of his hands, and presented them in the breast-plate of judgment unto his Father. And (lastly) he crowned himself with *holiness to the Lord,* consecrating his whole undertaking to the honour of his Father's holiness: now consider how great this man is. (2.) True believers are spiritual priests. The clean linen with which all their clothes of service must be made is *the righteousness of saints* (Rev. 19:8), and *Holiness to the Lord* must be so written upon their foreheads that all who converse with them may see, and say, that they bear the image of God's holiness, and are devoted to the praise of it.

Verses 32–43

Observe here, I. The builders of the tabernacle made very good despatch. It was not much more than five months from the beginning to the finishing of it. Though there was a great deal of fine work about it, such as is usually the work of time, embroidering and engraving, not only in gold, but in precious stones, yet they went through with it in a little time. Church-work is usually slow work, but they made quick work of this, and yet did it with the greatest exactness imaginable. For, 1. Many hands were employed, all unanimous, and not striving with each other. This expedited the business, and made it easy. 2. The workmen were taught of God, and so were kept from making blunders, which would have retarded them. 3. The people

were hearty and zealous in the work, and impatient till it was finished. God had prepared their hearts, and then *the thing was done suddenly,* 2 Chr. 29:36. Resolution and industry, and a cheerful application of mind, will, by the grace of God, bring a great deal of good work to pass in a little time, in less than one would expect.

II. They punctually observed their orders, and did not in the least vary from them. They did it *according to all that the Lord commanded Moses, v.* 32, 42. Note, God's work must be done, in every thing, according to his own will. His institutions neither need nor admit men's inventions to make them either more beautiful or more likely to answer the intention of them. *Add thou not unto his words.* God is pleased with willing worship, but not with will-worship.

III. They brought all their work to Moses, and submitted it to his inspection and censure, *v.* 33. He knew what he had ordered them to make; and now the particulars were called over, and all produced, that Moses might see both that they had made all, omitting nothing, and that they had made all according to the instructions given them, and that, if they had made a mistake in any thing, it might be forthwith rectified. Thus they showed respect to Moses, who was set over them in the Lord; not objecting that Moses did not understand such work, and therefore that there was no reason for submitting it to his judgment. No, that God who gave them so much knowledge as to do the work gave them also so much humility as to be willing to have it examined and compared with the model. Moses was in authority, and they would pay a deference to his place. *The spirit of the prophets is subject to the prophets.* And besides, though they knew how to do the work better than Moses, Moses had a better and more exact idea of the model than they had, and therefore they could not be well pleased with their own work, unless they had his approbation. Thus in all the services of religion we should *labour to be accepted of the Lord.*

IV. Moses, upon search, found all done according to the rule, *v.* 43. Moses, both for their satisfaction and for his own, did look upon all the work, piece by piece, and behold they had done it according to the pattern shown him, for the same Being that showed him the pattern guided their hand in the work. All the copies of God's grace exactly agree with the original of his counsels: what God works in us, and by us, is the fulfilling of the good pleasure of his own goodness; and when the mystery of God shall be finished, and all his performances come to be compared with his purposes, it will appear that behold all is done according to the counsel of his own will, not one iota or tittle of which shall fall to the ground, or be varied from.

V. Moses blessed them. 1. He commended them, and signified his approbation of all they had done. He did not find fault where there was none, as some do, who think they disparage their own judgment if they do not find something amiss in the best and most accomplished performance. In all this work it is probable there might have been found here and there a stitch amiss, and a stroke awry, which would have served for an over-curious and censorious critic to animadvert upon; but Moses was too candid to notice small faults where there were no great ones. Note, All governors must be a praise to those that do well, as well as a terror to evil-doers. Why should any take a pride in being hard to be pleased? 2. He not only praised them, but prayed for them. He blessed them as one having authority, for the less is blessed of the better. We read not of any wages that Moses paid them for their work, but this blessing he gave them. For, though ordinarily the labourer be worthy of his hire, yet in this case, 1. They wrought for themselves. The honour and comfort of God's tabernacle among them would be recompence enough. *If thou be wise, thou shalt be wise for thyself.* 2. They had their meat from heaven on free-cost, for themselves and their families, and their raiment waxed not old upon them; so that they neither needed wages nor had reason to expect any. *Freely you have received, freely give.* The obligations we lie under, both in duty and interest, to serve God, should be sufficient to quicken us to our work, though we had not a reward in prospect. But, 3. This blessing, in the name of the Lord, was wages enough for all their work. Those whom God employs he will bless, and those whom he blesses are blessed indeed. The blessing he commands is *life for evermore.*

CHAPTER 40

In this chapter, I. Orders are given for the setting up of the tabernacle and the fixing of all the appurtenances of it in their proper places (*v.* 1–8), and the consecrating of it (*v.* 9–11), and of the priests (*v.* 12–15). II. Care is taken to do all this, and as it was appointed to be done (*v.* 16–33). III. God takes possession of it by the cloud (*v.* 34, etc.).

Verses 1–15

The materials and furniture of the tabernacle had been viewed severally and approved, and now they must be put together. 1. God here directs Moses to set up the tabernacle and the utensils of it in their places. Though the work of the tabernacle was finished, and every thing ready for rearing, and the people, no doubt, were very desirous to see it up, yet Moses will not erect it till he has express orders for doing so. It is good to see God going before us in every step, Ps. 37:23. The time for doing this is fixed to *the first day of the first month* (*v.* 2), which wanted but fourteen days of a year since they came out of Egypt; and a good year's work there was done in it. Probably the work was made ready but just at the end of the year, so that the appointing of this day gave no delay, or next to none, to this good work. We must not put off any necessary duty under pretence of waiting for some remarkable day; the present season is the most convenient. But the tabernacle happening to be set up *on the first day of the first month* intimates that it is good to begin the year with some good work. Let him that is the first have the first; and let the things of his kingdom be first sought. In Hezekiah's time we find they began to sanctify the temple *on the first day of the first month,* 2 Chr. 29:17. The new moon (which by their computation was the first day of every month) was observed by them with some solemnity; and therefore this first new moon of the year was thus made remarkable. Note, When a new year begins, we should think of serving God more and better than we did the year before. Moses is particularly ordered to set up the tabernacle itself first, in which God would dwell and would be served (*v.* 2), then to put the ark in its place, and draw the veil before it (*v.* 3), then to fix the table, and the candlestick, and the altar of incense, without the veil (*v.* 4, 5), and to fix the hanging of the door before the door. Then in the court he must place the altar of burnt offering, and the laver (*v.* 6, 7); and, lastly, he must set up the curtains of the court, and a hanging for a court-gate. And all this would be easily done in one day, many hands no doubt being employed in it under the direction of Moses. 2. He directs Moses, when he had set up the tabernacle and all the furniture of it, to consecrate it and them, by anointing them with the oil which was prepared for the purpose, *ch.* 30:25, etc. It was there ordered that this should be done; here it was ordered that it should be done now, *v.* 9–11. Observe, Every thing was sanctified when it was put in its proper place, and not till then, for till then it was not fit for the use to which it was to be sanctified. As every thing is beautiful in its season, so is every thing in its place. 3. He directs him to consecrate Aaron and his sons. When the goods were brought into God's house, they were marked first, and then servants were hired to bear the vessels of the Lord; and those must be clean who were put into that office, *v.* 12–15. The law which was now ordered to be put in execution we had before, *ch.* 29. Thus in the visible church, which is God's tabernacle among men, it is requisite that there be ministers to keep the charge of the sanctuary, and that they receive the anointing.

Verses 16–33

When the tabernacle and the furniture of it were prepared, they did not put off the rearing of it till they came to Canaan, though they now hoped to be there very shortly; but, in obedience to the will of God, they set it up in the midst of their camp, while they were in the wilderness. Those that are unsettled in the world must not think that this will excuse them in their continued irreligion; as if it were enough to begin to serve God when they begin to be settled in the world. No; a tabernacle for God is a very needful and profitable companion even in a wilderness, especially considering that our carcases may fall in that wilderness, and we may be fixed in another world before we come to fix in this.

The rearing of the tabernacle was a good day's work; the consecrating of it, and of the priests, was attended to some days after. Here we have an account only of that new-year's-day's work. 1. Moses not only did all that God directed him to do, but in the order that God appointed; for God will be sought in the due order. 2. To each particular there is added an express reference to the divine appointment, which Moses governed himself by as carefully and conscientiously as the workmen did; and therefore, as before, so here it is repeated, *as the Lord commanded Moses,* seven times in less than fourteen verses. Moses himself, as great a man as he was, would not pretend to vary from the institution, neither to add to it nor diminish from it, in the least punctilio. Those that command others must remember that their Master also is in heaven, and they must do as they are commanded. 3. That which was to be veiled be veiled (*v.* 21), and that which was to be used he used immediately, for the instruction of the priests, that by seeing him do the several offices they might learn to do them the more dexterously. Though Moses was not properly a priest, yet he is numbered among the priests (Ps. 99:6), and the Jewish writers call him *the priest of the priests;* what he did he did by special warrant and direction from God, rather as a prophet, or law-giver, than as a priest. He set the wheels a going, and then left the work in the hands of the appointed ministry. (1.) When he had placed the table, he set the show-bread in order upon it (*v.* 23); for God will never have his table unfurnished. (2.) As soon as he had fixed the candlestick, *he lighted the lamps before the Lord, v.* 25. Even that dark dispensation would not admit of unlighted candles. (3.) The golden altar being put in its place, immediately he *burnt sweet incense thereon* (*v.* 27); for God's altar must be a smoking altar. (4.) The altar of the burnt-offering was no sooner set up in the court of the tabernacle than he had a *burnt-offering, and a meat-offering, ready to offer upon it, v.* 29. Some think, though this is mentioned here, it was not done till some time after; but it seems to me that he immediately began the ceremony of its consecration, though it was not completed for seven days. (5.) At the laver likewise, when he had fixed that, Moses himself washed his hands and feet. Thus, in all these instances, he not only showed the priests how to do their duty, but has taught us that God's gifts are intended for use, and not barely for show. Though the altars, and table, and candlestick, were fresh and new, he did not say it was a pity to sully them; no, he handselled them immediately. Talents were given to be occupied, not to be buried.

Verses 34–38

As when, in the creation, God had finished this earth, which he designed for man's habitation, he made man, and put him in possession of it, so when Moses had finished the tabernacle, which was designed for God's dwelling-place among men, God came and took possession of it. The *shechinah,* the divine eternal Word, though not yet made flesh, yet, as a prelude to that event, came and dwelt among them, Jn. 1:14. This was henceforward the *place of his throne,* and *the place of the soles of his feet* (Eze. 43:7); here he resided, here he ruled. By the visible tokens of God's coming among them to take possession of the tabernacle he testified both the return of his favour to them, which they had forfeited by the golden calf (*ch.* 33:7), and his gracious acceptance of all the expense they had been at, and all the care and pains they had taken about the tabernacle. Thus God owned them, showed himself well pleased with what they had done, and abundantly rewarded them. Note, God will dwell with those that prepare him a habitation. The broken and contrite heart, the clean and holy heart, that is furnished for his service, and devoted to his honour, shall be his *rest for ever;* here will Christ dwell by faith, Eph. 3:17. Where God has a throne and an altar in the soul, there is a living temple. And God will be sure to own and crown the operations of his own grace and the observance of his own appointments.

As God had manifested himself upon mount Sinai, so he did now in this newly-erected tabernacle. We read (*ch.* 24:16) that *the glory of the Lord abode upon mount Sinai,* which is said to be like *devouring fire* (*v.* 17), and that the *cloud covered it* on the outside, and the *glory of the Lord filled it* within, to which, probably there is an allusion in Zec. 2:5, where God promises to be a *wall of fire round about Jerusalem* (and the pillar of cloud was by night a pillar of fire) *and the glory in the midst of her.*

I. *The cloud covered the tent.* That same cloud which, as the chariot or pavilion of the *shechinah,* had come up before them out of Egypt and led them hither, now settled upon the tabernacle and hovered over it, even in the hottest and clearest day; for it was none of those clouds which the sun scatters. This cloud was intended to be, 1. A token of God's presence constantly visible day and night (*v.* 38) to all Israel, even to those that lay in the remotest corners of the camp, that they might never again make a question of it, *Is the Lord among us, or is he not?* That very cloud which had already been so pregnant with wonders in the Red Sea, and on mount Sinai, sufficient to prove God in it of a truth, was continually *in sight of all the house of Israel throughout all their journeys;* so that they were inexcusable if they believed not their own eyes. 2. A concealment of the tabernacle, and the glory of God in it. God did indeed dwell among them, but he dwelt in a cloud: *Verily thou art a God that hidest, thyself.* Blessed be God for the gospel of Christ, in which *we all with open face behold as in a glass,* not in a cloud, *the glory of the Lord.* 3. A protection of the tabernacle. They had sheltered it with one covering upon another, but, after all, the cloud that covered it was its best guard. Those that dwell in the house of the Lord are hidden there, and are safe under the divine protection, Ps. 27:4, 5. Yet this, which was then a peculiar favour to the tabernacle, is promised to every dwelling-place of mount Zion (Isa. 4:5); for *upon all the glory shall be a defence.* 4. A guide to the camp of Israel in their march through the wilderness, *v.* 36, 37. While the cloud continued on the tabernacle, they rested; when it removed, they removed and followed it, as being purely under divine direction. This is spoken of more fully, Num. 9:19; Ps. 78:14; 105:39. As before the tabernacle was set up the Israelites had the cloud for their guide, which appeared sometimes in one place and sometimes in another, but henceforward rested on the tabernacle and was to be found there only, so the church had divine revelation for its guide from the first, before the scriptures were written, but since the making up of that canon it rests in that as its tabernacle, and there only it is to be found, as in the creation the light which was made the first day, centered in the sun the fourth day. Blessed be God for the law and the testimony!

II. *The glory of the Lord filled the tabernacle, v.* 34, 35. The *shechinah* now made an awful and pompous entry into the tabernacle, through the outer part of which it passed into the most holy place, as the presence-chamber, and there seated itself between the cherubim. It was in light and fire, and (for aught we know) no otherwise, that the *shechinah* made itself visible; for *God is light; our God is a consuming fire.* With these the tabernacle was now filled, yet, as before the bush was not consumed, so now the curtains were not so much as singed by this fire; for to those that have received the anointing the terrible majesty of God is not destroying. Yet so dazzling was the light, and so dreadful was the fire, that Moses was *not able to enter into the tent of the congregation,* at the door of which he attended, till the splendour had a little abated, and the glory of the Lord retired within the veil, *v.* 35. This shows how terrible the glory and majesty of God are, and how unable the greatest and best of men are to stand before him. The divine light and fire, let forth in their full strength, will overpower the strongest heads and the purest hearts. But what Moses could not do, in that *he was weak through the flesh,* has been done by our Lord Jesus, whom God caused to draw near and approach, and who, as the forerunner, *has for us entered,* and has invited us to come boldly even to the mercy-seat. He was able to enter into the holy place not made with hands (Heb. 9:24); nay, he is himself the true tabernacle, filled with the glory of God (Jn. 1:14), even with the divine grace and truth prefigured by this fire and light. In him the shechinah took up its rest for ever, for in him *dwells all the fulness of the godhead bodily.* Blessed be God for Jesus Christ!

AN EXPOSITION, WITH PRACTICAL OBSERVATIONS, OF

THE THIRD BOOK OF MOSES, CALLED LEVITICUS

There is nothing historical in all this book of Leviticus except the account which it gives us of the consecration of the priesthood (*ch.* 8–9), of the punishment of Nadab and Abihu, by the hand of God, for offering strange fire (*ch.* 10), and of Shelomith's son, by the hand of the magistrate, for blasphemy (*ch.* 24). All the rest of the book is taken up with the laws, chiefly the ecclesiastical laws, which God gave to Israel by Moses, concerning their sacrifices and offerings, their meats and drinks, and divers washings, and the other peculiarities by which God set that people apart for himself, and distinguished them from other nations, all which were shadows of good things to come, which are realized and superseded by the gospel of Christ. We call the book *Leviticus,* from the Septuagint, because it contains the laws and ordinances of the *levitical priesthood* (as it is called, Heb. 7:11), and the ministrations of it. The Levites were principally charged with these institutions, both to do their part and to teach the people theirs. We read, in the close of the foregoing book, of the setting up of the tabernacle, which was to be the place of worship; and, as that was framed according to the pattern, so must the ordinances of worship be, which were there to be administered. In these the divine appointment was as particular as in the former, and must be as punctually observed. The remaining record of these abrogated laws is of use to us, for the strengthening of our faith in Jesus Christ, as *the Lamb slain from the foundation of the world,* and for the increase of our thankfulness to God, that by him we are freed from the yoke of the ceremonial law, and live in the times of reformation.

CHAPTER 1

This book begins with the laws concerning sacrifices, of which the most ancient were the burnt-offerings, about which God gives Moses instructions in this chapter. Orders are here given how that sort of sacrifice must be managed. I. If it was a bullock out of the herd (*v.* 3–9). II. If it was a sheep or goat, a lamb or kid, out of the flock (*v.* 10–13). III. If it was a turtle-dove or a young pigeon (*v.* 14–17). And whether the offering was more or less valuable in itself, if it was offered with an upright heart, according to these laws, it was accepted of God.

Verses 1–2

Observe here, 1. It is taken for granted that people would be inclined to bring offerings to the Lord. The very light of nature directs man, some way or other, to do honour to his Maker, and pay him homage as his Lord. Revealed religion supposes natural religion to be an ancient and early institution, since the fall had directed men to glorify God by sacrifice, which was an implicit acknowledgment of their having received all from God as creatures, and their having forfeited all to him as sinners. A conscience thoroughly convinced of dependence and guilt would be willing to come before God with *thousands of rams,* Mic. 6:6, 7. 2. Provision is made that men should not indulge their own fancies, nor become vain in their imaginations and inventions about their sacrifices, lest, while they pretended to honour God, they should really dishonour him, and do that which was unworthy of him. Every thing therefore is directed to be done with due decorum, by a certain rule, and so as that the sacrifices might be most significant both of the great sacrifice of atonement which Christ was to offer in the fulness of time and of the spiritual sacrifices of acknowledgment which believers should offer daily. 3. God gave those laws to Israel by Moses; nothing is more frequently repeated than this, *The Lord spoke unto Moses, saying, Speak unto the children of Israel.* God could have spoken it to the children of Israel himself, as he did the ten commandments; but he chose to deliver it to them by Moses, because they had desired he would no more speak to them himself, and he had designed that Moses should, above all the prophets, be a type of Christ, by whom God would in these last days speak to us, Heb. 1:2. By other prophets God sent messages to his people, but by Moses he gave them laws; and therefore he was fit to typify him to whom the Father has given all judgment. And, besides, the treasure of divine revelation was always to be put into earthen vessels, that our faith might be tried, and that the excellency of the power might be of God. 4. God spoke to him out of the tabernacle. As soon as ever the shechinah had taken possession of its new habitation, in token of the acceptance of what was done, God talked with Moses from the mercy-seat, while he attended without the veil, or rather at the door, hearing a voice only; and it is probable that he wrote what he heard at that time, to prevent any mistake, or a slip of memory, in the rehearsal of it. The tabernacle was set up to be a place of communion between God and Israel; there, where they performed their services to God, God revealed his will to them. Thus, by the word and by prayer, we now have fellowship with the Father, and with his Son Jesus Christ, Acts 6:4. When we speak to God we must desire to hear from him, and reckon it a great favour that he is pleased to speak to us. The Lord called to Moses, not to come near (under that dispensation, even Moses with terror from a burning mountain in thunder and lightning; but the remedial law of sacrifice was given more gently from a mercy-seat, because that was typical of the grace of the gospel, which is the ministration of life and peace.

Verses 3–9

If a man were rich and could afford it, it is supposed that he would bring his burnt-sacrifice, with which he designed to honour God, out of his herd of larger cattle. He that considers that God is the best that is will resolve to give him the best he has, else he gives him not the glory due unto his name. Now if a man determined to kill a bullock, not for an entertainment for his family and friends, but for a sacrifice to his God, these rules must be religiously observed: — 1. The beast to be offered must be a male, and without blemish, and the best he had in his pasture. Being designed purely for the honour of him that is infinitely perfect, it ought to be the most perfect in its kind. This signified the complete strength and purity that were in Christ the dying sacrifice, and the sincerity of heart and unblamableness of life that should be in Christians, who are presented to God as living sacrifices. But, literally, in Christ Jesus there is neither male nor female; nor is any natural blemish in the body a bar to our acceptance with God, but only the moral defects and deformities introduced by sin into the soul. 2. The owner must offer it voluntarily. What is done in religion, so as to please God, must be done by no other constraint than that of love. God accepts the willing people and the cheerful giver. Ainsworth and others read it, not as the principle, but as the end of offering: "Let him offer it *for his favourable acceptation before the Lord.* Let him propose this to himself as his end in bringing his sacrifice, and let his eye be fixed steadily upon that end — that he may be accepted of the Lord." Those only shall find acceptance who sincerely desire and design it in all their religious services, 2 Co. 5:9. 3. It must be offered at the door of the tabernacle, where the brazen altar of burnt-offerings stood, which sanctified the gift, and not elsewhere. He must offer it at the door, as one unworthy to enter, and acknowledging that there is no admission for a sinner into covenant and communion with God, but by sacrifice; but he must offer it at the tabernacle of the congregation, in token of his communion with the whole church of Israel even in this personal service. 4. The offerer must put his hand upon the head of his offering, *v.* 4. "He must put both his hands," say the Jewish doctors, "with all his might, between the horns of the beast," signifying thereby, (1.) The transfer of all his right to, and interest in, the beast, to God, actually, and by a manual delivery, resigning it to his service. (2.) An acknowledgment that he deserved to die, and would have been willing to die if God had required it, for the serving of his honour, and the obtaining of his favour. (3.) A dependence upon the sacrifice, as an instituted type of the great sacrifice on which the iniquity of us all was to be laid. The mystical signification of the sacrifices, and especially this rite, some think the apostle means by the doctrine of *laying on of hands* (Heb. 6:2), which typified evangelical faith. The offerer's putting his hand on the head of the offering was to signify his desire and hope that it might *be accepted from him to make atonement for him.* Though the burnt-offerings had not respect to any particular sin, as the sin-offering had, yet they were to make atonement for sin in general; and he that laid his hand on the head of a burnt-offering was to confess that *he had left undone what he ought to have done and had done that which he ought not to have done,* and to pray that, though he deserved to die himself, the death of his sacrifice might be accepted for the expiating of his guilt. 5. The sacrifice was to be killed by the priests of Levites, before the Lord, that is, in a devout religious manner, and with an eye to God and his honour. This signified that our Lord Jesus was to make his soul, or life, an offering for sin. Messiah the prince must be cut off as a sacrifice, *but not for himself,* Dan. 9:26. It signified also that in Christians, who are living sacrifices, the brutal part must be mortified or killed, the flesh crucified with its corrupt affections and lusts and all the appetites of the mere animal life. 6. The priests were to *sprinkle the blood upon the altar* (*v.* 5); for, the blood being the life, it was this that made atonement for the soul. This signified the direct and actual regard which our Lord Jesus had to the satisfaction of his Father's justice, and the securing of his injured honour, in the shedding of his blood; *he offered himself without spot to God.* It also signified the pacifying and purifying of our consciences by the sprinkling of the blood of Jesus Christ upon them by faith, 1 Pt. 1:2; Heb. 10:22. 7. The beast was to be flayed and decently cut up, and divided into its several joints or pieces, according to the art of the butcher; and then all the pieces, with the head and the fat (the legs and inwards being first washed), were to be burnt together upon the altar, *v.* 6–9. *"But to what purpose,"* would some say, *"was this waste?* Why should all this good meat, which might have been given to the poor, and have served their hungry families for food a great while, be burnt together to ashes?" So was the will of God; and it is not for us to object or to find fault with it. When it was burnt for the honour of God, in obedience to his command, and to signify spiritual blessings, it was really better bestowed, and better answered the end of its creation, than when it was used as food for man. We must never reckon that lost which is laid out for God. The burning of the sacrifice signified the sharp sufferings of Christ, and the devout affections with which, as a holy fire, Christians must offer up themselves their whole spirit, soul, and body, unto God. 8. This is said to be *an offering of a sweet savour,* or *savour of rest, unto the Lord.* The burning of flesh is unsavoury in itself; but this, as an act of obedience to a divine command, and a type of Christ, was well pleasing to God: he was reconciled to the offerer, and did himself take a complacency in that reconciliation. He rested, and was refreshed with these institutions of his grace, as, at first, with his works of creation (Ex. 31:17), rejoicing therein, Ps. 104:31. Christ's offering of himself to God is said to be of *a sweet-smelling savour* (Eph. 5:2), and the spiritual sacrifices of Christians are said to be *acceptable to God, through Christ,* 1 Pt. 2:5.

Verses 10–17

Here we have the laws concerning the burnt-offerings, which were of the flock or of the fowls. Those of the middle rank, that could not well afford to offer a bullock, would bring a sheep or a goat; and those that were not able to do that should be accepted of God if they brought a turtle-dove or a pigeon. For God, in his law and in his gospel, as well as in his providence, considers the poor. It is observable that those creatures were chosen for sacrifice which were most mild and gentle, harmless and inoffensive, to typify the innocence and meekness that were in Christ, and to teach the innocence and meekness that should be in Christians. Directions are here given, 1. Concerning the burnt-offerings of the flock, *v.* 10. The method of managing these is much the same with that of the bullocks; only it is ordered here that the sacrifice should be killed *on the side of the altar northward,* which, though mentioned here only, was probably to be observed concerning the former, and other sacrifices. Perhaps on that side of the altar there was the largest vacant space, and room for the priests to turn them in. It was of old observed that *fair weather comes out of the north,* and that *the north wind drives away rain;* and by these sacrifices the storms of God's wrath are scattered, and the light of God's countenance is obtained, which is more pleasant than the brightest fairest weather. 2. Concerning those of the fowls. They must be either turtle-doves (and, if so, "they must be *old* turtles," say the Jews), or *pigeons,* and, if so, they must be *young* pigeons. What was most acceptable at men's tables must be brought to God's altar. In the offering of these fowls, (1.) The head must be wrung off, "quite off," say some; others think only pinched, so as to kill the bird, and yet leave the head hanging to the body. But it seems more likely that it was to be quite separated, for it was to be burnt first. (2.) The blood was to be *wrung out at the side of the altar.* (3.) The garbages with the feathers were to be thrown by upon the dunghill. (4.) The body was to be opened, sprinkled with salt, and then burnt upon the altar. "This sacrifice of birds," the Jews say, "was one of the most difficult services the priests had to do," to teach those that minister in holy things to be as solicitous for the salvation of the poor as for that of the rich, and that the services of the poor are as acceptable to God, if they come from an upright heart, as the services of the rich, for he accepts *according to what a man hath,* and not *according to what he hath not,* 2 Co. 8:12. The poor man's turtle-doves, or young pigeons, are here said to be *an offering of a sweet-smelling savour,* as much as that of an ox or bullock that hath horns or hoofs. Yet, after all, to *love God with all our heart, and to love our neighbour as ourselves, is better than all burnt-offerings and sacrifices,* Mk. 12:33.

CHAPTER 2

In this chapter we have the law concerning the meat-offering. I. The matter of it; whether of raw flour with oil and incense (*v.* 1), or baked in the oven (*v.* 4), or upon a plate (*v.* 5, 6), or in a frying pan (*v.* 7). II. The management of it, of the flour (*v.* 2, 3), of the cakes (*v.* 8–10). III. Some particular rules concerning it, That leaven and honey must never be admitted (*v.* 11, 12), and salt never omitted in the meat-offering (*v.* 13). IV. The law concerning the offering of firstfruits in the ear (*v.* 14, etc.).

Verses 1–10

There were some meat-offerings that were only appendices to the burnt-offerings, as that which was offered with the daily sacrifice (Ex. 29:38, 39) and with the peace-offerings; these had drink-offerings joined with them (see Num. 15:4, 7, 9, 10), and in these the quantity was appointed. But the law of this chapter concerns those meat-offerings that were offered by themselves, whenever a man saw cause thus to express his devotion. The first offering we read of in scripture was of this kind (Gen. 4:3): *Cain brought of the fruit of the ground an offering.*

I. This sort of offering was appointed, 1. In condescension to the poor, and their ability, that those who themselves lived only upon bread and cakes might offer an acceptable offering to God out of that which was their own coarse and homely fare, and by making for God's altar, as the widow of Sarepta for his prophet, a little cake first, might procure such a blessing upon the handful of meal in the barrel, and the oil in the cruse, as that it should not fail. 2. As a proper acknowledgment of the mercy of God to them in their food. This was like a quitrent, by which they testified their dependence upon God, their thankfulness to him, and their expectations from him as their owner and bountiful benefactor, who giveth to all life, and breath, and food convenient. Thus must they honour the Lord with their substance, and, in token of their eating and drinking to his glory, must consecrate some of their meat and drink to his immediate service. Those that now, with a grateful charitable heart, deal out their bread to the hungry, and provide for the necessities of those that are destitute of daily food, and when they eat the fat and drink the sweet themselves send portions to those for whom nothing is prepared, offer unto God an acceptable meat-offering. The prophet laments it as one of the direful effects of famine that thereby the *meat-offering and drink-offering were cut off from the house of the Lord* (Joel 1:9), and reckoned it the greatest blessing of plenty that it would be the revival of them, Joel 2:14.

II. The laws of the meat-offerings were these: — 1. The ingredients must always be fine flour and oil, two staple commodities of the land of Canaan, Deu. 8:8. Oil was to them then in their food what butter is now to us. If it was undressed, the oil must be poured upon the flour (*v.* 1); if cooked, it must be mingled with the flour, *v.* 4, etc. 2. If it was flour unbaked, besides the oil it must have frankincense put upon it, which was to be burnt with it (*v.* 1, 2), for the perfuming of the altar; in allusion to this, gospel ministers are said to be *a sweet savour unto God,* 2 Co. 2:15. 3. If it was prepared, this might be done in various ways; the offerer might bake it, or fry it, or mix the flour and oil upon a plate, for the doing of which conveniences were provided about the tabernacle. The law was very exact even about those offerings that were least costly, to intimate the cognizance God takes of the religious services performed with a devout mind, even by the poor of his people. 4. It was to be presented by the offerer to the priest, which is called *bringing it to the Lord* (*v.* 8), for the priests were God's receivers, and were ordained to offer gifts. 5. Part of it was to be burnt upon the altar, for a memorial, that is, in token of their mindfulness of God's bounty to them, in giving them all things richly to enjoy. It was *an offering made by fire, v.* 2, 9. The consuming of it by fire might remind them that they deserved to have all the fruits of the earth thus burnt up, and that it was of the Lord's mercies that they were not. They might also learn that as *meats are for the belly, and the belly for meats,* so *God shall destroy both it and them* (1 Co. 6:13), and that *man lives not by bread alone.* This offering made by fire is here said to be *of a sweet savour unto the Lord;* and so are our spiritual offerings, which are made by the fire of holy love, particularly that of almsgiving, which is said to be *an odour of a sweet smell, a sacrifice acceptable, well pleasing to God* (Phil. 4:18), and *with such sacrifices God is well pleased,* Heb. 13:16. 6. The remainder of the meat-offering was to be given to the priests, *v.* 3, 10. *It is a thing most holy,* not to be eaten by the offerers, as the peace-offerings (which, though holy, were not most holy), but by the priests only, and their families. Thus God provided that those who served at the altar should live upon the altar, and live comfortably.

Verses 11–16

Here, I. Leaven and honey are forbidden to be put in any of their meat-offerings: *No leaven, nor any honey, in any offering made by fire, v.* 11. 1. The leaven was forbidden in remembrance of the unleavened bread they ate when they came out of Egypt. So much despatch was required in the offerings they made that it was not convenient they should stay for the leavening of them. The New Testament comparing pride and hypocrisy to leaven because they swell like leaven, comparing also malice and wickedness to leaven because they sour like leaven, we are to understand and improve this as a caution to take heed of those sins which will certainly spoil the acceptableness of our spiritual sacrifices. Pure hands must be lifted up without wrath, and all our gospel feasts kept with the unleavened bread of sincerity and truth. 2. Honey was forbidden, though Canaan flowed with it, because *to eat much honey is not good* (Prov. 25:16, 27); it turns to choler and bitterness in the stomach, though luscious to the taste. Some think the chief reason why those two things, leaven and honey, were forbidden, was because the Gentiles used them very much in their sacrifices, and God's people must not learn or use the way of the heathen, but his services must be the reverse of their idolatrous services; see Deu. 12:30, 31. Some make this application of this double prohibition: leaven signifies grief and sadness of spirit (Ps. 73:21), *My heart was leavened;* honey signifies sensual pleasure and mirth. In our service of God both these must be avoided, and a mean observed between those extremes; for the sorrow of the world worketh death, and a love to the delights of sense is a great enemy to holy love.

II. Salt is required in all their offerings, *v.* 13. The altar was the table of the Lord; and therefore, salt being always set on our tables, God would have it always used at his. It is called *the salt of the covenant,* because, as men confirmed their covenants with each other by eating and drinking together, at all which collations salt was used, so God, by accepting his people's gifts and feasting them upon his sacrifices, supping with them and they with him (Rev. 3:20), did confirm his covenant with them. Among the ancients salt was a symbol of friendship. The salt for the sacrifice was not brought by the offerers, but was provided at the public charge, as the wood was, Ezra 7:20–22. And there was a chamber in the court of the temple called *the chamber of salt,* in which they laid it up. *Can that which is unsavoury be eaten without salt?* God would hereby intimate to them that their sacrifices in themselves were unsavoury. The saints, who are living sacrifices to God, must have salt in themselves, for *every sacrifice must be salted with salt* (Mk. 9:49, 50), and our speech must be *always with grace* (Col. 4:6), so must all our religious performances be seasoned with that salt. Christianity is the salt of the earth.

III. Directions are given about the first-fruits. 1. The oblation of their first-fruits at harvest, of which we read, Deu. 26:2. These were offered to the Lord, not to be burnt upon the altar, but to be given to the priests as perquisites of their office, *v.* 12. And *you shall offer them* (that is, leaven and honey) in the oblation of the first-fruits, though they were forbidden in other meat-offerings; for they were proper enough to be eaten by the priests, though not to be burnt upon the altar. The loaves of the first-fruits are particularly ordered to be *baked with leaven,* Lev. 23:17. And we read of the first-fruits of honey brought to the house of God, 2 Chr. 31:5. 2. A meat-offering of their first-fruits. The former was required by the law; this was a free-will offering, *v.* 14–16. If a man, with a thankful sense of God's goodness to him in giving him hopes of a plentiful crop, was disposed to bring an offering in kind immediately out of his field, and present it to God, owning thereby his dependence upon God and obligations to him, (1.) Let him be sure to bring the first ripe and full ears, not such as were small and half-withered. Whatever was brought for an offering to God must be the best in its kind, though it were but green ears of corn. We mock God, and deceive ourselves, if we think to put him off with a corrupt thing while we have in our flock a male, Mal. 1:14. (2.) These green ears must be dried by the fire, that the corn, such as it was, might be beaten out of them. That is not expected from green ears which one may justly look for from those that have been left to grow fully ripe. If those that are young do God's work as well as they can, they shall be accepted, though they cannot do it so well as those that are aged and experienced. God makes the best of green ears of corn, and so must we. (3.) Oil and frankincense must be put upon it. Thus (as some allude to this) wisdom and humility must soften and sweeten the spirits and services of young people, and then their green ears of corn shall be acceptable. God takes a particular delight in the first ripe fruits of the Spirit and the expressions of early piety and devotion. Those that can but think and speak as children, yet, if they think and speak well, God will be well pleased with their buds and blossoms, and will never forget the kindness of their youth. (4.) It must be used as other meat-offerings, *v.* 16, compare *v.* 9. He shall *offer all the frankincense; it is an offering made by fire.* The fire and the frankincense seem to have had a special significancy. [1.] The fire denotes the fervency of spirit which ought to be in all our religious services. In every good thing we must be zealously affected. Holy love to God is the fire by which all our offerings must be made; else they are not of a sweet savour to God. [2.] The frankincense denotes the mediation and intercession of Christ, by which all our services are perfumed and recommended to God's gracious acceptance. Blessed be God that we have the substance of which all these observances were but shadows, the fruit that was hid under these leaves.

CHAPTER 3

In this chapter we have the law concerning the peace-offerings, whether they were, I. Of the heard, a bullock or a heifer (*v.* 1–5). Or, II. Of the flock, either a lamb (*v.* 6–11) or a goat (*v.* 12–17). The ordinances concerning each of these are much the same, yet they are repeated, to show the care we ought to take that all our services be done according to the appointment and the pleasure God takes in the services that are so performed. It is likewise to intimate what need we have of precept upon precept, and line upon line.

Verses 1–5

The burnt-offerings had regard to God as in himself the best of beings, most perfect and excellent; they were purely expressive of adoration, and therefore were wholly burnt. But the peace-offerings had regard to God as a benefactor to his creatures, and the giver of all good things to us; and therefore these were divided between the altar, the priest, and the owner. Peace signifies, 1. Reconciliation, concord, and communion. And so these were called *peace-offerings,* because in them God and his people did, as it were, feast together, in token of friendship. The priest, who was ordained for men in things pertaining to God, gave part of this peace-offering to God (that part which he required, and it was fit he should be first served), burning it upon God's altar; part he gave to the offerer, to be eaten by him with his family and friends; and part he took to himself, as the days-man that laid his hand upon them both. They could not thus eat together unless they were agreed; so that it was a symbol of friendship and fellowship between God and man, and a confirmation of the covenant of peace. 2. It signifies prosperity and all happiness: *Peace be to you* was as much as, *All good* be to you; and so the peace-offerings were offered either, (1.) By way of supplication or request for some good that was wanted and desired. If a man was in the pursuit or expectation of any mercy, he would back his prayer for it with a peace-offering, and probably put up the prayer when he laid his hand upon the head of his offering. Christ is our peace, our peace-offering; for through him alone it is that we can expect to obtain mercy, and an answer of peace to our prayers; and in him an upright prayer shall be acceptable and successful, though we bring not a peace-offering. The less costly our devotions are the more lively and serious they should be. Or, (2.) By way of thanksgiving for some particular mercy received. It is called *a peace-offering of thanksgiving,* for so it was sometimes; as in other cases *a vow, ch.* 7:15, 16. And some make the original word to signify *retribution.* When they had received any special mercy, and were enquiring what they should render, this they were directed to render to the God of their mercies as a grateful acknowledgment for the benefit done to them, Ps. 116:12. And we must offer to God the sacrifice of praise continually, by Christ our peace; and then this shall please the Lord better than an ox or bullock. Observe,

I. As to the matter of the peace-offering, suppose it was of the herd, it must be *without blemish;* and, if it was so, it was indifferent whether it was male or female, *v.* 1. In our spiritual offerings, it is not the sex, but the heart, that God looks at, Gal. 3:28.

II. As to the management of it. 1. The offerer was, by a solemn manumission, to transfer his interest in it to God (*v.* 2), and, with *his hand on the head* of the sacrifice, to acknowledge the particular mercies for which he designed this a thank-offering, or, if it was a vow, to make his prayer. 2. It must be killed; and, although this might be done in any part of the court, yet it is said to be *at the door of the tabernacle,* because the mercies received or expected were acknowledged to come from God, and the prayers or praises were directed to him, and both, as it were, through that door. Our Lord Jesus has said, *I am the door,* for he is indeed the door of the tabernacle. 3. The priest must *sprinkle the blood upon the altar,* for it was the blood that made atonement for the soul; and, though this was not a sin-offering, yet we must be taught that in all our offerings we must have an eye to Christ as the propitiation for sin, as those who know that the best of their services cannot be accepted unless through him their sins be pardoned. Penitent confessions must always go along with our thankful acknowledgments; and, whatever mercy we pray for, in order to it we must pray for the removal of guilt, as that which keeps good things from us. First *take away all iniquity,* and then *receive us graciously,* or *give good,* Hos. 14:2. 4. All the fat of the inwards, that which we call the tallow and suet, with the caul that encloses it and the kidneys in the midst of it, were to be taken away, and burnt upon the altar, as an offering *made by fire, v.* 3–5. And this was all that was sacrificed to the Lord out of the peace-offering; how the rest was to be disposed of we shall find, *ch.* 7:11, etc. It is ordered to be burnt upon the burnt-sacrifice, that is, the daily burnt-offering, the lamb which was offered every morning before any other sacrifice was offered; so that the fat of the peace-offerings was an addition to that, and a continuation of it. The great sacrifice of peace, that of the Lamb of God which takes away the sins of the world, prepares the altar for our sacrifices of praise, which are not accepted till we are reconciled. Now the burning of this fat is supposed to signify, (1.) The offering up of our good affections to God in all our prayers and praises. God must have the inwards; for we must pour out our souls, and lift up our hearts, in prayer, and must bless his name with all that is within us. It is required that we be inward with God in every thing wherein we have to do with him. The fat denotes the best and choicest, which must always be devoted to God, who has made for us a feast of fat things. (2.) The mortifying of our corrupt affections and lusts, and the burning up of them by the fire of divine grace, Col. 3:5. Then we are truly thankful for former mercies, and prepared to receive further mercy, when we part with our sins, and have our minds cleared from all sensuality by the *spirit of judgment* and the *spirit of burning,* Isa. 4:4.

Verses 6–17

Directions are here given concerning the peace-offering, if it was a sheep or a goat. Turtle-doves or young pigeons, which might be brought for whole burnt offerings, were not allowed for peace-offerings, because they have no fat considerable enough to be burnt upon the altar; and they would be next to nothing if they were to be divided according to the law of the peace-offerings. The laws concerning a lamb or goat offered for a peace offering are much the same with those concerning a bullock, and little now occurs here; but, 1. The rump of the mutton was to be burnt with the fat of the inwards upon the altar, the *whole rump* (*v.* 9), because in those countries it was very fat and large. Some observe from this that, be a thing ever so contemptible, God can make it honourable, by applying it to his service. Thus God is said to give more *abundant honour to that part which lacked,* 1 Co. 12:23, 24. 2. That which was burnt upon the altar is called the *food of the offering, v.* 11, 16. It fed the holy fire; it was acceptable to God as our food is to us; and since in the tabernacle God did, as it were, keep house among them, by the offerings on the altar he kept a good table, as Solomon in his court, 1 Ki. 4:22, etc. 3. Here is a general rule laid down, that *all the fat is the Lord's* (*v.* 16), and a law made thereupon, that they *should eat neither fat nor blood,* no, not in their private houses, *v.* 17. (1.) As for the *fat,* it is not meant of that which is interlarded with the meat (that they might eat, Neb. 8:10), but the fat of the inwards, the suet, which was always God's part out of the sacrificed beasts; and therefore they must not eat of it, no, not out of the beasts that they killed for their common use. Thus would God preserve the honour of that which was sacred to himself. They must not only not feed upon that fat which was to be the food of the altar, but not upon any like it, lest the *table of the Lord* (as the altar is called), if something were not reserved peculiar to it, should become contemptible, and *the fruit thereof, even its meat, contemptible,* Mal. 1:7, 12. (2.) The blood was universally forbidden likewise, for the same reason that the fat was, because it was God's part of every sacrifice. The heathen drank the blood of their sacrifices; hence we read of their *drink-offerings of blood,* Ps. 16:4. But God would not permit the blood, that made atonement, to be used as a common thing (Heb. 10:29), nor will he allow us, though we have the comfort of the atonement made, to assume to ourselves any share in the honour of making it. He that glories, let him glory in the Lord, and to his praise let all the blood be poured out.

CHAPTER 4

This chapter is concerning the sin-offering, which was properly intended to make atonement for a sin committed through ignorance, I. By the priest himself (*v.* 1–12). Or, II. By the whole congregation (*v.* 13–21). Or, III. By a ruler (*v.* 22–26). Or, IV. By a private person (*v.* 27, etc.).

Verses 1–12

The laws contained in the first three chapters seem to have been delivered to Moses at one time. Here begin the statutes of another session, another day. From the throne of glory between the cherubim God delivered these orders. And he enters now upon a subject more strictly new than those before. Burnt-offerings, meat-offerings, and peace-offerings, it should seem, had been offered before the giving of the law upon mount Sinai; those sacrifices the patriarchs had not been altogether unacquainted with (Gen. 8:20; Ex. 20:24), and in them they had respect to sin, to make atonement for it, Job 1:5. But the law being now added *because of transgressions* (Gal. 3:19), and having entered, that eventually *the offence might abound* (Rom. 5:20), they were put into a way of making atonement for sin more particularly by sacrifice, which was (more than any of the ceremonial institutions) *a shadow of good things to come,* but the substance is Christ, and that one offering of himself by which he put away sin and *perfected for ever those who are sanctified.*

I. The general case supposed we have, *v.* 2. Here observe, 1. Concerning sin in general, that it is described to be against *any of the commandments of the Lord;* for *sin is the transgression of the law,* the divine law. The wits or wills of men, their inventions or their injunctions, cannot make that to be sin which the law of God has not made to be so. It is said likewise, *if a soul sin,* for it is not sin if it be not some way or other the soul's act; hence it is called the *sin of the soul* (Mic. 6:7), and it is the soul that is injured by it, Prov. 8:36. 2. Concerning the sins for which those offerings were appointed. (1.) They are supposed to be overt acts; for, had they been required to bring a sacrifice for every sinful thought or word, the task had been endless. Atonement was made for those in the gross, on the day of expiation, once a year; but these are said to be done against the commandments. (2.) They are supposed to be sins of commission, things which ought not to be done. Omissions are sins, and must come into judgment; but what had been omitted at one time might be done at another, and so to obey was better than sacrifice: but a commission was past recall. (3.) They are supposed to be sins committed through ignorance. If they were done presumptuously, and with an avowed contempt of the law and the Law-maker, the offender was to be cut off, and there remained *no sacrifice for the sin,* Heb. 10:26, 27; Num. 15:30. But if the offender were either ignorant of the law, as in divers instances we may suppose many were (so numerous and various were the prohibitions), or were surprised into the sin unawares, the circumstances being such as made it evident that his resolution against the sin was sincere, but that he was overtaken in it, as the expression is (Gal. 6:1), in this case relief was provided by the remedial law of the sin-offering. And the Jews say, "Those crimes only were to be expiated by sacrifice, if committed ignorantly, for which the criminal was to have been cut off if they had been committed presumptuously."

II. The law begins with the case of the anointed priest, that is, the high priest, provided he should sin through ignorance; for *the law made men priests who had infirmity.* Though his ignorance was of all others least excusable, yet he was allowed to bring his offering. His office did not so far excuse his offence as that it should be forgiven him without a sacrifice; yet it did not so far aggravate it but that it should be forgiven him when he did bring his sacrifice. If he sin *according to the sin of the people* (so the case is put, *v.* 3), which supposes him in this matter to stand upon the level with other Israelites, and to have no benefit of his clergy at all. Now the law concerning the sin-offering for the high priest is, 1. That he must bring a bullock without blemish for a sin-offering (*v.* 3), as valuable an offering as that for the whole congregation (*v.* 14); whereas for any other ruler, or a common person, *a kid of the goats* should serve, *v.* 23, 28. This intimated the greatness of the guilt connected with the sin of a high priest. The eminency of his station, and his relation both to God and to the people, greatly aggravated his offences; see Rom. 2:21. 2. The hand of the offerer must be laid upon the head of the offering (*v.* 4), with a solemn penitent confession of the sin he had committed, putting it upon the head of the sin-offering, *ch.* 16:21. No remission without confession, Ps. 32:5; Prov. 28:13. It signified also a confidence in this instituted way of expiating guilt, as a figure of something better yet to come, which they could not stedfastly discern. He that laid his hand on the head of the beast thereby owned that he deserved to die himself, and that it was God's great mercy that he would please to accept the offering of this beast to die for him. The Jewish writers themselves say that neither the sin-offering nor the trespass-offering made atonement, except for those that repented and believed in their atonement. 3. The bullock must be killed, and a great deal of solemnity there must be in disposing of the blood; for it was *the blood that made atonement,* and *without shedding of blood* there was *no remission, v.* 5–7. Some of the blood of the high-priest's sin-offering was to be *sprinkled seven times before the veil,* with an eye towards the mercy-seat, though it was veiled: some of it was to be put upon the horns of the golden altar, because at that altar the priest himself ministered; and thus was signified the putting away of that pollution which from his sins did cleave to his services. It likewise serves to illustrate the influence which Christ's satisfaction has upon the prevalency of his intercession. The blood of his sacrifice is put upon the altar of his incense and sprinkled before the Lord. When this was done the remainder of the blood was poured at the foot of the brazen altar. By this rite, the sinner acknowledged that he deserved to have his blood thus poured out like water. It likewise signified the pouring out of the soul before God in true repentance, and typified our Saviour's *pouring out his soul unto death.* 4. The fat of the inwards was to be burnt upon the altar of burnt-offering, *v.* 8–10. By this the intention of the offering and of the atonement made by it was directed to the glory of God, who, having been dishonoured by the sin, was thus honoured by the sacrifice. It signified the sharp sufferings of our Lord Jesus, when he was made sin (that is, a sin-offering) for us, especially the sorrows of his soul and his inward agonies. It likewise teaches us, in conformity to the death of Christ, to crucify the flesh. 5. The head and body of the beast, skin and all, were to be carried *without the camp,* to a certain place appointed for that purpose, and there burnt to ashes, *v.* 11, 12. This was very significant, (1.) Of the duty of repentance, which is the putting away of sin as a detestable thing, which our soul hates. True penitents say to their idols, "Get you hence; what have we to do any more with idols?" The sin-offering is called *sin.* What they did to that we must do to our sins; the body of sin must be destroyed, Rom. 6:6. (2.) Of the privilege of remission. When God pardons sin he quite abolishes it, casts it behind his back. *The iniquity of Judah shall be sought for and not found.* The apostle takes particular notice of this ceremony, and applies it to Christ (Heb. 13:11–13), who suffered without the gate, in the place of a skull, where the ashes of dead men, as those of the altar, were poured out.

Verses 13–21

This is the law for expiating the guilt of a national sin, by a sin offering. If the leaders of the people, through mistake concerning the law, caused them to err, when the mistake was discovered an offering must be brought, that wrath might not come upon the whole congregation. Observe, 1. It is possible that the church may err, and that her guides may mislead her. It is here supposed that the whole congregation may sin, and sin through ignorance. God will always have a church on earth; but he never said it should be infallible, or perfectly pure from corruption on this side heaven. 2. When a sacrifice was to be offered for the whole congregation, the elders were to lay their hands upon the head of it (three of them at least), as representatives of the people and agents for them. The sin we suppose to have been some common custom, taken up and used by the generality of the people, upon presumption of its being lawful, which afterwards, upon search, appeared to be otherwise. In this case the commonness of the usage received perhaps by tradition from their fathers, and the vulgar opinion of its being lawful, would not so far excuse them from sin but that they must bring a sacrifice to make atonement for it. There are many bad customs and forms of speech which are thought to have no harm in them, and yet may bring guilt and wrath upon a land, which therefore it concerns the elders both to reform and to intercede with God for the pardon of, Joel 2:16. 3. The blood of this sin-offering, as of the former, was to be *sprinkled seven times before the Lord, v.* 17. It was not to be poured out there, but sprinkled only; for the cleansing virtue of the blood of Christ was then and still is sufficiently signified and represented by sprinkling, Isa. 52:15. It was to be sprinkled seven times. Seven is a number of perfection, because when God had made the world in six days he rested the seventh; so this signified the perfect satisfaction Christ made, and the complete cleansing of the souls of the faithful by it; see Heb. 10:14. The blood was likewise to be put upon the horns of the incense-altar, to which there seems to be an allusion in Jer. 17:1, where the sin of Judah is said to be *graven upon the horns of their altars.* If they did not forsake their sins, the putting of the blood of their sin-offerings upon the horns of their altars, instead of taking away their guilt, did but bind it on the faster, perpetuated the remembrance of it, and remained a witness against them. It is likewise alluded to in Rev. 9:13, where a voice is heard *from the four horns of the golden altar;* that is, an answer of peace is given to the prayers of the saints, which are acceptable and prevalent only by virtue of the blood of the sin-offering put upon the horns of that altar; compare Rev. 8:3. 4. When the offering is completed, it is said, *atonement is made, and the sin shall be forgiven, v.* 20. The promise of remission is founded upon the atonement. It is spoken here of the forgiveness of the sin of the whole congregation, that is, the turning away of those national judgments which the sin deserved. Note, The saving of churches and kingdoms from ruin is owing to the satisfaction and mediation of Christ.

Verses 22–26

Observe here, 1. That God takes notice of and is displeased with the sins of rulers. Those who have power to call others to account are themselves accountable to the ruler of rulers; for, as high as they are, there is a higher than they. This is intimated in that the commandment transgressed is here said to be the *commandment of the Lord his God, v.* 22. He is a prince to others, but let him know the Lord is a God to him. 2. The sin of the ruler which he committed through ignorance is supposed afterwards to come to his knowledge (*v.* 23), which must be either by the check of his own conscience or by the reproof of his friends, both which we should all, even the best and greatest, not only submit to, but be thankful for. What we have done amiss we should be very desirous to come to the knowledge of. *That which I see not, teach thou me, and show me wherein I have erred,* are prayers we should put up to God every day, that though through ignorance we fall into sin we may not through ignorance lie still in it. 3. The sin-offering for a ruler was to be *a kid of the goats,* not a bullock, as for the priest and the whole congregation; nor was the blood of his sin-offering to be brought into the tabernacle, as of the other two, but it was all bestowed upon the brazen altar (*v.* 25); nor was the flesh of it to be burnt, as that of the other two, without the camp, which intimated that the sin of a ruler, though worse than that of a common person, yet was not so heinous, nor of such pernicious consequence, as the sin of the high priest, or of the whole congregation. A kid of the goats was sufficient to be offered for a ruler, but a bullock for a tribe, to intimate that the ruler, though *major singulis — greater than each,* was *minor universis — less than the whole.* It is bad when great men give bad examples, but worse when all men follow them. 4. It is promised that the atonement shall be accepted and the sin forgiven (*v.* 26), that is, if he repent and reform; for otherwise God swore concerning Eli, a judge in Israel, that the iniquity of his house should not be purged with sacrifice nor offering for ever, 1 Sa. 3:14.

Verses 27–35

I. Here is the law of the sin-offering for a common person, which differs from that for a ruler only in this, that a private person might bring either a kid or a lamb, a ruler only a kid; and that for a ruler must be a male, for the other a female: in all the circumstances of the management of the offering they agreed. Observe, 1. The case supposed: *If any one of the common people sin through ignorance, v.* 27. The prophet supposes that they were not so likely as the great men to *know the way of the Lord, and the judgment of their God* (Jer. 5:4), and yet, if they sin through ignorance, they must bring a sin-offering. Note, Even sins of ignorance need to be atoned for by sacrifice. To be able to plead, when we are charged with sin, that we did it ignorantly, and through the surprise of temptation, will not bring us off if we be not interested in that great plea, *Christ hath died,* and entitled to the benefit of that. We have all need to pray with David (and he was a ruler) to be cleansed from *secret faults,* the errors which we ourselves do not understand or are not aware of, Ps. 19:12. 2. That the sins of ignorance committed by a single person, a common obscure person, did require a sacrifice; for, as the greatest are not above the censure, so the meanest are not below the cognizance of the divine justice. None of the common people, if offenders, were overlooked in a crowd. 3. That a sin-offering was not only admitted, but accepted, even from one of the common people, and an atonement made by it, *v.* 31, 35. Here rich and poor, prince and peasant, meet together; they are both alike welcome to Christ, and to an interest in his sacrifice, upon the same terms. See Job 34:19.

II. From all these laws concerning the sin-offerings we may learn, 1. To hate sin, and to watch against it. That is certainly a very bad thing to make atonement for which so many innocent and useful creatures must be slain and mangled thus. 2. To value Christ, the great and true sin-offering, whose blood cleanses from all sin, which it was not possible that the *blood of bulls and of goats should take away. Now, if any man sin,* Christ is *the propitiation* (1 Jn. 2:1, 2), not for Jews only, but for Gentiles. And perhaps there was some allusion to this law concerning sacrifices for sins of ignorance in that prayer of Christ's, just when he was offering up himself a sacrifice, *Father, forgive them, for they know not what they do.*

CHAPTER 5

This chapter, and part of the next, concern the trespass-offering. The difference between this and the sin-offering lay not so much in the sacrifices themselves, and the management of them, as in the occasions of the offering of them. They were both intended to make atonement for sin; but the former was more general, this applied to some particular instances. Observe what is here said, I. Concerning the trespass. If a man sin, 1. In concealing his knowledge, when he is adjured (*v.* 1). 2. In touching an unclean thing (*v.* 2, 3). 3. In swearing (*v.* 4). 4. In embezzling the holy things (*v.* 14–16). 5. In any sin of infirmity (*v.* 17–19). Some other cases there are, in which these offerings were to be offered (*ch.* 6:2–4; 14:12; 19:21; Num. 6:12). II. Concerning the trespass-offerings, 1. Of the flock (*v.* 5, 6). 2. Of fowls (*v.* 7–10). 3. Of flour (*v.* 11–13; but chiefly a ram without blemish (*v.* 15, etc.).

Verses 1–6

I. The offences here supposed are, 1. A man's concealing the truth when he was sworn as a witness to speak the truth, the whole truth, and nothing but the truth. Judges among the Jews had power to adjure not only the witnesses, as with us, but the person suspected (contrary to a rule of our law, that no man is bound to accuse himself), as appears by the high priest adjuring our Saviour, who thereupon answered, though before he stood silent, Mt. 26:63, 64. Now (*v.* 1), *If a soul sin* (that is, a person, for the soul is the man), if he *hear the voice of swearing* (that is, if he be adjured to testify what he knows, by an *oath* of the Lord upon him, 1 Ki. 8:31), if in such a case, for fear of offending one that either has been his friend or may be his enemy, he refuses to give evidence, or gives it but in part, *he shall bear his iniquity.* And that is a heavy burden, which, if some course be not taken to get it removed, will sink a man to the lowest hell. He that *heareth cursing* (that is, that is thus adjured) and betrayeth it not (that is, stifles his evidence, and does not utter it), he is a partner with the sinner, and *hateth his own soul;* see Prov. 29:24. Let all that are called out at any time to bear testimony think of this law, and be free and open in their evidence, and take heed of prevaricating. An oath of the Lord is a sacred thing, and not to be dallied with. 2. A man's touching any thing that was ceremonially unclean, *v.* 2, 3. If a man, polluted by such touch, came into the sanctuary inconsiderately, or if he neglected to wash himself according to the law, then he was to look upon himself as under guilt, and must bring his offering. Though his touching the unclean thing contracted only a ceremonial defilement, yet his neglect to wash himself according to the law was such an instance either of carelessness or contempt as contracted a moral guilt. If at first it be *hidden from him,* yet when he knows it he *shall be guilty.* Note, As soon as ever God by his Spirit convinces our consciences of any sin or duty we must immediately set in with the conviction, and prosecute it, as those that are not ashamed to own our former mistake. 3. Rash swearing. If a man binds himself by an oath that he will do or not do such a thing, and the performance of his oath afterwards proves either unlawful or impracticable, by which he is discharged from the obligation, yet he must bring an offering to atone for his fully in swearing so rashly, as David that he would kill Nabal.

And then it was that he must *say before the angel* that it *was an error,* Eccl. 5:6. *He shall be guilty in one of these* (*ch.* 5:4), guilty if he do not perform his oath, and yet, if the matter of it were evil, guilty if he do. Such wretched dilemmas as these do some men bring themselves into by their own rashness and folly; go which way they will their consciences are wounded, sin stares them in the face, so sadly are they *snared in the words of their mouth.* A more sad dilemma this is than that of the lepers, "If we sit still, we die; if we stir, we die." Wisdom and watchfulness beforehand would prevent these straits.

II. Now in these cases, 1. The offender must confess his sin and bring his offering (*v.* 5, 6); and the offering was not accepted unless it was accompanied with a penitential confession and a humble prayer for pardon. Observe, The confession must be particular, *that he hath sinned in that thing;* such was David's confession (Ps. 51:4), *I have done this evil;* and Achan's (Jos. 7:20), *Thus and thus have I done.* Deceit lies in generals; many will own in general they have sinned, for that all must own, so that it is not any particular reproach to them; but that they have sinned *in this thing* they stand too much upon their honour to acknowledge: but the way to be well assured of pardon, and to be well armed against sin for the future, is to be particular in our penitent confessions. 2. The priest must *make atonement for him.* As the atonement was not accepted without his repentance, so his repentance would not justify him without the atonement. Thus, in our reconciliation to God, Christ's part and ours are both needful.

Verses 7–13

Provision is here made for the poor of God's people, and the pacifying of their consciences under the sense of guilt. Those that were not able to bring a lamb might bring for a sin-offering a pair of *turtle-doves* or *two young pigeons;* nay, if any were so extremely poor that they were not able to procure these so often as they would have occasion, they might bring a pottle of fine flour, and this should be accepted. Thus the expense of the sin-offering was brought lower than that of any other offering, to teach us that no man's poverty shall ever be a bar in the way of his pardon. The poorest of all may have atonement made for them, if it be not their own fault. Thus the poor are evangelized; and no man shall say that he had not wherewithal to bear the charges of a journey to heaven. Now,

I. If the sinner brought two doves, one was to be offered for a sin-offering and the other for a burnt-offering, *v.* 7. Observe, 1. Before he offered the burnt-offering, which was for the honour and praise of God, he must offer the sin-offering, to make atonement. We must first see to it that our peace be made with God, and then we may expect that our services for his glory will be accepted. The sin-offering must make way for the burnt-offering. 2. After the sin-offering, which made atonement, came the burnt-offering, as an acknowledgment of the great mercy of God in appointing and accepting the atonement.

II. If he brought fine flour, a handful of it was to be offered, but without either oil or frankincense (*v.* 11), not only because this would make it too costly for the poor, for whose comfort this sacrifice was appointed, but because it was a sin-offering, and therefore, to show the loathsomeness of the sin for which it was offered, it must not be made grateful either to the taste by oil or to the smell by frankincense. The unsavouriness of the offering was to intimate that the sinner must never relish his sin again as he had done. God by these sacrifices did speak, 1. Comfort to those that had offended, that they might not despair, nor pine away in their iniquity; but, peace being thus made for them with God, they might have peace in him. 2. Caution likewise not to offend any more, remembering what an expensive troublesome thing it was to make atonement.

Verses 14–19

Hitherto in this chapter orders were given concerning those sacrifices that were both sin-offerings and trespass-offerings, for they go by both names, *v.* 6. Here we have the law concerning those that were properly and peculiarly *trespass-offerings,* which were offered to atone for trespasses done against a neighbour, those sins we commonly call trespasses. Now injuries done to another may be either in holy things or in common things; of the former we have the law in these verses; of the latter in the beginning of the next chapter. If a man *did harm* (as it is *v.* 16) *in the holy things of the Lord,* he thereby committed a trespass against the priests, the Lord's ministers, who were entrusted with the care of these holy things, and had the benefit of them. Now if a man did alienate or convert to his own use any thing that was dedicated to God, unwittingly, he was to bring this sacrifice; as suppose he had ignorantly made use of the tithes, or first-fruits, or first-born of his cattle, or (which, it should seem by *ch.* 22:14–16, is principally meant here) had eaten any of those parts of the sacrifices which were appropriated to the priests; this was a trespass. It is supposed to be done through mistake, or forgetfulness, for want either of care or zeal; for if it was done presumptuously, and in contempt of the law, the offender died without mercy, Heb. 10:28. But in case of negligence and ignorance this sacrifice was appointed; and Moses is told, 1. What must be done in case the trespass appeared to be certain. The trespasser must bring an offering to the Lord, which, in all those that were purely trespass-offerings, must be a *ram without blemish,* "of the second year," say the Jewish doctors. He must likewise make restitution to the priest, according to a just estimation of the thing which he had so alienated, adding a fifth part to it, that he might learn to take more heed next time of embezzling what was sacred to God, finding to his cost that there was nothing got by it, and that he paid dearly for his oversights. 2. What must be done in case it were doubtful whether he had trespassed or no; he had cause to suspect it, but he *wist it not* (*v.* 17), that is, he was not very certain; in this case, because it is good to be sure, he must bring his trespass-offering, and the value of that which he feared he had embezzled, only he was not to add the fifth part to it. Now this was designed to show the very great evil there is in sacrilege. Achan, that was guilty of it presumptuously, died for it; so did Ananias and Saphira. But this goes further to show the evil of it, that if a man had, through mere ignorance, and unwittingly, alienated the holy things, nay, if he did but suspect that he had done so, he must be at the expense, not only of a full restitution with interest, but of an offering, with the trouble of bringing it, and must take shame to himself, by making confession of it; so bad a thing is it to invade God's property, and so cautious should we be to abstain from all appearances of this evil. We are also taught here to be jealous over ourselves with a godly jealousy, to ask pardon for the sin, and make satisfaction for the wrong, which we do but suspect ourselves guilty of. In doubtful cases we should take and keep the safer side.

CHAPTER 6

The first seven verses of this chapter might fitly have been added to the foregoing chapter, being a continuation of the law of the trespass-offering, and the putting of other cases in which it was to be offered; and with this end the instructions God gave concerning the several kinds of sacrifices that should be offered: and then at *v.* 8 (which in the original begins a new section of the law) he comes to appoint the several rites and ceremonies concerning these sacrifices which had not been mentioned before. I. The burnt-offering (*v.* 8–13). II. The meat-offering (*v.* 11–18), particularly that at the consecration of the priest (*v.* 19–23). III. The sin-offering (*v.* 24, etc.).

Verses 1–7

This is the latter part of the law of the trespass-offering: the former part, which concerned trespasses about holy things, we had in the close of the foregoing chapter; this concerns trespasses in common things. Observe here,

I. The trespass supposed, *v.* 2, 3. Though all the instances relate to our neighbour, yet it is called a *trespass against the Lord,* because, though the injury be done immediately to our neighbour, yet an affront is thereby given to his Maker and our Master. He that speaks evil of his brother is said to speak evil of the law, and consequently of the Law-maker, Jam. 4:11. Though the person injured be ever so mean and despicable, and every way our inferior, yet the injury reflects upon that God who has made the command of loving our neighbour second to that of loving himself. The trespasses specified are, 1. Denying a trust: *If a man lie unto his neighbour in that which was delivered him to keep,* or, which is worse, which was lent him for his use. If we claim that as our own which is only borrowed, left in our custody, or committed to our care, this is a trespass *against the Lord,* who, for the benefit of human society, will have property and truth maintained. 2. Defrauding a partner: *If a man lie in fellowship,* claiming a sole interest in that wherein he has but a joint-interest. 3. Disowning a manifest wrong: *If a man* has the front to *lie in a thing taken away by violence,* which ordinarily cannot be hid. 4. Deceiving in commerce, or, as some think, by false accusation; if a man have *deceitfully oppressed* his neighbour, as some read it, either withholding what is due or extorting what is not. 5. Detaining what is found, and denying it (*v.* 3); if a man have *found that which was lost,* he must not call it his own presently, but endeavour to find out the owner, to whom it must be returned; this is doing as we would be done by: but he that *lies concerning it,* that falsely says he knows nothing of it, especially if he back this lie with a false oath, *trespasseth against the Lord,* who to every thing that is said is a witness, but in an oath he is the party appealed to, and highly affronted when he is called to witness to a lie.

II. The trespass-offering appointed. 1. *In the day of his trespass-offering* he must make satisfaction to his brother. This must be first done *if thy brother hath aught against thee: Because he hath sinned and is guilty,* (*v.* 4, 5), that is, is convicted of his guilt by his own conscience, and is touched with remorse for it; seeing himself guilty before God, let him faithfully restore all that he has got by fraud or oppression, with a fifth part added, to make amends to the owner for the loss and trouble he had sustained in the mean time; let him account both for debt and damages. Note, Where wrong has been done restitution must be made; and till it is made to the utmost of our power, or an equivalent accepted by the person wronged, we cannot have the comfort of the forgiveness of the sin; for the keeping of what is unjustly got avows the taking, and both together make but one continued act of unrighteousness. To repent is to undo what we have done amiss, which (whatever we pretend) we cannot be said to do till we restore what has been got by it, as Zaccheus (Lu. 19:8), and make satisfaction for the wrong done. 2. He must *then come and offer his gift,* must *bring his trespass-offering to the Lord* whom he had offended; and the priest must make an atonement for him, *v.* 6, 7. This trespass-offering could not, of itself, make satisfaction for sin, nor reconciliation between God and the sinner, but as it signified the atonement that was to be made by our Lord Jesus, when he should make his soul *an offering or sin,* a *trespass-offering;* it is the same word that is here used, Isa. 53:10. The trespasses here mentioned are trespasses still against the law of Christ, which insists as much upon justice and truth as ever the law of nature or the law of Moses did; and though now we may have them pardoned without a trespass-offering, yet not without true repentance, restitution, reformation, and a humble faith in the righteousness of Christ: and, if any make the more bold with these sins because they are not now put to the expense of a trespass-offering for them, they turn the grace of God into wantonness, and so bring upon themselves a swift destruction. The Lord is the avenger of all such, 1 Th. 4:6.

Verses 8–13

Hitherto we have had the instructions which Moses was directed to give to the people concerning the sacrifices; but here begin the instructions he was to give to the priests; he must *command Aaron and his sons, v.* 9. The priests were rulers in the house of God, but these rulers must be ruled; and those that had the command of others must themselves be commanded. Let ministers remember that not only commissions, but commands, were given to Aaron and his sons, who must be in subjection to them.

In these verses we have the law of the burnt-offering, as far as it was the peculiar care of the priests. The daily sacrifice of a lamb, which was offered morning and evening for the whole congregation, is here chiefly referred to.

I. The priest must take care of the ashes of the burnt-offering, that they be decently disposed of, *v.* 10, 11. He must clear the altar of them every morning, and put them on the east side of the altar, which was furthest from the sanctuary; this he must do in his linen garment, which he always wore when he did any service at the altar; and then he must shift himself, and put on other garments, either such as were his common wear, or (as some think) other priestly garments less honourable, and must *carry the ashes into a clean place without the camp.* Now, 1. God would have this done, for the honour of his altar and the sacrifices that were burnt upon it. Even the ashes of the sacrifices must be preserved, to testify the regard God had to it; by the burnt-offering *he* was honoured, and therefore thus *it* was honoured, and therefore thus *it* was honoured. And some think that this care which was taken of the ashes of the sacrifice typified the burial of our Saviour; his dead body (the ashes of his sacrifice) was carefully laid up in a garden, in a new sepulchre, which was a *clean place.* It was also requisite that the altar should be kept as clean as might be; the fire upon it would burn the better, and it is decent in a house to have a clean fireside. 2. God would have the priests themselves to keep it so, to teach them and us to stoop to the meanest services for the honour of God and of his altar. The priest himself must not only kindle the fire, but clean the hearth, and carry out the ashes. God's servants must think nothing below them but sin.

II. The priest must take care of the fire upon the altar, that it be kept *always burning.* This is much insisted on here (*v.* 9, 12), and this express law is given: *The fire shall ever be burning upon the altar, it shall never go out, v.* 13. We may suppose that no day passed without some extraordinary sacrifices, which were always offered between the morning and evening lamb; so that from morning to night the fire on the altar was kept up of course. But to preserve it *all night unto the morning* (*v.* 9) required some care. Those that keep good houses never let their kitchen fire go out; therefore God would thus give an instance of his good house-keeping. The first fire upon the altar came *from heaven* (*ch.* 9:24), so that by keeping that up continually with a constant supply of fuel all their sacrifices throughout all their generations might be said to be consumed with that fire from heaven, in token of God's acceptance. If, through carelessness, they should ever let it go out, they could not expect to have it so kindled again. Accordingly the Jews tell us that the fire never did go out upon the altar, till the captivity in Babylon. This is referred to Isa. 31:9, where God is said *to have his fire in Zion, and his furnace in Jerusalem.* By this law we are taught to keep up in our minds a constant disposition to all acts of piety and devotion, an habitual affection to divine things, so as to be always ready to every good word and work. We must not only not *quench the Spirit,* but we must *stir up the gift* that is in us. Though we be not always sacrificing, yet we must keep the fire of holy love always burning; and thus we must pray always.

Verses 14–23

The meat-offering was either that which was offered by the people or that by the priests at their consecration. Now,

I. As to the common meat-offering,

1. Only a handful of it was to be burnt upon the altar; all the rest was allowed to the priests for their food. The law of the burnt-offerings was such as imposed upon the priests a great deal of care and work, but allowed them little profit; for the flesh was wholly burnt, and the priests had nothing but the skin. But to make them amends the greatest part of the meat-offering was their own. The burning of a handful of it upon the altar (*v.* 15) was ordered before, *ch.* 2:2, 9. Here the remainder of it is consigned to the priests, the servants of God's house: *I have given it unto them for their portion of my offerings, v.* 17. Note, (1.) It is the will of God that his ministers should be well provided for with food convenient; and what is given to them he accepts as offered to himself, if it be done with a single eye. (2.) All Christians, being spiritual priests, do themselves share in the spiritual sacrifices they offer. It is not God that is the gainer by them; the handful burnt upon the altar was not worth speaking of, in comparison with the priests' share; we ourselves are the gainers by our religious services. Let God have all the frankincense, and the priests shall have the flour and the oil; what we give to God the praise and glory of we may take to ourselves the comfort and benefit of.

2. The laws concerning the eating of it were, (1.) That it must be *eaten unleavened, v.* 16. What was offered to God must have no leaven in it, and the priests must have it as the altar had it, and no otherwise. Thus must we keep the feasts of the Lord with the *unleavened bread of sincerity and truth.* (2.) It must be eaten in *the court of the tabernacle* (here called the *holy place*), in some room prepared by the side of the court for this purpose. It was a great crime to carry any of it out of the court. The very eating of it was a sacred rite, by which they were to honour God, and therefore it must be done in a religious manner, and with a holy reverence, which was preserved by confining it to the holy place. (3.) The males only must eat of it, *v.* 18. Of the less holy things, as the first-fruits and tithes, and the shoulder and breasts of the peace-offerings, the *daughters* of the priests might eat, for they might be carried out of the court; but this was of the most holy things, which being to be eaten only in the tabernacle, the *sons* of Aaron only might eat of it. (4.) The priests only that were clean might eat of it: *Every one that toucheth them shall be holy, v.* 18. Holy things for holy persons. Some read it, *Every thing that toucheth it shall be holy:* Al the furniture of the table on which these holy things were eaten must be appropriated to that use only, and never after used as common things.

II. As to the consecration meat-offering, which was offered for the priests themselves, it was to be *wholly burnt, and none of it eaten, v.* 23. It comes in here as an exception to the foregoing law. It should seem that this law concerning the meat-offering of initiation did not only oblige the high priest to offer it, and on that day only that he was anointed, and so for his successors in the day they were anointed; but the Jewish writers say that by this law every priest, on the day he first entered upon his ministry, was bound to offer this meat-offering, — that the high priest was bound to offer it every day of his life, from the day in which he was anointed, — and that it was to be offered besides the meat-offering that attended the morning and evening sacrifice, because it is said here to be a *meat-offering perpetual, v.* 20. Josephus says, "The high priest sacrificed twice every day at his own charges, and this was his sacrifice." Note, Those whom God has advanced above others in dignity and power ought to consider that he expects more from them than from others, and should attend to every intimation of service to be done for him. The meat-offering of the priest was to be baked as if it were to be eaten, and yet it must be wholly burnt. Though the priest that ministered was to be paid for serving the people, yet there was no reason that he should be paid for serving the high priest, who was the father of the family of the priests, and whom therefore any priest should take a pleasure in serving gratis. Nor was it fit that the priests should eat of the offerings of a priest; for as the sins of the people were typically transferred to the priests, which was signified by their eating of their offerings (Hos. 4:8), so the sins of the priests must be typically transferred to the altar, which therefore must eat up all their offerings. We are all undone, both ministers and people, if we must *bear our own iniquity;* nor could we have had any comfort or hope if God had not laid on his dear Son the iniquity of us all, and he is both the priest and the alter.

Verses 24–30

We have here so much of the law of the sin-offering as did peculiarly concern the priests that offered it. As, 1. That it must be killed *in the place where the burnt-offering was killed* (*v.* 25), that is, on the north side of the altar (*ch.* 1:11), which, some think typified the crucifying of Christ on mount Calvary, which was on the north side of Jerusalem. 2. That the priest who offered it for the sinner was (with his sons, or other priests, *v.* 29) to eat the flesh of it, after the blood and fat had been offered to God, in the *court of the tabernacle, v.* 26. Hereby they were to *bear the iniquity of the congregation,* as it is explained, *ch.* 10:17. 3. The blood of the sin-offering was with great reverence to be washed out of the clothes on which it happened to light (*v.* 27), which signified the awful regard we ought to have to the blood of Christ, not counting it a common thing; that blood must be sprinkled on the conscience, not on the raiment. 4. The vessel in which the flesh of the sin-offering was boiled must be broken if it were an earthen one, and, if a brazen one, well washed, *v.* 28. This intimated that the defilement was not wholly taken away by the offering, but did rather cleave to it, such was the weakness and deficiency of those sacrifices; but the blood of Christ thoroughly cleanses from all sin, and after it there needs no cleansing. 5. That all this must be understood of the common sin-offerings, not of those for the priest, or the body of the congregation, either occasional, or stated upon the day of atonement; for it had been before ordained, and was now ratified, that if the blood of the offering was brought into the holy place, as it was in those extraordinary cases, the flesh was not to be eaten, but burnt without the camp, *v.* 30. Hence the apostle infers the advantage we have under the gospel above what they had under the law; for though the blood of Christ was *brought into the tabernacle, to reconcile within the holy place,* yet we have a right by faith to *eat of the altar* (Heb. 13:10–12), and so to take the comfort of the great propitiation.

CHAPTER 7

Here is, I. The law of the trespass-offering (*v.* 1–7), with some further directions concerning the burnt-offering and the meat-offering (*v.* 8–10). II. The law of the peace-offering. The eating of it (*v.* 11–21), on which occasion the prohibition of eating fat or blood is repeated (*v.* 22–27), and the priests' share of it (*v.* 28–34). III. The conclusion of those institutions (*v.* 35, etc.).

Verses 1–10

Observe here, 1. Concerning the trespass-offering, that, being much of the same nature with the sin-offering, it was to be governed by the same rules, *v.* 6. When the blood and fat were offered to God to make atonement, the priests were to eat the flesh, as that of the sin-offering, in the holy place. The Jews have a tradition (as we have it from the learned bishop Patrick) concerning the sprinkling of the blood of the trespass-offering *round about upon the altar,* "That there was a scarlet line which went round about the altar exactly in the middle, and the blood of the burnt-offerings was sprinkled round about above the line, but that of the trespass-offerings and peace-offerings round about below the line." As to the flesh of the trespass-offering, the right to it belonged to the priest that offered it, *v.* 7. He that did the work must have the wages. This was an encouragement to the priests to give diligent attendance on the altar; the more ready and busy they were the more they got. Note, The more diligent we are in the services of religion the more we shall reap of the advantages of it. But any of the priests, and the males of their families, might be invited by him to whom it belonged to partake with him: *Every male among the priests shall eat thereof,* that is, may eat thereof, *in the holy place, v.* 6. And, no doubt, it was the usage to treat one another with those perquisites of their office, by which friendship and fellowship were kept up among the priests. Freely they had received, and must freely give. It seems the offerer was not himself to have any share of his trespass-offering, as he was to have of his peace-offering; but it was all divided between the altar and the priest. They offered peace-offerings in thankfulness for mercy, and then it was proper to feast; but they offered trespass-offerings in sorrow for sin, and then fasting was more proper, in token of holy mourning, and a resolution to abstain from sin. 2. Concerning the burnt-offering it is here appointed that the priest that offered it should have the skin (*v.* 8), which no doubt he might make money of. "This" (the Jews say) "is meant only for the burnt-offerings which were offered by particular persons; for the profit of the skins of the daily burnt-offerings for the congregation went to the repair of the sanctuary." Some suggest that this appointment will help us to understand God's clothing our first parents with *coats of skins,* Gen. 3:21. It is probable that the beasts whose skins they were were offered in sacrifice as whole burnt-offerings, and that Adam was the priest that offered them; and then God gave him the skins, as his fee, to make clothes of for himself and his wife, in remembrance of which the skins ever after pertained to the priest; and see Gen. 27:16. 3. Concerning the meat-offering, if it was dressed, it was fit to be eaten immediately; and therefore the priest that offered it was to have it, *v.* 9. If it was dry, there was not so much occasion for being in haste to use it; and therefore an equal dividend of it must be made among all the priests that were then in waiting, *v.* 10.

Verses 11–34

All this relates to the peace-offerings: it is the repetition and explication of what we had before, with various additions.

I. The nature and intention of the peace-offerings are here more distinctly opened. They were offered either, 1. In thankfulness for some special mercy received, such as recovery from sickness, preservation in a journey, deliverance at sea, redemption out of captivity, all which are specified in Ps. 107, and for them men are called upon to offer the sacrifice of thanksgiving, *v.* 22. Or, 2. In performance of some vow which a man made when he was in distress (*v.* 16), and this was less honourable than the former, though the omission of it would have been more culpable. Or, 3. In supplication for some special mercy which a man was in the pursuit and expectation of, here called a *voluntary offering.* This accompanied a man's prayers, as the former did his praises. We do not find that men were bound by the law, unless they had bound themselves by vow, to offer these peace-offerings upon such occasions, as they were to bring their sacrifices of atonement in case of sin committed. Not but that prayer and praise are as much our duty as repentance is; but here, in the expressions of their sense of mercy, God left them more to their liberty than in the expressions of their sense of sin — to try the generosity of their devotion, and that their sacrifices, being free-will offerings, might be the more laudable and acceptable; and, by obliging them to bring the sacrifices of atonement, God would show the necessity of the great propitiation.

II. The rites and ceremonies about the peace-offerings are enlarged upon.

1. If the peace-offering was offered for a thanksgiving, a meat-offering must be offered with it, cakes of several sorts, and wafers (*v.* 12), and (which was peculiar to the peace-offerings) leavened bread must be offered, not to be burnt upon the altar, that was forbidden (*ch.* 2:11), but to be eaten with the flesh of the sacrifice, that nothing might be wanting to make it a complete and pleasant feast; for unleavened bread was less grateful to the taste, and therefore, though enjoined in the passover for a particular reason, yet in other festivals leavened bread, which was lighter and more pleasant, was appointed, that men might feast at God's table as well as at their own. And some think that a meat-offering is required to be brought with every peace-offering, as well as with that of thanksgiving, by that law (*v.* 29) which requires an oblation with it, that the table might be as well furnished as the altar.

2. The flesh of the peace-offerings, both that which was the priest's share and that which was the offerer's must be eaten quickly, and not kept long, either raw, or dressed, cold. If it was a peace-offering for thanksgiving, it must be all eaten the same day (*v.* 16); if a vow, or voluntary offering, it must be eaten either the same day or the day after, *v.* 16. If any was left beyond the time limited, it was to be burnt (*v.* 17); and, if any person ate of what was so left their conduct should be animadverted upon as a very high misdemeanour, *v.* 18. Though they were not obliged to eat it in the holy place, as those offerings that are called most holy, but might take it to their own tents and feast upon it there, yet God would by this law make them to know a difference between that and other meat, and religiously to observe it, that whereas they might keep other meat cold in the house as long as they thought fit, and warm it again if they pleased, and eat it three or four days after, they might not do so with the flesh of their peace-offerings, but it must be eaten immediately. (1.) Because God would not have that holy flesh to be in danger of putrefying, or being fly-blown, to prevent which it must be salted with *fire* (as the expression is, Mk. 9:49) if it were kept; as, if it was used, it must be salted with salt. (2.) Because God would not have his people to be niggardly and sparing, and distrustful of providence, but cheerfully to enjoy what God gives them (Eccl. 8:15), and to do good with it, and not to be anxiously solicitous for the morrow. (3.) The flesh of the peace-offerings was God's treat, and therefore God would have the disposal of it; and he orders it to be used generously for the entertainment of their friends, and charitably for the relief of the poor, to show that he is a bountiful benefactor, *giving us all things richly to enjoy,* the bread of the day in its day. If the sacrifice was thanksgiving, they were especially obliged thus to testify their holy joy in God's goodness by their holy feasting. This law is made very strict (*v.* 18), that if the offerer did not take care to have all his offering eaten by himself or his family, his friends or the poor, within the time limited by the law, or, in the event of any part being left, to burn it (which was the most decent way of disposing of it, the sacrifices upon the altar being *consumed by fire*), then his offering should not be accepted, nor imputed to him. Note, All the benefit of our religious services is lost if we do not improve them, and conduct ourselves aright afterwards. They are not acceptable to God if they have not a due influence upon ourselves. If a man seemed generous in bringing a peace-offering, and yet afterwards proved sneaking and paltry in the using of it, it was as if he had never brought it; nay, *it shall be an abomination.* Note, There is no mean between God's acceptance and his abhorrence. If our persons and performances are sincere and upright, they are accepted; if not, they are an abomination, Prov. 15:8. He that eats it after the time appointed shall *bear his iniquity,* that is, he shall be *cut off from his people,* as it is explained (*ch.* 19:8), where this law is repeated. This law of eating the peace-offerings before the third day, that they might not putrefy, is applicable tot the resurrection of Christ after two days, that, being God's *holy one,* he might not see corruption, Ps. 16:10. And some think that it instructs us speedily, and without delay, to partake of Christ and his grace, feeding and feasting thereon by faith to-day, *while it is called to-day* (Heb. 3:13, 14), for it will be too late shortly.

3. But the flesh, and those that eat it, must be pure. (1.) The flesh must *touch no unclean thing;* if it did, it must not be eaten, but burnt, *v.* 19. If, in carrying it from the altar to the place where it was eaten, a dog touched it, or it touched a dead body or any other unclean thing, it was then unfit to be used in a religious feast. Every thing we honour the holy God with must be pure and carefully kept from all pollution. It is a case adjudged (Hag. 2:12) that the holy flesh could not by its touch communicate holiness to what was common; but by this law it is determined that by the touch of that which was unclean it received pollution from it, which intimates that the infection of sin is more easily and more frequently communicated than the savour of grace. (2.) It must not be eaten by any unclean person. When a person was upon any account ceremonially unclean it was at his peril if he presumed to eat of the flesh of the peace-offerings, *v.* 20, 21. Holy things are only for holy persons; the holiness of the food being ceremonial, those were incapacitated to partake of it who lay under any ceremonial uncleanness; but we are hereby taught to preserve ourselves pure from all the pollutions of sin, that we may have the benefit and comfort of Christ's sacrifice, 1 Pt. 2:1, 2. Our consciences must be purged from dead works, that we may be fit to *serve the living God,* Heb. 9:14. But if any dare to partake of the table of the Lord under the pollution of sin unrepented of, and so profane sacred things, they eat and drink *judgment to themselves,* as those did that ate of the peace-offerings (*v.* 20) and again (*v.* 21), that they *pertain unto the Lord:* whatever pertains to the Lord is sacred, and must be used with great reverence and not with unhallowed hands. *"Be you holy,* for God is holy, and you pertain to him."

4. The eating of blood and the fat of the inwards is here again prohibited; and the prohibition is annexed as before to the law of the peace-offerings, *ch.* 3:17. (1.) The prohibition of the fat seems to be confined to those beasts which were used for sacrifice, the bullocks, sheep, and goats: but of the roe-buck, the hart, and other clean beasts, they might eat the fat; for those only of which offerings were brought are mentioned here, *v.* 23–25. This was to preserve in their minds a reverence for God's altar, on which the fat of the inwards was burnt. The Jews say, "If a man eat so much as an olive of forbidden fat — if he do it presumptuously, he is in danger of being cut off by the hand of God — if ignorantly, he is to bring a sin-offering, and so to pay dearly for his carelessness." To eat of the flesh of that which died of itself, or was torn of beasts, was unlawful; but to eat of the fat of such was doubly unlawful, *v.* 24. (2.) The prohibition of blood is more general (*v.* 26, 27), because the fat was offered to God only by way of acknowledgment, but the blood *made atonement for the soul,* and so typified Christ's sacrifice much more than the burning of the fat did; to this therefore a greater reverence must be paid, till these types had their accomplishment in the offering up of the body of Christ once for all. The Jews rightly expound this law as forbidding only the *blood of the life,* as they express it, not that which we call the *gravy,* for of that they supposed it was lawful to eat.

5. The priest's share of the peace-offerings is here prescribed. Out of every beast that was offered for a peace-offering the priest that offered it was to have to himself the breast and the right shoulder, *v.* 30–34. Observe here, (1.) That when the sacrifice was killed the offerer himself must, with his own hands, present God's part of it, that he might signify thereby his cheerfully giving it up to God, and his desire that it might be accepted. He was with his own hands to *lift it up,* in token of his regard to God as the God of heaven, and then to *wave it to and fro,* in token of his regard to God as the Lord of the whole earth, to whom thus, as far as he could reach, he offered it, showing his readiness and wish to do him honour. Now that which was thus heaved and waved was the fat, and the breast, and the right shoulder, it was all offered to God; and then he ordered the fat to his altar, and the breast and shoulder to his priest, both being his receivers. (2.) That when the fat was burnt the priest took his part, on which he and his family were to feast, as well as the offerer and his family. In holy joy and thanksgiving, it is good to have our ministers to go before us, and to be our mouth to God. The melody is sweet when he that sows and those that reap rejoice together. Some observe a significancy in the parts assigned to the priests: the breast and the shoulder intimate the affections and the actions, which must be devoted to the honour of God by all his people and to the service also of the church by all his priests. Christ, our great peace-offering, feasts all his spiritual priests with the breast and shoulder, with the dearest love and the sweetest and strongest supports; for his is the wisdom of God and the power of God. When Saul was designed for a king Samuel ordered the shoulder of the peace-offering to be set before him (1 Sa. 9:24), which gave him a hint of something great and sacred intended for him. Jesus Christ is our great peace-offering; for he made himself a sacrifice, not only to atone for sin, and so to save us from the curse, but to purchase a blessing for us, and all good. By our joyfully partaking of the benefits of redemption we *feast upon the sacrifice,* to signify which the Lord's supper was instituted.

Verses 35–38

Here is the conclusion of these laws concerning the sacrifices, though some of them are afterwards repeated and explained. The are to be considered, 1. As a grant to the priests, *v.* 35, 36. In the day they were ordained to that work and office this provision was made for their comfortable maintenance. Note, God will take care that those who are employed for him be well paid and well provided for. Those that receive the anointing of the Spirit to minister unto the Lord shall have their portion, and it shall be a worthy portion, out of the offerings of the Lord; for God's work is its own wages, and there is a present reward of obedience in obedience. 2. As a statute for ever to the people, that they should bring these offerings according to the rules prescribed, and cheerfully give the priests their share out of them. God *commanded the children of Israel to offer their oblations,* *v.* 38. Note, The solemn acts religious worship are commanded. They are not things that we are left to our liberty in, and which we may do or not do at our pleasure; but we are under indispensable obligations to perform them in their season, and it is at our peril if we omit them. The observance of the laws of Christ cannot be less necessary than the observance of the laws of Moses was.

CHAPTER 8

This chapter gives us an account of the solemn consecration of Aaron and his sons to the priest's office. I. It was done publicly, and the congregation was called together to be witnesses of it (*v.* 1–4). II. It was done exactly according to God's appointment (*v.* 5). 1. They were washed and dressed (*v.* 6–9, 13). 2. The tabernacle and the utensils of it were anointed, and then the priests (*v.* 10–12). 3. A sin-offering was offered for them (*v.* 14–17). 4. A burnt-offering (*v.* 18–21). 5. The ram of consecration (*v.* 22–30). 6. The continuance of this solemnity for seven days (*v.* 31, etc.).

Verses 1–13

God had given Moses orders to consecrate Aaron and his sons to the priests' office, when he was with him the first time upon mount Sinai, Ex. 28 and 29, where we have also the particular instructions he had how to do it. Now here we have,

I. The orders repeated. What was there commanded to be done is here commanded to be done *now, v.* 2, 3. The tabernacle was newly set up, which, without the priests, would be as a candlestick without a candle; the law concerning sacrifices was newly given, but could not be observed without priests; for, though Aaron and his sons had been nominated to the office, they could not officiate, till they were consecrated, which yet must not be done till the place of their ministration was prepared, and the ordinances were instituted, that they might apply themselves to work as soon as ever they were consecrated, and might know that they were ordained, not only to the honour and profit, but to the business of the priesthood. Aaron and his sons were near relations to Moses, and therefore he would not consecrate them till he had further orders, lest he should seem too forward to bring honour into his family.

II. The congregation called together, *at the door,* that is, in the court *of the tabernacle, v.* 4. The elders and principal men of the congregation, who represented the body of the people, were summoned to attend; for the court would hold but a few of the many thousands of Israel. It was done thus publicly, 1. Because it was a solemn transaction between God and Israel; the priests were to be *ordained for men in things pertaining to God,* for the maintaining of a settled correspondence, and the negotiating of all affairs between the people and God; and therefore it was fit that both sides should appear, to own the appointment, at the door of the tabernacle of meeting. 2. The spectators of the solemnity could not but be possessed, by the sight of it, with a great veneration for the priests and their office, which was necessary among a people so wretchedly prone as these were to envy and discontent. It was strange that any of those who were witnesses of what was here done should afterwards say, as some of them did, *You take too much upon you, you sons of Levi;* but what would they have said if it had been done clandestinely? Note, It is very fit, and of good use, that ministers should be ordained publicly, *plebe praesente — in the presence of the common people,* according to the usage of the primitive church.

III. The commission read, *v.* 5. Moses, who was God's representative in this solemnity, produced his orders before the congregation: *This is the thing which the Lord commanded to be done.* Though God had crowned him king in Jeshurun, when he made his face to shine in the sight of all Israel, yet he did not institute or appoint any thing in God's worship but what God himself had commanded. The priesthood he delivered to them was that which he had received from the Lord. Note, All that minister about holy things must have an eye to God's command as their rule and warrant; for it is only in the observance of this that they can expect to be owned and accepted of God. Thus we must be able to say, in all acts of religious worship, *This is the thing which the Lord commanded to be done.*

IV. The ceremony performed according to the divine ritual. 1. Aaron and his sons were *washed with water* (*v.* 6), to signify that they ought now to purify themselves from all sinful dispositions and inclinations, and ever after to keep themselves pure. Christ washes those from their sins in his own blood whom he makes to our God kings and priests (Rev. 1:5, 6); and those that draw near to God must be washed in pure water, Heb. 10:22. Though they were ever so clean before and no filth was to be seen upon them, yet they must be washed, to signify their purification from sin, with which their souls were polluted, how clean soever their bodies were. 2. They were clothed with the holy garments, Aaron with his (*v.* 7–9), which typified the dignity of Christ our great high priest, and his sons with theirs (*v.* 13), which typified the decency of Christians, who are spiritual priests. Christ wears the breast-plate of judgment and the holy crown; for the church's high priest is her prophet and king. All believers are clothed with the robe of righteousness, and girt with the girdle of truth, resolution, and close application; and their heads are *bound,* as the word here is, with the bonnet or diadem of beauty, the beauty of holiness. 3. The high priest was anointed, and, it should seem, the holy things were anointed at the same time; some think that they were anointed before, but that the anointing of them is mentioned here because Aaron was anointed with the same oil with which they were anointed; but the manner of relating it here makes it more than probable that it was done at the same time, and that the seven days employed in consecrating the altar were coincident with the seven days of the priests' consecration. The tabernacle, and all its utensils, had some

of the anointing oil put upon them with Moses's finger (*v.* 10), so had the altar (*v.* 11); these were to sanctify the gold and the gift (Mt. 23:17–19), and therefore must themselves be thus sanctified; but he poured it out more plentifully upon the head of Aaron (*v.* 12), so that it ran down to the *skirts of his garments,* because his unction was to typify the anointing of Christ with the Spirit, which was not given by measure to him. Yet all believers also have received the anointing, which puts an indelible character upon them, 1 Jn. 2:27.

Verses 14–30

The covenant of priesthood must be made by sacrifice, as well as other covenants, Ps. 50:5. And thus Christ was consecrated by the sacrifice of himself, once for all. Sacrifices of each kind must be offered for the priests, that they might with the more tenderness and concern offer the gifts and sacrifices of the people, with compassion on the ignorant, and on *those that were out of the way,* not insulting over those for whom sacrifices were offered, remembering that they themselves had had sacrifices offered for them, being *compassed with infirmity.* 1. A bullock, the largest sacrifice, was offered for a sin-offering (*v.* 14), that hereby atonement might be made, and they might not bring any of the guilt of the sins of their former state into the new character they were now to put on. When Isaiah was sent to be a prophet, he was told to his comfort, *Thy iniquity is taken away,* Isa. 6:7. Ministers, that are to declare the remission of sins to others, should give diligence to get it made sure to themselves in the first place that their own sins are pardoned. Those to whom is *committed the ministry of reconciliation* must first be reconciled to God themselves, that they may deal for the souls of others as for their own. 2. A ram was offered for a burntoffering, *v.* 18–21. By this they gave to God the glory of this great honour which was now put upon them, and returned him praise for it, as Paul thanked Christ Jesus for *putting him into the ministry,* 1 Tim. 1:12. They also signified the devoting of themselves and all their services to the honour of God. 3. Another ram, called the *ram of consecration,* was offered for a peace-offering, *v.* 22, etc. The blood of it was part put on the priests, on their ears, thumbs, and toes, and part sprinkled upon the altar; and thus he did (as it were) marry them to the altar, upon which they must all their days give attendance. All the ceremonies about this offering, as those before, were appointed by the express command of God; and, if we compare this chapter with Ex. 29, we shall find that the performance of the solemnity exactly agrees with the precept there, and in nothing varies. Here, therefore, as in the account we had of the tabernacle and its vessels, it is again and again repeated, *As the Lord commanded Moses.* And thus Christ, when he sanctified himself with his own blood, had an eye to his Father's will in it. *As the Father gave me commandment so I do,* Jn. 14:31; 10:18; 6:38.

Verses 31–36

Moses, having done his part of the ceremony, now leaves Aaron and his sons to do theirs.

I. They must boil the flesh of their peace-offering, and eat it in the court of the tabernacle, and what remained they must burn with fire, *v.* 31, 32. This signified their thankful consent to the consecration: when God gave Ezekiel his commission, he told him to eat the roll, Eze. 3:1, 2.

II. They must not stir out of the court of the tabernacle for seven days, *v.* 33. The priesthood being a good warfare, they must thus learn to endure hardness, and to disentangle themselves from the affairs of this life, 2 Tim. 2:3, 4. Being consecrated to their service, they must *give themselves wholly to it,* and *attend continually to this very thing.* Thus Christ's apostles were appointed to *wait for the promise of the Father,* Acts 1:4. During this time appointed for their consecration, they were daily to repeat the same sacrifices which were offered the first day, *v.* 34. This shows the imperfection of the legal sacrifices, which, because they could not take away sin, were often repeated (Heb. 10:1, 2), but were here repeated seven times (a number of perfection), because they typified that *one offering, which perfected for ever those that were sanctified.* The work lasted seven days; for it was a kind of creation: and this time was appointed in honour of the sabbath, which, probably, was the last day of the seven, for which they were to prepare

during the six days. Thus the time of our life, like the six days, must be our preparation for the perfection of our consecration to God in the everlasting sabbath: they attended *day and night* (*v.* 35), and so constant should we be in our meditation on God's law, Ps. 1:2. They attended to *keep the charge of the Lord:* we have every one of us a charge to keep, an eternal God to glorify, an immortal soul to provide for, needful duty to be done, our generation to serve; and it must be our daily care to keep this charge, for it is the charge of the Lord our Master, who will shortly call us to an account about it, and it is at our utmost peril if we neglect it. Keep it *that you die not;* it is death, eternal death, to betray the trust we are charged with; by the consideration of this we must be kept in awe. *Lastly,* We are told (*v.* 36) that *Aaron and his sons did all that was commanded.* Thus their consecration was completed; and thus they set an example before the people of an exact obedience to the laws of sacrifices now newly given, and then they could with the better grace teach them. Thus the *covenant of peace* (Num. 25:12), *of life and peace* (Mal. 2:5), was made with Aaron and his sons; but after all the ceremonies that were used in their consecration there was one point of ratification which was reserved to be the honour and establishment of Christ's priesthood, which was this, that they were *made priests without an oath, but Christ with an oath* (Hab. 7:21), for neither such priests nor their priesthood could continue, but Christ's is a perpetual and unchangeable priesthood.

Gospel ministers are compared to those who served at the altar, for they *minister about holy things* (1 Co. 9:13), they are God's mouth to the people and the people's to God, the pastors and teachers Christ has appointed to continue in the church to the end of the world: they seem to be meant in that promise which points at gospel times (Isa. 66:21), *I will take of them for priests and for Levites.* No man may take this honour to himself, but he who upon trial is found to be clothed and anointed by the Spirit of God with gifts and graces to qualify him for it, and who with purpose of heart devotes himself entirely to the service, and is then by the *word and prayer* (for so every thing is sanctified), and the imposition of the hands of those that *give themselves to the word and prayer,* set apart to the office, and recommended to Christ as a servant and to the church as a steward and guide. And those that are thus solemnly dedicated to God ought not to depart from his service, but faithfully to abide in it all their days; and those that do so, and continue *labouring in the word and doctrine,* are to be accounted *worthy of double honour,* double to that of the Old-Testament priests.

CHAPTER 9

Aaron and his sons, having been solemnly consecrated to the priesthood, are in this chapter entering upon the execution of their office, the very next day after their consecration was completed. I. Moses (no doubt by direction from God) appoints a meeting between God and his priests, as the representatives of his people, ordering them to attend him, and assuring them that he would appear to them (*v.* 1–7). II. The meeting is held according to the appointment. 1. Aaron attends on God by sacrifice, offering a sin-offering and burnt-offering for himself (*v.* 8–14), and then the offerings for the people, whom he blessed in the name of the Lord (*v.* 15–22). 2. God signifies his acceptance, (1.) Of their persons, by showing them his glory (*v.* 23). (2.) Of their sacrifices, by consuming them with fire from heaven (*v.* 24).

Verses 1–7

Orders are here given for another solemnity upon the eighth day; for the newly-ordained priests were set to work immediately after the days of their consecration were finished, to let them know that they were not ordained to be idle: *He that desires the office of a bishop desires a good work,* which must be looked at with desire, more than the honour and benefit. The priests had not so much as one day's respite from service allowed them, that they might divert themselves, and receive the compliments of their friends upon their elevation, but were busily employed the very next day; for their consecration was the *filling of their hands.* God's spiritual priests have constant work cut out for them, which the duty of every day requires; and those that would give up their account with joy must redeem time; see Eze. 43:26, 27. Now, 1. Moses raises their expectation of a glorious appearance of God to them this day (*v.* 4): "To day the Lord will appear to you* that are the priests." And when all the congregation are gathered together, and *stand before the Lord,* he tells them (*v.* 6), *The* *glory of the Lord shall appear to you.* Though they had reason enough to believe God's acceptance of all that they had done according to his appointment, upon the general assurance we have that he is the *rewarder of those that diligently seek him* (even if he had not given them any sensible token of it), yet that if possible they and theirs might be effectually obliged to the service and worship of God, and might never turn aside to idols, the glory of God appeared to them, and visibly owned what they had done. We are not now to expect such appearances; we Christians walk more by faith, and less by sight, than they did. But we may be sure that God draws nigh to those who draw nigh to him, and that the offerings of faith are really acceptable to him, though, the sacrifices being spiritual, the tokens of the acceptance are, as it is fit they should be, spiritual likewise. To those who are duly consecrated to God he will undoubtedly manifest himself. 2. He puts both priests and people upon preparing to receive this favour which God designed them. *Aaron and his sons,* and *the elders of Israel,* are all summoned to attend, *v.* 1. Note, God will manifest himself in the solemn assemblies of his people and ministers; and those that would have the benefit and comfort of God's appearances must in them give their attendance. (1.) Aaron is ordered to prepare his offerings: *A young calf for a sin-offering, v.* 2. The Jewish writers suggest that a *calf* was appointed for a sin-offering to remind him of his sin in making the golden calf, by which he had rendered himself for ever unworthy of the honour of the priesthood, and which he had reason to reflect upon with sorrow and shame in all the atonements he made. (2.) Aaron must direct the people to get theirs ready. Hitherto Moses had told the people what they must do; but now Aaron, as high priest over the house of God, must be their teacher, *in things pertaining to God: Unto the children of Israel thou shalt speak, v.* 3. Now that he was to speak from them to God in the sacrifices (the language of which he that appointed them very well understood) he must speak from God to them in the laws about the sacrifices. Thus Moses would engage the people's respect and obedience to him, as one that was set *over them in the Lord, to admonish them.* (3.) Aaron must offer his own first, and then the people's, *v.* 7. Aaron must now *go to the altar,* Moses having shown him the way to it; and there, [1.] He must *make an atonement for himself;* for the high priest, being *compassed with infirmity, ought, as for the people, so also for himself, to offer for sins* (Heb. 5:2, 3), and for himself first; for how can we expect to be accepted in our prayers for others, if we ourselves be not reconciled to God? Nor is any service pleasing to God till the guilt of sin be removed by our interest in the great propitiation. Those that have the care of the souls of others are also hereby taught to look to their own in the first place; this charity must begin at home, though it must not end there. It is the charge to Timothy, to take care to save himself first, and then those that heard him, 1 Tim. 4:16. The high priest made atonement for himself, as one that was joined with sinners; but we have a high priest that was separated from sinners, and needed no atonement. When Messiah the prince was cut off as a sacrifice, it was not for himself; for he knew no sin. [2.] He must *make an atonement for the people,* by offering their sacrifices. Now that he was made a high priest he must lay to heart the concerns of the people, and this as their great concern, their reconciliation to God, and the putting away of sin which had separated between them and God. He must *make atonement as the Lord commanded.* See here the wonderful condescension of the mercy of God, that he not only allows an atonement to be made, but commands it; not only admits, but requires us to be reconciled to him. No room therefore is left to doubt but that the atonement which is commanded will be accepted.

Verses 8–22

These being the first offerings that ever were offered by the levitical priesthood, according to the newly-enacted law of sacrifices, the manner of offering them is particularly related, that it might appear how exactly they agreed with the institution. 1. Aaron with his own hands *slew the offering* (*v.* 8), and did the work of the inferior priests; for, great as he was, he must not think any service below him which he could do for the honour of God: and, as Moses had shown him how to do this work decently and dexterously, so he showed his sons, that they might do likewise; for this is the best way of teaching, and thus parents should instruct their children by example. Therefore as Moses before, so Aaron now offered some of each of the several sorts of sacrifices that were appointed, whose rites differed, that they might be *thoroughly furnished for every good work.* 2. He offered these *besides the burnt-sacrifice of the morning,* which was every day offered first, *v.* 17. Note, Our accustomed devotions morning and evening, alone and in our families, must not be omitted upon any pretence whatsoever, no, not when extraordinary services are to be performed; whatever is added, these must not be diminished. 3. It is not clear whether, when it is said that he burnt such and such parts of the sacrifices upon the altar (*v.* 10–20), the meaning is that he burnt them immediately with ordinary fire, as formerly, or that he laid them upon the altar ready to be burnt with the fire from heaven which they expected (*v.* 24), or whether, as bishop Patrick thinks, he burnt the offerings for himself with ordinary fire, but when they were burnt out he laid the people's sacrifices upon the altar, which were kindled and consumed by the fire of the Lord. I would rather conjecture, because it is said of all these sacrifices that *he burnt them* (except the burnt-offering for the people, of which it is said that he offered it *according to the manner, v.* 16, which seems to be equivalent), that he did not kindle the fire to burn them, but that then the fire from the Lord fastened upon them, put out the fire that he had kindled (as we know a greater fire puts out a less), and suddenly consumed the remainder, which the fire he had kindled would have consumed slowly. 4. When Aaron had done all that on his part was to be done about the sacrifices he *lifted up his hand towards the people, and blessed them, v.* 22. This was one part of the priest's work, in which he was a type of Christ, who came into the world to bless us, and when he was parted from his disciples, at his ascension, *lifted up his hands and blessed them,* and in them his whole church, of which they were the elders and representatives, as the great high priest of our profession. Aaron *lifted up his hands* in blessing them, to intimate whence he desired and expected the blessing to come, even from heaven, which is God's throne. Aaron could but crave a blessing, it is God's prerogative to command it. Aaron, when he had blessed, came down; Christ, when he blessed, went up.

Verses 23–24

We are not told what Moses and Aaron went into the tabernacle to do, *v.* 23. Some of the Jewish writers say, "They went in to pray for the appearance of the divine glory;" most probably they went in that Moses might instruct Aaron how to do the service that was to be done there — burn incense, light the lamps, set the show-bread, etc., that he might instruct his sons in it. But, when they came out, they both joined in blessing the people, who stood expecting the promised appearance of the divine glory; and it was now (when Moses and Aaron concurred in praying) that they had what they waited for. Note, God's manifestations of himself, of his glory and grace, are commonly given in answer to prayer. When Christ was praying the *heavens were opened,* Lu. 3:21. The glory of God appeared, not while the sacrifices were in offering, but when the priests prayed (as 2 Chr. 5:13), when they praised God, which intimates that the prayers and praises of God's spiritual priests are more pleasing to God than all burnt-offerings and sacrifices.

When the solemnity was finished, the blessing pronounced, and the congregation ready to be dismissed, in the close of the day, then God testified his acceptance, which gave them such satisfaction as was well worth waiting for.

I. *The glory of the Lord appeared unto all the people, v.* 23. What the appearance of it was we are not told; no doubt it was such as carried its own evidence along with it. The glory which *filled the tabernacle* (Ex. 40:34) now showed itself at the door of the tabernacle to those who attended there, as a prince shows himself to the expecting crowd, to gratify them. God hereby testified of their gifts, and showed them that he was worthy for whom they should do all this. Note, Those that diligently attend upon God in the way he has appointed shall have such a sight of his glory as shall be abundantly to their satisfaction. Those that dwell in God's house with an eye of faith may *behold the beauty of the Lord.*

II. *There came a fire out from before the Lord, and consumed the sacrifice, v.* 24. Here the learned bishop Patrick has a very probable conjecture, that Moses and Aaron staid in the tabernacle till it was time to offer the evening sacrifice, which Aaron did, but it is not mentioned, because it was done of course, and it was this which the *fire that came out from the Lord consumed.* Whether this fire came from heaven, or out of the most holy place, or from that visible appearance of the glory of God which all the people saw, it was a manifest token of God's acceptance of their service, as, afterwards, of Solomon's sacrifice, 2 Chr. 7:1, and Elijah's, 1 Ki. 18:38.

1. This fire did consume (or, as the word is, *eat up*) the present sacrifice. And two ways this was a testimony of acceptance: — (1.) It signified the turning away of God's wrath from them. God's wrath is a consuming fire; this fire might justly have fastened upon the people, and consumed them for their sins; but its fastening upon the sacrifice, and consuming that, signified God's acceptance of that as an atonement for the sinner. (2.) It signified God's entering into covenant and communion with them: they ate their part of the sacrifice, and the fire of the Lord ate up his part; and thus he did, as it were, *sup with them, and they with him,* Rev. 3:20.

2. This fire did, as it were, take possession of the altar. The fire was thus kindled in God's house, which was to continue as long as the house stood, as we read before, *ch.* 6:13. This also was a figure of good things to come. The Spirit descended upon the apostles in *fire* (Acts 2:3), so ratifying their commission, as this spoken of here did the priests'. And the descent of this holy fire into our souls to kindle in them pious and devout affections towards God, and such a holy zeal as burns up the flesh and the lusts of it, is a certain token of God's gracious acceptance of our persons and performances. That redounds to God's glory which is the work of his own grace in us. *Hereby we know that we dwell in God, and God in us, because he hath thus given us of his Spirit,* 1 Jn. 4:13. Now henceforward, (1.) All their sacrifices and incense must be offered with this fire. Note, Nothing goes to God but what comes from him. We must have grace, that holy fire, from the God of grace, else we cannot *serve him acceptably,* Heb. 12:28. (2.) The priests must keep it burning with a constant supply of fuel, and the fuel must be wood, the cleanest of fuel. Thus those to whom God has given grace must take heed of quenching the Spirit.

III. We are here told how the people were affected with this discovery of God's glory and grace; they received it, 1. With the highest joy: *They shouted;* so stirring up themselves and one another to a holy triumph, in the assurance now given them that they had God nigh unto them, which is spoken of the grandeur of their nation, Deu. 4:7. 2. With the lowest reverence: *They fell on their faces,* humbly adoring the majesty of that God who vouchsafed thus to manifest himself to them. That is a sinful fear of God which drives us from him; a gracious fear makes us bow before him. Very good impressions were made upon their minds for the present, but they soon wore off, as those commonly do which are made by that which is only sensible; while the influences of faith are durable.

CHAPTER 10

The story of this chapter is as sad an interruption to the institutions of the levitical law as that of the golden calf was to the account of the erecting of the tabernacle. Here is, I. The sin and death of Nadab and Abihu, the sons of Aaron (*v.* 1, 2). II. The quieting of Aaron under this sore affliction (*v.* 3). III. Orders given and observed about the funeral and mourning (*v.* 4–7). IV. A command to the priests not to drink wine when they went in to minister (*v.* 8–11). V. The care Moses took that they should go on with their work, notwithstanding the agitation produced by this event (*v.* 12, etc.).

Verses 1–2

Here is, I. The great sin that Nadab and Abihu were guilty of: and a great sin we must call it, how little soever it appears in our eye, because it is evident by the punishment of it that it was highly provoking to the God of heaven, whose judgment, we are sure, is according to truth. But what was their sin? All the account here given of it is that they *offered strange fire before the Lord, which he commanded them not* (*v.* 1), and the same Num. 3:4. 1. It does not appear the they had any orders to burn incense at all at this time. It is true their consecration was completed the day before, and it was part of their work, as priests, to serve at the altar of incense; but, it should seem, the whole service of this solemn day of inauguration was to be performed by Aaron himself, for he *slew the sacrifices* (ch. 9:8, 15, 18), and his sons were only to attend him (v. 9, 12, 18); therefore Moses and Aaron only *went into the tabernacle*, v. 23. But Nadab and Abihu were so proud of the honour they were newly advanced to, and so ambitious of doing the highest and most honourable part of their work immediately, that though the service of this day was extraordinary, and done by particular direction from Moses, yet without receiving orders, or so much as asking leave from him, they took their censers, and they would enter into the tabernacle, at the door of which they thought they had attended long enough, and would burn incense. And then their *offering strange fire* is the same with *offering strange incense*, which is expressly forbidden, Ex. 30:9. Moses, we may suppose, had the custody of the incense which was prepared for this purpose (Ex. 39:38), and they, doing this without his leave, had none of the incense which should have been offered, but common incense, so that the smoke of their incense came from a *strange fire*. God had indeed required the priests to burn incense, but, at this time, it was what he commanded them not; and so their crime was like that of Uzziah the king, 2 Chr. 26:16. The priests were to burn incense only when *it was their lot* (Lu. 1:9), and, at this time, it was not theirs. 2. Presuming thus to burn incense of their own without order, no marvel that they made a further blunder, and instead of taking of the fire from the altar, which was newly kindled from before the Lord and which henceforward must be used in offering both sacrifice and incense (Rev. 8:5), they took common fire, probably from that with which the flesh of the peace-offerings was boiled, and this they made use of in burning incense; not being holy fire, it is called *strange fire*; and, though not expressly forbidden, it was crime enough that God *commanded it not*. For (as bishop Hall well observes here) "It is a dangerous thing, in the service of God, to decline from his own institutions; we have to do with a God who is wise to prescribe his own worship, just to require what he has prescribed, and powerful to revenge what he has not prescribed." 3. Incense was always to be burned by only one priest at a time, but here they would both go in together to do it. 4. They did it rashly, and with precipitation. They *snatched* their censers, so some read it, in a light careless way, without due reverence and seriousness: when all the people *fell upon their faces*, before the *glory of the Lord*, they thought the dignity of their office was such as to exempt them from such abasements. The familiarity they were admitted to bred a contempt of the divine Majesty; and now that they were priests they thought they might do what they pleased. 5. There is reason to suspect that they were drunk when they did it, because of the law which was given upon this occasion, v. 8. They had been feasting upon the peace-offerings, and the drink-offerings that attended them, and so their heads were light, or, at least, their *hearts were merry with wine;* they *drank and forgot the law* (Prov. 31:5) and were guilty of this fatal miscarriage. 6. No doubt it was done presumptuously; for, if it had been done through ignorance, they would have been allowed the benefit of the law lately made, even for the priests, that they should bring a sin-offering, ch. 4:2, 3. But *the soul that doth aught presumptuously*, and in contempt of God's majesty, authority, and justice, *that soul shall be cut of*, Num. 15:30.

II. The dreadful punishment of this sin: *There went out fire from the Lord, and devoured them*, v. 2. This fire which consumed the sacrifices came the same way with that which had consumed the sacrifices (ch. 9:24), which showed what justice would have done to all the guilty people if infinite mercy had not found and accepted a ransom; and, if that fire struck such an awe upon the people, much more would this.

1. Observe the severity of their punishment. (1.) They *died*. Might it not have sufficed if they had been only struck with a leprosy, as Uzziah, or struck dumb, as Zechariah, and both by the altar of incense? No; they were both struck dead. The wages of this sin was death. (2.) They died *suddenly*, in the very act of their sin, and had not time so much

as to cry, "Lord, have mercy upon us!" Though God is long-suffering to us-ward, yet sometimes he makes quick work with sinners; sentence is executed speedily: presumptuous sinners bring upon themselves a swift destruction, and are justly denied even space to repent. (3.) They died *before the Lord;* that is, before the veil that covered the mercy-seat; for even mercy itself will not suffer its own glory to be affronted. Those that sinned before the Lord died before him. Damned sinners are said to be tormented *in the presence of the Lamb*, intimating that he does not interpose on their behalf, Rev. 14:10. (4.) They died *by fire*, as by fire they sinned. They slighted the fire that came from before the Lord to consume the sacrifices, and thought other fire would do every jot as well; and now God justly made them feel the power of that fire which they did not reverence. Thus those that hate to be refined by the fire of divine grace will undoubtedly be ruined by the fire of divine wrath. The fire did not burn them to ashes, as it had done the sacrifices, nor so much as singe their coats (v. 5), but, like lightning, struck them dead in an instant; by these different effects of the same fire God would show that it was no common fire, but kindled *by the breath of the Almighty*, Isa. 30:23. (5.) It is twice taken notice of in scripture that they *died childless*, Num. 3:4, and 1 Chr. 24:2. By their presumption they had reproached God's name, and God justly blotted out their names, and laid that honour in the dust which they were proud of.

2. But why did the Lord deal thus severely with them? Were they not the sons of Aaron, the saint of the Lord, nephews to Moses, the great favourite of heaven? Was not the holy anointing oil sprinkled upon them, as men whom God had set apart for himself? Had they not diligently attended during the seven days of their consecration, and *kept the charge of the Lord*, and might not that atone for this rashness? Would it not excuse them that they were young men, as yet unexperienced in these services, that it was the first offence, and done in a transport of joy for their elevation? And besides, never could men be worse spared: a great deal of work was now lately cut out for the priests to do, and the priesthood was confined to Aaron and his seed; he has but four sons; if two of them die, there will not be hands enough to do the service of the tabernacle; if they die childless, the house of Aaron will become weak and little, and the priesthood will be in danger of being lost for want of heirs. But none of all these considerations shall serve either to excuse the offence or bring off the offenders. For, (1.) The sin was greatly aggravated. It was a manifest contempt of Moses, and the divine law that was given by Moses. Hitherto it had been expressly observed concerning every thing that was done that they did it *as the Lord commanded Moses*, in opposition to which it is here said they did that *which the Lord commanded them not*, but they did it of their own heads. God was now teaching his people obedience, and to do every thing by rule, as becomes servants; for priests therefore to break rules and disobey was such a provocation as must by no means go unpunished. Their character made their sin more exceedingly sinful. For the sons of Aaron, his eldest sons, whom God had chosen to be immediate attendants upon him, for them to be guilty of such a piece of presumption, it cannot be suffered. There was in their sin a contempt of God's glory, which had now newly appeared in fire, as if that fire were needless, they had as good of their own before. (2.) Their punishment was a piece of necessary justice, now at the first settling of the ceremonial institutions. It is often threatened in the law that such and such offenders should be cut off from the people; and here God explained the threatening with a witness. Now that the laws concerning sacrifices were newly made, lest any should be tempted to think lightly of them because they descended to many circumstances which seemed very minute, these that were the first transgressors were thus punished, for warning to others, and to show how jealous God is in the matters of his worship. Thus he *magnified the law and made it honourable;* and let his priests know that the caution which so often occurs in the laws concerning them, that they must do so *that they die not*, was not a mere bugbear, but fair warning of their danger, if they did the work of the Lord negligently. And no doubt this exemplary piece of justice at first prevented many irregularities afterwards. Thus Ananias and Sapphira were punished, when they presumed to lie to the Holy

Ghost, that newly-descended fire. (3.) As the people's falling into idolatry, presently after the moral law was given, shows the weakness of the law and its insufficiency to take away sin, so the sin and punishment of these priests show the imperfection of that priesthood from the very beginning, and its inability to shelter any from the fire of God's wrath otherwise than as it was typical of Christ's priesthood, in the execution of which there never was, nor can be, any irregularity, or false step taken.

Verses 3–7

We may well think that when Nadab and Abihu were struck with death all about them were struck with horror, and every face, as well as theirs, gathered blackness. Great consternation, no doubt, seized them, and they were all full of confusion; but, whatever the rest were, Moses was composed, and knew what he said and did, not being displeased, as David was in a like case, 2 Sa. 6:8. But though it touched him in a very tender part, and was a dreadful damp to one of the greatest joys he ever knew, yet he kept possession of his own soul, and took care to keep good order and a due decorum in the sanctuary.

I. He endeavours to pacify Aaron, and to keep him in a good frame under this sad dispensation, v. 3. Moses was a brother that was born for adversity, and has taught us, by his example, with seasonable counsels and comforts to *support the weak*, and *strengthen the feeble-minded*. Observe here,

1. What it was that Moses suggested to his poor brother upon this occasion: *This is it that the Lord spoke*. Note, The most quieting considerations under affliction are those that are fetched from the word of God. So and so *the Lord hath said*, and it is not for us to gainsay it. Note, also, In all God's providences it is good to observe the fulfilling of scripture, and to compare God's word and his works together, which if we do we shall find an admirable harmony and agreement between them, and that they mutually explain and illustrate each other. But, (1.) Where did God speak this? We do not find the very words; but to this purport he had said (Ex. 19:22), *Let the priests who come near to the Lord sanctify themselves, lest the Lord break forth upon them*. Indeed the whole scope and tenour of his law spoke this, that being a holy God, and a sovereign Lord, he must always be worshipped with holiness and reverence, and exactly according to his own appointment; and, if any jest with him, it is at their peril. Much had been said to this purport, as Ex. 29:43, 44; 34:14; ch. 8:35. (2.) What was it that God spoke? It was this (the Lord by his grace speak it to all our hearts!) *I will be sanctified in those that come nigh me*, whoever they are, and *before all the people I will be glorified*. Note, *First*, Whenever we worship God, we come nigh unto him, as spiritual priests. This consideration ought to make us very reverent and serious in all acts of devotion, that in them we approach to God, and present ourselves before him. *Secondly*, It concerns us all, when we come nigh to God, to sanctify him, that is, to give him the praise of his holiness, to perform every religious exercise as those who believe that the God with whom we have to do is a holy God, a God of spotless purity and transcendent perfection, Isa. 8:13. *Thirdly*, When we sanctify God we glorify him, for his holiness is his glory; and, when we sanctify him in our solemn assemblies, we glorify him *before all the people*, confessing our own belief of his glory and desiring that others also may be affected with it. *Fourthly*, If God be not sanctified and glorified by us, he will be sanctified and glorified upon us. He will take vengeance on those that profane his sacred name by trifling with him. If his rent be not paid, it shall be distrained for. (3.) But what was this to the present case? What was there in this to quiet Aaron? Two things: — [1.] This must silence him, that his sons deserved their death; for they were thus cut off from their people because they did not sanctify and glorify God. The acts of necessary justice, how hard soever they may seem to bear upon the persons concerned, are not to be complained of, but submitted to. [2.] This must satisfy him, that the death of his sons redounded to the honour of God, and his impartial justice would for it be adored throughout all ages.

2. What good effects this had upon him: *Aaron held his peace*, that is, he patiently submitted to the holy will of God in this sad providence, was *dumb, and opened not his mouth*, because God did it. Something he was ready

to say by way of complaint (as losers think they may have leave to speak), but he wisely suppressed it, *laid his hand upon his mouth,* and said nothing, for fear lest he *should offend with his tongue,* now that his *heart was hot within him.* Note, (1.) When God corrects us or ours for sin, it is our duty to be silent under the correction, not to quarrel with God, arraign his justice, or charge him with folly, but to acquiesce in all that God does; not only bearing, but accepting, the punishment of iniquity, and saying, as Eli, in a case not much unlike this, *It is the Lord, let him do what seemeth him good,* 1 Sa. 3:18. *If our children have sinned against God* (as Bildad puts the case, Job 8:4), *and he have cast them away for their transgression,* though it must needs be grievous to think that the children of our love should be the children of God's wrath, yet we must awfully adore the divine justice, and make no exceptions against its processes. (2.) The most effectual arguments to quiet a gracious spirit under afflictions are those that are fetched from God's glory; this silenced Aaron. It is true he is a loser in his comforts by this severe execution, but Moses has shown him that God is a gainer in his glory, and therefore he has not a word to say against it: if God be sanctified, Aaron is satisfied. Far be it form him that he should honour his sons more than God, or wish that God's name, or house, or law, should be exposed to reproach or contempt for the preserving of the reputation of his family. No; now, as well as in the matter of the golden calf, Levi does not *acknowledge his brethren,* nor *know his own children;* and therefore *they shall teach Jacob thy judgments, and Israel thy law,* Deu. 33:9, 10. Ministers and their families are sometimes exercised with sore trials that they may be examples to the believers of patience and resignation to God, and they may comfort others with that with which they themselves have been comforted.

II. Moses gives orders about the dead bodies. It was not fit that they should be left to lie where they fell; yet their own father and brethren, the amazed spectators of this dismal tragedy, durst not offer to lift them up, no, not to see whether there was any life left in them; they must neither be diverted from nor unfitted for the great work that was now upon their hands. *Let the dead bury their dead,* but they must go on with their service; that is, "Rather let the dead be unburied, if there be nobody else to do it, than that work for God should be left undone by those whom he has called to it." But Moses takes care of this matter, that though they died by the hand of justice in the act of sin, yet they should be decently buried, and they were so, 5:4, 5. 1. Some of their nearest relations were employed in it, who were cousins-german to their father, and are here named, who would perform this office with tenderness and respect. They were Levites only, and might not have come into the sanctuary, no, not upon such an occasion as this, if they had not had a special command for it. 2. They carried them out of the camp to be burned, so far were they from burying them in the place of worship, or the court of it, according to our modern usage, though they died there, that they did not bury them, nor any of their dead, within the lines of their camp; as afterwards their burying places were out of their cities. The tabernacle was pitched in the midst of the camp, so that they could not carry these dead priests to their graves without carrying them through one of the squadrons of the camp; and doubtless it was a very awful affecting sight to the people. The names of Nadab and Abihu had become very great and honourable among them; none more talked of, nor more expected to appear abroad after the days of their consecration, to receive the honours and caresses of the crowd, whose manner it is to adore the rising sun; and next to Moses and Aaron, who were old and going off, Nadab and Abihu (who had been in the mount with God, Ex. 24:1) were looked upon as the great favourites of heaven, and the hopes of their people; and now on a sudden, when the tidings of the event had scarcely reached their ears, to see them both carried out dead, with the visible marks of divine vengeance upon them, as sacrifices to the justice of God, they could not choose but cry out, *Who is able to stand before this holy Lord God?* 1 Sa. 6:20. 3. They carried them out (and probably buried them) in their coats, and the garments of their priesthood, which they had lately put on, and perhaps were too proud of. Thus the impartiality of God's justice was proclaimed, and all the people were made to know that even the priests' garments would not protect an offender from the wrath of God. And it was easy to argue, "If they escape not when they transgress, can we expect to go unpunished?" And the priests' clothes being so soon made grave-clothes might intimate both that *the law worketh death,* and that in the process of time that priesthood itself should be abolished and buried in the grave of the Lord Jesus.

III. He gives directions about the mourning.

1. That the priests must not mourn. Aaron and his two surviving sons, though sad in spirit, must not use any outward expressions of sorrow upon this sad occasion, nor so much as follow the corpse one step from the door of the tabernacle, *v.* 7. It was afterwards forbidden to the high priest to use the ceremonies of mourning for the death of any friend whatsoever, though it were a father or mother (*ch.* 21:11); yet it was allowed at the same time to the inferior priests to mourn for their near relations, *v.* 2, 3. But here it was forbidden both to Aaron and his sons, because, (1.) They were now actually waiting, doing a great work, which must by no means cease (Neh. 6:3); and it was very much for the honour of God that their attendance on him should take place of their respects to their nearest relations, and that all services should give way to those of their ministry. By this they must make it to appear that they had a greater value and affection for their God and their work than for the best friend they had in the world; as Christ did, Mt. 12:47, 48. And we are hereby taught, when we are serving God in holy duties, to keep out minds, as much as may be, intent and engaged, and not to suffer them to be diverted by any worldly thoughts, or cares, or passions. Let us always attend upon the Lord without distraction. (2.) Their brethren were cut off for their transgression by the immediate hand of God, and therefore they must not mourn for them lest they should seem to countenance the sin, or impeach the justice of God in the punishment. Instead of lamenting their own loss, they must be wholly taken up in applauding the sentence, and subscribing to the equity of it. Note, The public concerns of God's glory ought to lie nearer our hearts than any private affections of our own. Observe, How Moses frightens them into this submission, and holds the rod over them to still their crying (*v.* 6): *"Lest you die* likewise, and *lest wrath come upon all the people,* who may be in danger of suffering for your irreverence, and disobedience, and ungoverned passions;" and again (*v.* 7), *lest you die.* See here what use we are to make of the judgments of God upon others; we must double our guard over ourselves, *lest we likewise perish.* The death, especially the sudden death, of others, instead of moving our passion, should compose us into a holy reverence of God, a cautious separation from all sin, and a serious expectation of our own death. The reason given them is because *the anointing oil of your God is upon you,* the honour of which must be carefully preserved by your doing the duty of your office with cheerfulness. Note, Those that through grace have *received the anointing* ought not to disturb themselves with the *sorrow of the world,* which *worketh death.* It was very hard, no doubt, for Aaron and his sons to restrain themselves upon such an extraordinary occasion from inordinate grief, but reason and grace mastered the passion, and they bore the affliction with an obedient patience: *They did according to the word of Moses,* because they knew it to be the word of God. Happy those who thus are themselves under God's government, and have their passions under their own government.

2. The people must mourn: *Let the whole house of Israel bewail the burning which the Lord has kindled.* The congregation must lament, not only the loss of their priests, but especially the displeasure of God which appeared in it. They must bewail the burning that was kindled, that it might not burn further. Aaron and his sons were in danger of being too much affected with the providence, and therefore they are forbidden to mourn: the house of Israel were in danger of being too little affected with it, and therefore they are commanded to lament. Thus nature must always be governed by grace, according as it needs to be either constrained or restrained.

Verses 8–11

Aaron having been very observant of what God said to him by Moses, now God does him the honour to speak to him immediately (*v.* 8): *The Lord spoke unto Aaron,* and the rather because what was now to be said Aaron might perhaps have taken amiss from Moses, as if he had suspected him to have been a gluttonous man and a winebibber, so apt are we to resent cautions as accusations; therefore God saith it himself to him, *Do not drink wine, nor strong drink, when you go into the tabernacle,* and this at their peril, *lest you die, v.* 9. Probably they had seen the ill effect of it in Nadab and Abihu, and therefore must take warning by them. Observe here, 1. The prohibition itself: *Do not drink wine nor strong drink.* At other times they were allowed it (it was not expected that every priest should be a Nazarite), but during the time of their ministration they were forbidden it. This was one of the laws in Ezekiel's temple (Eze. 44:21), and so it is required of gospel ministers that they be *not given to wine,* 1 Tim. 3:3. Note, Drunkenness is bad in any, but it is especially scandalous and pernicious in ministers, who of all men ought to have the clearest heads and the cleanest hearts. 2. The penalty annexed to the prohibition: *Lest you die; lest you die* when you are in drink, *and so that day come upon you unawares,* Lu. 21:34. Or, "Lest you do that which will make you liable to be cut off by the hand of God." The danger of death we are continually in should engage us to *be sober,* 1 Pt. 4:7. It is a pity that it should ever be used for the support of licentiousness, as it is by those who argue, *Let us eat and drink, for to-morrow we die.* 3. The reasons assigned for this prohibition. They must needs to be sober, else they could not duly discharge their office; they will be in danger of *erring through wine,* Isa. 28:7. They must be sure to keep sober, (1.) That they might themselves be able to distinguish, in their ministrations, between that which was sacred and that which was common, and might never confound them, *v.* 10. It concerns the Lord's ministers to put a difference between holy and unholy, both things and persons, that they may separate between *the precious and the vile,* Jer. 15:19. (2.) That they might be able to teach the people (*v.* 11), for that was a part of the priests' work (Deu. 33:10); and those that are addicted to drunkenness are very unfit to teach people God's statutes, both because those that live after the flesh can have no experimental acquaintance with the things of the Spirit, and because such teachers pull down with one hand what they build up with the other.

Verses 12–20

Moses is here directing Aaron to go on with his service after this interruption. Afflictions should rather quicken us to our duty than take us off from it. Observe (*v.* 12), He spoke unto Aaron and to his sons *that were left.* The notice taken of their survivorship intimates, 1. That Aaron should take comfort under the loss of two of his sons, from this consideration, that God had graciously spared him the other two, and that he had reason to be thankful for the remnant that was left, and all his sons were not dead, and, in token of his thankfulness to God, to go on cheerfully in his work. 2. That God's sparing them should be an engagement upon them to proceed in his service, and not to fly off from it. Here were four priests consecrated together, two were taken away, and two left; therefore the two that were left should endeavour to fill up the places of those that were gone, by double care and diligence in the services of the priesthood. Now,

I. Moses repeats the directions he had formerly given them about eating their share of the sacrifices, *v.* 12–14, 15. The priests must learn not only to *put a difference between the holy and the unholy,* as they had been taught (*v.* 10), but also to distinguish between that which was most holy and that which was only holy of the things that were to eat. That part of the meat-offering which remained to the priest was most holy, and therefore must be eaten in the courts of the tabernacle, and by Aaron *sons* only (*v.* 12, 13); but the breast and shoulder of the peace-offerings might be eaten in any decent place out of the courts of the tabernacle, and by the daughters of their families. The meat-offerings, being annexed to the burnt-offerings, were intended only and wholly for the glory of God; but the peace-offerings were ordained for the furtherance of men's joy and comfort; the former therefore were the more sacred, and to be had more in veneration. This distinction the priests must carefully observe, and take heed of making any blunders. Moses does not pretend to give any reasons for this difference, but refers to his instructions: *For so am I commanded, v.* 13. This was reason enough; he had *received of the Lord all that he delivered unto them,* 1 Co. 11:23.

II. He enquires concerning one deviation from the appointment, which it seems had happened upon this occasion, which was this: — There was a goat to be sacrificed as a *sin-offering or the people, ch.* 9:15. Now the law of the sin-offerings was that if the blood of them was brought into the holy place, as that of the sin-offerings for the priest was, then the flesh was to be burnt without the camp; otherwise it was to be eaten by the priest in the holy place, *ch.* 6:30. The meaning of this is here explained (*v.* 17), that the priests did hereby *bear the iniquity of the congregation,* that is, they were types of him who was to be made sin for us, and on whom God would *lay the iniquity of us all.* Now the blood of this goat was not brought into the holy place, and yet, it seems, it was burnt without the camp. Now observe here, 1. The gentle reproof Moses gives to Aaron and his sons for this irregularity. Here again Aaron sons are said to be those *that were left alive* (*v.* 16), who therefore ought to have taken warning; and Moses was *angry with them.* Though he was the meekest man in the world, it seems he could be angry; and when he thought God was disobeyed and dishonoured, and the priesthood endangered, he would be angry. Yet observe how very mildly he deals with Aaron and his sons, considering their present affliction. He only tells them *they should indeed have eaten it in the holy place,* but is willing to hear what they have to say for themselves, being loth to speak to the grief of those whom God had wounded.

2. The plausible excuse which Aaron makes for this mistake. Moses charged the fault upon Eleazar and Ithamar (*v.* 16), but it is probable that what they did was by Aaron direction, and therefore he apologized for it. He might have pleaded that this was a sin-offering for the congregation, and if it had been a bullock it must have been wholly burnt (*ch.* 4:21), and therefore why not now that it was a goat? But it seems it was otherwise ordered at this time, and therefore he makes his affliction his excuse, *v.* 19. Observe, (1.) How he speaks of affliction: *Such things have befallen me,* such sad things, which could not but go near his heart, and make it very happy. He was a high priest *taken from among men,* and could not put off natural affection when he put on the holy garments. He held his peace (*v.* 3), yet his sorrow was stirred, as David's, Ps. 39:2. Note, There may be a deep sense of affliction even where there is a sincere resignation to the will of God in the affliction. "*Such things* as never befel me before, and as I little expected now. My spirits cannot but sink, when I see my family sinking; I must needs be heavy, when God is angry:" thus it is easy to say a great deal to aggravate an affliction, but it is better to say little. (2.) How he makes this an excuse for his varying from the appointment about the sin-offering. He could not have eaten it but in his mourning, and with a sorrowful spirit; and would this have been accepted? He does not plead that his heart was so full of grief that he had no appetite for it, but that he feared it would not be accepted. Note, [1.] Acceptance with God is the great thing we should desire and aim at in all our religious services, particularly in the Lord's supper, which is our eating of the sin-offering. [2.] The sorrow of the world is a very great hindrance to our acceptable performance of holy duties, both as it is discomposing to ourselves, takes off our chariot-wheels and makes us drive heavily (1 Sa. 1:7, 8), and as it is displeasing to God, whose will it is that we should serve him cheerfully, Deu. 12:7. Mourner's bread was polluted, Hos. 9:4. See Mal. 3:14.

3. The acquiescence of Moses in this excuse: *He was content, v.* 20. Perhaps he thought it justified what they had done. God had provided that what could not be eaten might be burnt. Our unfitness for duty, when it is natural and not sinful, will have great allowances made for it; and God will have mercy and not sacrifice. At least he thought it did very much extenuate the fault; *the spirit indeed was willing, but the flesh was weak.* God by Moses showed that he considered his frame. It appeared that Aaron sincerely aimed at God's acceptance; and those that do so with an upright heart shall find he is not *extreme to mark what they do amiss.* Nor must we be severe in our animadversions upon every mistake, *considering ourselves, lest we also be tempted.*

CHAPTER 11

The ceremonial law is described by the apostle (Heb. 9:9, 10) to consist, not only "in gifts and sacrifices," which hitherto have been treated of in this book, but "in meats, and drinks, and divers washings" from ceremonial uncleanness, the laws concerning which begin with this chapter, which puts a difference between some sorts of flesh-meat and others, allowing some to be eaten as clean and forbidding others as unclean. "There is one kind of flesh of men." Nature startles at the thought of eating this, and none do it but such as have arrived at the highest degree of barbarity, and become but one remove from brutes; therefore there needed no law against it. But there is "another kind of flesh of beasts," concerning which the law directs here (*v.* 1–8), "another of fishes" (*v.* 9–12), "another of birds" (*v.* 13–19), and "another of creeping things," which are distinguished into two sorts, flying creeping things (*v.* 20–28) and creeping things upon the earth (*v.* 29–43). And the law concludes with the general rule of holiness, and reasons for it (*v.* 44, etc.).

Verses 1–8

Now that Aaron was consecrated a high priest over the house of God, God spoke to him with Moses, and appointed them both as joint-commissioners to deliver his will to the people. He spoke both to Moses and to Aaron about this matter; for it was particularly required of the priests that they should put a difference between clean and unclean, and teach the people to do so. After the flood, when God entered into covenant with Noah and his sons, he allowed them to eat flesh (Gen. 9:13), whereas before they were confined to the productions of the earth. But the liberty allowed to the sons of Noah is here limited to the sons of Israel. They might eat flesh, but not all kinds of flesh; some they must look upon as unclean and forbidden to them, others as clean and allowed them. The law in this matter is both very particular and very strict. But what reason can be given for this law? Why may not God's people have as free a use of all the creatures as other people? 1. It is reason enough that God would have it so: his will, as it is law sufficient, so it is reason sufficient; for his will is his wisdom. He saw good thus to try and exercise the obedience of his people, not only in the solemnities of his altar, but in matters of daily occurrence at their own table, that they might remember they were under authority. Thus God had tried the obedience of man in innocency, by forbidding him to eat of one particular tree. 2. Most of the meats forbidden as unclean are such as were really unwholesome, and not fit to be eaten; and those of them that we think wholesome enough, and use accordingly, as the rabbit, the hare, and the swine, perhaps in those countries, and to their bodies, might be hurtful. And then God in this law did by them but as a wise and loving father does by his children, whom he restrains from eating that which he knows will make them sick. Note, The Lord is for the body, and it is not only folly, but sin against God, to prejudice our health for the pleasing of our appetite. 3. God would thus teach his people to distinguish themselves from other people, not only in their religious worship, but in the common actions of life. Thus he would show them that they must not be numbered among the nations. It should seem there had been, before this, some difference between the Hebrews and other nations in their food, kept up by tradition; for the Egyptians and they would not eat together, Gen. 43:32. And even before the flood there was a distinction of beasts into clean and not clean (Gen. 7:2), which distinction was quite lost, with many other instances of religion, among the Gentiles. But by this law it is reduced to a certainty, and ordered to be kept up among the Jews, that thus, by having a diet peculiar to themselves, they might be kept from familiar conversation with their idolatrous neighbours, and might typify God's spiritual Israel, who not in these little things, but in the temper of their spirits, and the course of their lives, should be governed by a sober singularity, and not be conformed to this world. The learned observe further, That most of the creatures which by this law were to be abominated as unclean were such as were had in high veneration among the heathen, not so much for food as for divination and sacrifice to their gods; and therefore those are here mentioned as unclean, and an abomination, which yet they would not be in any temptation to eat, that they might keep up a religious loathing of that for which the Gentiles had a superstitious value. The swine, with the later Gentiles, was sacred to Venus, the owl to Minerva, the eagle to Jupiter, the dog to Hecate, etc., and all these are here made unclean. As to the beasts, there is a general rule laid down, that those which both part the hoof and chew the cud were clean, and those only: these are particularly mentioned in the repetition of this law (Deu. 14:4, 5), where it appears that the Israelites had variety enough allowed them, and needed not to complain of the confinement they were under. Those beasts that did not both *chew the cud and divide the hoof* were unclean, by which rule the flesh of swine, and of hares, and of rabbits, was prohibited to them, though commonly used among us. Therefore, particularly at the eating of any of these, we should give thanks for the liberty granted us in this matter by the gospel, which teaches us that *every creature of God is good,* and we are to *call nothing common or unclean.* Some observe a significancy in the rule here laid down for them to distinguish by, or at least think it may be alluded to. Meditation, and other acts of devotion done by the hidden man of the heart, may be signified by the chewing of the cud, digesting our spiritual food; justice and charity towards men, and the acts of a good conversation, may be signified by the *dividing of the hoof.* Now either of these without the other will not serve to recommend us to God, but both must go together, good affections in the heart and good works in the life: if either be wanting, we are not clean, surely we are not clean. Of all the creatures here forbidden as unclean, none has been more dreaded and detested by the pious Jews than swine's flesh. Many were put to death by Antiochus because they would not eat it. This, probably, they were most in danger of being tempted to, and therefore possessed themselves and their children with a particular antipathy to it, calling it not by its proper name, but *a strange thing.* It should seem the Gentiles used it superstitiously (Isa. 65:4), *they eat swine's flesh;* and therefore God forbids all use of it to his people, lest they should learn of their neighbours to make that ill use of it. Some suggest that the prohibition of these beasts as unclean was intended to be a caution to the people against the bad qualities of these creatures. We must not be filthy nor wallow in the mire as swine, nor be timorous and faint-hearted as hares, nor dwell in the earth as rabbits; let not man that is in honour make himself like these beasts that perish. The law forbade, not only the eating of them, but the very touching of them; for those that would be kept from any sin must be careful to avoid all temptations to it, and every thing that looks towards it or leads to it.

Verses 9–19

Here is, 1. A general rule concerning fishes, which were clean and which not. All that had fins and scales they might eat, and only those odd sorts of water-animals that have not were forbidden, *v.* 9, 10. The ancients accounted fish the most delicate food (so far were they from allowing it on fasting-days, or making it an instance of mortification to eat fish); therefore God did not lay much restraint upon his people in them; for he is a Master that allows his servants not only for necessity but for delight. Concerning the prohibited fish it is said, *They shall be an abomination to you* (*v.* 10–12), that is, "You shall count them unclean, and not only not eat of them, but keep at a distance from them." Note, Whatever is unclean should be to us an abomination; *touch not the unclean thing.* But observe, It was to be an abomination only to Jews; the neighbouring nations were under none of these obligations, nor are these things to be an abomination to us Christians. The Jews were honoured with peculiar privileges, and therefore, lest they should be proud of those, *Transeunt cum onere — They were likewise laid under peculiar restraints.* Thus God's spiritual Israel, as they are dignified above others by the gospel-covenant of adoption and friendship, so they must be mortified more than others by the gospel-commands of self-denial and bearing the cross. 2. Concerning fowls here is no general rule given, but a particular enumeration of those fowls that they must abstain from as unclean, which implies an allowance of all others. The critics here have their hands full to find out what is the true signification of the Hebrew words here used, some of which still remain uncertain, some sorts of fowls being peculiar to some countries. Were the law in force now, we should be concerned to know with certainty what are prohibited by it; and perhaps if we did, and were better acquainted with the nature of the fowls here mentioned, we should admire the knowledge of Adam, in giving them names expressive of their natures, Gen. 2:20. But the law being repealed, and the learning in a great measure lost, it is sufficient for us to observe that of the fowls here forbidden, (1.) Some are birds of prey, as the eagle, vulture, etc., and God would have his people to abhor every thing that is barbarous and cruel, and not to live by blood and rapine. Doves that are preyed upon were fit to be food for man and offerings to God; but kites and hawks that prey upon them must be looked upon as an abomination to God and man; for the condition of those that are persecuted for righteousness' sake appears to an eye of faith every way better than that of their persecutors. (2.) Others of them are solitary birds, that abide in dark and desolate places, as the owl and the pelican (Ps. 102:6), and the cormorant and raven (Isa. 34:11); for God's Israel should not be a melancholy people, nor affect sadness and constant solitude. (3.) Others of them feed upon that which is impure, as the stork on serpents, others of them on worms; and we must not only abstain from all impurity ourselves, but from communion with those that allow themselves in it. (4.) Others of them were used by the Egyptians and other Gentiles in their divinations. Some birds were reckoned fortunate, others ominous; and their soothsayers had great regard to the flights of these birds, all which therefore must be an abomination to God's people, who must not learn the way of the heathen.

Verses 20–42

Here is the law, 1. Concerning flying insects, as flies, wasps, bees, etc.; these they might not eat (*v.* 20), nor indeed are they fit to be eaten; but there were several sorts of locusts which in those countries were very good meat, and much used: John Baptist lived upon them in the desert, and they are here allowed them, *v.* 21, 22. 2. Concerning the creeping things on the earth; these were all forbidden (*v.* 29, 30, and again, *v.* 41, 42); for it was the curse of the serpent that *upon his belly he should go,* and therefore between him and man there was an enmity put (Gen. 3:15), which was preserved by this law. Dust is the meat of the creeping things, and therefore they are not fit to be man's meat. 3. Concerning the dead carcasses of all these unclean animals. (1.) Every one that touched them was to be unclean until the evening, *v.* 24–28. This law is often repeated, to possess them with a dread of every thing that was prohibited, though no particular reason for the prohibition did appear, but only the will of the Law-maker. Not that they were to be looked upon as defiling to the conscience, or that it was a sin against God to touch them, unless done in contempt of the law: in many cases, somebody must of necessity touch them, to remove them; but it was a *ceremonial* uncleanness they contracted, which for the time forbade them to come into the tabernacle, or to eat of any of the holy things, or so much as to converse familiarly with their neighbours. But the uncleanness continued only till the evening, to signify that all ceremonial pollutions were to come to an end by the death of Christ in the evening of the world. And we must learn, by daily renewing our repentance every night for the sins of the day, to cleanse ourselves from the pollution we contract by them, that we may not lie down in our uncleanness. Even unclean animals they might touch while they were alive without contracting any ceremonial uncleanness by it, as horses and dogs, because they were allowed to use them for service; but they might not touch them when they were dead, because they might not eat their flesh; and what must not be eaten must not be touched, Gen. 3:3. (2.) Even the vessels, or other things they fell upon, were thereby made unclean until the evening (*v.* 32), and if they were earthen vessels they must be broken, *v.* 33. This taught them carefully to avoid every thing that was polluting, even in their common actions. Not only the vessels of the sanctuary, but every pot in Jerusalem and Judah, must be *holiness to the Lord,* Zec. 14:20, 21. The laws in these cases are very critical, and the observance of them would be difficult, we should think, if every thing that a dead mouse or rat, for instance, falls upon must be unclean; and if it were an oven, or ranges for pots, they must all be broken down, *v.* 35. The exceptions also are very nice, *v.* 36, etc. All this was designed to exercise them to a constant care and exactness in their obedience, and to teach us, who by Christ are delivered from these burdensome observances, not to be less circumspect in the more weighty matters of the law. We ought as industriously to preserve our precious souls from the pollutions

of sin, and as speedily to cleanse them when they are polluted, as they were to preserve and cleanse their bodies and household goods from those ceremonial pollutions.

Verses 43–47

Here is, I. The exposition of this law, or a key to let us into the meaning of it. It was not intended merely for a bill of fare, or as the directions of a physician about their diet, but God would hereby teach them to sanctify themselves and to be holy, *v.* 44. That is, 1. They must hereby learn to put a difference between good and evil, and to reckon that it could not be all alike what they did, when it was not all alike what they ate. 2. To maintain a constant observance of the divine law, and to govern themselves by that in all their actions, even those that are common, which ought to be performed *after a godly sort,* 3 Jn. 6. Even eating and drinking must be by rule, and *to the glory of God,* 1 Co. 10:31. 3. To distinguish themselves from all their neighbours, as a people set apart for God, and obliged not to walk as the Gentiles: and all this is holiness. Thus these *rudiments of the world* were their tutors and governors (Gal. 4:2, 3), to bring them to that which is the revival of our first state in Adam and the earnest of our best state with Christ, that is, *holiness,* without which no man shall see the Lord. This is indeed the great design of all the ordinances, that by them we may sanctify ourselves and learn to be holy. Even This law concerning their food, which seemed to stoop so very low, aimed thus high, for it was the statute-law of heaven, under the Old Testament as well as the New, that *without holiness no man shall see the Lord.* The caution therefore (*v.* 43) is, *You shall not make yourselves abominable.* Note, By having fellowship with sin, which is abominable, we make ourselves abominable. That man is truly miserable who is in the sight of God abominable; and none are so but those that make themselves so. The Jewish writers themselves suggest that the intention of this law was to forbid them all communion by marriage, or otherwise, with the heathen, Deu. 7:2, 3. And thus the moral of it is obligatory on us, forbidding us to *have fellowship with the unfruitful works of darkness;* and, without this real holiness of the heart and life, *he that offereth an oblation is as if he offered swine's blood* (Isa. 66:3); and, if it was such a provocation for a man to eat swine's flesh himself, much more it must be so to offer swine's blood at God's altar; see Prov. 15:8. II. The reasons of this law; and they are all taken from the Law-maker himself, to whom we must have respect in all acts of obedience. 1. *I am the Lord your God,* v. 44. "Therefore you are bound to do thus, in pure obedience." God's sovereignty over us, and propriety in us, oblige us to do whatever he commands us, how much soever it crosses our inclinations. 2. *I am holy,* v. 44, and again, v. 45. If God be holy, we must be so, else we cannot expect to be accepted of him. His holiness is his glory (Ex. 15:11), and therefore it *becomes his house for ever,* Ps. 93:5. This great precept, thus enforced, though it comes in here in the midst of abrogated laws, is quoted and stamped for a gospel precept, 1 Pt. 1:16, where it is intimated that all these ceremonial restraints were designed to teach us that we must not *fashion ourselves according to our former lusts in our ignorance,* v. 14. 3. *I am the Lord that bringeth you out of the land of Egypt,* v. 45. This was a reason why they should cheerfully submit to distinguishing laws, having of late been so wonderfully dignified with distinguishing favours. He that had done more for them than for any other people might justly expect more from them. III. The conclusion of this statute: *This is the law of the beasts, and of the fowl,* etc., v. 46, 47. This law was to them a statute for ever, that is, as long as that economy lasted; but under the gospel we find it expressly repealed by a voice from heaven to Peter (Acts 10:15), as it had before been virtually set aside by the death of Christ, with the other ordinances that *perished in the using: Touch not, taste not, handle not,* Col. 2:21, 22. And now we are sure that *meat commends us not to God* (1 Co. 8:8), and that *nothing is unclean of itself* (Rom. 14:14), nor does that defile a man which goes into his mouth, but that which comes out from the heart, Mt. 15:11. Let us therefore, 1. Give thanks to God that we are not under this yoke, but that to us every creature of God is allowed as good, and nothing to be refused. 2. *Stand fast in the liberty wherewith Christ has made us free,* and take heed of those doctrines which *command*

to abstain from meats, and so would revive Moses again, 1 Tim. 4:3, 4. 3. Be strictly and conscientiously temperate in the use of the good creatures God has allowed us. If God's law has given us liberty, let us lay restraints upon ourselves, and never feed ourselves without fear, lest our table be a snare. *Set a knife to thy throat, if thou be a man given to appetite;* and *be not desirous of dainties* or varieties, Prov. 23:2, 3. Nature is content with little, grace with less, but lust with nothing.

CHAPTER 12

After the laws concerning clean and unclean food come the laws concerning clean and unclean persons; and the first is in this chapter concerning the ceremonial uncleanness of women in child-birth (*v.* 1–5). And concerning their purification from that uncleanness (*v.* 6, etc.).

Verses 1–5

The law here pronounces women lying-in ceremonially unclean. The Jews say, "The law extended even to an abortion, if the child was so formed as that the sex was distinguishable." 1. There was some time of strict separation immediately after the birth, which continued seven days for a son and fourteen for a daughter, *v.* 2, 5. During these days she was separated from her husband and friends, and those that necessarily attended her were ceremonially unclean, which was one reason why the males were not circumcised till the eighth day, because they participated in the mother's pollution during the days of her separation. 2. There was also a longer time appointed for their purifying; thirty-three days more (forty in all) if the birth were a male, and double that time if a female, *v.* 4, 5. During this time they were only separated from the sanctuary and forbidden to eat of the passover, or peace-offerings, or, if a priest's wife, to eat of any thing that was holy to the Lord. Why the time of both those was double for a female to what it was for a male I can assign no reason but the will of the Law-maker; in Christ Jesus no difference is made of male and female, Gal. 3:28; Col. 3:11. But this ceremonial uncleanness which the law laid women in child-bed under was to signify the pollution of sin which we are all conceived and born in, Ps. 51:5. For, if the root be impure, so is the branch, *Who can bring a clean thing out of an unclean?* If sin had not entered, nothing but purity and honour had attended all the productions of that great blessing, *Be fruitful and multiply;* but now that the nature of man is degenerated the propagation of that nature is laid under these marks of disgrace, because of the sin and corruption that are propagated with it, and in remembrance of the curse upon the woman that was first in the transgression. That *in sorrow* (to which it is here further added *in shame*) she should *bring forth children.* And the exclusion of the woman for so many days from the sanctuary, and all participation of the holy things, signified that our original corruption (that sinning sin which we brought into the world with us) would have excluded us for ever from the enjoyment of God and his favours if he had not graciously provided for our purifying.

Verses 6–8

A woman that had lain in, when the time set for her return to the sanctuary had come, was not to attend there empty, but must bring her offerings, *v.* 6. 1. A *burnt-offering;* a lamb if she was able, if poor, a pigeon. This she was to offer in thankfulness to God for his mercy to her, in bringing her safely through the pains of child-bearing and all the perils of child-bed, and in desire and hopes of God's further favour both to her and to the child. When a child is born there is joy and there is hope, and therefore it was proper to bring this offering, which was of a general nature; for what we rejoice in we must give thanks for, and what we are in hopes of we must pray for. But, besides this, 2. She must offer a *sin-offering,* which must be the same for poor and rich, a turtle-dove or a young pigeon; for, whatever difference there may be between rich and poor in the sacrifices of acknowledgment, that of atonement is the same for both. This sin-offering was intended either, (1.) To complete her purification from that ceremonial uncleanness which, though it was not in itself sinful, yet was typical of moral pollution; or, (2.) To make atonement for that which was really sin, either an inordinate desire of the blessing of children or discontent or impatience under the pains of child-bearing. It is only by

Christ, the great sin-offering, that the corruption of our nature is done away, and to that it is owing that we are not for ever excluded by it from the sanctuary, and from eating of the holy things. According to this law, we find that the mother of our blessed Lord, though he was not conceived in sin as others, yet *accomplished the days of purification,* and then presented her son to the Lord, being a first-born, and brought her own offering, *a pair of turtle-doves,* Lu. 2:22–24. So poor were Christ's parents that they were not able to bring a lamb for a burnt-offering; and so early was Christ *made under the law, to redeem those that were under it.* The morality of this law obliges those women that have received mercy from God in child-bearing with all thankfulness to own God's goodness to them, acknowledging themselves unworthy of it, and (which is the best purification of women that have been saved in child-bearing, 1 Tim. 2:15) to *continue in faith, and charity, and holiness, with sobriety;* for this shall please the Lord better than the turtle-doves or the young pigeons.

CHAPTER 13

The next ceremonial uncleanness is that of the leprosy, concerning which the law was very large and particular; we have the discovery of it in this chapter, and the cleansing of the leper in the next. Scarcely any one thing in all the levitical law takes up so much room as this. I. Rules are here given by which the priest must judge whether the man had the leprosy or no, according as the symptom was that appeared. 1. If it was a swelling, a scab, or a bright spot (*v.* 1–17). 2. If it was a bile (*v.* 18–23). 3. If it was in inflammation (*v.* 24–28). 4. If it was in the head or beard (*v.* 29–37). 5. If it was a bright spot (*v.* 38, 39). 6. If it was in a bald head (*v.* 40–44). II. Direction is given how the leper must be disposed of (*v.* 45, 46). III. Concerning the leprosy in garments (*v.* 47, etc.).

Verses 1–17

I. Concerning the plague of leprosy we may observe in general, 1. That it was rather an uncleanness than a disease; or, at least, so the law considered it, and therefore employed not the physicians but the priests about it. Christ is said to cleanse lepers, not to cure them. We do not read of any that died of the leprosy, but it rather buried them alive, by rendering them unfit for conversation with any but such as were infected like themselves. Yet there is a tradition that Pharaoh, who sought to kill Moses, was the first that ever was struck with this disease, and that he died of it. It is said to have begun first in Egypt, whence it spread into Syria. It was very well known to Moses, when he put his own hand into his bosom and took it out leprous. 2. That it was a plague inflicted immediately by the hand of God, and came not from natural causes, as other diseases; and therefore must be managed according to a divine law. Miriam's leprosy, and Gehazi's, and king Uzziah's, were all the punishments of particular sins: and, if generally it was so, no marvel there was so much care taken to distinguish it from a common distemper, that none might be looked upon as lying under this extraordinary token of divine displeasure but those that really were so. 3. That it is a plague not now known in the world; what is commonly called the leprosy is of a quite different nature. This seems to have been reserved as a particular scourge for the sinners of those times and places. The Jews retained the idolatrous customs they had learnt in Egypt, and therefore God justly caused this with some others of the diseases of Egypt to follow them. Yet we read of Naaman the Syrian, who was a leper, 2 Ki. 5:1. 4. That there were other breakings-out in the body which did very much resemble the leprosy, but were not it, which might make a man sore and loathsome and yet not ceremonially unclean. Justly are our bodies called vile bodies, which have in them the seeds of so many diseases, by which the lives of so many are made bitter to them. 5. That the judgment of it was referred to the priests. Lepers were looked upon as stigmatized by the justice of God, and therefore it was left to his servants the priests, who might be presumed to know his mark best, to pronounce who were lepers and who were not. All the Jews say, "Any priest, though disabled by a blemish to attend the sanctuary, might be a judge of the leprosy, provided the blemish were not in his eye. And he might" (they say) "take a common person to assist him in the search, but the priest only must pronounce the judgment." 6. That it was a figure of the moral pollution of men's minds by sin, which is the leprosy of the soul, defiling to the conscience, and from which Christ alone can cleanse us; for herein the power of his grace infinitely transcends that of the legal priesthood, that the priest could only convict the leper (for by the law is the knowledge of sin), but Christ can cure the leper, he can take away sin. *Lord, if thou wilt, thou canst make me clean,* which was more than the priests could do, Mt. 8:2. Some think that the leprosy signified, not so much sin in general as a state of sin, by which men are separated from God (their spot not being the spot of God's children), and scandalous sin, for which men are to be shut out from the communion of the faithful. It is a work of great importance, but of great difficulty, to judge of our spiritual state: we have all cause to suspect ourselves, being conscious to ourselves of sores and spots, but whether clean or unclean is the question. A man might have a scab (*v.* 6) and yet be clean: the best have their infirmities; but, as there were certain marks by which to know that it was a leprosy, so there are characters of such as are in the gall of bitterness, and the work of ministers is to declare the judgment of leprosy and to assist those that suspect themselves in the trial of their spiritual state, remitting or retaining sin. And hence the keys of the kingdom of heaven are said to be given to them, because they are to separate between the precious and the vile, and to judge who are fit as clean to partake of the holy things and who as unclean must be debarred from them.

II. Several rules are here laid down by which the judgment of the priest must be governed. 1. If the sore was but *skin-deep,* it was to be hoped it was not the *leprosy, v.* 4. But, if it was *deeper than the skin,* the man must be pronounced unclean, *v.* 3. The infirmities that consist with grace do not sink deep into the soul, but *the mind* still *serves the law of God,* and the *inward man delights in it,* Rom. 7:22, 25. But if the matter be really worse than it shows, and the inwards be infected, the case is dangerous. 2. If the sore *be at a stay,* and do not *spread,* it is no leprosy, *v.* 4, 5. But if it *spread much abroad,* and continue to do so after several inspections, the case is bad, *v.* 7, 8. If men do not grow worse, but a stop be put to the course of their sins and their corruptions be checked, it is to be hoped they will grow better; but if sin get ground, and they become worse every day, they are going downhill. 3. If there was *proud raw flesh* in the rising, the priest needed not to wait any longer, it was certainly a leprosy, *v.* 10, 11. Nor is there any surer indication of the badness of a man's spiritual state than the heart's rising in self-conceit, confidence in the flesh, and resistance of the reproofs of the word and strivings of the Spirit. 4. If the eruption, whatever it was, *covered all the skin* from head to foot, it was no leprosy (*v.* 12, 13); for it was an evidence that the vitals were sound and strong, and nature hereby helped itself, throwing out what was burdensome and pernicious. There is hope in the small-pox when they come out well: so if men freely confess their sins, and hide them not, there is no danger comparable to theirs that cover their sins. Some gather this from it, that there is more hope of the profane than of hypocrites. The publicans and harlots went into the kingdom of heaven before scribes and Pharisees. In one respect, the sudden breakings-out of passion, though bad enough, are not so dangerous as malice concealed. Others gather this, that, if we judge ourselves, we shall not be judged; if we see and own that there is *no health in us, no soundness in our flesh,* by reason of sin, we shall *find grace in the eyes of the Lord.* 5. The priest must take time in making his judgment, and not give it rashly. If the matter looked suspicious, he must shut up the patient seven days, and then seven days more, that his judgment might be *according to truth.* This teaches all, both ministers and people, not to be hasty in their censures, nor to judge any thing *before the time.* If *some men's sins go before unto judgment,* the sins of others *follow after,* and so men's good works; therefore let nothing be done *suddenly,* 1 Tim. 5:22, 24, 25. 6. If the person suspected was found to be clean, yet he must *wash his clothes* (*v.* 6), because he had been under the suspicion, and there had been in him that which gave ground for the suspicion. Even the prisoner that is acquitted must go down on his knees. We have need to be washed in the blood of Christ from our spots, though they be not leprosy-spots; for who can say, *I am pure from sin?* though there are those who through grace are *innocent from the great transgression.*

Verses 18–37

The priest is here instructed what judgment to make if there was any appearance of a leprosy, either, 1. In an old ulcer, or bile, that has been healed, *v.* 18, etc. When old sores, that seemed to be cured, break out again, it is to be feared there is a leprosy in them; such is the danger of those who, having escaped the pollutions of the world, are again *entangled therein and overcome.* Or, 2. In a burn by accident, for this seems to be meant, *v.* 24, etc. The burning of strife and contention often proves the occasion of the rising up and breaking out of that corruption which witnesses to men's faces that they are unclean. 3. In a scall-head. And in this commonly the judgment turned upon a very small matter. If the hair in the scall was black, it was a sign of soundness; if yellow, it was an indication of a leprosy, *v.* 30–37. The other rules in these cases are the same with those mentioned before. In reading of these several sorts of ailments, it will be good for us, 1. To lament the calamitous state of human life, which lies exposed to so many grievances. What troops of diseases are we beset with on every side! and they all entered by sin. 2. To give thanks to God if he has never afflicted us with any of these sores: if the constitution is healthful, and the body lively and easy, we are bound to glorify God with our bodies.

Verses 38–46

We have here,

I. Provisos that neither a *freckled skin* nor a *bald head* should be mistaken for a leprosy, *v.* 38–41. Every deformity must not forthwith be made a ceremonial defilement. Elisha was jeered for his *bald head* (2 Ki. 2:23); but it was the children of Bethel, that knew not the judgments of their God, who turned it to his reproach.

II. A particular brand set upon the leprosy if at any time it did appear in a *bald head: The plague is in his head, he is utterly unclean, v.* 44. If the leprosy of sin have seized the head, if the judgment be corrupted, and wicked principles which countenance and support wicked practices, be embraced, it is an *utter uncleanness,* from which few are ever cleansed. Soundness in the faith keeps the leprosy from the head, and saves conscience from being shipwrecked.

III. Directions what must be done with the convicted leper. When the priest, upon mature deliberation, had solemnly pronounced him unclean,

1. He must pronounce himself so, *v.* 45. He must put himself into the posture of a mourner and cry, *Unclean, unclean.* The leprosy was not itself a sin, but it was a sad token of God's displeasure and a sore affliction to him that was under it. It was a reproach to his name, put a full stop to his business in the world, cut him off from conversation with his friends and relations, condemned him to banishment till he was cleansed, shut him out from the sanctuary, and was, in effect, the ruin of all the comfort he could have in this world. Heman, it would seem, either was a leper or alludes to the melancholy condition of a leper, Ps. 88:8, etc. He must therefore, (1.) Humble himself under the mighty hand of God, not insisting upon his cleanness when the priest had pronounced him unclean, but justifying God and accepting the *punishment of his iniquity.* He must signify this by *rending his clothes, uncovering* his head, and *covering his upper lip,* all tokens of shame and confusion of face, and very significant of that self-loathing and self-abasement which should fill the hearts of penitents, the language of which is self-judging. Thus must we take to ourselves the shame that belongs to us, and with broken hearts call ourselves by our own name, *Unclean, unclean* — heart unclean, life unclean, unclean by original corruption, unclean by actual transgression — unclean, and therefore worthy to be for ever excluded from communion with God, and all hope of happiness in him. *We are all as an unclean thing* (Isa. 64:6) — unclean, and therefore undone, if infinite mercy do not interpose. (2.) He must give warning to others to take heed of coming near him. Wherever he went, he must cry to those he saw at a distance, *"I am unclean, unclean,* take heed of touching me." Not that the leprosy was catching, but by the touch of a leper ceremonial uncleanness was contracted. Every one therefore was concerned to avoid it; and the leper himself must give notice of the danger. And this was all that the law could do, in that it was weak through the flesh; it taught the leper to cry, *Unclean, unclean,* but the gospel has put another cry into the lepers' mouths, Lu. 17:12, 13, where we find ten lepers crying with a loud voice,

Jesus, Master, have mercy on us. The law only shows us our disease; the gospel shows us our help in Christ.

2. He must then be shut out of the camp, and afterwards, when they came to Canaan, out of the city, town, or village, where he lived, and *dwell alone* (*v.* 46), associating with none but those that were lepers like himself. When king Uzziah became a leper, he was banished from his palace, and *dwelt in a separate house,* 2 Chr. 26:21. And see 2 Ki. 7:3. This typified the purity which ought to be preserved in the gospel church, by the solemn and authoritative exclusion of scandalous sinners, that hate to be reformed, from the communion of the faithful. *Put away from among yourselves that wicked person,* 1 Co. 5:13.

Verses 47–59

This is the law concerning the plague of leprosy in a garment, whether linen or woollen. A leprosy in a garment, with discernible indications of it, the colour changed by it, the garment fretted, the nap worn off, and this in some one particular part of the garment, and increasing when it was shut up, and not to be got out by washing is a thing which to us now is altogether unaccountable. The learned confess that it was a sign and a miracle in Israel, an extraordinary punishment inflicted by the divine power, as a token of great displeasure against a person or family. 1. The process was much the same with that concerning a leprous person. The garment suspected to be tainted was not to be burnt immediately, though, it may be, there would have been no great loss of it; for in no case must sentence be given merely upon a surmise, but it must be *shown to the priest.* If, upon search, it was found that there was a *leprous spot* (the Jews say no bigger than a bean), it must be *burnt,* or at least that part of the garment in which the spot was, *v.* 52, 57. If the cause of the suspicion was gone, it must be *washed,* and then might be used, *v.* 58. 2. The signification also was much the same, to intimate the great malignity there is in sin: it not only defiles the sinner's conscience, but it brings a stain upon all his employments and enjoyments, all he has and all he does. *To those that are defiled and unbelieving is nothing pure,* Tit. 1:15. And we are taught hereby to hate even *the garments spotted with the flesh,* Jude 23. Those that make their clothes servants to their pride and lust may see them thereby tainted with a leprosy, and doomed to the fire, Isa. 3:18–24. But the ornament of *the hidden man of the heart is incorruptible,* 1 Pt. 3:4. The robes of righteousness never fret nor are moth-eaten.

CHAPTER 14

The former chapter directed the priests how to convict a leper of ceremonial uncleanness. No prescriptions are given for his cure; but, when God had cured him, the priests are in this chapter directed how to cleanse him. The remedy here is only adapted to the ceremonial part of his disease; but the authority Christ gave to his ministers was to cure the lepers, and so to cleanse them. We have here, I. The solemn declaration of the leper's being clean, with the significant ceremony attending it (*v.* 1–9). II. The sacrifices which he was to offer to God eight days after (*v.* 10–32). III. The management of a house in which appeared signs of a leprosy (*v.* 33–53). And the conclusion and summary of this whole matter (*v.* 54, etc.).

Verses 1–9

Here, I. It is supposed that the plague of the leprosy was not an incurable disease. Uzziah's indeed continued to the day of his death, and Gehazi's was entailed upon his seed; but Miriam's lasted only seven days: we may suppose that it often wore off in process of time. Though God contend long, he will *not contend for ever.*

II. The judgment of the cure, as well as that of the disease, was referred to the priest. He must go out of the camp to the leper, to see whether his leprosy was healed, *v.* 3. And we may suppose the priest did not contract any ceremonial uncleanness by coming near the leper, as another person would. It was in mercy to the poor lepers that the priests particularly had orders to attend them, for *the priests' lips should keep knowledge;* and those in affliction have need to be instructed both how to bear their afflictions and how to reap benefit by them, have need of the word, in concurrence with the rod, to bring them to repentance; therefore it is well for those that are sick if they have these messengers of the Lord of hosts with them, these interpreters, to *show unto them God's uprightness,* Job 33:23. When the leper was shut out, and could not go to the priests, it was well that the priests might come to him. *Is any sick? Let him send for the elders,* the min-

isters, Jam. 5:14. If we apply it to the spiritual leprosy of sin, it intimates that when we withdraw from those who walk disorderly, that they may be ashamed, we must not count them as enemies, but admonish them as brethren, 2 Th. 3:15. And also that when God by his grace has brought those to repentance who were shut out of communion for scandal, they ought with tenderness, and joy, and sincere affection, to be received in again. Thus Paul orders concerning the excommunicated Corinthian that when he had given evidences of his repentance they should forgive him, and comfort him, and *confirm their love towards him,* 2 Co. 2:7, 8. And ministers are entrusted by our Master with the declarative power of loosing as well as binding: both must be done with great caution and deliberation, impartially and without respect of persons, with earnest prayer to God for directions, and a sincere regard to the edification of the body of Christ, due care being always taken that sinners may not be encouraged by an excess of lenity, nor penitents discouraged by an excess of severity. Wisdom and sincerity are profitable to direct in this case.

III. If it was found that the leprosy was healed, the priest must declare it with a particular solemnity. The leper or his friends were to get ready two birds caught for this purpose (any sort of wild birds that were clean), and cedarwood, and scarlet, and hyssop; for all these were to be used in the ceremony. 1. A preparation was to be made of blood and water, with which the leper must be sprinkled. One of the birds (and the Jews say, if there was any difference, it must be the larger and better of the two) was to be killed over an earthen cup of spring water, so that the blood of the bird might discolour the water. This (as some other types) had its accomplishment in the death of Christ, when out of his pierced side there came water and blood, Jn. 19:34. Thus Christ comes into the soul for its cure and cleansing, *not by water only, but by water and blood,* 1 Jn. 5:6. 2. The living bird, with a little scarlet wool, and a bunch of hyssop, must be fastened to a cedar stick, dipped in the water and blood, which must be so sprinkled upon him that was to be cleansed, *v.* 6, 7. The cedar-wood signified the restoring of the leper to his strength and soundness, for that is a sort of wood not apt to putrefy. The scarlet wool signified his recovering a florid colour again, for the leprosy made him white as snow. And the hyssop intimated the removing of the disagreeable scent which commonly attended the leprosy. The cedar the stateliest plant, and hyssop the meanest, are here used together in this service (see 1 Ki. 4:33); for those of the lowest rank in the church may be of use in their place, as well as those that are most eminent, 1 Co. 12:2. Some make the slain bird to typify Christ *dying for our sins,* and the living bird Christ *rising again for our justification.* The dipping of the living bird in the blood of the slain bird intimated that the merit of Christ's death was that which made his resurrection effectual for our justification. He took his blood with him into the holy place, and there appeared a lamb as it had been slain. The cedar, scarlet wool, and hyssop, must all be dipped in the blood; for the word and ordinances, and all the operations of the Spirit, receive their efficacy for our cleansing from the blood of Christ. The leper must be sprinkled *seven times,* to signify a complete purification, in allusion to which David prays, *Wash me thoroughly,* Ps. 51:2. Naaman was directed to wash *seven times,* 2 Ki. 5:10. 3. The living bird was then to be let loose in the open field, to signify that the leper, being cleansed, was now no longer under restraint and confinement, but might take his liberty to go where he pleased. But this being signified by the flight of a bird towards heaven was an intimation to him henceforward to seek the things that are above, and not to spend this new life to which God had restored him merely in the pursuit of earthly things. This typified that glorious liberty of the children of God to which those are advanced who through grace are sprinkled from an evil conscience. Those whose souls before *bowed down to the dust* (Ps. 44:25), in grief and fear, now fly in the open firmament of heaven, and soar upwards upon the wings of faith and hope, and holy love and joy. 4. The priest must, upon this, pronounce him clean. It was requisite that this should be done with solemnity, that the leper might himself be the more affected with the mercy of God to him in his recovery, and that others might be satisfied to converse with him. Christ is our priest, to whom the Father

has committed all judgment, and particularly the judgment of the leprosy. By his definitive sentence impenitent sinners will have their everlasting portion assigned them with the unclean (Job 36:14), out of the holy city; and all that by his grace are cured and cleansed shall be received into the camp of the saints, into which no unclean thing shall enter. Those are clean indeed whom Christ pronounces so, and they need not regard what men say of them. But, though Christ was the *end of this law for righteousness,* yet being in the days of his flesh *made under the law,* which as yet stood unrepealed, he ordered those lepers whom he had cured miraculously to go and *show themselves to the priest,* and *offer for their cleansing according to the law,* Mt. 8:4; Lu. 17:14. The type must be kept up till it was answered by its antitype. 5. When the leper was pronounced clean, he must wash his body and his clothes, and shave *off all his hair* (*v.* 8), must still tarry seven days out of the camp, and on the seventh day must do it again, *v.* 9. The priest having pronounced him clean from the disease, he must make himself as clean as ever he could from all the remains of it, and from all other defilements, and he must take time to do this. Thus those who have the comfort of the remission of their sins, by the sprinkling of the blood of Christ upon their consciences, must with the utmost care and caution *cleanse themselves from all filthiness both of flesh and spirit,* and thoroughly *purge themselves from their old sins;* for *every one that hath this hope in him will* be concerned to *purify himself.*

Verses 10–20

Observe, I. To complete the purification of the leper, on the eighth day, after the former solemnity performed without the camp, and, as it should seem, before he returned to his own habitation, he was to attend *at the door of the tabernacle,* and was there to be *presented to the Lord,* with his offering, *v.* 11. Observe here, 1. That the mercies of God oblige us to present ourselves to him, Rom. 12:1. 2. When God has restored us to the liberty of ordinances again, after restraint by sickness, distance, or otherwise, we should take the first opportunity of testifying our respect to God, and our affection to his sanctuary, by a diligent improvement of the liberty we are restored to. When Christ had healed the impotent man, he soon after *found him in the temple,* Jn. 5:14. When Hezekiah asks, *What is the sign that I shall go up to the house of the Lord?* he means, "What is the sign that I shall recover?" intimating that if God restored him his health, so that he should be able to go abroad, the house of the Lord should be the first place he would go to. 3. When we present ourselves before the Lord we must present our offerings, devoting to God with ourselves all we have and can do. 4. Both we and our offerings must be presented before the Lord by the priest that made us clean, even our Lord Jesus, else neither we nor they can be accepted.

II. Three lambs the cleansed leper was to bring, with a meat-offering, and a log of oil, which was about half a pint. Now, 1. Most of the ceremony peculiar to this case was about the trespass-offering, the lamb for which was offered first, *v.* 12. And, besides the usual rites with which the trespass-offering was offered, some of the blood was to be put upon the ear, and thumb, and great toe, of the leper that was to be cleansed (*v.* 14), the very same ceremony that was used in the consecration of the priests, *ch.* 8:23, 24. It was a mortification to them to see the same purification necessary for them that was for a leper. The Jews say that the leper stood without the gate of the tabernacle and the priest within, and thus the ceremony was performed through the gate, signifying that now he was admitted with other Israelites to attend in the courts of the Lord's house again, and was as welcome as ever; though he had been a leper, and though perhaps the name might stick by him as long as he lived (as we read of one who probably was cleansed by our Lord Jesus, who yet afterwards is called *Simon the leper,* Mt. 26:6), yet he was as freely admitted as ever to communion with God and man. After the blood of the offering had been put with the priest's finger upon the extremities of the body, to include the whole, some of the oil that he brought, which was first waved and then sprinkled before the Lord, was in like manner put in the same places upon the blood. "The blood" (says the learned bishop Patrick) "seems to have been a token of forgiveness, the oil of healing," for God first *for-*

giveth our iniquities and then *healeth our diseases,* Ps. 103:3. See Isa. 38:17. Wherever the blood of Christ is applied for justification the oil of the Spirit is applied for sanctification; for these two are inseparable and both necessary to our acceptance with God. Nor shall our former leprosy, if it be healed by repentance, be any bar to these glorious privileges. Cleansed lepers are as welcome to the blood and the oil as consecrated priests. *Such were some of you, but you are washed.* When the leper was sprinkled the water must have blood in it (*v.* 5), when he was anointed the oil must have blood under it, to signify that all the graces and comforts of the Spirit, all his purifying dignifying influences, are owing to the death of Christ: it is by his blood alone that we are sanctified. 2. Besides this there must be a sin-offering and a burnt-offering, a lamb for each, *v.* 19, 20. By each of these offerings, it is said, the priests shall *make atonement for him.* (1.) His moral guilt shall be removed; the sin for which the leprosy was sent shall be pardoned, and all the sins he had been guilty of in his afflicted state. Note, The removal of any outward trouble is then doubly comfortable to us when at the same time God gives us some assurance of the forgiveness of our sins. If we *receive the atonement,* we have reason to rejoice, Rom. 5:11. (2.) His ceremonial pollution shall be removed, which had kept him from the participation of the holy things. And this is called *making an atonement for him,* because our restoration to the privileges of God's children, typified hereby, is owing purely to the great propitiation. When the atonement is made for him he shall be clean, both to his own satisfaction and to his reputation among his neighbours; he shall retrieve both his credit and his comfort, and both these true penitents become entitled to, both ease and honour, by their interest in the atonement. The burnt-offering, besides the atonement that was made by it, was a thankful acknowledgment of God's mercy to him: and the more immediate the hand of God was both in the sickness and in the cure the more reason he had thus to give glory to him, and thus, as our Saviour speaks (Mk. 1:44), to *offer for his cleansing* all *those things which Moses commanded for a testimony unto them.*

Verses 21–32

We have here the gracious provision which the law made for the cleansing of *poor lepers.* If they were not able to bring three lambs, and three tenth-deals of flour, they must bring one lamb, and one tenth-deal of flour, and, instead of the other two lambs, two turtle-doves or two young pigeons, *v.* 21, 22. Here see, 1. That the poverty of the person concerned would not excuse him if he brought no offering at all. Let none think that because they are poor God requires no service from them, since he has considered them, and demands that which it is in the power of the poorest to give. *"My son, give me thy heart,* and with that the *calves of thy lips* shall be accepted instead of the *calves of the stall."* 2. That God expected from those who were poor only according to their ability; *his commandments are not grievous,* nor does he make us to *serve with an offering.* The poor are as welcome to God's altar as the rich; and, if there be first a willing mind and an honest heart, two pigeons, when they are the utmost a man is able to get, are as acceptable to God as two lambs; for he requires *according to what a man has and not according to what he has not.* But it is observable that though a meaner sacrifice was accepted from the poor, yet the very same ceremony was used for them as was for the rich; for their souls are as precious and Christ and his gospel are the same to both. Let not us therefore have *the faith of our Lord Jesus Christ with respect of persons,* Jam. 2:1.

Verses 33–53

This is the law concerning the leprosy in a house. Now that they were in the wilderness they dwelt in tents, and had no houses, and therefore the law is made only an appendix to the former laws concerning the leprosy, because it related, not to their present state, but to their future settlement. The leprosy in a house is as unaccountable as the leprosy in a garment; but, if we see not what natural causes of it can be assigned, we may resolve it into the power of the God of nature, who here says, *I put the leprosy in a house* (*v.* 34), as his curse is said to *enter into a house,* and *consume it with the timber and stones thereof,* Zec. 5:4. Now, 1. It is supposed that even in Canaan itself, the land of promise, their houses might be infected with a leprosy. Though it was a holy land, this would not secure them from this plague, while the inhabitants were many of them so unholy. Thus a place and a name in the visible church will not secure wicked people from God's judgments. 2. It is likewise taken for granted that the owner of the house will make the priest acquainted with it, as soon as he sees the least cause to suspect the leprosy in his house: *It seemeth to me there is as it were a plague in the house, v.* 35. Sin, where that reigns in a house, is a plague there, as it is in a heart. And masters of families should be aware and afraid of the first appearance of gross sin in their families, and put away the iniquity, whatever it is, far from their tabernacles, Job 22:23. They should be jealous with a godly jealousy concerning those under their charge, lest they be drawn into sin, and take early advice, if it but seem that there is a plague in the house, lest the contagion spread, and many be by it defiled and destroyed. 3. If the priest, upon search, found that the leprosy had got into the house, he must try to cure it, by taking gout that part of the building that was infected, *v.* 40, 41. This was like cutting off a gangrened limb, for the preservation of the rest of the body. Corruption should be purged out in time, before it spread; for *a little leaven leaveneth the whole lump. If thy right hand offend thee, cut it off.* 4. If yet it remained in the house, the whole house must be pulled down, and all the materials carried to the dunghill, *v.* 44, 45. The owner had better be without a dwelling than live in one that was infected. Note, The leprosy of sin, if it be obstinate under the methods of cure, will at last be the ruin of families and churches. If Babylon will not be healed, she shall be forsaken and abandoned, and (according to the law respecting the leprous house), they shall not *take of her a stone for a corner, nor a stone for foundations,* Jer. 51:9, 26. The remainders of sin and corruption in our mortal bodies are like this leprosy in the house; after all our pains in scraping and plastering, we shall never be quite clear of it, till the earthly house of this tabernacle be dissolved and taken down; when we are dead we shall be free from sin, and not till then, Rom. 6:7. 5. If the taking out the infected stones cured the house, and the leprosy did not spread any further, then the house must be cleansed; not only aired, that it might be healthful, but purified from the ceremonial pollution, that it might be fit to be the habitation of an Israelite. The ceremony of its cleansing was much the same with that of cleansing a leprous person, *v.* 49, etc. This intimated that the house was smitten for the man's sake (as bishop Patrick expresses it), and he was to look upon himself as preserved by divine mercy. The houses of Israelites are said to be *dedicated* (Deu. 20:5), for they were a holy nation, and therefore they ought to keep their houses pure from all ceremonial pollutions, that they might be fit for the service of that God to whom they were devoted. And the same care should we take to reform whatever is amiss in our families, that we and our houses may serve the Lord; see Gen. 35:2. Some have thought the leprosy in the house was typical of the idolatry of the Jewish church, which did strangely cleave to it; for, though some of the reforming kings took away the infected stones, yet still it broke out again, till by the captivity of Babylon God took down the house, and carried it to an unclean land; and this proved an effectual cure of their inclination to idols and idolatrous worships.

Verses 54–57

This is the conclusion of this law concerning the leprosy. There is no repetition of it in Deuteronomy, only a general memorandum given (Deu. 24:8), *Take heed in the plague of leprosy.* We may see in this law, 1. The gracious care God took of his people Israel, for to them only this law pertained, and not to the Gentiles. When Naaman the Syrian was cured of his leprosy he was not bidden to show himself to the priest, though he was cured in Jordan, as the Jews that were cured by our Saviour were. Thus those who are entrusted with the key of discipline in the church judge those only *that are within;* but *those that are without God judgeth,* 1 Co. 5:12, 13. 2. The religious care we ought to take of ourselves, to keep our minds from the dominion of all sinful affections and dispositions, which are both their disease and their defilement, that we may be fit for the service of God. We ought also to avoid all bad company, and, as much as may be, to avoid coming with- in the danger of being infected by it. *Touch not the unclean thing, saith the Lord, and I will receive you,* 2 Co. 6:17.

CHAPTER 15

In this chapter we have laws concerning other ceremonial uncleannesses contracted either by bodily disease like that of the leper, or some natural incidents, and this either, I. In men (*v.* 1–18). Or, II. In women (*v.* 19–33). We need not be at all curious in explaining these antiquated laws, it is enough if we observe the general intention; but we have need to be very cautious lest sin take occasion by the commandment to become more exceedingly sinful; and exceedingly sinful it is when lust is kindled by sparks of fire from God's altar. The case is bad with the soul when it is putrefied by that which should purify it.

Verses 1–18

We have here the law concerning the ceremonial uncleanness that was contracted by running issues in men. It is called in the margin (*v.* 2) the *running of the reins:* a very grievous and loathsome disease, which was, usually the effect and consequent of wantonness and uncleanness, and a dissolute course of life, filling men's bones with the sins of their youth, and leaving them to mourn at the last, when all the pleasures of their wickedness have vanished, and nothing remains but the pain and anguish of a rotten carcase and a wounded conscience. And what fruit has the sinner then of those things whereof he has so much reason to be ashamed? Rom. 6:21. As modesty is *an ornament of grace to the head and chains about the neck,* so chastity is *health to the navel and marrow to the bones;* but uncleanness is a *wound and dishonour,* the consumption of the flesh and the body, and a sin which is often its own punishment more than any other. It was also sometimes inflicted by the righteous hand of God for other sins, as appears by David's imprecation of a curse upon the family of Joab, for the murder of Abner. 2 Sa. 3:29, *Let there not fail from the house of Joab one that hath an issue, or is a leper.* A vile disease for vile deserts. Now whoever had this disease upon him, 1. He was himself unclean, *v.* 2. He must not dare to come near the sanctuary, it was at his peril if he did, nor might he eat of the holy things. This signified the filthiness of sin, and of all the productions of our corrupt nature, which render us odious to God's holiness, and utterly unfit for communion with him. Out of a pure heart well kept are the issues of life (Prov. 4:23), but out of an unclean heart comes that which is defiling, Mt. 12:34, 35. 2. He made every person and thing unclean that he touched, or that touched him, *v.* 4–12. His bed, and his chair, and his saddle, and every thing that belonged to him, could not be touched without a ceremonial uncleanness contracted, which a man must remain conscious to himself of till sunset, and from which he could not be cleansed without washing his clothes, and bathing his flesh in water. This signified the contagion of sin, the danger we are in of being polluted by conversing with those that are polluted, and the need we have with the utmost circumspection to *save ourselves from this untoward generation.* 3. When he was cured of the disease, yet he could not be cleansed from the pollution without a sacrifice, for which he was to prepare himself by seven days' expectation after he was perfectly clear from his distemper, and by bathing in spring water, *v.* 13–15. This signified the great gospel duties of faith and repentance, and the great gospel privileges of the application of Christ's blood to our souls for our justification and his grace for our sanctification. God has promised to sprinkle clean water upon us, and to cleanse us from all our filthiness, and has appointed us by repentance to wash and make ourselves clean: he has also provided a sacrifice of atonement, and requires us by faith to interest ourselves in that sacrifice; for it is *the blood of Christ his Son that cleanses us from all sin,* and by which atonement is made for us, that we may have admission into God's presence and may partake of his favour.

Verses 19–33

This is concerning the ceremonial uncleanness which women lay under from their issues, both those that were regular and healthful, and according to the course of nature (*v.* 19–24), and those that were unseasonable, excessive, and the disease of the body; such was the bloody issue of that poor woman who was suddenly cured by touching the hem of Christ's garment, after she had lain twelve years under her distemper, and had spent her estate upon physicians and physic in vain. This made the woman that was afflicted with it unclean (*v.* 25) and every thing she touched unclean, *v.* 26, 27. And if she was cured, and found by seven days' trial that she was perfectly free from her issue of blood, she was to be cleansed by the offering of two turtle-doves or two young pigeons, to make an atonement for her, *v.* 28, 29. All wicked courses, particularly idolatries, are compared to the uncleanness of a *removed woman* (Eze. 36:17), and, in allusion to this, it is said of Jerusalem (Lam. 1:9), *Her filthiness is in her skirts*, so that (as it follows, *v.* 17) she was shunned as a menstruous woman.

I. The reasons given for all these laws (which we are ready to think might very well have been spared) we have, *v.* 31. 1. *Thus shall you separate the children of Israel* (for to them only and their servants and proselytes these laws pertained) *from their uncleanness;* that is, (1.) By these laws they were taught their privilege and honour, that they were *purified unto God a peculiar people*, and were intended by the holy God for a kingdom of priests, a holy nation; for that was a defilement to them which was not so to others. (2.) They were also taught their duty, which was to preserve the honour of their purity, and to keep themselves from all sinful pollutions. It was easy for them to argue that if those pollutions which were natural, unavoidable, involuntary, their affliction and not their sin, rendered them for the time so odious that they were not fit for communion either with God or man, much more abominable and filthy were they if they sinned against the light and law of nature, by drunkenness, adultery, fraud, and the like sins, which defile the very mind and conscience. And, if these ceremonial pollutions could not be done away but by sacrifice and offering, something greater and much more valuable must be expected and depended upon for the purifying of the soul from the uncleanness of sin. 2. Thus their dying in their uncleanness by the hand of God's justice, if while they were under any of these defilements they should come near the sanctuary, would be prevented. Note, It is a dangerous thing to die in our uncleanness; and it is our own fault if we do, since we have not only fair warning given us, by God's law, against those things that will defile us, but also such gracious provision made by his gospel for our cleansing if at any time we be defiled. 3. In all these laws there seems to be a special regard had to the honour of the tabernacle, to which none must approach in their uncleanness, that they *defile not my tabernacle*. Infinite Wisdom took this course to preserve in the minds of that careless people a continual dread of, and veneration for, the manifestations of God's glory and presence among them in his sanctuary. Now that the tabernacle of God was with men familiarity would be apt to breed contempt, and therefore the law made so many things of frequent incidence to be ceremonial pollutions, and to involve an incapacity of drawing near to the sanctuary (making death the penalty), that so they might not approach without great caution, and reverence, and serious preparation, and fear of being found unfit. Thus they were taught never to draw near to God but with an awful humble sense of their distance and danger, and an exact observance of every thing that was required in order to their safety and acceptance.

II. And what duty must we learn from all this? 1. Let us bless God that we are not under the yoke of these carnal ordinances, that, as nothing can destroy us, so nothing can defile us, but sin. Those may now partake of the Lord's supper who durst not then eat of the peace-offerings. And the defilement we contract by our sins of daily infirmity we may be cleansed from in secret by the renewed acts of repentance and faith, without bathing in water or bringing an offering to the door of the tabernacle. 2. Let us carefully abstain from all sin, as defiling to the conscience, and particularly from all fleshly lusts, *possessing our vessel in sanctification and honour, and not in the lusts of uncleanness*, which not only pollute the soul, but *war against it*, and threaten its ruin. 3. Let us all see how indispensably necessary real holiness is to our future happiness, and get our hearts purified by faith, that we may see God. Perhaps it is in allusion to these laws which forbade the unclean to approach the sanctuary that when it is asked, *Who shall stand in God's holy place?* it is answered, *He that hath clean hands and a pure heart* (Ps. 24:3, 4); for *without holiness no man shall see the Lord.*

CHAPTER 16

In this chapter we have the institution of the annual solemnity of the day of atonement, or expiation, which had as much gospel in it as perhaps any of the appointments of the ceremonial law, as appears by the reference the apostle makes to it, Heb. 9:7, etc. We had before divers laws concerning sin-offerings for particular persons, and to be offered upon particular occasions; but this is concerning the stated sacrifice, in which the whole nation was interested. The whole service of the day is committed to the high priest. I. He must never come into the most holy place but upon this day (*v.* 1, 2). II. He must come dressed in linen garments (*v.* 4). III. He must bring a sin-offering and a burnt-offering for himself (*v.* 3), offer his sin-offering (*v.* 6–11), then go within the veil with some of the blood of his sin-offering, burn incense, and sprinkle the blood before the mercy-seat (*v.* 12–14). IV. Two goats must be provided for the people, lots cast upon them, and, 1. One of them must be a sin-offering for the people (*v.* 5, 7–9), and the blood of it must be sprinkled before the mercy-seat (*v.* 15–17), and then some of the blood of both the sin-offerings must be sprinkled upon the altar (*v.* 18, 19). 2. The other must be a scape-goat (*v.* 10), the sins of Israel must be confessed over him, and then he must be sent away into the wilderness (*v.* 20–22), and he that brought him away must be ceremonially unclean (*v.* 26). V. The burnt-offerings were then to be offered, the fat of the sin-offerings burnt on the altar, and their flesh burnt without the camp (*v.* 23–25, 27, 28). VI. The people were to observe the day religiously by a holy rest and holy mourning for sin; and this was to be a statute for ever (*v.* 29, etc.).

Verses 1–4

Here is, I. The date of this law concerning the day of atonement: it was *after the death of the two sons of Aaron* (*v.* 1), which we read, *ch.* 10:1. 1. Lest Aaron should fear that any remaining guilt of that sin should cleave to his family, or (seeing the priests were so apt to offend) that some after-sin of his other sons should be the ruin of his family, he is directed how to make atonement for his house, that it might keep in with God; for the atonement for it would be the establishment of it, and preserve the entail of the blessing upon it. 2. The priests being warned by the death of Nadab and Abihu to approach to God with reverence and godly fear (without which they came at their peril), directions are here given how the nearest approach might be made, not only without peril, but to unspeakable advantage and comfort, if the directions were observed. When they were cut off for an undue approach, the rest must not say, "Then we will not draw near at all," but, "Then we will do it by rule." They died for their sin, therefore God graciously provides for the rest, that they die not. Thus God's judgments on some should be instructions to others.

II. The design of this law. One intention of it was to preserve a veneration for the most holy place, within the veil, where the *Shechinah*, or divine glory, was pleased to dwell between the cherubim: *Speak unto Aaron, that he come not at all times into the holy place, v.* 2. Before the veil some of the priests came every day to burn incense upon the golden altar, but within the veil none must ever come but the high priest only, and he but on one day in the year, and with great ceremony and caution. That place where God manifested his special presence must not be made common. If none must come into the presence-chamber of an earthly king uncalled, no, not the queen herself, upon pain of death (Esth. 4:11), was it not requisite that the same sacred respect should be paid to the Kings of kings? But see what a blessed change is made by the gospel of Christ; all good Christians have now *boldness to enter into the holiest*, through the veil, every day (Heb. 10:19, 20); and we *come boldly* (not as Aaron must, with fear and trembling) to the *throne of grace*, or mercy-seat, Heb. 4:16. While the manifestations of God's presence and grace were sensible, it was requisite that they should thus be confined and upon reserve, because the objects of sense the more familiar they are made the less awful or delightful they become; but now that they are purely spiritual it is otherwise, for the objects of faith the more they are conversed with the more do they manifest of their greatness and goodness: now therefore we are welcome to come at all times into the *holy place not made with hands*, for we are made to *sit together with Christ in heavenly places* by faith, Eph. 2:6. Then Aaron must not come near at all times, *lest he die;* we now must come near at all times that we may live: it is distance only that is our death. Then God appeared in the cloud upon the mercy-seat, but now with open face we behold, not in a dark cloud, but in a clear glass, the glory of the Lord, 2 Co. 3:18.

III. The person to whom the work of this day was committed, and that was the high priest only: *Thus shall Aaron come into the holy place, v.* 3. He was to do all himself upon the day of atonement: only there was a second provided to be his substitute or supporter, in case any thing should befal him, either of sickness or ceremonial uncleanness, that he could not perform the service of the day. All Christians are spiritual priests, but Christ only is the high priest, and he alone it is that makes atonement, nor needed he either assistant or substitute.

IV. The attire of the high priest in this service. He was not to be dressed up in his rich garments that were peculiar to himself: he was not to put on the ephod, with the precious stones in it, but only the linen clothes which he wore in common with the inferior priests, *v.* 4. That meaner dress did best become him on this day of humiliation; and, being thinner and lighter, he would in it be more expedite for the work or service of the day, which was all to go through his hands. Christ, our high priest, made atonement for sin in our nature; not in the robes of his own peculiar glory, but the linen garments of our mortality, clean indeed, but mean.

Verses 5–14

The Jewish writers say that for seven days before the day of expiation the high priest was to retire from his own house, and to dwell in a chamber of the temple, that he might prepare himself for the service of this great day. During those seven days he himself did the work of the inferior priests about the sacrifices, incense, etc., that he might have his hand in for this day: he must have the institution read to him again and again, that he might be fully apprised of the whole method. 1. He was to begin the service of the day very early with the usual morning sacrifice, after he had first washed his whole body before he dressed himself, and his hands and feet again afterwards. He then burned the daily incense, dressed the lamps, and offered the extraordinary sacrifice appointed for this day (not here, but Num. 29:8), a bullock, a ram, and seven lambs, all for burnt-offerings. This he is supposed to have done in his high priest's garments. 2. He must now put off his rich robes, bathe himself, put on the linen garments, and present unto the Lord his own bullock, which was to be a sin-offering for himself and his own house, *v.* 6. The bullock was set between the temple and the altar, and the offering of him mentioned in this verse was the making of a solemn confession of his sins and the sins of his house, earnestly praying for the forgiveness of them, and this with his hands on the head of the bullock. 3. He must then cast lots upon the two goats, which were to make (both together) one sin-offering for the congregation. One of these goats must be slain, in token of a satisfaction to be made to God's justice for sin, the other must be sent away, in token of the remission or dismission of sin by the mercy of God. Both must be presented together to God (*v.* 7) before the lot was cast upon them, and afterwards the scape-goat by itself, *v.* 10. Some think that goats were chosen for the sin-offering because, by the disagreeableness of their smell, the offensiveness of sin is represented: others think, because it was said that the demons which the heathens then worshipped often appeared to their worshippers in the form of goats, God therefore obliged his people to sacrifice goats, that they might never be tempted to sacrifice to goats. 4. The next thing to be done was to kill the bullock for the sin-offering for himself and his house, *v.* 11. "Now," say the Jews, "he must again put his hands on the head of the bullock, and repeat the confession and supplication he had before made, and kill the bullock with his own hands, to make atonement for himself first (for how could he make reconciliation for the sins of the people till he was himself first reconciled?) and for his house, not only his own family, but all the priests, who are called the *house of Aaron*," Ps. 135:19. This charity must begin at home, though it must not end there. The bullock being killed, he left one of the priests to stir the blood, that it might not thicken, and then, 5. He took a censer of burning coals (that would not smoke) in one hand, and a dish full of the sweet incense in the other, and then went into the holy of holies through the veil, and went up towards the ark, set the coals down upon the floor, and scattered the incense upon them, so that the room was immediately filled with smoke. The Jews say that he was to go in *side-ways*, that he might not look directly upon the ark where the divine glory was, till it was covered with smoke; then he must come out *backwards,* out of reverence to the divine majesty; and, after a short prayer, he was to hasten out of the sanctuary, to show himself to the people, that they might not suspect that he had misbehaved himself and died before the Lord. 6. He then fetched the blood of the bullock from the priest whom he had left stirring it, and took that in with him the second time into the holy of holies, which was now filled with the smoke of the incense, and sprinkled with his finger of that blood upon, or rather towards, the mercy-seat, once over against the top of it and then seven times towards the lower part of it, *v.* 14. But the drops of blood (as the Jews expound it) all fell upon the ground, and none touched the mercy-seat. Having done this, he came out of the most holy place, set the basin of blood down in the sanctuary, and went out.

Verses 15–19

When the priest had come out from the sprinkling the blood of the bullock before the mercy-seat, 1. He must next kill the goat which was the sin-offering for the people (*v.* 15) and go the third time into the holy of holies, to sprinkle the blood of the goat, as he had done that of the bullock; and thus he was to *make atonement for the holy place* (*v.* 16); that is, whereas the people by their sins had provoked God to take away those tokens of his favourable presence with them, and rendered even that holy place unfit to be the habitation of the holy God, atonement was hereby made for sin, that God, being reconciled to them, might continue with them. 2. He must then do the same for the outward part of the tabernacle that he had done for the inner room, by sprinkling the blood of the bullock first, and then that of the goat, without the veil, where the table and incense-altar stood, eight times each as before. The reason intimated is *because the tabernacle remained among them in the midst of their uncleanness, v.* 16. God would hereby show them how much their hearts needed to be purified, when even the tabernacle, only by standing in the midst of such an impure and sinful people, needed this expiation; and also that even their devotions and religious performances had much amiss in them, for which it was necessary that atonement should be made. During this solemnity, none of the inferior priests must come into the tabernacle (*v.* 17), but, by standing without, must own themselves unworthy and unfit to minister there, because their follies, and defects, and manifold impurities in their ministry, had made this expiation of the tabernacle necessary. 3. He must then put some of the blood, both of the bullock and of the goat mixed together, upon the horns of the altar that is before the Lord, *v.* 18, 19. It is certain that the altar of incense had this blood put upon it, for so it is expressly ordered (Ex. 30:10); but some think that this directs the high priest to the altar of burnt-offerings, for that also is here called the *altar before the Lord* (*v.* 12), because he is said to *go out* to it, and because it may be presumed that that also had need of an expiation; for to that the gifts and offerings of the children of Israel were all brought, from whose uncleanness the altar is here said to be hallowed.

Verses 20–28

The high priest having presented unto the Lord the expiatory sacrifices, by the sprinkling of their blood, the remainder of which, it is probable, he poured out at the foot of the brazen altar, 1. He is next to confess the sins of Israel, with both his hands upon the head of the scape-goat (*v.* 20, 21); and whenever hands were imposed upon the head of any sacrifice it was always done with confession, according as the nature of the sacrifice was; and, this being a sin-offering, it must be a confession of sin. In the latter and more degenerate ages of the Jewish church they had a set form of confession prepared for the high priest, but God here prescribed none; for it might be supposed that the high priest was so well acquainted with the state of the people, and had such a tender concern for them, that he needed not any form. The confession must be as particular as he could make it, not only of *all the iniquities of the children of Israel,* but *all their transgressions in all their sins.* In one sin there may be many transgressions, from the several aggravating circumstances of it; and in our confessions we should take notice of them, and not only say, *I have sinned,* but, with Achan, "Thus and thus have I done." By this confession he must *put the sins of Israel upon the head of the goat;* that is, exercising faith upon the divine appointment which constituted such a translation, he must transfer the punishment incurred from the sinners to the sacrifice, which would have been but a jest, nay, an affront to God, if he himself had not ordained it. 2. The goat was then to be sent away immediately by the hand of a fit person pitched upon for the purpose, into a wilderness, a land not inhabited; and God allowed them to make this construction of it, that the sending away of the goat was the sending away of their sins, by a free and full remission: *He shall bear upon him all their iniquities, v.* 22. The losing of the goat was a sign to them that *the sins of Israel should be sought for, and not found,* Jer. 50:20. The later Jews had a custom to tie one shred of scarlet cloth to the horns of the goat and another to the gate of the temple, or to the top of the rock where the goat was lost, and they concluded that if it turned white, as they say it usually did, the sins of Israel were forgiven, as it is written, *Though your sins have been as scarlet, they shall be as wool:* and they add that for forty years before the destruction of Jerusalem by the Romans the scarlet cloth never changed colour at all, which is a fair confession that, having rejected the substance, the shadow stood them in no stead. 3. The high priest must then put off his linen garments in the tabernacle, and leave them there, the Jews say never to be worn again by himself or any other, for they made new ones every year; and he must bathe himself in water, put on his rich clothes, and then offer both his own and the people's burnt-offerings, *v.* 23, 24. When we have the comfort of our pardon God must have the glory of it. If we have the benefit of the sacrifice of atonement, we must not grudge the sacrifices of acknowledgment. And, it should seem, the burning of the fat of the sin-offering was deferred till now (*v.* 25), that it might be consumed with the burnt-offerings. 4. The flesh of both those sin-offerings whose blood was taken within the veil was to be all burnt, not upon the altar, but at a distance without the camp, to signify both our putting away sin by true repentance, and the spirit of burning, and God's putting it away by a full remission, so that it shall never rise up in judgment against us. 5. He that took the scape-goat into the wilderness, and those that burned the sin-offering, were to be looked upon as ceremonially unclean, and must not come into the camp till they had washed their clothes and bathed their flesh in water, which signified the defiling nature of sin; even the sacrifice which was but made sin was defiling: also the imperfection of the legal sacrifices; they were so far from taking away sin that even *they* left some stain upon those that touched them. 6. When all this was done, the high priest went again into the most holy place to fetch his censer, and so returned to his own house with joy, because he had done his duty, and died not.

Verses 29–34

I. We have here some additional directions in reference to this great solemnity, particularly,

1. The day appointed for this solemnity. It must be observed yearly on *the tenth day of the seventh month, v.* 29. The seventh had been reckoned the first month, till God appointed that the month in which the children of Israel came out of Egypt should thenceforward be accounted and called the first month. Some have fancied that this tenth day of the seventh month was the day of the year on which our first parents fell, and that it was kept as a fast in remembrance of their fall. Dr. Lightfoot computes that this was the day on which Moses came the last time down from the mount, when he brought with him the renewed tables, and the assurances of God's being reconciled to Israel, and his face shone: that day must be a day of atonement throughout their generations; for the remembrance of God's forgiving them their sin about the golden calf might encourage them to hope that, upon their repentance, he would forgive them all trespasses.

2. The duty of the people on this day. (1.) They must rest from all their labours: *It shall be a sabbath of rest, v.* 31. The work of the day was itself enough, and a good day's work if it was done well; therefore they must do no other work at all. The work of humiliation for sin requires such a close application of mind, and such a fixed engagement of the whole man, as will not allow us to turn aside to any other work. The day of atonement seems to be that sabbath spoken of by the prophet (Isa. 58:13), for it is the same with the fast spoken of in the verses before. (2.) They must afflict their souls. They must refrain from all bodily refreshments and delights, in token of inward humiliation and contrition of soul for their sins. They all fasted on this day from food (except the sick and children), and laid aside their ornaments, and did not anoint themselves, as Daniel, *ch.* 10:3, 12. *David chastened his soul with fasting,* Ps. 35:13. And it signified the mortifying of sin and turning from it, *loosing the bands of wickedness,* Isa. 58:6, 7. The Jewish doctors advised that they should not on that day read those portions of scripture which were proper to affect them with delight and joy, because it was a day to afflict their souls.

3. The perpetuity of this institution: *It shall be a statute for ever, v.* 29, 34. It must not be intermitted any year, nor ever let fall till that constitution should be dissolved, and the type should be superseded by the antitype. As long as we are continually sinning, we must be continually repenting, and receiving the atonement. The law of afflicting our souls for sin is a statute for ever, which will continue in force till we arrive where all tears, even those of repentance, will be wiped from our eyes. The apostle observes it as an evidence of the insufficiency of the legal sacrifices to take away sin, and purge the conscience from it, that in them there was a *remembrance made of sin every year,* upon the day of atonement, Heb. 10:1–3. The annual repetition of the sacrifices showed that there was in them only a faint and feeble effort towards making atonement; it could be done effectually only by the *offering up of the body of Christ once for all,* and that once was sufficient; that sacrifice needed not to be repeated.

II. Let us see what there was of gospel in all this.

1. Here are typified the two great gospel privileges of the remission of sin and access to God, both which we owe to the mediation of our Lord Jesus. Here then let us see,

(1.) The expiation of guilt which Christ made for us. He is himself both the maker and the matter of the atonement; for he is, [1.] The priest, the high priest, that *makes reconciliation for the sins of the people,* Heb. 2:17. He, and he only, is *par negotio — fit for the work* and worthy of the honour: he is appointed by the Father to do it, who sanctified him, and sent him into the world for this purpose, that *God might in him reconcile the world to himself.* He undertook it, and for our sakes sanctified himself, and set himself apart for it, Jn. 17:19. The high priest's frequently bathing himself on this day, and performing the service of it in fine linen clean and white, signified the holiness of the Lord Jesus, his perfect freedom from all sin, and his being beautified and adorned with all grace. No man was to be with the high priest when he made atonement (*v.* 17); for our Lord Jesus was to *tread the wine-press alone,* and of the people there must be *none with him* (Isa. 63:3); therefore, when he entered upon his sufferings, *all his disciples forsook him and fled,* for it any of them had been taken and put to death with him it would have looked as if they had assisted in making the atonement; none but thieves, concerning whom there could be no such suspicion, must suffer with him. And observe what the extent of the atonement was which the high priest made: it was *for the holy sanctuary, for the tabernacle, for the altar, for the priests,* and *for all the people, v.* 33. Christ's satisfaction is that which atones for the sins both of ministers and people, the *iniquities of our holy* (and our unholy) *things;* the title we have to the privileges of ordinances, our comfort in them, and benefit by them, are all owing to the atonement Christ made. But, whereas the atonement which the high priest made pertained only to the congregation of Israel, Christ is the propitiation, not for their sins only, that are Jews, but for the sins of the whole Gentile world. And in this also Christ infinitely excelled Aaron, that Aaron needed to offer sacrifice for his own sin first, of which he was to make confession upon the head of his sin-offering; but our Lord Jesus had no sin of his own to answer for. *Such a high priest became us,* Heb. 7:26. And therefore, when he was baptized in Jordan, whereas others stood in the water *confessing their sins* (Mt. 3:6), he *went up straightway out of the water* (*v.* 16), having no sins to confess. [2.] As he is the high priest, so he is the sacrifice with which atonement is made; for he is all in all in our reconciliation to God. Thus he was prefigured by the two goats, which both made one offering: the slain goat was a type of Christ dying for our sins, the scape-goat a type of Christ rising again for our justification. It was directed by lot, the disposal whereof was of the Lord, which goat should be slain; for Christ was delivered *by the determinate counsel and foreknowledge of God. First,* The atonement is said to be completed by putting the sins of Israel upon the head of the goat. They deserved to have been abandoned and sent into a land of forgetfulness, but that punishment was here transferred to the goat that bore their sins, with reference to which God is said to have laid upon our Lord Jesus (the substance of all these shadows) *the iniquity of us all* (Isa. 53:6), and he is said to have *borne our sins,* even the punishment of them, *in his own body upon the tree,* 1 Pt. 2:24. Thus was he made sin for us, that is, a sacrifice for sin, 2 Co. 5:21. He suffered and died, not only for our good, but in our stead, and was forsaken, and seemed to be forgotten for a time, that we might not be forsaken and forgotten for ever. Some learned men have computed that our Lord Jesus was baptized of John in Jordan upon the tenth day of the seventh month, which was the very day of atonement. Then he entered upon his office as Mediator, and was immediately *driven of the Spirit into the wilderness,* a land not inhabited. *Secondly,* The consequence of this was that all the iniquities of Israel were *carried into a land of forgetfulness.* Thus Christ, the Lamb of God, *takes away the sin the of world,* by taking it upon himself, Jn. 1:29. And, when God forgives sin, he is said to remember it no more (Heb. 8:12), *to cast it behind his back* (Isa. 38:17), *into the depths of the sea* (Mic. 7:19), and to separate it *as far as the east is from the west,* Ps. 103:12.

(2.) The entrance into heaven which Christ made for us is here typified by the high priest's entrance into the most holy place. This the apostle has expounded (Heb. 9:7, etc.), and he shows, [1.] That heaven is the holiest of all, but not of that building, and that the way into it by faith, hope, and prayer, through a Mediator, was not then so clearly manifested as it is to us now by the gospel. [2.] That Christ our high priest entered into heaven at his ascension once for all, and as a public person, in the name of all his spiritual Israel, and through the veil of his flesh, which was rent for that purpose, Heb. 10:20. [3.] That he entered *by his own blood* (Heb. 9:12), taking with him to heaven the virtues of the sacrifice he offered on earth, and so sprinkling his blood, as it were, before the mercy-seat, where it speaks better things than the blood of bulls and goats could do. Hence he is said to appear in the midst of the throne as *a lamb that had been slain,* Rev. 5:6. And, though he had no sin of his own to expiate, yet it was by his own merit that he obtained for himself a restoration to his own ancient glory (Jn. 17:4, 5), as well as an eternal redemption for us, Heb. 9:12. [4.] The high priest in the holy place burned incense, which typified the intercession that Christ ever lives to make for us within the veil, in virtue of his satisfaction. And we could not expect to live, no, not before the mercy-seat, if it were not covered with the cloud of this incense. Mere mercy itself will not save us, without the interposition of a Mediator. The intercession of Christ is there set forth before God as incense, as *this incense.* And as the high priest interceded for himself first, then for his household, and then for all Israel, so our Lord Jesus, in the 17th of St. John (which was a specimen of the intercession he makes in heaven), recommended himself first to his Father, then his disciples who were his household, and then all that should believe on him through their word, as all Israel; and, having thus adverted to the uses and intentions of his offering, he was immediately seized and crucified, pursuant to these intentions. [5.] Herein the entry Christ made far exceeded Aaron's, that Aaron could not gain admission, no, not for his own sons, into the most holy place; but our Lord Jesus has consecrated for us also a *new and living way into the holiest,* so that we also have *boldness to enter,* Heb. 10:19, 20. [6.] The high priest was to come out again, but our Lord Jesus ever lives, making intercession, and always appears in the presence of God for us, whither as the forerunner he has for us entered, and where as agent he continues for us to reside.

2. Here are likewise typified the two great gospel duties of faith and repentance, by which we are qualified for the atonement, and come to be entitled to the benefit of it. (1.) By faith we must put our hands upon the head of the offering, relying on Christ as the Lord our Righteousness, pleading his satisfaction as that which was alone able to atone for our sins and procure us a pardon. *"Thou shalt answer, Lord, for me.* This is all I have to say for myself, *Christ has died, yea, rather has risen again;* to his grace and government I entirely submit myself, and in him I *receive the atonement,"* Rom. 5:11. (2.) By repentance we must afflict our souls; not only fasting for a time from the delights of the body, but inwardly sorrowing for our sins, and living a life of self-denial and mortification. We must also make a penitent confession of sin, and this with an eye to Christ, whom we have pierced, and mourning because of him; and with a hand of faith upon the atonement, assuring ourselves that, *if we confess our sins, God is faithful and just to forgive us our sins, and to cleanse us from all unrighteousness.*

Lastly, In the year of jubilee, the trumpet which proclaimed the liberty was ordered to be sounded in the close of the *day of atonement, ch.* 25:9. For the remission of our debt, release from our bondage, and our return to our inheritance, are all owing to the mediation and intercession of Jesus Christ. By the atonement we obtain rest for our souls, and all the glorious liberties of the children of God.

CHAPTER 17

After the law concerning the atonement to be made for all Israel by the high priest, at the tabernacle, with the blood of bulls and goats, in this chapter we have two prohibitions necessary for the preservation of the honour of that atonement. I. That no sacrifice should be offered by any other than the priests, nor any where but at the door of the tabernacle, and this upon pain of death (*v.* 1–9). II. That no blood should be eaten, and this under the same penalty (*v.* 10, etc.).

Verses 1–9

This statute obliged all the people of Israel to bring all their sacrifices to God's altar, to be offered there. And as to this matter we must consider,

I. How it stood before. 1. It was allowed to all people to build altars, and offer sacrifices to God, where they pleased. Wherever Abraham had a tent he built an altar, and every master of a family was a priest to his own family, as Job 1:5. 2. This liberty had been an occasion of idolatry. When every man was his own priest, and had an altar of his own, by degrees, as they became vain in their imaginations, they invented gods of their own, *and offered their sacrifices unto demons, v.* 7. The word signifies *rough* or *hairy goats,* because it is probable that in the shape the evil spirits often appeared to them, to invite their sacrifices and to signify their acceptance of them. For the devil, ever since he became a revolter from God and a rebel against him, has set up for a rival with him, and coveted to have divine honours paid him: he had the impudence to solicit our blessed Saviour to *fall down and worship him.* The Israelites themselves had learned in Egypt to sacrifice to demons. And some of them, it should seem, practised it even since the God of Israel had so gloriously appeared for them, and with them. They are said to *go a whoring after* these demons; for it was such a breach of their covenant with God as adultery is of the marriage covenant: and they were as strongly addicted to their idolatrous worships, and as hard to be reclaimed from them, as those that have given themselves over to fornication, to *work all uncleanness with greediness;* and therefore it is with reference to this that God calls himself *a jealous God.*

II. How this law settled it. 1. Some think that the children of Israel were by this law forbidden, while they were in the wilderness, to kill any beef, or mutton, or veal, or lamb, or goat, even for their common eating, but at the *door of the tabernacle,* where the blood and the fat were to be offered to God upon the altar, and the flesh to be returned back to the offerer to be eaten as a peace-offering, according to the law. And the statute is so worded (*v.* 3, 4) as to favour this opinion, for it speaks generally of killing any ox, or lamb, or goat. The learned Dr. Cudworth puts this sense upon it, and thinks that while they had their tabernacle so near them in the midst of their camp they ate no flesh but what had first been offered to God, but that when they were entering Canaan this constitution was altered (Deu. 12:21), and they were allowed to kill their beasts of the flock and herd at home, as well as the roebuck and the hart; only thrice a year they were to see God at his tabernacle, and to eat and drink before him there. And it is probable that in the wilderness they did not eat much flesh but that of their peace-offerings, preserving what cattle they had, for breed, against they came to Canaan; therefore they murmured for flesh, being weary of manna; and Moses on that occasion speaks as if they were very sparing of the *flocks and the herds,* Num. 11:4, 22. Yet it is hard to construe this as a temporary law, when it is expressly said to be a *statute for ever* (*v.* 7); and therefore, 2. It should seem rather to forbid only the killing of beasts for sacrifice any where but at God's altar. They must not offer sacrifice, as they had done, *in the open field* (*v.* 5), no, not to the true God, but it must be brought to the priest, to be offered on the altar of the Lord: and the solemnity they had lately witnessed, of consecrating both the priests and the altar, would serve for a good reason why they should confine themselves to both these that God had so signally appointed and owned. This law obliged not only the Israelites themselves, but the proselytes or strangers that were circumcised and sojourned among them, who were in danger of retaining an affection to their old ways of worship. If any should transgress this law, and offer sacrifice any where but at the tabernacle, (1.) The guilt was great: *Blood shall be imputed to that man; he hath shed blood, v.* 4. Though it was but a beast he had killed, yet, killing it otherwise than God had appointed, he was looked upon as a murderer. It is by the divine grant that we have the liberty to kill the inferior creatures, to the benefit of which we are not entitled, unless we submit to the limitations of it, which are that it be not done either with cruelty or with superstition, Gen. 9:3, 4. Nor was there ever any greater abuse done to the inferior creatures than when they were made either false gods or sacrifices to false gods, to which the apostle perhaps has special reference when he speaks of the vanity and bondage of corruption to which the creature was made subject, Rom. 8:20, 21, and compare *ch.* 1:23, 25. Idolatrous sacrifices were looked upon, not only as adultery, but as murder: he that *offereth them is as if he slew a man,* Isa. 66:3. (2.) The punishment should be severe: *That man shall be cut off from among his people.* Either the magistrate must do it if it were manifest and notorious, or, if not, God would take the work into his own hands, and the offender should be cut off by some immediate stroke of divine justice. The reasons why God thus strictly ordered all their sacrifices to be offered at one place were, [1.] For the preventing of idolatry and superstition. That sacrifices might be offered to God, and according to the rule, and without innovations, they must always be offered by the hands of the priests, who were servants in God's house, and under the eye of the high priest, who was ruler of the house, and took care to see every thing done according to God's ordinance. [2.] For the securing of the honour of God's temple and altar, the peculiar dignity of which would be endangered if they might offer their sacrifices any where else as well as there. [3.] For the preserving of unity and brotherly love among the Israelites, that meeting all at one altar, as all the children of the family meet daily at one table, they might live and love as brethren, and be as one man, of one mind in the Lord.

III. How this law was observed. 1. While the Israelites kept their integrity they had a tender and very jealous regard to this law, as appears by their zeal against the altar which was erected by the two tribes and a half, which they would by no means have left standing if they had not been satisfied that it was never designed, nor should ever be used, for sacrifice or offering, Jos. 22:12, etc. 2. The breach of this law was for many ages the scandalous and incurable corruption of the Jewish church, witness that complaint which so often occurs in the history even of the good kings, *Howbeit the high places were not taken away;* and it was an inlet to the grossest idolatries. 3. Yet this law was, in extraordinary cases, dispensed with. Gideon's sacrifice (Jdg. 6:26), Manoah's (Jdg. 13:19), Samuel's (1 Sa. 7:9; 9:13; 11:15), David's (2 Sa. 24:18), and Elijah's (1 Ki. 18:23), were accepted, though not offered at the usual place: but these were all either ordered by angels or offered by prophets; and some think that after the desolation of Shiloh, and before the building of the temple, while the ark and altar were unsettled, it was more allowable to offer sacrifice elsewhere.

IV. How the matter stands now, and what use we are to make of this law. 1. It is certain that the spiritual sacrifices we are now to offer are not confined to any one place. Our Saviour has made this clear (Jn. 4:21), and the apostle (1 Tim. 2:8), according to the prophecy, that *in every place incense should be offered,* Mal. 1:11. We have now no temple nor altar that sanctifies the gift, nor does the gospel unity lie in one place, but in one heart, and the *unity of the spirit.* 2. Christ is our altar, and the *true tabernacle* (Heb. 8:2; 13:10); in him God dwells among us, and it is in him that our sacrifices are acceptable to God, and in him only, 1 Pt. 2:5. To set up other mediators, or other altars, or other expiatory sacrifices, is, in effect, to set up other gods. He is the centre of unity, in whom all God's Israel meet. 3. Yet we are to have respect to the public worship of God, not *forsaking the assemblies of* his people, Heb. 10:25. The Lord loves *the gates of Zion more than all the dwellings of Jacob,* and so should we; see Eze. 20:40. Though God will graciously accept our family offerings, we must not therefore neglect the door of the tabernacle.

Verses 10–16

We have here, I. A repetition and confirmation of the law against eating blood. We have met with this prohibition twice before in the levitical law (*ch.* 3:17; 7:26), besides the place it had in the precepts of Noah, Gen. 9:4. But here, 1. The prohibition is repeated again and again, and reference had to the former laws to this purport (*v.* 12): *I said to the children of Israel, No soul of you shall eat blood;* and again (*v.* 14), *You shall eat the blood of no manner of flesh.* A great stress is laid upon it, as a law which has more in it than at first view one would think. 2. It is made binding, not only on the *house of Israel,* but on *the strangers that sojourned among them* (*v.* 10), which perhaps was one reason why it was thought advisable, for a time, to forbid blood to the Gentile converts, Acts 15:29. 3. The penalty annexed to this law is very severe (*v.* 10): *I will even set my face against that soul that eateth blood,* if he do it presumptuously, and *will cut him off;* and again (*v.* 14), *He shall be cut off.* Note, God's wrath will be the sinner's ruin. Write that man undone, for ever undone, against whom God sets his face; for what creature is able to confront the Creator? 4. A reason is given for this law (*v.* 11): because *it is the blood that makes atonement for the soul;* and *therefore* it was appointed to make atonement with, because *the life of the flesh is the blood.* The sinner deserved to die; therefore the sacrifice must die. Now, the blood being so the life that ordinarily beasts were killed for man's use by the drawing out of all their blood, God appointed the sprinkling or pouring out of the blood of the sacrifice upon the altar to signify that the life of the sacrifice was given to God instead of the sinner's life, and as a ransom or counter-price for it; therefore *without shedding of blood there was no remission,* Heb. 9:22. For this reason they must eat no blood, and, (1.) It was then a very good reason; for God would by this means preserve the honour of that way of atonement which he had instituted, and keep up in the minds of the people a reverent regard to it. The blood of the covenant being then a sensible object, no blood must be either eaten or trodden under foot as a common thing, as they must have no ointment nor perfume like that which God ordered them to make for himself. But, (2.) This reason is now superseded, which intimates that the law itself was ceremonial, and is now no longer in force: the blood of Christ who has come (and we are to look for no other) is that alone which makes atonement for the soul, and of which the blood of the sacrifices was an imperfect type: the coming of the substance supersedes the shadow. The blood of beasts is no longer the ransom, but Christ's blood only; and therefore there is not now that reason for abstaining from blood which there was then, and we cannot suppose it was the will of God that the law should survive the reason of it. The blood, provided it be so prepared as not to be unwholesome, is now allowed for the nourishment of our bodies, because it is no longer appointed to make an atonement for the soul. (3.) Yet it has still useful significancy. The life is in the blood; it is the vehicle of the animal spirits, and God would have his people to regard the life even of their beasts, and not to be cruel and hard-hearted, not to take delight in any thing that is barbarous. They must not be a blood-thirsty people. The blood then made atonement figuratively, now the blood of Christ makes atonement really and effectually; to this therefore we must have a reverent regard, and not use it as *a common thing,* for he will set his face against those that do so, and they shall be cut off, Heb. 10:29.

II. Some other precepts are here given as appendages to this law, and hedges about it, 1. They must cover the blood of that which they *took in hunting, v.* 13. They must not only not eat it, but must give it a decent burial, in token of some mystery which they must believe lay hidden in this constitution. the Jews look upon this as a very weighty precept and appoint that the blood should be covered with these words, *Blessed be he that hath sanctified us by his precepts, and commanded us to cover blood.* 2. They must not eat that which *died of itself* or was *torn of beasts* (*v.* 15), for the blood was either not at all, or not regularly, drawn out of them. God would have them to be curious in their diet, not with the curiosity that gratifies the sensual appetite, but with that which checks and restrains it. God would not have his children to eat every thing that came in their way with greediness, but to consider diligently what was before them, that they might learn in other things to ask questions for conscience' sake. Those that *flew upon the spoiled* sinned, 1 Sa. 14:32, 33. If a man did, through ignorance or inconsideration, eat the flesh of any beast not duly slain, he must *wash himself and his clothes,* else he *bore his iniquity, v.* 15, 16. The pollution was ceremonial, so was the purification from it; but if a man slighted the prescribed method of cleansing, or would not submit, he thereby contracted moral guilt. See the nature of a remedial law: he that obeys it has the benefit of it; he that does not, not only remains under his former guilt, but adds to that guilt of contemning the provisions made by divine grace for his relief, and sins against the remedy.

CHAPTER 18

Here is, I. A general law against all conformity to the corrupt usages of the heathen (*v.* 1–5). II. Particular laws, 1. Against incest (*v.* 6–18). 2. Against beastly lusts, and barbarous idolatries (*v.* 19–23). III. The enforcement of these laws from the ruin of the Canaanites (*v.* 24–30).

Verses 1–5

After divers ceremonial institutions, God here returns to the enforcement of moral precepts. The former are still of use to us as types, the latter still binding as laws. We have here, 1. The sacred authority by which these laws are enacted: *I am the Lord your God* (*v.* 1, 4, 30), and *I am the Lord, v.* 5, 6, 21. "The Lord, who has a right to rule all; your God, who has a peculiar right to rule you." Jehovah is the fountain of being, and therefore the fountain of power, whose we are, whom we are bound to serve, and who is able to punish all disobedience. "Your God to whom you have consented, in whom you are happy, to whom you lie under the highest obligations imaginable, and to whom you are accountable." 2. A strict caution to take heed of retaining the relics of the idolatries of Egypt, where they had dwelt, and of receiving the infection of the idolatries of Canaan, whither they were now going, *v.* 3. Now that God was by Moses teaching them his ordinances there was *aliquid dediscendum — something to be unlearned,* which they had sucked in with their milk in Egypt, a country noted for idolatry: *You shall not do after the doings of the land of Egypt.* It would be the greatest absurdity in itself to retain such an affection for their house of bondage as to be governed in their devotions by the usages of it, and the greatest ingratitude to God, who had so wonderfully and graciously delivered them. Nay, as if governed by a spirit of contradiction, they would be in danger, even after they had received these ordinances of God, of admitting the wicked usages of the Canaanites and of inheriting their vices with their land. Of this danger they are here warned, *You shall not walk in their ordinances.* Such a tyrant is custom that their practices are called *ordinances,* and they became rivals even with God's ordinances, and God's professing people were in danger of receiving law from them. 3. A solemn charge to them to *keep God's judgments, statutes, and ordinances, v.* 4, 5. To this charge, and many similar ones, David seems to refer in the many prayers and professions he makes relating to God's laws in the 119th Psalm. Observe here, (1.) The great rule of our obedience — God's statutes and judgments. These we must *keep to walk therein.* We must keep them in our books, and keep them in our hands, that we may practise them in our hearts and lives. *Remember God's commandments to do them,* Ps. 103:18. We must keep in them as our way to travel in, keep to them as our rule to work by, keep them as our treasure, as the apple of our eye, with the utmost care and value. (2.) The great advantage of our obedience: *Which if a man do, he shall live in them,* that is, "he shall be happy here and hereafter." We have reason to thank God, [1.] That this is still in force as a promise, with a very favourable construction of the condition. If we keep God's commandments in sincerity, though we come short of sinless perfection, we shall find that the way of duty is the way of comfort, and will be the way to happiness. Godliness has the *promise of life,* 1 Tim. 4:8. Wisdom has said, *Keep my commandments and live:* and *if through the Spirit we mortify the deeds of the body* (which are to us as the usages of Egypt were to Israel) *we shall live.* [2.] That it is not so in force in the nature of a covenant as that the least transgression shall for ever exclude us from this life. The apostle quotes this twice as opposite to the faith which the gospel reveals. It is the description of the *righteousness which is by the law, the man that doeth them shall live ev autois — in them* (Rom. 10:5), and is urged to prove that *the law is not of faith,* Gal. 3:12. The alteration which the gospel has made is in the last word: still *the man that does them shall live,* but not live *in them;* for the law could not give life, because we could not perfectly keep it; it was *weak through the flesh,* not in itself; but now *the man that does them* shall *live by the faith of the Son of God.* He shall owe his life to the grace of Christ, and not to the merit of his own works; see Gal. 3:21, 22. *The just shall live,* but they shall live *by faith,* by virtue of their union with Christ, who is their life.

Verses 6–18

These laws relate to the seventh commandment, and, no doubt, are obligatory on us under the gospel, for they are consonant to the very light and law of nature: one of the articles, that of a man's having his father's wife, the apostle speaks of as a sin *not so much as named among the Gentiles,* 1 Co. 5:1. Though some of the incests here forbidden were practised by some particular persons among the heathen, yet they were disallowed and detested, unless among those nations who had become barbarous, and were quite given up to vile affections. Observe,

I. That which is forbidden as to the relations here specified is *approaching to them to uncover their nakedness, v.* 6.

1. It is chiefly intended to forbid the marrying of any of these relations. Marriage is a divine institution; this and the sabbath, the eldest of all, of equal standing with man upon the earth: it is intended for the comfort of human life, and the decent and honourable propagation of the human race, such as became the dignity of man's nature above that of the beasts. It is *honourable in all,* and these laws are for the support of the honour of it. It was requisite that a divine ordinance should be subject to divine rules and restraints, especially because it concerns a thing wherein the corrupt nature of man is as apt as in any thing to be wilful and impetuous in its desires, and impatient of check. Yet these prohibitions, besides their being enacted by an incontestable authority, are in themselves highly reasonable and equitable. (1.) By marriage two were to become one flesh, therefore those that before were in a sense one flesh by nature could not, without the greatest absurdity, become one flesh by institution; for the institution was designed to unite those who before were not united. (2.) Marriage puts an equality between husband and wife. "Is she not thy companion taken out of thy side?" Therefore, if those who before were superior and inferior should intermarry (which is the case in most of the instances here laid down), the order of nature would be taken away by a positive institution, which must by no means be allowed. The inequality between master and servant, noble and ignoble, is founded in consent and custom, and there is no harm done if that be taken away by the equality of marriage; but the inequality between parents and children, uncles and nieces, aunts and nephews, either by blood or marriage, is founded in nature, and is therefore perpetual, and cannot without confusion be taken away by the equality of marriage, the institution of which, though ancient, is subsequent to the order of nature. (3.) No relations that are equals are forbidden, except brothers and sisters, by the whole blood or half blood, or by marriage; and in this there is not the same natural absurdity as in the former,

for Adam's sons must of necessity have married their own sisters; but it was requisite that it should be made by a positive law unlawful and detestable, for the preventing of sinful familiarities between those that in the days of their youth are supposed to live in a house together, and yet cannot intermarry without defeating one of the intentions of marriage, which is the enlargement of friendship and interest. If every man married his own sister (as they would be apt to do from generation to generation if it were lawful), each family would be a world to itself, and it would be forgotten that *we are members one of another.* It is certain that this has always been looked upon by the more sober heathen as a most infamous and abominable thing; and those who had not this law yet were herein a law to themselves. The making use of the ordinance of marriage for the patronizing of incestuous mixtures is so far from justifying them, or extenuating their guilt, that it adds the guilt of profaning an ordinance of God, and prostituting that to the vilest of purposes which was instituted for the noblest ends. But,

2. Uncleanness, committed with any of these relations out of marriage, is likewise, without doubt, forbidden here, and no less intended than the former: as also all lascivious carriage, wanton dalliance, and every thing that has the appearance of this evil. Relations must love one another, and are to have free and familiar converse with each other, but it must be with all purity; and the less it is suspected of evil by others the more care ought the persons themselves to take that *Satan do not get advantage against them,* for he is a very subtle enemy, and seeks all occasions against us.

II. The relations forbidden are most of them plainly described; and it is generally laid down as a rule that what relations of a man's own he is bound up from marrying the same relations of his wife he is likewise forbidden to marry, for they two are one. That law which forbids marrying a brother's wife (*v.* 16) had an exception peculiar to the Jewish state, that, if a man died without issue, his brother or next of kin should marry the widow, and raise up seed to the deceased (Deu. 25:5), for reasons which held good only in that commonwealth; and therefore now that those reasons have ceased the exception ceases, and the law is in force, that a man must in no case marry his brother's widow. That article (*v.* 18) which forbids a man to *take a wife to her sister* supposes a connivance at polygamy, as some other laws then did (Ex. 21:10; Deu. 21:15), but forbids a man's marrying two sisters, as Jacob did, because between those who had before been equal there would be apt to arise greater jealousies and animosities than between wives that were not so nearly related. If the sister of the wife be taken for the concubine, or secondary wife, nothing can be more vexing in her life, or as long as she lives.

Verses 19–30

Here is, I. A law to preserve the honour of the marriage-bed, that it should not be unseasonably used (*v.* 19), nor invaded by an adulterer, *v.* 20.

II. A law against that which was the most unnatural idolatry, causing their children to *pass through the fire to Moloch, v.* 21. Moloch (as some think) was the idol in and by which they worshipped the sun, that great fire of the world; and therefore in the worship of it they made their own children either sacrifices to this idol, burning them to death before it, or devotees to it, causing them to pass between two fires, as some think, or to be thrown through one, to the honour of this pretended deity, imagining that the consecrating of but one of their children in this manner to Moloch would procure good fortune for all the rest of their children. Did idolaters thus give their own children to false gods, and shall we think any thing too dear to be dedicated to, or to be parted with for, the true God? See how this sin of Israel (which they were afterwards guilty of, notwithstanding this law) is aggravated by the relation which they and their children stood in to God. Eze. 16:20, *Thou hast taken thy sons and thy daughters, whom thou hast borne unto me, and these thou hast sacrificed.* Therefore it is here called *profaning the name of their* God; for it looked as if they thought they were under greater obligations to Moloch than to Jehovah; for to him they offered their cattle only, but to Moloch their children.

III. A law against unnatural lusts, sodomy and bestiality, sins not to be named nor thought of without the utmost abhorrence imaginable, *v.* 22, 23. Other sins level men with the beasts, but these sink them much lower. That ever there should have been occasion for the making of these laws, and that since they are published they should ever have been broken, is the perpetual reproach and scandal of human nature; and the giving of men up to these vile affections was frequently the punishment of their idolatries; so the apostle shows, Rom. 1:24.

IV. Arguments against these and the like abominable wickednesses. He that has an indisputable right to command us, yet because he will deal with us as men, and *draw with the cords of a man,* condescends to reason with us. 1. Sinners defile themselves with these abominations: *Defile not yourselves in any of these things, v.* 24. All sin is defiling to the conscience, but these are sins that have a peculiar turpitude in them. Our heavenly Father, in kindness to us, requires of us that we keep ourselves clean, and do not wallow in the dirt. 2. *The souls that commit them shall be cut off, v.* 29. And justly; for, *if any man defile the temple of God, him shall God destroy,* 1 Co. 3:17. Fleshly lusts war against the soul, and will certainly be the ruin of it if God's mercy and grace prevent not. 3. *The land is defiled, v.* 25. If such wickednesses as these be practised and connived at, the land is thereby made unfit to have God's tabernacle in it, and the pure and holy God will withdraw the tokens of his gracious presence from it. It is also rendered unwholesome to the inhabitants, who are hereby infected with sin and exposed to plagues and it is really nauseous and loathsome to all good men in it, as the wickedness of Sodom was to the soul of righteous Lot. 4. These have been the abominations of the former inhabitants, v, 24, 27. Therefore it was necessary that these laws should be made, as antidotes and preservatives from the plague are necessary when we go into an infected place. And therefore they should not practise any such things, because the nations that had practised them now lay under the curse of God, and were shortly to fall by the sword of Israel. They could not but be sensible how odious those people had made themselves who wallowed in this mire, and how they stank in the nostrils of all good men; and shall a people sanctified and dignified as Israel was make themselves thus vile? When we observe how ill sin looks in others we should use this as an argument with ourselves with the utmost care and caution to preserve our purity. 5. For these and the like sins the Canaanites were to be destroyed; these filled the measure of the Amorites' iniquity (Gen. 15:16), and brought down that destruction of so many populous kingdoms which the Israelites were now shortly to be not only the spectators, but the instruments of: *Therefore I do visit the iniquity thereof upon it, v.* 25. Note, The tremendous judgments of God, executed on those that are daringly profane and atheistical, are intended as warnings to those who profess religion to take heed of every thing that has the least appearance of, or tendency towards, profaneness or atheism. Even the ruin of the Canaanites is an admonition to the Israelites not to do like them. Nay, to show that not only the Creator is provoked, but the creation burdened, by such abominations as these, it is added (*v.* 25), *The land itself vomiteth out her inhabitants.* The very ground they went upon did, as it were, groan under them, and was sick of them, and not easy till it had discharged itself of these *enemies of the Lord,* Isa. 1:24. This bespeaks the extreme loathsomeness of sin; sinful man indeed *drinks in iniquity like water,* but the harmless part of the creation even heaves at it, and rises against it. Many a house and many a town have spued out the wicked inhabitants, as it were, with abhorrence, Rev. 3:16. Therefore take heed, saith God, *that the land spue not you out also, v.* 28. It was secured to them, and entailed upon them, and yet they must expect that, if they made the vices of the Canaanites their own, with their land their fate would be the same. Note, Wicked Israelites are as abominable to God as wicked Canaanites, and more so, and will be as soon spued out, or sooner. Such a warning as was here given to the Israelites is given by the apostle to the Gentile converts, with reference to the rejected Jews, in whose room they were substituted (Rom. 11:19, etc.); they must take heed of falling *after the same example of unbelief,* Heb. 4:11. Apply it more generally; and let it deter us effectually from all sinful courses to consider how many they have been the ruin of. Lay the ear of faith to the gates of the bottomless pit, and hear the doleful shrieks and outcries of damned sinners, whom earth has spued out and hell has swallowed, that find themselves undone, for ever undone, by sin; and tremble lest this be your portion at last. God's threatenings and judgments should frighten us from sin.

V. The chapter concludes with a sovereign antidote against this infection: *Therefore you shall keep my ordinance that you commit not any one of these abominable customs, v.* 30. This is the remedy prescribed. Note, 1. Sinful customs are abominable customs, and their being common and fashionable does not make them at all the less abominable nor should we the less abominate them, but the more; because the more customary they are the more dangerous they are. 2. It is of pernicious consequence to admit and allow of any one sinful custom, because one will make way for many, *Uno absurdo dato, mille sequuntur — Admit but a single absurdity, you invite a thousand.* The way of sin is downhill. 3. A close and constant adherence to God's ordinances is the most effectual preservative from the infection of gross sin. The more we taste of the sweetness and feel of the power of holy ordinances the less inclination we shall have to the forbidden pleasures of sinners' abominable customs. It is the grace of God only that will secure us, and that grace is to be expected only in the use of the means of grace. Nor does God ever leave any to their own hearts' lusts till they have first left him and his institutions.

CHAPTER 19

Some ceremonial precepts there are in this chapter, but most of them are moral. One would wonder that when some of the lighter matters of the law are greatly enlarged upon (witness two long chapters concerning the leprosy) many of the weightier matters are put into a little compass: divers of the single verses of this chapter contain whole laws concerning judgment and mercy; for these are things which are manifest in every man's conscience; men's own thoughts are able to explain these, and to comment upon them. I. The laws of this chapter, which were peculiar to the Jews, are, 1. Concerning their peace-offerings (*v.* 5–8). 2. Concerning the gleanings of their fields (*v.* 9, 10). 3. Against mixtures of their cattle, seed, and cloth (*v.* 19). 4. Concerning their trees (*v.* 23–25). 5. Against some superstitious usages (*v.* 26–28). But, II. Most of these precepts are binding on us, for they are expositions of most of the ten commandments. 1. Here is the preface to the ten commandments, "I am the Lord," repeated fifteen times. 2. A sum of the ten commandments. All the first table in this, "Be you holy," (*v.* 2). All the second table in this, "Thou shalt love thy neighbour" (*v.* 18), and an answer to the question, "Who is my neighbour?" (*v.* 33, 34). 3. Something of each commandment. (1.) The first commandment implied in that which is often repeated here, "I am your God." And here is a prohibition of enchantment (*v.* 26) and witchcraft (*v.* 31), which make a god of the devil. (2.) Idolatry, against the second commandment, is forbidden, (*v.* 4). (3.) Profanation of God's name, against the third (*v.* 12). (4.) Sabbath-sanctification is pressed (*v.* 3, 30). (5.) Children are required to honour their parents (*v.* 3), and the aged (*v.* 32). (6.) Hatred and revenge are here forbidden, against the sixth commandment (*v.* 17, 18). (7.) Adultery (*v.* 20–22), and whoredom (*v.* 29). (8.) Justice is here required in judgment (*v.* 15), theft forbidden (*v.* 11), fraud and withholding dues (*v.* 13), and false weights (*v.* 35, 36). (9.) Lying (*v.* 11). Slandering (*v.* 14). Tale-bearing, and false-witness bearing (*v.* 16). (10.) The tenth commandment laying a restraint upon the heart, so does that (*v.* 17), "Thou shalt not hate thy brother in thy heart." And here is a solemn charge to observe all these statutes (*v.* 37). Now these are things which need not much help for the understanding of them, but require constant care and watchfulness for the observing of them. "A good understanding have all those that do these commandments."

Verses 1–10

Moses is ordered to deliver the summary of the laws *to all the congregation of the children of Israel* (*v.* 2); not to Aaron and his sons only, but to all the people, for they were all concerned to know their duty. Even in the darker ages of the law, that religion could not be of God which boasted of ignorance as its mother. Moses must make known God's statutes to all the congregation, and proclaim them through the camp. These laws, it is probable, he delivered himself to as many of the people as could be within hearing at once, and so by degrees at several times to them all. Many of the precepts here given they had received before, but it was requisite that they should be repeated, that they might be remembered. Precept must be upon precept, and line upon line, and all little enough. In these verses,

I. It is required that Israel be a holy people, because the God of Israel is a holy God, *v.* 2. Their being distinguished from all other people by peculiar laws and customs was intended to teach them a real separation from the world and the flesh, and an entire devotedness to God. And this is now the law of Christ (the Lord bring every thought within us into obedience to it!) *You shall be holy, for I am holy,* 1 Pt. 1:15, 16. We are the followers of the holy Jesus, and therefore must be, according to our capacity, consecrated to God's honour, and conformed to his nature and will. Israel was sanctified by the types and shadows (*ch.* 20:8), but we are *sanctified by the truth,* or substance of all those shadows, Jn. 17:17; Tit. 2:14.

II. That children be obedient to their parents: *"You shall fear every man his mother and his father, v.* 3. 1. The fear here required is the same with the honour commanded by the fifth commandment; see Mal. 1:6. It includes inward reverence and esteem, outward expressions of respect, obedience to the lawful commands of parents, care and endeavour to please them and make them easy, and to avoid every thing that may offend and grieve them, and incur their displeasure. The Jewish doctors ask, "What is this fear that is owing to a father?" And they answer, "It is not to stand in his way nor to sit in his place, not to contradict what he says nor to carp at it, not to call him by his name, either living or dead, but 'My Father,' or 'Sir;' it is to provide for him if he be poor, and the like." 2. Children, when they grow up to be men, must not think themselves discharged from this duty: every man, though he be a wise man, and a great man, yet must reverence his parents, because they are his parents. 3. The mother is put first, which is not usual, to show that the duty is equally owing to both; if the mother survive the father, still she must be reverenced and obeyed. 4. It is added, *and keep my sabbaths.* If God provides by his law for the preserving of the honour of parents, parents must use their authority over their children for the preserving of the honour of God, particularly the honour of his sabbaths, the custody of which is very much committed to parents by the fourth commandment, *Thou, and thy son, and thy daughter.* The ruin of young people has often been observed to begin in the contempt of their parents and the profanation of the sabbath day. Fitly therefore are these two precepts here put together in the beginning of this abridgment of the statutes: *"You shall fear, every man, his mother and his father, and keep my sabbaths.* Those are hopeful children, and likely to do well, that make conscience of honouring their parents and keeping holy the sabbath day. 5. The reason added to both these precepts is, *"I am the Lord your God;* the Lord of the sabbath and the God of your parents."

III. That God only be worshipped, and not by images (*v.* 4): *"Turn you not to idols,* to *Elilim,* to vanities, things of no power, no value, gods that are no gods. Turn not from the true God to false ones, from the mighty God to impotent ones, from the God that will make you holy and happy to those that will deceive you, debauch you, ruin you, and make you for ever miserable. Turn not your eye to them, much less your heart. *Make not to yourselves gods,* the creatures of your own fancy, nor think to worship the Creator by molten gods. You are the work of God's hands, be not so absurd as to worship gods *the work of your own hands."* Molten gods are specified for the sake of the molten calf.

IV. That the sacrifices of their peace-offerings should always be offered, and eaten, according to the law, *v.* 5–8. There was some particular reason, it is likely, for the repetition of this law rather than any other relating to the sacrifices. The eating of the peace-offerings was the people's part, and was done from under the eye of the priests, and perhaps some of them had kept the cold meat of their peace-offerings, as they had done the manna (Ex. 16:20), longer than was appointed, which occasioned this caution; see the law itself before, *ch.* 7:16–18. God will have his own work done in his own time. Though the sacrifice was offered according to the law, if it was not eaten according to the law, it was not accepted. Though ministers do their part, what the better if people do not theirs? There is work to be done after our spiritual sacrifices, in a due improvement of them; and, if this be neglected, all is in vain.

V. That they should leave the gleanings of their harvest and vintage for the poor, *v.* 9, 10. Note, Works of piety must be always attended with works of charity, according as our ability is. When they gathered in their corn, they must leave some standing in the corner of the field; the Jewish doctors say, "It should be a sixtieth part of the field;" and they must also leave the gleanings and the small clusters of their grapes, which at first were overlooked. This law, though not binding now in the letter of it, yet teaches us, 1. That we must not be covetous and griping, and greedy of every thing we can lay any claim to; nor insist upon our right in things small and trivial. 2. That we must be well pleased to see the poor supplied and refreshed with the fruit of our labours. We must not think every thing lost that goes beside ourselves, nor any thing wasted that goes to the poor. 3. That times of joy, such as harvest-time is, are proper times for charity; that, when we rejoice, the poor may rejoice with us, and when our hearts are blessing God their loins may bless us.

Verses 11–18

We are taught here,

I. To be honest and true in all our dealings, *v.* 11. God, who has appointed every man's property by his providence, forbids by his law the invading of that appointment, either by downright theft, *You shall not steal,* or by fraudulent dealing, "You shall not cheat, or deal falsely." Whatever we have in the world, we must see to it that it be honestly come by, for we cannot be truly rich, nor long rich, with that which is not. The God of truth, who requires truth in the heart (Ps. 51:6), requires it also in the tongue: *Neither lie one to another,* either in bargaining or common converse. This is one of the laws of Christianity (Col. 3:9): *Lie not one to another.* Those that do not speak truth do not deserve to be told truth; those that sin by lying justly suffer by it; therefore we are forbidden to *lie one to another;* for, if we lie to others, we teach them to lie to us.

II. To maintain a very reverent regard to the sacred name of God (*v.* 12), and not to call him to be witness either, 1. To a lie: *You shall not swear falsely.* It is bad to tell a lie, but it is much worse to swear it. Or, 2. To a trifle, and every impertinence: *Neither shalt thou profane the name of thy God,* by alienating it to any other purpose than that for which it is to be religiously used.

III. Neither to take nor keep any one's right from him, *v.* 13. We must not take that which is none of our own, either by fraud or robbery; nor detain that which belongs to another, particularly the *wages of the hireling,* let it not *abide with thee all night.* Let the day-labourer have his wages as soon as he has done his day's work, if he desire it. It is a great sin to deny the payment of it, nay, to defer it, to his damage, a sin that cries to heaven for vengeance, Jam. 5:4.

IV. To be particularly tender of the credit and safety of those that cannot help themselves, *v.* 14. 1. The credit of the deaf: *Thou shalt not curse the deaf;* that is, not only those that are naturally deaf, that cannot hear at all, but also those that are absent, and at present out of hearing of the curse, and so cannot show their resentment, return the affront, nor right themselves, and those that are patient, that seem as if they heard not, and are not willing to take notice of it, as David, Ps. 38:13. Do not injure any because they are unwilling, or unable, to avenge themselves, for God sees and hears, though they do not. 2. The safety of the blind we must likewise be tender of, and not put a stumbling-block before them; for this is to add affliction to the afflicted, and to make God's providence a servant to our malice. This prohibition implies a precept to help the blind, and remove stumbling-blocks out of their way. The Jewish writers, thinking it impossible that any should be so barbarous as to put a *stumbling-block in the way of the blind,* understood it figuratively, that it forbids giving bad counsel to those that are simple and easily imposed upon, by which they may be led to do something to their own prejudice. We ought to take heed of doing any thing which may occasion our weak brother to fall, Rom. 14:13; 1 Co. 8:9. It is added, as a preservative from these sins, *but fear thou God.* "Thou dost not fear the deaf and blind, they cannot right themselves; but remember it is the glory of God to help the helpless, and he will plead their cause." Note, The fear of God will restrain us from doing that which will not expose us to men's resentments.

V. Judges and all in authority are here commanded to give verdict and judgment without partiality (*v.* 15); whether they were constituted judges by commission or made so in a particular case by the consent of both parties, as referees or arbitrators, they must do no wrong to either side, but, to the utmost of their skill, must go according to the rules of equity, having respect purely to the merits of the cause, and not to the characters of the person. Justice must never be perverted, either, 1. In pity to the poor: *Thou shalt not respect the person of the poor,* Ex. 23:3. Whatever may be given to a poor man as an alms, yet let nothing be awarded him as his right but what he is legally entitled to, nor let his poverty excuse him from any just punishment for a fault. Or, 2. In veneration or fear of the mighty, in whose favour judges would be most frequently biased. The Jews say, "Judges were obliged by this law to be so impartial as not to let one of the contending parties sit while the other stood, nor permit one to say what he pleased and bid the other be short; see James 2:1–4.

VI. We are all forbidden to do any thing injurious to our neighbour's good name (*v.* 16), either, 1. In common conversation: *Thou shalt not go up and down as a tale-bearer.* It is as bad an office as a man can put himself into to be the publisher of every man's faults, divulging what was secret, aggravating crimes, and making the worst of every thing that was amiss, with design to blast and ruin men's reputation, and to sow discord among neighbours. The word used for a tale-bearer signifies a *pedlar,* or *petty chapman,* the interlopers of trade; for tale-bearers pick up ill-natured stories at one house and utter them at another, and commonly barter slanders by way of exchange. See this sin condemned, Prov. 11:13; 20:19; Jer. 9:4, 5; Eze. 22:9. Or, 2, In witness-bearing: Neither *shalt thou stand* as a witness *against the blood of thy neighbour,* if his blood be innocent, nor join in confederacy with such bloody men as those described," Prov. 1:11, 12. The Jewish doctors put this further sense upon it: "Thou shalt not stand by and see thy brother in danger, but thou shalt come in to his relief and succour, though it be with the peril of thy own life or limb;" they add, "He that can by his testimony clear one that is accused is obliged by this law to do it;" see Prov. 24:11, 12.

VII. We are commanded to rebuke our neighbour in love (*v.* 17): *Thou shalt in any wise rebuke thy neighbour.* 1. Rather rebuke him than hate him for an injury done to thyself. If we apprehend that our neighbour has any way wronged us, we must not conceive a secret grudge against him, and estrange ourselves from him, speaking to him neither bad nor good, as the manner of some is, who have the art of concealing their displeasure till they have an opportunity of a full revenge (2 Sa. 13:22); but we must rather give vent to our resentments with the meekness of wisdom, endeavour to convince our brother of the injury, reason the case fairly with him, and so put an end to the disgust conceived: this is the rule our Saviour gives in this case, Lu. 17:3. 2. Therefore rebuke him for his sin against God, because thou lovest him; endeavour to bring him to repentance, that his sin may be pardoned, and he may turn from it, and it may not be suffered to lie upon him. Note, Friendly reproof is a duty we owe to one another, and we ought both to give it and take it in love. *Let the righteous smite me, and it shall be a kindness,* Ps. 141:5. Faithful and useful are those *wounds of a friend,* Prov. 27:5, 6. It is here strictly commanded, *"Thou shalt in any wise* do it, and not omit it under any pretence." Consider, (1.) The guilt we incur by not reproving: it is construed here into a hating of our brother. We are ready to argue thus, "Such a one is a friend I love, therefore I will not make him uneasy by telling him of his faults;" but we should rather say, "therefore I will do him the kindness to tell him of them." Love covers sin from others, but not from the sinner himself. (2.) The mischief we do by not reproving: we *suffer sin upon him.* Must we help the ass of an enemy that has fallen under his burden, and shall we not help the soul of a friend? Ex. 23:5. And by *suffering sin upon him* we are in danger of *bearing sin for him,* as the margin reads it. If we reprove not the *unfruitful works of darkness,* we have fellowship with them, and become accessaries *ex post facto — after the fact,* Eph. 5:11. It is thy brother, thy neighbour, that is concerned; and he was a Cain that said, *Am I my brother's keeper?*

VIII. We are here required to put off all malice, and to put on brotherly love, *v.* 18. 1. We must be ill-affected to none: *Thou shalt not avenge, nor bear any grudge;* to the same purport with that *v.* 17, *Thou shalt not hate thy brother in thy heart;* for malice is murder begun. If our brother has done us an injury, we must not return it upon him, that is avenging; we must not upon every occasion upbraid him with it, that is bearing a grudge; but we must both forgive it and forget it, for thus we are forgiven of

God. It is a most ill-natured thing, and the bane of friendship, to retain the resentment of affronts and injuries, and to let that *word devour for ever.* 2. We must be well-affected to all: *Thou shalt love thy neighbour as thyself.* We often wrong ourselves, but we soon forgive ourselves those wrongs, and they do not at all lessen our love to ourselves; and in like manner we should love our neighbour. Our Saviour has made this the second great commandment of the law (Mt. 22:39), and the apostle shows how it is the summary of all the laws of the second table, Rom. 13:9, 10; Gal. 5:14. We must love our neighbour as truly as we love ourselves, and without dissimulation; we must evidence our love to our neighbour in the same way as that by which we evidence our love to ourselves, preventing his hurt, and procuring his good, to the utmost of our power. We must do to our neighbour as we would be done to ourselves (Mt. 7:12), putting *our souls into his soul's stead,* Job 16:4, 5. Nay, we must in many cases deny ourselves for the good of our neighbour, as Paul, 1 Co. 9:19, etc. Herein the gospel goes beyond even that excellent precept of the law; for Christ, by laying down his life for us, has taught us even to *lay down our lives for the brethren,* in some cases (1 Jn. 3:16), and so to love our neighbour better than ourselves.

Verses 19–29

Here is, I. A law against mixtures, *v.* 19. God in the beginning made the cattle *after their kind* (Gen. 1:25), and we must acquiesce in the order of nature God hath established, believing that is best and sufficient, and not covet monsters. *Add thou not unto his works, lest he reprove thee;* for it is the excellency of the work of God that nothing can, without making it worse, be either put to it or taken from it, Eccl. 3:14. As what God has joined we must not separate, so what he has separated we must not join. The sowing of mingled corn and the wearing of linsey-woolsey garments are forbidden, either as superstitious customs of the heathen or to intimate how careful they should be not to mingle themselves with the heathen nor to weave any of the usages of the Gentiles into God's ordinances. Ainsworth suggests that it was to lead Israel to the simplicity and sincerity of religion, and to all the parts and doctrines of the law and gospel in their distinct kinds. As faith is necessary, good works are necessary, but to mingle these together in the cause of our justification before God is forbidden, Gal. 2:16.

II. A law for punishing adultery committed with one that was a bondmaid that was espoused, *v.* 20–22. If she had not been espoused, the law appointed no punishment at all; being espoused, if she had not been a bondmaid, the punishment had been no less than death: but, being as yet a bondmaid (though before the completing of her espousals she must have been made free), the capital punishment is remitted, and they shall both be scourged; or, as some think, the woman only, and the man was to bring a sacrifice. It was for the honour of marriage, though but begun by betrothing, that the crime should be punished; but it was for the honour of freedom that it should not be punished as the debauching of a free woman was, so great was the difference then made between bond and free (Gal. 4:30); but the gospel of Christ knows no such distinction, Col. 3:11.

III. A law concerning fruit-trees, that for the first three years after they were planted, if they should happen to be so forward as to bear in that time, yet no use should be made of the fruit, *v.* 23–25. It was therefore the practice of the Jews to pluck off the fruit, as soon as they perceived it knit, from their young trees, as gardeners do sometimes, because their early bearing hinders their growing. If any did come to perfection, it was not to be used in the service either of God or man; but what they bore the fourth year was to be holy to the Lord, either given to the priests, or eaten before the Lord with joy, as their second tithe was, and thenceforward it was all their own. Now, 1. Some think this taught them not to follow the custom of the heathen, who, they say, consecrated the very first products of their fruit-trees to their idols, saying that otherwise all the fruits would be blasted. 2. This law in the case of fruit-trees seems to be parallel with that in the case of animals, that no creature should be accepted as an offering till it was past eight days old, nor till that day were children to be circumcised; see *ch.* 22:27. God would have the first-fruits of their trees, but, because for the first three years they were as inconsiderable as a lamb or a calf under eight days old, therefore God would not have them, for it is fit he should have every thing at its best; and yet he would not allow them to be used, because his first-fruits were not as yet offered: they must therefore be accounted as uncircumcised, that is, as an animal under eight days' old, not fit for any use. 3. We are hereby taught not to be over-hasty in catching at any comfort, but to be willing with patience to wait the time for the enjoyment of it, and particularly to acknowledge ourselves unworthy of the increase of the earth, our right to the fruits of which was forfeited by our first parents eating forbidden fruit, and we are restored to it only *by the word of God and prayer,* 1 Tim. 4:5.

IV. A law against the superstitious usages of the heathen, *v.* 26–28. 1. Eating upon the blood, as the Gentiles did, who gathered the blood of their sacrifices into a vessel for their demons (as they fancied) to drink, and then sat about it, eating the flesh themselves, signifying their communion with devils by their feasting with them. Let not this custom be used, for the blood of God's sacrifices was to be sprinkled on the altar, and then poured at the foot of it, and conveyed away. 2. Enchantment and divination, and a superstitious observation of the times, some days and hours lucky and others unlucky. Curious arts of this kind, it is likely, had been of late invented by the Egyptian priests, to amuse the people, and support their own credit. The Israelites had seen them practised, but must by no means imitate them. It would be unpardonable in those *to whom were committed the oracles of God* to ask counsel of the devil, and yet worse in Christians, to whom *the Son of God is manifested,* who has *destroyed the works of the devil.* For Christians to have their nativities cast, and their fortunes told them, to use spells and charms for the cure of diseases and the driving away of evil spirits, to be affected with the falling of the salt, a hare crossing the way, cross days, or the like, is an intolerable affront to the Lord Jesus, a support of paganism and idolatry, and a reproach both to themselves and to that worthy name by which they are called: and those must be grossly ignorant, both of the law and the gospel, that ask, "What harm is there in these things?" Is it no harm for those that have fellowship with Christ to have fellowship with devils, or to learn the ways of those that have? Surely *we have not so learned Christ.* 3. There was a superstition even in trimming themselves used by the heathen, which must not be imitated by the people of God: *You shall not round the corners of your heads.* Those that worshipped the hosts of heaven, in honour of them, cut their hair so as that their heads might resemble the celestial globe; but, as the custom was foolish itself, so, being done with respect to their false gods, it was idolatrous. 4. The rites and ceremonies by which they expressed their sorrow at their funerals must not be imitated, *v.* 28. They must not make cuts or prints in their flesh for the dead; for the heathen did so to pacify the infernal deities they dreamt of, and to render them propitious to their deceased friends. Christ by his sufferings has altered the property of death, and made it a true friend to every true Israelite; and now, as there needs nothing to make death propitious to us (for, if God be so, death is so of course), so we sorrow not as those that have no hope. Those whom the God of Israel had set apart for himself must not receive the image and superscription of these dunghill deities. *Lastly,* The prostituting of their daughters to uncleanness, which is here forbidden (*v.* 29), seems to have been practised by the heathen in their idolatrous worships, for with such abominations those unclean spirits which they worshipped were well pleased. And when lewdness obtained as a religious rite, and was committed in their temples, no marvel that the land became full of that wickedness, which, when it entered at the temple-doors, overspread the land like a mighty torrent, and bore down all the fences of virtue and modesty. The devil himself could not have brought such abominations into their lives if he had not first brought them into their worships. And justly were those given up to vile affections who forsook the holy God, and gave divine honours to impure spirits. Those that dishonour God are thus suffered to dishonour themselves and their families.

Verses 30–37

Here is, I. A law for the preserving of the honour of the time and place appropriated to the service of God, *v.* 30. This would be a means to secure them both from the idolatries and superstitions of the heathen and from all immoralities in conversation. 1. Sabbaths must be religiously observed, and not those times mentioned (*v.* 26) to which the heathen had a superstitious regard. 2. The sanctuary must be reverenced: great care must be taken to approach the tabernacle with that purity and preparation which the law required, and to attend there with that humility, decency, and closeness of application which became them in the immediate presence of such an awful majesty. Though now there is no place holy by divine institution, as the tabernacle and temple then were, yet this law obliges us to respect the solemn assemblies of Christians for religious worship, as being held under a promise of Christ's special presence in them, and to carry ourselves with a due decorum while in those assemblies we attend the administration of holy ordinances, Eccl. 5:1.

II. A caution against all communion with witches, and those that were in league with familiar spirits: *"Regard them not, seek not after them,* be not in fear of any evil from them nor in hopes of any good from them. Regard not their threatenings, or promises, or predictions; seek not to them for discovery or advice, for, if you do, you are defiled by it, and rendered abominable both to God and your own consciences." This was the sin that completed Saul's wickedness, for which he was rejected of God, 1 Chr. 10:13.

III. A charge to young people to show respect to the aged: *Thou shall rise up before the hoary head, v.* 32. Age is honourable, and he that is the Ancient of days requires that honour be paid to it. *The hoary head is a crown of glory.* Those whom God has honoured with the common blessing of long life we ought to honour with the distinguishing expressions of civility; and those who in age are wise and good are worthy of double honour: more respect is owing to such old men than merely to rise up before them; their credit and comfort must be carefully consulted, their experience and observations improved, and their counsels asked and hearkened to, Job 32:6, 7. Some, by the old man whose face or presence is to be honoured, understand the elder in office, as by the hoary head the elder in age;; both ought to be respected as fathers, and in the fear of God, who has put some of his honour upon both. Note, Religion teaches good manners, and obliges us to give honour to those to whom honour is due. It is an instance of great degeneracy and disorder in a land when *the child behaves himself proudly against the ancient, and the base against the honourable,* Isa. 3:5; Job 30:1, 12. It becomes the aged to receive this honour, and the younger to give it; for it is the ornament as well as duty of their youth to *order themselves lowly and reverently to all their betters.*

IV. A charge to the Israelites to be very tender of strangers, *v.* 33, 34. Both the law of God and his providence had vastly dignified Israel above any other people, yet they must not therefore think themselves authorized to trample upon all mankind but those of their own nation, and to insult them at their pleasure; no, *"Thou shall not vex a stranger, but love him as thyself,* and as one of thy own people." It is supposed that this stranger was not an idolater, but a worshipper of the God of Israel, though not circumcised, a proselyte of the gate at least, though not a proselyte of righteousness: if such a one sojourned among them, they must not vex him, nor oppress, nor over-reach him in a bargain, taking advantage of his ignorance of their laws and customs; they must reckon it as great a sin to cheat a stranger as to cheat an Israelite; "nay" (say the Jewish doctors) "they must not so much as upbraid him with his being a stranger, and his having been formerly an idolater." Strangers are God's particular care, as the widow and the fatherless are, because it is his honour to help the helpless, Ps. 146:9. It is therefore at our peril if we do them any wrong, or put any hardships upon them. Strangers shall be welcome to God's grace, and therefore we should do what we can to invite them to it, and to recommend religion to their good opinion. It argues a generous disposition, and a pious regard to God, as a common Father, to be kind to strangers; for those of different countries, customs, and languages, are all made of one blood. But here is a reason added peculiar to the Jews: *"For you were strangers in the land of Egypt.* God then favoured you, therefore do you now favour the strangers, and do to them as you then wished to be done to. You were strangers, and yet are now thus highly advanced; therefore you know not what these strangers may come to, whom you are apt to despise."

V. Justice in weights and measures is here commanded. That there should be no cheat in them, *v.* 35. That they should be very exact, *v.* 36. In weighing and measuring, we pretend a design to give all those their own whom we deal with; but, if the weights and measures be false, it is like a corruption in judgment, it cheats under colour of justice; and thus to deceive a man to his damage is worse than picking his pocket or robbing him on the highway. He that sells is bound to give the full of the commodity, and he that buys the full of the price agreed upon, which cannot be done without just balances, weights, and measures. *Let no man go beyond or defraud his brother,* for, though it be hidden from man, it will be found that *God is the avenger of all such.*

VI. The chapter concludes with a general command (*v.* 37): *You shall observe all my statutes, and do them.* Note, 1. We are not likely to do God's statutes, unless we observe them with great care and consideration. 2. Yet it is not enough barely to observe God's precepts, but we must make conscience of obeying them. What will it avail us to be critical in our notions, if we be not conscientious in our conversations? 3. An upright heart has respect to all God's commandments, Ps. 119:6. Though in many instances the hand fails in doing what should be done, yet the eye observes all God's statutes. We are not allowed to pick and choose our duty, but must aim at standing complete in all the will of God.

CHAPTER 20

The laws which before were made are in this chapter repeated and penalties annexed to them, that those who would not be deterred from sin by the fear of God might be deterred from it by the fear of punishment. If we will not avoid such and such practices because the law has made them sin (and it is most acceptable when we go on that principle of religion), surely we shall avoid them when the law has made them death, from a principle of self-preservation. In this chapter we have, I. Many particular crimes that are made capital. 1. Giving their children to Moloch (*v.* 1–5). 2. Consulting witches (*v.* 6, 27). 3. Cursing parents (*v.* 9). 4. Adultery (*v.* 10). 5. Incest (*v.* 11, 12, 14, 17, 19–21). 6. Unnatural lusts (*v.* 13, 15, 16, 18). II. General commands given to be holy (*v.* 7, 8, 22–26).

Verses 1–9

Moses is here directed to say that again to the children of Israel which he had in effect said before, *v.* 2. We are sure it was no vain repetition, but very necessary, that they might *give the more earnest heed to the things that were spoken,* and might believe them to be of great consequence, being so often inculcated. *God speaketh once, yea, twice,* and what he orders to be said again we must be willing to hear again, because *for us it is safe,* Phil. 3:1.

I. Three sins are in these verses threatened with death:—

1. Parents abusing their children, by sacrificing them to Moloch, *v.* 2, 3. There is the grossest absurdity that can be in all the rites of idolatry, and they are all a great reproach to men's reason; but none trampled upon all the honours of human nature as this did, the burning of children in the fire to the honour of a dunghill-god. It was a plain evidence that their gods were devils, who desired and delighted in the misery and ruin of mankind, and that the worshippers were worse than the beasts that perish, perfectly stripped, not only of reason, but of natural affection. Abraham's offering Isaac could not give countenance, much less could it give rise to this barbarous practice, since, though that was commanded, it was immediately countermanded. Yet such was the power of the god of this world over the children of disobedience that this monstrous piece of inhumanity was generally practised; and even the Israelites were in danger of being drawn into it, which made it necessary that this severe law should be made against it. It was not enough to tell them they might spare their children (the fruit of their body should never be accepted for the sin of their soul), but they must be told, (1.) That the criminal himself should be put to death as a murderer: *The people of the land shall stone him with stones* (*v.* 2), which was looked upon as the worst of capital punishments among the Jews. If the children were sacrificed to the malice of the devil, the parents must be sacrificed to the justice of God. And, if either the fact could not be proved or the magistrates did not do their duty, God would take the work into his own hands: *I will cut him off, v.* 3. Note, Those that escape punishment from men, yet shall not escape the righteous judgments of God; so wretchedly do those deceive themselves that promise themselves impunity in sin. How can those escape against whom God sets his face, that is, whom he frowns upon, meets as an enemy, and fights against? The heinousness of the crime is here set forth to justify the doom: it *defiles the sanctuary,* and *profanes the holy name* of God, for the honour of both which he is jealous. Observe, The malignity of the sin is laid upon that in it which was peculiar to Israel. When the Gentiles sacrificed their children they were guilty of murder and idolatry; but, if the Israelites did it, they incurred the additional guilt of defiling the sanctuary (which they attended upon even when they lay under this guilt, as if there might be an agreement between the temple of God and idols), and of *profaning the holy name of God,* by which they were called, as if he allowed his worshippers to do such things, Rom. 2:23, 24. (2.) That all his aiders and abetters should be cut off likewise by the righteous hand of God. If his neighbours concealed him, and would not come in as witnesses against him, — if the magistrates connived at him, and would not pass sentence upon him, rather pitying his folly than hating his impiety, — God himself would reckon with them, *v.* 4, 5. Misprision of idolatry is a crime cognizable in the court of heaven, and which shall not go unpunished: *I will set my face against that man* (that magistrate, Jer. 5:1) *and against his family.* Note, [1.] The wickedness of the master of a family often brings ruin upon a family; and he that should be the housekeeper proves the house-breaker. [2.] If magistrates will not do justice upon offenders, God will do justice upon them, because there is danger that many will *go a whoring after those* who do but countenance sin by winking at it. And, if the sins of leaders be leading sins, it is fit that their punishments should be exemplary punishments.

2. Children's abusing their parents, by cursing them, *v.* 9. If children should speak ill of their parents, or wish ill to them, or carry it scornfully or spitefully towards them, it was an iniquity to be punished by the judges, who were employed as conservators both of God's honour and of the public peace, which were both attacked by this unnatural insolence. See Prov. 30:17, *The eye that mocks at his father the ravens of the valley shall pick out,* which intimates that such wicked children were in a fair way to be not only hanged, but hanged in chains. This law of Moses Christ quotes and confirms (Mt. 15:4), for it is as direct a breach of the fifth commandment as wilful murder is of the sixth. The same law which requires parents to be tender of their children requires children to be respectful to their parents. He that despitefully uses his parents, the instruments of his being, flies in the face of God himself, the author of his being, who will not see the paternal dignity and authority insulted and trampled upon.

3. Persons abusing themselves by consulting such as have *familiar spirits, v.* 6. By this, as much as any thing, a man diminishes, disparages, and deceives himself, and so abuses himself. What greater madness can there be than for a man to go to a liar for information, and to an enemy for advice? Those do so who turn after those that deal in the black art, and know the depths of Satan. This is spiritual adultery as much as idolatry is, giving that honour to the devil which is due to God only; and the jealous God will give a bill of divorce to those that thus *go a whoring from him,* and will *cut them off,* they having first cut themselves off from him.

II. In the midst of these particular laws comes in that general charge, *v.* 7, 8, where we have,

1. The duties required; and they are two: — (1.) That in our principles, affections, and aims, we be holy: *Sanctify yourselves and be you holy.* We must cleanse ourselves from all the pollutions of sin, consecrate ourselves to the service and honour of God, and conform ourselves in every thing to his holy will and image: this is to *sanctify ourselves.* (2.) That in all our actions, and in the whole course of our conversation, we be obedient to the laws of God: *You shall keep my statutes.* By this only can we make it to appear that we have sanctified ourselves and are holy, even by our keeping God's commandments; *the tree is known by its fruit.* Nor can we *keep God's statutes,* as we ought, unless we first sanctify ourselves, and be holy. Make the tree good, and the fruit will be good.

2. The reasons to enforce these duties. (1.) *"I am the Lord your God;* therefore be holy, that you may resemble him whose people you are, and may be pleasing to him. Holiness becomes his house and household." (2.) *I am the Lord who sanctifieth you.* God sanctified them by peculiar privileges, laws, and favours, which distinguished them from all other nations, and dignified them as a people set apart for God. He gave them his word and ordinances to be means of their sanctification, and his good Spirit to instruct them; therefore they must be holy, else they received the grace of God herein in vain. Note, [1.] God's people are, and must be, persons of distinction. God has distinguished them by his holy covenant, and therefore they ought to distinguish themselves by their holy conversation. [2.] God's sanctifying us is a good reason why we should sanctify ourselves, that we may comply with the designs of his grace, and not walk contrary to them. If it be the Lord that sanctifies us, we may hope the work shall be done, though it be difficult: the manner of expression is like that, 2 Co. 5:5, *He that hath wrought us for the self-same thing is God.* And his grace is so far from superseding our care and endeavour that it most strongly engages and encourages them. *Work out your salvation, for it is God that worketh in you.*

Verses 10–21

Sins against the seventh commandment are here ordered to be severely punished. These are sins which, of all others, fools are most apt to make a mock at; but God would teach those the heinousness of the guilt by the extremity of the punishment that would not otherwise be taught it.

I. Lying with another man's wife was made a capital crime. The adulterer and the adulteress that had joined in the sin must fall alike under the sentence: they shall both be *put to death, v.* 10. Long before this, even in Job's time, this was reputed a *heinous crime* and an *iniquity to be punished by the judges,* Job 31:11. It is a presumptuous contempt of an ordinance of God, and a violation of his covenant, Prov. 2:17. It is an irreparable wrong to the injured husband, and debauches the mind and conscience of both the offenders as much as any thing. It is a sin which headstrong and unbridled lusts hurry men violently to, and therefore it needs such a powerful restraint as this. It is a sin which defiles a land and brings down God's judgments upon it, which disquiets families, and tends to the ruin of all virtue and religion, and therefore is fit to be animadverted upon by the conservators of the public peace: but see Jn. 8:3–11.

II. Incestuous connections, whether by marriage or not. 1. Some of them were to be punished with death, as a man's *lying with his father's wife, v.* 11. Reuben would have been put to death for his crime (Gen. 35:22) if this law had been then made. It was the sin of the incestuous Corinthian, for which he was to be *delivered unto Satan,* 1 Co. 5:1, 5. A man's debauching his daughter-in-law, or his mother-in-law, or his sister, was likewise to be punished with death, *v.* 12, 14, 17. 2. Others of them God would punish with the curse of barrenness, as a man's defiling his aunt, or his brother's wife (*v.* 19–21): *They shall die childless.* Those that keep not within the divine rules of marriage forfeit the blessings of marriage: *They shall commit whoredom, and shall not increase,* Hos. 4:10. Nay it is said, *They shall bear their iniquity,* that is, though they be not immediately cut off by the hand either of God or man for this sin, yet the guilt of it shall lie upon them, to be reckoned for another day, and not be purged with sacrifice or offering.

III. The unnatural lusts of sodomy and bestiality (sins not to be mentioned without horror) were to be punished with death, as they are at this day by our law, *v.* 13, 15, 16. Even the beast that was thus abused was to be killed with the sinner, who was thereby openly put to the greater shame: and the villany was thus represented as in the highest degree execrable and abominable, all occasions of the remembrance or mention of it being to be taken away. Even the unseasonable use of the marriage, if presumptuous, and in contempt of the law, would expose the offenders to the just judgment of God: they *shall be cut off, v.* 18. For this is the will of God, that *every man should possess his vessel* (and the wife is called the weaker vessel) *in sanctification and honour,* as becomes saints.

Verses 22–27

The last verse is a particular law, which comes in after the general conclusion, as if omitted in its proper place: it is for the putting of those to death that dealt with familiar spirits, *v.* 27. It would be an affront to God and to his lively oracles, a scandal to the country, and a temptation to ignorant bad people, to consult them, if such were known and suffered to live among them. Those that are in league with the devil have in effect made a covenant with death and an agreement with hell, and so shall their doom be.

The rest of these verses repeat and inculcate what had been said before; for to that unthinking forgetful people it was requisite that there should be line upon line, and that general rules, with their reasons, should be frequently insisted on, for the enforcement of particular laws, and making them more effectual. Three things we are here reminded of: —

I. Their dignity. 1. They had the *Lord for their God, v.* 24. They were his, his care, his choice, his treasure, his jewels, his kingdom of priests (*v.* 26): *That you should be mine.* Happy the people, and truly great, that are in such a case. 2. Their God was a holy God (*v.* 26), infinitely advanced above all others. His holiness is his glory, and it was their honour to be related to him, while their neighbours were the infamous worshippers of impure and filthy spirits. 3. The great God had separated them from other people (*v.* 24), and again, *v.* 26. Other nations were the common; they were the enclosure, beautified and enriched with peculiar privileges, and designed for peculiar honours; let them therefore value themselves accordingly, preserve their honour, and not lay it in the dust, by walking in the way of the heathen.

II. Their duty; this is inferred from their dignity. God had done more for them than for others, and therefore expected more from them than from others. And what is it that the Lord their God requires, in consideration of the great things done and designed? 1. *You shall keep all my statutes* (*v.* 22); and there was all the reason in the world that they should, for the statutes were their honour, and obedience to them would be their lasting comfort. 2. *You shall not walk in the manners of nations, v.* 23. Being separated from them, they must not associate with them, nor learn their ways. The manners of the nations were bad enough in them, but would be much worse in God's people. 3. You shall *put a difference between clean and unclean, v.* 25. This is holiness, to discern between things that differ, not to live at large, as if we might say and do any thing, but to speak and act with caution. 4. *You shall not make your souls abominable, v.* 25. Our constant care must be to preserve the honour, by preserving the purity, of our own souls, and never to do any thing to make them abominable to God and to our own consciences.

III. Their danger. 1. They were going into an infected place (*v.* 24): *You shall inherit their land,* a land *flowing with milk and honey,* which they would have the comfort of if they kept their integrity; but, withal, it was a land full of idols, idolatries, and superstitious usages, which they would be apt to fall in love with, having brought from Egypt with them a strange disposition to take that infection. 2. If they took the infection, it would be of pernicious consequence to them. The Canaanites were to be expelled for these very sins: *They committed all these things, therefore I abhorred them, v.* 23. See what an evil thing sin is; it provokes God to abhor his own creatures, whereas otherwise he delights in the work of his hands. And, if the Israelites trod in the steps of their impiety, they must expect that the land would spue them out (*v.* 22), as he had told them before, *ch.* 18:28. If God spared not the natural branches, but broke them off, neither would he spare those who were grafted in, if they degenerated. Thus the rejection of the Jews stands for a warning to all Christian churches to take heed lest the kingdom of God be taken from them. Those that sin like others must expect to smart like them; and their profession of relation to God will be no security to them.

CHAPTER 21

This chapter might borrow its title from Mal. 2:1, "And now, O you priests, this commandment is for you." It is a law obliging priests with the utmost care and jealousy to preserve the dignity of their priesthood. I. The inferior priests are here charged both concerning their mourning and concerning their marriages and their children (*v.* 1–9). II. The high priest is restrained more than any of them (*v.* 10–15). III. Neither the one nor the other must have any blemish (*v.* 16, etc.).

Verses 1–9

It was before appointed that the priests should teach the people the statutes God had given concerning the *difference between clean and unclean, ch.* 10:10, 11. Now here it is provided that they should themselves observe what they were to teach the people. Note, Those whose office it is to instruct must do it by example as well as precept, 1 Tim. 4:12. The priests were to draw nearer to God than any of the people, and to be more intimately conversant with sacred things, and therefore it was required of them that they should keep at a greater distance than others from every thing that was defiling and might diminish the honour of their priesthood.

I. They must take care not to disparage themselves in their mourning for the dead. All that mourned for the dead were supposed to come near the body, if not to touch it: and the Jews say, "It made a man ceremonially unclean to come within six feet of a dead corpse;" nay, it is declared (Num. 19:14) that all who come into the tent where the dead body lies shall be unclean seven days. Therefore all the mourners that attended the funeral could not but defile themselves, so as not to be fit to come into the sanctuary for seven days: for this reason it is ordered, 1. That the priests should never put themselves under this incapacity of coming into the sanctuary, unless it were for one of their nearest relations, *v.* 1–3. A priest was permitted to do it for a parent or a child, for a brother or an unmarried sister, and therefore, no doubt (though this is not mentioned) for the wife of his bosom; for Ezekiel, a priest, would have mourned for his wife if he had not been particularly prohibited, Eze. 24:17. By this allowance God put an honour upon natural affection, and favoured it so far as to dispense with the attendance of his servants for seven days, while they indulged themselves in their sorrow for the death of their dear relations; but, beyond this period, weeping must not hinder sowing, nor their affection to their relations take them off from the service of the sanctuary. Nor was it at all allowed for the death of any other, no, not of a *chief man among the people,* as some read it, *v.* 4. They must not defile themselves, no, nor for the high priest himself, unless thus akin to them. Though *there is a friend that is nearer than a brother,* yet the priests must not pay this respect to the best friend they had, except he were a relation, lest, if it were allowed for one, others should expect it, and so they should be frequently taken off from their work: and it is hereby intimated that there is a particular affection to be reserved for those that are thus near akin to us; and, when any such are removed by death, we ought to be affected with it, and lay it to heart, as the near approach of death to ourselves, and an alarm to us to prepare to follow. 2. That they must not be extravagant in the expressions of their mourning, no, not for their dearest relations, *v.* 5. Their mourning must not be either, (1.) Superstitious, according to the manner of the heathen, who cut off their hair, and let out their blood, in honour of the imaginary deities which presided (as they thought) in the congregation of the dead, that they might engage them to be propitious to their departed friends. Even the superstitious rites used of old at funerals are an indication of the ancient belief of the immortality of the soul, and its existence in a separate state: and though the rites themselves were forbidden by the divine law, because they were performed to false gods, yet the decent respect which nature teaches and which the law allows to be paid to the remains of our deceased friends, shows that we are not to look upon them as lost. Nor, (2.) Must it be passionate or immoderate. Note, God's ministers must be examples to others of patience under affliction, particularly that which touches in a very tender part, the death of their near relations. They are supposed to know more than others of the reasons why we must *not sorrow as those that have no hope* (1 Th. 4:13), and therefore they ought to be eminently calm and composed, that they may be able to comfort others with the same comforts wherewith they are themselves comforted of God. The people were forbidden to mourn for the dead with superstitious rites (*ch.* 19:27, 28), and what was unlawful to them was much more unlawful to the priest. The reason given for their peculiar care not to defile themselves we have (*v.* 6): *Because* they offered *the bread of their God,* even *the offerings of the Lord made by fire,* which were the provisions of God's house and table. They are highly honoured, and therefore must not stain their honour by making themselves slaves to their passions; they are continually employed in sacred service, and therefore must not be either diverted from or disfitted for the services they were called to. If they pollute themselves, they profane the name of their God on whom they attend: if the servants are rude and of ill behaviour, it is a reflection upon the master, as if he kept a loose and disorderly house. Note, All that either offer or eat the bread of our God must be holy in all manner of conversation, or else they profane that name which they pretend to sanctify.

II. They must take care not to degrade themselves in their marriage, *v.* 7. A priest must not marry a woman of ill fame, that either had been guilty or was suspected to have been guilty of uncleanness. He must not only not marry a harlot, though ever so great a penitent for her former whoredoms, but he must not marry one that was profane, that is, of a light carriage or indecent behaviour. Nay, he must not marry one that was divorced, because there was reason to think it was for some fault she was divorced. The priests were forbidden to undervalue themselves by such marriages as these, which were allowed to others, 1. Lest it should bring a present reproach upon their ministry, harden the profane in their profaneness, and grieve the hearts of serious people: the New Testament gives laws to ministers' wives (1 Tim. 3:11), that they be *grave and sober,* that *the ministry be not blamed.* 2. Lest it should entail a reproach upon their families; for the work and honour of the priesthood were to descend as an inheritance to their children after them. Those do not consult the good of their posterity as they ought who do not take care to marry such as are of good report and character. He that would seek *a godly seed* (as the expression is, Mal. 2:15) must first seek a godly wife, and take heed of a corruption of blood. It is added here (*v.* 8), *Thou shalt sanctify him,* and *he shall be holy unto thee.* "Not only thou, O Moses, by taking care that these laws be observed, but thou, O Israel, by all endeavours possible to keep up the reputation of the priesthood, which the priests themselves must do nothing to expose or forfeit. *He is holy to his God* (*v.* 7), therefore *he shall be holy unto thee.*" Note, We must honour those whom our God puts honour upon. Gospel ministers by this rule are to be *esteemed very highly in love for their works' sake* (1 Th. 5:13), and every Christian must look upon himself as concerned to be the guardian of their honour.

III. Their children must be afraid of doing any thing to disparage them (*v.* 9): *If the daughter of any priest play the whore,* her crime is great; she not only polluteth but *profaneth herself:* other women have not that honour to lose that she has, who, as one of a priest's family, has eaten of the holy things, and is supposed to have been better educated than others. Nay, *she profaneth her father;* he is reflected upon, and every body will be ready to ask, "Why did not he teach her better?" And the sinners in Zion will insult and say, "Here is your priest's daughter." Her punishment there must be peculiar: *She shall be burnt with fire,* for a terror to all priests' daughters. Note, The children of ministers ought, of all others, to take heed of doing any thing that is scandalous, because in them it is doubly scandalous, and will be punished accordingly by him whose name is *Jealous.*

Verses 10–15

More was expected from a priest than from other people, but more from the high priest than from other priests, because upon his head the *anointing oil was poured,* and he was *consecrated to put on the garments* (*v.* 10), both which were typical of the anointing and adorning of the Lord Jesus, with all the gifts and graces of the Holy Spirit, which he received without measure. It is called *the crown of the anointing oil of his God* (*v.* 12); for the anointing of the Spirit is, to all that have it, a *crown of glory,* and a *diadem of beauty.* The high priest being thus dignified,

I. He must not defile himself at all for the dead, no, nor for his nearest relations, *his father or his mother,* much less his child or brother, *v.* 11. 1. He must not use the common expressions of sorrow on those occasions, such as *uncov-*

ering his head, and rending his clothes (*v.* 10), so perfectly unconcerned must he show himself in all the crosses and comforts of this life: even his natural affection must be swallowed up in compassion to the ignorant, and a feeling of their infirmities, and a tender concern for the household of God, which he was made the ruler of. Thus being the holy one that was entrusted with the *thummim and the urim* he must not know *father or mother,* Deu. 33:8, 9. 2. He must not *go in to any dead body, v.* 11. If any of the inferior priests were under a ceremonial pollution, there were other priests that might supply their places; but, if the high priest were defiled, there would be a greater want of him. And the forbidding of him to go to any house of mourning, or attend any funeral, would be an indication to the people of the greatness of that dignity to which he was advanced. Our Lord Jesus, the great high priest of our profession, touched the dead body of Jairus's daughter, the bier of the widow's son, and the grave of Lazarus, to show that he came to altar the property of death, and to take off the terror of it, by breaking the power of it. Now that it cannot destroy it does not defile. 3. He must *not go out of the sanctuary* (*v.* 12); that is, whenever he was attending or officiating in the sanctuary, where usually he tarried in his own apartment all day, he must not go out upon any occasion whatsoever, nor cut short his attendance on the living God, no, not to pay his last respects to a dying relation. It was a profanation of the sanctuary to leave it, while his presence was requisite there, upon any such occasion; for thereby he preferred some other business before the service of God and the business of his profession, to which he ought to make every thing else give place. Thus our Lord Jesus would not leave off preaching to *speak with his mother and brethren,* Mt. 12:48.

II. He might not marry a widow (as other priests might), much less one divorced, or a harlot, *v.* 13, 14. The reason of this was to put a difference between him and other priests in this matter; and (as some suggest) that he might be a type of Christ, to whom the church was to be presented a *chaste virgin,* 2 Co. 11:2. See Eze. 44:22. Christ must have our first love, our pure love, our entire love; thus the *virgins love thee* (Cant. 1:3), and such only are fit to *follow the Lamb,* Rev. 14:4.

III. He might not profane his seed among his people, *v.* 15. Some understand it as forbidding him to marry any of an inferior rank, which would be a disparagement to his family. Jehoiada indeed married of his own tribe, but then it was into the royal family, 2 Chr. 22:11. This was not to teach him to be proud, but to teach him to be pure, and to do nothing unbecoming his office and the worthy name by which he was called. Or it may be a caution to him in disposing of his children; he must not profane his seed by marrying them unsuitably. Ministers' children are profaned if they be unequally yoked with unbelievers.

Verses 16–24

The priesthood being confined to one particular family, and entailed upon all the male issue of that family throughout their generations, it was very likely that some or other in after-ages that were born to the priesthood would have natural blemishes and deformities: the honour of the priesthood would not secure them from any of those calamities which are common to men. Divers blemishes are here specified; some that were ordinarily for life, as blindness; others that might be for a time, as a scurf or scab, and, when they were gone, the disability ceased. Now,

I. The law concerning priests that had blemishes was, 1. That they might *live upon the altar* (*v.* 22): *He shall eat* of the sacrifices with the other priests, even the *most holy things,* such as the show-bread and the sin-offerings, as well as the *holy things,* such as the tithes and first-fruits, and the priests' share of the peace-offerings. The blemishes were such as they could not help, and therefore, though they might not work, they must not starve. Note, None must be abused for their natural infirmities. Even the deformed child in the family must have its child's part. 2. Yet they must not *serve at the altar,* at either of the altars, nor be admitted to attend or assist the other priests in offering sacrifice or burning incense, *v.* 17, 21, 23. Great men choose to have such servants about them as are sightly, and it was fit that the great God should have such in his house then, when he was pleased to manifest his glory in external indications of it. But it was especially requisite that comely men should be chosen to minister about holy things, for the sake of the people, who were apt to judge according to outward appearance, and to think meanly of the service, how honourable soever it was made by the divine institution, of those that performed it looked despicably or went about it awkwardly. This provision God made for the preserving of the reputation of his altar, that it might not at any time fall under contempt. It was for the credit of the sanctuary that none should appear there who were any way disfigured, either by nature or accident.

II. Under the gospel, 1. Those that labour under any such blemishes as these have reason to thank God that they are not thereby excluded from offering spiritual sacrifices to God; nor, if otherwise qualified for it, from the office of the ministry. There is many a healthful beautiful soul lodged in a crazy deformed body. Yet, 2. We ought to infer hence how incapable those are to serve God acceptably whose minds are blemished and deformed by any reigning vice. Those are unworthy to be called Christians, and unfit to be employed as minsters, that are spiritually blind, and lame, and crooked, whose sins render them scandalous and deformed, so as that the offerings of the Lord are abhorred for their sakes. The deformities of Hophni and Phinehas were worse than any of the blemishes here mentioned. Let such therefore as are openly vicious be put out of the priesthood as polluted persons; and let all that are made to our God spiritual priests be before him *holy and without blemish,* and comfort themselves with this, that, though in this imperfect state they have spots that are the spots of God's children, yet they shall shortly appear before the throne of God *without spot, or wrinkle, or any such thing.*

CHAPTER 22

In this chapter we have divers laws concerning the priests and sacrifices all for the preserving of the honour of the sanctuary. I. That the priests should not eat the holy things in their uncleanness (*v.* 1–9). II. That no stranger who did not belong to some family of the priests should eat of the holy things (*v.* 10–13), and, if he did it unwittingly, he must make restitution, (*v.* 14–16). III. That the sacrifices which were offered must be without blemish (*v.* 17–25). IV. That they must be more than eight days old (*v.* 26–28), and that the sacrifices of thanksgiving must be eaten the same day they were offered (*v.* 29, etc.).

Verses 1–9

Those that had a natural blemish, though they were forbidden to do the priests' work, were yet allowed to eat of the holy things: and the Jewish writers say that "to keep them from idleness they were employed in the wood-room, to pick out that which was worm-eaten, that it might not be used in the fire upon the altar; they might also be employed in the judgment of leprosy:" but,

I. Those that were under any ceremonial uncleanness, which possibly they contracted by their own fault, might no so much as eat of the holy things while they continued in their pollution. 1. Some pollutions were permanent, as a leprosy or a running issue, *v.* 4. These separated the people from the sanctuary, and God would show that they were so far from being more excusable that really they were more abominable in a priest. 2. Others were more transient, as the touching of a dead body, or any thing else that was unclean, from which, after a certain time, a man was cleansed by bathing his flesh in water, *v.* 6. But whoever was thus defiled might not *eat of the holy things,* under pain of God's highest displeasure, who said, and ratified the saying, *That soul shall be cut off from my presence, v.* 3. Our being in the presence of God, and attending upon him, will be so far from securing us that it will but the more expose us to God's wrath, if we dare to draw nigh to him in our uncleanness. The destruction shall come *from the presence of the Lord* (2 Th. 1:9), as the fire by which Nadab and Abihu died came *from before the Lord.* Thus those who profane the holy word of God will be cut off by that word which they make so light of; it shall condemn them. They are again warned of their danger if they eat the holy thing in their uncleanness (*v.* 9), *lest they bear sin, and die therefore.* Note, (1.) Those contract great guilt who profane sacred things, by touching them with unhallowed hands. Eating the holy things signified an interest in the atonement; but, if they ate of them in their uncleanness, they were so far from lessening their guilt that they increased it: They shall *bear sin.* (2.) Sin is a burden which, if infinite mercy prevent not, will certainly sink those that bear it: They shall *die therefore.* Even priests may be ruined by their pollutions and presumptions.

II. As to the design of this law we may observe, 1. This obliged the priests carefully to preserve their purity, and to dread every thing that would defile them. The holy things were their livelihood; if they might not eat of them, how must they subsist? The more we have to lose of comfort and honour by our defilement, the more careful we should be to preserve our purity. 2. This impressed the people with a reverence for the holy things, when they saw the priests themselves *separated from them* (as the expression is, *v.* 2) so long as they were in their uncleanness. He is doubtless a God of infinite purity who kept his immediate attendants under so strict a discipline. 3. This teaches us carefully to watch against all moral pollutions, because by them we are unfitted to receive the comfort of God's sanctuary. Though we labour not under habitual deformities, yet actual defilements deprive us of the pleasure of communion with God; and therefore *he that is washed needeth to wash his feet* (Jn. 13:10), *to wash his hands,* and so to *compass the altar,* Ps. 26:6. Herein we have need to be jealous over ourselves, lest (as it is observably expressed here) we *profane God's holy name in those things which we hallow unto him, v.* 2. If we affront God in those very performances wherein we pretend to honour him, and provoke him instead of pleasing him, we shall make up but a bad account shortly; yet thus we do if we profane God's name, by doing that in our uncleanness which pretends to be hallowed to him.

Verses 10–16

The holy things were to be eaten by the priests and their families. Now,

I. Here is a law that no stranger should eat of them, that is, no person whatsoever but the priests only, and those that pertained to them, *v.* 10. The priests are charged with this care, not to *profane the holy things* by permitting the strangers to eat of them (*v.* 15) or *suffer them to bear the iniquity of trespass* (*v.* 16); that is, suffer them to bring guilt upon themselves, by meddling with that which they have no right to. Thus it is commonly understood. Note, We must not only be careful that we do not bear iniquity ourselves, but we must do what we can to prevent others bearing it. We must not only not suffer sin to *lie* upon our brother, but, if we can help it, we must not suffer it to *come* upon him. But perhaps there is another meaning of those words: the priests' eating the sin-offerings is said to signify their *bearing the iniquity of the congregation, to make an atonement for them, ch.* 10:17. Let not a stranger therefore eat of that holy thing particularly, and so pretend to *bear the iniquity of trespass;* for it is daring presumption for any to do that, but such as are appointed to do it. Those that set up other mediators besides Christ our priest, to *bear the iniquity of trespass,* sacrilegiously rob Christ of his honour, and invade his rights. When we warn people not to trust to their own righteousness, nor dare to appear before God in it, but to rely on Christ's righteousness only for peace and pardon, it is because we dare not *suffer them to bear the iniquity of trespass,* for we know it is too heavy for them.

II. Here is an explanation of the law, showing who were to be looked upon as belonging to the priest's family, and who not. 1. Sojourners and hired servants abode not in the house for ever; they were in the family, but not of it; and therefore they might not eat of the holy things (*v.* 10): but the servant that was born in the house or bought with money, being a heirloom to the family, though a servant, yet might eat of the holy things, *v.* 11. Note, Those only are entitled to the comforts of God's house who make it their *rest for ever,* and resolve to *dwell in it all the days of their life.* As for those who for a time only believe, to serve a present turn. They are looked upon but as sojourners and mercenaries, and have *no part nor lot in the matter.* 2. As to the children of the family, concerning the sons there could be no dispute, they were themselves priests, but concerning the daughters there was a distinction. While they continued in their father's house they might eat of the holy things; but, if they married such as were not priests, they lost their right (*v.* 12), for now they were cut off from the family of the priests. Yet if a priest's daughter became a widow, and had no children in whom she might preserve a distinct family, and returned to her father's house again, being neither wife nor mother, she should again be looked upon as a daughter, and might eat of the holy things. If those whom Providence has made sorrowful widows, and who are dislodged from the rest they had in the house of a husband, yet find it again in a father's house, they have reason to be thankful to the widows' God, who does not leave them comfortless. 3. Here is a demand of restitution to be made by him that had no right to the holy things, and yet should eat of them unwittingly, *v.* 14. If he did it presumptuously, and in contempt of the divine institution, he was liable to be cut off by the hand of God, and to be beaten by the magistrate; but, if he did it through weakness in inconsideration, he was to restore the value, adding a fifth part to it, besides which he was to bring an offering to atone for the trespass; see *ch.* 5:15, 16.

III. This law might be dispensed with in a case of necessity, as it was when David and his men ate of the showbread, 1 Sa. 21:6. And our Saviour justifies them, and gives a reason for it, which furnishes us with a lasting rule in all such cases, that *God will have mercy and not sacrifice,* Mt. 12:3, 4, 7. Rituals must give way to morals.

IV. It is an instruction to gospel ministers, who are *stewards of the mysteries of God,* not to admit all, without distinction, to *eat of the holy things,* but to take out the precious from the vile. Those that are scandalously ignorant or profane are strangers and aliens to the family of the Lord's priests; and it is not meet to take the children's bread and to cast it to such. Holy things are for holy persons, for those who are holy, at least, in profession, Mt. 7:6.

Verses 17–33

Here are four laws concerning sacrifices: —

I. Whatever was offered in sacrifice to God should be without blemish, otherwise it should not be accepted. This had often been mentioned in the particular institutions of the several sorts of offerings. Now here they are told what was to be accounted a blemish which rendered a beast unfit for sacrifice: if it was blind, or lame, had a wen, or the mange (*v.* 22), — if it was bruised, or crushed, or broken, or cut (*v.* 24), that is, as the Jewish writers understand it, if it was, in any of these ways, castrated, if bulls and rams were made into oxen and weathers, they might not be offered. Moreover a difference is made between what was brought as a free-will offering and what was brought as a vow, *v.* 23. And, though none that had any of the forementioned blemishes might be brought for either, yet if a beast had any thing superfluous or lacking (that is, as the Jews understand it, if there was a disproportion or inequality between those parts that are pairs, when one eye, or ear, or leg, was bigger than it should be, or less than it should be) — if there was no other blemish than this, it might be accepted for a free-will offering, to which a man had not before laid himself, nor had the divine law laid him, under any particular obligation; but for a vow it might not be accepted. Thus God would teach us to make conscience of performing our promises to him very exactly, and not afterwards to abate in quantity or value of what we had solemnly engaged to devote to him. What was, before the vow, in our own power, as in the case of a free-will offering, afterwards is not, Acts 5:4. It is again and again declared that no sacrifice should be accepted if it was thus blemished, *v.* 20, 21. According to this law great care was taken to search all the beasts that were brought to be sacrificed, that there might, to a certainty, be no blemish in them. A blemished sacrifice might not be accepted even *from the hand of a stranger,* though to such all possible encouragement should be given to do honour to the God of Israel, *v.* 25. By this it appears that strangers were expected to come to the house of God from a *far country* (1 Ki. 8:41, 42), and that they should be welcome, and their offerings accepted, as those of Darius, Ezra 6:9, 10; Isa. 56:6, 7. The heathen priests were many of them not so strict in this matter, but would receive sacrifices for their gods that were ever so scandalous; but let strangers know that the God of Israel would not be so served. Now, 1. This law was then necessary for the preserving of the honour of the sanctuary, and of the God that was there worshipped. It was fit that every thing that was employed for his honour should be the best of the kind; for, as he is the greatest and brightest, so he is the best of beings; and he that is the best must have the best. See how greatly and justly

displeasing the breach of this law was to the holy God, Mal. 1:8, 13, 14. 2. This law made all the legal sacrifices the fitter to be types of Christ, the great sacrifice from which all these derived their virtue. In allusion to this law, he is said to be *a Lamb without blemish* and *without spot,* 1 Pt. 1:19. As such a priest, so such a sacrifice, became us, who was harmless and undefiled. When Pilate declared, *I find no fault in this man,* he did thereby in effect pronounce the sacrifice without blemish. The Jews say it was the work of the sagan, or suffragan, high priest, to view the sacrifices, and see whether they were without blemish or no; when Christ suffered, Annas was in that office; but little did those who brought Christ to Annas first, by whom he was sent bound to Caiaphas, as a sacrifice fit to be offered (Jn. 18:13, 24), think that they were answering the type of this law. 3. It is an instruction to us to offer to God the best we have in our spiritual sacrifices. If our devotions are ignorant, and cold, and trifling, and full of distractions, we offer *the blind, and the lame, and the sick, for sacrifice;* but cursed be the deceiver that does so, for, while he thinks to put a cheat upon God, he puts a damning cheat upon his own soul.

II. That no beast should be offered in sacrifice before it was eight days old, *v.* 26, 27. It was provided before that the firstlings of their cattle, which were to be dedicated to God, should not be brought to him till after the eighth day, Ex. 22:30. Here it is provided that no creature should be offered in sacrifice till it was eight days old complete. Sooner than that it was not fit to be used at men's tables, and therefore not a God's altar. The Jews say, "It was because the sabbath sanctifies all things, and nothing should be offered to God till at least one sabbath had passed over it." It was in conformity to the law of circumcision, which children were to receive on the eighth day. Christ was sacrificed for us, not in his infancy, though then Herod sought to slay him, but in the prime of his time.

III. That the dam and her young should not both be killed in one day, whether in sacrifice or for common use, *v.* 28. There is such a law as this concerning birds, Deu. 22:6. This was forbidden, not as evil in itself, but because it looked barbarous and cruel to the brute creatures; like the tyranny of the king of Babylon, that slew Zedekiah's sons before his eyes, and then put out his eyes. It looked ill-natured towards the species to kill two generations at once, as if one designed the ruin of the kind.

IV. That the flesh of their thank-offerings should be eaten on the same day that they were sacrificed, *v.* 29, 30. This is a repetition of what we had before, *ch.* 7:15; 19:6, 7. The chapter concludes with such a general charge as we have often met with, to *keep God's commandments,* and not to *profane his holy name, v.* 31, 32. Those that profess God's name, if they do not make conscience of keeping his commandments, do but profane his name. The general reasons are added: God's authority over them — *I am the Lord;* his interest in them — I am *your God;* the title he had to them by redemption — "I *brought you out of the land of Egypt,* on purpose that I might be your God;" the designs of his grace concerning them — *I am the Lord that hallow you;* and the resolutions of his justice, if he had not honour from them, to *get himself honour* upon them — I will be *hallowed among the children of Israel.* God will be a loser in his glory by no man at last; but sooner or later will recover his right, either in the repentance of sinners or in their ruin.

CHAPTER 23

Hitherto the levitical law had been chiefly conversant about holy persons, holy things, and holy places; in this chapter we have the institution of holy times, many of which had been mentioned occasionally before, but here they are all put together, only the new moons are not mentioned. All the rest of the feasts of the Lord are, I. The weekly feast of the sabbath (*v.* 3). II. The yearly feasts, 1. The passover, and the feast of unleavened bread (*v.* 4–8), to which was annexed the offering of the sheaf of firstfruits (*v.* 9–14). 2. Pentecost (*v.* 15–22). 3. The solemnities of the seventh month. The feast of trumpets on the first day (*v.* 23–25), the day of atonement on the tenth day (*v.* 26–32), and the feast of tabernacles on the fifteenth (*v.* 33, etc.).

Verses 1–3

Here is, I. A general account of the holy times which God appointed (*v.* 2), and it is only his appointment that can make time holy; for he is the Lord of time, and as soon as ever he had set its wheels a-going it was he that sanctified and blessed one day above the rest, Gen. 2:3. Man may by his appointment make a good day (Esth. 9:19), but

it is God's prerogative to make a holy day; nor is any thing sanctified but by the stamp of his institution. As all inherent holiness comes from his special grace, so all adherent holiness from his special appointment. Now, concerning the holy times here ordained, observe, 1. They are called *feasts.* The day of atonement, which was one of them, was a fast; yet, because most of them were appointed for joy and rejoicing, they are in the general called feasts. Some read it, *These are my assemblies,* but that is co-incident with *convocations.* I would rather read it, These are *my solemnities;* so the word here used is translated (Isa. 33:20), where Zion is called the *city of our solemnities:* and, reading it so here, the day of atonement was as great a solemnity as any of them. 2. They are the feasts of the Lord *(my feasts),* observed to the honour of his name, and in obedience to his command. 3. They were proclaimed; for they were not to be observed by the priests only that attended the sanctuary, but by all the people. And this proclamation was the joyful sound concerning which we read, *Blessed are the people that know it,* Ps. 89:15. 4. They were to be sanctified and solemnized with holy convocations, that the services of these feasts might appear the more honourable and august, and the people the more unanimous in the performance of them; it was for the honour of God and his institutions, which sought not corners and the purity of which would be best preserved by the public administration of them; it was also for the edification of the people in love that the feasts were to be observed as holy convocations.

II. A repetition of the law of the sabbath in the first place. Though the annual feasts were made more remarkable by the general attendance at the sanctuary, yet these must not eclipse the brightness of the sabbath, *v.* 3. They are here told, 1. That on that day they must withdraw themselves from all the affairs and business of the world. It is a *sabbath of rest,* typifying our spiritual rest from sin, and in God: *You shall do no work therein.* On other holy days they were forbidden to do any servile work (*v.* 7), but on the sabbath, and the day of atonement (which is also called a sabbath), they were to do no work at all, no, not the dressing of meat. 2. On that day they must employ themselves in the service of God. (1.) It is a *holy convocation;* that is, "If it lie within your reach, you shall sanctify it in a religious assembly: let as many as can come to the door of the tabernacle, and let others meet elsewhere for prayer, and praise, and the reading of the law," as in the schools of the prophets, while prophecy continued, and afterwards in the synagogues. Christ appointed the New-Testament sabbath to be a holy convocation, by meeting his disciples once and again (and perhaps oftener) on the first day of the week. (2.) "Whether you have opportunity of sanctifying it in a holy convocation or not, yet let it be *the sabbath of the Lord in all your dwellings.* Put a difference between that day and other days in your families. It is the *sabbath of the Lord,* the day on which he rested from the work of creation, and on which he has appointed us to rest; let it be observed in all your dwellings, even now that you dwell in tents." Note, God's sabbaths are to be religiously observed in every private house, by every family apart, as well as by many families together in holy convocations. The sabbath of the Lord in our dwellings will be their beauty, strength, and safety; it will sanctify, edify, and glorify them.

Verses 4–14

Here again the feasts are called the *feasts of the Lord,* because he appointed them. Jeroboam's feast, which he *devised of his own heart* (1 Ki. 12:33), was an affront to God, and a reproach upon the people. These feasts were to be proclaimed in their seasons (*v.* 4), and the seasons God chose for them were in March, May and September (according to our present computation), not in winter, because travelling would then be uncomfortable, when the days were short, and the ways foul; not in the middle of summer, because then in those countries they were gathering in their harvest and vintage, and could be ill spared from their country business. Thus graciously does God consult our comfort in his appointments, obliging us thereby religiously to regard his glory in our observance of them, and not to complain of them as a burden. The solemnities appointed them were, 1. Many and returned frequently, which was intended to preserve in them a deep sense of

God and religion, and to prevent their inclining to the superstitions of the heathen. God kept them fully employed in his service, that they might not have time to hearken to the temptations of the idolatrous neighbourhood they lived in. 2. They were most of them times of joy and rejoicing. The weekly sabbath is so, and all their yearly solemnities, except the day of atonement. God would thus teach them that wisdom's ways are pleasantness, and engage them to his service by encouraging them to be cheerful in it and to sing at their work. Seven days were days of strict rest and holy convocations; the first day and the seventh of the feast of unleavened bread, the day of pentecost, the day of the feast of trumpets, the first day and the eighth of the feast of tabernacles, and the day of atonement: here were six for holy joy and one only for holy mourning. We are commanded to *rejoice evermore*, but not to be evermore weeping. Here is,

I. A repetition of the law of the passover, which was to be observed on the fourteenth day of the first month, in remembrance of their deliverance out of Egypt and the distinguishing preservation of their first-born, mercies never to be forgotten. This feast was to begin with the killing of the paschal lamb, *v*. 5. It was to continue seven days, during all which time they were to eat sad bread, that was unleavened (*v*. 6), and the first and last day of the seven were to be days of *holy rest* and *holy convocations, v*. 7, 8. They were not idle days spent in sport and recreation (as many that are called Christians spend their holy days), but offerings were *made by fire unto the Lord* at his altar; and we have reason to think that the people were taught to employ their time in prayer, and praise, and godly meditation.

II. An order for the offering of a sheaf of the first-fruits, upon the second day of the feast of unleavened bread; the first is called the *sabbath*, because it was observed as a sabbath (*v*. 11), and, on the morrow after, they had this solemnity. A sheaf or handful of new corn was brought to the priest, who was to heave it up, in token of his presenting it to the God of Heaven, and to wave it to and fro before the Lord, as the Lord of the whole earth, and this should be accepted for them as a thankful acknowledgment of God's mercy to them in clothing their fields with corn, and of their dependence upon God, and desire towards him, for the preserving of it to their use. For it was the expression both of prayer and praise, *v*. 11. A lamb for a burnt-offering was to be offered with it, *v*. 12. As the sacrifice of animals was generally attended with meat-offerings, so this sacrifice of corn was attended with a burnt-offering, that bread and flesh might be set together on God's table. They are forbidden to eat of their new corn till this handful was offered to God; for it was fit, if God and Israel feast together, that he should be served first. And the offering of this sheaf of first-fruits in the name of the whole congregation did, as it were, sanctify to them their whole harvest, and give them a comfortable use of all the rest; for then we may *eat our bread with joy* when we have, in some measure, performed our duty to God, and God has accepted our works, for thus all our enjoyments become clean to us. Now, 1. This law was given now, though there was no occasion for putting it in execution till they came to Canaan: in the wilderness they sowed no corn; but God's feeding them there with *bread from heaven* obliged them hereafter not to grudge him his share of their bread out of the earth. We find that when they came into Canaan the manna ceased upon the very day that the sheaf of first-fruits was offered; they had eaten of the old corn the day before (Jos. 5:11), and then on this day they offered the first-fruits, by which they became entitled to the new corn too (*v*. 12), so that there was no more occasion for manna. 1. This sheaf of first-fruits was typical of our Lord Jesus, who has risen from the dead as the *first-fruits of those that slept*, 1 Co. 15:20. That *branch of the Lord* (Isa. 4:2) was then presented to him, in virtue of the sacrifice of himself, the Lamb of God, and it was accepted for us. It is very observable that our Lord Jesus rose from the dead on the very day that the first-fruits were offered, to show that he was the substance of this shadow. 3. We are taught by this law to *honour the Lord with our substance, and with the first-fruits of all our increase*, Prov. 3:9. They were not to eat of their new corn till God's part was offered to him out of it (*v*. 14), for we must always begin with God, begin our lives with him, begin every day with him, begin every

meal with him, begin every affair and business with him; *seek first the kingdom of God.*

Verses 15–22

Here is the institution of the feast of *pentecost*, or *weeks*, as it is called (Deu. 16:9), because it was observed fifty days, or seven weeks, after the passover. It is also called the *feast of harvest*, Ex. 23:16. For as the presenting of the sheaf of first-fruits was an introduction to the harvest, and gave them liberty to put in the sickle, so they solemnized the finishing of their corn-harvest at this feast. 1. Then they offered a handful of ears of barley, now they offered *two loaves of wheaten bread, v*. 17. This was leavened. At the passover they ate unleavened bread, because it was in remembrance of the bread they ate when they came out of Egypt, which was unleavened; but now at pentecost it was leavened, because it was an acknowledgment of God's goodness to them in their ordinary food, which was leavened. 2. With that sheaf of first-fruits they offered only one lamb for a burnt-offering, but with these loaves of first-fruits they offered seven lambs, two rams, and one bullock, all for a burnt-offering, so giving glory to God, as the Lord of their land and the Lord of their harvest, by whose favour they lived and to whose praise they ought to live. They offered likewise a kid for a sin-offering, so taking shame to themselves as unworthy of the bread they ate, and imploring pardon for their sins, by which they had forfeited their harvest-mercies, and which they had been guilty of in the receiving of them. And lastly, two lambs for a sacrifice of peace-offerings, to beg a blessing upon the corn they had gathered in, which would be neither sure nor sweet to them without that blessing, Hag. 1:9. These were the only peace-offerings that were offered on the behalf of the whole congregation, and they were reckoned *most holy* offerings, whereas other peace-offerings were but *holy*. All these offerings are here appointed, *v*. 18–20. 3. That one day was to be kept with a holy convocation, *v*. 21. It was one of the days on which all Israel was to meet God and one another, at the place which the Lord should choose. Some suggest that whereas seven days were to make up the feast of unleavened bread there was only one day appointed for the feast of pentecost, because this was a busy time of the year with them, and God allowed them speedily to return to their work in the country. This annual feast was instituted in remembrance of the giving of the law upon mount Sinai, the fiftieth day after they came out of Egypt. That was the feast which they were told in Egypt must be observed to God in the wilderness, as a memorial of which ever after they kept this feast. But the period and perfection of this feast was the pouring out of the Spirit upon the apostles on the day of this feast (Acts 2:1), in which the law of faith was given, fifty days after Christ our passover was sacrificed for us. And on that day (as bishop Patrick well expresses it) the apostles, having themselves received the *first-fruits of the Spirit*, begat three thousand souls, through the word of truth, and presented them, as the first-fruits of the Christian church, to God and the Lamb.

To the institution of the feast of pentecost is annexed a repetition of that law which we had before (ch. 19:9), by which they were required to leave the gleanings of their fields, and the corn that grew on the ends of the butts, for the poor, *v*. 22. Probably it comes in here as a thing which the priests must take occasion to remind the people of, when they brought their first-fruits, intimating to them that to obey even in this small matter was better than sacrifice, and that, unless they were obedient, their offerings should not be accepted. It also taught them that the joy of harvest should express itself in charity to the poor, who must have their due out of what we have, as well as God his. Those that are truly sensible of the mercy they receive from God will without grudging show mercy to the poor.

Verses 23–32

Here is, I. The institution of the feast of trumpets, on the first day of the seventh month, *v*. 24, 25. That which was now the seventh month had been reckoned the first month, and the year of jubilee was still to begin with this month (ch. 25:8), so that this was their new year's day. It was to be as their other yearly sabbaths, a day of holy rest — *You shall do no servile work therein;* and a day of holy

work — *You shall offer an offering to the Lord;* concerning these particular directions were afterwards given, Num. 29:1. That which is here made peculiar to this festival is that it was *a memorial of blowing of trumpets*. They blew the trumpet every new moon (Ps. 81:3), but in the new moon of the seventh month it was to be done with more than ordinary solemnity; for they began to blow at sunrise and continued till sun-set. Now, 1. This is here said to be a *memorial*, perhaps of the sound of the trumpet upon mount Sinai when the law was given, which must never be forgotten. Some think that it was a memorial of the creation of the world, which is supposed to have been in autumn; for which reason this was, till now, the first month. The mighty word by which God made the world is called *the voice of his thunder* (Ps. 104:7); fitly therefore was it commemorated by blowing of trumpets, or a memorial of *shouting*, as the Chaldee renders it; for, when the *foundations of the earth were fastened, all the sons of God shouted for joy*, Job 38:6, 7. 2. The Jewish writers suppose it to have a spiritual signification. Now at the beginning of the year they were called by this sound of trumpet to shake off their spiritual drowsiness, to search and try their ways, and to amend them: the day of atonement was the ninth day after this; and thus they were awakened to prepare for that day, by sincere and serious repentance, that it might be indeed to them a day of atonement. And they say, "The devout Jews exercised themselves more in good works between the feast of trumpets and the day of expiation than at any other time of the year." 3. It was typical of the preaching of the gospel, by which joyful sound souls were to be called in to serve God and keep a spiritual feast to him. The conversion of the nations to the faith of Christ is said to be by the *blowing of a great trumpet*, Isa. 27:13.

II. A repetition of the law of the day of atonement, that is, so much of it as concerned the people. 1. They must on this day rest from all manner of work, and not only from servile works as on other annual festivals; it must be as strict a rest as that of the weekly sabbath, *v*. 28, 30, 31. The reason is: *For it is a day of atonement*. Note, The humbling of our souls for sin, and the making of our peace with God, is work that requires the whole man, and the closest application of mind imaginable, and all little enough. He that would do the work of a day of atonement in its day, as it should be done, had need lay aside the thoughts of every thing else. On that day God *spoke peace unto his people, and unto his saints;* and therefore they must lay aside all their worldly business, that they might the more clearly and the more reverently hear that voice of joy and gladness. Fasting days should be days of rest. 2. They must afflict their souls, and this upon pain of being cut off by the hand of God, *v*. 27, 29, 32. They must mortify the body, and deny the appetites of it, in token of their sorrow for the sins they had committed, and the mortifying of their indwelling corruptions. Every soul must be afflicted, because every soul was polluted, and guilty before God; while none have fulfilled the law of innocency none are exempt from the law of repentance, besides that every man must sigh and cry for the *abominations of the land*. 3. The entire day must be observed: *From even to even you shall afflict your souls* (*v*. 32), that is, "You shall begin your fast, and the expressions of your humiliation, in the *ninth day of the month at even*." They were to leave off all their worldly labour, and compose themselves to the work of the day approaching, some time before sun-set on the ninth day, and not to take any food (except children and sick people) till after sun-set on the tenth day. Note, The eves of solemn days ought to be employed in solemn preparation. When work for God and our souls is to be done, we should not straiten ourselves in time for the doing of it; for how can we spend our time better? Of this sabbath the rule here given is to be understood: *From even unto even shall you celebrate your sabbath.*

Verses 33–44

We have here, I. The institution of the feast of tabernacles, which was one of the three great feasts at which all the males were bound to attend, and celebrated with more expressions of joy than any of them.

1. As to the directions for regulating this feast, observe, (1.) It was to be observed on the fifteenth day of the seventh month (*v*. 34), but five days after the day of atone-

ment. We may suppose, though they were not all bound to attend on the day of atonement, as on the three great festivals, yet that many of the devout Jews came up so many days before the feast of tabernacles as to enjoy the opportunity of attending on the day of atonement. Now, [1.] The afflicting of their souls on the day of atonement prepared them for the joy of the feast of tabernacles. The more we are grieved and humbled for sin, the better qualified we are for the comforts of the Holy Ghost. [2.] The joy of this feast recompensed them for the sorrow of that fast; for those that *sow in tears* shall *reap in joy.* (2.) It was to continue eight days, the first and last of which were to be observed as sabbaths, days of holy rest and holy convocations, *v.* 35, 36, 39. The sacrifices to be offered on these eight days we have a very large appointment of, Num. 29:12, etc. (3.) During the first seven days of this feast all the people were to leave their houses, and the women and children in them, and to dwell in booths made of the boughs of thick trees, particularly palm trees, *v.* 40, 42. The Jews make the taking of the branches to be a distinct ceremony from the making of the booths. It is said, indeed (Neh. 8:15), that they *made their booths of the branches of trees,* which they might do, and yet use that further expression of joy, the carrying of palm-branches in their hands, which appears to have been a token of triumph upon other occasions (Jn. 12:13), and is alluded to, Rev. 7:9. The eighth day some make a distinct feast of itself, but it is called (Jn. 7:37) *that great day of the feast;* it was the day on which they returned from their booths, to settle again in their own houses. (4.) They were to *rejoice before the Lord God* during all the time of this feast, *v.* 40. The tradition of the Jews is that they were to express their joy by dancing, and singing hymns of praise to God, with musical instruments: and not the common people only, but the wise men of Israel, and their elders, were to do it in the court of the sanctuary: for (say they) the joy with which a man rejoices in doing a commandment is really a great service.

2. As to the design of this feast,

(1.) It was to be kept in remembrance of their dwelling in tents in the wilderness. Thus it is expounded here (*v.* 43): *That your generations may know,* not only by the written history, but by this ocular tradition, *that I made the children of Israel to dwell in booths.* Thus it kept in perpetual remembrance, [1.] The meanness of their beginning, and the low and desolate state out of which God advanced that people. Note, Those that are comfortably fixed ought often to call to mind their former unsettled state, when they were but little in their own eyes. [2.] The mercy of God to them, that, when they dwelt in tabernacles, God not only set up a tabernacle for himself among them, but, with the utmost care and tenderness imaginable, hung a canopy over them, even the cloud that sheltered them from the heat of the sun. God's former mercies to us and our fathers ought to be kept in everlasting remembrance. The eighth day was the great day of this feast, because then they returned to their own houses again, and remembered how, after they had long dwelt in tents in the wilderness, at length they came to a happy settlement in the land of promise, where they dwelt in goodly houses. And they would the more sensibly value and be thankful for the comforts and conveniences of their houses when they had been seven days dwelling in booths. It is good for those that have ease and plenty sometimes to learn what it is to endure hardness.

(2.) It was a feast of in-gathering, so it is called, Ex. 23:16. When they had gathered in the *fruit of their land* (*v.* 39), the vintage as well as the harvest, then they were to keep this feast in thankfulness to God for all the increase of the year; and some think that the eighth day of the feast had special reference to this ground of the institution. Note, The joy of harvest ought to be improved for the furtherance of our joy in God. *The earth is the Lord's and the fulness thereof,* and therefore whatever we have the comfort of he must have the glory of, especially when any mercy is perfected.

(3.) It was a typical feast. It is supposed by many that our blessed Saviour was born much about the time of this feast; then he left his mansions of light above to *tabernacle among us* (Jn. 1:14), and he dwelt in booths. And the worship of God under the New Testament is prophesied of under the notion of keeping the *feast of tabernacles,* Zec. 14:16. For, [1.] The gospel of Christ teaches us to dwell in tabernacles, to sit loose to this world, as those that have here no continuing city, but by faith, and hope and holy contempt of present things, to *go out to Christ without the camp,* Heb. 13:13, 14. [2.] It teaches us to rejoice before the Lord our God. Those are the circumcision, Israelites indeed, that always *rejoice in Christ Jesus,* Phil. 3:3. And the more we are taken off from this world the less liable we are to the interruption of our joys.

II. The summary and conclusion of these institutions.

1. God appointed these feasts (*v.* 37, 38), *besides the sabbaths and your free-will offerings.* This teaches us, (1.) That calls to extraordinary services will not excuse us from our constant stated performances. Within the days of the feast of tabernacles there must fall at least one sabbath, which must be as strictly observed as any other. (2.) That God's institutions leave room for free-will offerings. Not that we may invent what he never instituted, but we may repeat what he has instituted, ordinarily, the oftener the better. God is well pleased with a willing people.

2. Moses declared them to the children of Israel, *v.* 44. He let them know what God appointed, and neither more nor less. Thus Paul delivered to the churches what he had *received from the Lord.* We have reason to be thankful that the feasts of the Lord, declared unto us, are not so numerous, nor the observance of them so burdensome and costly, as theirs then were, but more spiritual and significant, and surer sweeter earnests of the everlasting feast, at the last in-gathering, which we hope to be celebrating to eternity.

CHAPTER 24

In this chapter we have, I. A repetition of the laws concerning the lamps and the show-bread (*v.* 1–9). II. A violation of the law against blasphemy, with the imprisonment, trial, condemnation, and execution, of the blasphemer (*v.* 10–14, with *v.* 23). III. The law against blasphemy reinforced (*v.* 15, 16), with sundry other laws (*v.* 17, etc.).

Verses 1–9

Care is here taken, and orders are given, for the decent furnishing of the candlestick and table in God's house.

I. The lamps must always be kept burning. The law for this we had before, Ex. 27:20, 21. It is here repeated, probably because it now began to be put in execution, when other things were settled. 1. The people were to provide oil (*v.* 2), and this, as every thing else that was to be used in God's service, must be of the best, *pure olive-oil, beaten,* probably it was double-strained. This was to *cause the lamps to burn;* all our English copies read it *lamps,* but in the original it is singular in *v.* 2 — to *cause the lamp to burn;* but plural in *v.* 4 — *he shall order the lamps.* The seven lamps made all one lamp, in allusion to which the blessed Spirit of grace is represented by *seven lamps of fire before the throne* (Rev. 4:5), for there are *diversities of gifts, but one Spirit,* 1 Co. 12:4. Ministers are as burning and shining lights in Christ's church, but it is the duty of people to provide comfortably for them, as Israel for the lamps. Scandalous maintenance makes a scandalous ministry. 2. The priests were to tend the lamps; they must snuff them, clean the candlestick, and supply them with oil, morning and evening, *v.* 3, 4. Thus it is the work of the ministers of the gospel to *hold forth that word of life,* not to set up new lights, but, by expounding and preaching the word, to make the light of it more clear and extensive. This was the ordinary way of keeping the lamps burning; but, when the church was poor and in distress, we find its lamps fed constantly with *oil from the good olives* immediately, without the ministry of priest or people (Zec. 4:2, 3); for, though God has tied us to means, he has not tied himself to them, but will take effectual care that his lamp never go out in the world for want of oil.

II. The table must always be kept spread. This was appointed before, Ex. 25:30. And here also, 1. The table was furnished with bread; not dainties nor varieties to gratify a luxurious palate, but twelve loaves or cakes of bread, *v.* 5, 6. Where there is plenty of bread there is no famine; and where bread is not there is no feast. There was a loaf for every tribe, for *in our Father's house there is bread enough.* They were all provided for by the divine bounty, and were all welcome to the divine grace. Even after the revolt of the ten tribes this number of loaves was continued (2 Chr. 13:11), for the sake of those few of each tribe that retained their affection to the temple and continued their attendance on it. 2. A handful of frankincense was put in a golden saucer, upon or by each row, *v.* 7. When the bread was removed, and given to the priests, this frankincense was burnt upon the golden altar (I suppose) over and above the daily incense: and this was for a memorial instead of the bread, an offering made by fire, as the handful of the meat-offering which was burnt upon the altar is called the *memorial thereof, ch.* 2:2. Thus a little was accepted as a humble acknowledgment, and all the loaves were consigned to the priests. All God's spiritual Israel, typified by the twelve loaves, are made through Christ a sweet savour to him, and their prayers are said to come up before God *for a memorial,* Acts 10:4. The word is borrowed from the ceremonial law. 3. Every sabbath it was renewed. When the loaves had stood there a week, the priests had them to eat with other holy things that were to be eaten in the holy place (*v.* 9), and new ones were provided at the public charge, and put in the room of them, *v.* 8. The Jews say, "The hands of those priests that put on were mixed with theirs that took off, that the table might be never empty, but the bread might be *before the Lord continually.*" God is never unprovided for the entertainment of those that visit him, as men often are, Lu. 11:5. Every one of those cakes contained two tenth-deals, that is, two omers of fine flour; just so much manna every Israelite gathered on the sixth day for the sabbath, Ex. 16:22. Hence some infer that this show-bread, which was set on the table on the sabbath, was intended as a memorial of the manna wherewith they were fed in the wilderness. Christ's ministers should provide new bread for his house every sabbath day, the production of their fresh studies in the scripture, that *their proficiency may appear to all,* 1 Tim. 4:1, 5.

Verses 10–23

Evil manners, we say, beget good laws. We have here an account of the evil manners of a certain nameless mongrel Israelite, and the good laws occasioned thereby.

I. The offender was the son of an Egyptian father and an Israelitish mother (*v.* 10); his mother was of the tribe of Dan, *v.* 11. Neither he nor his father is named, but his mother only, who was an Israelite. This notice is taken of his parentage either, 1. To intimate what occasioned the quarrel he was engaged in. The Jews say, "He offered to set up his tent among the Danites in the right of his mother, but was justly opposed by some or other of that tribe, and informed that his father being an Egyptian he had no part nor lot in the matter, but must look upon himself as a stranger." Or, 2. To show the common ill effect of such mixed marriages. When a daughter of Israel would marry an idolatrous malignant Egyptian, what could be the fruit of such a marriage but a blasphemer? For the children will be apt to take after the worse side, whichsoever it is, and will sooner learn of an Egyptian father to blaspheme than of an Israelitish mother to pray and praise.

II. The occasion of the offence was contention: He *strove with a man of Israel.* The mixed multitude of Egyptians that came up with Israel (Ex. 12:38) were in many ways hurtful to them, and this was one, they were often the authors of strife. The way to preserve the peace of the church is to preserve the purity of it. In this strife he broke out into ill language. Note, When quarrels begin we know not what mischief they will make before they end, nor how treat a matter a little fire may kindle. When men's passion is up they are apt to forget both their reason and their religion, which is a good reason why we should not be apt either to give or to resent provocation, but leave off strife before it be meddled with, because the beginning of it is *as the letting forth of water.*

III. The offence itself was blasphemy and cursing, *v.* 11. It is supposed that his cause came to be heard before the judges, who determined that he had no right to the privileges of an Israelite, his father being an Egyptian, and that, being enraged at the sentence, 1. He *blasphemed the name of the Lord.* He blasphemed *the name,* that is, he blasphemed God, who is known by his name only, not by his nature, or any similitude. Not as if God were a mere name, but his is a name above every name. The translators add *of the Lord,* which is implied, but not expressed, in the original, for the greater reverence of the divine Majesty: it is a shame that it should be found on record that the very name of Jehovah should be blasphemed; *tell it not in Gath.* It is a fond conceit of the superstitious Jews that his blasphemy was in pronouncing the name of *Jehovah,* which they call ineffable: he that made himself known by that name never forbade the calling of him by that name. It is probable that finding himself aggrieved by the divine appointment, which separated between the Israelites and strangers, he impudently reproached both the law and the Law-maker, and set him at defiance. 2. He cursed either God himself (and then his cursing was the same with blaspheming) or the person with whom he strove. Imprecations of mischief are the hellish language of hasty passion, as well as of rooted malice. Or perhaps he cursed the judges that gave sentence against him; he flew in the face of the court, and ridiculed the processes of it; thus he added sin to sin.

IV. The caution with which he was proceeded against for this sin. The witnesses or inferior judges brought him and his case (which was somewhat extraordinary) unto Moses (*v.* 11), according to the order settled (Ex. 18:22), and Moses himself would not give judgment hastily, but committed the offender into custody, till he had consulted the oracle in this case. Note, Judges must deliberate; both those that give the verdict and those that give the sentence must consider diligently what they do, and do nothing rashly, for *the judgment is God's* (Deu. 1:17), and before him there will be a rehearing of the cause. They waited to know what was *the mind of the Lord,* whether he was to be put to death by the hand of the magistrate or to be left to the judgment of God: or, rather, they wanted to know whether he should be stoned, as those were to be that only cursed their *parents* (*ch.* 20:9), or whether, the crime being so much greater, some sorer punishment should be inflicted on him. Note, Those that sit in judgment should sincerely desire, and by prayer and the use of all good means should endeavour to *know the mind of the Lord,* because they *judge for him* (2 Chr. 19:6) and to him they are accountable.

V. Sentence passed upon this offender by the righteous Judge of heaven and earth himself: *Let all the congregation stone him, v.* 14. God could have cut him off by an immediate stroke from heaven, but he would put this honour upon the institution of magistracy to make use of it for the supporting and vindicating of his own glory in the world. Observe, 1. The place of execution appointed: *Bring him forth without the camp.* To signify their detestation of the crime, they must thus cast out the criminal as an abominable branch, and separate him from them as an unclean thing and unworthy a place in the camp of Israel. 2. The executioners: *Let all the congregation* do it, to show their zeal for the honour of God's name. Every man should have a stone to throw at him that blasphemes God, reckoning himself nearly concerned in the reproaches cast on God, Ps. 69:9. Thus also the greater terror would be cast upon the congregation; those that once helped to stone a blasphemer would ever after dread every thing that bordered upon blasphemy, that looked like it or looked towards it. 3. The solemnity of the execution; before the congregation stoned him, the witnesses were to *lay their hands upon his head.* The Jews say that this was used in the execution of no criminals but blasphemers; and that it was done with words to this purport, *"Thy blood be upon thy own head, for thou thyself hast occasioned it.* Let no blame be laid on the law, judges, juries, or witnesses; *if thou scornest, thou alone shalt bear it."*

VI. A standing law made upon this occasion for the stoning of blasphemers, *v.* 15, 16. Magistrates are the guardians of both tables, and ought to be as jealous for the honour of God against those that speak contemptuously of his being and government as for the public peace and safety against the disturbers of them. 1. A great stress is laid upon this law, as in no case to be dispensed with: *He shall surely be put to death; they shall certainly stone him.* Those that lightly esteemed God's honour might think it hard to make a man an offender for a word (words are but wind); but God would let them know that they must not make light of such words as these, which come from malice against God in the heart of him that speaks, and must occasion either great guilt or great grief to those that hear. 2. It is made to extend to the strangers that sojourned among them, as well as those that were born in the land. God never made any law to compel strangers to be circumcised and embrace the Jewish religion (proselytes made by force would be no honour to the God of Israel), but he made a law to restrain strangers from speaking evil of the God of Israel. 3. He that was put to death for blasphemy is said to *bear his sin,* in the punishment of it; no sacrifice being appointed, on the head of which the sin might be transferred, he himself was to bear it upon his own head, as a sacrifice to divine justice. So *his own tongue fell upon him* (Ps. 64:8), and the tongue of a blasphemer will fall heavily.

VII. A repetition of some other laws annexed to this new law. 1. That murder should be punished with death (*v.* 17, and again *v.* 21), according to an ancient law in Noah's time (Gen. 9:6), and the very law of nature, Gen. 4:10. 2. That maimers should in like manner be punished by the law of retaliation, *v.* 19, 20. Not that men might in these cases be their own avengers, but they might appeal to the civil magistrate, who should award suffering to the injurious and satisfaction to the injured as should be thought fit in proportion to the hurt done. This law we had before, Ex. 22:4, 5. And it was more agreeable to that dispensation, in which were revealed the rigour of the law and what sin deserved, than to the dispensation we are under, in which are revealed the grace of the gospel and the remission of sins: and therefore our Saviour has set aside this law (Mt. 5:38, 39), not to restrain magistrates from executing public justice, but to restrain us all from returning personal injuries and to oblige us to forgive as we are and hope to be forgiven. 3. That hurt done wilfully to a neighbour's cattle should be punished by making good the damage, *v.* 18, 21. Thus the divine law took not only their lives, but their goods also under its protection. Those beasts which belonged to no particular person, but were, as our law speaks, *ferae naturae — of a wild nature,* it was lawful for them to kill; but not those which any man had a property in. Does God take care for oxen? Yes; for our sakes he does. 4. That strangers, as well as native Israelites, should be both entitled to the benefit of this law, so as not to suffer wrong, and liable to the penalty of this law in case they did wrong. And, it should seem, this is it that brings in these laws here, to show how equitable it was that strangers as well as Israelites should be punished for blasphemy, because strangers as well as Israelites were punishable for other crimes. And there may be this further reason for the recognition of these laws here, God would hereby show what provision he had made for man's safety, in punishing those that were injurious to him, which should be an argument with magistrates to be jealous for his honour, and to punish those that blasphemed his name. If God took care for their comfort, they ought to take care for his glory.

VIII. The execution of the blasphemer. Moses did, as it were, sign the warrant or it: He *spoke unto the children of Israel* to do it, and they *did as the Lord commanded Moses, v.* 23. This teaches that death is the wages of sin, and that blasphemy in particular is an *iniquity to be punished by the judges.* But, if those who thus profane the name of God escape punishment from men, yet the Lord our God will not suffer them to escape his righteous judgments. This blasphemer was the first that died by the law of Moses. Stephen, the first that died for the gospel, died by the abuse of this law; the martyr and the malefactor suffered the same death: but how vast the difference between them!

CHAPTER 25

The law of this chapter concerns the lands and estates of the Israelites in Canaan, the occupying and transferring of which were to be under the divine direction, as well as the management of religious worship; for, as the tabernacle was a holy house, so Canaan was a holy land; and upon that account, as much as any thing, it was the glory of all lands. In token of a peculiar title which God had to this land, and a right to dispose of it, he appointed, I. That every seventh year should be a year of rest from occupying the land, a sabbatical year (*v.* 1–7). In this God expected from them extraordinary instances of faith and obedience, and they might expect from God extraordinary instances of power and goodness in providing for them (*v.* 18–22). II. That every fiftieth year should be a year of jubilee, that is, 1. A year of release of debts and mortgages, and return to the possession of their alienated lands (*v.* 8–17). Particular directions are given, (1.) Concerning the sale and redemption of lands (*v.* 23–28). (2.) Of houses in cities and villages, with a proviso for Levite-cities (*v.* 29–34). 2. A year of release of servants and bond-slaves. (1.) Here is inserted a law for the kind usage of poor debtors (*v.* 35–38). (2). Then comes the law for the discharge of all Israelites that were sold for servants, in the year of jubilee, if they were not redeemed before. [1.] If they were sold to Israelites (*v.* 39–46). And, [2.] If sold to proselytes (*v.* 47–55). All these appointments have something moral and of perpetual obligation in them, though in the letter of them they were not only peculiar to the Jews, but to them only while they were in Canaan.

Verses 1–7

The law of Moses laid a great deal of stress upon the sabbath, the sanctification of which was the earliest and most ancient of all divine institutions, designed for the keeping up of the knowledge and worship of the Creator among men; that law not only revived the observance of the weekly sabbath, but, for the further advancement of the honour of them, added the institution of a sabbatical year: *In the seventh year shall be a sabbath of rest unto the land, v.* 4. And hence the Jews collect that vulgar tradition that after the world has stood six thousand years (a thousand years being to God as one day) it shall cease, and the eternal sabbath shall succeed — a weak foundation on which to build the fixing of that day and hour which it is God's prerogative to know. This sabbatical year began in September, at the end of harvest, the seventh month of their ecclesiastical year: and the law was, 1. That at the seed-time, which immediately followed the end of their in-gathering, they should sow no corn in their land, and that they should not in the spring dress their vineyards, and consequently that they should not expect either harvest or vintage the next year. 2. That what their ground did produce of itself they should not claim any property or use in, otherwise than from hand to mouth, but leave it for the poor, servants, strangers, and cattle, *v.* 5–7. It must be a sabbath of rest to the land; they must neither do any work about it, nor expect any fruit from it; all annual labours must be intermitted in the seventh year, as much as daily labours on the seventh day. The Jews say they "began not to reckon for the sabbatical year till they had completed the conquest of Canaan, which was in the eighth year of Joshua; the seventh year after that was the first sabbatical year, and so the fiftieth year was the jubilee." This year there was to be a general release of debts (Deu. 15:1, 2), and a public reading of the law in the feast (Deu. 31:10, 11), to make it the more solemn. Now, (1.) God would hereby show them that he was their landlord, and that they were tenants at will under him. Landlords are wont to stipulate with their tenants when they shall break up their ground, how long they shall till it, and when they shall let it rest: God would thus give, grant, and convey, that good land to them, under such provisos and limitations as should let them know that they were not proprietors, but dependents on their Lord. (2.) It was a kindness to their land to let it rest sometimes, and would keep it *in heart* (as our husbandmen express it) for posterity, whose satisfaction God would have them to consult, and not to use the ground as if it were designed only for one age. (3.) When they were thus for a whole year taken off from all country business, they would have the more leisure to attend the exercises of religion, and to get the knowledge of God and his law. (4.) They were hereby taught to be charitable and generous, and not to engross all to themselves, but to be willing that others should share with them in the gifts of God's bounty, which the earth brought forth of itself. (5.) They were brought to live in a constant dependence upon the divine providence, finding that, as man lives not by bread alone, so he has bread, not by his own industry alone, but, if God pleases, by the word of blessing from the mouth of God, without any care or pains of man, Mt. 4:4. (6.) They were reminded of the easy life man lived in paradise, when he ate of every good thing, not, as since, in the sweat of his face. Labour and toil came in with sin. (7.) They were taught to consider how the poor lived, that did neither sow nor reap, even by the blessing of God upon a little. (8.) This year of rest typified the spiritual rest which all believers enter into through Christ, our true Noah, who giveth us comfort and rest *concerning our work, and the toil of our hands, because of the ground which the Lord hath cursed,* Gen. 5:29. Through him we are eased of the burden of worldly care and labour, both being sanctified and sweetened to us, and we are enabled and encouraged to live by faith. And, as the fruits of this sabbath of the land were enjoyed in common, so the salvation wrought out by Christ is a common salvation; and this sabbatical year seems to have been revived in the

Christian church, when the believers had *all things common,* Acts 2:44.

Verses 8–22

Here is, I. The general institution of the jubilee, *v.* 8. etc. 1. When it was to be observed: after *seven sabbaths of years* (*v.* 8), whether the forty-ninth or fiftieth is a great question among learned men: that it should be the seventh sabbatical year, that is, the forty-ninth (which by a very common form of speech is called the fiftieth), seems to me most probable, and is, I think, made pretty clear and the objections removed by that learned chronologer Calvisius; but this is not a place for arguing the question. Seven sabbaths of weeks were reckoned from the passover to the feast of pentecost (or fiftieth day, for so pentecost signifies), and so seven sabbaths of years from one jubilee to another, and the seventh is called the fiftieth; and all this honour is put upon the sevenths for the sake of God's resting the seventh day from the work of creation. 2. How it was to be proclaimed, with sound of trumpet in all parts of the country (*v.* 5), both to give notice to all persons of it, and to express their joy and triumph in it; and the word *jobel,* or *jubilee,* is supposed to signify some particular sound of the trumpet distinguishable from any other; for the trumpet that gives an uncertain sound is of little service, 1 Co. 14:8. The trumpet was sounded in the close of the day of atonement; thence the jubilee commenced, and very fitly; when they had been humbling and afflicting their souls for sin, then they were made to hear this voice of *joy and gladness,* Ps. 11:8. When their peace was made with God, then liberty was proclaimed; for the removal of guilt is necessary to make way for the entrance of all true comfort, Rom. 5:1, 2. In allusion to this solemn proclamation of the jubilee, it was foretold concerning our Lord Jesus that he should *preach the acceptable year of the Lord,* Isa. 61:2. He sent his apostles to proclaim it with the trumpet of the everlasting gospel, which they were to preach to every creature. And it stands still foretold that at the last day the trumpet shall sound, which shall release the dead out of the bondage of the grave, and restore us to our possessions. 3. What was to be done in that year extraordinary; besides the common rest of the land, which was observed every sabbatical year (*v.* 11, 12), and the release of personal debts (Deu. 15:2, 3), there was to be the legal restoration of every Israelite to all the property, and all the liberty, which had been alienated from him since the last jubilee; so that never was any people so secured in their liberty and property (those glories of a people) as Israel was. Effectual care was taken that while they kept close to God these should not only not be taken from them by the violence of others, but not thrown away by their own folly. (1.) The property which every man had in his dividend of the land of Canaan could not be alienated any longer than till the year of jubilee, and then he or his should return to it, and have a title to it as undisputed, and the possession of it as undisturbed, as ever (*v.* 10, 13): "*You shall return every man to his possession;* so that if a man had sold or mortgaged his estate, or any part of it, it should then return to him or his heirs, free of all charge and encumbrance. Now this was no wrong to the purchaser, because the year of jubilee was fixed, and every man knew when it would come, and made his bargain accordingly. By our law indeed, if lands be granted to a man and his heirs, upon condition that he should never sell or alienate them, the grant is good, but the condition is void and repugnant: *Iniquum est ingenuis hominibus* (say the lawyers) *non esse liberam rerum suarum alienationem — It is unjust to prevent free men from alienating their own possessions.* Yet it is agreed in the books that if the king grant lands to a man in fee upon condition he shall not alienate, the condition is good. Now God would show his people Israel that their land was his, and they were his tenants; and therefore he ties them up that they shall not have power to sell, but only to make leases for any term of years, not going beyond the next jubilee. By this means it was provided, [1.] That their genealogies should be carefully preserved, which would be of use for clearing our Saviour's pedigree. [2.] That the distinction of tribes should be kept up; for, though a man might purchase lands in another tribe, yet he could not retain them longer than till the year of jubilee, and then they would revert of course. [3.] That

none should grow exorbitantly rich, by laying *house to house, and field to field* (Isa. 5:8), but should rather apply themselves to the cultivating of what they had than the enlarging of their possessions. The wisdom of the Roman commonwealth sometimes provided that no man should be master of above 500 acres. [4.] That no family should be sunk and ruined, and condemned to perpetual poverty. This particular care God took for the support of the honour of that people, and the preserving, not only of that good land to the nation in general, but of every man's share to his family in particular, for a perpetual inheritance, that it might the better typify that good part which shall *never be taken away* from those that have it.

(2.) The liberty which every man was born to, if it were sold or forfeited, should likewise return at the year of jubilee: *You shall return every man to his family, v.* 10. Those that were sold into other families thereby became strangers to their own; but in this year of redemption they were to return. This was typical of our redemption by Christ from the slavery of sin and Satan, and our restoration to the glorious liberty of the children of God. Some compute that the very year in which Christ died was a year of jubilee, and the last that ever was kept. But, however that be, we are sure it is the Son that *makes us free,* and then we are *free indeed.*

II. A law upon this occasion against oppression in buying and selling of land; neither the buyer nor the seller must overreach, *v.* 14–17. In short, the buyer must not give less, nor the seller take more, than the just value of the thing, considered as necessarily returning at the year of jubilee. It must be settled what the clear yearly value of the land was, and then how many years' purchase it was worth till the year of jubilee. But they must reckon only *the years of the fruits* (*v.* 15), and therefore must discount for the sabbatical years. It is easy to observe that the nearer the jubilee was the less must the value of the land be. *According to the fewness of the years thou shalt diminish the price.* But we do not find it so easy practically to infer thence that the nearer the world comes to its period the less value we should put upon the things of it: because *the time is short,* and the *fashion of the world passeth away,* let those that *buy be as though they possessed not.* One would put little value on an old house, that is ready to drop down. All bargains ought to be made by this rule, *You shall not oppress one another,* nor take advantage of one another's ignorance or necessity, *but thou shalt fear thy God.* Note, The fear of God reigning in the heart would effectually restrain us from doing any wrong to our neighbour in word or deed; for, though man be not, God is *the avenger* of those that *go beyond or defraud* their brethren, 1 Th. 4:6. Perhaps Nehemiah refers to this very law (*ch.* 5:15), where he tells us that he did not oppress those he had under his power, *because of the fear of God.*

III. Assurance given them that they should be no losers, but great gainers, by observing these years of rest. It is promised, 1. That they should be safe: *You shall dwell in the land in safety, v.* 18. and again, *v.* 19. The word signifies both outward safety and inward security and confidence of spirit, that they should be quiet both from evil and from the fear of evil. 2. That they should be rich: *You shall eat your fill.* Note, If we be careful to do our duty, we may cheerfully trust God with our comfort. 3. That they should not want food convenient that year in which they did neither sow nor reap: *I will command my blessing in the sixth year, and it shall bring forth fruit for three years, v.* 21. This was, (1.) A standing miracle, that, whereas at other times one year did but serve to bring in another, the productions of the sixth year should serve to bring in the ninth. Note, The blessing of God upon our provision will make a little go a great way, and *satisfy* even *the poor with bread,* Ps. 131:15. (2.) A lasting memorial of the manna which was given double on the sixth day for two days. (3.) It was intended for an encouragement to all God's people, in all ages, to trust him in the way of duty, and to cast their care upon him. There is nothing lost by faith and self-denial in our obedience.

Verses 23–38

Here is, I. A law concerning the real estates of the Israelites in the land of Canaan, and the transferring of them. 1. No land should be sold for ever from the family to whose lot it fell in the division of the land. And the reason given

is, *The land is mine, and you are strangers and sojourners with me, v.* 23. (1.) God having a particular propriety in this land, he would by this restraint keep them sensible of it. The possessions of good people, who, having given up themselves to God, have therewith given up all they have to him, are in a particular manner at his disposal, and his disposal of them must be submitted to. (2.) They being *strangers and sojourners with him* in that land, and having his tabernacle among them, to alienate their part of that land would be in effect to cut themselves off from their fellowship and communion with God, of which that was a token and symbol, for which reason Naboth would rather incur the wrath of a king than part with the inheritance of his fathers, 1 Ki. 21:3. 2. If a man was constrained through poverty to sell his land for the subsistence of his family, yet, if afterwards he was able, he might redeem it before the year of jubilee (*v.* 24, 26, 27), and the price must be settled according to the number of years since the sale and before the jubilee. 3. If the person himself was not able to redeem it, his next kinsman might (*v.* 25): *The redeemer thereof, he that is near unto him, shall come and shall redeem,* so it might be read. The kinsman is called *Goel,* the redeemer (Num. 5:8; Ruth 3:9), to whom belonged the right of redeeming the land. And this typified Christ, who assumed our nature, that he might be our *kinsman,* bone of our bone and flesh of our flesh, and, being the only kinsman we have that is able to do it, to him belonged the right of redemption. As for all our other kinsmen, their shoe must be plucked off (Ruth 4:6, 7); they cannot redeem. But Christ can and hath redeemed the inheritance which we by sin had forfeited and alienated, and made a new settlement of it upon all that by faith become allied to him. We know that this *Redeemer liveth,* Job 19:25. And some make this duty of the kinsman to signify the brotherly love that should be among Christians, inclining them to recover those that are fallen, and to restore them with the spirit of meekness. 4. If the land was not redeemed before the year of jubilee, then it should return of course to him that had sold or mortgaged it: *In the jubilee it shall go out, v.* 28. This was a figure of the free grace of God towards us in Christ, by which, and not by any price or merit of our own, we are restored to the favour of God, and become entitled to paradise, from which our first parents, and we in them, were expelled for disobedience. 5. A difference was made between houses in walled cities, and lands in the country, or houses in country villages. Houses in walled cities were more the fruits of their own industry than land in the country, which was the immediate gift of God's bounty; and therefore, if a man sold a house in a city, he might redeem it any time within a year after the sale, but otherwise it was confirmed to the purchaser for ever, and should not return, no, not at the year of the jubilee, *v.* 29, 30. This provision was made to encourage strangers and proselytes to come and settle among them. Though they could not purchase land in Canaan to them and their heirs, yet they might purchase houses in walled cities, which would be most convenient for those who were supposed to live by trade. But country houses could be disposed of no otherwise than as lands might. 6. A clause is added in favour of the Levites, by way of exception from these rules. (1.) Dwelling houses in the cities of the Levites might be redeemed at any time, and, if not redeemed, should revert in the year of jubilee (*v.* 32, 33), because the Levites had no other possessions than cities and their suburbs, and God would show that the Levites were his peculiar care; and it was for the interest of the public that they should not be impoverished, or wormed out of their inheritances. (2.) The fields adjoining to their cities (Num. 35:4, 5) might not be sold at any time, for they belonged, not to particular Levites, but to the city of the Levites, as a corporation, who could not alienate without a wrong to their tribe; therefore, if any of those fields were sold, the bargain was void, *v.* 34. Even the Egyptians took care to preserve the *land of the priests,* Gen. 47:22. And there is no less reason for the taking of the maintenance of the gospel ministry under the special protection of Christian governments.

II. A law for the relief of the poor, and the tender usage of poor debtors, and these are of more general and perpetual obligation than the former.

1. The poor must be relieved, *v.* 35. Here is, (1.) Our brother's poverty and distress supposed: *If thy brother be*

waxen poor; not only thy brother by nation as a Jew, but thy brother by nature as a man, for it follows, *though he be a stranger or a sojourner.* All men are to be looked upon and treated as brethren, for *we have all one Father,* Mal. 2:10. Though he is poor, yet still he is thy brother, and is to be loved and owned as a brother. Poverty does not destroy the relation. Though a son of Abraham, yet he may wax poor and fall into decay. Note, Poverty and decay are great grievances, and very common: *The poor you have always with you.* (2.) Our duty enjoined: *Thou shalt relieve him.* By sympathy, pitying the poor; by service, doing for them; and by supply, giving to them according to their necessity and thy ability.

2. Poor debtors must not be oppressed: *If thy brother be waxen poor,* and have occasion to borrow money of thee for the necessary support of his family, *take thou no usury of him,* either for money or victuals, *v.* 36, 37. And thus far this law binds still, but could never be thought binding where money is borrowed for purchase of lands, trade, or other improvements; for there it is reasonable that the lender share with the borrower in the profit. The law here is plainly intended for the relief of the poor, to whom it is sometimes as great a charity to lend freely as to give. Observe the arguments here used against extortion. (1.) God patronizes the poor: *"Fear thy God,* who will reckon with thee for all injuries done to the poor: thou fearest not them, but fear him." (2.) Relieve the poor, *that they may live with thee,* and some way or other they may be serviceable to thee. The rich can as ill spare the hands of the poor as the poor can the purses of the rich. (3.) The same argument is used to enforce this precept that prefaces all the ten commandments: *I am the Lord your God which brought you out of Egypt, v.* 38. Note, It becomes those that have received mercy to show mercy. If God has been gracious to us, we ought not to be rigorous with our brethren.

Verses 39–55

We have here the laws concerning servitude, designed to preserve the honour of the Jewish nation as a free people, and rescued by a divine power out of the house of bondage, into the glorious liberty of God's sons, his first-born. Now the law is,

I. That a native Israelite should never be made a bondman for perpetuity. If he was sold for debt, or for a crime, by the house of judgment, he was to serve but six years, and to go out the seventh; this was appointed, Ex. 21:2. But if he sold himself through extreme poverty, having nothing at all left him to preserve his life, and if it was to one of his own nation that he sold himself, in such a case it is here provided, 1. That he should not *serve as a bond-servant* (*v.* 39), nor be *sold with the sale of a bondman* (*v.* 42); that is, "it must not be looked upon that his master that bought him had as absolute a property in him as in a captive taken in war, that might be used, sold, and bequeathed, at pleasure, as much as a man's cattle; no, he shall serve thee as a *hired servant,* whom the master has the use of only, but not a despotic power over." And the reason is, *They are my servants, v.* 42. God does not make his servants slaves, and therefore their brethren must not. God had redeemed them out of Egypt, and therefore they must never be exposed to sale as bondmen. The apostle applies this spiritually (1 Co. 7:23), *You are bought with a price, be not the servants of men,* that is, "of the lusts of men, no, nor of your own lusts;" for, having *become the servants of God,* we must not *let sin reign in our mortal bodies,* Rom. 6:12, 22. 2. That while he did serve he should not be ruled with rigour, as the Israelites were in Egypt, *v.* 43. Both his work and his usage must be such as were fitting for a son of Abraham. Masters are still required to *give to their servants that which is just and equal,* Col. 4:1. They may be used, but must not be abused. Those masters that are always hectoring and domineering over their servants, taunting them and trampling upon them, that are unreasonable in exacting work and giving rebukes, and that rule them with a high hand, forget that their Master is in heaven; and what will they do when he rises up? as holy Job reasons with himself, Job 31:13, 14. 3. That at the year of jubilee he should *go out free,* he *and his children,* and should *return to his own family, v.* 41. This typified our redemption from the service of sin and Satan by the grace of God in Christ, whose *truth makes us free,* Jn. 7:32. The Jewish writers say that, for ten days before the jubilee-trumpet sounded, the servants that were to be discharged by it did express their great joy by feasting, and wearing garlands on their heads: it is therefore called the *joyful sound,* Ps. 89:15. And we are thus to rejoice in the liberty we have by Christ.

II. That they might purchase bondmen of the heathen nations that were round about them, or of those strangers that sojourned among them (except of those seven nations that were to be destroyed); and might claim a dominion over them, and entail them upon their families as an inheritance, for the year of jubilee should give no discharge to them, *v.* 44, 46. Thus in our English plantations the *negroes* only are used as slaves; how much to the credit of Christianity I shall not say. Now, 1. This authority which they had over the bondmen whom they purchased from the neighbouring nations was in pursuance of the blessing of Jacob, Gen. 27:29, *Let people serve thee.* 2. It prefigured the bringing in of the Gentiles to the service of Christ and his church. *Ask of me, and I will give thee the heathen for thy inheritance,* Ps. 2:8. And it is promised (Isa. 61:5), *Strangers shall stand and feed your flocks, and the sons of the alien shall be your vine-dressers;* see Rev. 2:26, 27. *The upright shall have the dominion in the morning,* Ps. 49:14. 3. It intimates that none shall have the benefit of the gospel jubilee but those only that are Israelites indeed, and the children of Abraham by faith: as for those that continue heathenish, they continue bondmen. See this turned upon the unbelieving Jews themselves, Gal. 4:25, where Jerusalem, when she had rejected Christ, is said to be *in bondage with her children.* Let me only add here that, though they are not forbidden to rule their bondmen with rigour, yet the Jewish doctors say, "It is the property of mercy, and way of wisdom, that a man should be compassionate, and not make his yoke heavy upon any servant that he has."

III. That if an Israelite sold himself for a servant to a wealthy proselyte that sojourned among them care should be taken that he should have the same advantages as if he had sold himself to an Israelite, and in some respects greater. 1. That he should not serve as a bondman, but as a hired servant, and not to be *ruled with rigour* (*v.* 53), *in thy sight,* which intimated that the Jewish magistrates should particularly have an eye to him, and, if he were abused, should take cognizance of it, and redress his grievances, though the injured servant did not himself complain. Also he was to go free at the year of jubilee, *v.* 54. Though the sons of strangers might serve them for ever, yet the sons of Israel might not serve strangers for ever; yet the servant here, having made himself a slave by his own act and deed, should not go out in the seventh year of release, but in the jubilee only. 2. That he should have this further advantage that he might be redeemed again before the year of jubilee, *v.* 48, 49. He that had sold himself to an Israelite might, if ever he was able, redeem himself, but his relations had no right to redeem him. "But if a man sold himself to a stranger," the Jews say, "his relations were urged to redeem him; if they did not, it was fit that he should be redeemed at the public charge," which we find done, Neh. 5:8. The price of his ransom was to be computed according to the prospect of the year of jubilee (*v.* 50–52), as in the redemption of land, *v.* 15, 16. The learned bishop Patrick quotes one of the Jewish rabbin for an evangelical exposition of that appointment (*v.* 48), *One of his brethren shall redeem him.* "This Redeemer," says the rabbi, *"is the Messiah, the Son of David."* They expected this Messiah to be their Redeemer out of their captivity, and to restore them to their own land again; but we welcome him as the Redeemer who shall come to Zion, and shall *turn away ungodliness from Jacob,* for he shall *save his people from their sins;* and under this notion there were those that *looked for redemption in Jerusalem.*

CHAPTER 26

This chapter is a solemn conclusion of the main body of the levitical law. The precepts that follow in this and the following book either relate to some particular matters or are repetitions and explications of the foregoing institutions. Now this chapter contains a general enforcement of all those laws by promises of reward in case of obedience on the one hand, and threatenings of punishment for disobedience on the other hand, the former to work upon hope, the latter on fear, those two handles of the soul, by which it is taken hold of and managed. Here is, I. A repetition of two or three of the principal of the commandments (*v.* 1, 2). II. An inviting promise of all good things, if they would but keep God's commandments (*v.* 3–13). III. A terrible threatening of ruining judgments which would be brought upon them if they were refractory and disobedient (*v.* 14–39). IV. A gracious promise of the return of mercy to those of them that would repent and reform (*v.* 40, etc.). Deu. 28 is parallel to this.

Verses 1–13

Here is, I. The inculcating of those precepts of the law which were of the greatest consequence, and by which were of the greatest consequence, and by which especially their obedience would be tried, *v.* 1, 2. They are the abstract of the second and fourth commandments, which, as they are by much the largest in the decalogue, so they are most frequently insisted on in other parts of the law. As, when a master has given many things in charge to his servant, he concludes with the repetition of those things which were of the greatest importance, and which the servant was most in danger of neglecting, bidding him, whatever he did, be sure to remember those, so here God by Moses, after many precepts, closes all with a special charge to observe these two great commandments. 1. "Be sure you never worship images, nor ever make any sort of images or pictures for a religious use," *v.* 1. No sin was more provoking to God than this, and yet there was none that they were more addicted to, and which afterwards proved of more pernicious consequence to them. Next to God's being, unity, and universal influence, it is necessary that we know and believe that he is an infinite Spirit; and therefore to represent him by an image in the making of it, to confine him to an image in the consecrating of it, and to worship him by an image in bowing down to it, *changes his truth into a lie* and *his glory into shame,* as much as any thing. 2. "Be sure you keep up a great veneration for sabbaths and religious assemblies," *v.* 2. As nothing tends more to corrupt religion than the use of images in devotion, so nothing contributes more to the support of it than *keeping the sabbaths* and *reverencing the sanctuary.* These make up very much of the instrumental part of religion, by which the essentials of it are kept up. Therefore we find in the prophets that, next to the sin of idolatry, there is no sin for which the Jews are more frequently reproved and threatened than the profanation of the sabbath day.

II. Great encouragements given them to live in constant obedience to all God's commandments, largely and strongly assuring them that if they did so they should be a happy people, and should be blessed with all the good things they could desire. Human governments enforce their laws with penalties to be inflicted for the breach of them; but God will be known as *the rewarder of those that seek and serve him.* Let us take a view of these great and precious promises, which, though they relate chiefly to the life which now is, and to the public national concerns of that people, were typical of the spiritual blessings entailed by the covenant of grace upon all believers through Christ. 1. Plenty and abundance of the fruits of the earth. They should have seasonable rain, neither too little nor too much, but what was requisite for their land, which was watered with the dew of heaven (Deu. 11:10, 11), that it might *yield its increase, v.* 4. The dependence which the fruitfulness of the earth beneath has upon the influences of heaven above is a sensible intimation to us that every good and perfect gift must be expected *from above,* from the *Father of lights.* It is promised that the earth should produce its fruits in such great abundance that they would be kept in full employment, during both the harvest and the vintage, to gather it in, *v.* 5. Before they had reaped their corn and threshed it, the vintage would be ready; and, before they had finished their vintage, it would be high time to begin their sowing. Long harvests are often with us the consequences of bad weather, but with them they should be the effects of a great increase. This signified the abundance of grace which should be poured out in gospel times, when the *ploughman should overtake the reaper* (Amos 9:13), and a great harvest of souls should be gathered in to Christ. The plenty should be so great that they should *bring forth the old* to be given away to the poor *because of the new,* to make room for it in their barns, which yet they would not *pull down to build greater,* as that rich fool (Lu. 12:18), for God gave them this abundance to be laid out, not be hoarded up from one year to another. *He that withholdeth corn, the people shall curse him,* Prov. 11:26. That promise (Mal. 3:10), *I will pour you out a blessing, that there shall not be room enough to receive it,* explains this, *v.* 10.

And that which crowns this blessing of plenty is (*v.* 5), You shall *eat your bread to the full,* which intimates that they should have, not only abundance, but content and satisfaction in it. They should have enough, and should know when they had enough. Thus *the meek shall eat and be satisfied,* Ps. 22:26. 2. Peace under the divine protection; "*You shall dwell in your land safely* (*v.* 5); both really save, and safe in your own apprehensions; you shall lie down to rest in the power and promise of God, and not only none shall hurt you, but none shall so much as *make you afraid,*" *v.* 6. See Ps. 4:8. They should not be infested with wild beasts, these should be *rid out of the land,* or, as it is promised (Job 5:23), should *be at peace with them.* Nor should they be terrified with the alarms of war: *Neither shall the sword go through your land.* This holy security is promised to all the faithful, Ps. 91:1, etc. Those must needs dwell in safety that *dwell in God,* Job 9:18, 19. 3. Victory and success in their wars abroad, while they had peace and tranquility at home, *v.* 7, 8. They are assured that the hand of God should so signally appear with them in their conquests that no disproportion of numbers should make against them: *Five of you* shall have courage to attack, and strength to *chase* and defeat, *a hundred,* as Jonathan did (1 Sa. 14:12), experiencing the truth of his own maxim (*v.* 6), that it is all one with the Lord to *save by many or by few.* 4. The increase of their people: *I will make you fruitful and multiply you, v.* 9. Thus the promise made to Abraham must be fulfilled, that his seed should be *as the dust of the earth;* and much more numerous they would have been if they had by their sin cut themselves short. It is promised to the gospel church that it shall be fruitful, Jn. 15:16. 5. The favour of God, which is the fountain of all good: *I will have respect unto you, v.* 9. If the eye of our faith be unto God, the eye of his favour will be unto us. More is implied than is expressed in that promise, *My soul shall not abhor you* (*v.* 11), as there is in that threatening, *My soul shall have no pleasure in him,* Heb. 10:38. Though there was that among them which might justly have alienated him from them, yet, if they would closely adhere to his institutions, he would not abhor them. 6. Tokens of his presence in and by his ordinances: *I will set my tabernacle among you, v.* 11. It was their honour and advantage that God's tabernacle was lately erected among them; but here he lets them know that the continuance and establishment of it depended upon their good behaviour. The tabernacle that was now set should be settled if they would be obedient, else not. Note, The way to have God's ordinances fixed among us, as a nail in a sure place, is to cleave closely to the institution of them. It is added (*v.* 12), "*I will walk among you,* with delight and satisfaction, as a man in his garden; I will keep up communion with you as a man walking with his friend." This seems to be alluded to, Rev. 2:1, where Christ is said to *walk in the midst of the golden candlesticks.* 7. The grace of the covenant, as the fountain and foundation, the sweetness and security, of all these blessings: *I will establish my covenant with you, v.* 9. Let them perform their part of the covenant, and God would not fail to perform his. All covenant-blessings are summed up in the covenant-relation (*v.* 12): *I will be your God, and you shall be my people;* and they are all grounded upon their redemption: *I am your God,* because *I brought you forth out of the land of Egypt, v.* 13. Having purchased them, he would own them, and never cast them off till they cast him off. He *broke their yoke,* and *made them go upright,* that is, their deliverance out of Egypt put them in a state both of ease and honour, that, being delivered out of the hands of their enemies, they might *serve God without fear,* each walking *in his uprightness.* When Israel rejected Christ, and was therefore rejected by him, their back is said to be *bowed down* always under the burden of their guilt, which was heavier than that of their bondage in Egypt, Rom. 11:10.

Verses 14–39

After God had set the blessing before them (the life and good which would make them a happy people if they would be obedient), he here sets the curse before them, the death and evil which would make them as miserable if they were disobedient. Let them not think themselves so deeply rooted as that God's power could not ruin them, nor so highly favoured as that his justice would not ruin them if they revolted from him and rebelled against him; no *You only have I known, therefore I will punish you* soonest and sorest. Amos 3:2. Observe,

I. How their sin is described, which would bring all this misery upon them. Not sins of ignorance and infirmity; God had provided sacrifices for those. Not the sins they repented of and forsook; but the sins that were presumptuously committed, and obstinately persisted in. Two things would certainly bring this ruin upon them: —

1. A contempt of God's commandments (*v.* 14): "*If you will not hearken to me* speaking to you by the law, nor *do all these commandments,* that is, desire and endeavour to do them, and, wherein you miss it, make use of the prescribed remedies." Thus their sin is supposed to begin in mere carelessness, and neglect, and omission. These are bad enough, but they make way for worse; for the people are brought in (*v.* 15) as, (1.) *Despising God's statutes,* both the duties enjoined and the authority enjoining them, thinking meanly of the law and the Law-maker. Note, Those are hastening apace to their own ruin who begin to think it below them to be religious. (2.) *Abhorring his judgments,* their very souls abhorring them. Note, Those that begin to despise religion will come by degrees to loathe it; and mean thoughts of it will ripen into ill thoughts of it; those that turn from it will turn against it, and their hearts will rise at it. (3.) *Breaking his covenant.* Though every breach of the commandment does not amount to a breach of the covenant (we were undone if it did), yet, when men have come to such a pitch of impiety as to despise and abhor the commandment, the next step will be to disown God, and all relation to him. Those that reject the precept will come at last to renounce the covenant. Observe, It is God's covenant which they break: he made it, but they break it. Note, If a covenant be made and kept between God and man, God must have all the honour; but, if ever it be broken, man must bear all the blame: on him shall this breach be.

2. A contempt of his corrections. Even their disobedience would not have been their destruction if they had not been obstinate and impenitent in it, notwithstanding the methods God took to reclaim them. Their contempt of God's word would not have brought them to ruin, if they had not added to that a contempt of his rod, which should have brought them to repentance. Three ways this is expressed: — (1.) "*If you will not for all this hearken to me, v.* 18, 21, 27. If you will not learn obedience by the things which you suffer, but be as deaf to the loud alarms of God's judgments as you have been to the close reasonings of his word and the secret whispers of your own consciences, you are obstinate indeed." (2.) "*If you walk contrary to me, v.* 21, 23, 27. All sinners walk contrary to God, to his truths, laws, and counsels; but those especially that are incorrigible under his judgments. The design of the rod is to humble them, and soften them, and bring them to repentance; but, instead of this, their hearts are more hardened and exasperated against God, and *in their distress* they *trespass yet more against him,* 2 Chr. 28:22. This is walking contrary to God. Some read it, "If you walk at all adventures with me, carelessly and presumptuously, as if you heeded not either what you do, whether it be right or wrong, or what God does with you, whether it be for you or against you, blundering on in wilful ignorance." (3.) *If you will not be reformed by these things.* God's design in punishing is to reform, by giving men sensible convictions of the evil of sin, and obliging them to seek unto him for relief: this is the primary intention; but those that will not be reformed by the judgments of God must expect to be ruined by them. Those have a great deal to answer for that have been long and often under God's correcting hand, and yet go on frowardly in a sinful way; sick and in pain, and yet not reformed; crossed and impoverished, and yet not reformed; broken with breach upon breach, yet *not returning to the Lord,* Amos 4:6, etc.

II. How the misery is described which their sin would bring upon them, under two heads: —

1. God himself would be against them; and this is the root and cause of all their misery. (1.) *I will set my face against you* (*v.* 17), that is, "I will set myself against you, set myself to ruin you." These proud sinners God will resist, and face those down that confront his authority. Or the face is put for the anger: "I will show myself highly displeased at you." (2.) *I will walk contrary to you* (*v.* 24, 28); *with the forward he will wrestle,* Ps. 28:26 [margin]. When God in his providence thwarts the designs of a people, which they thought well laid, crosses their purposes, breaks their measures, blasts their endeavours, and disappoints their expectations, then he walks contrary to them. Note, There is nothing got by striving with God Almighty, for he will break either the heart or the neck of those that contend with him, will bring them either to repentance or ruin. "I will walk at all adventures with you," so some read; "all covenant loving-kindness shall be forgotten, and I will leave you to common providence." Note, Those that cast off God deserve that he should cast them off. (3.) As they continued obstinate, the judgments should increase yet more upon them. If the first sensible tokens of God's displeasures do not attain their end, to humble and reform them, then (*v.* 18), *I will punish you seven times more,* and again (*v.* 21), *I will bring seven times more plagues,* and (*v.* 24), *I will punish you yet seven times,* and (*v.* 28), *I, even I, will chastise you seven times for your sins.* Note, If less judgments do not do their work, God will send greater; for, when he *judges, he will overcome.* If true repentance do not stay process, it will go on till execution be taken out. Those that are obstinate and incorrigible, when they have weathered one storm must expect another more violent; and, how severely soever they are punished, till they are in hell they must still say, "There is worse behind," unless they repent. If the *founder have* hitherto *melted in vain* (Jer. 6:29), the furnace will be heated *seven times hotter* (a proverbial expression, used Dan. 3:19), and again and again *seven times hotter;* and who among us can dwell with such devouring fire? God does not begin with the sorest judgments, to show that he is patient, and delights not in the death of sinners; but, if they repent not, he will proceed to the sorest, to show that he is righteous, and that he will not be mocked or set at defiance. (4.) Their misery is completed in that threatening: *My soul shall abhor you, v.* 30. That man is as miserable as he can be whom God abhors; for his resentments are just and effective. Thus *if any man draw back,* as these are supposed to do, *God's soul shall have no pleasure in him* (Heb. 10:38), and he will *spue them out of his mouth,* Rev. 3:16. It is spoken of as strange, and yet too true, *Hath thy soul loathed Zion?* Jer. 14:19.

2. The whole creation would be at war with them. All God's sore judgments would be sent against them; for he hath many arrows in his quiver. The threatenings here are very particular, because really they were prophecies, and he that foresaw all their rebellions knew they would prove so; see Deu. 31:16, 29. This long roll of threatening shows that evil pursues sinners. We have here,

(1.) Temporal judgments threatened. [1.] Diseases of body, which should be epidemical: *I will appoint over you,* as task-masters, to rule you with rigour, *terror, consumption, and the burning ague, v.* 16. What we translate *terror,* some think, signifies a particular disease, probably (says the learned bishop Patrick) the *falling sickness,* which is terror indeed: all chronical diseases are included in the consumption, and all acute diseases in the burning ague or fever. These consume the eyes, and cause sorrow both to those that are visited with them and to their friends and relations. Note, All diseases are God's servants; they do what he appoints them, and are often used as scourges wherewith he chastises a provoking people. The pestilence is threatened (*v.* 25) to meet them, when they are gathered together in their cities for fear of the sword. The greater the concourse of people is, the greater desolation does the pestilence make; and, when it gets among the soldiers that should defend a place, it is of most fatal consequence. [2.] Famine and scarcity of bread, which should be brought upon them several ways; as, *First,* By plunder (*v.* 16): *Your enemies shall eat it* up, and carry it off as the Midianites did, Jdg. 6:5, 6. *Secondly,* By unseasonable weather, especially the want of rain (*v.* 19): *I will make your heaven as iron,* letting fall no rain, but reflecting heat, and then the earth would of course be as dry and hard *as brass,* and their labour in ploughing and sowing would *be in vain* (*v.* 20); for the increase of the earth depends upon God's good providence more than upon man's good husbandry. This should be the breaking of the *staff of bread* (*v.* 26), which life leans upon, and is supported by, on which perhaps they had leaned more than upon God's blessing. There should be so great a dearth of corn that, whereas every family used to fill an oven of their own with household bread, now ten families should have to fill but one over, which would bring themselves and their children and servants to short allowance, so that they should *eat and not be satisfied.* The less they had the more craving should their appetites be. *Thirdly,* By the besieging of their cities, which would reduce them to such an extremity that they should *eat the flesh of their sons and daughters, v.* 29. [3.] War, and the prevailing of their enemies over them: "*You shall be slain before your enemies, v.* 17. Your choice men shall die in battle, and *those that hate you shall reign over you,* and justly, since you are not willing that the God that loved you should reign over you;" 2 Chr. 12:8. Miserable is that people whose enemies are their rulers and have got dominion over them, or whose rulers have become their enemies and under-hand seek the ruin of their interests. Thus God would *break the pride of their power, v.* 19. God had given them power over the nations; but when they, instead of being thankful for that power, and improving it for the service of God's kingdom, grew proud of it, and perverted the intentions of it, it was just with God to break it. Thus God would *bring a sword upon them to avenge the quarrel of his covenant, v.* 25. Note, God has a just quarrel with those that break covenant with him, for he will not be mocked by the treachery of perfidious men; and one way or other he will avenge this quarrel upon those that play at fast and loose with him. [4.] Wild beasts, lions, bears, and wolves, which should increase upon them, and tear in pieces all that come in their way (*v.* 22), as we read of two bears that in an instant killed forty-two children, 2 Ki. 2:24. This is one of the four sore judgments threatened Eze. 14:21, which plainly refers to this chapter. Man was made to have dominion over the creatures, and, though many of them are stronger than he, yet none of them could have hurt him, nay, all of them would have served him, if he had not first shaken off God's dominion, and so lost his own; and now the creatures are in rebellion against him that is in rebellion against his Maker, and, when the Lord of those hosts pleases, they are the executioners of his wrath and the ministers of his justice. [5.] Captivity, or dispersion: *I will scatter you among the heathen* (*v.* 33), *in your enemies' land, v.* 34. Never were any people so incorporated and united among themselves as they were; but for their sin God would scatter them, so that they should be lost among the heathen, from whom God had graciously distinguished them, but with whom they had wickedly mingled themselves. Yet, when they were scattered, divine justice had not done with them, but would draw out a sword after them, which would find them out, and follow them wherever they were. God's judgments, as they cannot be outfaced, so they cannot be outrun. [6.] The utter ruin and desolation of their land, which should be so remarkable that their very enemies themselves, who ha helped it forward, should in the review be astonished at it, *v.* 32. *First,* Their cities should be waste, forsaken, uninhabited, and all the buildings destroyed; those that escaped the desolations of war should fall to decay of themselves. *Secondly,* Their sanctuaries should be a desolation, that is, their synagogues where they met for religious worship every sabbath, as well as their tabernacle where they met thrice a year. *Thirdly,* The country itself should be desolate, not tilled or husbanded (*v.* 34, 35); then the land should enjoy its sabbaths, because they had not religiously observed the sabbatical years which God appointed them. They tilled their ground when God would have them let it rest; justly therefore were they driven out of it; and the expression intimates that the ground itself was pleased and easy when it was rid of the burden of such sinners, under which it had groaned, Rom. 8:20, etc. The captivity in Babylon lasted seventy years, and so long the land *enjoyed her sabbaths,* as is said (2 Chr. 36:21) with reference to this. [7.] The destruction of their idols, though rather a mercy than a judgment, yet, being a necessary piece of justice, is here mentioned, to show what would be the sin that would bring all these miseries upon them: *I will destroy your high places, v.* 30. Those that will not be parted from their sins by the commands of God shall be parted from them by his judgments; since they would not destroy their high places, God would. And, to upbraid them with the unreasonable fondness they had shown for their idols, it is foretold that their *carcases should be cast upon the carcases of their idols.* Those that are wedded to their lusts will sooner or later have enough of them. Their idols would not be able to help either themselves or their worshippers; but, those that made them being like them, they should both perish alike, and fall together as blind into the ditch.

(2.) Spiritual judgments are here threatened. These should seize the mind; for he that made the mind can, when he pleases, make his sword approach to it. It is here threatened, [1.] That they should find no acceptance with God: *I will not smell the savour of your sweet odours, v.* 31. Though the judgments of God upon them did not separate them and their sins, yet they extorted incense from them; but in vain — even their incense was an abomination, Isa. 1:13. [2.] That they should have no courage in their wars, but should be quite dispirited and disheartened. They should not only fear and flee (*v.* 17), but fear and *fall, when none pursued, v.* 36. A guilty conscience would be their continual terror, so that not only the sound of a trumpet, but the very *sound of a leaf, should chase them.* Note, Those that cast off the fear of God expose themselves to the fear of every thing else, Prov. 28:1. Their very fears should dash them *one against another, v.* 37, 38. And those that had increased one another's guilt would now increase one another's fears. [3.] That they should have no hope of the forgiveness of their sins (*v.* 39): *They shall pine away in their iniquity,* and *how should they then live?* Eze. 33:10. Note, It is a righteous thing with God to leave those to despair of pardon that have presumed to sin; and it is owing to free grace if we are not abandoned to pine away in the iniquity we were born in and have lived in.

Verses 40–46

Here the chapter concludes with gracious promises of the return of God's favour to them upon their repentance, that they might not (unless it were their own fault) *pine away in their iniquity.* Behold, with wonder, the riches of God's mercy to a people that had obstinately stood it out against the judgments of God, and would never think of surrendering till they were reduced to the last extremity. Yet *turn to strong-hold, you prisoners of hope,* Zec. 9:12. As bad as things are, they may be mended. *Yet there is hope in Israel.* Observe,

I. How the repentance which would qualify them for this mercy is described, *v.* 40, 41. The instances of it are three: — 1. Confession, by which they must give glory to God, and take shame to themselves. There must be a confession of sin, their own and their fathers', which they must lament the guilt of because they feel the smart of it; that thus they may cut off the entail of wrath. They must in their confession put sin under its worst character, as *walking contrary to God;* this is the sinfulness of sin, the worst thing in it, and which in our repentance we should especially bewail. There must also be a confession of wrath; they must overlook the instruments of their trouble and the second causes, and confess that God has *walked contrary to them,* and so *dealt with them according to their sins.* Such a confession as this we find made by Daniel just before the dawning of the day of their deliverance (*ch.* 9), and the like, Ezra 9 and Neh. 9:2. Remorse and godly sorrow for sin: *If their uncircumcised heart be humbled.* An impenitent, unbelieving, unhumbled heart, is called an *uncircumcised* heart, the heart of a Gentile that is a stranger to God, rather than the heart of an Israelite in covenant with him. True circumcision is *of the heart* (Rom. 2:29), without which the circumcision of the flesh avails nothing, Jer. 9:26. Now in repentance this uncircumcised heart was humbled, that is, it was truly broken and contrite for sin. Note, A humble heart under humbling providences prepares for deliverance and true comfort. 3. Submission to the justice of God in all his dealings; if they then *accept of the punishment of their iniquity* (*v.* 41 and again *v.* 43), that is, if they justify God and condemn themselves, patiently bear the punishment as that which they have well deserved, and carefully answer the ends o it as that which God has well designed, accept it as a kindness, take it as physic, and improve it, then they are penitents indeed.

II. How the mercy which they should obtain upon their repentance is described. 1. They should not be abandoned: *Though they have despised my judgments, yet, for all that, I will not cast them away, v.* 43, 44. He speaks as a tender Father that cannot find in his heart to disinherit a son that has been very provoking. *How shall I do it?* Hos. 11:8, 9. Till he had laid the foundations of a church for himself in the Gentile world, the Jewish church was not quite forsaken, nor cast away. 2. They should be remembered: *I will remember the land* with favour, which is grounded upon the promise before, *I will remember my covenant* (*v.* 42), which is repeated, *v.* 45. God is said *to remember the covenant* when he performs the promises of it, purely for his faithfulness' sake; not because there is any thing in us to recommend us to his favour, but because he will be as good as his word. This is the church's plea. Ps. 74:20, *Have respect unto the covenant.* He will remember the constitution of the covenant, which is such as leaves room for repentance, and promises pardon upon repentance; and the Mediator of the covenant, who was promised to Abraham, Isaac, and Jacob, and was sent, when the fulness of time came, in remembrance of that holy covenant. The word covenant is thrice repeated, to intimate that God is ever mindful of it and would have us to be so. The persons also with whom the covenant was made are mentioned in an unusual manner, *per modum ascensus — in the ascending line,* beginning with Jacob, to lead them gradually to the most ancient promise, which was made to the father of the faithful: thus (Mic. 7:20) he is said to perform the *truth to Jacob,* and the *mercy to Abraham.* He will for their sakes (*v.* 45), not their merit's sake, but their benefit's sake, remember the covenant of their ancestors, and upon that score show kindness to them, though most unworthy; they are therefore said to be, *as touching the election, beloved for the fathers' sake,* Rom. 11:28. Note, When those that have walked contrary to God in a way of sin return to him by sincere repentance, though he has walked contrary to them in a way of judgment he will return to them in a way of special mercy, pursuant to the covenant of redemption and grace. None are so ready to repent as God is to forgive upon repentance, through Christ, who is given for a covenant.

Lastly, These are said to be *the laws which the Lord made between him and the children of Israel, v.* 46. His communion with his church is kept up by his law. He manifests not only his dominion over them, but his favour to them, by giving them his law; and they manifest not only their holy fear, but their holy love, by the observance of it; and thus it is made between them, rather as a covenant than a law; for he draws with the cords of a man.

CHAPTER 27

The last verse of the foregoing chapter seemed to close up the statute-book; yet this chapter is added as an appendix. Having given laws concerning instituted services, here he directs concerning vows and voluntary services, the free-will offerings of their mouth. Perhaps some devout serious people among them might be so affected with what Moses had delivered to them in the foregoing chapter as in a pang of zeal to consecrate themselves, or their children, or estates to him: this, because honestly meant, God would accept; but, because men are apt to repent of such vows, he leaves room for the redemption of what had been so consecrated, at a certain rate. Here is, I. The law concerning what was sanctified to God, persons (*v.* 2–8), cattle, clean or unclean (*v.* 9–13), houses and lands (*v.* 15–25), with an exception of firstlings, (*v.* 26, 27). II. Concerning what was devoted (*v.* 28, 29). III. Concerning tithes (*v.* 30, etc.).

Verses 1–13

This is part of the law concerning singular vows, extraordinary ones, which though God did not expressly insist on, yet, if they were consistent with and conformable to the general precepts, he would be well pleased with. Note, We should not only ask, What must we do, but, What may we do, for the glory and honour of God? As the *liberal devises liberal things* (Isa. 32:8), so the pious devises pious things, and the enlarged heart would willingly do something extraordinary in the service of so good a Master as God is. When we receive or expect some singular mercy it is good to honour God with some singular vow.

I. The case is here put of persons vowed to God by a singular vow, *v.* 2. If a man consecrated himself, or a child, to the service of the tabernacle, to be employed there in some inferior office, as sweeping the floor, carrying out ashes, running of errands, or the like, *the person* so consecrated *shall be for the Lord,* that is, "God will graciously accept the good-will." *Thou didst well that it was in thy heart,* 2 Chr. 6:8. But forasmuch as he had no occasion to use their service about the tabernacle, a whole tribe being appropriated to the use of it, those that were thus vowed were to be redeemed, and the money paid for their redemption was employed for the repair of the sanctuary, or other uses of it, as appears by 2 Ki. 12:14, where it is called, in the margin, the *money of the souls of his estimation.* A book of rates is accordingly provided, by which the priests were to go in their estimation. Here is, 1. The rate of the middle-aged, between twenty and threescore, these were valued highest, because most serviceable; a male fifty shekels, and a female thirty, *v.* 3, 4. The females were then less esteemed, but not so in Christ; for in *Christ Jesus there is neither male nor female,* Gal. 3:28. Note, Those that are in the prime of their time must look upon themselves as obliged to do more in the service of God and their generation than can be expected either from minors, that have not yet arrived to their usefulness, or from the aged, that have survived it. 2. The rate of the youth between five years old and twenty was less, because they were then less capable of doing service, *v.* 5. 3. Infants under five years old were capable of being vowed to God by their parents, even before they were born, as Samuel was, but not to be presented and redeemed till a month old, that, as one sabbath passed over them before they were circumcised, so one new moon might pass over them before they were estimated; and their valuation was but small, *v.* 6. Samuel, who was thus vowed to God, was not redeemed, because he was a Levite, and a particular favourite, and therefore was employed in his childhood in the service of the tabernacle. 4. The aged are valued less than youth, but more than children, *v.* 7. And the Hebrews observe that the rate of an aged woman is two parts of three to that of an aged man, so that in that age the female came nearest to the value of the male, which occasioned (as bishop Patrick quotes it here) this saying among them, *That an old woman in a house is a treasure in a house.* Paul sets a great value upon the aged women, when he makes them *teachers of good things,* Tit. 2:3. 5. The poor shall be valued according to their ability, *v.* 8. Something they must pay, that they might learn not to be rash in vowing to God, for *he hath no pleasure in fools,* Eccl. 5:4. Yet not more than their ability, but *secundum tenementum — according to their possessions,* that they might not ruin themselves and their families by their zeal. Note, God expects and requires from men according to what they have, and not according to what they have not, Lu. 21:4.

II. The case is put of beasts vowed to God, 1. If it was a clean beast, such as was offered in sacrifice, it must not be redeemed, nor any equivalent given for it: *It shall be holy, v.* 9, 10. After it was vowed, it was not to be put to any common use, nor changed upon second thoughts; but it must be either offered upon the altar, or, if through any blemish it was not meet to be offered, he that vowed it should not take advantage of that, but the priests should have it for their own use (for they were God's receivers), or it should be sold for the service of the sanctuary. This teaches caution in making vows and constancy in keeping them when they are made; for *it is a snare to a man to devour that which is holy, and after vows to make enquiry,* Prov. 20:25. And to this that rule of charity seems to allude (2 Co. 9:7), *Every man, according as he purposeth in his heart, so let him give.* 2. If it was an unclean beast, it should go to the use of the priest at such a value; but he that vowed it, upon paying that value in money, and adding a fifth part more to it, might redeem it if he pleased, *v.* 11–13. It was fit that men should smart for their inconstancy. God has let us know his mind concerning his service, and he is not pleased if we do not know our own. God expects that those that deal with him should be at a point, and way what they will stand to.

Verses 14–25

Here is the law concerning real estates dedicated to the service of God by a singular vow.

I. Suppose a man, in his zeal for the honour of God, should *sanctify his house to God* (*v.* 14), the house must be valued by the priest, and the money got by the sale of it was to be converted to the use of the sanctuary, which by degrees came to be greatly enriched with *dedicated things,* 1 Ki. 15:15. But, if the owner be inclined to redeem it himself, he must not have it so cheap as another, but must add a fifth part to the price, for he should have considered before he had vowed it, *v.* 15. To him that was necessitous God would abate the estimation (*v.* 8); but to him that was fickle and humoursome, and whose second thoughts inclined more to the world and his secular interest than his first, God would rise in the price. Blessed be God, there is a way of sanctifying our houses to be holy unto the Lord, without either selling them or buying them. If we and our houses serve the Lord, if religion rule in them, and we put away iniquity far from them, and have a church in our house, holiness to the Lord is written upon it, it is his, and he will dwell with us in it.

II. Suppose a man should sanctify some part of his land to the Lord, giving it to pious uses, then a difference must be made between land that came to the donor by descent and that which came by purchase, and accordingly the case altered.

1. If it was the inheritance of his fathers, here called the *field of his possession,* which pertained to his family from the first division of Canaan, he might not give it all, no, not to the sanctuary; God would not admit such a degree of zeal as ruined a man's family. But he might sanctify or dedicate only some part of it, *v.* 16. And in that case, (1.) The land was to be valued (as our countrymen commonly compute land) by so many measures' sowing of barley. So much land as would take a *homer,* or *chomer,* of barley, which contained ten ephahs, Eze. 45:11 (not, as some have here mistaken it, an *omer,* which was but a tenth part of an ephah, Ex. 16:36), was valued at fifty shekels, a moderate price (*v.* 16), and that if it were sanctified immediately from the year of jubilee, *v.* 17. But, if some years after, there was to be a discount accordingly, even of that price, *v.* 18. And, (2.) When the value was fixed, the donor might, if he pleased, redeem it for sixty shekels the homer's sowing, which was with the addition of a fifth part: the money then went to the sanctuary, and the land reverted to him that had sanctified it, *v.* 19. But if he would not redeem it, and the priest sold it to another, then at the year of jubilee, beyond which the sale could not go, the land came to the priests, and was theirs for ever, *v.* 20, 21. Note, What is given to the Lord ought not to be given with a power of revocation; what is devoted to the Lord must be his for ever, by a perpetual covenant.

2. If the land was his own purchase, and came not to him from his ancestors, then not the land itself, but the value of it was to be given to the priests for pious uses, *v.* 22, 24. It was supposed that those who, by the blessing of God, had grown so rich as to become purchasers would think themselves obliged in gratitude to sanctify some part of their purchase, at least (and here they are not limited, but they might, if they pleased, sanctify the whole), to the service of God. For we ought to give *as God prospers us,* 1 Co. 16:2. Purchasers are in a special manner bound to be charitable. Now, forasmuch as purchased lands were by a former law to return at the year of jubilee to the family from which they were purchased, God would not have that law and the intentions of it defeated by making the lands *corban, a gift,* Mk. 7:11. But it was to be computed how much the land was worth for so many years as were from the vow to the jubilee; for only so long it was his own, and God *hates robbery for burnt-offerings.* We can never acceptably serve God with that of which we have wronged our neighbour. And so much money he was to give for the present, and keep the land in his own hands till the year of jubilee, when it was to return free of all encumbrances, even that of its being dedicated to him of whom it was bought. The value of the shekel by which all these estimations were to be made is here ascertained (*v.* 25); it shall be twenty gerahs, and every gerah was sixteen barley-corns. This was fixed before (Ex. 30:13); and, whereas there had been some alterations, it is again fixed in the laws of Ezekiel's visionary temple (Eze. 45:12), to denote that the gospel should reduce things to their ancient standard.

Verses 26–34

Here is, I. A caution given that no man should make such a jest of sanctifying things to the Lord as to sanctify any firstling to him, for that was his already by the law, *v.* 26. Though the matter of a general vow be that which we were before obliged to, as of our sacramental covenant, yet a singular vow should be of that which we were not, in such circumstances and proportions, antecedently bound to. The law concerning the firstlings of unclean beasts (*v.* 27) is the same with that before, *v.* 11, 12.

II. Things or persons devoted are here distinguished from things or persons that were only sanctified. 1. Devoted things were most holy to the Lord, and could neither revert nor be alienated, *v.* 28. They were of the same nature with those sacrifices which were called most holy, which none might touch but only the priests themselves. The difference between these and other sanctified things arose from the different expression of the vow. If a man dedicated any thing to God, binding himself with a solemn curse never to alienate it to any other purpose, then it was a thing devoted. 2. Devoted persons were to be put to death, *v.* 29. Not that it was in the power of any parent or master thus to devote a child or a servant to death; but it must be meant of the public enemies of Israel, who, either by the appointment of God or by the sentence of the congregation, were devoted, as the seven nations with which they must make no league. The city of Jericho in particular was thus devoted, Jos. 6:17. The inhabitants of Jabesh-Gilead were put to death for violating the curse pronounced upon those who came not up to Mizpeh, Jdg. 21:9, 10. Some think it was for want of being rightly informed of the true intent and meaning of this law that Jephtha sacrificed his daughter as one devoted, who might not be redeemed.

III. A law concerning tithes, which were paid for the service of God before the law, as appears by Abraham's payment of them, (Gen. 14:20), and Jacob's promise of them, Gen. 28:22. It is here appointed, 1. That they should pay tithe of all their increase, their corn, trees, and cattle, *v.* 30, 32. Whatsoever productions they had the benefit of God must be honoured with the tithe of, if it were titheable. Thus they acknowledged God to be the owner of their land, the giver of its fruits, and themselves to be his tenants, and dependents upon him. Thus they gave him thanks for the plenty they enjoyed, and supplicated his favour in the continuance of it. And we are taught in general to *honour the Lord with our substance* (Prov. 3:9), and in particular to support and maintain his ministers, and to be *ready to communicate* to them, Gal. 6:6; 1 Co. 9:11. And how this may be done in a fitter and more equal proportion than that of the tenth, which God himself appointed of old, I cannot see. 2. That which was once marked for tithe should not be altered, no, not for a better (*v.* 33), for Providence directed the rod that marked it. God would accept it though it were not the best, and they must not grudge it though it were, for it was what passed under the rod. 3. That it should not be redeemed, unless the owner would give a fifth part more for its ransom, *v.* 31. If men had the curiosity to prefer what was marked for tithe before any other part of their increase, it was fit that they should pay for their curiosity.

IV. The last verse seems to have reference to this whole book of which it is the conclusion: *These are the commandments which the Lord commanded Moses, for the children of Israel.* Many of these commandments are moral, and of perpetual obligation; others of them, which were ceremonial and peculiar to the Jewish economy, have notwithstanding a spiritual significancy, and are instructive to us who are furnished with a key to let us into the mysteries contained in them; for *unto us,* by those institutions, *is the gospel preached as well as unto them,* Heb. 4:2. Upon the whole matter, we may see cause to bless God that *we have not come to mount Sinai,* Heb. 12:18. 1. That we are not under the *dark shadows* of the law, but enjoy the clear light of the gospel, which shows us *Christ the end of the law for righteousness,* Rom. 10:4. The doctrine of our reconciliation to God by a Mediator is not clouded with the smoke of burning sacrifices, but cleared by the knowledge of *Christ and him crucified.* 2. That we are not under the *heavy yoke* of the law, and the carnal ordinances of it (as the apostle calls them, Heb. 9:10), imposed till the time of reformation, a yoke which *neither they nor their fathers were able to bear* (Acts 15:10), but under the sweet and easy institutions of the gospel, which pronounces those the *true worshippers that worship the Father in spirit and truth,* by Christ only, and in his name, who is our priest, temple, altar, sacrifice, purification, and all. Let us not therefore think that because we are not tied to the ceremonial cleansings, feasts, and oblations, a little care, time, and expense, will serve to honour God with. No, but rather have our hearts more enlarge with free-will offerings to his praise, more inflamed with holy love and joy, and more engaged in seriousness of thought and sincerity of intention. *Having boldness to enter into the holiest by the blood of Jesus, let us draw near with a true heart, and full assurance of faith,* worshipping God with so much the more cheerfulness and humble confidence, still saying, *Blessed be God for Jesus Christ!*

AN EXPOSITION, WITH PRACTICAL OBSERVATIONS, OF
THE FOURTH BOOK OF MOSES, CALLED NUMBERS

The titles of the five books of Moses, which we use in our Bibles, are all borrowed from the Greek translation of the Seventy, the most ancient version of the Old Testament that we know of. But the title of this book only we turn into English; in all the rest we retain the Greek word itself, for which difference I know no reason but that the Latin translators have generally done the same. Otherwise this book might as well have been called *Arithmoi*, the Greek title, as the first *Genesis*, and the second *Exodus;* or these might as well have been translated, and called, the first the *Generation*, or *Original*, the second the *Out-let*, or *Escape*, as this *Numbers*. — This book was thus entitled because of the numbers of the children of Israel, so often mentioned in this book, and so well worthy to give a title to it, because it was the remarkable accomplishment of God's promise to Abraham that his seed should be as the stars of heaven for multitude. It also relates to two numberings of them, one at mount Sinai (*ch.* 1), the other in the plains of Moab, thirty-nine years after (*ch.* 26). And not three men the same in the last account that were in the first. The book is almost equally divided between histories and laws, intermixed.

We have here, I. The histories of the numbering and marshalling of the tribes (*ch.* 1–4), the dedication of the altar and Levites (*ch.* 7, 8), their march (*ch.* 9, 10), their murmuring and unbelief, for which they were sentenced to wander forty years in the wilderness (*ch.* 11–14), the rebellion of Korah (*ch.* 16, 17), the history of the last year of the forty (*ch.* 20–26), the conquest of Midian, and the settlement of the two tribes (*ch.* 31, 32), with an account of their journeys (*ch.* 33), II. Divers laws about the Nazarites, etc. (*ch.* 5, 6); and again about the priests' charge, etc. (*ch.* 18, 19), feasts (*ch.* 28, 29), and vows (*ch.* 30), and relating to their settlement in Canaan (*ch.* 27, 34, 35, 36). An abstract of much of this book we have in a few words in Ps. 95:10, *Forty years long was I grieved with this generation;* and an application of it to ourselves in Heb. 4:1, *Let us fear lest we seem to come short.* Many considerable nations there were now in being, that dwelt in cities and fortified towns, of which no notice is taken, no account kept, by the sacred history: but very exact records are kept of the affairs of a handful of people, that dwelt in tents, and wandered strangely in a wilderness, because they were the children of the covenant. *For the Lord's portion is his people, Jacob is the lot of his inheritance.*

CHAPTER 1

Israel was now to be formed into a commonwealth, or rather a kingdom; for "the Lord was their King" (1 Sa. 12:12), their government a theocracy, and Moses under him was king in Jeshurun, Deu. 33:5. Now, for the right settlement of this holy state, next to the institution of good laws was necessary the institution of good order; and account therefore must be taken of the subjects of this kingdom, which is done in this chapter, where we have, I. Orders given to Moses to number the people (*v.* 1–4). II. Persons nominated to assist him herein (*v.* 5–16). III. The particular number of each tribe, as it was given in to Moses (*v.* 17–43). IV. The sum total of all together (*v.* 44–46). V. An exception of the Levites (*v.* 47, etc.).

Verses 1–16

I. We have here a commission issued out for the numbering of the people of Israel; and David, long after, paid dearly for doing it without a commission. Here is,

1. The date of this commission, *v.* 1. (1.) The place: it is given at God's court *in the wilderness of Sinai*, from his royal palace, *the tabernacle of the congregation.* (2.) The time: *In the second year* after they came up out of Egypt; we may call it the second year of that reign. The laws in Leviticus were given in the first month of that year; these orders were given in the beginning of the second month.

2. The directions given for the execution of it, *v.* 2, 3. (1.) None were to be numbered but the males, and those only such as were fit for war. None *under twenty years old;* for, though some such might have bulk and strength enough for military service, yet, in compassion to their tender years, God would not have them put upon it to bear arms. (2.) Nor were any to be numbered who through age, or bodily infirmity, blindness, lameness, or chronical diseases, were unfit for war. The church being militant, those only are reputed the true members of it that have enlisted themselves soldiers of Jesus Christ; for our life, our Christian life, is a warfare. (3.) The account was to be taken *according to their families*, that it might not only be known how many they were, and what were their names, but of what tribe and family, or clan, nay, of what particular house every person was; or, reckoning it the muster of an army, to what regiment every man belonged, that he might know his place himself and the government might know where to find him. They were numbered a little before this, when their poll-money was paid for the service of the tabernacle, Ex. 38:25, 26. But it should seem they were not then registered *by the house of their fathers*, as now they were. Their number was the same then that it was now: 603,550 men; for as many as had died since then, and were lost in the account, so many had arrived to be twenty years old, and were added to the account. Note, As *one generation passeth away another generation cometh.* As vacancies are daily made, so recruits are daily raised to fill up the vacancies, and Providence takes care that, one time or other, in one place or other, the births shall balance the burials, that the race of mankind and the holy seed may not be cut off and become extinct.

3. Commissioners are named for the doing of this work. Moses and Aaron were to preside (*v.* 3), and one man of every tribe, that was renowned in his tribe, and was presumed to know it well, was to assist in it — *the princes of the tribes, v.* 16. Note, Those that are honourable should study to be serv-

iceable; he that is great, let him be your minister, and show, by his knowing the public, that he deserves to be publicly known. The charge of this muster was committed to him who was the lord-lieutenant of that tribe. Now,

II. Why was this account ordered to be taken and kept? For several reasons. 1. To prove the accomplishment of the promise made to Abraham, that God would *multiply his seed exceedingly*, which promise was renewed to Jacob (Gen. 28:14), that *his seed should be as the dust of the earth.* Now it appears that there did not fail one tittle of that good promise, which was an encouragement to them to hope that the other promise of the land of Canaan for an inheritance should also be fulfilled in its season. When the number of a body of men is only guessed at, upon the view, it is easy for one that is disposed to cavil to surmise that the conjecture is mistaken, and that, if they were to be counted, they would not be found half so many; therefore God would have Israel numbered, that it might be upon record how vastly they were increased in a little time, that the power of God's providence and the truth of his promise may be seen and acknowledged by all. It could not have been expected, in any ordinary course of nature, that seventy-five souls (which was the number of Jacob's family when he went down into Egypt) should in 215 years (and it was no longer) multiply into so many hundred thousands. It is therefore to be attributed to an extraordinary virtue in the divine promise and blessing. 2. It was to intimate the particular care which God himself would take of his Israel, and which Moses and the inferior rulers were expected to take of them. God is called the *Shepherd of Israel*, Ps. 80:1. Now the shepherds always kept count of their flocks, and delivered them by number to their under-shepherds, that they might know if any were missing; in like manner God numbers his flock, that of all which he took into his fold he might lose none but upon a valuable consideration, even those that were sacrificed to his justice. 3. It was to put a difference between the true born Israelites and the mixed multitude that were among them; none were numbered but Israelites: all the world is but lumber in comparison with those jewels. Little account is made of others, but the saints God has a particular property in and concern for. *The Lord knows those that are his* (2 Tim. 2:19), *knows them by name*, Phil. 4:3. The hairs of their head are numbered ; but he will say to others, *"I never knew you*, never made any account of you." 4. It was in order to their being marshalled into several districts, for the more easy administration of justice, and their more regular march through the wilderness. It is a rout and a rabble, not an army, that is not mustered and put in order.

Verses 17–43

We have here the speedy execution of the orders given for the numbering of the people. It was begun the same day that the orders were given, *The first day of the second month;* compare *v.* 18 with *v.* 1. Note, When any work is to be done for God it is good to set about it quickly, while the sense of duty is strong and pressing. And, for aught that appears, it was but one day's work, for many other things were done between this and the twentieth day of this month, when they

removed their camp, ch. 10:11. Joab was almost ten months numbering the people in David's time (2 Sa. 24:8); but then they were dispersed, now they lived closely together; then Satan proposed the doing of it, now God commanded it. It was the sooner and more easily done now because it had been done but a little while ago, and they needed but review the old books, with the alterations since made, which probably they had kept an account of as they occurred.

In the particulars here left upon record, we may observe, 1. That the numbers are registered in words at length (as I may say), and not in figures; to every one of the twelve tribes it is repeated, for the greater ceremony and solemnity of the account, that they were numbered *by their generations, after their families, by the house of their fathers, according to the number of the names*, to show that every tribe took and gave in the account by the same rule and in the same method, though so many hands were employed in it, setting down the genealogy first, to show that their family descended from Israel, then the families themselves in their order, then dividing each family into the houses, or subordinate families, that branched from it, and under these the names of the particular persons, according to the rules of heraldry. Thus every man might know who were his relations or next of kin, on which some laws we have already met with did depend: besides that the nearer any are to us in relation the more ready we should be to do them good. 2. That they all end with hundreds, only Gad with fifty (*v.* 25), but none of the numbers descend to units or tens. Some think it was a special providence that ordered all the tribes just at this time to be even numbers, and no odd or broken numbers among them, to show them that there was something more than ordinary designed in their increase, there being this uncommon in the circumstance of it. It is rather probable that Moses having some time before appointed rulers of hundreds, and rulers of fifties (Ex. 18:25), they numbered the people by their respective rulers, which would bring the numbers to even hundreds or fifties. 3. That Judah is the must numerous of them all, more than double to Benjamin and Manasseh, and almost 12,000 more than any other tribe, *v.* 27. It was Judah whom *his brethren must praise* because from him Messiah the Prince was to descend; but, because that was a thing at a distance, God did in many ways honour that tribe in the mean time, particularly by the great increase of it, for his sake who was to spring out of Judah (Heb. 7:14) in the fulness of time. Judah was to lead the van through the wilderness, and therefore was furnished accordingly with greater strength than any other tribe. 4. Ephraim and Manasseh, the sons of Joseph, are numbered as distinct tribes, and both together made up almost as many as Judah; this was in pursuance of Jacob's adoption of them, by which they were equalled with their uncles Reuben and Simeon, Gen. 48:5. It was also the effect of the blessing of Joseph, who was to be a *fruitful bough*, Gen. 49:22. And Ephraim the younger is put first, and is more numerous than Manasseh, for Jacob had crossed hands, and foreseen ten thousands of Ephraim and thousands of Manasseh. The fulfilling of this confirms our faith in the spirit of prophecy with which the patriarchs were endued. 5. When they came down into Egypt Dan had but one son (Gen. 46:23), and so his tribe was but one family, *ch.* 26:42. Benjamin had then ten sons (Gen. 46:21), yet now the tribe of Dan is almost double in number to that of Benjamin. Note, The increasing and diminishing of families do not always go by probabilities. Some are multiplied greatly, and again are diminished, while others that were poor have families made them like a flock, Ps. 107:38, 39, 41; and see Job 12:23. 6. It is said of each of the tribes that those were numbered who were able to go forth to war, to remind them that they had wars before them, though now they were in peace and met with no opposition. *Let not him that girdeth on the harness boast as though he had put it off.*

Verses 44–46

We have here the sum total at the foot of the account; they were in all 600,000 fighting men, and 3550 over. Some think that when this was their number some months before (Ex. 38:26) the Levites were reckoned with them, but now that tribe was separated for the service of God, yet so many more had by this time attained to the age of twenty years as that still they were the same number, to show that whatever we part with for the honour and service of God it shall certainly be made up to us one way of other. Now we see what a vast body of men they were. Let us consider, 1. How much went to maintain all these (besides twice as many more, no question, of women and children, sick and aged, and the mixed multitude) for forty years together in the wilderness; and they were all at God's finding every day, having their food from the dew of heaven, and not from the fatness of the earth. O what a great and good housekeeper is our God, that has such numbers depending on him and receiving from him every day! 2. What work sin makes with a people; within forty years most of them would indeed have died of course for the common sin of mankind; for, when sin entered into the world, death came with it, and how great are the desolations which it makes in the earth! But, for the particular sin of unbelief and murmuring, all those that were now numbered, except two, laid their bones under their iniquity, and perished in the wilderness. 3. What a great multitude God's spiritual Israel will amount to at last; though at one time, and in one place, they seem to be but a little flock, yet when they come all together they shall be a great multitude, innumerable, Rev. 7:9. And, though the church's beginning be small, its latter end shall greatly increase. A little one shall become a thousand.

Verses 47–54

Care is here taken to distinguish from the rest of the tribes the tribe of Levi, which, in the matter of the golden calf, had distinguished itself, Ex. 32:26. Note, Singular services shall be recompensed with singular honours. Now,

I. It was the honour of the Levites that they were made guardians of the spiritualities; to them was committed the care of the tabernacle and the treasures thereof, both in their camps and in their marches. 1. When they moved the Levites were to take down the tabernacle, to carry it and all that belonged to it, and then to set it up again in the place appointed, *v.* 50, 51. It was for the honour of the holy things that none should be permitted to see them, or touch them, but those only who were called of God to the service. Thus we all are unfit and unworthy to have fellowship with God until we are first called by his grace *into the fellowship of his Son Jesus Christ our Lord,* and so, being the spiritual seed of that great high priest, are made *priests to our God;* and it is promised that God would take Levites to himself, even from the Gentiles, Isa. 66:21. 2. When they rested the Levites were to *encamp round about the tabernacle* (*v.* 50, 53), that they might be near their work, and resident upon their charge, always ready to attend, and that they might be a guard upon the tabernacle, to preserve it from being either plundered or profaned. They must pitch round about the tabernacle, *that there be no wrath upon the congregation,* as there would be if the tabernacle and the charge of it were neglected, or those crowded upon it that were not allowed to come near. Note, Great care must be taken to prevent sin, because the preventing of sin is the preventing of wrath.

II. It was their further honour that as Israel, being a holy people, was not *reckoned among the nations,* so they, being a holy tribe, were not reckoned among other Israelites, but numbered afterwards by themselves, *v.* 49. The service which the Levites were to do about the sanctuary is called (as we render it in the margin) a *warfare, ch.* 4:23. And, being engaged in that warfare, they were discharged from military services, and therefore not numbered with those that were to *go out to war.* Note, Those that minister about holy things should neither entangle themselves, nor be entangled, in secular affairs. The ministry is itself work enough for a whole man, and all little enough to be employed in it. It is an admonition to ministers to distinguish themselves by their exemplary conversation from common Israelites, not affecting to seem greater, but aiming to be really better, every way better than others.

CHAPTER 2

The thousands of Israel, having been mustered in the former chapter, in this are marshalled, and a regular disposition is made of their camp, by a divine appointment. Here is, I. A general order concerning it (*v.* 1, 2). II. Particular directions for the posting of each of the tribes, in four distinct squadrons, three tribes in each squadron. 1. In the van-guard on the east were posted Judah, Issachar, and Zebulun (*v.* 3–9). 2. In the right wing, southward, Reuben, Simeon, and Gad (*v.* 10–16). 3. In the rear, westward, Ephraim, Manasseh, and Benjamin, (*v.* 18–24). 4. In the left wing, northward, Dan, Asher, and Naphtali (*v.* 25–31). 5. The tabernacle in the centre (*v.* 17). III. The conclusion of this appointment (*v.* 32, etc.).

Verses 1–2

Here is the general appointment given both for their orderly encampment where they rested and their orderly march when they moved. Some order, it is possible, they had observed hitherto; they came out of Egypt in rank and file (Ex. 13:18), but now they were put into a better model. 1. They all dwelt in tents, and when they marched carried all their tents along with them, for *they found no city to dwell in,* Ps. 107:4. This represents to us our state in this world. It is a movable state (we are here to-day and gone to-morrow); and it is a military state: is not our life a warfare? We do but pitch our tents in this world, and have in it no continuing city. Let us, therefore, while we are pitching in this world, be pressing through it. 2. Those of a tribe were to pitch together, *every man by his own standard.* Note, It is the will of God that mutual love and affection, converse and communion, should be kept up among relations. Those that are of kin to each other should, as much as they can, be acquainted with each other; and the bonds of nature should be improved for the strengthening of the bonds of Christian communion. 3. Every one must know his place and keep in it; they were not allowed to fix where they pleased, nor to remove when they pleased, but God quarters them, with a charge to abide in their quarters. Note, It is God that *appoints us the bounds of our habitation,* and to him we must refer ourselves. *He shall choose our inheritance for us* (Ps. 47:4), and in his choice we must acquiesce, and not love to flit, nor be *as the bird that wanders from her nest.* 4. Every tribe had its standard, flag, or ensign, and it should seem every family had some particular ensign of their father's house, which was carried as with us the colours of each troop or company in a regiment are. These were of use for the distinction of tribes and families, and the gathering and keeping of them together, in allusion to which the preaching of the gospel is said to *lift up an ensign, to which the Gentiles shall seek,* and by which they shall pitch, Isa. 11:10, 12. Note, God is the God of order, and not of confusion. These standards made this mighty army seem more beautiful to its friends and more formidable to its enemies. The church of Christ is said to be as *terrible as an army with banners,* Cant. 6:10. It is uncertain how these standards were distinguished: some conjecture that the standard of each tribe was of the same colour with the precious stone in which the name of that tribe was written in the high priest's ephod, and that this was all the difference. Many of the modern Jews think there was some coat of arms painted in each standard, which had reference to the blessing of that tribe by Jacob. Judah bore a lion, Dan a serpent, Naphtali a hind, Benjamin a wolf, etc. Some of them say the four principal standards were, Judah a lion, Reuben a man, Joseph an ox, and Dan an eagle, making the appearances in Ezekiel's vision to allude it. Others say the name of each tribe was written in its standard. Whatever it was, no doubt it gave a certain direction. 5. They were to pitch about the tabernacle, which was to be in the midst of them, as the tent of pavilion of a general in the centre of an army. They must encamp round the tabernacle, (1.) That it might be equally a comfort and joy to them all, as it was a token of God's gracious presence with them. Ps. 46:5, *God is in the midst of her, she shall not be moved.* Their camp had reason to be hearty, when thus they had God in the heart of them. To have bread from heaven every day round about their camp, and fire from heaven, with other tokens of God's favour, in the midst of their camp, was abundantly sufficient to answer that question, *Is the Lord among us, or is he not? Happy art thou, O Israel!* It is probable that the doors of all their tents were made to look towards the tabernacle from all sides, for every Israelite should have his eyes always towards the Lord; therefore they worshipped at the tent-door. The tabernacle was in the midst of the camp, that it might be near to them; for it is a very desirable thing to have the solemn administrations of holy ordinances near us and within our reach. *The kingdom of God is among you.* (2.) That they might be a guard and defence upon the tabernacle and the Levites on every side. No invader could come near God's tabernacle without first penetrating the thickest of their squadrons. Note, If God undertake the protection of our comforts, we ought in our places to undertake the protection of his institutions, and stand up in defence of his honour, and interest, and ministers. 6. Yet they were to pitch afar off, in reverence to the sanctuary, that it might not seem crowded and thrust up among them, and that the common business of the camp might be no annoyance to it. They were also taught to keep their distance, lest too much familiarity should breed contempt. It is supposed (from Joshua 3:4) that the distance between the nearest part of the camp and the tabernacle (or perhaps between them and the camp of the Levites, who pitched near the tabernacle) was 2000 cubits, that is, 1000 yards, little more than half a measured mile with us; but the outer parts of the camp must needs be much further off. Some compute that the extent of their camp could be no less than twelve miles square; for it was like a movable city, with streets and lanes, in which perhaps the manna fell, as well as on the outside of the camp, that they might have it at their doors. In the Christian church we read of a throne (as in the tabernacle there was a mercy-seat) which is called a *glorious high throne from the beginning* (Jer. 17:12), and that throne surrounded by spiritual Israelites, twenty-four elders, double to the number of the tribes, *clothed in white raiment* (Rev. 4:4), and the banner over them is *Love;* but we are not ordered, as they were, to pitch afar off; no, we are invited to draw near, and come boldly. The saints of the Most High are said to be *round about him,* Ps. 76:11. God by his grace keep us close to him!

Verses 3–34

We have here the particular distribution of the twelve tribes into four squadrons, three tribes in a squadron, one of which was to lead the other two. Observe, 1. God himself appointed them their place, to prevent strife and envy among them. Had they been left to determine precedency among themselves, they would have been in danger of quarrelling with one another (as the disciples who strove *which should be greatest*); each would have had a pretence to be first, or at least not to be last. Had it been left to Moses to determine, they would have quarrelled with him, and charged him with partiality; therefore God does it, who is himself the fountain and judge of honour, and in his appointment all must acquiesce. If God in his providence advance others above us, and abase us, we ought to be as well satisfied in his doing it in that way as if he did it, as this was done here, by a voice out of the tabernacle; and this consideration, that it appears to be the will of God it should be so, should effectually silence all envies and discontents. And as far as our place comes to be our choice our Saviour has given us a rule in Lu. 14:8, *Sit not down in the highest room;* and another in Mt. 20:27, *He that will be chief, let him be your servant.* Those that are most humble and most serviceable are really most honourable. 2. Every tribe had a captain, a prince, or commander-in-chief, whom God himself nominated, the same that had been appointed to number them, *ch.* 1:5. Our being all the children of one Adam is so far from justifying the levellers, and taking away the distinction of place and honour, that even among the children of the same Abraham, the same

Jacob, the same Judah, God himself appointed that one should be captain of all the rest. There are *powers ordained of God,* and those to whom honour and fear are due and must be paid. Some observe the significancy of the names of these princes, at least, in general, how much God was in the thoughts of those that gave them their names, for most of them have *El, God,* at one end or other of their names. *Nethaneel, the gift of God; Eliab, my God a Father; Elizur, my God a rock; Shelumiel, God my peace; Eliasaph, God has added; Elishama, my God has heard: Gamaliel, God my reward; Pagiel, God has met me.* By this it appears that the Israelites in Egypt did not quite forget the name of their God, but, when they wanted other memorials, preserved the remembrance of it in the names of their children, and therewith comforted themselves in their affliction. 3. Those tribes were placed together under the same standard that were nearest of kin to each other; Judah, Issachar, and Zebulun, were the three younger sons of Leah, and they were put together; and Issachar and Zebulun would not grudge to be under Judah, since they were his younger brethren. Reuben and Simeon would not have been content in their place. Therefore Reuben, Jacob's eldest son, is made chief of the next squadron; Simeon, no doubt, is willing to be under him, and Gad, the son of Zilpah, Leah's handmaid, is fitly added to them in Levi's room: Ephraim, Manasseh, and Benjamin, are all the posterity of Rachel. Dan, the eldest son of Bilhah, is made a leading tribe, though the son of a concubine, that more abundant honour might be bestowed on that which lacked; and it was said, *Dan should judge his people,* and to him were added two younger sons of the handmaids. Thus unexceptionable was the order in which they were placed. 4. The tribe of Judah was in the first post of honour, encamped towards the rising sun, and in their marches led the van, not only because it was the most numerous tribe, but chiefly because from that tribe Christ was to come, who is the *Lion of the tribe of Judah,* and was to descend from the loins of him who was now nominated chief captain of that tribe. Nahshon is reckoned among the ancestors of Christ, Mt. 1:4. So that, when he went before them, Christ himself went before them in effect, as their leader. Judah was the first of the twelve sons of Jacob that was blessed. Reuben, Simeon, and Levi, were censured by their dying father; he therefore being first in blessing, though not in birth, is put first, to teach children how to value the smiles of their godly parents and dread their frowns. 5. The tribes of Levi pitched closely about the tabernacle, within the rest of their tribes, *v.* 17. They must defend the sanctuary, and then the rest of the tribes must defend them. Thus, in the vision which John saw of the glory of heaven, between the elders and the throne were four *living creatures full of eyes,* Rev. 4:6, 8. Civil powers should protect the religious interests of a nation, and be a defence upon that glory. 6. The camp of Dan (and so that tribe is called long after their settlement in Canaan (Jdg. 13:25), because celebrated for their military prowess), though posted in the left wing when they encamped, was ordered in their march to bring up the rear, *v.* 31. They were the most numerous, next to Judah, and therefore were ordered into a post which, next to the front, required the most strength, for as the strength is so shall the day be. *Lastly,* The children of Israel observed the orders given them, and did *as the Lord commanded Moses, v.* 34. They put themselves in the posts assigned them, without murmuring or disputing, and, as it was their safety, so it was their beauty; Balaam was charmed with the sight of it: *How goodly are thy tents, O Jacob! ch.* 24:5. Thus the gospel church, called the *camp of saints,* ought to be compact according to the scripture model, every one knowing and keeping his place, and then all that wish well to the church rejoice, *beholding their order,* Col. 2:5.

CHAPTER 3

This chapter and the next are concerning the tribe of Levi, which was to be mustered and marshalled by itself, and not in common with the other tribes, intimating the particular honour put upon them and the particular duty and service required from them. The Levites are in this chapter considered, I. As attendants on, and assistants to, the priests in the temple-service. And so we have an account, 1. Of the priests themselves (*v.* 1–4) and their work (*v.* 10). 2. Of the gift of the Levites to them (*v.* 5–9), in order to which they are mustered (*v.* 14–16), and the sum of them taken (*v.* 39). Each particular family of them is mustered, has its place assigned and its charge, the Gershonites (*v.* 17–26), the Kohathites (*v.* 27–32), the Merarites (*v.* 33–39). II. As equivalents for the first-born (*v.* 11–13). 1. The first-born are numbered, and the Levites taken instead of them, as far as the number of the Levites went (*v.* 40–45). 2. What first-born there were more than the Levites were redeemed (*v.* 46, etc.).

Verses 1–13

Here, I. The family of Aaron is confirmed in the priests' office, *v.* 10. They had been called to it before, and consecrated; here they are appointed to *wait on their priests' office:* the apostle uses this phrase (Rom. 12:7), *Let us wait on our ministry.* The office of the ministry requires a constant attendance and great diligence; so frequent are the returns of its work, and yet so transient its favourable opportunities, that it must be waited on. Here is repeated what was said before (*ch.* 1:51): *The stranger that cometh nigh shall be put to death,* which forbids the invading of the priest's office by any other person whatsoever; none must come nigh to minister but Aaron and his sons only, all others are strangers. It also lays a charge on the priests, as door-keepers in God's house, to take care that none should come near who were forbidden by the law; they must keep off all intruders, whose approach would be to the profanation of the holy things, telling them that if they came near it was at their peril, they would *die by the hand of God,* as Uzza did. The Jews say that afterwards there was hung over the door of the temple a golden sword (perhaps alluding to that flaming sword at the entrance of the garden of Eden), on which was engraven, *The stranger that cometh nigh shall be put to death.*

II. A particular account is given of this family of Aaron; what we have met with before concerning them is here repeated. 1. The consecration of the sons of Aaron, *v.* 3. They were all anointed to minister before the Lord, though it appeared afterwards, and God knew it, that two of them were wise and two were foolish. 2. The fall of the two elder (*v.* 4): they *offered strange fire,* and died for so doing, *before the Lord.* This is mentioned here in the preamble to the law concerning the priesthood, for a warning to all succeeding priests; let them know, by this example, that God is a jealous God, and will not be mocked; the holy anointing oil was an honour to the obedient, but not a shelter to the disobedient. It is here said, *They had no children,* Providence so ordering it, for their greater punishment, that none of their descendants should remain to be priests, and so bear up their name who had profaned God's name. 3. The continuance of the two younger: Eleazar and Ithamar ministered *in the sight of Aaron.* It intimates, (1.) The care they took about their ministration not to make any blunders; they kept under their father's eye, and took instruction from him in all they did, because, probably, Nadab and Abihu got out of their father's sight when they offered strange fire. Note, It is good for young people to act under the direction and inspection of those that are aged and experienced. (2.) The comfort Aaron took in it; it pleased him to see his younger sons behave themselves prudently and gravely, when his two elder had miscarried. Note, It is a great satisfaction to parents to *see their children walk in the truth,* 3 Jn. 4.

III. A grant is made of the Levites to be assistants to the priests in their work: *Give the Levites to Aaron, v.* 9. Aaron was to have a greater propriety in, and power over, the tribe of Levi than any other of the prices had in and over their respective tribes. There was a great deal of work belonging to the priests' office, and there were now only three pairs of hands to do it all, Aaron's and his two sons'; for it does not appear that they had either of them any children at this time, at least not any that were of age to minister, therefore God appoints the Levites to attend upon them. Note, Those whom God finds work for his will find help for. Here is, 1. The service for which the Levites were designed: they were to *minister to the priests* in their ministration to the Lord (*v.* 6), and to *keep Aaron's charge* (*v.* 7), as the deacons to the bishops in the evangelical constitution, serving at tables, while the bishops waited on their ministry. The Levites killed the sacrifices, and then the priests needed only to sprinkle the blood and burn the fat: the Levites prepared the incense, the priests burnt it. They were to keep, not only Aaron's charge, but the *charge of the whole congregation.* Note, It is a great trust that is reposed in ministers, not only for the glory of Christ, but for the good of his church; so that they must not only keep the charge of the great high priest, but must also be faithful to the souls of men, in trust for whom a dispensation is committed to them. 2. the consideration upon which the Levites were demanded; they were taken instead of the first-born. The preservation of the first-born of Israel, when all the first-born of the Egyptians (with whom they were many of them mingled) were destroyed, was looked upon by him who never makes any unreasonable demands as cause sufficient of the appropriating of all the first-born thenceforward to himself (*v.* 13): *All the first-born are mine.* That was sufficient to make them his, though he had given no reason for it, for he is the sole fountain and Lord of all beings and powers; but because all obedience must flow from love, and acts of duty must be acts of gratitude, before they were challenged into peculiar services they were crowned with peculiar favours. Note, When he that made us saves us we are thereby laid under further obligations to serve him and live to him. God's right to us by redemption corroborates the right he has to us by creation. Now because the first-born of a family are generally the favourites, and some would think it a disparagement to have their eldest sons servants to the priests, and attending before the door of the tabernacle, God took the tribe of Levi entire for his own, in lieu of the first-born, *v.* 12. Note, God's institutions put no hardships upon men in any of their just interests or reasonable affections. It was presumed that the Israelites would rather part with the Levites than with the first-born, and therefore God graciously ordered the exchange; yet for us he *spared not his own Son.*

Verses 14–39

The Levites being granted to Aaron to minister to him, they are here delivered to him by tale, that he might know what he had, and employ them accordingly. Observe,

I. By what rule they were numbered: *Every male from a month old and upward, v.* 15. The rest of the tribes were numbered only from twenty years old and upwards, and of them those only that were *able to go forth to war;* but into the number of the Levites they must take in both infants, and infirm; being exempted from the war, it was not insisted upon that they should be of age and strength for the wars. Though it appears afterwards that little more than a third part of the Levites were fit to be employed in the service of the tabernacle (about 8000 out of 22,000, *ch.* 4:47, 48), yet God would have them all numbered as retainers to his family; that none may think themselves disowned and rejected of God because they are not in a capacity of doing him that service which they see others do him. The Levites of a month old could not honour God and serve the tabernacle, as those that had grown up; yet out of the mouths of babes and sucklings the Levites' praise was perfected. Let not little children be hindered from being enrolled among the disciples of Christ, for such was the tribe of Levi, of such is the kingdom of heaven, that kingdom of priests. The redemption of the first-born was reckoned from a month old (*ch.* 18:15, 16), therefore from that age the Levites were numbered. They were numbered *after the house of their fathers,* not their *mothers,* for, if the daughter of a Levite married one of another tribe, her son was not a Levite; but we read of a spiritual priest to out God who inherited the unfeigned faith which dwelt in his mother and grandmother, 2 Tim. 1:5.

II. How they were distributed into three classes, according to the number of the sons of Levi, Gershon, Kohath, and Merari, and these subdivided into several families, *v.* 17–20.

1. Concerning each of these three classes we have an account, (1.) Of their number. The Gershonites were 7500. The Kohathites were 8600. The Merarites were 6200. The rest of the tribes had not their subordinate families numbered by themselves as those of Levi; this honour God put upon his own tribe. (2.) Of their post about the tabernacle on which they were to attend. The Gershonites pitched behind the tabernacle, westward, *v.* 23. The Kohathites on the right hand, southward, *v.* 29. The Merarites on the left hand, northward, *v.* 35. And, to complete the square, Moses and Aaron, with the priests, encamped in the front, eastward, *v.* 38. Thus was the tabernacle surrounded with its guards; and thus does the *angel of the Lord encamp round about those that fear him,* those living temples, Ps. 34:7. Every one knew his place, and must therein abide with God. (3.) Of their chief or head. As each class had

its own place, so each had its own prince. The commander of the Gershonites was Eliasaph (*v.* 24); of the Kohathites Elizaphan (*v.* 30), of whom we read (Lev. 10:4) that he was one of the bearers at the funeral of Nadab and Abihu; of the Merarites Zuriel, *v.* 35. (4.) Of their charge, when the camp moved. Each class knew their own business; it was requisite they should, for that which is every body's work often proves nobody's work. The Gershonites were charged with the custody and carriage of all the curtains and hangings and coverings of the tabernacle and court (*v.* 25, 26), the Kohathites of all the furniture of the tabernacle — the ark, altar, table, etc. (*v.* 31, 32), the Merarites of the heavy carriage, boards, bars, pillars, etc., *v.* 36, 37.

2. Here we may observe, (1.) That the Kohathites, though they were the second house, yet were preferred before the elder family of the Gershonites. Besides that Aaron and the priests were of that family, they were more numerous, and their post and charge more honourable, which probably was ordered to put an honour upon Moses, who was of that family. Yet, (2.) The posterity of Moses were not at all dignified or privileged, but stood upon the level with other Levites, that it might appear he did not seek the advancement of his own family, nor to entail any honours upon it either in church or state; he that had honour enough himself coveted not to have his name shine by that borrowed light, but rather to have the Levites borrow honour from his name. Let none think contemptibly of the Levites, though inferior to the priests, for Moses himself though it preferment enough for his sons to be Levites. Probably it was because the family of Moses were Levites only that in the title of this chapter, which is concerning that tribe (*v.* 1), Aaron is put before Moses.

III. The sum total of the numbers of this tribe. They are computed in all 22,000, *v.* 39. The sum of the particular families amounts to 300 more; if this had been added to the sum total, the Levites, instead of being 273 fewer than the first-born, as they were (*v.* 43), would have been twenty-seven more, and so the balance would have fallen the other way; but it is supposed that the 300 which were struck off from the account when the exchange was to be made were the first-born of the Levites themselves, born since their coming out of Egypt, which could not be put into the exchange, because they were already sanctified to God. But that which is especially observable here is that the tribe of Levi was by much the least of all the tribes. Note, God's part in the world is too often the smallest part. His chosen are comparatively a little flock.

Verses 40–51

Here is the exchange made of the Levites for the first-born. 1. The first-born were numbered from a month old, *v.* 42, 43. Those certainly were not reckoned who, though first-born, had become heads of families themselves, but those only that were under age; and the learned bishop Patrick is decidedly of opinion that none were numbered but those only that were born since their coming out of Egypt, when the first-born were sanctified, Ex. 13:2. If there were 22,000 first-born males, we may suppose as many females, and all these brought forth in the first year after they came out of Egypt, we must hence infer that in the last year of their servitude, even when it was in the greatest extremity, there were abundance of marriages made among the Israelites; they were not discouraged by the present distress, but married in faith, expecting that God would shortly visit them with mercy, and that their children, though born in bondage, should live in liberty and honour. And it was a token of good to them, an evidence that they were blessed of the Lord, that they were not only kept alive, but greatly increased, in a barren wilderness. 2. The number of the first-born, and that of the Levites, by a special providence, came pretty near to each other; thus, when he *divided the nations, he set the bounds of the people according to the number of the children of Israel,* Deu. 32:8. Known unto God are all his works beforehand, and there is an exact proportion between them, and so it will appear when they come to be compared. The Levites' cattle are said to be taken instead of the firstlings *of the cattle of the children of Israel,* that is, the Levites, with all their possessions, were devoted to God instead of the first-born and all theirs; for, when we give ourselves to God, all we have passes as appurtenances with the premises. 3. The small number of first-born which exceeded the number of the Levites (273 in all) were to be redeemed, at five shekels apiece, and the redemption-money given to Aaron; for it would not do well to have them added to the Levites. It is probable that in the exchange they began with the eldest of the first-born, and so downward, so that those were to be redeemed with money who were the 273 youngest of the first-born; more likely so than either that it was determined by lot or that the money was paid out of the public stock. The church is called the church of the *first-born,* which is redeemed, not as these were, with silver and gold, but, being devoted by sin to the justice of God, is ransomed with *the precious blood of the Son of God.*

CHAPTER 4

In the former chapter an account was taken of the whole tribe of Levi, in this we have an account of those of that tribe who were in the prime of their time for service, betwixt thirty and fifty years old. I. The serviceable men of the Kohathites are ordered to be numbered, and their charges are given them (*v.* 2–20). II. Of the Gershonites (*v.* 24–28). III. Of the Merarites (*v.* 29–33). IV. The numbers of each, and the sum total at last, are recorded (*v.* 34, etc.).

Verses 1–20

We have here a second muster of the tribe of Levi. As that tribe was taken out of all Israel to be God's peculiar, so the middle-aged men of that tribe were taken from among the rest to be actually employed in the service of the tabernacle. Now observe,

I. Who were to be taken into this number. All the males from thirty years old to fifty. Of the other tribes, those that were numbered to go forth to war were from twenty years old and upward, but of the Levites only from thirty to fifty; for the service of God requires the best of our strength, and the prime of our time, which cannot be better spent than to the honour of him who is the first and best. And a man may make a good soldier much sooner than a good minister. Now,

1. They were not to be employed till they were thirty years old, because till then they were in danger of retaining something childish and youthful and had not gravity enough to do the service, and wear the honour, of a Levite. They were entered as probationers at twenty-five years old, (*ch.* 8:24), and in David's time, when there was more work to be done, at twenty (1 Chr. 23:24, and so Ezra 3:8); but they must be five years learning and waiting, and so fitting themselves for service; nay, in David's time they were ten years in preparation, from twenty to thirty. John Baptist began his public ministry, and Christ his, at thirty years old. This is not in the letter of it obligatory on gospel ministers now, as if they must either not begin their work till thirty years old or must leave off at fifty; but it gives us two good rules: — (1.) That ministers must not be novices, 1 Tim. 3:6. It is a work that requires ripeness of judgment and great steadiness, and therefore those are very unfit for it who are but babes in knowledge and have not put away childish things. (2.) That they must learn before they teach, serve before they rule, and must *first be proved,* 1 Tim. 3:10.

2. They were discharged at fifty years old from the toilsome part of the service, particularly that of carrying the tabernacle; for that is the special service to which they are here ordained, and which there was most occasion for while they were in the wilderness. When they began to enter upon old age, they were dismissed, (1.) In favour to them, that they might no be over-toiled when their strength began to decay. Twenty years' good service was thought pretty well for one man. (2.) In honour to the work, that it might not be done by those who, through the infirmities of age, were slow and heavy. The service of God should be done when we are in the most lively active frame. Those do not consider this who put off their repentance to old age, and so leave the best work to be done in the worst time.

II. How their work is described. They are said to *enter into the host,* or warfare, *to do the work in the tabernacle.* The ministry is *a good work* (1 Tim. 3:1): ministers are not ordained to the honour only, but to the labour, not only to have the wages, but to do the work. It is also a *good warfare,* 1 Tim. 1:18. Those that enter into the ministry must look upon themselves as entered into the *host,* and approve themselves *good soldiers,* 2 Tim. 2:3. Now, as to the sons of Kohath in particular, here is,

1. Their service appointed them, in the removes of the tabernacle. Afterwards, when the tabernacle was fixed, they had other work assigned them; but this was the work of the day, which was to be done in its day. Observe, Wherever the camp of Israel went, the tabernacle of the Lord went with them, and care must be taken for the carriage of it. Note, Wherever we go, we must see to it that we take our religion along with us, and not forget that or any part of it. Now the Koliathites were to carry all the holy things of the tabernacle. They were charged with those things before (*ch.* 3:31), but here they have more particular instructions given them. (1.) Aaron, and his sons the priests, must pack up the things which the Kohathites were to carry, as here directed, *v.* 5, etc. God had before appointed that none should come into the most holy place, but only Aaron once a year with a cloud of incense (Lev. 16:2); and yet, the necessity of their unsettled state requiring it, that law is here dispensed with; for every time they removed Aaron and his sons went in to take down the ark, and make it up for carriage; for (as the learned bishop Patrick suggests) the *shechinah,* or display of the divine majesty, which was over the mercy-seat, removed for the present in the pillar of cloud, which was taken up, and then the ark was not dangerous to be approached. (2.) All the holy things must be covered, the ark and table with three coverings, all the rest with two. Even the ashes of the altar, in which the holy fire was carefully preserved and raked up, must have a purple cloth spread over them, *v.* 13. Even the brazen altar, though in the court of the sanctuary it stood open to the view of all, yet was covered in the carriage of it. All these coverings were designed, [1.] For safety, that these holy things might not be ruffled with the wind, sullied with the rain, nor tarnished with the sun, but that they might be preserved in their beauty; for *on all the glory shall be a defence.* The coverings of badgers' skins, being thick and strong, would keep out wet; and, while we are in our passage through the wilderness of this world, it concerns us to be fenced *for all weathers,* Isa. 4:5, 6. [2.] For decency and ornament. Most of these things had a cloth of blue, or purple, or scarlet, spread outmost; and the ark was covered with a cloth *wholly of blue* (*v.* 6), an emblem (say some) of the azure skies, which are spread like a curtain between us and the Majesty on high, Job 26:9. Those that are faithful to God should endeavour likewise to appear beautiful before men, that they may *adorn the doctrine of God our Saviour.* [3.] For concealment. It signified the darkness of that dispensation. That which is now brought to light by the gospel, and revealed to babes, was then hidden from the wise and prudent. They saw only the coverings, not the holy things themselves (Heb. 10:1); but now Christ has *destroyed the face of the covering,* Isa. 25:7. (3.) When all the holy things were covered, then the Kohathites were to carry them on their shoulders. These things that had staves were carried by their staves (*v.* 6, 8, 11, 14); those that had not were carried upon a bar, or bier, or bearing barrow, *v.* 10, 12. See how the tokens of God's presence in this world are movable things; but we look for a kingdom that cannot be moved.

2. Eleazar, now the eldest son of Aaron, is appointed overseer of the Kohathites in this service (*v.* 16); he must take care that nothing was forgotten, left behind, or displaced. As a priest he had more honour than the Levites, but then he had more care; and that care was a heavier burden, no doubt, upon his heart, than all the burdens that were laid upon their shoulders. It is much easier to do the work of the tabernacle than to discharge the trusts of it, to obey than to rule.

3. Great care must be taken to preserve the lives of these Levites, by preventing their unseasonable irreverent approach to the most holy things: *Cut you not off the Kohathites, v.* 18. Note, Those who do not what they can to keep others from sin do what they can to cut them off. [1.] The Kohathites must not see the holy things till the priests had covered them, *v.* 20. Even those that bore the vessels of the Lord saw not what they bore, so much were even those in the dark concerning the gospel whose office it was to expound the law. And, [2.] When the holy things were covered, they might not touch them, at least not the ark, called here *the holy thing,* upon pain of death, *v.* 15. Uzza was struck dead for the breach of this law. Thus were the Lord's ministers themselves then kept in fear, and that was a dispensation of terror, as well as darkness; but

now, through Christ, the case is altered; we have *seen with our eyes,* and our *hands have handles, the word of life* (1 Jn. 1:1), and we are encouraged to *come boldly to the throne of grace.*

Verses 21–33

We have here the charge of the other two families of the Levites, which, though not so honourable as the first, yet was necessary, and was to be done regularly. 1. The Gershonites were charged with all the drapery of the tabernacle, the curtains, and hangings, and the coverings of badgers' skins, *v.* 22–26. These they were to take down when the cloud removed, and the ark and the rest of the holy things were carried away, to pack up and bring with them, and then to set up again, where the cloud rested. Aaron and his sons allotted to them their respective charge: "You shall take care of such a curtain, and you of such a hanging, that every one may know his work, and there may be no confusion," *v.* 27. Ithamar particularly was to take the oversight of them, *v.* 28. 2. The Merarites were charged with the heavy carriage, the boards and bars, the pillars and sockets, the pins and cords, and these were delivered to them by name, *v.* 31, 32. An inventory was given them of every particular, that it might be forthcoming, and nothing to seek, when the tabernacle was to be set up again. Though these seemed of less importance than the other things pertaining to the sanctuary, yet there was this care taken of them, to teach us with the greatest exactness to preserve pure and entire all divine institutions, and to take care that nothing be lost. It also intimates the care God takes of his church, and every member of it; the good Shepherd *calls his own sheep by name,* Jn. 10:3. Here were thousands of men employed about these services, though a much less number would have served for the bearing of those burdens; but it was requisite that the tabernacle should be taken down, and set up, with great expedition, and many hands would make quick work, especially when every one knew his work. They had tents of their own to take care of, and to take along with them, but the young men under thirty, and the old men above fifty, might serve for them; nor is there any mention of them, for God's house must always be preferred before our own. Their care was preposterous who built and ceiled their own houses while God's house lay waste, Hag. 1:4, 9. The death of the saints is represented as the taking down of the tabernacle (2 Co. 5:1), and the putting of it off, 2 Pt. 1:14. The immortal soul, like the most holy things, is first covered and taken away, carried by angels, unseen, under the inspection of the Lord Jesus, our Eleazar. Care is also taken of the body — the skin and flesh, which are as the curtains, the bones and sinews which are as the bars and pillars; none of these shall be lost; commandment is given concerning the bones, a covenant made with the dust; these are in safe custody, and shall all be produced in the great day, when this tabernacle shall be set up again, and these vile bodies made like the glorious body of Jesus Christ.

Verses 34–49

We have here a particular account of the numbers of the three families of the Levites respectively, that is, of the effective men, between thirty years old and fifty. Observe, 1. The Kohathites were, in all, 8600 from a month old and upwards; but of these there were but 2750 serviceable men, not a third part. The Gershonites, in all, 7500, and of them but 2630 serviceable men, little more than a third part. Note, Of the many that add to the numbers of the church, there are comparatively but few that contribute to the service of it. So it has been, and so it is; many have a place in the tabernacle that do but little of the work of the tabernacle, Phil. 2:20, 21. 2. That the Merarites were but 6200 in all, and yet of these there were 3200 serviceable men, that is, more than half. The greatest burden lay upon that family, the boards, and pillars, and sockets; and God so ordered it that, though they were the fewest in number, yet they should have the most able men among them; for whatever service God calls men to he will furnish them for it, and give strength in proportion to the work, grace sufficient. 3. The whole number of the able men of the tribe of Levi who entered into God's host to war his warfare was but 8580, whereas the able men of the other tribes that entered into the host of Israel to war their warfare were many more. The least of the tribes had almost four times as many able men as the Levites, and some of them more than eight times as many; for those that are engaged in the service of this world, and war after the flesh, are many more than those that are devoted to the service of God, and *fight the good fight of faith.*

CHAPTER 5

In this chapter we have, I. An order, pursuant to the laws already made, for the removing of the unclean out of the camp (*v.* 1–4). II. A repetition of the laws concerning restitution, in case of wrong done to a neighbour (*v.* 5–8), and concerning the appropriating of the hallowed things to the priests (*v.* 9, 10). III. A new law made concerning the trial of a wife suspected of adultery, by the waters of jealousy (*v.* 11, etc.).

Verses 1–10

Here is, I. A command for the purifying of the camp, by turning out from within its lines all those that were ceremonially unclean, by issues, leprosies, or the touch of dead bodies, until they were cleansed according to the law, *v.* 2, 3.

1. These orders are executed immediately, *v.* 4. (1.) The camp was now newly-modelled and put in order, and therefore, to complete the reformation of it, it is next to be cleansed. Note, The purity of the church must be as carefully consulted and preserved as the peace and order of it. It is requisite, not only that every Israelite be confined to his own standard, but that every polluted Israelite be separated from it. *The wisdom from above is first pure, then peaceable.* (2.) God's tabernacle was now fixed in the midst of their camp, and therefore they must be careful to keep it clean. Note, The greater profession of religion any house or family make the more they are obliged to *put away iniquity far from their tabernacle,* Job 22:23. The person, the place, *in the midst of which God dwells,* must not be defiled; for, if it be, he will be affronted, offended, and provoked to withdraw, 1 Co. 3:16, 17.

2. This expulsion of the unclean out of the camp was to signify, (1.) What the governors of the church ought to do: they must *separate between the precious and the vile,* and purge out scandalous persons, as old leaven (1 Co. 5:8, 13), lest others should be infected and defiled, Heb. 12:15. It is for the glory of Christ and the edification of his church that those who are openly and incorrigibly profane and vicious should be put out and kept from Christian communion till they repent. (2.) What God himself will do in the great day: he will *thoroughly purge his floor,* and *gather out of his kingdom all things that offend.* As here the unclean were shut out of the camp, so into the new Jerusalem *no unclean thing shall enter,* Rev. 21:27.

II. A law concerning restitution, in case of wrong done to a neighbour. It is called *a sin that men commit* (*v.* 6), because it is common among men; *a sin of man,* that is, *a sin against man,* so it is thought it should be translated and understood. If a man overreach or defraud his brother in any matter, it is to be looked upon as a trespass against the Lord, who is the protector of right, the punisher of wrong, and who strictly charges and commands us to do justly. Now what is to be done when a man's awakened conscience charges him with guilt of this kind, and brings it to his remembrance though done long ago? 1. He must *confess his sin,* confess it to God, confess it to his neighbour, and so take shame to himself. If he have denied it before, though it go against the grain to own himself in a lie, yet he must do it; because his heart was hardened he denied it, therefore he has no other way of making it appear that his heart is now softened but by confessing it. 2. He must bring a sacrifice, a *ram of atonement,* *v.* 8. Satisfaction must be made for the offence done to God, whose law is broken, as well as for the loss sustained by our neighbour; restitution in this case is not sufficient without faith and repentance. 3. Yet the sacrifices would not be accepted till full amends were made to the party wronged, not only the principal, but a fifth part added to it, *v.* 7. It is certain that while that which is got by injustice is knowingly retained in the hands the guilt of the injustice remains upon the conscience, and is not purged by sacrifice nor offering, prayers not tears, for it is one and the same continued act of sin persisted in. This law we had before (Lev. 6:4), and it is here added that if the party wronged was dead, and he had no near kinsman who was entitled to the debt, or if it was any way uncertain to whom the restitution should be made, this should not serve for an excuse to detain what was unjustly gotten; to whomsoever it pertained, it was certainly none of his that got it by sin, and therefore it must be given to the priest, *v.* 8. If there were any that could make out a title to it, it must not be given to the priest (God hates robbery for burnt-offerings); but, if there were not, then it lapsed to the great Lord *(ob defectum sanguinis — for want of issue),* and the priests were his receivers. Note, Some work of piety or charity is a piece of necessary justice to be done by those who are conscience to themselves that they have done wrong, but know not how otherwise to make restitution; what is not our property will never be our profit.

III. A general rule concerning hallowed things given upon this occasion, that, whatever was given to the priest, *his it shall be, v.* 9, 10. 1. He that gave it was not to receive his gift again upon any pretence whatsoever. This law ratifies and confirms all grants for pious uses, that people might not give things to the priests in a fit of zeal, and then recall them in a fit of vexation. 2. The other priests should not come in sharers with that priest who then officiated, and to whom the hallowed thing, whatever it was, was given. Let him that was most ready and diligent in attending fare the better for it: if he do the work, let him have the pay, and much good may it do him.

Verses 11–31

We have here the law concerning the solemn trial of a wife whose husband was jealous of her. Observe,

I. What was the case supposed: That a man had some reason to suspect his wife to have committed adultery, *v.* 12–14. Here, 1. The sin of adultery is justly represented as an exceedingly sinful sin; it is going aside from God and virtue, and the good way, Prov. 2:17. It is committing a trespass against the husband, robbing him of his honour, alienating his right, introducing a spurious breed into his family to share with his children in his estate, and violating her covenant with him. It is being defiled; for nothing pollutes the mind and conscience more than this sin does. 2. It is supposed to be a sin which great care is taken by the sinners to conceal, which there is no witness of. *The eye of the adulterer waits for the twilight,* Job 24:15. And the adulteress takes her opportunity when *the good man is not at home,* Prov. 7:19. It would not covet to be secret if it were not shameful; and the devil who draws sinners to this sin teaches them how to cover it. 3. The *spirit of jealousy* is supposed to come upon the husband, of which Solomon says, It is the *rage of a man* (Prov. 6:34), and that it is *cruel as the grave,* Cant. 8:6. 4. "Yet" (say the Jewish writers) "he must make it appear that he has some just cause for the suspicion." The rule they give is, "If the husband have said unto his wife before witnesses, 'Be not thou in secret with such a man;' and, notwithstanding that admonition, it is afterwards proved that she was in secret with that man, though her father or her brother, then he may compel her to drink the bitter water." But the law here does not tie him to that particular method of proving the just cause of his suspicion; it might be otherwise proved. In case it could be proved that she had committed adultery, she was to be put to death (Lev. 20:10); but, if it was uncertain, then this law took place. Hence, (1.) Let all wives be admonished not to give any the least occasion for the suspicion of their chastity; it is not enough that they abstain from the evil of uncleanness, but they must abstain from all appearance of it, from every thing that looks like it, or leads to it, or may give the least umbrage to jealousy; for *how great a matter* may a *little fire kindle!* (2.) Let all husbands be admonished not to entertain any causeless or unjust suspicions of their wives. If charity in general, much more conjugal affection, teaches to *think no evil,* 1 Co. 13:5. It is the happiness of the virtuous woman that *the heart of her husband does safely trust in her,* Prov. 31:11.

II. What was the course prescribed in this case, that, if the suspected wife was innocent, she might not continue under the reproach and uneasiness of her husband's jealousy, and, if guilty, her sin might find her out, and others might hear, and fear, and take warning.

1. The process of the trial must be thus: — (1.) Her husband must *bring her to the priest,* with the witnesses that could prove the ground of his suspicion, and desire that she might be put upon her trial. The Jews say that the priest was first to endeavour to persuade her to confess

the truth, saying to this purport, "Dear daughter, perhaps thou wast overtaken by drinking wine, or wast carried away by the heat of youth or the examples of bad neighbours; come, confess the truth, for the sake of his great name which is described in the most sacred ceremony, and do not let it be blotted out with the bitter water." If she confessed, saying, "I am defiled," she was not put to death, but was divorced and lost her dowry; if she said, "I am pure," then they proceeded. (2.) He must bring a coarse offering of barley-meal, without oil or frankincense, agreeably to the present afflicted state of his family; for a great affliction it was either to have cause to be jealous or to be jealous without cause. It is an *offering of memorial,* to signify that what was to be done was intended as a religious appeal to the omniscience and justice of God. (3.) The priest was to prepare the water of jealousy, the holy water out of the laver at which the priests were to wash when they ministered; this must be brought in an *earthen vessel,* containing (they say) about a pint; and it must be an *earthen* vessel, because the coarser and plainer every thing was the more agreeable it was to the occasion. *Dust* must be put into the water, to signify the reproach she lay under, and the shame she ought to take to herself, putting her mouth in the dust; but dust from *the floor of the tabernacle,* to put an honour upon every thing that pertained to the place God had chosen to put his name there, and to keep up in the people a reverence for it; see Jn. 8:6. (4.) The woman was to be *set before the Lord,* at the east gate of the temple-court (say the Jews), and her head was to be uncovered, in token of her sorrowful condition; and there she stood for a spectacle to the world, that other women might learn not to do *after her lewdness,* Eze. 23:48. Only the Jews say, "Her own servants were not to be present, that she might not seem vile in their sight, who were to give honour to her; her husband also must be dismissed." (5.) The priest was to adjure her to tell the truth, and to denounce the curse of God against her if she were guilty, and to declare what would be the effect of her drinking the water of jealousy, *v.* 19–22. He must assure her that, if she were innocent, the water would do her no harm, *v.* 19. None need fear the curse of the law if they have not broken the commands of the law. But, if she were guilty, this water would be poison to her, it would make her *belly to swell and her thigh to rot,* and she should be a curse or abomination among her people, *v.* 21, 22. To this she must say, *Amen,* as Israel must do to the curses pronounced on mount Ebal, Deu. 27:15–26. Some think the *Amen,* being doubled, respects both parts of the adjuration, both that which freed her if innocent and that which condemned her if guilty. No woman, if she were guilty, could say *Amen* to this adjuration, and drink the water upon it, unless she disbelieved the truth of God or defied his justice, and had come to such a pitch of impudence and hard-heartedness in sin as to challenge God Almighty to do his worst, and choose rather to venture upon his curse than to give him glory by making confession; thus has whoredom *taken away the heart.* (6.) The priest was to write this curse in a scrip or scroll o parchment, *verbatim — word for word,* as he had expressed it, and then to wipe or scrape out what he had written into the water (*v.* 23), to signify that it was that curse which impregnated the water, and gave it its strength to effect what was intended. It signified that, if she were innocent, the curse should be blotted out and never appear against her, as it is written, Isa. 43:25, *I am he that blotteth out thy transgression,* and Ps. 51:9, *Blot out my iniquities;* but that, if she were guilty, the curse, as it was written, being infused into the water, would enter into her bowels with the water, even *like oil into her bones* (Ps. 109:18), as we read of a curse entering into a house, Zec. 5:4. (7.) The woman must then drink the water (*v.* 24); it is called *the bitter water,* some think because they put wormwood in it to make it bitter, or rather because it caused the curse. Thus sin is called *an evil thing and a bitter* for the same reason, because it *causeth the curse,* Jer. 2:19. If she had been guilty (and otherwise it did not cause the curse), she was made to know that though her stolen waters had been sweet, and her *bread eaten in secret pleasant,* yet the end was *bitter as wormwood,* Prov. 9:17, and *ch.* 5:4. Let all that meddle with forbidden pleasures know that they will be bitterness in the latter end. The Jews say that if, upon denouncing the curse, the woman was so terrified that she durst not drink the water, but confessed she was defiled, the priest flung down the water, and cast her offering among the ashes, and she was divorced without dowry: if she confessed not, and yet would not drink, they forced her to it; and, if she was ready to throw it up again, they hastened her away, that she might not pollute the holy place. (8.) Before she drank the water, the jealousy-offering was waved and offered upon the altar (*v.* 25, 26); a handful of it was burnt for a memorial, and the remainder of it eaten by the priest, unless the husband was a priest, and then it was scattered among the ashes. This offering in the midst of the transaction signified that the whole was an appeal to God, as a God that knows all things, and *from whom no secret is hid.* (9.) All things being thus performed according to the law, they were to wait the issue. The water, with a little dust put into it, and the scrapings of a written parchment, had no natural tendency at all to do either good or hurt; but if God was thus appealed to in the way of an instituted ordinance, though otherwise the innocent might have continued under suspicion and the guilty undiscovered, yet God would so far own his own institution as that in a little time, by the miraculous operation of Providence, the innocency of the innocent should be cleared, and the sin of the guilty should find them out. [1.] If the suspected woman was really guilty, the water she drank would be poison to her (*v.* 37), her belly would swell and her thigh rot by a vile disease for vile deserts, and she would *mourn at the last when her flesh and body were consumed,* Prov. 5:11. Bishop Patrick says, from some of the Jewish writers, that the effect of these waters appeared immediately, she grew pale, and her eyes ready to start out of her head. Dr. Lightfoot says that sometimes it appeared not for two or three years, but she bore no children, was sickly, languished, and rotted at last; it is probable that some indications appeared immediately. The rabbin say that the adulterer also died in the same day and hour that the adulteress did, and in the same manner too, that he belly swelled, and his secret parts rotted: a disease perhaps not much unlike that which in these latter ages the avenging hand of a righteous God has made the scourge of uncleanness, and with which whores and whoremongers infect, and plague, and ruin one another, since they escape punishment from men. The Jewish doctors add that the waters had this effect upon the adulteress only in case the husband had never offended in the same kind; but that, if he had at any time defiled the marriage-bed, God did not thus right him against his injurious wife; and that therefore in the latter and degenerate ages of the Jewish church, when uncleanness did abound, this way of trial was generally disused and laid aside; men, knowing their own crimes, were content not to know their wives' crimes. And to this perhaps may refer the threatening (Hos. 4:14), *I will not punish your spouses when they commit adultery, for you yourselves are separated with whores.* [2.] If she were innocent, the water she drank would be physic to her: *She shall be free, and shall conceive seed, v.* 28. The Jewish writers magnify the good effects of this water to the innocent woman, that, to recompense her for the wrong done to her by the suspicion, she should, after the drinking of these waters, be stronger and look better than ever; if she was sickly, she should become healthful, should bear a man-child, and have easy labour.

2. From the whole we may learn, (1.) That secret sins are known to God, and sometimes are strangely brought to light in this life; however, there is a day coming when God will, by Jesus Christ, as here by the priest, judge the *secrets of men according to the gospel,* Rom. 2:16. (2.) That, in particular, *Whoremongers and adulterers God will judge.* The violation of conjugal faith and chastity is highly provoking to the God of heaven, and sooner or later it will be reckoned for. Though we have not now the waters of jealousy to be a sensible terror to the unclean, yet we have a word from God which ought to be as great a terror, that if *any man defile the temple of God, him shall God destroy,* 1 Co. 3:17. (3.) That God will find out some way or other to clear the innocency of the innocent, and to bring forth their righteousness as the light. (4.) That to *the pure all things are pure,* but *to the defiled nothing* is so, Tit. 1:15. The same word is to some a *savour of life unto life, to others a savour of death unto death,* like those waters of jealousy, according as they receive it; the same providence is for good to some and for hurt to others, Jer. 24:5, 8, 9. And, whatsoever it is intended for, it *shall not return void.*

CHAPTER 6

In this chapter we have, I. The law concerning Nazarites, 1. What it was to which the vow of a Nazarite obliged him (*v.* 1–8). 2. A remedial law in case a Nazarite happened to be polluted by the touch of a dead body (*v.* 9–12). 3. The solemnity of his discharge when his time was up (*v.* 13–21). II. Instructions given to the priests how they should bless the people (*v.* 22, etc.).

Verses 1–21

After the law for the discovery and shame of those that by sin had made themselves vile, fitly follows this for the direction and encouragement of those who by their eminent piety and devotion had made themselves honourable, and distinguished themselves from their neighbours. It is very probable that there were those before the making of this law who went under the character of *Nazarites,* and were celebrated by that title as persons professing greater strictness and zeal in religion than other people; for the vow of a Nazarite is spoken of here as a thing already well known, but the obligation of it is reduced to a greater certainty than hitherto it had been. Joseph is called a Nazarite among his brethren (Gen. 49:26), not only because separate from them, but because eminent among them. Observe,

I. The general character of a Nazarite: it is a person *separated unto the Lord, v.* 2. Some were Nazarites for life, either by divine designation, as Samson (Jdg. 13:5), and John Baptist (Lu. 1:15), or by their parents' vow concerning them, as Samuel, 1 Sa. 1:11. Of these this law speaks not. Others were so for a certain time, and by their own voluntary engagement, and concerning them rules are given by this law. A woman might bind herself with the vow of a Nazarite, under the limitations we find, *ch.* 30:3, where the vow which the woman is supposed to vow unto the Lord seems to be meant especially of this vow. The Nazarites were, 1. Devoted to the Lord during the time of their Nazariteship, and, it is probable, spent much of their time in the study of the law, in acts of devotion, and instructing others. An air of piety was thereby put upon them, and upon their whole conversation. 2. They were separated from common persons and common things. Those that are consecrated to God must not be conformed to this world. They distinguished themselves, not only from others, but from what they themselves were before and after. 3. They separated themselves by vowing a vow. Every Israelite was bound by the divine law to love God with all his heart, but the Nazarites by their own act and deed bound themselves to some religious observances, as fruits and expressions of that love, which other Israelites were not bound to. Some such there were, whose spirits God stirred up to be in their day the ornaments of the church, the standard-bearers of religion, and patterns of piety. It is spoken of as a great favour to their nation that God *raised up of their young men for Nazarites,* Amos 2:11. The Nazarites were known in the streets and respected as *purer than snow, whiter than milk,* Lam. 4:7. Christ was called in reproach a Nazarene, so were his followers: but he was no Nazarite according to this law; he drank wine, and touched dead bodies, yet in his this type had its accomplishment, for in him all purity and perfection met; and every true Christian is a spiritual Nazarite, separated by vow unto the Lord. We find St. Paul, by the persuasion of his friends, in complaisance to the Jews, submitting to this law of the Nazarites; but at the same time it is declared that the Gentiles should *observe no such thing,* Acts 21:24, 25. It was looked upon as a great honour to a man to be a Nazarite, and therefore if a man speak of it as a punishment, saying for instance, "I will be a Nazarite rather than do so or so," he is (say the Jews) a wicked man; but he that vows unto the Lord in the way of holiness to be a Nazarite, lo, *the crown of his God is upon his head.*

II. The particular obligations that the Nazarites lay under. That the fancies of superstitious men might not multiply their restraints endlessly, God himself lays down the law for them, and gives them the rule of their profession.

1. They must have nothing to do with *the fruit of the vine, v.* 3, 4. They must drink no wine nor string drink, nor eat grapes, no, not the kernel nor the husk; they might not so much as eat a raisin. The learned Dr. Lightfoot has

a conjecture (Hor. Heb. in Luc. 1.15), that, as the ceremonial pollutions by leprosy and otherwise represented the sinful state of fallen man, so the institution of the order of Nazarites was designed to represent the pure and perfect state of man in innocency, and that the tree of knowledge, forbidden to Adam, was the vine, and for that reason it was forbidden to the Nazarites, and all the produce of it. Those who gave the Nazarites wine to drink did the tempter's work (Amos 2:12), persuading them to that forbidden fruit. That it was reckoned a perfection and praise not to drink wine appears from the instance of the Rechabites, Jer. 35:6. They were to *drink no wine,* (1.) That they might be examples of temperance and mortification. Those that separate themselves to God and to his honour must not gratify the desires of the body, but keep it under and bring it into subjection. Drinking *a little wine for the stomach's sake* is allowed, to help that, 1 Tim. 5:23. But drinking much wine for the *palate's sake,* to please that, does by no means become those who profess to walk not *after the flesh, but after the Spirit.* (2.) That they might be qualified to employ themselves in the service of God. They must not drink, lest they should *forget the law* (Prov. 31:5), lest they should *err through wine,* Isa. 28:7. Let all Christians oblige themselves to be very moderate in the use of wine and strong drink; for, if the love of these once gets the mastery of a man, he becomes a very easy prey to Satan. It is observable that because they were to drink no wine (which was the thing mainly intended) they were to eat nothing that came of the vine, to teach us with the utmost care and caution to avoid sin and every thing that borders upon it and leads to it, or may be a temptation to us. *Abstain from all appearance of evil,* 1 Th. 5:22.

2. They must not *cut their hair, v.* 5. They must neither poll their heads nor shave their beards; this was that mark of Samson's Nazariteship which we often read of in his story. Now, (1.) This signified a noble neglect of the body and the ease and ornament of it, which became those who, being separated to God, ought to be wholly taken up with their souls, to secure their peace and beauty. It signified that they had, for the present, renounced all sorts of sensual pleasures and delights, and resolved to live a life of self-denial and mortification. Mephibosheth in sorrow *trimmed not his beard,* 2 Sa. 19:24. (2.) Some observe that long hair is spoken of as a badge of subjection (1 Co. 11:5, etc.); so that the long hair of the Nazarites denoted their subjection to God, and their putting themselves under his dominion. (3.) By this they were known to all that met them to be Nazarites, and so it commanded respect. It made them look great without art; it was nature's crown to the head, and a testimony for them that they had preserved their purity. For, if they had been defiled, their hair must have been cut, *v.* 9. See Jer. 7:29.

3. They must not come near any dead body, *v.* 6, 7. Others might touch dead bodies, and contracted only a ceremonial pollution by it for some time; some must do it, else the dead must be unburied; but the Nazarites must not do it, upon pain of forfeiting all the honour of their Nazariteship. They must not attend the funeral of any relation, no, not father nor mother, any more than the high priest himself, because *the consecration of his God is upon his head.* Those that separate themselves to God must learn, (1.) To distinguish themselves, and do more than others. (2.) To keep their consciences pure from dead works, and not to touch the unclean thing. The greater profession of religion we make, and the more eminent we appear, the greater care we must take to avoid all sin, for we have so much the more honour to lose by it. (3.) To moderate their affections even to their near relations, so as not to let their sorrow for the loss of them break in upon their joy in God and submission to his will. See Mt. 8:21, 22.

4. All *the days of their separation* they must be *holy to the Lord, v.* 8. This was the meaning of those external observances, and without this they were of no account. The Nazarites must be devoted to God, employed for him, and their minds intent upon him; they must keep themselves pure in heart and life, and be in every thing conformable to the divine image and will; this is to be holy, this is to be a Nazarite indeed.

III. The provision that was made for the cleansing of a Nazarite, if he happened unavoidably to contract a ceremonial pollution by the touch of a dead body. No penalty is ordered by this law for the wilful breach of the fore-

going laws; for it was not supposed that a man who had so much religion as to make that vow could have so little as to break it presumptuously: nor could it be supposed that he should drink wine, or have his hair cut, but by his own fault; but purely by the providence of God, without any fault of his own, he might be near a dead body, and that is the case put (*v.* 9): *If a man die very suddenly by him, he has defiled the head of his consecration.* Note, Death sometimes takes men away very suddenly, and without any previous warning. A man might be well and dead in so little a time that the most careful Nazarite could not avoid being polluted by the dead body; so short a step is it sometimes, and so soon taken, from time to eternity. God prepare us for sudden death! In this case, 1. He must be purified from the ceremonial pollution he had contracted, as others must, upon the seventh day, *v.* 9. Nay, more was required for the purifying of the Nazarite than of any other person that had touched a dead body; he must bring a sin-offering and a burnt-offering, and an atonement must be *made for him, v.* 10, 11. This teaches us that sins of infirmity, and the faults we are overtaken in by surprise, must be seriously repented of, and that an application must be made of the virtue of Christ's sacrifice to our souls for the forgiveness of them every day, 1 Jn. 2:1, 2. It teaches us also that, if those who make an eminent profession of religion do any thing to sully the reputation of their profession, more is expected from them than others, for the retrieving both of their peace and of their credit. 2. He must begin the days of his separation again; for all that were past before his pollution, though coming ever so near the period of his time set, were lost, and not reckoned to him, *v.* 12. This obliged them to be very careful not to defile themselves by the dead, for that was the only thing that made them lose their time, and it teaches us that *if a righteous man turn away from his righteousness,* and defile himself with dead works, all his righteousness that he has done shall be lost to him, Eze. 33:13. It is all lost, all in vain, if he do not persevere, Gal. 3:4. He must begin again, and do his first works.

IV. The law for the solemn discharge of a Nazarite from his vow, when he had completed the time he fixed to himself. Before the expiration of that term he could not be discharged; before he vowed, it was in his own power, but it was too late after the vow to make enquiry. The Jews say that the time of a Nazarite's vow could not be less than thirty days; and if a man said, "I will be a Nazarite but for two days," yet he was bound for thirty; but it should seem Paul's vow was for only seven days (Acts 21:27), or, rather, then he observed the ceremony of finishing that vow of Nazariteship from which, being at a distance from the temple, he had discharged himself some years before at Cenchrea only by the ceremony of cutting his hair, Acts 18:18. When the time of the vowed separation was out, he was to be made free, 1. Publicly, *at the door of the tabernacle* (*v.* 13), that all might take notice of the finishing of his vow, and none might be offended if they saw him now drink wine, who had so lately refused. 2. It was to be done with sacrifices, *v.* 14. Lest he should think that by this eminent piece of devotion he had made God a debtor to him, he is appointed, even when he had finished his vow, to bring an offering to God; for, when we have done our utmost in duty to God, still we must own ourselves behind-hand with him. He must bring one of each sort of the instituted offerings. (1.) A burnt-offering, as an acknowledgment of God's sovereign dominion over him and all he had still, notwithstanding his discharge from this particular vow. (2.) A sin-offering. This, though mentioned second (*v.* 14), yet seems to have been offered first (*v.* 16), for atonement must be made for our sins before any of our sacrifices can be accepted. And it is very observable that even the Nazarite, who in the eye of men was *purer than snow* and *whiter than milk,* yet durst not appear before the holy God without a sin-offering. Though he had fulfilled the vow of his separation without any pollution, yet he must bring a sacrifice for sin; for there is guilt insensibly contracted by the best of men, even in their best works — some good omitted, some ill admitted, which, if we were dealt with in strict justice, would be our ruin, and in consequence of which it is necessary for us to receive the atonement, and plead it as our righteousness before God. (3.) A peace-offering, in thankfulness to God who had enabled him to fulfil his vow, and in supplication

to God for grace to preserve him from ever doing any thing unbecoming one that had been once a Nazarite, remembering that, though he was now freed from the bonds of his own vow, he still remained under the bonds of the divine law. (4.) To these were added the meat-offerings and drink-offerings, according to the manner (*v.* 15, 17), for these always accompanied the burnt-offerings and peace-offerings: and, besides these, a basket of unleavened cakes, and wafers. (5.) Part of the peace-offering, with a cake and wafer, was to be waved for a wave-offering (*v.* 19, 20); and this was a gratuity to the priest, who had it for his pains, after it had been first presented to God. (6.) Besides all this, he might bring his free-will offerings, *such as his hand shall get, v.* 21. More than this he might bring, but not less. And, to grace the solemnity, it was common upon this occasion to have their friends to be at *charges with them,* Acts 21:24. *Lastly,* One ceremony more was appointed, which was like the cancelling of the bond when the condition is performed, and that was the *cutting off of his hair,* which had been suffered to grow all the time of his being a Nazarite, and burning it in the fire over which the peace-offerings were boiling, *v.* 18. This intimated that his full performance of his vow was acceptable to God in Christ the great sacrifice, and not otherwise. Learn hence to *vow and pay to the Lord our God,* for *he has no pleasure in fools.*

Verses 22–27

Here, I. The priests, among other good offices which they were to do, are appointed solemnly to bless the people in the *name of the Lord, v.* 23. It was part of their work, Deu. 21:5. Hereby God put an honour upon the priests, for *the less is blessed of the better;* and hereby he gave great comfort and satisfaction to the people, who looked upon the priest as God's mouth to them. Though the priests of himself could do no more than beg a blessing, yet being an intercessor by office, and doing that in his name who commands the blessing, the prayer carried with it a promise, and he pronounced it as one having authority with his hands lifted up and his face towards the people. Now, 1. This was a type of Christ's errand into the world, which was to *bless us* (Acts 3:26), as the high priest of our profession. The last thing he did on earth was with uplifted hands to bless his disciples, Lu. 24:50, 51. The learned bishop Pearson observes it as a tradition of the Jews that the priests blessed the people only at the close of the morning sacrifice, not of the evening sacrifice, to show (says he) that in the last days, the days of the Messiah, which are (as it were) the evening of the world, the benediction of the law should cease, and the blessing of Christ should take place. 2. It was a pattern to gospel ministers, the masters of assemblies, who are in like manner to dismiss their solemn assemblies with a blessing. The same that are God's mouth to his people, to teach and command them, are his mouth likewise to bless them; and those that receive the law shall receive the blessing. The Hebrew doctors warn the people that they say not, "What availeth the blessing of this poor simple priest? For," say they, "the receiving of the blessing depends, not on the priest, but on the holy blessed God."

II. A form of blessing is here prescribed them. In their other devotions no form was prescribed, but this being God's command concerning benediction, that it might not look like any thing of their own, he puts the very words in their mouths, *v.* 24–26. Here observe, 1. That the blessing is commanded upon each particular person: *The Lord bless thee.* They must each of them prepare themselves to receive the blessing, and then they should find enough in it to make them every man happy. *Blessed shalt thou be,* Deu. 28:3. If we take the law to ourselves, we may take the blessing to ourselves, as if our names were inserted. 2. That the name *Jehovah* is three times repeated in it, and (as the critics observe) each with a different accent in the original; the Jews themselves think there is some mystery in this, and we know what it is, the New Testament having explained it, which directs us to expect the blessing from *the grace of our Lord Jesus Christ, the love of the Father, and the communion of the Holy Ghost,* each of which persons is Jehovah, and yet they are "not three Lords, but one Lord," 2 Co. 13:14. 3. That the favour of God is all in all in this blessing, for that is the fountain of all good. (1.) *The Lord bless thee!* Our blessing God is only our speaking well of him; his blessing us is doing well for us; those whom he blesses are blessed indeed. (2.) *The Lord make his face shine upon thee,* alluding to the shining of the sun upon the earth, to enlighten and comfort it, and to renew the face of it. "The Lord love thee and cause thee to know that he loves thee." We cannot but be happy if we have God's love; and we cannot but be easy if we know that we have it. (3.) *The Lord lift up his countenance upon thee.* This is to the same purport with the former, and it seems to allude to the smiles of a father upon his child, or of a man upon his friend whom he takes pleasure in. If God give us the assurances of his special favour and his acceptance of us, this will *put gladness into the heart,* Ps. 4:7, 8. 4. That the fruits of this favour conveyed by this blessing are protection, pardon, and peace. (1.) Protection from evil, v. 24. The Lord *keep thee,* for it is he that keeps Israel, and neither *slumbers nor sleeps* (Ps. 121:4), and all believers are *kept by the power of God.* (2.) Pardon of sin, v. 25. The Lord be *gracious,* or *merciful,* unto thee. (3.) Peace (v. 26), including all that good which goes to make up a complete happiness.

III. God here promises to ratify and confirm the blessing: *They shall put my name upon the children of Israel,* v. 27. God gives them leave to make use of his name in blessing the people, and to bless them as his people, called by his name. This included all the blessings they could pronounce upon them, to mark them for God's peculiar, the people of his choice and love. God's name upon them was their honour, their comfort, their safety, their plea. *We are called by thy name, leave us not.* It is added, *and I will bless them.* Note, A divine blessing goes along with divine institutions, and puts virtue and efficacy into them. What Christ says of the peace is true of the blessing, "Peace to this congregation," if the sons of peace and heirs of blessing be there, the peace, the blessing, shall rest upon them, Lu. 10:5, 6. For in *every place where God records his name* he will *meet his people and bless them.*

CHAPTER 7

God having set up house (as it were) in the midst of the camp of Israel, the princes of Israel here come a visiting with their presents, as tenants to their landlord, in the name of their respective tribes. I. They brought presents, 1. Upon the dedication of the tabernacle, for the service of that (v. 1–9). 2. Upon the dedication of the altar, for the use of that (v. 10–88). And, II. God graciously signified his acceptance of them (v. 89). The two foregoing chapters were the records of additional laws which God gave to Israel, this is the history of the additional services which Israel performed to God.

Verses 1–9

Here is the offering of the princes to the service of the tabernacle. Observe,

I. When it was; not till it was *fully set up,* v. 1. When all things were done both about the tabernacle itself, and the camp of Israel which surrounded it, according to the directions given, then they began their presents, probably about the eighth day of the second month. Note, Necessary observances must always take place of free-will offerings: first those, and then these.

II. Who it was that offered: *The princes of Israel, heads of the house of their fathers,* v. 2. Note, Those that are above others in power and dignity ought to go before others, and endeavour to go beyond them, in every thing that is good. The more any are advanced the more is expected from them, on account of the greater opportunity they have of serving God and their generation. What are wealth and authority good for, but as they enable a man to do so much the more good in the world?

III. What was offered: six wagons, with each of them a yoke of oxen to draw them, v. 3. Doubtless these wagons were agreeable to the rest of the furniture of the tabernacle and its appurtenances, the best of the kind, like the carriages which great princes use when they go in procession. Some think that God, by Moses, intimated to them what they should bring, or their own consideration perhaps suggested to them to make this present. Though God's wisdom had ordained all the essentials of the tabernacle, yet it seems these accidental conveniences were left to be provided by their own discretion, which was to set in order that which was wanting (Tit. 1:5), and these wagons were not refused, though no pattern of them was shown to Moses in the mount. Note, It must not be expected that the divine institution of ordinances should descend to all those circumstances which are determinable, and are fit

to be left alterable, by human prudence, that wisdom which is profitable to direct. Observe, No sooner is the tabernacle fully set up than this provision is made for the removal of it. Note, Even when we are but just settled in the world, and think we are beginning to take root, we must be preparing for changes and removes, especially for the great change. While we are here in this world, every thing must be accommodated to a militant and movable state. When the tabernacle was framing, the princes were very generous in their offerings, for then they brought *precious stones, and stones to be set* (Ex. 35:27), yet now they bring more presents. Note, Those that have done good should study to abound therein yet more and more, and not be *weary of well-doing.*

IV. How the offering was disposed of, and what use was made of it: the wagons and oxen were given to the Levites, to be used in carrying the tabernacle, both for their ease (for God would not have any of his servants overburdened with work), and for the more safe and right conveyance of the several parts of the tabernacle, which would be best kept together, and sheltered from the weather, in wagons. 1. The Gershonites, that had the light carriage, the curtains and hangings, had but two wagons, and two yoke of oxen (v. 7); when they had loaded these, they must carry the rest, if any remained, upon their shoulders. 2. The Merarites, that had the heavy carriage, and that which was most unwieldy, the boards, pillars, sockets, etc., had four wagons, and four yoke of oxen allotted them (v. 8); and yet, if they had not more wagons of their own, they would be obliged to carry a great deal upon their backs too, for the silver sockets alone weighed 100 talents, which was above four tons, and that was enough to load four wagons that were drawn but by one yoke of oxen a-piece. But each socket being a talent weight, which is about a man's burden (as appears, 2 Ki. 5:23) probably they carried those on their backs, and put the boards and pillars into the wagons. Observe here, How God wisely and graciously ordered the most strength to those that had the most work. Each had wagons *according to their service.* Whatever burden God in his providence lays upon us, he will by his sufficient grace proportion the strength to it, 1 Co. 10:13. 3. The Kohathites, that had the most sacred carriage, had no wagons at all, because they were to carry their charge upon their shoulders (v. 9), with a particular care and veneration. When in David's time they carried the ark in a cart, God made them to know to their terror, by the death of Uzza, that they did not *seek him in the due order.* See 1 Chr. 15:13.

Verses 10–89

We have here an account of the great solemnity of dedicating the altars, both that of burnt-offerings and that of incense; they had been sanctified before, when they were anointed (Lev. 8:10, 11), but now they were handselled, as it were, by the princes, with their free-will offerings. They began the use of them with rich presents, great expressions of joy and gladness, and extraordinary respect to those tokens of God's presence with them. Now observe here,

I. That the princes and great men were first and forwardest in the service of God. Those that are entitled to precedency should go before in good works, and that is true honour. Here is an example to the nobility and gentry, those that are in authority and of the first rank in their country; they ought to improve their honour and power, their estate and interest, for the promoting of religion, and the service of God, in the places where they live. It is justly expected that those who have more than others should do more good than others with what they have, else they are unfaithful stewards, and will not make up their *account with joy.* Nay, great men must not only with their wealth and power assist and protect those that serve God, but they must make conscience of being devout and religious themselves, and employing themselves in the exercises of piety, which will greatly redound to the honour of God (Ps. 138:4, 5), and have a good influence upon others, who will be the more easily persuaded to acts of devotion when they see them thus brought into reputation. It is certain that the greatest of men is less than the least of the ordinances of God; nor are the meanest services of religion any disparagement to those that make the greatest figure in the world.

II. The offerings they brought were very rich and valuable, so rich that some think there was not so great a difference in estate between them and others as that they were able to bear the expense of them themselves, but that the heads of each tribe contributed to the offering which their prince brought.

1. They brought some things to remain for standing service, twelve large silver dishes, each about sixty ounces weight, as many large silver cups, or bowls, of about thirty-five ounces — the former to be used for the meat-offerings, the latter for the drink-offerings — the former for the flesh of the sacrifices, the latter for the blood. The latter was God's table (as it were), and it was fit that so great a King should be served in plate. The golden spoons being filled with incense were intended, it is probable, for the service of the golden altar, for both the altars were anointed at the same time. Note, In works of piety and charity we ought to be generous according as our ability is. He that is the best should be served with the best we have. The Israelites indeed might well afford to part with their gold and silver in abundance to the service of the sanctuary, for they needed it not to buy meat and victual their camp, being daily fed with bread from heaven; nor did they need it to buy land, or pay their army, for they were shortly to be put in possession of Canaan.

2. They brought some things to be used immediately, offerings of each sort, burnt-offerings, sin-offerings, and a great many peace-offerings (on part of which they were to feast with their friends), and the meat-offerings that were to be annexed to them. Hereby they signified their thankful acceptance of, and cheerful submission to, all those laws concerning the sacrifices which God had lately by Moses delivered to them. And, though it was a time of joy and rejoicing, yet it is observable that still in the midst of their sacrifices we find a *sin-offering.* Since in our best services we are conscious to ourselves that there is a mixture of sin, it is fit that there should be even in our most joyful services a mixture of repentance. In all our approaches to God, we must by faith have an eye to Christ as the great sin-offering, and make mention of him.

3. They brought their offerings each on a separate day, in the order that they had been lately put into, so that the solemnity lasted twelve days. So God appointed (v. 11): *They shall bring their offering, each prince on his day,* and so they did. One sabbath must needs fall within the twelve days, if not two, but it should seem they did not intermit on the sabbath, for it was holy work, proper enough for a holy day. God appointed that it should thus be done on several days, (1.) That solemnity might be prolonged, and so might be universally taken notice of by all Israel, and the remembrance of it more effectually preserved. (2.) That an equal honour might thereby be put upon each tribe respectively; in Aaron's breast-plate each had his precious stone, so in this offering each had his day. (3.) Thus it would be done more decently and in order; God's work should not be done confusedly, and in a hurry; take time, and we shall have done the sooner, or at least we shall have done the better. (4.) God hereby signified how much pleased he is, and how much pleased we should be, with the exercises of piety and devotion. The repetition of them should be a continual pleasure to us, and we must not be weary of well doing. If extraordinary service be required to be done for twelve days together, we must not shrink from it, nor call it a task and a burden. (5.) The priests and Levites, having this occasion to offer the same sacrifices, and those some of every sort, every day, for so many days together, would have their hands well set in, and would be well versed in the laws concerning them. (6.) The peace-offerings were all to be eaten the same day they were offered, and two oxen, five rams, five he-goats, and five lambs, were enough for one day's festival; had there been more, especially if all had been brought on one day, there might have been danger of excess. The virtue of temperance must not be left, under pretence of the religion of feasting.

4. All their offerings were exactly the same, without any variation, though it is probable that neither the princes nor the tribes were all alike rich; but thus it was intimated that all the tribes of Israel had an equal share in the altar, and an equal interest in the sacrifices that were offered upon it. Though one tribe was posted more honourably in the camp than another, yet they and their services were

all alike acceptable to God. Nor must we have faith of our Lord Jesus Christ *with respect to persons,* Jam. 2:1.

5. Nahshon, the prince of the tribe of Judah, offered first, because God had given that tribe the first post of honour in the camp; and the rest of the tribes acquiesced, and offered in the same order in which God had appointed them to encamp. Judah, of which tribe Christ came, first, and then the rest; thus, in the dedication of souls to God, every man is presented in his own order, *Christ the first-fruits,* 1 Co. 15:23. Some observe that Nahshon is the only one that is not expressly called a prince (*v.* 12), which the Jews give this account of: he is not called a prince, that he might not be puffed up because he offered first; and all the others are called princes because they (though some of them of the elder house) submitted, and offered after him. Or, because the title of prince of Judah did more properly belong to Christ, for *unto him shall the gathering of the people be.*

6. Though the offerings were all the same, yet the account of them is repeated at large for each tribe, in the same words. We are sure there are no vain repetitions in scripture; what then shall we make of these repetitions? Might it not have served to say of this noble jury that the same offering which their foreman brought each on his day brought likewise? No, God would have it specified for each tribe: and why so? (1.) It was for the encouragement of these princes, and of their respective tribes, that each of their offerings being recorded at large no slight might seem to be put upon them; for rich and poor meet together before God. (2.) It was for the encouragement of all generous acts of piety and charity, by letting us know that what is so given is lent to the Lord, and he carefully records it, with every one's name prefixed to his gift, because what is so given he will pay again, and even a *cup of cold water* shall have its *reward.* He is not unrighteous, to forget either the cost or the *labour of love,* Heb. 6:10. We find Christ taking particular notice of what was cast into the treasury, Mk. 12:41. Though what is offered be but little, though it be a contribution to the charity of others, yet if it be according to our ability it shall be recorded, that it may be recompensed in the resurrection of the just.

7. The sum total is added at the foot of the account (*v.* 84–88), to show how much God was pleased with the mention of his freewill-offerings, and what a great deal they amounted to in the whole, when every prince brought in his quota! How greatly would the sanctuary of God be enriched and beautified if all would in their places do their part towards it, by exemplary purity and devotion, extensive charity, and universal usefulness!

8. God signified his gracious acceptance of these presents that were brought him, by speaking familiarly to Moses, as a man speaks to his friend, from off the mercy-seat (*v.* 89, *ch.* 12:8); and in speaking to him he did in effect speak to all Israel, showing them this token for good, Ps. 103:7. Note, By this we may know that God hears and accepts our prayers if he gives us grace to hear and receive his word, for thus our communion with him is maintained and kept up. I know not why we may not suppose that upon each of the days on which these offerings were brought (probably while the priests and offerers were feasting upon the peace-offerings) Moses was in the tabernacle, receiving some of those laws and orders which we have already met with in this and the foregoing book. And here the excellent bishop Patrick observes that God's speaking to Moses thus by an audible articulate voice, as if he had been clothed with a holy body, might be looked upon as an earnest of the incarnation of the Son of God in the fulness of time, when the Word should be made flesh, and speak in the language of the sons of men. For, however God *at sundry times and in divers manners spoke unto the fathers, he has in these last days spoken unto us by his Son.* And that he who now spoke to Moses, as the *shechinah* or divine Majesty, from between the cherubim, was the eternal Word, the second person in the Trinity, was the pious conjecture of many of the ancients; for all God's communion with man is by his Son, by whom he made the world, and rules the church, and who *is the same yesterday, to-day, and for ever.*

CHAPTER 8

This chapter is concerning the lamps or lights of the sanctuary. I. The burning lamps in the candlestick, which the priests were charged to tend (*v.* 1–4). II. The living lamps (if I may so call them), The Levites, who as ministers were burning and shining lights. The ordination of the priests we had an account of, Lev. 8. Here we have an account of the ordination of the Levites, the inferior clergy. 1. How they were purified (*v.* 5–8). 2. How they were parted with by the people (*v.* 9, 10). 3. How they were presented to God in lieu of the firstborn (*v.* 11–18). 4. How they were consigned to Aaron and his sons, to be ministers to them (*v.* 19). 5. How all these orders were duly executed (*v.* 20–22). And, lastly, the age appointed for their ministration (*v.* 23, etc.).

Verses 1–4

Directions were given long before this for the making of the golden candlestick (Ex. 25:31), and it was made according to the pattern shown to Moses in the mount, Ex. 38:17. But now it was that the lamps were first ordered to be lighted, when other things began to be used. Observe, 1. Who must light the lamps; Aaron himself, he *lighted the lamps, v.* 3. As the people's representative to God, he thus did the office of a servant in God's house, lighting his Master's candle; as the representative of God to the people, he thus gave them the intimations of God's will and favour, thus expressed (Ps. 18:28), *Thou wilt light my candle;* and thus Aaron himself was now lately directed to bless the people, *The Lord make his face to shine upon thee, ch.* 6:25. The commandment is a *lamp,* Prov. 6:23. The scripture is *a light shining in a dark place,* 2 Pt. 1:19. And a dark place indeed even the church would be without it, as the tabernacle (which had no window in it) without the lamps. Now the work of ministers is to light these lamps, by expounding and applying the word of God. The priest lighted the middle lamp from the fire of the altar, and the rest of the lamps he lighted one from another, which (says Mr. Ainsworth) signifies that the fountain of all light and knowledge is in Christ, who has the *seven spirits of God* figured by the *seven lamps of fire* (Rev. 4:5), but that in the expounding of scripture one passage must borrow light from another. He also supposes that, *seven* being a number of perfection, by the seven branches of the candlestick is shown the full perfection of the scriptures, which are able to make us wise to salvation. 2. To what end the lamps were lighted, that they might give light *over against the candlestick,* that is, to that part of the tabernacle where the table stood, with the show-bread upon it, over against the candlestick. They were not lighted like tapers in an urn, to burn to themselves, but to give light to the other side of the tabernacle, for therefore candles are lighted, Mt. 5:15. Note, The lights of the world, the lights of the church, must shine as lights. Therefore we have light, that we may give light.

Verses 5–26

We read before of the separating of the Levites from among the children of Israel when they were numbered, and the numbering of them by themselves (*ch.* 3:6, 15), that they might be employed in the service of the tabernacle. Now here we have directions given for their solemn ordination (*v.* 6), and the performance of it, *v.* 20. All Israel must know that they took not this honour to themselves, but were called of God to it; nor was it enough that they were distinguished from their neighbours, but they must be solemnly devoted to God. Note, All that are employed for God must be dedicated to him, according as the degree of employment is. Christian musts be baptized, ministers must be ordained; we must first give ourselves unto the Lord, and then our services. Observe in what method this was done:

I. The Levites must be cleansed, and were so. The rites and ceremonies of their cleansing were to be performed, 1. By themselves. They must *wash their clothes,* and not only bathe, but *shave all their flesh,* as the leper was to do when he was cleansed, Lev. 14:8. They must *cause a razor to pass over all their flesh,* to clear themselves from that defilement which would not wash off. Jacob, whom God loved, was a smooth man; it was Esau that was hairy. The great pains they were to take with themselves to make themselves clean teaches all Christians, and ministers particularly, by repentance and mortification, to *cleanse themselves from all filthiness of flesh and spirit,* that they may *perfect holiness.* Those must be clean that bear the vessels of the Lord. 2. By Moses. He must *sprinkle the water of purifying upon them,* which was prepared by divine direction. This signified the application of the blood of Christ to our souls by faith, to purify us from an evil conscience, that we may be fit to serve the living God. It is our duty to cleanse ourselves, and God's promise that he will cleanse us.

II. The Levites, being thus prepared, must be brought before the Lord in a solemn assembly of all Israel, and the *children of Israel* must *put their hands upon them* (*v.* 10), so transferring their interest in them and in their service (to which, as a part, the whole body of the people was entitled) to God and to his sanctuary. They presented them to God *as living sacrifices, holy and acceptable,* to perform a *reasonable service;* and therefore, as the offerers in all other cases did, *they laid their hands upon them,* desiring that their service might be accepted in lieu of the attendance of the whole congregation, particularly the first-born, which they acknowledge God might have insisted on. This will not serve to prove a power in the people to ordain ministers; for this imposition of hands by the children of Israel upon the Levites did not make them ministers of the sanctuary, but only signified the people's parting with that tribe out of their militia, and civil incorporations, in order to their being made ministers by Aaron, who was to offer them before the Lord. All the congregation of the children of Israel could not lay hands on them, but it is probable that the rulers and elders did it as the representative body of the people. Some think that the first-born did it because in their stead the Levites were consecrated to God. Whatever God calls for from us to serve his own glory by, we must cheerfully resign it, lay our hands upon it, not to detain it but to surrender it, and let it go to him that is entitled to it.

III. Sacrifices were to be offered for them, a sin-offering first (*v.* 12), and then a burnt-offering, to make an *atonement for the Levites,* who, as the parties concerned, were to lay their hands upon the head of the sacrifices. See here, 1. That we are all utterly unworthy and unfit to be admitted into and employed in the service of God, till atonement be made for sin, and thereby our peace made with God. That interposing cloud must be scattered before there can be any comfortable communion settled between God and our souls. 2. That it is by sacrifice, by Christ the great sacrifice, that we are reconciled to God, and made fit to be offered to him. It is by him that Christians are sanctified to the work of their Christianity, and ministers to the work of their ministry. The learned bishop Patrick's notion of the sacrifice offered by the Levites is that the Levites were themselves considered as an expiatory sacrifice, for they were given to *make atonement for the children of Israel,* (*v.* 19), and yet not being devoted to death, any more than the first-born were, these two sacrifices were substituted in their stead, upon which therefore they were to lay their hands, that the sin which the children of Israel laid upon them (*v.* 10) might be transferred to these beasts.

IV. The Levites themselves were *offered before the Lord* for an *offering of the children of Israel, v.* 11. Aaron gave them up to God, as being first given up by themselves, and by the children of Israel. The original word signifies a *wave-offering,* not that they were actually waved, but they were presented to God as the God of heaven, and the Lord of the whole earth, as the wave-offerings were. And in calling them wave-offerings it was intimated to them that they must continually lift up themselves towards God in his service, lift up their eyes, lift up their hearts, and must move to and fro with readiness in the business of their profession. They were not ordained to be idle, but to be active and stirring.

V. God here declares his acceptance of them: *The Levites shall be mine, v.* 14. God took them instead of the first-born (*v.* 16–18), of which before, *ch.* 3:41. Note, What is in sincerity offered to God shall be graciously owned and accepted by him. And his ministers who have obtained mercy of him to be faithful have particular marks of favour and honour put upon them: *they shall be mine,* and then (*v.* 15) they shall *go in to do the service of the tabernacle.* God takes them for his own, that they may serve him. All that expect to share in the privileges of the tabernacle must resolve to do the service of the tabernacle. As, on the one hand, none of God's creatures are his necessary servants (he needs not the service of any of them), so, on the other hand, none are taken merely as honorary servants, to do nothing. All whom God owns he employs; angels themselves have their services.

VI. They are then given as a gift to Aaron and his sons

(*v.* 19), yet so as that the benefit accrued to the children of Israel. 1. The Levites must act under the priests as attendants on them, and assistants to them, in the service of the sanctuary. Aaron offers them to God (*v.* 11), and then God gives them back to Aaron, *v.* 19. Note, Whatever we give up to God, he will give back to us unspeakably to our advantage. Our hearts, our children, our estates, are never more ours, more truly, more comfortably ours, than when we have offered them up to God. 2. They must act for the people. They were taken to *do the service of the children of Israel,* that is, not only to do the service which they should do, but to serve their interests, and do that which would really redound to the honour, safety, and prosperity of the whole nation. Note, Those that faithfully perform the service of God do one of the best services that can be done to the public; God's ministers, while they keep within the sphere of their office and conscientiously discharge the duty of it, must be looked upon as some of the most useful servants of their country. The children of Israel can as ill spare the tribe of Levi as any of their tribes. But what is the service they do the children of Israel? It follows, it is to *make an atonement for them, that there be no plague among them.* It was the priests' work to make atonement by sacrifice, but the Levites made atonement by attendance, and preserved the peace with heaven which was made by sacrifice. If the service of the priests in the tabernacle had been left to all the first-born of Israel promiscuously, it would have been either neglected or done unskillfully and irreverently, being done by those that were not so closely tied to it, nor so diligently trained to it, nor so constantly used to it, as the Levites were; and this would bring *a plague among the children of Israel* — meaning, perhaps, the death of the first-born themselves, which was the last and greatest of the plagues of Egypt. To prevent this, and to preserve the atonement, the Levites were appointed to do this service, who should be bred up to it under their parents from their infancy, and therefore would be well versed in it; and so the children of Israel, that is, the first-born, should not need to come nigh to the sanctuary; or, when any Israelites had occasion, the Levites would be ready to instruct them, and introduce them, and so prevent any fatal miscarriage or mistake. Note, It is a very great kindness to the church that ministers are appointed to go before the people in the things of God, as guides, overseers, and rulers, in religious worship, and to make that their business. When Christ ascended on high, he *gave these gifts,* Eph. 4:8, 11, 12.

VII. The time of their ministration is fixed. 1. They were to enter upon the service at twenty-five years old, *v.* 24. They were not charged with the carrying of the tabernacle and the utensils of it till they were thirty years old, *ch.* 4:3. But they were entered to be otherwise serviceable at twenty-five years old, a very good age for ministers to begin their public work at. The work then required that strength of body and the work now requires that maturity of judgment and steadiness of behaviour which men rarely arrive at till about that age; and novices are in danger of being lifted up with pride. 2. They were to have a writ of ease at fifty years old; then they were to return from the warfare, as the phrase is (*v.* 25), not cashiered with disgrace, but preferred rather to the rest which their age required, to be loaded with the honours of their office, as hitherto they had been with the burdens of it. They shall *minister with their brethren in the tabernacle,* to direct the junior Levites, and set them in; and they shall *keep the charge,* as guards upon the avenues of the tabernacle, to see that no stranger intruded, nor any person in his uncleanness, but they shall not be put upon any service which may be a fatigue to them. If God's grace provide that men shall have ability according to their work, man's prudence should take care that men have work only according to their ability. The aged are most fit for trusts, and to keep the charge; the younger are most fit for work, and to do the service. Those that have *used the office of a servant well purchase to themselves a good degree,* 1 Tim. 3:13. Yet indeed gifts are not tied to ages (Job 32:9), but *all these worketh that one and the self-same Spirit.* Thus was the affair of the Levites settled.

CHAPTER 9

This chapter is, I. Concerning the great ordinance of the passover; 1. Orders given for the observance of it, at the return of the year (*v.* 1–5). 2. Provisos added in regard to such as should be ceremonially unclean, or otherwise disabled, at the time when the passover was to be kept (*v.* 6–14). II. Concerning the great favour of the pillar of cloud, which was a guide to Israel through the wilderness (*v.* 15, etc.).

Verses 1–14

Here we have,

I. An order given for the solemnization of the passover, the day twelvemonth after they came out of Egypt, on the fourteenth day of the first month of the second year, some days before they were numbered, for that was done in the beginning of the second month. Observe, 1. God gave particular orders for the keeping of this passover, otherwise (it should seem) they would not have kept it, for, in the first institution of this ordinance, it was appointed to be kept when they should *come into the land of promise,* Ex. 12:25. And, no passover till they came to Canaan, Jos. 5:10. This was an early indication of the abolishing of the ceremonial institutions at last, that, so soon after they were first appointed, some of them were suffered to lie asleep for so many years. The ordinance of the Lord's supper (which came in the room of the passover) was not thus intermitted or set aside in the first days of the Christian church, though those were days of greater difficulty and distress than Israel knew in the wilderness; nay, in the times of persecution, the Lord's supper was celebrated more frequently than afterwards. The Israelites in the wilderness could not forget their deliverance out of Egypt, their present state was a constant memorandum of it to them. All the danger was when they came to Canaan; there therefore they had need to be reminded of the *rock out of which they were hewn.* However, because the first passover was celebrated in a hurry, and was rather the substance itself than the sign, it was the will of God that at the return of the year, when they were more composed, and better acquainted with the divine law, they should observe it again, that their children might more distinctly understand the solemnity and the better remember it hereafter. Calvin supposes that they were obliged to keep it now, and notes it as an instance of their carelessness that they had need to be reminded of an institution which they so lately received. 2. Moses faithfully transmitted to the people the orders given him, *v.* 4. Thus Paul delivered to the churches what he *received of the Lord* concerning the gospel passover, 1 Co. 11:23. Note, Magistrates must be monitors, and ministers must *stir up men's minds by way of remembrance* to that which is good. 3. The people observed the orders given them, *v.* 5. Though they had lately kept the feast of dedication (*ch.* 7), yet they did not desire to excuse themselves with that from keeping this feast. Note, Extraordinary performances must not supersede or jostle out or stated services. They kept the passover even in the wilderness: though our condition be solitary and unsettled, yet we must keep up our attendance on God by holy ordinances as we have opportunity, for in them we may find the best conversation and the best repose. Thus is God' Israel provided for in a desert.

II. Instructions given concerning those that were ceremonially unclean when they were to eat the passover. The law of the passover required every Israelite to eat of it. Some subsequent laws had forbidden those that had contracted any ceremonial pollution to eat of the holy things; those whose minds and consciences are defiled by sin are utterly unfit for communion with God, and cannot partake, with any true comfort, of the gospel passover, till they are cleansed by true repentance and faith: and a sad dilemma they are in; if they come not to holy ordinances, they are guilty of a contempt of them; if they do come in their pollution, they are guilty of a profanation of them. They must therefore wash, and then *compass God's altar.* Now,

1. Here is the case that happened in Israel when this passover was to be kept: *Certain men were defiled by the dead body of a man* (*v.* 6), and they lay under that defilement seven days (*ch.* 19:11), and in that time might not eat of the holy things, Lev. 7:20. This was not their iniquity, but their infelicity: some persons must touch dead bodies, to bury them out of sight, and therefore they could, with the better grace, bring their complaint to Moses.

2. The application made to Moses by the person concerned, *v.* 7. Note, It is people's wisdom, in difficult cases concerning sin and duty, to consult with their ministers whom God has set over them, and to *ask the law at their mouth,* Mal. 2:7. These means we must use in pursuance of our prayers to God to lead us in a plain path. Observe with what trouble and concern these men complained that they were kept back from offering to the Lord. They did not complain of the law as unjust, but lamented their unhappiness that they fell under the restraint of it at this time, and desired some expedient might be found out for their relief. Note, It is a blessed thing to see people hungering and thirsting after God's ordinances, and to hear them complaining of that which prevents their enjoyment of them. It should be a trouble to us when by any occasion we are kept back from bringing our offering in the solemnities of a sabbath or a sacrament, as it was to David when he was banished from the altar, Ps. 42:1, 2.

3. The deliberation of Moses in resolving this case. Here seemed to be law against law; and, though it is a rule that the latter law must explain the former, yet he pitied these Israelites that were thus deprived of the privilege of the passover, and therefore took time to consult the oracles, and to know what was the mind of God in this case: *I will hear what the Lord will command concerning you, v.* 8. Ministers must take example hence in resolving cases of conscience. (1.) They must not determine rashly, but take time to consider, that every circumstance may be duly weighted, the case viewed in a true light, and spiritual things compared with spiritual. (2.) They must ask counsel at God's mouth, and not determine according to the bias of their own fancy or affection, but impartially, according to the mind of God, to the best of their knowledge. We have no such oracle to consult as Moses had, but we must have recourse to *the law and the testimony,* and speak according to that rule; and if, in difficult cases, we take time to spread the matter in particular before God by humble believing prayer, we have reason to hope that the Spirit who is promised to *lead us into all truth* will enable us to direct others *in the good and right way.*

4. The directions which God gave in this case, and in other similar cases, explanatory of the law of the passover. The disagreeable accident produced good laws. (1.) Those that happened to be ceremonially unclean at the time when the passover should be eaten were allowed to eat it that day month, when they were clean; so were those that happened to be *in a journey afar off, v.* 10, 11. See here, [1.] That when we are to attend upon God in solemn ordinances it is very necessary both that we be clean and that we be composed. [2.] That that may excuse the deferring of a duty for a time which yet will not justify us in the total neglect and omission of it. He that is at variance with his brother may *leave his gift before the altar,* while he goes to be *reconciled to his brother;* but when he has done his part towards it, whether it be effected or no, he must *come again and offer his gift,* Mt. 5:23, 24. This secondary passover was to be kept on the same day of the month with the first, because the ordinance was a memorial of their deliverance on that day of the month. Once we find the whole congregation keeping the passover on this fourteenth day of the second month, in Hezekiah's time (2 Chr. 30:15), which perhaps may help to account for the admission of some that were not clean to the eating of it. Had the general passover been kept in the first month, the unclean might have been put off till the second; but, that being kept in the second month, they had no warrant to eat it in the third month, and therefore, rather than not eat of it at all, they were admitted, though not cleansed *according to the purification of the sanctuary, v.* 19, 20. (2.) Whenever the passover was kept in the second month, all the rites and ceremonies of it must be strictly observed, *v.* 12. They must not think that, because the time was dispensed with, any part of the solemnity of it might be abated; when we cannot do as we would we must do the utmost we can in the service of God. (3.) This allowance in a case of necessity would be no means countenance or indulge any in their neglect to keep the passover at the time appointed, when they were not under the necessity, *v.* 13. When a person is under no incapacity to eat the passover in the appointed time, if he neglects it then, upon the presumption of the liberty granted by this law, he puts an affront upon God, impiously abuses his kindness, and he shall certainly *bear his sin,* and *be cut off from his people.* Note, As those who against their minds are forced to absent themselves from God's ordin-

ances may comfortably expect the favours of God's grace under their affliction, so those who of choice absent themselves may justly expect the tokens of God's wrath for their sin. *Be not deceived, God is not mocked.* (4.) Here is a clause added in favour of strangers, *v.* 14. Though it was requisite that the stranger who would join with them in eating the passover should be circumcised as a proselyte to their religion (Ex. 12:48, 49), yet this kind admission of those that were not native Israelites to eat the passover was an intimation of the favour designed for the poor Gentiles by Christ. As then there was one law, so in the days of the Messiah there should be one gospel, for the stranger and for him that was born in the land; for *in every nation he that fears God and works righteousness is accepted of him,* and this was a truth before Peter perceived it, Acts 10:34, 35.

Verses 15–23

We have here the history of the cloud; not a natural history: *who knows the balancings of the clouds?* but a divine history of a cloud that was appointed to be the visible sign and symbol of God's presence with Israel.

I. When the tabernacle was finished this cloud, which before had hung on high over their camp, settled upon the tabernacle, and covered it, to show that God manifests his presence with his people in and by his ordinances; there he makes himself known, and to them we must look if we would *see the beauty of the Lord,* Ps. 27:4; Eze. 37:26, 27. Thus God glorified his own appointments, and signified his acceptance of his people's love and obedience.

II. That which appeared as a cloud by day appeared as a fire all night. Had it been a cloud only, it would not have been visible by night; and, had it been a fire only, it would have been scarcely discernible by day; but God would give them sensible demonstrations of the constancy of his presence with them, and his care of them, and that he *kept them night and day,* Isa. 27:3; Ps. 121:6. And thus we are taught to *set God always before us,* and to see him near us both night and day. Something of the nature of that divine revelation which the Old-Testament church was governed by might also be signified by these visible signs of God's presence, the cloud denoting the darkness and the fire the terror of that dispensation, in comparison with the more clear and comfortable discoveries God has made of his glory in the face of Jesus Christ.

III. This pillar of cloud and fire directed and determined all the motions, marches, and encampments, of Israel in the wilderness. 1. As long as the cloud rested upon the tabernacle, so long they continued in the same place, and never stirred; though no doubt they were very desirous to be pressing forward in their journey towards Canaan, where they longed to be and hoped to be quickly, yet as long as the cloud rested, if it was a month or a year, so long they rested, *v.* 22. Note, He that believeth doth not make haste. There is no time lost while we are waiting God's time. It is as acceptable a piece of submission to the will of God to sit still contentedly when our lot requires it as to work for him when we are called to it. 2. When the cloud was taken up, they removed, how comfortably soever they were encamped, *v.* 17. Whether it moved by day or night, they delayed not to attend its motions (*v.* 21), and probably there were some appointed to stand sentinel day and night within sight of it, to give timely notice to the camp of its beginning to stir, and this called *keeping the charge of the Lord.* The people, being thus kept at a constant uncertainty, and having no time fixed for stopping or removing, were obliged to hold themselves in constant readiness to march upon very short warning. And for the same reason we are kept at uncertainty concerning the time of our putting off the earthly house of this tabernacle, that we may be always ready to *remove at the commandment of the Lord.* 3. As long and as far as the cloud moved, so long and so far they marched, and just where it abode they pitched their tents about it, and God's tent under it, *v.* 17. Note, It is uncomfortable staying when God has departed, but very safe and pleasant going when we see God go before us and resting where he appoints us to rest. This is repeated again and again in these verses, because it was a constant miracle, and often repeated, and what never failed in all their travels, and because it is a matter which we should take particular notice of as very significant and instructive. It is mentioned long after by David (Ps. 105:39), and by the people of God after their captivity, Neh. 9:19. And the guidance of this cloud is spoken of as signifying the guidance of the blessed Spirit. Isa. 63:14, *The Spirit of the Lord caused him to rest, and so didst thou lead thy people.* This teaches us, (1.) The particular care God takes of his people. Nothing could be more expressive and significant of God's tenderness of Israel than the guidance of this cloud was; it led them by the *right way* (Ps. 107:7), went on their pace: God did by it, as it were, cover them with his feathers. We are not now to expect such sensible tokens of the divine presence and guidance as this was, but the promise is sure to all God's spiritual Israel that he will *guide them by his counsel* (Ps. 73:24), *even unto death* (Ps. 48:14), that all the children of God shall be *led by the Spirit of God* (Rom. 8:14), that he will *direct the paths* of those who in *all their ways acknowledge him,* Prov. 3:6. There is a particular providence conversant about all their affairs, to direct and overrule them for the best. *The steps of a good man are ordered by the Lord,* Ps. 37:23. (2.) The particular regard we ought to have to God in all our ways. In our affections and actions we must follow the direction of his word and Spirit; all the motions of our souls must be guided by the divine will; at the commandment of the Lord our hearts should always move and rest; in all our affairs we must follow Providence, reconciling ourselves to all its disposals, and bringing our mind to our condition, whatever it is. The people of Israel, having the cloud for their guide, were eased of the trouble of holding councils of war, to consider when and whither they should march, which might have occasioned strifes and debates among them: nor needed they to send spies before to inform them of the posture of the country, or pioneers to clear the way, or officers to mark out their camp; the pillar of cloud did all this for them: and those that by faith commit their works to the Lord, though they are bound to the prudent use of means, yet may in like manner be easy in the expectation of the event. *"Father, thy will be done;* dispose of me and mine as thou pleasest; here I am, desirous to be found *waiting on my God continually,* to journey and rest at *the commandment of the Lord.* What thou wilt, and where thou wilt, only let me be thine, and always in the way of my duty."

CHAPTER 10

In this chapter we have, I. Orders given about the making and using of silver trumpets, which seems to have been the last of all the commandments God gave upon mount Sinai, and one of the least, yet not without its significancy (*v.* 1–10). II. The history of the removal of Israel's camp from mount Sinai, and their orderly march into the wilderness of Paran (*v.* 11–28). III. Moses's treaty with Hobab, his brother-in-law (*v.* 29–32). IV. Moses's prayer at the removing and resting of the ark (*v.* 33, etc.).

Verses 1–10

We have here directions concerning the public notices that were to be given to the people upon several occasions by sound of trumpet. In a thing of this nature, one would think, Moses needed not to have been taught of God: his own reason might teach him the conveniency of trumpets; but the constitution of Israel was to be in every thing divine, and therefore even in this matter, small as it seems. Moses is here directed, 1. About the making of them. They must be made of silver; not cast but of beaten work (as some read it), the matter and shape, no doubt, very fit for the purpose. He was now ordered to make but two, because there were but two priests to use them. But in Solomon's time we read of 120 *priests sounding with trumpets,* 2 Chr. 5:12. The form of these trumpets is supposed to have been much like ours at this day. 2. Who were to make use of them; not any inferior person, but the priests themselves, the *sons of Aaron, v.* 8. As great as they were, they must not think it a disparagement to them to be trumpeters in the house of God; the meanest office there was honourable. This signified that the Lord's ministers should *lift up their voice like a trumpet,* to show people their sins (Isa. 58:1), to call them to Christ, Isa. 27:13. 3. Upon what occasions the trumpets were to be sounded. (1.) For the *calling of assemblies, v.* 2. Thus they are told to blow the trumpet in Zion for the calling of a solemn assembly together, to sanctify a fast, Joel 2:15. Public notice ought to be given of the time and place of religious assemblies; for the invitation to the benefit or ordinances is general: *whoever will, let him come.* wisdom cries in the chief places of concourse. But, that the trumpet might not *give an uncertain sound,* they are directed, if only the princes and elders were to meet, to blow but one of the trumpets; less should serve to call *them* together, who ought to be examples of forwardness in any thing that is good: but, if the body of the people were to be called together, both the trumpets must be sounded, that they might be heard at the greater distance. In allusion to this, they are said to be blessed that *hear the joyful sound* (Ps. 89:15), that is, that are invited and called upon to wait upon God in public ordinances, Ps. 122:1. And the general assembly at the great day will be summoned by *the sound of the archangel's trumpet,* Mt. 24:31. (2.) For the *journeying of the camps,* to give notice when each squadron must move; for no man's voice could reach to give the word of command: soldiers with us that are well disciplined may be exercised by beat of drums. When the trumpets were blown for this purpose, they must*sound an alarm* (*v.* 5), a broken, quavering, interrupted sound, which was proper to excite and encourage the minds of people in their marches against their enemies; whereas a continued equal sound was more proper for the calling of the assembly together (*v.* 7): yet when the people were called together to deprecate God's judgments we find an alarm sounded, Joel 2:1. At the first sounding, Judah's squadron marched, at the second Reuben's, at the third Ephraim's, at the fourth Dan's, *v.* 5, 6. And some think that this was intended to sanctify their marches, for thus were proclaimed by the priests, who were God's mouth to the people, not only the divine orders given them to move, but the divine blessing upon them in all their motions. He that hath ears, let him hear that *God is with them of a truth.* King Abijah valued himself and his army very much upon this (2 Chr. 13:12), *God himself is with us for our captain and his priests with sounding trumpets.* (3.) For the animating and encouraging of their armies, when they went out in battle (*v.* 9): *"If you go to war, blow with the trumpets,* signifying thereby your appeal to heaven for the decision of the controversy, and your prayer to God to give you victory; and God will own this his own institution, and *you shall be remembered before the Lord your God."* God will take notice of this sound of the trumpet, and be engaged to fight their battles, and let all the people take notice of it, and be encouraged to fight his, as David, when he heard *a sound of a going upon the tops of the mulberry trees.* Not that God needed to be awaked by sound of trumpet any more than Christ needed to be awaked by his disciples in the storm, Mt. 8:25. But where he intends mercy it is his will that we should solicit it; ministers must stir up the good soldiers of Jesus Christ to fight manfully against sin, the world, and the devil, by assuring them that Christ is the *captain of their salvation,* and will *tread Satan under their feet.* (4.) For the solemnizing of their sacred feasts, *v.* 10. One of their feasts was called *a memorial of the blowing of trumpets,* Lev. 23:23, etc. And it should seem they were thus to grace the solemnity of all their feasts (Ps. 81:3), and their sacrifices (2 Chr. 29:27), to intimate with what joy and delight they performed their duty to God, and to raise the minds of those that attended the services to a holy triumph in the God they worshipped. And then their performances were for a *memorial before God;* for he takes pleasure in our religious exercises when we take pleasure in them. Holy work should be done with holy joy.

Verses 11–28

Here is, I. A general account of the removal of the camp of Israel from mount Sinai, before which mountain it had lain now about a year, in which time and place a great deal of memorable business was done. Of this removal, it should seem, God gave them notice some time before (Deu. 1:6, 7): *You have dwelt long enough in this mountain, turn you and take your journey towards the land of promise.* The apostle tells us that *mount Sinai genders to bondage* (Gal. 4:24), and signifies the law there given, which is of use indeed as a schoolmaster to bring us to Christ, yet we must not rest in it, but advance towards the joys and liberties of the children of God, for our happiness is conferred not by the law, but by promise. Observe, 1. The signal given (*v.* 11): *The cloud was taken up,* and we may suppose it stood for some time, till they were ready to march; and a great deal of work it was to take down all those tents, and pack up all those goods that they had there; but every family being employed about its own, and all at the same time, many hands made quick work of it. 2. The march began: *They took their journey according to the commandment of the Lord,* and just as the cloud led them, *v.* 13. Some think that mention is thus frequently made in this and the foregoing chapter of the *commandment of the Lord,* guiding and governing them in all their travels, to obviate the calumny and reproach which were afterwards thrown upon Israel, that they tarried so long in the wilderness, because they had lost themselves there, and could not find the way out. No, the matter was not so; in every stage, in every step, they were under divine direction; and, if they knew not where they were, yet he that led them knew. Note, Those that have given up themselves to the direction of God's word and Spirit steer a steady course, even when they seem to be bewildered. While they are sure they cannot lose their God and guide, they need not fear losing their way. 3. The place they rested in, after three days' march: They went *out of the wilderness of Sinai,* and rested *in the wilderness of Paran.* Note, All our removals in this world are but from one wilderness to another. The changes which we think will be for the better do not always prove so; while we carry about with us, wherever we go, the common infirmities of human nature, we must expect, wherever we go, to meet with its common calamities; we shall never be at rest, never at home, till we come to heaven, and all will be well there.

II. A particular draught of the order of their march, according to the late model. 1. Judah's squadron marched first, *v.* 14–16. The leading standard, now lodged with that tribe, was an earnest of the sceptre which in David's time should be committed to it, and looked further to the captain of our salvation, of whom it was likewise foretold that *unto him should the gathering of the people be.* 2. Then came those two families of the Levites which were entrusted to carry the tabernacle. As soon as ever the cloud was taken up, the tabernacle was taken down, and packed up for removing, *v.* 17. And here the six wagons came laden with the more bulky part of the tabernacle. This frequent removing of the tabernacle in all their journeys signified the movableness of that ceremonial dispensation. That which was so often shifted would at length vanish away, Heb. 8:13. 3. Reuben's squadron marched forward next, taking place after Judah, *according to the commandment of the Lord, v.* 18–20. 4. Then the Kohathites followed with their charge, the sacred furniture of the tabernacle, *in the midst of the camp,* the safest and most honourable place, *v.* 21. And they (that is, says the margin, the Gershonites and Merarites) did *set up the tabernacle against they came;* and perhaps it is expressed thus generally because, if there was occasion, not those Levites only, but the other Israelites that were in the first squadron, lent a hand to the tabernacle to hasten the rearing of it up, even before they set up their own tents. 5. Ephraim's squadron followed next after the ark (*v.* 22–24), to which some think the psalmist alludes when he prays (Ps. 80:2), *Before Ephraim, Benjamin, and Manasseh,* the three tribes that composed this squadron, *stir up thy strength* (and the ark is called his strength, Ps. 78:61), *and come and save us.* 6. Dan's squadron followed last, *v.* 25–27. It is called the *rearward,* or *gathering host,* of all the camps, because it gathered up all that were left behind; not the women and children (these we may suppose were taken care of by the heads of their families in their respective tribes), but all the unclean, the mixed multitude, and all that were weak and feeble, and cast behind in their march. Note, He that leadeth Joseph like a flock has a tender regard to the hindmost (Eze. 34:16), that cannot keep pace with the rest, and *of all that are given him he will lose none,* Jn. 17:11.

Verses 29–36

Here is, I. An account of what passed between Moses and Hobab, now upon this advance which the camp of Israel made towards Canaan. Some think that Hobab was the same with Jethro, Moses's father-in-law, and that the story, Ex. 18, should come in here; it seems more probable that Hobab was the son of Jethro, *alias* Reuel, or Raguel (Ex. 2:18), and that when the father, being aged, went to his own land (Ex. 18:27), he left his son Hobab with Moses, as Barzillai left Chimham with David; and the same word signifies both a *father-in-law* and a *brother-in-law.* Now this Hobab staid contentedly with Israel while they encamped at mount Sinai, near his own country; but, now that they were removing, he was for going back to his own country and kindred, and his father's house. Here is, 1. The kind invitation Moses gives him to go forward with them to Canaan, *v.* 29. He tempts him with a promise that they would certainly be kind to him, and puts God's word in for security: *The Lord hath spoken good concerning Israel.* As if he had said, "Come, cast in thy lot among us, and thou shalt fare as we fare; and we have the promise of God that we shall fare well." Note, Those that are bound for the heavenly Canaan should invite and encourage all their friends to go along with them, for we shall have never the less of the treasures of the covenant, and the joys of heaven, for others coming in to share with us. And what argument can be more powerful with us to take God's people for our people than this, that God *hath spoken good concerning them?* It is good having fellowship with those that have fellowship with God (1 Jn. 1:3), and going with those with whom God is, Zec. 8:23. 2. Hobab's inclination, and present resolution, to go back to his own country, *v.* 30. One would have thought that he who had seen so much of the special presence of God with Israel, and such surprising tokens of his favour to them, would not have needed much invitation to embark with them. But his refusal must be imputed to the affection he had for his native air and soil, which was not overpowered, as it ought to have been, by a believing regard to the promise of God and a value for covenant blessings. He was indeed a son of Abraham's loins (for the Midianites descended from Abraham by Keturah), but not an heir of Abraham's faith (Heb. 11:8), else he would not have given Moses this answer. Note, The things of this world, which are seen, draw strongly from the pursuit of the things of the other world, which are not seen. The magnetic virtue of this earth prevails with most people above the attractives of heaven itself. 3. The great importunity Moses used with him to alter his resolution, *v.* 31, 32. He urges, (1.) That he might be serviceable to them: *"We are to encamp in the wilderness"* (a country well known to Hobab), *"and thou mayest be to us instead of eyes,* not to show us where we must encamp, nor what way we must march" (which the cloud was to direct), "but to show us the conveniences and inconveniences of the place we march through and encamp in, that we may make the best use we can of the conveniences, and the best fence we can against the inconveniences." Note, It will very well consist with our trust in God's providence to make use of the help of our friends in those things wherein they are capable of being serviceable to us. Even those that were led by miracle must not slight the ordinary means of direction. Some think that Moses suggests this to Hobab, not because he expected much benefit from his information, but to please him with the thought of being some way useful to so great a body, and so to draw him on with them, by inspiring him with an ambition to obtain that honour. Calvin gives quite another sense of this place, very agreeably with the original, which yet I do not find taken notice of by any since. *"Leave us not, I pray thee,* but come along, to share with us in the promised land, *for therefore hast thou known our encampment in the wilderness, and hast been to us instead of eyes;* and we cannot make thee amends for sharing with us in our hardships, and doing us so many good offices, unless thou go with us to Canaan. Surely for this reason thou didst set out with us that thou mightest go on with us." Note, Those that have begun well should use that as a reason for their persevering, because otherwise they lose the benefit and recompence of all they have done and suffered. (2.) That they would be kind to him: *What goodness the Lord shall do to us, the same we will do to thee, v.* 32. Note, [1.] We can give only what we receive. We can do no more service and kindness to our friends than God is pleased to put it into the power of our hand to do. This is all we dare promise, to do good as God shall enable us. [2.] Those that share with God's Israel in their labours and hardships shall share with them in their comforts and honours. Those that are wiling to take their lot with them in the wilderness shall have their lot with them in Canaan; *if we suffer with them we shall reign with them,* 2 Tim. 2:12; Lu. 22:28, 29.

We do not find any reply that Hobab here made to Moses, and therefore we hope that his silence gave consent, and he did not leave them, but that, when he perceived he might be useful, he preferred that before the gratifying of his own inclination; in this case he left us a good example. And we find (Jdg. 1:16; 1 Sa. 15:6) that his family was no loser by it.

II. An account of the communion between God and Israel in this removal. They left *the mount of the Lord* (*v.* 33), that Mount Sinai where they had seen his glory and heard his voice, and had been taken into covenant with him (they must not expect that such appearances of God to them as they had there been blessed with should be constant); they departed from that celebrated mountain, which we never read of in scripture any more, unless with reference to these past stories; now farewell, Sinai; *Zion* is the mountain of which God has said. *This is my rest for ever* (Ps. 132:14), and of which we must say so. But when they left the *mount of the Lord* they took with them the *ark of the covenant of the Lord,* by which their stated communion with God was to be kept up. For,

1. By it God did *direct their paths.* The ark of the covenant went before them, some think in *place,* at least in this removal; others think only in *influence;* though it was carried in the midst of the camp, yet the cloud that hovered over it directed all their motions. The ark (that is, the God of the ark) is said to *search out a resting place* for them; not that God's infinite wisdom and knowledge need to make searches, but every place they were directed to was as convenient for them as if the wisest man they had among them had been employed to go before them, and mark out their camp to the best advantage. thus Canaan is said to be a land which God *spied out,* Eze. 20:6.

2. By it they did *in all their ways acknowledge God,* looking upon it as a token of God's presence; when that moved, or rested, they had their eye up unto God. Moses, as the mouth of the congregation, lifted up a prayer, both at the removing and at the resting of the ark; thus their going out and coming in were sanctified by prayer, and it is an example to us to begin and end every day's journey, and every day's work, with prayer.

(1.) Here is his prayer when the ark set forward: *Rise up, Lord, and let thy enemies be scattered, v.* 35. They were now in a desolate country, but they were marching towards an enemy's country, and their dependence was upon God for success and victory in their wars, as well as for direction and supply in the wilderness. David used this prayer long after (Ps. 68:1), for he also fought the Lords' battles. Note, [1.] There are those in the world that are enemies to God, and haters of him: secret and open enemies; enemies to his truths, his laws, his ordinances, his people. [2.] The scattering and defeating of God's enemies is a thing to be earnestly desired, and believingly expected, by all the Lord's people. This prayer is a prophecy. Those that persist in rebellion against God are hasting towards their own ruin. [3.] For the scattering and defeating of God's enemies, there needs no more but God's arising. *When God arose to judgment,* the work was soon done, Ps. 76:8, 9. "Rise, Lord, as the sun riseth to scatter the shadows of the night." Christ's rising from the dead scattered his enemies, Ps. 68:18.

(2.) His prayer when the ark rested, *v.* 36. [1.] That God would cause his people to rest. So some read it, *"Return, O Lord, the many thousands of Israel,* return them to their rest again after this fatigue." Thus it is said (Isa. 63:14), *The Spirit of the Lord caused him to rest.* Thus he prays that God would give Israel success and victory abroad, and peace and tranquillity at home. [2.] That God himself would take up his rest among them. So we read it: *Return to the thousands of Israel,* the *ten thousand thousand,* so the word is. Note, *First,* The church of God is a great body; there are many thousands belonging to God's Israel. *Secondly,* We ought in our prayers to concern ourselves for this body. *Thirdly,* The welfare and happiness of the Israel of God consist in the continual presence of God among them. Their safety consists not in their numbers, though they are thousands, many thousands, but in the favour of God, and his gracious return to them and residence with them. These thousands are cyphers; he is the figure: and upon this account, *Happy art thou, O Israel! who is like unto thee, O people!*

CHAPTER 11

Hitherto things had gone pretty well in Israel; little interruption had been given to the methods of God's favour to them since the matter of the golden calf; the people seemed teachable in marshalling and purifying the camp, the princes devout and generous in dedicating the altar, and there was good hope that they would be in Canaan presently. But at this chapter begins a melancholy scene; the measures are all broken, God has turned to be their enemy, and fights against them — and it is sin that makes all this mischief. I. Their murmurings kindled a fire among them, which yet was soon quenched by the prayer of Moses (*v.* 1–3). II. No sooner was the fire of judgment quenched than the fire of sin breaks out again, and God takes occasion from it to magnify both his mercy and his justice. 1. The people fret for want of flesh (*v.* 4–9). 2. Moses frets for want of help (*v.* 10–15). Now, (1.) God promises to gratify them both, to appoint help for Moses (*v.* 16, 17), and to give the people flesh (*v.* 18–23). And, (2.) He presently makes good both these promises. For, [1.] The Spirit of God qualifies the seventy elders for the government (*v.* 24–30). [2.] The power of God brings quails to feast the people (*v.* 31, 32). Yet [3.] The justice of God plagued them for their murmurings (*v.* 33, etc.).

Verses 1–3

Here is, I. The people's sin. They *complained, v.* 1. *They were, as it were, complainers.* So it is in the margin. There were some secret grudgings and discontents among them, which as yet did not break out in an open mutiny. But how great a matter did this little fire kindle! They had received from God excellent laws and ordinances, and yet no sooner had they departed from the mount of the Lord than they began to quarrel with God himself. See in this, 1. The sinfulness of sin, which takes occasion from the commandment to be the more provoking. 2. The weakness of the law through the flesh, Rom. 8:3. The law discovered sin, but could not destroy it; checked it, but could not conquer it. They *complained.* Interpreters enquire what they complained of; and truly, when they were furnished with so much matter for thanksgiving, one may justly wonder where they found any matter for complaint; it is probable that those who complained did not all agree in the cause. Some perhaps complained that they were removed from Mount Sinai, where they had been at rest so long, others that they did not remove sooner: some complained of the weather, others of the ways: some perhaps thought three days' journey was too long a march, others thought it not long enough, because it did not bring them into Canaan. When we consider how their camp was guided, guarded, graced, what good victuals they had and good company, and what care was taken of them in their marches that their feet should not swell nor their clothes wear (Deu. 8:4), we may ask, "What could have been done more for a people to make them easy?" And yet they complained. Note, Those that are of a fretful discontented spirit will always find something or other to quarrel with, though the circumstances of their outward condition be ever so favourable.

II. God's just resentment of the affront given to him by this sin: *The Lord heard it,* though it does not appear that Moses did. Note, God is acquainted with the secret frettings and murmurings of the heart, though they are industriously concealed from men. What he took notice of his was much displeased with, and his *anger was kindled.* Note, Though God graciously gives us leave to complain to him when there is cause (Ps. 142:2), yet he is justly provoked, and takes it very ill, if we complain of him when there is no cause: such conduct in our inferiors provokes us.

III. The judgment wherewith God chastised them for this sin: *The fire of the Lord burnt among them,* such flashes of fire from the cloud as had consumed Nadab and Abihu. The fire of their wrath against God burned in their minds (Ps. 39:3), and justly does the fire of God's wrath fasten upon their bodies. We read of their murmurings several times, when they came first out of Egypt, Ex. 15, 16, and 17. But we do not read of any plagues inflicted on them for their murmurings, as there were now; for now they had had great experience of God's care of them, and therefore now to distrust him was so much the more inexcusable. Now a *fire was kindled against Jacob* (Ps. 78:21), but, to show how unwilling God was to contend with them, it fastened on those only that were *in the uttermost parts of the camp.* Thus God's judgments came upon them gradually, that they might take warning.

IV. Their cry to Moses, who was their tried intercessor, *v.* 2. *When he slew them, then they sought him,* and made their application to Moses to stand their friend. Note, 1. When we complain without cause, it is just with God to give us cause to complain. 2. Those that slight God's friends when they are in prosperity would be glad to make them their friends when they are in distress. *Father Abraham, send Lazarus.*

V. The prevalency of Moses's intercession for them: *When Moses prayed unto the Lord* (he was always ready to stand in the gap to turn away the wrath of God) God had respect to him and his offering, and *the fire was quenched.* By this it appears that God delights not in punishing, for, when he has begun his controversy, he is soon prevailed with to let it fall. Moses was one of those worthies who *by faith quenched the violence of fire.*

VI. A new name given hereupon to the place, to perpetuate the shame of a murmuring people and the honour of a righteous God; the place was called *Taberah,* a *burning* (*v.* 3), that others might hear, and fear, and take warning not to sin as they did, lest they should smart as they did, 1 Co. 10:10.

Verses 4–15

These verses represent things sadly unhinged and out of order in Israel, both the people and the prince uneasy.

I. Here is the people fretting, and speaking against God himself (as it is interpreted, Ps. 78:19), notwithstanding his glorious appearances both to them and for them. Observe,

1. Who were the criminals. (1.) The *mixed multitude* began, they *fell a lusting, v.* 4. The rabble that came with them out of Egypt, expecting only the land of promise, but not a state of probation in the way to it. They were hangers on, who took hold of the skirts of the Jews, and would go with them only because they knew not how to live at home, and were disposed to seek their fortunes (as we say) abroad. These were the scabbed sheep that infected the flock, the leaven that leavened the whole lump. Note, A few factious, discontented, ill-natured people, may do a great deal of mischief in the best societies, if great care be not taken to discountenance them. Such as these are an *untoward generation,* from which it is our wisdom to *save ourselves,* Acts 2:40. (2.) Even *the children of Israel* took the infection, as we are informed, *v.* 4. The holy seed joined themselves to the people of these abominations. The mixed multitude here spoken of were not numbered with the children of Israel, but were set aside as a people God made no account of; and yet the children of Israel, forgetting their own character and distinction, herded themselves with them and learned their way, as if the scum and outcasts of the camp were to be the privy-counsellors of it. The children of Israel, a people near to God and highly privileged, yet drawn into rebellion against him! O how little honour has God in the world, when even the people which he formed for himself, to show forth his praise, were so much a dishonour to him! Therefore let none think that their external professions and privileges will be their security either against Satan's temptations to sin or God's judgments for sin. See 1 Co. 10:1, 2, 12.

2. What was the crime: they lusted and murmured. Though they had been lately corrected for this sin, and many of them overthrown for it, as God overthrew Sodom and Gomorrah, and the smell of the fire was still in their nostrils, yet they returned to it. See Prov. 27:22. (1.) They magnified the plenty and dainties they had had in Egypt (*v.* 5), as if God had done them a great deal of wrong in taking them thence. While they were in Egypt they sighed by reason of their burdens, for their lives were made bitter to them with hard bondage; and yet now they talk of Egypt as if they had all lived like princes there, when this serves as a colour for their present discontent. But with what face can they talk of eating fish in Egypt freely, or for nought, as if it cost them nothing, when they paid so dearly for it with their hard service? They *remember the cucumbers, and the melons, and the leeks, and the onions, and the garlick* (precious stuff indeed to be fond of!), but they do not remember the brick-kilns and the task-masters, the voice of the oppressor and the smart of the whip. No, these are forgotten by these ungrateful people. (2.) They were sick of the good provision God had made for them, *v.* 6. It was bread from heaven, angels' food. To show how unreasonable their complaint was, it is here described, *v.* 7–9. It was good for food, and pleasant to the eye, every grain like an orient pearl; it was wholesome food and nourishing; it was not to be called *dry bread,* for it tasted like fresh oil; it was agreeable (the Jews say, Wisd. 16:20) to every man's palate, and tasted as he would have it; and, though it was still the same, yet, by the different ways of dressing it, it yielded them a grateful variety; it cost them no money, nor care, for it fell in the night, while they slept; and the labour of gathering it was not worth speaking of; they lived upon free quarter, and yet could talk of Egypt's cheapness and the fish they ate there freely. Nay, which was much more valuable than all this, the manna came from the immediate power and bounty of God, not from common providence, but from special favour. It was, as God's compassion, new every morning, always fresh, not as their food who live on shipboard. While they lived on manna, they seemed to be exempted from the curse which sin has brought on man, that in the *sweat of his face should he eat bread.* And yet they speak of manna with such scorn, as if it were not good enough to be meat for swine: *Our soul is dried away.* They speak as if God dealt hardly with them in allowing them no better food. At first they admired it (Ex. 16:15): *What is this?* "What a curious precious thing is this!" But now they despised it. Note, Peevish discontented minds will find fault with that which has no fault in it but that it is too good for them. It is very provoking to God to undervalue his favours, and to put a *but* upon our common mercies. Nothing but manna! Those that might be very happy often make themselves very miserable by their discontents. (3.) They could not be satisfied unless they had flesh to eat. They brought flocks and herds with them in great abundance out of Egypt; but either they were covetous, and could not find in their hearts to kill them, lest they should lessen their flocks (they must have flesh as cheap as they had bread, or they would not be pleased), or else they were curious, beef and mutton would not please them; they must have something more nice and delicate, like the fish they did eat in Egypt. Food would not serve; they must be feasted. They had feasted with God upon the peace-offerings which they had their share of; but it seems God did not keep a table good enough for them, they must have daintier bits than any that came to his altar. Note, It is an evidence of the dominion of the carnal mind when we are solicitous to have all the delights and satisfactions of sense wound up to the height of pleasurableness. *Be not desirous of dainties,* Prov. 23:1–3. If God gives us food convenient, we ought to be thankful, though we do not eat the fat and drink the sweet. (4.) They distrusted the power and goodness of God as insufficient for their supply: *Who will give us flesh to eat?* taking it for granted that God could not. Thus this question is commented upon, Ps. 78:19, 20, *Can he provide flesh also?* though he had given them flesh with their bread once, when he saw fit (Ex. 16:13), and they might have expected that he would do it again, and in mercy, if, instead of murmuring, they had prayed. Note, It is an offence to God to let our desires go beyond our faith. (5.) They were eager and importunate in their desires; they *lusted a lust,* so the word is, lusted greatly and greedily, till they wept again for vexation. So childish were the children of Israel, and so humoursome, that they cried because they had not what they would have and when they would have it. They did not offer up this desire to God, but would rather be beholden to any one else than to him. We should not indulge ourselves in any desire which we cannot in faith turn into prayer, as we cannot when we *ask meat for our lust,* Ps. 78:18. For this sin the *anger of the Lord was kindled greatly against them,* which is written for our admonition, that we should not *lust after evil things as they lusted,* 1 Co. 10:6. (6.) Flesh is good food, and may lawfully be eaten; yet they are said to lust after evil things. What is lawful of itself becomes evil to us when it is what God does not allot to us and yet we eagerly desire it.

II. Moses himself, though so meek and good a man, is uneasy upon this occasion: *Moses also was displeased.* Now, 1. It must be confessed that the provocation was very great. These murmurings of theirs reflected great dishonour upon God, and Moses laid to heart the reproaches cast on himself; they knew that he did his utmost for their good, and that he neither did nor could do any thing without a divine appointment; and yet to be thus continually teased and clamoured against by an unreasonable ungrateful people would break in upon the temper even of Moses himself. God considered this, and therefore we do not find that he chided him for his uneasiness. 2. Yet Moses expressed himself otherwise than became him upon this provocation, and came short of his duty both to God and Israel in these expostulations. (1.) He undervalues the honour God had put upon him, in making him the illustrious minister of his power and grace, in the deliverance and guidance of that peculiar people, which might have been sufficient to balance the burden. (2.) He complains too much of a sensible grievance, and lays too near his heart a little noise and fatigue. If he could not bear the toil of government, which was but running with the footman, how would he bear the terrors of war, which was contending with horses? He might easily have furnished himself with considerations enough to enable him to slight their clamours, and make nothing of them. (3.) He magnifies his own performances, that *all the burden of the people lay upon him;* whereas God himself did in effect ease him of all the burden. Moses needed not to be in care to provide quarters for them, or victuals; God did all. And, if any difficult case happened, he needed not to be in any perplexity, while he had the oracle to consult, and in it the divine wisdom to direct him, the divine authority to back him and bear him out, and almighty power itself to dispense rewards and punishments. (4.) He is not so sensible as he ought to be of the obligation he lay under, by virtue of the divine commission and command, to do the utmost he could for his people, when he suggests that because they were not the children of his body therefore he was not concerned to take a fatherly care of them, though God himself, who might employ him as he pleased, had appointed him to be a father to them. (5.) He takes too much to himself when he asks, *Whence should I have flesh to give them* (v. 13), as if he were the housekeeper, and not God. *Moses gave them not the bread,* Jn. 6:32. Nor was it expected that he should give them the flesh, but as an instrument in God's hand; and if he meant, "Whence should God have it for them?" he too much limited the power of the Holy One of Israel. (6.) He speaks distrustfully of the divine grace when he despairs of being *able to bear all this people,* v. 14. Had the work been much less, he could not have gone through it in his own strength; but had it been much greater, through God strengthening him, he might have done it. (7.) It was worst of all passionately to wish for death, and desire to be killed out of hand, because just at this time his life was made a little uneasy to him, v. 15. Is this Moses? Is this the meekest of all the men on the earth? The best have their infirmities, and fail sometimes in the exercise of that grace for which they are most eminent. But God graciously overlooked Moses's passion at this time, and therefore we must not be severe in our animadversions upon it, but pray, *Lord, lead us not into temptation.*

Verses 16–23

We have here God's gracious answer to both the foregoing complaints, wherein his goodness takes occasion from man's badness to appear so much the more illustrious.

I. Provision is made for the redress of the grievances Moses complains of. If he find the weight of government lie too heavy upon him, though he was a little too passionate in his remonstrance, yet he shall be eased, not by being discarded from the government himself, as he justly might have been if God had been extreme to mark what he said amiss, but by having assistants appointed him, who should be, as the apostle speaks (1 Co. 12:28), *helps, governments* (that is, helps in government), not at all to lessen or eclipse his honour, but to make the work more easy to him, and to *bear the burden of the people with him.* And that this provision might be both agreeable and really serviceable,

1. Moses is directed to nominate the persons, v. 16. The people were too hot and heady and tumultuous to be entrusted with the election; Moses must please himself in the choice, that he may not afterwards complain. The number he is to choose is seventy men, according to the number of the souls that went down into Egypt. He must choose such as he knew to be elders, that is, wise and experienced men. Those that had acquitted themselves best, as *rulers of thousands and hundreds* (Ex. 18:25), purchase to themselves now this good degree. "Choose such as thou knowest to be elders indeed, and not in name only, officers that execute their office." We read of the same number of elders (Ex. 24:1) that went up with Moses to Mount Sinai, but they were distinguished only for that occasion, these for a perpetuity; and, according to this constitution, the Sanhedrim, or great council of the Jews, which in after ages sat at Jerusalem, and was the highest court of judgment among them, consisted of seventy men. Our Saviour seems to have had an eye to it in the choice of seventy disciples, who were to be assistants to the apostles, Lu. 10.

2. God promises to qualify them. If they were not found fit for the employ, they should be made fit, else they might prove more a hindrance than a help to Moses, v. 17. Though Moses had talked too boldly with God, yet God does not therefore break off communion with him; he bears a great deal with us, and we must with one another: *I will come down* (said God) *and talk with thee,* when thou art more calm and composed; *and I will take of the same spirit* of wisdom, and piety, and courage, *that is upon thee,* and *put it upon them.* Not that Moses had the less of the Spirit for their sharing, nor that they were hereby made equal with him; Moses was still unequalled (Deu. 34:10), but they were clothed with a spirit of government proportionable to their place, and with a spirit of prophecy to prove their divine call to it, the government being a Theocracy. Note, (1.) Those whom God employs in any service he qualifies for it, and those that are not in some measure qualified cannot think themselves duly called. (2.) All good qualifications are from God; every *perfect gift is from the Father of lights.*

II. Even the humour of the discontented people shall be gratified too, that every mouth may be stopped. They are ordered to *sanctify themselves* (v. 18), that is, to put themselves into a posture to receive such a proof of God's power as should be a token both of mercy and judgment. *Prepare to meet thy God, O Israel,* Amos 4:12.

1. God promises (shall I say?) — he threatens rather, that they shall have their fill of flesh, that for a month together they shall not only be fed, but feasted, with flesh, besides their daily manna; and, if they have not a better government of their appetites than now it appears they have they shall be surfeited with it (v. 19, 20): You shall eat *till it come out at your nostrils, and become loathsome to you.* See here, (1.) The vanity of all the delights of sense; they will cloy, but not satisfy: spiritual pleasures are the contrary. As the world passes away, so do the lusts of it, 1 Jn. 2:17. What was greedily coveted in a little time comes to be nauseated. (2.) What brutish sins (and worse than brutish) gluttony and drunkenness are; they put a force upon nature, and make that the sickness of the body which should be its health; they are sins that are their own punishments, and yet not the worst that attend them. (3.) What a righteous thing it is with God to make that loathsome to men which they have inordinately lusted after. God could make them despise flesh as much as they had despised manna.

2. Moses objects the improbability of making good this word, v. 21, 22. It is an objection like that which the disciples made, Mk. 8:4, *Whence can a man satisfy these men?* Some excuse Moses here, and construe what he says as only a modest enquiry which way the supply must be expected; but it savours too much of diffidence and distrust of God to be justified. He objects the number of the people, as if he that provided bread for them all could not, by the same unlimited power, provide flesh too. He reckons it must be the flesh either of beasts or fishes, because they are the most bulky animals, little thinking that the flesh of birds, little birds, should serve the purpose. God sees not as man sees, but his thoughts are above ours. He objects the greediness of the people's desires in that word, *to suffice them.* Note, Even true and great believers sometimes find it hard to trust God under the discouragements of second causes, and *against hope to believe in hope.* Moses himself could scarcely forbear saying, *Can God furnish a table in the wilderness?* when this had become the common cry. No doubt this was his infirmity.

3. God gives a short but sufficient answer to the objection in that question, *Has the Lord's hand waxed short?* v. 23. If Moses had remembered *the years of the right hand of the Most High,* he would not have started all these difficulties; therefore God reminds him of them, intimating that this objection reflected upon the divine power, of which he himself had been so often, not only the witness, but the instrument. Had he forgotten what wonders the divine power had wrought for that people, when it inflicted the plagues of Egypt, divided the sea, broached the rock, and rained bread from heaven? Had that power abated? Was God weaker than he used to be? Or was he tired with what he had done? Whatever our unbelieving hearts may suggest to the contrary, it is certain, (1.) That God's hand is not short; his power cannot be restrained in the exerting of itself by any thing but his own will; with him nothing is impossible. That hand is not short which meas-

ures the waters, metes out the heavens (Isa. 40:12), and grasps the winds, Prov. 30:4. (2.) That it has not waxed short. He is as strong as ever he was, *fainteth not, neither is weary.* And this is sufficient to silence all our distrusts when means fail us, *Is any thing too hard for the Lord?* God here brings Moses to this first principle, sets him back in his lesson, to learn the ancient name of God, *The Lord God Almighty,* and puts the proof upon the issue: *Thou shalt see whether my word shall come to pass or not.* This magnifies God's word above all his name, that his works never come short of it. If he speaks, it is done.

Verses 24–30

We have here the performance of God's word to Moses, that he should have help in the government of Israel.

I. Here is the case of the seventy privy-counsellors in general. Moses, though a little disturbed by the tumult of the people, yet was thoroughly composed by the communion he had with God, and soon came to himself again. And according as the matter was concerted, 1. He did his part; he presented the seventy elders before the Lord, round the tabernacle (v. 24), that they might there stand ready to receive the grace of God, in the place where he manifested himself, and that the people also might be witnesses of their solemn call. Note, Those that expect favour from God must humbly offer themselves and their service to him. 2. God was not wanting to do his part. *He gave of his Spirit to the seventy elders* (v. 25), which enabled those whose capacities and education set them but on a level with their neighbours of a sudden to say and do that which was extraordinary, and which proved them to be actuated by divine inspiration: they prophesied, and did not cease all that day, and (some think) only that day. They discoursed to the people of the things of God, and perhaps commented upon the law they had lately received with admirable clearness, and fulness, and readiness, and aptness of expression, so that all who heard them might see and say that *God was with them of a truth;* see 1 Co. 14:24, 25. Thus, long afterwards, Saul was marked for the government by the gift of prophecy, which came upon him for a day and a night, 1 Sa. 10:6, 11. When Moses was to fetch Israel out of Egypt, Aaron was appointed to be his prophet, Ex. 7:1. But, now that God had called Aaron to other work, in his room Moses has seventy prophets to attend him. Note, Those are fittest to rule in God's Israel that are well acquainted with divine things and are apt to teach to edification.

II. Here is the particular case of two of them, *Eldad* and *Medad,* probably two brothers.

1. They were nominated by Moses to be assistants in the government, but they *went not out unto the tabernacle* as the rest did, v. 26. Calvin conjectures that the summons was sent them, but that it did not find them, they being somewhere out of the way; so that, though they were written, yet they were not called. Most think that they declined coming to the tabernacle out of an excess of modesty and humility; being sensible of their own weakness and unworthiness, they desired to be excused from coming into the government. Their principle was their praise, but their practice in not obeying orders was their fault.

2. The Spirit of God found them out in the camp, where they were hidden among the stuff, and there they prophesied, that is, they exercised their gift of praying, preaching, and praising God, in some private tent. Note, The Spirit of God is not tied to the tabernacle, but, *like the wind, blows where he listeth,* Jn. 3:8. *Whither can we go from that Spirit?* There was a special providence in it that these two should be absent, for thus it appeared that it was indeed a divine Spirit which the elders were actuated by, and that Moses gave them not that Spirit, but God himself. They modestly declined preferment, but God forced it upon them; nay, they have the honour of being *named,* which the rest have not: for those that humble themselves shall be exalted, and those are most fit for government who are least ambitious of it.

3. Information of this was given to Moses (v. 27): "*Eldad and Medad do prophesy in the camp;* there is a conventicle in such a tent, and Eldad and Medad are holding forth there, from under the inspection and presidency of Moses, and out of the communion of the rest of the elders." Whoever the person was that brought the tidings, he seems to have looked upon it as an irregularity.

4. Joshua moved to have them silenced: *My lord Moses, forbid them, v.* 28. It is probable that Joshua himself was one of the seventy, which made him the more jealous for the honour of their order. He takes it for granted that they were not under any necessitating impulse, *for the spirit of the prophets is subject to the prophets,* and therefore he would have them either not to prophesy at all or to come to the tabernacle and prophesy in concert with the rest. He does not desire that they should be punished for what they had done, but only restrained for the future. This motion he made from a good principle, not out of any personal dislike to Eldad and Medad, but out of an honest zeal for that which he apprehended to be the unity of the church, and concern for the honour of God and Moses.

5. Moses rejected the motion, and reproved him that made it (*v.* 29): "*Enviest thou for my sake?* Thou knowest not what manner of spirit thou art of." Though Joshua was Moses's particular friend and confidant, though he said this out of a respect to Moses, whose honour he was very loth to see lessened by the call of those elders, yet Moses reproves him, and in him all that show such a spirit. (1.) We must not secretly grieve at the gifts, graces, and usefulness of others. It was the fault of John's disciples that they envied Christ's honour because it shaded their master's, Jn. 3:26, etc. (2.) We must not be transported into heats against the weaknesses and infirmities of others. Granting that Eldad and Medad were guilty of an irregularity, yet Joshua was too quick and too warm upon them. Our zeal must always be tempered with the meekness of wisdom: the righteousness of God needs not the wrath of man, Jam. 1:20. (3.) We must not make even the best and most useful men heads of a party. Paul would not have his name made use of to patronise a faction, 1 Co. 1:12, 13. (4.) We must not be forward to condemn and silence those that differ from us, as if they did not follow Christ because they do not follow *him with us,* Mk. 9:38. Shall we reject those whom Christ has owned, or restrain any from doing good because they are not in every thing of our mind? Moses was of another spirit; so far from silencing these two, and quenching the Spirit in them, he wished *all the Lord's people were prophets,* that is, that he would *put his Spirit upon them.* Not that he would have any set up for prophets that were not duly qualified, or that he expected that the Spirit of prophecy should be made thus common; but thus he expresses the love and esteem he had for *all the Lord's people,* the complacency he took in the gifts of others, and how far he was from being displeased at Eldad and Medad's prophesying from under his eye. Such an excellent spirit as this blessed Paul was of, rejoicing that Christ was preached, though it was by those who therein intended to *add affliction to his bonds,* Phil. 1:16. We ought to be pleased that God is served and glorified, and good done, though to the lessening of our credit and the credit of our way.

6. The elders, now newly ordained, immediately entered upon their administration (*v.* 30); when their call was sufficiently attested by their prophesying, they went with Moses to the camp, and applied themselves to business. Having received the gift, they *ministered the same as good stewards.* And now Moses was pleased that he had so many to share with him in his work and honour. And, (1.) Let the testimony of Moses be credited by those who desire to be in power, that government is a burden. It is a burden of care and trouble to those who make conscience of the duty of it; and to those who do not it will prove a heavier burden in the day of account, when they fall under the doom of the unprofitable servant that buried his talent. (2.) Let the example of Moses be imitated by those that are in power; let them not despise the advice and assistance of others, but desire it, and be thankful for it, not coveting to monopolize wisdom and power. In the multitude of counsellors there is safety.

Verses 31–35

God, having performed his promise to Moses by giving him assessors in the government, thereby proving the power he has over the spirits of men by his Spirit, he here performs his promise to the people by giving them flesh, proving thereby his power over the inferior creatures and his dominion in the kingdom of nature. Observe, 1. How the people were gratified with flesh in abundance: *A wind* (a south-east wind, as appears, Ps. 78:26) *brought quails, v.* 31. It is uncertain what sort of animals they were; the psalmist calls them *feathered fowl,* or *fowl of wing.* The learned bishop Patrick inclines to agree with some modern writers, who think they were *locusts,* a delicious sort of food well known in those parts, the rather because they were brought with a wind, lay in heaps, and were dried in the sun for use. Whatever they were, they answered the intention, they served for a month's feast for Israel, such an indulgent Father was God to his froward family. Locusts, that had been a plague to fruitful Egypt, feeding upon the fruits, were a blessing to a barren wilderness, being themselves fed upon. 2. How greedy they were of this flesh that God sent them. They *flew upon the spoil* with an unsatiable appetite, not regarding what Moses had told them from God, that they would surfeit upon it, 5:32. Two days and a night they were at it, gathering flesh, till every master of a family had brought home ten homers (that is, ten ass-loads) at least. David longed for the water of the well of Bethlehem, but would not drink it when he had it, because it was obtained by venturing; much more reason these Israelites had to refuse this flesh, which was obtained by murmuring, and which, they might easily perceive, by what Moses said, was given them in anger; but those that are under the power of a carnal mind will have their lusts fulfilled, though it be to the certain damage and ruin of their precious souls. 3. How dearly they paid for their feasts, when it came into the reckoning: *The Lord smote them with a very great plague* (*v.* 33), some bodily disease, which probably was the effect of their surfeit, and was the death of many of them, and those, it is likely, the ringleaders in the mutiny. Note, God often grants the desires of his own people in love. He *gave them their request,* but *sent leanness into their soul,* Ps. 16:15. By all that was said to them they *were not estranged from their lusts,* and therefore, *while the meat was in their mouths, the wrath of God came upon them,* Ps. 78:30, 31. What we inordinately desire, if we obtain it (we have reason to fear), will be some way or other a grief and cross to us. God satiated them first, and then plagued them, (1.) To save the reputation of his own power, that it might not be said, "He would not have cut them off had he been able to supply them." And, (2.) To show us the meaning of the prosperity of sinners; it is their preparation for ruin, they are fed as an ox for the slaughter. *Lastly,* The remembrance of this is preserved in the name given to the place, *v.* 34. Moses called it *Kibroth-hattaavah,* the *graves of lusters* or *of lust.* And well it had been if these graves of Israel's lusters had proved the graves of Israel's lust: the warning was designed to be so, but it had not its due effect, for it follows (Ps. 78:32), *For all this, they sinned still.*

CHAPTER 12

In the foregoing chapter we had the vexation which the people gave to Moses; in this we have his patience tried by his own relations. I. Miriam and Aaron, his own brother and sister, affronted him (*v.* 1–3). II. God called them to an account for it (*v.* 4–9). III. Miriam was smitten with a leprosy for it (*v.* 10). IV. Aaron submits, and Moses meekly intercedes for Miriam (*v.* 11–13). V. She is healed, but put to shame for seven days (*v.* 14–16). And this is recorded to show that the best persons and families have both their follies and their crosses.

Verses 1–3

Here is, I. The unbecoming passion of Aaron and Miriam: they *spoke against Moses, v.* 1. If Moses, that received so much honour from God, yet received so many slights and affronts from men, shall any of us think such trials either strange or hard, and be either provoked or discouraged by them? But who would have thought that disturbance should be created to Moses, 1. From those that were themselves serious and good; nay, that were eminent in religion, Miriam a prophetess, Aaron the high priest, both of them joint-commissioners with Moses for the deliverance of Israel? Mic. 6:4, *I sent before thee Moses, Aaron, and Miriam.* 2. From those that were his nearest relations, his own brother and sister, who shone so much by rays borrowed from him? Thus the spouse complains (Cant. 1:6), *My mother's children were angry with me;* and quarrels among relations are in a special manner grievous. *A brother offended is harder to be won than a strong city.* Yet this helps to confirm the call of Moses, and shows that his advancement was purely by the divine favour, and not by any compact or collusion with his kindred, who themselves grudged his advancement. Neither did many of our Saviour's kindred believe on him, Jn. 7:5. It should seem that Miriam began the quarrel, and Aaron, not having been employed or consulted in the choice of the seventy elders, was for the present somewhat disgusted, and so was the sooner drawn in to take his sister's part. It would grieve one to see the hand of Aaron in so many trespasses, but it shows that *the law made men priests who had infirmity.* Satan prevailed first with Eve, and by her with Adam; see what need we have to take heed of being drawn into quarrels by our relations, for we know not how great a matter a little fire may kindle. Aaron ought to have remembered how Moses stood his friend when God was angry with him for making the golden calf (Deu. 9:20), and not to have rendered him evil for good. Two things they quarrelled with Moses about: — (1.) About his marriage: some think a late marriage with a Cushite or Arabian; others because of Zipporah, whom on this occasion they called, in scorn, an Ethiopian woman, and who, they insinuated, had too great an influence upon Moses in the choice of these seventy elders. Perhaps there was some private falling out between Zipporah and Miriam, which occasioned some hot words, and one peevish reflection introduced another, till Moses and Aaron came to be interested. (2.) About his government; not the mismanagement of it, but the monopolizing of it (*v.* 2): "*Hath the Lord spoken only by Moses?* Must *he* alone have the choice of the persons on whom the spirit of prophecy shall come? *Hath he not spoken also by us?* Might not we have had a hand in that affair, and preferred our friends, as well as Moses his?" They could not deny that God had spoken by Moses, but it was plain he had sometimes spoken also by them; and that which they intended was to make themselves equal with him, though God had so many ways distinguished him. Note, Striving to be greatest is a sin which easily besets disciples themselves, and it is exceedingly sinful. Even those that are well preferred are seldom pleased if others be better preferred. Those that excel are commonly envied.

II. The wonderful patience of Moses under this provocation. *The Lord heard it* (*v.* 2), but Moses himself took no notice of it, for (*v.* 3) he was very meek. He had a great deal of reason to resent the affront; it was ill-natured and ill-timed, when the people were disposed to mutiny, and had lately given him a great deal of vexation with their murmurings, which would be in danger of breaking out again when thus headed and countenanced by Aaron and Miriam; but he, *as a deaf man, heard not.* When God's honour was concerned, as in the case of the golden calf, no man more zealous than Moses; but, when his own honour was touched, no man more meek: as bold as a lion in the cause of God, but as mild as a lamb in his own cause. God's people are the *meek of the earth* (Zep. 2:3), but some are more remarkable than others for this grace, as Moses, who was thus fitted for the work he was called to, which required all the meekness he had and sometimes more. And sometimes the unkindness of our friends is a greater trial of our meekness than the malice of our enemies. Christ himself records his own meekness (Mt. 11:29, *I am meek and lowly in heart*), and the copy of meekness which Christ has set was without a blot, but that of Moses was not.

Verses 4–9

Moses did not resent the injury done him, nor complain of it to God, nor make any appeal to him; but God resented it. He hears all we say in our passion, and is a swift witness of our hasty speeches, which is a reason why we should resolutely bridle our tongues, that we speak not ill of others, and why we should patiently stop our ears, and not take notice of it, if others speak ill of us. *I heard not, for thou wilt hear,* Ps. 38:13–15. The more silent we are in our own cause the more is God engaged to plead it. The accused innocent needs to say little if he knows the judge himself will be his advocate.

I. The cause is called, and the parties are summoned forthwith to attend at the door of the tabernacle, *v.* 4, 5. Moses had often shown himself jealous for God's honour, and now God showed himself jealous for his reputation; for *those that honour God he will honour,* nor will he ever be behind-hand with any that appear for him. Judges of old sat in the gate of the city to try causes, and so on this occasion the *shechinah* in the cloud of glory stood *at the door of the tabernacle,* and Aaron and Miriam, as delinquents, were called to the bar.

II. Aaron and Miriam were made to know that great as they were they must not pretend to be equal to Moses, nor set up as rivals with him, v. 6–8. Were they prophets of the Lord? Of Moses it might be truly said, *He more.* 1. It was true that God put a great deal of honour upon the prophets. However men mocked them and misused them, they were the favourites and intimates of heaven. God *made himself known to them,* either by dreams when they were asleep or by visions when they were awake, and by them made himself known to others. And those are happy, those are great, truly great, truly happy, to whom God *makes himself known,* Now he does it not by dreams and visions, as of old, but by the *Spirit of wisdom and revelation,* who makes known those things to babes which *prophets and kings* desired to see and might not. Hence in the last days, the days of the Messiah, the *sons and daughters* are said to *prophesy* (Joel 2:28), because they shall be better acquainted with the mysteries of the kingdom of grace than even the prophets themselves were; see Heb. 1:1, 2. 2. Yet the honour put upon Moses was far greater (v. 7): *My servant Moses is not so,* he excels them all. To recompense Moses for his meekly and patiently bearing the affronts which Miriam and Aaron gave him, God not only cleared him, but praised him; and took that occasion to give him an encomium which remains upon record to his immortal honour; and thus shall those that are reviled and persecuted for righteousness' sake have a *great reward in heaven,* Christ will confess them before his Father and the holy angels. (1.) Moses was a man of great integrity and tried fidelity. He is *faithful in all my house.* This is put first in his character, because grace excels gifts, love excels knowledge, and sincerity in the service of God puts a greater honour upon a man and recommends him to the divine favour more than learning, abstruse speculations, and an ability to *speak with tongues.* This is that part of Moses's character which the apostle quotes when he would show that Christ was greater than Moses, making it out that he was so in this chief instance of his greatness; for Moses was faithful only *as a servant,* but Christ *as a son,* Heb. 3:2, 5, 6. God entrusted Moses to deliver his mind in all things to Israel; Israel entrusted him to treat for them with God; and he was faithful to both. He said and did every thing in the management of that great affair as became an honest good man, that aimed at nothing else but the honour of God and the welfare of Israel. (2.) Moses was therefore honoured with clearer discoveries of God's mind, and a more intimate communion with God, than any other prophet whatsoever. He shall, [1.] Hear more from God than any other prophet, more clearly and distinctly: *With him will I speak mouth to mouth,* or *face to face* (Ex. 30:11), *as a man speaks to his friend,* whom he discourses with freely and familiarly, and without any confusion or consternation, such as sometimes other prophets were under; as Ezekiel, and John himself, when God spoke to them. By other prophets God sent to his people reproofs, and predictions of good or evil, which were properly enough delivered in dark speeches, figures, types, and parables; but by Moses he gave laws to his people, and the institution of holy ordinances, which could by no means be delivered by dark speeches, but must be expressed in the plainest and most intelligible manner. [2.] He shall see more of God than any other prophet: *The similitude of the Lord shall behold,* as he hath seen it in Horeb, when God proclaimed his name before him. Yet he saw only the similitude of the Lord, angels and glorified saints always behold the face of our Father. Moses had the spirit of prophecy in a way peculiar to himself, and which set him far above all other prophets; yet *he that is least in the kingdom of heaven is greater than he,* much more does our Lord Jesus infinitely excel him, Heb. 3:1, etc.

Now let Miriam and Aaron consider who it was that they insulted: *Were you not afraid to speak against my servant Moses? Against my servant, against Moses?* so it runs in the original. "How dare you abuse any servant of mine, especially such a servant as Moses, who is a friend, a confidant, and steward of the house?" How durst they speak to the grief and reproach of one whom God had so much to say in commendation of? Might they not expect that God would resent it, and take it as an affront to himself? Note, We have reason to be afraid of saying or doing any thing against the servants of God; it is at our peril if we do, for God will plead their cause, and reckon that what

touches them touches the apple of his eye. It is a dangerous thing to *offend Christ's little ones,* Mt. 18:6. Those are presumptuous indeed that *are not afraid to speak evil of dignities,* 2 Pt. 2:10.

III. God, having thus shown them their fault and folly, next shows them his displeasure (v. 9): *The anger of the Lord was kindled against them,* of which perhaps some sensible indications were given in the change of the colour of the cloud, or some flashes of lightning from it. But indeed it was indication enough of his displeasure that he departed, and would not so much as hear their excuse, for he needed not, *understanding their thoughts afar off;* and thus he would show that he was displeased. Note, The removal of God's presence from us is the surest and saddest token of God's displeasure against us. Woe unto us if he depart; and he never departs till we by our sin and folly drive him from us.

Verses 10–16

Here is, I. God's judgment upon Miriam (v. 10): *The cloud departed from off* that part of *the tabernacle,* in token of God's displeasure, and presently Miriam became leprous; when God goes, evil comes; expect no good when God departs. The leprosy was a disease often inflicted by the immediate hand of God as the punishment of some particular sin, as on Gehazi for lying, on Uzziah for invading the priest's office, and here on Miriam for scolding and making mischief among relations. The plague of the leprosy, it is likely, appeared in her face, so that it appeared to all that saw her that she was struck with it, with the worst of it, she was leprous as snow; not only so white, but so soft, the solid flesh losing its consistency, as that which putrefies does. Her foul tongue (says bishop Hall) is justly punished with a foul face, and her folly in pretending to be a rival with Moses is made manifest to all men, for every one sees his face to be glorious, and hers to be leprous. While Moses needs a veil to hide his glory, Miriam needs one to hide her shame. Note, Those distempers which any way deform us ought to be construed as a rebuke to our pride, and improved for the cure of it, and under such humbling providences we ought to be very humble. It is a sign that the heart is hard indeed if the flesh be mortified, and yet the lusts of the flesh remain unmortified. It should seem that this plague upon Miriam was designed for an exposition of the law concerning the leprosy (Lev. 13), for it is referred to upon the rehearsal of that law, Deu. 24:8, 9. Miriam was struck with a leprosy, but not Aaron, because she was first in the transgression, and God would put a difference between those that mislead and those that are misled. Aaron's office, though it saved him not from God's displeasure, yet helped to secure him from this token of his displeasure, which would not only have suspended him for the present from officiating, when (there being no priests but himself and his two sons) he could ill be spared, but it would have rendered him and his office mean, and would have been a lasting blot upon his family. Aaron as priest was to be the judge of the leprosy, and his performing that part of his office upon this occasion, when he *looked upon Miriam, and behold she was leprous,* was a sufficient mortification to him. He was struck through her side, and could not pronounce her leprous without blushing and trembling, knowing himself to be equally obnoxious. This judgment upon Miriam is improvable by us as a warning to take heed of putting any affront upon our Lord Jesus. If she was thus chastised for speaking against Moses, what will become of those that sin against Christ?

II. Aaron's submission hereupon (v. 11, 12); he humbles himself to Moses, confesses his fault, and begs pardon. He that but just now joined with his sister in speaking against Moses is here forced for himself and his sister to make a penitent address to him, and in the highest degree to magnify him (as if he had the power of God to forgive and heal) whom he had so lately vilified. Note, Those that trample upon the saints and servants of God will one day be glad to make court to them; at furthest, in the other world, as the foolish virgins to the wise for a little oil, and the rich man to Lazarus for a little water; and perhaps in this world, as Job's friend to him for his prayers, and here Aaron to Moses. Rev. 3:9. In his submission, 1. He confesses his own and his sister's sin, v. 11. He speaks respectfully to Moses,

of whom he had spoken slightly, calls him his lord, and now turns the reproach upon himself, speaks as one ashamed of what he had said: *We have sinned, we have done foolishly.* Those sin, and do foolishly, who revile and speak evil of any, especially of good people or of those in authority. Repentance is the unsaying of that which we have said amiss, and it had better be unsaid than that we be undone by it. 2. He begs Moses's pardon: *Lay not this sin upon us.* Aaron was to bring his gift to the altar, but, knowing that his brother had something against him, he of all men was concerned to reconcile himself to his brother, that he might be qualified to offer his gift. Some think that this speedy submission which God saw him ready to make was that which prevented his being struck with a leprosy as his sister was. 3. He recommends the deplorable condition of his sister to Moses's compassionate consideration (v. 12): *Let her not be as one dead,* that is, "Let her not continue so separated from conversation, defiling all she touches, and even to putrefy above ground as one dead." He eloquently describes the misery of her case, to move his pity.

III. The intercession made for Miriam (v. 13): He *cried unto the Lord* with a loud voice, because the cloud, the symbol of his presence, was removed and stood at some distance, and to express his fervency in this request, *Heal her now, O Lord, I beseech thee.* By this he made it to appear that he did heartily forgive her the injury she had one him, that he had not accused her to God, nor called for justice against her; so far from this that, when God in tenderness to his honour had chastised her insolence, he was the first that moved for reversing the judgment. By this example we are taught to *pray for those that despitefully use us;* and not to take pleasure in the most righteous punishment inflicted either by God or man on those that have been injurious to us. Jeroboam's withered hand was restored at the special instance and request of the prophet against whom it had been stretched out, 1 Ki. 13:6. So Miriam here was healed by the prayer of Moses, whom she had abused, and Abimelech by the prayer of Abraham, Gen. 20:17. Moses might have stood off, and have said, "She is served well enough, let her govern her tongue better next time;" but, not content with being able to say that he had not prayed for the inflicting of the judgment, he prays earnestly for the removal of it. This pattern of Moses, and that of our Saviour, *Father, forgive them,* we must study to conform to.

IV. The accommodating of this matter so as that mercy and justice might meet together. 1. Mercy takes place so far as that Miriam shall be healed; Moses forgives her, and God will. See 2 Co. 2:10. But, 2. Justice takes place so far as that Miriam shall be humbled (v. 14): *Let her be shut out from the camp seven days,* that she herself might be made more sensible of her fault and penitent for it, and that her punishment might be the more public, and all Israel might take notice of it and take warning by it not to mutiny. If Miriam the prophetess be put under such marks of humiliation for one hasty word spoken against Moses, what may we expect for our murmurings? *If this be done in a green tree, what shall be done in the dry?* See how people debase and diminish themselves by sin, stain their glory, and lay their honour in the dust. When Miriam praised God, we find her at the head of the congregation and one of the brightest ornaments of it, Ex. 15:20. Now that she quarrelled with God we find her expelled as the filth and off-scouring of it. A reason is given for her being put out of the camp for seven days, because thus she ought to *accept of the punishment of her iniquity.* If her father, her earthly father, had but spit in her face, and so signified his displeasure against her, would she not be so troubled and concerned at it, and so sorry that she had deserved it, as to shut herself up for some time in her room, and not come into his presence, or show her face in the family, being ashamed of her own folly and unhappiness? If such reverence as this be owing to the fathers of our flesh, when they correct us, much more ought we to humble ourselves under the mighty hand of the Father of spirits, Heb. 12:9. Note, When we are under the tokens of God's displeasure for sin, it becomes us to take shame to ourselves, and to lie down in that shame, owning that *to us belongs confusion of face.* If by our own fault and folly we expose ourselves to the reproach and contempt of men, the just censures of the church, or the rebukes of the divine Providence, we must confess that our Father justly spits in our face, and be ashamed.

V. The hindrance that this gave to the people's progress: *The people journeyed not till Miriam was brought in again, v.* 15. God did not remove the cloud, and therefore they did not remove their camp. This was intended, 1. As a rebuke to the people, who were conscious to themselves of having sinned after the similitude of Miriam's transgression, in speaking against Moses: thus far therefore they shall share in her punishment, that it shall retard their march forward towards Canaan. Many things oppose us, but nothing hinders us in the way to heaven as sin does. 2. As a mark of respect to Miriam. If the camp had removed during the days of her suspension, her trouble and shame had been the greater; therefore, in compassion to her, they shall stay till her excommunication be taken off, and she taken in again, it is probable with the usual ceremonies of the cleansing of lepers. Note, Those that are under censure and rebuke for sin ought to be treated with a great deal of tenderness, and not be over-loaded, no, not with the shame they have deserved, not *counted as enemies* (2 Th. 3:15), but *forgiven and comforted,* 2 Co. 2:7. Sinners must be cast out with grief, and penitents taken in with joy. When Miriam was absolved and re-admitted, the people went forward into the wilderness of Paran, which joined up to the south border of Canaan, and thither their next remove would have been if they had not put a bar in their own way.

CHAPTER 13

It is a memorable and very melancholy story which is related in this and the following chapter, of the turning back of Israel from the borders of Canaan, when they were just ready to set foot in it, and the sentencing of them to wander and perish in the wilderness for their unbelief and murmuring. It is referred to Ps. 95:7, etc., and improved for warning to Christians, Heb. 3:7, etc. In this chapter we have, I. The sending of twelve spies before them into Canaan (*v.* 1–16). II. The instructions given to these spies (*v.* 17–20). III. Their executing their commission according to their instructions, and their return from the search (*v.* 21–25). IV. The report they brought back to the camp of Israel (*v.* 26, etc.).

Verses 1–20

Here we have, I. Orders given to send spies to search out the land of Canaan. It is here said, God directed Moses to send them (*v.* 1, 2), but it appears by the repetition of the story afterwards (Deu. 1:22) that the motion came originally from the people; they came to Moses, and said, *We will send men before us;* and it was the fruit of their unbelief. They would not take God's word that it was a good land, and that he would, without fail, put them in possession of it. They could not trust the pillar of cloud and fire to show them the way to it, but had a better opinion of their own politics than of God's wisdom. How absurd was it for them to send to spy out a land which God himself had spied out for them, to enquire the way into it when God himself had undertaken to show them the way! But thus we ruin ourselves by giving more credit to the reports and representations of sense than to divine revelation; we walk by sight, not by faith; whereas, *if we will receive the witness of men,* without doubt *the witness of God is greater.* The people making this motion to Moses, he (perhaps not aware of the unbelief at the bottom of it) consulted God in the case, who bade him gratify the people in this matter, and send spies before them: "Let them walk in their own counsels." Yet God was no way accessory to the sin that followed, for the sending of these spies was so far from being the cause of the sin that if the spies had done their duty, and the people theirs, it might have been the confirmation of their faith, and of good service to them.

II. The persons nominated that were to be employed in this service (*v.* 4, etc.), one of each tribe, that it might appear to be the act of the people in general; and rulers, person of figure in their respective tribes, some of the rulers of thousands or hundreds, to put the greater credit upon their embassy. This was designed for the best, but it proved to have this ill effect that the quality of the persons occasioned the evil report they brought up to be the more credited and the people to be the more influenced by it. Some think that they are all named for the sake of two good ones that were among them, Caleb and Joshua. Notice is taken of the change of Joshua's name upon this occasion, *v.* 16. He was Moses's minister, but had been employed, though of the tribe of Ephraim, as general of the forces that were sent out against Amalek. The name by which he was generally called and known in his own tribe was *Oshea,* but Moses called him *Joshua,* in token of his affection to him and power over him; and now, it should seem, he ordered others to call him so, and fixed that to be his name henceforward. *Oshea* signifies a prayer for salvation, *Save thou; Joshua* signifies a promise of salvation, *He will save,* in answer to that prayer: so near is the relation between prayers and promises. Prayers prevail for promises, and promises direct and encourage prayers. Some think that Moses designed, by taking the first syllable of the name Jehovah and prefixing it to his name, which turned *Hoshea* into *Jehoshua,* to put an honour upon him, and to encourage him in this and all his future services with the assurances of God's presence. Yet after this he is called *Hoshea,* Deu. 32:44. *Jesus* is the same name with *Joshua,* and it is the name of our Lord Christ, of whom Joshua was a type as successor to Moses, Israel's captain, and conqueror of Canaan. There was another of the same name, who was also a type of Christ, Zec. 6:11. Joshua was the saviour of God's people from the powers of Canaan, but Christ is their Saviour from the powers of hell.

III. The instructions given to those spies. They were sent into the land of Canaan the nearest way, to traverse the country, and to take account of its present state, *v.* 17. Two heads of enquiry were given them in charge, 1. Concerning the land itself: *See what that is* (*v.* 18, and again, *v.* 19), see whether it be *good or bad,* and (*v.* 20) *whether it be fat or lean.* All parts of the earth do not share alike in the blessing of fruitfulness; some countries are blessed with a richer soil than others. Moses himself was well satisfied that Canaan was a very good land, but he sent these spies to bring an account of it for the satisfaction of the people; as John Baptist sent to Jesus, to ask whether he was the Christ, not to inform himself, but to inform those he sent. They must take notice whether the air was healthful or no, what the soil was, and what the productions; and, for the better satisfaction of the people, they must bring with them some of the fruits. 2. Concerning the inhabitants — their number, few or many — their size and stature, whether strong able-bodied men or weak, — their habitations, whether they lived in tents or houses, whether in open villages or in walled towns, — whether the woods were standing as in those countries that are uncultivated, through the unskillfulness and slothfulness of the inhabitants, or whether the woods were cut down, and the country made champaign, for the convenience of tillage. These were the things they were to enquire about. Perhaps there had not been of late years such commerce between Egypt and Canaan as there was in Jacob's time, else they might have informed themselves of these things without sending men on purpose to search. See the advantage we may derive from books and learning, which acquaint those that are curious and inquisitive with the state of foreign countries, at a much greater distance than Canaan was now from Israel, without this trouble and expense.

IV. Moses dismisses the spies with this charge, *Be of good courage,* intimating, not only that they should be themselves encouraged against the difficulties of this expedition, but that they should bring an encouraging account to the people and make the best of every thing. It was not only a great undertaking they were put upon, which required good management and resolution, but it was a great trust that was reposed in them, which required that they should be faithful.

Verses 21–25

We have here a short account of the survey which the spies made of the promised land. 1. They went quite through it, from Zin in the south, to Rehob, near Hamath, in the north, *v.* 21. See *ch.* 34:3, 8. It is probable that they did not go altogether in a body, lest they should be suspected and taken up, which there would be the more danger of if the Canaanites knew (and one would think they could not but know) how near the Israelites were to them; but they divided themselves into several companies, and so passed unsuspected, as way-faring men. 2. They took particular notice of Hebron (*v.* 22), probably because near there was the field of Machpelah, where the patriarchs were buried (Gen. 23:2), whose dead bodies did, as it were, keep possession of that land for their posterity. To this sepulchre they made a particular visit, and found the adjoining city in the possession of the sons of Anak, who are here named. In that place where they expected the greatest encouragements they met with the greatest discouragements. Where the bodies of their ancestors kept possession for them the giants kept possession against them. *They ascended by the south, and came to Hebron,* that is, "Caleb," say the Jews, "in particular," for to his being there we find express reference, Jos. 14:9, 12, 13. But that others of the spies were there too appears by their description of the Anakim, *v.* 33. 3. They brought a bunch of grapes with them, and some other of the fruits of the land, as a proof of the extraordinary goodness of the country. Probably they furnished themselves with these fruits when they were leaving the country and returning. The cluster of grapes was so large and so heavy that they hung it upon a bar, and carried it between two of them, *v.* 23, 24. The place whence they took it was, from this circumstance, called the *valley of the cluster,* that famous cluster which was to Israel both the earnest and the specimen of all the fruits of Canaan. Such are the present comforts which we have in communion with God, foretastes of the fulness of joy we expect in the heavenly Canaan. We may see by them what heaven is.

Verses 26–33

It is a wonder how the people of Israel had patience to stay forty days for the return of their spies, when they were just ready to enter Canaan, under all the assurances of success they could have from the divine power, and a constant series of miracles that had hitherto attended them; but they distrusted God's power and promise, and were willing to be held in suspense by their own counsels, rather than be brought to a certainty by God's covenant. How much do we stand in our own light by our unbelief! Well, at length the messengers return, but they agree not in their report.

I. The major part discourage the people from going forward to Canaan; and justly are the Israelites left to this temptation, for putting so much confidence in the judgment of men, when they had the word of God to trust to. It is a righteous thing with God to give those up to strong delusions who will not receive his truth in the love of it.

1. Observe their report. (1.) They could not deny but that the land of Canaan was a very fruitful land; the bunch of grapes they brought with them was an ocular demonstration of it, *v.* 27. God had promised them a land flowing with milk and honey, and the evil spies themselves own that it is such a land. Thus even out of the mouth of adversaries will God be glorified and the truth of his promise attested. And yet afterwards they contradict themselves, when they say (*v.* 32), *It is a land that eateth up the inhabitants thereof;* as if, though it had milk, and honey, and grapes, yet it wanted other necessary provision; some think that there was a great plague in the country at the time they surveyed it, which they ought to have imputed to the wisdom of the divine Providence, which thus lessened the numbers of their enemies, to facilitate their conquests; but they invidiously imputed it to the unwholesomeness of the air, and thence took occasion to disparage the country. For this unreasonable fear of a plague in Canaan, they were justly cut off immediately by a *plague in the wilderness, ch.* 14:37. But, (2.) They represented the conquest of it as altogether impracticable, and that it was to no purpose to attempt it. The people are strong (*v.* 28), men of a *great stature* (*v.* 32), *stronger than we, v.* 31. The cities are represented as impregnable fortresses: they *are walled* and *very great, v.* 28. But nothing served their ill purpose more than a description of the giants, on whom they lay a great stress: *We saw the children of Anak there* (*v.* 28), and again, we *saw the giants,* those men of a prodigious size, the *sons of Anak,* who *come of the giants, v.* 33. They spoke as if they were ready to tremble at the mention of them, as they had done at the sight of them. "O these tremendous giants! when we were near them, *we were in our own sight as grasshoppers,* not only little and weak, but trembling and daunted." Compare Job 39:20, *Canst thou make him afraid as a grasshopper?* "Nay, and *so we were in their sight;* they looked upon us with as much scorn and disdain as we did upon them with fear and trembling." So that upon the whole matter they gave it in as their judgment, *We are not able to go up against them* (*v.* 31), and therefore must think of taking some other course.

2. Now, even if they had been to judge only by human

probabilities, they could not have been excused from the imputation of cowardice. Were not the hosts of Israel very numerous? 600,000 effective men, well marshalled and modelled, closely embodied, and entirely united in interest and affection, constituted as formidable an army as perhaps was ever brought into the field; many a less has done more than perhaps the conquering of Canaan was, witness Alexander's army. Moses, their commander-in-chief, was wise and brave; and if the people had put on resolution, and behaved themselves valiantly, what could have stood before them? It is true the Canaanites were strong, but they were dispersed (*v.* 29): *Some dwell in the south and others in the mountains;* so that by reason of their distance they could not soon get together, and by reason of their divided interests they could not long keep together, to oppose Israel. The country being plentiful would subsist an army, and, though the cities were walled, if they could beat them in the field the strong-holds would fall of course into their hands. And, lastly, as for the giants, their overgrown stature would but make them the better mark, and the bulkiest men have not always the best mettle.

3. But, though they deserved to be posted for cowards, this was not the worst, the scripture brands them for unbelievers. It was not any human probabilities they were required to depend upon, but, (1.) They had the manifest and sensible tokens of God's presence with them, and the engagement of his power for them. The Canaanites were stronger than Israel; suppose they were, but were they stronger than the God of Israel? We are not able to deal with them, but is not God Almighty able? Have we not him in the midst of us? Does not he go before us? And is any thing too hard for him? Were we as grasshoppers before the giants, and are not they less than grasshoppers before God? Their cities are walled against us, but can they be walled against heaven? Besides this, (2.) They had had very great experience of the length and strength of God's arm, lifted up and made bare on their behalf. Were not the Egyptians as much stronger than they as the Canaanites were? And yet, without a sword drawn by Israel or a stroke struck, the chariots and horsemen of Egypt were quite routed and ruined; the Amalekites took them at great disadvantages, and yet they were discomfited. Miracles were at this time their daily bread; were there nothing else, an army so well victualled as theirs was, so constantly, so plentifully, and all on free cost, would have a might advantage against any other force. Nay, (3.) They had particular promises made them of victory and success in their wars against the Canaanites. God had given Abraham all possible assurances that he would put his seed into possession of that land, Gen. 15:18; 17:8. He had expressly promised them by Moses that he would *drive out the Canaanites* from *before them* (Ex. 33:2), and that he would do it *by little and little,* Ex. 23:30. And, after all this, for them to say, *We are not able to go up against them,* was in effect to say, "God himself is not able to make his words good." It was in effect to give him the lie, and to tell him he had undertaken more than he could perform. We have a short account of their sin, with which they infected the whole congregation, Ps. 106:24. They *despised the land, they believed not his word.* Though, upon search, they had found it as good as he had said, *a land flowing with milk and honey,* yet they would not believe it as sure as he had said, but despaired of having it, though eternal truth itself had engaged it to them. And now this is the representation of the evil spies.

II. Caleb encouraged them to go forward, though he was seconded by Joshua only (*v.* 30): *Caleb stilled the people,* whom he saw already put into a ferment even *before Moses* himself, whose shining face could not daunt them, when they began to grow unruly. *Caleb* signifies *all heart,* and he answered his name, was hearty himself, and would have made the people so if they would have hearkened to him. If Joshua had begun to stem the tide, he would have been suspected of partiality to Moses, whose minister he was; and therefore he prudently left it to Caleb's management at first, who was of the tribe of Judah, the leading tribe, and therefore the fittest to be heard. Caleb had seen and observed the strength of the inhabitants as much as his fellows, and upon the whole matter, 1. He speaks very confidently of success: *We are well able to overcome them,* as strong as they are. 2. He animates the people to go on, and, his lot lying in the van, he speaks as one resolved to lead them on with bravery: *"Let us go up at once,* one bold step, one bold stroke more, will do our business; it is all our own if we have but courage to make it so: *Let us go up and possess it."* He does not say, "Let us go up and conquer it;" he looks upon that to be as good as done already; but, "Let us go up and possess it; there is nothing to be done but to enter, and take the possession which God our great Lord is ready to give us." Note, *The righteous are bold as a lion.* Difficulties that lie in the way of salvation dwindle and vanish before a lively active faith in the power and promise of God. *All things are possible,* if they be but promised, *to him that believes.*

CHAPTER 14

This chapter gives us an account of that fatal quarrel between God and Israel upon which, for their murmuring and unbelief, he swore in his wrath that they should not enter into his rest. Here is, I. The mutiny and rebellion of Israel against God, upon the report of the evil spies (*v.* 1–4). II. The fruitless endeavour of Moses and Aaron, Caleb and Joshua, to still the tumult (*v.* 5–10). III. Their utter ruin justly threatened by an offended God (*v.* 11, 12). IV. The humble intercession of Moses for them (*v.* 13–19). V. A mitigation of the sentence in answer to the prayer of Moses; they shall not all be cut off, but the decree goes forth ratified with an oath, published to the people, again and again repeated, that this whole congregation should perish in the wilderness, and none of them enter Canaan but Caleb and Joshua only (*v.* 20–35). VI. The present death of the evil spies (*v.* 36–39). VII. The rebuke given to those who attempted to go forward notwithstanding (*v.* 40–45). And this is written for our admonition, that we "fall not after the same example of unbelief."

Verses 1–4

Here we see what mischief the evil spies made by their unfair representation. We may suppose that these twelve that were impanelled to enquire concerning Canaan had talked it over among themselves before they brought in their report in public; and Caleb and Joshua, it is likely, had done their utmost to bring the rest over to be of their mind, and if they would but have agreed that Caleb, according to his pose, should have spoken for them all, as their foreman, all had been well; but the evil spies, it should seem, wilfully designed to raise this mutiny, purely in opposition to Moses and Aaron, though they could not propose any advantage to themselves by it, unless they hoped to be captains and commanders of the retreat into Egypt they were now meditating. But what came of it? Here in these verses we find those whom they studied to humour put into a vexation, and, before the end of the chapter, brought to ruin. Observe,

I. How the people fretted themselves: *They lifted up their voices and cried* (*v.* 1); giving credit to the report of the spies rather than to the word of God, and imagining their condition desperate, they laid the reins on the neck of their passions, and could keep no manner of temper. Like foolish froward children, they fall a crying, yet know not what they cry for. It would have been time enough to cry out when the enemy had beaten up their quarters, and they had seen the sons of Anak at the gate of their camp; but those that cried when nothing hurt them deserved to have something given them to cry for. And, as if all had been already gone, they sat down and *wept that night.* Note, Unbelief, or distrust of God, is a sin that is its own punishment. Those that do not trust God are continually vexing themselves. The world's mourners are more than God's, and the *sorrow of the world worketh death.*

II. How they flew in the face of their governors — *murmured against Moses and Aaron,* and in them reproached the Lord, *v.* 2, 3. The congregation of elders began the discontent (*v.* 1), but the contagion soon spread through the whole camp, for *the children of Israel murmured.* Jealousies and discontents spread like wildfire among the unthinking multitude, who are easily taught to *despise dominions, and to speak evil of dignities.* 1. They look back with a causeless discontent. They wish that they had died in Egypt with the first-born that were slain there, or in the wilderness with those that lately died of the plague for lusting. See the prodigious madness of unbridled passions, which make men prodigal even of that which nature accounts most dear, life itself. Never were so many months spent so pleasantly as these which they had spent since they came out of Egypt, loaded with honours, compassed with favours, and continually entertained with something or other that was surprising; and yet, as if all these things had not made it worth their while to live, they wished they had died in Egypt. And such a light opinion they had of God's tremendous judgments executed on their neighbours for their sin that they wished they had shared with them in their plagues, rather than run the hazard of making a descent upon Canaan. They wish rather to die criminals under God's justice than live conquerors in his favour. Some read it, *O that we had died in Egypt, or in the wilderness! O that we might die!* They wish to die, for fear of dying; and have not sense enough to reason as the poor lepers, when rather than die upon the spot they ventured into an enemy's camp, *If they kill us, we shall but die,* 2 Ki. 7:4. How base were the spirits of these degenerate Israelites, who, rather than die (if it come to the worst) like soldiers on the bed of honour, with their swords in their hands, desire to die like rotten sheep in the wilderness. 2. They look forward with a groundless despair, taking it for granted (*v.* 3) that if they went on they must fall by the sword, and pretend to lay the cause of their fear upon the great care they had for their wives and children, who, they conclude, will be a prey to the Canaanites. And here is a most wicked blasphemous reflection upon God himself, as if he had brought them hither on purpose that they might fall by the sword, and that their wives and children, those poor innocents, should be a prey. Thus do they, in effect, charge that God who is love itself with the worst of malice, and eternal Truth with the basest hypocrisy, suggesting that all the kind things he had said to them, and done for them, hitherto, were intended only to decoy them into a snare, and to cover a secret design carried on all along to ruin them. Daring impudence! But what will not that tongue speak against heaven that is set on fire of hell? The devil keeps up his interest in the hearts of men by insinuating to them ill thoughts of God, as if he desired the death of sinners, and delighted in the hardships and sufferings of his own servants, whereas he knows his thoughts to usward (whether we know them so or no) to be *thoughts of good, and not of evil,* Jer. 29:11.

III. How they came at last to this desperate resolve, that, instead of going forward to Canaan, they would go back again to Egypt. The motion is first made by way of query only (*v.* 3): *Were it not better for us to return into Egypt?* But the ferment being high, and the spirits of the people being disposed to entertain any thing that was perverse, it soon ripened to a resolution, without a debate (*v.* 4): *Let us make a captain and return to Egypt;* and it is lamented long after (Neh. 9:17) that *in their rebellion they appointed a captain to return to their bondage;* for they knew Moses would not be their captain in this retreat. Now, 1. It was the greatest folly in the world to wish themselves in Egypt, or to think that if they were there it would be better with them than it was. If they durst not go forward to Canaan, yet better be as they were than go back to Egypt. What did they want? What had they to complain of? They had plenty, and peace, and rest, were under a good government, had good company, had the tokens of God's presence with them, and enough to make them easy even in the wilderness, if they had but hearts to be content. But whither were they thus eager to go to better themselves? To Egypt! Had they so soon forgotten the sore bondage they were in there? Would they be again under the tyranny of their taskmasters, and at the drudgery of making brick? And, after all the plagues which Egypt had suffered for their sakes, could they expect any better treatment there than they had formerly, and not rather much worse? In how little time (not a year and a half) have they forgotten all the sighs of their bondage, and all the songs of their deliverance! Like brute-beasts, they mind only what is present, and their memories, with the other powers of reason, are sacrificed to their passions. See Ps. 106:7. We find it threatened (Deu. 28:68), as the completing of their misery, that they should be brought into Egypt again, and yet this is what they here wish for. Sinners are enemies to themselves; and those that walk not in God's counsels consult their own mischief and ruin. 2. It was a most senseless ridiculous thing to talk of returning thither through the wilderness. Could they expect that God's cloud would lead them or his manna attend them? And, if they did not, the thousands of Israel must unavoidably be lost and perish in the wilderness. Suppose the difficulties of conquering Canaan were as great as they imagined, those of returning to Egypt were much greater. In this let us see, (1.) The folly of discontent and impatience under the crosses of our outward condition. We are uneasy at that which is, complain of our place and lot, and we would shift; but is there any place or condition in this world that has not something in it to make us uneasy if we are disposed to be so? The way to better our condition is to get our spirits into a better frame; and instead of asking, "Were it not better to go to Egypt?" ask, "Were it not better to be content, and make the best of that which is?" (2.) The folly of apostasy from the ways of God. Heaven is the Canaan set before us, a land flowing with milk and honey; those that bring up ever so ill a report of it cannot but say that it is indeed a good land, only it is hard to get to it. Strict and serious godliness is looked upon as an impracticable thing, and this deters many who began well from going on; rather than undergo the imaginary hardships of a religious life, they run themselves upon the certain fatal consequences of a sinful course; and so they transcribe the folly of Israel, who, when they were within a step of Canaan, would make a captain, and return to Egypt.

Verses 5–10

The friends of Israel here interpose to save them if possible from ruining themselves, but in vain. The physicians of their state would have healed them, but they would not be healed; their watchmen gave them warning, but they would not take warning, and so their blood is upon their own heads.

I. The best endeavours were used to still the tumult, and, if now at last they would have understood the things that belonged to their peace, all the following mischief would have been prevented.

1. Moses and Aaron did their part, *v.* 5. Though it was against them that they murmured (*v.* 2), yet they bravely overlooked the affront and injury done them, and approved themselves faithful friends to those who were outrageous enemies to them. The clamour and noise of the people were so great that Moses and Aaron could not be heard; should they order any of their servants to proclaim silence, the angry multitude would perhaps be the more clamorous; and therefore, to gain audience in the sight of all the assembly, they fell on their faces, thus expressing, (1.) Their humble prayers to God to still the noise of this sea, the noise of its waves, even the tumult of the people. (2.) The great trouble and concern of their own spirits. They fell down as men astonished and even thunder-struck, amazed to see a people throw away their own mercies: to see those so ill-humoured who were so well taught. And, (3.) Their great earnestness with the people to cease their murmurings; they hoped to work upon them by this humble posture, and to prevail with them not to persist in their rebellion; Moses and Aaron beseech them, as though by them God himself did beseech them, to be reconciled unto God. What they said to the people Moses relates in the repetition of this story. Deu. 1:29, 30, *Be not afraid; the Lord your God shall fight for you.* Note, Those that are zealous friends to precious souls will stoop to any thing for their salvation. Moses and Aaron, notwithstanding the posts of honour they are in, prostrate themselves to the people to beg of them not to ruin themselves.

2. Caleb and Joshua did their part: they rent their clothes in a holy indignation at the sin of the people, and a holy dread of the wrath of God, which they saw ready to break out against them. it was the greater trouble to these good men because the tumult was occasioned by those spies with whom they had been joined in commission; and therefore they thought themselves obliged to do what they could to still the storm which their fellows had raised. No reasoning could be more pertinent and pathetic than theirs was (*v.* 7–9), and they spoke as with authority.

(1.) They assured them of the goodness of the land they had surveyed, and that it was really worth venturing for, and not a land that *ate up the inhabitants,* as the evil spies had represented it. It is an *exceedingly good land* (*v.* 7); it is *very, very good,* so the word is; so that they had no reason to *despise this pleasant land.* Note, If men were but thoroughly convinced of the desirableness of the gains of religion, they would not stick at the services of it.

(2.) They made nothing of the difficulties that seemed to lie in the way of their gaining the possession of it: *"Fear not the people of the land, v.* 9. Whatever formidable ideas have been given you of them, the lion is not so fierce as he is painted. *They are bread for us,"* that is, "they are set before us rather to be fed upon than to be fought with, so easily, so pleasantly, and with so much advantage to ourselves shall we master them." Pharaoh is said to have been given them for meat (Ps. 74:14), and the Canaanites will be so too. They show that, whatever was suggested to the contrary, the advantage was clear on Israel's side. For, [1.] Though the Canaanites dwell in walled cities, they are naked: *Their defence has departed from them;* that common providence which preserves the rights of nations has abandoned them, and will be no shelter nor protection to them. The other spies took notice of their strength, but these of their wickedness, and thence inferred that God had forsaken them, and therefore *their defence had departed.* No people can be safe when they have provoked God to leave them. [2.] Though Israel dwell in tents they are fortified: *The Lord is with us,* and his name is a strong tower; *fear them not.* Note, While we have the presence of God with us, we need not fear the most powerful force against us.

(3.) They showed them plainly that all the danger they were in was from their own discontents, and that they would succeed against all their enemies if they did not make God their enemy. On this point alone the cause would turn (*v.* 8): *"If the Lord delight in us,* as certainly he does, and will if we do not provoke him, *he will bring us into this good land;* we shall without fail get it in possession by his favour, and the light of his countenance (Ps. 44:3), if we do not forfeit his favour and by our own follies turn away our own mercies." It has come to this issue (*v.* 9): *Only rebel not you against the Lord.* Note, Nothing can ruin sinners but their own rebellion. If God leave them, it is because they drive him from them; and they die because they will die. None are excluded the heavenly Canaan but those that exclude themselves. And, now, could the case have been made more plain? could it have been urged more closely? But what was the effect?

II. It was all to no purpose; they were deaf to this fair reasoning; nay, they were exasperated by it, and grew more outrageous: *All the congregation bade stone them with stones, v.* 10. The rulers of the congregation, and the great men (so bishop Patrick), ordered the common people to fall upon them, and knock their brains out. Their case was sad indeed when their leaders thus *caused them to err.* Note, It is common for those whose hearts are *fully set in them to do evil* to rage at those who give them good counsel. Those who hate to be reformed hate those that would reform them, and count them their enemies because they tell them the truth. Thus early did Israel begin to misuse the prophets, and *stone those that were sent to them,* and it was this that filled the measure of their sin, Mt. 23:37. *Stone them with stones!* Why, what evil have they done? No crime can be laid to their charge; but the truth is *these two witnesses tormented those* that were obstinate in their infidelity, Rev. 11:10. Caleb and Joshua had but just said, *The Lord is with us; fear them not* (*v.* 9): and, if Israel will not apply those encouraging words to their own fears, those that uttered them know how to encourage themselves with them against this enraged multitude that spoke of stoning them, as David in a like cause, 1 Sa. 30:6. Those that cannot prevail to edify others with their counsels and comforts should endeavour at least to edify themselves. Caleb and Joshua knew they appeared for God and his glory, and therefore doubted not but God would appear for them and their safety. And they were not disappointed, for immediately *the glory of the Lord appeared,* to the terror and confusion of those that were for stoning the servants of God. When they reflected upon God (*v.* 3), his glory appeared not to silence their blasphemies; but, when they threatened Caleb and Joshua, they touched the apple of his eye, and his glory appeared immediately. Note, Those who faithfully expose themselves for God are sure to be taken under his special protection, and shall be hidden from the rage of men, either under heaven or in heaven.

Verses 11–19

Here is, I. The righteous sentence which God gave against Israel for their murmuring and unbelief, which, though afterwards mitigated, showed what was the desert of their sin and the demand of injured justice, and what would have been done if Moses had not interposed. When the glory of the Lord *appeared in the tabernacle* we may suppose that Moses took it for a call to him immediately to come and attend there, as before the tabernacle was erected he went up to the mount in a similar case, Ex. 32:30. Thus, while the people were studying to disgrace him, God publicly put honour upon him, as the man of his counsel. Now here we are told what God said to him there.

1. He showed him the great evil of the people's sin, *v.* 11. What passed between God and Israel went through the hands of Moses: when they were displeased with God they told Moses of it (*v.* 2); when God was displeased with them he told Moses too, *revealing his secret to his servant the prophet,* Amos 3:7. Two things God justly complains of to Moses: — (1.) Their sin. They *provoke me,* or (as the word signifies) they *reject, reproach, despise* me, for *they will not believe me.* This was the bitter root which bore the gall and wormwood. It was their unbelief that made this a day of provocation in the wilderness, Heb. 3:8. Note, Distrust of God, of his power and promise, is itself a very great provocation, and at the bottom of many other provocations. Unbelief is a great sin (1 Jn. 5:10), and a root sin, Heb. 3:12. (2.) Their continuance in it: *How long will they do so?* Note, The God of heaven keeps an account how long sinners persist in their provocations; and the longer they persist the more he is displeased. The aggravations of their sin were, [1.] Their relation to God: *This people,* a peculiar people, a professing people. The nearer any are to God in name and profession, the more he is provoked by their sins, especially their unbelief. [2.] The experience they had had of God's power and goodness, in *all the signs* which he *had shown among them,* by which, one would think, he had effectually obliged them to trust him and follow him. The more God has done for us the greater is the provocation if we distrust him.

2. He showed him the sentence which justice passed upon them for it, *v.* 12. "What remains now but that I should make a full end of them? It will soon be done. *I will smite them with the pestilence,* not leave a man of them alive, but wholly blot out their name and race, and so disinherit them, and be no more troubled with them. *Ah, I will ease me of my adversaries.* They wish to die; and let them die, and neither root nor branch be left of them. Such rebellious children deserve to be disinherited." And if it be asked, "What will become of God's covenant with Abraham then?" here is an answer, "I shall be preserved in the family of Moses: *I will make of thee a greater nation."* Thus, (1.) God would try Moses, whether he still continued that affection for Israel which he formerly expressed upon a like occasion, in preferring their interests before the advancement of his own family; and it is proved that Moses was still of the same public spirit, and could not bear the thought of raising his own name upon the ruin of the name of Israel. (2.) God would teach us that he will not be a loser by the ruin of sinners. If Adam and Eve had been cut off and disinherited, he could have made another Adam and another Eve, and have glorified his mercy in them, as here he could have glorified his mercy in Moses, though Israel had been ruined.

II. The humble intercession Moses made for them. Their sin had made a fatal breach in the wall of their defence, at which destruction would certainly have entered if Moses had not seasonably stepped in and made it good. Here he was a type of Christ, who interceded for his persecutors, and *prayed for those* that *despitefully used* him, leaving us an example to his own rule, Mt. 5:44.

1. The prayer of his petition is, in one word, *Pardon, I beseech thee, the iniquity of this people* (*v.* 19), that is, "Do not bring upon them the ruin they deserve." This was Christ's prayer for those that crucified him, *Father forgive them.* The pardon of a national sin, as such, consists in the turning away of the national punishment; and that is it for which Moses is here so earnest.

2. The pleas are many, and strongly urged.

(1.) He insists most upon the plea that is taken from the glory of God, *v.* 13–16. With this he begins, and somewhat abruptly, taking occasion from that dreadful word, *I will disinherit them. Lord* (says he), *then the Egyptians shall hear it.* God's honour lay nearer to his heart than any interests of his own. Observe how he *orders this cause* before God. He pleads, [1.] That the eyes both of Egypt and Canaan were upon them, and great expectations were raised concerning them. They could not but have heard *that thou, Lord, art among this people, v.* 14. The neighbouring countries rang of it, how much this people were the particular care of heaven, so as never any people under the sun were. [2.] That if they should be cut off great notice would be taken of it. "The *Egyptians will hear it* (*v.* 13), for they have their spies among us, and they will *tell it to the inhabitants of the land*" (*v.* 14); for there was great correspondence between Egypt and Canaan, although not by the way of this wilderness. "If this people that have made so great a noise be all consumed, if their mighty pretensions come to nothing, and their light go out in a snuff, it will be told with pleasure in Gath, and published in the streets of Askelon; and what construction will the heathen put upon it? It will be impossible to make them understand it as an act of God's justice, and as such redounding to God's honour; *brutish men know not this* (Ps. 92:6): but they will impute it to the failing of God's power, and so turn it to his reproach, *v.* 16. They will say, He slew them in the wilderness because he was not able to bring them to Canaan, his arm being shortened, and his stock of miracles being spent. Now, Lord, let not one attribute be glorified at the expense of another; rather let mercy *rejoice against judgment* than that almighty power should be impeached." Note, The best pleas in prayer are those that are taken from God's honour; for they agree with the first petition of the Lord's Prayer, *Hallowed be thy name. Do not disgrace the throne of thy glory.* God pleads it with himself (Deu. 32:27), *I feareth the wrath of the enemy;* and we should use it as an argument with ourselves to walk so in every thing as to give no occasion to the enemies of the Lord to blaspheme, 1 Tim. 6:1.

(2.) He pleads God's proclamation of his name at Horeb (*v.* 17, 18): *Let the power of the Lord be great.* Power is here put for pardoning mercy; it is his power over his own anger. If he should destroy them, God's power would be questioned; if he should continue and complete their salvation, notwithstanding the difficulties that arose, not only from the strength of their enemies, but from their own provocations, this would greatly magnify the divine power: what cannot he do who could make so weak a people conquerors and such an unworthy people favourites? The more danger there is of others reproaching God's power the more desirous we should be to see it glorified. To enforce this petition, he refers to the word which God had spoken: *The Lord is long-suffering and of great mercy.* God's goodness had there been spoken of as his glory; God gloried in it, Ex. 34:6, 7. Now here he prays that upon this occasion he would glorify it. Note, We must take our encouragement in prayer from the word of God, upon which he has *caused us to hope,* Ps. 119:49. "Lord, be and do *according as thou hast spoken;* for hast thou spoken, and wilt thou not make it good?" Three things God had solemnly made a declaration of, which Moses here fastens upon, and improves for the enforcing of his petition: — [1.] The goodness of God's nature in general, that he is long-suffering, or slow to anger, and of great mercy; not soon provoked, but tender and compassionate towards offenders. [2.] His readiness in particular to pardon sin: *Forgiving iniquity and transgression,* sins of all sorts. [3.] His unwillingness to proceed to extremity, even when he does punish. For in this sense the following words may be read: *That will by no means make quite desolate, in visiting the iniquity of the fathers upon the children.* God had indeed said in the second commandment that he would thus visit, but here he promises not to make a full end of families, churches, and nations, at once; and so it is very applicable to this occasion, for Moses cannot beg that God would not at all punish this sin (it would be too great an encouragement to rebellion if he should set no mark of his displeasure upon it), but that he would not *kill all this people as one man, v.* 15. He does not ask that they may not be corrected, but that they may not be disinherited. And this proclamation of God's name was the more apposite to his purpose because it was made upon occasion of the pardoning of their sin in making the golden calf. This sin which they had now fallen into was bad enough, but it was not idolatry.

(3.) He pleads past experience: *As thou hast forgiven this people from Egypt, v.* 19. This seemed to make against him. Why should those be forgiven any more who, after they had been so often forgiven, revolted yet more and more, and seemed hardened and encouraged in their rebellion by the lenity and patience of their God, and the frequent pardons they had obtained? Among men it would have been thought impolitic to take notice of such a circumstance in a request of this nature, as it might operate

to the prejudice of the petitioner: but, as in other things so in pardoning sin, God's thoughts and ways are infinitely above ours, Isa. 55:9. Moses looks upon it as a good plea, *Lord, forgive, as thou hast forgiven.* It will be no more a reproach to thy justice, nor any less the praise of thy mercy, to forgive now, than it has been formerly. Therefore the *sons of Jacob are not consumed,* because they have to do with a *God that changes not,* Mal. 3:6.

Verses 20–35

We have here God's answer to the prayer of Moses, which sings both of mercy and judgment. It is given privately to Moses (*v.* 20–25), and then directed to be made public to the people, *v.* 26–35. The frequent repetitions of the same things in it speak these resolves to be unalterable. Let us see the particulars.

I. The extremity of the sentence is receded from (*v.* 20): "*I have pardoned,* so as not to cut them all off at once, and disinherit them." See the power of prayer, and the delight God takes in putting an honour upon it. He designed a pardon, but Moses shall have the praise of obtaining it by prayer: it shall be done *according to thy word;* thus, as a prince, he has power with God, and prevails. See what countenance and encouragement God gives to our intercessions for others, that we may be public-spirited in prayer. Here is a whole nation rescued from ruin by the effectual fervent prayer of one righteous man. See how ready God is to forgive sin, and how easy to be entreated: *Pardon,* says Moses (*v.* 19), *I have pardoned,* says God, *v.* 20. David found him thus swift to show mercy, Ps. 32:5. *He deals not with us after our sins,* Ps. 103:10.

II. The glorifying of God's name is, in the general, resolved upon, *v.* 21. It is said, it is sworn, *All the earth shall be filled with the glory of the Lord.* Moses in his prayer had shown a great concern for the glory of God. "Let me alone," says God, "to secure that effectually, and to advance it, by this dispensation." All the world shall see how God hates sin even in his own people, and will reckon for it, and yet how gracious and merciful he is, and how slow to anger. Thus when our Saviour prayed, *Father, glorify thy name,* he was immediately answered, *I have glorified it, and will glorify it yet again,* Jn. 12:28. Note, Those that sincerely seek God's glory may be sure of what they seek. God having turned this prayer for the glorifying of himself into a promise, we may turn it into praise, in concert with the angels, Isa. 6:3, *The earth is full of his glory.*

III. The sin of this people which provoked God to proceed against them is here aggravated, *v.* 22, 27. It is not made worse than really it was, but is shown to be exceedingly sinful. It was an evil congregation, each bad, but altogether in congregation, very bad. 1. They tempted God — tempted his power, whether he could help them in their straits — his goodness, whether he would — and his faithfulness, whether his promise would be performed. They tempted his justice, whether he would resent their provocations and punish them or no. They dared him, and in effect challenged him, as God does the idols (Isa. 41:23), to do *good,* or do *evil.* 2. They murmured against him. This is much insisted on, *v.* 27. As they questioned what he would do, so they quarrelled with him for every thing he did or had done, continually fretting and finding fault. It does not appear that they murmured at any of the laws or ordinances that God gave them (though they proved a heavy yoke), but they murmured at the conduct they were under, and the provision made for them. Note, It is much easier to bring ourselves to the external services of religion, and observe all the formalities of devotion, than to live a life of dependence upon, and submission to, the divine Providence in the course of our conversation. 3. They did this after they had seen God's miracles in Egypt and in the wilderness, *v.* 2. They would not believe their own eyes, which were witnesses for God that he was in the midst of them of a truth. 4. They had repeated the provocations ten times, that is, very often: the Jewish writers reckon this exactly the tenth time that the body of the congregation had provoked God. First, at the Red Sea, Ex. 14:11. In Marah, Ex. 15:23, 24. In the wilderness of Sin, Ex. 16:2. At Rephidim, Ex. 17:1, 2. The golden calf, Ex. 32. Then at Taberah. Then at Kibroth-Hattaavah, ch. 11. And so this was the tenth. Note, God keeps an account how often we repeat our provocations, and will sooner or later set them in order before us. 5. They had not heark-

ened to his voice, though he had again and again admonished them of their sin.

IV. The sentence passed upon them for this sin. 1. That they should not see the promised land (*v.* 23), nor *come into it, v.* 30. He swore in his wrath that they should not *enter into his rest,* Ps. 95:11. Note, Disbelief of the promise is a forfeiture of the benefit of it. Those that despise the pleasant land shall be shut out of it. The promise of God should be fulfilled to their posterity, but not to them. 2. That they should immediately *turn back into the wilderness, v.* 25. Their next remove should be a retreat. They must face about, and instead of going forward to Canaan, on the very borders of which they now were, they must withdraw towards the Red Sea again. *To-morrow turn you;* that is, "Very shortly you shall be brought back to that vast howling wilderness which you are so weary of. And it is time to shift for your own safety, for the *Amalekites lie in wait in the valley,* ready to attack you if you march forward." Of them they had been distrustfully afraid (ch. 13:29), and now with them God justly frightened them. *The fear of the wicked shall come upon him.* 3. That all those who had now grown up to men's estate should die in the wilderness, not all at once, but by degrees. They wished that they might die in the wilderness, and God said *Amen* to their passionate wish, and made their sin their ruin, *snared them in the words of their mouth,* and *caused their own tongue to fall upon them,* took them at their word, and determined that their *carcases should fall in the wilderness, v.* 28, 29, and again, *v.* 32, 35. See with what contempt they are spoken of, now that they had by their sin made themselves vile; the mighty men of valour were but carcases, when the Spirit of the Lord had departed from them. They were all as dead men. Their fathers had such a value for Canaan that they desired to have their dead bodies carried thither to be buried, in token of their dependence upon God's promise that they should have that land for a possession: but these, having despised that good land and disbelieved the promise of it, shall not have the honour to be buried in it, but shall have their graves in the wilderness. 4. That in pursuance of this sentence they should wander to and fro in the wilderness, like travellers that have lost themselves, for forty years; that is, so long as to make it full forty years from their coming out of Egypt to their entrance into Canaan, *v.* 33, 34. Thus long they were kept wandering, (1.) To answer the number of the days in which the spies were searching the land. They were content to wait forty days for the testimony of men, because they could not take God's word; and therefore justly are they kept forty years waiting for the performance of God's promise. (2.) That hereby they might be brought to repentance, and find mercy with God in the other world, whatever became of them in this. Now they had time to bethink themselves, and to consider their ways; and the inconveniences of the wilderness would help to humble them and prove them, and *show them what was in their heart,* Deu. 8:2. Thus long they *bore their iniquities,* feeling the weight of God's wrath in the punishment. They were made to groan under the burden of their own sin that brought it upon them, which was *too heavy for them to bear.* (3.) That they might sensibly feel what a dangerous thing it is for God's covenant-people to break with him: "*You shall know my breach of promise,* both the causes of it, that it is procured by your sin" (for God never leaves any till they first leave him), "and the consequences of it, that it will produce your ruin; you are quite undone when you are thrown out of covenant." (4.) That a new generation might in this time be raised up, which could not be done all of a sudden. And the children, being brought up under the tokens of God's displeasure against their fathers, and so *bearing their whoredoms* (that is, the punishment of their sins, especially their idolatry about the golden calf, which God now remembered against them), might take warning not to tread in the steps of their fathers' disobedience. And their wandering so long in the wilderness would make Canaan at last the more welcome to them. It should seem that upon occasion of this sentence Moses penned the ninetieth Psalm, which is very apposite to the present state of Israel, and wherein they are taught to pray that since this sentence could not be reversed it might be sanctified, and they might learn to *apply their hearts unto wisdom.*

V. The mercy that was mixed with this severe sentence.

1. Mercy to Caleb and Joshua, that though they should wander with the rest in the wilderness, yet they, and only they of all that were now above twenty years old, should survive the years of banishment, and live to enter Canaan. Caleb only is spoken of (*v.* 24), and a particular mark of honour put upon him, both, (1.) In the character given of him: he had *another spirit,* different from the rest of the spies, an *after-spirit,* which furnished him with second thoughts, and he *followed the Lord fully,* kept close to his duty, and went through with it, though deserted and threatened; and, (2.) In the recompence promised to him: *Him will I bring in due time into the land whereinto he went.* Note, [1.] It ought to be the great care and endeavour of every one of us to follow the Lord fully. We must, in a course of obedience to God's will and of service to his honour, follow him universally, without dividing, — uprightly, without dissembling, — cheerfully, without disputing, — and constantly, without declining; and this is following him fully. [2.] Those that would follow God fully must have another spirit, another from the spirit of the world, and another from what their own spirit has been. They must have the spirit of Caleb. [3.] Those that follow God fully in times of general apostasy God will own and honour by singular preservations in times of general calamity. The heavenly Canaan shall be the everlasting inheritance of those that follow the Lord fully. When Caleb is again mentioned (*v.* 30) Joshua stands with him, compassed with the same favours and crowned with the same honours, having stood with him in the same services.

2. Mercy to the children even of these rebels. They should have a seed preserved, and Canaan secured to that seed: *Your little ones,* now under twenty years old, *which you,* in your unbelief, *said should be a prey, them will I bring in, v.* 31. They had invidiously charged God with a design to ruin their children, *v.* 3. But God will let them know that he can put a difference between the guilty and the innocent, and cut them off without touching their children. Thus the promise made to Abraham, though it seemed to fail for a time, was kept from failing for evermore; and, though God chastened their transgressions with a rod, yet his *loving kindness he would not utterly take away.*

Verses 36–45

Here is, I. The sudden death of the ten evil spies. While the sentence was passing upon the people, before it was published, they *died of the plague before the Lord, v.* 36, 37. Now,

1. God hereby showed his particular displeasure against those who *sinned and made Israel to sin.* (1.) They sinned themselves, in bringing up a slander upon the land of promise. Note, Those greatly provoke God who misrepresent religion, cast reproach upon it, and raise prejudices in men's minds against it, or give occasion to those to do so who seek occasion. Those that represent the service of God as mean and despicable, melancholy and uncomfortable, hard and impracticable, needless and unprofitable, bring up an *evil report* upon the good land, *pervert the right ways of the Lord,* and in effect give him the lie. (2.) They *made Israel to sin.* They designedly *made all the congregation murmur* against God. Note, Ring-leaders in sin may expect to fall under particular marks of the wrath of God, who will severely reckon for the blood of souls, which is thus spilt.

2. God hereby showed what he could have done with the whole congregation, and gave an earnest of the execution of the sentence now passed upon them. He that thus cut off one of a tribe could have cut off their whole tribes suddenly, and would do it gradually. Note, The remarkable deaths of notorious sinners are earnests of the final perdition of ungodly men, 2 Pt. 2:5, 6. Thus the wrath of God is revealed, that sinners may hear and fear.

II. The special preservation of Caleb and Joshua: *They lived still, v.* 38. It is probable that all the twelve spies stood together, for the eyes of all Israel were now upon them; and therefore it is taken notice of as very remarkable, and which could not but be affecting to the whole congregation, that when the ten evil spies fell down dead of the plague, a malignant infectious distemper, yet these two that stood among them lived, and were well. God hereby confirmed their testimony, and put those to confusion that spoke of stoning them. He likewise gave them an assur-

ance of their continued preservation in the wilderness, when thousands should fall on their right hand and on their left, Ps. 91:7. Death never misses his mark, nor takes any by oversight that were designed for life, though in the midst of those that were to die.

III. The publication of the sentence to all the people, *v.* 36. He told them all what the decree was which had gone forth concerning them, and which could not be reversed, that they must all die in the wilderness, and Canaan must be reserved for the next generation. It was a very great disappointment, we may well think, to Moses himself, who longed to be in Canaan, as well as to all the people; yet he acquiesced, but they wept and mourned greatly. The assurance which Moses had of God's being glorified by this sentence gave him satisfaction, while the consciousness of their own guilt, and their having procured it to themselves, gave them the greatest vexation. They wept for nothing (*v.* 1), and now they have cause given them to weep; so justly are murmurers made mourners. If they had mourned for the sin when they were faithfully reproved for it (*v.* 9), the sentence would have been prevented; but now that they mourned for the judgment only their grief came too late, and did them no service; they *found no place for repentance, though they sought it carefully with tears,* Heb. 12:17. Such mourning as this there is in hell, but the tears will not quench the flames, no, nor cool the tongue.

IV. The foolish fruitless attempts of some of the Israelites to enter Canaan, notwithstanding the sentence.

1. They were now eager to go forward towards Canaan, *v.* 40. They were up early, mustered all their force, got together in a body, and begged of Moses to lead them on against the enemy, and now there is no more talk among them of making a captain to return into Egypt. They confess their fault: *We have sinned;* they profess reformation: *Lo, we be here, and will go up.* They now desire the land which they had despised, and put a confidence in the promise which they had distrusted. Thus when God judges he will overcome, and, first or last, will convince sinners of the evil of all their ungodly deeds, and hard speeches, and force them to recall their own words. But, though God was glorified by this recantation of theirs, they were not benefited by it, because it came too late. The decree had gone forth, the consumption was determined; they did not seek the Lord while he might be found, and now he would not be found. O, if men would but be as earnest for heaven while their day of grace lasts as they will be when it is over, would be as solicitous to provide themselves with oil while the bridegroom tarries as they will be when the bridegroom comes, how well were it for them!

2. Moses utterly disallows their motion, and forbids the expedition they were meditating: *Go not up, v.* 41–43. (1.) He gives them warning of the sin; it is *transgressing the commandment of the Lord,* who had expressly ordered them, when they did move, to move back towards the Red Sea. Note, That which has been duty, in its season, when it comes to be mistimed may be turned into sin. It is true the command he refers to was in the nature of a punishment, but he that has not obeyed the law is obliged to submit to the penalty, for the Lord is our Judge as well as Lawgiver. (2.) He gives them this warning of the danger: "*It shall not prosper,* never expect it." Note, It is folly to promise ourselves success in that which we undertake contrary to the mind of God. "*The Canaanites are before you* to attack you, and *the Lord is not among you* to protect you and fight for you, and therefore look to yourselves *that you be not smitten before your enemies.*" Those that are out of the way of their duty are from under God's protection, and go at their peril. It is dangerous going where we cannot expect God should go along with us. Nay, he plainly foresees and foretels their defeat: *You shall fall by the sword* of the Amalekites and Canaanites (who were to have fallen by their sword); *Because you are turned away from the Lord,* from following the guidance of his precept and promise, *therefore the Lord will not be with you.* Note, God will certainly leave those that leave him; and those that are left of him lie exposed to all misery.

3. They venture notwithstanding. Never was people so perverse and so desperately resolved in every thing to walk contrary to God. God bade them go, and they would not; he forbade them, and they would. Thus is the *carnal mind enmity to God: They presumed to go up unto the hill-top,*

v. 44. Here, (1.) They struggled against the sentence of divine justice, and would press on in defiance of it. (2.) They slighted the tokens of God's presence, for they would go though they left Moses and the ark of the covenant behind them. They had distrusted God's strength, and now they presume upon their own without his.

4. The expedition speeds accordingly, *v.* 45. The enemy had posted themselves upon the top of the hill, to make good that pass against the invaders, and, being informed by their scouts of their approach, sallied out upon them, and defeated them, and it is probable that many of the Israelites were killed. Now the sentence began to be executed that their *carcases should fall in the wilderness.* Note, That affair can never end well that begins with sin. The way to obtain peace with our friends, and success against our enemies, is to make God our friend, and keep ourselves in his love. The Jews, like these their ancestors, when they had rejected Christ's righteousness, attempted to establish their own, and it sped as this.

CHAPTER 15

This chapter, which is mostly concerning sacrifice and offering, comes in between the story of two rebellions (one *ch.* 14, the other *ch.* 16), to signify that these legal institutions were typical of the gifts which Christ was to receive even for the rebellious, Ps. 68:18. In the foregoing chapter, upon Israel's provocation, God had determined to destroy them, and in token of his wrath had sentenced them to perish in the wilderness. But, upon Moses' intercession, he said, "I have pardoned;" and, in token of that mercy, in this chapter he repeats and explains some of the laws concerning offerings, to show that he was reconciled to them, notwithstanding the severe dispensation they wee under, and would not unchurch them. Here is, I. The law concerning the meat-offerings and drink-offerings (*v.* 1–12) both for Israelites and for strangers (*v.* 13–16), and a law concerning the heave-offerings of the first of their dough (*v.* 17–21). II. The law concerning sacrifices for sins of ignorance (*v.* 22–29). III. The punishment of presumptuous sins (*v.* 30, 31), and an instance given in the sabbath-breaker (*v.* 32–36). IV. A law concerning fringes, for memorandums, upon the borders of their garments (*v.* 37, etc.).

Verses 1–21

Here we have,

I. Full instructions given concerning the meat-offerings and drink-offerings, which were appendages to all the sacrifices of animals. The beginning of this law is very encouraging: *When you come into the land of your habitation which I give unto you,* they you shall do so and so, *v.* 2. This was a plain intimation, not only that God was reconciled to them notwithstanding the sentence he had passed upon them, but that he would secure the promised land to their seed notwithstanding their proneness to rebel against him. They might think some time or other they should be guilty of a misdemeanour that would be fatal to them, and would exclude them for ever, as the last had done for one generation; but this intimates an assurance that they should be kept from provoking God to such a degree as would amount to a forfeiture; for this statute takes it for granted that there were some of them that should in due time come into Canaan. The meat-offerings were of two sorts; some were offered alone, and we have the law concerning those, Lev. 2:1, etc. Others were added to the burnt-offerings and peace-offerings, and constantly attended them, and about these direction is here given. It was requisite, since the sacrifices of acknowledgment (specified in *v.* 3) were intended as the food of God's table, that there should be a constant provision of bread, oil, and wine, whatever the flesh-meat was. The caterers or purveyors for Solomon's temple provided *fine flour,* 1 Ki. 4:22. And it was fit that God should keep a good house, that his table should be furnished with bread as well as flesh, and that his cup should run over. In my Father's house there is bread enough. Now the intent of this law is to direct what proportion the meat-offering and drink-offering should bear to several sacrifices to which they were annexed. If the sacrifice was a lamb or a kid, then the meat-offering must be a tenth-deal of flour, that is, an omer, which contained about five pints; this must be mingled with oil, the fourth part of a hin (a hin contained about five quarts), and the drink-offering must be the same quantity of wine, about a quart and half a pint, *v.* 3–5. If it was a ram, the meat-offering was doubled, two tenth-deals of flour, about five quarts, and a third part of a hin of oil (which was to them as butter is to us) mingled with it; and the same quantity of wine for a drink-offering, *v.* 6, 7. If the sacrifice was a bullock, the meat-offering was to be trebled, three omers, with five pints of oil, and the same quantity of wine for a drink-offering, v. 8–10. And thus for each sacrifice, whether offered by a particular person or at the common charge. Note, Our religious services should be governed, as by other rules, so by the rule of proportion.

II. Natives and strangers are here set upon a level, in this as in other matters (v. 13–16): *"One law shall be for you and for the stranger* that is proselyted to the Jewish religion." Now, 1. This was an invitation to the Gentiles to become proselytes, and to embrace the faith and worship of the true God. In civil things there was a difference between strangers and true-born Israelites, but not in the things of God; *as you are, so shall the stranger be before the Lord,* for with him there is no respect of persons. See Isa. 56:3. 2. This was an obligation upon the Jews to be kind to strangers, and not to oppress them, because they saw them owned and accepted of God. Communion in religion is a great engagement to mutual affection, and should slay all enmities. 3. It was a mortification to the pride of the Jews, who are apt to be puffed up with their birthright privileges. "We are Abraham's seed." God let them know that the sons of the stranger were as welcome to him as the sons of Jacob; no man's birth or parentage shall turn either to his advantage or his prejudice in his acceptance with God. This likewise intimated that, as believing strangers should be accounted Israelites, so unbelieving Israelites should be accounted strangers. 4. It was a happy presage of the calling of the Gentiles, and of their admission into the church. If the law made so little difference between Jew and Gentile, much less would the gospel make, which broke down the partition-wall, and reconciled both to God in one sacrifice, without the observance of the legal ceremonies.

III. A law for the offering of the first of their dough unto the Lord. This, as the former, goes upon the comfortable supposition of their having *come into the promised land,* v. 18. Now that they lived upon manna they needed not such an express acknowledgment of God's title to their daily bread, and their dependence upon him for it, the thing spoke for itself; but in Canaan, where they should eat the fruit of their own industry, God required that he should be owned as their landlord and their great benefactor. They must not only offer him the first-fruits and tenths of the corn in their fields (these had already been reserved); but when they had it in their houses, in their kneading trough, when it was almost ready to be set upon their tables, God must have a further tribute of acknowledgment, part of their dough (the Jews say a fortieth part, at least, of the whole lump) must be heaved or offered up to God (v. 20, 21), and the priest must have it for the use of his family. Thus they must own their dependence upon God for their daily bread, even when they had it in the house with them; they must then wait on God for the comfortable use of it; for we read of that which was brought home, and yet God did blow upon it, and it came to little, Hag. 1:9. Christ has taught us to pray not, *Give us this year our yearly harvest,* but *Give us this day our daily bread.* God by this law said to the people, as the prophet long afterwards said to the widow of Sarepta (1 Ki. 17:13), *Only make me thereof a little cake first.* This offering was expressly kept up by the laws of Ezekiel's visionary temple, and it is a commandment with promise of family-mercies (Eze. 44:30): *You shall give unto the priest the first of your dough, that he may cause the blessing to rest in thy house;* for, when God has had his dues out of our estates, we may expect the comfort of what falls to our share.

Verses 22–29

We have here the laws concerning sacrifices for sins of ignorance; the Jews understand it of idolatry, or false worship, through the error of their teachers. The case here supposed is that they *had not observed all these commandments,* v. 22, 23. If they had failed in the offerings of their acknowledgment, and had not brought them according to the law, then they must bring an offering of atonement, yea, though the omission had been through forgetfulness or mistake. If they failed in one part of the ceremony, they must make it up by the observance of another part, which was in the nature of a remedial law. 1. The case is put of a national sin, committed through ignorance, and become customary through a vulgar error (v. 24) — *the congregation,* that is, the body of the people, for so it is explained (v. 25): *All the congregation of the children of Israel.* The

ceremonial observances were so numerous, and so various, that, it might easily be supposed, some of them by degrees would be forgotten and disused, as particularly that immediately before concerning the heave-offering of their dough: now if, in process of time, upon consulting the law, there should appear to have been a general neglect of that or any other appointment, then a sacrifice must be offered for the whole congregation, and the oversight shall be forgiven (v. 25, 26) and not punished, as it deserved, with some national judgment. The offering of the sacrifice *according to the manner,* or *ordinance,* plainly refers to a former statute, of which this is the repetition; and the same bullock which is there called *a sin-offering* (Lev. 4:13, 21) is here called *a burnt-offering* (v. 24), because it was wholly burnt, though not upon the altar, yet without the camp. And here is the addition of a *kid of the goats for a sin-offering.* According to this law, we find that Hezekiah made atonement for the errors of his father's reign, by *seven bullocks, seven rams, seven lambs, and seven he-goats,* which he offered as a *sin-offering for the kingdom, and for the sanctuary, and for Judah* (2 Chr. 29:21), and *for all Israel,* v. 24. And we find the like done after the return out of captivity, Ezra 8:35. 2. It is likewise supposed to be the case of a particular person: *If any soul sin through ignorance* (v. 27), neglecting any part of his duty, he must bring his offering, as was appointed, Lev. 4:27, etc. Thus atonement shall be made *for the soul that sins, when he sins through ignorance,* v. 28. Observe, (1.) Sins committed ignorantly need to have atonement made for them; for, though ignorance will in a degree excuse, it will not justify those that might have known their Lord's will and did it not. David prayed to be cleansed from his *secret faults,* that is, those sins which he himself was not aware of, the errors he did not understand, Ps. 19:12. (2.) Sins committed ignorantly shall be forgiven, through Christ the great sacrifice, who, when he offered up himself once for all upon the cross, seemed to explain the intention of his offering in that prayer, *Father, forgive them, for they know not what they do.* And Paul seems to allude to this law concerning sins of ignorance (1 Tim. 1:13), *I obtained mercy, because I did it ignorantly and in unbelief.* And it looked favourable upon the Gentiles that this law of atoning for sins of ignorance is expressly made to extend to those who were strangers to the commonwealth of Israel (v. 29), but supposed to be *proselytes of righteousness.* Thus the blessing of Abraham comes upon the Gentiles.

Verses 30–36

Here is, I. The general doom passed upon presumptuous sinners. 1. Those are to be reckoned presumptuous sinners that sin *with a high hand,* as the original phrase is (v. 30), that is, that avowedly confront God's authority, and set up their own lust in competition with it, that sin for sinning-sake, in contradiction to the precept of the law, and in defiance of the penalty, that fight against God, and dare him to do his worst; see Job 15:25. It is not only to sin against knowledge, but to sin designedly against God's will and glory. 2. Sins thus committed are exceedingly sinful. He that thus breaks the commandment, (1.) *Reproaches the Lord* (v. 30); he says the worst he can of him, and most unjustly. The language of presumptuous sin is, "Eternal truth is not fit to be believed, the Lord of all not fit to be obeyed, and almighty power not fit to be either feared or trusted." It imputes folly to Infinite Wisdom, and iniquity to the righteous Judge of heaven and earth; such is the malignity of wilful sin. (2.) He *despises the word of the Lord,* v. 31. There are those who, in many instances, come short of fulfilling the word, and yet have a great value for it, and count the law honourable; but presumptuous sinners despise it, thinking themselves too great, too good, and too wise, to be ruled by it. *What is the Almighty that we should serve him?* Whatever the sin itself is, it is contumacy that incurs the anathema. It is rebellion added to the sin that is as witch-craft, and stubbornness as idolatry. 3. The sentence passed on such is dreadful. There remains no sacrifice for those sins; the law provided none: *That soul shall be cut off from among his people* (v. 30), *utterly cut off* (v. 31); and that God may be for ever justified, and the sinner for ever confounded, *his iniquity shall be upon him,* and there needs no more to sink him to the lowest hell. Thus the Jewish doctors understand it, that *the iniquity shall cleave to the soul, after it is cut off, and that man*

shall *give an account of his sin at the great day of judgment.* Perhaps the kind of offence might be such as did not expose the offender to the censure of the civil magistrate, but, if it was done presumptuously, God himself would take the punishment of it into his own hands, and into them it is a fearful thing to fall. In the New Testament we find the like sentence of exclusion from all benefit by the great sacrifice passed upon the blasphemy against the Holy Ghost, and a total apostasy from Christianity.

II. A particular instance of presumption in the sin of sabbath-breaking. 1. The offence was the gathering of sticks on the sabbath day (v. 32), which, it is probable, were designed to make a fire of, whereas they were commanded to bake and seeth what they had occasion for the day before, Ex. 16:23. This seemed but a small offence, but it was a violation of the law of the sabbath, and so was a tacit contempt of the Creator, to whose honour the sabbath was dedicated, and an incursion upon the whole law, which the sabbath was intended as a hedge about. And it appears by the context to have been done presumptuously, and in affront both of the law and to the Law-maker. 2. The offender was secured, v. 33, 34. Those that found him *gathering sticks,* in their zeal for the honour of the sabbath, *brought him to Moses and Aaron, and all the congregation,* which intimates that being the sabbath day the congregation was at that time gathered to Moses and Aaron, to receive instruction from them, and to join with them in religious worship. It seems, even common Israelites, though there was much amiss among them, yet would not contentedly see the sabbath profaned, which was a good sign that they had not quite forsaken God, nor were utterly forsaken of him. 3. God was consulted, *because it was not declared what should be done to him.* The law had already made the profanation of the sabbath a capital crime (Ex. 31:14, *ch.* 35:2); but they were in doubt, either concerning the offence (whether this that he had done should be deemed a profanation or no) or concerning the punishment, which death he should die. God was the Judge, and before him they brought this cause. 4. Sentence was passed; the prisoner was adjudged a sabbath-breaker, according to the intent of that law, and as such he must be put to death; and to show how great the crime was, and how displeasing to God, and that others might hear and fear and not do in like manner presumptuously, that death is appointed him which was looked upon as most terrible: He must be *stoned with stones,* v. 35. Note, God is jealous for the honour of his sabbaths, and will not hold those guiltless, whatever men do, that profane them. 5. Execution was done pursuant to the sentence, v. 36. He was *stoned* to death *by the congregation.* As many as could were employed in the execution, that those, at least, might be afraid of breaking the sabbath, who had thrown a stone at this sabbath-breaker. This intimates that the open profanation of the sabbath is a sin which ought to be punished and restrained by the civil magistrate, who, as far as overt acts go, is keeper of both tables. See Neh. 13:17. One would think there could be no great harm in gathering a few sticks, on what day soever it was, but God intended the exemplary punishment of him that did so for a standing warning to us all, to make conscience of keeping holy the sabbath.

Verses 37–41

Provision had been just now made by the law for the pardon of sins of ignorance and infirmity; now here is an expedient provided for the preventing of such sins. They are ordered to make fringes upon the borders of their garments, which were to be memorandums to them of their duty, that they might not sin through forgetfulness. 1. The sign appointed is a fringe of silk, or thread, or worsted, or the garment itself ravelled at the bottom, and a blue riband bound on the top of it to keep it tight, v. 38. The Jews being a peculiar people, they were thus distinguished from their neighbours in their dress, as well as in their diet, and taught by such little instances of singularity not to be conformed to the way of the heathen in greater things. Thus likewise they proclaimed themselves Jews wherever they were, as those that were not ashamed of God and his law. Our Saviour, being made under the law, wore these fringes; hence we read of the hem or border, of his garment, Mt. 9:20. These borders the Pharisees enlarged, that they might be thought more holy and devout than other people. The phylacteries were different things; these were their own invention, the fringes were a divine institution. The Jews at this day wear them, saying, when they put them on, *Blessed be he who has sanctified us unto himself, and commanded us to wear fringes.* 2. The intention of it was to remind them that they were a peculiar people. They were not appointed for the trimming and adorning of their clothes, but *to stir up their pure minds by way of remembrance* (2 Pt. 3:1), that they might *look upon the fringe and remember the commandments.* Many look upon their ornaments to feed their pride, but they must look upon these ornaments to awaken their consciences to a sense of their duty, that their religion might constantly beset them, and that they might carry it about with them, as they did their clothes, wherever they went. If they were tempted to sin, the fringe would be a monitor to them not to break God's commandments: If a duty was forgotten to be done in its season, the fringe would remind them of it. This institution, though it is not an imposition upon us, is an instruction to us, always to *remember the commandments of the Lord our God,* that we *may do them,* to treasure them up in our memories, and to apply them to particular cases as there is occasion to use them. It was intended particularly to be a preservative from idolatry: that you *seek not after your own heart, and your own eyes,* in your religious worship. Yet it may extend also to the whole conversation, for nothing is more contrary to God's honour, and our own true interest, than to *walk in the way of our heart* and in *the sight of our eyes;* for the *imagination of the heart is evil,* and so is the *lust of the eyes.*

After the repetition of some ceremonial appointments, the chapter closes with that great and fundamental law of religion, *Be holy unto your God,* purged from sin, and sincerely devoted to his service; and that great reason for all the commandments is again and again inculcated, *I am the Lord your God.* Did we more firmly believe, and more frequently and seriously consider, that God is the Lord, and our God and Redeemer, we should see ourselves bound in duty, interest, and gratitude, to keep all his commandments.

CHAPTER 16

The date of the history contained in this chapter is altogether uncertain. Probably these mutinies happened after their removal back again from Kadesh-barnea, when they were fixed (if I may so speak) for their wandering in the wilderness, and began to look upon that as their settlement. Presently after new laws given follows the story of a new rebellion, as if sin took occasion from the commandment to become more exceedingly sinful. Here is, I. A daring and dangerous rebellion raised against Moses and Aaron, by Korah, Dathan, and Abiram (*v.* 1–15). 1. Korah and his accomplices contend for the priesthood against Aaron (*v.* 3). Moses reasons with them, and appeals to God for a decision of the controversy (*v.* 4–11). 2. Dathan and Abiram quarrel with Moses, and refuse to obey his summons, which greatly grieves him (*v.* 12–15). II. A solemn appearance of the pretenders to the priesthood before God, according to order, and a public appearance of the glory of the Lord, which would have consumed the whole congregation if Moses and Aaron had not interceded (*v.* 16–22). III. The deciding of the controversy, and the crushing of the rebellion, by the cutting off of the rebels. 1. Those in their tents were buried alive (*v.* 23–34). 2. Those at the door of the tabernacle were consumed by fire (*v.* 35), and their censers preserved for a memorial (*v.* 37–40). IV. A new insurrection of the people (*v.* 41–43). 1. God stayed in the insurrection by a plague (*v.* 45). 2. Aaron stayed the plague by offering incense (*v.* 46–50). The manner and method of recording this story plainly show the ferment to have been very great.

Verses 1–11

Here is, I. An account of the rebels, who and what they were, not, as formerly, the mixed multitude and the dregs of the people, who are therefore never named, but men of distinction and quality, that made a figure. Korah was the ring-leader: he formed and headed the faction; therefore it is called *the gainsaying of Korah,* Jude 11. He was cousin-german to Moses, they were brothers' children, yet the nearness of the relation could not restrain him from being insolent and rude to Moses. Think it not strange if a man's foes be *those of his own house.* With him joined Dathan and Abiram, chief men of the tribe of Reuben, the eldest son of Jacob. Probably Korah was disgusted both at the preferment of Aaron to the priesthood and the constituting of Elizaphan to the head of the Kohathites (*ch.* 3:30); and perhaps the Reubenites were angry that the tribe of Judah had the first post of honour in the camp. *On* is mentioned (*v.* 1) as one of the heads of the faction, but never after in the whole story, either because, as some think, he repented and left them, or because he did not make himself so remarkable as Dathan and Abiram did. The Kohathites encamped on the same side of the tabernacle that the Reubenites did, which perhaps gave Korah an opportunity of drawing them in, whence the Jews say, *Woe to the wicked man, and woe to his neighbour,* who is in danger of being infected by him. And, these being themselves *men of renown,* they seduced into the conspiracy *two hundred and fifty princes of the assembly* (*v.* 2); probably they were first-born, or at least heads of families, who, before the elevation of Aaron, had themselves ministered in holy things. Note, The pride, ambition, and emulation, of great men, have always been the occasion of a great deal of mischief both in churches and states. God by his grace make great men humble, and so give peace in our time, O Lord! Famous men, and men of renown, as these are described to be, were the great sinners of the old world, Gen. 6:4. The fame and renown which they had did not content them; they were high, but would be higher, and thus the famous men became infamous.

II. The rebels' remonstrance, *v.* 3. That which they quarrel with is the settlement of the priesthood upon Aaron and his family, which they think an honour too great for Moses to give and Aaron to accept, and so they are both charged with usurpation: *You take too much upon you;* or, "Let it suffice you to have domineered thus long, and now think of resigning your places to those who have as good a title to them and are as well able to manage them." 1. They proudly boast of the holiness of the congregation, and the presence of God in it. "They are *holy, every one of them,* and as fit to be employed in offering sacrifice as Aaron is, and as masters of families formerly were, and *the Lord is among them,* to direct and own them." Small reason they had to boast of the people's purity, or of God's favour, as the people had been so frequently and so lately polluted with sin, and were now under the marks of God's displeasure, which should have made them thankful for priests to mediate between them and God; but, instead of that, they envy them. 2. They unjustly charge Moses and Aaron with taking the honour they had to themselves, whereas it was evident, beyond contradiction, that they were called of God to it, Heb. 5:4. So that they would either have no priests at all, nor any government, none to preside either in civil or sacred things, none over the congregation, none above it, or they would not acquiesce in that constitution of the government which God had appointed. See here, (1.) What spirit levellers are of, and those that despise dominions, and resist the powers that God has set over them; they are proud, envious, ambitious, turbulent, wicked, and unreasonable men. (2.) What usage even the best and most useful men may expect, even from those they have been serviceable to. If those be represented as usurpers that have the best titles, and those as tyrants that govern best, let them recollect that Moses and Aaron were thus abused.

III. Moses's conduct when their remonstrance was published against him. How did he take it?

1. He *fell on his face* (*v.* 4), as before, *ch.* 14:5. Thus he showed how willing he would have been to yield to them, and how gladly he would have resigned his government, if it would have consisted with his duty to God and his fidelity to the trust reposed in him. Thus also he applied to God, by prayer, for direction what to say and to do upon this sad occasion. He would not speak to them till he had thus humbled and composed his own spirit (which could not but begin to be heated), and had received instruction from God. The *heart of the wise* in such a case *studies to answer,* and asks counsel at God's mouth.

2. He agrees to refer the case to God, and leave it to him to decide it, as one well assured of the goodness of his title, and yet well content to resign, if God thought fit, to gratify this discontented people with another nomination. An honest cause fears not a speedy trial; even to-morrow let it be brought on, *v.* 5–7. Let Korah and his partisans bring their censers, and offer incense before the Lord, and, if he testify his acceptance of them, well and good; Moses is now as willing that all the Lord's people should be priests, if God so pleased, as before that they should all be prophets, *ch.* 11:29. But if God, upon an appeal to him, determine (as no doubt he would) for Aaron, they would find it highly dangerous to make the experiment: and therefore he puts it off till to-morrow, to try whether, when they had slept upon it, they would desist, and let fall their pretensions.

3. He argues the case fairly with them, to still the mutiny with fair reasoning, if possible, before the appeal came to God's tribunal, for then he knew it would end in the confusion of the complainants.

(1.) He calls them *the sons of Levi, v.* 7, and again *v.* 8. They were of his own tribe, nay, they were of God's tribe; it was therefore the worse in them thus to mutiny both against God and against him. It was not long since the sons of Levi had bravely appeared on God's side, in the matter of the golden calf, and got immortal honour by it; and shall those that were then the only innocents now be the leading criminals, and lose all the honour they had won? Could there be such chaff on God's floor? Levites, and yet rebels?

(2.) He retorts their charge upon themselves. They had unjustly charged Moses and Aaron with taking too much upon them, though they had done no more than what God put upon them; nay, says Moses, *You take too much upon you, you sons of Levi.* Note, Those that take upon them to control and contradict God's appointment take too much upon them. It is enough for us to submit; it is too much to prescribe.

(3.) He shows them the privilege they had as Levites, which was sufficient for them, they needed not to aspire to the honour of the priesthood, *v.* 9, 10. He reminds them how great the honour was to which they were preferred, as Levites. [1.] They were *separated from the congregation of Israel,* distinguished from them, dignified above them; instead of complaining that Aaron's family was advanced above theirs, they ought to have been thankful that their tribe was advanced above the rest of the tribes, though they had been in all respects upon the level with them. Note, It will help to keep us from envying those that are above us duly to consider how many there are below us. Instead of fretting that any are preferred before us in honour, power, estate, or interest, in gifts, graces, or usefulness, we have reason to bless God if we, who are less than the least, are not put among the very last. Many perhaps who deserve better are not preferred so well. [2.] They were separated to very great and valuable honours, *First,* To *draw near to God,* nearer than the common Israelites, though they also were a people near unto him; the nearer any are to God the greater is their honour. *Secondly, To do the service of the tabernacle.* It is honour enough to bear the vessels of the sanctuary, and to be employed in any part of the service of the tabernacle. God's service is not only perfect freedom, but high preferment. *Thirdly,* To *stand before the congregation to minister unto them.* Note, Those are truly great that serve the public, and it is the honour of God's ministers to be the church's ministers; nay, which adds to the dignity put upon them, [3.] It was the God of Israel himself that separated them. It was his act and deed to put them into their place, and therefore they ought not to have been discontented: and he it was likewise that put Aaron into his place, and therefore they ought not to have envied him.

(4.) He convicts them of the sin of undervaluing those privileges: *Seemeth it a small thing unto you?* As if he had said, "It ill becomes you of all men to grudge Aaron the priesthood, when at the same time that he was advanced to that honour you were designed for another honour dependent upon it, and shine with rays borrowed from him." Note, [1.] The privilege of drawing near to the God of Israel is not a small thing in itself, and therefore must not appear small to us. To those who neglect opportunities of drawing near to God, who are careless and formal in it, to whom it is a task and not a pleasure, we may properly put this question: "Seemeth it a small thing to you that God has made you a people near unto him?" [2.] Those who aspire after and usurp the honours forbidden them put a great contempt upon the honours allowed them. We have each of us as good a share of reputation as God sees fit for us, and sees us fit for, and much better than we deserve; and we ought to rest satisfied with it, and not, as these, *exercise ourselves in things too high for us: Seek you the priesthood also?* They would not *own* that they sought it, but Moses saw that they had this in their eye; the law had provided very well for those that served at the altar, and therefore they would put in for the office.

(5.) He interprets their mutiny to be a rebellion against God (*v.* 11); while they pretended to assert the holiness and liberty of the Israel of God, they really took up arms against the God of Israel: *You are gathered together against the Lord.* Note, Those that strive against God's ordinances and providences, whatever they pretend, and whether they are aware of it or no, do indeed strive with their Maker. Those resist the prince who resist those that are commissioned by him: for, alas! says Moses, *What is Aaron, that you murmur against him?* If murmurers and complainers would consider that the instruments they quarrel with are but instruments whom God employs, and that they are but what he makes them, and neither more nor less, better nor worse, they would not be so bold and free in their censures and reproaches as they are. Those that found the priesthood, as it was settled, a blessing, must give all the praise to God; but if any found it a burden they must not therefore quarrel with Aaron, who is but what he is made, and does but as he is bidden. Thus he interested God in the cause, and so might be sure of speeding well in his appeal.

Verses 12–22

Here is, I. The insolence of Dathan and Abiram, and their treasonable remonstrance. Moses had heard what Korah had to say, and had answered it; now he summons Dathan and Abiram to bring in their complaints (*v.* 12); but they would not obey his summons, either because they could not for shame say that to his face which they were resolved to say, and then it is an instance of some remains of modesty in them; or, rather, because they would not so far own his authority, and then it is an instance of the highest degree of impudence. They spoke the language of Pharaoh himself, who set Moses at defiance, but they forgot how dearly he paid for it. Had not their heads been wretchedly heated, and their hearts hardened, they might have considered that, if they regarded not these messengers, Moses could soon in God's name send messengers of death for them. But thus the God of this world *blinds the minds of those that believe not.* But by the same messengers they send their articles of impeachment against Moses; and the charge runs very high. 1. They charge him with having done them a great deal of wrong in bringing them out of Egypt, invidiously calling that *a land flowing with milk and honey, v.* 13. Onions, and garlick, and fish, they had indeed plenty of in Egypt, but it never pretended to milk and honey; only they would thus banter the promise of Canaan. Ungrateful wretches, to represent that as an injury to them which was really the greatest favour that ever was bestowed upon any people! 2. They charge him with a design upon their lives, that he intended to *kill them in the wilderness,* though they were so well provided for. And, if they were sentenced to die in the wilderness, they must thank themselves. Moses would have healed them, and they would not be healed. 3. They charge him with a design upon their liberties, that he meant to enslave them, by *making himself a prince over them.* A prince over them! Was he not a tender father to them? nay, their devoted servant for the Lord's sake? Had they not their properties secured, their order preserved, and justice impartially administered? Did they not live in ease and honour? And yet they complain as if Moses's yoke were heavier than Pharaoh's. And did Moses make himself a prince? Far from it. How gladly would he have declined the office at first! How gladly would he have resigned it many a time since! And yet he is thus put under the blackest characters of a tyrant and a usurper. 4. They charge him with cheating them, raising their expectations of a good land, and then defeating them (*v.* 14): *Thou hast not brought us,* as thou promisedst us, *into a land that floweth with milk and honey;* and pray whose fault was that? He had brought them to the borders of it, and was just ready, under God, to put them in possession of it; but they thrust it away from them, and shut the door against themselves; so that it was purely their own fault that they were not now in Canaan, and yet Moses must bear the blame. Thus when the *foolishness of man perverteth his way his heart fretteth against the Lord,* Prov. 19:3. 5. They charge him in the general with unfair dealing, that he put *out the eyes of these men,* and then meant to lead them blindfold as he pleased. The design of all he did for them was to open their eyes, and yet they insinuate that he intended to put out their eyes, that they might not see themselves imposed upon. Note, The wisest and best cannot please

every body, nor gain the good word of all. Those often fall under the heaviest censures who have merited the highest applause. Many a good work Moses had shown them from the Father, and for which of these do they reproach him?

II. Moses's just resentment of their insolence, *v.* 15. Moses, though the meekest man, yet, finding God reproached in him, *was very wroth;* he could not bear to see a people ruining themselves for whose salvation he had done so much. In this discomposure,

1. He appeals to God concerning his own integrity; whereas they basely reflected upon him as ambitious, covetous, and oppressive, in making himself a prince over them, God was his witness, (1.) That he never got any thing by them: *I have not taken one ass from them,* not only not by way of bribery and extortion, but not by way of recompence or gratuity for all the good offices he had done them; he never took the pay of a general, or the salary of a judge, much less the tribute of a prince. He got more in his estate when he kept Jethro's flock than when he came to be king in Jeshurun. (2.) That they never lost any thing by him: *Neither have I hurt any one of them,* no, not the least, no, not the worst, no, not those that had been most peevish and provoking to him: he never abused his power to the support of wrong. Note, Those that have never blemished themselves need not fear being slurred by others: when men condemn us we may be easy, if our own hearts condemn us not.

2. He begs of God to plead his cause, and clear him, by showing his displeasure at the incense which Korah and his company were to offer, with whom Dathan and Abiram were in confederacy. Lord, says he, *Respect not thou their offering.* Herein he seems to refer to the history of Cain, lately written by his own hand, of whom it is said that to him and his offering God had not respect, Gen. 4:5. These that *followed the gainsaying of Korah walked in the way of Cain* (these are put together, Jude 11), and therefore he prays that they might be frowned upon as Cain was, and put to the same confusion.

III. Issue joined between Moses and his accusers. 1. Moses challenges them to appear with Aaron next morning, at the time of offering up the morning incense, and refer the matter to God's judgment, *v.* 16, 17. Since he could not convince them by his calm and affectionate reasoning, he is ready to enter into bonds to stand God's award, not doubting but that God would appear, to decide the controversy. This reference he had agreed to before (*v.* 6, 7), and here adds only one clause, which bespeaks his great condescension to the plaintiffs, that Aaron, against whose advancement they excepted, though now advanced by the divine institution to the honour of burning incense within the tabernacle, yet, upon this trial, should put himself into the place of a probationer, and stand upon the level with Korah, at the door of the tabernacle; nay, and Moses himself would stand with them, so that the complainant shall have all the fair dealing he can desire; and thus *every mouth shall be stopped.* 2. Korah accepts the challenge, and makes his appearance with Moses and Aaron *at the door of the tabernacle,* to make good his pretensions, *v.* 18, 19. If he had not had a very great stock of impudence, he could not have carried on the matter thus far. Had not he lately seen Nadab and Abihu, the consecrated priests, struck dead for daring to offer incense with unhallowed fire? and could he and his accomplices expect to fare any better in offering incense with unhallowed hands? Yet, to confront Moses and Aaron, in the height of his pride he thus bids defiance to Heaven, and pretends to demand the divine acceptance without a divine warrant; thus wretchedly is the heart hardened through the deceitfulness of sin. They *took every man his censer.* Perhaps these were some of the censers which these heads of families had made use of at their family-altars, before this part of religious service was confined to the priesthood and the altar in the tabernacle (and they would bring them into use and reputation again); or they might be common chafing-dishes, which were for their ordinary use. Now to attend the solemn trial, and to be witness of the issue, one would have thought Moses should have *gathered the congregation against the rebels,* but it seems Korah gathered them against Moses (*v.* 19), which intimates that a great part of the congregation sided with Korah, were at his beck, and wished him success, and that Korah's hopes were very high

of carrying the point against Aaron; for, had he suspected the event, he would not have coveted to make the trial thus public: but little did he think that he was now calling the congregation together to be the witnesses of his own confusion! Note, Proud and ambitious men, while they are projecting their own advancement, often prove to have been hurrying on their own shameful fall.

IV. The judgment set, and the Judge taking the tribunal, and threatening to give sentence against the whole congregation. 1. The *glory of the Lord appeared, v.* 19. The same glory that appeared to instal Aaron in his office at first (Lev. 9:23) now appeared to confirm him in it, and to confound those that oppose him, and set up themselves in competition with him. The *Shechinah,* or divine Majesty, the glory of the eternal Word, which ordinarily dwelt between the cherubim within the veil, now was publicly seen over the door of the tabernacle, to the terror of the whole congregation; for, though they saw no manner of similitude, yet probably the appearances of the light and fire were such as plainly showed God to be angry with them; as when he appeared, *ch.* 14:10. Nothing is more terrible to those who are conscious of guilt than the appearances of divine glory; for such a glorious Being must needs be a formidable enemy. 2. God threatened to *consume them all in a moment,* and, in order to that, bade Moses and Aaron stand from among them, *v.* 21. God thus showed what their sin deserved, and how very provoking it was to him. See what a dangerous thing it is to have fellowship with sinners, and in the least to partake with them. Many of the congregation, it is likely, came only for company, following the crowd, or for curiosity, to see the issue, yet not coming, as they ought to have done, to bear their testimony against the rebels, and openly to declare for God and Moses, they had like to have been all consumed in a moment. If we follow the herd into which the devil has entered, it is at our peril.

V. The humble intercession of Moses and Aaron for the congregation, *v.* 22. 1. Their posture was importuning: they *fell on their faces,* prostrating themselves before God, as supplicants in good earnest, that they might prevail for sparing mercy. Though the people had treacherously deserted them, and struck in with those that were in arms against them, yet they approved themselves faithful to the trusts reposed in them, as shepherds of Israel, who were to stand in the breach when they saw the flock in danger. Note, If others fail in their duty to us, this does not discharge us from our duty to them, nor take off the obligations we lie under to seek their welfare. 2. Their prayer was a pleading prayer, and it proved a prevailing one. Now God would have *destroyed them* if Moses had not *turned away his wrath* (Ps. 106:23); yet far be it from us to imagine that Moses was more considerate or more compassionate than God in such a case as this: but God saw fit to show his just displeasure against the sin of sinners by the sentence, and at the same time to show his gracious condescension to the prayers of the saints, by the revocation of the sentence at the intercession of Moses. Observe in the prayer, (1.) The title they give to God: *The God of the spirits of all flesh.* See what man is; he is a spirit in flesh, a soul embodied, a creature wonderfully compounded of heaven and earth. See what God is; he is the God of the spirits of all mankind. *He forms the spirit,* Zec. 12:1. He *fathers it,* Heb. 12:9. He has an ability to fashion it (Ps. 33:15), and authority to dispose of it, for he has said, *All souls are mine,* Eze. 18:4. They insinuate hereby that though, as *the God of the spirits of all flesh,* he might in sovereignty consume this congregation in a moment, yet it was to be hoped that he would in mercy spare them, not only because they were the work of his own hands, and he had a propriety in them, but because, being the *God of spirits,* he knew their frame, and could distinguish between the leaders and the led, between those who sinned maliciously and those who were drawn in by their wiles, and would make a difference accordingly in his judgments. (2.) The argument they insist on; it is much the same with that which Abraham urged in his intercession for Sodom (Gen. 18:23): *Wilt thou destroy the righteous with the wicked?* Such is the plea here: *Shall one man sin and wilt thou be wroth with all the congregation?* Not but that it was the sin of them all to join in this matter, but the great transgression was his that first hatched the treason. Note, Whatever God may do in sovereignty and strict justice, we have reason to hope that he will not destroy a congregation for the sin of one, but that, *righteousness and peace* having *kissed each other* in the undertaking of the Redeemer, *mercy shall rejoice against judgment.* Moses knew that all the congregation must perish in the wilderness by degrees, yet he is thus earnest in prayer that they might not be consumed at once, and would reckon it a favour to obtain a reprieve. *Lord, let it alone this year.*

Verses 23–34

We have here the determining of the controversy with Dathan and Abiram, who rebelled against Moses, as in the next paragraph the determining of the controversy with Korah and his company, who would be rivals with Aaron. It should seem that Dathan and Abiram had set up a spacious tabernacle in the midst of the tents of their families, where they kept court, met in council, and hung out their flag of defiance against Moses; it is here called *the tabernacle of Korah, Dathan, and Abiram, v.* 24, 27. There, as in the place of rendezvous, Dathan and Abiram staid, when Korah and his friends went up to the tabernacle of the Lord, waiting the issue of their trial; but here we are told how they had their business done, before that trial was over. For God will take what method he pleases in his judgments.

I. Public warning is given to the congregation to withdraw immediately from the tents of the rebels. 1. God bids Moses speak to this purport, *v.* 24. This was in answer to Moses's prayer. He had begged that God would not *destroy the whole congregation.* "Well," says God, "I will not, provided they be so wise as to shift for their own safety, and get out of the way of danger. If they will quit the rebels, well and good, they shall not perish with them; otherwise, let them take what follows." Note, We cannot expect to reap benefit by the prayers of our friends for our salvation, unless we ourselves be diligent and faithful in making use of the means of salvation; for God never promised to save by miracles those that would not save themselves by means. Moses that had prayed for them must preach this to them, and warn them to *flee from this wrath to come.* 2. Moses accordingly repairs to the head-quarters of the rebels, leaving Aaron at the door of the tabernacle, *v.* 25. Dathan and Abiram had contumaciously refused to come up to him (*v.* 12), yet he humbly condescends to go down to them, to try if he could yet convince and reclaim them. Ministers must thus with meekness instruct those that oppose themselves, and not think it below them to stoop to those that are most stubborn, for their good. Christ himself stretches out his hand to a rebellious and gainsaying people. The seventy elders of Israel attend Moses and his guard, to secure him from the insolence of the rabble, and by their presence to put an honour upon him, and if possible to strike an awe upon the rebels. It is our duty to contribute all we can to the countenance and support of injured innocency and honour. 3. Proclamation is made that all manner of persons, as they tendered their own safety, should forthwith *depart from the tents of these wicked men* (*v.* 26), and thus should signify that they deserted their cause and interest, detested their crimes and counsels, and dreaded the punishment coming upon them. Note, Those that would not perish with sinners must *come out from among them,* and be separate. In vain do we pray, *Gather not our souls with sinners,* if we save not ourselves from the *untoward generation.* God's people are called out of Babylon, lest they share both in her sins and in her plagues, Rev. 18:4.

II. The congregation takes the warning, but the rebels themselves continue obstinate, *v.* 27. 1. God, in mercy, inclined the people to forsake the rebels: *They got up from the tabernacle of Korah, Dathan, and Abiram,* both those whose lot it was to pitch near them (who doubtless with themselves removed their families, and all their effects) and those also who had come from all parts of their camp to see the issue. It was in answer to the prayer of Moses that God thus stirred up the hearts of the congregation to shift for their own preservation. Note, To those whom God will save he gives repentance, that they may *recover themselves out of the snare of the devil.* Grace to separate from evil doers is one of the things that accompany salvation. 2. God, in justice, left the rebels to the obstinacy and hardness of their own hearts. Though they saw themselves abandoned by all their neighbours, and set up as a mark to the ar-

rows of God's justice, yet instead of falling down and humbling themselves before God and Moses, owning their crime and begging pardon, instead of fleeing and dispersing themselves to seek for shelter in the crowd, they impudently *stood in the doors of their tents,* as if they would out-face God himself, and dare him to his worst. Thus were their hearts hardened to their own destruction, and they were fearless when their case was most fearful. But what a pity was it that their little children, who were not capable of guilt or fear, should by the presumption of their parents be put in this audacious posture! Happy they who are taught betimes to bow before God, and not as those unhappy little ones to stand it out against him!

III. Sentence is solemnly pronounced upon them by Moses in the name of the Lord, and the decision of the controversy is put upon the execution of that sentence by the almighty power of God. Moses, by divine instinct and direction, when the eyes of all Israel were fastened upon him, waiting the event, moved with a just and holy indignation at the impudence of the rebels, boldly puts the whole matter to a surprising issue, *v.* 28–30. 1. If the rebels die a common death, he will be content to be called and counted an impostor; not only if they die a natural death, but if they die by any sort of judgment that has formerly been executed on other malefactors. "If they die by the plague, or by fire from heaven, or by the sword, then say, God has disowned Moses;" but, 2. "If the earth open and swallow them up" (a punishment without precedent), "then let all the house of Israel know assuredly that I am God's servant, sent by him, and employed for him, and that those that fight against me fight against him." The judgment itself would have been proof enough of God's displeasure against the rebels, and would have given all men to *understand that they had provoked the Lord;* but when it was thus solemnly foretold and appealed to by Moses beforehand, when there was not the least previous indication of it from without, the convincing evidence of it was much the stronger, and it was put beyond dispute that he was not only a servant but a favourite of Heaven, who was so intimately acquainted with the divine counsels, and could obtain such extraordinary appearances of the divine power in his vindication.

IV. Execution is immediately done. It appeared that God and his servant Moses understood one another very well; for, as soon as ever Moses had spoken the word, God did the work, the earth *clave asunder* (*v.* 31), *opened her mouth, and swallowed them all up,* them and theirs (*v.* 32), and then *closed upon them, v.* 33. This judgment was, 1. Unparalleled. God, in it, *created a new thing,* did what he never did before; for he has many arrows in his quiver; and there are diversities of operations in wrath as well as mercy. Dathan and Abiram thought themselves safe because they were at a distance from the *shechinah,* whence the fire of the Lord had sometimes issued, *qui procul à Jove* (they say) *procul à fulmine — he who is far from Jove is far from the thunderbolt.* But God made them to know that he was not tied up to one way of punishing; the earth, when he pleases, shall serve his justice as effectually as the fire. 2. It was very terrible to the sinners themselves to go down alive into their own graves, to be dead and buried in an instant, to go down thus to the bars of the pit when they were in their *full strength wholly at ease and quiet.* 3. It was severe upon their poor children, who, for the greater terror of the judgment, and fuller indication of the divine wrath, perished as parts of their parents, in which, though we cannot particularly tell how bad they might be to deserve it or how good God might be otherwise to them to compensate it, yet of this we are sure in the general, that Infinite Justice did them no wrong. *Far be it from God that he should do iniquity.* 4. It was altogether miraculous. The cleaving of the earth was as wonderful, and as much above the power of nature, as the cleaving of the sea, and the closing of the earth again more so than the closing of the waters. God has all the creatures at his command, and can make any of them, when he pleases, instruments of his justice; nor will any of them be our friends if he be our enemy. God now confirmed to Israel what Moses had lately taught them in that prayer of his, Ps. 90:11, *Who knows the power of thy anger?* He has, when he pleases, *strange punishments for the workers of iniquity,* Job 31:3. Let us therefore conclude, *Who is able to stand before this holy Lord God?* 5. It was very

significant. They *set their mouths against the heavens,* and *their throat was an open sepulchre;* justly therefore does the earth open her mouth upon them and swallow them up. They made a rent in the congregation; justly therefore is the earth rent under them. Presumptuous sinners, that hate to be reformed, are a burden to the earth, the whole creation groans under them, which here was signified by this, that the earth sunk under these rebels, as weary of bearing them and being under them. And, considering how the earth is still in like manner loaded with the weight of iniquity, we have reason to wonder that this was the only time it ever sunk under its load. 6. It was typical of the eternal ruin of sinners who die impenitent, who, perhaps in allusion to this, are said to *sink down into the pit* (Ps. 9:15) and to *go down quickly into hell,* Ps. 55:15. But David, even when he *sinks in deep mire,* yet prays in faith, *Let not the pit shut her mouth upon me,* as it does on the damned, between whom and life there is a gulf fixed, Ps. 69:2–15. His case was bad, but not, like this, desperate.

V. All Israel is alarmed at the judgment: *They fled at the cry of them, v.* 34. They cried for help when it was too late. Their doleful shrieks, instead of fetching their neighbours in to their relief, drove them so much the further off; for knowing their own guilt, and one another's, they hastened one another, saying, *Lest the earth swallow us up also.* Note, Others' ruins should be our warnings. Could we by faith hear the outcries of those that have gone down to the bottomless pit, we should give more diligence than we do to escape for our lives, lest we also come into that condemnation.

Verses 35–40

We must now look back to the door of the tabernacle, where we left the pretenders to the priesthood with their censers in their hands ready to offer incense; and here we find,

I. Vengeance taken on them, *v.* 35. It is probable that when the earth opened in the camp to swallow up Dathan and Abiram *a fire went out from the Lord and consumed the 250 men that offered incense,* while Aaron that stood with them was preserved alive. This punishment was not indeed so new a thing as the former, for Nadab and Abihu thus died; but it was not less strange or dreadful, and in it it appeared, 1. That *our God is a consuming fire.* Is thunder a sensible indication of the terror of his voice? Lightning is also the power of his hand. We must see in this his fiery indignation which devours the adversaries, and infer from it what a fearful thing it is to *fall into the hands of the living God,* Heb. 10:27–31. 2. That it is at our peril if we meddle with that which does not belong to us. God is jealous of the honour of his own institutions, and will not have them invaded. It is most probable that Korah himself was consumed with those 250 that presumed to offer incense; for the priesthood was the thing he aimed at, and therefore we have reason to think that he would not quit his post at the door of the tabernacle. But, behold, those are made sacrifices to the justice of God who flattered themselves with the hopes of being priests. Had they been content with their office as Levites, which was sacred and honourable, and better than they deserved, they might have lived and died with joy and reputation; but, like the angels that sinned, *leaving their first estate,* and aiming at the honours that were not appointed them, they were thrust down to *Hades,* their censers struck out of their hands, and their breath out of their bodies, by a burning which typified *the vengeance of eternal fire.*

II. Care is taken to perpetuate the remembrance of this vengeance. No mention is made of the taking up of their carcases: the scripture leaves them as dung upon the face of the earth; but orders are given about their censers, 1. That they be secured, because they are hallowed. Eleazar is charged with this, *v.* 37. Those invaders of the priesthood had proceeded so far, by the divine patience and submission, as to kindle their incense with fire from off the altar, which they were suffered to use by way of experiment: but, as soon as they had kindled their fire, God kindled another, which put a fatal final period to their pretensions; now Eleazar is ordered to scatter the fire, with the incense that was kindled with it, in some unclean place without the camp, to signify God's abhorrence of their offering as a polluted thing: *The sacrifice of the wicked is an abomination to the Lord.* But he is to gather up the censers out of the mingled burning, God's fire and theirs, because *they are hallowed.* Having been once put to a holy use, and that by God's own order (though only for trial) they must not return to common service; so some understand it: rather, *they are devoted,* they are an anathema; and therefore, as all devoted things, they must be made some way or other serviceable to the glory of God. 2. That they be used in the service of the sanctuary, not as censers, which would rather have put honour upon the usurpers whose disgrace was intended; nor was there occasion for brazen censers, the golden altar was served with golden ones; but they must be beaten into *broad plates for a covering of the brazen altar, v.* 38–40. These pretenders thought to have ruined the altar, by laying the priesthood in common again; but to show that Aaron's office was so far from being shaken by their impotent malice that it was rather confirmed by it, their censers, which offered to rival his, were used both for the adorning and for the preserving of the altar at which he ministered. Yet this was not all; this covering of the altar must be a *memorial to the children of Israel,* throughout their generations, of this great event. Though there was so much in it astonishing, and though Moses was to record it in his history, yet there was danger of its being forgotten in process of time; impressions that seem deep are not always durable; therefore it was necessary to appoint this record of the judgment, that the Levites who attended this altar, and had their inferior services appointed them, might learn to keep within their bounds, and be afraid of transgressing them, lest they should be made like Korah and his company, who were Levites, and would have been priests. These censers were preserved *in terrorem,* that others might hear and fear, and do no more presumptuously. Thus God has provided that his wonderful works, both in mercy and judgment, should be had in everlasting remembrance, that the end of them may be answered, and they may serve for instruction and admonition to those *on whom the ends of the world are come.*

Verses 41–50

Here is, I. A new rebellion raised the very next day against Moses and Aaron. Be astonished, O heavens, at this, and wonder, O earth! Was there ever such an instance of the incurable corruption of sinners? *On the morrow* (v. 41) the body of the people mutinied. 1. Though they were so lately terrified by the sight of the punishment of the rebels. The shrieks of those sinking sinners, those sinners against their own souls, were yet sounding in their ears, the smell of the fire yet remained, and the gaping earth was scarcely thoroughly closed, and yet the same sins were re-acted and all these warnings slighted. 2. Though they were so lately saved from sharing in the same punishment, and the survivors were *as brands plucked out of the burning,* yet they fly in the face of Moses and Aaron, to whose intercession they owed their preservation. Their charge runs very high: *You have killed the people of the Lord.* Could any thing have been said more unjustly and maliciously? They canonize the rebels, calling those the people of the Lord who died in arms against him. They stigmatize divine justice itself. It was plain enough that Moses and Aaron had no hand in their death (they did what they could to save them), so that in charging them with murder they did in effect charge God himself with it. The continued obstinacy of this people, notwithstanding the terrors of God's law as it was given on Mount Sinai, and the terrors of his judgments as they were here executed on the disobedient, shows how necessary the grace of God is to the effectual change of men's hearts and lives, without which the most likely means will never attain the end. Love will do what fear could not.

II. God's speedy appearance against the rebels. When they had *gathered against Moses and Aaron,* perhaps with a design to depose or murder them, they *looked towards the tabernacle,* as if their misgiving consciences expected some frowns thence, and, *behold, the glory of the Lord appeared* (v. 42), for the protection of his servants, and the confusion of his and their accusers and adversaries. Moses and Aaron thereupon came before the tabernacle, partly for their own safety (there they took sanctuary from the strife of tongues, Ps. 27:5; 31:20), and partly for advice, to know what was the mind of God upon this occasion, v. 43. Justice hereupon declares that they deserve to be con-

sumed *in a moment, v.* 45. Why should those live another day who hate to be reformed, and whose rebellions are their daily practices? Let just vengeance take place and do its work, and the trouble will soon be over; only Moses and Aaron must first be secured.

III. The intercession which Moses and Aaron made for them. Though they had as much reason, one would think, as Elias had to make intercession against Israel (Rom. 11:2), yet they forgive and forget the indignities offered them, and are the best friends their enemies have. 1. They both *fell on their faces,* humbly to intercede with God for mercy, knowing how great the provocation was. This they had done several times before, upon similar occasions; and, though the people had basely requited them for it, yet, God having graciously accepted them, they still have recourse to the same method. This is praying always. 2. Moses, perceiving that the *plague had begun in the congregation* of the rebels (that is, that body of them which was gathered against Moses), sent Aaron by an act of his priestly office to make atonement for them, v. 46. And Aaron readily went and burned incense between the living and the dead, not to purify the infected air, but to pacify an offended God, and so stayed the progress of the judgment. By this it appeared, (1.) That Aaron was a very good man, and a man that had a true love for the children of his people, though they hated and envied him. Though God was now avenging his quarrel and pleading the cause of his priesthood, yet he interposes to turn away God's wrath. Nay, forgetting his age and gravity, he ran into the midst of the congregation to help them. He did not say, "Let them smart awhile, and then, when I come, I shall be the more welcome;" but, as one tender of the life of every Israelite, he makes all possible speed into the gap at which death was entering. Moses and Aaron, who had been charged with killing the people of the Lord, might justly have upbraided them now; could they expect those to be their saviours whom they had so invidiously called their murderers? But those good men have taught us here by their example not to be sullen towards those that are peevish with us, nor to take the advantage which men give us by their provoking language to deny them any real kindness which it is in the power of our hands to do them. We must render good for evil. (2.) That Aaron was a very bold man — bold to venture into the midst of an enraged rabble that were gathered together against him, and who, for aught he knew, might be the more exasperated by the plague that had begun — bold to venture into the midst of the infection, where the arrows of death flew thickest, and hundreds, nay thousands, were falling on the right hand and on the left. To save their lives he put his own into his hand, not counting it dear to him, so that he might but fulfil his ministry. (3.) That Aaron was a man of God, and *ordained for men, in things pertaining to God.* His call to the priesthood was hereby abundantly confirmed and set above all contradiction; God had not only saved his life when the intruders were cut off, but now made him an instrument for saving Israel. Compare the censer of Aaron here with the *censers of those sinners against their own souls.* Those provoked God's anger, this pacified it; those destroyed men's lives, this saved them; no room therefore is left to doubt of Aaron's call to the priesthood. Note, Those make out the best title to public honours that lay out themselves the most for public good and obtain mercy of the Lord to be faithful and useful. If any man will be great, let him make himself the servant of all. (4.) That Aaron was a type of Christ, who came into the world to make an atonement for sin and to turn away the wrath of God from us, and who, by his mediation and intercession, *stands between the living and the dead,* to secure his chosen Israel to himself, and save them out of the midst of a world infected with sin and the curse.

IV. The result and issue of the whole matter. 1. God's justice was glorified in the death of some. Great execution the sword of the Lord did in a very little time. Though Aaron made all the haste he could, yet, before he could reach his post of service, there were 14,700 men laid dead upon the spot, v. 49. There were but few comparatively that died about the matter of Korah, the ring-leaders only were made examples; but, the people not being led to repentance by the patience and forbearance of God with them, justice is not now so sparing of the blood of Israelites. They complained of the death of a few hundreds as

an unmerciful slaughter made among the *people of the Lord,* but here God silences that complaint by the slaughter of many thousands. Note, Those that quarrel with less judgments prepare greater for themselves; for when God judges he will overcome. 2. His mercy was glorified in the preservation of the rest. God showed them what he could do by his power, and what he might do in justice, but then showed them what he would do in his love and pity: he would, notwithstanding all this, preserve them a people to himself in and by a mediator. The cloud of Aaron's incense coming from his hand stayed the plague. Note, It is much for the glory of God's goodness that many a time even in wrath he remembers mercy. And, even when judgments have been begun, prayer puts a stop to them; so ready is he to forgive, and so little pleasure does he take in the death of sinners.

CHAPTER 17

Enough had been done in the chapter before to quash all pretensions of the families of the tribe of Levi that would set up in competition with Aaron, and to make it appear that Aaron was the head of the tribe; but it seems, when that matter was settled, the princes of the rest of the tribes began to murmur. If the head of a tribe must be a priest, why not the head of some other tribe than that of Levi? He that searches the heart knew this thought to be in the breast of some of them, and before it broke out into any overt act graciously anticipated it, to prevent bloodshed; and it is done by miracle in this chapter, not a miracle of wrath, as before, but of grace. I. The matter is put upon trial by the bringing of twelve rods, one for each prince, before the Lord (v. 1–7). II. Upon trial, the matter is determined by the miraculous blossoming of Aaron's rod (v. 8, 9). III. The decision of the controversy is registered by the preservation of the rod (v. 10, 11). IV. The people acquiesce in it with some reluctance (v. 12, 13).

Verses 1–7

Here we have, I. Orders given for the bringing in of a rod for every tribe (which was peculiarly significant, for the word here used for a rod sometimes signifies a tribe, as particularly *ch.* 34:13), that God by a miracle, wrought on purpose, might make it known on whom he had conferred the honour of the priesthood. 1. It seems then the priesthood was a preferment worth seeking and striving for, even by the princes of the tribes. It is an honour to the greatest of men to be employed in the service of God. Yet perhaps these contended for it rather for the sake of the profit and power that attended the office than for the sake of that in it which was divine and sacred. 2. It seems likewise, after all that had been done to settle this matter, there were those who would be ready upon any occasion to contest it. They would not acquiesce in the divine appointment, but would make an interest in opposition to it. They strive with God for the dominion; and the question is whose will shall stand. God will rule, but Israel will not be ruled; and this is the quarrel. 3. It is an instance of the grace of God that, having wrought divers miracles to punish sin, he would work one more on purpose to prevent it. God has effectually provided that the obstinate shall be left inexcusable, and every mouth shall be stopped. Israel were very prone to murmur both against God and against their governors. "Now," said God, *"I will make to cease from me the murmurings of the children of Israel, v.* 5. If any thing will convince them, they shall be convinced; and, if this will not convince them, nothing will." This was to be to them, as Christ said the sign of the prophet Jonas (that is, his own resurrection) should be to the men of that generation, the highest proof of his mission that should be given them. The directions are, (1.) That twelve rods or staves should be brought in. It is probable that they were not now fresh cut out of a tree, for then the miracle would not have been so great; but that they were the staves which the princes ordinarily used as ensigns of their authority (of which we read *ch.* 21:18), old dry staves, that had no sap in them, and it is probable that they were all made of the almond-tree. It should seem they were but twelve in all, with Aaron's, for, when Levi comes into the account, Ephraim and Manasseh make but one, under the name of Joseph. (2.) That the name of each prince should be written upon his rod, that every man might know his own, and to prevent contests. Writing is often a good preservative against strife, for what is written may be appealed to. (3.) That they should be laid up in the tabernacle, for one night, before the testimony, that is, before the ark, which, with its mercy seat, was a symbol, token, or testimony, of God's presence with them. (4.) They were to expect, being told it before, that the rod of the tribe, or prince, whom God chose to the priesthood, should bud and blossom, *v.* 5. It was requisite that they should be told of it, that it might appear not to be casual, but according to the counsel and will of God.

II. The preparing of the rods accordingly. The princes brought them in, some of them perhaps fondly expecting that the choice would fall upon them, and all of them thinking it honour enough to be competitors with Aaron, and to stand candidates, even for the priesthood (*v.* 7); and *Moses laid them up before the Lord.* He did not object that the matter was sufficiently settled already, and enough done to convince those that were not invincibly hardened in their prejudices. He did not undertake to determine the controversy himself, though it might easily have been done; nor did he suggest that it would be to no purpose to offer satisfaction to a people that were willingly blind. But, since God will have it so, he did his part, and lodged the case before the Lord, to whom the appeal was made by consent, and left it with him.

Verses 8–13

Here is, I. The final determination of the controversy concerning the priesthood by a miracle, *v.* 8, 9. The rods or staves were brought out from the most holy place where they were laid up, and publicly produced before the people; and, while all the rest of the rods remained as they were, Aaron's rod only, of a dry stick, became a living branch, budded, and blossomed, and yielded almonds. In some places there were buds, in others blossoms, in others fruit, at the same time. This was miraculous, and took away all suspicion of a fraud, as if in the night Moses had taken away Aaron's rod, and put a living branch of an almond tree in the room of it; for no ordinary branch would have buds, blossoms, and fruits upon it, all at once. Now,

1. This was a plain indication to the people that Aaron was chosen to the priesthood, and not any other of the princes of the tribes. Thus he was distinguished from them and manifested to be under the special blessing of heaven, which sometimes yields increase where there is neither planting nor watering by the hand of man. Bishop Hall here observes that fruitfulness is the best evidence of a divine call, and that the plants of God's setting, and the boughs cut off from them, will flourish. See Ps. 92:12–14. The trees of the Lord, though they seem dry trees, are full of sap.

2. It was a very proper sign to represent the priesthood itself, which was hereby confirmed to Aaron. (1.) That it should be fruitful and serviceable to the church of God. It produced not only blossoms, but almonds; for the priesthood was designed, not only for an honour to Aaron, but for a blessing to Israel. Thus Christ ordained his apostles and ministers that they should go and bring forth fruit, and that their *fruit should remain,* Jn. 15:16. (2.) That there should be a succession of priests. Here were not only almonds for the present, but buds and blossoms promising more hereafter. Thus has Christ provided in his church that a seed should serve him from generation to generation. (3.) That yet this priesthood should not be perpetual, but in process of time, like the branches and blossoms of a tree, should fail and wither. The flourishing of the almond-tree is mentioned as one of the signs of old age, Eccl. 12:5. This character was betimes put upon the Mosaic priesthood, which soon became old and *ready to vanish away,* Heb. 8:13.

3. It was a type and figure of Christ and his priesthood: for he is *the man, the branch,* that is to be *a priest upon his throne,* as it follows (Zec. 6:12); and he was to *grow up before God,* as this before the ark, *like a tender plant, and a root out of a dry ground,* Isa. 53:2.

II. The record of this determination, by the preserving of the rod before the testimony, *in perpetuam rei memoriam — that it might be had in perpetual remembrance, v.* 10, 11. It is probable that the buds, and blossoms, and fruit, continued fresh; the same divine power that produced them in a night preserved them for ages, at least so long as it was necessary for a token against the rebels. So it was a standing miracle, and the continuance of it was an undeniable proof of the truth of it. Even the leaf of God's trees shall not wither, Ps. 1:3. This rod was preserved, as the censers were, to *take away their murmurings, that they die not.* Note, 1. The design of God in all his providences, both mercies and judgments, and in the memorials of them, is to take away sin, and to prevent it. These things are done, these things written, *that we sin not,* 1 Jn. 2:1. Christ was *manifested to take away sin.* 2. What God does for the taking away of sin is done in real kindness to us, *that we die not.* All the bitter potions he gives, and all the sharp methods he uses with us, are for the cure of a disease which otherwise would certainly be fatal. Bishop Hall observes here that the tables of the law, the pot of manna, and Aaron's rod, were preserved together in or about the ark (the apostle takes notice of them all three together, Heb. 9:4), to show to after-ages how the ancient church was taught, and fed, and ruled; and he infers how precious the doctrine, sacraments, and government, of the church are to God and should be to us. The rod of Moses was used in working many miracles, yet we do not find that this was preserved, for the keeping of it would serve only to gratify men's curiosity; but the rod of Aaron, which carried its miracle along with it, was carefully preserved, because that would be of standing use to convince men's consciences, to silence all disputes about the priesthood, and to confirm the faith of God's Israel in his institutions. Such is the difference between the sacraments which Christ has appointed for edification and the relics which men have devised for superstition.

III. The outcry of the people hereupon (*v.* 12, 13): *Behold, we die, we perish, we all perish. Shall we be consumed with dying?* This may be considered as the language either, 1. Of a repining people quarrelling with the judgments of God, which, by their own pride and obstinacy, they had brought upon themselves. They seem to speak despairingly, as if God was a hard Master, that sought advantage against them, and took all occasions to pick quarrels with them, so that if they trod every so little awry, if they stepped ever so little beyond their bounds, they must die, they must perish, they must all perish, basely insinuating that God would never be satisfied with their blood and ruin, till he had made an end of them all and they were consumed with dying. Thus they seem to be like a *wild bull in a net, full of the fury of the Lord* (Isa. 51:20), fretting that God was too hard for them and that they were forced to submit, which they did only because they could not help it. Note, It is a very wicked thing to fret against God when we are in affliction, and in our distress thus to trespass yet more. If we die, if we perish, it is owing to ourselves, and the blame will lie upon our own heads. Or, 2. Of a repenting people. Many interpreters take it as expressing their submission: "Now we see that it is the will of God we should keep our distance, and that it is at our peril if we draw nearer than is appointed. We submit to the divine will in this appointment; we will not contend any more, lest we all perish:" and they engage Moses to intercede for them, that they may not be all consumed with dying. Thus the point was gained, and in this matter God quite took away their murmurings, and henceforward they acquiesced. Note, When God judges he will overcome, and, one way or other, will oblige the most obstinate gainsayers to confess their folly sooner or later, and that wherein they dealt proudly he was above them. *Vicisti Galilaee — O Galilaean, thou hast conquered!*

CHAPTER 18

Aaron being now fully established in the priesthood abundantly to his own satisfaction, and to the satisfaction of the people (which was the good that God brought out of the evil opposition made to him), in this chapter God gives him full instructions concerning his office or rather repeats those which he had before given him. He tells him, I. What must be his work and the care and charge committed to him, and what assistance he should have the Levites in that work (*v.* 1–7). II. What should be his and the Levites' wages for this work. 1. The perquisites or fees peculiar to the priests (*v.* 8–19). 2. The settled maintenance of the Levites (*v.* 20–24). III. The portion which must be paid to the priests out of the Levites' maintenance (*v.* 25–32). Thus every one knew what he had to do, and what he had to live upon.

Verses 1–7

The coherence of this chapter with that foregoing is very observable.

I. The people, in the close of that chapter, had complained of the difficulty and peril that there were in drawing near to God, which put them under some dreadful apprehensions that the tabernacle in the midst of them, which they hoped would have been their joy and glory, would rather be their terror and ruin. Now, in answer to this complaint, God here gives them to understand by Aaron that the priests should come near for them as their representatives; so that, though the people were obliged to keep their distance, yet that should not at all redound to their disgrace or prejudice, but their comfortable communion with God should be kept up by the interposition of the priests.

II. A great deal of honour God had now lately put upon Aaron; his rod had budded and blossomed, when the rods of the rest of the princes remained dry, and destitute both of fruit and ornament. Now lest Aaron should be puffed up with the abundance of the favours that were done him, and the miracles that were wrought for the support of him in his high station, God comes to him to remind him of the burden that was laid upon him, and the duty required from him as a priest. He would see reason not to be proud of his preferment, but to receive the honours of his office with reverence and holy trembling, when he considered how great was the charge committed to him, and how hard it would be for him to give a good account of it. *Be not high-minded, but fear.*

1. God tells him of the danger that attended his dignity, *v.* 1. (1.) That both the priests and Levites *(thou, and thy sons, and thy father's house)* should *bear the iniquity of the sanctuary;* that is, if the sanctuary were profaned by the intrusion of strangers, or persons in their uncleanness, the blame should lie upon the Levites and priests, who ought to have kept them off. Though the sinner that thrust in presumptuously should die in his iniquity, yet his blood should be required at the hands of the watchmen. Or it may be taken more generally: "If any of the duties or offices of the sanctuary be neglected, if any service be not done in its season or not according to the law, if any thing be lost or misplaced in the removal of the sanctuary, you shall be accountable for it, and answer it at your peril." (2.) That the priests should themselves *bear the iniquity of the priesthood;* that is, if they either neglected any part of their work or permitted any other persons to invade their office, and take their work out of their hands, they should bear the blame of it. Note, The greater the trust is of work and power that is committed to us the greater is our danger of contracting guilt, by falsifying and betraying that trust. This is a good reason why we should neither be envious at others' honours nor ambitious ourselves of high places, because great dignity exposes us to great iniquity. Those that are entrusted with the charge of the sanctuary will have a great deal to answer for. Who would covet the care of souls who considers the account that must be given of that care?

2. He tells him of the duty that attended his dignity. (1.) That he and his sons must *minister before the tabernacle of witness* (*v.* 2); that is (as bishop Patrick explains it), *before the most holy place,* in which the ark was, on the outside of the veil of that tabernacle, but within the door of the tabernacle, of the congregation. They were to attend the golden altar, the table, and candlestick, which no Levite might approach to. *You shall serve, v.* 7. Not, "You shall rule" (it was never intended that they should lord it over God's heritage), but "You shall serve God and the congregation." Note, The priesthood is a service. *If any desire the office of a bishop he desires a good work.* Ministers must remember that they are ministers, that is, servants, of whom it is required that they be humble, diligent, and faithful. (2.) That the Levites must assist him and his sons, and minister to them in all the *service of the tabernacle* (*v.* 2–4), though they must by no means come nigh the vessels of the sanctuary, nor at the altar meddle with the great services of burning the fat and sprinkling the blood. Aaron's family was very small, and, as it increased, the rest of the families of Israel would increase likewise, so that the hands of the priests neither were now nor were likely to be sufficient for all the service of the tabernacle; therefore (says God) *the Levites shall be joined to thee, v.* 2, and again *v.* 4, where there seems to be an allusion to the name of Levi, which signifies *joined.* Many of the Levites had of late set themselves against Aaron, but henceforward God promises that they should be heartily joined to him in interest and affection, and should no more contest with him. It was a good sign to Aaron that God owned him when he inclined the hearts of those concerned to own him too. The Levites are said to be given as a gift to the priests, *v.* 6. Note, We are to value it as a great gift of the divine bounty to have those joined to us that will be helpful and serviceable to us in the service of God. (3.) That both priests

and Levites must carefully watch against the profanation of sacred things. The Levites must *keep the charge of the tabernacle,* that *no stranger* (that is, none who upon any account was forbidden to come) might *come nigh* (*v.* 4), and that upon pain of death, *v.* 7. And the priests must *keep the charge of the sanctuary* (*v.* 5), must instruct the people, and admonish them concerning the due distance they were to keep, and not suffer them to break the bounds set them, as Korah's company had done, that there be *no wrath any more upon the children of Israel.* Note, The preventing of sin is the preventing of wrath; and the mischief sin has done should be a warning to us for the future to watch against it both in ourselves and others.

Verses 8–19

The priest's service is called a *warfare;* and who goes a warfare at his own charges? As they were well employed, so they were well provided for, and well paid. None shall serve God for nought. All believers are spiritual priests, and God has promised to take care of them; they shall *dwell in the land,* and *verily they shall be fed,* and shall not *want any good thing.* Godliness has the *promise of the life that now is.* And from this plentiful provision here made for the priests the apostle infers that it is the duty of Christian churches to maintain their ministers; those that *served at the altar lived upon the altar.* So those that preach the gospel should *live upon the gospel,* and live comfortably, 1 Co. 9:13, 14. Scandalous maintenance makes scandalous ministers. Now observe, 1. That much of the provision that was made for them arose out of the sacrifices which they themselves were employed to offer. They had the skins of almost all the sacrifices, which they might sell, and they had a considerable share out of the meat-offerings, sin-offerings, etc. Those that had the charge of the offerings had the benefit, *v.* 8. Note, God's work is its own wages, and his service carries its recompence along with it. Even in keeping God's commandments there is great reward. The present pleasures of religion are part of its pay. 2. That they had not only a good table kept for them, but money likewise in their pockets for the redemption of the first-born, and those firstlings of cattle which might not be offered in sacrifice. Thus their maintenance was such as left them altogether *disentangled from the affairs of this life;* they had no grounds to occupy, no land to till, no vineyards to dress, no cattle to tend, no visible estate to take care of, and yet had a more plentiful income than any other families whatsoever. Thus God ordered it that they might be the more entirely addicted to their ministry, and not diverted from it, nor disturbed in it, by any worldly care or business (the ministry requires a whole man); and that they might be examples of living by faith, not only in God's providence, but in his ordinance. They lived from hand to mouth, that they might learn to take no thought for the morrow; sufficient for the day would be the provision thereof: and they had no estates to leave their children, that they might by faith leave their children, that they might by faith leave them to the care of that God who had *fed them all their lives long.* 3. Of the provision that was made for their tables some is said to be *most holy* (*v.* 9, 10), which was to be eaten by the priests themselves, and in the court of the tabernacle only; but other perquisites were less holy, of which their families might eat, at their own houses, provided they were clean, *v.* 11–13. See Lev. 21:10, etc. 4. It is commanded that the *best of the oil,* and *the best of the wine and wheat,* should be offered for the *first-fruits unto the Lord,* which the priest were to have, *v.* 12. Note, We must always serve and honour God with the best we have, for he is the best, and best deserves it; he is the first, and therefore must have the first ripe. Those that think to save charges by putting God off with the refuse do but deceive themselves, for *God is not mocked.* 5. All this is given to the priests *by reason of the anointing, v.* 8. It was not for the sake of their personal merits above other Israelites that they had these tributes paid to them, be it known unto them; but purely for the sake of the office to which they were anointed. Thus all the comforts that are given to the Lord's people are given them by reason of the anointing which they have received. It is said to be given them *by an ordinance for ever* (*v.* 8), and it is a *covenant of salt for ever, v.* 19. As long as the priesthood should continue this should continue to be the maintenance of it, that this lamp might not go out for want of oil to keep it burning. Thus provision is made that a gospel ministry should continue till Christ comes, by an ordinance for ever. *Lo, I am with you* (that is their maintenance and support) *always, even to the end of the world.* Thanks be to the Redeemer, it is the word which he has *commanded to a thousand generations.*

Verses 20–32

Here is a further account of the provision that was made both for the Levites and for the priests, out of the country.

I. They must have *no inheritance in the land;* only cities to dwell in were afterwards allowed them, but no ground to occupy: *Thou shalt not have any part among them, v.* 20. It is repeated again *v.* 23, and again *v.* 24, *Among the children of Israel they shall have no inheritance,* either by purchase or descent. God would have them comfortably provided for, but would not have their families over-rich, lest they should think themselves above that work which their wages supposed and obliged them constantly to attend upon. As Israel was a peculiar people, and not to be numbered among the nations, so Levi was a peculiar tribe, and not to be settled as the rest of the tribes, but in all respects distinguished from them. A good reason is given why they must have *no inheritance in the land,* for, says God, *I am thy part, and thy inheritance.* Note, Those that have God for their inheritance and their portion for ever ought to look with a holy contempt and indifference upon the inheritances of this world, and not covet their portion in it. *"The Lord is my portion, therefore will I hope in him,* and not depend upon any thing I have on this earth," Lam. 3:24. The Levites shall have no inheritance, and yet they shall live very comfortably and plentifully — to teach us that Providence has various ways of supporting those that live in a dependence upon it; the fowls reap not, and yet are fed, the lilies spin not, and yet are clothed, the Levites have no inheritance in Israel, and yet live better than any other tribe. The repetition of that caution, that *no Israelite should approach the tabernacle,* comes in suitable, though somewhat abruptly, *v.* 22. It seems set in opposition to that order concerning the priests and Levites that they should have *no inheritance in Israel,* to show how God dispenses his favours variously. The Levites have the honour of attending the tabernacle, which is denied the Israelites; but then the Israelites have the honour of inheritances in Canaan, which is denied the Levites; thus each is kept from either envying or despising the other, and both have reason to rejoice in their lot. The Israelites must not *come nigh the tabernacle,* but then the Levites must have *no inheritance in the land;* if ministers expect that people should keep in their sphere, and not intermeddle with sacred offices, let them keep in theirs, and not entangle themselves in secular affairs.

II. But they must both have tithes of the land. Besides the first-fruits which were appropriated to the priests, which, the Jews say, were to be a fiftieth part, or at least a sixtieth, the tithe also was appropriated. 1. The Levites had the tithes of the people's increase (*v.* 21): *I have given* (whose the whole is) *all the tenths in Israel,* of all the productions of the land, to *the children of Levi,* to be divided among them in just proportions, *for their service which they serve.* The Levites were the smallest tribe of the twelve, and yet, besides all other advantages, they had a tenth part of the yearly profits, without the trouble and expense of ploughing and sowing; such care did God take of those that were devoted to his service; not only that they might be well maintained, but that they might be honoured with a national acknowledgment of the good services they did to the public, and owned as God's agents and receivers; for that which was a heave-offering, or an offering lifted heavenward unto the Lord, was by him consigned to the Levites. 2. The priests had the tenths of the Levites' tithes settled upon them. The order for this Moses is directed to give to the Levites, whom God would have to pay it with cheerfulness, rather than the priests to demand it with authority: *Speak to the Levites* that it be *offered by them,* rather than levied upon them. Now observe, (1.) The Levites were to give God his dues out of their tithes, as well as the Israelites out of their increase. They were God's tenants, and rent was expected from them, nor were they exempted by their office. Thus now, ministers must be charitable out of what they receive; and the more freely they have received the more freely they must give, and be examples of liberality. *You shall offer a heave-offering to the Lord, v.* 26. Those that are employed to assist the devotions of others must be sure to pay their own, as a heave-offering to the Lord. Prayers and praises lifted up to God, or rather the heart lifted up in them, are now our heave-offerings. This (says God) shall be *reckoned to you as though it were the corn of the threshing-floor;* that is, though it was not the fruit of their ground, nor of their own labour, as the tithes of other Israelites were, yet being of such as they had it should be accepted, to the sanctifying of all the rest. (2.) This was to be given *to Aaron the priest* (*v.* 28), and to his successors the high priests, to be divided and disposed of in such proportions as they should think fit among the inferior priests. Most of the profits of the priests' office, which were appointed in the former part of the chapter, arising from the sacrifices, those priests had the benefit of who constantly attended at the altar; but, forasmuch as there were many priests employed in the country to teach and rule, those tithes taken by the Levites, it is probable, were directed by the high priest for their maintenance. It is the probable conjecture of the learned bishop Patrick that the tenth of this last tenth was reserved for the high priest himself, to support his state and dignity; for otherwise we read not of any peculiar provision made for him. (3.) When the Levites had thus paid the tenth of their income, as a heave-offering to the Lord, they had themselves the comfortable enjoyment of the other nine parts (*v.* 30): "When you have thus *heaved the best from it* (for still God's part must be the best) then you shall *eat the rest,* not as a holy thing, but with the same freedom that the other Israelites eat their part with, *in every place, you and your households," v.* 31. See here what is the way to have the comfort of all our worldly possessions so as to bear no sin by reason of them, as it follows, *v.* 32. [1.] We must be sure that what we have be got honestly and in the service of God. It is *your reward for your service;* that meat is the best eating that is first earned; but, if any *will not work, neither shall he eat,* 2 Th. 3:10. And that seems to be spoken of as having a particular comfort and satisfaction in it which is the reward of faithful service done in the tabernacle of the congregation. [2.] We must be sure that God has his dues out of it. Then we have the comfort of our substance when we have honoured the Lord with it. The *you shall bear no sin by reason of it,* when *you have heaved the best from it.* This intimates that we must never feed ourselves without fear, lest our table become a snare, and we bear sin by reason of it; and that therefore we are concerned to *give alms of such things as we have,* that all may be clean and comfortable to us.

CHAPTER 19

This chapter is only concerning the preparing and using of the ashes which were to impregnate the water of purification. The people had complained of the strictness of the law, which forbade their near approach to the tabernacle, *ch.* 17:13. In answer to this complaint, they are here directed to purify themselves, so as that they might come as far as they had occasion without fear. Here is, I. The method of preparing these ashes, by the burning of a red heifer, with a great deal of ceremony (*v.* 1–10). II. The way of using them. 1. They were designed to purify persons from the pollution contracted by a dead body (*v.* 11–16). 2. They were to be put into running water (a small quantity of them), with which the person to be cleansed must be purified (*v.* 17–22). And that this ceremonial purification was a type and figure of the cleansing of the consciences of believers from the pollutions of sin appears by the apostle's discourse, Heb. 9:13, 14, where he compares the efficacy of the blood of Christ with the sanctifying virtue that was in "the ashes of a heifer sprinkling the unclean."

Verses 1–10

We have here the divine appointment concerning the solemn burning of a red heifer to ashes, and the preserving of the ashes, that of them might be made, not a beautifying, but a purifying, water, for that was the utmost the law reached to; it offered not to adorn as the gospel does, but to cleanse only. This burning of the heifer, though it was not properly a sacrifice of expiation, being not performed at the altar, yet was typical of the death and sufferings of Christ, by which he intended, not only to satisfy God's justice, but to purify and pacify our consciences, that we may have peace with God and also peace in our own bosoms, to prepare for which Christ died, not only like the bulls and goats at the altar, but like the heifer without the camp.

I. There was a great deal of care employed in the choice of the heifer that was to be burnt, much more than in the choice of any other offering, *v.* 2. It must not only be without blemish, typifying the spotless purity and sinless perfection of the Lord Jesus, but it must a red heifer, because of the rarity of the colour, that it might be the more remarkable: the Jews say, "If but two hairs were black or white, it was unlawful." Christ, as man, was the Son of Adam, *red earth,* and we find him red in his apparel, red with his own blood, and red with the blood of his enemies. And it must be one on which never came yoke, which was not insisted on in other sacrifices, but thus was typified the voluntary offer of the Lord Jesus, when he said, *Lo, I come,* He was bound and held with no other cords than those of his own love. This heifer was to be provided at the expense of the congregation, because they were all to have a joint interest in it; and so all believers have in Christ.

II. There was to be a great deal of ceremony in the burning of it. The care of doing it was committed to Eleazar, not to Aaron himself, because it was not fit that he should do any thing to render himself ceremonially unclean, no, not so much as *till the evening* (*v.* 8); yet it being an affair of great concern especially in the significancy of it, it was to be performed by him that was next to Aaron in dignity. The chief priests of that time had the principal hand in the death of Christ. Now,

1. The heifer was to be slain without the camp, as an impure thing, which bespeaks the insufficiency of the methods prescribed by the ceremonial law to take away sin. So far were they from cleansing effectually that they were themselves unclean; as if the pollution that was laid upon them continued to cleave to them. Yet, to answer this type, our Lord Jesus, being made sin and a curse for us, *suffered without the gate,* Heb. 13:12.

2. Eleazar was to *sprinkle the blood directly before the door of the tabernacle,* and looking steadfastly towards it, *v.* 4. This made it in some sort an expiation; for the sprinkling of the blood before the Lord was the chief solemnity in all the sacrifices of atonement; therefore, though this was not done at the altar, yet, being done towards the sanctuary, it was intimated that the virtue and validity of it depended upon the sanctuary, and were derived from it. This signified the satisfaction that was made to God by the death of Christ, our great high priest, who *by the eternal Spirit* (and the Spirit is called the finger of God, as Ainsworth observes, Lu. 11:20) *offered himself without spot unto God;* directly before the sanctuary, when he said, *Father, into thy hands I commit my spirit.* It also signifies how necessary it was to the purifying of our hearts that satisfaction should be made to divine justice. This sprinkling of the blood put virtue into the ashes.

3. The heifer was to be *wholly burnt, v.* 5. This typified the extreme sufferings of our Lord Jesus, both in soul and body, as a sacrifice made by fire. The priest was to cast into the fire, while it was burning, cedarwood, hyssop, and scarlet, which were used in the cleansing of lepers (Lev. 14:6, 7), that the ashes of these might be mingled with the ashes of the heifer, because they were designed for purification.

4. The ashes of the heifer (separated as well as they could from the ashes of the wood wherewith it was burnt) were to be carefully gathered up by the hand of a clean person, and (as the Jews say) pounded and sifted, and so laid up for the use of the congregation, as there was occasion (*v.* 9), not only for that generation, but for posterity; for the ashes of this one heifer were sufficient to season as many vessels of water as the people of Israel would need for many ages. The Jews say that this one served till the captivity, nearly 1000 years, and that there was never another heifer burnt till Ezra's time, after their return, to which tradition of theirs, grounded (I suppose) only upon the silence of their old records, I see no reason we have to give credit, since in the later times of their church, of which they had more full records, they find eight burnt between Ezra's time and the destruction of the second temple, which was about 500 years, These ashes are said to be laid up here as *a purification for sin,* because, though they were intended to purify only from ceremonial uncleanness, yet they were a type of that purification for sin which our Lord Jesus made by his death. Ashes mixed with water are used in scouring, but these had their virtue purely from the divine institution, and their accomplishment and perfection in Christ, who is *the end of this law for righteousness.* Now observe, (1.) That the water of purification was made so by the ashes of a heifer, whose blood was sprinkled before the sanctuary; so that which cleanses our consciences is the abiding virtue of the death of Christ; it is his blood that *cleanses from all sin,* 1 Jn. 1:7. (2.) That the ashes were sufficient for all the people. There needed not to be a fresh heifer slain for every person or family that had occasion to be purified, but this one was enough for all, even for the strangers that sojourned among them (*v.* 10); so there is virtue enough in the blood of Christ for all that repent and believe the gospel, for every Israelite, and not for their sins only, but for *the sins of the whole world,* 1 Jn. 2:2. (3.) That these ashes were capable of being preserved without waste to many ages. No bodily substance is so incorruptible as ashes are, which (says bishop Patrick) made these a very fit emblem of the everlasting efficacy of the sacrifice of Christ. He is able to save, and, in order to that, able to cleanse, to the uttermost, both of person and times. (4.) These ashes were laid up as a stock or treasure, for the constant purification of Israel from their pollutions; so the blood of Christ is laid up for us in the word and sacraments, as an inexhaustible fountain of merit, to which by faith we may have recourse daily for the purging of our consciences; see Zec. 13:1.

5. All those that were employed in this service were made ceremonially unclean by it; even Eleazar himself, though he did but sprinkle the blood, *v.* 7. *He that burned the heifer was unclean* (*v.* 8), and he that *gathered up the ashes* (*v.* 10); so all that had a hand in putting Christ to death contracted guilt by it: his betrayer, his prosecutors, his judge, his executioner, all did what they did with wicked hands, though it was *by the determinate counsel and foreknowledge of God* (Acts 2:23); yet some of them were, and all might have been cleansed by the virtue of that same blood which they had brought themselves under the guilt of. Some make this to signify the imperfection of the legal services, and their insufficiency to take away sin, inasmuch as those who prepared for the purifying of others were themselves polluted by the preparation. The Jews say, This is a mystery which Solomon himself did not understand, that the same thing should pollute those that were clean and purify those that were unclean. But (says bishop Patrick) it is not strange to those who consider that all the sacrifices which were offered for sin were therefore looked upon as impure, because the sins of men were laid upon them, as all our sins were upon Christ, who therefore is said to be *made sin for us,* 2 Co. 5:21.

Verses 11–22

Directions are here given concerning the use and application of the ashes which were prepared for purification. they were laid up to be laid out; and therefore, though now one place would serve to keep them in, while all Israel lay so closely encamped, yet it is probable that afterwards, when they came to Canaan, some of these ashes were kept in every town, for there would be daily use for them. Observe,

I. In what cases there needed a purification with these ashes. No other is mentioned here than the ceremonial uncleanness that was contracted by the touch of a dead body, or of the bone or grave of a dead man, or being in the tent or house where a dead body lay, *v.* 11, 14–16. This I look upon to have been one of the greatest burdens of the ceremonial law, and one of the most unaccountable. He that touched the carcase of an unclean beast, or any living man under the greatest ceremonial uncleanness, was made unclean by it only *till the evening,* and needed only common water to purify himself with; but he that came near the dead body of man, woman, or child, much bear the reproach of his uncleanness seven days, must twice be purified with the water of separation, which he could not obtain without trouble and charge, and till he was purified must not come near the sanctuary upon pain of death.

1. This was strange, considering, (1.) that whenever any died (and we are in deaths oft) several persons must unavoidable contract this pollution, the body must be stripped, washed, wound up, carried out, and buried, and this could not be done without many hands, and yet all defiled, which signifies that in our corrupt and fallen state there is none that lives and sins not; we cannot avoid being polluted by the defiling world we pass through, and we offend daily, yet the impossibility of our being sinless does not make sin the less polluting. (2.) that taking care of the dead, to see them decently buried, is not only necessary, but a very good office, and an act of kindness, both to the honour of the dead and the comfort of the living, and yet uncleanness was contracted by it, which intimates that the pollutions of sin mix with and cleave to our best services. *There is not a just man upon earth that doeth good and sinneth not;* we are apt some way or other to do amiss even in our doing good. (3.) That this pollution was contracted by what was done privately in their own houses, which intimates (as bishop Patrick observes) that God sees what is done in secret, and nothing can be concealed from the divine Majesty. (4.) This pollution might be contracted, and yet a man might never know it, as by the touch of a grave which appeared not, of which our Saviour says, Those that *walk over it are not aware of it* (Lu. 11:44), which intimates the defilement of the conscience by sins of ignorance, and the cause we have to cry out, "Who can understand his errors?" and to pray, "Cleanse us from secret faults, faults which we ourselves do not see ourselves guilty of."

2. But why did the law make a dead corpse such a defiling thing? (1.) Because death is the *wages of sin, entered into the world* by it, and reigns by the power of it. Death to mankind is another thing from what it is to other creatures: it is a curse, it is the execution of the law, and therefore the defilement of death signifies the defilement of sin. (2.) Because the law could not conquer death, nor abolish it and alter the property of it, as the gospel does by bringing life and immortality to light, and so introducing a better hope. Since our Redeemer was dead and buried, death is no more destroying to the Israel of God, and therefore dead bodies are no more defiling; but while the church was under the law, to show that it *made not the comers thereunto perfect,* the pollution contracted by dead bodies could not but form in their minds melancholy and uncomfortable notions concerning death, while believers now through Christ can triumph over it. *O grave! where is thy victory?* Where is thy pollution?

II. How the ashes were to be used and applied in these cases. 1. A small quantity of the ashes must be put into a cup of spring water, and mixed with the water, which thereby was made, as it is here called, a *water of separation,* because it was to be sprinkled on those who were separated or removed from the sanctuary by their uncleanness. As the ashes of the heifer signified the merit of Christ, so the running water signified the power and grace of the blesses Spirit, who is compared to rivers of living water; and it is by his operation that the righteousness of Christ is applied to us for our cleansing. Hence we are said to be washed, that is, sanctified and justified, not only in the name of the Lord Jesus, but by the *Spirit of our God,* 1 Co. 6:11; 1 Pt. 1:2. Those that promise themselves benefit by the righteousness of Christ, while they submit not to the grace and influence of the Spirit, do but deceive themselves, for we cannot put asunder what God has joined, nor be purified by the ashes otherwise than in the running water. 2. This water must be applied by a bunch of hyssop dipped in it, with which the person or thing to be cleansed must be sprinkled (*v.* 18), in allusion to which David prays, *Purge me with hyssop.* Faith is the bunch of hyssop wherewith the conscience is sprinkled and the heart purified. Many might be sprinkled at once, and the water with which the ashes were mingled might serve for many sprinklings, till it was all spent; and a very little lighting upon a man served to purify him, if done with that intention. In allusion to this application of the water of separation by sprinkling, the blood of Christ is said to be the *blood of sprinkling* (Heb. 12:24), and with it were are said to be *sprinkled from an evil conscience* (Heb. 10:22), that is, we are freed from the uneasiness that arises from a sense of our guilt. And it is foretold that Christ, by his baptism, shall *sprinkle many nations,* Isa. 52:15. 3. The unclean person must be sprinkled with this water on *the third day* after his pollution, and *on the seventh day, v.* 12–19. The days were reckoned (we may suppose) from the last time of his touching or coming near the dead body; for he would not begin the days of his cleansing while he was still under a necessity of repeating the pollution; but when the dead body was buried, so that there was no further occasion of meddling with it, then he began to reckon his days. Then, and then only, we may with comfort apply Christ's merit to our souls, when we have forsaken sin, and cease all *fellowship with the unfruitful works of* death and *darkness.* The repetition of the sprinkling teaches us often to renew the actings of repentance and faith, wash as Naaman, *seven times;* we need to do that often which is so necessary to be well done. 4. Though the pollution contracted was only ceremonial, yet the neglect of the purification prescribed would turn into moral guilt: *He that shall be unclean* and shall *not purify himself, that soul shall be cut off, v.* 20. Note, It is a dangerous thing to contemn divine institutions, though they may seem minute. A slight wound, if neglected, may prove fatal; a sin we call little, if not repented of, will be our ruin, when great sinners that repent shall find mercy. Our uncleanness separates us from God, but it is our being unclean and not purifying ourselves that will separate us for ever from him: it is not the wound that is fatal, so much as the contempt of the remedy. 5. Even he that *sprinkled the water of separation,* or *touched* it, or *touched the unclean person,* must be *unclean till the evening,* that is, must not come near the sanctuary on that day, *v.* 21, 22. Thus God would show them the imperfection of those services, and their insufficiency to purify the conscience, that they might look for the Messiah, who in the fulness of time should by the eternal Spirit offer himself without spot unto God, and so *purge our consciences from dead works* (that is, from sin, which defiles like a dead body, and is therefore called a *body of death*), that we may have liberty of access to the sanctuary, to serve the living God with living sacrifices.

CHAPTER 20

At this chapter begins the history of the fortieth year (which was the last year) of the Israelites' wandering in the wilderness. And since the beginning of their second year, when they were sentenced to perform their quarantine in the desert, there to wear away the tedious revolution of forty years, there is little recorded concerning them till this last year, which brought them to the borders of Canaan, and the history of this year is almost as large as the history of the first year. This chapter gives an account of, I. The death of Miriam (*v.* 1). II. The fetching of water out of the rock, in which observe, 1. The distress Israel was in, for want of water (*v.* 2). 2. Their discontent and murmuring in that distress (*v.* 3–5). 3. God's pity and power engaged for their supply with water out of the rock (*v.* 6–9). 4. The infirmity of Moses and Aaron upon this occasion (*v.* 10, 11). 5. God's displeasure against them (*v.* 12, 13). III. The negotiation with the Edomites. Israel's request (*v.* 14–17), and the repulse the Edomites gave them (*v.* 18–21). IV. The death of Aaron the high priest upon Mount Hor, the instalment of Eleazar in his room, and the people's mourning for him (*v.* 2, etc.).

Verses 1–13

After thirty-eight years' tedious marches, or rather tedious rests, in the wilderness, backward towards the Red Sea, the armies of Israel now at length set their faces towards Canaan again, and had come not far off from the place where they were when, by the righteous sentence of divine Justice, they were made to begin their wanderings. Hitherto they had been led about as in a maze or labyrinth, while execution was doing upon the rebels that were sentenced; but they were now brought into the right way again: they abode in Kadesh (*v.* 1), not Kadesh-barnea, which was near the borders of Canaan, but another Kadesh on the confines of Edom, further off from the land of promise, yet in the way to it from the Red Sea, to which they had been hurried back. Now,

I. Here dies Miriam, the sister of Moses and Aaron, and as it should seem older than either of them. She must have been so if she was that sister that was set to watch Moses when he was put into the ark of bulrushes, Ex. 2:4. *Miriam died there, v.* 1. She was a prophetess, and had been an instrument of much good to Israel, Mic. 6:4. When Moses and Aaron with their rod went before them, to work wonders for them, Miriam with her timbrel went before them in praising God for these wondrous works (Ex. 15:20), and therein did them real service; yet she had once been a murmurer (*ch.* 12:1), and must not enter Canaan.

II. Here there is another Meribah. one place we met with before of that name, in the beginning of their march through the wilderness, which was so called *because of the chiding of the children of Israel,* Ex. 17:7. And now we have another place, at the latter end of their march, which bears the same name for the same reason: *This is the water of Meribah, v.* 13. What was there done was here re-acted.

1. *There was no water for the congregation, v.* 2. The water out of the rock of Rephidim had followed them while there was need of it; but it is probable that for some time they had been in a country where they were supplied in an ordinary way, and when common providence supplied them it was fit that the miracle should cease. But in this place it fell out that there was no water, or not sufficient for the congregation. Note, We live in a wanting world, and, wherever we are, must expect to meet with some inconvenience or other. It is a great mercy to have plenty of water, a mercy which if we found the want of we should own the worth of.

2. Hereupon they murmured, mutinied (*v.* 2), *gathered themselves together,* and took up arms *against Moses and Aaron.* They chid with them (*v.* 3), spoke the same absurd and brutish language that their fathers had done before them. (1.) They wished they had died as malefactors by the hands of divine justice, rather than thus seem for a while neglected by the divine mercy: *Would God that we had died when our brethren died before the Lord!* Instead of giving God thanks, as they ought to have done, for sparing them, they not only despise the mercy of their reprieve, but quarrel with it, as if God had done them a great deal of wrong in giving them their lives for a prey, and snatching them as brands out of the burning. But they need not wish that they had died with their brethren, they are here taking the ready way to die like their brethren in a little while. *Woe unto those that desire the day of the Lord,* Amos 5:18. (2.) They were angry that they were brought out of Egypt, and led through this wilderness, *v.* 4, 5. They quarrelled with Moses for that which they knew was the Lord's doing; they represented that as an injury which was the greatest favour that ever was done to any people. They prefer slavery before liberty, the house of bondage before the land of promise; and though, the present want was of water only, yet, now that they are disposed to find fault, it shall be looked upon as an insufferable hardship put upon them that they have not vines and figs. It was an aggravation of their crime, [1.] that they had smarted so long for the discontents and distrusts of their fathers. *They had borne their whoredoms* now almost *forty years in the wilderness* (*ch.* 14:33); and yet they ventured in the same steps, and, as is charged upon Belshazzar, *humbled not their hearts, though they knew all this,* Dan. 5:22. [2.] That they had had such long and constant experience of God's goodness to them, and of the tenderness and faithfulness of Moses and Aaron. [3.] That Miriam was now lately dead; and, having lost one of their leaders, they ought to have been more respectful to those that were left; but, as if they were resolved to provoke God to leave them as sheep without any shepherd, they grow outrageous against them: instead of condoling with Moses and Aaron for the death of their sister, they add affliction to their grief.

3. Moses and Aaron made them no reply, but retired to the door of the tabernacle to know God's mind in this case, *v.* 6. There they *fell on their faces,* as formerly on the like occasion, to deprecate the wrath of God and to entreat direction from him. Here is no mention of any thing they said; they knew that God heard the murmurings of the people, and before him they humbly prostrate themselves, making intercessions with *groanings that cannot be uttered.* There they lay waiting for orders *Speak, Lord, for thy servants hear.*

4. God appeared, to determine the matter; not on his tribunal of justice, to sentence the rebels according to their deserts; no, he *will not return to destroy Ephraim* (Hosea 11:9), will *not always chide;* see Gen. 8:21. But he appeared, (1.) On his throne of glory, to silence their unjust murmuring (*v.* 6): The *glory of the Lord appeared,* to *still the tumult of the people,* by striking an awe upon them. Note, A believing sight of the glory of the Lord would be an effectual check to our lusts and passions, and would keep our mouths as with a bridle. (2.) On his throne of grace, to satisfy their just desires. It was requisite that they should have water, and therefore, thought the manner of their petitioning for it was irregular and disorderly, yet God did not take that advantage against them to deny it to them, but gave immediate orders for their supply, *v.* 8. Moses must a second time in God's name command water out of a rock for them, to show that God is as able as ever to supply his people with good things, even in their greatest straits an in the utmost failure of second causes. Almighty power can bring water out of a rock, has done it, and can again, for his arm is not shortened. Lest it should be thought that there was something peculiar in the former rock itself, some secret spring which nature hid before in it, God here bids him broach another, and does not, as then, direct him which he must apply to, but lets him make use of which he pleased, or the first he came to; all alike to Omnipotence. [1.] God bids him take the rod, that famous rod with which he summoned the plagues of Egypt, and divided the sea, that, having that in his hand, both he and the people might be reminded of the great things God had formerly done for them, and might be encouraged to trust in him now. This rod, it seems, was kept in the tabernacle (*v.* 9), for it was the *rod of God,* the *rod of his strength,* as the gospel is called (Ps. 110:2), perhaps in allusion to it. [2.] God bids him gather the assembly, not the elders only, but the people, to be witnesses of what was done, that by their own eyes they might be convinced and made ashamed of their unbelief. There is no fallacy in God's works of wonder, and therefore they shun not the light, nor the inspection and enquiry of many witnesses. [3.] He bids him speak to the rock, which would do as it was bidden, to shame the people who had been so often spoken to, and would not hear nor obey. Their hearts were harder than this rock, not so tender, not so yielding, not so obedient. [4.] He promises that the rock should give forth water (*v.* 8), and it did so (*v.* 11): *The water came out abundantly.* This is an instance, not only of the power of God, that he could thus fetch *honey out of the rock,* and *oil out of the flinty rock,* but of his mercy and grace, that he would do it for such a provoking people. This was a new generation (most of the old stock were by this time worn off), yet they were as bad as those that went before them; murmuring ran in the blood, yet the entail of the divine favour was not cut off, but in this instance of it the divine patience shines as brightly as the divine power. He is God and not man, in sparing and pardoning; nay, he not only here gave them the drink which they drank of in common with their beasts (*v.* 8, 11), but in it he made them to drink spiritual drink, which typified spiritual blessings, *for that rock was Christ.*

5. Moses and Aaron acted improperly in the management of this matter, so much so that God in displeasure told them immediately that they should not have the honour of bringing Israel into Canaan, *v.* 10–12.

(1.) This is a strange passage of story, yet very instructive. [1.] It is certain that God was greatly offended, and justly, for he is never angry without cause. Though they were his servants, and had obtained mercy to be faithful, though they were his favourites, and such as he had highly honoured, yet for something they thought, or said, or did, upon this occasion, he put them under the disgrace and mortification of dying, as other unbelieving Israelites did, short of Canaan. And no doubt the crime deserved the punishment. [2.] Yet it is uncertain what it was in this management that was so provoking to God. The fault was complicated. *First,* They did not punctually observe their orders, but in some things varied from their commission; God bade them *speak to the rock,* and they spoke *to the people,* and *smote the rock,* which at this time they were not ordered to do, but they thought speaking would not do. When, in distrust of the power of the word, we have recourse to the secular power in matters of pure conscience, we do, as Moses here, smite the rock to which we should only speak, *Secondly,* They assumed too much of the glory of this work of wonder to themselves: *Must we fetch water?* as if it were done by some power or worthiness of theirs. Therefore it is charged upon them (*v.* 12) that *they did not sanctify God,* that is, they did not give him that glory of this miracle which was due unto his name. *Thirdly,* Unbelief was the great transgression (*v.* 12): *You believed me not;* nay, it is called *rebelling against God's commandment, ch.* 27:14. The command was to bring water out of the rock, but they rebelled against this command, by distrusting it, and doubting whether it would take effect or no. They speak doubtfully: *Must we fetch water?* And probably they did in some other ways discover an uncertainty in their own minds whether water would come or no for such a rebellious generation as this was. And perhaps they the rather questioned it, though God had promised it, because the glory of the Lord did not appear before them upon this rock, as it had done upon the rock in Rephidim, Ex. 17:6. They would not take God's word without a sign. Dr. Lightfoot's notion of their unbelief is that they doubted whether now at last, when the forty years had expired, they should enter Canaan, and whether they must not for the murmurings of the people be condemned to another period of toil, because a new rock was now opened for their supply, which they took for an indication of their longer stay. And, if so, justly were they kept out of Canaan themselves, while the people entered at the time appointed. *Fourthly,* They said and did all in heat and passion; this is the account given of the sin (Ps. 106:33): *They provoked his spirit, so that he spoke unadvisedly with his lips.* It was in his passion that he called them *rebels.* It is true they were so; God had called them so; and Moses afterwards, in the way of a just reproof (Deu. 9:24), calls them so without offence; but now it came from a provoked spirit, and was spoken unadvisedly: it was too much like *Raca,* and *Thou fool.* His smiting the rock twice (it should seem, not waiting at all for the eruption of the water upon the first stroke) shows that he was in a heat. The same thing said and done with meekness may be justifiable which when said and done in anger may be highly culpable; see Jam. 1:20. *Fifthly,* That which aggravated all the rest, and made it the more provoking, was that it was public, *before the eyes of the children of Israel,* to whom they should have been examples of faith, and hope, and meekness. We find Moses guilty of sinful distrust, *ch.* 11:22, 23. That was private between God and him, and therefore was only checked. But his was public; it dishonoured God before Israel, as if he grudged them his favours, and discouraged the people's hope in God, and therefore this was severely punished, and the more because of the dignity and eminency of those that offended.

(2.) From the whole we may learn, [1.] That the best of men have their failings, even in those graces that they are most eminent for. The man Moses was very meek, and yet here he sinned in passion; wherefore *let him that thinks he stands take heed lest he fall.* [2.] That God judges not as man judges concerning sins; we might think that there was not much amiss in what Moses said and did, yet God saw cause to animadvert severely upon it. He knows the frame of men's spirits, what temper they are of, and what temper they are in upon particular occasions, and from what thoughts and intents words and actions do proceed; and we are sure that therefore *his judgment is according to truth,* when it agrees not with ours. [3.] that God not only takes notice of, and is displeased with, the sins of his people, but that the nearer any are to him the more offensive are their sins, Amos 3:2. It should seem, the Psalmist refers to this sin of Moses and Aaron (Ps. 99:8): *Thou wast a God that forgavest them, though thou tookest vengeance on their inventions.* As many are spared in this life and punished in the other, so many are punished in this life and saved in the other. [4.] That, when our heart is hot within us, we are concerned to take heed that we offend not with our tongue. Yet, [5.] It is an evidence of the sincerity of Moses, and his impartiality in writing, that he himself left this upon record concerning himself, and drew not a veil over his own infirmity, by which it appeared that in what he wrote, as well as what he did, he sought God's glory more than his own.

Lastly, The place is hereupon called *Meribah, v.* 13. It is called *Meribah-Kadesh* (Deu. 32:51), to distinguish it from the other Meribah. It is the *water of strife;* to perpetuate the remembrance of the people's sin, and Moses's, and yet of God's mercy, who supplied them with water, and owned and honoured Moses notwithstanding. Thus he was sanctified in the, as the *Holy One of Israel,* so he is called when his mercy rejoices against judgment, Hos. 11:9. Moses and Aaron did not sanctify God as they ought in the eyes of Israel (*v.* 12), but God was sanctified in them; for he will not be a loser in his honour by any man. If he be not glorified by us, he will be glorified upon us.

Verses 14-21

We have here the application made by Israel to the Edomites. The nearest way to Canaan from the place where Israel now lay encamped was through the country of Edom. Now,

I. Moses sends ambassadors to treat with the king of Edom for leave to pass through his country, and gives them instructions what to say, *v.* 14-17. 1. They are to claim kindred with the Edomites: *Thus saith thy brother Israel.* Both nations descended from Abraham and Isaac, their common ancestors; Esau and Jacob, the two fathers of their respective nations, were twin-brothers; and therefore, for

relation-sake, they might reasonably expect this kindness from them; nor needed the Edomites to fear that their brother Israel had any ill design upon them, or would take any advantages against them. 2. They are to give a short account of the history and present state of Israel, which, they take it for granted, the Edomites were no strangers to. And in this there was a double plea: — (1.) Israel had been abused by the Egyptians, and therefore ought to be pitied and succoured by their relations: *"The Egyptians vexed us and our fathers,* but we may hope our brethren the Edomites will not be so vexatious." (2.) Israel had been wonderfully saved by the Lord, and therefore ought to be countenanced and favoured (*v.* 16): *"We cried unto the Lord, and he sent an angel,* the angel of his presence, the angel of the covenant, the eternal Word, who had *brought us forth out of Egypt,* and led us hither." It was therefore the interest of the Edomites to ingratiate themselves with a people that had so great an interest in heaven and were so much its favourites, and it was at their peril if they offered them any injury. It is our wisdom and duty to be kind to those whom God is pleased to own, and to take his people for our people. *Come in, thou blessed of the Lord.* 3. They are humbly to beg a passport through their country. Though God himself, in the pillar of cloud and fire, was Israel's guide, in following which they might have justified their passing through any man's ground against all the world, yet God would have this respect paid to the Edomites, to show that no man's property ought to be invaded under colour of religion. Dominion is founded in providence, not in grace. Thus when Christ was to pass through a village of the Samaritans, to whom his coming was likely to be offensive, he *sent messengers before his face* to ask leave, Lu. 9:52. Those that would receive kindness must not disdain to request it. 4. They are to give security for the good behaviour of the Israelites in this march, that they would keep in the king's high road, that they would commit no trespass upon any man's property, either in ground or water, that they would not so much as make use of a well without paying for it, and that they would make all convenient speed, as fast as they could well go on their feet, *v.* 17, 19. Nothing could be offered more fair and neighbourly.

II. The ambassadors returned with a denial, *v.* 18. Edom, that is, the king of Edom, as protector of his country, said, *Thou shalt not pass by me;* and, when the ambassadors urged it further, he repeated the denial (*v.* 20) and threatened, if they offered to enter his country, it should be at their peril; he raised his trained bands to oppose them. *Thus Edom refused to give Israel passage.* This was owing, 1. To their jealousy of the Israelites; they feared they should receive promises. And truly, had this numerous army been under any other discipline and command than that of the righteous God himself, who would no more suffer them to do wrong than to take wrong, there might have been cause for this jealousy; but what could they fear from a nation that had *statutes and judgments so righteous?* 2. It was owing to the old enmity which Esau bore to Israel. If they had no reason to fear damage by them, yet they were not willing to show so much kindness to them. Esau hated Jacob because of the blessing, and now the hatred revived, when the blessing was ready to be inherited. God would hereby discover the ill-nature of the Edomites to their shame, and try the good-nature of the Israelites to their honour: they *turned away from him,* and did not take this occasion to quarrel with him. Note, We must not think it strange if the most reasonable requests be denied by unreasonable men, and if those be affronted by men whom God favours. *I as a deaf man heard not.* After this indignity which the Edomites offered to Israel God gave them a particular caution *not to abhor an Edomite* (Deu. 23:7), though the Edomites had shown such an abhorrence of them, to teach us in such cases not to meditate revenge.

Verses 22-29

The chapter began with the funeral of Miriam, and it ends with the funeral of her brother Aaron. When death comes into a family, it often strikes double. Israel had not improved the former affliction they were under, by the death of the prophetess, and therefore, soon after, God took away their priest, to try if they would lay that to heart. This happened at the very next stage, when they removed to Mount Hor, fetching a compass round the Edomites'

country, leaving it on their left hand. Wherever we go, death attends us, and the graves are ready for us.

I. God bids Aaron die, *v.* 24. God takes Moses and Aaron aside, and tells them, *Aaron shall be gathered to his people.* These two dear brothers are told that they must part. Aaron the elder must die first, but Moses is not likely to be long after him; so that it is but for a while, a little while, that they are parted. 1. There is something of displeasure in these orders. Aaron must not enter Canaan, because he had failed in his duty at the waters of strife. The mention of this, no doubt, went to the heart of Moses, who knew himself, perhaps, at that time, to be the guiltier of the two. 2. There is much of mercy in them. Aaron, though he dies for his transgression, is not put to death as a malefactor, by a plague, or fire from heaven, but dies with ease and in honour. He is not *cut off from his people,* as the expression usually is concerning those that die by the hand of divine justice, but he is *gathered to his people,* as one that died in the arms of divine grace. 3. There is much of type and significancy in them. Aaron must not enter Canaan, to show that the Levitical priesthood could make nothing perfect: that must be done by the bringing in of a better hope. Those priests could not continue by reason of sin and death, but the priesthood of Christ, being undefiled, is unchangeable, and to this, which abides for ever, Aaron must resign all his honour, Heb. 7:23-25.

II. Aaron submits, and dies in the method and manner appointed, and, for aught that appears, with as much cheerfulness as if he had been going to bed.

1. He puts on his holy garments to take his leave of them, and goes up with his brother and son to the top of Mount Hor, and probably some of the elders of Israel with him, *v.* 27. They went up *in the sight of all the congregation,* who, it is likely, were told on what errand they went up; by this solemn procession Aaron lets Israel know that he is neither afraid nor ashamed to die, but, when the bridegroom comes, can trim his lamp and go forth to meet him. His going up the hill to die signified that the death of saints (and Aaron is called *the saint of the Lord*) is their ascension; they rather go up than go down to death.

2. Moses, whose hands had first clothed Aaron with his priestly garments, now strips him of them; for, in reverence to the priesthood, it was not fit that he should die in them. Note, Death will strip us; naked we came into the world, and naked we must go out. We shall see little reason to be proud of our clothes, our ornaments, or marks of honour, if we consider how soon death will strip us of our glory, divest us of all our offices and honours, and take the crown off from our head.

3. Moses immediately puts the priestly garments upon Eleazar his son, clothes him with his father's robe, and *strengthens him with his girdle,* Isa. 22:21. Now, (1.) This was a great comfort to Moses, by whose hand the law of the priesthood was given to see that it should be kept up in a succession, and that a lamp was ordained for the anointed, which should not be extinguished by death itself. This was a happy earnest and indication to the church of the care God would take that as one generation of ministers and Christians (spiritual priests) passes away another generation should come up instead of it. (2.) It was a great satisfaction to Aaron to see his son, who was dear to him, thus preferred, and his office, which was dearer, thus preserved and secured, and especially to see in this a figure of Christ's everlasting priesthood, in which alone his would be perpetuated. *Now,* Lord, might Aaron say, *let thy servant depart in peace, for my eyes have seen thy salvation.* (3.) It was a great kindness to the people. The installing of Eleazar before Aaron was dead would prevent those who bore ill-will to Aaron's family from attempting to set up another upon his death, in competition with his son. What could they do when the matter was already settled? It would likewise encourage those among them that feared God, and be a token for good to them, that he would not leave them, nor suffer his faithfulness to fail.

4. *Aaron died there.* Quickly after he was stripped of his priestly garments, he laid himself down and died contentedly; for a good man would desire, if it were the will of God, not to outlive his usefulness. Why should we covet to continue any longer in this world than while we may do God and our generation some service in it?

5. Moses and Eleazar, with those that attended them, buried Aaron where he died, as appears by Deu. 10:6, and

then *came down from the mount.* And now, when they came down, and had left Aaron behind, it might be proper for them to think that he had rather gone up to the better world and had left them behind.

6. All the congregation *mourned for Aaron thirty days, v.* 29. Though the loss was well made up in Eleazar, who, being in the prime of life, was fitter from public service that Aaron would have been if he had lived, yet it was a debt owing to their deceased high priest to mourn for him. While he lived, they were murmuring at him upon all occasions, but now that he was dead they mourned for him. Thus many are taught to lament the loss of those mercies which they would not learn to be thankful for the enjoyment of. Many good men have had more honour done to their memories than ever they had to their persons, witness those that were persecuted while they lived, but when they were dead had their sepulchres garnished.

CHAPTER 21

The armies of Israel now begin to emerge out of the wilderness, and to come into a land inhabited, to enter upon action, and take possession of the frontiers of the land of promise. A glorious campaign this chapter gives us the history of, especially in the latter part of it. Here is, I. The defeat of Arad the Canaanite (*v.* 1–3). II. The chastisement of the people with fiery serpents for their murmurings, and the relief granted them upon their submission by a brazen serpent (*v.* 4–9). III. Several marches forward, and some occurrences by the way (*v.* 10–20). IV. The celebrated conquest of Sihon king of the Amorites (*v.* 21–32), and of Og king of Bashan (*v.* 33–35), and possession taken of their land.

Verses 1–3

Here is, 1. The descent which Arad the Canaanite made upon the camp of Israel, hearing that they came *by the way of the spies;* for, though the spies which Moses had sent thirty-eight years before then passed and repassed unobserved, yet their coming, and their errand, it is likely, were afterwards known to the Canaanites, gave them an alarm, and induced them to keep an eye upon Israel and get intelligence of all their motions. Now, when they understood that they were facing about towards Canaan, this Arad, thinking it policy to keep the war at a distance, made an onset upon them and fought with them. But it proved that he meddled to his own hurt; had he sat still, his people might have been last destroyed of all the Canaanites, but now they were the first. Thus those that are *overmuch wicked die before their time,* Eccl. 7:17. 2. His success at first in this attempt. His advance-guards picked up some straggling Israelites, and took them prisoners, *v.* 1. This, no doubt, puffed him up, and he began to thin that he should have the honour of crushing this formidable body, and saving his country from the ruin which it threatened. It was likewise a trial to the faith of the Israelites and a check to them for their distrusts and discontents. 3. Israel's humble address to God upon this occasion, *v.* 2. It was a temptation to them to murmur as their fathers did, and to despair of getting possession of Canaan; but God, who thus tried them by his providence, enabled them by his grace to quit themselves well in the trial, and to trust in him for relief against this fierce and powerful assailant. They, by their elders, in prayer for success, *vowed a vow.* Noe, When we are desiring and expecting mercy from God we should bind our souls with a bond that we will faithfully do our duty to him, particularly that we will honour him with the mercy we are in the pursuit of. Thus Israel here promised to destroy the cities of these Canaanites, as devoted to God, and not to take the spoil of them to their own use. If God would give them victory, he should have all the praise, and they would not make a gain of it to themselves. When we are in this frame we are prepared to receive mercy. 4. The victory which the Israelites obtained over the Canaanites, *v.* 3. A strong party was sent out, probably under the command of Joshua, which not only drove back these Canaanites, but followed them to their cities, which probably lay on the edge of the wilderness, and utterly destroyed them, and so returned to the camp. *Vincimur in praelie, sed non in bello — We lose a battle, but we finally triumph.* What is said of the tribe of God is true of all God's Israel, a troop may overcome them, but they shall overcome at the last. The place was called *Hormah,* as a memorial of the destruction, for the terror of the Canaanites, and probably for warning to posterity not to attempt the rebuilding of these cities, which were destroyed as devoted to God and sacrifices to divine justice. And it appears from the instance of Jericho that the law concerning such cities was that they should never be rebuilt. There seems to be an allusion to this name in the prophecy of the fall of the New Testament Babylon (Rev. 16:16), where its forces are said to be gathered together to a place called *Armageddon — the destruction of a troop.*

Verses 4–9

Here is, I. The fatigue of Israel by a long march round the land of Edom, because they could not obtain passage through it the nearest way: *The soul of the people was much discouraged because of the way, v.* 4. Perhaps the way was rough and uneven, or foul and dirty; or it fretted them to go far about, and that they were not permitted to force their passage through the Edomites' country. Those that are of a fretful discontented spirit will always find something or other to make them uneasy.

II. Their unbelief and murmuring upon this occasion, *v.* 5. Though they had just now obtained a glorious victory over the Canaanites, and were going on conquering and to conquer, yet they speak very discontentedly of what God had done for them and distrustfully of what he would do, vexed that they were brought out of Egypt, that they had not bread and water as other people had by their own care and industry, but by miracle, they knew not how. They have *bread enough and to spare;* and yet they complain *there is no bread,* because, though they eat angels' food, yet they are weary of it; manna itself is loathed, and called *light bread,* fit for children, not for men and soldiers. What will those be pleased with whom manna will not please? Those that are disposed to quarrel will find fault where there is no fault to be found. Thus those who have long enjoyed the means of grace are apt to surfeit even on the heavenly manna, and to call it light bread. But let not the contempt which some cast upon the word of God cause us to value it the less: it is the bread of life, substantial bread, and will nourish those who by faith feed upon it to eternal life, whoever calls it light bread.

III. The righteous judgment which God brought upon them for their murmuring, *v.* 6. He sent *fiery serpents among them,* which bit or stung many of them to death. The wilderness through which they had passed was all along infested with those fiery serpents, as appears, Deu. 8:15. but hitherto God had wonderfully preserved his people from receiving hurt by them, till now that they murmured, to chastise them for which these animals, which hitherto had shunned their camp, now invade it. Justly are those made to feel God's judgments that are not thankful for his mercies. These serpents are called *fiery,* from their colour, or from their rage, or from the effects of their bitings, inflaming the body, putting it immediately into a high fever, scorching it with an insatiable thirst. They had unjustly complained for want of water (*v.* 5), to chastise them for which God sends upon them this thirst, which no water would quench. Those that cry without cause have justly cause given them to cry out. They distrustfully concluded that they must *die in the wilderness,* and God took them at their word, chose their delusions, and brought their unbelieving fears upon them; many of them did die. They had impudently flown in the face of God himself, and the *poison of asps was under their lips,* and now these fiery serpents (which, it should seem, were flying serpents, Isa. 14:29) flew in their faces and poisoned them. They in their pride had lifted themselves up against God and Moses, and now God humbled and mortified them, by making these despicable animals a plague to them. That artillery is now turned against them which had formerly been made use of in their defence against the Egyptians. He that brought quails to feast them let them know that he could bring serpents to bite them; the whole creation is at war with those that are in arms against God.

IV. Their repentance and supplication to God under this judgment, *v.* 7. They confess their fault: *We have sinned.* They are particular in their confession: *We have spoken against the Lord, and against thee.* It is to be feared that they would not have owned the sin if they had not felt the smart; but they relent under the rod; *when he slew them, then they sought him.* They beg the prayers of Moses for them, as conscious to themselves of their own unworthiness to be heard, and convinced of the great interest which Moses had in heaven. How soon is their tone altered! Those who had just before quarrelled with him as their worst enemy now make their court to him as their best friend, and choose him for their advocate with God. Afflictions often change men's sentiments concerning God's people, and teach them to value those prayers which, at a former period, they had scorned. Moses, to show that he had heartily forgiven them, blesses those who had cursed him, and *prays for those who had despitefully used him* Herein he was a type of Christ, who interceded for his persecutors, and a pattern to us to go and do likewise, and thus to show that we *love our enemies.*

V. The wonderful provision which God made for their relief. He did not employ Moses in summoning the judgment, but, that he might recommend him to the good affection of the people, he made him instrumental in their relief, *v.* 8, 9. God ordered Moses to make the representation of a fiery serpent, which he did, in brass, and set it up on a very long pole, so that it might be seen from all parts of the camp, and every one that was stung with a fiery serpent was healed by looking up to this serpent of brass. The people prayed that God would *take away the serpents from them* (*v.* 7), but God saw fit not to do this: for he gives effectual relief in the best way, though not in our way. Thus those who did not die for their murmuring were yet made to smart for it, that they might the more feelingly repent and humble themselves for it; they were likewise made to receive their cure from God, by the hand of Moses, that they might be taught, if possible, never again to speak against God and Moses. This method of cure was altogether miraculous, and the more wonderful if what some naturalists say be true, that looking upon bright and burnished brass is hurtful to those that are stung with fiery serpents. God can bring about his purposes by contrary means. The Jews themselves say that it was not the sight of the brazen serpent that cured them, but, in looking up to it, they looked up to God as the Lord that healed them. But there was much of gospel in this appointment. Our Saviour has told us so (Jn. 3:14, 15), that *as Moses lifted up the serpent in the wilderness so the Son of man must be lifted up,* that *whosoever believeth in him should not perish.* Observe then a resemblance,

1. Between their disease and ours. The devil is the old serpent, a fiery serpent, hence he appears (Rev. 12:3) as a *great red dragon.* Sin is the biting of this fiery serpent; it is painful to the startled conscience, and poisonous to the seared conscience. Satan's temptations are called his *fiery darts,* Eph. 6:16. Lust and passion inflame the soul, so do the terrors of the Almighty, when they *set themselves in array.* At the last, sin *bites like a serpent* and *stings like an adder;* and even its sweets are turned into the gall of asps.

2. Between their remedy and ours. (1.) It was God himself that devised and prescribed this antidote against the fiery serpents; so our salvation by Christ was the contrivance of Infinite Wisdom; God himself has found the ransom. (2.) It was a very unlikely method of cure; so our salvation by the death of Christ is *to the Jews a stumbling-block and to the Greeks foolishness.* It was Moses that *lifted up the serpent in the wilderness,* so the law is a schoolmaster to bring us to Christ, and Moses wrote of him, John *v.* 46. Christ was lifted up by the rulers of the Jews, who were the successors of Moses. (3.) That which cured was shaped in the likeness of that which wounded. So Christ, though perfectly free from sin himself, yet was *made in the likeness of sinful flesh* (Rom. 8:3), so like that it was taken for granted that this man was a sinner, Jn. 9:24. (4.) The brazen serpent was lifted up; so was Christ. He was lifted up upon the cross (Jn. 12:33, 34), for his was made a spectacle to the world. He was lifted up by the preaching of the gospel. The word here used for a *pole* signifies a *banner,* or *ensign,* for Christ crucified *stands for an ensign of the people,* Isa. 11:10. Some make the lifting up of the serpent to be a figure of Christ's triumphing over Satan, the old serpent, whose head he bruised, when in his cross he made an open show of the principalities and powers which he had spoiled and destroyed, Col. 2:15.

3. Between the application of their remedy and ours. They looked and lived, and we, if we believe, shall not perish; it is by faith that we look unto Jesus, Heb. 12:2. *Look unto me, and be you saved,* Isa. 45:22. We must be sensible of our wound and of our danger by it, receive the record which God has given concerning his Son, and rely upon the assurance he has given us that we shall be healed

and saved by him if we resign ourselves to his direction. The brazen serpent's being lifted up would not cure if it was not looked upon. If any pored on their wound, and would not look up to the brazen serpent, they inevitably died. If they slighted this method of cure, and had recourse to natural medicines, and trusted to them, they justly perished; so if sinners either despise Christ's righteousness or despair of benefit by it their wound will, without doubt, be fatal. But whoever looked up to this healing sign, though from the outmost part of the camp, though with a weak and weeping eye, was certainly healed; so whosoever believes in Christ, though as yet but weak in faith, shall not perish. There are weak brethren *for whom Christ died.* Perhaps for some time after the serpent was set up the camp of Israel was molested by the fiery serpents; and it is the probable conjecture of some that they carried this brazen serpent along with them through the rest of their journey, and set it up wherever they encamped, and, when they settled in Canaan, fixed it somewhere within the borders of the land; for it is not likely that the children of Israel went so far off as this was into the wilderness to burn incense to it, as we find they did, 2 Ki. 18:4. Even those that are delivered from the eternal death which is the wages of sin must expect to feel the pain and smart of it as long as they are here in this world; but, if it be not our own fault, we may have the brazen serpent to accompany us, to be still looked up to upon all occasions, by bearing about with us continually the dying of the Lord Jesus.

Verses 10-20

We have here an account of the several stages and removals of the children of Israel, till they came into the plains of Moab, out of which they at length passed over Jordan into Canaan, as we read in the beginning of Joshua. Natural motions are quicker the nearer they are to their centre. The Israelites were now drawing near to the promised rest, and now they *set forward,* as the expression is, *v.* 10. It were well if we would do thus in our way to heaven, rid ground in the latter end of our journey, and the nearer we come to heaven be so much the more active and abundant in the work of the Lord. Two things especially are observable in the brief account here given of these removals: —

1. The wonderful success which God blessed his people with, near the brooks of Arnon, *v.* 13-15. They had now compassed the land of Edom (which they were not to invade, nor so much as to disturb, Deu. 2:4, 5), and had come to the border of Moab. It is well that there are more ways than one to Canaan. The enemies of God's people may retard their passage, but cannot prevent their entrance into the promised rest. Care is taken to let us know that the Israelites in their march religiously observed the orders which God gave them to use no hostility against the Moabites (Deu. 2:9), because they were the posterity of righteous Lot; therefore they pitched on the other side of Arnon (*v.* 13), that side which was now in the possession of the Amorites, one of the devoted nations, though formerly it had belonged to Moab, as appears here, *v.* 26, 27. This care of theirs not to offer violence to the Moabites is pleaded by Jephtha long afterwards, in his remonstrance against the Ammonites (Jdg. 11:15, etc.), and turned to them for a testimony. What their achievements were, now that they pitched on the banks of the river Arnon, we are not particularly told, but are referred to the *book of the wars of the Lord,* perhaps that book which was begun with the history of the war with the Amalekites, Ex. 17:14. *Write it* (said God) *for a memorial in a book,* to which were added all the other battles which Israel fought, in order, and, among the rest, their actions on the river Arnon, at *Vaheb* in *Suphah* (as our margin reads it) and other places on that river. Or, *it shall be said* (as some read it) *in the rehearsal,* or commemoration, *of the wars of the Lord, what he did in the Red Sea,* when he brought Israel out of Egypt, and what he did *in the brooks of Arnon,* just before he brought them into Canaan. Note, In celebrating the memorials of God's favours to us, it is good to observe the series of them, and how divine goodness and mercy have constantly followed us, even from the Red Sea to the brooks of Arnon. In every stage of our lives, nay, in every step, we should take notice of what God has wrought for us; what he did at such a time, and what in such a place, ought to be distinctly remembered.

2. The wonderful supply which God blessed his people with at *Beer* (*v.* 16), which signifies the *well* or *fountain.* It is said (*v.* 10) they pitched in *Oboth,* which signifies *bottles,* so called perhaps because there they filled their bottles with water, which should last them for some time; but by this time, we may suppose, it was with them as it was with Hagar (Gen. 21:15), *The water was spent in the bottle;* yet we do not find that they murmured, and therefore God, in compassion to them, brought them to a well of water, to encourage them to wait on him in humble silence and expectation and to believe that he would graciously take cognizance of their wants, though they did not complain of them. In this world, we do at the best but pitch in *Oboth,* where our comforts lie in close and scanty vessels; when we come to heaven we shall remove to *Beer,* the well of life, the fountain of living waters. Hitherto we have found, when they were supplied with water, they asked it in unjust discontent, and God gave it in just displeasure; but here we find, (1.) That God gave it in love (*v.* 16): *Gather the people together,* to be witnesses of the wonder, and joint-sharers in the favour, *and I will give them water.* Before they prayed, God granted, and anticipated them with the blessings of his goodness. (2.) That they received it with joy and thankfulness, which made the mercy doubly sweet to them, *v.* 17. Then they sang this song, to the glory of God and the encouragement of one another, *Spring up, O well!* Thus they pray that it may spring up, for promised mercies must be fetched in by prayer; they triumph that it does spring up, and meet it with their joyful acclamations. With joy must we *draw water out of the wells of salvation,* Isa. 11:3. As the brazen serpent was a figure of Christ, who is lifted up for our cure, so is this well a figure of the Spirit, who is poured forth for our comfort, and from whom flow to us *rivers of living waters,* Jn. 7:38. Does this well spring up in our souls? We should sing to it; take the comfort to ourselves, and give the glory to God; stir up this gift, sing to it, *Spring up, O well!* thou *fountain of gardens,* to water my soul (Cant. 4:15), plead the promise, which perhaps alludes to this story (Isa. 41:17, 18), *I will make the wilderness wells of water.* (3.) That whereas before the remembrance of the miracle was perpetuated in the names given to the places, which signified the people's strife and murmuring, now it was perpetuated in a song of praise, which preserved on record the manner in which it was done (*v.* 18): *The princes digged the well,* the seventy elders, it is probable, *by direction of the lawgiver* (that is, Moses, under God) *with their staves;* that is, with their staves they made holes in the soft and sandy ground, and God caused the water miraculously to spring up in the holes which they made. Thus the pious Israelites long afterwards, *passing through the valley of Baca,* a dry and thirsty place, made wells, and God by rain from heaven filled the pools, Ps. 84:6. Observe, [1.] God promised to give them water, but the must open the ground to receive it, and give it vent. God's favours must be expected in the use of such means as lie within our power, but still the excellency of the power is of God. [2.] The nobles of Israel were forward to set their hands to this work, and used their staves, probable those that were the ensigns of their honour and power, for the public service, and it is upon record to their honour. And we may suppose that it was a great confirmation to them in their offices, and a great comfort to the people, that they were made use of by the divine power as instruments to this miraculous supply. By this it appeared that the spirit of Moses, who must shortly die, rested in some measure upon the nobles of Israel. Moses did not strike the ground himself, as formerly the rock, but gave them direction to do it, that their staves might share in the honour of his rod, and they might comfortably hope that when he should leave them yet God would not, but that they also in their generation should be public blessings, and might expect the divine presence with them as long as they acted by the direction of the lawgiver. For comfort must be looked for only in the way of duty; and, if we would share in divine joys, we must carefully follow the divine direction.

Verses 21-35

We have here an account of the victories obtained by Israel over Sihon and Og, which must be distinctly considered, not only because they are here distinctly related, but because long afterwards the memorial of them is distinctly celebrated, and they are severally assigned as instances of everlasting mercy. He slew *Sihon king of the Amorites, for his mercy endureth for ever, and Og the king of Bashan, for his mercy endureth for ever,* Ps. 136:19, 20.

I. Israel sent a peaceable message to Sihon king of the Amorites (*v.* 21), but received an unpeaceable return, worse than that of the Edomites to the like message, *ch.* 20:18, 20. For the Edomites only refused them a passage, and stood upon their own defence to keep them out; but Sihon went out with his forces *against Israel in the wilderness,* out of his own borders, without any provocation given him (*v.* 23), and so ran himself upon his own ruin. Jephtha intimates that he was prompted by his politics to do this (Jdg. 11:20); *Sihon trusted not Israel to pass through his coast;* but his politics deceived him, for Moses says, *God hardened his spirit and made his heart obstinate, that he might deliver him into the hand of Israel,* Deu. 2:30. The enemies of God's church are often infatuated in those very counsels which they think most wisely taken. Sihon's army was routed, and not only so, but all his country came into the possession of Israel, *v.* 24, 25. This seizure is justified, 1. Against the Amorites themselves, for they were the aggressors, and provoked the Israelites to battle; and yet, perhaps, that would not have been sufficient to entitle Israel to their land, but that God himself, the King of nations, the Lord of the whole earth, had given them a grant of it. The Amorites formed one of the devoted nations whose land God had promised to Abraham and his seed, which promise should be performed when the iniquity of the Amorites should be full, Gen. 15:16. Jephtha insists upon this grant as their title, Jdg. 11:23, 24. The victory which God gave them over the Amorites put them in possession, and then, the promise made to their fathers having given them a right, by virtue of that they kept possession. 2. Against the Moabites, who had formerly been the lords-proprietors of this country. If they should ever lay claim to it, and should plead that God himself had provided that *none of their land should be given to Israel for a possession* (Deu. 2:9), Moses here furnishes posterity with a replication to their plea, and Jephtha makes use of it against the Amorites 260 years afterwards, when Israel's title to this country was questioned. (1.) The justification itself is that though it was true this country had belonged to the Moabites, yet the Amorites had taken it from them some time before, and were now in full and quiet possession of it, *v.* 26. The Israelites did not take it out of the hands of the Moabites, they had before lost it to the Amorites, and were constrained to give up their pretensions to it; and, when Israel had taken it from the Amorites, they were under no obligation to restore it to the Moabites, whose title to it was long since extinguished. See here the uncertainty of worldly possessions, how often they change their owners, and how soon we may be deprived of them, even when we think ourselves most sure of them; *they make themselves wings.* It is our wisdom therefore to secure the good part which cannot be taken away from us. See also the wisdom of the divine Providence and its perfect foresight, by which preparation is made long before for the accomplishment of all God's purposes in their season. This country being designed in due time for Israel, it is beforehand put into the hand of the Amorites, who little think that they have it but as trustees till Israel come of age, and then must surrender it. We understand not the vast reaches of Providence, but known unto God are all his works, as appears in this instance, that he *set the bounds of the people according to the number of the children of Israel,* Deu. 32:8. All that land which he intended for his chosen people he put into the possession of the devoted nations, that were to be driven out. (2.) For proof of the allegation, he refers to the authentic records of the country, for so their proverbs or songs were, one of which he quotes some passages out of (*v.* 27-30), which sufficiently proves what is vouched for, namely, [1.] That such and such places that are here named, though they had been in the possession of the Moabites, had by right of war become the dominion of Sihon king of the Amorites. Heshbon had become his city, and he obtained such a quiet possession of it that it was built and prepared for him (*v.* 27), and the country to Dibon and Nophah was likewise subdued, and annexed to the kingdom of the Amorites, *v.* 30, [2.] That the Moabites were utterly disabled ever to regain the possession. Even Ar of Moab, though not taken or attempted by Sihon, but still remaining the metropolis of Moab, yet was so wasted by this loss that is would never be able to make head, *v.* 28. The Moabites were undone, and even Chemosh their god had given them up, as unable to rescue them out of the hands of Sihon, *v.* 29. By all this it appears that the Moabites' claim to this country was barred for ever. There may be a further reason for inserting this Amorite poem, namely, to show that the triumphing of the wicked is short. Those that had conquered the Moabites, and insulted over them, were now themselves conquered and insulted over by the Israel of God. It is very probable that the same Sihon, king of the Amorites, that had got this country from the Moabites, now lost it to the Israelites; for, though it is said to be taken from a former king of Moab (*v.* 26), yet not by a former king of the Amorites; and then it shows how sometimes justice makes men to see the loss of that which they got by violence, and were puffed up with the gain of. They are *exalted but for a little while,* Job 24:24.

II. Og king of Bashan, instead of being warned by the fate of his neighbours to make peace with Israel, is instigated by it to make war with them, which proves in like manner to be his destruction. Og was also an Amorite, and therefore perhaps thought himself better able to deal with Israel than his neighbours were, and more likely to prevail, because of his own gigantic strength and stature, which Moses takes notice of, Deu. 3:11, where he gives a more full account of this story. Here observe, 1. That the Amorite begins the war (*v.* 33): He *went out to battle against Israel.* His country was very rich and pleasant. Bashan was famous for the best timber (witness the oaks of Bashan), and the best breed of cattle, witness the bulls and kine of Bashan, and the lambs and rams of that country, which are celebrated, Deu. 32:14. Wicked men do their utmost to secure themselves and their possessions against the judgments of God, but all in vain, when their day comes, on which they must fall. 2. That God interests himself in the cause, bids Israel not to fear this threatening force, and promises a complete victory: "*I have delivered him into thy hand* (*v.* 34): the thing is as good as done already, it is all thy own, enter and take possession." Giants are but worms before God's power. 3. That Israel is more than a conqueror, not only routs the enemies' army, but gains the enemies' country, which afterwards was part of the inheritance of the two tribes and a half that were first seated on the other side Jordan. God gave Israel these successes, while Moses was yet with them, both for his comfort (that he might see the beginning of that glorious work, which he must not live to see the finishing of) and for the encouragement of the people in the war of Canaan under Joshua. Though this was to them in comparison but as the day of small things, yet it was an earnest of great things.

CHAPTER 22

At this chapter begins the famous story of Balak and Balaam, their attempt to curse Israel, and the baffling of that attempt; God's people are long afterwards told to remember what Balak the king of Moab consulted, and what Balaam the son of Beor answered him, that they might know the righteousness of the Lord, Mic. 6:5. In this chapter we have, I. Balak's fear of Israel, and the plot he had to get them cursed (*v.* 1–4). II. The embassy he sent to Balaam, a conjurer, to fetch him for that purpose, and the disappointment he met with in the first embassy (*v.* 5–14). III. Balaam's coming to him upon his second message (*v.* 15–21). IV. The opposition Balaam met with by the way (*v.* 22–35). V. The interview at length between Balak and Balaam (*v.* 36, etc.).

Verses 1–14

The children of Israel have at length finished their wanderings in the wilderness, out of which they went up (ch. 21:18), and are now encamped in the plains of Moab near Jordan, where they continued till they passed through Jordan under Joshua, after the death of Moses. Now we have here,

I. The fright which the Moabites were in upon the approach of Israel, *v.* 2–4. They needed not to fear any harm from them if they knew (and it is probable that Moses let them know) the orders God had given to Israel not to contend with the Moabites, nor to use any hostility against them, Deu. 2:9. But, if they had any notice of this, they were jealous that it was but a sham, to make them secure, that they might be the more easily conquered. Notwithstanding the old friendship between Abraham and Lot, the Moabites resolved to ruin Israel if they could, and therefore they will take it for granted, without any ground for the suspicion, that Israel resolves to ruin them. Thus it is common for those that design mischief to pretend that mischief is designed against them; and their groundless jealousies must be the colour of their causeless malice. They hear of their triumphs over the Amorites (*v.* 2), and think that their own house is in danger when their neighbour's is on fire. They observe their multitudes (*v.* 3): *They were many;* and hence infer how easily they would conquer their country, and all about them if some speedy and effectual course were not taken to stop the progress of their victorious arms: "They shall *lick up* or devour us, and *all that are round about us,* as speedily and irresistibly *as the ox eats up the grass"* (*v.* 4), owning themselves to be an unequal match for so formidable an enemy. Therefore they were sorely afraid and distressed themselves; thus were the wicked *in great fear where no fear was,* Ps. 53:5. These fears they communicated to their neighbours, the elders of Midian, that some measures might be concerted between them for their common safety; for, if the kingdom of Moab fall, the republic of Midian cannot stand long. The Moabites, if they had pleased, might have made a good use of the advances of Israel, and their successes against the Amorites. They had reason to rejoice, and give God and Israel thanks for freeing them from the threatening power of Sihon king of the Amorites, who had taken from them part of their country, and was likely to overrun the rest. They had reason likewise to court Israel's friendship, and to come in to their assistance; but having forsaken the religion of their father Lot, and being sunk into idolatry, they hated the people of the God of Abraham, and were justly infatuated in their counsels and given up to distress.

II. The project which the king of Moab formed to get the people of Israel cursed, that is, to set God against them, who, he perceived, hitherto fought for them. He trusted more to his arts than to his arms, and had a notion that if he could but get some prophet or other, with his powerful charms, to imprecate evil upon them, and to pronounce a blessing upon himself and his forces, then, though otherwise too weak, he should be able to deal with them. This notion arose, 1. Out of the remains of some religion; for it owns a dependence upon some visible sovereign powers that rule in the affairs of the children of men and determine them, and an obligation upon us to make application to these powers. 2. Out of the ruins of the true religion; for if the Midianites and Moabites had not wretchedly degenerated from the faith and worship of their pious ancestors, Abraham and Lot, they could not have imagined it possible to do any mischief with their curses to a people who alone adhered to the service of the true God, from whose service they had themselves revolted.

III. The court which he made to Balaam the son of Beor, a famous conjurer, to engage him to curse Israel. The Balaam lived a great way off, in that country whence Abraham came, and where Laban lived; but, though it was probable that there were many nearer home that were pretenders to divination, yet none had so great a reputation for success as Balaam, and Balak will employ the best he can hear of, though he send a great way for him, so much is his heart upon this project. And to gain him, 1. He makes him his friend, complaining to him, as his confidant, of the danger he was in from the numbers and neighbourhood of the camp of Israel: *They cover the face of the earth,* and they *abide over against me, v.* 5. 2. In effect he makes him his god, by the great power he attributes to his word: *He whom thou blessest is blessed,* and *he whom thou cursest is cursed, v.* 6. The learned bishop Patrick inclines to think, with many of the Jewish writers, that Balaam had been a great prophet, who, for the accomplishment of his predictions and the answers of his prayers, both for good and evil, had been looked upon justly as a man of great interest with God; but that, growing proud and covetous, God departed from him, and then, to support his sinking credit, he betook himself to diabolical arts. He is called a *prophet* (2 Pt. 2:16,) because he had been one, or perhaps he had raised his reputation from the first by his magical charms, as Simon Magus, who bewitched the people so far that he was called *the great power of God,* Acts 8:10. Curses pronounced by God's prophets in the name of the Lord have wonderful effects, as Noah's (Gen. 9:25), and Elisha's, 2 Ki. 2:24. But the curse *causeless shall not come* (Prov. 26:2), no more than Goliath's, when he *cursed David by his gods,* 1 Sa. 17:43. Let us desire to have the prayers of God's ministers and people for us, and dread having them against us; for they are greatly regarded by him who blesseth indeed and curseth indeed. But Balak cannot rely upon these compliments as sufficient to prevail with Balaam, the main inducement is yet behind (*v.* 7): they took *the rewards of divination in their hand, the wages of unrighteousness,* which he *loved,* 2 Pt. 2:15.

IV. The restraint God lays upon Balaam, forbidding him to curse Israel. It is very probable that Balaam, being a curious inquisitive man, was no stranger to Israel's case and character, but had heard that God was with them of a truth, so that he ought to have given the messengers their answer immediately, that he would never curse a people whom God had blessed; but he lodges the messengers, and takes a night's time to consider what he shall do, and to receive instructions from God, *v.* 8. When we enter into a parley with temptations we are in great danger of being overcome by them. In the night God comes to him, probably in a dream, and enquires what business those strangers had with him. He knows it, but he will know it from him. Balaam gives him an account of their errand (*v.* 9–11), and God thereupon charges him not to go with them, or attempt to curse that blessed people, *v.* 12. Thus God sometimes, for the preservation of his people, was pleased to speak to bad men, as to Abimelech (Gen. 20:3), and to Laban, Gen. 31:24. And we read of some that were workers of iniquity, and yet in Christ's name prophesied, and *did many wondrous works.* Balaam is charged not only not to go to Balak, but not to offer to curse this people, which he might have attempted at a distance; and the reason is given: *They are blessed.* This was part of the blessing of Abraham (Gen. 12:3), *I will curse him that curseth thee;* so that an attempt to curse them would be not only fruitless, but perilous. Israel had often provoked God in the wilderness, yet he will not suffer their enemies to curse them, for he *rewards them not according to their iniquities.* The blessedness of those whose sin is covered comes upon them, Rom. 4:6, 7.

V. The return of the messengers without Balaam. 1. Balaam is not faithful in returning God's answer to the messengers, *v.* 13. He only tells them, *the Lord refuseth to give me leave to go with you.* He did not tell them, as he ought to have done, that Israel was a blessed people, and must by no means be cursed; for then the design would have been crushed, and the temptation would not have been renewed: but he, in effect, desired them to give his humble service to Balak, and let him know that he applauded his project, and would have been very glad to gratify him, but that truly he had the character of a prophet, and must not go without leave from God, which he had not yet obtained, and therefore for the present he must be excused. Note, Those are a fair mark for Satan's temptation that speak diminishingly of divine prohibitions, as if they amounted to no more than the denial of a permission, and as if to go against God's law were only to go without his leave. 2. The messengers are not faithful in returning Balaam's answer to Balak. All the account they give of it is, *Balaam refuseth to come with us* (*v.* 14), intimating that he only wanted more courtship and higher proffers; but they are not willing Balak should know that God had signified his disallowance of the attempt. Thus are great men wretchedly abused by the flatteries of those about them, who do all they can to prevent their seeing their own faults and follies.

Verses 15–21

We have here a second embassy sent to Balaam, to fetch him over to curse Israel. It were well for us if we were as earnest and constant in prosecuting a good work, notwithstanding disappointments, as Balak was in pursuing this ill design. The enemies of the church are restless and unwearied in their attempts against it; but he that sits in heaven laughs at them. Observe,

I. The temptation Balak laid before Balaam. He contrived to make this assault more vigorous than the former. It is very probable that he sent double money in the hands of his messengers; but, besides that, now he tempted him with honours, laid a bait not only for his covetousness, but for his pride and ambition. How earnestly should we beg of God daily to mortify in us these two limbs of the old man! Those that know how to look with a holy contempt upon worldly wealth and preferment will find it not so hard a matter as most men do to keep a good conscience. See how artfully Balak managed the temptation. 1. The messengers he sent were *more,* and *more honourable, v.* 15. He sent to this conjurer with as great respect and deference to his quality as if he had been a sovereign prince, apprehending perhaps that Balaam had thought himself slighted in the fewness and meanness of the former messengers. 2. The request was very urgent. This powerful prince becomes a suitor to him: *"Let nothing, I pray thee, hinder thee* (*v.* 16), no, not God, nor conscience, nor any fear either of sin or shame." 3. The proffers were high: *"I will promote thee to very great honour* among the princes of Moab;" nay, he gives him a blank, and he shall write his own terms: *I will do whatsoever thou sayest,* that is, "I will give thee whatever thou desirest, and observe whatever thou orderest; thy word shall be a law to me," *v.* 17. Thus sinners stick at no pains, spare no cost, and care not how low they stoop, for the gratifying either of their luxury or of their malice; shall we then be stiff and strait-handed in our compliance with the laws of virtue? God forbid.

II. Balaam's seeming resistance of, but real yielding to, this temptation. We may here discern in Balaam a struggle between his convictions and his corruptions. 1. His convictions charged him to adhere to the command of God, and he spoke their language, *v.* 18. Nor could any man have said better: *"If Balak would give me his house full of silver and gold,* and that is more than he can give or I can ask, *I cannot go beyond the word of the Lord my God."* See how honourably he speaks of God; he is *Jehovah, my God.* Note, Many call God theirs that are not his, not *truly* because not *only* his; *they swear by the Lord, and by Malcham.* See how respectfully he speaks of the word of God, as one resolved to stick to it, and in nothing to vary from it, and how slightly of the wealth of this world, as if gold and silver were nothing to him in comparison with the favour of God; and yet, at the same time, the searcher of hearts knew that he loved the wages of unrighteousness. Note, It is an easy thing for bad men to speak very good words, and with their mouth to make a show of piety. There is no judging of men by their words. God knows the heart. 2. His corruptions at the same time strongly inclined him to go contrary to the command. He seemed to refuse the temptation, *v.* 18. But even then he expressed no abhorrence of it, as Christ did when he had the kingdoms of the world offered him *(Get thee hence Satan),* and as Peter did when Simon Magus offered him money: *Thy money perish with thee.* But it appears (*v.* 19) that he had a strong inclination to accept the proffer; for he would further attend, to know what God would say to him, hoping that he might alter his mind and give him leave to go. This was a vile reflection upon God Almighty, as if he could change his mind, and now at last suffer those to be cursed whom he had pronounced blessed, and as if he would be brought to allow what he had already declared to be evil. Surely he thought God *altogether such a one as himself.* He had already been told what the will of God was, in which he ought to have acquiesced, and not to have desired a re-hearing of that cause which was already so plainly determined. Note, It is a very great affront to God, and a certain evidence of the dominion of corruption in the heart, to beg leave to sin.

III. The permission God gave him to go, *v.* 20. God came to him, probably by an anger, and told him he might, if he pleased, go with Balak's messengers. *So he gave him up to his own heart's lust.* "Since thou hast such a mind to go, even go, yet know that *the journey thou undertakest shall not be for thy honour;* for, though thou hast leave to go, thou shalt not, as thou hopest, have leave to curse, *for the word which I shall say unto thee, that thou shalt do."* Note, God has wicked men in a chain; *hitherto they shall come* by his permission, but no further that he does permit them. Thus he makes the wrath of man to praise him, yet, at the same time, restrains the remainder of it. It was in anger that God said to Balaam, "Go with them," and we have reason to think that Balaam himself so understood it, for we do not find him pleading this allowance when God reproved him for going. Note, As God sometimes denies the prayers of his people in love, so sometimes he grants the desires of the wicked in wrath.

IV. His setting out in the journey, *v.* 21. God gave him leave to go *if the men called him,* but he was so fond of the journey that we do not find he staid for their calling him, but he himself *rose up in the morning,* got every thing ready with all speed, and *went with the princes of Moab,* who were proud enough that they had carried their point. The apostle describes Balaam's sin here to be that he *ran greedily into an error for reward,* Jude 11. The love of money is the root of all evil.

Verses 22–35

We have here an account of the opposition God gave to Balaam in his journey towards Moab; probably the princes had gone before, or gone some other way, and Balaam had pointed out where he would meet them, or where they should stay for him, for we read nothing of them in this part of our narrative, only that Balaam, like a person of some quality, was attended with his two men — honour enough, one would think, for such a man, he needed not be beholden to Balak for promotion.

I. Here is God's displeasure against Balaam for undertaking this journey: God's *anger was kindled because he went, v.* 22. Note, 1. The sin of sinners is not to be thought the less provoking to God because he permits it. We must not think that, because God does not by his providence restrain men from sin, therefore he approves of it, or that it is therefore not hateful to him; he suffers sin, and yet is angry at it. 2. Nothing is more displeasing to God than malicious designs against his people; he that touches them touches the apple of his eye.

II. The way God took to let Balaam know his displeasure against him: *An angel stood in the way for an adversary.* Now God fulfilled his promise to Israel (Ex. 23:22), *I will be an enemy to thy enemies.* The holy angels are adversaries to sin, and perhaps are employed more than we are aware of in preventing it, particularly in opposing those that have any ill designs against God's church and people, for whom Michael our prince stands up, Dan. 12:1; 10:21. What a comfort is this to all that wish well to the Israel of God, that he never suffers wicked men to form an attempt against them, without sending his holy angels forth to break the attempt and secure his little ones! When the prophet saw the four horns that scattered Judah, at the same time he saw four carpenters that were to fray those horns, Zec. 1:18, etc. When the *enemy comes in like a flood the Spirit of the Lord will lift up a standard against him.* This angel was an adversary to Balaam, because Balaam counted him his adversary; otherwise those are really our best friends, and we are so to reckon them, that stop our progress in a sinful way. The angel stood with his sword drawn (*v.* 23), *a flaming sword,* like that in the hands of the cherubim (Gen. 3:24), *turning every way.* Note, The holy angels are at war with those with whom God is angry, for they are the ministers of his justice. Observe,

1. Balaam had notice given him of God's displeasure, by the ass, and this *did not startle him.* The *ass saw the angel, v.* 23. How vainly did Balaam boast that he was a man whose *eyes were open,* and that he *saw the visions of the Almighty* (*ch.* 24:3, 4), when the ass he rode on saw more than he did, his eyes being blinded with covetousness and ambition and dazzled with the rewards of divination! Note, Many have God against them, and his holy angels, but are not aware of it. The *ass knows his owner,* sees his danger, but Balaam does *not know, does not consider,* Isa. 1:3. *Lord, when thy hand is lifted up, they will not see,* Isa. 26:11. Let none be puffed up with a conceit of visions and revelations, when even an ass saw an angel; yet let those be ashamed of their own sottishness, worse than that of the beasts that perish, who, when they are told of the sword of God's wrath drawn against them, while they persist in wicked ways, yet will go on: the ass understood the law of self-preservation better than so; for, to save both herself and her senseless rider, (1.) She *turned aside out of the way, v.* 23. Balaam should have taken the hint of this, and considered whether he was not out of the way of his duty; but, instead of this, he *beat her into the way again.* Thus those who by wilful sin are running headlong into perdition are angry at those that would prevent their ruin. (2.) She had not gone much further before she saw the angel again, and the, to avoid him, *ran up to a wall,* and *crushed her rider's foot, v.* 24, 25. How many ill accidents are we liable to in travelling upon the road, from which if we are preserved we must own our obligations to the divine Providence, which by the ministry of angels *keeps us in all our ways, lest we dash our foot against a stone;* but, if we at any time meet with a disaster, it should put us upon enquiring whether our way be right in the sight of God or no. The crushing of Balaam's foot, though it was the saving of his life, provoked him so much that he smote his ass the second time, so angry are we apt to be at that which, though a present uneasiness, yet is a real kindness. (3.) Upon the next encounter with the angel, the ass fell down under Balaam, *v.* 26, 27. He ought to have considered that there was certainly something extraordinary in this; for his ass was not restive, nor did she use to serve him thus: but it is common for those whose hearts are *fully set in them to do evil* to push on violently, and break through all the difficulties which Providence lays in their way to give check to them and to stop them in their career. Balaam the third time smote his ass, though she had now done him the best piece of service that ever she did him, saving him from the sword of the angel, and by her falling down teaching him to do likewise. (4.) When all this would not work upon him, God opened the mouth of the ass, and she spoke to him once and again; and yet neither did this move him: *The Lord opened the mouth of the ass, v.* 28. This was a great miracle, quite above the power of nature, and wrought by the power of the God of nature, who made man's mouth, and taught him to speak, for otherwise (since we learn to speak purely by imitation, and therefore those that are born deaf are consequently dumb) the first man would never have spoken, nor any of his seed. He that made man speak could, when he pleased, make the ass to *speak with man's voice,* 2 Pt. 2:16. Here Mr. Ainsworth observes that the devil, when he tempted our first parents to sin, employed a subtle serpent, but that God, when he would convince Balaam, employed a silly ass, a creature dull and sottish to a proverb; for Satan corrupts men's minds by the *craftiness of those that lie in wait to deceive,* but Christ has *chosen the foolish things of the world to confound the wise.* By a dumb ass God rebukes the madness of the prophet, for he will never want reprovers, but when he pleases can make the stones cry out as witnesses to him, Lu. 19:40; Hab. 2:11. [1.] The ass complained of Balaam's cruelty (*v.* 28): *What have I done unto thee, that thou hast smitten me?* Note, The righteous God will not see the meanest and weakest abused; but either they shall be enabled to speak in their own defence or he will some way or other speak for them. If God would not suffer a beast to be wronged, much less a man, a Christian, a child of his own. We cannot *open the mouth of the dumb,* as God did here, but we may and must *open our mouth for the dumb,* Prov. 31:8; Job 31:13. The ass's complaint was just: *What have I done?* Note, When we are prompted to smite any with hand or tongue, we should consider what they have done unto us, and what provocation they have given us. We hear it not, but thus the whole creation groans, being burdened, Rom. 8:22. It was much that Balaam was not astonished to hear his ass speak, and put to confusion: but some think that it was no new thing to him (being a conjurer) to be thus spoken to by his familiars; others rather think that his brutish headstrong passion so blinded him that he could not observe or consider the strangeness of the thing. Nothing besots men worse than unbridled anger. Balaam in his fury *wished he had a sword to kill his ass with, v.* 29. See his impotency; can he think by his curses to do mischief to Israel that has it not in his power to kill his own ass? This he cannot do, yet he fain would; and what would he get by that, but make himself so much the poorer (as many do), to gratify his passion and revenge? Such was the madness of this false prophet. Here bishop Hall observes, It is ill falling into the hands of those whom the brute-creatures find unmerciful; for *a good man regardeth the life of his beast.* [2.] The ass reasoned with him, *v.* 30. God enabled not only a dumb creature to speak, but a dull creature to speak to the purpose. Three things she argues with him from: — *First,* His propriety in her: *Am not I thy ass?* Note, 1. God has given to man a dominion over the creatures: they are *delivered into his hand* to be used, and *put under his feet* to be ruled. 2. Even wicked people have a title to the possessions God gives to them, which they are not to be wronged of. 3. The dominion God has given us over the creatures is a good reason why we should not abuse them. We are their lords, and therefore must not be tyrants. *Secondly,* Her serviceableness to him: *On which thou hast rid-*

den. Note, It is good for us often to consider how useful the inferior creatures are, and have been, to us, that we may be thankful to God, and tender of them. *Thirdly,* That she was not wont to do so by him, and had never before crushed his foot, nor fallen down under him; he might therefore conclude there was something more than ordinary that made her do so now. Note, 1. The rare occurrence of an offence should moderate our displeasure against an offender. 2. When the creatures depart from their wonted obedience to us, we should enquire the cause within ourselves, and be humbled for our sin.

2. Balaam at length had notice of God's displeasure by the angel, and this did startle him. When God opened his eyes *he saw the angel* (*v.* 31), and then he himself *fell flat upon his face,* in reverence of that glorious messenger, and in fear of the sword he saw in his hand. God has many ways of breading and bringing down the hard and unhumbled heart. (1.) The angel reproved him for his outrageousness (*v.* 32, 33): *Wherefore hast thou smitten thy ass?* Whether we consider it or no, it is certain that God will call us to account for the abuses done to his creatures. Nay, he shows him how much more reason he had to smite upon his breast, and to condemn himself, than to fly out thus against his ass (*"Thy way is perverse before me,* and then how canst thou expect to prosper?"), and how much wiser his ass was than himself, and how much beholden he was to her that she turned aside; it was for his safety, and not for her own, for had she gone on he had been slain, and she had been saved alive. Note, When our eyes are opened we shall see what danger we are in in a sinful way, and how much it was for our advantage to be crossed in it, and what fools we were to quarrel with our crosses which helped to save our lives. (2.) Balaam then seemed to relent (*v.* 34): *"I have sinned,* sinned in undertaking this journey, sinned in pushing on so violently;" but he excused it with this, that he saw not the angel; yet, now that he did see him, he was willing to go back again. That which was displeasing to God was not so much his going as his going with a malicious design against Israel, and a secret hope that notwithstanding the proviso with which his permission was clogged he might prevail to curse them, and so gratify Balak, and get preferment under him. It does not appear that he was sensible of this wickedness of his heart, or willing to own it, but, when he finds he cannot go forward, he will be content (since there is no remedy) to go back. Here is no sign that his heart is turned, but, if his hands are tied, he cannot help it. Thus many leave their sins only because their sins have left them. There seems to be a reformation of the life, but what will this avail if there be no renovation of the heart? (3.) The angel however continued his permission: *"Go with the men, v.* 35. Go, if thou hast a mind to be made a fool of, and to be shamed before Balak, and all the princes of Moab. *Go, only the word that I shall speak unto thee, that thou shalt speak,* whether thou wilt or no," for this seems not to be a precept, but a prediction of the event, that he should not only not be able to curse Israel, but should be forced to bless them, which would be more for the glory of God and his own confusion than if he had turned back. Thus God gave him fair warning, but he would not take it; he *went with the princes of Balak.* For the iniquity of Balaam's covetousness God was wroth, and smote him, but he *went on frowardly,* Isa. 57:17.

Verses 36–41

We have here the meeting between Balak and Balaam, confederate enemies to God's Israel; but here they seem to differ in their expectations of the success. 1. Balak speaks of it with confidence, not doubting but to gain his point now that Balaam had come. In expectation of this, he went out to meet him, even to the utmost border of his country (*v.* 36), partly to gratify his own impatient desire to see one he had such great expectations from, and partly to do honour to Balaam, and so to engage him with his utmost power to serve him. See what respect heathen princes paid to those that had but the name and face of prophets, and pretended to have any interest in heaven; and how welcome one was that came with his mouth full of curses. What a shame is it then that the ambassadors of Christ are so little respected by most, so much despised by some, and that those are so coldly entertained who bring tidings of peace and a blessing! Balak has now nothing to complain of but that Balaam did not come sooner, *v.* 37. And he thinks that he should have considered the importunity Balak had used, *Did I not earnestly send to thee?* (and the importunity of people inferior to kings has prevailed with many against their inclinations), and that he should also have considered Balak's intentions concerning him: *Am not I able to promote thee to honour?* Balak, as king, was in his own kingdom the fountain of honour, and Balaam should have his choice of all the preferments that were in his gift; he therefore thinks himself affronted by Balaam's delays, which looked as if he thought the honours he prepared not worthy his acceptance. Note, Promotion to honour is a very tempting bait to many people; and it were well if we would be drawn into the service of God by the honour he sets before us. Why do we delay to come unto him? Is *not he able to promote us to honour?* 2. Balaam speaks doubtfully of the issue, and bids Balak not depend to much upon him (*v.* 38): *"Have I now any power at all to say any thing?* I have come, but what the nearer am I? Gladly would I curse Israel; but I must not, I cannot, God will not suffer me." He seems to speak with vexation at the hook in his nose and the bridle in his jaws, such as Sennacherib was tied up with, Isa. 37:29. 3. They address themselves with all speed to the business. Balaam is nobly entertained over night, a sacrifice of thanksgiving is offered to the gods of Moab, for the safe arrival of this welcome guest, and his is treated with a feast upon the sacrifice, *v.* 40. And the next morning, that no time might be lost, Balak takes Balaam in his chariot to the high places of his kingdom, not only because their holiness (such as it was), he thought, might give some advantage to his divinations, but their height might give him a convenient prospect of the camp of Israel, which was to be the butt or mark at which he must shoot his envenomed arrows. And now Balaam is really as solicitous to please Balak as ever he had pretended to be to please God. See what need we have to pray every day, *Our Father in heaven, lead us not into temptation.*

CHAPTER 23

In this chapter we have Balak and Balaam busy at work to do Israel a mischief, and, for ought that appears, neither Moses nor the elders of Israel know any thing of the matter, nor are in a capacity to break the snare; but God, who keeps Israel, and neither slumbers nor sleeps, baffles the attempt, without any intercession or contrivance of theirs. Here is, I. The first attempt to curse Israel. 1. The preparation made for it by sacrifice (*v.* 1–3). 2. The contrary instruction God gave Balaam (*v.* 4, 5). 3. The blessing Balaam was compelled to pronounce upon Israel, instead of a curse (*v.* 7–10). 4. The great disappointment of Balak (*v.* 11, 12). II. The second attempt, in the same manner made, and in the same manner frustrated (*v.* 13–26). III. Preparations made for a third attempt (*v.* 27–30), the issue of which we have in the next chapter.

Verses 1–12

Here is, I. Great preparation made for the cursing of Israel. That which was aimed at was to engage the God of Israel to forsake them, and either to be on Moab's side or to stand neuter. O the sottishness of superstition, to imagine that God will be at men's beck! Balaam and Balak think to bribe him with altars and sacrifices, offered without any warrant or institution of his: as if he would *eat the flesh of bulls or drink the blood of goats.* Ridiculous nonsense, to think that these would please God, and gain his favour, when there could be in them no exercise either of faith or obedience! Yet, it should seem, they offered these sacrifices to the God of heaven the supreme *Numen — Divinity,* and not to any of their local deities. But the multiplying of altars was an instance of their degeneracy from the religion of their ancestors, and their apostasy to idolatry; for those that multiplied altars multiplied gods. *Ephraim made many altars to sin,* Hos. 8:11. *Thus they liked not to retain God in their knowledge, but became vain in their imaginations;* and yet presumptuously expected hereby to gain God over to them from Israel, who had his sanctuary among them, and his anointed altar. Observe here, 1. How very imperious Balaam was, proud to have the command of a king and to give law to princes. Such is the spirit of that wicked one who exalts himself above all that is called God, or that is worshipped. With what authority does Balaam give orders! *Build me here* (in the place I have pitched upon) *seven altars,* of stone or turf. Thus he covers his malice against Israel with a show of devotion, but his sacrifice was an abomination, being brought with such a *wicked mind,* Prov. 21:27. That which he aimed at was not to honour God with the sacrifices of righteousness, but to enrich himself with the wages of unrighteousness. 2. How very obsequious Balak was. The altars were presently built, and the sacrifices prepared, the best of the sort, *seven bullocks and seven rams.* Balak makes no objection to the charge, nor does he snuff at it, or think it either a weariness or a disparagement to *stand by his burnt-offering* as Balaam ordered him.

II. The turning of the curse into a blessing, by the overruling power of God, in love to Israel, which is the account Moses gives of it, Deu. 23:5.

1. God puts the blessing into the mouth of Balaam. While the sacrifices were burning, Balaam retired; he *went solitary,* into some dark grove on the top of the high place, *v.* 3, marg. Thus much he knew, that solitude gives a good opportunity for communion with God; those that would meet with him must retire from the world, and the business and conversation of it, and love to be private, reckoning themselves never less alone than when alone, because the Father is with them. Enter therefore into thy closet, and shut the door, and be assured that God will meet thee if thou *seek him in the due order.* But Balaam retired with a peradventure only, having some thoughts that God might meet him; but being conscious to himself of guilt, and knowing that God had lately met him in anger, he had reason to speak doubtfully: *Peradventure the Lord will come to meet me, v.* 3. *But let not such a man think that he shall receive any* favour from God. Nay, it should seem, though he pretended to go and meet with God, he really designed to use enchantments; see *ch.* 24:1. But, whatever he intended. God designed to serve his own glory by him, and therefore *met Balaam, v.* 4. *What communion has light with darkness?* No friendly communion, we may be sure. Balaam's way was still perverse, and God was still an adversary to him; but, Balak having chosen him for his oracle, God would constrain him to utter such a confession, to the honour of god and Israel, as should render those for ever inexcusable who should appear in arms against them. When Balaam was aware that God met him, probably by an angel, he boasted of his performances: *I have prepared seven altars, and offered upon every altar a bullock and a ram.* How had he done it? It cost him nothing; it was done at Balak's expense; yet, (1.) He boasts of it, as if he had done some mighty thing. The acts of devotion which are done in hypocrisy are commonly reflected upon with pride and vain glory. Thus the Pharisee went up to the temple to boast of his religion, Lu. 18:11, 12. (2.) He insists upon it as a reason why God should gratify him in his desire to curse Israel, as if now he had made God his debtor, and might draw upon him for what he pleased. He thinks God is so much beholden to him for these sacrifices that the least he can do in recompense for them is to sacrifice his Israel to the malice of the king of Moab. Note, It is a common cheat that wicked people put upon themselves, to think that by the shows of piety they may prevail with God to countenance them, and connive at them, in their greatest immoralities, especially in persecution, Isa. 66:5. However, thought the sacrifice was an abomination, God took the occasion of Balaam's expectation to *put a word into his mouth* (*v.* 5); *for the answer of the tongue if from the Lord,* and thus he would show how much those are mistaken who say, *With our tongue we will prevail, our lips are our own,* Ps. 12:4. He that made man's mouth knows how to manage it, and to serve his own purposes by it. This speaks terror to daring sinners, that *set their mouth against the heavens. God can make their own tongues to fall upon them,* Ps. 64:8. And it speaks comfort to God's witnesses, whom at any time he calls out to appear for him; if God put a word into the mouth of Balaam, who would have defied God and Israel, surely he will not be wanting to those who desire to glorify God and edify his people by their testimony, but it *shall be given them in that same hour what they should speak.*

2. Balaam pronounces the blessing in the ears of Balak. He found him *standing by his burnt-sacrifice* (*v.* 6), closely attending it, and earnestly expecting the success. those that wold have an answer of peace from God must abide by the sacrifice, and *attend on the Lord without distraction, not weary in well doing.* Balaam, having fixed himself in the place appointed for his denouncing curses against Israel, which perhaps he had drawn up in form ready to

deliver, takes up his parable, and it proves a blessing, *v.* 7. He pronounces Israel safe and happy, and so blesses them.

(1.) He pronounces them safe, and out of the reach of his envenomed darts. [1.] He owns that the design was to curse them, that Balak sent for him out of his own country, and that he came, with that intent, *v.* 7. The message sent to him was, *Come, curse me Jacob, and come, defy Israel.* Balak intended to make war upon them, and he would have Balaam to bless his arms, and to prophesy and pray for the ruin of Israel. [2.] He owns the design defeated, and his own inability to accomplish it. He could not so much as give them an ill word or an ill wish: *How shall I curse those whom God has not cursed? v.* 8. Not that therefore he would not do it, but therefore he could not do it. this is a fair confession, *First,* Of the weakness and impotency of his own magic skill, for which others valued him so much, and doubtless he valued himself no less. He was the most celebrated man of that profession, and yet owns himself baffled. God had warned the Israelites not to use divination (Lev. 19:31), and this providence gave them a reason for that law, by showing them the weakness and folly of it. As they had seen the magicians of Egypt befooled, so, here, the great conjurer of the east. See Isa. 47:12–14. *Secondly,* It is a confession of the sovereignty and dominion of the divine power. He owns that he could do no more than God would suffer him to do, for God could overrule all his purposes, and turn his counsels headlong. *Thirdly,* It is a confession of the inviolable security of the people of God. Note, 1. God's Israel are owned and blessed of him. He has not cursed them, for they are delivered from the curse of the law; he has not defied them, nor rejected or abandoned them, though mean and vile. 2. Those that have the good-will of Heaven have the ill-will of hell; the serpent and this seed have an enmity to them. 3. Though the enemies of God's people may prevail far against them, yet they cannot curse them; that is, they cannot do them any real mischief, much less a ruining mischief, for they cannot *separate them from the love of God,* Rom. 8:39.

(2.) He pronounces them happy in three things: —

[1.] Happy in their peculiarity, and distinction from the rest of the nations: *From the top of the rock I see him, v.* 9. And it seems to have been a great surprise to him that whereas, it is probable, they were represented to him as a rude and disorderly rabble, that infested the countries round about in rambling parties, he was them a regular incorporated camp, in which appeared all the marks of discipline and good order; he saw them a people dwelling alone, and foresaw they would continue so, and their singularity would be their unspeakable honour. Persons of quality we call person of *distinction;* this was Israel's praise, though their enemies turned it to their reproach, that they differed from all the neighbouring nations, not only in their religion and sacred rites, but in their diet, and dress, and common usages, as a people called out of the world, and not to be conformed to it. They never lost their reputation till they *mingled among the heathen,* Ps. 106:35. Note, It is the duty and honour of those that are dedicated to God to be separated from the world, and not to walk according to the course and custom of it. Those who make conscience of peculiar duties may take the comfort of peculiar privileges, which it is probable Balaam has an eye to here. God's Israel shall not stand upon a level with other nations, but be dignified above them all, as a people near to God, and set apart for him.

[2.] Happy in their numbers, not so few and despicable as they were represented to him, but an innumerable company, which made them both honourable and formidable (*v.* 10): *Who can count the dust of Jacob?* The number of the people was the thing that Balak was vexed at (*ch.* 22:3): *Moab was afraid of them, because they were many;* and God does here by Balaam promote that fear and vexation, foretelling their further increase. Balak would have him see *the utmost part of the people* (*ch.* 22:41), hoping the more he saw of them the more he would be exasperated against them, and throw about his curses with the more keenness and rage; but it proved quite contrary: instead of being angry at their numbers, he admired them. The better acquainted we are with God's people the better opinion we have of them. He takes notice of the number, *First,* Of the *dust of Jacob;* that is, the people of Jacob, concerning whom it was foretold that they should be as the dust for number, Gen. 28:14. Thus he owns the fulfilling of the promise made to the fathers, and expects that it should be yet further accomplished. Perhaps it was part of David's fault in numbering the people that he offered to count the dust of Jacob, which God had said should be innumerable. *Secondly,* Of the *fourth part of Israel,* alluding to the form of their camp, which was cast into four squadrons, under four standards. Note, God's Israel are a very great body, his spiritual Israel are so, and they will appear to be so when they shall all be gathered together unto him in the great day, Rev. 7:9.

[3.] Happy in their end: *Let me die the death of the righteous* Israelites, that are in covenant with God, and let my *last end, or future state, be like theirs, or my recompence,* namely, in the other world. Here, *First,* It is taken for granted that death is the end of all men; the righteous themselves must die: and it is good for us to think of this with application, as Balaam himself does here, speaking of his own death. *Secondly,* he goes upon the supposition of the soul's immortality, and a different state on the other side death, to which this is a noble testimony, and an evidence of its being anciently known and believed. For how could the death of the righteous be more desirable than the death of the wicked upon any other account than as it involved happiness in another world, since in the manner and circumstances of dying we see *all things come alike to all? Thirdly,* He pronounces the righteous truly blessed, not only while they live, but when they die, which makes their death not only more desirable than the death of others, but even more desirable than life itself; for in that sense his wish may be taken. Not only, "When I do die, let me die the death of the righteous;" but, "I could even now be willing to die, on condition that I might *die the death of the righteous,* and reach my end this moment, provided it might be like his." Very near the place where Balaam now was, on one of the mountains of Moab, not long after this, Moses died, and to that perhaps God, who put this word into his mouth, designed it should have a reference, that by it Moses might be encouraged to go up and die such a death as Balaam himself wished to die. *Fourthly,* He shows his opinion of religion to be better than his resolution; there are many who desire to die the death of the righteous, but do not endeavour to live the life of the righteous. Gladly would they have their end like theirs, but not their way. They would be saints in heaven, but not saints on earth. This is the *desire of the slothful, which kills him, because his hands refuse to labour.* This of Balaam's is only a wish, not a prayer, and it is a vain wish, being only a wish for the end, without any care for the means. Thus far this blessing goes, even to death, and beyond it, as far as the last end. Now,

III. We are told, 1. How Balak fretted at it, *v.* 11. He pretended to honour the Lord with his sacrifices, and to wait for the answer God would send him; and yet, when it did not prove according to his mind, he forgot God, and flew into a great passion against Balaam, as if it had been purely his doing: *"What hast thou done unto me!* How hast thou disappointed me!" Sometimes God makes the enemies of his church a vexation one to another, while he that sits in heaven laughs at them, and the efforts of their impotent malice. 2. How Balaam was forced to acquiesce in it. He submits because he cannot help it, and yet humours the thing with no small address, as if he had been peculiarly conscientious, answering Balak with the gravity of a prophet: *Must I not take heed to speak that which the Lord has put in my mouth? v.* 12. Thus a confession of God's overruling power is extorted from a wicked prophet, to the further confusion of a wicked prince.

Verses 13–30

Here is, I. Preparation made the second time, as before, for the cursing of Israel. 1. The place is changed, *v.* 13. Balak fancied that Balaam, having so full a prospect of the whole camp of Israel, *from the top of the rocks* (*v.* 9), was either so enamoured with the beauty of it that he would not curse them or so affrighted with the terror of it that he durst not; and therefore he would bring him to another place, form which he might see only some part of them, which would appear more despicable, and that part at least which would lie in view he hoped he might obtain leave to curse, and so by degrees he should get ground against them, intending, no doubt, if he had gained this point, to make his attack on that part of the camp of Israel which Balaam now had in his eye, and into which he was to throw the fireballs of his curses. See how restless and unwearied the church's enemies are in their malicious attempts to ruin it; they leave no stone unturned, no project untried, to compass it. O that we were as full of contrivance and resolution in prosecuting good designs for the glory of God! 2. The sacrifices are repeated, new altars are built, a bullock and a ram offered on every altar, and Balak attends his sacrifice as closely as ever, *v.* 14, 15. Were we thus earnest to obtain the blessing as Balak was to procure a curse (designedly upon Israel, but really upon himself and his people), we should not grudge the return both of the charge and of the labour of religious exercises. 3. Balaam renews his attendance on God, and God meets him the second time, and puts another word into his mouth, not to reverse the former, but to ratify it, *v.* 16, 17. If God said not to Balaam, *Seek in vain,* much less will he say so to *any of the seed of Jacob,* who shall surely find him, not only as Balaam, their instructor and oracle, but their bountiful rewarder. When Balaam returned Balak was impatient to know what message he had: *"What hath the Lord spoken?* Are there any better tidings yet, any hopes of speeding?" This should be our enquiry when we come to hear the word of God. See Jer. 23:35.

II. A second conversion of the curse into a blessing by the overruling power of God; and this blessing is both larger and stronger than the former, and quite cuts off all hopes of altering it. Balak having been so forward to ask what the Lord had spoken (*v.* 17), Balaam now addresses himself particularly to him (*v.* 18): *Rise up, Balak, and hear.* It was a message from God that he had to deliver, and it is required of Balak, though a king, that he attend (*hear* and *hearken,* with a close application of mind, let not a word slip), and also that he attend with reverence: *Rise up, and hear.* His successor Eglon, when he was to receive a message from God, *rose out of his seat,* Jdg. 3:20.

1. Two things Balaam in this discourse informs Balak of, sorely to his grief and disappointment: —

(1.) That he had no reason to hope that he should ruin Israel.

[1.] It would be to no purpose to attempt to ruin them, and he would deceive himself if he expected it, for three reasons: —

First, Because God is unchangeable: *God is not a man that he should lie, v.* 19. Men change their minds, and therefore break their words; they lie, because they repent. But God does neither. He never changes his mind, and therefore never recalls his promise. Balaam had owned (*v.* 8) that he could not alter God's counsel, and thence he infers here that God himself would not alter it; such is the imperfection of man, and such the perfection of God. It is impossible for God to lie, Heb. 6:18. And, when in scripture he is said to *repent,* it is not meant of any change of his mind (for *he is in one mind, and who can turn him?*) but only of the change of his way. This is a great truth, that with God there is no *variableness nor shadow of turning.* Now here, 1. He appeals to Balak himself concerning it: *"Hath he said, and shall he not do it?* Said it in his own purpose, and shall he not perform it in his providence, according to the counsel of his will? Hath he spoken in his word, in his promise, and shall he not make it good? Can we think otherwise of God than that he is unchangeably one with himself and true to his word? All his decrees are unalterable, and all his promises inviolable." 2. He applies this general truth to the case in hand (*v.* 20): *He hath blessed and I cannot reverse it,* that is, "I cannot prevail with him to reverse it." Israel were of old a blessed people, a seed that the Lord had blessed; the blessing of Abraham came upon them; they were born under the blessing of the covenant, and born to the blessing of Canaan, and therefore they could not be cursed, unless you could suppose that the God of eternal truth should break his word, and become false to himself and his people.

Secondly, Because Israel are at present unblamable: *he has not beheld iniquity in Jacob, v.* 21. Not but that there was iniquity in Jacob, and God saw it; but, 1. There was not such a degree of iniquity as might provoke God to abandon them and give them up to ruin. As bad as they were, they were not so bad as this. 2. There was no idolatry among them, which is in a particular manner called iniquity and perverseness; we have found nothing of that kind in Israel since the golden calf, and therefore, though they were in other instances very provoking, yet God would not cast them off. Balaam knew that nothing would separate between them and God but sin. While God saw no reigning sin among them, he would send no destroying curse among them; and therefore, as long as they kept in with God, he despaired of ever doing them any mischief. Note, While we keep from sin we keep from harm. Some give another sense of those words; they read it thus: *He has not beheld wrong offered to Jacob, nor will he see any grievance done to Israel,* that is, "He has not nor will he permit it, or allow it; he will not see Israel injured, but he will right them, and avenge their quarrel." Note, God will not bear to see any injury done to his church and people; for what is done against them he takes as done against himself, and will reckon for it accordingly.

Thirdly, Because the power of both was irresistible. He shows Balak that there was no contending with them, it was to no purpose to attempt it; for, 1. They had the presence of God with them: *"The Lord his God is with him* in a particular manner, and not provoked to withdraw from him." 2. They had the joy of that presence, and were always made to triumph in it: *The shout* or alarm *of a king is among them.* They shout against their enemies, as sure of victory and success, glorying continually in God as their King and conqueror for them. 3. They had had the experience of the benefit of God's presence with them, and his power engaged for them; for God *brought them out of Egypt, v.* 22. The power which had done that could never be restrained, never resisted; and, having begun so gloriously, he would no doubt finish gloriously. 4. While they had God's presence with them they had the strength of a unicorn, able to make head against all that opposed them. See *ch.* 24:8. Such is the strength which the God of Israel gives unto his people.

[2.] From all this he infers that it was to no purpose for him to think of doing them a mischief by all the arts he could use, *v.* 23. *First,* He owns himself baffled. Surely there is no enchantment against Jacob so as to prevail. The curses of hell can never take place against the blessings of heaven. Not but that attempts of this kind would be made, but they would certainly be fruitless and ineffectual. Some observe that *Jacob* denotes the church low and afflicted, *Israel* denotes it prosperous and advanced; but be the church high or low, be her friends few or many, let second causes smile or frown, it comes all to one: no weapon formed against it shall prosper. Note, God easily can, and certainly will, baffle and disappoint all the devices and designs of the powers of darkness against his church, so that they shall not prevail to destroy it. *Secondly,* He foresees that this would be remembered in time to come. *According to this time,* that is, with reference to this we are now about, it shall be said concerning Jacob and Israel, and said by them, *What hath God wrought!* What great things hath God done for his people! It shall be said with wonder, joy, and thankfulness, and a challenge to the neighbouring nations to produce any similar instances of the care of their gods for them. Note, The defeating of the designs of the church's enemies ought to be had in everlasting remembrance to the glory of God. *There is none like unto the God of Jeshurun.* What Balaam says here concerning the pre-eminence of the God of Israel above all the gods of the Gentiles perhaps Moses refers to when he says (Deu. 32:31), *Their rock is not as our rock, even our enemies themselves being judges,* Balaam particularly. Balak therefore has no hopes of ruining Israel. But,

(2.) Balaam shows him that he had more reason to fear being ruined by them, for they were likely to make bloody work among his neighbours; and, if he and his country escaped, it was not because he was too great for them to meddle with, but because he fell not within their commission *v.* 24. Behold, and tremble; the people that now have lain for some time closely encamped do but repose themselves for a while like a lion couchant, but shortly they *shall rise up as a great lion,* a lion rampant, that *shall not lie down till he eat of the prey, and drink the blood of the slain.* This seems to point at the victories he foresaw they would obtain over the Canaanites, that they would never lay down their arms till they had made a complete conquest of the land they had now in view; and, when his neighbour's house was on fire, he had reason to think his own in danger.

2. Now what was the issue of this disappointment?

(1.) Balak and Balaam were both of them sick of the cause. [1.] Balak is now willing to have his conjurer silenced. Since he cannot say what he would have him, he wishes him to say nothing: *"Neither curse them at all nor bless them at all, v.* 25. If thous canst not curse them, I beseech thee not to bless them. If thou canst no assist and encourage my forces, yet do not oppose and dispirit them" Note, God can make those that depart from him weary of the *multitude of their counsels,* Isa. 47:13; 57:10. [2.] Balaam is still willing to own himself overruled, and appeals to what he had said in the beginning of this enterprise (*ch.* 22:38): *All that the Lord speaketh, that I must do, v.* 26. This sows, *First,* In general, that the way of man is not in himself; there are many devices in man's heart, but God's counsels shall stand. *Secondly,* In particular, that, as no weapon formed against the church shall prosper, so every tongue that rises against her in judgment god will control and condemn, Isa. 54:17.

(2.) Yet they resolve to make another attempt. They think it scorn to be baffled, and therefore pursue the design, though it be only to their further confusion. And now the third time, [1.] They change the place. Balak is at last convinced that it is not Balaam's fault, on whom, before, he had laid the blame, but that really he was under a divine check, and therefore now he hopes to bring him to a place whence God might at least permit him to curse them, *v.* 27. Probably he and Balaam were the more encouraged thus to repeat their attempt because God had the second time allowed Balaam to go, though he had forbidden him the first time. Since by repeated trials they had carried that point, they hope in like manner to carry this. Thus because sinners are borne with, and sentence against their evil works is not executed speedily, their hearts are the more fully set in them to do evil. The place to which Balak now took Balaam was the top of Peor, the most eminent high place in all his country, where, it is probable, Baal was worshipped, and it was thence called *Baal-peor.* He chose this place with a hope, either, *First,* That it being the residence (as he fancied) of Baal, the god of Moab, Jehovah the God of Israel would not, or could not, come hither to hinder the operation; or, *Secondly,* That, it being a place acceptable to his god, it would be so to the Lord, and there he would be brought into a good humour. Such idle conceits have foolish men of God, and so vain are their imaginations concerning him. Thus the Syrians fancied the Lord to be God of the hills, but not of the valleys (1 Ki. 20:28), as if he were more powerful in one place than he is in every place. [2.] They repeat their sacrifice, seven bullocks and seven rams, upon seven altars, *v.* 29, 30. Thus do they persevere in their expensive oblations, though they had no promise on which to build their hopes of speeding. Let not us therefore, who have a promise that the vision at the end shall speak and not lie, be discouraged by delays, but continue instant in prayer, and not faint, Lu. 18:1.

CHAPTER 24

This chapter continues and concludes the history of the defeat of the counsels of Balak and Balaam against Israel, not by might, nor by power, but by the Spirit of the Lord of hosts; and as great an instance it is of God's power over the children of men, and his favour towards his own children, as any of the victories recorded in the book of the wars of the Lord. What preparation was made the third time for the cursing of Israel we read of in the close of the foregoing chapter. In this chapter we are told, I. What the blessing was into which that intended curse was turned (*v.* 1–9). II. How Balak dismissed Balaam from his service thereupon (*v.* 10–13). III. The predictions Balaam left behind him concerning Israel, and some of the neighbouring nations (*v.* 14, etc.).

Verses 1–9

The blessing itself which Balaam here pronounces upon Israel is much the same with the two we had in the foregoing chapter; but the introduction to it is different.

I. The method of proceeding here varies much in several instances. 1. Balaam laid aside the enchantments which he had hitherto depended on, used no spells, or charms, or magic arts, finding they did him no service; it was to no purpose to deal with the devil for a curse, when it was plain that God was determined immovably to bless, *v.* 1. Sooner or later God will convince men of their folly in seeking after lying vanities, which cannot profit. To what purpose should he seek for enchantment? He knew that God was out of the reach of them. 2. He did not now retire into a solitary place as before, but set his face directly towards the wilderness where Israel lay encamped; and, since there is no remedy, but they must be blessed, he will design nothing else, but will submit by compulsion. 3. Now *the Spirit of God came upon him,* that is, the Spirit of prophecy, as upon Saul to prevent him from taking David, 1 Sa. 19:23. He spoke not his own sense, but the language of the Spirit that came upon him. 4. He used a different preface now from what he had used before (*v.* 3, 4), much like that of David (2 Sa. 23:1–3), yet savouring very much (as some think) of pride and vain-glory, taking all the praise of this prophecy to himself, and magnifying himself as one of the cabinet-council of heaven. Two things he boasts of: — (1.) The favour God did him in making known himself to him. He *heard the words of God, and saw the vision of the Almighty.* God himself had met him and spoken to him (*ch.* 23:16), and with this he was greatly puffed up. Paul speaks with humility of his visions and revelations (2 Co. 12:1), but Balaam speaks of his with pride. (2.) His own power to receive and bear those revelations. He fell into a trance indeed, as other prophets did, but he had his eyes open. This he mentions twice; but the words in the original are not the same. The *man whose eyes were shut,* some think it may be read so (*v.* 39), but now *having his eyes open, v.* 4. When he attempted to curse Israel, he owns, he was in a mistake, but now he began to see his error, and yet still he remained blinded by covetousness and ambition, those foolish and hurtful lusts. Note, [1.] Those that oppose God and his people will sooner or later be made to see themselves wretchedly deceived. [2.] Many have their eyes open that have not their hearts open, are enlightened, but not sanctified; and that knowledge which puffs men up with pride will but serve to light them to hell, whither many go with their eyes open.

II. Yet the blessing is for substance the same with those before. Several things he admires in Israel: —

1. Their beauty (*v.* 5): *How goodly are thy tents, O Jacob!* Though they dwelt not in stately palaces, but in coarse and homely tents, and these, no doubt, sadly weather-beaten, yet Balaam sees a beauty in those tents, because of their admirable order, according to their tribes, *v.* 2. Nothing recommends religion more to the good opinion of those that look upon it at a distance than the unity and harmony of its professors, Ps. 133:1. The amiableness of this people, and the great reputation they should gain among their neighbours, are compared (*v.* 6) to the beauty and sweetness of fruitful valleys and fine gardens, flourishing trees and fragrant spices. Note, Those whose eyes are open see the saints on the earth to be excellent ones, and their delight is accordingly in them. *The righteous,* doubtless, *is more excellent than his neighbour.* They are *trees which the Lord has planted;* that is their excellency. The branches of righteousness are the planting of the Lord. See Hos. 14:5–7.

2. Their fruitfulness and increase. This may be intended by those similitudes (*v.* 6) of the valleys, gardens, and trees, as well as by those expressions (*v.* 7), *He shall pour the water out of his buckets;* that is, God shall water them with his blessing like rain from heaven, and then his *seed shall be in many waters.* Compare Hos. 2:23, *I will sow her unto me in the earth.* And waters are in scripture put for *peoples, and multitudes, and nations.* This has been fulfilled in the wonderful increase of that nation and their vast multitude even in their dispersion.

3. Their honour and advancement. As the multitude of the people is the honour of the prince, so the magnificence of the prince is the honour of the people; Balaam therefore foretells that their *king shall be higher than Agag.* Agag, it is probable, was the most potent monarch in those parts; Balaam knew of none more considerable than he was; he rose above the rest of his neighbours. But Balaam foretells that Israel's chief commander, who, after Moses, was Joshua, should be more great and honourable than ever Agag was, and make a far better figure in history. Saul, their first king, triumphed over Agag, though, it is said, *he came delicately.*

4. Their power and victory, *v.* 8. (1.) He looks back upon what they had done, or rather what had been done for them: *God brought them forth out of Egypt;* this he had spoken of before, *ch.* 23:22. The wonders that attended their deliverance out of Egypt contributed more to their honour, and the terror of their adversaries, than any thing

else, Jos. 2:10. He that brought them out of Egypt will not fail to bring them into Canaan, for, *as for God, his work is perfect.* (2.) He looks down upon their present strength. Israel hath, as it were, *the strength of a unicorn,* of which creature it is said (Job 39:9, 10), *Will he be willing to serve thee, or abide by thy crib? Canst thou bind him with his band in the furrow?* "No, Israel is too powerful to be checked or held in by my curses or thy armies." (3.) He looks forward to their future conquests: *He shall eat up the nations his enemies;* that is, "he shall not only destroy and devour them as easily and irresistibly as a lion does his prey, but he shall himself be strengthened, and fattened, and enriched, by their spoils."

5. Their courage and security: *He lay down as a lion, as a great lion, v.* 9. Now he does so in the plains of Moab, and asks no leave of the king of Moab, nor is he in fear of him; shortly will he do so in Canaan. When he has torn his prey, he will take his repose, *quiet from the fear of evil,* and bid defiance to all his neighbours; for who shall stir up a sleeping lion? It is observed of lions (as the learned bishop Patrick takes notice here) that they do not retire into places of shelter to sleep, but lie down any where, knowing that none dares meddle with them: thus secure were Israel in Canaan, chiefly in the days of David and Solomon; and thus is *the righteous bold as a lion* (Prov. 28:1), not to assault others, but to repose themselves, because *God maketh them to dwell in safety,* Ps. 4:8.

6. Their interest, and influence upon their neighbours. Their friends, and those in alliance with them, were happy: *Blessed is he that blesseth thee;* those that do them any kindness will certainly fare the better for it. But their enemies, and those in arms against them, were certainly miserable: *Cursed is he that curseth thee;* those that do them any injury do it at their peril; for God takes what is done to them, whether good or evil, as done to himself. Thus he confirms the blessing of Abraham (Gen. 12:3), and speaks as if *therefore* he did at this time bless Israel, and not curse them, because he desired to share in the blessing of Israel's friends and dreaded the curse on Israel's enemies.

Verses 10–14

We have here the conclusion of this vain attempt to curse Israel, and the total abandonment of it. 1. Balak made the worst of it. He broke out into a rage against Balaam (*v.* 10), expressed both in words and gesture the highest degree of vexation at the disappointment; he smote his hands together, for indignation, to see all his measures thus broken, and his project baffled. He charged Balaam with putting upon him the basest affront and cheat imaginable: "*I called thee to curse my enemies,* and thou hast shown thyself in league with them, and in their interests, for thou hast *blessed them these three times,* though, by appointing the altars to be built and sacrifices to be offered, thou madest be believe thou wouldest certainly curse them." Hereupon he forbade him his presence, expelled him his country, upbraided him with the preferments he had designed to bestow upon him, but now would not (*v.* 11): "*The Lord hath kept thee back from honour.* See what thou gettest by pleasing the Lord, instead of pleasing me; thou has hindered thy preferment by it." Thus those who are any way losers by their duty are commonly upbraided with it, as fools, for preferring it before their interest in the world. Whereas, if Balaam had been voluntary and sincere in his adherence to the word of the Lord, though he lost the honour Balak designed him by it, God would have made that loss up to him abundantly to his advantage. 2. Balaam made the best if it. (1.) He endeavours to excuse the disappointment. And a very good excuse he has for it, that God restrained him from saying what he would have said, and constrained him to say what he would not; and that this was what Balak ought not to be displeased at, not only because he could not help it, but because he had told Balak before what he must depend upon. *v.* 12, 13. Balak could not say that he had cheated him, since he had given him fair notice of the check he found himself under. (2.) He endeavours to atone for it, *v.* 14. Though he cannot do what Balak would have him do, yet, [1.] He will gratify his curiosity with some predictions concerning the nations about him. It is natural to us to be pleased with prophecy, and with this he hopes to pacify the angry prince. [2.] He will satisfy him with an assurance that, whatever this formidable people should do to his people, it should not be till the latter days; so that he, for his part, needed not to fear any mischief or molestation from them; the *vision was for a great while to come,* but in his days there should be peace. [3.] He will put him into a method of doing Israel a mischief without the ceremonies of enchantment and execration. This seems to be implied in that word: *I will advertise thee;* for it properly signifies, *I will counsel thee.* What the counsel was is not set down here, because it was given privately, but we are told afterwards what it was, *ch.* 31:16. He counselled him to entice the Israelites to idolatry, Rev. 2:14. Since he could not have leave from God to curse them, he puts him in a way of getting help from the devil to tempt them. *Flectere si nequeo superos, Acheronta movebo — If I cannot move heaven, I will solicit hell.*

Verses 15–25

The office of prophets was both to bless and to prophesy in the name of the Lord. Balaam, as a prophet, per force had blessed Israel; here he foretels future events.

I. His preface is much the same as that, *v.* 3, 4. He personates a true prophet admirably well, God permitting and directing him to do so, because, whatever he was, the prophecy itself was a true prophecy. He boasts, 1. That his *eyes are open* (*v.* 15), for prophets were *in old time called seers* (1 Sa. 9:9), because they must speak what they had seen, and therefore, before they opened their lips, it was necessary that they should have their eyes open. 2. That he has *heard the words of God,* which many do that do not heed them, nor hear God in them. 3. That he *knew the knowledge of the Most High;* this is added here. A man may be full of the knowledge of God and yet utterly destitute of the grace of God, may receive the truth in the light of it and yet be a stranger to the love of it. 4. That *he saw the vision of the Almighty,* but not so as to be *changed into the same image.* He calls God the *Most High,* and the *Almighty;* no man could speak more honourably of him, nor seem to put a greater value upon his acquaintance with him, and yet he had no true fear of him, love to him, or faith in him, so far may a man go towards heaven, and yet come short.

II. Here is his prophecy concerning him that should be the crown and glory of his people Israel, who is, 1. David in the type, who *not now,* not quickly, but in process of time, should *smite the corners of Moab.* (*v.* 17), and take possession of Mount Seir, and under whom the forces of Israel should *do valiantly, v.* 18. This was fulfilled when David smote Moab, and *measured them with a line,* so that *the Moabites became David' servants,* 2 Sa. 8:2. And at the same time the Edomites likewise were brought into obedience to Israel, *v.* 14. But, 2. Our Lord Jesus, the promised Messiah, is chiefly pointed at in the antitype, and of him it is an illustrious prophecy; it was the will of God that notice should thus be given of his coming, a great while before, not only to the people of the Jews, but to other nations, because his gospel and kingdom were to extend themselves so far beyond the borders of the land of Israel. It is here foretold, (1.) That while: "*I shall see him, but not now;* I do see him in vision, but at a very great distance, through the interposing space of 1500 years at least." Or understand it thus: — Balaam, a wicked man, shall see Christ, but shall not see him nigh, nor see him as Job, who saw him *as his Redeemer,* and saw him for himself, Job 19:25, 27. When he comes in the clouds *every eye shall see him,* but many will see him (as the rich man in hell saw Abraham) *afar off.* (2.) That he shall come out of Jacob, and Israel, as a star and a sceptre, the former denoting his glory and lustre, and the *bright and morning star,* the latter his power and authority; it is *he that shall have dominion.* Perhaps this prophecy of Balaam (one of the children of the east) concerning a star that should arise out of Jacob, as the indication of a sceptre arising in Israel, being preserved by a tradition of that country, gave occasion to the wise men, who were of the east too, upon the sight of an unusual star over the land of Judea, to enquire for him that was *born king of the Jews,* Mt. 2:2. (3.) That his kingdom shall be universal, and victorious over all opposition, which was typified by David's victories over Moab and Edom. But the Messiah shall destroy, or, as some read it, *shall rule over, all the children of Seth.* (*v.* 17), that is, all the children of men, who descend from Seth, the son of Adam, the descendants of the rest of Adam's sons being cut off by the deluge. Christ shall be king, not only of Jacob and Israel, but of all the world; so that all the children of Seth shall be either governed by his golden sceptre or dashed in pieces by his iron rod. He shall set up a universal rule, authority, and power, of his own, and shall put down all opposing rule, 1 Co. 15:24. He shall *unwall all the children of Seth;* so some read it. He shall take down all their defences and carnal confidences, so that they shall either admit his government or lie open to his judgments. (4.) That his Israel shall do valiantly; the subjects of Christ, animated by his might, shall maintain a spiritual was with the powers of darkness, and be more than conquerors. *The people that do know their God shall be strong, and do exploits,* Dan. 11:32.

III. Here is his prophecy concerning the Amalekites and Kenites, part of whose country, it is probable, he had now in view. 1. The Amalekites were now the *chief of the nations* (*v.* 20), therefore Agag was spoken of (*v.* 7) as an eminent prince, and they were the first that engaged Israel when they came out of Egypt; but the time will come when that nation, as great as it looks now, will be totally ruined and rooted out: *His latter end shall be that he perish for ever.* Here Balaam confirms that doom of Amalek which Moses had read (Ex. 17:14, 16), where God had sworn that he would have *perpetual war with Amalek.* Note, Those whom God is at war with will certainly perish for ever; for when God judges he will overcome. 2. The Kenites were now the securest of the nations; their situation was such as that nature was their engineer, and had strongly fortified them: "*Thou puttest thy nest* (like the eagle) *in a rock, v.* 21. Thou thinkest thyself safe, and yet the *Kenites shall be wasted* (*v.* 22) and gradually brought to decay, till they be carried away captive by the Assyrians," which was done at the captivity of the ten tribes. Note, Bodies politic, like natural bodies, though of the strongest constitutions, will gradually decay, and come to ruin at last; even a nest in a rock will be no perpetual security.

IV. Here is a prophecy that looks as far forward as the Greeks and Romans, for theirs is supposed to be meant by the *coast of Chittim, v.* 24.

1. The introduction to this parable; this article of his prophecy is very observable (*v.* 23): *Alas! who shall live when God doeth this?* Here he acknowledges all the revolutions of states and kingdoms to be the Lord's doing: *God doeth this;* whoever are the instruments, he is the supreme director. But he speaks mournfully concerning them, and has a very melancholy prospect of these events: *Who shall live?* Either, (1.) These events are so distant, and so far off to come, that it is hard to say *who shall live till they come;* but, whoever shall live to see them, there will be amazing turns. Or, (2.) They will be so dismal, and make such desolations, that scarcely any will escape or be left alive; who shall live when death rides in triumph? Rev. 6:8. Those that live then will be as brands plucked out of the fire, and will have their lives given them as a prey. God fit us for the worst of times!

2. The prophecy itself is observable. Both Greece and Italy lie much upon the sea, and therefore their armies were sent forth mostly in ships. Now he seems here to foretell, (2.) That the forces of the Grecians should humble and bring down the Assyrians, who were united with the Persians, which was fulfilled when the eastern country was overcome, or overrun rather, by Alexander. (2.) That theirs and the Roman forces should afflict the Hebrews, or Jews, who were called *the children of Eber;* this was fulfilled in part when the Grecian empire was oppressive to the Jewish nation, but chiefly when the Roman empire ruined it and put a period to it. But, (3.) That Chittim, that is, the Roman empire, in which the Grecian was at length swallowed up, should itself perish for ever, when the stone cut out of the mountain without hands shall consume all these kingdoms, and particularly the *feet of iron and clay,* Dan. 2:34. Thus (says Dr. Lightfoot) Balaam, instead of cursing the church, curses Amalek the first, and Rome the last, enemy of the church. And *so let all thy enemies perish, O Lord!*

CHAPTER 25

Israel, having escaped the curse of Balaam, here sustains a great deal of damage and reproach by the counsel of Balaam, who, it seems, before he left Balak, put him into a more effectual way than that which Balak thought of to separate between the Israelites and their God. "The Lord will not be prevailed with by Balaam's charms to ruin them; try if they will not be prevailed with by the charms of the daughters of Moab to ruin themselves." None are more fatally bewitched than those that are bewitched by their own lusts. Here is, I. The sin of Israel; they were enticed by the daughters of Moab both to whoredom and to idolatry (v. 1–3). II. The punishment of this sin by the hand of the magistrate (v. 4, 5) and by the immediate hand of God (v. 9). III. The pious zeal of Phinehas in slaying Zimri and Cozbi, two impudent sinners (v. 6, 8, 14, 15). IV. God's commendation of the zeal of Phinehas (v. 10–13). V. Enmity put between the Israelites and the Midianites, their tempters, as at first between the woman and the serpent (v. 16, etc.).

Verses 1–5

Here is, I. The sin of Israel, to which they were enticed by the daughters of Moab and Midian; they were guilty both of corporal and spiritual whoredoms, for *Israel joined himself unto Baal-peor, v.* 3. Not all, nor the most, but very many, were taken in this snare. Now concerning this observe, 1. That Balak, by the advice of Balaam, *cast this stumbling-block before the children of Israel,* Rev. 2:14. Note, Those are our worst enemies that draw us to sin, for that is the greatest mischief any man can do us. If Balak had drawn out his armed men against them to fight them, Israel had bravely resisted, and no doubt had been more than conquerors; but now that he sends his beautiful women among them, and invites them to his idolatrous feasts, the Israelites basely yield, and are shamefully overcome: those are smitten with this harlots that could not be smitten with his sword. Note, We are more endangered by the charms of a smiling world than by the terrors of a frowning world. 2. That the daughters of Moab were their tempters and conquerors. Ever since Eve was first in the transgression the fairer sex, though the weaker, has been a snare to many; yea strong men have been wounded and slain by the lips of the strange woman (Prov. 7:26), witness Solomon, whose wives were shares and nets to him Eccl. 7:26. 3. That whoredom and idolatry went together. They first defiled and debauched their consciences, by committing lewdness with the women, and then were easily drawn, in complaisance to them, and in contempt of the God of Israel, to bow down to their idols. And they were more likely to do so if, as it is commonly supposed, and seems probable by the joining of them together, the uncleanness committed was a part of the worship and service performed to Baal-peor. Those that have broken the fences of modesty will never be held by the bonds of piety, and those that have dishonoured themselves by fleshly lusts will not scruple to dishonour God by idolatrous worships, and for this they are justly given up yet further to vile affections. 4. That by eating of the idolatrous sacrifices they *joined themselves to Baal-peor* to whom they were offered, which the apostle urges as a reason why Christians should not *eat things offered to idols,* because thereby they had fellowship with the devils to whom they were offered, 1 Co. 10:20. It is called *eating the sacrifices of the dead* (Ps. 106:28), not only because the idol itself was a dead thing, but because the person represented by it was some great hero, who since his death was deified, as saints in the Roman church are canonized. 5. It was great aggravation of the sin that *Israel abode in Shittim,* where they had the land of Canaan in view, and were just ready to enter and take possession of it. It was the highest degree of treachery and ingratitude to be false to their God, whom they had found so faithful to them, and to eat of idol-sacrifices when they were ready to be feasted so richly on God's favours.

II. God's just displeasure against them for this sin. Israel's whoredoms did that which all Balaam's enchantments could not do, they set God against them; now he was *turned to be their enemy, and fought against them.* So many of the people, nay, so many of the princes, were guilty, that the sin became national, and for it God was wroth with the whole congregation. 1. A plague immediately broke out, for we read of the staying of it (v. 8), and of the number that died of it (v. 9), but no mention of the beginning of it, which therefore must be implied in those words (v. 3), *The anger of the Lord was kindled against Israel.* It is said expressly (Ps. 106:29), *The plague broke in.* Note, Epidemical diseases are the fruits of God's anger, and the just punishments of epidemical sins; one infection follows the other. The plague, no doubt, fastened on those that were most guilty, who were soon made to pay dearly for their forbidden pleasures; and though now God does not always plague such sinners, as he did here, yet that word of God

will be fulfilled, *If any man defile the temple of God, him shall God destroy,* 1 Co. 3:17. 2. The ringleaders are ordered to be put to death by the hand of public justice, which will be the only way to stay the plague (v. 4): *Take the heads of the people* (that is, of that part of the people that went out of the camp of Israel into the country of Moab, to join in their idolatries) — *take them and hang them up before the sun,* as sacrifices to God's justice, and for a terror to the rest of the people. The judges must first order them to be *slain with the sword* (v. 5), and their dead bodies must be hanged up, that the stupid Israelites, seeing their leaders and princes so severely punished for their whoredom and idolatry, without any regard to their quality, might be possessed with a sense of the evil of the sin and the terror of God's wrath against them. Ringleaders in sin ought to be made examples of justice.

Verses 6–15

Here is a remarkable contest between wickedness and righteousness, which shall be most bold and resolute; and righteousness carries the day, as no doubt it will at last.

I. Never was vice more daring than it was in Zimri, *a prince of a chief house* in the tribe of Simeon. Such a degree of impudence in wickedness had he arrived at that he publicly appeared leading a Midianitish harlot (and a harlot of quality too like himself, a *daughter of a chief house in Midian*) in the sight of Moses, and all the good people of Israel. He did not think it enough to go out with his harlot to worship the gods of Moab, but, when he had done that, he brought her with him to dishonour the God of Israel. He not only owned her publicly as his friend, and higher in his favour then any of the daughters of Israel, but openly went with her *into the tent, v.* 8. The word signifies such a booth or place of retirement as was designed and fitted up for lewdness. Thus he *declared his sin as Sodom,* as was so far from blushing for it that he rather prided himself in it, and gloried in his shame. All the circumstances concurred to make it exceedingly sinful, exceedingly shameful. 1. It was an affront to the justice of the nation, and bade defiance to that. The judges were ordered to put the criminals to death, but he thought himself too great for them to meddle with, and, in effect, bade them touch him if they durst. He had certainly cast off all fear of God who stood in no awe of the powers which he had ordained to be *a terror to evil-doers.* 2. It was an affront to the religion of the nation, and put a contempt upon that. Moses, and the main body of the congregation, who kept their integrity, *were weeping at the door of the tabernacle,* lamenting the sin committed and deprecating the plague begun; they were *sanctifying a fast* in a solemn assembly, weeping *between the porch and the altar,* to turn away the wrath of God from the congregation. Then comes Zimri among them, with his harlot in his hand, to banter them, and, in effect, to tell them that he was resolved to fill the measure of sin as fast as they emptied it.

II. Never was virtue more daring than it was in Phinehas. Being aware of the insolence of Zimri, which it is probable, all the congregation took notice of, in a holy indignation at the offenders he rises up from his prayers, takes his sword or half-pike, follows those impudent sinners into their tent, and stabs them both, v. 7, 8. It is not at all difficult to justify Phinehas in what he did; for, being now heir-apparent to the high-priesthood, no doubt he was one of those judges of Israel whom Moses had ordered, by the divine appointment, to slay all those whom they knew to have joined themselves to Baal-peor, so that this gives no countenance at all to private persons, under pretence of zeal against sin, to put offenders to death, who ought to be prosecuted by due course of law. The civil magistrate is the avenger, to *execute wrath upon him that doeth evil,* and no private person may take his work out of his hand. Two ways God testified his acceptance of the pious zeal of Phinehas: — 1. He immediately put a stop to the plague, v. 8. Their weeping and praying prevailed not till this piece of necessary justice was done. If magistrates do not take care to punish sin, God will; but their justice will be the best prevention of his judgment, as in the case of Achan, Jos. 7:13. 2. He put an honour upon Phinehas. Though he did no more than it was his duty to do as a judge, yet because he did it with extraordinary zeal against sin, and for the honour of God and Israel, and did it when the other judges, out of respect to Zimri's character as a

prince, were afraid, and declined doing it, therefore God showed himself particularly well pleased with him, and it *was counted to him for righteousness,* Ps. 106:31. There is nothing lost by venturing for God. If Zimri's relations bore him a grudge for it, and his friends might censure him as indiscreet in this violent and hasty execution, what needed he care, while God accepted him? In a good thing we should be zealously affected. (1.) Phinehas, upon this occasion, though a young man, is pronounced his country's patriot and best friend, v. 11. He has *turned away my wrath from the children of Israel.* So much does God delight in showing mercy that he is well pleased with those that are instrumental in turning away his wrath. This is the best service we can do to our people; and we may contribute something towards it by our prayers, and by our endeavours in our places to *bring the wickedness of the wicked to an end.* (2.) The priesthood is entailed by covenant upon his family. It was designed him before, but now it was confirmed to him, and, which added much to the comfort and honour of it, it was made the recompence of his pious zeal, v. 12, 13. It is here called *an everlasting priesthood,* because it should continue to the period of the Old-Testament dispensation, and should then have its perfection and perpetuity in the unchangeable priesthood of Christ, who is *consecrated for evermore.* By the *covenant of peace* given him, some understand in general a promise of long life and prosperity, and all good; it seems rather to be meant particularly of the covenant of priesthood, for that is called the *covenant of life and peace* (Mal. 2:5), and was made for the preservation of peace between God and his people. Observe how the reward answered the service. By executing justice he had *made an atonement for the children of Israel* (v. 13), and therefore he and his shall henceforward be employed in making atonement by sacrifice. He *was zealous for his God,* and therefore he shall have the covenant of *an everlasting priesthood.* Note, It is requisite that ministers should be not only for God, but zealous for God. It is required of them that they do more than others for the support and advancement of the interests of God's kingdom among men.

Verses 16–18

God had punished the Israelites for their sin with a plague; as a Father he corrected his own children with a rod. But we read not that any of the Midianites died of the plague; God took another course with them, and punished them with the sword of an enemy, not with the rod of a father. 1. Moses, though the meekest man, and far from a spirit of revenge, is ordered to *vex the Midianites and smite them, v.* 17. Note, We must set ourselves against that, whatever it is, which is an occasion of sin to us, though it be a right eye or a right hand that thus offends us, Mt. 5:29, 30. This is that holy indignation and revenge which godly sorrow worketh, 2 Co. 7:11. 2. The reason given for the meditating of this revenge is because they *vex you with their wiles, v.* 18. Note, Whatever draws us to sin should be a vexation to us, as a thorn in the flesh. The mischief which the Midianites did to Israel by enticing them to whoredom must be remembered and punished with as much severity as that which the Amalekites did in fighting with them when they came out of Egypt, Ex. 17:14. God will certainly reckon with those that do the devil's work in tempting men to sin. See further orders given in this matter, ch. 31:2.

CHAPTER 26

This book is called Numbers, from the numberings of the children of Israel, of which it gives an account. Once they were numbered at Mount Sinai, in the first year after they came out of Egypt, which we had an account of, *ch.* 1 and 2. And now a second time they were numbered in the plains of Moab, just before they entered Canaan, and of this we have an account in this chapter. We have, I. Orders given for the doing of it (v. 1–4). II. A register of the families and numbers of each tribe (v. 5–50), and the sum total (v. 51). III. Direction given to divide the land among them (v. 52–56). IV. The families and numbers of the Levites by themselves (v. 57–62). V. Notice taken of the fulfilling of the threatening in the death of all those that were first numbered (v. 63–65), and to this there seems to have been a special regard in the taking and keeping of this account.

Verses 1–4

Observe here, 1. That Moses did not number the people but when God commanded him. David in his time did it without a command, and paid dearly for it. God was Israel's king, and he would not have this act of authority done but by his express orders. Moses, perhaps, by this time, had heard of the blessing with which Balaam was constrained, sorely against his will, to bless Israel, and particularly the notice he took of their numbers; and he was sufficiently pleased with that general testimony borne to this instance of their strength and honour by an adversary, though he knew not their numbers exactly, till God now appointed him to take the sum of them. 2. Eleazar was joined in commission with him, as Aaron had been before, by which God honoured Eleazar before the elders of his people, and confirmed his succession. 3. It was presently after the plague that this account was ordered to be taken, to show that though God had in justice contended with them by that sweeping pestilence, yet he had not made a full end, nor would he utterly cast them off. God's Israel shall not be ruined, though it be severely rebuked. 4. They were now to go by the same rule that they had gone by in the former numbering, counting those only that were able to go forth to war, for this was the service now before them.

Verses 5–51

This is the register of the tribes as they were now enrolled, in the same order that they were numbered in *ch.* 1. Observe,

I. The account that is here kept of the families of each tribe, which must not be understood of such as we call families, those that live in a house together, but such as were the descendants of the several sons of the patriarchs, by whose names, in honour of them, their posterity distinguished themselves and one another. The families of the twelve tribes are thus numbered: — Of Dan but one, for Dan had but one son, and yet that tribe was the most numerous of all except Judah, *v.* 42, 43. Its beginning was small, but its latter end greatly increased. Zebulun was divided into three families, Ephraim into four, Issachar into four, Naphtali into four, and Reuben into four; Judah, Simeon, and Asher, had five families apiece, Gad and Benjamin seven apiece, and Manasseh eight. Benjamin brought ten sons into Egypt (Gen. 46:21), but three of them, it seems either died childless or their families were extinct, for here we find seven only of those names preserved, and that whole tribe none of the most numerous; for Providence, in the building up of families and nations, does not tie itself to probabilities. *The barren hath borne seven, and she that hath many children has waxed feeble,* 1 Sa. 2:5.

II. The numbers of each tribe. And here our best entertainment will be to compare these numbers with those when they were numbered at Mount Sinai. The sum total was nearly the same; they were now 1820 fewer than they were then; yet seven of the tribes had increased in number. Judah had increased 1900, Issachar 9900, Zebulun 3100, Manasseh 20, 500, Benjamin 10,200, Dan 1700, and Asher 11,900. But the other five had decreased more than to balance that increase. Reuben had decreased 2770, Simeon 37,100, Gad 5150, Ephraim 8000, and Naphtali 8000. In this account we may observe, 1. that all the three tribes that were encamped under the standard of Judah, who was the ancestor of Christ, had increased, for his church shall be edified and multiplied. 2. That none of the tribes had increased so much as that of Manasseh, which in the former account was the smallest of all the tribes, only 32,200, while here it is one of the most considerable; and that of his brother Ephraim, which there was numerous, is here one of the least. Jacob had crossed hands upon their heads, and had preferred Ephraim before Manasseh, which perhaps the Ephraimites had prided themselves too much in, and had trampled upon their brethren the Manassites; but, when the Lord saw that Manasseh was despised, he thus multiplied him exceedingly, for it is his glory to help the weakest, and raise up those that are cast down. 3. That none of the tribes decreased so much as Simeon did; from 59,300, it such to 22,200, little more than a third part of what it was. One whole family of that tribe (namely Ohad, mentioned Ex. 6:15) was extinct in the wilderness. Hence Simeon is not mentioned in Moses's blessing (Deu. 33), and the lot of that tribe in Canaan was inconsiderable, only a canton out of Judah's lot, Jos. 19:9. Some conjecture that most of those 24,000 who were cut off by the plague for the iniquity of Peor were of that tribe; for Zimri, who was a ringleader in that iniquity, was a prince of that tribe, many of whom therefore were influenced by his example to *follow his pernicious ways.*

III. In the account of the tribe of Reuben mention is made of the rebellion of Dathan and Abiram, who were of that tribe, in confederacy with Korah a Levite, *v.* 9–11. Though the story had been largely related but a few chapters before, yet here it comes in again, as fit to be had in remembrance and thought of by posterity, whenever they looked into their pedigree and pleased themselves with the antiquity of their families and the glory of their ancestors, that they might call themselves a seed of evil doers. Two things are here said of them: — 1. That they had been *famous in the congregation, v.* 9. Probably they were remarkable for their ingenuity, activity, and fitness for business: — *That Dathan and Abiram* that might have been advanced in due time under God and Moses; but their ambitious spirits put them upon striving against God and Moses, and when they quarrelled with the one they quarrelled with the other. And what was the issue? 2. Those that might have been famous were made infamous: they *became a sign, v.* 10. They were made monuments of divine justice; God, in their ruin, showed himself glorious in holiness, and so they were set up for a warning to all others, in all ages, to take heed of treading in the steps of their pride and rebellion. Notice is here taken of the preservation of the *children of Korah* (*v.* 11); they *died not,* as the children of Dathan and Abiram did, doubtless because they kept themselves pure from the infection, and would not join, no, not with their own father, in rebellion. If we partake not of the sins of sinners, we shall not partake of their plagues. These sons of Korah were afterwards, in their posterity, eminently serviceable to the church, being employed by David as singers in the house of the Lord; hence many psalms are said to be for *the sons of Korah:* and perhaps they were made to bear his name so long after, rather than the name of any other of their ancestors, for warning to themselves, and as an instance of the power of God, which brought those choice fruits even out of that bitter root. The children of families that have been stigmatized should endeavour, by their eminent virtues, to roll away the reproach of their fathers.

Verses 52–56

If any ask why such a particular account is kept of the tribes, and families, and numbers, of the people of Israel, here is an answer for them; as they were multiplied, so they were portioned, not by common providence, but by promise; and, for the support of the honour of divine revelation, God will have the fulfilling of the promise taken notice of both in their increase and in their inheritance. When Moses had numbered the people God did not say, *By these shall the land be conquered;* but, taking that for granted, he tells him, *Unto these shall the land be divided.* "These that are now registered as the sons of Israel shall be admitted (as it were by copy of court-roll) heirs of the land of Canaan." Now, in the distributing, or quartering, of these tribes, 1. The general rule of equity is here prescribed to Moses, that to many he should give more, and to few he should give less (*v.* 54); yet, alas! *he* was so far from giving any to others that he must not have any himself, but this direction given to him was intended for Joshua his successor. 2. The application of this general rule was to be determined *by lot* (*v.* 55); notwithstanding it seems thus to be left to the prudence of their prince, yet the matter must be finally reserved to the providence of their God, in which they must all acquiesce, how much soever it contradicted their policies or inclination: *According to the lot shall the possession be divided.* As the God of nations, so the God of Israel in particular, reserves it to himself to *appoint the bounds of our habitation.* And thus Christ, our Joshua, when he was urged to appoint one of his disciples *to his right hand,* another *to his left* in his kingdom, acknowledged the sovereignty of his Father in the disposal: *It is not mine to give.* Joshua must not dispose of inheritances in Canaan according to his own mind. *But it shall be given to those for whom it is prepared of my Father.*

Verses 57–62

Levi was God's tribe, a tribe that was to have no inheritance with the rest in the land of Canaan, and therefore was not numbered with the rest, but by itself; so it had been numbered in the beginning of this book at Mount Sinai, and therefore came not under the sentence passed upon all that were then numbered, that none of them should enter Canaan but Caleb and Joshua; for of the Levites that were not numbered with them, nor were to go forth to war, Eleazar and Ithamar, and perhaps others who were above twenty years old then (as appears, *ch.* 4:16, 28), entered Canaan; and yet this tribe, now at its second numbering, had increased but 1000, and was still one of the smallest tribes. Mention is made here of the death of Nadab and Abihu for offering strange fire, as before of the sin and punishment of Korah, because *these things happened to them for ensamples.*

Verses 63–65

That which is observable in this conclusion of the account is the execution of the sentence passed upon the murmurers (*ch.* 14:29), that not one of those who *were numbered from twenty years old and upwards* (and that the Levites were not, but either from a month old or from thirty years old to fifty) should enter Canaan, except Caleb and Joshua. In the muster now made particular directions, no doubt, were given to those of each tribe that were employed in taking the account, to compare these rolls with the former, and to observe whether there were any now left of those that were numbered at Mount Sinai, and it appeared that there was not one man numbered now that was numbered then except Caleb and Joshua, *v.* 64, 65. Herein appeared, 1. The righteousness of God, and his faithfulness to his threatenings, when once the *decree has gone forth.* He *swore in his wrath,* and what he had sworn he performed. Better all those carcasses, had they been ten times as many, should fall to the ground, than the word of God. Though the rising generation was mixed with the, and many of the guilty and condemned criminals long survived the sentence, even to the last year of the forty, yet they were cut off by some means or other before this muster was made. Those whom God has condemned cannot escape either by losing themselves in a crowd or by the delay of execution. 2. The goodness of God to this people, notwithstanding their provocations. Though that murmuring race was cut off, yet God raised up another generation, which was as numerous as they, that, though they perished, yet the name of Israel might not be cut off, lest the inheritance of the promise should be lost for want of heirs. And, though the number fell a little short what it was at Mount Sinai, yet those now numbered had this advantage, that they were all middle-aged men, between twenty and sixty, in the prime of their time for service; and during the thirty-eight years of their wandering and wasting in the wilderness they had an opportunity of acquainting themselves with the laws and ordinances of God, having no business, civil or military, to divert them from those sacred studies, and having Moses and Aaron to instruct them, and God's good Spirit, Neh. 9:20. 3. The truth of God, in performing his promise made to Caleb and Joshua. They were to be preserved from falling in this common ruin, and they were so. The arrows of death, though they fly in the dark, do not fly at random, even when they fly thickest, but are directed to the mark intended, and no other. All that are written among the living shall have their lives given them for a prey, in the most dangerous times. Thousands may fall on their right hand, and ten thousands on their left, but they shall escape.

CHAPTER 27

Here is, I. The case of Zelophehad's daughters determined (*v.* 1–11). II. Notice given to Moses of his death approaching (*v.* 12–14). III. Provision made of a successor in the government, 1. By the prayer of Moses (*v.* 15–17). 2. By the appointment of God (*v.* 18, etc.).

Verses 1–11

Mention is made of the case of these daughters of Zelophehad in the chapter before, *v.* 33. It should seem, by the particular notice taken of it, that it was a singular case, and that the like did not at this time occur in all Israel, that the head of a family had no sons, but daughters only. Their case is again debated (*ch.* 36) upon another article of it; and, according to the judgments given in their case, we find them put in possession, Jos. 17:3, 4. One would suppose that their personal character was such as added weight to their case, and caused it to be so often taken notice of.

Here is, I. Their case stated by themselves, and their petition upon it presented to the highest court of judicature, which consisted of Moses as king, the princes as lords, and the congregation, or elders of the people who were chose their representatives, as the commons, *v.* 2. This august assembly sat near the *door of the tabernacle,* that in difficult cases they might consult the oracle. To them these young ladies made their application; for it is the duty of magistrates to *defend the fatherless,* Ps. 82:3. We find not that the had any advocate to speak for them, but they managed their own cause ingeniously enough, which they could do the better because it was plain and honest, and spoke for itself. Now observe,

1. What it is they petition for: That they might have a possession in the land of *Canaan, among the brethren of their father, v.* 4. What God had said to Moses (*ch.* 26:53) he had faithfully made known to the people, that the land of Canaan was to be divided among those that were now numbered; these daughters knew that they were not numbered, and therefore by this rule must expect no inheritance, and the family of their father must be looked upon as extinct, and written childless, though he had all these daughters: this they thought hard, and therefore prayed to be admitted heirs to their father, and to have an inheritance in his right. If they had had a brother, they would not have applied to Moses (as one did to Christ, Lu. 12:13) for an order to inherit with him. But, having no brother, they beg for a possession. Herein they discovered, (1.) A strong faith in the power and promise of God concerning the giving of the land of Canaan to Israel. Though it was yet unconquered, untouched, and in the full possession of the natives, yet they petition for their share in it as if it were all their own already. See Ps. 60:6, 7, *God has spoken in his holiness,* and the *Gilead is mine, Manasseh is mane.* (2.) An earnest desire of a place and name in the land of promise, which was a type of heaven; and if they had, as some think, an eye to that, and by this claim laid hold on eternal life, they were five wise virgins indeed; and their example should quicken us with all possible diligence to make sure our title to the heavenly inheritance, in the disposal of which, by the covenant of grace, no difference is made between male and female, Gal. 3:28. (3.) A true respect and honour for their father, whose name was dear and precious to them now that he was gone, and they were therefore solicitous that it should not be *done away from among his family.* There is a debt which children owe to the memory of their parents, required by the fifth commandment: *Honour thy father and mother.*

2. What their plea is: That their father did not die under any attainder which might be thought to have corrupted his blood and forfeited his estate, but he *died in his own sin* (*v.* 3), not engaged in any mutiny or rebellion against Moses, particularly not in that of Korah and his company, nor in any way concerned in the sins of others, but chargeable only with the common iniquities of mankind, for which to his own Master he was to stand or fall, but laid not himself open to any judicial process before Moses and the princes. He was never convicted of any thing that might be a bar to his children's claim. It is a comfort to parents, when they come to die, if, though they smart themselves for their own sin, yet they are not conscious to themselves of any of those iniquities which God visits upon the children.

II. Their case determined by the divine oracle. Moses did not presume to give judgment himself, because, though their pretensions seemed just and reasonable, yet his express orders were to divide the land among those that were numbered, who were the males only; he therefore *brings their cause before the Lord,* and waits for his decision (*v.* 5), and God himself gives the judgment upon it. He takes cognizance of the affairs, not only of nations, but of private families, and orders them in judgment, according to the counsel of his own will. 1. The petition is granted (*v.* 7): *They speak right, give them a possession.* Those that seek an inheritance in the land of promise shall have what they seek, and other things shall be added to them. These are claims which God will countenance and crown. 2. The point is settled for all future occasions. These daughters of Zelophehad consulted, not only their own comfort and the credit of their family, but the honour and happiness of their sex likewise; for on this particular occasion a general law was made that, in case a man had no son, his estate should go to his daughters (*v.* 8); not to the eldest, as the eldest son, but to them all in copartnership, share and share alike. Those that in such a case deprive their daughters of their right, purely to keep up the name of their family, unless a valuable consideration be allowed them, may make the entail of their lands surer than the entail of a blessing with them. Further directions are given for the disposal of inheritances, *v.* 9–11. "If a man have no issue at all, his estate shall go to his brethren; if no brethren, then to his father's brethren; and, if there be no such, then to his next kinsman." With this the rules of our law exactly agree: and though the Jewish doctors here will have it understood that if a man have no children his estate shall go to his father, if living, before his brethren, yet there is nothing of that in the law, and our common law has an express rule against it, That an estate cannot ascend lineally; so that if a person purchase lands in fee-simple, and die without issue in the life-time of his father, his father cannot be his heir. See how God makes heirs, and in his disposal we must acquiesce.

Verses 12–14

Here, 1. God tells Moses of his fault, his speaking unadvisedly with his lips at the waters of strife, where he did not express, so carefully as he ought to have done, a regard to the honour both of God and Israel, *v.* 14. Though Moses was a servant of the Lord, a faithful servant, yet once he *rebelled against God's commandment,* and failed in his duty; and though a very honourable servant, and highly favoured, yet he shall hear of his miscarriage, and all the world shall hear of it too, again and again; for God will show his displeasure against sin, even in those that are nearest and dearest to him. Those that are *in reputation for wisdom and honour* have need to be constantly careful of their words and ways, lest at any time they say or do that which may be a diminution to their comfort, or to their credit, or both, a great while after. 2. He tells Moses of his death. His death was the punishment of his sin, and yet notice is given him of it in such a manner as might best serve to sweeten and mollify the sentence, and reconcile him to it. (1.) Moses must die, but he shall first have the satisfaction of seeing the land of promise, *v.* 12. God did not intend with this sight of Canaan to tantalize him, or upbraid him with his folly in doing that which cut him short of it, nor had it any impression of that kind upon him, but God appointed it and Moses accepted it as a favour, his sight (we have reason to think) being wonderfully strengthened and enlarged to take such a full and distinct view of it as did abundantly gratify his innocent curiosity. This sight of Canaan signified his believing prospect of the better country, that is, the heavenly, which is very comfortable to dying saints. (2.) Moses must die, but death does not *cut him off;* it only gathers him to his people, brings him to rest with the holy patriarchs that had gone before him. Abraham, and Isaac, and Jacob, were *his people,* the people of his choice and love, and to them death gathered him. (3.) Moses must die, but only as Aaron died before him, *v.* 13. And Moses had seen how easily and cheerfully Aaron had put off the priesthood first and then the body; let not Moses therefore be afraid of dying; it was but to be *gathered to his people,* as Aaron was gathered. Thus the death of our near and dear relations should be improved by us, [1.] As an engagement to us to think often of dying. We are not better than our fathers or brethren; if they are gone, we are going; if they are gathered already, we must be gathered very shortly. [2.] As an encouragement to us to think of death without terror, and even to please ourselves with the thoughts of it. It is but to die as such and such died, if we live as they lived; and their *end was peace, they finished their course with joy;* why then should we fear any evil in that melancholy valley?

Verses 15–23

Here, I. Moses prays for a successor. When God had told him that he must die, though it appears elsewhere that he solicited for a reprieve for himself (Deu. 3:24, 25), yet, when this could not be obtained, he begged earnestly that the work of God might be carried on, though he might not have the honour of finishing it. Envious spirits do not love their successors, but Moses was not one of these. We should concern ourselves, both in our prayers and in our endeavours, for the rising generation, that religion may flourish, and the interests of God's kingdom among men may be maintained and advanced, when we are in our graves. In this prayer Moses expresses, 1. A tender concern for the people of Israel: *That the congregation of the Lord be not as sheep which have no shepherd.* Our Saviour uses this comparison in his compassions for the people when they wanted good ministers, Mt. 9:36. Magistrates and ministers are the shepherds of a people; if these be wanting, or be not as they should be, people are apt to wander and be scattered abroad, are exposed to enemies, and in danger of wanting food and of hurting one another, *as sheep having no shepherd.* 2. A believing dependence upon God, as the *God of the spirits of all flesh.* He is both the former and the searcher of spirits, and therefore can either find men fit or make them fit to serve his purposes, for the good of his church. Moses prays to God, not to send an angel, but to *set a man over the congregation,* that is, to nominate and appoint one whom he would qualify and own as ruler of his people Israel. Before God gave this blessing to Israel, he stirred up Moses to pray for it: thus Christ, before he sent forth his apostles, called to those about him *to pray the Lord of the harvest that he would send forth labourers into his harvest,* Mt. 9:38.

II. God, in answer to his prayer, appoints him a successor, even Joshua, who had long since signalized himself by his courage in fighting Amalek, his humility in ministering to Moses, and his faith and sincerity in witnessing against the report of the evil spies; this is the man whom God pitches upon to succeed Moses: *A man in whom is the Spirit, the Spirit of grace* (he is a good man, fearing God and hating covetousness, and acting from principle), the *spirit of government* (he is fit to do the work and discharge the trusts of his place), a spirit of conduct and courage; and he had also the *spirit of prophecy,* for the Lord often *spoke unto him,* Jos. 4:1; 6:2; 7:10. Now here,

1. God directs Moses how to secure the succession to Joshua. (1.) He must ordain him: *Lay thy hand upon him, v.* 18. This was done in token of Moses' transferring the government to him, as the laying of hands on the sacrifice put the offering in the place and stead of the offerer; also in token of God's conferring the blessing of the Spirit upon him, which Moses obtained by prayer. It is said (Deu. 34:9), *Joshua was full of the spirit of wisdom, for Moses had laid his hands on him.* This rite of imposing hands we find used in the New Testament in the setting apart of gospel ministers, denoting a solemn designation of them to the office and an earnest desire that God would qualify them for it and own them in it. It is the offering of them to Christ and his church for living sacrifices. (2.) He must present him to Eleazar and the people, set him before them, that they might know him to be designed of God for this great trust and consent to that designation. (3.) He must *give him a charge, v.* 19. He must be charged with the people of Israel, who were delivered into his hand as sheep into the hand of a shepherd, and for whom he must be accountable. He must be strictly charged to do his duty to them; though they were under his command, he was under God's command, and from him must receive charge. The highest must know that there is a higher than they. This charge must be given him *in their sight,* that it might be the more affecting to Joshua, and that the people, seeing the work and care of their prince, might be the more engaged to assist and encourage him. (4.) He must *put some of his honour upon him, v.* 20. Joshua at the most had but some of the honour of Moses, and in many instances came short of him; but this seems to be meant of his taking him now, while he lived, into partnership with him in the government and admitting him to act with authority as his assistant. It is an honour to be employed for God and his church; some of this honour must be put upon Joshua, that the people, being used to obey him while Moses lived, might the more cheerfully do it afterwards. (5.) He must appoint Eleazar the high priest, with this breast-plate of judgment, to be his privy-council (*v.* 21): *He shall stand before Eleazar,* by him to consult the oracle, ready to receive and observe all the instructions that should be given him by it. This was a direction to Joshua. Though he was full of the Spirit, and had all this honour put upon him, yet he must do nothing without asking counsel of God, not leaning to his own understanding. It was also a great encouragement to him. To govern Israel, and to con-

quer Canaan, were two hard tasks, but God assures him that in both he should be under a divine conduct; and in every difficult case God would advise him to that which should be for the best. Moses had recourse to the oracle of God himself, but Joshua and the succeeding judges must use the ministry of the high priest, and consult the judgment of urim, which, the Jews say, might not be enquired of but by the king or the head of the sanhedrim, or by the agent or representative of the people, for them, and in their name. Thus the government of Israel was now purely divine, for both the designation and direction of their princes were entirely so. *At the word of the priest,* according to the *judgment of urim,* Joshua and all Israel must go out and come in; and no doubt God, who thus guided, would preserve both their going out and their coming in. Those are safe, and may be easy, that follow God, and in all their ways acknowledge him.

2. Moses does according to these directions, *v.* 22, 23. He cheerfully ordained Joshua, (1.) Though it was a present lessening to himself, and amounted almost to a resignation of the government. He was very willing that the people should look off from him, and gaze on the rising sun. (2.) Though it might appear a perpetual slur upon his family. It would not have been so much his praise if he had thus resigned his honour to a son of his own; but with his own hands first to ordain Eleazar high priest, and then Joshua, one of another tribe, chief ruler, while his own children had no preferment at all, but were left in the rank of common Levites, this was such an instance of self-denial and submission to the will of God as was more his glory than the highest advancement of his family could have been; for it confirms his character as the meekest man upon earth, and faithful to him that appointed him in all his house. This (says the excellent bishop Patrick) shows him to have had a principle which raised him above all other lawgivers, who always took care to establish their families in some share of that greatness which they themselves possessed; but hereby it appeared that Moses acted not from himself, because he acted not for himself.

CHAPTER 28

Now that the people were numbered, orders given for the dividing of the land, and a general of the forces nominated and commissioned, one would have expected that the next chapter should begin the history of the campaign, or at least should give us an account of the ordinances of war; no, it contains the ordinances of worship, and provides that now, as they were on the point of entering Canaan, they should be sure to take their religion along with them, and not forget this, in the prosecution of their wars (*v.* 1, 2). The laws are here repeated and summed up concerning the sacrifices that were to be offered, I. Daily (*v.* 3–8). II. Weekly (*v.* 9, 10). III. Monthly (*v.* 11–15). IV. Yearly. 1. At the passover (*v.* 16–25). 2. At pentecost (*v.* 26–31). And the next chapter is concerning the annual solemnities of the seventh month.

Verses 1–8

Here is, I. A general order given concerning the offerings of the Lord, which were to be brought in their season, *v.* 2. These laws are here given afresh, not because the observance of them was wholly disused during their thirty-eight years' wandering in the wilderness (we cannot think that they were so long without any public worship, but that at least the daily lamb was offered morning and evening, and doubled on the sabbath day; so bishop Patrick conjectures; but that many of the sacrifices were then omitted is plainly intimated, Amos *v.* 25, quoted by Stephen, Acts 7:42. *Did you offer unto me sacrifices and offerings in the wilderness forty years, O house of Israel?* It is implied, "No, you did not." But, whether the course of sacrifices had been interrupted or no, God saw fit now to repeat the law of sacrifices, 1. Because this was a new generation of men, that were most of them unborn when the former laws were given; therefore, that they might be left without excuse, they have not only these laws written, to be read to them, but again repeated from God himself, and put into a less compass and a plainer method. 2. Because they were now entering upon war, and might be tempted to think that while they were engaged in that they should be excused from offering sacrifices. *Inter arma silent leges — law is little regarded amidst the clash of arms.* No, says God, *my bread for my sacrifices* even now *shall you observe to offer, and that in the due season.* They were peculiarly concerned to keep their peace with God when they were at war with their enemies. In the wilderness they were solitary, and quite separate from all other people, and

therefore there they needed not so much their distinguishing badges, nor would their omission of sacrifices be so scandalous as when they came into Canaan, when they mingled with other people. 3. Because possession was now to be given them of the land of promise, that land flowing with milk and honey, where they would have plenty of all good things. "Now" (says God), "When you are feasting yourselves, forget not to offer the bread of your God." Canaan was given to them upon this condition, that they should *observe God's statutes,* Ps. 105:44, 45.

II. The particular law of the daily sacrifice, a lamb in the morning and a lamb in the evening, which, for the constancy of it as duly as the day came, is called a *continual burnt-offering* (*v.* 3), which intimates that when we are bidden to *pray always, and to pray without ceasing,* it is intended that at least every morning and every evening we offer up our solemn prayers and praises to God. This is said to be *ordained in Mount Sinai* (*v.* 6), when the other laws were given. The institution of it we have, Ex. 29:38. Nothing is here added in the repetition of the law, but that the wine to be poured out in the drink-offering is ordered to be *strong wine* (*v.* 7), the riches and most generous and best-bodied wine they could get. Though it was to be poured out upon the altar, and not drunk (they therefore might be ready to think the worst would serve to be so thrown away), yet God requires the strongest, to teach us to serve God with the best we have. The wine must be strong (says Ainsworth) because it was a figure of the blood of Christ, the memorial of which is still left to the church in wine, and of the blood of the martyrs, which was poured out as a drink-offering upon the *sacrifice and service of our faith,* Phil. 2:17.

Verses 9–15

The new moons and the sabbaths are often spoken of together, as great solemnities in the Jewish church, very comfortable to the saints then, and typical of gospel grace. Now we have here the sacrifices appointed, 1. For the sabbaths. Every sabbath day the offering must be doubled; besides the two lambs offered for the daily burnt-offering, there must be two more offered, one (it is probable) added to the morning sacrifice, and the other to the evening, *v.* 9, 10. This teaches us to double our devotions on sabbath days, for so the duty of the day requires. The sabbath rest is to be observed, in order to a more close application to the sabbath work, which ought to fill up sabbath time. In Ezekiel's temple-service, which points at gospel times, the sabbath offerings were to be six lambs and a ram, with their meat-offerings, and drink-offerings (Eze. 46:4, 5), to intimate not only the continuance, but the advancement, of sabbath sanctification in the days of the Messiah. This is *the burnt-offering of the sabbath in his sabbath,* so it is in the original, *v.* 10. We must do every sabbath day's work in its day, studying to redeem every minute of sabbath time as those that believe it precious; and not thinking to put off one sabbath's work to another, for sufficient to every sabbath is the service thereof. 2. For the new moons. Some suggest that, as the sabbath was kept with an eye to the creation of the world, so the new moons were sanctified with an eye to the divine providence, which *appoints the moon for seasons,* guiding the revolutions of time by its changes, and governing sublunary bodies (as many think) by its influences. Though we observe not any feast of new moons, yet we must not forget to give God the glory of all the precious things put forth by the moon which he has *established for ever, a faithful witness in heaven,* Ps. 89:37. The offerings in the new moons were very considerable, two bullocks, a ram, and seven lambs, with the meat-offerings and drink-offerings that were to attend them (*v.* 11, etc.), besides a sin-offering, *v.* 15. For, when we give glory to God by confessing his mercies, we must give glory to him likewise by confessing our own sins; and, when we rejoice in the gifts of common providence, we must make the sacrifice of Christ, that great gift of special grace, the fountain and spring-head of our joy. Some have questioned whether the new moons were to be reckoned among their feasts; but why should they not, when, besides the special sacrifices which were then to be offered, they rested from servile works (Amos 8:5), *blew the trumpets* (*ch.* 10:10), and went to the prophets *to hear the word?* 2 Ki. 4:23. And the worship performed in the new moons is made typical of gospel solemnities, Isa. 66:23.

Verses 16–31

Here is, I. The appointment of the pass-over sacrifices; not that which was the chief, the paschal lamb (sufficient instructions had formerly been given concerning that), but those which were to be offered upon the seven days of unleavened bread, which followed it, *v.* 17–25. The first and last of those seven days were to be sanctified as sabbaths, by a holy rest and a holy convocation, and on each of the seven days they were to be liberal in their sacrifices, in token of their great and constant thankfulness for their deliverance out of Egypt: *Two bullocks, a ram, and seven lambs.* A gospel conversation, in gratitude for *Christ our passover* who was sacrificed, is called the *keeping of this feast* (1 Co. 5:8); for it is not enough that we purge out the *leavened bread* of malice and wickedness, but we must *offer the bread of our God, even the sacrifice of praise, continually,* and continue herein unto the end. 2. The sacrifices are likewise appointed which were to be offered at the feast of pentecost, here called the *day of the first-fruits, v.* 26. In the feast of unleavened bread they offered a *sheaf of their first-fruits* of barley (which with them was first ripe) to the priest (Lev. 23:10), as an introduction to the harvest; but now, about seven weeks after, they were to bring a *new meat-offering to the Lord,* at the end of harvest, in thankfulness to God, who had not only given, *but preserved to their use, the kindly fruits of the earth, so as that in due time they did enjoy them.* It was at this feast that *the Spirit was poured out* (Acts 2:1, etc.), and thousands were converted by the preaching of the apostles, and were presented to Christ, to be *a kind of first-fruits of his creatures.* The sacrifice that was to be offered with the loaves of the first-fruits was appointed, Lev. 23:18. But over and above, besides that and besides the daily offerings, they were to offer *two bullocks, one ram, and seven lambs, with a kid for a sin-offering, v.* 27–30. When God sows plentifully upon us he expects to reap accordingly from us. Bishop Patrick observes that no *peace-offerings* are appointed in this chapter, which were chiefly for the benefit of the offerers, and therefore in them they were left more to themselves; but *burnt-offerings* were purely for the honour of God, were confessions of his dominion, and typified evangelical piety and devotion, by which the soul is wholly offered up to God in the flames of holy love; and *sin-offerings* were typical of Christ's sacrifice of himself, *by which we and our services are perfected and sanctified.*

CHAPTER 29

This chapter appoints the offerings that were to be made by fire unto the Lord in the three great solemnities of the seventh month. I. In the feast of trumpets on the first day of that month (*v.* 1–6). II. In the day of atonement on the tenth day (*v.* 7–11). III. In the feast of tabernacles on the fifteenth day and the seven days following (*v.* 12–38). And then the conclusion of these ordinances (*v.* 39, 40).

Verses 1–11

There were more sacred solemnities in the seventh month than in any other month of the year, not only because it had been the first month till the deliverance of Israel out of Egypt (which, falling in the month Abib, occasioned that to be thenceforth made the *beginning of the months* in all ecclesiastical computations), but because still it continued the first month in the civil reckonings of the jubilees and years of release, and also because it was the time of vacation between harvest and seedtime, when they had most leisure to attend the sanctuary, which intimates that, though God will dispense with sacrifices in consideration of works of necessity and mercy, yet the more leisure we have from the pressing occasions of this life the more time we should spend in the immediate service of God. 1. We have here the appointment of the sacrifices that were to be offered on the first day of the month, the day of *blowing the trumpets,* which was a preparative for the two great solemnities of holy mourning on the day of atonement and of holy joy in the feast of tabernacles. The intention of divine institutions is well answered when one religious service helps to fit us for another and all for heaven. The *blowing of the trumpets* was appointed, Lev. 23:24. Here the people are directed what sacrifices to offer on that day, of which there was not then any mention made. Note, Those who would know the mind of God in the scripture must compare one part of the scripture with another, and put those parts together that have reference to the same thing, for the latter discoveries of divine light explain what was dark and supply what was defective in the former, *that the man of God may be perfect.* The sacrifices then to be offered are particularly ordered here (*v.* 2–6), and care taken that these should not supersede the daily oblation and that of the new moon. It is hereby intimated that we must not seek occasions to abate our zeal in God's service, nor be glad of an excuse to omit a good duty, but rather rejoice in an opportunity of accumulating and doing more than ordinary in religion. If we perform family-worship, we must not think that this will excuse us from our secret devotions; nor that on the days we go to church we need not worship God alone and with our families; but we should *always abound in the work of the Lord.* 2. On the *day of atonement.* Besides all the services of that day, which we had the institution of, Lev. 16, and which, one would think, required trouble and charge enough, here are burnt-offerings ordered to be offered, *v.* 8–10. For in our faith and repentance, those two great gospel graces which were signified by that day's performances, we must have an eye to the glory and honour of God, which was purely intended in the burnt-offerings; there was likewise to be a *kid of the goats for a sin-offering, besides the great sin-offering of atonement* (*v.* 11), which intimates that there are so many defects and faults, even in the exercises and expressions of our repentance, that we have need of an interest in a sacrifice to expiate the guilt even of that part of our holy things. Though we must not repent that we have repented, yet we must repent that we have not repented better. It likewise intimated the imperfection of the legal sacrifices, and their insufficiency to take away sin, that on the very day the *sin-offering of atonement* was offered, yet there must be another sin-offering. But *what the law could not do, in that it was weak,* that Christ has done.

Verses 12–40

Soon after the day of atonement, that day in which men were to afflict their souls, followed the feast of tabernacles, in which they were to rejoice before the Lord; for those that *sow in tears* shall soon *reap in joy.* To the former laws about this feast, which we had, Lev. 23:34, etc., here are added directions about the *offerings by fire,* which they were to offer unto the Lord during the *seven days of that feast,* Lev. 23:36. Observe here, 1. Their days of rejoicing were to be days of sacrifices. A disposition to be cheerful does us no harm, nor is any bad symptom, when it is so far from unfitting us for the duties of God's immediate service that it encourages and enlarges our hearts in them. 2. All the days of their dwelling in booths they must offer sacrifices. While we are here in a tabernacle-state, it is our interest as well as duty constantly to keep up communion with God; nor will the unsettledness of our outward condition excuse us in our neglect of the duties of God's worship. 3. The sacrifices for each of the seven days, though differing in nothing but the number of the bullocks, are severally and particularly appointed, which yet is no vain repetition; for God would thus teach them to be very exact in those observances, and to keep an eye of faith fixed upon the institution in every day's work. It likewise intimates that the repetition of the same services, if performed with an upright heart, and with a continued fire of pious and devout affection, is no weariness to God, and therefore we ought not to snuff at it, or to say, *Behold, what a weariness it is to us!* 4. The number of bullocks (which were the most costly part of the sacrifice) decreased every day. On the first day of the feast they were to offer thirteen, on the second day but twelve, on the third day eleven, etc. So that on the seventh they offered seven; and the last day, though it was the great day of the feast, and celebrated with a holy convocation, yet they were to offer but one bullock; and, whereas on all the other days they offered two rams and fourteen lambs, on this they offered but one ram and seven lambs. Such was the will of the Law-maker, and that is reason enough for the law. Some suggest that God herein considered the infirmity of the flesh, which is apt to grudge the charge and expense of religion; it is therefore ordered to grow less and less, that they might not complain as if God had *made them to serve with an offering,* Isa. 43:23. Or it is hereby intimated to them that the legal dispensation should wax old, and vanish away at last; and the multitude of their sacrifices should end in one great sacrifice, infinitely more worthy than all of them. It was on the last day of the feast, after all these sacrifices had been ordered, that our Lord Jesus stood and cried to those who still thirsted after righteousness (being sensible of the insufficiency of these sacrifices to justify them) *to come unto him and drink,* Jn. 7:37. 5. The meat-offerings and drink-offerings attended all the sacrifices, *according to their number, after the manner.* Be there ever so much flesh, it is no feast without bread and drink, therefore these must never be omitted at God's altar, which was his table. We must not think that doing much in religion will be accepted if we do not do it well, and after the manner that God has appointed. 6. Every day there must be a sin-offering presented, as we observed in the other feasts. Our burnt-offerings of praise cannot be accepted of God unless we have an interest in the great sacrifice of propitiation which Christ offered when for us he made himself a sin-offering. 7. Even when all these sacrifices were offered, yet the continual burnt-offering must not be omitted either morning or evening, but each day this must be offered first in the morning and last in the evening. No extraordinary services should jostle out our stated devotions. 8. Though all these sacrifices were required to be presented by the body of the congregation, at the common charge, yet, besides these, particular persons were to glorify God with their vows and their free-will offerings, *v.* 39. When God commanded that this *they must do,* he left room for the generosity of their devotion, a great deal more they *might do,* not inventing other worships, but abounding in these, as 2 Chr. 30:23, 24. Large directions had been given in Leviticus concerning the offerings of all sorts that should be brought by particular persons according to the providences of God concerning them and the graces of God in them. Though every Israelite had an interest in these common sacrifices, yet he must not think that these will serve instead of his vows and his free-will offerings. Thus our ministers' praying with us and for us will not excuse us from praying for ourselves.

CHAPTER 30

In this chapter we have a law concerning vows, which had been mentioned in the close of the foregoing chapter. I. Here is a general rule laid down that all vows must be carefully performed (*v.* 1, 2). II. Some particular exceptions to this rule. 1. That the vows of daughters should not be binding unless allowed by the father (*v.* 3–5). Nor, 2. The vows of wives unless allowed by the husband (*v.* 6, etc.).

Verses 1–2

This law was delivered to the heads of the tribes that they might instruct those who were under their charge, explain the law to them, give then necessary cautions, and call them to account, if there were occasion, for the breach of their vows. Perhaps the heads of the tribes had, upon some emergency of this kind, consulted Moses, and desired by him to know the mind of God, and here they are told it: *This is the thing which the Lord has commanded* concerning vows, and it is a command still in force.

1. The case supposed is that a person vows a vow unto the Lord, making God a party to the promise, and designing his honour and glory in it. The matter of the vow is supposed to be something lawful: no man can be by his own promise bound to do that which he is already by the divine precept prohibited from doing. Yet it is supposed to be something which, in such and such measures and degrees, was not a necessary duty antecedent to the vow. A person might vow to bring such and such sacrifices at certain times, to give such and such a sum or such a proportion in alms, to forbear such meats and drinks which the law allowed, to fast and afflict the soul (which is specified *v.* 13) at other times besides the day of atonement. And many similar vows might be made in an extraordinary heat of holy zeal, in humiliation for some sin committed or for the prevention of sin, in the pursuit of some mercy desired or in gratitude for some mercy received. It is of great use to make such vows as these, provided they be made in sincerity with due caution. Vows (say the Jewish doctors) are *the hedge of separation,* that is, a fence to religion. He that vows is here said to *bind his soul with a bond.* It is a vow to God, who is a spirit, and to him the soul, with all its powers, must be bound. A promise to man is a bond upon the estate, but a promise to God is a bond upon the soul. Our sacramental vows, by which we are bound to no more than what was before our duty, and which neither father nor husband can disannul, are bonds upon the soul, and by them we must feel ourselves bound out from all sin and bound up to the whole will of God. Our occasional vows concerning that which before was *in our own power* (Acts 5:4), when they are made, are bonds upon the soul likewise. 2. The command given is that these vows be conscientiously performed: *He shall not break his word,* though afterwards he may change his mind, but he shall do according to what he has said. *Margin, He shall not profane his word.* Vowing is an ordinance of God; if we vow in hypocrisy we profane that ordinance: it is plainly determined, *Better not vow than vow and not pay,* Eccl. 5:5. *Be not deceived, God is not mocked.* His promises to us are *yea and amen,* let not ours to him be *yea and nay.*

Verses 3–16

It is here taken for granted that all such persons as are *sui juris — at their own disposal,* and are likewise of sound understanding and memory, are bound to perform whatever they vow that is lawful and possible; but, if the person vowing be under the dominion and at the disposal of another, the case is different. Two cases much alike are here put and determined: —

I. The case of a daughter in her father's house: and some think, probably enough, that it extends to a son likewise, while he is at home with his father, and under tutors and governors. Whether the exception may thus be stretched I cannot say. *Non est distinguendum, ubi lex non distinguit — We are not allowed to make distinctions which the law does not.* The rule is general, If a man vow, he must pay. But for a daughter it is express: her vow is nugatory or in suspense till her father knows it, and (it is supposed) knows it from her; for, when it comes to his knowledge, it is in his power either to ratify or nullify it. But in favour of the vow, 1. Even his silence shall suffice to ratify it: If he *hold his peace, her vows shall stand, v.* 4. *Qui tacet, consentire videtur — Silence gives consent.* Hereby he allows his daughter the liberty she has assumed, and, as long as he says nothing against her vow, she shall be bound by it. But, 2. His protestation against it shall perfectly disannul it, because it is possible that such vow may by prejudicial to the affairs of the family, break the father's measures, perplex the provision made for his table if the vow related to meats, or lessen the provision made for his children if the vow would be more expensive than his estate would bear; however, it was certain that it was an infringement of his authority over his child, and therefore, if he disallow it, she is discharged, and *the Lord shall forgive her,* that is, she shall not be charged with the guilt of violating her vow; she showed her good-will in making the vow, and, if her intentions therein were sincere, she shall be accounted better than sacrifice. This shows how great a deference children owe to their parents, and how much they ought to honour them and be obedient to them. It is for the interest of the public that the paternal authority be supported; for, when children are countenanced in their disobedience to their parents (as they were by the tradition of the elders, Mt. 15:5, 6), they soon become in other things *children of Belial.* If this law be not to be extended to children's marrying without their parents' consent so far as to put it in parents' power to annul the marriage and dissolve the obligation (as some have thought it does), yet certainly it proves the sinfulness of it, and obliges the children that have thus done foolishly to repent and humble themselves before God and their parents.

II. The case of a wife is much the same. As for a woman that is a widow or divorced, she has neither father nor husband to control her, so that, whatever vows she binds her soul with, they shall *stand against her* (*v.* 9), it is at her peril if she run back; but a wife, who has nothing that she can strictly call her own, but with her husband's allowance, cannot, without that, make any such vow. 1. The law is plain in case of a wife that continues so long after the vow. If her husband allow her vow, though only by silence, it must stand, *v.* 6, 7. If he disallow it, since her obligation to that which she had vowed arose purely from her own act, and not from any prior command of God, her obligation to her husband shall take place of it, for to him she ought to be in subjection *as unto the Lord;* and now it is so far from being her duty to fulfil her vow that it would be her sin to disobey her husband, whose consent perhaps she ought to have asked before she made the vow; therefore she needs *forgiveness, v.* 8. 2. The law is the same in case of a wife that soon after becomes a widow, or is put away. Though, if she return to her father's house, she does not therefore so come again under his authority as that he has power to disannul hew vows (*v.* 9), yet if the vow was made while she was in the house of her husband, and her husband disallowed it, it was made void and of no effect for ever, and she does not return under the law of her vow when she is loosed from the law of her husband. This seems to be the distinct meaning of *v.* 10–14, which otherwise would be but a repetition of *v.* 6–8. But it is added (*v.* 15) that, if the husband make void the vows of his wife, he shall *bear her iniquity;* that is, if the thing she had vowed was really good, for the honour of God and the prosperity of her own soul, and the husband disallowed it out of covetousness, or humour, or to show his authority, though she be discharged from the obligation of her vow, yet he will have a great deal to answer for. Now here it is very observable how carefully the divine law consults the good order of families, and preserves the power of superior relations, and the duty and reverence of inferiors. It is fit that every man should *bear rule in his own house,* and have his wife and children in subjection with all gravity; and rather than this great rule should be broken, or any encouragement given to inferior relations to break those bonds asunder, God himself would quit his right, and release the obligations even of a solemn vow; so much does religion strengthen the ties of all relations, and secure the welfare of all societiesd, that in it the *families of the earth are blessed.*

CHAPTER 31

This chapter belongs to "the book of the wars of the Lord," in which it is probable it was inserted. It is the history of a holy war, a war with Midian. Here is, I. A divine command for the war (*v.* 1, 2). II. The undertaking of the war (*v.* 3–6). III. The glorious success of it (*v.* 7–12). IV. Their triumphant return from the war. 1. The respect Moses paid to the soldiers (*v.* 13). 2. The rebuke he gave them for sparing the women (*v.* 14–18). 3. The directions he gave them for the purifying of themselves and their effects (*v.* 19–24). 4. The distribution of the spoil they had taken, one half to the soldiers, the other to the congregation, and a tribute to the Lord out of each (*v.* 25–47). 5. The free-will offering of the officers (*v.* 48, etc.).

Verses 1–6

Here, I. The Lord of hosts gives orders to Moses to make war upon the Midianites, and his commission no doubt justified this war, though it will not serve to justify the like without such commission. The Midianites were the posterity of Abraham by Ketuarah, Gen. 25:2. Some of them settled south of Canaan, among whom Jethro lived, and they retained the worship of the true God; but these were settled east of Canaan, and had fallen into idolatry, neighbours to, and in confederacy with, the Moabites. Their land was not designed to be given to Israel, nor would Israel have meddled with them if they had not made themselves obnoxious to their resentment by sending their bad women among them to draw them to whoredom and idolatry. This was the provocation, this was the quarrel. For this (says God) *avenge Israel of the Midianites, v.* 2. 1. God would have the Midianites chastised, an inroad made upon that part of their country which lay next to the camp of Israel, and which was probably more concerned in that mischief than the Moabites, who therefore were let alone. God will have us to reckon those our worst enemies that draw us to sin, and to avoid them; and since *every man is tempted when he is drawn aside of his own lusts,* and these are the Midianites which ensnare us with their wiles, on them we should avenge ourselves, not only make no league with them, but make war upon them by living a life of mortification. God had taken vengeance on his own people for yielding to the Midianites' temptations; now the Midianites, that gave the temptation, must be reckoned with, for *the deceived and the deceiver are his* (Job 12:16), both accountable to his tribunal; and, though *judgment begin at the house of God,* it shall not end there, 1 Pt. 4:17. There is a day coming when vengeance will be taken on those that have introduced errors and corruptions into the church, and the devil that deceived men will be *cast into the lake of fire.* Israel's quarrel with Amalek, that fought against them, was not avenged till long after: but their quarrel with Midian, that debauched them, was speedily avenged, for they were looked upon as much more the dangerous and malicious enemies. 2. God would have it done by Moses, in his life-time, that he who had so deeply resented that injury might have the satisfaction of seeing it avenged. "See this execution done upon the enemies of God and Israel, and *afterwards thou shalt be gathered to thy people.*" This was the only piece of service of this kind that Moses must further do, and then he has accomplished, as a hireling, his day, and shall have his *quietus — enter into rest:* hitherto his usefulness must come, and no further; the wars of Canaan must be carried on by another hand. Note, God sometimes removes useful men when we think they can be ill spared; but this ought to satisfy us, that they are never removed till they have done the work which was appointed them.

II. Moses gives orders to the people to prepare for this expedition, *v.* 3. He would not have the whole body of the camp to stir, but they must *arm some of themselves to the war,* such as were either most fit or most forward, and *avenge the Lord of Midian.* God said, *Avenge Israel;* Moses says, *Avenge the Lord;* for the interests of God and Israel are united, and the cause of both is one and the same. And if God, in what he does, shows himself jealous for the honour of Israel, surely Israel, in what they do, ought to show themselves jealous for the glory of God. Then only we can justify the avenging of ourselves when it is the vengeance of the Lord that we engage in. Nay, for this reason we are forbidden to avenge ourselves, because God has said, *Vengeance is mine, I will repay.*

III. A detachment is drawn out accordingly for this service, 1000 *out of every tribe,* 12,000 in all, a small number in comparison with what they could have sent, and it is probable small in comparison with the number of the enemies they were sent against. But God would teach them that it is all one to him *to save by many or by few,* 1 Sa. 14:6.

IV. Phinehas the son of Eleazar is sent along with them. It is strange that no mention is made of Joshua in this great action. If he was general of these forces, who do we not find him leading them out? If he tarried at home, why do we not find him meeting them with Moses at their return? It is probable, each tribe having a captain of its own thousand, there was no general, but they proceeded in the order of their march through the wilderness, Judah first, and the rest in their posts, under the command of their respective captains, spoken of *v.* 48. But, the war being a holy war, Phinehas was their common head, not to supply the place of a general, but, by the oracle of God, to determine the resolves of their counsels of war, in which the captains of thousands would all acquiesce, and according to which they would act in conjunction. He therefore took with him the holy instruments or vessels, probably the breast-plate of judgment, by which God might he consulted in any emergency. Though he was not yet the high priest, yet he might be delegated *pro hac vice — for this particular occasion,* to bear the urim and thummim, as 1 Sa. 23:6. And there was a particular reason for sending Phinehas to preside in this expedition; he has already signalized himself for his zeal against the Midianites and their cursed arts to ensnare Israel when he slew Cozbi, a daughter of a chief house in Midian, for her impudence in the matter of Peor, *ch.* 25:15. He that had so well used the sword of justice against a particular criminal was best qualified to guide the sword of war against the whole nation. *Thou hast been faithful over a few things, I will make thee ruler over many things.*

Verses 7–12

Here is, 1. The descent which this little army of Israelites made, under the divine commission, conduct, and command, upon the country of Midian. They *warred against the Midianites.* It is very probable that they first published their manifesto, showing the reasons of the war, and requiring them to give up the ringleaders of the mischief to justice; for such afterwards was the *law* (Deu. 20:10), and such the *practice,* Jdg. 20:12, 13. But the Midianites justifying what they had done, and standing by those that had done it, the Israelites attacked them with fire and sword, and all the pious fury with which their zeal for God and their people inspired them. 2. The execution (the military execution) they did in this descent. (1.) *They slew all the males* (*v.* 7), that is, all they met with as far as they went; they put them all to the sword, and gave no quarter. But that they did not slay all the males of the nation is certain, for we find the Midianites a powerful and formidable enemy to Israel in the days of Gideon; and they were the Midianites of this country, for they are reckoned with the *children of the east,* Jdg. 6:3. (2.) They *slew the kings of Midian* the same that are called *elders of Midian* (*ch.* 22:4), and the *dukes of Sihon,* Jos. 13:21. Five of these princes are here named, one of whom is *Zur,* probably the same Zur whose daughter Cosbi was, *ch.* 25:15. (3.) They slew Balaam. Many conjectures there are as to what brought Balaam among the Midianites at this time; it is probable that the Midianites, having intelligence of the march of this army of Israelites against them, hired Balaam to come and assist them with his enchantments, that if he could not prevail to act offensively in their favour, by cursing the armies of Israel, yet he might act defensively, by blessing the country of Midian. Whatever was the occasion of his being there, God's overruling providence brought him thither, and there his just vengeance found him. Had he himself believed what he said of the happy state of Israel, he would not have herded thus with the enemies of Israel; but justly does he die the death of the wicked (though he pretended to desire that of the righteous), and go *down slain to the pit with the uncircumcised,* who rebelled thus against the convictions of his own conscience. The Midianites' wiles were Balaam's projects, it was therefore just that he should perish with them, Hos. 4:5. Now was *his* folly made manifest to all men, who foretold the fate of others, but foresaw not his own. (4.) They took all the *women and children captives, v.* 9. (5.) They *burnt their cities and goodly castles* (*v.* 10), not designing to inhabit them themselves (that country was out of their line), but they thus prevented those who had made their escape from sheltering themselves in their own country and settling there again. Some understand it of their idol-temples; it was fit that they should share in this vengeance. (6.) They plundered the country, and carried off all the cattle and valuable goods, and so returned to the camp of Israel laden with a very rich booty, *v.* 9, 11, 12. Thus (as when they came out of Egypt) they were enriched with the spoils of their enemies, and furnished with stock for the good land into which God was bringing them.

Verses 13–24

We have here the triumphant return of the army of Israel from the war with Midian, and here,

I. They were met with great respect, *v.* 13. Moses himself, notwithstanding his age and gravity, walked out of the camp to congratulate them on their victory, and to grace the solemnity of their triumphs. Public successes should be publicly acknowledged, to the glory of God, and the encouragement of those that have jeoparded their lives in their country's cause.

II. They were severely reproved for saving the women alive. It is very probable that Moses had commanded them to kill the women, at least this was implied in the general order to avenge Israel of the Midianites; the execution having reference to that crime, their drawing them in to the worship of Peor, it was easy to conclude that the women, who were the principal criminals, must not be spared. What! says Moses, *have you saved the women alive? v.* 15. He was moved with a holy indignation at the sight of them. *These were those that caused the children of Israel to commit this trespass;* and therefore, 1. It is just that they should die. The law in case of whoredom was, *The adulterer and adulteress should surely be put to death.* God had put to death the adulterers of Israel by the plague, and now it was fit that the adulteresses of Midian, especially since they had been the tempters, should be put to death by the sword. 2. "It is dangerous to let them live; they will be still tempting the Israelites to uncleanness, and so your captives will be your conquerors and a second time your destroyers." Severe orders are therefore given that all the grown women should be slain in cold blood, and only the female children spared.

III. They were obliged to purify themselves, according to the ceremony of the law, and to abide without the camp seven days, till their purification was accomplished. For, 1. They had imbrued their hands in blood, by which though they had not contracted any moral guilt, the war being just and lawful, yet they were brought under a ceremonial uncleanness, which rendered them unfit to come near the tabernacle till they were purified. Thus God would preserve in their minds a dread and detestation of murder. David must not build the temple because he had been a *man of war, and had shed blood,* 1 Chr. 28:3. 2. They could not but have touched dead bodies, by which they were polluted, and that required they should be purified with the water of separation, *v.* 19, 20, 24.

IV. They must likewise purify the spoil they had taken, the captives (*v.* 19) and all the goods, *v.* 21–23. What would bear the fire must pass through the fire, and what would not must be washed with water. These things had been use by Midianites, and, having now come into the possession of Israelites, it was fit that they should be sanctified to the service of that holy nation and the honour of their holy God. To us now every thing is sanctified by the word and prayer, if we are sanctified by the Spirit, who is compared both to fire and water. *To the pure all things are pure.*

Verses 25–47

We have here the distribution of the spoil which was taken in this expedition against Midian. God himself directed how it should be distributed, and Moses and Eleazar did according to the directions, and thus unhappy contests among themselves were prevented and the victory was made to turn to the common benefit. It was fit that he who gave them the prey should order the disposal of it. All we have is from God, and therefore must be subject to his will.

I. The prey is ordered to be divided into two parts, one for the 12,000 men that undertook the war, and the other for the congregation. The prey that was divided seems to have been only the captives and the cattle; as for the plate, and jewels, and other goods, every man kept what he took, as is intimated, *v.* 50–53. That only was distributed which would be of use for the stocking of that good land into which they were going. Now observe, 1. That the one half of the prey was given to the whole congregation, Moses allotting to each tribe its share, and then leaving it to the heads of the tribes to divide their respective shares among themselves, according to their families. The war was undertaken on the behalf of the whole congregation; they would all have been ready to *go to the help of the Lord against the mighty,* if they had been so ordered, and they did help, it is likely, by their prayers; and therefore God appoints that those that *tarried at home should divide the spoil,* Ps. 68:12. David, in his time, made it a *statute and an ordinance for Israel,* that, as his part is that *goes down to the battle, so shall his part be that tarrieth by the stuff,* 1 Sa. 30:24, 25. Those that are employed in public trusts must not think to benefit themselves only by their toils and hazards, but must aim at the advantage of the community. 2. That yet the 12,000 that went to the battle had as much for their share as the whole congregation (which were fifty times as many) had for theirs; so that the particular persons of the soldiery had a much better share than any of their brethren that tarried at home: and good reason they should. The greater pains we take, and the greater hazards we run, in the service of God and our generation, the greater will our recompence be at last; for *God is not unrighteous to forget the work and labour of love.*

II. God was to have a tribute out of it, as an acknowledgment of his sovereignty over them in general, and that he was their king to whom *tribute was due,* and particularly of his interest in this war and the gains of it, he having given them their success; and that the priests, the Lord's receivers, might have something added to the provision made for their maintenance. Note, Whatever we have, God must have his dues out of it. And here (as before) the soldiers are favoured above the rest of the congregation, for out of the people's share God required one in fifty, but out of the soldier's share only one in 500, because the people got theirs easily, without any peril or fatigue. The less opportunity we have of honouring God with our personal services the more it is expected we should honour him with our substance. The tribute out of the soldiers' half was given to the priests (*v.* 29), that out of the people's half was given to the Levites, *v.* 30. For the priests were taken from among the Levites, as these soldiers from among the people, for special and hazardous service, and their pay was proportioned accordingly.

Verses 48–54

Here is a great example of piety and devotion in the officers of the army, the colonels, that are called *captains of thousands,* and the inferior officers that were *captains of hundreds;* they came to Moses as their general and

commander-in-chief, and, though he was now going off the stage they very humbly and respectfully addressed themselves to him, calling themselves his *servants;* the honours they had won did not puff them up, so as to make them forget their duty to him. Observe in their address to them, 1. The pious notice they take of God's wonderful goodness to them in this late expedition, in preserving not only their own lives, but the lives of all the men of war that they had under their charge; so that, upon the review of their muster-roll, it appeared there was not one missing, *v.* 49. This was very extraordinary, and perhaps cannot be paralleled in any history. So many thousands of lives jeoparded in the high places of the field, and not one lost, either by the sword of the enemy or by any disease or disaster. This was *the Lord's doing,* and cannot but be marvellous in the eyes of those that consider how the lives of all men, especially soldiers, are continually in their hands. It is an evidence of the tender feeling which these commanders had for their soldiers, and that their lives were very precious to them, that they looked upon it as a mercy to themselves that none of those under their charge miscarried. *Of all that were given them they had lost none;* so precious also is the blood of Christ's subjects and soldiers to him, Ps. 72:14. 2. The pious acknowledgment they make for this favour: *Therefore we have brought an oblation to the Lord, v.* 50. The oblation they brought was out of that which *every man had gotten,* and it was gotten honestly by a divine warrant. Thus every man should lay by *according as God has prospered him,* 1 Co. 16:2. For where God sows plentifully in the gifts of his bounty he expects to reap accordingly in the fruits of our piety and charity. The tabernacle first, and the temple afterwards, were beautified and enriched with the spoils taken from the enemies of Israel; as by David (2 Sa. 8:11, 12), and his captains, 1 Chr. 26:26, 27. We should never take any thing to ourselves, in war or trade, which we cannot in faith consecrate a part of to God, who *hates robbery for burnt-offerings;* but, when God has remarkably preserved and prospered us, he expects that we should make some particular return of gratitude to him. As to this oblation, (1.) The captains offered it to *make an atonement for their souls, v.* 50. Instead of coming to Moses to demand a recompence for the good service they had done in *avenging the Lord of Midian,* or to set up trophies of their victory for the immortalizing of their own names, they bring an oblation to *make atonement for their souls,* being conscious to themselves, as the best men must be even in their best services, that they had been defective in their duty, not only in that instance for which they were reproved (*v.* 14), but in many others; *for there is not a just man upon the earth that doeth good and sinneth not.* (2.) Moses accepted it, and laid it up in the tabernacle *as a memorial for the children of Israel* (*v.* 54), that is, a monument of God's goodness to them, that they might be encouraged to trust in him in their further wars, and a monument of their gratitude to God (sacrifices are said to be memorials), that he, being well pleased with this thankful acknowledgment of favours bestowed, might continue and repeat his mercies to them.

CHAPTER 32

In this chapter we have, I. The humble request of the tribes of Reuben and Gad for an inheritance on that side Jordan where Israel now lay encamped (*v.* 1–5). II. Moses's misinterpretation of their request (*v.* 6–15). III. Their explication of it, and stating it aright (*v.* 16–19). IV. The grant of their petition under the provisos and limitations which they themselves proposed (*v.* 20, etc.).

Verses 1–15

Israel's tents were now pitched in the plains of Moab, where they continued many months, looking back upon the conquests they had already made of the land of Sihon and Og, and looking forward to Canaan, which they hoped in a little while to make themselves masters of. While they made this stand, and were at a pause, this great affair of the disposal of the conquests they had already made was here concerted and settled, not by any particular order or appointment of God, but at the special instance and request of two of the tribes, to which Moses, after a long debate that arose upon it, consented. For even *then,* when so much was done by the extraordinary appearances of divine Providence, many things were left to the direction of human prudence; for God, in governing both the world

and the church, makes use of the reason of men, and serves his own purposes by it.

I. Here is a motion made by the Reubenites and the Gadites, that the land which they had lately possessed themselves of, and which in the right of conquest belonged to Israel in common, might be assigned to them in particular for their inheritance: upon the general idea they had of the land of promise, they supposed this would be about their proportion. Reuben and Gad were encamped under the same standard, and so had the better opportunity of comparing notes, and settling this matter between themselves. In the first verse the children of Reuben are named first, but afterwards the children of Gad (*v.* 2, 25, 31), either because the Gadites made the first motion and were most forward for it, or because they were the better spokesmen and had more of the art of management, Reuben's tribe still lying under Jacob's sentence, *he shall not excel.* Two things common in the world induced these tribes to make this choice and this motion upon it, the *lust of the eye* and the *pride of life,* 1 Jn. 2:16. 1. The *lust of the eye.* This land which they coveted was not only beautiful for situation, and pleasant to the eye, but it was good for food, food for cattle; and they had a great multitude of cattle, above the rest of the tribes, it is supposed because they brought more out of Egypt, than the rest did; but that was forty years before, and stocks of cattle increase and decrease in less time than that; therefore I rather think they had been better husbands of their cattle in the wilderness, had tended them better, had taken more care of the breed, and not been so profuse as their neighbours in eating the *lambs out of the flock* and the *calves out of the midst of the stall.* Now they, having these large stocks, coveted land proportionable. Many scriptures speak of Bashan and Gilead as places famous for cattle; they had been so already, and therefore these tribes hoped they would be so to them, and whatever comes of it here they desire to take their lot. The judicious Calvin thinks there was much amiss in the principle they went upon, and that they consulted their own private convenience more than the public good, that they had not such regard to the honour and interest of Israel, and the promise made to Abraham of the land of Canaan (strictly so called), as they ought to have had. And still it is too true that many *seek their own things* more than the *things of Jesus Christ* (Phil. 2:21), and that many are influenced by their secular interest and advantage to take up short of the heavenly Canaan. Their spirits agree too well with this world, and with the things that are seen, that are temporal; and they say, "It is good to be here," and so lose what is hereafter for want of seeking it. Lot thus chose *by the sight of the eye,* and smarted for his choice. Would we choose our portion aright we must look above the things that are seen. 2. Perhaps there was something of the *pride of life* in it. Reuben was the first-born of Israel, but he had lost his birthright. Several of the tribes, and Judah especially, had risen above him, so that he could not expect the best lot in Canaan; and therefore, to save the shadow of a birthright, when he had forfeited the substance, he here catches at the first lot, though it was out of Canaan, and far off from the tabernacle. Thus Esau sold his birthright, and yet got to be served first with an inheritance in Mount Seir. The tribe of Gad descended from the first-born of Zilpah, and were like pretenders with the Reubenites; and Manasseh too was a first-born, but knew he must be eclipsed by Ephraim his younger brother, and therefore he also coveted to get precedency.

II. Moses's dislike of this motion, and the severe rebuke he gives to it, as a faithful prince and prophet.

1. It must be confessed that *prima facie — at first sight,* the thing looked ill, especially the closing words of their petition: *Bring us not over Jordan, v.* 5 (1.) It seems to proceed from a bad principle, a contempt of the land of promise, which Moses himself was so desirous of a sight of, a distrust too of the power of God to dispossess the Canaanites, as if a lot in a land which they knew, and which was already conquered, was more desirable than a lot in a land they knew not, and which was yet to be conquered: one bird in the hand is worth two in the bush. There seemed also to be covetousness in it; for that which they insisted on was that it was convenient for their cattle. It argued likewise a neglect of their brethren, as if they cared not what became of Israel, while they themselves were well provided for. (2.) It might have been of bad consequence.

The people might have taken improper hints from it, and have suggested that they were few enough, when they had their whole number, to deal with the Canaanites, but how unequal would the match be if they should drop two tribes and a half (above a fifth part of their strength) on this side Jordan. It would likewise be a bad precedent; if they must have the land thus granted them as soon as it was conquered, other tribes might make the same pretensions and claims, and so the regular disposition of the land by lot would be anticipated.

2. Moses is therefore very warm upon them, which is to be imputed to his pious zeal against sin, and not to any peevishness, the effect of old age, for his meekness abated not, any more than his natural force. (1.) He shows them what he apprehended to be evil in this motion, that it would discharge the heart of their brethren, *v.* 6, 7. "What!" (says he, with a holy indignation at their selfishness) *"shall your brethren go to war,* and expose themselves to all the hardships and hazards of the field, and *shall you sit here* at your ease? No, do not deceive yourselves, you shall never be indulged by me in this sloth and cowardice." It ill becomes any of God's Israel to sit down unconcerned in the difficult and perilous concernments of their brethren, whether public or personal. (2.) He reminds them of the fatal consequences of the unbelief and faintheartedness of their fathers, when they were just ready to enter Canaan, as they themselves now were. He recites the story very particularly (*v.* 8–13): *"Thus did your fathers,* whose punishment should be a warning to you to take heed of sinning after the similitude of their transgression." (3.) He gives them fair warning of the mischief that would be likely to follow upon this separation which they were about to make from the camp of Israel; they would be in danger of bringing wrath upon the whole congregation, and hurrying them all back again into the wilderness (*v.* 14, 15): *"You have risen up in your fathers' stead* to despise the pleasant land and reject it as they did, when we hoped you had risen up in their stead to possess it." It was an encouragement to Moses to see what an increase of men there was in these tribes, but a discouragement to see that it was withal an increase of sinful men, treading in the steps of their fathers' impiety. It is sad to see the rising generation in families and countries not only no better, but worse than that which went before it; and what comes of it? Why, *it augments the fierce anger of the Lord;* not only continues that fire, but increases it, and fills the measure, often till it overflows in a deluge of desolation. Note, If men did but consider as they ought, what would be the end of sin, they would be afraid of the beginnings of it.

Verses 16–27

We have here the accommodating of the matter between Moses and the two tribes, about their settlement on this side Jordan. Probably the petitioners withdrew, and considered with themselves what answer they should return to the severe reproof Moses had given them; and, after some consultation, they return with this proposal, that their men of war should go and assist their brethren in the conquest of Canaan, and they would leave their families and flocks behind them in this land: and thus they might have their request, and no harm would be done. Now it is uncertain whether they designed this at first when they brought their petition or no. If they did, it is an instance how often that which is honestly meant is unhappily misinterpreted; yet Moses herein was excusable, for he had reason to suspect the worst of them, and the rebuke he gave them was from the abundance of his care to prevent sin. But, if they did not, it is an instance of the good effect of plain dealing; Moses, by showing them their sin, and the danger of it, brought them to their duty without murmuring or disputing. They object not that their brethren were able to contend with the Canaanites without their help, especially since they were sure of God's fighting for them; but engage themselves to stand by them.

I. Their proposal is very fair and generous, and such as, instead of disheartening, would rather encourage their brethren. 1. That their *men of war,* who were fit for service, would go *ready armed before the children of Israel* into the land of Canaan. So far would they be from deserting them that, if it were thought fit, they would lead them on, and be foremost is all dangerous enterprises. So far were they from either distrusting or despising the conquest of Canaan that they would assist in it with the utmost readiness and resolution. 2. That they would leave behind them their families and cattle (which would otherwise be but the incumbrance of their camp), and so they would be the more serviceable to their brethren, *v.* 16. 3. That they would not return to their possessions till the conquest of Canaan was completed, *v.* 18. Their brethren should have their best help as long as they needed it. 4. That yet they would not expect any share of the land that was yet to be conquered (*v.* 19): *"We will not desire to inherit with them,* nor, under colour of assisting them in the war, put in for a share with them in the land; no, we will be content with our inheritance on this side Jordan, and there will be so much the more on yonder side for them."

II. Moses thereupon grants their request, upon consideration that they would adhere to their proposals. 1. He insists much upon it that they should never lay down their arms till their brethren laid down theirs. They promised to go armed *before the children of Israel, v.* 17. "Nay," says Moses, "you shall go armed *before the Lord, v.* 20, 21. It is God's cause more than your brethren's, and to him you must have an eye, and not to them only." *Before the Lord,* that is, before the ark of the Lord, the token of his presence, which, it should seem, they carried about with them in the wars of Canaan, and immediately before which these two tribes were posted, as we find in the order of their march, *ch.* 2:10, 17. 2. Upon this condition he grants them this land for their possession, and tells them they shall be *guiltless before the Lord and before Israel, v.* 22. They should have the land, and neither sin nor blame should cleave to it, neither sin before God nor blame before Israel; and, whatever possessions we have, it is desirable thus to come guiltless to them. But, 3. He warns them of the danger of breaking their word: "If you fail, you *sin against the Lord* (*v.* 23), and not against your brethren only, and *be sure your sin will find you out;"* that is, "God will certainly reckon with you for it, though you may make a light matter of it." Note, Sin will, without doubt, find out the sinner sooner or later. It concerns us therefore to find our sins out, that we may repent of them and forsake them, lest our sins find us out to our ruin and confusion.

III. They unanimously agree to the provisos and conditions of the grant, and do, as it were, give bond for performance, by a solemn promise: *Thy servants will do as my lord commandeth, v.* 25. Their brethren had all contributed their assistance to the conquest of this country, which they desired for a possession, and therefore they owned themselves obliged in justice to help them in the conquest of that which was to be their possession. Having received kindness, we ought to return it, though it was not so conditioned when we received it. We may suppose that this promise was understood, on both sides, so as not to oblige all that were numbered of these tribes to go over armed, but those only that were fittest for the expedition, who would be most serviceable, while it was necessary that some should be left to till the ground and guard the country; and accordingly we find that about 40,000 of the two tribes and a half went over armed (Jos. 4:13), whereas their whole number was about 100,000.

Verses 28–42

Here, 1. Moses settles this matter with Eleazar, and with Joshua who was to be his successor, knowing that he himself must not live to see it perfected, *v.* 28–30. He gives them an estate upon condition, leaving it to Joshua, if they fulfilled the condition, to declare the estate absolute: "If *they will not go over with you,"* he does not say "you shall give them no inheritance at all," but "you shall not give them this inheritance which they covet. if their militia will not come over with you, compel the whole tribes to come over, and let them take their lot with their brethren, and fare as they fare; *they shall have possessions in Canaan,* and let them not expect that the lot will favour them." Hereupon they repeat their promise to adhere to their brethren, *v.* 31, 32. 2. Moses settles them in the land they desired. He gave it to them for a possession, *v.* 33. Here is the first mention of the half tribe of Manasseh coming in with them for a share; probably they had not joined with them in the petition, but, the land when it came to be apportioned proving to be too much for them, this half tribe had a lot among them, perhaps at their request, or by divine direction, or because they had signalized themselves in the conquest of this country: for the children of Machir, a stout and warlike family, had taken Gilead and dispossessed the Amorites, *v.* 39. "Let them win it and wear it, get it and take it." And, they being celebrated for their courage and bravery, it was for the common safety to put them in this frontier-country. Concerning the settlement of these tribes observe, (1.) They built the cities, that is, repaired them, because either they had been damaged by the war or the Amorites had suffered them to go to decay. (2.) They changed the names of them (*v.* 38), either to show their authority, that the change of the names might signify the change of their owners, or because their names were idolatrous, and carried in them a respect to the dunghill-deities that were there worshipped. Nebo and Baal were names of their gods, which they were forbidden to make mention of (Ex. 23:13), and which, by changing the names of these cities, they endeavoured to bury in oblivion; and God promises to take away the names of Baalim out of the mouths of his people, Hos. 2:17.

Lastly, It is observable that, as these tribes were now first placed before the other tribes, so, long afterwards, they were displaced before the other tribes. We find that they were carried captive into Assyria some years before the other tribes, 2 Ki. 15:29. Such a proportion does Providence sometimes observe in balancing prosperity and adversity; he sets the one over-against the other.

CHAPTER 33

In this chapter we have, I. A particular account of the removals and encampments of the children of Israel, from their escape out of Egypt to their entrance into Canaan, forty-two in all, with some remarkable events that happened at some of those places (*v.* 1–49). II. A strict command given them to drive out all the inhabitants of the land of Canaan, which they were not going to conquer and take possession of (*v.* 50–56). So that the former part of the chapter looks back upon their march through the wilderness, the latter looks forward to their settlement in Canaan.

Verses 1–49

This is a review and brief rehearsal of the travels of the children of Israel through the wilderness. It was a memorable history and well worthy to be thus abridged, and the abridgment thus preserved, to the honour of God that led them and for the encouragement of the generations that followed. Observe here,

I. How the account was kept: *Moses wrote their goings out, v.* 2. When they began this tedious march, God ordered him to keep a journal or diary, and to insert in it all the remarkable occurrences of their way, that it might be a satisfaction to himself in the review and an instruction to others when it should be published. It may be of good use to private Christians, but especially to those in public stations, to preserve in writing an account of the providences of God concerning them, the constant series of mercies they have experienced, especially those turns and changes which have made some days of their lives more remarkable. Our memories are deceitful and need this help, that we may *remember all the way which the Lord our God has led us in this wilderness,* Deu. 8:2.

II. What the account itself was. It began with their departure out of Egypt, continued with their march through the wilderness, and ended in the plains of Moab, where they now lay encamped.

1. Some things are observed here concerning their departure out of Egypt, which they are reminded of upon all occasions, as a work of wonder never to be forgotten. (1.) That they *went forth with their armies* (*v.* 1), rank and file, as an army with banners. (2.) Under the hand of Moses and Aaron, their guides, overseers, and rulers, under God. (3.) *With a high hand,* because God's hand was high that wrought for them, *and in the sight of all the Egyptians, v.* 3. They did not steal away clandestinely (Isa. 52:12), but in defiance of their enemies, to whom God had made them such a burdensome stone that they neither could, nor would, nor durst, oppose them. (4.) They went forth while the Egyptians were burying, or at least preparing to bury, their first-born, *v.* 4. They had a mind good enough, or rather bad enough, still to have detained the Israelites their prisoners, but God found them other work to do. They would have God's first-born buried alive, but God set them a burying their own first-born. (5.) To all the plagues of Egypt it is added here that *on their gods also the Lord executed judgments.* Their idols which they worshipped, it is probable, were broken down, as Dagon after-

wards before the ark, so that they could not consult them about this great affair. To this perhaps there is reference, Isa. 19:1, *The idols of Egypt shall be moved at his presence.*

2. Concerning their travels towards Canaan. Observe, (1.) They were continually upon the remove. When they had pitched a little while in one place they departed from that to another. Such is our state in this world; we have here no continuing city. (2.) Most of their way lay through a wilderness, uninhabited, untracked, unfurnished even with the necessaries of human life, which magnifies the wisdom and power of God, by whose wonderful conduct and bounty the thousands of Israel not only subsisted for forty years in that desolate place, but came out at least as numerous and vigorous as they went in. At first they pitched *in the edge of the wilderness* (v. 6), but afterwards in the heart of it; by less difficulties God prepares his people for greater. We find them in the wilderness of Etham (v. 8), of Sin (v. 11), of Sinai, v. 15. Our removals in this world are but from one wilderness to another. (3.) They were led to and fro, forward and backward, as in a maze or labyrinth, and yet were all the while under the direction of the pillar of cloud and fire. He led them about (Deu. 32:10), and yet led them the right way, Ps. 107:7. The way which God takes in bringing his people to himself is always the best way, though it does not always seem to us the nearest way. (4.) Some events are mentioned in this journal, as their want of water at Rephidim (v. 14), the death of Aaron (v. 38, 39), the insult of Arad (v. 40); and the very name of *Kibroth-hattaavah — the graves of lusts* (v. 16), has a story depending upon it. Thus we ought to keep in mind the providences of God concerning us and our families, us and our land, and the many instances of that divine care which has led us, and fed us, and kept us, all our days hitherto. Shittim, the place where the people sinned in the matter of Peor (ch. 25:1), is here called *Abel-shittim. Abel* signifies *mourning* (as Gen. 50:11), and probably this place was so called from the mourning of the good people of Israel on account of that sin and of God's wrath against them for it. It was so great a mourning that it gave a name to the place.

Verses 50–56

While the children of Israel were in the wilderness their total separation from all other people kept them out of the way of temptation to idolatry, and perhaps this was one thing intended by their long confinement in the wilderness, that thereby the idols of Egypt might be forgotten, and the people aired (as it were) and purified from that infection, and the generation that entered Canaan might be such as never knew those depths of Satan. But now that they were to pass over Jordan they were entering again into that temptation, and therefore, 1. They are here strictly charged utterly to destroy all remnants of idolatry. They must not only *drive out the inhabitants of the land,* that they may possess their country, but they must deface all their idolatrous pictures and images, and *pull down all their high places,* v. 52. They must not preserve any of them, no, not as monuments of antiquity to gratify the curious, nor as ornaments of their houses, nor toys for their children to play with, but they must destroy all, both in token of their abhorrence and detestation of idolatry and to prevent their being tempted to worship those images, and the false gods represented by them, or to worship the God of Israel by such images or representations. 2. They were assured that, if they did so, God would by degrees put them in full possession of the land of promise, v. 53, 54. If they would keep themselves pure from the idols of Canaan, God would enrich them with the wealth of Canaan. Learn not their way, and then fear not their power. 3. They were threatened that, if they spared either the idols or the idolaters, they should be beaten with their own rod and their sin would certainly be their punishment. (1.) They would foster snakes in their own bosoms, v. 55. The remnant of the Canaanites, if they made any league with them, though it were but a cessation of arms, would be *pricks in their eyes and thorns in their sides,* that is, they would be upon all occasions vexatious to them, insulting them, robbing them, and, to the utmost of their power, making mischief among them. We must expect trouble and affliction from that, whatever it is, which we sinfully indulge; that which we are willing should tempt us we shall find will vex us. (2.) The righteous God would turn that wheel

upon the Israelites which was to have crushed the Canaanites: *I shall do to you as I thought to do unto them,* v. 56. It was intended that the Canaanites should be dispossessed; but if the Israelites fell in with them, and learned their way, they should be dispossessed, for God's displeasure would justly be greater against them than against the Canaanites themselves. Let us hear this, and fear. If we do not drive sin out, sin will drive us out; if we be not the death of our lusts, our lusts will be the death of our souls.

CHAPTER 34

In this chapter God directs Moses, and he is to direct Israel, I. Concerning the bounds and borders of the land of Canaan (v. 1–15). II. Concerning the division and distribution of it to the tribes of Israel (v. 16, etc.).

Verses 1–15

We have here a particular draught of the line by which the land of Canaan was meted, and bounded, on all sides. God directs Moses to settle it here, not as a geographer in his map, merely to please the curious, but as a prince in his grant, that it may be certainly known what passes, and is conveyed, by the grant. There was a much larger possession promised them, which in due time they would have possessed if they had been obedient, reaching even to the river Euphrates, Deu. 11:24. And even so far the dominion of Israel did extend in David's time and Solomon's, 2 Chr. 9:26. But this which is here described is Canaan only, which was the lot of the nine tribes and a half, for the other two and a half were already settled, v. 14, 15. Now concerning the limits of Canaan observe,

I. That it was limited within certain bounds: for God *appoints the bounds of our habitation,* Acts 17:26. The borders are set them, 1. That they might know whom they were to dispossess, and how far the commission which was given them extended (ch. 33:53), that they should *drive out the inhabitants.* Those that lay within these borders, and those only, they must destroy; hitherto their bloody sword must go, and no further. 2. That they might know what to expect the possession of themselves. God would not have his people to enlarge their desire of worldly possessions, but to know when they have enough, and to rest satisfied with it. The Israelites themselves must not be *placed alone in the midst of the earth,* but must leave room for their neighbours to live by them. God sets bounds to our lot; let us then set bounds to our desires, and bring our mind to our condition.

II. That it lay comparatively in a very little compass: as it is here bounded, it is reckoned to be but about 160 miles in length and about fifty in breadth; perhaps it did not contain more than half as much ground as England, and yet this is the country which was promised to the father of the faithful and was the possession of the seed of Israel. This was that little spot of ground in which only, for many ages, *God was known, and his name was great,* Ps. 76:1. This was the vineyard of the Lord, the garden enclosed; but, as it is with gardens and vineyards, the narrowness of the extent was abundantly compensated by the extraordinary fruitfulness of the soil, otherwise it could not have subsisted so numerous a nation as did inhabit it. See here then, 1. How small a part of the world God has for himself. Though the *earth is his, and the fullness thereof,* yet few have the knowledge of him and serve him; but those few are happy, very happy, because fruitful to God. 2. How small a share of the world God often gives to his own people. Those that have their portion in heaven have reason to be content with a small pittance of this earth; but, as here, what is wanting in quantity is made up in quality; *a little that a righteous man has,* having it from the love of God and with his blessing, is far better and more comfortable *than the riches of many wicked,* Ps. 37:16.

III. It is observable what the bounds and limits of it were. 1. Canaan was itself a *pleasant land* (so it is called Dan. 8:9), and yet it bordered upon wilderness and seas, and was surrounded with divers melancholy prospects. Thus the vineyard of the church is compassed on all hands with the desert of this world, which serves as a foil to it, to make it appear the more beautiful for situation. 2. Many of its borders were its defences and natural fortifications, to render the access of enemies the more difficult, and to intimate to Israel that the God of nature was their protector, and with his favour would *compass them as with a shield.* 3. The border reached to the *river of Egypt* (v. 5), that the

sight of that country which they could look into out of their own might remind them of their bondage there, and their wonderful deliverance thence. 4. Their border is here made to begin at the *Salt Sea* (v. 3), and there it ends, v. 12. This was the remaining lasting monument of the destruction of Sodom and Gomorrah. That pleasant fruitful vale in which these cities stood became a lake, which was never stirred by any wind, bore no vessels, was replenished with no fish, no living creature of any sort being found in it, therefore called the *Dead Sea.* This was part of their border, that it might be a constant warning to them to take heed of those sins which had been the ruin of Sodom; yet the iniquity of Sodom was afterwards found in Israel (Eze. 16:49), for which Canaan was made, though not a salt sea as Sodom, yet a barren soil, and continues so to this day. 5. Their western border was the *Great Sea* (v. 6), which is now called the *Mediterranean.* Some consider this sea itself to have been a part of their possession, and that by virtue of this grant, they had the dominion of it, and, if they had not forfeited it by sin, might have rode masters of it.

Verses 16–29

God here appoints commissioners for the dividing of the land to them. The conquest of it is taken for granted, though as yet there was never a stroke struck towards it. Here is no nomination of the generals and commanders-in-chief that should carry on the war; for they were to get the land in possession, *not by their own sword or bow, but by the power and favour of God;* and so confident must they be of victory and success while God fought for them that the persons must now be named who should be entrusted with the dividing of the land, that is, who should preside in casting the lots, and determine controversies that might arise, and see that all was done fairly. 1. The principal commissioners, who were of the *quorum,* were Eleazar and Joshua (v. 17), typifying Christ, who, as priest and king, divides the heavenly Canaan to the spiritual Israel; yet, as they were to go by the lot, so Christ acknowledges the disposal must be by the will of the Father, Mt. 20:23. Compare, Eph. 1:11. 2. Besides these, that there might be no suspicion of partiality, a prince of each tribe was appointed to inspect this matter, and to see that the tribe he served for was in no respect injured. Public affairs should be so managed as not only to give their right to all, but, if possible, to give satisfaction to all that they have justice done them., It is a happiness to a land to have the princes of their people meet together, some out of every tribe, to concert the affairs that are of common concern, a constitution which is the abundant honour, ease, and safety, of the nation that is blessed with it. 3. Some observe that the order of the tribes here very much differs from that in which they hitherto, upon all occasions, been named, and agrees with the neighbourhood of their lots in the division of the land. Judah, Simeon, and Benjamin, the first three here named, lay close together; the inheritance of Dan lay next them on one side, that of Ephraim and Manasseh on another side; Zebulun and Issachar lay abreast more northerly, and, lastly, Asher and Naphtali most northward of all, as is easy to observe in looking over a map of Canaan; this (says bishop Patrick) is an evidence that Moses was guided by a divine Spirit in his writings. Known unto God are all his works beforehand, and what is new and surprising to us he perfectly foresaw, without any confusion or uncertainty.

CHAPTER 35

Orders having been given before for the dividing of the land of Canaan among the lay-tribes (as I may call them), care is here taken for a competent provision for the clergy, the tribe of Levi, which ministered in holy things. I. Forty-eight cities were to be assigned them, with their suburbs, some in every tribe (v. 1–8). II. Six cities out of these were to be for cities of refuge, for any man that killed another unawares (v. 9–15). In the law concerning these observe, 1. In what case sanctuary was not allowed, namely, that of wilful murder (v. 16–21). 2. In what cases it was allowed (v. 22–24). 3. What was the law concerning those that took shelter in these cities of refuge (v. 25, etc.).

Verses 1–8

The laws about the tithes and offerings had provided very plentifully for the maintenance of the Levites, but it was not to be thought, nor indeed was it for the public good, that when they came to Canaan they should all live about the tabernacle, as they had done in the wilderness, and therefore care must be taken to provide habitations for them, in which they might live comfortably and usefully. It is this which is here taken care of.

I. Cities were allotted them, with their suburbs, *v.* 2. They were not to have any ground for tillage; they needed not to *sow, nor reap, nor gather into barns,* for their heavenly Father fed them with the tithe of the increase of other people's labours, that they might the more closely attend to the study of the law, and might have more leisure to teach the people; for they were not fed thus easily that they might live in idleness, but that they might give themselves wholly to the business of their profession, and not be entangled in the affairs of this life. 1. Cities were allotted them, that they might live near together, and converse with one another about the law, to their mutual edification; and that in doubtful cases they might consult one another, and in all cases strengthen one another's hands. 2. These cities had suburbs annexed to them for their cattle (*v.* 3), a thousand cubits from the wall was allowed them for out-houses to keep their cattle in, and then two thousand more for fields to graze their cattle in, *v.* 4, 5. Thus was care taken that they should not only live, but live plentifully, and have all desirable conveniences about them, that they might not be looked upon with contempt by their neighbours.

II. These cities were to be assigned them out of the possessions of each tribe, *v.* 8. 1. That each tribe might thus make a grateful acknowledgment to God out of their real as well as out of their personal estates (for what was given to the Levites was accepted as given to the Lord) and thus their possessions were sanctified to them. 2. That each tribe might have the benefit of the Levites' dwelling among them, to *teach them the good knowledge of the Lord;* thus that light was diffused through all parts of the country, and none were left to sit in darkness, Deu. 33:10, *They shall teach Jacob thy judgments.* Jacob's curse on Levi's anger was, *I will scatter them in Israel,* Gen. 49:7. But that curse was turned into a blessing, and the Levites, by being thus scattered, were put into a capacity of doing so much the more good. It is a great mercy to a country to be replenished in all parts with faithful ministers.

III. The number allotted them was forty-eight in all, four out of each of the twelve tribes, one with another. Out of the united tribes of Simeon and Judah nine, out of Naphtali three, and four apiece out of the rest, as appears, Jos. 21. Thus were they blessed with a good ministry, and that ministry with a comfortable maintenance, not only in tithes, but in glebe-lands. And, though the gospel is not so particular as the law was in this matter, yet it expressly provides that he that is *taught in the word* should *communicate unto him that teaches in all good things,* Gal. 6:6.

Verses 9–34

We have here the orders given concerning the cities of refuge, fitly annexed to what goes before, because they were all Levites' cities. In this part of the constitution there is a great deal both of good law and pure gospel.

I. Here is a great deal of good law, in the case of murder and manslaughter, a case of which the laws of all nations have taken particular cognizance. It is here enacted and provided, consonant to natural equity,

1. That wilful murder should be punished with death, and in that case no sanctuary should be allowed, no ransom taken, nor any commutation of the punishment accepted: The *murderer shall surely be put to death, v.* 16. It is supposed to be done *of hatred* (*v.* 20), or *in enmity* (*v.* 21), upon a sudden provocation (for our Saviour makes rash anger, as well as malice prepense, to be murder, Mt. 5:21, 22), whether the person be murdered with an instrument of iron (*v.* 16) or wood (*v.* 18), or with a stone thrown at him (*v.* 17, 20); nay, if he smite him with his hand in enmity, and death ensue, it is murder (*v.* 21); and it was an ancient law, consonant to the law of nature, that *whoso sheds man's blood, by man shall his blood be shed,* Gen. 9:6. Where wrong has been done restitution must be made; and, since the murderer cannot restore the life he has wrongfully taken away, his own must be exacted from him in lieu of it, not (as some have fancied) to satisfy the manes or ghost of the person slain, but to satisfy the law and the justice of a nation; and to be a warning to all others not to do likewise. It is here said, and it is well worthy the consideration of all princes and states, *that blood defiles* not only the conscience of the murderer, who is thereby proved *not to have eternal life abiding in him* (1 Jn. 3:15), but also the land in which it is shed; so very offensive is it to God and all good men, and the worst of nuisances. And it is added that *the land cannot be cleansed* from the blood of the murdered, but by the blood of the murderer, *v.* 33. If murderers escape punishment from men, those that suffer them to escape will have a great deal to answer for, and God will nevertheless not suffer them to escape his righteous judgments. Upon the same principle it is provided that no satisfaction should be taken for the *life of a murderer* (*v.* 31): *If a man would give all the substance of his house* to the judges, to the country, or to the avenger of blood, to atone for his crime, it must *utterly be contemned.* The redemption of the life is so precious that it cannot be obtained by the *multitude of riches* (Ps. 49:6–8), which perhaps may allude to this law. A rule of law comes in here (which is a rule of our law in cases of treason only) that no man shall be put to death upon the testimony of one witness, but it was necessary there should be two (*v.* 30); this law is settled in all capital cases, Deu. 17:6; 19:15. And, *lastly,* not only the prosecution, but the execution, of the murderer, is committed to the next of kin, who, as he was to be the redeemer of his kinsman's estate if it were mortgaged, so he was to be the *avenger of his blood if he were murdered* (*v.* 19): *The avenger of blood himself shall slay the murderer,* if he be convicted by the *notorious evidence of the fact,* and he needed not to have recourse by a judicial process to the court of judgment. But if it were uncertain who the murderer was, and the proof doubtful, we cannot think that his bare suspicion, or surmise, would empower him to do that which the judges themselves could not do but upon the testimony of two witnesses. Only if the fact were plain then the next heir of the person slain might himself, in a just indignation, slay the murderer wherever he met him. Some think this must be understood to be after the lawful judgment of the magistrate, and so the Chaldee says, "He shall slay him, *when he shall be condemned unto him by judgment;*" but it should seem, by *v.* 24, that the judges interposed only in a doubtful case, and that if the person on whom he took vengeance was indeed the murderer, and a wilful murderer, the avenger was innocent (*v.* 27), only, if it proved otherwise, it was at his peril. Our law allows an appeal to be brought against a murderer by the widow, or next heir, of the person murdered, yea, though the murderer have been acquitted upon an indictment; and, if the murderer be found guilty upon that appeal, execution shall be awarded at the suit of the appellant, who may properly be called *the avenger of blood.*

2. But if the homicide was not voluntary, nor done designedly, if it was *without enmity, or lying in wait* (*v.* 22), not *seeing* the person or not *seeking his harm* (*v.* 23), which our law calls chance-medley, or homicide *per infortunium — through misfortune,* in this case there were cities of refuge appointed for the manslayer to flee to. By our law this incurs a forfeiture of goods, but a pardon is granted of course upon the special matter found. Concerning the cities of refuge the law was, (1.) That, if a man killed another, in these cities he was safe, and under the protection of the law, till he had his trial *before the congregation,* that is, before the judges in open court. If he neglected thus to surrender himself, it was at his peril; if the avenger of blood met him elsewhere, or overtook him loitering in his way to the city of refuge, and slew him, his blood was upon his own head, because he did not make use of the security which God had provided for him. (2.) If, upon trial, it were found to be willful murder, the city of refuge should no longer be a protection to him; it was already determined: *Thou shalt take him from my altar, that he may die,* Ex. 21:14. (3.) But if it were found to be by error or accident, and that the stroke was given without any design upon the life of the person slain or any other, then the man-slayer should continue safe in *the city of refuge,* and the avenger of blood might not meddle with him, *v.* 25. There he was to remain in banishment from his own house and patrimony *till the death of the high priest;* and, if at any time he went out of that city or the suburbs of it, he put himself out of the protection of the law, and the avenger of blood, if he met him, might slay him, *v.* 26–28. Now, [1.] By the preservation of the life of the man-slayer God would teach us that men ought not to suffer for that which is rather their unhappiness than their crime, rather the act of Providence than their own act, for *God delivered him into his hand,* Ex. 21:13. [2.] By the banishment of the man-slayer from his own city, and his confinement to the city of refuge, where he was in a manner a prisoner, God would teach us to conceive a dread and horror of the guilt of blood, and to be very careful of life, and always afraid lest by oversight or negligence we occasion the death of any. [3.] By the limiting of the time of the offender's banishment to the death of the high priest, an honour was put upon that sacred office. The high priest was to be looked upon as so great a blessing to his country that when he died their sorrow upon that occasion should swallow up all other resentments. The cities of refuge being all of them Levites' cities, and the high priest being the head of that tribe, and consequently having a peculiar dominion over these cites, those that were confined to them might properly be looked upon as his prisoners, and so his death must be their discharge; it was, as it were, at his suit that the delinquent was imprisoned, and therefore at his death it fell. *Actio moritur cum persona — The suit expires with the party.* Anisworth has another notion of it, That as the high priests, while they lived, by their service and sacrificing made atonement for sin, wherein they prefigured Christ's satisfaction, so, at their death, those were released that had been exiled for casual murder, which typified redemption in Israel. [4.] By the abandoning of the prisoner to the avenger of blood, in case he at any time went out of the limits of the city of refuge, they were taught to adhere to the methods which Infinite Wisdom prescribed for their security. It was for the honour of a remedial law that it should be so strictly observed. How can we expect to be saved if we neglect the salvation, which is indeed a great salvation!

II. Here is a great deal of good gospel couched under the type and figure of the cities of refuge; and to them the apostle seems to allude when he speaks of our *fleeing for refuge to the hope set before is* (Heb. 6:18), and being *found in Christ,* Phil. 3:9. We never read in the history of the Old Testament of any use made of these cities of refuge, any more than of other such institutions, which yet, no doubt, were made use of upon the occasions intended; only we read of those that, in dangerous cases, took hold of *the horns of the altar* (1 Ki. 1:50; 2:28); for the altar, wherever that stood, was, as it were the capital *city of refuge.* But the law concerning these cities was designed both to raise and to encourage the expectations of those who looked for redemption in Israel, which should be to those who were convinced of sin, and in terror by reason of it, as the cities of refuge were to the man-slayer. Observe, 1. There were several cities of refuge, and they were so appointed in several parts of the country that the man-slayer, wherever he dwelt in the land of Israel, might in half a day reach one or other of them; so, though there is but one Christ appointed for our refuge, yet, wherever we are, he is a refuge at hand, a very present help, for *the word is nigh us* and Christ in the word. 2. The man-slayer was safe in any of these cities; so in Christ believers that flee to him, and rest in him, are protected from the wrath of God and the curse of the law. *There is no condemnation to those that are in Christ Jesus,* Rom. 8:1. Who shall condemn those that are thus sheltered? 3. They were all Levites' cities; it was a kindness to the poor prisoner that though he might not go up to the place where the ark was, yet he was in the midst of Levites, who would teach him the good knowledge of the Lord, and instruct him how to improve the providence he was now under. It might also be expected that the Levites would comfort and encourage him, and bid him welcome; so it is the work of gospel ministers to bid poor sinners welcome to Christ, and to assist and counsel those that through grace are in him. 4. Even strangers and sojourners, though they were not native Israelites, might take the benefit of these cities of refuge, *v.* 15. So in Christ Jesus no difference in made between Greek and Jew; even the *sons of the stranger* that by faith flee to Christ shall be safe in him. 5. Even the suburbs or borders of the city were a sufficient security to the offender, *v.* 26, 27. So there is virtue even in the hem of Christ's garment for the healing and saving of poor sinners. If we cannot reach to a full assurance, we may comfort ourselves in a good hope through grace. 6. The protection which the man-slayer found in the city of refuge was not owing to the strength of its walls, or gates, or bars, but purely to the divine appointment; so it is the word of the gospel that gives souls safety in Christ, *for him hath God the Father sealed.* 7. If the offender was ever caught struggling out of the borders of his city of refuge, or stealing home to his house again, he lost the benefit of his protection, and lay exposed to the avenger of blood; so those that are in Christ must abide in Christ, for it is at their peril if they forsake him and wander from him. *Drawing back is to perdition.*

CHAPTER 36

We have in this chapter the determination of another question that arose upon the case of the daughters of Zelophehad. God had appointed that they should inherit, *ch.* 27:7. Now here, I. An inconvenience is suggested, in case they should marry into any other tribe (*v.* 1–4). II. It is prevented by a divine appointment that they should marry in their own tribe and family (*v.* 5–7), and this is settled for a rule in like cases (*v.* 8, 9); and they did marry accordingly to some of their own relations (*v.* 10–12), and with this the book concludes (*v.* 13).

Verses 1–4

We have here the humble address which the heads of the tribe of Manasseh made to Moses and the princes, on occasion of the order lately made concerning the daughters of Zelophehad. The family they belonged to was part of that half of the tribe of Manasseh which we yet to have their lot within Jordan, not that half that was already settled; and yet they speak of the land of their possession, and the inheritance of their fathers, with as great assurance as if they had it already in their hands, knowing whom they had trusted. In their appeal observe, 1. They fairly recite the former order made in this case, and do not move to have that set aside, but are very willing to acquiesce in it (*v.* 2): *The Lord commanded to give the inheritance of Zelophehad to his daughters;* and they are very well pleased that it should be so, none of them knowing but that hereafter it might be the case of their own families, and then their daughters would have the benefit of this law. 2. They represent the inconvenience which might, possibly, follow hereupon, if the daughters of Zelophehad should see cause to marry into any other tribes, *v.* 3. And it is probable that this was not a bare surmise, or supposition, but that they knew, at this time, great court was made to them by some young gentlemen of other tribes, because they were heiresses, that they might get footing in this tribe, and so enlarge their own inheritance. This truly is often aimed at more than it should be in making marriages, not the meetness of the person, but the convenience of the estate, to *lay house to house, and field to field. Wisdom indeed is good with an inheritance;* but what is an inheritance good for in that relation without wisdom? But here, we may presume, the personal merit of these daughters recommended them as well as their fortunes; however, the heads of their tribe foresaw the mischief that would follow, and brought the case to Moses, that he might consult the oracle of God concerning it. The difficulty they start God could have obviated and provided against in the former order given in this case; but to teach us that we must, in our affairs, not only attend God's providence, but make use of our own prudence, God did not direct in it till the themselves that were concerned wisely foresaw the inconvenience, and piously applied to Moses for a rule in it. For though they were chief fathers in their families, and might have assumed a power to overrule these daughters of Zelophehad in disposing of themselves, especially their father being dead and the common interest of their tribe being concerned in it, yet they chose rather to refer the matter to Moses, and it issued well. We should not covet to be judges in our own case, for it is difficult to be so without being partial. It is easier in many cases to take good advice than to give it, and it is a satisfaction to be under direction. Two things they aimed at in their representation: — (1.) To preserve the divine appointment of inheritances. They urged the command (*v.* 2), that the land should be given by lot to the respective tribes, and urged that it would break in upon the divine appointment if such a considerable part of the lot of Manasseh should, by their marriage, be transferred to any other tribe; for the issue would be denominated from the father's tribe, not the mother's. This indeed would not lessen the lot of the particular persons of that tribe (they would have their own still), but it would lessen the lot of the tribe in general, and render it less strong and considerable; they therefore thought themselves concerned for the reputation of their tribe, and perhaps were the more jealous for it because it was already very much weakened by the sitting down of the one half of it on this side Jordan. (2.) To prevent contests and quarrels among posterity. If those of other tribes should come among them perhaps it might occasion some contests. They would be apt to give and receive disturbance, and their title might, in process of time, come to be questioned; and how great a matter would this fire kindle! It is the wisdom and duty of those that have estates in the world to settle them, and dispose of them, so as that no strife and contention may arise about them among posterity.

Verses 5–13

Here is, I. The matter settled by express order from God between the daughters of Zelophehad and the rest of the tribe of Manasseh. The petition is assented to, and care taken to prevent the inconvenience feared: *The tribe of the sons of Joseph hath said well, v.* 5. Thus those that consult the oracles of God concerning the making of their heavenly inheritance sure shall not only be directed what to do, but their enquiries shall be graciously accepted, and they shall have not only their *well done,* but their *well said,* good and faithful servant. Now the matter is thus accommodated: these heiresses must be obliged to marry, not only within their own tribe of Manasseh, but within the particular family of the Hepherites, to which they did belong. 1. They are not determined to any particular persons; there was choice enough in the family of their father: *Let them marry to whom they think best.* As children must preserve the authority of their parents, and not marry against their minds, so parents must consult the affections of their children in disposing of them, and not compel them to marry such as they cannot love. Forced marriages are not likely to prove blessings. 2. Yet they are confined to their own relations, that their inheritance may not go to another family. God would have them know that the land being to be divided by lot, the disposal whereof was of the Lord, they could not mend, and therefore should not alter, his appointment. The inheritances must not *remove from tribe to tribe* (*v.* 7), lest there should be confusion among them, their estates entangled, and their genealogies perplexed. God would not have one tribe to be enriched by the straitening and impoverishing of another, since they were all alike the seed of Abraham his friend.

II. The law, in this particular case, was made perpetual, and to be observed whenever hereafter the like case should happen, *v.* 8. Those that were not heiresses might marry into what tribe they pleased (though we may suppose that, ordinarily, they kept within their own tribe), but those that were must either quit their claim to the inheritance or marry one of their own family, that each of the tribes might keep to its own inheritance, and one tribe might not encroach upon another, but throughout their generations there might remain immovable the ancient landmarks, set, not by their fathers, but by the *God of their fathers.*

III. The submission of the daughters of Zelophehad to this appointment. How could they but marry well, and to their satisfaction, when God himself directed them? They married their father's brothers' sons, *v.* 10–12. By this it appears, 1. That the marriage of cousin-germans is not in itself unlawful, nor within the degrees prohibited, for then God would not have countenanced these marriages. But, 2. That ordinarily it is not advisable; for, if there had not been a particular reason for it (which cannot hold in any case now, inheritances being not disposed of as then by the special designation of Heaven), they would not have married such near relations. The world is wide, and he that walks uprightly will endeavour to walk surely.

IV. The conclusion of this whole book, referring to the latter part of it: *These are the judgments which the Lord commanded in the plains of Moab* (*v.* 13), these foregoing, ever since *ch.* 26, most of which related to their settlement in Canaan, into which they were now entering. Whatever new condition God is by his providence bringing us into, we must beg of him to teach us the duty of it, and to enable us to do it, that we may do the work of the day in its day, of the place in its place.

AN EXPOSITION, WITH PRACTICAL OBSERVATIONS, OF

THE FIFTH BOOK OF MOSES, CALLED DEUTERONOMY

This book is a repetition of very much both of the history and of the laws contained in the three foregoing books, which repetition Moses delivered to Israel (both by word of mouth, that it might affect, and by writing, that it might abide) a little before his death. There is no new history in it but that of the death of Moses in the last chapter, nor any new revelation to Moses, for aught that appears, and therefore the style here is not, as before, *The Lord spoke unto Moses, saying.* But the former laws are repeated and commented upon, explained and enlarged, and some particular precepts added to them, with copius reasonings for the enforcing of them: in this Moses was divinely inspired and assisted, so that this is as truly the word of the Lord by Moses as that which was spoken to him with an audible voice *out of the tabernacle of the congregation,* Lev. 1:1. The Greek interpreters call it *Deuteronomy,* which signifies the *second law,* or a *second edition of the law,* not with amendments, for there needed none, but with additions, for the further direction of the people in divers cases not mentioned before. Now, I. It was much for the honour of the divine law that it should be thus repeated; how great were the things of that law which was thus inculcated, and how inexcusable would those be by whom they were *counted as a strange thing!* Hos. 8:12. II. There might be a particular reason for the repeating of it now; the men of that generation to which the law was first given were all dead, and a new generation had sprung up, to whom God would have it repeated by Moses himself, that, if possible, it might make a lasting impression upon them. Now that they were just going to take possession of the land of Canaan, Moses must read the articles of agreement to them, that they might know upon what terms and conditions they were to hold and enjoy that land, and might understand that they were upon their good behaviour in it. III. It would be of great use to the people to have those parts of the law thus gathered up and put together which did more immediately concern them and their practice; for the laws which concerned the priests and Levites, and the execution of their offices, are not repeated: it was enough for them that they were once delivered. But, in compassion to the infirmities of the people, the laws of more common concern are delivered a second time. *Precept must be upon precept, and line upon line,* Isa. 28:10. The great and needful truths of the gospel should be often pressed upon people by the ministers of Christ. *To write the same things* (says Paul, Phil. 3:1) *to me indeed is not grievous, but for you it is safe.* What God has spoken once we have need to hear twice, to hear many times, and it is well if, after all, it be duly perceived and regarded. In three ways this book of Deuteronomy was magnified and made honourable: — 1. The king was to write a copy of it with his own hand, and to read therein all the days of his life, *ch.* 17, 18, 19. 2. It was to be written upon great stones plastered, at their passing over Jordan, *ch.* 27:2, 3. 3. It was to be read publicly every seventh year, at the feast of tabernacles, by the priests, in the audience of all Israel, *ch.* 31:9, etc. The gospel is a kind of Deuteronomy, a second law, a remedial law, a spiritual law, a law of faith; by it we are under the law of Christ, and it is a law that *makes the comers thereunto perfect.*

This book of Deuteronomy begins with a brief rehearsal of the most remarkable events that had befallen the Israelites since they came from Mount Sinai. In the fourth chapter we have a most pathetic exhortation to obedience. In the twelfth chapter, and so on to the twenty-seventh, are repeated many particular laws, which are enforced (*ch.* 27 and 28) with promises and threatenings, blessings and curses, formed into a covenant, *ch.* 29 and 30. Care is taken to perpetuate the remembrance of these things among them (*ch.* 31), particularly by a song (*ch.* 32), and so Moses concludes with a blessing, *ch.* 33. All this was delivered by Moses to Israel in the last month of his life. The whole book contains the history but of two months; compare *ch.* 1:3 with Jos. 4:19, the latter of which was the thirty days of Israel's mourning for Moses; see how busy that great and good man was to do good when he knew that his time was short, how quick his motion when he drew near his rest. Thus we have more recorded of what our blessed Saviour said and did in the last week of his life than in any other. The last words of eminent persons make or should make deep impressions. Observe, for the honour of this book, that when our Saviour would answer the devil's temptations with, *It is written,* he fetched all his quotations out of this book, Mt. 4:4, 7, 10.

CHAPTER 1

The first part of Moses's farewell sermon to Israel begins with this chapter, and is continued to the latter end of the fourth chapter. In the first five verses of this chapter we have the date of the sermon, the place where it was preached (*v.* 1, 2, 5), and the time when (*v.* 3, 4). The narrative in this chapter reminds them, I. Of the promise God made them of the land of Canaan (*v.* 6–8). II. Of the provision made of judges for them (*v.* 9–18). III. Of their unbelief and murmuring upon the report of the spies (*v.* 19–33). IV. Of the sentence passed upon them for it, and the ratification of that sentence (*v.* 34, etc.).

Verses 1–8

We have here, I. The date of this sermon which Moses preached to the people of Israel. A great auditory, no question, he had, as many as could crowd within hearing, and particularly all the elders and officers, the representatives of the people; and, probably, it was on the sabbath day that he delivered this to them. 1. The place were they were now encamped was *in the plain, in the land of Moab* (*v.* 1, 5), where they were just ready to enter Canaan, and engage in a war with the Canaanites. Yet he discourses not to them concerning military affairs, the arts and stratagems of war, but concerning their duty to God; for, if they kept themselves in his fear and favour, he would secure to them the conquest of the land: their religion would be their best policy. 2. The time was near the end of the fortieth year since they came out of Egypt. So long God had *borne their manners,* and they had *borne their own iniquity* (Num. 14:34), and now that a new and more pleasant scene was to be introduced, as a token for good, Moses repeats the law to them. Thus, after God's controversy with them on account of the golden calf, the first and surest sign of God's being reconciled to them was the *renewing of the tables.* There is no better evidence and earnest of God's favour than his putting his law in our hearts, Ps. 147:19, 20.

II. The discourse itself. In general, Moses spoke unto them *all that the Lord had given him in commandment* (*v.* 3), which intimates, not only that what he now delivered was for substance the same with what had formerly been commanded, but that it was what God now commanded him to repeat. He gave them this rehearsal and exhortation purely by divine direction; God appointed him to leave this legacy to the church. He begins his narrative with their removal from Mount Sinai (*v.* 6), and relates here, 1. The orders which God gave them to decamp, and proceed in their march (*v.* 6, 7): *You have dwelt long enough in this mount.* This was the mount *that burned with fire* (Heb. 12:18), and *gendered to bandage,* Gal. 4:24. Thither God brought them to humble them, and by the terrors of the law to prepare them for the land of promise. There he kept them about a year, and then told them they had *dwelt long enough* there, they must go forward. Though God brings his people into trouble and affliction, into spiritual trouble and affliction of mind, he knows when they have dwelt long enough in it, and will certainly find a time, the fittest time, to advance them from the terrors of the spirit of adoption. See Rom. 8:15. 2. The prospect which he gave them of a happy and early settlement in Canaan: *Go to the land of the Canaanites* (*v.* 7); enter and take possession, it is all your own. *Behold I have set the land before you, v.* 8. When God commands us to go forward in our Christian course he sets the heavenly Canaan before us for our encouragement.

Verses 9–18

Moses here reminds them of the happy constitution of their government, which was such as might make them all safe and easy if it was not their own fault. When good laws were given them good men were entrusted with the execution of them, which, as it was an instance of God's goodness to them, so it was of the care of Moses concerning them; and, it should seem, he mentions it here to recommend himself to them as a man that sincerely sought their welfare, and so to make way for what he was about to say to them, wherein he aimed at nothing but their good. In this part of his narrative he insinuates to them,

I. That he greatly rejoiced in the increase of their numbers. He owns the accomplishment of God's promise to Abraham (*v.* 10): *You are as the stars of heaven for multitude;* and prays for the further accomplishment of it (*v.* 11): *God make you a thousand times more.* This prayer comes in in a parenthesis, and a good prayer prudently put in cannot be impertinent in any discourse of divine things, nor will a pious ejaculation break the coherence, but rather strengthen and adorn it. But how greatly are his desires enlarged when he prays that they might be made a thousand times more than they were! We are not straitened in the power and goodness of God, why should we be straitened in our own faith and hope, which ought to be as large as the promise? larger they need not be. It is from the promise that Moses here takes the measures of his prayer: *The Lord bless you as he hath promised you.* And why might he not hope that they might become a thousand times more than they were now when they were now ten thousand times more than they were when they went down into Egypt, about 250 years ago? Observe, When they were under the government of Pharaoh the increase of their numbers was envied, and complained of as a grievance (Ex. 1:9); but now, under the government of Moses, it was rejoiced in, and prayed for as a blessing. The consideration of this might give them occasion to reflect with shame upon their own folly when they had talked of making a captain and returning to Egypt.

II. That he was not ambitious of monopolizing the honour of the government, and ruling them himself alone, as an absolute monarch, *v.* 9. Though he was a man as well worthy of that honour, and as well qualified for the business, as ever any man was, yet he was desirous that others might be taken in as assistants to him in the business and consequently sharers with him in the honour: *I cannot myself alone bear the burden, v.* 12. Magistracy is a burden. Moses himself, though eminently gifted for it, found it lay heavily on his shoulders; nay, the best magistrates complain most of the burden, and are most desirous of help, and most afraid of undertaking more than they can perform.

III. That he was not desirous to prefer his own creatures, or such as should underhand have a dependence upon him; for he leaves it to the people to choose their own judges, to whom he would grant commissions, not *durant bene placito — to be turned out when he pleased;* but *quam diu se bene gesserint — to continue so long as they approved themselves faithful. Take you wise men, that are known to be so among your tribes, and I will make them rulers, v.* 13. Thus the apostles directed the multitude to choose overseers of the poor, and then they ordained them,. Acts 6:3, 6. He directs them to *take wise men and understanding,* whose personal merit would recommend them. The rise and origin of this nation were so late that none of them could pretend to antiquity of race, and nobility of birth, above their brethren; and, having all lately come out of slavery in Egypt, it is probable that one family was not much richer than another; so that their choice must be directed purely by the qualifications of wisdom, experience, and integrity. "Choose those," says Moses, "whose praise is in your tribes, and with all my heart *I will make them rulers.*" We must not grudge that God's work be done by other hands than ours, provided it be done by good hands.

IV. That he was in this matter very willing to please the people; and, though he did not in any thing aim at their applause, yet in a thing of this nature he would not act without their approbation. And they agreed to the proposal: *The thing which thou hast spoken is good, v.* 14. This he mentions to aggravate the sin of their mutinies and discontents after this, that the government they quarrelled with was what they themselves had consented to; Moses would have pleased them if they would have been pleased.

V. That he aimed to edify them as well as to gratify them; for,

1. He appointed men of good characters (*v.* 15), *wise men and men known,* men that would be faithful to their trust and to the public interest.

2. He gave them a good charge, *v.* 16, 17. Those that are advanced to honour must know that they are charged with business, and must give account another day of their charge. (1.) He charges them to be diligent and patient: *Hear the causes.* Hear both sides, hear them fully, hear them carefully; for nature has provided us with two ears, and *he that answereth a matter before he heareth it, it is folly and shame to him.* The ear of the learner is necessary to the tongue of the learned, Isa. 50:4. (2.) To be just and impartial: *Judge righteously.* Judgment must be given according to the merits of the cause, without regard to the quality of the parties. The natives must not be suffered to abuse the strangers any more that the strangers to insult the natives or to encroach upon them; the great must not be suffered to oppress the small, nor to crush them, any more than the small, to rob the great, or to affront them. No faces must be known in judgment, but unbribed unbiased equity must always pass sentence. (3.) To be resolute and courageous: *"You shall not be afraid of the face of man;* be not overawed to do an ill thing, either by the clamours of the crowd or by the menaces of those that have power in their hands." And he gave them a good reason to enforce this charge: *"For the judgment is God's.* You are God's vicegerents, you act for him, and therefore must act like him; you are his representatives, but if you judge unrighteously, you misrepresent him. The judgment is his, and therefore he will protect you in doing right, and will certainly call you to account if you do wrong."

3. He allowed them to bring all difficult cases to him, and he would always be ready to hear and determine, and to make both the judges and the people easy. *Happy art thou. O Israel!* in such praise as Moses was.

Verses 19–46

Moses here makes a large rehearsal of the fatal turn which was given to their affairs by their own sins, and God's wrath, when, from the very borders of Canaan, the honour of conquering it, and the pleasure of possessing it, the whole generation was hurried back into the wilderness, and their carcases fell there. It was a memorable story; we read it Num. 13 and 14, but divers circumstances are found here which are not related there.

I. He reminds them of their march from Horeb to Kadesh-barnea (*v.* 19), through *that great and terrible wilderness.* This he takes notice of, 1. To make them sensible of the great goodness of God to them, in guiding them through so great a wilderness, and protecting them from the mischiefs they were surrounded with in such a terrible wilderness. The remembrance of our dangers should make us thankful for our deliverances. 2. To aggravate the folly of those who, in their discontent, would have gone back to Egypt through the wilderness, though they had forfeited, and had no reason to expect, the divine guidance, in such a retrograde motion.

II. He shows them how fair they stood for Canaan at that time, *v.* 20, 21. He told them with triumph, the land is *set before you, go up and possess it.* He lets them see how near they were to a happy settlement when they put a bar in their own door, that their sin might appear the more exceedingly sinful. It will aggravate the eternal ruin of hypocrites that they were *not far from the kingdom of God* and yet came short, Mk. 12:34.

III. He lays the blame of sending the spies upon them, which did not appear in Numbers, there it is said (*ch.* 13:1, 2) that the Lord directed the sending of them, but here we find that the people first desired it, and God, in permitting it, gave them up to their counsels: *You said, We will send men before us, v.* 22. Moses had given them God's word (*v.* 20, 21), but they could not find in their hearts to rely upon that: human policy goes further with them than divine wisdom, and they will needs light a candle to the sun. As if it were not enough that they were sure of a God before them, they must send men before them.

IV. He repeats the report which the spies brought of the goodness of the land which they were sent to survey, *v.* 24, 25. The blessings which God has promised are truly valuable and desirable, even the unbelievers themselves being judges: never any looked into the holy land, but they must own it a good land. Yet they represented the difficulties of conquering it as insuperable (*v.* 28); as if it were in vain to think of attacking them either by battle, "for the people are taller than we," or by siege, "for the cities are walled up to heaven," an hyperbole which they made use of to serve their ill purpose, which was to dishearten the people, and perhaps they intended to reflect on the God of heaven himself, as if they were able to defy him, like the Babel-builders, the top of whose tower must reach to heaven, Gen. 11:4. Those places only are walled up to heaven that are compassed with God's favour as with a shield.

V. He tells them what pains he took with them to encourage them, when their brethren had said so much to discourage them (*v.* 29): *Then I said unto you, Dread not.* Moses suggested enough to have stilled the tumult, and to have kept them with their faces towards Canaan. He assured them that God was present with them, and president among them, and would certainly *fight for them, v.* 30. And for proof of his power over their enemies he refers them to what they had seen done in Egypt, where their enemies had all possible advantages against them and yet were humbled and forced to yield, *v.* 30. And for proof of God's goodwill to them, and the real kindness which he intended them, he refers them to what *they had seen in the wilderness* (*v.* 31, 33), through which they had been guided by the eye of divine wisdom in a pillar of cloud and fire (which guided both their motions and their rests), and had been carried in the arms of divine grace with as much care and tenderness as were ever shown to any child borne in the arms of a nursing father. And was there any room left to distrust this God? Or were they not the most ungrateful people in the world, who, after such sensible proofs of the divine goodness, *hardened their hearts in the day of temptation?* Moses had complained once that God had charged him to carry this people *as a nursing father doth the sucking child* (Num. 11:12); but here he owns that it was God that so carried them, and perhaps this is alluded to (Acts 13:18), where he is said to *bear them,* or to *suffer their manners.*

VI. He charges them with the sin which they were guilty of upon this occasion. Though those to whom he was now speaking were a new generation, yet he lays it upon them: *You rebelled, and you murmured;* for many of these were then in being, though under twenty years old, and perhaps were engaged in the riot; and the rest inherited their fathers' vices, and smarted for them. Observe what he lays to their charge. 1. Disobedience and rebellion against God's law: *You would not go up, but rebelled, v.* 26. The rejecting of God's favours is really a rebelling against his authority. 2. Invidious reflections upon God's goodness. They basely suggested: *Because the Lord hated us, he brought us out of Egypt, v.* 27. What could have been more absurd, more disingenuous, and more reproachful to God? 3. An unbelieving heart at the bottom of all this: *You did not believe the Lord your God, v.* 32. All your disobedience to God's laws, and distrust of his power and goodness, flow from a disbelief of his word. A sad pass it has come to with us when the God of eternal truth cannot be believed.

VII. He repeats the sentence passed upon them for this sin, which now they had seen the execution of. 1. They were all condemned to die in the wilderness, and none of them must be suffered to enter Canaan except Caleb and Joshua, *v.* 34–38. So long they must continue in their wanderings in the wilderness that most of them would drop off of course, and the youngest of them should be cut off. Thus *they could not enter in because of unbelief.* It was not the breach of any of the commands of the law that shut them out of Canaan, no, not the golden calf, but their disbelief of that promise which was typical of gospel grace, to signify that no sin will ruin us but unbelief, which is a sin against the remedy. 2. Moses himself afterwards fell under God's displeasure for a hasty word which they provoked him to speak: *The Lord was angry with me for your sakes, v.* 37. Because all the old stock must go off, Moses himself must not stay behind. Their unbelief let death into the camp, and, having entered, even Moses falls within his commission. 3. Yet here is mercy mixed with wrath. (1.) That, though Moses might not bring them into Canaan, Joshua should (*v.* 38): *Encourage him;* for he would be discouraged from taking up a government which he saw Moses himself fall under the weight of; but let him be assured that he shall accomplish that for which he is raised up: *He shall cause Israel to inherit it.* Thus *what the law could not do, in that it was weak,* Jesus, our Joshua, does by bringing in the better hope. (2.) That, though this generation should not enter into Canaan, the next should, *v.* 39. As they had been chosen for their fathers' sakes, so their children might justly have been rejected for their sakes. But *mercy rejoiceth against judgement.*

VIII. He reminds them of their foolish and fruitless attempt to get this sentence reversed when it was too late. 1. They tried it by their reformation in this particular; whereas they had refused to go up against the Canaanites, now they would go up, aye, that they would, in all haste, and they girded on their weapons of war for that purpose, *v.* 41. Thus, when the door is shut, and the day of grace is over, there will be found those that stand without and knock. But this, which looked like a reformation, proved but a further rebellion. God, by Moses, prohibited the attempt (*v.* 42): *yet they went presumptuously up to the hill* (*v.* 43), acting now in contempt of the threatening, as before in contempt of the promise, as if they were governed by a spirit of contradiction; and it sped accordingly (*v.* 44): they were chased and destroyed; and, by this defeat which they suffered when they provoked God to leave them, they were taught what success they might have had if they had kept themselves in his love. 2. They tried by their prayers and tears to get the sentence reversed: *They returned and wept before the Lord, v.* 45. While they were fretting and quarrelling, it is said (Num. 14:1): *They wept that night;* those were tears of rebellion *against* God, these were tears of repentance and humiliation *before* God. Note, Tears of discontent must be wept over again; the sorrow of the world worketh death, and is to be repented of; it is not so with godly sorrow, *that* will end in joy. But their weeping was all to no purpose. *The Lord would not harken to your voice,* because you would not harken to his; the decree had gone forth, and, like Esau, they found no place of repentance, though they sought it carefully with tears.

CHAPTER 2

Moses, in this chapter, proceeds in the rehearsal of God's providences concerning Israel in their way to Canaan, yet preserves not the record of any thing that happened during their tedious march back to the Red Sea, in which they wore out almost thirty-eight years, but passes that over in silence as a dark time, and makes his narrative to begin again when they faced about towards Canaan (*v.* 1–3), and drew towards the countries that were inhabited, concerning which God here gives them direction. I. What nations they must not give any disturbance to. 1. Not to the Edomites (*v.* 4–8). 2. Not to the Moabites (*v.* 9), of the antiquities of whose country, with that of the Edomites, he gives some account (*v.* 10–12). And here comes in an account of their passing the river Zered (*v.* 13–16). 3. Not to the Ammonites, of whose country here is some account given (*v.* 17–23). II. What nations they should attack and conquer. They must begin with Sihon, king of the Amorites (*v.* 24, 25). And accordingly, 1. They had a fair occasion of quarrelling with him (*v.* 26–32). 2. God gave them a complete victory over him (*v.* 33, etc.).

Verses 1–7

Here is, I. A short account of the long stay of Israel in the wilderness: *We compassed Mount Seir many days, v.* 1. Nearly *thirty-eight* years they wandered in the deserts of Seir; probably in some of their rests they staid several years, and never stirred; God by this not only chastised them for their murmuring and unbelief, but, 1. Prepared them for Canaan, by humbling them for sin, teaching them to mortify their lusts, to follow God, and to comfort themselves in him. It is a work of time to make souls meet for heaven, and it must be done by a long train of exercises. 2. He prepared the Canaanites for destruction. All this time the measure of their iniquity was filling up; and, though it might have been improved by them as a space to repent in, it was abused by them to the hardening of their hearts. Now that the host of Israel was once repulsed, and after that was so long entangled and seemingly lost in the wilderness, they were secure, and thought the danger was over from that quarter, which would make the next attempt of Israel upon them the more dreadful.

II. Orders given them to turn towards Canaan. Though God contend long, he will not contend for ever. Though Israel may be long kept waiting for deliverance or enlargement, it will come at last: *The vision is for an appointed time, and at the end it shall speak, and not lie.*

III. A charge given them not to annoy the Edomites.

1. They must not offer any hostility to them as enemies: *Meddle not with them, v.* 4, 5. (1.) They must not improve the advantage they had against them, by the fright they would be put into upon Israel's approach: *"They shall be afraid of you,* knowing your strength and numbers, and the power of God engaged for you; but think not that, because their fears make them an easy prey, you may therefore prey upon them; no, *take heed to yourselves."* There is need of great caution and a strict government of our own spirits, to keep ourselves from injuring those against whom we have an advantage. Or this caution is given to the princes; they must not only not meddle with the Edomites themselves, but not permit any of the soldiers to meddle with them. (2.) They must not avenge upon the Edomites the affront they gave them in refusing them passage through their country, Num. 20:21. Thus, before God brought Israel to destroy their enemies in Canaan, he taught them to forgive their enemies in Edom. (3.) They must not expect to have any part of their land given them for a possession: Mount Seir was already settled upon the Edomites, and they must not, under pretence of God's covenant and conduct, think to seize for themselves all they could lay hands on. Dominion is not founded in grace. God's Israel shall be well placed, but must not expect to be *placed alone in the midst of the earth,* Isa. 5:8.

2. They must trade with them as neighbours, buy meat and water of them, and pay for what they bought, *v.* 6. Religion must never be made a cloak for injustice. The reason given (*v.* 7), is, "God hath blessed thee, and hitherto thou hast lacked nothing; and therefore," (1.) "Thou needest not beg; scorn to be beholden to Edomites, when thou hast a God all-sufficient to depend upon. Thou hast wherewithal to pay for what thou callest for (thanks to the divine blessing!); use therefore what thou hast, use it cheerfully, and do not sponge upon the Edomites." (2.) "Therefore thou must not steal. Thou hast experienced the care of the divine providence concerning thee, in confidence of which for the future, and in a firm belief of its sufficiency, never use any indirect methods for thy supply. Live by the faith and not by thy sword."

Verses 8–23

It is observable here that Moses, speaking of the Edomites (*v.* 8), calls them, *"our brethren, the children of Esau."* Though they had been unkind to Israel, in refusing them a peaceable passage through their country, yet he calls them brethren. For, though our relations fail in their duty to us, we must retain a sense of the relation, and not be wanting in our duty to them, as there is occasion. Now in these verses we have,

I. The account which Moses gives of the origin of the nations of which he had here occasion to speak, the Moabites, Edomites, and Ammonites. We know very well, from other parts of his history, whose posterity they were; but here he tells us how they came to those countries in which Israel found them; they were not the *aborigines,* or first planters. But, 1. The Moabites dwelt in a country which had belonged to a numerous race of giants, called *Emim* (that is, *terrible ones*), as tall as the Anakim, and perhaps more fierce, *v.* 10, 11. 2. The Edomites in like manner dispossessed the Horim from Mount Seir, and took their country (*v.* 12. and again *v.* 22), of which we read, Gen. 36:20. 3. The Ammonites likewise got possession of a country that had formerly been inhabited by giants, called *Zamzummim, crafty men,* or *wicked men* (*v.* 20, 21), probably the same that are called *Zuzim,* Gen. 14:5. He illustrates these remarks by an instance older than any of these; the Caphtorim (who were akin to the Philistines, Gen. 10:14) drove the Avim out of their country, and took possession of it, *v.* 23. The learned bishop Patrick supposes these Avites, being expelled hence, to have settled in Assyria, and to be the same people we read of under that name, 2 Ki. 17:31. Now these revolutions are recorded, (1.) To show how soon the world was peopled after the flood, so well peopled that, when a family grew numerous, they could not find a place to settle in, at least in that part of the world, but they must drive out those that were already settled. (2.) To show that the race is not to the swift, nor the battle to the strong. Giants were expelled by those of ordinary stature; for probably these giants, like those before the flood (Gen. 6:4), were notorious for impiety and oppression, which brought the judgments of God upon them, against which their great strength would be on defence. (3.) To show what uncertain things worldly possessions are, and how often they change their owners; it was so of old, and ever will be so. Families decline, and from them estates are transferred to families that increase; so little constancy or continuance is there in these things. (4.) To encourage the children of Israel, who were now going to take possession of Canaan, against the difficulties they would meet with, and to show the unbelief of those that were afraid of the sons of Anak, to whom the giants, here said to be conquered, are compared, *v.* 11, 21. If the providence of God had done this for the Moabites and Ammonites, much more would his promise do it for Israel his peculiar people.

II. The advances which Israel made towards Canaan. They *passed by the way of the wilderness of Moab* (*v.* 8), and then went over the brook or vale of Zered (*v.* 13), and there Moses takes notice of the fulfilling of the word which God had spoken concerning them, that none of those that were numbered at Mount Sinai should see the land that God had promised, Num. 14:23. According to that sentence, now that they began to set their faces towards Canaan, and to have it in their eye, notice is taken of their being all destroyed and consumed, and not a man of them left, *v.* 14. Common providence, we may observe, in about thirty-eight years, ordinarily raises a new generation, so that in that time few remain of the old one; but here it was entirely new, and none at all remained but Caleb and Joshua: *for indeed the hand of the Lord was against them, v.* 15. Those cannot but waste, until they were consumed, who have the hand of God against them. Observe, Israel is not called to engage with the Canaanites till all the men of war, the veteran regiments, that had been used to hardship, and had learned the art of war from the Egyptians, *were consumed and dead from among the people* (*v.* 16), that the conquest of Canaan, being effected by a host of new-raised men, trained up in a wilderness, the excellency of the power might the more plainly appear to be *of God and not of men.*

III. The caution given them not to meddle with the Moabites or Ammonites, whom they must not disseize, nor so much as disturb in their possessions: *Distress them not, nor contend with them, v.* 9. Though the Moabites aimed to ruin Israel (Num. 22:6), yet Israel must not aim to ruin them. If others design us a mischief, this will not justify us in designing them a mischief. But why must not the Moabites and Ammonites be meddled with? 1. Because they were the *children of Lot* (*v.* 9, 19), righteous Lot, who kept his integrity in Sodom. Note, Children often fare the better in this world for the piety of their ancestors: the seed of the upright, though they degenerate, yet are blessed with temporal good things. 2. Because the land they were possessed of was what God had given them, and he did not design it for Israel. Even wicked men have a right to their worldly possessions, and must not be wronged. The tares are allowed their place in the field, and must not be rooted out until the harvest. God gives and preserves outward blessings to wicked men, to show that these are not the best things, but he has better in store for his own children.

Verses 24–37

God having tried the self-denial of his people in forbidding them to meddle with the Moabites and Ammonites, and they having quietly passed by those rich countries, and, though superior in number, not made any attack upon them, here he recompenses them for their obedience by giving them possession of the country of Sihon king of the Amorites. If we forbear what God forbids, we shall receive what he promises, and shall be no losers at last by our obedience, though it may seem for the present to be to our loss. Wrong not others, and God shall right thee.

I. God gives them commission to seize upon the country of Sihon king of Heshbon, *v.* 24, 25. This was then God's way of disposing of kingdoms, but such particular grants are not now either to be expected or pretended. In this commission observe, 1. Though God assured them that the land should be their own, yet they must bestir themselves, and contend in battle with the enemy. What God gives we must endeavour to get. 2. God promises that when they fight he will fight for them. Do you *begin to possess it, and I will begin to put the dread of you* upon them. God would dispirit the enemy and so destroy them, would magnify Israel and so terrify all those against whom they were commissioned. See Ex. 15:14.

II. Moses sends to Sihon a message of peace, and only begs a passage through his land, with a promise to give his country no disturbance, but the advantage of trading for ready money with so great a body, *v.* 26–29. Moses herein did neither disobey God, who bade him contend with Sihon, nor dissemble with Sihon; but doubtless it was by divine direction that he did it, that Sihon might be left inexcusable, though God hardened his heart. This may illustrate the method of God's dealing with those to whom he gives his gospel, but does not give grace to believe it.

III. Sihon began the war (*v.* 32), God having *made his heart obstinate,* and hidden from his eyes the thing that belonged to his peace (*v.* 30), that he might deliver him into the hand of Israel. Those that meddle with the people of God meddle to their own hurt; and God sometimes ruins his enemies by their own resolves. See Mic. 4:11–13; Rev. 16:14.

IV. Israel was victorious. 1. They put all the Amorites to the sword, men, women, and children (*v.* 33, 34); this they did as the executioners of God's wrath; now the measure of the Amorites' iniquity was full (Gen. 15:16), and the longer it was in the filling the sorer was the reckoning at last. This was one of the devoted nations. They died, not as Israel's enemies, but as sacrifices to divine justice, in the offering of which sacrifices Israel was employed, as a kingdom of priests. The case being therefore extraordinary, it ought not to be drawn into a precedent for military executions, which make no distinction and give no quarter: those will have *judgment without mercy that show no mercy.* 2. They took possession of all they had; their cities (*v.* 34), their goods (*v.* 35), and their land, *v.* 36. The wealth of the sinner is laid up for the just. What a new world did Israel now come into! Most of them were born, and had lived all their days, in a vast howling wilderness, where they knew not what either fields or cities were, had no houses to dwell in, and neither sowed nor reaped; and now of a sudden to become masters of a country so well built, so well husbanded, this made them amends for their long waiting, and yet it was but the earnest of a great deal more. Much more joyful will the change be which holy souls will experience when they remove out of the wilderness of this world to the *better country, that is, the heavenly, to the city that has foundations.*

CHAPTER 3

Moses, in this chapter, relates, I. The conquest of Og, king of Bashan, and the seizing of his country (*v.* 1–11). II. The distribution of these new conquests to the two tribes and a half (*v.* 12–17). Under certain provisos and limitations (*v.* 18–20). III. The encouragement given to Joshua to carry on the war which was so gloriously begun (*v.* 21, 22). IV. Moses's request to go over into Canaan (*v.* 23–25), with the denial of that request, but the grant of an equivalent (*v.* 26, etc.).

Verses 1–11

We have here another brave country delivered into the hand of Israel, that of Bashan; the conquest of Sihon is often mentioned together with that of Og, to the praise of God, the rather because in these Israel's triumphs began, Ps. 135:11; 136:19, 20. See,

I. How they got the mastery of Og, a very formidable prince, 1. Very strong, for he was of the remnant of the giants (*v.* 11); his personal strength was extraordinary, a monument of which was preserved by the Ammonites in his bedstead, which was shown as a rarity in their chief city. You might guess at his weight by the materials of his bedstead; it was iron, as if a bedstead of wood were too weak for him to trust to: and you might guess at his stature by the dimensions of it; it was nine cubits long and four cubits broad, which, supposing a cubit to be but half a yard (and some learned men have made it appear to be somewhat more), was four yards and a half long, and two yards broad; and if we allow his bedstead to be two cubits longer than himself, and that is as much as we need allow, he was three yards and a half high, double the stature of an ordinary man, and every way proportionable, yet they smote him, *v.* 3. Note, when God pleads his people's cause he can deal with giants as with grasshoppers. No man's might can secure him against the Almighty. The army of Og was very powerful, for he had the command of sixty fortified cities, besides the unwalled towns, *v.* 5. Yet all this was nothing before God's Israel, when they came with commission to destroy him. 2. He was very bold and daring: He *came out against Israel to battle, v.* 1. It was wonderful that he did not take warning by the ruin of Sihon, and send to desire conditions of peace; but he trusted to his own strength, and so was hardened to his destruction. Note, Those that are not awakened by the judgments of God upon others, but persist in their defiance of heaven, are ripening apace for the like judgments upon themselves, Jer. 3:8. God bade Moses not fear him, *v.* 2. If Moses himself was so strong in faith as not to need the caution, yet it is probable that the people needed it, and for them these fresh assurances are designed; *"I will deliver him into thy hand;* not only deliver thee out of his hand, that he shall not be thy ruin, but deliver him *into thy hand,* that thou shalt be his ruin, and make him pay dearly for his attempt." He adds, *Thou shalt do to him as thou didst to Sihon,* intimating that they ought to be encouraged by their former victory to trust in God for another victory, for he is God, and changeth not.

II. How they got possession of Bashan, a very desirable country. They took all the cities (*v.* 4), and all the spoil of them, *v.* 7. They made them all their own, *v.* 10. So that now they had in their hands all that fruitful country which lay east of Jordan, from *the river Arnon unto Hermon, v.* 8. Their conquering and possessing these countries was intended, not only for the encouragement of Israel in the wars of Canaan, but for the satisfaction of Moses before his death. Since he must not live to see the completing of their victory and settlement, God thus gives him a specimen of it. Thus the Spirit is given to those that believe as the *earnest of their inheritance,* until the redemption of the purchased possession.

Verses 12–20

Having shown how this country which they were now in was conquered, in these verses he shows how it was settled upon the Reubenites, Gadites, and half the tribe of Manasseh, which we had the story of before, Num. 32. Here is the rehearsal. 1. Moses specifies the particular parts of the country that were allotted to each tribe, especially the distribution of the lot to the half tribe of Manasseh, the subdividing of which tribe is observable. Joseph was divided into Ephraim and Manasseh; Manasseh was divided into one half on the one side Jordan and the other half on the other side: that on the east side Jordan was again divided into two great families, which had their several allotments: Jair, *v.* 14, Machir, *v.* 15. And perhaps Jacob's prediction of the smallness of that tribe was now accomplished in these divisions and subdivisions. Observe that Bashan is here called *the land of the giants,* because it had been in their possession, but Og was the last of them. These giants, it seems, had lost their country, and were rooted out of it sooner than any of their neighbours; for those who, presuming upon their strength and stature, had their hand against every man, had every man's hand against them, and went down slain to the pit, though they were the terror of the mighty in the land of the living. 2. He repeats the condition of the grant which they had already agreed to, *v.* 18–20. That they should send a strong detachment over Jordan to lead the van in the conquest of Canaan, who should not return to their families, at least not to settle (though for a time they might retire thither into winter quarters, at the end of a campaign), till they had seen their brethren in as full possession of their respective allotments as they themselves were now in of theirs. They must hereby be taught not to *look at their own things only, but at the things of others,* Phil. 2:4. It ill becomes an Israelite to be selfish, and to prefer any private interest before the public welfare. When we are rest we should desire to see our brethren at rest too, and should be ready to do what we can towards it; for we are not born for ourselves, but are members one of another. A good man cannot rejoice much in the comforts of his family unless withal he sees *peace upon Israel,* Ps. 128:6.

Verses 21–29

Here is I. The encouragement which Moses gave to Joshua, who was to succeed him in the government, *v.* 21, 22. He commanded him not to fear. This those that are aged and experienced in the service of God should do all they can to strengthen the hands of those that are young, and setting out in religion. Two things he would have him consider for his encouragement: — 1. What God has done. Joshua had seen what a total defeat God had given by the forces of Israel to these two kings, and thence he might easily infer, *so shall the Lord do to all the rest of the kingdoms* upon which we are to make war. He must not only infer thence that thus the Lord can do with them all, for his arm is not shortened, but thus he will do, for his purpose is not changed; he that has begun will finish; *as for God, his work is perfect.* Joshua had seen it with his own eyes. And the more we have seen of the instances of divine wisdom, power, and goodness, the more inexcusable we are if we *fear what flesh can do unto us.* 2. What God had promised. The *Lord your God he shall fight for you;* and that cause cannot but be victorious which the Lord of hosts fights for. *If God be for us, who can be against us* so as to prevail? We reproach our leader if we follow him trembling.

II. The prayer which Moses made for himself, and the answer which God gave to that prayer.

1. His prayer was that, if it were God's will, he might go before Israel over Jordan into Canaan. At that time, when he had been encouraging Joshua to fight Israel's battles, taking it for granted that he must be their leader, he was touched with an earnest desire to go over himself, which expresses itself not in any passionate and impatient complaints, or reflections upon the sentence he was under, but in humble prayers to God for a gracious reversing of it. *I besought the Lord.* Note, We should never allow any desires in our hearts which we cannot in faith offer up to God by prayer; and what desires are innocent, let them be presented to God. We have not because we ask not. Observe,

(1.) What he pleads here. Two things: — [1.] The great experience which he had had of God's goodness to him in what he had done for Israel: *"Thou hast begun to show thy servant thy greatness.* Lord, perfect what thou hast begun. Thou hast given me to see thy glory in the conquest of these two kings, and the sight has affected me with wonder and thankfulness. O let me see more of the outgoings of my God, my King! This great work, no doubt, will be carried on and completed; let me have the satisfaction of seeing it." Note, the more we see of God's glory in his works the more we shall desire to see. *The works of the Lord are great,* and therefore are sought out more and more *of all those that have pleasure therein.* [2.] The good impressions that had been made upon his heart by what he had seen: For *what God is there in heaven or earth that can do according to thy works?* The more we are affected with what we have seen of God, of his wisdom, power, and goodness, the better we are prepared for further discoveries. Those shall see the works of God that admire him in them. Moses had thus expressed himself concerning God and his works long before (Ex. 15:11), and he still continues of the same mind, that there are no works worthy to be compared with God's works, Ps. 86:8.

(2.) What he begs: *I pray thee let me go over, v.* 25. God had said he should not go over; yet he prays that he might, not knowing but that the threatening was conditional, for it was not ratified with an oath, as that concerning the people was, that they should not enter. Thus Hezekiah prayed for his own life, and David for the life of his child, after both had ben expressly threatened; and the former prevailed, though the latter did not. Moses remembered the time when he had by prayer prevailed with God to recede from the declarations which he had made of his wrath against Israel, Ex. 32:14. And why might he not hope in like manner to prevail for himself? *Let me go over and see the good land.* Not, "Let me go over and be a prince and a ruler there;" he seeks not his own honour, is content to resign the government to Joshua; but, "Let me go to be a spectator of thy kindness to Israel, to see what I believe concerning the goodness of the land of promise." How pathetically does he speak of Canaan, that *good land,* that *goodly mountain!* Note, Those may hope to obtain and enjoy God's favours that know how to value them. What he means by *that goodly mountain* we may learn from Ps. 78:54, where it is said of God's Israel that *he brought them to the border of his sanctuary, even to this mountain which his right hand had purchased,* where it is plainly to be understood of the whole land of Canaan, yet with an eye to the sanctuary, the glory of it.

2. God's answer to this prayer had in it a mixture of mercy and judgment, that he might sing unto God of both.

(1.) There was judgment in the denial of his request, and that in something of anger too: *The Lord was wroth with me for your sakes, v.* 26. God not only sees sin in his people, but is much displeased with it; and even those that are delivered from the wrath to come may yet lie under the tokens of God's wrath in this world, and may be denied some particular favour which their hearts are much set upon. God is a gracious, tender, loving Father; but he is angry with his children when they do amiss, and denies them many a thing that they desire and are ready to cry for. But how was he wroth with Moses *for the sake of Israel?* Either, [1.] For that sin which they provoked him to; see Ps. 106:32, 33. Or, [2.] The removal of Moses at that time, when he could so ill be spared, was a rebuke to all Israel, and a punishment of their sin. Or, [3.] It was for their sakes, that it might be a warning to them to take heed of offending God by passionate and unbelieving speeches at any time, after the similitude of his transgression; for, if *this were done to such a green tree, what should be done to the dry?* He acknowledges that God would not hear him. God had often heard him for Israel, yet he would not hear him for himself. It was the prerogative of Christ, the great Intercessor, to be heard always; yet of him his enemies said, *He saved others, himself he could not save,* which the Jews would not have upbraided him with had they considered that Moses, their great prophet, prevailed for others, but for himself he could not prevail. Though Moses, being one of the wrestling seed of Jacob, did not seek in vain, yet he had not the thing itself which he sought for. God may accept our prayers, and yet not grant us the very thing we pray for.

(2.) Here is mercy mixed with this wrath in several things: — [1.] God quieted the spirit of Moses under the decree that had gone forth by that word (*v.* 26), *Let it suffice thee.* With this word, no doubt, a divine power went to reconcile Moses to the will of God, and to bring him to acquiesce in it. If God does not by his providence give us what we desire, yet, if by his grace he makes us content without it, it comes much to one. *"Let it suffice thee* to have God for they father, and heaven for thy portion, though thou hast not every thing thou wouldest have in this world. Be satisfied with this, *God is all-sufficient."* [2.] He put an honour upon his prayer in directing him not to insist upon this request: *Speak no more to me of this matter.* It intimates that what God does not think fit to grant we should not think fit to ask, and that God takes such a pleasure in the prayer of the upright that it is no pleasure to him, no, not in any particular instance, to give a denial to it. [3.] He promised him a sight of Canaan *from the top of Pisgah, v.* 27. Though he should not have the possession of it, he should have the prospect of it; not to tantalize him, but such a sight of it as would yield him true satisfaction, and would enable him to form a very clear and pleasing idea of that promised land. Probably Moses had not only his sight preserved for other purposes, but greatly enlarged for this purpose; for, if he had not had such a sight of it as others could not have from the same place, it would have been no particular favour to Moses, nor the matter of a promise. Even great believers, in this present state, see heaven but at a distance. [4.] He provided him a successor, one who should support the honour of Moses and carry on and complete that glorious work which the heart of Moses was so much upon, the bringing of Israel to Canaan, and settling them there (*v.* 28): *Charge Joshua and encourage him* in this work. Those to whom God gives a charge, he will be sure to give encouragement to. And it is a comfort to the church's friends (when they are dying and going off) to see God's work likely to be carried on by other hands, when they are silent in the dust.

CHAPTER 4

In this chapter we have, I. A most earnest and pathetic exhortation to obedience, both in general, and in some particular instances, backed with a great variety of very pressing arguments, repeated again and again, and set before them in the most moving and affectionate manner imaginable (*v.* 1–40). II. The appointing of the cities of refuge on that side Jordan (*v.* 41–43). III. The particular description of the place where Moses delivered the following repetition of the law (*v.* 44, etc.).

Verses 1–40

This most lively and excellent discourse is so entire, and the particulars of it are so often repeated, that we must take it altogether in the exposition of it, and endeavour to digest it into proper heads, for we cannot divide it into paragraphs.

I. In general, it is the use and application of the foregoing history; it comes in by way of inference from it: *Now therefore harken, O Israel, v.* 1. This use we should make of the review of God's providences concerning us, we should by them be quickened and engaged to duty and obedience. The histories of the years of ancient times should in like manner be improved by us.

II. The scope and drift of his discourse is to persuade them to keep close to God and to his service, and not to forsake him for any other god, nor in any instance to decline from their duty to him. Now observe what he says to them, with a great deal of divine rhetoric, both by way of exhortation and direction, and also by way of motive and argument to enforce his exhortations.

1. See here how he charges and commands them, and shows them *what is good, and what the Lord requires of them.*

(1.) He demands their diligent attention to the word of God, and to the statutes and judgments that were taught them: *Hearken, O Israel.* He means, not only that they must now give him the hearing, but that whenever the book of the law was read to them, or read by them, they should be attentive to it. "Hearken to the statutes, as containing the great commands of God and the great concerns of your own souls, and therefore challenging your utmost attention." At Horeb God had *made them hear his words* (*v.* 10), hear them with a witness; the attention which was then constrained by the circumstances of the delivery ought ever after to be engaged by the excellency of the things themselves. What God so *spoke once,* we should *hear twice,* hear often.

(2.) He charges them to preserve the divine law pure and entire among them, *v.* 2. Keep it pure, and do not add to it; keep it entire, and do not diminish from it. Not in practice, so some: "You shall not add by committing the evil which the law forbids, nor diminish by omitting the good which the law requires." Not in opinion, so others: "You shall not add your own inventions, as if the divine institutions were defective, nor introduce, much less impose, any rites of religious worship other than what God has appointed; nor shall you diminish, or set aside, any thing that is appointed, as needless or superfluous." God's work is perfect, nothing can be put to it, nor taken from it, without making it the worse. See Eccl. 3:14. The Jews understand it as prohibiting the alteration of the text or letter of the law, even in the least jot or tittle; and to their great care and exactness herein we are very much indebted, under God, for the purity and integrity of the Hebrew code. We find a fence like this made about the New Testament in the close of it, Rev. 22:18, 19.

(3.) He charges them to keep God's *commandments* (*v.* 2), to *do them* (*v.* 5, 14), to *keep and do them* (*v.* 6), to *perform the covenant, v.* 13. Hearing must be in order to doing, knowledge in order to practice. God's commandments were the way they must keep in, the rule they must keep to; they must govern themselves by the moral precepts, perform their devotion according to the divine ritual, and administer justice according to the judicial law. He concludes his discourse (*v.* 40) with this repeated charge: *Thou shalt keep his statutes and his commandments which*

I command thee. What are laws made for but to be observed and obeyed?

(4.) He charges them to be very strict and careful in their observance of the law (*v.* 9): *Only take heed to thyself, and keep thy soul diligently;* and (*v.* 15), *Take you therefore good heed unto yourselves;* and again (*v.* 23), *Take heed to yourselves.* Those that would be religious must be very cautious, and walk circumspectly. Considering how many temptations we are compassed about with, and what corrupt inclinations we have in our own bosoms, we have great need to look about us and to keep our hearts with all diligence. Those cannot walk aright that walk carelessly and at all adventures.

(5.) He charges them particularly to take heed of the sin of idolatry, that sin which of all others they would be most tempted to by the customs of the nations, which they were most addicted to by the corruption of their hearts, and which would be most provoking to God and of the most pernicious consequences to themselves: *Take good heed,* lest in this matter *you corrupt yourselves, v.* 15, 16. Two sorts of idolatry he cautions them against: — [1.] The worship of images, however by them they might intend to worship the true God, as they had done in the golden calf, so changing the *truth of God into a lie* and his *glory into shame.* The second commandment is expressly directed against this, and is here enlarged upon, *v.* 15–18. "Take heed *lest you corrupt yourselves,"* that is, "lest you debauch yourselves;" for those that think to make images of God form in their minds such notions of him as must needs be an inlet to all impieties; and it is intimated that it is a spiritual adultery. "And take heed lest you destroy yourselves. If any thing ruin you, this will be it. Whatever you do, make no similitude of God, either in a human shape, *male of female,* or in the shape of any *beast or fowl, serpent or fish;"* for the heathen worshipped their gods by images of all these kinds, being either not able to form, or not willing to admit, that plain demonstration which we find, Hos. 8:6: *The workman made it, therefore it is not God.* To represent an infinite Spirit by an image, and the great Creator by the image of a creature, is the greatest affront we can put upon God and the greatest cheat we can put upon ourselves. As an argument against their making images of God, he urges it very much upon them that when God made himself known to them at Horeb he did it by a voice of words which sounded in their ears, to teach them that *faith comes by hearing,* and God in the word is nigh us; but no image was presented to their eye, for to see God as he is is reserved for our happiness in the other world, and to see him as he is not will do us hurt and no good in this world. You saw *no similitude* (*v.* 12), *no manner of similitude, v.* 15. Probably they expected to have seen some similitude, for they were ready to *break through unto the Lord to gaze,* Ex. 19:21. But all they saw was *light* and *fire,* and nothing that they could make an image of, God an infinite wisdom so ordering his manifestation of himself because of the *peril of idolatry.* It is said indeed of Moses that he *beheld the similitude of the Lord* (Num. 12:8), God allowing him that favour because he was above the temptation of idolatry; but for the people who had lately come from admiring the idols of Egypt, they must see no resemblance of God, lest they should have pretended to copy it, and so should have received the second commandment in vain; "for" (says bishop Patrick) "they would have thought that this forbade them only to make any representation of God besides that wherein he showed himself to them, in which they would have concluded it lawful to represent him." Let this be a caution to us to take heed of making images of God in our fancy and imagination when we are worshipping him, lest thereby we corrupt ourselves. There may be idols in the heart, where there are none in the sanctuary. [2.] The worship of the sun, moon, and stars, is another sort of idolatry which they were cautioned against, *v.* 19. This was the most ancient species of idolatry and the most plausible, drawing the adoration to those creatures that not only are in a situation above us, but are most sensibly glorious in themselves and most generally serviceable to the world. And the plausibleness of it made it the more dangerous. It is intimated here, *First,* How strong the temptation is to sense; for the caution is, *Lest thou shouldest be driven to worship them* by the strong impulse of a vain imagination and the impetuous torrent of the customs of the nations. The heart is supposed to *walk after the eye,* which, in our corrupt and degenerate state, it is very apt to do. *"When thou seest the sun, moon, and stars,* thou wilt so admire their height and brightness, their regular motion and powerful influence, that thou wilt be strongly tempted to give that glory to them which is due to him that made them, and made them what they are to us — gave them their beings, and made them blessings to the world." It seems there was need of a great deal of resolution to arm them against this temptation, so weak was their faith in an invisible God and an invisible world. *Secondly,* Yet he shows how weak the temptation would be to those that would use their reason; for these pretended deities, the *sun, moon, and stars,* were only blessings which the Lord their God, whom they were obliged to worship, had imparted to all nations. It is absurd to worship them, for they are man's servants, were made and ordained to give light on earth; and shall we serve those that were made to serve us? The sun, in Hebrew is called *shemesh,* which signifies a *servant,* for it is the minister-general of this visible world, and holds the candle to all mankind; let it not then be worshipped as a lord. Moreover, they are God's gifts; he has imparted them; whatever benefit we have by them, we owe it to him; it is therefore highly injurious to him to give that honour and praise to them which is due to him only.

(6.) He charges them to teach their children to observe the laws of God: *Teach them to thy sons, and thy sons' sons* (*v.* 9), *that they may teach their children, v.* 10. [1.] Care must be taken in general to preserve the entail of religion among them, and to transmit the knowledge and worship of God to posterity; for the kingdom of God in Israel was designed to be perpetual, if they did not forfeit the privilege of it. [2.] Parents must, in order hereunto, particularly take care to teach their own children the fear of God, and to train them up in an observance of all his commandments.

(7.) He charges them never to forget their duty: *Take heed lest you forget the covenant of the Lord your God, v.* 23. Though God is ever mindful of the covenant, we are apt to forget it; and this is at the bottom of all our departures from God. We have need therefore to watch against all those things which would put the covenant out of our minds, and to watch over our own hearts, lest at any time we let it slip; and so we must take heed lest at any time we forget our religion, lest we lose it or leave it off. Care and caution, and holy watchfulness, are the best helps against a bad memory. These are the directions and commands he gives them.

2. Let us see now what are the motives or arguments with which he backs these exhortations. How does he order the cause before them, and fill his mouth with arguments! He has a great deal to say on God's behalf. Some of his topics are indeed peculiar to that people, yet applicable to us. But, upon the whole, it is evident that religion has reason on its side, the powerful charms of which all that are irreligious wilfully stop their ears against.

(1.) He urges the greatness, glory, and goodness, of God. Did we consider what a God he is with whom we have to do, we should surely make conscience of our duty to him and not dare to sin against him. He reminds them here, [1.] That the Lord Jehovah is the *one and only living and true God.* This they must *know and consider, v.* 39. There are many things which we know, but are not the better for, because we do not consider them, we do not apply them to ourselves, nor draw proper inferences from them. This is a truth so evident that it cannot but be known, and so influential that, if it were duly considered, it would effectually reform the world, *That the Lord Jehovah he is God,* an infinite and eternal Being, self-existent and self-sufficient, and the fountain of all being, power, and motion — that he is *God in heaven above,* clothed with all the glory and Lord of all the hosts of the upper world, and that he is God *upon earth beneath,* which, though distant from the throne of his glory, is not out of the reach of his sight or power, and though despicable and mean is not below his care and cognizance. And *there is none else,* no true and living God but himself. All the deities of the heathen were counterfeits and usurpers; nor did any of them so much as pretend to be universal monarchs in heaven and earth, but only local deities. The Israelites, who worshipped no other than the supreme *Numen — Divinity,* were for ever inexcusable if they either changed their God or neglected him. [2.] That he is a *consuming fire, a jealous God, v.* 24. Take heed of offending him, for, *First,* He has a jealous eye to discern an affront; he must have your entire affection and adoration, and will by no means endure a rival. God's jealousy over us is a good reason for our godly jealousy over ourselves. *Secondly,* He has a heavy hand to punish an affront, especially in his worship, for therein he is in a special manner jealous. He is a *consuming fire;* his wrath against sinners is so; it is dreadful and destroying, it is a *fiery indignation* which will *devour the adversaries,* Heb. 10:27. Fire consumes that only which is fuel for it, so the wrath of God fastens upon those only who, by their own sin, have fitted themselves for destruction, 1. Cor. 3:13; Isa. 27:4. Even in the New Testament we find the same argument urged upon us as a reason why we should serve *God with reverence* (Heb. 12:28, 29), because though he is our God, and a rejoicing light to those that serve him faithfully, yet he is a consuming fire to those that trifle with him. *Thirdly,* That yet he is *a merciful God, v.* 31. It comes in here as an encouragement to repentance, but might serve as an inducement to obedience, and a consideration proper to prevent their apostasy. Shall we forsake a merciful God, who will never forsake us, as it follows here, if we be faithful unto him? Whither can we go to better ourselves? Shall we forget the covenant of our God, who will not *forget the covenant of our fathers?* Let us be held to our duty by the bonds of love, and prevailed with by the mercies of God to cleave to him.

(2.) He urges their relation to this God, his authority over them and their obligations to him. "The commandments you are to keep and do are not mine," says Moses, "not my inventions, not my injunctions, but they are the commandments of the Lord, framed by infinite wisdom, enacted by sovereign power. He is the *Lord God of your fathers* (*v.* 1), so that you are his by inheritance: your fathers were his, and you were born in his house. He is the *Lord your God* (*v.* 2), so that you are his by your own consent. He is the *Lord my God* (*v.* 5), so that I treat with you as his agent and ambassador;" and in his name Moses delivered unto them all that, and that only, which he had received from the Lord.

(3.) He urges the wisdom of being religious: *For this is your wisdom in the sight of the nations, v.* 6. In keeping God's commandments, [1.] They would act wisely for themselves; *This is your wisdom.* It is not only agreeable to right reason, but highly conducive to our true interest; this is one of the first and most ancient maxims of divine revelation. *The fear of the Lord, that is wisdom,* Job 28:28. [2.] They would answer the expectations of their neighbours, who, upon reading or hearing the precepts of the law that was given them, would conclude that certainly the people that were governed by this law were a wise and understanding people. Great things may justly be looked for from those who are guided by divine revelation, and unto whom are committed the oracles of God. They must needs be wiser and better than other people; and so they are if they are ruled by the rules that are given them; and if they are not, though reproach may for their sakes be cast upon the religion they profess, yet it will in the end certainly return upon themselves to their eternal confusion. Those that enjoy the benefit of divine light and laws ought to conduct themselves so as to support their own reputation for wisdom and honour (see Eccl. 10:1), that God may be glorified thereby.

(4.) He urges the singular advantages which they enjoyed by virtue of the happy establishment they were under, *v.* 7, 8. Our communion with God (which is the highest honour and happiness we are capable of in this world) is kept up by the word and prayer; in both these Israel were happy above any people under heaven. [1.] Never were any people so privileged in speaking to God, *v.* 7. He was nigh unto them in all that they called upon him for, ready to answer their enquiries and resolve them by his oracle, ready to answer their requests and to grant them by a particular providence. When they had cried unto God for bread, for water, for healing, they had found him near them, to succour and relieve them, a very present help, and in the midst of them (Ps. 46:1, 5), his ear open to their prayers. Observe, *First,* It is the character of God's Israel that on all occasions they call upon him, in every thing they make their requests known to God. They do nothing but what they consult him in, they desire nothing but what they come to him for. *Secondly,* Those that call upon God shall certainly find him within call, and ready to give an answer of peace to every prayer of faith; see Isa. 58:9, *"Thou shalt cry,* as the child for a nurse, *and he shall say, Here I am,* what does my dear child cry for?" *Thirdly,* This is a privilege which makes the Israel of God truly great and honourable. What can go further than this to magnify a people or a person? Is any name more illustrious than that of Israel, *a prince with God? What nation is there so great?* Other nations might boast of greater numbers, larger territories, and more ancient incorporations; but none could boast of such an interest in heaven as Israel had. They had their gods, but not so nigh to them as Israel's God was; they could not help them in a time of need, as 1 Ki. 18:27. [2.] Never were any people so privileged in hearing from God, by the statutes and judgments which were set before them, *v.* 8. This also was the grandeur of Israel above any people. *What nation is there so great, that hath statutes and judgments so righteous?* Observe, *First,* That all these statutes and judgments of the divine law are infinitely just and righteous, above the statutes and judgments of any of the nations. The law of God is far more excellent that the law of nations. No law so consonant to natural equity and the unprejudiced dictates of right reason, so consistent with itself in all the parts of it, and so conducive to the welfare and interest of mankind, as the scripture-law is, Ps. 119:128. *Secondly,* The having of these statutes and judgments set before them is the true and transcendent greatness of any nation or people. See Ps. 147:19, 20. It is an honour to us that we have the Bible in reputation and power among us. It is an evidence of a people's being high in the favour of God, and a means of making them high among the nations. Those that magnify the law shall be magnified by it.

(5.) He urges God's glorious appearances to them at Mount Sinai, when he gave them this law. This he insists much upon. Take heed *lest thou forget the day that thou stoodest before the Lord thy God in Horeb, v.* 10. Some of them were now alive that could remember it, though they were then under twenty years of age, and the rest of them might be said to stand there in the loins of their fathers, who received the law and entered into covenant there, not for themselves only, but for their children, to whom God had an eye particularly in giving the law, that they might teach it to their children. Two things they must remember, and, one would think, they could never forget them: — [1.] What they saw at Mount Sinai, *v.* 11. They saw a strange composition of fire and darkness, both dreadful and very awful; and they must needs be a striking foil to each other; the darkness made the fire in the midst of it look the more dreadful. Fires in the night are the most frightful, and the fire made the darkness that surrounded it look the more awful; for it must needs be a strong darkness which such a fire did not disperse. In allusion to this appearance upon Mount Sinai, God is said to show himself for his people, and against his and their enemies, in fire and darkness together, Ps. 18:8, 9. He tells them again (*v.* 36) what they saw, for he would have them never forget it: *He showed thee his great fire.* One flash of lightning, that fire from heaven, strikes an awe upon us; and some have observed that most creatures naturally turn their faces towards the lightning, as ready to receive the impressions of it; but how dreadful then must a constant fire from heaven be! It gave an earnest of the day of judgment, in which *the Lord Jesus shall be revealed in flaming fire.* As he reminds them of what they saw, so he tells them what they saw not; no manner of similitude, from which they might form either an idea of God in their fancies or an image of God in their high places. By what we see of God sufficient ground is given us to believe him to be a Being of infinite power and perfection, but no occasion given us to suspect him to have a body such as we have. [2.] What they heard at Mount Sinai (*v.* 12): *"The Lord spoke unto you* with an intelligible voice, in your own language, and you heard it." This he enlarges upon towards the close of his discourse, *v.* 32, 33, 36. *First, They heard the voice of God, speaking out of heaven.* God manifests himself to all the world in the works of creation, without speech or language, and yet their voice is heard (Ps. 19:1–3); but to Israel he made himself known by speech and language, condescending to the weakness of the church's infant state. Here was the *voice of one crying in the wilderness, to prepare the way of the Lord. Secondly,* They heard it *out of the midst of the fire,* which showed that it was God himself that spoke to them, for who else could dwell with devouring fire? God spoke to Job out of the whirlwind, which was terrible; but to Israel out of the fire, which was more terrible. We have reason to be thankful that he does not thus speak to us, but by men like ourselves, *whose terror shall not make us afraid,* Job 33:6, 7. *Thirdly,* They heard it and yet lived, *v.* 33. It was a wonder of mercy that the fire did not devour them, or that they did not die for fear, when Moses himself trembled. *Fourthly,* Never any people heard the like. He bids them enquire of former days and distant places, and they would find this favour of God to Israel without precedent or parallel, *v.* 32. This singular honour done them called for singular obedience from them. It might justly be expected that they should do more for God than other people, since God had done so much more for them.

(6.) He urges God's gracious appearances for them, in bringing them out of Egypt, from the iron furnace, where they laboured in the fire, forming them into a people, and then taking them to be his own people, a *people of inheritance* (*v.* 20); this he mentions again, *v.* 34, 37, 38. Never did God do such a thing for any people; the rise of this nation was quite different from that of all other nations. [1.] They were thus dignified and distinguished, not for any thing in them that was deserving or inviting, but because God had a kindness for their fathers: he chose them. See the reasons of free grace; we are not beloved for our own sakes, but for his sake who is the great trustee of the covenant. [2.] They were delivered out of Egypt by miracles and signs, in mercy to them and in judgment upon the Egyptians, against whom God stretched out his arm, which was signified by Moses's stretching out his hand in summoning the plagues. [3.] They were designed for a happy settlement in Canaan, *v.* 38. Nations must be driven out from before them, to make room for them, to show how much dearer they were to God than any other people were. Egyptians and Canaanites must both be sacrificed to Israel's honour and interest. Those that stand in Israel's light, in Israel's way, shall find it is at their peril.

(7.) He urges God's righteous appearance against them sometimes for their sins. He specifies particularly the matter of Peor, *v.* 3, 4. This had happened very lately: their eyes had seen but the other day the sudden destruction of those that joined themselves to Baal-peor and the preservation of those that clave to the Lord, from which they might easily infer the danger of apostasy from God and the benefit of adherence to him. He also takes notice again of God's displeasure against himself: *The Lord was angry with me for your sakes, v.* 21, 22. He mentions this to try their ingenuousness, whether they would really be troubled for the great prejudice which they had occasioned to their faithful friend and leader. Others' sufferings for our sakes should grieve us more than our own.

(8.) He urges the certain advantage of obedience. This argument he begins with (*v.* 1): *That you may live, and go in and possess the land;* and this he concludes with (*v.* 40): *That it may go well with thee, and with thy children after thee.* He reminds them that they were upon their good behaviour, that their prosperity would depend upon their piety. If they kept God's precepts, he would undoubtedly fulfil his promises.

(9.) He urges the fatal consequences of their apostasy from God, that it would undoubtedly be the ruin of their nation. This he enlarges upon, *v.* 25–31. Here, [1.] He foresees their revolt from God to idols, that in process of time, when they had remained long in the land and were settled upon their lees, they *would corrupt themselves, and make a graven image;* this was the sin that would most easily beset them, *v.* 25. [2.] He foretels the judgments of God upon them for this: *You shall utterly be destroyed* (*v.* 26), *scattered among the nations, v.* 27. And their sin should be made their punishment (*v.* 28): *"There shall you serve gods, the work of men's hands,* be compelled to serve them, whether you will or no, or, through your own sottishness and stupidity, you will find no better succours to apply yourselves in your captivity." Those that cast off the duties of religion in their prosperity cannot expect the comforts of it when they come to be in distress. Justly are they then sent to the *gods whom they have served,* Jdg. 10:14. [3.] Yet he encourages them to hope that God would reserve mercy for them in the latter days, that he would by his judgments upon them bring them to repentance, and take them again into covenant with himself, *v.* 29–31. Here observe, *First,* That whatever place we are in we may *thence seek the Lord our God,* though ever so remote from our own land or from his holy temple. There is no part of this earth that has a gulf fixed between it and heaven. *Secondly,* Those, and those only, shall find God to their comfort, who seek him with all their heart, that is, who are entirely devoted to him, earnestly desirous of his favour and solicitous to obtain it. *Thirdly,* Afflictions are sent to engage and quicken us to see God, and, by the grace of God working with them, many are thus reduced to their right mind, "When these things shall come upon thee, it is to be hoped that thou wilt *turn to the Lord they God,* for thou seest what comes of turning from him;" see Dan. 9:11, 12. *Fourthly,* God's faithfulness to his covenant encourages us to hope that he will not reject us, though we be driven to him by affliction. If we at length remember the covenant, we shall find that he has not forgotten it.

Now let all these arguments be laid together, and then say whether religion has not reason on its side. None cast off the government of their God but those that have first abandoned the understanding of a man.

Verses 41–49

Here is, 1. The nomination of the cities of refuge on that side Jordan where Israel now lay encamped. Three cities were appointed for that purpose, one in the lot of Reuben, another in that of Gad, and another in that of the half tribe of Manasseh, *v.* 41–43. What Moses could do for that people while he was yet with them he did, to give example to the rulers who were settled that they might observe them the better when he was gone. 2. The introduction to another sermon that Moses preached to Israel, which we have in the following chapters. Probably it was preached the next sabbath day after, when the congregation attended to receive instruction. He had in general exhorted them to obedience in the former chapter; here he comes to repeat the law which they were to observe, for he demands a universal but not an implicit obedience. How can we do our duty if we do not know it? Here therefore he sets the law before them as the rule they were to work by, the way they were to walk in, sets it before them as the glass in which they were to see their natural face, that, looking into this perfect law of liberty, they might continue therein. *These are the testimonies, the statutes, and the judgments,* the moral, ceremonial, and judicial laws, which had been enacted before, when Israel had newly come out of Egypt, and were now repeated, *on this side Jordan, v.* 44–46. The place where Moses gave them these laws in charge is here particularly described. (1.) It was over-against Beth-peor, an idol-temple of the Moabites, which perhaps Moses sometimes looked towards, with a particular caution to them against the infection of that and other such like dangerous places. (2.) It was upon their new conquests, in the very land which they had got out of the hands of Sihon and Og, and were now actually in possession of, *v.* 47. Their present triumphs herein were a powerful argument for obedience.

CHAPTER 5

In this chapter we have the second edition of the ten commandments. I. The general intent of them; they were in the nature of a covenant between God and Israel (*v.* 1–5). II. The particular precepts are repeated (*v.* 6–21), with the double delivery of them, both by word and writing (*v.* 22). III. The settling of the correspondence thenceforward between God and Israel, by the mediation and ministry of Moses. 1. It was Israel's humble petition that it might be so (*v.* 23–27). 2. It was God's gracious grant that it should be so (*v.* 28–31). And hence he infers the obligation they were under to obedience (*v.* 32, 33).

Verses 1–5

Here, 1. Moses summons the assembly. He *called all Israel;* not only the elders, but, it is likely, as many of the people as could come within hearing, *v.* 1. The greatest of them were not above God's command, nor the meanest of them below his cognizance; but they were all bound to do. 2. He demands attention: *"Hear, O Israel;* hear and heed, hear and remember, hear, that you may learn, and keep, and do; else your hearing is to no purpose." When we hear the word of God we must set ourselves to learn it, that we may have it ready to us upon all occasions, and what we have learned we must put in practice, for that is the end of hearing and learning; not to fill our heads with notions, or our mouths with talk, but to rectify and direct our affections and conversations. 3. He refers them to the covenant made with them in Horeb, as that which they must govern themselves by. See the wonderful condescension of divine grace in turning the command into a covenant, that we might be the more strongly bound to obedience by our own consent and the more encouraged in it by the divine promise, both which are supposed in the covenant. The promises and threatenings annexed to some of the precepts, as to the second, third, and fifth, make them amount to a covenant. Observe, (1.) The parties to this covenant. God made it, *not with our fathers,* not with Abraham, Isaac, and Jacob; to them God gave the *covenant of circumcision* (Acts 7:8), but not that of the ten commandments. The light of divine revelation shone gradually, and the children were made to know more of God's mind than their fathers had done. "The covenant was made with us, or our immediate parents that represented us, before Mount Sinai, and transacted for us." (2.) The publication of this covenant. God himself did, as it were, read the articles to them (*v.* 4): He *talked with you face to face; word to word,* so the Chaldee. Not in dark visions, as of old he spoke to the fathers (Job 4:12, 13), but openly and clearly, and so that all the thousands of Israel might hear and understand. He spoke to them, and then received the answer they returned to him: thus was it transacted *face to face.* (3.) The mediator of the covenant: *Moses stood between God and them,* at the foot of the mount (*v.* 5), and carried messages between them both for the settling of the preliminaries (Ex. 19) and for the changing of the ratifications, Ex. 24. Herein Moses was a type of Christ, who *stands between God and man, to show us the word of the Lord,* a blessed days-man, that has laid his hand upon us both, so that we may both hear from God and speak to him without trembling.

Verses 6–22

Here is the repetition of the ten commandments, in which observe, 1. Though they had been spoken before, and written, yet they are again rehearsed; for precept must be upon precept, and line upon line, and all little enough to keep the word of God in our minds and to preserve and renew the impressions of it. We have need to have the same things often inculcated upon us. See Phil. 3:1. 2. There is some variation here from that record (Ex. 20), as there is between the Lord's prayer as it is in Mt. 6 and as it is Lu. 11. In both it is more necessary that we tie ourselves to the things than to the words unalterably. 3. The most considerable variation is in the fourth commandment. In Ex. 20 the reason annexed is taken from the creation of the world; here it is taken from their deliverance out of Egypt, because that was typical of our redemption by Jesus Christ, in remembrance of which the Christian sabbath was to be observed: *Remember that thou wast a servant, and God brought thee out, v.* 15. And Therefore, (1.) "It is fit that thy servants should be favoured by the sabbath-rest; for thou knowest the heart of a servant, and how welcome one day's ease will be after six days' labour." (2.) "It is fit that thy God should be honoured by the sabbath-work, and the religious services of the day, in consideration of the great things he has done for thee." In the resurrection of Christ we were brought into the glorious liberty of the children of God, *with a mighty hand and an outstretched arm;* therefore, by the gospel-edition of the law, we are directed to observe the first day of the week, in remembrance of that glorious work of power and grace. 4. It is added in the fifth commandment, *That it may go well with thee,* which addition the apostle quotes, and puts first (Eph. 6:3), *that it may be well with thee, and that thou mayest live long.* If there be instances of some that have been very dutiful to their parents, and yet have not lived long upon earth, we may reconcile it to the promise by this explication of it, Whether they live long or no, it shall go well with them, either in this world or in a better. See Eccl. 8:12. 5. The last five commandments are connected or coupled together, which they are not in Exodus: *Neither shalt thou commit adultery, neither shalt thou steal, etc.,* which intimate that God's commands are all of a piece: the same authority that obliges us to one obliges us to another; and we must not be partial in the law, but have respect to all God's commandments, for he that *offends in*

one point is guilty of all, Jam. 2:10, 11. 6. That these commandments were given with a great deal of awful solemnity, *v.* 22. (1.) They were spoken with *a great voice out of the fire, and thick darkness.* That was a dispensation of terror, designed to make the gospel of grace the more welcome, and to be a specimen of the terrors of the judgment-day, Ps. 50:3, 4. (2.) *He added no more.* What other laws he gave them were sent by Moses, but no more were spoken in the same manner that the ten commandments were. *He added no more,* therefore we must not add: the law of the Lord is perfect. (3.) *He wrote them in two tables of stone,* that they might be preserved from corruption, and might be transmitted pure and entire to posterity, for whose use they were intended, as well as for the present generation. These being the heads of the covenant, the chest in which the written tables were deposited was called the *ark of the covenant.* See Rev. 11:19.

Verses 23–33

Here, I. Moses reminds them of the agreement of both the parties that were now treating, in the mediation of Moses.

1. Here is the consternation that the people were put into by that extreme terror with which the law was given. They owned that they could not bear it any more: "*This great fire will consume us;* this dreadful voice will be fatal to us; we shall certainly die if we hear it any more," *v.* 25. They wondered that they were not already struck dead with it, and took it for an extraordinary instance of the divine power and goodness, not only that they were thus spoken to, but that they were enabled to bear it. For *who ever heard the voice of the living God, as we have, and lived?* God's appearances have always been terrible to man, ever since the fall: but Christ, having taken away sin, invites us to come boldly to the throne of grace.

2. Their earnest request that God would henceforth speak to them by Moses, with a promise that they would hear what he said as from God himself, and do it, *v.* 27. It seems by this, (1.) That they expected to receive further commands from God and were willing to hear more from him. (2.) That they thought Moses able to bear those discoveries of the divine glory which they by reason of guilt were sensible of their inability to stand up under. They believed him to be a favourite of Heaven, and also one that would be faithful to them; yet at other times they murmured at him, and but a little before this were ready to stone him, Ex. 17:4. See how men's convictions correct their passions. (3.) That now they were in a good mind, under the strong convictions of the word they heard. Many have their consciences startled by the law that have them not purified; fair promises are extorted from them, but no good principles fixed and rooted in them.

3. God's approbation of their request. (1.) He commends what they said, *v.* 28. They spoke it to Moses, but God took notice of it; for there is not a word in our tongue but he knows it. He acknowledges, *They have well said.* Their owning the necessity of a mediator to deal between them and God was well said. Their desire to receive further directions from God by Moses, and their promise to observe what directions should be given them, were well said. And what is well said shall have its praise with God, and should have with us. What is good, as far as it goes, let it be commended. (2.) He wishes they were but sincere in it: *O that there were such a heart in them! v.* 29. [1.] Such a heart as they should have, a heart to fear God, and keep his commandments for ever. Note, The God of heaven is truly and earnestly desirous of the welfare and salvation of poor sinners. He has given abundant proof that he is so: he gives us time and space to repent, by his mercies invites us to repentance, and waits to be gracious; he has sent his Son to redeem us, published a general offer of pardon and life, promised his Spirit to those that pray for him, and has said and sworn that he has no pleasure in the ruin of sinners. [2.] Such a heart as they now had, or one would think they had. Note, It would be well with many if there were always such a heart in them as there seems to be sometimes, when they are under conviction of sin, or the rebukes of Providence, or when they come to look death in the face: *How gracious will they be when these pangs come upon them!* O that there were always such a heart in them! (3.) He appoints Moses to be his messenger to them, to receive the law from his mouth and to communicate it to

them, *v.* 31. Here the matter was settled by consent of both parties that God should hence-forward speak to us by men like ourselves, by Moses and the prophets, by the apostles and the evangelists, and, if we believe not these, neither should we be persuaded though God should speak to us as he did to Israel at Mount Sinai, or send expresses from heaven or hell.

II. Hence he infers a charge to them to observe and do all that God had commanded them, *v.* 32, 33. Seeing God had shown himself so tender of them, and so willing to consider their frame and gratify them in what they desired, and withal so ready to make the best of them, — seeing they themselves had desired to have Moses for their teacher, who was now teaching them, — and seeing they had promised so solemnly, and under the influence of so many good causes and considerations, that they would hear and do, he charges them to *walk in all the ways that God had commanded them,* assuring them that it would be highly for their advantage to do so. The only way to be happy is to be holy. *Say to the righteous, It shall be well with them.*

CHAPTER 6

Moses, in this chapter, goes on with his charge to Israel, to be sure to keep up their religion in Canaan. It is much the same with *ch.* 4. I. His preface is a persuasive to obedience (*v.* 1–3). II. He lays down the great principles of obedience. The first truth to be believed, That God is one (*v.* 4). The first duty to be done, To love him with all our heart (*v.* 5). III. He prescribes the means for keeping up religion (*v.* 6–9). IV. He cautions them against those things which would be the ruin of religion — abuse of plenty (*v.* 10–12), inclination to idolatry (*v.* 14, 15), and gives them some general precepts (*v.* 13, 16–18). V. He directs them what instructions to give their children (*v.* 20, etc.).

Verses 1–3

Observe here, 1. That Moses taught the people all that, and that only, which God commanded him to teach them, *v.* 1. Thus Christ's ministers are to teach his churches *all that he has commanded,* and neither more nor less, Mt. 28:20. 2. That the end of their being taught was that they might do as they were taught (*v.* 1), might *keep God's statutes* (*v.* 2), and *observe to do them, v.* 3. Good instructions from parents and ministers will but aggravate our condemnation if we do not live up to them. 3. That Moses carefully endeavoured to fix them for God and godliness, now that they were entering upon the land of Canaan, that they might be prepared for the comforts of that land, and fortified against the snares of it, and now that they were setting out in the world might set out well. 4. That the fear of God in the heart will be the most powerful principle of obedience: *That thou mightest fear the Lord thy God, to keep all his statutes, v.* 2. 5. The entail of religion in a family, or country, is the best entail: it is highly desirable that not we only, but our children, and our children's children, may fear the Lord. 6. Religion and righteousness advance and secure the prosperity of any people. Fear God, and it shall be well with thee. Those that are well taught, if they do what they are taught, shall be well fed too, as Israel in the *land flowing with milk and honey, v.* 3.

Verses 4–16

Here is, I. A brief summary of religion, containing the first principles of faith and obedience, *v.* 4, 5. These two verses the Jews reckon one of the choicest portions of scripture: they write it in their phylacteries, and think themselves not only obliged to say it at least twice every day, but very happy in being so obliged, having this saying among them, *Blessed are we, who every morning and evening say, Hear, O Israel, the Lord our God is one Lord.* But more blessed are we if we duly consider and improve,

1. What we are here taught to believe concerning God: that *Jehovah our God is one Jehovah.* (1.) That the God whom we serve is Jehovah, a Being infinitely and eternally perfect, self-existent, and self-sufficient. (2.) That he is the one only living and true God; he only is God, and he is but one. The firm belief of this self-evident truth would effectually arm them against all idolatry, which was introduced by that fundamental error, that there are gods many. It is past dispute that there is one God, and there *is no other but he,* Mk. 12:32. Let us therefore have no other, nor desire to have any other. Some have thought there is here a plain intimation of the trinity of persons in the unity of the Godhead; for here is the name of God three times, and yet all declared to be one. Happy they that have this

one Lord for their God; for they have but one master to please, but one benefactor to seek to. It is better to have one fountain that a thousand cisterns, one all-sufficient God than a thousand insufficient ones.

2. What we are here taught concerning the duty which God requires of man. It is all summed up in this as its principle, *Thou shalt love the Lord thy God with all thy heart.* He had undertaken (*v.* 2) to teach them to fear God; and, in pursuance of his undertaking, he here teaches them to love him, for the warmer our affection to him the greater will be our veneration for him; the child that honours his parents no doubt loves them. Did ever any prince make a law that his subjects should love him? Yet such is the condescension of the divine grace that this is made the first and great commandment of God's law, that we love him, and that we perform all other parts of our duty to him from a principle of love. *My son, give me thy heart.* We must highly esteem him, be well pleased that there is such a Being, well pleased in all his attributes, and relations to us: our desire must be towards him, our delight in him, our dependence upon him, and to him we must be entirely devoted. It must be a constant pleasure to us to think of him, hear from him, speak to him, and serve him. We must love him, (1.) As the Lord, the best of beings, most excellent and amiable in himself. (2.) As our God, a God in covenant with us, our Father, and the most kind and bountiful of friends and benefactors. We are also commanded to love God *with all our heart, and soul, and might;* that is, we must love him, [1.] With a sincere love; not in word and tongue only, saying we love him when our hearts are not with him, but inwardly, and in truth, solacing ourselves in him. [2.] With a strong love; the heart must be carried out towards him with great ardour and fervency of affection. Some have hence though that we should avoid saying (as we commonly express ourselves) that we will do this or that with all our heart, for we must not do any thing with all our heart but love God; and that this phrase, being here used concerning that sacred fire, should not be unhallowed. He that is our all must have our all, and none but he. [3.] With a superlative love; we must love God above any creature whatsoever, and love nothing besides him but what we love for him and in subordination to him. [4.] With an intelligent love; for so it is explained, Mk. 12:33. To love him with all the heart, and with all the understanding, we must know him, and therefore love him as those that see good cause to love him. [5.] With an entire love; he is one, and therefore our hearts must be united in this love, and the whole stream of our affections must run towards him. O that this love of God may be shed abroad in our hearts!

II. Means are here prescribed for the maintaining and keeping up of religion in our hearts and houses, that it might not wither and go to decay. And they are these: — 1. Meditation: *These words which I command thee shall be in thy heart, v.* 6. Though the words alone without the things will do us no good, yet we are in danger of losing the things if we neglect the words, by which ordinarily divine light and power are conveyed to the heart. God's words must be laid up on our heart, that our thoughts may be daily conversant with them and employed about them, and thereby the whole soul may be brought to abide and act under the influence and impression of them. This immediately follows upon the law of loving God with all your heart; for those that do so will lay up his word in their hearts both as an evidence and effect of that love and as a means to preserve and increase it. He that loves God loves his Bible. 2. The religious education of children (*v.* 7): *"Thou shalt teach them diligently to thy children;* and by communicating thy knowledge thou wilt increase it." Those that love the Lord God themselves should do what they can to engage the affections of their children to him, and so to preserve the entail of religion in their families from being cut off. *Thou shalt whet them diligently upon thy children,* so some read it; frequently repeat these things to them, try all ways of instilling them into their minds, and making them pierce into their hearts; as, in whetting a knife, it is turned first on this side, then on that. "Be careful and exact in teaching thy children; and aim, as by whetting, to sharpen them, and put an edge upon them. Teach them to thy children, not only those of thy own body" (say the Jews) "but all those that are anyway under thy care and tuition." Bishop Patrick well observes here that Moses thought his law so very plain and easy that every father might be able to instruct his sons in it and every mother her daughters. Thus that good thing which is committed to us we must carefully transmit to those that come after us, that it may be perpetuated. 3. Pious discourse. "Thou shalt talk of these things, with due reverence and seriousness, for the benefit not only of thy children, but of thy other domestics, thy friends and companions, as thou sittest in thy house at work, or at meat, or at rest, or to receive visits, and when thou walkest by the way for diversion, or for conversation, of in journeys, when at night thou art retiring from thy family to lie down for sleep, and when in the morning thou hast risen up and returnest to thy family again. Take all occasions to discourse with those about thee of divine things; not of unrevealed mysteries, or matters of doubtful disputation, but of the plain truths and laws of God, and the things that belong to our peace." So far is it from being reckoned a diminution to the honour of sacred things to make them subject of our familiar discourse that they are recommended to us to be talked of; for the more conversant we are with them the more we shall admire them and be affected with them, and may thereby be instrumental to communicate divine light and heat. 4. Frequent reading of the word: *They shall be as frontlets between thy eyes, and thou shalt write them upon the posts of thy house, v.* 8, 9. It is probable that at that time there were few written copies of the whole law, only at the feasts of tabernacles the people had it read to them; and therefore God appointed them, at least for the present, to write some select sentences of the law, that were most weighty and comprehensive, upon their walls, or in scrolls of parchment to be worn about their wrists; and some think that hence the phylacteries so much used among the Jews took rise. Christ blames the Pharisees, not for wearing them, but for affecting to have them broader than other people's, Mt. 23:5. But when Bibles came to be common among them there was less occasion for this expedient. It was prudently and piously provided by the first reformers of the English church that then, when Bibles were scarce, some select portions of scripture should be written on the walls and pillars of the churches, which the people might make familiar to them, in conformity to this direction, which seems to have been binding in the letter of it to the Jews as it is to us in the intent of it, which is that we should endeavour by all means possible to make the word of God familiar to us, that we may have it ready to us upon all occasions, for our restraint from sin and our direction and excitement to our duty. It must be as that which is *graven on the palms of our hands,* always before our eyes. See Prov. 7:1–3. It is also intimated that we must never be ashamed to own our religion, nor to own ourselves under the check and government of it. Let it be written on our gates, and let every one that goes by our door read it, that we believe Jehovah to be God alone, and believe ourselves bound to *love him with all our hearts.*

III. A caution is here given not to forget God in a day of prosperity and plenty, *v.* 10–12. Here, 1. He raises their expectations of the goodness of their God, taking it for granted that he would bring them into the good land that he had promised (*v.* 10), that they should no longer dwell in tents as shepherds and poor travellers, but should settle in great and goodly cities, should no longer wander in a barren wilderness, but should enjoy houses will furnished and gardens well planted (*v.* 11), and all this without any care and expense of their own, which he here lays a great stress upon — *Cities which thou buildest not, houses which thou filledst not, etc.,* both because it made the mercy really much more valuable that what they had come to them so cheaply, and yet, if they did not actually consider it, the mercy would be the less esteemed, for we are most sensible of the value of that which has cost us dear. When they came so easily by the gift they would be apt to grow secure, and unmindful of the giver. 2. He engages their watchfulness against the badness of their own hearts: *Then beware,* when thou liest safe and soft, *lest thou forget the Lord, v.* 12. Note, (1.) In a day of prosperity we are in great danger of forgetting God, our dependence upon him, our need of him, and our obligations to him. When the world smiles we are apt to make our court to it, and expect our happiness in it, and so we forget him that his our only portion and rest. Agur prays against this temptation (Prov. 30:9): *Lest I be full and deny thee.* (2.) There is therefore need of great care and caution at such a time, and a strict watch over our own hearts. *"Then beware;* being warned of your danger, stand upon your guard against it. *Bind the words of God for a sign upon thy hand,* for this end to prevent thy forgetting God. When thou art settled in Canaan forget not thy deliverance out of Egypt; but look to the *rock out of which thou wast hewn.* When thy latter end has greatly increased, remember the smallness of thy beginnings."

IV. Some special precepts and prohibitions are here given, which are of great consequence. 1. They must upon all occasions give honour to God (*v.* 13): *Fear him and serve him* (for, if he be a Master, we must both reverence him and do his work); *and swear by his name,* that is, they must not upon any occasion appeal to any other, as the discerner of truth and avenger of wrong. Swear by him only, and not by an idol, or any other creature. Swear by his name in all treaties and covenants with the neighbouring nations, and do not compliment them so far as to swear by their gods. Swearing by his mane is sometimes put for an open profession of his name. Isa. 45:23, *Every tongue shall swear,* is expounded (Rom. 14:11), *Every tongue shall confess to God.* 2. They must not upon any occasion give that honour to other gods (*v.* 14): *You shall not go after other gods,* that is, "You shall not serve nor worship them;" for therein they went astray, they went a whoring from the true God, who in this, more than in any thing, is *jealous god* (*v.* 15): and the learned bishop Patrick observes here, out of Maimonides, that we never find, either in the law or the prophets, *anger,* or *fury,* or *jealousy,* or *indignation,* attributed to God but upon occasion of idolatry. 3. They must take heed of dishonouring God by *tempting him* (*v.* 16): *You shall not tempt the Lord your God,* that is, "You shall not in any exigence distrust the power, presence, and providence of God, nor quarrel with him," which, if they indulged an evil heart of unbelief, they would take occasion to do in Canaan as well as in the wilderness. No change of condition will cure a disposition of murmur and fret. Our Saviour uses this caution as an answer to one of Satan's temptations, with application to himself, Mt. 4:7, *Thou shalt not tempt the Lord thy God,* either by despairing of his power and goodness while we keep in the way of our duty, or by presuming upon it when we turn aside out of that way.

Verses 17–25

Here, I. Moses charges them to keep God's commandments themselves: *You shall diligently keep God's commandments, v.* 17–19. Note, It requires a great deal of care and pains to keep up religion in the power of it in our hearts and lives. Negligence will ruin us; but we cannot be saved without diligence. To induce them to this, he here shows them, 1. That this would be very acceptable to God: it is *right and good in the sight of the Lord;* and that is right and good indeed that is, so in *God's sight.* If we have any regard to the favour of our Creator as our felicity, and the law of our creation as our rule, we shall be religious. 2. That it would be very advantageous and profitable to themselves. It would secure to them the possession of the land of Canaan, prosperity there, and constant victory over those that stood in their way. In short, "Do well, and it shall be *well with thee."*

II. He charges them to instruct their children in the commands of God, not only that they might in their tender years intelligently and affectionately join in religious services, but that afterwards they might in their day keep up religion, and convey it to those that should come after them. Now,

1. Here is a proper question which it is supposed the children would ask (*v.* 20): *"What mean the testimonies and the statutes?* What is the meaning of the feasts we observe, the sacrifices we offer, and the many peculiar customs we keep up?" Observe, (1.) All divine institutions have a certain meaning, and there is something great designed in them. (2.) It concerns us to know and understand the meaning of them, that we may perform a reasonable service and may not *offer the blind for sacrifice.* (3.) It is good for children betimes to enquire into the true intent and meaning of the religious observances they are trained up in. If any are thus inquisitive in divine things it is a good sign that they are concerned about them, and a good means

of their attaining to a great acquaintance with them. *Then shall we know* if thus we *follow on to know.*

2. Here is a full answer put into the parents' mouths to be given to this good question. Parents and teachers must give instruction to those under their charge, though they do not ask it, nay, though they have an aversion to it; much more must they be ready to answer questions, and to give instruction when it is desired; for it may be hoped that those who ask it will be willing to receive it. Did the children ask the meaning of God's laws? Let them be told that they were to be observed, (1.) In a grateful remembrance of God's former favours to them, especially their deliverance out of Egypt, *v.* 21–23. The children must be often told of the deplorable state their ancestors were in when they were bondmen in Egypt, the great salvation God wrought for them in fetching them out thence, and that God, in giving them these peculiar statutes, meant to perpetuate the memorial of that work of wonder, by which they were formed into a peculiar people. (2.) As the prescribed condition of his further favours (*v.* 24): *The Lord commanded us all these statutes for our good.* Note, God commands us nothing but what is really for our good. It is our interest as well as our duty to be religious. [1.] It will be our life: *That he might preserve us alive,* which is a great favour, and more than we could expect, considering how often we have forfeited life itself. Godliness has the promise of the continuance and comfort of the life that now is as far as it is for God's glory. [2.] It will be our righteousness. Could we perfectly fulfil but that one command of loving God with all our heart, soul, and might, and could we say, "We have never done otherwise," this would be so our righteousness as to entitle us to the benefits of the covenant of innocency; had we continued in every thing that is written in the book of the law to do it, the law would have justified us. But this we cannot pretend to, therefore our sincere obedience shall be accepted through a Mediator to denominate us, as Noah was, *righteous before God,* Gen. 7:1; Lu. 1:6; and 1 Jn. 3:7. The Chaldee reads it, *There shall be a reward to us if we observe to do these commandments;* for, without doubt, in keeping God's commandments there is great reward.

CHAPTER 7

Moses in this chapter exhorts Israel, I. In general, to keep God's commandments (*v.* 11, 12). II. In particular, and in order to that, to keep themselves pure from all communion with idolaters. 1. They must utterly destroy the seven devoted nations, and not spare them, or make leagues with them (*v.* 1, 2, 16, 24). 2. They must by no means marry with the remainders of them (*v.* 3, 4). 3. They must deface and consume their altars and images, and not so much as take the silver and gold of them to their own use (*v.* 5, 25, 26). To enforce this charge, he shows that they were bound to do so, (1.) In duty. Considering [1.] Their election to God (*v.* 6). [2.] The reason of that election (*v.* 7, 8). [3.] The terms they stood upon with God (*v.* 9, 10). (2.) In interest. It is here promised, [1.] In general, that, if they would serve God, he would bless and prosper them (*v.* 12–15). [2.] In particular, that if they would drive out the nations, that they might not be a temptation to them, God would drive them out, that they should not be any vexation to them (*v.* 17, etc.).

Verses 1–11

Here is, I. A very strict caution against all friendship and fellowship with idols and idolaters. Those that are taken into communion with God must have no communication with the unfruitful works of darkness. These things they are charged about for the preventing of this snare now before them.

1. They must *show them no mercy, v.* 1, 2. Bloody work is here appointed them, and yet it is God's work, and good work, and in its time and place needful, acceptable, and honourable.

(1.) God here engages to do his part. It is spoken of as a thing taken for granted that God would *bring them into the land of promise,* that he would cast out the nations before them, who were the present occupants of that land; no room was left to doubt of that. His power is irresistible, and therefore he can do it; his promise is inviolable, and therefore he will do it. Now, [1.] These devoted nations are here named and numbered (*v.* 1), *seven* in all, and seven to one are great odds. They are specified, that Israel might know the bounds and limits of their commission: hitherto their severity must come, but no further; nor must they, under colour of this commission, kill all that came in their way; no, here must its waves be stayed. The confining of this commission to the nations here mentioned plainly intimates that after-ages were not to draw this into a precedent; this will not serve to justify those barbarous laws which give no quarter. How agreeable soever this method might be, when God himself prescribed it, to that dispensation under which such multitudes of beasts were killed and burned in sacrifice, now that all sacrifices of atonement are perfected in, and superseded by, the great propitiation made by the blood of Christ, human blood has become perhaps more precious than it was, and those that have most power yet must not be prodigal of it. [2.] They are here owned to be greater and mightier than Israel. They had been long rooted in this land, to which Israel came strangers; they were more numerous, had men much more bulky and more expert in war than Israel had; yet all this shall not prevent their being cast out before Israel. The strength of Israel's enemies magnifies the power of Israel's God, who will certainly be too hard for them.

(2.) He engages them to do their part. Thou shalt *smite them, and utterly destroy them, v.* 2. If God cast them out, Israel must not take them in, no, not as tenants, nor tributaries, nor servants. Not covenant of any kind must be made with them, no mercy must be shown them. This severity was appointed, [1.] By way of punishment for the wickedness they and their fathers had been guilty of. The iniquity of the Amorites was now full, and the longer it had been in the filling the sorer was the vengeance when it came at last. [2.] In order to prevent the mischiefs they would do to God's Israel if they were left alive. The people of these abominations must not be mingled with the holy seed, lest they corrupt them. Better that all these lives should be lost from the earth than that religion and the true worship of God should be lost in Israel. Thus we must deal with our lusts that was against our souls; God has delivered them into our hands by that promise, *Sin shall not have dominion over you,* unless it be your own faults; let not us them make covenants with them, nor show them any mercy, but mortify and crucify them, and utterly destroy them.

2. They must make no marriages with those of them that escaped the sword, *v.* 3, 4. The families of the Canaanites were ancient, and it is probable that some of them were called *honourable,* which might be a temptation to the Israelites, especially those of them that were of least note in their tribes, to court an alliance with them, to ennoble their blood; and the rather because their acquaintance with the country might be serviceable to them in the improvement of it: but religion, and the fear of God, must overrule all these considerations. To intermarry with them was *therefore* unlawful, because it was dangerous; this very thing had proved of fatal consequence to the old world (Gen. 6:2), and thousands in the world that now is have been undone by irreligious ungodly marriages; for there is more ground of fear in mixed marriages that the good will be perverted than of hope that the bad will be converted. The event proved the reasonableness of this warning: *They will turn away thy son from following me.* Solomon paid dearly for his folly herein. We find a national repentance for this sin of marrying strange wives, and care taken to reform (Ezra 9, 10; and Neh. 13), and a New-Testament caution not to be *unequally yoked with unbelievers,* 2 Co. 6:14. Those that in choosing yokefellows keep not at least within the bounds of a justifiable profession of religion cannot promise themselves helps meet for them. One of the Chaldee paraphrases adds here, as a reason of this command (*v.* 3), *For he that marries with idolaters does in effect marry with their idols.*

3. They must destroy all the relics of their idolatry, *v.* 5. Their altars and pillars, their groves and graven images, all must be destroyed, both in a holy indignation against idolatry and to prevent infection. This command was given before, Ex. 23:24; 34:13. A great deal of good work of this kind was done by the people, in their pious zeal (2 Chr. 31:1), and by good Josiah (2 Chr. 34:3, 7), and with this may be compared the burning of the conjuring books, Acts 19:19.

II. Here are very good reasons to enforce this caution.

1. The choice which God had made of this people for his own, *v.* 6. There was such a covenant and communion established between God and Israel as was not between him and any other people in the world. Shall they by their idolatries dishonour him who had thus honoured them? Shall they slight him who had thus testified his kindness for them? Shall they put themselves upon the level with other people, when God had thus dignified and advanced them above all people? Had God taken them to be a special people to him, and no other but them, and will not they take God to be a special God to them, and no other but him?

2. The freeness of that grace which made this choice. (1.) There was nothing in them to recommend or entitle them to this favour. *In multitude of the people is the king's honour,* Prov. 14:28. But their number was inconsiderable; they were only seventy souls when they went down into Egypt, and, though greatly increased there, yet there were many other nations more numerous: *You were the fewest of all people, v.* 7. The author of the Jerusalem Targum passes too great a compliment upon his nation in his reading this, *You were humble in spirit, and meek above all people;* quite contrary: they were rather stiff-necked and ill-natured above all people. (2.) God fetched the reason of it purely from himself, *v.* 8. [1.] He loved you *because he would love you.* Even so, Father, because it seemed good in thy eyes. All that God loves he loves freely, Hos. 14:4. Those that perish perish by their own merits, but all that are saved are saved by prerogative. [2.] He has done his work because he would keep his word. "He has brought you out of Egypt in pursuance of the oath sworn to your fathers." Nothing in them, or done by them, did or could make God a debtor to them; but he had made himself a debtor to his own promise, which he would perform notwithstanding their unworthiness.

3. The tenour of the covenant into which they were taken; it was in short this, That as they were to God so God would be to them. They should certainly find him, (1.) Kind to his friends, *v.* 9. "The Lord thy God is not like the gods of the nations, the creatures of fancy, subjects fit enough for loose poetry, but no proper objects of serious devotion; no, he is God, God indeed, God alone, the faithful God, able and ready not only to fulfil his own promises, but to answer all the just expectations of his worshippers, and he will certainly keep covenant and mercy," that is, "show mercy according to covenant, to *those that love him and keep his commandments"* (and in vain do we pretend to love him if we do not make conscience of his commandments); "and this" (as is here added for the explication of the promise in the second commandment) "not only to thousands of persons, but to thousands of generations — so inexhaustible the fountain, so constant are the streams!" (2.) Just to his enemies: He *repays those that hate him, v.* 10. Note, [1.] Wilful sinners are haters of God; for the carnal mind is enmity against him. Idolaters are so in a special manner, for they are in league with his rivals. [2.] Those that hate God cannot hurt him, but certainly ruin themselves. He will repay them to their face, in defiance of them and all their impotent malice. His arrows are said to be *made ready against the face of them,* Ps. 21:12. Or, He will bring those judgments upon them which shall appear to themselves to be the just punishment of their idolatry. Compare Job 21:19, *He rewardeth him, and he shall know it.* Though vengeance seem to be slow, yet it is not slack. The wicked and sinner shall be *recompensed in the earth,* Prov. 11:31. I cannot pass the gloss of the Jerusalem Targum upon this place, because it speaks the faith of the Jewish church concerning a future state: *He recompenses to those that hate him the reward of their good works in this world, that he may destroy them in the world to come.*

Verses 12–26

Here, I. The caution against idolatry is repeated, and against communion with idolaters: "Thou shalt consume the people, and not serve their gods." *v.* 16. We are in danger of having fellowship with the works of darkness if we take pleasure in fellowship with those that do those works. Here is also a repetition of the charge to destroy the images, *v.* 25, 26. The idols which the heathen had worshipped were an abomination to God, and therefore must be so to them: all that truly love God hat what he hates. Observe how this is urged upon them: *Thou shalt utterly detest it, and thou shalt utterly abhor it;* such a holy indignation as this must we conceive against sin, that *abominable thing which the Lord hates.* They must not retain the images to gratify their covetousness: *Thou shalt not desire the silver nor gold that is on them,* nor think it a pity to have that destroyed. Achan paid dearly for converting that to his own use which was an anathema. Nor must they retain them to gratify their curiosity: "Neither shalt thou bring it into thy house, to be hung up as an ornament, or preserved as a monument of antiquity. No, to the fire with it, that is the fittest place for it." Two reasons are given for this caution: — 1. *Lest thou be snared therein* (*v.* 25), that is, "Lest thou be drawn, ere thou art aware, to like it and love it, to fancy it and pay respect to it" 2. *Lest thou be a cursed thing like it, v.* 26. Those that make images are said to be like the, stupid and senseless; here they are said to be in a worse sense like them, accursed of God and devoted to destruction. Compare these two reasons together, and observe that whatever brings us into a snare brings us under a curse.

II. The promise of God's favour to them, if they would be obedient, is enlarged upon with a most affecting copiousness and fluency of expression, which intimates how much it is both God's desire and our own interest that we be religious. All possible assurance is here given them,

1. That, if they would sincerely endeavour to do their part of the covenant, God would certainly perform his part. He shall *keep the mercy which he swore to thy fathers, v.* 12. Let us be constant in our duty, and we cannot question the constancy of God's mercy.

2. That if they would love God and serve him, and devote themselves and theirs to him, he would love them, and bless them, and multiply them greatly, *v.* 13, 14. What could they desire more to make them happy? (1.) *"He will love thee."* He began in love to us (1 Jn. 4:10), and, if we return his love in filial duty, then, and then only, we may expect the continuance of it, Jn. 14:21. (2.) "He will bless thee with the tokens of his love above all people." If they would distinguish themselves from their neighbours by singular services, God would dignify them above their neighbours by singular blessings. (3.) "He will *multiply thee."* Increase was the ancient blessing for the peopling of the world, once and again (Gen. 1:28; 9:1), and here for the peopling of Canaan, that little world by itself. The increase both of their families and of their stock is promised: they should neither have estates without heirs nor heirs without estates, but should have the complete satisfaction of having many children and plentiful provisions and portions for them.

3. That, if they would keep themselves pure from the idolatries of Egypt, God would keep them clear form the *diseases of Egypt, v.* 15. It seems to refer not only to those plagues of Egypt by the force of which they were delivered, but to some other epidemical country disease (as we call it), which they remembered the prevalency of among the Egyptians, and by which God had chastised them for their national sins. Diseases are God's servants; they go where he sends them, and do what he bids them. It is therefore good for the health of our bodies to mortify the sin of our souls.

4. That, if they *would* cut off the devoted nations, they *should* cut them off, and none should be able to stand before them. Their duty in this matter would itself be their advantage: *Thou shalt consume all the people which the Lord thy God shall deliver thee* — this is the precept (*v.* 16); and *the Lord thy God shall deliver them unto thee, and shall destroy them* — this is the promise, *v.* 23. Thus we are commanded not to let sin reign, not to indulge ourselves in it nor give countenance to it, but to hate it and strive against it; and then God has promised that *sin shall not have dominion over us* (Rom. 6:12,14), but that we shall be more than conquerors over it. The difficulty and doubtfulness of the conquest of Canaan having been a stone of stumbling to their fathers, Moses here animates them against those things which were most likely to discourage them, bidding them not to be *afraid of them, v.* 18, and again, *v.* 21. (1.) Let them not be disheartened by the number and strength of their enemies: *Say not, They are more than I, how can I dispossess them? v.* 17. We are apt to think that the most numerous must needs be victorious: but, to fortify Israel against this temptation, Moses reminds them of the destruction of Pharaoh and all the power of Egypt, *v.* 18, 19. They had seen the great *temptations,* or *miracles* (so the Chaldee reads it), the signs and wonders, wherewith God had brought them out of Egypt, in order to his bringing them into Canaan, and thence might easily infer that God *could* dispossess the Canaanites (who, though formidable enough, had not such advantages against Israel as the Egyptians had; he that had done the greater could do the less), and that he *would* dispossess them, otherwise his bringing Israel out of Egypt had been no kindness to them. He that begun would finish. Thou shalt therefore *well remember* this, *v.* 18. The word and works of God are well remembered when they are improved as helps to our faith and obedience. That is well laid up which is ready to us when we have occasion to use it. (2.) Let them not be disheartened by the weakness and deficiency of their own forces; for God will send them in auxiliary troops of *hornets,* or *wasps,* as some read it (*v.* 20), probably larger than ordinary, which would so terrify and molest their enemies (and perhaps be the death of many to them) that their most numerous armies would become an easy prey to Israel. God plagued the Egyptians with flies, but the Canaanites with hornets. Those who take not warning by less judgments on others may expect greater on themselves. But the great encouragement of Israel was that they had God among them, a *mighty God and terrible, v.* 21. And if God be for us, if God be with us, we need not fear the power of any creature against us. (3.) Let them not be disheartened by the slow progress of their arms, nor think that the Canaanites would never be subdued if they were not expelled the first year; no, they must be *put out by little and little,* and not *all at once, v.* 22. Note, We must not think that, because the deliverance of the church and the destruction of its enemies are not effected immediately, therefore they will never be effected. God will do his own work in his own method and time, and we may be sure that they are always the best. Thus corruption is driven out of the hearts of believers *by little and little.* The work of sanctification is carried on gradually; but that judgment will at length be brought forth into a complete victory. The reason here given (as before, Ex. 23:29, 30) is, *Lest the beast of the field increase upon thee.* The earth God has given to the children of men; and therefore there shall rather be a remainder of Canaanites to keep possession till Israel become numerous enough to replenish it than that it should be a habitation of dragons, and a court for *the wild beasts of the desert,* Isa. 34:13, 14. Yet God could have prevented this mischief from the beasts, Lev. 26:6. But pride and security, and other sins that are the common effects of a settled prosperity, were enemies more dangerous than the beasts of the field, and these would be apt to increase upon them. See Judges 3:1, 4.

CHAPTER 8

Moses had charged parents in teaching their children to whet the word of God upon them (*ch.* 6:7) by frequent repetition of the same things over and over again; and here he himself takes the same method of instructing the Israelites as his children, frequently inculcating the same precepts and cautions, with the same motives or arguments to enforce them, that what they heard so often might abide with them. In this chapter Moses gives them, I. General exhortations to obedience (*v.* 1, 6). II. A review of the great things God had done for them in the wilderness, as a good argument for obedience (*v.* 2–5, 15, 16). III. A prospect of the good land into which God would now bring them (*v.* 7–9). IV. A necessary caution against the temptations of a prosperous condition (*v.* 10–14, and 17, 18). V. A fair warning of the fatal consequences of apostasy from God (*v.* 19, 20).

Verses 1–9

The charge here given them is the same as before, to keep and do all God's commandments. Their obedience must be, 1. Careful: *Observe to do.* 2. Universal: To *do all the commandments, v.* 1. And, 3. From a good principle, with a regard to God as the Lord, and their God, and particularly with a holy fear of him (*v.* 6), from a reverence of his majesty, a submission to his authority, and a dread of his wrath. To engage them to this obedience, besides the great advantages of it, which he sets before them (that they should *live and multiply,* and all should be well with them, *v.* 1), he directs them,

I. To look back upon the wilderness through which God had now brought them: *Thou shalt remember all the way which the Lord thy God led thee these forty years in the wilderness, v.* 2. Now that they had come of age, and were entering upon their inheritance, they must be reminded of the discipline they had been under during their minority and the method God had taken to train them up for himself. The wilderness was the school in which they had been for forty years boarded and taught, under tutors and governors; and this was a time to bring it all to remembrance. The occurrences of these last forty years were very memorable and well worthy to be remembered, very useful and profitable to be remembered, as yielding a complication of arguments for obedience; and they were recorded on purpose that they might be remembered. As the feast of the passover was a memorial of their deliverance out of Egypt, so was the feast of tabernacles of their passage through the wilderness. Note, It is very good for us to remember all the ways both of God's providence and grace, by which he has led us hitherto through this wilderness, that we may be prevailed with cheerfully to serve him and trust in him. Here let us set up our Ebenezer.

1. They must remember the straits they were sometimes brought into, (1.) For the mortifying of their pride; it was to *humble* them, that they might not be exalted above measure with the abundance of miracles that were wrought in their favor, and that they might not be secure, and confident of being in Canaan immediately. (2.) For the manifesting of their perverseness: to *prove* them, that they and others might know (for God himself perfectly knew it before) all that was in their heart, and might see that God chose them not for any thing in them that might recommend them to his favour, for their whole carriage was untoward and provoking. Many commandments God gave them which there would have been no occasion for if they had not been led through the wilderness, as those relating to the manna (Ex. 16:28); and God thereby tried them, as our first parents were tried by the trees of the garden, whether they would keep God's commandments or not. Or God thereby proved them whether they would trust his promises, the word which he commanded to a thousand generations, and, in dependence on his promises, obey his precepts.

2. They must remember the supplies which were always granted them.

(1.) God himself took particular care of their food, raiment, and health; and what would they have more? [1.] They had manna for food (*v.* 3): *God suffered them to hunger,* and the *fed them with manna,* that the extremity of their want might make the supply the more acceptable, and God's goodness to them therein the more remarkable. God often brings his people low, that he may have the honour of helping them. And thus the manna of heavenly comforts is given to those that *hunger and thirst after righteousness,* Mt. 5:6. *To the hungry soul every bitter thing is sweet.* It is said of the manna that it was a sort of food which neither *they nor their fathers knew.* And again, *v.* 16. If they knew there was such a thing that fell sometimes with the dew in those countries, as some think they did, yet it was never known to fall in such vast quantities, so constantly, and at all seasons of the year, so long, and only about a certain place. These things were altogether miraculous, and without precedent; *the Lord created a new thing* for their supply. And hereby he taught them the *man liveth not by bread alone.* Though God has appointed bread for the strengthening of man's heart, and that is ordinarily made the staff of life, yet God can, when he pleases, command support and nourishment without it, and make something else, very unlikely, to answer the intention as well. We might live upon air if it were sanctified for that use by *the word of God;* for the means God ordinarily uses he is not tied to, but can perform his kind purposes to his people without them. Our Saviour quotes this scripture in answer to that temptation of Satan, *Command that these stones be made bread.* "What need of that?" says Christ; "my heavenly Father can keep me alive without bread," Mt. 4:3,4. Let none of God's children distrust their Father, nor take any sinful indirect course for the supply of their own necessities; some way or other, God will provide for them in the way of duty and honest diligence, *and verily they shall be fed.* It may be applied spiritually; the *word of God,* as it is the revelation of God's will and grace duly received and entertained by faith, is the food of the soul, the life which is supported by that is the life of the man, and not only that life which is supported by bread. The manna typified Christ, *the bread of life.* He is *the Word of God;* by him we live. The Lord evermore give us that bread which endures to eternal life, and let us not be put off with the *meat that perisheth!* [2.] The same clothes served them from Egypt to Canaan, at least the generality of them. Though they had no change of raiment, yet it was always new, and waxed not old upon them, *v.* 4. This was a standing miracle, and the greater if, as the Jews say, they grew with them, so as to be always fit for them. But it is plain that they brought out of Egypt bundles of clothes on their shoulders (Ex. 12:34), which they might barter with each other as there was occasion; and these, with what they wore, sufficed till they came into a country where they could furnish themselves with new clothes.

(2.) By the method God took of providing food and raiment for them [1.] He humbled them. It was a mortification to them to be tied for forty years together to the same meat, without any varieties, and to the same clothes, in the same fashion. Thus he taught them that the good things he designed for them were figures of better things, and that the happiness of man consists not in being clothed in *purple or fine linen*, and in *faring sumptuously every day*, but in being taken into covenant and communion with God, and in *learning his righteous judgements*. God's law, which was given to Israel in the wilderness, must be to them instead of food and raiment. [2.] He proved them, whether they could trust him to provide for them when means and second causes failed. Thus he taught them to live in a dependence upon Providence, and not to perplex themselves with care *what they should eat and drink*, and *wherewithal they should be clothed*. Christ would have his disciples learn the same lesson (Mt. 6:25), and took a like method to teach it to them, when he *sent them out without purse or scrip*, and yet took care that they *lacked nothing*, Lu. 22:35. [3.] God took care of their health and ease. Though they travelled on foot in a dry country, the way rough and untrodden, yet their *feet swelled not*. God preserved them from taking hurt by the inconveniences of their journey; and mercies of this kind we ought to acknowledge. Note, Those that follow God's conduct are not only safe but easy. Our feet swell not while we keep in the way of duty; it is the *way of transgression* that *is hard*, Prov. 13:15. God had promised to *keep the feet of his saints*, 1 Sa. 2:9.

3. They must also remember the rebukes they had been under, *v.* 5. During these years of their education they had been kept under a strict discipline, and not without need. *As a man chasteneth his son*, for his good, and because he loves him, *so the Lord thy God chasteneth thee*. God is a loving tender Father to all his children, yet when there is occasion they shall feel the smart of the rod. Israel did so: they were chastened that they might not be condemned, chastened with the rod of men. Not as a man wounds and slays his enemies whose destruction he aims at, but as a man chastens his son whose happiness and welfare he designs: so did their God chasten them; he chastened and taught them, Ps. 94:12. This they must *consider in their heart*, that is, they must own it from their own experience that God had corrected them with a fatherly love, for which they must return to him a filial reverence and compliance. Because God has chastened thee as a father, *therefore* (*v.* 6) *thou shalt keep his commandments*. This use we should make of all our afflictions; by them let us be engaged and quickened to our duty. Thus they are directed to look back upon the wilderness.

II. He directs them to look forward to Canaan, into which God was now bringing them. Look which way we will, both our reviews and our prospects will furnish us with arguments for obedience. Observe,

1. The land which they were now going to take possession of is here described to be a very good land, having every thing in it that was desirable, *v.* 7–9. (1.) It was *well-watered, like Eden, the garden of the Lord*. It was *a land of brooks of water, of fountains and depths*, which contributed to the fruitfulness of the soil. Perhaps there was a greater plenty of water there now than in Abraham's time, the Canaanites having found and digged wells; so that Israel reaped the fruit of their industry as well as of God's bounty. (2.) The ground produced great plenty of all good things, not only for the necessary support, but for the convenience and comfort of human life. In their fathers' land they had bread enough; it was corn land, a land of wheat and barley, where, with the common care and labour of the husbandman, they might eat bread without scarceness. It was a fruitful land, that was never turned into barrenness but for the iniquity of those that dwelt therein. They had not only water enough to quench their thirst, but vines, the fruit whereof was ordained to make glad the heart. And, if they were desirous of dainties, they needed not to send to far countries for them, when their own was so well stocked with fig-trees, and pomegranates, olives of the best kind, and honey, or *date-trees*, as some think it should be read. (3.) Even the bowels of its earth were very rich, though it should seem that *silver and gold they had none;* of these the princes of Sheba should bring presents (Ps. 72:10, 15); yet they had plenty of those more serviceable metals, iron and brass. Iron-stone and mines of brass were found in their hills. See Job 28:2.

2. These things are mentioned, (1.) To show the great difference between that wilderness through which God had led them and the good land into which he was bringing them. Note, Those that bear the inconveniences of an afflicted state with patience and submission, are humbled by them and prove well under them, are best prepared for better circumstances. (2.) To show what obligations they lay under to keep God's commandments, both in gratitude for his favours to them and from a regard to their own interest, that the favours might be continued. The only way to keep possession of this good land would be to keep in the way of their duty. (3.) To show what a figure it was of good things to come. Whatever others saw, it is probable that Moses in it saw a type of the better country: The gospel church is the New-Testament Canaan, watered with the Spirit in his gifts and graces, planted with the trees of righteousness, bearing the fruits of righteousness. Heaven is the good land, in which there is nothing wanting, and where there is a fulness of joy.

Verses 10–20

Moses, having mentioned the great plenty they would find in the land of Canaan, finds it necessary to caution them against the abuse of that plenty, which was a sin they would be the more prone to new that they came into the vineyard of the Lord, immediately out of a barren desert.

I. He directs them to the duty of a prosperous condition, *v.* 10. They are allowed to eat even to fulness, not to surfeiting no excess; but let them always remember their benefactor, the founder of their feast, and never fail to give thanks after meat: *Then thou shalt bless the Lord thy God*. 1. They must take heed of eating or drinking so much as to indispose themselves for this duty of blessing God, rather aiming to serve God therein with so much the more cheerfulness and enlargement. 2. They must not have any fellowship with those that, when they had eaten and were full, blessed false gods, as the Israelites themselves had done in their worship of the golden calf, Ex. 32:6. 3. Whatever they had the comfort of God must have the glory of. As our Saviour has taught us to bless before we eat (Mt. 14:19, 20), so we are here taught to bless after meat. That is our *Hosannah — God bless;* this is our *Hallelujah — Blessed be God. In every thing we must give thanks*. From this law the religious Jews took up a laudable usage of blessing God, not only at their solemn meals, but upon other occasions; if they drank a cup of wine they lifted up their hands and said, *Blessed be he that created the fruit of the vine to make glad the heart*. If they did but smell at a flower, they said, *Blessed be he that made this flower sweet*. 4. When they gave thanks for the fruits of the land they must give thanks for the fruits of the land itself, which was given them by promise From all our comfortable enjoyments we must take occasion to thank God for our comfortable settlements; and I know not but we of this nation have as much reason as they had to give thanks for a good land.

II. He arms them against the temptations of a prosperous condition, and charges them to stand upon their guard against them: "When thou art settled in goodly houses of thy own building," *v.* 12 (for though God gave them houses which they builded not, *ch.* 6:10, these would not serve them, they must have larger and finer), — "and when thou hast grown *rich in cattle, in silver, and in gold* (*v.* 13), as Abraham (Gen. 13:2), — when *all thou hast is multiplied*," 1. "Then take heed of pride. Beware *lest then thy heart be lifted up*," *v.* 14. When the estate rises, the mind is apt to rise with it, in self-conceit, self-complacency, and self-confidence. Let us therefore strive to keep the spirit low in a high condition; humility is both the ease and the ornament of prosperity. Take heed of saying, so much as in thy heart, that proud word, *My power, even the might of my hand, hath gotten me this wealth*, *v.* 17. Note, We must never take the praise of our prosperity to ourselves, nor attribute it to our ingenuity or industry; for bread is not always *to the wise*, nor *riches to men of understanding*, Eccl. 9:11. It is spiritual idolatry thus to *sacrifice to our own net*, Hab. 1:16. 2. "Then take heed of forgetting God." This follows upon the *lifting up on the heart;* for it is *through the pride of the countenance* that the *wicked seek not after God*, Ps. 10:4. Those that admire themselves despise God. (1.) "Forget not thy duty to God." *v.* 11. We forget God if we keep not his commandments; we forget his authority over us, and our obligations to him and expectations from him, if we are not obedient to his laws. When men grow rich they are tempted to think religion a needless thing. They are happy without it, think it a thing below them and too hard upon them. Their dignity forbids them to stoop, and their liberty forbids them to serve. But we are basely ungrateful if the better God is to us the worse we are to him. (2.) "Forget not God's former dealings with thee. Thy deliverance out of Egypt, *v.* 14. The provision he made for thee in the wilderness, that great and terrible wilderness." They must never forget the impressions which the horror of that wilderness made upon them; see Jer. 2:6, where it is called the very *shadow of death*. There God preserved them from being destroyed by the fiery serpents and scorpions, though sometimes he made use of them for their correction: there he kept them from perishing for want of water, following them with water out of a rock of flint (*v.* 15), out of which (says bishop Patrick) one would rather have expected fire than water. There he fed them with manna, of which before (*v.* 3), taking care to keep them alive, that he might *do them good at their latter end*, *v.* 16. Note, God reserves the best till the last for his Israel. However he may seem to deal hardly with them by the way, he will not fail to do them good at their latter end. (3.) "Forget not God's hand in thy present prosperity, *v.* 18. Remember it is he that giveth thee wealth; for he *giveth thee power to get wealth*." See here how God's giving and our getting are reconciled, and apply it to spiritual wealth. It is our duty to get wisdom, and above all our gettings to get understanding; and yet it is God's grace that gives wisdom, and when we have got it we must not say, It was the might of our hand that got it, but must own it was God that gave us power to get it, and therefore to him we must give the praise and consecrate the use of it. The *blessing of the Lord* on the *hand of the diligent* makes rich both for this world and for the other. He *giveth thee power to get wealth*, not so much to gratify thee, and make thee easy, as that he may establish his covenant. All God's gifts are in pursuance of his promises.

III. He repeats the fair warning he had often given them of the fatal consequences of their apostasy from God, *v.* 19, 20. Observe, 1. How he describes the sin; it is forgetting God, and then worshipping other gods. What wickedness will not those fall into that keep thoughts of God out of their minds? And, when once the affections are displaced from God, they will soon be misplaced upon lying vanities. 2. How he denounces wrath and ruin against them for it: "If you do so, *you shall surely perish*, and the power and might of your hands, which you are so proud of, cannot help you. Nay, you shall perish as the nations that are driven out before you. God will make no more account of you, notwithstanding his covenant with you and your relation to him, than he does of them, if you will not be obedient and faithful to him." Those that follow others in sin will certainly follow them to destruction. If we do as sinners do, we must expect to fare as sinners fare.

CHAPTER 9

The design of Moses in this chapter is to convince the people of Israel of their utter unworthiness to receive from God those great favours that were now to be conferred upon them, writing this, as it were, in capital letters at the head of their charter, "Not for your sake, be it known unto you," Eze. 36:32. I. He assures them of victory over their enemies (*v.* 1–3). II. He cautions them not to attribute their successes to their own merit, but to God's justice, which was engaged against their enemies, and his faithfulness, which was engaged to their fathers (*v.* 4–6). III. To make it evident that they had no reason to boast of their own righteousness, he mentions their faults, shows Israel their transgressions, and the house of Jacob their sins. In general, they had been all along a provoking people (*v.* 7–24). In particular, 1. In the matter of the golden calf, the story of which he largely relates (*v.* 8–21). 2. He mentions some other instances of their rebellion (*v.* 22, 23). And, 3. Returns, at *v.* 25, to speak of the intercession he had made for them at Horeb, to prevent their being ruined for the golden calf.

Verses 1–6

The call to attention (*v.* 1), *Hear, O Israel*, intimates that this was a new discourse, delivered at some distance of time after the former, probably the next sabbath day.

I. Moses represents to the people the formidable strength of the enemies which they were now to encounter, *v.* 1. The nations they were to dispossess were mightier than themselves, not a rude and undisciplined rout, like the natives of America, that were easily made a prey of. But, should they besiege them, they would find their cities well fortified, according as the art of fortification then was; should they engage them in the field, they would find the people great and tall, of whom common fame had reported that there was no standing before them, *v.* 2. This representation is much the same with that which the evil spies had made (Num. 13:28, 33), but made with a very different intention: that was designed to drive them from God and to discourage their hope in him; this to drive them to God and to engage their hope in him, since no power less than that which is almighty could secure and prosper them.

II. He assures them of victory, by the presence of God with them, notwithstanding the strength of the enemy, *v.* 3. "Understand therefore what thou must trust to for success, and which way thou must look; it is the Lord thy God that goes before thee, not only as thy captain, or commander-in-chief, to give direction, but as a consuming fire, to do execution among them. Observe, He shall destroy them, and then thou shalt drive them out. Thou canst not drive them out, unless he destroy them and bring them down. But he will not destroy them and bring them down, unless thou set thyself in good earnest to drive them out." We must do our endeavour in dependence upon God's grace, and we shall have that grace if we do our endeavour.

III. He cautions them not to entertain the least thought of their own righteousness, as if that had procured them this favour at God's hand: "Say not. *For my righteousness* (either with regard to my good character or in recompence for any good service) *the Lord hath brought me in to possess this land* (*v.* 4); never think it is for thy righteousness or the uprightness of thy heart, that it is in consideration either of thy good conversation or of they good disposition," *v.* 5. And again (*v.* 6) it is insisted on, because it is hard to bring people from a conceit of their own merit, and yet very necessary that it be done: "*Understand* (know it, and believe it, and consider it) that *the Lord thy God giveth thee not this land for thy righteousness.* Hadst thou been to come to it upon that condition, thou wouldst have been for ever shut out of it, *for thou art a stiff-necked people.*" Note, Our gaining possession of the heavenly Canaan, as it must be attributed to God's power and not to our own might, so it must be ascribed to God's grace and not to our own merit: in Christ we have both righteousness and strength; in him therefore we must glory, and not in ourselves, or any sufficiency of our own.

IV. He intimates to them the true reasons why God would take this good land out of the hands of the Canaanites, and settle it upon Israel, and they are borrowed from his own honour, not from Israel's deserts. 1. He will be honoured in the destruction of idolaters; they are justly looked upon as haters of him, and therefore he will visit their iniquity upon them. It is *for the wickedness of these nations* that God *drives them out, v.* 4, and again, *v.* 5. All those whom God rejects are rejected for their own wickedness: but none of those whom he accepts are accepted for their own righteousness. 2. He will be honoured in the performance of his promise to those that are in covenant with him: God swore to the patriarchs, who loved him and left all to follow him, that he would give this land to their seed; and therefore he would *keep that promised mercy for thousands of those that loved him and kept his commandments;* he would not suffer his promise to fail. It was for their fathers' sakes that they were beloved, Rom. 11:28. Thus boasting is for ever excluded. See Eph. 1:9, 11.

Verses 7–29

That they might have no pretence to think that God brought them to Canaan *for their righteousness,* Moses here shows them what a miracle of mercy it was that they had not long ere this been destroyed in the wilderness: "*Remember, and forget not, how thou provokedst the Lord thy God* (*v.* 7); so far from purchasing his favour, thou hast many a time laid thyself open to his displeasure." Their fathers' provocations are here charged upon them; for, if God had dealt with their fathers according to their deserts, this generation would never have been, much less would they have entered Canaan. We are apt to forget our provocations, especially when the smart of the rod is over, and have need to be often put in mind of them, that we may never entertain any conceit of our own righteousness. Paul argues from the guilt which all mankind is under to prove that we cannot be *justified before God* by our own works, Rom. 3:19, 20. If our works condemn us, they will not justify us. Observe, 1. They had been a provoking people ever since they came out of Egypt, *v.* 7. *Forty years long,* from first to last, were God and Moses grieved with them. It is a very sad character Moses now at parting leaves of them: *You have been rebellious since the day I knew you, v.* 24. No sooner were they formed into a people than there was a faction formed among them, which upon all occasions made head against God and his government. Though the Mosaic history records little more than the occurrences of the first and last year of the forty, yet it seems by this general account that the rest of the years were not much better, but one continued provocation. 2. Even in Horeb they made a calf and worshipped it, *v.* 8, etc. That was a sin so heinous, and by several aggravations made so exceedingly sinful, that they deserved upon all occasions to be upbraided with it. It was done in the very place where the law was given by which they were expressly forbidden to worship God by images, and while the mountain was yet burning before their eyes, and Moses had gone up to fetch them the law in writing. They *turned aside quickly, v.* 16. 3. God was very angry with them for their sin. Let them not think that God overlooked what they did amiss, and gave them Canaan for what was good among them. No, God had determined to destroy them (*v.* 8), could easily have done it, and would have been no loser by it; he even desired Moses to let him alone that he might do it, *v.* 13, 14. By this it appeared how heinous their sin was, for God is never angry with any above what there is cause for, as men often are. Moses himself, though a friend and favourite, trembled at the revelation of God's wrath from heaven against their ungodliness and unrighteousness (*v.* 19): *I was afraid of the anger of the Lord,* afraid perhaps not for them only, but for himself, Ps. 119:120. 4. They had by their sin broken covenant with God, and forfeited all the privileges of the covenant, which Moses signified to them by *breaking the tables, v.* 17. A bill of divorce was given them, and thenceforward they might justly have been abandoned for ever, so that their mouth was certainly stopped from pleading any righteousness of their own. God had, in effect, disowned them, when he said to Moses (*v.* 12), "They are thy people, they are none of mine, nor shall they be dealt with as mine." 5. Aaron himself fell under God's displeasure for it, though he was the saint of the Lord, and was only brought by surprise or terror to be confederate with them in the sin: *The Lord was very angry with Aaron, v.* 20. No man's place or character can shelter him from the wrath of God if he have *fellowship with the unfruitful works of darkness.* Aaron, that should have made atonement for them if the iniquity could have been purged away by sacrifice and offering, did himself fall under the wrath of God: so little did they consider what they did when they drew him in. 6. It was with great difficulty and very long attendance that Moses himself prevailed to turn away the wrath of God, and prevent their utter ruin. He fasted and prayed full forty days and forty nights before he could obtain their pardon, *v.* 18. And some think twice forty days (*v.* 25), because it is said, *as I fell down before,* whereas his errand in the first forty was not of that nature. Others think it was but one forty, though twice mentioned (as also in *ch.* 10:10); but this was enough to make them sensible how great God's displeasure was against them, and what a narrow escape they had for their lives. And in this appears the greatness of God's anger against all mankind that no less a person than his Son, and no less a price than his own blood, would serve to turn it away. Moses here tells them the substance of his intercession for them. He was obliged to own their stubbornness, and their wickedness, and their sin, *v.* 27. Their character was bad indeed when he that appeared an advocate for them could not give them a good word, and had nothing else to say in their behalf but that God had done great things for them, which really did but aggravate their crime (*v.* 26), — that they were the posterity of good ancestors (*v.* 27), which might also have been turned upon him, as making the matter worse and not better, — and that the Egyptians would reproach God, if he should destroy them, as unable to perfect what he had wrought for them (*v.* 28), a plea which might easily enough have been answered: no matter what the Egyptians say, while the heavens declare God's righteousness; so that the saving of them from ruin at that time was owing purely to the mercy of God, and the importunity of Moses, and not to any merit of theirs, that could be offered so much as in mitigation of their offence. 7. To affect them the more with the destruction they were then at the brink of, he describes very particularly the destruction of the calf they had made, *v.* 21. He calls it their *sin:* perhaps not only because it had been the matter of their sin, but because the destroying of it was intended for a testimony against their sin, and an indication to them what the sinners themselves did deserve. Those that made it were like unto it, and would have had no wrong done them if they had been thus stamped to dust, and consumed, and scattered, and no remains of them left. It was infinite mercy that accepted the destruction of the idol instead of the destruction of the idolaters. 8. Even after this fair escape that they had, in many other instances they provoked the Lord again and again. He needed only to name the places, for they carried the memorials either of the sin or of the punishment in their names (*v.* 22): at *Taberah, burning,* where God set fire to them for their murmuring, — at *Massah, the temptation,* where they challenged almighty power to help them, — and at *Kibroth-hattaavah, the graves of lusters,* where the dainties they coveted were their poison; and, after these, their unbelief and distrust at Kadesh-barnea, of which he had already told them (*ch.* 1), and which he here mentions again (*v.* 23), would certainly have completed their ruin if they had been dealt with according to their own merits.

Now let them lay all this together, and it will appear that whatever favour God should hereafter show them, in subduing their enemies and putting them in possession of the land of Canaan, it was not for their righteousness. It is good for us often to remember against ourselves, with sorrow and shame, our former sins, and to review the records conscience keeps of them, that we may see how much we are indebted to free grace, and may humbly own that we never merited at God's hand any thing but wrath and the curse.

CHAPTER 10

Moses having, in the foregoing chapter, reminded them of their own sin, as a reason why they should not depend upon their own righteousness, in this chapter he sets before them God's great mercy to them, notwithstanding their provocations, as a reason why they should be more obedient for the future. I. He mentions divers tokens of God's favour and reconciliation to them, never to be forgotten. (1.) The renewing of the tables of the covenant (*v.* 1–5). (2.) Giving orders for their progress towards Canaan (*v.* 6, 7). (3.) Choosing the tribe of Levi for his own (*v.* 8, 9). (4.) And continuing the priesthood after the death of Aaron (*v.* 6). (5.) Owning and accepting the intercession of Moses for them (*v.* 10, 11). II. Hence he infers what obligations they lay under to fear, and love, and serve God, which he presses upon them with many motives (*v.* 12, etc.).

Verses 1–11

There were four things in and by which God showed himself reconciled to Israel and made them truly great and happy, and in which God's goodness took occasion from their badness to make him the more illustrious: —

I. He gave them his law, gave it to them in writing, as a standing pledge of his favour. Though the tables that were first written were broken, because Israel had broken the commandments, and God might justly break the covenant, yet when his anger was turned away the tables were renewed, *v.* 1, 2. Note, God's putting his law in our reconciliation to God and the best earnest of our happiness in him. Moses is told to hew the tables; for the law prepares the heart by conviction and humiliation for the grace of God, but it is only that grace that then writes the law in it. Moses made *an ark of shittim-wood* (*v.* 3), a plain chest, the same, I suppose, in which the tables were afterwards preserved: but Bezaleel is said to make it (Ex. 37:1), because he afterwards finished it up and overlaid it with gold. Or Moses is said to make it because, when he went up the second time into the mount, he ordered it to be made by Bezaleel against he came down. And it is observable that for this reason the ark was the first thing that God gave orders about, Ex. 25:10. And this left an earnest to the congregation that the tables should not miscarry this second time, as they had done the first. God will send his law and gospel to those whose hearts are prepared as arks to receive them. Christ is the ark in which now our salvation is kept safely, that it may not be lost as it was in the first Adam, when he had it in his own hand. Observe, 1. What it was that God wrote on the two tables, the ten commandments (*v.* 4), or *ten words,* intimating in how little a compass they were contained: they were not ten volumes, but ten words: it was the same with the first writing, and both the same that he spoke in the mount. The second edition needed no correction nor amendment, nor did what he wrote differ form what he spoke. The written word is as truly the word of God as that which he spoke to his servants the prophets. 2. What care was taken of it. These two tables, thus engraven, were faithfully laid up in the ark. *And there they be,* said Moses, pointing it is probable towards the sanctuary, *v.* 5. That good thing which was committed to him he transmitted to them, and left it pure and entire in their hands; now let them look to it at their peril. Thus we may say to the rising generation, "God has entrusted us with Bibles, sabbaths, sacraments, etc., as tokens of his presence and favour, and there they be; we lodge them with you," 2 Tim. 1:13, 14.

II. He led them forward towards Canaan, though they in their hearts turned back towards Egypt, and he might justly have chosen their delusions, *v.* 6, 7. He brought them to a land of *rivers of waters,* out of a dry and barren wilderness. Sometimes God supplied their wants by the ordinary course of nature: when that failed, then by miracles; and yet after this, when they were brought into a little distress, we find them distrusting God and murmuring, Num. 20:3, 4.

III. He appointed a standing ministry among them, to deal for them in holy things. At that time when Moses went up a second time to the mount, or soon after, he had orders to separate the tribe of Levi to God, and to his immediate service, they having distinguished themselves by their zeal against the worshippers of the golden calf, *v.* 8, 9. The Kohathites carried the ark; they and the other Levites stood *before the Lord,* to minister to him in all the offices of the tabernacle; and the priests, who were of that tribe, were to bless the people. This was a standing ordinance, which had now continued almost forty years, even unto this day; and provision was made for the perpetuating of it by the settled maintenance of that tribe, which was such as gave them great encouragement in their work, and no diversion from it. *The Lord is his inheritance.* Note, A settled ministry is a great blessing to a people, and a special token of God's favour. And, since the particular priests could not continue by reason of death, God showed his care of the people in securing a succession, which Moses takes notice of here, *v.* 6. When *Aaron died,* the priesthood did not die with him, but *Eleazar his son ministered in his stead,* and took care of the ark, in which the tables of stone, those precious stones, were deposited, that they should suffer no damage; there they be, and he has the custody of them. Under the law, a succession in the ministry was kept up, by an entail of the office on a certain tribe and family. But now, under the gospel, when the effusion of the Spirit is more plentiful and powerful, the succession is kept up by the Spirit's operation on men's hearts, qualifying men for, and inclining men to, that work, some in every age, that the name of Israel may not be blotted out.

IV. He accepted Moses as an advocate or intercessor for them, and therefore constituted him their prince and leader (*v.* 10, 11): *The Lord hearkened to me and said, Arise, go before the people.* It was a mercy to them that they had such a friend, so faithful both to him that appointed him and to those for whom he was appointed. It was fit that he who had saved them from ruin, by his intercession with heaven, should have the conduct and command of them. And herein he was a type of Christ, who, as he ever lives making intercession for us, so he has *all power both in heaven and in earth.*

Verses 12–22

Here is a most pathetic exhortation to obedience, inferred from the premises, and urged with very powerful arguments and a great deal of persuasive rhetoric. Moses brings it in like an orator, with an appeal to his auditors *And now, Israel, what doth the Lord thy God require of thee? v.* 12. Ask what he requires; as David (Ps. 116:12), *What shall I render?* When we have received mercy from God it becomes us to enquire what returns we shall make to him. Consider what he requires, and you will find it is nothing but what is highly just and reasonable in itself and of unspeakable benefit and advantage to you. Let us see here what he does require, and what abundant reason there is why we should do what he requires.

I. We are here most plainly directed in our duty to God, to our neighbour, and to ourselves.

1. We are here taught our duty to God, both in the dispositions and affections of our souls and in the actions of our lives, our principles and our practices. (1.) We must *fear the Lord our God, v.* 12, and again *v.* 20. We must adore his majesty, acknowledge his authority, stand in awe of his power, and dread his wrath. This is gospel duty, Rev. 14:6, 7. (2.) We must love him, be well pleased that he is, desire that he may be ours, and delight in the contemplation of him and in communion with him. Fear him as a great God, and our Lord, love him as a good God, and our Father and benefactor. (3.) We must walk in his ways, that is, the ways which he has appointed us to walk in. The whole course of our conversation must be conformable to his holy will. (4.) We must *serve him* (*v.* 20), *serve him with all our heart and soul* (*v.* 12), devote ourselves to his honour, put ourselves under his government, and lay out ourselves to advance all the interests of his kingdom among men. And we must be hearty and zealous in his service, engage and employ our inward man in his work, and what we do for him we must do cheerfully and with a good will. (5.) We must *keep his commandments and his statutes, v.* 13. Having given up ourselves to his service, we must make his revealed will our rule in every thing, perform all he prescribes, forbear all the forbids, firmly believing that all the statutes he commands us are for our good. Besides the reward of obedience, which will be our unspeakable gain, there are true honour and pleasure in obedience. It is really for our present good to be meek and humble, chaste and sober, just and charitable, patient and contented; these make us easy, and safe, and pleasant, and truly great. (6.) We must give honour to God, in swearing by *his name* (*v.* 20); so give him the honour of his omniscience, his sovereignty, his justice, as well as of his necessary existence. *Swear by his name,* and not by the name of any creature, or false god, whenever an oath for confirmation is called for. (7.) To him we must cleave, *v.* 20. Having chosen him for our God, we must faithfully and constantly abide with him and never forsake him. Cleave to him as one we love and delight in, trust and confide in, and from whom we have great expectations.

2. We are here taught our duty to our neighbour (*v.* 19): *Love the stranger;* and, if the stranger, much more our brethren, as ourselves. If the Israelites that were such a peculiar people, so particularly distinguished from all people, must be kind to strangers, much more must we, that are not enclosed in such a pale; we must have a tender concern for all that share with us in the human nature, and *as we have opportunity;* (that is, according to their necessities and our abilities) we must *do good to all men.* Two arguments are here urged to enforce this duty: — (1.) God's common providence, which extends itself to all nations of men, they being all *made of one blood.* God *loveth the stranger* (*v.* 18), that is, he gives to all life, and breath, and all things, even to those that are Gentiles, and *strangers to the commonwealth of Israel* and to Israel's God. He knows those perfectly whom we know nothing of. He gives *food and raiment* even to those to whom he has not shown his word and statutes. God's common gifts to mankind oblige us to honour all men. Or the expression denotes the particular care which Providence takes of strangers in distress, which we ought to praise him for (Ps. 146:9, The *Lord preserveth the strangers*), and to imitate him, to serve him, and concur with him therein, being forward to make ourselves instruments in his hand of kindness to strangers. (2.) The afflicted condition which the Israelites themselves had been in, when they were strangers in Egypt. Those that have themselves been in distress, and have found mercy with God, should sympathize most feelingly with those that are in the like distress and be ready to show kindness to them. The people of the Jews, notwithstanding these repeated commands given them to be kind to strangers, conceived a rooted antipathy to the Gentiles, whom they looked upon with the utmost disdain, which made them envy the grace of God and the gospel of Christ, and this brought a final ruin upon themselves.

3. We are here taught our duty to ourselves (*v.* 16): *Circumcise the foreskin of your hearts.* that is, "Cast away from you all corrupt affections and inclinations, which hinder you from fearing and loving God. *Mortify the flesh* with the lusts of it. Away with all filthiness and superfluity of naughtiness, which obstruct the free course of the word of God to your hearts. Rest not in the circumcision of the body, which was only the sign, but be circumcised in heart, which is the thing signified." See Rom. 2:29. The command of Christ goes further than this, and obliges us not only to cut off the foreskin of the heart, which may easily be spared, but to cut off the right hand and to pluck out the right eye that is an offence to us; the more spiritual the dispensation is the more spiritual we are obliged to be, and to go the closer in mortifying sin. And *be no more stiff-necked,* as they had been hitherto, *ch.* 9:24. "Be not any longer obstinate against divine commands and corrections, but ready to comply with the will of God in both." The circumcision of the heart makes it ready to yield to God, and draw in his yoke.

II. We are here most pathetically persuaded to our duty. Let but reason rule us, and religion will.

1. Consider the greatness and glory of God, and therefore fear him, and from that principle serve and obey him. What is it that is thought to make a man great, but great honour, power, and possessions? Think then how great the Lord our God is, and greatly to be feared. (1.) He has great honour, a name above every name. He is *God of gods,* and *Lord of lords, v.* 17. Angels are called *gods,* so are magistrates, and the Gentiles had *gods many, and lords many,* the creatures of their own fancy; but God is infinitely above all these nominal deities. What an absurdity would it be for them to worship other gods when the God to whom they had sworn allegiance was the God of gods! (2.) He has great power. He is a *mighty God and terrible* (*v.* 17), *who regardeth not persons.* He has the power of a conqueror, and so he is terrible to those that resist him and rebel against him. He has the power of a judge, and so he is just to all those that appeal to him or appear before him. And it is as much the greatness and honour of a judge to be impartial in his justice, without respect to persons or bribes, as it is to a general to be terrible to the enemy. Our God is both. (3.) He has great possessions. Heaven and earth are his (*v.* 14), and all the hosts and stars of both. Therefore he is able to bear us out in his service, and to make up the losses we sustain in discharging our duty to him. And yet therefore he has no need of us, nor any thing we have or can do; we are undone without him, but he is happy without us, which makes the condescensions of his grace, in accepting us and our services, truly admirable. Heaven and earth are his possession, and yet *the Lord's portion is his people.*

2. Consider the goodness and grace of God, and therefore love him, and from that principle serve and obey him. His goodness is his glory as much as his greatness. (1.) He is good to all. Whomsoever he finds miserable, to them he will be found merciful: He *executes the judgment of the fatherless and widow, v.* 18. It is his honour to help the helpless, and to succour those that most need relief and that men are apt to do injury to, or at least to put a light upon. See Ps. 68:4, 5; 146:7, 9. (2.) But *truly God is good to Israel* in a special obligations to him: *"He is they praise, and he is thy God, v.* 21. *Therefore* love him and serve him, because of the relation wherein he stands to thee. He is thy God, a God in covenant with thee, and as such he is thy praise," that is [1.] "He puts honour upon thee; he is the God in whom, all the day long, thou mayest boast that thou knowest him, and art known of him. If he is thy God, he is thy glory." [2.] "He expects honour from thee. *He is thy praise,"* that is "he is the God whom thou art bound to praise; if he has not praise from thee, whence may he expect it?" He *inhabits the praises of Israel.* Consider, *First,* The gracious choice he made of Israel, *v.* 15. "He had a delight in thy fathers, and therefore chose their seed." Not that there was any thing in them to merit his favour, or to recommend them to it, but so it seemed good in his eyes. He would be kind to them, though he had no need

of them. *Secondly,* The great things he had done for Israel, *v.* 21, 22. He reminds them not only of what they had heard with their ears, and which their fathers had told them of, but of what they had seen with their eyes, and which they must tell their children of, particularly that within a few generations seventy souls (for they were no more when Jacob went down into Egypt) increased to a great nation, *as the stars of heaven for multitude.* And the more they were in number the more praise and service God expected from them; yet it proved, as in the old world, that when they began to multiply they corrupted themselves.

CHAPTER 11

With this chapter Moses concludes his preface to the repetition of the statutes and judgments which they must observe to do. He repeats the general charge (*v.* 1), and, having in the close of the foregoing chapter begun to mention the great things God had done among them, in this, I. He specifies several of the great works God had done before their eyes (*v.* 2–7). II. He sets before them, for the future, life and death, the blessing and the curse, according as they did, or did not, keep God's commandments, that they should certainly prosper if they were obedient, should be blessed with plenty of all good things (*v.* 8–15), and with victory over their enemies, and the enlargement of their coast thereby (*v.* 22–25). But their disobedience would undoubtedly be their ruin (*v.* 16, 17). III. He directs them what means to use that they might keep in mind the law of God (*v.* 18–21). And, IV. Concludes all with solemnly charging them to choose which they would have, the blessing or the curse (*v.* 26, etc.).

Verses 1–7

Because *God has made thee as the stars of heaven for multitude* (so the preceding chapter concludes), *therefore thou shalt love the Lord thy God* (so this begins). Those whom God has built up into families, whose beginning was small, but whose latter end greatly increases, should use that as an argument with themselves why they should serve God. Thou shalt *keep his charge,* that is, the oracles of his word and ordinances of his worship, with which they were entrusted and for which they were accountable. It is a phrase often used concerning the office of the priests and Levites, for all Israel was a kingdom of priests, a holy nation. Observe the connection of these two: *Thou shalt love the Lord* and *keep his charge,* since love will work in obedience, and that only is acceptable obedience which flows from a principle of love. 1 Jn. 5:3.

Mention is made of the great and terrible works of God which their *eyes had seen, v.* 7. This part of his discourse Moses addresses to the *seniors* among the people, the elders in age; and probably the elders in office were so, and were now his immediate auditors: there were some among them that could remember their deliverance out of Egypt, all above fifty, and to them he speaks this, not to the children, who knew it by hearsay only, *v.* 2. Note, God's mercies to us when we were young we should remember and retain the impressions of when we are old; what our eyes have seen, especially in our early days, has affected us, and should be improved by us long after. They had seen what terrible judgments God had executed upon the enemies of Israel's peace, 1. Upon Pharaoh and the Egyptians that enslaved them. What a fine country was ruined and laid waste by one plague after another, to force Israel's enlargement! *v.* 3. What a fine army was entirely drowned in the Red Sea, to prevent Israel's being re-enslaved! *v.* 4. Thus did he give *Egypt for their ransom,* Isa. 43:3. Rather shall that famous kingdom be destroyed than that Israel shall not be delivered. 2. Upon Dathan and Abiram that embroiled them. Remember *what he did in the wilderness* (*v.* 5), by how many necessary *chastisements* (as they are called, *v.* 2) they were kept from ruining themselves, particularly when those daring Reubenites defied the authority of Moses and headed a dangerous rebellion against God himself, which threatened the ruin of a whole nation, and might have ended in that if the divine power had not immediately crushed the rebellion by burying the rebels alive, them and *all that was in their possession, v.* 6. What was done against them, though misinterpreted by the disaffected party (Num. 16:41), was really done in mercy to Israel. To be saved from the mischiefs of insurrections at home is as great a kindness to a people, and therefore lays them under as strong obligations, as protection from the invasion of enemies abroad.

Verses 8–17

Still Moses urges the same subject, as loth to conclude till he had gained his point. *"If thou wilt enter into life,* if thou wilt enter into Canaan, a type of that life, and find it a good land indeed to thee, *keep the commandments: Keep all the commandments which I command you this day;* love God, and serve him with all your heart."

I. Because this was the way to get and keep possession of the promised land. 1. It was the way to get possession (*v.* 8): *That you may be strong* for war, and so *go in and possess it.* So little did they know either of hardship or hazard in the wars of Canaan that he does not say they should go in and fight for it; no, they had nothing in effect to do but go in and possess it. He does not go about to teach them the art of war, how to draw the bow, and use the sword, and keep ranks, that they might be strong, and go in and possess the land; no, but let them keep God's commandments, and their religion, while they are true to it, will be their strength, and secure their success. (2.) It was the way to keep possession (*v.* 9): *That you may prolong your days in this land* that your eye is upon. Sin tends to the shortening of the days of particular persons and to the shortening of the days of a people's prosperity; but obedience will be a lengthening out of their tranquillity.

II. Because the land of Canaan, into which they were going, had a more sensible dependence upon the blessing of heaven than the land of Egypt had, *v.* 10–12. Egypt was a country fruitful enough, but it was all flat, and was watered, not as other countries with rain (it is said of Egypt, Zec. 14:18, that it *has no rain*), but by the overflowing of the river Nile at a certain season of the year, to the improving of which there was necessary a great deal of the art and labour of the husbandman, so that in Egypt a man must bestow as much cost and pains upon a field as upon a garden of herbs. And this made them the more apt to imagine that the power of their own hands got them this wealth. But the land of Canaan was an uneven country, a land of hills and valleys, which not only gave a more pleasing prospect to the eye, but yielded a greater variety of soils for the several purposes of the husbandman. It was a land that had no great rivers in it, except Jordan, but *drank water of the rain of heaven,* and so, 1. Saved them a great deal of labour. While the Egyptians were ditching and guttering in the fields, up to the knees in mud, to bring water to their land, which otherwise would soon become like the heath in the wilderness, the Israelites could sit in their houses, warm and easy, and leave it to God to water their land with the former and the latter rain, which is called *the river of God* (Ps. 65:9), perhaps in allusion to, and contempt of, the river of Egypt, which that nation was so proud of. Note, The better God has provided, by our outward condition, for our ease and convenience, the more we should abound in his service: the less we have to do for our bodies the more we should do for God and our souls. 2. So he directed them to look upwards to God, who *giveth us rain form heaven and fruitful seasons* (Acts 14:17), and promised to be himself as *the dew unto Israel,* Hos. 14:5. Note, (1.) Mercies bring with them the greatest comfort and sweetness when we see them coming from heaven, the immediate gifts of divine Providence. (2.) The closer dependence we have upon God the more cheerful we should be in our obedience to him. See how Moses here magnifies the land of Canaan above all other lands, that the *eyes of God were always upon it,* that is, they should be so, to see that nothing was wanting, while they kept close to God and duty; its fruitfulness should be not so much the happy effect of its soil as the immediate fruit of the divine blessing; this may be inferred from its present state, for it is said to be at this day, now that God has departed from it, as barren a spot of ground as perhaps any under heaven. Call it not *Naomi:* call it *Marah.*

III. Because God would certainly bless them with an abundance of all good things if they would love him and serve him (*v.* 13–15): *I will give you the rain of your land in due season,* so that they should neither want it when the ground called for it nor have it in excess; but they should have the former rain, which fell at seed-time, and the latter rain, which fell before the harvest, Amos 4:7. This represented all the seasonable blessings which God would bestow upon them, especially spiritual comforts, which should come *as the latter and former, rain,* Hos. 6:3. And the earth thus watered produced, 1. Fruits for the service of man, *corn and wine, and oil,* Ps. 104:13–15. 2. Grass for the cattle, that they also might be serviceable to man, that *he might eat of them and be full, v.* 15. Godliness hath here the *promise of the life that now is;* but the favour of God shall put gladness into the heart, more than the increase of corn, and wine, and oil will.

IV. Because their revolt from God to idols. would certainly be their ruin: *Take heed that your hearts be not deceived, v.* 16, 17. All that forsake God to set their affection upon, or pay their devotion to, any creature, will find themselves wretchedly deceived to their own destruction; and this will aggravate it that it was purely for want of taking heed. A little care would have prevented their being imposed upon by the great deceiver. To awaken them to take heed, Moses here tells them plainly that if they should *turn aside to other gods,* 1. They would provoke the wrath of God against them; and *who knows the power of that anger?* 2. Good things would be turned away from them; the heaven would withhold its rain, and then of course the earth would not yield its fruit. 3. Evil things would come upon them; they would perish quickly form off this good land. And the better the land was the more grievous it would be to perish from it. The goodness of the land would not be their security, when the badness of the inhabitants had made them ripe for ruin.

Verses 18–25

Here, I. Moses repeats the directions he had given for the guidance and assistance of the people in their obedience, and for the keeping up of religion among them (*v.* 18–20), which is much to the same purport with what we had before, *ch.* 6:6, etc. Let us all be directed by the three rules here given: — 1. Let our hearts be filled with the word of God: *Lay up these words in your heart and in your soul.* The heart must be the treasury or storehouse in which the word of God must be laid up, to be used upon all occasions. We cannot expect good practices in the conversation, unless there be good thoughts, good affections, and good principles, in the heart. 2. Let our eyes be fixed upon the word of God. "Bind these words for a sign *upon your hand,* which is always in view (Isa. 49:16), *and as frontlets between your eyes,* which you cannot avoid the sight of; let them be as ready and familiar to you, and have your eye as constantly upon them, as if they were *written upon your door-posts,* and could not be overlooked either when you go out or when you come in." Thus we must *lay God's judgments before us,* having a constant regard to them, as the guide of our way, as the rule of our work, Ps. 119:30. 3. Let our tongues be employed about the word of God. Let it be the subject of our familiar discourse, wherever we are; especially with our children, who must be taught the service of God, as the one thing needful, much more needful than either the rules of decency or the calling they must live by in this world. Great care and pains must be taken to acquaint children betimes, and to affect them, with the word of God and the wondrous things of his law. Nor will any thing contribute more to the prosperity and perpetuity of religion in a nation than the good education of children: if the seed be holy, it is the substance of a land.

II. He repeats the assurances he had before given them, in God's name, of prosperity and success if they were obedient. 1. They should have a happy settlement, *v.* 21. Their days should be multiplied; and, when they were fulfilled, the days of their children likewise should be many, as the days of heaven, that is, Canaan should be sure to them and their heirs for ever, as long as the world stands, if they did not by their own sin throw themselves out of it. 2. It should not be in the power of their enemies to give them any disturbance, nor make them upon any account uneasy. "If you will *keep God's commandments,* and be careful to do your duty (*v.* 22), God will not only crown the labours of the husbandman with plenty of the fruits of the earth, but he will own and succeed the more glorious undertakings of the men of war. Victory shall attend your arms; which way soever they turn, God will drive out these nations, and put you in possession of their land," *v.* 23, 24. Their territories should be enlarged to the utmost extent of the promise, Gen. 15:18. And all their neighbours should stand in awe of them, *v.* 25. Nothing contributes more to the making of a nation considerable abroad, valuable to its friends and formidable to its enemies, than religion reigning in it; for who can be against those that have God for them? And he is certainly for those that are sincerely for him, Prov. 14:34.

Verses 26–32

Here Moses concludes his general exhortations to obedience; and his management is very affecting, and such as, one would think, should have engaged them for ever to God, and should have left impressions upon them never to be worn out.

I. He sums up all his arguments for obedience in two words, *the blessing and the curse* (*v.* 26), that is, the rewards and the punishments, as they stand in the promises and the threatenings, which are the great sanctions of the law, taking hold of hope and fear, those two handles of the soul, by which it is caught, held, and managed. These two, the blessing and the curse, he set before them, that is, 1. He explained them, that they might know them; he enumerated the particulars contained both in the blessing and in the curse, that they might see the more fully how desirable the blessing was, and how dreadful the curse. 2. He confirmed them, that they might believe them, made it evident to them, by the proofs he produced of his own commission, that the blessing was not a fool's paradise, nor the curse a bugbear, but that both were real declarations of the purpose of God concerning them. 3. He charged them to choose which of these they would have, so fairly does he deal with them, and so far is he from *putting out the eyes of these men,* as he was charged, Num. 16:14. They and we are plainly told on what terms we stand with Almighty God. (1.) If we be obedient to his laws, we may be sure of a blessing, *v.* 27. But, (2.) If we be disobedient, we may be as sure of a curse, *v.* 28. *Say you to the righteous* (for God has said it, and all the world cannot unsay it) that *it shall be well with them: but woe to the wicked, it shall be ill with them.*

II. He appoints a public and solemn proclamation to be made of the blessing and curse which he had set before them, upon the two mountains of Gerizim and Ebal, *v.* 29, 30. We have more particular directions for this solemnity in *ch.* 27:11, etc., and an account of the performance of it, Jos. 8:33, etc. It was to be done, and was done, immediately upon their coming into Canaan, that when they first took possession of that land they might know upon what terms they stood. The place where this was to be done is particularly described by Moses, though he never saw it, which is one circumstance among many that evidences his divine instructions. It is said be near the *plain,* or *oaks,* or *meadows,* of *Moreh,* which was one of the first places that Abraham came to in Canaan; so that in sending them thither, to hear the blessing and the curse, God reminded them of the promise he made to Abraham in that very place, Gen. 12:6, 7. The mention of this appointment here serves, 1. For the encouragement of their faith in the promise of God, that they should be masters of Canaan quickly. Do it (says Moses) on the other side Jordan (*v.* 30), for you may be confident *you shall pass over Jordan, v.* 31. The institution of this service to be done in Canaan was an assurance to them that they should be brought into possession of it, and a token like that which God gave to Moses (Ex. 3:12): *You shall serve God upon this mountain.* And, 2. It serves for an engagement upon them to be obedient, that they might escape that curse, and obtain that blessing, which, besides what they had already heard, they must shortly be witnesses to the solemn publication of (*v.* 32): "*You shall observe to do the statutes and judgements,* that you may not in that solemnity be witnesses against yourselves."

CHAPTER 12

Moses at this chapter comes to the particular statues which he had to give in charge to Israel, and he begins with those which relate to the worship of God, and particularly those which explain the second commandment, about which God is in a special manner jealous. I. They must utterly destroy all relics and remains of idolatry (*v.* 1–3). II. They must keep close to the tabernacle (*v.* 4, 5). The former precept was intended to prevent all false worship, the latter to preserve the worship God had instituted. By this latter law, 1. They are commanded to bring all their offerings to the altar of God, and all their holy things to the place which he should choose (*v.* 6, 7, 11, 12, 14, 18, 26–28). 2. They are forbidden, in general, to do as they now did in the wilderness (*v.* 8–11), and as the Canaanites had done (*v.* 29–32), and, in particular, to eat the hallowed things at their own houses (*v.* 13, 17, 18), or to forsake the instituted ministry (*v.* 19). 3. They are permitted to eat flesh as common food at their own houses, provided they do not eat the blood (*v.* 15, 16, and again, *v.* 20–26).

Verses 1–4

From those great original truths, That there is a God, and that there is but one God, arise those great fundamental laws, That that God is to be worshipped, and he only, and that therefore we are to have no other God before him: this is the first commandment, and the second is a guard upon it, or a hedge about it. To prevent a revolt to false gods, we are forbidden to worship the true God in such a way and manner as the false gods were worshipped in, and are commanded to observe the instituted ordinances of worship that we may adhere to the proper object of worship. For this reason Moses is very large in his exposition of the second commandment. What is contained in this and the four following chapters mostly refers to that. *These are statutes and judgments* which they must *observe to do* (*v.* 1), 1. In the days of their rest and prosperity, when they should be masters of Canaan. We must not think that our religion is instituted only to be our work in the years of our servitude, our entertainment in the places of our solitude, and our consolation in affliction; no, when we come to possess a good land, still we must keep up the worship of God in Canaan as well as in a wilderness, when we have grown up as well as when we are children, when we are full of business as well as when we have nothing else to do. 2. *All the days,* as long as you *live upon the earth.* While we are here in our state of trial, we must continue in our obedience, even to the end, and never leave our duty, nor grow weary of well-doing. Now,

I. They are here charged to abolish and extirpate all those things that the Canaanites had served their idol-gods with, *v.* 2, 3. Here is no mention of idol-temples, which countenances the opinion some have, that the tabernacle Moses reared in the wilderness was the first habitation that ever was made for religious uses, and that from it temples took their rise. But the places that had been used, and were now to be levelled, were enclosures for their worship on *mountains and hills* (as if the height of the ground would give advantage to the ascent of their devotions), and under green trees, either because pleasant or because awful: whatever makes the mind easy and reverent, contracts and composes it, was thought to befriend devotion. The solemn shade and silence of a grove are still admired by those that are disposed to contemplation. But the advantage which these retirements gave to the Gentiles in the worship of their idols was that they concealed those works of darkness which could not bear the light; and therefore they must all be destroyed, with the altars, pillars, and images, that had been used by the natives in the worship of their gods, so as that the very names of them might be buried in oblivion, and not only not be remembered with respect, but not remembered at all. They must thus consult, 1. The reputation of their land; let it never be said of this holy land that it had been thus polluted, but let all these dunghills be carried away, as things they were ashamed of. 2. The safety of their religion; let none be left remaining, lest profane unthinking people, especially in degenerate ages, should make use of them in the service of the God of Israel. Let these pest-houses be demolished, as things they were afraid of. He begins the statutes that relate to divine worship with this, because there must first be an abhorrence of that which is evil before there can be a steady adherence to that which is good, Rom. 12:9. The kingdom of God must be set up, both in persons and places, upon the ruins of the devil's kingdom; for they cannot stand together, nor can there be any communion between Christ and Belial.

II. They are charged not to transfer the rites and usages of idolaters into he worship of God; no, not under colour of beautifying and improving it (*v.* 4): *You shall not do so to the Lord your god,* that is, "you must not think to do honour to him by offering sacrifices on mountains and hills, erecting pillars, planting groves, and setting up images; no, you must not indulge a luxurious fancy in your worship, nor think that whatever pleases that will please God: *he is above all gods,* and will not be worshipped as other gods are."

Verses 5–32

There is not any one particular precept (as I remember) in all the law of Moses so largely pressed and inculcated as this, by which they are all tied to bring their sacrifices to that one altar which was set up in the court of the tabernacle, and there to perform all the rituals of their religion; for, as to moral services, then, no doubt, as now, men might pray every where, as they did in their synagogues. The command to do this, and the prohibition of the contrary, are here repeated again and again, as we teach children: and yet we are sure that there is in scripture no vain repetition; but all this stress is laid upon it, 1. Because of the strange proneness there was in the hearts of the people to idolatry and superstition, and the danger of their being seduced by the many temptations which they would be surrounded with. 2. Because of the great use which the observance of this appointment would be of to them, both to prevent the introducing of corrupt customs into their worship and to preserve among them unity and brotherly love, that, meeting all in one place, they might continue both of one way and of one heart. 3. Because of the significancy of this appointment. They must keep to one place, in token of their belief of those two great truths, which we find together (1 Tim. 2:5), That *there is one God,* and *one Mediator between God and man.* It not only served to keep up the notion of the unity of the Godhead, but was an intimation to them (though they could not stedfastly discern it) of the one only way of approach to God and communion with him, in and by the Messiah.

Let us now reduce this long charge to its proper heads.

I. It is here promised that when they were settled in Canaan, when they had *rest from their enemies, and dwelt in safety,* God would choose a certain place, which he would appoint to be the centre of their unity, to which they should bring all their offerings, *v.* 10, 11. Observe, 1. If they just be tied to one place, they should not be left in doubt concerning it, but should certainly know what place it was. Had Christ intended, under the gospel, to make any one place such a seat of power as Rome pretends to be, we should not have been left so destitute of instruction as we are concerning the appointed place. 2. God does not leave it to them to choose the place, lest the tribes should have quarrelled about it, each striving, for their secular advantage, to have it among them; but he reserves the choice to himself, as he does the designation of the Redeemer and the institution of holy ordinances. 3. He does not appoint the place now, as he had appointed mounts Gerizim and Ebal, for the pronouncing of the blessings and curses (*ch.* 11:29), but reserves the doing of it till hereafter, that hereby they might be made to expect further directions from heaven, and a divine conduct, after Moses should be removed. The place which God would choose is said to be the place where he would put his name, that is, which he would have to be called his, where his honour should dwell, where he would manifest himself to his people, and make himself known, as men do by their names, and where he would receive addresses, by which his name is both praised and called upon. It was to be his habitation, where, as King of Israel, he would keep court, and be found by all those that reverently sought him. The ark was the token of God's presence, and where that was put there God put his name, and that was his habitation. It contained the tables of the law; for none must expect to receive favours from God's hand but those that are willing to *receive the law from his mouth.* The place which God first chose for the ark to reside in was Shiloh; and, after that place had sinned away its honours, we find the ark at Kirjath-jearim and other places; but at length, in David's time, it was fixed at Jerusalem, and God said concerning Solomon's temple, more expressly than ever he had said concerning any other place, *This I have chosen for a house of sacrifice,* 2 Chr. 7:12. Compare 2 Chr. 6:5. Now, under the gospel, we have no temple that sanctifies the gold, no altar that sanctifies the gift, but Christ only; and, as to the places of worship, the prophets foretold that *in every place* the spiritual *incense should be offered,* Mal. 1:11. And our Saviour has declared that those are accepted as true worshippers who worship God in sincerity and truth, without regard either to this mountain or Jerusalem, Jn. 4:23.

II. They are commanded to bring all their burnt-offerings and sacrifices to this place that God would choose (*v.* 6 and again *v.* 11): *Thither shall you bring all that I command you;* and (*v.* 14), *There thou shalt offer thy burnt offerings;* and (*v.* 27), *The flesh and the blood must be offered upon the altar of the Lord thy God.* And of their peace-offerings, here called their *sacrifices,* though they were to *eat the flesh,* yet *the blood* was to be *poured out upon the altar.* By this they were taught that sacrifices and offerings God did not desire, nor accept, for their own sake, nor for any intrinsic worth in them, as natural expressions of homage and adoration; but that they received their virtue purely from that altar on which they were offered, as it typified Christ; whereas prayers and praises, as much more necessary and valuable, were to be offered every day by the people of God wherever they were. A devout Israelite might honour God, and keep up communion with him, and obtain mercy from him, though he had not an opportunity, perhaps, for many months together, of bringing a sacrifice to his altar. But this signified the obligation we Christians are under to offer up all our spiritual sacrifices to God in the name of Jesus Christ, hoping for acceptance only upon the score of his mediation, 1 Pt. 2:5.

III. They are commanded to feast upon their hallowed things before the Lord, with holy joy. They must not only bring to the altar the sacrifices which were to be offered to God, but hey must bring to the place of the altar all those things which they were appointed by the law to eat and drink, to the honour of God, in token of their communion with him, *v.* 6. Their, *tithes, and heave-offerings of their hand,* that is, their first-fruits, their vows, and *free-will-offerings,* and firstlings, all those things which were to be religiously made use of either by themselves or by the priests and Levites, must be brought to the place which God would choose; as all the revenues of the crown, from all parts of the kingdom, are brought into the exchequer. And (*v.* 7): *There you shall eat before the Lord, and rejoice in all that you put your hands unto;* and again (*v.* 12), *You shall rejoice before the Lord, you, and your sons, and your daughters.* Observe here, 1. That what we do in the service of God and to his glory redounds to our benefit, if it be not our own fault. Those that sacrifice to God are welcome to eat before him, and to feast upon their sacrifices: he *sups with us,* and *we with him,* Rev. 3:20. If we glorify God, we edify ourselves, and cultivate our own minds, through the grace of God, by the increase of our knowledge and faith, the enlivening of devout affections, and the confirming of gracious habits and resolutions: thus is the soul nourished. 2. That work for God should be done with holy joy and cheerfulness. You shall *eat and rejoice, v.* 7, and again, *v.* 12 and *v.* 18. (1.) Now while they were before the Lord they must rejoice, *v.* 12. It is the will of God that we should serve him with gladness; none displeased him more than those that *covered his altar with tears.* Mal. 2:13. See what a good Master we serve, who has made it our duty to sing at our work. Even the children and servants must rejoice with them before God, that the services of religion might be a pleasure to them, and not a task or drudgery. (2.) They must *carry away with them* the grateful relish of that delight which they found in communion with God; they must rejoice in all that they *put their hands unto, v.* 7. Some of the comfort which they must take with them into their common employments; and, being thus strengthened in soul, whatever they did they must do it heartily and cheerfully. And this holy pious joy in God and his goodness, with which we are to rejoice evermore, would be the best preservative against the sin and snare of *vain and carnal mirth* and a relief against the *sorrows of the world.*

IV. They are commanded to be kind to the Levites. Did they feast with joy? The Levites must feast with them, and rejoice with them, *v.* 12, and again, *v.* 18; and a general caution (*v.* 19), *Take heed that thou forsake not the Levite as long as thou livest.* There were Levites that attended the altar as assistants to the priests, and these must not be forsaken, that is, the service they performed must be constantly adhered to; no other altar must be set up than that which God appointed; for that would be to forsake the Levites. But this seems to be spoken of the Levites that were dispersed in the country to instruct the people in the law of God, and to assist them in their devotions; for it is *the Levite within their gates* that they are here commanded to make much of. It is a great mercy to have Levites near us, within our gates, that we may ask the law at their mouth, and at our feasts to be a check upon us, to restrain excesses. And it is the duty of people to be kind to their ministers that give them good instructions and set them good examples. As long as we live we shall need their assistance, till we come to that world where ordinances will be superseded; and therefore *as long as we live* we must not forsake the Levites. The reason given (*v.* 12) is because *the Levite has no part nor inheritance with you,* so that he cannot grow rich by husbandry or trade; let him therefore share with you in the comfort of your riches. They must give the Levites their tithes and offerings, settled on them by the law, because they had no other maintenance.

V. They are allowed to eat common flesh, but not the flesh of their offerings, in their own houses, wherever they dwelt. What was any way devoted to God they must not eat at home, *v.* 13, 17. But what was not so devoted they might kill and eat of at their pleasure, *v.* 15. And this permission is again repeated, *v.* 20–22. It should seem that while they were in the wilderness they did not eat the flesh of any of those kinds of beasts that were used in sacrifice, but what was killed at the door of the tabernacle, and part of it presented to God as a peace-offering, Lev. 17:3, 4. But when they came to Canaan, where they must live at a great distance from the tabernacle, they might kill what they pleased for their own use of their flocks and herds, without bringing part to the altar. This allowance is very express, and repeated, lest Satan should take occasion from that law which forbade the eating of their sacrifices at their own houses to suggest to them, as he did to our first parents, hard thoughts of God, as if he grudged them: *Thou mayest eat whatsoever thy soul lusteth after.* There is a natural regular appetite, which it is lawful to gratify with temperance and sobriety, not taking too great a pleasure in the gratification, nor being uneasy if it be crossed. The unclean, who might not eat of the holy things, yet might eat of the same sort of flesh when it was only used as common food. The distinction between clean persons and unclean was sacred, and designed for the preserving of the honour of their holy feasts, and therefore must not be brought into their ordinary meals. This permission has a double restriction: — 1. They must eat according to the blessing which God had given them, *v.* 15. Note, It is not only our wisdom, but our duty, to live according to our estates, and not to spend above what we have. As it is unjust on the one hand to hoard what should be laid out, so it is much more unjust to lay out more than we have; for what is not our own must needs be another's, who is thereby robbed and defrauded. And this, I say, is much more unjust, because it is easier afterwards to distribute what has been unduly spared, and so to make a sort of restitution for the wrong, than it is to repay to wife, and children, and creditors, what has been unduly spent. Between these two extremes let wisdom find the mean, and then let watchfulness and resolution keep it. 2. They must not eat blood (*v.* 16, and again, *v.* 23): *Only be sure that thou eat not the blood* (*v.* 24), *Thou shalt not eat it;* and (*v.* 25), *Thou shalt not eat it, that it may go well with thee.* When they could not bring the blood to the altar, to pour it out there before the Lord, as belonging to him, they must pour it out upon the earth, as not belonging to them, because it was the life, and therefore, as an acknowledgment, belonged to him who gives life, and, as an atonement, belonged to him to whom life is forfeited. Bishop Patrick thinks one reason why they were forbidden thus strictly the eating of blood was to prevent the superstitions of the old idolaters about the blood of their sacrifices, which they thought their demons delighted in, and by eating of which they imagined that they had communion with them.

VI. They are forbidden to keep up either their own corrupt usages in the wilderness or the corrupt usages of their predecessors in the land of Canaan.

1. They must not keep up those improper customs which they had got into in the wilderness, and which were connived at in consideration of the present unsettledness of their condition (*v.* 8, 9): *You shall not do after all the things that we do here this day.* Never was there a better governor than Moses, and one would think never a better opportunity of keeping up good order and discipline than now among the people of Israel, when they lay so closely encamped under the eye of their governor; and yet it seems there was much amiss and many irregularities had crept in among them. We must never expect to see any society perfectly pure and right, and as it should be till we come to the heavenly Canaan. They had sacrifices and religious worship, courts of justice and civil government, and, by the stoning of the man that *gathered sticks on the sabbath day,* it appears there was great strictness used in guarding the most weighty matters of the law; but being frequently upon the remove, and always at uncertainty, (1.) They could none of them observe the solemn feasts, and the rites of cleansing, with the exactness that the law required. And, (2.) Those among them that were disposed to do amiss had opportunity given them to do it unobserved by the frequent interruptions which their removals gave to the administration of justice. But (says Moses) when you come to Canaan, you *shall not do as we do here.* Note, When the people of God are in an unsettled condition, that may be tolerated and dispensed with which would by no means be allowed at another time. Cases of necessity are to be considered while the necessity continues; but that must not be done in Canaan which was done in the wilderness. While a house is in the building a great deal of dirt and rubbish are suffered to lie by it, which must all be taken away when the house is built. Moses was now about to lay down his life and government, and it was a comfort to him to foresee that Israel would be better in the next reign than they had been in his.

2. They must not worship the Lord by any of those rites or ceremonies which the notions of Canaan had made use of in the service of their gods, *v.* 29–32. They must not so much as enquire into the modes and forms of idolatrous worship. What good would it do to them to *know those depths of Satan?* Rev. 2:24. It is best to be ignorant of that which there is danger of being infected by. They must not introduce the customs of idolaters, (1.) Because it would be absurd to make those their patterns whom God had made their slaves and captives, cut off, and destroyed from before them. The Canaanites had not flourished and prospered so much in the service of their gods as that the Israelites should be invited to take up their customs. Those are wretchedly besotted indeed who will walk in the way of sinners, after they have seen their end. (2.) Because some of their customs were most barbarous and inhuman, and such as trampled, not only upon the light and law of nature, but upon natural affection itself, as *burning their sons and their daughters in the fire to their gods* (*v.* 31), the very mention of which is sufficient to make it odious, and possess us with a horror of it. (3.) Because their idolatrous customs were an abomination to the Lord, and the translating of them into his worship would make even that an abomination and an affront to him by which they should give him honour, and by which they hoped to obtain his favour. The case is bad indeed when the sacrifice itself has become an abomination, Prov. 15:8. He therefore concludes (*v.* 32) with the same caution concerning the worship of God which he had before given concerning the word of God (*ch.* 4:2): *"You shall not add thereto* any inventions of your own, under pretence of making the ordinance either more significant or more magnificent, *nor diminish from it,* under pretence of making it more easy and practicable, or of setting aside that which may be spared; but observe to do all that, and that only, which God has commanded." We may then hope in our religious worship to obtain the divine acceptance when we observe the divine appointment. God will have his own work done in his own way.

CHAPTER 13

Moses is still upon that necessary subject concerning the peril of idolatry. In the close of the foregoing chapter he had cautioned them against the peril that might arise from their predecessors the Canaanites. In this chapter he cautions them against the rise of idolatry from among themselves; they must take heed lest any should draw them to idolatry, I. By the pretence of prophecy (*v.* 1–5). II. By the pretence of friendship and relation (*v.* 6–11). III. By the pretence of numbers (*v.* 12–18). But in all these cases the temptation must be resolutely resisted and the tempters punished and cut off.

Verses 1–5

Here is, I. A very strange supposition, *v.* 1, 2. 1. It is strange that there should arise any among themselves, especially any pretending to vision and prophecy, who should instigate them to *go and serve other gods.* Was it possible that any who had so much knowledge of the methods of divine revelation as to be able to personate a prophet should yet have so little knowledge of the divine nature and will as to go himself and entice his neighbours *after other gods?* Could an Israelite ever be guilty of such impiety? Could a man of sense ever be guilty of such absurdity? We see it in our own day, and therefore may think it the less strange; multitudes that profess both learning and religion yet exciting both themselves and others, not only to worship God by images, but to give divine honour to saints and angels, which is no better than *going after other gods to serve them;* such is the power of strong delusions. 2. It is yet more strange that the sign or wonder given for the confirmation of this false doctrine should come to pass. Can it be thought that God himself should give any countenance to such a vile proceeding? Did ever a false prophet work a true miracle? It is only supposed here for two reasons: — (1.) To strengthen the caution here given against hearkening to such a one. "Though it were possible that he should work a true miracle, yet you must not believe him if he tell you that you must serve other gods, for the divine law against that is certainly perpetual and unalterable." The supposition is like that in Gal. 1:8, *If we, or an angel from heaven, preach any other gospel to you* — which does not prove it possible that an angel should preach another gospel, but strongly expresses the certainty and perpetuity of that which we have received. So here, (2.) It is to fortify them against the danger of impostures and lying wonders (2 Th. 2:9): "Suppose the credentials he produces be so artfully counterfeited that you cannot discern the cheat, nor disprove them, yet, if they are intended to draw you to the service of other gods, that alone is sufficient to disprove them; no evidence can be admitted against so clear a truth as that of the unity of the Godhead, and so plain a law as that of worshipping the *one only living and true God."* We cannot suppose that the God of truth should set his seal of miracles to a lie, to so gross a lie as is supposed in that temptation, *Let us go after other gods.* But if it be asked, Why is this false prophet permitted to counterfeit this broad seal? It is answered here (*v.* 3): *"The Lord you God proveth you.* He suffers you to be set upon by such a temptation to try your constancy, that both those that are perfect and those that are false and corrupt may be made manifest. It is to prove you; therefore see that you acquit yourselves well in the trial, and stand your ground."

II. Here is a very necessary charge given in this case, 1. Not to yield to the temptation: *"Thou shalt not hearken to the worlds of that prophet, v.* 3. Not only thou shalt not do the thing he tempts thee to, but thou shalt not so much as patiently hear the temptation, but reject it with the utmost disdain and detestation. Such a suggestion as this is not to be so much as parleyed with, but the ear must be stopped against it. *Get thee behind me, Satan."* Some temptations are so grossly vile that they will not bear a debate, nor may we so much as give them the hearing. What follows (*v.* 4), *You shall walk after the Lord,* may be looked upon, (1.) As prescribing a preservative from the temptation: "Keep close to your duty, and you keep out of harm's way. God never leaves us till we leave him." Or, (2.) As furnishing us with an answer to the temptation; say, "It is written, *Thou shalt walk after the Lord,* and *cleave unto him;* and therefore what have I to do with idols?"

2. Not to spare the tempter, *v.* 5. That prophet shall be *put to death,* both to punish him for the attempt he has made (the seducer must die, though none were seduced by him — a design upon the crown is treason) and to prevent his doing further mischief. This is called *putting away the evil.* There is no way of removing the guilt but by removing the guilty; if such a criminal be not punished, those that should punish him make themselves responsible. And thus the *mischief must be put away;* the infection must be kept from spreading by cutting off the gangrened limb, and putting away the mischief-makers. such Dangerous diseases as these must be taken in time.

Verses 6–11

Further provision is made by this branch of the statute against receiving the infection of idolatry from those that are near and dear to us.

I. It is the policy of the tempter to send his solicitations by the hand of those whom we love, whom we least suspect of any ill design upon us, and whom we are desirous to please and apt to conform ourselves to. The enticement here is supposed to come from a brother or child that are near by nature, from a wife or friend that are near by choice, and are to us *as our own souls, v.* 6. Satan tempted Adam by Eve and Christ by Peter. We are therefore concerned to stand upon our guard against a bad proposal when the person that makes it can pretend to an interest in us, that we many never sin against God in compliment to the best friend we have in the world. The temptation is supposed to be private: he will *entice thee secretly,* implying that idolatry is a work of darkness, which dreads the light and covets to be concealed, and in which the sinner promises himself, and the tempter promises him, secrecy and security. Concerning the false gods proposed to be served, 1. The tempter suggests that the worshipping of these gods was the common practice of the world; and, if they limited their adorations to an invisible Deity, they were singular, and like nobody, for these gods were the *gods of the people round about them,* and indeed of all the nations of the earth, *v.* 7. This suggestion draws many away from religion and godliness, that it is an unfashionable thing; and they make their court to the world and the flesh because these are the *gods of the people that are round about them.* 2. Moses suggests, in opposition to this, that it had not been the practice of their ancestors; they are gods which *thou hast not known, thou nor thy fathers.* Those that are born of godly parents, and have been educated in pious exercises, when they are enticed to a vain, loose, careless way of living should remember that those are ways which *they have not known, they nor their fathers.* And will they thus degenerate?

II. It is our duty to prefer God and religion before the best friends we have in the world. 1. We must not, in complaisance to our friends, break God's law (*v.* 8): *"Thou shalt not consent to him.* nor go with him to his idolatrous worship, no, not for company, or curiosity, or to gain a better interest in is affections." It is a general rule, *If sinners entice thee, consent thou not,* Prov. 1:10. 2. We must not, in compassion to our friends, obstruct the course of God's justice. He that attempts such a thing must not only be looked upon as an enemy, or dangerous person, whom one should be afraid of, and swear the peace against, but as a criminal or traitor, whom, in zeal for our sovereign Lord, his crown and dignity, we are bound to inform against, and cannot conceal without incurring the guilt of a great misprision (*v.* 9): *Thou shalt surely kill him.* By this law the persons enticed were bound to the seducer, and to give evidence against him before the proper judges, that he might suffer the penalty of the law, and that without delay, which the Jews say is here intended in that phrase, as it is in the Hebrew, *killing thou shalt kill him.* Neither the prosecution nor the execution must be deferred; and he that was first in the former must be first in the latter, to show that he stood to his testimony: *"Thy hand shall be first upon him,* to mark him out as an anathema, and then the hands of all the people, to put him away as an accursed thing." The death he must die was that which was looked upon among the Jews as the severest of all deaths. He must be stoned: and his accusation written is that he has sought to thrust thee away, by a kind of violence, *from the Lord they God, v.* 10. Those are certainly our worst enemies that would *thrust us from God,* our best friend; and whatever draws us to sin, separates between us and God, is a design upon our life, and to be resented accordingly, And, lastly, here is the good effect of this necessary execution (*v.* 11): *All Israel shall hear and fear.* They *ought to hear and fear;* for the punishment of crimes committed is designed *in terrorem — to terrify,* and so to prevent their repetition. And it is to be hoped they will hear and fear, and by the severity of the punishment, especially when it is at the prosecution of a father, a brother, or a friend, will be made to conceive a horror of the sin, as exceedingly sinful, and to be afraid of incurring the like punishment themselves. *Smite the scorner* that sins presumptuously, *and the simple,* that is in danger of sinning carelessly, *will beware.*

Verses 12–18

Here the case is put of a city revolting from its allegiance to the God of Israel, *and serving other gods.*

I. The crime is supposed to be committed, 1. By one of the cities of Israel, that lay within the jurisdiction of their courts. The church then *judged those only that were within,* 1 Co. 5:12, 13. And, even when they were ordered to preserve their religion in the first principles of it by fire and sword to propagate it. Those that are born within the allegiance of a prince, if they take up arms against him, are dealt with as traitors, but foreign invaders are not so. The city that is here supposed to have become idolatrous is one that formerly worshipped the true God, but had now withdrawn to other gods, which intimates how great the crime is, and how sore the punishment will be, of those that, *after they have known the way of righteousness, turn aside from it,* 2 Pt. 2:21. 2. It is supposed to be committed by the generality of the inhabitants of the city, for we may conclude that, if a considerable number did retain their integrity, those only that were guilty were to be destroyed, and the city was to be spared for the sake of the righteous in it; for *will not the Judge of all the earth do right?* No doubt he will. 3. They are supposed to be drawn to idolatry by *certain men, the children of Belial,* men that would endure no yoke (so it signifies), that neither fear God nor regard man, but shake off all restraints of law and conscience, and are perfectly lost to all manner of virtue; these are those that say, "Let us serve other gods," that will not only allow, but will countenance and encourage, our immoralities. Belial is put for *the devil* (2 Co. 6:15), and the children of Belial are his children. These withdraw the inhabitants of the city; for a little of this old leaven, when it is entertained, soon leavens the whole lump.

II. The cause is ordered to be tried with a great deal of care (*v.* 14): *Thou shalt enquire and make search.* They must not proceed upon common fame, or take the information by hearsay, but must examine the proofs, and not give judgment against them unless the evidence was clear and the charge fully made out. God himself, before he destroyed Sodom, is said to have come down to see whether its crimes were according to the clamour, Gen. 18:21. In judicial processes it is requisite that time, and care, and pains, be taken to find out the truth, and that search be made without any passion, prejudice, or partiality. The Jewish writers say that, though particular persons who were idolaters might be judged by the inferior courts, the defection of a city was to be tried by the great Sanhedrim; and, if it appeared that they were thrust away to idolatry, two learned men were sent to them to admonish and reclaim them. If they repented, all would be well; if not, then all Israel must go up to war against them, to testify their indignation against idolatry and to stop the spreading of the contagion.

III. If the crime were proved, and the criminals were incorrigible, the city was to be wholly destroyed. If there were a few righteous men in it, no doubt they would remove themselves and their families out of such a dangerous place, and then all the inhabitants, men, women, and children, must be put to the sword (*v.* 15), all the spoil of the city, both shop-goods and the furniture of houses, must be brought into the marketplace and burned, and the city itself must be laid in ashes and never built again, *v.* 16. The soldiers are forbidden, upon pain of death, to convert any of the plunder to their own use, *v.* 17. It was a devoted thing, and dangerous to meddle with, as we find in the case of Achan. Now, 1. God enjoins this severity of show what a jealous God he is in the matters of his worship, and how great a crime it is to serve other gods. Let men know that God will not give his glory to another, nor his praise to graven images. 2. He expects that magistrates, having their honour and power from him, should be concerned for his honour, and use their power for *terror to evil doers,* else they bear the sword in vain. 3. The faithful worshippers of the true God must take all occasions to show their just indignation against idolatry, much more against atheism, infidelity, and irreligion. 4. It is here intimated that the best expedient for the turning away of God's anger from a land is to execute justice upon the *wicked of the land* (*v.* 17), that the Lord may *turn from the fierceness of his anger,* which was ready to break out against the whole nation, for the wickedness of that one apostate city. It is promised that, if they would thus root wickedness out of their land, God would multiply them. They might think it impolitic, and against the interest of their nation, to ruin a whole city for a crime relating purely to religion, and that they should be more sparing of the blood of Israelites: "Fear not the" (says Moses), "God will multiply you the more; the body of your nation will lose nothing by the letting out of this corrupt blood." *Lastly,* Though we do not find this law put in execution in all the history of the Jewish church (Gibeah was destroyed, not for idolatry, but immorality), yet for the neglect of the execution of it upon the inferior cities that served idols God himself, by the army of the Chaldeans, put it in execution upon Jerusalem, the head city, which, for is apostasy from God, was utterly destroyed and laid waste, and lay in ruins seventy years. Though idolaters may escape punishment from men (nor is this law in the letter of it binding now, under the gospel), yet the Lord our God will not suffer them to escape his righteous judgements. The New Testament speaks of communion with idolaters as a sin which, above any other, *provokes the Lord to jealousy,* and dares him as if we were *stronger than he,* 1 Co. 10:21, 22.

CHAPTER 14

Moses in this chapter teaches them, I. To distinguish themselves from their neighbours by a singularity, 1. In their mourning (*v.* 1, 2). 2. In their meat (*v.* 3–21). II. To devote themselves unto God, and, in token of that, to give him his dues out of their estates, the yearly tithe, and that every third year, for the maintenance of their religious feasts, the Levites, and the poor (*v.* 22, etc.).

Verses 1–21

Moses here tells the people of Israel,

I. How God had dignified them, as a peculiar people, with three distinguishing privileges, which were their honour, and figures of those spiritual blessings in heavenly things with which God has in Christ blessed us. 1. Here is election: *The Lord hath chosen thee,* v: 2. Not for their own merit, nor for any good works foreseen, but because he would magnify the riches of his power and grace among them. He did not choose them because they were by their own dedication and subjection a peculiar people to him above other nations, but he chose them that they might be so by his grace; and thus were believers chosen, Eph, 1:4. 2. Here is adoption (*v.* 1): "*You are the children of the Lord your God,* formed by him into a people, owned by him as his people, nay, his family, *a people near unto him,* nearer than any other." *Israel is my son, my first-born;* not because he needed children, but because they were orphans, and needed a father. Every Israelite is indeed a child of God, a partaker of his nature and favour, his love and blessing *Behold what manner of love the Father has bestowed upon us!* 3. Here is sanctification (*v.* 2): "*Thou art a holy people,* separated and set apart for God, devoted to his service, designed for his praise, governed by a holy law, graced by a holy tabernacle, and the holy ordinances relating to it." God's people are under the strongest obligations to be holy, and, if they are holy, are indebted to the grace of God that makes them so. The Lord has set them apart for himself, and qualified them for his service and the enjoyment of him, and so has made them holy to himself.

II. How they ought to distinguish themselves by a sober singularity from all the nations that were about them. And, God having thus advanced them, let not them debase themselves by admitting the superstitious customs of idolaters, and, by making themselves like them, put themselves upon the level with them. *Be you the children of the Lord your God;* so the Seventy read it, as a command, that is, "Carry yourselves as becomes the children of God, and do nothing to disgrace the honour and forfeit the privileges of the relation." In two things particularly they must distinguish themselves: —

1. In their mourning: *You shall not cut yourselves, v.* 1. This forbids (as some think), not only their cutting themselves at their funerals, either to express their grief or with their own blood to appease the infernal deities, but their wounding and mangling themselves in the worship of their gods, as Baal's prophets did (1 Ki. 18:28), or their marking themselves by incisions in their flesh for such and such deities, which in them, above any, would be an inexcusable crime, who in the sign of circumcision bore about with them in their bodies the marks of the Lord Jehovah. So that, (1.) They are forbidden to deform or hurt their own bodies upon any account. Methinks this is like a parent's change to his little children, that are foolish, careless, and wilful, and are apt to play with knives: *Children, you shall not cut yourselves.* This is the intention of those commands which oblige us to deny ourselves; the true meaning of them, if we understood them aright, would appear to be, *Do yourselves no harm.* And this also is the design of those providences which most cross us, to remove from us those things by which we are in danger of doing ourselves harm. Knives are taken from us, lest we should cut ourselves. Those that are dedicated to God as a holy people must do nothing to disfigure themselves; the body is for the Lord, and is to be used accordingly. (2.) They are forbidden to disturb and afflict their own minds with inordinate grief for the loss of near and dear relations: "You shall not express or exasperate you sorrow, even upon the most mournful occasions, by cutting yourselves, and making baldness between your eyes, like men enraged, or resolvedly hardened in sorrow for the dead, as those that have no hope," 1 Th. 4:13. It is an excellent passage which Mr. Ainsworth here quotes from one of the Jewish writers, who understands this as a law against immoderate grief for the death of our relations. *If your father* (for instance) *die, you shall not cut yourselves,* that is, *you shall not sorrow more than is meet, for you are not fatherless, you have a Father, who is great, living, and permanent, even the holy blessed God,* whose children you are, *v.* 1. *But an infidel* (says he), *when his father dies, hath no father that can help him in time of need; for he hath said to a stock, Thou art my father, and to a stone, Thou hast brought me forth* (Jer. 2:27); *therefore he weeps, cuts himself, and makes himself bald.* We that have a God to hope in, and a heaven to hope for, must bear up ourselves with that hope under every burden of this kind.

2. They must be singular in their meat. Observe,

(1.) Many sorts of flesh which were wholesome enough, and which other people did commonly eat, they must religiously abstain from as unclean. This law we had before Lev. 11:2, where it was largely opened. It seems plainly, by the connection here, to be intended as a mark of peculiarity; for their observance of it would cause them to be taken notice of in all mixed companies as a separate people, and would preserve them from mingling themselves with, and conforming themselves to, their idolatrous neighbours. [1.] Concerning beasts, here is a more particular enumeration of those which they were allowed to eat then was in Leviticus, to show that they had no reason to complain of their being restrained from eating swines' flesh, and hares, and rabbits (which were all that were then forbidden, but are now commonly used), when they were allowed so great a variety, not only of that which we call butcher's meat (*v.* 4), which alone was offered in sacrifice, but of venison, which they had great plenty of in Canaan, *the hart, and the roe-buck, and the fallow deer* (*v.* 5), which, though never brought to God's altar, was allowed them at their own table. See *ch.* 12:22. When of all these (as Adam of *every tree of the garden*) they might freely eat, those were inexcusable who, to gratify a perverse appetite, or (as should seem) in honour of their idols, and in participation of their idolatrous sacrifices, *ate swines' flesh, and had broth of abominable things* (made so by this law) *in their vessels,* Isa. 65:4. [2.] Concerning fish there is only one general rule given, that whatsoever had not fins and scales (as shell-fish and eels, besides leeches and other animals in the water that are not proper food) was *unclean and forbidden, v.* 9, 10. [3.] No general rule is given concerning fowl, but those are particularly mentioned that were to be unclean to them, and there are few or none of them which are here forbidden that are now commonly eaten; and whatsoever is not expressly forbidden is allowed, *v.* 11–20. *Of all clean fowls you may eat.* [4.] They are further forbidden, *First,* To eat the flesh of any creature that died of itself, because the blood was not separated from it, and, besides the ceremonial uncleanness which it lay under (from Lev. 11:39), it is not wholesome food, nor ordinarily used among us, except by the poor. *Secondly,* To *seethe a kid in its mother's milk,* either to gratify their own luxury, supposing it a dainty bit, or in conformity to some superstitious custom of the heathen. The Chaldee paraphrasts read it, *Thou shalt not eat flesh-meats and milk-meats together;* and so it would forbid the use of butter as sauce to any flesh.

(2.) Now as to all these precepts concerning their food, [1.] It is plain in the law itself that they belonged only to the Jews, and were not moral, nor of perpetual use, because not of universal obligation; for what they might not eat themselves they might give to a stranger, a proselyte of the gate, that had renounced idolatry, and therefore was permitted to live among them, though not circumcised; or they might sell it to an alien, a mere Gentile, that came into their country for trade, but might not settle it, *v.* 21. They might feed upon that which an Israelite might not touch, which is a plain instance of their peculiarity, and their being a holy people. [2.] It is plain in the gospel that they are now antiquated and repealed. For *every creature of God is good, and nothing now to be refused,* or *called common and unclean,* 1 Tim. 4:4.

Verses 22–29

We have here a part of the statute concerning tithes. The productions of the ground were twice tithed, so that, putting both together, a fifth part was devoted to God out of their increase, and only four parts of five were for their own common use; and they could not but own they paid an easy rent, especially since God's part was disposed of to their own benefit and advantage. The first tithe was for the maintenance of their Levites, who taught them the good knowledge of God, and ministered to them in holy things; this is supposed as anciently due, and is entailed upon the Levites as an inheritance, by that law, Num. 18:24, etc. But it is the second tithe that is here spoken of, which was to be taken out of the remainder when the Levites had had theirs.

I. They are here charged to separate it, and set it apart for God: *Thou shalt truly tithe all the increase of they seed, v.* 22. The Levites took care of their own, but the separating of this was left to the owners themselves, the law encouraging them to be honest by reposing a confidence in them, and so trying their fear of God. They are commanded to tithe *truly,* that is, to be sure to do it, and to do it faithfully and carefully, that God's part might not be diminished either with design or by oversight. Note, We must be sure to give God his full dues out of our estates; for, being but stewards of them, it is required that we be faithful, as those that must give account.

II. They are here directed how to dispose of it when they had separated it. Let every man lay by as God prospers him and gives him success, and then let him lay out in pious uses as God gives him opportunity; and it will be the easier to lay out, and the proportion will be more satisfying, when first we have laid by. This second tithe may be disposed of,

1. In works of piety, for the first two years after the year of release. They must bring it up, either in kind or in the full value of it, to the place of the sanctuary, and there must spend it in holy feasting before the Lord. If they could do it with any convenience, they must bring it in kind (*v.* 23); but, if not, they might turn it into money (*v.* 24, 25), and that money must be laid out in something to feast upon before the Lord. The comfortable cheerful using of what God has given us, with temperance and sobriety, is really the honouring of God with it. Contentment, holy joy, and thankfulness, make every meal a religious feast. The end of this law we have (*v.* 23): *That thou mayest learn to fear the Lord thy God always;* it was to keep them right and firm to their religion, (1.) By acquainting them with the sanctuary, the holy things, and the solemn services that were there performed. What they read the appointment of their Bibles, it would do them good to see the observance of in the tabernacle; it would make a deeper impression upon them, which would keep them out of the snares of the idolatrous customs. Note, It will have a good influence upon our constancy in religion *never to forsake the assembling of ourselves together,* Heb. 10:25. By the comfort of the communion of saints, we may be kept to our communion with God. (2.) By using them to the most pleasant and delightful services of religion. Let them *rejoice before the Lord, that they may learn to fear him always.* The more pleasure we find in the ways of religion the more likely we shall be to persevere in those ways. One thing they must remember in their pious entertainments — to bid their Levites welcome to them. Thou shalt not *forsake the Levites* (*v.* 27): "Let him never be a stranger to thy table, especially when thou eatest before the Lord."

2. Every third year this tithe must be disposed of at home in works of charity (*v.* 28, 29): *Lay it up within they own gates,* and let it be given to the poor, who, knowing the provision this law had made for them, no doubt would come to seek it; and, that they might make the poor familiar to them and not disdain their company, they are here directed to welcome them to their houses. "Thither let them come, and eat and be satisfied." In this charitable distribution of the second tithe they must have an eye to the poor ministers and add to their encouragement by entertaining them, then to poor strangers (not only for the supply of their necessities, but to put a respect upon them, and so to invite them to turn proselytes), and then to the

fatherless and widow, who, though perhaps they might have a competent maintenance left them, yet could not be supposed to live so plentifully and comfortably as they had done in months past, and therefore they were to countenance them, and help to make them easy by inviting them to this entertainment. God has a particular care for widows and fatherless, and he requires that we should have the same. It is his honour, and will be ours, to help the helpless. And if we thus serve God, and do good with what we have, it is promised here that the Lord our God will *bless us in all the work of our hand.* Note, (1.) The blessing of God is all in all to our outward prosperity, and, without that blessing, the work of our hands which we do will bring nothing to pass. (2.) The way to obtain that blessing is to be diligent and charitable. The blessing descends upon the working hand: "Except not that God should bless thee in thy idleness and love of ease, but in all the work of they hand." It is the hand of the diligent, with the blessing of God upon it, that makes rich, Prov. 10:4, 22. And it descends upon the giving hand; he that thus scatters certainly increases, and the liberal soul will be made fat. It is an undoubted truth, though little believed, that to be charitable to the poor, and to be free and generous in the support of religion and any good work, is the surest and safest way of thriving. What is lent to the Lord will be repaid with abundant interest. See Eze. 44:30.

CHAPTER 15

In this chapter Moses gives orders, I. Concerning the release of debts, every seventh year (*v.* 1–6), with a caution that this should be no hindrance to charitable lending (*v.* 7–11). II. Concerning the release of servants after seven years' service (*v.* 12–18). III. Concerning the sanctification of the firstlings of cattle to God (*v.* 19, etc.).

Verses 1–11

Here is, I. A law for the relief of poor debtors, such (we may suppose) as were insolvent. Every seventh year was a year of release, in which the ground rested from being tilled and servants were discharged from their services; and, among other acts of grace, this was one, that those who had borrowed money, and had not been able to pay it before, should this year be released from it; and though, if they were able, they were afterwards bound in conscience to repay it, yet thenceforth the creditor should never recover it by law. Many good expositors think it only forbids the exacting of the debt in the year of release, because, no harvest being gathered in that year, it could not be expected that men should pay their debts then, but that afterwards it might be sued for and recovered: so that the release did not extinguish the debt, but only stayed the process for a time. But others think it was a release of the debt for ever, and this seems more probable, yet under certain limitations expressed or implied. It is supposed (*v.* 3) that the debtor was an Israelite (an alien could not take the benefit of this law) and that he was poor (*v.* 4), that he did not borrow for trade or purchase, but for the subsistence of his family, and that now he could not pay it without reducing himself to poverty and coming under a necessity of seeking relief in other countries, which might be his temptation to revolt from God. The law is not that the creditor shall not receive the debt if the debtor, or his friends for him, can pay it; but he shall not exact it by a legal process. The reasons of this law are, 1. To put an honour upon the sabbatical year: *Because it is called the Lord's release, v.* 2. That was Gods year for their land, as the weekly sabbath was God's day for themselves, their servants, and cattle; and, as by the resting of their ground, so by the release of their debts, God would teach them to depend upon his providence. This year of release typified the grace of the gospel, in which is proclaimed the acceptable year of the Lord, and by which we obtain the release of our debts, that is, the pardon of our sins, and we are taught to forgive injuries, as we are and hope to be forgiven of God. 2. It was to prevent the falling of any Israelite into extreme poverty: so the margin reads (*v.* 4), *To the end there shall be no poor among you,* none miserably and scandalously poor, to the reproach of their nation and religion, the reputation of which they ought to preserve. 3. God's security is here given by a divine promise that, whatever they lost by their poor debtors, it should be made up to them in the blessing of God upon all they had and did, *v.* 4–6. Let them take care to do their duty, and then God would bless them with such great increase that what they might lose by bad debts, if they generously remitted them, should not be missed out of their stock at the year's end. Not only, *the Lord shall bless thee* (*v.* 4), but he *doth bless thee, v.* 6. It is altogether inexcusable if, though God had given us abundance, so that we have not only enough but to spare, yet we are rigorous and server in our demands from our poor brethren; for our abundance should be the supply of their wants, that at least there may not be such an inequality as is between two extremes, 2 Co. 8:14. They must also consider that their land was God's gift to them, that all their increase was the fruit of God's blessing upon them, and therefore they were bound in duty to him to use and dispose of their estates as he should order and direct them. And, *lastly,* If they would remit what little sums they had lent to their poor brethren, it is promised that they should be able to lend great sums to their rich neighbours, *even to many nations* (*v.* 6), and should be enriched by those loans. Thus the nations should become subject to them, and dependent on them, as *the borrower is servant to the lender,* Prov. 22:7. To be able to lend, and not to have need to borrow, we must look upon as a great mercy, and a good reason why we should do good with what we have, lest we provoke God to turn the scales.

II. Here is a law in favour of poor borrowers, that they might not suffer damage by the former law. Men would be apt to argue, *If the case of a man be so with his debtor* that if the debt be not paid before the year of release it shall be lost, it were better not to lend. "No," says this branch of the statute, "thou shalt not think such a thought." 1. It is taken for granted that there would be poor among them, who would have occasion to borrow (*v.* 7), and that there would never cease to be some such objects of charity (*v.* 7), and that there would never cease to be some such objects of charity (*v.* 11): *The poor shall never cease out of thy land,* though not such as were reduced to extreme poverty, yet such as would be behind-hand, and would have occasion to borrow; of such poor he here speaks, and such we have always with us, so that a charitable disposition may soon find a charitable occasion. 2. In such a case we are here commanded to lend or give, according to our ability and the necessity of the case: *Thou shalt not harden thy heart, nor shut thy hand, v.* 7. If the hand be shut, it is a sign the heart is hardened; for, *if the clouds were full of rain, they would empty themselves,* Eccl. 11:3. Bowels of compassion would produce liberal distributions, Jam. 2:15, 16. Thou shalt not only stretch out thy hand to him to reach him something, but thou shalt *open thy hand wide unto him,* to *lend him sufficient, v.* 8. Sometimes there is as much charity in prudent lending as in giving, as it obliges the borrower to industry and honesty and may put him into a way of helping himself. We are sometimes tempted to think, when an object of charity presents itself, we may choose whether we will give any thing or nothing, little or much; whereas it is here an express precept (*v.* 11), *I command thee,* not only to give, but to *open thy hand wide,* to give liberally. 3. Here is a caveat against that objection which might arise against charitable lending from the foregoing law for the release of debts (*v.* 9): *Beware that there be not a thought,* a covetous ill-natured thought, *in thy Belial heart, "The year of release is at hand,* and therefore I will not lend what I must then be sure to lose;" lest thy poor brother, whom thou refusest to lend to, complain to God, and it will be a sin, a great sin, to thee. Note, (1.) The law is spiritual and lays a restraint upon the thoughts of the heart. We mistake if we think thoughts are free from the divine cognizance and check. (2.) That is a wicked heart indeed that raises evil thoughts from the good law of God, as theirs did who, because God had obliged them to the charity of forgiving, denied the charity of giving. (3.) We must carefully watch against all those secret suggestions which would divert us from our duty or discourage us in it. Those that would keep from the act of sin must keep out of their minds the very thought of sin. (4.) When we have an occasion of charitable lending, if we cannot trust the borrower, we must trust God, and lend, hoping for nothing again in this world, but expecting it will be recompensed in the resurrection of the just, Lu. 6:35; 14:14. (5.) It is a dreadful thing to have the cry of the poor against us, for God has his ear open to that cry, and, in compassion to them, will be sue to reckon with those that deal hardly with them. (6.) That which we think is our prudence often proves sin to us; he that refused to lend because the year of release was at hand thought he did wisely, and that men would *praise him as doing well for himself,* Ps. 49:18. But he is here told that he did wickedly, and that God would condemn him as doing ill to his brother; and we are sure that the *judgment of God is according to truth,* and that what he says is sin to us will certainly be ruin to us if it be not repented of.

III. Here is a command to give cheerfully whatever we give in charity: *"Thy heart shall not be grieved when thou givest, v.* 10. Be not loth to part with thy money on so good an account, nor think it lost; grudge not a kindness to they brother; and distrust not the providence of God, as if thou shouldest want that thyself which thou givest in charity; but, on the contrary, let it be a pleasure and a satisfaction of soul to thee to think that thou art honouring God with thy substance, doing good, making thy brother easy, and laying up for thyself a good security for the time to come. What thou doest do freely, for God *loves a cheerful giver,"* 2 Co. 9:7.

IV. Here is a promise of a recompence in this life: *"For this thing the Lord thy God shall bless thee."* Covetous people say "Giving undoes us;" no, giving cheerfully in charity will enrich us, it will *fill the barns with plenty* (Prov. 3:10) and the soul with true comfort, Isa. 58:10, 11.

Verses 12–18

Here is, I. A repetition of the law that had been given concerning Hebrew servants who had sold themselves for servants, or were sold by their parents through extreme poverty, or were sold by the court of judgment for some crime committed. The law was, 1. That they should serve but six years, and in the seventh should go out free, *v.* 12. Compare Ex. 21:2. And, if the year of jubilee happened before they served out their time, that would be their discharge. God's Israel were a free people, and must not be compelled to perpetual slavery; thus are God's spiritual Israel called unto liberty. 2. That if, when their six years' service had expired, they had no mind to go out free, but would rather continue in service, as having less care, though taking more pains, than their masters, in this case they must lay themselves under an obligation to serve for ever, that is, for life, by having *their ears bored to the door-posts, v.* 16, 17. Compare Ex. 21:6. If hereby a man disgraced himself with some, as of a mean and servile spirit, that had not a due sense of the honour and pleasure of liberty, yet, we may suppose, with others he got reputation, as of a quiet contented spirit, humble, and diligent, and loving, and not *given to change.*

II. Here is an addition to this law, requiring them to put some small stock into their servants' hands to set up with for themselves, when they sent them out of their service, *v.* 13, 14. It was to be supposed that they had nothing of their own, and that their friends had little or nothing for them, else they else they would have been redeemed before they were discharged by law; they had no wages for their service, and all they got by their labour was their masters', so that their liberty would do them little good, having nothing to begin the world with; therefore their masters are here commanded to furnish them liberally with corn and cattle. No certain measure is prescribed: that is left to the generosity of the master, who probably would have respect to the servant's merit and necessity; but the Jewish writers say, "He could not give less than the value of thirty shekels of silver, but as much more as he pleased" The maid-servants, though they were not to have their ears bored if they were disposed to stay, yet, if they went out free, they were to have a gratuity given them; for to this those words refer, *Unto thy maid-servant thou shalt do likewise, v.* 17. The reasons for this are taken from the law of gratitude. They must do it, 1. In gratitude to God, who had not only brought them out of Egypt (*v.* 15), but brought them out greatly enriched with the spoils of the Egyptians. Let them not send their servants out empty, for they were not sent empty out of the house of bondage. God's tender care of us and kindness to us oblige us to be careful of, and kind to, those that have a dependence upon us. Thus we must *render according to the benefit done unto us.* 2. In gratitude to their servants, *v.* 18. "Grudge not to give him a little out of thy abundance, for *he has been worth a double hired servant unto thee.* The days of the hireling at most were but three years (Isa. 16:14), but he has served thee six years, and, unlike the hired servant, without any wages." Masters and landlords ought to consider what need they have of, and what ease and advantage they have by, their servants and tenants, and should not only be just but kind to them. To these reasons it is added, as before in this chapter (*v.* 4, 6, 10), *The Lord they God shall bless thee.* Then we may expect family blessings, the springs of family-prosperity, when we make conscience of our duty to our family-relations.

Verses 19–23

Here is, 1. A repetition of the law concerning the firstlings of their cattle, that, if they were males, they were to be *sanctified to the Lord* (*v.* 19), in remembrance of, and in thankfulness for, the sparing of the first-born of Israel, when the first-born of the Egyptians, both of man and beast, were slain by the destroying angel (Ex. 13:2, 15); on the eighth day it was to be given to God (Ex. 22:30), and to be divided between the priest and the altar, Num. 18:17, 18. 2. An addition to that law, for the further explication of it, directing them what to do with the firstlings, (1.) That were females: "Thou shalt *do no work with the* female *firstlings of the cow,* nor shear those of the sheep" (*v.* 19); of them the learned bishop Patrick understands it. Though the female firstlings were not so entirely sanctified to God as the males, nor so early as at eight days old, yet they were not to be converted by the owners to their own use as the other cattle, but must be offered to God as peace-offerings, or used in a religious feast, at the year's end, *v.* 20. *Thou shalt eat it before the Lord thy God,* as directed *ch.* 12:18. (2.) But what must they do with that which was blemished, ill-blemished? *v.* 21. Were it male or female, it must not be brought near the sanctuary, nor used either for sacrifice or for holy feasting, for it would not be fit to honour God with, nor to typify Christ, who is a *Lamb without blemish;* yet it must not be reared, but killed and eaten at their own houses as common food (*v.* 22), only they must be sure *not to eat it with the blood, v.* 23. The frequent repetition of this caution intimates what need the people had of it, and what stress God laid upon it. What a mercy it is that we are not under this yoke! We are not dieted as they were; we make no difference between a first calf, or lamb, and the rest that follow. Let us therefore realize the gospel meaning of this law, devoting ourselves and the first of our time and strength to God, as a kind of first-fruits of his creatures, and using all our comforts and enjoyments to his praise and under the direction of his law, as we have them all by his gift.

CHAPTER 16

In this chapter we have, I. A repetition of the laws concerning the three yearly feasts; in particular, that of the passover (*v.* 1–8). That of pentecost (*v.* 9–12). That of tabernacles (*v.* 13–15). And the general law concerning the people's attendance on them (*v.* 16, 17). II. The institution of an inferior magistracy, and general rules of justice given to those that were called into office (*v.* 18–20). III. A caveat against groves and images (*v.* 21, 22).

Verses 1–17

Much of the communion between God and his people Israel was kept up, and a face of religion preserved in the nation, by the three yearly feasts, the institution of which, and the laws concerning them, we have several times met with already; and here they are repeated.

I. The law of the passover, so great a solemnity that it made the whole month, in the midst of which it was placed, considerable: *Observe the month Abib, v.* 1. Though one week only of this month was to be kept as a festival, yet their preparations before must be so solemn, and their reflections upon it and improvements of it afterwards so serious, as to amount to an observance of the whole month. The month of Abib, or of *new fruits,* as the Chaldee translates it, answers to our March (or part of March and part of April), and was by a special order from God, in remembrance of the deliverance of Israel out of Egypt, made the *beginning of their year* (Ex. 12:2), which before was reckoned to begin in September. This month they were to keep the passover, in remembrance of their being *brought out of Egypt by night, v.* 1. The Chaldee paraphrasts expound it, "Because they came out of Egypt by daylight," there being an express order that they should not stir out of their doors till morning, Ex. 12:22. One of them expounds it thus: *"He brought thee out of Egypt,* and did wonders *by night."* The other, "and thou shalt eat the passover *by night."* The laws concerning it are, 1. That they must be sure to sacrifice the passover in the place that God should choose (*v.* 2), and in no other place, *v.* 5–7. The passover was itself a sacrifice; hence Christ, as our passover, is said to be *sacrificed for us* (1 Co. *v.* 7), and many other sacrifices were offered during the seven days of the feast (Num. 28:19, etc.), which are included here, for they are said to be sacrificed *of the flock and the herd,* whereas the passover itself was only of the flock, either a lamb or a kid: now no sacrifice was accepted but from the altar that sanctified it; it was therefore necessary that they should to up to the place of the altar, for, though the paschal lamb was entirely eaten by the owners, yet it must be killed in the court, the blood sprinkled, and the inwards burned upon the altar. By confining them to the appointed rule, from which they would have been apt to vary, and to introduce foolish inventions of their own, had they been permitted to offer these sacrifices within their own gates, from under the inspection of the priests. They were also hereby directed to have their eye up unto God in the solemnity, and the *desire of their hearts towards the remembrance of his name,* being appointed to attend where he had chosen *to place his name, v.* 2 and 6. But, when the solemnity was over, they might *turn and go unto their tents, v.* 7. Some think that they might, if they pleased, return the very morning after the paschal lamb was killed and eaten, the priests and Levites being sufficient to carry on the rest of the week's work; but the first day of the seven is so far from being the day of their dispersion that it is expressly appointed for a *holy convocation* (Lev. 23:7; Num. 28:18); therefore we must take it as Jonathan's paraphrase expounds it, *in the morning after the end of the feast thou shalt go to thy cities.* And it was the practice to keep together the whole week, 2 Chr. 35:17. 2. That they must eat unleavened bread for seven days, and no leavened bread must be seen in all their coasts, *v.* 3, 4, 8. The bread they were confined to is here called *bread of affliction,* because neither grateful to the taste nor easy of digestion, and therefore proper to signify the heaviness of their spirits in their bondage and to keep in remembrance the haste in which they came out, the case being so urgent that they could not stay for the leavening of the bread they took with them for their march. The Jewish writers tell us that the custom at the passover supper was that the master of the family broke this unleavened bread, and gave to every one a piece of it, saying, *This is* (that is, this signifies, represents, or commemorates, which explains that saying of our Saviour, *This is my body) the bread of affliction which your fathers did eat in the land of Egypt.* The gospel meaning of this feast of unleavened bread the apostle gives us, 1 Co. 5:7. *Christ our passover being sacrificed for us,* and we having participated in the blessed fruits of that sacrifice to our comfort, *let us keep the feast* in a holy conversation, free from *the leaven of malice* towards our brethren and hypocrisy towards God, and *with the unleavened bread of sincerity* and love. *Lastly,* Observe, concerning the passover, for what end it was instituted: *"That thou mayest remember the day when thou camest forth out of Egypt,* not only on the day of the passover, or during the seven days of the feast, but *all the days of thy life* (*v.* 3), as a constant inducement to obedience." Thus we celebrate the memorial of Christ's death at certain times, that we may remember it at all times, as a reason why we should *live to him that died for us and rose again.*

II. Seven weeks after the passover the feast of pentecost was to be observed, concerning which they are here directed, 1. Whence to number their seven weeks, *from the time thou beginnest to put the sickle to the corn* (*v.* 9), that is, from the morrow after the first day of the feast of unleavened bread, for on that day (though it is probable the people did not begin their harvest till the feast was ended) messengers were sent to reap a sheaf of barley, which was to be offered to God as the first-fruits, Lev. 23:10. Some think it implies a particular care which Providence would take of their land with respect to the weather, that their harvest should be always ripe and ready for the sickle just at the same time. 2. How they were to keep this feast. (1.) They must *bring an offering unto God, v.* 10. It is here called a *tribute of a free-will-offering.* It was required of them as a tribute to their Sovereign Lord and owner, under whom they held all they had; and yet because the law did not determine the *quantum,* but it was left to every man's generosity to bring what he chose, and whatever he brought he must give cheerfully, it is therefore called a *free-will offering.* It was a grateful acknowledgment of the goodness of God to them in the mercies of these corn-harvests now finished, and therefore must be *according as God had blessed them.* Where God sows plentifully he expects to reap accordingly. (2.) They must rejoice before God, *v.* 11. Holy joy is the heart and soul of thankful praises, which are as the language and expression of holy joy. They must rejoice in their receivings from God, and in their returns of service and sacrifice to him; our duty must be our delight as well as our enjoyments. They must have their very servants to rejoice with them, "for remember (*v.* 12) that *thou wast a bond-man,* and wouldest have been very thankful if thy taskmasters would have given thee some time and cause for rejoicing; and thy God did bring thee out to keep a feast with gladness; therefore be pleasant with thy servants, and make them easy." And, it should seem, those general words, *thou shalt observe and do these statutes,* are added here for a particular reason, because this feast was kept in remembrance of the giving of the law upon Mount Sinai, fifty days after they came out of Egypt; now the best way of expressing our thankfulness to God for his favour to us in giving us his law is to *observe and do according to the precepts* of it.

III. They must keep the feast of tabernacles, *v.* 13–15. Here is no repetition of the law concerning the sacrifices that were to be offered in great abundance at this feast (which we had at large, Num. 29:12, etc.), because the care of these belonged to the priests and Levites, who had not so much need of a repetition as the people had, and because the spiritual part of the service, which consisted in holy joy, was most pleasing to God, and was to be the perpetual duty of a gospel conversation, of which this feast was typical. Observe what stress is laid upon it here: *Thou shalt rejoice in thy feast* (*v.* 14), *and, because the Lord shall bless thee, thou shalt surely rejoice, v.* 15. Note, 1. It is the will of God that his people should be a cheerful people. If those that were under the law must rejoice before God, much more must we that are under the grace of the gospel, which makes it our duty, not only as here to rejoice in our feasts, but to *rejoice evermore, to rejoice in the Lord always.* 2. When we rejoice in God ourselves we should do what we can to assist others also to rejoice in him, by comforting the mourners and supplying the necessitous, that even *the stranger, the fatherless, and the widow may rejoice with us.* See Job 29:13. 3. We must rejoice in God, not only because of what we have received and are receiving from him daily, but because of what he has promised, and we expect to receive yet further from him: because *he shall bless thee,* therefore *thou shalt rejoice.* Those that make God their joy may *rejoice in hope,* for he is faithful that has promised.

IV. The laws concerning the three solemn feasts are summed up (*v.* 16, 17), as often before, Ex. 23:16, 17; 34:23. The general commands concerning them are, 1. That all the males must then make their personal appearance before God, that by their frequent meeting to worship God, at the same place, and by the same rule, they might be kept faithful and constant to that holy religion which was established among them. 2. That none must appear before God empty, but every man must bring some offering or other, in token of a dependence upon God and gratitude to him. And God was not unreasonable in his demands; let every man but give as he was able, and no more was expected. The same is still the rule of charity, 1 Co. 16:2. Those that give to their power shall be accepted, but those that give beyond their power are accounted worthy of double honour (2 cor. 8:3), as the poor widow that gave *all she had,* Lu. 21:4.

Verses 18–22

Here is, I. Care taken for the due administration of justice among them, that controversies might be determined, matters in variance adjusted, the injured redressed, and the injurious punished. While they were encamped in the wilderness, they had *judges and officers* according to their numbers, rulers of thousands and hundreds, Ex. 17:25. When they came to Canaan, they must have them according to their towns and cities, in all their gates; for the courts of judgment sat in the gates. Now, 1. Here is a commission given to these inferior magistrates: "Judges to try and pass sentence, and officers to execute their sentences, shalt thou make thee." However the persons were pitched upon, whether by the nomination of their sovereign or by the election of the people, *the power were ordained of God,* Rom. 13:1. And it was a great mercy to the people thus to have justice brought to their doors, that it might be more expeditious and less expensive, a blessing which we of this nation ought to be very thankful for. Pursuant to this law, besides the great sanhedrim that sat at the sanctuary, consisting of seventy elders and a president, there was in the larger cities, such as had in them above 120 families, a court of twenty-three judges, in the smaller cities a court of three judges. See this law revived by Jehoshaphat, 2 Chr. 19:5, 8. 2. Here is a command given to these magistrates to do justice in the execution of the trust reposed in them. Better not judge at all than not judge with just judgment, according to the direction of the law and the evidence of the fact. (1.) The judges are here cautioned not to do wrong to any (*v.* 19), nor to take any gifts, which would tempt them to do wrong. This law had been given before, Ex. 23:8. (2.) They are charged to do justice to all: *"That which is altogether just shalt thou follow, v.* 20. Adhere to the principles of justice, act by the rules of justice, countenance the demands of justice, imitate the patterns of justice, and pursue with resolution that which appears to be just. *Justice, justice, shalt thou follow."* This is that which the magistrate is to have in his eye, on this he must be intent, and to this all personal regards must be sacrificed, to do *right to all* and *wrong to none.*

II. Care taken for the preventing of all conformity to the idolatrous customs of the heathen, *v.* 21, 22. They must not only not join with the idolaters in their worships, not visit their groves, nor bow before the images which they had set up, but, 1. They must not plant a grove, nor so much as a tree, near God's altar lest they should make it look like the altars of the false gods. They made groves the places of their worship either to make it secret (but that which is true and good desires the light rather), or to make it solemn, but the worship of the true God has enough in itself to make it so and needs not the advantage of such a circumstance. 2. They must not set up any image, statue, or pillar, to the honour of God, for it is a thing which the Lord hates; nothing belies or reproaches him more, or tends more to corrupt and debauch the minds of men, than representing and worshipping by an image that God who is an infinite and eternal Spirit.

CHAPTER 17

The charge of this chapter is, I. Concerning the purity and perfection of all those animals that were offered in sacrifice (*v.* 1). II. Concerning the punishment of those that worshipped idols (*v.* 2–7). III. Concerning appeals from the inferior courts to the great sanhedrim (*v.* 8–13). IV. Concerning the choice and duty of a king (*v.* 14, etc.).

Verses 1–7

Here is, I. A law for preserving the honour of God's worship, by providing that no creature that had any blemish should be offered in sacrifice to him, *v.* 1. This caveat we have often met with: *Thou shalt not sacrifice that which has any blemish,* which renders it unsightly, or *any evil matter or thing* (as the following word night better be rendered), any sickness or weakness, though not discernible at first view; it is an abomination to God. God is the best of beings, and therefore whatsoever he is served with ought to be the best in its kind. And the Old-Testament sacrifices in a special manner must be so, because they were types of Christ, who is a *Lamb without blemish or spot* (1 Pt. 1:19), perfectly pure from all sin and all appearance of it. In the latter times of the Jewish church, when by the captivity in Babylon they were cured of idolatry, yet they were charged with profaneness in the breach of this law, with *offering the blind, and the lame, and the sick for sacrifice,* Mal. 1:8.

II. A law for the punishing of those that worshipped false gods. It was made a capital crime to seduce others to idolatry (*ch.* 13), here it is made no less to be seduced. If the *blind thus mislead the blind, both must fall into the ditch.* Thus God would possess them with a dread of that sin, which they must conclude exceedingly sinful when so many sanguinary laws were made against it, and would deter those from it that would not otherwise be persuaded against it; and yet the law, which works death, proved ineffectual. See here,

1. What the crime was against which this law was levelled, serving or worshipping other gods, *v.* 3. That which was the most ancient and plausible idolatry is specified, worshipping the sun, moon, and stars; and, if that was so detestable a thing, much more was it so to worship stocks and stones, or the representations of mean and contemptible animals. Of this it is said, (1.) That it is what God had not commanded. He had again and again forbidden it; but it is thus expressed to intimate that, if there had been no more against it, this had been enough (for in the worship of God his institution and appointment must be our rule and warrant), and that God never commanded his worshippers to debase themselves so far as to do homage to their fellow-creatures: had God commanded them to do it, they might justly have complained of it as a reproach and disparagement to them; yet, when he has forbidden it, they will, from a spirit of contradiction, put this indignity upon themselves. (2.) That it is *wickedness in the sight of God, v.* 2. Be it ever so industriously concealed, he sees it, and, be it ever so ingeniously palliated, he hates it: it is a sin in itself exceedingly heinous, and the highest affront that can be offered to Almighty God. (3.) That it is a transgression of the covenant. It was on this condition that God took them to be his peculiar people, that they should serve and worship him only as their God, so that if they gave to any other the honour which was due to him alone that covenant was void, and all the benefit of it forfeited. Other sins were transgressions of the command, but this was a transgression of the covenant. It was spiritual adultery, which breaks them marriage bond. (4.) That it is abomination in Israel, *v.* 4. Idolatry was bad enough in any, but it was particularly abominable in Israel, a people so blessed with peculiar discoveries of the will and favour of the only true and living God.

2. How it must be tried. Upon information given of it, or any ground of suspicion that any person whatsoever, man or woman, had served other gods, (1.) Enquiry must be made, *v.* 4. Though it appears not certain at first, it may afterwards upon search appear so; and, if it can possibly be discovered, it must not be unpunished; if not, yet the very enquiry concerning it would possess the country with a dread of it. (2.) Evidence must be given in, *v.* 6. How heinous and dangerous soever the crime is, yet they must not punish any for it, unless there were good proof against them, by two witnesses at least. They must not, under pretence of honouring God, wrong an innocent man. This law, which requires two witnesses in case of life, we had before, Num. 35:30; it is quoted, Mt. 18:16.

3. What sentence must be passed and executed. So great a punishment as death, so great a death as stoning, must be inflicted on the idolater, whether man or woman, for the infirmity of the weaker sex would be no excuse, *v.* 5. The place of execution must be the gate of the city, that the shame might be the greater to the criminal and the warning the more public to all others. The hands of the witnesses, in this as in other cases, must be first upon him, that is, they must cast the first stone at him, thereby avowing their testimony, and solemnly imprecating the guilt of his blood upon themselves if their evidence were false. This custom might be of use to deter men from false-witness bearing. The witnesses are really, and therefore it was required that they should be actually, the death of the malefactor. But they must be followed, and the execution completed, by the hands of all the people, who were thus to testify their detestation of the crime and to *put the evil away from among them,* as before, *ch.* 13:9.

Verses 8–13

Courts of judgment were ordered to be erected in every city (*ch.* 16:18), and they were empowered to hear and determine causes according to law, both those which we call pleas of the crown and those between party and party; and we may suppose that ordinarily they ended the matters that were brought before them, and their sentence was definitive; but, 1. It is here taken for granted that sometimes a case might come into their court too difficult for those inferior judges to determine, who could not be thought to be so learned in the laws as those that presided in the higher courts; so that (to speak in the language of our law) they must find a special verdict, and take time to advise before the giving of judgment (*v.* 8): *If there arise a matter too hard for thee in judgment,* which it would be no dishonour to the judges to own the difficulty of, — suppose it between *blood and blood,* the blood of a person which cried and the blood of him that was charged with the murder which was demanded, when it was doubtful upon the evidence whether it was wilful or casual, — or between *plea and plea,* the plea (that is, the bill or declaration) of the plaintiff and the plea of the defendant, — or between *stroke and stroke,* in actions of assault and battery; in these and similar cases, thought the evidence were plain, yet doubts might arise about the sense and meaning of the law and the application of it to the particular case. 2. These difficult cases, which hitherto had been brought to Moses, according to Jethro's advice, were, after his death, to be brought to the supreme power, wherever it was lodged, whether in a judge (when there was such an extraordinary person raised up and qualified for that great service, as Othniel, Deborah, Gideon, etc.) or in the high-priest (when he was by the eminency of his gifts called of God to preside in public affairs, as Eli), or, if no single person were marked by heaven for this honour, then in the priests and Levites (or in the priests, who were Levites of course), who not only attended the sanctuary, but met in council to receive appeals from the inferior courts, who might reasonably be supposed, not only to be best qualified by their learning and experience, but to have the best assistance of the divine Spirit for the deciding of doubts, *v.* 9, 11, 12. They are not appointed to consult the urim and thummim, for it is supposed that these were to be consulted only in cases relating to the public, either the body of the people or the prince; but in ordinary cases the wisdom and integrity of those that sat at the stern must be relied on, their judgment had not the divine authority of an oracle, yet besides the moral certainty it had, as the judgment of knowing, prudent, and experienced men, it had the advantage of a divine promise, implied in those words (*v.* 9), *They shall show thee the sentence of judgment;* it had also the support of a divine institution, by which they were made the supreme judicature of the nation. 3. The definitive sentence given by the judge, priest, or great council, must be obeyed by the parties concerned, upon pain of death: *Thou shalt do according to their sentence* (*v.* 10); thou shalt observe to do it, thou shalt not *decline from it* (*v.* 11), *to the right hand nor to the left.* Note, It is for the honour of God and the welfare of a people that the authority of the higher power be supported and the due order of government observed, that those be obeyed who are appointed to rule, and that every soul be subject to them in all those things that fall within their commission. Though the party thought himself injured by the sentence (as every man is apt to be partial in is own cause), yet he must needs be subject, must stand to the award, how unpleasing soever, and bear, or lose, or pay, according to it, not only for wrath, but also for conscience' sake. But if an inferior judge contradict the sentence of the higher court and will not execute the orders of it, or a private person refuse to conform to their sentence, the contumacy must be punished with death, though the matter were ever so small in which the opposition was made: *That man shall die, and all the people shall hear and fear, v.* 12, 13. See here, (1.) The evil of disobedience. Rebellion and stubbornness, from a spirit of contradiction and opposition of God, or those in authority under him, from a principle of contempt and self-willedness, are as witchcraft and idolatry. To differ in opinion from weakness and infirmity may be excused and must be borne with; but to do so presumptuously, in pride and wickedness (as the ancient translations explain it), this is to take up arms against the government, and is an affront to him by whom the powers that be are ordained. (2.) The design of punishment: that others may hear and fear, and not do the like. Some would be so considerate as to infer the heinousness of the offence from the grievousness of the penalty, and therefore would detest it; and others would so far consult their own safety as to cross their humours by conforming to the sentence rather than to sin against their own heads, and forfeit their lives by going contrary to it. From this law the apostle infers the greatness of the punishment of which those will be thought worthy that trample on the authority of the Son of God, Heb. 10:28, 29.

Verses 14–20

After the laws which concerned subjects fitly followed the laws which concern kings; for those that rule others must themselves remember that they are under command. Here are laws given,

I. To the electors of the empire, what rules they must go by in making their choice, *v.* 14, 15. 1. It is here supposed that the people would, in process of time, be desirous of a king, whose royal pomp and power would be thought to make their nation look great among their neighbours. Their having a king is neither promised as a mercy nor commanded as a duty (nothing could be better for them than the divine regimen they were under), but it is permitted them if they desired it. If they would but take care to have the ends of government answered, and God's laws duly observed and put in execution, they should not be tied to any one form of government, but should be welcome to have a king. Though something irregular is supposed to be the principle of the desire, that they might be like the nations (whereas God in many ways distinguished them from the nations), yet God would indulge them in it, because he intended to serve his own purposes by it, in making the regal government typical of the kingdom of the Messiah. 2. They are directed in their choice. If they will have a king over them, as God foresaw they would (though it does not appear that ever the motion was made till almost 400 years after), then they must, (1.) Ask counsel at God's mouth, and make him king whom God shall choose; and happy it was for them that they had an oracle to consult in so weighty an affair, and a God to choose for them who knows infallibly what every man is and will be. Kings are God's vicegerents, and therefore it is fit that he should have the choosing of them: God had himself been in a particular manner Israel's King, and if they set another over them, under him, it was necessary that he should nominate the person. Accordingly, when the people desired a king, they applied to Samuel a prophet of the Lord; and afterwards David, Solomon, Jeroboam, Jehu, and others, were chosen by the prophets; and the people are reproved for not observing this law, Hos. 8:4: *They have set up kings but not by me.* In all cases God's choice, if we can but know it, should direct, determine, and overrule ours. (2.) They must not choose a foreigner under pretence of strengthening their alliances, or of the extraordinary fitness of the person, lest a strange king should introduce strange customs of usages, contrary to those that were established by the divine law; but he must be *one from among thy brethren,* that he may be a type of Christ, who is bone of our bone, Heb. 2:14.

II. Laws are here given to the prince that should be elected for the due administration of the government.

1. He must carefully avoid every thing that would divert him from God and religion. Riches, honours, and pleasures are the three great hindrances of godliness *(the lusts of the flesh, the lusts of the eye, and the pride of life),* especially to those in high stations: against these therefore the king is here warned. (1.) He must not gratify the love of honour by multiplying horses, *v.* 16. He that rode upon a horse (a stately creature) in a country where asses and mules were generally used looked very great; and therefore though he might have horses for his own saddle, and chariots, yet he must not set *servants on horseback* (Eccl. 10:7) nor have many horses for his officers and guards (when God was their King, his judges rode on asses, Jdg. 5:10; 12:14), nor must he multiply horses for war, lest he should trust too much to them, Ps. 20:7; 33:17; Hos. 14:3. The reason here given against his multiplying horses is because it would produce a greater correspondence with Egypt (which furnished Canaan with horses, 1 Ki. 10:28, 29) than it was fit the Israel of God should have, who were brought thence with such a high hand: *You shall return no more that way,* for fear of being infected with the idolatries of Egypt (Lev. 18:3), to which they were very prone. Note, We should take heed of that commerce or conversation by which we are in danger of being drawn into sin. If Israel must not return to Egypt, they must not trade with Egypt; Solomon got no good by it. (2.) He must not gratify the love of pleasure by multiplying wives (*v.* 17), as Solomon did to his undoing (1 Ki. 11:1), that his heart, being set upon them, turn not away from business, and every thing that is serious, and especially from the exercise of piety and devotion, to which nothing is a greater enemy than the indulgence of the flesh. (3.) He must not gratify the love of riches by greatly multiplying silver and gold. A competent treasure is allowed him, and he is not forbidden to be good husband of it, but, [1.] He must not greatly multiply money, so as to oppress his people by raising it (as Solomon seems to have done, 1 Ki. 12:4), nor so as to deceive himself, by trusting to it, and setting his heart upon it, Ps. 62:10. [2.] He must not multiply it to himself. David multiplied silver and gold, but it was for the service of God (1 Chr. 29:4), not for himself; for his people, not for his own family.

2. He must carefully apply himself to the law of God, and make that his rule. This must be to him better than all riches, honours, and pleasures, than many horses or many wives, better than thousands of gold and silver.

(1.) He must write himself a copy of the law out of the original, which was in the custody of the priests that attended the sanctuary, *v.* 18. Some think that he was to write only this book of Deuteronomy, which is an abstract of the law, and the precepts of which, being mostly moral and judicial, concerned the king more than the laws in Leviticus and Numbers, which, being ceremonial, concerned chiefly the priests. Others think that he was to transcribe all the five books of Moses, which are called *the law,* and which were preserved together as the foundation of their religion. Now, [1.] Though the king might be presumed to have very fair copies by him from his ancestors, yet, besides those, he must have one of his own: it might be presumed that theirs were worn with constant use; he must have a fresh one to begin the world with. [2.] Though he had secretaries about him whom he might employ to write this copy, and who perhaps could write a better hand than he, yet he must do it himself, with his own hand, for the honour of the law, and that he might think no act of religion below him, to inure himself to labour and study, and especially that he might thereby be obliged to take particular notice of every part of the law and by writing it might imprint it in his mind. Note, It is of great use for each of us to write down what we observe as most affecting and edifying to us, out of the scriptures and good books, and out of the sermons we hear. A prudent pen may go far towards making up the deficiencies of the memory, and the furnishing of the treasures of the good householder with things new and old. [3.] He must do this even when he sits upon the throne of his kingdom, provided that he had not done it before. When he begins to apply himself to business, he must apply himself to this in the first place. He that sits upon the throne of a kingdom cannot but have his hands full. The affairs of his kingdom both at home and abroad call for a large share of his time and thoughts, and yet he must write himself a copy of the law. Let not those who call themselves men of business think that this will excuse them from making religion their business; nor let great men think it any disparagement to them to write for themselves those *great things of God's law which he hath written to them,* Hos. 8:12.

(2.) Having a Bible by him of his own writing, he must not think it enough to keep it in his cabinet, but he must *read therein all the days of his life, v.* 19. It is not enough to have Bibles, but we must use them, use them daily, as the duty and necessity of everyday require: our souls must have their constant meals of that manna; and, if well digested, it will be true nourishment and strength to them. As the body is receiving benefit by its food continually, and not only when it is eating, so is the soul, by the word of God, if it *meditate therein day and night,* Ps. 1:2. And we must persevere in the use of the written word of God as long as we live. Christ's scholars never learn above their Bibles, but will have a constant occasion for them till they come to that world where knowledge and love will both be made perfect.

(3.) His writing and reading were all nothing if he did not reduce to practice what he wrote and read, *v.* 19, 20. The word of God is not designed merely to be and entertaining subject of speculation, but to be a commanding rule of conversation. Let him know, [1.] What dominion his religion must have over him, and what influence it must have upon him. *First,* It must possess him with a very reverent and awful regard to the divine majesty and authority. He must learn (and thus the most learned must by ever learning) *to fear the Lord his God;* and, as high as he is, he must remember that God is above him, and, whatever fear his subjects owe to him, that, and much more, he owes to God as his King. *Secondly,* It must engage him to a constant observance of the law of God, and a conscientious obedience to it, as the effect of that fear. He must keep *all the words of this law* (he is *custos utriusque tabulae — the keeper of both tables*), not only take care that others do them, but do them himself as a humble servant to the God of heaven and a good example to his inferiors. *Thirdly,* It must keep him humble. How much soever he is advanced, let him keep his spirit low, and let the *fear of his God prevent the contempt of his brethren;* and let not his heart *be lifted up above them,* so as to carry himself haughtily or disdainfully towards them, and to trample upon them. Let him not conceit himself better than they because he is greater and makes a fairer show; but let him remember that he is the *minister of God to them for good* (*major singulis,* but *minor universis — greater than any one,* but *less than the whole*). It must prevent his errors, either *on he right hand or on the left* (for there are errors on both hands), and keep him right, in all instances, to his God and to his duty. [2.] What advantage his religion would be of to him. Those that fear God and keep his commandments will certainly fare the better for it in this world. The greatest monarch in the world may receive more benefit by religion than by all the wealth and power of his monarchy. It will be of advantage, *First,* To his person: *He shall prolong his days in his kingdom.* We find in the history of the kings of Judah that, generally, the best reigns were the longest, except when God shortened them for the punishment of the people, as Josiah's. *Secondly,* To his family: his children shall also prosper. Entail religion upon posterity, and God will entail a blessing upon it.

CHAPTER 18

In this chapter, I. The rights and revenues of the church are settled, and rules given concerning the Levites' ministration and maintenance (*v.* 1–8). II. The caution against the idolatrous abominable customs of the heathen is repeated (*v.* 9–14). III. A promise is given them of the spirit of prophecy to continue among them, and to centre at last in Christ the great prophet (*v.* 15–18). IV. Wrath threatened against those that despise prophecy (*v.* 19) or counterfeit it (*v.* 20), and a rule given for the trial of it (*v.* 21, 22).

Verses 1–8

Magistracy and ministry are two divine institutions of admirable use for the support and advancement of the *kingdom of God among men.* Laws concerning the former we had in the close of the foregoing chapter, directions are in this given concerning the latter. Land-marks are here set between the estates of the priests and those of the people.

I. Care is taken that the priests entangle not themselves with the affairs of this life, nor enrich themselves with the wealth of this world; they have better things to mind. They *shall have no part nor inheritance with Israel,* that is, no share either in the spoils taken in war or in the land that was to be divided by lot, *v.* 1. Their warfare and husbandry are both spiritual, and enough to fill their hands both with work and profit and to content them. *The Lord is their inheritance, v.* 2. Note, Those that have God for their inheritance, according to the new covenant, should not be greedy of great things in the world, neither gripe what they have nor grasp at more, but look upon all present things with the indifference which becomes those that believe God to be all-sufficient.

II. Care is likewise taken that they want not any of the comforts and conveniences of this life. Though God, who is a Spirit, is their inheritance, it does not therefore follow that they must live upon the air; no,

1. The people must provide for them. They must have their *due from the people, v.* 3. Their maintenance must not depend upon the generosity of the people, but they must be by law entitled to it. He that is taught in the word ought in justice to communicate to him that teaches him; and he that has the benefit of solemn religious assemblies ought to contribute to the comfortable support of those that preside in such assemblies. (1.) The priests who in their courses served at the altar had their share of the sacrifices, namely, the peace-offerings, that were brought while they were in waiting: besides the breast and shoulder, which were appointed them before (Lev. 7:32–34), the cheeks and maw are here ordered to be given them; so far was the law from diminishing what was already granted that it gave them an augmentation (2.) The first-fruits which arose within such a precinct were brought in, as it should seem, to the priests that resided among them, for their maintenance in the country; the first of their corn

and wine for food, and the first of their fleece for clothing (*v.* 4); for the priests who were employed to teach others ought themselves to learn, having food and raiment, to be therewith content. The first-fruits were devoted to God, and he constituted the priests his receivers; and if God reckons what is, in general, given to the poor, lent to him, to be repaid with interest, much more what is, in particular, given to the poor, lent to him, to be repaid with interest, much more what is, in particular, given to poor ministers. There is a good reason given for this constant charge upon their estates (*v.* 5), because the Levites were *chosen of God,* and his choice must be owned and countenanced, and those honoured by us whom he honours; and *because they stood to minister,* and ought to be recompensed for their attendance and labour, especially since it was *in the name of the Lord,* by his warrant, in his service, and for his praise, and this charge entailed upon their seed for ever; those who were thus engaged and thus employed ought to have all due encouragement given them, as some of the most needful useful members of their commonwealth.

2. The priests must not themselves stand in one another's light. If a priest that by the law was obliged to serve at the altar only in his turn, and was paid for that, should, out of his great affection to the sanctuary, devote himself to a constant attendance there, and quit the ease and pleasure of the city in which he had his lot for the satisfaction of serving the altar, the priests whose turn it was to attend must admit him both to join in the work and to share in the wages, and not grudge him either the honour of the one or the profit of the other, though it might seem to break in upon them, *v.* 6–8. Note, A hearty pious zeal to serve God and his church, though it may a little encroach upon a settled order, and there may be somewhat in it that looks irregular, yet ought to be gratified and not discouraged. He that appears to have a hearty affection to the sanctuary, and loves dearly to be employed in the service of it, *in God's name let him minister;* he shall be as welcome to God as the Levites whose course it was to minister, and should be so to them. The settling of the courses was intended rather to secure those to the work that were not willing to do so much than to exclude any that were willing to do more. And he that thus serves as a volunteer shall have as good pay as the pressed men, *besides that which comes of the sale of his patrimony.* The church of Rome obliges those who leave their estates to go into a monastery to bring the produce of their estates with them into the common stock of the monastery, for gain is their godliness; but here it is ordered that the pious devotee should reserve to himself the produce of his patrimony, for religion and the ministry were never appointed of God, however they have been abused by men, to serve a secular interest.

Verses 9–14

One would not think there had been so much need as it seems there was to arm the people of Israel against the infection of the idolatrous customs of the Canaanites. Was it possible that a people so blessed with divine institutions should ever admit the brutish and barbarous inventions of men and devils? Were they in any danger of making those their tutors and directors in religion whom God had made their captives and tributaries? It seems they were in danger, and therefore, after many similar cautions, they are here charged not to do after the abominations of those nations, *v.* 9.

I. Some particulars are specified; as, 1. The consecrating of their children to Moloch, an idol that represented the sun, by making them to *pass through the fire,* and sometimes consuming them as sacrifices in the fire, *v.* 10. See the law against this before, Lev. 18:21. 2. Using arts of divination, to get the unnecessary knowledge of things to come, *enchantments, witchcrafts, charms, etc.,* by which the power and knowledge peculiar to God were attributed to the devil, to the great reproach both of God's counsels and of his providence, *v.* 10, 11. one would wonder that such arts and works of darkness, so senseless and absurd, so impious and profane, could be found in a country where divine revelation shone so clearly; yet we find remains of them even where Christ's holy religion is known and professed; such are the powers and policies of the *rulers of the darkness of this world.* But let those give heed to fortune-tellers, or go to wizards for the discovery of things secret, that use spells for the cure of diseases, are in any league or acquaintance with familiar spirits, or form a confederacy with those that are — let them know that they can have no fellowship with God while thus they have fellowship with devils. It is amazing to think that there should by any pretenders of this kind in such a land and day of light as we live in.

II. Some reasons are given against their conformity to the customs of the Gentiles. 1. Because it would make them abominable to God. The things themselves being hateful to him, those that do them are an abomination; and miserable is that creature that has become odious to its Creator, *v.* 12. See the malignity and mischievousness of sin; that must needs be an evil thing indeed which provokes the God of mercy to detest the work of his own hands. 2. Because these abominable practices had been the ruin of the Canaanites, of which ruin they were not only the witnesses but the instruments. It would be the most inexcusable folly, as well as the most unpardonable impiety, for them to practise themselves those very things for which they had been employed so severely to chastise others. Did the land spue out the abominations of the Canaanites, and shall Israel lick up the vomit? 3. Because they were *better taught, v.* 13, 14. It is an argument like that of the apostle against Christians walking as the Gentiles walked (Eph. 4:17, 18, 20): *You have not so learned Christ.* "It is true these nations, whom God *gave up to their own hearts' lusts, and suffered to walk in their own ways* (Acts 14:16), did thus corrupt themselves; but thou art not thus abandoned by the grace of God: *the Lord thy God had not suffered thee to do so;* thou art instructed in divine things, and hast fair warning given thee of the evil of those practices; and therefore, whatever others do, it is expected that thou shouldest be *perfect with the Lord thy God,*" that is, "that thou shouldest give divine honours to him, to him only, and to no other, and not mix any of the superstitious customs of the heathen with his institutions." One of the Chaldee paraphrasts here takes notice of God's furnishing them with the oracle of urim and thummim, as a preservative from all unlawful arts of divination. Those were fools indeed who would go to consult the father of lies when they had such a ready way of consulting the God of truth.

Verses 15–22

Here is, I. The promise of the great prophet, with a command to receive him, and hearken to him. Now,

1. Some think it is the promise of a succession of prophets, that should for many ages be kept up in Israel. Besides the priests and Levites, their ordinary ministers, whose office it was to teach Jacob God's law, they should have prophets, extraordinary ministers, to reprove them for their faults, remind them of their duty, and foretel things to come, judgments for warning and deliverances for their comfort. Having these prophets, (1.) They need not use divinations, nor consult with familiar spirits, for they might enquire of God's prophets even concerning their private affairs, as Saul did when he was in quest of his father's asses, 1 Sa. 9:6. (2.) They could not miss the way of their duty through ignorance or mistake, nor differ in their opinions about it, having prophets among them, whom, in every difficult doubtful case, they might advise with and appeal to. These prophets were like unto Moses in some respects, though far inferior to him, Deu. 34:10.

2. Whether a succession of prophets be included in this promise or not, we are sure that it is primarily intended as a promise of Christ, and it is the clearest promise of him that is in all the law of Moses. It is expressly applied to our Lord Jesus as the Messiah promised (Acts 3:22; 7:37), and the people had an eye to this promise when they said concerning him, *This is of a truth that prophet that should come into the world* (Jn. 6:14); and it was his Spirit that spoke in all the other prophets, 1 Pt. 1:11. Observe,

(1.) What it is that is here promised concerning Christ. What God promised Moses at Mount Sinai (which he relates, *v.* 18), he promised the people (*v.* 15) in God's name. [1.] That there should come a prophet, great above all the prophets, by whom God would make known himself and his will to the children of men more fully and clearly than ever he had done before. He is the *light of the world,* as prophecy was of the Jewish church, Jn. 8:12. He is the Word, by whom God speaks to us, Jn. 1:1; Heb. 1:2. [2.] That God would *raise him up from the midst of them.* In his birth he should be one of that nation, should live among them and be sent to them. In his resurrection he should be *raised up at Jerusalem,* and thence his doctrine should go forth to all the world: thus God, having raised up his Son Christ Jesus, sent him to bless us. [3.] That he should be like unto Moses, only as much above him as the other prophets came short of him. Moses was such a prophet as was a law-giver to Israel and their deliverer out of Egypt, and so was Christ: he not only teaches, but rules and saves. Moses was the founder of a new dispensation by signs and wonders and mighty deeds, and so was Christ, by which he proved himself a teacher come from God. Was Moses faithful? So was Christ; Moses as a servant, but Christ as a Son. [4.] That God would put his words in his mouth, *v.* 18. What messages God had to send to the children of men he would send them by him, and give him full instructions what to say and do as a prophet. Hence our Saviour says, *My doctrine is not mine* originally, *but his that sent me,* Jn. 7:16. So that this great promise is performed; this Prophet has come, even Jesus; it is he that should come, and we are to look for no other.

(2.) The agreeableness of this designed dispensation to the people's avowed choice and desire at Mount Sinai, *v.* 16, 17. There God had spoken to them in thunder and lightning, out of the midst of the fire and thick darkness. Every word made their ears tingle and their hearts tremble, so that the whole congregation was ready to die with fear. In this fright, they begged hard that God would not speak to them in this manner any more (they could not bear it, it would overwhelm and distract them), but that he would speak to them by men like themselves, by Moses now, and afterwards by other prophets like unto him. "Well," says God, "it shall be so; they shall be spoken to by men, whose *terrors shall not make them afraid;*" and, to crown the favour beyond what they were able to ask or think, in the fulness of time the Word itself was made flesh, and they saw his glory as of the *only-begotten of the Father,* not, as at Mount Sinai, full of majesty and terror, *but full of grace and truth,* Jn. 1:14. Thus, in answer to the request of those who were struck with amazement by the law, God promised the incarnation of his Son, though we may suppose it far from the thoughts of those that made that request.

(3.) A charge and command given to all people to hear and believe, hear and obey, this great prophet here promised: *Unto him you shall hearken* (*v.* 15); and whoever will not hearken to him shall be surely and severely reckoned with for his contempt (*v.* 19): *I will require it of him.* God himself applied this to our Lord Jesus in the *voice that came out of the excellent glory,* Mt. 17:5, *Hear you him,* that is, this is he concerning whom it was said by Moses of old, *Unto him you shall hearken;* and Moses and Elias then stood by and assented to it. The sentence here passed on those that hearken not to this prophet is repeated and ratified in the New Testament. *He that believeth not the Son, the wrath of God abideth on him,* Jn. 3:36. *And how shall we escape if we turn away from him that speaketh from heaven?* Heb. 12:25. The Chaldee paraphrase here reads it, *My Word shall require it of him,* which can be no other than a divine person, Christ the eternal Word, to whom the Father has committed all judgement, and by whom he will at the last day judge the world. Whoever turns a deaf ear to Jesus Christ shall find that it is at his peril; the same that is the prophet is to be his judge, Jn. 12:48.

II. Here is a caution against false prophets, 1. By way of threatening against the pretenders themselves, *v.* 20. Whoever sets up for a prophet, and produces either a commission from the true God, shall be deemed and adjudged guilty of high treason against the crown and dignity of the King of kings, and that traitor shall be put to death (*v.* 20), namely, by the judgment of the great sanhedrim, which, in process of time, sat at Jerusalem; and therefore our Saviour says that a prophet could not perish but at Jerusalem, and lays the blood of the prophets at Jerusalem's door (Lu. 13:33, 34), whom therefore God himself would punish; yet *there* false prophets were supported. 2. By way of direction to the people, that they might not be imposed upon by pretenders, of which there were many, as appears, Jer. 23:25; Eze. 13:6; 1 Ki. 22:6. It is a very proper question which they are supposed to ask, *v.* 21. Since it is so great a duty to hearken to the true prophets, and yet there is so much danger of being misled by false prophets, *how shall we know the word which the Lord has not spoken?*

By what marks may we discover a cheat? Note, It highly concerns us to have a right touchstone wherewith to try the word we hear, that we may know what that word is which the Lord has not spoken. Whatever is directly repugnant to sense, to the light and law of nature, and to the plain meaning of the written word, we may be sure is not that which the Lord has spoken; nor that which gives countenance and encouragement to sin, or has a manifest tendency to the destruction of piety or charity: far be it from God that he should contradict himself. The rule here given in answer to this enquiry was adapted chiefly to that state, *v.* 22. If there was any cause to suspect the sincerity of a prophet, let them observe that if he gave them any sign, or foretold something to come, and the event was not according to his prediction, they might be sure he was not sent of God. This does not refer so much to the foretelling of mercies and judgments (though as to these, and the difference between the predictions of mercies and judgments, there is a rule of discerning between truth and falsehood laid down by the prophet, Jer. 28:8, 9), but rather to the giving of signs on purpose to confirm their mission. Though the sign did come to pass, yet this would not serve to prove their mission if they called them to serve other gods; this point had been already settled, Deu. 13:1–3. But, if the sign did not come to pass, this would serve to disprove their mission. "When Moses cast his rod upon the ground (it is bishop Patrick's explanation of this), and said it would become a serpent, if it had not accordingly been turned into a serpent, Moses had been a false prophet: if, when Elijah called for fire from heaven to consume the sacrifice, none had come, he had been no better than the prophets of Baal." Samuel's mission was proved by this, that *God let none of his words fall to the ground,* 1 Sa. 3:19, 20. And by the miracles Christ wrought, especially by that great sign he gave of his resurrection the third day, which came to pass as he foretold, it appeared that he was a teacher come from God. *Lastly,* They are directed not to be afraid of a false prophet; that is, not to be afraid of the judgments such a one might denounce to amuse people and strike terror upon them; nor to be afraid of executing the law upon him when, upon a strict and impartial scrutiny, it appeared that he was a false prophet. This command not to fear a false prophet implies that a true prophet, who proved his commission by clear and undeniable proofs, was to be feared, and it was at their peril if they offered him any violence or put any slight upon him.

CHAPTER 19

The laws which Moses had hitherto been repeating and urging mostly concerned the acts of religion and devotion towards God; but here he comes more fully to press the duties of righteousness between man and man. This chapter relates, I. To the sixth commandment, "Thou shalt not kill" (*v.* 1–13). II. To the eighth commandment, "Thou shalt not steal" (*v.* 14). III. To the ninth commandment, "Thou shalt not bear false witness," (*v.* 15, etc.).

Verses 1–13

It was one of the precepts given to the sons of Noah that *whoso sheddeth man's blood by man shall his blood be shed,* that is, by the avenger of blood, Gen. 9:6. Now here we have the law settled between blood and blood, between the blood of the murdered and the blood of the murderer, and effectual provision made,

I. That the cities of refuge should be a protection to him that slew another casually, so that he should not die for that as a crime which was not his voluntary act, but only his unhappiness. The appointment of these cities of refuge we had before (Ex. 21:13), and the law laid down concerning them at large, Num. 35:10, etc. It is here repeated, and direction is given concerning three things: —

1. The appointing of three cities in Canaan for this purpose. Moses had already appointed three on that side Jordan which he saw the conquest of; and now he bids them, when they should be settled in the other part of the country, to appoint three more, *v.* 1–3, 7. The country was to be divided into three districts, as near by as might be equal, and a city of refuge in the centre of each so that every corner of the land might have one within reach. Thus Christ is not a refuge at a distance, which we must ascend to heaven or go down to the deep for, but the word is nigh us, and Christ in the word, Rom. 10:8. The gospel brings salvation *to our door,* and there it knocks for admission. To make the flight of the delinquent the more easy, the way must be prepared that led to the city of refuge. Probably they had causeways or street-ways leading to those cities, and the Jews say that the magistrates of Israel, upon one certain day in the year, sent out messengers to see that those roads were in good repair, and they were to remove stumbling-blocks, mend bridges that were broken, and, where two ways met, they were to set up a Mercurial post, with a finger to point the right way, on which was engraven in great letters, *Miklat, Miklat — Refuge, Refuge.* In allusion to this, gospel ministers are to show people the way to Christ, and to assist and direct them in flying by faith to him for refuge. They must be ready to remove their prejudices, and help them over their difficulties. And, blessed be God, *the way of holiness,* to all that seek it faithfully, is a highway so plain that *the wayfaring men, though fools, shall not err therein.*

2. The use to be made of these cities, *v.* 4–6. (1.) It is supposed that it might so happen that a man might be the death of his neighbour without any design upon him either from a sudden passion or malice prepense, but purely by accident, as by the flying off of an axe-head, which is the instance here given, with which every case of this kind was to be compared, and by it adjudged. See how human life lies exposed daily, and what deaths we are often in, and what need therefore we have to be always ready, our souls being continually in our hands. How are the sons of men *snared in an evil time, when it falls suddenly upon them!* Eccl. 9:12. An evil time indeed it is when this happens not only to the slain but to the slayer. (2.) It is supposed that the relations of the person slain would be forward to avenge the blood, in affection to their friend and in zeal for public justice. Though the law did not allow the avenging of any other affront or injury with death, yet the avenger of blood, the blood of a relation, shall have great allowances made for the heat of his heart upon such a provocation as that, and his killing only, should not be accounted murder if he did it before he got to the city of refuge, though it is owned he was not worthy of death. Thus would God possess people with a great horror and dread of the sin of murder: if mere chance-medley did thus expose a man, surely he that wilfully does violence to the blood of any person, whether from an old grudge or upon a sudden provocation, must flee to the pit, and *let no man stay him* (Prov. 28:17); yet the New Testament represents the sin of murder as more heinous and more dangerous than even this law does. 1 Jn. 3:15, *You know that no murderer has eternal life abiding in him.* (3.) It is provided that, if an avenger of blood should be so unreasonable as to demand satisfaction for blood shed by accident only, then the city of refuge should protect the slayer. Sins of ignorance indeed do expose us to the wrath of God, but there is relief provided, if by faith and repentance we make use of it. Paul that had been a persecutor obtained mercy, because he did it ignorantly; and Christ prayed for his crucifiers, *Father, forgive them, for they know not what they do.*

3. The appointing of three cities more for this use in case God should hereafter enlarge their territories and the dominion of their religion, that all those places which came under the government of the law of Moses in other instances might enjoy the benefit of that law in this instance, *v.* 8–10. Here is, (1.) An intimation of God's gracious intention to enlarge their coast, as he had promised to their fathers, if they did not by their disobedience forfeit the promise, the condition of which is here carefully repeated, that, if it were not performed, the reproach might lie upon them, and not on God. He promised to give it, *if thou shalt keep all these commandments;* not otherwise. (2.) A direction to them to appoint three cities more in their new conquests, which, the number intimates, should be as large as their first conquests were; wherever the border of Israel went this privilege must attend it, that *innocent blood be not shed, v.* 10. Though God is the saviour and preserver of all men, and has a tender regard to all lives, yet the blood of Israelites is in a particular manner precious to him, Ps. 72:14. The learned Ainsworth observes that the Jewish writers themselves own that, the condition not being performed, the promise of the enlarging of their coast was never fulfilled; so that there was no occasion for ever adding these three cities of refuge; yet the holy blessed God (say they) *did not command it in vain, for in the days of Messiah the prince* three other cities shall be added to these six: they expect it to be fulfilled in the letter, but we know that in Christ it has its spiritual accomplishment, for the borders of the gospel Israel are enlarged according to the promise, and in Christ, *the Lord our righteousness,* refuge is provided for those that by faith flee to him.

II. It is provided that the cities of refuge should be no sanctuary or shelter to a wilful murderer, but even thence he should be fetched, and delivered to the avenger of blood, *v.* 11–13. 1. This shows that wilful murder must never be protected by the civil magistrate; he bears the sword of justice in vain if he suffers those to escape the edge of it that lie under the guilt of blood, which he by office is the avenger of. During the dominion of the papacy in our own land, before the Reformation, there were some churches and religious houses (as they called them) that were made sanctuaries for the protection of all sorts of criminals that fled to them, wilful murderers not excepted, so that (as Stamford says, in his *Pleas of the Crown, lib.* II. *c.* 38) the government follows not Moses but Romulus, and it was not till about the latter end of Henry VIII's time that this privilege of sanctuary for wilful murder was taken away, when in that, as in other cases, the word of God came to be regarded more than the dictates of the see of Rome. And some have thought it would be a completing of that instance of reformation if the benefit of clergy were taken away for man-slaughter, that is, the killing of a man upon a small provocation, since this law allowed refuge only in case of that which our law calls chance-medley. 2. It may be alluded to to show that in Jesus Christ there is no refuge for presumptuous sinners, that *go on still in their trespasses.* If we thus *sin wilfully,* sin and go on in it, there *remains no sacrifice,* Heb. 10:26. Those that flee to Christ from their sins shall be safe in him, but not those that expect to be sheltered by him in their sins. Salvation itself cannot save such: divine justice will fetch them even from the city of refuge, the protection of which they are not entitled to.

Verses 14–21

Here is a statute for the preventing of frauds and perjuries; for the divine law takes care of men's rights and properties, and has made a hedge about them. Such a friend is it to human society and men's civil interest.

I. A law against frauds, *v.* 14. 1. Here is an implicit direction given to the first planters of Canaan to fix land-marks, according to the distribution of the land to the several tribes and families by lot. Note, It is the will of God that every one should know his own, and that all good means should be used to prevent encroachments and the doing and suffering of wrong. When right is settled, care must be taken that it be not afterwards unsettled, and that, if possible, no occasion of dispute may arise. 2. An express law to posterity not to remove those land-marks which were thus fixed at first, by which a man secretly got that to himself which was his neighbour's. This, without doubt, is a moral precept, and still binding, and to us it forbids, (1.) The invading of any man's right, and taking to ourselves that which is not our own, by any fraudulent arts or practices, as by forging, concealing, destroying, or altering deeds and writings (which are our land-marks, to which appeals are made), or by shifting hedges, meer-stones, and boundaries. Though the land-marks were set by the hand of man, yet he was a thief and a robber by the law of God that removed them. Let every man be content with his own lot, and just to his neighbours, and then we shall have no land-marks removed. (2.) It forbids the sowing of discord among neighbours, and doing any thing to occasion strife and law-suits, which is done (and it is very ill done) by confounding those things which should determine disputes and decide controversies. And, (3.) It forbids breaking in upon the settled order and constitution of civil government, and the altering of ancient usages without just cause. This law supports the honour of prescriptions. *Consuetudo facit jus — Custom is to be held as law.*

II. A law against perjuries, which enacts two things: — 1. That a single witness should never be admitted to give evidence in a criminal cause, so as that sentence should be passed upon his testimony, *v.* 15. This law we had before, Num. 35:30, and in this book, *ch.* 17:6. This was enacted in favour to the prisoner, whose life and honour should not lie at the mercy of a particular person that had a pique against him, and for caution to the accuser not to say that which he could not corroborate by the testimony of another. It is a just shame which this law puts upon mankind as false and not to be trusted; every man is by it suspected: and it is the honour of God's grace that the record he has given concerning his Son is confirmed both in heaven and in earth by *three witnesses*, 1 Jn. 5:7. *Let God be true and every man a liar*, Rom. 3:4. 2. That a false witness should incur the same punishment which was to have been inflicted upon the person he accused. *If two, or three*, or many witnesses, concurred in a false testimony, they were all liable to be prosecuted upon this law. (2.) The person wronged or brought into peril by the false testimony is supposed to be the appellant, *v.* 17. And yet if the person were put to death upon the evidence, and afterwards it appeared to be false, any other person, or the judges themselves, *ex officio — by virtue of their office*, might call the false witness to account. (3.) Causes of this kind, having more than ordinary difficulty in them, were to be brought before the supreme court, *The priests and judges*, who are said to be *before the Lord*, because, as other judges sat in the gates of their cities, so these at the gate of the sanctuary, *ch.* 17:12. (4.) There must be great care in the trial, *v.* 18. A diligent inquisition must be made into the characters of the persons, and all the circumstances of the case, which must be compared, that the truth might be found out, which, where it is thus faithfully and impartially enquired into, Providence, it may be hoped, will particularly advance the discovery of. (5.) If it appeared that a man had knowingly and maliciously borne false witness against his neighbour, though the mischief he designed him thereby was not effected, he must undergo the same penalty which his evidence would have brought his neighbour under, *v.* 19. *Nec lex est justior ulla — Nor could any law be more just.* If the crime he accused his neighbour of was to be punished with death, the false witness must be put to death; if with stripes, he must be beaten; if with a pecuniary mulct, he was to be fined the sum. And because to those who considered not the heinousness of the crime, and the necessity of making this provision against it, it might seem hard to punish a man so severely for a few words' speaking, especially when no mischief did actually follow, it is added: *Thy eye shall not pity, v.* 21. No man needs to be more merciful than God. The benefit that will accrue to the public from this severity will abundantly recompense it: *Those that remain shall hear and fear, v.* 20. Such exemplary punishments will be warnings to others not to attempt any such mischief, when they see how he that *made the pit and digged it has fallen into the ditch which he made.*

CHAPTER 20

This chapter settles the militia, and establishes the laws and ordinances of war, I. Relating to the soldiers. 1. Those must be encouraged that were drawn up to battle (*v.* 1-4). 2. Those must be dismissed and sent back again whose private affairs called for their attendance at home (*v.* 5-7), or whose weakness and timidity unfitted them for service in the field (*v.* 8, 9). II. Relating to the enemies they made war with. 1. The treaties they must make with the cities that were far off (*v.* 10-15). 2. The destruction they must make of the people into whose land they were going (*v.* 16-18). 3. The care they must take, in besieging cities, not to destroy the fruit-trees (*v.* 19, 20).

Verses 1–9

Israel was at this time to be considered rather as a camp than as a kingdom, entering upon an enemy's country, and not yet settled in a country of their own; and, besides the war they were now entering upon in order to their settlement, even after their settlement they could neither protect nor enlarge their coast without hearing the alarms of war. It was therefore needful that they should have directions given them in their military affairs; and in these verses they are directed in managing, marshalling, and drawing up their own forces. And it is observable that the discipline of war here prescribed is so far from having any thing in it harsh or severe, as is usual in martial law, that the intent of the whole is, on the contrary, to encourage the soldiers, and to make their service easy to them.

I. Those that were disposed to fight must be encouraged and animated against their fears.

1. Moses here gives a general encouragement, which the leaders and commanders in the war must take to themselves: "*Be not afraid of them, v.* 1. Though the enemy have ever so much the advantage by their numbers (being more than thou), and by their cavalry (their armies being much

made up of horses and chariots, which thou art not allowed to multiply), yet decline not coming to a battle with them, dread not the issue, nor doubt of success." Two things they must encourage themselves with in their wars, provided they kept close to their God and their religion, otherwise they forfeited these encouragements: — (1.) The presence of God with them: "*The Lord thy God is with thee*, and therefore thou art not in danger, nor needest thou be afraid." See Isa. 41:10. (2.) The experience they and their fathers had had of God's power and goodness in *bringing them out of the land of Egypt*, in defiance of Pharaoh and all his hosts, which was not only in general a proof of the divine omnipotence, but to them in particular a pledge of what God would do further for them. He that saved them from those greater enemies would not suffer them to be run down by those that were every way less considerable, and thus to have all he had done for them undone again.

2. This encouragement must be particularly addressed to the common soldiers by a priest appointed, and, the Jews say, anointed, for that purpose, whom they call *the anointed of the war*, a very proper title for our anointed Redeemer, the captain of our salvation: This priest, in God's name, was to animate the people; and who so fit to do that as he whose office it was as priest to pray for them? For the best encouragements arise from the precious promises made to the prayer of faith. This priest must, (1.) Charge them not to be afraid (*v.* 3), for nothing weakens the hands so much as that which makes the heart tremble, *v.* 3. There is need of precept upon precept to this purport, as there is here: *Let not your hearts be tender* (so the word is), to receive all the impressions of fear, but let a believing confidence in the power and promise of God harden them. *Fear not, and do not make haste* (so the word is), for he that believeth doth not make more haste than good speed. "Do not make haste either rashly to anticipate your advantages or basely to fly off upon every disadvantage." (2.) He must assure them of the presence of God with them, to own and plead their righteous cause, and not only to save them from their enemies, but to give them victory over them, *v.* 4. Note, Those have no reason to fear that have God with them. The giving of this encouragement by a priest, one of the Lord's ministers, intimates, [1.] That it is very fit that armies should have chaplains, not only to pray for them, but to preach to them, both to reprove that which would hinder their success and to raise their hopes of it. [2.] That it is the work of Christ's ministers to encourage his good soldiers in their spiritual conflict with the world and the flesh, and to assure them of a conquest, yea, more than a conquest, through Christ that loved us.

II. Those that were indisposed to fight must be discharged, whether the indisposition did arise,

1. From the circumstances of a man's outward condition; as, (1.) If he had lately built or purchased a new house, and had not taken possession of it, had not dedicated it (*v.* 5), that is, made a solemn festival for the entertainment of his friends, that came to him to welcome him to his house; let him go home and take the comfort of that which God had blessed him with, till, by enjoying it for some time, he become less fond of it, and consequently less disturbed in the war by the thoughts of it, and more willing to lie and leave it. For this is the nature of all our worldly enjoyments, that they please us best at first; after a while we see the vanity of them. Some think that this dedication of their houses was a religious act, and that they took possession of them with prayers and praises, with a solemn devoting of themselves and all their enjoyments to the service and honour of God. David penned the 30th Psalm on such an occasion, as appears by the title. Note, He that has a house of his own should dedicate it to God by setting up and keeping up the fear and worship of God in it, that he may have a church in his house; and nothing should be suffered to divert a man from this. Or, (2.) If a man had been at a great expense to *plant a vineyard*, and longed to *eat of the fruit* of it, which for the first three years he was forbidden to do by the law (Lev. 19:23, etc.), let him go home, if he has a mind, and gratify his own humour with the fruits of it, *v.* 6. See how indulgent God is to his people in innocent things, and how far from being a hard Master. Since we naturally covet to eat the labour of our hands, rather than an Israelite should be crossed therein, his service in war shall be dispensed with., Or, (3.)

If a man had made up his mind to be married, and the marriage were not solemnized, he was at liberty to return (*v.* 7), as also to tarry at home for one year after marriage (*ch.* 24:5), for the terrors of war would be disagreeable to a man who had just welcomed the soft scene of domestic attachment. And God would not be served in his wars by pressed men, that were forced into the army against their will, but they must all be perfectly volunteers. Ps. 110:3, *Thy people shall be willing.* In running the Christian race, and fighting the good fight of faith, we must *lay aside every weight*, and all that which would clog and divert our minds and make us unwilling. The Jewish writers agree that this liberty to return was allowed only in those wars which they made voluntarily (as bishop Patrick expresses it), not those which were made by the divine command against Amalek and the Canaanites, in which every man was bound to fight.

2. If a man's indisposition to fight arose from the weakness and timidity of his own spirit, he had leave to return from the war, *v.* 8. This proclamation Gideon made to his army, and it detached above two-thirds of them, Jdg. 7:3. Some make the fearfulness and faintheartedness here supposed to arise from the terrors of an evil conscience, which would make a man afraid to look death and danger in the face. It was then thought that men of loose and profligate lives would not be good soldiers, but must needs be both cowards in an army and curses to it, the shame and trouble of the camp; and therefore those who were conscious to themselves of notorious guilt were shaken off. But it seems rather to be meant of a natural fearfulness. It was partly in kindness to them that they had their discharge (for, though shamed, they were eased); but much more in kindness to the rest of the army, who were hereby freed from the incumbrance of such as were useless and unserviceable, while the danger of infection from their cowardice and flight was prevented. This is the reason here given: *Lest his brethren's heart fail as well as his heart.* Fear is catching, and in an army is of most pernicious consequence. We must take heed that we *fear not the fear of those that are afraid*, Isa. 8:12.

III. It is here ordered that, when all the cowards were dismissed, then captains should be nominated (*v.* 9), for it was in a special manner necessary that the leaders and commanders should be men of courage. That reform therefore must be made when the army was first mustered and marshalled. The soldiers of Christ have need of courage, that they may quit themselves like men, and endure hardness like good soldiers, especially the officers of his army.

Verses 10–20

They are here directed what method to take in dealing with the cities (these only are mentioned, *v.* 10, but doubtless the armies in the field, and the nations they had occasion to deal with, are likewise intended) upon which they made war. They must not make a descent upon any of their neighbours till they had first given them fair notice, by a public manifesto, or remonstrance, stating the ground of their quarrel with them. In dealing with the worst of enemies, the laws of justice and honour must be observed; and, as the sword must never be taken in hand without cause, so not without cause shown. War is an appeal, in which the merits of the cause must be set forth.

I. Even to the proclamation of war must be subjoined a tender of peace, if they would accept of it upon reasonable terms. That is (say the Jewish writers), "upon condition that they renounce idolatry, worship the God of Israel, as proselytes of the gate that were not circumcised, pay to their new masters a yearly tribute, and submit to their government:" on these terms the process of war should be stayed, and their conquerors, upon this submission, were to be their protectors, *v.* 10, 11. Some think that even the seven nations of Canaan were to have this offer of peace made to them; and the offer was no jest or mockery, though *it was of the Lord to harden their hearts* that they should not accept it, Jos. 11:20. Others think that they are excluded (*v.* 16) not only from the benefit of that law (*v.* 13) which confines military execution to the males only, but from the benefit of this also, which allows not to make war till peace was refused. And I see not how they could proclaim peace to those who by the law were to be utterly rooted out, and to whom they were to show no mercy, *ch.* 7:2. But for any other nation which they made war upon, for the enlarging of their coast, the avenging of any wrong done, or the recovery of any right denied, they must first proclaim peace to the. Let this show, 1. God's grace in dealing with sinners: though he might most justly and easily destroy them, yet, having no pleasure in their ruin, he proclaims peace, and beseeches them to be reconciled; so that those who lie most obnoxious to his justice, and ready to fall as sacrifices to it, if they make him an answer of peace, and open to him, upon condition that they will be tributaries and servants to him, shall not only be saved from ruin, but incorporated with his Israel, as fellow-citizens with the saints. 2. Let it show us our duty in dealing with our brethren: if any quarrel happen, let us not only be ready to hearken to the proposals of peace, but forward to make such proposals. We should never make use of the law till we have first tried to accommodate matters in variance amicably, and without expense and vexation. *We* must be for peace, whoever are for war.

II. If the offers of peace were not accepted, then they must proceed to push on the war. And let those to whom God offers peace know that if they reject the offer, and take not the benefit of it within the time limited, judgment will rejoice against mercy in the execution as much as now mercy rejoices against judgment in the reprieve. In this case, 1. There is a promise implied that they should be victorious. It is taken for granted that *the Lord their God would deliver it into their hands, v.* 13. Note, Those enterprises which we undertake by a divine warrant, and prosecute by divine direction, we may expect to succeed in. If we take God's method, we shall have his blessing. 2. They are ordered, in honour to the public justice, to put all the soldiers to the sword, for them I understand by *every male* (*v.* 13), all that bore arms (as all then did that were able); but the spoil they are allowed to take to themselves (*v.* 14), in which were reckoned the women and children. Note, A justifiable property is acquired in that which is won in lawful war. God himself owns the title: *The Lord thy God gives it thee;* and therefore he must be owned in it, Ps. 44:3.

III. The nations of Canaan are excepted from the merciful provisions made by this law. Remnants might be left of the cities that were very far off (*v.* 15), because by them they were not in so much danger of being infected with idolatry, nor was their country so directly and immediately intended in the promise; but of the cities which were given to Israel for an inheritance no remnants must be left of their inhabitants (*v.* 16), for it put a slight upon the promise to admit Canaanites to share with them in the peculiar land of promise; and for another reason they must be utterly destroyed (*v.* 17), because, since it could not be expected that they should be cured of their idolatry, if they were left with that plague-sore upon them they would be in danger of infecting God's Israel, who were too apt to take the infection: *They will teach you to do after their abominations* (*v.* 18), to introduce their customs into the worship of the God of Israel, and by degrees to forsake him and to worship false gods; for those that dare violate the second commandment will not long keep to the first. Strange worships open the door to strange deities.

IV. Care is here taken that in the besieging of cities there should not be any destruction made of fruit-trees, *v.* 19–20. In those times, when besiegers forced their way, not as now with bombs and cannon-ball, but with battering rams, they had occasion for much timber in carrying on their sieges: now because, in the heat of war, men are not apt to consider, as they ought, the public good, it is expressly provided that fruit-trees should not be used as timber-trees. That reason, *for the tree of the field is man's* (the word *life* we supply), all the ancient versions, the Septuagint, Targums, etc., read, *For is the tree of the field a man?* Or *the tree of the field is not a man, that it should come against thee in the siege,* or *retire from thee into the bulwark.* "Do not brutishly vent thy rage against the trees that can do thee no harm." But our translation seems most agreeable to the intent of the law, and it teaches us, 1. That God is a better friend to man than man is to himself; and God's law, which we are apt to complain of as a heavy yoke, consults our interest and comfort, while our own appetites and passions, of which we are so indulgent, are really enemies to our welfare. The intent of many of the divine precepts is to restrain us from destroying that which is our life and food. 2. That armies and their commanders are not allowed to make what desolation they please in the countries that are the seat of war. Military rage must always be checked and ruled with reason. War, though carried on with ever so much caution, is destructive enough, and should not be made more so than is absolutely necessary. Generous spirits will show themselves tender, not only of men's lives, but of their livelihoods; for, though *the life is more than meat,* yet it will soon be nothing without meat. 3. The Jews understand this as a prohibition of all wilful waste upon any account whatsoever. No fruit-tree is to be destroyed unless it be barren, and cumber the ground. "Nay," they maintain, "whoso wilfully breaks vessels, tears clothes, stops wells, pulls down buildings, or destroys meat, transgresses this law: *Thou shalt not destroy.*" Christ took care that the broken meat should be gathered up, that nothing might be lost. Every creature of God is good, and, as nothing is to be refused, so nothing is to be abused. We may live to want what we carelessly waste.

CHAPTER 21

In this chapter provision is made, I. For the putting away of the guilt of blood from the land, when he that shed it had fled from justice (*v.* 1–9). II. For the preserving of the honour of a captive maid (*v.* 10–14). III. For the securing of the right of a first-born son, though he were not a favourite (*v.* 15–17). IV. For the restraining and punishing of a rebellious son (*v.* 18–21). V. For the maintaining of the honour of human bodies, which must not be hanged in chains, but decently buried, even the bodies of the worst malefactors (*v.* 22, 23).

Verses 1–9

Care had been taken by some preceding laws for the vigorous and effectual persecution of a wilful murderer (*ch.* 19:11 etc.), the putting of whom to death was the putting away of the guilt of blood from the land; but if this could not be done, the murderer not being discovered, they must not think that the land was in no danger of contracting any pollution because it was not through any neglect of theirs that the murderer was unpunished; no, a great solemnity is here provided for the putting away of the guilt, as an expression of their dread and detestation of that sin.

I. The case supposed is that *one is found slain, and it is not known who slew him, v.* 1. The providence of God has sometimes wonderfully brought to light these hidden works of darkness, and by strange occurrences the sin of the guilty has found them out, insomuch that it has become a proverb, *Murder will out.* But it is not always so; now and then the devil's promises of secresy and impunity in this world are made good; yet it is but for a while: there is a time coming when secret murders will be discovered; the *earth shall disclose her blood* (Isa. 26:21), upon the inquisition which justice makes for it; and there is an eternity coming when those that escaped punishment from men will lie under the righteous judgment of God. And the impunity with which so many murders and other wickednesses are committed in this world makes it necessary that there should be a day of judgment, to *require that which is past,* Eccl. 3:15.

II. Directions are given concerning what is to be done in this case. Observe,

1. It is taken for granted that a diligent search had been made for the murderer, witnesses examined, and circumstances strictly enquired into, that if possible they might find out the guilty person; but if, after all, they could not trace it out, not fasten the charge upon any, then, (1.) The *elders of the next city* (that had a court of three and twenty in it) were to concern themselves about this matter. If it were doubtful which city was next, the great sanhedrim were to send commissioners to determine that matter by an exact measure, *v.* 2, 3. Note, Public persons must be solicitous about the public good; and those that are in power and reputation in cities must lay out themselves to redress grievances, and reform what is amiss in the country and neighbourhood that lie about them. Those that are next to them should have the largest share of their good influence, as ministers of God for good. (2.) The priests and Levites must assist and preside in this solemnity (*v.* 5), that they might direct the management of it in all points according to the law, and particularly might be the people's mouth to God in the prayer that was to be put up on this sad occasion, *v.* 8. God being Israel's King, his ministers must be their magistrates, and by their word, as the mouth of the court and learned in the laws, every controversy must be tried. It was Israel's privilege that they had such guides, overseers, and rulers, and their duty to make use of them upon all occasions, especially in sacred things, as this was. (3.) They were to bring a heifer down into a rough and unoccupied valley, and to kill it there, *v.* 3, 4. This was not a sacrifice (for it was not brought to the altar), but a solemn protestation that thus they would put the murderer to death if they had him in their hands. The heifer must be one that had not drawn in the yoke, to signify (say some) that the murderer was a son of Belial; it must be brought into a rough valley, to signify the horror of the fact, and that the defilement which blood brings upon a land turns it into barrenness. And the Jews say that unless, after this, the murderer was found out, this valley where the heifer was killed was never to be tilled nor sown. (4.) The elders were to *wash their hands in water* over the heifer that was killed, and to profess, not only that they had not shed this innocent blood themselves, but that they knew not who had (*v.* 6, 7), nor had knowingly concealed the murderer, helped him to make his escape, or been any way aiding or abetting. To this custom David alludes, Ps. 26:6, *I will wash my hands in innocency;* but if Pilate had any eye to it (Mt. 27:24) he wretchedly misapplied it when he condemned Christ, knowing him to be innocent, and yet acquitted himself from the guilt of innocent blood. *Protestatio non valet contra factum — Protestations are of no avail when contradicted by fact.* (5.) The priests were to pray to God for the country and nation, that God would be merciful to them, and not bring upon them the judgments which the connivance at the sin of murder would deserve. It might be presumed that the murderer was either one of their city or was now harboured in their city; and therefore they must pray that they might not fare the worse for his being among them, Num. 16:22. *Be merciful, O Lord, to thy people Israel, v.* 8. Note, When we hear of the wickedness of the wicked we have need to cry earnestly to God for mercy for our land, which groans and trembles under it. We must empty the measure by our prayers which others are filling by their sins. Now,

2. This solemnity was appointed, (1.) That it might give occasion to common and public discourse concerning the murder, which perhaps might some way or other occasion the discovery of it. (2.) That it might possess people with a dread of the guilt of blood, which defiles not only the conscience of him that sheds it (this should engage us all to pray with David, *Deliver me from blood-guiltiness*), but the land in which it is shed; it cries to the magistrate for justice on the criminal, and, if that cry be not heard, it cries to heaven for judgment on the land. If there must be so much care employed to save the land from guilt when the murderer was not known, it was certainly impossible to secure it from guilt if the murderer was known and yet protected. All would be taught, by this solemnity, to use their utmost care and diligence to prevent, discover, and punish murder. Even the heathen mariners dreaded the guilt of blood, Jon. 1:14. (3.) That we might all learn to take heed of partaking in other men's sins, and making ourselves accessory to them *ex post facto — after the fact,* by countenancing the sin or sinner, and not witnessing against it in our places. We have *fellowship with the unfruitful works of darkness* if we do not reprove them rather, and bear our testimony against them. The repentance of the church of Corinth for the sin of one of their members produced such a carefulness, such a clearing of themselves, such a holy indignation, fear, and revenge (2 Co. 7:11), as were signified by the solemnity here appointed.

Verses 10–14

By this law a soldier is allowed to marry his captive if he pleased. For the hardness of their hearts Moses gave them this permission, lest, if they had not had liberty given them to marry such, they should have taken liberty to defile themselves with them, and by such wickedness the camp would have been troubled. The man is supposed to have a wife already, and to take this wife for a secondary wife, as the Jews called them. This indulgence of men's inordinate desires, in which their hearts walked after their eyes, is by no means agreeable to the law of Christ, which therefore in this respect, among others, far exceeds in glory the law of Moses. The gospel permits not him that has one wife to take another, for *from the beginning it was not so.* The gospel forbids looking upon a woman, though a beautiful one, to lust after her, and commands the mortifying and denying of all irregular desires, though it be as uneasy as the cutting off of a right hand; so much does our holy religion, more than that of the Jews, advance the honour and support the dominion of the soul over the body, the spirit over the flesh, consonant to the glorious discovery it makes of life and immortality, and the better hope.

But, though military men were allowed this liberty, yet care is here taken that they should not abuse it, that is,

I. That they should not abuse themselves by doing it too hastily, though the captive was ever so desirable: *"If thou wouldest have her to thy wife* (v. 10, 11), it is true thou needest not ask her parents' consent, for she is thy captive, and is at thy disposal. But, 1. Thou shalt have no familiar intercourse till thou hast married her."* This allowance was designed to gratify, not a filthy brutish lust, in the heat and fury of its rebellion against reason and virtue, but an honourable and generous affection to a comely and amiable person, though in distress; therefore he may make her his wife if he will, but he must not *deal with her as with a harlot.* 2. "Thou shalt not marry her of a sudden, but keep her a full month in thy house," v. 12, 13. This he must do either, (1.) That he may try to take his affection off from her; for he must know that, though in marrying her he does not do ill (so the law then stood), yet in letting her alone he does much better. Let her therefore shave her head, that he might not be enamoured with her locks, and *let her nails grow* (so the margin reads it), to spoil the beauty of her hand. *Quisquid amas cupias non placuisse nimis — We should moderate our affection for those things which we are tempted to love inordinately.* Or rather, (2.) This was done in token of her renouncing idolatry, and becoming a proselyte to the Jewish religion. The shaving of her head, the paring of her nails, and the changing of her apparel, signified her putting off her former conversation, which was corrupt in her ignorance, that she might become a new creature. She must remain in his house to be taught the good knowledge of the Lord and the worship of him: and the Jews say that if she refused, and continued obstinate in idolatry, he must not marry her. Note, The professors of religion must not be unequally yoked with unbelievers, 2 Co. 6:14.

II. That they should not abuse the poor captive. 1. She must have time to *bewail her father and mother,* from whom she was separated, and without whose consent and blessing she is now likely to be married, and perhaps to a common soldier of Israel, though in her country ever so nobly born and bred. To force a marriage till these sorrows were digested, and in some measure got over, and she was better reconciled to the land of her captivity by being better acquainted with it, would be very unkind. She must not bewail her idols, but be glad to part with them; to her near and dear relations only her affection must be thus indulged. 2. If, upon second thoughts, he that had brought her to his house with a purpose to marry her changed his mind and would not marry her, he might not make merchandise of her, as of his other prisoners, but must give her liberty to return, if she pleased, to her own country, because he had humbled her and afflicted her, by raising expectations and then disappointing them (v. 14); having made a fool of her, he might not make a prey of her. This intimates how binding the laws of justice and honour are, particularly in the pretensions of love, the courting of affections, and the promises of marriage, which are to be looked upon as solemn things, that have something sacred in them, and therefore are not to be jested with.

Verses 15–17

This law restrains men from disinheriting their eldest sons out of mere caprice, and without just provocation.

I. The case here put (v. 15) is very instructive. 1. It shows the great mischief of having more wives than one, which the law of Moses did not restrain, probably in hopes that men's own experience of the great inconvenience of it in families would at last put an end to it and make them a law to themselves. Observe the supposition here: If a man have two wives, it is a thousand to one but one of them is beloved and the other hated (that is, manifestly loved less) as Leah was by Jacob, and the effect of this cannot but be strifes and jealousies, envy, confusion, and every evil work, which could not but create a constant uneasiness and vexation to the husband, and involve him both in sin and trouble. Those do much better consult their own

ease and satisfaction who adhere to God's law than those who indulge their own lusts. 2. It shows how Providence commonly sides with the weakest, and *gives more abundant honour to that part which lacked;* for the first-born son is here supposed to be *hers that was hated;* it was so in Jacob's family: because *the Lord saw that Leah was hated,* Gen. 29:31. The great householder wisely gives to each his dividend of comfort; if one had the honour to be the beloved wife, it often proved that the other had the honour to be the mother of the first-born.

II. The law in this case is still binding on parents; they must give their children their right without partiality. In the case supposed, the eldest son, though the son of the less-beloved wife, must have his birthright privilege, which was a double portion of the father's estate, because he was the beginning of his strength that is, in him his family began to be strengthened and his quiver began to be filled with the *arrows of a mighty man* (Ps. 127:4), and therefore the right of the first-born is his, v. 16, 17. Jacob had indeed deprived Reuben of his birthright, and given it to Joseph, but it was because Reuben had forfeited the birthright by his incest, not because he was the *son of the hated;* now, lest that which Jacob did justly should be drawn into a precedent for others to do the same thing unjustly, it is here provided that when the father makes his will, or otherwise settled his estate, the child shall not fare the worse for the mother's unhappiness in having less of her husband's love, for that was not the child's fault. Note, (1.) Parents ought to make no other difference in dispensing their affections among their children than what they see plainly God makes in dispensing his grace among them. (2.) Since it is the providence of God that makes heirs, the disposal of providence in that matter must be acquiesced in and not opposed. No son should be abandoned by his father till he manifestly appear to be abandoned of God, which is hard to say of any while there is life.

Verses 18–23

Here is, I. A law for the punishing of a rebellious son. Having in the former law provided that parents should not deprive their children of their right, it was fit that it should next be provided that children withdraw not the honour and duty which are owing to their parents, for there is no partiality in the divine law. Observe,

1. How the criminal is here described. He is a *stubborn and rebellious son, v.* 18. No child was to fare the worse for the weakness of his capacity, the slowness or dulness of his understanding, but for his wilfulness and obstinacy. If he carry himself proudly and insolently towards his parents, contemn their authority, slight their reproofs and admonitions, disobey the express commands they give him for his own good, hate to be reformed by the correction they give him, shame their family, grieve their hearts, waste their substance, and threaten to ruin their estate by riotous living — this is a *stubborn and rebellious son.* He is particularly supposed (v. 20) to be a *glutton or a drunkard.* This intimates either, (1.) That these were sins which his parents did in a particular manner warn him against, and therefore that in these instances there was a plain evidence that he did not obey their voice. Lemuel had this charge from his mother, Prov. 31:4. Note, In the education of children, great care should be taken to suppress all inclinations to drunkenness, and to keep them out of the way of temptations to it; in order hereunto they should be possessed betimes with a dread and detestation of that beastly sin, and taught betimes to deny themselves. Or, (2.) That his being a *glutton and a drunkard* was the cause of his insolence and obstinacy towards his parents. Note, There is nothing that draws men into all manner of wickedness, and hardens them in it, more certainly and fatally than drunkenness does. When men take to drink they forget the law, they forget all law (Prov. 31:5), even that fundamental law of honouring parents.

2. How this criminal is to be proceeded against. His own father and mother are to be his prosecutors, v. 19, 20. They might not put him to death themselves, but they must complain of him to the elders of the city, and the complaint must needs be made with a sad heart: *This our son is stubborn and rebellious.* Note, Those that give up themselves to vice and wickedness, and will not be reclaimed, forfeit their interest in the natural affections of the nearest rela-

tions; the instruments of their being justly become the instruments of their destruction. The children that forget their duty must thank themselves and not blame their parents if they are regarded with less and less affection. And, how difficult soever tender parents now find it to reconcile themselves to the just punishment of their rebellious children, in the day of the revelation of the righteous judgment of God all natural affection will be so entirely swallowed up in divine love that they will acquiesce even in the condemnation of those children, because God will be therein for ever glorified.

3. What judgment is to be executed upon him: he must publicly *stoned to death by the men of his city, v.* 21. And thus, (1.) The paternal authority was supported, and God, our common Father, showed himself jealous for it, it being one of the first and most ancient streams derived from him that is the fountain of all power. (2.) This law, if duly executed, would *early destroy the wicked of the land.* (Ps. 101:8), and prevent the spreading of the gangrene, by cutting off the corrupt part betimes; for those that were bad members of families would never make good members of the commonwealth. (3.) It would strike an awe upon children, and frighten them into obedience to their parents, if they would not otherwise be brought to their duty and kept in it: *All Israel shall hear.* The Jews say, "The elders that condemned him were to send notice of it in writing all the nation over, *In such a court, such a day, we stoned such a one, because he was a stubborn and rebellious son."* And I have sometimes wished that as in all our courts there is an exact record kept of the condemnation of criminals, *in perpetuam rei memoriam — that the memorial may never be lost,* so there might be public and authentic notice given in print to the kingdom of such condemnations, and the executions upon them, by the elders themselves, *in terrorem — that all may hear and fear.*

II. A law for the burying of the bodies of malefactors that were hanged, v. 22. The hanging of them by the neck till the body was dead was not used at all among the Jews, as with us; but of such as were stoned to death, if it were for blasphemy, or some other very execrable crime, it was usual, by order of the judges, to hang up the dead bodies upon a post for some time, as a spectacle to the world, to express the ignominy of the crime, and to strike the greater terror upon others, that they might not only hear and fear, but see and fear. Now it is here provided that, whatever time of the day they were thus hanged up, at sun-set they should be taken down and buried, and not left to hang out all night; sufficient (says the law) *to such a man is this punishment;* hitherto let it go, but no further. Let the malefactor and his crime be hidden in the grave. Now, 1. God would thus preserve the honour of human bodies and tenderness towards the worst of criminals. The time of exposing dead bodies thus is limited for the same reason that the number of stripes was limited by another law: *Lest thy brother seem vile unto thee.* Punishing beyond death God reserves to himself; as for man, there is no more that he can do. Whether therefore the hanging of malefactors in chains, and setting up their heads and quarters, be decent among Christians that look for the resurrection of the body, may perhaps be worth considering. 2. Yet it is plain there was something ceremonial in it; by the law of Moses the touch of a dead body was defiling, and therefore dead bodies must not be left hanging up in the country, because, by the same rule, this would defile the land. But, 3. There is one reason here given which has reference to Christ. *He that is hanged is accursed of God,* that is, it is the highest degree of disgrace and reproach that can be done to a man, and proclaims him under the curse of God as much as any external punishment can. Those that see him thus hang between heaven and earth will conclude him abandoned of both and unworthy of either; and therefore let him not hang all night, for that would carry it too far. Now the apostle, showing how Christ has redeemed us from the curse of the law by being himself made a curse for us, illustrates it by comparing the brand here put on him that was hanged on a tree with the death of Christ, Gal. 3:13. Moses, by the Spirit, uses this phrase of being *accursed of God,* when he means no more than being treated most ignominiously, that it might afterwards be applied to the death of Christ, and might show that in it he underwent the curse of the law for us, which is a great enhancement of his love and a great encouragement to our faith in him. And (as the excellent bishop Patrick well observes) this passage is applied to the death of Christ, not only because he bore our sins and was exposed to shame, as these malefactors were that were accursed of God, but because he was in the evening taken down from the cursed tree and buried (and that by the particular care of the Jews, with an eye to this law, Jn. 19:31), in token that now, the guilt being removed, the law was satisfied, as it was when the malefactor had hanged till sun-set; it demanded no more. Then he ceased to be a curse, and those that were his. And, as the land of Israel was pure and clean when the dead body was buried, so the church is washed and cleansed by the complete satisfaction which thus Christ made.

CHAPTER 22

The laws of this chapter provide, I. For the preservation of charity and good neighbourship, in the care of strayed or fallen cattle (*v.* 1–4). II. For the preservation of order and distinction, that men and women should not wear one another's clothes (*v.* 5), and that other needless mixtures should be avoided (*v.* 9–11). III. For the preservation of birds (*v.* 6, 7). IV. Of life (*v.* 8). V. Of the commandments (*v.* 12). VI. Of the reputation of a wife abused, if she were innocent (*v.* 13–19), but for her punishment if guilty (*v.* 20, 21). VII. For the preservation of the chastity of wives (*v.* 22). Virgins betrothed (*v.* 23–27), or not betrothed (*v.* 28, 29). And, lastly, against incest (*v.* 30).

Verses 1–4

The kindness that was commanded to be shown in reference to an enemy (Ex. 23:4, etc.) is here required to be much more done for a neighbour, though he were not an Israelite, for the law is consonant to natural equity. 1. That strayed cattle should be brought back, either to the owner or to the pasture out of which they had gone astray, *v.* 1, 2. This must be done in pity to the very cattle, which, while they wandered, were exposed; and in civility and respect to the owner, nay, and in justice to him, for it was doing as we would be done by, which is one of the fundamental laws of equity. Note, Religion teaches us to be neighbourly, and to be ready to do all good offices, as we have opportunity, to all men. In doing this, (1.) They must not mind trouble, but, if they knew who the owner was, must take it back themselves; for, if they should only send notice to the owner to come and look after it himself, some mischief might befal it ere he could reach it. (2.) They must not mind expense, but, if they knew not who the owner was, must take it home and feed it till the owner was found. If such care must be taken of a neighbour's ox or ass going astray, much more of himself going astray from God and his duty; we should do our utmost to convert him (Jam. 5:19), and restore him, considering ourselves, Gal. 6:1. 2. That lost goods should be brought to the owner, *v.* 3. The Jews say, "He that found the lost goods was to give public notice of them by the common crier three or four times," according to the usage with us; if the owner could not be found, he that found the goods might convert them to his own use; but (say some learned writers in this case) he would do very well to give the value of the goods to the poor. 3. That cattle in distress should be helped, *v.* 4. This must be done both in compassion to the brute-creatures (for a *merciful man regardeth the life of a beast,* though it be not his own) and in love and friendship to our neighbour, not knowing how soon we may have occasion for his help. If one member may say to another, "I have at present no need of thee," it cannot say, "I never shall."

Verses 5–12

Here are several laws in these verses which seem to stoop very low, and to take cognizance of things mean and minute. Men's laws commonly do not so: *De minimis non curat lex — The law takes no cognizance of little things;* but because God's providence extends itself to the smallest affairs, his precepts do so, that even in them we may be *in the fear of the Lord,* as we are under his eye and care. And yet the significancy and tendency of these statutes, which seem little, are such that, notwithstanding their minuteness, being fond among the things of God's law, which he has written to us, they are to be accounted great things.

I. The distinction of sexes by the apparel is to be kept up, for the preservation of our own and our neighbour's chastity, *v.* 5. *Nature itself teaches* that a difference be made between them in *their hair* (1 Co. 11:14), and by the same rule in their clothes, which therefore ought not to be confounded, either in ordinary wear or occasionally. To befriend a lawful escape or concealment it may be done, but whether for sport or in the acting of plays is justly questionable. 1. Some think it refers to the idolatrous custom of the Gentiles: in the worship of Venus, women appeared in armour, and men in women's clothes; this, as other such superstitious usages, is here said to be *an abomination to the Lord.* 2. It forbids the confounding of the dispositions and affairs of the sexes: men must not be effeminate, nor do the women's work in the house, nor must women be viragos, pretend to *teach, or usurp authority,* 1 Tim. 2:11, 12. Probably this confounding of garments had been used to gain opportunity of committing uncleanness, and is therefore forbidden; for those that would be kept from sin must keep themselves from all occasions of it and approaches to it.

II. In taking a bird's-nest, the dam must be let go, *v.* 6, 7. The Jews say, "This is the least of all the commandments of the law of Moses," and yet the same promise is here made to the observance of it that is made to the keeping of the fifth commandment, which is one of the greatest, *that it may be well with thee, and that thou mayest prolong thy days;* for, as disobedience in a small matter shows a very great contempt of the law, so obedience in a small matter shows a very great regard to it. He that let go a bird out of his hand (which was worth two in the bush) purely because God bade him, in that made it to appear that he *esteemed all God's precepts concerning all things to be right,* and that he could deny himself rather than sin against God. But *doth God take care* for birds? 1 Co. 9:9. Yes, certainly; and perhaps to this law our Saviour alludes. Lu. 12:6, *Are not five sparrows sold for two farthings, and not one of them is forgotten before God?* This law, 1. Forbids us to be cruel to the brute-creatures, or to take a pleasure in destroying them. Though God has made us *wiser than the fowls of heaven,* and given us *dominion over them,* yet we must not abuse them nor rule them with rigour. *Let go the dam* to breed again; *destroy it not, for a blessing is in it,* Isa. 65:8. 2. It teaches us compassion to those of our own kind, and to abhor the thought of every thing that looks barbarous, and cruel, and ill-natured, especially towards those of the weaker and tender sex, which always ought to be treated with the utmost respect, in consideration of the sorrows wherein they bring forth children. It is spoken of as an instance of the most inhuman cruelty that *the mother was dashed to pieces upon her children* (Hos. 10:14), and that the *women with child were ripped open,* Amos 1:13. 3. It further intimates that we must not take advantage against any, from their natural affection and the tenderness of their disposition, to do them an injury. The dam could not have been taken if her concern for her eggs or young (unlike to the ostrich) had not detained her upon the next when otherwise she could easily have secured herself by flight. Now, since it is a thousand pities that she should fare the worse for that which is her praise, the law takes care that she shall be let go. The remembrance of this may perhaps, some time or other, keep us from doing a hard or unkind thing to those whom we have at our mercy.

III. In building a house, care must be taken to make it safe, that none might receive mischief by falling from it, *v.* 8. The roofs of their houses were flat for people to walk on, as appears by many scriptures; now lest any, through carelessness, should fall off them, they must compass them with battlements, which (the Jews say) must be three feet and a half high; if this were not done, and mischief followed, the owner, by his neglect, brought the guilt of blood upon his house. See here, 1. How precious men's lives are to God, who protects them, not only by his providence, but by his law. 2. How precious, therefore, they ought to be to us, and what care we should take to prevent hurt from coming to any person. The Jews say that by the equity of this law they were obliged (and so are we too) to fence, or remove, every thing by which life may be endangered, as to cover draw-wells, keep bridges in repair, and the like, lest, if any perish through our omission, their blood be required at our hand.

IV. Odd mixtures are here forbidden, *v.* 9, 10. Much of this we met with before, Lev. 19:19. There appears not any thing at all of moral evil in these things, and therefore we now make no conscience of sowing wheat and rye together, ploughing with horses and oxen together, and of wearing linsey-woolsey garments; but hereby is forbidden either, 1. A conformity to some idolatrous customs of the heathen. Or, 2. That which is contrary to the plainness and purity of an Israelite. They must not gratify their own vanity and curiosity by putting those things together which the Creator in infinite wisdom had made asunder: they must not be unequally yoked with unbelievers, nor mingle themselves with the unclean, as an ox with an ass. Nor must their profession and appearance in the world be motley, or party-coloured, but all of a piece, all of a kind.

V. The law concerning fringes upon their garments, and memorandums of the commandments, which we had before (Num. 15:38, 39), is here repeated, *v.* 12. By these they were distinguished from other people, so that it might be said, upon the first sight There goes an Israelite, which taught them not to be ashamed of their country, nor the peculiarities of their religion, how much soever their neighbours looked upon them and it with contempt: and they were also put in mind of the precepts upon the particular occasions to which they had reference; and perhaps this law is repeated here because the precepts immediately foregoing seemed so minute that they were in danger of being overlooked and forgotten. The fringes will remind you not to make your garments of linen and woollen, *v.* 11.

Verses 13–30

These laws relate to the seventh commandment, laying a restraint by laying a penalty upon those fleshly lusts which war against the soul.

I. If a man, lusting after another woman, to get rid of his wife slander her and falsely accuse her, as not having the virginity she pretended to when he married her, upon the disproof of his slander he must be punished, *v.* 13–19. What the meaning of that evidence is by which the husband's accusation was to be proved false the learned are not agreed, nor is it at all necessary to enquire — those for whom this law was intended, no doubt, understood it: it is sufficient for us to know that this wicked husband, who had thus endeavoured to ruin the reputation of his own wife, was to be scourged, and fined, and bound out from ever divorcing the wife he had thus abused, *v.* 18, 19. Upon his dislike of her he might have divorced her if he had pleased, by the permission of the law (*ch.* 24:1), but then he must have given her her dowry: if therefore to save that, and to do her the greater mischief, he would thus destroy her good name, it was fit that he should be severely punished for it, and for ever after forfeit the permission to divorce her. Observe, 1. The nearer any are in relation to us the greater sin it is to belie them and blemish their reputation. It is spoken of as a crime of the highest nature to *slander thy own mother's son* (Ps. 50:20), who is next to thyself, much more to slander thy own wife, or thy own husband, that is thyself: it is an ill bird indeed that defiles its own nest. 2. Chastity is honour as well as virtue, and that which gives occasion for the suspicion of it is as great a reproach and disgrace as any whatsoever: in this matter therefore, above any thing, we should be highly tender both of our own good name and that of others. 3. Parents must look upon themselves as concerned to vindicate the reputation of their children, for it is a branch of their own.

II. If the woman that was married as a virgin was not found to be one she was to be stoned to death at her father's door, *v.* 20, 21. If the uncleanness had been committed before she was betrothed it would not have been punished as a capital crime; but she must die for the abuse she put upon him whom she married, being conscious to herself of being defiled, while she made him believe her to be a chaste and modest woman. But some think that her uncleanness was punished with death only in case it was committed after she was betrothed, supposing there were few come to maturity but what were betrothed, though not yet married. Now, 1. This gave a powerful caution to young women to flee fornication, since, however concealed before, so as not to mar their marriage, it would very likely be discovered afterwards, to their perpetual infamy and utter ruin. 2. It is intimated to parents that they must by all means possible preserve their children's chastity, by giving them good advice and admonition, setting them good examples, keeping them from bad company, praying for them, and laying them under needful restraints, because, if the children committed lewdness, the parents must have the grief and shame of the execution at their own door. That phrase of *folly wrought in Israel* was used concerning this very crime in the case of Dinah, Gen. 34:7. All sin is folly, uncleanness especially; but, above all, uncleanness in Israel, by profession a holy people.

III. If any man, single or married, lay with a married woman, they were both to be put to death, *v.* 22. This law we had before, Lev. 20:10. For a married man to lie with a single woman was not a crime of so high a nature, nor was it punished with death, because not introducing a spurious brood into families under the character of legitimate children.

IV. If a damsel were betrothed and not married, she was from under the eye of her intended husband, and therefore she and her chastity were taken under the special protection of the law. 1. If her chastity were violated by her own consent, she was to be put to death, and her adulterer with her, *v.* 23, 24. And it shall be presumed that she consented if it were done in the city, or in any place where, had she cried out, help might speedily have come in to prevent the injury offered her. *Qui tacet, consentire videtur — Silence implies consent.* Note, It may be presumed that those willingly yield to a temptation (whatever they pretend) who will not use the means and helps they might be furnished with to avoid and overcome it. Nay, her being found in the city, a place of company and diversion, when she should have kept under the protection of her father's house, was an evidence against her that she had not that dread of the sin and the danger of it which became a modest woman. Note, Those that needlessly expose themselves to temptation justly suffer for the same, if, ere they are aware, they be surprised and caught by it. Dinah lost her honour to gratify her curiosity with a sight of the *daughters of the land.* By this law the Virgin Mary was in danger of being made a public example, that is, of being stoned to death, but that God, by an angel, cleared the matter to Joseph. 2. If she were forced, and never consented, he that committed the rape was to be put to death, but the damsel was to be acquitted, *v.* 24–27. Now if it were done in the field, out of the hearing of neighbours, it shall be presumed that she cried out, but there was none to save her; and, besides, her going into the field, a place of solitude, did not so much expose her. Now by this law it is intimated to us, (1.) That we shall suffer only for the wickedness we do, not for that which is done to us. That is no sin which has not more or less of the will in it. (2.) That we must presume the best concerning all persons, unless the contrary do appear; not only charity, but equity teaches us to do so. Though none heard her cry, yet, because none could hear it if she did, it shall be taken for granted that she did. This rule we should go by in judging of persons and actions: *believe all things, and hope all things.* (3.) That our chastity should be as dear to us as our life when that is assaulted, it is not at all improper to cry *murder, murder,* for, *as when a man riseth against his neighbour and slayeth him, even so is this matter.* (4.) By way of allusion to this, see what we are to do when Satan sets upon us with his temptations: wherever we are, let us cry aloud to heaven for help *(Succurre, Domine, vim patior — Help me, O Lord, for I suffer violence),* and there we may be sure to be heard, and answered, as Paul was, *My grace is sufficient for thee.*

V. If a damsel not betrothed were thus abused by violence, he that abused her should be fined, the father should have the fine, and, if he and the damsel did consent, he should be bound to marry her, and never to divorce her, how much soever she was below him, and how unpleasing soever she might afterwards be to him, as Tamar was to Amnon after he had forced her, *v.* 28, 29. This was to deter men from such vicious practices, which it is a shame that we are necessitated to read and write of.

VI. The law against a man's marrying his father's widow, or having any undue familiarity with his father's wife, is here repeated (*v.* 30) from Lev. 18:8. And, probably, it is intended (as bishop Patrick notes) for a short memorandum to them carefully to observe all the laws there made against incestuous marriages, that being specified which is the most detestable of all; it is that of which the apostle says, *It is not so much as named among the Gentiles,* 1 Co. 5:1.

CHAPTER 23

The laws of this chapter provide, I. For the preserving of the purity and honour of the families of Israel, by excluding such as would be a disgrace to them (*v.* 1–8). II. For the preserving of the purity and honour of the camp of Israel when it was abroad (*v.* 9–14). III. For the encouraging and entertaining of slaves who fled to them (*v.* 15, 16). IV. Against whoredom (*v.* 17, 18). V. Against usury (*v.* 19, 20). IV. Against the breach of vows (*v.* 21–23). VII. What liberty a man might take in his neighbour's field and vineyard, and what not (*v.* 23, 25).

Verses 1–8

Interpreters are not agreed what is here meant by *entering into the congregation of the Lord,* which is here forbidden to eunuchs and to bastards, Ammonites and Moabites, for ever, but to Edomites and Egyptians only till the third generation. 1. Some think they are hereby excluded from communicating with the people of God in their religious services. Though eunuchs and bastards were owned as members of the church, and the Ammonites and Moabites might be circumcised and proselyted to the Jewish religion, yet they and their families must lie for some time under marks of disgrace, remembering the rock whence they were hewn, and must not come so near the sanctuary as others might, nor have so free a communion with Israelites. 2. Others think they are hereby excluded from bearing office in the congregation: none of these must be elders or judges, lest the honour of the magistracy should thereby be stained. 3. Others think they are excluded only from marrying with Israelites. Thus the learned bishop Patrick inclines to understand it; yet we find that when this law was put in execution after the captivity they separated from Israel, not only the strange wives, but all the mixed multitude, see Neh. 13:1 — 2. With the daughters of these nations (though out of the nations of Canaan), it should seem, the men of Israel might marry, if they were completely proselyted to the Jewish religion; but with the men of these nations the daughters of Israel might not marry, nor could the men be naturalized otherwise than as here provided.

It is plain, in general, that disgrace is here put,

I. Upon bastards and eunuchs, *v.* 1, 2. By bastards here the Jewish writers understand, not all that were born of fornication, or out of marriage, but all the issue of those incestuous mixtures which are forbidden, Lev. 18. And, though it was not the fault of the issue, yet, to deter people from those unlawful marriages and unlawful lusts, it was very convenient that their posterity should thus be made infamous. By this rule Jephthah, though the son of a harlot, a strange woman (Jdg. 11:1, 2), yet was not a bastard in the sense of this law. And as for the eunuchs, though by this law they seemed to be cast out of the vineyard as dry trees, which they complain of (Isa. 56:3), yet it is here promised (*v.* 5) that if they took care of their duty to God, as far as they were admitted, by keeping his sabbaths and choosing the things that pleased him, the want of this privilege should be made up to them with such spiritual blessings as would entitle them to an everlasting name.

II. Upon Ammonites and Moabites, the posterity of Lot, who, for his outward convenience, had separated himself from Abraham, Gen. 13:11. And we do not find that he or his ever joined themselves again to the children of the covenant. They are here cut off *to the tenth generation,* that is, (as some think it is explained), for ever. Compare Neh. 13:1. The reason of this quarrel which Israel must have with them, so as not to *seek their peace* (*v.* 6), is because of the unkindness they had now lately done to the camp of Israel, notwithstanding the orders God had given not to distress or vex them, *ch.* 2:9, 19. 1. It was bad enough that they did not *meet them with bread and water in the way* (*v.* 4), that they did not as allies, or at least as neutral states, bring victuals into their camp, which they should have been duly paid for. It was well that God's Israel did not need their kindness, God himself following them with bread and water. However this omission of the Ammonites should be remembered against their nation in future ages. Note, God will certainly reckon, not only with those that oppose his people, but with those that do not help and further them, when it is in the power of their hand to do it. The charge at the great day is for an omission: *I was hungry, and you gave me no meat.* 2. The Moabites had done worse, they hired Balaam to curse Israel, *v.* 4. It is true *God turned the curse into a blessing* (*v.* 5), not only changing the word in Balaam's mouth, but making that really turn to the honour and advantage of Israel which was designed for their ruin. But though the design was defeated, and overruled for good, the Moabites' wickedness was not the less provoking. God will deal with sinners, but according to their endeavours, Ps. 28:4.

III. The Edomites and Egyptians had not so deep a mark of displeasure put upon them as the Moabites and Ammonites had. If an Edomite or Egyptian turned proselyte, his grand-children should be looked upon as members of the congregation of the Lord to all intents and purposes, *v.* 7, 8. We should think that the Edomites had been more injurious to the Israelites than the Ammonites, and deserved as little favour from them (Num. 20:20), and yet "*Thou shalt not abhor an Edomite,* as thou must an Ammonite, for he is thy brother." Note, The unkindness of near relations, though by many worst taken, yet should with us, for that reason, because of the relation, be first forgiven. And then, as to the Egyptians, here is a strange reason given why they must not be abhorred: "*Thou wast a stranger in their land,* and therefore, though hardly used there, be civil to them, for old acquaintance' sake." They must not remember their bondage in Egypt for the keeping up of any ill will to the Egyptians, but only for the magnifying of Gods power and goodness in their deliverance.

Verses 9–14

Israel was now encamped, and this vast army was just entering upon action, which was likely to keep them together for a long time, and therefore it was fit to give them particular directions for the good ordering of their camp. And the charge is in one word to be *clean.* They must take care to keep their camp pure from moral, ceremonial, and natural pollution.

I. From moral pollution (*v.* 9): *When the host goes forth against thy enemy* then look upon thyself as in a special manner engaged to *keep thyself from every evil thing.* 1. The soldiers themselves must take heed of sin, for sin takes off the edge of valour; guilt makes men cowards. Those that put their lives in their hands are concerned to make and keep their peace with God, and preserve a conscience void of offence; then may they look death in the face without terror. Soldiers, in executing their commission, must keep themselves from gratifying the lusts of malice, covetousness, or uncleanness, for these are wicked things — must keep themselves from the idols, or accursed things, they found in the camps they plundered. 2. Even those that tarried at home, the body of the people, and every particular person, must at that time especially keep from every wicked thing, lest by sin they provoke God to withdraw his presence from the host, and give victory to the enemy for the correcting of his own people. Times of war should be times of reformation, else how can we expect God should hear and answer our prayers for success? Ps. 66:18. See 1 Sa. 7:3.

II. From ceremonial pollution, which might befal a person when unconscious of it, for which he was bound to wash his flesh in water, and look upon himself as *unclean until the evening,* Lev. 15:16. A soldier, notwithstanding the constant service and duty he had to do in the camp, must be so far from looking upon himself as discharged from the observance of this ceremony that more was required from him than at another time; had he been at his own house, he needed only to wash his flesh, but, being in the army, he must go abroad out of the camp, as one concerned to keep it pure and ashamed of his own impurity, and not return till after sunset, *v.* 10, 11. By this trouble and reproach, which even involuntary pollutions exposed men to, they were taught to keep up a very great dread of all fleshly lusts. It were well if military men would consider this.

III. From natural pollution; the camp of the Lord must have nothing offensive in it, *v.* 12–14. It is strange that the divine law, or at least the solemn order and direction of Moses, should extend to a thing of this nature; but the design of it was to teach them, 1. Modesty and decorum; nature itself teaches them thus to distinguish themselves from beasts that know no shame. 2. Cleanliness, and, though not niceness, yet neatness, even in their camp. Filthiness is offensive to the senses God has endued us with, prejudicial to the health, a wrong to the comfort of human life, and an evidence of a careless slothful temper of mind.

3. Purity from the pollutions of sin; if there must be this care taken to preserve the body clean and sweet, much more should we be solicitous to keep the mind so. 4. A reverence of the divine majesty. This is the reason here given: *For the Lord thy God walketh* by his ark, the special token of his presence, *in the midst of thy camp;* with respect to that external symbol this external purity is required, which (though not insisted on in the letter when that reason ceases) teaches us to preserve inward purity of soul, in consideration of the eye of God, which is always upon us. By this expression of respect to the presence of God among them, they were taught both to fortify themselves against sin and to encourage themselves against their enemies with the consideration of that presence. 5. A regard one to another. The filthiness of one is noisome to many; this law of cleanliness therefore teaches us not to do that which will be justly offensive to our brethren and grieve them. It is a law against nuisances.

Verses 15–25

Orders are here given about five several things which have no relation one to another: —

I. The land of Israel is here made a sanctuary, or city of refuge, for servants that were wronged and abused by their masters, and fled thither for shelter from the neighbouring countries, *v.* 15, 16. We cannot suppose that they were hereby obliged to give entertainment to all the unprincipled men that ran from service; Israel needed not (as Rome at first did) to be thus peopled. But, 1. They must not deliver up the trembling servant to his enraged master, till upon trial it appeared that the servant has wronged his master and was justly liable to punishment. Note, It is an honourable thing to shelter and protect the weak, provided they be not wicked. God allows his people to patronise the oppressed. The angel bid Hagar return to her mistress, and Paul sent Onesimus back to his master Philemon, because they had neither of them any cause to go away, nor was either of them exposed to any danger in returning. But the servant here is supposed to escape, that is, to run for his life, to the people of Israel, of whom he had heard (as Benhadad of the kings of Israel, 1 Ki. 20:31) that they were a merciful people, to save himself from the fury of a tyrant; and in that case to deliver him up is to throw a lamb into the mouth of a lion. 2. If it appeared that the servant was abused, they must not only protect him, but, supposing him willing to embrace their religion, they must give him all the encouragement that might be to settle among them. Care is taken both that he should not be imposed up on in the place of his settlement — let it be *that which he shall choose* and *where it liketh him best,* and that he should not exchange one hard master for many — *thou shalt not oppress him.* Thus would he soon find a comfortable difference between the land of Israel and other lands, and would choose it to be his rest for ever. Note, Proselytes and converts to the truth should be treated with particular tenderness, that they may have no temptation to return.

II. The land of Israel must be no shelter for the unclean; no whore, no Sodomite, must be suffered to live among them (*v.* 17, 18), neither a whore nor a whoremonger. No houses of uncleanness must be kept either by men or women. Here is, 1. A good reason intimated why there should be no such wickedness tolerated among them: they were Israelites. This seems to have an emphasis laid upon it. For a daughter of Israel to be a whore, or a son of Israel a whoremaster, is to reproach the stock they are come of, the people they belong to, and the God they worship. It is bad in any, but worst in Israelites, a holy nation, 2 Sa. 13:12. 2. A just mark of displeasure put upon this wickedness, that the hire of a whore, that is, the money she gets by her whoring, and the price of a dog, that is, of the Sodomite, pimp, or whoremaster (so I incline to understand it, for such are called *dogs,* Rev. 22:15), the money he gets by his lewd and villainous practices, no part of it shall be *brought into the house of the Lord* (as the hire of prostitutes among the Gentiles was into their temples) *for any vow.* This intimates, (1.) That God would not accept of any offering at all from such wicked people; they had nothing to bring an offering of but what they got by their wickedness, and therefore their sacrifice could not but be *an abomination to the Lord,* Prov. 15:8. (2.) That they should not think, by making and paying vows, and bring-

ing offerings to the Lord, to obtain leave to go on in this sin, as (it should seem) some that followed that trade suggested to themselves, when their offerings were admitted. Prov. 7:14, 15, *This day have I paid my vows, therefore came I forth to meet thee.* Nothing should be accepted in commutation of penance. (3.) That we cannot honour God with our substance unless it be honestly and honourably come by. It must not only be considered what we give, but how we got it; God hates robbery for burnt-offerings, and uncleanness too.

III. The matter of usury is here settled, *v.* 19, 20. (1.) They must not lend upon usury to an Israelite. They had and held their estates immediately from and under God, who, while he distinguished them from all other people, might have ordered, had he so pleased, that they should have all things in common among themselves; but instead of that, and in token of their joint interest in the good land he had given them, he only appointed them, as there was occasion, to lend to one another without interest, which among them would be little or no loss to the lender, because their land was so divided, their estates were so settled, and there was so little of merchandise among them, that it was seldom or never that they had occasion to borrow any great sums, only what was necessary for the subsistence of their families when the fruits of their ground had met with any disaster, or the like; and, in such a case, for a small matter to insist upon usury would have been very barbarous. Where the borrower gets, or hopes to get, it is just that the lender should share in the gain; but to him that borrows for his necessary food pity must be shown, and we must lend, hoping for nothing again, if we have wherewithal to do it, Lu. 6:35. (2.) They might lend upon usury to a stranger, who was supposed to live by trade, and (as we say) by turning the penny, and therefore got by what he borrowed, and came among them in hopes to do so. By this it appears that usury is not in itself oppressive; for they must not oppress a stranger, and yet might exact usury from him.

IV. The performance of the vows wherewith we have bound our souls is here required; and it is a branch of the law of nature, *v.* 21–23. (1.) We are here left at our liberty whether we will make vows or no: *If thou shalt forbear to vow* (some particular sacrifice and offering, more than was commanded by the law), *it shall be no sin to thee.* God had already signified his readiness to accept a free-will offering thus vowed, though it were but a little fine flour (Lev. 2:4, etc.), which was encouragement enough to those who were so inclined. But lest the priests, who had the largest share of those vows and voluntary offerings, should sponge upon the people, by pressing it upon them as their duty to make such vows, beyond their ability and inclination, they are here expressly told that it should not be reckoned a sin in them if they did not make any such vows, as it would be if they omitted any of the sacrifices that God had particularly required. For (as bishop Patrick well expresses it) God would have men to be easy in his service, and all their offerings to be free and cheerful. (2.) We are here laid under the highest obligations, when we have made a vow, to perform it, and to perform it speedily: *"Thou shalt not be slack to pay it,* lest if it be delayed beyond the first opportunity the zeal abate, the vow be forgotten, or something happen to disable thee for the performance of it. *That which has gone out of thy lips* as a solemn and deliberate vow must not be recalled, but *thou shalt keep and perform it,* punctually and fully." The rule of the gospel goes somewhat further than this. 2 Co. 9:7, *Every one, according as he purposeth in his heart,* though it have not gone out of his lips, *so let him give.* Here is a good reason why we should pay our vows, that if we do not *God will require it of us,* will surely and severely reckon with us, not only for lying, but for going about to mock him, who cannot be mocked. See Eccl. 5:4.

V. Allowance is here given, when they passed through a cornfield or vineyard, to pluck and eat of the corn or grapes that grew by the road-side, whether it was done for necessity or delight, only they must carry none away with them, *v.* 24, 25. Therefore the disciples were not censured for plucking the ears of corn (it was well enough known that the law allowed it), but for doing it on the sabbath day, which the tradition of the elders had forbidden. Now, 1. This law intimated to them what great plenty of corn and wine they should have in Canaan, so much that

a little would not be missed out of their fruits: they should have enough for themselves and all their friends. 2. It provided for the support of poor travellers, to relieve the fatigue of their journey, and teaches us to be kind to such. The Jews say, "This law was chiefly intended in favour of labourers, who were employed in gathering in their harvest and vintage; their mouths must not be muzzled any more than that of the ox when he treads out the corn." 3. It teaches us not to insist upon property in a small matter, of which it is easy to say, *What is that between me and thee?* It was true the grapes which the passenger ate were none of his own, nor did the proprietor give them to him; but the thing was of so small value that he had reason to think were he present, he would not deny them to him, anymore than he himself would grudge the like courtesy, and therefore it was no theft to take them. 4. It used them to hospitality, and teaches us to be ready to distribute, willing to communicate, and not to think every thing lost that is given away. Yet, 4. It forbids us to abuse the kindness of our friends, and to take the advantage of fair concessions to make unreasonable encroachments: we must not draw an ell from those that give but an inch. They may eat of their neighbour's grapes; but it does not therefore follow that they may carry away.

CHAPTER 24

In this chapter we have, I. The toleration of divorce (*v.* 1–4). II. A discharge of new-married men from the war (*v.* 5). III. Laws concerning pledges (*v.* 6, 10–13, 17). IV. Against man-stealing (*v.* 7). V. Concerning the leprosy (*v.* 8, 9). VI. Against the injustice of masters towards their servants (*v.* 14, 15). Judges in capital causes (*v.* 16), and civil concerns (*v.* 17, 18). VII. Of charity to the poor (*v.* 19, etc.).

Verses 1–4

This is that permission which the Pharisees erroneously referred to as a precept, Mt. 19:7, *Moses commanded to give a writing of divorcement.* It was not so; our Saviour told them that he only suffered it because of the hardness of their hearts, lest, if they had not had liberty to divorce their wives, they should have ruled them with rigour, and it may be, have been the death of them. It is probable that divorces were in use before (they are taken for granted, Lev. 21:14), and Moses thought it needful here to give some rules concerning them. 1. That a man might not divorce his wife unless he *found some uncleanness in her, v.* 1. It was not sufficient to say that he did not like her, or that he liked another better, but he must show cause for his dislike; something that made her disagreeable and unpleasant to him, though it might not make her so to another. This uncleanness must mean something less than adultery; for, for that, she was to die; and less than the suspicion of it, for in that case he might give her the waters of jealousy; but it means either a light carriage, or a cross froward disposition, or some loathsome sore or disease; nay, some of the Jewish writers suppose that an offensive breath might be a just ground for divorce. Whatever is meant by it, doubtless it was something considerable; so that their modern doctors erred who allowed divorce for every cause, though ever so trivial, Mt. 19:3. 2. That it must be done, not by word of mouth, for that might be spoken hastily, but by writing, and that put in due form, and solemnly declared, before witnesses, to be his own act and deed, which was a work of time, and left room for consideration, that it might not be done rashly. 3. That the husband must give it into the hand of his wife, and send her away, which some think obliged him to endow her and make provision for her, according to her quality and such as might help to marry her again; and good reason he should do this, since the cause of quarrel was not her fault, but her infelicity. 4. That being divorced it was lawful for her to marry another husband, *v.* 2. The divorce had dissolved the bond of marriage as effectually as death could dissolve it; so that she was as free to marry again as if her first husband had been naturally dead. 5. That if her second husband died, or divorced her, then still she might marry a third, but her first husband should never take her again (*v.* 3, 4), which he might have done if she had not married another; for by that act of her own she had perfectly renounced him for ever, and, as to him, was looked upon as defiled, though not as to another person. The Jewish writers say that this was to prevent a most vile and wicked practice which the Egyptians had of changing wives; or perhaps it was intended to prevent men's rashness in putting away their wives; for the wife that was divorced would be apt, in revenge, to marry another immediately, and perhaps the husband that divorced her, how much soever he though to better himself by another choice, would find the next worse, and something in her more disagreeable, so that he would wish for his first wife again. "No" (says this law) "you shall not have her, you should have kept her when you had her." Note, It is best to be content with such things as we have, since changes made by discontent often prove for the worse. The uneasiness we know is commonly better, though we are apt to think it worse, than that which we do not know. By the strictness of this law God illustrates the riches of his grace in his willingness to be reconciled to his people that had gone a whoring from him. Jer. 3:1, *Thou hast played the harlot with many lovers, yet return again to me.* For his thoughts and ways are above ours.

Verses 5–13

Here is, I. Provision made for the preservation and confirmation of love between new-married people, *v.* 5. This fitly follows upon the laws concerning divorce, which would be prevented if their affection to each other were well settled at first. If the husband were much abroad from his wife the first year, his love to her would be in danger of cooling, and of being drawn aside to others whom he would meet with abroad; therefore his service to his country in war, embassies, or other public business that would call him from home, shall be dispensed with, *that he may cheer up the wife that he has taken.* Note, 1. It is of great consequence that love be kept up between husband and wife, and that every thing be very carefully avoided which might make them strange one to another, especially at first; for in that relation, where there is not the love that should be, there is an inlet ready to abundance of guilt and grief. 2. One of the duties of that relation is to cheer up one another under the cares and crosses that happen, as helpers of each other's joy; for a cheerful heart does good like a medicine.

II. A law against man-stealing, *v.* 7. It was not death by the law of Moses to steal cattle or goods; but to steal a child, or a weak and simple man, or one that a man had in his power, and to make merchandize of him, this was a capital crime, and could not be expiated, as other thefts, by restitution — so much is *a man better than a sheep,* Mt. 12:12. It was a very heinous offence, for, 1. It was robbing the public of one of its members. 2. It was taking away a man's liberty, the liberty of a free-born Israelite, which was next in value to his life. 3. It was driving a man out from the inheritance of the land, to the privileges of which he was entitled, and bidding him go serve other gods, as David complains against Saul, 1 Sa. 26:19.

III. A memorandum concerning the leprosy, *v.* 8, 9. 1. The laws concerning it must be carefully observed. The laws concerning it we had, Lev. 13:14. They are here said to be commanded to the *priests and Levites,* and therefore are not repeated in a discourse to the people; but the people are here charged, in case of leprosy, to apply to the priest according to the law, and to abide by his judgment, so far as it agreed with the law and the plain matter of fact. The plague of leprosy being usually a particular mark of God's displeasure for sin, he in whom the signs of it did appear ought not to conceal it, nor cut out the signs of it, nor apply to the physician for relief; but he must go to the priest, and follow his directions. Thus those that feel their consciences under guilt and wrath must not cover it, nor endeavour to shake off their convictions, but by repentance, and prayer, and humble confession, take the appointed way to peace and pardon. 2. The particular case of Miriam, who was smitten with leprosy for quarrelling with Moses, must not be forgotten. It was an explication of the law concerning the leprosy. Remember that, and, (1.) "Take heed of sinning after the similitude of her transgression, by despising dominions and speaking evil of dignities, lest you thereby bring upon yourselves the same judgment." (2.) "If any of you be smitten with a leprosy, expect not that the law should be dispensed with, nor think it hard to be shut out of the camp and so made a spectacle; there is no remedy: Miriam herself, though a prophetess and the sister of Moses, was not exempted, but was forced to submit to this severe discipline when she was under this divine rebuke." Thus David, Hezekiah, Peter, and other great men, when they had sinned, humbled themselves, and took to themselves shame and grief; let us not expect to be reconciled upon easier terms.

IV. Some necessary orders given about pledges for the security of money lent. They are not forbidden to take such securities as would save the lender from loss, and oblige the borrower to be honest; but, 1. They must not take the millstone for a pledge (*v.* 6), for with that they ground the corn that was to be bread for their families, or, if it were a public mill, with it the miller got his livelihood; and so it forbids the taking of any thing for a pledge by the want of which a man was in danger of being undone. Consonant to this is the ancient common law of England, which provides that no man be distrained of the utensils or instruments of his trade or profession, as the axe of a carpenter, or the books of a scholar, or beasts belonging to the plough, as long as there are other beasts of which distress may be made (*Coke, 1 Inst. fol.* 47). This teaches us to consult the comfort and subsistence of others as much as our own advantage. That creditor who cares not though his debtor and his family starve, nor is at all concerned what become of them, so he may but get his money or secure it, goes contrary, not only to the law of Christ, but even to the law of Moses too. 2. They must not go into the borrower's house to fetch the pledge, but must stand without, and he must bring it, *v.* 10, 11. *The borrower* (says Solomon) *is servant to the lender;* therefore lest the lender should abuse the advantage he has against him, and improve it for his own interest, it is provided that he shall take not what he pleases, but what the borrower can best spare. A man's house is his castle, even the poor man's house is so, and is here taken under the protection of the law. 3. That a poor man's bed-clothes should never be taken for a pledge, *v.* 12, 13. This we had before, Ex. 22:26, 27. If they were taken in the morning, they must be brought back again at night, which is in effect to say that they must not be taken at all. "Let the poor debtor sleep in his own raiment, and bless thee," that is, "pray for thee, and praise God for thy kindness to him." Note, Poor debtors ought to be sensible (more sensible than commonly they are) of the goodness of those creditors that do not take all the advantage of the law against them, and to repay their kindnesses by their prayers for them, when they are not in a capacity to repay it in any other way. "Nay, thou shalt not only have the prayers and good wishes of thy poor brother, but *it shall be righteousness to thee before the Lord thy God,*" that is, "It shall be accepted and rewarded as an act of mercy to thy brother and obedience to thy God, and an evidence of thy sincere conformity to the law. Though it may be looked upon by men as an act of weakness to deliver up the securities thou hast for thy debt, yet it shall be looked upon by thy God as an act of goodness, which shall in no wise lose its reward."

Verses 14–22

Here, I. Masters are commanded to be just to their poor servants, *v.* 14, 15. 1. They must not oppress them, by overloading them with work, by giving them undue and unreasonable rebukes, or by withholding from them proper maintenance. A servant, though a stranger to the commonwealth of Israel, must not be abused: "For *thou wast a bondman* in the land where thou wast a stranger (*v.* 18), and thou knowest what a grievous thing it is to be oppressed by a task-master, and therefore, in tenderness to those that are servants and strangers, and in gratitude to that God who set thee at liberty and settled thee in a country of thy own, *thou shalt not oppress a servant.*" Let not masters be tyrants to their servants, for their Master is in heaven. See Job 31:13. 2. They must be faithful and punctual in paying them their wages: *"At his day thou shalt give him his hire,* not only pay it in time, without further delay. As soon as he had done his day's work, if he desire it, let him have his day's wages," as those labourers (Mt. 20:8) *when evening had come.* he that works by day-wages is supposed to live from hand to mouth, and cannot have to-morrow's bread for his family till be is paid for this day's labour. If the wages be withheld, (1.) It will be grief to the servant, for, poor man, he *sets his heart upon it,*. or, as the word is, he *lifts up his soul to it,* he is earnestly desirous of it, as the reward of his work (Job 7:2), and depends upon it as the gift of God's providence for the maintenance of his family. A compassionate master, though it should be somewhat inconvenient to himself, would not disappoint the expectation of a poor servant that was so fond to think of receiving his wages. But that is not the worst. (2.) It will be guilt to the master. "The injured servant will cry against thee to the Lord; since he has no one else to appeal to, he will lodge his appeal in the court of heaven, and it will be sin to thee." Or, if he do not complain, the cause will speak for itself, the *"hire of the labourers which is kept back by fraud* will itself *cry,"* Jam. 5:4. It is a greater sin than most people think it is, and will be found so in the great day, to put hardships upon poor servants, labourers, and workmen, that we employ. God will do them right if men do not.

II. Magistrates and judges are commanded to be just in their administrations. 1. In those which we call *pleas of the crown* a standing rule is here given, that *the fathers shall not be put to death for the children, nor the children for the fathers, v.* 16. If the children make themselves obnoxious to the law, let them suffer for it, but let not the parents suffer either for them or with them; it is grief enough to them to see their children suffer: if the parents be guilty, let them die for their own sin; but though God, the sovereign Lord of life, sometimes visits the iniquity of the fathers upon the children, especially the sin of idolatry, and when he deals with nations in their national capacity, yet he does not allow men to do so. Accordingly, we find Amaziah sparing the children, even when the fathers were put to death for killing the king, 2 Ki. 14:6. It was in an extraordinary case, and no doubt by special direction from heaven, that Saul's sons were put to death for his offence, and they died rather as sacrifices than as malefactors, 2 Sa. 21:9, 14. 2. In common pleas between party and party, great care must be taken that none whose cause was just should fare the worse for their weakness, nor for their being destitute of friends, as strangers, fatherless, and widows (*v.* 17): *"Thou shalt not pervert their judgment,* nor force them to give their very raiment for a pledge, by defrauding them of their right." Judges must be advocates for those that cannot speak for themselves and have no friends to speak for them.

III. The rich are commanded to be kind and charitable to the poor. Many ways they are ordered to be so by the law of Moses. The particular instance of charity here prescribed is that they should not be greedy in gathering in their corn, and grapes, and olives, so as to be afraid of leaving any behind them, but be willing to overlook some, and let the poor have the gleanings, *v.* 19–22. 1. "Say not, 'It is all my own, and why should not I have it?' But learn a generous contempt of property in small matters. One sheaf or two forgotten will make thee never the poorer at the year's end, and it will do somebody good, if thou have it not." 2. "Say not, '*What I give I will give,* and know whom I give it to, why should I leave it to be gathered by I know not whom, that will never thank me.' But trust God's providence with the disposal of thy charity, perhaps that will direct it to the most necessitous." Or, "Thou mayest reasonably think it will come to the hands of the most industrious, that are forward to seek and gather that which this law provides for them." 3. "Say not, 'What should the poor do with grapes and olives? It is enough for them to have bread and water;' for, since they have the same senses that the rich have, why should not they have some little share of the delights of sense?" Boaz ordered handfuls of corn to be left on purpose for Ruth, and God blessed him. All that is left is not lost.

CHAPTER 25

Here is, I. A law to moderate the scourging of malefactors (*v.* 1–3). II. A law in favour of the ox the treads out the corn (*v.* 4). III. For the disgracing of him that refused to marry his brother's widow (*v.* 5–10). IV. For the punishment of an immodest woman (*v.* 11, 12). V. For just weights and measures (*v.* 13–16). VI. For the destroying of Amalek (*v.* 17, etc.).

Verses 1–4

Here is, I. A direction to the judges in scourging malefactors, *v.* 1–3. 1. It is here supposed that, if a man be charged with a crime, the accuser and the accused (*Actor* and *Reus*) should be brought face to face before the judges, that the controversy may be determined. 2. If a man were accused of a crime, and the proof fell short, so that the charge could not be made out against him by the evidence, then he was to be acquitted: *"Thou shalt justify the righteous,"* that is, "him that appears to the court to be so." If the accusation be proved, then the conviction of the accused is a justification of the accuser, as righteous in the prosecution. 3. If the accused were found guilty, judgment must be given against him: "Thou shalt *condemn the wicked;*" for to justify the wicked is as much an abomination to the Lord as it is to condemn the righteous, Prov. 17:15. 4. If the crime were not made capital by the law, then the criminal must be beaten. A great many precepts we have met with which have not any particular penalty annexed to them, the violation of most of which, according to the constant practice of the Jews, was punished by scourging, from which no person's rank or quality did exempt him if he were a delinquent, but with this proviso, that he should never be upbraided with it, nor should it be looked upon as leaving any mark of infamy or disgrace upon him. The directions here given for the scourging of criminals are, (1.) That it be done solemnly; not tumultuously through the streets, but in open court before the judge's face, and with so much deliberation as that the stripes might be numbered. The Jews say that while execution was in doing the chief justice of the court read with a loud voice Deu. 28:58, 59, and 29:9, and concluded with those words (Ps. 78:38), *But he, being full of compassion, forgave their iniquity.* Thus it was made a sort of religious act, and so much the more likely to reform the offender himself and to be a warning to others. (2.) That it be done in proportion to the crime, *according to his fault,* that some crimes might appear, as they are, more heinous than others, the criminal being *beaten with many stripes,* to which perhaps there is an allusion, Lu. 12:47, 48. (3.) That how great soever the crime were the number of stripes should never exceed *forty, v.* 3. Forty *save one* was the common usage, as appears, 2 Co. 11:24. It seems, they always gave Paul as many stripes as ever they gave to any malefactor whatsoever. They abated one for fear of having miscounted (though one of the judges was appointed to number the stripes), or because they would never go to the utmost rigour, or because the execution was usually done with a whip of three lashes, so that thirteen stripes (each one being counted for three) made up thirty-nine, but one more by that reckoning would have been forty-two. The reason given for this is, *lest thy brother should seem vile unto thee.* He must still be looked upon as *a brother* (2 Th. 3:15), and his reputation as such was preserved by this merciful limitation of his punishment. It saves him from seeming vile to his brethren, when God himself by his law takes this care of him. Men must not be treated as dogs; nor must those seem vile in our sight to whom, for aught we know, God may yet give grace to make them precious in his sight.

II. A charge to husbandmen not to hinder their cattle from eating when they were working, if meat were within their reach, *v.* 4. This instance of the beast that trod out the corn (to which there is an allusion in that of the prophet, Hos. 10:11) is put for all similar instances. That which makes this law very remarkable above its fellows (and which countenances the like application of other such laws) is that it is twice quoted in the New Testament to show that it is the duty of the people to give their ministers a comfortable maintenance, 1 Co. 9:9, 10, and 1 Tim. 5:17, 18. It teaches us in the letter of it to make much of the brute-creatures that serve us, and to allow them not only the necessary supports for their life, but the advantages of their labour; and thus we must learn not only to be just, but kind, to all that are employed for our good, not only to maintain but to encourage them, especially those that labour among us in the word and doctrine, and so are employed for the good of our better part.

Verses 5–12

Here is, I. The law settled concerning the marrying of the brother's widow. It appears from the story of Judah's family that this had been an ancient usage (Gen. 38:8), for the keeping up of distinct families. The case put is a case that often happens, of a man's dying without issue, it may be in the prime of his time, soon after his marriage, and while his brethren were yet so young as to be unmarried. Now in this case, 1. The widow was not to marry again into any other family, unless all the relations of her husband did refuse her, that the estate she was endowed with might not be alienated. 2. The husband's brother, or next of kin, must marry her, partly out of respect to her, who, having forgotten her own people and her father's house,

should have all possible kindness shown her by the family into which she was married; and partly out of respect to the deceased husband, that though he was dead and gone he might not be forgotten, nor lost out of the genealogies of his tribe; for the first-born child, which the brother or next kinsman should have by the widow, should be denominated from him that was dead, and entered in the genealogy as his child, *v.* 5, 6. Under that dispensation we have reason to think men had not so clear and certain a prospect of living themselves on the other side death as we have now, to whom *life and immortality are brought to light by the gospel;* and therefore they could not but be the more desirous to live in their posterity, which innocent desire was in some measure gratified by this law, an expedient being found out that, though a man had no child by his wife, yet *his name should not be put out of Israel,* that is, out of the pedigree, or, which is equivalent, remain there under the brand of childlessness. The Sadducees put a case to our Saviour upon this law, with a design to perplex the doctrine of the resurrection by it (Mt. 22:24, etc.), perhaps insinuating that there was no need of maintaining the immortality of the soul and a future state, since the law had so well provided for the perpetuating of men's names and families in the world. But, 3. If the brother, or next of kin, declined to do this good office to the memory of him that was gone, what must be done in that case? Why, (1.) He shall not be compelled to do it, *v.* 7. If he like her not, he is at liberty to refuse her, which, some think, was not permitted in this case before this law of Moses. Affection is all in all to the comfort of the conjugal relation; this is a thing which cannot be forced, and therefore the relation should not be forced without it. (2.) Yet he shall be publicly disgraced for not doing it. The widow, as the person most concerned for the name and honour of the deceased, was to complain to the elders of his refusal; if he persist in it, she must *pluck off his shoe, and spit in his face,* in open court (or, as the Jewish doctors moderate it, spit *before* his face), thus to fasten a mark of infamy upon him, which was to remain with his family after him, *v.* 8–10. Note, Those justly suffer in their own reputation who do not do what they ought to preserve the name and honour of others. He that would not build up his brother's house deserved to have this blemish put upon his own, that it should be called *the house of him that had his shoe loosed,* in token that he deserved to go barefoot. In the case of Ruth we find this law executed (Ruth 4:7), but because, upon the refusal of the next kinsman, there was another ready to perform the duty of a husband's brother, it was that other that plucked off the shoe, and not the widow — Boaz, and not Ruth.

II. A law for the punishing of an immodest woman, *v.* 11, 12. The woman that by the foregoing law was to complain against her husband's brother for not marrying her, and to spit in his face before the elders, needed a good measure of assurance; but, lest the confidence which that law supported should grow to an excess unbecoming the sex, here is a very severe but just law to punish impudence and immodesty. 1. The instance of it is confessedly scandalous to the highest degree. A woman could not do it unless she were perfectly lost to all virtue and honour. 2. The occasion is such as might in part excuse it; it was to help her husband out of the hands of one that was too hard for him. Now if the doing of it in a passion, and with such a good intention, was to be so severely punished, much more when it was done wantonly and in lust. 3. The punishment was that her hand should be cut off; and the magistrates must not pretend to be more merciful than God: *Thy eye shall not pity her.* Perhaps our Saviour alludes to this law when he commands us to *cut off the right hand* that *offends us,* or is an occasion of sin to us. Better put the greatest hardships that can be upon the body than ruin the soul for ever. Modesty is the hedge of chastity, and therefore ought to be very carefully preserved and kept up by both sexes.

Verses 13–19

Here is, I. A law against deceitful weights and measures: they must not only not use them, but they must not have them, not have them in the bag, not have them in the house (*v.* 13, 14); for, if they had them, they would be strongly tempted to use them. They must not have a great weight and measure to buy by and a small one to sell by, for that

was to cheat both ways, when either was bad enough; as we read of those that made the *ephah* small, in which they measured the corn they sold, and the *shekel* great, by which they weighed the money they received for it, Amos 8:5. But *thou shalt have a perfect and just weight, v.* 15. That which is the rule of justice must itself be just; if that be otherwise, it is a constant cheat. This had been taken care of before, Lev. 19:35, 36. This law is enforced with two very good reasons: — 1. That justice and equity will bring down upon us the blessing of God. The way to have our days lengthened, and to prosper, is to be just and fair in all our dealings *Honesty is the best policy.* 2. That fraud and injustice will expose us to the curse of God, *v.* 16. Not only unrighteousness itself, but all that do unrighteously, are an *abomination to the Lord.* And miserable is that man who is abhorred by his Maker. How hateful, particularly, all the arts of deceit are to God, Solomon several times observes, Prov. 11:1; 20:10, 23; and the apostle tells us *that the Lord is the avenger of all such* as overreach and *defraud in any matter,* 1 Th. 4:6.

II. A law for the rooting out of Amalek. Here is a *just weight* and a *just measure,* that, as Amalek had measured to Israel, so it should be measure to Amalek again.

1. The mischief Amalek did to Israel must be here remembered, *v.* 17 18. When it was first done it was ordered to be recorded (Ex. 17:14–16), and here the remembrance of it is ordered to be preserved, not in personal revenge (for that generation which suffered by the Amalekites was gone, so that those who now lived, and their posterity, could not have any personal resentment of the injury), but in a zeal for the glory of God (which was insulted by the Amalekites), that *throne of the Lord* against which the hand of Amalek was stretched out. The carriage of the Amalekites towards Israel is here represented, (1.) As very base and disingenuous. They had no occasion at all to quarrel with Israel, nor did they give them any notice, by a manifesto or declaration of war; but took them at an advantage, when they had just come out of the house of bondage, and, for aught that appeared to them, were only going to *sacrifice to God in the wilderness.* (2.) As very barbarous and cruel; for they smote those that were more feeble, whom they should have succoured. The greatest cowards are commonly the most cruel; while those that have the courage of a man will have the compassion of a man. (3.) As very impious and profane: they feared not God. If they had had any reverence for the majesty of the God of Israel, which they saw a token of in the cloud, or any dread of his wrath, which they lately heard of the power of over Pharaoh, they durst not have made this assault upon Israel. Well, here was the ground of the quarrel: and it shows how God takes what is done against his people as done against himself, and that he will particularly reckon with those that discourage and hinder young beginners in religion, that (as Satan's agents) set upon the weak and feeble, either to divert them or to disquiet them, and offend his little ones.

2. This mischief must in due time be revenged, *v.* 19. When their wars were finished, by which they were to settle their kingdom and enlarge their coast, then they must *make war upon Amalek* (*v.* 19), not merely to chase them, but to consume them, to *blot out the remembrance of Amalek.* It was an instance of God's patience that he deferred the vengeance so long, which should have led the Amalekites to repentance; yet an instance of fearful retribution that the posterity of Amalek, so long after, were destroyed for the mischief done by their ancestors to the Israel of God, that all the world might see, and say, that he who *toucheth them toucheth the apple of his eye.* It was nearly 400 years after this that Saul was ordered to put this sentence in execution (1 Sa. 15), and was rejected of God because he did not do it effectually, but spared some of that devoted nation, in contempt, not only of the particular orders he received from Samuel, but of this general command here given by Moses, which he could not be ignorant of. David afterwards made some destruction of them; and the Simeonites, in Hezekiah's time, smote the rest that remained (1 Chr. 4:43); for when God judges he will overcome.

CHAPTER 26

With this chapter Moses concludes the particular statutes which he thought fit to give Israel in charge at his parting with them; what follows is by way of sanction and ratification. In this chapter, I. Moses gives them a form of confession to be made by him that offered the basket of his first-fruits (*v.* 1–11). II. The protestation and prayer to be made after the disposal of the third year's tithe (*v.* 12–15). III. He binds on all the precepts he had given them, 1. By the divine authority: "Not I, but the Lord thy God has commanded thee to do these statutes" (*v.* 16). 2. By the mutual covenant between God and them (*v.* 17, etc.).

Verses 1–11

Here is, I. A good work ordered to be done, and that is the presenting of a basket of their first-fruits to God every year, *v.* 1, 2. Besides the *sheaf of first-fruits,* which was offered for the whole land, on the morrow after the passover (Lev. 23:10), every man was to bring for himself a basket of first-fruits at the feast of pentecost, when the harvest was ended, which is therefore called the *feast of first-fruits* (Ex. 34:22), and is said to be kept with a *tribute of free-will-offering,* Deu. 16:10. But the Jews say, "The first-fruits, if not brought then, might be brought any time after, between that and winter." When a man went into the field or vineyard at the time when the fruits were ripening, he was to mark that which he observed most forward, and to lay it by for first-fruits, wheat, barley, grapes, figs, pomegranates, olives, and dates, some of each sort must be put in the same basket, with leaves between them, and presented to God in the place which he should choose. Now from this law we may learn, 1. To acknowledge God as the giver of all those good things which are the support and comfort of our natural life, and therefore to serve and honour him with them. 2. To deny ourselves. What is first ripe we are most fond of; those that are nice and curious expect to be served with each fruit at its first coming in. *My soul desired the first ripe fruits,* Micah 7:1. When therefore God appointed them to lay those by for him he taught them to prefer the glorifying of his name before the gratifying of their own appetites and desires. 3. To give to God the first and best we have, as those that believe him to be the first and best of beings. Those that consecrate the days of their youth, and the prime of their time, to the service and honour of God, bring him their first-fruits, and with such offerings he is well pleased. *I remember the kindness of thy youth.*

II. Good words put into their mouths to be said in the doing of this good work, as an explication of the meaning of this ceremony, that it might be a reasonable service. The offerer must begin his acknowledgment before he delivered his basket to the priest, and then must go on with it, when the priest had set down the basket before the altar, as a present to God their great landlord, *v.* 3, 4.

1. He must begin with a receipt in full for the good land which God had given them (*v.* 3): *I profess that I have come* now at last, after forty years' wandering, *unto the country which the Lord swore to give us.* This was most proper to be said when they came first into Canaan; probably when they had been long settled there they varied from this form. Note, When God has made good his promises to us he expects that we should own it, to the honour of his faithfulness; this is like giving up the bond, as Solomon does, 1 Ki. 8:56, *There has not failed one word of all his good promise.* And our creature-comforts are doubly sweet to us when we see them flowing from the fountain of the promise.

2. He must remember and own the mean origin of that nation of which he was a member. How great soever they were now, and he himself with them, their beginning was very small, which ought thus to be kept in mind throughout all the ages of their church by this public confession, that they might not be proud of their privileges and advantages, but might for ever be thankful to that God whose grace chose them when they were so low and raised them so high. Two things they must own for this purpose: — (1.) The meanness of their common ancestor: *A Syrian ready to perish was my father, v.* 5. Jacob is here called an *Aramite,* or *Syrian,* because he lived twenty years in Padan-Aram; his wives were of that country, and his children were all born there, except Benjamin; and perhaps the confessor means not Jacob himself, but that son of Jacob who was the father of his tribe. However it be, both father and sons were more than once ready to perish, by Laban's severity, Esau's cruelty, and the famine in the land, which last was the occasion of their going down into Egypt. *Laban the Syrian sought to destroy my father* (so the Chaldee), *had almost destroyed him,* so the Arabic. (2.) The mis-

erable condition of their nation in its infancy. They sojourned in Egypt as strangers, they served there as slaves (*v.* 6), and that a great while: as their father was called a *Syrian,* they might be called *Egyptians;* so that their possession of Canaan being so long discontinued they could not pretend any tenant-right to it. A poor, despised, oppressed people they were in Egypt, and therefore, though now rich and great, had no reason to be proud, or secure, or forgetful of God.

3. He must thankfully acknowledge God's great goodness, not only to himself in particular, but to Israel in general. (1.) In bringing them out of Egypt, *v.* 7, 8. It is spoken of here as an act of pity — *he looked on our affliction;* and an act of power — *he brought us forth with a mighty hand.* This was a great salvation, fit to be remembered upon all occasions, and particularly upon this; they need not grudge to bring a basket of first-fruits to God, for to him they owed it that they were not now bringing in the tale of bricks to their cruel task-masters. (2.) In settling them in Canaan: *He hath given us this land, v.* 9. Observe, He must not only give thanks for his own lot, but for the land in general which was given to Israel; not only for this year's profits, but for the ground itself which produced them, which God had graciously granted to his ancestors and entailed upon his posterity. Note, The comfort we have in particular enjoyments should lead us to be thankful for our share in public peace and plenty; and with present mercies we should bless God for the former mercies we remember and the further mercies we expect and hope for.

4. He must offer to God his basket of first-fruits (*v.* 10): "I have *brought the first-fruits of the land* (like a peppercorn) as a quit-rent for *the land which thou hast given me.*" Note, Whatever we give to God, it is but *of his own* that we *give him,* 1 Chr. 29:14. And it becomes us, who receive so much from him, to study what we shall render to him. The basket he set before God; and the priests, as God's receivers, had the first-fruits, as perquisites of their place and fees for attending, Num. 18:12.

III. The offerer is here appointed, when he has finished the service, 1. To give glory to God: *Thou shalt worship the Lord thy God.* His first-fruits were not accepted without further acts of adoration. A humble, reverent, thankful heart is that which God looks at and requires, and, without this, all we can put in a basket will not avail. *If a man would give all the substance of his house* to be excused from this, or in lieu of it, *it would utterly be contemned.* 2. To take the comfort of it to himself and family: *Thou shalt rejoice in every good thing, v.* 11. It is the will of God that we should be cheerful, not only in our attendance upon his holy ordinances, but in our enjoyments of the gifts of his providence. Whatever good thing God gives us, it is his will that we should make the most comfortable use we can of it, yet still tracing the streams to the fountain of all comfort and consolation.

Verses 12–15

Concerning the disposal of their tithe the third year we had the law before, *ch.* 14:28, 29. The second tithe, which in the other two years was to be spent in extraordinaries at the feasts, was to be spent the third year at home, in entertaining the poor. Now because this was done from under the eye of the priests, and a great confidence was put in the people's honesty, that they would dispose of it according to the law, to the *Levite, the stranger, and the fatherless* (*v.* 12), it is therefore required that when at the next feast after they appeared *before the Lord* they should there testify (as it were) upon oath, in a religious manner, that they had fully administered, and been true to their trust.

I. They must make a solemn protestation to this purport, *v.* 13, 14. 1. That no hallowed things were hoarded up: "*I have brought them away out of my house,* nothing now remains there but my own part." 2. That the poor, and particularly poor ministers, poor strangers, and poor widows, had had their part according to the commandment. It is fit that God, who by his providence gives us all we have, should by his law direct the using of it, and, though we are not now under such particular appropriations of our revenue as they then were, yet, in general, we are commanded to give alms of such things as we have; and then, and not otherwise, all things are clean to us. *Then*

we may take the comfort of our enjoyments, when God has thus had his dues out of them. This is a commandment which must not be transgressed, no, not with an excuse of its being forgotten, *v.* 13. 3. That none of this tithe had been misapplied to any common use, much less to any ill use. This seems to refer to the tithe of the other two years, which was to be eaten by the owners themselves; they must profess, (1.) That they had not eaten of it in their mourning, when, by their mourning for the dead, they were commonly unclean; or they had not eaten of it grudgingly, as those that all their days eat in darkness. (2.) That they had not sacrilegiously alienated it to any common use, for it was not their own. And, (3.) That they had not given it for the dead, for the honour of their dead gods, or in hope of making it beneficial to their dead friends. Now the obliging of them to make this solemn protestation at the three years' end would be an obligation upon them to deal faithfully, knowing that they must be called upon thus to purge themselves. It is our wisdom to keep conscience clear at all times, that when we come to give up our account we may lift up our face without spot. The Jews say that this protestation of their integrity was to be made with a low voice, because it looked like a self-commendation, but that the foregoing confession of God's goodness was to be made with a loud voice to his glory. He that durst not make this protestation must bring his *trespass-offering,* Lev. 5:15.

II. To this solemn protestation they must add a *solemn prayer* (*v.* 15), not particularly for themselves, but for *God's people Israel;* for in the common peace and prosperity every particular person prospers and has peace. We must learn hence to be public-spirited in prayer, and to wrestle with God for blessings for the land and nation, our English Israel, and for the universal church, which we are directed to have an eye to in our prayers, as the *Israel of God,* Gal. 6:16. In this prayer we are taught, 1. To look up to God as in a holy habitation, and thence to infer that holiness becomes his house, and that he will be sanctified in those that are about him. 2. To depend upon the favour of God, and his gracious cognizance, as sufficient to make us and our people happy. 3. To reckon it wonderful condescension in God to case an eye even upon so great and honourable a body as Israel was. It is looking down. 4. To be earnest with God for a blessing upon his people Israel, and upon the *land which he has given us.* For how should the earth yield its increase, or, if it does, what comfort can we take in it, unless therewith *God, even our own God, gives us his blessing?* Ps. 67:6.

Verses 16–19

Two things Moses here urges to enforce all these precepts: — 1. That they were the commands of God, *v.* 16. They were not the dictates of his own wisdom, nor were they enacted by any authority of his own, but infinite wisdom framed them, and the power of the King of kings made them binding to them: "*The Lord thy God commands thee,* therefore thou art bound in duty and gratitude to obey him, and it is at thy peril if thou disobey. They are his laws, therefore thou shalt do them, for to that end were they given thee: do them and not dispute them, do them and not draw back from them; do them not carelessly and hypocritically, but with thy heart and soul, thy whole heart and thy whole soul." 2. That their covenant with God obliged them to keep these commands. He insists not only upon God's sovereignty over them, but his propriety in them, and the relation wherein they stood to him. The covenant is mutual, and it binds to obedience both ways. (1.) That we may perform our part of the covenant, and answer the intentions of that (*v.* 17): "*Thou hast avouched* and solemnly owned and confessed *the Lord Jehovah to be thy God,* thy Prince and Ruler. As he is so by an incontestable right, so he is by thy own consent." They did this implicitly by their attendance on his word, had done it expressly (Ex. 24), and were now to do it again before they parted, *ch.* 29:1. Now this obliges us, in fidelity to our word, as well as in duty to our Sovereign, to *keep his statutes and his commandments.* We really forswear ourselves, and perfidiously violate the most sacred engagements, if, when we have taken the Lord to be our God, we do not make conscience of obeying his commands. (2.) That God's part of the covenant also may be made good, and the intentions of that answered (*v.* 18, 19): The *Lord has avouched,* not only taken, but publicly owned thee to be his *segullah,* his *peculiar people, as he has promised thee,* that is, according to the true intent and meaning of the promise. Now their obedience was not only the condition of this favour, and of the continuance of it (if they were not obedient, God would disown them, and cast them off), but it was also the principal design of this favour. "He has avouched thee on purpose *that thou shouldest keep his commandments,* that thou mightest have both the best directions and the best encouragements in religion." Thus we are *elected to obedience* (1 Pt. 1:2), *chosen that we should be holy* (Eph. 1:4), purified, a peculiar people, that we might not only do good works, but be zealous in them, Tit. 2:14. Two things God is here said to design in avouching them to be his peculiar people (*v.* 19), to make them high, and, in order to that, to make them holy; for holiness is true honour, and the only way to everlasting honour. [1.] To make them high above all nations. The greatest honour we are capable of in this world is to be taken into covenant with God, and to live in his service. They should be, *First,* High *in praise;* for God would accept them, which is true praise, Rom. 2:29. Their friends would admire them, Zep. 3:19, 20. *Secondly,* High *in name,* which, some think, denotes the continuance and perpetuity of that praise, *a name that shall not be cut off. Thirdly,* High *in honour,* that is, in all the advantages of wealth and power, which would make them great above their neighbours. See Jer. 13:11. [2.] That they might be a holy people, separated for God, devoted to him, and employed continually in his service. This God aimed at in taking them to be his people; so that, if they did not keep his commandments, they received all this grace in vain.

CHAPTER 27

Moses having very largely and fully set before the people their duty, both to God and one another, in general and in particular instances, — having shown them plainly what is good, and what the law requires of them, — and having in the close of the foregoing chapter laid them under the obligation both of the command and the covenant, he comes in this chapter to prescribe outward means, I. For the helping of their memories, that they might not forget the law as a strange thing. They must write all the words of this law upon stones (*v.* 1–10). II. For the moving of their affections, that they might not be indifferent to the law as a light thing. Whey they came into Canaan, the blessings and curses which were the sanctions of the law, were to be solemnly pronounced in the hearing of all Israel, who were to say Amen to them (*v.* 11–26). And if such a solemnity as this would not make a deep impression upon them, and affect them with the great things of God's law, nothing would.

Verses 1–10

Here is, I. A general charge to the people to keep God's commandments; for in vain did they know them, unless they would do them. This is pressed upon them, 1. With all authority. *Moses with the elders of Israel,* the rulers of each tribe (*v.* 1), and again, *Moses and the priests the Levites* (*v.* 9); so that the charge is given by Moses who was king in Jeshurun, and by their lords, both spiritual and temporal, in concurrence with him. Lest they should think that it was Moses only, an old and dying man, that made such ado about religion, or the priests and Levites only, whose trade it was to attend religion and who had their maintenance out of it, the elders of Israel, whom God had placed in honour and power over them, and who were men of business in the world and likely to be so long so when Moses was gone, *they* commanded their people to *keep God's law.* Moses, having put some of his honour upon them, joins them in commission with himself, in giving this charge, as Paul sometimes in his epistles joins with himself Silvanus and Timotheus. Note, All that have any interest in others, or power over them, should use it for the support and furtherance of religion among them. Though the supreme power of a nation provide ever so good laws for this purpose, if inferior magistrates in their places, and ministers in theirs, and masters of families in theirs, do not execute their offices, it will all be to little effect. 2. With all importunity. They press it upon them with the utmost earnestness (*v.* 9, 10): *Take heed and hearken, O Israel.* It is a thing that requires and deserves the highest degree of caution and attention. They tell them of their privilege and honour: *"This day thou hast become the people of the Lord thy God,* the Lord having avouched thee to be his own, and being now about to put thee in possession of Canaan which he had long promised as *thy God* (Gen. 17:7, 8), and which if he had failed to do in due time, he would have been ashamed to be called thy God, Heb. 11:16. Now thou art more than ever his people, therefore *obey his voice."* Privileges should be improved as engagements to duty. Should not a people be ruled by their God?

II. A particular direction to them with great solemnity to register *the words of this law,* as soon as they came into Canaan. It was to be done but once, and at their entrance into the land of promise, in token of their taking possession of it under the several provisos and conditions contained in this law. There was a solemn ratification of the covenant between God and Israel at Mount Sinai, when an altar was erected, with twelve pillars, and the book of the covenant was produced, Ex. 24:4. That which is here appointed is a somewhat similar solemnity.

1. They must set up a monument on which they must *write the words of this law.* (1.) The monument itself was to be very mean, only rough unhewn stone plastered over; not polished marble or alabaster, nor brass tables, but common plaster upon stone, *v.* 2. The command is repeated (*v.* 4), and orders are given that it be written, not very finely, to be admired by the curious, but very plainly, that he who runs may read it, Hab. 2:2. The word of God needs not to be set off by the art of man, nor embellished with the *enticing words of man's wisdom.* But, (2.) The inscription was to be very great: *All the words of this law, v.* 3, and again, *v.* 8. Some understand it only of the covenant between God and Israel, mentioned *ch.* 26:17, 18. Let this help be set up for a witness, like that memorial of the covenant between Laban and Jacob, which was nothing but a heap of stones thrown hastily together, upon which they did eat together in token of friendship (Gen. 31:46, 47), and that stone which Joshua set up, Jos. 24:26. Others think that the curses of the covenant in this chapter were written upon this monument, the rather because it was set up in Mount Ebal, *v.* 4. Others think that the whole book of Deuteronomy was written upon this monument, or at least the statutes and judgments from *ch.* 12 to the end of *ch.* 26. And it is not improbable that the heap might be so large as, taking in all the sides of it, to contain so copious an inscription, unless we will suppose (as some do) that the ten commandments only were here written, as an authentic copy of the close rolls which were laid up in the ark. They must write this when they had gone into Canaan, and yet Moses says (*v.* 3), *"Write it that thou mayest go in,"* that is, "that thou mayest go in with comfort, and assurance of success and settlement, otherwise it were well for thee not to go in at all. Write it as the conditions of thy entry, and own that thou comest in upon these terms and no other: since Canaan is given by promise, it must be held by obedience."

2. They must also set up an altar. By the words of the law which were written upon the plaster, God *spoke to them;* by the altar, and the sacrifices offered upon it, they spoke to God; and thus was communion kept up between them and God. The word and prayer must go together. Though they might not, of their own heads, set up any altar besides that at the tabernacle, yet, but the appointment of God, they might upon a special occasion. Elijah built a temporary altar of twelve unhewn stones, similar to this, when he brought Israel back to the covenant which was now made, 1 Ki. 18:31, 32. Now, (1.) This altar must be made of such stones as they found ready upon the field, not newly cut out of the rock, much less squared artificially: *Thou shalt not lift up any iron tool upon them, v.* 5. Christ, our altar, is a *stone cut out of the mountain without hands* (Dan. 2:34, 35), and therefore *refused by the builders,* as having no form or comeliness, but accepted of God the Father, and made the head of the corner. (2.) Burnt-offerings and peace-offerings must be offered upon this altar (*v.* 6,7), that by them they might give glory to God and obtain favour. Where the law was written, an altar was set up close by it, to signify that we could not look with any comfort upon the law, being conscious to ourselves of the violation of it, if it were not for the great sacrifice by which atonement is made for sin; and the altar was set up on Mount Ebal, the mount on which those tribes stood that said *Amen* to the curses, to intimate that through Christ we are *redeemed from the curse of the law.* In the Old Testament the words of the law are written, with the curse annexed, which would fill us with horror and amazement if we had not in the New Testament (which is bound up with it) an altar erected close by it, which gives us everlasting consolation. (3.) They must eat there, and *rejoice before the Lord their God, v.* 7. This signified, [1.] The consent they gave to the covenant; for the parties to a covenant ratified the covenant by feasting together. They were partakers of the altar, which was God's table, as his servants and tenants, and such they acknowledged themselves, and, being put in possession of this good land, bound themselves to pay the rent and to do the services reserved by the royal grant. [2.] The comfort they took in the covenant; they had reason to rejoice in the law, when they had an altar, a remedial law, so near it. It was a great favour to them, and a token for good, that God *gave them his statutes;* and that they were owned as the people of God, and the *children of the promise,* was what they had reason to rejoice in, though, when this solemnity was to be performed, they were not put in full possession of Canaan; but God has *spoken in his holiness,* and then *I will rejoice, Gilead is mine, Manasseh is mine;* all my own.

Verses 11–26

When the law was written, to be *seen and read by all men,* the sanctions of it were to be published, which, to complete the solemnity of their covenanting with God, they were deliberately to declare their approbation of. This they were before directed to do (*ch.* 11:29, 30), and therefore the appointment here begins somewhat abruptly, *v.* 12. There were, it seems, in Canaan, that part of it which afterwards fell to the lot of Ephraim (Joshua's tribe), two mountains that lay near together, with a valley between, one called *Gerizim* and the other *Ebal.* On the sides of these two mountains, which faced one another, all the tribes were to be drawn up, six on one side and six on the other, so that in the valley, at the foot of each mountain, they came pretty near together, so near as that the priests standing betwixt them might be heard by those that were next them on both sides; then when silence was proclaimed, and attention commanded, one of the priests, or perhaps more at some distance from each other, pronounced with a loud voice one of the curses here following, and all the people that stood on the side and foot of Mount Ebal (those that stood further off taking the signal from those that stood nearer and within hearing) said *Amen;* then the contrary blessing was pronounced, "Blessed is he that doth not so or so," and then those that stood on the side, and at the foot, of Mount Gerizim, said *Amen.* This could not but affect them very much with the blessings and curses, the promises and threatenings, of the law, and not only acquaint all the people with them, but teach them to apply them to themselves.

I. Something is to be observed, in general, concerning this solemnity, which was to be done, but once and not repeated, but would be talked of to posterity,. 1. God appointed which tribes should stand upon Mount Gerizim and which on Mount Ebal (*v.* 12, 13), to prevent the disputes that might have arisen if they had been left to dispose of themselves. The six tribes that were appointed for blessing were all the children of the free women, for to such the promise belongs, Gal. 4:31. Levi is here put among the rest, to teach ministers to apply to themselves the blessing and curse which they preach to others, and by faith to set their own *Amen* to it. 2. Of those tribes that were to say *Amen* to the blessings it is said, *They stood to bless the people,* but of the other, *They stood to curse,* not mentioning the people, as loth to suppose that any of this people whom God had taken for his own should lay themselves under the curse. Or, perhaps, the different mode of expression intimates that there was to be but one blessing pronounced in general upon the people of Israel, as a happy people, and that should ever be so, *if they were obedient;* and to this blessing the tribes on Mount Gerizim were to say *Amen* — "Happy art thou, O Israel, and mayest thou ever be so;" but then the curses come in as exceptions from the general rule, and we know *exceptio firmat regulam — the exception confirms the rule.* Israel is a blessed people, but, if there be any particular persons even among them that do such and such things as are mentioned, let them know that they have no part nor lot in the matter, but are under a curse. This shows how ready God is to bestow the blessing; if any fall under the curse, they may thank themselves, they bring it upon their own heads. 3. The Levites or priests, such of them as were appointed for that purpose, were to pronounce the curses as well as the blessings. They were ordained to bless (*ch.* 10:8), the priests did it daily, Num. 6:23. But they *must separate between the precious and the vile;* they must not give that blessing promiscuously, but must declare it to whom it did not belong, lest those who had no right to it themselves should think to share in it by being in the crowd. Note, Ministers must preach the terrors of the law as well as the comforts of the gospel; must not only allure people to their duty with the promises of a blessing, but awe them to it with the threatenings of a curse. 4. The curses are here expressed, but not the blessings; for as many as were under the law were under the curse, but it was a honour reserved for Christ to bless us, and so to do that for us which *the law could not do, in that it was weak.* In Christ's sermon upon the mount, which was the true Mount Gerizim, we have blessings only, Mt. 5:3, etc. 5. To each of the curses the people were to say *Amen.* It is easy to understand the meaning of *Amen* to the blessings. The Jews have a saying to encourage people to say *Amen* to the public prayers, *Whosoever answereth* Amen, *after him that blesseth, he is as he that blesseth.* But how could they say *Amen* to the curses? (1.) It was a profession of their faith in the truth of them, that these and the like curses were not bug-bears to frighten children and fools, but the real declarations of the wrath of God against the ungodliness and unrighteousness of men, not one *iota* of which shall fall to the ground. (2.) It was an acknowledgment of the equity of these curses; when they said *Amen,* they did in effect say, not only, *It is certain it shall be so,* but, *It is just it should be so.* Those who do such things deserve to fall and lie under the curse. (3.) It was such an imprecation upon themselves as strongly obliged them to have nothing to do with those evil practices upon which the curse is here entailed. "Let God's wrath fall upon us if ever we do such things." We read of those that entered into a curse (and with us that is the usual form of a solemn oath) to *walk in God's law* Neh. 10:29. Nay, the Jews say (as the learned bishop Patrick quotes them), "All the people, by saying this *Amen,* became bound for one another, that they would observe God's laws, by which every man was obliged, as far as he could, to prevent his neighbour from breaking these laws, and to reprove those that had offended, lest they should bear sin and the curse for them."

II. Let us now observe what are the particular sins against which the curses are here denounced.

1. Sins against the second commandment. This flaming sword is set to keep that commandment first, *v.* 15. Those are here cursed, not only that worship images, but that make them or keep them, if they be such (or like such) as idolaters used in the service of their gods. Whether it be a graven image or a molten image, it comes all to one, *it is an abomination to the Lord,* even though it be not set up in public, but in a secret place, — though it be not actually worshipped, nor is it said to be designed for worship, but reserved there with respect and a constant temptation. He that does this may perhaps escape punishment from men, but he cannot escape the curse of God.

2. Against the fifth commandment, *v.* 16. The contempt of parents is a sin so heinous that it is put next to the contempt of God himself. If a man abused his parents, either in word or deed, he fell under the sentence of the magistrate, and must be *put to death,* Ex. 21:15, 17. But to set light by them in his heart was a thing which the magistrate could not take cognizance of, and therefore it is here laid under the curse of God, who knows the heart. Those are cursed children that carry themselves scornfully and insolently towards their parents.

3. Against the eighth commandment. The curse of God is here fastened, (1.) Upon an unjust neighbour that *removes the land-marks, v.* 17. See *ch.* 19:14. Upon an unjust counsellor, who, when his advice is asked, maliciously directs his friend to that which he knows will be to his prejudice, which is *making the blind to wander out of the way,* under pretence of directing him in the way, than which nothing can be either more barbarous or more treacherous, *v.* 18. Those that seduce others from the way of God's commandments, and entice them to sin, bring this curse upon themselves, which our Saviour has explained, Mt. 15:14, *The blind lead the blind, and both shall fall into the ditch.* (3.) Upon an unjust judge, that *perverteth the judgment of the stranger, fatherless, and widow,* whom he should protect and vindicate, *v.* 19. These are supposed to be poor and friendless (nothing to be got by doing them a kindness, nor any thing lost by disobliging them), and therefore judges may be tempted to side with their adversaries against right and equity; but cursed are such judges.

4. Against the seventh commandment. Incest is a cursed sin, with a *sister, a father's wife, or a mother-in-law, v.* 20, 22, 23. These crimes not only exposed men to the sword of the magistrate (Lev. 20:11), but, which is more dreadful, to the wrath of God; bestiality likewise, *v.* 21.

5. Against the sixth commandment. Two of the worst kinds of murder are here specified: — (1.) Murder unseen, when a man does not set upon his neighbour as a fair adversary, giving him an opportunity to defend himself, but *smites him secretly* (*v.* 24), as by poison or otherwise, when he sees not who hurts him. See Ps. 10:8, 9. Though such secret murders may go undiscovered and unpunished, yet the curse of God will follow them. (2.) Murder under colour of law, which is the greatest affront to God, for it makes an ordinance of his to patronise the worst of villains, and the greatest wrong to our neighbour, for it ruins his honour as well as his life: cursed therefore is he that will be hired, or bribed, to accuse, or to convict, or to condemn, and so *to slay, an innocent person, v.* 25. See Ps. 15:5.

6. The solemnity concludes with a general curse upon him *that confirmeth not,* or, as it might be read, that *performeth not, all the words of this law to do them, v.* 26. By our obedience to the law we set our seal to it, and so confirm it, as by our disobedience we do what lies in us to disannul it, Ps. 119:126. The apostle, following all the ancient versions, reads it, *Cursed is every one that continues not,* Gal. 3:10. Lest those who were guilty of other sins, not mentioned in this commination, should think themselves safe from the curse, this last reaches all; not only those who do the evil which the law forbids, but those also who omit the good which the law requires: to this we must all say *Amen,* owning ourselves under the curse, justly to have deserved it, and that we must certainly have perished for ever under it, if Christ had not *redeemed us from the curse of the law, by being made a curse for us.*

CHAPTER 28

This chapter is a very large exposition of two words in the foregoing chapter, the blessing and the curse. Those were pronounced blessed in general that were obedient, and those cursed that were disobedient; but, because generals are not so affecting, Moses here descends to particulars, and describes the blessing and the curse, not in their fountains (these are out of sight, and therefore the most considerable, yet least considered, the favour of God the spring of all the blessings, and the wrath of God the spring of all the curses), but in their streams, the sensible effects of the blessing and the curse, for they are real things and have real effects. I. He describes the blessings that should come upon them if they were obedient; personal, family, and especially national, for in that capacity especially they are here treated with (*v.* 1–14). II. He more largely describes the curses which would come upon them if they were disobedient; such as would be, 1. Their extreme vexation (*v.* 15–44). 2. Their utter ruin and destruction at last (*v.* 45–68). This chapter is much to the same purport with Lev. 26, setting before them life and death, good and evil; and the promise, in the close of that chapter, of their restoration, upon their repentance, is here likewise more largely repeated, *ch.* 30. Thus, as they had precept upon precept in the repetition of the law, so they had line upon line in the repetition of the promises and threatenings. And these are both there and here delivered, not only as sanctions of the law, what should be conditionally, but as predictions of the event, what would be certainly, that for a while the people of Israel would be happy in their obedience, but that at length they would be undone by their disobedience; and therefore it is said (*ch.* 30:1) that all those things would come upon them, both the blessing and the curse.

Verses 1–14

The blessings are here put before the curses, to intimate, 1. That God is slow to anger, but swift to show mercy: he has said it, and sworn, that he would much rather we would obey and live than sin and die. It is his delight to bless. 2. That though both the promises and the threatenings are designed to bring and hold us to our duty, yet it is better that we be allured to that which is good by a filial hope of God's favour than that we be frightened to it by a servile fear of his wrath. That obedience pleases best which comes from a principle of delight in God's goodness. Now,

I. We have here the conditions upon which the blessing is promised. 1. It is upon condition that they *diligently hearken to the voice of God* (*v.* 1, 2), that they hear God speaking to them by his word, and use their utmost endeavours to acquaint themselves with his will, *v.* 13. 2. Upon condition that they *observe and do all his commandments* (and in order to obedience there is need of observation) and that they*keep the commandments of God* (*v.* 9) and walk in his ways. Not only do them for once, but keep them for ever; not only set out in his ways, but walk in them to the end. 3. Upon condition that they should not *go aside either to the right hand or to the left,* either to superstition on the one hand, or profaneness on the other; and particularly that they should not go after other gods (*v.* 14), which was the sin that of all others they were most prone to, and God would be most displeased with. Let them take care to keep up religion, both the form and power of it, in their families and nation, and God would not fail to bless them.

II. The particulars of this blessing.

1. It is promised that the providence of God should prosper them in all their outward concerns. These blessings are said to *overtake them, v.* 2. Good people sometimes, under the sense of their unworthiness, are ready to fly from the blessing and to conclude that it belongs not to them,; but the blessing shall find them out and follow them notwithstanding. Thus in the great day the blessing will overtake the righteous that say, *Lord, when saw we thee hungry and fed thee?* Mt. 25:37. Observe,

(1.) Several things are enumerated in which God by his providence would bless them: — [1.] They should be safe and easy; a blessing should rest upon their persons wherever they were, *in the city,* or *in the field, v.* 3. Whether their habitation was in town or country, whether they were husbandmen or tradesmen, whether their business called them into the city or into the field, they should be preserved from the dangers and have the comforts of their condition. This blessing should attend them in their journeys, going out and coming in, *v.* 6. Their persons should be protected, and the affair they went about should succeed well. Observe here, What a necessary and constant dependence we have upon God both for the continuance and comfort of this life. We need him at every turn, in all the various movements of life; we cannot be safe if he withdraw his protection, nor easy if he suspend his favour; but, if he bless us, go where we will it is well with us. [2.] Their families should be built up in a numerous issue: blessed *shall be the fruit of thy body* (*v.* 4), and in that the Lord shall *make thee plenteous* (*v.* 11), in pursuance of the promise made to Abraham, that his seed should be *as the stars of heaven* for multitude, and that God would be a God to them, than which a greater blessing, and more comprehensive, could not be entailed upon the fruit of their body. See Isa. 61:9. [3.] They should be rich, and have an abundance of all the good things of this life, which are promised them, not merely that they might have the pleasure of enjoying them, but (as bishop Patrick observes out of one of the Jewish writers) that they might have wherewithal to honour God, and might be helped and encouraged to serve him cheerfully and to proceed and persevere in their obedience to him. A blessing is promised, *First,* On all they had without doors, corn and cattle in the field (*v.* 4, 11), their cows and sheep particularly, which would be blessed for the owners' sakes, and made blessings to them. In order to this, it is promised that God would give them *rain in due season,* which is called his *good treasure* (*v.* 12), because with this river of God the earth is enriched, Ps. 65:9. Our constant supplies we must see coming from God's good treasure, and own our obligations to him for them; if he withhold his rain, the fruits both of the ground and of the cattle soon perish. *Secondly,* On all they had within doors, the basket and the store (*v.* 5), the store-houses or barns, *v.* 8. When it is brought home, God will bless it, and not blow upon it as sometimes he does, Hag. 1:6, 9. We depend upon God and his blessing, not only for our yearly corn out of the field, but for our daily bread out of our basket and store, and therefore are taught to pray for it every day. [4.] They should have success in all their employments, which would be a constant satisfaction to them: *"The Lord shall command the blessing* (and it is he only that can command it) upon thee, not only in all thou hast, but in all thou doest, all *that thou settest thy hand to," v.* 8. This intimated that even when they were rich they must not be idle, but must find some good employment or other to set their hand to, and God would own their industry, and *bless the work of their hand* (*v.* 12); for that which *makes rich,* and keeps so, is *the blessing of the Lord* upon *the hand of the diligent,* Prov. 10:4, 22. [5.] They should have honour among their neighbours (*v.* 1): *The Lord thy God will set thee on high above all nations.* He made them so, by taking them into covenant with himself, *ch.* 26:19. And he would make them more and more so by their outward prosperity, if they would not by sin disparage themselves. Two things should help to make them great among the nations: — *First,* Their wealth (*v.* 12): "*Thou shalt lend to many nations* upon interest" (which they were allowed to take form the neighbouring nations), "but thou shalt not have occasion to borrow." This would give them great influence with all about them; for the borrower is servant to the lender. It may be meant of trade and commerce, that they should export abundantly more than they should import, which would keep the balance on their side. *Secondly,* Their power (*v.* 13): "*The Lord shall make thee the head,* to give law to all about thee, to exact tribute, and to arbitrate all controversies." Every sheaf should bow to theirs, which would make them so considerable that *all the people of the earth* would be *afraid of them* (*v.* 10), that is, would reverence their true grandeur, and dread making them their enemies. The flourishing of religion among them, and the blessing of God upon them, would make them formidable to all their neighbours, terrible as an army with banners. [6.] They should be victorious over their enemies, and prosper in all their wars. If any were so daring as to rise up against them to oppress them, or encroach upon them, it should be at their peril, they should certainly fall before them, *v.* 7. The forces of the enemy, though entirely drawn up to come against them one way, should be entirely routed, and flee before them seven ways, each making the best of his way.

(2.) From the whole we learn (though it were well if men would believe it) that religion and piety are the best friends to outward prosperity. Though temporal blessings do not take up so much room in the promises of the New Testament as they do in those of the Old, yet it is enough that our Lord Jesus has given us his word (and surely we may take his word) that if we *seek first the kingdom of God, and the righteousness thereof, all other things* shall be added to us, as far as Infinite Wisdom sees good; and who can desire them further? Mt. 6:33.

2. It is likewise promised that the grace of God should *establish them a holy people, v.* 9. Having taken them into covenant with himself, he would keep them in covenant; and, provided they used the means of stedfastness, he would give them the grace of steadfastness, that they should not depart from him. Note, Those that are sincere in holiness God will establish in holiness; and he is *of power to do it,* Rom. 16:25. He that is holy shall be holy still; and those whom God establishes in holiness he thereby establishes a people to himself, for a long as we keep close to God he will never forsake us. This establishment of their religion would be the establishment of their reputation (*v.* 10): *All the people of the earth shall see,* and own, *that thou art called by the name of the Lord,* that is, "that thou art a most excellent and glorious people, under the particular care and countenance of the great God. They shall be made to know that a people called by the name Jehovah are without doubt the happiest people under the sun, even their enemies themselves being judges." The favourites of Heaven are truly great, and, first or last, it will be made to appear that they are so, if not in this world, yet at that day when those who confess Christ now shall be confessed by him before men and angels, as those whom he delights to honour.

Verses 15–44

Having viewed the bright side of the cloud, which is towards the obedient, we have now presented to us the dark side, which is towards the disobedient. If we do not keep God's commandments, we not only come short of the blessing promised, but we lay ourselves under the curse, which is as comprehensive of all misery as the blessing is of all happiness. Observe,

I. The equity of this curse. It is not a curse causeless, nor for some light cause; God seeks not occasion against us, nor is he apt to quarrel with us. That which is here mentioned as bringing the curse is, 1. Despising God, refusing to *hearken to his voice* (*v.* 15), which bespeaks the highest contempt imaginable, as if what he said were not worth the heeding, or we were not under any obligation to him. 2. Disobeying him, *not doing his commandments,* or not observing to do them. None fall under his curse but those that rebel against his command. 3. Deserting him. "It is because of the *wickedness of thy doings,* not only whereby thou hast slighted me, but *whereby thou hast forsaken me," v.* 20. God never casts us off till we first cast him off. It intimates that their idolatry, by which they forsook the true God for false gods, would be their destroying sin more than any other.

II. The extent and efficacy of this curse.

1. In general, it is declared, "*All these curses shall come upon thee* from above, *and shall overtake thee;* though thou endeavour to escape them, it is to no purpose to attempt it, they shall follow thee whithersoever thou goest, and seize thee, overtake thee, and overcome thee," *v.* 15. It is said of the sinner, when God's wrath is in pursuit of him, that he *would fain flee out of his hand* (Job 27:22), but he cannot; if he *flee from the iron weapon,* yet *the bow of steel shall* reach him and *strike him through.* There is no running from God but by running to him, no fleeing from his justice but by fleeing to his mercy. See Ps. 21:7, 8. (1.) Wherever the sinner goes, the curse of God follows him; wherever he is, it rests upon him. He is cursed *in the city* and *in the field, v.* 16. The strength of the city cannot shelter him from it, the pleasant air of the country is no fence against these pestilential steams. He is cursed (*v.* 19) when he comes in, for the curse is *upon the house of the wicked* (Prov. 3:33), and he is cursed when he goes out, for he cannot leave that curse behind him, nor get rid of it, which has entered into his bowels like water and like oil into his bones. (2.). Whatever he has is under a curse: *Cursed is the ground for his sake,* and all that is on it, or comes out of it, and so he is cursed from the ground, as Cain, Gen. 4:11. The *basket and store* are cursed, *v.* 17, 18. All his enjoyments being forfeited by him are in a manner forbidden to him, as cursed things, which he has no title to. To those whose *mind and conscience are defiled* every thing else is so, Tit. 1:15. They are all embittered to him; he cannot take any true comfort in them, for the wrath of God mixes itself with them, and he is so far from having any security of the continuance of them that, if his eyes be open, he may see them all condemned and ready to be confiscated, and with them all his joys and all his hopes gone for ever. (3.) Whatever he does is under a curse too. It is a curse in all that *he sets his hand to* (*v.* 20), a constant disappointment, which those are subject to that set their hearts upon the world, and expect their happiness in it, and which cannot but be a constant vexation. This curse is just the reverse of the blessing in the former part of the chapter. Thus whatever bliss there is in heaven there is not only the want of it, but the contrary to it, in hell. Isa. 65:13, *My servants shall eat, but you shall be hungry.*

2. Many particular judgments are here enumerated, which would be the fruits of the curse, and with which God would punish the people of the Jews for their apostasy and disobedience. These judgments threatened are of divers kinds, for God has many arrows in his quiver, *four sore judgments* (Eze. 14:21), and many more. They are represented as very terrible, and the descriptions of them are exceedingly lively and affecting, that men, knowing these terrors of the Lord, might, if possible, be persuaded. The threatenings of the same judgment are several times repeated, that they might make the more deep and lasting impressions, and to intimate that, if men persisted in their disobedience, the judgment which they thought was over, and of which they said, "Surely the bitterness of it is past," would return with double force; for when God judges he will overcome. (1.) Bodily diseases are here threatened, that they should be epidemical in their land. These God sometimes makes use of for the chastisement and improvement of his own people. *Lord, behold, he whom thou lovest is sick.* But here they are threatened to be brought upon his enemies as tokens of his wrath, and designed for their ruin. So that according to the temper of our spirits, under sickness, accordingly it is to us a blessing or a curse. But, whatever sickness may be to particular persons, it is certain that epidemical diseases raging among a people are national judgments, and are so to be accounted. He here threatens, [1.] Painful diseases (*v.* 35), a sore botch, beginning in the legs and knees, but spreading, like Job's boils, from heat to foot. [2.] Shameful diseases (*v.* 27), the botch of Egypt (such boils and blains as the Egyptians had been plagued with, when God brought Israel from among them), and the emerods and scab, vile diseases, the just punishment of those who by sin had made themselves vile. [3.] Mortal diseases, the pestilence (*v.* 21), the consumption (put for all chronical diseases), and the fever (for all acute diseases), *v.* 22. See Lev. 26:16. And all incurable, *v.* 27. (2.) Famine, and scarcity of provisions; and this, [1.] For want of rain (*v.* 23, 24): *Thy heaven over thy head,* that part that is over thy land, *shall be as* dry *as brass,* while the heavens over other countries shall distil their dews; and, when the heaven is as brass, the earth of course will be as iron, so hard and unfruitful. Instead of rain, the dust shall be blown out of the highways into the field, and spoil the little that there is of the fruits of the earth. [2.] By destroying insects. The locust should destroy the corn, so that they should not have so much as their *seed again, v.* 38, 42. And the fruit of the vine, which should make glad their hearts, should all be worm-eaten, *v.* 39. and the olive, some way or other, should be made to *cast its fruit, v.* 40. The heathen use many superstitious customs in honour of their idol-gods for preserving the fruits of the earth; but Moses tells Israel that the only way they had to preserve them was to keep God's commandments; for he is a God that will not be sported with, like their idols, but will be served in spirit and truth. This threatening we find fulfilled in Israel, 1 Ki. 17:1; Jer. 14:1, etc.; Joel 1:4. (3.) That they should be smitten before their enemies in war, who, it is likely, would be the more cruel to them, when they had them at their mercy, for the severity they had used against the nations of Canaan, which their neighbours in after-ages would be apt to remember against them, *v.* 25. It would make their flight the more shameful, and the more grievous, that they might have triumphed over their enemies if they had but been faithful to their God. The carcases of those that were slain in war, or died in captivity among strangers, should be *meat for the fowls* (*v.* 26); and an Israelite, having forfeited the favour of his God, should have so little humanity shown him as that *no man should drive them away,* so odious would God's curse make him to all mankind. (4.) That they should be infatuated in all their counsels, so as not to discern their own interest, nor bring any thing to pass for the public good: *The Lord shall smite thee with madness and blindness, v.* 28, 29. Note, God's judgments can reach the minds of men to fill them with darkness and horror, as well as their bodies and estates; and those are the sorest of all judgments which make men a terror to themselves, and their own destroyers. That which they contrived to secure themselves by should still turn to their prejudice. Thus we often find that the allies they confided in *distressed them* and *strengthened them not,* 2 Chr. 28:20. Those that will not walk in God's counsels are justly left to be ruined by their own; and those that are wilfully blind to their duty deserve to be made blind to their interest, and, seeing they *loved darkness rather than light,* let them *grope at noon-day* as in the dark. (5.) That they should be plundered of all their enjoyments, stripped of all by the proud and imperious conqueror, such as Benhadad was to Ahab, 1 Ki. 20:5, 6. Not only their houses and vineyards should be taken from them, but their wives and children, *v.* 30, 32. Their dearest comforts, which they took most pleasure in, and promised themselves most from, should be the entertainment and triumph of their enemies. As they had dwelt in houses which they built not, and eaten of vineyards which they planted not (*ch.* 6:10, 11), so others should do by them. Their oxen, asses, and sheep, like Job's, should be taken away before their eyes, and they should not be able to recover them, *v.* 31. And all the fruit of their land and labours should be devoured and eaten up by the enemy; so that they and theirs would want necessaries, while their enemies were revelling with that which they had laboured for. (6.) That they should be carried captives into a far country; nay, into *all the kingdoms of the earth, v.* 25. Their sons and daughters, whom they promised themselves comfort in, should go into captivity (*v.* 41), and they themselves at length, and their king in whom they promised themselves safety and settlement, *v.* 36. This was fully accomplished when the ten tribes first were carried captive into Assyria (2 Ki. 17:6), and not long after the two tribes into Babylon, and two of their kings, 2 Ki. 24:14, 15; 25:7, 21. That which is mentioned as an aggravation of their captivity is that they should go into an unknown country, the language and customs of which would be very uncouth, and their treatment among them

barbarous, and there they should *serve other gods,* that is, be compelled to do so by their enemies, as they were in Babylon, Dan. 3:6. Note, God often makes men's sin their punishment, and chooses their delusions. You shall *serve other gods,* that is, "You shall serve those that do serve them;" a nation is often in scripture called by the name of its gods, as Jer. 48:7. They had made idolaters their associates, and now god made idolaters their oppressors. (7.) That those who remained should be insulted and tyrannized over by strangers, *v.* 43, 44. So the ten tribes were by the colonies which the king of Assyria sent to take possession of their land, 2 Ki. 17:24. Or this may be meant of the gradual encroachments which the strangers within their gates should make upon them, so as insensibly to worm them out of their estates. We read of the fulfilling of this, Hos. 7:9, *Strangers have devoured his strength.* Foreigners ate the bread out of the mouths of trueborn Israelites, by which they were justly chastised for introducing strange gods. (8.) That their reputation among their neighbours should be quite sunk, and those that had been a name, and a praise, should be an astonishment, a proverb, and a by-word, *v.* 37. Some have observed the fulfilling of this threatening in their present state; for, when we would express the most perfidious and barbarous treatment, we say, *None but a Jew would have done so.* Thus is sin a reproach to any people. (9.) To complete their misery, it is threatened that they should be put quite out of the possession of their minds by all these troubles (*v.* 34): *Thou shalt be mad for the sight of thy eyes,* that is, quite bereaved of all comfort and hope, and abandoned to utter despair. Those that walk by sight, and not by faith, are in danger of losing reason itself, when every thing about them looks frightful; and their condition is woeful indeed that are *mad for the sight of their eyes.*

Verses 45-68

One would have thought that enough had been said to possess them with a dread of that *wrath of God* which is *revealed from heaven against the ungodliness and unrighteousness of men.* But to show how deep the treasures of that wrath are, and that still there is more and worse behind, Moses, when one would have thought that he had concluded this dismal subject, begins again, and adds to this roll of curses many similar words: as Jeremiah did to his, Jer. 36:32. It should seem that in the former part of this commination Moses foretells their captivity in Babylon, and the calamities which introduced and attended that, by which, even after their return, they were brought to that low and poor condition which is described, *v.* 44. That their enemies should be *the head,* and they *the tail:* but here, in this latter part, he foretels their last destruction by the Romans and their dispersion thereupon. And the present deplorable state of the Jewish nation, and of all that have incorporated themselves with them, by embracing their religion, does so fully and exactly answer to the prediction in these verses that it serves for an incontestable proof of the truth of prophecy, and consequently of the divine authority of the scripture. And, this last destruction being here represented as more dreadful than the former, it shows that their sin, in rejecting Christ and his gospel, was more heinous and more provoking to God than idolatry itself, and left them more under the power of Satan; for their captivity in Babylon cured them effectually of their idolatry in seventy years' time; but under this last destruction now for above 1600 years they continue incurably averse to the Lord Jesus. Observe,

I. What is here said in general of the wrath of God, which should light and lie upon them for their sins.

1. That, if they would not be *ruled by the commands of God,* they should certainly be *ruined by his curse, v.* 45, 46. Because thou didst not *keep his commandments* (especially that of hearing and obeying the great prophet), *these curses shall come upon thee,* as upon a people appointed to destruction, the generation of God's wrath: and they shall be *for a sign* and *for a wonder.* It is amazing to think that a people so long the favourites of Heaven should be so perfectly abandoned and cast off, that a people so closely incorporated should be so universally dispersed, and yet that a people so scattered in all nations should preserve themselves distinct and not mix with any, but like Cain be fugitives and vagabonds, and yet marked to be known.

2. That, if they would not serve God with cheerfulness, they should be compelled to *serve their enemies* (*v.* 47, 48), that they might know the difference (2 Chr. 12:8), which, some think, is the meaning of Eze. 20:24, 25, *Because they despised my statutes, I gave them statutes that were not good.* Observe here, (1.) It is justly expected from those to whom God gives an abundance of the good things of this life that they should serve him. What does he maintain us for out that we may do his work, and be some way serviceable to his honour? (2.) The more God gives us the more cheerfully we should serve him; our abundance should be oil to the wheels of our obedience. God is a Master that will be served with gladness, and delights to hear us sing at our work. (3.) If, when we receive the gifts of God's bounty, we either do not serve him at all or serve him with reluctance, it is a righteous thing with him to make us know the hardships of want and servitude. Those deserve to have cause given them to complain who complain without a cause. *Tristis es et felix — Happy, and yet not easy!* Blush at thy own folly and ingratitude.

3. That, if they would not *give glory to God* by a reverential obedience, he would get *him honour upon them* by *wonderful* plagues, *v.* 58, 59. Note, (1.) God justly expects from us that we should fear his fearful name; and, which is strange, that name which is here proposed as the object of our fear is, THE LORD THY GOD, which is very fitly here put in our Bibles in capital letters; for nothing can sound more truly august. As nothing is more comfortable, so nothing more awful, than this, that he with whom we have to do is Jehovah, a being infinitely perfect and blessed, and the author of all being; and that he is our God, our rightful Lord and owner, from whom we are to receive laws and to whom we are to give account: this is great, and greatly to be feared. (2.) We may justly expect from God that, if we do not fear his fearful name, we shall feel his fearful plagues; for one way or other God will be feared. All God's plagues are dreadful, but some are wonderful, carrying in them extraordinary signatures of divine power and justice, so that a man, upon the first view of them, may say, *Verily, there is a God that judgeth in the earth.*

II. How the destruction threatened is described. Moses is here upon the same melancholy subject that our Saviour is discoursing of to his disciples in his farewell sermon (Mt. 24), namely, The destruction of Jerusalem and the Jewish nation. Observe,

1. Five things are here foretold as steps to their ruin: —

(1.) That they should be invaded by a foreign enemy (v 49, 50): *A nation from far,* namely, the Romans, *as swift as the eagle hastening to the prey.* Our Saviour makes use of this similitude, in foretelling this destruction, that *where the carcase is there will the eagles be gathered together,* Mt. 24:28. And bishop Patrick observes (to make the accomplishment the more remarkable) that the ensign of the Roman armies was an eagle. This nation is said to be of a fierce countenance, an indication of a fierce nature, stern and severe, that would not pity the weakness and infirmity either of little children or of old people.

(2.) That the country should be laid waste, and all the fruits of it eaten up by this army of foreigners, which is the natural consequence of an invasion, especially when it is made, as that by the Romans was, for the chastisement of rebels: He *shall eat the fruits of thy cattle and land* (*v.* 51), so that the inhabitants should be starved, while the invaders were fed to the full.

(3.) That their cities should be besieged, and that such would be the obstinacy of the besieged, and such the vigour of the besiegers, that they would be reduced to the last extremity, and at length fall into the hands of the enemy, *v.* 52. No place, though ever so well fortified, no, not Jerusalem itself, though it held out long, would escape. Two of the common consequences of a long siege are here foretold: — [1.] A miserable famine, which would prevail to such a degree that, for want of food, they should *kill and eat their own children, v.* 53. Men should do so, notwithstanding their hardiness, and ability to bear hunger; and, though obliged by the law of nature to provide for their own families, yet should refuse to give to the wife and children that were starving any of the child that was barbarously butchered, *v.* 54, 55. Nay, women, ladies of quality, notwithstanding their natural niceness about their food, and their natural affection to their children, yet, for

want of food, should so far forget all humanity as to kill and eat them, *v.* 56, 57. Let us observe, by the way, how hard this fate must needs be to the tender and delicate women, and learn not to indulge ourselves in tenderness and delicacy, because we know not what we may be reduced to before we die; the more nice we are, the harder it will be to us to bear want, and the more danger we shall be in or sacrificing reason, and religion, and natural affection itself, to the clamours and cravings of an unmortified and ungoverned appetite. This threatening was fulfilled in the letter of it, more than once, to the perpetual reproach of the Jewish nation: never was the like done either by Greek or barbarian, but in the siege of Samaria, a woman *boiled her own son,* 2 Ki. 6:28, 29. And it is spoken of as commonly done among them in the siege of Jerusalem by the Babylonians, Lam. 4:10. And, in the last siege by the Romans, Josephus tells us of a noble woman that killed and ate her own child, through the extremity of the famine, and when she had eaten one half secretly (*v.* 57), that she might have it to herself, the mob, smelling meat, got into the house, to whom she showed the other half, which she had kept till another time, inviting them to share with her. What is too barbarous for those to do that are abandoned of God! [2.] Sickness is another common effect of a strait and long siege, and that is here threatened: *Sore sickness, and of long continuance, v.* 59. These should attend the Jews wherever they went afterwards, the diseases of Egypt, leprosies, botches, and foul ulcers, *v.* 60. Nay, as if the particular miseries here threatened were not enough, he concludes with an *et cetera, v.* 61. The Lord will bring upon thee every sickness, and every plague, though it be *not written in the book of this law.* Those that fall under the curse of God will find that the one half was not told them of the weight and terror of that curse.

(4.) That multitudes of them should perish, so that they should become *few in number, v.* 62. It was a nation that God had wonderfully increased, so that they were *as the stars of heaven for multitude;* but, for their sin, they were *diminished and brought low,* Ps. 107:38, 39. It is computed that in the destruction of the Jewish nation by the Romans, as appears by the account Josephus gives of it, above two millions fell by the sword at several places, besides what perished by famine and pestilence; so that the whole country was laid waste and turned into a wilderness. That is a terrible word (*v.* 63), *As the Lord rejoiced over you to do you good, so he will rejoice over you to destroy you.* Behold here *the goodness and severity of God:* mercy here shines brightly in the pleasure God takes in doing good — he rejoices in it; yet justice here appears no less illustrious in the pleasure he takes in destroying the impenitent; not as it is the making of his creatures miserable, but as it is the asserting of his own honour and the securing of the ends of his government. See what a malignant mischievous thing sin is, which (as I may say) makes it necessary for the God of infinite goodness to rejoice in the destruction of his own creatures, even those that had been favourites.

(5.) That the remnant should be scattered throughout the nations This completes their woe: *The Lord shall scatter thee among all people, v.* 64. This is remarkably fulfilled in their present dispersion, for there are Jews to be fond almost in all countries that are possessed either by Christians or Mahometans, and in such numbers that it has been said, If they could unite in one common interest, they would be a very formidable body, and able to deal with the most powerful states and princes; but they abide under the power of this curse, and are so scattered that they are not able to incorporate. It is here foretold that in this dispersion, [1.] They should have no religion, or none to any purpose, should have no temple, nor altar, nor priesthood, for they should *serve other gods.* Some think this has been fulfilled in the force put upon the Jews in popish countries to worship the images that are used in the Romish church, to their great vexation. [2.] They should have no rest, no rest of body: *The sole of thy foot shall not have rest* (*v.* 65), but be continually upon the remove, either in hope of gain or fear of persecution; all wandering Jews: no rest of the mind (which is much worse), but a trembling heart (*v.* 65); *no assurance of life* (*v.* 66); weary both of light and darkness, which are, in their turns, both welcome to a quiet mind, but to them both day and night would be a terror, *v.* 67. Such was once the condition of

Job (Job 7:4), but to them this should be constant and perpetual; that blindness and darkness which the apostle speaks of as having happened to Israel, and that guilt which *bowed down their back always* (Rom. 11:8–10), must needs occasion a constant restlessness and amazement. Those are a torment to themselves, and to all about them, that fear day and night and are always uneasy. Let good people strive against it, and not give way to that fear which has torment; and let wicked people not be secure in their wickedness, for their hearts cannot endure, nor can their hands be strong, when the terrors of God set themselves in array against them. Those that say *in the morning, O that it were evening,* and *in the evening, O that it were morning,* show, *First,* A constant fret and vexation, chiding the hours for lingering and complaining of the length of every minute. Let time be precious to us when we are in prosperity, and then it will not be so tedious to us when we are in afflictions as otherwise it would. *Secondly,* A constant fright and terror, afraid in the morning of the *arrow that flieth by day,* and therefore wishing the day over; but what will this do for them? When evening comes, the trembling heart is no less apprehensive of the *terror by night,* Ps. 91. 5, 6. Happy they whose minds, being stayed on God, are *quiet from the fear of evil!* Observe here, The terror arises not only from the sight of the eyes, but from the fear of the heart, not only from real dangers, but from imaginary ones; the causes of fear, when they come to be enquired into, often prove to be only the creatures of the fancy.

2. In the close, God threatens to leave them as he found them, in a *house of bondage* (*v.* 68): *The Lord shall bring thee into Egypt again,* that is into such a miserable state as they were in when they were slaves to the Egyptians, and ruled by them with rigour. God had brought them out of Egypt, and had said, *They shall see it no more again* (*ch.* 17:16); but now they should be reduced to the same state of slavery that they had been in there. To be sold to strangers would be bad enough, but much worse to be sold to their enemies. Even slaves may be valued as such, but a Jew should have so ill a name for all that is base that when he was exposed to sale no man would buy him, which would make his master that had him to sell the more severe with him. Thirty Jews (they say) have been sold for one small piece of money, as they sold our Saviour for thirty pieces.

3. Upon the whole matter, (1.) The accomplishment of these predictions upon the Jewish nation shows that Moses spoke by the Spirit of God, who certainly foresees the ruin of sinners, and gives them warning of it, that they may prevent it by a true and timely repentance, or else be left inexcusable. (2.) Let us all hence learn to stand in awe and not to sin. I have heard of a wicked man, who, upon reading the threatenings of this chapter, was so enraged that he tore the leaf out of the Bible, as Jehoiakim cut Jeremiah's roll; but to what purpose is it to deface a copy, while the original remains upon record in the divine counsels, by which it is unalterably determined that *the wages of sin is death,* whether men will hear or whether they will forbear?

CHAPTER 29

The first words of this chapter are the contents of it, "These are the words of the covenant" (*v.* 1), that is, these that follow. Here is, I. A recital of God's dealings with them, in order to the bringing of them into this covenant (*v.* 2–8). II. A solemn charge to them to keep the covenant (*v.* 9). III. An abstract of the covenant itself (*v.* 12, 13). IV. A specification of the persons taken into the covenant (*v.* 10, 11, 14, 15). V. An intimation of the great design of this covenant against idolatry, in a parenthesis (*v.* 16, 17). VI. A most solemn and dreadful denunciation of the wrath of God against such persons as promise themselves peace in a sinful way (*v.* 18–28). VII. The conclusion of this treaty, with a distinction between things secret and things revealed (*v.* 29).

Verses 1–9

Now that Moses had largely repeated the commands which the people were to observe as their part of the covenant, and the promises and threatenings which God would make good (according as they behaved themselves) as part of the covenant, the whole is here summed up in a federal transaction. The covenant formerly made is here renewed, and Moses, who was before, is still, the mediator of it (*v.* 1): *The Lord commanded Moses to make it.* Moses himself, though king in Jeshurun, could not make the covenant any otherwise than as God gave him instructions. It does not lie in the power of ministers to fix the terms of the covenant; they are only to dispense the seals of it. This is said to be *besides the covenant made in Horeb;* for, though the covenant was the same, yet it was a new promulgation and ratification of it. It is probable that some now living, though not of age to be mustered, were of age to consent for themselves to the covenant made at Horeb, and yet it is here renewed. Note, Those that have solemnly covenanted with God should take all opportunities to do it again, as those that like their choice too well to change. But the far greater part were a new generation, and therefore the covenant must be made afresh with them, for it is fit that the covenant should be renewed to the children of the covenant.

I. It is usual for indentures to begin with a recital; this does so, with a rehearsal of the great things God had done for them, 1. As an encouragement to them to believe that God would indeed be to them a God, for he would not have done so much for them if he had not designed more, to which all he had hitherto done was but a preface (as it were) or introduction; nay, he had shown himself a God in what he had hitherto done for them, which might raise their expectations of something great and answering the vast extent and compass of that pregnant promise, that God would be to them a God. 2. As an engagement upon them to be to him an obedient people, in consideration of what he had done for them.

II. For the proof of what he here advances he appeals to their own eyes (*v.* 2): *You have seen all that the Lord did.* Their own senses were incontestable evidence of the matter of fact, that God had done great things for them; and then their own reason was a no less competent judge of the equity of his inference from it: *Keep therefore the words of this covenant, v.* 9.

III. These things he specifies, to show the power and goodness of God in his appearances for them. 1. Their deliverance out of Egypt, *v.* 2, 3. The amazing signs and miracles by which Pharaoh was plagued and compelled to dismiss them, and Israel was tried (for they are called *temptations*) whether they would trust God to secure them from, and save them by, those plagues. 2. Their conduct through the wilderness for forty years, *v.* 5, 6. There they were led, and clad, and fed, by miracles; though the paths of the wilderness were not only unknown but untrodden, yet God kept them from being lost there; and (as bishop Patrick observes) those very shoes which by the appointment of God they put on in Egypt, at the passover, when the were ready to march (Ex. 12:11), never wore out, but served them to Canaan: and though they lived not upon bread which strengthens the heart, and wine which rejoices it, but upon manna and rock-water, yet they were men of strength and courage, mighty men, and able to go forth to war. By these miracles they were made to know that the Lord was God, and by these mercies that he was their God. 3. The victory they had lately obtained of Sihon and Og, and that good land which they had taken possession of, *v.* 7, 8. Both former mercies and fresh mercies should be improved by us as inducements to obedience.

IV. By way of inference from these memoirs,

1. Moses laments their stupidity: *Yet the Lord has not given you a heart to perceive, v.* 4. This does not lay the blame of their senselessness, and sottishness, and unbelief, upon God, as if they had stood ready to receive his grace and had begged for it, but he had denied them; no, but it fastens the guilt upon themselves. "The Lord, who is the Father of spirits, a God in covenant with you, and who had always been so rich in mercy to you, no doubt would have crowned all his other gifts with this, he would have given you a heart to perceive and eyes to see if you had not by your own frowardness and perverseness frustrated his kind intentions, and received his grace in vain." Note, (1.) The hearing ear, the seeing eye, and the understanding heart, are the gift of God. All that have them have them from him. (2.) God gives not only food and raiment, but wealth and large possessions, to many to whom he does not give grace. Many enjoy the gifts who have not hearts to perceive the giver, nor the true intention and use of the gifts. (3.) God's readiness to do us good in other things is a plain evidence that if we have not grace, that best of gifts, it is our own fault and not his; he would have gathered us and we would not.

2. Moses charges them to be obedient: *Keep therefore, and do, v.* 9. Note, We are bound in gratitude and interest, as well as duty and faithfulness, to *keep the words of the covenant.*

Verses 10–29

It appears by the length of the sentences here, and by the copiousness and pungency of the expressions, that Moses, now that he was drawing near to the close of his discourse, was very warm and zealous, and very desirous to impress what he said upon the minds of this unthinking people. To bind them the faster to God and duty, he here, with great solemnity of expression (to make up the want of the external ceremony that was used Ex. 24:4 etc.), concludes a bargain (as it were) between them and God, an everlasting covenant, which God would not forget and they must not. He requires not their explicit consent, but lays the matter plainly before them, and then leaves it between God and their own consciences. Observe,

I. The parties to this covenant. 1. It is the Lord their God they are to covenant with, *v.* 12. To him they must give up themselves, to him they must join themselves. "It is his oath; he has drawn up the covenant and settled it; he requires your consent to it; he has sworn to you and to him you must be sworn." This requires us to be sincere and serious, humble and reverent, in our covenant-transactions with God, remembering how great a God he is with whom we are covenanting, who has a perfect knowledge of us and an absolute dominion over us. 2. They are all to be taken into covenant with him. They were all summoned to attend (*v.* 2), and did accordingly, and are told (*v.* 10) what was the design of their appearing before God now in a body — they were to enter into covenant with him. (1.) Even their great men, the captains of their tribes, their elders and officers, must not think it any disparagement to their honour, or any diminution of their power, to put their necks under the yoke of this covenant, and to draw in it. They must rather enter into the covenant first, to set a good example to their inferiors. (2.) Not the men only, but their wives and children, must come into this covenant; though they were not numbered and mustered, yet they must be *joined to the Lord, v.* 11. Observe, Even little ones are capable of being taken into covenant with God, and are to be admitted with their parents. Little children, so little as to be carried in arms, must be brought to Christ, and shall be blessed by him, for *of such* was and *is the kingdom of God.* (3.) Not the men of Israel only, but the stranger that was in their camp, provided he was so far proselyted to their religion as to renounce all false gods, was taken into this covenant with the God of Israel, forasmuch as he also, though a stranger, was to be looked upon in this matter as a *son of Abraham,* Lu. 19:9. This was an early indication of favour to the Gentiles, and of the kindness God had in store for them. (4.) Not the freemen only, but the hewers of wood and drawers of water, the meanest drudge they had among them. Note, As none are too great to come under the bonds of the covenant, so none are too mean to inherit the blessings of the covenant. In Christ no difference is made between *bond and free,* Col. 3:11. *Art thou called being a servant? Care not for it,* 1 Co. 7:21. (5.) Not only those that were now present before God in this solemn assembly, but those also that were not here with them were taken into covenant (*v.* 15): *As with him that standeth here with us* (so bishop Patrick thinks it should be rendered) *so also with him, that is not here with us this day;* that is, [1.] Those that tarried at home were included; though detained either by sickness or necessary business, they must not therefore think themselves disengaged; no, every Israelite shares in the common blessings. Those that tarry at home divide the spoil, and therefore every Israelite must own himself bound by the consent of the representative body. Those who cannot go up to the house of the Lord must keep up a spiritual communion with those that do, and be present in spirit when they are absent in body. [2.] The generations to come are included. Nay, one of the Chaldee paraphrasts reads it, *All the generations that have been from the first days of the world, and all that shall arise to the end of the whole world, stand with us here this day.* And so, taking this covenant as a typical dispensation of the covenant of grace, it is a noble testimony to the Mediator of that covenant, who is *the same yesterday, to-day, and for ever.*

II. The summary of this covenant. All the precepts and all the promises of the covenant are included in the covenant-relation between God and them, v. 13. That they should be appointed, raised up, *established, for a people to him,* to observe and obey him, to be devoted to him and dependent on him, and that he should be to them a God, according to the tenour of the covenant made with their fathers, to make them holy, high, and happy Their fathers are here named, *Abraham, Isaac,* and *Jacob,* as examples of piety, which those were to set themselves to imitate who expected any benefit from the covenant made with them. Note, A due consideration of the relation we stand in to God as our God, and of the obligation we lie under as a people to him, is enough to bring us to all the duties and all the comforts of the covenant.

III. The principal design of the renewing of this covenant at this time was to fortify them against temptations to idolatry. Though other sins will be the sinner's ruin, yet this was the sin that was likely to be *their* ruin. Now concerning this he shows,

1. The danger they were in of being tempted to it (v. 16, 17): *"You know we have dwelt in the land of Egypt,* a country addicted to idolatry; and it were well if there were not among you some remains of the infection of that idolatry; we have *passed by other nations,* the Edomites, Moabites, *etc.* and have *seen their abominations* and *their idols,* and some among you, it may be, have liked them too well, and still hanker after them, and would rather worship a wooden god that they can see than an infinite Spirit whom they never saw." It is to be hoped that there were those among them who, the more they saw of these abominations and idols, the more they hated them; but there were those that were smitten with the sight of them, saw the accursed things and coveted them.

2. The danger they were in if they yielded to the temptation. He gives them fair warning: it was at their peril if they forsook God to serve idols. If they would not be bound and held by the precepts of the covenant, they would find that the curses of the covenant would be strong enough to bind and hold them.

(1.) Idolatry would be the ruin of particular persons and their families, v. 18–21, where observe,

[1.] The sinner described, v. 18. *First,* He is one whose *heart turns away from his God;* there the mischief begins, in the *evil heart of unbelief,* which inclines men to *depart from the living God* to dead idols. Even to this sin men are tempted when they are drawn aside by their own lusts and fancies. Those that begin to turn from God, by neglecting their duty to him, are easily drawn to other gods: and those that serve other gods do certainly turn away from the true God; for he will admit of no rivals: he will be all or nothing. *Secondly,* He is a *root that bears gall and wormwood;* that is, he is a dangerous man, who, being himself poisoned with bad principles and inclinations, with a secret contempt of the God of Israel and his institutions and a veneration for the gods of the nations, endeavours, by all arts possible, to corrupt and poison others and draw them to idolatry: this is a man whose fruit is *hemlock* (so the word is translated, Hos. 10:4) and *wormwood;* it is very displeasing to God, and will be, to all that are seduced by him, *bitterness in the latter end.* This is referred to by the apostle, Heb. 12:15, where he is in like manner cautioning us to take heed of those that would seduce us from the Christian faith; they are the weeds or tares in a field, which, if let alone, will overspread the whole field. A little of this leaven will be in danger of infecting the whole lump.

[2.] His security in the sun. He promises himself impunity, though he persists in his impiety, v. 19. Though he *hears the words of the curse,* so that he cannot plead ignorance of the danger, as other idolaters, yet even then he *blesses himself in his own heart,* thinks himself safe from the wrath of the God of Israel, under the protection of his idol-gods, and *therefore says,* "I shall have peace, though I be governed in my religion, not by God's institution, but by my own imagination, to add drunkenness to thirst, one act of wickedness to another." Idolaters were like drunkards, violently set upon their idols themselves and industrious to draw others in with them. Revellings commonly accompanied their idolatries (1 Pt. 4:3), so that this speaks a woe to drunkards (especially the drunkards of Ephraim), who, when they are awake, being thirsty, *seek it yet again,* Prov. 23:35. And those that made themselves drunk in hon-

our of their idols were the worst of drunkards. Note, *First,* There are many who are under the curse of God and yet bless themselves; but it will soon be found that in blessing themselves they do but deceive themselves. *Secondly,* Those are ripe for ruin, and there is little hope of their repentance, who have made themselves believe that they shall have peace though they go on in a sinful way. *Thirdly,* Drunkenness is a sin that hardens the heart, and debauches the conscience, as much as any other, a sin to which men are strangely tempted themselves even when they have lately felt the mischiefs of it, and to which they are strangely fond of drawing others, Hab. 2:15. And such an ensnaring sin is idolatry.

[3.] God's just severity against him for the sin, and for the impious affront he put upon God in saying he should have peace though he went on, so giving the lie to eternal truth, Gen. 3:4. There is scarcely a threatening in all the book of God that sounds more dreadful than this. O that presumptuous sinners would read it and tremble! For it is not a bug-bear to frighten children and fools, but a real declaration of the wrath of God against the ungodliness and the unrighteousness of men, v. 20, 21. *First, The Lord shall not spare him.* The days of his reprieve, which he abuses, will be shortened, and no mercy remembered in the midst of judgment. *Secondly,* The *anger of the Lord, and his jealousy,* which is the fiercest anger, *shall smoke against him,* like the smoke of a furnace. *Thirdly,* The *curses written* shall *lie upon him,* not only light upon him to terrify him, but abide upon him, to sink him to the lowest hell, Jn. 3:36. *Fourthly, His name shall be blotted out,* that is, he himself shall be cut off, and his memory shall rot and perish with him. *Fifthly,* He shall be *separated unto evil,* which is the most proper notion of a curse; he shall be cut off from all happiness and all hope of it, and marked out for misery without remedy. And *(lastly)* All this *according to the curses of the covenant,* which are the most fearful curses, being the just revenges of abused grace.

(2.) Idolatry would be the ruin of their nation; it would bring plagues upon the land that connived at this root of bitterness and received the infection; as far as the sin spread, the judgment should spread likewise.

[1.] The ruin is described. It begins with plagues and sicknesses (v. 22), to try if they will be reclaimed by less judgments; but, if not, it ends in a total overthrow, like that of Sodom, v. 23. As that valley, which had been like the garden of the Lord for fruitfulness, was turned into a lake of salt and sulphur, so should the land of Canaan be made desolate and barren, as it has been ever since the last destruction of it by the Romans. The lake of Sodom bordered closely upon the land of Israel, that by it they might be warned against the iniquity of Sodom; but, not taking the warning, they were made as like to Sodom in ruin as they had been in sin.

[2.] The reason of it is enquired into, and assigned. *First,* It would be enquired into by the *generations to come* (v. 22), who would find the state of their nation in all respects the reverse of what it had been, and, when they read both the history and the promise, would be astonished at the change. The stranger likewise, and the nations about them, as well as particular persons, would ask, *Wherefore hath the Lord done thus unto this land? v.* 24. Great desolations are thus represented elsewhere as striking the spectators with amazement, 1 Ki. 9:8, 9; Jer. 22:8,9. It was time for the neighbours to tremble when judgment thus *began at the house of God,* 1 Pt. 4:17. The emphasis of the question is to be laid upon *this land,* the land of Canaan, this good land, the glory of all lands, this land flowing with milk and honey. A thousand pities that such a good land as this should be made desolate, but this is not all; it is this *holy* land, the land of Israel, a people in covenant with God; it is Immanuel's land, a land where God was known and worshipped, and yet thus wasted. Note, 1. It is no new thing for God to bring desolating judgments upon a people that in profession are near to him, Amos 3:2. 2. He never does this without a good reason. 3. It concerns us to enquire into the reason, that we may give glory to God and take warning to ourselves. *Secondly,* The reason is here assigned, in answer to that enquiry. The matter would be so plain that all men would say, It was because they *forsook the covenant of the Lord God of their fathers, v.* 25. Note, God never forsakes any till they first forsake him. But those that desert the God of their fathers are justly cast

out of the inheritance of their fathers. They went and *served other gods* (v. 26), gods that they had no acquaintance with, nor lay under any obligation to either in duty of gratitude; for God has not given the creatures to be served by us, but to serve us; nor have they done any good to us (as some read it), more than what God has enabled them to do; to the Creator therefore we are debtors, and not to the creatures. It was for this that God was angry with them (v. 27), and *rooted them out in anger, v.* 28. So that, how dreadful soever the desolation was, the Lord was righteous in it, which is acknowledged, Dan. 9:11–14. "Thus" (says Mr. Ainsworth) "the law of Moses leaves sinners under the curse, and *rooted out of the Lord's land;* but the grace of Christ towards penitent believing sinners plants them again *upon their land, and they shall no more be pulled up,* being kept by the power of God," Amos 9:15.

[3.] He concludes his prophecy of the Jews' rejection just as St. Paul concludes his discourse on the same subject, when it began to be fulfilled (Rom. 11:33), *How unsearchable are God's judgments, and his ways past finding out!* So here (v. 29), *Secret things belong to the Lord our God.* Some make it to be one sentence, *The secret things of the Lord our God are revealed to us and to our children,* as far as we are concerned to know them, and *he hath not dealt so with other nations:* but we make it two sentences, by which, *First,* We are forbidden curiously to enquire into the secret counsels of God and to determine concerning them. A full answer is given to that question, *Wherefore has the Lord done thus to this land?* sufficient to justify God and admonish us. But if any ask further why God would be at such a vast expense of miracles to form such a people, whose apostasy and ruin he plainly foresaw, why he did not by his almighty grace prevent it, or what he intends yet to do with them, let such know that these are questions which cannot be answered, and therefore are not fit to be asked. It is presumption in us to pry into the *Arcana imperii — the mysteries of government,* and to enquire into the reasons of state which *it is not for us to know.* See Acts 1:7; Jn. 21:22; Col. 2:18. *Secondly,* We are directed and encouraged diligently to enquire into that which God has made known: things *revealed belong to us and to our children.* Note, 1. Though God has kept much of his counsel secret, yet there is enough revealed to satisfy and save us. He has *kept back nothing that is profitable for us,* but that only which it is good for us to be ignorant of. 2. We ought to acquaint ourselves, and our children too, with the things of God that are revealed. We are not only allowed to search into them, but are concerned to do so. They are things which we and ours are nearly interested in. They are the rules we are to live by, the grants we are to live upon; and therefore we are to learn them diligently ourselves, and to teach them diligently to our children. 3. All our knowledge must be in order to practice, for this is the end of all divine revelation, not to furnish us with curious subjects of speculation and discourse, with which to entertain ourselves and our friends, *but that we may do all the words of this law,* and be blessed in our deed.

CHAPTER 30

One would have thought that the threatenings in the close of the foregoing chapter had made a full end of the people of Israel, and had left their case for ever desperate; but in this chapter we have a plain intimation of the mercy God had in store for them in the latter days, so that mercy at length rejoices against judgment, and has the last word. Here we have, I. Exceedingly great and precious promises made to them, upon their repentance and return to God (v. 1-10). II. The righteousness of faith set before them in the plainness and easiness of the commandment that was now given them (v. 11-14). III. A fair reference of the whole matter to their choice (v. 15, etc.).

Verses 1–10

These verses may be considered either as a conditional promise or as an absolute prediction.

I. They are chiefly to be considered as a conditional promise, and so they belong to all persons and all people, and not to Israel only; and the design of them is to assure us that the greatest sinners, if they repent and be converted, shall have their sins pardoned, and be restored to God's favour. This is the purport of the covenant of grace, it leaves room for repentance in case of misdemeanour, and promises pardon upon repentance, which the covenant of innocency did not. Now observe here,

1. How the repentance is described which is the con-

dition of these promises. (1.) It begins in *serious consideration, v.* 1. "Thou shalt call to mind that which thou hadst forgotten or not regarded." Note, Consideration is the first step towards conversion. Isa. 46:8, *Bring to mind, O you transgressors.* The prodigal son came to himself first, and then to his father. That which they should call to mind is the blessing and the curse. If sinners would but seriously consider the happiness they have lost by sin and the misery they have brought themselves into, and that by repentance they may escape that misery and recover that happiness, they would not delay to *return to the Lord their God.* The prodigal *called to mind the blessing and the curse* when he considered his present poverty and the plenty of bread *in his father's house,* Lu. 15:17. (2.) It consists in sincere conversion. The effect of the consideration cannot but be godly sorrow and shame, Eze. 6:9; 7:16. But that which is the life and soul of repentance, and without which the most passionate expressions are but a jest, is *returning to the Lord our God, v.* 2. If thou turn (*v.* 10) *with all thy heart and with all thy soul.* We must return to our allegiance to God as our Lord and ruler, our dependence upon him as our Father and benefactor, our devotedness to him as our highest end, and our communion with him as our God in covenant. We must return to God from all that which stands in opposition to him or competition with him. In this return to God we must be upright — with the heart and soul, and universal — with all the heart and all the soul. (3.) It is evidenced by a constant obedience to the holy will of God: If thou shalt *obey his voice (v.* 2), thou and thy children; for it is not enough that we do our duty ourselves, but we must train up and engage our children to do it. Or this comes in as the condition of the entail of the blessing upon their children, provided their children kept close to their duty. [1.] This obedience must be with an eye to God: Thou shalt *obey his voice* (*v.* 8), and hearken to it, *v.* 10. [2.] It must be sincere, and cheerful, and entire: *With all thy heart, and with all thy soul, v.* 2. [3.] It must be from a principle of love, and that love must be *with all thy heart and with all thy soul, v.* 6. It is the heart and soul that God looks at and requires; he will have these or nothing, and these entire or not at all. [4.] It must be universal: *According to all that I command thee, v.* 2, and again v 8, *to do all his commandments;* for he that allows himself in the breach of one commandment involves himself in the guilt of contemning them all, James 2:10. An upright heart has *respect to all God's commandments,* Ps. 119:6.

2. What the favour is which is promised upon this repentance. Though they are brought to God by their trouble and distress, in the nations whither they were driven (*v.* 1), yet God will graciously accept of them notwithstanding; for on this errand afflictions are sent, to bring us to repentance. Though they are *driven out to the utmost parts of heaven,* yet thence their penitent prayers shall reach God's gracious ear, and there his favour shall find them out, *v.* 4. *Undique ad caelos tantundem est viae — From every place there is the same way to heaven.* This promise Nehemiah pleads in his prayer for dispersed Israel, Neh. 1:9. It is here promised, (1.) That God would have compassion upon them, as proper objects of his pity, *v.* 3. Against sinners that go on in sin God has indignation (*ch.* 29:20), but on those that repent and bemoan themselves he has compassion, Jer. 31:18, 20. True penitents may take great encouragement from the compassions and tender mercies of our God, which never fail, but overflow. (2.) That he would *turn their captivity, and gather them from the nations whither they were scattered* (*v.* 3), though ever so remote, *v.* 4. One of the Chaldee paraphrasts applies this to the Messiah, explaining it thus: *The word of the Lord shall gather you by the hand of Elias the great priest, and shall bring you by the hand of the king Messiah;* for this was God's covenant with him, that he should *restore the preserved of Israel,* Isa. 49:6. And this was the design of his death, to *gather into one the children of God that were scattered abroad,* Jn. 11:51, 52. *To him shall the gathering of the people be.* (3.) That he would *bring them into their land again, v.* 5. Note, Penitent sinners are not only delivered out of their misery, but restored to true happiness in the favour of God. The land they are brought into to possess it is , though not the same, yet in some respects better than that which our first father Adam possessed, and out of which he was expelled. (4.) That he would *do them good* (*v.* 5) and *rejoice over them for good, v.* 9. For there is joy in heaven upon the repentance and conversion of sinners: the father of the prodigal *rejoiced over him for good.* (5.) That he would multiply them (*v.* 5), and that, when they grew numerous, every mouth might have meat: he would *make them plenteous in every work of their hand, v.* 9. National repentance and reformation bring national plenty, peace, and prosperity. It is promised, *The Lord will make thee plenteous* in the fruit of thy cattle and land, for good. Many have plenty for hurt; the prosperity of fools destroys them. Then it is for good when with it God gives us grace to use it for his glory. (6.) That he would transfer the curses they had been under to their enemies, *v.* 7. When God was gathering them in to re-establish them they would meet with much opposition; but the same curses that had been a burden upon them should become a defence to them, by being turned upon their adversaries. The cup of trembling should be taken out of their hand, and put into the hand of those that afflicted them, Isa. 51:22, 23. (7.) That he would give them his grace to change their hearts, and rule there (*v.* 6): *The Lord thy God will circumcise thy heart, to love the Lord.* Note, [1.] The heart must be circumcised to love God. The filth of the flesh must be put away; and the foolishness of the heart, as the Chaldee paraphrase expounds it. See Col. 2:11, 12; Rom. 2:29. Circumcision was a seal of the covenant; the heart is then *circumcised to love God* when it is strongly engaged and held by that bond to this duty. [2.] It is the work of God's grace to circumcise the heart, and to shed abroad the love of God there; and this grace is given to all that repent and seek it carefully. Nay, that seems to be rather a promise than a precept (*v.* 8): *Thou shalt return and obey the voice of the Lord.* He that requires us to return promises grace to enable us to return: and it is our fault if that grace be not effectual. herein the covenant of grace is well ordered, that whatsoever is required in the covenant is promised. *Turn you at my reproof: behold, I will pour out my Spirit,* Prov. 1:23.

3. It is observable how Moses here calls God *the Lord thy God* twelve times in these ten verses, intimating, (1.) That penitents may take direction and encouragement in their return to God from their relation to him. Jer. 3:22, *"Behold, we come unto thee, for thou art the Lord our God;* therefore to thee we are bound to come, whither else should we go? And therefore we hope to find favour with thee." (2.) That those who have revolted from God, if they return to him and do their first works, shall be restored to their former state of honour and happiness. *Bring hither the first robe.* In the threatenings of the former chapter he is all along called the *Lord,* a God of power and the Judge of all: but, in the promises of this chapter, *the Lord thy God,* a God of grace, and in covenant with thee.

II. This may also be considered as a prediction of the repentance and restoration of the Jews: *When all these things shall have come upon thee* (*v.* 1), the blessing first, and after that the curse, then the mercy in reserve shall take place. Though their hearts were wretchedly hardened, yet the grace of God could soften and change them; and then, though their case was deplorably miserable, the providence of God would redress all their grievances. Now, 1. It is certain that this was fulfilled in their return from their captivity in Babylon. It was a wonderful instance of their repentance and reformation that Ephraim, who had been joined to idols, renounced them, and said, *What have I to do any more with idols?* That captivity effectually cured them of idolatry; and then God planted them again in their own land and did them good. But, 2. Some think that it is yet further to be accomplished in the conversion of the Jews who are now dispersed, their repentance for the sin of their fathers in crucifying Christ, their return to God through him, and their accession to the Christian church. But, *alas! who shall live when God doth this?*

Verses 11–14

Moses here urges them to obedience from the consideration of the plainness and easiness of the command.

I. This is true of the law of Moses. They could never plead in excuse of their disobedience that God had enjoined them that which was either unintelligible or impracticable, impossible to be known or to be done (*v.* 11): *It is not hidden from thee.* That is, not send messengers to heaven (*v.* 12), to enquire what thou must do to please God; nor needest thou *go beyond sea* (*v.* 13), as the philosophers did, that travelled through many and distant regions in pursuit of learning; no, thou art not put to that labour and expense; nor is the commandment within the reach of those only that have a great estate or a refined genius, but it is *very nigh unto thee, v.* 14. It is written in thy books, made plain upon tables, so that he that runs may read it; thy priests' lips keep this knowledge, and, when any difficulty arises, thou mayest *ask the law at their mouth,* Mal. 2:7. It is not communicated in a strange language; but it is in thy mouth, that is, in the vulgar tongue that is commonly used by thee, in which thou mayest hear it read, and talk of it familiarly among thy children. It is not wrapped up in obscure phrases or figures to puzzle and amuse thee, or in hieroglyphics, but it is in thy heart; it is delivered in such a manner as that it is level to thy capacity, even to the capacity of the meanest." 2. "It is not too *hard* nor *heavy* for thee:" so the Septuagint reads it, *v.* 11. Thou needest not say, "As good attempt to climb to heaven, or flee upon the wings of the morning to the uttermost part of the sea, as go about to do all the words of this law:" no, the matter is not so; it is no such intolerable yoke as some ill-minded people represent it. It was indeed a heavy yoke in comparison with that of Christ (Acts 15:10), but not in comparison with the idolatrous services of the neighbouring nations. God appeals to themselves that he had not *made them to serve with an offering, nor wearied them with incense,* Isa. 43:23; Mic. 6:3. But he speaks especially of the moral law, and its precepts: "That is very nigh thee, consonant to the law of nature, which would have been found in every man's heart, and every man's mouth, if he would but have attended to it. There is that in thee which *consents to the law that it is good,* Rom. 7:16. Thou hast therefore no reason to complain of any insuperable difficulty in the observance of it."

II. This is true of the gospel of Christ, to which the apostle applies it, and makes it the language of the *righteousness which is of faith,* Rom. 10:6–8. And many think this is principally intended by Moses here; for he *wrote of Christ,* Jn. 5:46. This is God's commandment now under the gospel that we *believe in the name of his Son Jesus Christ,* 1 Jn. 3:23. If we ask, as the blind man did, *Lord, who is he?* or where is he, that we may believe on him? (Jn. 9:36), this scripture gives an answer, We need not go up to heaven, to fetch him thence, for he has come down thence in his incarnation; nor down to the deep, to fetch him thence, for thence he has come up in his resurrection. But the word is nigh us, and Christ in that word; so that if we believe with the heart that the promises of the incarnation and resurrection of the Messiah are fulfilled in our Lord Jesus, and receive him accordingly, and confess him with our mouth, we have then Christ with us, and we shall be saved. He is near, very near, that justifies us. The law was plain and easy, but the gospel much more so.

Verses 15–20

Moses here concludes with a very bright light, and a very strong fire, that, if possible, what he had been preaching of might find entrance into the understanding and affections of this unthinking people. What could be said more moving, and more likely to make deep and lasting impressions? The manner of his treating with them is so rational, so prudent, so affectionate, and every way so apt to gain the point, that it abundantly shows him to be in earnest, and leaves them inexcusable in their disobedience.

I. He states the case very fairly. He appeals to themselves concerning it whether he had not laid the matter as plainly as they could wish before them. 1. Every man covets to obtain life and good, and to escape death and evil, desires happiness and dreads misery. "Well," says he, "I have shown you the way to obtain all the happiness you can desire and to avoid all misery. Be obedient, and all shall be well, and nothing amiss." Our first parents ate the forbidden fruit, in hopes of getting thereby the knowledge of good and evil; but it was a miserable knowledge they got, of good by the loss of it, and of evil by the sense of it; yet such is the compassion of God towards man that, instead of giving him to his own delusion, he has favoured him by his word with such a knowledge of good and evil as will make him for ever happy if it be not his own fault. 2. Every man is moved and governed in his actions by hope and fear, hope of good and fear of evil, real of apparent.

"Now," says Moses, "I have tried both ways; if you will be either drawn to obedience by the certain prospect of advantage by it, or driven to obedience by the no less certain prospect of ruin in case you be disobedient — if you will be wrought upon either way, you will be kept close to God and your duty; but, if you will not, you are utterly inexcusable." Let us, then, hear the conclusion of the whole matter. (1.) If they and theirs would love God and serve him, they should live and be happy, *v.* 16. If they would love God, and evidence the sincerity of their love by keeping his commandments — if they would make conscience of keeping his commandments, and do it from a principle of love — then God would do them good, and they should be as happy as his love and blessing could make them. (2.) If they or theirs should at any time turn from God, desert his service, and worship other gods this would certainly be their ruin, *v.* 17, 18. Observe, It is not for every failure in the particulars of their duty that ruin is threatened, but for apostasy and idolatry: though every violation of the command deserved the curse, yet the nation would be destroyed by that only which is the violation of the marriage covenant. The purport of the New Testament is much the same; this, in like manner, sets before us life and death, good and evil; *He that believes shall be saved; he that believes not shall be damned,* Mk. 16:16. And this faith includes love and obedience. *To those who by patient continuance in well doing seek for glory, honour, and immortality,* God will give *eternal life. But to those that are contentious, and do not obey the truth, but obey unrighteousness* (and so, in effect, worship other gods and serve them), will be rendered the indignation and wrath of an immortal God, the consequence of which must needs be the tribulation and anguish of an immortal soul, Rom. 2:7–9.

II. Having thus stated the case, he fairly puts them to their choice, with a direction to them to choose well. He appeals to heaven and earth concerning his fair and faithful dealing with them, *v.* 19. They could not but own that whatever was the issue he had delivered his soul; therefore, that they might deliver theirs, he bids them choose life, that is, choose to do their duty, which would be their life. Note, 1. Those shall have life that choose it: those that choose the favour of God and communion with him for their felicity, and prosecute their choice as they ought, shall have what they choose. 2. Those that come short of life and happiness must thank themselves; they would have had it if they had chosen it when it was put to their choice: but they die because they *will* die; that is, because they do not like the life promised upon the terms proposed.

III. In the last verse, 1. He shows them, in short, what their duty is, *to love God,* and to love him as *the Lord,* a Being most amiable, and as *their God,* a God in covenant with them; and, as an evidence of this love, to *obey his voice* in every thing, and by a constancy in this love and obedience to *cleave to him,* and never to forsake him in affection or practice. 2. He shows them what reason there was for this duty, inconsideration, (1.) Of their dependence upon God: *He is thy life, and the length of thy days.* He gives life, preserves life, restores life, and prolongs it by his power though it is a frail life, and by his patience though it is a forfeited life: he sweetens life with his comforts, and is the sovereign Lord of life; *in his hand our breath is.* Therefore we are concerned to keep ourselves in his love; for it is good having him our friend, and bad having him our enemy. (2.) Of their obligation to him for the promise of Canaan made to their fathers and ratified with an oath. And, (3.) Of their expectations from him in performance of that promise: "Love God, and serve him, that thou mayest dwell in that land of promise which thou mayest be sure he can give, and uphold to thee who is *thy life and the length of thy days.*" All these are arguments to us to continue in love and obedience to the God of our mercies.

CHAPTER 31

In this chapter Moses, having finished his sermon, I. Encourages both the people who were now to enter Canaan (*v.* 1–6), and Joshua who was to lead them (*v.* 7, 8, 23). And, II. He takes care for the keeping of these things always in their remembrance after his decease, 1. By the book of the law which was, (1.) Written. (2.) Delivered into the custody of the priests (*v.* 9, and 24–27). (3.) Ordered to be publicly read every seventh year (*v.* 10–13). 2. By a song which God orders Moses to prepare for their instruction and admonition. (1.) He calls Moses and Joshua to the door of the tabernacle (*v.* 14, 15). (2.) He foretels the apostasy of Israel in process of time, and the judgments they would thereby bring upon themselves (*v.* 16–18). (3.) He prescribes the following song to be a witness against them (*v.* 19–21). (4.) Moses wrote it (*v.* 22). And delivered it to Israel, with an intimation of the design of it, as he had received it from the Lord (*v.* 28, etc.).

Verses 1–8

Loth to part (we say) *bids oft farewell.* Moses does so to the children of Israel: not because he was loth to go to God, but because he was loth to leave them, fearing that when he had left them they would leave God. He had finished what he had to say to them by way of counsel and exhortation: here he calls them together to give them a word of encouragement, especially with reference to the wars of Canaan, in which they were now to engage. It was a discouragement to them that Moses was to be removed at a time when he could so ill be spared: though Joshua was continued to fight for them in the valley, they would want Moses to intercede for them on the hill, as he did, Ex. 17:10. But there is no remedy: *Moses can no more go out and come in, v.* 2. Not that he was disabled by any decay either of body or mind; for his *natural force was not abated, ch.* 24:7. But he cannot any longer discharge his office; for, 1. He is 120 *years old,* and it is time for him to think of resigning his honour and returning to his rest. He that had arrived at so great an age then, when seventy or eighty was the ordinary stint, as appears by the prayer of Moses (Ps. 90:10), might well think that he had accomplished as a hireling his day. 2. He is under a divine sentence: *Thou shalt not go over Jordan.* Thus a full stop was put to his usefulness; hitherto he must go, hitherto he must serve, but no further. So God had appointed it and Moses acquiesces: for I know not why we should any of us desire to live a day longer than while God has work for us to do; nor shall we be accountable for more time than is allotted us. But, though Moses must not go over himself, he is anxious to encourage those that must.

I. He encourages the people; and never could any general animate his soldiers upon such good grounds as those on which Moses here encourages Israel. 1. He assures them of the constant presence of God with them (*v.* 3): *The Lord thy God.* that has led thee and kept thee hitherto *will go over before thee;* and those might follow boldly who were sure that they had God for their leader. He repeats it again (*v.* 6) with an emphasis: *"The Lord thy God,* the great Jehovah, who is thine in covenant, *he it is,* he and no less, he and no other, *that goes before thee;* not only who by his promise has assured thee that he *will go before thee;* but by his ark, the visible token of his presence, shows thee that he *does* actually *go before thee."* And he repeats it with enlargement: "Not only he goes over before thee at first, to bring thee in, but he will continue with thee all along, with thee and thine; *he will not fail thee nor forsake thee;* he will not disappoint thy expectations in any strait, nor will he ever desert thy interest; be constant to him, and he will be so to thee." This is applied by the apostle to all God's spiritual Israel, for the encouragement of their faith and hope; unto us is this gospel preached, as well as unto them *He will never fail thee, nor forsake thee,* Heb. 13:5. 2. He commends Joshua to them for a leader: *Joshua, he shall go over before thee, v.* 3. One whose conduct, and courage, and sincere affection to their interest, they had had long experience of; and one whom God had ordained and appointed to be their leader, and therefore, no doubt, would own and bless, and make a blessing to them. See Num. 27:18. Note, It is a great encouragement to a people when, instead of some useful instruments that are removed, God raises up others to carry on his work. 3. He ensures their success. The greatest generals, supported with the greatest advantages, must yet own the issues of war to be doubtful and uncertain; the battle is not always to the strong nor to the bold; an ill accident unthought of may turn the scale against the highest hopes. But Moses had warrant from God to assure Israel that, notwithstanding the disadvantages they laboured under, they should certainly be victorious. A coward will fight when he is sure to be a conqueror. God undertakes to do the work — *he will destroy these nations;* and Israel shall do little else than divide the spoil — *thou shalt possess them, v.* 3. Two things might encourage their hopes of this: — (1.) The victories they had already obtained over Sihon and Og (*v.* 4), from which they might infer both the power of God, that he could do what he had done, and the purpose of God, that he would finish what he had begun to do. Thus must we improve our experience. (2.) The command God had given them to destroy the Canaanites (*ch.* 7:2; 12:2), to which he refers here (*v.* 5, that you *may do unto them according to all which I have commanded you),* and from which they might infer that, if God had commanded them to destroy the Canaanites, no doubt he would put it into the power of their hands to do it. Note, What God has made our duty we have reason to expect opportunity and assistance from him for the doing of. So that from all this he had reason enough to bid them *be strong and of a good courage, v.* 6. While they had the power of God engaged for them they had no reason to fear all the powers of Canaan engaged against them.

II. He encourages Joshua, *v.* 7, 8. Observe, 1. Though Joshua was an experienced general, and a man of approved gallantry and resolution, who had already signalized himself in many brave actions, yet Moses saw cause to bid him *be of good courage,* now that he was entering upon a new scene of action; and Joshua was far from taking it as an affront, or as a tacit questioning of his courage, to be thus charged, as sometimes we find proud and peevish spirits invidiously taking exhortations and admonitions for reproaches and reflections. Joshua himself is very well pleased to be admonished by Moses to be strong and of good courage. 2. He gives him this charge *in the sight of all Israel,* that they might be the more observant of him whom they saw thus solemnly inaugurated, and that he might set himself the more to be an example of courage to the people who were witnesses to this charge here given to him as well as to themselves. 3. He gives him the same assurances of the divine presence, and consequently of a glorious success, that he had given the people. God would be with him, would not forsake him, and therefore he should certainly accomplish the glorious enterprise to which he was called and commissioned: *Thou shalt cause them to inherit the land* of promise. Note, Those shall speed well that have God with them; and therefore they ought to *be of good courage.* Through God let us do valiantly, for through him we shall do victoriously; if we resist the devil, he shall flee, and God shall *shortly tread him under our feet.*

Verses 9–13

The law was given by Moses; so it is said, Jn. 1:17. He was not only entrusted to deliver it to that generation, but to transmit it to the generations to come; and here it appears that he was faithful to that trust.

I. *Moses wrote this law, v.* 9. The learned bishop Patrick understands this of all the five books of Moses, which are often called the *law;* he supposes that though Moses had written most of the Pentateuch before, yet he did not finish it till now; now he put his last hand to that sacred volume. Many think that the law here (especially since it is called *this law,* this grand abridgment of the law) is to be understood of this book of Deuteronomy; all those discourses to the people which have taken up this whole book, he, being in them divinely inspired, wrote them as the word of God. He wrote this law, 1. That those who had heard it might often review it themselves, and call it to mind. 2. That it might be the more safely handed down to posterity. Note, The church has received abundance of advantage from the writing, as well as from the preaching, of divine things; faith comes not only by hearing, but by reading. The same care that was taken of the law, thanks be to God, is taken of the gospel too; soon after it was preached it was written, that it might reach to those on whom the ends of the world shall come.

II. Having written it, he committed it to the care and custody of the priests and elders. He delivered one authentic copy to the priests, to be laid up by the ark (*v.* 26), there to remain as a standard by which all other copies must be tried. And it is supposed that he gave another copy to the elders of each tribe, to be transcribed by all of that tribe that were so disposed. Some observe that the elders, as well as the priests, were entrusted with the law, to intimate that magistrates by the power, as well as ministers by their doctrine, are to maintain religion, and to take care that the law be not broken nor lost.

III. He appointed the public reading of this law in a general assembly of all Israel every seventh year. The pious Jews (it is very probable) read the laws daily in their families, and *Moses of old time was read in the synagogue every sabbath day,* Acts 15:21. But once in seven years, that the law might be the more magnified and made honourable, it must be read in a general assembly. Though we read the word in private, we must not think it needless to hear it read in public. Now here he give direction,

1. When this solemn reading of the law must be, that the time might add to the solemnity; it must be done, (1.) In the year of release. In that year the land rested, so that they could the better spare time to attend this service. Servants who were then discharged, and poor debtors who were then acquitted from their debts, must know that, having the benefit of the law, it was justly expected they should yield obedience to it, and therefore give up themselves to be God's servants, because he had loosed their bonds. The year of release was typical of gospel grace, which therefore is called the *acceptable year of the Lord;* for our remission and liberty by Christ engage us to keep his commandments, Lu. 1:74, 75. (2.) At the feast of tabernacles in that year. In that feast they were particularly required to *rejoice before God,* Lev. 23:40. Therefore then they must read the law, both to qualify their mirth and keep it in due bounds, and to sanctify their mirth, that they might make the law of God the matter of their rejoicing, and might read it with pleasure and not as a task.

2. To whom it must be read: To *all Israel* (v. 11), *men, women, and children, and the strangers,* v. 12. The women and children were not obliged to go up to the other feasts, but to this only in which the law was read. Note, It is the will of God that all people should acquaint themselves with his word. It is a rule to all, and therefore should be read to all. It is supposed that, since all Israel could not possibly meet in one place, nor could one man's voice reach them all, as many as the courts of the Lord's house would hold met there, and the rest at the same time in their synagogues. The Jewish doctors say that the hearers were bound to *prepare their hearts,* and to hear *with fear and reverence, and with joy and trembling,* as in the day *when the law was given on Mount Sinai;* and, though there were *great and wise men who knew the whole law very well,* yet they were bound to *hear with great attention;* for he that *reads is the messenger of the congregation to cause the words of God to be heard.* I wish those that hear the gospel read and preached would consider this.

3. By whom it must be read: *Thou shalt read it* (v. 11), "Thou, O Israel," by a proper person appointed for that purpose; or, "Thou, O Joshua," their chief ruler; accordingly we find that he did read the law himself, Jos. 8:34, 35. So did Josiah, 2 Chr. 34:30, and Ezra, Neh. 8:3. And the Jews say that the king himself (when they had one) was the person that read in the courts of the temple, that a pulpit was set up for that purpose in the midst of the court, in which the king stood, that the book of the law was delivered to him by the high priest, that he stood up to receive it, uttered a prayer (as every one did that was to read the law in public) before he read; and then, if he pleased, he might sit down and read. But if he read standing it was thought the more commendable, as (they say) king Agrippa did. Here let me offer it as a conjecture that Solomon is called the *preacher,* in his Ecclesiastes, because he delivered the substance of that book in a discourse to the people, after his public reading of the law in the feast of tabernacles, according to this appointment here.

4. For what end it must be thus solemnly read. (1.) That the present generation might hereby keep up their acquaintance with the law of God, v. 12. They must hear, that they may learn, and *fear God, and observe to do their duty.* See here what we are to aim at in hearing the word; we must hear, that we may learn and grow in knowledge; and every time we read the scriptures we shall find that there is still more and more to be learned out of them. We must learn, that we may fear God, that is, that we may be duly affected with divine things; and must fear God, that we may *observe and do the words of his law;* for in vain do we pretend to fear him if we do not obey him. (2.) That the rising generation might betimes be leavened with religion (v. 13); not only that those who know something may thus know more, but that *the children who have not known any thing* may betimes know this, how much it is their interest as well as duty to fear God.

Verses 14–21

Here, I. Moses and Joshua are summoned to attend the divine majesty at the door of the tabernacle, v. 14. Moses is told again that he must shortly die; even those that are most ready and willing to die have need to be often reminded of the approach of death. In consideration of this, he must come himself to meet God; for whatever improves our communion with God furthers our preparation for death. He must also bring Joshua with him to be presented to God for a successor, and to receive his commission and charge. Moses readily obeys the summons, for he was not one of those that look with an evil eye upon their successors, but, on the contrary, rejoiced in him.

II. God graciously gives them the meeting: *He appeared in the tabernacle* (as the shechinah used to appear) *in a pillar of a cloud,* v. 15. This is the only time in all this book that we read of the glory of God appearing, whereas we often read of it in the three foregoing books, which perhaps signifies that in the latter days, under the evangelical law, such visible appearances as these of the divine glory are not to be expected, but we must take heed to the more sure word of prophecy.

III. He tells Moses that, after his death, the covenant which he had taken so much pains to make between Israel and their God would certainly be broken. 1. That Israel would *forsake God,* v. 16. And we may be sure that if the covenant between God and man be broken the blame must lie on man, it is he that breaks it; we have often observed it, That God never leaves any till they first leave him. Worshipping the gods of the Canaanites (who had been the natives, but henceforward were to be looked upon as the strangers of that land) would undoubtedly be counted a deserting of God, and, like adultery, a violation of the covenant. Thus still those are revolters from Christ, and will be so adjudged, who either make a god of their money by reigning covetousness or a god of their belly by reigning sensuality. Those that *turn to other gods* (v. 18) forsake their own mercies. This apostasy of theirs is foretold to be the effect of their prosperity (v. 20): *They shall have eaten and filled themselves;* this is all they will aim at in eating, to gratify their own appetites, and then they will wax fat, grow secure and sensual; their security will take off their dread of God and his judgments; and their sensuality will incline them to the idolatries of the heathen, which *made provision for the flesh to fulfil the lusts of it.* Note, God has a clear and infallible foresight of all the wickedness of the wicked, and has often covenanted with those who *he knew would deal very treacherously* (Isa. 48:8), and conferred many favours on those who he knew would deal very ungratefully. 2. That then God would forsake Israel; and justly does he cast those off who had so unjustly cast him off (v. 17): *My anger shall be kindled against them, and I will forsake them.* His providence would forsake them, no longer to protect and prosper them, and then they would become a prey to all their neighbours. His spirit and grace would forsake them, no longer to teach and guide them, and then they would be more and more bigoted, besotted, and hardened in their idolatries. Thus *many evils and troubles would befal them.* (v. 17, 21), which would be such manifest indications of God's displeasure against them that they themselves would be constrained to own it: *Have not these evils come upon us because our God is not among us?* Those that have sinned away their God will find that thereby they pull all mischiefs upon their own heads. But that which completed their misery was that God would *hide his face from them in that day,* that day of their trouble and distress, v. 18. Whatever outward troubles we are in, if we have but the light of God's countenance, we may be easy. But, if God hide his face from us and our prayers, we are undone.

IV. He directs Moses to deliver them a song, in the composing of which he should be divinely inspired, and which should remain a standing testimony for God as faithful to them in giving them warning, and against them as persons false to themselves in not taking the warning, v. 19. The written word in general, as well as this song in particular, is a witness for God against all those that break covenant with him. It shall be for a testimony, Mt. 24:14. The wisdom of man has devised many ways of conveying the knowledge of good and evil, by laws, histories, prophecies, proverbs, and, among the rest, by songs; each has its advantages. And the wisdom of God has in the scrip-

ture made use of them all, that ignorant and careless men might be left inexcusable. 1. This song, if rightly improved, might be a means to prevent their apostasy; for in the inditing of it God had an eye to their present imagination, now, *before they were brought into the land of promise,* v. 21. God knew very well that there were in their hearts such gross conceits of the deity, and such inclinations of idolatry, that they would be tinder to the sparks of that temptation; and therefore in this song he gives them warning of their danger that way. Note, The word of God is a *discerner of the thoughts and intents of men's hearts,* and meets with them strangely by its reproofs and corrections, Heb. 4:12. Compare 1 Co. 14:25. Ministers who preach the word know not the imaginations men go about, but God, whose word it is, knows perfectly. 2. If this song did not prevent their apostasy, yet it might help to bring them to repentance, and to recover them from their apostasy. When their troubles come upon them, this *song shall not be forgotten,* but may serve as a glass to show them their own faces, that they may humble themselves, and return to him from whom they have revolted. Note, Those for whom God has mercy in store he may leave to fall, yet he will provide means for their recovery. Medicines are prepared before-hand for their cure.

Verses 22–30

Here, I. The charge is given to Joshua, which God has said (v. 14) he would give him. The same in effect that Moses had given him. The same in effect that Moses had given him (v. 7): *Be strong and of a good courage,* v. 23. Joshua had now heard from God so much of the wickedness of the people whom he was to have the conduct of as could not but be a discouragement to him: "Nay," says God, "how bad soever they are, thou shalt go through thy understanding, for *I will be with thee.* Thou shalt put them into possession of Canaan. If they afterwards by their sin throw themselves out of it again, that will be no fault of thine, nor any dishonour to thee, therefore *be of good courage."*

II. The solemn delivery of the book of the law to the Levites, to be deposited in the side of the ark, is here again related (v. 24–26), of which before, v. 9. Only they are here directed where to treasure up this precious original, not in the ark (there only the two tables were preserved), but in another box *by the side of the ark.* It is probable that this was the very book that was found in the house of the Lord (having been somehow or other misplaced) in the days of Josiah (2 Chr. 34:14), and so perhaps the following words here, *that it may be a witness against thee,* may particularly point at that event, which happened so long after; for the finding of this very book occasioned the public reading of it by Josiah himself, for a witness against a people who were then almost ripe for their ruin by the Babylonians.

III. The song which follows in the next chapter is here delivered to Moses, and by him to the people. He wrote it first (v. 22), as the Spirit of God indited it, and then *spoke it in the ears of all the congregation* (v. 30), and taught it to them (v. 22), that is, gave out copies of it, and ordered the people to learn it by heart. It was delivered by word of mouth first, and afterwards in writing, to the elders and officers, as the representatives of their respective tribes (v. 28), by them to be transmitted to their several families and households. It was delivered to them with a solemn appeal to heaven and earth concerning the fair warning which was given them by it of the fatal consequences of their apostasy from God, and with a declaration of the little joy and little hope Moses had in and concerning them. 1. He declares what little joy he had had of them while he was with them, v. 27. It is not in a passion that he says, *I know thy rebellion* (as once he said unadvisedly, *Hear now, you rebels),* but it is the result of a long acquaintance with them: *you have been rebellious against the Lord.* Their rebellions against himself he makes no mention of: these he had long since forgiven and forgotten; but they must be made to hear of their rebellions against God, that they may be ever repented of and never repeated. 2. What little hopes he had of them now that he was leaving them. From what God had now said to him (v. 16) more than from his own experience of them, though that was discouraging enough, he tells them (v. 29), *I know that after my death you will utterly corrupt yourselves.* Many a sad thought, no doubt, it occasioned to this good man, to foresee the apostasy and ruin of a people he had taken so much pains with, in order to them good and make them happy; but this was his comfort, that he had done his duty, and that God would be glorified, if not in their settlement, yet in their dispersion. Thus our Lord Jesus, a little before his death, foretold the rise of false Christs and false prophets (Mt. 24:24), notwithstanding which, and all the apostasies of the latter times, we may be confident that *the gates of hell shall not prevail against the church,* for the *foundation of God stands sure.*

CHAPTER 32

In this chapter we have, I. The song which Moses, by the appointment of God, delivered to the children of Israel, for a standing admonition to them, to take heed of forsaking God. This takes up most of the chapter, in which we have, 1. The preface (*v.* 1, 2). 2. A high character of God, and, in opposition to that, a bad character of the people of Israel (*v.* 3–6). 3. A rehearsal of the great things God had done for them, and in opposition to that an account of their ill carriage towards him (*v.* 7–18). 4. A prediction of the wasting destroying judgments which God would bring upon them for their sins, in which God is here justified by the many aggravations of their impieties (*v.* 19–33). 5. A promise of the destruction of their enemies and oppressors at last, and the glorious deliverance of a remnant of Israel (*v.* 36–43). II. The exhortation with which Moses delivered this song to them (*v.* 41–47). III. The orders God gives to Moses to go up to Mount Nebo and die (*v.* 48, etc.).

Verses 1–6

Here is, I. A commanding preface or introduction to this song of Moses, *v.* 1, 2. He begins, 1. With a solemn appeal to heaven and earth concerning the truth and importance of what he was about to say, and the justice of the divine proceedings against a rebellious and backsliding people, for he had said (*ch.* 31:28) that he would in this song call heaven and earth to record against them. Heaven and earth would sooner hear than this perverse and unthinking people; for they revolt not from the obedience to their Creator, but *continue to this day, according to his ordinances, as his servants* (Ps. 119:89–91), and therefore will rise up in judgment against rebellious Israel. Heaven and earth will be witnesses against sinners, witnesses of the warning given them and of their refusal to take the warning (see Job 20:27); the *heaven shall reveal his iniquity, and the earth shall rise up against him.* Or heaven and earth are here put for the inhabitants of both, angels and men; both shall agree to justify God in his proceedings against Israel, and to *declare his righteousness,* Ps. 50:6; see Rev. 19:1, 2. 2. he begins with a solemn application of what he was about to say to the people (*v.* 2): *My doctrine shall drop as the rain.* "It shall be a beating sweeping rain to the rebellious;" so one of the Chaldee paraphrasts expounds the first clause. Rain is sometimes sent for judgment, witness that with which the world was deluged; and so the word of God, while to some it is reviving and refreshing — a *savour of life unto life,* is to others terrifying and killing — a *savour of death unto death.* It shall be as a sweet and comfortable dew to those who are rightly prepared to receive it. Observe, (1.) The subject of this song is doctrine; he had given them a song of praise and thanksgiving (Ex. 15), but this is a song of instruction, for in psalms, and hymns, and spiritual songs, we are not only to give glory to god, but to *teach and admonish one another,* Col. 3:16. Hence many of David's psalms are entitled *Maschil — to give instruction.* (2.) This doctrine is fitly compared to rain and showers which come from above, to make the earth fruitful, and *accomplish that for which they are sent.* (Isa. 55:10, 11), and depend not upon the wisdom or will of man, Mic. 5:7. It is a mercy to have this rain come often upon us, and our duty to *drink it in,* Heb. 6:7. (3.) He promises that his doctrine shall drop and distil as the dew, and the small rain, which descend silently and without noise. The word preached is likely to profit when it comes gently, and sweetly insinuates itself into the hearts and affections of the hearers. (4.) He bespeaks their acceptance and entertainment of it, and that it might be as sweet, and pleasant, and welcome to them as rain to the *thirsty earth,* Ps. 72:6. And the word of God is likely to do us good when it is thus acceptable. (5.) The learned bishop Patrick understands it as a prayer that his words which were sent from heaven to them might sink into their hearts and soften them, as the rain softens the earth, and so make them fruitful in obedience.

II. An awful declaration of the greatness and righteousness of God, *v.* 3, 4.

1. He begins with this, and lays it down as his first principle, (1.) To preserve the honour of God, that no reproach might be cast upon him for the sake of the wickedness of his people Israel; how wicked and corrupt soever those are who are called by his name, he is just, and right, and all that is good, and is not to be thought the worse of for their badness. (2.) To aggravate the wickedness of Israel, who knew and worshipped such a holy god, and yet were themselves so unholy. And, (3.) To justify God in his dealings with them; we must abide by it, that God is righteous, even when his *judgments are a great deep,* Jer. 12:1; Ps. 36:6.

2. Moses here sets himself to *publish the name of the Lord* (*v.* 3), that Israel, knowing what a God he is whom they had avouched for theirs, might never be such fools as to exchange him for a false god, a dunghill god. He calls upon them therefore to ascribe greatness to him. It will be of great use to us for the preventing of sin, and the preserving of us in the way of our duty, always to keep up high and honourable thoughts of God, and to take all occasions to express them: *Ascribe greatness to our God.* We cannot add to his greatness, for it is infinite; but we must acknowledge it, and give him the glory of it. Now, when Moses would set forth the greatness of God, he does it, not by explaining his eternity and immensity, or describing the brightness of his glory in the upper world, but by showing the faithfulness of his word, the perfection of his works, and the wisdom and equity of all the administrations of his government; for in these his glory shines most clearly to us, and these are the things revealed concerning him, which *belong to us and our children, v.* 4. (1.) *He is the rock.* So he is called six times in this chapter, and the Septuagint all along translates it *theos, God.* The learned Mr. Hugh Broughton reckons that God is called the *rock* eighteen times (besides in this chapter) in the Old Testament (though in some places we translate it *strength),* and charges it therefore upon the papists that they make St. Peter a god when they make him the rock on which the church is built. God is the rock, for he is in himself immutable immovable, and he is to all that seek him and fly to him an impenetrable shelter, and to all that trust in him an everlasting foundation. (2.) *His work is perfect.* His work of creation was so, *all very good;* his works of providence are so, or will be so in due time, and when the mystery of God shall be finished the perfection of his works will appear to all the world. Nothing that God does can be mended, Eccl. 3:14. God was now perfecting what he had promised and begun for his people Israel, and from the perfection of this work they must take occasion to give him the glory of the perfection of all his works. The best of men's works are imperfect, they have their flaws and defects, and are left unfinished; but, *as for God, his work is perfect;* if he begin, he will make an end. (3.) *All his ways are judgment.* The ends of his ways are all righteous, and he is wise in the choice of the means in order to those ends. *Judgment* signifies both *prudence* and *justice. The ways of the Lord are right,* Hos. 14:9. (4.) He is *a God of truth,* whose word we may take and rely upon, for he cannot lie who is faithful to all his promises, nor shall his threatenings fall to the ground. (5.) He is *without iniquity,* one who never cheated any that trusted in him, never wronged any that appealed to his justice, nor ever was hard upon any that cast themselves upon his mercy. (6.) *Just and right is he.* As he will not wrong any by punishing them more than they deserve, so he will not fail to recompense all those that serve him or suffer for him. He is indeed just and right; for he will effectually take care that none shall lose by him. Now what a bright and amiable idea does this one verse give us of the God whom we worship; and what reason have we then to love him and fear him, to live a life of delight in him, dependence on him, and devotedness to him! This is *our rock, and there is no unrighteousness in him;* nor can there be, Ps. 92:15.

III. A high charge exhibited against the Israel of God, whose character was in all respects the reverse of that of the *God of Israel, v.* 5. 1. *They have corrupted themselves.* Or, *It has corrupted itself;* the body of the people has: *the whole head sick, and the whole heart faint.* God did not corrupt them, for *just and right is he;* but they are themselves the sole authors of their own sin and ruin; and both are included in this word. *They have debauched themselves;* for every man is tempted when he is drawn away of his own lust. And *they have destroyed themselves,* Hos. 13:9. If thou scornest, thou alone shalt bear the guilt and grief, Prov. 9:12. 2. *Their spot is not the spot of his children.* Even God's children have their spots, while they are in this imperfect state; for if we say we have no sin, no spot, we deceive ourselves. But the sin of Israel was none of those; it was not an infirmity which they strove against, watched and prayed against, but an evil which their hearts were fully set in them to do. For, 3. They were a *perverse and crooked generation,* that were actuated by a spirit of contradiction, and therefore would do what was forbidden because it was forbidden, would set up their own humour and fancy in opposition to the will of God, were impatient of reproof, hated to be reformed, and *went on frowardly in the way of their heart.* The Chaldee paraphrase reads this verse thus: *They have scattered* or changed *themselves, and not him, even the children that served idols, a generation that has depraved its own works, and alienated itself.* Idolaters cannot hurt God, nor do any damage to his works, nor make him a stranger to this world. See Job 35:6. No, all the hurt they do is to themselves and their own works. The learned bishop Patrick gives another reading of it: *Did he do him any hurt?* That is, "Is God the rock to be blamed for the evils that should befal Israel? No, *His children are their blot,"* that is, "All the evil that comes upon them is the fruit of their children's wickedness; for the whole generation of them is crooked and perverse." All that are ruined ruin themselves; they die because they will die.

IV. A pathetic expostulation with this provoking people for their ingratitude (*v.* 6): *"Do you thus requite the Lord?* Surely you will not hereafter be so base and disingenuous in your carriage towards him as you have been." 1. He reminds them of the obligations God had laid upon them to serve him, and to cleave to him. He had been a Father to them, had begotten them, fed them, carried them, nursed them, and borne their manners; and would they spurn at the bowels of a Father? He had bought them, had been at a vast expense of miracles to bring them out of Egypt, had given *men for them,* and *people for their life,* Isa. 43:4. *"Is not he thy Father, thy owner* (so some), that has an incontestable propriety in thee?" and *the ox knoweth his owner.* "he has made thee, and brought thee into being, established thee and kept thee in being; has he not done so? Can you deny the engagements you lie under to him, in consideration of the great things he has done and designed for you?" And are not our obligations, as baptized Christians, equally great and strong to our Creator that made us, our Redeemer that bought us, and our Sanctifier that has established us. 2. Hence he infers the evil of deserting him and rebelling against him. For, (1.) It was base ingratitude: *"Do you thus require the Lord?* Are these the returns you make him for all his favours to you? The powers you have from him will you employ them against him?" See Mic. 6:3, 4; Jn. 10:32. This is such monstrous villany as all the world will cry shame of: call a man ungrateful, and you can call him no worse. (2.) It was prodigious madness: *O foolish people and unwise!* Fools, and double fools! *who has bewitched you?* Gal. 3:1. "Fools indeed, to disoblige one on whom you have such a necessary dependence! To forsake your own mercies for lying vanities!" Note, All wilful sinners, especially sinners in Israel, are the most unwise and the most ungrateful people in the world.

Verses 7–14

Moses, having in general represented God to them as their great benefactor, whom they were bound in gratitude to observe and obey, in these verses gives particular instances of God's kindness to them and concern for them. 1. Some instances were ancient, and for proof of them he appeals to the records (*v.* 7): *Remember the days of old;* that is, "Keep in remembrance the history of those days, and of the wonderful providences of God concerning the old world, and concerning your ancestors Abraham, Isaac, and Jacob; you will find a constant series of mercies attending them, and how long since things were working towards that which has now come to pass." Note, The authentic histories of ancient times are of singular use, and especially the history of the church in its infancy, both the

Old-Testament and the New-Testament church. 2. Others were more modern, and for proof of them he appeals to their fathers and elders that were now alive and with them. Parents must diligently teach their children, not only the word of God, his laws (*ch.* 6:7), and the meaning of his ordinances (Ex. 12:26, 27), but his works also, and the methods of his providence. See Ps. 78:3, 4, 6, 7. And children should desire the knowledge of those things which will be of use to engage them to their duty and to direct them in it.

Three things are here enlarged upon as instances of God's kindness to his people Israel, and strong obligations upon them never to forsake him: —

I. The early designation of the land of Canaan for their inheritance; for herein it was a type and figure of our heavenly inheritance, that it was of old ordained and prepared in the divine counsels, *v.* 8. Observe,

1. When the earth was divided among the sons of men, in the days of Peleg, after the flood, and each family had its lot, in which it must settle, and by degrees grow up into a nation, then God had Israel in his thoughts and in his eye; for, designing this good land into which they were now going to be in due time an inheritance for them, he ordered that the posterity of Canaan, rather than any other of the families then in being, should be planted there in the mean time, to keep possession, as it were, till Israel was ready for it, because those families were under the curse of Noah, by which they were condemned to servitude and ruin (Gen. 9:25), and therefore would be the more justly, honourably, easily, and effectually, rooted out, when the fulness of time should come that Israel should take possession. Thus he set the bounds of that people with an eye to the designed number of the children of Israel, that they might have just as much as would serve their turn. And some observe that Canaan himself, and his eleven sons (Gen. 10:15, etc.), make up just the number of the twelve tribes of Israel. Note, (1.) The wisdom of God has appointed the bounds of men's habitation, and determined both the place and time of our living in the world, Acts 17:26. When he *gave the earth to the children of men* (Ps. 115:16), it was not that every man might catch as he could; no, he divides to nations their inheritance, and will have every one to know his own, and not to invade another's property. (2.) Infinite wisdom has a vast reach, and designs beforehand what is brought to pass long after. *Known unto God are all his works* from the beginning to the end (Acts 15:18), but they are not so to us, Eccl. 3:11. (3.) The great God, in governing the world, and ordering the affairs of states and kingdoms, has a special regard to his church and people, and consults their good in all. See 2 Chr. 16:9, and Isa. 45:4. The Canaanites thought they had as good and sure a title to their land as any of their neighbours had to theirs; but God intended that they should only be tenants, till the Israelites, their landlords, came. Thus God serves his own purposes of kindness to his people, by those that neither know him nor love him, *who mean not so, neither doth their heart think so,* Isa. 10:7; Mic. 4:12.

2. The reason given for the particular care God took for this people, so long before they were either born or thought of (as I may say), in our world, does yet more magnify the kindness, and make it obliging beyond expression (*v.* 9): *For the Lord's portion is his people.* All the world is his. He is owner and possessor of heaven and earth, but his church is his in a peculiar manner. It is his demesne, his vineyard, his garden enclosed. He has a particular delight in it: it is the beloved of his soul, in it he walks, he dwells, it is his rest for ever. He has a particular concern for it, keeps it as the apple of his eye. He has particular expectations from it, as a man has from his portion, has a much greater rent of honour, glory, and worship, from that distinguished remnant, than from all the world besides. That God should be his people's portion is easy to be accounted for, for he is their joy and felicity; but how they should be his portion, who neither needs them nor can be benefited by them, must be resolved into the wondrous condescensions of free grace. *Even so, Father, because it seemed good in thy eyes* so to call and to account them.

II. The forming of them into a people, that they might be fit to enter upon this inheritance, like an heir of age, at the time appointed of the Father. And herein also Canaan was a figure of the heavenly inheritance; for, as it was from eternity proposed and designed for all God's spiritual Israel, so they are, in time (and it is a work of time), fitted and made meet for it, Col. 1:12. The deliverance of Israel out of slavery, by the destruction of their oppressors, was attended with so many wonders obvious to sense, and had been so often spoken of, that it needed not to be mentioned in this song; but the gracious works God wrought upon them would be less taken notice of than the glorious works he had wrought for them, and therefore he chooses rather to advert to them. A great deal was done to model this people, to cast them into some shape, and to fit them for the great things designed for them in the land of promise; and it is here most elegantly described.

1. *He found him in a desert land, v.* 10. This refers, no doubt, to the wilderness through which God brought them to Canaan, and in which he took so much pains with them; it is called *the church in the wilderness,* Acts 7:38. There it was born, and nursed, and educated, that all might appear to be divine and from heaven, since they had there no communication with any part of this earth either for food or learning. But, because he is said to *find* them there, it seems designed also to represent both the bad state and the bad character of that people when God began first to appear for them. (1.) Their condition was forlorn. Egypt was to them a desert land, and a waste howling wilderness, for they were bond-slaves in it, and cried by reason of their oppression, and were perfectly bewildered and at a loss for relief; there God found them, and thence he fetched them. And, (2.) Their disposition was very unpromising. So ignorant were the generality of them in divine things, so stupid and unapt to receive the impressions of them, so peevish and humoursome, so froward and quarrelsome, and withal so strangely addicted to the idolatries of Egypt, that they might well be said to be found in a desert land; for one might as reasonably expect a crop of corn from a barren wilderness as any good fruit of service to God from a people of such a character. Those that are renewed and sanctified by grace should often remember what they were by nature.

2. *He led him about and instructed him.* When God had them in the wilderness he did not bring them directly to Canaan, but made them go a great way about, and so he instructed them; that is, (1.) by this means he took time to instruct them, and gave them commandments as they were able to receive them. Those whose business it is to instruct others must not expect it will be done of a sudden; learners must have time to learn. (2.) By this means he tried their faith, and patience, and dependence upon God, and inured them to the hardships of the wilderness, and so instructed them. Every stage had something in it that was instructive; even when he chastened them, he thereby *taught them out of his law.* It is said (Ps. 107:7) that he *led them forth by the right way;.* and yet here that he *led them about;* for God always leads his people the right way, however to us it may seem circuitous: so that the furthest way about proves, if not the nearest way, yet the best way home to Canaan. How God instructed them is explained long after (Neh. 9:13), *Thou gavest them right judgments and true laws, good statutes, and commandments;* and especially (*v.* 20), *Thou gavest them also thy good Spirit to instruct them;* and he instructs effectually. We may well imagine how unfit that people would have been for Canaan had they not first gone through the discipline of the wilderness.

3. *He kept him as the apple of his eye,* with all the care and tenderness that could be, from the malignant influences of an open sky and air, and all the perils of an inhospitable desert. The pillar of cloud and fire was both a guide and a guard to them.

4. He did that for them which the eagle does for her nest of young ones, *v.* 11, 12. The similitude was touched, Ex. 19:4, *I bore you on eagles' wings;* here it is enlarged upon. The eagle is observed to have a strong affection for her young, and to show it, not only as other creatures by protecting them and making provision for them, but by educating them and teaching them to fly. For this purpose she stirs them out of the nest where they lie dozing, flutters over them, to show them how they must use their wings, and then accustoms them to fly upon her wings till they have learnt to fly upon their own. This, by the way, is an example to parents to train up their children to business, and not to indulge them in idleness and the love of ease. God did thus by Israel; when they were in love with their slavery, and loth to leave it, God, by Moses, stirred them up to aspire after liberty, and many a time kept them from returning to the house of bondage. He carried them out of Egypt, led them into the wilderness, and now at length had led them through it. *The Lord alone did lead him,* he needed not any assistance, nor did he take any to be partner with him in the achievement, which was a good reason why they should serve the Lord only and no other, so much as in partnership, much less in rivalship with him. There was no strange god with him to contribute to Israel's salvation, and therefore there should be none to share in Israel's homage and adoration, Ps. 81:9.

III. The settling of them in a good land. This was done in part already, in the happy planting of the two tribes and a half, an earnest of what would speedily and certainly be done for the rest of the tribes. 1. They were blessed with glorious victories over their enemies (*v.* 13): *He made him ride on the high places of the earth,* that is, he brought him on with conquest, and brought him home with triumph. he rode over the high places or strong holds that were kept against him, sat in ease and honour upon the fruitful hills of Canaan. In Egypt they looked mean, and were so, in poverty and disgrace; but in Canaan they looked great, and were so, advanced and enriched; they rode in state, as a people whom the King of kings delighted to honour. 2. With great plenty of all good things. Not only the ordinary increase of the field, but, which was uncommon, *Honey out of the rock, and oil out of the flinty rock,* which may refer either, (1.) To their miraculous supply of fresh water out of the rock that followed them in the wilderness, which is called *honey and oil,* because the necessity they were reduced to made it as sweet and acceptable as honey and oil at another time. Or, (2.) To the great abundance of honey and oil they should find in Canaan, even in those parts that were least fertile. The rocks in Canaan should yield a better increase than the fields and meadows of other countries. Other productions of Canaan are mentioned, *v.* 14. Such abundance and such variety of wholesome food (and every thing the best in its kind) that every meal might be a feast if they pleased: excellent bread made of the best corn, here called the *kidneys of the wheat* (for a grain of wheat is not unlike a kidney), butter and milk in abundance, the flesh of cattle well fed, and for their drink, no worse than the *pure blood of the grape;* so indulgent a Father was God to them, and so kind a benefactor. Ainsworth makes the plenty of good things in Canaan to be a figure of the fruitfulness of Christ's kingdom, and the heavenly comforts of his word and Spirit: for the children of his kingdom he has butter and milk, the sincere milk of the word; and strong meat for strong men, with the wine that makes glad the heart.

Verses 15–18

We have here a description of the apostasy of Israel from God, which would shortly come to pass, and to which already they had a disposition. One would have thought that a people under so many obligations to their God, in duty, gratitude, and interest, would never have turned from him; but, alas! they *turned aside quickly.* Here are two great instances of their wickedness, and each of them amounted to an apostasy from God: —

I. Security and sensuality, pride and insolence, and the other common abuses of plenty and prosperity, *v.* 15. These people were called *Jeshurun — an upright people* (so some), *a seeing people,* so others: but they soon lost the reputation both of their knowledge and of their righteousness; for, being well-fed, 1. They *waxed fat,* and *grew thick,* that is, they indulged themselves in all manner of luxury and gratifications of their appetites, as if they had nothing to do but to *make provision for the flesh, to fulfil the lusts of it.* They *grew fat,* that is, they grew big and unwieldy, unmindful of business, and unfit for it; dull and stupid, careless and senseless; and this was the effect of their plenty. Thus *the prosperity of fools destroys them,* Prov. 1:32. Yet this was not the worst of it. 2. They *kicked;* they grew proud and insolent, and *lifted up the heel* even against God himself. If God rebuked them, either by his prophets or by his providence, they *kicked against the goad,* as an *untamed heifer,* or a *bullock unaccustomed to the yoke,* and in their rage persecuted the prophets, and flew in the face of providence itself. And thus he *forsook God that made him* (not paying due respect to his creator, nor answering the ends of his creation), and put an intolerable contempt upon *the rock of his salvation*, as if he were not indebted to him for any past favours, nor had any dependence upon him for the future. Those that make a god of themselves and a god of their bellies, in pride and wantonness, and cannot bear to be told of it, certainly thereby forsake God and show how lightly they esteem him.

II. Idolatry was the great instance of their apostasy, and which the former led them to, as it made them sick of their religion, self-willed, and fond of changes. Observe,

1. What sort of gods they chose and offered sacrifice to, when they forsook the God that made them, *v.* 16, 17. This aggravated their sin that those very services which they should have done to the true God they did, (1.) To *strange gods*, that could not pretend to have done them any kindness, or laid them under any obligation to them, gods that they had no knowledge of, nor could expect any benefit by, for they were strangers. Or they are called *strange gods*, because they were other than the one only true God, to whom they were betrothed and ought to have been faithful. (2.) To *new gods, that came newly up*; for even in religion, the antiquity of which is one of its honours, vain minds have strangely affected novelty, and, in contempt of the Ancient of days, have been fond of new gods. A new god! can there be a more monstrous absurdity? Would we find the right way to rest, we must ask for the *good old way*, Jer. 6:16. It was true their fathers had worshipped *other gods* (Jos. 24:2), and perhaps it had been some little excuse if the children had returned to them; but to serve *new gods whom their fathers feared not*, and to like them the better for being new, was to open a door to endless idolatries. (3.) They were such as were no gods at all, but mere counterfeits and pretenders; their names the invention of men's fancies, and their images the work of men's hands. Nay, (4.) They were devils. So far from being *gods, fathers* and *benefactors* to mankind, they really were *destroyers* (so the word signifies), such as aimed to do mischief. If there were any spirits or invisible powers that possessed their idol-temples and images, they were evil spirits and malignant powers, whom yet they did not need to worship for fear they should hurt them, as they say the Indians do; for those that faithfully worship God are out of the devil's reach: nay, the devil can destroy those only that sacrifice to him. How mad are idolaters, who forsake the *rock of salvation* to run themselves upon the *rock of perdition!*

2. What a great affront this was to Jehovah their God. (1.) It was justly interpreted a forgetting of him (*v.* 18): *Of the Rock that begat thee thou art unmindful.* Mindfulness of God would prevent sin, but, when the world is served and the flesh indulged, God is forgotten; and can any thing be more base and unworthy than to forget the God that is the author of our being, by whom we subsist, and in whom we live and move? And see what comes of it, Isa. 17:10,11, *Because thou hast forgotten the God of thy salvation, and hast not been mindful of the Rock of thy strength*, though the strange slips be pleasant plants at first, yet the harvest at last *will be a heap in the day of grief and of desperate sorrow.* There is nothing got by forgetting God. (2.) It was justly resented as an inexcusable offence: *They provoked him to jealousy and to anger* (*v.* 16), for their idols were abominations to him. See here God's displeasure against idols, whether they be set up in the heart or in the sanctuary. [1.] He is jealous of them, as rivals with him for the throne in the heart. [2.] He hates them, as enemies to his crown and government. [3.] He is, and will be, very angry with those that have any respect or affection for them. Those consider not what they do that provoke God; for *who knows the power of his anger?*

Verses 19–25

The method of this song follows the method of the predictions in the foregoing chapter, and therefore, after the revolt of Israel from God, described in the foregoing verses, here follow immediately the resolves of divine Justice concerning them; we deceive ourselves if we think that God will be thus mocked by a foolish faithless people, that play fast and loose with him.

I. He had delighted in them, but now he would reject them with detestation and disdain, *v.* 19. When the Lord saw their treachery, and folly, and base ingratitude, he abhorred them, he despised them, so some read it. Sin makes us odious in the sight of the holy God; and no sinners are so loathsome to him as those that he has called, and that have called themselves, his sons and his daughters, and yet have been provoking to him. Note, The nearer any are to God in profession the more noisome are they to him if they are defiled in a sinful way, Ps. 106:39, 40.

II. He had given them the tokens of his presence with them and his favour to them; but now he would withdraw and *hide his face from them, v.* 20. His *hiding his face* signifies his great displeasure; they had *turned their back* upon God, and now God would turn his back upon them (compare Jer. 18:17 with Jer. 2:27); but here it denotes also the slowness of God's proceedings against them in a way of judgment. They began in their apostasy with omissions of good, and so proceeded to commissions of evil. In like manner God will first suspend his favours, and let them see what the issue of that will be, what a friend they lose when they provoke God to depart, and will try whether this will bring them to repentance. Thus we find God hiding himself, as it were, in expectation of the event, Isa. 57:17. To justify himself in leaving them he shows that they were such as there was no dealing with; for, 1. They were froward and a people that could not be pleased, or obstinate in sin, and that could not be convinced and reclaimed. 2. They were faithless, and a people that could not be trusted. When he saved them, and took them into covenant, he said, *Surely they are children that will not lie* (Isa. 63:8); but when they proved otherwise, *children in whom is no faith*, they deserved to be abandoned, and that the God of truth should have no more to do with them.

III. He had done every thing to make them easy and to please them, but now he would do that against them which should be most vexatious to them. The punishment here answers the sin, *v.* 21. 1. They had provoked God with despicable deities which were not gods at all, but vanities, creatures of their own imagination, that could not pretend either to merit or to repay the respects of their worshippers; the more vain and vile the gods were after which they went a whoring the greater was the offence to that great and good God whom they set them up in competition with and contradiction to. This put two great evils into their idolatry, Jer. 2:13. 2. God would therefore plague them with despicable enemies, that were worthless, weak, and inconsiderable, and not deserving the name of a people, which was a great mortification to them, and aggravated the oppressions they groaned under The more base the people were that tyrannised over them the more barbarous they would be (none so insolent as a beggar on horseback), besides that it would be infamous to Israel, who had so often triumphed over great and mighty nations, to be themselves trampled upon by the weak and foolish, and to come under the curse of Canaan, who was to be a servant of servants. But God can make the weakest instrument a scourge to the strongest sinner; and those that by sin insult their might Creator are justly insulted by the meanest of their fellow-creatures. This was remarkably fulfilled in the days of the judges, when they were sometimes oppressed by the very Canaanites themselves, whom they had subdued, Jdg. 4:2. But the apostle applies it to the conversion of the Gentiles, who had been a people not in covenant with God, and foolish in divine things, yet were brought into the church, sorely to the grief of the Jews, who upon all occasions showed a great indignation at it, which was both their sin and their punishment, as envy always is, Rom. 10:19.

IV. He had planted them in a good land, and replenished them with all good things; but now he would strip them of all their comforts, and bring them to ruin. The judgments threatened are very terrible, *v.* 22–25. 1. The fire of God's anger shall consume them, *v.* 22. Are they proud of their plenty? It shall burn up the increase of the earth. Are they confident of their strength? It shall destroy the very foundations of their mountains: there is no fence against the judgments of God when they come with commission to lay all waste. It shall burn to the lowest hell, that is, it shall bring them to the very depth of misery in this world, which yet would be but a faint resemblance of the complete and endless misery of sinners in the other world. The damnation of hell (as our Saviour calls it) is the fire of God's anger, fastening upon the guilty conscience of a sinner, to its inexpressible and everlasting torment, Isa. 30:33. 2. The arrows of God's judgments shall be spent upon them, till his quiver is quite exhausted, *v.* 23. The judgments of God, like arrows, fly swiftly (Ps. 64:7), reaching those at a distance who flatter themselves with hopes of escaping them, Ps. 21:8, 12. They come from an unseen hand, but wound mortally, for God never misses his mark, 1 Ki. 22:34. The particular judgments here threatened are, (1.) Famine: *they shall be burnt*, or *parched, with hunger.* (2.) Pestilence and other diseases, here called *burning heat and bitter destruction.* (3.) The insults of the inferior creatures: *the teeth of beasts and the poison of serpents, v.* 24. (4.) War and the fatal consequences of it, *v.* 25. [1.] Perpetual frights. When the *sword is without*, there cannot but be *terror within.* 2 Co. 7:5, *Without were fightings, within were fears.* Those who cast off the fear of God are justly exposed to the fear of enemies. [2.] Universal deaths. The sword of the Lord, when it is sent to lay all waste, will destroy without distinction; neither the strength of the young man nor the beauty of the virgin, neither the innocency of the suckling nor the gravity or infirmity of the man of gray hairs, will be their security from the sword when it devours one as well as another. Such devastation does war make, especially when it is pushed on by men as ravenous as wild beasts and as venomous as serpents, *v.* 24. See here what mischief sin does, and reckon those fools that make a mock at it.

Verses 26–38

After many terrible threatenings of deserved wrath and vengeance, we have here surprising intimations of mercy, undeserved mercy, which rejoices against judgment, and by which it appears that God has *no pleasure in the death of sinners*, but would rather they should *turn and live.*

I. In jealousy for his own honour, he will not *make a full end* of them, *v.* 26–28. 1. It cannot be denied but that they deserved to be utterly ruined, and that their *remembrance should be made to cease from among men*, so that the name of an Israelite should never be known but in history; *for they were a nation void of counsel* (v, 28), the most sottish inconsiderate people that ever were, that would not believe the gory of God, though they saw it, nor understand his loving kindness, though they tasted it and lived upon it. Of those who could cast off such a God, such a law, such a covenant, for vain and dunghill-deities, it might truly be said, There is *no understanding in them.* 2. It would have been an easy thing with God to ruin them and blot out the remembrance of them; when the greatest part of them were cut off by the sword, it was but scattering the remnant into some remote obscure corners of the earth, where they should never have been heard of any more, and the thing had been done. See Eze. 5:12. God can destroy those that are most strongly fortified, disperse those that are most closely united, and bury those names in perpetual oblivion that have been most celebrated. 3. Justice demanded it: *I said I would scatter them.* It is fit those should be cut off from the earth that have cut themselves off from their God; why should they not be dealt with according to their deserts? 4. Wisdom considered the pride and insolence of the enemy, which would take occasion from the ruin of a people that had been so dear to God, and for whom he had done such great things, to reflect upon God and to imagine that because they had got the better of Israel they had carried the day against the God of Israel: The *adversaries will say, Our hand is high*, high indeed, when it has been too high for those whom God himself fought for; nor will they consider that *the Lord has done all this*, but will dream that they have done it in despite of him, as if the God of Israel were as weak and impotent, and as easily run down, as the pretended deities of other nations. 5. In consideration of this, Mercy prevails for the sparing of a remnant and the saving of that unworthy people from utter ruin: *I feared the wrath of the enemy.* It is an expression after the manner of men; it is certain that God fears no man's wrath, but he acted in this matter as if he had feared it. Those few good people in Israel that had a concern for the honour of God's name *feared the wrath of the enemy* in this instance more than in any other, as Joshua (Jos. 7:9), and David often; and, because they feared it, God himself is said to fear it. He needed not Moses to plead it with him, but reminded himself of it: *What will the Egyptians say?* Let all those whose hearts tremble for the ark of God and his Israel comfort themselves with this, that God will *work for his own name,* and will not suffer it to be profaned and polluted: how much soever we deserve to be disgraced, God will never *disgrace the throne of his glory.*

II. In concern for their welfare, he earnestly desires their conversion; and, in order to that, their serious consideration of their latter end, *v.* 29. Observe, 1. Though God had pronounced them a foolish people and of no understanding, yet he wishes they were wise, as Deu. 5:29, *O that there were such a heart in them!* and Ps. 94:8, *You fools, when will you be wise?* God delights not to see sinners ruin themselves, but desires they will help themselves; and, if they will, he is ready to help them. 2. It is a great piece of wisdom, and will contribute much to the return of sinners to God, seriously to consider the latter end, or the future state. It is here meant particularly of that which God by Moses had foretold concerning this people in the latter days: but it may be applied more generally. We ought to understand and consider, (1.) The latter end of life, and the future state of the soul. To think of death as our removal from a world of sense to a world of spirits, the final period of our state of trial and probation, and our entrance upon an unchangeable state of recompence and retribution. (2.) The latter end of sin, and the future state of those that live and die in it. O that men would consider the happiness they will lose, and the misery they will certainly plunge themselves into, if they *go on still in their trespasses, what will be in the end thereof,* Jer. 5:31. Jerusalem forgot this, and therefore *came down wonderfully,* Lam. 1:9.

III. He calls to mind the great things he had done for them formerly, as a reason why he should not quite cast them off. This seems to be the meaning of that (*v.* 30, 31), "How should one Israelite have been too hard for a thousand Canaanites, as they have been many a time, but that God, who is greater than all gods, fought for them!" And so it corresponds with that, Isa. 63:10, 11. When he was *turned to be their enemy,* as here, *and fought against them* for their sins, *then he remembered the days of old,* saying, *Where is he that brought them out of the sea?* So here, his arm begins to awake as in the days of old *against the wrath of the enemy,* Ps. 138:7. there was a time when the enemies of Israel were sold by their own rock, that is, their own idol-gods, who could not help them, but betrayed them, because Jehovah, the God of Israel, had shut them up as sheep for the slaughter. For the enemies themselves must own that their gods were a very unequal match for the God of Israel. *For their vine is of the vine of Sodom, v.* 32, 33. This must be meant of the enemies of Israel, who fell so easily before the sword of Israel because they were ripe for ruin, and the measure of their iniquity was full. Yet these verses may be understood of the strange prevalency of the enemies of Israel against them, when God made use of them as the *rod of his anger,* Isa. 10:5, 6. "How should one Canaanite chase a thousand Israelites" (as it is threatened against those that trust to Egypt for help, Isa. 30:17, *One thousand shall flee at the rebuke of one*) "unless Israel's rock had deserted them and given them up." For otherwise, however they may impute their power *to their gods* (Hab. 1:11), as the Philistines imputed their victory to Dagon, it is certain the enemies' rock could not have prevailed against the rock of Israel; God would soon have subdued their enemies (Ps. 81:14), but that the wickedness of Israel delivered them into their hands. For their vine, that is, Israel's, is of the *vine of Sodom, v.* 32, 33. They were planted a choice vine, wholly a right seed, but by sin had become the *degenerate plant of a strange vine* (Jer. 2:21), and not only transcribed the iniquity of Sodom, but outdid it, Eze. 16:48. God called them his *vineyard,* his *pleasant plant,* Isa. 5:7. But their fruits were, 1. Very offensive, and displeasing to God, bitter as gall. 2 Very malignant, and pernicious one to another, *like the cruel venom of asps.* Some understand this of their punishment; their sin would be *bitterness in the latter end* (2 Sa. 2:26), it would *bite like a serpent and sting like an adder,* Job 20:14, Prov. 23:32.

IV. He resolves upon the destruction of those at last that had been their persecutors and oppressors. When the cup of trembling goes round, the king of Babel shall pledge it at last, Jer. 25:26, and see Isa. 51:22, 23. The day is coming when the judgment that began at the house of God shall end with the sinner and ungodly, 1 Pt. 4:17, 18. God will in due time bring down the church's enemies.

1. In displeasure against their wickedness, which he takes notice of, and keeps an account of, *v.* 34, 35. "Is not this implacable fury of theirs against Israel *laid up in store with me,* to be reckoned for hereafter, when it shall be made to appear that *to me belongs vengeance?*" Some understand it of the sin of Israel, especially their persecuting the prophets, which was laid up in store against them from the *blood of righteous Abel,* Mt. 23:35. However it teaches us that the wickedness of the wicked is all laid up in store with God. (1.) He observes it, Ps. 90:8. He knows both what the vine is and what the grapes are, what is the temper of the mind and what are the actions of life. (21.) He keeps a record of it both in his own omniscience and in the sinner's conscience; and this is *sealed up among his treasures,* which denotes both safety and secresy: these books cannot be lost, nor will they be opened till the great day. See Hos. 13:12. (3.) He often delays the punishment of sin for a great while; it is laid up in store, till the measure be full, and the day of divine patience has expired. See Job 21:28–30. (4.) There is a day of reckoning coming, when all the treasures of guilt and wrath will be broken up, and the sin of sinners shall surely find them out. [1.] The thing itself will certainly be done, for the Lord is a *God to whom vengeance belongs,* and therefore he will repay, Isa. 59:18. This is quoted by the apostle to show the severity of God's wrath against those that revolt from the faith of Christ, Heb. 10:30. [2.] It will be done in due time, in the best time; nay, it will be done in a short time. *The day of their calamity is at hand;* and, though it may seem to tarry, it lingers not, it slumbers not, but makes haste. *In one hour,* shall the judgment of Babylon come.

2. He will do it in compassion to his own people, who, though they had greatly provoked him, yet stood in relation to him, and their misery appealed to his mercy (*v.* 36): *The Lord shall judge his people,.* that is, judge for them against their enemies, plead their cause, and break the yoke of oppression under which they had long groaned, *repenting himself for his servants;* not changing his mind, but changing his way, and fighting for them, as he had fought against them, *when he sees that their power is gone.* This plainly points at the deliverances God wrought for Israel by the judges out of the hands of those to whom he had sold them for their sins (see Jdg. 2:11–18), and how *his soul was grieved for the misery of Israel* (Jdg. 10:16), and this when they were reduced to the last extremity. God helped them when they could not help themselves; for there was *none shut up or left;* that is, none that dwelt either in cities or walled towns, in which they were shut up, nor any that dwelt in scattered houses in the country, in which they were left at a distance from neighbours. Note, God's time to appear for the deliverance of his people is when things are at the worst with them. God tries his people's faith, and stirs up prayer, by letting things go to the worst, and then magnifies his own power, and fills the faces of his enemies with shame and the hearts of his people with so much the greater joy, by rescuing them out of extremity as *brands out of the burning.*

3. He will do it in contempt and to the reproach of idol-gods, *v.* 37, 38. *Where are their gods?* Two ways it may be understood: (1.) That God would do that for his people which the idols they had served could not do for them. They had forsaken God, and been very liberal in their sacrifices to idols, had brought to their altars the *fat of their sacrifices* and the *wine of their drink-offerings,* which they supposed their deities to feed upon and on which they feasted with them. "Now," says God, "will these gods you have made your court to, at so great an expense, help you in your distress, and so repay you for all your charges in their service? *Go get you to the gods you have served, and let them deliver you,* Jdg. 10:14. This is intended to convince them of their folly in forsaking a God that could help them for gods that could not, and so to bring them to repentance and qualify them for deliverance. When the adulteress shall *follow after her lovers* and *not overtake them,* pray to her idols and receive no kindness from them, *then she shall say, I will go and return to my first husband,* Hos. 2:7. See Isa. 16:12; Jer. 2:27, 28. Or, (2.) That God would do that against his enemies which the idols they had served could not save them from, Sennacherib and Nebuchadnezzar boldly challenged the God of Israel to deliver his worshippers (Isa. 37:10; Dan. 3:15), and he did deliver them, to the confusion of their enemies. But the God of Israel challenged Bel and Nebo to deliver their worshippers, to rise up and help them, and to be their protection (Isa. 47:12, 13); but they were so far from helping them that they themselves, that is, their images, which was all that was of them, *went into captivity,* Isa. 46:1, 2. Note, Those who trust to any rock but God will find it sand in the day of their distress; it will fail them when they most need it.

Verses 39–43

This conclusion of the song speaks three things:

I. Glory to God, *v.* 39. "See now upon the whole matter, *that I, even I, am he.* Learn this from the destruction of idolaters, and the inability of their idols to help them." The great God here demands the glory, 1. Of a self-existence: *I, even I, am he.* Thus Moses concludes with that name of God by which he was first made to know him (Ex. 3:14), *"I am that I am.* I am he that I have been, that I will be, that I have promised to be, that I have threatened to be; all shall find me true to my word." The Targum of Uzzielides paraphrases it thus: *When the Word of the Lord shall reveal himself to redeem his people, he shall say to all people, See that I now am what I am, and have been, and I am what I will be,* which we know very well how to apply to him who said to John, *I am he who is, and was, and is to come,* Rev. 1:8. These words, *I even I, am he,* we meet with often in those chapters of Isaiah where God is encouraging his people to hope for their deliverance out of Babylon, Isa. 41:4; 43:11, 13, 25, 46:4. 2. Of a sole supremacy. "There *is no god with me.* None to help with me, none to cope with me." See Isa. 43:10, 11. 3. Of an absolute sovereignty, a universal agency: *I kill, and I make alive;* that is, all evil and all good come from his hand to providence; he forms both the light of life and the darkness of death, Isa. 45:7; Lam. 3:37, 38. Or, He kills and wounds his enemies, but heals and makes alive his own people, kills and wounds with his judgments those that revolt from him and rebel against him; but, when they return and repent, he heals them, and makes them alive with his mercy and grace. Or it denotes his incontestable authority to dispose of all his creatures, and the beings he has given them, so as to serve his own purposes by them: *Whom he will he slays, and whom he will he keeps alive,* when his judgments are abroad. Or thus, Though he kill, yet he makes alive again: *though he cause grief, yet will he have compassion,* Lam. 3:32. Though he have *torn,* he will *heal us,* Hos. 6:1, 2. The Jerusalem Targum reads it, *I kill those that are alive in this world, and make those alive in the other world that are dead.* And some of the Jewish doctors themselves have observed that death, and a life after it, that is, eternal life, is intimated in these words. 4. Of an irresistible power, which cannot be controlled: *Neither is there any that can deliver out of my hand* those that I have marked for destruction. As no exception can be made against the sentence of God's justice, so no escape can be made from the executions of his power.

II. Terror to his enemies, *v.* 40–42. Terror indeed to those that hate him, as all those do that serve other gods, that persist in wilful disobedience to the divine law, and that malign and persecute his faithful servants. These are those to whom God will render vengeance, those his enemies that will not have him to reign over them. In order to alarm such in time to repent and return to their allegiance, the wrath of God is here revealed from heaven against them. 1. The divine sentence is ratified with an oath (*v.* 40): He *lifts up his hand to heaven,* the habitation of his holiness; this was an ancient and very significant sign used in swearing, Gen. 14:22. And, since he could swear by no greater, he swears by himself and his own life. Those are miserable without remedy that have the word and oath of God against them. The Lord hath sworn, and will not repent, that the sin of sinners shall be their ruin if they go on in it. 2. Preparation is made for the execution: The *glittering sword is whet.* See Ps. 7:12. It is a sword *bathed in heaven,* Isa. 34:5. While the sword is in whetting, space is given to the sinner to repent and make his peace, which, if he neglects, will render the wound the deeper. And, as the sword is whet, so the hand that is to wield it takes hold on judgment with a resolution to go through with it. 3. The execution itself will be very terrible: The *sword shall devour flesh* in abundance, and the *arrows* be made *drunk with blood,* such vast quantities of it shall be shed, the blood of the slain in battle, and of the captives, to whom no quarter shall be given, but who shall be put under military execution. When he begins revenge he will make an end; for in this also his work is perfect. The critics are much perplexed with the last clause, *From the beginning of revenges upon the enemy.* The learned bishop Patrick (that great master) thinks it may admit this reading, *From the king to the slave of the enemies,* Jer. 50:35–37. When the sword of God's wrath is drawn it will make bloody work, blood to the horse-bridles, Rev. 14:20.

III. Comfort to his own people (*v.* 43): *Rejoice, O you nations, with his people.* He concludes the song with words of joy; for in God's Israel there is a remnant whose end will be peace. God's people will rejoice at last, will rejoice everlastingly. Three things are here mentioned as the matter of joy: — 1. The enlarging of the church's bounds. The apostle applies the first words of this verse to the conversion of the Gentiles. Rom. 15:10, *Rejoice you Gentiles with his people.* See what the grace of God does in the conversion of souls, it brings them to rejoice with the people of God; for true religion brings us acquainted with true joy, so great a mistake are those under that think it tends to make men melancholy. 2. The avenging of the church's controversies upon her adversaries. He will make inquisition for *the blood of his servants,* and it shall appear how precious it is to him; for those that spilt it shall have blood given them to drink. 3. The mercy God has in store for his church, and for all that belong to it: He will be *merciful to his land, and to his people,* that is, to all every where that fear and serve him. Whatever judgments are brought upon sinners, it shall go well with the people of God; in this let Jews and Gentiles rejoice together.

Verses 44–52

Here is, I. The solemn delivery of this song to the children of Israel, *v.* 44, 45. Moses spoke it to as many as could hear him, while Joshua, in another assembly, at the same time, delivered it to as many as his voice would reach. Thus coming to them from the mouth of both their governors, Moses who was laying down the government, and Joshua who was taking it up, they would see they were both in the same mind, and that, though they changed their commander, there was no change in the divine command; Joshua, as well as Moses, would be a witness against them if ever they forsook God.

II. An earnest charge to them to mind these and all the rest of the good words that Moses had said to them. How earnestly does he long after them all, how very desirous that the word of God might make deep and lasting impressions upon them, how jealous over them with a godly jealousy, lest they should at any time let slip these great things!

1. The duties he charges upon them are, (1.) Carefully to attend to these themselves: "Set your hearts both to the laws, and to the promises and threatenings, the blessings and curses, and now at last to this song. Let the mind be closely applied to the consideration of these things; be affected with them; be intent upon your duty, and cleave to it with full purpose of heart." (2.) Faithfully to transmit these things to those that should come after them: "What interest you have in your children, or influence upon them, use it for this purpose; and *command them* (as your father Abraham did, Gen. 18:19) *to observe to do all the words of this law.*" Those that are good themselves cannot but desire that their children may be so likewise, and that posterity may keep up religion in their day and the entail of it may not be cut off.

2. The arguments he uses to persuade them to make religion their business and to persevere in it are, (1.) The vast importance of the things themselves which he had charged upon them (*v.* 47): *"It is not a vain thing, because it is your life.* It is not an indifferent thing, but of absolute necessity; it is not a trifle, but a matter of consequence, a matter of life and death; mind it, and you are made for ever; neglect it, and you are for ever undone." O that men were but fully persuaded of this, that religion is their life, even the life of their souls! (2.) The vast advantage it would be of to them: *Through this thing you shall prolong your days* in Canaan, which is a typical promise of that eternal life which Christ has assured us those shall enter into that keep the commandments of God, Mt. 19:17.

III. Orders given to Moses concerning his death. Now that this renowned witness for God had finished his testimony, he must go up to Mount Nebo and die; in the prophecy of Christ's two witnesses there is a plain allusion to Moses and Elias (Rev. 11:6), and perhaps their removal, being by martyrdom, is no less glorious than the removal either of Moses or Elias. Orders were given to Moses that self-same day, *v.* 48. Now that he had done his work, why should he desire to live a day longer? He had indeed formerly prayed that he might go over Jordan, but now he is entirely satisfied, and, as God had bidden him, *saith no more of that matter.* 1. God here reminds him of the sin he had been guilty of, for which he was excluded Canaan (*v.* 51), that he might the more patiently bear the rebuke because he had sinned, and that now he might renew his sorrow for that unadvised word, for it is good for the best of men to die repenting of the infirmities they are conscious to themselves of. It was an omission that was thus displeasing to God; he did *not sanctify God,* as he ought to have done, *before the children of Israel,* he did not carry himself with a due decorum in executing the orders he had then received. 2. He reminds him of the death of his brother Aaron (*v.* 50), to make his own the more familiar and the less formidable. Note, It is a great encouragement to us, when we die, to think of our friends that have gone before us through that darksome valley, especially of Christ, our elder brother and great high priest. 3. He sends him up to a high hill, thence to take a view of the land of Canaan and then die, *v.* 49, 50. The remembrance of his sin might make death terrible, but the sight God gave him of Canaan took off the terror of it, as it was a token of God's being reconciled to him, and a plain indication to him that though his sin shut him out of the earthly Canaan, yet it should not deprive him of that better country which in this world can only be seen, and that with an eye of faith. Note, Those may die with comfort and ease whenever God calls for them (notwithstanding the sins they remember against themselves) who have a believing prospect and a well-grounded hope of eternal life beyond death.

CHAPTER 33

Yet Moses has not done with the children of Israel; he seemed to have taken final leave of them in the close of the foregoing chapter, but still he has something more to say. He had preached them a farewell sermon, a very copious and pathetic discourse. After sermon he had given out a psalm, a long psalm; and now nothing remains but to dismiss them with a blessing; that blessing he pronounces in this chapter in the name of the Lord, and so leaves them. I. He pronounces them all blessed in what God had done for them already, especially in giving them his law (*v.* 2–5). II. He pronounces a blessing upon each tribe, which is both a prayer for and a prophecy of their felicity. 1. Reuben (*v.* 6). 2. Judah (*v.* 7). 3. Levi (*v.* 8–11). 4. Benjamin (*v.* 42). 5. Joseph (*v.* 13–17). 6. Zebulun and Issachar (*v.* 18, 19). 7. Gad (*v.* 20, 21). 8. Dan (*v.* 22). 9. Naphtali (*v.* 23). 10. Asher (*v.* 24, 25). III. He pronounces them all in general blessed upon the account of what God would be to them, and do for them if they were obedient (*v.* 26, etc.).

Verses 1–5

The first verse is the title of the chapter: it is a blessing. In the foregoing chapter he had thundered out the terrors of the Lord against Israel for their sin; it was a chapter like Ezekiel's roll, full of lamentation, and mourning, and woe. Now to soften that, and that he might not seem to part in anger, he here subjoins a blessing, and leaves his peace, which should descend and rest upon all those among them that were the sons of peace. Thus Christ's last work on earth was to bless his disciples (Lu. 24:50), like Moses here, in token of parting as friends. Moses blessed them, 1. As a prophet — a *man of God.* Note, It is a very desirable thing to have an interest in the prayers of those that have an interest in heaven; it is a *prophet's reward.* In this blessing Moses not only expresses his good wishes to this people, but by the spirit of prophecy foretels things to come concerning them. 2. As a parent to Israel; for so good princes are to their subjects. Jacob upon his death-bed blessed his sons (Gen. 49:1), in conformity to whose example Moses here blesses the tribes that were descended from them, to show that though they had been very provoking yet the entail of the blessing was not cut off. The doing of this immediately before his death would not only be the more likely to leave an impression upon them, but would be an indication of the great good-will of Moses to them, that he desired their happiness, though he must die and not share in it.

He begins his blessing with a lofty description of the glorious appearances of God to them in giving them the law, and the great advantage they had by it.

I. There was a visible and illustrious discovery of the divine majesty, enough to convince and for ever silence atheists and infidels, to awaken and affect those that were most stupid and careless, and to put to shame all secret inclinations to other gods, *v.* 2. 1. His appearance was glorious: he shone forth like the sun when he goes forth in his strength. Even Seir and Paran, two mountains at some distance, were illuminated by the divine glory which appeared on Mount Sinai, and reflected some of the rays of it, so bright was the appearance, and so much taken notice of by the adjacent countries. To this the prophet alludes, to set forth the wonders of the divine providence, Hab. 3:3, 4; Ps. 18:7–9. The Jerusalem Targum has a strange gloss upon this, that, "when God came down to give the law, he offered it on Mount Seir to the Edomites, but they refused it, because they found in it, *Thou shalt not kill.* Then he offered it on Mount Paran to the Ishmaelites, but they also refused it, because they found in it, *Thou shalt not steal;* and then he came to Mount Sinai and offered it to Israel, and they said, *All that the Lord shall say we will do.*" I would not have transcribed so groundless a conceit but for the antiquity of it. 2. His retinue was glorious; he came with his holy myriads, as Enoch had long since foretold he should come in the last day to judge the world, Jude 14. These were the angels, those *chariots of God in the midst of which* the Lord was, on *that holy place,* Ps. 68:17. They attended the divine majesty, and were employed as his ministers in the solemnities of the day. Hence the law is said to *be given by the disposition of angels,* Acts 7:53; Heb. 2:2.

II. He gave them his law, which is, 1. Called *a fiery law,* because it was given them *out of the midst of the fire* (Deu. 4:33), and because it works like fire; if it be received, it is melting, warming, purifying, and burns up the dross of corruption; if it be rejected, it hardens, sears, torments, and destroys. The Spirit descended in cloven tongues as of fire; for the gospel also is a fiery law. 2. It is said to *go from his right hand,* either because he wrote it on tables of stone, or to denote the power and energy of the law and the divine strength that goes along with it, that it may not return void. Or it came as a gift to them, and a precious gift it was, a right-hand blessing. 3. It was an instance of the special kindness he had for them: *Yea, he loved the people* (*v.* 32), and therefore, though it was a fiery law, yet it is said to *go for them* (*v.* 2), that is, in favour to them. Note, The law of God written in the heart is a certain evidence of the love of God shed abroad there: we must reckon God's law one of the gifts of his grace. Yea, he embraced the people, or *laid them in his bosom;* so the word signifies, which denotes not only the dearest love, but the most tender and careful protection. *All his saints are in his hand.* Some understand it particularly of his supporting them and preserving them alive at Mount Sinai, when the terror was so great that Moses himself quaked; they heard the voice of God and lived, *ch.* 4:33. Or it denotes his forming them into a people by his law; he moulded and fashioned them as a potter does the clay. Or they were in his hand to be covered and protected, used and disposed of, as the seven stars were in the hand of Christ, Rev. 1:16. Note, God has all his saints in his hand; and, though there are *ten thousands of his saints* (*v.* 2), yet his hand, with which he measures the waters, is large enough, and strong enough, to hold them all, and we may be sure that *none can pluck them out of his hand,* Jn. 10:28.

III. He disposed them to receive the law which he gave them: *They sat down at thy feet,* as scholars at the feet of their master, in token of reverence, in attendance and humble submission to what is taught; so Israel sat at the foot of Mount Sinai, and promised to hear and do whatever God should say. They were *struck to thy feet,* so some read it; namely, by the terrors of Mount Sinai, which greatly humbled them for the present, Ex. 20:19. Every one then stood ready to receive God's words, and did so again when the law was publicly read to them, as Jos. 8:34. It is a great privilege when we have heard the words of God to have opportunity of hearing them again. Jn. 17:26, *I have declared thy name, and will declare it.* So Israel not only had received the law, but should still receive it by their prayers, and other lively oracles. The people are taught (*v.* 4, 5), in gratitude for the law of God, always to keep up an honourable remembrance both of the law itself and of Moses by whom it was given. Two of the Chaldee paraphrasts read it, *The children of Israel said, Moses commanded us a law.* And the Jews say that as soon as a child was able to speak his father was obliged to teach him these words: *Moses commanded us a law, even the inheritance of the congregation of Jacob.*

1. They are taught to speak with great respect of the law, and to call it *the inheritance of the congregation of Jacob.* They looked upon it, (1.) As peculiar to them, and that by which they were distinguished from other nations, who neither had the knowledge of it (Ps. 147:20), nor, if they had, were under those obligations to observe it that Israel were under: and therefore (says bishop Patrick), "when the Jews conquered any country, they did not force any to embrace the law of Moses, but only to submit to the seven precepts of Noah." (2.) As entailed upon them; for so inheritances are to be transmitted to their posterity. And, (3.) As their wealth and true treasure. Those that enjoy the word of God and the means of grace have reason to say, We have a goodly heritage. He is indeed a rich man in whom the word of Christ dwells richly. Perhaps the law is called their *inheritance* because it was given them with their inheritance, and we so annexed to it that the forsaking of the law would be a forfeiture of the inheritance. See Ps. 119:111.

2. They are taught to speak with great respect of Moses; and they were the more obliged to keep up his name because he had not provided for the keeping of it up in his family; his posterity were never called the *sons of Moses,* as the priests were the *sons of Aaron.* (1.) They must own Moses a great benefactor to their nation, in that he *commanded them the law;* for, though it came from the hand of God, it went through the hand of Moses. (2.,) *He was king in Jeshurun. Having commanded them the law,* as long as he lived he took care to see it observed and put in execution; and they were very happy in having such a king, who ruled them, and went in and out before them at all times, but did in a special manner look great when the *heads of the people were gathered together* in parliament, as it were, and Moses was president among them. Some understand this of God himself; he did then declare himself their King when he gave them the law, and he continued so long as they were *Jeshurun,* an upright people, and till they rejected him, 1 Sa. 12:12. But it seems rather to be understood of Moses. A good government is a great blessing to any people, and what they have reason to be very thankful for; and that constitution is very happy which as Israel's, which as ours, divides the power between the king in Jeshurun and the heads of the tribes, when they are gathered together.

Verses 6–7

Here is, I. The blessing of Reuben. Though Reuben had lost the honour of his birthright, yet Moses begins with him; for we should not insult over those that are disgraced, nor desire to perpetuate marks of infamy upon any, though ever so justly fastened at first, *v.* 6. Moses desires and foretels, 1. The preserving of this tribe. Though a frontier tribe on the other side Jordan, yet, *"Let it live,* and not be either ruined by its neighbours or lost among them." And perhaps he refers to those chosen men of that tribe who, having had their lot assigned them already, left their families in it, and were now ready to *go over armed before their brethren,* Num. 32:27. "Let them be protected in this noble expedition, and have their heads covered in the day of battle." 2. Let it be a numerous tribe; though their other honours be lost, so that they shall not excel, yet let them multiply." *Let Reuben live and not die, though his men be few;* so bishop Patrick, thinks it may be rendered. "Though he must not expect to flourish (Gen. 49:4), yet let him not perish." All the Chaldee paraphrasts refer this to the other world: *Let Reuben live in life eternal, and not die the second death,* so Onkelos. *Let Reuben live in this world, and not die that death which the wicked die in the world to come,* so Jonathan and the Jerusalem Targum.

II. The blessing of Judah, which is put before Levi because our *Loud sprang out of Judah,* and (as Dr. Lightfoot says) because of the dignity of the kingdom above the priesthood. The blessing (*v.* 7) may refer either, 1. To the whole tribe in general. Moses prays for, and prophesies, the great prosperity of that tribe., That God would hear his prayers (see an instance, 2 Chr. 13:14, 15), settle him in his lot, prosper him in all his affairs, and give him victory over his enemies. It is taken for granted that the tribe of Judah would be both a praying tribe and an active tribe. "Lord," says Moses, "hear his prayers, and give success to all his undertakings: *let his hands be sufficient for him* both in husbandry and in war." The voice of prayer should always be attended with the hand of endeavour, and then we may expect prosperity. Or, 2. It may refer in particular to David, as a type of Christ, that God *would hear his prayers,* Ps. 20:1 (and Christ was *heard always,* Jn. 11:42), that he would give him victory over his enemies, and success in his great undertakings. See Ps. 89:20 etc. And that prayer that God would *bring him to his people* seems to refer to Jacob's prophecy concerning Shiloh, That *to him should the gathering of the people be,* Gen. 49:10. The tribe of Simeon is omitted in the blessing, because Jacob had left it under a brand, and it had never done any thing, as Levi had done, to retrieve its honour. It was lessened in the wilderness more than any other of the tribes; and Zimri, who was so notoriously guilty in the matter of Peor but the other day, was of that tribe. Or, because the lot of Simeon was an appendage to that of Judah, that tribe is included in the blessing of Judah. Some copies of the Septuagint join Simeon with Reuben: *Let Reuben live and not die; and let Simeon be many in number.*

Verses 8–11

In blessing the tribe of Levi, Moses expresses himself more at large, not so much because it was his own tribe (for he takes no notice of his relation to it) as because it was God's tribe. The blessing of Levi has reference.

I. To the high priest, here called God's *holy one* (*v.* 8), because his office was holy, in token of which, *Holiness to the Lord* was written upon his forehead. 1. He seems to acknowledge that God might justly have displaced Aaron and his seed, for his sin at Meribah, (Ex. 17:7), which might be very remarkable, and which God might have an eye to in conferring the priesthood upon him, though no mention is made of it there. All the Chaldee paraphrasts agree that it was a trial in which he was *found perfect and faithful,* and *stood in the trial;* therefore not that, Num. 20:2. He prays that the office of the high priest might ever remain: *Let thy thummim and thy urim be with him.* It was given him for some eminent piece of service, as appears, Mal. 2:5. "Lord, let it never be taken from him." Notwithstanding this blessing, the urim and thummim were lost in the captivity, and never restored under the second temple. But this prayer has its full accomplishment in Jesus Christ, God's Holy One, and our great high priest, of whom Aaron was a type: with him who had lain in the Father's bosom from eternity the urim and thummim shall remain; for he is the wonderful and everlasting counsellor. Some translate the thummim and urim appellatively, the rather because the usual order is here inverted, and here only. *Thummim* signifies *integrity,* and *Urim illumination:* Let these be with thy holy one, that is, "Lord, let the high priest ever be both an upright man and an understanding man." A good prayer to be put up for the ministers of the gospel, that they may have clear heads and honest hearts; light and sincerity make a complete minister.

II. To the inferior priests and Levites, *v.* 9–11.

1. He commends the zeal of this tribe for God when they sided with Moses (and so with God) against the worshippers of the golden calf (Ex. 32:26 etc.), and, being employed in cutting off the ring-leaders in that wickedness, they did it impartially: the best friends they had in the world, though as dear to them as their next relations, they did not spare if they were idolaters. Note, Our regard to God and to his glory ought always to prevail above our regard to any creature whatsoever. And those who not only keep themselves pure from the common iniquities of the times and places in which they live, but, as they are capable, bear testimony against them, and *stand up for God against the evil-doers,* shall have special marks of honour put upon them. Perhaps Moses may have an eye to the sons of Korah, who refused to join with their father in his gain-saying, Num. 26:11. Also to Phinebas, who *executed judgment,* and *stayed the plague.* And indeed the office of the priests and Levites, which engaged their constant attendance, at least in their turns, at God's altar, laid them under a necessity of being frequently absent from their families, which they could not take such care of, nor make such provision for, as other Israelites might. This was the constant self-denial they submitted to, that they might *observe God's word,* and keep the *covenant of priesthood.* Note, Those that are called to minister in holy things must sit loose to the relations and interests that are dearest to them in this world, and prefer the gratifying of the best friend they have, Acts 21:13; 20:24. Our Lord Jesus knew not his mother and his brethren when they would have taken him off from his work, Mt. 12:48.

2. He confirms the commission granted to this tribe to minister in holy things, which was the recompence of their zeal and fidelity, *v.* 10. (1.) They were to deal for God with the people: *"They shall teach Jacob thy judgments and Israel thy laws,* both as preachers in thy religious assemblies, reading and expounding the law (Neh. 8:7, 8), and as judges, determining doubtful and difficult cases that were brought before them," 2 Chr. 17:8, 9. The priests' lips kept this knowledge for the use of the people, who were to ask the law at their mouth, Mal. 2:7. Even Haggai, a prophet, consulted the priests in a case of conscience, Hag. 2:11, etc. Note, Preaching is necessary, not only for the first planting of churches, but for the preserving and edifying of churches when they are planted. See Eze. 44:23, 24. (2.) They were to deal for the people with God, in burning incense to the praise and glory of God, and offering sacrifices to make atonement for sin and to obtain the divine favour. This was the work of the priests, but the Levites attended and assisted in it. Those that would have benefit by their incense and offerings must diligently and faithfully observe their instructions.

3. He prays for them, *v.* 11. (1.) That God would prosper them in their estates, and make that which was allotted them for their maintenance comfortable to them. *Bless, Lord, his substance.* The provision made for them was very plentiful, and came to them easily, and yet they could have no joy of it unless God blessed it to them; and, since God himself was their portion, a particular blessing might be expected to attend this portion. *Bless, Lord, his virtue;* so some read it. "Lord, increase thy graces in them, and make them more and more fit for their work." (2.) That he would accept them in their services: *"Accept the work of his hands,* both for himself and for the people for whom he ministers." Acceptance with God is that which we should all aim at, and be ambitious of, in all our devotions, whether men accept us or no (2 Co. 5:9), and it is the most valuable blessing we can desire either for ourselves or others. (3.) That he would take his part against all his enemies: *Smite through the loins of those that rise against him.* He supposes that God's ministers would have many enemies: some would hate their persons for their faithfulness, and would endeavour to do them a mischief; others would envy them their maintenance, and endeavour sacrilegiously to deprive them of it; others would oppose them in the execution of their office and not submit to the sentence of the priests; and some would aim to overthrow the office itself. Now he prays that God would blast all such attempts, and return the mischief upon the heads of the authors. This prayer is a prophecy that God will certainly reckon with those that are enemies to his ministers, and will keep up a ministry in his church to the end of time, in spite of all the designs of the gates of hell against it. Saul rose up against the Lord's priests (1 Sa. 22:18), and this filled the measure of his sin.

Verses 12–17

Here is, I. The blessing of Benjamin, *v.* 12. Benjamin is put next to Levi, because the temple, where the priests' work lay, was just upon the edge of the lot of this tribe; and it is put before Joseph because of the dignity of Jerusalem (part of which was in this tribe) above Samaria, which was in the tribe of Ephraim, and because Benjamin adhered to the house of David, and to the temple of the Lord, when the rest of the tribes deserted both with Jeroboam. 1. Benjamin is here called the *beloved of the Lord,* and the father of this tribe was Jacob's beloved son, the *son of his right hand.* Note, Those are blessed indeed that are beloved of the Lord. Saul the first king, and Paul the great apostle, were both of this tribe. 2. He is here assured of the divine protection: he shall *dwell safely.* Note, Those are safe whom God loves, Ps. 91:1. 3. It is here intimated that the temple in which God would dwell should be built in the borders of this tribe. Jerusalem the holy city was in the lot of this tribe (Jos. 18:28); and though Zion, the city of David, is supposed to belong to Judah, yet Mount Moriah, on which the temple was built, was in Benjamin's lot. God is *therefore* said to dwell *between his shoulders,* because the temple stood on that mount, as the head of a man upon his shoulders. And by this means Benjamin was covered all the day long under the protection of the sanctuary (Ps. 125:2), which is often spoken of as a place of refuge, Ps. 27:4, 5; Neh. 6:10. Benjamin, dwelling by the temple of God, *dwelt in safety by him.* Note, It is a happy thing to be in the neighbourhood of the temple. This situation of Benjamin, it is likely, was the only thing that kept that tribe in adherence with Judah to the divine institutions, when the other ten tribes apostatized. Those have corrupt and wicked hearts indeed who, the nearer they are to the church, are so much the further from God.

II. The blessing of Joseph, including both Manasseh and Ephraim. In Jacob's blessing (Gen. 49) that of Joseph is the largest, and so it is here; and thence Moses here borrows the title he gives to Joseph (*v.* 16), that he was *separated from his brethren,* or, as it might be read, *a Nazarite among them,* both in regard of his piety, wherein it appears, by many instances, he excelled them all, and of his dignity in Egypt, where he was both their ruler and benefactor. His brethren separated him from them by making him a slave, but God distinguished him from them by making him a prince. Now the blessings here prayed for, and prophesied of, for this tribe, are great plenty and great power.

1. Great plenty, *v.* 13–16. In general: *Blessed of the Lord be his land.* Those were very fruitful countries that fell into the lot of Ephraim and Manasseh, yet Moses prays they might be watered with the blessing of God, which makes rich, and on which all fruitfulness depends. Now,

(1.) He enumerates many particulars which he prays may contribute to the wealth and abundance of those two tribes, looking up to the Creator for the benefit and serviceableness of all the inferior creatures, for they are all that to us which he makes them to be. He prays, [1.] For seasonable rains and dews, *the precious things of heaven;* and so precious they are, though but pure water, that without them the fruits of the earth would all fail and be cut off. [2.] For plentiful springs, which help to make the earth fruitful, called here *the deep that coucheth beneath;* both are the *rivers of God* (Ps. 65:9), and he made particularly the *fountains of waters,* Rev. 14:7. [3.] For the benign influences of the heavenly bodies (*v.* 14), *for the precious fruits* (the word signifies that which is most excellent, and the best in its kind) put forth by the quickening heat of the sun, and the cooling moisture of the moon. "Let them have the yearly fruits in their several months, according to the course of nature, in one month olives, in another dates," etc. So some understand it. [4.] For the fruitfulness even of their hills and mountains, which in other countries used to be barren (*v.* 15): Let them have *the chief things of the ancient mountains;* and, if the mountains be fruitful, the fruits on them will be first and best ripened. They are called ancient mountains, not because prior in time to other mountains, but because , like the first-born, they were superior in worth and excellency; and lasting hills, not only because as other mountains they were immovable (Hab. 3:6), but because the fruitfulness of them should continue. [5.] For the productions of the lower grounds (*v.* 16): *For the precious things of the earth.* Though the earth itself seems a useless worthless lump of matter, yet there are precious things produced out of it, for the support and comfort of human life. Job 28:5. *Out of it cometh bread,* because out of it came our bodies, and to it they must return. But what are the *precious things of the earth* to a soul that came from God and must return to him? Or what is its fulness to the fulness that is in Christ, whence we receive grace for grace? Some make these precious things here prayed for to be figures of *spiritual blessings in heavenly things by Christ,* the gifts, graces, and comforts of the Spirit.

(2.) He crowns all with the good-will, or favourable acceptance, of him that *dwelt in the bush* (*v.* 16), that is, of God, that God who appeared to Moses in the bush that burned and was not consumed (Ex. 3:2), to give him his commission for the bringing of Israel out of Egypt. Though God's glory appeared there but for a while, yet it is said to dwell there, because it continued as long as there was occasion for it: *the good-will of the shechinah in the bush;* so it might be read, for *shechinah* signifies *that which dwelleth;* and, though it was but a little while a dweller in the bush, yet it continued to dwell with the people of Israel. *My dweller in the bush;* so it should be rendered; that was an appearance of the divine Majesty to Moses only, in token of the particular interest he had in God, which he desires to improve for the good of this tribe. Many a time God has appeared to Moses, but now that he is just dying he seems to have the most pleasing remembrance of that which was the first time, when his acquaintance with the visions of the Almighty first began, and his correspondence with heaven was first settled: that was a time of love never to be forgotten. It was at the bush that God declared himself *the God of Abraham, Isaac, and Jacob,* and so confirmed the promise made to the fathers, that promise which reached as far as the resurrection of the body and eternal life, as appears by our Saviour's argument from it, Lu. 20:37. So that, when he prays for the good-will of him that *dwelt in the bush,* he has an eye to the covenant then and there renewed, on which all our hopes of God's favour must be bottomed. Now he concludes this large blessing with a prayer for the favour or good-will of God, [1.] Because that is the fountain and spring-head of all these blessings; they are gifts of God's good-will; they are so to his own people, whatever they are to others. Indeed when Ephraim (a descendant from Joseph) slid back from God, *as a backsliding heifer,* those fruits of his country were so far from being the gifts of God's good-will that they were intended but to fatten him for the slaughter, *as a lamb in a large place,* Hos. 4:16, 17. [2.] Because that is the comfort and sweetness of all these blessings; then we have joy of them when we taste God's good-will in them. [3.] Because that is better than all these, infinitely better; for if we have but the favour and good-will of God we are happy, and may be easy in the want of all these things, and may rejoice in the God of our salvation *though the fig-tree do not blossom, and there be no fruit in the vine,* Hab. 3:17, 18.

2. Great power Joseph is here blessed with, *v.* 17. Here are three instances of his power foretold: (1.) His authority among his brethren: *His glory is like the firstling of his bullock,* or young bull, which is a stately creature, and therefore was formerly used as an emblem of royal majesty. Joshua, who was to succeed Moses, was of the tribe of Ephraim the son of Joseph, and his glory was indeed illustrious, and he was an honour to his tribe. In Ephraim was the royal city of the ten tribes afterwards. And of Manasseh were Gideon, Jephthah, and Jair, who were all ornaments and blessings to their country. Some think he is compared to the firstling of the bullock because the birthright which Reuben lost devolved upon Joseph (1 Chr. 5:1, 2), and to the firstling of *his* bullock, because Bashan, which was in the lot of Manasseh, was famous for bulls and cows, Ps. 22:12; Amos 4:1. (2.) His force against his enemies and victory over them: *His horns are like the horn of a unicorn,* that is, "The forces he shall bring into the field shall be very strong and formidable, and *with them he shall push the people,*" that is, "He shall overcome all that stand in his way." It appears from the Ephraimites' contests, both with Gideon (Jdg. 8:1) and with Jephthah (Jdg. 12:1), that they were a warlike tribe and fierce. Yet we find the children of Ephraim, when they had forsaken the covenant of God, though they were *armed, turning back in the day of battle* (Ps. 78:9, 10); for, though here pronounced *strong and bold as unicorns,* when God had departed from them they became as weak as other men. (3.) The numbers of his people, in which Ephraim, though the younger house, exceeded, Jacob having, in the foresight of the same thing, crossed hands, Gen. 48:19. *They are the ten thousands of Ephraim, and the thousands of Manasseh.* Jonathan's Targum applies it to the ten thousands of Canaanites conquered by Joshua, who was of the tribe of Manasseh. And the gloss of the Jerusalem Targum upon the former part of this verse is observable, that "as the firstlings of the bullock were never to be worked, nor could the unicorn ever be tamed, so Joseph should continue free; and they would have continued free if they had not by sin sold themselves."

Verses 18–21

Here we have, I. The blessings of Zebulun and Issachar put together, for they were both the sons of Jacob by Leah, and by their lot in Canaan they were neighbours; it is foretold,

1. That they should both have a comfortable settlement and employment, *v.* 18. Zebulun must rejoice, for he shall have cause to rejoice; and Moses prays that he may have cause in his going out, either to war (for *Zebulun jeoparded their lives in the high places of the field,* Jdg. 5:18), or rather to sea, for Zebulun was a *haven of ships,* Gen. 49:13. And Issachar must rejoice in his tents, that is, in his business at home, his husbandry, to which the men of that tribe generally confined themselves, because they saw that rest was good, and when the sea was rough the land was pleasant, Gen. 49:14, 15. Observe here, (1.) That the providence of God, as it variously appoints the bounds of men's habitation, some in the city and some in the country, some in the seaports and some in the inland towns, so it wisely disposes men's inclinations to different employments for the good of the public, as each member of the body is situated and qualified for the service of the whole. The genius of some men leads them to a book, of others to the sea, of others to the sword; some are inclined to rural affairs, others to trade, and some have a turn for mechanics; and it is well it is so. *If the whole body were an eye, where were the hearing?* 1 Co. 12:17. It was for the common good of Israel that the men of Zebulun were merchants and that the men of Issachar were husbandmen. (2.) That whatever our place and business are it is our wisdom and duty to accommodate ourselves to them, and it is a great happiness to be well pleased with them. Let Zebulun rejoice in his going out; let him thank God for the gains and make the best of the losses and inconveniences of his merchandise, and not despise the meanness, nor envy the quietness, of Issachar's tents. Let *Issachar rejoice in his tents,* let him be well pleased with the retirements and content with the small profits of his country seats, and not grudge that he has not Zebulun's pleasure of travelling and profit of trading. Every business has both its conveniences and inconveniences, and therefore whatever Providence has made our business we ought to bring our minds to it; and it is really a great happiness, whatever our lot is, to be easy with it. *This is the gift of God,* Eccl. 5:19.

2. That they should both be serviceable in their places to the honour of God and the interests of religion in the nation (*v.* 19): *They shall call the people to the mountain,* that is, to the *temple,* which Moses foresaw should be built upon a mountain. I see not why this should be confined (as it is by most interpreters) to Zebulun; if both Zebulun and Issachar received the comforts of their respective employments, why may we not suppose that they both took care to give God the glory of them? Two things they shall do for God: —

(1.) They shall invite others to his service. *Call the people to the mountain.* [1.] Zebulun shall improve his acquaintance and commerce with the neighbouring nations, to whom he goes out, for this noble purpose, to propagate religion among them, and to invite them into the service of the God of Israel. Note, Men of great business, or large conversation, should wisely and zealously endeavour to recommend the practice of serious godliness to those with whom they converse and among whom their business lies. Such are blessed, for they are blessings. It were well if the enlargement of trade with foreign countries might be made to contribute to the spreading of the gospel. This prophecy concerning Zebulun perhaps looks as far as the preaching of Christ and his apostles, which began in the land of Zebulun (Mt. 4:14, 15); then they *called the people to the mountain,* that is, to the kingdom of the Messiah, which is called the *mountain of the Lord's house,* Isa. 2:2. [2.] Issachar that tarries at home, and dwells in tents, shall call upon his neighbours to go up to the sanctuary at the times appointed for their solemn feasts, either because they should be more zealous and forward than their neighbours (and it has been often observed that though those that with Zebulun dwell in the haven of ships, which are places of concourse, have commonly more of the *light* of religion, those that with Issachar dwell in tents in the country have more of the *life* and *heat* of it), and may therefore with their zeal provoke those to a holy emulation that have more knowledge (Ps. 122:1); or because they were more observant of the times appointed for their feasts than others were. One of the Chaldee paraphrasts reads the foregoing verse, *Rejoice, Issachar, in the tents of thy schools,* supposing they would many of them be scholars, and would use their learning for that purpose, according to the revolutions of the year, to give notice of the times of the feasts; for almanacs were not then so common as they are now. And Onkelos more particularly, *Rejoice, Issachar, when thou goest to compute the times of the solemnities at Jerusalem;* for then *the tribes of Israel shall be gathered to the mountain of the house of the sanctuary.* So he reads the beginning of this verse; and many think this is the meaning of that character of the men of Issachar in David's time, That *they had understanding of the times to know what Israel ought to do,* 1 Chr. 12:32. And the character which follows (*v.* 33) of the men of Zebulun, that they were such as *went forth to battle, expert in war,* perhaps may explain the blessing of that tribe here. Note, Those that have not opportunity as Zebulun had of bringing into the church those that are without may yet be very serviceable to its interest by helping to quicken, encourage, and build up, those that are within. And it is good work to call people to God's ordinances, to put those in remembrance that are forgetful, and to stir up those that are slothful, who will follow, but care not to lead.

(2.) They shall not only invite others to the service of God, but they shall abound in it themselves: *There they shall offer sacrifices of righteousness.* They shall not send others to the temple and stay at home themselves, under pretence that they cannot leave their business; but, when they stir up others to *go speedily to pray before the Lord,* they shall say, *We will go also,* as it is Zec. 8:21. Note, The good we exhort others to we should ourselves be examples of. And, when they come to the temple, they shall not appear before the Lord empty, but shall bring for the honour and service of God according as he has prospered them, 1 Co. 16:2. [1.] It is here foretold that both these tribes should grow rich. Zebulun that goes abroad shall *suck of the abundance of the seas,* which are full breasts to the merchants, while Issachar, that tarries at home, shall enrich himself with *treasures hid in the sands,* either the fruits of the earth or the underground treasures of metals and minerals, or (because the word for sand here signifies properly the sand of the sea) the rich things thrown up by the sea, for the lot of Issachar reached to the sea-side. Perhaps their success in *calling the people to the mount* is intimated by their *sucking of the abundance of the seas,* for we have a like phrase used for the bringing in of the nations to the church (Isa. 60:5), *The abundance of the sea shall be converted unto thee,* and (*v.* 16), *Thou shalt suck the milk of the Gentiles.* It is foretold, [2.] That these tribes, being thus enriched, should *consecrate their gain unto the Lord, and their substance unto the Lord of the whole earth,* Mic. 4:13. The *merchandise* of Zebulun, and the *hire* of Issachar, shall be *holiness to the Lord* (Isa. 23:18), for thereof they shall *offer sacrifices of righteousness,* that is, sacrifices according to the law. Note, We must serve and honour God with what we have; and where he sows plentifully he expects to reap accordingly. Those that *suck of the abundance of the seas, and of the treasures hid in the sand,* ought to offer sacrifices of righteousness proportionable.

II. The blessing of the tribe of Gad comes next, *v.* 20, 21. This was one of the tribes that was already seated on that side Jordan where Moses now was. Now,

1. He foretels what this tribe would be, *v.* 20. (1.) That it would be enlarged, as at present it had a spacious allotment; and he gives God the glory both of its present and of its future extent: *Blessed be he that enlargeth Gad.* We find how this tribe was enlarged by their success in a war which it seems they carried on very religiously against the Hagarites, 1 Chr. 5:19, 20, 22. Note, God is to have the glory of all our enlargements. (2.) That it would be a valiant and victorious tribe, would, if let alone, dwell secure and fearless as a lion; but, if provoked, would, like a lion, *tear the arm with the crown of the head;* that is, would pull in pieces all that stood in his way, both the arm (that is, the strength) and the crown of the head (that is, the policy and authority) of his enemies. In David's time there were Gadites whose faces were *as the faces of lions,* 1 Chr. 12:8. Some reckon Jehu to be of this tribe, because the first mention we have of him is at Ramoth Gilead, which belonged to Gad, and they think this may refer to his valiant acts.

2. He commends this tribe for what they had done and were now doing, *v.* 21. (1.) They had done very wisely for themselves, when they chose their lot with the first, in a country already conquered: *He provided the first part for himself;* though he had a concern for his brethren, yet his charity began at home, and he was willing to see himself first served, first settled. The Gadites were the first and most active movers for an allotment on that side Jordan, and therefore are still mentioned before the Reubenites in the history of that affair, Num. 32:2. And thus, while the other tribes had their portion assigned them by Joshua the conqueror, Gad and his companions had theirs from Moses the law-giver, and in it they were seated by law; or (as the word is) *covered* or protected by a special providence which watched over those that were left behind, while the men of war went forward with their brethren. Note, *Men will praise thee when thou doest well for thyself* (when thou providest first for thyself, as Gad did), Ps. 49:18. And God will praise thee when thou doest well for thy soul, which is indeed thyself, and providest the first part for that in a portion from the law-giver. (2.) They were now doing honestly and bravely for their brethren; for they *came with the heads of the people,* before whom they went armed over Jordan, to *execute the justice of the Lord* upon the Canaanites, under the conduct of Joshua, to whom we afterwards find they solemnly vowed obedience, Jos. 1:12, 16. This was what they undertook to do when they had their lot assigned them, Num. 32:27. This they did, Jos. 4:12. And, when the wars of Canaan were ended, Joshua dismissed them with a blessing, Jos. 22:7. Note, It is a blessed and honourable thing to be helpful to our brethren in their affairs, and particularly to assist in executing the justice of the Lord by suppressing that which is provoking to him: it was this that was counted to Phinehas for righteousness.

Verses 22–25

Here is, I. The blessing of Dan, *v.* 22. Jacob in his blessing had compared him to a serpent for subtlety; Moses compares him to a lion for courage and resolution: and what could stand before those that had the head of a serpent and the heart of a lion? He is compared to the lions that leaped from Bashan, a mountain noted for fierce lions, whence they came down to leap upon their prey in the plains. This may refer either, 1. To the particular victories obtained by Samson (who was of this tribe) over the Philistines. *The Spirit of the Lord began to move him in the camp of Dan* when he was very young, as *a lion's whelp,* so that in his attacks upon the Philistines he surprised them, and overpowered them by main strength, as a lion does his prey; and one of his first exploits was the rending of a lion. Or, 2. To a more general achievement of that tribe, when a party of them, upon information brought them of the security of Laish, which lay in the furthest part of the land of Canaan from them, surprised it, and soon made themselves masters of it. See Jdg. 18:27. And, the mountains of Bashan lying not far from that city, probably thence they made their descent upon it; and therefore are here said to *leap from Bashan.*

II. The blessing of Naphtali, *v.* 23. He looks upon this tribe with wonder, and applauds it: "O Naphtali, thou art happy, thou shalt be so, mayest thou be ever so!" Three things make up the happiness of this tribe: — 1. Be thou *satisfied with favour.* Some understand it of the favour of men, their good-will and good word. Jacob had described this tribe to be, generally, courteous obliging people, giving goodly words, as the loving hind, Gen. 49:21. Now what should they get by being so? Moses here tells them they should have an interest in the affections of their neighbours, and be satisfied with favour. Those that are loving shall be beloved. But others understand it of the favour of God, and with good reason; for that only is the favour that is satisfying to the soul and puts true gladness into the heart. Those are happy indeed that have the favour of God; and those shall have it that place their satisfaction in it, and reckon that, in having that, they have enough and desire no more. 2. Be thou *full with the blessing of the Lord,* that is, not only with those good things that are the fruits of the blessing (corn, and wine, and oil), but with the blessing itself; that is, the grace of God, according to his promise and covenant. Those who have that blessing may well reckon themselves full: they need nothing else to make them happy. "The portion of the tribe of Naphtali" (the Jews say) "was so fruitful, and the productions so forward, though it lay north, that those of that tribe were generally the first that brought their first-fruits to the temple; and so they had first the blessing from the priest, which was the blessing of the Lord." Capernaum, in which Christ chiefly resided, lay in this tribe. 3. Be thou *in possession of the sea and the south;* so it may be read, that is, of that sea which shall lie south of thy lot, that was the sea of Galilee, which we so often read of in the gospels, directly north of which the lot of this tribe lay, and which was of great advantage to this tribe, witness the wealth of Capernaum and Bethsaida, which lay within this tribe, and upon the shore of that sea. See how Moses was guided by a spirit of prophesy in these blessings; for before the lot was cast into the lap he foresaw and foretold how the disposal of it would be.

III. The blessing of Asher, *v.* 24, 25. Four things he prays for and prophecies concerning this tribe, which carries blessedness in its name; for Leah called the father of it *Asher,* saying *Happy am I,* Gen. 30:13. 1. The increase of their numbers. They were now a numerous tribe, Num. 26:47. "Let it be more so: *Let Asher be blessed with children.*" Note, Children, especially children of the covenant, are blessings, not burdens. 2. Their interest in their neighbours: *Let him be acceptable to his brethren.* Note, It is a very desirable thing to have the love and good-will of those we live among: it is what we should pray to God for, who has all hearts in his hand; and what we should endeavour to gain by meekness and humility, and a readiness, as we have ability and opportunity, to do good to all men. 3. The richness of their land. (1.) Above ground: *Let him dip his foot in oil,* that is, "Let him have such plenty of it in his lot that he may not only anoint his head with it, but, if he please, wash his feet in it," which was not commonly done; yet we find our blessed Saviour so acceptable to his brethren that his feet were anointed with the most precious ointment, Lu. 7:46. (2.) Under ground: *Thy shoes shall be iron and brass,* that is, "Thou shalt have great plenty of these metals (mines of them) in thy own ground, which by an uncommon blessing shall have both its surface and its bowels rich:" or, if they had them not as the productions of their own country, they should have them imported from abroad; for the lot of this tribe lay on the seacoast. The Chaldee paraphrasts understand this figuratively: "Thou shalt be strong and bright, as iron and brass." 4. The continuance of their strength and vigour: *As thy days, so shall thy strength be.* Many paraphrase it thus, "The strength of thy old age shall be like that of thy youth; thou shalt not feel a decay, nor be the worse for the wearing, but shalt renew thy youth; as if not thy shoes only, but thy bones, were iron and brass." The day is often in scripture put for the events of the day; and, taking it so here, it is a promise that God would graciously support them under their trials and troubles, whatever they were. And so it is a promise sure to all the spiritual seed of Abraham, that God will wisely proportion their graces and comforts to the services and sufferings he calls them out to. Have they work appointed them? They shall have strength to do it. Have they burdens appointed them? They shall have strength to bear them; and never be *tempted above that they are able.* Faithful is he that has thus promised, and hath caused us to hope in this promise.

Verses 26–29

These are the last words of all that ever Moses, that great writer, that great dictator, either wrote himself or had written from his dictation; they are therefore very remarkable, and no doubt we shall find them very improving. Moses, the man of God (who had as much reason as ever any mere man had to know both), with his last breath magnifies both the God of Israel and the Israel of God. They are both incomparable in his eye; and we are sure that in this his judgment of both his eye did not wax dim.

I. No God like the God of Israel. None of the gods of the nations were capable of doing that for their worshippers which Jehovah did for his: *There is none like unto the God of Jeshurun, v.* 26. Note, When we are expecting that God should bless us in doing well for us we must bless him by speaking well of him: and one of the most solemn ways of praising God is by acknowledging that there is none like him. Now, 1. This was the honour of Israel. Every nation boasted of its god; but none had such a God to boast of as Israel had. 2. It was their happiness that they were taken into covenant with such a God. Two things he takes notice of as proofs of the incontestable pre-eminence of the God of Jeshurun above all other gods: (1.) His sovereign power and authority: *He rides upon the heavens,* and with the greatest state and magnificence on the skies. Riding on the heavens denotes his greatness and glory, in which he manifests himself to the upper world, and the use he makes of the influences of heaven, and the productions of the clouds, in bringing to pass his own counsels in this lower world: he manages and directs them as a man does the horse he rides on. When he has any thing to do for his people he *rides upon the heavens* to do it; for he does it swiftly and strongly: no enemy can either anticipate or obstruct the progress of him that rides on the heavens. (2.) His boundless eternity; he is the eternal God, and his arms are *everlasting, v.* 27. The gods of the heathen were but lately invented, and would shortly perish; but the God of Jeshurun is eternal: he was before all worlds, and will be when time and days shall be no more. See Hab. 1:12.

II. No people like the Israel of God. Having pronounced each tribe happy, in the close he pronounces all together very happy, so happy in all respects that there was no nation under the sun comparable to them (*v.* 29): *Happy art thou, O Israel,* a people whose God is the Lord, on that account truly happy, and *none like unto thee.* If Israel honour God as a non-such God, he will favour them so as to make them a non-such people, the envy of all their neighbours and the joy of all their well-wishers. *Who is like unto thee, O people? Behold, thou art fair, my love,* says Christ of his spouse. To which she presently returns, *Behold thou art fair, my beloved. What one nation* (no, not all the nations together) is *like thy people Israel?* 2 Sa. 7:23. What is here said of the church of Israel and the honours and privileges of it is certainly to be applied to *the church of the first-born,* that are written in heaven. The Christian church is the Israel of God, as the apostle calls it (Gal. 6:16), on which there shall be peace, and which is dignified above all societies in the world, as Israel was.

1. Never were people so well seated and sheltered (*v.* 27): *The eternal God is thy refuge.* Or, as the word signifies, "thy *habitation,* or *mansion-house,* in which thou art safe, and easy, and at rest, as a man in his own house." Every Israelite indeed is at home in God; the soul returns to him, and reposes in him as its resting-place (Ps. 116:7), its hiding-place, Ps. 32:7. And those that make him their habitation shall have all the comforts and benefits of a habitation in him, Ps. 91:1. Moses had an eye to God as the habitation of Israel when they were wandering in the wilderness (Ps. 90:1): *Lord, thou hast been our dwelling-place in all generations.* And now that they were going to settle in Canaan they must not change their habitation; still they will need, and still they shall have, the eternal God for their dwelling-place; without him Canaan itself would be a wilderness, and a land of darkness.

2. Never were people so well supported and borne up: *Underneath are the everlasting arms;* that is, the almighty power of God is engaged for the protection and consolation of all that trust in him, in their greatest straits and distresses, and under the heaviest burdens. The everlasting arms shall support, (1.) The interests of the church in general, that they shall not sink, or be run down; underneath the church is that rock of ages on which it is built, and against which the gates of hell shall never prevail, Mt. 16:18. (2.) The spirits or particular believers, so that, though they may be oppressed, they shall not be overwhelmed by any trouble. How low soever the people of God are at any time brought, everlasting arms are underneath them to keep the spirit from sinking, from fainting, and the faith from failing, even when they are pressed above measure. The everlasting covenant, and the everlasting consolations that flow from it, are indeed everlasting arms, with which believers have been wonderfully sustained, and kept cheerful in the worst of times; divine grace is sufficient for them, 2 Co. 12:9.

3. Never were people so well commanded and led on to battle: *"He shall thrust out the enemy from before thee* by his almighty power, which will make room for thee; and by a commission which will bear thee out he shall say, *Destroy them."* They were now entering upon a land that was in the full possession of a strong and formidable people, and who, being its first planters, looked upon themselves as its rightful owners; how shall Israel justify, and how shall they accomplish, the expulsion of them? (1.) God will give them a commission to destroy the Canaanites, and that will justify them, and bear them out in it, against all the world. He that is sovereign Lord of all lives and all lands not only allowed and permitted, but expressly commanded and appointed the children of Israel both to take possession of the land of Canaan and to put the sword to the people of Canaan, which, being thus authorized, they might not only lawfully but honourably do, without incurring the least stain or imputation of theft by the one or murder by the other. (2.) God will give them power and ability to destroy them; nay, he will in effect do it to their hands: he will *thrust out the enemy from before them;* for the very fear of Israel shall put them to flight. God *drive out the heathen to plant his people,* Ps. 44:2. Thus believers are more than conquerors over their spiritual enemies, through Christ that loved them. The captain of our salvation *thrust out the enemy from before us* when he overcame the world and spoiled principalities and powers on the cross; and the word of command to us is, *"Destroy them;* pursue the victory, and you shall divide the spoil."

4. Never were people so well secured and protected (*v.* 28): *Israel shall then dwell in safety alone.* Those that dwell in God, and make his name their strong tower, *dwell in safety;* the *place of their defence is the munitions of rocks,* Isa. 33:16. They shall dwell in safety alone. (1.) Though alone. Though they contract no alliances with their neighbours, nor have any reason to expect help or succour from any of them, yet they shall dwell in safety; they shall really be safe, and they shall think themselves so. (2.) Because alone. They shall dwell in safety as long as they continue pure, and unmixed with the heathen, a singular and peculiar people. Their distinction from other nations, though it made them *like a speckled bird* (Jer. 12:9), and exposed them to the ill-will of those about them, yet was really their preservation from the mischief their neighbours wished them, as it kept them under the divine protection. All that keep close to God shall be kept safely by him. It is promised that in the kingdom of Christ *Israel shall dwell safely,* Jer. 23:6.

5. Never were people so well provided for: *The fountain of Jacob* (that is, the present generation of that people, which is as the fountain to all the streams that shall hereafter descend and be derived from it) shall now presently be fixed upon a good land. *The eye of Jacob* (so it might be read, for the same word signifies a fountain and an eye) *is upon the land of corn and wine,* that is, where they now lay encamped they had Canaan in their eye, it was just before their faces, on the other side the river, and they would have it in their hands and under their feet quickly. This land upon which they had set their eye was blessed both with the fatness of the earth and the dew of heaven; it was a *land of corn and wine,* substantial and useful productions: also his heavens (as if the heavens were particularly designed to be blessings to that land) *shall drop down dew,* without which, though the soil were ever so good, the corn and wine would soon fail. Every Israelite indeed has his eye, the eye of faith, upon the better country, the heavenly Canaan, which is richly replenished with better things than corn and wine.

6. Never were people so well helped. If they were in any strait, God himself rode upon the heavens for *their help, v.* 26. And they were *a people saved by the Lord, v.* 29. If they were in danger of any harm, or in want of any good, they had an eternal God to go to, an almighty power to trust to; nothing could hurt those whom God helped, nor was it possible that the people should perish which *was saved by the Lord.* Those that are added to the gospel Israel are *such as shall be saved,* Acts 2:47.

7. Never were people so well armed. God himself was the shield of their help by whom they were armed defensively, and sufficiently guarded against all assailants: and he was the *sword of their excellency,* by whom they were armed offensively, and made both formidable and successful in all their wars. God is called the *sword of their excellency* because, in fighting for them, he made them to excel other people, or because in all he did for them he had an eye to his sanctuary among them, which is called the *excellency of Jacob,* Ps. 47:4; Eze. 24:21; Amos 6:8. Those in whose hearts is the excellency of holiness have God himself for their shield and sword — are defended by the whole armour of God; his word is their sword, and faith in it is their shield, Eph. 6:16, 17.

8. Never were people so well assured of victory over their enemies: *They shall be found liars unto thee;* That is, "shall be forced to submit to thee sorely against their will, so that it will be but a counterfeit submission; yet the point shall be gained, for thou shalt *tread upon their necks"* (so the Septuagint), which we find done, Jos. 10:24. "Thou shalt tread down their strong-holds, be they ever so high, and trample upon their palaces and temples, though esteemed ever so sacred. *If thy enemies be found liars to thee"* (so some read it), *"thou shalt tread upon their high places;* if they will not be held by the bonds of leagues and treaties, they shall be broken by the force of war." Thus shall the God of peace tread Satan under the feet of all believers, and shall *do it shortly,* Rom. 16:20.

Now lay all this together, and then you will say, *Happy art thou, O Israel! Who is like unto thee, O people!* Thrice happy the people whose God is the Lord.

CHAPTER 34

Having read how Moses finished his testimony, we are told here how he immediately after finished his life. This chapter could not be written by Moses himself, but was added by Joshua or Eleazar, or, as bishop Patrick conjectures, by Samuel, who was a prophet, and wrote by divine authority what he found in the records of Joshua, and his successors the judges. We have had an account of his dying words, here we have an account of his dying work, and that is work we must all do shortly, and it had need be well done. Here is, I. The view Moses had of the land of Canaan just before he died (*v.* 1–4). II. His death and burial (*v.* 5, 6). III. His age (*v.* 7). IV. Israel's mourning for him (*v.* 8). V. His successor (*v.* 9). VI. His character (*v.* 10, etc.).

Verses 1–4

Here is, I. Moses climbing upwards towards heaven, as high as the top of Pisgah, there to die; for that was the place appointed, *ch.* 32:49, 50. Israel lay encamped upon the flat grounds in the plains of Moab, and thence he went up, according to order, to the mountain of Nebo, to the highest point or ridge of that mountain, which was called *Pisgah, v.* 1. Pisgah is an appellative name for all such eminences. It should seem, Moses went up alone to the top of Pisgah, *alone without help* — a sign that his natural force was not abated when on the last day of his life he could walk up to the top of a high hill without such supporters as once he had when his hands were heavy (Ex. 17:12), *alone without company.* When he had made an end of blessing Israel, we may suppose, he solemnly took leave of Joshua, and Eleazar, and the rest of his friends, who probably brought him to the foot of the hill; but then he gave them such a charge as Abraham gave to his servants at the foot of another hill: *Tarry you here while I go yonder and die:* they must not see him die, because they must not know of his sepulchre. But, whether this were so or not, he went up to the top of Pisgah, 1. To show that he was willing to die. When he knew the place of his death, he was so far from avoiding it that he cheerfully mounted a steep hill to come at it. Note, Those that through grace are well acquainted with another world, and have been much conversant with it, need not be afraid to leave this. 2. To show that he looked upon death as his ascension. The soul of a man, of a good man, when it leaves the body, *goes upwards* (Eccl. 3:21), in conformity to which motion of the soul, the body of Moses shall go along with it as far upwards as its earth will carry it. When God's servants are sent for out of the world, the summons runs thus, *Go up and die.*

II. Moses looking downward again towards this earth, to see the earthly Canaan into which he must never enter, but therein by faith looking forwards to the heavenly Canaan into which he should now immediately enter. God had threatened that he should not come into the possession of Canaan, and the threatening is fulfilled. But he had also promised that he should have a prospect of it, and the promise is here performed: *The Lord showed him* all that good land, *v.* 1. 1. If he went up alone to the top of Pisgah, yet he *was not alone, for the Father was with him,* Jn. 16:32. If a man has any friends, he will have them about him when he lies a dying. But if, either through God's providence or their unkindness, it should so happen that we should then be alone, we need *fear no evil* if the great and good Shepherd be with us, Ps. 23:4. 2. Though his sight was very good, and he had all the advantage of high ground that he could desire for the prospect, yet he could not have seen what he now saw, all Canaan from end to end (reckoned about fifty or sixty miles), if his sight had not been miraculously assisted and enlarged, and therefore it is said, *The Lord showed it to him.* Note, All the pleasant prospects we have of the better country we are beholden to the grace of God for; it is he that gives the *spirit of wisdom* as well as the *spirit of revelation,* the eye as well as the object. This sight which God here gave Moses of Canaan, probably, the devil designed to mimic, and pretended to out-do, when in an airy phantom he showed to our Saviour, whom he had placed like Moses upon an *exceedingly high mountain,* all the kingdoms of the world and the glory of them, not gradually, as here, first one country and then another, but all in a moment of time. 3. He saw it at a distance. Such a sight the Old-Testament saints had of the kingdom of the Messiah; they *saw it afar off.* Thus Abraham, long before this, saw Christ's day; and, being fully persuaded of it, embraced it in the promise, leaving others to embrace it in the performance, Heb. 11:13. Such a sight believers now have, through grace, of the bliss and glory of their future state. The word and ordinances are to them what Mount Pisgah was to Moses; from them they have comfortable prospects of the glory to be revealed, and rejoice in hope of it. 4. He saw it, but must never enjoy it. As God sometimes takes his people away from the evil to come, so at other times he takes them away from the good to come, that is, the good which shall be enjoyed by the church in the present world. Glorious things are spoken of the kingdom of Christ in the latter days, its advancement, enlargement, and flourishing state; we foresee it, but we are not likely to live to see it. Those that shall come after us, we hope will enter that promised land, which is a comfort to us when we find our own carcases falling in this wilderness. See 2 Ki. 7:2. 5. He saw all this just before his death. Sometimes God reserves the brightest discoveries of his grace to his people to be the support of their dying moments. Canaan was *Immanuel's land* (Isa. 8:8), so that in viewing it he had a view of the blessings we enjoy by Christ. It was a type of heaven (Heb. 11:16), which faith is the substance and evidence of. Note, Those may leave this world with a great deal of cheerfulness that die in the faith of Christ, and in the hope of heaven, and with Canaan in their eye. Having thus seen the salvation of God, we may well say, *Lord, now let thou thy servant depart in peace.*

Verses 5–8

Here is, I. The death of Moses (*v.* 5): *Moses the servant of the Lord died.* God told him he must not go over Jordan, and, though at first he prayed earnestly for the reversing of the sentence yet God's answer to his prayer sufficed him, and now he *spoke no more of that matter, ch.* 3:26. Thus our blessed Saviour prayed that the cup might pass from him, yet, since it might not, he acquiesced with, *Father, thy will be done.* Moses had reason to desire to live a while longer in the world. He was old, it is true, but he had not yet *attained to the years of the life of his fathers;* his father Amram lived to be 137; his grandfather Kohath 133; his great grandfather Levi 137; Ex. 6:16–20. And why must Moses, whose life was more serviceable than any of theirs, die at 120, especially since he felt not the decays of age, but was as fit for service as ever? Israel could ill spare him at this time; his conduct and his converse with God would be as great a happiness to them in the conquest of Canaan as the courage of Joshua. It bore hard upon Moses himself, when he had gone through all the fatigues of the wilderness, to be prevented from enjoying the pleasures of Canaan; when he had borne the burden and heat of the day, to resign the honour of finishing the work to another, and that not his son, but his servant, who must enter into his labours. We may suppose that this was not pleasant to flesh and blood. But *the man Moses was very meek;* God will have it so, and he cheerfully submits. 1. He is here called *the servant of the Lord,* not only as a good man (all the saints are God's servants), but as a useful man, eminently useful, who had served God's counsels in bringing Israel out of Egypt, and leading them through the wilderness. It was more his honour to be the *servant of the Lord.* than to be king in Jeshurun. 12. Yet he dies. Neither his piety nor his usefulness would exempt him from the stroke of death. God's servants must die that they may rest from their labours, receive their recompense, and make room for others. When God's servants are removed, and must serve him no longer on earth, they go to serve him better, to serve him *day and night in his temple.* 3. He dies in the land of Moab, short of Canaan, while as yet he and his people were in an unsettled condition and had not entered into their rest. In the heavenly Canaan there will be no more death. 4. He dies *according to the word of the Lord. At the mouth of the Lord;* so the word is. The Jews say, "with a kiss from the mouth of God." No doubt, he died very easily (it was an *euthanasia — a delightful death*), there were no bands in his death; and he had in his death a most pleasing taste of the love of God to him: but that he *died at the mouth of the Lord* means no more but that he died in compliance with the will of God. Note, The servants of the Lord, when they have done all their other work, must die at last, in obedience to their Master, and be freely willing to go home whenever he sends for them, Acts 21:13.

II. His burial, *v.* 6. It is a groundless conceit of some of the Jews that Moses was translated to heaven as Elijah was, for it is expressly said that he *died and was buried;* yet probably he was raised to meet Elias, to grace the solemnity of Christ's transfiguration. 1. God himself buried him, namely, by the ministry of angels, which made this funeral, though very private, yet very magnificent. Note, God takes care of the dead bodies of his servants; as their death is precious, so is their dust, not a grain of it shall be lost, but the covenant with it shall be remembered. When Moses was dead, God buried him; when Christ was dead, God raised him, for the law of Moses was to have an end, but not the gospel of Christ. Believers are dead to the law that they might be married to another, even *to him who is raised from the dead,* Rom. 7:4. It should seem Michael, that is, Christ (as some think), had the burying of Moses, for by him the Mosaical ordinances were abolished and taken out of the way, *nailed to his cross,* and buried in his grave, Col. 2:14. 2. He was buried in a valley *over against Beth-peor.* How easily could the angels that buried him have conveyed him over Jordan and buried him with the patriarchs in the cave of Machpelah! But we must learn not be over-solicitous about the place of our burial. If the soul be at rest with God, the matter is not great where the body rests. One of the Chaldee paraphrasts says, "He was buried over against Beth-peor, that, whenever Baal-peor boasted of the Israelites being joined to him, the grave of Moses over against his temple might be a check to him." 3. The particular place was not known, lest the children of Israel, who were so very prone to idolatry, should have enshrined and worshipped the dead body of Moses, that great founder and benefactor of their nation. It is true that we read not, among all the instances of their idolatry, that they worshipped relics, the reason of which perhaps was because they were thus prevented from worshipping Moses, and so could not for shame worship any other. Some of the Jewish writers say that the body of Moses was concealed, that necromancers, who enquired of the dead, might not disquiet him, as the witch of Endor did Samuel, to *bring him up.* God would not have the name and memory of his servant Moses thus abused. Many think this was the contest between Michael and the devil about the body of Moses, mentioned Jude 90. The devil would make the place known that it might be a snare to the people, and Michael would not let him. Those therefore who are for giving divine honours to the relics of departed saints side with the devil against Michael our prince.

III. His age, *v.* 7. His life was prolonged, 1. To old age. He was 120 years old, which, though far short of the years of the patriarchs, yet much exceeded the years of most of his contemporaries, for the ordinary age of man had been lately reduced to seventy, Ps. 90:10. The years of the life of Moses were three forties. The first forty he lived a courtier, at ease and in honour in Pharaoh's court; the second forty he lived a poor desolate shepherd in Midian; the third forty he lived a king in Jeshurun, in honour and power, but encumbered with a great deal of care and toil: so changeable is the world we live in, and alloyed with such mixtures; but the world before us is unmixed and unchangeable. 2. To a good old age: *His eye was not dim* (as Isaac's, Gen. 27:1, and Jacob's, Gen. 48:10), *nor was his natural force abated;* there was no decay either of the strength of his body or of the vigour and activity of his mind, but he could still speak, and write, and walk as well as ever. His understanding was as clear, and his memory as strong, as ever. "His visage was not wrinkled," say some of the Jewish writers; "he had lost never a tooth," say others; and many of them expound it of the shining of his face (Ex. 34:30), that that continued to the last. This was the general reward of his services; and it was in particular the effect of his extraordinary meekness, for that is a grace which is, as much as any other, *health to the navel and marrow to the bones.* Of the moral law which was given by Moses, though the condemning power be vacated to true believers, yet the commands are still binding, and will be to the end of the world; the eye of them is not waxen dim, for they shall discern the thoughts and intents of the heart, nor is their natural force or obligation abated but still we are *under the law to Christ.*

IV. The solemn mourning that there was for him, *v.* 8. It is a debt owing to the surviving honour of deceased worthies to follow them with our tears, as those who loved and valued them, are sensible of our loss of them, and are truly humbled for those sins which have provoked God to deprive us of them; for penitential tears very fitly mix with these. Observe, 1. Who the mourners were: *The children of Israel.* They all conformed to the ceremony, whatever it was, though some of them perhaps, who were ill-affected to his government, were but mock-mourners; yet we may suppose there were those among them who had formerly quarrelled with him and his government, and perhaps had been of those who spoke of stoning him, who now were sensible of their loss, and heartily lamented him when he was removed from them, though they knew not how to value him when he was with them. Thus those who had murmured were made to learn doctrine, Isa. 29:24. Note, The loss of good men, especially good governors, is to be much lamented and laid to heart: those are stupid who do not consider it. 2. How long they mourned: *Thirty days.* So long the formality lasted, and we may suppose there were some in whom the mourning continued much longer. Yet the *ending of the days of weeping and mourning* for Moses is an intimation that, how great soever our losses have been, we must not abandon ourselves to perpetual grief; we must suffer the wound at least to heal up in time. If we hope to go to heaven rejoicing, why should we resolve to go to the grave mourning? The ceremonial law of Moses is dead and buried in the grave of Christ; but the Jews have not yet ended the days of their mourning for it.

Verses 9–12

We have here a very honourable encomium passed both on Moses and Joshua; each has his praise, and should have. It is ungrateful so to magnify our living friends as to forget the merits of those that are gone, to whose memories there is a debt of honour due: all the respect must not be paid to the rising sun; and, on the other hand, it is unjust so to cry up the merits of those that are gone as to despise the benefit we have in those that survive and succeed them. Let God be glorified in both, as here.

I. Joshua is praised as a man admirably qualified for the work to which he was called, *v.* 9. Moses brought Israel to the borders of Canaan and then died and left them, to signify that *the law made nothing perfect,* Heb. 7:19. It brings men into a wilderness of conviction, but not into the Canaan of rest and settled peace. It is an honour reserved for Joshua (our Lord Jesus, of whom Joshua was a type) to do that for us which *the law could not do, in that it was weak through the flesh,* Rom. 8:3. Through him we enter into rest, the spiritual rest of conscience and eternal rest in heaven. Three things concurred to clear Joshua's call to this great undertaking: — 1. God fitted him for it: *He was full of the spirit of wisdom;* and so he had need who had such a peevish people to rule, and such a politic people to conquer. conduct is as requisite in a general as courage. Herein Joshua was a type of Christ, in whom are hidden the treasures of wisdom. 2. Moses, by the divine appointment, had ordained him to it: *He had laid his hands upon him,* so substituting him to be his successor, and praying to God to qualify him for the service to which he had called him; and this comes in as a reason why God gave him a more than ordinary *spirit of wisdom,* because his designation to the government was God's own act (those whom God employs he will in some measure make fit for the employment) and because this was the thing that Moses had asked of God for him when he laid his hands on him. When the bodily presence of Christ withdrew from his church, he prayed the Father to send another Comforter, and obtained what he prayed for. 3. The people cheerfully owned him and submitted to him. Note, An interest in the affections of people is a great advantage, and a great encouragement to those that are called to public trusts of what kind soever. It was also a great mercy to the people that when Moses was dead they were not as sheep having no shepherd, but had one ready among them in whom they did unanimously, and might with the highest satisfaction, acquiesce.

II. Moses is praised (*v.* 10–12), and with good reason. 1. He was indeed a very great man, especially upon two accounts: — (1.) His intimacy with the God of nature: *God knew him face to face,* and so he knew God. See Num. 12:8. He saw more of the glory of God than any (at least of the Old-Testament saints) ever did. He had more free and frequent access to God, and was spoken to not in dreams, and visions, and slumberings on the bed, but when he was awake and standing before the cherubim. Other prophets, when God appeared and spoke to them, were struck with terror (Dan. 10:7), but Moses, whenever he received a divine revelation, preserved his tranquillity. (2.) His interest and power in the kingdom of nature. The miracles of judgment he wrought in Egypt before Pharaoh, and the miracles of mercy he wrought in the wilderness before Israel, served to demonstrate that he was a particular favourite of Heaven, and had an extra-ordinary commission to act as he did on this earth. Never was there any man whom Israel had more reason to love, or whom the enemies of Israel had more reason to fear. Observe, The historian calls the miracles Moses wrought *signs and wonders,* done with *a mighty hand and great terror,* which may refer to the terrors of Mount Sinai, by which God fully ratified Moses's commission and demonstrated it beyond exception to be divine, and this *in the sight of all Israel.*

2. He was greater than any other of the prophets of the Old Testament. Though they were men of great interest in heaven and great influence upon earth, yet they were none of them to be compared with this great man; none of them either so evidenced or executed a commission from heaven as Moses did. This encomium of Moses seems to have been written long after his death, yet then there had not arisen any prophet *like unto Moses,* nor did there arise any such between that period and the *sealing up of the vision and prophecy.* by Moses God gave the law, and moulded and formed the Jewish church; by the other prophets he only sent particular reproofs, directions, and predictions. The last of the prophets concludes with a charge *to remember the law of Moses,* Mal. 4:4. Christ himself often appealed to the writings of Moses, and vouched him for a witness, as one that *saw his day* at a distance *and spoke of him.* But, as far as the other prophets came short of him, our Lord Jesus went beyond him. His doctrine was more excellent, his miracles were more illustrious, and his communion with his Father was more intimate, for he *had lain in his bosom from eternity,* and by him God does now in these last days speak to us. Moses was faithful as a servant, but Christ as a Son. The history of Moses leaves him buried in the plains of Moab, and concludes with the period of his government; but the history of our Saviour leaves him sitting *at the right hand of the Majesty on high,* and we are assured that *of the increase of his government and peace there shall be no end.* The apostle, in his epistle to the Hebrews, largely proves the pre-eminence of Christ above Moses, as a good reason why we that are Christians should be obedient, faithful, and constant, to that holy religion which we make profession of. God, by his grace, make us all so!

AN EXPOSITION, WITH PRACTICAL OBSERVATIONS, OF THE BOOK OF JOSHUA

I. We have now before us the history of the Jewish nation in this book and those that follow it to the end of the book of Esther. These books, to he end of the books of the Kings, the Jewish writers call *the first book of the prophets,* to bring them within the distribution of the books of the *Old Testament,* into the Law, the Prophets, and the Chetubim, or Hagiographa, Lu. 24:44. The rest they make part of the Hagiographa. For, though history is their subject, it is justly supposed that prophets were their penmen. To those books that are purely and properly *prophetical* the name of the prophet is prefixed, because the credibility of the prophecies depended much upon the character of the prophets; but these historical books, it is probable, were collections of the authentic records of the nation, which some of the prophets (and the Jewish church was for many ages more or less continually blessed with such) were divinely directed and helped to put together for the service of the church to the end of the world; as their other officers, so their historiographers, had their authority *from heaven.* — It should seem that though the substance of the several histories was written when the events were fresh in memory, and written under a divine direction, yet, under the same direction, they were put into the form in which we now have them by some other hand, long afterwards, probably all by the same hand, or about the same time. The grounds of the conjecture are, 1. Because former writings are so often referred to, as the Book of Jasher (Jos. 10:13, and 2 Sa. 1:18), the Chronicles of the Kings of Israel and Judah, and the books of Gad, Nathan, and Iddo. 2. Because the days when the things were done are spoken of sometimes as days long since passed; as 1 Sa. 9:9, *He that is now called a prophet was formerly called a seer.* And, 3. Because we so often read of things remaining *unto this day;* as stones (Jos. 4:9; 7:26; 8:29; 10:27; 1 Sa. 6:18), names of places (Jos. 5:9; 7:26; Jdg. 1:26; 15:19; 18:12; 2 Ki. 14:7), rights and possessions (Jdg. 1:21; 1 Sa. 27:6), customs and usages (1 Sa. 5:5; 2 Ki. 17:41), which clauses have been since added to the history by the inspired collectors for the confirmation and illustration of it to those of their own age. And, if one may offer a mere conjecture, it is not unlikely that the historical books, to the end of the Kings, were put together by Jeremiah the prophet, a little before the captivity; for it is said of Ziklag (1 Sa. 27:6) that it pertains to the *kings of Judah* (which style began after Solomon and ended in the captivity) *unto this day.* And it is still more probable that those which follow were put together by Ezra the scribe, some time after the captivity. However, though we are in the dark concerning their authors, we are in no doubt concerning their authority; they were a part of the oracles of God, which were committed to the Jews, and were so received and referred to by our Saviour and the apostles.

In the five books of Moses we had a very full account of the rise, advance, and constitution, of the Old-Testament church, the family out of which it was raised, the promise, that great charter by which it was incorporated, the miracles by which it was built up, and the laws and ordinances by which it was to be governed, from which one would conceive and expectation of its character and state very different from what we find in this history. A nation that had statutes and judgments so righteous, one would think, should have been very holy; and a nation what had promises so rich should have been very happy. But, alas! a great part of the history is a melancholy representation of their sins and miseries; for *the law made nothing perfect,* but this was to be done by the *bringing in of the better hope.* And yet, if we compare the history of the Christian church with its constitution, we shall find the same cause for wonder, so many have been its errors and corruptions; for neither does the *gospel make any thing perfect* in this world, but leaves us still in expectation of a *better hope* in the future state.

II. We have next before us the *book of Joshua,* so called, perhaps, not because it was written *by* him, for that is uncertain. Dr. Lightfoot thinks that Phinehas wrote it. Bishop Patrick is clear that Joshua wrote it himself. However that be, it is written *concerning* him, and, if any other wrote it, it was collected out of his journals or memoirs. It contains the history of Israel under the command and government of Joshua, how he presided as general of their armies, 1. In their entrance into Canaan, *ch.* 1–5. 2. In their conquest of Canaan, *ch.* 6–12. 3. In the distribution of the land of Canaan among the tribes of Israel, *ch.* 22–24. In all which he was a great example of wisdom, courage, fidelity, and piety, to all that are in places of public trust. But this is not all the use that is to be made of this history. We may see in it, 1. *Much of God* and *his providence* — his power in the kingdom of nature, his justice in punishing the Canaanites when the *measure of their iniquity was full,* his faithfulness to his covenant with the patriarchs, and his kindness to his people Israel, notwithstanding their provocations. We may see him as the Lord of Hosts *determining the issues of war,* and as the director of the lot, *determining the bounds of men's habitations.* 2. *Much of Christ* and *his grace.* Though Joshua is not expressly mentioned in the New Testament as a type of Christ, yet all agree that he was a very eminent one. He bore our Saviour's name, as did also another type of him, Joshua the high priest, Zec. 6:11, 12. The Septuagint, giving the name of Joshua a Greek termination, call him all along *Iēsous, Jesus,* and so he is called Acts 7:45, and Heb. 4:8. Justin Martyr, one of the first writers of the Christian church *(Dialog. cum Tryph.* p. mihi 300), makes that promise in Ex. 23:20, *My angel shall bring thee into the place I have prepared,* to point at Joshua; and these words, *My name is in him,* to refer to this, that his names should be the same with that of the Messiah. It signifies, *He shall save.* Joshua saves God's people from the Canaanites; our Lord Jesus saves them *from their sins.* Christ, as Joshua, is the *captain of our salvation,* a *leader and commander of the people,* to tread Satan under their feet, to put them in possession of the heavenly Canaan, and to *give them rest,* which (it is said, Heb. 4:8) Joshua did not.

CHAPTER 1

The book begins with the history, not of Joshua's life (many remarkable passages of that we had before in the books of Moses) but of his reign and government. In this chapter, I. God appoints him to the government in the stead of Moses, gives him an ample commission, full instructions, and great encouragements (*v.* 1–9). II. He accepts the government, and addresses himself immediately to the business of it, giving orders to the officers of the people in general (*v.* 10, 11) and particularly to the two tribes and a half (*v.* 12–15). III. The people agree to it, and take an oath of fealty to him (*v.* 16–18). A reign which thus began with God could not but be honourable to the prince and comfortable to the subject. The last words of Moses are still verified, "Happy art thou, O Israel! Who is like unto thee, O people?" Deu. 33:29.

Verses 1–9

Honour is here put upon Joshua, and great power lodged in his hand, by him that is the fountain of honour and power, and by whom kings reign. Instructions are given him by Infinite Wisdom, and encouragements by the God of all consolation. God had before spoken to Moses concerning him (Num. 27:18), but now he speaks to him (*v.* 1), probably as he spoke to Moses (Lev. 1:1) *out of the tabernacle of the congregation,* where Joshua had with Moses presented himself (Deu. 31:14), to learn the way of attending there. Though Eleazar had the breast-plate of judgment, which Joshua was directed to consult as there was occasion (Num. 27:21), yet, for his greater encouragement, God here speaks to him immediately, some think in a dream or vision (as Job 33:15); for though God has tied us to instituted ordinances, in them to attend him, yet he has not tied himself to them, but that he may without them make himself known to his people, and speak to their hearts otherwise than by their ears. Concerning Joshua's call to the government observe here,

I. The time when it was given him: *After the death of Moses.* As soon as ever Moses was dead, Joshua took upon him the administration, by virtue of his solemn ordination in Moses's life-time. An interregnum, though but for a few days, might have been of bad consequence; but it is probable that God did not speak to him to go forward towards Canaan till after the thirty days of mourning for Moses were ended; not, as the Jews say, because the sadness of his spirit during those days unfitted him for communion with God (he sorrowed not as one that had no hope), but by this solemn pause, and a month's adjournment of the public councils, even now when time was so very precious to them, God would put an honour upon the memory of Moses, and give time to the people not only to lament their loss of him, but to repent of their miscarriages towards him during the forty years of his government.

II. The place Joshua had been in before he was thus preferred. He was Moses's minister, that is, an immediate attendant upon his person and assistant in business. The Septuagint translates it *hypourgos*, a workman under Moses, under his direction and command. Observe, 1. He that was here called to honour had been long bred to business. Our Lord Jesus himself took upon him the form of a servant, and then God highly exalted him. 2. He was trained up in subjection and under command. Those are fittest to rule that have learnt to obey. 3. He that was to succeed Moses was intimately acquainted with him, that he might *fully know his doctrine and manner of life, his purpose and long-suffering* (2 Tim. 3:10), might take the same measures, walk in the same spirit, in the same steps, having to carry on the same work. 4. He was herein a type of Christ, who might therefore be called Moses's minister, because he was made under the law and fulfilled all the righteousness of it.

III. The call itself that God gave him, which is very full.

1. The consideration upon which he was called to the government: *Moses my servant is dead, v.* 2. All good men are God's servants; and it is no disparagement, but an honour, to the greatest of men to be so: angels themselves are his ministers. Moses was called to extraordinary work, was a steward in God's house, and in the discharge of the trusts reposed in him he served not himself but God who employed him; he was faithful as a servant, and with an eye to the Son, as is intimated, Heb. 3:5, where what he did is said to be for a *testimony of the things that should be spoken after.* God will own his servants, will confess them in the great day. But Moses, though God's servant, and one that could ill be spared, is dead; for God will change hands, to show that whatever instruments he uses he is not tied to any. Moses, when he has done his work as a servant, dies and goes to *rest from his labours, and enters into the joy of his Lord.* Observe, God takes notice of the death of his servants. It is precious in his sight, Ps. 116:15.

2. The call itself. *Now therefore arise.* (1.) "Though Moses is dead, the work must go on; therefore arise, and go about it." Let not weeping hinder sowing, nor the withering of the most useful hands be the weakening of ours; for, when God has work to do, he will either find or make instruments fit to carry it on. Moses the *servant* is dead, but God the *Master* is not: he lives for ever. (2.) "Because Moses is dead, therefore the work devolves upon thee as his successor, for hereunto thou wast appointed. Therefore there is need of thee to fill up his place; up, and be doing." Note, [1.] The removal of useful men should quicken survivors to be so much the more diligent in doing good. Such and such are dead, and we must die shortly, therefore let us work while it is day. [2.] It is a great mercy to a people, if, when useful men are taken away in the midst of their usefulness, others are raised up in their stead to go on where they broke off. Joshua must arise to finish what Moses began. Thus the latter generations enter into the labours of the former. And thus Christ, our Joshua, does that for us which could never be done by the law of Moses, —*justifies* (Acts 13:39), and *sanctifies,* Romans 8:3. The life of Moses made way for Joshua, and prepared the people for what was to be done by him. Thus the law is a schoolmaster to bring us to Christ: and then the death of Moses made room for Joshua; thus we are dead to the law, our first husband, that we may be *married to Christ,* Rom. 7:4.

3. The particular service he was now called out to: *"Arise, go over this Jordan,* this river which you have in view, and on the banks of which you lie encamped." This was a trial to the faith of Joshua, whether he would give orders to make preparation for passing the river when there was no visible way of getting over it, at least not at this place and at this time, when *all the banks were overflown, ch.* 3:15. He had no pontoons or bridge of boats by which to convey them over, and yet he must believe that God, who had ordered them over, would open a way for them. Going over Jordan was going into Canaan; thither Moses might not, could not, bring them, Deu. 31:2. Thus the honour of bringing the many sons to glory is reserved for Christ the *captain of our salvation,* Heb. 2:10.

4. The grant of the land of Canaan to the children of Israel is here repeated (*v.* 2–4): *I do give it them.* To the patriarchs it was promised, *I will give it;* but, now that the fourth generation had expired, the iniquity of the Amorites was full, and the time had come for the performance of the promise, it is actually conveyed, and they are put in possession of that which they had long been in expectation of: "I do give it, enter upon it, it is all your own; nay (*v.* 3), *I have given it;* though it be yet unconquered, it is as sure to you as if it were in your hands." Observe, (1.) The persons to whom the conveyance is made: *To them, even to the children of Israel* (*v.* 2), because they are the seed of Jacob, who was called *Israel* at the time when this promise was made to him, Gen. 35:10, 12. The children of Israel, though they had been very provoking in the wilderness, yet, for their fathers' sakes, should have the entail preserved. And it was the children of the murmurers that God said should enter Canaan, Num. 14:31. (2.) The land itself that is conveyed: From the river Euphrates eastward, to the Mediterranean Sea westward, *v.* 4. Though their sin cut them short of this large possession, and they never replenished all the country within the bounds here mentioned, yet, had they been obedient, God would have given them this and much more. Out of all these countries, and many others, there were in process of time proselytes to the Jewish religion, as appears, Acts 2:5, etc. If their church was enlarged, though their nation was not multiplied, it cannot be said that the promise was of no effect. And, if this promise had not its full accomplishment in the letter, believers might thence infer that it had a further meaning, and was to be fulfilled in the kingdom of the Messiah, both that of grace and that of glory. (3.) The condition is here implied upon which this grant is made, in those words, *as I said unto Moses,* that is, "upon the terms that Moses told you of many a time, *if you will keep my statutes,* you shall go in and possess that good land. Take it under those provisos and limitations, and not otherwise." The precept and promise must not be separated. (4.) It is intimated with what ease they should gain the possession of this land, if it were not their own fault, in these words, *"Every place that the sole of your foot shall tread upon* (within the following bounds) shall be your own. Do but set your foot upon it and you have it."

5. The promises God here makes to Joshua for his encouragement. (1.) That he should be sure of the presence of God with him in this great work to which he was called (*v.* 5): *"As I was with Moses,* to direct and strengthen him, to own and prosper him, and give him success in bringing Israel out of Egypt and leading them through the wilderness, so I will be with thee to enable thee to settle them in Canaan." Joshua was sensible how far he came short of Moses in wisdom and grace; But what Moses did was done by virtue of the presence of God with him, and, though Joshua had not always the same presence of mind that Moses had, yet, if he had always the same presence of God, he would do well enough. Note, it is a great comfort to the rising generation of ministers and Christians that the same grace which was sufficient for those that went before them shall not be wanting to them if they be not wanting to themselves in the improvement of it. It is repeated here again (*v.* 9). *"The Lord thy God is with thee* as a God of power, and that power engaged for thee whithersoever thou goest." Note, Those that go where God sends them shall have him with them wherever they go and they need desire no more to make them easy and prosperous. (2.) That the presence of God should never be withdrawn from him: *I will not fail thee, nor forsake thee, v.* 5. Moses had assured him of this (Deu. 31:8), that, though he must now leave him, God never would: and here God himself confirms that word of his servant Moses (Isa. 44:26), and engages never to leave Joshua. We need the presence of God, not only when we are beginning our work to set us in, but in the progress of it to further us with a continual help. If that at any time fail us, we are gone; this we may be sure, that *the Lord is with us while we are with him.* This promise here made to Joshua is applied to all believers, and improved as an argument against covetousness, Heb. 13:5, *Be content with such things as you have, for he hath said, I will never leave thee.* (3.) That he should have victory over all the enemies of Israel (*v.* 5): *There shall not any man* that comes against thee *be able to stand before thee.* Note, There is no standing before those that have God on their side. *If he be for us, who can be against us?* God promises him clear success — the enemy should not make any head against him; and constant success — all the days of his life. However it might be with Israel when he was gone, all his reign should be graced with triumphs. What Joshua had himself encouraged the people with long ago (Num. 14:9) God here encourages him with. (4.) That he should himself have the dividing of this land among the people of Israel, *v.* 6. It was a great encouragement to him in beginning this work that he was sure to see it finished and his labour should not be in vain. Some make it a reason why he should arm himself with resolution, and be of good courage, because of the bad character of the people whom he must cause to inherit that land. He knew well what a froward discontented people they were, and how unmanageable they had been in his predecessor's time; let him therefore expect vexation from them and be of good courage.

6. The charge or command he gives to Joshua, which is, (1.) That he conform himself in every thing to the law of God, and make this his rule *v.* 7, 8. God does, as it were, put the book of the law into Joshua's hand; as, when Joash was crowned, they *gave him the testimony,* 2 Ki. 11:12. And concerning this book he is charged, [1.] To *meditate therein day and night,* that he might understand it and have it ready in him upon all occasions. If ever any man's business might have excused him from meditation, and other acts of devotion, one would think Joshua's might at this time. It was a great trust that was lodged in his hands; the care of it was enough to fill him, if he had had ten souls, and yet he must find time and thoughts for meditation. Whatever affairs of this world we have to mind, we must not neglect the one thing needful. [5.] Not to let it depart out of his mouth; that is, all his orders to the people, and his judgments upon appeals made to him, must be consonant to the law of God; upon all occasions he must *speak according to this rule,* Isa. 8:20. Joshua was to maintain and carry on the work that Moses had begun, and therefore he must not only complete the salvation Moses had wrought for them, but must uphold the holy religion he had established among them. There was no occasion to make new laws; but *that good thing which was committed to him* he must carefully and faithfully keep, 2 Tim. 1:14. [3.] He must *observe to do according to all this law.* To this end he must meditate therein, not for contemplation sake only, or to fill his head with notions, or that he might find something to puzzle the priests with, but that he might, both as a man and as a magistrate, observe to do *according to what was written* therein; and several things were written there which had particular reference to the business he had now before him, as the laws concerning their wars, the destroying of the Canaanites and the dividing of Canaan; etc.; these he must religiously observe. Joshua was a man of great power and authority, yet he must himself be under command and do as he is bidden. No man's dignity or dominion, how great soever, sets him above the law of God. Joshua must not only govern by law, and take care that the people observed the law, but he must observe it himself, and so by his own example maintain the honour and power of it. *First,* He must do what was written. It is not enough to hear and read the word, to commend and admire it, to know and remember it, to talk and discourse of it, but we must do it. *Secondly,* He must do according to what was written, exactly observing the law as his copy, and doing, not only that which was there required, but in all circumstances according to the appointment. *Thirdly,* He must do according to all that was written, without exception or reserve, having a *respect to all God's commandments,* even those which are most displeasing to flesh and blood. *Fourthly,* He must observe to do so, observe the checks of conscience, the hints of providence; and all the advantages of opportunity. Careful observance is necessary to universal obedience. *Fifthly,* He must *not turn from it,* either in

his own practice or in any act of government, to the right hand or to the left, for there are errors on both hands, and virtue is in the mean. *Sixthly,* He must be *strong and courageous,* that he might do according to the law. So many discouragements there are in the way of duty that those who will proceed and persevere in it must put on resolution. And, *lastly,* to encourage him in his obedience, he assures him that then he shall *do wisely* (as it is in the margin) and *make his way prosperous, v.* 7, 8. Those that make the word of God their rule, and conscientiously walk by that rule, shall both do well and speed well; it will furnish them with the best maxims by which to order their conversation (Ps. 111:10); and it will entitle them to the best blessings: God shall *give them the desire of their heart.*

(2.) That he encourage himself herein with the promise and presence of God, and make these his stay (*v.* 6): *Be strong and of a good courage.* And again (*v.* 7), as if this was the one thing needful: *Only be strong and very courageous.* And he concludes with this (*v.* 9): *Be strong and of a good courage; be not afraid, neither be thou dismayed.* Joshua had long since signalized his valour, in the war with Amalek, and in his dissent from the report of the evil spies; and yet God sees fit thus to inculcate this precept upon him. Those that have grace have need to be called upon again and again to exercise grace and to improve in it. Joshua was humble and low in his own eyes, not distrustful of God, and his power, and promise, but diffident of himself, and of his own wisdom, and strength, and sufficiency for the work, especially coming after so great a man as Moses; and therefore God repeats this so often, "*Be strong and of a good courage;* let not the sense of thy own infirmities dishearten thee; God is all-sufficient. *Have not I commanded thee?*" [1.] "I have commanded the work to be done, and therefore it shall be done, how invincible soever the difficulties may seem that lie in the way." Nay, [2.] "I have commanded, called, and commissioned, thee to do it, and therefore will be sure to own thee, and strengthen thee, and bear thee out in. it." Note, When we are in the way of our duty we have reason to be strong and very courageous; and it will help very much to animate and embolden us if we keep our eye upon the divine warrant, hear God saying, "*Have not I commanded thee?* I will therefore help thee, succeed thee, accept thee, reward thee." Our Lord Jesus, as Joshua here, was borne up under his sufferings by a regard to the will of God and the *commandment he had received from his Father,* Jn. 10:18.

Verses 10–15

Joshua, being settled in the government, immediately applies himself to business; not to take state or to take his pleasure, but to further the work of God among, the people over whom God had set him. As he that desires the office of a minister (1 Tim. 3:1), so he that desires the office of a magistrate, desires a work, a good work; neither is preferred to be idle.

I. He issues out orders to the people to provide for a march; and they had been so long encamped in their present post that it would be a work of some difficulty to decamp. The officers of the people that commanded under Joshua in their respective tribes and families attended him for orders, which they were to transmit to the people. Inferior magistrates are as necessary and as serviceable to the public good in their places as the supreme magistrate in his. What could Joshua have done without officers? We are therefore required to be subject, not only to *the king as supreme, but to governors as to those that are sent by him,* 1 Pt. 2:13, 14. By these officers, 1. Joshua gives public notice that they were *to pass over Jordan within three days.* These orders, I suppose, were not given till after the return of the spies that were sent to bring an account of Jericho, though the story of that affair follows, *ch.* 2. And perhaps that was such an instance of his jealousy, and excessive caution, as made it necessary that he should be so often bidden as he was to be strong and of a good courage. Observe with what assurance Joshua says to the people, because God had said it to him, You shall pass over Jordan, and *shall possess* the land. We greatly honour the truth of God. 2. He gives them directions to prepare victuals, not to prepare transport vessels. He that bore Egypt upon eagle's wings would in like manner bear them into Canaan, to bring them to himself, Ex. 19:4. But those

that were desirous to have other victuals besides the manna, which had not yet ceased, must prepare it and have it ready against the time appointed. Perhaps, though the manna did not quite cease till they came into Canaan (*ch.* 5:12), yet since they had come *into a land inhabited* (Ex. 16:35), where they might be furnished in part with other provisions, it did not fall so plentifully, nor did they gather so much as when they had it first given to them in the wilderness, but decreased gradually, and therefore they are ordered to provide other victuals, in which perhaps was included all other things necessary to their march. And some of the Jewish writer, considering that having manna they needed not to provide other victuals, understand it figuratively, that they must *repent of their sins,* and make their *peace with God,* and resolve to live a new life, that they might be ready to receive this great favour. See Ex. 19:10, 11.

II. He reminds the two tribes and a half of the obligations they were under to go over Jordan with their brethren, though they left their possessions and families on this side. Interest would make the other tribes glad to go over Jordan, but in these it was an act of self-denial, and against the grain; therefore it was needful to produce the agreement which Moses had made with them, when he gave them their possession before their brethren (*v.* 13): *Remember the word which Moses commanded you.* Some of them perhaps were ready to think now that Moses was dead, who they thought was too hard upon them in this matter, they might find some excuse or other to release themselves from this engagement, or might prevail with Joshua to dispense with them; but he holds them to it, and lets them know that, though Moses was dead, his commands and their promises were still in full force. He reminds them, 1. Of the advantages they had received in being first settled: "*The Lord your God hath given you rest.* He has given your minds rest; you know what you have to trust to, and are not as the rest of the tribes waiting the issue of the war first and then of the lot. He has also given your families rest, your wives and children, whose settlement is your satisfaction. He has given you rest by giving you this land, this good land, of which you are in full and quiet possession." Note, When God by his providence has given us rest we ought to consider how we may honour him with the advantages of it, and what service we may do to our brethren who are unsettled, or not so well settled as we are When God had given David rest (2 Sa. 7:1), see how restless he was till he had *found out a habitation* for the ark, Ps. 132:4, 5. When God has given us rest, we must take heed of slothfulness and of settling upon our lees. 2. He reminds them of their agreement to help their brethren in the wars of Canaan till God had in like manner given them rest, *v.* 14, 15. This was, (1.) Reasonable in itself. So closely were all the tribes incorporated that they must needs look upon themselves as members one of another. (2.) It was enjoined them by Moses, the servant of the Lord; he commanded them to do this, and Joshua his successor would see his commands observed. (3.) It was the only expedient they had to save themselves from the guilt of a great sin in settling on that side Jordan, a sin which would one time or other find them out, Num. 32:23. (4.) It was the condition of the grant Moses had made them of the land they were possessed of, so that they could not be sure of a good title to, or a comfortable enjoyment of, *the land of their possession,* as it is here called (*v.* 15), if they did not fulfil the condition. (5.) They themselves had covenanted and agreed thereunto (Num. 32:25): *Thy servants will do as my Lord commandeth.* Thus we all lie under manifold obligations to strengthen the hands one of another, and not to seek our own welfare only, but one another's.

Verses 16–18

This answer was given not by the two tribes and a half only (though they are spoken of immediately before), but by the *officers of all the people* (*v.* 10), as their representatives, concurring with the divine appointment, by which Joshua was set over them, and they did it heartily, and with a great deal of cheerfulness and resolution.

I. They promise him obedience (*v.* 16), not only as subjects to their prince, but as soldiers to their general, of whose particular orders they are to be observant. He that hath *soldiers under him saith to this man, Go, and he goeth; and to another, Come, and he cometh,* Mt. 8:9. Thus the

people of Joshua; *"All that thou commandest us we will readily do,* without murmuring or disputing; and whithersoever thou sends us, though upon the most difficult and perilous expedition, we will go." We must thus swear allegiance to our Lord Jesus, as the captain of our salvation, and bind ourselves to do what he commands us by his word, and to go where he sends us by his providence. And since Joshua, being humbly conscious to himself how far short he came of Moses, feared he should not have such an influence upon the people and such an interest in them as Moses had, they here promise that they will be as obedient to him as ever they had been to Moses, *v.* 17. To speak truth, they had no reason to boast of their obedience to Moses; he had found them a stiff-necked people, Deu. 9:24. But they meant that they would be as observant of Joshua as they should have been, and as some of them were (and the generality of them at least sometimes) of Moses. Note, We must not so magnify those that are gone, how eminent soever they were, either in the magistracy or in the ministry, as to be wanting in the honour and duty we owe to those that survive and succeed them, though in gifts they may come short of them. Obedience for conscience' sake will continue, though Providence change the hands by which it rules and acts.

II. They pray for the presence of God with him (*v.* 17): *"Only the Lord thy God be with thee,* to bless and prosper thee, and give thee success, *as he was with Moses."* Prayers and supplications are to be made for all in authority, 1 Tim. 2:1, 2. And the best thing we can ask of God for our magistrates is that they may have the presence of God with them; this will make them blessings to us, so that in seeking this for them we consult our own interest. A reason is here intimated why they would obey him as they had obeyed Moses, because they believed (and in faith prayed) that God's presence would be with him as it was with Moses. Those that we have reason to think have favour from God should have honour and respect from us. Some understand it as a limitation of their obedience: "We will obey only as far as we perceive the Lord is with thee, but no further. while thou keepest close to God we will keep close to thee; hitherto shall our obedience come, but no further." But they were so far from having any suspicion of Joshua's deviating from the divine rule that there needed not such a proviso.

III. They pass an act to make it death for any Israelite to disobey Joshua's orders, or *rebel against his commandment, v.* 18. Perhaps if such a law had been made in Moses's time it might have prevented many of the rebellions that were formed against him; for most men fear the sword of the magistrate more than the justice of God. Yet there was a special reason for the making of this law now that they were entering upon the wars of Canaan; for in times of war the severity of military discipline is more necessary than at other times. Some think that in this statute they had an eye to that law concerning the prophet God would raise up like unto Moses, which they think, though it refer chiefly to Christ, yet takes in Joshua by the way as a type of him, that whosoever would not hearken to him should be *cut off from his people.* Deu. 18:19, *I will require it of him.*

IV. They animate him to go on with cheerfulness in the work to which God had called him; and, in desiring that he would be strong and of a good courage, they did in effect promise him that they would do all they could, by an exact, bold, and cheerful observance of all his orders, to encourage him. It very much heartens those that lead in a good work to see those that follow follow with a good will. Joshua, though of approved valour, did not take it as an affront, but as a great kindness, for the people to bid him be strong and of a good courage.

CHAPTER 2

In this chapter we have an account of the scouts that were employed to bring an account to Joshua of the posture of the city of Jericho. Observe here, I. How Joshua sent them (*v.* 1). II. How Rahab received them, and protected them, and told a lie for them (*v.* 2–7), so that they escaped out of the hands of the enemy. III. The account she gave them of the present posture of Jericho, and the panic-fear they were struck with upon the approach of Israel (*v.* 8–11). IV. The bargain she made with them for the security of herself and her relations in the ruin she saw coming upon her city (*v.* 12–21). V. Their safe return to Joshua, and the account they gave him of their expedition (*v.* 22–24). And that which makes this story most remarkable is that Rahab, the person principally concerned in it, is twice celebrated in the New Testament as a great believer (Heb. 11:31) and as one whose faith proved itself by good works, James 2:25.

Verses 1–7

In these verses we have,

I. The prudence of Joshua, in sending spies to observe this important pass, which was likely to be disputed at the entrance of Israel into Canaan (v. 1). Go *view the land, even Jericho.* Moses had sent spies (Num. 13) Joshua himself was one of them and it proved of ill consequence. Yet Joshua now sent spies, not, as the former were sent, to survey the whole land, but Jericho only; not to bring the account to the whole congregation, but to Joshua only, who, like a watchful general, was continually projecting for the public good, and, was particularly careful to take the first step well and not to stumble at the threshold. It was not fit that Joshua should venture over Jordan, to make his remarks *incognito — in disguise;* but he sends two men (two young men, says the Septuagint), to view the land, that from their report he might take his measures in attacking Jericho. Observe, 1. There is no remedy, but great men must see with other people's eyes, which makes it very necessary that they be cautious in the choice of those they employ, since so much often depends upon their fidelity. 2. Faith in God's promise ought not to supersede but encourage our diligence in the use of proper means. Joshua is sure he has God with him, and yet sends men before him. We do not trust God, but tempt him, if our expectations slacken our endeavours. 3. See how ready these men were to go upon this hazardous enterprise. Though they put their lives in their hands yet they ventured in obedience to Joshua their general, in zeal for the service of the camp, and in dependence upon the power of that God who, being the keeper of Israel in general, is the protector of every particular Israelite in the way of his duty.

II. The providence of God directing the spies to the house of Rahab. How they got over Jordan we are not told; but into Jericho they came, which was about seven or eight miles from the river, and there seeking for a convenient inn were directed to the house of Rahab, here called a *harlot,* a woman that had formerly been of ill fame, the reproach of which stuck to her name, though of late she had repented and reformed. Simon the leper (Mt. 26:6), though cleansed from his leprosy, wore the reproach of it in his name at long as he lived; so Rahab the harlot; and she is so called in the New Testament, where both her faith and her good works are praised, to teach us, 1. That the greatness of sin is no bar to pardoning mercy if it be truly repented of in time. We read of publicans and harlots entering into the kingdom of the Messiah, and being welcomed to all the privileged of that kingdom, Mt. 21:31. 2. That there are many who before their conversion were very wicked and vile, and yet afterwards come to great eminence in faith and holiness. 3. Even those that through grace have repented of the sins of their youth must expect to bear the reproach of them, and when they hear of their old faults must renew their repentance, and, as an evidence of that, hear of them patiently. God's Israel, for aught that appears, had but one friend, but one well-wisher in all Jericho, and that was Rahab a harlot. God has often served his own purposes and his church's interests by men of different morals. Had these scouts gone to any other house than this they would certainly have been betrayed and put to death without mercy. But God knew where they had a friend that would be true to them, though they did not, and directed them thither. Thus that which seems to us most contingent and accidental is often over-ruled by the divine providence to serve its great ends. And those that faithfully acknowledge God in their ways he will *guide with his eye.* See Jer. 36:19, 26.

III. The piety of Rahab in receiving and protecting these Israelites. Those that keep public-houses entertain all comers, and think themselves obliged to be civil to their guests. But Rahab showed her guests more than common civility, and went upon an uncommon principle in what she did; it was *by faith* that she received those with peace against whom her king and country had denounced war, Heb. 11:31. 1. She bade them welcome to her house; they lodged there, though it appears by what she said to them (v. 9) she knew both whence they came and what their business was. 2. Perceiving that they were observed com-

ing into the city, and that umbrage was taken at it, she hid them upon the roof of the house, which was flat, and covered them with stalks of flax (v. 6), so that, if the officers should come thither to search for them, there they might lie undiscovered. By these stalks of flax, which she herself had lain in order upon the roof to dry in the sun, in order to the beating of it and making it ready for the wheel, it appears she had one of the good characters of the virtuous woman, however in others of them she might be deficient, that she *sought wool and flax, and wrought willingly with her hands,* Prov. 31:13. From this instance of her honest industry one would hope that, whatever she had been formerly, she was not now a harlot. 3. When she was examined concerning them, she denied they were in her house, turned off the officers that had a warrant to search for them with a sham, and so secured them. No marvel that the king of Jericho sent to enquire after them (v. 2, 3); he had cause to fear when the enemy was at his door, and his fear made him suspicious and jealous of all strangers. He had reason to demand from Rahab that she should *bring forth the men* to be dealt with as spies; but Rahab not only disowned that she knew them, or knew where they were, but, that no further search might be made for them in the city, told the pursuers they had gone away again and in all probability might be overtaken, v. 4, 5. Now, (1.) We are sure this was a good work: it is canonized by the apostle (James 2:25), where she is said to be *justified by works,* and this is specified, that *she received the messengers, and sent them out another way,* and she did it by faith, such a faith as set her above the fear of man, even of the wrath of the king. She believed, upon the report she had heard of the wonders wrought for Israel, that their God was the only true God, and that therefore their declared design upon Canaan would undoubtedly take effect and in this faith she sided with them, protected them, and courted their favour. Had she said, "I believe God is yours and Canaan yours, but I dare not show you any kindness," her faith had been dead and inactive, and would not have justified her. But by this it appeared to be both alive and lively, that she exposed herself to the utmost peril, even of life, in obedience to her faith. Note, Those only are true believers that can find in their hearts to venture for God; and those that by faith take the Lord for their God take his people for their people, and cast in their lot among them. Those that have God for their refuge and hiding-place must testify their gratitude by their readiness to shelter his people when there is occasion. *Let my outcasts dwell with thee,* Isa. 16:3, 4. And we must be glad of an opportunity of testifying the sincerity and zeal of our love to God by hazardous services to his church and kingdom among men. But, (2.) There is that in it which it is not easy to justify, and yet it must be justified, or else it could not be so good a work as to justify her. [1.] It is plain that she betrayed her country by harbouring the enemies of it, and aiding those that were designing its destruction, which could not consist with her allegiance to her prince and her affection and duty to the community she was a member of. But that which justifies her in this is that *she knew the Lord had given Israel this land* (v. 9), knew it by the incontestable miracles God had wrought for them, which confirmed that grant; and her obligations to God were higher than her obligations to any other. If she knew *God had given them this land,* it would have been a sin to join with those that hindered them from possessing it. But, since no such grant of any land to any people can now be proved, this will by no means justify any such treacherous practices against the public welfare. [2.] It is plain that she deceived the officers that examined her with an untruth — That she knew not whence the men were, that they had gone out, that she knew not whither they had gone. What shall we say to this? If she had either told the truth or been silent, she would have betrayed the spies, and this would certainly have been a great sin; and it does not appear that she had any other way of concealing them than by this ironical direction to the officers to pursue them another way, which if they would suffer themselves to be deceived by, let them be deceived. None are bound to accuse themselves, or their friends, of that which, though enquired after as a crime, they know to be a virtue. This case was altogether extraordinary, and therefore cannot be drawn into a precedent; and that may be justified here which would be by no means lawful in a com-

mon case. Rahab knew, by what was already done on the other side Jordan, that no mercy was to be shown to the Canaanites, and thence inferred that, if mercy was not owing them, truth was not; those that might be destroyed might be deceived. Yet divines generally conceive that it was a sin, which however admitted of this extenuation, that being a Canaanite she was not better taught the evil of lying; but God accepted her faith and pardoned her infirmity. However it was in this case, we are sure it is our duty to speak every man the truth to his neighbour, to dread and detest lying, and never to *do evil, that* evil, *that good may come of it,* Rom. 3:8. But God accepts what is sincerely and honestly intended, though there be a mixture of frailty and folly in it, and is not extreme to mark what we do amiss. Some suggest that what she said might possibly be true of some other men.

Verses 8–21

The matter is here settled between Rahab and the spies respecting the service she was now to do for them, and the favour they were afterwards to show to her. She secures them on condition that they should secure her.

I. She gives them, and by them sends to Joshua and Israel, all the encouragement that could be desired to make their intended descent upon Canaan. this was what they came for, and it was worth coming for. Having got clear of the officers, she comes up to them to the *roof of the house* where they lay hid, finds them perhaps somewhat dismayed at the peril they apprehended themselves in from the officers, and scarcely recovered from the fright, but has that to say to them which will give them abundant satisfaction. 1. She lets them know that the report of the great things God had done for them had come to Jericho (v. 10), not only that they had an account of their late victories obtained over the Amorites in the neighbouring country, on the other side of the river, but that their miraculous deliverance out of Egypt, and passage through the Red Sea, a great way off, and forty years ago, were remembered and talked of afresh in Jericho, to the amazement of every body. Thus *this* Joshua and his fellows were *men wondered at,* Zec. 3:8. See how God *makes his wonderful works to be remembered* (Ps. 111:4), so that *men shall speak of the might of his terrible acts,* Ps. 145:6. 2. She tells them what impressions the tidings of these things had made upon the Canaanites: Your *terror has fallen upon us* (v. 9); *our hearts did melt,* v. 11. If she kept a public house, this would give her an opportunity of understanding the sense of various companies and of travellers from other parts of the country, so that they could not know this any way better than by her information; and it would be of great use to Joshua and Israel to know it; it would put courage into the most cowardly Israelite to hear how their enemies were dispirited, and it was easy to conclude that those who now fainted before them would infallibly fall before them, especially because it was the accomplishment of a promise God had made them, that he would *lay the fear and dread of them upon all this land* (Deu. 11:25), and so it would be an earnest of the accomplishment of all the other promises God had made to them. Let not the stout man glory in his courage, any more than the strong man in his strength; for God can weaken both mind and body. Let not God's Israel be afraid of their most powerful enemies; for their God can, when he pleases, make their most powerful enemies afraid of them. Let none think to harden their hearts against God and prosper; for he that made man's soul can at any time make the sword of his terrors approach to it. 3. She hereupon makes profession of her faith in God and his promise; and perhaps *there was not found so great faith* (all things considered), no, *not in Israel,* as in this woman of Canaan. (1.) who believes God's power and dominion over all the world (v. 11): "Jehovah your God, whom you worship and call upon, is so far above all gods that he is the only true God; for *he is God in heaven above and in earth beneath,* and is served by all the hosts of both." A vast distance there is between heaven and earth, yet both are equally under the inspection and government of the great Jehovah. Heaven is not above his power, nor is earth below his cognizance. (2.) She believes his promise to his people Israel (v. 9): *I know that the Lord hath given you the land.* The king of Jericho had heard as much as she had of the great things God had done for Israel, yet he cannot infer thence that the Lord had given them this land, but resolves to hold it out against them to the last extremity; for the most powerful means of conviction will not of themselves attain the end without divine grace, and by that grace Rahab the harlot, who had only heard of the wonders God had wrought, speaks with more assurance of the truth of the promise made to the fathers than all the elders of Israel had done who were eye-witnesses of those wonders, many of whom perished through unbelief of this promise. *Blessed are those that have not seen, and yet have believed;* so Rahab did. *O woman, great is thy faith!*

II. She engaged them to take her and her relations under their protection, that they might not perish in the destruction of Jericho, *v.* 12, 13. Now, 1. It was an evidence of the sincerity and strength of her faith concerning the approaching revolution in her country that she was so solicitous to make an interest for herself with the Israelites, and courted their kindness. She foresaw the conquest of her country, and in the belief of that bespoke in time the favour of the conquerors. Thus Noah, being *moved with fear, prepared an ark to the saving of his house, and the condemning of the world,* Heb. 11:7. Those who truly believe the divine revelation concerning the ruin of sinners, and the grant of the heavenly land to God's Israel, will give diligence to flee from the wrath to come, and to lay hold of eternal life, by joining themselves to God and to his people. 2. The provision she made for the safety of her relations, as well as for her own, is a laudable instance of natural affection, and an intimation to us in like manner to do all we can for the salvation of the souls of those that are dear to us, and, with ourselves, to bring them, if possible, into the bond of the covenant. No mention is made of her husband and children, but only her parents, and brothers, and sisters, for whom, though she was herself a housekeeper, she retained a due concern. 3. Her request that they would swear unto her by Jehovah is an instance of her acquaintance with the only true God, and her faith in him and devotion towards him, one act of which is religiously to *swear by his name.* 4. Her petition is very just and reasonable, that, since she had protected them, they should protect her, and since her kindness to them extended to their people, for whom they were now negotiating, their kindness to her should take in all hers. It was the least they could do for one that had saved their lives with the hazard of her own. Note, Those that show mercy may expect to find mercy. Observe, She does not demand any preferment by way of reward for her kindness to them, though they lay so much at her mercy that she might have made her own terms, but only indents for her Life, which in a general destruction would be a singular favour. Thus God promised Ebed-Melech, in recompence for his kindness to Jeremiah, that in the worst of times he should have *his life for a prey,* Jer. 39:18. Yet this Rahab was afterwards advanced to be a princess in Israel, the wife of Salmon, and one of the ancestors of Christ, Mt. 1:5. Those that faithfully serve Christ and suffer for him he will not only protect, but prefer, and will do for them *more than they are able to ask or think.*

III. They solemnly engaged for her preservation in the common destruction (*v.* 14): *"Our life for yours.* We will take as much care of your lives as of our own, and would as soon hurt ourselves as any of you." Nay, they imprecate God's judgments on themselves if they should violate their promise to her. She had pawned her life for theirs, and now they in requital pawn their lives for hers, and (as public persons) with them they pawn the public faith and the credit of their nation, for they plainly interest all Israel in the engagement in those words, *When the Lord has given us the land,* meaning not themselves only, but the people whose agents they were. No doubt they knew themselves sufficiently authorized to treat with Rahab concerning this matter, and were confident that Joshua would ratify what they did, else they had not dealt honestly; the general law that they should make no covenant with the Canaanites (Deu. 7:2) did not forbid them to take under their protection a particular person, that had heartily come into their interests and had done them real kindnesses. The law of gratitude is one of the laws of nature. Now observe here, 1. The promises they made her. In general, *"We will deal kindly and truly with thee, v.* 14. We will not only be kind in promising now, but true in performing what we promise; and not only true in performing just what we promise, but kind in out-doing thy demands and expectations." The goodness of God is often expressed by his kindness and truth (Ps. 117:2), and in both these we must be followers of him. In particular, *"If a hand be upon any in the house with thee,* his *blood shall be on our head," v.* 19. If hurt come through our carelessness to those whom we are obliged to protect, we thereby contract guilt, and blood will be found a heavy load. 2. The provisos and limitations of their promises. Though they were in haste, and it may be in some confusion, yet we find them very cautious in settling this agreement and the terms of it, not to bind themselves to more than was fit for them to perform. Note, Covenants must be made with care, and we must swear in judgment, lest we find ourselves perplexed and entangled when it is too late *after vows to make enquiry.* Those that will be conscientious in keeping their promises will be cautious in making them, and perhaps may insert conditions which others may think frivolous. Their promise is here accompanied with three provisos, and they were necessary ones. They will protect Rahab, and all her relations always, provided, (1.) That she tie the scarlet cord with which she was now about to let them down in the window of her house, *v.* 18. This was to be a mark upon the house, which the spies would take care to give notice of to the camp of Israel, that no soldier, how hot and eager soever he was in military executions, might offer any violence to the house that was thus distinguished. This was like the blood sprinkled upon the door-post, which secured e first-born from the destroying angel, and, being of the same colour, some allude to this also to represent the safety of believers under the protection of the blood of Christ sprinkled on the conscience. The same cord that she made use of for the preservation of these Israelites was to be made use of for her preservation. What we serve and honour God with we may expect he will bless and make comfortable to us. (2.) That she should have all those whose safety she had desired in the house with her and keep them there, and that, at the time of taking the town, none of them should dare to stir out of doors, *v.* 18, 19. This was a *necessary* proviso, for Rahab's kindred could not be distinguished any other way than by being in her distinguished house; should they mingle with their neighbours, there was no remedy, but the sword would devour *one as well as another.* It was a *reasonable* proviso that, since they were saved purely for Rahab's sake, her house should have the honour of being their castle, and that, if they would not *perish with those that believed not,* they should thus far believe the certainty and severity of the ruin coming upon their city as to retire into a place made safe by promise, as Noah into the ark and Lot into Zoar, and should *save themselves from this untoward generation,* by separating from them. It was likewise a *significant* proviso, intimating to us that those who are added to the church that they may be saved must keep close to the society of the faithful, and, having *escaped the corruption that is in the world through lust,* must take heed of being again entangled therein. (3.) That she should keep counsel (*v.* 14, 20): *If thou utter this our business,* that is, "If thou betray us when we are gone, or if thou make this agreement public, so as that others tie scarlet lines in their windows and so confound us, then we will be clear of thy oath." Those are unworthy of *the secret of the Lord* that know now how to keep it to themselves when there is occasion.

IV. She then took effectual care to secure her new friends, and *sent them out another way,* James 2:25. Having fully understood the bargain they made with her, and consented to it (*v.* 21), she then *let them down by a cord* over the city wall (*v.* 15), the situation of her house befriending them herein: thus Paul made his escape out of Damascus, 2 Co. 11:33. She also directed them which way to go for their own safety, being better acquainted with the country than they were, *v.* 16. she directs them to leave the high road, and abscond in the mountains till the pursuers returned, for till then they could not safely venture over Jordan. those that are in the way of God and their duty may expect that Providence will protect them, but this will not excuse them from taking all prudent methods for their own safety. God will keep us, but then we must not wilfully expose ourselves. Providence must be trusted, but not tempted. Calvin thinks that their charge to Rahab to keep this matter secret, and not to utter it, was intended for her safety, lest she, boasting of her security from the sword of Israel, should, before they came to protect her, fall into the hands of the king of Jericho and be put to death for treason: thus do they prudently advise her for her safety, as she advised them for theirs. And it is good advice, which we should at any time be thankful for, to *take heed to ourselves.*

Verses 22–24

We have here the safe return of the spies Joshua had sent, and the great encouragement they brought with them to Israel to proceed in their descent upon Canaan. Had they been disposed to discourage the people, as the evil spies did that Moses sent, they might have told them what they had observed of the height and strength of the walls of Jericho, and the extraordinary vigilance of the king of Jericho, and how narrowly they escaped out of his hands; but they were of another spirit, and, depending themselves upon the divine promise, they animated Joshua likewise. 1. Their return in safety was itself an encouragement to Joshua, and a token for good. that God provided for them so good a friend as Rahab was in an enemy's country, and that notwithstanding the rage of the king of Jericho and the eagerness of the pursuers they had come back in peace, was such an instance of God's great care concerning them for Israel's sake as might assure the people of the divine guidance and care they were under, which should undoubtedly make the progress of their arms glorious. He that so wonderfully protected their scouts would preserve their men of war, and cover their heads in the day of battle. 2. The report they brought was much more encouraging (*v.* 24): *"All the inhabitants of the country,* though resolved to stand it out, yet *do faint because of us,* they have neither wisdom to yield nor courage to fight," whence they conclude, *"Truly the Lord has delivered into our hands all the land,* it is all our own; we have nothing to do, in effect, but to take possession." Sinners' frights are sometimes sure presages of their fall. If we resist our spiritual enemies they will flee before us, which will encourage us to hope that in due time we shall be more than conquerors.

CHAPTER 3

This chapter, and that which follows it, give us the history of Israel's passing through Jordan into Canaan, and a very memorable history it is. Long afterwards, they are told to remember what God did for them between Shittim (whence they decamped, *v.* 1). and Gilgal, where they next pitched, *ch.* 4:19, Mic. 6:5, that they might know the righteousness of the Lord. By Joshua's order they marched up to the river's side (*v.* 1), and then almighty power led them through it. They passed through the Red Sea unexpectedly, and in their flight by night, but they have notice some time before of their passing through Jordan, and their expectations raised. I. The people are directed to follow the ark (*v.* 2–4). II. They are commanded to sanctify themselves (*v.* 5). III. The priests with the ark are ordered to lead the van (*v.* 6). IV. Joshua is magnified and made commander in chief (*v.* 7, 8). V. Public notice is given of what God is about to do for them (*v.* 9–13). IV. The thing is done, Jordan is divided, and Israel brought safely through it (*v.* 14–17). This was the Lord's doing, and it is marvellous in our eyes.

Verses 1–6

Rahab, in mentioning to the spies the *drying up of the Red Sea* (*ch.* 2:10), the report of which terrified the Canaanites more than anything else, intimates that those on that side the water expected that Jordan, that great defence of their country, would in like manner give way to them. Whether the Israelites had any expectation of it does not appear. God often *did things for them which they looked not for,* Isa. 64:3. Now here we are told,

I. That they *came to Jordan and lodged there, v.* 1. Though they were not yet told how they should pass the river, and were unprovided for the passing of it in any ordinary way, yet they went forward in faith, having been told (*ch.* 1:11) that they should pass it. We must go on in the way of our duty though we foresee difficulties, trusting God to help us through them when we come to them. Let us proceed as far as we can, and depend on divine sufficiency for that which we find ourselves not sufficient for. In this march Joshua led them, and particular notice is taken of his early rising as there is afterwards upon other occasions (*ch.* 6:12; 7:16; 8:10), which intimates how little he loved his ease, how much he loved his business, and what care and pains he was willing to take in it. Those that would bring great tings to pass must rise early. *Love not sleep, lest thou come to poverty.* Joshua herein set a good example to the officers under him, and taught them to rise early, and to all that are in public stations especially to attend continually to the duty of their place.

II. That the people were directed to follow the ark. Officers were appointed to go through the host to give these directions (*v.* 2), that every Israelite might know both what to do and what to depend upon.

1. They might depend upon the ark to lead them; that is, upon God himself, of whose presence the ark was an instituted sign and token. It seems, the pillar of cloud and fire was removed, else that would have led them, unless we suppose that it now hovered over the ark and so they had a double guide: honour was put upon the ark, and a defence upon that glory. It is called here the *ark of the covenant of the Lord their God.* What greater encouragement could they have than this, that the Lord was their God, a God in covenant with them? Here was the *ark of the covenant;* if God be ours, we need not fear any evil. He was nigh to them, present with them, went before them: what could come amiss to those that were thus guided, thus guarded? Formerly the ark was carried in the midst of the camp, but now it went before them to *search out a resting-place* for them (Num. 10:33), and, as it were, to give them livery and seisin of the promised land, and put them in possession of it In the ark the tables of the law were, and over it the mercy-seat; for the divine law and grace reigning in the heart are the surest pledges of God's presence and favour, and those that would be led to the heavenly Canaan must take the law of God for their guide *(if thou wilt enter into life keep the commandments)* and have the great propitiation in their eye, *looking for the mercy of our Lord Jesus Christ unto eternal life.*

2. They might depend upon the priests and Levites, who were appointed for that purpose to carry the ark before them. The work of ministers is to hold forth the word of life, and to take care of the administration of those ordinances which are the tokens of God's presence and the instruments of his power and grace; and herein they must go before the people of God in their way to heaven.

3. The people must follow the ark: *Remove from your place and go after it,* (1.) As those that are resolved never to forsake it. Wherever God's ordinances are, there we must be; if they flit, we must remove and go after them. (2.) As those that are entirely satisfied in its guidance, that it will lead in the best way to the best end; and therefore, *Lord, I will follow thee whithersoever thou goest.* This must be all their car, to attend the motions of the ark, and follow it with an implicit faith. Thus must we walk after the rule of the word and the direction of the Spirit in every thing, so shall *peace be upon us,* as it now was upon the Israel of God. They must follow the priests as far as they carried the ark, but no further; so we must follow our ministers only as they follow Christ.

4. In following the ark, they must *keep their distance, v.* 4. They must none of them come within a thousand yards of the ark. (1.) They must thus express their awful and reverent regard to that token of God's presence, lest its familiarity with them should breed contempt. This charge to them not to come near was agreeable to that dispensation of darkness, bondage, and terror: but we now through Christ have access with boldness. (2.) Thus it was made to appear that the ark was able to protect itself, and needed not to be guarded by the men of war, but was itself a guard to them. With what a noble defiance of the enemy did it leave all it its friends half a mile behind except the unarmed priests that carried it as perfectly sufficient for its own safety and theirs that fallowed it! (3.) Thus it was the better seen by those that were to be led by it: *That you may know the way by which you must go,* seeing it, as it were, chalked out or tracked by the ark. Had they been allowed to come near it, they would have surrounded it, and none would have had the sight of it but those that were close to it; but, as it was put at such a distance before them, they would all have the satisfaction of seeing it, and would be animated by the sight. And it was with good reason that this provision was made for their encouragement: *For you have not passed this way heretofore.* This had been the character of all their way through the wilderness, it was an untrodden path, but this especially through Jordan. While we are here we must expect and prepare for unusual events, to pass ways that we have not passed before, and much more when we go hence; our way through the *valley of the shadow of death* is a way we have not gone before, which makes it the more formidable. But, if we have the assurance of God's presence, we need not fear; that will furnish us with such strength as we never had when we come to do a work we never did.

III. They were commanded to sanctify themselves, that they might be prepared to attend the ark; and with good reason: For *to-morrow the Lord will do wonders among you, v.* 5. See how magnificently he speaks of God's works: he *doeth wonders,* and is therefore to be adored, admired, and trusted in. See how intimately acquainted Joshua was with the divine counsels: he could tell before-hand what god would do, and when. See what preparation we must make to receive the discoveries of God's glory and the communications of his grace: we must sanctify ourselves. This we must do when we are to attend the ark, and God by it is about to do wonders among us; we must separate ourselves from all other cares, devote ourselves to God's honour, and *cleanse ourselves from all filthiness of flesh and spirit.* The people of Israel were now entering into the holy land, and therefore must sanctify themselves. God was about to give them uncommon instances of his favour, which by meditation and prayer they must compose their minds to a very careful observation of, that they might give God the glory, and take to themselves the comfort, of these appearances.

IV. The priests were ordered to take up the ark and carry it *before the people, v.* 6. It was the Levites' work ordinarily to carry the ark, Num. 4:15. But on this great occasion the priests were ordered to do it. And they did as they were commanded, *took up the ark,* and did not think themselves disparaged, *went before the people,* and did not thing themselves exposed; the ark they carried was both their honour and their defence. And now we may suppose that prayer of Moses used, when the ark set forward (Num. 10:35), *Rise up, Lord and let they enemies be scattered.* Magistrates are here instructed to stir up ministers to their work, and to make use of their authority for the furtherance of religion. Ministers must likewise learn to go before in the way of God, and not to shrink nor draw back when dangers are before them. They mus expect to be most struck at, but they *know whom they have trusted.*

Verses 7–13

We may observe here how God honours Joshua, and by this wondrous work he is about to do designs to make Israel know that he is their governor, and then how Joshua honours God and endeavours by it to make Israel know that he is their God. Thus those that honour God he will honour, and those whom he has advanced should do what they can in their places to exalt him.

I. God speaks to Joshua to put honour upon him, *v.* 7, 8. 1. It was a great honour God id him that he spoke to him as he had done to Moses from off the mercy-seat, before the priests removed it with the ark. This would make Joshua easy in himself and great among the people, that God was pleased to speak so familiarly to him. 2. that he designed to *magnify him in the sight of all Israel.* He had told him before that he would be with him (*ch.* 1:5), and that comforted him, but now all Israel shall see it, and this would magnify him. Those are truly great with whom God is and whom he employs and owns in his service. God magnified him because he would have the people magnify him. Pious magistrates are to be highly honoured and esteemed as public blessings, and the more we see of God with them the more we should honour them. by the dividing of the red Sea Israel was convinced that God was with Moses in bringing them out of Egypt; therefore they are said to be *baptized unto Moses in the sea,* 1 Co. 10:2. and upon that occasion they *believed him,* Ex. 14:31. And now, by the dividing of Jordan, they shall be convinced that God is in like manner with Joshua in bringing them into Canaan. God had magnified Joshua before on several occasions, but now he began to magnify him as the successor of Moses in the government. Some have observed that it was at the banks of Jordan that God began to magnify Joshua, and at the same place he began to magnify our Lord Jesus as Mediator; for John was baptizing at Bethabara, *the house of passage,* and there it was that when our Saviour was baptized it was proclaimed concerning him, *This is my beloved Son.* 3. That by him he gave orders to the priests themselves, though they were his immediate attendants (*v.* 8): *Thou shalt command the priests,* that is, "Thou shalt make known to them the divine command in this matter, and take care that they observe it, to stand still at the brink of Jordan while the waters part, that it may appear to be *at the presence of the Lord,* of the mighty God of Jacob, that Jordan is *driven back,"* Ps. 114:5, 7. God could have divided the river without the priests, but they could not without him. The priests must herein set a good example to the people, and teach them to do their utmost in the service of God, and trust him for help in time of need.

II. Joshua speaks to the people, and therein honours God.

1. He demands attention (*v.* 9): *"Come hither* to me, as many as can come within hearing, and, before you see the works, *hear the words of the Lord your God,* that you may compare them together and they may illustrate each other." He had commanded them to sanctify themselves, and therefore calls them to *hear the word of God,* for that is the ordinary means of sanctification, Jn. 17:17.

2. He now tells them, at length, by what way they should pass over Jordan, by the stopping of its streams (*v.* 13): *The waters of Jordan shall be cut off.* God could by a sudden and miraculous frost have congealed the surface, so that they might all have gone over upon the ice; but that being a thing sometimes done even in that country by the ordinary power of nature (Job 38:30), it would not have been such an honour to Israel's God, nor such a terror to Israel's enemies; it must therefore be done in such a way as had no precedent but the dividing of the Red Sea: and that miracle is here repeated, to show that God has the same power to finish the salvation of his people that he had to begin it, for he is the *Alpha* and the *Omega;* and that *the word of the Lord* (as the Chaldee reads it, *v.* 7), the essential, eternal Word, was as truly with Joshua as he was with Moses. And by the dividing of the waters from the waters, and the making of the dry land to appear which had been covered, God would remind them of that in which Moses by revelation had instructed them concerning the work of creation (Gen. 1:6, 9), that by what they now saw their belief of that which they there read might be assisted, and they might know that the God whom they worshipped was the same God that made the world and that it was the same power that was engaged and employed for them.

3. The people having been directed before to follow the ark are here told that it should *pass before them into Jordan, v.* 11. Observe, (1.) The ark of the covenant must be their guide. during the reign of Moses, the cloud was their guide, but now, in Joshua's reign, the ark; both were visible signs of God's presence and presidency, but divine grace under the Mosaic dispensation was wrapt up as in a cloud and covered with a veil, while by Christ, our Joshua, it is revealed in the ark of the covenant unveiled. (2.) It is called *the ark of the covenant of the Lord of all the earth.* "He that is your God (*v.* 9), in covenant with you, is the *Lord of all the earth,* has both right and power to command, control, use, and dispose of all nations and of all creatures. He is the *Lord of all the earth,* therefore he needs not you, nor can he be benefited by you; therefore it is your honour and happiness to have him in covenant with you: if he be yours, all the creatures are at your service, and when he pleases shall be employed for you." When we are praising and worshipping God as Israel's God, and ours through Christ, we must remember that he is the *Lord of the whole earth,* and reverence him and trust in him accordingly. Some observe an accent in the original, which they think directs us to translate it somewhat more emphatically, *Behold the ark of the covenant, even the ark of the Lord, or even of the covenant of the Lord of all the earth.* (3.) They are told that the ark should *pass before them into Jordan.* God would not appoint them to go any where but where he himself would go before them and go with them; and they might safely venture, even into Jordan itself, if the ark of the covenant led them. While we make God's precepts our rule, his promises our stay, and his providence our guide, we need not dread the greatest difficulties we may meet with in the way of duty. That promise is sure to all the seed (Isa. 43:2), *When thou passes through the waters I will be with thee, and through the rivers they shall not overflow thee.*

4. From what God was now about to do for them he infers an assurance of what he would yet further do. This he mentions first, so much was his heart upon it, and so

great a satisfaction did it give him (*v.* 10): *"Hereby you shall know that the living God* (the true God, and God of power, not one of the dead gods of the heathen) *is among you,* though you see him not, nor are to have any image of him, is among you to give you law, secure your welfare, and receive your homage, — is among you in this great undertaking now before you; and therefore you shall, nay, he himself *will, without fail, drive out from before you the Canaanites."* So that the dividing of Jordan was intended to be to them, (1.) A sure token of God's presence with them. By this they could not but *know that God was among them,* unless their unbelief was as obstinate against the most convincing evidence as that of their fathers was, who presently after God had divided the Red Sea before them, impudently asked, *Is the Lord among us, or is he not?* Ex. 17:7. (2.) A sure pledge of the conquest of Canaan. "If the living God is among you, *expelling he will expel* (so the Hebrew phrase is) *from before you the Canaanites."* He will do it certainly, and do it effectually. What should hinder him? What can stand in his way before whom rivers are divided and dried up? The forcing of the lines was certain presage of the ruin of all their hosts: how could they stand their ground when Jordan itself was driven back? When they had not courage to dispute this pass, but trembled at the approach of the *mighty God of Jacob* (Ps. 114:7), what opposition could they ever make after this? This assurance which Joshua here gives them was so well grounded that it would enable one Israelite to chase a thousand Canaanites, and two to put then thousand to flight; and it would be abundantly strengthened by remembering the song of Moses, dictated forty years before, which plainly foretold the dividing of Jordan and the influence it would have upon the driving out of the Canaanites. Ex. 15:15–17, *"The inhabitants of Canaan shall melt away,* and so be effectually driven out; they shall be as still as a stone till thy people pass over, and then thou shalt bring them in and plant them." Note, God's glorious appearances for his church and people ought to be improved by us for the encouragement of our faith and hope for the future. *As for God, his work is perfect.* If Jordan's flood cannot keep them our, Canaan's force cannot turn them out again.

5. He directs them to get twelve men ready, one of each tribe, who must be within call to receive such orders as Joshua should afterwards give them, *v.* 12. It does not appear that they were to attend the priests, and walk with them when they carried the ark, that they might more immediately be witnesses of the wonders done by it, as some think; but they were to be at hand for the service they were called to, *ch.* 4:4, etc.

Verses 14–17

Here we have a short and plain account of the dividing of the river Jordan, and the passage of the children of Israel through it. The story is not garnished with the flowers of rhetoric (gold needs not to be painted), but it tell us, in short, matter of fact.

I. That this river was now broader and deeper than usually it was at other times of the year, *v.* 15. The melting of the snow on the mountains of Lebanon, near which this river had its rise, was the occasion that at the time of harvest, barley-harvest, which was the spring of the year, Jordan overflowed all his banks. This great flood, just at that time (which Providence might have restrained for once, of which he might have ordered them to cross at another time of the year) very much magnified the power of God and his kindness to Israel. Note, Though the opposition given to the salvation of God's people have all imaginable advantages, yet god can and will conquer it. Let the banks of Jordan be filled to the brink, filled till they run over, it is as easy to Omnipotence to divide them, and dry them up, as if they were ever so narrow, ever so shallow; it is all one with the Lord.

II. That as soon as ever the feet of the priests dipped in the brim of the water the stream stopped immediately, as if a sluice had been led down to dam it up, *v.* 15, 16. So that the waters above swelled, stood on a heap, and ran back, and yet, as it should seem did not spread, but congealed, which unaccountable rising of the river was observed with amazement by those that live upward upon it many miles off, and the remembrance of it remained among them long after: the waters on the other side this invisible dam ran down of course, and left the bottom of the river dry as far downward, it is likely, as they swelled upward. When they passed through the red Sea, the waters were a wall on either hand, here only on the right-hand. Note, The God of nature can, when he pleases, change the course of nature, and alter its properties, can turn fluids into solids, *waters into standing rocks,* as, on the contrary, *rocks into standing waters,* to serve his own purposes. See Ps. 114:5, 8. What cannot God do? What will he not do for the perfecting of his peoples, salvation? Sometimes he *cleaves the earth with rivers* (Hab. 3:9), and sometimes, as here, cleaves the rivers without earth. It is easy to imagine how, when the course of this strong rapid stream was arrested on a sudden, *the waters roared and were troubled,* so that the mountains seemed to *shake with the swelling thereof* (Ps. 46:3), how *the floods lifted up their voice, the floods lifted up their waves,* while the Lord on high showed himself *mightier than the noise of* these *many waters,* Ps. 93:3, 4. With reference to this the prophet asks, *Was the Lord displeased against the rivers? was thine anger against the rivers?* Hab. 3:8. No, *Thou wentest forth for the salvation of thy people, v.* 13. In allusion to this, it is foretold, among the great things God will do for the gospel church in the latter days, that the great river Euphrates shall be dried up, that *the way of the kings of the east may be prepared,* Rev. 16:12. When the time has come for Israel's entrance into the land of promise all difficulties shall be conquered, *mountains shall become plains* (Zec. 4:7) and rivers become dry, for the *ransomed of the Lord to pass over.* When we have finished our pilgrimage through this wilderness, death will be like this Jordan between us and the heavenly Canaan, but the ark of the covenant has prepare us a way through it; it is the last enemy that shall be destroyed.

III. That *the people passed over right against Jericho,* which was, 1. An instance of their boldness, and a noble defiance of their enemies. Jericho was one of the strongest cities, and yet they dared to face it at their first entrance. 2. It was an encouragement to them to venture through Jordan, for Jericho was a goodly city and the country about it extremely pleasant; and, having that in view as their own, what difficulties could discourage them from taking possession? 3. It would increase the confusion and terror of their enemies, who no doubt strictly observed their motions, and were the amazed spectators of this work of wonders.

IV. That the priests *stood still in the midst of Jordan while all the people passed over, v.* 17. There the ark was appointed to be, to show that the same power that parted the waters kept them parted as long as there was occasion; and had not the divine presence, of which the ark was a token, been their security, the waters would have returned upon them and buried them. there the priests were appointed to stand still, 1. To try their faith, whether they could venture to take their post, when god assigned it to them, with mountains of water over their heads. As they made a bold step when they set the first foot into Jordan, so now they made a bold stand when they tarried longest in Jordan; but they knew they carried their own protection with them. Note, Ministers in times of peril should be examples of courage and confidence in the divine goodness. 2. It was to encourage the faith of the people, that they might go triumphantly into Canaan, and *fear no evil,* no, not in this *valley of the shadow of death* (for so the divided river was), being assured of God's presence, which interposed between them and the greatest danger, between them and the proud waters, which otherwise had gone over their souls. Thus in the greatest dangers the saints are *comforted* with *his rod and his staff,* Ps. 23:4.

CHAPTER 4

This chapter gives a further account of the miraculous passage of Israel through Jordan. I. The provision that was made at that time to preserve the memorial of it, by twelve stones set up in Jordan (*v.* 9) and other twelve stones taken up out of Jordan (*v.* 1–8). II. The march of the people through Jordan's channel, the two tribes first, then all the people, and the priests that bore the ark last (*v.* 10–14). III. The closing of the waters again upon their coming up with the ark (*v.* 15–19). IV. The erecting of the monument in Gilgal, to preserve the remembrance of this work of wonder to posterity (*v.* 20–24).

Verses 1–9

We may well imagine how busy Joshua and all the men of war were while they were passing over Jordan, when besides their own marching into an enemy's country, and in the face of the enemy, which could not but occasion them many thoughts of hear, they had their wives, and children, and families, their cattle, and tents, and all their effects, bag and baggage, to convey by this strange and untrodden path, which we must suppose either very muddy or very stony, troublesome to the weak and frightful to the timorous, the descent to the bottom of the river and the ascent out of it steep, so that every man must needs have his head full of care and his hands full of business, and Joshua more than any of them. And yet, in the midst of all his hurry, care must be taken to perpetuate the memorial of this wonderous work of God, and this care might not be adjourned to a time of greater leisure. Note, How much soever we have to do of business for ourselves and our families, we must not neglect nor omit what we have to do for the glory of God and the serving of his honour, for that is our best business. Now,

I. God gave orders for the preparing of this memorial. Had Joshua done it without divine direction, it might have looked like a design to perpetuate his own name and honour, nor would it have commanded so sacred and venerable a regard from posterity as now, when god himself appointed it. Note, God's works of wonder ought to be kept in everlasting remembrance, and means devise for the preserving of the memorial of them. Some of the Israelites that passed over Jordan perhaps were so stupid, and so little affected with this great favour of God to them, that they felt no concern to have it remembered; while others, it may be, were so much affected with it, and had such deep impressions made upon them by it, that they thought there needed no memorial of it to be erected, the heart and tongue of every Israelite in every age would be a living lasting monument of it. But God, knowing their frame, and how apt they had been soon to forget his works, ordered an expedient for the keeping of this in remembrance to all generations, that those who could not, or would not, read the record of it in the sacred history, might come to the knowledge of it by the monument set up in remembrance of it, of which the common tradition of the country would be an explication; it would likewise serve to corroborate the proof of the matter of fact, and would remain a standing evidence of it to those who in after-ages might question the truth of it. A monument is to be erected, and, 1. Joshua, as chief captain, must five direction about it (*v.* 1): *When all the people had clean passed over Jordan,* not even the feeble, that were the hindmost of them, left behind, so that God had done his work completely, and every Israelite got safe into Canaan, then God spoke unto Joshua to provide materials for this monument. It is the pious conjecture of the learned bishop Patrick that Joshua had gone into some place of retirement to return thanks immediately for this wonderful mercy, and then god met him, and spoke thus to him. Or, perhaps, it was by Eleazar the priest that God gave these and other instructions to Joshua; for, though he is not mentioned here, yet, when Joshua was ordained by the imposition of hands to this great trust, god appointed that Eleazar should *ask counsel for him after the judgment of Urim, and at his word Joshua and all the children of Israel must go out and come in,* Num. 27:21. 2. One man out of each tribe, and he a chosen man, must be employed to prepare materials for this monument, that each tribe might have the story told them by one of themselves, and each tribe might contribute something to the glory of God thereby (*v.* 2, 4): *Out of ever tribe a man.* Not the Levites only, but every Israelite must, in his place, help to *make known to the sons of men God's mighty acts,* Ps. 145:12. The two tribes, though seated already in their possession, yet, sharing in the mercy, must lend a hand to the memorial of it. 3. The stones that must be set up for this memorial are ordered to be taken out of the midst of the cannel (where, probably, there lay abundance of great stones), and as near as might be from the very place where the priests stood *with the ark, v.* 3, 5. This intended monument deserved to be made of stones curiously cut with the finest and most exquisite art, but these stones out of the bottom of the river were more natural and more apt indications of the miracle. let posterity know by this that Jordan was driven back, for these very stones were then fetched out of it. In the institution of signs, God always chose that which was most proper and significant, rather than that which is pompous or curious; for *God hath chosen the foolish things of the world.* These twelve men, after they got over Jordan, must be sent back to the place where the ark stood, being permitted to come near it (which others might not) for this service: *"Pass over before the ark* (v. 5), that is, into the presence of the ark, which now stands in the midst of Jordan, and thence fetch these stones." 4. the use of these stones is here appointed for a sign (v. 6), a memorial, v. 7. They would give occasion to the children to ask their parents in time to come, *How came these stones hither?* (probably the land about not being stony), and then the parents would inform them, as they themselves had been informed, that in this place Jordan was divided by the almighty power of God, to give Israel passage into Canaan, as Joshua enlarges on this head, v. 22, etc.

II. According to these orders the thing was done. 1. Twelve stones were taken up out of the midst of Jordan, and carried in the sight of the people to the place where they had their head-quarters that night, v. 8. It is probable that the stones they took were as big as they could well carry, and as near as might be of a size and shape. But whether they went away with them immediately to the place, of whether they staid to attend the ark, and kept pace with the solemn procession of that, to grace its triumphant entry in to Canaan, is not certain. By these stones which they were ordered to take up God did, as it were, give them livery and seisin of this good land; it is all their own, let them enter and take possession; therefore what these twelve did the children of Israel are said to do (v. 8), because they were the representatives of their respective tribes. In allusion to this, we may observe that when the Lord Jesus, our Joshua, having overcome the sharpness of death and dried up that Jordan, had opened the kingdom of heaven to all believers, he appointed his twelve apostles according to the number of the tribes of Israel, by the memorial of the gospel to transmit the knowledge of this to remote places and future ages. 2. Other twelve stones (probably much larger than the other, for we read not that they were each of them one man's load) were set up *in the midst of Jordan* (v. 9), piled up so high in a heap or pillar as that the top of it might be seen above the water when the river was low, or seen in the water when it was clear, or at least the noise of commotion of the water passing over it would be observable, and the bargemen would avoid it, as they do a rock. Some way or other, it is likely, it was discernible, so as to notify the very place where the ark stood, and to serve for a duplicate to the other monument, which was to set up on dry land in Gilgal, for the confirming of its testimony and the preserving of its tradition. The sign being doubled, no doubt the thing was certain.

Verses 10–19

The inspired historian seems to be so well pleased with his subject here that he is loth to quit it, and is therefore very particular in his narrative, especially in observing how closely Joshua pursued the orders God gave him, and that he did nothing without divine direction, finishing all that *the Lord had commanded* him (v. 10), which is also said to be what *Moses commanded.* We read not of any particular commands that Moses gave to Joshua about this matter: the thing was altogether new to him. It must therefore be understood of the general instructions Moses had given him to follow the divine direction, to deliver that to the people which he *received of the Lord,* and to take all occasions to remind them of their duty to God, as the best return for his favours to them. This which Moses, who was now dead and gone, had said to him, he had in mind at this time, and *did accordingly.* It is well for us to have the good instructions that have been given us ready to us when we have occasion for them.

I. *The people hasted and passed over,* v. 10. Some understand this of the twelve men that carried the stones, but it seems rather to be meant of the body of the people, for, though an account was given of their passing over (v. 1), yet here it is repeated for the sake of this circumstance, which was to be added, that they passed over *in haste,* either because Joshua by their officers ordered them to make haste, for it was to be but one day's work and they must not *leave a hoof behind,* or perhaps it was their own inclination that hastened them. 1. Some hasted because

they were not able to trust God. They were afraid the waters should return upon them, being conscious of guilt, and diffident of the divine power and goodness. 2. Others because they were not willing to tempt God to continue the miracle longer than needs must, nor would they put the patience of the priests that bor the ark too much to the stretch by unnecessary delay. 3. Others because they were eager to be in Canaan, and would thus show how much they longed after that pleasant land. 4. Those that considered least, yet hasted because others did. He that believeth doth not make haste to *anticipate* God's counsels, but he makes haste to *attend* them, Isa. 28:16.

II. The two tribes and a half led the van, v. 12, 13. So they had promised when they had their lot given them on that side Jordan, Num. 32:27. And Joshua had lately reminded them of their promise, ch. 1:12–15. It was fit that those who had the first settlement should be the first in the encounter of difficulties, the rather because they had not the incumbrance of families with them as the other tribes had, and they were all chose men, and fit for service, ready armed. It was a good providence that they had so strong a body to lead them on, and would be an encouragement to the rest. And the two tribes had no reason to complain: the post of danger is the post of honour.

III. When all the people had got clear to the other side, the priests with the ark came up out of Jordan. This, one would think, should have been done of course; their own reason would tell them that now there was no more occasion for them, and yet they did not stir a step till Joshua ordered them to move, and Joshua did not order them out of Jordan till God directed him to do so, v. 15–17. so observant were they of Joshua, and he of God, which was their praise, as it was their happiness to be under such good direction. How low a condition soever God may at any time bring his priests or people to, let them patiently wait, till by his providence he shall call them up out of it, as the priests here were called to come up out of Jordan, and let them not be weary of waiting, while they have the tokens of God's presence with them, even the ark of the covenant, in the depth of their adversity.

IV. As soon as ever the priests and the ark had come up out of Jordan, the waters of the river, which had stood on a heap, gradually flowed down according to their nature and usual course, and soon filled the channel again, v. 18. This makes it yet more evident that the stop which had now been given to the river was not from any secret natural cause, but purely from the power of God's presence, and for the sake of his Israel; for when Israel's turn was served, and the token of God's presence was removed, immediately the water went forward again; so that if it be asked, *What ailed thee, O Jordan! that thou wast driven back?* It must be answered, It was purely in obedience to the God of Israel, and in kindness to the Israel of God. There is therefore none *like unto the God of Jeshurun; happy also art thou, O Israel! who is like unto thee, O people?* Some observe here, by way of allusion, that when the ark, and the priests that bor it, are removed from any place, the flood-gates are drawn up, the defence has departed, and an inundation of judgments is to be expected shortly. Those that are unchurched will soon be undone. The glory has departed if the ark is taken.

V. Notice is taken of the honour put upon Joshua by all this (v. 14): *On that day the Lord magnified Joshua,* both by the fellowship he admitted him to with himself, speaking to him upon all occasions and being ready to be consulted by him, and by the authority he confirmed him in over both priests and people. Those that honour God he will honour, and when he will magnify a man, as he had said he would magnify Joshua (ch. 3:7), he will do it effectually. Yet it was not for Joshua's sake only that he was thus magnified, but to put him in a capacity of doing so much the more service to Israel, for hereupon they feared him as they feared Moses. Se here what is the best and surest way to command the respect of inferiors, and to gain their reverence and observance, not by blustering and threatening, and carrying it with a high hand, but by holiness and love, and all possible indications of a constant regard to their welfare, and to God's will and honour. Those are feared in the best manner, and to the best purpose, who make it to appear that God is with them, and that they set him before them. Those that are sanctified are

truly magnified, and are worthy of double honour. Favourites of heaven should be looked on with awe.

VI. An account is kept of the time of this great event (v. 19): it was *on the tenth day of the first month,* just forty years since they came out of Egypt, wanting five days. God had said in his wrath that they should wander forty years in the wilderness, but, to make up that forty, we must take in the first year, which was then past, and had been a year of triumph in their deliverance out of Egypt, and this last, which had been a year of triumph likewise on the other side Jordan, so that all the forty were not years of sorrow; and at last he brought them into Canaan five days before the forty years were ended, to show how little pleasure God takes in punishing, how swift he is to show mercy, and that *for the elects' sake the days* of trouble *are shortened,* Mt. 24:22. God ordered it so that they should enter Canaan four days before the annual solemnity of the passover, and on the very day when the preparation for it was to begin (Ex. 12:3), because he would have their entrance into Canaan Graced and sanctified with that religious feast, and would have them then to be reminded of their deliverance out of Egypt, that, comparing them together, God might be glorified as the *Alpha* and *Omega* of their bliss.

Verses 20–24

The twelve stones which were *laid down in Gilgal* (v. 8) are here set up either one upon another, yet so as that they might be distinctly counted, or one by another in rows; for after they were fixed they ar not call *a heap of stones,* but *these stones.*

I. It is here taken for granted that posterity would enquire into the meaning of them, supposing them intended for a memorial: *Your children shall ask their fathers* (for who else should they ask?) *What mean these stones?* Notes, Those that will be wise when they are old must be inquisitive when they are young. Our Lord Jesus, though he had in himself the fulness of knowledge, has by his example taught children and young people to hear and ask questions, Lu. 2:46. Perhaps when John was baptizing in Jordan at Bethabara (the house of passage, where the people passed over) he pointed at these very stones, while saying (Mt. 3:9) *God is able of these stones* (which were at first set up by the twelve tribes) *to raise up children unto Abraham.* The stones being the memorial of the miracle, the children's question gave occasion for the improvement of it; but our Saviour says (Lu. 10:40), *If the* children *should hold their peace, the stones would immediately cry out;* for one way or other the Lord will be glorified in his works of wonder.

II. The parents are here directed what answer to give to this enquiry (v. 22): *"You shall let your children know* that which you have yourselves learned from the written word and from your fathers." Note, It is the duty of parents to acquaint their children betimes with the word and works of God, that they may be trained up in the way they should go.

1. They must let their children know that Jordan was driven back before Israel, who *went through it upon dry land,* and that this was the very place where they passed over. They saw how deep and strong a stream Jordan now was, but the divine power put a stop to it, even when it overflowed all its banks — "and this for you, that live so long after." Note, God's mercies to our ancestors were mercies to us; and we should take all occasions to revive the remembrance of the great things God did for our fathers *in the days of old.* The place thus marked would be a memorandum to them: Israel came over this Jordan. A local memory would be of use to them, and the sight of the place remind them of that which was done there; and not only the inhabitants of that country, but strangers and travellers, would look upon these stones and receive instruction. Many, upon the sight of the stones, would go to their Bibles, and there read the history of this wondrous work; and some perhaps, upon reading the history, though living at a distance, would have the curiosity to go and see the stones.

2. They must take that occasion to tell their children of the drying up of the Red Sea forty years before: *As the Lord your God did to the Red Sea.* Note. (1.) It greatly magnifies later mercies to compare them with former mercies, for, by making the comparison, it appears that god is the same yesterday, to-day, and for ever. (2.) Later mercies

should bring to remembrance former mercies, and revive our thankfulness for them.

3. They must put them in the way of making a good use of these works of wonder, the knowledge whereof was thus carefully transmitted to them, *v.* 24. (1.) The power of God was hereby magnified. All the world was or might be convinced that *the hand of the Lord is mighty,* that nothing is too hard for God to do; nor can any power, no, not that of nature itself, obstruct what God will effect. The deliverances of God's people are instructions to all people, and fair warnings not to contend with Omnipotence. (2.) The people of God were engaged and encouraged to persevere in his service *"That you might fear the Lord your God,* and consequently do your duty to him, and this for ever," or *all days (margin),* "every day, all the days of your lives, and your seed throughout your generations." The remembrance of this wonderful work should effectually restrain them from the worship of other gods, and constrain them to abide and abound in the service of their own God. Note, In all the instructions and informations parents give their children, they should have this chiefly in their eye, to teach and engage them to *fear God for ever.* Serious godliness is the best learning.

CHAPTER 5

Israel have now got over Jordan, and the waters which had opened before them, to favour their march forward, are closed again behind them, to forbid their retreat backward. They have now got footing in Canaan, and must apply themselves to the conquest of it, in order to which this chapter tells us, I. How their enemies were dispirited (*v.* 1). II. What was done at their first landing to assist and encourage them. 1. The covenant of circumcision was renewed (*v.* 2–9). 2. The feast of the passover was celebrated (*v.* 10). 3. Their camp was victualled with the corn of the land, whereupon the manna ceased (*v.* 11, 12). 4. The captain of the Lord's host himself appeared to Joshua to animate and direct him (*v.* 13–15).

Verses 1–9

A vast show, no doubt, the numerous camp of Israel made in the plains of Jericho, where now they had pitched their tents. *Who can count the dust of Jacob?* That which had long been the *church in the wilderness has now come up from the wilderness, leaning upon her beloved, and looks forth as the morning, fair as the moon, clear as the sun, and terrible as an army with banners.* How terrible she was in the eyes of her enemies we are here told, *v.* 1. How fair and clear she was made in the eyes of her friends, by the rolling away of the reproach of Egypt, we are told in the following verses.

I. Here is the fright which the Canaanites were put into by their miraculously passing over Jordan, *v.* 1. The news of it was soon dispersed all the country over, not only as a prodigy in itself, but as an alarm to all the kings and kingdoms of Canaan. Now, as when Babylon was taken, *One post runs to meet another, and one messenger to meet another,* to carry the amazing tidings to every corner of their land, Jer. 51:31. And here we are told what impressions the tidings made upon the kings of this land: *Their heart melted* like wax before the fire, *neither was there spirit in them any more.* This intimates that, though the heart of the people generally had fainted before (as Rahab owned, *ch.* 2:9), yet the kings had till now kept up their spirits pretty well, had promised themselves that, being in possession, their country populous, and their cities fortified, they should be able to make their part good against the invaders; but when they heard not only that they had come over Jordan, and that this defence of their country was broken through, but that they had come over by a miracle, the God of nature manifestly fighting for them, *their hearts failed them* too, they gave up the cause for gone, and were now at their wits' end. And, 1. they had reason enough to be afraid; Israel itself was a formidable body, and much more so when God was its head, a God of almighty power. What can make head against them if Jordan be driven back before them? 2. God impressed these fears upon them, and dispirited them, as he had promised (Ex. 23:27), *I will send my fear before thee.* God can make the wicked to fear *where no fear is* (Ps. 53:5.), much more where there is such cause for fear as was here. He that made the soul can, when he pleases, make his sword thus to approach to it and kill it with his terrors.

II. The opportunity which this gave to the Israelites to circumcise those among them that were uncircumcised: *At that time* (*v.* 2), when the country about them was in that great consternation, God ordered Joshua to circumcise the children of Israel, for at that time it might be done with safety even in an enemy's country; their hearts being melted, their hands were tied, that they could not take this advantage against them as Simeon and Levi did against the Shechemites, to come upon them *when they were sore.* Joshua could not be sure of this, and therefore, if he had ordered this general circumcision just at this time of his own head, he might justly have been censured as imprudent; for, how good soever the thing was in itself, in the eye of reason it was not seasonable at this time, and might have been of dangerous consequence; but, when God commanded him to do it, he must not *consult with flesh and blood;* he that bade them to do it would, no doubt, protect them and bear them out in it. Now observe,

1. The occasion there was for this general circumcision. (1.) All that came out of Egypt were circumcised, *v.* 5. while they had peace in Egypt doubtless they circumcised their children the eighth day according to the law. But after they began to be oppressed, especially when the edict was made for the destruction of their male infants, the administration of this ordinance was interrupted; many of them were uncircumcised, of whom there was a general circumcision, either during the time of the three days' darkness, as Dr. Lightfoot conjectures, or a year after, just before their eating the second passover at Mount Sinai, and in order to that solemnity (Num. 9:2) as many think. And it is with reference to that general circumcision that this is called a *second, v.* 2. But the learned Masius thinks it refers to the general circumcision of Abraham's family when that ordinance was first instituted, Gen. 17:23. That first confirmed the promise of the land of Canaan, this second was a thankful celebration of the performance of that promise. But, (2.) All that were *born in the wilderness,* namely, after their walking in the wilderness, became by the divine sentence a judgment upon them for their disobedience, as is intimated by that repetition of the sentence, *v.* 6. Al that were born since that fatal day on which God swore in his wrath that none of that generation should *enter into his rest* were uncircumcised. But what shall we say to this? Had not God enjoined it to Abraham, under a very severe penalty, that every man-child of his seed should be circumcised on the eighth day? Gen. 17:9–14. Was it not the seal of the everlasting covenant? Was not so great a stress laid upon it when they were coming out of Egypt that when, immediately after the first passover, the law concerning that feast was made perpetual, this was one clause of it, that no uncircumcised person should eat of it, but should be deemed as a stranger? and yet, under the government of Moses himself, to have all their children that were born for thirty-eight years together left uncircumcised is unaccountable. So great an omission could not be general but by divine direction. Now, [1.] Some think circumcision was omitted because it was needless: it was appointed to be a mark of distinction between the Israelites and other nations, and therefore in the wilderness, where they were so perfectly separated from all and mingled with none, there was no occasion for it. [2.] Others think that they did not look upon the precept of circumcision as obligatory till they came to settle in Canaan; for in the covenant made with them at Mount Sinai nothing was said about circumcision, neither was it of Moses but *of the fathers* (Jn. 7:22), and with particular reference to the grant of the land of Canaan, Gen. 17:8. [3.] Others think that God favourably dispensed with the observance of this ordinance in consideration of the unsettledness of their state, and their frequent removals while they were in the wilderness. It was requisite that children after they were circumcised should rest for some time while they were sore, and stirring them might be dangerous to them; God therefore would have mercy and not sacrifice. This reason is generally acquiesced in, but to me it is not satisfactory, for sometimes they staid a year in a place (Num. 9:22), if not much longer, and in their removals the little children, though sore, might be wrapped so warm, and carried so easy, as to receive no damage, and might certainly be much better accommodated than the mothers in travail or while lying in. Therefore, [4.] To me it seems to have been a continued token of God's displeasure against them for their unbelief and murmuring. Circumcision was originally a seal of the promise of the land of Canaan, as we observed before. It was in the believing hope of that good land that the patriarchs circumcised their children; but when God had *sworn in his wrath* concerning the men of was who came out of Egypt that they should be consumed in the wilderness, and never enter Canaan, nor come within sight of it (as that sentence is here repeated, *v.* 6, reference being made to it), as a further ratification of that sentence, and to be a constant memorandum of it to them, all that fell under that sentence, and were to fall by it, were forbidden to circumcise their children, by which they were plainly told that, whatever others might, they should never have the benefit of that promise of which circumcision was the seal. And this was such a significant indication of God's wrath as the breaking of the tables of the covenant was when Israel had broken the covenant by making the golden calf. It is true that there is no express mention of this judicial prohibition in the account of that sentence; but an intimation of it in Num. 14:33, *Your children shall bear your whoredoms.* It is probable the children of Caleb and Joshua were circumcised, for they were excepted out of that sentence, and of Caleb it is particularly said, *To him will I give the land, and to his children* (Deu. 1:36), which was the very promise that circumcision was the seal of: and Joshua is here told to circumcise the people, not his own family. Whatever the reason was, it seems that this great ordinance was omitted in Israel for almost forty years together, which is a plain indication that it was not of absolute necessity, nor was to be of perpetual obligation, but should in the fulness of time be abolished, as now it was for so long a time suspended.

2. The orders given to Joshua for this general circumcision (*v.* 2): *Circumcise again the children of Israel,* not the same person, but the body of the people. Why was this ordered to be done now? Answ. (2.) Because now the promise of which circumcision was instituted to be the seal was performed. The seed of Israel was brought safely into the land of Canaan. "Let them therefore hereby own the truth of that promise which their fathers had disbelieved, and could not find in their hearts to trust to." (2.) Because now the threatening of which the suspending of circumcision for thirty-eight years was the ratification was fully executed by the expiring of the forty years. That *warfare is accomplished, that iniquity is pardoned* (Isa. 40:2), and therefore now the seal of the covenant is revived again. But why was it not done sooner? why not while they were resting some months in the plains of Moab? why not during the thirty days of their mourning for Moses? Why was it not deferred longer, till they had made some progress in the conquest of Canaan, and had gained a settlement there, at least till they had entrenched themselves, and fortified their camp? why must it be done the very next day after they had come over Jordan? Answ. Because divine Wisdom saw that to be the fittest time, just when the forty years were ended, and they had entered Canaan; and the reasons which human wisdom would have offered against it were easily overruled. [1.] God would hereby show that the camp of Israel was not governed by the ordinary rules and measures of war, but by immediate direction from God, who by thus exposing them, in the most dangerous moments, magnified his own power in protecting them even then. And this great instance of security, in disabling themselves for action just when they were entering upon action, proclaimed such confidence in the divine care for their safety as would increase their enemies' fears, much more when their scouts informed them not only of the thing itself that was done, but of the meaning of it, that it was a seal of the grant of this land to Israel. [2.] God would hereby animate his people Israel against the difficulties they were now to encounter, by confirming his covenant with them, which gave them unquestionable assurance of victory and success, and the full possession of the land of promise. [3.] God would hereby teach them, and us with them, in all great undertakings to *begin with God,* to make sure of his favour, by offering ourselves to him *a living sacrifice* (for that was signified by the blood of circumcision), and then we may expect to prosper in all we do. [4.] The reviving of circumcision, after it had been so long disused, was designed to revive the observance of other institutions, the omission of which had been connived at in the wilderness. This command to circumcise them was to remind them of that which Moses had told them (Deu. 21:8), that when they should have come *over Jordan* they must not do as they had done *in the wilderness,* but must come under a stricter discipline. It was

said concerning many of the laws God had given them that they must observe them *in the land* to which they were going, Deu. 6:1; 12:1. [5.] This *second* circumcision, as it is here called, was typical of the spiritual circumcision with which the Israel of God, when they enter into the gospel rest, are circumcised; it is the learned bishop Pierson's observation that this circumcision being performed under the direction of Joshua, Moses' successor, it points to *Jesus as the true circumciser,* the author of *another circumcision* than that *of the flesh,* commanded by the law, even the *circumcision of the heart* (Rom. 2:29), called the *circumcision of Christ,* Col, 2:11.

3. The people's obedience to these orders. Joshua *circumcised the children of Israel* (*v.* 3), not himself with his own hands, but he commanded that it should be done, and took care that it was done: it might soon be despatched, for it was not necessary that it should be done by a priest or Levite, but any one might be employed to do it. All those that were under twenty years old when the people were numbered at Mount Sinai, and not being numbered with them fell not by the fatal sentence, were circumcised, and by them all the rest might be circumcised in a little time. The people had promised to hearken to Joshua as they had hearkened to Moses (*ch.* 1:17), and here they gave an instance of their dutifulness by submitting to this painful institution, and not calling him for the sake of it a bloody governor, as Zipporah because of the circumcision called Moses a bloody husband.

4. The names given to the place where this was done, to perpetuate the memory of it. (1.) It was called *the hill of the foreskins, v.* 3. Probably the foreskins that were cut off were laid on a heap, and covered with earth, so that they made a little hillock. (2.) It was called *Gilgal,* from a word which signifies to take away, from that which God said to Joshua (*v.* 9), *This day have I rolled away the reproach of Egypt.* God is jealous for the honour of his people, his own honour being so much interested in it; and, whatever reproach they may lie under for a time, first or last it will certainly be rolled away, and every tongue that riseth up against them he will condemn. [1.] Their circumcision rolled away the reproach of Egypt. they were hereby owned to be the free-born children of God, having the seal of the covenant in their flesh, and so the reproach of their bondage in Egypt was removed. They were tainted with the idolatry of Egypt, and that was their reproach; but now that they were circumcised it was to be hoped they would be so entirely devoted to God that the reproach of their affection to Egypt would be rolled away. [2.] Their coming safely to Canaan rolled away the reproach of Egypt, for it silenced that spiteful suggestion of the Egyptians, that *for mischief they were brought out, the wilderness had shut them in,* Ex. 14:3. Their wandering so long in the wilderness confirmed the reproach, but now that they had entered Canaan in triumph that reproach was done away. When God glorifies himself in perfecting the salvation of his people he not only silences the reproach of their enemies, but rolls it upon themselves.

Verses 10–12

We may well imagine that the people of Canaan were astonished, and that when they observed the motions of the enemy they could not but think them very strange. When soldiers take the field they are apt to think themselves excused from religious exercises (they have not time nor thought to attend to them), yet Joshua opens the campaign with one act of devotion after another. What was afterwards said to another Joshua might truly be said to this, *Hear now, O Joshua! thou and thy fellows that sit before thee are men wondered at* (Zec. 3:8), and yet indeed he took the right method. that is likely to end well which begins with God. Here is,

I. A solemn passover kept, at the time appointed by the law, *the fourteenth day of the first month,* and in the same place where they were circumcised, *v.* 10. While they were wandering in the wilderness they were denied the benefit and comfort of this ordinance, as a further token of God's displeasure; but now, in answer to the prayer of Moses upon the passing of that sentence Ps. 90:15, God comforted them again, after the time that he had afflicted them, and therefore now that joyful ordinance is revived again. Now that they had entered into Canaan it was very seasonable to remember those wondrous works of divine power and goodness by which they were brought out of Egypt. The finishing of mercies should bring to mind the beginning of them; and when it is perfect day we must not forget how welcome the morning-light was when we had long waited for it. The solemn passover followed immediately after the solemn circumcision; thus, when those that received the word were baptized, immediately we find them *breaking bread,* Acts 2:41, 42. They dept this passover in the plains of Jericho, as it were in defiance of the Canaanites that were round about them and enraged against them, and yet could not give them any disturbance. Thus God gave them an early instance of the performance of that promise that when they went up to keep the feasts their land should be taken under the special protection of the divine Providence. Ex. 34:24, *Neither shall any man desire thy land.* He now *prepared a table before them in the presence of their enemies,* Ps. 23:5.

II. Provision made for their camp of the *corn of the land,* and the *ceasing of the manna* thereupon, *v.* 11, 12. Manna was a wonderful mercy to them when they needed it. But it was the mark of a wilderness state; it was the food of children; and therefore, though it was angel's food, and not to be complained of a light bread, yet it would be more acceptable to them to eat of the *corn of the land,* and this they are now furnished with.

1. The country people, having retired for safety into Jericho, had left their barns and fields, and all that was in them, which served for the subsistence of this great army. And the supply came very seasonably, for, (1.) After the passover they were to keep *the feast of unleavened bread,* which they could not do according to the appointment when they had nothing but manna to live upon; and perhaps this was one reason why it was intermitted in the wilderness. But now they found old corn enough in the barns of the Canaanites to supply them plentifully for that occasion; thus *the wealth of the sinner is laid up for the just,* and little did those who laid it up think *whose all these things should be which they had provided.* (2.) On the morrow after the passover-sabbath they were to *wave the sheaf of first-fruits before the Lord,* Lev. 23:10, 11. And this they were particularly ordered to do when they *came into the land which God would vice them:* and they were furnished for this with the *fruit of the land that year* (*v.* 12), which was then growing and beginning to be ripe. Thus they were well provided for, both with *old and new corn, as good householders.* See Mt. 13:52. And as soon as ever the fruits of this good land came to their hands they had an opportunity of honouring God with them, and employing them in his service according to his appointment. And thus, *behold, all things were clean* and comfortable *to them.* Calvin is of opinion that they had dept the passover every year in its season during their wandering in the wilderness, though it is not mentioned, and that God dispensed with their being uncircumcised, as he did, notwithstanding that, admit them to offer other sacrifices. but some gather from Amos *v.* 25 that after the sentence passed upon them there were no sacrifices offered till they came to Canaan, and consequently no passover was kept. And it is observable that after that sentence (Num. 14) the law which follows (Num. 15) concerning sacrifices begins thus: *"When you shall have come into the land of your habitations"* you shall do so and so.

2. Notice is taken of the ceasing of the manna as soon as ever they had eaten the *old corn of the land,* (1.) To show that it did not come by chance or common providence, as snow or hail does, but by the special designation of divine wisdom and goodness; for, as it came just when they needed it, so it continued as long as they had occasion for it and no longer. (2.) To teach us not to expect extraordinary supplies when supplies may be had in an ordinary way. If God had dealt with Israel according to their deserts, the manna would have ceased when they called it light bread; but as long as they needed it God continued it, though they despised it; and now that they needed it not God withdrew it, though perhaps some of them desired it. He is a wise Father, who knows the necessities of his children, and accommodates his gifts to *them,* not to their humours. The word and ordinances of God are spiritual manna, with which God nourishes his people in this wilderness, and, though often forfeited, yet they are continued while we are here; but when we come to the heavenly Canaan this manna will cease, for we shall no longer have need of it.

Verses 13–15

We have hitherto found God often speaking to Joshua, but we read not till now of any appearance of God's glory to him; now that his difficulties increased his encouragements were increased in proportion. Observe,

I. The time when he was favoured with this vision. It was immediately after he had performed the great solemnities of circumcision and the passover; then God made himself known to him. Note, We may then expect the discoveries of the divine grace when we are found in the way of our duty and are diligent and sincere in our attendance on holy ordinances.

II. The place where he had this vision. It was *by Jericho; in Jericho,* so the word is; in it by faith and hope, though as yet he had not begun to lay siege to it; in it in thought and expectation; or in the fields of Jericho, hard by the city. There, it should seem, he was all alone, fearless of danger, because sure of the divine protection. There he was (some think) meditating and praying; and to those who are so employed God often graciously manifests himself. Or perhaps there he was to take a view of the city, to observe its fortifications, and contrive how to attack it; and perhaps he was at a loss within himself how to make his approaches, when God came and directed him. Note, God will *help those that help themselves. Vigilantibus non dormientibus succurrit lex — The law succours those who watch, not those who sleep.* Joshua was in his post as a general, when God came and made himself known as Generalissimo.

III. The appearance itself. Joshua, as is usual with those that are full of thought and care, was looking downwards, his eyes fixed on the ground, when of a sudden he was surprised with the appearance of a man who stood before him at some little distance, which obliged him to lift up his eyes, and gave a diversion to his musings, *v.* 13. He appeared to him as a man, but a considerable man, and one fit to be taken notice of. Now, 1. We have reason to think that this man was the Son of God, the eternal Word, who, before he assumed the human nature for a perpetuity, frequently appeared in a human shape. So bishop Patrick thinks, consonant to the judgment of the fathers. Joshua gave him divine honours, and he received them, which a created angel would not have done, and he is called *Jehovah, ch.* 6:2. 2. He here appeared as a soldier, with *his sword drawn in his hand.* To Abraham in his tent he appeared as a traveller; to Joshua in the field as a man of war. Christ will be to his people what their faith expects and desires. Christ had his sword drawn, which served, (1.) To justify the war Joshua was engaging in, and to show him that it was of God, who gave him commission to kill and slay. If the sovereign draw the sword, this proclaims war, and authorizes the subject to do so too. The sword is then well drawn when Christ *draws it, and gives the banner to those that fear him, to be displayed because of the truth,* Ps. 60:4. (2.) To encourage him to carry it on with vigour; for Christ's sword drawn in his hand denotes how ready he is for the defence and salvation of his people, who through him shall do valiantly. His sword turns every way.

IV. The bold question with which Joshua accosted him; he did not send a servant, but stepped up to him himself, and asked, *Art thou for us or for our adversaries?* which intimates his readiness to entertain him if he were for them, and to fight him if he were against them. This shows, 1. His great courage and resolution. He was not ruffled by the suddenness of the appearance, nor daunted with the majesty and bravery which no doubt appeared in the countenance of the person he saw; but, with a presence of mind that became so great a general, put this fair question to him. God had bidden Joshua be courageous, and by this it appears that he was so; for what God by his word requires of his people he does by his grace work in them. 2. His great concern for the people and their cause; so heartily has he embarked in the interests of Israel that none shall stand by him with the face of a man but he will know whether he be a friend or a foe. It should seem, he suspected him for an enemy, a Goliath that had come to *defy the armies of the living God,* and to give him a challenge. Thus apt are we to look upon that as against us which is most for us. The question plainly implies that the cause between the Israelites and the Canaanites, between Christ and Beelzebub, will not admit of a neutrality. *He that is not with us is against us.*

V. The account he gave of himself, *v.* 14. "Nay, not for your adversaries, you may be sure, but *as captain of the host of the Lord have I now come,* not only for you as a friend, but over you as commander in chief." Here were now, as of old (Gen. 32:2), *Mahanaim, two hosts,* a host of Israelites ready to engage the Canaanites and a host of angels to protect them therein, and he, as captain of both, conducts the host of Israel and commands the host of angels to their assistance. Perhaps in allusion to this Christ is called the *captain of our salvation* (Heb. 2:10), *and a leader and commander to the people,* Isa. 55:4. Those cannot but be victorious that have such a captain. He now came as captain to review the troops, to animate them, and to give the necessary orders for the besieging of Jericho.

VI. The great respect Joshua paid him when he understood who he was; it is probable that he perceived, not only by what he said but by some other sensible indications, that he was a divine person, and not a man. 1. Joshua paid homage to him: He *fell on his face to the earth and did worship.* Joshua was himself general of the forces of Israel, and yet he was far from looking with jealousy upon this stranger, who produced a commission as captain of the Lord's host above him; he did not offer to dispute his claims, but cheerfully submitted to him as his commander. It will become the greatest of men to be humble and reverent in their addresses to God. 2. He begged to receive commands and directions from him: *What saith my Lord unto his servant?* His former question was not more bold and soldier-like than this was pious and saintlike; nor was it any disparagement to the greatness of Joshua's spirit thus to humble himself when he had to do with God: even crowned heads cannot bow to low before the throne of the Lord Jesus, who is *King of kings,* Ps. 2:10,11; 72:10, 11; Rev. 19:16. Observe, (1.) The relation he owns between himself and Christ, that Christ was his Lord and himself his servant and under his command, Christ his Captain and himself a soldier under him, to do as he is bidden, Mt. 8:9. Note, The foundation of all acceptable obedience is laid in a sincere dedication of ourselves, as servants to Jesus Christ as *our Lord,* Ps. 16:2. (2.) The enquiry he makes pursuant to this relation: *What saith my Lord?* which implies an earnest desire to know the will of Christ, and a cheerful readiness and resolution to do it. Joshua owns himself an inferior officer, and stands to receive orders. This temper of mind shows him fit for the post he was in; for those know best how to command that know how to obey.

VII. The further expressions of reverence which this divine captain required from Joshua (*v.* 15): *Loose thy shoe from off thy foot,* in token of reverence and respect (which with us are signified by uncovering the head), and as an acknowledgment of a divine presence, which, while it continued there, did in a manner sanctify the place and dignify it. We are accustomed to say of a person for whom we have a great affection that we love the very ground he treads upon; thus Joshua must show his reverence for this divine person, he must not tread the ground he stood on with his dirty shoes, Eccl. 5:1. Outward expressions of inward reverence, and a religious awe of God, well become us, and are required of us, whenever we approach to him in solemn ordinances. Bishop Patrick well observes here that the very same orders that God gave to Moses at the bush, when he was sending him to bring Israel out of Egypt (Ex. 3:5), her here gives to Joshua, for the confirming of his faith in the promise he had lately given him, that as he had been with Moses so he would be with him, *ch.* 1:5. Had Moses such a presence of God with him as, when it became sensible, sanctified the ground? So had Joshua.

And *(lastly)* Hereby he prepares him to receive the instructions he was about to give him concerning the siege of Jericho, which this captain of the Lord's host had now come to give Israel possession of.

CHAPTER 6

Joshua opened the campaign with the siege of Jericho, a city which could not trust so much to the courage of its people as to act offensively, and to send out its forces to oppose Israel's landing and encamping, but trusted so much to the strength of its walls as to stand upon its defence, and not to surrender, or desire conditions of peace. Now here we have the story of the taking of it, I. The directions and assurances which the captain of the Lord's host gave concerning it (*v.* 1–5). II. The trial of the people's patient obedience in walking round the city six days (*v.* 6–14). III. The wonderful delivery of it into their hands the seventh day, with a solemn charge to them to use it as a devoted thing (*v.* 15–21 and 24). IV. The preservation of Rahab and her relations (*v.* 22, 23, 25). V. A curse pronounced upon the man that should dare to rebuild this city (*v.* 26, 27). An abstract of this story we find among the trophies of faith, Heb. 11:30. "By faith the walls of Jericho fell down, after they were compassed about seven days."

Verses 1–5

We have here a contest between God and the men of Jericho, and their different resolutions, upon which it is easy to say whose word shall prevail.

I. Jericho resolves Israel shall *not* be its master, *v.* 1. It was *straitly shut up, because of the children of Israel.* It *did shut up, and it was shut up* (so it is in the margin); it *did shut up* itself, being strongly fortified both by art and nature, and it *was shut up* by the obstinacy and resolution of the inhabitants, who agreed never to surrender nor so much as sound a parley; none went out as deserters or to treat of peace, nor were any admitted in to offer peace. Thus were they infatuated, and their hearts hardened to their own destruction — the miserable case and character of all those that *strengthen themselves against the Almighty,* Job 15:25.

II. God resolves Israel *shall* be its master, and that quickly, The captain of the Lord's host, here called *Jehovah,* taking notice how strongly Jericho was fortified and how strictly guarded, and knowing Joshua's thoughts and cares about reducing it, and perhaps his fears of a disgrace there and of stumbling at the threshold, gave him here all the assurance he could desire of success (*v.* 2): *See, I have given into thy hand Jericho.* Not, *"I will do it,* but, *I have done it;* it is all thy own, as sure as if it were already in thy possession." It was designed that this city, being the first-fruits of Canaan, should be entirely devoted to God, and that neither Joshua nor Israel should ever be one mite the richer for it, and yet it is here said to be *given into their hand;* for we must reckon that most our own which we have an opportunity of honouring God with and employing in his service. Now. 1. The captain of the Lord's host gives directions how the city should be besieged. No trenches are to be opened, no batteries erected, nor battering rams drawn up, nor any military preparations made; but the ark of God must be carried by the priests round the city once a day for six days together, and seven times the seventh day, attended by the men of war in silence, the priests all the while blowing with trumpets of rams' horns, *v.* 3, 4. This was all they were to do. 2. He assures them that on the seventh day before night they should, without fail, be masters of the town. Upon a signal given, they must all shout, and immediately the wall should fall down, which would not only expose the inhabitants, but so dispirit them that they would not be able to make any resistance, *v.* 5. God appointed this way, (1.) To magnify his own power, that he might be *exalted in his own strength* (Ps. 21:13), not in the strength of instruments. God would hereby yet further make bare his own almighty arm for the encouragement of Israel and the terror and confusion of the Canaanites. (2.) To put an honour upon his ark, the instituted token of his presence, and to give a reason for the laws by which the people were obliged to look upon it with the most profound veneration and respect. When, long after this, the ark was brought into the camp without orders from God, it was looked upon as a profanation of it, and the people paid dearly for their presumption, 1 Sa. 4:3, etc. but now that it was done by the divine appointment it was an honour to the ark of God, and a great encouragement to the faith of Israel. (3.) It was likewise to put honour upon the priests, who were appointed upon this occasion to carry the ark and sound the trumpets. Ordinarily the priests were excused from war, but that this privilege, with other honours and powers that the law had given them, might not be grudged them, in this service they are principally employed, and so the people are made sensible what blessings they were to the public and how well worthy of all the advantages conferred upon them. (4.) It was to try the faith, obedience, and patience, of the people, to try whether they would observe a precept which to human policy seemed foolish to obey and believe a promise which in human probability seemed impossible to be performed. They were also proved whether they could patiently bear the reproaches of their enemies and patiently wait for the salvation of the Lord. Thus by faith, not by force, the walls of Jericho fell down. (5.) It was to encourage the hope of Israel with reference to the remaining difficulties that were before them. That suggestion of the evil spies that Canaan could never be conquered because the cities were *walled up to heaven* (Deu. 1:28) would by this be for ever silenced. The strongest and highest walls cannot hold out against Omnipotence; they needed not to fight, and therefore needed not to fear, because God fought for them.

Verses 6–16

We have here an account of the cavalcade which Israel made about Jericho, the orders Joshua gave concerning it, as he had received them from the Lord and their punctual observance of these orders. We do not find that he gave the people the express assurances God had given him that he would deliver the city into their hands; but he tried whether they would obey orders with a general confidence that it would end well, and we find them very observant both of God and Joshua.

I. Wherever the ark went the people attended it, *v.* 9. The armed men went before it to clear the way, not thinking it any disparagement to them, though they were men of war, to be pioneers to the ark of God. If any obstacle should be found in crossing the roads that led to the city (which they must do in walking round it) they would remove it; if any opposition should be made by the enemy, they would encounter it, that the priests' march with the ark might be easy and safe. It is an honour to the greatest men to do any good office to the ark and to serve the interests of religion in their country. The *rereward,* either another body of armed men, or Dan's squadron, which marched last through the wilderness, or, as some think, the multitude of the people who were not armed or disciplined for war (as many of them as would) followed the ark, to testify their respect to it, to grace the solemnity, and to be witnesses of what was done. Every faithful zealous Israelite would be willing to undergo the same fatigues and run the same hazard with the priests that bore the ark.

II. Seven priests went immediately before the ark, having trumpets in their hands, with which they were continually sounding, *v.* 4, 5, 9, 13. The priests were God's ministers, and thus in his name, 1. They proclaimed war with the Canaanites, and so stuck a terror upon them; for by terrors upon their spirits they were to be conquered and subdued. Thus God's ministers, by the solemn declarations of his wrath against all ungodliness and unrighteousness of men, must blow the trumpet in Zion, and sound an alarm in the holy mountain, that the sinners in Zion may be afraid. They are God's heralds to denounce war against all those that go on still in their trespasses, but say, "We shall have peace, though we go on." 2. They proclaimed God's gracious presence with Israel, and so put life and courage into them. It was appointed that when they went to war the priests should encourage them with the assurance of God's presence with them, Deu. 20:2–4. And particularly their blowing with trumpets was to be a sign to the people that they should be remembered before the Lord Their God in the day of battle, Num. 10:9. It encouraged Abijah, 2 Chr. 13:12. Thus God's ministers, by sounding the Jubilee trumpet of the everlasting gospel, which proclaims liberty and victory, must encourage the good soldiers of Jesus Christ in their spiritual warfare.

III. The trumpets they used were not those silver trumpets which were appointed to be made for their ordinary service, but trumpets of rams' horns, bored hollow for the purpose, as some think. These trumpets were of the basest matter, dullest sound, and least show, that the excellency of the power might be of God. Thus by the foolishness of preaching, fitly compared to the sounding of these rams' horns, the devil's kingdom is thrown down; and the *weapons of our warfare,* though they are not carnal nor seem to a carnal eye likely to bring any thing to pass, are yet *mighty through God to the pulling down of strong-holds,* 2 Co. 10:4, 5. The word here is *trumpets of Jobel,* that is, such trumpets as they used to blow withal in the year of jubilee; so many interpreters understand it, as signifying the complete liberty to which Israel was now brought, and the bringing of the land of Canaan into the hands of its just and rightful owners.

IV. All the people were commanded to be silent, not to speak a word, nor make any noise (v. 10), that they might the more carefully attend to the sound of the sacred trumpets, which they were now to look upon as the voice of God among them; and it does not become us to speak when God is speaking. It likewise intimates their reverent expectation of the event. Zec. 2:13, *Be silent, O all flesh, before the Lord.* Ex. 14:14, *God shall fight, and you shall hold your peace.*

V. They were to do this once a day for six days together and seven times the seventh day, and they did so, v. 14, 15. God could have caused the walls of Jericho to fall upon the first surrounding of them, but they must go round them thirteen times before they fall, that they might be kept waiting patiently for the Lord. Though they had lately come into Canaan, and their time was very precious (for they had a great deal of work before them), yet they must linger so many days about Jericho, seeming to do nothing, nor to make any progress in their business. As promised deliverances must be expected in God's way, so they must be expected in his time. *He that believes does not make haste,* not more haste than God would have him make. *Go yet seven times,* before any thing hopeful appears, 1 Ki. 18:43.

VI. One of these days must needs be a sabbath day, and the Jews say that it was the last, but this is not certain; however, if he that appointed them to rest on the other sabbath days appointed them to walk on this, that was sufficient to justify them in it; he never intended to bind himself by his own laws, but that when he pleased he might dispense with them. The impotent man went upon this principle when he argued (John v. 11), *He that made me whole* (and therefore has a divine power) *said unto me, Take up thy bed.* And, in this case here, it was an honour to the sabbath day, by which our time is divided into weeks, that just seven days were to be spent in this work, and seven priests were employed to sound seven trumpets, this number being, on this occasion, as well as many others, made remarkable, in remembrance of the six day's work of creation and the seventh day's rest from it. And, besides, the law of the sabbath forbids our own work, which is servile and secular, but this which they did was a religious act. It is certainly no breach of the sabbath rest to do the sabbath work, for the sake of which the rest was instituted; and what is the sabbath work but to attend the ark in all its motions?

VII. They continued to do this during the time appointed, and seven times the seventh day, though they saw not any effect of it, believing that *at the end the vision would speak and not lie,* Hab. 2:3. If we persevere in the way of duty, we shall lose nothing by it in the long run. It is probable they walked at such a distance from the walls as to be out of the reach of the enemies' arrows and out of the hearing of their scoffs. We may suppose the oddness of the thing did at first amuse the besieged, but by the seventh day they had grown secure, feeling no harm from that which perhaps they looked upon as an enchantment. Probably they bantered the besiegers, as those mentioned in Neh. 4:2, *"What do these feeble Jews?* Is this the people we thought so formidable? Are these their methods of attack?"* Thus they cried peace and safety, that the destruction might be the more terrible when it came. *Wicked men* (says bishop Hall) *think God in jest when he is preparing for their judgment;* but they will be convinced of their mistake when it is too late.

VIII. At last they were to give a shout, and did so, and immediately the walls fell, v. 16. This was a shout for mastery, a triumphant shout; the *shout of a king is among them,* Num. 23:21. This was a shout of faith; they believed that the walls of Jericho would fall, and by this faith the walls were thrown down. It was a shot of prayer, an echo to the sound of the trumpets which proclaimed the promise that God would remember them; with one accord, as one man, they cry to heaven for help, and help comes in. Some allude to this to show that we must never expect a complete victory over our own corruptions till the very evening of our last day, and then we shall shout in triumph over them, *when we come to the number and measure of our perfection,* as bishop Hall expresses it. *A good heart* (says he) *groans under the sense of his infirmities, fain would be rid of them, and strives and prays, but, when all is done, until the end of the seventh day it cannot be;*

then judgment shall be brought forth unto victory. And at the end of time, when our Lord shall descend from heaven with a shout, and the sound of a trumpet, Satan's kingdom shall be completely ruined, and not till then, when all opposing rule, principality, and power, shall be effectually and eternally put down.

Verses 17–27

The people had religiously observed the orders given them concerning the besieging of Jericho, and now at length Joshua had told them (v. 16), *"The Lord hath given you the city,* enter and take possession." Accordingly in these verses we have,

I. The rules they were to observe in taking possession. God gives it to them, and therefore may direct it to what uses and intents, and clog it with what provisos and limitations he thinks fit. It is given to them to be devoted to God, as the first and perhaps the worst of all the cities of Canaan. 1. The city must be burnt, and all the lives in it sacrificed without mercy to the justice of God. All this they knew was included in those words, v. 17. The city shall be a *cherem,* a devoted thing, at and all therein, to the Lord. No life in it might be ransomed upon any terms; they must all be surely *put to death,* Lev. 27:29. So he appoints from whom as creatures they had received their lives, and to whom as sinners they had forfeited them; and who may dispute his sentence? *Is God unrighteous, who thus taketh vengeance?* God forbid we should entertain such a thought! There was more of God seen in the taking of Jericho than of any other of the cities of Canaan, and therefore that must be more than any other devoted to him. And the severe usage of this city would strike a terror upon all the rest and melt their hearts yet more before Israel. Only, when this severity is ordered, Rahab and her family are excepted: *She shall live and all that are with her.* She had distinguished herself from her neighbours by the kindness she showed to Israel, and therefore shall be distinguished from them by the speedy return of that kindness. 2. All the treasure of it, the money and plate and valuable goods, must be consecrated to the service of the tabernacle, and brought into the stock of dedicated things, the Jews say because the city was taken on the sabbath day. Thus God would be honoured by the beautifying and enriching of his tabernacle; thus preparation was made for the extraordinary expenses of his service; and thus the Israelites were taught not to set their hearts upon worldly wealth nor to aim at heaping up abundance of it for themselves. God had promised them a land *flowing with milk and honey,* not a land abounding with silver and gold; for he would have them live comfortably in it, that they might serve him cheerfully, but not covet either to trade with distant countries or to hoard for after times. He would likewise have them to reckon themselves enriched in the enriching of the tabernacle, and to think that which was laid up in God's house as truly their honour and wealth as if it had been laid up in their own. 3. A particular caution is given them to take heed of meddling with the forbidden spoil; for what was devoted to God, if they offered to appropriate it to their own use, would prove accursed to them; therefore (v. 18) *"In any wise keep yourselves from the accursed thing;* you will find yourselves inclined to reach towards it, but check yourselves, and frighten yourselves from having any thing to do with it." He speaks as if he foresaw the sin of Achan, which we have an account of in the next chapter, when he gives this reason for the caution, *lest you make the camp of Israel a curse and trouble it,* as it proved that Achan did.

II. The entrance that was opened to them into the city by the sudden fall of the walls, or at least that part of the wall over against which they then were when they gave the shout (v. 20): *The wall fell down flat,* and probably killed abundance of people, the guards that stood sentinel upon it, or others that crowded about it, to look at the Israelites that were walking round. We read of thousands killed by the fall of a wall, 1 Ki. 20:30. that which they trusted to for defence proved their destruction. The sudden fall of the wall, no doubt, put the inhabitants into such a consternation that they had no strength nor spirit to make any resistance, but they became an easy prey to the sword of Israel, and saw to how little purpose it was to shut their gates against a people that had *the Lord on the head of them,* Mic. 2:13. Note, The God of heaven easily can, and

certainly will, break down all the opposing power of his and his church's enemies. Gates of brass and bars of iron are, before him, but as straw and rotten wood, Isa. 45:1, 2. *Who will bring me into the strong city? Wilt not thou, O God?* Ps. 60:9, 10. Thus shall Satan's kingdom fall, nor shall any prosper that harden themselves against God.

III. The execution of the orders given concerning this devoted city. All that breathed were put to the sword; not only the men that were found in arms, but the women, and children, and old people. Though they cried for quarter, and begged ever so earnestly for their lives, there was no room for compassion, pity must be forgotten: they *utterly destroyed all, v. 21.* If they had not had a divine warrant under the seal of miracles for this execution, it could not have been justified, nor can it justify the like now, when we are sure no such warrant can be produced. But, being appointed by the righteous Judge of heaven and earth to do it, who is not unrighteous in taking vengeance, they are to be applauded in doing it as the faithful ministers of his justice. Work for God was then bloody work; and *cursed was he that did it deceitfully, keeping back his sword from blood,* Jer. 48:10. But the spirit of the gospel is very different, for Christ came not to destroy men's lives but to save them, Lu. 9:56. Christ's victories were of another nature. The cattle were put to death with the owners, as additional sacrifices to the divine justice. The cattle of the Israelites, when slain at the altar, were accepted as sacrifices *for* them, but the cattle of these Canaanites were required to be slain as sacrifices *with* them, for their iniquity was not to be purged with sacrifice and offering: both were for the glory of God. 2. The city was *burnt with fire, and all that was in it, v. 24.* The Israelites, perhaps, when they had taken Jericho, a large and well-built city, hoped they should have that for their head-quarters; but God will have them yet to dwell in tents, and therefore fires this nest, lest they should nestle in it. 3. All the silver and gold, and all those vessels which were capable of being purified by fire, were brought into the treasury of the house of the Lord; not that he needed it but that he would be honoured by it, as the Lord of hosts, of their hosts in particular, the God that gave the victory and therefore might demand the spoil, either the whole, as here, or, as sometimes, a tenth, Heb. 7:4.

IV. The preservation of Rahab the harlot, or inn-keeper, who *perished not with those that believed not,* Heb. 11:31. The public faith was engaged for her safety by the two spies, who acted therein as public persons; and therefore, though the hurry they were in at the taking of the town was no doubt very great, yet Joshua took effectual care for her preservation. The same persons that she had secured were employed to secure her, v. 22, 23. They were best able to do it who knew her and her house, and they were fittest to do it, that it might appear it was for the sake of her kindness to them that she was thus distinguished and had her life given her for a prey. All her kindred were saved with her; like Noah she *believed to the saving of her house;* and thus faith in Christ *brings salvation to the house,* Acts 16:31. Some ask how her house, which is said to have been *upon the wall* (ch. 2:15), escaped falling with the wall; we are sure it did escape, for she and her relations were safe in it, either though it joined so near to the wall as to be said to be *upon it,* yet it was so far off as not to fall either with the wall or under it; or, rather, that part of the wall on which her house stood fell not. Now being preserved alive, 1. She was left for some time without the camp to be purified from the Gentile superstition, which she was to renounce, and to be prepared for her admission as a proselyte. 2. She was in due time incorporated with the church of Israel, and she and her posterity dwelt in Israel, and her family was remarkable long after. We find her the wife of Salmon, prince of Judah, mother of Boaz, and named among the ancestors of our Saviour, Mt. 1:5. Having received Israelites in the name of Israelites, she had an Israelite's reward. Bishop Pierson observes that Joshua's saving Rahab the harlot, and admitting her into Israel, were a figure of Christ's receiving into his kingdom, and entertaining there, the publicans and the harlots, Mt. 21:31. Or it may be applied to the conversion of the Gentiles.

V. Jericho is condemned to a perpetual desolation, and a curse pronounced upon the man that at any time hereafter should offer to rebuild it (v. 26): *Joshua adjured them,* that is, the elders and people of Israel, not only by their own consent, obliging themselves and their posterity never to rebuild this city, but by the divine appointment, God himself having forbidden it under the sever penalty here annexed. 1. God would hereby show the weight of a divine curse; where it rests there is no contending with it nor getting from under it; it brings ruin without remedy or repair. 2. He would have it to remain in its ruins a standing monument of his wrath against the Canaanites when the measure of their iniquity was full, and of his mercy to his people when the time had come for their settlement in Canaan. The desolations of their enemies were witnesses of his favour to them, and would upbraid them with their ingratitude to that God who had done so much for them. The situation of the city was very pleasant, and probably its nearness to Jordan was an advantage to it, which would tempt men to build upon the same spot; but they are here told it is at their peril if they do it. Men build for their posterity, but he that builds Jericho shall have no posterity to enjoy what he builds; his eldest son shall die when he begins the work, and if he take not warning by that stroke to desist, but will go on presumptuously, the finishing of his work shall be attended with the funeral of his youngest, and we must suppose all the rest cut off between. This curse, not being a *curse causeless*, did come upon that man who long after rebuilded Jericho (1 Ki. 16:34), but we are not to think it made the place ever the worse when it was built, or brought any hurt to those that inhabited it. We find Jericho afterwards graced with the presence, not only of those two great prophets Elijah and Elisha, but of our blessed Saviour himself, Lu. 18:35; 19:1; Mt. 20:29. Note, It is a dangerous thing to attempt the building up of that which God will have to be destroyed. See Mal. 1:4.

Lastly, All this magnified Joshua and raised his reputation (*v.* 27); it made him not only acceptable to Israel, but formidable to the Canaanites, because it appeared that God was with him of a truth: the Word of the Lord was with him, so the Chaldee, even Christ himself, the same that was with Moses. Nothing can more raise a man's reputation, nor make him appear more truly great, than to have the evidences of God's presence with him.

CHAPTER 7

More than once we have found the affairs of Israel, even when they were in the happiest posture and gave the most hopeful prospects, perplexed and embarrassed by sin, and a stop thereby put to the most promising proceedings. The golden calf, the murmuring at Kadesh, and the iniquity of Peor, had broken their measures and given them great disturbance; and in this chapter we have such another instance of the interruption given to the progress of their arms by sin. But it being only the sin of one person or family, and soon expiated, the consequences were not so mischievous as of those other sins; however it served to let them know that they were still upon their good behaviour. We have here, I. The sin of Achan in meddling with the accursed thing (*v.* 1). II. The defeat of Israel before Ai thereupon (*v.* 2–5). III. Joshua's humiliation and prayer on occasion of that sad disaster (*v.* 6–9). IV. The directions God gave him for the putting away of the guilt which had provoked God thus to contend with them (*v.* 10–15). V. The discovery, trial, conviction, condemnation, and execution, of the criminal, by which the anger of God was turned away (*v.* 16–26). And by this story it appears that, as the laws, so Canaan itself, "made nothing perfect," the perfection both of holiness and peace to God's Israel is to be expected in the heavenly Canaan only.

Verses 1–5

The story of this chapter begins with a *but. The Lord was with Joshua, and his fame was noised through all that country,* so the foregoing chapter ends, and it left no room to doubt but that he would go on as he had begun *conquering and to conquer.* He did right, and observed his orders in every thing. *But the children of Israel committed a trespass,* and so set God against them; and then even Joshua's name and fame, his wisdom and courage, could do them no service. If we lose our God, we lose our friends, who cannot help us unless God be for us. Now here is,

I. Achan sinning, *v.* 1. Here is only a general mention made of the sin; we shall afterwards have a more particular account of it from his own mouth. The sin is here said to be *taking of the accursed thing,* in disobedience to the command and in defiance of the threatening, *ch.* 6:18. In the sacking of Jericho orders were given that they should neither spare any lives nor take any treasure to themselves; we read not of the breach of the former prohibition (there were none to whom they showed any mercy), but of the latter: compassion was put off and yielded to the law, but covetousness was indulged. The love of the world is that root of bitterness which of all others is most hardly rooted up. Yet the history of Achan is a plain intimation that he of all the thousands of Israel was the only delinquent in this matter. Had there been more in like manner guilty, no doubt we should have heard of it: and it is strange there were no more. The temptation was strong. It was easy to suggest what a pity it was that so many things of value should be burnt; to what purpose is this waste? In plundering cities, every man reckons himself entitled to what he can lay his hands on. It was easy to promise themselves secrecy and impunity. Yet by the grace of God such impressions were made upon the minds of the Israelites by the ordinances of God, circumcision and the passover, which they had lately been partakers of, and by the providences of God which had been concerning them, that they stood in awe of the divine precept and judgment, and generously denied themselves in obedience to their God. And yet, though it was a single person that sinned, the children of Israel are said *to commit the trespass,* because one of their body did it, and he was not as yet separated from them, nor disowned by them. They did it, that is, by what Achan did guilt was brought upon the whole society of which he was a member. This should be a warning to us to take heed of sin ourselves, lest by it many be defiled or disquieted (Heb. 12:15), and to take heed of having fellowship with sinners, and of being in league with them, lest we share in their guilt. Many a careful tradesman has been broken by a careless partner. And it concerns us to watch over one another for the preventing of sin, because others' sins may redound to our damage.

II. The camp of Israel suffering for the same: *The anger of the Lord was kindled against Israel;* he saw the offence, though they did not, and takes a course to make them see it; for one way or other, sooner or later, secret sins will be brought to light; and, if men enquire not after them, God will, and with his enquiries will awaken theirs. man a community is under guilt and wrath and is not aware of it till the fire breaks out: here it broke out quickly. 1. Joshua sends a detachment to seize upon the next city that was in their way, and that was Ai. Only 3000 men were sent, advice being brought him by his spies that the place was inconsiderable, and needed no greater force for the reduction of it, *v.* 2, 3. Now perhaps it was a culpable assurance, or security rather that led them to send so small a party on this expedition; it might also be an indulgence of the people in the love of ease, for they will not have all *the people to labour thither.* Perhaps the people were the less forward to go upon this expedition because they were denied the plunder of Jericho; and these spies were willing they should be gratified. Whereas when the town was to be taken, though God by his own power would throw down the walls, yet they must *all labour thither* and *labour there* too, in walking round it. It did not bode well at all that God's Israel began to think much of their labour, and contrived how to spare their pains. It is required that we *work out our salvation,* though it is *God that works in us.* It has likewise often proved of bad consequence to make too light of an enemy. *They are but few* (say the spies), but, as few as they were, they were too many for them. It will awaken our care and diligence in our Christian warfare to consider that *we wrestle with principalities and powers.* 2. The party he sent, in their first attack upon the town, were repulsed with some loss (*v.* 4, 5): *They fled before the men of Ai,* finding themselves unaccountably dispirited, and their enemies to sally out upon them with more vigour and resolution than they expected. In their retreat they had about thirty-six men cut off: no great loss indeed out of such a number, but a dreadful surprise to those who had no reason to expect any other in any attack than clear, cheap, and certain victory. And now, as it proves, it is well there were but 3000 that fell under this disgrace. Had the body of the army been there, they would have been no more able to keep their ground, now they were under guilt and wrath, than this small party, and to them the defeat would have been much more grievous and dishonourable. However, it was bad enough as it was, and served, (1.) To humble God's Israel, and to teach them always to *rejoice with trembling. Let not him that girdeth on the harness boast as he that putteth if off.* (2.) To harden the Canaanites, and to make them the more secure notwithstanding the terrors they had been struck with, that their ruin, when it came, might be the more dreadful. (3.) To be an evidence of God's displeasure against Israel, and a call to them to *purge out the old leaven.* And this was principally intended in their defeat. 3. The retreat of this party in disorder put the whole camp of Israel into a fright: *The hearts of the people melted,* not so much for the loss as for the disappointment. Joshua had assured them that *the living God would without fail drive out the Canaanites from before them, ch.* 3:10. How can this event be reconciled to that promise? To every thinking man among them it appeared an indication of God's displeasure, and an omen of something worse, and therefore no marvel it put them into such a consternation; if *God turn to be their enemy and fight against them,* what will become of them? True Israelites tremble when God is angry.

Verses 6–9

We have here an account of the deep concern Joshua was in upon this sad occasion. He, as a public person, interested himself more than any other in this public loss, and is therein an example to princes and great men, and teaches them to lay much to heart the calamities that befal their people: he is also a type of Christ, to whom the blood of his subjects is precious, Ps. 72:14. Observe,

I. How he grieved: He *rent his clothes* (*v.* 6), in token of great sorrow for this public disaster, and especially a dread of God's displeasure, which was certainly the cause of it. Had it been but the common chance of war (as we are too apt to express it), it would not have become a general to droop thus under it; but, when God was angry, it was his duty and honour to feel thus. One of the bravest soldiers that ever was owned that his *flesh trembled for fear of God,* Ps. 119:120. As one *humbling himself under the mighty had of God, he fell to the earth upon his face,* not thinking it any disparagement to him to lie thus low before the great God, to whom he directed this token of reverence, by keeping his eye towards *the ark of the Lord.* The elders of Israel, being interested in the cause and influenced by his example, prostrated themselves with him, and, in token of deep humiliation, *put dust upon their heads,* not only as mourners, but as penitents; not doubting but it was for some sin or other that God did thus contend with them (though they knew not what it was), they *humbled themselves* before God, and thus deprecated the progress of his wrath. This they continued *until even-tide,* to show that it was not the result of a sudden feeling, but proceeded from a deep conviction of their misery and danger if God were any way provoked to depart from them. Joshua did not fall foul upon his spies for their misinformation concerning the strength of the enemy, nor upon the soldiers for their cowardice, though perhaps both were blameworthy, but *his eye is up to God;* for *is there any evil in the camp and he has not done it?* His eye is upon God as displeased, and that troubles him.

II. How he prayed, or pleaded rather, humbly expostulating the case with God, not sullen, as David when *the Lord had made a breach upon Uzzah,* but much affected; his spirit seemed to be somewhat ruffled and discomposed, yet not so as to be put out of frame for prayer; but, by giving vent to his trouble in a humble address to God, he keeps his temper and it ends well. 1. Now he wishes they had all taken up with the lot of the two tribes on the other side Jordan, *v.* 7. He thinks it would have been better to have staid there and been cut short than come hither to be cut off. This savours too much of discontent and distrust of God, and cannot be justified, though the surprise and disappointment to one deeply concerned for the public interest may in part excuse it. Those words, *wherefore hast thou brought us over Jordan to destroy us?* are too like what the murmurers often said (Ex. 14:11, 12; 16:3; 17:3; Num. 14:2, 3); but he that searches the heart knew they came from another spirit, and therefore was not extreme to mark what he said amiss. Had Joshua considered that this disorder which their affairs were put into no doubt proceeded from something amiss, which yet might easily be redressed, and all set to rights again (as often in his predecessor's time), he would not have spoken of it as a thing taken for granted that they were *delivered into the hands of the Amorites to be destroyed.* God knows what he does, though we do not; but this we may be sure of, he never did nor ever will do us any wrong. 2. He speaks as one quite at a loss concerning the meaning of this event

(v. 8): "What shall I say, what construction can I put upon it, when Israel, thy own people, for whom thou hast lately done such great things and to whom thou hast promised the full possession of this land, when they turn their backs before their enemies" (their necks, so the word is), "when they not only flee before them, but fall before them, and become a prey to them? What shall we think of the divine power? Is the Lord's arm shortened? Of the divine promise? Is his word yea and nay? Of what God has done for us? Shall this be all undone again and prove in vain?" Note, The methods of Providence are often intricate and perplexing, and such as the wisest and best of men know not what to say to; but they shall know hereafter, Jn. 13:7. 3. He pleads the danger Israel was now in of being ruined. He gives up all for lost: "The Canaanites will environ us round, concluding that now our defence having departed, and the scales being turned in their favour, we shall soon be as contemptible as ever we were formidable, and they will cut off our name from the earth," v. 9. Thus even good men, when things go against them a little, are too apt to fear the worst, and make harder conclusions than there is reason for. But his comes in here as a plea: "Lord, let not Israel's name, which has been so dear to thee and so great in the world, be cut off." 4. He pleads the reproach that would be cast on God, and that if Israel were ruined his glory would suffer by it. They will cut off our name, says he, yet, as if he had corrected himself for insisting upon that, it is no great matter (thinks he) what becomes of our little name (the cutting off of that will be a small loss), but what wilt thou do for thy great name? this he looks upon and laments as the great aggravation of the calamity. He feared it would reflect on God, his wisdom and power, his goodness and faithfulness; what would the Egyptians say? Note, Nothing is more grievous to a gracious soul than dishonour done to God's name. This also he insists upon as a plea for the preventing of his fears and for a return of God's favour; it is the only word in all his address that has any encouragement in it, and he concludes with it, leaving it to this issue, Father, glorify thy name. The name of God is a great name, above every name; and, whatever happens, we ought to believe that he will, and pray that he would, work for his own name, that this may not be polluted. This should be our concern more than any thing else. On this we must fix our eye as the end of all our desires, and from this we must fetch our encouragement as the foundation of all our hopes. We cannot urge a better plea than this, Lord, What wilt thou do for thy great name? Let God in all be glorified, and then welcome his whole will.

Verses 10–15

We have here God's answer to Joshua's address, which, we may suppose, came from the oracle over the ark, before which Joshua had prostrated himself, v. 6. Those that desire to know the will of God must attend with their desires upon the lively oracles, and wait at wisdom's gates for wisdom's dictates, Prov. 8:34. And let those that find themselves under the tokens of God's displeasure never complain of him, but complain to him, and they shall receive an answer of peace. The answer came immediately, while he was yet speaking (Isa. 65:24), as that to Daniel, Dan. 9:20, etc.

I. God encourages Joshua against his present despondencies, and the black and melancholy apprehensions he had of the present posture of Israel's affairs (v. 10): "Get thee up, suffer not thy spirits to droop and sink thus; wherefore liest thou thus upon thy face?" No doubt Joshua did well to humble himself before God, and mourn as he did, under the tokens of his displeasure; but now God told him it was enough, he would not have him continue any longer in that melancholy posture, for God delights not in the grief of penitents when they afflict their souls further than as it qualifies them for pardon and peace; the days even of that mourning must be ended. Arise, shake thyself from the dust, Isa. 53:2. Joshua continued his mourning till eventide (v. 6), so late that they could do nothing that night towards the discovery of the criminal, but were forced to put it off till next morning. Daniel (Dan. 9:21), and Ezra (Ezra 9:5, 6), continued their mourning only till the time of the evening sacrifice; that revived them both: but Joshua went past that time, and therefore is thus roused: "Get thee up, do not lie all night there." Yet we find that Moses fell down

before the Lord forty days and forty nights, to make intercession for Israel, Deu. 9:18. Joshua must get up because he has other work to do than to lie there; the accursed thing must be discovered and cast out, and the sooner the better; Joshua is the man that must do it, and therefore it is time for him to lay aside his mourning weeds, and put on his judge's robes, and clothe himself with zeal as a cloak. Weeping must not hinder sowing, nor one duty of religion jostle out another. Every thing is beautiful in its season. Shechaniah perhaps had an eye to this in what he said to Ezra upon a like occasion. See Ezra 10:2–4.

II. He informs him of the true and only cause of this disaster, and shows him wherefore he contended with them (v. 11): Israel hath sinned. "Think not that God's mind is changed, his arm shortened, or his promise about to fail; no, it is sin, it is sin, that great mischief-maker, that has stopped the current of divine favours and has made this breach upon you." The sinner is not named, though the sin is described, but it is spoken of as the act of Israel in general, till they have fastened it upon the particular person, and their godly sorrow have so wrought a clearing of themselves, as theirs did, 2 Co. 7:11. Observe how the sin is here made to appear exceedingly sinful. 1. They have transgressed my covenant, an express precept with a penalty annexed to it. It was agreed that God should have all the spoil of Jericho, and they should have the spoil of the rest of the cities of Canaan; but, in robbing God of his part, they transgressed this covenant. 2. They have even taken of the devoted thing, in contempt of the curse which was so solemnly denounced against him that should dare to break in upon God's property, as if that curse had nothing in it formidable. 3. They have also stolen; they did it clandestinely, as if they could conceal it from the divine omniscience, and they were ready to say, The Lord shall not see, or will not miss so small a matter out of so great a spoil. Thus thou thoughtest I was altogether such a one as thyself. 4. They have dissembled also. Probably, when the action was over, Joshua called all the tribes, and asked them whether they had faithfully disposed of the spoil according to the divine command, and charged them, if they knew of any transgression, that they should discover it, but Achan joined with the rest in a general protestation of innocency, and kept his countenance, like the adulterous woman that eats and wipes her mouth, and says, I have done no wickedness. Nay, 5. They have put the accursed thing among their own goods, as if they had as good a title to that as to any thing they have, never expecting to be called to an account, nor designing to make restitution. All this Joshua, though a wise and vigilant ruler, knew nothing of, till God told him, who knows all the secret wickedness that is in the world, which men know nothing of God could at this time have told him who the person was that had done this thing, but he does not, (1.) To exercise the zeal of Joshua and Israel, in searching out the criminal. (2.) To give the sinner himself space to repent and make confession. Joshua no doubt proclaimed it immediately throughout the camp that there was such a transgression committed, upon which, if Achan had surrendered himself, and penitently owned his guilt, and prevented the scrutiny, who knows but he might have had the benefit of that law which accepted of a trespass-offering, with restitution, from those that had sinned through ignorance in the holy things of the law? Lev. 5:15, 16. But Achan never discovering himself till the lot discovered him evidenced the hardness of his heart, and therefore he found no mercy.

III. He awakens him to enquire further into it, by telling him, 1. That this was the only ground for the controversy God had with them, this, and nothing else; so that when this accursed thing was put away he needed not fear, all would be well, the stream of their successes, when this one obstruction was removed, would run as strong as ever. 2. That if this accursed thing were not destroyed they could not expect the return of God's gracious presence; in plain terms, neither will I be with you any more as I have been, except you destroy the accursed, that is, the accursed person, who is made so by the accursed thing. That which is accursed will be destroyed; and those whom God has entrusted to bear the sword bear it in vain if they make it not a terror to that wickedness which brings these judgments of God on a land. By personal repentance and reformation, we destroy the accursed thing in our own hearts, and, unless we do this, we must never expect the favour

of the blessed God. Let all men know that it is nothing but sin that separates between them and God, and, if it be not sincerely repented of and forsaken, it will separate eternally.

IV. He directs him in what method to make this enquiry and prosecution. 1. He must sanctify the people, now over-night, that is, as it is explained, he must command them to sanctify themselves, v. 13. And what can either magistrates or ministers do more towards sanctification? They must put themselves into a suitable frame to appear before God and submit to the divine scrutiny, must examine themselves, now that God was coming to examine them, must prepare to meet their God. They were called to sanctify themselves when they were to receive the divine law (Ex. 19), and now also when they were to come under the divine judgment; for in both God is to be attended with the utmost reverence. "There is an accursed thing in the midst of you, and therefore sanctify yourselves," that is, Let all that are innocent be able to clear themselves, and be the more careful to cleanse themselves. The sin of others may be improved by us as furtherances of our sanctification, as the scandal of the incestuous Corinthian occasioned a blessed reformation in that church, 2 Co. 7:11. 2. He must bring them all under the scrutiny of the lot (v. 14); the tribe which the guilty person was of should first be discovered by lot, then the family, then the household, and last of all the person. The conviction came upon him thus gradually that he might have some space given him to come in and surrender himself; for God is not willing that any should perish, but that all should come to repentance. Observe, The Lord is said to take the tribe, and family, and household, on which the lot fell, because the disposal of the lot is of the Lord, and, however casual it seems, is under the direction of infinite wisdom and justice; and to show that when the sin of sinners finds them out God is to be acknowledged in it; it is he that seizes them, and the arrests are in his name. God hath found out the iniquity of thy servants, Gen. 44:16. It is also intimated with what a certain and unerring judgment the righteous God does and will distinguish between the innocent and the guilty, so that though for a time they seem involved in the same condemnation, as the whole tribe did when it was first taken by the lot, yet he who has his fan in his hand will effectually provide for the taking out of the precious from the vile; so that though the righteous be of the same tribe, and family, and household, with the wicked, yet they shall never be treated as the wicked, Gen. 18:25. 3. When the criminal was found out he must be put to death without mercy (Heb. 10:28), and with all the expressions of a holy detestation, v. 15. He and all that he has must be burnt with fire, that there might be no remainders of the accursed thing among them; and the reason given for this severe sentence is because the criminal has, (1.) Given a great affront to God: He has transgressed the covenant of the Lord, who is jealous particularly for the honour of the holy covenant. (2.) He has done a great injury to the church of God: He has wrought folly in Israel, has shamed that nation which is looked upon by all its neighbours to be a wise and understanding people, has infected that nation which is sanctified to God, and troubled that nation of which he is the protector. These being crimes so heinous in their nature, and of such pernicious consequence and example, the execution, which otherwise would have come under the imputation of cruelty, is to be applauded as a piece of necessary justice. It was sacrilege; it was invading God's rights, alienating his property, and converting to a private use that which was devoted to his glory and appropriated to the service of his sanctuary — this was the crime to be thus severely punished, for warning to all people in all ages to take heed how they rob God.

Verses 16–26

We have in these verses,

I. The discovery of Achan by the lot, which proved a perfect lot, though it proceeded gradually. Though we may suppose that Joshua slept the better, and with more ease and satisfaction, when he knew the worst of the disease of that body of which, under God, he was the head, and was put into a certain method of cure, yet he rose up early in the morning (v. 16), so much was his heart upon it, to put away the accursed thing. We have found Joshua upon other occasions an early riser; here it shows his zeal and vehement desire to see Israel restored to the divine favour. In the scrutiny observe, 1. That the guilty tribe was that of Judah, which was, and was to be, of all the tribes, the most honourable and illustrious; this was an alloy to their dignity, and might serve as a check to their pride: many there were who were its glories, but here was one that was its reproach. Let not the best families think it strange if there be those found in them, and descending from them, that prove their grief and shame. Judah was to have the first and largest lot in Canaan; the more inexcusable is one of that tribe it, not content to wait for his own share, he break in upon God's property. The Jews' tradition is that when the tribe of Judah was taken the valiant men of that tribe drew their swords, and professed they would not sheathe them again till they saw the criminal punished and themselves cleared who knew their own innocency. 2. That the guilty person was at length fastened upon, and the language of the lot was, *Thou art the man, v.* 18. It was strange that Achan, being conscious to himself of guilt, when he saw the lot come nearer and nearer to him, had not either the wit to make an escape or the grace to make a confession; but *his heart was hardened through the deceitfulness of sin,* and it proved to be *to his own destruction.* We may well imagine how his countenance changed, and what horror and confusion seized him when he was singled out as the delinquent, when the eyes of all Israel were fastened upon him, and every one was ready to say, *Have we found thee, O our enemy?* See here, (1.) The folly of those that promise themselves secrecy in sin: the righteous God has many ways of bringing to light the hidden works of darkness, and so bringing to shame and ruin those that continue their fellowship with those unfruitful works. *A bird of the air,* when God pleases, shall *carry the voice,* Eccl. 10:20. See Ps. 94:7, etc. (2.) How much it is our concern, when God is contending with us, to find out what the cause of action is, what the particular sin is, that, like Achan, troubles our camp. We must thus examine ourselves and carefully review the records of conscience, that we may find out the accursed thing, and pray earnestly with holy Job, *Lord, show me wherefore thou contendest with me.* Discover the traitor and he shall be no longer harboured.

II. His arraignment and examination, *v.* 19. Joshua sits judge, and, though abundantly satisfied of his guilt by the determination of the lot, yet urges him to make a penitent confession, that his soul might be saved by it in the other world, though he could not give him any encouragement to hope that he should save his life by it. Observe, 1. How He accosts him with the greatest mildness and tenderness that could be, like a true disciple of Moses. He might justly have called him "thief," and "rebel," "Raca," and "thou fool," but he call him "son;" he might have adjured him to confess, as the high priest did our blessed Saviour, or threatened him with the torture to extort a confession, but for love's sake he rather beseeches him: *I pray thee make confession.* This is an example to all not to insult over those that are in misery, though they have brought themselves into it by their own wickedness, but to treat even offenders with the spirit of meekness, not knowing, what we ourselves should have been and done if God had put us into the hands of our own counsels. It is likewise an example to magistrates, in executing justice, to govern their own passions with a strict and prudent hand, and never suffer themselves to be transported by them into any indecencies of behaviour or language, no, not towards those that have given the greatest provocations. *The wrath of man worketh not the righteousness of God.* Let them remember *the judgment is God's, who is Lord of his anger.* This is the likeliest method of bringing offenders to repentance. 2. What he wishes him to do, to confess the fact, to confess it to God, the party offended by the crime; Joshua was to him in god's stead, so that in confessing to him he confessed to God. Hereby he would satisfy Joshua and the congregation concerning that which was laid to his charge; his confession would also be an evidence of his repentance, and a warning to others to take heed of sinning after the similitude of his transgression: but that which Joshua aims at herein is that God might be honoured by it, as the Lord, the God of infinite knowledge and power, from whom no secrets are hid; and as the God of Israel, who, as he does particularly resent affronts given to his Israel, so he does the affronts given him by Israel. Note, In confessing sin, as we take shame to ourselves, so we give glory to God as righteous God, owning him justly displeased with us, and as a good God, who will not improve our confessions as evidences against us, but is faithful and just to forgive when we are brought to own that he would be faithful and just if he should punish. By sin we have injured God in his honour. Christ by his death has made satisfaction for the injury; but it is required that we by repentance show our good will to his honour, and, as far as in us lies, give glory to him. Bishop Patrick quotes the Samaritan chronicle, making Joshua to say here to Achan, *Lift up thy eyes to the king of heaven and earth, and acknowledge that nothing can be hidden from him who knoweth the greatest secrets.*

III. His confession, which now at last, when he saw it was to no purpose to conceal his crime, was free and ingenuous enough, *v.* 20, 21. Here is, 1. A penitent acknowledgment of fault. "Indeed I have sinned; what I am charged with is too true to be denied and too bad to be excused. I own it, I lament it; the Lord is righteous in bringing it to light, for indeed I have sinned." This is the language of a penitent that is sick of his, and whose conscience is loaded with it. "I have nothing to accuse any one else of, but a great deal to say against myself; it is with me that the accursed thing is found; I am the man who has *perverted that which was right and it profited me not."* And that wherewith he aggravates the sin is that it was committed *against the Lord God of Israel.* He was himself an Israelite, a sharer with the rest of that exalted nation in their privileges, so that, in offending *the God of Israel,* he offended his own God, which laid him under the guilt of the basest treachery and ingratitude imaginable. 2. A particular narrative of the fact: *Thus and thus have I done.* God had told Joshua in general that a part of the devoted things was alienated, but is to him to draw from Achan an account of the particulars; for, one way or other, God will make sinners' *own tongues to fall upon them* (Ps. 64:8); if ever he bring them to repentance, they will be their own accusers, and their awakened consciences will be instead of a thousand witnesses. Note, It becomes penitents, in the confession of their sins to God, to be very particular; not only, "I have sinned," but, "In this and that instance I have sinned," reflecting with regret upon all the steps that led to the sin and all the circumstances that aggravated it and made it exceedingly sinful: *thus and thus have I done.* He confesses, (1.) To the things taken. In plundering a house in Jericho he found a goodly Babylonish garment; the word signifies a robe, such as princes wore when they appeared in state, probably it belonged to the King of Jericho; it was far fetched, as we translate it, from Babylon. A garment of divers colours, so some render it. Whatever it was, in his eyes it made a very glorious show. "A thousand pities" (thinks Achan) "that it should be burnt; then it will do nobody any good; if I take it for myself, it will serve me many a year for my best garment." Under these pretences, he makes bold with this first, and things it no harm to save it from the fire; but, his hand being thus in, he proceeds to take a bag of money, *two hundred shekels,* that is one hundred ounces of silver, and a w*wedge of gold* which weighed *fifty shekels,* that is twenty-five ounces. He could not plead that, in taking these, he saved them *from the fire* (for the *silver and gold* were to be laid up in *the treasury*); but those that make a slight excuse to serve in daring to commit one sin will have their hearts so hardened by it that they will venture upon the next without such an excuse; for the way of sin is downhill. See what a peer prize it was for which Achan ran this desperate hazard, and what an unspeakable loser he was by the bargain. See Mt. 16:26. (2.) He confesses the manner of taking them. [1.] the sin began in the eye. he saw these fine things, as Eve saw the forbidden fruit, and was strangely charmed with the sight. See what comes of suffering the heart to walk after the eyes, and what need we have to make this covenant with our eyes, that if they wander they shall be sure to weep for it. *Look not thou upon the wine that is red,* upon the woman that is fair; close the right eye that thus offense thee, to prevent the necessity of plucking it out, and casting it from thee, Mt. *v.* 28, 29. [2.] It proceeded out of the heart. He owns, *I coveted them.* thus lust conceived and brought forth this sin. Those that would be kept from sinful actions must mortify and check in themselves sinful desires, particularly the desire of worldly wealth, which we more particularly call *covetousness.* O what a world of evil is the love money the root of! Had Achan looked upon these things with an eye of faith, he would have seen them accursed things, and would have dreaded them, but, looking upon them with an eye of sense only, he saw them goodly things, and coveted them. It was not the looking, but the lusting that ruined him. [3.] When he had committed it he was very industrious to conceal it. Having taken of the forbidden treasures, fearing lest any search should be made for prohibited goods, he *hid them in the earth,* as one that resolved to keep what he had gotten, and never to make restitution. Thus does Achan confess the whole matter, that God might be justified in the sentence passed upon him. See the *deceitfulness of sin;* that which is pleasing in the commission is bitter in the reflection; at the last it bites like a serpent. Particularly, see what comes of ill-gotten goods, and how those will be cheated that rob God. Job 20:15, *He hath swallowed down riches, and he shall vomit them up again.*

IV. His conviction. God had convicted him by the lot; he had convicted himself by his own confession; but, that no room might be left for the most discontented Israelite to object against the process, Joshua has him further convicted by the searching of his tent, in which the goods were found which he confessed to. Particular notice is taken of the haste which the messengers made that were sent to search: They *ran to the tent* (*v.* 22), not only to show their readiness to obey Joshua's orders, but to show how uneasy they were till the camp was cleared of the accursed thing, that they might regain the divine favour. Those that feel themselves under wrath find themselves concerned not to defer the putting away of sin. Delays are dangerous, and it is not time to trifle. When the stolen goods were brought they were *laid out before the Lord* (*v.* 23), that all Israel might see how plain the evidence was against Achan, and might adore the strictness of God's judgments in punishing so severely the stealing of such small things, and yet the justice of his judgments in maintaining his right to devoted things, and might be afraid of ever offending in the like kind. In laying them out before the Lord they acknowledged his title to them, and waited to receive his directions concerning them. Note, Those that think to put a cheat upon God do but deceive themselves; what is taken from him he will recover (Hos. 2:9) and he will be a loser by no man at last.

V. His condemnation. Joshua passes sentence upon him (*v.* 25): *Why hast thou troubled us?* There is the ground of the sentence. *O, how much hast thou troubled us!* so some read it. He refers to what was said when the warning was given not to meddle with the accursed thing (*ch.* 6:18), *lest you make the camp of Israel a curse and trouble it.* Note, Sin is a very troublesome thing, not only to the sinner himself, but to all about him. *He that is greedy of gain,* as Achan was, *troubles his own house* (Prov. 15:27) and all the communities he belongs to. Now (says Joshua) *God shall trouble thee.* See why Achan was so severely dealt with, not only because he had robbed God, but because he had troubled Israel; over his head he had (as it were) this accusation written, "Achan, *the troubler of Israel,"* as Ahab, 1 Ki. 18:18. This therefore is his doom: *God shall trouble thee.* Note, the righteous God will certainly *recompense tribulation to those that trouble* his people, 2 Th. 1:6. Those that are troublesome shall be troubled. Some of the Jewish doctors, from that word which determines the troubling of him to *this day,* infer that therefore he should not be troubled in the world to come; the flesh was destroyed that spirit might be saved, and, if so, the dispensation was really less severe than it seemed. In the description both of his sin and of his punishment, by the trouble that was in both, there is a plain allusion to his name Achan, or, as he is called, 1 Chr. 2:7, *Achar,* which signifies *trouble.* He did too much answer his name.

VI. His execution. No reprieve could be obtained; a gangrened member must be cut off immediately. When he is proved to be an anathema, and the troubler of the camp, we may suppose all the people cry out against him, *Away with him, away with him! Stone him, stone him!* Here is,

1. The place of execution. They brought him out of the camp, in token of their putting *far from them that wicked person,* 1 Co. *v.* 13. When our Lord Jesus was made a curse for us, that by his trouble we might have peace, he suffered as an accursed thing *without the gate,* bearing our

reproach, Heb. 13:12, 13. The execution was at a distance, that the camp which was disturbed by Achan's sin might not be defiled by his death.

2. The persons employed in his execution. It was the act of all Israel, *v.* 24, 25. They were all spectators of it, that they might see and fear. Public executions are public examples. Nay, they were all consenting to his death, and as many as could were active in it, in token of the universal detestation in which they held his sacrilegious attempt, and their dread of God's displeasure against them.

3. The partakers with him in the punishment; for *he perished not alone in his iniquity, ch.* 22:20. (1.) The stolen goods were destroyed with him, the garment burnt, as it should have been with the rest of the combustible things in Jericho, and the silver and gold defaced, melted, lost, and buried, in the ashes of the rest of his goods under *the heap of stones,* so as never to be put to any other use. (2.) All his other goods were destroyed likewise, not only his tent, and the furniture of that, but his *oxen, asses, and sheep,* to show that goods gotten unjustly, especially if they be gotten by sacrilege, will not only turn to no account, but will blast and waste the rest of the possessions to which they are added. The eagle in the fable, that stole flesh from the altar, brought a coal of fire with it, which burnt her nest, Hab. 2:9, 10; Zec. 5:3, 4. Those lose their own that grasp at more than their own. (3.) His sons and daughters were put to death with him. Some indeed think that they were *brought out* (*v.* 24) only to be the spectators of their father's punishment, but most conclude that they died with him, and that they must be meant *v.* 25, where it is said they *burned them with fire, after they had stoned them with stones.* God had expressly provided that magistrates should not put the children to death for the fathers'; but he did not intend to bind himself by that law, and in this case he had expressly ordered (*v.* 15) that the criminal, and all that he had, should be burnt. Perhaps his sons and daughters were aiders and abettors in the villany, had helped to carry off the accursed thing. It is very probable that they assisted in the concealment, and that he could not hide them in the midst of his tent but they must know and keep his counsel, and so they became accessaries *ex post facto — after the fact;* and, if they were ever so little partakers in the crime, it was son heinous that they were justly sharers in the punishment. However God was hereby glorified, and the judgment executed was thus made the more tremendous.

4. The punishment itself that was inflicted on him. He was stoned (some think as a sabbath breaker, supposing that the sacrilege was committed on the sabbath day), and then his dead body was burnt, as an accursed thing, of which there should be no remainder left. The concurrence of all the people in this execution teaches us how much it is the interest of a nation that all in it should contribute what they can, in their places, to the suppression of vice and profaneness, and the reformation of manners; *sin is a reproach to any people,* and therefore every Israelite indeed will have a stone to throw at it.

5. The pacifying of God's wrath hereby (*v.* 26): *The Lord turned from the fierceness of his anger.* The putting away of sin by true repentance and reformation, as it is the only way, so it is a sure and most effectual way, to recover the divine favour. Take away the cause, and the effect will cease.

VII. The record of his conviction and execution. Care was taken to preserve the remembrance of it, for warning and instruction to posterity. 1. A heap of stones was raised on the place where Achan was executed, every one perhaps of the congregation throwing a stone to the heap, in token of his detestation of the crime. 2. A new name was given to the place; it was called the*Valley of Achor,* or *trouble.* This was a perpetual brand of infamy upon Achan's name, and a perpetual warning to all people not to invade God's property. By this severity against Achan, the honour of Joshua's government, now in the infancy of it, was maintained, and Israel, at their entrance upon the promised Canaan, were reminded to observe, at their peril, the provisos and limitations of the grant by which they held it. The *Valley of Achor* is said to be given for a *door of hope,* because when we put away the accursed thing then there begins to be hope in Israel, Hos. 2:15; Ezra 10:2.

CHAPTER 8

The embarrassment which Achan's sin gave to the affairs of Israel being over, we have them here in a very good posture again, the affairs both of war and religion. Here is, I. The glorious progress of their arms in the taking of Ai, before which they had lately suffered disgrace. 1. God encourages Joshua to attack it, with the assurance of success, and directs him what method to take (*v.* 1, 2). 2. Joshua gives orders accordingly to the men of war (*v.* 3–8). 3. The stratagem is managed as it was projected, and succeeds as it was desired (*v.* 9–22). 4. Joshua becomes master of this city, puts all the inhabitants to the sword, burns it, hangs the king, but gives the plunder to the soldiers (*v.* 23–29). II. The great solemnity of writing and reading the law before a general assembly of all Israel, drawn up for that purpose upon the two mountains of Gerizim and Ebal, according to an order which Moses had received from the Lord, and delivered to them (*v.* 30–35). Thus did they take their work before them, and make the business of their religion to keep pace with their secular business.

Verses 1–2

Israel were very happy in having such a commander as Joshua, but Joshua was more happy in having such a director as God himself; when any difficulty occurred, he needed not to call a council of war who had *God so nigh unto him,* not only to answer, but even to anticipate, his enquiries. It should seem, Joshua was now at a stand, had scarcely recovered the discomposure he was put into by the trouble Achan gave them, and could not think, without fear and trembling, of pushing forward, lest there should be in the camp another Achan; then God spoke to him, either by vision, as before (*ch.* 5), or by the breastplate of judgment. Note, When we have faithfully put away sin, that accursed thing, which *separates between us and God,* then, and not till then, we may expect to hear from God to our comfort; and God's directing us how to go on in our Christian work and warfare is a good evidence of his being reconciled to us. Observe here,

I. The encouragement God gives to Joshua to proceed: *Fear not, neither be thou dismayed, v.* 1. This intimates that the sin of Achan, and the consequences of it, had been a very great discouragement to Joshua, and made his heart almost ready to fail. Corruptions within the church weaken the hands, and damp the spirits, of her guides and helpers, more than oppositions from without; treacherous Israelites are to be dreaded more than malicious Canaanites. But God bids Joshua not be dismayed; the same power that keeps Israel from being ruined by their enemies shall keep them from ruining themselves. To animate him, 1. He assures him of success against Ai, tells him it is all his own; but he must take it as god's gift: *I have given it into thy hands,* which secured him both title and possession, and obliged him to give God the glory of both, Ps. 44:3. 2. He allows the people to take the spoil to themselves. Here the spoil was not consecrated to God as that of Jericho, and therefore there was no danger of the people's committing such a trespass as they had committed there. Observe, How Achan who caught at forbidden spoil lost that, and life, and all, but the rest of the people who had conscientiously refrained from the accursed thing were quickly recompensed for their obedience with the spoil of Ai. the way to have the comfort of what God allows us is to forbear what he forbids us. No man shall lose by his self-denial; let God have his dues first, and then all will be clean to us and sure, 1 Ki. 17:13. God did not bring them to these *goodly cities,* and *houses filled with all good things,* to tantalize them with the sight of that which they might not touch; but, having received the first-fruits from Jericho, the spoil of Ai, and of all the cities which thenceforward came into their hands, they might take for a prey to themselves.

II. The direction he gives him in attacking Ai. It must not be such a work of time as the taking of Jericho was; this would have prolonged the war too much. Those that had patiently waited seven days for Jericho shall have Ai given them in one day. Nor was it, as that, to be taken by miracle, and purely by the act of God, but now their own conduct and courage must be exercised; having seen God work for them, they must now bestir themselves. God directs him, 1. to take all the people, that they might all be spectators of the action and sharers in the spoil. Hereby God gave him a tacit rebuke for sending so small a detachment against Ai in the former attempt upon it, *ch.* 7:4. 2. To lay an ambush behind the city; this was a method which perhaps Joshua would not have thought of at this time, if God had not directed him to it; and though now we are not to expect direction, as here, by visions, voices, or oracles, yet, whenever those who are entrusted with public councils take prudent measures for the public good, it must be acknowledged that god puts it into their hears; he that teaches the husbandman discretion no doubt teaches statesman and general.

Verses 3–22

We have here an account of the taking of Ai by stratagem. The stratagem here used, we are sure, was lawful and good; God himself appointed it, and we have no reason to think but that the like is lawful and good in other wars. Here was no league broken, no treaty of peace, that the advantage was gained; no, these are sacred things, and not to be jested with, nor used to serve a turn; truth, when once it is plighted, becomes a debt even to the enemy. But in this stratagem here was no untruth told; nothing was concealed but their own counsels, which no enemy ever pretended a right to be entrusted with; nothing was dissembled, nothing counterfeited but a retreat, which was no natural or necessary indication at all of their inability to maintain their onset, or of any design not to renew it. The enemy ought to have been upon their guard, and to have kept within the defence of their own walls. Common prudence, had they been governed by it, would have directed them not to venture on the pursuit of an army which they saw was so far superior to them in numbers, and leave their city unguarded; but *(si populus vult decipi, decipiatur — if the people will be deceived, let them)* if the Canaanites will be so easily imposed upon, and in pursuit of God's Israel will break through all the laws of policy and good management, the Israelites are not at all to be blamed for taking advantage of their fury and thoughtlessness; nor is it any way inconsistent with the character God is pleased to give of them, that they are *children that will not lie.* Now in the account here given of this matter,

I. There is some difficulty in adjusting the numbers that were employed to effect it. Mention is made (*v.* 3) of 30,000 that were *chosen and sent away by night,* to whom the charge was given to surprise the city as soon as ever they perceived it was evacuated, *v.* 4, 7, 8. And yet afterwards (*v.* 12) it is said, Joshua *took* 5000 *men and set them to lie in ambush* behind the city, and that *ambush entered the city,* and *set it on fire, v.* 19. Now, 1. Some think there were two parties sent out to lie in ambush, 30,000 first, and afterwards 5000 to guard the roads, and to intercept those that were first sent out; and that Joshua made his open attack upon the city with all the thousands of Israel. So the learned bishop Patrick, insisting upon God's command (*v.* 1) to take *all the people of war with him.* But, 2. Others think that all the people were taken only to encamp before the city, and that out of them Joshua chose out 30,000 men to be employed in the action, out of which he sent out 5000 to lie in ambush, which were as many as could be supposed to march *incognito — without being discovered* (more would have been seen, and thus the design would have been broken) and that then with the other 25,000 he made the open attack, as Masius thinks, or with the 30,000, which, as Calvin thinks, he kept entire for that purpose, having, besides them, sent out 5000 for an ambuscade. And those 5000 (they think) must be meant by those (*v.* 3) whom he *sent away by night,* with orders to lie in wait behind the city, though the particular number is not specified till *v.* 12. If we admit such a seeming disturbance in the order of the narrative (of which, perhaps, similar instances might be cited from the other scripture histories), it seems most probable that there was but one ambushment, which consisted only of 5000, enough for such a purpose.

II. Yet the principal parts of the story are plain enough, that a detachment being secretly marched behind the city, on the other side to that on which the main body of the army lay (the situation of the country, it is probable, favouring their concealment), Joshua, and the forces with him, faced the city; the garrison made a vigorous sally out upon them, whereupon they withdrew, gave ground, and retreated in some seeming disorder towards the wilderness, which being perceived by the men of Ai, they drew out all the force they had to pursue them. This gave a fair opportunity for those that lay in ambush to make themselves masters of the city, whereof when they had given notice by a smoke to Joshua, he, with all his force, returned upon the pursuers, who now, when it was too late, were aware of the snare they were drawn into, and, their retreat being intercepted, they were every man of them cut off. The like artifice we find used, Jdg. 20:30, etc. Now in this story we may observe,

1. What a brave commander Joshua was. See, (1.) His conduct and prudence. God gave him the hint (*v.* 2) that he should lay an ambush behind the city, but left him to himself to order the particulars, which he did admirably well. Doubtless *wisdom strengthens the wise more than ten mighty men,* Eccl. 7:19. (2.) His care and industry (*v.* 10): *He rose up early in the morning,* that he might lose no time, and to show how intent his mind was upon his business. Those that would maintain their spiritual conflicts must not love their ease. (3.) His courage and resolution; though an army of Israelites had been repulsed before Ai, yet he resolves to lead them on in person the second time, *v.* 5. Being himself also an elder, he took the elders of Israel with him to make this attack upon the city (*v.* 10), as if he were going rather to sit in judgment upon them as criminals than to fight them as enemies. (4.) His caution and consideration (*v.* 13): He *went that night into the midst of the valley,* to make the necessary dispositions for an attack, and to see that every thing was in good order. It is the pious conjecture of the learned bishop Patrick that he went into the valley alone, to pray to God for a blessing upon his enterprise, and he did not seek in vain. (5.) His constancy and perseverance; when he had stretched out his spear towards the city (*v.* 18, a spear almost as fatal and formidable to the enemies of Israel as the rod of Moses was) he never drew back his hand till the work was done. His hands in fighting, like Moses's in interceding, were steady till the going down of the sun. Those that have stretched out their hands against their spiritual enemies must never draw them back. *Lastly,* What Joshua did in the stratagem is applicable to our Lord Jesus, of whom he was a type. Joshua conquered by yielding, as if he had himself been conquered; so our Lord Jesus, when he bowed his head and gave up the ghost, seemed as if death and triumphed over him, and as if he and all his interests had been routed and ruined; but in his resurrection he rallied again and gave the powers of darkness a total defeat; he broke the serpent's head, by suffering him to bruise his heel. A glorious stratagem!

2. What an obedient people Israel was. What *Joshua commanded them to do, according to the commandment of the Lord* (*v.* 8), they did it without murmuring or disputing. Those that were sent to lie in ambush between Beth-el and Ai (two cities confederate against them) were in a post of danger, and had they been discovered might all have been cut off, and yet they ventured; and, when the body of the army retreated and fled, it was both disgraceful and perilous, and yet, in obedience to Joshua, they did it.

3. What an infatuated enemy the king of Ai was, (1.) That he did not by his scouts discover those that lay in ambush behind the city, *v.* 14. Some observe it as a remarkable instance of the power of God in making men blind to their own interest, and the things that belong to their peace, that *he wist not that there were liers in wait against him.* Those are most in danger who are least aware that they are so. (2.) That when Israel seemed to fly he drew out all his forces to pursue them, and left none to guard his city and to secure his retreat, *v.* 17. Thus the church's enemies often run themselves into destruction by their own fury and the violence of their rage against the Israel of God. Pharaoh plunged himself into the Red Sea by the eagerness with which he pursued Israel. (3.) That from the killing of thirty-six men out of 3000, when Israel made the former attack upon his city, he should infer the total routing of so great an army as now he had to deal with (*v.* 6): *They flee before us as at the first.* See how the prosperity of fools destroys them and hardens them to their ruin. God had made use of the men of Ai as a scourge to chastise his people for meddling with the accursed thing, and this had puffed them up with a conceit that they must have the honour of delivering their country from these formidable invaders; but they were soon made to see their mistake, and that when the Israelites had reconciled themselves to their God they could have no power against them. God had made use of them only for the rebuking of Israel, with a purpose, when the correction was over, to throw the rod itself into the fire; *howbeit, they meant not so,* but *it was in their heart to destroy and cut off,* Isa. 10:5–7.

4. What a complete victory Israel obtained over them by the favour and blessing of God. Each did his part: the divided forces of Israel, by signals agreed on, understood one another, and every thing succeeded according to the project; so that the men of Ai, even when they were most confident of victory, found themselves surrounded, so that they had neither spirit to resist nor room to fly, but were under a fatal necessity of yielding their lives to the destroyers. And now it is hard to say whether the shouts of the men of Israel, or the shrieks of the men of Ai, were the louder, but easy to imagine what terror and confusion they were filled with, when their highest assurances sunk so suddenly into the heaviest despair. Note, The triumphing of the wicked is short, Job 20:5. They are *exalted for a little while,* that their fall and ruin may be the sorer, Job 24:24. See how easily, how quickly, the scale turns against those that have not God on their side.

Verses 23–29

We have here an account of the improvement which the Israelites made of their victory over Ai. 1. They put all to the sword, not only in the field, but in the city, man, woman, and child, none of them remained, *v.* 24. God, the righteous Judge, had passed this sentence upon them for their wickedness, so that the Israelites were only the ministers of his justice and the executioners of his doom. Once in this story, and but once, mention is made of the men of Beth-el, as confederates with the men of Ai, *v.* 17. Though they had a king of their own, and were not subjects to the king of Ai (for the king of Beth-el is reckoned among the thirty-one kings that Joshua destroyed, *ch.* 12:16), yet Ai being a stronger place they threw themselves into that, for their own safety, and the strengthening of their neighbours' hands, and so (we may presume) were all cut off with them; thus that by which they hoped to prevent their own ruin hastened it. The whole number of the slain, it seems, was but 12,000, and inconsiderable body to make head against all the thousands of Israel; but those whom God will destroy he infatuates. Here it is said (*v.* 26) that *Joshua drew not his hand back wherewith he stretched out the spear* (*v.* 18) till the slaughter was completed. Some think the spear he stretched out was not to slay the enemies, but to animate and encourage his own soldiers, some flag or ensign being hung out at the end of this spear; and they observe it as an instance of his self-denial that though the fire of courage wherewith his breast was filled would have pushed him forward, sword in hand, into the hottest of the action, yet, in obedience to God, he kept the inferior post of a standard-bearer, and did not quit it till the work was done. By the spear stretched out, he directed the people to expect their help from God, and to him to give the praise. 2. They plundered the city and took all the spoil to themselves, *v.* 27. Thus the wealth of the sinner is laid up for the just; the spoil they brought out of Egypt, by borrowing of their neighbours, was much of it expended upon the tabernacle they had reared in the wilderness, for which they are now reimbursed with interest. The spoil here taken, it is probable, was all brought together, and distributed by Joshua in due proportions, as that of the Midianites was, Num. 31:26, etc. It was not seized with irregularity or violence, for God is the God or order and equity, and not of confusion. 3. They laid the city in ashes, and left it to remain so, *v.* 28. Israel must yet dwell in tents, and therefore this city, as well as Jericho, must be burnt. And, though there was no curse entailed upon him that should rebuild it, yet, it seems, it was not rebuilt unless it be the same with Aijah, which we read of, long after, Neh. 11:31. Some think it was not rebuilt because Israel had received a defeat before it, the remembrance of which should be buried in the ruins of the city. 4. The king of Ai was taken prisoner and cut off, not by the sword of war as a soldier, but by the sword of justice as a malefactor. Joshua ordered him to be hanged, and his dead body thrown at the gate of his own city, *under a heap of stone, v.* 23, 29. Some particular reason, no doubt, there was for this severity against the king of Ai; it is likely he had been notoriously wicked and vile, and a blasphemer of the God of Israel, perhaps upon occasion of the repulse he had given to the forces of Israel in their first onset. Some observe that his dead body was thrown at the gate where he had been wont to sit in judgment that so much the greater contempt might thereby be poured upon the dignity he had been proud of, and he might be punished for the unrighteous decrees he had made in the very place where he had made them. Thus the Lord is known by the judgments which he executes.

Verses 30–35

This religious solemnity of which we have here an account comes in somewhat surprisingly in the midst of the history of the wars of Canaan. After the taking of Jericho and Ai, we should have expected that the next news would be of their taking possession of the country, the pushing on of their victories in other cities, and the carrying of the war into the bowels of the nation, now that they had made themselves masters of these frontier towns. But here a scene opens of quite another nature; the camp of Israel is drawn out into the field, not to engage the enemy, but to offer sacrifice, to hear the law read, and to say *Amen* to the blessings and the curses. Some think this was not done till after some of the following victories were obtained which were read of, *ch.* 10 and 11. But it should seem by the maps that Shechem (near to which these two mountains Gerizim and Ebal were) was not so far off from Ai but that when they had taken that they might penetrate into the country as far as those two mountains, and therefore I would not willingly admit a transposition of the story; and the rather because, as it comes in here, it is a remarkable instance, 1. Of the zeal of Israel for the service of God and for his honour. Though never was war more honourable, more pleasant, or more gainful, nor ever was war more sure of victory, or more necessary to a settlement (for they had neither houses nor lands of their own till they had won them by the sword, no, not Joshua himself), yet all the business of the war shall stand still, while they make a long march to the place appointed, and there attend this solemnity. God appointed them to do this when they should have got over Jordan, and they did it as soon as possibly they could, though they might have had a colourable pretence to put it off. Note, We must not think to defer our covenanting with God till we are settled in the world, or must any business put us by from minding and pursuing the one thing needful. The way to prosper is to begin with God, Mt. 6:33. 2. It is an instance of the care of God concerning his faithful servants and worshippers. Though they were in an enemy's country, as yet unconquered, yet in the service of God they were safe, as Jacob when in this very country he was going to Beth-el to pay his vows: *the terror of God was upon the cities round about,* Gen. 35:5. Note, When we are in the way of duty God takes us under his special protection.

Twice Moses had given express orders for this solemnity; once Deu. 11:29, 30, where he seems to have pointed to the very place where it was to be performed; and again Deu. 27:2, etc. It was a federal transaction: the covenant was now renewed between God and Israel upon their taking possession of the land of promise, that they might be encouraged in the conquest of it, and might know upon what terms they held it, and come under fresh obligations to obedience. In token of the covenant,

I. They built an altar, and offered sacrifice to God (*v.* 30, 31), in token of their dedication of themselves to God, as living sacrifices to his honour, in and by a Mediator, who is the altar that sanctifies this gift. This altar was erected on Mount *Ebal,* the mount on which the curse was put (Deu. 11:29), to signify that there, where by the law we had reason to expect a curse, by Christ's sacrifice of himself for us and his mediation we have peace with God; he has redeemed us from the curse of the law by being made a *curse for us,* Gal. 3:13. Even where it was said, by the curse, *You are not my people,* there it is said, through Christ the altar, *You are the children of the living God,* Hos. 1:10. The curses pronounced on Mount Ebal would immediately have been executed if atonement had not been made by sacrifice. By the sacrifices offered on this altar they did likewise give God the glory of the victories they had already obtained, as Ex. 17:15. Now that they had had the comfort of them, in the spoils of Ai, it was fit that God should have the praise of them. And they also implored his favour for their future success; for supplications as well as thanksgivings were intended in their peace-offerings. The way to prosper in all that we put our hand to is to take God along with us, and in all our ways to acknowledge him by prayer, praise, and dependence. The altar they built was of rough unhewn stone, according to the law (Ex. 20:25), for that which is most plain and natural, and least artful and affected, in the worship of God, he is best pleased with. Man's device can add no beauty to God's institutions.

II. They received the law from God; and this those must do that would find favour with him, and expect to have their offerings accepted; for, if we turn away our ear from hearing the law, our prayers will be an abomination. When God took Israel into covenant he gave them his law, and they, in token of their consent to the covenant, subjected themselves to the law. Now here,

1. The law of the ten commandments was written upon stones in the presence of all Israel, as an abridgment of the whole, *v.* 32. This copy was not graven in the stone, as that which was reserved in the ark: That was to be done only by the finger of God; it is his prerogative to write the law in the heart. But the stones were plastered, and it was written upon the plaster, Deu. 27:4, 8. It was written, that all might see what it was that they consented to, and that it might be a standing remaining testimony to posterity of God's goodness in giving them such good laws, and a testimony against them if they were disobedient to them. It is a great mercy to any people to have the law of God in writing, and it is fit that the written law should be exposed to common view in a known tongue, that it may be seen and read of all men.

2. The blessings and the curses, the sanctions of the law, were publicly read, and the people (we may suppose), according to Moses's appointment, said *Amen* to them, *v.* 33, 34.

(1.) The auditory was very large. [1.] The greatest prince was not excused. The elders, officers, and judges, are not above the cognizance of the law, but will come under the blessing or the curse, according as they are or are not obedient to it, and therefore they must be present to consent to the covenant and to go before the people therein. [2.] The poorest stranger was not excluded. Here was a general naturalization of them: as well the stranger as he that was born among them was taken into covenant. This was an encouragement to proselytes, and a happy presage of the kindnesses intended for the poor Gentiles in the latter days.

(2.) The tribes were posted, as Moses directed, six towards Gerizim and six towards Ebal. And the ark in the midst of the valley was between them, for it was the *ark of the covenant;* and in it were shut up the close rolls of that law which was copied out and shown openly upon the stones. The covenant was commanded, and the command covenanted. the priests that attended the ark, or some of the Levites that attended them, after the people had all taken their places, and silence was proclaimed, pronounced distinctly the blessings and the curses, as Moses had drawn them up, to which the tribes said *Amen;* and yet it is here only said that they should *bless the people,* for the blessing was that which was first and chiefly intended, and which God designed in giving the law. If they fell under the curse, that was their own fault. And it was really a blessing to the people that they had this matter laid so plainly before them, *life and death, good and evil;* he *had not dealt so with other nations.*

3. The law itself also containing the precepts and prohibitions was read (*v.* 35), it should seem by Joshua himself, who did not think it below him to be a reader in the congregation of the Lord. In conformity to this example, the solemn reading of the law, which was appointed once in seven years (Deu. 31:10, 11), was performed by their king or chief magistrate. It is here intimated what a general publication of the law this was. (1.) Every word was read; even the minutest precepts were not omitted, nor the most copious abridged; not one iota or tittle of the law shall pass away, and therefore none was, in reading, skipped over, under pretence of want of time, or that any part was needless or not proper to be read. It was not many weeks since Moses had preached the whole book of *Deuteronomy* to them, yet Joshua must now read it all over again; it is good to hear twice what God has spoken once (Ps. 62:11) and to review what had been delivered to us, or to have it repeated, that we may not let it slip. (2.) Every Israelite was present, even *the women and the little ones* that all might know and do their duty. Note, Masters of families should bring their wives and children with them to the solemn assemblies for religious worship. All that are capable of learning must come to be *taught out of the law.* The strangers also attended with them; for wherever we are, though but as strangers, we should improve every opportunity of acquainting ourselves with God and his holy will.

CHAPTER 9

Here is in this chapter, I. The impolite confederacy of the kings of Canaan against Israel (*v.* 1, 2). II. The polite confederacy of the inhabitants of Gibeon with Israel, 1. How it was subtly proposed and petitioned for by the Gibeonites pretending to come from a far country (*v.* 3–13). 2. How it was unwarily consented to by Joshua and the Israelites, to the disgust of the congregation when the fraud was discovered (*v.* 14–18). 3. How the matter was adjusted to the satisfaction of all sides, by giving these Gibeonites their lives because they had covenanted with them, yet depriving them of their liberties because the covenant was not fairly obtained (*v.* 19–27).

Verses 1–2

Hitherto the Canaanites had acted defensively; the Israelites were the aggressors upon Jericho and Ai. But here the kings of Canaan are in consultation to attack Israel, and concert matters for a vigorous effort of their united forces to check the progress of their victorious arms. Now, 1. It was strange they did not do this sooner. They had notice long since of their approach; Israel's design upon Canaan was no secret; one would have expected that a prudent concern for their common safety would put them upon taking some measures to oppose their coming over Jordan, and maintain that pass against them, or to give them a warm reception as soon as they were over. It was strange they did not attempt to raise the siege of Jericho, or at least fall in with the men of Ai, when they had given them a defeat. But they were, either through presumption or despair, wonderfully infatuated and at their wits' end. Many know not the things that belong to their peace till they are hidden from their eyes. 2. It was more strange that they did it now. Now that the conquest of Jericho had given such a pregnant proof of God's power, and that of Ai of Israel's policy, one would have thought the end of their consultation should be, not to fight with Israel, but to make peace with them, and to gain the best terms they could for themselves. This would have been their wisdom (Lu. 14:32), but their minds were blinded, and their hearts hardened to their destruction. Observe, (1.) What induced them now at last to enter upon this consultation. When they *heard thereof* (*v.* 1), not only of the conquest of Jericho and Ai, but of the convention of the states of Mount Ebal, of which we have an account immediately before, — when they heard that Joshua, as if he thought himself already completely master of the country, had had all his people together, and had read the laws to them by which they must be governed, and taken their promises to submit to those laws, — then they perceived the Israelites were in good earnest, and thought it was high time for them to bestir themselves. The pious devotion of God's people sometimes provokes and exasperates their enemies more than any thing else. (2.) How unanimous they were in their resolves. Though they were many kings of different nations, Hittites, Amorites, Perizzites, etc., doubtless of different interests, and that had often been at variance one with another, yet they determined, *nemine contradicente — unanimously,* to unite against Israel. O that Israel would learn this of Canaanites, to sacrifice private interests to the public welfare, and to lay aside all animosities among themselves, that they may cordially unite against the common enemies of God's kingdom among men!

Verses 3–14

Here, I. The Gibeonites desire to make peace with Israel, being alarmed by the tidings they heard of the destruction of Jericho, *v.* 3. Other people heard those tidings, and were irritated thereby to make war upon Israel; but the Gibeonites heard them and were induced to make peace with them. Thus the discovery of the glory and grace of God in the gospel is to some a *savour of life unto life, but to others a savour of death unto death,* 2 Co. 2:16. The same sun softens wax and hardens clay. I do not remember that we read any where of a king of Gibeon. Had their government been at this time in a single person, perhaps his heart would have been too high to yield to Israel, and he would have joined with the rest of the kings against Israel. But these four united cities (mentioned *v.* 17) seem to have been governed by elders, or senators (*v.* 11), who consulted the common safety more than their own personal dignity. The inhabitants of Gibeon did well for themselves. We have,

II. The method they took to compass it. They knew that all the inhabitants of the land of Canaan were to be cut off; perhaps they had some spies in the congregation at Ebal, when the law was read, who observed and brought them notice of the command given to Israel (Deu. 7:1–3), that they should *show no mercy* to the Canaanites, give them no quarter in battle, which made them afraid of fighting them, and that they should *make no covenant with them,* which made them despair of gaining any advantage by treating with them; and therefore there was no way of saving their lives from the sword of Israel unless they could, by disguising themselves, make Joshua believe that they came from some very country, which the Israelites were not commanded to make war upon nor forbidden to *make peace with,* but were particularly appointed to *offer peace to,* Deu. 20:10, 15. Unless they could be admitted under this notion, they saw there was but one way with them: they must submit to the fate of Jericho and Ai. Though the neighbouring princes *knew that all the men thereof were mighty* (ch 10:2), and they knew it themselves, yet they durst not contend with Israel, who had an Almighty God on their side. This therefore is the only game they have to play, and observe,

1. They play it very artfully and successfully. Never was any such thing more craftily managed.

(1.) They come under the character of ambassadors from a foreign state, which they thought would please the princes of Israel, and make them proud of the honour of being courted by distant countries: we find Hezekiah fond of those that came to him from a far country (Isa. 39:3); they were not used to be thus courted.

(2.) They pretended to have undergone the fatigues of a very long journey, and produced what passed for an ocular demonstration of it. It should seem it was then usual for those that undertook long journeys to take with them, as we do now for long voyages, all manner of provision in kind, the country not being furnished as ours is now with houses of entertainment, for the convenience of which, when we have occasion to make use of them, we have reason to be very thankful. Now they here pretended that their provision, when they brought it from home, was fresh and new, but now it appeared to be old and dry, whereas it might well be presumed they had not loitered, but made the best of their way; so that hence it must be inferred that they came, as they said they did, from a very far country: their sacks or portmanteaus were old; the wine was all drunk, and the bottles in which it had been were broken; their shoes and clothes were worse than those of the Israelites in forty years, and their bread was mouldy, *v.* 4, 5, and again, *v.* 12, 13. Thus God's Israel have often been deceived and imposed upon with a show of antiquity. But (as bishop Hall expresses it) *errors are never the older for being patched,* and so seeming old; but those that will be caught with this Gibeonitish stratagem prove they have not consulted with God. And thus there are those who make themselves poor with the badges of want and distress and yet have great riches (Prov. 13:7), or at least have no need of relief, by which fraud charity is misplaced and diverted from those that are real objects of it.

(3.) When they were suspected, and more strictly examined as to whence they came, they industriously declined telling the name of their country, till the agreement was settled. [1.] The men of Israel suspected a fraud (*v.* 7): *"Peradventure you dwell among us,* and then we may not, we must not, make any league with you." This might have discouraged the Gibeonites from urging the matter any further, concluding that if the peace were made the Israelites would not think themselves obliged to keep it, having thus solemnly protested against it in case they *dwelt among them;* but, knowing that there was no hope at all if they stood it out, they bravely ventured a submission. "Who knows but the people of Israel may save us alive, though thus inveigled into a promise; and if we tell them at last we shall but die." [2.] Joshua put the questions to them, *Who are you? and whence come you?* He finds himself concerned to stand upon his guard against secret fraud as well as against open force. We in our spiritual warfare must *stand against the wiles of the devil,* remembering he is a subtle serpent as well as a roaring lion. In all leagues of relation and friendship we must first try and then trust, lest we repent at leisure agreements made in haste. [3.] They would not tell whence they came; but still repeat the same thing: *We have come from a very far country, v.* 9. They will have it thought that it is a country Joshua knows nothing of nor ever heard of, and therefore would be never the wiser if they should tell him the name of it.

(4.) They profess a respect for the God of Israel, the more to ingratiate themselves with Joshua, and we charitably believe they were sincere in this profession: *"We have come because of the name of the Lord thy God* (*v.* 9), because of what we have heard of that name, which has convinced us that it is *above every name,* and because we have a desire towards that name and the remembrance of it, and would gladly come under its protection."

(5.) They fetch their inducements from what had been done some time before in Moses's reign, the tidings whereof might easily be supposed ere this to have reached distant regions, the plagues of Egypt and the destruction of Sihon and Og (*v.* 9, 10), but prudently say nothing of the destruction of Jericho and Ai (though this was the true inducement, *v.* 3), because they will have it supposed that they came from home long before those conquests were made. We need not be long to seek for reasons why we should submit to the God of Israel; we may be furnished either with new or old, which we will.

(6.) They make a general submission — *We are our servants;* and humbly sue for a general agreement — *Make a league with us, v.* 11. They insist not upon terms, but will be glad of peace upon any terms; nor will the case admit of delays, lest the fraud be discovered; they would fain have the bargain struck up immediately; if Joshua will but *make a league* with them, they have all they come for, and they hope their ragged clothes and clouted shoes will be no exception against them. God and Israel reject none for their poverty. But,

2. There is a mixture of good and evil in their conduct. (1.) Their falsehood cannot be justified, nor ought it to be drawn into a precedent. We must not do evil that good may come. Had they owned their country but renounced the idolatries of it, resigning the possession of it to Israel and themselves to the God of Israel, we have reason to think Joshua would have been directed by the oracle of God to spare their lives, and they needed not to have made these pretensions. It is observable that when they had once said, *We have come from a far country* (*v.* 6), they found themselves necessitated to say it again (*v.* 9), and to say what was utterly false concerning their bread, their bottles, and their clothes (*v.* 12, 13), for one lie is an inlet to another, and that to a third, and so on. The way of that sin is down-hill. But, (2.) Their faith and prudence are to be greatly commended. Our Lord commended even the unjust steward, because he had done wisely and well for himself, Lu. 16:8. In submitting to Israel, they submitted to the God of Israel, which implied a renunciation of the god they had served, a resignation to the laws of true religion. They had heard enough to convince them of the infinite power of the God of Israel, and thence might infer his other perfections of wisdom and goodness; and how can we do better for ourselves than surrender at discretion to infinite wisdom, and cast ourselves upon the mercy of a God of infinite goodness. The submission of these Gibeonites was the more laudable because it was, [1.] Singular. Their neighbours took another course, and expected they should join with them. [2.] Speedy. They did not stay till Israel had besieged their cities; then it would have been too late to capitulate; but when they were at some distance they desired conditions of peace. Thy way to avoid a judgment is to meet it by repentance. Let us imitate these Gibeonites, and make our peace with God in the rags of humiliation, godly sorrow, and mortification, so our iniquity shall not be our ruin. Let us be servants to Jesus, our blessed Joshua, and make a league with him and the Israel of God, and we shall live.

Verses 15–21

Here is, I. The treaty soon concluded with the Gibeonites, *v.* 15. The thing was not done with much formality, but in short, 1. They agreed to let them live, and more the Gibeonites did not ask. In a common war this would have been but a small matter to be granted; but in the wars of Canaan, which were to make a general destruction, it was a great favour to a Canaanite to have his *life given him for a prey,* Jer. 45:5. 2. This agreement was made not by Joshua only, but by the princes of the congregation in conjunction with him. Though Joshua had an extraordinary call to the government, and extraordinary qualifications for it, yet he would not act in an affair of this nature without the counsel and concurrence of the princes, who were neither kept in the dark nor kept under foot, but were treated by him as sharers in the government. 3. It was ratified by an oath; they swore unto them, not by any of the gods of Canaan, but by the God of Israel only, *v.* 19. Those that mean honestly do not startle at assurances, but satisfy those with whom they treat, and glorify God by calling him to witness to the sincerity of their intentions. 4. Nothing appears to have been culpable in all this but that it was done rashly; they took of their victuals, by which they satisfied themselves that it was indeed old and dry, but did not consider that his was no proof of their bringing it fresh from home; so that, making use of their senses only, but not their reason, *they received the men* (as the margin reads it) *because of their victuals,* perceiving perhaps, upon the view and taste of their bread, not only that now it was old, but that it had been fine and very good at first, whence they inferred that they were persons of some quality, and therefore the friendship of their country was not to be despised. But *they asked not counsel at the mouth of the Lord.* They had the Urim and Thummim with them, which they might have advised with in this difficult case, and which would have told them no lie, would have led them into no error; but they relied so much on their own politics that they thought it needless to bring the matter to the oracle. Joshua himself was not altogether without blame herein. Note, We make more haste than good speed in any business when we stay not to take God along with us, and by the word and prayer to consult him. Many a time we see cause to reflect upon it with regret that such and such an affair miscarried, because we *asked not counsel at the mouth of the Lord;* would we acknowledge him in all our ways, we should find them more safe, easy, and successful.

II. The fraud soon discovered, by which this league was procured. *A lying tongue is but for a moment,* and truth will be the daughter of time. Within three days they found, to their great surprise, that the cities which these ambassadors had treated for were very near them, but one night's foot-march from the camp at Gilgal, *ch.* 10:9. Either their own scouts or the parties that sallied out to acquaint themselves with the country, or perhaps some deserters that came over to them from the enemy, informed them of the truth in this matter. Those that suffer themselves to be deceived by the wiles of Satan will soon be undeceived to their confusion, and will find that near, even at the door, which they imagined was very far off.

III. The disgust of the congregation at this. They did indeed submit to the restraints which this league laid upon them, and smote not the cities of the Gibeonites, neither slew the persons nor seized the prey; but it vexed them to have their hands thus tied, and they *murmured against the princes* (*v.* 18) it is to be feared, more from a jealousy for their own profit than from a zeal for the fulfilling of God's command, though some of them perhaps had a regard to that. Many are forward to arraign and censure the actions of princes while they are ignorant of the springs of those actions and are incompetent judges of the reasons of state that govern them. While therefore we are satisfied in general that those who are over us aim at nothing but the public good, and sincerely seek the welfare of their people, we ought to make the best of what they do and not exercise ourselves in things above us.

IV. The prudent endeavour of the princes to pacify the discontented congregation, and to accommodate the matter; herein all the princes concurred and were unanimous, which doubtless disposed the people to acquiesce.

1. They resolved to spare the lives of the Gibeonites, for so they had expressly sworn to do (*v.* 15), to let them live. (1.) The oath was lawful, else it had not bound them any more than Herod's oath bound him to cut off John Baptist's head; it is true God had appointed them to destroy all the Canaanites, but the law must be construed, *in favorem vitae — with some tender allowance,* to mean those only that stood it out and would not surrender their country to them, and not to bind them so far to put off the sense of honour and humanity as to slay those who had never lifted up a hand against them nor ever would, but before they were reduced to any extremity, or ever attempted any act of hostility, with one consent humbled themselves; the *kings of Israel were certainly more merciful kings than to do so* (1 Ki. 20:31), and the God of Israel a more merciful God than to order it so. *Satis est prostrasse leoni — It is enough to have laid the lion prostrate.* And besides, the reason of the law is the law; the mischief designed to be prevented by that law was the infecting of the Israelites with their idolatry, Deu. 7:4. But if the Gibeonites renounce their idolatry, and become friends and servants to the house of God, the danger is effectually prevented, the reason of the law ceases, and consequently the obligation of it, especially to a thing of this nature. The conversion of sinners shall prevent their ruin. (2.) The oath being lawful, both the princes and the people for whom they transacted were bound by it, bound in conscience, bound in honour to the God of Israel, by whom they had sworn, and whose name would have been blasphemed by the Canaanites if they had violated this oath. They speak as those that *feared an oath* (Eccl. 9:2), when they argued thus: *We will let them live, lest wrath be upon us, because of the oath which we swore, v.* 20. He that ratifies a promise with an oath imprecates the divine vengeance if he wilfully break his promise, and has reason to expect that divine justice will take him at his word. God is not mocked, and therefore oaths are not to be jested with. The princes would keep their word, [1.] Though they lost by it. A citizen of Zion *swears to his own hurt and changes not,* Ps. 15:4. Joshua and the princes, when they found it was to their prejudice that they had thus bound themselves, did not apply to Eleazar for a dispensation, much less did they pretend that no faith is to be kept with heretics, with Canaanites; no, they were strangers to the modern artifices of the Romish church to elude the most sacred bonds, and even to sanctify perjuries [2.] Though the people were uneasy at it, and their discontent might have ended in a mutiny, yet the princes would not violate their engagement to the Gibeonites; we must never be over-awed, either by majesty or multitude, to do a sinful thing, and go against our consciences. [3.] Though they were drawn into this league by a wile, and might have had a very plausible pretence to declare it null and void, yet they adhered to it. They might have pleaded that though those were the men with whom they exchanged the ratifications, yet these were not the cities intended in the league; they had promised to spare certain cities, without names, that were very far off, and upon the express consideration of their being so; but these were very near, and therefore not the cities that they covenanted with. And many learned men have thought that they were so grossly imposed upon by the Gibeonites that it would have been lawful for them to have recalled their promise, but to preserve their reputation, and to keep up in Israel a veneration of an oath, they would stand to it; but it is plain that they thought themselves indispensably obliged by it, and were apprehensive that the wrath of God would fall upon them if they broke it. And, however their adherence to it might be displeasing to the congregation, it is plain that it was acceptable to God; for when, in pursuance of this league, they undertook the protection of the Gibeonites, God gave them the most glorious victory that ever they had in all their wars (*ch.* 10), and long afterwards severely avenged the wrong Saul did to the Gibeonites in violation of this league, 2 Sa. 21:1. Let this convince us all how religiously we ought to perform our promises, and make good our bargains; and what conscience we ought to make of our words when they are once given. If a covenant obtained by so many lies and deceits might not be broken, shall we think to evade the obligation of those that have been made with all possible honesty and fairness? If the fraud of others will not justify or excuse our falsehood, certainly the honesty of others in dealing with us will aggravate and condemn our dishonesty in dealing with them.

2. Though they spared their lives, yet they seized their liberties, and sentenced them to be *hewers of wood and drawers of water to the congregation, v.* 21. By this proposal the discontented congregation was pacified; for, (1.) Those who were angry that the Gibeonites lived might be

content when they saw them condemned to that which, in the general apprehension, is worse than death, perpetual servitude. (2.) Those who were angry that they were not spoiled might be content when their serving the congregation would be more to the public advantage than their best effects could be; and, in short, the Israelites would be not losers either in honour or profit by this peace with the Gibeonites; convince them of this, and they will be satisfied.

Verses 22–27

The matter is here settled between Joshua and the Gibeonites, and an explanation of the league agreed upon. We may suppose that now, not the messengers who were first sent, but the elders of Gibeon, and of the cities that were dependent upon it, were themselves present and treated with, that the matter might be fully compromised.

I. Joshua reproves them for their fraud, *v.* 22. And they excuse it as well as they can, *v.* 24. 1. Joshua gives the reproof very mildly: *Wherefore have you beguiled us?* He does not load them with any ill names, does not give them any harsh provoking language, does not call them, as they deserved to be called, *base liars,* but only asks them, *Why have you beguiled us?* Under the greatest provocations, it is our wisdom and duty to keep our temper, and to bridle our passion; a just cause needs not anger to defend it, and a bad one is made never the better by it. 2. They make the best excuse for themselves, that the thing would bear, *v.* 24. They found by the word of God that sentence of death was passed upon them (the command was to *destroy all the inhabitants of the land,* without exception), and they found by the works of God already wrought that there was no opposing the execution of this sentence; they considered that God's sovereignty is incontestable, his justice inflexible, his power irresistible, and therefore resolved to try what his mercy was, and found it was not in vain to cast themselves upon it. They do not go about to justify their lie, but in effect beg pardon for it, pleading it was purely to save their lives that they did it, which every man that finds in himself the force of the law of self-preservation will therefore make great allowances for, especially in such a case as this, where the fear was not merely of the power of man (if that were all, one might flee from that to the divine protection), but of the power of God himself, which they saw engaged against them.

II. Joshua condemns them to servitude, as a punishment of their fraud (*v.* 23), and they submit to the sentence (*v.* 25), and for aught that appears both sides are pleased.

1. Joshua pronounces them perpetual bondmen. They had purchased their lives with a lie, but, that being no good consideration, he obliges them to hold their lives under the rent and reservation of their continual labours, in hewing wood and drawing water, the meanest and most toilsome employments. Thus their lie was punished; had they dealt fairly and plainly with Israel, perhaps they would have had more honourable conditions granted them, but now, since they gain their lives with ragged clothes and clouted shoes, the badges of servitude, they are condemned for ever to wear such, so must their doom be. And thus the ransom of their lives is paid; dominion is acquired by the preservation of a life that lies at mercy *(servus dicitur a servando — a servant is so called from the act of saving);* they owe their service to those to whom they owe their lives. Observe how the judgment is given against them. (1.) Their servitude is made a curse to them. "Now you are cursed with the ancient curse of Canaan," from whom these Hivites descended, *a servant of servants shalt thou be,* Gen. 9:25. What shall be done to the false tongue but this? Cursed shall it be. (2.) Yet this curse is turned into a blessing; they must be servants, but it shall be for *the house of my God.* The princes would have them slaves *unto all the congregation* (*v.* 21), at least they chose to express themselves so, for the pacifying of the people that were discontented; but Joshua mitigates the sentence, both in honour to God and in favour to the Gibeonites: it would be too hard upon them to make them every man's drudge; if they must be *hewers of wood and drawers of water,* than which there cannot be a greater disparagement, especially to those who are citizens of a royal city, and *all mighty men* (*ch.* 10:2), yet they shall be so to *the house of my God,* than which there cannot be a greater preferment: David himself could have wished to be a door-keeper there. Even servile work becomes honourable when it is done for the house of our God and the offices thereof. [1.] They were hereby excluded from the liberties and privileges of true-born Israelites, and a remaining mark of distinction was put upon their posterity throughout all their generations. [2.] They were hereby employed in such services as required their personal attendance upon *the altar of God in the place which he should choose* (*v.* 27), which would bring them to the knowledge of the law of God, keep them strictly to that holy religion to which they were proselyted, and prevent their revolt to the idolatries of their fathers. [3.] This would be a great advantage to the priests and Levites to have so many, and those mighty men, constant attendants upon them, and engaged by office to do all the drudgery of the tabernacle. A great deal of wood must be hewed for fuel for God's house, not only to keep the fire burning continually upon the altar, but to boil the flesh of the peace-offerings, etc. And a great deal of water must be drawn for the divers washings which the law prescribed. These and other such servile works, such as washing the vessels, carrying out ashes, sweeping the courts, etc., which otherwise the Levites must have done themselves, these Gibeonites were appointed to do. [4.] They were herein servants to the congregation too; for whatever promotes and helps forward the worship of God is real service to the commonwealth. It is the interest of every Israelite that the altar of God be well attended. Hereby also the congregation was excused from much of that servile work which perhaps would otherwise have been expected from some of them. God had made a law that the Israelites should never make any of their brethren bondmen; if they had slaves, they must be of the heathen that were round about them, Lev. 25:44. Now in honour of this law, and of Israel that was honoured by it, God would not have the drudgery, no, not of the tabernacle itself, to be done by Israelites, but by Gibeonites, who were afterwards called *Nethinim,* men given to the Levites, as the Levites were to the priests (Num. 3:9), to minister to them in the service of God. [5.] This may be looked upon as typifying the admission of the Gentiles into the gospel church. Now they were taken in upon their submission to be under-officers, but afterwards God promises that he will *take of them for priests and Levites,* Isa. 66:21.

2. They submit to this condition, *v.* 25. Conscious of a fault in framing a lie whereby to deceive the Israelites, and sensible also how narrowly they escaped with their lives and what a kindness it was to have them spared, they acquiesce in the proposal: *Do as it seemeth right unto thee.* Better live in servitude, especially such servitude, than not live at all. Those of the very meanest and most despicable condition are described to be *hewers of wood and drawers of water,* Deu. 29:11. But skin for skin, liberty, and labour, and *all that a man has, will he give for his life,* and no ill bargain. Accordingly the matter was determined. (1.) Joshua delivered them out of the hands of the Israelites that they should not be slain, *v.* 26. It seems there were those who would have fallen upon them with the sword if Joshua had not interposed with his authority; but wise generals know when to sheathe the sword, as well as when to draw it. (2.) He then delivered them again into the hands of the Israelites to be enslaved, *v.* 27. They were not to keep possession of their cities, for we find afterwards that three of them fell to the lot of Benjamin and one to that of Judah; nor were they themselves to be at their own disposal, but, as bishop Patrick thinks, were dispersed into the cities of the priests and Levites, and came up with them in their courses to serve at the altar, out of the profits of which, it is probable, they were maintained. And thus Israel's bondmen became the Lord's freemen, for his service in the meanest office is liberty, and his work is its own wages. And this they got by their early submission. Let us, in like manner, submit to our Lord Jesus, and refer our lives to him, saying, *"We are in thy hand, do unto us as seemeth good and right unto thee;* only save our souls, and we shall not repent it:" if he appoint us to bear his cross, and draw in his yoke, and serve at his altar, this shall be afterwards neither shame nor grief to us, while the meanest office in God's service will entitle us to a *dwelling in the house of the Lord all the days of our life.*

CHAPTER 10

We have in this chapter an account of the conquest of the kings and kingdoms of the southern part of the land of Canaan, as, in the next chapter, of the reduction of the northern parts, which together completed the glorious successes of the wars of Canaan. In this chapter we have an account, I. Of the routing of their forces in the field, in which observe, 1. Their confederacy against the Gibeonites (*v.* 1–5). 2. The Gibeonites' request to Joshua to assist them (*v.* 6). 3. Joshua's speeds march under divine encouragement for their relief (*v.* 7–9). 4. The defeat of the armies of these confederate kings (*v.* 10, 11). 5. The miraculous prolonging of the day by the standing still of the sun in favour of the conquerors (*v.* 12–14). II. Of the execution of the kings that escaped out of the battle (*v.* 15–27). III. Of the taking of the particular cities, and the total destruction of all that were found in them. Makkedah (*v.* 28)). Libnah (*v.* 29, 30). Lachish (*v.* 31, 32) and the king of Gezer that attempted its rescue (*v.* 33). Eglon (*v.* 34, 35). Hebron (*v.* 36, 37). Debir (*v.* 38, 39). And the bringing of all that country into the hands of Israel (*v.* 40–42). And, lastly, the return of the army to the head-quarters (*v.* 43).

Verses 1–6

Joshua and the hosts of Israel had now been a good while in the land of Canaan, and no great matters were effected; they were made masters of Jericho by a miracle, of Ai by stratagem, and of Gibeon by surrender, and that was all; hitherto the progress of their victories had not seemed proportionable to the magnificence of their entry and the glory of their beginnings. Those among them that were impatient of delays, it is probable, complained of Joshua's slowness, and asked why they did not immediately penetrate into the heart of the country, before the enemy could rally their forces to make head against them, why they stood trifling, while they were so confident both of their title and of their success. Thus Joshua's prudence, perhaps, was censured as slothfulness, cowardice, and want of spirit. But, 1. Canaan was not to be conquered in a day. God had said that *by little and little* he would drive out the Canaanites, Ex. 23:30. He that believeth will not make haste, or conclude that the promise will never be performed because it is not performed so soon as he expected. 2. Joshua waited for the Canaanites to be the aggressors; let them first make an onset upon Israel, or the allies of Israel, and then their destruction will be, or at least will appear to be, the more just and more justifiable. Joshua had warrant sufficient to set upon them, yet he stays till they strike the first stroke, that he might provide for honest things in the sight, not only of God, but of men; and they would be the more inexcusable in their resistance, now that they had seen what favour the Gibeonites found with Israel. 3. It was for the advantage of Israel to sit still awhile, that the forces of these little kings might unite in one body, and so might the more easily be cut off at one blow. This God had in his eye when he put it into their hearts to combine against Israel; though they designed thereby to strengthen one another, that which he intended was to gather them as sheaves into the floor, to fall together under the flail, Mic. 4:12. Thus oftentimes that seeming paradox proves wholesome counsel, *Stay awhile, and we shall have done the sooner.*

After Israel had waited awhile for an occasion to make war upon the Canaanites, a fair one offers itself. 1. Five kings combine against the Gibeonites. Adoni-zedec king of Jerusalem was the first mover and ring-leader of this confederacy. He had a good name (it signifies *lord of righteousness*), being a descendant perhaps from Melchizedek, *king of righteousness;* but, notwithstanding the goodness of his name and family, it seems he was a bad man, and an implacable enemy to the posterity of that Abraham to whom his predecessor, Melchizedek, was such a faithful friend. He called upon his neighbours to join against Israel either because he was the most honourable prince, and had the precedency among these kings (perhaps they had some dependence upon him, at least they paid a deference to him, as the most public, powerful, and active man they had among them), or because he was first or most apprehensive of the danger his country was in, not only by the conquest of Jericho and Ai, but the surrender of Gibeon, which, it seems, was the chief thing that alarmed him, it being one of the most considerable frontier towns they had. Against Gibeon therefore all the force he would raise must be leveled. *Come,* says he, *and help me, that we may smite Gibeon.* This he resolves to do, either, (1.) In policy, that he might retake the city, because it was a strong city, and of great consequence to this country in whose hands it was; or, (2.) In passion, that he might chastise the citizens for making peace with Joshua, pretending that they had perfidiously betrayed their country and strengthened the common enemy, whereas they had really done the greatest kindness imaginable to their country, by setting them a good example, if they would have followed it. Thus Satan and his instruments make war upon those that make peace with God. *Marvel not if the world hate you,* and treat those as deserters who are converts to Christ. 2. The Gibeonites send notice to Joshua of the distress and danger they are in, *v.* 6. Now they expect benefit from the league they had made with Israel, because, though it was obtained by deceit, it was afterwards confirmed when the truth came out. They think Joshua obliged to help them, (1.) In conscience, because they were his servants; not in compliment, as they had said in their first address (*ch.* 9:8), *We are thy servants,* but in reality made servants to the congregation; and it is the duty of masters to take care of the poorest and meanest of their servants, and not to see them wronged when it is in the power of their hand to right them. Those that pay allegiance may reasonably expect protection. Thus David pleads with God (Ps. 119:94), *I am thine, save me;* and so may we, if indeed we be his. (2.) In honour, because the ground of their enemies' quarrel with them was the respect they had shown to Israel, and the confidence they had in a covenant with them. Joshua cannot refuse to help them when it is for their affection to him, and to the name of his God, that they are attacked. David thinks it a good plea with God (Ps. 69:7), *For thy sake I have borne reproach.* When our spiritual enemies set themselves in array against us, and threaten to swallow us up, let us, by faith and prayer, apply to Christ, our Joshua, for strength and succour, as Paul did, and we shall receive the same answer of peace, *My grace is sufficient for thee,* 2 Co. 12:8, 9.

Verses 7–14

Here, I. Joshua resolves to assist the Gibeonites, and God encourages him in this resolve. 1. He ascended from Gilgal (*v.* 7), that is, he designed, determined, and prepared for, this expedition to relieve Gibeon, for it is probable it was before he stirred a step that God spoke to him to encourage him. It was generous and just in Joshua to help his new allies, though perhaps the king of Jerusalem, when he attacked them, little thought that Joshua would be so ready to help them, but expected he would abandon them as Canaanites, the rather because they had obtained their league with him by fraud; therefore he speaks with assurance (*v.* 4) of smiting Gibeon. But Joshua knew that his promise to let them live obliged him, not only not to slay them himself, but not to stand by and see them slain when it was in the power of his hand to prevent it, Prov. 24:11, 12. He knew that when they embraced the faith and worship of the God of Israel they came to trust under the shadow of his wings (Ruth 2:12), and therefore, as his servants, he was bound to protect them. 2. God animated him for his undertaking, (*v.* 8): *Fear not,* that is, (1.) "Doubt not of the goodness of thy cause and the clearness of thy call; though it be to assist Gibeonites, thou art in the way of duty, and God is with thee of a truth." (2.) "Dread not the power of the enemy; though so many kings are confederate against thee, and are resolved to make their utmost efforts for the reduction of Gibeon, and it may be will fight desperately in a desperate cause, yet let not this discourage thee, *I have delivered them into thy hand;*" and those can make neither resistance nor escape whom God has marked for destruction.

II. Joshua applies himself to execute this resolve, and God assists him in the execution. Here we have,

1. The great industry of Joshua, and the power of God working with it for the defeat of the enemy. In this action, (1.) Joshua showed his good-will in the haste he made for the relief of Gibeon (*v.* 9): *He came unto them suddenly,* for the extremity was such as would not admit delay. If one of the tribes of Israel had been in danger, he could not have shown more care or zeal for its relief than here for Gibeon, remembering in this, as in other cases, there must be one law for the stranger that was proselyted and for him that was born in the land. Scarcely had the confederate princes got their forces together, and sat down before Gibeon, when Joshua was upon them, the surprise of which would put them into the greatest confusion. Now that the enemy were actually drawn up into a body, which had all as it were but one neck, despatch was as serviceable to his cause as before delay was, while he waited for this general rendezvous; and now that things were ripe for execution no man more expeditious than Joshua, who before had seemed slow. Now it shall never be said, *He left that to be done to-morrow which he could do to-day.* When Joshua found he could not reach Gibeon in a day, lest he should lose any real advantages against the enemy, or so much as seem to come short or to neglect his new allies, he marched all night, resolving not to give sleep to his eyes, nor slumber to his eye-lids, till he had accomplished this enterprise. It was well the forces he took with him were mighty men of valour, not only able-bodied men, but men of spirit and resolution, and hearty in the cause, else they neither could nor would have borne this fatigue, but would have murmured at their leader and would have asked, "Is this the rest we were promised in Canaan?" But they well considered that the present toil was in order to a happy settlement, and therefore were reconciled to it. Let the *good soldiers of Jesus Christ* learn hence to *endure hardness, in following the Lamb whithersoever he goes,* and not think themselves undone if their religion lose them now and then a night's sleep; it will be enough to rest when we come to heaven. But why needed Joshua to put himself and his men so much to the stretch? Had not God promised him that without fail he would *deliver the enemies into his hand?* It is true he had; but God's promises are intended, not to slacken and supersede, but to quicken and encourage our endeavours. He that believeth doth not make haste to anticipate providence, but doth make haste to attend it, with a diligent, not a distrustful, speed. (2.) God showed his great power in defeating the enemies whom Joshua so vigorously attacked, *v.* 10, 11. Joshua had a very numerous and powerful army with him, hands enough to despatch a dispirited enemy, so that the enemy might have been scattered by the ordinary fate of war; but God himself would appear in this great and decisive battle, and draw up the artillery of heaven against the Canaanites, to demonstrate to this people that they *got not this land in possession by their own sword, neither did their own arm save them, but God's right hand and his arm,* Ps. 44:3. *The Lord discomfited them before Israel.* Israel did what they could, and yet God did all. [1.] It must needs be a very great terror and confusion to the enemy to perceive that heaven itself fought against them; for who can contest with, flee from, or fence against, the powers of heaven? They had affronted the true God and robbed him of his honour by worshipping the host of heaven, giving that worship to the creature which is due to the Creator only; and now the host of heaven fights against them, and even that part of the creation which they had idolized is at war with them, and even triumphs in their ruin, Jer. 8:2. There is no way of making any creature propitious to us, no, not by sacrifice nor offering, but only by making our peace with God and keeping ourselves in his love. This had been enough to make them an easy prey to the victorious Israelites, yet this was not all. [2.] Besides the terror struck upon them, there was a great slaughter made of them by hail-stones, which were so large, and came down with such a force, that more were killed by the hail-stones than by the sword of the Israelites, though no doubt they were busy. God himself speaks to Job of treasures, or magazines, of snow and hail, which he has *reserved for the day of battle and war* (Job 38:22, 23), and here they are made use of to destroy the Canaanites. Here was hail, shot from God's great ordnance, that, against whomsoever it was directed, was sure to hit (and never glanced upon the Israelites mixed with them), and wherever it hit was sure to kill. See here how miserable those are that have God for their enemy, and how sure to perish; it is a fearful thing to fall into his hands, for there is no fleeing out of them. Some observe that Beth-horon lay north of Gibeon, Azekah and Makkedah lay south, so that they fled each way but, which way soever they fled, the hail-stones pursued them, and met them at every turn.

2. The great faith of Joshua, and the power of God crowning it with the miraculous arrest of the sun, that the day of Israel's victories might be prolonged, and so the enemy totally defeated. The hail-stones had their rise no higher than the clouds, but, to show that Israel's help came from above the clouds, the sun itself, who by his constant motion serves the whole earth, by halting when there was occasion served the Israelites, and did them a kindness. *The sun and moon stood still in their habitation, at the light of thy arrows* which gave the signal, Hab. 3:11.

(1.) Here is the prayer of Joshua that the sun might stand still. I call it his prayer, because it is said (*v.* 12) *he spoke to the Lord;* as Elijah, though we read (1 Ki. 17:1) only of his prophesying of the drought, yet is said (James 5:17) to pray for it. Observe, [1.] An instance of Joshua's unwearied activity in the service of God and Israel, that though he had marched all night and fought all day, and, one might expect, would be inclined to repose himself and get a little sleep, and give his army some time to rest — that, like the hireling, he would earnestly desire the shadow, and bid the night welcome, when he had done such a good day's work — yet, instead of this, he wishes for nothing so much as the prolonging of the day. Note, Those that *wait on the Lord* and work for him *shall renew their strength, shall run and not be weary, shall walk and not faint,* Isa. 40:31. [2.] An instance of his great faith in the almighty power of God, as above the power of nature, and able to control and alter the usual course of it. No doubt Joshua had an extraordinary impulse or impression upon his spirit, which he knew to be of divine origin, prompting him to desire that this miracle might be wrought upon this occasion, else it would have been presumption in him to desire or expect; the prayer would not have been granted by the divine power, if it had not been dictated by the divine grace. God wrought this faith in him, and then said, *"According to thy faith,* and thy prayer of faith, *be it unto thee."* It cannot be imagined, however, that such a thing as this should have entered into his mind if God had not put it there; a man would have had a thousand projects in his head for the completing of the victory before he would have thought of desiring the sun to stand still; but even in the Old-Testament saints *the Spirit made intercession according to the will of God.* What God will give he inclines the hearts of his praying people to ask, and for what he will do he will be enquired of, Eze. 36:37. Now, *First,* It looked great for Joshua to say, *Sun, stand thou still.* His ancestor Joseph had indeed dreamed that the sun and moon did homage to him; but who would have thought that, after it had been fulfilled in the figure, it should be again fulfilled in the letter to one of his posterity? The prayer is thus expressed with authority, because it was not an ordinary prayer, such as is directed and supported only by God's common providence or promise, but the prayer of a prophet at this time divinely inspired for this purpose; and yet it intimates to us the prevalency of prayer in general, so far as it is regulated by the word of God, and may remind us of that honour put upon prayer (Isa. 45:11), *Concerning the work of my hands command you me.* He bids the sun stand still upon Gibeon, the place of action and the seat of war, intimating that what he designed in this request was the advantage of Israel against their enemies; it is probable that the sun was now declining, and that he did not call for the lengthening out of the day until he observed it hastening towards it period. He does likewise, in the name of the King of kings, arrest the moon, perhaps because it was requisite for the preserving of the harmony and good order of the spheres that the course of the rest of the heavenly bodies should be stayed likewise, otherwise, while the sun shone, he needed not the moon; and here he mentions the valley of Ajalon, which was near to Gibeon, because there he was at that time. *Secondly,* It was bold indeed to say so before Israel, and argues a very strong assurance of faith. If the event had not answered the demand, nothing could have been a greater slur upon him; the Israelites would have concluded he was certainly going mad, or he would never have talked so extravagantly. But he knew very well God would own and answer a petition which he himself directed to be drawn up and presented, and therefore was not afraid to say before all Israel, calling them to observe this work of wonder, *Sun, stand thou still,* for he was confident in him whom he had trusted. He believed the almighty power of God, else he could not have expected that the sun, going on in its strength, driving in a full career, and *rejoicing as a strong man to run a race,* should be stopped in an instant. He believed the sovereignty of God in the kingdom of nature, else he could not have expected that the established law and course of nature should be changed and interrupted, the ordinances of heaven, and the constant usage according to these ordinances, broken in upon. And he believed God's particular favour to Israel above all people under the sun, else he could not have expected that, to favour them upon an emergency with a double day, he should (which must follow of course) amaze and terrify so great a part of the terrestrial globe with a double night at the same time. It is true, he *causeth the sun to shine upon the just and the unjust;* but for this once the unjust shall wait for it beyond the usual time, while, in favour to righteous Israel, it stands still.

(2.) The wonderful answer to this prayer. No sooner said than done (*v.* 13): *The sun stood still, and the moon staid.* Notwithstanding the vast distance between the earth and the sun, at the word of Joshua the sun stopped immediately; for the same God that rules in heaven above rules at the same time on this earth, and, when he pleases, even *the heavens shall hear the earth,* as here. Concerning this great miracle it is here said, [1.] *That it continued a whole day,* that is, the sun continued as long again above the horizon as otherwise it would have done. It is commonly supposed to have been about the middle of summer that this happened, when, in that country, it was about fourteen hours between sun and sun, so that this day was about twenty-eight hours long; yet, if we suppose it to have been at that time of the year when the days are at the shortest, it will be the more probable that Joshua should desire and pray for the prolonging of the day. [2.] That hereby the people had full time to avenge themselves of their enemies, and to give them a total defeat. We often read in history of battles which the night put an end to, the shadows of which favoured the retreat of the conquered; to prevent this advantage to the enemy in their flight, the day was doubled, that the hand of Israel might *find out all their enemies;* but the eye and hand of God can find them out without the help of the sun's light, for to him *the night shineth as the day,* Ps. 139:12. Note, Sometimes God completes a great salvation in a little time, and makes but one day's work of it. Perhaps this miracle is alluded to Zec. 14:6, 7, where the day of God's fighting against the nations is said to be *one day,* and that *at evening time it shall be light,* as here. And, [3.] That there was *never any day like it,* before or since, in which God put such an honour upon faith and prayer, and upon Israel's cause; never did he so wonderfully comply with the request of a man, nor so wonderfully fight for his people. [4.] This is said to be written *in the book of Jasher,* a collection of state-poems, in which the poem made upon this occasion was preserved among the rest; probably the same with that *book of the wars of the Lord* (Num. 21:14), which afterwards was continued and carried on by one Jasher. Those words, *Sun, stand thou still upon Gibeon, and thou moon in the valley of Ajalon,* sounding metrical, are supposed to be taken from the narrative of this event as it was found in the book of Jasher. Not that the divine testimony of the book of Joshua needed confirmation from the book of Jasher, a human composition; but to those who had that book in their hands it would be of use to compare this history with it, which warrants the appeals the learned make to profane history for corroborating the proofs of the truth of sacred history. [5.] But surely this stupendous miracle of the standing still of the sun was intended for something more than merely to give Israel so much the more time to find out and kill their enemies, which, without this, might have been done the next day. *First,* God would hereby magnify Joshua (*ch.* 3:7), as a particular favourite, and one whom he did delight to honour, being a type of him who has all power both in heaven and in earth and whom the winds and the seas obey. *Secondly,* He would hereby notify to all the world what he was doing for his people Israel here in Canaan; the sun, the eye of the world, must be fixed for some hours upon Gibeon and the valley of Ajalon, as if to contemplate the great works of God there for Israel, and so to engage the children of men to look that way, and to *enquire of this wonder done in the land,* 2 Chr. 32:31. Proclamation was hereby made to all the neighbouring nations. *Come, behold the works of the Lord* (Ps. 46:8), and say, *What nation is there so great as Israel is, who has God so nigh unto them?* One would have supposed that this would bring such real ambassadors as the Gibeonites pretended to be from a very far country, to court the friendship of Israel because of the name of the Lord their God. *Thirdly,* He would hereby convince and confound those idolaters that worshipped the sun and moon and gave divine honours to them, by demonstrating that they were subject to the command of the God of Israel, and that, as high as they were, he was above them; and thus he would fortify his people against temptations to this idolatry, which he foresaw they would be addicted to (Deu. 4:19), and which, notwithstanding this, they afterwards corrupted themselves with. *Fourthly,* This miracle signified (it is the learned bishop Pierson's notion) that in the latter days, when the light of the world was tending towards a light of darkness, the *Sun of righteousness,* even our Joshua, should arise (Mal. 4:2), give check to the approaching night, and be the true light. To which let me add that when Christ conquered our spiritual enemies upon the cross the miracle wrought on the sun was the reverse of this; it was then darkened as if it had gone down at noon, for Christ needed not the light of the sun to carry on his victories: he then made darkness his pavilion. And, *Lastly,* The arresting of the sun and moon in this day of battle prefigured the turning of the sun into darkness, and the moon into blood, in the last great and terrible day of the Lord.

Verses 15–27

It was a brave appearance, no doubt, which the five kings made when they took the field for the reducing of Gibeon, and a brave army they had following them; but they were all routed, put into disorder first, and then brought to destruction by the hail-stones. And now Joshua thought, his work being done, he might go with his army into quarters of refreshment. Accordingly it was resolved, perhaps in a council of war, that they should presently return *to the camp at Gilgal* (*v.* 15), till they should receive orders from God to take possession of the country they had now conquered; but he soon finds he has more work cut out for him. The victory must be pursued, that the spoils might be divided. Accordingly he applies himself to it with renewed vigour.

I. The forces that had dispersed themselves must be followed and smitten. When tidings were brought to Joshua where the kings were he ordered a guard to be set upon them for the present (*v.* 18), *reserving them* for another *day of destruction,* and to be *brought forth to a day of wrath,* Job 21:30. He directs his men to pursue the common soldiers, as much as might be, to prevent their escaping to the garrisons, which would strengthen them, and make the reduction of them the more difficult, *v.* 19. Like a prudent general, he does that first which is most needful, and defers his triumphs till he has completed his conquests; nor was he in such haste to insult over the captive kings but that he would first prevent the rallying again of their scattered forces. The result of this vigorous pursuit was, 1. That a very great slaughter was made of the enemies of God and Israel. And, 2. The field was cleared of them, so that none remained but such as got into fenced cities, where they would not long be safe themselves, nor were they capable of doing any service to the cities that sheltered them, unless they could have left their fears behind them. 3. *None moved his tongue against any of the children of Israel, v.* 21. This expression intimates, (1.) Their perfect safety and tranquillity; some think it should be read (from Ex. 11:7), *Against any of the children of Israel did not a dog move his tongue;* no, not against any one man of them. They were not threatened by any danger at all after their victory, no, not so much as the barking of a dog. Not one single Israelite (for the original makes it so particular) was brought into any distress, either in the battle or in the pursuit. (2.) Their honour and reputation; no man had any reproach to cast upon them, nor an ill word to give them. God not only tied the hands, but stopped the mouths, of their enraged enemies, and put lying lips to silence. (3.) The Chaldee paraphrase makes it an expression of their unalloyed joy for this victory, reading it, *There was no hurt nor loss to the children of Israel, for which any man should afflict his soul.* When the army came to be reviewed after the battle, there was none slain, none wounded, none missing. Not one Israelite had occasion to lament either the loss of a friend or the loss of a limb, so cheap, so easy, so glorious, was this victory.

II. The kings that had hidden themselves must now be called to an account, as rebels against the Israel of God, to whom, by the divine promise and grant, this land did of right belong and should have been surrendered upon demand. See here,

1. How they were secured. The cave which they fled to, and trusted in for a refuge, became their prison, in which they were clapped up, till Joshua sat in judgment on them, *v.* 18. It seems they all escaped both the hail-stones and the sword, God so ordering it, not in kindness to them, but that they might be reserved for a more solemn and terrible execution; as, for this cause, Pharaoh survived the plagues of Egypt, and was made to stand, that God might in him *show his power,* Ex. 9:16. They all fled, and met at the same place, Providence directing them; and now those who were lately consulting against Israel were put upon new counsels to preserve themselves and agreed to take shelter in the same cave. The information brought to Joshua of this is an evidence that there were those of the country, who knew the holes and fastnesses of it, that were in his interests. And the care Joshua took to keep them there when they were there, as it is an instance of his policy and presence of mind, even in the heat of action, so, in the result of their project, it shows how those not only deceive themselves, but destroy themselves, who think to hide themselves from God. Their refuge of lies will but bind them over to God's judgment.

2. How they were triumphed over. Joshua ordered them to be brought forth out of the cave, set before him as at the bar, and their names called over, *v.* 22, 23. And when they either were bound and cast upon the ground unable to help themselves, or threw themselves upon the ground, humbly to beg for their lives, he called for the general officers and great men, and commanded them to trample upon these kings, and set their feet upon their necks, not in sport and to make themselves and the company merry, but with the gravity and decorum that became the ministers of the divine justice who were not herein to gratify any pride or passion of their own, but to give glory to the God of Israel as higher than the highest, who *treads upon princes as mortar* (Isa. 41:25), and *is terrible to the kings of the earth,* Ps. 76:12. The thing does indeed look barbarous, thus to insult over men in misery, who had suddenly fallen from the highest pitch of honour into this disgrace. It was hard for crowned heads to be thus trodden upon, not by Joshua himself (that might better have been borne), at least not by him only, but by all the captains of the army. Certainly it ought not to be drawn into a precedent, for the case was extraordinary, and we have reason to think it was by divine direction and impulse that Joshua did this. (1.) God would hereby punish the abominable wickedness of these kings, the measure of whose iniquity was now full. And, by this public act of justice done upon these ringleaders of the Canaanites in sin, he would possess his people with the greater dread and detestation of those sins of *the nations that God cast out from before them,* which they would be tempted to imitate. (2.) He would hereby have the promise by Moses made good (Deu. 33:29), *Thou shalt tread upon their high places,* that is, their great men, which should the rather be speedily fulfilled in the letter because they are the very last words of Moses that we find upon record. (3.) He would hereby encourage the faith and hope of his people Israel in reference to the wars that were yet before them. Therefore Joshua said (*v.* 25): *Fear not, nor be dismayed.* [1.] "Fear not these kings, nor any of theirs, as if there were any danger of having this affront now put upon them in after-time revenged upon yourselves, a consideration which keeps many from being insolent towards those they have at their mercy, because they know not how soon the uncertain fate of war may turn the same wheel upon themselves; but you need not fear that any should rise up ever to revenge this quarrel." [2.] "Fear not any other kings, who may at any time be in confederacy against you, for you see these brought down, whom you thought formidable. *Thus shall the Lord do to all your enemies;* now that they begin to fall, to fall so low that you may set your feet on their necks, you may be confident that they shall not prevail, but shall *surely fall before you,"* Esth. 6:13. (4.) He would hereby give a type and figure of Christ's victories over the powers of darkness, and believers' victories through him. All the enemies of the Redeemer shall be *made his footstool,* Ps. 110:1. And see Ps. 18:40. The *kings of the earth set themselves* against him (Ps. 2:2), but sooner or later we shall see all things put under Him (Heb. 2:8), and *principalities*

and powers made a show of, Col. 2:15. And in these triumphs we are more than conquerors, may *tread upon the lion and adder* (Ps. 91:13), may *ride on the high places of the earth* (Isa. 58:14), and may be confident that *the God of peace shall tread Satan under our feet,* shall do it shortly and do it effectually, Rom. 16:20. See Ps. 149:8, 9.

3. How they were put to death. Perhaps, when they had undergone that terrible mortification of being trodden upon by the captains of Israel, they were ready to say, as Agag, *Surely the bitterness of death is past,* and that *sufficient unto them was this punishment which was inflicted by many;* but their honours cannot excuse their lives, their forfeited devoted lives. Joshua smote them with the sword, and then hanged up their bodies till evening, when they were taken down, and thrown *into the cave in which they had hidden themselves, v.* 26, 27. That which they thought would have been their shelter was made their prison first and then their grave; so shall we be disappointed in that which we flee to from God: yet to good people the grave is still *a hiding-place,* Job 14:13. If these five kings had humbled themselves in time, and had begged peace instead of waging war, they might have saved their lives; but now the decree had gone forth, and they *found no place for repentance,* or the reversal of the judgment; it was too late to expect it, though perhaps *they sought it carefully with tears.*

Verses 28–43

We are here informed how Joshua improved the late glorious victory he had obtained and the advantages he had gained by it, and to do this well is a general's praise.

I. Here is a particular account of the several cities which he immediately made himself master of. 1. The cities of three of the kings whom he had conquered in the field he went and took possession of, Lachish (*v.* 31, 32), Eglon (*v.* 34, 35), and Hebron, *v.* 36, 37. The other two, Jerusalem and Jarmuth, were not taken at this time; perhaps his forces were either so much fatigued with what they had done or so well content with what they had got that they had no mind to attack those places, and so they let slip the fairest opportunity they could ever expect of reducing them with ease, which afterwards was not done without difficulty, Jdg. 1:8; 2 Sa. 5:6. 2. Three other cities, and royal cities too, he took: Makkedah, into the neighbourhood of which the five kings had fled, which brought Joshua and his forces thither in pursuit of them, and so hastened its ruin (*v.* 28), Libnah (*v.* 29, 30), and Debir, *v.* 38, 39. 3. One king that brought in his forces for the relief of Lachish, that had lost its king, proved to meddle to his own hurt; it was Horam king of Gezer, who, either in friendship to his neighbours or for his own security, offered to stop the progress of Joshua's arms, and was cut off with all his forces, *v.* 33. Thus wicked men are often snared in their counsels, and, by opposing God in the way of his judgments, bring them the sooner on their own heads.

II. A general account of the country which was hereby reduced and brought into Israel's hands (*v.* 40–42), that part of the land of Canaan of which they first got possession, which lay south of Jerusalem, and afterwards fell, for the most part, to the lot of the tribe of Judah. Observe in this narrative,

1. The great speed Joshua made in taking these cities, which, some think, is intimated in the manner of relating it, which is quick and concise. He flew like lightning from place to place; and though they all stood it out to the last extremity, and none of these cities opened their gates to him, yet in a little time he got them all into his hands, summoned them, and seized them, the same day (*v.* 28), or in two days, *v.* 32. Now that they were struck with fear, by the defeat of their armies and the death of their kings, Joshua prudently followed his blow. See what a great deal of work may be done in a little time, if we will but be busy and improve our opportunities.

2. The great severity Joshua used towards those he conquered. He gave no quarter to man, woman, nor child, put to the sword *all the souls* (*v.* 28, 30, 32, 35, etc.), *utterly destroyed all that breathed* (*v.* 40), and *left none remaining.* Nothing could justify this military execution but that herein they did *as the Lord God of Israel commanded* (*v.* 40), which was sufficient not only to bear them out, and save them for the imputation of cruelty, but to sanctify what they did, and make it an acceptable piece of service

to his justice. God would hereby, (1.) Manifest his hatred of the idolatries and other abominations which the Canaanites had been guilty of, and leave us to judge how great the provocation was which they had given him by the greatness of the destruction which was brought upon them when the measure of their iniquity was full. (2.) He would hereby magnify his love to his people Israel, in giving so many men for them, and *people for their life,* Isa. 43:4. When the *heathen are to be cast out to make room for this vine* (Ps. 80:8) divine justice appears more prodigal than ever of human blood, that the Israelites might find themselves for ever obliged to spend their lives to the glory of that God who had sacrificed so many of the lives of his creatures to their interest. (3.) Hereby was typified the final and eternal destruction of all the impenitent implacable enemies of the Lord Jesus, who, having slighted the riches of his grace, must for ever feel the weight of his wrath, and shall *have judgment without mercy. Nations that forget God shall be turned into hell,* and no reproach at all to God's infinite goodness.

3. The great success of this expedition. The spoil of these cities was now divided among the men of war that plundered them; and the cities themselves, with the land about them, were shortly to be divided among the tribes, for the Lord *fought for Israel, v.* 42. They could not have gotten the victory if God had not undertaken the battle; then we conquer when God fights for us; and, *if he be for us, who can be against us?*

CHAPTER 11

This chapter continues and concludes the history of the conquest of Canaan; of the reduction of the southern parts we had an account in the foregoing chapter, after which we may suppose Joshua allowed his forces some breathing-time; now here we have the story of the war in the north, and the happy success of that war. I. The confederacy of the northern crowns against Israel (*v.* 1–5). II. The encouragement which God gave to Joshua to engage them (*v.* 6). III. His victory over them (*v.* 7–9). IV. The taking of their cities (*v.* 10–15). V. The destruction of the Anakim (*v.* 21, 22). VI. The general conclusion of the story of this war (*v.* 16–20, 23).

Verses 1–9

We are here entering upon the story of another campaign that Joshua made, and it was a glorious one, no less illustrious than the former in the success of it, though in respect of miracles it was inferior to it in glory. The wonders God then wrought for them were to animate and encourage them to act vigorously themselves. Thus the war carried on by the preaching of the gospel against Satan's kingdom was at first forwarded by miracles; but, the war being by them sufficiently proved to be of God, the managers of it are now left to the ordinary assistance of divine grace in the use of the sword of the Spirit, and must not expect hail-stones nor the standing still of the sun. In this story we have,

I. The Canaanites taking the field against Israel. They were the aggressors, God hardening their hearts to begin the war, that Israel might be justified beyond exception in destroying them. Joshua and all Israel had returned to the camp at Gilgal, and perhaps these kings knew no other than that they intended to sit down content with the conquest they had already made, and yet they prepare war against them. Note, Sinners bring ruin upon their own heads, so that *God will be justified when he speaks,* and they alone shall bear the blame for ever. Judah had now *couched as a lion gone up from the prey;* if the northern kings rouse him up, it is at their peril, Gen. 49:9. Now, 1. Several nations joined in this confederacy, some *in the mountains* and some *in the plains, v.* 2. Canaanites from east and west, Amorites, Hittites, Perizzites, etc. (*v.* 3), of different constitutions and divided interests among themselves, and yet they here unite against Israel as against a common enemy. Thus are the *children of this world* more unanimous, and therein *wiser, than the children of light.* The oneness of the church's enemies should shame the church's friends out of their discords and divisions, and engage them to be one. 2. The head of this confederacy was *Jabin king of Hazor* (*v.* 1), as Adoni-zedec was of the former; it is said (*v.* 10) Hazor had been the *head of all those kingdoms,* which could not have revolted without occasioning ill-will; but this was forgotten and laid aside upon this occasion, by consent of parties, Lu. 23:12. When they had all drawn up their forces together, every kingdom bringing in its quota, they were a very great army, much

greater than the former, *as the sand on the sea shore in multitude,* and upon this account much stronger and more formidable, that they had horses and chariots very many, which we do not find the southern kings had; hereby they had a great advantage against Israel, for their army consisted only of foot, and they never brought horses nor chariots into the field. Josephus tells us that the army of the Canaanites consisted of 300,000 foot, 10,000 horses, and 20,000 chariots. *Many there be that rise up* against God's Israel; doubtless their numbers made them very confident of success, but it proved that so much the greater slaughter was made of them.

II. The encouragement God gave to Joshua to give them the meeting, even upon the ground of their own choosing (*v.* 6): *Be not afraid because of them.* Joshua was remarkable for his courage — it was his master grace, and yet it seems he had need to be again and again cautioned not to be afraid. Fresh dangers and difficulties make it necessary to fetch in fresh supports and comforts from the word of God, which we have always nigh unto us, to be made use of in every time of need. Those that have God on their side need not be disturbed at the number and power of their enemies; *more are those that are with us than those that are against us;* those have the hosts of the Lord that have the Lord of hosts engaged for them. For his encouragement, 1. God assures him of success, and fixes the hour: *To-morrow about this time,* when an engagement (it is probable) was expected and designed on both sides, *I will deliver them up slain.* Though they were to be slain by the sword of Israel, yet it is spoken of as God's work, that he would deliver them up. 2. He appoints him to *hough their horses, hamstring* them, *lame* them, and *burn their chariots,* not only that Israel might not use them hereafter, but that they might not fear them now, their God designing this contempt to be put upon them. Let Israel look upon their chariots but as rotten wood designed for the fire, and their horses of war as disabled things, scarcely good enough for the cart. This encouragement which God here gave to Joshua no doubt he communicated to the people, who perhaps were under some apprehensions of danger from this vast army, notwithstanding the experience they had had of God's power engaged for them. And the wisdom and goodness of God are to be observed, (1.) In infatuating the counsels of the enemy, that all the kings of Canaan, who were not dispersed at such a distance from each other but that they might have got all together in a body, did not at first confederate against Israel, but were divided into the southern and northern combination, and so became the less formidable. And, (2.) In preparing his people to encounter the greater force, by breaking the less. They first engage with five kings together, and now with many more. God proportions our trials to our strength and our strength to our trials.

III. Joshua's march against these confederate forces, *v.* 7. He *came upon them suddenly,* and surprised them in their quarters. He made this haste, 1. That he might put them into the greater confusion, by giving them an alarm, when they little thought he was near them. 2. That he might be sure not to come short of the honour God had fixed, to give him the meeting at the enemies' camp, *to-morrow about this time.* It is fit we should keep time with God.

IV. His success, *v.* 8. He obtained the honour and advantage of a complete victory; he smote them and chased them, in the several ways they took in their flight; some fled towards Zidon, which lay to the northwest, others towards Mizpeh, eastward, but the parties Joshua sent out pursued them each way. So *the Lord delivered them into the hand of Israel;* they would not deliver themselves into the hands of Israel to be made proselytes and tributaries, and so offered up to God's grace (Rom. 15:16), and therefore God delivered them into their hands to be made sacrifices to his justice; for God will be honoured by us or upon us.

V. His obedience to the orders given him, in destroying the horses and chariots (*v.* 9), which was an instance, 1. Of his subjection to the divine will, as one under authority, that must do as he is bidden. 2. Of his self-denial, and crossing his own genius and inclination in compliance with God's command. 3. Of his confidence in the power of God engaged for Israel, which enabled them to despise the chariots and horses which others trusted in, Ps. 20:7; 33:17. 4. Of his care to keep up in the people the like confidence in God, by taking that from them which they would be tempted to trust too much to. This was *cutting off a right hand.*

Verses 10–14

We have here the same improvement made of this victory as was made of that in the foregoing chapter. 1. The destruction of Hazor is particularly recorded, because in it, and by the king thereof, this daring design against Israel was laid, *v.* 10, 11. The king of Hazor, it seems, escaped with his life out of the battle, and thought himself safe when he had got back into his own city, and Joshua had gone in pursuit of the scattered troops another way. But it proved that that which he thought would be for his welfare was his trap; in it *he was taken as in an evil net;* there he was slain, and his city, for his sake, burned. Yet we find that the remains of it being not well looked after by Israel the Canaanites rebuilt it, and settled there under another king of the same name, Jdg. 4:2. 2. The rest of the cities of that part of the country are spoken of only in general, that Joshua got them all into his hands, but did not burn them as he did Hazor, for Israel was to dwell in *great and goodly cities which they builded not* (Deu. 6:10) and in these among the rest. And here we find Israel rolling in blood and treasure. (1.) In the blood of their enemies; *they smote all the souls* (*v.* 1), *neither left they any to breathe* (*v.* 14), that there might be none to infect them with the abominations of Canaan, and none to disturb them in the possession of it. The children were cut off, lest they should afterwards lay claim to any part of this land in the right of their parents. (2.) In the wealth of their enemies. The spoil, and the cattle, they *took for a prey to themselves, v.* 14. As they were enriched with the spoil of their oppressors when they came out of Egypt, wherewith to defray the charges of their apprenticeship in the wilderness, so they were now enriched with the spoil of their enemies for a stock wherewith to set up in the land of Canaan. Thus is the wealth of the sinner laid up for the just.

Verses 15–23

We have here the conclusion of this whole matter.

I. A short account is here given of what was done in four things: — 1. The obstinacy of the Canaanites in their opposition to the Israelites. It was strange that though it appeared so manifestly that God fought for Israel, and in every engagement the Canaanites had the worst of it, yet they stood it out to the last; not one city made peace with Israel, but the Gibeonites only, who understood the things that belonged to their peace better than their neighbours, *v.* 19. It is intimated that other cities might have made as good terms for themselves, without ragged clothes and clouted shoes, if they would have humbled themselves, but they never so much as *desired conditions of peace.* We here are told whence this unaccountable infatuation came: *It was of the Lord to harden their hearts, v.* 20. As Pharaoh's heart was hardened by his own pride and wilfulness first, and afterwards by the righteous judgment of God, to his destruction, so were the hearts of these Canaanites. To punish them for all their other follies, God left them to this, to make those their enemies whom they might have made their friends. This was it that ruined them: they *came against Israel in battle,* and gave the first blow, and therefore *might have no favour* shown them. Those know not what they do who give the provocation to divine justice, or the authorized instruments of it. *Are we stronger than God?* Observe here, That hardness of heart is the ruin of sinners. Those that are stupid and secure, and heedless of divine warnings, are already marked for destruction. What hope is there of those concerning whom God has said, *Go, make their hearts fat?* 2. The constancy of the Israelites in prosecuting this war (*v.* 18): *Joshua made war a long time;* some reckon it five years, others seven, that were spent in subduing this land: so long God would train up Israel to war, and give them repeated instances of his power and goodness in every new victory that he gave them. 3. The conquest of the Anakim at last, *v.* 21, 22. Either this was done as they met with them where they were dispersed, as some think, or rather it should seem the Anakim had retired to their fastnesses, and so were hunted out and cut off at last, after all the rest of Israel's enemies. The mountains of Judah and Israel were the habitations of those mountains of men; but not their height, nor the strength of their caves, nor the difficulty of the passes to them, could secure, no, not these mighty men, from the sword of Joshua. The cutting off of the sons of Anak is particularly mentioned because these had been such a terror to the spies forty years before, and their bulk and strength had been thought an insuperable difficulty in the way of the reducing of Canaan, Num. 13:28, 33. Even that opposition which seemed invincible was got over. Never let the sons of Anak be a terror to the Israel of God, for even their day will come to fall. Giants are dwarfs to Omnipotence; yet this struggle with the Anakim was reserved for the latter end of the war, when the Israelites had become more expert in the arts of war, and had had more experience of the power and goodness of God. Note, God sometimes reserves the sharpest trials of his people by affliction and temptation for the latter end of their days. Therefore *let not him that girds on the harness boast as he that puts it off.* Death, that tremendous son of Anak, is the last enemy that is to be encountered; but it is *to be destroyed,* 1 Co. 15:26. Thanks be to God, who will give us the victory. 4. The end and issue of this long war. The Canaanites were rooted out, not perfectly (as we shall find after in the book of Judges), but in a good measure; they were not able to make any head either, (1.) So as to keep the Israelites out of possession of the land: *Joshua took all that land, v.* 16, 17. And we may suppose the people dispersed themselves and their families into the countries they had conquered, at least those that lay nearest to the head-quarters at Gilgal, until an orderly distribution should be made by lot, that every man might know his own. Or, (2.) So as to keep them in action, or give them any molestation (*v.* 23): *The land rested from war.* It ended not in a peace with the Canaanites (that was forbidden), but in a peace from them. There is a rest, a rest from war, remaining for the people of God, into which they shall enter when their warfare is accomplished.

II. That which was now done is here compared with that which had been said to Moses. God's word and his works, if viewed and considered together, will mutually illustrate each other. It is here observed in the close, 1. That all the precepts God had given to Moses relating to the conquest of Canaan were obeyed on the people's part, at least while Joshua lived. See how solemnly this is remarked (*v.* 15): *As the Lord commanded Moses his servant,* by whose hand the law was given, *so did Moses command Joshua,* for Moses was faithful, as a law-giver, to him that appointed him; he did his part, and then he died: but were the commands of Moses observed when he was in his grave? Yes, they were: *So did Joshua,* who was, in his place, as faithful as Moses in his. *He left nothing undone* (Heb. he *removed nothing) of all that the Lord commanded Moses.* Those that leave their duty undone do what they can to remove or make void the command of God, by which they are bound to do it; but Joshua, by performing the precept, *confirmed* it, as the expression is, Deu. 27:26. Joshua was himself a great commander, and yet nothing was more his praise than his obedience. Those that rule others at their will must themselves be ruled by the divine will; then their power is indeed their honour, and not otherwise. The pious obedience for which Joshua is here commended respects especially the command to destroy the Canaanites, and to *break down their altars and burn their images,* Deu. 7:2–5; Ex. 23:24; 34:13. Joshua, in his zeal for the Lord of hosts, spared neither the idols nor the idolaters. Saul's disobedience, or rather his partial obedience, to the command of God, for the utter destruction of the Amalekites, cost him his kingdom. It should seem Joshua himself gives this account of his most careful and punctual observance of his orders in the execution of his commission, that in all respects he had done as Moses commanded him; and then it intimates that he had more pleasure and satisfaction in reflecting upon his obedience to the commands of God in all this war, and valued himself more upon that, than upon all the gains and triumphs with which he was enriched and advanced. 2. That all the promises God had given to Moses relating to this conquest were accomplished *on his part, v.* 23. Joshua *took the whole land,* conquered it, and took possession of it, *according to all that the Lord said unto Moses.* God had promised to drive out the nations before them (Ex. 33:2; 34:11), and to *bring them down,* Deu. 9:3. And now it was done. There failed not one word of the promise. Our successes and enjoyments are then doubly sweet and comfortable to us when we see them flowing to us from the promise (this is *according to what the Lord said),* as our obedience is then acceptable to God when it has an eye to the precept. And, if we make conscience of our duty, we need not question the performance of the promise.

CHAPTER 12

This chapter is a summary of Israel's conquests. I. Their conquests under Moses, on the other side Jordan (for we now suppose ourselves in Canaan) eastward, which we had the history of, Num. 21:24, etc. And here the abridgment of that history (*v.* 1–6). II. Their conquests under Joshua, on this side Jordan, westward. 1. The country they reduced (*v.* 7, 8). 2. The kings they subdued, thirty-one in all (*v.* 9–24). And this comes in here, not only as a conclusion of the history of the wars of Canaan (that we might at one view see what they had got), but as a preface to the history of the dividing of Canaan, that all that might be put together which they were not to make a distribution of.

Verses 1–6

Joshua, or whoever else is the historian before he comes to sum up the new conquests Israel had made, in these verses receives their former conquests in Moses's time, under whom they became masters of the great and potent kingdoms of Sihon and Og. Note, Fresh mercies must not drown the remembrance of former mercies, nor must the glory of the present instruments of good to the church be suffered to eclipse and diminish the just honour of those who have gone before them, and who were the blessings and ornaments of their day. Joshua's services and achievements are confessedly great, but let not those under Moses be overlooked and forgotten, since God was the same who wrought both, and both put together proclaim him the Alpha and Omega of Israel's great salvation. Here is, 1. A description of this conquered country, the measure and bounds of it in general (*v.* 1): *From the river Arnon* in the south, to *Mount Hermon* in the north. In particular, here is a description of the kingdom of Sihon (*v.* 2, 3), and that of Og, *v.* 4, 5. Moses had described this country very particularly (Deu. 2:36; 3:4, etc.), and this description here agrees with his. King Og is said to dwell at Ashtaroth and Edrei (*v.* 4), probably because they were both his royal cities; he had palaces in both, and resided sometimes in one and sometimes in the other; one perhaps was his summer seat and the other his winter seat. But Israel took both from him, and made one grave to serve him that could not be content with one palace. 2. The distribution of this country. Moses assigned it to the two tribes and a half, at their request, and divided it among them (*v.* 6), of which we had the story at large, Num. 32. The dividing of it when it was conquered by Moses is here mentioned as an example to Joshua what he must do now that he had conquered the country on this side Jordan. Moses, in his time, gave to one part of Israel a very rich and fruitful country, but it was on the outside of Jordan; but Joshua gave to all Israel the holy land, the mountain of God's sanctuary, within Jordan: so the law conferred upon some few of God's spiritual Israel external temporal blessings, which were earnests of good things to come; but our Lord Jesus, the true Joshua, has provided for all the children of promise spiritual blessings — the privileges of the sanctuary, and the heavenly Canaan. The triumphs and grants of the law were glorious, but those of the gospel far exceed in glory.

Verses 7–24

We have here a breviate of Joshua's conquests.

I. The limits of the country he conquered. It lay between Jordan on the east and the Mediterranean Sea on the west, and extended from Baal-gad near Lebanon in the north to Halak, which lay upon the country of Edom in the south, *v.* 7. The boundaries are more largely described, Num. 34:2, etc. But what is here said is enough to show that God had been as good as his word, and had given them possession of all he had promised them by Moses, if they would but have kept it.

II. The various kinds of land that were found in this country, which contributed both to its pleasantness and to its fruitfulness, *v.* 8. There were mountains, not craggy, and rocky, and barren, which are frightful to the traveller and useless to the inhabitants, but fruitful hills, such as put forth *precious things* (Deu. 33:15), which charmed the spectator's eye and filled the owner's hand. And valleys, not mossy and boggy, but *covered with corn,* Ps. 65:13. There were plains, and springs to water them; and even in that rich land there were wildernesses too, or forests, which were not so thickly inhabited as other parts, yet had towns and houses in them, but served as foils to set off the more pleasant and fruitful countries.

III. The several nations that had been in possession of this country — Hittites, Amorites, Canaanites, etc., all of them descended from Canaan, the accursed son of Ham, Gen. 10:15–18. Seven nations they are called (Deu. 7:1), and so many are there reckoned up, but here six only are mentioned, the Girgashites being either lost or left out, though we find them, Gen. 10:16 and 15:21. Either they were incorporated with some other of these nations, or, as the tradition of the Jews is, upon the approach of Israel under Joshua they all withdrew and went into Africa, leaving their country to be possessed by Israel, with whom they saw it was to no purpose to contend, and therefore they are not named among the nations that Joshua subdued.

IV. A list of the kings that were conquered and subdued by the sword of Israel, some in the field, others in their own cities, thirty-one in all, and very particularly named and counted, it should seem, in the order in which they were conquered; for the catalogue begins with the kings of Jericho and Ai, then takes in the king of Jerusalem and the princes of the south that were in confederacy with him, and then proceeds to those of the northern association. Now, 1. This shows what a very fruitful country Canaan then was, which could support so many kingdoms, and in which so many kings chose to throng together rather than disperse themselves into other countries, which we may suppose not yet inhabited, but where, though they might find more room, they could not expect such plenty and pleasure: this was the land God spied out for Israel; and yet at this day it is one of the most barren, despicable, and unprofitable countries in the world: such is the effect of the curse it lies under, since its possessors rejected Christ and his gospel, as was foretold by Moses, Deu. 29:23. 2. It shows what narrow limits men's ambition was then confined to. These kings contented themselves with the government, each of them, of one city and the towns and villages that pertained to it; and no one of them, for aught that appears, aimed to make himself master of the rest, but, when there was occasion, all united for the common safety. Yet it should seem that what was wanting in the extent of their territories was made up in the absoluteness of their power, their subjects being all their tenants and vassals, and entirely at their command. 3. It shows how good God was to Israel, in giving them victory over all these kings, and possession of all these kingdoms, and what obligations he hereby laid upon them to *observe his statutes and to keep his laws,* Ps. 105:44, 45. Here were thirty-one kingdoms, or seigniories, to be divided among nine tribes and a half of Israel. Of these there fell to the lot of Judah the kingdoms of Hebron, Jarmuth, Lachish, Eglon, Debir, Arad, Libnan, and Adullam, eight in all, besides part of the kingdom of Jerusalem and part of Geder. Benjamin had the kingdoms of Jericho, Ai, Jerusalem, Makkedah, Beth-el, and the nations of Gilgal, six in all. Simeon had the kingdom of Hormah and part of Geder. Ephraim had the kingdoms of Gezer and Tirzah. Manasseh (that half-tribe) had the kingdoms of Tappuah and Hepher, Taanach and Megiddo. Asher had the kingdoms of Aphek and Achshaph. Zebulun had the kingdoms of Lasharon, Shimron-meron, and Jokneam. Naphtali had the kingdoms of Madon, Hazor, and Kedesh. And Issachar had that of Dor. These were some of the great and famous kings that God smote, *for his mercy endureth for ever; and gave their land for a heritage, even a heritage unto Israel his servant, for his mercy endureth for ever,* Ps. 136:17, etc.

CHAPTER 13

At this chapter begins the account of the dividing of the land of Canaan among the tribes of Israel by lot, a narrative not so entertaining and instructive as that of the conquest of it, and yet it is thought fit to be inserted in the sacred history, to illustrate the performance of the promise made to the fathers, that this land should be given to the seed of Jacob, to them and not to any other. The preserving of this distribution would be of great use to the Jewish nation, who were obliged by the law to keep up this first distribution, and not to transfer inheritances from tribe to tribe, Num. 36:9. It is likewise of use to us for the explaining of other scriptures: the learned know how much light the geographical description of a country gives to the history of it. And therefore we are not to skip over these chapters of hard names as useless and not to be regarded; where God has a mouth to speak and a hand to write we should find an ear to hear an eye to read; and God give us a heart to profit! In this chapter, I. God informs Joshua what parts of the country that were intended in the grant to Israel yet remained unconquered, and not got in possession (*v.* 1–6). II. He appoints him, notwithstanding, to make a distribution of what was conquered (*v.* 7). III. To complete this account, here is a repetition of the distribution Moses had made of the land on the other side Jordan; in general (*v.* 8–14), in particular, the lot of Reuben (*v.* 15-23), of Gad (*v.* 24–28), of the half tribe of Manasseh (*v.* 29–33).

Verses 1–6

Here, I. God puts Joshua in mind of his old age, *v.* 1. 1. It is said that Joshua was *old and stricken in years,* and he and Caleb were at this time the only old men among the thousands of Israel, none except them of all those who were numbered at Mount Sinai being now alive. He had been a man of war from his youth (Ex. 17:10); but now he yielded to the infirmities of age, with which it is in vain for the stoutest to think of contesting. It should seem Joshua had not the same strength and vigour in his old age that Moses had; all that come to old age do not find it alike good; generally, the days of old age are evil days, and such as there is no pleasure in, nor expectation of service from. 2. God takes notice of it to him: *God said to him, Thou art old.* Note, It is good for those who are *old and stricken in years* to be put in remembrance of their being so. Some have *gray hairs here and there upon them, and perceive it not* (Hos. 7:9); they do not care to think of it, and therefore need to be told of it, that they may be quickened to do the work of life, and make preparation for death, which is coming towards them apace. But God mentions Joshua's age and growing infirmities, (1.) As a reason why he should now lay by the thoughts of pursuing the war; he cannot expect to see an end of it quickly, for there remained much land, more perhaps than he thought, to be possessed, in several parts remote from each other: and it was not fit that at his age he should be put upon the fatigue of renewing the war, and carrying it to such distant places; no, it was enough for him that he had reduced the body of the country. "Let him be gathered to rest with honour and the thanks of his people for the good services he had done them, and let the conquering of the skirts of the country be left for those that shall come after." As he had entered into the labours of Moses, so let others enter into his, and bring forth the top-stone, the doing of which was reserved for David long after. Observe, God considers the frame of his people, and would not have them burdened with work above their strength. It cannot be expected that old people should do as they have done for God and their country. (2.) As a reason why he should speedily apply himself to the dividing of that which he had conquered. That work must be done, and done quickly; it was necessary that he should preside in the doing of it, and therefore, he being *old and stricken in years,* and not likely to continue long, let him make this his concluding piece of service to God and Israel. All people, but especially old people, should set themselves to do that quickly which must be done before they die, lest death prevent them, Eccl. 9:10.

II. He gives him a particular account of the land that yet remained unconquered, which was intended for Israel, and which, in due time, they should be masters of if they did not put a bar in their own door. Divers places are here mentioned, some in the south, as the country of the Philistines, governed by five lords, and the land that lay towards Egypt (*v.* 2, 3), some westward, as that which lay towards the Sidonians (*v.* 4), some eastward, as all Lebanon (*v.* 5), some towards the north, as that in the entering in of Hamath, *v.* 5. Joshua is told this, and he made the people acquainted with it, 1. That they might be the more affected with God's goodness to them in giving them this good land, and might thereby be engaged to love and serve him; for, if this which they had was too little, God would moreover *give them such and such things,* 2 Sa. 12:8. 2. That they might not be tempted to make any league, or contract any dangerous familiarity with these their neighbours so as to learn their way, but might rather be jealous of them, as a people that kept them from their right and that they had just cause of quarrel with. 3. That they might keep themselves in a posture for war, and not think of putting off the harness so long as there remained any land to be possessed. Nor must we lay aside our spiritual armour, nor be off our watch, till our victory be completed in the kingdom of glory.

III. He promises that he would make the Israelites masters of all those countries that were yet unsubdued, though Joshua was old and not able to do it, old and not likely to live to see it done. Whatever becomes of us, and however we may be laid aside as despised broken vessels, God will do his own work in his own time (*v.* 6): *I will drive them out.* The original is emphatic: *"It is I that will do it,* I that can do it when thou are dead and gone, and will do it if Israel be not wanting to themselves." "I will do it by my Word," so the Chaldee here, as in many other places, "by the eternal Word, the captain of the hosts of the Lord." This promise that he would drive them out from before the children of Israel plainly supposes it as the condition of the promise that the children of Israel must themselves attempt their extirpation, must go up against them, else they could not be said to be driven out before them; if afterwards Israel, through sloth, or cowardice, or affection to these idolaters, sit still and let them alone, they must blame themselves, and not God, if they be not driven out. We must work out our salvation, and then God will work in us and work with us; we must resist our spiritual enemies, and then God will tread them under our feet; we must go forth to our Christian work and warfare, and then God will go forth before us.

Verses 7–33

Here we have, I. Orders given to Joshua to assign to each tribe its portion of this land, including that which was yet unsubdued, which must be brought into the lot, in a believing confidence that it should be conquered when Israel was multiplied so as to have occasion for it (*v.* 7): *Now divide this land.* Joshua thought all must be conquered before any must be divided. "No," said, God, "there is as much conquered as will serve your turn for the present; divide this, and make your best of it, and wait for the remainder hereafter." Note, We must take the comfort of what we have, though we cannot compass all we would have. Observe,

1. The land must be divided among the several tribes, and they must not always live in common, as now they did. Which way soever a just property is acquired, it is the will of that God who has given the earth to the children of men that there should be such a thing, and that every man should know his own, and not invade that which is another's. The world must be governed, not by force, but right, by the law of equity, not of arms.

2. That it must be divided for an inheritance, though they got it by conquest. (1.) The promise of it came to them as an inheritance from their fathers; the land of promise pertained to the children of promise, who were thus beloved for their fathers' sakes, and in performance of the covenant with them. (2.) The possession of it was to be transmitted by them, as an inheritance to their children. Frequently, what is got by force is soon lost again; but Israel, having an incontestable title to this land by the divine grant, might see it hereby secured as an inheritance to their seed after them, and that God kept this mercy for thousands.

3. That Joshua must not divide it by his own will. Though he was a very wise, just, and good man, it must not be left to him to give what he pleased to each tribe; but he must do it by lot, which referred the matter wholly to God, and to his determination, for he it is that appoints the bounds of our habitation, and every man's judgment must proceed from him. But Joshua must preside in this affair, must manage this solemn appeal to Providence, and see that the lot was drawn fairly and without fraud, and that every tribe did acquiesce in it. The lot indeed *causeth contention to cease,* Prov. 18:18. But, if upon this lot any controversy should arise, Joshua by his wisdom and authority must determine it, and prevent any ill consequences of it. Joshua must have the honour of dividing the land, (1.) Because he had undergone the fatigue of conquering it: and when, through his hand, each tribe received its allotment, they would thereby be made the more sensible of their obligations to him. And what a pleasure must it needs be to a man of such a public spirit as Joshua was to see the people that were so dear to him eating of the labour of his hands! (2.) That he might be herein a type of Christ, who has not only conquered for us the gates of hell, but has opened to us the gates of heaven, and, hav-

ing purchased the eternal inheritance for all believers, will in due time put them all in possession of it.

II. An account is here given of the distribution of the land on the other side Jordan among the Reubenites, and Gadites, and half the tribe of Manasseh. Observe,

1. How this account is introduced. It comes in, (1.) As the reason why this land within Jordan must be divided only to the nine tribes and a half, because the other two and a half were already provided for. (2.) As a pattern to Joshua in the work he had now to do. He had seen Moses distribute that land, which would give him some aid in distributing this, and thence he might take his measure; only this was to be done by lot, but it should seem Moses did that himself, according to the wisdom given unto him. (3.) As an inducement to Joshua to hasten the dividing of this land, that the nine tribes and a half might not be kept any longer than was necessary out of their possession, since their brethren of the two tribes and a half were so well settled in theirs; and God their common Father would not have such a difference made between his children.

2. The particulars of this account.

(1.) Here is a general description of the country that was given to the two tribes and a half, *which Moses gave them, even as Moses gave them, v.* 8. The repetition implies a ratification of the grant by Joshua. Moses settled this matter, and, as Moses settled it, so shall it rest; Joshua will not, under any pretence whatsoever, go about to alter it. And a reason is intimated why he would not, because Moses was the servant of the Lord, and acted in this matter by secret direction from him and was faithful as a servant. Here we have, [1.] The fixing of the boundaries of this country, by which they were divided from the neighbouring nations, *v.* 9, etc. Israel must know their own and keep to it, and may not, under pretence of their being God's peculiar people, encroach upon their neighbours, and invade their rights and properties, to which they had a good and firm title by providence, though not, as Israel, a title by promise. [2.] An exception of one part of this country from Israel's possession, though it was in their grant, namely, the Geshurites and the Maachathites, *v.* 13. They had not leisure to reduce all the remote and obscure corners of the country in Moses's time, and afterwards they had no mind to it, being easy with what they had. Thus those who are not straitened in God's promises are yet straitened in their own faith, and prayers, and endeavours.

(2.) A very particular account of the inheritances of these two tribes and a half, how they were separated from each other, and what cites, with the towns, villages, and fields, commonly known and reputed to be appurtenances to them, belonged to each tribe. This is very fully and exactly set down in order that posterity might, in reading this history, be the more affected with the goodness of God to their ancestors, when they found what a large and fruitful country, and what abundance of great and famous cities, he put them in possession of (God's grants look best when we descend to the particulars); and also that the limits of every tribe being punctually set down in this authentic record disputes might be prevented, and such contests between the tribes as commonly happen where boundaries have not been adjusted nor this matter brought to a certainty. And we have reason to think that the register here prescribed and published of the lot of each tribe was of great use to Israel in after-ages, was often appealed to, and always acquiesced in, for the determining of *meum* and *tuum — mine* and *thine.*

[1.] We have here the lot of the tribe of Reuben, Jacob's first-born, who, though he had lost the dignity and power which pertained to the birthright, yet, it seems, had the advantage of being first served. Perhaps those of that tribe had an eye to this in desiring to be seated on that side Jordan, that, since they could not expect the benefit of the best lot, they might have the credit of the first. Observe, *First,* In the account of the lot of this tribe mention is made of the slaughter, 1. Of Sihon, king of the Amorites, who reigned in this country, and might have kept it and his life if he would have been neighbourly, and have suffered Israel to pass through his territories, but, by attempting to oppose them, justly brought ruin upon himself, Num. 21:21, etc. 2. Of the princes of Midian, who were slain afterwards in another war (Num. 31:8), and yet are here called *dukes of Sihon,* and are said to be *smitten with him,* because they were either tributaries to him, or, in his opposition to Israel, confederates with him, and hearty in his interests, and his fall made way for theirs not long after. 3. Of Balaam particularly, that would, if he could, have cursed Israel, and was soon after recompensed *according to the wickedness of his endeavour* (Ps. 28:4), for he fell with those that set him on. This was recorded before (Num. 31:8), and is here repeated, because the defeating of Balaam's purpose to curse Israel was the turning of that curse into a blessing, and was such an instance of the power and goodness of God as was fit to be had in everlasting remembrance. See Mic. 6:5. *Secondly,* Within the lot of this tribe was that Mount Pisgah from the top of which Moses took his view of the earthly Canaan and his flight to the heavenly. And not far off thence Elijah was when he was fetched up to heaven in a chariot of fire. The separation of this tribe from the rest, by the river Jordan, was that which Deborah lamented; and the preference they gave to their private interests above the public was what she censured, Jdg. 5:15, 16. In this tribe lay Heshbon and Sibmah, famed for their fruitful fields and vineyards. See Isa. 16:8, 9; Jer. 47:32. This tribe, with that of Gad, was sorely shaken by Hazael king of Syria (2 Ki. 10:33), and afterwards dislodged and carried into captivity, twenty years before the general captivity of the ten tribes by the king of Assyria, 1 Chr. 5:26.

[2.] The lot of the tribe of Gad, *v.* 24–28. This lay north of Reuben's lot; the country of Gilead lay in this tribe, so famous for its balm that it is thought strange indeed if there be no balm in Gilead, and the cities of Jabesh-Gilead and Ramoth-Gilead which we often read of in scripture. Succoth and Penuel, which we read of in the story of Gideon, were in this tribe; and that forest which is called the *wood of Ephraim* (from the slaughter Jephthah made there of the Ephraimites), in which Absalom's rebellious army was beaten, while his father David lay at Mahanaim, one of the frontier-cities of this tribe, *v.* 26. Sharon, famous for roses, was in this tribe. And within the limits of this tribe lived those Gadarenes that loved their swine better than their Saviour, fitter to be called *Girgashites* than *Israelites.*

[3.] The lot of the half-tribe of Manasseh, *v.* 29–31. Bashan, the kingdom of Og, was in this allotment, famous for the best timber, witness the oaks of Bashan — and the best breed of cattle, witness the bulls and rams of Bashan. This tribe lay north of Gad, reached to Mount Hermon, and had in it part of Gilead. Mispeh was in this half-tribe, and Jephthah was one of its ornaments; so was Elijah, for in this tribe was Thisbe, whence he is called the Tishbite; and Jair was another. In the edge of the tribe stood Chorazin, honoured with Christ's wondrous works, but ruined by his righteous woe for not improving them.

[4.] Twice in this chapter it is taken notice of that to the tribe of Levi *Moses gave no inheritance* (*v.* 14, 33), for so God had appointed, Num. 18:20. If they had been appointed to a lot entire by themselves, Moses would have served them first, not because it was his own tribe, but because it was God's; but they must be provided for in another manner; their habitations must be scattered in all the tribes, and their maintenance brought out of all the tribes, and God himself was the portion both of their inheritance and of their cup, Deu. 10:9; 18:2.

CHAPTER 14

Here is, I. The general method that was taken in dividing the land (*v.* 1–5). II. The demand Caleb made of Hebron, as his by promise, and therefore not to be put into the lot with the rest (*v.* 6–12). And Joshua's grant of that demand (*v.* 13–15). This was done at Gilgal, which was as yet their head-quarters.

Verses 1–5

The historian, having in the foregoing chapter given an account of the disposal of the countries on the other side Jordan, now comes to tell us what they did with the countries in the land of Canaan. They were not conquered to be left desert, *a habitation for dragons, and a court for owls,* Isa. 34:13. No, the Israelites that had hitherto been closely encamped in a body, and the greatest part of them such as never knew any other way of living, must now disperse themselves to replenish these new conquests. It is said of the earth, *God created it not in vain; he formed it to be inhabited,* Isa. 45:18. Canaan would have been subdued in vain if it had not been inhabited. Yet every man might not go and settle where he pleased, but as there seems to have been in the days of Peleg an orderly and regular division of the habitable earth among the sons of Noah (Gen. 10:25, 32), so there was now such a division of the land of Canaan among the sons of Jacob. God had given Moses directions how this distribution should be made, and those directions are here punctually observed. See Num. 26:53, etc.

I. The managers of this great affair were Joshua the chief magistrate, Eleazar the chief priest, and ten princes, one of each of the tribes that were now to have their inheritance, whom God himself had nominated (Num. 34:17, etc.) some years before; and, it should seem, they were all now in being, and attended this service, that every tribe, having a representative of its own, might be satisfied that there was fair dealing, and might the more contentedly sit down by its lot.

II. The tribes among whom this dividend was to be made were nine and a half. 1. Not the two and a half that were already seated (*v.* 3), though perhaps now that they saw what a good land Canaan was, and how effectually it was subdued, they might some of them repent their choice, and wish they had now been to have their lot with their brethren, upon which condition they would gladly have given up what they had on the other side Jordan; but it could not be admitted: they had made their election without power of revocation, and so must their doom be; they themselves have decided it, and they must adhere to their choice. 2. Not the tribe of Levi; this was to be otherwise provided for. God had distinguished them from, and dignified them above, the other tribes, and they must not now mingle themselves with them, nor cast in their lot among them, for this would entangle them in the affairs of this life, which would not consist with a due attendance on their sacred function. But, 3. Joseph made two tribes, Manasseh and Ephraim, pursuant to Jacob's adoption of Joseph's two sons, and so the number of the tribes was kept up to twelve, though Levi was taken out, which is intimated here (*v.* 4): *The children of Joseph were two tribes, therefore they gave no part to Levi,* they being twelve without them.

III. The rule by which they went was the lot, *v.* 2. *The disposal* of that is *of the Lord,* Prov. 16:33. It was here used in an affair of weight, and which could not otherwise be accommodated to universal satisfaction, and it was used in a solemn religious manner as an appeal to God, by consent of parties. In dividing by lot, 1. They referred themselves to God, and to his wisdom and sovereignty, believing him fitter to determine for them than they for themselves. Ps. 47:4, *He shall choose our inheritance for us.* 2. They professed a willingness to abide by the determination of it; for every man must take what is his lot, and make the best of it. In allusion to this we are said to *obtain an inheritance in Christ* (Eph. 1:11), *eklērōthēmen — we have obtained it by lot,* so the word signified; for it is obtained by a divine designation. Christ, our Joshua, gives eternal life to *as many as were given him,* Jn. 17:2.

Verses 6–15

Before the lot was cast into the lap for the determining of the portions of the respective tribes, the particular portion of Caleb was assigned to him. He was now, except Joshua, not only the oldest man in all Israel, but was twenty years older than any of them, for all that were above twenty years old when he was forty were dead in the wilderness; it was fit therefore that this phoenix of his age should have some particular marks of honour put upon him in the dividing of the land. Now,

I. Caleb here presents his petition, or rather makes his demand, to have Hebron given him for a possession (*this mountain* he calls it, *v.* 12), and not to have that put into the lot with the other parts of the country. To justify his demand, he shows that God had long since, by Moses, promised him *that very mountain;* so that God's mind being already made known in this matter it would be a vain and needless thing to consult it any further by casting lots, by which we are to appeal to God in those cases only which cannot otherwise be decided, not in those which, like this, are already determined. Caleb is here called the *Kenezite,* some think from some remarkable victory obtained by him over the Kenezites, as the Romans gave their great generals titles from the countries they conquered, as Africanus, Germanicus, etc. Observe,

1. To enforce his petition, (1.) He brings the children of Judah, that is, the heads and great men of that tribe,

along with him, to present it, who were willing thus to pay their respects to that ornament of their tribe, and to testify their consent that he should be provided for by himself, and that they would not take it as any reflection upon the rest of this tribe. Caleb was the person whom God had chosen out of that tribe to be employed in dividing the land (Num. 34:19), and therefore, lest he should seem to improve his authority as a commissioner for his own private advantage and satisfaction, he brings his brethren along with him, and waiving his own power, seems rather to rely upon their interest. (2.) He appeals to Joshua himself concerning the truth of the allegations upon which he grounded his petition: *Thou knowest the thing, v.* 6. (3.) He makes a very honourable mention of Moses, which he knew would not be at all unpleasing to Joshua: *Moses the man of God (v.* 6), and the *servant of the Lord, v.* 7. What Moses said he took as from God himself, because Moses was his mouth and his agent, and therefore he had reason both to desire and expect that it should be made good. What can be more earnestly desired than the tokens of God's favour? And what more confidently expected than the grants of his promise?

2. In his petition he sets forth,

(1.) The testimony of his conscience concerning his integrity in the management of that great affair on which it proved the fare of Israel turned, the spying out of the land. Caleb was one of the twelve that were sent out on that errand (v. 7), and he now reflected upon it with comfort, and mentioned it, not in pride, but as that which, being the consideration of the grant, was necessary to be inserted in the plea, [1.] That he made his report as it was in his heart, that is, he spoke as he thought when he spoke so honourably of the land of Canaan, so confidently of the power of God to put them in possession of it, and so contemptibly of the opposition that the Canaanites, even the Anakim themselves, could make against them, as we find he did, Num. 13:30; 14:7–9. He did not do it merely to please Moses, or to keep the people quiet, much less from a spirit of contradiction to his fellows, but from a full conviction of the truth of what he said and a firm belief of the divine promise. [2.] That herein he *wholly followed the Lord his God,* that is, he kept close to his duty, and sincerely aimed at the glory of God in it. He conformed himself to the divine will with an eye to the divine favour. He had obtained this testimony from God himself (Num. 14:24), and therefore it was not vain-glory in him to speak of it, any more than it is for those who have *God's Spirit witnessing with their spirits* that they are the children of God humbly and thankfully to tell others for their encouragement what God has done for their souls. Note, Those that follow God fully when they are young shall have both the credit and comfort of it when they are old, and the reward of it for ever in the heavenly Canaan. [3.] That he did this when all his brethren and companions in that service, except Joshua, did otherwise. They *made the heart of the people melt* (v. 8), and how pernicious the consequences of it were was very well known. It adds much to the praise of following God if we adhere to him when others desert and decline from him. Caleb needed not to mention particularly Joshua's conduct in this matter; it was sufficiently known, and he would not seem to flatter him; it was enough to say (v. 6), *Thou knowest what the Lord spoke concerning me and thee.*

(2.) The experience he had had of God's goodness to him ever since to this day. Though he had wandered with the rest in the wilderness, and had been kept thirty-eight years out of Canaan as they were, for that sin which he was so far from having a hand in that he had done his utmost to prevent it, yet, instead of complaining of this, he mentioned, to the glory of God, his mercy to him in two things: — [1.] That he was kept alive in the wilderness, not only notwithstanding the common perils and fatigues of that tedious march, but though all that generation of Israelites, except himself and Joshua, were one way or other cut off by death. With what a grateful sense of God's goodness to him does he speak it! (v. 10). *Now behold* (behold and wonder) *the Lord hath kept me alive these forty and five years,* thirty-eight years in the wilderness, through the plagues of the desert, and seven years in Canaan through the perils of war! Note, *First,* While we live, it is God that keeps us alive; by his power he protects us from death, and by his bounty supplies us continually

with the supports and comforts of life. He *holdeth our soul in life. Secondly,* The longer we live the more sensible we should be of God's goodness to us in keeping us alive, his care in prolonging our frail lives, his patience in prolonging our forfeited lives. Has he kept me alive these forty-five years? Is it about that time of life with us? Or is it more? Or is it less? We have reason to say, *It is of the Lord's mercies that we are not consumed.* How much are we indebted to the favour of God, and what shall we render? Let the life thus kept by the providence of God be devoted to his praise. *Thirdly,* The death of many others round about us should make us the more thankful to God for sparing us and keeping us alive. Thousands falling on our right hand and our left and yet ourselves spared. These distinguishing favours impose on us strong obligations to singular obedience. [2.] That he was fit for business, now that he was in Canaan. Though eighty-five years old, yet as hearty and lively as when he was forty (v. 11): *As my strength was then, so is it now.* This was the fruit of the promise, and out-did what was said; for God not only gives what he promises, but he gives more: life by promise shall be life, and health, and strength, and all that which will make the promised life a blessing and comfort. Moses had said in his prayer (Ps. 90:10) that at *eighty years old* even their *strength is labour and sorrow,* and so it is most commonly. But Caleb was an exception to the rule; his strength at eighty-five was ease and joy: this he got by *following the Lord fully.* Caleb here takes notice of this to the glory of God, and as an excuse for his asking a portion which he must fetch out of the giants' hands. Let not Joshua tell him he *knew not what he asked;* could he get the possession of that which he begged for a title to? "Yes," says he, "why not? I am as fit for war now as ever I was." (3.) The promise Moses had made him in God's name that he should have *this mountain, v.* 9. This promise is his chief plea, and that on which he relies. As we find it (Num. 14:24) it is general, *him will I bring into the land whereunto he went, and his seed shall possess it;* but it seems it was more particular, and Joshua knew it; both sides understood this mountain for which Caleb was now a suitor to be intended. This was the place from which, more than any other, the spies took their report, for here they met with the sons of Anak (Num. 13:22), the sight of whom made such an impression upon them, v. 3. We may suppose that Caleb, observing what stress they laid upon the difficulty of conquering Hebron, a city garrisoned by the giants, and how thence they inferred that the conquest of the whole land was utterly impracticable, in opposition to their suggestions, and to convince the people that he spoke as he thought, bravely desired to have that city which they called *invincible* assigned to himself for his own portion: "I will undertake to deal with that, and, if I cannot get it for my inheritance, I will be without." "Well," said Moses, "it shall be thy own then, win it and wear it." Such a noble heroic spirit Caleb had, and so desirous was he to inspire his brethren with it, that he chose this place only because it was the most difficult to be conquered. And, to show that his soul did not decay any more than his body, now forty-five years after he adheres to his choice and is still of the same mind.

(4.) The hopes he had of being master of it, though the sons of Anak were in possession of it (v. 12): *If the Lord will be with me, then I shall be able to drive them out.* The city of Hebron Joshua had already reduced (ch. 10:37), but the mountain which belonged to it, and which was inhabited by the sons of Anak, was yet unconquered; for though the cutting off of the Anakim from Hebron was mentioned ch. 11:21, because the historian would relate all the military actions together, yet it seems it was not conquered till after they had begun to divide the land. Observe, He builds his hopes of driving out the sons of Anak upon the presence of God with him. He does not say, "Because I am now as strong for war as I was at forty, therefore I shall drive them out," depending upon his personal valour; nor does he depend upon his interest in the war-like tribe of Judah, who attended him now in making this address, and no doubt would assist him; nor does he court Joshua's aid, or put it upon that, "If thou wilt be with me I shall gain my point." But, *If the Lord will be with me.* Here, [1.] He seems to speak doubtfully of God's being with him, not from any distrust of his goodness or faithfulness. He had spoken without the least hesitation of God's presence

with Israel in general (Num. 14:9); *the Lord is with us.* But for himself, from a humble sense of his own unworthiness of such a favour, he chooses to express himself thus, *If the Lord will be with me.* The Chaldee paraphrase reads it, *If the Word of the Lord be my helper,* that Word which is God, and in the fulness of time was made flesh, and is the captain of our salvation. [2.] But he expresses without the least doubt his assurance that if God were with him he should be able to dispossess the sons of Anak. "If God be with us, *If God be for us, who can be against us,* so as to prevail?" It is also intimated that if God were not with him, though all the forces of Israel should come in to his assistance, he should not be able to gain his point. Whatever we undertake, God's favourable presence with us is all in all to our success; this therefore we must earnestly pray for, and carefully make sure of, by keeping ourselves in the love of God; and on this we must depend, and from this take our encouragement against the greatest difficulties.

3. Upon the whole matter, Caleb's request is (v. 12), *Give me this mountain,* (1.) Because it was formerly in God's promise, and he would let Israel know how much he valued the promise, insisting upon *this mountain, whereof the Lord spake in that day,* as most desirable, though perhaps as good a portion might have fallen to him by lot in common with the rest. Those that live by faith value that which is given by promise far above that which is given by providence only. (2.) Because it was now in the Anakim's possession, and he would let Israel know how little he feared the enemy, and would by his example animate them to push on their conquests. Herein Caleb answered his name, which signifies *all heart.*

II. Joshua grants his petition (v. 13): *Joshua blessed him,* commended his bravery, applauded his request, and gave him what he asked. He also prayed for him, and for his good success in his intended undertaking against the sons of Anak. Joshua was both a prince and a prophet, and upon both accounts it was proper for him to give Caleb his blessing, for *the less is blessed of the better.* Hebron was settled on Caleb and his heirs (v. 14), *because he wholly followed the Lord God of Israel.* And happy are we if we follow him. Note, Singular piety shall be crowned with singular favours. Now, 1. We are here told what Hebron had been, the city of Arba, a great man among the Anakim (v. 15); we find it called *Kirjath-arba* (Gen. 23:2), as the place where Sarah died. Hereabouts Abraham, Isaac, and Jacob lived most of their time in Canaan, and near to it was the cave of Machpelah, where they were buried, which perhaps had led Caleb hither when he went to spy out the land, and had made him covet this rather than any other part for his inheritance. 2. We are afterwards told what Hebron was. (1.) It was one of the cities belonging to priests (Jos. 21:13), and a *city of refuge,* Jos. 20:7. When Caleb had it, he contented himself with the country about it, and cheerfully gave the city to the priests, the Lord's ministers, thinking it could not be better bestowed, no, not upon his own children, nor that it was the less his own for being thus devoted to God. (2.) It was a royal city, and, in the beginning of David's reign, the metropolis of the kingdom of Judah; thither the people resorted to him, and there he reigned seven years. Thus highly was Caleb's city honoured; it is a pity there should have been such a blemish upon his family long after as Nabal was, who was *of the house of Caleb,* 1 Sa. 25:3. But the best men cannot entail their virtues.

CHAPTER 15

Though the land was not completely conquered, yet being (as was said in the close of the foregoing chapter) as rest from war for the present, and their armies all drawn out of the field to a general rendezvous at Gilgal, there they began to divide the land, though the work was afterwards perfected at Shiloh, ch. 18:1, etc. In this chapter we have the lot of the tribe of Judah, which in this, as in other things, had the precedency. I. The borders or bounds of the inheritance of Judah (v. 1–12). II. The particular assignment of Hebron and the country thereabout to Caleb and his family (v. 13–19). III. The names of the several cities that fell within Judah's lot (v. 20–63).

Verses 1–12

Judah and Joseph were the two sons of Jacob on whom Reuben's forfeited birth-right devolved. Judah had the dominion entailed on him, and Joseph the double portion, and therefore these two tribes were first seated, Judah in the southern part of the land of Canaan and Joseph in the northern part, and on them the other seven did attend, and had their respective lots as appurtenances to these two; the lots of Benjamin, Simeon, and Dan, were appendant to Judah, and those of Issachar and Zebulun, Naphtali and Asher, to Joseph. These two were first set up to be provided for, it should seem, before there was such an exact survey of the land as we find afterwards, *ch.* 18:9. It is probable that the most considerable parts of the northern and southern countries, and those that lay nearest to Gilgal, and which the people were best acquainted with, were first put into two portions, and the lot was cast upon them between these two principal tribes, of the one of which Joshua was, and of the other Caleb, who was the first commissioner in this writ of partition; and, by the decision of that lot, the southern country, of which we have an account in this chapter, fell to Judah, and the northern, of which we have an account in the two following chapters, to Joseph. And when this was done there was a more equal dividend (either in quantity or quality) of the remainder among the seven tribes. And this, probably, was intended in that general rule which was given concerning this partition (Num. 33:54), *to the more you shall give the more inheritance, and to the fewer you shall give the less,* and *every man's inheritance shall be where his lot falleth;* that is, "You shall appoint two greater portions which shall be determined by lot to those more numerous tribes of Judah and Joseph, and then the rest shall be less portions to be allotted to the less numerous tribes." The former was done in Gilgal, the latter in Shiloh.

In these verses, we have the borders of the lot of Judah, which, as the rest, is said to be *by their families,* that is, with an eye to the number of their families. And it intimates that Joshua and Eleazar, and the rest of the commissioners, when they had by lot given each tribe its portion, did afterwards (it is probable by lot likewise) subdivide those larger portions, and assign to each family its inheritance, and then to each household, which would be better done by this supreme authority, and be apt to give less disgust than if it had been left to the inferior magistrates of each tribe to make that distribution. The borders of this tribe are here largely fixed, yet not unalterably, for a good deal of that which lies within these bounds was afterwards assigned to the lots of Simeon and Dan. 1. The eastern border was all, and only, the Salt Sea, *v.* 5. Every sea is salt, but this was of an extraordinary and more than natural saltness, the effects of that fire and brimstone with which Sodom and Gomorrah were destroyed in Abraham's time, whose ruins lie buried in the bottom of this dead water, which never either was moved itself or had any living thing in it. 2. The southern border was that of the land of Canaan in general, as will appear by comparing *v.* 1–4 with Num. 34:3–5. So that this powerful and warlike tribe of Judah guarded the frontiers of the whole land, on that side which lay towards their old sworn enemies (though their two fathers were twin-brethren), the Edomites. Our Lord therefore, who *sprang out of Judah,* and whose *the kingdom is, shall judge the mount of Esau,* Obad. 21. 3. The northern border divided it from the lot of Benjamin. In this, mention is made of *the stone of Bohan* a Reubenite (*v.* 6), who probably was a great commander of those forces of Reuben that came over Jordan, and died in the camp at Gilgal, and was buried not far off under this stone. The valley of Achor likewise lies upon this border (*v.* 7), to remind the men of Judah of the trouble which Achan, one of their tribe, gave to the congregation of Israel, that they might not be too much lifted up with their services. This northern line touched closely upon Jerusalem (*v.* 8), so closely as to include in the lot of this tribe Mount Zion and Mount Moriah, though the greater part of the city lay in the lot of Benjamin. 4. The west border went near to the great sea at first (*v.* 12), but afterwards the lot of the tribe of Dan took off a good part of Judah's lot on that side; for the lot was only to determine between Judah and Joseph, which should have the north and which the south, and not immovably to fix the border of either. Judah's inheritance had its boundaries determined. Though it was a powerful warlike tribe, and had a great interest in the other tribes, yet they must not therefore be left to their own choice, to enlarge their possessions at pleasure, but must live so as that their neighbours might live by them. Those that are placed high yet must not think to be *placed alone in the midst of the earth.*

Verses 13–19

The historian seems pleased with every occasion to make mention of Caleb and to do him honour, because he had honoured God in following him fully. Observe,

I. The grant Joshua made him of the mountain of Hebron for his inheritance is here repeated (*v.* 13), and it is said to be given him. 1. *According to the commandment of the Lord to Joshua.* Though Caleb, in his petition, had made out a very good title to it by promise, yet, because God had ordered Joshua to divide the land by lot, he would not in this one single instance, no, not to gratify his old friend Caleb, do otherwise, without orders from God, whose oracle, it is probable, he consulted upon this occasion. In every doubtful case it is very desirable to know the mind of God, and to see the way of our duty plain. 2. It is said to be a part *among the children of Judah;* though it was assigned him before the lot of that tribe came up, yet it proved, God so directing the lot, to be in the heart of that tribe, which was graciously ordered in kindness to him, that he might not be as one separated from his brethren and surrounded by those of other tribes.

II. Caleb having obtained this grant, we are told,

1. How he signalized his own valour in the conquest of Hebron (*v.* 14): *He drove thence the three sons of Anak,* he and those that he engaged to assist him in this service. This is mentioned here to show that the confidence he had expressed of success in this affair, through the presence of God with him (*ch.* 14:12), did not deceive him, but the event answered his expectation. It is not said that he *slew these giants,* but he *drove them thence,* which intimates that they retired upon his approach and fled before him; the strength and stature of their bodies could not keep up the courage of their minds, but with the countenances of lions they had the hearts of trembling hares. Thus does God often *cut off the spirit of princes* (Ps. 76:12), *take away the heart of the chief of the people* (Job 12:24), and so shame the confidence of the proud; and thus if we resist the devil, that roaring lion, though he fall not, yet he will flee.

2. How he encouraged the valour of those about him in the conquest of Debir, *v.* 15, etc. It seems, though Joshua had once made himself master of Debir (*ch.* 10:39), yet the Canaanites had regained the possession in the absence of the army, so that the work had to be done a second time; and when Caleb had completed the reduction of Hebron, which was for himself and his own family, to show his zeal for the public good, as much as for his own private interest, he pushes on his conquest to Debir, and will not lay down his arms till he sees that city also effectually reduced, which lay but ten miles southward from Hebron, though he had not any particular concern in it, but the reducing of it would be to the general advantage of his tribe. Let us learn hence not to seek and mind our own things only, but to concern and engage ourselves for the welfare of the community we are members of; we are not born for ourselves, nor must we *live to ourselves.*

(1.) Notice is taken of the name of this city. It had been called *Kirjath-sepher, the city of a book,* and *Kirjath-sannah* (*v.* 49), which some translate *the city of learning* (so the Septuagint *Polis grammatōn*), whence some conjecture that it had been a university among the Canaanites, like Athens in Greece, in which their youth were educated; or perhaps the books of their chronicles or records, or the antiquities of the nation, were laid up there; and, it may be, this was it that made Caleb so desirous to see Israel master of this city, that they might get acquainted with the ancient learning of the Canaanites.

(2.) The proffer that Caleb made of his daughter, and a good portion with her, to any one that would undertake to reduce that city, and to command the forces that should be employed in that service, *v.* 16. Thus Saul promised a daughter to him that would kill Goliath (1 Sa. 17:25), neither of them intending to force his daughter to marry such as she could not love, but both of them presuming upon their daughters' obedience, and submission to their fathers' will, though it might be contrary to their own humour or inclination. Caleb's family was not long honourable and wealthy, but religious; he that himself *followed the Lord fully* no doubt taught his children to do so, and therefore it could not but be a desirable match to any young gentleman. Caleb, in making the proposal, aims, [1.] To do service to his country by the reducing of that important place; and, [2.] To marry a daughter well, to a man of learning, that would have a particular affection for *the city of books,* and a man of war, that would be likely to serve his country, and do worthily in his generation. Could he but marry his child to a man of such a character, he would think her well bestowed, whether the share in the lot of his tribe were more or less.

(3.) The place was bravely taken by Othniel, a nephew of Caleb, whom probably Caleb had thoughts of when he made the proffer, *v.* 17. This Othniel, who thus signalized himself when he was young, had long after, in his advanced years, the honour to be both a deliverer and a judge in Israel, the first single person that presided in their affairs after Joshua's death. It is good for those who are setting out in the world to begin betimes with that which is great and good, that, excelling in service when they are young, they may excel in honour when they grow old.

(4.) Hereupon (all parties being agreed) Othniel married his cousin-german Achsah, Caleb's daughter. It is probable that he had a kindness for her before, which put him upon this bold undertaking to obtain her. Love to his country, an ambition of honour, and a desire to find favour with the princes of his people, might not have engaged him in this great action, but his affection for Achsah did. This made it intolerable to him to think that any one should do more to win her favour than he would, and so inspired him with this generous fire. Thus is love strong as death, and jealousy cruel as the grave.

(5.) Because the historian is now upon the dividing of the land, he gives us an account of Achsah's portion, which was in land, as more valuable because enjoyed by virtue of the divine promise, though we may suppose the conquerors of Canaan, who had had the spoil of so many rich cities, were full of money too. [1.] Some land she obtained by Caleb's free grant, which was allowed while she married within her own tribe and family, as Zelophehad's daughters did. He *gave her a south land, v.* 19. Land indeed, but *a south land,* dry, and apt to be parched. [2.] She obtained more upon her request; she would have had her husband to ask for a field, probably some particular field, or champaign ground, which belonged to Caleb's lot, and joined to that south land which he had settled upon his daughter at marriage. She thought her husband had the best interest in her father, who, no doubt, was extremely pleased with his late glorious achievement, but he thought it was more proper for her to ask, and she would be more likely to prevail; accordingly she did, submitting to her husband's judgment, though contrary to her own; and she managed the undertaking with great address. *First,* She took the opportunity when her father brought her home to the house of her husband, when the satisfaction of having disposed of his daughter so well would make him think nothing too much to do for her. *Secondly,* She *lighted off her ass,* in token of respect and reverence to her father, whom she would honour still, as much as before her marriage. She *cried* or *sighed* from off her ass, so the Septuagint and the vulgar Latin read it; she expressed some grief and concern, that she might give her father occasion to ask her what she wanted. *Thirdly,* She calls it *a blessing,* because it would add much to the comfort of her settlement; and she was sure that, since she married not only with her father's consent, but in obedience to his command, he would not deny her his blessing. *Fourthly,* She asks only for the *water,* without which the ground she had would be of little use either for tillage or pasture, but she means the field in which the springs of water were. The modesty and reasonableness of her quest gave it a great advantage. Earth without water would be like a tree without sap, or the body of an animal without blood; therefore, when God *gathered the waters into one place,* he wisely and graciously left some in every place, that the earth might be enriched for the service of man. See Ps. 104:10, etc. Well, Achsah gained her point; her father gave her what she asked, and perhaps more, for *he gave her the upper springs and the nether springs,* two fields so called from the springs that were in them, as we commonly distinguish between the higher field and the lower field. Those who understand it but of one field, watered both with the rain of heaven and the springs that issued out of the bowels of the earth, give countenance to the allusion we commonly make to this, when we pray for spiritual and heavenly blessings which relate to our souls as blessings of the upper springs, and those which relate to the body and the life that now is as blessings of the nether springs.

From this story we learn, 1. That it is no breach of the tenth commandment moderately to desire those comforts and conveniences of this life which we see attainable in a fair and regular way. 2. That husbands and wives should mutually advise, and jointly agree, about that which is for the common good of their family; and much more should they concur in asking of their heavenly Father the best blessings, those of the upper springs. 3. That parents must never think that lost which is bestowed upon their children for their real advantage, but must be free in giving them portions as well as maintenance, especially when they are dutiful. Caleb had sons (1 Chr. 4:15), and yet gave thus liberally to his daughter. Those parents forget themselves and their relation who grudge their children what is convenient for them when they can conveniently part with it.

Verses 20–63

We have here a list of the several cities that fell within the lot of the tribe of Judah, which are mentioned by name, that they might know their own, and both keep it and keep to it, and might neither through cowardice nor sloth lose the possession of what was their own.

I. The cities are here named, and numbered in several classes, which they then could account for the reason of better than we can now. Here are, 1. Some that are said to be the uttermost cities *towards the coast of Edom, v.* 21–32. Here are thirty-eight named, and yet said to be *twenty-nine* (*v.* 32), because nine of these were afterwards transferred to the lot of Simeon, and are reckoned as belonging to that, as appears by comparing *ch.* 19:2, etc.; therefore those only are counted (though the rest are named) which remained to Judah. 2. Others that are said to be *in the valley* (*v.* 33) are counted to be fourteen, yet fifteen are named; but it is probable that Gederah and Gederathaim were either two names or two parts of one and the same city. 3. Then sixteen are named without any head of distinction, *v.* 37–41, and nine more, *v.* 42–44. 4. Then the three Philistine-cities, Ekron, Ashdod, and Gaza, *v.* 45–47. 5. Cities *in the mountains,* eleven in all (*v.* 48–51), nine more (*v.* 52–54), ten more (*v.* 55–57), six more (*v.* 58, 59), then two (*v.* 60), and six in the wilderness, a part of the country not so thick of inhabitants as some others were.

II. Now here, 1. We do not find Bethlehem, which was afterwards the city of David, and was ennobled by the birth of our Lord Jesus in it. But that city, which at the best was but *little among the thousands of Judah* (Mic. 5:2), except that it was thus dignified, was now so little as not to be accounted one of the cities, but perhaps was one of the villages not named. Christ came to give honour to the places he was related to, not to receive honour from them. 2. Jerusalem is said to continue in the hands of the Jebusites (*v.* 63), *for the children of Judah could not drive them out,* through their sluggishness, stupidity, and unbelief. Had they attempted it with vigour and resolution, we have reason to think God would not have been wanting to them to give them success; but they could not do it, because they would not. Jerusalem was afterwards to be the holy city, the royal city, the city of the great King, the brightest ornament of all the land of Israel. God has designed it should be so. It may therefore be justly looked upon as a punishment of their neglect to conquer other cities which God had given them that they were so long kept out of this. 3. Among the cities of Judah (in all 114) we meet with Libnah, which in Joram's days revolted, and probably set up for a free independent state (2 Ki. 8:22), and Lachish, where king Amaziah was slain (1 Ki. 14:19); it led the dance in idolatry (Mic. 1:13); it was the *beginning of sin to the daughter of Zion.* Giloh, Ahithophel's town, is here mentioned, and Tekoa, of which the prophet Amos was, and near which Jehoshaphat obtained that glorious victory, 2 Chr. 20:20, etc., and Maresha, where Asa was a conqueror. Many of the cities of this tribe occur in the history of David's troubles. Adullam, Ziph, Keilah, Maon, Engedi, Ziklag, here reckoned in this tribe, were places near which David had most of his haunts; for, though sometimes Saul drove him out from the inheritance of the Lord, yet he kept as close to it as he could. The wilderness of Judah he frequented much, and in it John Baptist preached, and there the kingdom of heaven commenced, Mt. 3:1. The riches of this country no doubt answered Jacob's blessing of this tribe, that he should *wash his garments in wine,* Gen. 49:11. And, in general, *Judah, thou art he whom thy brethren shall praise,* not envy.

CHAPTER 16

It is a pity that this and the following chapter should be separated, for both of them give us the lot of the children of Joseph, Ephraim and Manasseh, who, next to Judah, were to have the post of honour, and therefore had the first and best portion in the northern part of Canaan, as Judah now had in the southern part. In this chapter we have, I. A general account of the lot of these two tribes together (*v.* 1–4). II. The borders of the lot of Ephraim in particular (*v.* 5–10). That of Manasseh following in the next chapter.

Verses 1–4

Though Joseph was one of the younger sons of Jacob, yet he was his eldest by his most just and best beloved wife Rachel, was himself *his best beloved son,* and had been the greatest ornament and support of his family, kept it from perishing in a time of famine, and had been the *shepherd and stone of Israel,* and therefore his posterity were very much favoured by the lot. Their portion lay in the very heart of the land of Canaan. It extended from Jordan in the east (*v.* 1) to the sea, the Mediterranean Sea, in the west, so that it took up the whole breadth of Canaan from side to side; and no question the fruitfulness of the soil answered the blessings both of Jacob and Moses, Gen. 49:25, 26, and Deu. 33:13, etc. The portions allotted to Ephraim and Manasseh are not so particularly described as those of the other tribes; we have only the limits and boundaries of them, not the particular cities in them, as before we had the cities of Judah and afterwards those of the other tribes. For this no reason can be assigned, unless we may suppose that Joshua being himself of the children of Joseph they referred it to him alone to distribute among them the several cities that lay within their lot, and therefore did not bring in the names of their cities to the great council of their princes who sat upon this affair, by which means it came to pass that they were not inserted with the rest in the books.

Verses 5–10

Here, 1. The border of the lot of Ephraim is set down, by which it was divided on the south from Benjamin and Dan, who lay between it and Judah, and on the north from Manasseh; for east and west it reached from Jordan to the great sea. The learned, who aim to be exact in drawing the line according to the directions here, find themselves very much at a loss, the description being short and intricate. The report of those who in these latter ages have travelled those countries will not serve to clear the difficulties, so vastly unlike is it now to what it was then; not only cities have been so destroyed as that no mark nor footstep of them remains, but brooks are dried up, rivers alter their courses, and *even the mountain falling cometh to nought, and the rock is removed out of his place,* Job 14:18. Unless I could hope to solve the doubts that arise upon this draught of the border of Ephraim, it is to no purpose to mention them: no doubt it was then perfectly understood, so as that the first intention of recording it was effectually answered, which was to notify the ancient landmarks, which posterity must by no means remove. 2. Some separate cities are spoken of, that lay not within these borders, at least not if the line was drawn direct, but lay within the lot of Manasseh (*v.* 9), which might better be read, *and there were separate cities for the children of Ephraim among the inheritance of the children of Manasseh,* because it proved that Manasseh could spare them, and Ephraim had need of them, and it might be hoped that no inconvenience would arise from this mixture of these two tribes together, who were both the sons of Joseph, and should *love as brethren.* And by this it appears that though, when the tribes were numbered in the plains of Moab, Manasseh had got the start of Ephraim in number, for Manasseh was then 52,000, and Ephraim but 32,000 (Num. 26:34, 37), yet by the time they were well settled in Canaan the hands were crossed again, and the blessing of Moses was verified, Deu. 33:17, *They are the ten thousands of Ephraim and they are the thousands of Manasseh.* Families and kingdoms are diminished and increased, increased and diminished again, as God pleases. 3. A brand is put upon the Ephraimites, that they did not drive out the Canaanites from Gezer (*v.* 10), either through carelessness or cowardice, either for want of faith in the promise of God, that he would give them success if they would make a vigorous effort, or for want of zeal for the command of God, which obliged them *utterly to drive out the Canaanites,* and to make no peace with them. And, though they hoped to satisfy the law by putting them under tribute, yet (as Calvin thinks) this made the matter worse, for it shows that they spared them out of covetousness, that they might be profited by their labours, and by dealing with them for their tribute they were in danger of being infected with their idolatry; yet some think that, when they brought them under tribute, they obliged them to renounce their idols, and to observe the seven precepts of the sons of Noah; and I should think so, but that we find in the sequel of the story that the Israelites were so far from restraining idolatry in others that they soon fell into it themselves. Many famous places were within this lot of the tribe of Ephraim, though not mentioned here. In it were Ramah, Samuel's city (called in the New Testament *Arimathea,* of which Joseph was, that took care of our Saviour's burial), and Shiloh, where the tabernacle was first set up. Tirzah also, the royal city of Jeroboam and his successors, and Deborah's palm-tree, under which she judged Israel, were in this tribe. Samaria, built by Omri after the burning of the royal palace of Tirzah, was in this tribe, and was long the royal city of the kingdom of the ten tribes; not far from it were Shechem, and the mountains Ebal and Gerizim, and Sychar, near which was Jacob's well, where Christ talked with the woman of Samaria. We read much of Mount Ephraim in the story of the Judges, and of a city called *Ephraim,* it is probable in this tribe, to which Christ retired, Jn. 11:54. The whole kingdom of the ten tribes is often, in the prophets, especially in Hosea, called *Ephraim.*

CHAPTER 17

The half tribe of Manasseh comes next to be provided for; and here we have, I. The families of that tribe that were to be portioned (*v.* 1–6). II. The country that fell to their lot (*v.* 7–13). III. The joint request of the two tribes that descended from Joseph, for the enlargement of their lot, and Joshua's answer to that request (*v.* 14–18).

Verses 1–6

Manasseh was itself but one half of the tribe of Joseph, and yet was divided and subdivided. 1. It was divided into two parts, one already settled on the other side Jordan, consisting of those who were the posterity of Machir, *v.* 1. This Machir was born to Manasseh in Egypt; there he had signalized himself as a man of war, probably in the contests between the Ephraimites and the men of Gath, 1 Chr. 7:21. His warlike disposition descended to his posterity, and therefore Moses gave them Gileaxdand Bashan, on the other side Jordan, of which before, *ch.* 13:31. It is here said that the lot came to Manasseh, *for he was the first-born of* Joseph. Bishop Patrick thinks it should be translated, *though he was the first-born of* Joseph, and then the meaning is plain, that the second lot was for Manasseh, because, though he was the first-born, yet Jacob had preferred Ephraim before him. See the names of those heads of the families that settled on the other side Jordan, 1 Chr. 5:24. 2. That part on this side Jordan as subdivided into ten families, *v.* 5. There were six sons of Gilead here named (*v.* 2), the same that are recorded Num. 26:30–32, only that he who is there called *Jezeer* is here called *Abiezer.* Five of these sons had each of them their portion; the sixth, which was Hepher, had his male line cut off in his son Zelophehad, who left daughters only, five in number, of whom we have often read, and these five had each of them a portion; though perhaps, they claiming under Hepher, all their five portions were but equal to one of the portions of the five sons. Or if Hepher had other sons besides Zelophehad, in whom the name of his family was kept up, their posterity married to the daughters of Zelophehad the elder brother, and in their right had these portions assigned them. See Num. 36:12. Here is, (1.) The claim which the daughters of Zelophehad made, grounded upon the command God gave to Moses concerning them, *v.* 4. They had themselves, when they were young, pleaded their own cause before Moses, and obtained the grant of an inheritance with their brethren, and now they would not lose the benefit of that grant for want of speaking to Joshua, but seasonably put in their demand themselves, as it should seem, and not their husbands for them. (2.) The assignment of their portions according to their claim. Joshua knew very well what God had ordered in their case, and did not object that they having not served in the wars of Canaan there was no reason why they should share in the possessions of Canaan, but readily *gave them as inheritance among the brethren of their father.* And now they reaped the benefit of their own pious zeal and prudent forecast in this matter. Thus those who take care in the wilderness of this world to make sure to themselves a place in the inheritance of the saints in light will certainly have the comfort of it in the other world, while those that neglect it now will lose it for ever.

Verses 7–13

We have here a short account of the lot of this half tribe. It reached from Jordan on the east to the great sea on the west; on the south it lay all along contiguous to Ephraim, but on the north it abutted upon Asher and Issachar. Asher lay north-west, and Issachar north-east, which seems to be the meaning of that (*v.* 10), that they (that is, Manasseh and Ephraim, as related to it, both together making the tribe of Joseph) met in Asher on the north and Issachar on the east, for Ephraim itself reached not those tribes. Some things are particularly observed concerning this lot: — 1. That there was great communication between this tribe and that of Ephraim. The city of Tappuah belonged to Ephraim, but the country adjoining to Manasseh (*v.* 8); there were likewise many cities of Ephraim that lay within the border of Manasseh (*v.* 9), of which before, *ch.* 16:9. 2. That Manasseh likewise had cities with their appurtenances in the tribes of Issachar and Asher (*v.* 11), God so ordering it, that though every tribe had its peculiar inheritance, which might not be alienated from it, yet they should thus intermix one with another, to keep up mutual acquaintance and correspondence among the tribes, and to give occasion for the doing of good offices one to another, as became those who, though of different tribes, were all one Israel, and were bound to love as brethren. 3. That they suffered the Canaanites to live among them, contrary to the command of God, serving their own ends by conniving at them, for they made them tributaries, *v.* 12, 13. The Ephraimites had done the same (*ch.* 16:10), and from them perhaps the Manassites learned it, and with their example excused themselves in it. The most remarkable person of this half tribe in after-time was Gideon, whose great actions were done within this lot. He was of the family of Abiezer; Cesarea was in this lot, and Antipatris, famed in the latter ages of the Jewish state.

Verses 14–18

Here, I. The children of Joseph quarrel with their lot; if they had had any just cause to quarrel with it, we have reason to think Joshua would have relieved them, by adding to it, or altering it, which it does not appear he did. It is probable, because Joshua was himself of the tribe of Ephraim, they promised themselves that they should have some particular favour shown them, and should not be confined to the decision of the lot so closely as the other tribes; but Joshua makes them know that in the discharge of his office, as a public person, he had no more regard to his own tribe than to any other, but would administer impartially, without favour or affection, wherein he has left an excellent example to all in public trusts. It was a very competent provision that was made for them, as much, for aught that appears, as they were able to manage, and yet they call it in disdain but *one lot,* as if that which was assigned to them both was scarcely sufficient for one. The word for *complainers* (Jude 16) is *mempsimoiroi,* blamers of their lot: — 1. That they were very numerous, through the blessing of God upon them (*v.* 14): *I am a great people, for the Lord has blessed me;* and we have reason to hope that he that hath sent mouths will send meat. *"I am a great people,* and in so small a lot shall not have *room to thrive."* Yet observe, when they speak thankfully of their present increase, they do not speak confidently of the continuance of it. "The Lord has blessed me hitherto, however he may see fit to deal with me for the future." The uncertainty of what may be must not make us unthankful for what has been and is done in kindness to us. 2. That a good part of that country which had now fallen to their lot was in the hands of the Canaanites, and that they were formidable enemies, who brought into the field of battle *chariots of iron* (*v.* 16), that is, chariots with long scythes fastened to the sides of them, or the axle-tree, which made great destruction of all that came in their way, mowing them down like corn. They urge that though they had a good portion assigned them, yet it was in bad hands, and they could not come to the possession of it, wishing to have their lot in those countries that were more thoroughly reduced than this was.

II. Joshua endeavours to reconcile them to their lot. He owns they were a *great people,* and being two tribes ought to have more than *one lot only* (*v.* 17), but tells them that what had fallen to their share would be a sufficient lot for them both, if they would but work and fight. They desired a lot in which they might indulge themselves in ease and luxury. "No," says Joshua, "you must not count upon that; *in the sweat of thy face shalt thou eat bread* is a sentence in force even in Canaan itself." He retorts their own argument, that they were a *great people.* "If so, you are the better able to help yourselves, and have the less reason to expect help from others. If thou hast many mouths to be filled, thou hast twice as many hands to be employed; earn, and then eat." 1. He bids them work for more (*v.* 15): *"Get thee up to the wood-country,* which is within thy own border, and let all hands be set to work to cut down the trees, rid the rough lands, and make them, with art and industry, good arable ground." Note, Many wish for larger possessions who do not cultivate and make the best of what they have, think they should have more talents given them who do not trade with those with which they are entrusted. Most people's poverty is the effect of their idleness; would they dig, they need not beg. 2. He bids them fight for more (*v.* 17, 18), when they pleaded that they could not come at the wood-lands he spoke of because in the valley between them and it were Canaanites whom they durst not enter the lists with. "Never fear them," said Joshua, "thou hast God on thy side, and *thou shalt drive out the Canaanites,* if thou wilt set about it in good earnest, *though they have iron chariots."* We straiten ourselves by apprehending the difficulties in the way of our enlargement to be greater than really they are. What can be insuperable to faith and holy resolution?

CHAPTER 18

In this chapter we have, I. The setting up of the tabernacle at Shiloh (*v.* 1). II. The stirring up of the seven tribes that were yet unsettled to look after their lot, and the putting of them in a method for it, by Joshua (*v.* 2–7). III. The distributing of the land into seven lots, by certain men employed for that purpose (*v.* 8, 9). IV. The determining of these seven portions to the seven tribes yet unprovided for by lot (*v.* 10). V. The particular lot of the tribe of Benjamin, the borders of it (*v.* 11–20). And the cities contained in it (*v.* 21–28). The other six tribes we shall find well provided for in the next chapter.

Verse 1

In the midst of the story of the dividing of the land comes in this account of the setting up of the tabernacle, which had hitherto continued in its old place in the centre of their camp; but now that three of the four squadrons that used to surround it in the wilderness were broken and diminished, those of Judah, Ephraim, and Reuben, by the removal of those tribes to their respective possessions, and that of Dan only remained entire, it was time to think of removing the tabernacle itself into a city. Many a time the priests and Levites had taken it down, carried it, and set it up again in the wilderness, according to the directions given them (Num. 4:5, etc.); but now they must do it for good and all, not one of the stakes thereof must any more be removed, nor any of the cords thereof broken, Isa. 33:20. Observe,

I. The place to which the tabernacle was removed, and in which it was set up. It was *Shiloh,* a city in the lot of Ephraim, but lying close upon the lot of Benjamin. Doubtless God himself did some way or other direct them to this place, for he had promised to *choose the place* where he would make *his name to dwell,* Deu. 12:11. It is most probable God made known his mind in this matter by the judgment of Urim. This place was pitched upon, 1. Because it was in the heart of the country, nearer the centre than Jerusalem was, and therefore the more convenient for the meeting of all Israel there from the several parts of the country; it had been in the midst of their camp in the wilderness, and therefore must now be in the midst of their nation, as that which sanctified the whole, and was *the glory in the midst of them.* See Ps. 46:5. 2. Because it was in the lot of that tribe of which Joshua was, who was now their chief magistrate, and it would be both for his honour and convenience and for the advantage of the country to have it near him. The testimony of Israel and the thrones of judgment do well together, Ps. 122:4, 5. 3. Some think there was an eye to the name of the place, *Shiloh* being the name by which the Messiah was known in dying Jacob's prophecy (Gen. 49:10), which prophecy, no doubt, was well known among the Jews; the setting up of the tabernacle in Shiloh gave them a hint that in that Shiloh whom Jacob spoke of all the ordinances of this worldly sanctuary should have their accomplishment in a greater and more perfect tabernacle, Heb. 9:1, 11. And Dr. Lightfoot thinks that the place where the tabernacle was set up was therefore called *Shiloh,* because of the peaceableness of the land at this time; as afterwards in Salem was his temple, which also signifies *peaceable.*

II. The solemn manner of doing it: *The whole congregation assembled together* to attend the solemnity, to do honour to the ark of God, as the token of his presence, and to bid it welcome to its settlement. Every Israelite was interested in it, and therefore all testified their joy and satisfaction upon this occasion. See 2 Sa. 6:15. It is probable those tribes that were yet encamped when the tabernacle was removed to Shiloh decamped from Gilgal and pitched about Shiloh, for every true Israelite will desire to fix where God's tabernacle fixed. Mention is made, on this occasion, of the land being subdued before them, to intimate that the country, hereabouts at least, being thoroughly reduced, they met with no opposition, nor were they apprehensive of any danger, but thought it time to make this grateful acknowledgment of God's goodness to them in the constant series of successes with which he had blessed them. It was a good presage of a comfortable settlement to themselves in Canaan, when their first care was to see the ark well settled as soon as they had a safe place ready to settle it in. Here the ark continued about 300 years, till the sins of Eli's house forfeited the ark, lost it and ruined Shiloh, and its ruins were long after made use of as warnings to Jerusalem. *Go, see what I did to Shiloh,* Jer. 7:12; Ps. 78:60.

Verses 2–10

Here, I. Joshua reproves those tribes which were yet unsettled that they did not bestir themselves to gain a settlement in the land which God had given them. Seven tribes were yet unprovided for, though sure of an inheritance, yet uncertain where it should be, and it seems in no great care about it, *v.* 2. And with them Joshua reasons (*v.* 3): *How long are you slack?* 1. They were too well pleased with their present condition, liked well enough to live in a body together, the more the merrier, and, like the Babel-builders, had no mind to be scattered abroad and break good company. The spoil of the cities they had taken served them to live plentifully upon for the present, and they banished the thoughts of time to come. Perhaps the tribes of Judah and Joseph, who had already received their inheritance in the countries next adjoining, were generous in entertaining their brethren who were yet unprovided for, so that they went from one good house to another among their friends, with which, instead of grudging that they were postponed, they were so well pleased that they cared not for going to houses of their own. 2. They were slothful and dilatory. It may be they wished the thing done, but had not spirit to stir in it, or move towards the doing of it, though it was so much for their own advantage; like the sluggard, that *hides his hand in his bosom, and it grieves him to bring it to his mouth again.* The countries that remained to be divided lay at a distance, and some parts of them in the hands of the Canaanites. If they go to take possession of them, the cities must be rebuilt or repaired, they must drive their flocks and herds a great way, and carry their wives and children to strange places, and this will not be done without care and pains, and breaking through some hardships; thus *he that observes the wind shall not sow, and he that regards the clouds shall not reap,* Eccl. 11:4. Note, Many are diverted from real duties, and debarred from real comforts, by seeming difficulties. God by his grace has given us a title to a good land, the heavenly Canaan, but we are *slack to take possession;* we enter not into that rest, as we might by faith, and hope, and holy joy; we live not in heaven, as we might by setting our affections on things above and having our conversation there. How long shall it be thus with us? How long shall we thus stand in our own light, and *forsake our own mercies* for lying vanities? Joshua was sensible of the inconveniences of this delay, that, while they neglected to take possession of the land that was conquered, the Canaanites were recovering strength and spirit, and fortifying themselves in the places that were yet in their hands, which would make the total expulsion of them the more difficult. They would lose their advantages by not following their blow; and therefore, *as an eagle stirreth up her nest,* so Joshua stirs them up to take possession of their lot. He is ready to do his part, if they will but do theirs.

II. He puts them in a way to settle themselves.

1. The land that remained must be surveyed, an account taken of the cities, and the territories belonging to them, *v.* 4. These must be divided into seven equal parts, as near as they could guess at their true value, which they must have an eye to, and not merely to the number of the cities and extent of the country. Judah is fixed on the south and Joseph on the north of Shiloh, to protect the tabernacle (*v.* 5), and therefore they need not describe their country, but those countries only that were yet undisposed of. He gives a reason (*v.* 7) why they must divide it into seven parts only, because the Levites were to have no temporal estate (as we say), but their benefices only, which were entailed upon their families: *The priesthood of the Lord is their inheritance,* and a very honourable, comfortable, plentiful inheritance it was. Gad and Reuben, with half of the tribe of Manasseh, were already fixed, and needed not to have any further care taken of them. Now, (1.) The surveyors were three men out of each of the seven tribes that were to be provided for (*v.* 4), one-and-twenty in all, who perhaps for greater expedition, because they had already lost time, divided themselves into three companies, one of each tribe in each company, and took each their district to survey. The matter was thus referred equally, that there might be neither any partiality used in making up the seven lots, nor any shadow of suspicion given, but all might be satisfied that they had right done them. (2.) The survey was accordingly made, and brought in to Joshua, *v.* 8, 9. Josephus says it was seven months in the doing. And we must in it observe, [1.] The faith and courage of the persons employed: abundance of Canaanites remained in the land, and all raging against Israel, *as a bear robbed of her whelps;* the business of these surveyors would soon be known, and what could they expect but to be way-laid, and have their brains knocked out by the fierce observers? But in obedience to Joshua's command, and in dependence upon God's power, they thus put their lives in their hands to serve their country. [2.] The good providence of God in protecting them from the many deaths they were exposed to, and bringing them all safely again to the host at Shiloh. When we are in the way of our duty we are under the special protection of the Almighty.

2. When it was surveyed, and reduced to seven lots, then Joshua would, by appeal to God, and direction from him, determine which of these lots should belong to each tribe (*v.* 6): *That I may cast lots for you here* at the tabernacle (because it was a sacred transaction) *before the Lord our God,* to whom each tribe must have an eye, with thankfulness for the conveniences and submission to the inconveniences of their allotment. What we have in the world we must acknowledge God's property in, and dispose of it as before him, with justice, and charity, and dependence upon Providence. The heavenly Canaan is described to us in a book, the book of the scriptures, and there are in it mansions and portions sufficient for all God's spiritual Israel. Christ is our Joshua that divides it to us. On him we must attend, and to him we must apply for an inheritance with the saints in light. See Jn. 17:2, 3.

Verses 11–28

We have here the lot of the tribe of Benjamin, which Providence cast next to Joseph on the one hand, because Benjamin was own and only brother to Joseph, and was little Benjamin (Ps. 68:27), that needed the protection of great Joseph, and yet had a better protector, for *the Lord shall cover him all the day long,* Deu. 33:12. And it was next to Judah on the other hand, that this tribe might hereafter unite with Judah in an adherence to the throne of David and the temple at Jerusalem. Here we have, 1. The exact borders and limits of this tribe, which we need not be exact in the explication of. As it had Judah on the south and Joseph on the north, so it had Jordan on the east and Dan on the west. The western border is said to *compass the corner of the sea southward* (*v.* 14), whereas no part of the lot of this tribe came near to the great sea. Bishop Patrick thinks the meaning is that it ran along in a parallel line to the great sea, though at a distance. Dr. Fuller suggests that since it is not called *the great sea,* but only *the sea,* which often signifies any lake or mere, it may be meant of the pool of Gibeon, which may be called *a corner* or *canton* of the sea; it is called the *great waters of Gibeon* (Jer. 41:12), and it is compassed by the western border of this tribe. 2. The particular cities in this tribe, not all, but the most considerable. Twenty-six are here named. Jericho is put first, though dismantled, and forbidden to be rebuilt as a city with gates and walls, because it might be built and inhabited as a country village, and so was not useless to this tribe. Gilgal, where Israel first encamped when Saul was made king (1 Sa. 11:15), was in this tribe. It was afterwards a very profane place. Hos. 9:15, *All their wickedness is in Gilgal.* Beth-el was in this tribe, a famous place. Though Benjamin adhered to the house of David, yet Beth-el, it seems, was in the possession of the house of Joseph (Jdg. 1:23–25), and there Jeroboam set up one of his calves. In this tribe was Gibeon, where the altar was in the beginning of Solomon's time, 2 Chr. 1:3. Gibeah likewise, that infamous place where the Levite's concubine was abused. Mizpeh, and near it Samuel's Ebenezer, and also Anathoth, Jeremiah's city, were in this tribe, as was the northern part of Jerusalem. Paul was the honour of this tribe (Rom. 11:1; Phil. 3:5); but where his land lay we know not: he sought the better country.

CHAPTER 19

In the description of the lots of Judah and Benjamin we have an account both of the borders that surrounded them and of the cities contained in them. In that of Ephraim and Manasseh we have the borders, but not the cities; in this chapter Simeon and Dan are described by their cities only, and not their borders, because they lay very much within Judah, especially the former; the rest have both their borders described and their cities names, especially frontiers. Here is, I. The lot of Simeon (*v.* 1–9). II. Of Zebulun (*v.* 10–16). III. Of Issachar (*v.* 17–23). IV. Of Asher (*v.* 24–31). V. Of Naphtali (*v.* 32–39). VI. Of Dan (*v.* 40–48). Lastly, The inheritance assigned to Joshua himself and his own family (*v.* 49–51).

Verses 1–9

Simeon's lot was drawn after Judah's, Joseph's, and Benjamin's, because Jacob had put that tribe under disgrace; yet it is put before the two younger sons of Leah and the three sons of the handmaids. Not one person of note, neither judge nor prophet, was of this tribe, that we know of.

I. The situation of their lot was within that of Judah (*v.* 1) and was taken from it, *v.* 9. It seems, those that first surveyed the land thought it larger than it was, and that it would have held out to give every tribe in proportion as large a share as they had carved out for Judah; but, upon a more strict enquiry, it was found that it would not reach (*v.* 9): *The part of the children of Judah was too much for them,* more than they needed, and more, as it proved, than fell to their share. Yet God did not by the lot lessen it, but left it to their prudence and care afterwards to discover and rectify the mistake, which when they did, 1. The men of Judah did not oppose the taking away of the cities again, which by the first distribution fell within their border, when they were convinced that they had more than their proportion. In all such cases errors must be excepted and a review admitted if there be occasion. Though, in strictness, what fell to their lot was their right against all the world, yet they would not insist upon it when it appeared that another tribe would want what they had to spare. Note, We must look on the things of others, and not on our own only. The abundance of some must supply the wants of others, that there may be somewhat of an equality, for which there may be equity where there is not law. 2. That which was thus taken off from Judah to be put into a new lot Providence directed to the tribe of Simeon, that Jacob's prophecy concerning this tribe might be fulfilled, *I will divide them in Jacob.* The cities of Simeon were scattered in Judah, with which tribe they were surrounded, except on that side towards the sea. This brought them into a confederacy with the tribe of Judah (Jdg. 1:3), and afterwards was a happy occasion of the adherence of many of this tribe to the house of David, at the time of the revolt of the ten tribes to Jeroboam. 2 Chr. 15:9, *out of Simeon they fell to* Asa *in abundance.* It is good being in a good neighbourhood.

II. The cities within their lot are here named. Beersheba, or Sheba, for these names seem to refer to the same place, is put first. Ziklag, which we read of in David's story, is one of them. What course they took to enlarge their borders and make room for themselves we find 1 Chr. 4:39, etc.

Verses 10–16

This is the lot of Zebulun, who, though born of Leah after Issachar, yet was blessed by Jacob and Moses before him; and therefore it was so ordered that his lot was drawn before that of Issachar, north of which it lay and south of Asher. 1. The lot of this tribe was washed by the great sea on the west, and by the sea of Tiberias on the east, answering Jacob's prophecy (Gen. 49:13), *Zebulun shall be a haven of ships,* trading ships on the great sea and fishing ships on the sea of Galilee. 2. Though there were some places in this tribe which were made famous in the Old Testament, especially *Mount Carmel,* on which the famous trial was between God and Baal in Elijah's time, yet it was made much more illustrious in the New Testament; for within the lot of this tribe was Nazareth, where our blessed Saviour spent so much of his time on earth, and from which he was called *Jesus of Nazareth,* and *Mount Tabor* on which he was transfigured, and that coast of the sea of Galilee on which Christ preached so many sermons and wrought so many miracles.

Verses 17–23

The lot of Issachar ran from Jordan in the east to the great sea in the west, Manasseh on the south, and Zebulun on the north. A numerous tribe, Num. 26:25. Tola, one of the judges, was of this tribe, Jdg. 10:1. So was Baasha, one of the kings of Israel, 1 Ki. 15:27. The most considerable places in this tribe were, 1. Jezreel, in which was Ahab's palace, and near it Naboth's vineyard. 2. Shunem, where lived that good Shunamite that entertained Elisha. 3. The river Kishon, on the banks of which, in this tribe, Sisera was beaten by Deborah and Barak. 4. The mountains of Gilboa, on which Saul and Jonathan were slain, which were not far from Endor, where Saul consulted the witch. 5. The valley of Megiddo, where Josiah was slain near Hadad-rimmon, 2 Ki. 23:29; Zec. 12:11.

Verses 24–31

The lot of Asher lay upon the coast of the great sea. We read not of any famous person of this tribe but Anna the prophetess, who was a constant resident in the temple at the time of our Saviour's birth, Lu. 2:36. Nor were there many famous places in this tribe. Aphek (mentioned *v.* 30) was the place near which Benhadad was beaten by Ahad, 1 Ki. 20:30. But close adjoining to this tribe were the celebrated sea-port towns of Tyre and Sidon, which we read so much of. Tyre is called here *that strong city* (*v.* 29), but Bishop Patrick thinks it was not the same Tyre that we read of afterwards, for that was built on an island; this old strong city was on the continent. And it is conjectured by some that into these two strong-holds, Sidon and Tzor, or Tyre, many of the people of Canaan fled and took shelter when Joshua invaded them.

Verses 32–39

Naphtali lay furthest north of all the tribes, bordering on Mount Libanus. The city of Leshem, or Liash, lay on the utmost edge of it to the north, and therefore when the Danites had made themselves masters of it, and called it *Dan,* the length of Canaan from north to south was reckoned from Dan to Beersheba. It had Zebulun on the south, Asher on the west, and Judah upon Jordan, probably a city of that name, and so distinguished from the tribe of Judah on the east. It was in the lot of this tribe, near the waters of Merom, that Joshua fought and routed Jabin, *ch.* 11:1. etc. In this tribe stood Capernaum and Bethsaida, on the north end of the sea of Tiberias, in which Christ did so many mighty works; and the mountain (as is supposed) on which Christ preached, Mt. 5:1.

Verses 40–48

Dan, though commander of one of the four squadrons of the camp of Israel, in the wilderness, that which brought up the rear, yet was last provided for in Canaan, and his lot fell in the southern part of Canaan, between Judah on the east and the land of the Philistines on the west, Ephraim on the north and Simeon on the south. Providence ordered this numerous and powerful tribe into a post of danger, as best able to deal with those vexatious neighbours the Philistines, and so it was found in Samson. Here is an account, 1. Of what fell to this tribe by lot, Zorah, and Eshtaol, and the camp of Dan thereabouts, of which we read in the story of Samson. And near there was the valley of Eshcol, whence the spies brought the famous bunch of grapes. Japho, or Joppa was in this lot. 2. Of what they got by their own industry and valour, which is mentioned here (*v.* 47), but related at large, Jdg. 18:7, etc.

Verses 49–51

Before this account of the dividing of the land is solemnly closed up, in the last verse, which intimates that the thing was done to the satisfaction of all, here is an account of the particular inheritance assigned to Joshua. 1. He was last served, though the eldest and greatest man of all Israel, and who, having commanded in the conquest of Canaan, might have demanded the first settlement in it for himself and his family. But he would make it to appear that in all he did he sought the good of his country, and not any private interest of his own. He was content to be unfixed till he saw them all settled; and herein is a great example to all in public places to prefer the common welfare before their particular satisfaction. Let the public be first served. 2. He had his lot *according to the word of the Lord.* It is probable that, when God by Moses told Caleb what inheritance he should have (*ch.* 14:9), he gave the like promise to Joshua, which he had an eye to in making his election: this made his portion doubly pleasant, that he had it, not as the rest by common providence, but by special promise. 3. He chose it in Mount Ephraim, which belonged to his own tribe, with which he thereby put himself in common, when he might by prerogative have chosen his inheritance in some other tribe, as suppose that of Judah, and thereby have distinguished himself from them. Let no man's preferment or honour make him ashamed of his family or country, or estrange him from it. The tabernacle was set up in the lot of Ephraim, and Joshua would forecast not to be far from that. 4. The *children of Israel* are said to *give it to him* (*v.* 49), which bespeaks his humility, that he would not take it to himself without the people's consent and approbation, as if he would thereby own himself, though *major singulis — greater than any one,* yet *minor universis — less than the whole assemblage,* and would hold even the estate of his family, under God, by the grant of the people. 5. It was a city that must be built before it was fit to be dwelt in. While others dwelt in houses which they built not, Joshua must erect for himself (that he might be a pattern of industry and contentment with mean things) such buildings as he could hastily run up, without curiosity or magnificence. Our Lord Jesus thus came and dwelt among us, not in pomp but poverty, providing rest for us, yet himself not having where to lay his head. *Even Christ pleased not himself.*

CHAPTER 20

This short chapter is concerning the cities of refuge, which we often read of in the writings of Moses, but this is the last time that we find mention of them, for now that matter was thoroughly settled. Here is, I. The law God gave concerning them (*v.* 1–6). II. The people's designation of the particular cities for that use (*v.* 7–9). And this remedial law was a figure of good things to come.

Verses 1–6

Many things were by the law of Moses ordered to be done when they came to Canaan and this among the rest, the appointing of sanctuaries for the protecting of those that were guilty of casual murder, which was a privilege to all Israel, since no man could be sure but some time or other it might be his own case; and it was for the interest of the land that the blood of an innocent person, whose hand only was guilty but not his heart, should not be shed, no, not by the avenger of blood: of this law, which was so much for their advantage, God here reminds them, that they might remind themselves of the other laws he had given them, which concerned his honour. 1. Orders are given for the appointing of these cities (*v.* 2), and very seasonably at this time when the land was newly surveyed, and so they were the better able to divide the coasts of it into three parts, as God had directed them, in order to the more convenient situation of these cities of refuge, Deu. 19:3. Yet it is probable that it was not done till after the Levites had their portion assigned them in the next chapter, because the cities of refuge were all to be Levites' cities. As soon as ever God had given them cities of rest, he bade them appoint cities of refuge, to which none of them knew but they might be glad to escape. Thus God provided, not only for their ease at all times, but for their safety in times of danger, and such times we must expect and prepare for in this world. And it intimates what God's spiritual Israel have and shall have, in Christ and heaven, not only rest to repose themselves in, but refuge to secure themselves in. And we cannot think these cities of refuge would have been so often and so much spoken of in the law of Moses, and have had so much care taken about them (when the intention of them might have been effectually answered, as it is in our law, by authorizing the courts of judgment to protect and acquit the manslayer in all those cases wherein he was to have privilege of sanctuary), if they were not designed to typify the relief which the gospel provides for poor penitent sinners, and their protection from the curse of the law and the wrath of God, in our Lord Jesus, to whom believers flee for refuge (Heb. 6:18), and in whom they are found (Phil. 3:9) as in a sanctuary, where they are privileged from arrests, and *there is now no condemnation to them,* Rom. 8:1. 2. Instructions are given for the using of these cities. The laws in this matter we had before, Num. 35:10, etc., where they were opened at large. (1.) It is supposed that a man might possibly kill a person, it might be his own child or dearest friend, unawares and unwittingly (*v.* 3), not only whom he hated not, but whom he truly loved beforetime (*v.* 5); for *the way of man is not in himself.* What reason have we to thank God who has kept us both from slaying and from being slain by accident! In this case, it is supposed that the relations of the person slain would demand the life of the slayer, as a satisfaction to that ancient law that *whoso sheds man's blood, by man shall his blood be shed.* (2.) It is provided that if upon trial it appeared that the murder was done purely by accident, and not by design, either upon an old grudge or a sudden passion, then the slayer should be sheltered from the avenger of blood in any one of these cities, *v.* 4–6. By this law he was entitled to a dwelling in that city, was taken into the care of the government of it, but was confined to it, as prisoner at large; only, if he survived the high priest, then, and not till then, he might return to his own city. And the Jews say, "If he died before the high priest in the city of his refuge and exile, and was buried there, yet, at the death of the high priest, his bones should be removed with respect to the place of his fathers' sepulchres."

Verses 7–9

We have here the nomination of the cities of refuge in the land of Canaan, which was made by the advice and authority of Joshua and the princes (*v.* 7); and upon occasion of the mention of this is repeated the nomination of the other three in the lot of the other two tribes and a half, which was made by Moses (Deu. 4:43), but (as bishop Patrick thinks) they had not the privilege till now. 1. They are said to *sanctify* these cities, that is the original word for *appointed, v.* 7. Not that any ceremony was used to signify the consecration of them, only they did by a public act of court solemnly declare them cities of refuge, and as such sacred to the honour of God, as the protector of exposed innocency. If they were sanctuaries, it was proper to say they were *sanctified.* Christ, our refuge, was sanctified by his Father; nay, for our sakes he sanctified himself, Jn. 17:19. 2. These cities (as those also on the other side Jordan) stood in the three several parts of the country, so conveniently that a man might (they say) in half a day reach some one of them from any corner of the country. Kedesh was in Naphtali, the most northern tribe, Hebron in Judah, the most southern, and Shechem in Ephraim, which lay in the middle, about equally distant from the other two. God is a refuge at hand. 3. They were all Levites' cities, which put an honour upon God's tribe, making them judges in those cases wherein divine Providence was so nearly concerned, and protectors to oppressed innocency. It was also a kindness to the poor refugee, that when he might not go up to the house of the Lord, nor tread his courts, yet he had the servants of God's house with him, to instruct him, and pray for him, and help to make up the want of public ordinances. If he must be confined, it shall be to a Levite-city, where he may, if he will, improve his time. 4. These cities were upon hills to be seen afar off, for a city on a hill cannot be hid; and this would both direct and encourage the poor distressed man that was making that way; and, though therefore his way at last was up-hill, yet this would comfort him, that he would be in his place of safety quickly, and if he could but get into the suburbs of the city he was well enough off. 5. Some observe a significancy in the names of these cities with application to Christ our refuge. I delight not in quibbling upon names, yet am willing to take notice of these. *Kedesh* signifies *holy,* and our refuge is the holy Jesus. *Shechem, a shoulder,* and the government is upon his shoulder. *Hebron, fellowship,* and believers are called into the fellowship of Christ Jesus our Lord. *Bezer, a fortification,* for he is a strong-hold to all those that trust in him. *Ramoth, high* or *exalted,* for him hath God exalted with his own right hand. *Golan, joy* or *exultation,* for in him all the saints are justified, and shall glory. *Lastly,* Besides all these, the horns of the altar, wherever it was, were a refuge to those who took hold of them, if the crime were such as that sanctuary allowed. This is implied in that law (Ex. 21:14), that a wilful murderer shall be taken from God's altar to be put to death. And we find the altar used for this purpose. 1 Ki. 1:50; 2:28. Christ is our altar, who not only *sanctifies the gift,* but protects the giver.

CHAPTER 21

It had been often said that the tribe of Levi should have "no inheritance with their brethren," no particular part of the country assigned them, as the other tribes had, no, not the country about Shiloh, which one might have expected to be appropriated to them as the lands of the church; but, though they were not thus cast into a country by themselves, it appears, by the provision made for them in this chapter, that they were no losers, but the rest of the tribes were very much gainers, by their being dispersed. We have here, I. The motion they made to have their cities assigned them, according to God's appointment (*v.* 1, 2). II. The nomination of the cities accordingly out of the several tribes, and the distribution of them to the respective families of this tribe (*v.* 3–8). III. A catalogue of the cities, forty-eight in all (*v.* 9–42). IV. A receipt entered in full of all that God had promised to his people Israel (*v.* 43–45).

Verses 1–8

Here is, I. The Levites' petition presented to this general convention of the states, now sitting at Shiloh, *v.* 1, 2. Observe, 1. They had not their lot assigned them till they made their claim. There is an inheritance provided for all the saints, that royal priesthood, but then they must petition for it. *Ask, and it shall be given you.* Joshua had quickened the rest of the tribes who were slack to put in their claims, but the Levites, it may be supposed, knew their duty and interest better than the rest, and were therefore forward in this matter, when it came to their turn, without being called upon. They build their claim upon a very good foundation, not their own merits nor services, but the divine precept: *"The Lord commanded by the hand of Moses to give us cities,* commanded you to grant them, which implied a command to us to ask them." Note, The maintenance of ministers is not an arbitrary thing, left purely to the good-will of the people, who may let them starve if they please; no, as the God of Israel commanded that the Levites should be well provided for, so has the Lord Jesus, the King of the Christian church, ordained, and a perpetual ordinance it is that *those who preach the gospel should live of the gospel* (1 Co. 9:14), and should live comfortably. 2. They did not make their claim till all the rest of the tribes were provided for, and then they did it immediately. There was some reason for it; every tribe must first know their own, else they would not know what they gave the Levites, and so it could not be such a reasonable service as it ought to be. But it is also an instance of their humility, modesty, and patience (and Levites should be examples of these and other virtues), that they were willing to be served last, and they fared never the worse for it. Let not God's ministers complain if at any time they find themselves postponed in men's thoughts and cares, but let them make sure of the favour of God and the honour that comes from him, and then they may well enough afford to bear the slights and neglects of men.

II. The Levites' petition granted immediately, without any dispute, the princes of Israel being perhaps ashamed that they needed to be called upon in this matter, and that the motion had not been made among themselves for the settling of the Levites. 1. The children of Israel are said to give the cities for the Levites. God had appointed how many they should be in all, forty-eight. It is probable that Joshua and the princes, upon consideration of the extent and value of the lot of each tribe as it was laid before them, had appointed how many cities should be taken out of each; and then the fathers of the several tribes themselves agreed which they should be, and therefore are said to give them, as an offering, to the Lord; so God had appointed. Num. 35:8, *Every one shall give of his cities to the Levites.* Here God tried their generosity, and it was found to praise and honour, for it appears by the following catalogue that the cities they gave to the Levites were generally some of the best and most considerable in each tribe. And it is probable that they had an eye to the situation of them, taking care they should be so dispersed as that no part of the country should be too far distant from a Levites' city. 2. They gave them *at the commandment of the Lord,* that is, with an eye to the command and in obedience to it, which was it that sanctified the grant. They gave the number that God commanded, and it was well this matter was settled that the Levites might not ask more nor the Israelites offer less. They gave them also with their suburbs, or glebe-lands, belonging to them, so many cubits by measure from the walls of the city, as God had commanded (Num. 35:4, 5), and did not go about to cut them short. 3. When the forty-eight cities were pitched upon, they were divided into four lots, as they lay next together, and then by lot were determined to the four several families of the tribe of Levi. When the Israelites had surrendered the cities into the hand of God, he would himself have the distributing of them among his servants. (1.) The family of Aaron, who were the only priests, had for their share the thirteen cities that were given by the tribes of Judah, Simeon, and Benjamin, *v.* 4. God in wisdom ordered it thus, that though Jerusalem itself was not one of their cities, it being as yet in the possession of the Jebusites (and those generous tribes would not mock the Levites, who had another warfare to mind, with a city that must be recovered by the sword before it could be enjoyed), yet the cities that fell to their lot were those which lay next to Jerusalem, because that was to be, in process of time, the holy city, where their business would chiefly lie. (2.) The Kohathite-Levites (among whom were the posterity of Moses, though never distinguished from them) had the cities that lay in the lot of Dan, which lay next to Judah, and in that of Ephraim, and the half-tribe of Manasseh, which lay next to Benjamin. So those who descended from Aaron's father joined nearest to Aaron's sons. (3.) Gershon was the eldest son of Levi, and therefore, though the younger house of the Kohathites was preferred before his, yet his children had the precedency of the other family of Merari, *v.* 6. (4.) The Merarites, the youngest house, had their lot last, and it lay furthest off, *v.* 7. The rest of the sons of Jacob had a lot for every tribe only, but Levi, God's tribe, had a lot for each of its families; for there is a particular providence directing and attending the removals and settlements of ministers, and appointing where those shall fix who are to be the lights of the world.

Verses 9–42

We have here a particular account of the cities which were given to the children of Levi out of the several tribes, not only to be occupied and inhabited by them, as tenants to the several tribes in which they lay — no, their interest in them was not dependent and precarious, but to be owned and possessed by them as lords and proprietors, and as having the same title to them that the rest of the tribes had to their cities or lands, as appears by the law which preserved the house in the Levites' cities from being alienated any longer than till the year of jubilee, Lev. 25:32, 33. Yet it is probable that the Levites having only the cities and suburbs, while the land about pertained to the tribes in which they lay, those of that tribe, for the convenience of occupying that land, might commonly rent houses of the Levites, as they could spare them in their cities, and so live among them as their tenants. Several things may be observed in this account, besides what was observed in the law concerning it, Num. 35.

I. That the Levites were dispersed into all the tribes, and not suffered to live all together in any one part of the country. This would find them all with work, and employ them all for the good of others; for ministers, of all people, must neither be idle nor live to themselves or to one another only. Christ left his twelve disciples together in a body, but left orders that they should in due time disperse themselves, that they might *preach the gospel to every creature.* The mixing of the Levites thus with the other tribes would be an obligation upon them to walk circumspectly, and as became their sacred function, and to avoid every thing that might disgrace it. Had they lived all together, they would have been tempted to wink at one another's faults, and to excuse one another when they did amiss; but by this means they were made to see the eyes of all Israel upon them, and therefore saw it their concern to walk so as that their ministry might in nothing be blamed nor their high character suffer by their ill carriage.

II. That every tribe of Israel was adorned and enriched with its share of Levites' cities in proportion to its compass, even those that lay most remote. They were all God's people, and therefore they all had Levites among them. 1. To show kindness to, as God appointed them, Deu. 12:19; 14:29. They were God's receivers, to whom the people might give their grateful acknowledgments of God's goodness, as the occasion and disposition were. 2. To receive advice and instruction from; when they could not go up to the tabernacle, to consult those who attended there, they might go to a Levites' city, and be taught the good knowledge of the Lord. Thus God set up a candle in every room of his house, to give light to all his family; as those that attended the altar *kept the charge of the Lord,* to see that no divine appointment was neglected there, so those that were scattered in the country had their charge too, which was to see that no idolatrous superstitious usages were introduced at a distance and to watch for the souls of God's Israel. Thus did God graciously provide for the keeping up of religion among them, and that they might have the word nigh them; yet, blessed be God, we, under the gospel, have it yet nigher, not only Levites in every county, but Levites in every parish, whose office it is still to teach the people knowledge, and to go before them in the things of God.

III. That there were thirteen cities, and those some of the best, appointed for the priests, the sons of Aaron, *v.* 19. Aaron left but two sons, Eleazar and Ithamar, yet his family was now so much increased, and it was foreseen that it would in process of time grow so numerous, as to replenish all these cities, though a considerable number must of necessity be resident wherever the ark and the altar were. We read in both Testaments of such numbers of priests that we may suppose none of all the families of Israel that came out of Egypt increased afterwards so much as that of Aaron did; and the promise afterwards to the house of Aaron is, *God shall increase you more and more, you and your children,* Ps. 115:12, 14. He will raise up a *seed to serve him.*

IV. That some of the Levites' cities were afterwards famous upon other accounts. Hebron was the city in which David began his reign, and in Manhanaim, another Levites' city (*v.* 38), he lay, and had his headquarters when he fled from Absalom. The first Israelite that ever wore the title of king (namely, Abimelech, the son of Gideon) reigned in Shechem, another Levites' city, *v.* 21.

V. That the number of them in all was more than of most of the tribes, except Judah, though the tribe of Levi was one of the least of the tribes, to show how liberal God is, and his people should be, to his ministers; yet the disproportion will not appear so great as at first it seems, if we consider that the Levites had cities only with their suburbs to dwell in, but the rest of the tribes, besides their cities (and those perhaps were many more than are named in the account of their lot), had many unwalled towns and villages which they inhabited, besides country houses.

Upon the whole, it appears that effectual care was taken that the Levites should live both comfortably and usefully: and those, whether ministers or others, for whom Providence has done well, must look upon themselves as obliged thereby to do good, and, according as their capacity and opportunity are, to serve their generation.

Verses 43–45

We have here the conclusion of this whole matter, the foregoing history summed up, and, to make it appear the more bright, compared with the promise of which it was the full accomplishment. God's word and his works mutually illustrate each other. The performance makes the promise appear very true and the promise makes the performance appear very kind.

I. God had promised to give the seed of Abraham the land of Canaan for a possession, and now at last he performed this promise (*v.* 43): *They possessed it, and dwelt therein.* Though they had often forfeited the benefit of that promise, and God had long delayed the performance of it, yet at last all difficulties were conquered, and Canaan was their own. And the promise of the heavenly Canaan is as sure to all God's spiritual Israel, for it is the promise of him that cannot lie.

II. God had promised to give them rest in that land, and now they had rest round about, rest from the fatigues of their travel through the wilderness (which tedious march, perhaps, was long in their bones), rest from their wars in Canaan, and the insults which their enemies there had at first offered them. They now dwelt, not only in habitations of their own, but those quiet and peaceable ones; though there were Canaanites that remained, yet none that had either strength or spirit to attack them, nor so much as give them an alarm. This rest continued till they by their own sin and folly put thorns into their own beds and their own eyes.

III. God had promised to give them victory and success in their wars, and this promise likewise was fulfilled: *There stood not a man before them, v.* 44. They had the better in every battle, and which way soever they turned their forces they prospered. It is true there were Canaanites now remaining in many parts of the land, and such as afterwards made head against them, and became very formidable. But, 1. As to the present remains of the Canaanites, they were no contradiction to the promise, for God had said he would not drive them out all at once, but by *little and little,* Ex. 23:30. They had now as much in their full possession as they had occasion for and as they had hands to manage, so that the Canaanites only kept possession of some of the less cultivated parts of the country against the beasts of the field, till Israel, in process of time, should become numerous enough to replenish them. 2. As to the after prevalency of the Canaanites, that was purely the effect of Israel's cowardice and slothfulness, and the punishment of their sinful inclination to the idolatries and other abominations of the heathen, whom the Lord would have cast out before them but that they harboured and indulged them. So that the foundation of God stands sure. Israel's experience of God's fidelity is here upon record, and is an acquittance under their hands to the honour of God, the vindication of his promise which had been so often distrusted, and the encouragement of all believers to the end of the world: *There failed not any good thing,* no, nor *aught* of any good thing (so full is it expressed), *which the Lord had spoken unto the house of Israel,* but in due time *all came to pass, v.* 45. Such an acknowledgment as this, here subscribed by Joshua in the name of all Israel, we afterwards find made by Solomon, and all Israel did in effect say *Amen* to it, 1 Ki. 8:56. The inviolable truth of God's promise, and the performance of it to the utmost, are what all the saints have been ready to bear their testimony to; and, if in any thing the performance has seemed to come short, they have been as ready to own that they themselves must bear all the blame.

CHAPTER 22

Many particular things we have read concerning the two tribes and a half, though nothing separated them from the rest of the tribes except the river Jordan, and this chapter is wholly concerning them. I. Joshua's dismission of the militia of those tribes from the camp of Israel, in which the had served as auxiliaries, during all the wars of Canaan, and their return thereupon to their own country (*v.* 1–9). II. The altar they built on the borders of Jordan, in token of their communion with the land of Israel (*v.* 10). III. The offence which the rest of the tribes took at this altar, and the message they sent thereupon (*v.* 11–20). IV. The apology which the two tribes and a half made for what they had done (*v.* 21–29). V. The satisfaction which their apology gave to the rest of the tribes (*v.* 30–34). And (which is strange), whereas in most differences that happen there is a fault on both sides, on this there was fault on no side; none (for aught that appears) were to be blamed, but all to be praised.

Verses 1–9

The war being ended, and ended gloriously, Joshua, as a prudent general, disbands his army, who never designed to make war their trade, and sends them home, to enjoy what they had conquered, and to beat their swords into plough-shares and their spears into pruning-hooks; and particularly the forces of these separate tribes, who had received their inheritance on the other side Jordan from Moses upon this condition, that their men of war should assist the other tribes in the conquest of Canaan, which they promised to do (Num. 32:32), and renewed the promise to Joshua at the opening of the campaign, Jos. 1:16. And, now that they had performed their bargain, Joshua publicly and solemnly in Shiloh gives them their discharge. Whether this was done, as it was placed, not till after the land was divided, as some think, or whether after the war was ended, and before the division was made, as others think (because there was no need of their assistance in dividing the land, but only in conquering it, nor were there any of their tribes employed as commissioners in that affair, but only of the other ten, Num. 34:18, etc.), this is certain, it was not done till after Shiloh was made the head-quarters (*v.* 2), and the land was begun to be divided before they removed from Gilgal, *ch.* 14:6.

It is probable that this army of Reubenites and Gadites, which had led the van in all the wars of Canaan, had sometimes, in the intervals of action, and when the rest of the army retired into winter-quarters, some of them at least, made a step over Jordan, for it was not far, to visit their families, and to look after their private affairs, and perhaps tarried at home, and sent others in their room more serviceable; but still these two tribes and a half had their quota of troops ready, 40,000 in all, which, whenever there was occasion, presented themselves at their respective posts, and now attended in a body to receive their discharge. Though their affection to their families, and concern for their affairs, could not but make them, after so long an absence, very desirous to return, yet, like good soldiers, they would not move till they had orders from their general. So, though our heavenly Father's house above be ever so desirable (it is bishop Hall's allusion), yet must we stay on earth till our warfare be accomplished, wait for a due discharge, and not anticipate the time of our removal.

I. Joshua dismisses them to the *land of their possession, v.* 4. Those that were first in the assignment of their lot were last in the enjoyment of it; they got the start of their brethren in title, but their brethren were before them in full possession; so *the last shall be first, and the first last,* that there may be something of equality.

II. He dismisses them with their pay; for who goes a warfare at his own charge? *Return with much riches unto your tents, v.* 8. Though all the land they had helped to conquer was to go to the other tribes, yet they should have their share of the plunder, and had so, and this was all the pay that any of the soldiers expected; for the wars of Canaan bore their own charges. "Go," says Joshua, "go home to your tents," that is, "your houses," which he calls *tents,* because they had been so much used to tents in the wilderness; and indeed the strongest and stateliest houses in this world are to be looked upon but as tents, mean and movable in comparison with our house above. "Go home *with much riches,* not only cattle, the spoil of the country, but silver and gold, the plunder of the cities, and," 1. "Let your brethren whom you leave behind have your good word, who have allowed you your share in full, though the land is entirely theirs, and have not offered to make any drawback. Do not say that you are losers by us." 2. "Let your brethren whom you go to, who abode by the stuff, have some share of the spoil: *Divide the spoil with your brethren,* as that was divided which was taken in the war with Midian, Num. 31:27. Let your brethren that have wanted you all this while be the better for you when you come home."

III. He dismisses them with a very honourable character. Though their service was a due debt, and the performance of a promise, and they had done no more than was their duty to do, yet he highly commends them; not only gives them up their bonds, as it were, now that they had fulfilled the condition, but applauds their good services. Though it was by the favour of God and his power that Israel got possession of this land, and he must have all the glory, yet Joshua thought there was a thankful acknowledgment due to their brethren who assisted them, and whose sword and bow were employed for them. God must be chiefly eyed in our praises, yet instruments must not be altogether overlooked. He here commends them, 1. For the readiness of their obedience to their commanders, *v.* 2. When Moses was gone, they remembered and observed the charge he had given them; and all the orders which Joshua, as general of the forces, had issued out, they had carefully obeyed, went, and came, and did, as he appointed, Mt. 8:9. It is as much as any thing the soldier's praise to observe the word of command. 2. For the constancy of their affection and adherence to their brethren: *You have not left them these many days.* How many days he does not say, nor can we gather it with certainty from any other place. Calvisius and others of the best chronologers compute that the conquering and dividing of the land was the work of about six or seven years, and so long these separate tribes attended their camp, and did them the best service they could. Note, It will be the honour of those that have espoused the cause of God's Israel, and twisted interests with them, to adhere to them, and never to leave them till God has given them rest, and then they shall rest with them. 3. For the faithfulness of their obedience to the divine law. They had not only done their duty to Joshua and Israel, but, which was best of all, they had made conscience of their duty to God: *You have kept the charge,* or, as the word is, *You have kept the keeping,* that is, "You have carefully and circumspectly kept the *commandment of the Lord your God,* not only in this particular instance of continuing in the service of Israel to the end of the war, but, in general, you have kept up religion in your part of the camp, a rare and excellent thing among soldiers, and where it is worthy to be praised."

IV. He dismisses them with good counsel, not to cultivate their ground, fortify their cities, and, now that their hands were inured to war and victory, to invade their neighbours, and so enlarge their own territories, but to keep up serious godliness among them in the power of it. They were not political but pious instructions that he gave them, *v.* 5. 1. In general, to *take diligent heed to do the commandment and the law.* Those that have the commandment have it in vain unless they *do* the commandment; and it will not be done aright (so apt are we to turn aside, and so industrious are our spiritual enemies to turn us aside) unless we take heed, diligent heed. 2. In particular, to *love the Lord our God,* as the best of beings, and the best of friends; and as far as this principle rules in the heart, and is the spring of its pulses, there will be a constant care and sincere endeavour to *walk in his ways,* in all his ways, even those that are narrow and up-hill, in every particular instance, in all manner of conversation to *keep his commandments,* at all times and in all conditions with purpose of heart to *cleave unto him,* and to serve him and his honour, and the interest of his kingdom among men, *with all our heart and with all our soul.* What good counsel was here given to them is given to us all. God give us grace to take it!

V. He dismisses them with a blessing (*v.* 6), particularly the half tribe of Manasseh, to which Joshua, as an Ephraimite, was somewhat nearer akin than to the other two, and who perhaps were the more loth to depart because they left one half of their own tribe behind them, and therefore, bidding often farewell, and lingering behind, had a second dismission and blessing, *v.* 7. Joshua not only prayed for them as a friend, but blessed them as a father in the name of the Lord, recommending them, their families, and affairs, to the grace of God. Some by the blessing Joshua gave them understand the presents he made them, in recompence of their services; but Joshua being a prophet, and having given them one part of a prophet's reward in the instructions he gave them (*v.* 5), no doubt we must understand this of the other, even the prayers he made for them, as one having authority, and as God's vicegerent.

VI. Being thus dismissed, they returned to *the land of their possession* in a body (*v.* 9), ferry-boats being, it is likely, provided for their repassing Jordan. Though masters of families may sometimes have occasion to be absent, long absent, from their families, yet, when their business abroad is finished, they must remember home is their place, from which they ought not to wander as a bird from her nest.

Verses 10–20

Here is, I. The pious care of the separated tribes to keep their hold of Canaan's religion, even when they were leaving Canaan's land, that they might not be as the *sons of the stranger, utterly separated from God's people,* Isa. 56:3. In order to this, they built a great altar on the borders of Jordan, to be a witness for them that they were Israelites, and as such *partakers of the altar of* the Lord, 1 Co. 10:18. When they came to Jordan (*v.* 10) they did not consult how to preserve the remembrance of their own exploits in the wars of Canaan, and the services they had done their brethren, by erecting a monument to the immortal honour of the two tribes and a half; but their relation to the church of God, together with their interest in the communion of saints, is that which they are solicitous to preserve and perpetuate the proofs and evidences of; and therefore without delay, when the thing was first proposed by some among them, who, though glad to think that they were going towards home, were sorry to think that they were going from the altar of God, immediately they erected this altar, which served as a bridge to keep up their fellowship with the other tribes in the things of God. Some think they built this altar on the Canaan-side of Jordan, in the lot of Benjamin, that, looking over the river, they might see the figure of the altar at Shiloh, when they could not conveniently go to it; but it is more likely that they built it on their own side of the water, for what had they to do to build on another man's land without his consent? And it is said to be *over-against* the land of Canaan; nor would there have been any cause of suspecting it designed for sacrifice if they had not built it among themselves. This altar was very innocently and honestly designed, but it would have been well if, since it had in it an appearance of evil, and might be an occasion of offence to their brethren, they had consulted the oracle of God about it before they did it, or at least acquainted their brethren with their purpose, and given them the same explication of their altar before, to prevent their jealousy, which they did afterwards, to remove it. Their zeal was commendable, but it ought to have been guided with discretion. There was no need to hasten the building of an altar for the purpose for which they intended this, but they might have taken time to consider and take advice; yet, when their sincerity was made to appear, we do not find that they were blamed for their rashness. God does, and men should, overlook the weakness of an honest zeal.

II. The holy jealousy of the other tribes for the honour of God and his altar at Shiloh. Notice was immediately brought to the princes of Israel of the setting up of this altar, *v.* 11. And they, knowing how strict and severe that law was which required them to offer all their sacrifices in the place which God should choose, and not elsewhere (Deu. 12:5–7), were soon apprehensive that the setting up of another altar was an affront to the choice which God had lately made of a place to put his name in, and had a direct tendency to the worship of some other God. Now,

1. Their suspicion was very excusable, for it must be confessed the thing, *prima facie — at first sight,* looked ill, and seemed to imply a design to set up and maintain a competitor with the altar at Shiloh. It was no strained *innuendo* from the building of an altar to infer an intention to offer sacrifice upon it, and that might introduce idolatry and end in a total apostasy from the faith and worship of the God of Israel. So great a matter might this fire kindle. God is jealous for his own institutions, and therefore we should be so too, and afraid of every thing that looks like, or leads to, idolatry.

2. Their zeal, upon this suspicion, was very commendable, *v.* 12. When they apprehended that these tribes, which by the river Jordan were separated from them, were separating themselves from God, they took it as the greatest injury that could be done to themselves, and showed a readiness, if it were necessary, to put their lives in their hands in defence of the altar of God, and to take up arms for the chastising and reducing of these rebels, and to prevent the spreading of the infection, if no gentler methods would serve, by cutting off from their body the gangrened member. They all gathered together, and Shiloh was the place of their rendezvous, because it was in defence of the divine charter lately granted to that place that they now appeared; their resolution was as became a kingdom of priests, who, being devoted to God and his service, did not

acknowledge their brethren nor know their own children, Deu. 33:9. They would immediately go up to war against them if it appeared they had revolted from God, and were in rebellion against him. Though they were bone of their bone, had been companions with them in tribulation in the wilderness, and serviceable to them in the wars of Canaan, yet, if they turn to serve other gods, they will treat them as enemies, not as sons of Israel, but as children of whoredoms, for so God had appointed, Deu. 13:12, etc. They had but lately sheathed their swords, and retired from the perils and fatigues of war to the rest God had given them, and yet they are willing to begin a new war rather than be any way wanting in their duty to restrain, repress, and revenge, idolatry, and every step towards it — a brave resolution, and which shows them hearty for their religion, and, we hope, careful and diligent in the practice of it themselves. Corruptions in religion are best dealt with at first, before they get head and plead prescription.

3. Their prudence in the prosecution of this zealous resolution is no less commendable. God had appointed them, in cases of this nature, to enquire and make search (Deu. 13:14), that they might not wrong their brethren under pretence of righting their religion; accordingly they resolve here not to send forth their armies, to wage war, till they had first sent their ambassadors to enquire into the merits of the cause, and these men of the first rank, one out of each tribe, and Phinehas at the head of them to be their spokesman, v. 13, 14. Thus was their zeal for God tempered, guided, and governed by the meekness of wisdom. He that knows all things, and hates all evil things, would not punish the worst of criminals but he would first go down and see, Gen. 18:21. Many an unhappy strife would be prevented, or soon healed by an impartial and favourable enquiry into that which is the matter of the offence. The rectifying of mistakes and misunderstandings, and the setting of misconstrued words and actions in a true light, would be the most effectual way to accommodate both private and public quarrels, and bring them to a happy period.

4. The ambassadors' management of this matter came fully up to the sense and spirit of the congregation concerning it, and bespeaks much both of zeal and prudence.

(1.) The charge they draw up against their brethren is indeed very high, and admits no other excuse than that it was in their zeal for the honour of God, and was now intended to justify the resentments of the congregation at Shiloh and to awaken the supposed delinquents to clear themselves, otherwise they might have suspended their judgment, or mollified it at least, and not have taken it for granted, as they do here (v. 16), that the building of this altar was a trespass against the God of Israel, and a trespass no less heinous than the revolt of soldiers from their captain (you turn from following the Lord), and the rebellion of subjects against their sovereign: that you might rebel this day against the Lord. Hard words. It is well they were not able to make good their charge. Let not innocency think it strange to be thus misrepresented and accused. They laid to my charge things that I knew not.

(2.) The aggravation of the crime charged upon their brethren is somewhat far-fetched: Is the iniquity of Peor too little for us? v. 17. Probably that is mentioned because Phinehas, the first commissioner in this treaty, had signalized himself in that matter (Num. 25:7), and because we may suppose they were not about the very place in which that iniquity was committed on the other side Jordan. It is good to recollect and improve those instances of the wrath of God, revealed from heaven against the ungodliness and unrighteousness of men, which have fallen out in our own time, and which we ourselves have been eye-witnesses of. He reminds them of the iniquity of Peor, [1.] As a very great sin, and very provoking to God. The building of this altar seemed but a small matter, but it might lead to an iniquity as bad as that of Peor, and therefore must be crushed in its first rise. Note, The remembrance of great sins committed formerly should engage us to stand upon our guard against the least occasions and beginnings of sin; for the way of sin is down-hill. [2.] As a sin that the whole congregation had smarted for: "There was a plague in the congregation of the Lord, of which, in one day, there died no fewer than 24,000; was not that enough for ever to warn you against idolatry? What! will you bring upon yourselves another plague? Are you so mad upon an idolatrous altar that you will run yourselves thus upon the sword's point

of God's judgments? Does not our camp still feel from that sin and the punishment of it? We are not cleansed from it unto this day; there are remaining sparks," First, "Of the infection of that sin; some among us so inclined to idolatry that if you set up another altar they will soon take occasion from that, whether you intend it or no, to worship another God." Secondly, "Of the wrath of God against us for that sin. We have reason to fear that, if we provoke God by another sin to visit, he will remember against us the iniquity of Peor, as he threatened to do that of the golden calf, Ex. 32:34. And dare you wake the sleeping lion of divine vengeance?" Note, It is a foolish and dangerous thing for people to think their former sins little, too little for them, as those do who add sin to sin, and so treasure up wrath against the day of wrath. Let therefore the time past suffice, 1 Pt. 4:3.

(3.) The reason they give for their concerning themselves so warmly in this matter is very sufficient. They were obliged to it, in their own necessary defence, by the law of self-preservation: "For, if you revolt from God to-day, who knows but to-morrow his judgments may break in upon the whole congregation (v. 18), as in the case of Achan? v. 20. He sinned, and we all smarted for it, by which we should receive instruction, and from what God did then infer what he may do, and fear what he will do, if we do not witness against your sin, who are so many, and punish it." Note, The conservators of the public peace are obliged, in justice to the common safety, to use their power for the restraining and suppressing of vice and profaneness, lest, if it be connived at, the sin thereby become national, and bring God's judgments upon the community. Nay, we are all concerned to reprove our neighbour when he does amiss, lest we bear sin for him, Lev. 19:17.

(4.) The offer they make is very fair and kind (v. 19), that if they thought the land of their possession unclean, for want of an altar, and therefore could not be easy without one, rather than they should set up another in competition with that at Shiloh they should be welcome to come back to the land where the Lord's tabernacle was, and settle there, and they would very willingly straiten themselves to make room for them. By this they showed a sincere and truly pious zeal against schism, that rather than their brethren should have any occasion to set up a separate altar, though their pretence for it, as here supposed, was very weak and grounded upon a great mistake, yet they were willing to part with a considerable share of the land which God himself had by the lot assigned them, to comprehend them and take them in among them. This was the spirit of Israelites indeed.

Verses 21–29

We may suppose there was a general convention called of the princes and great men of the separate tribes, to give audience to these ambassadors; or perhaps the army, as it came home, was still encamped in a body, and not yet dispersed; however it was, there were enough to represent the two tribes and a half, and to give their sense. Their reply to the warm remonstrance of the ten tribes is very fair and ingenuous. They do not retort their charge, upbraid them with the injustice and unkindness of their threatenings, nor reproach them for their rash and hasty censures, but give them a soft answer which turns away wrath, avoiding all those grievous words which stir up anger; they demur not to their jurisdiction, nor plead that they were not accountable to them for what they had done, nor bid them mind their own business, but, by a free and open declaration of their sincere intention in what they did, free themselves from the imputation they were under, and set themselves right in the opinion of their brethren, to do which they only needed to state the case and put the matter in a true light.

I. They solemnly protest against any design to use this altar for sacrifice or offering, and therefore were far from setting it up in competition with the altar at Shiloh, or from entertaining the least thought of deserting that. They had indeed set up that which had the shape and fashion of an altar, but they had not dedicated it to a religious use, had had no solemnity of its consecration, and therefore ought not to be charged with a design to put it to any such use. To gain credit to this protestation here is,

1. A solemn appeal to God concerning it, with which they begin their defence, intending thereby to give glory

to God first, and then to give satisfaction to their brethren, v. 22. (1.) A profound awe and reverence of God are expressed in the form of their appeal: The Lord God of gods, the Lord God of gods, he knows. Or, as it might be read somewhat closer to the original, The God of gods, Jehovah, the God of gods, Jehovah, he knows, which bespeaks his self-existence and self-sufficiency; he is Jehovah, and has sovereignty and supremacy over all beings and powers whatsoever, even those that are called gods, or that are worshipped. This brief confession of their faith would help to obviate and remove their brethren's suspicion of them, as if they intended to desert the God of Israel, and worship other gods: how could those entertain such a thought who believed him to be God over all? Let us learn hence always to speak of God with reverence and seriousness, and to mention his name with a solemn pause. Those who make their appeals to heaven with a slight, careless, "God knows," have reason to fear lest they take his name in vain, for it is very unlike this appeal. (2.) It is a great confidence of their own integrity which they express in the matter of their appeal. They refer the controversy to the God of gods, whose judgment, we are sure, is according to truth, such as the guilty have reason to dread and the upright to rejoice in. "If it be in rebellion or transgression that we have built this altar, to confront the altar of the Lord at Shiloh, to make a party, or to set up any new gods or worships," [1.] "He knows it (v. 22), for he is perfectly acquainted with the thoughts and intents of the heart, and particularly with all inclinations to idolatry (Ps. 44:20, 21); this is in a particular manner before him. We believe he knows it, and we cannot by any arts conceal it from him." [2.] "Let him require it, as we know he will, for he is a jealous God." Nothing but a clear conscience would have thus imprecated divine justice to avenge the rebellion if there had been any. Note, First, In every thing we do in religion, it highly concerns us to approve ourselves to God in our integrity therein, remembering that he knows the heart. Secondly, When we fall under the censures of men, it is very comfortable to be able with a humble confidence to appeal to God concerning our sincerity. See 1 Co. 4:3, 4.

2. A sober apology presented to their brethren: Israel, he shall know. Though the record on high, and the witness in our bosoms, are principally to be made sure for us, yet there is a satisfaction besides which we owe to our brethren who doubt concerning our integrity, and which we should be ready to give with meekness and fear. if our sincerity be known to God, we should study likewise to let others know it by its fruits, especially those who, though they mistake us, yet show a zeal for the glory of God, as the ten tribes here did.

3. A serious abjuration or renunciation of the design which they were suspected to be guilty of. With this they conclude their defence (v. 29): "God forbid that we should rebel against the Lord, as we own we should if we had set up this altar for burnt-offerings; no, we abhor the thought of it. We have as great a value and veneration for the altar of the Lord at Shiloh as any of the tribes of Israel have, and are as firmly resolved to adhere to it and constantly to attend it; we have the same concern that you have for the purity of God's worship and the unity of his church; far be it, far be it from us, to think of turning away from following God."

II. They fully explain their true intent and meaning in building this altar; and we have all the reason in the world to believe that it is a true representation of their design, and not advanced now to palliate it afterwards, as we have reason to think that these same persons meant very honestly when they petitioned to have their lot on that side Jordan, though then also is was their unhappiness to be misunderstood even by Moses himself. In their vindication, they make it out that the building of this altar was so far from being a step towards a separation from their brethren, and from the altar of the Lord at Shiloh, that, on the contrary, it was really designed for a pledge and preservative of their communion with their brethren and with the altar of God, and a token of their resolution to do the service of the Lord before him (v. 27), and to continue to do so.

1. They gave an account of the fears they had lest, in process of time, their posterity, being seated at such a distance from the tabernacle, should be looked upon and treated as strangers to the commonwealth of Israel (v. 24);

it was for fear of this thing, and the word signifies a great perplexity and solicitude of mind which they were in, until they eased themselves by this expedient. As they were returning home (and we may suppose it was not thought of before, else they would have made Joshua acquainted with their purpose), some of them in discourse started this matter, and the rest took the hint, and represented to themselves and one another a very melancholy prospect of what might probably happen in after-ages, that their children would be looked upon by the other tribes as having no interest in the altar of God and the sacrifices there offered. Now indeed they were owned as brethren, and were as welcome at the tabernacle as any other of the tribes; but what if their children after them should be disowned? They, by reason of their distance, and the interposition of Jordan, which it was not easy at all times to pass and re-pass, could not be so numerous and constant in their attendance on the three yearly feasts as the other tribes, to make a continual claim to the privileges of Israelites, and would therefore be looked upon as inconsiderable members of their church, and by degrees would be rejected as not members of it at all: *So shall your children* (who in their pride will be apt to monopolize the privileges of the altar) *make our children* (who perhaps will not be so careful as they ought to be to keep hold of those privileges) *cease from fearing the Lord.* Note, (1.) Those that are cut off from public ordinances are likely to lose all religion, and will by degrees cease from fearing the Lord. Though the form and profession of godliness are kept up by many without the life and power of it, yet the life and power of it will not long be kept up without the form and profession. You take away grace if you take away the means of grace. (2.) Those who have themselves found the comfort and benefit of God's ordinances cannot but desire to preserve and perpetuate the entail of them upon their seed, and use all possible precautions that their children after them may not be *made to cease from following the Lord,* or be looked upon as having no part in him.

2. The project they had to prevent this, *v.* 26–28. "Therefore, to secure an interest in the altar of God to those who shall come after us, and to prove their title to it, *we said, Let us build an altar, to be a witness between us and you,*" that, having this copy of the altar in their custody, it might be produced as an evidence of their right to the privilege of the original. Every one that saw this altar, and observed that it was never used for sacrifice and offering, would enquire what was the meaning of it, and this answer would be given to that enquiry, that it was built by those separate tribes, in token of their communion with their brethren and their joint-interest with them in the altar of the Lord. Christ is the great altar that sanctifies every gift; the best evidence of our interest in him will be the pattern of his Spirit in our hearts, and our conformity to him. If we can produce this it will be a testimony for us that we have *a part in the Lord,* and an earnest of our perseverance in following him.

Verses 30–34

We have here the good issue of this controversy, which, if there had not been on both sides a disposition to peace, as there was on both sides a zeal for God, might have been of ill consequence; for quarrels about religion, for want of wisdom and love, often prove the most fierce and most difficult to be accommodated. But these contending parties, when the matter was fairly stated and argued, were so happy as to understand one another very well, and so the difference was presently compromised.

I. The ambassadors were exceedingly pleased when the separate tribes had given in a protestation of the innocency of their intentions in building this altar. 1. The ambassadors did not call in question their sincerity in that protestation, did not say, "You tell us you design it not for sacrifice and offering, but who can believe you? What security will you give us that it shall never be so used?" No. *Charity believes all things, hopes all things,* believes and hopes the best, and is very loth to give the lie to any. 2. They did not upbraid them with the rashness and unadvisedness of this action, did not tell them, "If you would do such a thing, and with this good intention, yet you might have had so much respect for Joshua and Eleazar as to have advised with them, or at least have made them acquainted with it, and so have saved the trouble and ex-

pense of this embassy." But a little want of consideration and good manners should be excused and overlooked in those who, we have reason to think, mean honestly. 3. Much less did they go about to fish for evidence to make out their charge, because they had once exhibited it, but were glad to have their mistake rectified, and were not at all ashamed to own it. Proud and peevish spirits, when they have passed an unjust censure upon their brethren, though ever so much convincing evidence be brought of the injustice of it, will stand to it, and can by no means be persuaded to retract it. These ambassadors were not so prejudiced; their brethren's vindication pleased them, *v.* 30. They looked upon their innocency as a token of God's presence (*v.* 31), especially when they found that what was done was so far from being an indication of their growing cool to the altar of God that, one the contrary, it was a fruit of their zealous affection to it: *You have delivered the children of Israel out of the hand of the Lord,* that is, "You have not, as we feared, delivered them into the hand of the Lord, or exposed them to his judgments by the trespass we were jealous of."

II. The congregation was abundantly satisfied when their ambassadors reported to them their brethren's apology for what they had done. It should seem they staid together, at least by their representatives, until they heard the issue (*v.* 32); and when they understood the truth of the matter it pleased them (*v.* 33), and they *blessed God.* Note, Our brethren's constancy in religion, their zeal for the power of godliness, and their keeping the *unity of the Spirit* in faith and love, notwithstanding the jealousies conceived of them as breaking the unity of the church, are things which we should be very glad to be satisfied of, and should make the matter both of our rejoicing and of our thanksgiving; let God have the glory of it, and let us take the comfort of it. Being thus satisfied, they laid down their arms immediately, and were so far from any thoughts of prosecuting the war they had been meditating against their brethren that we may suppose them wishing for the next feast, when they should meet them at Shiloh.

III. The separate tribes were gratified, and, since they had a mind to preserve among them this pattern of the altar of God, though there was not likely to be that occasion for it which they fancied, yet Joshua and the princes let them have their humour, and did not give orders for the demolishing of it, though there was as much reason to fear that it might in process of time be an occasion of idolatry as there was to hope that ever it might be a preservation from idolatry. Thus did *the strong bear the infirmities of the weak.* Only care was taken that they having explained the meaning of their altar, that it was intended for no more than a testimony of their communion with the altar at Shiloh, this explanation should be recorded, which was done according to the usage of those times by giving a name to it signifying so much (*v.* 34); they called it *Ed, a witness* to that, and no more, a witness of the relation they stood in to God and Israel, and of their concurrence with the rest of the tribes in the same common faith, *that Jehovah he is God,* he and no other. It was a witness to posterity of their care to transmit their religion pure and entire to them, and would be a witness against them if ever they should forsake God and turn from following after him.

CHAPTER 23

In this and the following chapter we have two farewell sermons, which Joshua preached to the people of Israel a little before his death. Had he designed to gratify the curiosity of succeeding ages, he would rather have recorded the method of Israel's settlement in their new conquests, their husbandry, manufacturers, trade, customs, courts of justice, and the constitutions of their infant commonwealth, which one would wish to be informed of; but that which he intended in the registers of this book was to entail on posterity a sense of religion and their duty to God; and therefore, overlooking these things which are the usual subjects of a common history, he here transmits to his reader the methods he took to persuade Israel to be faithful to their covenant with their God, which might have a good influence on the generations to come who should read those reasonings, as we may hope they had on that generation which then heard them. In this chapter we have, I. A convention of the states called (*v.* 1, 2), probably to consult about the common concerns of their land, and to set in order that which, after some years' trial, being left to their prudence, was found wanting. II. Joshua's speech to them as the opening, or perhaps at the concluding, of the sessions, to hear which was the principal design of their coming together. In it, 1. Joshua reminds them of what God had done for them (*v.* 3, 4, 9, 14), and what he was ready to do yet further (*v.* 5, 10). 2. He exhorts them carefully and resolutely to persevere

in their duty to God (*v.* 6, 8, 11). III. He cautions them against all familiarity with their idolatrous neighbours (*v.* 7). IV. He gives them fair warning of the fatal consequences of it, if they should revolt from God and turn to idols (*v.* 12, 13, 15, 16). In all this he showed himself zealous for his God, and jealous over Israel with a godly jealousy.

Verses 1–10

As to the date of this edict of Joshua,

I. No mention at all is made of the place where this general assembly was held; some think it was at Timnath-serah, Joshua's own city, where he lived, and whence, being old, he could not well remove. But it does not appear that he took so much state upon him; therefore it is more probable this meeting was at Shiloh, where the tabernacle of meeting was, and to which place, perhaps, all the males that could had now come up to worship before the Lord, at one of the three great feasts, which Joshua took the opportunity of, for the delivering of this charge to them.

II. There is only a general mention of the time when this was done. It was *long after the Lord had given them rest,* but it is not said how long, *v.* 1. It was, 1. So long as that Israel had time to feel the comforts of their rest and possessions in Canaan, and to enjoy the advantages of that good land. 2. So long as that Joshua had time to observe which ways their danger lay of being corrupted, namely, by their intimacy with the Canaanites that remained, against which he is therefore careful to arm them.

III. The persons to whom Joshua made this speech: *To all Israel, even their elders, etc.* So it might be read, *v.* 2. They could not all come within hearing, but he called for all the elders, that is, the privy-counsellors, which in later times constituted the great Sanhedrim, the heads of the tribes, that is, the noblemen and gentlemen of their respective countries, the judges learned in the laws, that tried criminals and causes, and gave judgment upon them, and, lastly, the officers or sheriffs, who were entrusted with the execution of those judgments. These Joshua called together, and to them he addressed himself, 1. That they might communicate what he said, or at least the sense and substance of it, to those under them in their respective countries, and so this charge might be dispersed through the whole nation. 2. Because, if they would be prevailed upon to serve God and cleave to him, they, by their influence on the common people, would keep them faithful. If great men be good men, they will help to make many good.

IV. Joshua's circumstances when he gave them this charge: He *was old and stricken in age* (*v.* 1), probably it was in the last year of his life, and he lived to be 110 years old, *ch.* 24:29. And he himself takes notice of it, in the first words of is discourse, *v.* 2. When he began to be old, some years ago, God reminded him of it (*ch.* 13:1): *Thou art old.* But now he did himself feel so much of the decays of age that he needed not to be told of it, he readily speaks of it himself: *I am old and stricken in age.* He uses it, 1. As an argument with himself to give them this charge, because being old he could expect to be but a little while with them, to advise and instruct them, and therefore (as Peter speaks, 2 Pt. 1:13) *as long as he is in this tabernacle* he will take all opportunities to *put them in remembrance* of their duty, knowing by the increasing infirmities of age that he must shortly put off this tabernacle, and desiring that after his decease they might continue as good as they were now. When we see death hastening towards us, this should quicken us to do the work of life with all our might. 2. As an argument with them to give heed to what he said. he was old and experienced, and therefore to be the more regarded, for days should speak; he had grown old in their service, and had spent himself for their good, and therefore was to be the more regarded by them. He was old and dying; they would not have him long to preach to them; therefore let them observe what he said now, and lay it up in store for the time to come.

V. The discourse itself, the scope of which is to engage them if possible, them and their seed after them, to persevere in the true faith and worship of the God of Israel.

1. He puts them in mind of the great things God had done for them, now in his days, and under his administration, for here he goes no further back. And for the proof of this he appeals to their own eyes (*v.* 3): "*You have seen all that the Lord your God has done;* not what I have done, or what you have done (we were only instruments in God's

hand), but what God himself has done by me and for you." (1.) Many great and mighty nations (as the rate of nations then went) were driven out from as fine a country as any was at that time upon the face of the earth, to make room for Israel. "You see *what he has done to these nations,* who were his creatures, the work of his hands, and whom he could have made new creatures and fit for his service; yet see what destruction he has made of them *because of you* (*v.* 2), how he has *driven them out from before you* (*v.* 9), as if they were of no account with him, though great and strong in comparison with you." (2.) They were not only driven out (this they might have been, and yet sent to some other country less rich to begin a new plantation there, suppose to that wilderness in which Israel had wandered so long, and so they would only have exchanged seats with them), but they were trodden down before them; though they held out against them with the greatest obstinacy that could be, yet they were subdued before them, which made the possessing of their land so much the more glorious to Israel and so much the more illustrious an instance of the power and goodness of the God of Israel (*v.* 3): *"The Lord your God* has not only led you, and fed you, and kept you, but he has fought for you as a man of war," by which title he was known among them when he first brought them out of Egypt, Ex. 15:3. So clear and cheap were all their victories, during the course of this long war, that *no man had been able to stand before them* (*v.* 9), that is, to make head against them, so as to put them in fear, create them any difficulty, or give any check to the progress of their victorious arms. In every battle they carried the day, and in every siege they carried the city; their loss before Ai was upon a particular occasion, was inconsiderable, and only served to show them on what terms they stood with God; but, otherwise, never was army crowned with such a constant uninterrupted series of successes as the armies of Israel were in the wars of Canaan. (3.) They had not only conquered the Canaanites, but were put in full possession of their land (*v.* 4): *"I have divided to you by lot these nations,* both those which are cut off and those which remain, not only that you may spoil and plunder them, and live at discretion in their country for a time, but to be a sure and lasting inheritance for your tribes. You have it not only under your feet, but in your hands."

2. He assures them of God's readiness to carry on and complete this glorious work in due time. It is true some of the Canaanites did yet remain, and in some places were strong and daring, but this should be no disappointment to their expectations; when Israel was so multiplied as to be able to replenish this land God would expel the Canaanites to the last man, provided Israel would pursue their advantages and carry on the war against them with vigour (*v.* 5): *"The Lord your God will drive them from out of your sight,* so that there shall not be a Canaanite to be seen in the land; and even that part of the country which is yet in their hands you shall possess." If it were objected that the men of war of the several tribes being dispersed to their respective countries, and the army disbanded, it would be difficult to get them together when there was occasion to renew the war upon the remainder of the Canaanites, in answer to this he tells them what little need they had to be in care about the numbers of their forces (*v.* 10): *One man of you shall chase a thousand,* as Jonathan did, 1 Sa. 14:13. "Each tribe may venture for itself, and for the recovery of its own lot, without fearing disadvantage by the disproportion of numbers; for the Lord your God, whose all power is, both to inspirit and to dispirit, and who has all the creatures at his beck, *he it is that fighteth for you;* and how many do you reckon him for?"

3. He hereupon most earnestly charges them to adhere to their duty, to go on and persevere in the good ways of the Lord wherein they had so well set out. He exhorts them,

(1.) To be very courageous (*v.* 6): "God fighteth for you against your enemies, do you therefore *behave yourselves valiantly* for him. Keep and do with a firm resolution *all that is written in the book of the law.*" He presses upon them no more than what they were already bound to. "Keep with care, do with diligence, and eye what is written with sincerity."

(2.) To be very cautious: "Take heed of missing it, either on the right hand or on the left, for there are errors and extremes on both hands. Take heed of running either into a profane neglect of any of God's institutions or into a superstitious addition of any of your own inventions." They must especially take heed of all approaches towards idolatry, the sin to which they were first inclined and would be most tempted, *v.* 7. [1.] They must not acquaint themselves with idolaters, nor come among them to visit them or be present at any of their feasts or entertainments, for they could not contract any intimacy nor keep up any conversation with them, without danger of infection. [2.] They must not show the least respect to any idol, nor *make mention of the name of their gods,* but endeavour to bury the remembrance of them in perpetual oblivion, that the worship of them may never be revived. "Let the very name of them be forgotten. Look upon idols as filthy detestable things, not to be named without the utmost loathing and detestation." The Jews would not suffer their children to name swine's flesh, because it was forbidden, lest the name of it should occasion their desiring it; but, if they had occasion to speak of it, they must call it *that strange thing.* It is a pity that among Christians the names of the heathen gods are so commonly used, and made so familiar as they are, especially in plays and poems: let those names which have been set up in rivalship with God be for ever loathed and lost. [3.] They must not countenance others in showing respect to them. They must not only not swear by them themselves, but they must not cause others to swear by them, which supposes that they must not make any covenants with idolaters, because they, in the confirming of their covenants, would swear by their idols; never let Israelites admit such an oath. [4.] They must take heed of these occasions of idolatry, lest by degrees they should arrive at the highest step of it, which was serving false gods, and bowing down to them, against the letter of the second commandment.

(3.) To be very constant (*v.* 8): *Cleave unto the Lord your God,* that is, "delight in him, depend upon him, devote yourselves to his glory, and continue to do so to the end, *as you have done unto this day,* ever since you came to Canaan;" for, being willing to make the best of them, he looks not so far back as the iniquity of Peor. There might be many things amiss among them, but they had not forsaken the Lord their God, and it is in order to insinuate his exhortation to perseverance with the more pleasing power that he praises them. "Go on and prosper, for the Lord is with you while you are with him." Those that command should commend; the way to make people better is to make the best of them. "You have cleaved to the Lord unto this day, therefore go on to do so, else you lose the praise and recompence of what you have wrought. Your righteousness will not be mentioned unto you if you turn from it."

Verses 11–16

Here, I. Joshua directs them what to do, that they might persevere in religion, *v.* 11. Would we cleave to the Lord, and not forsake him, 1. We must always stand upon our guard, for many a precious soul is lost and ruined through carelessness: "Take heed therefore, *take good heed to yourselves,* to your *souls* (so the word is), that the inward man be kept clean from the pollutions of sin, and closely employed in the service of God." God has given us precious souls with this charge, "Take good heed to them, keep them with all diligence, above all keepings." 2. What we do in religion we must do from a principle of love, not by constraint or from a slavish fear of God, but of choice and with delight. *"Lord the Lord your God,* and you will not leave him."

II. He urges God's fidelity to them as an argument why they should be faithful to him (*v.* 14): *"I am going the way of all the earth,* I am old and dying." To die is to go a journey, a journey to our long home; it is the way of all the earth, the way that all mankind must go, sooner or later. Joshua himself, though so great and good a man, and one that could so ill be spared, cannot be exempted from this common lot. He takes notice of it here that they might look upon these as his dying words, and regard them accordingly. Or thus: *"I am dying,* and leaving you. *Me you have not always;* but if you cleave to the Lord he will never leave you." Or thus, "Now that I am near my end it is proper to look back upon the years that are past; and, in the review, I find, and you *yourselves know it in all your hearts and in all your souls,* by a full conviction on the clearest evidence, and the thing has made an impression upon you" — (that knowledge does us good which is seated, not in the head only, but in the heart and soul, and with which we are duly affected) — "you know that *not one thing hath failed of all the good things which the Lord spoke concerning you"* (and he spoke a great many); see *ch.* 21:45. God had promised them victory, rest, plenty, his tabernacle among them, etc., and *not one thing had failed* of all he had promised. "Now," said he, "has God been thus true to you? Be not you false to him." It is the apostle's argument for perseverance (Heb. 10:23), *He is faithful that has promised.*

III. He gives them fair warning what would be the fatal consequences of apostasy (*v.* 12, 13, 15, 16): "If you go back, know for a certainty it will be your ruin." Observe,

1. How he describes the apostasy which he warns them against. The steps of it would be (*v.* 12) growing intimate with idolaters, who would craftily wheedle them, and insinuate themselves into their acquaintance, now that they had become lords of the country, to serve their own ends. The next step would be intermarrying with them, drawn to it by their artifices, who would be glad to bestow their children upon these wealthy Israelites. And the consequence of that would be (*v.* 16) *serving other gods* (which were pretended to be the ancient deities of the country) and bowing down to them. Thus the way of sin is downhill, and those who have fellowship with sinners cannot avoid having fellowship with sin. This he represents, (1.) As a base and shameful desertion; "it is going back from what you have so well begun," *v.* 12. (2.) As a most perfidious breach of promise (*v.* 16): "It is a transgression of *the covenant of the Lord your God, which he commanded you,* and which you yourselves set your hand to." Other sins were transgressions of the law God commanded them, but this was a transgression of the covenant he commanded them, and amounted to a breach of the relation between God and them and a forfeiture of all the benefits of the covenant.

2. How he describes the destruction which he warns them of. He tells them, (1.) That these remainders of the Canaanites, if they should harbour them, and indulge them, and join in affinity with them, would be snares and traps to them, both to draw them to sin (not only to idolatry, but to all immoralities, which would be the ruin, not only of their virtue, but of their wisdom and sense, their spirit and honour), and also to draw them into foolish bargains, unprofitable projects, and all manner of inconveniences; and having thus by underhand practices decoyed them into one mischief or other, so as to gain advantages against them, they would then act more openly, and be *scourges in their sides* and *thorns in their eyes,* would perhaps kill or drive away their cattle, burn or steal their corn, alarm or plunder their houses, and would be all ways possible be vexatious to them; for, whatever pretences of friendship they might make, a Canaanite, unless proselyted to the faith and worship of the true God, would in every age hate the very name and sight of an Israelite. See how the punishment would be made to answer the sin, nay, how the sin itself would be the punishment. (2.) That the anger of the Lord would be kindled against them. Their making leagues with the Canaanites would not only give those idolaters the opportunity of doing them a mischief, and be the fostering of snakes in their bosoms, but it would likewise provoke God to become their enemy, and would kindle the fire of his displeasure against them. (3.) That all the threatenings of the word would be fulfilled, as the promise had been, for the God of eternal truth is faithful to both (*v.* 15): *"As all good things have come upon you* according to the promise, so long as you have kept close to God, so all evil things will come upon you according to the threatening, if you forsake him." Moses had *set before them good and evil;* they had experienced the good, and were now in the enjoyment of it, and the evil would as certainly come if they were disobedient. As God's promises are not a fool's paradise, so his threatenings are not bugbears. (4.) That it would end in the utter ruin of their church and nation, as Moses had foretold. This is three times mentioned here. Your enemies will vex you *until you perish from off this good land, v.* 13. Again, "God will plague you *until he have destroyed you from off this good land, v.* 15. Heaven and earth will concur to root you out, so that (*v.* 16) *you shall perish from off the good land."* It

will aggravate their perdition that the land from which they shall perish is a good land, and a land which God himself had given them, and which therefore he would have secured to them if they by their wickedness had not thrown themselves out of it. Thus the goodness of the heavenly Canaan, and the free and sure grant God has made of it, will aggravate the misery of those that shall for ever be shut out and perish from it. Nothing will make them see how wretched they are so much as to see how happy they might have been. Joshua thus sets before them the fatal consequences of their apostasy, that, *knowing the terror of the Lord,* they might be persuaded *with purpose of heart to cleave to him.*

CHAPTER 24

This chapter concludes the life and reign of Joshua, in which we have, I. The great care and pains he took to confirm the people of Israel in the true faith and worship of God, that they might, after his death, persevere therein. In order to this he called another general assembly of the heads of the congregation of Israel (*v.* 1) and dealt with them. 1. By way of narrative, recounting the great things God had done for them and their fathers (*v.* 2–13). 2. By way of charge to them, in consideration thereof, to serve God (*v.* 14). 3. By way of treaty with them, wherein he aims to bring them, (1.) To make religion their deliberate choice; and they did so, with reasons for their choice (*v.* 15–18). (2.) To make it their determinate choice, and to resolve to adhere to it (*v.* 19–24). 4. By way of covenant upon that treaty (*v.* 25–28). II. The conclusion of this history, with, 1. The death and burial of Joshua (*v.* 29, 30) and Eleazar (*v.* 33), and the mention of the burial of Joseph's bones upon that occasion (*v.* 32). 2. A general account of the state of Israel at that time (*v.* 31).

Verses 1–14

Joshua thought he had taken his last farewell of Israel in the solemn charge he gave them in the foregoing chapter, when he said, *I go the way of all the earth;* but God graciously continuing his life longer than expected, and renewing his strength, he was desirous to improve it for the good of Israel. He did not say, "I have taken my leave of them once, and let that serve;" but, having yet a longer space given him, he summons them together again, that he might try what more he could do to engage them for God. Note, We must never think our work for God done till our life is done; and, if he lengthen out our days beyond what we thought, we must conclude it is because he has some further service for us to do.

The assembly is the same with that in the foregoing chapter, the *elders, heads, judges, and officers of Israel, v.* 1. But it is here made somewhat more solemn than it was there.

I. The place appointed for their meeting is *Shechem,* not only because that lay nearer to Joshua than Shiloh, and therefore more convenient now that he was infirm and unfit for travelling, but because it was the place where Abraham, the first trustee of God's covenant with this people, settled at his coming to Canaan, and where God appeared to him (Gen. 12:6, 7), and near which stood mounts Gerizim and Ebal, where the people had renewed their covenant with God at their first coming into Canaan, Jos. 8:30. Of the promises God had made to their fathers, and of the promises they themselves had made to God, this place might serve to put them in mind.

II. They presented themselves not only before Joshua, but before God, in this assembly, that is, they came together in a solemn religious manner, as into the special presence of God, and with an eye to his speaking to them by Joshua; and it is probable the service began with prayer. It is the conjecture of interpreters that upon this great occasion Joshua ordered the ark of God to be brought by the priests to Shechem, which, they say, was about ten miles from Shiloh, and to be set down in the place of their meeting, which is therefore called (*v.* 26) *the sanctuary of the Lord,* the presence of the ark making it so at that time; and this was done to grace the solemnity, and to strike an awe upon the people that attended. We have not now any such sensible tokens of the divine presence, but are to believe that *where two or three are gathered together* in Christ's name he is as really in the midst of them as God was where the ark was, and they are indeed presenting themselves before him.

III. Joshua spoke to them in God's name, and as from him, in the language of a prophet (*v.* 2): *"Thus saith the Lord,* Jehovah, the great God, and the God of Israel, your God in covenant, whom therefore you are bound to hear and give heed to." Note, The word of God is to be received by us as his, whoever is the messenger that brings it, whose greatness cannot add to it, nor his meanness diminish from it. His sermon consists of doctrine and application.

1. The doctrinal part is a history of the great things God had done for his people, and for their fathers before them. God by Joshua recounts the marvels of old: "I did so and so." They must know and consider, not only that such and such things were done, but that God did them. It is a series of wonders that is here recorded, and perhaps many more were mentioned by Joshua, which for brevity's sake are here omitted. See what God had wrought. (1.) He brought Abraham out of Ur of the Chaldees, *v.* 2, 3. He and his ancestors had served other gods there, for it was the country in which, though celebrated for learning, idolatry, as some think, had its rise; there *the world by wisdom knew not God.* Abraham, who afterwards was the friend of God and the great favourite of heaven, was bred up in idolatry, and lived long in it, till God by his grace snatched him as a brand out of that burning. Let them remember that rock out of which they were hewn, and not relapse into that sin from which their fathers by a miracle of free grace were delivered. "I took him," says God, "else he had never come out of that sinful state." Hence Abraham's justification is made by the apostle an instance of God's *justifying the ungodly,* Rom. 4:5. (2.) He brought him to Canaan, and built up his family, led him through the land to Shechem, where they now were, multiplied his seed by Ishmael, who begat twelve princes, but at last gave him Isaac the promised son, and in him multiplied his seed. When Isaac had two sons, Jacob and Esau, God provided an inheritance for Esau elsewhere in Mount Seir, that the land of Canaan might be reserved entire for the seed of Jacob, and the posterity of Esau might not pretend to a share in it. (3.) He delivered the seed of Jacob out of Egypt with a high hand (*v.* 5, 6), and rescued them out of the hands of Pharaoh and his host at the Red Sea, *v.* 6, 7. The same waters were the Israelites' guard and the Egyptians' grave, and this in answer to prayer; for, though we find in the story that they in that distress murmured against God (Ex. 14:11, 12), notice is here taken of their *crying to God;* he graciously accepted those that prayed to him, and overlooked the folly of those that quarrelled with him. (4.) He protected them in the wilderness, where they are here said, not to *wander,* but to *dwell for a long season, v.* 7. So wisely were all their motions directed, and so safely were they kept, that even there they had as certain a dwelling-place as if they had been in a walled city. (5.) He gave them the land of the Amorites, on the other side Jordan (*v.* 8), and there defeated the plot of Balak and Balaam against them, so that Balaam could not curse them as he desired, and therefore Balak durst not fight them as he designed, and as, because he designed it, he is here said to have done it. The turning of Balaam's tongue to bless Israel, when he intended to curse them, is often mentioned as an instance of the divine power put forth in Israel's favour as remarkable as any, because in it God proved (and does still, more than we are aware of) his dominion over the powers of darkness, and over the spirits of men. (6.) He brought them safely and triumphantly into Canaan, delivered the Canaanites into their hand (*v.* 11), *sent hornets before them,* when they were actually engaged in battle with the enemy, which with their stings tormented them and with their noise terrified them, so that they became a very easy prey to Israel. These dreadful swarms first appeared in their war with Sihon and Og, the two kings of the Amorites, and afterwards in their other battles, *v.* 12. God had promised to do this for them, Ex. 23:27, 28. And here Joshua takes notice of the fulfilling of that promise. See Ex. 23:27, 28; Deu. 7:20. These hornets, it should seem, annoyed the enemy more than the artillery of Israel, and therefore he adds, *not with thy sword nor bow.* It was purely the Lord's doing. *Lastly,* They were now in the peaceable possession of a good land, and lived comfortably upon the fruit of other people's labours, *v.* 13.

2. The application of this history of God's mercies to them is by way of exhortation to fear and serve God, in gratitude for his favour, and that it might be continued to them, *v.* 14. Now therefore, in consideration of all this, (1.) *"Fear the Lord,* the Lord and his goodness, Hos. 3:5. Reverence a God of such infinite power, fear to offend him and to forfeit his goodness, keep up an awe of his majesty, a deference to his authority, a dread of his displeasure, and a continual regard to his all-seeing eye upon you." (2.) "Let your practice be consonant to this principle, and serve him both by the outward acts of religious worship and every instance of obedience in your whole conversation, and this *in sincerity and truth,* with a single eye and an upright heart, and inward impressions answerable to outward expressions." This is the *truth in the inward part,* which God requires, Ps. 51:6. For what good will it do us to dissemble with a God that searches the heart? (3.) *Put away the strange gods,* both Chaldean and Egyptian idols, for those they were most in danger of revolting to. It should seem by this charge, which is repeated (*v.* 23), that there were some among them that privately kept in their closets the images or pictures of these dunghill-deities, which came to their hands from their ancestors, as heir-looms of their families, though, it may be, they did not worship them; these Joshua earnestly urges them to throw away: "Deface them, destroy them, lest you be tempted to serve them." Jacob pressed his household to do this, and at this very place; for, when they gave him up the little images they had, he buried them *under the oak which was by Shechem,* Gen. 35:2, 4. Perhaps the oak mentioned here (*v.* 26) was the same oak, or another in the same place, which might be well called the *oak of reformation,* as there were idolatrous oaks.

Verses 15–28

Never was any treaty carried on with better management, nor brought to a better issue, than this of Joshua with the people, to engage them to serve God. The manner of his dealing with them shows him to have been in earnest, and that his heart was much upon it, to leave them under all possible obligations to cleave to him, particularly the obligation of a choice and of a covenant.

I. Would it be any obligation upon them if they made the service of God their choice? — he here puts them to their choice, not as if it were antecedently indifferent whether they served God or nor, or as if they were at liberty to refuse his service, but because it would have a great influence upon their perseverance in religion if they embraced it with the reason of men and with the resolution of men. These two things he here brings them to.

1. He brings them to embrace their religion rationally and intelligently, for it is a reasonable service. The will of man is apt to glory in its native liberty, and, in a jealousy for the honour of this, adheres with most pleasure to that which is its own choice and is not imposed upon it; therefore it is God's will that this service should be, not our chance, or a force upon us, but our choice. Accordingly,

(1.) Joshua fairly puts the matter to their choice, *v.* 15. Here, [1.] He proposes the candidates that stand for the election. The Lord, Jehovah, on one side, and on the other side either the gods of their ancestors, which would pretend to recommend themselves to those that were fond of antiquity, and that which was received by tradition from their fathers, or the *gods of their neighbours,* the Amorites, in *whose land they dwelt,* which would insinuate themselves into the affections of those that were complaisant and fond of good fellowship. [2.] He supposes there were those to whom, upon some account or other, it would *seem evil to serve the Lord.* There are prejudices and objections which some people raise against religion, which, with those that are inclined to the world and the flesh, have great force. It seems evil to them, hard and unreasonable, to be obliged to deny themselves, mortify the flesh, take up their cross, etc. But, being in a state of probation, it is fit there should be some difficulties in the way, else there were no trial. [3.] He refers it to themselves: *"Choose you whom you will serve,* choose this day, now that the matter is laid thus plainly before you, speedily bring it to a head, and do not stand hesitating." Elijah, long after this, referred the decision of the controversy between Jehovah and Baal to the consciences of those with whom he was treating, 1 Ki. 18:21. Joshua's putting the matter here to this issue plainly intimates two things: — *First,* That it is the will of God we should every one of us make religion our serious and deliberate choice. Let us state the matter impartially to ourselves, weigh things in an even balance, and then determine for that which we find to be really true and good. Let us resolve upon a life of serious godliness, not merely because we know no other way, but because really, upon search, we find no better. *Secondly,* That religion has so much self-evident reason and righteousness on its side that it may safely be referred to every man that allows himself a free thought either to choose or refuse it; for the merits of the cause are so plain that no considerate man can do otherwise but choose it. The case is so clear that it determines itself. Perhaps Joshua designed, by putting them to their choice, thus to try if there were any among them who, upon so fair an occasion given, would show a coolness and indifference towards the service of God, whether they would desire time to consider and consult their friends before they gave in an answer, and if any such should appear he might set a mark upon them, and warn the rest to avoid them. [4.] He directs their choice in this matter by an open declaration of his own resolutions: "But as for me and my house, whatever you do, we will serve the Lord, and I hope you will all be of the same mind." Here he resolves, *First,* For himself: *As for me, I will serve the Lord.* Note, The service of God is nothing below the greatest of men; it is so far from being a diminution and disparagement to princes and those of the first rank to be religious that it is their greatest honour, and adds the brightest crown of glory to them. Observe how positive he is: "I will serve God." It is no abridgment of our liberty to bind ourselves with a bond to God. *Secondly,* For *his house,* that is, his family, his children and servants, such as were immediately under his eye and care, his inspection and influence. Joshua was a ruler, a judge in Israel, yet he did not make his necessary application to public affairs an excuse for the neglect of family religion. Those that have the charge of many families, as magistrates and ministers, must take special care of their own (1 Tim. 3:4, 5): *I and my house* will serve God. 1. "Not my house, without me." He would not engage them to that work which he would not set his own hand to. As some who would have their children and servants good, but will not be so themselves; that is, they would have them go to heaven, but intend to go to hell themselves. 2. "Not I, without my house." He supposes he might be forsaken by his people, but in his house, where his authority was greater and more immediate, there he would over-rule. Note, When we cannot bring as many as we would to the service of God we must bring as many as we can, and extend our endeavours to the utmost sphere of our activity; if we cannot reform the land, let us put away iniquity far from our own tabernacle. 3. "First I, and then my house." Note, Those that lead and rule in other things should be first in the service of God, and go before in the best things. *Thirdly,* He resolves to do this whatever others did. Though all the families of Israel should revolt from God, and serve idols, yet Joshua and his family will stedfastly adhere to the God of Israel. Note, Those that resolve to serve God must not mind being singular in it, nor be drawn by the crowd to forsake his service. Those that are bound for heaven must be willing to swim against the stream, and must not do as the most do, but as the best do.

(2.) The matter being thus put to their choice, they immediately determine it by a free, rational, and intelligent declaration, for the God of Israel, against all competitors whatsoever, *v.* 16–18. Here, [1.] They concur with Joshua in his resolution, being influenced by the example of so great a man, who had been so great a blessing to them (*v.* 18): *We also will serve the Lord.* See how much good great men might do, if they were but zealous in religion, by their influence on their inferiors. [2.] They startle at the thought of apostatizing from God (*v.* 16): *God forbid;* the word intimates the greatest dread and detestation imaginable. "Far be it, far be it from us, that we or ours should ever *forsake the Lord to serve other gods.* We must be perfectly lost to all sense of justice, gratitude, and honour, ere we can harbour the least thought of such a thing." Thus must our hearts rise against all temptations to desert the service of God. *Get thee behind me, Satan.* [3.] They give very substantial reasons for their choice, to show that they did not make it purely in compliance to Joshua, but from a full conviction of the reasonableness and equity of it. They make this choice for, and in consideration, *First,* Of the many great and very kind things God had done for them, bringing them out of Egypt through the wilderness into Canaan, *v.* 17, 18. Thus they repeat to themselves Joshua's sermon, and then express their sincere compliance with the intentions of it. *Secondly,* Of the relation they stood in to God, and his covenant with them: "We *will serve the Lord* (v. 18), *for he is our God,* who has gracious-

ly engaged himself by promise to us, and to whom we have by solemn vow engaged ourselves."

2. He brings them to embrace their religion resolutely, and to express a full purpose of heart to cleave to the Lord. Now that he has them in a good mind he follows his blow, and drives the nail to the head, that it might, if possible, be a nail in a sure place. Fast bind, fast find.

(1.) In order to this he sets before them the difficulties of religion, and that in it which might be thought discouraging (*v.* 19, 20): *You cannot serve the Lord, for he is a holy God,* or, as it is in the Hebrew, *he is the holy Gods,* intimating the mystery of the Trinity, three in one; *holy, holy, holy,* holy Father, holy Son, holy Spirit. *He will not forgive.* And, *if you forsake him, he will do you hurt.* Certainly Joshua does not intend hereby to deter them from the service of God as impracticable and dangerous. But, [1.] He perhaps intends to represent here the suggestions of seducers, who tempted Israel from their God, and from the service of him; with such insinuations as these, that he was a hard master, his work impossible to be done, and he not to be pleased, and, if displeased, implacable and revengeful, — that he would confine their respects to himself only, and would not suffer them to show the least kindness for any other, — and that herein he was very unlike the gods of the nations, which were easy, and neither holy nor jealous. It is probable that this was then commonly objected against the Jewish religion, as it has all along been the artifice of Satan every since he tempted our first parents thus to misrepresent God and his laws, as harsh and severe; and Joshua by his tone and manner of speaking might make them perceive he intended it as an objection, and would put it to them how they would keep their ground against the force of it. Or, [2.] He thus expresses his godly jealousy over them, and his fear concerning them, that, notwithstanding the profession they now made of zeal for God and his service, they would afterwards draw back, and if they did they would find him just and jealous to avenge it. Or, [3.] He resolves to let them know the worst of it, and what strict terms they must expect to stand upon with God, that they might sit down and count the cost. "*You cannot serve the Lord,* except you put away all other gods for he is holy and jealous, and will by no means admit a rival, and therefore you must be very watchful and careful, for it is at your peril if you desert his service; better you had never known it." Thus, though our Master has assured us that *his yoke is easy,* yet lest, upon the presumption of this, we should grow remiss and careless, he has also told us that the gate is strait, and the way narrow, that leads to life, that we may therefore strive to enter, and not seek only. "*You cannot serve God and Mammon;* therefore, if you resolve to serve God, you must renounce all competitors with him. You cannot serve God in your own strength, nor will he forgive your transgressions for any righteousness of your own; but *all the seed of Israel must be justified and must glory in the Lord alone as their righteousness* and *strength,*" Isa. 45:24, 25. They must therefore come off from all confidence in their own sufficiency, else their purposes would be to no purpose. Or, [4.] Joshua thus urges on them the seeming discouragements which lay in their way, that he might sharpen their resolutions, and draw from them a promise yet more express and solemn that they would continue faithful to God and their religion. He draws it form them that they might catch at it the more earnestly and hold it the faster.

(2.) Notwithstanding this statement of the difficulties of religion, they declare a firm and fixed resolution to continue and persevere therein (*v.* 21): "*Nay, but we will serve the Lord.* We will think never the worse of him for his being a holy and jealous God, nor for his confining his servants to worship himself only. Justly will he consume those that forsake him, but we never will forsake him; not only we have a good mind to serve him, and we hope we shall, but we are at a point, we cannot bear to hear any *entreaties to leave him or to turn from following after him* (Ruth 1:16); in the strength of divine grace we are resolved that we will serve the Lord." This resolution they repeat with an explication (v. 24): "*The Lord our God will we serve,* not only be called his servants and wear his livery, but our religion shall rule us in every thing, *and his voice will we obey.*" And in vain do we *call him Master and Lord, if we do not the things which he saith,* Lu. 6:46. This last promise they make in answer to the charge Joshua gave them

(v. 23), that, in order to their perseverance, they should, [1.] Put away the images and relics of the strange gods, and not keep any of the tokens of those other lovers in their custody, if they resolved their *Maker should be their husband;* they promise, in this, to obey his voice. [2.] That they should *incline their hearts to the God of Israel,* use their authority over their own hearts to engage them for God, not only to set their affections upon him, but to settle them so. These terms they agree to, and thus, as Joshua explains the bargain, they strike it: *The Lord our God will we serve.*

II. The service of God being thus made their deliberate choice, Joshua binds them to it by a solemn covenant, *v.* 25. Moses had twice publicly ratified this covenant between God and Israel, at Mount Sinai (Ex. 24) and in the plains of Moab, Deu. 29:1. Joshua had likewise done it once (*ch.* 8:31, etc.) and now the second time. It is here called a *statute* and an *ordinance,* because of the strength and perpetuity of its obligation, and because even this covenant bound them to no more than what they were antecedently bound to by the divine command. Now, to give it the formalities of a covenant, 1. He calls witnesses, no other than themselves (*v.* 22): *You are witnesses that you have chosen the Lord.* He promises himself that they would never forget the solemnities of this day; but, if hereafter they should break this covenant, he assures them that the professions and promises they had now made would certainly rise up in judgment against them and condemn them; and they agreed to it: *We are witnesses;* let us be judged out of our own mouths if ever we be false to our God." 2. He put it in writing, and inserted it, as we find it here, in the sacred canon: He *wrote it in the book of the law* (v. 26), in that original which was laid up in the side of the ark, and thence, probably, it was transcribed into the several copies which the princes had for the use of each tribe. There it was written, that their obligation to religion by the divine precept, and that by their own promise, might remain on record together. 3. He erected a memorandum of it, for the benefit of those who perhaps were not conversant with writings, *v.* 26, 27. He *set up a great stone under an oak,* as a monument of this covenant, and perhaps wrote an inscription upon it (by which stones are made to speak) signifying the intention of it. When he says, *It hath heard* what was past, he tacitly upbraids the people with the hardness of their hearts, as if this stone had heard to as good purpose as some of them; and, if they should forget what was no done, this stone would so far preserve the remembrance of it as to reproach them for their stupidity and carelessness, and be a witness against them.

The matter being thus settled, Joshua dismissed this assembly of the grandees of Israel (*v.* 28), and took his last leave of them, well satisfied in having done his part, by which he had delivered his soul; if they perished, their blood would be upon their own heads.

Verses 29–33

This book, which began with triumphs, here ends with funerals, by which all the glory of man is stained. We have here 1. The burial of Joseph, *v.* 32. He died about 200 years before in Egypt, but *gave commandment concerning his bones,* that they should not rest in their grave until Israel had rest in the land of promise; now therefore the children of Israel, who had brought this coffin full of bones with them out of Egypt, carried it along with them in all their marches through the wilderness (the two tribes of Ephraim and Manasseh, it is probable, taking particular care of it), and kept it in their camp till Canaan was perfectly reduced, now at last they deposited it in that piece of ground which his father gave him near Shechem, Gen. 48:22. Probably it was upon this occasion that Joshua called for all Israel to meet him at Shechem (*v.* 1), to attend Joseph's coffin to the grave there, so that the sermon in this chapter served both for Joseph's funeral sermon and his own farewell sermon; and if it was, as is supposed, in the last year of his life, the occasion might very well remind him of his own death being at hand, for he was not just at the same age that his illustrious ancestor Joseph had arrived at when he died, 110 *years old;* compare *v.* 29 with Gen. 50:26. 2. The death and burial of Joshua, *v.* 29, 30. We are not told how long he lived after the coming of Israel into Canaan. Dr. Lightfoot thinks it was about seventeen years; but the Jewish chronologers generally say it was about twenty-seven or twenty-eight years. He is here called the *servant of the Lord,* the same title that was given to Moses (*ch.* 1:1) when mention was made of his death; for, though Joshua was in many respects inferior to Moses, yet in this he was equal to him, that, according as his work was, he approved himself a diligent and faithful servant of God. And he that traded with his two talents had the same approbation that he had who traded with his five. *Well done, good and faithful servant.* Joshua's burying-place is here said to be *on the north side of the hill Gaash,* or *the quaking hill;* the Jews say it was so called because it trembled at the burial of Joshua, to upbraid the people of Israel with their stupidity in that they did not lament the death of that great and good man as they ought to have done. Thus at the death of Christ, our Joshua, the earth quaked. The learned bishop Patrick observes that there is no mention of any days of mourning being observed for Joshua, as there were for Moses and Aaron, in which, he says, St. Hierom and others of the fathers think there is a mystery, namely, that under the law, when life and immortality were not brought to so clear a light as they are now, they had reason to mourn and weep for the death of their friends; but now that Jesus, our Joshua, has opened the kingdom of heaven, we may rather rejoice. 3. The death and burial of Eleazar the chief priest, who, it is probable, died about the same time that Joshua did, as Aaron in the same year with Moses, *v.* 33. The Jews say that Eleazar, a little before he died, called the elders together, and gave them a charge as Joshua had done. He was buried in a hill that pertained to Phinehas his son, which came to him, not by descent, for then it would have pertained to his father first, nor had the priests any cities in Mount Ephraim, but either it fell to him by marriage, as the Jews conjecture, or it was freely bestowed upon him, to build a country seat on, by some pious Israelite that was well-affected to the priesthood, for it is here said to have been *given him;* and there he buried his dear father. 4. A general idea given us of the state of Israel at this time, *v.* 31. While Joshua lived, religion was kept up among them under his care and influence; but soon after he and his contemporaries died it went to decay, so much oftentimes does one head hold up: how well is it for the gospel church that Christ, our Joshua, is still with it, by his Spirit, and will be always, even *unto the end of the world!*

AN EXPOSITION, WITH PRACTICAL OBSERVATIONS, OF

THE BOOK OF JUDGES

This is called the Hebrew *Shepher Shophtim,* the *Book of Judges,* which the Syriac and Arabic versions enlarge upon, and call it, *The Book of the Judges of the Children of Israel;* the judgments of that nation being peculiar, so were their judges, whose office differed vastly from that of the judges of other nations. The Septuagint entitles it only *Kritai, Judges.* It is the history of the *commonwealth of Israel,* during the government of the judges from Othniel to Eli, so much of it as God saw fit to transmit to us. It contains the history (according to Dr. Lightfoot's computation) of 299 years, reckoning to Othniel of Judah forty years, to Ehud of Benjamin eighty years, to Barak of Naphtali forty years, to Gideon of Manasseh forty years, to Abimelech his son three years, to Tola of Issachar twenty-three, to Jair of Manasseh twenty-two, to Jephtha of Manasseh six, to Ibzan of Judah seven, to Elon of Zebulun ten, to Abdon of Ephriam eight, to Samson of Dan twenty, in all 299. As for the years of their servitude, as were Eglon is said to oppress them eighteen years and Jabin twenty years, and so some others, those must be reckoned to fall in with some or other of the years of the judges. The judges here appear to have been of eight several tribes; that honour was thus diffused, until at last it cèntred in Judah. Eli and Samuel, the two judges that fall not within this book, were of Levi. It seems, there was no judge of Reuben or Simeon, Gad or Asher. The history of these judges in their order we have in this book to the end of *ch.* 16. And then in the last five chapters we have an account of some particular memorable events which happened, as the story of Ruth did (Ruth 1:1) *in the days when the judges ruled,* but it is not certain in which judge's days; but they are put together at the end of the book, that the thread of the general history might not be interrupted. Now as to the state of the commonwealth of Israel during this period, I. They do not appear here either so great or so good as one might have expected the character of such a peculiar people would be, that were governed by such laws and enriched by such promises. We find them wretchedly corrupted, and wretchedly oppressed by their neighbours about them, and nowhere in all the book, either in war or council, do they make any figure proportionable to their glorious entry into Canaan. What shall we say to it? God would hereby show us the lamentable imperfection of all persons and things under the sun, that we may look for complete holiness and happiness in the other world, and not in this. Yet, II. We may hope that though the historian in this book enlarges most upon their provocations and grievances, yet there was a face of religion upon the land; and, however there were those among them that were drawn aside to idolatry, yet the tabernacle-service, according to the law of Moses, was kept up, and there were many that attended it. Historians record not the common course of justice and commerce in a nation, taking that for granted, but only the wars and disturbances that happen; but the reader must consider the other, to balance the blackness of them. III. It should seem that in these times each tribe had very much its government in ordinary within itself, and acted separately, without one common head, or council, which occasioned many differences among themselves, and kept them from being or doing any thing considerable. IV. The government of the judges was not constant, but occasional; when it is said that after Ehud's victory *the land rested eighty years,* and after Barak's *forty,* it is not certain that they lived, much less that they governed, so long; but they and the rest were raised up and animated by the Spirit of God to do particular service to the public when there was occasion, to *avenge Israel of their enemies,* and to purge Israel of their idolatries, which are the two things principally meant by their judging Israel. Yet Deborah, as a prophetess, was attended for judgment by all Israel, before there was occasion for her agency in war, *ch.* 4:4. V. During the government of the judges, God was in a more especial manner Israel's king; so Samuel tells them when they were resolved to throw off this form of government, 1 Sa. 12:12. God would try what his own law and the constitutions of that would do to keep them in order, and it proved that when *there was no king in Israel every man did that which was right in his own eyes;* he therefore, towards the latter end of this time, made the government of the judges more constant and universal that it was at first, and at length gave them David, a king after his own heart; then, and not till then, Israel began to flourish, which should make us very thankful for magistrates both supreme and subordinate, for they are *ministers of God unto us for good.* Four of the judges of Israel are canonized (Heb. 11:32), Gideon, Barak, Samson, and Jephtha. The Learned bishop Patrick thinks the prophet Samuel was the penman of this Book.

CHAPTER 1

This chapter gives us a particular account what sort of progress the several tribes of Israel made in the reducing of Canaan after the death of Joshua. He did (as we say) break the neck of that great work, and put it into such a posture that they might easily have perfected it in due time, if they had not been wanting to themselves; what they did in order hereunto, and wherein they came short, we are told. I. The united tribes o Judah and Simeon did bravely. 1. God appointed Judah to begin (*v.* 1, 2). 2. Judah took Simeon to act in conjunction with him (*v.* 3). 3. They succeeded in their enterprises against Bezek (*v.* 4–7), Jerusalem (*v.* 8). Hebron and Debir (*v.* 9–15), Hormah, Gaza, and other places (*v.* 17–19). 4. Yet where there were chariots of iron their hearts failed them (*v.* 19). Mention is made of the Kenites settling among them (*v.* 16). II. The other tribes, in comparison with these, acted a cowardly part. 1. Benjamin failed (*v.* 21). 2. The house of Joseph did well against Beth-el (*v.* 22–26), but in other places did not improve their advantages, nor Manasseh (*v.* 27, 28), nor Ephraim (*v.* 29). 3. Zebulun spared the Canaanites (*v.* 30). 4. Asher truckled worse than any of them to the Canaanites (*v.* 31, 32). 5. Naphtali was kept out of the full possession of several of his cities (*v.* 33). 6. Dan was straitened by the Amorites (*v.* 34). No account is given of Issachar, nor of the two tribes and a half on the other side Jordan.

Verses 1–8

Here, I. The children of Israel consult the oracle of God for direction which of all the tribes should first attempt to clear their country of the Canaanites, and to animate and encourage the rest. It was *after the death of Joshua.* While he lived he directed them, and all the tribes were obedient to him, but when he died he left no successor in the same authority that he had; but the people must consult the breast-plate of judgment, and thence receive the word of command; for God himself, as he was their King, so he was the Lord of their hosts. The question they ask is, *Who shall go up first? v.* 1. By this time, we may suppose, they were so multiplied that the places they were in possession of began to be too strait for them, and they must thrust out the enemy to make room; now they enquire who should first take up arms. Whether each tribe was ambitious of being first, and so strove for the honour of it, or whether each was afraid of being first, and so strove to decline it, does not appear; but by common consent the matter was referred to God himself, who is the fittest both to dispose of honours and to cut out work.

II. God appointed that Judah should go up first, and promised him success (*v.* 2): *"I have delivered the land into his hand,* to be possessed, and therefore will deliver the enemy into his hand, that keeps him out of possession, to be destroyed." And why must Judah be first in this undertaking? 1. Judah was the most numerous and powerful tribe, and therefore let Judah venture first. Note, God appoints service according to the strength he has given. Those that are most able, from them most work is expected. 2. Judah was first in dignity, and therefore must be first in duty. He it is whom *his brethren must praise,* and therefore he it is who must lead in perilous services. Let the burden of honour and the burden of work go together. 3. Judah was first served; the lot came up for Judah first, and therefore Judah must first fight. 4. Judah was the tribe out of which our Lord was to spring: so that in Judah, Christ, the Lion of the tribe of Judah, went before them. Christ engaged the powers of darkness first, and foiled them, which animates us for our conflicts; and it is in him that we are *more than conquerors.* Observe, The service and the success are put together: "Judah shall go up; let him do his part, and then he shall find that *I have delivered the land into his hand."* His service will not avail unless God give the success; but God will not give the success unless he vigorously apply himself to the service.

III. Judah hereupon prepares to go up, but courts his brother and neighbour the tribe of Simeon (the lot of which tribe fell within that of Judah and was assigned out of it) to join forces with him, *v.* 3. Observe here, 1. That the strongest should not despise but desire the assistance even of those that are weaker. Judah was the most considerable of all the tribes, and Simeon the least considerable, and yet Judah begs Simeon's friendship, and prays an aid from him; the head cannot say to the foot, *I have no need of thee,* for we are *members one of another.* 2. Those that crave assistance must be ready to give assistance: *Come with me into my lot,* and then *I will go with thee into thine.* It becomes Israelites to help one another against Canaanites; and all Christians, even those of different tribes, should strengthen one another's hands against the common interests of Satan's kingdom. Those who thus help one another in love have reason to hope that God will graciously help them both.

IV. The confederate forces of Judah and Simeon take the field: *Judah went up* (*v.* 4), and Simeon with him, *v.* 3. Caleb, it is probable, was commander-in-chief of this expedition; for who so fit as he who had both an old man's head and a young man's hand, the experience of age and the vigour of youth? Jos. 14:10, 11. It should seem too, by what follows (*v.* 10, 11), that he was not yet in possession of his own allotment. It was happy for them that they had such a general as, according to his name, was all heart. Some think that the Canaanites had got together into a body, a formidable body, when Israel consulted who should go and *fight against them,* and that they then began to stir when they heard of the death of Joshua, whose name had been so dreadful to them; but, if so, it proved they did but meddle to their own hurt.

V. God gave them great success. Whether they invaded the enemy, or the enemy first gave them the alarm, *the Lord delivered them into their hand, v.* 4. Though the army of Judah was strong and bold, yet the victory is attributed to God: he *delivered the Canaanites into their hand;* having given them authority, he here gives them ability to destroy them — put it in their power, and so tried their obedience to his command, which was *utterly to cut them off.* Bishop Patrick observes upon this that we meet not with such religious expressions in the heathen writers, concerning the success of their arms, as we have here and elsewhere in this sacred history. I wish such pious acknowledgments of the divine providence had not grown into disuse at this time with many that are called Christians. Now, 1. We are told how the army of the Canaanites was routed in the field, in or near Bezek, the place where they drew up, which afterwards Saul made the place of a general rendezvous (1 Sa. 11:8); they slew 10,000 men, which blow, if followed, could not but be a very great weakening to those that were already brought so very low. 2. How their king was taken and mortified. His name was Adoni-bezek, which signifies, *lord of Bezek.* There have been those that called their lands by *their own names* (Ps. 49:11), but here was one (and there has been many another) that called himself by his land's name. He was taken prisoner after the battle, and we are here told how they used him; they cut off his thumbs, to disfit him for fighting, and his great toes, that he might not be able to run away, *v.* 6. It had been barbarous thus to triumph over a man in misery, and that lay at their mercy, but that he was a devoted Canaanite, and one that had in like manner abused others, which probably they had heard of. Josephus says, "They cut off his hands and his feet," probably supposing those more likely to be mortal wounds than only the cutting off of his thumbs and his great toes. But this indignity which they did him extorted from him an acknowledgment of the righteousness of God, *v.* 7. Here observe, (1.) What a great man this Adoni-bezek had been, how great in the field, where armies fled before him, how great at home, where kings were *set with the dogs of his flock;* and yet now himself a prisoner, and reduced to the extremity of meanness and disgrace. See how changeable this world is, and how slippery its high places are. Let not the highest be proud, nor the strongest secure, for they know not how low they may be brought before they die. (2.) What desolations he had made among his neighbours: he had wholly subdued seventy kings, to such a degree as to have them his prisoners; he that was the chief person in a city was then called a *king,* and the greatness of their title did but aggravate their disgrace, and fired the pride of him that insulted over them. We cannot suppose that Adoni-bezek had seventy of these petty princes at once his slaves; but first and last, in the course of his reign, he had thus deposed and abused so many, who perhaps were many of them kings of the same cities that successively opposed him, and whom he thus treated to please his own imperious barbarous fancy, and for a terror to others. It seems the Canaanites had been wasted by civil wars, and those bloody ones, among themselves, which would very much facilitate the conquest of them by Israel. "Judah," says Dr. Lightfoot, "in conquering Adoni-bezek, did, in effect, conquer seventy kings." (3.) How justly he was teated as he had treated others. Thus the righteous God sometimes, in his providence, makes the punishment to answer the sin, and observes an equality in his judgments; the spoiler shall be spoiled, and the *treacherous dealer dealt treacherously* with, Isa. 33:1. And those that *showed no mercy* shall have *no mercy shown* them, Jam. 2:13. See Rev. 13:10; 18:6. (4.) How honestly he owned the righteousness of God herein: *As I have done, so God has requited me.* See the power of conscience, when God by his judgments awakens it, how it brings sin to remembrance, and subscribes to the justice of God. He that in his pride had set God at defiance now yields to him, and reflects with as much regret upon the kings under his table as ever he had looked upon them with pleasure when he had them there. He seems to own that he was better dealt with than he had dealt with his prisoners; for though the Israelites maimed him (according to the law of retaliation, an *eye for an eye,* so a thumb for a thumb), yet they did not put him *under the table* to be fed with the crumbs there, because, though the other might well be looked upon as an act of justice, this would have savoured more of pride and haughtiness than did become an Israelite.

VI. Particular notice is taken of the conquest of Jerusalem, *v.* 8. Our translators judge it spoken of here as done formerly in Joshua's time, and only repeated on occasion of Adoni-bezek's dying there, and therefore read it, "they had fought against Jerusalem," and put this verse in a parenthesis; but the original speaks of it as a thing now done, and this seems most probable because it is said to be done by the children of Judah in particular, not by all Israel in general, whom Joshua commanded. Joshua indeed conquered and slew Adoni-zedec, king of Jerusalem (Jos. 10), but we read not there of his taking the city; probably, while he was pursing his conquests elsewhere, this Adoni-bezek, a neighbouring prince, got possession of it, whom Israel having conquered in the field, the city fell into their hands, and they slew the inhabitants, except those who retreated into the castle and held out there till David's time, and they *set the city on fire,* in token of their detestation of the idolatry wherewith it had been deeply infected, yet probably not so utterly as to consume it, but to leave convenient habitations for as many as they had to put into the possession of it.

Verses 9–20

We have here a further account of that glorious and successful campaign which Judah and Simeon made. 1. The lot of Judah was pretty well cleared of the Canaanites, yet not thoroughly. Those that *dwelt in the mountain* (the mountains that were round about Jerusalem) were driven out (*v.* 9, 19), but those in the valley kept their ground against them, having *chariots of iron,* such as we read of, Jos. 17:16. Here the men of Judah failed, and thereby spoiled the influence which otherwise their example hitherto might have had on the rest of the tribes, who followed them in this instance of their cowardice, rather than in all the other instances of their courage. They had iron chariots, and therefore it was thought not safe to attack them: but had not Israel God on their side, *whose chariots are thousands of angels* (Ps. 68:17), before whom these iron chariots would be but as stubble to the fire? Had not God expressly promised by the oracle (*v.* 2) to give them success against the Canaanites in this very expedition, without excepting those that had iron chariots? Yet they suffered their fears to prevail against their faith, they could not trust God under any disadvantages, and therefore durst not face the iron chariots, but meanly withdrew their forces, when with one bold stroke they might have completed their victories; and it proved of pernicious consequence. They did run well, what hindered them? Gal. 5:7. 2. Caleb was put in possession of Hebron, which, though given him by Joshua ten or twelve years before (as Dr. Lightfoot computes), yet being employed in public service, for the settling of the tribes, which he preferred before his own private interests, it seems he did not till now make himself master of; so well content was that good man to serve others, while he left himself to be served last; few are like-minded, for *all seek their own,* Phil. 2:20, 21. Yet now the men of Judah all came in to his assistance for the reducing of Hebron (*v.* 10), slew the sons of Anak, and put him in possession of it, *v.* 20. They gave Hebron unto Caleb. And now Caleb, that he might return the kindness of his countrymen, is impatient to see Debir reduced and put into the hands of the men of Judah, to expedite which he proffers his daughter to the person that will undertake to command in the siege of that important place, *v.* 11, 12. Othniel bravely undertakes it, and wins the town and the lady (*v.* 13), and by his wife's interest and management with her father gains a very good inheritance for himself and his family, *v.* 14, 15. We had this passage before, Jos. 15:16–19, where it was largely explained and improved. 3. Simeon got ground of the Canaanites in his border, *v.* 17, 18. In the eastern part of Simeon's lot, they destroyed the Canaanites in Zephath, and called it *Hormah — destruction,* adding this to some other devoted cities not far off, which they had some time ago, with good reason, called by that name, Num. 21:2, 3. And this perhaps was the complete performance of the vow they them made that they would utterly destroy these cities of the Canaanites in the south. In the western part they took Gaza, Askelon, and Ekron, cities of the Philistines; they gained present possession of the cities, but, not destroying the inhabitants, the Philistines in process of time recovered the cities, and proved inveterate enemies to the Israel of God, and no better could come of doing their work by the halves. 4. The Kenites gained a settlement in the tribe of Judah, choosing it there rather than in any other tribe, because it was the strongest, and there they hoped to be safe and quiet, *v.* 16. These were the posterity of Jethro, who either went with Israel when Moses invited them (Num. 10:29) or met them about the same place when they came up from their wanderings in the wilderness thirty-eight years after, and went with them then to Canaan, Moses having promised them that they should fare as Israel fared, Num. 10:32. They had at first seated themselves in the *city of palm-trees,* that is, Jericho, a city which never was to be rebuilt, and therefore the fitter for those who *dwelt in tents,* and did not mind building. But afterwards they removed into the wilderness of Judah, either out of their affection to that place, because solitary and retired, or out of their affection to that tribe, which perhaps had been in a particular manner kind to them. Yet we find the tent of Jael, who was of that family, far north, in the lot of Naphtali, when Sisera took shelter there, *ch.* 4:17. This respect Israel showed them, to let them fix where they pleased, being a quiet people, who, wherever they were, were content with a little. Those that molested none were molested by none. *Blessed are the meek, for* thus *they shall inherit the earth.*

Verses 21–36

We are here told upon what terms the rest of the tribes stood with the Canaanites that remained.

I. Benjamin neglected to drive the Jebusites out of that part of the city of Jerusalem which fell to their lot, *v.* 21. Judah had set them a good example, and gained them great advantages by what they did (*v.* 9), but they did not follow the blow for want of resolution.

II. The house of Joseph,

1. Bestirred themselves a little to get possession of Bethel, *v.* 22. That city is mentioned in the tribe of Benjamin, Jos. 18:22. Yet it is spoken of there (*v.* 13) as a city in the borders of that tribe, and, it should seem, the line went through it, so that one half of it only belonged to Benjamin, the other half to Ephraim; and perhaps the activity of the Ephraimites at this time, to recover it from the Canaanites, secured it entirely to them henceforward, or at least the greatest part of it, for afterwards we find it so much under the power of the ten tribes (and Benjamin was none of them) that Jeroboam set up one of his calves in it. In this account of the expedition of the Ephraimites against Beth-el observe,

(1.) Their interest in the divine favour: *The Lord was with them,* and would have been with the other tribes if they would have exerted their strength. The Chaldee reads it here, as in many other places, *The Word of the Lord was their helper,* namely, Christ himself, the captain of the Lord's host, now that they acted separately, as well as when they were all in one body.

(2.) The prudent measures they took to gain the city. They sent spies to observe what part of the city was weakest, or which way they might make their attack with most advantage, *v.* 23. These spies got very good information from a man they providentially met with, who showed them a private way into the town, which was left unguarded because, being not generally known, no danger was suspected on that side. And here, [1.] He is not to be blamed for giving them this intelligence if he did it from a conviction that *the Lord was with them,* and that by his donation the land was theirs of right, any more than Rahab was for entertaining those whom she knew to be enemies of her country, but friends of God. Nor, [2.] Are those to be blamed who *showed him mercy,* gave him and his family not only their lives, but liberty to go wherever they pleased: for one good turn requires another. But, it seems, he would not join himself to the people of Israel, he feared them rather than loved them, and therefore he removed after a colony of the Hittites, which, it should seem, had gone into Arabia and settled there upon Joshua's invasion of the country; with them this man chose to dwell, and among them he built a city, a small one, we may suppose, such as planters commonly build, and in the name of it preserved the ancient name of his native city, *Luz, an almondtree,* preferring this before its new name, which carried religion in it, *Bethel — the house of God.*

(3.) Their success. The spies brought or sent notice of the intelligence they had gained to the army, which improved their advantages, surprised the city, and put them all to the sword, *v.* 25. But,

2. Besides this achievement, it seems, the children of Joseph did nothing remarkable (1.) Manasseh failed to drive out the Canaanites from several very considerable cities in their lot, and did not make any attempt upon them, *v.* 27. But the Canaanites, being in possession, were resolved not to quit it; they would dwell in that land, and Manasseh had not resolution enough to offer to dispossess them; as if there was no meddling with them unless they were willing to resign, which it was not to be expected they ever would be. Only as Israel got strength they got ground, and served themselves, both by their contributions and by their personal services, *v.* 28, 35. (2.) Ephraim likewise, though a powerful tribe, neglected Gezer a considerable city, and suffered the Canaanites to *dwell among them* (*v.* 29), which, some think, intimates their allowing them a quiet settlement, and indulging them with the privileges of an unconquered people, not so much as making them tributaries.

III. Zebulun, perhaps inclining to the sea-trade, for it was foretold that it should be a haven for ships, neglected to reduce Kitron and Nahalol (*v.* 30), and only made the inhabitants of those places tributaries to them.

IV. Asher quitted itself worse than any of the tribes (*v.* 31, 32), not only in leaving more towns than any of them in the hands of the Canaanites, but in submitting to the Canaanites instead of making them tributaries; for so the manner of expression intimates, that the Asherites dwelt among the Canaanites, as if the Canaanites were the more numerous and the more powerful, would still be lords of the country, and the Israelites must be only upon sufferance among them.

V. Naphtali also permitted the Canaanites to live among them (*v.* 33), only by degrees they got them so far under as to exact contributions from them.

VI. Dan was so far from extending his conquests where his lot lay that, wanting spirit to make head against the Amorites, he was forced by them to retire into the mountains and inhabit the cities there, but durst not venture into the valley, where, it is probable, the chariots of iron were, *v.* 34. Nay, and some of the cities in the mountains were kept against them, *v.* 35. Thus were they straitened in their possessions, and forced to seek for more room at Laish, a great way off, *ch.* 18:1, etc. In Jacob's blessing Judah is compared to a lion, Dan to a serpent; now observe how Judah with his lion-like courage prospered and prevailed, but Dan with all his serpenting subtlety could get no ground; craft and artful management do not always effect the wonders they pretend to. What Dan came short of doing, it seems, his neighbours the Ephraimites in part did for him; they put the Amorites under tribute, *v.* 35.

Upon the whole matter it appears that the people of Israel were generally very careless both of their duty and interest in this thing; they did not what they might have done to expel the Canaanites and make room for themselves. And, 1. It was owing to their slothfulness and cowardice. They would not be at the pains to complete their conquests; like the sluggard, that dreamed of a lion in the way, a lion in the streets, they fancied insuperable difficulties, and frightened themselves with winds and clouds from sowing and reaping. 2. It was owing to their covetousness; the Canaanites' labour and money would do them more good (they thought) than their blood, and therefore they were willing to let them live among them, that they might make a hand of them. 3. They had not that dread and detestation of idolatry which they ought to have had; they thought it a pity to put these Canaanites to the sword, though the measure of their iniquity was full, thought it would be no harm to let them live among them, and that they should be in no danger from them. 4. The same thing that kept their fathers forty years out of Canaan kept them now out of the full possession of it, and that was unbelief. Distrust of the power and promise of God lost them their advantages, and ran them into a thousand mischiefs.

CHAPTER 2

In this chapter we have, I. A particular message which God sent to Israel by an angel, and the impression it made upon them (*v.* 1–5). II. A general idea of the state of Israel during the government of the judges, in which observe, 1. Their adherence to God while Joshua and the elders lived (*v.* 6–10). 2. Their revolt afterwards to idolatry (*v.* 11–13). 3. God's displeasure against them, and his judgments upon them for it (*v.* 14, 15). 4. His pity towards them, shown in raising them up deliverers (*v.* 16–18). 5. Their relapse into idolatry after the judgment was over (*v.* 17–19). 6. The full stop God in anger put to their successes (*v.* 20–23). These are the contents, not only of this chapter, but of the whole book.

Verses 1–5

It was the privilege of Israel that they had not only a law in general sent them from heaven, once for all, to direct them into and keep them in the way of happiness, but that they had particular messages sent them from heaven, as there was occasion, for reproof, for correction, and for instruction in righteousness, when at any time they turned aside out of that way. Besides the written word which they had before them to read, they often *heard a word behind them, saying, This is the way,* Isa. 30:21. Here begins that way of God's dealing with them. When they would not hear Moses, let it be tried whether they will hear the prophets. In these verses we have a very awakening sermon that was preached to them when they began to cool in their religion.

I. The preacher was an *angel of the Lord* (*v.* 1), not a prophet, not Phinehas, as the Jews conceit; gospel ministers are indeed called *angels of the churches,* but the Old-Testament prophets are never called angels of the Lord; no doubt this was a messenger we from heaven. Such extraordinary messengers we sometimes find in this book employed in the raising up of the judges that delivered Israel, as Gideon and Samson; and now, to show how various are the good offices they do for God's Israel, here is one sent to preach to them, to prevent their falling into sin and trouble. This extraordinary messenger was sent to command, if possible, the greater regard to the message, and to affect the minds of a people whom nothing seemed to affect but what was sensible. The learned bishop Patrick is clearly of opinion that this was not a created angel, but the Angel of the covenant, the same that appeared to Joshua as *captain of the hosts of the Lord,* who was God himself. Christ himself, says Dr. Lightfoot; who but God and Christ could say, *I made you to go up out of Egypt?* Joshua had lately admonished them to take heed of entangling themselves with the Canaanites, but they regarded not the words of a dying man; the same warning therefore is here brought them by the living God himself, the Son of God appearing as an angel. If they slight his servants, surely they will reverence his Son. This angel of the Lord is said to come up from Gilgal, perhaps not walking on the earth, but flying swiftly, as the angel Gabriel did to Daniel, in the open firmament of heaven; but, whether walking or flying, he seemed to come from Gilgal for a particular reason. Gilgal was long their headquarters after they came into Canaan, many signal favours they had there received from God, and there the covenant of circumcision was renewed (Mic. 6:5), of all which it was designed they should be reminded by his coming from Gilgal. The remembrance of *what we have received and heard* will prepare us for a warning to hold fast, Rev. 3:2, 3.

II. The persons to whom this sermon was preached were *all the children of Israel, v.* 4. A great congregation for a great preacher! They were assembled either for war, each tribe sending in its forces for some great expedition, or rather for worship, and then the place of their meeting must be Shiloh, where the tabernacle was, at which they were all to come together three times a year. When we attend upon God in instituted ordinances we may expect to hear from him, and to receive his gifts at his own gates. The place is called *Bochim* (*v.* 1), because it gained that name upon this occasion. All Israel needed the reproof and warning here given, and therefore it is spoken to them all.

III. The sermon itself is short, but very close. God here tells them plainly, 1. What he had done for them, *v.* 1. He had brought them out of Egypt, a land of slavery and toil, into Canaan, a land of rest, liberty, and plenty. The miseries of the one served as a foil to the felicities of the other. God had herein been kind to them, true to the oath sworn to their fathers, had given such proofs of his power as left them inexcusable if they distrusted it, and such engagements to his service as left them inexcusable if they deserted it. 2. What he had promised them: *I said, I will never break my covenant with you.* When he took them to be his peculiar people, it was not with any design to cast them off again, or to change them for another people at his pleasure; let them but be faithful to him, and they should find him unchangeably constant to them. He told them plainly that the covenant he entered into with them should never break, unless it broke on their side. 3. What were his just and reasonable expectations from them (*v.* 2): that being taken into covenant with God they should make no league with the Canaanites, who were both his enemies and theirs, — that having set up his altar they should throw down their altars, lest they should be a temptation to them to serve their gods. Could any thing be demanded more easy? 4. How they had in this very thing, which he had most insisted on, disobeyed him: "But you have not in so small a matter obeyed my voice." In contempt of their covenant with God, and their confederacy with each other in that covenant, they made leagues of friendship with the idolatrous devoted Canaanites, and connived at their altars, though they stood in competition with God's. *"Why have you done this?* What account can you give of this perverseness of yours at the bar of right reason? What apology can you make for yourselves, or what excuse can you offer?" Those that throw off their communion with God, and have fellowship with the unfruitful works of darkness, know not what they do now, and will have nothing to say for themselves in the day of account shortly. 5. How they must expect to smart by and by for this their folly, *v.* 3. Their tolerating the Canaanites among them would, (1.) Put a period to their victories: *"You* will not drive them out," says God, "and therefore *I* will not;" thus their sin was made their punishment. Thus those who indulge their lusts and corruptions, which they should mortify, forfeit the grace of God, and it is justly withdrawn from them. If we will not resist the devil, we cannot expect that God should tread him under our feet. (2.) It would involve them in continual troubles. "They shall be thorns in your sides to gore you, which way soever you turn, always doing you one mischief or other." Those deceive themselves who expect advantage by friendship with those that are enemies to God. (3.) It would (which was worst of all) expose them to constant temptation and draw them to sin. "Their gods" (their *abominations,* so the Chaldee) "will be a snare to you; you will find yourselves wretchedly entangled in an affection to them, and it will be your ruin," so some read it. Those that approach sin are justly left to themselves to fall into sin and to perish in it. God often makes men's sin their punishment; and thorns and snares are *in the way of the froward,* who will walk contrary to God.

IV. The good success of this sermon is very remarkable: The people *lifted up their voice and wept, v.* 4. 1. The angel had told them of their sins, for which they thus expressed their sorrow: the lifted up their voice in confession of sin, crying out against their own folly and ingratitude, and wept, as those that were both ashamed of themselves and angry at themselves, as having acted so directly contrary both to their reason and to their interest. 2. The angel had threatened them with the judgments of God, of which they thus expressed their dread: they lifted up their voice in prayer to God to turn away his wrath from them, and wept for fear of that wrath. They relented upon this alarm, and their hearts melted within them, and trembled at the word, and not without cause. This was good, and a sign that the word they heard made an impression upon them: it is a wonder sinners can ever read their Bible with dry eyes. But this was not enough; they wept, but we do not find that they reformed, that they went home and destroyed all the remains of idolatry and idolaters among them. Many are melted under the word that harden again before they are cast into a new mould. However, this general weeping, (1.) Gave a new name to the place (*v.* 5): they called it *Bochim, Weepers,* a good name for our religious assemblies to answer. Had they kept close to God and their duty, no voice but that of singing would have been heard in their congregation; but by their sin and folly the had made other work for themselves, and now nothing is to be heard but the voice of weeping. (2.) It gave occasion for a solemn sacrifice: They *sacrificed there unto the Lord,* having (as is supposed) met at Shiloh, where God's altar was. They offered sacrifice to turn away God's wrath, and to obtain his favour, and in token of their dedication of themselves to him, and to him only, making a covenant by this sacrifice. The disease being thus taken in time, and the physic administered working so well, one would have hoped a cure might be effected. But by the sequel of the story it appears to have been too deeply rooted to be wept out.

Verses 6–23

The beginning of this paragraph is only a repetition of what account we had before of the people's good character during the government of Joshua, and of his death and burial (Jos. 24:29, 30), which comes in here again only to make way for the following account, which this chapter gives, of their degeneracy and apostasy. The angel had foretold that the Canaanites and their idols would be a snare to Israel; now the historian undertakes to show that they were so, and, that this may appear the more clear, he looks back a little, and takes notice, 1. Of their happy settlement in the land of Canaan. Joshua, having distributed this land among them, dismissed them to the quiet and comfortable possession of it (*v.* 6): *He sent them away,* not only every tribe, but *every man to his inheritance,* no doubt giving them his blessing. 2. Of their continuance in the faith and fear of God's holy name as long as Joshua lived, *v.* 7. As they went to their possessions with good resolutions to cleave to God, so they persisted for some time in these good resolutions, as long as they had good rulers that set them good examples, gave them good instructions, and reproved and restrained the corruptions that crept in among them, and as long as they had fresh in remembrance the great things God did for them when he brought them into Canaan: those that had seen these wonders had so much sense as to believe their own eyes, and so much reason as to serve that God who had appeared so gloriously on their behalf; but those that followed, because they had not seen, believed not. 3. Of the death and burial of Joshua, which gave a fatal stroke to the interests of religion among the people, *v.* 8, 9. Yet so much sense they had of their obligations to him that they did him honour at his death, and buried him in *Timnath-heres;* so it is called here, not, as in Joshua, *Timnath-serah. Heres* signifies the *sun,* a representation of which, some think, was set upon his sepulchre, and gave name to it, in remembrance of the sun's standing still at his word. So divers of the Jewish writers say; but I much question whether an image of the sun would be allowed to the honour of Joshua at that time, when, by reason of men's general proneness to worship the sun, it would be in danger of being abused to the dishonour of God. 4. Of the rising of a new generation, *v.* 10. All that generation in a few years wore off, their good instructions and examples died and were buried with them, and there arose another generation of Israelites who had so little sense of religion, and were in so little care about it, that, notwithstanding all the advantages of their education, one might truly say that they knew not the Lord, knew him not aright, knew him not as he had revealed himself, else they would not have forsaken him. They were so entirely devoted to the world, so intent upon the business of it or so indulgent of the flesh in ease and luxury, that they never minded the true God and his holy religion, and so were easily drawn aside to false gods and their abominable superstitions.

And so he comes to give us a general idea of the series of things in Israel during the time of the judges, the same repeated in the same order.

I. The people of Israel forsook the God of Israel, and gave that worship and honour to the dunghill deities of the Canaanites which was due to him alone. *Be astonished, O heavens! at this, and wonder, O earth! Hath a nation,* such a nation, so well fed, so well taught, *changed its God,* such a God, a God of infinite power, unspotted purity, inexhaustible goodness, and so very jealous of a competitor, for stocks and stones that could do neither good nor evil? Jer. 2:11, 12. Never was there such an instance of folly, ingratitude, and perfidiousness. Observe how it is described here, *v.* 11–13. In general, *they did evil,* nothing could be more evil, that is, more provoking to God, nor more prejudicial to themselves, and it was *in the sight of the Lord;* all evil is before him, but he takes special notice of the sin of having any other god. In particular, 1. They *forsook the Lord* (*v.* 12, and again *v.* 13); this was one of the two great evils they were guilty of, Jer. 2:13. They had been joined to the Lord in covenant, but now they forsook him, as a wife *treacherously departs from her husband.* "They forsook the worship of the Lord," so the Chaldee: for those that forsake the worship of God do in effect forsake God himself. It aggravated this that he was *the God of their fathers,* so that they were *born in his house,* and therefore bound to serve him; and that he *brought them out of the land of Egypt,* he *loosed their bonds,* and upon that account also they were obliged to serve him. 2. When they forsook the only true God they did not turn atheists, nor were they such fools as to say, *There is no God;* but they followed other gods: so much remained of pure nature as to own a God, yet so much appeared of corrupt nature as to multiply gods, and take up with any, and to follow the fashion, not the rule, in religious worship. Israel had the honour of being a peculiar people and dignified above all others, and yet so false were they to their own privileges that they were fond of the gods *of the people that were round about them.* Baal and Ashtaroth, he-gods and she-gods; they made their court to sun and moon, Jupiter and Juno. *Baalim* signifies *lords,* and *Ashtaroth blessed ones,* both plural, for when they forsook Jehovah, who is one, they had gods many and lords many, as a luxuriant fancy pleased to multiply them. Whatever they took for their gods, they served them and bowed down to them, gave honour to them and begged favours from them.

II. The God of Israel was hereby provoked to anger, and delivered them up into the hand of their enemies, *v.* 14, 15. He was wroth with them, for he is a jealous God and true to the honour of his own name; and the way he took to punish them for their apostasy was to make those their tormentors whom they yielded to as their tempters. They made themselves as mean and miserable by forsaking God as they would have been great and happy if they had continued faithful to him. 1. The scale of victory turned against them. After they forsook God, whenever they took the sword in hand they were as sure to be beaten as before they had been sure to conquer. Formerly their enemies could not stand before them, but, wherever they went, the hand of the Lord was for them; when they began to cool in their religion, God suspended his favour, stopped the progress of their successes, and would not drive out their enemies any more (*v.* 3), only suffered them to keep their ground; but now, when they had quite revolted to idolatry, the war turned directly against them, and they *could not any longer stand before their enemies.* God would rather give the success to those that had never known nor owned him than to those that had done both, but had now deserted him. Wherever they went, they might perceive that God himself had *turned to be their enemy, and fought against them,* Isa. 63:10. 2. The balance of power then turned against them of course. Whoever would might spoil them, whoever would might oppress them. God sold them into the hands of their enemies; not only he delivered them up freely, as we do that which we have sold, but he did it upon a valuable consideration, that he might get himself honour as a jealous God, who would not spare even his own peculiar people when they provoked him. He sold them as insolvent debtors are sold (Mt. 18:25), by their sufferings to make some sort of reparation to his glory for the injury it sustained by their apostasy. Observe how their punishment, (1.) Answered what they had done. They served the gods of *the nations that were round about them,* even the meanest, and God made then serve the princes of the nations that were round about them, even the meanest. He that is company for every fool is justly made a fool of by every company. (2.) How it answered what God has spoken. The hand of heaven was thus turned against them, *as the Lord had said,* and *as the Lord had sworn* (*v.* 15), referring to the curse and death set before them in the covenant, with the blessing and life. Those that have found God true to his promises may thence infer that he will be as true to his threatenings.

III. The God of infinite mercy took pity on them in their distresses, though they had brought themselves into them by their own sin and folly, and wrought deliverance for them. Nevertheless, though their trouble was the punishment of their sin and the accomplishment of God's word, yet they were in process of time saved out of their trouble, *v.* 16–18. Here observe, 1. The inducement of their deliverance. It came purely from God's pity and tender compassion; the reason was fetched from within himself. It is not said, *It repented them because of their iniquities* (for it appears, *v.* 17, that many of them continued unreformed), but, *It repented the Lord because of their groanings;* though it is not so much the burden of sin as the burden of affliction that they are said to groan under. It is true they deserved to perish for ever under his curse, yet, this being the day of his patience and our probation, he does not stir up all his wrath. He might in justice have abandoned them, but he could not for pity do it. 2. The instruments of their deliverance. God did not send angels from heaven to rescue them, nor bring in any foreign power to their aid, but raised up judges from among themselves, as there was occasion, men to whom God gave extraordinary qualifications for, and calls to, that special service for which they were designed, which was to reform and deliver Israel, and whose great attempts he crowned with wonderful success: *The Lord was with the judges* when he raised them up, and so they became saviours. Observe, (1.) In the days of the greatest degeneracy and distress of the church there shall be some whom God will either find or make to redress its grievances and set things to rights. (2.) God must be acknowledged in the seasonable rising up of useful men for public service. He endues men with wisdom and courage, gives them hearts to act and venture. All that are in any way the blessings of their country must be looked upon as the gifts of God. (3.) Whom God calls he will own, and give them his presence; whom he raises up he will be with. (4.) The judges of a land are its saviours.

IV. The degenerate Israelites were not effectually and thoroughly reformed, no, not by their judges, *v.* 17–19. 1. Even while their judges were with them, and active in the work of reformation, there were those that *would not hearken to their judges,* but at that very time *went a whoring after other gods,* so mad were they upon their idols, and so obstinately *bent to backslide.* They had been espoused to God, but broke the marriage-covenant, and went a whoring after these gods. Idolatry is spiritual adultery, so vile, and base, and perfidious a thing is it, and so hardly are those reclaimed that are addicted to it. 2. Those that in the times of reformation began to amend *yet turned quickly out of the way* again, and became as bad as ever. The way they turned out of was that which their godly ancestors walked in, and set them out in; but they soon started from under the influence both of their fathers' good example and of their own good education. The wicked children of godly parents do so, and will therefore have a great deal to answer for. However, *when the judge was dead,* they looked upon the dam which checked the stream of their idolatry as removed, and then it flowed down again with so much the more fury, and the next age seemed to be rather the worse for the attempts that had been made towards reformation, *v.* 19. *They corrupted themselves more than their fathers,* strove to outdo them in multiplying strange gods and inventing profane and impious rites of worship, as it were in contradiction to their reformers. *They ceased not* from, or, as the word is, *they would not let fall,* any of their own doings, grew not ashamed of those idolatrous services that were most odious nor weary of those that were most barbarous, would not so much as diminish one step of their hard and stubborn way. Thus those that have forsaken the good ways of God, which they have once known and professed, commonly grow most daring and desperate in sin, and have their hearts most hardened.

V. God's just resolution hereupon was still to continue the rod over them, 1. Their sin was sparing the Canaanites, and this in contempt and violation of the covenant God had made with them and the commands he had given them, *v.* 20. 2. Their punishment was that the Canaanites were spared, and so they were beaten with their own rod. They were not all delivered into the hand of Joshua while he lived, *v.* 23. Our Lord Jesus, though he *spoiled principalities and powers,* yet did not complete his victory at first. *We see not yet all things put under him;* there are remains of Satan's interest in the church, as there were of the Canaanites in the land; but our Joshua lives for ever, and will in the great day perfect his conquest. After Joshua's death, little was done for a long time against the Canaanites: Israel indulged them, and grew familiar with them, and therefore God would not drive them out any more, *v.* 21. If they will have such inmates as these among them, let them take them, and see what will come of it. God chose their delusions, Isa. 66:4. Thus men cherish and indulge their own corrupt appetites and passions, and, instead of mortifying them, make provision for them, and therefore God justly leaves them to themselves under the power of their sins, which will be their ruin. *So shall their doom be; they themselves have decided it.* These remnants of the Canaanites were left to prove Israel (*v.* 22), *whether they would keep the way of the Lord or not;* not that God might know them, but that they might know themselves. It was to try, (1.) Whether they could resist the temptations to idolatry which the Canaanites would lay before them. God had told them they could not, Deu. 7:4. But they thought they could. "Well," said God, "I will try you;" and, upon trial, it was found that the tempters' charms were far too strong for them. God has told us how deceitful and desperately wicked our hearts are, but we are not willing to believe it till by making bold with temptation we find it too true by sad experience. (2.) Whether they would make a good use of the vexations which the remaining natives would give them, and the many troubles they would occasion them, and would thereby be convinced of sin and humbled for it, reformed, and driven to God and their duty, whether by continual alarms from them they would be kept in awe and made afraid of provoking God.

CHAPTER 3

In this chapter, I. A general account of Israel's enemies is premised, and of the mischief they did them (*v.* 1–7). II. A particular account of the brave exploits done by the first three of the judges. 1. Othniel, whom God raised up to fight Israel's battles, and plead their cause against the king of Mesopotamia (*v.* 8–11). 2. Ehud, who was employed in rescuing Israel out of the hands of the Moabites, and did it by stabbing the king of Moab (*v.* 12–30). 3. Shamgar, who signalized himself in an encounter with the Philistines (*v.* 31).

Verses 1–7

We are here told what remained of the old inhabitants of Canaan. 1. There were some of them that kept together in united bodies, unbroken (*v.* 3): *The five lords of the Philistines,* namely, Ashdod, Gaza, Askelon, Gath, and Ekron, 1 Sa. 6:17. Three of these cities had been in part reduced (*ch.* 1:18), but it seems the Philistines (probably with the help of the other two, which strengthened their confederacy with each other thenceforward) recovered the possession of them. These gave the greatest disturbance to Israel of any of the natives, especially in the latter times of the judges, and they were never quite reduced until David's time. There was a particular nation called *Canaanites,* that kept their ground with the Sidonians, upon the coast of the great sea. And in the north the Hivites held much of Mount Lebanon, it being a remote corner, in which perhaps they were supported by some of the neighbouring states. But, besides these, 2. There were every where in all parts of the country some scatterings of the nations (*v.* 5), Hittites, Amorites, etc., which, by Israel's foolish connivance and indulgence, were so many, so easy, and so insolent, that the *children of Israel* are said to *dwell among them,* as if the right had still remained in the Canaanites, and the Israelites had been taken in by their permission and only as tenants at will.

Now concerning these remnants of the natives observe,

I. How wisely God permitted them to remain. It is mentioned in the close of the foregoing chapter as an act of God's justice, that he let them remain for Israel's correction. But here another construction is put upon it, and it appears to have been an act of God's *wisdom,* that he let them remain for Israel's real advantage, that those who *had not known the wars of Canaan* might *learn war, v.* 1, 2. It was the will of God that the people of Israel should be inured to war, 1. Because their country was *exceedingly rich and fruitful,* and abounded with dainties of all sorts, which, if they were not sometimes made to know hardship, would be in danger of sinking them into the utmost degree of luxury and effeminacy. They must sometimes wade in blood, and not always in milk and honey, lest even their men of war, by the long disuse of arms, should become as soft and as nice as the *tender and delicate woman, that would not set so much as the sole of her foot to the ground for tenderness and delicacy,* a temper as destructive to every thing that is good as it is to every thing that is great, and therefore to be carefully watched against by all God's Israel. 2. Because their country lay very much in the midst of enemies, by whom they must expect to be insulted; for God's heritage was a *speckled bird; the birds round about were against her,* Jer. 12:9. It was therefore necessary they should be well disciplined, that they might defend their coasts when invaded, and might hereafter enlarge their coast as God had promised them. The art of war is best learnt by experience, which not only acquaints men with martial discipline, but (which is no less necessary) inspires them with a martial disposition. It was for the interest of Israel to breed soldiers, as it is the interest of an island to breed sea-men, and therefore God left Canaanites among them, that, by the less difficulties and hardships they met with in encountering them, they might be prepared for greater, and, by *running with the footmen,* might learn *to contend with horses,* Jer. 12:5. Israel was a figure of the church militant, that must fight its way to a triumphant state. The soldiers of Christ must endure hardness, 2 Tim. 2:3. Corruption is therefore left remaining in the hearts even of good Christians, that they may learn war, may keep on the *whole armour of God,* and stand continually upon their guard. The learned bishop Patrick offers another sense of *v.* 2: *That they might know to teach them war,* that is, they shall know what it is to be left to themselves. Their fathers fought by a divine power. God taught their hands to war and their fingers to fight; but now that they have forfeited his favour let them learn what it is to fight like other men.

II. How wickedly Israel mingled themselves with those that did remain. One thing God intended in leaving them among them was *to prove Israel* (*v.* 4), that those who were faithful to the God of Israel might have the honour of resisting the Canaanites' allurements to idolatry, and that those who were false and insincere might be discovered, and might fall under the shame of yielding to those allurements. Thus in the Christian churches there must needs be heresies, *that those who are perfect may be made manifest,* 1 Co. 11:19. Israel, upon trial, proved bad. 1. They joined in marriage with the Canaanites (*v.* 6), though they could not advance either their honour or their estate by marrying with them. They would mar their blood instead of mending it, and sink their estates instead of raising them, by such marriages. 2. Thus they were brought to join in worship with them; they served their *gods* (*v.* 6), *Baalim and the groves* (*v.* 7), that is, the images that were worshipped in groves of thick trees, which were a sort of natural temples. In such unequal matches there is more reason to fear that the bad will corrupt the good than to hope that the good will reform the bad, as there is in laying two pears together, the one rotten and the other sound. When they inclined to worship other gods they *forgot the Lord their God.* In complaisance to their new relations, they talked of nothing by Baalim and the groves, so that by degrees they lost the remembrance of the true God, and forgot there was such a Being, and what obligations they lay under to him. In nothing is the corrupt memory of man more treacherous than in this, that it is apt to forget God; because out of sight, he is out of mind; and here begins all the wickedness that is in the world: they *have perverted their way,* for they have *forgotten the Lord their God.*

Verses 8–11

We now come to the records of the government of the particular judges, the first of which was Othniel, in whom the story of this book is knit to that of Joshua, for even in Joshua's time Othniel began to be famous, by which it appears that it was not long after Israel's settlement in Canaan before their purity began to be corrupted and their peace (by consequence) disturbed. And those who have taken pains to enquire into the sacred chronology are generally agreed that the Danites' idolatry, and the war with the Benjamites for abusing the Levite's concubine, though related in the latter end of this book, happened about this time, under or before the government of Othniel, who, though a judge, was not such a king in Israel as would keep men from doing what was *right in their own eyes.* In this short narrative of Othniel's government we have,

I. The distress that Israel was brought into for their sin, *v.* 8. God being justly displeased with them for plucking up the hedge of their peculiarity, and laying themselves in common with the nations, plucked up the hedge of their protection and laid them open to the nations, set them to sale as goods he would part with, and the first that laid hands on them was Chushan-rishathaim, king of that Syria which lay between the two great rivers of Tigris and Euphrates, thence called *Mesopotamia,* which signifies *in the midst of rivers.* It is probable that this was a warlike prince, and, aiming to enlarge his dominions, he invaded the two tribes first on the other side Jordan that lay next him, and afterwards, perhaps by degrees, penetrated into the heart of the country, and as far as he went put them under contribution, exacting it with rigour, and perhaps quartering soldiers upon them. Laban, who oppressed Jacob with a hard service, was of this country; but it lay at such a distance that one could not have thought Israel's trouble would come from such a far country, which shows so much the more of the hand of God in it.

II. Their return to God in this distress: *When he slew them, then they sought him* whom before they had slighted. The *children of Israel,* even the generality of them, *cried unto the Lord, v.* 9. At first they made light of their trouble, and thought they could easily shake off the yoke of a prince at such a distance; but, when it continued eight years, they began to feel the smart of it, and then those cried under it who before had laughed at it. Those who in the day of their mirth had cried to Baalim and Ashtaroth now that they are in trouble cry to the Lord from whom they had revolted, whose justice brought them into this trouble, and whose power and favour could alone help them out of it. Affliction makes those cry to God with importunity who before would scarcely speak to him.

III. God's return in mercy to them for their deliverance. Though need drove them to him, he did not therefore reject their prayers, but graciously raised up a deliverer, or *saviour,* as the word is. Observe, 1. Who the deliverer was. It was Othniel, who married Caleb's daughter, one of the old stock that had *seen the works of the Lord,* and had himself, no question, kept his integrity, and secretly lamented the apostasy of his people, but waited for a divine call to appear publicly for the redress of their grievances. He was now, we may suppose, far advanced in years, when God raised him up to this honour, but the decays of age were no hindrance to his usefulness when God had work for him to do. 2. Whence he had his commission, not of man, nor by man; but *the Spirit of the Lord came upon him* (*v.* 10), the spirit of wisdom and courage to qualify him for the service, and a spirit of power to excite him to it, so as to give him and others full satisfaction that it was the will of God he should engage in it. The Chaldee says, *The spirit of prophecy remained on him.* 3. What method he took. He first judged Israel, reproved them, called them to account for their sins, and reformed them, and then went out to war. This was the right method. Let sin at home be conquered, that worst of enemies, and then enemies abroad will be the more easily dealt with. Thus let Christ be our Judge and Law-giver, and then *he will save us,* and on no other terms, Isa. 33:22. 4. What good success he had. He prevailed to break the yoke of the oppression, and, as it should seem, to break the neck of the oppressor; for it is said, *The Lord delivered Chushan-rishathaim into his hand.* Now was Judah, of which tribe Othniel was, *as a lion's whelp gone up from the prey.* 5. The happy consequence of Othniel's good services. The land, though not getting ground, yet had rest, and some fruits of the reformation, forty years; and the benefit would have been perpetual if they had kept close to God and their duty.

Verses 12–30

Ehud is the next of the judges whose achievements are related in this history, and here is an account of his actions.

I. When Israel sins again God raises up a new oppressor, *v.* 12–14. It was an aggravation of their wickedness that they did evil again after they had smarted so long for their former iniquities, promised so fair when Othniel judged them, and received so much mercy from God in their deliverance. What, and after all this, again to break his commandments! Was the disease obstinate to all the methods of cure, both corrosives and lenitives? It seems it was. Perhaps they thought they might make the more bold with their old sins because they saw themselves in no danger from their old oppressor; the powers of that kingdom were weakened and brought low. But God made them know that he had variety of rods wherewith to chastise them: He *strengthened Eglon king of Moab against them.* This oppressor lay nearer to them than the former, and therefore would be the more mischievous to them; God's judgments thus approached them gradually, to bring them to repentance. When Israel dwelt in tents, but kept their integrity, Balak king of Moab, who would have strengthened himself against them, was baffled; but now that they had forsaken God, and worshipped the gods of the nations round about them (and perhaps those of the Moabites among the rest), here was another king of Moab, whom God strengthened against them, put power into his hands, though a wicked man, that he might be a scourge to Israel. The staff in his hand with which he beat Israel was God's indignation; *howbeit he meant not so, neither did his heart think so,* Isa. 10:6, 7. Israelites did ill, and, we may suppose, Moabites did worse; yet because God commonly punishes the sins of his own people in this world, that, the flesh being destroyed, the spirit may be saved, Israel is weakened and Moab strengthened against them. God would not suffer the Israelites, when they were the stronger, to distress the Moabites, nor give them any disturbance, though they were idolaters (Deu. 2:9); yet now he suffered the Moabites to distress Israel, and strengthened them on purpose that they might: *Thy judgments, O God! are a great deep.* The king of Moab took to his assistance the Ammonites and Amalekites (*v.* 13), and this strengthened him; and we are here told how they prevailed. 1. They beat them in the field: They *went and smote Israel* (*v.* 13), not only those tribes that lay next them on the other side Jordan, who, though first settled, being frontier-tribes, were most disturbed; but those also within Jordan, for they made themselves masters of *the city of palm-trees,* which, it is probable, was a strong-hold erected near the place where Jericho had stood, for that was so called (Deu. 34:3), into which the Moabites put a garrison, to be a bridle upon Israel, and to secure the passes of Jordan, for the preservation of the communication with their own country. It was well for the Kenites that they had left this city (*ch.* 1:16) before it fell into the hands of the enemy. See how quickly the Israelites lost that by their own sin which they had gained by miracles of divine mercy. 2. They made them to serve (*v.* 14), that is, exacted tribute from them, either the fruits of the earth in kind or money in lieu of them. They neglected the service of God, and did not pay him his tribute; thus therefore did God recover from them that *wine and oil,* that silver and gold, which they prepared for Baal, Hos. 2:8. What should have been paid to the divine grace, and was not, was distrained for, and paid to the divine justice. The former servitude (*v.* 8) lasted but eight years, this eighteen; for, if less troubles do not do the work, God will send greater.

II. When Israel prays again God raises up a new deliverer (*v.* 15), named *Ehud.* We are here told,

1. That he was a Benjamite. The city of palm-trees lay within the lot of this tribe, by which it is probable that they suffered most, and therefore stirred first to shake off the yoke. It is supposed by the chronologers that the Israelites' war with Benjamin for the wickedness of Gibeah, by which that whole tribe was reduced to 600 men, happened before this, so that we may well think that tribe to be now the weakest of all the tribes, yet out of it God raised up this deliverer, in token of his being perfectly reconciled to them, to manifest his own power in ordaining strength out of weakness, and that he might bestow *more abundant honour upon that part which lacked,* 1 Co. 12:24.

2. That he was left-handed, as it seems many of that tribe were, *ch.* 20:16. Benjamin signifies *the son of the right hand,* and yet multitudes of them were left-handed; for men's natures do not always answer their names. The LXX. say he was an *ambi-dexter,* one that could use both hands alike, supposing that this was an advantage to him in the action he was called to; but the Hebrew phrase, that he was *shut of his right hand,* intimates that, either through disease of disuse, he made little or no use of that, but of his left hand only, and so was the less fit for war, because he must needs handle his sword but awkwardly; yet God chose this left-handed man to be the man of his right hand, whom he would *make strong for himself,* Ps. 80:17. It was *God's right hand* that gained Israel the victory (Ps. 44:3), not the right hand of the instruments he employed.

3. We are here told what Ehud did for the deliverance of Israel out of the hands of the Moabites. He saved the oppressed by destroying the oppressors, when the measure of their iniquity was full and the set time to favour Israel had come.

(1.) He put to death Eglon the king of Moab; I say, *put him to death,* not murdered or assassinated him, but as a judge, or minister of divine justice, executed the judgments of God upon him, as an implacable enemy to God and Israel. This story is particularly related.

[1.] He had a fair occasion of access to him. Being an ingenious active man, and fit to stand before kings, his people chose him to carry a present in the name of all Israel, over and above their tribute, to their great lord the king of Moab, that they might find favour in his eyes, *v.* 15. The present is called *mincha* in the original, which is the word used in the law for the offerings that were presented to God to obtain his favour; these the children of Israel had not offered in their season to the God that loved them; and now, to punish them for their neglect, they are laid under a necessity of bringing their offerings to a heathen prince that hated them. Ehud went on his errand to Eglon, offered his present with the usual ceremony and expressions of dutiful respect, the better to colour what he intended and to prevent suspicion.

[2.] It should seem, from the first, he designed to be the death of him, God putting it into his heart, and letting him know also that the motion was from himself, by the Spirit that came upon him, the impulses of which carried with them their own evidence, and so gave him full satisfaction both as to the lawfulness and the success of this daring attempt, of both which he would have had reason enough to doubt. If he be sure that God bids him do it, he is sure both that he may do it and that he shall do it; for a command from God is sufficient to bear us out, and bring us off, both against our consciences and against all the world. That he compassed and imagined the death of this tyrant appears by the preparation he made of a weapon for the purpose, a short dagger, but half a yard long, like a bayonet, which might easily be concealed under his clothes (*v.* 16), perhaps because none were suffered to come near the king with their swords by their sides. This he wore on his right thigh, that it might be the more ready to his left hand, and might be the less suspected.

[3.] He contrived how to be alone with him, which he might the more easily be now that he had not only made himself known to him, but ingratiated himself by the present, and the compliments which perhaps, on this occasion, he had passed upon him. Observe, how he laid his plot. *First,* He concealed his design even from his own attendants, brought them part of the way, and then ordered them to go forward towards home, while he himself, as if he had forgotten something behind him, went back to the king of Moab's court, *v.* 18. There needed but one hand to do the execution; had more been engaged they could not so safely have kept counsel, nor so easily have made an escape. *Secondly,* He returned from the quarries by Gilgal (*v.* 19), from the *graven images* (so it is in the margin) which were with Gilgal, set up perhaps by the Moabites with the twelve stones which Joshua had set up there. Some suggest that the sight of these idols stirred up in him such an indignation against the king of Moab as put him upon the execution of that design which otherwise he had thought to let fall for the present. Or, perhaps, he came so far as to these images, that, telling from what place he returned, the king of Moab might be the more apt to believe he had a message from God. *Thirdly,* He begged a private audience, and obtained it in a withdrawing-room, here called a *summer parlour.* He told the king he had a secret errand to him, who thereupon ordered all his attendants to withdraw, *v.* 19. Whether he expected to receive some private instructions from an oracle, or some private informations concerning the present state of Israel, as if Ehud would betray his country, it was a very unwise thing for him to be all alone with a stronger and one whom he had reason to look upon as an enemy; but those that are marked for ruin are infatuated, and their *hearts hid from understanding;* God deprives them of discretion.

[4.] When he had him alone he soon dispatched him. His summer parlour, where he used to indulge himself in ease and luxury, was the place of his execution. *First,* Ehud demands his attention to *a message from God* (*v.* 20), and that message was a dagger. God sends to us by the judgments of his hand, as well as by the judgments of his mouth. *Secondly,* Eglon pays respect to a message from God. Though a king, though a heathen king, though rich and powerful, though now tyrannizing over the people of God, though a fat unwieldy man that could not easily rise nor stand long, though in private and what he did was not under observation, yet, when he expected to receive orders form heaven, he rose out of his seat; whether it was low and easy, or whether it was high and stately, he quitted it, and stood up when God was about to speak to him, thereby owning God his superior. This shames the irreverence of many who are called Christians, and yet, when a message from God is delivered to them, study to show, by all the marks of carelessness, how little they regard it. Ehud, in calling what he had to do *a message from God,* plainly avouches a divine commission for it; and God's inclining Eglon to stand up to it did both confirm the commission and facilitate the execution. *Thirdly,* The message was delivered, not to his ear, but immediately, and literally, to his heart, into which the fatal knife was thrust, and was left there, *v.* 21, 22. His extreme fatness made him unable to resist or to help himself; probably it was the effect of his luxury and excess; and, when *the fat closed up the blade,* God would by this circumstance show how those that pamper the body do but prepare for their own misery. However, it was an emblem of his carnal security and senselessness. His heart was a fat as grease, and in that he thought himself enclosed. See Ps. 119:70; 17:10. Eglon signifies a *calf,* and he fell like a fatted calf, by the knife, an acceptable sacrifice to divine justice. Notice is taken of the coming out of the dirt or dung, that the death of this proud tyrant may appear the more ignominious and shameful. He that had been so very nice and curious about his own body, to keep it easy and clean, shall now be found wallowing in his own blood and excrements. Thus does God pour contempt upon princes. Now this act of Ehud's may justify itself because he had special direction from God to do it, and it was agreeable to the usual method which, under that dispensation, God took to avenge his people of their enemies, and to manifest to the world his own justice. But it will by no means justify any now in doing the like. No such commissions are now given, and to pretend to them is to blaspheme God, and made him patronize the worst of villanies. Christ bade Peter sheathe the sword, and we find not that he bade him draw it again.

[5.] Providence wonderfully favoured his escape, when he had done the execution. *First,* The tyrant fell silently, without any shriek or out-cry, which might have been overheard by his servants at a distance. How silently does he go down to the pit, choked up, it may be, with his own fat, which stifled his dying groans, though he had made so great a noise in the world, and had been *the terror of the mighty in the land of the living! Secondly,* The heroic executioner of this vengeance, with such a presence of mind as discovered not only no consciousness of guilt, but a strong confidence in the divine protection, shut the doors after him, took the key with him, and passed through the guards with such an air of innocence, and boldness, and unconcernedness, as made them not at all to suspect his having done any thing amiss. *Thirdly,* The servants that attended in the antechamber, coming to the door of the inner parlour, when Ehud had gone, to know their master's pleasure, and finding it locked and all quiet, concluded he had lain down to sleep, had covered his feet upon his couch, and gone to consult his pillow about the message he had received, and to dream upon it (*v.* 24), and therefore would not offer to open the door. Thus by their care not to disturb his sleep they lost the opportunity of revenging his death. See what comes of men's taking state too much, and obliging those about them to keep their distance; some time or other it may come against them more than they think of. *Fourthly,* The servants at length opened the door, and found their master had *slept indeed his long sleep, v.* 25. The horror of this tragical spectacle, and the confusion it must needs put them into, to reflect upon their own inconsideration in not opening the door sooner, quite put by the thoughts of sending pursuers after him that had done it, whom now they despaired of overtaking. *Lastly,* Ehud by this means made his escape to Sierath, *a thick wood;* so some, *v.* 26. It is not said any where in this story what was the place in which Eglon lived now; but, there being no mention of Ehud passing and repassing Jordan, I am inclined to think that Eglon had left his own country of Moab, on the other side Jordan, and made his principal residence at this time in the city of palm-trees, within the land of Canaan, a richer country than his own, and that there he was slain, and then the quarries by Gilgal were not far off him. There where he had settled himself, and thought he had sufficiently fortified himself to lord it over the people of God, there he was cut off, and proved to be fed for the slaughter *like a lamb in a large place.*

(2.) Ehud, having slain the king of Moab, gave a total rout to the forces of the Moabites that were among them, and so effectually shook off the yoke of their oppression. [1.] He raised an army immediately in Mount Ephraim, at some distance form the headquarters of the Moabites, and headed them himself, *v.* 27. The trumpet he blew was indeed a jubilee-trumpet, proclaiming liberty, and a joyful sound it was to the oppressed Israelites, who for a long time had heard no other trumpets than those of their enemies. [2.] Like a pious man, and as one that did all this in faith, he took encouragement himself, and gave encouragement to his soldiers, from the power of God engaged for them (*v.* 28): *"Follow me, for the Lord hath delivered your enemies into your hands;* we are sure to have God with us, and therefore may go on boldly, and shall go on triumphantly." [3.] Like a politic general, he first secured the fords of Jordan, set strong guards upon all those passes, to cut off the communications between the Moabites that were in the land of Israel (for upon them only his design was) and their own country on the other side Jordan, that if, upon the alarm given them, they resolved to fly, they might not escape thither, and, if they resolved to fight, they might not have assistance thence. Thus he shut them up in that land as their prison in which they were pleasing themselves as their palace and paradise. [4.] He then fell upon them, and put them all to the sword, 10,000 of them, which it seems was the number appointed to keep Israel in subjection (*v.* 29): *There escaped not a man* of them. And they were the best and choicest of all the king of Moab's forces, all lusty men, men of bulk and stature, and not only able-bodied, but high spirited too, and men of valour, *v.* 29. But neither their strength nor their courage stood them in any stead when the set time had come for God to deliver them into the hand of Israel. [5.] The consequence of this victory was that the power of the Moabites was wholly broken in the land of Israel. The country was cleared of these oppressors, and *the land had rest eighty years, v.* 30. We may hope that there was likewise a reformation among them, and a check give to idolatry, by the influence of Ehud which continued a good part of this time. It was a great while for the land to rest, fourscore years; yet what is that to the saints' everlasting rest in the heavenly Canaan?

Verse 31

When it is said *the land had rest eighty years,* some think it meant chiefly of that part of the land which lay eastward on the banks of Jordan, which had been oppressed by the Moabites; but it seems, by this passage here, that the other side of the country which lay south-west was in that time infested by the Philistines, against whom Shamgar made head. 1. It seems Israel needed deliverance, for *he delivered Israel;* how great the distress was Deborah afterwards related in her song (*ch.* 5:6), that *in the days of Shamgar the highways were unoccupied,* etc.; that part of the country which lay next to the Philistines was so infested with plunderers that people could not travel the roads in safety, but were in danger of being set upon and robbed, nor durst they dwell in the unguarded villages, but were forced to take shelter in the fortified cities. 2. God raised him up to deliver them, as it should seem, while Ehud was yet living, but superannuated. So inconsiderable were the enemies for number that it seems the killing of 600 of them amounted to a deliverance of Israel, and so many he slew with an ox-goad, or, as some read it, *a plough-share.* It is probable that he was himself following the plough when the Philistines made an inroad upon the country to ravage it, and God put it into his heart to oppose them; the impulse being sudden and strong, and having neither sword nor spear to do execution with, he took the instrument that was next at hand, some of the tools of his plough, and with that killed so many hundred men and came off unhurt. See here, (1.) That God can make those eminently serviceable to his glory and his church's good whose extraction, education, and employment, are very mean and obscure. He that has the residue of the Spirit could, when he pleased, make ploughmen judges and generals, and fishermen apostles. (2.) It is no matter how weak the weapon is if God direct and strengthen the arm. An ox-goad, when God pleases, shall do more than Goliath's sword. And sometimes he chooses to work by such unlikely means, that the excellency of the power may appear to be of God.

CHAPTER 4

The method of the history of Deborah and Barak (the heroes in this chapter) is the same with that before Here is, I. Israel revolted from God (*v.* 1). II. Israel oppressed by Jabin (*v.* 2, 3). III. Israel judged by Deborah (*v.* 4, 5). IV. Israel rescued out of the hands of Jabin. 1. Their deliverance is concerted between Deborah and Barak (*v.* 6, 9). 2. It is accomplished by their joint-agency. Barak takes the field (*v.* 10). Sisera, Jabin's general, meets him (*v.* 12, 13). Deborah encourages him (*v.* 14). And God gives him a complete victory. The army routed (*v.* 15, 16). The general forced to flee (*v.* 17). And where he expected shelter he had his life stolen from him by Jael while he was asleep (*v.* 18–21), which completes Barak's triumph (*v.* 22). and Israel's deliverance (*v.* 23, 24).

Verses 1–3

Here is, I. Israel backsliding from God: They again *did evil in his sight,* forsook his service, and worshipped idols; for this was the sin which now most easily beset them, *v.* 1. See in this, 1. The strange strength of corruption, which hurries men into sin notwithstanding the most frequent experience of its fatal consequences. The bent to backslide is with great difficulty restrained. 2. The common ill effects of a long peace. The land had rest eighty years, which should have confirmed them in their religion; but, on the contrary, it made them secure and wanton, and indulgent of those lusts which the worship of the false gods was calculated for the gratification of. Thus *the prosperity of fools destroys them. Jeshurun waxeth fat and kicketh.* 3. The great loss which a people sustains by the death of good governors. *The did evil, because Ehud was dead.* So it may be read. He kept a strict eye upon them, restrained and punished every thing that looked towards idolatry, and kept them close to God's service. But, when he was gone, they revolted, fearing him more than God.

II. Israel oppressed by their enemies. When they forsook God, he forsook them; and then they became an easy prey to every spoiler. They alienated themselves from God as if he were none of theirs; and then God alienated them as none of his. Those that threw themselves out of God's service threw themselves out of his protection. *What has my beloved to do in my house* when she has thus played the harlot? Jer. 11:15. He *sold them into the hand of Jabin, v.* 2. This Jabin reigned in Hazor, as another of the same name, and perhaps his ancestor, had done before him, whom Joshua routed and slew, and burnt his city, Jos. 11:1, 10. But it seems, in process of time, the city was rebuilt, the power regained, the loss retrieved, and, by degrees, the king of Hazor becomes able to tyrannize over Israel, who by sin had lost all their advantage against the Canaanites. This servitude was longer than either of the former, and much more grievous. Jabin, and his general Sisera, did mightily oppress Israel. That which aggravated the oppression was, 1. That this enemy was nearer to them than any of the former, in their borders, in their bowels, and by this means had the more opportunity to do them a mischief. 2. That they were the natives of the country, who bore an implacable enmity to them, for invading and dispossessing them, and when they had them in their power would be so much the more cruel and mischievous towards them in revenge of the old quarrel. 3. That these Canaanites had formerly been conquered and subdued by Israel, were of old sentenced to be their servants (Gen. 9:25), and might now have been under their feet, and utterly incapable of giving them any disturbance, if their own slothfulness, cowardice, and unbelief, had not suffered them thus to get head. To be oppressed by those whom their fathers had conquered, and whom they themselves had foolishly spared, could not but be very grievous.

III. Israel returning to their God: They *cried unto the Lord,* when distress drove them to him, and they saw no other way of relief. Those that slight God in their prosperity will find themselves under a necessity of seeking him when they are in trouble.

Verses 4–9

The year of the redeemed at length came, when Israel was to be delivered out of the hands of Jabin, and restored again to their liberty, which we may suppose the northern tribes, that lay nearest to the oppressors and felt most the effects of his fury, did in a particular manner cry to God for. *For the oppression of the poor, and the sighing of the needy, now will* God *arise.* Now here we have,

I. The preparation of the people for their deliverance, by the prophetic conduct and government of Deborah, *v.* 4, 5. Her name signifies a *bee;* and she answered her name by her industry, sagacity, and great usefulness to the public, her sweetness to her friends and sharpness to her enemies. She is said to be *the wife of Lapidoth;* but, the termination not being commonly found in the name of a man, some make this the name of a place: she was *a woman of Lapidoth.* Others take it appellatively, Lapidoth signifies *lamps.* The Rabbin say she had employed herself in making wicks for the lamps of the tabernacle; and, having stooped to that mean office for God, she was afterwards thus preferred. Or she was a woman of *illuminations,* or of *splendours,* one that was extraordinarily knowing and wise, and so came to be very eminent and illustrious. Concerning her we are here told, 1. That she was intimately acquainted with God; she was *a prophetess,* one that was instructed in divine knowledge by the immediate inspiration of the Spirit of God, and had gifts of wisdom, to which she attained not in an ordinary way: she *heard the words of God,* and probably *saw the visions of the Almighty.* 2. That she was entirely devoted to the service of Israel. She judged Israel at the time that Jabin oppressed them; and perhaps, being a woman, she was the more easily permitted by the oppressor to do it. She judged, not as a princess, by an civil authority conferred upon her, but as a prophetess, and as God's mouth to them, correcting abuses and redressing grievances, especially those which related to the worship of God. The children of Israel came up to her from all parts for judgment, not so much for the deciding of controversies between man and man as for advice in the reformation of what was amiss in things pertaining to God. Those among them who before had secretly lamented the impieties and idolatries of their neighbours, but knew not where to apply for the restraining of them, now made their complaints to Deborah, who, by the sword of the Spirit, showing them the judgment of God, reduced and reclaimed many, and excited and animated the magistrates in their respective districts to put the laws in execution. It is said she *dwelt,* or, as some read it, she *sat* under a palm-tree, called ever after from her *the palm-tree of Deborah.* Either she had her house under that tree, a mean habitation which would couch under a tree, or she had her judgment-seat in the open air, under the shadow of that tree, which was an emblem of the justice she sat there to administer, which will thrive and grow against opposition, as palms under pressures. Josephus says that the children of Israel came to Deborah, to desire her to pray to God for them, that they might be delivered out of the hand of Jabin; and Samuel is said at one particular time to judge Israel in Mizpeh, that is, to bring them back again to God, when they made the same address to him upon a like occasion, 1 Sa. 7:6, 8.

II. The project laid for their deliverance. When the children of Israel *came to her for judgment,* with her they found salvation. So those that seek to God for grace shall have grace and peace, grace and comfort, grace and glory. She was not herself fit to command an army in person, being a woman; but she nominated one that was fit, Barak of Naphtali, who, it is probable, had already signalized himself in some rencounters with the forces of the oppressor, living near him (for Hazor and Harosheth lay within the lot of that tribe), and thereby had gained a reputation and interest among his people. Some struggles, we may suppose, that brave man had made towards the shaking off of the yoke, but could not effect it till he had his commission and instructions from Deborah. He could do nothing without her head, nor she without his hands; but both together made a complete deliverer, and effected a complete deliverance. The greatest and best are not self-sufficient, but need one another.

1. By God's direction, she orders Barak to raise an army, and engage Jabin's forces, that were under Sisera's command, *v.* 6, 7. Barak, it may be, had been meditating some great attempt against the common enemy; a spark of generous fire was glowing in his breast, and he would fain do something to the purpose for his people and for the cities of his God. But two things discouraged him:

(1.) He wanted a commission to levy forces; this therefore Deborah here gives him under the broad seal of heaven, which, as a prophetess, she had a warrant to affix to it: *"Hath not the Lord God of Israel commanded it?* Yet, certainly he has; take my word for it." Some think she intends this as an appeal to Barak's own heart. "Has not God, by a secret whisper to thyself, given thee some intimation of his purpose to make use of thee as an instrument in his hands to save Israel? Hast not thou felt some impulse of this kind upon thy own spirit?" If so, the spirit of prophesy in Deborah confirms the spirit of a soldier in Barak: *Go and draw towards Mount Tabor.* [1.] She directs him what number of men to raise — 10,000; and let him not fear that these will be too few, when God hath said he will by them save Israel. [2.] Whence he should raise them — only out of his own tribe, and that of Zebulun next adjoining. These two counties should furnish him with an army sufficient; he need not stay to go further. And, [3.] She orders him where to make his rendezvous — at Mount Tabor, in his own neighbourhood.

(2.) When he had an army raised, he knew not how he should have an opportunity of engaging the enemy, who perhaps declined fighting, having heard that Israel, if they had but courage enough to make head against any enemy, seldom failed of success. "Well," says Deborah, in the name of "God, *I will draw unto thee Sisera and his army.*" She assured him that the matter should be determined by one pitched battle, and should not be long in the doing. [1.] In mentioning the power of the enemy, Sisera, a celebrated general, bold and experienced, his chariots, his iron chariots, and his multitude of soldiers, she obliged Barak to fortify himself with the utmost degree of resolution; for the enemy he was to engage was a very formidable one. It is good to know the worst, that we may provide accordingly. But, [2.] In fixing the very place to which Sisera would draw his army, she gave him a sign, which might help to confirm his faith when he came to engage. it was a contingent things, and depended upon Sisera's own will; but, when afterwards Barak should see the event falling out just as Deborah had foretold, he might thence infer that certainly in the rest she said she spoke under a divine direction, which would be a great encouragement to him, especially because with this, [3.] She gave him an express promise of success *I will* (that is, God will, in whose name I speak) *deliver them into thy hand;* so that when he saw them drawn up against him, according to Deborah's word, he might be confident that, according to her word, he should soon see them fallen before him. Observe, God *drew them to him* only that he might *deliver them into his hand.* When Sisera drew his forces together, he designed the destruction of Israel; but God *gathered them as sheaves into the floor,* for their own destruction, Mic. 4:11, 12. *Assemble yourselves, and you shall be broken to pieces,* Isa. 8:9. See Rev. 19:17, 18.

2. At Barak's request, she promises to go along with him to the field of battle. (1.) Barak insisted much upon the necessity of her presence, which would be to him better than a council of war (*v.* 8): *"If thou wilt go with me* to direct and advise me, and in every difficult case to let me know God's mind, *then I will go* with all my heart, and not fear the chariots of iron; otherwise not." Some make this to be the language of a weak faith; he could not take her word unless he had her with him in pawn, as it were, for performance. It seems rather to arise from a conviction of the necessity of God's presence and continual direction, a pledge and earnest of which he would reckon Deborah's presence to be, and therefore begged thus earnestly for it. *"If thou go not up with me,* in token of God's going with me, *carry me not up hence."* Nothing would be a greater satisfaction to him than to have the prophetess with him to animate the soldiers and to be consulted as an oracle upon all occasions. (2.) Deborah promised to go with him, *v.* 9. No toil nor peril shall discourage her from doing the utmost that becomes her to do for the service of her country. She would not send him where she would not go herself. Those that in God's name call others to their duty should be very ready to assist them in it. Deborah was the weaker vessel, yet had the stronger faith. But though she agrees to go with Barak, if he insists upon it, she gives him a hint proper enough to move a soldier not to insist upon it: *The journey thou undertakest* (so confident was she of the success that she called his engaging in war but the undertaking of a journey) *shall not be for thy honour;* not so much for thy honour as if thou hadst gone by thyself; for *the Lord shall sell Sisera* (now his turn comes to be sold as Israel was, *v.* 2, by way of reprisal) *"into the hands of a woman;"* that is, [1.] The world would ascribe the victory to the hand of Deborah: this he might himself foresee. [2.] God (to correct his weakness) would complete the victory by the hand of Jael, which would be some eclipse to his glory. But Barak values the satisfaction of his mind, and the good success of his enterprise, more than his honour; and therefore will by no means drop his request. He dares not fight unless he have Deborah with him, to direct him and pray for him. She therefore stood to her word with a masculine courage; this noble heroine *arose and went with Barak.*

Verses 10–16

Here, I. Barak beats up for volunteers, and soon has his quota of men ready, *v.* 10. Deborah had appointed him to raise an army of 10,000 men (*v.* 6), and so many he has presently *at his feet,* following him, and subject to his command. God is said to call us *to his feet* (Isa. 41:2), that is, into obedience to him. Some think it intimates that they were all footmen, and so the armies of the Jews generally were, which made the disproportion of strength between them and the enemy (who had horses and chariots) very great, and the victory the more illustrious; but the presence of God and his prophetess was abundantly sufficient to balance that disproportion. Barak had his men *at his feet,* which intimates their cheerfulness and readiness to attend him whithersoever he went, Rev. 14:4. Though the tribes of Zebulun and Naphtali were chiefly depended on, yet it appears by Deborah's song that some had come in to him from other tribes (Manasseh and Issachar), and more were expected that came not, from Reuben, Dan, and Asher, *ch.* 5:14–17. But these are overlooked here; and we are only told that to make his 10,000 men effective indeed *Deborah went up with him.* The 11th verse, concerning the removal of Heber, one of the families of the Kenites, out of the wilderness of Judah, in the south, where those families had fixed themselves (*ch.* 1:16), into the northern country, comes in for the sake of what was to follow concerning the exploit of Jael, a wife of that family.

II. Sisera, upon notice of Barak's motions, takes the field with a very numerous and powerful army (*v.* 12, 13): *They showed Sisera,* that is, it was shown to him. Yet some think it refers to the Kenites, mentioned immediately before, *v.* 11. They gave Sisera notice of Barak's rendezvous, there being peace at this time between Jabin and that family, *v.* 17. Whether they intended it as a kindness to him or no, it served to accomplish what God had said by Deborah (*v.* 7): *I will draw unto thee Sisera.* Sisera's confidence was chiefly in his chariots; therefore particular notice is taken of them, 900 *chariots of iron,* which, with the scythes fastened to their axle-trees, when they were driven into an army of footmen, did terrible execution. So ingenious have men been in inventing methods of destroying one another, to gratify those lusts *from which come wars and fightings.*

III. Deborah gives orders to engage the enemy, *v.* 14. Josephus says that when Barak saw Sisera's army drawn up, and attempting to surround the mountain on the top of which he and his forces lay encamped, his heart quite failed him, and he determined to retire to a place of greater safety; but Deborah animated him to make a descent upon Sisera, assuring him that this was the day marked out in the divine counsels for his defeat. "Now they appear most threatening they are ripe for ruin. The thing is as sure to be done as if it were done already: *The Lord hath delivered Sisera into thy hand."* See how the work and honour of this great action are divided between Deborah and Barak; she, as the head, *gives the word,* he, as the hand, *does the work.* Thus does God dispense his gifts variously, 1 Co. 12:4, etc. But, though ordinarily *the head of the woman is the man* (1 Co. 11:3), he that has the residue of the Spirit was pleased to cross hands, and to put the head upon the woman's shoulders, choosing the weak things of the world to shame the mighty, that no flesh might glory in his presence. It was well for Barak that he had Deborah with him; for she made up what was defective, 1. In his conduct, by telling him, *This is the day.* 2. In his courage, by assuring him of God's presence: *"Has not the Lord gone out before thee?* Darest not thou follow when thou hast God himself for thy leader?" Note, (1.) In every undertaking it is good to be satisfied that God goes before us, that we are in the way of our duty and under his direction. (2.) If we have ground to hope that God goes before us, we ought to go on with courage and cheerfulness. Be not dismayed at the difficulties thou meetest with in resisting Satan, in serving God, or suffering for him; for *has not the Lord gone out before thee?* Follow him fully then.

IV. God himself routs the enemy's army, *v.* 15. Barak, in obedience to Deborah's orders, went down into the valley, though there upon the plain the iron chariots would have so much the more advantage against him, quitting his fastnesses upon the mountain in dependence upon the divine power; for *in vain is salvation hoped for from hills and mountains; in the Lord alone is the salvation of his people,* Jer. 3:23. And he was not deceived in his confidence: *The Lord discomfited Sisera.* It was not so much the bold and surprising alarm which Barak gave their camp that dispirited and dispersed them, but God's terror seized their spirits and put them into an unaccountable confusion. *The stars,* it seems, fought against them, *ch.* 5:20. Josephus says that a violent storm of hail which beat in their faces gave them this rout, disabled them, and drove them back; so that they became a very easy prey to the army of Israel, and Deborah's words were made good: *"The Lord has delivered them into thy hand;* it is now in thy power to do what thou wilt with them."

V. Barak bravely improves his advantage, follows the blow with undaunted resolution and unwearied diligence, prosecutes the victory, pursues the scattered forces, even to their general's head-quarters at Harosheth (*v.* 16), and spares none whom God had delivered into his hand to be destroyed: *There was not a man left.* When God goes before us in our spiritual conflicts we must bestir ourselves; and, when by grace he gives us some success against the enemies of our souls, we must improve it by watchfulness and resolution, and carry on the holy war with vigour.

Verses 17–24

We have seen the army of the Canaanites totally routed. It is said (Ps. 83:9, 10, where the defeat of this army is pleaded as a precedent for God's doing the like in after times) that they became *as dung for the earth.* Now here we have,

I. The fall of their general, Sisera, captain of the host, in whom, it is likely, Jabin their king put an entire confidence, and therefore was not himself present in the action. Let us trace the steps of this mighty man's fall.

1. He quitted his chariot, and took to his feet, *v.* 15, 17. His chariots had been his pride and his confidence; and we may suppose he had therefore despised and defied the armies of the living God, because they were all on foot, and had neither chariot nor horse, as he had. Justly therefore is he thus made ashamed of his confidence, and forced to quit it, and thinks himself then most safe and easy when he has got clear of his chariot, though we may well suppose it the best made, and best drawn, of any of them. Thus are those disappointed who rest on the creature; like a broken reed, it not only breaks under them, but runs into their hand, and pierceth them with many sorrows. The idol may quickly become a burden (Isa. 46:1), and what we were sick for God can make us sick of. How miserable doth Sisera look now he is dismounted! It is hard to say whether he blusheth or trembleth more. Put not your trust in princes, if they may so soon be brought to this, if he who but lately trusted to his arms with so much assurance must now trust to his heels only with so little.

2. He fled for shelter to the tents of the Kenites, having no strong-hold, nor any place of is own in reach to retire to. The mean and solitary way of the Kenites' living, perhaps, he had formerly despised and ridiculed, and the more because religion was kept up among them; yet now he is glad to put himself under the protection of one of these tents: and he chooses the wife's tent or apartment, either because less suspected, or because it happened to be next to him, and the first he came to, *v.* 17. And that which encouraged him to go thither was that at this time there was peace between his master and the house of Heber: not that there was any league offensive and defensive between them, only at present there were no indications of hostility. Jabin did them no harm, did not oppress them as he did the Israelites, their plain, quiet, harmless way of living making them not suspected nor feared, and perhaps God so ordering it as a recompence for their constant adherence to the true religion. Sisera thought he might therefore be safe among them; not considering that, though they themselves suffered not by Jabin's power, they heartily sympathized with the Israel of God that did.

3. Jael invited him in, and bade him very welcome. Probably she stood at the tent door, to enquire what news from the army, and what the success of the battle which was fought not far off. (1.) She invited him in. Perhaps she stood waiting for an opportunity to show kindness to any distressed Israelite, if there should be occasion for it; but seeing Sisera come in great haste, panting and out of breath, she invited him to come and repose himself in her tent, in which, while she seemed to design the relieving of his fatigue, perhaps she really intended the retarding of his flight, that he might fall into the hands of Barak, who was not in a hot chase after him (*v.* 18), and it may well questioned whether she had at first any thought of taking away his life, but rather God afterwards put it into her heart. (2.) She made very much of him, and seemed mighty careful to have him easy, as her invited guest. Was he weary? she finds him a very convenient place to repose himself in, and recruit his strength. Was he thirsty? well he might. Did he want a little water to cool his tongue?

the best liquor her tent afforded was at his service, and that was milk (*v.* 19), which, we may suppose, he drank heartily of, and, being refreshed with it, was the better disposed to sleep. Was he cold, or afraid of catching cold? or did he desire to be hid from the pursuers, if they should search that tent? she covered him with a mantle, *v.* 18. All expressions of care for his safety. Only when he desired her to tell a lie for him, and to say he was not there, she declined making any such promise, *v.* 20. We must not sin against God, no, not to oblige those we would show ourselves most observant of. *Lastly,* We must suppose she kept her tent as quiet as she could, and free from noise, that he might sleep the sooner and the faster. And now was Sisera least safe when he was most secure. How uncertain and precarious is human life! and what assurance can we have of it, when it may so easily be betrayed by those with whom it is trusted, and those may prove its destroyers who we hoped would be its protectors! It is best making God our friend, for he will not deceive us.

4. When he lay fast asleep she drove a long nail through his temples, so fastened his head to the ground, and killed him, *v.* 21. And, though this was enough to do the business, yet, to make sure work (if we translate it rightly, *ch.* 5:26), she cut off his head, and left it nailed there. Whether she designed this or no when she invited him into her tent does not appear; probably the thought was darted into her mind when she saw him lie so conveniently to receive such a fatal blow; and, doubtless, the thought brought with it evidence sufficient that it came not from Satan as a murderer and destroyer, but from God as a righteous judge and avenger, so much of brightness and heavenly light did she perceive in the inducements to it that offered themselves, the honour of God and the deliverance of Israel, and nothing of the blackness of malice, hatred, or personal revenge. (1.) It was a divine power that enabled her to do it, and inspired her with a more than manly courage. What if her hand should shake, and she should miss her blow? What if he should awake when she was attempting it? Or suppose some of his own attendants should follow him, and surprise her in the face, how dearly would she and all hers be made to pay for it? Yet, obtaining help of God, she did it effectually. (2.) It was a divine warrant that justified her in the doing of it; and therefore, since no such extraordinary commissions can now be pretended, it ought not in any case to be imitated. The laws of friendship and hospitality must be religiously observed, and we must abhor the thought of betraying any whom we have invited and encouraged to put a confidence in us. And, as to this act of Jael (like that of Ehud in the chapter before), we have reason to think she was conscious of such a divine impulse upon her spirit to do it as did abundantly satisfy herself (and it ought therefore to satisfy us) that it was well done. God's judgments are a great deep. The instrument of this execution was a nail of the tent, that is, one of the great pins with which the tent, or the stakes of it, were fastened. They often removing their tents, she had been used to drive these nails, and therefore knew how to do it the more dexterously on this great occasion. he that thought to destroy Israel with his many iron chariots is himself destroyed with one iron nail. Thus do the weak things of the world confound the mighty. See here Jael's glory and Sisera's shame. The great commander dies, [1.] In his sleep, fast asleep, and weary. It comes in as a reason why he stirred not, to make resistance. So fettered was he in the chains of sleep that he could not find his hands. Thus *the stout-hearted are spoiled at thy rebuke, O God of Jacob! they are cast into a dead sleep,* and so are made to sleep their last, Ps. 76:5, 6. Let not the strong man then glory in his strength; for when he sleeps where is it? It is weak, and he can do nothing; a child may insult him then, and steal his life from him; and yet if he sleep not he is soon spent and weary, and can do nothing either. Those words which we here put in a parenthesis *(for he was weary)* all the ancient versions read otherwise: *he struggled* (or started, as we say) *and died,* so the Syriac and Arabic, *Exagitans sese mortuus est. He fainted and died,* so the LXX. *Consocians morte soporem,* so the vulgar Latin, joining sleep and death together, seeing they are so near akin. *He fainted and died.* He dies, [2.] With his head nailed to the ground, an emblem of his earthly-mindedness. *O curve in terram animoe!* His ear (says bishop Hall) was fastened close to the earth, as if his body had been listening what had become of his soul. He dies, [3.] By the hand of a woman. This added to the shame of his death before men; and had he but known it, as Abimelech (*ch.* 9:54), we may well imagine how much it would have added to the vexation of his own heart.

II. The glory and joy of Israel hereupon. 1. Barak their leader finds his enemy dead, (*v.* 22), and no doubt, he was very well pleased to find his work done so well to his hand, and so much to the glory of God and the confusion of his enemies. had he stood too nicely upon a point of honour, he would have resented it as an affront to have the general slain by any hand but his; but now he remembered that this diminution of his honour he was sentenced to undergo, for insisting upon Deborah's going with him *(the Lord shall sell Sisera into the hand of a woman),* though then it was little thought that the prediction would be fulfilled in such a way as this. 2. Israel is completely delivered out of the hands of Jabin king of Canaan, *v.* 23, 24. They not only shook off his yoke by this day's victory, but they afterwards prosecuted the war against him, till they had destroyed him, he and his nation being by the divine appointment devoted to ruin and not to be spared. The Israelites, having soundly smarted for their foolish pity in not doing it before, resolved now it is in their power to indulge them no longer, but to make a thorough riddance of them, as a people to whom to show mercy was as contrary to their own interest as it was to God's command; and probably it is with an eye to the sentence they were under that this enemy is named three times here in these last two verses, and called *king of Canaan;* for as such he was to be destroyed; and so thoroughly was he destroyed that I do not remember to read of the kings of Canaan any more after this. The children of Israel would have prevented a great deal of mischief if they had sooner destroyed these Canaanites, as God had both commanded and enabled them; but better be wise late, and buy wisdom by experience, than never wise.

CHAPTER 5

This chapter contains the triumphal song which was composed and sung upon occasion of that glorious victory which Israel obtained over the forces of Jabin king of Canaan and the happy consequences of that victory. Probably it was usual then to publish poems upon such occasions, as now; but this only is preserved of all the poems of that age of the judges, because dictated by Deborah a prophetess, designed for a psalm of praise then, and a pattern of praise to after-ages, and it gives a great deal of light to the history of these times. I. It begins with praise to God (*v.* 2, 3). II. The substance of this song transmits the memory of this great achievement. 1. Comparing God's appearances for them on this occasion with his appearances to them on Mount Sinai (*v.* 4, 5). 2. Magnifying their deliverance from the consideration of the calamitous condition they had been in (*v.* 6–8). 3. Calling those to join in praise that shared in the benefits of the success (*v.* 9–13). 4. Reflecting honour upon those tribes that were forward and active in that war, and disgrace on those that declined the service (*v.* 14–19, 23). 5. Taking notice how God himself fought for them (*v.* 20–22). 6. Celebrating particularly the honour of Jael, that slew Sisera, on which head the song is very large (*v.* 24–30). It concludes with a prayer to God (*v.* 31).

Verses 1–5

The former chapter let us know what great things God had done for Israel; in this we have the thankful returns they made to God, that all ages of the church might learn that work of heaven to praise God.

I. God is praised by a song, which is, 1. A very natural expression of rejoicing. *Is any merry? Let him sing;* and holy joy is the very soul and root of praise and thanksgiving. God is pleased to reckon himself glorified by our joy in him, and in his wondrous works. His servants' joy is his delight, and their sons are melody to him. 2. A very proper expedient for spreading the knowledge and perpetuating the remembrance of great events. Neighbours would learn this song one of another and children of their parents; and by that means those who had not books, or could not read, yet would be made acquainted with these works of God; and *one generation* would thus *praise God's works to another,* and *declare his mighty acts,* Ps. 145:4, etc.

II. Deborah herself penned this song, as appears by *v.* 7: *Till I Deborah arose.* And the first words should be rendered, *Then she sang, even Deborah.* 1. She used her gifts as a prophetess in composing the song, and the strain throughout is very fine and lofty, the images are lively, the expressions elegant, and an admirable mixture there is in it of sweetness and majesty. No poetry is comparable to the sacred poetry. And, 2. We may supposed she used her power as a princess, in obliging the conquering army of Israel to learn and sing this son. She expects not that they should, by their poems, celebrate her praises and magnify here, but requires that in this poem they should join with her in celebrating God's praises and magnifying him. She had been the first wheel in the action, and now is so in the thanksgiving.

III. It was sung on that day, not the very day that the fight was, but on that occasion, and soon after, as soon as a thanksgiving day could conveniently be appointed. When we have received mercy from God, we ought to be speedy in our returns of praise, while the impressions of the mercy are fresh. It is rent to be paid at the day.

1. She begins with a general Hallelujah: *Praise* (or *bless,* for that is the word) *you the Lord, v.* 2. The design of the song is to give glory to God; this therefore is put first, to explain and direct all that follows, like the first petition of the Lord's prayer, *Hallowed be thy name.* Two things God is here praised for: — (1.) The vengeance he took on Israel's enemies, for the avenging of Israel upon their proud and cruel oppressors, recompensing into their bosoms all the injuries they had done to his people. *The Lord is known* as a righteous God, and the God to whom vengeance belongs *by the judgments which he executeth.* (2.) The grace he gave to Israel's friends, *when the people willingly offered themselves* to serve in this war. God is to have the glory of all the good offices that are at any time done us; and the more willingly they are done the more is to be observed of that grace which gives both to will and to do. For these two things she resolves to leave this song upon record, to the honour of the everlasting God (*v.* 3): *I, even I, will sing unto the Lord,* Jehovah, that God of incontestable sovereignty and irresistible power, even to *the Lord God of Israel,* who governs all for the good of the church.

2. She calls to the great ones of the world, that sit at the upper end of its table, to attend to her song, and take notice of the subject of it: *Hear, O you kings! give ear, O you princes!* (1.) She would have them know that as great and as high as they were there was one above them with whom it is folly to contend, and to whom it was their interest to submit, that horses and chariots are vain things for safety. (2.) She would have them to join with her in praising the God of Israel, and no longer to praise their counterfeit deities, as Belshazzar did. Dan. 5:4, *He praised the gods of gold and silver.* She bespeaks them as the psalmist (Ps. 2:10, 11), *Be wise now therefore, O you kings! serve the Lord with fear.* (3.) She would have them take warning by Sisera's fate, and not dare to offer any injury to the people of God, whose cause, sooner or later, God will plead with jealousy.

3. She looks back upon God's former appearances, and compares this with them, the more to magnify the glorious author of this great salvation. What God is doing should bring to our mind what he has done; for he is the same yesterday, to-day, and for ever (*v.* 4): *Lord, when thou wentest our of Seir.* This may be understood either, (1.) Of the appearances of God's power and justice against the enemies of Israel to subdue and conquer them; and so Hab. 3:3, 4, etc., is parallel to it, where the destruction of the church's enemies is thus described. When God had led his people Israel from the country of Edom he brought down under their feet Sihom and Og, striking them and their armies with such terror and amazement that they seemed apprehensive heaven and earth were coming together. Their hearts melted, as if all the world had been melting round about them. Or it notes the glorious displays of the divine majesty; and the surprising effects of the divine power, enough to make the earth tremble, the heavens drop like snow before the sun, and the mountains to melt. Compare Ps. 18:7. God's counsels are so far from being hindered by any creature that, when the time of their accomplishment comes, that which seemed to stand in their way will not only yield before them, but be made to serve them. See Isa. 64:1, 2. Or, (2.) It is meant of the appearances of God's glory and majesty to Israel, when he gave them his law at Mount Sinai. It was then literally true, *the earth trembled, and the heavens dropped,* etc. Compare Deu. 33:2; Ps. 68:7, 8. Let all the kings and princes know that this is the God whom Deborah praises, and not such mean and impotent deities as they paid their homage to. The Chaldee paraphrase applies it to the giving of the law, but has a strange descant on those words, *the mountains*

melted. Tabor, Hermon, and Carmel, contended among themselves: one said, Let the divine majesty dwell upon me; the other said, Let it dwell upon me; but God made it to dwell upon Mount Sinai, the meanest and least of all the mountains. I suppose it means the least valuable, because barren and rocky.

Verses 6–11

Here, I. Deborah describes the distressed state of Israel under the tyranny of Jabin, that the greatness of their trouble might make their salvation appear the more illustrious and the more gracious (*v.* 6): *From the days of Shamgar,* who did something towards the deliverance of Israel from the Philistines, to the days of Jael, the present day, in which Jael has so signalized herself, the country has been in a manner desolate. 1. No trade. For want of soldiers to protect men of business in their business from the incursions of the enemy, and for want of magistrates to restrain and punish thieves and robbers among them (men of broken fortunes and desperate spirits, that, having no employment, took to rob on the highroad), all commerce ceased, and the highways were unoccupied; no caravans of merchants, as formerly. 2. No travelling. Whereas in times when there was some order and government the travellers might be safe in the open roads, and the robbers were forced to lurk in the by-ways, no, on the contrary, the robbers insulted on the open roads without check, and the honest travellers were obliged to sculk and walk through by-ways, in continual frights. 3. No tillage. The fields must needs be laid waste and unoccupied when the inhabitants of the villages, the country farmers, ceased from their employment, quitted their houses which were continually alarmed and plundered by the banditti, and were obliged to take shelter for themselves and their families in walled and fenced cities. 4. No administration of justice. There was war in the gates where their courts were kept, *v.* 8. So that it was not till this salvation was wrought that *the people of the Lord* durst *go down to the gates, v.* 11. The continual incursions of the enemy deprived the magistrates of the dignity, and the people of the benefit, of their government. 5. No peace to him that went out nor to him that came in. The gates through which they passed and repassed were infested by the enemy; nay, the places of drawing water were alarmed by the archers — a mighty achievement to terrify the drawers of water. 6. Neither arms nor spirit to help themselves with, not a *shield nor spear seen among forty thousand, v.* 8. Either they were disarmed by their oppressors, or they themselves neglected the art of war; so that, though they had spears and shields, they were not to be seen, but were thrown by and suffered to rust, they having neither skill nor will to use them.

II. She shows in one word what it was that brought all this misery upon them: *They chose new gods, v.* 8. It was their idolatry that provoked God to give them up thus into the hands of their enemies. The Lord their God was one Lord, but this would not content them: they must have more, many more, still more. Their God was the Ancient of days, still the same, and therefore they grew weary of him, and must have new gods, which they were as fond of as children of new clothes, names newly invented, heroes newly canonized. Their fathers, when put to their choice, chose the Lord for their God (Jos. 24:21), but they would not abide by that choice, they must have gods of their own choosing.

III. She takes notice of God's great goodness to Israel in raising up such as should redress these grievances. Herself first (*v.* 7): *Till that I Deborah arose,* to restrain and punish those who disturbed the public peace, and protect men in their business, and then the face of things was changed for the better quickly; those beasts of prey retired upon the breaking forth of this joyful light, and *man went forth again to his work and labour,* Ps. 104:22, 23. Thus she became a mother in Israel, a nursing mother, such was the affection she bore to her people, and such the care and pains she took for the public welfare. Under her there were other governors of Israel (*v.* 9), who, like her, had done their part as governors to reform the people, and then, like her, offered themselves willingly to serve in the war, not insisting upon the exemption which their dignity and office entitled them to, when the had so fair an opportunity of appearing in their country's cause; and no doubt the example of the governors influenced the people in like manner *willingly to offer themselves, v.* 2. Of these governors she says, *My heart is towards them,* that is, "I truly love and honour them; they have won my heart for ever; I shall never forget them." Note, Those are worthy of double honour that recede voluntarily from the demands of their honour to serve God and his church.

IV. She calls upon those who had a particular share in the advantages of this great salvation to offer up particular thanks to God for it, *v.* 10, 11. Let every man speak as he found of the goodness of God in this happy change of the posture of public affairs. 1. *You that ride on white asses,* that is, the nobility and gentry. Horses were little used in that county; they had, it is probable, a much better breed of asses than we have; but persons of quality, it seems, were distinguished by the colour of the asses they rode on; the white being more rare were therefore more valued. Notice is taken of Abdon's sons and grandsons riding on ass-colts, as indicating them to be men of distinction, *ch.* 12:14. Let such as are by this salvation restored, not only to their liberty as other Israelites, but to their dignity, speak God's praises. 2. Let those that *sit in judgment* be sensible of it, and thankful for it as a very great mercy, that they may sit safely there, that the sword of justice is not struck out of their hand by the sword of war. 3. Let those that *walk by the way,* and meet with none there to make them afraid, speak to themselves in pious meditations, and to their fellow-travellers in religious discourses, of the goodness of God in ridding the roads of those banditti that had so long infested them. 4. Let those that draw in peace, and have not their wells taken from them, or stopped up, nor are in danger of being caught by the enemy when they go forth to draw, there, where they find themselves so much more safe and easy than they have been, *there let them rehearse the acts of the Lord,* not Deborah's acts, nor Barak's, but the Lord's, taking notice of his hand making peace in their borders, and creating a defence upon all the glory. This *is the Lord's doing.* Observe in these acts of his, (1.) Justice executed on his daring enemies. They are the righteous acts of the Lord. See him pleading a righteous cause, and sitting in the throne judging aright, and give him glory as the Judge of all the earth. (2.) Kindness shown to his trembling people, *the inhabitants of the villages,* who lay most open to the enemy, had suffered most, and were most in danger, Eze. 38:11. It is the glory of God to protect those that are most exposed, and to help the weakest. Let us all take notice of the share we in particular have in the public peace and tranquility, the inhabitants of the villages especially, and give God the praise of it.

Verses 12–23

Here, I. Deborah stirs up herself and Barak to celebrate this victory in the most solemn manner, to the glory of God and the honour of Israel, for the encouragement of their friends and the greater confusion of their enemies, *v.* 12. 1. Deborah, as a prophetess, must do it by a song, to compose and sing which she excites herself: *Awake, awake,* and again, *awake, awake,* which intimates the sense she had of the excellency and difficulty of the work; it needed and well deserved the utmost liveliness and vigour of soul in the performance of it; all the powers and faculties of the soul in their closest intensity and application ought to be employed in it. Thus too she expresses the sense she had of her own infirmity, and aptness to flag and remit in her zeal in this work. Note, Praising God is work that we should awake to, and awake ourselves to, Ps. 108:2. 2. Barak, as a general, must do it by a triumph: *Lead thy captivity captive.* Though the army of Sisera was cut off in the field, and no quarter given, yet we may suppose in the prosecution of the victory, when the war was carried into the enemy's country, many not found in arms were seized and made prisoners of war. These she would have led in chains after Barak, when he made his public entry into his own city, to grace his triumphs; not as if it should be any pleasure to him to trample upon his fellow-creatures, but thus he must give glory to God, and serve that great purpose of his government which is to *look upon those that are proud and to abase them.*

II. She gives good reason for this praise and triumph, *v.* 13. This glorious victory had made the remnant of Israel, and Deborah in particular, look very great, a circumstance which they owed entirely to God. 1. The Israelites had become few and inconsiderable, and yet to them God gave dominion over nobles. Many of them were cut off by the enemy, many died of grief, and perhaps some had removed their families and effects into foreign parts; yet those few that remained, by divine assistance, with one brave and generous effort, not only shook off the yoke of oppression from their own neck, but got power over their oppressors. As long as any of God's Israel remain (and a remnant God will have in the worst of times) there is hope, be it ever so small a remnant, for God can make him that remains, though it should be but one single person, triumph over the most proud and potent. 2. Deborah was herself of the weaker sex, and the sex that from the fall had been sentenced to subjection, and yet the Lord that is himself higher than the highest authorized her to rule over the mighty men of Israel, who willingly submitted to her direction, and enabled her to triumph over the mighty men of Canaan, who fell before the army she commanded; so wonderfully did he *advance the low estate of his handmaid.* "The Lord made me, a woman, to have dominion over mighty men." A despised stone is made *head of the corner. This is* indeed the *Lord's doing, and marvellous in our eyes.*

III. She makes particular remarks on the several parties concerned in this great action, taking notice who fought against them, who fought for them, and who stood neuter.

1. Who fought against them. The power of the enemy must be taken notice of, that the victory may appear the more glorious. Jabin and Sisera had been mentioned in the history, but here it appears further, (1.) That Amalek was in league with Jabin, and sent him in assistance, or endeavoured to do it. Ephraim is here said to act against Amalek (*v.* 14), probably intercepting and cutting off some forces of the Amalekites that were upon their march to join Sisera. Amalek had helped Moab to oppress Israel (*ch.* 3:13) and now had helped Jabin; they were inveterate enemies to God's people — their hand had always *been against the throne of the Lord* (Ex. 17:16); and therefore they were the more dangerous. (2.) That others of the kings of Canaan, who had somewhat recovered themselves since their defeat by Joshua, joined with Jabin, and strengthened his army with their forces, having the same implacable enmity to Israel that he had, and those kingdoms, when they were in their strength, having been subject to that of Hazor, Jos. 11:10. These kings *came and fought, v.* 19. Israel had no king; their enemies had many, whose power and influence, especially acting in confederacy, made them very formidable; and yet Israel, having the Lord for their King, was too hard for them all. It is said of these kings that *they took no gain of money,* they were not mercenary troops hired into the service of Jabin (such often fail in an extremity), but they were volunteers and hearty in the cause against Israel: they *desired not the riches of silver,* so the Chaldee, but only the satisfaction of helping to ruin Israel. Acting upon this principle, they were the more formidable, and would be the more cruel.

2. Who fought for them. The several tribes that assisted in this great exploit are here spoken of with honour; for, though God is chiefly to be glorified, instruments must have their due praise, for the encouragement of others: but, after all, it was heaven that turned the scale.

(1.) Ephraim and Benjamin, those tribes among whom Deborah herself lived, bestirred themselves, and did bravely, by her influence upon them; for her palm-tree was in the tribe of Ephraim, and very near to that of Benjamin (*v.* 14): *Out of Ephraim was there a root,* and life in the root, against Amalek. There was in Ephraim a mountain called *the mount of Amalek,* mentioned, *ch.* 12:15, which, some think, is here meant, and some read it, *there was a root in Amalek,* that is, in that mountain, a strong resolution in the minds of that people to make head against the oppressors, which was the root of the matter. Herein Benjamin had set them a good example among his people. "Ephraim moved *after thee, Benjamin;*" though Benjamin was the junior tribe, and much inferior, especially at this time, to Ephraim, both in number and wealth, yet when they led Ephraim followed in appearing for the common cause. If we be not so bold as to lead, yet we must not be so proud and sullen as not to follow even our inferiors in a good work. Ephraim was a at a distance from the place of action, and therefore could not send forth many of its boughs to the service; but Deborah, who was one of them, knew there was a root of them, that they were hearty well-wishers to the cause. Dr. Lightfoot gives quite another sense of this. Joshua, of Ephraim, had been a root of such victories against Amalek (Ex. 17), and Ehud of Benjamin lately against Amalek and Moab.

(2.) The ice being broken by Ephraim and Benjamin, Machir (the half-tribe of Manasseh beyond Jordan) and Zebulun sent in men that were very serviceable to this great design. When an army is to be raised, especially under such disadvantages as Barak now experienced from the long disuse of arms and the dispiritedness of the people, it is of great consequence to be furnished, [1.] With men of courage for officers, and such the family of Machir furnished them with, for thence came down *governors.* The children of Machir were particularly famous for their valour in Moses' time (Num. 32:39), and it seems it continued in their family, the more because they were seated in the frontiers. [2.] With men of learning and ingenuity for secretaries of war, and with such they were supplied out of Zebulun: thence came men *that handle the pen of the writer,* clerks that issued out orders, wrote circular letters, drew commissions, mustered their men, and kept their accounts. Thus must every man, *according as he has received the gift, minister the same,* for the public good (1 Pt. 4:10); the eyes see, and the ears hear, for the whole body. I know it is generally understood of the forwardness even of the scholars of this tribe, who studied the law and expounded it, to take up arms in this cause, though they were better skilled in books than in the art of war. So Sir Richard Blackmore paraphrases it: —

The scribes of Zebulun and learned men,
To wield the sword, laid down the pen.

(3.) Issachar did good service too; though he *saw that rest was good,* and therefore *bowed his shoulder to bear,* which is the character of that tribe (Gen. 49:15), yet they disdained to bear the yoke of Jabin's tribute, and now preferred the generous toils of war to a servile rest. Though it should seem there were not many common soldiers enlisted out of that tribe, yet *the princes of Issachar were with Deborah and Barak* (*v.* 15), probably, as a great council of war to advise upon emergencies. And, it should seem, these princes of Issachar did in person accompany Barak into the field of battle. Did he go on foot? They footed it with him, not consulting their honour or ease. Did he go into the valley, the place of most danger? They exposed themselves with him, and were still at his right hand to advise him: for the men of Issachar were men that *had understanding of the times,* 1 Chr. 12:32.

(4.) Zebulun and Naphtali were the most bold and active of all the tribes, not only out of a particular affection to Barak their countryman, but because, they lying nearest to Jabin, the yoke of oppression lay heavier on their necks than on those of any other tribe. Better die in honour than live in bondage; and therefore, in a pious zeal for God and their country, they *jeoparded their lives unto the death in the high places of the field, v.* 18. With what heroic bravery did they charge and push on even upon the chariots of iron, despising danger, and setting death itself at defiance in so good a cause!

(5.) The stars from heaven appeared, or acted at least, on Israel's side (*v.* 20): *The stars in their courses,* according to the order and direction of him who is the great Lord of their hosts, *fought against Sisera,* by their malignant influences, or by causing the storms of hail and thunder which contributed so much to the rout of Sisera's army. The Chaldee reads it, *from heaven, from the place where the stars go forth, war was waged against Sisera,* that is, the power of the God of heaven was engaged against him, making use of the ministration of the angels of heaven. Some way or other, the heavenly bodies (not arrested, as when the sun stood still at Joshua's word, but going on in their courses) fought against Sisera. Those whom God is an enemy to the whole creation is at war with. Perhaps the flashes of lightning by which the stars fought was that which frightened the horses, so as that they pranced till their very hoofs were broken (*v.* 22), and probably overturned the chariots of iron which they drew or turned them back upon their owners.

(6.) The river of Kishon fought against their enemies. It swept away multitudes of those that hoped to make their escape through it, *v.* 21. Ordinarily, it was but a shallow river, and, being in their own country, we may suppose they well knew its fords and safest passages, and yet now, probably by the great rain that fell, it was so swollen, and the stream so deep and strong, that those who attempted to pass it were drowned, being feeble and faint, and unable to make their way through it. And then were the horse-hoofs broken by means of the *plungings.* So it is in the margin, *v.* 22. The river of Kishon is called *that ancient river* because described or celebrated by ancient historians or poets, or rather because it was designed of old, in the counsel of God, to serve his purposes against Sisera at this time, and did so, as if it had been made on purpose; thus *the water of the old pool* God is said to have fashioned long ago for that use to which it was put, Isa. 22:11.

(7.) Deborah's own soul fought against them; she speaks of it with a holy exultation (*v.* 21): *O, my soul, thou hast trodden down strength.* She did it by exciting others to do it, and assisting them, which she did with all her heart. Also by her prayers; as Moses conquered Amalek by lifting up his hand, so Deborah vanquished Sisera by lifting up her heart. And when the soul is employed in holy exercises, and heart-work is made of them, through the grace of God the strength of our spiritual enemies will be trodden down and will fall before us.

3. In this great engagement she observes who stood *neuter,* and did not side with Israel as might have been expected. It is strange to find how many, even of those who were called Israelites, basely deserted this glorious cause and declined to appear. No mention is made of Judah nor Simeon among the tribes concerned, because they, lying so very remote from the scene of action, had not an opportunity to appear, and therefore it was not expected from them; but for those that lay near, and yet would not venture, indelible marks of disgrace are here put upon them, as they deserved.

(1.) Reuben basely declined the service, *v.* 15, 16. Justly had he long ago been deprived of the privileges of the birth-right, and still does his dying father's doom stick by him: *unstable as water, he shall not excel.* Two things hindered them from engaging: — [1.] Their divisions. This jarring string she twice strikes upon to their shame: *For the divisions of Reuben* (or in these divisions) *there were great thoughts,* impressions, and searchings *of heart.* Not only for their division from Canaan by the river Jordan, which needed not to have hindered them had they been hearty in the cause, for Gilead abode beyond Jordan, and yet from Machir of Gilead came down governors; but it means either that they were divided among themselves, could not agree who should go or who should lead, each striving to gain the posts of honour and shun those of danger, some unhappy contests in their tribe kept them from uniting together, and with their brethren, for the common good, or that they were divided in their opinion of this war from the rest of the tribes, thought the attempt either not justifiable or not practicable, and therefore blamed those that engaged in it and did themselves decline it. This occasioned great searchings of heart among the rest, especially when the had reason to suspect that, whatever Reuben pretended, his sitting still now proceeded from a cooling of his affections to his brethren and an alienation of mind from them, which occasioned them many sad thoughts. It grieves us to see our mother's children angry with us for doing our duty and looking strange upon us when we most need their friendship and assistance. [2.] Their business in the world: *Reuben abode among the sheepfolds,* a warmer and safer place than the camp, pretending they could not conveniently leave the sheep they tended; he loved to *hear the bleatings of the flocks,* or, as some read it, the *whistlings* of the flocks, the music which the shepherds made with their oaten reeds or pipes, and the pastorals which they sung; these Reuben preferred before the martial drum and trumpet. Thus many are kept from doing their duty by the fear of trouble, the love of ease, and an inordinate affection to their worldly business and advantage. Narrow selfish spirits care not what becomes of the interests of God's church, so they can but get, keep, and save money. *All seek their own,* Phil. 2:21.

(2.) Dan and Asher did the same, *v.* 17. These two lay on the sea-coast, and, [1.] Dan pretended he could not leave his ships but they would be exposed, and therefore *I pray thee have me excused.* Those of that tribe perhaps pleaded that their sea-trade disfitted them for land-service and diverted them from it; but Zebulun also was a haven for ships, a sea-faring tribe, and yet was forward and active in this expedition. There is no excuse we make to shift off duty but what some or other have broken through and set aside, whose courage and resolution will rise up against us and shame us. [2.] Asher pretended he must stay at home to repair the breaches which the sea had in some places made upon his land, and to fortify his works against the encroachments of it, or he abode in his creeks, or small havens, where his trading vessels lay to attend them. A little thing will serve those for a pretence to stay at home who have no mind to engage in the most necessary services because there are difficulty and danger in them.

(3.) But above all Meroz is condemned, and a curse pronounced upon the inhabitants of it, *Because they came not to the help of the Lord, v.* 23. Probably this was some city that lay near the scene of action, and therefore the inhabitants had a fair opportunity of showing their obedience to God and their concern for Israel, and of doing a good service to the common cause; but they basely declined it, for fear of Jabin's iron chariots, being willing to sleep in a whole skin. The Lord needed not their help; he made it to appear he could do his work without them; but no thanks to them: for aught they knew the attempt might have miscarried for want of their hand, and therefore they are cursed for *not coming to the help of the Lord,* when it was in effect proclaimed, *Who is on the Lord's side?* The cause between God and the mighty (the principalities and powers of the kingdom of darkness) will not admit of neutrality. God looks upon those as against him that are not with him. This curse is pronounced by the *angel of the Lord,* our Lord Jesus, the captain of the Lord's host (and *those whom he curses are cursed indeed),* and further than we have warrant and authority from him we may not curse. He that will richly reward all his good soldiers will certainly and severely punish all cowards and deserters. This city of Meroz seems to have been at this time a considerable place, since something great was expected from it; but probably, after the angel of the Lord had pronounced this curse upon it, it dwindled, and, like the fig-tree which Christ cursed, withered away, so that we never read of it after this in scripture.

Verses 24–31

Deborah here concludes this triumphant song,

I. With the praises of Jael, her sister-heroine, whose valiant act had completed and crowned the victory. She had mentioned her before (*v.* 6) as one that would have served her country if it had been in her power; now she applauds her as one that did serve it admirably well when it was in her power. Her poetry is finest and most florid here in the latter end of the song. How honourably does she speak of Jael (*v.* 24), who preferred her peace with the God of Israel before her peace with the king of Canaan, and though not a native of Israel (for aught that appears) yet heartily espoused the cause of Israel in this critical conjuncture, jeoparded her life as truly as if she had been in the high places of the field, and bravely fought for those whom she saw God fought for! *Blessed shall she be above women in the tent.* Note, Those whose lot is cast in the tent, in a very low and narrow sphere of activity, if they serve God in that according to their capacity, shall in no wise lose their reward. Jael in the tent wins as rich a blessing as Barak in the field. Nothing is more confounding, grievous, and shameful, than disappointment, and Deborah here does most elegantly describe two great disappointments, the shame of which was typical of sinners' everlasting shame.

1. Sisera found a fatal enemy where he expected a firm and faithful friend. (1.) Jael showed him the kindness of a friend, and perhaps at that time intended no other than kindness, until God, by an immediate impulse upon her mind (which impulses then were to be regarded, and carried so much of their own evidence with them that they might be relied upon, but cannot now be pretended to), directed her to do otherwise, *v.* 25. He asked only for fair water to quench his thirst, but she, not only to show her housewifery and good housekeeping, but to express her respect to him, *gave him milk* and *brought forth butter,* that is (say some interpreters), milk which had the butter taken from it; we call it butter-milk. No (say others), it was

milk that had the butter still in it; we call it cream. Whichsoever it was, it was probably the best her house afforded; and, to set it off, she brought it *in a lordly dish,* such as she called so, the finest she had, and better than she ordinarily used at her town table. This confirmed Sisera's opinion of her friendship, and made him sleep the faster and the more secure. But, (2.) She proved his mortal enemy, gave him his death's stroke: it is curiously described, *v.* 26, 27. [1.] How great does Jael look, *hammering Sisera,* as it is in the margin, mauling that proud man who had been so long the terror of the mighty, and sending him down slain to the pit with *his iniquities upon his bones!* Eze. 32:27. She seems to have gone about it with no more terror nor concern than if she had been going to nail one of the boards or bars of her tent, so confident was she of divine aid and protection. We read it she *smote off his head,* probably with his own sword, which, now that his head was nailed through, she durst take from his side, but not before, for fear of waking him. But because there was no occasion for cutting off his head, nor was it mentioned in the history, many think it should be read, *she struck through his head.* That head which had been proudly lifted up against God and Israel, and in which had been forged bloody designs for the destruction of God's people, Jael finds a soft place in, and into that with a good will strikes her nail. [2.] How mean does Sisera look, fallen at Jael's feet! *v.* 27. At the feet of this female executioner he bowed, he fell; all his struggles for life availed not; she followed her blow until he fell down dead. There lies extended the deserted carcase of that proud man, not on the bed of honour, not in the high places of the field, not having any glorious wound to show from a glittering sword, or a bow of steel, but in the corner of a tent, at the feet of a woman, with a disgraceful wound by a sorry nail struck through his head. Thus is shame the fate of proud men. And this is a very lively representation of the ruin of those sinners whose prosperity slays them; it flatters and caresses them with milk and butter in a lordly dish, as if it would make them easy and happy, but it nails their heads and hearts too to the ground in earthly-mindedness, and pierces them through with many sorrows; its flatteries are fatal, and sink them at last into destruction and perdition, 1 Tim. 6:9, 10.

2. Sisera's mother had the tidings brought her of her son's fall and ruin when she was big with expectation of his glorious and triumphant return, *v.* 28–30, where we have, (1.) Her fond desire to see her son come back in triumph: *Why is his chariot so long in coming?* She speaks this, not so much out of a concern for his safety, or any jealousy of his having miscarried (she had no fear of that, so confident was she of his success), but out of a longing for his glory, which with a feminine weakness she was passionately impatient to see, chiding the lingering chariot, and expostulating concerning the delays of it, little thinking that her unhappy son had been, before this, forced to quit that chariot which they were so proud of, and which she thought came so slowly. *The chariots of his glory had now become the shame of his house,* Isa. 22:18. Let us take heed of indulging such desires as these towards any temporal good thing, particularly towards that which cherishes vain-glory, for this was what she here doted on. Eagerness and impatience in our desires do us a great deal of prejudice, and make it intolerable to us to be crossed. But towards the second coming of Jesus Christ, and the glories of that day, we should thus stand affected *(Come, Lord Jesus, come quickly),* for here we cannot be disappointed. (2.) Her foolish hope and confidence that he would come at last in so much the greater pomp. Her wise ladies answered her, and thought they gave a very good account of the delay; yea, she *(in her wisdom,* says the Chaldee) tauntingly made answer to herself, *"Have they not sped?* No doubt they have, and that which delays them is that they are *dividing the prey,* which is so much that it is a work of time to make a distribution of it." In the spoil they pleased themselves with the thought of, observe, [1.] How impudently, and to the reproach and scandal of their sex, these ladies boast of the multitude of damsels which the soldiers would have the abusing of. [2.] How childishly they pleased themselves with the hope of seeing Sisera himself in a gaudy mantle of *divers colours;* how charmingly would it look! *of divers colours of needle-work,* plundered out of the wardrobe of some Israelitish lady; it is repeated again, as that which pleased their fancy above any thing, *of divers colours of needle-work on both sides,* and therefore very rich; such pieces of embroidery they hoped Sisera would have to present his mother and the ladies with. Thus apt are we to deceive ourselves with great expectations and confident hopes of honour, and pleasure, and wealth in this world, by which we prepare for ourselves the shame and grief of a disappointment. And thus does God often bring ruin on his enemies when they are most elevated.

II. She concludes all with a prayer to God, 1. For the destruction of all his foes: *"So,* so shamefully, so miserably, *let all thy enemies perish, O Lord;* let all that hope to triumph in Israel's ruin be thus disappointed and triumphed over. *Do to them all as unto Sisera,"* Ps. 83:9. Though our enemies are to be prayed for, God's enemies, as such, are to be prayed against; and, when we see some of God's enemies remarkably humbled and brought down, this is an encouragement to us to pray for the downfall of all the rest. Deborah was a prophetess, and this prayer was a prediction that in due time all God's enemies shall perish, Ps. 92:9. None ever hardened his heart against God and prospered. 2. For the exaltation and comfort of all his friends. "But let those that love him, and heartily wish well to his kingdom among men, be *as the sun when he goeth forth in his strength;* let them shine so bright, appear so glorious in the eye of the world, cast such benign influences, be as much out of the reach of their enemies, who curse the rising sun because it scorches them; let them *rejoice as a strong man to run a race,* Ps. 19:5. Let them, as burning and shining lights in their places, dispel the mists of darkness, and shine with more and more lustre and power *unto the perfect day."* Prov. 4:18. Such shall be the honour, and such the joy, of all that love God in sincerity, and for ever they shall *shine as the sun in the firmament of our Father.*

The victory here celebrated with this song was of such happy consequence to Israel that for the best part of one age they enjoyed the peace which it opened the way to: *The land had rest forty years,* that is, so long it was from this victory to the raising up of Gideon. And well would it have been if, when the churches and the tribes had rest, they had been edified, *and had walked in the fear of the Lord.*

CHAPTER 6

Nothing that occurred in the quiet and peaceable times of Israel is recorded; the forty years' rest after the conquest of Jabin is passed over in silence; and here begins the story of another distress and another deliverance, by Gideon, the fourth of the judges. Here is, I. The calamitous condition of Israel, by the inroads of the Midianites (*v.* 1–6). II. The message God sent them by a prophet, by convincing them of sin, to prepare them for deliverance (*v.* 7–10). III. The raising up of Gideon to be their deliverer. 1. A commission which God sent him by the hand of an angel, and confirmed by a sign (*v.* 11–24). 2. The first-fruits of his government in the reform of his father's house (*v.* 25–32). 3. The preparations he made for a war with the Midianites, and the encouragement given him by a sign (*v.* 33–40).

Verses 1–6

We have here, I. Israel's sin renewed: *They did evil in the sight of the Lord, v.* 1. The burnt child dreads the fire; yet this perverse unthinking people, that had so often smarted sorely for their idolatry, upon a little respite of God's judgments return to it again. *This people hath a revolting rebellious heart,* not kept in awe by the terror of God's judgments, nor engaged in honour and gratitude by the great things he had done for them to keep themselves in his love. The providence of God will not change the hearts and lives of sinners.

II. Israel's troubles repeated. This would follow of course; let all that sin expect to suffer; let all that return to folly expect to return to misery. *With the froward God will show himself froward* (Ps. 18:26), and will walk contrary to those that walk contrary to him, Lev. 26:21, 24. Now as to this trouble, 1. It arose from a very despicable enemy. God delivered them into the hand of Midian (*v.* 1), not Midian in the south where Jethro lived, but Midian in the east that joined to Moab (Num. 22:4), a people that all men despised as uncultivated and unintelligent; hence we read not here of any king, lord, or general, that they had, but the force with which they destroyed Israel was an undisciplined mob; and, which made it the more grievous, they were a people that Israel had formerly subdued, and in a manner destroyed (see Num. 31:7), and yet by this time (nearly 200 years after) the poor remains of them were so multiplied, and so magnified, that they were capable of being made a very severe scourge to Israel. Thus *God moved them to jealousy with those who were not a people,* even a foolish nation, Deu. 32:21. The meanest creature will serve to chastise those that have made the great Creator their enemy. And, when those we are authorized to rule prove rebellious and disobedient to us, it concerns us to enquire whether we have not been so to our sovereign Ruler. 2. It arose to a very formidable height (*v.* 2): *The hand of Midian prevailed,* purely by their multitude. God had promised to increase Israel as the sand on the sea shore; but their sin stopped their growth and diminished them, and then their enemies, though otherwise every way inferior to them, overpowered them with numbers. They came upon them as *grasshoppers for multitude* (*v.* 5), not in a regular army to engage them in the field, but in a confused swarm to plunder the country, quarter themselves upon it, and enrich themselves with its spoils — bands of robbers, and no better. And sinful Israel, being separated by sin from God, had not spirit to make head against them. Observe the wretched havoc that these Midianites made with their bands of plunderers in Israel. Here we have, (1.) The Israelites imprisoned, or rather imprisoning themselves, in dens and caves, *v.* 2. This was owing purely to their own timorousness and faint-heartedness, that they would rather fly than fight; it was the effect of a guilty conscience, which made them tremble at the shaking of a leaf, and the just punishment of their apostasy from God, who thus fought against them with those very terrors with which he would otherwise have fought for them. Had it not been for this, we cannot but think Israel a match for the Midianites, and able enough to make head against them; but the heart that departs from God is lost, not only to that which is good, but to that which is great. Sin dispirits men, and makes them sneak into dens and caves. The day will come when chief captains and mighty men will call in vain to rocks and mountains to hide them. (2.) The Israelites impoverished, greatly impoverished, *v.* 6. The Midianites and the other children of the east that joined with them to live by spoil and rapine (as long before the Sabeans and Chaldeans did that plundered Job, freebooters) made frequent incursions into the land of Canaan. This fruitful land was a great temptation to them; and the sloth and luxury into which the Israelites had sunk by forty years' rest made them and their substance an easy prey to them. They came up against them (*v.* 3), pitched their camps among them (*v.* 4), and brought their cattle with them, particularly camels innumerable (*v.* 5), not a flying party to make a sally upon them and be gone presently, but they resolved to force their way, and penetrated through the heart of the country as far as Gaza on the western side, *v.* 4. They let the Israelites alone to sow their ground, but towards harvest they came and seized all, and ate up and destroyed it, both grass and corn, and when they went away took with them the sheep and oxen, so that in short they left no sustenance for Israel, except what was privately taken by the rightful owners into the dens and caves. Now here we may see, [1.] The justice of God in the punishment of their sin. They had neglected to honour God with their substance in tithes and offerings, and had prepared that for Baal with which God should have been served, and now God justly sends an enemy to take it away *in the season thereof,* Hos. 2:8, 9. [2.] The consequence of God's departure from a people; when he goes all good goes and all mischiefs break in. When Israel kept in with God, they reaped what others sowed (Jos. 24:13; Ps. 105:44); but now that God had forsaken them others reaped what they sowed. Let us take occasion from this to bless God for our national peace and tranquillity, that we *eat the labour of our hands.*

III. Israel's sense of God's hand revived at last. Seven years, year after year, did the Midianites make these inroads upon them, each we may suppose worse than the other (*v.* 1), until at last, all other succours failing, *Israel cried unto the Lord* (*v.* 6), for crying to Baal ruined them, and would not help them. When God judges he will overcome; and sinners shall be made either to bend or break before him.

Verses 7–10

Observe here, I. The cognizance God took of the cries of Israel, when at length they were directed towards him.

Though in their prosperity they had neglected him and made court to his rivals, and though they never looked towards him until they were driven to it by extremity, yet, upon their complain and prayer, he intended relief for them. Thus would he show how ready he is to forgive, how swift he is to show mercy, and how inclinable to hear prayer, that sinners may be encouraged to return and repent, Ps. 130:4.

II. The method God took of working deliverance for them.

1. Before he sent an angel to raise them up a saviour he sent a prophet to reprove them for sin, and to bring them to repentance, *v.* 8. This prophet is not named, but he was a man, a prophet, not an angel, as *ch.* 2:1. Whether this prophet took an opportunity of delivering his message to the children of Israel when they had met together in a general assembly, at some solemn feast or other great occasion, or whether he went from city to city and from tribe to tribe, preaching to this purport, is not certain; but his errand was to convince them of sin, that, in their crying to the Lord, they might confess that with sorrow and shame, and not spend their breath in only complaining of their trouble. They cried to God for a deliverer, and God sent them a prophet to instruct them, and to make them ready for deliverance. Note, (1.) We have reason to hope God is designing mercy for us if we find he is by his grace preparing us for it. If to those that are sick he sends a messenger, an interpreter, by whom he *shows unto man his uprightness, then he is gracious,* and grants a recovery, Job 33:23, 24. (2.) The sending of prophets to a people, and the furnishing of a land with faithful ministers, is a token for good, and an evidence that God has mercy in store for them. He thus turns us to him, and then causes his face to shine, Ps. 80:19.

2. We have here the heads of the message which this prophet delivered in to Israel, in the name of the Lord.

(1.) He sets before them the great things God had done for them (*v.* 8, 9): *Thus saith the Lord God of Israel;* they had worshipped the *gods of the nations,* as if they had had no God of their own to worship and therefore might choose whom they pleased; but they are here reminded of one whom they had forgotten, who was known by the title of *the God of Israel,* and to him they must return. They had turned to other gods, as if their own had been either incapable or unwilling to protect them, and therefore they are told what he did for their fathers, in whose loins they were, the benefit of which descended and still remained to this their ungrateful seed. [1.] He brought them out of Egypt, where otherwise they would have continued in perpetual poverty and slavery. [2.] He *delivered them out of the hands of all that oppressed them;* this is mentioned to intimate that the reason why they were not now delivered out of the hands of the oppressing Midianites was not for want of any power or good-will in God, but because by their iniquity they had sold themselves, and God would not redeem them until they by repentance revoked the bargain. [3.] He put them in quiet possession of this good land; this not only aggravated their sin, and affixed the brand of base ingratitude to it, but it justified God, and cleared him from blame upon account of the trouble they were now in. They could not say he was unkind, for he had given all possible proofs of his designing well for them; if ill befel them notwithstanding, they must thank themselves.

(2.) He shows the easiness and equity of God's demands and expectations from them (*v.* 10): *"I am the Lord your God,* to whom you lie under the highest obligations, *fear not the gods of the Amorites,"* that is, "do not worship them, nor show any respect to them; do not worship them for fear of their doing you any hurt, for what hurt can they do you while I am your God? Fear God, and you need not fear them."

(3.) He charges them with rebellion against God, who had laid this injunction upon them: *But you have not obeyed my voice.* The charge is short, but very comprehensive; this was the malignity of all their sin, it was disobedience to God; and therefore it was this that brought those calamities upon them under which they were now groaning, pursuant to the threatenings annexed to his commands. He intends hereby to bring them to repentance; and our repentance is then right and genuine when the sinfulness of sin, as disobedience to God, is that in it which we chiefly lament.

Verses 11–24

It is not said what effect the prophet's sermon had upon the people, but we may hope it had a good effect, and that some of them at least repented and reformed upon it; for here, immediately after, we have the dawning of the day of their deliverance, by the effectual calling of Gideon to take upon him the command of their forces against the Midianites.

I. The person to be commissioned for this service was Gideon, the son of Joash, *v.* 14. The father was now living, but he was passed by, and this honour put upon the son, for the father kept up in his own family the worship of Baal (*v.* 25), which we may suppose this son, as far as was in his power, witnessed against. He was of the half tribe of Manasseh that lay in Canaan, of the family of Abiezer; the eldest house of that tribe, Jos. 17:2. Hitherto the judges were raised up out of that tribe which suffered most by the oppression, and probably it was so here.

II. The person that gave him the commission was an *angel of the Lord;* it should seem not a created angel, but the Son of God himself, the eternal Word, the Lord of the angels, who then appeared upon some great occasions in human shape, as a prelude (says the learned bishop Patrick) to what he intended in the fulness of time, when he would take our nature upon him, as we say, for good and all. This angel is here called *Jehovah,* the incommunicable name of God (*v.* 14, 16), and he said, *I will be with thee.*

1. This divine person appeared here to Gideon, and it is observable how he found him, (1.) Retired — all alone. God often manifests himself to his people when they are out of the noise and hurry of this world. Silence and solitude befriend our communion with God. (2.) Employed in threshing wheat, with a *staff* or *rod* (so the word signifies), such as they used in beating out fitches and cummin (Isa. 28:27), but now used for wheat, probably because he had but little to thresh, he needed not the oxen to tread it out. It was not then looked upon as any diminution to him, though he was a person of some account and a *mighty man of valour,* to lay his hand to the business of the husbandman. He had many servants (*v.* 27), and yet would not himself live in idleness. We put ourselves in the way of divine visits when we employ ourselves in honest business. Tidings of Christ's birth were brought to the shepherds when they were keeping their flocks. The work he was about was an emblem of that greater work to which he was now to be called, as the disciples' fishing was. From threshing corn he is fetched to thresh the Midianites, Isa. 41:15. (3.) Distressed; he was threshing his wheat, not in the threshing-floor, the proper place, but *by the wine-press,* in some private unsuspected corner, for fear of the Midianites. He himself shared in the common calamity, and now the angel came to animate him against Midian when he himself could speak so feelingly of the heaviness of their yoke. The day of the greatest distress is God's time to appear for his people's relief.

2. Let us now see what passed between the angel and Gideon, who knew not with certainty, till after he was gone, that he was an angel, but supposed he was a prophet.

(1.) The angel accosted him with respect, and assured him of the presence of God with him, *v.* 12. He calls him a *mighty man of valour,* perhaps because he observed how he threshed his corn with all his might; and seest thou a man diligent in his business? whatever his business is, he shall *stand before kings.* He that is faithful in a few things shall be ruler over many. Gideon was a man of a brave active spirit, and yet buried alive in obscurity, through the iniquity of the times; but he is here animated to undertake something great, like himself, with that word, *The Lord is with thee,* or, as the Chaldee reads it, *the Word of the Lord is thy help.* It was very sure that the Lord was with him when this angel was with him. By this word, [1.] He gives him his commission. If we have God's presence with us, this will justify us and bear us out in our undertakings. [2.] He inspires him with all necessary qualifications for the execution of his commission. "The Lord is with thee to guide and strengthen thee, to animate and support thee." [3.] He assures him of success; for, *if God be for us, who can* prevail *against us?* If he be with us, nothing can be wanting to us. The presence of God with us is all in all to our prosperity, whatever we do. Gideon was a mighty man of valour, and yet he could bring nothing to pass without the presence of God, and that presence is enough to make any man mighty in valour and to give a man courage at any time.

(2.) Gideon gave a very melancholy answer to this joyful salutation (*v.* 13): *O my Lord! if the Lord be with us* (which the Chaldee reads, *Is the Shechinah of the Lord our help?* making that the same with *the Word of the Lord) why then has all this befallen us?* "all this trouble and distress from the Midianites' incursions, which force me to thresh wheat here by the wine-press — all this loss, and grief, and fright; and *where are all the miracles which our fathers told us of?"* Observe, In his reply he regards not the praise of his own valour, nor does this in the least elevate him or give him any encouragement, though it is probable the angel adapted what he said to that which Gideon was at the same time thinking of; while his labouring hands were employed about his wheat, his working head and daring heart were meditating Israel's rescue and Midian's ruin, with which thought he that knows the heart seasonably sets in, calls him a man of valour for his brave projects, and open him a way to put them in execution; yet Gideon, as if not conscious to himself of any thing great or encouraging in his own spirit, fastens only on the assurance the angel had given him of God's presence, as that by which they held all their comfort. Observe, The angel spoke in particular to him: *The Lord is with thee;* but he expostulates for all: *If the Lord be with us,* herding himself with the thousands of Israel, and admitting no comfort but what they might be sharers in, so far is he from the thoughts of monopolizing it, though he had so fair an occasion given him. Note, Public spirits reckon that only an honour and joy to themselves which puts them in a capacity of serving the common interests of God's church. Gideon was a mighty man of valour, but as yet weak in faith, which makes it hard to him to reconcile to the assurances now given him of the presence of God, [1.] The distress to which Israel was reduced: *Why has all this* (and *all this* was no little) *befallen us?* Note, It is sometimes hard, but never impossible, to reconcile cross providences with the presence of God and his favour. [2.] The delay of their deliverance: *"Where are all the miracles which our fathers told us of?* Why does not the same power which delivered our fathers from the yoke of the Egyptians deliver us out of the hands of the Midianites?" As if because God did not immediately work miracles for their deliverance, though they had by their sins forfeited his favour and help, it must be questioned whether ever he had wrought the miracles which their fathers told them of, or, if he had, whether he had now the same wisdom, and power, and good-will to his people, that he had had formerly. This was his weakness. We must not expect that the miracles which were wrought when a church was in the forming, and some great truth in the settling, should be continued and repeated when the formation and settlement are completed: no, nor that the mercies God showed to our fathers that served him, and kept close to him, should be renewed to us, if we degenerate and revolt from him. Gideon ought not to have said either, *First,* That *God had delivered them into the hands of the Midianites,* for by their iniquities they had sold themselves, or, *Secondly,* That now they were in their hands he had forsaken them, for he had lately sent them a prophet (*v.* 8), which was a certain indication that he had not forsaken them.

(3.) The angel gave him a very effectual answer to his objections, by giving him a commission to deliver Israel out of the hands of the Midianites, and assuring him of success therein, *v.* 14. Now the angel is called *Jehovah,* for he speaks as one having authority, and not as a messenger. [1.] There was something extraordinary in the look he now gave to Gideon; it was a gracious favourable look, which revived his spirits that dropped, and silenced his fears, such a look as that with which God's *countenance beholds the upright,* Ps. 11:7. He looked upon him, and smiled at the objections he made, which he gave him no direct answer to, but girded and clothed him with such power as would shortly enable him to answer them himself, and make him ashamed that ever he had made them. It was a speaking look, like Christ's upon Peter (Lu. 22:61), a powerful look, a look that strangely darted new light and life into Gideon's breast, and inspired him with a generous heat, far above what he felt before. [2.] But there was much more in what he said to him. *First,* He commissioned him to appear and act as Israel's deliverer. Such a one the few thinking people in the nation, and Gideon among the rest, were now expecting to be raised up, according to God's former method, in answer to the cries of oppressed Israel; and now Gideon is told, "Thou art the man: *Go in this thy might,* this might wherewith thou art now threshing wheat; go and employ it to a nobler purpose; *I will make thee a thresher of men."* Or, rather, "this might wherewith thou art now endued by this look." God gave him his commission by giving him all the qualifications that were necessary for the execution of it, which is more than the mightiest prince and potentate on earth can do for those to whom he gives commissions. God's fitting men for work is a sure and constant evidence of his calling them to it. "Go, not in thy might, that which is natural, and of thyself, depend not on thy own valour; but go in *this* thy might, this which thou hast now received, *go in the strength of the Lord God,* that is, the strength with which thou must strengthen thyself." *Secondly,* He assured him of success. This was enough to put courage into him; he might be confident he should not miscarry in the attempt; it should not turn either to his own disgrace or the damage of his people (as baffled enterprises do), but to his honour and their happiness: *Thou shalt save Israel from the hand of the Midianites,* and so shalt not only be an eye-witness, but a glorious instrument, of such wonders as thy *fathers told thee of.* Gideon, we may suppose, looked as one astonished at this strange and surprising power conferred upon him, and questions whether he may depend upon what he hears: the angel ratifies his commission with a *teste meipso — an appeal to his own authority;* there needed no more. *"Have not I commanded thee* — I that have all power in heaven and earth, and particular authority here as Israel's King, giving commissions immediately — *I* who *am that I am,* the same that sent Moses?" Ex. 3:14.

(4.) Gideon made a very modest objection against this commission (*v.* 15): *O my Lord! wherewith shall I save Israel?* This question bespeaks him either, [1.] Distrustful of God and his power, as if, though God should be with him, yet it were impossible for him to save Israel. True faith is often weak, yet it shall not be rejected, but encouraged and strengthened. Or, [2.] Inquisitive concerning the methods he must take: "Lord, I labour under all imaginable disadvantages for it; if I must do it, thou must put me in the way." Note, Those who receive commissions from God must expect and seek for instructions from him. Or rather, [3.] Humble, self-diffident, and self-denying. The angel had honoured him, but see how meanly he speaks of himself: "My family is comparatively poor in Manasseh" (impoverished, it may be, more than other families by the Midianites), "and I am the least, that have the least honour and interest, *in my father's house;* what can I pretend to do? I am utterly unfit for the service, and unworthy of the honour." Note, God often chooses to do great things by those that are little, especially that are so in their own eyes. God delights to advance the humble.

(5.) This objection was soon answered by a repetition of the promise that God would be with him, *v.* 16. "Object not thy poverty and meanness; such things have indeed often hindered men in great enterprises, but what are they to a man that has the presence of God with him, which will make up all the deficiencies of honour and estate. *Surely I will be with thee,* to direct and strengthen thee, and put such a reputation upon thee that, how weak soever thy personal interest is, thou shalt have soldiers enough to follow thee, and be assured *thou shalt smite the Midianites as one men,* as easily as if they were but one man and as effectually. All the thousands of Midian shall be as if they had but one neck, and thou shalt have the cutting of it off."

(6.) Gideon desires to have his faith confirmed touching this commission; for he would not be over-credulous of that which tended so much to his own praise, would not venture upon an undertaking so far above him, and in which he must engage many more, but he would be well satisfied himself of his authority, and would be able to give satisfaction to others as to him who gave him that authority. He therefore humbly begs of this divine person, whoever he was, [1.] That he would give him a sign, *v.* 17. And, the commission being given him out of the common road of providence, he might reasonably expect it should be confirmed by some act of God out of the common course of nature: "Show me a sign to assure me of the truth of this concerning which thou talkest with me, that it is something more than talk, and that thou art in earnest." Now, under the dispensation of the Spirit, we are not to expect signs before our eyes, such as Gideon here desired, but must earnestly pray to God that, if *we have found grace in his sight,* he would show us a sign in our heart, by the powerful operations of his Spirit there, *fulfilling the work of faith,* and perfecting what is lacking in it. [2.] In order hereunto, that he would accept of a treat, and so give him a further and longer opportunity of conversation with him, *v.* 18. Those who know what it is to have communion with God desire the continuance of it, and are loth to part, praying with Gideon, *Depart not hence, I pray thee.* That which Gideon desired in courting his stay was that he might bring out some provision of meat for this stranger. He did not take him into the house to entertain him there, perhaps because his father's house were not well affected to him and his friends, or because he desired still to be in private with this stranger, and to converse with him alone (therefore he calls not for a servant to bring the provision, but fetches it himself), or because thus his father Abraham entertained angels unawares, not in his tent, but under a tree, Gen. 18:8. Upon the angel's promise to stay to dinner with him, he hastened to bring out a kid, which, it is likely, was ready boiled for his own dinner, so that in making it ready he had nothing to do but to put it in the basket (for here was no sauce to serve it up in, nor the dish garnished) and the broth in a vessel, and so he presented it, *v.* 19. Hereby he intended, *First,* To testify his grateful and generous respects to this stranger, and, in him, to God who sent him, as one that studied what he should render. He had pleaded the poverty of his family (*v.* 15) to excuse himself from being a general, but not here to excuse himself from being hospitable. Out of the little which the Midianites had left him he would gladly spare enough to entertain a friend, especially a messenger from heaven. *Secondly,* To try who and what this extraordinary person was. What he brought out is called his *present, v.* 18. It is the same word that is used for a meat-offering, and perhaps that word is used which signifies both because Gideon intended to leave it to this divine person to determine which it should be when he had it before him: whether a feast or a meat-offering, and accordingly he would be able to judge concerning him: if he ate of it as common meat, he would suppose him to be a man, a prophet; if otherwise, as it proved, he should know him to be an angel.

(7.) The angel gives him a sign in and by that which he had kindly prepared for his entertainment. For what we offer to God for his glory, and in token of our gratitude to him, will be made by the grace of God to turn to our own comfort and satisfaction. The angel ordered him to take the flesh and bread out of the basket, and lay it upon a hard and cold rock, and to pour out the broth upon it, which, if he brought it hot, would soon be cold there; and *Gideon did so* (*v.* 20), believing that the angel appointed it, not in contempt of his courtesy, but with an intention to give him a sign, which he did, abundantly to his satisfaction. For, [1.] He turned the *meat into an offering made by fire, of a sweet savour* unto himself, showing hereby that he was not a man who needed meat, but the Son of God who was to be served and honoured by sacrifice, and who in the fulness of time was to make himself a sacrifice. [2.] He brought fire *out of the rock,* to consume this sacrifice, summoning it, not by striking the rock, as we strike fire out of a flint, but by a gentle touch given to the offering with the end of his staff, *v.* 21. Hereby he gave him a sign that he had *found grace in his sight,* for God testified his acceptance of sacrifices by kindling them, if public, with fire from heaven, as those of Moses and Elias, if private, as this, with fire out of the earth, which was equivalent: both were the effect of divine power; and this acceptance of his sacrifice evidenced the acceptance of his person, confirmed his commission, and perhaps was intended to signify his success in the execution of it, that he and his army should be a surprising terror and consumption to the Midianites, like this fire out of the rock. [3.] He *departed out of his sight* immediately, did not walk off as a man, but vanished and disappeared as a spirit. Here was as much of a sign as he could wish.

(8.) Gideon, though no doubt he was confirmed in his faith by the indications given of the divinity of the person who had spoken to him, yet for the present was put into a great fright by it, till God graciously pacified him and removed his fears. [1.] Gideon speaks peril to himself (*v.* 22): *When he perceived that he was an angel* (which was not till he had departed, as the two disciples knew not it was Jesus they had been talking with till he was going, Lu. 24:31), then he cried out, *Alas! O Lord God!* be merciful to me, I am undone, for *I have seen an angel,* as Jacob, who wondered that his life was preserved when he had seen God, Gen. 32:30. Ever since man has by sin exposed himself to God's wrath and curse an express from heaven has been a terror to him, as he scarcely dares to expect good tidings thence; at least, in this world of sense, it is a very awful thing to have any sensible conversation with that world of spirits to which we are so much strangers. Gideon's courage failed him now. [2.] God speaks peace to him, *v.* 23. It might have been fatal to him, but he assures him it should not. The Lord had *departed out of his sight, v.* 21. But though he must no longer walk by sight he might still live by faith, that faith which comes by hearing; for the Lord said to him, with an audible voice (as bishop Patrick thinks) these encouraging words, *"Peace be unto thee,* all is well, and be thou satisfied that it is so. Fear not; he that came to employ thee did not intend to slay thee; *thou shalt not die."* See how ready God is to revive the hearts of those that tremble at his word and presence, and to give those that stand in awe of his majesty assurances of his mercy.

3. The memorial of this vision which Gideon set up was a monument in form of an altar, the rather because it was by a kind of sacrifice upon a rock, without the solemnity of an altar, that the angel manifested his acceptance of him; then an altar was unnecessary (the angel's staff was sufficient to sanctify the gift without an altar), but now it was of use to preserve the remembrance of the vision, which was done by the name Gideon gave to this memorial, *Jehovah-shalom* (*v.* 24) — *The Lord peace.* This is, (1.) The title of the Lord that spoke to him. Compare Gen. 16:13. The same that is the *Lord our righteousness* is *our peace* (Eph. 2:14), our reconciler and so our Saviour. Or, (2.) The substance of what he said to him: *"The Lord spoke peace,* and created that fruit of the lips, bade me be easy when I was in that agitation." Or, (3.) A prayer grounded upon what he had said, so the margin understands it: *The Lord send peace,* that is, rest from the present trouble, for still the public welfare lay nearest his heart.

Verses 25–32

Here, I. Orders are given to Gideon to begin his government with the reformation of his father's house, *v.* 25, 26. A correspondence being settled between God and Gideon, by the appearance of the angel to him, it was kept up in another way; the same night after he had seen God, when he was full of thoughts concerning what had passed, which probably he had not yet communicated to any, *The Lord said unto him* in a dream, *Do so and so.* Note, God's visits, if gratefully received, shall be graciously repeated. Bid God welcome, and he will come again. Gideon is appointed, 1. To throw down Baal's altar, which it seems hi father had, either for his own house or perhaps for the whole town. See the power of God's grace, that he could raise up a reformer, and the condescensions of his grace, that he would raise up a deliverer, out of the family of one that was a ring-leader in idolatry. But Gideon must not now think it enough not to worship at that altar, which we charitably hope he had not done, but he must throw it down; not consecrate the same altar to God (tit is bishop Hall's observation), but utterly demolish it. God first commands down the monuments of superstition, and then enjoins his own service. He must likewise *cut down the grove that was by it,* the plantation of young trees, designed to beautify the place. The learned bishop Patrick, by the grove, understands the image in the grove, probably the image of Ashtaroth (for the word for a grove is *Ashereh*), which stood upon or close by the altar. 2. The erect an altar to God, *to Jehovah his God,* which probably was to be notified by an inscription upon the altar to that purport — to Jehovah, Gideon's God, or Israel's. It would have been an improper thing for him to build an altar, even to the God of Israel, especially for burnt-offering and sacrifice, and would have been construed into a contempt of the altar at Shiloh, if God, who has not tied up himself to his own laws, had not bidden him to do it. But now it was his duty and honour to be thus employed. God directs him to the place where he should build it, on the *top of the rock*, perhaps in the same place in which the angel had appeared to him, near to the altar he had already built: and he must not do it in a hurry, but with the decency that became a religious action *(in an orderly manner,* as it is in the margin), according to the ancient law for altars raised on particular occasions, that they must be of earth not of hewn stone. The word here used for the rock on which the altar was to be built signifies a fortress, or strong-hold, erected, some think, to secure them from the Midianites; if so, it was no security while the altar of Baal was so near it, but it was effectually fortified when an altar to the Lord was built on the top of it, for that is the best defence upon our glory. On this altar, (1.) He was to offer sacrifice. Two bullocks he must offer: his father's *young bullock, and the second bullock of seven years old,* so it should rather be read, not *even* the second as we read it. The former, we may suppose, he was to offer for himself, the latter *for the sins of the people* whom he was to deliver. It was requisite he should thus make peace with God, before he made war on Midian. Till sin be pardoned through the great sacrifice, no good is to be expected. These bullocks, it is supposed, were intended for sacrifices on the altar of Baal, but were now converted to a better use. Thus, when the *strong man armed* is overcome and dispossessed, the stronger than he divides the spoil, seizes that for himself *which was prepared for Baal.* Let him come *whose right it is,* and *give it to him.* (2.) Ball's grove, or image, or whatever it was that was the sanctity or beauty of his altar, must not only be burnt, but must be used as fuel for God's altar, to signify not only that whatever sets up itself in opposition to God shall be destroyed, but that the justice of God will be glorified in its destruction. God ordered Gideon to do this, [1.] To try his zeal for religion, which it was necessary he should give proofs of before he took the field, to give proof of his valour there. [2.] That some steps might hereby to taken towards Israel's reformation, which must prepare the way for their deliverance. Sin, the cause, must be taken away, else how should the trouble, which was but the effect, come to an end? And it might be hoped that this example of Gideon's, who was now shortly to appear so great a man, would be followed by the rest of the cities and tribes, and the destruction of this one altar of Baal would be the destruction of many.

II. Gideon was *obedient to the heavenly vision, v.* 27. He that was to command the Israel of God must be subject to the God of Israel, without disputing, and, as a type of Christ, must first *save his people from their sins,* and then save them from their enemies. 1. He had servants of his own, whom he could confide in, who, we may suppose, like him, had kept their integrity, and had *not bowed the knee to Baal,* and therefore were forward to assist him in destroying the altar of Baal. 2. He did not scruple taking his father's bullock and offering it to God without his father's consent, because God, who expressly commanded him to do so, had a better title to it than his father had, and it was the greatest real kindness he could do to his father to prevent his sin. 3. He expected to incur the displeasure of his father's household by it, and the ill-will of his neighbours, yet he did it, remembering how much it was Levi's praise that, in the cause of God, *he said to his father and mother, I have not seen him,* Deu. 33:9. And, while he was sure of the favour of God, he feared not the anger of men; he that bade him do it would bear him out. Yet, 4. Though he feared not their resentment when it was done, to prevent their resistance in the doing of it he prudently chose to do it by night, that he might not be disturbed in these sacred actions. And some think it was the same night in which God spoke to him to do it, and that, as soon as ever he had received the orders, he immediately applied himself to the execution of them, and finished before morning.

III. He was brought into peril of his life for doing it, *v.* 28–30. 1. It was soon discovered what was done. Gideon, when he had gone through with the business, did not desire the concealment of it, nor could it be hid, for the men of the city *rose early in the morning,* as it should seem, to say their matins at Baal's altar, and so to begin the day with their god, such a one as he was, a shame to those who say the true God is their God, and yet, in the morning, direct no prayer to him, nor look up. 2. It was soon discovered who had done it. Strict enquiry was made. Gideon was known to be disaffected to the worship of Baal, which brought him into suspicion, and positive proof immediately came against him: "Gideon, no doubt, *has done this thing."* 3. Gideon being found guilty of the fact, to such a pitch of impiety had these degenerate Israelites arrived that they take it for law he must die for the same, and require his own father (who, by patronising their idolatry, had given them too much cause to expect he would comply with them herein) to deliver him up: *Bring out thy son, that he may die.* Be astonished, O heavens! at this, and tremble, O earth! By the law of God the worshippers of Baal were to die, but these wicked men impiously turn the penalty upon the worshippers of the God of Israel. How prodigiously mad were they upon their idols! Was it not enough to offer the choicest of their bullocks to Baal, but must the bravest youth of their city fall as a sacrifice to that dunghill-deity, when they pretended he was provoked? How soon will idolaters become persecutors!

IV. He was rescued out of the hands of his persecutors by his own father, *v.* 31.

1. There were those that stood against Gideon, that not only appeared at the first to make a demand, but insisted on it, and would have him put to death. Notwithstanding the heavy judgments they were at this time under for their idolatry, yet they hated to be reformed, and walked contrary to God even when he was walking contrary to them.

2. Yet then *Joash stood for him;* he was one of the chief men of the city. Those that have power may do a great deal for the protection of an honest man and an honest cause, and when they so use their power they are ministers of God for good.

(1.) This Joash had patronised Baal's altar, yet now protects him that had destroyed it, [1.] Out of natural affection to his son, and perhaps a particular esteem for him as a virtuous, valiant, valuable, young man, and never the worse for not joining with him in the worship of Baal. Many that have not courage enough to keep their integrity themselves yet have so much conscience left as makes them love and esteem those that do. If Joash had a kindness for Baal, yet he had a greater kindness for his son. Or, [2.] Out of a care for the public peace. The mob grew riotous, and, he feared, would grow more so, and therefore, as some think, he bestirred himself to repress the tumult: "Let it be left to the judges; it is not for you to pass sentence upon any man;" he that offers it, *let him be put to death:* he means not as an idolater, but as a disturber of the peace, and the mover of sedition. Under this same colour Paul was rescued at Ephesus from those that were as zealous for Diana as these were for Baal, Acts 19:40. Or, [3.] Out of a conviction that Gideon had done well. His son, perhaps, had reasoned with him, or God, who has all hearts in his hands, had secretly and effectually influenced him to appear thus against the advocates for Baal, though he had complied with them formerly in the worship of Baal. Note, It is good to appear for God when we are called to it, though there be few or none to second us, because God can incline the hearts of those to stand by us from whom we little expect assistance. Let us do our duty, and then trust God with our safety.

(2.) Two things Joash urges: — [1.] That it was absurd for them to plead for Baal. "Will you that are Israelites, the worshippers of the one only living and true God, plead for Baal, a false god? Will you be so sottish, so senseless? Those whose fathers' god Baal was, and who never knew any other, are more excusable in pleading for him than you are, that are in covenant with Jehovah, and have been trained up in the knowledge of him. You that have smarted so much for worshipping Baal, and have brought all this mischief and calamity upon yourselves by it, will you yet plead for Baal?" Note, It is bad to commit sin, but it is great wickedness indeed to plead for it, especially to plead for Baal, that idol, whatever it is, which possesses that room in the heart which God should have. [2.] That it was needless for them to plead for Baal. If he were not a god, as was pretended, they could have nothing to say for him; if he were, he was able to plead for himself, as the God of Israel had often done by fire from heaven, or some other judgment against those who put contempt upon him. Here is a fair challenge to Baal to *do either good or evil,* and the result convinced his worshippers of their folly in praying to one to help them that could not avenge himself; after this Gideon remarkably prospered, and thereby it appeared how unable Baal was to maintain his own cause.

(3.) Gideon's father hereupon gave him a new name (*v.* 32); he called him *Jerubbaal:* "Let Baal plead; let him plead against him if he can; if he have any thing to say for himself against his destroyer, let him say it." This name was a standing defiance to Baal: "Now that Gideon is taking up arms against the Midianites that worship Baal, let him defend his worshippers if he can." It likewise gave honour to Gideon (a sworn enemy to that great usurper, and that had carried the day against him), that encouragement to his soldiers, that they fought under one that fought for God against this great competitor with him for the throne. It is the probable conjecture of the learned that that Jerombalus whom Sanchoniathon (one of the most ancient of all the heathen writers) speaks of as *a priest of the god Jao* (a corruption of the name *Jehovah),* and one to whom he was indebted for a great deal of knowledge, was this Jerubbaal. He is called *Jerubbesheth* (2 Sa. 11:12), *Baal,* a *lord,* being fitly turned into *Besheth, shame.*

Verses 33–40

Here we have, I. The descent which the enemies of Israel made upon them, *v.* 33. A vast number of Midianites, Amalekites, and Arabians, got together, and came over Jordan, none either caring or daring to guard that important and advantageous pass against them, and they made their headquarters in the valley of Jezreel, in the heart of Manasseh's tribe, not far from Gideon's city. Some think that the notice they had of Gideon's destroying Baal's altar brought them over, and that they came to plead for Baal and to make that a pretence for quarrelling with Israel; but it is more likely that it was now harvest-time, when they had been wont each year to make such a visit as this (*v.* 3), and that they were expected when Gideon was threshing, *v.* 11. God raised up Gideon to be ready against this terrible blow came. Their success so many years in these incursions, the little opposition they had met with and the great booty they had carried off, made them now both very eager and very confident. But it proved that *the measure of their iniquity was full* and the year of recompence had come; they must now *make an end to spoil* and *must be spoiled,* and they are *gathered as sheaves to the floor* (Mic. 4:12, 13), for Gideon to thresh.

II. The preparation which Gideon makes to attack them in their camp, *v.* 34, 35. 1. God by his Spirit put life into Gideon: *The Spirit of the Lord clothes Gideon* (so the word is), clothed him as a robe, to put honour upon him, clothed him as a coat of mail, to put defence upon him. Those are well clad that are thus clothed. *A spirit of fortitude from before the Lord clothed Gideon;* so the Chaldee. He was of himself a mighty man of valour; yet personal strength and courage, though vigorously exerted, would not suffice for this great action; he must have the *armour of God* upon him, and this is what he must depend upon: *The Spirit of the Lord clothed him* in an extraordinary manner. Whom God calls to his work he will qualify and animate for it. 2. Gideon with his trumpet put life into his neighbours, God working with him; he *blew a trumpet,* to call in volunteers, and more came in than perhaps he expected. (1.) The men of Abiezer, though lately enraged against him for throwing down the altar of Baal, and though they had condemned him to death as a criminal, were now convinced of their error, bravely came in to his assistance, and submitted to him as their general: *Abiezer was gathered after him, v.* 34. So suddenly can God turn the hearts even of idolaters and persecutors. (2.) Distant tribes, even Asher and Naphtali, which lay most remote, though strangers to him, obeyed his summons, and sent him in the best of their forces, *v.* 35. Though they lay furthest from the danger, yet, considering that if their neighbours were over-run by the Midianites their own turn would be next, they were forward to join against a common enemy.

III. The signs which God gratified him with, for the confirming both of his own faith and that of his followers; and perhaps it was more for their sakes than for his own that he desired them. Or, perhaps, he desired by these to be satisfied whether this was the time of his conquering the Midianites, or whether he was to wait for some other opportunity. Observe, 1. His request for a sign (*v.* 36, 37): "Let me by this *know that thou wilt save Israel by my hand, let a fleece of wool,* spread in the open air, be *wet with the dew,* and let the ground about it be dry." The purport of this is, *Lord, I believe, help thou my unbelief.* He found his own faith weak and wavering, and therefore begged of God by this sign to perfect what was lacking in it. We may suppose that God, who intended to give him these signs, for the glorifying of his own power and goodness, put it into his heart to ask them. Yet, when he repeated his request for a second sign, the reverse of the former, he did it with a very humble apology, deprecating God's displeasure, because it looked so like a peevish humoursome distrust of God and dissatisfaction with the many assurances he had already given him (*v.* 39): *Let not thy anger be hot against me.* Though he took the boldness to ask another sign, yet he did it with such fear and trembling as showed that the familiarity God had graciously admitted him to did not breed any contempt of God's glory, nor presumption on God's goodness. Abraham had given him an example of this, when God gave him leave to be very free with him (Gen. 18:30, 32), *O let not the Lord be angry, and I will speak.* God's favour must be sought with great reverence, a due sense of our distance, and a religious fear of his wrath. 2. God's gracious grant of his request. See how tender God is of true believers though they be weak, and how ready to condescend to their infirmities, that the bruised reed may not be broken nor the smoking flax quenched. Gideon would have *the fleece wet* and the *ground dry;* but then, lest any should object, "It is natural for wool, if ever so little moisture fall, to drink it in and retain it, and therefore there was nothing extraordinary in this," though the quantity wrung out was sufficient to obviate such an objection, yet he desires that next night the ground might be wet and the fleece dry, and it is done, so willing is God to *give to the heirs of promise strong consolation* (Heb. 6:17, 18), even by two immutable things. He suffers himself, not only to be prevailed with by their importunities, but even to be prescribed to by their doubts and dissatisfactions. These signs were, (1.) Truly miraculous, and therefore abundantly serving to confirm his commission. It is said of the dew that it is *from the Lord,* and *tarrieth not for man, nor waiteth for the sons of men* (Micah 5:7); and yet God here in this matter *hearkened to the voice of a man;* as to Joshua, in directing the course of the sun, so to Gideon in directing that of the dew, by which it appears that it falls not by chance, but by providence. The latter sign inverted the former, and, to please Gideon, it was wrought backward and forward, whence Dr. Fuller observes that *heaven's real miracles will endure turning, being inside and outside both alike.* (2.) Very significant. He and his men were going to engage the Midianites; could God distinguish between a small fleece of Israel and the vast floor of Midian? Yes, by this he is made to know that he can. Is Gideon desirous that the dew of divine grace might descend upon himself in particular? He sees the fleece wet with dew to assure him of it. Does he desire that God will be as the dew to all Israel? Behold, all the ground is wet. Some make this fleece an emblem of the Jewish nation, which, when time was, was wet with the dew of God's word and ordinances, while the rest of the world was dry; but since the rejection of Christ and his gospel they are dry *as the heath in the wilderness,* while the nations about are *as a watered garden.*

CHAPTER 7

This chapter presents us with Gideon in the field, commanding the army of Israel, and routing the army of the Midianites, for which great exploit we found in the former chapter how he was prepared by his converse with God and his conquest of Baal. We are here told, I. What direction God gave to Gideon for the modelling of his army, by which it was reduced to 300 men (*v.* 1, 8). II. What encouragement God gave to Gideon to attack the enemy, by sending him secretly into their camp to hear a Midianite tell his dream (*v.* 9–15). III. How he formed his attack upon the enemy's camp with his 300 men, not to fight them, but to frighten them (*v.* 16–20). IV. The success of this attack; it put them to flight, and gave them a total rout, the disbanded forces, and their other neighbours, then coming in to his assistance (*v.* 21–25). It is a story that shines very brightly in the book of the wars of the Lord.

Verses 1–8

Here, I. Gideon applies himself with all possible care and industry to do the part of a good general, in leading on the hosts of Israel against the Midianites (*v.* 1): *He rose up early,* as one whose heart was upon his business, and

who was afraid of losing time. Now that he is sure God is with him he is impatient of delay. He pitched near a famous well, that his army might not be distressed for want of water, and gained the higher ground, which possibly might be some advantage to him, for the Midianites *were beneath him in the valley.* Note, Faith in God's promises must not slacken, but rather quicken, our endeavours. When we are sure God goes before us, then we must bestir ourselves, 2 Sa. 5:24.

II. God provides that the praise of the intended victory may be reserved wholly to himself, by appointing 300 men only to be employed in this service.

1. The army consisted of 32,000 men, a small army in comparison with what the Midianites had now brought into the field; Gideon was ready to think them too few, but God comes to him, and tells him they are *too many, v.* 2. Not but that those did well who offered themselves willingly to this expedition, but God saw fit not to make use of all that came. We often find God bringing great things to pass by a few hands, but this was the only time that he purposely made them fewer. Had Deborah lately blamed those who *came not to the help of the Lord,* and yet in the next great action must those be turned off that do come? Yes; (1.) God would hereby show that when he employed suitable instruments in his service he did not need them, but could do his work without them, so that he was not indebted to them for their service, but they to him for employing them. (2.) He would hereby put those to shame for their cowardice who had tamely submitted to the Midianites, and durst not make head against them, because of the disproportion of their numbers. They now saw that, if they had but made sure of the favour of God, one of them might have chased a thousand. (3.) He would hereby silence and exclude boasting. This is the reason here given by him who knows the pride that is in men's hearts: *Lest Israel vaunt themselves against me.* Justly were those denied the honour of the success. *My own hand hath saved me* is a word that must never come out of the mouth of such as shall be saved. *He that glories must glory in the Lord,* and all flesh must be silent before him.

2. Two ways God took to lessen their numbers: — (1.) He ordered all that would own themselves timorous and faint-hearted to be dismissed, *v.* 3. They were now encamped on a mountain close to the enemy, called *Mount Gilead,* from Gilead, the common ancestor of these families of Manasseh, which were seated on this side Jordan (Num. 26:30), and thence they might see perhaps the vast numbers of the enemy; those therefore who were disheartened at the sight were left to their liberty, to go back if they pleased. There was a law for making such a proclamation as this, Deu. 20:8. But Gideon perhaps thought that concerned only those wars which were undertaken for the enlarging of their coast, not, as this, for their necessary defence against an invader; therefore Gideon would not have proclaimed this if God, who knew how his forces would hereby be diminished, had not commanded him. Cowards would be as likely as any, after the victory, to take the honour of it from God, and therefore God would not do them the honour to employ them in it. One would have thought there would be scarcely one Israelite to be found that against such an enemy as the Midianites, and under such a leader as Gideon, would own himself fearful; yet above two parts of three took advantage of this proclamation, and filed off, when they saw the strength of the enemy and their own weakness, not considering the assurances of the divine presence which their general had received of the Lord, and, it is likely, delivered unto them. Some think the oppression they had been under so long had broken their spirits, others, more probably, that consciousness of their own guilt had deprived them of their courage. Sin stared them in the face, and therefore they durst not look death in the face. Note, Fearful faint-hearted people are not fit to be employed for God; and, among those that are enlisted under the banner of Christ, there are more such than we think there are. (2.) He directed the cashiering of all that remained except 300 men, and he did it by a sign: *The people are yet too many* for me to make use off, *v.* 4. See how much God's thoughts and ways are above ours. Gideon himself, it is likely, thought they were too few, though they were as many as Barak encountered Sisera with (*ch.* 4:14); and, had he not forced his way through the discouragement by dint of faith, he

himself would have started back from so hazardous an enterprise, and have made the best of his own way back. But God saith, they are *too many,* and, when diminished to a third part, they are yet *too many,* which may help us to understand those providences which sometimes seem to weaken the church and its interests: its friends are too many, too mighty, too wise, for God to work deliverance by; God is taking a course to lessen them, that he may be *exalted in his own strength.* Gideon is ordered to bring his soldiers to the watering, probably to the well of Harod (*v.* 1) and the stream that ran from it; he, or some appointed by him, must observe how they drank. We must suppose they were all thirsty, and were inclined to drink; it is likely he told them they must prepare to enter upon action immediately, and therefore must refresh themselves accordingly, not expecting, after this, to drink any thing else but the blood of their enemies. Now some, and no doubt the most, would kneel down on their knees to drink, and put their mouths to the water as horses do, and so they might get their full draught. Others, it may be, would not make such a formal business of it, but as a dog laps with his tongue, a lap and away, so they would hastily take up a little water in their hands, and cool their mouths with that, and be gone. Three hundred and no more there were of this latter sort, that drank in haste, and by those God tells Gideon he would rout the Midianites, *v.* 7. By the former distinction none were retained but hearty men, that were resolved to do their utmost for retrieving the liberties of Israel; but by this further distinction it was provided that none should be made use of but, [1.] Men that were hardy, that could endure long fatigue, without complaining of thirst or weariness, that had not in them any dregs either of sloth or luxury. [2.] Men that were hasty, that thought it long till they were engaged with the enemy, preferring the service of God and their country before their necessary refreshment; such as these God chooses to employ, that are not only well affected, but zealously affected in a good thing. And also because these were the smaller number, and therefore the least likely to effect what they were designed for, God would by them save Israel. It was a great trial to the faith and courage of Gideon, when God bade him let all the rest of the people but these 300 *go every man to his place,* that is, go where they pleased out of his call, and from under his command; yet we may suppose those that were hearty in the cause, though now set aside, did not go so far out of hearing but that they were ready to follow the blow, when the 300 had broken the ice, though this does not appear. Thus strangely was Gideon's army purged, and modelled, and reduced, instead of being recruited, as one would think in so great an action it both needed and deserved to be. Now,

3. Let us see how this little despicable regiment, on which the stress of the action must lie, was accoutred and fitted out. Had these 300 been double-manned with servants and attendants, and double-armed with swords and spears, we should have thought them the more likely to bring something to pass. But, instead of making them more serviceable by their equipment, they are made less so. For, (1.) Every soldier turns butler: They *took victuals in their hands* (*v.* 8), left their bag and baggage behind, and every man burdened himself with his own provision, which was a trial of their faith, whether they could trust God when they had no more provisions with them than they could carry, and a trial of their diligence, whether they would carry as much as they had occasion for. This was indeed living from hand to mouth. (2.) Every soldier turns trumpeter. The regiments that were cashiered left their trumpets behind them for the use of these 300 men, who were furnished with these instead of weapons of war, as if they had been going rather to a game than to a battle.

Verses 9–15

Gideon's army being diminished as we have found it was, he must either fight by faith or not at all; God therefore here provides recruits for his faith, instead of recruits for his forces.

I. He furnishes him with a good foundation to build his faith upon. Nothing but a word from God will be a footing for faith. He has this as full and express as he can desire, *v.* 9. 1. A word of command to warrant the action, which otherwise seemed rash and indiscreet, and unbecoming a wise general: *Arise, get thee down* with this handful of men *unto the host.* 2. A word of promise to assure him of the success, which otherwise seemed very improbable: *I have delivered it into thy hand;* it is all thy own. This *word of the Lord* came to him the same night, when he was (we may suppose) greatly agitated and full of care how he should come off; *in the multitude of his thoughts within him these comforts did delight his soul.* Divine consolations are given in to believers not only strongly but seasonably.

II. He furnishes him with a good prop to support his faith with. 1. He orders him to be his own spy, and now in the dead of the night to go down privately into the host of Midian, and see what intelligence he could gain: *"If thou fear to go down* to fight, go first only with thy own servant (*v.* 10) and *hear what they say"* (*v.* 11); and it is intimated to him that he should hear that which would greatly strengthen his faith. God knows the infirmities of his people, and what great encouragement they may sometimes take from a small matter; and therefore, knowing beforehand what would occur to Gideon, in that very part of the camp to which he would go down, he orders him to go down and hearken to what they said, that he might the more firmly believe what God said. He must take with him *Phurah his servant,* one that he could confide in, probably one of the ten that had helped him to break down the altar of Baal. He must take him and no one else with him, must take him with him to be a witness of what he should hear the Midianites say, that out of the mouth of these two witnesses, when the matter came to be reported to Israel, the word might be established. He must take his servant with him, because two are better than one and a little help is better than none. 2. Being so, he orders him the sight of something that was discouraging. It was enough to frighten him to discern, perhaps by moon-light, the vast numbers of the enemy (*v.* 12), the men like grasshoppers for multitude, and they proved no better than grasshoppers for strength and courage; the camels one could not count, any more than the sand. But, 3. He causes him to hear that which was to him a very good omen; and when he had heard it he went back again immediately, supposing he now had what he was sent thither for. He overheard two soldiers of the enemy, that were comrades, talking; probably they were in bed together, waking in the night. (1.) One of them tells his dream, and as our dreams generally are, and therefore not worth telling again, it is a very foolish one. He dreamed that he saw a barley-cake come rolling down the hill into the camp of the Midianites, and "methought," says he (for so we speak in telling our dreams), "this rolling cake struck one of our tents" (perhaps one of the chief of their tents) "and with such violence that" (would you think it?) "it overturned the tent, forced down the stakes, and broke the cords at one blow, so that the tent lay along and buried its inhabitants," *v.* 13. *In multitudes of dreams there are divers vanities,* says Solomon, Eccl. 5:7. One would wonder what odd incoherent things are often put together by a ludicrous fancy in our dreams. (2.) The other, it may be between sleeping and waking, undertakes to interpret this dream, and the interpretation is very far-fetched: *This is nothing else save the sword of Gideon, v.* 14. Our expositors now can tell us how apt the resemblance was, that Gideon, who had threshed corn for his family, and made cakes for his friend (*ch.* 6:11–19), was fitly represented by a cake, — that he and his army were as inconsiderable as a cake made of a little flour, as contemptible as a barley-cake, hastily got together as a cake suddenly baked upon the coals, and as unlikely to conquer this great army as a cake to overthrow a tent. But, after all, do *not interpretations belong to God?* He put it into the head of the one to dream and into the mouth of the other to give the sense of it; if Gideon had heard the dream only, and he and his servant had been left to interpret it themselves, it had so little significancy in it that it would have done him little service; but, having the interpretation from the mouth of an enemy, it not only appeared to come from God, who has all men's hearts and tongues in his hand, but it was likewise an evidence that the enemy was quite dispirited, and that the name of Gideon had become so formidable to them that it disturbed their sleep. The victory would easily be won which was already so tamely yielded: *Into his hand hath God delivered Midian.* Those were not likely to fight who saw God fighting against them.

Lastly, Gideon, observing the finger of God pointing him to this very place, at this very time, to hear this dream and the interpretation of it, was exceedingly encouraged by it against the melancholy apprehensions he had upon the reducing of his army. He was very well pleased to hear himself compared to a barley-cake, when it proved to effect such great things. Being hereby animated, we are told (*v.* 15), 1. How he gave God the glory of it; he worshipped immediately, bowed his head, or, it may be, lifted up his eyes and hands, and in a short ejaculation thanked God for the victory he was now sure of, and for this encouragement to expect it. Wherever we are, we may speak to God, and worship him, and find a way open heavenward. God must have the praise of that which is encouraging to our faith, and his providence must be acknowledged in those events which, though minute and seemingly accidental, prove serviceable to us. 2. How he gave his friends a share in the encouragements he had received: *Arise,* prepare to march presently; *the Lord has delivered Midian into your hand.*

Verses 16–22

Here is, I. The alarm which Gideon gave to the hosts of Midian in the dead time of the night; for it was intended that those who had so long been a terror to Israel, and had so often frightened them, should themselves be routed and ruined purely by terror.

1. The attack here made was, in many circumstances, like that which Abraham made upon the army that had taken Lot captive. The number of men was much the same: Abraham had 318, Gideon 300; they both divided their forces, both made their attack by night, and were both victorious under great disadvantages (Gen. 14:14, 15); and Gideon is not only a son of Abraham (so were the Midianites by Keturah) but an heir of his faith. Gideon, (1.) Divided his army, small as it was, into three battalions (*v.* 16), one of which he himself commanded (*v.* 19), because great armies (and such a one he would make a show of) were usually divided into the right wing, and left wing, and the body of the army. (2.) He ordered them all to do as he did, *v.* 17. He told them now, it is very likely, what they must do, else the thing was so strange that they would scarcely have done it of a sudden, but he would, by doing it first, give notice to them when to do it, as officers exercise their soldiers with the word of command or by beat of drum: *Look on me, and do likewise.* Such is the word of command which our Lord Jesus, the captain of our salvation, gives his soldiers; for he has *left us an example,* with a charge to follow it: *As I do, so shall you do.* (3.) He made his descent in the night, when they were secure and least expected it, which would put them into great consternation, and when the smallness of his army would not be discovered. In the night all frights are most frightful, especially in the dead of the night, as this was, a little after midnight, when the middle watch began, and the alarm would wake them out of their sleep. We read of *terror by night* as very terrible (Ps. 91:5), and *fear in the night,* Cant. 3:8. (4.) That which Gideon aimed at was to frighten this huge host, to give them not only a fatal rout, but a very shameful one. He accoutred his army with every man a trumpet in his right hand, and an earthen pitcher, with a torch in it, in his left, and he himself thought it no disparagement to him to march before them thus armed. He would make but a jest of conquering this army, and goes out against them rather as against a company of children than against a host of soldiers. *The virgin, the daughter of Zion, hath despised thee,* and *laughed thee to scorn,* Isa. 37:22. The fewness of his men favoured his design; for, being so few, they marched to the camp with the greater secresy and expedition, so that they were not discovered till they were close by the camp; and he contrived to give the alarm when they had just mounted the guards (*v.* 19), that the sentinels, being then wakeful, might the sooner disperse the alarm through the camp, which was the best service they could do him. Three ways Gideon contrived to strike a terror upon this army, and so put them into confusion. [1.] With a great noise. Every man must blow his trumpet in the most terrible manner he could and clatter an earthen pitcher to pieces at the same time; probably each dashed his pitcher to his next man's, and so they were broken both together, which would not only make a great crash, but was a figure of what would be the effects of the fright, even the Midianites' killing one another. [2.] With a great blaze. The lighted torches were hid in the pitchers, like *a candle under a bushel,* until they came to the camp, and then, being taken out all together of a sudden, would make a glaring show, and run through the camp like a flash of lightning. Perhaps with these they set some of the tents on the outside of the camp on fire, which would very much increase the confusion. [3.] With a great shout. Every man must cry, *For the Lord, and for Gideon,* so some think it should be read in *v.* 18, for there the sword is not in the original, but it is in *v.* 20, *The sword of the Lord, and of Gideon.* It should seem, he borrowed the word from the Midianite's dream (*v.* 14): it is *the sword of Gideon.* Finding his name was a terror to them, he thus improves it against them, but prefixes the name of Jehovah, as the figure without which his own was but an insignificant cypher. This would put life into his own men, who might well take courage when they had such a God as Jehovah, and such a man as Gideon, both to *fight for,* and to *fight for them;* well might those follow who had such leaders. It would likewise put their enemies into a fright, who had of old heard of Jehovah's great name, and of late of Gideon's. The sword of the Lord is all in all to the success of the sword of Gideon, yet the sword of Gideon must be employed. Men the instruments, and God the principal agent, must both be considered in their places, but men, the greatest and best, always in subserviency and subordination to God. This army was to be defeated purely by terrors, and these are especially the *sword of the Lord.* These soldiers, if they had swords by their sides, that was all, they had none in their hands, but they gained the victory by shouting "The sword." So the church's enemies are routed by *a sword out of the mouth,* Rev. 19:21. 2. These soldiers, if they had swords by their sides, that was all, they had none in their hands, but they gained the victory by shouting "The sword." So the church's enemies are routed by *a sword out of the mouth,* Rev. 19:21.

2. This method here taken of defeating the Midianites may be alluded to, (1.) As typifying the destruction of the devil's kingdom in the world by the preaching of the everlasting gospel, the sounding of that trumpet, and the holding forth of that light out of earthen vessels, for such the ministers of the gospel are, in whom the treasure of that light is deposited, 2 Co. 4:6, 7. Thus God chose the *foolish things of the world to confound the wise,* a barley-cake to overthrow the tents of Midian, that the *excellency of the power might be of God only;* the gospel is a sword, not in the hand, but in the mouth, the sword *of the Lord and of Gideon,* of God and Jesus Christ, him that sits on the throne and the Lamb. (2.) As representing the terrors of the great day. So the excellent bishop Hall applies it; if these pitchers, trumpets, and firebrands, did so daunt and dismay the proud troops of Midian and Amalek, who shall be able to stand before the last terror, when the trumpet of the archangel shall sound, the elements shall be on a flame, the heavens pass away with a great noise, and the Lord himself shall descend with a shout!

II. The wonderful success of this alarm. The Midianites were shouted out of their lives, as the walls of Jericho were shouted down, that Gideon might see what he lately despaired of ever seeing, the *wonders that their fathers told them of.* Gideon's soldiers observed their orders, and *stood every man in his place round about the camp* (*v.* 21), sounding his trumpet to excite them to fight one another, and holding out his torch to light them to their ruin. They did not rush into the host of Midian, as greedy either of blood or spoil, but patiently stood still to *see the salvation of the Lord,* a salvation purely of his own working. Observe how the design took effect. 1. They feared the Israelites. *All the host* immediately took the alarm; it flew like lightning through all their lines, and *they ran, and cried, and fled, v.* 21. There was something natural in this fright. We may suppose they had not had intelligence of the great diminution of Gideon's army, but rather concluded that since their last advices it had been growing greater and greater; and therefore they had reason to suspect, knowing how odious and grievous they had made themselves and what bold steps had been taken towards the throwing off of their yoke, that it was a very great army which was to be ushered in with all those trumpeters and torch-bearers. But there was more of a supernatural power impressing this terror upon them. God himself gave it the setting on, to show how that promise should have been fulfilled if they had not forfeited it, *One of you shall chase a thousand.* See the power of imagination, and how much it may become a terror at some times, as at other times it is a pleasure. 2. They fell foul upon one another: *The Lord set every man's sword against his fellow, v.* 22. In this confusion, observing the trumpeters and torch-bearers to stand still without their camp, they concluded the body of the army had already entered and was in the midst of them, and therefore every one ran at the next he met, though a friend, supposing him an enemy, and one such mistake as this would occasion many, for then he that slew him would certainly be taken for an enemy, and would be dispatched immediately. It is our interest to preserve such a command of our own spirits as never to *be afraid with any amazement,* for we cannot conceive what mischiefs we thereby plunge ourselves into. See also how God often makes the enemies of his church instruments to destroy one another; it is a pity the church's friends should ever be thus infatuated. 3. They fled for their lives. Perhaps when day-light came they were sensible of their mistake in fighting with one another, and concluded that by this fatal error they had so weakened themselves that now it was impossible to make any head against Israel, and therefore made the best of their way towards their own country, though, for aught that appears, the 300 men kept their ground. *The wicked flee when none pursueth,* Prov. 28:1. *Terrors make him afraid on every side, and drive him to his feet,* Job 18:11.

Verses 23–25

We have here the prosecution of this glorious victory. 1. Gideon's soldiers that had been dismissed, and perhaps had begun to disperse themselves, upon notice of the enemies' flight got together again, and vigorously pursued those whom they had not courage to face. The men of Israel out of Naphtali and Asher who did this (*v.* 23) were not such as now came from those distant countries, but the same that had enlisted themselves (*ch.* 6:35), but had been cashiered. Those who were fearful and afraid to fight (*v.* 3) now took heart, when the worst was over, and were ready enough to divide the spoil, though backward to make the onset. Those also that might not fight though they had a mind to it, and were disbanded by order from God, did not as those, 2 Chr. 25:10, 13, *return in great anger,* but waited for an opportunity of doing service in pursuing the victory, though they were denied the honour of helping to force the lines. 2. The Ephraimites, upon a summons from Gideon, came in unanimously, and secured the passes over Jordan, by the several fords, to cut off the enemies' retreat into their own country, that they might be entirely destroyed, to prevent the like mischief to Israel another time. Now that they had begun to fall, it was easy to say, Down with them, Esth. 6:13. They *took the waters* (*v.* 24), that is, posted themselves along the river side, so that the Midianites, who fled from those who pursued them, fell into the hands of those that waited to intercept them. Here were *fear, and the pit, and the snare,* Isa. 24:17. 3. Two of the chief commanders of the host of Midian were taken and slain by the Ephraimites on this side Jordan, *v.* 25. Their names perhaps signified their nature, *Oreb* signifies a *raven,* and *Zeeb* a *wolf (corvus* and *lupus).* These in their flight had taken shelter, one *in a rock* (Isa. 2:21; Rev. 6:15), the other by a *wine-press,* as Gideon for fear of them had lately hid his corn by a wine-press, *ch.* 6:11. But the places of their shelter were made the places of their slaughter, and the memory of it was preserved to posterity in the names of the places, to their perpetual infamy: *Here fell the princes of Midian.*

CHAPTER 8

This chapter gives us a further account of Gideon's victory over the Midianites, with the residue of the story of his life and government. I. Gideon prudently pacifies the offended Ephraimites (*v.* 1–3). II. He bravely pursues the flying Midianites (*v.* 4, 10–12). III. He justly chastises the insolence of the men of Succoth and Penuel, who basely abused him (*v.* 5–9), and were reckoned with for it (*v.* 13–17). IV. He honourably slays the two kings of Midian (*v.* 18–21). V. After all this he modestly declines the government of Israel (*v.* 22, 23). VI. He foolishly gratified the superstitious humour of his people by setting up an ephod in his own city, which proved a great snare (*v.* 24–27). VII. He kept the country quiet for forty years (*v.* 28). VIII. He died in honour, and left a numerous family behind him (*v.* 29–32). IX. Both he and his God were soon forgotten by ungrateful Israel (*v.* 33–35).

Verses 1–3

No sooner were the Midianites, the common enemy, subdued, than, through the violence of some hot spirits, the children of Israel were ready to quarrel among themselves; an unhappy spark was struck, which, if Gideon had not with a great deal of wisdom and grace extinguished immediately, might have broken out into a flame of fatal consequence. The Ephraimites, when they brought the heads of Oreb and Zeeb to Gideon as general, instead of congratulating him upon his successes and addressing him with thanks for his great services, as they ought to have done, picked a quarrel with him and grew very hot upon it.

I. Their accusation was very peevish and unreasonable: *Why didst thou not call us when thou wentest to fight with the Midianites? v.* 1. Ephraim was brother to Manasseh, Gideon's tribe, and had the pre-eminence in Jacob's blessing and in Moses's, and therefore was very jealous of Manasseh, lest that tribe should at any time eclipse the honour of theirs. Hence we find Manasseh against Ephraim and Ephraim against Manasseh, Isa. 9:21. *A brother offended is harder to be won than a strong city, and their contentions are as the bars of a castle,* Prov. 18:19. But how unjust was their quarrel with Gideon! They were angry that he did not send for them to begin the attack upon Midian, as well as to follow the blow. Why were they not called to lead the van? The post of honour, they thought, belonged to them. But, 1. Gideon was called of God, and must act as he directed; he neither took the honour to himself nor did he himself dispose of honours, but left it to God to do all. So that the Ephraimites, in this quarrel, reflected upon the divine conduct; and what was Gideon that they *murmured against him?* 2. Why did not the Ephraimites offer themselves willingly to the service? They knew the enemy was in their country, and had heard of the forces that were raising to oppose them, to which they ought to have joined themselves, in zeal for the common cause, though they had not a formal invitation. Those seek themselves more than God that stand upon a point of honour to excuse themselves from doing real service to God and their generation. In Deborah's time there was a root of Ephraim, *ch.* 5:14. Why did not this appear now? The case itself called them, they needed not wait for a call from Gideon. 3. Gideon had saved their credit in not calling them. If he had sent for them, no doubt may of them would have gone back with the faint-hearted, or been dismissed with the lazy, slothful, and intemperate; so that by not calling them he prevented the putting of those slurs upon them. Cowards will seem valiant when the danger is over, but those consult their reputation who try not their courage when danger is near.

II. Gideon's answer was very calm and peaceable, and was intended not so much to justify himself as to please and pacify them, *v.* 2, 3. He answers them, 1. With a great deal of meekness and temper. He did not resent the affront, nor answer anger with anger, but mildly reasoned the case with them, and he won as true honour by this command which he had over his own passion as by his victory over the Midianites. *He that is slow to anger is better than the mighty.* 2. With a great deal of modesty and humility, magnifying their performances above his own: *Is not the gleaning of the grapes of Ephraim,* who picked up the stragglers of the enemy, and cut off those of them that escaped, *better than the vintage of Abiezer* — a greater honour to them, and better service to the country, than the first attack Gideon made upon them? The destruction of the church's enemies is compared to a vintage, Rev. 14:18. In this he owns their gleanings better than his gatherings. The improving of a victory is often more honourable, and of greater consequence, than the winning of it; in this they had signalized themselves, and their own courage and conduct, or, rather, God had dignified them; for thought, to magnify their achievements, he is willing to diminish his own performances, yet he will not take any flowers from God's crown to adorn theirs with: *"God has delivered into your hands the princes of Midian,* and a great slaughter has been made of the enemy by your numerous hosts, and *what was I able to do* with 300 men, *in comparison of you* and your brave exploits?" Gideon stands here a very great example of self-denial, and this instance shows us, (1.) That humility of deportment is the best way to remove envy. It is true even right works are often envied, Eccl. 4:4. Yet they are not so apt to be so when those who do them appear not to be proud of them. Those are malignant indeed who seek to cast down from their excellency those that humble and abase themselves, (2.) It is likewise the surest method of ending strife, for *only by pride comes contention,* Prov. 13:10. (3.) Humility is most amiable and admirable in the midst of great attainments and advancements. Gideon's conquests did greatly set off his condescensions. (4.) It is the proper act of humility to *esteem others better than ourselves,* and *in honour to prefer one another.*

Now what was the issue of this controversy? The Ephraimites had *chidden with him sharply* (*v.* 1), forgetting the respect due to their general and one whom God had honoured, and giving vent to their passion in a very indecent liberty of speech, a certain sign of a weak and indefensible cause. Reason runs low when the chiding flies high. But Gideon's *soft answer turned away their wrath,* Prov. 15:1. *Their anger was abated towards him, v.* 3. It is intimated that they retained some resentment, but he prudently overlooked it and let it cool by degrees. Very great and good men must expect to have their patience tried by the unkindnesses and follies even of those they serve and must not think it strange.

Verses 4–17

In these verses we have,

I. Gideon, as a valiant general, pursuing the remaining Midianites, and bravely following his blow. A very great slaughter was made of the enemy at first: 120,000 *men that drew the sword, v.* 10. Such a terrible execution did they make among themselves, and so easy a prey were they to Israel. But, it seems, the two kings of Midian, being better provided than the rest for an escape, with 15,000 men got over Jordan before the passes could be secured by the Ephraimites, and made towards their own country. Gideon thinks he does not fully execute his commission to save Israel if he let them escape. He is not content to chase them out of the country, but he will *chase them out of the world,* Job 18:18. This resolution is here pushed on with great firmness, and crowned with great success.

1. His firmness was very exemplary. He effected his purpose under the greatest disadvantages and discouragements that could be. (1.) He took none with him but his 300 men, who now laid aside their trumpets and torches, and betook themselves to their swords and spears. God had said, *By these 300 men will I save you* (*ch.* 7:7); and, confiding in that promise, Gideon kept to them only, *v.* 4. He expected more from 300 men, supported by a particular promise, than from so many thousands supported only by their own valour. (2.) They were *faint, and yet pursuing,* much fatigued with what they had done, and yet eager to do more against the enemies of their country. Our spiritual warfare must thus be prosecuted with what strength we have, though we have but little; it is many a time the true Christina's case, fainting and yet pursuing. (3.) Though he met with discouragement from those of his own people, was jeered for what he was doing, as going about what he could never accomplish, yet he went on with it. If those that should be our helpers in the way of our duty prove hindrances to us, let not this drive us off from it. Those know not how to value God's acceptance that know not how to despise the reproaches and contempts of men. (4.) He made a very long march by *the way of those that dwelt in tents* (*v.* 11), either because he hoped to find them kinder to him than the men of Succoth and Penuel, that dwelt in walled towns (sometimes there is more generosity and charity found in country tents than in city palaces), or because that was a road in which he would be least expected, and therefore that way it would be the greater surprise to them. It is evident he spared no pains to complete his victory. Now he found it an advantage to have his 300 men such as could bear hunger, and thirst, and toil. It should seem, he set upon the enemy by night, as he had done before, for *the host was secure.* The security of sinners often proves their ruin, and dangers are most fatal when least feared.

2. His success was very encouraging to resolution and industry in a good cause. He routed the army (*v.* 11), and took the two kings prisoners, *v.* 12. Note, The fear of the wicked shall come upon him. Those that think to run *from the sword of the Lord and of Gideon* do but run *upon* it.

If he *flee from the iron weapon,* yet *the bow of steel shall strike him through;* for *evil pursueth sinners.*

II. Here is Gideon, as a righteous judge, chastising the insolence of the disaffected Israelites, the men of Succoth and the men of Penuel, both in the tribe of Gad, on the other side Jordan.

1. Their crime was great. Gideon, with a handful of feeble folk was pursuing the common enemy, to complete the deliverance of Israel. His way led him through the city of Succoth first and afterwards of Penuel. He expected not that the magistrates should meet him in their formalities, congratulate him upon his victory, present him with the keys of their city, and give him a treat, much less that they should send forces in to his assistance, though he was entitled to all this; but he only begs some necessary food for his soldiers that were ready to faint for want, and he does it very humbly and importunately: *Give, I pray you, loaves of bread unto the people that follow me, v.* 5. The request would have been reasonable if they had been but poor travellers in distress; but considering that they were soldiers, *called, and chose, and faithful* (Rev. 17:14), men whom God had greatly honoured and to whom Israel was highly obliged, who had done great service to their country and were now doing more, — that they were conquerors, and had power to put them under contribution, — and that they were fighting God's battles and Israel's, — nothing could be more just than that their brethren should furnish them with the best provisions their city afforded. But the princes of Succoth neither *feared God nor regarded man.* For, (1.) In contempt of God, they refused to answer the just demands of him whom God had raised up to save them, affronted him, bantered him, despised the success he had already been honoured with, despaired of the success of his present undertaking, did what they could to discourage him in prosecuting the war, and were very willing to believe that the remaining forces of Midian, which they had now seen march through their country, would be too hard for him: *Are the hands of Zebah and Zalmunna now in thy hand?* "No, nor ever will be," so they conclude, judging by the disproportion of numbers. (2.) The bowels of their compassion were shut up against their brethren; they were as destitute of love as they were of faith, would not give morsels of bread (so some read it) to those that were ready to perish. Were these princes? were these Israelites? unworthy either title, base and degenerate men! Surely they were worshippers of Baal, or in the interests of Midian. The men of Penuel gave the same answer to the same request, defying *the sword of the Lord and of Gideon, v.* 8.

2. The warning he gave them of the punishment of their crime was very fair. (1.) He did not punish it immediately, because he would not lose so much time from the pursuit of the enemy that were flying from him, because he would not seem to do it in a neat of passion, and because he would do it more to their shame and confusion when he had completed his undertaking, which they thought impracticable. But, (2.) He told them how he would punish it (*v.* 7, 9), to show the confidence he had of success in the strength of God, and that, if they had the least grain of grace and consideration left, they might upon second thoughts repent of their folly, humble themselves, and contrive how to atone for it, by sending after him succours and supplies, which if they had done, no doubt, Gideon would have pardoned them. God gives notice of danger, and space to repent, that sinners may *flee from the wrath to come.*

3. The warning being slighted, the punishment, though very severe, was really very just.

(1.) The princes of Succoth were first made examples. Gideon got intelligence of their number, seventy-seven men, their names, and places of abode, which were described in writing to him, *v.* 14. And, to their great surprise, when they thought he had scarcely overtaken the Midianites, he returned a conqueror. His 300 men were now the ministers of his justice; they secured all these princes, and brought them before Gideon, who showed them his royal captives in chains. "These are the men you thought me an unequal match for, and would give me no assistance in the pursuit of," *v.* 15. And he punished them with thorns and briers, but, it should seem, not unto death. With these, [1.] He tormented their bodies, either by scourging or by rolling them in the thorns and briers; some way or other he *tore their flesh, v.* 7. Those shall have judgment without mercy that have shown no mercy. Perhaps he observed them to be soft and delicate men, who despised him and his company for their roughness and hardiness, and therefore Gideon thus mortified them for their effeminacy. [2.] He instructed their minds: With these *he taught the men of Succoth, v.* 16. The correction he gave them was intended, not for destruction, but wholesome discipline, to make them wiser and better for the future. *He made them know* (so the word is), made them know themselves and their folly, God and their duty, made them know who Gideon was, since they would not know by the success wherewith God had crowned him. Note, Many are taught with the briers and thorns of affliction that would not learn otherwise. God gives *wisdom* by *the rod and reproof, chastens* and *teaches,* and by correction *opens the ear to discipline.* Our blessed Saviour, though he was a Son, yet *learnt obedience by the things which he suffered,* Heb. 5:8. Let every *pricking brier,* and *grieving thorn,* especially when it becomes a *thorn in the flesh,* be thus interpreted, thus improved. "By this God designs to teach me; what good lesson shall I learn?"

(2.) The doom of the men of Penuel comes next, and it should seem he used them more severely than the other, for good reason, no doubt, *v.* 17. [1.] He *beat down their tower,* of which they gloried, in which they trusted, perhaps scornfully advising Gideon and his men rather to secure themselves in that than to pursue the Midianites. What men make their pride is justly by its ruin made their shame. [2.] He *slew the men of the city,* not all, perhaps not the elders or princes, but those that had affronted him, and those only. He slew some of the men of the city that were most insolent and abusive, for terror to the rest, and *so he taught the men of Penuel.*

Verses 18–21

Judgment began *at the house of God,* in the just correction of the men of Succoth and Penuel, who were Israelites, but it did not end there. The kings of Midian, when they had served to demonstrate Gideon's victories, and grace his triumphs, must now be reckoned with. 1. They are indicted for the murder of Gideon's brethren some time ago at Mount Tabor. When the children of Israel, for fear of the Midianites, made themselves *dens in the mountains* (*ch.* 6:2), those young men, it is likely, took shelter in that mountain, where they were found by these two kings, and most basely and barbarously slain in cold blood. When he asks them *what manner of men they were* (*v.* 18), it is not because he was uncertain of the thing, or wanted proof of it; he was not so little concerned for his brethren's blood as not to enquire it out before now, nor were these proud tyrants solicitous to conceal it. But he puts that question to them that by their acknowledgment of the more than ordinary comeliness of the persons they slew their crime might appear the more heinous, and consequently their punishment the more righteous. They could not but own that, though they were found in a mean and abject condition, yet they had an unusual greatness and majesty in their countenances, not unlike Gideon himself at this time: they *resembled the children of a king,* born for something great. 2. Being found guilty of this murder by their own confession, Gideon, though he might have put them to death as Israel's judge for the injuries done to that people in general, as Oreb and Zeeb (*ch.* 7:25), yet chooses rather to put on the character of an *avenger of blood,* as next of kin to the persons slain: *They were my brethren, v.* 19. Their other crimes might have been forgiven, at least Gideon would not have slain them himself, let them have answered it to the people; but *the voice of his brethren's blood cries,* cries *to him,* now it is in the power of his hand to avenge it, and therefore there is no remedy — by him must *their blood be shed,* though they were kings. Little did they think to hear of this so long after; but murder seldom goes unpunished even in this life. 3. The execution is done by Gideon himself with his own hand, because he was the *avenger of blood;* he bade his son slay them, for he was a near relation to the persons murdered, and fittest to be his father's substitute and representative, and he would thus train him up to the acts of justice and boldness, *v.* 20. But, (1.) The young man himself desired to be excused; he feared, though they were bound and could make no resistance, *because he was yet a youth,* and not used to such work: courage does not always run in the blood. (2.) The prisoners themselves desired that Gideon would excuse it (*v.* 21), begged that, if they must die, they might die *by his own hand,* which would be somewhat more honourable to them, and more easy; for by his great strength they would sooner be dispatched and rid out of their pain. *As is the man, so is his strength.* Either they mean it of themselves (they were men of such strength as called for a better hand than that young man's to overpower quickly) or of Gideon, "Thou art at thy full strength; he has not yet come to it; therefore be thou the executioner." From those that are grown up to maturity, it is expected that what they do in any service be done with so much the more strength. Gideon dispatched them quickly, and seized the *ornaments that were on their camels' necks, ornaments like the moon,* so it is in the margin, either badges of their royalty or perhaps of their idolatry, for Ashteroth was represented by the moon, as Baal by the sun. With there he took all their other ornaments, as appears *v.* 26, where we find that he did not put them to so good a use as one would have wished. The destruction of these two kings, and that of the two princes (*ch.* 7:25) is long afterwards pleaded as a precedent in prayer for the ruin of others of the church's enemies, Ps. 83:11, *Make their nobles like Oreb and Zeeb, and all their princes as Zebah and Zalmunna,* let them all be but off in like manner.

Verses 22–28

Here is, I. Gideon's laudable modesty, after his great victory, in refusing the government which the people offered him. 1. It was honest in them to offer it: *Rule thou over us, for thou hast delivered us, v.* 22. They thought it very reasonable that he who had gone through the toils and perils of their deliverance should enjoy the honour and power of commanding them ever afterwards, and very desirable that he who in this great and critical juncture had had such manifest tokens of God's presence with him should ever afterwards preside in their affairs. Let us apply it to the Lord Jesus: he hath delivered us out of the hands of our enemies, our spiritual enemies, the worst and most dangerous, and therefore it is fit he should rule over us; for how can we be better ruled than by one that appears to have so great an interest in heaven and so great a kindness for this earth? We are delivered that we may *serve him without fear,* Lu. 1:74, 75. 2. It was honourable in him to refuse it: *I will not rule over you, v.* 23. What he did was with a design to serve them, not to rule them — to make them safe, easy, and happy, not to make himself great or honourable. And, as he was not ambitious of grandeur himself, so he did not covet to entail it upon his family: *"My son shall not rule over you,* either while I live or when I am gone, *but the Lord shall* still *rule over you,* and constitute your judges by the special designation of his own Spirit, as he has done." This intimates, (1.) His modesty, and the mean opinion he had of himself and his own merits. He thought the honour of doing good was recompence enough for all his services, which needed not to be rewarded with the honour of bearing sway. *He that is greatest, let him be your minister.* (2.) His piety, and the great opinion he had of God's government. Perhaps he discerned in the people a dislike of the theocracy, or divine government, a desire of a king like the nations, and thought they availed themselves of his merits as a colourable pretence to move for this change of government. But Gideon would by no means admit it. No good man can be pleased with any honour done to himself which ought to be peculiar to God. *Were you baptized in the name of Paul?* 1 Co. 1:13.

II. Gideon's irregular zeal to perpetuate the remembrance of this victory by an ephod made of the choicest of the spoils. 1. He asked the men of Israel to give him the ear-rings of their prey; for such ornaments they stripped the slain of in abundance. These he demanded, either because they were the finest gold, and therefore fittest for a religious use, or because they had had as ear-rings some superstitious signification, which he thought too well of. Aaron called for the ear-rings to make the golden calf of, Ex. 32:2. These Gideon begged *v.* 24. And he had reason enough to think that those who offered him a crown, when he declined it, would not deny him their ear-rings, when he begged them, nor did they, *v.* 25. 2. He himself added the spoil he took from the kings of Midian, which, it should seem, had fallen to his share, *v.* 26. The generals had that part of the prey which was most splendid, the *prey of divers colours, ch.* 5:30. 3. Of this he made an ephod, *v.* 27. It was plausible enough, and might be well intended to preserve a memorial of so divine a victory in the judge's own city. But it was a very unadvised thing to make that memorial to be an ephod, a sacred garment. I would gladly put the best construction that can be upon the actions of good men, and such a one we are sure Gideon was. But we have reason to suspect that this ephod had, as usual, a teraphim annexed to it (Hos. 3:4), and that, having an altar already built by divine appointment (*ch.* 6:26), which he erroneously imagined he might still use for sacrifice, he intended this for an oracle, to be consulted in doubtful cases. So the learned Dr. Spencer supposes. Each tribe having now very much its government within itself, they were too apt to covet their religion among themselves. We read very little of Shiloh, and the ark there, in all the story of the Judges. Sometimes by divine dispensation, and much oftener by the transgression of men, that law which obliged them to worship only at that one altar seems not to have been so religiously observed as one would have expected, any more than afterwards, when in the reigns even of very good kings *the high places were not taken away,* from which we may infer that that law had a further reach as a type of Christ, by whose mediation alone all our services are accepted. Gideon therefore, through ignorance or inconsideration, sinned in making this ephod, though he had a good intention in it. Shiloh, it is true, was not far off, but it was in Ephraim, and that tribe had lately disobliged him (*v.* 1), which made him perhaps not care to go so often among them as his occasions would lead him to consult the oracle, and therefore he would have one nearer home. However this might be honestly intended, and at first did little hurt, yet in process of time, (1.) *Israel went a whoring after it,* that is, they deserted God's altar and priesthood, being fond of change, and prone to idolatry, and having some excuse for paying respect to this ephod, because so good a man as Gideon had set it up, and by degrees their respect to it grew more and more superstitious. Note, Many are led into false ways by one false step of a good man. The beginning of sin, particularly of idolatry and will-worship, *is as the letting forth of water,* so it has been found in the fatal corruptions of the church of Rome; therefore *leave it off before it be meddled with.* (2.) It became a snare to Gideon himself, abating his zeal for the house of God in his old age, and much more to his house, who were drawn by it into sin, and it proved the ruin of the family.

III. Gideon's happy agency for the repose of Israel, *v.* 28. The Midianites that had been so vexatious gave them no more disturbance. Gideon, though he would not assume the honour and power of a king, governed as a judge, and did all the good offices he could for his people; so that *the country was in quietness forty years.* Hitherto the times of Israel had been reckoned by forties. Othniel judged forty years, Ehud eighty — just two forties, Barak forty, and now Gideon forty, providence so ordering it to bring in mind the forty years of their wandering in the wilderness. *Forty years long was I grieved with this generation.* And see Eze. 4:6. After these, Eli ruled forty years (1 Sa. 4:18), Samuel and Saul forty (Acts 13:21), David forty, and Solomon forty. Forty years is about an age.

Verses 29–35

We have here the conclusion of the story of Gideon. 1. He lived privately, *v.* 29. He was not puffed up with his great honours, did not covet a palace or castle to dwell in, but retired to the house he had lived in before his elevation. Thus that brave Roman Who was called from the plough upon a sudden occasion to command the army when the action was over returned to his plough again. 2. His family was multiplied. He had many wives (therein he transgressed the law); by them he had seventy sons (*v.* 30), but by a concubine he had one whom he named *Abimelech* (which signifies, *my father a king),* that proved the ruin of his family, *v.* 31. 3. He died in honour, in a good old age, when he had lived as long as he was capable of serving God and his country; and who would desire to live any longer? And he was *buried in the sepulchre of his fathers.* 4. After his death the people corrupted themselves, and went all to naught. As soon as ever Gideon was dead, who had kept them close to the worship of the God of Israel, they found themselves under no restraint, and then they *went a whoring after Baalim, v.* 33. They went a whoring first after another ephod (*v.* 27), for which irregularity Gideon had himself given them too much occasion, and now they went a whoring after another god. False worships made way for false deities. They now chose a new god (*ch.* 5:8), a god of a new name, *Baal-berith* (a goddess, say some); Berith, some think, was Berytus, the place where the Phoenicians worshipped this idol. The name signifies *the Lord of a covenant.* Perhaps he was so called because his worshippers joined themselves by covenant to him, in imitation of Israel's covenanting with God; for the devil is God's ape. In this revolt of Israel to idolatry they showed, (1.) Great ingratitude to God (*v.* 34): *They remembered not the Lord,* not only who had delivered them into the hands of their enemies, to punish them for their idolatry, but who had also *delivered them out of the hands of their enemies,* to invite them back again into his service; both the judgments and the mercies were forgotten, and the impressions of them lost. (2.) Great ingratitude to Gideon, *v.* 35. A great deal of *goodness he had shown unto Israel,* as a father to his country, for which they ought to have been kind to his family when he was gone, for that is one way by which we ought to show ourselves grateful to our friends and benefactors, and may be returning their kindnesses when they are in their graves. But Israel showed not this kindness to Gideon's family, as we shall find in the next chapter. No wonder if those who forget their God forget their friends.

CHAPTER 9

The apostasy of Israel after the death of Gideon is punished, not as the former apostasies by a foreign invasion, or the oppressions of any neighbouring power, but by intestine broils among themselves, which in this chapter we have the story of; and it is hard to say whether their sin or their misery appears most in it. It is an account of the usurpation and tyranny of Abimelech, who was base son to Gideon; so we must call him, and not more modishly his natural son: he was so unlike him. We are here told, I. How he thrust himself into the government at Shechem, his own city, by subtlety and cruelty, particularly by the murder of all his brethren (*v.* 1–6). II. How his doom was read in a parable by Jothan, Gideon's youngest son (*v.* 7–21). III. What strifes there were between Abimelech and his friends the Shechemites (*v.* 22–41). IV. How this ended in the ruin of the Shechemites (*v.* 42–49), and of Abimelech himself (*v.* 50–57). Of this meteor, this ignis fatuus of a prince, that was not a protector but a plague to his country, we may say, as once was said of a great tyrant, that he came in like a fox, ruled like a lion, and died like a dog. "For the transgression of a land, such are the princes thereof."

Verses 1–6

We are here told by what arts Abimelech got into authority, and made himself great. His mother perhaps had instilled into his mind some towering ambitious thoughts, and the name his father gave him, carrying royalty in it, might help to blow up these sparks; and now that he has buried his father nothing will serve his proud spirit but he will succeed him in the government of Israel, directly contrary to his father's will, for he had declared *no son of his should rule over them.* He had no call from God to this honour as his father had, nor was there any present occasion for a judge to deliver Israel as there was when his father was advanced; but his own ambition must be gratified, and its gratification is all he aims at. Now observe here,

I. How craftily he got his mother's relations into his interests. Shechem was a city in the tribe of Ephraim, of great note. Joshua had held his last assembly there. If that city would but appear for him, and set him up, he thought it would go far in his favour. There he had an interest in the family of which his mother was, and by them he made an interest in the leading men of the city. It does not appear that any of them had an eye to him as a man of merit, who had any thing to recommend him to such a choice, but the motion came first from himself. None would have dreamed of making such a one king, if he had not dreamed of it himself. And see here, 1. How he wheedled them into the choice, *v.* 2, 3. He basely suggested that Gideon having left seventy sons, who made a good figure and had a good interest, they were designing to keep the power which their father had in their hands, and by a joint-influence to reign over Israel. "Now," says he, "you had better have one king than more, than many, than so many. Affairs of state are best managed by a single person," *v.* 2. We have no reason to think that all or any of Gideon's sons had the least intention to reign over Israel (they were of their father's mind, that *the Lord should reign over them,* and they were not called of him), yet this he insinuates to pave the way to his own pretensions. Note, Those who design ill themselves are commonly most apt to suspect that others design ill. As for himself, he only puts them in mind of his relation to them *(verbum sapienti — A word to the wise is sufficient): Remember that I am your bone and your flesh.* The plot took wonderfully. The magistrates of Shechem were pleased to think of their city being a royal city and the metropolis of Israel, and therefore they *inclined to follow him; for they said, "He is our brother,* and his advancement will be our advantage." 2. How he got money from them to bear the charges of his pretensions (*v.* 4): *They gave him seventy pieces of silver;* it is not said what the value of these pieces was; so many shekels are less, and so many talents more, than we can well imagine; therefore it is supposed they were each a pound weight: but they gave this money out of the house of Baal-berith, that is, out of the public treasury, which, out of respect to their idol, they deposited in his temple to be protected by him; or out of the offerings that had been made to that idol, which they hoped would prosper the better in his hands for its having been consecrated to their god. How unfit was he to reign over Israel, because unlikely to defend them, who, instead of restraining and punishing idolatry, thus early made himself a pensioner to an idol! 3. What soldiers he enlisted. He hired into his service vain and light persons, the scum and scoundrels of the country, men of broken fortunes, giddy heads, and profligate lives; none but such would own him, and they were fittest to serve his purpose. Like leader like followers.

II. How cruelly he got his father's sons out of the way.

1. The first thing he did with the rabble he headed was to kill all his brethren at once, publicly and in cold blood, threescore and ten men, one only escaping, all slain upon one stone. See in this bloody tragedy, (1.) The power of ambition what beasts it will turn men into, how it will break through all the ties of natural affection and natural conscience, and sacrifice that which is most sacred, dear, and valuable, to its designs. Strange that ever it should enter into the heart of a man to be so very barbarous! (2.) The peril of honour and high birth. Their being the sons of so great a man as Gideon exposed them thus and made Abimelech jealous of them. We find just the same number of Ahab's sons slain together at Samaria, 2 Ki. 10:1, 7. The grand seigniors have seldom thought themselves safe while any of their brethren have been unstrangled. Let none then envy those of high extraction, or complain of their own meanness and obscurity. The lower the safer.

2. Way being thus made for Abimelech's election, the men of Shechem proceeded to choose him king, *v.* 6. God was not consulted whether they should have any king at all, much less who it should be; here is no advising with the priest or with their brethren of any other city or tribe, though it was designed that he should reign over Israel, *v.* 22. But, (1.) The Shechemites, as if they were the people and wisdom must die with them, did all; they aided and abetted him in the murder of his brethren (*v.* 24), and then they *made him king.* The men of Shechem (that is, the great men, the chief magistrates of the city), and the house of Millo (that is, the common-council, the *full house* or *house of fulness,* as the word signifies), those that met in their guildhall (we read often of the house of Millo, or state-house in Jerusalem, or the city of David, 2 Sa. 5:9; 2 Ki. 12:20), these gathered together, not to prosecute and punish Abimelech for this barbarous murder, as they ought to have done, he being one of their citizens, but to *make him king. Pretium sceleris tulit hic diadema — His wickedness was rewarded with a diadem.* What could they promise themselves from a king that laid the foundation of his kingdom in blood? (2.) The rest of the Israelites were so very sottish as to sit by unconcerned. They took no care to give check to this usurpation, to protect the sons of Gideon, or to avenge their death, but tamely submitted to the bloody tyrant, as men who with their religion had lost their reason, and all sense of honour and liberty, justice and gratitude. How vigorously had their fathers appeared to avenge the death of the Levite's concubine, and yet so wretchedly degenerate are they now as not to attempt the avenging of the death of Gideon's sons; it is for this that they are charged with ingratitude (*ch.* 8:35): *Neither showed they kindness to the house of Jerubbaal.*

Verses 7–21

We have here the only testimony that appears to have been borne against the wicked confederacy of Abimelech and the men of Shechem. It was a sign they had provoked God to depart from them that neither any prophet was sent nor any remarkable judgment, to awaken this stupid people, and to stop the progress of this threatening mischief. Only Jotham, the youngest son of Gideon, who by a special providence escaped the common ruin of his family (*v.* 5), dealt plainly with the Shechemites, and his speech, which is here recorded, shows him to have been a man of such great ingenuity and wisdom, and really such an accomplished gentleman, that we cannot but the more lament the fall of Gideon's sons. Jotham did not go about to raise an army out of the other cities of Israel (in which, one would think, he might have made a good interest for his father's sake), to avenge his brethren's death, much less to set up himself in competition with Abimelech, so groundless was the usurper's suggestion that the sons of Gideon aimed at dominion (*v.* 2); but he contents himself with giving a faithful reproof to the Shechemites, and fair warning of the fatal consequences. He got an opportunity of speaking to them from the top of Mount Gerizim, the mount of blessings, at the foot of which probably the Shechemites were, upon some occasion or other, gathered together (Josephus says, solemnizing a festival), and it seems they were willing to hear what he had to say.

I. His preface is very serious: *"Hearken unto me, you men of Shechem, that God may hearken unto you, v.* 7. As ever you hope to obtain God's favour, and to be accepted of him, give me a patient and impartial hearing." Note, Those who expect God to hear their prayers must be willing to hear reason, to hear a faithful reproof, and to hear the complaints and appeals of wronged innocency. If we *turn away our ear from hearing the law, our prayer will be an abomination,* Prov. 28:9.

II. His parable is very ingenious — that when the trees were disposed to choose a king the government was offered to those valuable trees the olive, the fig-tree, and the vine, but they refused it, choosing rather to serve than rule, to do good than bear sway. But the same tender being made to the bramble he accepted it with vain-glorious exultation. The way of instruction by parables is an ancient way, and very useful, especially to give reproofs by.

1. He hereby applauds the generous modesty of Gideon, and the other judges who were before him, and perhaps of the sons of Gideon, who had declined accepting the state and power of kings when they might have had them, and likewise shows that it is in general the temper of all wise and good men to decline preferment and to choose rather to be useful than to be great. (1.) There was no occasion at all for the trees to choose a king; they are all the *trees of the Lord which he has planted* (Ps. 104:16) and which therefore he will protect. Nor was there any occasion for Israel to talk of setting a king over them; for *the Lord was their king.* (2.) When they had it in their thoughts to choose a king they did not offer the government to the stately cedar, or the lofty pine, which are only for show and shade, and not otherwise useful till they are cut down, but to the fruit-trees, the vine and the olive. Those that bear fruit for the public good are justly respected and honoured by all that are wise more than those that affect to make a figure. For a good useful man some *would even dare to die.* (3.) The reason which all these fruit-trees gave for their refusal was much the same. The olive pleads (*v.* 9), *Should I leave my wine,* wherewith both God and man are served and honoured? for oil and wine were used both at God's altars and at men's tables. And *shall I leave my sweetness, saith the fig-tree, and my good fruit* (*v.* 11), *and go to be promoted over the trees?* or, as the margin reads it, *go up and down for the trees?* It is intimated, [1.] That government involves a man in a great deal both of toil and care; he that is promoted over the trees must go up and down for them, and make himself a perfect drudge to business. [2.] That those who are preferred to places of public trust and power must resolve to forego all their private interests and advantages, and sacrifice them to the good of the community. The fig-tree must lose its sweetness, its sweet retirement, sweet repose, and sweet conversation and contemplation, if it go to be *promoted over the trees,* and must undergo a constant fatigue. [3.] That those who are advanced to honour and dignity are in great danger of losing their fatness and fruitfulness. Preferment is apt to make men proud and slothful, and thus spoil their usefulness, with which in a lower sphere they honoured God and man, for which reason those that desire to do good are afraid of being too great.

2. He hereby exposes the ridiculous ambition of Abimelech, whom he compares to the bramble or thistle, *v.* 14. He supposes the trees to make their court to him: *Come thou and reign over us,* perhaps because he knew not that the first motion of Abimelech's preferment came from himself (as we found, *v.* 2), but thought the Shechemites had proposed it to him; however, supposing it so, his folly in accepting it deserved to be chastised. The bramble is a worthless plant, not to be numbered among the trees, useless and fruitless, nay, hurtful and vexatious, scratching and tearing, and doing mischief; it began with the curse, and its end is to be burned. Such a one was Abimelech, and yet chosen to the government *by the trees, by all the trees;* this election seems to have been more unanimous than any of the others. Let us not think it strange if we see *folly set in great dignity* (Eccl. 10:6), and the *vilest men exalted* (Ps. 12:8), and men blind to their own interest in the choice of their guides. The bramble, being chosen to the government, takes no time to consider whether he should accept it or no, but immediately, as if he had been born and bred to dominion, hectors, and assures them they shall find him as he found them. See what *great swelling words of vanity* he speaks (*v.* 15), what promises he makes to his faithful subjects: *Let them come and trust in my shadow:* a goodly shadow to trust in! How unlike to *the shadow of a great rock in a weary land,* which a good magistrate is compared to! Isa. 32:2. Trust in his shadow! — more likely to be scratched if they came near him — more likely to be injured by him than benefited. Thus men *boast of a false gift.* Yet he threatens with as much confidence as he promises: If you be not faithful, *let fire come out of the bramble* (a very unlikely thing to emit fire) and *devour the cedars of Lebanon* — more likely to catch fire, and be itself devoured.

III. His application is very close and plain. In it, 1. He reminds them of the many good services his father had done for them, *v.* 17. He fought their battles, at the hazard of his own life, and to their unspeakable advantage. It was a shame that they needed to be put in mind of this. 2. He aggravates their unkindness to his father's family. They had not *done to him according to the deserving of his hands, v.* 16. Great merits often meet with very ill returns. especially to posterity, when the benefactor if forgotten, as Joseph was among the Egyptians. Gideon had left many sons that were an honour to his name and family, and these they had barbarously murdered; one son he had left that was the blemish of his name and family, for he was *the son of his maid-servant,* whom all that had any respect to Gideon's honour would endeavour to conceal, yet him they made their king. In both they put the utmost contempt imaginable upon Gideon. 3. He leaves it to the event to determine whether they had done well, whereby he lodges the appeal with the divine providence. (1.) If they prospered long in this villany, he would give them leave to say they had done well, *v.* 19. "If your conduct towards the house of Gideon be such as can be justified at any bar of justice, honour, or conscience, much good may it do you with your new king." But, (2.) If they had, as he was sure they had, dealt basely and wickedly in this matter, let them never expect to prosper, *v.* 20. Abimelech and the Shechemites, that had strengthened one another's hands in this villany, would certainly be a plague and ruin one to another. Let none expect to do ill and fare well.

Jotham, having given them this admonition, made a shift to escape with his life, *v.* 21. Either they could not reach him or they were so far convinced that they would not add the guilt of his blood to all the rest. But, for fear of Abimelech, he lived in exile, in some remote obscure place. Those whose extraction and education are ever so high know not to what difficulties and straits they may be reduced.

Verses 22–49

Three years Abimelech reigned, after a sort, without any disturbance; it is not said, He judged Israel, or did any service at all to his country, but so long he enjoyed the title and dignity of a king; and not only the Shechemites, but many other places, paid him respect. They must have been fond of a king that could please themselves with such a one as this. But the triumphing of the wicked is short. *Within three years, as the years of a hireling, all this glory shall be contemned,* and laid in the dust, Isa. 16:14. The ruin of these confederates in wickedness was from the righteous hand of the God to whom vengeance belongs. *He sent an evil spirit between Abimelech and the Shechemites* (*v.* 23), that is, they grew jealous one of another and ill-affected one to another. He slighted those that set him up, and perhaps countenanced other cities which now began to come into his interests more than he did theirs; and then they grew uneasy at his government, blamed his conduct, and quarrelled at his impositions. This was from God. He permitted the devil, that great mischief-maker, to sow discord between them, and he is *an evil spirit,* whom God not only keeps under his check, but sometimes serves his own purposes by. Their own lusts were evil spirits; they are devils in men's own hearts; from them come wars and fightings. These God gave them up to, and so might be said to *send the evil spirits between them.* When men's sin is made their punishment, though God is not the author of the sin, yet the punishment is from him. The quarrel God had with Abimelech and the Shechemites was for the murder of the sons of Gideon (*v.* 24): *That the cruelty done to them might come and their blood be laid* as a burden *upon Abimelech that slew them, and the men of Shechem that helped him.* Note, 1. Sooner or later God will make inquisition for blood, innocent blood, and will return it on the heads of those that shed it, who shall have blood given them to drink, for they are worthy. 2. Accessaries shall be reckoned with, as well as principals, in that and other sins. The Shechemites that countenanced Abimelech's pretensions, aided and abetted him in his bloody project, and avowed the fact by making him king after he had done it, must fall with him, fall by him, and fall first. 3. Those that combine together to do wickedly are justly dashed in pieces one against another. Blood cannot be a lasting cement to any interest.

I. The Shechemites began to affront Abimelech, perhaps they scarcely knew why or wherefore, but they were given to change. 1. They *dealt treacherously with him, v.* 23. It is not said, They repented of their sin in owning him. Had they done so, it would have been laudable to disown him; but they did it only upon some particular pique conceived against him by their pride or envy. Those that set him up were the first that deserted him and endeavoured to dethrone him. It is not strange that those who were ungrateful to Gideon were unfaithful to Abimelech; for what will hold those that will not be held by the obligation of such merits as Gideon's? Note, It is just with God that those who tempt others to be cone perfidious should afterwards be themselves betrayed by those whom they have taught to be perfidious. 2. They aimed to seize him when he was at Arumah (*v.* 41), his country-seat. Expecting him to come to town, they *set liers in wait for him* (*v.* 25), who should make him their prisoner whom they had lately made their prince. Those who were thus posted, he not coming, took the opportunity of robbing travellers, which would help to make the people more and more uneasy under Abimelech, when they saw he could not or would not protect them from highway-men. 3. They entertained one Gaal, and set him up as their head in opposition to Abimelech, *v.* 26. This Gaal is said to be the son of *Ebed,* which signifies *a servant,* perhaps denoting the meanness of his extraction. As Abimelech was by the mother's side, so he by the father's, the son of a servant. Here was one bramble contesting with another. We have reason to suspect that this Gaal was a native Canaanite, because he courts the Shechemites into subjection to the men of Hamor, who was the ancient lord of this city in Jacob's time. He was a bold ambitious man, served their purpose admirably well when they were disposed to quarrel with Abimelech, and they also served his purpose; so he went over to them to blow the coals, and they *put their confidence in him.* 4. They did all the despite they could to Abimelech's name, *v.* 27. They made themselves very merry in his absence, as those who were glad he was out of the way, and who, now that they had another to head them, were in hopes to get clear of him; nay, they *went into the house of their god,* to solemnize their feast of ingathering, and there *they did eat, and drink, and cursed*

Abimelech, not only said all the ill they could of him in their table-talk and the song of their drunkards, but wished all the ill they could to him over their sacrifices, praying to their idol to destroy him. They drank healths to his confusion, and with as loud huzzas as ever they had drunk them to his prosperity. That very temple whence they had fetched money to set him up with did they now meet in to curse him and contrive his ruin. Had they deserted their idol-god with their image-king, they might have hoped to prosper; but, while they still cleave to the former, the latter shall cleave to them to their ruin. How should Satan cast out Satan? 5. They pleased themselves with Gaal's vaunted defiance of Abimelech, *v.* 28, 29. They loved to hear that impudent upstart speak scornfully, (1.) Of Abimelech, though calling him in disdain *Shechem,* or *a Shechemite,* he reflected upon their own city. (2.) Of his good father likewise, Gideon: *Is not he the son of Jerubbaal?* So he calls him, perhaps in an impious indignation at his name and memory for throwing down the altar of Baal, turning that to his reproach which was his praise. (3.) Of his prime minister of state, *Zebul his officer, and ruler of the city.* "We may well be ashamed to serve them, and need not be afraid to oppose them." Men of turbulent ambitious spirits thus *despise dominion, and speak evil of dignities.* Gaal aimed not to recover Shechem's liberty, only to change their tyrant: *"O that this people were under my hand!* What I would do! I would challenge Abimelech to try titles for the crown;" and it should seem he desired his friends to send him word that he was ready to dispute it with him whenever he pleased: *"Increase thy army, and come out.* Do thy worst; let the point be determined by the sword." This pleased the Shechemites, who were now as sick of Abimelech as ever they had been fond of him. Men of no conscience will be men of no constancy.

II. Abimelech turned all his force upon them, and, in a little time, quite ruined them. Observe the steps of their overthrow.

1. The Shechemites' counsels were betrayed to Abimelech by Zebul his confidant, the ruler of the city, who continued hearty for him. *His anger was kindled* (*v.* 30), and the more because Gaal had spoken slightly of him (*v.* 28), for perhaps, if he had complimented and caressed him now that things were in this ferment, he might have gained him to his interest; but he, being disobliged, sends notice to Abimelech of all that was said and done in Shechem against him, *v.* 31. Betrayers are often betrayed by some among themselves, and the cursing of the king is sometimes strangely carried by a bird of the air. He prudently advises him to come against the city immediately, and lose no time, *v.* 32, 33. He thinks it best that he should march his forces by night into the neighbourhood, surprise the city in the morning, and then make the best of his advantages. How could the Shechemites hope to speed in their attempt when the ruler of their city was in the interests of their enemy? They knew it, and yet took no care to secure him.

2. Gaal, that headed their faction, having been betrayed by Zebul, Abimelech's confidant, was most wretchedly bantered by him. Abimelech, according to Zebul's advice, drew all his forces down upon Shechem by night, *v.* 34. Gaal, in the morning, went out *to the gate* (*v.* 35) to see what posture things were in, and to enquire, What news? Zebul, as a ruler of the city, met him there as a friend. Abimelech and his forces beginning to move towards the city, Gaal discovers them (*v.* 36), takes notice of their approach to Zebul that was standing with him, little thinking that he had sent for them and was now expecting them. "Look," says he, "do not I see a body of men coming down from the mountain towards us? Yonder they are," pointing to the place. "No, no," says Zebul; "thy eye-sight deceives thee; it is but *the shadow of the mountains* which thou takest to be an army." By this he intended, (1.) To ridicule him, as a man of no sense or spirit, and therefore very unfit for what he pretended to, as a man that might easily be imposed upon and made to believe any thing, and that was so silly and so cowardly that he apprehended danger where there was none, and was ready to fight with a shadow. (2.) To detain him, and hold him in talk, while the forces of Abimelech were coming up, that thereby they might gain advantage. But when Gaal, being content to believe those he now saw to be but the shadow of the mountains (perhaps the mountains of Ebal and Gerizim, which lay close by the city), was undeceived by the discovery of two other companies that marched apace towards the city, then Zebul took another way to banter him, upbraiding him with what he had said but a day or two before, in contempt of Abimelech (*v.* 38): *Where is now thy mouth,* that foul mouth of thine, *wherewith thou saidst, Who is Abimelech?* Note, Proud and haughty people are often made in a little time to change their note, and to dread those whom they had most despised. Gaal had, in a bravado, challenged Abimelech to *increase his army and come out;* but now Zebul, in Abimelech's name, challenges him: *Go out, and fight with them,* if thou darest. Justly are the insolent thus insulted over.

3. Abimelech routed Gaal's forces that sallied out of the town, *v.* 39, 40. Gaal, disheartened no doubt by Zebul's hectoring him, and perceiving his interest weaker than he thought it was, though he marched out against Abimelech with what little force he had, was soon put to the worst, and obliged to retire into the city with great precipitation. In this action the Shechemites' loss was considerable: *Many were overthrown and wounded,* the common effect of popular tumults, in which the inconsiderate multitude are often drawn into fatal snare by those that promise them glorious success.

4. Zebul that night expelled Gaal, and the party he had brought with him into Shechem, out of the city (*v.* 41), sending him to the place whence he came. For though the generality of the city continued still averse to Abimelech, as appears by the sequel of the story, yet they were willing to part with Gaal, and did not oppose his expulsion, because, though he had talked big, both his skill and courage had failed him when there was occasion for them. Most people judge of men's fitness for business by their success, and he that does not speed well is concluded not to do well. Well, Gaal's interest in Shechem is soon at an end, and he that had talked of removing Abimelech is himself removed, nor do we ever hear of him any more. *Exit Gaal — Gaal retires.*

5. Abimelech, the next day, set upon the city, and quite destroyed it, for their treacherous dealings with him. Perhaps Abimelech had notice of their expelling Gaal, who had headed the faction, with which they thought he would have been satisfied, but the crime was too keep to be thus atoned for, and his resentments were too keen to be pacified by so small an instance of submission, besides that it was more Zebul's act than theirs; by it their hands were weakened, and therefore he resolved to follow his blow, and effectually to chastise their treachery. (1.) He had intelligence brought him that the people of Shechem had come out *into the field, v.* 42. Some think into the field of business to plough and sow (having lately gathered in their harvest), or to perfect their harvest, for it was only their vintage that they had made an end of (*v.* 27), and then it intimates that they were secure. And because Abimelech had retired (*v.* 41) they thought themselves in no danger from him, and then the issue of it is an instance of sudden destruction coming upon those that cry, Peace and safety. Others think they went out into the field of battle; though Gaal was driven out, they would not lay down their arms, but put themselves into a posture for another engagement with Abimelech, in which they hoped to retrieve what they had lost the day before, (2.) He himself, with a strong detachment, cut off the communication between them and the city, *stood in the entering of the gate* (*v.* 44), that they might neither make their retreat into the city nor receive any succours from the city, and then sent two companies of his men, who were too strong for them, and they put them all to the sword, *ran upon those that were in the fields and slew them.* When we go out about our business we are not sure that we shall come home again; there are deaths both in the city and in the field. (3.) He then fell upon the city itself, and, with a rage reaching up to heaven, though it was the place of his nativity, laid it in ruins, slew all the people, beat down all the buildings, and, in token of his desire that it might be a perpetual desolation, sowed it with salt, that it might remain a lasting monument of the punishment of perfidiousness. Yet Abimelech prevailed not to make its desolations perpetual; for it was afterwards rebuilt, and became so considerable a place that all Israel came thither to make Rehoboam king, 1 Ki. 12:1. And the place proved an ill omen. Abimelech intended hereby to punish the Shechemites for their serving him formerly in the murder of Gideon's sons. Thus, when God makes use of men as instruments in his hand to do his work, he means one thing and they another, Isa. 10:6, 7. They design to maintain their honour, but God to maintain his.

6. Those that retired into a strong-hold of their idol-temple were all destroyed there. These are called *the men of the tower of Shechem* (*v.* 46, 47), some castle that belonged to the city, but lay at some distance from it. They, hearing of the destruction of the city, withdrew into a hold of the temple, trusting, it is likely, not so much to its strength as to its sanctity; they put themselves under the protection of their idol: for thus *all people will walk in the name of their god,* and shall not we then choose to dwell in the house of the Lord all the days of our life? For *in the time of trouble he shall hide us in his pavilion,* Ps. 27:5. The *name of the Lord is a strong tower,* Prov. 18:10. But that which they hoped would be for their welfare proved to them a snare and a trap, as those will certainly find that run to idols for shelter; it will prove a refuge of lies. When Abimelech had them altogether penned up in that hold he desired no more. That barbarous project immediately came into his head of setting fire to the strong-hold, and, so to speak, burning all the birds together in the nest. He kept the design to himself, but set all his men on work to expedite the execution of it, *v.* 48, 49. He ordered them all to follow him, and do as he did: as his father had said to his men (*ch.* 7:17), *Look on me, and do likewise;* so saith he to his, as becomes a general that will not be wanting to give both the plainest direction and the highest encouragement that can be to his soldiers: *What you have seen me do make haste to do, as I have done.* Not *Ite illuc — Go thither;* but *Venite huc — Come hither.* The officers in Christ's army should thus teach by their example, Phil. 4:9. He and they fetched each of them a bough from a wood not far off, laid all their boughs together under the wall of this tower, which it is probable was of wood, set fire to their boughs, and so burnt down their hold and all that were in it, who were either burnt or stifled with the smoke. What inventions men have to destroy one another! Whence come these cruel wars and fightings but from their lusts? Some think that the men of the tower of Shechem were the same with the house of Millo, and then Jotham's just imprecation was answered in the letter: *Let fire come out from* Abimelech, and devour not only in general the men of Shechem, but in particular the house of Millo, *v.* 20. About 1000 men and women perished in these flames, many of whom, it is probable, were no way concerned in the quarrel between Abimelech and the Shechemites, nor meddled with either side, yet, in this civil war, they came to this miserable end; for men of factious turbulent spirits *perish not alone in their iniquity,* but involve many more, that follow them in their simplicity, in the same calamity with them.

Verses 50–57

We have seen the ruin of the Shechemites completed by the hand of Abimelech; and now it comes to his turn to be reckoned with who was their leader in villany. Thebez was a small city, probably not far from Shechem, dependent upon it, and in confederacy with it. Now,

I. Abimelech attempted the destruction of this city (*v.* 50), drove all the inhabitants of the town into the castle, or citadel, *v.* 51. When he had them there he did not doubt but he should do the same execution here that he had lately done at the strong-hold of the temple of Baal-berith, not considering that the tower of an idol-temple lay more exposed to divine vengeance than any other tower. He attempted to set fire to this tower, at least to burn down the door, and so force an entrance, *v.* 52. Those who have escaped and succeeded well in one desperate attempt are apt to think the like attempt another time not desperate. This instance was long after quoted to show how dangerous it is to come near the call of a besieged city, 2 Sa. 11:20, etc. But God infatuates those whom he will ruin.

II. In the attempt he was himself destroyed, having his brains knocked out with a piece of a millstone, *v.* 57. *No doubt this man was a murderer, whom, though he had escaped* the dangers of the war with Shechem, yet *vengeance suffered not to live,* Acts 28:4. *Evil pursues sinners,* and sometimes overtakes them when they are not only secure, but triumphant. Thebez, we may suppose, was a weak inconsiderable place, compared with Shechem. Abimelech, having conquered the greater, makes no doubt of being master of the less without any difficulty, especially when he had taken the city, and had only the tower to deal with; yet he lays his bones by that, and there is all his honour buried. Thus are the *mighty things of the world* often confounded by the weakest and those things that are most made light of. See here what rebukes those are justly put under many times by the divine providence that are unreasonable in their demands of satisfaction for injuries received. Abimelech had some reason to chastise the Shechemites, and he had done it with a witness; but when he will carry his revenges further, and nothing will serve but that Thebez also must be sacrificed to his rage, he is not only disappointed there, but destroyed; *for verily there is a God that judges in the earth.* Three circumstances are worthy of observation in the death of Abimelech: — 1. That he was slain with a stone, as he had slain his brethren all *upon one stone.* 2. That he had his skull broken. Vengeance aimed at that guilty head which had worn the usurped crown. 3. That the stone was cast upon him by a woman, *v.* 53. He saw the stone come; it was therefore strange he did not avoid it, but, no doubt, this made it so much the greater mortification to him to see from what hand it came. Sisera died by a woman's hand and knew it not; but Abimelech not only fell by the hand of a woman but knew it, and, when he found himself ready to breathe his last, nothing troubled him so much as this, that it should be said, A woman slew him. See, (1.) His foolish pride, in laying so much to heart this little circumstance of his disgrace. Here was no care taken about his precious soul, no concern what would become of that, no prayer to God for his mercy; but very solicitous he is to patch up his shattered credit, when there is no patching his shattered skull. "O let it never be said that such a mighty man as Abimelech was killed by a woman!" The man was dying, but his pride was alive and strong, and the same vain-glorious humour that had governed him all along appears now at last. *Qualis vita, finis ita — As was his life, such was his death.* As God punished his cruelty by the manner of his death, so he punished his pride by the instrument of it. (2.) His foolish project to avoid this disgrace; nothing could be more ridiculous; his own servant must run him through, not to rid him the sooner out of his pain, but *that men say not, A woman slew him.* Could he think that this would conceal what the woman had done, and not rather proclaim it the more? Nay, it added to the infamy of his death, for hereby he became a self-murderer. Better have it said, *A woman slew him,* than that it should be said, His servant slew him by his own order; yet now both will be said of him to his everlasting reproach. And it is observable that this very thing which Abimelech was in such care to conceal appears to have been more particularly remembered by posterity than most passages of his history; for Joab speaks of it as that which he expected David would reproach him with, for coming so *nigh the wall,* 2 Sa. 11:21. The ignominy we seek to avoid by sin we do but perpetuate the remembrance of.

III. The issue of all is that Abimelech being slain, 1. Israel's peace was restored, and an end was put to this civil war; for those that followed him *departed every man to his place, v.* 55. 2. God's justice was glorified (*v.* 56, 57): *Thus God* punished *the wickedness of Abimelech, and of the men of Shechem,* and fulfilled Jotham's curse, for it was not a *curse causeless.* Thus he preserved the honour of his government, and gave warning to all ages to expect blood for blood. *The Lord is known by the judgments which he executes,* when *the wicked is snared in the work of his own hands.* Though wickedness may prosper awhile, it will not prosper always.

CHAPTER 10

In this chapter we have, I. The peaceable times Israel enjoyed under the government of two judges, Tola and Jair (*v.* 1–5). II. The troublesome times that ensued. 1. Israel's sin that brought them into trouble (*v.* 6). 2. The trouble itself they were in (*v.* 7–9). III. Their repentance and humiliation for sin, their prayers and reformation, and the mercy they found with God thereupon (*v.* 10–16). IV. Preparation made for their deliverance out of the hand of their oppressors (*v.* 17, 18).

Verses 1–5

Quiet and peaceable reigns, though the best to live in, are the worst to write of, as yielding least variety of matter for the historian to entertain his reader with; such were the reigns of these two judges, Tola and Jair, who make but a small figure and take up but a very little room in this history. But no doubt they were both *raised up of God* to serve their country in the quality of judges, not pretending, as Abimelech had done, to the grandeur of kings, nor, like him, taking the honour they had to themselves, but being called of God to it. 1. Concerning Tola it is said that he arose after Abimelech to defend Israel, *v.* 1. After Abimelech had debauched Israel by his wickedness, disquieted and disturbed them by his restless ambition, and, by the mischiefs he brought on them, exposed them to enemies from abroad, God animated this good man to appear for the reforming of abuses, the putting down of idolatry, the appeasing of tumults, and the healing of the wounds given to the state by Abimelech's usurpation. Thus he saved them from themselves, and guarded them against their enemies. He was of the tribe of Issachar, a tribe disposed to serve, for he *bowed his shoulder to bear* (Gen. 49:14, 15), yet one of that tribe is here raised up to rule; for those that humble themselves shall be exalted. He bore the name of him that was ancestor to the first family of that tribe; of the sons of Issachar Tola was the first, Gen. 46:13; Num. 26:23. It signifies a *worm,* yet, being the name of his ancestor, he was not ashamed of it. Though he was of Issachar, yet, when he was raised up to the government, he came and dwelt in Mount Ephraim, which was more in the heart of the country, that the people might the more conveniently resort to him for judgment. He judged Israel twenty-three years (*v.* 2), kept things in good order, but did not any thing very memorable. 2. Jair was a Gileadite, so was his next successor Jephthah, both of that half tribe of the tribe of Manasseh which lay on the other side Jordan; though they seemed separated from their brethren, yet God took care, while the honour of the government was shifted from tribe to tribe and before it settled in Judah, that those who lay remote should sometimes share in it, *putting more abundant honour on that part which lacked.* Jair bore the name of a very famous man of the same tribe who in Moses's time was very active in reducing this country, Num. 32:41; Jos. 13:30. That which is chiefly remarkable concerning this Jair is the increase and honour of his family: *He had thirty sons, v.* 4. And, (1.) They had good preferments, for they *rode on thirty ass colts;* that is, they were judges itinerant, who, as deputies to their father, rode from place to place in their several circuits to administer justice. We find afterwards that Samuel made his sons judges, though he could not make them good ones, 1 Sa. 8:1–3. (2.) They had good possessions, every one a city, out of those that were called, from their ancestor of the same name with their father, *Havoth-jair — the villages of Jair;* yet they are called *cities,* either because those young gentlemen to whom they were assigned enlarged and fortified them, and so improved them into cities, or because they were as well pleased with their lot in those country towns as if they had been cities compact together and fenced with gates and bars. Villages are cities to a contented mind.

Verses 6–9

While those two judges, Tola and Jair, presided in the affairs of Israel, things went well, but afterwards,

I. Israel returned to their idolatry, that sin which did most easily beset them (*v.* 6): *They did evil again in the sight of the Lord,* from whom they were unaccountably bent to backslide, as a *foolish people and unwise.* 1. They worshipped many gods; not only their old demons Baalim and Ashtaroth, which the Canaanites had worshipped, but, as if they would proclaim their folly to all their neighbours, they served the gods of Syria, Zidon, Moab, Ammon, and the Philistines. It looks as if the chief trade of Israel had been to import deities from all countries. It is hard to say whether it was more impious or impolitic to do this. By introducing these foreign deities, they rendered themselves mean and despicable, for no nation that had any sense of honour changed their gods. Much of the wealth of Israel, we may suppose, was carried out, in offerings to the temples of the deities in the several countries whence they came, on which, as their mother-churches, their temples in Israel were expected to own their dependence; the priests and devotees of those sorry deities would follow their gods, no doubt, in crowds into the land of Israel, and, if they could not live in their own country, would take root there, and so *strangers would devour their strength.* If they did it in compliment to the neighbouring nations, and to ingratiate themselves with them, justly were they disappointed; for those nations which by their wicked arts they sought to make their friends by the righteous judgments of God became their enemies and oppressors. *In quo quis peccat, in eo punitur — Wherein a person offends, therein he shall be punished.* 2. They did not so much as admit the God of Israel to be one of those many deities they worshipped, but quite cast him off: They *forsook the Lord, and served not him* at all. Those that think to serve both God and Mammon will soon come entirely to forsake God, and to serve Mammon only. If God have not all the heart, he will soon have none of it.

II. God renewed his judgments upon them, bringing them under the power of oppressing enemies. Had they *fallen into the hands of the Lord* immediately, they might have found that *his mercies were great;* but God let them *fall into the hands of man,* whose tender mercies are cruel. He *sold them into the hands of the Philistines* that lay southwest of Canaan, and of the Ammonites that lay northeast, both at the same time; so that between those two millstones they were miserably *crushed,* as the original word is (*v.* 8) for *oppressed.* God had appointed that, if any of the cities of Israel should revolt to idolatry, the rest should make war upon them and cut them off, Deu. 13:12, etc. They had been jealous enough in this matter, almost to an extreme, in the case of the altar set up by the two tribes and a half (Jos. 22); but now they had grown so very bad that when one city was infected with idolatry the next took the infection and instead of punishing it, imitated and out-did it; and therefore, since those that should have been revengers to *execute wrath on those that did* this *evil* were themselves guilty, or *bore the sword in vain,* God brought the neighbouring nations upon them, to chastise them for their apostasy. The oppression of Israel by the Ammonites, the posterity of Lot, was, 1. Very long. It continued eighteen years. Some make those years to be part of the judgeship of Jair, who could not prevail to reform and deliver Israel as he would. Others make them to commence at the death of Jair, which seems the more probable because that part of Israel which was most infested by the Ammonites was Gilead, Jair's own country, which we cannot suppose to have suffered so much while he was living, but that part at least would be reformed and protected. 2. Very grievous. They vexed them and oppressed them. It was a great vexation to be oppressed by such a despicable people as the children of Ammon were. They began with those tribes that lay next them on the other side Jordan, here called *the land of the Amorites* (*v.* 8) because the Israelites had so wretchedly degenerated, and had made themselves so like the heathen, that they had become, in a manner, perfect Amorites (Eze. 16:3), or because by their sin they forfeited their title to this land, so that it might justly be looked upon as *the land of the Amorites* again, from whom they took it. But by degrees they pushed forward, came over Jordan, and invaded Judah, and Benjamin, and Ephraim (*v.* 9), three of the most famous tribes of Israel, yet thus insulted when they had forsaken God, and unable to make head against the invader. Now the threatening was fulfilled that they should be *slain before their enemies,* and should have *no power to stand before them,* Lev. 26:17, 37. Their *ways and their doings procure this to themselves;* they have sadly degenerated, and so they come to be sorely distressed.

Verses 10–18

Here is, I. A humble confession which Israel make to God in their distress, *v.* 10. Now they own themselves guilty, like a malefactor upon the rack, and promise reformation, like a child under the rod. They not only complain of the distress, but acknowledge it is their own sin that has brought them into the distress; therefore God is righteous, and they have no reason to repine. They confess their omissions, for in them their sin began — "We have forsaken our God," and their commissions — "We have served Baalim, and herein have done foolishly, treacherously, and very wickedly."

II. A humbling message which God thereupon sends to Israel, whether by an angel (as *ch.* 2:1) or by a prophet (as *ch.* 6:8) is not certain. It was kind that God took notice of their cry, and did not turn a deaf ear to it and send them no answer at all; it was kind likewise that when they began to repent he sent them such a message as was proper to increase their repentance, that they might be qualified and prepared for deliverance. Now in this message, 1. He upbraids them with their great ingratitude, reminds them of the great things he had done for them, delivering them from such and such enemies, the Egyptians first, out of whose land they were rescued, the Amorites whom they conquered and into whose land they entered, and since their settlement there, when the Ammonites had joined with the Moabites to oppress them (*ch.* 3:13), when the Philistines were vexatious in the days of Shamgar, and afterwards other enemies had given them trouble, upon their petition God had wrought many a great salvation for them, *v.* 11, 12. Of their being oppressed by the Zidonians and the Maonites we read not elsewhere. God had in justice corrected them, and in mercy delivered them, and therefore might reasonably expect that either through fear or through love they would adhere to him and his service. Well therefore might the word cut them to the heart (*v.* 13), "Yet *you have forsaken me* that have brought you out of your troubles and *served other gods* that brought you into your troubles." Thus did they *forsake their own mercies* for *their own delusions.* 2. He shows them how justly he might now abandon them to ruin, by abandoning them to the *gods that they had served.* To awaken them to a thorough repentance and reformation, he lets them see, (1.) Their folly in serving Baalim. They had been at a vast expense to obtain the favour of such gods as could not help them when they had most need of their help: *"Go, and cry unto the gods which you have chosen* (*v.* 14), try what they can do for you now. You have worshipped them as gods — try if they have now either a divine power or a divine goodness to be employed for you. You paid your homage to them as your kings and lords — try if they will now protect you. You brought your sacrifices of praise to their altars as your benefactors, imagining that they gave you your corn, and wine, and oil, but a friend indeed will be a friend in need; what stead will their favour stand you in now?" Note, It is necessary, in true repentance, that there be a full conviction of the utter insufficiency of all those things to help us and do us any kindness which we have idolized and set upon the throne in our hearts in competition with God. We must be convinced that the pleasures of sense on which we have doted cannot be our satisfaction, nor the wealth of the world which we have coveted be our portion, that we cannot be happy or easy any where but in God. (2.) Their misery and danger in forsaking God. "See what a pass you have brought yourselves to; now you can expect no other than that I should say, *I will deliver you no more,* and what will become of you then?" *v.* 13. This he tells them, not only as what he *might* do, but as what he *would* do if they rested in a confession of what they had done amiss, and did not put away their idols and amend for the future.

III. A humble submission which Israel hereupon made to God's justice, with a humble application to his mercy, *v.* 15. *The children of Israel met together,* probably in a solemn assembly at the door of the tabernacle, received the impressions of the message God had sent them, were not driven by it to despair, though it was very threatening, but resolve to lie at God's feet, and, if they perish, they will perish there. They not only repeat their confession, *We have sinned,* but, 1. They surrender themselves to God's justice: *Do thou unto us whatsoever seemeth good unto thee.* Hereby they own that they deserved the severest tokens of God's displeasure and were sure he could do them no wrong, whatever he laid upon them; they humbled themselves under his mighty and heavy hand, and *accepted of the punishment of their iniquity,* which Moses had made the condition of God's return in mercy to them, Lev. 26:41. Note, True penitents dare and will refer themselves to God to correct them as he thinks fit, knowing that their sin is highly malignant in its deserts, and that God is not rigorous or extreme in his demands. 2. They supplicate for God's mercy: *Deliver us only, we pray thee, this day,* from this enemy. They acknowledge what they deserved, yet pray to God not to deal with them according to their deserts. Note, We must submit to God's justice with a hope in his mercy.

IV. A blessed reformation set on foot hereupon. They brought forth fruits meet for repentance (*v.* 16): *They put away the gods of strangers* (as the word is), strange gods, and worshipped by those nations that were strangers to the commonwealth of Israel and to the covenants of promise, and they *served the Lord.* Need drove them to him. They knew it was to no purpose to go to the gods whom they had served, and therefore returned to the God whom they had slighted. This is true repentance not only for sin, but from sin.

V. God's gracious return in mercy to them, which is expressed here very tenderly (*v.* 16): *His soul was grieved for the misery of Israel.* Not that there is any grief in God (he has infinite joy and happiness in himself, which cannot be broken in upon by either the sins or the miseries of his creatures), nor that there is any change in God: he *is in one mind, and who can turn him?* But his goodness is his glory. By it he proclaims his name, and magnifies it above all names; and, as he is pleased to put himself into the relation of a father to his people that are in covenant with him, so he is pleased to represent his goodness to them by the compassions of a father towards his children; for, as he is the Father of lights, so he is the Father of mercies. As the disobedience and misery of a child are a grief to a tender father, and make him feel very sensibly from his natural affection, so the provocations of God's people are a grief to him (Ps. 95:10), he is *broken with their whorish heart* (Eze. 6:9); their troubles also are a grief to him; so he is pleased to speak when he is pleased to appear for the deliverance of his people, changing his way and method of proceeding, as tender parents when they begin to relent towards their children with whom they have been displeased. Such are the tender mercies of our God, and so far is he from having any pleasure in the death of sinners.

VI. Things are now working towards their deliverance from the Ammonites' oppression, *v.* 17, 18. God had said, "I will deliver you no more;" but now they are not what they were, they are other men, they are new men, and now he will deliver them. That threatening was denounced to convince and humble them, and, now that it had taken its desired effect, it is revoked in order to their deliverance. 1. The Ammonites are hardened to their own ruin. They gathered together in one body, that they might be destroyed at one blow, Rev. 16:16. 2. The Israelites are animated to their own rescue. They assembled likewise, *v.* 17. During their eighteen years' oppression, as in their former servitudes, they were run down by their enemies, because they would not incorporate; each family, city, or tribe, would stand by itself, and act independently, and so they all became an easy prey to the oppressors, for want of a due sense of a common interest to cement them: but, whenever they got together, they did well; so they did here. When God's Israel become as one man to advance a common good and oppose a common enemy what difficulty can stand before them? The people and princes of Gilead, having met, consult first about a general that should command in chief against the Ammonites. Hitherto most of the deliverers of Israel had an extraordinary call to the office, as Ehud, Barak, Gideon; but the next is to be called in a more common way, by a convention of the states, who enquired out a fit man to command their army, found out one admirably well qualified for the purpose, and God owned their choice by putting his Spirit upon him (*ch.* 11:29); so that this instance is of use for direction and encouragement in after-ages, when extraordinary calls are no longer to be expected. Let such be impartially chosen to public trust and power as God has qualified, and then God will graciously own those who are thus chosen.

CHAPTER 11

This chapter gives as the history of Jephthah, another of Israel's judges, and numbered among the worthies of the Old Testament, that by faith did great things (Heb. 11:32), though he had not such an extraordinary call as the rest there mentioned had. Here we have, I. The disadvantages of his origin (*v.* 1–3). II. The Gileadites' choice of him to be commander-in-chief against the Ammonites, and the terms he made with them (*v.* 4–11). III. His treaty with the king of Ammon about the rights of the two nations, that the matter might be determined, if possible, without bloodshed (*v.* 12–28). IV. His war with the Ammonites, which he enters upon with a solemn vow (*v.* 29–31), prosecutes with bravery (*v.* 32), and ends with a glorious victory (*v.* 33). V. The straits he was brought into at his return to his own house by the vow he had made (*v.* 34–40).

Verses 1–3

The princes and people of Gilead we left, in the close of the foregoing chapter, consulting about the choice of a general, having come to this resolve, that whoever would undertake to lead their forces against the children of Ammon should by common consent be head over all the inhabitants of Gilead. The enterprise was difficult, and it was fit that so great an encouragement as this should be proposed to him that would undertake it. Now all agreed that Jephthah, the Gileadite, was a mighty man of valour, and very fit for that purpose, none so fit as he, but he lay under three disadvantages: — 1. He was *the son of a harlot* (*v.* 1), of *a strange woman* (*v.* 2), one that was neither a wife nor a concubine; some think his mother was a Gentile; so Josephus, who calls him *a stranger by the mother's side.* An Ishmaelite, say the Jews. If his mother was a harlot, that was not his fault, however it was his disgrace. Men ought not to be reproached with any of the infelicities of their parentage or extraction, so long as they are endeavouring by their personal merits to roll away the reproach. The son of a harlot, if born again, born from above, shall be accepted of God, and be as welcome as any other to the glorious liberties of his children. Jephthah could not read in the law the brand there put on the Ammonites, the enemies he was to grapple with, that they should *not enter into the congregation of the Lord,* but in the same paragraph he met with that which looked black upon himself, that a bastard should be in like manner excluded, Deu. 23:2, 3. But if that law means, as most probably it does, only those that are born of incest, not of fornication, he was not within the reach of it. 2. He had been driven from his country by his brethren. His father's legitimate children, insisting upon the rigour of the law, thrust him out from having any inheritance with them, without any consideration of his extraordinary qualifications, which merited a dispensation, and would have made him a mighty strength and ornament of their family, if they had overlooked his being illegitimate and admitted him to a child's part, *v.* 2. One would not have thought this abandoned youth was intended to be Israel's deliverer and judge, but God often humbles those whom he designs to exalt, and makes that *stone the head of the corner which the builders refused;* so Joseph, Moses, and David, the three most eminent of the shepherds of Israel, were all thrust out by men, before they were called of God to their great offices. 3. He had, in his exile, headed a rabble, *v.* 3. Being driven out by his brethren, his great soul would not suffer him either to dig or beg, but by his sword he must live; and, being soon noted for his bravery, those that were reduced to such straits, and animated by such a spirit, enlisted themselves under him. *Vain men* they are here called, that is, men that had run through their estates and had to seek for a livelihood. These went out with him, not to rob or plunder, but to hunt wild beasts, and perhaps to make incursions upon those countries which Israel was entitled to, but had not as yet come to the possession of, or were some way or other injured by. This is the man that must save Israel. That people had by their idolatry made themselves children of whoredoms, and aliens from God and his covenant, and therefore, though God upon their repentance will deliver them, yet, to mortify them and remind them of their sin, he chooses to do it by a bastard and an exile.

Verses 4–11

Here is, I. The distress which the children of Israel were in upon the Ammonites' invasion of their country, *v.* 4. Probably this was the same invasion with that mentioned, *ch.* 10:17, when *the children of Ammon* were *gathered together and encamped in or against Gilead.* And those words, *in process of time,* refer to what goes immediately before of the expulsion of Jephthah; many days after he had been thus thrust out in disgrace was he fetched back again with honour.

II. The court which the elders made to Jephthah hereupon to come and help them. They did not write or send a messenger to him, but went themselves to fetch him, resolving to have no denial, and the exigence of the case was such as would admit no delay. Their errand to him was, *Come, and be our captain, v.* 6. They knew none among themselves that was able to undertake that great trust, but in effect confessed themselves unfit for it; they know him to be a bold man, and inured to the sword, and therefore he must be the man. See how God prepared men for the service he designs them for, and makes their troubles work for their advancement. If Jephthah had not been put to his shifts by his brethren's unkindness, he would not have had such occasion as this gave him to exercise and improve his martial genius, and so to signalize himself and become famous. *Out of the eater comes forth meat.* The children of Israel were assembled and encamped, *ch.* 10:17. But an army without a general is like a body without a head; therefore *Come,* say they, *and be our captain, that we may fight.* See the necessity of government; though they were hearty enough in the cause, yet they owned they could not fight without a captain to command them. So necessary is it to all societies that there be a *pars imperans* and a *pars subdita, some to rule* and *others to obey,* that any community would humbly beg the favour of being commanded rather than that every man should be his own master. Blessed be God for government, for a good government.

III. The objections Jephthah makes against accepting their offer: *Did you not hate me, and expel me? v.* 7. It should seem that his brethren were some of these elders, or these elders by suffering his brethren to abuse him, and not righting him as they ought to have done (for their business is to *defend the poor and fatherless,* Ps. 82:3, 4), had made themselves guilty of his expulsion, and he might justly charge them with it. Magistrates, that have power to protect those that are injured, if they neglect to redress their grievances are really guilty of inflicting them. "You hated me and expelled me, and therefore how can I believe that you are sincere in this proposal, and how can you expect that I should do you any service?" Not but that Jephthah was very willing to serve his country, but he thought fit to give them a hint of their former unkindness to him, that they might repent of their sin in using him so ill, and might for the future be the more sensible of their obligations. Thus Joseph humbled his brethren before he made himself known to them. The particular case between the Gileadites and Jephthah was a resemblance of the general state of the case between Israel and God at this time. They had thrust God out by their idolatries, yet in their distress begged his help; he told them how justly he might have rejected them, and yet graciously delivered them. So did Jephthah. Many slight God and good men till they come to be in distress, and then they are desirous of God's mercy and good men's prayers.

IV. Their urgency with him to accept the government they offer him, *v.* 8. "Therefore because we formerly did thee that wrong, and to show thee that we repent of it and would gladly atone for it, we *turn again to thee now,* to put such an honour upon thee as shall balance that indignity." Let this instance be, 1. A caution to us not to despise or trample upon any because they are mean, nor to be injurious to any that we have advantage against, because, whatever we think of them now, the time may come when we may have need of them, and may be glad to be beholden to them. It is our wisdom to make no man our enemy, because we know not how soon our distresses may be such as that we may be highly concerned to make him our friend. 2. An encouragement to men of worth that are slighted or ill-treated. Let them bear it with meekness and cheerfulness, and leave it to God to make their light shine out of obscurity. Fuller's remark on this story, in his "Pisgah Sight," is this: "Virtue once in an age will work her own advancement, and, when such as hate it chance to need it, they will be forced to prefer it," and then the honour will appear the brighter.

V. The bargain he makes with them. He had mentioned the injuries they had formerly done him, but, perceiving their repentance, his spirit was too great and generous to mention them any more. God had forgiven Israel the affronts they had put upon him (*ch.* 10:16), and therefore Jephthah will forgive. Only he thinks it prudent to make his bargain wisely for the future, since he deals with men that he had reason to distrust. 1. He puts to them a fair question, *v.* 9. He speaks not with too much confidence of his success, knowing how justly God might suffer the Ammonites to prevail for the further punishment of Israel; but puts an *if* upon it. Nor does he speak with any confidence at all in himself; if he do succeed, it is *the Lord that delivers them into his hand,* intending hereby to remind his countrymen to look up to God, as arbitrator of the controversy and the giver of victory, for so *he* did. "Now if, by the blessing of God, I come home a conqueror, tell me plainly *shall I be your head?* If I deliver you, under God, shall I, under him, reform you?" The same question is put to those who desire salvation by Christ. "If he save you, will you be willing that he shall rule you? for on no other terms will he save you. If he make you happy, shall he make you holy? If he be your helper, shall he be your head?" 2. They immediately give him a positive answer (*v.* 10): "We will *do according to thy words;* command us in war, and thou shalt command us in peace." They do not take time to consider of it. The case was too plain to need a debate, and the necessity too pressing to admit a delay. They knew they had power to conclude a treaty for those whom they represented, and therefore bound it with an oath, *The Lord be witness between us.* They appeal to God's omniscience as the judge of their present sincerity, and to his justice as an avenger if afterwards they should prove false. *The Lord be a hearer,* so the word is. Whatever we speak, it concerns us to remember that God is a hearer, and to speak accordingly. Thus was the original contract ratified between Jephthah and the Gileadites, which all Israel, it should seem, agreed to afterwards, for it is said (*ch.* 12:7), *he judged Israel.* He hereupon went with them (*v.* 11) to the place where they were all assembled (*ch.* 10:17), and there by common consent they *made him head and captain,* and so ratified the bargain their representatives had made with him, that he should be not only captain now, but head for life. Jephthah, to obtain this little honour, was willing to expose his life for them (*ch.* 12:3), and shall we be discouraged in our Christian warfare by any of the difficulties we may meet with in it, when Christ himself has promised *a crown of life to him that overcometh?*

VI. Jephthah's pious acknowledgment of God in this great affair (*v.* 11): *He uttered all his words before the Lord in Mizpeh,* that is, upon his elevation, he immediately retired to his devotions, and in prayer spread the whole matter before God, both his choice to the office and his execution of the office, as one that had his eye ever towards the Lord, and would do nothing without him, that leaned not to his own understanding or courage, but depended on God and his favour. He utters before God all his thoughts and cares in this matter; for God gives us leave to be free with him. 1. "Lord, the people have made me their head; wilt thou confirm the choice, and own me as thy people's head under thee and for thee?" God justly complains of Israel (Hos. 8:4), *they have set up kings, but not by me.* "Lord," said Jephthah, "I will be no head of their making without thee. I will not accept the government unless thou give me leave." Had Abimelech done this, he might have prospered. 2. "Lord, they have made me their captain, to go before them in this war with the Ammonites; shall I have thy presence? Wilt thou go before me? If not, carry me not up hence. Lord, satisfy me in the justice of the cause. Assure me of success in the enterprise." This is a rare example, to be imitated by all, particularly by great ones; in all our ways let us acknowledge God, seek his favour, ask counsel at his mouth, and take him along with us; so shall we make our way prosperous. Thus Jephthah opened the campaign with prayer. That was likely to end gloriously which began thus piously.

Verses 12–28

We have here the treaty between Jephthah, now judge of Israel, and the king of the Ammonites (who is not named), that the controversy between the two nations might, if possible, be accommodated without the effusion of blood.

I. Jephthah, as one having authority, sent to the king of Ammon, who in this war was the aggressor, to demand his reasons for invading the land of Israel: *"Why hast thou come to fight against me in my land? v.* 12. Had I come first into thy land to disturb thee in thy possession, this would have been reason enough for fighting against me, for how must force be repelled but by force? but what hast thou to do to come thus in a hostile manner into *my land?"* so he calls it, in the name both of God and Israel. Now this fair demand shows, 1. That Jephthah did not delight in war, though he was a mighty man of valour, but was willing to prevent it by a peaceable accommodation. If he could by reason persuade the invaders to retire, he would not compel them to do it by the sword. War should be the last remedy, not to be used till all other methods of ending matters in variance have been tried in vain, *ratio ultima regum — the last resource of kings.* This rule should be observed in going to law. The sword of justice, as well as the sword of war, must not be appealed to till the contending parties have first endeavoured by gentler means to understand one another, and to accommodate matters in variance, 1 Co. 6:1. 2. That Jephthah did delight in equity, and designed no other than to do justice. If the children of Ammon could convince him that Israel had done them wrong, he was ready to restore the rights of the Ammonites. If not, it was plain by their invasion that they did Israel wrong, and he was ready to maintain the rights of the Israelites. A sense of justice should guide and govern us in all our undertakings.

II. The king of the Ammonites now gives in his demand, which he should have published before he had invaded Israel, *v.* 13. His pretence is, "Israel took away my lands long since; now therefore restore those lands." We have reason to think the Ammonites, when they made this descent upon Israel, meant no other than to spoil and plunder the country, and enrich themselves with the prey, as they had done formerly under Eglon (*ch.* 3:13) when no such demand as this was made, though the matter was then fresh; but when Jephthah demanded the cause of their quarrel, and they could not for shame own what was their true intent and meaning, some old musty records were searched, or some ancient traditions enquired into, and from them this reason was drawn to serve the present turn, for a colourable pretence of equity in the invasion. Even those that do the greatest wrong yet have such a conviction in their consciences of justice that they would seem to do right. *Restore those lands.* See upon what uncertain terms we hold our worldly possessions; what we think we have the surest hold of may be challenged from us, and wrested out of our hands. Those that have got to the heavenly Canaan need not fear having their titles questioned.

III. Jephthah gives in a very full and satisfactory answer to this demand, showing it to be altogether unjust and unreasonable, and that the Ammonites had no title to this country that lay between the rivers Arnon and Jabbok, now in the possession of the tribes of Reuben and Gad. As one very well versed in the history of his country, he shows,

1. That Israel never took any land away either from the Moabites or Ammonites. He puts them together because they were brethren, the children of Lot, near neighbours, and of united interests, having the same god, Chemosh, and perhaps sometimes the same king. The lands in question Israel took away, not from the Moabites or Ammonites (they had particular orders from God not to meddle with them nor any thing they had, Deu. 2:9, 19, and religiously observed their orders), but they found them in the possession of Sihon king of the Amorites, and out of his hand they took them justly and honourably, as he will show afterwards. If the Amorites, before Israel came into that country, had taken these lands from the Moabites or Ammonites, as it should seem they had (Num. 21:26; Jos. 13:25), Israel was not concerned to enquire into that or answer for it. If the Ammonites had lost these lands and their title to them, the children of Israel were under no obligation to recover the possession for them. Their business was to conquer for themselves, not for other people. This is his first plea, "Not guilty of the trespass."

2. That they were so far from invading the property of any other nations than the devoted posterity of cursed Canaan (one of the branches of which the Amorites were, Gen. 10:16) that they would not so much as force a passage through the country either of the Edomites, the seed of Esau, or of the Moabites, the seed of Lot; but even after a very tedious march through the wilderness, with which they were sadly tired (*v.* 16), when the king of Edom first, and afterwards the king of Moab, denied them the courtesy of a way through their country (*v.* 17), rather than give them any offence or annoyance, weary as they were, they put themselves to the further fatigue of compassing both the land of Edom and that of Moab, and came not within the border of either, *v.* 18. Note, Those that behave themselves inoffensively may take the comfort of it, and plead it against those that charge them with injustice and wrong doing. Our *righteousness will answer for us in time to come*

(Gen. 30:33) and will *put to silence the ignorance of foolish men,* 1 Pt. 2:15.

3. That in that war in which they took this land out of the hands of Sihon king of the Amorites he was the aggressor, and not they, *v.* 19, 20. They sent a humble petition to him for leave to go through his land, willing to give him any security for their good behaviour in their march. *"Let us pass* (say they) *unto our place,* that is, to the land of Canaan, which is the only place we call ours, and to which we are pressing forward, not designing a settlement here." But Sihon not only denied them this courtesy, as Edom and Moab had done (had he only done so, who knows but Israel might have gone about some other way?) but he mustered all his forces, and fought against Israel (*v.* 20), not only shut them out of his own land, but would have cut them off from the face of the earth (Nub. 21:23, 24), aimed at nothing less than their ruin, *v.* 20. Israel therefore, in their war with him, stood in their own just and necessary defence, and therefore, having routed his army, might justly, in further revenge of the injury, seize his country as forfeited. Thus Israel came to the possession of this country, and doubted not to make good their title to it; and it is very unreasonable for the Ammonites to question their title, for the Amorites were the inhabitants of that country, and it was purely their land and their coasts that the Israelites then made themselves masters of, *v.* 21, 22.

4. He pleads a grant from the crown, and claims under that, *v.* 23, 24. It was not Israel (they were fatigued with their long march, and were not fit for action so soon), but it was the Lord God of Israel, who is King of nations, whose the earth is and the fulness thereof, he it was that dispossessed the Amorites and planted Israel in their room. God gave them the land by an express and particular conveyance, such as vested the title in them, which they might make good against all the world. Deu. 2:24, *I have given into thy hand Sihon and his land;* he gave it to them, by giving them a complete victory over the present occupants, notwithstanding the great disadvantages they were under. "Can you think that God gave it to us in such an extraordinary manner with design that we should return it to the Moabites or Ammonites again? No, we put a higher value upon God's favours than to part with them so easily." To corroborate this plea, he urges an argument *ad hominem — directed to the man: Wilt not thou possess that which Chemosh thy god giveth thee?* He not only appeals to the common resolutions of men to hold their own against all the world, but to the common religion of the nations, which, they thought, obliged them to make much of that which their gods gave them. Not that Jephthah thought Chemosh a god, only he is *thy god,* and the worshippers even of those dunghill deities that could do neither good nor evil yet thought themselves beholden to them for all they had (Hos. 2:12, *These are my rewards which my lovers have given me;* and see Jdg. 16:24) and made this a reason why they would hold it fast, that their gods gave it to them. "This thou thinkest a good title, and shall not we?" The Ammonites had dispossessed those that dwelt in their land before them; they thought they did it by the help of Chemosh their god, but really it was Jehovah the God of Israel that did it for them, as is expressly said, Deu. 2:19, 21. "Now," says Jephthah, "we have as good a title to our country as you have to yours." Note, One instance of the honour and respect we owe to God, as our God, is rightly to possess that which he gives us to possess, receive it from him, use it for him, keep it for his sake, and part with it when he calls for it. He has given it to us to possess, not to enjoy. He himself only must be enjoyed.

5. He pleads prescription. (1.) Their title had not been disputed when they first entered upon it, *v.* 25. "Balak who was then king of Moab, from whom the greatest part of these lands had been taken by the Amorites, and who was most concerned and best able to oppose us, if he had had any thing to object against our settlement there, yet sat still, and never offered to strive against Israel." He knew that for his own part he had fairly lost it to the Amorites and was not able to recover it, and could not but acknowledge that Israel had fairly won it of the Amorites, and therefore all his care was to secure what was left: he never pretended a title to what was lost. See Num. 22:2, 3. "He then acquiesced in God's way of disposing of kingdoms, and wilt not thou now?" (2.) Their possession had never yet been disturbed, *v.* 26. He pleads that they had kept this country as their own now about 300 years, and the Ammonites in all that time had never attempted to take it from them, no, not when they had it in their power to oppress them, *ch.* 3:13, 14. So that, supposing their title had not been clear at the first (which yet he had proved it was), yet, no claim having been made for so many generations, the entry of the children of Ammon, without doubt, was barred for ever. A title so long unquestioned shall be presumed unquestionable.

6. By these arguments Jephthah justifies himself and his own cause ("I have not sinned against thee in taking or keeping what I have no right to; if I had, I would instantly make restitution"), and condemns the Ammonites: *"Thou doest me wrong to war against me,* and must expect to speed accordingly," *v.* 27. It seems to me an evidence that the children of Israel, in the days of their prosperity and power (for some such days they had in the times of the judges) had conducted themselves very inoffensively to all their neighbours and had not been vexatious or oppressing to them (either by way of reprisal or under colour of propagating their religion), that the king of the Ammonites, when he would seek an occasion of quarrelling with them, was forced to look 300 years back for a pretence. It becomes the people of God thus to be blameless and harmless, and without rebuke.

7. For the deciding of the controversy, he puts himself upon God and his sword, and the king of Ammon joins issue with him (*v.* 27, 28): *The Lord the Judge be judge this day.* With this solemn reference of the matter to the Judge of heaven and earth he designs either to deter the Ammonites from proceeding and oblige them to retire, when they saw the right of the cause was against them, or to justify himself in subduing them if they should go on. Note, War is an appeal to heaven, to God the Judge of all, to whom the issues of it belong. If doubtful rights be disputed, he is hereby requested to determine them. If manifest rights be invaded or denied, he is hereby applied to for the vindicating of what is just and the punishing of wrong. As the sword of justice was made for lawless and disobedient persons (1 Tim. 1:9), so was the sword of war made for lawless and disobedient princes and nations. In war therefore the eye must be ever up to God, and it must always be thought a dangerous thing to desire or expect that God should patronise unrighteousness.

Neither Jephthah's apology, nor his appeal, wrought upon the king of the children of Ammon; they had found the sweets of the spoil of Israel, in the eighteen years wherein they had oppressed them (*ch.* 10:8), and hoped now to make themselves masters of the tree with the fruit of which they had so often enriched themselves. He hearkened not to the words of Jephthah, his heart being hardened to his destruction.

Verses 29–40

We have here Jephthah triumphing in a glorious victory, but, as an alloy to his joy, troubled and distressed by an unadvised vow.

I. Jephthah's victory was clear, and shines very brightly, both to his honour and to the honour of God, his in pleading and God's in owning a righteous cause. 1. God gave him an excellent spirit, and he improved it bravely, *v.* 29. When it appeared by the people's unanimous choice of him for their leader that he had so clear a call to engage, and by the obstinate deafness of the king of Ammon to the proposals of accommodation that he had so just a cause to engage in, then the Spirit of the Lord came upon him, and very much advanced his natural faculties, enduing him with power from on high, and making him more bold and more wise than ever he had been, and more fired with a holy zeal against the enemies of his people. Hereby God confirmed him in his office, and assured him of success in his undertaking. Thus animated, he loses no time, but with an undaunted resolution takes the field. Particular notice is taken of the way by which he advanced towards the enemy's camp, probably because the choice of it was an instance of that extraordinary discretion with which the Spirit of the Lord had furnished him; for those who sincerely walk after the Spirit shall be led forth the right way. 2. God gave him eminent success, and he bravely improved that too (*v.* 32): *The Lord delivered the Ammonites into his hand,* and so gave judgment upon the appeal in favour of the righteous cause, and made those feel the force of war that would not yield to the force of reason; for he *sits in the throne, judging right.* Jephthah lost not the advantages given him, but pursued and completed his victory. Having routed their forces in the field, he pursued them to their cities, where he put to the sword all he found in arms, so as utterly to disable them from giving Israel any molestation, *v.* 33. But it does not appear that he utterly destroyed the people, as Joshua had destroyed the devoted nations, nor that he offered to make himself master of the country, though their pretensions to the land of Israel might have given him colour to do so: only he took care that they should be effectually subdued. Though others' attempting wrong to us will justify us in the defence of our own right, yet it will not authorize us to do them wrong.

II. Jephthah's vow is dark, and much in the clouds. When he was going out from his own house upon this hazardous undertaking, in prayer to God for his presence with him he makes a secret but solemn vow or religious promise to God, that, if God would graciously bring him back a conqueror, whosoever or whatsoever should first come out of his house to meet him it should be devoted to God, and offered up for a burnt-offering. At his return, tidings of his victory coming home before him, his own and only daughter meets him with the seasonable expressions of joy. This puts him into a great confusion; but there was no remedy: after she had taken some time to lament her own infelicity, she cheerfully submitted to the performance of his vow. Now,

1. There are several good lessons to be learnt out of this story. (1.) That there may be remainders of distrust and doubting even in the hearts of true and great believers. Jephthah had reason enough to be confident of success, especially when he found *the Spirit of the Lord come upon him,* and yet, now that it comes to the settling, he seems to hesitate (*v.* 30): *If thou wilt without fail deliver them into my hand,* then I will do so and so. And perhaps the snare into which his vow brought him was designed to correct the weakness of his faith, and a fond conceit he had that he could not promise himself a victory unless he proffered something considerable to be given to God in lieu of it. (2.) That yet it is very good, when we are in the pursuit or expectation of any mercy, to make vows to God of some instance of acceptable service to him, not as a purchase of the favour we desire, but as an expression of our gratitude to him and the deep sense we have of our obligations to render according to the benefit done to us. The matter of such a singular vow (Lev. 27:2) must be something that has a plain and direct tendency either to the advancement of God's glory, and the interests of his kingdom among men, or to the furtherance of ourselves in his service, and in that which is antecedently our duty. (3.) That we have great need to be very cautious and well advised in the making of such vows, lest, by indulging a present emotion even of pious zeal, we entangle our own consciences, involve ourselves in perplexities, and are forced at last to *say before the angel that it was an error,* Eccl. 5:2–6. *It is a snare to a man* hastily to *devour that which is holy,* without due consideration *quid valeant humeri, quid ferre recusent — what we are able or unable to effect,* and without inserting the needful provisos and limitations which might prevent the entanglement, and then after vows to make the enquiry which should have been made before, Prov. 20:25. Let Jephthah's harm be our warning in this matter. See Deu. 23:22. (4.) That what we have solemnly vowed to God we must conscientiously perform, if it be possible and lawful, though it be ever so difficult and grievous to us. Jephthah's sense of the powerful obligation of his vow must always be ours (*v.* 35): *"I have opened my mouth unto the Lord* in a solemn vow, *and I cannot go back,"* that is, "I cannot recall the vow myself, it is too late, nor can any power on earth dispense with it, or give me up my bond." The thing was my own, and *in my own power* (Acts 5:4), but now it is not. *Vow and pay,* Ps. 76:11. We deceive ourselves if we think to mock God. If we apply this to the consent we have solemnly given, in our sacramental vows, to the covenant of grace made with poor sinners in Christ, what a powerful argument will it be against the sins we have by those vows bound ourselves out from, what a strong inducement to

the duties we have hereby bound ourselves up to, and what a ready answer to every temptation! *"I have opened my mouth to the Lord,* and *I cannot go back;* I must therefore go forward. I have sworn, and I must, I will, perform it. Let me not dare to play fast and loose with God." (5.) That it well becomes children obediently and cheerfully to submit to their parents in the Lord, and particularly to comply with their pious resolutions for the honour of God and the keeping up of religion in their families, though they be harsh and severe, as the Rechabites, who for many generations religiously observed the commands of Jonadab their father in forbearing wine, and Jephthah's daughter here, who, for the satisfying of her father's conscience, and for the honour of God and her country, yielded herself as one devoted (*v.* 36): *"Do to me according to that which hath proceeded out of thy mouth;* I know I am dear to thee, but am well content that God should be dearer." The father might disallow any vow made by the daughter (Num. 30:5), but the daughter could not disallow or disannul, no, not such a vow as this, made by the father. This magnifies the law of the fifth commandment. (6.) That our friends' grievances should be our griefs. Where she went to bewail her hard fate the virgins, her companions, joined with her in her lamentations, *v.* 38. With those of her own sex and age she used to associate, who no doubt, now that her father had on a sudden grown so great, expected, shortly after his return, to dance at her wedding, but were heavily disappointed when they were called to retire to the mountains with her and share in her griefs. Those are unworthy the name of friends that will only rejoice with us, and not weep with us. (7.) That heroic zeal for the honour of God and Israel, though alloyed with infirmity and indiscretion, is worthy to be had in perpetual remembrance. It well became the daughters of Israel by an annual solemnity to preserve the honourable memory of Jephthah's daughter, who made light even of her own life like a noble heroine, when God had taken vengeance on Israel's enemies, *v.* 36. Such a rare instance of one that preferred the public interest before life itself was never to be forgotten. Her sex forbade her to follow to the war, and so to expose her life in battle, in lieu of which she hazards it much more (and perhaps apprehended that she did so, having some intimation of his vow, and did it designedly; for he tells her, *v.* 35, *Thou hast brought me very low)* to grace his triumphs. So transported was she with the victory as a common benefit that she was willing to be herself offered up as a thank-offering for it, and would think her life well bestowed when laid down on so great an occasion. She thinks it an honour to die, not as a sacrifice of atonement for the people's sins (that honour was reserved for Christ only), but as a sacrifice of acknowledgment for the people's mercies. (8.) From Jephthah's concern on this occasion, we must learn not to think it strange if the day of our triumphs in this world prove upon some account or other the day of our griefs, and therefore must always rejoice with trembling; we hope for a day of triumph hereafter which will have no alloy.

2. Yet there are some difficult questions that do arise upon this story which have very much employed the pens of learned men. I will say but little respecting them, because Mr. Poole has discussed them very fully in his English annotations.

(1.) It is hard to say what Jephthah did to his daughter in performance of his vow. [1.] Some think he only shut her up for a nun, and that it being unlawful, according to one part of his vow (for they make it disjunctive), to offer her up for a burnt-offering, he thus, according to the other part, engaged her to *be the Lord's,* that is, totally to sequester herself from all the affairs of this life, and consequently from marriage, and to employ herself wholly in the acts of devotion all her days. That which countenances this opinion is that she is *said to bewail her virginity* (*v.* 37, 38) and that *she knew no man, v.* 39. But, if he sacrificed her, it was proper enough for her to bewail, not her death, because that was intended to be for the honour of God, and she would undergo it cheerfully, but that unhappy circumstance of it which made it more grievous to her than any other, because she was her father's only child, in whom he hoped his name and family would be built up, that she was unmarried, and so left no issue to inherit her father's honour and estate; therefore it is particularly taken notice of (*v.* 34) that besides her he had neither son nor daughter. But that which makes me think Jephthah did not go about thus to satisfy his vow, or evade it rather, is that we do not find any law, usage, or custom, in all the Old Testament, which does in the least intimate that a single life was any branch or article of religion, or that any person, man or woman, was looked upon as the more holy, more the Lord's, or devoted to him, for living unmarried: it was no part of the law either of the priests or of the Nazarites. Deborah and Huldah, both prophetesses, are both of them particularly recorded to have been married women. Besides, had she only been confined to a single life, she needed not to have desired these two months to bewail it in: she had her whole life before her to do that, if she saw cause. Nor needed she to take such a sad leave of her companions; for those that are of that opinion understand what is said in *v.* 40 of their coming to *talk with her,* as our margin reads it, four days in a year. Therefore, [2.] It seems more probable that he offered her up for a sacrifice, according to the letter of his vow, misunderstanding that law which spoke of persons devoted by the curse of God as if it were to be applied to such as were devoted by men's vows (Lev. 27:29, *None devoted shall be redeemed, but shall surely be put to death*), and wanting to be better informed of the power the law gave him in this case to redeem her. Abraham's attempt to offer up Isaac perhaps encouraged him, and made him think, if God would not accept this sacrifice which he had vowed, he would send an angel to stay his hand, as he did Abraham's. If she came out designedly to be made a sacrifice, as who knows but she might? perhaps he thought that would make the case the plainer. *Volenti non sit injuria — No injury is done to a person by that to which he himself consents.* He imagined, it may be, that where there was neither anger nor malice there was no murder, and that his good intention would sanctify this bad action; and, since he had made such a vow, he thought better to kill his daughter than break his vow, and let Providence bear the blame, that brought her forth to meet him.

(2.) But, supposing that Jephthah did sacrifice his daughter, the question is whether he did well. [1.] Some justify him in it, and think he did well, and as became one that preferred the honour of God before that which was dearest to him in this world. He is mentioned among the eminent believers who by faith did great things, Heb. 11:32. And this was one of the great things he did. It was done deliberately, and upon two months' consideration and consultation. He is never blamed for it by any inspired writer. Though it highly exalts the paternal authority, yet it cannot justify any in doing the like. He was an extraordinary person. *The Spirit of the Lord came upon him.* Many circumstances, now unknown to us, might make this altogether extraordinary, and justify it, yet not so as that it might justify the like. Some learned men have made this sacrifice a figure of Christ the great sacrifice: he was of unspotted purity and innocency, as she a chaste virgin; he was devoted to death by his Father, and so made a curse, or an anathema, for us; he submitted himself, as she did, to his Father's will: *Not as I will, but as thou wilt.* But, [2.] Most condemn Jephthah; he did ill to make so rash a vow, and worse to perform it. He could not be bound by his vow to that which God had forbidden by the letter of the sixth commandment: *Thou shalt not kill.* God had forbidden human sacrifices, so that it was (says Dr. Lightfoot) in effect a sacrifice to Moloch. And, probably, the reason why it is left dubious by the inspired penman whether he sacrificed her or no was that those who did afterwards offer their children might not take any encouragement from this instance. Concerning this and some other such passages in the sacred story, which learned men are in the dark, divided, and in doubt about, we need not much perplex ourselves; what is necessary to our salvation, thanks be to God, is plain enough.

CHAPTER 12

In this chapter we have, I. Jephthah's rencounter with the Ephraimites, and the blood shed on that unhappy occasion (*v.* 1–6), and the conclusion of Jephthah's life and government (*v.* 7). II. A short account of three other of the judges of Israel: Ibzan (*v.* 8–10), Elon (*v.* 11, 12), Abdon (*v.* 13–15).

Verses 1–7

Here Is, I. The unreasonable displeasure of the men of Ephraim against Jephthah, because he had not called them in to his assistance against the Ammonites, that they might share in the triumphs and spoils, *v.* 1. Pride was at the bottom of the quarrel. Only by that comes contention. Proud men think all the honours lost that go beside themselves, and then *who can stand before envy?* The Ephraimites had the same quarrel with Gideon (*ch.* 8:1), who was of Manasseh on their side Jordan, as Jephthah was of Manasseh on the other side Jordan. Ephraim and Manasseh were hearer akin than any other of the tribes, being both the sons of Joseph, and yet they were more jealous one of another than any other of the tribes. Jacob having crossed hands, and given Ephraim the preference, looking as far forward as the kingdom of the ten tribes, which Ephraim was the head of, after the revolt from the house of David, that tribe, not content with that honour in the promise, was displeased if Manasseh had any honour done it in the mean time. It is a pity that kindred or relationship, which should be an inducement to love and peace, should be ever an occasion (as it often proves) of strife and discord. *A brother offended is harder to be won than a strong city, and contentions among brethren are as the bars of a castle.* The anger of the Ephraimites at Jephthah was, 1. Causeless and unjust. Why *didst thou not call us to go with thee?* For a good reason. Because it was the men of Gilead that had made him their captain, not the men of Ephraim, so that he had no authority to call them. Had his attempt miscarried for want of their help, they might justly have blamed him for not desiring it. But when the work was done, and done effectually, the Ammonites being subdued and Israel delivered, there was no harm done, though their hands were not employed in it. 2. It was cruel and outrageous. They get together in a tumultuous manner, pass over Jordan as far as Mizpeh in Gilead, where Jephthah lived, and no less will satisfy their fury but they will burn his house and him in it. *Cursed be their anger, for it was fierce.* Those resentments that have the least reason for them have commonly the most rage in them. Jephthah was now a conqueror over the common enemies of Israel, and they should have come to congratulate him, and return him the thanks of their tribe for the good services he had done; but we must not think it strange if we receive ill from those from whom we deserve well. Jephthah was now a mourner for the calamity of his family upon his daughter's account, and they should have come to condole with him and comfort him; but barbarous men take a pleasure in adding affliction to the afflicted. In this world, the end of one trouble often proves the beginning of another; nor must we ever *boast as though we had put off the harness.*

II. Jephthah's warm vindication of himself. He did not endeavour to pacify them, as Gideon had done in the like case; the Ephraimites were now more outrageous than they were them, and Jephthah had not so much of a meek and quiet spirit as Gideon had. Whether they would be pacified or no, Jephthah takes care,

1. To justify himself, *v.* 2, 3. He makes it out that they had no cause at all to quarrel with him, for, (1.) It was not in pursuit of glory that he had engaged in this war, but for the necessary defence of his country, with which the children of Ammon greatly strove. (2.) He had invited the Ephraimites to come and join with him, though he neither needed them nor was under any obligation to pay that respect to them, but they had declined the service: *I called you, and you delivered me not out of their hands.* Had that been true which they charged him with, yet it would not have been a just ground of quarrel; but it seems it was false, and, as the matter of fact now appears, he had more cause to quarrel with them for deserting the common interests of Israel in a time of need. It is no new thing for those who are themselves most culpable to be most clamorous in accusing the innocent. (3.) The enterprise was very hazardous, and they had more reason to pity him than to be angry with him: *I put my life in my hands,* that is, "exposed myself to the utmost peril in what I did, having so small an army." The honour they envied was bought dearly enough; they needed not to grudge it to him; few of them would have ventured so far for it. (4.) He does not take the glory of the success to himself (that would have been invidious), but gives it all to God: *"The Lord delivered them into my hands.* If God was pleased so far to make use of me for his glory, why should you be offended at that? Have you any reason to *fight against me?* Is not

that in effect to fight against God, in whose hand I have been only an unworthy instrument?"

2. When this just answer (though not so soft an answer as Gideon's) did not prevail to turn away their wrath, he took care both to defend himself from their fury and to chastise their insolence with the sword, by virtue of his authority as Israel's judge. (1.) The Ephraimites had not only quarrelled with Jephthah, but, when his neighbours and friends appeared to take his part, they had abused them, and given them foul language; for I adhere to our translation, and so take it, *v.* 4. They said in scorn, "You Gileadites that dwell here on the other side Jordan are but fugitives of Ephraim, the scum and dregs of the tribes of Joseph, of which Ephraim is the chief, the refuse of the family, and are so accounted among the Ephraimites and among the Manassites. Who cares for you? All your neighbours know what you are, no better than fugitives and vagabonds, separated from your brethren, and driven hither into a corner." The Gileadites were as true Israelites as any other, and at this time had signalized themselves, both in the choice of Jephthah and in the war with Ammon, above all the families of Israel, and yet are most basely and unjustly called *fugitives.* It is an ill thing to fasten names or characters of reproach upon persons or countries, as is common, especially upon those that lie under outward disadvantages: it often occasions quarrels that prove of ill consequence, as it did here. See likewise what a mischievous thing an abusive tongue is, that calls ill names, and gives scurrilous language: it *sets on fire the course of nature, and is set on fire of hell* (Jam. 3:6), and many a time cuts the throat of him that uses it, as it did here, Ps. 64:8. If these Ephraimites could have denied themselves the poor satisfaction of calling the Gileadites *fugitives,* they might have prevented a great deal of bloodshed; for *grievous words stir up anger,* and who knows how great a matter a little of that fire may kindle? (2.) This affront raises the Gileadites' blood, and the indignity done to themselves, as well as to their captain, must be revenged. [1.] They routed them in the field, *v.* 4. They fought with Ephraim, and, Ephraim being but a rude unheaded rabble, smote Ephraim, and put them to flight. [2.] They cut off their retreat, and so completed their revenge, *v.* 5, 6. The Gileadites, who perhaps were better acquainted with the passages of Jordan than the Ephraimites were, secured them with strong guards, who were ordered to slay every Ephraimite that offered to pass the river. Here was, *First,* Cruelty enough in the destruction of them. Sufficient surely was *the punishment which was inflicted by many;* when they were routed in the field, there needed not this severity to cut off all that escaped. Shall the sword devour for ever? Whether Jephthah is to be praised for this I know not; perhaps he saw it to be a piece of necessary justice. *Secondly,* Cunning enough in the discovery of them. It seems the Ephraimites, though they spoke the same language with other Israelites, yet had got a custom in the dialect of their country to pronounce the Hebrew letter *Shin* like *Samech,* and they had so strangely used themselves to it that they could not do otherwise, no, not to save their lives. We learn to speak by imitation; those that first used *s* for *sh,* did it either because it was shorter or because it was finer, and their children learnt to speak like them, so that you might know an Ephraimite by it; as in England we know a west-country man or a north-country man, nay, perhaps a Shropshire man, and a Cheshire man, by his pronunciation. *Thou art a Galilean, and thy speech betrays thee.* By this the Ephraimites were discovered. If they took a man that they suspected to be an Ephraimite, but he denied it, they bade him say *Shibboleth;* but either he *could not,* as our translation reads it, or he did not heed, or frame, or direct himself, as some read, to pronounce it aright, but said *Sibboleth,* and so was known to be an Ephraimite, and was slain immediately. *Shibboleth* signifies a *river or stream:* "Ask leave to go over Shibboleth, the river." Those that were thus cut off made up the whole number of slaughtered Ephraimites forty-two thousand, *v.* 6. Thus another mutiny of that angry tribe was prevented.

3. Now let us observe the righteousness of God in the punishment of these proud and passionate Ephraimites, which in several instances answered to their sin. (1.) They were proud of the honour of their tribe, gloried in this, that they were Ephraimites; but how soon were they brought to be ashamed or afraid to own their country! *Art thou an Ephraimite?* No, now rather of any tribe than that. (2.) They had gone in a rage over Jordan to burn Jephthah's house with fire, but now they came back to Jordan as sneakingly as they had passed it furiously, and were cut off from ever returning to their own houses. (3.) They had upbraided the Gileadites with the infelicity of their country, lying at such a distance, and now they suffered by an infirmity peculiar to their own country, in not being able to pronounce *Shibboleth.* (4.) They had called the Gileadites, unjustly, fugitives, and now they really and in good earnest became fugitives themselves; and in the Hebrew the same word (*v.* 5) is used of the Ephraimites that escaped, or that fled, which they had used in scorn of the Gileadites, calling them *fugitives.* He that rolls the stone of reproach unjustly upon another, let him expect that it will justly return upon himself.

III. Here is the end of Jephthah's government. He judged Israel but six years, and then died, *v.* 7. Perhaps the death of his daughter sunk him so that he never looked up afterwards, but it shortened his days, and he went to his grave mourning.

Verses 8–15

We have here a short account of the short reigns of three more of the judges of Israel, the first of whom governed but seven years, the second ten, and the third eight. *For the transgression of a land, many are the princes thereof,* many in a short time, successively (Prov. 28:2), good men being removed in the beginning of their usefulness and by the time that they have applied themselves to their business.

I. Ibzan of Bethlehem, most probably Bethlehem of Judah, David's city, not that in Zebulun, which is only mentioned once, Jos. 19:15. He ruled but seven years, but by the number of his children, and his disposing of them all in marriage himself, it appears that he lived long; and probably the great increase of his family, and the numerous alliances he made, added to his personal merits, made him the more fit to be either chosen by the people as Jephthah was, or called of God immediately, as Gideon was, to be Israel's judge, to keep up and carry on the work of God among them. That which is remarkable concerning him is, 1. That he had many children, sixty in all, a quiver full of these arrows. Thus was Bethlehem of old famous for increase, the very city where *he* was to be born whose spiritual seed should be *as the stars of heaven.* 2. That he had an equal number of each sex, thirty sons and thirty daughters, a thing which does not often happen in the same family, yet, in the great family of mankind, he that at first made two, male and female, by his wise providence preserves a succession of both in some sort of equality as far as is requisite to the keeping up of the generations of men upon earth. 3. That he took care to marry them all. His daughters he sent abroad, *et maritis dedit,* so the vulgar Latin adds — *he provided husbands for them;* and, as it were in exchange, and both ways, strengthening his interest, he *took in thirty daughters from abroad for his sons.* The Jews say, Every father owes three things to his son: to teach him to read the law, give him a trade, and get him a wife. What a difference was there between Ibzan's family and that of his immediate predecessor Jephthah! Ibzan has sixty children and all married, Jephthah but one, a daughter, that dies or lives unmarried. Some are increased, others are diminished: both are the Lord's doing.

II. Elon of Zebulun, in the north of Canaan, was next raised up to preside in public affairs, to administer justice, and to reform abuses. Ten years he continued a blessing to Israel, and then died, *v.* 11, 12. Dr. Lightfoot computes that in the beginning of his time the forty years' oppression by the Philistines began (spoken of *ch.* 13:1), and about that time Samson was born. Probably, his residence being in the north, the Philistines who bordered upon the southern parts of Canaan took the opportunity of making incursions upon them.

III. Abdon, of the tribe of Ephraim, succeeded, and in him that illustrious tribe begins to recover its reputation, having not afforded any person of note since Joshua; for Abimelech the Shechemite was rather a scandal to it. This Abdon was famous for the multitude of his offspring (*v.* 14): he had forty sons and thirty grandsons, all of whom he lived to see grown up, and they rode on seventy ass-colts either as judges and officers or as gentlemen and persons of distinction. It was a satisfaction to him thus to see his children's children, but it is feared he did not see peace upon Israel, for by this time the Philistines had begun to break in upon them. Concerning this, and the rest of these judges that have ever so short an account given of them, yet notice is taken where they were buried (*v.* 7, 10, 12, 15), perhaps because the inscriptions upon their monuments (for such were anciently used, 2 Ki. 23:17) would serve for the confirmation and enlargement of their story, and might be consulted by such as desired further information concerning them. Peter, having occasion to speak of David, says, *His sepulchre is with us unto this day,* Acts 2:29. Or it is intended for the honour of the places where they laid their bones, but may be improved for the lessening of our esteem of all worldly glory, of which death and the grave will stain the pride. These judges, that were as gods to Israel, died like men, and all their honour was laid in the dust.

It is very strange that in the history of all these judges, some of whose actions are very particularly related, there is not so much as once mention made of the high priest, or any other priest or Levite, appearing either for counsel or action in any public affair, from Phinehas (Jdg. 20:28) to Eli, which may well be computed 250 years; only the names of the high priests at that time are preserved, 1 Chr. 6:4–7; and Ezra 7:3–5. How can this strange obscurity of that priesthood for so long a time, now in the beginning of its days, agree with that mighty splendour with which it was introduced and the figure which the institution of it makes in the law of Moses? Surely it intimates that the institution was chiefly intended to be typical, and that the great benefits that seemed to be promised by it were to be chiefly looked for in its antitype, the everlasting priesthood of our Lord Jesus, in comparison of the superior glory of which that priesthood had no glory, 2 Co. 3:10.

CHAPTER 13

At this chapter begins the story of Samson, the last of the judges of Israel whose story is recorded in this book, and next before Eli. The passages related concerning him are, from first to last, very surprising and uncommon. The figure he makes in this history is really great, and yet vastly different from that of his predecessors. We never find him at the head either of a court or of an army, never upon the throne of judgment nor in the field of battle, yet, in his own proper person, a great patriot of his country, and a terrible scourge and check to its enemies and oppressors; he was an eminent believer (Heb. 11:32) and a glorious type of him who with his own arm wrought salvation. The history of the rest of the judges commences from their advancement to that station, but Samson's begins with his birth, nay, with his conception, no less than an angel from heaven ushers him into the world, as a pattern of what should be afterwards done to John Baptist and to Christ. This is related in this chapter. I. The occasion of raising up this deliverer was the oppression of Israel by the Philistines (*v.* 1). II. His birth is foretold by an angel to his mother (*v.* 2–5). III. She relates the prediction to his father (*v.* 6, 7). IV. They both together have it again from the angel (*v.* 8–14), whom they treat with respect (*v.* 15–18), and who, to their great amazement, discovers his dignity at parting (*v.* 19–23). V. Samson is born (*v.* 24, 25).

Verses 1–7

The first verse gives us a short account, such as we have too often met with already, of the great distress that Israel was in, which gave occasion for the raising up of a deliverer. They did evil, as they had done, *in the sight of the Lord,* and then God delivered them, as he had done, into the hands of their enemies. If there had been no sin, there would have needed no Saviour; but sin was suffered to abound, that grace might much more abound. The enemies God now sold them to were the Philistines, their next neighbours, that lay among them, the first and chief of the nations which were devoted to destruction, but which God *left to prove them* (*ch.* 3:1, 3), *the five lords of the Philistines,* an inconsiderable people in comparison with Israel (they had but five cities of any note), and yet, when God made use of them as the staff in his hand, they were very oppressive and vexatious. And this trouble lasted longer than any yet: it continued forty years, though probably not always alike violent. When Israel was in this distress Samson was born; and here we have his birth foretold by an angel. Observe,

I. His extraction. He was of the tribe of Dan, *v.* 2. *Dan* signifies a *judge* or *judgment,* Gen. 30:6. And probably it was with an eye to Samson that dying Jacob foretold, *Dan shall judge his people,* that is, "he shall produce a judge for his people, though one of the sons of the handmaids, as one, as well as any one, of the tribes of Israel," Gen. 49:16. The lot of the tribe of Dan lay next to the country of the Philistines, and therefore one of that tribe was most fit to be made a bridle upon them. His parents had been long childless. Many eminent persons were born of mothers that had been kept a great while in the want of the blessing of children, as Isaac, Joseph, Samuel, and John Baptist, that the mercy might be the more acceptable when it did come. *Sing, O barren! thou that didst not bear,* Isa. 54:1. Note, Mercies long waited for often prove signal mercies, and it is made to appear that they were worth waiting for, and by them others may be encouraged to continue their hope in God's mercy.

II. The glad tidings brought to his mother, that she should have a son. The messenger was an *angel of the Lord* (*v.* 3), yet appearing as a man, with the aspect and garb of a prophet, or man of God. And this angel (as the learned bishop Patrick supposes, on *v.* 18) was the Lord himself, that is, the *Word of the Lord,* who was to be the Messiah, for his name is called *Wonderful, v.* 18, and *Jehovah, v.* 19. The great Redeemer did in a particular manner concern himself about this typical redeemer. It was not so much for the sake of Manoah and his wife, obscure Danites, that this extraordinary message was sent, but for Israel's sake, whose deliverer he was to be, and not only so (his services to Israel not seeming to answer to the grandeur of his entry) but for the Messiah's sake, whose type he was to be, and whose birth must be foretold by an angel, as his was. The angel, in the message he delivers, 1. Takes notice of her affliction: *Behold now, thou art barren and bearest not.* Hence she might gather he was a prophet, that though a stranger to her, and one she had never seen before, yet he knew this to be her grievance. He tells her of it, not to upbraid her with it, but because perhaps at this time she was actually thinking of this affliction and bemoaning herself as one written childless. God often sends in comfort to his people very seasonably, when they feel most from their troubles. "*Now* thou art barren, but thou shalt not be always so," as she feared, "nor long so." 2. He assures her that she should *conceive and bear a son* (*v.* 3) and repeats the assurance, *v.* 5. To show the power of a divine word, the strongest man that ever was was a child of promise, as Isaac, born by force and virtue of a promise, and faith in that promise, Heb. 11:11; Gal. 4:23. Many a woman, after having been long barren, has borne a son by providence, but Samson was by promise, because a figure of the promised seed, so long expected by the faith of the Old-Testament saints, 3. He appoints that the child should be a Nazarite from his birth, and therefore that the mother should be subject to the law of the Nazarites (though not under the vow of a Nazarite) and should *drink no wine or strong drink* so long as this child was to have its nourishment from her, either in the womb or at the breast, *v.* 4, 5. Observe, This deliverer of Israel must be in the strictest manner devoted to God and an example of holiness. It is spoken of as a kindness to the people that God raised up of their young men for Nazarites, Amos 2:11. Other judges had corrected their apostasies from God, but Samson must appear as one, more than any of them, consecrated to God; and, notwithstanding what we read of his faults, we have reason to think that being a Nazarite of God's making he did, in the course of his conversation, exemplify, not only the ceremony, but the substance of that *separation to the Lord* in which the Nazariteship did consist, Num. 6:2. Those that would save others must by singular piety distinguish themselves. Samuel, who carried on Israel's deliverance from the Philistines, was a Nazarite by his mother's vow (1 Sa. 1:11), as Samson by the divine appointment. The mother of this deliverer must therefore deny herself, and not eat any unclean thing; what was lawful at another time was now to be forborne. As the promise tried her faith, so this precept tried her obedience; for God requires both from those on whom he will bestow his favours. Women with child ought conscientiously to avoid whatever they have reason to think will be any way prejudicial to the health or good constitution of the fruit of their body. And perhaps Samson's mother was to refrain from wine and strong drink, not only because he was designed for a Nazarite, but because he was designed for a man of great strength, which his mother's temperance would contribute to. 4. He foretels the service which this child should do to his country: *He shall begin to deliver Israel.* Note, It is very desirable that our children may be not only devoted entirely to God themselves, but instrumental for the good of others, and the service of their generation — not recluses, candles *under a bushel,* but *on a candlestick.* Observe, *He shall begin* to deliver Israel. This intimated that the oppression of the Philistines should last long, for Israel's deliverance from it should not so much as begin, not one step be taken towards it, till this child, who was now unborn, should have grown up to a capacity of beginning it. And yet he must not complete the deliverance: he shall only *begin* to deliver Israel, which intimates that the trouble should still be prolonged. God chooses to carry on his work gradually and by several hands. One lays the foundation of a good work, another builds, and perhaps a third brings forth the top stone. Now herein Samson was a type of Christ, (1.) As a Nazarite to God, a Nazarite from the womb. For, though our Lord Jesus was not a Nazarite himself, yet he was typified by the Nazarites, as being perfectly pure from all sin, not so much as conceived in it, and entirely devoted to his Father's honour. Of the Jewish church, *as concerning the flesh, Christ came,* because to them pertained the promise of him, Rom. 9:4, 5. By virtue of that promise,. he long lay as it were in the womb of that church, which for many ages was pregnant of him, and therefore, like Samson's mother, during that pregnancy was made a holy nation and a peculiar people, and strictly forbidden to *touch any unclean thing for his sake,* who in the fulness of time was to come from them. (2.) As a deliverer of Israel; for he is Jesus a Saviour, who saves his people from their sins. But with this difference: Samson did only begin to deliver Israel (David was afterwards raised up to complete the destruction of the Philistines), but our Lord Jesus is both Samson and David too, both the *author and finisher of our faith.*

III. The report which Manoah's wife, in a transport of joy, brings in all haste to her husband, of this surprising message *v.* 6, 7. The glad tidings were brought her when she was alone, perhaps religiously employed in meditation or prayer; but she could not, she would not, conceal them from her husband, but gives him an account, 1. Of the messenger. It was a man of God, *v.* 6. His countenance she could describe; it was very awful: he had such a majesty in his looks, such a sparkling eye, such a shining face, so powerfully commanding reverence and respect, that according to the idea she had of an angel he had the very countenance of one. But his name she can give no account of, nor to what tribe or city of Israel he belonged, for he did not think fit to tell her, and, for her part, the very sight of him struck such an awe upon her that she durst not ask him. She was abundantly satisfied that he was a servant of God; his person and message she thought carried their own evidence along with them, and she enquired no further. 2. Of the message. She gives him a particular account both of the promise and of the precept (*v.* 7), that he also might believe the promise and might on all occasions be a monitor to her to observe the precept. Thus should yoke-fellows communicate to each other their experiences of communion with God, and their improvements in acquaintance with him, that they may be helpful to each other in *the way that is called holy.*

Verses 8–14

We have here an account of a second visit which the angel of God made to Manoah and his wife.

I. Manoah earnestly prayed for it, *v.* 8. He was not incredulous of the story his wife told him; he knew she was a virtuous woman, and therefore the *heart of her husband did safely trust in her;* he knew she would not go about to impose upon him, much less was he, as Josephus unworthily represents him, jealous of his wife's conversation with this stranger; but, 1. He takes it for granted that this child of promise shall in due time be given them, and speaks without hesitation of *the child that shall be born.* There was *not found so great faith,* no, not in Zechariah, a priest, then in waiting at the altar of the Lord, and to whom the angel himself appeared, as was in this honest Danite. Things hidden from the wise and prudent, who value themselves upon the niceness of their enquiries, are often revealed unto babes, who know how to prize God's gifts and to take God's word. *Blessed are those that have not seen and yet,* as Manoah here, *have believed.* 2. All his care is *what they should do to the child* that should be born. Note, Good men are more solicitous and desirous to know the duty that is to be done by them than to know the events that shall occur concerning them; for duty is ours, events are God's. Solomon enquires concerning the good men should *do,* not the good they should *have,* Eccl. 2:3. 3. He therefore prays to God to send the same blessed messenger again, to give them further instructions concerning the management of this Nazarite, fearing lest his wife's joy for the promise might have made her forget some part of the precept, in which he was desirous to be fully informed, and lie under no mistake: *"Lord, let the man of God come again unto us,* for we desire to be better acquainted with him." Note, Those that have heard from heaven cannot but wish to hear more thence, again and again to meet with the man of God. Observe, He does not go or send his servants abroad, to find out this man of God, but seeks him upon his knees, prays to God to send him, and, thus seeking, finds him. Would we have God's messengers, the ministers of his gospel, to bring a word proper for us, and for our instruction? *Entreat the Lord* to send them to us, to teach us, Rom. 15:30, 32.

II. God graciously granted it: *God hearkened to the voice of Manoah, v.* 9. Note, God will not fail some way or other to guide those by his counsel that are sincerely desirous to know their duty, and apply themselves to him to teach them, Ps. 25:8, 9.

1. The angel appears the second time also to the wife, when she is sitting alone, probably tending the flocks, or otherwise well employed in the field where she has retired. Solitude is often a good opportunity of communion with God; good people have thought themselves never less alone than when alone, if God be with them.

2. She goes in all haste to call her husband, doubtless humbly beseeching the stay of this blessed messenger till she should return and her husband with her, *v.* 10, 11. She did not desire him to go with her to her husband, but would fetch her husband to him. Those that would meet with God must attend where he is pleased to manifest himself. "Oh," says she, overjoyed, "my dear love, thy prayers are answered — yonder is the man of God, come to make us another visit — he that came the other day," or, as some read it, *this* day, for *other* is not in the original, and it is probable enough that both these visits were on the same day, and at the same place, and that the second time she sat expecting him. The man of God is very willing she should call her husband, Jn. 4:16. Those that have an acquaintance with the things of God themselves should invite others to the same acquaintance, Jn. 1:45, 46. Manoah is not disgusted that the angel did not this second time appear to him, but very willingly goes after his wife to the man of God. To atone (as it were) for the first fatal miscarriage, when Eve earnestly pressed Adam to that which was evil, and he too easily yielded to her, let yoke-fellows excite one another to love and good works; and, if the wife will lead, let not the husband think it any disparagement to him to follow her in that which is virtuous and praiseworthy.

3. Manoah having come to the angel, and being satisfied by him that he was the same that had appeared to his wife, does, with all humility, (1.) Welcome the promise (*v.* 12): *Now let thy words come to pass;* this was the language, not only of his desire, but of his faith, like that of the blessed Virgin, Lu. 1:38. *"Be it according to thy word.* Lord, I lay hold on what thou hast said, and depend upon it; *let it come to pass."* (2.) Beg that the prescriptions given might be repeated: *How shall we order the child?* The directions were given to his wife, but he looks upon himself as concerned to assist her in the careful management of this promised seed, according to order; for the utmost care of both the parents, and their constant joint endeavour, are little enough to be engaged for the good ordering of children that are devoted to God and to be brought up for him. Let not one devolve it on the other, but both do their best. Observe from Manoah's enquiry, [1.] In general, that, when God is pleased to bestow any mercy upon us, our great care must be how to use it well, and as we ought, because it is then only a mercy indeed when it is rightly managed. God has given us bodies, souls, estates; how shall we order them, that we may answer the intent of the donor, and give a good account of them? [2.] In particular, those to whom God has given children must be very careful how they order them, and what they do unto them, that they may drive out the foolishness that is *bound up in their hearts,* form their minds and manners well betimes,

and *train them in the way wherein they should go.* Herein pious parents will beg divine assistance. "Lord, teach us how we may order our children, that they may be Nazarites, and living sacrifices to thee."

4. The angel repeats the directions he had before given (*v.* 13, 14): *Of all* that I forbad *let her beware;* and *all that I commanded her let her observe.* Note, There is need of a good deal both of caution and observation, for the right ordering both of ourselves and of our children. Beware and observe; take heed not only of drinking *wine* or *strong drink,* but of *eating any thing that cometh of the vine.* Those that would preserve themselves pure must keep at a distance from that which borders upon sin or leads to it. When she was with child of a Nazarite, she must not eat *any unclean thing;* so those *in whom Christ is formed* must carefully *cleanse themselves from all filthiness of flesh and spirit,* and do nothing to the prejudice of that new man.

Verses 15–23

We have here an account,

I. Of what further passed between Manoah and the angel at this interview. It was in kindness to him that while the angel was with him it was concealed from him that he was an angel; for, had he known it, it would have been such a terror to him that he durst not have conversed with him as he did (*v.* 16): *He knew not that he was an angel.* So Christ *was in the world, and the world knew him not. Verily thou art a God that hidest thyself.* We could not bear the sight of the divine glory unveiled. God having determined to speak to us by men like ourselves, prophets and ministers, even when he spoke by his angels, or by his Son, they appeared in the likeness of men, and were taken but for men of God. Now,

1. The angel declined to accept his treat, and appointed him to turn it into a sacrifice. Manoah, being desirous to show some token of respect and gratitude to this venerable stranger who had brought them these glad tidings, begged he would take some refreshment with him (*v.* 15): We will soon *make ready a kid for thee.* Those that welcome the message will be kind to the messengers for his sake that sends them, 1 Th. 5:13. But the angel told him (*v.* 16) he would *not eat of his bread,* any more than he would of Gideon's, but, as there, directed him to offer it to God, *ch.* 6:20, 21. Angels need not meat nor drink; but the glorifying of God is their meat and drink, and it was Christ's, Jn. 4:34. And we in some measure do the will of God as they do it if, though we cannot live without meat and drink, yet we eat and drink to the glory of God, and so turn even our common meals into sacrifices.

2. The angel declined telling him his name, and would not so far gratify his curiosity. Manoah desired to know his name (*v.* 17), and of what tribe he was, not as if he doubted the truth of his message, but that they might return his visit, and be better acquainted with him (it is good to increase and improve our acquaintance with good men and good ministers); and he has a further design: *"That when thy sayings come to pass, we may do thee honour,* celebrate thee as a true prophet, and recommend others to thee for divine instructions, — that we may call the child that shall be born after thy name, and so do thee honour, — or that we may send thee a present, honouring one whom God has honoured." But the angel denies his request with something of a check to his curiosity (*v.* 18): *Why askest thou thus after my name?* Jacob himself could not prevail for this favour, Gen. 32:29. Note, We have not what we ask when we ask we know not what. Manoah's request was honestly meant and yet was denied. God told Moses his name (Ex. 3:13, 14), because there was a particular occasion for his knowing it, but here there was no occasion. What Manoah asked for instruction in his duty he was readily told (*v.* 12, 13), but what he asked to gratify his curiosity was denied. God has in his word given us full directions concerning our duty, but never designed to answer all the enquiries of a speculative head. He gives him a reason for his refusal: *It is secret.* The names of angels were not as yet revealed, to prevent the idolizing of them. After the captivity, when the church was cured of idolatry, angels made themselves known to Daniel by their names, Michael and Gabriel; and to Zacharias the angel told his name unasked (Lu. 1:19): *I am Gabriel.* But here it is *secret,* or it is *wonderful,* too wonderful for us. One of Christ's names is *Wonderful,* Isa. 9:6. His name was long a secret, but by the gospel it is brought to light: *Jesus a Saviour.* Manoah must not ask because he must not know. Note, (1.) There are secret things which belong not to us, and which we must content ourselves to be in the dark about while we are here in this world. (2.) We must therefore never indulge a vain curiosity in our enquiries concerning these things, Col. 2:18. *Nescire velle quae Magister maximus docere non vult erudita inscitia est — To be willingly ignorant of those things which our great Master refuses to teach us is to be at once ignorant and wise.*

3. The angel assisted and owned their sacrifice, and, at parting, gave them to understand who he was. He had directed them to offer their burnt-offering to the Lord, *v.* 16. Praises offered up to God are the most acceptable entertainment of the angels; see Rev. 22:9, *worship God.* And Manoah, having so good a warrant, though he was no priest and had no altar, turned his meat into a meat offering, and *offered it upon a rock to the Lord* (*v.* 19), that is, he brought and laid it to be offered. "Lord, here it is, do what thou pleasest with it." Thus we must bring our hearts to God as living sacrifices, and submit them to the operation of his Spirit. All things being now ready, (1.) *The angel did wondrously,* for his name was *Wonderful.* Probably the wonder he did was the same with what he had done for Gideon, he made fire to come either down from heaven or up out of the rock to consume the sacrifice. (2.) He ascended up towards heaven *in the flame of the sacrifice, v.* 20. By this it appeared that he was not, as they thought, a mere man, but a messenger immediately from heaven. Thence certainly he descended, for thither he ascended, Jn. 3:13; 6:62. This signified God's acceptance of the offering and intimates to what we owe the acceptance of all our offerings, even to the mediation of the angel of the covenant, that other angel, who puts *much incense to the prayers of saints* and *so offers them before the throne,* Rev. 8:3. Prayer is the ascent of the soul to God. But it is Christ in the heart by faith that makes it an offering of a sweet-smelling savour: without him our services are offensive smoke, but, in him, acceptable flame. We may apply it to Christ's sacrifice of himself for us; he ascended in the flame of his own offering, for *by his own blood he entered in once into the holy place,* Heb. 9:12. While the angel did this, it is twice said (*v.* 19, 20) *that Manoah and his wife looked on.* This is a proof of the miracle: the matter of fact was true, for out of the mouth of these two eyewitnesses the report of it is established. The angel did all that was done in the sacrifice; they did but look on; yet doubtless, when the angel ascended towards heaven, their hearts ascended with him in thanksgiving for the promise which came thence and in expectation of the performance to come thence too. Yet, when the angel has ascended, they dared not, as those that were the witnesses of Christ's ascension, stand gazing up into heaven, but in holy fear and reverence they fell on their faces to the ground. And now, [1.] They *knew that it was an angel, v.* 21. It was plain it was not the body of a man they saw, since it was not chained to the earth, nor prejudiced by fire; but ascended, and ascended in flame, and therefore with good reason they conclude it was an angel; for he *maketh his angels spirits, and his ministers a flame of fire.* [2.] But he did not any more appear to them; it was for a particular occasion, now over, that he was sent, not to settle a constant correspondence, as with prophets. They must remember and observe what the angel had said and not expect to hear more.

II. We have an account of the impressions which this vision made upon Manoah and his wife. While the angel did wondrously, they looked on, and said nothing (so it becomes us carefully to observe the wondrous works of God, and to be silent before him); but when he had gone, having finished his work, they had time to make their reflections. 1. In Manoah's reflection upon it there is *great fear, v.* 22. He had spoken with great assurance of the son they should shortly be the joyful parents of (*v.* 8, 12), and yet is now put into such a confusion by that very thing which should have strengthened and encouraged his faith that he counts upon nothing but their being both cut off immediately: *We shall surely die.* It was a vulgar opinion generally received among the ancient Jews that it was present death to see God or an angel; and this notion quite overcome his faith for the present, as it did Gideon's, *ch.* 6:22. 2. In his wife's reflection upon it there is great faith, *v.* 23. Here the weaker vessel was the stronger believer, which perhaps was the reason why the angel chose once and again to appear to her. Manoah's heart began to fail him, but his wife, as a help meet for him, encouraged him. Two are better than one, for, if one fall into dejections and despondencies, the other will help to raise him up. Yoke-fellows should piously assist each other's faith and joy as there is occasion. None could argue better than Manoah's wife does here: *We shall surely die,* said her husband; "Nay," said she, "we need not fear that; let us never turn that against us which is really for us. We shall not die unless God be pleased to kill us: our death must come from his hand and his pleasure. Now the tokens of his favour which we have received forbid us to think that he designs our destruction. Had he thought fit to kill us, (1.) He would not have accepted our sacrifice, and signified to us his acceptance of it by *turning it to ashes,* Ps. 20:3, *margin.* The sacrifice was the ransom of our lives, and the fire fastening upon that was a plain indication of the turning away of his wrath from us. The sacrifice of the wicked is an abomination, but you see ours is not so. (2.) He would not have shown us all these things, these strange sights, now at a time when there is little or no open vision (1 Sa. 3:1), nor would he have given these exceedingly great and precious promises of a son that shall be a Nazarite and a deliverer of Israel — he would not have told us such things as these if he had been pleased to kill us. We need not fear the withering of those roots out of which such a branch is yet to spring." Note, Hereby it appears that God designs not the death of sinners that he has accepted the great sacrifice which Christ offered up for their salvation, has put them in a way of obtaining his favour, and has assured them of it upon their repentance. Had he been pleased to kill them, he would not have done so. And let those good Christians who have had communion with God in the word and prayer, to whom he has graciously manifested himself, and who have had reason to think God has accepted their works, take encouragement thence in a cloudy and dark day. "God would not have done what he has done for my soul if he had designed to forsake me, and leave me to perish at last; for his work is perfect, nor will he mock his people with his favours." Learn to reason as Manoah's wife did, "If God had designed me to perish under his wrath, he would not have given me such distinguishing tokens of his favour." *O woman! great is thy faith.*

Verses 24–25

Here is, 1. Samson's birth. The woman that had been long barren bore a son, according to the promise; for no word of God shall fall to the ground. Hath he spoken, and shall he not make it good? 2. His name, *Samson,* has been derived by some, from *Shemesh, the sun,* turned into a diminutive, *sol exiguus — the sun in miniature,* perhaps because, being born like Moses to be a deliverer, he was like him exceedingly fair, his face shone like a little sun; or his parents so named him in remembrance of the shining countenance of that man of God who brought them the notice of him; though they knew not his name, yet thus, now that his sayings had come to pass, they did him honour. A little sun, because a Nazarite born (for the Nazarites were as *rubies* and *sapphires,* Lam. 4:7, and because of his great strength. The sun is compared to a *strong man* Ps. 19:5); why should not a strong man then be compared to the sun when he goes forth in his strength? A little sun, because the glory of, and a light to, his people Israel, a type of Christ, the Sun of righteousness. 3. His childhood. He grew more than is usual in strength and stature, far out-grew other children of his age; and not in that only, but in other instances, it appeared that the Lord blessed him, qualified him, both in body and mind, for something great and extraordinary. Children of promise shall have the blessing. 4. His youth. When he grew up a little *the Spirit of the Lord began to move him, v.* 25. This was an evidence that the Lord blessed him. Where God gives his blessing he gives his Spirit to qualify for the blessing. Those are blessed indeed in whom the Spirit of grace begins to work betimes, in the days of their childhood. If the *Spirit be poured out upon our offspring,* they will spring up as *willows by the water courses,* Isa. 44:3, 4. The Spirit of God moved Samson in the camp of Dan, that is, in the general muster of the trained bands of that tribe, who probably had formed a camp between Zorah and Eshtaol, near the place where he lived, to oppose the incursions of the Philistines; there Samson, when a child, appeared among them, and signalized himself by some very brave actions, excelling them all in manly exercises and trials of strength: and probably he showed himself more than ordinarily zealous against the enemies of his country, and discovered more of a public spirit than could be expected in a child. The Spirit moved him *at times,* not at all times, but as the wind blows, when he listed, to show that what he did was not from himself, for then he could have done it at any time. Strong men think themselves greatly animated by wine (Ps. 78:65), but Samson drank no wine, and yet excelled in strength and courage, and every thing that was bold and brave, for he had the Spirit of God moving him; therefore *be not drunk with wine, but be filled with the Spirit,* who will come to those that are sober and temperate.

CHAPTER 14

The idea which this chapter gives us of Samson is not what one might have expected concerning one who, by the special designation of heaven, was a Nazarite to God and a deliverer of Israel; and yet really he was both. Here is, I. Samson's courtship of a daughter of the Philistines, and his marriage to her (*v.* 1–5, 7, 8). II. His conquest of a lion, and the prize he found in the carcase of it (*v.* 5, 6, 8, 9). III. Samson's riddle proposed to his companions (*v.* 10–14) and unriddled by the treachery of his wife (*v.* 15–18). IV. The occasion this gave him to kill thirty of the Philistines (*v.* 19) and to break off his new alliance (*v.* 20).

Verses 1–9

Here, I. Samson, under the extraordinary guidance of Providence, seeks an occasion of quarrelling with the Philistines, by joining in affinity with them — a strange method, but the truth is Samson was himself a riddle, a paradox of a man, did that which was really great and good, by that which was seemingly weak and evil, because he was designed not to be a pattern to us (who must walk by rule, not by example), but a type of him who, though he knew no sin, was made sin for us, and appeared *in the likeness of sinful flesh,* that he might *condemn* and *destroy sin in the flesh,* Rom. 8:3.

1. As the negotiation of Samson's marriage was a common case, we may observe, (1.) That is was weakly and foolishly done of him to set his affections upon a daughter of the Philistines; the thing appeared very improper. Shall one that is not only an Israelite, but a Nazarite, devoted to the Lord, covet to become one with a worshipper of Dagon? Shall one marked for a patriot of his country match among those that are its sworn enemies? He saw this woman (*v.* 1), and she *pleased him well, v.* 3. It does not appear that he had any reason to think her wise or virtuous, or in any way likely to be a help-meet for him; but he saw something in her face that was very agreeable to his fancy, and therefore nothing will serve but she must be his wife. He that in the choice of a wife is guided only by his eye, and governed by his fancy, must afterwards thank himself if he find a Philistine in his arms. (2.) Yet it was wisely and well done not to proceed so much as to make his addresses to her till he had first made his parents acquainted with the matter. He told them, and desired them to *get her for him to wife, v.* 2. Herein he is an example to all children. Conformably to the law of the fifth commandment, children ought not to marry, nor to move towards marrying, without the advice and consent of their parents; those that do (as bishop Hall here expresses it) *wilfully unchild themselves, and exchange natural affections for violent.* parents have a property in their children as parts of themselves. In marriage this property is transferred; for such is the law of the relation that *a man shall leave his father and his mother and cleave to his wife.* It is therefore not only unkind and ungrateful, but very unjust, to alienate this property without their concurrence; whoso thus *robbeth his father or mother,* stealing himself from them, who is nearer and dearer to them than their goods, *and* yet *saith, It is no transgression, the same is the companion of a destroyer,* Prov. 28:24. (3.) His parents did well to dissuade him from yoking himself thus unequally with unbelievers. Let those who profess religion, but are courting an affinity with the profane and irreligious, matching into families where they have reason to think the fear of God is not, nor the worship of God, let them hear their reasoning, and apply it to themselves: *"Is there never a woman among the daughters of thy brethren,* or, if none of our tribe, *never a one among all thy people,* never an Israelite, that pleases thee, or that thou canst think worthy of thy affection, that thou shouldest marry a Philistine?" In the old world the sons of God corrupted and ruined themselves, their families, and that truly primitive church, by marrying with the *daughters of men,* Gen. 6:2. God had forbidden the people of Israel to marry with the devoted nations, one of which the Philistines were, Deu. 7:3. (4.) If there had not been a special reason for it, it certainly would have been improper in him to insist upon his choice, and in them to agree to it at last. Yet their tender compliance with his affections may be observed as an example to parents not to be unreasonable in crossing their children's choices, nor to deny their consent, especially to those that have seasonably and dutifully asked it, without some very good cause. As children must *obey their parents in the Lord,* so parents must not *provoke their children to wrath, lest they be discouraged.* This Nazarite, in his subjection to his parents, asking their consent, and not proceeding till he had it, was not only an example to all children, but a type of the holy child Jesus, who *went down with his parents to Nazareth* (thence called a *Nazarene)* and was subject to them, Lu. 2:51.

2. But this treaty of marriage is expressly said to be *of the Lord, v.* 4. Not only that God afterwards overruled it to serve his designs against the Philistines, but that he put it into Samson's heart to make this choice, that he *might have occasion against the Philistine.* It was not a thing evil in itself for him to marry a Philistine. It was forbidden because of the danger of receiving hurt by idolaters; where there was not only no danger of that kind, but an opportunity hoped for of doing that hurt to them which would be good service to Israel, the law might well be dispense with. It was said (*ch.* 13:25) that *the Spirit of the Lord began to move him at times,* and we have reason to think he himself perceived that Spirit to move him at this time, when he made this choice, and that otherwise he would have yielded to his parents' dissuasives, nor would they have consented at last if he had not satisfied them it was *of the Lord.* This would bring him into acquaintance and converse with the Philistines, by which he might have such opportunities of galling them as otherwise he could not have. It should seem, the way in which the Philistines oppressed Israel was, not by great armies, but by the clandestine incursions of their giants and small parties of their plunderers. In the same way therefore Samson must deal with them; let him but by this marriage get among them, and he would be a *thorn in their sides.* Jesus Christ, having to deliver us from this present evil world, and to cast out the prince of it, did himself visit it, though full of pollution and enmity, and, by assuming a body, did in some sense join in affinity with it, that he might destroy our spiritual enemies, and his own arm might work the salvation.

II. Samson, by a special providence, is animated and encouraged to attack the Philistines. That being the service for which he was designed, God, when he called him to it, prepared him for it by two occurrences: —

1. By enabling him, in one journey to Timnath, to *kill a lion, v.* 5, 6. Many decline doing the service they might do because they *know not their own strength.* God let Samson know what he could do in the strength of the *Spirit of the Lord,* that he might never be afraid to look the greatest difficulties in the face. David, who was to complete the destruction of the Philistines, must try his hand first upon *a lion and a bear,* that thence he might infer, as we may suppose Samson did, that the uncircumcised Philistine should be as one of them, 1 Sa. 17:36. (1.) Samson's encounter with the lion was hazardous. It was a young lion, one of the fiercest sort, that set upon him, roaring for his prey, and setting his eye particularly upon him; *he roared in meeting him,* so the word is. He was all alone in the vineyards, whither he had rambled from his father and mother (who kept the high road), probably to eat grapes. Children consider not how they expose themselves to the roaring lion that seeks to devour when, out of a foolish fondness for liberty, they wander from under the eye and wing of their prudent pious parents. Nor do young people consider what lions lurk in the vineyards, the vineyards of red wines, as dangerous as snakes under the green grass. Had Samson met with this lion in the way, he might have had more reason to expect help both from God and man than here in the solitary vineyards, out of his road. But there was a special providence in it, and the more hazardous the encounter was, (2.) The victory was so much the more illustrious. It was obtained without any difficulty: he strangled the lion, and tore his throat as easily as he would have strangled a kid, yet without any instrument, not only no sword nor bow, but not so much as a staff or knife; he had *nothing in his hand.* Christ engaged the roaring lion, and conquered him in the beginning of his public work (Mt. 4:1, etc.), and afterwards spoiled principalities and powers, triumphing over them *in himself,* as some read it, not by any instrument. He was *exalted in his own strength.* That which added much to the glory of Samson's triumph over the lion was that when he had done this great exploit he did not boast of it, did *not so much as tell his father nor mother* that which many a one would soon have published through the whole country. Modesty and humility make up the brightest crown of great performances.

2. By providing him, the next journey, with honey in the carcase of this lion, *v.* 8, 9. When he came down the next time to solemnize his nuptials, and his parents with him, he had the curiosity to turn aside into the vineyard where he had killed the lion, perhaps that with the sight of the place he might affect himself with the mercy of that great deliverance, and might there solemnly give thanks to God for it. It is good thus to *remind ourselves* of God's former favours to us. There he found the carcase of the lion; the birds or beasts of prey, it is likely, had eaten the flesh, and in the skeleton a swarm of bees had knit, and made a hive of it, and had not been idle, but had there laid up a good stock of honey, which was one of the staple commodities of Canaan; such plenty there was of it that the land is said to *flow with milk and honey.* Samson, having a better title than any man to the hive, seizes the honey with his hands. This supposes an encounter with the bees; but he that dreaded not lion's paws had no reason to fear *their* stings. As by his victory over the lion he was emboldened to encounter the Philistine-giants, if there should be occasion, notwithstanding their strength and fierceness, so by dislodging the bees he was taught not to fear the multitude of the Philistines; though they *compassed him about like bees, yet in the name of the Lord he should destroy them,* Ps. 118:12. Of the honey he here found, (1.) He ate himself, asking no questions for conscience' sake; for the dead bones of an unclean beast had not that ceremonial pollution in them that the bones of a man had. John Baptist, that Nazarite of the New Testament, lived upon wild honey. (2.) He gave to his parents, and they did eat; he did not eat all himself. *Hast thou found honey? eat so much as is sufficient for thee,* and no more, Prov. 25:16. He let his parents share with him. Children should be grateful to their parents with the fruits of their own industry, and so *show piety at home,* 1 Tim. 5:4. Let those that by the grace of God have found sweetness in religion themselves communicate their experience to their friends and relations, and invite them to come and share with them. He told not his parents whence he had it, lest they should scruple eating it. Bishop Hall observes here that *those are less wise and more scrupulous than Samson that decline the use of God's gifts because they find them in ill vessels.* Honey is hone still, though in a dead lion. Our Lord Jesus having conquered Satan, that roaring lion, believers find honey in the carcase, abundant strength and satisfaction, enough for themselves and for all their friends, from that victory.

Verses 10–20

We have here an account of Samson's wedding feast and the occasion it gave him to fall foul upon the Philistines.

I. Samson conformed to the custom of the country in making a festival of his nuptial solemnities, which continued seven days, *v.* 10. Though he was a Nazarite, he did not affect, in a thing of this nature, to be singular, but did *as the young men used to do* upon such occasions. It is no part of religion to go contrary to the innocent usages of the places where we live: nay, it is a reproach to religion when those who profess it give just occasion to others to call them covetous, sneaking, and morose. A good man should strive to make himself, in the best sense, a good companion.

II. His wife's relations paid him the accustomed respect of the place upon that occasion, and brought him thirty young men to keep him company during the solemnity, and to attend him as his grooms-men (*v.* 11): *When they saw him,* what a comely man he was, and what an ingenuous graceful look he had, they brought him these to do him honour, and to improve by his conversation while he staid among them. Or, rather, when they saw him, what a strong stout man he was, they brought these, seemingly to be his companions, but really to be a guard upon him, or spies to observe him. Jealous enough they were of him, but would have been more so had they known of his victory over the lion, which therefore he had industriously concealed. The favours of Philistines have often some mischief or other designed in them.

III. Samson, to entertain the company, propounds a riddle to them, and lays a wager with them that they cannot find it out in seven days, *v.* 12–14. The usage, it seems, was very ancient upon such occasions, when friends were together, to be innocently merry, not to spend all the time in dull eating and drinking, as bishop Patrick expresses it, or in other gratifications of sense, as music, dancing, or shows, but to propose questions, by which their learning and ingenuity might be tried and improved. This becomes men, wise men, that value themselves by their reason; but very unlike to it are the infamous and worse than brutish entertainments of this degenerate age, which send nothing round but the glass and the health, till reason is drowned, and wisdom sunk. Now, 1. Samson's riddle was his own invention, for it was his own achievement that gave occasion for it: *Out of the eater came forth meat, and out of the strong came forth sweetness.* Read my riddle, what is this? Beasts of prey do not yield meat for man, yet *food came from the devourer;* and those creatures that are strong when they are alive commonly smell strong and are every way offensive when they are dead, as horses, and yet *out of the strong,* or out of *the bitter,* so the Syriac and Arabic read it, *came sweetness.* If they had but so much sense as to consider what eater is most strong, and what meat is most sweet, they would have found out the riddle, and neither lions nor honey were such strangers to their country that the thoughts of them needed to be out of the way; and the solving of the riddle would have given him occasion to tell them the entertaining story on which it was founded. This riddle is applicable to many of the methods of divine providence and grace. When God, by an overruling providence, brings good out of evil to his church and people, — when that which threatened their ruin turns to their advantage, — when their enemies are made serviceable to them, and the wrath of men turns to God's praise, — then comes *meat out of the eater* and *sweetness out of the strong.* See Phil. 1:12. 2. His water was more considerable to him than to them, because he was one against thirty partners. It was not a wager laid upon God's providence, or upon the chance of a die or a card, but upon their ingenuity, and amounted to no more than an honorary recompence of wit and a disgrace upon stupidity.

IV. His companions, when they could not expound the riddle themselves, obliged his wife to get from him the exposition of it, *v.* 15. Whether they were really of a dull capacity, or whether under a particular infatuation at this time, it was strange that none of the thirty could in all this time stumble upon so plain a thing as that, *What is sweeter than honey* and *what stronger than a lion?* It should seem that in wit, as well as manners, they were barbarous — barbarous indeed to threaten the bride that, if she would not use means with the bridegroom to let them into the meaning of it, they would *burn her and her father's house with fire.* Could any thing be more brutish? It was base enough to turn a jest into earnest, and those were unworthy of conversation that would grow so outrageous rather than confess their ignorance and lose so small a wager; nor would it save their credit at all to tell the riddle when they were told it. It was yet more villainous to engage Samson's wife to be a traitor to her own husband, and to pretend a greater interest in her than he had. Now that she was married she must *forget her own people.* Yet most inhuman of all was it to threaten, if she could not prevail, to burn her and all her relations with fire, and all for fear of losing each of them the value of a shirt and a coat: *Have you called us to take what we have?* Those must never lay wagers that cannot lose more tamely and easily than thus.

V. His wife, by unreasonable importunity, obtains from him a key to his riddle. It was *on the seventh day,* that is, the seventh day of the week (as Dr. Lightfoot conjectures), but the fourth day of the feast, that they solicited her to entice her husband (*v.* 15), and she did it, 1. With great art and management (*v.* 16), resolving not to believe he loved her, unless he would gratify her in this thing. She knew he could not bear to have his love questioned, and therefore, if any thing would work upon him, that would: *"Thou dost but hate me, and lovest me not,* if thou deniest me;" whereas he had much more reason to say, "Thou dost but *hate me,* and *lovest me not,* if thou insistest on it." And, that she might not make this the test of his affection, he assures her he had not told his own parents, notwithstanding the confidence he reposed in them. If this prevail not, she will try the powerful eloquence of tears: she *wept before him* the rest of *the days of the feast,* choosing rather to mar the mirth, as the bride's tears must needs do, than not gain her point, and oblige her countrymen, *v.* 17. 2. With great success. At last, being quite wearied with her importunity, he told her what was the meaning of his riddle, and though we may suppose she promised secresy, and that if he would but let her know she would tell nobody, she immediately told it to the *children of her people;* nor could he expect better from a Philistine, especially when the interests of her country were ever so little concerned. See Mic. 7:5, 6. The riddle is at length *unriddled* (*v.* 18): *What is sweeter than honey,* or a better meat? Prov. 24:13. *What is stronger than a lion,* or a greater devourer? Samson generously owns they had won the wager, though he had good reason to dispute it, because they had not declared the riddle, as the bargain was (*v.* 12), but it had been declared to them. But he only thought fit to tell them of it: *If you had not ploughed with my heifer,* made use of your interest with my wife, *you would not have found out my riddle.* Satan, in his temptations, could not do us the mischief he does if he did not plough with the heifer of our own corrupt nature.

VI. Samson pays his wager to these Philistines with the spoils of others of their countrymen, *v.* 19. He took this occasion to quarrel with the Philistines, went down to Ashkelon, one of their cities, where probably he knew there was some great festival observed at this time, to which many flocked, out of whom he picked out thirty, slew them, and took their clothes, and gave them to those that had expounded the riddle; so that, in balancing the account, it appeared that the Philistines were the losers, for one of the lives they lost was worth all the suits of clothes they won: the body is more than raiment. *The Spirit of the Lord came upon him,* both to authorize and to enable him to do this.

VII. This proves a good occasion of weaning Samson from his new relations. He found how his companions had abused him and how his wife had betrayed him, and therefore *his anger was kindled, v.* 19. Better be angry with Philistines than in love with them, because, when we join ourselves to them, we are most in danger of being ensnared by them. And, meeting with this ill usage among them, he *went up to his father's house.* It were well for us if the unkindnesses we meet with from the world, and our disappointments in it, had but this good effect upon us, to oblige us by faith and prayer to return to our heavenly Father's house and rest there. The inconveniences that occur in our way should make us love home and long to be there. No sooner had he gone than his wife was disposed of to another, *v.* 20. Instead of begging his pardon for the wrong she had done him, when he justly signified his resentment of it only by withdrawing in displeasure for a time, she immediately marries him that was the chief of the guests, the friend of the bridegroom, whom perhaps she loved too well, and was too willing to oblige, when she got her husband to tell her the riddle. See how little confidence is to be put in man, when those may prove our enemies whom we have used as our friends.

CHAPTER 15

Samson, when he courted an alliance with the Philistines, did but seek an occasion against them, *ch.* 14:4. Now here we have a further account of the occasions he took to weaken them, and to avenge, not his own, but Israel's quarrels, upon them. Everything here is surprising; if any thing be thought incredible, because impossible, it must be remembered that with God nothing is impossible, and it was by the Spirit of the Lord coming upon him that he was both directed to and strengthened for those unusual ways of making war. I. From the perfidiousness of his wife and her father, he took occasion to burn their corn (*v.* 1–5). II. From the Philistines' barbarous cruelty to his wife and her father, he took occasion to smite them with a great slaughter (*v.* 6–8). III. From the treachery of his countrymen, who delivered him bound to the Philistines, he took occasion to kill 1000 of them with the jaw-bone of an ass (*v.* 9–17). IV. From the distress he was then in for want of water, God took occasion to show him favour in a seasonable supply (*v.* 18–20).

Verses 1–8

Here is, I. Samson's return to his wife, whom he had left in displeasure; not hearing perhaps that she was given to another, when time had a little cooled his resentments, he came back to her, *visited her with a kid, v.* 1. The value of the present was inconsiderable, but it was intended as a token of reconciliation, and perhaps was then so used, when those that had been at variance were brought together again; he sent this, that he might sup with her in her apartments, and she with him, on his provision, and so they might be friends again. It was generously done of Samson, though he was the party offended and the superior relation, to whom therefore she was bound in duty to sue for peace and to make the first motion of reconciliation. When differences happen between near relations, let hose be ever reckoned the wisest and the best that are most forward to forgive and forget injuries and most willing to stoop and yield for peace' sake.

II. The repulse he met with. Her father forbade him to come near her; for truly he had married her to another, *v.* 2. He endeavours, 1. To justify himself in this wrong: *I verily thought that thou hadst utterly hated her.* A very ill opinion he had of Samson, measuring that Nazarite by the common temper of the Philistines; could he think worse of him than to suspect that, because he was justly angry with his wife, he utterly hated her, and, because he had seen cause to return to his father's house for a while, therefore he had abandoned her for ever? Yet this is all he had to say in excuse of this injury. Thus he made the worst of jealousies to patronize the worst of robberies. But it will never bear us out in doing ill to say, "We thought others designed ill." 2. He endeavours to pacify Samson by offering him his younger daughter, whom, because the handsomer, he thought Samson might accept, in full recompence for the wrong. See what confusions those did admit and bring their families to that were not governed by the fear and law of God, marrying a daughter this week to one and next week to another, giving a man one daughter first and then another. Samson scorned his proposal; he knew better things than *to take a wife to her sister,* Lev. 18:18.

III. The revenge Samson took upon the Philistines for this abuse. Had he designed herein only to plead his own cause he would have challenged his rival, and would have chastised him and his father-in-law only. But he looks upon himself as a public person, and the affront as done to the whole nation of Israel, for probably they put this slight upon him because he was of that nation, and pleased themselves with it, that they had put such an abuse upon an Israelite; and therefore he resolves to do the Philistines a displeasure, and does not doubt but this treatment which he had met with among them would justify him in it (*v.* 3): *Now shall I be more blameless than the Philistines.* He had done what became him in offering to be reconciled to his wife, but, she having rendered it impracticable, now they could not blame him if he showed his just resentment. Note, When differences arise we ought to do our duty in order to the ending of them, and then, whatever the ill consequences of them may be, we shall be blameless. Now the way Samson took to be revenged on them was by setting their corn-fields on fire, which would be a great weakening and impoverishing to the country, *v.* 4, 5. 1. The method he took to do it was very strange. He sent 150 couple of foxes, tied tail to tail, into the corn-fields; every couple had a stick of fire between their tails, with which, being terrified, they ran into the corn for shelter, and so set fire to it; thus the fire would break out in many places at the same time, and therefore could not be conquered, especially if this was done, as it is probable it was, in the night. He might have employed men to do it, but perhaps he could not find Israelites enough that had courage to do it, and he himself could do it but in one place at a time, which would not effect his purpose. We never find Samson, in any of his exploits, making use of any person whatsoever, either servant or soldier, therefore, in this project, he chose to make use of foxes as his incendiaries. They had injured Samson by their subtlety and malice, and now Samson returns the injury by subtle foxes and mischievous fire-brands. By the meanness and weakness of the animals he employed, he designed to put contempt upon the enemies he fought against. This stratagem is often alluded to to show how the church's adversaries, that are of different interests and designs among themselves, that look and draw contrary ways in other things, yet have often united in a fire-brand, some cursed project or other, to waste the church of God, and particularly to kindle the fire of division in it. 2. The mischief he hereby did to the Philistines was very great. It was in the time of wheat harvest (*v.* 1), so that the straw being dry it soon burnt the shocks of corn that were cut, and *the standing corn, and the vineyards and olives.* This was a waste of the good creatures, but where other acts of hostility are lawful destroying the forage is justly reckoned to be so: if he might take away their lives, he might take away their livelihood. And God was righteous in it: the *corn, and the wine, and the oil,* which they had prepared for Dagon, to be a meat-offering to him, were thus, in the season thereof, made a burnt-offering to God's justice.

IV. The Philistines' outrage against Samson's treacherous wife and her father. Understanding that they had provoked Samson to do this mischief to the country, the rabble set upon them and burnt them with fire, perhaps in their own house, *v.* 6. Samson himself they durst not attack, and therefore, with more justice than perhaps they themselves designed in it, they wreak their vengeance upon those who, they could not but own, had given him cause to be angry. Instead of taking vengeance upon Samson, they took vengeance for him, when he, out of respect to the relation he had stood in to them, was not willing to do it for himself. See his hand in it *to whom vengeance belongs.* Those that deal treacherously shall be spoiled and dealt treacherously with; and *the Lord is known by these judgments which he executes,* especially when, as here, he makes use of his people's enemies as instruments for revenging one upon another his people's quarrels. When a barbarous Philistine sets fire to a treacherous one, the *righteous may rejoice to see the vengeance,* Ps. 58:10, 11. Thus shall *the wrath of man praise God,* Ps. 76:10. The Philistines had threatened Samson's wife, that, if she would not get the riddle out of him, they would *burn her and her father's house with fire, ch.* 14:15. She, to save herself and oblige her countrymen, betrayed her husband; and what came of it? The very thing that she feared, and sought by sin to avoid, came upon her; she and her father's house were burnt with fire, and her countrymen, whom she sought to oblige by the wrong she did to her husband, brought this evil upon her. The mischief we seek to escape by any unlawful practices we often pull upon our own heads. *He that will* thus *save his life shall lose it.*

V. The occasion Samson took hence to do them a yet greater mischief, which touched their bone and their flesh, *v.* 7, 8. *"Though you have done this* to them, and thereby shown what you would do to me if you could, yet that shall not deter me from being further vexatious to you." Or, "Though you think, by doing this, you have made me satisfaction for the affront I received among you, yet I have Israel's cause to plead as a public person, and for the wrongs done to them *I will be avenged on you,* and, if you will then forbear your insults, I will cease, aiming at no more than the deliverance of Israel." So he *smote them hip and thigh with a great stroke,* so the word is. We suppose the wounds he gave them to have been mortal, as wounds in the hip or thigh often prove, and therefore translate it, *with a great slaughter.* Some think he only lamed them, disabled them for service, as horses were houghed or ham-strung. It seems to be a phrase used to express a desperate attack; he killed them pellmell, or routed them horse and foot. He smote them with his hip upon thigh, that is, with the strength he had, not in his arms and hands, but in his hips and thighs, for he kicked and spurned at them, and so mortified them, *trod them in his anger,* and *trampled them in his fury,* Isa. 63:3. And, when he had done, he retired to a natural fortress in the top of the rock Etam, where he waited to see whether the Philistines would be tamed by the correction he had given them.

Verses 9–17

Here is, I. Samson violently pursued by the Philistine. They went up in a body, a more formidable force than they had together when Samson smote them hip and thigh; and they pitched in Judah, and spread themselves up and down the country, to find out Samson, who they heard had come this way, *v.* 9. When the men of Judah, who had tamely submitted to their yoke, pleaded that they had paid their tribute, and that none of their tribe had given them any offence, they freely own they designed nothing in this invasion but to seize Samson; they would fight *neither against small nor great,* but only that judge of Israel (*v.* 10), to *do to him as he has done to us,* that is, to smite his hip and thigh, as he did ours — *an eye for an eye.* Here was an army sent against one man, for indeed he was himself an army. Thus a whole band of men was sent to seize our Lord Jesus, that blessed Samson, though a tenth part would have served now that his hour had come, and ten times as many would have done nothing if he had not yielded.

II. Samson basely betrayed and delivered up by the men of Judah, *v.* 11. Of Judah were they? Degenerate branches of that valiant tribe! Utterly unworthy to carry in their standard *the lion of the tribe of Judah.* Perhaps they were disaffected to Samson because he was not of their tribe. Out of a foolish fondness for their forfeited precedency, they would rather be oppressed by Philistines than rescued by a Danite. Often has the church's deliverance been obstructed by such jealousies and pretended points of honour. Rather it was because they stood in awe of the Philistines, and were willing, at any rate, to get them out of their country. If their spirits had not been perfectly cowed and broken by their sins and troubles, and they had not been given up to a spirit of slumber, they would have taken this fair opportunity to shake off the Philistine's yoke. If they had had the least spark of ingenuousness and courage remaining in them, having so brave a man as Samson was to head them, they would now have made one bold struggle for the recovery of their liberty; but no marvel if those that had debased themselves to hell in the worship of their dung-hill gods (Isa. 57:9) thus debased themselves to the dust, in submission to their insulting oppressors. Sin dispirits men, nay, it infatuates them, and hides from their eyes the things that belong to their peace. Probably Samson went into the border of that country to offer his service, *supposing his brethren would have understood how that God by his hand would deliver them,* as Moses did, Acts 7:25. But they thrust him from them, and very disingenuously, 1. Blamed him for what he had done against the Philistines, as if he had done them a great injury. Such ungrateful returns have those often received that have done the best service imaginable to their country. Thus our Lord Jesus did many good works, and for these they were ready to stone him. 2. They begged of him that he would suffer them to bind him, and deliver him up to the Philistines. Cowardly unthankful wretches! Fond of their fetters and in love with servitude! Thus the Jews delivered up our Saviour, under pretence of a fear lest the Romans should come and take away their place and nation. With what a sordid servile spirit do they argue, *Knowest thou not that the Philistines rule over us?* And whose fault was that? They knew they had no right to rule over them, nor would they have been sold into their hands if they had not first *sold themselves to work wickedness.*

III. Samson tamely yielding to be bound by his countrymen, and delivered into the hands of his enraged enemies, *v.* 12, 13. Now easily could he have beaten them off, and kept the top of his rock against these 3000 men, and none of them all could, or durst, have laid hands on him; but he patiently submitted, 1. That he might give an example of great meekness, mixed with great strength and courage; as one that had rule over his own spirit, he knew how to yield as well as how to conquer. 2. That, by being delivered up to the Philistine, he might have an opportunity of making a slaughter among them. 3. That he might be a type of Christ, who, when he had shown what he could do, in striking those down that came to seize him, yielded to be bound and led as a *lamb to the slaughter.* Samson justified himself in what he had done against the Philistines: *"As they did to me, so I did to them;* it was a piece of necessary justice, and they ought not to retaliate it upon me, for they began." He covenants with the men of Judah that, if he put himself into their hands, they should

not fall upon him themselves, because then he should be tempted to fall upon them, which he was very loth to do. This they promised him (*v.* 13), and then he surrendered. The men of Judah, being his betrayers, were in effect his murderers; they would not kill him themselves, but they did that which was worse, they delivered him into the hands of the uncircumcised Philistines, who they knew would do worse than kill him, would abuse and torment him to death. Perhaps they thought, as some think Judas did when he betrayed Christ, that he would by his great strength deliver himself out of their hands; but no thanks to them if he had delivered himself, and, if they thought he would do so, they might of themselves have thought this again, that he could and would deliver them too if they would adhere to him and make him their head. Justly is their misery prolonged who, to oblige their worst enemies, thus abuse their best friend. Never were men so infatuated except those who thus treated our blessed Saviour.

IV. Samson making his part good against the Philistines, even when he was delivered into their hands, fast pinioned with two new cords. The Philistines, when they had him among them, *shouted against him* (*v.* 14), so triumphing in their success, and insulting over him. If God had not tied their hands faster than the men of Judah had tied his, they would have shot at him (as their archers did at Saul) to dispatch him immediately, rather than have shouted at him, and given him time to help himself. But their security and joy were a presage of their ruin. When they shouted against him as a man run down, confident that all was their own, then the *Spirit of the Lord came upon him,* came mightily upon him, inspired him with more than ordinary strength and resolution. Thus fired, 1. He presently got clear of his bonds. The two new cords, upon the first struggle he gave, broke, and were *melted* (as the original word is) from off his hands, no doubt to the great amazement and terror of those that shouted against him, whose shouts were hereby turned into shrieks. Observe, When the *Spirit of the Lord came upon him, his cords were loosed. Where the Spirit of the Lord is there is liberty,* and those are free indeed who are thus freed. This typified the resurrection of Christ by the power of the Spirit of holiness. In it he loosed the bands of death, and its cords, the grave-clothes, fell from his hands without being loosed, as Lazarus's were, because it was impossible that the mighty Saviour should be holden of them; and thus he triumphed over the powers of darkness that shouted against him, as if they had him sure. 2. He made a great destruction among the Philistines, who all gathered about him to make sport with him, *v.* 15. See how poorly he was armed: he had no better weapon than the jaw-bone of an ass, and yet what execution he did with it! he never laid it out of his hand till he had with it laid 1000 Philistines dead upon the spot; and thus that promise was more than accomplished. *One of you shall chase a thousand,* Jos. 23:10. A jaw-bone was an inconvenient thing to grasp, and, one would think, might easily be wrested out of his hand, and a few such blows as he gave with it might have crushed and broken it, and yet it held good to the last. Had it been the jaw-bone of a lion, especially that which he himself had slain, it might have helped to heighten his fancy and to make him think himself the more formidable; but to take the bone of that despicable animal was to do wonders by *the foolish things of the world,* that the *excellency of the power might be of God and not of man.* One of David's worthies slew 300 Philistines at once, but it was *with a spear,* 1 Chr. 11:11. Another slew of them till his hand was weary and stuck to his sword, 2 Sa. 23:10. But they all came short of Samson. What could be thought too hard, too much, for him to do, on whom the Spirit of the Lord came mightily! *Through God we shall do valiantly.* It was strange the men of Judah did not now come in to his aid: cowards can strike a falling enemy. But he was to be a type of him that *trod the wine-press alone.*

V. Samson celebrating his own victory, since the men of Judah would not do even that for him. He composed a short song, which he sang to himself, for the daughters of Israel did not meet him, as afterwards they did Saul, to sing, with more reason, *Samson hath slain his thousands.* The burden of this song was, *With the jaw-bone of an ass, heaps upon heaps, have I slain a thousand men, v.* 16. The same word in Hebrew *(chamor)* signifies both an *ass* and a *heap,* so that this is an elegant paronomasia, and represents the Philistines falling as tamely as asses. He also gave a name to the place, to perpetuate the Philistines' disgrace, *v.* 17. *Ramath-lehi,* the *lifting up of the jaw-bone.* Yet he did not vain-gloriously carry the bone about with him for a show, but threw it away when he had done with it. So little were relics valued then.

Verses 18–20

Here is, I. The distress which Samson was in after this great performance (*v.* 18): *He was sore athirst.* It was a natural effect of the great heat he had been in, and the great pains he had taken; his zeal consumed him, ate him up, and made him forget himself, till, when he had time to pause a little, he found himself reduced to the last extremity for want of water and ready to faint. Perhaps there was a special hand of God in it, as there was in the whole transaction; and God would hereby keep him from being proud of his great strength and great achievements, and let him know that he was but a man, and liable to the calamities that are common to men. And Josephus says, It was designed to chastise him for not making mention of God and his hand in his memorial of the victory he had obtained, but taking all the praise to himself: *I have slain a thousand men;* now that he is ready to die for thirst he is under a sensible conviction that his own arm could not have saved him, without God's right hand and arm. Samson had drunk largely of the blood of the Philistines, but blood will never quench any man's thirst. Providence so ordered it that there was no water near him, and he was so fatigued that he could not go far to seek it; the men of Judah, one would think, should have met him, now that he had come off a conqueror, *with bread and wine,* as Melchizedek did Abram, to atone for the injury they had done him; but so little notice did they take of their deliverer that he was ready to perish for want of a draught of water. Thus are the greatest slights often put upon those that do the greatest services. Christ on the cross, said, *I thirst.*

II. His prayer to God in this distress. Those that forget to attend God with their praises may perhaps be compelled to attend him with their prayers. Afflictions are often sent to bring unthankful people to God. Two things he pleads with God in this prayer, 1. His having experienced the power and goodness of God in his late success: *Thou hast given this great deliverance into the hand of thy servant.* He owns himself God's servant in what he had been doing: "Lord, wilt thou not own a poor servant of thine, that has spent himself in thy service? *I am thine, save me."* He calls his victory a *deliverance,* a *great* deliverance; for, if God had not helped him, he had not only not conquered the Philistines, but had been swallowed up by them. He owns it to come from God, and now corrects his former error in assuming it too much to himself; and this he pleads in his present strait. Note, Past experiences of God's power and goodness are excellent pleas in prayer for further mercy. "Lord, thou hast delivered often, wilt thou not deliver still? 2 Co. 1:10. Thou hast begun, wilt thou not finish? Thou hast done the greater, wilt thou not do the less?" Ps. 56:13. 2. His being now exposed to his enemies: *"Lest I fall into the hands of the uncircumcised,* and then they will triumph, will *tell it in Gath, and in the streets of Ashkelon;* and will it not redound to God's dishonour of his champion become so easy a prey to the uncircumcised?" The best pleas are those taken from God's glory.

III. The seasonable relief God sent him. God heard his prayer, and sent him water, either out of the bone or out of the earth through the bone, *v.* 19. That bone which he had made an instrument of God's service God, to recompense him, made an instrument of his supply. But I rather incline to our marginal reading: *God clave a hollow place that was in Lehi:* the place of this action was, from the jaw-bone, called *Lehi;* even before the action we find it so called, *v.* 9, 14. And there, in that field, or hill, or plain, or whatever it was, that was so called, God caused a fountain suddenly and seasonably to open just by him, and water to spring up out of it in abundance, which continued a well ever after. Of this fair water he drank, and his spirits revived. We should be more thankful for the mercy of water did we consider how ill we can spare it. And this instance of Samson's relief should encourage us to trust in God, and seek to him, for, when he pleases, he can *open rivers in high places.* See Isa. 41:17, 18.

IV. The memorial of this, in the name Samson gave to this upstart fountain, *Enhakkore, the well of him that cried,* thereby keeping in remembrance both his own distress, which occasioned him to cry, and God's favour to him, in answer to his cry. Many a spring of comfort God opens to his people, which may fitly be called by this name; it is *the well of him that cried.* Samson had given a name to the place which denoted him great and triumphant — *Ramath-lehi,* the *lifting up of the jaw-bone;* but here he gives it another name, which denotes him needy and dependent.

V. The continuance of Samson's government after these achievements, *v.* 20. At length Israel submitted to him whom they had betrayed. Now it was past dispute that God was with him, so that henceforward they all owned him and were directed by him as their judge. *The stone which the builders refused became the head-stone.* It intimates the low condition of Israel that the government was dated by *the days of the Philistines;* yet it was a mercy to Israel that, though they were oppressed by a foreign enemy, yet they had a judge that preserved order and kept them from ruining one another. Twenty years his government continued, according to the usages of the judges' administration; but of the particulars we have no account, save of the beginning of his government in this chapter and the end of it in the next.

CHAPTER 16

Samson's name (we have observed before) signifies a little sun (solparvus); we have seen this sun rising very bright, and his morning ray strong and clear; and, nothing appearing to the contrary, we take it for granted that the middle of the day was proportionably illustrious, while he judged Israel twenty years; but the melancholy story of this chapter gives us such an account of his evening as did not commend his day. This little sun set under a cloud, and yet, just in the setting, darted forth one such strong and glorious beam as made him even then a type of Christ, conquering by death. Here is, I. Samson greatly endangered by his familiarity with one harlot, and hardly escaping (*v.* 1–3). II. Samson quite ruined by his familiarity with another harlot, Delilah. Observe, 1. How he was betrayed to her by his own lusts (*v.* 4). 2. How he was betrayed by her to his sworn enemies, the Philistines, who, (1.) By her means got it out of him at last where his great strength lay (*v.* 5–17). (2.) Then robbed him of his strength, by taking from his head the crown of his separation (*v.* 18–20). (3.) Then seized him, blinded him, imprisoned him, abused him, and, at a solemn festival, made a show of him (*v.* 21–25). But, lastly, he avenged himself of them by pulling down the theatre upon their heads, and so dying with them (*v.* 26–31).

Verses 1–3

Here is, 1. Samson's sin, *v.* 1. His taking a Philistine to wife, in the beginning of his time, was in some degree excusable, but to join himself to a harlot that he accidentally saw among them was such a profanation of his honour as an Israelite, as a Nazarite, that we cannot but blush to read it. *Tell it not in Gath.* This vile impurity makes the graceful visage of this Nazarite *blacker than a coal,* Lam. 4:7, 8. We find not that Samson had any business in Gaza; if he went thither in quest of a harlot it would make one willing to hope that, as bad as things were otherwise, there were no prostitutes among the daughters of Israel. Some think he went thither to observe what posture the Philistines were in, that he might get some advantages against them; if so, he forgot his business, neglected that, and so fell into this snare. His sin began in his eye, with which he should have made a covenant; he saw there one in the *attire of a harlot,* and the lust which conceived brought forth sin: he *went in unto her.* 2. Samson's danger. Notice was sent to the magistrates of Gaza, perhaps by the treacherous harlot herself, that Samson was in the town, *v.* 2. Probably he came in a disguise, or in the dusk of the evening, and went into an inn or public-house, which happened to be kept by this harlot. The gates of the city were hereupon shut, guards set, all kept quiet, that Samson might suspect no danger. Now they thought they had him in a prison, and doubted not but to be the death of him the next morning. O that all those who indulge their sensual appetites in drunkenness, uncleanness, or any fleshly lusts, would see themselves thus surrounded, waylaid, and marked for ruin, by their spiritual enemies! The faster they sleep, and the more secure they are, the greater is their danger. 3. Samson's escape, *v.* 3. He rose at midnight, perhaps roused by a dream, in slumberings upon the bed (Job 33:15), by his guardian angel, or rather by the checks of his own conscience. He arose with a penitent abhorrence (we hope) of the sin he was now committing, and of himself because of it, and with a pious resolution not to return to it, — rose under an apprehension of the danger he was in, that he was as one that slept upon the top of a mast, — rose with such thoughts as these: "Is this a bed fit for a Nazarite to sleep in? Shall a temple of the living God be thus polluted? Can I be safe under this guilt?" It was bad that he lay down without such checks; but it would have been worse if he had lain still under them. He makes immediately towards the gate of the city, probably finds the guards asleep, else he would have made them sleep their last, stays not to break open the gates, but plucks up the posts, takes them, gates and bar and all, all very large and strong and a vast weight, yet he carries them on his back several miles, *up to the top of a hill,* in disdain of their attempt to secure him with gates and bars, designing thus to render himself more formidable to the Philistines and more acceptable to his people, thus to give a proof of the great strength God had given him and a type of Christ's victory over death and the grave. He not only rolled away the stone from the door of the sepulchre, and so came forth himself, but carried away the gates of the grave, bar and all, and so left it, ever after, an open prison to all that are his; it shall not, it cannot, always detain them. *O death! where is thy sting?* Where are thy gates? Thanks be to him that not only gained a victory for himself, but giveth us the victory!

Verses 4–17

The burnt child dreads the fire; yet Samson, that has more than the strength of a man, in this comes short of the wisdom of a child; for, though he had been more than once brought into the highest degree of mischief and danger by the love of women and lusting after them, yet he would not take warning, but is here again taken in the same snare, and this third time pays for all. Solomon seems to refer especially to this story of Samson when, in his caution against uncleanness, he gives this account of a whorish woman (Prov. 7:26), that *she hath cast down many wounded, yea, many strong men have been slain by her;* and (Prov. 6:26) that *the adulteress will hunt for the precious life.* This bad woman, that brought Samson to ruin, is here named *Delilah,* an infamous name, and fitly used to express the person, or thing, that by flattery or falsehood brings mischief and destruction on those to whom kindness is pretended. See here,

I. The affection Samson had for Delilah: he loved her, *v.* 4. Some think she was his wife, but then he would have had her home to his own house; others that he courted her to make her his wife; but there is too much reason to suspect that it was a sinful affection he had for her, and that he lived in uncleanness with her. Whether she was an Israelite or a Philistine is not certain. If an Israelite, which is scarcely probable, yet she had the heart of a Philistine.

II. The interest which the lords of the Philistines made with her to betray Samson, *v.* 5. 1. That which they told her they designed was to humble him, or afflict him; they would promise not to do him any hurt, only they would disable him not to do them any. And so much conscience it should seem they made of this promise that even then, when he lay ever so much at their mercy, they would not kill him, no, not when the razor that cut his hair might sooner and more easily have cut his throat. 2. That which they desired, in order hereunto, was to know where his great strength lay, and by what means he might be bound. Perhaps they imagined he had some spell or charm which he carried about with him, by the force of which he did these great things, and doubted not but that, if they could get this from him, he would be manageable; and therefore, having had reason enough formerly to know which was his blind side, hoped to find out his riddle a second time by ploughing with his heifer. They engaged Delilah to get it out of him, telling her what a kindness it would be to them, and perhaps assuring her it should not be improved to any real mischief, either to him or her. 3. For this they bid high, promised to give her each of them 1100 pieces of silver, 5500 in all. So many shekels amounted to above 1000*l.* sterling; with this she was hired to betray one she pretended to love. See what horrid wickedness the love of money is the root of. Our blessed Saviour was thus betrayed by one whom he called *friend,* and with a kiss too, for filthy lucre. No marvel if those who are unchaste, as Delilah, be unjust; such as lose their honesty in one instance will in another.

III. The arts by which he put her off from time to time, and kept his own counsel a great while. She asked him *where his great strength lay,* and whether it were possible for him to be bound and afflicted (*v.* 6), pretending that she only desired he would satisfy her curiosity in that one thing, and that she thought it was impossible he should be bound otherwise than by her charms.

1. When she urged him very much, he told her, (1.) That he might be bound with *seven green withs, v.* 7. The experiment was tried (*v.* 8), but it would not do: he *broke the withs* as easily *as a thread of tow is broken when it toucheth the fire, v.* 9. (2.) When she still continued her importunity (*v.* 10) he told her that with two new ropes he might be so cramped and hampered that he might be as easily dealt with as any other man, *v.* 11. This experiment was tried too, but it failed: the *new ropes* broke from off his arm *like a thread, v.* 12. (3.) When she still pressed him to communicate the secret, and upbraided him with it as an unkindness that he had bantered her so long, he then told her that the weaving of the seven locks of his head would make a great alteration in him, *v.* 13. This came nearer the matter than any thing he had yet said, but it would not do: his strength appeared to be very much in his hair, when, upon the trial of this, purely by the strength of his hair, he carried away the *pin of the beam* and *the web.*

2. In the making of all these experiments, it is hard to say whether there appears more of Samson's weakness or Delilah's wickedness. (1.) Could any thing be more wicked than her restless and unreasonable importunity with him to discover a secret which she knew would endanger his life if ever it were lodged any where but in his own breast? What could be more base and disingenuous, more false and treacherous, than to lay his head in her lap, as one whom she loved, and at the same time to design the betraying of him to those by whom he was mortally hated? (2.) Could any thing be more weak than for him to continue a parley with one who, he so plainly saw, was aiming to do him a mischief, — that he should lend an ear so long to such an impudent request, that she might know how to do him a mischief, — that when he perceived liers in wait for him in the chamber, and that they were ready to apprehend him if they had been able, he did not immediately quit the chamber, with a resolution never to come into it any more, — nay, that he should again lay his head in that lap out of which he had been so often roused with that alarm, *The Philistines are upon thee, Samson?* One can hardly imagine a man so perfectly besotted, and void of all consideration, as Samson now was; but whoredom is one of those things that *take away the heart.* It is hard to say what Samson meant in suffering her to try so often whether she could weaken and afflict him; some think he did not certainly know himself where his strength lay, but, it should seem, he did know, for, when he told her that which would disable him indeed, it is said, *He told her all his heart.* It seems, he designed to banter her, and to try if he could turn it off with a jest, and to baffle the *liers in wait,* and make fools of them; but it was very unwise in him that he did not quit the field as soon as ever he perceived that he was not able to keep the ground.

IV. The disclosure he at last made of this great secret; and, if the disclosure proved fatal to him, he must thank himself, who had not power to keep his own counsel from one that manifestly sought his ruin. *Surely in vain is the net spread in the sight of any bird,* but in Samson's sight is the net spread, and yet he is taken in it. If he had not been blind before the Philistines put out his eyes, he might have seen himself betrayed. Delilah signifies a *consumer;* she was so to him. Observe, 1. How she teazed him, telling him she would not believe he loved her, unless he would gratify her in this matter (*v.* 15): *How canst thou say, I love thee, when they heart is not with me?* That is, "when thou canst not trust me with the counsels of they heart?" Passionate lovers cannot bear to have their love called in question; they would do any thing rather than their sincerity should be suspected. Here therefore Delilah had this fond fool (excuse me that I call him so) at an advantage. This expostulation is indeed grounded upon a great truth, that those only have our love, not that have our good words or our good wishes, but that have our hearts. That is love without dissimulation; but it is falsehood and flattery in the highest degree to say we love those with whom our hearts are not. How can we say we love either our brother, whom we have seen, or God, whom we have not seen, if our hearts be not with him? She continued many days vexatious to him with her importunity, so that he had no pleasure of his life with her (*v.* 16); why then did he not leave her? It was because he was captivated to her by the power of love, falsely so called, but truly lust. This bewitched and perfectly intoxicated him, and by the force of it see, 2. How she conquered him (*v.* 17): He *told her all his heart.* God left him to himself to do this foolish thing, to punish him for indulging himself in the lusts of uncleanness. The angel that foretold his birth said nothing of his great strength, but only that he should be a Nazarite, and particularly that *no razor should come upon his head, ch.* 13:5. His consecration to God was to be his strength, for he was to be *strengthened according to the glorious power of that Spirit which wrought in him mightily,* that his strength, by promise, not by nature, might be a type and figure of the spiritual strength of believers, Col. 1:11, 29. Therefore the badge of his consecration was the pledge of his strength; if he lose the former, he knows he forfeits the latter. "If I be shaven, I shall no longer be a Nazarite, and then my strength will be lost." The making of his bodily strength to depend so much on his hair, which could have no natural influence upon it either one way or other, teaches us to magnify divine institutions, and to expect God's grace, and the continuance of it, only the use of those means of grace wherein he has appointed us to attend upon him, the word, sacraments, and prayer. In these earthen vessels is this treasure.

Verses 18–21

We have here the fatal consequences of Samson's folly in betraying his own strength; he soon paid dearly for it. A *whore is a deep ditch; he that is abhorred of the Lord shall fall therein.* In that pit Samson sinks. Observe, 1. What care Delilah took to make sure of the money for herself. She now perceived, by the manner of his speaking, that he had *told her all his heart,* and the lords of the Philistines that hired her to do this base thing are sent for; but they must be sure to bring *the money in their hands, v.* 18. The wages of unrighteousness are accordingly produced, unknown to Samson. It would have grieved one's heart to have seen one of the bravest men then in the world sold and bought, as a *sheep for the slaughter;* how does this instance sully all the glory of man, and forbid the strong man ever to boast of his strength! 2. What course she took to deliver him up to them according to the bargain. Many in the world would, for the hundredth part of what was here given Delilah, sell those that they pretend the greatest respect for. *Trust not in a friend then, put no confidence in a guide.* See what a treacherous method she took (*v.* 19): She *made him sleep upon her knees.* Josephus says, She gave him some intoxicating liquor, which laid him to sleep. What opiates she might steal into his cup we know not, but we cannot suppose that he knowingly drank wine or strong drink, for that would have been a forfeiture of his Nazariteship as much as the cutting off of his hair. She pretended the greatest kindness even when she designed the greatest mischief, which yet she could not have compassed if she had not made him sleep. See the fatal consequences of security. Satan ruins men by rocking them asleep, flattering them into a good opinion of their own safety, and so bringing them to mind nothing and fear nothing, and then he robs them of their strength and honour and leads them captive at his will. When we sleep our spiritual enemies do not. When he was asleep she had a person ready to cut off his hair, which he did so silently and so quickly that it did not awake him, but plainly afflicted him; even in his sleep, his spirit manifestly sunk upon it. I think we may suppose that if this ill turn had been done to him in his sleep by some spiteful body, without his being himself accessory to it, as he was here, it would not have had this strange effect upon him; but it was his own wickedness that corrected him. It was his iniquity, else it would not have been so much his infelicity. 3. What little concern he himself was in at it, *v.* 20. He could not but miss his hair as soon as he awoke, and yet said, *"I will shake myself as at other times* after sleep," or, "as at other times when the Philistines were upon me, to make my part good against them." Perhaps he thought to shake himself the more easily, and that his head would feel the lighter, now that his hair was cut, little thinking how much heavier the burden of guilt was than that of hair. He soon found in himself some change, we have reason to think so, and yet *wist not that the Lord had departed from him:* he did not consider that this was the reason of the change. Note, Many have lost the favourable presence of God and are not aware of it; they have provoked God to withdraw from them, but are not sensible of their loss, nor ever complain of it. Their souls languish and grow weak, their gifts wither, every thing goes cross with them; and yet they impute not this to the right cause: they are not aware that *God has departed from them,* nor are they in any care to reconcile themselves to him or to recover his favour. When God has departed we cannot do as at other times. 4. What improvement the Philistines soon made of their advantages against him, *v.* 21. The Philistines took him when God had departed from him. Those that have thrown themselves out of God's protection become an easy prey to their enemies. If we sleep in the lap of our lusts, we shall certainly wake in the hands of the Philistines. It is probable they had promised Delilah not to kill him, but they took an effectual course to disable him. The first thing they did, when they had him in their hands and found they could manage him, was to *put out his eyes,* by *applying fire to them,* says the Arabic version. They considered that his eyes would never come again, as perhaps his hair might, and that the strongest arms could do little without eyes to guide the, and therefore, if now they blind him, they for ever blind him. His eyes were the inlets of his sin: he saw the harlot at Gaza, and went in unto her (*v.* 1), and now his punishment began there. Now that the Philistines had blinded him he had time to remember how his own lust had blinded him. The best preservative of the eyes is to turn them away from beholding vanity. *They brought him down to Gaza,* that there he might appear in weakness where he had lately given such proofs of his strength (*v.* 3), and be a jest to those to whom he had been a terror. They *bound him with fetters of brass* who had before been held in the cords of his own iniquity, and he did *grind in the prison,* work in their bridewell, either for their profit or his punishment, or for both. The devil does thus by sinners, *blinds the minds of those who believe not,* and so enslaves them, and secures them in his interests. Poor Samson, how hast thou fallen! How is thy honour laid in the dust! How has the glory and defence of Israel become the drudge and triumph of the Philistines! *The crown has fallen from his head; woe unto him, for he hath sinned.* Let all take warning by his fall carefully to preserve their purity, and to watch against all fleshly lusts; for all our glory has gone, and our defence departed form us, when the covenant of our separation to God, as spiritual Nazarites, is profaned.

Verses 22–31

Though the last stage of Samson's life was inglorious, and one could wish there were a veil drawn over it, yet this account here given of his death may be allowed to lessen, though it does not quite roll away, the reproach of it; for there was honour in his death. No doubt he greatly repented of his sin, the dishonour he had by it done to God and his forfeiture of the honour God had put upon him; for that God was reconciled to him appears, 1. By the return of the sign of his Nazariteship (*v.* 22): *His hair began to grow again, as when he was shaven,* that is, to be as thick and as long as when it was cut off. It is probable that their general thanksgiving to Dagon was not long deferred, before which Samson's hair had thus grown, by which, and the particular notice taken of it, it seems to have been extraordinary, and designed for a special indication of the return of God's favour to him upon his repentance. For the growth of his hair was neither the cause nor the sign of the return of his strength further than as it was the badge of his consecration, and a token that God accepted him as a Nazarite again, after the interruption, without those ceremonies which were appointed for the restoration of a lapsed Nazarite, which he had not now the opportunity of performing, Num. 6:9. It is strange that the Philistines in whose hands he was were not jealous of the growth of his hair again, and did not cut it; but perhaps they were willing his great strength should return to him, that they might have so much the more work out of him, and now that he was blind they were in no fear of any hurt from him. 2. By the use God made of him for the destruction of the enemies of his people, and that at a time when it would be most for the vindication of the honour of God, and not immediately for the defence and deliverance of Israel. Observe,

I. How insolently the Philistines affronted the God of Israel, 1. By the sacrifices they offered to Dagon, his rival. This Dagon they call their *god,* a god of their own making, represented by an image, the upper part of which was in the shape of a man, the lower part of a fish, purely the creature of fancy; yet it served them to set up in opposition to the true and living God. To this pretended deity they ascribe their success (*v.* 23, 24): *Our god has delivered Samson our enemy, and the destroyer of our country, into our hands.* So they dreamed, though he could do neither good nor evil. They knew Delilah had betrayed him, and they had paid her for doing it, yet they attribute it to their god, and are confirmed by it in their belief of his power to protect them. All people will thus walk in the name of their gods: they will give them the praise of their achievements; and shall not we pay this tribute to our God whose kingdom ruleth over all? Yet, considering what wicked arts they used to get Samson into their hands, it must be confessed it was only such a dunghill-deity as Dagon that was fit to be made a patron of the villany. Sacrifices were offered, and songs of praise sung, on the general thanksgiving day, for this victory obtained over one man; there were great expressions of joy, and all to the honour of Dagon. Much more reason have we to give the praise of all our successes to our God. *Thanks be to him who causeth us to triumph in Christ Jesus!* 2. By the sport they made with Samson, God's champion, they reflected on God himself. When they were merry with wine, to make them more merry Samson must be fetched to make sport for them (*v.* 25, 27), that is, for them to make sport with. Having sacrificed to their god, and eaten and drunk upon the sacrifice, they rose up to play, according to the usage of idolaters (1 Co. 10:7), and Samson must be the fool in the play. They made themselves and one another laugh to see how, being blind, he stumbled and blundered. It is likely they *smote this judge of Israel upon the cheek* (Mic. 5:1), and said, *Prophesy who smote thee.* It was an instance of their barbarity to trample thus upon a man in misery, at the sight of whom awhile ago they would have trembled. It put Samson into the depth of misery, and as a sword in his bones were their reproaches, when they said, *Where is now thy God?* Nothing could be more grievous to so great a spirit; yet, being a penitent, his godly sorrow makes him patient, and he accepts the indignity as the punishment of his iniquity. How unrighteous soever the Philistines were, he could not but own that God was righteous. He had sported himself in his own deceivings and with his own deceivers, and justly are the Philistines let loose upon him to make sport with him. Uncleanness is a sin that makes men vile, and exposes them to contempt. *A wound and dishonour shall he get* whose heart is deceived by a woman, and *his reproach shall not be wiped away.* Everlasting shame and contempt will be the portion of those that are blinded and bound by their own lusts. The devil that deceived them will insult over them.

II. How justly the God of Israel brought sudden destruction upon them by the hands of Samson. Thousands of the Philistines had got together, to attend their lords in the sacrifices and joys of this day, and to be the spectators of this comedy; but it proved to them a fatal tragedy, for they were all slain, and buried in the ruins of the house: whether it was a temple or a theatre, or whether it was some slight building run up for the purpose, is uncertain. Observe,

1. Who were destroyed: All the *lords of the Philistines* (*v.* 27), who had by bribes corrupted Delilah to betray Samson to them. Evil pursued those sinners. Many of the people likewise, to the number of 3000, and among them a great many women, one of whom, it is likely, was that harlot of Gaza mentioned, *v.* 1. Samson had been drawn into sin by the Philistine women, and now a great slaughter is made among them, as was by Moses's order among the women of Midian, because it was they that *caused the children of Israel to trespass against the Lord in the matter of Peor,* Num. 31:16.

2. When they were destroyed. (1.) When they were merry, secure, and jovial, and far from apprehending themselves in any danger. When they saw Samson lay hold of the pillars, we may suppose, his doing so served them for a jest, and they made sport with that too: *What will this feeble Jew do?* How are sinners brought to desolation in a moment! They are lifted up in pride and mirth, that their fall may be the more dreadful. Let us never envy the mirth of wicked people, but infer from this instance that their triumphing is short and their joy but for a moment. (2.) It was when they were praising Dagon their god, and giving that honour to him which is due to God only, which is no less than treason against the King of kings, his crown and dignity. Justly therefore is the blood of these traitors mingled with their sacrifices. Belshazzar was cut off when he was praising his man-made gods, Dan. 5:4. (3.) It was when they were making sport with an Israelite, a Nazarite, and insulting over him, persecuting him whom God had smitten. Nothing fills the measure of the iniquity of any person or people faster than mocking and misusing the servants of God, yea, though it is by their own folly that they are brought low. Those know not what they do, nor whom they affront, that make sport with a good man.

3. How they were destroyed. Samson pulled the house down upon them, God no doubt putting it into his heart, as a public person, thus to avenge God's quarrel with them, Israel's, and his own. (1.) He gained strength to do it by prayer, *v.* 28. That strength which he had lost by sin he, like a true penitent, recovers by prayer; as David, who, when he had provoked the Spirit of grace to withdraw, prayed (Ps. 51:12), *Restore unto me the joy of thy salvation, and uphold me with thy free Spirit.* We may suppose that this was only a mental prayer, and that his voice was not heard (for it was made in a noisy clamorous crowd of Philistines); but, though his voice was not heard of men, yet his prayer was heard of God and graciously answered, and though he lived not to give an account himself of this his prayer, as Nehemiah did of his, yet God not only accepted it in heaven, but, by revealing it to the inspired penmen, provided for the registering of it in his church. He prayed to God to remember him and strengthen him this once, thereby owning that his strength for what he had already done he had from God, and begged it might be afforded to him once more, to give them a parting blow. That it was not from a principle of passion or personal revenge, but from a holy zeal for the glory of God and Israel, that he desired to do this, appears from God's accepting and answering the prayer. Samson died praying, so did our blessed Saviour; but Samson prayed for vengeance, Christ for forgiveness. (2.) He gained opportunity to do it by leaning on the two pillars which were the chief supports of the building, and were, it seems, so near together that he could take hold of them both at one time, *v.* 26, 29. Having hold of them, he bore them down with all his might, crying aloud, *Let me die with the Philistines, v.* 30. *Animamque in vulnere ponit — While inflicting the wound he dies.* The vast concourse of people that were upon the roof looking down through it to see the sport, we may suppose, contributed to the fall of it. A weight so much greater than ever it was designed to carry might perhaps have sunk of itself, at least it made the fall more fatal to those within: and indeed few of either could escape being either stifled or crushed to death. This was done, not by any natural strength of Samson, but by the almighty power of God, and is not only marvellous, but miraculous, in our eyes. Now in this, [1.] The Philistines were greatly mortified. All their lords and great men were killed, and abundance of their people, and this in the midst of their triumph; the temple of Dagon (as many think the house was) was pulled down, and Dagon buried in it. This would give a great check to the insolence of the survivors, and, if Israel had but had so much sense and spirit left them as to improve the advantages of this juncture, they might now have thrown off the Philistines' yoke. [2.] Samson may very well be justified, and brought in not guilty of any sinful murder either of himself or the Philistines. He was a public person, a declared enemy to the Philistines, against whom he might therefore take all advantages. They were now in the most barbarous manner making war upon him; all present were aiding and abetting, and justly die with him. Nor was he *felo de se,* or *a self-murderer,* in it; for it was not his own life that he aimed at, though he had too much reason to be weary of it, but the lives of Israel's enemies, for the reaching of which he bravely resigned his own, *not counting it dear to him, so that he might finish his course* with honour. [3.] God was very much glorified in pardoning Samson's great transgressions, of which this was an evidence. It has been said that the prince's giving a commission to one convicted amounts to a pardon. Yet, *though he was a God that forgave him, he took vengeance of his inventions* (Ps. 99:8), and, by suffering his champion to die in fetters, warned all to take heed of those lusts which war against the soul. However, we have good reason to hope that though Samson died with the Philistines he had not his everlasting portion with them. *The Lord knows those that are his.* [4.] Christ was plainly typified. He pulled down the devil's kingdom, as Samson did Dagon's temple; and, when he died, he obtained the most glorious victory over the powers of darkness. Then when his arms were stretched out upon the cross, as Samson's to the two pillars, he gave a fatal shake to the gates of hell, and, *through death, destroyed him that had the power of death, that is, the devil* (Heb. 2:14, 15), and herein exceeded Samson, that he not only died with the Philistines, but rose again to triumph over them.

Lastly, The story of Samson concludes, 1. With an account of his burial. His own relations, animated by the glories that attended his death, came and found out his body among the slain, brought it honourably to his own country, and buried it in the place of his fathers' sepulchres, the Philistines being in such a consternation that they durst not oppose it. 2. With the repetition of the account we had before of the continuance of his government: *He judged Israel twenty years;* and, if they had not been as mean and sneaking as he was brave and daring, he would have left them clear of the Philistines' yoke. They might have been easy, safe, and happy, if they would but have given God and their judges leave to make them so.

CHAPTER 17

All agree that what is related in this and the rest of the chapters to the end of this book was not done, as the narrative occurs, after Samson, but long before, even soon after the death of Joshua, in the days of Phinehas the son of Eleazar, *ch.* 20:28. But it is cast here into the latter part of the book that it might not interrupt the history of the Judges. That it might appear how happy the nation was in the judges it is here shown how unhappy they were when there was none. I. Then idolatry began in the family of Micah, *ch.* 17. II. Then it spread itself into the tribe of Dan, *ch.* 18. III. Then villany was committed in Gibeah of Benjamin, *ch.* 19. IV. Then that whole tribe was destroyed for countenancing it, *ch.* 20. V. Then strange expedients were adopted to keep up that tribe, *ch.* 21. Therefore blessed be God for the government we are under! In this chapter we are told how Micah an Ephraimite furnished himself, 1. With an image for his god (*v.* 1–6). 2. With a Levite, such a one as he was, for his priest (*v.* 7–13).

Verses 1–6

Here we have, I. Micah and his mother quarrelling. 1. The son robs the mother. The old woman had hoarded, with long scraping and saving, a great sum of money, 1100 pieces of silver. It is likely she intended, when she died, to leave it to her son: in the mean time it did her good to look upon it, and to count it over. The young man had a family of children grown up, for he had one of age to be a priest, *v.* 5. He knows where to find his mother's cash, thinks he has more need of it than she has, cannot stay till she dies, and so takes it away privately for his own use. Though it is a fault in parents to withhold from their children that which is meet, and lead them into temptation to wish them in their graves, yet even this will by no means excuse the wickedness of those children that steal from their parents, and think all their own that they can get from them, though by the most indirect methods. 2. The mother curses the son, or whoever had taken her money. It should seem she suspected her son; for, when she cursed, she spoke in his cars so loud, and with so much passion and vehemence, as made both his ears to tingle. See what mischief the love of money makes, how it destroys the duty and comfort of every relation. It was the love of money that made Micah so undutiful to his mother as to rob her, and made her so unkind and void of natural affection to her son as to curse him if he had it and concealed it. Outward losses drive good people to their prayers, but bad people to their curses. This woman's silver was her god before it was made thither into a graven or a molten image, else the loss of it would not have put her into such a passion as caused her quite to forget and break through all the laws of decency and piety. It is a very foolish thing for those that are provoked to throw their curses about *as a mad-*

man that casteth fire-brands, arrows, and death, since they know not but they may light upon those that are most dear to them.

II. Micah and his mother reconciled. 1. The son was so terrified with his mother's curses that he restored the money. Though he had so little grace as to take it, he had so much left as not to dare to keep it when his mother had sent a curse after it. He cannot believe his mother's money will do him any good without his mother's blessing, nor dares he deny the theft when he is charged with it, nor retain the money when it is demanded by the right owner. It is best not to do evil, but it is next best, when it is done, to undo it again by repentance, confession, and restitution. Let children be afraid of having the prayers of their parents against them; for, though the curse causeless shall not come, yet that which is justly deserved may be justly feared, even though it was passionately and indecently uttered. 2. The mother was so pleased with her son's repentance that she recalled her curses, and turned them into prayers for her son's welfare: *Blessed be thou of the Lord, my son.* When those that have been guilty of a fault appear to be free and ingenuous in owning it they ought to be commended for their repentance, rather than still be condemned and upbraided for their fault.

III. Micah and his mother agreeing to turn their money into a god, and set up idolatry in their family; and this seems to have been the first instance of the revolt of any Israelite from God and his instituted worship after the death of Joshua and the elders that out-lived him, and is therefore thus particularly related. And though this was only the worship of the true God by an image, against the *second* commandment, yet this opened the door to the worship of other gods, Baalim and the groves, against the *first and great* commandment. Observe,

1. The mother's contrivance of this matter. When the silver was restored she pretended she had *dedicated it to the Lord* (*v.* 3), either before it was stolen, and then she would have this thought to be the reason why she was so much grieved at the loss of it and imprecated evil on him that had taken it, because it was a dedicated and therefore an accursed thing, or after it was stolen she had made a vow that, if she could retrieve it, she would dedicate it to God, and then she would have the providence that had so far favoured her as to bring it back to her hands to be an owning of her vow. "Come," said she to her son, "the money is mine, but thou hast a mind to it; let it be neither mine nor thine, but let us both agree to make it into an image for a religious use." Had she put it to a use that was indeed for the service and honour of God, this would have been a good way of accommodating the matter between them; but, as it was, the project was wicked. Probably this old woman was one of those that came out of Egypt, and would have such images made as she had seen there; now that she began to dote she called to remembrance the follies of her youth, and perhaps told her son that this way of worshipping God by images was, to her knowledge, the old religion.

2. The son's compliance with her. It should seem, when she first proposed the thing he stumbled at it, knowing what the second commandment was; for, when she said (*v.* 3) she designed it for her son to make an image of, yet he restored it to his mother (being loth to have a hand in making the image), and she gave it to the founder and had the thing done, blaming him perhaps for scrupling at it, *v.* 4. But, when the images were made, Micah, by his mother's persuasion, was not only well reconciled to them, but greatly pleased and in love with them; so strangely bewitching was idolatry, and so much supported by *traditions received from their parents,* 1 Pt. 1:18; Jer. 44:17. But observe how the old woman's covetousness prevailed, in part, above her superstition. She had wholly dedicated the silver to make the graven and molten images (*v.* 3), all the 1100 pieces; but, when it came to be done, she made less than a fifth part serve, even 200 *shekels, v.* 4. She thought that enough, and indeed it was too much to give for an image that is a teacher of lies. Had it been devoted truly to the honour of God, he would not thus have been put off with part of the price, but would have signified his resentment of the affront, as he did in the case of Ananias and Sapphira. Now observe,

(1.) What was the corruption here introduced, *v.* 5. The man Micah had *a house of gods, a house of God,* so the

Septuagint, for so he thought it, as good as that at Shiloh, and better, because his own, of his own inventing and at his own disposal; for people love to have their religion under their girdle, to manage it as they please. *A house of error,* so the Chaldee, for really it was so, a deviation from the way of truth and an inlet to all deceit. Idolatry is a great cheat, and one of the worst of errors. That which he aimed at in the progress of his idolatry, whether he designed it at first or no, was to mimic and rival both God's oracles and his ordinances. [1.] His oracles; for he made *teraphim,* little images which he might advise with as there was occasion, and receive informations, directions, and predictions from. What the *urim* and *thummim* were to the prince and people these *teraphim* should be to his family; yet he could not think that the true God would own them, or give answers by them, and therefore depended upon such demons as the heathen worshipped to inspire them and make them serviceable to him. Thus, while the honour of Jehovah was pretended (*v.* 3), yet, his institution being relinquished, these Israelites unavoidably lapsed into downright idolatry and demon-worship. [2.] His ordinances. Some room or apartment in the house of Micah was appointed for the temple or house of God; an ephod, or holy garment, was provided for his priest to officiate in, in imitation of those used at the tabernacle of God, and one of his sons he consecrated, probably the eldest, to be his priest. And, when he had set up a graven or molten image to represent the object of his worship, no marvel if a priest of his own getting and his own making served to be the manager of it. Here is no mention of any altar, sacrifice, or incense, in honour of these silver gods, but, having a priest, it is probable he had all these, unless we suppose that, at first, his gods were intended only to be advised with, not to be adored, like Laban's teraphim; but the beginning of idolatry, as of other sins, is *like the letting forth of water:* break the dam, and you bring a deluge. Here idolatry began, and it spread like a fretting leprosy. Dr. Lightfoot would have us observe that as 1100 pieces of silver were here devoted to the making of an idol, which ruined religion, especially in the tribe of Dan (as we shall presently find), which was Samson's tribe, so 1100 pieces of silver were given by each Philistine lord for the ruin of Samson.

(2.) What was the cause of this corruption (*v.* 6): *There was no king in Israel,* no judge or sovereign prince to take cognizance of the setting up of these images (which, doubtless, the country about soon resorted to), and to give orders for the destroying of them, none to convince Micah of his error and to restrain and punish him, to take this disease in time, by which the spreading of the infection might have been happily prevented. Every man did that which was *right in his own eyes,* and then they soon did that which was *evil in the sight of the Lord.* When they were without a king to keep good order among them, God's house was forsaken, his priests were neglected, and all went to ruin among them. See what a mercy government is, and what reason there is that not only *prayers and intercessions, but giving of thanks,* should *be made for kings and all in authority,* 1 Tim. 2:1, 2. Nothing contributes more, under God, to the support of religion in the world, than the due administration of those two great ordinances, magistracy and ministry.

Verses 7–13

We have here an account of Micah's furnishing himself with a Levite for his chaplain, either thinking his son, because the heir of his estate, too good to officiate, or rather, because not of God's tribe, not good enough. Observe,

I. What brought this Levite to Micah. By his mother's side he was of the family of Judah, and lived at Bethlehem among his mother's relations (for that was not a Levites' city), or, upon some other account, as a stranger or inmate, sojourned there, *v.* 7. Thence he went to *sojourn where he could find a place,* and in his travels came to the house of Micah in Mount Ephraim, *v.* 8. Now, 1. Some think it was his unhappiness that he was under a necessity of removing, either because he was persecuted and abused, or rather neglected and starved, at Bethlehem. God had made plentiful provision for the Levites, but the people withheld their dues, and did not help them into the possession of the cities assigned to them; so that they were reduced to straits, and no care was taken for their

relief. Israel's forsaking God began with forsaking the Levites, which therefore they are warned against, Deu. 12:19. It is a sign religion is going to decay when good ministers are neglected and at a loss for a livelihood. But, 2. It seems rather to have been his fault and folly, that he loved to wander, threw himself out where he was, and forfeited the respect of his friends, and, having a roving head, would go to seek his fortune, as we say. We cannot conceive that things had yet come to such a pass among them that a Levite should be poor, unless it was his own fault. As those are fit to be pitied that would fix but may not, so those are fit to be punished that might fix but will not. Unsettledness being, one would think, a constant uneasiness, it is strange that any Israelite, especially any Levite, should affect it.

II. What bargain Micah made with him. Had he not been well enough content with his son for his priest, he would have gone or sent abroad to enquire out a Levite, but now he only takes hold of one that drops into his hands, which showed that he had no great zeal in the matter. It is probable that this rambling Levite had heard, in the country, of Micah's house of *gods, his graven and molten image,* which, if he had had any thing of the spirit of a Levite in him, would have brought him thither to reprove Micah for his idolatry, to tell how directly contrary it was to the law of God, and how it would bring the judgments of God upon him; but instead of this, like a base and degenerate branch of that sacred tribe, thither he goes to offer his service, with, *Have you any work for a Levite?* for I am out of business, and *go to sojourn where I may find a place;* all he aimed at was to get bread, not to do good, *v.* 9. Micah courts him into his family (*v.* 10), and promises him, 1. Good preferment: *Be unto me a father and a priest.* Though a young man, and taken up at the door, yet, if he take him for a priest, he will respect him as a father, so far is he from setting him among his servants. He asks not for his credentials, takes no time to enquire how he behaved in the place of his last settlement, considers not whether, though he was a Levite, yet he might not be of such a bad character as to be a plague and scandal to his family, but thinks, though he should be ever so great a rake, he might serve for a priest to a graven image, like Jeroboam's priest of the *lowest of the people,* 1 Ki. 12:31. No marvel if those who can make any thing serve for a god can also make any thing serve for a priest. 2. A tolerable maintenance. He will allow him *meat, and drink, and clothes, a double suit,* so the word is in the margin, a better and a worse, one for every day's wear and one for holy days, and ten shekels, about twenty-five shillings, a year for spending money — a poor salary in comparison of what God provided for the Levites that behaved well; but those that forsake God's service will never better themselves, nor find a better master. The ministry is the best calling but the worst trade in the world.

III. The Levite's settlement with him (*v.* 11): He was *content to dwell with the man;* though his work was superstitious and his wages were scandalous, he objected against neither, but thought himself happy that he had lighted on so good a house. Micah, thinking himself holier than any of his neighbours, presumed to consecrate this Levite, *v.* 12. As if his building, furnishing, and endowing this chapel authorized him, not only to appoint the person that should officiate there, but to confer those orders upon him which he had no right to give nor the other to receive. And now he shows him respect as a father and tenderness as a son, and is willing thus to make up the deficiency of the coin he gave him.

IV. Micah's satisfaction in this (*v.* 13): *Now know I that the Lord will do me good* (that is, he hoped that his new establishment would gain reputation among his neighbours, which would turn to his advantage, for he would share in the profit of his altar; or, rather, he hoped that God would countenance and bless him in all he put his hand unto) *because I have a Levite to be my priest.* 1. He thought it was a sign of God's favour to him and his images that he had so opportunely sent a Levite to his door. Thus those who please themselves with their own delusions, if Providence unexpectedly bring any thing to their hands that furthers them in their evil way, are too apt to infer thence that God is pleased with them. 2. He thought now that the error of his priesthood was amended all was well, though he still retained his graven and molten image.

Note, Many deceive themselves into a good opinion of their state by a partial reformation. They think they are as good as they should be, because, in some one particular instance, they are not so bad as they have been, as if the correcting of one fault would atone for their persisting in all the rest. 3. He thought the making of a Levite into a priest was a very meritorious act, which really was a presumptuous usurpation, and every provoking to God. Men's pride, and ignorance, and self-flattery, will undertake, not only to justify, but magnify and sanctify, the most daring impieties and invasions upon the divine prerogatives. With much reason might Micah have said, "Now may I fear that God will curse me, because I have debauched one of his own tribe, and drawn him into the worship of a graven image;" yet for this he hopes God will do him good. 4. He thought that having a Levite in the house with him would of course entitle him to the divine favour. Carnal hearts are apt to build too much upon their external privileges, and to conclude that God will certainly do them good because they are born of godly parents, dwell in praying families, are linked in society with those that are very good, and sit under a lively ministry; whereas all this is but like having a Levite to be their priest, which amounts to no security at all that God will do them good, unless they be good themselves, and make a good use of these advantages.

CHAPTER 18

How idolatry crept into the family of Micah we read in the preceding chapter, how it was translated thence into the tribe of Dan we have an account in this chapter, and how it gained a settlement in a city of note; for how great a matter does a little fire kindle! The tribe of Dan had their lot assigned them last of all the tribes, and, it happening to be too strait for them, a considerable city in the utmost corner of Canaan northward was added to it. "Let them get it, and take it;" it was called Laish or Leshem, Jos. 19:47. Now here we are told, I. How they sent spies to bring them an account of the place, who, by the way, got acquainted with Micah's priest (*v.* 1–6). II. What an encouraging report these spies brought back (*v.* 7–10). III. What forces were sent to conquer Laish (*v.* 11–13). IV. How they, by the way, plundered Micah of his gods (*v.* 14–26). V. How easily they conquered Laish (*v.* 27–29), and, when they had it, set up the graven image in it (*v.* 30, 31).

Verses 1–6

Here is, 1. The eye which these Danites had upon Laish, not the whole tribe of Dan, but one family of them, to whose lot, in the subdivision of Canaan, that city fell. Hitherto this family had sojourned with their brethren, who had taken possession of their lot, which lay between Judah and the Philistines, and had declined going to their own city, because there was *no king in Israel* to rule over them, *v.* 1. It lay a great way off, separate from the rest of their tribe; it was entirely in the enemy's hand, and therefore they would sponge upon their brethren rather than go far to provide for themselves. But at length necessity forced them to arouse themselves, and they began to think of an inheritance to dwell in. It is better to have a little of one's own than always to hang upon others. 2. The enquiry which this family of the Danites made concerning Laish: They sent *five men to search the land* (*v.* 2), that they might know the character of the country, whether it was an inheritance worth going so far for, and the posture of the people, whether the making of themselves masters of it was a thing practicable, what force was necessary in order thereunto, and which was the best way of making an attack upon it. The men they sent were men of valour, who, if they fell into their enemies' hands, knew how to look danger in the face. It is prudent to look before we leap. Dan had the subtlety of *a serpent by the way* (Gen. 49:17), as well as the courage of a *lion's whelp, leaping from Bashan,* Deu. 33:22. 3. The acquaintance which their spies got with Micah's priest, and the use they made of that acquaintance. It seems, they had know this Levite formerly, he having in his rambles been sometimes in their country; and, though his countenance might be altered, they knew him again by his voice, *v.* 3. They were surprised to find him so far off, enquired what brought him thither, and he told them (*v.* 4) what business he had there, and what encouragement. They, understanding that he had an oracle in his custody, desired he would tell them whether they should prosper in their present undertaking, *v.* 5. See their carelessness and regardlessness of God and his providence; they would not have enquired of the Lord at all if this Levite's mentioning the teraphim he had with him had not put it into their heads. Many never think of religion but just when it falls in their way and they cannot avoid it, like chance customers. See their ignorance of the divine law, that they thought God, who had forbidden the religious use of graven images, would yet own them in consulting an image, and give them an answer of peace. *Should he be enquired of by them?* Eze. 14:3. They seem to have had a greater opinion of Micah's teraphim than of God's urim; for they had passed by Shiloh, and, for aught that appears, had not enquired there of God's high priest, but Micah's shabby Levite shall be an oracle to them. He betakes himself to his usual method of consulting his teraphim; and, whether he himself believed it or no, he humoured the thing so well that he made them believe he had an answer from God encouraging them to go on, and assuring them of good success (*v.* 6): *"Go in peace,* you shall be safe, and may be easy, for *before the Lord is your way,"* that is, "he approves it" (as the Lord is said to *know the way of the righteous* with acceptation), "and therefore he will make it prosperous, his eye will be upon you for good, he will direct your way, and preserve your *going out and coming in."* Note, Our great care should be that our way be such as God approves, and, if it be so, we may *go in peace.* If God care for us, on him let us cast our care, and be satisfied that we cannot miss our way if he *go before us.*

Verses 7–13

Here is, I. The observation which the spies made upon the city of Laish, and the posture of its inhabitants, *v.* 7. Never was place so ill governed and so ill guarded, which would make it a very easy prey to the invader.

1. It was ill governed, for every man might be as bad as he would, and there was no magistrate, no *heir of restraint* (as the word is), that might so much as *put them to shame in any thing,* much less *put them to death,* so that by the most impudent immoralities they provoked God's wrath, and by all manner of mutual mischiefs weakened and consumed one another. See here, (1.) What the office of magistrates is. They are to be *heirs of restraint,* that is, to preserve a constant entail of power, as heirs to an inheritance, in the places where they are, for the restraining of that which is evil. They are *possessors of restraint,* entrusted with their authority for this end, that they may check and suppress every thing that is vicious and be *a terror to evil doers.* It is only God's grace that can renew men's depraved minds and turn their hearts; but the magistrate's power may restrain their bad practices and tie their hands, so that the wickedness of the wicked may not be either so injurious or so infectious as otherwise it would be. Though the sword of justice cannot cut up the root of bitterness, it may cut off its branches and hinder its growth and spreading, that vice may not go without a check, for then it becomes daring and dangerous, and the community shares in the guilt. (2.) See what method must be used for the restraint of wickedness. Sinners must be put to shame, that those who will not be restrained by the shamefulness of the sin before God and their own consciences may be restrained by the shamefulness of the punishment before men. All ways must be tried to dash sin out of countenance and cover it with contempt, to make people ashamed of their idleness, drunkenness, cheating, lying, and other sins, by making reputation always appear on virtue's side. (3.) See how miserable, and how near to ruin, those places are that either have no magistrates or none that bear the sword to any purpose; the wicked then *walk on every side,* Ps. 12:8. And how happy we are in good laws and a good government.

2. It was ill guarded. The people of Laish were careless, quiet, and secure, their gates left open, their walls out of repair, because under no apprehension of danger in any way, though their wickedness was so great that they had reason to fear divine vengeance every day. It was a sign that the Israelites, through their sloth and cowardice, were not now such a terror to the Canaanites as they were when they first came among them, else the city of Laish, which probably knew itself to be assigned to them, would not have been so very secure. Though they were an open and inland town, they *lived secure, like the Zidonians* (who were surrounded with the sea and were well fortified both by art and nature), but were *far from the Zidonians,* who therefore could not come in to their assistance, nor help to defend them from the danger which, by debauching their manners, they had helped to bring them into. And, *lastly,* they had *no business with any man,* which bespeaks either the idleness they affected (they followed no trade, and so grew lazy and luxurious, and utterly unable to defend themselves) or the independency they affected: they scorned to be either in subjection to or alliance with any of their neighbours, and so they had none to protect them nor bring in any aid to them. They cared for nobody and therefore nobody cared for them. Such as these were the men of Laish.

II. The encouragement which they consequently gave to their countrymen that sent them to prosecute their design upon this city, *v.* 8–10. Probably the Danites had formed notions of the insuperable difficulties of the enterprise, thought it impossible ever to make themselves masters of Laish, and therefore had kept themselves so long out of the possession of it, perhaps suggesting likewise to one another, in their unbelief, that it was not a country worth going so far and running such a risk for, which jealousies the spies (and they were not, in this, evil spies) had an eye to in their report. 1. They represent the place as desirable: "If you will trust our judgments, *we have seen the land,* and we are agreed in our verdict upon the view, that, behold, *it is very good* (*v.* 9), better than this mountainous country into which we are here crowded by the Philistines. You need not doubt of living comfortably in it, for it is a place *where there is no want of any thing,"* *v.* 10. See what a good land Canaan was, that this city which lay furthest of all northward, in the utmost corner of the country, stood on such a fruitful spot. 2. They represent it as attainable. They do not at all question but, with God's blessing, they may soon get possession of it; for *the people are secure, v.* 10. And the more secure always the less safe. "God *has given it into your hands,* and you may have it for the taking." They stir them up to the undertaking: *"Arise, that we may go up against them,* let us go about it speedily and resolutely." They expostulate with them for their delays, and chide them out of their sluggishness: *Are you still? Be not slothful to go.* Men need to be thus stirred up to mind even their interest. Heaven is *a very good land, where there is no want of any thing;* our God has, by the promise, *given it into our hands;* let us not then be slothful in making it sure, and *laying hold on eternal life,* but *strive to enter.*

III. The Danites' expedition against Laish. This particular family of them, to whose lot that city fell, now at length make towards it, *v.* 11–13. The military men were but 600 in all, not a hundredth part of that tribe, for when they entered Canaan the Danites were above 64,000, Num. 26:43. It was strange that none of their brethren of their own tribe, much less of any other, came in to their assistance; but it was long after Israel came to Canaan before there appeared among them any thing of a public spirit, or concern for a common interest, which was the reason why they seldom united in a common head, and this kept them low and inconsiderable. It appears (by *v.* 21) that these 600 were the whole number that went to settle there, for they had their families and effects with them, their *little ones and cattle,* so confident were they of success. The other tribes gave them a free passage through their country. Their first day's march brought them to Kirjath-jearim (*v.* 12), and such rare things had military encampments now become in Israel that the place where they rested that night was thence called *Mahaneh-dan, the camp of Dan,* and probably the place whence they began their march between Zorah and Eshtaol was called by the same name, and is meant, *ch.* 13:25. The second day's march brought them to Mount Ephraim, near Micah's house (*v.* 13), and there we must pause awhile.

Verses 14–26

The Danites had sent out their spies to find out a country for them, and they sped well in their search; but here, now that they came to the place (for till this brought it to their mind it does not appear that they had mentioned it to their brethren), they oblige them with a further discovery — they can tell them where there are gods: "Here, *in these houses,* there are an ephod, and teraphim, and a great many fine things for devotion, such as we have not the like in our country; *now therefore consider what you have to do, v.* 14. We consulted them, and had a good answer from them; they are worth having, nay, they are worth stealing (that is, having upon the worst terms), and, if we can but make ourselves masters of these gods, we may the better hope to prosper, and make ourselves masters of Laish." So far they were in the right, that it was desirable to have God's presence with them, but wretchedly mistaken when they took these images (which were fitter to be used in a puppet-play than in acts of devotion) for tokens of God's presence. They thought an oracle would be pretty company for them in their enterprise, and instead of a council of war to consult upon every emergency; and, the place they were going to settle in being so far from Shiloh, they thought they had more need of a *house of gods* among themselves than Micah had that lived so near to it. They might have made as good an ephod and teraphim themselves as these were, and such as would have served their purpose every whit as well; but the reputation which they found them in possession of (though they had had that reputation but a while) amused them into a strange veneration for this *house of gods,* which they would soon have dropped if they had had so much sense as to enquire into its origin, and examine whether there were any thing divine in its institution. Being determined to take these gods along with them, we are here told how they stole the images, cajoled the priest, and frightened Micah from attempting to rescue them.

I. The five men that knew the house and the avenues to it, and particularly the chapel, went in and fetched out the images, with the ephod, and teraphim, and all the appurtenances, while the 600 kept the priest in talk at the gate, *v.* 16–18. See what little care this sorry priest took of his gods; while he was sauntering at the gate, and gazing at the strangers, his treasure (such as it was) was gone. See how impotent these sorry gods were, that could not keep themselves from being stolen. It is mentioned as the reproach of idols that they *themselves had gone into captivity,* Isa. 46:2. O the sottishness of these Danites! How could they imagine those gods should protect them that could not keep themselves from being stolen? Yet because they went by the name of gods, as if it were not enough that they had with them the presence of the invisible God, nor that they stood in relation to the tabernacle, where there were even visible tokens of his presence, nothing will serve them but they must have *gods to go before them,* not of their own making indeed, but, which was as bad, of their own stealing. Their idolatry began in theft, a proper prologue for such an opera. In order to the breaking of the second commandment, they begin with the eighth, and take their neighbour's goods to make them their gods. The holy God *hates robbery for burnt-offerings,* but the devil loves it. Had these Danites seized the images to deface and abolish them, and the priest to punish him, they would have done like Israelites indeed, and would have appeared jealous for their God as their fathers had done (Jos. 22:16); but to take them for their own use was such a complicated crime as showed that they neither feared God nor regarded man, but were perfectly lost both to godliness and honesty.

II. They set upon the priest, and flattered him into a good humour, not only to let the gods go, but to go himself along with them; for without him they knew not well how to make use of the gods. Observe, 1. How they tempted him, *v.* 19. They assured him of better preferment with them than what he now had. It would be more honour and profit to be chaplain to a regiment (for they were no more, though they called themselves a *tribe)* than to be only a domestic chaplain to a private gentleman. Let him go with them, and he shall have more dependants on him, more sacrifices brought to his altar, and more fees for consulting his teraphim, than he had here. 2. How they won him. A little persuasion served: *His heart was glad, v.* 20. The proposal took well enough with his rambling fancy, which would never let him stay long at a place, and gratified his covetousness and ambition. He had no reason to say but that he was well off where he was; Micah had not *deceived him, nor changed his wages.* He was not moved with any remorse of conscience for attending on a graven image: had he gone away to Shiloh to minister to the Lord's priests, according to the duty of a Levite, he might have been welcome there (Deu. 18:6), and his removal would have been commendable; but, instead of this, he takes the images with him, and carries the infection of the idolatry into a whole city. It would have been very unjust and ungrateful to Micah if he had only gone away himself, but it was much more so to take the images along with him, which he knew the heart of Micah was set upon. Yet better could not be expected from a treacherous Levite. What house can be sure of him who has forsaken the house of the Lord? Or what friend will he be true to that has been false to his God? He could not pretend that he was under compulsive force, for he was *glad in his heart* to go. If ten shekels won him (as bishop Hall expresses it), eleven would lose him; for what can hold those that have made shipwreck of a good conscience? *The hireling flees because he is a hireling.* The priest and his gods went in *the midst of the people.* There they placed him, that they might secure him either from going back himself, if his mind should change, or from being fetched back by Micah; or perhaps this post was assigned to him in imitation of the order of Israel's march through the wilderness, in which the ark and the priests went in the midst of their camp.

III. They frightened Micah back when he pursued them to recover his gods. As soon as ever he perceived that his chapel was plundered, and his chaplain had run away from him, he mustered all the forces he could and pursued the robbers, *v.* 22. His neighbours, and perhaps tenants, that used to join with him in his devotions, were forward to help him on this occasion; they got together, and pursued the robbers, who, having their children and cattle before them (*v.* 21), could make no great haste, so that they soon overtook them, hoping by strength of reason to recover what was stolen, for the disproportion of their numbers was such that they could not hope to do it by strength of arm. The pursuers called after them, desiring to speak a word with them; those in the rear (where it is probable they posted the fiercest and strongest of their company, expecting there to be attacked) turned about and asked Micah what ailed him that he was so much concerned, and what he would have, *v.* 23. He argues with them, and pleads his right, which he thought should prevail; but they, in answer, plead their might, which, it proved, did prevail; for it is common that might overcomes right.

1. He insists upon the wrong they had certainly done him (*v.* 24): "*You have taken away my gods,* my images of God, which I have an incontestable title to, for I made them myself, and which I have such an affection for that I am undone if I lose them; for what have I more that will do me any good if these be lost?" Now, (1.) This discovers to us the folly of idolaters, and the power that Satan has over them. What a folly was it for him to call those his *gods* which he had made, when he only that made us is to be worshipped by us as a God! Folly indeed to set his heart upon such silly idle things, and to look upon himself as undone when he had lost them! (2.) This may discover to us our spiritual idolatry. That creature which we place our happiness in, which we set our affections inordinately upon, and which we can by no means find in our hearts to part with, of which we say, "What have we more?" *that* we make an idol of. That is put in God's place, and is a usurper, which we are concerned about as if our life and comfort, our hope and happiness, and our all, were bound up in it. But, (3.) If all people will thus walk in the name of their god, shall we not be in like manner affected towards our God, the true God? Let us reckon the having of an interest in God and communion with him incomparably the richest portion, and the loss of God the sorest loss. Woe unto us if he depart, for what have we more? Deserted souls that are lamenting after the Lord may well wonder, as Micah did, that you should ask what ails them; for the tokens of God's favour are suspended, his comforts are withdrawn, and what have they more?

2. They insist upon the mischief they would certainly do him if he prosecuted his demand. They would not hear reason, nor do justice, nor so much as offer to pay him the prime cost he had been at upon those images, nor promise to make restitution of what they had taken when they had served their present purpose with them in this expedition and had time to copy them and make others like them for themselves: much less had they any compassion for a loss he so bitterly lamented. They would not so much as give him good words, but resolved to justify their robbery with murder if he did not immediately let fall his claims, *v.* 25. "Take heed *lest angry fellows run upon thee, and thou lose thy life,* and that is worse than losing thy gods." Wicked and unreasonable men reckon it a great provocation to be asked to do justice, and support themselves by their power against right and reason. Micah's crime is asking his own, yet, for this, he is in danger of losing his life and the lives of his household. Micah has not courage enough to venture his life for the rescue of his gods, so little opinion has he of their being able to protect him and bear him out, and therefore tamely gives them up (*v.* 26): *He turned and went back to his house;* and if the loss of his idols did but convince him (as, one would think, it should) of their vanity and impotency, and his own folly in setting his heart upon them, and send him back to the true God from whom he had revolted, he that lost them had a much better bargain than those that by force of arms carried them off. If the loss of our idols cure us of the love of them, and make us say, *What have we to do any more with idols?* the loss will be unspeakable gain. See Isa. 2:20; 30:22.

Verses 27–31

Here is, I. Laish conquered by the Danites. They proceeded on their march, and, because they met with no disaster, perhaps concluded they had not done amiss in robbing Micah. Many justify themselves in their impiety by their prosperity. Observe, 1. What posture they found the people of Laish in, both those of the city and those of the country about. They were quiet and secure, not jealous of the five spies that had been among them to search out the land, nor had they any intelligence of the approach of this enemy, which made them a very easy prey to this little handful of men that came upon them, *v.* 27. Note, Many are brought to destruction by their security. Satan gets advantage against us when we are careless and off our watch. Happy therefore is the man that feareth always. 2. What a complete victory they obtained over them: They *put all the people to the sword,* and burnt down so much of the city as they thought fit to rebuild (*v.* 27, 28), and, for aught that appears, herein they met with no resistance; for the measure of the iniquity of the Canaanites was full, that of the Danites was but beginning to fill. 3. How the conquerors settled themselves in their room, *v.* 28, 29. They built the city, or much of it, anew (the old buildings having gone to decay), and *called the name of it Dan,* to be a witness for them that, though separated so far off from their brethren, they were nevertheless Danites by birth, which might hereafter, by reason of their distance, be called in question. We should feel concerned not to lose the privilege of our relation to God's Israel, and therefore should take all occasions to own it and preserve the remembrance of it to ours after us.

II. Idolatry immediately set up there. God had graciously performed his promise, in putting them in possession of that which fell to their lot, obliging them thereby to be faithful to him who had been so to them. They *inherited the labour of the people, that they might observe his statues,* Ps. 105:44, 45. But the first thing they do after they are settled is to break his statues. As soon as they began to settle themselves they *set up the graven image* (*v.* 30), perversely attributing their success to that idol which, if God had not been infinitely patient, would have been their ruin. Thus a prosperous idolater goes on to offend, *imputing this his power unto his god,* Hab. 1:11. Their Levite, who officiated as priest, is at length *named* here — *Jonathan, the son of Gershom, the son of Manasseh.* The word *Manasseh,* in the original, has the letter *n,* set over the head, which, some of the Jewish rabbin say, is an intimation that it should be left out, and then *Manasseh* will be *Moses,* and this Levite, they say, was grandson to the famous Moses, who indeed had a son named Gershom; but, say they, the historian, in honour of Moses, by a half interposition of that letter, turned the name into Manasseh. The vulgar Latin reads it *Moses.* And if indeed Moses had a grandson that was rakish, and was picked up as a fit tool to be made use of in the setting up of idolatry, it is not the only instance (would to God it were!) of the unhappy degenerating of the posterity of great and good men. Children's children are not always the crown of old men. But the learned bishop Patrick takes this to be an idle conceit of the rabbin, and supposes this Jonathan to be of some other family of the Levites. How long these corruptions continued we are told in the close. 1. That the posterity of this Jonathan continued to act as priests to this family of Dan that was seated at Laish, and in the country about, till the captivity, *v.* 30. After Micah's image was removed this family retained the character of priests, and had respect paid them as such by that city, and it is very probable that Jeroboam had an eye to them when he set up one of his calves there (which they could welcome at Can, and put some reputation upon, when the priests of the Lord would have nothing to do with them), and that this family officiated as some of his priests. 2. That these images continued till Samuel's time, for so long *the ark of God was at Shiloh;* and it is probable that in him time effectual care was taken to suppress and abolish this idolatry. See how dangerous it is to admit an infection, for spiritual distempers are not so soon cured as caught.

CHAPTER 19

The three remaining chapters of this book contain a most tragical story of the wickedness of the men of Gibeah, patronised by the tribe of Benjamin, for which that tribe was severely chastised and almost entirely cut off by the rest of the tribes. This seems to have been done not long after the death of Joshua, for it was when there was no king, no judge, in Israel (*v.* 1, and 21:25), and Phinehas was then high priest, 20:28. These particular iniquities, the Danites' idolatry, and the Benjamites' immorality, let in that general apostasy, 3:7. The abuse of the Levite's concubine is here very particularly related. I. Her adulterous elopement from him (*v.* 1, 2). II. His reconciliation to her, and the journey he took to fetch her home (*v.* 3). III. Her father's kind entertainment of him (*v.* 4–9). IV. The abuse he met with at Gibeah, where, being benighted, he was forced to stop. 1. He was neglected by the men of Gibeah (*v.* 10–15) and entertained by an Ephraimite that sojourned among them (*v.* 16–21). 2. They set upon him in his quarters, as the Sodomites did on Lot's quests (*v.* 22–24). 3. They villainously forced his concubine to death (*v.* 25–28). V. The course he took to send notice of this to all the tribes of Israel (*v.* 29, 30).

Verses 1–15

The domestic affairs of this Levite would not have been related thus largely but to make way for the following story of the injuries done him, in which the whole nation interested themselves. Bishop Hall's first remark upon this story is, *That there is no complain of a public ordered state but there is a Levite at one end of it, either as an agent or as a patient.* In Micah's idolatry a Levite was active; in the wickedness of Gibeah a Levite was passive; *no tribe shall sooner feel the want of government than that of Levi;* and, in all the book of Judges, no mention is made of any of that tribe, but of these two. This Levite was of Mount Ephraim, *v.* 1. He married a wife of Bethlehem-Judah. She is called his *concubine,* because she was not endowed, for perhaps he had nothing to endow her with, being himself a sojourner and not settled; but it does not appear that he had any other wife, and the margin calls her *a wife, a concubine, v.* 1. She came from the same city that Micah's Levite came from, as if Bethlehem-Judah owed a double ill turn to Mount Ephraim, for she was as bad for a Levite's wife as the other for a Levite.

I. This Levite's concubine played the whore and eloped from her husband, *v.* 2. The Chaldee reads it only that she *carried herself insolently to him,* or *despised him,* and, he being displeased at it, *she went away from him,* and (which was not fair) was received and entertained at her father's house. Had her husband turned her out of doors unjustly, her father ought to have pitied her affliction; but, when she treacherously departed from her husband to embrace the bosom of a stranger, her father ought not to have countenanced her sin. Perhaps she would not have violated her duty to her husband if she had not known too well where she should be kindly received. Children's ruin is often owing very much to parents' indulgence.

II. The Levite went himself to court her return. It was a sign there was no king, no judge, in Israel, else she would have been prosecuted and put to death as an adulteress; but, instead of that, she is addressed in the kindest manner by her injured husband, who takes a long journey on purpose to beseech her to be reconciled, *v.* 3. If he had put her away, it would have been a crime in him to return to her again, Jer. 3:1. But, she having gone away, it was a virtue in him to forgive the offence, and, though the party wronged, to make the first motion to her to be friends again. It is part of the character of the wisdom from above that it is gentle and easy to be entreated. He spoke *friendly* to her, or *comfortably* (for so the Hebrew phrase of *speaking to the heart* commonly signifies), which intimates that she was in sorrow, penitent fore what she had done amiss, which probably he heard of when he came to fetch her back. Thus God promises concerning adulterous Israel (Hos. 2:14), *I will bring her into the wilderness, and speak comfortably to her.*

III. Her father made him very welcome, and, by his extraordinary kindness to him, endeavoured to atone for the countenance he had given his daughter in withdrawing from him, and to confirm him in his disposition to be reconciled to her. 1. He entertains him kindly, *rejoices to see him* (*v.* 3), treats him generously for three days, *v.* 4. And the Levite, to show that he was perfectly reconciled, accepted his kindness, and we do not find that he upbraided him or his daughter with what had been amiss, but was as easy and as pleasant as at his first wedding-feast. It becomes all, but especially Levites, to forgive as God does. Every thing among them gave a hopeful prospect of their living comfortably together for the future; but, could they have foreseen what befel them within one day or two, how would all their mirth have been embittered and turned into mourning! When the affairs of our families are in the best posture we ought to rejoice with trembling, because we know not what troubles one day may bring forth. We cannot foresee what evil is near us, but we ought to consider what may be, that we may not be secure, as if to-morrow must needs be as this day and *much more abundant,* Isa. 56:12. 2. He is very earnest for his stay, as a further demonstration of his hearty welcome. The affection he had for him, and the pleasure he took in his company, proceeded, (1.) From a civil regard to him as his son-in-law and an ingrafted branch of his own house. Note, Love and duty are due to those to whom we are related by marriage as well as to those who are bone of our bone: and those that show kindness as this Levite did may expect to receive kindness as he did. And, (2.) From a pious respect to him as a Levite, a servant of God's house; if he was such a Levite as he should be (and nothing appears to the contrary) he is to be commended for courting his stay, finding his conversation profitable, and having opportunity to learn from him the *good knowledge of the Lord,* hoping also that *the Lord will do him good because he has a Levite* to be his son-in-law, and will bless him for his sake. [1.] He forces him to stay the fourth day, and this was kind; not knowing when they might be together again, he engages him to stay as long as he possibly could. The Levite, though nobly treated, was very urgent to be gone. A good man's heart is where his business is; for *as a bird that wanders from her nest so is the man that wanders form his place.* It is a sign a man has either little to do at home, or little heart to do what he has to do, when he can take pleasure in being long abroad where he has nothing to do. It is especially good to see a Levite willing to go home to his few sheep in the wilderness. Yet this Levite was overcome by importunity and kind persuasion to stay longer than he intended, *v.* 5–7. We ought to avoid the extreme of an over-easy yielding, to the neglect of our duty on the one hand, and that of moroseness and wilfulness, to the neglect of our friends and their kindness on the other hand. Our Saviour, after his resurrection, was prevailed upon to stay with his friends longer than he at first intimated to be his purpose, Lu. 24:28, 29. [2.] He forces him to stay till the afternoon of the fifth day, and this, as it proved, was unkind, *v.* 8, 9. He would by no means let him go before dinner, promises him he shall have dinner early, designing thereby, as he had done the day before, to detain him another night; but the Levite was intent on the *house of the Lord at Shiloh* (*v.* 18), and, being impatient to get thither, would stay no longer. Had they set out early, they might have reached some better lodging-place than that which they were now constrained to take up with, nay, they might have got to Shiloh. Note, Our friends' designed kindnesses often prove, in the event, real injuries; what is meant for our welfare becomes a trap. *Who knows what is good for a man in this life?* The Levite was unwise in setting out so late; he might have got home better if he had staid a night longer and taken the day before him.

IV. In his return home he was forced to lodge at Gibeah, a city in the tribe of Benjamin, afterwards called *Gibeah of Saul,* which lay on his road towards Shiloh and Mount Ephraim. When it drew towards night, and the shadows of the evening were stretched out, they began to think (as it behoves us to do when we observe the day of our life hastening towards a period) where they must lodge. When night came they could not pursue their journey. *He that walketh in darkness knoweth not whither he goes.* They could not but desire rest, for which the night was intended, as the day for labour. 1. The servant proposed that they should lodge in Jebus, afterwards Jerusalem, but as yet in the possession of Jebusites. "Come," said the servant, "let us lodge in this city of the Jebusites," *v.* 11. And, if they had done so, it is probable they would have had much better usage than they met with in Gibeah of Benjamin. Debauched and profligate Israelites are worse and much more dangerous than Canaanites themselves. But the master, as became one of God's tribe, would by no means quarter, no, not one night, in a city of strangers (*v.* 12), not because he questioned his safety among them, but he was not willing, if he could possibly avoid it, to have so much intimacy and familiarity with them as a night's lodging came to, nor to be so much beholden to them. By shunning this place he would witness against the wickedness of those that contracted friendship and familiarity with these devoted nations. Let Israelites, Levites especially, associate with Israelites, and not with the *sons of the stranger.* 2. Having passed by Jebus, which was about five or six miles from Bethlehem (the place whence they came), and not having daylight to bring them to Ramah, they stopped at Gibeah (*v.* 13–15); there they sat down in the street, nobody offering them a lodging. In these countries, at that time, there were no inns, or public-houses, in which, as with us, travellers might have entertainment for their money, but they carried entertainment along with them, as this Levite did (*v.* 19), and depended upon the courtesy and hospitality of the inhabitants for a lodging. Let us take occasion hence, when we are in journeys, to thank God for this, among other conveniences of travelling, that there are inns to entertain strangers, and in which they may be welcome and well accommodated for their money. Surely there is no country in the world wherein one may stay at home with more satisfaction, or go abroad with more comfort, than in our own nation. This traveller, though a Levite (and to those of that tribe God had particularly commanded his people to be kind upon all occasions), met with very cold entertainment at Gibeah: *No man took them into his house.* If they had any reason to think he was a Levite perhaps that made those ill-disposed people the more shy of him. There are those who will have this laid to their charge at the great day, *I was a stranger and you took me not in.*

Verses 16–21

Though there as not one *of* Gibeah, yet it proved there was one *in* Gibeah, that showed some civility to this distressed Levite, who was glad that any one took notice of him. It was strange that some of those wicked people, who, when it was dark, designed so ill to him and his concubine, did not, under pretence of kindness, invite them in, that they might have a fairer opportunity of perpetrating their villany; but either they had not wit enough to be so designing, or not wickedness enough to be so deceiving. Or, perhaps, none of them separately thought of such a wickedness, till in the black and dark night they got together to contrive what mischief they should do. Bad people in confederacy make one another much worse than any of them would be by themselves. When the Levite, and his wife, and servant, were beginning to fear that they must lie in the street all night (and as good have laid in a den of lions) they were at length invited into a house, and we are here told,

I. Who that kind man was that invited them. 1. He was a man of Mount Ephraim, and only sojourned in Gibeah, *v.* 16. Of all the tribes of Israel, the Benjamites had most reason to be kind to poor travellers, for their ancestor, Benjamin, was born upon the road, his mother being then upon a journey, and very near to this place, Gen. 35:16, 17. Yet they were hard-hearted to a traveller in distress, while an honest Ephraimite had compassion on him, and, no doubt, was the more kind to him, when, upon enquiry, he found that he was his countryman, of Mount Ephraim likewise. He that was himself but a sojourner in Gibeah was the more compassionate to a wayfaring man, for he *knew the heart of a stranger,* Ex. 23:9; Deu. 10:19. Good people, that look upon themselves but as strangers and sojourners in this world, should for this reason be tender to one another, because they all belong to the same better country and are not at home here. 2. He was an old man, one that retained some of the expiring virtue of an Israelite. The rising generation was entirely corrupted; if there was any good remaining among them, it was only with those that were old and going off. 3. He was coming home from his work out of the field at eventide. The evening calls home labourers, Ps. 104:23. But, it should seem, this was the only labourer that this evening brought home to Gibeah. The rest had given themselves up to sloth and luxury, and no marvel there was among them, as in Sodom, abundance of uncleanness, when there was among them, as in Sodom, abundance of idleness, Eze. 16:49. But he that was honestly diligent in his business all day was disposed to be generously hospitable to these poor strangers at night. Let men *labour, that they may have to give,* Eph. 4:28. It appears from *v.* 21 that he was a man of some substance, and yet had been himself at work in the field. No man's estate will privilege him in idleness.

II. How free and generous he was in his invitation. He did not stay till they applied to him to beg for a night's lodging; but when he saw them (*v.* 17) enquired into their circumstances, and anticipated them with his kindness. Thus our good God answers before we call. Note, A charitable disposition expects only opportunity, not importunity, to do good, and will succour upon sight, unsought unto. Hence we read of a *bountiful eye,* Prov. 22:9. If Gibeah was like Sodom, this old man was like Lot in Sodom, who *sat in the gate* to invite strangers, Gen. 19:1. Thus *Job opened his doors to the traveller,* and would not suffer him to *lodge in the street,* Job 31:32. Observe, 1. How ready he was to give credit to the Levite's account of himself when he saw no reason at all to question the truth of it. Charity is not apt to distrust, but *hopeth all things* (1 Co. 13:7) and will not make use of Nabal's excuse for his churlishness to David, *Many servants now-a-days break away from their masters,* 1 Sa. 25:10. The Levite, in his account of himself, professed that he was now going *to the house of the Lord* (*v.* 18), for there he designed to attend, either with a trespass-offering for the sins of his family, or with a peace-offering for the mercies of his family, or both, before he went to his own house. And, if the men of Gibeah had any intimation of his being bound that way, probably they would therefore be disinclined to entertain him. The Samaritans would not receive Christ because his face was towards Jerusalem, Lu. 9:53. But for this reason, because he was a Levite and was now going to the house of the Lord, this good old man was the more kind to him. Thus he received a disciples *in the name of a disciple,* a servant of God for his Master's sake. 2. How free he was to give him entertainment. The Levite was himself provided with all necessaries (*v.* 19), wanted nothing but a lodging, but his generous host would be himself at the charge of his entertainment (*v.* 20): *Let all thy wants be upon me;* so he *brought him into his house, v.* 21. Thus God will, some way or other, raise up friends for his people and ministers, even when they seem forlorn.

Verses 22–30

Here is, I. The great wickedness of the men of Gibeah. One could not imagine that ever it should enter into the heart of men that had the use of human reason, of Israelites that had the benefit of divine revelation, to be so very wicked. "Lord, what is man!" said David, "what a *mean* creature is he!" "Lord, what is man," may we say upon the reading of this story, "what a vile creature is he, when he is given up to his own heart's lusts!" The sinners are here called *sons of Belial,* that is, ungovernable men, men that would endure no yoke, children of the devil (for he is Belial), resembling him, and joining with him in rebellion against God and his government. Sons of Benjamin, of whom Moses had said, *The beloved of the Lord shall dwell in safety by him* (Deu. 33:12), have become such sons of Belial that an honest man cannot lodge in safety among them. The sufferers were a Levite and his wife, and that kind man that gave them entertainment. We are strangers upon earth, and must expect strange usage. It is said *they were making their hearts merry* when this trouble came upon them, *v.* 22. If the mirth was innocent, it teaches us of what uncertain continuance all our creature comforts and enjoyments are; when we are ever so well pleased with our friends, we know not how near our enemies are; nor, if it be well with us this hour, can we be sure it will be so the next. If the mirth was sinful and excessive, let it be a warning to us to keep a strict guard upon ourselves, that we grow not intemperate in the use of lawful things, nor be transported into indecencies by our cheerfulness; for *the end of that mirth is heaviness.* God can soon change the note of those that are making their hearts merry, and turn their laughter into mourning and their joy into heaviness. Let us see what the wickedness of these Benjamites was.

1. They made a rude and insolent assault, in the night, upon the habitation of an honest man, that not only lived peaceably among them, but kept a good house and was a blessing and ornament to their city. They beset the house round, and, to the great terror of those within, beat as hard as they could at the door, *v.* 22. A man's house is his castle, in which he ought to be both safe and quiet, and, where there is law, it is taken under the special protection of it; but there was no king in Israel to keep the peace and secure honest men from the sons of violence.

2. They had a particular spite at the strangers that were within their gates, that only desired a night's lodging among them, contrary to the laws of hospitality, which all civilized nations have accounted sacred, and which the master of the house pleaded with them (*v.* 23): *Seeing that this man has come into my house.* Those are base and abject spirits indeed that will trample upon the helpless, and use a man the worse for his being a stranger, whom they know no ill of.

3. They designed in the most filthy and abominable manner (not to be thought of without horror and detestation) to abuse the Levite, whom perhaps they had observed to be young and comely: *Bring him forth that we may know him.* We should certainly have concluded they meant only to enquire whence he came, and to know his character, but that the good man of the house, who understood their meaning too well, by his answer lets us know that they designed the gratification of that most unnatural and worse than brutish lust which was expressly forbidden by the law of Moses, and called an *abomination,* Lev. 18:22. Those that are guilty of it are ranked in the New Testament among the worst and vilest of sinners (1 Tim. 1:10), and such as *shall not inherit the kingdom of God,* 1 Co. 6:9. Now, (1.) This was the sin of Sodom, and is thence called *Sodomy.* The Dead Sea, which was the standing monument of God's vengeance upon Sodom, for its filthiness, was one of the boundaries of Canaan, and lay not many miles off from Gibeah. We may suppose the men of Gibeah had seen it many a time, and yet would not take warning by it, but did worse than Sodom (Eze. 16:48), and sinned just *after the similitude of their transgression.* Who would have expected (says bishop Hall) such extreme abomination to come out of the loins of Jacob? Even the worst pagans were saints to them. What did it avail them that they had the ark of God in Shiloh when they had Sodom in their streets — God's law in their fringes, but the devil in their hearts? Nothing but hell itself can yield a worse creature than a depraved Israelite. (2.) This was the punishment of their idolatry, that sin to which they were, above all others, most addicted. Because they liked not to retain God in their knowledge, therefore he gave them up to these vile affections, by which they dishonoured themselves as they had by their idolatry dishonoured him and turned his glory into shame, Rom. 1:24, 28. See and admire, in this instance, the patience of God. Why were not these sons of Belial struck blind, as the Sodomites were? Why were not fire and brimstone rained from heaven upon their city? It was because God would leave it to Israel to punish them by the sword, and would reserve his own punishment of them for the future state, in which those that *go after strange flesh* shall *suffer the vengeance of eternal fire,* Jude 7.

4. They were deaf to the reproofs and reasoning of the good man of the house, who, being well acquainted (we may suppose) with the story of Lot and the Sodomites, set himself to imitate Lot, *v.* 23, 24. Compare Gen. 19:6–8. He went out to them as Lot did, spoke civilly to them, called them brethren, begged of them to desist, pleaded the protection of his house which his guests were under, and represented to them the great wickedness of their attempt: "Do not so wickedly, so very wickedly." He calls it *folly* and *a vile thing.* But in one thing he conformed too far to Lot's example (as we are apt in imitating good men to follow them even in their false steps), in offering them his daughter to do what they would with. He had not power thus to prostitute his daughter, nor ought he to have done this evil that good might come. But this wicked proposal of his may be in part excused from the great surprise and terror he was in, his concern for his guests, and his having too close a regard to what Lot did in the like case, especially not finding that the angels who were by reproved him for it. And perhaps he hoped that his mentioning this as a more natural gratification of their lust would have sent them back to their common harlots. But *they would not hearken to him, v.* 25. Headstrong lusts are like the deaf adder that stoppeth her ear; they sear the conscience and make it insensible.

5. They got the Levite's wife among them, and abused her to death, *v.* 25. They slighted the old man's offer of his daughter to their lust, either because she was not handsome or because they knew her to be one of great gravity and modesty: but, when the Levite brought them his concubine, they took her with them by force to the place appointed for their filthiness. Josephus, in his narrative of this story, makes her to be the person they had a design upon when they beset the house, and says nothing of their villainous design upon the Levite himself. They saw her (he says) in the street, when they came into the town, and were smitten with her beauty; and perhaps, though she was reconciled to her husband, her looks did not bespeak her to be one of the most modest. Many bring mischief of this kind upon themselves by their loose carriage and behaviour; a little spark may kindle a great fire. One would think the Levite should have followed them, to see what became of his wife, but it is probable he durst not, lest they should do him a mischief. In the miserable end of this woman, we may see the righteous hand of God punishing her for her former uncleanness, when she played the whore against her husband, *v.* 2. Though her father had countenanced her, her husband had forgiven her, and the fault was forgotten now that the quarrel was made up, yet God remembered it against her when he suffered these wicked men thus wretchedly to abuse her; how unrighteous soever they were in their treatment of her, in permitting it the Lord was righteous. Her punishment answered her sin, *Culpa libido fuit, poena libido fuit — Lust was her sin, and lust was her punishment.* By the law of Moses she was to have been put to death for her adultery. She escaped that punishment from men, yet vengeance pursued her; for, if there was no king in Israel, yet there was a God in Israel, a God that judgeth in the earth. We must not think it enough to make our peace with men, whom by our sins we have wronged, but are concerned, by repentance and faith, to make our peace with God, who sees not as men see, nor makes so light of sin as men often do. The justice of God in this matter does not at all extenuate the horrid wickedness of these men of Gibeah, than which nothing could be more barbarous and inhuman.

II. The notice that was sent of this wickedness to all the tribes of Israel. The poor abused woman made towards her husband's lodgings as soon as ever the approach of the day-light obliged these sons of Belial to let her go (for these works of darkness hate and dread the light), *v.* 25. Down she fell at the door, with her hands on the threshold, begging pardon (as it were) for her former transgression, and in that posture of a penitent, with her mouth in the dust, she expired. There he found her (*v.* 26, 27), supposed her asleep, or overcome with shame and confusion for what had happened, but soon perceived she was dead (*v.* 28), took up her dead body, which, we may suppose, had all over it marks of the hands, the blows, and other abuses, she had received. On this sad occasion he waived his purpose of going to Shiloh, and went directly home. He that went out in hopes to return rejoicing came in again melancholy and disconsolate, sat down and considered, "Is this an injury fit to be passed by?" He cannot call for fire from heaven to consume the men of Gibeah, as those angels did who were, after the same manner, insulted by the Sodomites. There was no king in Israel, nor (for aught that appears) any sanhedrim, or great council, to appeal to, and demand justice from. Phinehas is high priest, but he attends closely to the business of the sanctuary, and will be no judge or divider. He has therefore no other way left him than to appeal to the people: let the community be judge. Though they had no general stated assembly of all the tribes, yet it is probable that each tribe had a meeting of their chiefs within itself. To each of the tribes, in their respective meetings, he sent by special messengers a remonstrance of the wrong that was done him, in all its aggravating circumstances, and with it a piece of his wife's dead body (*v.* 29), both to confirm the truth of the story and to affect them the more with it. He divided it into twelve pieces, *according to the bones,* so some read it, that is, by the joints, sending one to each tribe, even to Benjamin among the rest, with the hope that some among them would be moved to join in punishing so great a villany, and the more warmly because committed by some of their own tribe. It did indeed look very barbarous thus to mangle a dead body, which, having been so wretchedly dishonoured, ought to have been decently interred; but the Levite designed hereby, not only to represent their barbarous usage of his wife, whom they had better have cut in pieces thus than have used as they did, but also to express his own passionate concern and thereby to excite the like in them. And it had the desired effect. All that saw the pieces of the dead body, and were told how the matter was, expressed the same sentiments upon it. 1. That the men of Gibeah had been guilty of a very heinous piece of wickedness, the like to which had never been known before in Israel, *v.* 30. It was a complicated crime, loaded and blackened with all possible aggravations. They were not such fools as to make a mock at this sin, or turn the story off with a jest. 2. That a general assembly of all Israel should be called, to debate what was fit to be done for the punishment of this wickedness, that a stop might be put to this threatening inundation of debauchery, and the wrath of God might not be poured upon the whole nation for it. It is not a common case, and therefore they stir up one another to come together upon the occasion with this: *Consider of it, take advice, and speak your minds.* We have here the three great rules by which those that sit in council ought to go in every arduous affair. (1.) Let every man retire into himself, and weigh the matter impartially and fully in his own thoughts, and seriously and calmly consider it, without prejudice on either side, before he speaks upon it. (2.) Let them freely talk it over, and every man take advice of his friend, know his opinion and his reasons, and weigh them. (3.) Then let every man speak his mind, and give his vote according to his conscience. In the multitude of such counsellors there is safety.

CHAPTER 20

Into the book of the wars of the Lord the story of this chapter must be brought, but it looks as sad and uncomfortable as any article in all that history; for there is nothing in it that looks in the least bright or pleasant but the pious zeal of Israel against the wickedness of the men of Gibeah, which made it on their side a just and holy war; but otherwise the obstinacy of the Benjamites in protecting their criminals, which was the foundation of the war, the vast loss which the Israelites sustained in carrying on the war, and (though the righteous cause was victorious at last) the issuing of the war in the almost utter extirpation of the tribe of Benjamin, make it, from first to last, melancholy. And yet this happened soon after the glorious settlement of Israel in the land of promise, upon which one would have expected every thing to be prosperous and serene. In this chapter we have, I. The Levite's cause heard in a general convention of the tribes (*v.* 1–7). II. A unanimous resolve to avenge his quarrel upon the men of Gibeah (*v.* 8–11). III. The Benjamites appearing in defence of the criminals (*v.* 12–17). IV. The defeat of Israel in the first and second day's battle (*v.* 18–25). V. Their humbling themselves before God upon that occasion (*v.* 26–28). VI. The total rout they gave the Benjamites in the third engagement, by a stratagem, by which they were all cut off, except 600 men (*v.* 29–48). And all this the effect of the indignities done to one poor Levite and his wife; so little do those that do iniquity consider what will be the end thereof.

Verses 1–11

Here is, I. A general meeting of all the congregation of Israel to examine the matter concerning the Levite's concubine, and to consider what was to be done upon it, *v.* 1, 2. It does not appear that they were summoned by the authority of any one common head, but they came together by the consent and agreement, as it were, of one common heart, fired with a holy zeal for the honour of God and Israel. 1. The place of their meeting was *Mizpeh;* they gathered together unto the Lord there, for Mizpeh was so very near to Shiloh that their encampment might very well be supposed to reach from Mizpeh to Shiloh. Shiloh was a small town, and therefore, when there was a general meeting of the people to represent themselves before God, they chose Mizpeh for their head-quarters, which was the next adjoining city of note, perhaps because they were not willing to give that trouble to Shiloh which so great an assembly would occasion, it being the resident of the priests that attended the tabernacle. 2. The persons that met were all Israel, from Dan (the city very lately so called, *ch.* 18:29) in the north to Beersheba in the south, with the land of Gilead (that is, the tribes on the other side Jordan), all *as one man,* so unanimous were they in their concern for the public good. Here was an assembly of the people of God, not a convocation of the Levites and priests, though a Levite was the person principally concerned in the cause, but an assembly of the people, to whom the Levite referred himself with an *Appello populum — I appeal to the people.* The *people of God were* 400,000 *footmen that drew the sword,* that is, were armed and disciplined, and fit for service, and some of them perhaps such as had *known the wars of Canaan, ch.* 3:1. In this assembly of all Israel, the chief (or corners) of the people (for rulers are the corner-stones of the people, that keep all together) presented themselves as the representatives of the rest. They rendered themselves at their respective posts, at the head of the thousands and hundreds, the fifties and tens, over which they presided; for so much order and government, we may suppose, at least, they had among them, though they had no general or commander-in-chief. So that here was, (1.) A general congress of the states for counsel. The chief of the people presented themselves, to lead and direct in this affair. (2.) A general rendezvous of the militia for action, all that drew sword and were men of war (*v.* 17), not hirelings nor pressed men, but the best freeholders, that went at their own charge. Israel were above 600,000 when they came into Canaan, and we have reason to think they were at this time much increased, rather than diminished; but then all between twenty and sixty were military men, now we may suppose more than the one half exempted from bearing arms to cultivate the land; so that these were as the trained bands. The militia of the two tribes and a half were 40,000 (Jos. 4:13), but the tribes were many more.

II. Notice given to the tribe of Benjamin of this meeting (*v.* 3): *They heard that the children of Israel had gone up to Mizpeh.* Probably they had a legal summons sent them to appear with their brethren, that the cause might be fairly debated, before any resolutions were taken up upon it, and so the mischiefs that followed would have been happily prevented; but the notice they had of this meeting rather hardened and exasperated them than awakened them to think of the things that belonged to their peace and honour.

III. A solemn examination of the crime charged upon the men of Gibeah. A very horrid representation of it had been made by the report of the messengers that were sent to call them together, but it was fit it should be more closely enquired into, because such things are often made worse than really they were; a committee therefore was appointed to examine the witnesses (upon oath, no doubt) and to report the matter. It is only the testimony of the Levite himself that is here recorded, but it is probable his servant, and the old man, were examined, and gave in their testimony, for that more than one were examined appears by the original (*v.* 3), which is, *Tell you us;* and the law was that none should be put to death, much less so many, upon the testimony of one witness only. The Levite gives a particular account of the matter: that he came into Gibeah only as a traveller to lodge there, not giving the least shadow of suspicion that he designed them any ill turn (*v.* 4), and that the men of Gibeah, even those that were of substance among them, that should have been a protection to the stranger within their gates, riotously set upon the house where he lodged, and *thought to slay him;* he could not, for shame relate the demand which they, without shame, made, *ch.* 19:22. They declared their sin as Sodom, even the sin of Sodom, but his modesty would not suffer him to repeat it; it was sufficient to say they would have slain him, for he would rather have been slain than have submitted to their villany; and, if they had got him into their hands, they would have abused him to death, witness what they had done to his concubine: They have *forced her that she is dead, v.* 5. And, to excite in his countrymen an indignation at this wickedness, he had sent pieces of the mangled body to all the tribes, which had fetched them together to bear their testimony against the *lewdness and folly committed in Israel, v.* 6. All lewdness is folly, but especially lewdness in Israel. For those to defile their own bodies who have the honourable seal of the covenant in their flesh, for those to defy the divine vengeance to whom it is so clearly revealed from heaven — Nabal is their name, and folly is with them. He concludes his declaration with an appeal to the judgment of the court (*v.* 7): *You are all children of Israel,* and therefore you *know law and judgment,* Esth. 1:13. "You are a holy people to God, and have a dread of every thing which will dishonour our God and defile the land; you are of the same community, members of the same body, and therefore likely to feel from the distempers of it; you are children of Israel, that ought to take particular care of the Levites, God's tribe, among you, and therefore give your advice and counsel what is to be done."

IV. The resolution they came to hereupon, which was that, being now together, they would not disperse till they had seen vengeance taken upon this wicked city, which was the reproach and scandal of their nation. Observe, 1. Their zeal against the lewdness that was committed. They would not return to their houses, how much soever their families and their affairs at home wanted them, till they had vindicated the honour of God and Israel, and recovered with their swords, if it could not be had otherwise, that satisfaction for the crime which the justice of the nation called for, *v.* 8. By this they showed themselves children of Israel indeed, that they preferred the public interest before their private concerns. 2. Their prudence in sending out a considerable body of their forces to fetch provisions for the rest, *v.* 9, 10. One of ten, and he chosen by lot, 40,000 in all, must go to their respective countries, whence they came, to fetch bread and other necessaries for the subsistence of this great army; for when they came from home they took with them provisions only for a journey to Mizpeh, not for an encampment (which might prove long) before Gibeah. This was to prevent their scattering to forage for themselves, for, if they had done this, it would have been hard to get them all together again, especially all in so good a mind. Note, When there appears in people a pious zeal for any good work it is best to strike while the iron is hot, for such zeal is apt to cool quickly if the prosecution of the work be delayed. Let it never be said that we left that good work to be done to-morrow which we could as well have done to-day. 3. Their unanimity in these counsels, and the execution of them. The resolution was voted, *Nemine contradicente — Without a dissenting voice* (*v.* 8); it was one and all; and, when it was put in execution, they were *knit together as one man, v.* 11. This was their glory and strength, that the several tribes had no separate interests when the common good was concerned.

Verses 12–17

Here is, I. The fair and just demand which the tribes of Israel, now encamped, sent to the tribe of Benjamin, to deliver up the malefactors of Gibeah to justice, *v.* 12, 13. If the tribe of Benjamin had come up, as they ought to have done, to the assembly, and agreed with them in their resolution, there would have been none to deal with but the men of Gibeah only, but they, by their absence, taking part with the criminals, application must be made to them all. The Israelites were zealous against the wickedness that was committed, yet they were discreet in their zeal, and did not think it would justify them in falling upon the whole tribe of Benjamin unless they, by refusing to give up the criminals, and protecting them against justice, should make themselves guilty, *ex post facto — as accessaries after the fact.* They desire them to consider how great the wickedness was that was committed (*v.* 12), and that it was done among them: and how necessary it was therefore that they should either punish the malefactors with death themselves, according to the law of Moses, or deliver them up to the general assembly, to be so much the more publicly and solemnly punished, that evil might be put away from Israel, the national guilt removed, the infection stopped by cutting off the gangrened part, and national judgments prevented; for the sin was so very like that of the Sodomites that they might justly fear, if they did not punish it, God would rain hail from heaven upon them, as he did, not only upon Sodom, but the neighbouring cities. If the Israelites had not made this reasonable demand, they would have had much more reason to lament the following desolations of Benjamin. All methods of accommodation must be used before we go to war or go to law. The demand was like that of Joab's to Abel, 2 Sa. 20:20, 21. "Only deliver up the traitor, and we will lay down our arms." On these terms, and no other, God will be at peace with us, that we part with our sins, that we mortify and crucify our lusts, and then all shall be well; his anger will be turned away.

II. The wretched obstinacy and perverseness of the men of Benjamin, who seem to have been as unanimous and zealous in their resolutions to stand by the criminals as the rest of the tribes were to punish them, so little sense had they of their honour, duty, and interest. 1. They were so prodigiously vile as to patronise the wickedness that was committed: They *would not hearken to the voice of their brethren* (v. 13), either because those of that tribe were generally more vicious and debauched at this time than the rest of the tribes, and therefore would not bear to have that punished in others of which they knew themselves guilty (some of the most fruitful and pleasant parts of Canaan fell to the lot of this tribe; their land, like that of Sodom, was *as the garden of the Lord*, which perhaps helped to make the inhabitants, like the men of Sodom, wicked, and *sinners before the Lord exceedingly*, Gen. 13:10, 13), or because (as bishop Patrick suggests) they took it ill that the other tribes should meddle with their concerns; they would not do that which they knew was their duty because they were reminded of it by their brethren, by whom they scorned to be taught and controlled. If there were any wise men among them that would have complied with the demand made, yet they were overpowered by the majority, who thus made the crime of the men of Gibeah their own. Thus we have *fellowship with the unfruitful works of darkness* if we say *A confederacy* with those that have, and make ourselves guilty of other men's sins by countenancing and defending them. It seems there is no cause so bad but it will find some patrons, some advocates, to appear for it; but *woe be to those by whom such offences come*. Those will have a great deal to answer for that obstruct the course of necessary justice, and strengthen the hands of the wicked, by saying, *O wicked man! thou shalt not die.*

2. They were so prodigiously vain and presumptuous as to make head against the united force of all Israel. Never, surely, were men so wretchedly infatuated as they were when they took up arms in opposition, (1.) To so good a cause as Israel had. How could they expect to prosper when they fought against justice, and consequently against the just God himself, against those that had the high priest and the divine oracle on their side, and so acted in downright rebellion against the sacred and supreme authority of the nation. (2.) To so great a force as Israel had. The disproportion of their numbers was much greater than that, Lu. 14:31, 32, where he that had but 10,000 durst not meet him that came against him with 20,000, and therefore desired conditions of peace. There the enemy was but two to one, here above fifteen to one; yet they despised conditions of peace. All the forces they could bring into the field were but 26,000 men, besides 700 men of Gibeah (v. 15); yet with these they will dare to face 400,000 men of Israel, v. 17. Thus sinners are infatuated to their own ruin, and provoke him to jealousy who is infinitely stronger than they, 1 Co. 10:22. But it should seem they depended upon the skill of their men to make up what was wanting in numbers, especially a regiment of slingers, 700 men, who, though left-handed, were so dexterous at slinging stones that they would not be a hair's breadth beside their mark, v. 16. But these good marksmen were very much out in their aim when they espoused this bad cause. *Benjamin* signifies *the son of the right hand*, yet we find his posterity left-handed.

Verses 18–25

We have here the defeat of the men of Israel in their first and second battle with the Benjamites.

I. Before their first engagement they asked counsel of God concerning the order of their battle and were directed, and yet they were sorely beaten. They did not think it was proper to ask of God whether they should go up at all against Benjamin (the case was plain enough, the men of Gibeah must be punished for their wickedness, and Israel must inflict the punishment or it will not be done), but "Who shall go first?" (v. 18), that is, "Who shall be general of our army?" for, which soever tribe was appointed to go first, the prince of that tribe must be looked upon as commander-in-chief of the whole body. For, if they had

meant it of the order of their march only, it would have been proper to ask, "Who shall go next?" and then, "Who next?" But, if they know that Judah must go first, they know they must all observe the orders of the prince of that tribe. This honour was done to Judah because our Lord Jesus was to spring from that tribe, who was in all things to have the pre-eminence. The tribe that went up first had the most honourable post, but withal the most dangerous, and probably lost most in the engagement. Who would strive for precedency that sees the peril of it? Yet though Judah, that strong and valiant tribe, goes up first, and all the tribes of Israel attend them, *little Benjamin* (so he is called, Ps. 68:27), is too hard for them all. The whole army lays siege to Gibeah, v. 19. The Benjamites advance to raise the siege, and the army prepares to give them a warm reception (v. 20). But between the Benjamites that attacked them in the front with incredible fury, and the men of Gibeah that sallied out upon their rear, they were put into confusion and lost 22,000 men, v. 21. Here were no prisoners taken, for there was no quarter given, but all put to the sword.

II. Before their second engagement they again *asked counsel of God*, and more solemnly than before; for they *wept before the Lord until evening* (v. 23), lamenting the loss of so many brave men, especially as it was a token of God's displeasure and would give occasion to the Benjamites to triumph in the success of their wickedness. Also at this time they did not ask who should go up first, but whether they should go up at all. The intimate a reason why they should scruple to do it, especially now that Providence had frowned upon them, because Benjamin was their brother, and a readiness to lay down their arms if God should so order them. God bade them go up; he allowed the attempt, for, though Benjamin was their brother, he was a gangrened member of their body and must be cut off. Upon this they encouraged themselves, perhaps more in their own strength than in the divine commission, and made a second attempt upon the forces of the rebels, in the same place where the former battle was fought (v. 22), with the hope of retrieving their credit upon the same spot of ground where they had lost it, which they would not superstitiously change, as if there were any thing unlucky in the place. But they were this second time repulsed, with the loss of 18,000 men, v. 25. The former day's loss and this amounted to 40,000, which was just a tenth part of the whole army, and the same number that they had drawn out by lot to fetch victuals, v. 10. They decimated themselves for that service, and now God again decimated them for the slaughter. But what shall we say to these things, that so just and honourable a cause should thus be put to the worst once and again? Were they not fighting God's battle against sin? Had they not his commission? What, and yet miscarry thus! 1. God's judgments are a great deep, and his way is in the sea. *Clouds and darkness are* often *round about* him, *but judgment and justice are* always *the habitation of his throne*. We may be sure of the righteousness, when we cannot see the reasons, of God's proceedings. 2. God would hereby show them, and us in them, that *the race is not to the swift nor the battle to the strong*, that we are not to confide in numbers, which perhaps the Israelites did with too much assurance. We must never lay the weight on an arm of flesh, which only the Rock of ages will bear. 3. God designed hereby to correct Israel for their sins. They did well to show such a zeal against the wickedness of Gibeah: but *were there not with them, even with them, sins against the Lord their God?* Those must be made to know their own iniquity that are forward in condemning the iniquity of others. Some think it was a rebuke to them for not witnessing against the idolatry of Micah and the Danites, by which their religion was corrupted, as they now did against the lewdness of Gibeah and the Benjamites, by which the public peace was disturbed, though God had particularly ordered them to levy war upon idolaters, Deu. 13:12, etc. 4. God would hereby teach us not to think it strange if a good cause should suffer defeat fore a while, nor to judge of the merits of it by the success of it. The interest of grace in the heart, and of religion in the world, may be foiled, and suffer great loss, and seem to be quite run down, but judgment will be brought forth to victory at last. *Vincimur in praelio, sed non in bello — We are foiled in a battle, but not in the whole campaign.* Right may fall, but it shall arise.

Verses 26–48

We have here a full account of the complete victory which the Israelites obtained over the Benjamites in the third engagement: the righteous cause was victorious at last, when the managers of it amended what had been amiss; for, when a good cause suffers, it is for want of good management. Observe then how the victory was obtained, and how it was pursued.

I. How the victory was obtained. Two things they had trusted too much to in the former engagements — the goodness of their cause and the superiority of their numbers. It was true that they had both right and strength on their side, which were great advantages; but they depended too much upon them, to the neglect of those duties to which now, this third time, when they see their error, they apply themselves.

1. They were previously so confident of the goodness of their cause that they thought it needless to address themselves to God for his presence and blessing. They took it for granted that God would bless them, nay, perhaps they concluded that he owed them his favour, and could not in justice withhold it, since it was in defence of virtue that they appeared and took up arms. But God having shown them that he was under no obligation to prosper their enterprise, that he neither needed them nor was tied to them, that they were more indebted to him for the honour of being ministers of his justice than he to them for the service, now they became humble petitioners for success. Before they only consulted God's oracle, *Who shall go up first?* And, *Shall we go up?* But now they implored his favour, fasted and prayed, and *offered burnt-offerings and peace-offerings* (v. 26), to make an atonement for sin and an acknowledgment of their dependence upon God, and as an expression of their desire towards him. We cannot expect the presence of God with us, unless we thus seek it in the way he has appointed. And when they were in this frame, and thus sought the Lord, then he not only ordered them to go up against the Benjamites the third time, but gave them a promise of victory: *Tomorrow I will deliver them into thy hand,* v. 28.

2. They were previously so confident of the greatness of their strength that they thought it needless to use any art, to lay any ambush, or form a stratagem, not doubting but to conquer purely by a strong hand; but now they saw it was requisite to use some policy, as if they had an enemy to deal with them that had been superior in number; accordingly, they set *liers in wait* (v. 29), and gained their point, as their fathers did before Ai (Jos. 8), stratagems of that kind being most likely to take effect after a previous defeat, which has flushed the enemy, and made the pretended flight the less suspected. The management of this artifice is here very largely described. The assurance God had given them of success in this day's action, instead of making them remiss and presumptuous, set all heads and hands on work for the effecting of what God had promised.

(1.) Observe the method they took. The body of the army faced the city of Gibeah, as they had done before, advancing towards the gates, v. 30. The Benjamites, the body of whose army was now quartered at Gibeah, sallied out upon them, and charged them with great bravery. The besiegers gave back. retired with precipitation, as if their hearts failed them upon the sight of the Benjamites, which they were willing to believe, proudly imagining that by their former success they had made themselves very formidable. Some loss the Israelites sustained in this counterfeit flight, about thirty men being cut off in their rear, v. 31, 39. But, when the Benjamites were all drawn out of the city, the ambush seized the city (v. 37), gave a signal to the body of the army (v. 38, 40), which immediately turned upon them (v. 41), and, it should seem, another considerable party that was posted at Baal-tamar came upon them at the same time (v. 33); so that the Benjamites were quite surrounded, which put them into the greatest consternation that could be. A sense of guilt now disheartened them, and the higher their hopes had been raised the more grievous was this confusion. At first *the battle was sore* (v. 34), the Benjamites fought with fury; but, when they saw what a snare they were drawn into, they thought one pair of heels (as we say) was worth two pair of hands, and they made the best of their way *towards the wilderness* (v. 42); but in vain: *the battle overtook them*, and, to complete their distress, *those who came out of the cities of Israel,* that waited to see the event of the battle, joined with their pursuers, and helped to cut them off. Every man's hand was against them.

(2.) Observe in this story, [1.] That the Benjamites, in the beginning of the battle, were confident that the day was their own: *They are smitten down before us, v.* 32, 39. Sometimes God suffers wicked men to be lifted up in successes and hopes, that their fall may be the sorer. See how short their joy is, and their triumphing but for a moment. *Let not him that girdeth on the harness boast,* except he has reason to boast in God. [2.] Evil was near them and they did not know it, *v.* 34. But (*v.* 41) they saw, when it was too late to prevent it, *that evil had come upon them.* What evils may at any time be near us we cannot tell, but the less they are feared the heavier they fall. Sinners will not be persuaded to see evil near them, but how dreadful will it be when it comes and there is no escaping! 1 Th. 5:3. [3.] Though the men of Israel played their parts so well in this engagement, yet the victory is ascribed to God (*v.* 35): *The Lord smote Benjamin before Israel.* The battle was his, and so was the success. [4.] They *trode down the men of Benjamin with ease* when God fought against them, *v.* 43. It is an easy thing to trample upon those who have made God their enemy. See Mal. 4:3.

II. How the victory was prosecuted and improved in a military execution done upon these sinners against their own souls. 1. Gibeah itself, that nest of lewdness, was destroyed in the first place. The ambush that entered the city by surprise *drew themselves along,* that is, dispersed themselves into the several parts of it, which they might easily do, now that all the men of war had sallied out and very presumptuously left it defenceless; and they smote all they found, even women and children, *with the sword* (*v.* 37), and set fire to the city, *v.* 40. Sin brings ruin upon cities. 2. The army in the field was quite routed and cut off: 18,000 men of valour lay dead upon the spot, *v.* 44. 3. Those that escaped from the field were pursued, and cut off in their flight, to the number of 7000, *v.* 45. It is to no purpose to think of out-running divine vengeance. *Evil pursues sinners,* and it will overtake them. 4. Even those that tarried at home were involved in the ruin. They *let their sword devour for ever,* not considering that *it would be bitterness in the latter end,* as Abner pleads long after, when he was at the head of an army of Benjamites, probably with an eye to this very story, 2 Sa. 2:25, 26. They put to the sword all that breathed, and set fire to *all the cities, v.* 48. So that of all the tribe of Benjamin, for aught that appears, there remained none alive but 600 men that took shelter in the rock Rimmon, and lay close there four months, *v.* 47. Now, (1.) It is difficult to justify this severity as it was Israel's act. The whole tribe of Benjamin was culpable; but must they therefore be treated as devoted Canaanites? That it was done in the heat of war, that this was the way of prosecuting victories which the sword of Israel had been accustomed to, that the Israelites were extremely exasperated against the Benjamites for the slaughter they had made among them in the two former engagements, will go but a little way to excuse the cruelty of this execution. It is true they had sworn that whosoever did not come up to Mizpeh should be *put to death, ch.* 21:5. But that, if it was a justifiable oath, yet extended only to the men of war; the rest were not expected to come. Yet, (2.) It is easy to justify the hand of God in it. Benjamin had sinner against him, and God had threatened that, if they forgot him, they should *perish as the nations* that were before them perished (Deu. 8:20), who were all in this manner cut off. (3.) It is easy likewise to improve it for warning against the beginnings of sin: they are *like the letting forth of water, therefore leave it off before it be meddled with,* for we know not *what will be in the end thereof.* The eternal ruin of souls will be worse, and more fearful, than all these desolations of a tribe. This affair of Gibeah is twice spoken of by the prophet Hosea as the beginning of the corruption of Israel and a pattern to all that followed (Hos. 9:9): *They have deeply corrupted themselves as in the days of Gibeah;* and (Hos. 10:9), *Thou hast sinned from the days of Gibeah;* and it is added that *the battle in Gibeah against the children of iniquity did not* (that is, did not *at first)* overtake them.

CHAPTER 21

The ruins of the tribe of Benjamin we read of in the foregoing chapter; now here we have, I. The lamentation which Israel made over these ruins (*v.* 1–4, 6, 15). II. The provision they made for the repair of them out of the 600 men that escaped, for whom they procured wives, 1. Of the virgins of Jabesh-Gilead, when they destroyed that city for not sending its forces to the general rendezvous (*v.* 5, 7–14). 2. Of the daughters of Shiloh (*v.* 16–25). And so this melancholy story concludes.

Verses 1–15

We may observe in these verses,

I. The ardent zeal which the Israelites had expressed against the wickedness of the men of Gibeah, as it was countenanced by the tribe of Benjamin. Occasion is here given to mention two instances of their zeal on this occasion, which we did not meet with before: — 1. While the general convention of the states was gathering together, and was waiting for a full house before they would proceed, they bound themselves with the great execration, which they called the *Cherum,* utterly to destroy all those cities that should not send in their representatives and their quota of men upon this occasion, or had sentenced those to that curse who should thus refuse (*v.* 5); for they would look upon such refusers as having no indignation at the crime committed, no concern for the securing of the nation from God's judgments by the administration of justice, nor any regard to the authority of a common consent, by which they were summoned to meet. 2. When they had met and heard the cause they made another solemn oath that none of all the thousands of Israel then present, nor any of those whom they represented (not intending to bind their posterity), should, if they could help it, *marry a daughter* to a Benjamite, *v.* 1. This was made an article of the war, not with any design to extirpate the tribe, but because in general they would treat those who were then actors and abettors of this villany in all respects as they treated the devoted nations of Canaan, whom they were not only obliged to destroy, but with whom they were forbidden to marry; and because, in particular, they judged those unworthy to match with a daughter of Israel that had been so very barbarous and abusive to one of the tender sex, than which nothing could be done more base and villainous, nor a more certain indication given of a mind perfectly lost to all honour and virtue. We may suppose that the Levite's sending the mangled pieces of his wife'[s body to the several tribes helped very much to inspire them with all this fury, and much more than a bare narrative of the fact, though ever so well attested, would have done, so much does the eye affect the heart.

II. The deep concern which the Israelites did express for the destruction of the tribe of Benjamin when it was accomplished. Observe,

1. The tide of their anger at Benjamin's crime did not run so high and so strong before but the tide of their grief for Benjamin's destruction ran as high and as strong after: *They repented for Benjamin their brother, v.* 6, 15. They did not repent of their zeal against the sin; there is a holy indignation against sin, the fruit of godly sorrow, which is *to salvation, not to be repented of,* 2 Co. 7:10, 11. But they repented of the sad consequences of what they had done, that they had carried the matter further than was either just or necessary. It would have been enough to destroy all they found in arms; they needed not to have cut off the husbandmen and shepherds, the women and children. Note, (1.) There may be over-doing in well-doing. Great care must be taken in the government of our zeal, lest that which seemed supernatural in its causes prove unnatural in its effects. That is no good divinity which swallows up humanity. Many a war is ill ended which was well begun. (2.) Even necessary justice is to be done with compassion. God does not punish with delight, nor should men. (3.) Strong passions make work for repentance. What we say and do in a heat our calmer thoughts commonly wish undone again. (4.) In a civil war (according to the usage of the Romans) no victories ought to be celebrated with triumphs, because, which soever side gets, the community loses, as here *there is a tribe cut off from Israel.* What the better is the body for one member's crushing another? Now,

2. How did they express their concern? (1.) By their grief for the breach that was made. They came to the house of God, for thither they brought all their doubts, all their counsels, all their cares, and all their sorrows. There was to be heard on this occasion, not the voice of joy and praise, but only that of lamentation, and mourning, and woe: They *lifted up their voices and wept sore* (*v.* 2), not so much for the 40,000 whom they had lost (these would not be so much missed out of eleven tribes), but for the entire destruction of one whole tribe; for this was the complaint they poured out before God (*v.* 3): *There is one tribe lacking.* God had taken care of every tribe; their number twelve was that which they were known by; every tribe had his station appointed in the camp, and his stone in the high priest's breast-plate; every tribe had his blessing both from Jacob and Moses; and it would be an intolerable reproach to them if they should drop any out of this illustrious jury, and lose one out of twelve, especially Benjamin, the youngest, who was particularly dear to Jacob their common ancestor, and whom all the rest ought to have been in a particular manner tender of. Benjamin is not; what then will become of Jacob? Benjamin is become a Benoni, the son of the right hand a son of sorrow! In this trouble they built an altar, not in competition, but in communion with the appointed altar at the door of the tabernacle, which was not large enough to contain all the sacrifices they designed; for they offered burnt offerings and peace offerings, to give thanks for their victory, yet to atone for their own folly in the pursuit of it, and to implore the divine favour in their present strait. Every thing that grieves us should bring us to God. (2.) By their amicable treaty with the poor distressed refugees that were hidden in the rock Rimmon, to whom they sent an act of indemnity, assuring them, upon the public faith, that they would now no longer treat them as enemies, but receive them as brethren, *v.* 13. The falling out of friends should thus be the renewing of friendship. Even those that have sinned, if at length they repent, must be forgiven and comforted, 2 Co. 2:7. (3.) By the care they took to provide wives for them, that their tribe might be built up again, and the ruins of it repaired. Had the men of Israel sought themselves, they would have been secretly pleased with the extinguishing of the families of Benjamin, because then the land allotted to them would escheat to the rest of the tribes, *ob defectum sanguinis — for want of heirs,* and be easily seized for want of occupants; but those have not the spirit of Israelites who aim to raise themselves upon the ruins of their neighbours. They were so far from any design of this kind that all heads were at work to find out ways and means for the rebuilding of this tribe. All the women and children of Benjamin were slain: they had sworn not to marry their daughters to any of them; it was against the divine law that they should match with the Canaanites; to oblige them to that would be, in effect, to bid them *go and serve other gods.* What must they do then for wives for them? While the poor distressed Benjamites that were hidden in the rock feared their brethren were contriving to ruin them, they were at the same time upon a project to prefer them; and it was this: — [1.] There was a piece of necessary justice to be done upon the city of Jabesh-Gilead, which belonged to the tribe of Gad, on the other side Jordan. It was found upon looking over the muster-roll (which was taken, *ch.* 20:2) that none appeared from that city upon the general summons (*v.* 8, 9), and it was then resolved, before it appeared who were absent, that whatever city of Israel should be guilty of such a contempt of the public authority and interest that city should be an anathema; Jabesh-Gilead lies under that severe sentence, which might by no means be dispensed with. Those that had spared the Canaanites in many places, who were devoted to destruction by the divine command, could not find in their hearts to spare their brethren that were devoted by their own curse. Why did they not now send men to root the Jebusites out of Jerusalem, to avoid whom the poor Levite had been forced to go to Gibeah? *ch.* 19:11, 12. Men are commonly more zealous to support their own authority than God's. A detachment is therefore sent of 12,000 men, to execute the sentence upon Jabesh-Gilead. Having found that when the whole body of the army went against Gibeah the people were thought too many for God to deliver them into their hands, on this expedition they sent but a few, *v.* 10. Their commission is to put all to the sword, men, women, and children (*v.* 11), according to that law (Lev. 27:29), *Whatsoever is devoted of men,* by those that have power to do it, *shall surely be put to death.* [2.] An expedient is hence

formed for providing the Benjamites with wives. When Moses sent the same number of men to avenge the Lord on Midian, the same orders were given as here, that all married women should be slain with their husbands, as one with them, but that the virgins should be saved alive, Num. 31:17, 18. That precedent was sufficient to support the distinction here made between a wife and a virgin, *v.* 11,
12. 400 virgins that were marriageable were found in Jabesh-Gilead, and these were married to so many of the surviving Benjamites, *v.* 14. Their fathers were not present when the vow was made not to marry with Benjamites, so that they were not under any colour of obligation by it: and besides, being a prey taken in war, they were at the disposal of the conquerors. Perhaps the alliance now contracted between Benjamin and Jabesh-Gilead made Saul, who was a Benjamite, the more concerned for that place (1 Sa. 11:4), though then inhabited by new families.

Verses 16–25

We have here the method that was taken to provide the 200 Benjamites that remained with wives. And, though the tribe was reduced to a small number, they were only in care to provide each man with one wife, not with more under pretence of multiplying them the faster. They may not bestow their daughters upon them, but to save their oath, and yet marry some of their daughters to them, they put them into a way of taking them by surprise, and marrying them, which should be ratified by their parents' consent, *ex post facto — afterwards.* The less consideration is used before the making of a vow, the more, commonly, there is need of afterwards for the keeping of it.

I. That which gave an opportunity for the doing of this was a public ball at Shiloh, in the fields, at which all the young ladies of that city and the parts adjacent that were so disposed met to dance, in honour of a *feast of the Lord* then observed, probably the feast of tabernacles (*v.* 19), for that feast (bishop Patrick says) was the only season wherein the Jewish virgins were allowed to dance, and that not so much for their own recreation as to express their holy joy, as David when he danced before the ark, otherwise the present melancholy posture of public affairs would have made dancing unseasonable, as Isa. 22:12, 13. The dancing was very modest and chaste. It was not mixed dancing; no men danced with these daughters of Shiloh, nor did any married women so far forget their gravity as to join with them. However their dancing thus in public made them an easy prey to those that had a design upon them, whence bishop Hall observes that the *ambushes of evil spirits carry away many souls from dancing to a fearful desolation.*

II. The elders of Israel gave authority to the Benjamites to do this, to *lie in wait in the vineyards* which surrounded the green they used to dance on, and, when they were in the midst of their sport, to come upon them, and catch every man a wife for himself, and carry them straight away to their own country, *v.* 20, 21. They knew that none of their own daughters would be there, so that the parents of these virgins could not be said to give them, for they knew nothing of the matter. A sorry *salvo* is better than none, to save the breaking of an oath: it were much better to be cautious in making vows, that there be not occasion afterwards, as there was here, *to say before the angel that it was an error.* Here was a very preposterous way of match-making, when both the mutual affection of the young people and the consent of the parents must be presumed to come after; the case was extraordinary, and may by no means be drawn into a precedent. Over hasty marriages often occasion a leisurely repentance; and what comfort can be expected from a match made either by force or fraud? The virgins of Jabesh-Gilead were taken out of the midst of blood and slaughter, but these of Shiloh out of the midst of mirth and joy; the former had reason to be thankful that they had their lives for a prey, and the latter, it is to be hoped, had no cause to complain, after a while, when they found themselves matched, not to men of broken and desperate fortunes, as they seemed to be, who were lately fetched out of a cave, but to men of the best and largest estates in the nation, as they must needs be when the lot of the whole tribe of Benjamin, which consisted of 45,600 men (Num. 26:41), came to be divided again among 600, who had all by survivorship.

III. They undertook to pacify the fathers of these young women. As to the infringement of their paternal authority, they would easily forgive it when they considered to what fair estates their daughters were matched and what mothers in Israel they were likely to be; but the oath they were bound by, not to give their daughters to Benjamites, might perhaps stick with some of them, whose consciences were tender, yet, as to that, this might satisfy them: — 1. That the necessity was urgent (*v.* 22): *We reserved not to each man his wife,* owning now that they did ill to destroy all the women, and desiring to atone for their too rigorous construction of their vow to destroy them by the most favourable construction of their vow not to match with them. "And therefore for our sakes, who were too severe, let them keep what they have got." For, 2. In strictness it was not a breach of their vow; they had sworn not to give them their daughters, but they had not sworn to fetch them back if they were forcibly taken, so that if there was any fault the elders must be responsible, not the parents. And *Quod fieri non debuit, factum valet — That which ought not to have been done is yet valid when it is done.* The thing was done, and is ratified only by connivance, according to the law, Num. 30:4.

Lastly, In the close of all we have, 1. The settling of the tribe of Benjamin again. The few that remained returned to the inheritance of that tribe, *v.* 23. And soon after from among them sprang Ehud, who was famous in his generation, the second judge of Israel, *ch.* 3:15. 2. The disbanding and dispersing of the army of Israel, *v.* 24. They did not set up for a standing army, nor pretend to make any alterations or establishments in the government; but when the affair was over for which they were called together, they quietly departed in God's peace, every man to his family. Public services must not make us think ourselves above our own private affairs and the duty of providing for our own house. 3. A repetition of the cause of these confusions, *v.* 25. Though God was their King, every man would be his own master, as if there was no king. Blessed be God for magistracy.

AN EXPOSITION, WITH PRACTICAL OBSERVATIONS, OF

THE BOOK OF RUTH

This short history of the domestic affairs of one particular family fitly follows the book of Judges (the events related here happening in the days of the judges), and fitly goes before the books of Samuel, because in the close it introduces David; yet the Jews, in their Bibles, separate it from both, and make it one of the five *Megilloth,* or *Volumes,* which they put together towards the latter end, in this order: *Solomon's Song, Ruth, Lamentations, Ecclesiastes,* and *Esther.* It is probable that Samuel was the penman of it. It relates not miracles nor laws, wars nor victories, nor the revolutions of states, but the affliction first and afterwards the comfort of Naomi, the conversion first and afterwards the preferment of Ruth. Many such events have happened, which perhaps we may think as well worthy to be recorded; but these God saw fit to transmit the knowledge of to us; and even common historians think they have liberty to choose their subject. The design of this book is, I. To lead to providence, to show us how conversant it is about our private concerns, and to teach us in them all to have an eye to it, acknowledging God in all our ways and in all events that concern us. See 1 Sa. 2:7, 8; Ps. 113:7–9. II. To lead to Christ, who descended from Ruth, and part of whose genealogy concludes the book, whence it is fetched into Mt. 1. In the conversion of Ruth the Moabitess, and the bringing of her into the pedigree of the Messiah, we have a type of the calling of the Gentiles in due time into the fellowship of Christ Jesus our Lord. The afflictions of Naomi and Ruth we have an account of, *ch.* 1. Instances of their industry and humility, *ch.* 2. The bringing of them into an alliance with Boaz, *ch.* 3. And their happy settlement thereby, *ch.* 4. And let us remember the scene is laid in Bethlehem, the city where our Redeemer was born.

CHAPTER 1

In this chapter we have Naomi's afflictions. I. As a distressed housekeeper, forced by famine to remove into the land of Moab (*v.* 1, 2). II. As a mournful widow and mother, bewailing the death of her husband and her two sons (*v.* 3–5). III. As a careful mother-in-law, desirous to be kind to her two daughters, but at a loss how to be so when she returns to her own country (*v.* 6–13). Orpah she parts with in sorrow (*v.* 14). Ruth she takes with her in fear (*v.* 15–18). IV. As a poor woman sent back to the place of her first settlement, to be supported by the kindness of her friends (*v.* 19–22). All these things were melancholy and seemed against her, and yet all were working for good.

Verses 1–5

The first words give all the date we have of this story. It was *in the days when the judges ruled* (*v.* 1), not in those disorderly times when *there was no king in Israel;* but under which of the judges these things happened we are not told, and the conjectures of the learned are very uncertain. It must have been towards the beginning of the judges' time, for Boaz, who married Ruth, was born of Rahab, who received the spies in Joshua's time. Some think it was in the days of Ehud, others of Deborah; the learned bishop Patrick inclines to think it was in the days of Gideon, because in his days only we read of a famine by the Midianites' invasion, Judges 6:3, 4. While the judges were ruling, some one city and some another, Providence takes particular cognizance of Bethlehem, and has an eye to a King, to Messiah himself, who should descend from two Gentile mothers, Rahab and Ruth. Here is,

I. A famine in the land, in the land of Canaan, that land *flowing with milk and honey.* This was one of the judgments which God had threatened to bring upon them for their sins, Lev. 26:19, 20. He has many arrows in his quiver. In the days of the judges they were oppressed by their enemies; and, when by that judgment they were not reformed, God tried this, for when he *judges he will overcome.* When the land had rest, yet it had not plenty; even in Bethlehem, which signifies *the house of bread,* there was scarcity. A *fruitful land is turned into barrenness,* to correct and restrain the luxury and wantonness of those that dwell therein.

II. An account of one particular family distressed in the famine; it is that of *Elimelech.* His name signifies *my God a king,* agreeable to the state of Israel when the judges ruled, for the Lord was their King, and comfortable to him and his family in their affliction, that God was theirs and that he reigns for ever. His wife was *Naomi,* which signifies my *amiable* or *pleasant* one. But his sons' names were *Mahlon* and *Chilion, sickness* and *consumption,* perhaps because weakly children, and not likely to be longlived. Such are the productions of our pleasant things, weak and infirm, fading and dying.

III. The removal of this family from Bethlehem into the country of Moab on the other side Jordan, for subsistence, because of the famine, *v.* 1, 2. It seems there was plenty in the country of Moab when there was scarcity of bread in the land of Israel. Common gifts of providence are often bestowed in greater plenty upon those that are strangers to God than upon those that know and worship him. *Moab is at ease from his youth,* while Israel *is emptied from vessel to vessel* (Jer. 48:11), not because God loves Moabites better, but because they have *their portion in this life.*

Thither Elimelech goes, not to settle for ever, but to sojourn for a time, during the dearth, as Abraham, on a similar occasion, went into Egypt, and Isaac into the land of the Philistines. Now here, 1. Elimelech's care to provide for his family, and his taking his wife and children with him, were without doubt commendable. *If any provide not for his own, he hath denied the faith,* 1 Tim. 5:8. When he was in his straits he did not forsake his house, go seek his fortune himself, and leave his wife and children to shift for their own maintenance; but, as became a tender husband and a loving father, where he went he took them with him, not as the ostrich, Job 39:16. But, 2. I see not how his removal into the country of Moab, upon this occasion, could be justified. Abraham and Isaac were only sojourners in Canaan, and it was agreeable to their condition to remove; but the seed of Israel were now fixed, and ought not to remove into the territories of the heathen. What reason had Elimelech to go more than any of his neighbours? If by any ill husbandry he had wasted his patrimony, and sold his land or mortgaged it (as it should seem, *ch.* 4:3, 4), which brought him into a more necessitous condition than others, the law of God would have obliged his neighbours to relieve him (Lev. 25:35); but that was not his case, for he went out full, *v.* 21. By those who tarried at home it appears that the famine was not so extreme but that there was sufficient to keep life and soul together; and his charge was but small, only two sons. But if he could not be content with the short allowance that his neighbours took up with, and *in the day of famine could not be satisfied* unless he kept as plentiful a table as he had done formerly, if he could not live in hope that there would come years of plenty again in due time, or could not with patience wait for those years, it was his fault, and he did by it dishonour God and the good land he had given them, *weaken the hands of his brethren,* with whom he should have been willing to take his lot, and set an ill example to others. If all should do as he did Canaan would be dispeopled. Note, It is an evidence of a discontented, distrustful, unstable spirit, to be weary of the place in which God hath set us, and to be for leaving it immediately whenever we meet with any uneasiness or inconvenience in it. It is folly to think of escaping that cross which, being laid in our way, we ought to take up. It is our wisdom to make the best of that which is, for it is seldom that changing our place is mending it. Or, if he would remove, why to the country of Moab? If he had made enquiry, it is probable he would have found plenty in some of the tribes of Israel, those, for instance, on the other side Jordan, that bordered on the land of Moab; if he had had that zeal for God and his worship, and that affection for his brethren which became an Israelite, he would not have persuaded himself so easily to go and sojourn among Moabites.

IV. The marriage of his two sons to two of the daughters of Moab after his death, *v.* 4. All agree that this was ill done. The Chaldee says, *They transgressed the decree of the word of the Lord in taking strange wives.* If they would not stay unmarried till their return to the land of Israel, they were not so far off but that they might have fetched themselves wives thence. Little did Elimelech think, when he went to sojourn in Moab, that ever his sons would thus join in affinity with Moabites. But those that bring young people into bad acquaintance, and take them out of the way of public ordinances, though they may think them well-principled and armed against temptation, know not what they do, nor *what will be the end thereof.* It does not appear that the women they married were proselyted to the Jewish religion, for Orpah is said to return to her gods (*v.* 15); the gods of Moab were hers still. It is a groundless tradition of the Jews that Ruth was the daughter of Eglon king of Moab, yet the Chaldee paraphrast inserts it; but this and their other tradition, which he inserts likewise, cannot agree, that Boaz who married Ruth was the same with Ibzan, who judged Israel 200 years after Eglon's death, Jdg. 12.

V. The death of Elimelech and his two sons, and the disconsolate condition Naomi was thereby reduced to. Her husband died (*v.* 3) and her two sons (*v.* 5) soon after their marriage, and the Chaldee says, *Their days were shortened,* because they transgressed the law in marrying strange wives. See here, 1. That wherever we go we cannot out-run death, whose fatal arrows fly in all places. 2. That we cannot expect to prosper when we go out of the way of our duty. *He that will save his life* by any indirect course *shall lose it.* 3. That death, when it comes into a family, often makes breach upon breach. One is taken away to prepare another to follow soon after; one is taken away, and that affliction is not duly improved, and therefore God sends another of the same kind. When Naomi had lost her husband she took so much the more complacency and put so much the more confidence in her sons. Under the shadow of these surviving comforts she thinks she shall live among the heathen, and exceedingly glad she was of these gourds; but behold they wither presently, *green and growing up in the morning, cut down and dried up* before night, buried soon after they were married, for neither of them left any children. So uncertain and transient are all our enjoyments here. It is therefore our wisdom to make sure of those comforts that will be made sure and of which death cannot rob us. But how desolate was the condition, and how disconsolate the spirit, of poor Naomi, when the woman *was left of her two sons and her husband!* When *these two things, loss of children and widowhood, come upon her in a moment,* come upon her *in their perfection, by whom shall she be comforted?* Isa. 47:9; 51:19. It is God alone who has wherewithal to comfort those who are thus cast down.

Verses 6–18

See here, I. The good affection Naomi bore to the land of Israel, *v.* 6. Though she could not stay in it while the famine lasted, she would not stay out of it when the famine ceased. Though the country of Moab had afforded her shelter and supply in a time of need, yet she did not intend it should be her rest for ever; no land should be that but the holy land, in which the sanctuary of God was, of which he had said, *This is my rest for ever.* Observe,

1. God, at last, returned in mercy to his people; for, though he contend long, he will not contend always. As the judgment of oppression, under which they often groaned in the time of the judges, still came to an end, after a while, when God had raised them up a deliverer, so here the judgment of famine: At length God graciously *visited his people in giving them bread.* Plenty is God's gift, and it is his visitation which by bread, the staff of life, *holds our souls in life.* Though this mercy be the more striking when it comes after famine, yet if we have constantly enjoyed it, and never knew what famine meant, we are not to think it the less valuable.

2. Naomi then returned, in duty to her people. She had often enquired of their state, what harvests they had and how the markets went, and still the tidings were discouraging; but like the prophet's servant, who, having looked seven times and seen no sign of rain, at length discerned a cloud no bigger than a man's hand, which soon overspread the heavens, so Naomi at last has good news brought her of plenty in Bethlehem, and then she can think of no other than returning thither again. Hew new alliances in the country of Moab could not make her forget her relation to the land of Israel. Note, Though there be a reason for our being in bad places, yet, when the reason ceases, we must by no means continue in them. Forced absence from God's ordinances, and forced presence with wicked people, are great afflictions; but when the force ceases, and such a situation is continued of choice, then it becomes a great sin. It should seem she began to think of returning immediately upon the death of her two sons, (1.) Because she looked upon that affliction to be a judgment upon her family for lingering in the country of Moab; and hearing this to be the *voice of the rod, and of him that appointed it,* she obeys and returns. Had she returned upon the death of her husband, perhaps she might have saved the life of her sons; but, *when God judgeth he will overcome,* and, if one affliction prevail not to awaken us to a sight and sense of sin and duty, another shall. When death comes into a family it ought to be improved for the reforming of what is amiss in the family: when relations are taken away from us we are put upon enquiry whether, in some instance or other, we are not out of the way of our duty, that we may return to it. God *calls our sins to remembrance,* when he *slays a son,* 1 Ki. 17:18. And, if he thus hedge up our way with thorns, it is that he may oblige us to say, We will *go and return to our first husband,* as Naomi here to her country, Hos. 2:7. (2.) Because the land of Moab had now become a melancholy place to her. It is with little pleasure that she can breathe in that air in which her husband and sons had expired, or go on that ground in which they lay buried out of her sight, but not out of her thoughts; now she will go to Canaan again. Thus God takes away from us the comforts we stay ourselves too much upon and solace ourselves too much in, here in the land of our sojourning, that we may think more of our home in the other world, and by faith and hope may hasten towards it. Earth is embittered to us, that heaven may be endeared.

II. The good affection which her daughters-in-law, and one of them especially, bore to her, and her generous return of their good affection.

1. They were both so kind as to accompany her, some part of the way at least, when she returned towards the land of Judah. Her two daughters-in-law did not go about to persuade her to continue in the land of Moab, but, if she was resolved to go home, would pay her all possible civility and respect at parting; and this was one instance of it: they would *bring her on her way,* at least to the utmost limits of their country, and help her to carry her luggage as far as they went, for it does not appear that she had any servant to attend her, *v.* 7. By this we see both that Naomi, as became an Israelite, had been very kind and obliging to them and had won their love, in which she is an example to all mothers-in-law, and that Orpah and Ruth had a just sense of her kindness, for they were willing to return it thus far. It was a sign they had dwelt together in unity, though *those* were dead by whom the relation between them came. Though they retained an affection for the gods of Moab (*v.* 15), and Naomi was still faithful to the God of Israel, yet that was no hindrance to either side from love and kindness, and all the good offices that the relation required. Mothers-in-law and daughters-in-law are too often at variance (Mt. 10:35), and therefore it is the more commendable if they live in love; let all who sustain this relation aim at the praise of doing so.

2. When they had gone a little way with her Naomi, with a great deal of affection, urged them to go back (*v.* 8, 9): *Return each to her mother's house.* When they were dislodged by a sad providence from the house of their husbands it was a mercy to them that they had their parents yet living, that they had their houses to go to, where they might be welcome and easy, and were not turned out to the wide world. Naomi suggests that their own mothers would be more agreeable to them than a mother-in-law, especially when their own mothers had houses and their mother-in-law was not sure she had a place to lay her head in which she could call her own. She dismisses them,

(1.) With commendation. This is a debt owing to those who have conducted themselves well in any relation, they ought to have the praise of it: *You have dealt kindly with the dead and with me,* that is, "You were good wives to your husbands that are gone, and have been good daughters to me, and not wanting to your duty in either relation." Note, When we and our relations are parting, by death or otherwise, it is very comfortable if we have both their testimony and the testimony of our own consciences for us that while we were together we carefully endeavoured to do our duty in the relation. This will help to allay the bitterness of parting; and, while we are together, we should labour so to conduct ourselves as that when we part we may not have cause to reflect with regret upon our miscarriages in the relation.

(2.) With prayer. It is very proper for friends, when they part, to part with prayer. She sends them home with her blessing; and the blessing of a mother-in-law is not to be slighted. In this blessing she twice mentions the name *Jehovah,* Israel's God, and the only true God, that she might direct her daughters to look up to him as the only fountain of all good. To him she prays in general that he would recompense to them the kindness they had shown to her and hers. It may be expected and prayed for in faith that God will deal kindly with those that have dealt kindly with their relations. *He that watereth shall be watered also himself.* And, in particular, that they might be happy in marrying again: *The Lord grant that you may find rest, each of you in the house of her husband.* Note, [1.] It is very fit that, according to the apostle's direction (1 Tim. 5:14), the younger women, and he speaks there of young widows, should *marry, bear children,* and *guide the house.* And it is a pity that those who have approved themselves good wives should not again be blessed with good husbands, especially those that, like these widows, have no children. [2.] The married state is a state of rest, such rest as this world affords, rest in the house of a husband, more than can be expected in the house of a mother or a mother-in-law. [3.] This rest is God's gift. If any content and satisfaction be found in our outward condition, God must be acknowledged in it. There are those that are unequally yoked, that find little rest even in the house of a husband. Their affliction ought to make those the more thankful to whom the relation is comfortable. Yet let God be the rest of the soul, and no perfect rest thought of on this side heaven.

(3.) She dismissed them with great affection: *She kissed them,* wished she had somewhat better to give them, but silver and gold she had none. However, this parting kiss shall be the seal of such a true friendship as (though she never see them more) she will, while she lives, retain the pleasing remembrance of. If relations must part, let them thus part in love, that they may (if they never meet again in this world) meet in the world of everlasting love.

3. The two young widows could not think of parting with their good mother-in-law, so much had the good conversation of that pious Israelite won upon them. They not only lifted up their voice and wept, as loth to part, but they professed a resolution to adhere to her (*v.* 10): *"Surely we will return with thee unto thy people,* and take our lot with thee." It is a rare instance of affection to a mother-in-law and an evidence that they had, for her sake, conceived a good opinion of the people of Israel. Even Orpah, who afterwards went back to her gods, now seemed resolved to go forward with Naomi. The sad ceremony of parting, and the tears shed on that occasion, drew from her this protestation, but it did not hold. Strong passions, without a settled judgment, commonly produce weak resolutions.

4. Naomi sets herself to dissuade them from going along with her, *v.* 11–13.

(1.) Naomi urges her afflicted condition. If she had had any sons in Canaan, or any near kinsmen, whom she could have expected to marry the widows, to *raise up seed* to those that were gone, and to redeem the mortgaged estate of the family, it might have been some encouragement to them to hope for a comfortable settlement at Bethlehem. But she had no sons, nor could she think of any near kinsman likely to do the kinsman's part, and therefore argues that she was never likely to have any sons to be husbands for them, for she was too old to have a husband; it became here age to think of dying and going out of the world, not of marrying and beginning the world again. Or, if she had a husband, she could not expect to have children, nor, if she had sons, could she think that these young widows would stay unmarried till her sons that should yet be born would grow up to be marriageable. Yet this was not all: she could not only not propose to herself to marry them like themselves, but she knew not how to maintain them like themselves. The greatest grievance of that poor condition to which she was reduced was that she was not in a capacity to do for them as she would: *It grieveth me* more *for your sakes* than for my own *that the hand of the Lord has gone out against me.* Observe, [1.] She judges herself chiefly aimed at in the affliction, that God's quarrel was principally with her: *"The hand of the Lord has gone out against me.* I am the sinner; it is with me that God has a controversy; it is with me that he is contending; I take it to myself." This well becomes us when we are under affliction; though many others share in the trouble, yet we must hear the voice of the rod as if it spoke only against us and to us, not billeting the rebukes of it at other people's houses, but taking them to ourselves. [2.] She laments most the trouble that redounded to them from it. She was the sinner, but they were the sufferers: *It grieveth me much for your sakes.* A gracious generous spirit can better bear its own burden than it can bear to see it a grievance to others, or others in any way drawn into trouble by it. Naomi could more easily want herself than see her daughters want. "Therefore *turn again, my daughters,* for, alas! I am in no capacity to do you any kindness." But,

(2.) Did Naomi do well thus to discourage her daughters from going with her, when, by taking them with her, she might save them from the idolatry of Moab and bring them to the faith and worship of the God of Israel? Naomi, no doubt, desired to do so. But, [1.] If they did come with her, she would not have them to come upon her account. Those that take upon them a profession of religion only in complaisance to their relations, to oblige their friends, or for the sake of company, will be converts of small value and of short continuance. [2.] If they did come with her, she would have them to make it their deliberate choice, and to sit down first and count the cost, as it concerns those to do that may take up a profession of religion. It is good for us to be told the worst. Our Saviour took this course with him who, in the heat of zeal, spoke that bold word, *Master, I will follow thee whithersoever thou goest.* "Come, come," says Christ, "canst thou fare as I fare? *The Son of man has not where to lay his head;* know this, and then consider whether thou canst find in thy heart to take thy lot with him," Mt. 8:19, 20. Thus Naomi deals with her daughters-in-law. Thoughts ripened into resolves by serious consideration are likely to be kept always in the imagination of the heart, whereas what is soon ripe is soon rotten.

5. Orpah was easily persuaded to yield to her own corrupt inclination, and to go back to her country, her kindred, and her father's house, now when she stood fair for an effectual call from it. They both *lifted up their voice and wept again* (*v.* 14), being much affected with the tender things that Naomi had said. But it had a different effect upon them: to Orpah it was a savour of death unto death; the representation Naomi had made of the inconveniences they must count upon if they went forward to Canaan sent her back to the country of Moab, and served her as an excuse for her apostasy; but, on the contrary, it strengthened Ruth's resolution, and her good affection to Naomi, with whose wisdom and goodness she was never so charmed as she was upon this occasion; thus to her it was a savour of life unto life. (1.) *Orpah kissed her mother-in-law,* that is, took an affectionate leave of her, bade her farewell for ever, without any purpose to follow her hereafter, as he that said he would follow Christ when he had buried his father or bidden those farewell that were at home. Orpah's kiss showed she had an affection for Naomi and was loth to part from her; yet she did not love her well enough to leave her country for her sake. Thus many have a value and affection for Christ, and yet come short of salvation by him, because they cannot find in their hearts to forsake other things for him. They love him and yet leave him, because they do not love him enough, but love other things better. Thus the young man that went away from Christ went away sorrowful, Mt. 19:22. But, (2.) *Ruth clave unto her.* Wether, when she came from home, she was resolved to go forward with her or no does not appear; perhaps she was before determined what to do, out of a sincere affection for the God of Israel and to his law, of which, by the good instructions of Naomi, she had some knowledge.

6. Naomi persuades Ruth to go back, urging, as a further inducement, her sister's example (*v.* 15): *Thy sister-in-law has gone back to her people,* and therefore of course gone back *to her gods;* for, whatever she might do while she lived with her mother-in-law, it would be next to impossible for her to show any respect to the God of Israel when she went to live among the worshippers of Chemosh. Those that forsake the communion of saints, and return to the people of Moab, will certainly break off their communion with God, and embrace the idols of Moab. Now, *return thou after thy sister,* that is, "If ever thou wilt return, return now. This is the greatest trial of thy constancy; stand this trial, and thou art mine for ever." Such offences as that of Orpah's revolt must needs come, that those who are perfect and sincere may be made manifest, as Ruth was upon this occasion.

7. Ruth puts an end to the debate by a most solemn profession of her immovable resolution never to forsake her, nor to return to her own country and her old relations again, *v.* 16, 17.

(1.) Nothing could be said more fine, more brave, than this. She seems to have had another spirit, and another speech, now that her sister had gone, and it is an instance of the grace of God inclining the soul to the resolute choice of the better part. *Draw me* thus, and *we will run after thee.* Her mother's dissuasions made her the more resolute; as when Joshua said to the people, *You cannot serve the Lord,* they said it with the more vehemence, *Nay, but we will.* [1.] She begs of her mother-in-law to say no more against her going: *"Entreat me not to leave thee, or to return from following after thee;* for all thy entreaties now cannot shake that resolution which thy instructions formerly have wrought in me, and therefore let me hear no more of them." Note, It is a great vexation and uneasiness to those that are resolved for God and religion to be tempted and solicited to alter their resolution. Those that would not think of it would not hear of it. *Entreat me not.* The margin reads it, *Be not against me.* Note, We are to reckon those against us, and really our enemies, that would hinder us in our way to the heavenly Canaan. Our relations they may be, but they cannot be our friends, that would dissuade us from and discourage us in the service of God and the work of religion. [2.] She is very particular in her resolution to cleave to her and never to forsake her; and she speaks the language of one resolved for God and heaven. She is so in love, not with her mother's beauty, or riches, or gaiety (all these were withered and gone), but with her wisdom, and virtue, and grace, which remained with her, even in her present poor and melancholy condition, that she resolves to cleave to her. *First,* She will travel with her: *Whither thou goest I will go,* though to a country I never saw and in a low and ill opinion of which I have been trained up; though far from my own country, yet with thee every road shall be pleasant. *Secondly,* She will dwell with her: *"Where thou lodgest I will lodge,* though it be in a cottage, nay, though it be no better a lodging than Jacob had when he had the stones for his pillow. Where thou settest up thy staff I will set up mine, be it where it may." *Thirdly,* She will twist interest with her: *Thy people shall be my people.* From Naomi's character she concludes certainly that the great nation was a wise and an understanding people. She judges of them all by her good mother, who, wherever she went, was a credit to her country (as all those should study to be who profess relation to the better country, that is, the heavenly), and therefore she will think herself happy if she may be reckoned one of them. "Thy people shall be mine to associate with, to be conformable to, and to be concerned for." *Fourthly,* She will join in religion with her. Thus she determined to be hers *usque ad aras — to the very altars: "Thy God shall be my God,* and farewell to all the gods of Moab, which are vanity and a lie. I will adore the God of Israel, the only living and true God, trust in him alone, serve him, and in every thing be ruled by him;" this is to take the Lord for our God. *Fifthly,* She will gladly die in the same bed: *Where thou diest will I die.* She takes it for granted they must both die, and that in all probability Naomi, as the elder, would die first, and resolves to continue in the same house, if it might be, till her days also were fulfilled, intimating likewise a desire to partake of her happiness in death; she wishes to die in the same place, in token of her dying after the same manner. "Let me die the death of righteous Naomi, and let my last end be like hers." *Sixthly,* She will desire to be buried in the same grave, and to lay her bones by hers: *There will I be buried,* not desiring to have so much as her dead body carried back to the country of Moab, in token of any remaining kindness for it; but, Naomi and she having joined souls, she desires they may mingle dust, in hopes of rising together, and being together for ever in the other world. [3.] She backs her resolution to adhere to Naomi with a solemn oath: *The Lord do so to me, and more also* (which was an ancient form of imprecation), *if aught but death part thee and me.* An oath for confirmation was an end of this strife, and would leave a lasting obligation upon her never to forsake that good way she was now making choice of. *First,* It is implied that death would separate between them for a time. She could promise to die and be buried in the same place, but not at the same time; it might so happen that she might die first, and this would part them. Note, Death parts those whom nothing else will part. A dying hour is a parting hour, and should be so thought of by us and prepared for. *Secondly,* It is resolved that nothing else should part them; not any kindness from her own family and people, nor any hope of preferment among them, not any unkindness from Israel, nor the fear of poverty and disgrace among them. "No, I will *never leave thee.*" Now,

(2.) This is a pattern of a resolute convert to God and religion. Thus must we be at a point. [1.] We must take the Lord for our God. "This God is *my God for ever and ever;* I have avouched him for mine." [2.] When we take God for our God we must take his people for our people in all conditions; though they be a poor despised people, yet, if they be his, they must be ours. [3.] Having cast in our lot among them, we must be willing to take our lot with them and to fare as they fare. We must submit to the same yoke and draw in it faithfully, take up the same cross and carry it cheerfully, go where God will have us to go, though it should be into banishment, and lodge where he will have us to lodge, though it be in a prison, die where he will have us die, and lay our bones in the graves of the upright, who enter into peace and rest in their beds, though they be but the *graves of the common people.* [4.] We must resolve to continue and persevere, and herein our adherence to Christ must be closer than that of Ruth to Naomi. She resolved that nothing but death should separate them; but we must resolve that death itself shall not separate us from our duty to Christ, and then we may be sure that death itself shall not separate us from our happiness in Christ. [5.] We must bind our souls with a bond never to break these pious resolutions, and swear unto the Lord that we will cleave to him. Fast bind, fast find. He that means honestly does not startle at assurances.

8. Naomi is hereby silenced (*v.* 18): *When she saw that Ruth was stedfastly minded to go with her* (which was the very thing she aimed at in all that she had said, to make her of a stedfast mind in going with her), when she saw that she had gained her point, she was well satisfied, and *left off speaking to her.* She could desire no more than that solemn protestation which Ruth had just now made. See the power of resolution, how it puts temptation to silence. Those that are unresolved, and go in religious ways without a stedfast mind, tempt the tempter, and stand like a door half open, which invites a thief; but resolution shuts and bolts the door, resists the devil, and forces him to flee.

The Chaldee paraphrase thus relates the debate between Naomi and Ruth: — Ruth said, *Entreat me not to leave thee,* for *I will be a proselyte.* Naomi said, *We are commanded to keep sabbaths and good days, on which we may not travel above 2000 cubits* — a sabbath-day's journey. *Well,* said Ruth, *whither thou goest I will go.* Naomi said, *We are commanded not to tarry all night with Gentiles. Well,* said Ruth, *where thou lodgest I will lodge.* Naomi said, *We are commanded to keep 613 precepts. Well,* said Ruth, *whatever thy people keep I will keep, for they shall be my people.* Naomi said, *We are forbidden to worship any strange god. Well,* said Ruth, *thy God shall be my God.* Naomi said, *We have four sorts of deaths for malefactors, stoning, burning, strangling, and slaying with the sword. Well,* said Ruth, *where thou diest I will die. We have,* said Naomi, *houses of sepulchre. And there,* said Ruth, *will I be buried.*

Verses 19–22

Naomi and Ruth, after many a weary step (the fatigue of the journey, we may suppose, being somewhat relieved by the good instructions Naomi gave to her proselyte and the good discourse they had together), came at last to Bethlehem. And they came very seasonably, *in the beginning of the barley-harvest,* which was the first of their harvests, that of wheat following after. Now Naomi's own eyes might convince her of the truth of what she had heard in the country of Moab, that *the Lord had visited his people in giving them bread,* and Ruth might see this good land in its best state; and now they had opportunity to provide for winter. Our *times are in God's hand,* both the events and the time of them. Notice is here taken,

I. Of the discomposure of the neighbours upon this occasion (*v.* 19): *All the city was moved about them.* Her old acquaintance gathered about her, to enquire concerning her state, and to bid her welcome to Bethlehem again. Or perhaps they were *moved about her,* lest she should be a charge to the town, she looked so bare. By this it appears that she had formerly lived respectably, else there would not have been so much notice taken of her. If those that have been in a high and prosperous condition break, or fall into poverty or disgrace, their fall is the more remarkable. And they said, *Is this Naomi?* The *women* of the city said it, for the word is feminine. Those with whom she had formerly been intimate were surprised to see her in this condition; she was so much broken and altered with her afflictions that they could scarcely believe their own eyes, nor think that this was the same person whom they had formerly seen, so fresh, and fair, and gay: *Is this Naomi?* So unlike is the rose when it is withered to what it was when it was blooming. What a poor figure does Naomi make now, compared with what she made in her prosperity! If any asked this question in contempt, upbraiding her with her miseries ("is this she that could not be content to fare as her neighbours did, but must ramble to a strange country? see what she has got by it!"), their temper was very base and sordid. Nothing more barbarous than to triumph over those that are fallen. But we may suppose that the generality asked it in compassion and commiseration: "Is this she that lived so plentifully, and kept so good a house, and was so charitable to the poor? *How has the gold become dim!*" Those that had seen the magnificence of the first temple wept when they saw the meanness of the second; so these here. Note, Afflictions will make great and surprising changes in a little time. When we see how sickness and old age alter people, change their countenance and temper, we may think of what the Bethlehemites said: *"Is this Naomi?* One would not take it to be the same person." God, by his grace, fit us for all such changes, especially the great change!

II. Of the composure of Naomi's spirit. If some upbraided her with her poverty, she was not moved against them, as she would have been if she had been poor and proud; but, with a great deal of pious patience, bore that and all the other melancholy effects of her affliction (*v.* 20, 21): *Call me not Naomi, call me Mara,* etc. *"Naomi* signifies *pleasant* or *amiable;* but all my pleasant things are laid waste; call me *Mara, bitter* or *bitterness,* for I am now a woman of a sorrowful spirit." Thus does she bring her mind to her condition, which we all ought to do when our condition is not in every thing to our mind. Observe,

1. The change of her state, and how it is described, with a pious regard to the divine providence, and without any passionate murmurings or complaints. (1.) It was a very sad and melancholy change. She *went out full;* so she thought herself when she had her husband with her and two sons. Much of the fulness of our comfort in this world arises from agreeable relations. But she now *came home again empty,* a widow and childless, and probably had sold her goods, and of all the effects she took with her brought home no more than the clothes on her back. So uncertain is all that which we call fulness in the creature, 1 Sa. 2:5. Even in the fulness of that sufficiency we may be in straits. But there is a fulness, a spiritual and divine fulness, which we can never be emptied of, a good part which shall not be *taken from those that have it.* (2.) She acknowledges the hand of God, his mighty hand, in the affliction. "It is the Lord that has *brought me home again empty;* it is the Almighty that has afflicted me." Note, Nothing conduces more to satisfy a gracious soul under an affliction than the consideration of the hand of God in it. *It is the Lord,* 1 Sa. 3:18; Job 1:21. Especially to consider that he who afflicts us is *Shaddai,* the *Almighty,* with whom it is folly to contend and to whom it is our duty and interest to submit. It is that name of God by which he enters into covenant with his people: *I am God Almighty, God All-sufficient,* Gen. 17:1. He afflicts as a God in covenant, and his all-sufficiency may be our support and supply under all our afflictions. He that empties us of the creature knows how to fill us with himself. (3.) She speaks very feelingly of the impression which the affliction had made upon her: He has *dealt very bitterly with me.* The cup of affliction is a bitter cup, and even that which afterwards *yields the peaceable fruit of righteousness,* yet, for the present, is *not joyous, but grievous,* Heb. 12:11. Job complains, *Thou writest bitter things against me,* Job 13:26. (4.) She owns the affliction to come from God as a controversy: *The Lord hath testified against me.* Note, When God corrects us he *testifies against us* and contends with us (Job 10:17), intimating that he is displeased with us. Every rod has a voice, the voice of a witness.

2. The compliance of her spirit with this change: *"Call me not Naomi,* for I am no more pleasant, either to myself or to my friends; *but call me Mara,* a name more agreeable to my present state." Many that are debased and impoverished yet affect to be called by the empty names and titles of honour they have formerly enjoyed. Naomi did not so. Her humility regards not a glorious name in a dejected state. If God deal bitterly with her, she will accommodate herself to the dispensation, and is willing to be called *Mara, bitter.* Note, It well becomes us to have our hearts humbled under humbling providences. When our condition is brought down our spirits should be brought down with it. And then our troubles are sanctified to us when we thus comport with them; for it is not an affliction itself, but an affliction rightly borne, that does us good. *Perdidisti tot mala, si nondum misera esse didicisti — So many calamities have been lost upon you if you have not yet learned how to suffer.* Sen. ad Helv. *Tribulation works patience.*

CHAPTER 2

There is scarcely any chapter in all the sacred history that stoops so low as this to take cognizance of so mean a person as Ruth, a poor Moabitish widow, so mean an action as her gleaning corn in a neighbour's field, and the minute circumstances thereof. But all this was in order to her being grafted into the line of Christ and taken in among his ancestors, that she might be a figure of the espousals of the Gentile church to Christ, Isa. 54:1. This makes the story remarkable; and many of the passages of it are instructive and very improvable. Here we have, I. Ruth's humility and industry in gleaming corn, Providence directing her to Boaz's field (*v.* 1–3). II. The great favour which Boaz showed to her in many instances (*v.* 4–16). III. The return of Ruth to her mother-in-law (*v.* 18–23).

Verses 1–3

Naomi had now gained a settlement in Bethlehem among her old friends; and here we have an account,

I. Of her rich kinsman, Boaz, *a mighty man of wealth, v.* 1. The Chaldee reads it, *mighty in the law.* If he was both, it was a most rare and excellent conjunction, to be mighty in wealth and mighty in the scriptures too; those that are so are mighty indeed. He was grandson of Nahshon, who was prince of the tribe of Judah in the wilderness, and son of Salmon, probably a younger son, by Rahab, the harlot of Jericho. He carries might in his name, *Boaz — in him is strength;* and he was of the family of Elimelech, that family which was now reduced and brought so low. Observe, 1. Boaz, though a rich and great man, had poor relations. Every branch of the tree is not a top-branch. Let not those that are great in the world be ashamed to own their kindred that are mean and despised, lest they be found therein proud, scornful, and unnatural. 2. Naomi, though a poor contemptible widow, had rich relations, whom yet she boasted not of, nor was burdensome to, nor expected any thing from when she returned to Bethlehem in distress. Those that have rich relations, while they themselves are poor, ought to know that it is the wise providence of God that makes the difference (in which we ought to acquiesce), and that to be proud of our relation to such is a great sin, and to trust to it is great folly.

II. Of her poor daughter-in-law, Ruth. 1. Her condition was very low and poor, which was a great trial to the faith and constancy of a young proselyte. The Bethlehemites would have done well if they had invited Naomi and her daughter-in-law first to one good house and then to another (it would have been a great support to an aged widow and a great encouragement to a new convert); but, instead of tasting the dainties of Canaan, they have no way of getting necessary food but by gleaning corn, and otherwise, for aught that appears, they might have starved. Note, *God has chosen the poor of this world;* and poor they are likely to be, for, though God has chosen them, commonly men overlook them. 2. Her character, in this condition, was very good (*v.* 2): *She said to Naomi,* not, "Let me now go to the land of Moab again, for there is no living here, here there is want, but *in my father's house there is bread enough.*" No, she is *not mindful of the country from which she came out,* otherwise she had now a fair occasion to return. The God of Israel shall be her God, and, though he slay her, yet will she trust in him and never forsake him. But her request is, *Let me go to the field, and glean ears of corn.* Those that are well born, and have been well brought up, know not what straits they may be reduced to, nor what mean employments they may be obliged to get their bread by, Lam. 4:5. When the case is thus melancholy, let Ruth be remembered, who is a great example, (1.) Of humility. When Providence had made her poor she did not say, "To glean, which is in effect to beg, I am ashamed," but cheerfully stoops to the meanness of her circumstances and accommodates herself to her lot. High spirits can more easily starve than stoop; Ruth was none of those. She does not tell her mother she was never brought up to live upon crumbs. Though she was not brought up to it, she is brought down to it, and is not uneasy at it. Nay, it is her own motion, not her mother's injunction. Humility is one of the brightest ornaments of youth, and one of the best omens. Before Ruth's honour was this humility. Observe how humbly she speaks of herself, in her expectation of leave to glean: Let me glean after him *in whose sight I shall find grace.* She does not say, "I will go and glean, and surely nobody will deny me the liberty," but, "I will go and glean, in the hope that somebody will allow me the liberty." Note, Poor people must not demand kindness as a debt, but humbly ask it, and take it as a favour, though in ever so small a matter. It becomes the poor to use entreaties. (2.) Of industry. She does not say to her mother-in-law, "Let me now go a visiting to the ladies of the town, or go a walking in the fields to take the air and be merry; I cannot sit all day moping with you." No, it is not sport, but business, that her heart is upon: *"Let me go and glean ears of corn,* which will turn to some good account." She was one of those virtuous women that love not to eat the bread of idleness, but love to take pains. This is an example to young people. Let them learn betimes to labour, and, *what their hand finds to do, do it with their might.* A disposition to diligence bodes well both for this world and the other. Love not sleep, love not sport, love not sauntering; but love business. It is also an example to poor people to work for their living, and not beg that which they are able to earn. We must not be shy of any honest employment, though it be mean, *ergon ouden oneidos — No labour is a reproach.* Sin is a thing below us, but we must not think any thing else so That Providence calls us to. (3.) Of regard to her mother. Though she was but her mother-in-law, and though, being loosed by death from the law of her husband, she might easily suppose herself thereby loosed from the law of her husband's mother, yet she is dutifully observant of her. She will not go out without letting her know and asking her leave. This respect young people ought to show to their parents and governors; it is part of the honour due to them. She did not say, "Mother, if you will go with me, I will go glean:" but, "Do you sit at home and take your ease, and I will go abroad, and take pains." *Juniores ad labores — Youth should work.* Let young people take advice from the aged, but not put them upon toil. (4.) Of dependence upon Providence, intimated in that, I will *glean after him in whose sight I shall find grace.* She knows not which way to go, nor whom to enquire for, but will trust Providence to raise her up some friend or other that will be kind to her. Let us always keep us good thoughts of the divine providence, and believe that while we do well it will do well for us. And it did well for Ruth; for when she went out alone, without guide or companion, to glean, *her hap was to light on the field of Boaz, v.* 3. To her it seemed casual. She knew not whose field it was, nor had she any reason for going to that more than any other, and therefore it is said to be *her hap;* but Providence directed her steps to this field. Note, God wisely orders small events; and those that seem altogether contingent serve his own glory and the good of his people. Many a great affair is brought about by a little turn, which seemed fortuitous to us, but was directed by Providence with design.

Verses 4–16

Now Boaz himself appears, and a great deal of decency there appears in his carriage both towards his own servants and towards this poor stranger.

I. Towards his own servants, and those that were employed for him in reaping and gathering in his corn. Harvest-time is busy time, many hands must then be at work. Boaz that had much, being a mighty man of wealth, had much to do, and consequently many to work under him and to live upon him. *As goods are increased those are increased that eat them, and what good has the owner thereof save the beholding of them with his eyes?* Boaz is here an example of a good master.

1. He had a servant that was set over the reapers, *v.* 6. In great families it is requisite there should be one to oversee the rest of the servants, and appoint to each their portion both of work and meat. Ministers are such servants in God's house, and it is requisite that they be both wise and faithful, and *show their Lord all things,* as he here, *v.* 6.

2. Yet he came himself to his reapers, to see how the work went forward, if he found any thing amiss to rectify it, and to give further orders what should be done. This was both for his own interest (he that wholly leaves his business to others will have it done by the halves; the master's eye makes a fat horse) and it was also for the encouragement of his servants, who would go on the more cheerfully in their work when their master countenanced them so far as to make them a visit. Masters that live at ease should think with tenderness of those that toil for them and bear the burden and heat of the day.

3. Kind and pious salutations were interchanged between Boaz and his reapers.

(1.) He said to them, *The Lord be with you;* and they replied, *The Lord bless thee, v.* 4. Hereby they expressed, [1.] Their mutual respect to each other; he to them as good servants, and they to him as a good master. When he came to them he did not fall a chiding them, as if he came only to find fault and exercise his authority, but he prayed for them: *"The Lord be with you,* prosper you, and give you health and strength, and preserve you from any disaster." Nor did they, as soon as ever he was out of hearing, fall a cursing him, as some ill-natured servants that hate their master's eye, but they returned his courtesy: *"The Lord bless thee,* and make our labours serviceable to thy prosperity." Things are likely to go on well in a house where there is such good-will as this between master and servants. [2.] Their joint-dependence upon the divine providence. They express their kindness to each other by praying one for another. They show not only their courtesy, but their piety, and acknowledgement that all good comes from the presence and blessing of God, which therefore we should value and desire above any thing else both for ourselves and others.

(2.) Let us hence learn to use, [1.] Courteous salutations, as expressions of a sincere good-will to our friends. [2.] Pious ejaculations, lifting up our hearts to God for his favour, in such short prayers as these. Only we must take heed that they do not degenerate into formality, lest in them we *take the name of the Lord our God in vain;* but, if we be serious in them, we may in them keep up our communion with God, and fetch in mercy and grace from him. It appears to have been the usual custom thus to wish reapers good speed, Ps. 129:7, 8.

4. He took an account from his reapers concerning a stranger he met with in the field, and gave necessary orders concerning her, that they should not touch her (*v.* 9) nor reproach her, *v.* 15. Masters must take care, not only that they do no hurt themselves, but that they suffer not their servants and those under them to do hurt. He also ordered them to be kind to her, and *let fall some of the handfuls on purpose for her.* Though it is fit that masters should restrain and rebuke their servants' wastefulness, yet they should not tie them up from being charitable, but give them allowance for that, with prudent directions.

II. Boaz was very kind to Ruth, and showed her a great deal of favour, induced to it by the account he had of her, and what he observed concerning her, God also inclining his heart to countenance her. Coming among his reapers, he observed this stranger among them, and got intelligence from his steward who she was, and here is a very particular account of what passed concerning her.

1. The steward gave to Boaz a very fair account of her, proper to recommend her to his favour, *v.* 6, 7. (1.) That she was a stranger, and therefore one of those that by the law of God were to *gather the gleanings of the harvest,* Lev. 19:9, 10. She is the Moabitish damsel. (2.) That she was allied to his family; she came back with Naomi, the wife of Elimelech, a kinsman of Boaz. (3.) That she was a proselyte, for she came out of the country of Moab to settle in the land of Israel. (4.) That she was very modest, and had not gleaned till she had asked leave. (5.) That she was very industrious, and had continued close to her work from morning even until now. And the poor that are industrious and willing to take pains are fit to be encouraged. Now, in the heat of the day, she tarried a little in the house or booth that was set up in the field for shelter from the weather to repose herself, and some suggest that it is probably she retired for her devotion. But she soon came back to her work, and, except that little intermission, kept close to it all day, though it was not what she had been used to. Servants should be just in the character and reports they give to their masters, and take heed they do not misrepresent any person, nor without cause discourage their master's charity.

2. Boaz was hereupon extremely civil to her in divers instances. (1.) He ordered her to attend his reapers in every field they gathered in and not to glean in the field of another, for she should not need to go any where else to better herself (*v.* 8): *Abide here fast by my maidens;* for those of her own sex were the fittest company for her. (2.) He charged all his servants to be very tender of her and respectful to her, and no doubt they would be so to one to whom they saw their master kind. She was a stranger, and it is probably her language, dress, and mien differed much from theirs; but he charged them that they should not in any thing affront her, or be abusive to her, as rude servants are too apt to be to strangers. (3.) He bade her welcome to the entertainment he had provided for his own servants. He ordered her, not only to drink of the water which was drawn for them (for that seems to be the liquor he means, *v.* 9, drawn from the famous well of Beth-lehem which was by the gate, the water of which David longed for, 2 Sa. 23:15), but *at meal-time to come and eat of their bread* (*v.* 14), yea, and she should be welcome to their sauce too: *Come, dip thy morsel in the vinegar,* to make it savoury; for God allows us not only nourishing but relishing food, not for necessity only, but for delight. And for encouragement o her, and direction to the servants, he, himself, happening to be present when the reapers sat down to meat, *reached her parched corn* to eat. It is no disparagement to the finest hand to be *reached forth to the needy* (Prov. 31:20), and to be employed in serving the poor. Observe, Boaz was not scanty in his provision for his reapers, but sent them so much more than enough for themselves as would be entertainment for a stranger. Thus *there is that scattereth and yet increaseth.* (4.) He commended her for her dutiful respect to her mother-in-law, which, though he did not know her by sight, yet he had heard of (*v.* 11): *It has been fully shown me all that thou hast done unto thy mother-in-law.* Note, Those that do well ought to have the praise of it. But that which especially he commended her for was that she had left her own country, and had become a proselyte to the Jewish religion; for so the Chaldee expounds it: "Thou hast come to be proselyted, and to dwell among *a people whom thou knowest not."* Those that leave all, to embrace the true religion, are worthy of double honour. (5.) He prayed for her (*v.* 12): *The Lord recompense thy work.* Her strong affection to the commonwealth of Israel, to which she was by birth an alien, was such a work of the divine grace in her as would certainly be crowned with a full reward by him *under whose wings she had come to trust.* Note, Those that by faith come under the wings of the divine grace, and have a full complacency and confidence in that grace, may be sure of a full recompence of reward for their so doing. From this expression, the Jews describe a proselyte to be one that is *gathered under the wings of the divine majesty.* (6.) He encouraged her to go on in her gleaning, and did not offer to take her off from that; for the greatest kindness we can do our poor relations is to assist and encourage their industry. Boaz ordered his servants to let her glean among the sheaves, where other gleaners were not allowed to come, and not to reproach her, that is, not to call her *thief,* or to suspect her of taking more than was allowed her, *v.* 15. All this shows Boaz to have been a man of a generous spirit, and one that, according to the law, considered the heart of a stranger.

3. Ruth received his favours with a great deal of humility and gratitude, and conducted herself with as much propriety in her place as he did himself in his, but little thinking that she should shortly be the mistress of that field she was now gleaning in. (1.) She paid all possible respect to him, and gave him honour, according to the usage of the country (*v.* 10): *She fell on her face, and bowed herself to the ground.* Note, Good breeding is a great ornament to religion; and we must render *honour to whom honour is due.* (2.) She humbly owned herself unworthy of his favours: *"I am a stranger* (*v.* 10) and *not like one of thy handmaids* (*v.* 13), not so well dressed nor so well taught, not so neat nor so handy." Note, It well becomes us all to think meanly of ourselves, and to take notice of that in ourselves which is diminishing, esteeming others better than ourselves. (3.) She gratefully acknowledged his kindness to her; though it was no great expense to him, nor much more than what he was obliged to by the divine law, yet she magnifies and admires it: *Why have I found grace in thy eyes? v.* 10. (4.) She begs the continuance of his good-will: *Let me find favour in they sight* (*v.* 13), and owns that what he had said had been a cordial to her: *Thou hast comforted me, for that thou hast spoken friendly to me.* Those that are great, and in high places, know not how much good they may do to their inferiors with a kind look or by speaking friendly to them; and so small an expense, one would think, they should not grudge, when it shall be put upon the score of their charity. (5.) When Boaz gave her her dinner with his reapers she only ate so much as would suffice her, and left the rest, and immediately rose up to glean, *v.* 14, 15. She did not, under pretence either of her want or of her labour, eat more than was convenient for her, nor so much as to unfit her for work in the afternoon. Temperance is a friend to industry; and we must eat and drink to strengthen us for business, not to indispose us to it.

Verses 17–23

Here, I. Ruth finishes her day's work, *v.* 17. 1. She took care not to lose time, for she gleaned until evening. We must not be weary of well-doing, because in due season we shall reap. She did not make an excuse to sit still, or go home, till the evening. Let us *work the works of him that sent us, while it is day.* She scarcely used, much less did she abuse, the kindness of Boaz; for, though he ordered his servants to leave handfuls for her, she continued to glean the scattered ears. 2. She took care not to lose what she had gathered, but threshed it herself, that she might the more easily carry it home, and might have it ready for use. *The slothful man roasteth not that which he took in hunting,* and so loseth the benefit of it, *but the substance of a diligent man is precious,* Prov. 12:27. Ruth had gathered it ear by ear, but, when she had put it all together, it was an ephah of barley, about four pecks. Many a little makes a great deal. It is an encouragement to industry that in all labour, even that of gleaning, there is profit, but the *talk of the lips tendeth only to penury.* When she had got her corn into as little compass as she could, she took it up herself, and carried it into the city, though, had she asked them, it is likely some of Boaz's servants would have done that for her. We should study to be as little as possible troublesome to those that are kind to us. She did not think it either too hard or too mean a service to carry her corn herself into the city, but was rather pleased with what she had gotten by her own industry, and careful to secure it; and let us thus take care that we *lose not those things which we have wrought,* which we have gained, 2 Jn. 8.

II. She paid her respects to her mother-in-law, went straight home to her and did not go to converse with Boaz's servants, *showed her what she had gleaned,* that she might see she had not been idle.

1. She entertained her with what she had left of the good dinner Boaz had given her. She gave to her what she had reserved, after she was sufficed (*v.* 18), which refers to *v.* 14. If she had any thing better than another, her mother should have part with her. Thus, having shown industry abroad, she showed piety at home; so children's maintaining their parents is called (1 Tim. 5:4), and it is part of the honour due to them by the fifth commandment, Mt. 15:6.

2. She gave her an account of her day's work, and how a kind providence had favoured her in it, which made it very comfortable to her; for the gleanings that a righteous man hath are better than the harvests of many wicked, Ps. 37:16. (1.) Naomi asked her where she had been: *Where hast thou gleaned to-day?* Note, Parents should take care to enquire into the ways of their children, how, and where, and in what company they spend their time. This may prevent many extravagancies which children, left to themselves, run into, by which they bring both themselves and their parents to shame. If we are not our brethren's, yet surely we are our children's keepers: and we know what a son Adonijah proved, that had never been chidden. Parents should examine their children, not to frighten nor discourage them, not so as to make them hate home or tempt them to tell a lie, but to commend them if they have done well, and with mildness to reprove and caution them if they have done otherwise. It is a good question for us to ask ourselves in the close of every day, *"Where have I gleaned to-day?* What improvements have I made in knowledge and grace? What have I done or obtained that will turn to a good account?" (2.) Ruth gave her a particular account of the kindness she had received from Boaz (*v.* 19) and the hopes she had of further kindness from him, he having ordered her to attend his servants throughout all the harvest, *v.* 21. Note, Children should look upon themselves as accountable to their parents and to those that are over them, and not think it a disparagement to them to be examined; let them *do that which is good,* and they shall have praise of the same. Ruth told her mother what kindness Boaz had shown her, that she might take some occasion or another to acknowledge it and return him thanks; but she did not tell her how Boaz had commended her, *v.* 11. Humility teaches us, not only not to praise ourselves, but not to be forward to publish others' praises of us. (3.) We are here told what Naomi said to it. [1.] She prayed heartily for him that had been her daughter's benefactor, even before she knew who it was (*v.* 19): *Blessed be he,* whoever he was, *that did take knowledge of thee,* shooting the arrow of prayer at a venture. But more particularly when she was told who it was (*v.* 20): *Blessed be he of the Lord.* Note, The poor must pray for those that are kind and liberal to them, and thus requite them, when they are not capable of making them any other requital. Let the loins of the poor bless those that refresh them, Job 29:13; 31:20. And he that hears the cries of the poor against their oppressors (Ex. 22:27), it may be hoped, will hear the prayers of the poor for their benefactors. She now remembered the former kindnesses Boaz had shown to her husband and sons, and joins those to this: he has not *left off his kindness to the living and to the dead.* If we generously show kindness even to those that seem to have forgotten our former favours, perhaps it may help to revive the remembrance even of those which seem buried. [2.] She acquainted Ruth with the relation their family was in to Boaz: *The man is near of kin to us.* It should seem she had been so long in Moab that she had forgotten her kindred in the land of Israel, till by this providence God brought it to her mind. At least she had not told Ruth of it, though it might have been some encouragement to a young proselyte. Unlike to humble Naomi are many, who, though fallen into decay themselves, are continually boasting of their great relations. Nay, Observe the chain of thought here, and in it a chain of providences, bringing about what was designed concerning Ruth. Ruth names Boaz as one that had been kind to her. Naomi bethinks herself who that should be, and presently recollects herself: *"The man is near of kin to us;* now that I hear his name, I remember him very well." This thought brings in another: "He is *our next kinsman,* our *goel,* that has the right to redeem our estate that was mortgaged, and therefore from him we may expect further kindness. He is the likeliest man in all Bethlehem to set us up." Thus God brings things to our mind, sometimes on a sudden, that prove to have a wonderful tendency to our good. [3.] She appointed Ruth to continue her attendance in the fields of Boaz (*v.* 22): *"Let them not meet thee in any other field,* for that will be construed a contempt of his courtesy." Our blessed Saviour is our *Goel;* it is he that has a right to redeem. If we expect to receive benefit by him, let us closely adhere to him, and his fields, and his family; let us not go to the world and its fields for that which is to be had with him only, and which he has encouraged us to expect from him. Has the Lord dealt bountifully with us? Let us not be found in any other field, nor seek for happiness and satisfaction in the creature. Tradesmen take it ill if those that are in their books go to another shop. We lose divine favours if we slight them. Some think Naomi gave her daughter-in-law a tacit rebuke; she had spoken (*v.* 21) of keeping fast by the young *men.* "Nay," said Naomi (*v.* 22), *"It is good that thou go out with his maidens; they* are fitter company for thee than the *young men."* But they are too critical. Ruth spoke of the young men because they were the principal labourers, and to them Boaz had given directions concerning her; and Naomi takes it for granted that, while she attended the young men, her society would be with the maidens, as was fit. Ruth dutifully observed her mother's directions; she continued to glean, to the end, not only of barley-harvest, but of the wheat-harvest, which followed it, that she might gather food in harvest to serve for winter, Prov. 6:6–8. She also kept fast by the maidens of Boaz, with whom she afterwards cultivated an acquaintance, which might do her service, *v.* 23. But she constantly came to her mother at night in due time, as became a virtuous woman, that was for working days, and not for merry nights. And when the harvest was ended (as bishop Patrick expounds it) she did not gad abroad, but kept her aged mother company at home. Dinah went out to see the daughters of the land, and we know what a disgrace her vanity ended in. Ruth kept at home, and helped to maintain her mother, and went out on no other errand than to get provision for her, and we shall find afterwards what preferment her humility and industry ended in. *Seest thou a man diligent in his business?* Honour is before him.

CHAPTER 3

We found it very easy, in the former chapter, to applaud the decency of Ruth's behaviour, and to show what good use we may make of the account given us of it; but in this chapter we shall have much ado to vindicate it from the imputation of indecency, and to save it from having an ill use made of it; but the goodness of those times was such as saved what is recorded here from being ill done, and yet the badness of these times is such as that it will not justify any now in doing the like. Here is, I. The directions Naomi gave to her daughter-in-law how to claim Boaz for her husband (*v.* 1–5). II. Ruth's punctual observance of those directions (*v.* 6, 7). III. The kind and honourable treatment Boaz gave her (*v.* 8–15). IV. Her return to her mother-in-law (*v.* 16–18).

Verses 1–5

Here is, I. Naomi's care for her daughter's comfort is without doubt very commendable, and is recorded for imitation. She had no thoughts of marrying herself, *ch.* 1:12. But, though she that was old had resolved upon a perpetual widowhood, yet she was far from the thoughts of confining her daughter-in-law to it, that was young. Age must not make itself a standard to youth. On the contrary, she is full of contrivance how to get her well married. Her wisdom projected that for her daughter which her daughter's modesty forbade her to project for herself, *v.* 1. This she did 1. In justice to the dead, to raise up seed to those that were gone, and so to preserve the family from being extinct. 2. In kindness and gratitude to her daughter-in-law, who had conducted herself very dutifully and respectfully to her. *"My daughter"* (said she, looking upon her in all respects as her own), *"shall I not seek rest for thee,"* that is, a settlement in the married state; "shall I not get thee a good husband, *that it may be well with thee,"* that is, "that thou mayest live plentifully and pleasantly, and not spend all thy days in the mean and melancholy condition we now live in?" Note, (1.) A married state is, or should be, a state of rest to young people. Wandering affections are then fixed, and the heart must be at rest. It is at rest in the house of a husband, and in his heart, *ch.* 1:9. Those are giddy indeed that marriage does not compose. (2.) That which should be desired and designed by those that enter into the married state is *that it may be well with them,* in order to which it is necessary that they choose well; otherwise, instead of being a rest to them, it may prove the greatest uneasiness. Parents, in disposing of their children, must have this in their eye, *that it may be well with them.* And be it always remembered *that is best for us which is best for our souls.* (3.) It is the duty of parents to seek this rest for their children, and to do all that is fit for them to do, in due time, in order to it. And the more dutiful and respectful they are to them, though they can the worse spare them, yet they should the rather prefer them, and the better.

II. The course she took in order to her daughter's preferment was very extraordinary and looks suspicious. If there was any thing improper in it, the fault must lie upon Naomi, who put her daughter upon it, and who knew, or should know, the laws and usages of Israel better than Ruth. 1. It was true that Boaz, being near of kin to the deceased, and (for aught that Naomi knew to the contrary) the nearest of all now alive, was obliged by the divine law to marry the widow of Mahlon, who was the eldest son of Elimelech, and was dead without issue (*v.* 2): *"Is not Boaz of our kindred,* and therefore bound in conscience to take care of our affairs?" This may encourage us to lay ourselves by faith at the feet of Christ, that he is our near kinsman; having taken our nature upon him, he is *bone of our bone and flesh of our flesh.* 2. It was a convenient time to remind him of it, now that he had got so much acquaintance with Ruth by her constant attendance on his reapers during the whole harvest, which was now ended; and he also, by the kindness he had shown to Ruth in smaller matters, had encouraged Naomi to hope that he would not be unkind, much less unjust, in this greater. And she thought it was a good opportunity to apply to him when he made a winnowing-feast at his threshing-floor (*v.* 2), then and there completing the joy of the harvest, and treating his workmen like a kind master: *He winnoweth barley to-night,* that is, he makes his entertainment to-night. As Nabal and Absalom had feasts at their sheep-shearing, so Boaz at his winnowing. 3. Naomi thought Ruth the most proper person to do it herself; and perhaps it was the usage in that country that in this case the woman should make the demand; so much is intimated by the law, Deu. 25:7–9. Naomi therefore orders her daughter-in-law to make herself clean and neat, not to make herself fine (*v.* 3): *"Wash thyself and anoint thee,* not paint thee (as Jezebel), put on thy raiment, but not the attire of a harlot, and go down to the floor," whither, it is probable, she was invited to the supper there made; but she must not make herself known, that it, not make her errand known (she herself could not but be very well known among Boaz's reapers) till the company had dispersed and Boaz had retired. And upon this occasion she would have an easier access to him in private than she could have at his own house. And thus far was well enough. But, 4. Her coming to lie down at his feet, when he was asleep in his bed, had such an appearance of evil, was such an approach towards it, and might have been such an occasion of it, that we know not well how to justify it. Many expositors think it unjustifiable, particularly the excellent Mr. Poole. We must not to evil that good may come. It is dangerous to bring the spark and the tinder together; for how great a matter may a little fire kindle! All agree that it is not to be drawn into a precedent; neither our laws nor our times are the same that were then; yet I am willing to make the best of it. If Boaz was, as they presumed, the next kinsman, she was his wife before God (as we say), and there needed but little ceremony to complete the nuptials; and Naomi did not intend that Ruth should approach to him any otherwise than as his wife. She knew Boaz to be not only an old man (she would not have trusted to that alone in venturing her daughter-in-law so near him), but a grave sober man, a virtuous and religious man, and one that feared God. She knew Ruth to be a modest woman, *chaste, and a keeper at home,* Tit. 2:5. The Israelites had indeed been once debauched by the daughters of Moab (Num. 25:1), but this Moabitess was none of those daughters. Naomi herself designed nothing but what was honest and honourable, and her charity (which *believeth all things* and *hopeth all things*) banished and forbade all suspicion that either Boaz or Ruth would attempt any thing but what was likewise honest and honourable. If what she advised had been then as indecent and immodest (according to the usage of the country) as it seems now to us, we cannot think that if Naomi had had so little virtue (which yet we have no reason to suspect) she would also have had so little wisdom as to put her daughter upon it, since that alone might have marred the match, and have alienated the affections of so grave and good a man as Boaz from her. We must therefore think that the thing did not look so ill then as it does now. Naomi referred her daughter-in-law to Boaz for further directions. When she had thus made her claim, Boaz, who was more learned in the laws, would *tell her what she must do.* Thus must we lay ourselves at the feet of our Redeemer, to receive from him our doom. *Lord, what wilt thou have me to do?* Acts 9:6. We may be sure, if Ruth had apprehended any evil in that which her mother advised her to, she was a woman of too much virtue and too much sense to promise as she did (*v.* 5): *All that thou sayest unto me I will do.* Thus must *the younger submit to the elder,* and to their grave and prudent counsels, when they have nothing worth speaking of to object against it.

Verses 6–13

Here is, I. Boaz's good management of his common affairs. It is probable, according to the common usage, 1. When his servants winnowed, he was with them, and had his eye upon them, to prevent, not their stealing any of his corn (he had no reason to fear that), but their waste of it through carelessness in the winnowing of it. Masters may sustain great losses by servants that are heedless, though they be honest, which is a reason why men should be diligent to *know the state of their own flocks,* and look well to them. 2. When he had more than ordinary work to be done, he treated his servants with extraordinary entertainments, and, for their encouragement, did *eat and drink with them.* It well becomes those that are rich and great to be generous to, and also to be familiar with, those that are under them, and employed for them. 3. When Boaz had supped with his workmen, and been awhile pleasant with them, he *went to bed in due time,* so early that by midnight he had his first sleep (*v.* 8), and thus he would be fit for his business betimes next morning. All that are good husbands will keep good hours, and not indulge themselves nor their families in unseasonable mirth. The Chaldee paraphrase tell us (*v.* 7) that *Boaz ate and drank and his heart was good* (and so the Hebrew word is), *and he blessed the name of the Lord, who had heard his prayers, and taken away the famine from the land of Israel.* So that he went sober to bed, his heart was in a good frame, and not overcharged with surfeiting and drunkenness. And he did not go to bed without prayer. Now that he had eaten and was full he blessed the Lord, and now that he was going to rest he committed himself to the divine protection; it was well he did, for he had an unusual temptation before him, though he knew not of it. 4. He had his bed or couch laid *at the end of the heap of corn;* not because he had set his heart upon it, nor only that he might watch and keep it safe from thieves, but it was too late to go home to the city, and here he would be near his work, and ready for it next morning, and he would show that he was not nice or curious in his lodging, neither took state nor consulted his ease, but was, like his father Jacob, a plain man, that, when there was occasion, could make his bed in a barn, and, if need were, sleep contentedly in the straw.

II. Ruth's good assurance in the management of her affair. She observed her mother's orders, went and laid herself down, not by his side, but overcross his bed's feet, in her clothes, and kept awake, waiting for an opportunity to tell her errand. When he awaked in the night, and perceived there was somebody at his feet, and enquired who it was, she told him her name and then her errand (*v.* 9), that she came to put herself under his protection, as the person appointed by the divine law to be her protector: *"Thou art he that has a right to redeem* a family and an estate from perishing, and therefore *let this ruin be under thy hand:* and *spread thy skirt over me* — be pleased to espouse me and my cause." Thus must we by faith apply ourselves to Jesus Christ as our next kinsman, that is able to redeem us, come under his wings, as we are invited (Mt. 23:37), and beg of him to *spread his skirt over us.* "Lord Jesus, take me into thy covenant and under thy care. *I am oppressed, undertake for me."*

III. The good acceptance Ruth gained with Boaz. What she did had no ill-effect, either one way or other, so that Naomi was not mistaken in her good opinion of her kinsman. He knew her demand was just and honourable, and treated her accordingly, and did not *deal with* his *sister as with a harlot,* Gen. 34:31. For,

1. He did not offer to violate her chastity, though he had all the opportunity that could be. The Chaldee paraphrase thus descants upon it: — He *subdued his concupiscence, and did not approach to her, but did as Joseph the Just, who would not come near to his Egyptian mistress, and as Phaltiel the Pious, who, when Saul had given him Michal, David's wife* (1 Sa. 25:44), *put a sword between himself and her, that he might not touch her.* Boaz knew it was not any sinful lust that brought her thither, and therefore bravely maintained both his own honour and hers.

2. He did not put any ill construction upon what she did, did not reproach her as an impudent woman and unfit to make an honest man a wife. She having approved herself well in the fields, and all her conduct having been modest and decent, he would not, from this instance, entertain the least suspicion of her character nor seem to do so, perhaps blaming himself that he had not offered the service of a kinsman to these distressed widows, and saved her this trouble, and ready to say as Judah concerning his daughter-in-law, *She is more righteous than I.* But on the contrary,

(1.) He commended her, spoke kindly to her, called her his *daughter,* and spoke honourably of her, as a woman of eminent virtue. She had shown in this instance more kindness to her mother-in-law, and to the family into which she had matched, than in any instance yet. It was very kind to leave her own country and come along with her mother to the land of Israel, to dwell with her, and help to maintain her. For this he had blessed her (*ch.* 2:12); but now he says, Thou hast *shown more kindness in the latter end than at the beginning* (*v.* 10), in that she consulted not her own fancy, but her husband's family, in marrying again. She received not the addresses of *young men* (much less did she seek them) *whether poor or rich,* but was willing to marry as the divine law directed, though it was to an old man, because it was for the honour and interest of the family into which she had matched, and for which she had an entire kindness. Young people must aim, in disposing of themselves, not so much to please their own eye as to please God and their parents.

(2.) He promised her marriage (*v.* 11): *"Fear not* that I will slight thee, or expose thee; no, *I will do all that thou requirest,* for it is the same that the law requires, from the next of kin, and I have no reason to decline it, *for all the city of my people doth know that thou art a virtuous woman," v.* 11. Note, [1.] Exemplary virtue ought to have its due praise (Phil. 4:8), and it will recommend both men and women to the esteem of the wisest and best. Ruth was a poor woman, and poverty often obscures the lustre of virtue; yet Ruth's virtues, even in a mean condition, were generally taken notice of and could not be hid; nay, her virtues took away the reproach of her poverty. If poor people be but good people, they shall have honour from God and man. Ruth had been remarkable for her humility, which paved the way to this honour. The less she proclaimed her own goodness the more did her neighbours take notice of it. [2.] In the choice of yoke-fellows, virtue should especially be regarded, known approved virtue. Let religion determine the choice, and it will certainly crown the choice and make it comfortable. *Wisdom is better than gold,* and, when it is said to be *good with an inheritance,* the meaning is that an inheritance is worth little without it.

(3.) He made his promise conditional, and could not do otherwise, for it seems there was a kinsman that was nearer than he, to whom the right of redemption did belong, *v.* 12. This he knew, but we may reasonably suppose Naomi (who had been long abroad, and could not be exact in the pedigree of her husband's family) was ignorant of it, otherwise she would never have sent her daughter to make her claim of Boaz. Yet he does not bid her go herself to this other kinsman; this would have been to put too great a hardship upon her: but he promises, [1.] That he would himself propose it to the other kinsman, and know his mind. The Hebrew word for a widow signifies *one that is dumb.* Boaz will therefore *open his mouth for the dumb* (Prov. 31:8), and will say that for this widow which she knew not how to say for herself. [2.] That, if the other kinsman refused to do the kinsman's part, he would do it, would marry the widow, redeem the land, and so repair the family. This promise he backs with a solemn oath, for it was a conditional contract of marriage (*v.* 13): *As the Lord liveth.* Thus keeping the matter in suspense, he bade her wait till morning. Bishop Hall thus sums up this matter in his contemplations: — "Boaz, instead of touching her as a wanton, blesseth her as a father, encourageth her as a friend, promiseth her as a kinsman, rewards her as a patron, and sends her away laden with hopes and gifts, no less chaste, more happy, than she came. O admirable temperance, worthy the progenitor of him in whose lips and heart there was no guile!"

Verses 14–18

We are here told, I. How Ruth was dismissed by Boaz. It would not have been safe for her to go home in the dead of the night; therefore *she lay at his feet* (not by his side) *until morning.* But as soon as ever the day broke, that she had light to go home by, she got away, *before one could know another,* that, if she were seen, yet she might not be known to be abroad so unseasonably. She was not shy of being known to be a gleaner in the field, nor ashamed of that mark of her poverty. But she would not willingly be known to be a night-walker, for her virtue was her greatest honour, and that which she most valued. Boaz dismissed her, 1. With a charge to keep counsel (*v.* 14): *Let it not be known that a woman came into the floor,* and lay all night so near to Boaz; for, though they needed not to care much what people said of them while they were both conscious to themselves of an unspotted purity, yet, because few could have come so near the fire as they did and not have been scorched, had it been known it would have occasioned suspicions in some and reflections from others. Good people would have been troubled, and bad people would have triumphed, and therefore *let it not be known.* Note, We must always take care, not only to keep a good conscience, but to keep a good name: either we must not do that which, though innocent, is liable to be misinterpreted, or, if we do, we must not *let it be known.* We must avoid not only sin, but scandal. There was likewise a particular reason for concealment here. If this matter should take wind, it might prejudice the freedom of the other kinsman's choice, and he would make this his reason for refusing Ruth, that Boaz and she had been together. 2. He dismissed her with a good present of corn, which would be very acceptable to her poor mother at home, and an evidence for her that he had not sent her away in dislike, which Naomi might have suspected if he had sent her away empty. He gave it to her in her *veil,* or *apron,* or *mantle,* gave it to her by measure. Like a prudent corn-master, he kept an account of all he delivered out. It was *six measures,* that is six omers as is supposed, ten of which made an ephah; whatever the measure was, it is probable he gave her as much as she could well carry, *v.* 15. And the Chaldee says, *Strength was given her from the Lord to carry it;* and adds that now *it was told her by the spirit of prophecy that from her should descend six of the most righteous men of their age,* namely, *David, Daniel, his three companions, and the king Messiah.*

II. How she was welcomed by her mother-in-law. She asked her, *"Who art thou, my daughter?* Art thou a bride or no? Must I give thee joy?" So Ruth told her how the matter stood (*v.* 17), whereupon her mother, 1. Advised her to be satisfied in what was done: *Sit still, my daughter, till thou know how the matter will fall* (*v.* 18) — *how it is decreed in heaven,* so the Chaldee reads it, for marriages are made there. She had done all that was fit for her to do, and now she must patiently wait the issue and not be perplexed about it. Let us learn hence to cast our care upon providence, to follow that and attend the motions of it, composing ourselves into an expectation of the event, with a resolution to acquiesce in it, whatever it be. Sometimes that proves best done for us that is least our own doing. *"Sit still,* therefore, *and see how the matter will fall,* and say, Let it fall how it will, I am ready for it." 2. She assured her that Boaz, having undertaken this matter, would approve himself a faithful careful friend: *He will not be at rest till he have finished the matter.* Though it was a busy time with him in his fields and his floor, yet, having undertaken to serve his friend, he would not neglect the business. Naomi believes that Ruth has won his heart, and that therefore he will not be easy till he knows whether she be his or no. This she gives as a reason why Ruth should sit still and not perplex herself about it, that Boaz had undertaken it, and he would be sure to manage it well. Much more reason have good Christians to be *careful for nothing,* but *cast their care on God,* because he has promised to *care for them:* and what need have we to care if he do? *Sit still, and see how the matter will fall,* for *the Lord will perfect that which concerns thee,* and will make it to work for good to thee, Ps. 37:4, 5; 138:8. *Your strength is to sit still,* Isa. 30:7.

CHAPTER 4

In this chapter we have the wedding between Boaz and Ruth, in the circumstances of which there was something uncommon, which is kept upon record for the illustration, not only of the law concerning the marrying of a brother's widow (Deu. 25:5, etc.), for cases help to expound laws, but of the gospel too, for from this marriage descended David, and the Son of David, whose espousals to the Gentile church were hereby typified. We are here told, I. How Boaz got clear of his rival, and fairly shook him off (*v.* 1–8). II. How his marriage with Ruth was publicly solemnized, and attended with the good wishes of his neighbours (*v.* 9–12). III. The happy issue that descended from this marriage, Obed, the grandfather of David (*v.* 13–17). And so the book concludes with the pedigree of David (*v.* 18–22). Perhaps it was to oblige him that the blessed Spirit directed the inserting of this story in the sacred canon, he being desirous that the virtues of his great-grandmother Ruth, together with her Gentile extraction and the singular providences that attended her, should be transmitted to posterity.

Verses 1–8

Here, 1. Boaz calls a court immediately. It is probable he was himself one of the elders (or aldermen) of the city; for he was a mighty man of wealth. Perhaps he was father of the city, and sat chief; for he seems here to have gone up to the gate as one having authority, and not as a common person; like Job, *ch.* 29:7, etc. We cannot suppose him less than a magistrate in his city who was grandson to Nahshon, prince of Judah; and his lying at the end of a heap of corn in the threshing-floor the night before was not at all inconsistent, in those days of plainness, with the honour of his sitting judge in the gate. But why was Boaz so hasty, why so fond of the match? Ruth was not rich, but lived upon alms; not honourable, but a poor stranger. She was never said to be beautiful; if ever she had been so, we may suppose that weeping, and travelling, and gleaning, had withered her lilies and roses. But that which made Boaz in love with her, and solicitous to expedite the affair, was that all her neighbours agreed she was a virtuous woman. This set her price with him *far above rubies* (Prov. 31:10); and therefore he thinks, if by marrying her he might do her a real kindness, he should also do himself a very great kindness. He will therefore bring it to a conclusion immediately. It was not court-day, but he got ten men of the elders of the city to meet him in the town-hall over the gate, where public business used to be transacted, *v.* 2. So many, it is probable, by the custom of the city, made a full court. Boaz, though a judge, would not be judge in his own cause, but desired the concurrence of other elders. Honest intentions dread not a public cognizance. 2. He summons his rival to come and hear the matter that was to be proposed to him (*v.* 1): *"Ho, such a one,* sit down here." He called him by his name, no doubt, but the divine historian thought not fit to record it, for, because he refused to raise up the name of the dead, he deserved not to have his name preserved to future ages in this history. Providence favoured Boaz in ordering it so that this kinsman should come by thus opportunely, just when the matter was ready to be proposed to him. Great affairs are sometimes much furthered by small circumstances, which facilitate and expedite them. 3. He proposes to the other kinsman the redemption of Naomi's land, which, it is probable, had been mortgaged for money to buy bread with when the famine was in the land (*v.* 3): *"Naomi has a parcel of land to sell,* namely, the equity of the redemption of it out of the hands of the mortgagee, which she is willing to part with;" or, as some think, it was her jointure for her life, and, wanting money, for a small matter she would sell her interest to the heir at law, who was fittest to be the purchaser. This he gives the kinsman legal notice of (*v.* 4), that he might have the refusal of it. Whoever had it must pay for it, and Boaz might have said, "My money is as good as my kinsman's; if I have a mind to it, why may not I buy it privately, since I had the first proffer of it, and say nothing to my kinsman?" No, Boaz, though fond enough of the purchase, would not do so mean a thing as to take a bargain over another man's head that was nearer a-kin to it; and we are taught by his example to be not only just and honest, but fair and honourable, in all our dealings, and to do nothing which we are unwilling should see the light, but be above-board. 4. The kinsman seemed forward to redeem the land till he was told that, if he did that, he must marry the widow, and then he flew off. He liked the land well enough, and probably caught at that the more greedily because he hoped that the poor widow being under a necessity of selling he have so much the better bargain: *"I will redeem it"* (said he) "with all my heart," thinking it would be a fine addition to his estate, *v.* 4. But Boaz told him there was a young widow in the case, and, if he have the land, he must take her with it, *Terra transit cum onere — The estate passes with this incumbrance;* either the divine law or the usage of the country would oblige him to it, or Naomi insisted upon it that she would not sell the land but upon this condition, *v.* 5. Some think this does not relate to the law of marrying the brother's widow (for that seems to oblige only the children of the same father, Deu. 25:5, unless by custom it was afterwards made to extend to the next of kin), but to the law of redemption of inheritances (Lev. 25:24, 25), for it is a *goel,* a *redeemer,* that is here enquired for; and if so it was not by the law, but by Naomi's own resolution, that the purchaser was to marry the widow. However it was, this kinsman, when he heard the conditions of the bargain, refused it (*v.* 6): *"I cannot redeem it for myself.* I will not meddle with it upon these terms, lest I mar my own inheritance." The land, he thought, would be an improvement of his inheritance, but not the land with the woman; that would mar it. Perhaps he thought it would be a disparagement to him to marry such a poor widow that had come from a strange country, and almost lived upon alms. He fancied it would be a blemish to his family, it would mar his blood, and disgrace his posterity. Her eminent virtues were not sufficient in his eye to counterbalance this. The Chaldee paraphrase makes his reason for this refusal to be that he had another wife, and, if he should take Ruth, it might occasion strife and contention in his family, which would mar the comfort of his inheritance. Or he thought she might bring him a great many children, and they would all expect shares out of his estate, which would scatter it into too many hands, so that the family would make the less figure. This makes many shy of the great redemption: they are not willing to espouse religion. They have heard well of it, and have nothing to say against it; they will give it their good word, but at the same time they will give their good word with it; they are willing to part with it, and cannot be bound to it, for fear of marring their own inheritance in this world. Heaven they could be glad of, but holiness they can dispense with; it will not agree with the lusts they have already espoused, and therefore, let who will purchase heaven at that rate, they cannot. 5. The right of redemption is fairly resigned to Boaz. If this nameless kinsman lost a good bargain, a good estate, and a good wife too, he may thank himself for not considering it better, and Boaz will thank him for making his way clear to that which he valued and desired above any thing. In those ancient times it was not the usage to pass estates by writings, as afterwards (Jer. 32:10, etc.), but by some sign or ceremony, as with us by livery and seisin, as we commonly call it, that is, the delivery of seisin, seisin of a house by giving the key, of land by giving turf and a twig. The ceremony here used was, he that surrendered *plucked off his shoe* (the Chaldee says it was *the glove of his right hand*) and gave it to him to whom he made the surrender, intimating thereby that, whatever right he had to tread or go upon the land, he conveyed and transferred it, upon a valuable consideration, to the purchaser: this was a *testimony in Israel, v.* 7. And it was done in this case, *v.* 8. If this kinsman had been bound by the law to marry Ruth, and his refusal had been a contempt of that law, Ruth must have *plucked off his shoe* and *spit in his face,* Deu. 25:9. But, though his relation should in some measure oblige him to the duty, yet the distance of his relation might serve to excuse him from the penalty, or Ruth might very well dispense with it, since his refusal was all she desired from him. But bishop Patrick, and the best interpreters, think this had no relation to that law, and that the drawing off of the shoe was not any disgrace as there, but a confirmation of the surrender, and an evidence that it was not fraudulently nor surreptitiously obtained. Note, Fair and open dealing in all matters of contract and commerce is what all those must make conscience of that would approve themselves Israelites indeed, without guile. How much more honourably and honestly does Boaz come by this purchase than if he had secretly undermined his kinsman, and privately struck up a bargain with Naomi, unknown to him. Honesty will be found the best policy.

Verses 9–12

Boaz now sees his way clear, and therefore delays not to perform his promise made to Ruth that he would do the kinsman's part, but in the gate of the city, before the elders and all the people, publishes a marriage-contract between himself and Ruth the Moabitess, and therewith the purchase of all the estate that belonged to the family of Elimelech. If he had not been (*ch.* 2:1) *a mighty man of wealth,* he could not have compassed this redemption, nor done this service to his kinsman's family. What is a great estate good for, but that it enables a man to do so much the more good in his generation, and especially to those of his own household, if he have but a heart to use it so! Now concerning this marriage it appears,

I. That it was solemnized, or at least published, before many witnesses, *v.* 9, 10. "You are witnesses," 1. "That I have bought the estate. Whoever has it, or any part of it, mortgaged to him, let him come to me and he shall have his money, according to the value of the land," which was computed by the number of years to the year of jubilee (Lev. 25:15), when it would have returned of course to Elimelech's family. The more public the sales of estates are the better they are guarded against frauds. 2. "That I have purchased the widow to be my wife." He had no portion with her; what jointure she had was encumbered, and he could not have it without giving as much for it as it was worth, and therefore he might well say he purchased her; and yet, being a virtuous woman, he reckoned he had a good bargain. *House and riches are the inheritance of fathers,* but a prudent wife is more valuable, is from the Lord as a special gift. He designed, in marrying her, to preserve the memory of the dead, that the name of Mahlon, though he left no son to bear it up, might not be cut off from the gate of his place, but by this means might be preserved, that it should be inserted in the public register that Boaz married Ruth the widow of Mahlon, the son of Elimelech, which posterity, whenever they had occasion to consult the register, would take particular notice of. And this history, being preserved for the sake of that marriage and the issue of it, proved an effectual means to perpetuate the name of Mahlon, even beyond the thought or intention of Boaz, to the world's end. And observe that because Boaz did this honour to the dead, as well as this kindness to the living, God did him the honour to bring him into the genealogy of the Messiah, by which his family was dignified above all the families of Israel; while the other kinsman, that was so much afraid of diminishing himself, and marring his inheritance, by marrying the widow, has his name, family, and inheritance, buried in oblivion and disgrace. A tender and generous concern for the honour of the dead and the comfort of poor widows and strangers, neither of which can return the kindness (Lu. 14:14), is sure what God will be well pleased with and will surely recompense. Our Lord Jesus is our *Goel,* our *Redeemer,* our everlasting Redeemer. He looked, like Boaz, with compassion on the deplorable state of fallen mankind. At a vast expense he redeemed the heavenly inheritance for us, which by sin was mortgaged, and forfeited into the hands of divine justice, and which we should never have been able to redeem. He likewise purchased a peculiar people, whom he would espouse to himself, though strangers and foreigners, like Ruth, poor and despised, that the name of that dead and buried race might not be cut off for ever. He ventured the marring of his own inheritance, to do this, for, *though he was rich, yet for our sakes he became poor;* but he was abundantly recompensed for it by his Father, who, because he thus humbled himself, hath *highly exalted him, and given him a name above every name.* Let us own our obligations to him, make sure our contract with him, and study all our days how to do him honour. Boaz, by making a public declaration of this marriage and purchase, not only secured his title against all pretenders, as it were by a fine with proclamations, but put honour upon Ruth, showed that he was not ashamed of her, and her parentage and poverty, and left a testimony against clandestine marriages. It is only that which is evil that hates the light and comes not to it. Boaz called witnesses to what he did, for it was what he could justify, and would never disown; and such regard was then had, even to the contemned crowd, that not only the elders, but all the people that were in the gate, passing and re-passing, were appealed to (*v.* 9), and hearkened to (*v.* 11) when they said, *We are witnesses.*

II. That it was attended with many prayers. The elders and all the people, when they witnessed to it, wished well to it, and blessed it, *v.* 11, 12. Ruth, it should seem, was now sent for; for they speak of her (*v.* 12) as present: *This young woman;* and, he having taken her to wife, they look upon her as already come into his house. And very heartily they pray for the new-married couple.

1. The senior elder, it is likely, made this prayer, and the

rest of the elders, with the people, joined in it, and therefore it is spoken of as made by them all; for in public prayers, though but one speaks, we must all pray. Observe, (1.) Marriages ought to be blessed, and accompanied with prayer, because every creature and every condition are that to us, and no more, that God makes them to be. It is civil and friendly to wish all happiness to those who enter into that condition; and what good we desire we should pray for from the fountain of all good. The minister who gives himself to the word and prayer, as he is the fittest person to exhort, so he is the fittest to bless and pray for those that enter into this relation. (2.) We ought to desire and pray for the welfare and prosperity one of another, so far from envying or grieving at it.

2. Now here, (1.) They prayed for Ruth: *The Lord make the woman that has come into thy house like Rachel and Leah,* that is, "God make her a good wife and a fruitful mother." Ruth was a virtuous woman, and yet needed the prayers of her friends, that by the grace of God she might be made a blessing to the family she had come into. They prayed that she might be like Rachel and Leah, rather than like Sarah and Rebekah, for Sarah had but one son, and Rebekah but one that was in covenant, the other was Esau, who was rejected; but Rachel and Leah did *build up the house of Israel:* all their children were in the church, and their offspring was numerous. "May she be a flourishing, fruitful, faithful *vine by thy house side.*" (2.) They prayed for Boaz, that he might continue to do worthily in the city to which he was an ornament, and might there be more and more famous. They desired that the wife might be a blessing in the private affairs of the house, and the husband a blessing in the public business of the town, that she in her place, and he in his, might be wise, virtuous, and successful. Observe, The way to be famous is to do worthily. Great reputation must be obtained by great merits. It is not enough not to do unworthily, to be harmless and inoffensive, but we must do worthily, be useful and serviceable to our generation. Those that would be truly illustrious must in their places shine as lights. (3.) They prayed for the family: *"Let thy house be like the house of Pharez,"* that is, "let it be very numerous, let it greatly increase and multiply, as the house of Pharez did." The Bethlehemites were of the house of Pharez, and knew very well how numerous it was; in the distribution of the tribes, that grandson of Jacob had the honour which none of the rest had but Manasseh and Ephraim, that his posterity was subdivided into two distinct families, Hezron and Hamul, Num. 26:21. Now they prayed that the family of Boaz, which was one branch of that stock, might in process of time become as numerous and great as the whole stock now was.

Verses 13–22

Here is, I. Ruth a wife. Boaz took her, with the usual solemnities, to his house, and *she became his wife* (*v.* 13), all the city, no doubt, congratulating the preferment of a virtuous woman, purely for her virtues. We have reason to think that Orpah, who returned from Naomi to her people and her gods, was never half so well preferred as Ruth was. He that forsakes all for Christ shall find more than all with him; it shall be recompensed a hundred-fold in this present time. Now Orpah wished she had gone with Naomi too; but she, like the other kinsman, stood in her own light. Boaz had prayed that this pious proselyte might receive a full reward of her courage and constancy from the God of Israel, *under whose wings she had come to trust;* and now he became an instrument of that kindness, which was an answer to his prayer, and helped to make his own words good. Now she had the command of those servants with whom she had associated and of those fields in which she had gleaned. Thus sometimes *God raiseth up the poor out of the dust, to set them with princes,* Ps. 113:7, 8.

II. Ruth a mother: *The Lord gave her conception;* for *the fruit of the womb is his reward,* Ps. 127:3. It is one of the keys he hath in his hand; and he sometimes makes the barren woman that had been long so to be *a joyful mother of children,* Ps. 113:9; Isa. 54:1.

III. Ruth still a daughter-in-law, and the same that she always was, to Naomi, who was so far from being forgotten that she was a principal sharer in these new joys. The good women that were at the labour when this child was born congratulated Naomi upon it more than either Boaz or Ruth, because she was the match-maker, and it was the family of her husband that was hereby built up. See here, as before, what an air of devotion there was then even in the common expressions of civility among the Israelites. Prayer to God attended the birth of the child. What a pity it is that such pious language should either be disused among Christians or degenerate into a formality. *"Blessed be the Lord* that has sent thee this grandson," *v.* 14, 15. 1. Who was the preserver of the name of her family, and who, they hoped, would be famous, because his father was so. 2. Who would be hereafter dutiful and kind to her, so they hoped, because his mother was so. If he would but take after her, he would be a comfort to his aged grandmother, a restorer of her life, and, if there should be occasion, would have wherewithal to be the nourisher of her old age. It is a great comfort to those that are going into years to see any of those that descend from them growing up, that are likely, by the blessing of God, to be a stay and support to them, when the years come wherein they will need such, and of which they will say they have no pleasure in them. Observe, They say of Ruth that she loved Naomi, and therefore was better to her than seven sons. See how God in his providence sometimes makes up the want and loss of those relations from whom we expected most comfort in those from whom we expected least. The bonds of love prove stronger than those of nature, and there is a *friend that sticks closer than a brother;* so here there was a daughter-in-law better than an own child. See what wisdom and grace will do. Now here, (1.) The child is named by the neighbours, *v.* 17. The good women would have it called *Obed, a servant,* either in remembrance of the meanness and poverty of the mother or in prospect of his being hereafter a servant, and very serviceable, to his grandmother. It is no dishonour to those that are ever so well born to be servants to God, their friends, and their generation. The motto of the princes of Wales is *Ich dien — I serve.* (2.) The child is nursed by the grandmother, that is, dry-nursed, when the mother had weaned him from the breast, *v.* 16. She laid it in her bosom, in token of her tender affection to it and care of it. Grandmothers are often the most fond.

IV. Ruth is hereby brought in among the ancestors of David and Christ, which was the greatest honour. The genealogy is here drawn from Pharez, through Boaz and Obed, to David, and so leads towards the Messiah, and therefore it is not an endless genealogy.

AN EXPOSITION, WITH PRACTICAL OBSERVATIONS, OF

THE FIRST BOOK OF SAMUEL

This book, and that which follows it, bear the name of *Samuel* in the title, not because he was the penman of them (except of so much of them as fell within his own time, to the twenty-fifth chapter of the first book, in which we have an account of his death), but because the first book begins with a large account of him, his birth and childhood, his life and government; and the rest of these two volumes that are denominated from him contains the history of the reigns of *Saul* and *David,* who were both anointed by him. And, because the history of these two kings takes up the greatest part of these books, the Vulgar latin calls them the *First* and *Second Books of the Kings,* and the two that follow the *Third* and *Fourth,* which the titles in our English Bibles take notice of with an *alias: otherwise called the First Book of the Kings,* etc. The Septuagint calls them the first and second Book *of the Kingdoms.* It is needless to contend about it, but there is no occasion to vary from the Hebrew verity. These two books contain the history of the last two of the judges, *Eli* and *Samuel,* who were not, as the rest, men of war, but priests (and so much of them is an appendix to the book of Judges), and of the first two of the kings, *Saul* and *David,* and so much of them is an entrance upon the history of the kings. They contain a considerable part of the sacred history, are sometimes referred to in the New Testament, and often in the titles of David's Psalms, which, if placed in their order, would fall in these books. It is uncertain who was the penman of them; it is probable that Samuel wrote the history of his own time, and that, after him, some of the prophets that were with David (Nathan as likely as any) continued it. This first book gives us a full account of Eli's fall and Samuel's rise and good government, *ch.* 1–8. Of Samuel's resignation of the government and Saul's advancement and mal-administration, *ch.* 9–15. The choice of David, his struggles with Saul, Saul's ruin at last, and the opening of the way for David to the throne, *ch.* 16–31. And these things are written for our learning.

CHAPTER 1

The history of Samuel here begins as early as that of Samson did, even before he was born, as afterwards the history of John the Baptist and our blessed Saviour. Some of the scripture-worthies drop out of the clouds, as it were, and their first appearance is in their full growth and lustre. But others are accounted for from the birth, and from the womb, and from the conception. What God says of the prophet Jeremiah is true of all: "Before I formed thee in the belly I knew thee," Jer. 1:5. But some great men were brought into the world with more observation than others, and were more early distinguished from common persons, as Samuel for one. God, in this matter, acts as a free agent. The story of Samson introduces him as a child of promise, Jdg. 13. But the story of Samuel introduces him as a child of prayer. Samson's birth was foretold by an angel to his mother; Samuel was asked of God by his mother. Both together intimate what wonders are produced by the word and prayer. Samuel's mother was Hannah, the principal person concerned in the story of this chapter. I. Here is her affliction — she was childless, and this affliction aggravated by her rival's insolence, but in some measure balanced by her husband's kindness (*v.* 1–8). II. The prayer and vow she made to God under this affliction, in which Eli the high priest at first censured her, but afterwards encouraged her (*v.* 9–18). III. The birth and nursing of Samuel (*v.* 19–23) IV. The presenting of him to the Lord (*v.* 24–28).

Verses 1–8

We have here an account of the state of the family into which Samuel the prophet was born. His father's name was Elkanah, a Levite, and of the family of the Kohathites (the most honourable house of that tribe) as appears, 1 Chr. 6:33, 34. His ancestor Zuph was an Ephrathite, that is, of Bethlehem-Judah, which was called *Ephrathah,* Ruth, 1:2. There this family of the Levites was first seated, but one branch of it, in process of time, removed to Mount Ephraim, from which Elkanah descended. Micah's Levite came from Bethlehem to Mount Ephraim, Jdg. 17:8. Perhaps notice is taken of their being originally Ephrathites to show their alliance to David. This Elkanah lived at Ramah, or Ramathaim, which signifies *the double Ramah,* the higher and lower town, the same with Arimathea of which Joseph was, here called *Ramathaim-zophim.* Zophim signifies *watchmen;* probably they had one of the schools of the prophets there, for prophets are called *watchmen:* the Chaldee paraphrase calls Elkanah *a disciple of the prophets.* But it seems to me that it was in Samuel that prophecy revived, before his time there being, for a great while, no open vision, *ch.* 3:1. Nor is there any mention of a prophet of the Lord from Moses to Samuel, except Jdg. 6:8. So that we have no reason to think that there was any nursery or college of prophets here till Samuel himself founded one, *ch.* 19:19, 20. This is the account of Samuel's parentage, and the place of his nativity. Let us now take notice of the state of the family.

I. It was a devout family. All the families of Israel should be so, but Levites' families in a particular manner. Ministers should be patterns of family religion. Elkanah went up at the solemn feasts to the tabernacle at Shiloh, to *worship and to sacrifice to the Lord of hosts.* I think this is the first time in scripture that God is called *the Lord of hosts — Jehovah Sabaoth,* a name by which he was afterwards very much called and known. Probably Samuel the prophet was the first that used this title of God, for the comfort of Israel, when in his time their hosts were few and feeble and those of their enemies many and mighty; then it would be a support to them to think that the God they served was Lord of hosts, of all the hosts both of heaven and earth; of them he has a sovereign command, and makes what use he pleases of them. Elkanah was a country Levite, and, for aught that appears, had not any place or office which required his attendance at the tabernacle, but he went up as a common Israelite, with his own sacrifices, to encourage his neighbours and set them a good example. When he sacrificed he worshipped, joining prayers and thanksgivings with his sacrifices. In this course of religion he was constant, for he went up yearly. And that which made it the more commendable in him was, 1. That there was a general decay and neglect of religion in the nations. Some among them worshipped other gods, and the generality were remiss in the service of the God of Israel, and yet Elkanah kept his integrity; whatever others did, his resolution was that he and his house should serve the Lord. 2. That Hophni and Phinehas, the sons of Eli, were the men that were now chiefly employed in the service of the house of God; and they were men that conducted themselves very ill in their place, as we shall find afterwards; yet Elkanah went up to sacrifice. God had then tied his people to one place and one altar, and forbidden them, under any pretence whatsoever, to worship elsewhere, and therefore, in pure obedience to that command, he attended at Shiloh. If the priests did not do their duty, he would do his. Thanks be to God, we, under the gospel, are not tied to any one place or family; but the pastors and teachers whom the exalted Redeemer has given to his church are those only whose ministration tends to the *perfecting of the saints* and the *edifying of the body of Christ,* Eph. 4:11, 12. None have dominion over our faith; but our obligation is to those that are the helpers of our holiness and joy, not to any that by their scandalous immoralities, like Hophni and Phinehas, make the sacrifices of the Lord to be abhorred, though still the validity and efficacy of the sacraments depend not on the purity of him that administers them.

II. Yet it was a divided family, and the divisions of it carried with them both guilt and grief. Where there is piety, it is a pity but there should be unity. The joint-devotions of a family should put an end to divisions in it.

1. The original cause of this division was Elkanah's marrying two wives, which was a transgression of the original institution of marriage, to which our Saviour reduces it. Mt. 19:5, 8, *From the beginning it was not so.* It made mischief in Abraham's family, and Jacob's, and here in Elkanah's. How much better does the law of God provide for our comfort and ease in this world than we should, if we were left to ourselves! It is probable that Elkanah married Hannah first, and, because he had not children by her so soon as he hoped, he married Peninnah, who bore him children indeed, but was in other things a vexation to him. Thus are men often beaten with rods of their own making.

2. That which followed upon this error was that the two wives could not agree. They had different blessings: Peninnah, like Leah, was fruitful and had many children, which should have made her easy and thankful, though she was but a second wife, and was less beloved; Hannah, like Rachel, was childless indeed, but she was very dear to her husband, and he took all occasions to let both her and others know that she was so, and many a *worthy portion he gave her* (*v.* 5), and this should have made her easy and thankful. But they were of different tempers: Peninnah could not bear the blessing of fruitfulness, but she grew haughty and insolent; Hannah could not bear the affliction of barrenness, but she grew melancholy and discontented: and Elkanah had a difficult part to act between them.

(1.) Elkanah kept up his attendance at God's altar notwithstanding this unhappy difference in his family, and took his wives and children with him, that, if they could not agree in other things, they might agree to worship God together. If the devotions of a family prevail not to put an end to its divisions, yet let not the divisions put a stop to the devotions.

(2.) He did all he could to encourage Hannah, and to keep up her spirits under her affliction, *v.* 4, 5. At the feast he offered peace-offerings, to supplicate for peace in his family; and when he and his family were to eat their share of the sacrifice, in token of their communion with God and his altar, though he carved to Peninnah and her children competent portions, yet to Hannah he gave a worthy portion, the choicest piece that came to the table, the piece (whatever it was) that used to be given on such occasions to those that were most valued; this he did in token of his love to her, and to give all possible assurances of it. Observe, [1.] Elkanah loved his wife never the less for her being barren. *Christ loves his church,* notwithstanding her infirmities, her barrenness; and *so ought men to love their wives,* Eph. 5:25. To abate our just love to any relation for the sake of any infirmity which they cannot help, and which is not their sin but their affliction, is to make God's providence quarrel with his precept, and very unkindly to add affliction to the afflicted. [2.] He studied to show his love so much the more because she was afflicted, insulted, and low-spirited. It is wisdom and duty to support the weakest, and to hold up those that are run down. [3.] He showed his great love to her by the share he gave her of his peace-offerings. Thus we should testify our affection to our friends and relations, by abounding in prayer for them. The better we love them the more room let us give them in our prayers.

(3.) Peninnah was extremely peevish and provoking. [1.] She upbraided Hannah with her affliction, despised her because she was barren, and gave her taunting language, as one whom Heaven did not favour. [2.] She envied the interest she had in the love of Elkanah, and the more kind he was to her the more was she exasperated against her, which was all over base and barbarous. [3.] She did this most when they *went up to the house of the Lord,* perhaps because then they were more together than at other times, or because then Elkanah showed his affection most to Hannah. But it was very sinful at such a time to show her malice, when pure hands were to be lifted up at God's altar without wrath and quarrelling. It was likewise very unkind at that time to vex Hannah, not only because then they were in company, and others would take notice of it, but then Hannah was to mind her devotions, and desired to be most calm and composed, and free from disturbance. The great adversary to our purity and peace is then most industrious to ruffle us when we should be most composed. When the *sons of God* come to *present themselves before the Lord Satan* will be sure to *come among them,* Job 1:6. [4.] She continued to do this from year to year, not once or twice, but it was her constant practice; neither deference to her husband nor compassion to Hannah could break her of it. [5.] That which she designed was to make her fret, perhaps in hopes to break her heart, that she might possess her husband's heart solely, or because she took a pleasure in her uneasiness, nor could Hannah gratify her more than by fretting. Note, It is an evidence of a base disposition to delight in grieving those that are melancholy and of a sorrowful spirit, and in putting those out of humour that are apt to fret and be uneasy. We ought to bear one another's burdens, not add to them.

(4.) Hannah (poor woman) could not hear the provocation: *She wept, and did not eat, v.* 7. It made her uneasy to herself and to all her relations. She did not eat of the feast; her trouble took away her appetite, made her unfit for any company, and a jar in the harmony of family-joy. It was of the *feast upon the sacrifice* that she *did not eat,* for they were not to *eat of the holy things in their mourning,* Deu. 26:14; Lev. 10:19. Yet it was her infirmity so far to give way to the sorrow of the world as to unfit herself for holy joy in God. Those that are of a fretful spirit, and are apt to lay provocations too much to heart, are enemies to themselves, and strip themselves very much of the comforts both of life and godliness. We find that God took notice of this ill effect of discontents and disagreements in the conjugal relation, that the parties aggrieved *covered the altar of the Lord with tears, insomuch that he regarded not the offering,* Mal. 2:13.

(5.) Elkanah said what he could to her to comfort her. She did not upbraid him with his unkindness in marrying another wife as Sarah did, nor did she render to Peninnah railing for railing, but took the trouble wholly to herself, which made her an object of much compassion. Elkanah showed himself extremely grieved at her grief (*v.* 8): *Hannah, why weepest thou?* [1.] He is much disquieted to see her thus overwhelmed with sorrow. Those that by marriage are made one flesh ought thus far to be of one spirit too, to share in each other's troubles, so that one cannot be easy while the other is uneasy. [2.] He gives her a loving reproof for it: *Why weepest thou? And why is thy heart grieved?* As many as God loves he rebukes, and so should we. He puts her upon enquiring into the cause of her grief. Though she had just reason to be troubled, yet let her consider whether she had reason to be troubled to such a degree, especially so much as to be taken off by it from eating of the holy things. Note, Our sorrow upon any account is sinful and inordinate when it diverts us from our duty to God and embitters our comfort in him, when it makes us unthankful for the mercies we enjoy and distrustful of the goodness of God to us in further mercies, when it casts a damp upon our joy in Christ, and hinders us from doing the duty and taking the comfort of our particular relations. [3.] He intimates that nothing should be wanting on his part to balance her grief: *"Am not I better to thee than ten sons?* Thou knowest thou hast my entire affection, and let that comfort thee." Note, We ought to take notice of our comforts, to keep us from grieving excessively for our crosses; for our crosses we deserve, but our comforts we have forfeited. If we would keep the balance even, we must look at that which is for us, as well as at that which is against us, else we are unjust to Providence and unkind to ourselves. *God hath set the one over-against the other* (Eccl. 7:14) and so should we.

Verses 9–18

Elkanah had gently reproved Hannah for her inordinate grief, and here we find the good effect of the reproof.

I. It brought her to her meat. She ate and drank, *v.* 9. She did not harden herself in sorrow, nor grow sullen when she was reproved for it; but, when she perceived her husband uneasy that she did not come and eat with them, she cheered up her own spirits as well as she could, and came to table. it is as great a piece of self-denial to control our passions as it is to control our appetites.

II. It brought her to her prayers. It put her upon considering, "Do I well to be angry? Do I well to fret? What good does it do me? Instead of binding the burden thus upon my shoulders, had I not better easy myself of it, and cast it upon the Lord by prayer?" Elkanah had said, *Am not I better to thee than ten sons?* which perhaps occasioned her to think within herself, "Whether *he* be so or no, *God* is, and therefore to him will I apply, and before him will I pour out my complaint, and try what relief that will give me." If ever she will make a more solemn address than ordinary to the throne of grace upon this errand, now is the time. They are at Shiloh, at the door of the tabernacle, where God had promised to meet his people, and which was the *house of prayer.* They had recently offered their peace-offerings, to obtain the favour of God and all good and in token of their communion with him; and, taking the comfort of their being accepted of him, they had feasted upon the sacrifice; and now it was proper to put up her prayer in virtue of that sacrifice, for the peace-offerings, for by it not only atonement is made for sin, but the audience and acceptance of our prayers and an answer of peace to them are obtained for us: to that sacrifice, in all our supplications, we must have an eye. Now concerning Hannah's prayer we may observe,

1. The warm and lively devotion there was in it, which appeared in several instances, for our direction in prayer. (1.) She improved the present grief and trouble of her spirit for the exciting and quickening of her pious affections in prayer: *Being in bitterness of soul, she prayed, v.* 10. This good use we should make of our afflictions, they should make us the more lively in our addresses to God. Our blessed Saviour himself, *being in an agony, prayed more earnestly,* Lu. 22:44. (2.) She mingled tears with her prayers. It was not a dry prayer: she wept sore. Like a true Israelite, she *wept and made supplication* (Hos. 12:4), with an eye to the tender mercy of our God, who knows the troubled soul. The prayer came from her heart, as the tears from her eyes. (3.) She was very particular, and yet very modest, in her petition. She begged a child, a man-child, that it might be fit to serve in the tabernacle. God gives us leave, in prayer, not only to ask good things in general, but to mention that special good thing which we most need and desire. Yet she says not, as Rachel, *Give me children,* Gen. 30:1. She will be very thankful for *one.* (4.) She made a solemn vow, or promise, that if God would give her a son she would *give him up to God, v.* 11. He would be by birth a Levite, and so devoted to the service of God, but he should be by her vow a Nazarite, and his very childhood should be sacred. It is probable she had acquainted Elkanah with her purpose before, and had had his consent and

approbation. Note, Parents have a right to dedicate their children to God, as living sacrifices and spiritual priests; and an obligation is thereby laid upon them to serve God faithfully *all the days of their life.* Note further, It is very proper, when we are in pursuit of any mercy, to bind our own souls with a bond, that, if God give it us, we will devote it to his honour and cheerfully use it in his service. Not that hereby we can pretend to merit the gift, but thus we are qualified for it and for the comfort of it. In hope of mercy, let us promise duty. (5.) She spoke all this so softly that none could hear her. Her lips moved, but *her voice was not heard, v.* 13. Hereby she testified her belief of God's knowledge of the heart and its desires. Thoughts are words to him, nor is he one of those gods that must be *cried aloud to,* 1 Ki. 18:27. It was likewise an instance of her humility and holy shamefacedness in her approach to God. She was none of those that *made her voice to be heard on high,* Isa. 58:4. It was a secret prayer, and therefore, though made in a public place, yet was thus made secretly, and not, as the Pharisees prayed, *to be seen of men.* It is true prayer is not a thing we have reason to be ashamed of, but we must avoid all appearances of ostentation. Let what passes between God and our souls be kept to ourselves.

2. The hard censure she fell under for it. Eli was now high priest, and judge in Israel; he sat upon a seat in the temple, to oversee what was done there, *v.* 9. The tabernacle is here called the *temple,* because it was now fixed, and served all the purposes of a temple. There Eli sat to receive addresses and give direction, and somewhere (it is probable in a private corner) he espied Hannah at her prayers, and by her unusual manner fancied she was drunken, and spoke to her accordingly (*v.* 14): *How long wilt thou be drunken?* — the very imputation that Peter and the apostles fell under when the Holy Ghost *gave them utterance,* Acts 2:13. Perhaps in this degenerate age it was no strange thing to see drunken women at the door of the tabernacle; for otherwise, one would think, the vile lust of Hophni and Phinehas could not have found so easy a prey there, *ch.* 2:22. Eli took Hannah for one of these. It is one bad effect of the abounding of iniquity, and its becoming fashionable, that it often gives occasion to suspect the innocent. When a disease is epidemical every one is suspected to be tainted with it. Now, (1.) This was Eli's fault; and a great fault it was to pass so severe a censure without better observation or information. If his own eyes had already become dim, he should have employed those about him to enquire. Drunkards are commonly noisy and turbulent, but this poor woman was silent and composed. His fault was the worse that he was the priest of the Lord, who should have had *compassion on the ignorant,* Heb. 5:2. Note, It ill becomes us to be rash and hasty in our censures of others, and to be forward to believe people guilty of bad things, while either the matter of fact on which the censure is grounded is doubtful and unproved or is capable of a good construction. Charity commands us to hope the best concerning all, and forbids censoriousness. Paul had very good information when he did but *partly believe* (1 Co. 11:18), hoping it was not so. Especially we ought to be cautious how we censure the devotions of others, lest we call that *hypocrisy, enthusiasm,* or *superstition,* which is really the fruit of an honest zeal, and it is accepted of God. (2.) It was Hannah's affliction; and a great affliction it was, added to all the rest, vinegar to the wounds of her spirit. She had been reproved by Elkanah because she would not eat and drink, and now to be reproached by Eli as if she had eaten and drunk too much was very hard. Note, It is no new thing for those that do well to be ill thought of, and we must not think it strange if at any time it be our lot.

3. Hannah's humble vindication of herself from this crime with which she was charged. She bore it admirably well. She did not retort the charge and upbraid him with the debauchery of his own sons, did not bid him look at home and restrain them, did not tell him how ill it became one in his place thus to abuse a poor sorrowful worshipper at the throne of grace. When we are at any time unjustly censured we have need to set a double watch before the door of our lips, that we do not recriminate, and return censure for censure. Hannah thought it enough to vindicate herself, and so must we, *v.* 15, 16. (1.) In justice to herself, she expressly denies the charge, speaks to him with all possible respect, calls him, *My lord,* intimates how very desirous she was to stand right in his opinion and how loth to lie under his censure. "No, my lord, it is not as you suspect; I have drunk neither wine nor strong drink, not any at all" (though it was proper enough to be given to one of such a *heavy heart,* Prov. 31:6), "much less to any excess; therefore *count not thy handmaid for a daughter of Belial."* Note, Drunkards are children of Belial (women-drunkards, particularly), children of the wicked one, children of disobedience, children that will not endure the yoke (else they would not be drunk), more especially when they are actually drunk. Those that cannot govern themselves will not bear that any one else should. Hannah owns that the crime would have been very great if she had indeed been guilty of it, and he might justly have shut her out of the courts of God's house; but the very manner of her speaking in her own defence was sufficient to demonstrate that she was not drunk. (2.) In justice to him, she gives an account of her present behaviour, which had given occasion to his suspicion: *"I am a woman of a sorrowful spirit,* dejected and discomposed, and that is the reason I do not look as other people; the eyes are red, not with wine, but with weeping. And at this time I have not been talking to myself, as drunkards and fools do, but I have been pouring out my soul before the Lord, who hears and understands the language of the heart, and this out of the abundance of my complaint and grief." She had been more than ordinarily fervent in prayer to God, and this, she tells him, was the true reason of the transport and disorder she seemed to be in. Note, When we are unjustly censured we should endeavour, not only to clear ourselves, but to satisfy our brethren, by giving them a just and true account of that which they misapprehended.

4. The atonement Eli made for his rash unfriendly censure, by a kind and fatherly benediction, *v.* 17. He did not (as many are apt to do in such a case) take it for an affront to have his mistake rectified and to be convinced of his error, nor did it put him out of humour. But, on the contrary, he now encouraged Hannah's devotions as much as before he had discountenanced them; not only intimated that he was satisfied of her innocency by those words, *Go in peace,* but, being high priest, as one having authority he blessed her in the name of the Lord, and, though he knew not what the particular blessing was that she had been praying for, yet he puts his *Amen* to it, so good an opinion had he now conceived of her prudence and piety: *The God of Israel grant thee thy petition,* whatever it is, *that thou hast asked of him.* Note, By our meek and humble carriage towards those that reproach us because they do not know us, we may perhaps make them our friends, and turn their censures of us into prayers for us.

5. The great satisfaction of mind with which Hannah now went away, *v.* 18. She begged the continuance of Eli's good opinion of her and his good prayers for her, and then she went her way and did eat of what remained of the peace-offerings (none of which was to be left until the morning), *and her countenance was no more sad,* no more as it had been, giving marks of inward trouble and discomposure; but she looked pleasant and cheerful, and all was well. Why, what had happened? Whence came this sudden happy change? She had by prayer committed her case to God and left it with him, and now she was no more perplexed about it. She had prayed for herself, and Eli had prayed for her; and she believed that God would either give her the mercy she had prayed for or make up the want of it to her some other way. Note, Prayer is heart's-ease to a gracious soul; the seed of Jacob have often found it so, being confident that God will never say unto them, *Seek you me in vain,* see Phil. 4:6, 7. Prayer will smooth the countenance; it should do so.

Verses 19–28

Here is, I. The return of Elkanah and his family to their own habitation, when the days appointed for the feast were over, *v.* 19. Observe how they improved their time at the tabernacle. Every day they were there, even that which was fixed for their journey home, they worshipped God; and they rose up early to do it. It is good to begin the day with God. Let him that is the first have the first. They had a journey before them, and a family of children to take with them, and yet they would not stir till they had worshipped God together. Prayer and provender do not hinder a journey. They had spent several days now in religious worship, and yet they attended once more. We should not be weary of well-doing.

II. The birth and name of this desired son. At length the Lord remembered Hannah, the very thing she desired (*v.* 11), and more she needed not desire, that was enough, for then she conceived and bore a son. Though God seem long to forget his people's burdens, troubles, cares, and prayers, yet he will at length make it to appear that they are not out of his mind. This son the mother called *Samuel, v.* 20. Some make the etymology of this name to be much the same with that of *Ishmael — heard of God,* because the mother's prayers were remarkably heard, and he was an answer to them. Others, because of the reason she gives for the name, make it to signify *asked of God.* It comes nearly to the same; she designed by it to perpetuate the remembrance of God's favour to her in answering her prayers. Thus she designed, upon every mention of his name, to take the comfort to herself and to give God the glory of that gracious condescension. Note, Mercies in answer to prayer are to be remembered with peculiar expressions of thankfulness, as Ps. 116:1, 2. How many seasonable deliverances and supplies may we call *Samuels, asked of God;* and whatever is so we are in a special manner engaged to devote to him. Hannah intended by this name to put her son in mind of the obligation he was under to be the Lord's, in consideration of this, that he was asked of God and was at the same time dedicated to him. A child of prayer is in a special manner bound to be a good child. Lemuel's mother reminds him that he was the *son of her vows,* Prov. 31:2.

III. The close attendance Hannah gave to the nursing of him, not only because he was dear to her, but because he was devoted to God, and for him she nursed him herself, and did not hang him on another's breast. We ought to take care of our children, not only with an eye to the law of nature as they are ours, but with an eye to the covenant of grace as they are given up to God. See Eze. 16:20, 21. This sanctifies the nursing of them, when it is done as unto the Lord. Elkanah went up every year to worship at the tabernacle, and particularly to perform his vow, perhaps some vow he had made distinct from Hannah's if God would give him a son by her, *v.* 21. But Hannah, though she felt a warm regard for the courts of God's house, begged leave of her husband to stay at home; for the women were not under any obligation to go up to the three yearly feasts, as the men were. However Hannah had been accustomed to go, but now desired to be excused, 1. Because she would not be so long absent from her nursery. *Can a woman forget her sucking child?* We may suppose she kept constantly at home, for, if she had gone any where, she would have gone to Shiloh. Note, God will have mercy and not sacrifice. Those that are detained from public ordinances by the nursing and tending of little children may take comfort from this instance, and believe that, if they do that with an eye to God, he will graciously accept them therein, and though they tarry at home they shall divide the spoil. 2. Because she would not go up to Shiloh till her son was big enough, not only to be taken thither, but to be left there; for, if once she took him thither, she thought she could never find in her heart to bring him back again. Note, Those who are stedfastly resolved to pay their vows may yet see good cause to defer the payment of them. *Every thing is beautiful in its season.* No animal was accepted in sacrifice till it had been for some time under the dam, Lev. 22:27. Fruit is best when it is ripe. Elkanah agrees to what she proposes (*v.* 23): *Do what seemeth thee good.* So far was he from delighting to cross her that he referred it entirely to her. *Behold how good and pleasant a thing it is,* when yoke-fellows thus draw even in the yoke, and accommodate themselves to one another, each thinking well of what the other does, especially in works of piety and charity. He adds a prayer: *Only the Lord establish his word,* that is, "God preserve the child through the perils of his infancy, that the solemn vow which God signified his acceptance of, by giving us the child, may be performed in its season, and so the whole matter may be accomplished." Note, Those that have in sincerity devoted their children to God may with comfort pray for them, that God will establish the word sealed to them at the same time that they were sealed for him.

IV. The solemn entering of this child into the service of the sanctuary. We may take it for granted that he was presented to the Lord at forty days old, as all the first-born were (Lu. 2:22, 23): but this is not mentioned, because there was nothing in it singular; but now that he was weaned he was presented, not to be redeemed. Some think it was as soon as he was weaned from the breast, which, the Jews say, was not till he was three years old; it is said she gave him suck till she had weaned him, *v.* 23. Others think it was not till he was weaned from childish things, at eight or ten years old. But I see no inconvenience in admitting such an extraordinary child as this into the tabernacle at three years old, to be educated among the children of the priests. It is said (*v.* 24), *The child was young,* but, being intelligent above his years, he was no trouble. None can begin too soon to be religious. *The child was a child,* so the Hebrew reads it, in his learning-age. For *whom shall he teach knowledge* but *those that are* newly *weaned from the milk and drawn from the breasts?* Isa. 28:9. Observe how she presented her child, 1. With a sacrifice; no less than three bullocks, with a meat-offering for each, *v.* 24. A bullock, perhaps, for each year of the child's life. Or one for a burnt-offering, another for a sin-offering, and the third of a peace-offering. So far was she from thinking that, by presenting her son to God, she made God her debtor, that she thought it requisite by these slain offerings to seek God's acceptance of her living sacrifice. All our covenants with God for ourselves and ours must be made by sacrifice, the great sacrifice. 2. With a grateful acknowledgement of God's goodness in answer to prayer. This she makes to Eli, because he had encouraged her to hope for an answer of peace (*v.* 26, 27): *"For this child I prayed.* Here it was obtained by prayer, and here it is resigned to the prayer-hearing God. You have forgotten me, my lord, but I who now appear so cheerful am the woman, the very same, that three years ago stood by thee here weeping and praying, and this was the child I prayed for." Answers of prayer may thus be humbly triumphed in, to the glory of God. Here is a living testimony for God. "I am his witness that he is gracious (see Ps. 66:16–19); for this mercy, this comfort, I prayed, *and the Lord has given me my petition."* See Ps. 34:2, 4, 6. Hannah does not remind Eli of it by adverting to the suspicion he had formerly expressed; she does not say, "I am the woman whom you passed that severe censure upon; what do you think of me now?" Good men ought not to be upbraided with their infirmities and oversights. They have themselves repented of them; let them hear no more of them. 3. With a full surrender of all her interest in this child unto the Lord (*v.* 28): *I have lent him to the Lord as long as he liveth.* And she repeats it, because she will never revoke it: *He shall be* (a deodand) *lent* or given *to the Lord.* Not that she designed to call for him back, as we do what we lend, but she uses this word *Shaol, lent,* because it is the same word that she had used before (*v.* 20, *I asked* him of the Lord), only in another conjugation. And (*v.* 27) the Lord gave me the petition which *I asked* (*Shaalti,* in Kal), therefore *I have lent him* (*Hishilti,* the same word in Hiphil), and so it gives another etymology of his name *Samuel,* not only *asked of God,* but *lent to God.* And observe, (1.) Whatever we give to God, it is what we have first asked and received from him. All our gifts to him were first his gifts to us. *Of thy own, Lord, have we given thee,* 1 Chr. 29:14, 16. (2.) Whatever we give to God may upon this account be said to be *lent* to him, that though we may not recall it, as a thing lent, yet he will certainly repay it, with interest, to our unspeakable advantage, particularly what is given *to his poor,* Prov. 19:17. When by baptism we dedicate our children to God, let us remember that they were his before by a sovereign right, and that they are ours still so much the more to our comfort. Hannah resigns him to the Lord, not for a certain term of years, as children are sent apprentices, but *durante vita — as long as he liveth, he shall be lent unto the Lord,* a Nazarite for life. Such must our covenant with God be, a marriage-covenant; as long as live we must be his, and never forsake him.

Lastly, The child Samuel did his part beyond what could have been expected from one of his years; for of him that seems to be spoken, *He worshipped the Lord there,* that is *he said his prayers.* He was no doubt extraordinarily forward (we have known children that have discovered some sense of religion very young), and his mother, designing him for the sanctuary, took particular care to train him up to that which was to be his work in the sanctuary. Note, Little children should learn betimes to worship God. Their parents should instruct them in his worship and bring them to it, put them upon engaging in it as well as they can, and God will graciously accept them and teach them to do better.

CHAPTER 2

In this chapter we have, I. Hannah's song of thanksgiving to God for his favour to her in giving her Samuel (*v.* 1–10). II. Their return to their family, with Eli's blessing (*v.* 11, 20). The increase of their family (*v.* 21). Samuel's growth and improvement (*v.* 11, 18, 21, 26), and the care Hannah took to clothe him (*v.* 19). III. The great wickedness of Eli's sons (*v.* 12–17, 22). IV. The over-mild reproof that Eli gave them for it (*v.* 23–25). V. The justly dreadful message God sent him by a prophet, threatening the ruin of his family for the wickedness of his sons (*v.* 27–36).

Verses 1–10

We have here Hannah's thanksgiving, dictated, not only by the spirit of prayer, but by the spirit of prophecy. Her petition for the mercy she desired we had before (*ch.* 1:11), and here we have her return of praise; in both *out of the abundance of a heart* deeply affected (in the former with her own wants, and in the latter with God's goodness) *her mouth spoke.* Observe in general, 1. When she had received mercy from God she owned it, with thankfulness to his praise. Not like the nine lepers, Lu. 17:17. Praise is our rent, our tribute. We are unjust if we do not pay it. 2. The mercy she had received was an answer to prayer, and therefore she thought herself especially obliged to give thanks for it. What we win by prayer we may wear with comfort, and must wear with praise. 3. Her thanksgiving is here called a prayer: *Hannah prayed;* for thanksgiving is an essential part of prayer. In every address to God we must express a grateful regard to him as our benefactor. Nay, and thanksgiving for mercies received shall be accepted as a petition for further mercy. 4. From this particular mercy which she had received from God she takes occasion, with an elevated and enlarged heart, to speak glorious things of God and of his government of the world for the good of his church. Whatever at any time gives rise to our praises in this manner they should be raised. 5. Her prayer was mental. *Her voice was not heard;* but in her thanksgiving she spoke, that all might hear her. She made her supplication *with groanings that could not be uttered,* but now her lips were opened to *show forth God's praise.* 6. This thanksgiving is here left upon record for the encouragement of those of the weaker sex to attend the throne of grace. God will regard their prayers and praises. The virgin Mary's song has great affinity with this of Hannah, Lu. 1:46. Three things we have in this thanksgiving: —

I. Hannah's triumph in God, in his glorious perfections, and the great things he had done for her, *v.* 1–3. Observe,

1. What great things she says of God. She takes little notice of the particular mercy she was now rejoicing in, does not commend Samuel for the prettiest child, the most toward and sensible for his age that she ever saw, as fond parents are too apt to do. No, she overlooks the gift, and praises the giver; whereas most forget the giver and fasten only on the gift. Every stream should lead us to the fountain; and the favours we receive from God should raise our admiration of the infinite perfections there are in God. There may be other Samuels, but no other Jehovah. *There is none beside thee.* Note, God is to be praised as a peerless being, and of unparalleled perfection. This glory is due unto his name, to own not only that there is *none like him, but that there is none besides him.* All others were pretenders, Ps. 18:31. Four of God's glorious attributes Hannah here celebrates the glory of: — (1.) His unspotted purity. This is that attribute which is most praised in the upper world, by those that always behold his face, Isa. 6:3; Rev. 4:8. When Israel triumphed over the Egyptians God was praised *as glorious in holiness,* Ex. 15:11. So here, in Hannah's triumph, *There is none holy as the Lord.* It is the rectitude of his nature, his infinite agreement with himself, and the equity of his government and judgment in all the administrations of both. At the remembrance of this we ought to give thanks. (2.) His almighty power: *Neither is there any rock* (or *any strength,* for so the word is sometimes rendered) *like our God.* Hannah had experienced a mighty support by staying herself upon him, and therefore speaks as she had found, and seems to refer to that of Moses, Deu. 32:31. (3.) His unsearchable wisdom: *The Lord,* the Judge of all, *is a God of knowledge;* he clearly and perfectly sees into the character of every person and the merits of every cause, and he gives knowledge and understanding to those that seek them of him. (4.) His unerring justice: *By him actions are weighed.* His own are so, in his eternal counsels; the actions of the children of men are so, in the balances of his judgment, so that he will *render to every man according to his work,* and is not mistaken in what any man is or does.

2. How she solaces herself in these things. What we give God the glory of we may take the comfort of. Hannah does so, (1.) In holy joy: *My heart rejoiceth in the Lord;* not so much in her son as in her God; he is to be the gladness of our joy (Ps. 43:4), and our joy must not terminate in any thing short of him: *"I rejoice in thy salvation;* not only in this particular favour to me, but in the salvation of thy people Israel, those salvations especially which this child will be an instrument of, and that, above all, by Christ, which those are but the types of." (2.) In holy triumph: *"My horn is exalted;* not only is my reputation saved by my having a son, but greatly raised by having such a son." We read of some of the singers whom David appointed to lift up the horn, an instrument of music, in praising God (1 Chr. 25:5), so that, *My horn is exalted* means this, "My praises are very much elevated to an unusual strain." *Exalted in the Lord;* God is to have the honour of all our exaltations, and in him must we triumph. *My mouth is enlarged,* that is, "Now I have wherewith to answer those that reproached me." He that has his quiver full of arrows, his house full of children, shall not be ashamed to *speak with the enemy in the gate,* Ps. 127:5.

3. How she herewith silences those that set up themselves as rivals with God and rebels against him (*v.* 3): *Talk no more so exceedingly proudly.* Let not Peninnah and her children upbraid her any more with her confidence in God and praying to him: at length she found it not in vain. See Mic. 7:10, *Then she that is my enemy shall see it, and shame shall cover her that said, Where is thy God?* Or perhaps it was below her to take so much notice of Peninnah, and her malice, in this song; but this is intended as a check to the insolence of the Philistines, and other enemies of God and Israel, that *set their mouth against the heavens,* Ps. 73:9. "Let this put them to silence and shame; he that has thus judged for me against my adversary will judge for his people against all theirs."

II. The notice she takes of the wisdom and sovereignty of the divine providence, in its disposals of the affairs of the children of men; such are the vicissitudes of them, and such the strange and sudden turns and revolutions of them, that it is often found a very short step between the height of prosperity and the depth of adversity. *God has* not only *set the one over against the other* (Eccl. 7:14), but the one very near the other, and no gulf fixed between them, that we may *rejoice as though we rejoiced not* and *weep as though we wept not.*

1. The strong are soon weakened and the weak are soon strengthened, when God pleases, *v.* 4. On the one hand, if he speak the word, *the bows of the mighty men are broken;* they are disarmed, disabled to do as they have before done and as they have designed to do. Those have been worsted in battle who seemed upon all accounts to have the advantage on their side, and thought themselves sure of victory. See Ps. 46:9; 37:15, 17. Particular persons are soon weakened by sickness and age, and they find that the bow does not long abide in strength; many a mighty man who has gloried in his might has found it a deceitful bow, that failed him when he trusted to it. On the other hand, if the Lord speak the word, those who stumble through weakness, who were so feeble that they could not go straight or steady, are *girded with strength,* in body and mind, and are able to bring great things to pass. Those who were weakened by sickness return to their vigour (Job 33:25), and those who were brought down by sorrow shall recover their comfort, which will *confirm the weak hands and the feeble knees,* Isa. 35:3. Victory turns in favour of that side that was given up for gone, and even *the lame take the prey,* Isa. 33:23.

2. The rich are soon impoverished and the poor strangely enriched on a sudden, *v.* 5. Providence sometimes does so blast men's estates and cross their endeavours, and with a fire not blown consume their increase, that those who were full (their barns full, and their bags full, their *houses full of good things,* Job 22:18, and their *bellies full of these hidden treasures,* Ps. 17:14) have been reduced to such straits and extremities as to want the necessary supports of life, and to *hire out themselves for bread,* and they must dig, since to *beg they are ashamed. Riches flee away* (Prov. 23:5), and leave those miserable who, when they had them, placed their happiness in them. To those that have been full and free poverty must needs be doubly grievous. But, on the other hand, sometimes Providence so orders it that *those who are hungry cease,* that is, cease to hire out themselves for bread as they have done. Having, by God's blessing on their industry, got beforehand in the world, and enough to live upon at ease, *they shall hunger no more, not thirst any more.* This is not to be ascribed to fortune, nor merely to men's wisdom or folly. *Riches are not to men of understanding, nor favour to men of skill* (Eccl. 9:11), nor is it always men's own fault that they become poor, but (*v.* 7) *the Lord maketh some poor and maketh others rich;* the impoverishing of one is the enriching of another, and it is God's doing. To some he gives power to get wealth, from others he takes away power to keep the wealth they have. Are we poor? God made us poor, which

is a good reason why we should be content, and reconcile ourselves to our condition. Are we rich? God made us rich, which is a good reason why we should be thankful, and serve him cheerfully in the abundance of good things he gives us. It may be understood of the same person; those that were rich God makes poor, and after awhile makes rich again, as Job; he gave, he takes away, and then gives again. Let not the rich be proud and secure, for God can soon make them poor; let not the poor despond and despair, for God can in due time enrich them again.

3. Empty families are replenished and numerous families diminished and made few. This is the instance that comes close to the occasion of the thanksgiving: *The barren hath borne seven,* meaning herself, for, though at present she had but one son, yet that one being a Nazarite, devoted to God and employed in his immediate service, he was to her as good as seven. Or it is the language of her faith. Now that she had one she hoped for more, and was not disappointed; she had five more (*v.* 21), so that if we reckon Samuel but for two, as we well may, she has the number she promised herself: the *barren hath borne seven,* while, on the other hand, *she that hath many children has waxed feeble,* and hath left bearing. She says no more. Peninnah is now mortified and crest-fallen. The tradition of the Jews is that when Hannah bore one child Peninnah buried two. There are many instances both of the increase of families that were inconsiderable and the extinguishing of families that made a figure, Job 22:23; Ps. 107:38, etc.

4. God is the sovereign Lord of life and death (*v.* 6): *The Lord killeth and maketh alive.* Understand it, (1.) Of God's sovereign dominion and universal agency, in the lives and deaths of the children of men. He presides in births and burials. Whenever any die it is God that directs the arrows of death. *The Lord killeth.* Death is his messenger, strikes whom and when he bids; none are brought to the dust but it is he that brings them down, for in his hand are the *keys of death and the grave,* Rev. 1:18. Whenever any are born it is he that *makes them alive. None knows what is the way of the spirit,* but this we know, that it comes from the *Father of spirits.* Whenever any are recovered from sickness, and delivered from imminent perils, it is God that bringeth up; for *to him belong the issues from death.* (2.) Of the distinction he makes between some and others: *He killeth* some, and *maketh,* that is, keepeth, others *alive* that were in the same danger (in war, suppose, or pestilence), two in a bed together, it may be, one taken by death and the other left alive. *Even so, Father, because it seemed good in thy eyes.* Some that were most likely to live are brought down to the grave, and others that were as likely to die are brought up; for living and dying do not go by likelihoods. God's providences towards some are killing, ruining to their comforts, and towards others at the same time reviving. (3.) Of the change he makes with one and the same person: *He killeth and bringeth down to the grave,* that is, he brings even to death's door, and then revives and raises up, when even life was despaired of and a sentence of death received, 2 Co. 1:8, 9. *He turns to destruction,* and then says, *Return,* Ps. 110:3. Nothing is too hard for God to do, no, not the quickening of the dead, and putting life into dry bones.

5. Advancement and abasement are both from him. He brings some low and lifts up others (*v.* 7), humbles the proud and gives grace and honour to the lowly, lays those in the dust that would vie with the God above them and trample upon all about them (Job 40:12, 13), but lifts up those with his salvation that humble themselves before him, Jam. 4:10. Or it may be understood of the same persons: those whom he had brought low, when they are sufficiently humbled, he lifteth up. This is enlarged upon, *v.* 8. *He raiseth up the poor out of the dust,* a low and mean condition, nay, from the dunghill, a base and servile condition, loathed, and despised, *to set them among princes.* See Ps. 113:7, 8. Promotion comes not by chance, but from the counsel of God, which often prefers those that were very unlikely and that men thought very unworthy. Joseph and Daniel, Moses and David, were thus strangely advanced, from a prison to a palace, from a sheephook to a sceptre. The princes they are set among may be tempted to disdain them, but God can establish the honour which he gives thus surprisingly, and make them even to *inherit the throne of glory.* Let not those whom Providence has thus preferred be upbraided with the dust and dunghill they are raised out of, for the meaner their beginnings were the more they are favoured, and God is glorified, in their advancement, if it be by lawful and honourable means.

6. A reason is given for all these dispensations which obliges us to acquiesce in them, how surprising soever they are: *For the pillars of the earth are the Lord's.* (1.) If we understand this literally, it intimates God's almighty power, which cannot be controlled. He upholds the whole creation, founded the earth, and still sustains it by the word of his power. What cannot he do in the affairs of families and kingdoms, far beyond our conception and expectation, *who hangs the earth upon nothing?* Job 26:7. But, (2.) If we understand it figuratively, it intimates his incontestable sovereignty, which cannot be disputed. The princes and great ones of the earth, the directors of states and governments, are the *pillars of the earth,* Ps. 75:3. On these hinges the affairs of the world seem to turn, but they are the Lord's, Ps. 47:9. From him they have their power, and therefore he may advance whom he pleases; and who may say, *What doest thou?*

III. A prediction of the preservation and advancement of all God's faithful friends, and the destruction of all his and their enemies. Having testified her joyful triumph in what God had done, and is doing, she concludes with joyful hopes of what he would do, *v.* 9, 10. Pious affections (says bishop Patrick) in those days rose many times to the height of prophecy, whereby God continued in that nation his true religion, in the midst of their idolatrous inclinations. This prophecy may refer, 1. More immediately to the government of Israel by Samuel, and by David whom he was employed to anoint. The Israelites, God's saints, should be protected and delivered; the Philistines, their enemies, should be conquered and subdued, and particularly by *thunder, ch.* 7:10. Their dominions should be enlarged, king David strengthened and greatly exalted, and Israel (that in the time of the judges had made so small a figure and had much ado to subsist) should now shortly become great and considerable, and give law to all its neighbours. An extraordinary change that was; and the birth of Samuel was, as it were, the dawning of that day. But, 2. We have reason to think that this prophecy looks further, to the kingdom of Christ, and the administration of that kingdom of grace, of which she now comes to speak, having spoken so largely of the kingdom of providence. And here is the first time that we meet with the name *Messiah,* or *his Anointed.* The ancient expositors, both Jewish and Christian, make it to look beyond David, to the Son of David. Glorious things are here spoken of the kingdom of the Mediator, both before and since his incarnation; for the method of the administration of it, both by the eternal Word and by that Word made flesh, is much the same. Concerning that kingdom we are here assured, (1.) That all the loyal subjects of it shall be carefully and powerfully protected (*v.* 9): *He will keep the feet of his saints.* There are a people in the world that are God's saints, his select and sanctified ones; and he will keep their feet, that is, all that belongs to them shall be under his protection, down to their very feet, the lowest part of the body. If he will keep their feet, much more their head and hearts. Or he will keep their feet, that is, he will secure the ground they stand on, and establish their goings; he will set a guard of grace upon their affections and actions, that their feet may neither wander out of the way nor stumble in the way. When their feet are ready to slip (Ps. 73:2) *his mercy holdeth them up* (Ps. 94:18) and *keepeth them from falling,* Jude 24. While we keep God's ways he will keep our feet. See Ps. 37:23, 24. (2.) That all the powers engaged against it shall not be able to effect the ruin of it. By strength shall no man prevail. God's strength is engaged for the church; and, while it is so, man's strength shall not prevail against it. The church seems destitute of strength, her friends few and feeble, but prevalency does not go by human strength, Ps. 33:16. God neither needs it for him (Ps. 147:10) nor dreads it against him. (3.) That all the enemies of it will certainly be broken and brought down: *The wicked shall be silent in darkness, v.* 9. They shall be struck both blind and dumb, not be able to see their way nor have any thing to say for themselves. Damned sinners are sentenced to utter darkness, and in it they will be for ever speechless, Mt. 22:12, 13. The wicked are called *the adversaries of the Lord,* and it is foretold (*v.* 10) that they *shall be broken to pieces.* Their designs against his kingdom among men will all be dashed, and they themselves destroyed; how can those speed better that are in arms against Omnipotence? See Lu. 19:27. God has many ways of doing it, and, rather than fail, from *heaven shall he thunder upon them,* and so, not only put them in terror and consternation, but bring them to destruction. Who can stand before God's thunderbolts? (4.) That the conquests of this kingdom shall extend themselves to distant regions: *The Lord shall judge the ends of the earth.* David's victories and dominions reached far, but the *uttermost parts of the earth* are promised to the Messiah for his *possession* (Ps. 2:8), to be either reduced to his golden sceptre or ruined by his iron rod. God is Judge of all, and he will judge for his people against his and their enemies, Ps. 110:5, 6. (5.) That the power and honour of Messiah the prince shall grow and increase more and more: *He shall give strength unto his king,* for the accomplishing of his great undertaking (Ps. 89:21, and see Lu. 22:43), strengthen him to go through the difficulties of his humiliation, and in his exaltation he will *lift up the head* (Ps. 110:7), lift up the horn, the power and honour, of his *anointed,* and *make him higher than the kings of the earth,* Ps. 89:27. This crowns the triumph, and is, more than any thing, the matter of her exultation. Her *horn is exalted* (*v.* 1) because she foresees the horn of the Messiah will be so. This secures the hope. The subjects of Christ's kingdom will be safe, and the enemies of it will be ruined, for the anointed, the Lord Christ, is girded with strength, and is able to save and destroy unto the uttermost.

Verses 11–26

In these verses we have the good character and posture of Elkanah's family, and the bad character and posture of Eli's family. The account of these two is observably interwoven throughout this whole paragraph, as if the historian intended to set the one over against the other, that they might set off one another. The devotion and good order of Elkanah's family aggravated the iniquity of Eli's house; while the wickedness of Eli's sons made Samuel's early piety appear the more bright and illustrious.

I. Let us see how well things went in Elkanah's family and how much better than formerly. 1. Eli dismissed them from the house of the Lord, when they had entered their little son there, with a blessing, *v.* 20. He blessed as one having authority: *The Lord give thee* more children *of this woman, for the loan that is lent to the Lord.* If Hannah had then had many children, it would not have been such a generous piece of piety to part with one out of many for the service of the tabernacle; but when she had but one, an only one whom she loved, her Isaac, to present him to the Lord was such an act of heroic piety as should by no means lose its reward. As when Abraham had offered Isaac he received the promise of a numerous issue (Gen. 22:16, 17), so did Hannah, when she had presented Samuel unto the Lord a living sacrifice. Note, What is lent to the Lord will certainly be repaid with interest, to our unspeakable advantage, and oftentimes in kind. Hannah resigns one child to God, and is recompensed with five; for Eli's blessing took effect (*v.* 21): *She bore three sons and two daughters.* There is nothing lost by lending to God or losing for him; it shall be repaid *a hundred-fold,* Mt. 19:29. 2. They returned to their own habitation. This is twice mentioned, *v.* 11, and again *v.* 20. It was very pleasant to attend at God's house, to bless him, and to be blessed of him. But they have a family at home that must be looked after, and thither they return, cheerfully leaving the dear little one behind them, knowing they left him in a good place; and it does not appear that he cried after them, but was as willing to stay as they were to leave him, so soon did he *put away childish things* and behave like a man. 3. They kept up their constant attendance at the house of God with their *yearly sacrifice, v.* 19. They did not think that their son's ministering there would excuse them, or that that offering must serve instead of other offerings; but, having found the benefit of drawing near to God, they would omit no appointed season for it, and now they had one loadstone more in Shiloh to draw them thither. We may suppose they went thither to see their child oftener than once a year, for it was not ten miles from Ramah; but their annual visit is taken notice of because then they brought their yearly sacrifice, and then Hannah fitted up her son (and some think oftener than once a year) with a new suit of clothes, *a little coat* (*v.* 19) and every thing belonging to it. She undertook to find him with clothes during his apprenticeship at the tabernacle, and took care he should be well provided, that he might appear the more decent and sightly in his ministration, and to encourage him in his towardly beginnings. Parents must take care that their children want nothing that is fit for them, whether they are with them or from them; but those that are dutiful and hopeful, and minister to the Lord, must be thought worthy of double care and kindness. 4. The child Samuel did very well. Four separate times he is mentioned in these verses, and two things we are told of: — (1.) The service he did to the Lord. He did well indeed, for he *ministered to the Lord* (*v.* 11, 18) according as his capacity was. He learned his catechism and was constant to his devotions, soon learned to read, and took a pleasure in the book of the law, and thus he *ministered to the Lord.* He ministered before Eli, that is, under his inspection, and as he ordered him, not before Eli's sons; all parties were agreed that they were unfit to be his tutors. Perhaps he attended immediately on Eli's person, was ready to him to fetch and bring as he had occasion, and that is called *ministering to the Lord.* Some little services perhaps he was employed in about the altar, though much under the age appointed by the law for the Levites' ministration. He could light a candle, or hold a dish, or run on an errand, or shut a door; and, because he did this with a pious disposition of mind it is called *ministering to the Lord,* and great notice is taken of it. After awhile he did his work so well that Eli appointed that he should minister with a *linen ephod* as the priests did (though he was no priest), because he saw that God was with him. Note, Little children must learn betimes to *minister to the Lord.* Parents must train them up to it, and God will accept them. Particularly let them learn to pay respect to their teachers, as Samuel to Eli. None can begin too soon to be religious. See Ps. 8:2, and Mt. 21:15, 16. (2.) The blessing he received from the Lord: He *grew before the Lord,* as a tender plant (*v.* 21), *grew on* (*v.* 26) in strength and stature, and especially in wisdom and understanding and fitness for business. Note, Those young people that serve God as well as they can will obtain grace to improve, that they may serve him better. Those that are planted in God's house shall *flourish,* Ps. 92:13. *He was in favour with the Lord and with man.* Note, It is a great encouragement to children to be tractable, and virtuous, and good betimes, that if they be both God and man will love them. Such children are the darlings both of heaven and earth. What is here said of Samuel is said of our blessed Saviour, that great example, Lu. 2:52.

II. Let us now see how ill things went in Eli's family, though seated at the very door of the tabernacle. The nearer the church the further from God.

1. The abominable wickedness of Eli's sons (*v.* 12): *The sons of Eli were sons of Belial.* It is emphatically expressed. Nothing appears to the contrary but that Eli himself was a very good man, and no doubt had educated his sons well, giving them good instructions, setting them good examples, and putting up many a good prayer for them; and yet, when they grew up, they proved *sons of Belial,* profane wicked men, and arrant rakes: *They knew not the Lord.* They could not but have a notional knowledge of God and his law, a form of knowledge (Rom. 2:20), yet, because their practice was not conformable to it, they are spoken of as wholly ignorant of God; they lived as if they knew nothing at all of God. Note, Parents cannot give grace to their children, nor does it run in the blood. Many that are sincerely pious themselves live to see those that come from them notoriously impious and profane; *for the race is not to the swift.* Eli was high priest and judge in Israel. His sons were priests by their birth. Their character was sacred and honourable, and obliged them, for their reputation-sake, to observe decorum. They were resident at the fountain-head both of magistracy and ministry, and yet they were *sons of Belial,* and their honour, power, and learning, made them so much the worse. They did not go to *serve other gods,* as those did that lived at a distance from the altar, for from the house of God they had their wealth and dignity; but, which was worse, they managed the service of God as if he had been one of the dunghill deities of the heathen. It is hard to say which dishonours God more, idolatry or profaneness, especially the profaneness of the priests. Let us see the wickedness of Eli's sons; and it is a sad sight.

(1.) They profaned the offerings of the Lord, and made a gain to themselves, or rather a gratification of their own luxury, out of them. God had provided competently for them out of the sacrifices. *The offerings of the Lord made by fire* were a considerable branch of their revenue, but not enough to please them; they served not the God of Israel, but their own bellies (Rom. 16:18), being such as the prophet calls *greedy dogs that can never have enough,* Isa. 56:11. [1.] They robbed the offerers, and seized for themselves some of their part of the sacrifice of the peace-offerings. The priests had for their share the *wave-breast* and the *heave shoulder* (Lev. 7:34), but these did not content them; when the flesh was boiling for the offerer to feast upon religiously with his friends, they sent a servant with a flesh-hook of three teeth, a trident, and that must be stuck into the pot, and whatever that brought up the priest must have (*v.* 13, 14), and the people, out of their great veneration, suffered this to grow into a custom, so that after awhile prescription was pleaded for this manifest wrong. [2.] They stepped in before God himself, and encroached upon his right too. *As if it were a small thing to weary men, they wearied my God also,* Isa. 7:13. Be it observed, to the honour of Israel, that though the people tamely yielded to their unwarrantable demands from them, yet they were very solicitous that God should not be robbed: *Let them not fail to burn the fat presently, v.* 16. Let the altar have its due, for that is the main matter. Unless God have the fat, they can feast with little comfort upon the flesh. It was a shame that the priests should need to be thus admonished by the people of their duty; but they regarded not the admonition. The priest will be served first, and will take what he thinks fit of the fat too, for he is weary of boiled meat, he must have roast, and, in order to that, they must give it to him raw; and if the offerer dispute it, though not in his own favour (let the priest take what he pleases of his part) but in favour of the altar (let them be sure to *burn the fat* first), even the priest's servant had grown so very imperious that he would either have it now or take it by force, than which there could not be a greater affront to God nor a greater abuse to the people. The effect was, *First,* That God was displeased: *The sin of the young men was very great before the Lord, v.* 17. Nothing is more provoking to God than the profanation of sacred things, and men serving their lusts with the offerings of the Lord. *Secondly,* That religion suffered by it: *Men abhorred the offerings of the Lord.* All good men abhorred their management of the offerings, and too many insensibly fell into a contempt of the offerings themselves for their sakes. It was the people's sin to think the worse of God's institutions, but it was the much greater sin of the priests that gave them occasion to do so. Nothing brings a greater reproach upon religion than ministers' covetousness, sensuality, and imperiousness. In the midst of this sad story comes in the repeated mention of Samuel's devotion. *But Samuel ministered before the Lord,* as an instance of the power of God's grace, in preserving him pure and pious in the midst of this wicked crew; and this helped to keep up the sinking credit of the sanctuary in the minds of the people, who, when they had said all they could against Eli's sons, could not but admire Samuel's seriousness, and speak well of religion for his sake.

(2.) They debauched the women that came to worship at the door of the tabernacle, *v.* 22. They had wives of their own, but were like *fed horses,* Jer. 5:8. To have gone to the harlots' houses, the common prostitutes, would have been abominable wickedness, but to use the interest which as priests they had in those women that had devout dispositions and were religiously inclined, and to bring them to commit their wickedness, was such horrid impiety as one can scarcely think it possible that men who called themselves priests should ever be guilty of. *Be astonished, O heavens! at this, and tremble, O earth!* No words can sufficiently express the villany of such practices as these.

2. The reproof which Eli gave his sons for this their wickedness: *Eli was very old* (*v.* 22) and could not himself inspect the service of the tabernacle as he had done, but left all to his sons, who, because of the infirmities of his age, slighted him, and did what they would. However, he was told of the wickedness of his sons, and we may well imagine what a heart-breaking it was to him, and how much it added to the burdens of his age; but it should seem he did not so much as reprove them till he heard of their debauching the women, and then he thought fit to give them a check. Had he rebuked them for their greediness and luxury, this might have been prevented. Young people should be told of their faults as soon as it is perceived that they begin to be extravagant, lest their hearts be hardened. Now concerning the reproof he gave them observe,

(1.) That it was very just and rational. That which he said was very proper. [1.] He tells them that the matter of fact was too plain to be denied and too public to be concealed: *"I hear of your evil dealings by all this people, v.* 23. It is not the surmise of one or two, but the avowed testimony of many; all your neighbours cry out shame on you, and bring their complaints to me, expecting that I should redress the grievance." [2.] He shows them the bad consequences of it, that they not only sinned, but made Israel to sin, and would have the people's sin to answer for as well as their own: "You that should turn men from iniquity (Mal. 2:6), *you make the Lord's people to transgress,* and corrupt the nation instead of reforming it; you tempt people to go and serve other gods when they see the God of Israel so ill served." [3.] He warns them of the danger they brought themselves into by it, *v.* 25. He intimates to them what God afterwards told him, that the *iniquity* would not be *purged with sacrifice nor offering, ch.* 3:14. *If one man sin against another,* the judge (that is, the priest, who was appointed to be the judge in many cases, Deu. 17:9) *shall judge him,* shall undertake his cause, arbitrate the matter, and make atonement for the offender; *but if a man sin against the Lord* (that is, if a priest profane the holy things of the Lord, if a man that deals with God for others do himself affront him) *who shall entreat for him?* Eli was himself a judge, and had often made intercession for transgressors, but, says he, "You that *sin against the Lord,"* that is, "against the law and honour of God, in those very things which immediately pertain to him, and by which reconciliation is to be made, how can I entreat for you?" Their condition was deplorable indeed when their own father could not speak a good word for them, nor could have the face to appear as their advocate. Sins against the remedy, the atonement itself, are most dangerous, *treading under foot the blood of the covenant,* for then there *remains no more sacrifice,* Heb. 10:26.

(2.) It was too mild and gentle. He should have rebuked them sharply. Their crimes deserved sharpness; their temper needed it; the softness of his dealing with them would but harden them the more. The animad-version was too easy when he said, *It is no good report.* he should have said, "It is a shameful scandalous thing, and not to be suffered!" Whether it was because he loved them or because he feared them that he dealt thus tenderly with them, it was certainly an evidence of his want of zeal for the honour of God and his sanctuary. He bound them over to God's judgment, but he should have taken cognizance of their crimes himself, as high priest and judge, and have restrained and punished them. What he said was right, but it was not enough. Note, It is sometimes necessary that we put an edge upon the reproofs we give. There are those that must be saved *with fear,* Jude 23. 3. Their obstinacy against this reproof. His lenity did not at all work upon them: They *hearkened not to their father,* though he was also a judge. They had no regard either to his authority or to his affection, which was to them *an evident token of perdition;* it was *because the Lord would slay them.* They had long hardened their hearts, and now God, in a way of righteous judgment, hardened their hearts, and seared their consciences, and withheld from them the grace they had resisted and forfeited. Note, Those that are deaf to the reproofs of wisdom are manifestly marked for ruin. The Lord has *determined to destroy them,* 2 Chr. 25:16. See Prov. 29:1. Immediately upon this, Samuel's tractableness is again mentioned (*v.* 26), to shame their obstinacy: *The child Samuel grew.* God's grace is his own; he denied it to the sons of the high priest and gave it to the child of an obscure country Levite.

Verses 27–36

Eli reproved his sons too gently, and did not threaten them as he should, and therefore God sent a prophet to him to reprove him sharply, and to threaten him, because, by his indulgence of them, he had strengthened their hands in their wickedness. If good men be wanting in their duty, and by their carelessness and remissness contribute any thing to the sin of sinners, they must expect both to hear of it and to smart for it. Eli's family was now nearer to God than all *the families of the earth, and therefore he will punish them,* Amos 3:2. The message is sent to Eli himself, because God would bring him to repentance and save him; not to his sons, whom he had determined to destroy. And it might have been a means of awakening him to do his duty at last, and so to have prevented the judgment, but we do not find it had any great effect upon him. The message this prophet delivers from God is very close.

I. He reminds him of the great things God had done for the house of his fathers and for his family. He appeared to Aaron in Egypt (Ex. 4:27), in the house of bondage, as a token of further favour which he designed for him, *v.* 27. He advanced him to the priesthood, entailed it upon his family, and thereby dignified it above any of the families of Israel. He entrusted him with honourable work, to offer on God's altar, *to burn incense,* and to wear that ephod in which was the breast-plate of judgment. He settled upon him an honourable maintenance, a share out of *all the offerings made by fire, v.* 28. What could he have done more for them, to engage them to be faithful to him? Note, The distinguishing favours we have received from God, especially those of the spiritual priesthood, are great aggravations of sin, and will be remembered against us in the day of account, if we profane our crown and betray our trusts, Deu. 32:6; 2 Sa. 12:7, 8.

II. He exhibits a high charge against him and his family. His children did wickedly, and he connived at it, and thereby involved himself in the guilt; the indictment therefore runs against them all, *v.* 29. 1. His sons had impiously profaned the holy things of God: *"You kick at my sacrifice which I have commanded;* not only trample upon the institution as a mean thing, but spurn at it as a thing you hate to be tied up to." They did the utmost despite imaginable to the offerings of the Lord when they committed all that outrage and rapine about them that we read of, and violently plundered the pots on which, in effect, *Holiness to the Lord* was written (Zec. 14:20), and took that to themselves which God had appointed to be burnt on his altar. 2. Eli had bolstered them up in it, by not punishing their insolence and impiety: "Thou for thy part *honourest thy sons above me,"* that is, "thou hadst rather see my offerings disgraced by their profanation of them than see thy sons disgraced by a legal censure upon them for so doing, which ought to have been inflicted, even to suspension and deprivation *ab officio et beneficio — of their office and its emoluments."* Those that allow and countenance their children in any evil way, and do not use their authority to restrain and punish them, do in effect *honour them more than God,* being more tender of their reputation than of his glory and more desirous to humour them than to honour him. 3. They had all shared in the gains of the sacrilege. It is to be feared that Eli himself, though he disliked and reproved the abuses they committed, yet did not forbear to eat of the roast meat they sacrilegiously got, *v.* 15. He was a *fat heavy man* (*ch.* 4:18), and therefore it is charged upon the whole family (though Hophni and Phinehas were principally guilty), *You make yourselves fat with the chief of all the offerings.* God gave them sufficient to feed them, but that would not suffice; they made themselves fat, and served their lusts with that which God was to be served with. See Hos. 4:8.

III. He declares the cutting off of the entail of the high priesthood from his family (*v.* 30): *"The Lord God of Israel,* who is jealous for his own honour and Israel's, says, and lets thee know it, that thy commission is revoked and superseded." *I said, indeed, that thy house, and the house of thy father* Ithamar (for from that younger son of Aaron Eli descended), *should walk before me for ever.* Upon what occasion the dignity of the high priesthood was transferred from the family of Eleazar to that of Ithamar does not appear; but it seems this had been done, and Eli stood fair to have that honour perpetuated to his posterity. But observe, the promise carried its own condition along with it: *They shall walk before me forever,* that is, "they shall have the honour, provided they faithfully do the service." *Walking before God* is the great condition of the covenant, Gen. 17:1. Let them set me before their face, and I will set them before my face continually (Ps. 41:12), otherwise not. But now the Lord says, *Be it far from me.* "Now that you cast me off you can expect no other than that I should cast you off; you will not walk before me as you should, and therefore you shall not." Such wicked and abusive servants God will discard, and turn out of his service. Some think there is a further reach in this recall of the grant, and that it was not only to be fulfilled shortly in the deposing of the posterity of Eli, when Zadok, who descended from Eleazar, was put in Abiathar's room, but it was to have its complete accomplishment at length in the total abolition of the Levitical priesthood by the priesthood of Christ.

IV. He gives a good reason for this revocation, taken from a settled and standing rule of God's government, according to which all must expect to be dealt with (like that by which Cain was tried, Gen. 4:7): *Those that honour me I will honour, and those that despise me shall be lightly esteemed.*

1. Observe in general, (1.) That God is the fountain of honour and dishonour; he can exalt the meanest and put contempt upon the greatest. (2.) As we deal with God we must expect to be dealt with by him, and yet more favourably than we deserve. See Ps. 18:25, 26.

2. Particularly, (1.) Be it spoken, to the everlasting reputation of religion or of serious godliness, that it gives honour to God and puts honour upon men. By it we seek and serve the glory of God, and he will be behind-hand with none that do so, but here and hereafter will secure their glory. The way to be truly great is to be truly good. If we humble and deny ourselves in any thing to honour God, and have a single eye to him in it, we may depend upon this promise, he will put the best honour upon us. See Jn. 12:26. (2.) Be it spoken, to the everlasting reproach of impiety or profaneness, that this does dishonour to God (despises the greatest and best of beings, whom angels adore) and will bring dishonour upon men, for those that do so shall be lightly esteemed; not only God will lightly esteem them (that perhaps they will not regard, as those that honour him value his honour, of whom therefore it is said, *I will honour them*), but they shall be lightly esteemed by all the world; the very honour they are proud of shall be laid in the dust; they shall see themselves despised by all mankind, their names a reproach; when they are gone, their memory shall rot, and, when they rise again, it shall be to everlasting shame and contempt. The dishonour which their impotent malice puts upon God and his omnipotent justice will return upon their own heads, Ps. 79:12.

V. He foretels the particular judgments which should come upon his family, to its perpetual ignominy. A curse should be entailed upon his posterity, and a terrible curse it is, and shows how jealous God is in the matters of his worship and how ill he takes it when those who are bound by their character and profession to preserve and advance the interests of his glory are false to their trust, and betray them. If God's ministers be vicious and profane, *of how much sorer punishment will they be thought worthy,* here and for ever, than other sinners! Let such read the doom here passed on Eli's house, and tremble. It is threatened,

1. That their power should be broken (*v.* 31): *I will cut off thy arm, and the arm of thy father's house.* They should be stripped of all their authority, should be deposed, and have no influence upon the people as they had had. God *would make them contemptible and base.* See Mal. 2:8, 9. The sons had abused their power to oppress the people and encroach upon their rights, and the father had not used his power, as he ought to have done, to restrain and punish them, and therefore it was justly threatened that the arm should be cut off which was not stretched out as it should have been.

2. That their lives should be shortened. He was himself an old man; but instead of using the wisdom, gravity, experience, and authority of his age, for the service of God and the support of religion, he had suffered the infirmities of age to make him more cool and remiss in his duty, and therefore it is here threatened that none of his posterity should live to be old, *v.* 31, 32. It is twice spoken: *"There shall not be an old man in thy house for ever;"* and again (*v.* 33), *"All the increase of thy house,* from generation to generation, *shall die in the flower of their age,* when they are in the midst of the years of their service," so that though the family should not be extinct, yet it should never be considerable, nor should any member of it come to be eminent in his day. Bishop Patrick relates, out of some of the Jewish writers, that long after this, there being a family in Jerusalem none of which commonly lived above eighteen years, upon search it was found that they descended from the house of Eli, on which this sentence was passed.

3. That all their comforts should be embittered. (1.) The comfort they had in the sanctuary, in its wealth and prosperity: *Thou shalt see an enemy in my habitation.* This was fulfilled in the Philistines' invasions and the mischiefs they did to Israel, by which the country was impoverished (*ch.* 13:19), and no doubt the priests' incomes were thereby very much impaired. The captivity of the ark was such an act of hostility committed upon God's habitation as broke Eli's heart. As it is a blessing to a family to see *peace upon Israel* (Ps. 128:5, 6), so the contrary is a sore judgment upon a family, especially a family of priests. (2.) The comfort of their children: *"The man of thine whom I shall not cut off by an untimely death* shall live to be a blot and burden to the family, a scandal and vexation to his relations; he shall be to *consume thy eyes* and *grieve thy heart,* for his foolishness or his sickliness, his wickedness or his poverty." Grief for a dead child is great, but for a bad child often greater.

4. That their substance should be wasted and they should be reduced to extreme poverty (*v.* 36): *"He that is left* alive *in thy house* shall have little joy of his life, for want of a livelihood; he shall come and crouch to the succeeding family for a subsistence." (1.) He shall beg for the smallest alms — *a piece of silver* (and the word signifies the *least* piece) and *a morsel of bread.* See how this answered the sin. Eli's sons must have the best pieces of flesh, but their sons will be glad of *a morsel of bread.* Note, Want is the just punishment of wantonness. Those who could not be content without dainties and varieties are brought, they or theirs, to want necessaries, and the Lord is righteous in thus visiting them. (2.) He shall beg for the meanest office: *Put me into somewhat belonging to the priesthood* (as it is in the original); *make me as one of the hired servants,* the fittest place for a prodigal. Plenty and power are forfeited when they are abused. They should not be able to pretend to any good preferment, not to any place at the altar, but should petition for some poor employment, be the work ever so hard and the wages ever so small, so they might but get bread. This, it is probable, was fully accomplished when Abiathar, who was of Eli's race, was deposed by Solomon for treason, and he and his turned out of office in the temple (1 Ki. 2:26, 27), by which it is easy to think his posterity were reduced to the extremities here described.

5. That God would shortly begin to execute these judgments in the death of Hophni and Phinehas, the sad tidings of which Eli himself should live to hear: *This shall be a sign to thee, v.* 34. When thou hearest it, say, "Now the word of God begins to operate; here is one threatening fulfilled, from which I infer that all the rest will be fulfilled in their order." Hophni and Phinehas had many a time sinned together, and it is here foretold that they should die together both in one day. Bind these tares in a bundle for the fire. This was fulfilled, *ch.* 4:11.

VI. In the midst of all these threatenings against the house of Eli, here is mercy promised to Israel (*v.* 35): *I will raise me up a faithful priest.* 1. This was fulfilled in Zadoc, of the family of Eleazar, who came into Abiathar's place in the beginning of Solomon's reign, and was faithful to his trust; and the high priests were of his posterity as long as the Levitical priesthood continued. Note, The wickedness of ministers, though it destroy themselves, yet it shall not destroy the ministry. How bad soever the officers are, the office shall continue always to the end of the world. If some betray their trust, yet others shall be raised up that will be true to it. God's work shall never fall to the ground for want of hands to carry it on. The high priest is here said to *walk before God's anointed* (that is, David and his seed) because he wore the breastplate of judgment, which he was to consult, not in common cases, but for the king, in the affairs of state. Note, Notwithstanding the degeneracy we see and lament in many families, God will secure to himself a succession. If some grow worse than their ancestors, others, to balance that, shall grow better. 2. It has its full accomplishment in the priesthood of Christ, that merciful and faithful high priest whom God raised up when the Levitical priesthood was thrown off, who in all things did his father's mind, and for whom God will build a sure house, build it on a rock, so that the gates of hell cannot prevail against it.

CHAPTER 3

In the foregoing chapter we had Samuel a young priest, though by birth a Levite only, for he ministered before the Lord in a linen ephod; in this chapter we have him a young prophet, which was more, God in an extraordinary manner revealing himself to him, and in him reviving, if not commencing, prophecy in Israel. Here is, I. God's first manifestation of himself in an extraordinary manner to Samuel (*v.* 1–10). II. The message he sent by him to Eli (*v.* 11–14). III. The faithful delivery of that message to Eli, and his submission to the righteousness of God in it (*v.* 15–18). IV. The establishment of Samuel to be a prophet in Israel (*v.* 19–21).

Verses 1–10

To make way for the account of God's revealing himself first to Samuel, we are here told, 1. How industrious Samuel was in serving God, according as his place and capacity were (*v.* 1): *The child Samuel,* though but a child, *ministered unto the Lord before Eli.* It was an aggravation of the wickedness of Eli's sons that the child Samuel shamed them. They rebelled against the Lord, but Samuel ministered to him; they slighted their father's admonitions, but Samuel was observant of them; he ministered before Eli, under his eye and direction. It was the praise of Samuel that he was so far from being influenced by their bad example that he did not in the least fall off, but improved and went on. And it was a preparative for the honours God intended him; he that was thus faithful in a little was soon after entrusted with much more. Let those that are young be humble and diligent, which they will find the surest way to preferment. Those are fittest to rule who have learnt to obey. 2. How scarce a thing prophecy then was, which made the call of Samuel to be the greater surprise to himself and the greater favour to Israel: *The word of the Lord was precious in those days.* Now and then a man of God was employed as a messenger upon an extraordinary occasion (as *ch.* 2:27), but there were no settled prophets, to whom the people might have recourse for counsel, nor from whom they might expect the discoveries of the divine will. And the rarity of prophecy made it the more precious in the account of all those that knew how to put a right value upon it. It was precious, for what there was (it seems) was private: *There was no open vision,* that is, there were none that were publicly known to have visions. Perhaps the impiety and impurity that prevailed in the tabernacle, and no doubt corrupted the whole nation, had provoked God, as a token of his displeasure, to withdraw the Spirit of prophecy, till the decree had gone forth for the raising up of a more faithful priest, and then, as an earnest of that, this faithful prophet was raised up.

The manner of God's revealing himself to Samuel is here related very particularly, for it was uncommon.

I. Eli had retired. Samuel had waited on him to his bed, and the rest that attended the service of the sanctuary had gone, we may suppose, to their several apartments (*v.* 2): *Eli had laid down in his place;* he went to bed betimes, being unfit for business and soon weary of it, and perhaps loving his ease too well. Probably he kept his chamber much, which gave his sons the greater liberty. And he sought retirement the more because his eyes began to wax dim, an affliction which came justly upon him for winking at his sons' faults.

II. Samuel had laid down to sleep, in some closet near to Eli's room, as his page of the back-stairs, ready within call if the old man should want any thing in the night, perhaps to read to him if he could not sleep. He chose to take Samuel into this office rather than any of his own family, because of the towardly disposition he observed in him. When his own sons were a grief to him, his little servitor was his joy. Let those that are afflicted in their children thank God if they have any about them in whom they are comforted. *Samuel had laid down ere the lamp of God went out, v.* 3. It should seem he lay somewhere so near the holy place that he went to bed by that light, before any of the lamps in the branches of the candlestick went out (for the main lamp never went out), which probably was towards midnight. Till that time Samuel had been employing himself in some good exercise or other, reading and prayer, or perhaps cleaning or making ready the holy place; and then went softly to his bed. Then we may expect God's gracious visits, when we are constant and diligent in our duty.

III. God called him by name, and he took it for Eli's call, and ran to him, *v.* 4, 5. Samuel lay awake in his bed, his thoughts, no doubt, well employed (as David's Ps. 63:6), when the Lord called to him, bishop Patrick thinks out of the most holy place, and so the Chaldee paraphrase reads it, *A voice was heard out of the temple of the Lord;* but Eli, though it is likely he lay nearer, heard it not; yet possibly it might come some other way. Hereupon we have an instance, 1. Of Samuel's industry, and readiness to wait on Eli; supposing it was he that called him, he hastened out of his warm bed and ran to him, to see if he wanted any thing, and perhaps fearing he was not well. "Here am I," said he — a good example to servants, to come when they are called; and to the younger, not only to submit to the elder, but to be careful and tender of them. 2. Of his infirmity, and unacquaintedness with the visions of the Almighty, that he took that to be only Eli's call which was really the call of God. Such mistakes as these we make oftener than we think of. God calls to us by his word, and we take it to be only the call of the minister, and answer it accordingly; he calls to us by his providences, and we look only at the instruments. His voice cries, and it is but here and there a man of wisdom that understands it to be his voice. Eli assured him he did not call him, yet did not chide him for disturbing him with being over-officious, did not call him a *fool,* and tell him he dreamed, but mildly bade him lie down again, he had nothing for him to do. If servants must be ready at their masters' call, masters also must be tender of their servants' comfort: that thy *man-servant and thy maid-servant* may *rest as well as thou.* So *Samuel went and lay down.* God calls many by the ministry of the word, and they say, as Samuel did, "Here am I;" but not looking at God, nor discerning his voice in the call, the impressions of it are soon lost; they lie down again, and their convictions come to nothing.

IV. The same call was repeated, and the same mistake made, a second and third time, *v.* 6–9. 1. God continued to call the child *yet again* (*v.* 6), and *again the third time, v.* 8. Note, The call which divine grace designs to make effectual shall be repeated till it is so, that is, till we come at the call; for the purpose of God, according to which we are called, shall certainly stand. 2. Samuel was still ignorant that it was the Lord that called him (*v.* 7): *Samuel did not yet know the Lord.* He knew the written word, and was acquainted with the mind of God in that, but he did not yet apprehend the way in which God reveals himself to his servants the prophets, especially by a *still small voice;* this was altogether new and strange to him. Perhaps he would have been sooner aware of a divine revelation had it come in a dream or a vision; but this was a way he had not only not known himself, but not heard of. Those that have the greatest knowledge of divine things must remember the time when they were as babes, unskilful in the word of righteousness. *When I was a child I understood as a child.* Yet let us not despise the day of small things. *Thus did Samuel* (so the margin reads it) *before he knew the Lord, and before the word of the Lord was revealed unto him;* thus he blundered one time after another, but afterwards he understood his duty better. The witness of the Spirit in the hearts of the faithful is often thus mistaken, by which means they lose the comfort of it; and the strivings of the Spirit with the consciences of sinners are likewise often mistaken, and so the benefit of their convictions is lost. *God speaketh once, yea, twice, but man perceiveth it not,* Job 33:14. 3. Samuel went to Eli this second and third time, the voice perhaps resembling his, and the child being very near to him; and he tells Eli, with great assurance, *"Thou didst call me* (*v.* 6–8), it could be no one else." Samuel's disposition to come when he was called, though but by Eli, proving him dutiful and active, qualified him for the favour now to be shown him; God chooses to employ such. But there was a special providence in it, that he should go thus often to Eli; for hereby, at length, *Eli perceived that the Lord had called the child, v.* 8. And, (1.) This would be a mortification to him, and he would apprehend it to be a step towards his family's being degraded, that when God had something to say he should choose to say it to the child Samuel, his servant that waited on him, and not to him. And it would humble him the more when afterwards he found it was a message to himself, and yet sent to him by a child. He had reason to look upon this as a further token of God's displeasure. (2.) This would put him upon enquiring what it was that God said to Samuel, and would abundantly satisfy him of the truth and certainty of what should be delivered, and no room would be left for him to suggest that it was but a fancy of Samuel's; for before the message was delivered he himself perceived that God was about to speak to him, and yet must not know what it was till he had it from Samuel himself. Thus even the infirmities and mistakes of those whom God employs are overruled by infinite Wisdom, and made serviceable to his purposes.

V. At length Samuel was put into a posture to receive a message from God, not to be lodged with himself and go no further, but, that he might be a complete prophet, to be published and made an open vision. 1. Eli, perceiving that it was the voice of God that Samuel heard, gave him instructions what to say, *v.* 9. This was honestly done, that though it was a disgrace to him for God's call to pass him by, and be directed to Samuel, yet he put him in the way how to entertain it. Had he been envious of this honour done to Samuel, he would have done what he could to deprive him of it, and, since he did not perceive it himself, would have bidden him lie down and sleep, and never heed it, it was but a dream; but he was of a better spirit than to act so; he gave him the best advice he could, for the forwarding of his advancement. Thus the elder should, without grudging, do their utmost to assist and improve the younger that are rising up, though they see themselves likely to be darkened and eclipsed by them. Let us never be wanting to inform and instruct those that are coming after us, even such as will soon be preferred before us, Jn. 1:30. The instruction Eli gave him was, when God called the next time, to say, *Speak, Lord, for they servant heareth.* He must call himself God's servant, must desire to know the mind of God. *"Speak, Lord,* speak to me, speak now:" and he must prepare to hear, and promise to attend: *Thy servant heareth.* Note, Then we may expect that God will speak to us, when we set ourselves to hearken to what he says, Ps. 85:8; Hab. 2:1. When we come to read the word of God, and to attend on the preaching of it, we should come thus disposed, submitting ourselves to the commanding light and power of it: *Speak, Lord, for thy servant heareth.* 2. It should seem that God spoke the fourth time in a way somewhat different from the other; though the call was, as at other times, a call to him by name, yet now *he stood and called,* which intimates that there was now some visible appearance of the divine glory to Samuel, a vision that stood before him, like that before Eliphaz, though he *could not discern the form thereof,* Job 4:16. This satisfied him that it was not Eli that called; for he now *saw the voice that spoke with him,* as it is expressed, Rev. 1:12. Now also the call was doubled — *Samuel, Samuel,* as if God delighted in the mention of his name, or to intimate that now he should be made to understand who spoke to him. *God hath spoken once, twice have I heard this,* Ps. 62:11. It was an honour to him that God was pleased to *know him by name* (Ex. 33:12), and then his call was powerful and effectual when he called him by name, and so brought it particularly to him, as *Saul, Saul.* Thus God called to Abraham by name, Gen. 22:1. 3. Samuel said, as he was taught, *Speak, for thy servant heareth.* Note, Good words should be put into children's mouths betimes, and apt expressions of pious and devout affections, by which they may be prepared for a better acquaintance with divine things, and trained up to a holy converse with them. Teach young people what they shall say, for *they cannot order their speech by reason of darkness.* Samuel did not now rise and run as before when he thought Eli called, but lay still and listened. The more sedate and composed our spirits are the better prepared they are for divine discoveries. Let all tumultuous thoughts and passions be kept under, and every thing be quiet and serene in the soul, and then we are fit to hear from God. All must be silent when he speaks. But observe, Samuel left out one word; he did not say, *Speak, Lord,* but only, *Speak, for thy servant heareth,* way was made for the message he was now to receive, and Samuel was brought acquainted with the words of God and visions of the Almighty, and this *ere the lamp of God went out* (*v.* 3) *in the temple of the Lord,* which some of the Jewish writers put a mystical sense upon; before the fall of Eli, and the eclipsing of the Urim and Thummim for some time thereby, God called Samuel, and made him an oracle, whence they have an observation among their doctors, *That the sun riseth, and the sun goeth down* (Eccl. 1:5), that is, say they, Ere God maketh the sun of one righteous man to set, he makes the sun of another righteous man to rise. *Smith ex Kimchi.*

Verses 11–18

Here is, I. The message which, after all this introduction, God delivered to Samuel concerning Eli's house. God did not come to him now to tell him how great a man he should be in his day, what a figure he should make, and what a blessing he should be in Israel. Young people have commonly a great curiosity to be told their fortune, but God came to Samuel, not to gratify his curiosity, but to employ him in his service and send him on an errand to another person, which was much better; and yet the matter of this first message, which no doubt made a very great impression upon him, might be of good use to him afterwards, when his own sons proved, though not so bad as Eli's, yet not so good as they should have been, *ch.* 8:3. The message is short, not nearly so long as that which the man of God brought, *ch.* 2:27. For, Samuel being a child, it could not be expected that he should remember a long message, and God considered his frame. The memories of children must not be overcharged, no, not with divine things. But it is a sad message, a message of wrath, to ratify the message in the former chapter, and to bind on the sentence there pronounced, because perhaps Eli did not give so much regard to that as he ought to have done. Divine threatenings, the less they are heeded, the surer they will come and the heavier they will fall. Reference is here had to what was there said concerning both the sin and the punishment.

1. Concerning the sin: it is the *iniquity that he knoweth, v.* 13. The man of God told him of it, and many a time his own conscience had told him of it. O what a great deal of guilt and corruption is there in us concerning which we may say, "It is the iniquity *which our own heart knoweth,* we are conscious to ourselves of it!" In short, the iniquity was this: *His sons made themselves vile, and he restrained them not.*

Or, as it is in the Hebrew, he *frowned not upon them.* If he did show his dislike of their wicked courses, yet not to that degree that he ought to have done: he did reprove them, but he did not punish them, for the mischief they did, nor deprive them of their power to do mischief, which as a father, high priest, and judge, he might have done. Note, (1.) Sinners do by their own wickedness make themselves vile. They debauch themselves (for *every man is tempted when he is drawn aside of his own lusts,* Jam. 1:14) and thereby they debase themselves, and make themselves not only mean, but odious to the holy God and holy men and angels. Sin is a vile thing, and degrades men more than any thing, Ps. 15:4. Eli's sons made light of God, and made his offerings vile in the people's eyes; but the shame returned into their own bosom: they *made themselves vile.* (2.) Those that do not restrain the sins of others, when it is in the power of their hand to do it, make themselves partakers of the guilt, and will be charged as accessaries: Those in authority will have a great deal to answer for if they make not the sword they bear a *terror to evil workers.*

2. Concerning the punishment: it is *that which I have spoken concerning his house,* v. 12 and 13. *I have told him that I will judge his house for ever,* that is, that a curse should be entailed upon his family from generation to generation. The particulars of this curse we had before; they are not here repeated, but it is added, (1.) That when that sentence began to be executed it would be very dreadful and amazing to all Israel (v. 11): *Both the ears of every one that hears it shall tingle.* Every Israelite would be struck with terror and astonishment to hear of the slaying of Eli's sons, the breaking of Eli's neck, and the dispersion of Eli's family. Lord, how terrible art thou in thy judgments! If this be done in a green tree, what shall be done in the dry? Note, God's judgments upon others should affect us with a holy fear, Ps. 119:120. (2.) That these direful first-fruits of the execution would be certain earnests of the progress and full accomplishment of it: *When I begin I will* proceed and *make an end* of all that I have threatened, v. 12. It is intimated that it might possibly be some time before he would begin, but let them not call that forbearance an acquittance, nor that reprieve a pardon; for when at length he does begin he will make thorough work of it, and, though he stay long, he will strike home. (3.) That no room should be left for hope that this sentence might be reversed and the execution stayed or mitigated, v. 14. [1.] God would not revoke the sentence, for he backed it with an oath: *I have sworn to the house of Eli;* and God will not go back from what he has sworn either in mercy or judgment. [2.] He would never come to a composition for the forfeiture: "The *iniquity of Eli's house shall not be purged with sacrifice nor offering for ever.* No atonement shall be made for the sin, nor any abatement of the punishment." This was the imperfection of the legal sacrifices, that there were iniquities which they did not reach, which they would not purge; *but the blood of Christ cleanseth from all sin,* and secures all those that by faith are interested in it from that eternal death which is the wages of sin.

II. The delivery of this message to Eli. Observe,

1. Samuel's modest concealment of it, v. 15. (1.) He *lay till the morning,* and we may well suppose he lay awake pondering on what he had heard, repeating it to himself, and considering what use he must make of it. After we have received the spiritual food of God's word, it is good to compose ourselves, and give it time to digest. (2.) He opened the doors of the house of the Lord, in the morning, as he used to do, being up first in the tabernacle. That he should do so at other times was an instance of extraordinary towardliness in a child, but that he should do so this morning was an instance of great humility. God had highly honoured him above all the children of his people, yet he was not proud of the honour, nor puffed up with it, did not think himself too great and too good to be employed in these mean and servile offices, but, as cheerfully as ever, went and opened the doors of the tabernacle. Note, Those to whom God manifests himself he makes and keeps low in their own eyes, and willing to stoop to any thing by which they may be serviceable to his glory, though but as door-keepers in his house. One would have expected that Samuel would be so full of his vision as to forget his ordinary service, that he would go among his companions, as one in an ecstasy, to tell them what converse he had had with God this night; but he modestly keeps it to himself, tells the vision to no man, but silently

goes on in his business. Our secret communion with God is not to be proclaimed upon the house-tops. (3.) *He feared to show Eli the vision.* If he was afraid Eli would be angry with him and chide him, then we have cause to suspect that Eli used to be as severe with this towardly child as he was indulgent to his own wicked sons, and this will bear hard upon him. But we will suppose it was rather because he was afraid to grieve and trouble the good old man that he was so shy. If he had run immediately with the tidings to Eli, this would have looked as if he desired the woeful day and hoped to build his own family upon the ruin of Eli's; therefore it became him not to be forward to declare the vision. No good man can take pleasure in bringing evil tidings, especially not Samuel to Eli, the pupil to the tutor whom he loves and honours.

2. Eli's careful enquiry into it, v. 16, 17. As soon as ever he heard Samuel stirring he called for him, probably to his bed-side; and, having before perceived that God had spoken to him, he obliged him, not only by importunity (*I pray thee, hide it not from me),* but, finding him timorous and backward, by an adjuration likewise — *God do so to thee, and more also, if thou hide any thing from me!* He had reason enough to fear that the message prophesied no good concerning him, but evil; and yet, because it was a message from God, he could not contentedly be ignorant of it. A good man desires to be acquainted with all the will of God, whether it make for him or against him. His adjuration — *God do so to thee, if thou hide any thing from me* — may intimate the fearful doom of unfaithful watchmen; if they warn not sinners, they bring upon themselves that wrath and curse which they should have denounced, in God's name, against those that *go on still in their trespasses.*

3. Samuel's faithful delivery of his message at last (v. 18): *He told him every whit.* When he saw that he must tell him he never minced the matter, nor offered to make it better than it was, to blunt that which was sharp, or to gild the bitter pill, but delivered the message as plainly and fully as he received it, *not shunning to declare the whole counsel of God.* Christ's ministers must deal thus faithfully.

4. Eli's pious acquiescence in it. He did not question Samuel's integrity, was not cross with him, nor had he any thing to object against the equity of the sentence. He did not complain of the punishment, as Cain did, that it was greater than he either deserved or could bear, but patiently submitted, and accepted the punishment of his iniquity. *It is the Lord, let him do what seemeth him good.* He understood the sentence to intend only a temporal punishment, and the entail of disgrace and poverty upon his posterity, and not a final separation of them from the favour of God, and therefore he cheerfully submitted, did not repine, because he knew the demerits of his family; nor did he now intercede for the reversing of the sentence, because God had ratified it with a solemn oath, of which he would not repent. He therefore composes himself into a humble resignation to God's will, as Aaron, in a case not much unlike. Lev. 10:3, *He held his peace.* In a few words, (1.) He lays down this satisfying truth, *"It is the Lord;* it is he that pronounces the judgment, from whose bar there lies no appeal and against whose sentence there lies no exception. It is he that will execute the judgment, whose power cannot be resisted, his justice arraigned, nor his sovereignty contested. *It is the Lord,* who will thus sanctify and glorify himself, and it is highly fit he should. *It is the Lord,* with whom there is no unrighteousness, who never did nor ever will do any wrong to any of his creatures, nor exact more than their iniquity deserves." (2.) He infers from it this satisfying conclusion: "*Let him do what seemeth him good.* I have nothing to say against his proceedings. He is righteous in all his ways and holy in all his works, and therefore *his will be done. I will bear the indignation of the Lord, because I have sinned against him."* Thus we ought to quiet ourselves under God's rebuke, and never to strive with our Maker.

Verses 19–21

Samuel being thus brought acquainted with the visions of God, we have here an account of the further honour done him as a prophet.

I. God did him honour. Having begun to favour him, he carried on and crowned his own work in him: *Samuel*

grew, for the Lord was with him, v. 19. All our increase in wisdom and grace is owing to the presence of God with us; this is all in all to our growth. God honoured Samuel, 1. By further manifestations of himself to him. Samuel had faithfully delivered the message he was entrusted with, and therefore God employed him again in his service: *The Lord revealed himself again to Samuel in Shiloh, v.* 21. Note, God will graciously repeat his visits to those that receive them aright. 2. By fulfilling what he spoke by him: *God did let none of his words fall to the ground, v.* 19. Whatever Samuel said, as a prophet, it proved true, and was accomplished in its season. Probably there were some remarkable instances of the truth of Samuel's predictions that happened soon after, which confirmed those that were afterwards to be fulfilled, and gave general satisfaction as to his mission. God will *confirm the word of his servants,* and *perform the counsel of his messengers* (Isa. 44:26), and will do what he hath said.

II. Israel did him honour. They all knew and owned *that Samuel was established to be a prophet, v.* 20. 1. He grew famous; all that came up to Shiloh to worship took notice of him, and admired him, and talked of him when they returned home. Early piety will be the greatest honour of young people, and bring them, as much as any thing, and as soon, into reputation. Those that honour God he will honour. 2. He grew useful and very serviceable to his generation. He that began betimes to *be* good soon came to *do* good. His established commission from God, and established reputation with the people, gave him a great opportunity of shining as a light in Israel. When old Eli was rejected, young Samuel was established; for God will never leave himself without a witness nor his church without a guide.

CHAPTER 4

The predictions in the foregoing chapters concerning the ruin of Eli's house here begin to be fulfilled; how long after does not appear, but certainly not long. Such sinners God often makes quick work with. Here is, I. The disgrace and loss Israel sustained in an encounter with the Philistines (v. 1, 2). II. Their foolish project to fortify themselves by bringing the ark of God into their camp upon the shoulders of Hophni and Phinehas (v. 3, 4), which made them secure (v. 5) and struck a fear into the Philistines, but such a fear as roused them (v. 6–9). III. The fatal consequences of it: Israel was beaten, and the ark taken prisoner (v. 10, 11). IV. The tidings of this brought to Shiloh, and the sad reception of those tidings. 1. The city was put into confusion (v. 12, 13). 2. Eli fainted away, fell, and broke his neck (v. 14–18). 3. Upon hearing what had occurred his daughter-in-law fell in labour, bore a son, but died immediately (v. 19–22). These were the things which would make the ears of those that heard them to tingle.

Verses 1–9

The first words of this paragraph, which relate to Samuel, that *his word came to all Israel,* seem not to have any reference to the following story, as if it was by any direction of his that the Israelites went out against the Philistines. Had they consulted him, though but newly initiated as a prophet, his counsel might have stood them in more stead than the presence of the ark did; but perhaps the princes of Israel despised his youth, and would not have recourse to him as an oracle, and he did not as yet interpose in public affairs; nor do we find any mention of his name henceforward till some years after (ch. 7:3), only *his word came to all Israel,* that is, people from all parts that were piously disposed had recourse to him as a prophet and consulted him. Perhaps it is meant of his prophecy against the house of Eli. This was generally known and talked of, and all that were serious and observing compared the events here related, when they came to pass, with the prophecy, and saw it accomplished in them. Here is,

I. A war entered into with the Philistines, v. 1. It was an attempt to throw off the yoke of their oppression, and would have succeeded better if they had first repented and reformed, and so begun their work at the right end. It is computed that this was about the middle of the forty years' dominion that the Philistines had over Israel (Jdg. 13:1) and soon after the death of Samson; so bishop Patrick, who thinks the slaughter he made at his death might encourage this attempt; but Dr. Lightfoot reckons it forty years after Samson's death, for so long Eli judged, v. 18.

II. The defeat of Israel in that war, v. 2. Israel, who were the aggressors, were smitten, and had 4000 men killed upon the spot. God had promised that one of them should chase a thousand; but now, on the contrary, *Israel is smit-*

ten before the Philistines. Sin, the accursed thing, was in the camp, and gave their enemies all the advantage against them they could wish for.

III. The measures they concerted for another engagement. A council of war was called, and, instead of resolving to fast and pray and amend their lives, so ill taught were they (and no wonder when they had such teachers) that, 1. They quarrelled with God for appearing against them (*v.* 3): *Wherefore has the Lord smitten us?* If they meant this as an enquiry into the cause of God's displeasure, they needed not go far to find that out. It was plain enough; Israel had sinned, though they were not willing to see it and own it. But it rather seems that they expostulate boldly with God about it, are displeased at what God has done, and dispute the matter with him. They own the hand of God in their trouble (so far was right): "It is the Lord that has smitten us;" but, instead of submitting to it, they quarrel with it, and speak as those that are angry at him and his providence, and not aware of any just provocation they have given him: "Wherefore shall we, that are Israelites, be smitten before the Philistines? How absurd and unjust is it!" Note, The foolishness of man perverts his way, and then his heart *frets against the Lord* (Prov. 19:3) and finds fault with him. 2. They imagined that they could oblige him to appear for them the next time by bringing the ark into their camp. The elders of Israel were so ignorant and foolish as to make the proposal (*v.* 3), and the people soon put it in execution, *v.* 4. They sent to Shiloh for the ark, and Eli had not courage enough to detain it, but sent his ungodly sons, Hophni and Phinehas, along with it, at least permitted them to go, though he knew that wherever they went the curse of God went along with them. Now see here, (1.) The profound veneration the people had for the ark. "O send for that, and it will do wonders for us." The ark was, by institution, a visible token of God's presence. God had said that he would dwell *between the cherubim,* which were over the ark and were carried along with it; now they thought that, by paying a great respect to this sacred chest, they should prove themselves to be Israelites indeed, and effectually engage God Almighty to appear in their favour. Note, It is common for those that have estranged themselves from the vitals of religion to discover a great fondness for the rituals and external observances of it, for those that even deny the power of godliness not only to have, but to have in admiration, the form of it. The temple of the Lord is cried up, and the ark of the Lord stickled for with a great deal of seeming zeal by multitudes that have no regard at all for the Lord of the temple and the God of the ark, as if a fiery concern for the name of Christianity would atone for a profane contempt of the thing. And yet indeed they did but make an idol of the ark, and looked upon it to be as much an image of the God of Israel as those idols which the heathen worshipped were of their gods. To worship the true God, and not to worship him as God, is in effect not to worship him at all. (2.) Their egregious folly in thinking that the ark, if they had it in their camp, would certainly *save them out of the hand of their enemies,* and bring victory back to their side. For, [1.] When the ark set forward Moses prayed, *Rise up, Lord, and let thy enemies be scattered,* well knowing that it was not the ark moving with them, but God appearing for them, that must give them success; and here were no proper means used to engage God to favour them with his presence; what good then would the ark do them, the shell without the kernel? [2.] They were so far from having God's leave to remove his ark that he had plainly enough intimated to them in his law that when they were settled in Canaan his ark should be settled in the place that he should choose (Deu. 12:5, 11), and that they must come to it, not it to them. How then could they expect any advantage by it when they had not a just and legal possession of it, nor any warrant to remove it from its place? Instead of honouring God by what they did, they really affronted him. Nay, [3.] If there had been nothing else to invalidate their expectations from the ark, how could they expect it should bring a blessing when Hophni and Phinehas were the men that carried it? It would have given too much countenance to their villany if the ark had done any kindness to Israel while it was in the hands of those graceless priests.

IV. The great joy there was in the camp of Israel when the ark was brought into it (*v.* 5): *They shouted, so that the earth rang again.* Now they thought themselves sure of victory, and therefore gave a triumphant shout before the battle, as if the day was without fail their own, intending, by this mighty shout, to animate themselves and their own forces, and to intimidate their adversaries. Note, Carnal people triumph much in the external privileges and performances of religion, and build much upon them, as if these would infallibly save them, and as if the ark, God's throne, in the camp, would bring them to heaven, though the world and the flesh should be upon the throne in the heart.

V. The consternation into which the bringing of the ark into the camp of Israel put the Philistines. The two armies lay so near encamped that the Philistines heard the shout the Israelites gave on this great occasion. They soon understood what it was they triumphed in (*v.* 6), and were afraid of the consequences. For, 1. It had never been done before in their days: *God has come into their camp,* and therefore *woe unto us* (*v.* 7), and again, *woe unto us, v.* 8. The name of the God of Israel was formidable even to those that worshipped other gods, and some apprehensions even the infidels had of the danger of contending with them. Natural conscience suggests this, that those are in a woeful condition who have God against them. Yet see what gross notions they had of the divine presence, as if the God of Israel were not as much in the camp before the ark came thither, which may very well be excused in them, since the notions the Israelites themselves had of that presence were no better. "O," say they, "this is a new design upon us, more frightful than all their stratagems, for *there has not been such a thing heretofore;* this was the most effectual course they could take to dispirit our men and weaken their hands." 2. When it had been done in the days of old, it had wrought wonders: *These are the gods that smote the Egyptians with all the plagues in the wilderness, v.* 8. Here they were as much out in their history as in their divinity: the plagues of Egypt were inflicted before the ark was made and before Israel came into the wilderness; but some confused traditions they had of wonders wrought by or for Israel when this ark was carried before them, which they attributed, not to Jehovah, but to the ark. Now, say they, *Who shall deliver us out of the hand of these mighty gods?* taking the ark for God, as well they might when the Israelites themselves idolized it. Yet, it should seem, they scarcely believed themselves when they spoke thus formidably of *these mighty gods,* but only bantered; for instead of retreating, or proposing conditions of peace, which they would have done had they been really convinced of the power of Israel's God, they stirred up one another to fight so much the more stoutly; this surprising difficulty did but sharpen their resolution (*v.* 9): *Be strong, and quit yourselves like men.* The commanders inspired bold and generous thoughts into the minds of their soldiers when they bade them remember how they had lorded it over Israel, and what an intolerable grief and shame it would be if they flinched now, and suffered Israel to lord it over them.

Verses 10–11

Here is a short account of the issue of this battle.

I. Israel was smitten, the army dispersed and totally routed, not retiring into the camp, as before (*v.* 2) when they hoped to rally again, but returning to their tents, every man shifting for his own safety and making the best of his way home, despairing to make head any more; and 30,000 were slain in the field of battle, *v.* 10. Israel was put to the worse, 1. Though they had the better cause, were the people of God and the Philistines were uncircumcised; they stood up in necessary defence of their just rights and liberties against invaders, and yet they failed of success, for *their rock had sold them.* A good cause often suffers for the sake of the bad men that undertake it. 2. Though they had the greater confidence, and were the more courageous. They shouted, while the Philistines trembled, and yet, when God pleased so to order it, the Philistines' terrors were turned into triumphs, and Israel's shouts into lamentations. 3. Though they had the ark of God with them. External privileges will secure none that abuse them and do not live up to them. The ark in the camp will add nothing to its strength when there is an Achan in it.

II. The ark itself was taken by the Philistines; and Hophni and Phinehas, who it is likely kept close to it, and when it was in danger ventured far in the defense of it, because by it they got their living, were *both slain, v.* 11. To this sad even the Psalmist refers, Ps. 78:61. 64, *He delivered his strength into captivity, and his glory into the enemy's hands. Their priests fell by the sword.* 1. The slaughter of the priests, considering their bad character, was no great loss to Israel, but it was a dreadful judgment upon the house of Eli. The word which God had spoken was fulfilled in it (*ch.* 2:34): *This shall be a sign unto thee,* an earnest of the judgments threatened, *thy two sons shall die both in one day,* and so shall all *the increase of thy house die in the flower of their age, v.* 33. If Eli had done his duty, and *put them, as polluted, from the priesthood* (Neh. 7:64), they might have lived, though in disgrace; but now God takes the work into his own hands, and chases them out of the world by the sword of the uncircumcised. *The Lord is known by those judgments which he executeth.* It is true the sword devours one as well as another, but these were waited for of the sword, marked for vengeance. They were out of the place; what had they to do in the camp? When men leave the way of their duty they shut themselves out of God's protection. But this was not all; they had betrayed the ark, by bringing it into danger, without a warrant from God, and this filled the measure of their iniquities. But, 2. The taking of the ark was a very great judgment upon Israel, and a certain token of God's hot displeasure against them. Now they are made to see their folly in trusting to their external privileges which they had by their wickedness forfeited them, and fancying that the ark would save them when God had departed from them. Now they are made to reflect, with the utmost regret, upon their own rashness and presumption in bringing the ark into the camp and so exposing it, and wish a thousand times they had left it where God had fixed it. Now they are convinced that God will not be prescribed to by vain and foolish men, and that though he has bound us to his ark he has not bound himself to it, but will rather deliver it into the hands of his sworn enemies than suffer it to be profaned by his false friends, and countenance their superstition. Let none think to shelter themselves from the wrath of God under the cloak of a visible profession, for there will be those cast into outer darkness that have *eaten and drunk in Christ's presence.*

Verses 12–18

Tidings are here brought to Shiloh of the fatal issue of their battle with the Philistines. Bad news flies fast. This soon spread through all Israel; every man that fled to his tent brought it, with too plain a proof of it, to his neighbours. But no place was so nearly concerned as Shiloh. Thither therefore an express posted away immediately; it was a man of Benjamin; the Jews fancy it was Saul. *He rent his clothes, and put earth upon his head,* by these signs to proclaim the sorrowful news to all that saw him as he ran, and to show how much he himself was affected with it, *v.* 12. He went straight to Shiloh with it; and here we are told,

I. How the city received it. *Eli sat in the gate* (*v.* 13, 18), but the messenger was loth to tell him first, and therefore passed him by, and told it in the city, with all the aggravating circumstances; and now *both the ears of every one that heard it tingled,* as was foretold, *ch.* 3:11. Their hearts trembled, and every face gathered blackness. *All the city cried out* (*v.* 13), and well they might, for, besides that this was a calamity to all Israel, it was a particular loss to Shiloh, and the ruin of that place; for, though the ark was soon rescued out of the hands of the Philistines, yet it never returned to Shiloh again; their candlestick was removed out of its place, because they had *left their first love,* and their city dwindled, and sunk, and came to nothing. Now God *forsook the tabernacle of Shiloh,* they having driven him from them; and the tribe of Ephraim, which had for 340 years been blessed with the presence of the ark in it, lost the honour (Ps. 78:60, 67), and, some time after, it was transferred to the tribe of Judah, the *Mount Sion which he loved,* as it follows (*v.* 68), because the men of Shiloh knew not *the day of their visitation.* This abandoning of Shiloh Jerusalem is long afterwards reminded of, and told to take warning by, Jer. 7:12, *"Go see what I did to Shiloh.* From this day, this fatal day, let the desolations of Shiloh be dated." They had therefore reason enough to cry out when they heard that the ark was taken.

II. What a fatal blow it was to old Eli. Let us see, 1. With what fear he expected the tidings. Though old, and blind, and heavy, yet he could not keep his chamber when he was sensible the glory of Israel lay at stake, but placed himself by the way-side, to receive the first intelligence; for *his heart trembled for the ark of God, v.* 13. His careful thoughts represented to him what a dishonour it would be to God, and what an irreparable loss to Israel, if the ark should fall into the Philistines' hands, with what profane triumphs the tidings would be told in Gath and published in the streets of Ashkelon. He also apprehended what imminent danger there was of it. Israel had forfeited the ark (his own sons especially) and the Philistines would aim at it; and now the threatening comes to his mind, that he should *see an enemy in God's habitation* (*ch.* 2:32); and perhaps his own heart reproached him for not using his authority to prevent the carrying of the ark into the camp. All these things made him tremble. Note, All good men lay the interests of God's church nearer their hearts than any secular interest or concern of their own, and cannot but be in pain and fear for them if at any time they are in peril. How can we be easy if the ark be not safe? 2. With what grief he received the tidings. Though he could not see, he could hear the *tumult* and *crying of the city,* and perceived it to be the voice of lamentation, and mourning, and woe; like a careful magistrate, he asks, *What means the noise of this tumult? v.* 14. He is told there is an express come from the army, who relates the story to him very distinctly, and with great confidence, having himself been an eye-witness of it, *v.* 16, 17. The account of the defeat of the army, and the slaughter of a great number of the soldiers, was very grievous to him as a judge; the tidings of the death of his two sons, of whom he had been so indulgent, and who, he had reason to fear, died impenitent, touched him in a tender part as a father; yet it was not for these that his heart trembled: there is a greater concern upon his spirit, which swallows up the less; he does not interrupt the narrative with any passionate lamentations for his sons, like David for Absalom, but waits for the end of the story, not doubting but that the messenger, being an Israelite, would, without being asked, say something of the ark; and if he could but have said, "Yet the ark of God is safe, and we are bringing that home," his joy for that would have overcome his grief for all the other disasters, and have made him easy; but, when the messenger concludes his story with, *The ark of God is taken,* he is struck to the heart, his spirits fail, and, it should seem, he swooned away, fell off his seat, and partly with the fainting, and partly with the fall, he died immediately, and never spoke a word more. His heart was broken first, and then his neck. So fell the high priest and judge of Israel, so fell his heavy head when he had lived within two of 100 years, so fell the crown from his head when he had judged Israel about forty years: thus did his sun set under a cloud, thus were the folly and wickedness of those sons of his, whom he had indulged, his ruin at last. Thus does God sometimes set marks of his displeasure in this life upon good men who have misconducted themselves, that others may hear, and fear, and take warning. A man may die miserably and yet not die eternally, may come to an untimely end and yet the end be peace. Dr. Lightfoot observes that Eli died the death of an unredeemed ass, whose neck was to be broken, Ex. 13:13. Yet we must observe, to Eli's praise, that it was the loss of the ark that was his death, not the slaughter of his sons. He does, in effect, say, "Let me fall with the ark, for what pious Israelite can live with any comfort when God's ordinances are removed?" Farewell all in this world, even life itself, if the ark be gone.

Verses 19–22

We have here another melancholy story, that carries on the desolations of Eli's house, and the sorrowful feeling which the tidings of the ark's captivity excited. It is concerning the wife of Phinehas, one of those ungracious sons of Eli that had brought all this mischief on Israel. It cost her her life, though young, as well as that of her father-in-law, that was old; for many a green head, as well as many a hoary head, has been brought by sorrow to the grave: it worketh death. By what is here related of her it appears,

I. That she was a woman of a very tender spirit. Providence so ordered it that, just at this time, she was near her time; and our Saviour hath said, *Woe to those that are with child,* or *give suck,* in such days as these, Mt. 24:19. So little joy will there then be in the birth, even of a man-child, that it will be said, *Blessed are the wombs that bear not,* Lu. 23:29. The amazing news coming at this unhappy juncture, it put her into labour, as great frights or other strong passions sometimes do. When she heard of the death of her father-in-law whom she reverenced, and her husband whom, bad as he was, she loved, but especially of the loss of the ark, *she travailed, for her pains came* thickly *upon her* (*v.* 19), and the tidings so seized her spirits, at a time when they needed all possible supports, that, though she had strength to bear the child, she, soon after, fainted and died away, being very willing to let life go when she had lost the greatest comforts of her life. Those who are drawing near to that trying hour have need to treasure up for themselves comforts from the covenant of grace, to balance, not only the usual sorrows, but any thing extraordinary that may add to the grief which they do not foresee. Faith, at such a time, will keep from fainting, Ps. 27:13.

II. That she was a woman of a very gracious spirit though matched to a wicked husband. Her concern for the death of her husband and father-in-law was an evidence of her natural affection; but her much greater concern for the loss of the ark was an evidence of her pious and devout affection to God and sacred things. The former helped to hasten her travail, but it appears by her dying words that the latter lay nearer her heart (*v.* 22): *She said, The glory has departed from Israel,* not lamenting so much the sinking of that particular family to which she was related as the general calamity of Israel in the captivity of the ark. This, this was it that was her grief, that was her death.

1. This made her regardless of her child. The women that attended her, who it is likely were some of the first rank in the city, encouraged her, and, thinking that he concern was mostly about the issue of her pains, when the child was born, *said unto her, Fear not,* now the worst is past, *for thou has borne a son* (and perhaps it was her first-born), *but she answered not, neither did she regard it.* The sorrows of her travail, if she had no other, would have been *forgotten, for joy that a man-child was born into the world.* Jn. 16:21. But what is that joy, (1.) To one that feels herself dying? No joy but that which is spiritual and divine will stand us in any stead then. Death is too serious a thing to admit the relish of any earthly joy; it is all flat and sapless then. (2.) What is it to one that is lamenting the loss of the ark? Small comfort could she have of a child born in Israel, in Shiloh, when the ark is lost, and is a prisoner in the land of the Philistines. What pleasure can we take in our creature-comforts and enjoyments if we want God's word and ordinances, especially if we want the comfort of his gracious presence and the light of his countenance? *As vinegar upon nitre, so is he that sings songs* so such *heavy hearts.*

2. This made her give her child a name which should perpetuate the remembrance of the calamity and her sense of it. She has nothing to say to the child, only it being her province, now that her husband was dead, to name the child, she orders them to call it *I-chabod,* that is, *Where is the glory?* Or, *Alas for the glory!* or, *There is no glory* (*v.* 21), which she thus explains with her dying lips (*v.* 22): *"The glory has departed from Israel; for the ark of God is taken.* Call the child inglorious, for so he is; the beauty of Israel is lost, and there appears no hope of ever retrieving it; never let the name of an Israelite, must less a priest, carry glory in it any more, now that the ark is taken." Note, (1.) The purity and plenty of God's ordinances, and the tokens of his presence in them, are the glory of any people, much more so than their wealth, and trade, and interest, among the nations. 2. Nothing is more cutting, more killing, to a faithful Israelite, than the want and loss of these. If God go, the glory goes, and all good goes. Woe unto us if he depart!

CHAPTER 5

It is now time to enquire what has become of the ark of God; we cannot but think that we shall hear more of that sacred treasure. I should have thought the next news would have been that all Israel, from Dan to Beer-sheba, had gathered together as one man, with a resolution to bring it back, or die in the attempt; but we find not any motion made of that kind, so little was there of zeal or courage left among them. Nay, we do not find that they desired a treaty with the Philistines about the ransom of it, or offered any thing in lieu of it. "It is gone, and let it go." Many have softness enough to lament the loss of the ark that have not hardiness enough to take one step towards the recovery of it, any more than Israel here. If the ark will help itself it may, for they will not help it. Unworthy they were of the name of Israelites that could thus tamely part with the glory of Israel. God would therefore take the work into his own hands and plead his own cause, since men would not appear for him. We are told in this chapter, I. How the Philistines triumphed over the ark (*v.* 1, 2), and, II. How the ark triumphed over the Philistines, 1. Over Dagon their god (*v.* 3–5). 2. Over the Philistines themselves, who were sorely plagued with emerods, and made weary of the ark; the men of Ashdod first (*v.* 6, 7), then the men of Gath (*v.* 8, 9), and lastly those of Ekron, which forced them at length upon a resolution to send the ark back to the land of Israel; for when God judgeth he will overcome.

Verses 1–5

Here is, I. The Philistines' triumph over the ark, which they were the more pleased, the more proud, to be now masters of, because before the battle they were possessed with a great fear of it, *ch.* 4:7. When they had it in their hands God restrained them, that they did not offer any violence to it, did not break it to pieces, as the Israelites were ordered to do by the idols of the heathen, but showed some respect to it, and carefully carried it to a place of safety. Whether their curiosity led them to open it, and to read what was written with the finger of God on the two tables of stone that were in it, we are not told; perhaps they looked no further than the golden outside and the cherubim that covered it, like children that are more affected with the fine binding of their bibles than with the precious matter contained in them. They carried it to Ashdod, one of their five cities, and that in which Dagon's temple was; there they placed the ark of God, *by Dagon* (*v.* 2), either 1. As a sacred thing, which they designed to pay some religious respect to, in conjunction with Dagon; for the gods of the heathen were never looked upon as averse to partners. Though the nations would not change their gods, yet they would multiply them and add to them. But they were mistaken in the God of Israel when, in putting his ark by Dagon's image, they intended to do him honour; for he is not worshipped at all if he is not worshipped alone. *The Lord our God is one Lord.* Or rather, 2. They placed it there as a trophy of victory, in honour of Dagon their god, to whom no doubt they intended to offer a great sacrifice, as they had done when they had taken Samson (Jdg. 16:23, 24), boasting that as then they had triumphed over Israel's champion so now over Israel's God. What a reproach was this to God's great name! what a *disgrace to the throne of his glory!* Shall the ark, the symbol of God's presence, be a prisoner to Dagon, a dunghill deity? (1.) So it is, because God will show of how little account the ark of the covenant is if the covenant itself be broken and neglected; even sacred signs are not things that either he is tied to or we can trust to. (2.) So it is for a time, that God may have so much the more glory, in reckoning with those that thus affront him, and get him honour upon them. Having punished Israel, that betrayed the ark, by giving it into the hands of the Philistines, he will next deal with those that abused it, and will fetch it out of their hands again. Thus even the *wrath of man shall praise him;* and he is bringing about his own glory even when he seems to neglect it, Ps. 76:10. Out of the eater shall come forth meat.

II. The ark's triumph over Dagon. Once and again Dagon was made to fall before it. If they designed to do honour to the ark, God thereby showed that he valued not their honour, nor would he accept it; for he will be worshipped, not *with* any god, but *above* all gods. *He owes a shame* (as bishop Hall expresses it) *to those who will be making matches betwixt himself and Belial.* But they really designed to affront it, and though for some hours Dagon stood by the ark, and it is likely stood above it (the ark, as its footstool), yet the next morning, when the worshippers of Dagon came to pay their devotions to his shrine, they found their triumphing short, Job 20:5.

1. Dagon, that is, the image (for that was all the god), had *fallen upon his face to the earth before the ark, v.* 3. God had seemed to forget the ark, but see how the Psalmist speaks of his appearing, at last, to vindicate his own honour. When he had delivered his strength into captivity, and all seemed going to ruin, *then the Lord awaked as one out of sleep, and like a mighty man that shouteth by reason of wine,* Ps. 78:59–65. And therefore he prevented the utter desolations of the Jewish church, because he *feared the wrath of the enemy,* Deu. 32:26, 27. Great care was taken, in setting up the images of their gods, to fix

them. The prophet takes notice of it, Isa. 41:7, *He fastened it with nails that it should not be moved;* and again, Isa. 46:7. And yet Dagon's fastenings stood him in no stead. The ark of God triumphs over him upon his own dunghill, in his own temple. Down he comes before the ark, directly towards it (though the ark was set on one side of him), as it were, pointing to the conqueror, to whom he is constrained to yield and do homage. Note, The kingdom of Satan will certainly fall before the kingdom of Christ, error before truth, profaneness before godliness, and corruption before grace in the hearts of the faithful. When the interests of religion seem to be run down and ready to sink, yet even then we may be confident that the day of their triumph will come. Great is the truth, and will prevail. Dagon by falling prostrate before the ark of God, which was a posture of adoration, did as it were direct his worshippers to pay their homage to the God of Israel, as *greater than all gods.* See Ex. 18:11.

2. The priests, finding their idol on the floor, make all the haste they can, before it be known, to set him in his place again. A sorry silly thing it was to make a god of, which, when it was down, wanted help to get up again; and sottish wretches those were that could pray for help from that idol that needed, and in effect implored, their help. How could they attribute their victory to the power of Dagon when Dagon himself could not keep his own ground before the ark? But they are resolved Dagon shall be their god still, and therefore set him in his place. Bishop Hall observes hence, It is just with God that those who want grace shall want wit too; and it is the work of superstition to turn men into the stocks and stones they worship. *Those that make them are like unto them.* What is it that the great upholders of the antichristian kingdom are doing at this day but heaving Dagon up, and labouring to set him in his place again, and healing the deadly wound that has been given to the beast? but if the reformation be the cause of God, before which it has begun to fall, it shall not prevail, but shall surely fall before it.

3. The next night Dagon fell the second time, *v.* 4. They rose early, either, as usual, to make their addresses to their god, or earlier than usual, being impatient to know whether Dagon had kept his standing this night; and, to their great confusion, they find his case worse now than before. Whether the matter of which the image was made was apt to break or no, so it was that the head and hands were *cut off upon the threshold,* so that nothing remained but the stump, or, as the margin reads it, *the fishy part of* Dagon; for (as many learned men conjecture) the upper part of this image was in a human shape, the lower in the shape of a fish, as mermaids are painted. Such strong delusions were idolaters given up to, so vain were they in their imaginations, and so wretchedly darkened were their foolish hearts, as to worship the images, not only of creatures, but of nonentities, the mere figments of fancy. Well, the misshapen monster is by this fall made to appear, (1.) Very ridiculous, and worthy to be despised. A pretty figure Dagon made now, when the fall had anatomized him, and shown how the human part and the fishy part were artificially put together, which perhaps the ignorant devotees had been made to believe was done by miracle! (2.) Very impotent, and unworthy to be prayed to or trusted in; for his losing his head and hands proved him utterly destitute both of wisdom and power, and for ever disabled either to advise or act for his worshippers. This they got by setting Dagon in his place again; they had better have let him alone when he was down. But those can speed no better that contend with God, and will set up that which he is throwing down, Mal. 1:4. God, by this, magnified his ark and made it honourable, when they vilified and made it contemptible. He also showed what will be the end of all that which is set up in opposition to him. *Gird yourselves,* but *you shall be broken to pieces,* Isa. 8:9.

4. The threshold of Dagon's temple was ever looked upon as sacred, and not to be trodden on, *v.* 5. Some think that reference is had to this superstitious usage of Dagon's worshippers in Zep. 1:9, where God threatens to punish those who, in imitation of them, leaped over the threshold. One would have thought that this incontestable proof of the ark's victory over Dagon would convince the Philistines of their folly in worshipping such a senseless thing, and that henceforward they would pay their homage to the conqueror; but, instead of being reformed, they were hardened in their idolatry, and, as evil men and seducers are wont to do, became worse and worse, 2 Tim. 3:13. Instead of despising Dagon, for the threshold's sake that beheaded him, they were almost ready to worship the threshold because it was the block on which he was beheaded, and will never set their feet on that on which Dagon lost his head, shaming those who *tread under foot the blood of the covenant* and trample on things truly sacred. Yet this piece of superstition would help to perpetuate the remembrance of Dagon's disgrace; for, with the custom, the reason would be transmitted to posterity, and the children that should be born, enquiring why the threshold of Dagon's temple must not be trodden on, would be told that Dagon fell before the ark of the Lord. Thus God would have honour even out of their superstition. We are not told that they repaired the broken image; it is probable that they sent the art of God away first, and then they patched it up again, and set it in its place; for, it seems, they *cannot deliver their souls, nor say, Is there not a lie in our right hand?* Isa. 44:20.

Verses 6–12

The downfall of Dagon (if the people had made a good use of it, and had been brought by it to repent of their idolatries and to humble themselves before the God of Israel and seek his face) might have prevented the vengeance which God here proceeds to take upon them for the indignities done to his ark, and their obstinate adherence to their idol, in defiance of the plainest conviction. *Lord, when thy hand is lifted up they will not see, but they shall see,* Isa. 26:11. And, if they will not see the glory, they shall feel the weight, of God's hand, for so the Philistines did. *The hand of the Lord was heavy upon them* (*v.* 6), and he not only convinced them of their folly, but severely chastised their insolence. 1. *He destroyed them,* that is, cut many of them off by sudden death, those, we may suppose, that had most triumphed in the captivity of the ark. This is distinguished from the disease with which others were smitten. At Gath it is called *a great destruction* (*v.* 9), *a deadly destruction, v.* 11. And it is expressly said (*v.* 12) that those who were *smitten with the emerods were the men that died not* by the other *destruction,* which probably was the pestilence. They boasted of the great slaughter which their sword had made among the Israelites, *ch.* 4:10. But God lets them know that though he does not see fit to draw Israel's sword against them (they were unworthy to be employed), yet God had a sword of his own, with which he could make a no less dreadful execution among them, which if he whet, and *his hand take hold on judgment, he will render vengeance to his enemies,* Deu. 32:41, 42. Note, Those that contend with God, his ark, and his Israel, will infallibly be ruined at last. If conviction conquer not, destruction shall. 2. Those that were not destroyed *he smote with emerods* (*v.* 6), *in their secret parts* (*v.* 9), so grievous that (*v.* 12) the *cry went up to heaven,* that is, it might be heard a great way off, and perhaps, in the extremity of their pain and misery, they cried, not to Dagon, but to the God of heaven. The Psalmist, speaking of this sore judgment upon the Philistines, describes it thus: God *smote his enemies in the hinder parts,* and *put them to a perpetual reproach,* Ps. 78:66. The emerods (which we call the piles, and perhaps it was then a more grievous disease than it is now) is threatened among the judgments that would be the fruit of the curse, Deu. 28:27. It was both a painful and shameful disease; a vile disease for vile deserts. By it God would humble their pride, and put contempt upon them, as they had done upon his ark. The disease was epidemical, and perhaps, among them, a new disease. *Ashdod was smitten, and the coasts thereof,* the country round. For contempt of God's ordinances, *many are weak and sick, and many sleep,* 1 Co. 11:30. 3. The men of Ashdod were soon aware that it was *the hand of God, the God of Israel, v.* 7. Thus they were constrained to acknowledge his power and dominion, and confess themselves within his jurisdiction, and yet they would not renounce Dagon and submit to Jehovah; but rather, now that he touched their bone and their flesh, and in a tender part, they were ready to curse him to his face, and instead of making their peace with him, and courting the stay of his ark upon better terms, they desired to get clear of it, as the Gadarenes, who, when they had lost their swine, desired Christ to *depart out of their coasts.* Carnal hearts, when they smart under the judgments of God, would rather, if it were possible, put him far from them than enter into covenant and communion with him, and make him their friend. Thus the men of Ashdod resolve, *The ark of the God of Israel shall not abide with us.* 4. It is resolved to change the place of its imprisonment. A great council was called, and the question proposed to all the lords was, "What shall be we with the ark?" And at last it was agreed that it should be carried to Gath, *v.* 8. Some superstitious conceit they had that the fault was in the place, and that the ark would be better pleased with another lodging, further off from Dagon's temple; and therefore, instead of returning it, as they should have done, to its own place, they contrive to send it to another place. *Gath* is pitched upon, a place famed for a race of giants, but their strength and stature are no fence against the pestilence and the emerods: the men of that city were smitten, *both great and small* (*v.* 9), both dwarfs and giants, all alike to God's judgments; none so great as to over-top them, none so small as to be over-looked by them. 5. They were all at last weary of the ark, and very willing to get rid of it. It was sent from Gath to Ekron, and, coming by order of council, the Ekronites could not refuse it, but were much exasperated against their great men for sending them such a fatal present (*v.* 10): *They have sent it to us to slay us and our people.* The ark had the tables of the law in it; and nothing more welcome to faithful Israelites than the word of God (to them it is *a savour of life unto life*), but to uncircumcised Philistines, that persist in enmity to God, nothing more dreadful nor unwelcome: to them it is *a savour of death unto death.* A general assembly is instantly called, to advise about *sending the ark again to its place, v.* 11. While they are consulting about it, the hand of God is doing execution; and their contrivances to evade the judgment do but spread it. Many drop down dead among them. Many more are raging ill of the emerods, *v.* 12. What shall they do? Their triumphs in the captivity of the ark are soon turned into lamentations, and they are as eager to quit it as ever they had been to seize it. Note, God can easily make Jerusalem a burdensome stone to all that heave at it, Zec. 12:3. Those that fight against God will soon have enough of it, and, first or last, will be made to know that none ever hardened their hearts against him and prospered. The wealth that is got by fraud and injustice, especially that which is got by sacrilege and robbing God, though swallowed greedily, and rolled under the tongue as a sweet morsel, must be vomited up again; for, till it be, the sinner shall not *feel quietness in his belly,* Job 20:15–20.

CHAPTER 6

In this chapter we have the return of the ark to the land of Israel, whither we are now gladly to attend it, and observe, I. How the Philistines dismissed it, by the advice of their priests (*v.* 1–11), with rich presents to the God of Israel, to make an atonement for their sin (*v.* 3–5), and yet with a project to bring it back, unless Providence directed the kine, contrary to their inclination, to go to the land of Israel (*v.* 8, 9). II. How the Israelites entertained it. 1. With great joy and sacrifices of praise (*v.* 12–18). 2. With an over-bold curiosity to look into it, for which many of them were struck dead, the terror of which moved them to send it forward to another city (*v.* 19–21).

Verses 1–9

The first words of the chapter tell us how long the captivity of the ark continued — it was *in the country of the Philistines seven months. In the field of the Philistines* (so it is in the original), from which some gather that, having tried it in all their cities, and found it a plague to the inhabitants of each, at length they sent it into the open fields, upon which mice sprang up out of the ground in great multitudes, and destroyed the corn which was now nearly ripe and marred the land. With that judgment they were plagued (*v.* 5), and yet it is not mentioned in the foregoing chapter; so God let them know that wherever they carried the ark, so long as they carried it captive, they should find it a curse to them. *Cursed shalt thou be in the city, and cursed in the field,* Deu. 28:16. But, most take it to signify, as we render it, *The country of the Philistines.* Now, 1. Seven months Israel was punished with the absence of the ark, that special token of God's presence. How bare did the tabernacle look without it! How was the holy city now a desolation, and the holy land a wilderness! A melancholy time no doubt it was to the good people among them, particularly to Samuel; but they had this to comfort themselves with, as we have in the like distress when we are deprived of the comfort of public ordinances, that, wherever the ark is, *the Lord is in his holy temple, the Lord's throne is in heaven,* and by faith and prayer we may have access with boldness to him there. We may have God nigh unto us when the ark is at a distance. 2. Seven months the Philistines were punished with the presence of the ark; so long it was a plague to them, because they would not send it home sooner. Note, Sinners lengthen out their own miseries by obstinately refusing to part with their sins. Egypt's plagues would have been fewer than ten if Pharaoh's heart had not been hardened not to let the people go. But at length it is determined that the ark must be sent back; there is no remedy, they are undone if they detain it.

I. The priests and the diviners are consulted about it, *v.* 2. They were supposed to be best acquainted both with the rules of wisdom and with the rites of worship and atonement. And the Israelites being their neighbours, and famed above all people for the institutions of their religion, they had no doubt the curiosity to acquaint themselves with their laws and usages; and therefore it was proper to ask them, *What shall we do to the ark of Jehovah?* All nations have had a regard to their priests, as the men whose lips keep knowledge. Had the Philistines diviners? We have divines, of whom we should enquire wherewith we shall *come before the Lord* and *bow ourselves before the most high God.*

II. They give their advice very fully, and seem to be very unanimous in it. It was a wonder they did not, as friends to their country, give it, *ex officio — officially,* before they were asked. 1. They urge it upon them that it was absolutely necessary to send the ark back, from the example of Pharaoh and the Egyptians, *v.* 6. Some, it may be, were loth to yield, and were willing to try it out with the ark awhile longer, and to them they apply themselves: *Wherefore do you harden your hearts, as the Egyptians and Pharaoh did?* It seems they were well acquainted with the Mosaic history, and could cite precedents out of it. This good use we should make of the remaining records of God's judgments upon obstinate sinners, we should by them be warned not to harden our hearts as they did. It is much cheaper to learn by other people's experience than by our own. The Egyptians were forced at last to let Israel go; therefore let the Philistines yield in time to let the ark go. 2. They advise that, when they sent it back, they should send a trespass-offering with it, *v.* 3. Whatever the gods of other nations were, they knew the God of Israel was a jealous God, and how strict he was in his demands of sin-offerings and trespass-offerings from his own people; and therefore, since they found how highly he resented the affront of holding his ark captive, those with whom he had such a quarrel must *in any wise return him a trespass-offering,* and they could not expect to be healed upon any other terms. Injured justice demands satisfaction. So far natural light instructed men. But when they began to contrive what that satisfaction should be, they became wretchedly vain in their imaginations. But those who by wilful sin have imprisoned the truth in unrighteousness, as the Philistines did the ark (Rom. 1:18), may conclude that there is no making their peace with him whom they have thus injured but by a sin-offering; and we know but one that can take away sin. 3. They direct that this trespass-offering should be an acknowledgement of the punishment of their iniquity, by which they might take shame to themselves as conquered and yielding, and guilty before God, and might *give glory to the God of Israel* as their mighty conqueror and most just avenger, *v.* 5. They must make images of the *emerods,* that is, of the swellings and sores with which they had been afflicted, so making the reproach of that shameful disease perpetual by their own act and deed (Ps. 78:66), also images of the *mice that had marred the land,* owning thereby the almighty power of the God of Israel, who could chastise and humble them, even in the day of their triumph, by such small and despicable animals. These images must be made of gold, the most precious metal, to intimate that they would gladly purchase their peace with the God of Israel at any rate, and would not think it bought too dearly with gold, *with much fine gold.* The *golden emerods* must be, in number, five, according to the *number of the lords,* who, it is likely, were all afflicted with them, and were content thus to own it; it was advised that the *golden mice* should be five too,

but, because the whole country was infested with them, it should seem, upon second thoughts, they sent more of them, *according to the number both of the fenced cities and of the country villages, v.* 18. Their priests reminded them that *one plague was on them all;* they could not blame one another, for they were all guilty, which they were plainly told by being all plagued. Their proposal to offer a trespass-offering for their offence was conformable enough to divine revelation at that time; but to send such things as these for trespass-offerings was very foreign, and showed them grossly ignorant of the methods of reconciliation appointed by the law of Moses; for there it appears all along that it is blood, and not gold, that makes atonement for the soul. 4. They encourage them to hope that hereby they would take an effectual course to get rid of the plague: *You shall be healed, v.* 3. For, it seems, the disease obstinately resisted all the methods of cure their physicians had prescribed. "Let them therefore send back the ark, and then," say they, *"It shall be known to you why his hand is not removed from you,* that is, by this it will appear whether it is for your detaining the ark that you are thus plagued; for, if it be, upon your delivering it up the plague will cease." God has sometimes put his people upon making such a trial, whether their reformation would not be their relief. *Prove me now herewith, saith the Lord of hosts,* Mal. 3:10; Hag. 2:18, 19. Yet they speak doubtfully (*v.* 5): *Peradventure he will lighten his hand from off you;* as if now they began to think that the judgment might come from God's hand, and yet not be removed immediately upon the restitution of the ark; however that was the likeliest way to obtain mercy. Take away the cause and the effect will cease. 5. Yet they put them in a way to make a further trial whether it was the hand of the God of Israel that had smitten them with these plagues or no. They must, in honour of the ark, put it on a new cart or carriage, to be drawn by two milch-cows, that had calves daily sucking them (*v.* 7), unused to draw, and inclined to home, both for the sake of the crib where they were fed and of the calves they nourished, and, besides, altogether unacquainted with the road that led towards the land of Israel. They must have no one to lead or drive them, but must take their own way, which, in all reason, one might expect, would be home again; and yet, unless the God of Israel, after all the other miracles he has wrought, will work one more, and by an invisible power lead these cows, contrary to their natural instinct and inclination, to the land of Israel, and particularly to Beth-shemesh, they will retract their former opinion, and will believe it was not the hand of God that smote them, but it was a chance that *happened to them, v.* 8, 9. Thus did God suffer himself to be tempted and prescribed to, after he had been otherwise affronted, by these uncircumcised Philistines. Would they have been content that the honour of Dagon, their god, should be put upon such an issue as this? See how willing bad men are to shift off their convictions of the hand of God upon them, and to believe, when they are in trouble, that it is *a chance that happens to them;* and, if so, the rod has no voice which they are concerned to hear or heed.

Verses 10–18

We are here told,

I. How the Philistines dismissed the ark, *v.* 10, 11. They were made as glad to part with it as ever they had been to take it. As God had fetched Israel out of the house of bondage, so now he fetched the ark out of its captivity, in such a manner as that *Egypt was glad when they departed,* Ps. 105:38. 1. They received no money or price for the ransom of it, as they hoped to do, even beyond a king's ransom. Thus it is prophesied of Cyrus (Isa. 45:13), *He shall let go my captives, not for price nor reward.* Nay, 2. They gave jewels of gold, as the Egyptians did to the Israelites, to be rid of it. Thus the ark that was carried into the land of the Philistines, a trophy of their victory, carried back with it trophies of its own, and lasting monuments of the disgrace of the Philistines. Note, God will be no loser in his glory, at last, by the successes of the church's enemies against his ark, but will get himself honour from those that seek to do dishonour to him.

II. How the kine brought it to the land of Israel, *v.* 12. They *took the straight way to Beth-shemesh,* the next city of the land of Israel, and a priests' city, *and turned not*

aside. This was a wonderful instance of the power of God over the brute-creatures, and, all things considered, no less than a miracle, that cattle unaccustomed to the yoke should draw so even, so orderly, and still go forward, — that, without any driver, they should go from home, to which all tame creatures have a natural inclination, and from their own calves, to which they had a natural affection, — that, without any director, they should go the straight road to Beth-shemesh, a city eight or ten miles off, never miss the way, never turn aside into the fields to feed themselves, nor turn back home to feed their calves. They went on lowing for their young ones, by which it appeared that they had not forgotten them, but that nature was sensible of the grievance of going from them; the power of the God of nature therefore appeared so much the greater, in overruling one of the strongest instincts of nature. These two kine, says Dr. Lightfoot, knew their owner, their great owner (Isa. 1:3), whom Hophni and Phinehas knew not, to which I may add they brought home the ark to shame the stupidity of Israel, that made no attempt to fetch it home. God's providence is conversant about the motions even of brute-creatures, and serves its own purposes by them. The lords of the Philistines, with a suitable retinue no doubt, went after them, wondering at the power of the God of Israel; and thus those who thought to triumph over the ark were made to go like menial servants after it.

III. How it was welcomed to the land of Israel: *The men of Beth-shemesh were reaping their wheat-harvest, v.* 13. They were going on with their worldly business, and were in no care about the ark, made no enquiries what had become of it; if they had, it is likely they might have had private intelligence beforehand of its coming, and might have gone to meet it, and conduct it into their own border. But they were as careless as the people that *ceiled their own houses* and *let God's house lie waste.* Note, God will in his own time effect the deliverance of his church, not only though it be fought against by its enemies, but though it be neglected by its friends. Some observe that the returning ark found the men of Beth-shemesh, not idling or sporting in the streets of the city, but busy, reaping their corn in their fields, and well employed. Thus the tidings of the birth of Christ were brought to the shepherds when they were *keeping their flock by night.* The devil visits idle men with his temptations. God visits industrious men with his favours. The same invisible hand that directed the kine to the land of Israel brought them into the field of Joshua, and in that field they stood, some think for the owner's sake, on whom, being a very good man, they suppose God designed to put this honour. I rather think it was for the sake of the great stone in that field, which was convenient to put the ark upon, and which is spoken of, *v.* 14, 15, 18. Now, 1. When the reapers *saw the ark, they rejoiced* (*v.* 13); their joy for that was greater than the joy of harvest, and therefore they left their work to bid it welcome. When the Lord turned again the captivity of his ark they were *like men that dream; then was their mouth filled with laughter,* Ps. 126:1, 2. Though they had not zeal and courage enough to attempt the rescue or ransom of it, yet, when it did come, they bade it heartily welcome. Note, The return of the ark, and the revival of holy ordinances, after days of restraint and trouble, cannot but be matter of great joy to every faithful Israelite. 3. They offered up the kine for a burnt-offering, to the honour of God, and made use of the wood of the cart for fuel, *v.* 14. Probably the Philistines intended these, when they sent them, to be a part of their trespass-offering, to make atonement, *v.* 3, 7. However, the men of Beth-shemesh looked upon it as proper to make this use of them, because it was by no means fit that ever they should be put to any other use; never shall that cart carry any common thing that has once carried that sacred symbol of the divine presence: and the kine had been under such an immediate guidance of heaven that God had, as it were, already laid claim to them; they were servants to him, and therefore must be sacrifices to him, and no doubt were accepted, though females, whereas, in strictness, every burnt-offering was to be a male. 3. They deposited the ark, with a chest of jewels that the Philistines presented, upon the great stone in the open field, a cold lodging for the ark of the Lord and a very mean one; yet better so than in Dagon's temple, or in the hands of the Philistines. It is desirable to see the ark in its habitation in all the circumstances of solemnity and splendour; but better have it upon a great stone, and in the fields of the wood, than be without it. The intrinsic grandeur of instituted ordinances ought not to be diminished in our eyes by the meanness and poverty of the place where they are administered. As the burning of the cart and cows that brought home the ark might be construed to signify their hopes that it should never be carried away again out of the land of Israel, so the setting of it upon a great stone might signify their hopes that it should be established again upon a firm foundation. The church is built upon a rock. 4. They offered the sacrifices of thanksgiving to God, some think upon the great stone, more probably upon an altar of earth made for the purpose, *v.* 15. And, the case being extraordinary, the law for offering at the altar in the court of the tabernacle was dispensed with, and the more easily because Shiloh was now dismantled; God himself had forsaken it, and the ark, which was its chief glory, they had with them here. Beth-shemesh, though it lay within the lot of the tribe of Dan, yet belonged to Judah, so that this accidental bringing of the ark hither was an indication of its designed settlement there, in process of time; for, when God *refused the tabernacle of Joseph, he chose the tribe of Judah,* Ps. 78:67, 68. It was one of those cities which were assigned out of the lot of Judah to the *sons of Aaron,* Jos. 21:16. Whither should the ark go but to a priests' city? And it was well they had those of that sacred order ready (for though they are here called *Levites, v.* 15, yet it should seem they were priests) both to take down the ark and to offer the sacrifices. 5. The lords of the Philistines returned to Ekron, much affected, we may suppose, with what they had seen of the glory of God and the zeal of the Israelites, and yet not reclaimed from the worship of Dagon; for how seldom *has a nation changed its gods, though they were no gods!* Jer. 2:11. Though they cannot but think the God of Israel *glorious in holiness and fearful in praises,* yet they are resolved they will think Baal-zebub, the god of Ekron, at least as good as he, and to him they will cleave because he is theirs. 6. Notice is taken of the continuance of the great stone in the same place; there it is *unto this day* (*v.* 18), because it remained a lasting memorial of this great event, and served to support the traditional history by which it was transmitted to posterity. The fathers would say to the children, "This is the stone upon which the ark of God was set when it came out of the Philistines' hands, a thing never to be forgotten."

Verses 19–21

Here is, 1. The sin of the men of Beth-shemesh: *They looked into the ark of the Lord, v.* 19. Every Israelite had heard great talk of the ark, and had been possessed with a profound veneration for it; but they had been told that it was lodged within a veil, and even the high priest himself might not look upon it but once a year, and then through a cloud of incense. Perhaps this made many say (as we are apt to covet that which is forbidden) what a great deal they would give for a sight of it. Some of these Beth-shemites, we may suppose, for that reason, *rejoiced to see the ark* (*v.* 13) more than for the sake of the public. Yet this did not content them; they might see it, but they would go further, they would take off the covering, which it is likely was nailed or screwed on, and look into it, under pretence of seeing whether the Philistines had not taken the two tables out of it or some way damaged them, but really to gratify a sinful curiosity of their own, which intruded into those things that God had thought fit to conceal from them. Note, It is a great affront to God for vain men to pry into and meddle with the secret things which belong not to them, Deu. 29:29; Col. 2:18. We were all ruined by an ambition of forbidden knowledge. That which made this looking into the ark a great sin was that it proceeded from a very low and mean opinion of the ark. The familiarity they had with it upon this occasion bred contempt and irreverence. Perhaps they presumed upon their being priests; but the dignity of the ministerial office will be so far from excusing that it will aggravate a careless and irreverent treatment of holy things. They should, by their example, have taught others to keep their distance and look upon the ark with a holy awe. Perhaps they presumed upon the kind entertainment they had given the ark, and the sacrifices they had now offered to welcome it home with, for which they thought the ark was indebted to them, and they might be allowed to repay themselves with the satisfaction of looking into it. But let no man think that his service done for God will justify him in any instance of disrespect or irreverence towards the things of God. Or it may be they presumed upon the present mean circumstances the ark was in, newly come out of captivity, and unsettled; now that it stood upon a cold stone, they thought they might make free with it; they should never have such another opportunity of being familiar with it. It is an offence to God if we think meanly of his ordinances because of the meanness of the manner of their administration. Had they looked with an understanding eye upon the ark, and not judged purely by outward appearance, they would have thought that the ark never shone with greater majesty than it did not. It had triumphed over the Philistines, and come out of its house of bondage (like Christ out of the grave) by its own power; had they considered this, they would not have looked into it thus, as a common chest. 2. Their punishment for this sin: *He smote the men of Beth-shemesh, many of them, with a great slaughter.* How jealous is God for the honour of his ark! He will not suffer it to be profaned. *Be not deceived, God is not mocked.* Those that will not fear his goodness, and reverently use the tokens of his grace, shall be made to feel his justice, and sink under the tokens of his displeasure. Those that pry into what is forbidden, and come too near to holy fire, will find it is at their peril. *He smote* 50,070 *men.* This account of the numbers smitten is expressed in a very unusual manner in the original, which, besides the improbability that there should be so many guilty and so many slain, occasions many learned men to question whether we take the matter aright. In the original it is, *He smote in* (or among) *the people three score and ten men, fifty thousand men.* The Syriac and Arabic read it, *five thousand and seventy men.* The Chaldee reads it, *seventy men of the elders, and fifty thousand of the common people. Seventy men as valuable as* 50,000, so some, because they were priests. Some think the seventy men were the Beth-shemites that were slain for looking into the ark, and the 50,000 were those that were slain by the ark, in the land of the Philistines. *He smote seventy men,* that is, *fifty out of a thousand,* which was one in twenty, a half decimation; so some understand it. The Septuagint read it much as we do, *he smote seventy men, and fifty thousand men.* Josephus says only seventy were smitten. 3. The terror that was struck upon the men of Beth-shemesh by this severe stroke. They said, as well they might, *Who is able to stand before this holy Lord God? v.* 20. Some think this expresses their murmuring against God, as if he had dealt hardly and unjustly with them. Instead of quarrelling with themselves and their own sins, they quarrelled with God and his judgments; as *David was displeased,* in a case not much dissimilar, 2 Sa. 6:8, 9. I rather think it intimates their awful and reverent adoration of God, as the Lord God, as a holy Lord God, and as a God before whom none is able to stand. This they infer from that tremendous judgment, "Who is able to stand before the God of the ark?" To stand before God to worship him (blessed be his name) is not impossible; we are through Christ invited, encouraged, and enabled to do it, but to stand before God to contend with him we are not able. Who is able to stand before the throne of his immediate glory, and look full upon it? 1 Tim. 6:16. Who is able to stand before the tribunal of his enflexible justice, and make his part good there? Ps. 130:3; 143:2. Who is able to stand before the arm of his provoked power, and either resist or bear the strokes of it? Ps. 76:7. 4. Their desire, hereupon, to be rid of the ark. They asked, *To whom shall he go up from us? v.* 20. They should rather have asked, "How may we make our peace with him, and recover his favour?" Mic. 6:6, 7. But they begin to be as weary of the ark as the Philistines had been, whereas, if they had treated it with due reverence, who knows but it might have taken up its residence among them, and they had all been blessed for the ark's sake? But thus, when the word of God works with terror on sinners' consciences, they, instead of taking the blame and shame to themselves, quarrel with the word, and put it from them, Jer. 6:10. They sent messengers to the elders of Kirjath-jearim, a strong city further up in the country, and begged of them to come and fetch the ark up thither, *v.* 21. They durst not touch it to bring it thither themselves, but stood aloof from it as a dangerous thing. Thus do foolish men run from one extreme to the other, from presumptuous boldness to slavish shyness. Kirjath-jearim, that is, *the city of woods,* belonged to Judah, Jos. 15:9, 60. It lay in the way from Beth-shemesh to Shiloh, so that when they sent to them to fetch it, we may suppose, they intended that the elders of Shiloh should fetch it thence, but God intended otherwise. Thus was it sent from town to town, and no care taken of it by the public, a sign that there was no king in Israel.

CHAPTER 7

In this chapter we have, I. The eclipsing of the glory of the ark, by its privacy in Kirjath-jearim for many years (*v.* 1, 2). II. The appearing of the glory of Samuel in his public services for the good of Israel, to whom he was raised up to be a judge, and he was the last that bore that character. This chapter gives us all the account we have of him when he was in the prime of his time; for what we had before was in his childhood (*ch.* 2 and 3); what we have of him after was in his old age (8:1). We have him here active, 1. In the reformation of Israel from their idolatry (*v.* 3, 4). 2. In the reviving of religion among them (*v.* 5, 6). 3. In praying for them against the invading Philistines (*v.* 7–9), over whom God, in answer to his prayer, gave them a glorious victory (*v.* 10, 11). 4. In erecting a thankful memorial of that victory (*v.* 12). 5. In the improvement of that victory (*v.* 13, 14). 6. In the administration of justice (*v.* 15–17). And these were the things for which God was preparing the designing him, in the early vouchsafements of his grace to him.

Verses 1–2

Here we must attend the ark to Kirjath-jearim, and then leave it there, to hear not a word more of it except once (*ch.* 14:18), till David fetched it thence, about forty years after, 1 Chr. 13:6.

I. We are very willing to attend it thither, for the men of Beth-shemesh have by their own folly made that a burden which might have been a blessing; and gladly would we see it among those to whom it will be a *savour of life unto life,* for in every place where it has been of late it has been a *savour of death unto death.* Now,

1. The men of Kirjath-jearim cheerfully bring it among them, *v.* 1. *They came,* at the first word, *and fetched up the ark of the Lord.* Their neighbours the Beth-shemites, were not more glad to get rid of it than they were to receive it, knowing very well that what slaughter the ark had made at Beth-shemesh was not an act of arbitrary power, but of necessary justice, and those that suffered by it must blame themselves, not the ark; we may depend upon the word which God hath said (Jer. 25:6), *Provoke me not, and I will do you no hurt.* Note, The judgments of God on those who profane his ordinances should not make us afraid of the ordinances, but of profaning them and making an ill use of them.

2. They carefully provided for its decent entertainment among them, as a welcome guest, with true affection, and, as an honourable guest, with respect and reverence.

(1.) They provided a proper place to receive it. They had no public building to adorn with it, but they lodged it in the house of Abinadab, which stood upon the highest ground, and, probably, was the best house in their city; or perhaps the master of it was the most eminent man they had for piety, and best affected to the ark. The men of Beth-shemesh left it exposed upon a stone in the open field, and, though it was a city of priests, none of them received it into his house; but the men of Kirjath-jearim, though common Israelites, gave it house-room, and no doubt the best-furnished room in the house to which it was brought. Note, [1.] God will find out a resting-place for his ark; if some thrust it from them, yet the hearts of others shall be inclined to receive it. [2.] It is no new thing for God's ark to be thrust into a private house. Christ and his apostles preached from house to house when they could not have public places at command. [3.] Sometimes priests are shamed and out-done in religion by common Israelites.

(2.) They provided a proper person to attend it: *They sanctified Eleazar his son to keep it;* not the father, either because he was aged and infirm, or because he had the affairs of his house and family to attend, from which they would not take him off. But the son, who, it is probable, was a very pious devout young man, and zealously affected towards the best things. His business was to keep the ark, not only from being seized by malicious Philistines, but from being touched or looked into by too curious Israelites. He was to keep the room clean and decent in which the ark was, that, though it was in an obscure place, it might no look like a neglected thing, which no man looked after. It does not appear that this Eleazar was of the tribe of Levi, much less of the house of Aaron, nor was it needful that he should, for here was no altar either for sacrifice or incense, only we may suppose that some devout Israelites would come and pray before the ark, and those that did so he was there ready to attend and assist. For this purpose they sanctified him, that is, by his own consent, they obliged him to make this his business, and to give a constant attendance to it; they set him apart for it in the name of all their citizens. This was irregular, but was excusable because of the present distress. When the ark has but recently come out of captivity we cannot expect it to be on a sudden in its usual solemnity, but must take things as they are, and make the best of them.

II. Yet we are very loth to leave it here, wishing it well at Shiloh again, but that is made desolate (Jer. 7:14), or at least wishing it at Nob, or Gibeon, or wherever the tabernacle and the altars are; but, it seems, it must lie by the way for want of some public-spirited men to bring it to its proper place. 1. The time of its continuance here was long, very long, above forty years it lay in these fields of the wood, a remote, obscure, private place, unfrequented and almost unregarded (*v.* 2): *The time that the ark abode in Kirjath-jearim was long,* even till David fetched it thence. It was very strange that all the time that Samuel governed the ark was never brought to its place in the holy of holies, an evidence of the decay of holy zeal among them. God suffered it to be so, to punish them for their neglect of the ark when it was in its place and to show that the great stress which the institution laid upon the ark was but typical of Christ, and those *good things to come which cannot be moved,* Heb. 9:23; 12:27. It was a just reproach to the priests that one not of their order was sanctified to keep the ark. 2. Twenty years of this time had passed before the house of Israel was sensible of the want of the ark. The Septuagint read it somewhat more clearly than we do; *and it was twenty years, and* (that is, when) *the whole house of Israel looked up again after the Lord.* So long the ark remained in obscurity, and the Israelites were not sensible of the inconvenience, nor ever made any enquiry after it, what has become of it; though, while it was absent from the tabernacle, the token of God's special presence was wanting, nor could they keep the day of atonement as it should be kept. They were content with the altars without the ark; so easily can formal professors rest satisfied in a round of external performances, without any tokens of God's presence or acceptance. But at length they bethought themselves, and began to lament after the lord, stirred up to it, it is probable, by the preaching of Samuel, with which an extraordinary working of the Spirit of God set in. A general disposition to repentance and reformation now appears throughout all Israel, and they begin to *look unto him whom they had slighted, and to mourn,* Zec. 12:10. Dr. Lightfoot thinks this was a matter and time as remarkable as almost any we read of in scripture; and that the great conversion, Acts 2 and 3, is the only parallel to it. Note, (1.) Those that know how to value God's ordinances cannot but reckon it a very lamentable thing to want them. (2.) True repentance and conversion begin in lamenting after the Lord; we must be sensible that by sin we have provoked him to withdraw and are undone if we continue in a state of distance from him, and be restless till we have recovered his favour and obtained his gracious returns. It was better with the Israelites when they wanted the ark, and were lamenting after it, than when they had the ark, and were prying into it, or priding themselves in it. Better see people longing in the scarcity of the means of grace than loathing in the abundance of them.

Verses 3–6

We may well wonder where Samuel was and what he was doing all this while, for we have not had him so much as named till now, since *ch.* 4:1, not as if he were unconcerned, but his labours among his people are not mentioned till there appears the fruit of them. When he perceived that they began to *lament after the Lord* he struck while the iron was hot, and two things he endeavoured to do for them, as a faithful servant of God and a faithful friend to the Israel of God: —

I. He endeavoured to separate between them and their idols, for *there* reformation must begin. He *spoke to all the house of Israel* (*v.* 3), going, as it should seem, from place

to place, an itinerant preacher (for we find not that they were gathered together till *v.* 5), and wherever he came this was his exhortation, *"If you do indeed return to the Lord,* as you seem inclined to do, by your lamentations for your departure from him and his from you, then know, 1. That you must renounce and abandon your idols, *put away the strange gods,* for your God will admit no rival; put them away from you, each one from himself, nay, and put them *from among you,* do what you can, in your places, to rid them out of the country. Put away Baalim, the strange gods, and Ashtaroth, the strange goddesses," for such also they had. Or Ashtaroth is particularly named because it was the best-beloved idol, and that which they were most wedded to. Note, True repentance strikes at the darling sin, and will with a peculiar zeal and resolution put away that, the sin which most *easily besets us.* 2. "That you must make a solemn business of returning to God, and do it with a serious consideration and a stedfast resolution, for both are included in *preparing the heart,* directing, disposing, establishing, the heart unto the Lord. 3. That you must be wholly for God, for him and no other, *serve him only,* else you do not serve him at all so as to please him. 4. That this is the only way and a sure way to prosperity and deliverance. Take this course, and *he will deliver you out of the hand of the Philistines;* for it was because you forsook him and served other gods that he delivered you into their hands." This was the purport of Samuel's preaching, and it had a wonderfully good effect (*v.* 4): *They put away Baalim and Ashtaroth,* not only quitted the worship of them, but destroyed their images, demolished their altars, and quite abandoned them. *What have we to do any more with idols?* Hos. 14:8; Isa. 30:22.

II. He endeavoured to engage them for ever to God and his service. Now that he had them in a good mind he did all he could to keep them in it.

1. He summons all Israel, at least by their elders, as their representatives, to meet him at Mizpeh (*v.* 5), and there he promises to pray for them. And it was worth while for them to come from the remotest part of the country to join with Samuel in seeking God's favour. Note, Ministers should pray for those to whom they preach, that God by his grace would make the preaching effectual. And, when we come together in religious assemblies, we must remember that it is as much our business there to join in public prayers as it is to hear a sermon. He would pray for them that, by the grace of God, they might be parted from their idols, and that then, by the providence of God, they might be delivered from the Philistines. Ministers would profit their people more if they did but pray more for them.

2. They obey his summons, and not only come to the meeting, but conform to the intentions of it, and appear there very well disposed, *v.* 6.

(1.) *They drew water and poured it out before the Lord,* signifying, [1.] Their humiliation and contrition for sin, owning themselves as water spilt upon the ground, which cannot be gathered up again (2 Sa. 14:14), so mean, so miserable, before God, Ps. 22:14. The Chaldee reads it, *They poured out their hearts in repentance before the Lord.* They wept rivers of tears, and sorrowed after a godly sort, for it was before the Lord and with an eye to him. [2.] Their earnest prayers and supplications to God for mercy. The soul is, in prayer, poured out before God, Ps. 62:8. [3.] Their universal reformation; they thus expressed their willingness to part with all their sins, and to retain no more of the relish or savour of them than the vessel does of the water that is poured out of it. They were free and full in their confession, and fixed in their resolution to cast away from them *all their transgressions.* Israel is now *baptized from their idols,* so Dr. Lightfoot. [4.] Some think it signifies their joy in the hope of God's mercy, which Samuel had assured them of. This ceremony was used with that signification at the feast of tabernacles, Jn. 7:37, 38, and see Isa. 12:3. Taking it in this sense, it must be read, *They drew water after they had fasted.* In the close of their humiliation they thus expressed their hope of pardon and reconciliation.

(2.) *They fasted,* abstained from food, afflicted their souls, so expressing repentance and exciting devotion.

(3.) They made a public confession: *We have sinned against the Lord,* so giving glory to God and taking shame to themselves. And, if we thus confess our sins, we shall find our God *faithful and just to forgive us our sins.*

3. Samuel judged them at that time in Mizpeh, that is, he assured them, in God's name, of the pardon of their sins, upon their repentance, and that God was reconciled to them. It was a judgment of absolution. Or he received informations against those that did not leave their idols, and proceeded against them according to law. Those that would not judge themselves he judged. Or now he settled courts of justice among them, and appointed the terms and circuits which he observed afterwards, *v.* 16. Now he set those wheels a-going; and, whereas he began to act as a magistrate, to prevent their relapsing into those sins which now they seemed to have renounced.

Verses 7–12

Here, I. The Philistines invade Israel (*v.* 7), taking umbrage from that general meeting for repentance and prayer as if it had been a rendezvous for war, and, if so, they thought it prudent to keep the war out of their own country. They had no just cause for this suspicion; but those that seek to do mischief to others will be forward to imagine that others design mischief to them. Now see here, 1. How evil sometimes seems to come out of good. The religious meeting of the Israelites at Mizpeh brought trouble upon them from the Philistines, which perhaps tempted them to wish they had staid at home and to blame Samuel for calling them together. But we may be in God's way and yet meet with distress; nay, when sinners begin to repent and reform, they must expect that Satan will muster all his force against them, and set his instruments on work to the utmost to oppose and discourage them. But, 2. How good is, at length, brought out of that evil. Israel could never be threatened more seasonably than at this time, when they were repenting and praying, nor could they have been better prepared to receive the enemy; nor could the Philistines have acted more impolitely for themselves than to make war upon Israel at this time, when they were making their peace with God. But God permitted them to do it, that he might have an opportunity immediately of crowning his people's reformation with tokens of his favour, and of confirming the words of his messenger, who had assured them that if they repented God would *deliver them out of the hand of the Philistines.* Thus he makes man's wrath to praise him, and serves the purposes of his grace to his people even by the malicious designs of their enemies against them, Mic. 4:11, 12.

II. Israel cleaves closely to Samuel, as their best friend, under God, in this distress; though he was no military man, nor ever celebrated as a mighty man of valour, yet, being afraid of the Philistines, for whom they thought themselves an unequal match, they engaged Samuel's prayers for them: *Cease not to cry unto the Lord our God for us, v.* 8. They were here unarmed, unprepared for war, come together to fast and pray, not to fight; prayers and tears therefore being all the weapons many of them are now furnished with, to these they have recourse. And, knowing Samuel to have a great interest in heaven, they earnestly beg of him to improve it for them. They had reason to expect it, because he had promised to *pray for them* (*v.* 5), had promised them deliverance from the Philistines (*v.* 3), and they had been observant of him in all that which he had spoken to them from the Lord. Thus those who sincerely submit to Christ, as their lawgiver and judge, need not doubt of their interest in his intercession. They were very solicitous that Samuel should not cease to pray for them: what military preparations were to be made they would undertake them, but let him continue instant in prayer, perhaps remembering that when Moses did but let down his hand ever so little Amalek prevailed. O what a comfort is it to all believers that our great intercessor above never ceases, is never silent, for he *always appears in the presence of God for us!*

III. Samuel intercedes with God for them, and does it *by sacrifice, v.* 9. He took a sucking lamb, and offered it for a *burnt-offering, a whole burnt-offering, to the Lord,* and, while the sacrifice was in burning, with the smoke of it his prayers ascended up to heaven for Israel. Observe, 1. He made intercession with a sacrifice. Christ intercedes in the virtue of his satisfaction, and in all our prayers we must have an eye to his great oblation, depending upon that for audience and acceptance. Samuel's sacrifice without his prayer would have been an empty shadow, his prayer without the sacrifice would not have been so prevalent, but both together teach us what great things we may expect from God in answer to those prayers which are made with faith in Christ's sacrifice. 2. It was a burnt-offering, which was offered purely for the glory of God, so intimating that the great plea he relied on in his prayer was taken from the honour of God. "Lord, help thy people now for thy name's sake." When we endeavour to give glory to God we may hope he will, in answer to our prayers, work for his own glory. 3. It was but one sucking lamb that he offered; for it is the integrity and intention of the heart that God looks at, more than the bulk or number of the offerings. This one lamb (typifying the Lamb of God) was more acceptable than thousands of rams or bullocks would have been without faith and prayer. Samuel was no priest, but he was a Levite and a prophet; the case was extraordinary, and what he did was by special direction, and therefore was accepted of God. And justly was this reproach put upon the priests because they had corrupted themselves.

IV. God gave a gracious answer to Samuel's prayer (*v.* 9): *The Lord heard him.* He was himself a *Samuel, asked of God,* and many a Samuel, many a mercy in answer to prayer, God gave him. Sons of prayer should be famous for praying, as *Samuel was among those that call upon his name,* Ps. 99:6. The answer was a real answer: the Philistines were discomfited (*v.* 10, 11), totally routed, and that in such a manner as highly magnified the prayer of Samuel, the power of God, and the valour of Israel. 1. The prayer of Samuel was honoured; for at the very time when he was offering up his sacrifice, and his prayer with it, the battle began, and turned immediately against the Philistines. Thus *while he was yet speaking God heard,* and answered in thunder, Isa. 65:24. God showed that it was Samuel's prayer and sacrifice that he had respect to, and hereby let Israel know that as in a former engagement with the Philistines he had justly chastised their presumptuous confidence in the presence of the ark, on the shoulders of two profane priests, so now he graciously accepted their humble dependence upon the prayer of faith from the mouth and heart of a pious prophet. 2. The power of God was greatly honoured; for he took the work into his own hand, and discomfited them, not with great hail-stones, which would kill them (as Jos. 10:11), but with a great thunder, which frightened them and put them into such terror and consternation that they fainted away, and became a very easy prey to the sword of Israel, before whom, being thus confounded, they were smitten. Josephus adds that the earth quaked under them when first they made the onset and in many places opened and swallowed them up, and that, besides the terror of the thunder, their faces and hands were burnt with lightning, which obliged them to shift for themselves by flight. And, being thus driven to their heels by the immediate hand of God (whom they feared not so much as they had feared his ark, *ch.* 4:7), then, 3. Honour was put upon the hosts of Israel; they were made use of for the completing of the victory, and had the pleasure of triumphing over their oppressors: *They pursued the Philistines, and smote them.* How soon did they find the benefit of their repentance, and reformation, and return to God! Now that they have thus engaged him for them none of their enemies can stand before them.

V. Samuel erected a thankful memorial of this victory, to the glory of God and for the encouragement of Israel, *v.* 12. He set up an *Eben-ezer, the stone of help.* If ever the people's hard hearts should lose the impressions of this providence, this stone would either revive the remembrance of it, and make them thankful, or remain a standing witness against them for their unthankfulness. 1. The place where this memorial was set up was the same where, twenty years before, the Israelites were smitten before the Philistines, for that was beside Eben-ezer, *ch.* 4:1. The sin which procured that defeat formerly being pardoned upon their repentance, the pardon was sealed by this glorious victory in the very same place where they then suffered loss; see Hos. 1:10. 2. Samuel himself took care to set up this monument. He had been instrumental by prayer to obtain the mercy, and therefore he thought himself in a special manner obliged to make this grateful acknowledgement of it. 3. The reason he gives for the name is, *Hitherto the Lord hath helped us,* in which he speaks thankfully of what was past, giving the glory of the victory to God only, who had added this to all his former favours; and yet he speaks somewhat doubtfully for the future: "Hitherto things have done well, but what God may yet do with us we know not, *that* we refer to him; but let us praise him for what he has done." Note, The beginnings of mercy and deliverance are to be acknowledged by us with thankfulness so far as they go, though they be not completely finished, nay, though the issue seem uncertain. *Having obtained help from God, I continue hitherto,* says blessed Paul, Acts 26:22.

Verses 13–17

We have here a short account of the further good services that Samuel did to Israel. Having parted them from their idols, and brought them home to their God, he had put them into a capacity of receiving further benefits by his ministry. Having prevailed in that, he becomes, in other instances, a great blessing to them; yet, writing it himself, he is brief in the relation. We are not told here, but it appears (2 Chr. 35:18) that in the days of Samuel the prophet the people of Israel kept the ordinance of the passover with more than ordinary devotion, notwithstanding the distance of the ark and the desolations of Shiloh. Many good offices, no doubt, he did for Israel, but here we are only told how instrumental he was, 1. In securing the public peace (*v.* 13): *"In his days the Philistines came no more into the coast of Israel,* made no inroads or incursions upon them; they perceived that God now fought for Israel and that his hand was against the Philistines, and this kept them in awe, and restrained the remainder of their wrath." Samuel was a protector and deliverer to Israel, not by dint of sword, as Gideon, nor by strength of arm, as Samson, but by the power of prayer to God and carrying on a work of reformation among the people. Religion and piety are the best securities of a nation. 2. In recovering the public rights, *v.* 14. By his influence Israel had the courage to demand the cities which the Philistines had unjustly taken from them and had long detained; and the Philistines, not daring to contend with one that had so great an interest in heaven, tamely yielded to the demand, and restored (some think) even Ekron and Gath, two of the capital cities, though afterwards they retook them; others think some small towns that lay between Ekron and Gath, which were forced out of the Philistines' hands. This they got by their reformation and religion, they got ground of their enemies and got forward in their affairs. It is added, *There was peace between Israel and the Amorites,* that is, the Canaanites, the remains of the natives. Not that Israel made any league with them, but they were quiet, and not so mischievous to Israel as they had sometimes been. Thus *when a man's ways please the Lord he maketh even his enemies to be at peace with him* and give him no disturbance, Prov. 16:7. 3. In administering public justice (*v.* 15, 16): *He judged Israel;* as a prophet he taught them their duty and reproved them for their sins, which is called *judging,* Eze. 20:4; 22:2. Moses judged Israel when he *made them know the statutes of God and his laws* (Ex. 18:16); and thus Samuel judged them to the last, even after Saul was made king; so he promised them then, when Saul was inaugurated (*ch.* 12:23), *I will* not cease to *teach you the good and the right way.* As a magistrate, he received appeals from the inferior courts and gave judgment upon them, tried causes and determined them, tried prisoners and acquitted or condemned them, according to the law. This he did all his days, till he grew old and past service, and resigned to Saul; and afterwards he exercised authority when application was made to him; nay, he judged even Agag, and Saul himself. But when he was in his prime he rode the circuit, for the convenience of the country, at least of that part of it which lay most under his influence. He kept courts at Beth-el, Gilgal, and Mizpeh, all in the tribe of Benjamin; but his constant residence was at Ramah, his father's city, and there he judged Israel, thither they resorted to him from all parts with their complaints, *v.* 17. 4. In keeping up the public exercises of religion; for there, where he lived, he built an altar to the Lord, not in contempt of the altar that was at Nob, or Gibeon, or wherever the tabernacle was; but divine justice having laid Sholoh waste, and no other place being yet chosen for them to bring their offerings to (Deu. 12:11), he looked upon the law which confined them to one place to be for the present suspended, and therefore, being a prophet, and under divine direction, he did as the patriarchs did, he built an altar where he lived, both for the use of his own family and for the good of the country that resorted to it. Great men should use their wealth, power, and interest, for the keeping up of religion in the places where they live.

CHAPTER 8

Things went so very well with Israel, in the chapter before, under Samuel's administration, that, methinks, it is a pity to find him so quickly, as we do in this chapter, old, and going off, and things working towards a revolution. But so it is; Israel's good days seldom continue long. We have here, I. Samuel decaying (*v.* 1). II. His sons degenerating (*v.* 2, 3). III. Israel discontented with the present government and anxious to see a change. For 1. They petition Samuel to set a king over them (*v.* 4, 5). 2. Samuel brings the matter to God (*v.* 6). 3. God directs him what answer to give them, by way of reproof (*v.* 7, 8), and by way of remonstrance, setting forth the consequences of a change of the government, and how uneasy they would soon be under it (*v.* 9–18). 4. They insist upon their petition (*v.* 19, 20). 5. Samuel promises them, from God, that they shall shortly be gratified (*v.* 21, 22). Thus hard is it for people to know when they are well off.

Verses 1–3

Two sad things we find here, but not strange things: — 1. A good and useful man growing old and unfit for service (*v.* 1): *Samuel was old,* and could not judge Israel, as he had done. He is not reckoned to be past sixty years of age now, perhaps not so much; but he was a man betimes, was full of thoughts and cared when he was a child, which perhaps hastened the infirmities of age upon him. The fruits that are the first ripe keep the worst. He had spent his strength and spirits in the fatigue of public business, and now, if he think to shake himself as at other times, he finds he is mistaken: old age has cut his hair. Those that are in the prime of their time ought to be busy in doing the work of life: for, as they go into years, they will find themselves less disposed to it and less able for it. 2. The children of a good man turning aside, and not treading in his steps. Samuel had given his sons so good an education, and they had given him such good hopes of their doing well, and gained such a reputation in Israel, that he made them judges, assistants to him awhile, and afterwards deputies under him at Beersheeba, which lay remote from Ramah, *v.* 2. Probably the southern countries petitioned for their residence there, that they might not be necessitated to travel far with their causes. We have reason to think that Samuel gave them their commissions, not because they were his sons (he had no ambition to entail the government upon his family, any more than Gideon had), but because, for aught that yet appeared, they were men very fit for the trust; and none so proper to ease the aged judge, and take some of the burden off him, as *(coeteris paribus — other things being equal)* his own sons, who no doubt were respected for their good father's sake, and, having such an advantage at setting out, might soon have been great if they had but been good. But, alas! *his sons walked not in his ways* (*v.* 3), and, when their character was the reverse of his, their relation to so good a man, which otherwise would have been their honour, was really their disgrace. *Degeneranti genus opprobrium — A good extraction is a reproach to him that degenerates from it.* Note, Those that have the most grace themselves cannot give grace to their children. It has often been the grief of good men to see their posterity, instead of treading in their steps, trampling upon them, and, as Job speaks, *marring their path.* Nay, many that have begun well, promised fair, and set out in the right path, so that their parents and friends have had great hopes of them, yet afterwards have turned aside to by-paths, and been the grief of those of whom they should have been the joy. When Samuel's sons were made judges, and settled at a distance form him, then they discovered themselves. Thus, (1.) Many that have been well educated, and have conducted themselves well while they were under their parents' eye, when they have gone abroad into the world and set up for themselves have proved bad. Let none therefore be secure either of themselves or theirs, but depend on divine grace. (2.) Many that have done well in a state of meanness and subjection have been spoiled by preferment and power. Honours change men's minds, and too often for the worse. It does not appear that Samuel's sons were so profane and vicious as Eli's sons; but, whatever they were in other respects, they were corrupt judges, they *turned aside after lucre,* after *the mammon of unrighteousness,* so the Chaldee reads it. Note, *The love of money is the root of all evil.* It is pernicious in any, but especially in judges. Samuel had taken no bribes (*ch.* 12:3), but his sons had, though, no doubt, he warned them against it when he made them judges; and then they perverted judgment. In determining controversies, they had an eye to the bribe, not to the law, and enquired who bid highest, not who had right on his side. It is sad with a people when the public justice that should do them right, being perverted, does them the greatest wrong.

Verses 4–22

We have here the starting of a matter perfectly new and surprising, which was the setting up of kingly government in Israel. Perhaps the thing had been often talked of among them by those that were given to change and affected that which looked great. But we do not find that it was ever till now publicly proposed and debated. Abimelech was little better than a titular king, though he is said to reign over Israel (Judges 9:22), and perhaps his fall had for a great while rendered the title of king odious in Israel, as that of Tarquinius did among the Romans; but, if it had, by this time the odium was worn off, and some bold steps are here taken towards so great a revolution as that amounted to. Here is,

I. The address of the elders to Samuel in this matter (*v.* 4, 5): They *gathered themselves together,* by common consent; and not in a riotous tumultuous manner, but with the respect due to his character, they came to him to his house as Ramah with their address, which contained,

1. A remonstrance of their grievances: in short, *Thou art old, and thy sons walk not in thy ways.* Many a fairer occasion that people had had to ask a king, when they were oppressed by their neighbours or embroiled at home for want of *a king in Israel,* but a small thing will serve factious spirits for a colour to desire a change. (1.) It was true that Samuel was old; but if that made him less able to ride the circuit, and sit long on the bench, yet it made him the more wise and experienced, and, upon that account, the fitter to rule. If he was old, had he not grown old in their service? And it was very unkind, ungrateful, nay, and unjust, to cast him off when he was old, who had spent his days in doing them good. God had saved his youth from being despicable (*ch.* 3:20), yet they make his old age so, which should have been counted worthy of double honour. If old people be upbraided with their infirmities, and laid aside for them, let them not think it strange; Samuel himself was so. (2.) It was true that his sons did not walk in his ways; the more was his grief, but they could not say it was his fault: he had not, like Eli, indulged them in their badness, but was ready to receive complaints against them. And, if that had been the thing desired, we may well suppose, upon the making out of the charge of bribery against them he would have superseded their commissions and punished them. But this would not content the elders of Israel; they had another project in their head.

2. A petition for the redress of these grievances, by setting a king over them: *Make us a king to judge us like all the nations.* Thus far it was well, that they did not rise up in rebellion against Samuel and set up a king for themselves, *vi et armis — by force;* but they applied to Samuel, God's prophet, and humbly begged of him to do it. But it appears by what follows that it was an evil proposal and ill made, and was displeasing to God. God designed them a king, a man after his own heart, when Samuel was dead; but they would anticipate God's counsel, and would have one now that Samuel was old. They had a prophet to judge them, that had immediate correspondence with heaven, and therein they were great and happy above any nation, none having God *so nigh unto them* as they had, Deu. 4:7. But this would not serve; they must have a king to judge them with external pomp and power, like *all the nations.* A poor prophet in a mantle, though conversant in the visions of the Almighty, looked mean in the eyes of those who judged by outward appearance; but a king in a purple robe, with his guards and officers of state, would look great: and such a one they must have. They knew it was in vain to court Samuel to take upon him the title and dignity of a king, but he must appoint them one. They do not say, "Give us a king that is wise and good, and will judge better than thy sons do," but, "Give us a king," any body that will but make a figure. Thus foolishly did they forsake their own mercies, and, under pretence of advancing the dignity of their nation to that of their neighbours,

did really thrust themselves down from their own excellency, and profane their crown by *casting it to the ground.*

II. Samuel's resentment of this address, *v.* 6. Let us see how he took it. 1. It cut him to the heart. Probably it was a surprise to him, and he had not any intimation before of their design, which made it the more grievous. The thing displeased Samuel; not when they upbraided him with his own infirmities and his children's irregularities (he could patiently bear what reflected on himself and his own family), but it *displeased him when they said, Give us a king to judge us,* because that reflected upon God and his honour. 2. It drove him to his knees; he gave them no answer for the present, but took time to consider of what they proposed, and prayed unto the Lord for direction what to do, spreading the case before him and leaving it with him, and so making himself easy. Samuel was a man much in prayer, and we are encouraged *in every thing to make our requests known to God,* Phil. 4:6. When any thing disturbs us, it is our interest, as well as our duty, to show before God our trouble, and he gives us leave to be humbly free with him.

III. The instruction God gave him concerning this matter. Those that in straits seek to God shall find him nigh unto them, and ready to direct them. He tells him,

1. That which would be an allay to his displeasure. Samuel was much disturbed at the proposal: it troubled him greatly to see his prophetic office thus slighted, and all the good turns he had done to Israel thus ungratefully returned; but God tells him he must not think it either hard or strange. (1.) He must not think it hard that they had put this slight upon him, for they had herein put a slight upon God himself: "*They have not rejected thee* only, but *they have rejected me.* I share with thee in the affront," *v.* 7. Note, If God interest himself in the indignities that are done us, and the contempts that are put upon us, we may well afford to bear them patiently; nor need we think the worse of ourselves if *for his sake we bear reproach* (Ps. 69:7), but rather rejoice and count it an honour, Col. 1:24. Samuel must not complain that they were weary of his government, though just and gentle, for really they were weary of God's government; this was what they disliked: *They have rejected me, that I should not reign over them.* God *reigns over the heathen* (Ps. 47:8), over all the world, but the government of Israel had hitherto been, in a more peculiar manner than ever any government was, a Theocracy, a divine government; their judges had their call and commission immediately from God; the affairs of their nation were under his peculiar direction. As the constitution, so the administration of their government, was by *Thus saith the Lord;* this method they were weary of, though it was their honour and safety, above any thing, so long as they kept in with God. They were indeed so much the more exposed to calamities if they provoked God to anger by sin, and found they could not transgress at so cheap a rate as other nations could, which perhaps was the true reason why they desired to stand upon the same terms with God that other nations did. (2.) He must not think it strange, nor marvel at the matter, for they do as they always have done: *According to all the works which they have done, since the day that I brought them out of Egypt, so do they unto thee, v.* 8; They had at first been so very respectful and obsequious to Samuel that he began to hope they were cured of their old stubborn disposition; but now he found himself deceived in them, and must not be surprised at it. They had always been rude to their governors, witness Moses and Aaron; nay, *They have forsaken me and served other gods;* the greatness of their crime, in affecting new gods, may make this crime of affecting new governors seem little. Samuel might expect they would deal treacherously, for they were called *transgressors from the womb,* Isa. 48:8. This had been *their manner from their youth up,* Jer. 22:21.

2. He tells him that which would be an answer to their demand. Samuel would not have known what to say if God had not instructed him. Should he oppose the motion, it would bespeak a greater fondness of power and dominion than did become a prophet, and an indulgence of his sons. Should he yield to the motion, it would look like the betraying of his trust, and he would become accessory to all the bad consequences of a change. Aaron sinned in gratifying the people when they said, *Make us gods;* Samuel dares not therefore comply with them when they say, *Make*

us a king, but he gives them, with assurance, the answer God sent them.

(1.) He must tell them that *they shall have a king. Hearken to the voice of the people, v.* 7, and again, *v.* 9. Not that God was pleased with their request, but, as sometimes he crosses us in love, so at other times he gratifies us in wrath; he did so here. When they said, *Give us a king and princes he gave them a king in his anger* (see Hos. 13:10, 11), as he gave them quails, Ps. 106:15; 78:29. God bade Samuel humour them in this matter, [1.] That they might be beaten with their own rod, and might feel, to their cost, the difference between his government and the government of a king; see 2 Chr. 12:8. It soon appeared how much worse their condition was, in all respects, under Saul, than it had been under Samuel. [2.] To prevent something worse. If they were not gratified, they would either rise in rebellion against Samuel or universally revolt from their religion and admit the gods of the nations, that they might have kings like them. Rather than so, let them have a king. [3.] God knows how to bring glory to himself out of it, and to serve his own wise purposes even by their foolish counsels.

(2.) But he must tell them, withal, that when they have a king they will soon have enough of him, and will, when it is too late, repent of their choice. This he must *protest solemnly to them* (*v.* 9), that, if they would have a king to rule them, as the eastern kings ruled their subjects, they would find the yoke exceedingly heavy. They looked only at the pomp or magnificence of a king, and thought that would make their nation great and considerable among its neighbours, and would strike a terror upon their enemies; but he must bid them consider how they would like to bear the charges of that pomp, and how they would endure that arbitrary power which the neighbouring kings assumed. Note, Those that set their hearts inordinately upon any thing in this world ought, for the moderating of their desires, to consider the inconveniences as well as the conveniences that will attend it, and to set the one over against the other in their thoughts. Those that submit to the government of the world and the flesh are told plainly what hard masters they are, and what a tyranny the dominion of sin is; and yet they will exchange God's government for it.

IV. Samuel's faithful delivery of God's mind to them, *v.* 10. He *told them all the words of the Lord,* how ill he resented it, that he construed it a rejecting of him, and compared it with their serving other gods, — that he would grant their request if they insisted on it, but withal had ordered him to represent to them the certain consequences of their choice, that they would be such that if they had any reason left them, and would allow themselves to consult their own interest, they would withdraw their petition, and beg to continue as they were. Accordingly he lays before them, very particularly, what would be, not the right of a king in general, but *the manner of the king that should reign over them,* according to the pattern of the nations, *v.* 11. Samuel does not speak (as bishop Patrick expounds it) of a just and honest right of a king to do these things, for his right is quite otherwise described in that part of Moses's law which concerns the king's duty, but such a right as the kings of the nations had then acquired. *This shall be the manner of the king,* that is, "thus he must support his dignity at the expense of that which is dearest to you, and thus he will abuse his power, as those that have power are apt to do; and, having the militia in his hand, you will be under a necessity of submitting to him."

1. If they will have such a king as the nations have, let them consider, (1.) That king must have a great retinue, abundance of servants to wait on him, grooms to look after his chariots and horses, gentlemen to ride about with him, and footmen to run before his chariots. This is the chief grandeur of princes, and the imaginary glory of great men, to have a multitude of attendants. And whence must he have these? "Why, he will take your sons, who are free-born, have a liberal education, and whom you now have at your own disposal, and will *appoint them for himself," v.* 11. They must wait upon him, and be at his beck; those that used to work for their parents and themselves must work for him, *ear his ground, and reap his harvest* (*v.* 12), and count it their preferment too, *v.* 16. This would be a great change. (2.) He must keep a great table; he will not be content to dine with his neighbours upon a sacrifice,

as Samuel used to do (*ch.* 9:13); but he must have a variety of dainty dishes, forced meats, and sweet-meats, and delicate sauces; and who must prepare him these? "Why, he will take your daughters, the most ingenious and handy of them, whom you hoped to prefer to houses and tables of their own; and, whether you be willing or no, they must be his confectioners, and cooks, and bakers, and the like." (3.) "He must needs have a standing army, for guards and garrisons; and your sons, instead of being elders of your cities, and living in quiet and honour at home, must be captains over thousands and captains over fifties, and must be disposed of at the pleasure of the sovereign." (4.) "You may expect that he will have great favourites, whom, having dignified and ennobled, he must enrich, and give them estates suitable to their honour; and which way can he do that, but out of your inheritances? *v.* 14. *He will take your fields and vineyards,* which descended to you from your ancestors, and which you hoped to leave to your posterity after you, *even the best of them;* and will not only take them to himself (you could bear that better), but he will *give them to his servants,* who will be your masters, and bear rule over that for which you have laboured, How will you like that?" (5.) "He must have great revenues to maintain his grandeur and power with; and whence must he have them but from you? He will take the tenth of the fruits of your ground (*v.* 15), and your cattle, *v.* 17. You think the tenths, the double tenths, which the law of God has appointed for the support of the church, grievous enough, and grudge the payment of them; but, if you have a king, there must issue another tenth out of your estates, which will be levied with more rigour, for the support of the royal dignity. Consider the expense with the magnificence, and whether it will quit cost."

2. These would be their grievances, and, (1.) They would have none but God to complain to. Once they complained to the prince himself, and were answered, according to the manner of the king, Your *yoke is heavy, and I will add to it,* 1 Ki. 12:11. (2.) When they complained to God he *would not hear them, v.* 18. Nor could they expect that he should, both because they had been deaf to his calls and admonitions, and this trouble, in particular, they had brought upon themselves by rejecting him, and would not believe when he told them what would come of it. Note, When we bring ourselves into distress by our own irregular desires and projects we justly forfeit the comfort of prayer and the benefit of divine aids, and, if God be not better to us than we deserve, must have our relief in our own hands, and then it is bad with us.

V. The people's obstinacy in their demand, *v.* 19, 20. One would think such a representation of the consequences as this was, coming from God himself, who can neither deceive by his word nor be deceived in his knowledge, should have prevailed with them to waive their request: but their hearts were upon it, right or wrong, good or evil: *"We will have a king over us,* whatever God or Samuel say to the contrary; we will have a king, whatever it cost us, and whatever inconvenience we bring upon ourselves or our posterity by it." See their folly. 1. They were quite deaf to reason and blind to their own interest. They could not answer Samuel's arguments against it, nor deny the force of them, and yet they grow more violent in their request, and more insolent. Before it was, "Pray, *make us a king;"* now it is, *"Nay, but we will have a king;* yea, that we will, because we will; nor will we bear to have any thing said against it." See the absurdity of inordinate desires, and how they rob men of their reason. 2. They could not stay God's time. God had intimated to them in the law that, in due time, Israel should have a king (Deu. 17:14, 15), and perhaps they had some intimation that the time was at hand; but they are all in haste: "We, in our day, will have this king over us." Could they but have waited ten or twelve years longer they would have had David, a king of God's giving in mercy, and all the calamities that attended the setting up of Saul would have been prevented. Sudden resolves and hasty desires make work for a long and leisurely repentance. 3. That which they aimed at in desiring a king was not only, as before, that they might be like the nations, and levelled with the one above whom God had so far advanced them, but that they might have one to judge them, and to go out before them when they took the field, and to fight their battles. Foolish people and unwise! Could they ever desire a battle better fought for them that the last was, by Samuel's prayer and God's thunder? *ch.* 7:10. Was victory hereby too sure to them? And were they fond of trying the chance of war at the same uncertainty that others did? So sick, it seems, were they of their privileges: and what was the issue? Their first king was slain in a battle, which none of their judges ever were; so was Josiah, one of the last and best.

VI. The dismissing of them with an intimation that very shortly they should have what they asked. 1. *Samuel rehearsed all their words in the ears of the Lord, v.* 21. Not but that God perfectly knew it, without Samuel's report; but thus he dealt faithfully between God and Israel, as a prophet, returning the answer to him that sent him; and thus he waited on God for further direction. God is fully acquainted with the state of the case we are in care and doubt about, but he will know it from us. His rehearsing it *in the ears of the Lord* intimates that it was done in private; for the people were not disposed to join with him in prayer to God for direction in this matter; also it bespeaks a holy familiarity, to which God graciously admits his people: they speak in the ears of the Lord, as one friend whispers with another; their communion with God is *meat they have to eat which the world knows not of,* Jn. 4:32. 2. God gave direction that they should have a king, since they were so inordinately set upon it (*v.* 22): *"Make them a king,* and let them make their best of him, and thank themselves if that very pomp and power which they are so eager to see their sovereign in be their plague and burden." *So he gave them up to their own hearts' lusts.* Samuel told them this, but sent them home for the present, *every man to his city;* for the designation of the person must be left to God; they had now no more to do. When God saw fit to notify the choice to Samuel they should hear further from him; in the mean time let them keep the peace and expect the issue.

CHAPTER 9

Samuel had promised Israel, from God, that they should have a king; it is strange that the next news is not of candidates setting up for the government, making an interest in the people, or recommending themselves to Samuel, and, by him, to God, to be put in nomination. Why does not the prince of the tribe of Judah, whoever he is, look about him now, remembering Jacob's entail of the sceptre on that tribe? Is there never a bold aspiring man in Israel, to say, "I will be king, if God will choose me?" No, none appears, whether it is owing to a culpable mean-spiritedness or a laudable humility I know not; but surely it is what can scarcely be paralleled in the history of any kingdom; a crown, such a crown, set up, and nobody bids for it. Most governments began in the ambition of the prince to rule, but Israel's in the ambition of the people to be ruled. Had any of those elders who petitioned for a king afterwards petitioned to be king, I should have suspected that person's ambition to have been at the bottom of the motion; but now (let them have the praise of what was good in them) it was not so. God having, in the law, undertaken to choose their king (Deu. 17:15), they all sit still, till they hear from heaven, and that they do in this chapter, which begins the story of Saul, their first king, and, by strange steps of Providence, brings him to Samuel to be anointed privately, and so to be prepared for an election by lot, and a public commendation to the people, which follows in the next chapter. Here is, I. A short account of Saul's parentage and person (*v.* 1, 2). II. A large and particular account of the bringing of him to Samuel, to whom he had been before altogether a stranger. 1. God, by revelation, had told Samuel to expect him (*v.* 15, 16). 2. God, by providence, led him to Samuel. (1.) Being sent to seek his father's asses, he was at a loss (*v.* 3–5). (2.) By the advice of his servant, he determined to consult Samuel (*v.* 6–10). (3.) By the direction of the young maidens, he found him out (*v.* 11–14). (4.) Samuel, being informed of God concerning him (*v.* 17), treated him with respect in the gate (*v.* 18–21), in the dining-room (*v.* 22–24), and at length in private, where he prepared him to hear the surprising news that he must be king (*v.* 25–27). And these beginnings would have been very hopeful and promising if it had not been that the sin of the people was the spring of this great affair.

Verses 1–2

We are here told, 1. What a good family Saul was of, *v.* 1. He was of the tribe of Benjamin; so was the New-Testament Saul, who also was called *Paul,* and he mentions it as his honour, for Benjamin was a favourite, Rom. 11:1; Phil. 3:5. That tribe had been reduced to a very small number by the fatal war with Gibeah, and much ado there was to provide wives for those 600 men that were the poor remains of it out of that diminished tribe, which is here called, with good reason, *the smallest of the tribes of Israel, v.* 21. Saul sprang as a root out of a dry ground. That tribe, though fewest in number, was first in dignity, *God giving more abundant honour to that part which lacked,* 1 Co. 12:24. His father was *Kish, a mighty man of power,* or, as the margin reads it, *in substance;* in spirit bold, in body strong, in estate wealthy. The whole lot of the tribe of Benjamin coming to be distributed among 600 men, we may suppose their inheritances were much larger than theirs who were of other tribes, an advantage which somewhat helped to balance the disadvantage of the smallness of their number. 2. What a good figure Saul made, *v.* 2. No mention is here made of his wisdom or virtue, his learning or piety, or any of the accomplishments of his mind, but that he was a tall, proper, handsome man, that had a good face, a good shape, and a good presence, graceful and well proportioned: *Among all the children of Israel there was not a goodlier person than he;* and, as if nature had marked him for preeminence and superiority, he was taller by the head and shoulders than any of the people, the fitter to be a match for the giants of Gath, the champions of the Philistines. When God chose a king after his own heart he pitched upon one that was not at all remarkable for the height of his stature, nor any thing in his countenance but the innocence and sweetness that appeared there, *ch.* 16:7, 12. But when he chose a king after the people's heart, who aimed at nothing so much as stateliness and grandeur, he pitched upon this huge tall man, who, if he had no other good qualities, yet would look great. It does not appear that he excelled in strength so much as he did in stature; Samson did, and him they slighted, bound, and betrayed into the hands of the Philistines; justly therefore are they now put off with one who, though of uncommon height, is weak as other men. They would have a king like the nations, and the nations commonly chose portly men for their kings.

Verses 3–10

Here is, I. A great man rising from small beginnings. It does not appear that Saul had any preferment at all, or was in any post of honour or trust, till he was chosen king of Israel. Most that are advanced rise gradually, but Saul, from the level with his neighbours, stepped at once into the throne, according to that of Hannah, He *raiseth up the poor out of the dust, to set them among princes,* 1 Sa. 2:8. Saul, it should seem, though he was himself married and had children grown up, yet lived in his father's house, and was subject to him. Promotion comes not by chance nor human probabilities, but God is the Judge.

II. A great event arising from small occurrences. How low does the history begin! Having to trace Saul to the crown, we find him first employed as meanly as any we meet with called out to preferment.

1. Saul's father sends him with one of his servants to seek some asses that he had lost. It may be they had no way then to give public notice of such a number of asses strayed or stolen out of the grounds of Kish the Benjamite. A very good law they had to oblige men to bring back an ox or an ass that went astray, but it is to be feared that was, as other good laws, neglected and forgotten. It is easy to observe here that those who have must expect to lose, that it is wisdom to look after what is lost, that no man should think it below him to know the state of his flocks, that children should be forward to serve their parents' interests. Saul readily went to *seek his father's asses, v.* 3, 4. His taking care of the asses is to be ascribed, not so much to the humility of his spirit as to the plainness and simplicity of those times. But his obedience to his father in it was very commendable. *Seest thou a man diligent in his business,* and dutiful to his superiors, willing to stoop and willing to take pains? he does as Saul stand fair for preferment. The servant of Kish would be faithful only as a servant, but Saul as a son, in his own business, and therefore he was sent with him. Saul and his servants travelled far (probably on foot) in quest of the asses, but in vain: they found them not. He missed of what he sought, but had no reason to complain of the disappointment, for he met with the kingdom, which he never dreamed of.

2. When he could not find them, he determined to return to his father (*v.* 5), in consideration of his father's tender concern for him, being apprehensive that if they staid out any longer his aged father would begin to fear, as Jacob concerning Joseph, that an evil beast had devoured them or some mischief had befallen them; he will *leave caring for the asses,* as much as he was in care about them, and *will take thought for us.* Children should take care that they do nothing to grieve or frighten their parents, but be tender of their tenderness.

3. His servant proposed (for, it should seem, he had more religion in him than his master) that, since they were

now at Ramah, they should call on Samuel, and take his advice in this important affair. Observe here, (1.) They were close by the city where Samuel lived, and that put it into their heads to consult him (*v.* 6): *There is in this city a man of God.* Note, Wherever we are we should improve our opportunities of acquainting ourselves with those that are wise and good. But there are many that will consult a man of God, if he comes in their way, that would not go a step out of their way to get wisdom. (2.) The servant spoke very respectfully concerning Samuel, though he had not personal knowledge of him, but by common fame only: *He is a man of God, and an honourable man.* Note, Men of God are honourable men, and should be so in our eyes. Acquaintance with the things of God, and serviceableness to the kingdom of God, put true honour upon men, and make them great. This was the honour of Samuel, as a man of God, that *all he saith comes surely to pass.* This was observed concerning him when he was a young prophet (*ch.* 3:19), *God did let none of his words fall to the ground;* and still it held true. (3.) They agreed to consult him concerning *the way that they should go; peradventure he can show us.* All the use they would make of the man of God was to be advised by him whether they should return home, or, if there were any hopes of finding the asses, which way they must go next — a poor business to employ a prophet about! Had they said, "Let us give up the asses for lost, and, now that we are so near the man of God, let us go and learn from him the good knowledge of God, let us consult him how we may order our conversations aright, and enquire the law at his mouth, since we may not have such another opportunity, and then we shall not lose our journey" — the proposal would have been such as became Israelites; but to make prophecy, that glory of Israel, serve so mean a turn as this, discovered too much what manner of spirit they were of. Note, Most people would rather be told their fortune than told their duty, how to be rich than how to be saved. If it were the business of the men of God to direct for the recovery of lost asses, they would be consulted much more than they are now that it is their business to direct for the recovery of lost souls; so preposterous is the care of most men! (4.) Saul was thoughtful what present they should bring to the man of God, what fee they should give him for his advice (*v.* 7): *What shall we bring the man?* They could not present him, as Jeroboam's wife did Ahijah, with loaves and cakes (1 Ki. 14:3), for their bread was spent; but the servant bethought himself that he had in his pocket the fourth part of a shekel, about seven-pence halfpenny in value, and *that* he would give to the man of God to direct them, *v.* 8. "That will do," says Saul; *"let us go," v.* 10. Some think that when Saul talked of giving Samuel a fee he measured him by himself, or by his sons, as if he must be hired to do an honest Israelite a kindness, and was like the false prophets, that *divined for money,* Mic. 3:11. He came to him as a fortune-teller, rather than as a prophet, and therefore thought the fourth part of a shekel was enough to give him. But it rather seems to be agreeable to the general usage of those times, as it is to natural equity, that those who sowed spiritual things should reap not only eternal things from him that employs them, but temporal things from those for whom they are employed. Samuel needed not their money, nor would he have denied them his advice if they had not brought it (it is probable, when he had it, he gave it to the por); but they brought it to him as a token of their respect and the value they put upon his office; nor did he refuse it, for they were able to give it, and, though it was but little, it was the widow's mite. But Saul, as he never thought of going to the man of God till the servant proposed it, so, it should seem, he mentioned the want of a present as an objection against their going; he would not own that he had money in his pocket, but, when the servant generously offered to be at the charge, then, "Well, said," says Saul; "come, let us go." Most people love a cheap religion, and like it best when they can devolve the expense of it on others. (5.) The historian here takes notice of the name then given to the prophets: they called them *Seers,* or *seeing men* (*v.* 9), not but that the name *prophet* was then used, and applied to such persons, but that of seers was more in use. Note, Those that are prophets must first be seers; those who undertake to speak to others of the things of God must have an insight into those things themselves.

Verses 11–17

Here, I. Saul, by an ordinary enquiry, is directed to Samuel, *v.* 11–14. Gibeah of Saul was not twenty miles from Ramah where Samuel dwelt, and was near to Mizpeh where he often judged Israel, and yet, it seems, Saul had lived so very privately, and had taken so little notice of public affairs, that he had never seen Samuel, for when he met him (*v.* 18) he did not know him, so that there was no cause to suspect any secret compact or collusion between them in this matter. *I knew him not,* says John Baptist concerning Christ, Jn. 1:31. Yet I do not think it any commendation to Saul that he was a stranger to Samuel. However,

1. The maid-servants of Ramah, whom they met with at the places of drawing water, could give him and his servant intelligence concerning Samuel; and very particular they were in their directions, *v.* 12, 13. We should always be ready to give what assistance we can to those that are enquiring after God's prophets, and to further them in their enquiries. Even the maid-servants could tell them, (1.) That there was a sacrifice that day in the high place, it being either an ordinary festival or an extraordinary day of prayer and thanksgiving, with which sacrifices were joined. The tabernacle being deprived of the ark, the altar there had not now the reputation it formerly had, nor were they confined to it, as they would be when God had again chosen a place to put his name in; and therefore now other places were allowed. Samuel had built an altar at Ramah (*ch.* 7:17), and here we have him making use of that altar. (2.) That Samuel came that day to the city, either from his circuit or from his country seat. He was such a public person that his movements were generally known. (3.) That this was just the time of their meeting to feast before the Lord upon the sacrifice: "About this time you will find him in the street going up to the high place." They knew the hour of the solemn feast. (4.) That the people would not eat till Samuel came, not only because he was the worthiest person, and they ought in good manners to stay for him, and he was, as some think, the maker of this feast, the sacrifice being offered at his charge and upon his account; but because, as a man of God, whoever made the feast, *he* must bless the sacrifice, that is, those parts of the sacrifice which they feasted upon, which may be considered, [1.] As a common meal, and so this is an instance of the great duty of craving a blessing upon our meat before we partake of it. We cannot expect benefit from our food without that blessing, and we have no reason to expect that blessing if we do not pray for it. Thus we must give glory to God as our benefactor, and own our dependence upon him and our obligations to him. Or, [2.] As a religious assembly. When the sacrifice was offered, which was the ceremony, Samuel blessed it, that is, he prayed over it, and offered up spiritual sacrifices with it, which were the substance; and afterwards, when the holy duties were performed, they did eat. Let the soul first be served. The feast upon the sacrifice being a sacred rite, it was requisite that it should in a particular manner be blessed, as is the Christian eucharist. They feasted in token of their reconciliation to God by virtue of the sacrifice, and their participation of the benefits of it; and Samuel blessed the feast, that is, he prayed to God to grace the solemnity with his special presence, that it might answer those great ends. Bishop Hall observes what a particular account those maid-servants could give of the usages of those sacred feasts, and infers from it that, "where there is the practice and example of piety in the better sort, there will be a reflection of it upon the meanest. It is no small advantage to live in religious places; for we shall be much to blame if all goodness fall beside us."

2. Saul and his servant followed the directions given them, and very opportunely met Samuel going to the high place, the synagogue of the city, *v.* 14. This seemed purely accidental, but the divine providence ordered it for the forwarding of this great event. The wise God serves very great and certain purposes by very small and casual occurrences. A sparrow falls not to the ground without our Father.

II. Samuel, by an extraordinary revelation, is informed concerning Saul. He was a seer, and therefore must see this in a way peculiar to himself.

1. God had told him, the day before, that he would, at this time, send him the man that should serve the people of Israel for such a king as they wished to have, *like all the nations, v.* 15, 16. He *told him in his ear,* that is, privately, by a secret whisper to his mind, or perhaps by a still small voice, some soft and gentle sounds conveyed to his ear, probably when he was praying in secret for direction in that and other affairs of the nation. He had spoken *in the ears of the Lord* (*ch.* 8:21), and now God *spoke in his ear,* in token of friendship and familiarity, for *he revealeth his secret to his servants the prophets,* as secrets in their ear, Amos 3:7. God told him before, that it might not be a surprise to him; and perhaps it was in expectation of it that he appointed the feast and the sacrifice, for the imploring of God's blessing upon this great and important affair, though he might keep the particular occasion in his own breast, God having only told it to him in his ear. The Hebrew phrase is, *He uncovered the ear of Samuel,* to which some allude for the explication of the way of God's revealing himself to us; he not only speaks, but *uncovers our ear.* We have naturally a covering on our ears, so that we perceive not what God says (Job 33:14), but, when God will manifest himself to a soul, he uncovers the ear, says, *Ephphratha, Be opened;* he takes *the veil from off the heart,* 2 Co. 3:16. Though God had, in displeasure, granted their request for a king, yet here he speaks tenderly of Israel; for even in *wrath he remembers mercy.* (1.) He calls them again and again his people; though a peevish and provoking people, yet mine still. (2.) He sends them a man to be captain over them, that they might not be a body without a head, and to *save them out of the hand of the Philistines,* which perhaps was more than many of them aimed at in desiring a king. (3.) He does it with a gracious respect to them and to their cry: *I have looked upon my people,* and *their cry has come unto me.* He gratified them with what they cried for, as the tender mother humours the froward child, lest it should break its heart. And (as bishop Patrick observes), though he would not hear their cry to relieve them against the oppression of their kings (*ch.* 8:18), yet he was so gracious as to make those kings instruments of their deliverance from the oppression of their neighbours, which was more than they had reason to expect.

2. When Saul came up towards him in the street God again whispered Samuel in the ear (*v.* 17): *Behold the man whom I spoke to thee of!* Saul being a man of unusual stature, it is natural to think that Samuel fixed his eye upon him at a distance, and perhaps looked the more wistfully towards him because the hour had now come when God would send him the man that should be king of Israel, and he fancied this might be he; but, that he might be fully satisfied, God told him expressly, *That is the man* that shall *restrain* (for magistrates are heirs of restraint) *my people Israel.*

Verses 18–27

Providence having at length brought Samuel and Saul together, we have here an account of what passed between them in the gate, at the feast, and in private.

I. In the gate of the city; passing through that, Saul found him (*v.* 18), and, little thinking that he was Samuel himself, asked him the way to Samuel's house: *Tell me where the seer's house is;* for there he expected to find him. See how mean a figure Samuel made, though so great a man: he took not any state, had no attendants, no ensigns of honour carried before him, nor any distinguishing habit, no, not when he went to church, but appeared, in all respects, so much a common person that Saul, though he was told he should meet him, never suspected that it was he, but, as if he looked more like a porter than a prophet, asked him the way to the seer's house. Thus is great worth oftentimes hidden under a very despicable appearance. Samuel knew that it was not the house, but the man, that he wanted, and therefore answered him, *"I am the seer,* the person you enquire for," *v.* 19. Samuel knew him before he knew Samuel; thus, though all that are called to the kingdom of glory are brought to know God, yet first they were known of him, Gal. 4:9. Now, 1. Samuel obliges him to stay with him till the next day. The greatest part of this day had been spent in sacrificing, and the rest of it was to be spent in holy feasting, and therefore, *"To-morrow I will let thee go,* and not sooner; now *go up before me to the high place;* let us pray together, and then we will talk together." Saul had nothing in his mind but to find his asses, but Samuel would take him off from that care, and dispose him to the exercises of piety; and therefore bids him *go to the high place,* and go before him, because, it may be, some business obliged Samuel to call by the way. 2. He satisfies him about his asses (*v.* 20): *Set not thy mind on them,* be not in further care about them; *they are found.* By this Saul might perceive that he was a prophet, that he could give him an answer to the enquiry which he had not yet made, and tell him what he thought; and thence he might infer, if a man of God can do this, much more doth God himself *understand our thoughts afar off.* 3. He surprises him with an intimation of preferment before him: *"On whom is all the desire of Israel?* Is it not a king that they are set upon, and there is never a man in Israel that will suit them as thou wilt." It does not appear that the country had as yet any eye upon him for the government, because they had left it wholly to God to choose for them; but such a one as he they wished for, and his advancement would be the advancement of his family and relations, as Abner, and others. 4. To this strange intimation Saul returns a very modest answer, *v.* 21. Samuel, he thought, did but banter him, because he was a tall man, but a very unlikely man to be a king; for, though the historian says (*v.* 1) his father was a *mighty man of power,* yet he himself speaks diminishingly of his tribe and family. "Benjamin, the youngest of Jacob's sons, when grown up to be a man, was called a *little one* (Gen. 44:20); that tribe was diminished by the war of Gibeah; and *I am a Benjamite, my family the least,"* probably a younger house, not in any place of honour or trust, no, not in their own tribe. Gideon had expressed himself thus, Jdg. 6:15. A humble disposition is a good presage of preferment.

II. At the public feast; thither Samuel took him and his servant. Though the advancement of Saul would be the deposing of Samuel, yet that good prophet was so far from envying him, or bearing him any ill-will for it, that he was the first and forwardest man to do him honour, in compliance with the will of God. If this be the man whom God has chosen, though he be none of Samuel's particular friends or confidants, yet he is heartily welcome to his table, nay, to his bosom. We may suppose it was no unseasonable kindness to Saul to give him a meal's meat, for it seems, by what he said (*v.* 7), that all their meat and money were spent. But this was not all. Samuel treats him not as a common person, but a person of quality and distinction, to prepare both him and the people for what was to follow. Two marks of honour he put upon him: — 1. He set him *in the best place,* as more honourable than any other of the guests, to whom he said, *Give this man place,* Lu. 14:9. Though we may suppose the magistrates were there, who in their own city would claim precedency, yet the master of the feast made Saul and his servant too (who, if Saul was a king, must be respected as his prime minister of state) *sit in the chief place, v.* 22. Note, Civil respects must be paid to those who in civil things have the precedency given them by the divine providence. 2. He presented him with the *best dish,* which, having had notice from heaven the day before of his coming (*v.* 16), he had designed for him, and ordered the cook to secure for him, when he gave orders for inviting the guests and making preparation for them. And what should this precious dish be, which was so very carefully reserved for the king-elect? One would expect it should be something very nice and delicate. No, it was a plain shoulder of mutton (*v.* 23, 24). The right shoulder of the peace-offerings was to be given to the priests, who were God's receivers (Lev. 7:32); the next in honour to that was the left shoulder, which probably was always allotted to those that sat at the upper end of the table, and was wont to be Samuel's mess at other times; so that his giving it to Saul now was an implicit resignation of his place to him. Some observe a significancy in this dish. The shoulder denotes strength, and the breast, which some think went with it, denotes affection: he that was king had *the government upon his shoulder,* for he must bear the weight of it; and the people in his bosom, for they must be dear to him.

III. What passed between them in private. Both that evening and early the next morning Samuel communed with Saul upon the flat roof of the house, *v.* 25, 26. We may suppose Samuel now told him the whole story of the people's desire of a king, the grounds of their desire, and God's grant of it, to all which Saul, living very privately, was perhaps a stranger; he satisfied him that he was the person God had pitched upon for the government; and whereas Saul would object that Samuel was in possession, and he would not for all the world take it out of his hands, Samuel, we may suppose, gave him all the assurance he could desire of his willingness to resign. Early in the morning he sent him towards home, brought him part of the way, bade him send his servant before, that they might be private (*v.* 27), and there, as we find in the beginning of the next chapter, he anointed him, and therein showed him the *word of the Lord,* that is, gave him full satisfaction that he was the person chosen to be king, for he would not jest with that sacred rite. It is by the *unction of the Holy Ghost* that Christ, the great prophet, *shows us the word of the Lord.* 1 Jn. 2:27, *the same anointing teacheth you of all things.*

CHAPTER 10

We left Samuel and Saul walking together, probably some private way over the fields down from Ramah, perhaps in the paths of the vineyards, and Saul expecting to hear from Samuel the word of God. Now here we have, I. The anointing of Saul then and there (*v.* 1). The signs Samuel gave him (*v.* 2–6). And instructions (*v.* 7–8). II. The accomplishment of those signs to the satisfaction of Saul (*v.* 9–13). III. His return to his father's house (*v.* 14–16). IV. His public election by lot, and solemn inauguration (*v.* 17–25). V. His return to his own city (*v.* 26, 27). It is a great work that is here a doing, the setting up not only of a monarch, but of monarchy itself, in Israel; and therefore in all the advances towards it much of God is seen.

Verses 1–8

Samuel is here executing the office of a prophet, giving Saul full assurance from God that he should be king, as he was afterwards, according to these prophecies which went before of him.

I. He *anointed him* and *kissed him, v.* 1. This was not done in a solemn assembly, but it was done by divine appointment, which made up the want of all external solemnities, nor was it ever the less valid for its being done in private, under a hedge, or, as the Jews say, by *a fountain.* God's institutions are great and honourable, though the circumstances of their administration be ever so mean and despicable. 1. Samuel, by anointing Saul, assured him that it was God's act to make him king: *Is it not because the Lord hath anointed thee?* And, in token of that, the high priest was anointed to his office, to signify the conferring of those gifts upon him that were requisite for the discharge of its duties, and the same was intimated in the anointing of kings; for whom God calls he qualifies, and suitable qualifications furnish good proof of a commission. These sacred unctions, then used, pointed at the great Messiah, or anointed one, the king of the church, and high priest of our profession, who was anointed with the oil of the Spirit, not by measure, but without measure, and above all the priests and princes of the Jewish church. It was common oil, no doubt, which Samuel used, and we read not of his blessing it or praying over it. But it was only a vial of oil that he anointed him with, the vessel brittle, because his kingdom would soon be cracked and broken, and the quantity small, because he had but little of the Spirit conferred upon him to what David had, who was therefore anointed with a horn of oil, as were Solomon and Jehu with a box of oil. 2. By kissing him, he assured him of his own approbation of the choice, not only his consent to it, but his complacency in it, though it abridged his power and eclipsed his glory and the glory of his family. *"God has anointed thee,"* says Samuel, *"to be king,* and I am satisfied and very well pleased, in pledge of which take this kiss." It was likewise a kiss of homage and allegiance; hereby he not only owns him to be king, but his king, and in this sense we are commanded to *kiss the Son,* Ps. 2:12. God has anointed him, and therefore we must thus acknowledge him and do homage to him. In Samuel's explication of the ceremony, he reminds him, (1.) Of the nature of the government to which he is called. He was anointed to be a captain, a commander indeed, which bespeaks honour and power, but a commander in war, which bespeaks care, and toil, and danger. (2.) Of the origin of it: *The Lord hath anointed thee.* By him he ruled, and therefore must rule for him, in dependence on him, and with an eye to his glory. (3.) Of the end of it. It is over his inheritance, to take care of that, protect it, and order all the affairs of it for the best, as a steward whom a great man sets over his estate, to manage it for his service and give an account of it to him.

II. For his further satisfaction he gives him some signs, which should come to pass immediately, this very day; and they were such as would not only confirm the word of Samuel in general, and prove him a true prophet, but would confirm this word to Saul in particular, that he should be king. 1. He should presently meet with some that would bring him intelligence from home of the care his father's house was in concerning him, *v.* 2. These he would meet hard by Rachel's sepulchre. The first place Samuel directed him to was a sepulchre, the sepulchre of one of his ancestors, for Rachel died in travail with Benjamin; there he must read a lecture of his own mortality, and now that he had a crown in his eye must think of his grave, in which all his honour would be laid in the dust. Here two men would meet him, perhaps sent on purpose to look after him, and would tell him the asses were found, and his father was in pain concerning him, saying, *What shall I do for my son?* He would reckon it happened well that he met with these messengers; and it is good to eye Providence in favourable conjunctures (though the matter be minute) and to be encouraged to trust it in greater matters. 2. He should next meet with others going to Bethel, where, it should seem, there was a high place for religious worship, and these men were bringing their sacrifices thither, *v.* 3, 4. It was a token for good to one that was designed for the government of Israel, wherever he came, to meet with people going to worship God. It is supposed that those kids and loaves, and the bottle of wine which the three men had with them, were designed for sacrifice, with the meat-offerings and drink-offerings that were to attend the sacrifice; yet Samuel tells Saul that they will give him two of their loaves, and he must take them. Such a present would look to us now like the relieving of a beggar. Saul must hereafter remember the time when he received alms, and must therefore be humble and charitable to the poor. But perhaps it would then be construed a fit present for a prince; and, as such, Saul must receive it, the first present that was brought to him, by such as knew not what they did, nor why they did it, but God put it into their hearts, which made it the more fit to be a sign to him. These two loaves, which were the first tribute paid to this newly-anointed king, might serve for an admonition to him not to spend the wealth of his crown in luxury, but still to be content with plain food. Bread is the staff of life. 3. The most remarkable sign of all would be his joining with a company of prophets that he should meet with, under the influence of a spirit of prophecy, which should at that time come upon him. What God works in us by his Spirit serves much more for the confirming of faith than any thing wrought for us by his providence. He here (*v.* 5, 6) tells him, (1.) Where this would happen: *At the hill of God,* where there was a *garrison of the Philistines,* which is supposed to be near Gibeah, his own city, for there was the Philistines' garrison, *ch.* 13:3. Perhaps it was one of the articles of Samuel's agreement with them that they should have a garrison there, or, rather, after they were subdued in the beginning of his time they got ground again, so far as to force this garrison into that place, and thence God raised up the man that should chastise them. There was a place that was called the *hill of God,* because of one of the schools of the prophets built upon it; and such respect did even Philistines themselves pay to religion that a garrison of their soldiers suffered a school of God's prophets to live peaceably by them, and did not only not dislodge them, but not restrain nor disturb the public exercises of their devotion. (2.) Upon what occasion; he should meet *a company of prophets with music before them, prophesying,* and with them he should join himself. These prophets were not (as it should seem) divinely inspired to foretel things to come, nor did God reveal himself to them by dreams and visions, but they employed themselves in the study of the law, in instructing their neighbours, and in the acts of piety, especially in praising God, wherein they were wonderfully assisted and enlarged by the Spirit of God. It was happy for Israel that they had not only prophets, but companies of prophets, who gave them good instructions and set them good examples, and helped very much to keep up religion among them. Now the word of the Lord was not precious, as it had been when Samuel was first raised up, who had been instrumental in founding these colleges, or religious houses, whence, it is probable, the synagogues took their rise. What a pity was it that Israel should be weary of the government of such a man, who though he had not, as a man of war, expelled the Philistines, yet (which was a greater kindness to Israel) had, as a man of God, settled the schools of the prophets! Music was then used as a proper means to dispose the mind to receive the impressions of the good Spirit, as it did Elisha's, 2 Ki. 3:15. But we have no reason to look for the same benefit by it now, unless we saw it as effectual as it was then in Saul's case, to drive away the evil spirit. These prophets had been at the high place, probably offering sacrifice, and now they came back singing psalms. We should come from holy ordinances with our hearts greatly enlarged in holy joy and praise. See Ps. 138:5. Saul should find himself strongly moved to join with them, and should be turned thereby *into another man* from what he had been while he lived in a private capacity. The Spirit of God, by his ordinances, changes men, wonderfully transforms them; Saul, by praising God in the communion of saints, became another man, but whether a new man or no may be questioned.

III. He directs him to proceed in the administration of his government as Providence should lead him, and as Samuel should advise him. 1. He must follow Providence in ordinary cases (*v.* 7): *"Do as occasion shall serve thee.* Take such measures as thy own prudence shall direct thee." But, 2. In an extraordinary strait that would hereafter befal him at Gilgal, and would be the most critical juncture of all, when he would have special need of divine aids, he must wait for Samuel to come to him, and must tarry *seven days* in expectation of him, *v.* 8. How his failing in this matter proved his fall we find afterwards, *ch.* 13:11. It was now a plain intimation to him that he was upon his good behaviour, and, though a king, must act under the direction of Samuel, and do as he should order him. The greatest of men must own themselves in subjection to God and his word.

Verses 9–16

Saul has now taken his leave of Samuel, much amazed, we may well suppose, at what has been done to him, almost ready to question whether he be awake or no, and whether it be not all a dream. Now here we are told,

I. What occurred by the way, *v.* 9. Those signs which Samuel had given him came to pass very punctually; but that which gave him the greatest satisfaction of all was this, he found immediately that God had given him *another heart.* A new fire was kindled in his breast, such as he had never before been acquainted with: seeking the asses is quite out of his mind, and he thinks of nothing but fighting the Philistines, redressing the grievances of Israel, making laws, administering justice, and providing for the public safety; these are the things that now fill his head. He finds himself raised to such a pitch of boldness and bravery as he never thought he should be conscious of. He has no longer the heart of a husbandman, which is low, and mean, and narrow, and concerned only about his corn and cattle; but the heart of a statesman, a general, a prince. Whom God calls to any service he will make fit for it. If he advance to another station, he will give another heart, to those who sincerely desire to serve him with their power.

II. What occurred when he came near home. They came to *the hill* (*v.* 10), that is, to *Gibeah,* or *Geba,* which signifies *a hill,* and so the Chaldee here takes it as a proper name; he met with the prophets as Samuel had told him, and the Spirit of God came upon him, strongly and suddenly (so the word signifies), but not so as to rest and abide upon him. It came on so as to go off quickly. However, for the present, it had a strange effect upon him; for he immediately joined with the prophets in their devotion, and that with as much decorum and as great a transport of affection as any of them: *He prophesied among them.* Now,

1. His prophesying was publicly taken notice of, *v.* 11, 12. He was now among his acquaintance, who, when they saw him among the prophets, called one another to come and see a strange sight. This would prepare them to accept him as a king, though one of themselves, when they had seen how God had advanced him to the honour of a prophet. The seventy elders prophesied before they were made judges, Num. 11:25. Now, (1.) They all wondered to see Saul among the prophets: *What is this that has come to the son of Kish?* Though this school of the prophets was near his father's house, yet he had never associated with them, nor shown them any respect, perhaps had sometimes spoken slightly of them; and now to see him prophesying among them was a surprise to them, as it was long after when his namesake, in the New Testament, preached that gospel which he had before persecuted, Acts 9:21. Where God gives another heart it will soon show itself. (2.) One of them, that was wiser than the rest, asked, *"Who is their father,* or instructor? Is is not God? Are they not all taught of him? Do they not all owe their gifts to him? And is he limited? Cannot he make Saul a prophet, as well as any of them, if he please?" Or, "Is not Samuel their father?" Under God, he was so; and Saul had now lately been with him, which, by his servant, he might know. No marvel for him to prophesy who lay last night under Samuel's roof. (3.) It became a proverb, commonly used in Israel, when they would express their wonder at a bad man's either becoming good, or at least being found in good company, *Is Saul among the prophets?* Note, Saul among the prophets is a wonder to a proverb. Let not the worst be despaired of, yet let not an external show of devotion, and a sudden change for the present, be too much relied on; for Saul among the prophets was Saul still.

2. His being anointed was kept private. When he had done prophesying, (1.) It should seem he uttered all his words before the Lord, and recommended the affair to his favour, for he went straight *to the high place* (*v.* 13), to give God thanks for his mercies to him and to pray for the continuance of those mercies. But, (2.) He industriously concealed from his relations what had passed. His uncle, who met with him either at the high place or as soon as he came home, examined him, *v.* 14. Saul owned, for his servant knew it, that they had been with Samuel, and that he told them the asses were found, but said not a word of *the kingdom, v.* 14, 15. This was an instance, [1.] Of his humility. Many a one would have been so elated with this surprising elevation as to proclaim it upon the house-top. But Saul, though he might please himself with it in his own breast, did not pride himself in it among his neighbours. The heirs of the kingdom of glory are well enough pleased that *the world knows them not,* 1 Jn. 3:1. [2.] Of his prudence. Had he been forward to proclaim it, he would have been envied, and he knew not what difficulty that might have created him. Samuel had communicated it to him as a secret, and he knows how to keep counsel. Thus it appears that he had another heart, a heart fit for government. [3.] Of his dependence upon God. He does not go about to make an interest for himself, but leaves it to God to carry on his own work by Samuel, and, for his own part, sits still, to see how the matter will fall.

Verses 17–27

Saul's nomination to the throne is here made public, in a general assembly of the elders of Israel, the representatives of their respective tribes at Mizpeh. It is probable that this convention of the states was called as soon as conveniently it might, after Saul was anointed, for, if there must be a change in their government, the sooner the better: it might be of bad consequence to be long in the doing. The people having met in a solemn assembly, in which God was in a peculiar manner present (and therefore it is said they were *called together unto the Lord, v.* 17), Samuel acts for God among them.

I. He reproves them for casting off the government of a prophet, and desiring that of a captain. 1. He shows them (*v.* 18) how happy they had been under the divine government; when God ruled them, he *delivered them out of the hand of those that oppressed them,* and what would they desire more? Could the mightiest man of valour do that for them which the Almighty God had done? 2. He likewise shows them (*v.* 19) what an affront they had put upon God (who had himself saved them *out of all their tribulations,* by his own power, and by such as he had immediately called and qualified) in desiring a king to save them. He tells them in plain terms, *"You have this day rejected your God;* you have in effect done it: so he construes it, and he might justly, for your so doing, reject you." Those that can live better by sense than by faith, that stay themselves upon an arm of flesh rather than upon the almighty arm, forsake a fountain of living waters for broken cisterns. And some make their obstinacy in this matter to be a presage of their rejecting Christ, in casting off whom they cast off God, that he should not reign over them.

II. He puts them upon choosing their king by lot. He knew whom God had chosen, and had already anointed him, but he knew also the peevishness of that people, and that there were those among them who would not acquiesce in the choice if it depended upon his single testimony; and therefore, that every tribe and every family of the chosen tribe might please themselves with having a chance for it, he calls them to the lot, *v.* 19. Benjamin is taken out of all the tribes (*v.* 20), and out of that tribe Saul the son of Kish, *v.* 21. By this method it would appear to the people, as it already appeared to Samuel, that Saul was appointed of God to be king; for *the disposal of the lot is of the Lord.* It would also prevent all disputes and exceptions; for *the lot causeth contentions to cease, and parteth between the mighty.* When the tribe of Benjamin was taken, they might easily foresee that they were setting up a family that would soon be put down again; for dying Jacob had, by the spirit of prophecy, entailed the dominion upon Judah. Judah is the tribe that must *rule as a lion; Benjamin* shall only *ravin as a wolf,* Gen. 49:10, 27. Those therefore that knew the scriptures could not be very fond of the doing of that which they foresaw must, ere long, be undone again.

III. It is with much ado, and not without further enquiries of the Lord, that Saul is at length produced. When the lot fell upon him, every one expected he should answer to his name at the first call, but, instead of that, none of his friends could find him (*v.* 21), he had *hidden himself among the stuff* (*v.* 22), so little fond was he now of that power which yet, when he was in possession of, he could not without the utmost indignation think of parting with.

1. He withdrew, in hopes that, upon his not appearing, they would proceed to another choice, or thus to express his modesty; for, by what had already passed, he knew he must be the man. We may suppose he was at this time really averse to take upon him the government, (1.) Because he was conscious to himself of unfitness for so great a trust. He had not been bred up to books, or arms, or courts, and feared he should be guilty of some fatal blunder. (2.) Because it would expose him to the envy of his neighbours that were ill-affected towards him. (3.) Because he understood, by what Samuel had said, that the people sinned in asking a king, and it was in anger that God granted their request. (4.) Because the affairs of Israel were at this time in a bad posture; the Philistines were strong, the Ammonites threatening: and he must be bold indeed that will set sail in a storm.

2. But the congregation, believing that choice well made which God himself made, would leave no way untried to find him out on whom the lot fell. *They enquired of the Lord,* either by the high priest, and his breast-plate of judgment, or by Samuel, and his spirit of prophecy; and the Lord directed them where they should find him, hidden among the carriages, and thence *they fetched him, v.* 23. Note, None will be losers at last by their humility and modesty. Honour, like the shadow, follows those that flee from it, but flees from those that pursue it.

IV. Samuel presents him to the people, and they accept him. He needed not to mount the bench, or scaffold, to be seen; when he stood upon even ground with the rest he was seen above them all, for he was taller than any of them by *head and shoulders, v.* 23. "Look you," said Samuel, "what a king God has chosen for you, just such a one as you wished for; *there is none like him among all the people,* that has so much majesty in his countenance and such a graceful stateliness in his mien; he is in the crowd like a cedar among the shrubs. Let your own eyes be judges, is he not a brave and gallant man?" The people hereupon signified their approbation of the choice, and their acceptance of him; they *shouted and said, Let the king live,* that is, "Let him long reign over us in health and prosperity." Subjects were wont to testify their affection and allegiance to their prince by their good wishes, and those turned (as our translation does this) into addresses to God. Ps. 72:15, *Prayer shall be made for him continually.* See Ps. 20:1. Samuel had told them they would soon be weary of their king, but, in the mind they are now in, they will never be so: *Let the king live.*

V. Samuel settles the original contract between them, and leaves it upon record, *v.* 25. He had before told them *the manner of the king* (*ch.* 8:11), how he would abuse his power; now he tells them *the manner of the kingdom,* or rather the law, or judgment, or constitution, of it, what power the prince might challenge and the utmost of the property the subject might claim. He fixed the land-marks between them, that neither might encroach upon the other. Let them rightly understand one another at first, and let the agreement remain in black and white, which will tend to preserve a good understanding between them ever after. The learned bishop Patrick thinks he now repeated and registered what he had told them (*ch.* 8:11) of the arbitrary power their kings would assume, that it might hereafter be a witness against them that they had drawn the calamity upon themselves, for they were warned what it would come to and yet they would have a king.

VI. The convention was dissolved when the solemnity was over: *Samuel sent every man to his house.* Here were no votes passed, nor, for aught that appears, so much as a motion made, for the raising of money to support the dignity of their new-elected king; if therefore he afterwards thinks fit to take what they do not think fit to give (which yet it was necessary that he should have), they must thank themselves. They went every man to his house, pleased with the name of a king over them, and *Saul also went home to Gibeah,* to his father's house, not puffed up with the name of a kingdom under him. At Gibeah he had no palace, no throne, no court, yet thither he goes. If he must be a king, as one mindful of the rock out of which he was hewn, he will make his own city the royal city, nor will he be ashamed (as too many are when they are preferred) of his mean relations. Such a humble spirit as this puts a beauty and lustre upon great advancements. The condition rising, and the mind not rising with it, behold how good and pleasant it is! But,

1. How did the people stand affected to their new king? The generality of them, it should seem, did not show themselves much concerned: They *went every man to his own house.* Their own domestic affairs lay nearer their hearts than any interests of the public; this was the general temper. But, (1.) There were some so faithful as to attend him: *A band of men whose hearts God had touched, v.* 26. Not the body of the people, but a small company, who because they were fond of their own choice of a king, or because they had so much more sense than their neighbours as to conclude that if he was a king he ought to be respected accordingly, went with him to Gibeah, as his life-guard. They were those *whose hearts God had touched,* in this instance, to do their duty. Note, Whatever good there is in us, or is done by us, at any time, it must be ascribed to the grace of God. If the heart bend at any time the right way, it is because he has touched it. One touch is enough, when it is divine. (2.) There were others so spiteful as to affront him; children of Belial, men that would endure no yoke, that would be pleased with nothing that either God or Samuel did; they *despised him* (*v.* 27) for the meanness of his tribe and family, the smallness of his estate, and the privacy of his education; and they said, *How shall this man save us?* Yet they did not propose any man more likely; nor, whomsoever they had, must their salvation come from the man, but from God. They would not join with their neighbours in testifying an affection to him and his government, by bringing him presents, or addressing him upon his accession to the crown. Perhaps those discontented spirits were most earnest for a king, and yet, now that they had one, they quarrelled with him, because he was not altogether such a one as themselves. It was reason enough for them not to like him because others did. Thus differently are men affected to our exalted Redeemer. God hath set him king upon the holy hill of Sion. There is a remnant that submit to him, rejoice in him, bring him presents, and follow him wherever he goes; and they are those *whose hearts God has touched,* whom he has *made willing in the day of his power.* But there are others who despise him, who ask, *How shall this man save us?* They are offended in him, stumble at his external meanness, and they will be broken by it.

2. How did Saul resent the bad conduct of those that were disaffected to his government? *He held his peace.* Margin, *He was as though he had been deaf.* He was so far from resenting it that he seemed not to take notice of it, which was an evidence of his humility and modesty, and the mercifulness of his disposition, and also that he was well satisfied with his title to the crown; for those are commonly most jealous of their honour, and most revengeful of affronts, that gain their power by improper means. Christ held his peace when he was affronted, for it was the day of his patience; but there is a day of recompence coming.

CHAPER 11

In this chapter we have the first-fruits of Saul's government, in the glorious rescue of Jabesh-Gilead out of the hands of the Ammonites. Let not Israel thence infer that therefore they did well to ask a king (God could and would have saved them without one); but let them admire God's goodness, that he did not reject them when they rejected him, and acknowledge his wisdom in the choice of the person whom, if he did not find fit, yet he made fit, for the great trust he called him to, and enabled, in some measure, to merit the crown by his public services, before it was fixed on his head by the public approbation. Here is, I. The great extremity to which the city of Jabesh-Gilead, on the other side of Jordan, was reduced by the Ammonites (*v.* 1–3). II. Saul's great readiness to come to their relief, whereby he signalized himself (*v.* 4–10). III. The good success of his attempt, by which God signalized him (*v.* 11). IV. Saul's tenderness, notwithstanding this, towards those that had opposed him (*v.* 12, 13). V. The public confirmation and recognition of his election to the government (*v.* 14, 15).

Verses 1–4

The Ammonites were bad neighbours to those tribes of Israel that lay next them, though descendants from just Lot, and, for that reason, dealt civilly with by Israel. See Deu. 2:19. Jephthah, in his time, had humbled them, but now the sin of Israel had put them into a capacity to make head again, and avenge that quarrel. The city of Jabesh-Gilead had been, some ages ago, destroyed by Israel's sword of justice, for not appearing against the wickedness of Gibeah (Judges 21:10); and now being replenished again, probably by the posterity of those that then escaped the sword, it is in danger of being destroyed by the Ammonites, as if some bad fate attended the place. Nahash, king of Ammon (1 Chr. 19:1) laid siege to it. Now here,

I. The besieged beat a parley (*v.* 1): *"Make a covenant with us, and we will* surrender upon terms, and *serve thee."* They had lost the virtue of Israelites, else they would not have thus lost the valour of Israelites, nor tamely yielded to serve an Ammonite, without one bold struggle for themselves. Had they not broken their covenant with God, and forsaken his service, they needed not thus to have courted a covenant with a Gentile nation, and offered themselves to serve them.

II. The besiegers offer them base and barbarous conditions; they will spare their lives, and take them to be their servants, upon condition that they shall *put out their right eyes, v.* 2. The Gileadites were content to part with their liberty and estates for the ransom of their blood; and, had the Ammonites taken them at their word, the matter would have been so settled immediately, and the Gileadites would not have sent out for relief. But their abject concessions make the Ammonites more insolent in their demands, and they cannot be content to have them for their servants, but, 1. They must torment them, and put them to pain, exquisite pain, for so the thrusting out of an eye would do. 2. They must disable them for war, and render them incapable, though not of labour (that would have been a loss to their lords), yet of bearing arms; for in those times they fought with shields in their left hands, which covered their left eye, so that a soldier without his right eye was in effect blind. 3. They must put a *reproach upon all Israel,* as weak and cowardly, that would suffer the inhabitants of one of their chief cities to be thus miserably used, and not offer to rescue them.

III. The besieged desire, and obtain, seven days' time to consider of this proposal, *v.* 3. If Nahash had not granted them this respite, we may suppose the horror of the proposal would have made them desperate, and they would rather have died with their swords in their hands than have surrendered to such merciless enemies: therefore Nahash, not imagining it possible that, in so short a time, they should have relief, and being very secure of the advantages he thought he had against them, in a bravado gave them seven days, that the reproach upon Israel, for not rescuing them, might be the greater, and his triumphs the more illustrious. But there was a providence in it, that his security might be his infatuation and ruin.

IV. Notice is sent of this to Gibeah. They said they would send messengers *to all the coasts of Israel* (*v.* 3), which made Nahash the more secure, for that, he thought, would be a work of time, and none would be forward to appear if they had not one common head; and perhaps Nahash had not yet heard of the new-elected king. But the messengers, either of their own accord or by order from their masters, went straight to Gibeah, and, not finding Saul within, told their news to the people, who fell a weeping upon hearing it, *v.* 4. They would sooner lament their brethren's misery and danger than think of helping them, shed their tears for them than shed their blood. They wept, as despairing to help the men of Jabesh-Gilead, and fearing lest, if that frontier-city should be lost, the enemy would penetrate into the very bowels of their country, which now appeared in great hazard.

Verses 5–11

What is here related turns very much to the honour of Saul, and shows the happy fruits of that other spirit with which he was endued. Observe here,

I. His humility. Though he was anointed king, and accepted by his people, yet he did not think it below him to know the state of his own flocks, but went himself to see them, and came in the evening, with his servants, *after the herd out of the field, v.* 5. This was an evidence that he was not puffed up with his advancement, as those are most apt to be that are raised from a mean estate. Providence had not yet found him business as a king; he left all to Samuel; and therefore, rather than be idle, he would, for the present, apply himself to his country business again. Though the sons of Belial would, perhaps, despise him the more for it, such as were virtuous and wise, and loved business themselves, would think never the worse of him. He had no revenues settled upon him for the support of his dignity, and he was desirous not to be burdensome to the people, for which reason, like Paul, he worked with his hands; for, if he neglect his domestic affairs, how must he maintain himself and his family? Solomon gives it as a reason why men should look well to their herds because *the crown doth not endure to every generation,* Prov. 27:23, 24. Saul's did not; he must therefore provide something surer.

II. His concern for his neighbours. When he perceived them in tears, he asked, *"What ails the people that they weep?* Let me know, that, if it be a grievance which can be redressed, I may help them, and that, if not, I may weep with them." Good magistrates are in pain if their subjects are in tears.

III. His zeal for the safety and honour of Israel. When he heard of the insolence of the Ammonites, and the distress of a city, a mother in Israel, *the Spirit of God came upon him,* and put great thoughts into his mind, *and his anger was kindled greatly, v.* 6. He was angry at the insolence of the Ammonites, angry at the mean and sneaking spirit of the men of Jabesh-Gilead, angry that they had not sent him notice sooner of the Ammonites' descent and the extremity they were likely to be reduced to. He was angry to see his neighbours weeping, when it was fitter for them to be preparing for war. It was a brave and generous fire that was now kindled in the breast of Saul, and such as became his high station.

IV. The authority and power he exerted upon this important occasion. He soon let Israel know that, though he had retired to his privacy, he had a care for the public, and knew how to command men into the field, as well as how to drive cattle out of the field, *v.* 5, 7. He sent a summons to all the coasts of Israel, to show the extent of his power beyond his own tribe, even to all the tribes, and ordered all the military men forthwith to appear in arms at a general rendezvous in Bezek. Observe, 1. His modesty, in joining Samuel in commission with himself. He would not execute the office of a king without a due regard to that of a prophet. 2. His mildness in the penalty threatened against those that should disobey his orders. He hews a yoke of oxen in pieces, and sends the pieces to the several cities of Israel, threatening, with respect to him who should decline the public service, not, "Thus shall it be done to *him,*" but, "Thus shall it be done to his *oxen.*" God had threatened it as a great judgment (Deu. 28:31), *Thy ox shall be slain before thy eyes, and thou shalt not eat thereof.* It was necessary that the command should be enforced with some penalty, but this was not nearly so severe as that which was affixed to a similar order by the whole congregation, Jdg. 21:5. Saul wished to show that his government was more gentle than that which they had been under. The effect of this summons was that the militia, or trained bands, of the nation, *came out as one man,* and the reason given is, because *the fear of the Lord fell upon them.* Saul did not affect to make them fear him, but they were influenced to observe his orders by the fear of God and a regard to him who had made Saul their king and them members one of another. Note, Religion and the fear of God will make men good subjects, good soldiers, and good friends to the public interests of the country. Those that fear God will make conscience of their duty to all men, particularly to their rulers.

V. His prudent proceedings in this great affair, *v.* 8. He numbered those that came in to him, that he might know his own strength, and how to distribute his forces in the best manner their numbers would allow. It is the honour of princes to know the number of their men, but it is the honour of the King of kings that *there is not any number of his armies,* Job 25:3. In this muster, it seems, Judah, though numbered by itself, made no great figure; for, as it was one tribe of twelve, so it was but an eleventh part of the whole number, 30,330, though the rendezvous was at Bezek, in that tribe. They wanted the numbers, or the courage, or the zeal for which that tribe used to be famous; so low was it, just before the sceptre was brought into it in David.

VI. His faith and confidence, and (grounded thereon) his courage and resolution, in this enterprise. It should seem that those very messengers who brought the tidings from Jabesh-Gilead Saul sent into the country to raise the militia, who would be sure to be faithful and careful in their own business, and them he now sends back to their distressed countrymen, with this assurance (in which, it is probable, Samuel encouraged him): *"To-morrow,* by such an hour, before the enemy can pretend that the seven days have expired, *you shall have deliverance, v.* 9. Be you ready to do your part, and we will not fail to do ours. Do you sally out upon the besiegers, while we surround them." Saul knew he had a just cause, a clear call, and God on his side, and therefore doubted not of success. This was good news to the besieged Gileadites, whose right eyes had wept themselves dry for their calamities, and now began to fail with looking for relief and to ache in expectation of the doom of the ensuing day, when they must look their last; the greater the exigence the more welcome the deliverance. When they heard it they were glad, relying on the assurances that were sent to them. And they sent into the enemies' camp (*v.* 10) to tell them that next day they would be ready to meet them, which the enemies understood as an intimation that they despaired of relief, and so were made the more secure by it. If they took not care, by sending out scouts, to rectify their own mistake, they must thank themselves if they were surprised: the besieged were under no obligation to give them notice of the help they were assured of.

VII. His industry and close application to this business. If he had been bred up to war from his youth, and had led regiments as often as he had followed droves, he could not have gone about an affair of this nature more dexterously nor more diligently. When the Spirit of the Lord comes upon men it will make them expert even without experience. A vast army (especially in comparison with the present usage) Saul had now at his foot, and a long march before him, nearly sixty miles, and over Jordan too. No cavalry in his army, but all infantry, which he divides into three battalions, *v.* 11. And observe, 1. With what incredible swiftness he flew to the enemy. In a day and a night he came to the place of action, where his own fate, and that of Israel, must be determined. He had passed his word, and would not break it; nay, he was better than his word, for he promised help next day, *by that time the sun was hot* (*v.* 9), but brought it before day, *in the morning-watch, v.* 11. Whom God helps he *helps right early,* Ps. 46:5. 2. With what incredible bravery he flew upon the enemy. Betimes in the morning, when they lay dreaming of the triumphs they expected that day over the miserable inhabitants of Jabesh-Gilead, before they were aware he was in the midst of their host; and his men, being marched against them in three columns, surrounded them on every side, so that they could have neither heart nor time to make head against them.

Lastly, To complete his honour, God crowned all these virtues with success. Jabesh-Gilead was rescued, and the Ammonites were totally routed; he had now the day before him to complete his victory in, and so complete a victory it was that those who remained, after a great slaughter, were scattered so that *two of them were not left together* to encourage or help one another, *v.* 11. We may suppose that Saul was the more vigorous in this matter, 1. Because there was some alliance between the tribe of Benjamin and the city of Jabesh-Gilead. That city had declined joining with the rest of the Israelites to destroy Gibeah, which was then punished as their crime, but perhaps was now remembered as their kindness, when Saul of Gibeah came with so much readiness and resolution to relieve Jabesh-Gilead. Yet that was not all; two-thirds of the Benjamites that then remained were provided with wives from that city (Jdg. 21:14), so that most of the mothers of Benjamin were daughters of Jabesh-Gilead, for which city Saul, being a Benjamite, had therefore a particular kindness; and we find they returned his kindness, *ch.* 31:11, 12. 2. Because it was the Ammonites' invasion that induced the people to desire a king (so Samuel says, *ch.* 12:12), so that if he had not done his part, in this expedition, he would have disappointed their expectations, and for ever forfeited their respect.

Verses 12–15

We have here the improvement of the glorious victory which Saul had obtained, not the improvement of it abroad, though we take it for granted that the men of Jabesh-Gilead, having so narrowly saved their right eyes, would with them now discern the opportunity they had of avenging themselves upon these cruel enemies and disabling them from ever straitening them in like manner again; now shall they be avenged on the Ammonites for their right eyes condemned, as Samson on the Philistines for his two eyes put out, Jdg. 16:28. But the account here given is of the improvement of this victory at home.

I. The people took this occasion to show their jealousy for the honour of Saul, and their resentment of the indignities done him. Samuel, it seems, was present, if not in the action (it was too far for him to march) yet to meet them when they returned victorious; and to him, as judge, the motion was made (for they knew Saul would not be judge in his own cause) that the sons of Belial that would not have him to reign over them should be brought forth and slain, *v.* 12. Saul's good fortune (as foolish men commonly call it) went further with them to confirm his title than either his choice by lot or Samuel's anointing him. They had not courage thus to move for the prosecution of those that opposed him when he himself looked mean, but, now that his victory made him look great, nothing would serve but they must be put to death.

II. Saul took this occasion to give further proofs of his clemency, for, without waiting for Samuel's answer, he himself quashed the motion (*v.* 13): *There shall not a man be put to death this day,* no, not those men, those bad men, that had abused him, and therein reflected on God himself, 1. Because it was a day of joy and triumph: *"To day the Lord has wrought salvation in Israel;* and, since God has been so good to us all, let us not be harsh one to another. Now that God has made the heart of Israel in general so glad, let not us make sad the hearts of any particular Israelites." 2. Because he hoped they were by this day's work brought to a better temper, were now convinced that this man, under God, could save them, now honoured him whom before they had despised; and, if they are but reclaimed, he is secured from receiving any disturbance by them, and therefore his point is gained. If an enemy be made a friend, that will be more to our advantage than to have him slain. And all good princes consider that their power is for edification, not for destruction.

III. Samuel took this occasion to call the people together *before the Lord in Gilgal, v.* 14, 15. 1. That they might publicly give God thanks for their late victory. There they *rejoiced greatly,* and, that God might have the praise of that which they had the comfort of, they *sacrificed to him,* as the giver of all their successes, *sacrifices of peace-offerings.* 2. That they might confirm Saul in the government, more solemnly than had been yet done, that he might not retire again to his obscurity. Samuel would have the kingdom renewed; he would renew his resignation, and the people should renew their approbation, and so in concurrence with, or rather in attendance upon, the divine nomination, they made Saul king, making it their own act and deed to submit to him.

CHAPTER 12

We left the general assembly of the states together, in the close of the foregoing chapter; in this chapter we have Samuel's speech to them, when he resigned the government into the hands of Saul, in which, I. He clears himself from all suspicion or imputation of mismanagement, while the administration was in his hands (*v.* 1–5). II. He reminds them of the great things God had done for them and for their fathers (*v.* 6–13). III. He sets before them good and evil, the blessing and the curse (*v.* 14, 15). IV. He awakens them to regard what he said to them, by calling to God for thunder (*v.* 16–19). V. He encourages them with hopes that all should be well (*v.* 20–25). This is his farewell sermon to that august assembly and Saul's coronation sermon.

Verses 1–5

Here, I. Samuel gives them a short account of the late revolution, and of the present posture of their government, by way of preface to what he had further to say to them, *v.* 1, 2. 1. For his own part, he had spent his days in their service; he began betimes to be useful among them, and had continued long so: *"I have walked before you,* as a guide to direct you, as a shepherd that leads his flock (Ps. 80:1), *from my childhood unto this day."* As soon as he was illuminated with the light of prophecy, in his early days, he began to be a burning and shining light to Israel; "and now my best days are done: *I am old and gray-headed;"* therefore they were the more unkind to cast him off, yet therefore he was the more willing to resign, finding the weight of government heavy upon his stooping shoulders. He was old, and therefore the more able to advise them, and the more observant they should have been of what he said, for *days shall speak* and *the multitude of years shall teach wisdom;* and there is a particular reverence due to the aged, especially aged magistrates and aged ministers. "I am old, and therefore not likely to live long, perhaps may never have an opportunity of speaking to you again, and therefore take notice of what I say." 2. As for his sons, *"Behold"* (says he), *"they are with you,* you may, if you please, call them to an account for any thing they have done amiss. They are present with you, and have not, upon this revolution, fled from their country. They are upon the level with you, subjects to the new king as well as you; if you can prove them guilty of any wrong, you may prosecute them now by a due course of law, punish them, and oblige them to make restitution." 3. As for their new king, Samuel had gratified them in setting him over them (*v.* 1): *"I have hearkened to your voice in all that you said to me,* being desirous to please you, if possible, and make you easy, though to the discarding of myself and family; and now will you hearken to me, and take my advice?" The change was now perfected: *"Behold, the king walketh before you"* (*v.* 2); he appears in public, ready to serve you in public business. Now that you have made yourselves like the nations in your civil government, and have cast off the divine administration in that, take heed lest you make yourselves like the nations in religion and cast off the worship of God.

II. He solemnly appeals to them concerning his own integrity in the administration of the government (*v.* 3): *Witness against me, whose ox have I taken?* Observe,

1. His design in this appeal. By this he intended, (1.) To convince them of the injury they had done him in setting him aside, when they had nothing amiss to charge him with (his government had no fault but that it was too cheap, too easy, too gentle), and also of the injury they had done themselves in turning off one that did not so much as take an ox or an ass from them, to put themselves under the power of one that would take from them their fields and vineyards, nay, and their very sons and daughters (*ch.* 8:11), so unlike would the manner of the king be from Samuel's manner. (2.) To preserve his own reputation. Those that heard of Samuel's being rejected as he was would be ready to suspect that certainly he had done some evil thing, or he would never have been so ill treated; so that it was necessary for him to make this challenge, that it might appear upon record that it was not for any iniquity in his hands that he was laid aside, but to gratify the humour of a giddy people, who owned they could not have a better man to rule them, only they desired a bigger man. There is a just debt which every man owes to his own good name, especially men in public stations, which is to guard it against unjust aspersions and suspi-

cions, that we may finish our course with honour as well as joy. (3.) As he designed hereby to leave a good name behind him, so he designed to leave his successor a good example before him; let him write after his copy, and he will write fair. (4.) He designed, in the close of his discourse, to reprove the people, and therefore he begins with a vindication of himself; for he that will, with confidence, tell another of his sin, must see to it that he himself be clear.

2. In the appeal itself observe,

(1.) What it is that Samuel here acquits himself from. [1.] He had never, under any pretence whatsoever, taken that which was not his own, ox or ass, had never distrained their cattle for tribute, fines, or forfeitures, nor used their service without paying for it. [2.] He had never defrauded those with whom he dealt, nor oppressed those that were under his power. [3.] He had never taken bribes to pervert justice, nor was ever biassed by favour for affection to give judgment in a cause against his conscience.

(2.) How he calls upon those that had slighted him to bear witness concerning his conduct: "*Here I am; witness against me.* If you have any thing to lay to my charge, do it *before the Lord and the king,* the proper judges." He puts honour upon Saul, by owning himself accountable to him if guilty of any wrong.

III. Upon this appeal he is honourably acquitted. He did not expect that they would do him honour at parting, though he well deserved it, and therefore mentioned not any of the good services he had done them, for which they ought to have applauded him, and returned him the thanks of the house; all he desired was that they should do him justice, and that they did (*v.* 4) readily owning, 1. That he had not made his government oppressive to them, nor used his power to their wrong. 2. That he had not made it expensive to them: *Neither hast thou taken aught of any man's hand* for the support of thy dignity. Like Nehemiah, he did *not require the bread of the governor* (Neh. 5:18), had not only been righteous, but generous, had *coveted no man's silver, or gold, or apparel,* Acts 20:33.

IV. This honourable testimony borne to Samuel's integrity is left upon record to his honour (*v.* 5): "*The Lord is witness,* who searcheth the heart, *and his anointed is witness,* who trieth overt acts;" and the people agree to it: "*He is witness.*" Note, The testimony of our neighbours, and especially the testimony of our own consciences for us, that we have in our places lived honestly, will be our comfort under the slights and contempts that are put upon us. Demetrius is a happy man, that has a *good report of all men and of the truth itself,* 3 Jn. 12.

Verses 6–15

Samuel, having sufficiently secured his own reputation, instead of upbraiding the people upon it with their unkindness to him, sets himself to instruct them, and keep them in the way of their duty, and then the change of the government would be the less damage to them.

I. He reminds them of the great goodness of God to them and to their fathers, gives them an abstract of the history of their nation, that, by the consideration of the great things God had done for them, they might be for ever engaged to love him and serve him. "Come," says he (*v.* 7), "stand still, stand in token of reverence when God is speaking to you, stand still in token of attention and composedness of mind, and give me leave to reason with you." Religion has reason on its side, Isa. 1:18. The work of ministers is to reason with people, not only to exhort and direct, but to persuade, to convince men's judgments, and so to gain their wills and affections. Let reason rule men, and they will be good. He reasons of the righteous acts of the Lord, that is, "both the benefits he hath bestowed upon you, in performance of his promises, and the punishments he has inflicted on you for your sins." His favours are called *his righteous acts* (Jdg. 5:11), because in them he is just to his own honour. He not only puts them in mind of what God had done for them in their days, but of what he had done of old, in the days of their fathers, because the present age had the benefit of God's former favours. We may suppose that his discourse was much larger than as here related. 1. he reminds them of their deliverance out of Egypt. Into that house of bondage Jacob and his family came down poor and little; when they were oppressed they cried unto God, who advanced Moses and Aaron, from mean beginnings, to be their deliverers, and

the founders of their state and settlement in Canaan, *v.* 6, 8. 2. He reminds them of the miseries and calamities which their fathers brought themselves into by forgetting God and serving other gods, *v.* 9. They enslaved themselves, for they were sold as criminals and captives into the hand of oppressors. They exposed themselves to the desolation of war, and their neighbours fought against them. 3. He reminds them of their fathers' repentance and humiliation before God for their idolatries: *They said, We have sinned, v.* 10. Let not them imitate the sins of their fathers, for what they had done amiss they had many a time wished undone again. In the day of their distress they had sought unto God, and had promised to serve him; let their children then reckon that good at all times which they found good in bad times. 4. He reminds them of the glorious deliverances God had wrought for them, the victories he had blessed them with, and their happy settlements, many a time, after days of trouble and distress, *v.* 11. He specifies some of their judges, Gideon and Jephthah, great conquerors in their time; among the rest he mentions Bedan, whom we read not of any where else: he might be some eminent person, that was instrumental of salvation to them, though not recorded in the book of Judges, such a one as Shamgar, of whom it is said that he *delivered* Israel, but not that he *judged* them, Jdg. 3:31. Perhaps this Bedan guarded and delivered them on one side, at the same time when some other of the judges appeared and acted for them on another side. Some think it was the same with Jair (so the learned Mr. Poole), others the same with Samson, who was Ben Dan, a son of Dan, of that tribe, and the Spirit of the Lord came upon him Be-Dan, inn Dan, in the camp of Can. Samuel mentions himself, not to his own praise, but to the honour of God, who had made him an instrument of subduing the Philistines. 5. At last he puts them in mind of God's late favour to the present generation, in gratifying them with a king, when they would prescribe to God by such a one to save them out of the hand of Nahash king of Ammon, *v.* 12, 13. Now it appears that this was the immediate occasion of their desiring a king: Nahash threatened them; they desired Samuel to nominate a general; he told them that God was commander-in-chief in all their wars and they needed no other, that what was wanting in them should be made up by his power: *The Lord is your king.* But they insisted on it, *Nay, but a king shall reign over us.* "And now," said he, "you have a king, a king of your own asking — let that be spoken to your shame; but a king of God's making — let that be spoken to his honour and the glory of his grace." God did not cast them off, even when they in effect cast him off.

II. He shows them that they are now upon their good behaviour, they and their king. Let them not think that they had now cut themselves off from all dependence upon God, and that now, having a king of their own, the making of their own fortunes (as men foolishly call it) was in their own hands; no, still their judgment must proceed from the Lord. He tells them plainly,

1. That their obedience to God would certainly be their happiness, *v.* 14. If they would not revolt from God to idols, nor rebel against him by breaking his commandments, but would persevere in their allegiance to him, would fear his wrath, serve his interests, and obey his will, then they and their king should certainly be happy; but observe how the promise is expressed: *Then you shall continue following the Lord your God;* that is, (1.) "You shall continue in the way of your duty to God, which will be your honour and comfort." Note, To those that are sincere in their religion God will give grace to persevere in it: those that follow God faithfully will be divinely strengthened to continue following him. And observe, Following God is a work that is its own wages. It is the matter of a promise as well as of a precept. (2.) "You shall continue under the divine guidance and protection: *You shall be after the Lord,* so it is in the original, that is, "he will go before you to lead and prosper you, and make your way plain. *The Lord is with you while you are with him.*"

2. That their disobedience would as certainly be their ruin (*v.* 15): "*If you rebel,* think not that your having a king will secure you against God's judgments, and that having in this instance made yourselves *like the nations* you may sin at as cheap a rate as they can. No, *the hand of the Lord will be against you, as it was against your fathers* when they offended him, in the days of the judges." We mistake

if we think that we can evade God's justice by shaking off his dominion. If God shall not rule us, yet he will judge us.

Verses 16–25

Two things Samuel here aims at: —

I. To convince the people of their sin in desiring a king. They were now rejoicing before God in and with their king (*ch.* 11:15), and offering to God the sacrifices of praise, which they hoped God would accept; and this perhaps made them think that there was no harm in their asking a king, but really they had done well in it. Therefore Samuel here charges it upon them as their sin, as wickedness, *great wickedness in the sight of the Lord.* Note, Though we meet with prosperity and success in a way of sin, yet we must not therefore think the more favourably of it. They have a king, and if they conduct themselves well their king may be a very great blessing to them, and yet Samuel will have them perceive and see that their *wickedness was great in asking a king.* We must never think well of that which God in his law frowns upon, though in his providence he may seem to smile upon it. Observe,

1. The expressions of God's displeasure against them for asking a king. At Samuel's word, God sent prodigious thunder and rain upon them, at a season of the year when, in that country, the like was never seen or known before, *v.* 16–18. Thunder and rain have natural causes and sometimes terrible effects. But Samuel made it to appear that this was designed by the almighty power of God on purpose to convince them that they had done very *wickedly in asking a king;* not only by its coming in an unusual time, in wheat-harvest, and this on a fair clear day, when there appeared not to the eye any signs of a storm, but by his giving notice of it before. Had there happened to be thunder and rain at the time when he was speaking to them, he might have improved it for their awakening and conviction, as we may in a like case; but, to make it no less than a miracle, before it came, (1.) He spoke to them of it (*v.* 16, 17): *Stand and see this great thing.* He had before told them to *stand and hear* (*v.* 7); but, because he did not see that his reasoning with them affected them (so stupid were they and unthinking), now he bids them *stand and see.* If what he said in a *still small voice* did not reach their hearts, nor his doctrine which dropped as the dew, they shall hear God speaking to them in dreadful claps of thunder and the great rain of his strength. He appealed to this as a sign: "*I will call upon the Lord, and he will send thunder, will* send it just now, to confirm the word of his servant, and to make you see that I spoke truly when I told you that God was angry with you for *asking a king.*" And the event proved him a true prophet; the sign and wonder came to pass. (2.) He spoke to God for it. Samuel called unto the Lord, and, in answer to his prayer, even while he was yet speaking, *the Lord sent thunder and rain.* By this Samuel made it to appear, not only what a powerful influence God has upon this earth, that he could, of a sudden, when natural causes did not work towards it, produce this dreadful rain and thunder, and bring them out of his treasures (Ps. 135:7), but also what a powerful interest he had in heaven, that God would thus *hearken to the voice of a man* (Jos. 10:14) and answer him *in the secret place of thunder,* Ps. 81:7. Samuel, that son of prayer, was still famous for success in prayer. Now by this extraordinary thunder and rain sent on this occasion, [1.] God testified his displeasure against them in the same way in which he had formerly testified it, and at the prayer of Samuel too, against the Philistines. *The Lord discomfited them with a great thunder, ch.* 7:10. Now that Israel rebelled, and vexed his Holy Spirit, he turned to be their enemy, and fought against them with the same weapons which, not long before, had been employed against their adversaries, Isa. 63:10. [2.] He showed them their folly in desiring a king to save them, rather than God or Samuel, promising themselves more from an arm of flesh than from the arm of God or from the power of prayer. Could their king *thunder with a voice like God?* Job 40:9. Could their prince command such forces as the prophet could by his prayers? [3.] He intimated to them that how serene and prosperous soever their condition seemed to be now that they had a king, like the weather in wheat-harvest, yet, if God pleased, he could soon change the face of their heavens, and persecute them with his tempest, as the Psalmist speaks.

2. The impressions which this made upon the people. It startled them very much, as well it might. (1.) *They greatly feared the Lord and Samuel.* Though when they had a king they were ready to think they must fear him only, God made them know that *he is greatly to be feared* and his prophets for his sake. Now they were rejoicing in their king, God taught them to rejoice with trembling. (2.) They owned their sin and folly in desiring a king: *We have added to all our sins this evil, v.* 19. Some people will not be brought to a sight of their sins by any gentler methods than storms and thunders. Samuel did not extort this confession from them till the matter was settled and the king confirmed, lest it should look as if he designed by it rather to establish himself in the government than to bring them to repentance. Now that they were *flattering themselves in their own eyes, their iniquity was found to be hateful,* Ps. 36:2. (3.) They earnestly begged Samuel's prayers (*v.* 19): *Pray for thy servants, that we die not.* They were apprehensive of their danger from the wrath of God, and could not expect that he should hear their prayers for themselves, and therefore they entreat Samuel to pray for them. Now they see their need of him whom awhile ago they slighted. Thus many that will not have *Christ to reign over them* would yet be glad to have him intercede for them, to turn away the wrath of God. And the time may come when those that have despised and ridiculed praying people will value their prayers, and desire a share in them. *"Pray"* (say they) *"to the Lord thy God;* we know not how to call him ours, but, if thou hast any interest in him, improve it for us."

II. He aims to confirm the people in their religion, and engage them for ever to cleave unto the Lord. The design of his discourse is much the same with Joshua's, *ch.* 23 and 24.

1. He would not that the terrors of the Lord should frighten them from him, for they were intended to frighten them to him (*v.* 20): *"Fear not; though you have done all this wickedness,* and though God is angry with you for it, yet do not therefore abandon his service, nor *turn from following him." Fear not,* that is, "despair not, fear not with amazement, the weather will clear up after the storm. Fear not; for, though God will frown upon his people, yet he will not forsake them (*v.* 22) *for his great name's sake;* do not you forsake him then." Every transgression in the covenant, though it displease the Lord, yet does not throw us out of covenant, and therefore God's just rebukes must not drive us from our hope in his mercy. The fixedness of God's choice is owing to the freeness of it; we may therefore hope he will not forsake his people, because it has *pleased him to make them his people.* Had he chosen them for their good merits, we might fear he would cast them off for their bad merits; but, choosing them *for his name's sake,* for his name's sake he will not leave them.

2. He cautions them against idolatry: *"Turn not aside* from God and the worship of him" (*v.* 20, and again *v.* 21); "for if you turn aside from God, whatever you turn aside to, you will find it is a vain thing, that can never answer your expectations, but will certainly deceive you if you trust to it; it is a broken reed, a broken cistern." Idols could not profit those that sought to them in their wants, nor deliver those that sought to them in their straits, for they were vain, and not what they pretended to be. *An idol is nothing in the world,* 1 Co. 8:4.

3. He comforts them with an assurance that he would continue his care and concern for them, *v.* 23. They desired him to pray for them, *v.* 19. He might have said, "Go to Saul, the king that you have put in my room," and get him to pray for you; but so far is he from upbraiding them with their disrespect to him that he promised them much more than they asked. (1.) They asked it of him as a favour; he promised it as a duty, and startles at the thought of neglecting it. *Pray for you!* says he, *God forbid that I should sin against the Lord in not doing it.* Note, It is a sin against God not to pray for the Israel of God, especially for those of them that are under our charge: and good men are afraid of the guilt of omissions. (2.) They asked him to pray for them at this time, and upon this occasion, but he promised to continue his prayers for them and to cease as long as he lived. Our rule is to *pray without ceasing;* we sin if we restrain prayer in general, and in particular if we cease praying for the church. (3.) They asked him only to pray for them, but he promised to do more for them, not only to pray for them, but to teach them; though they were not willing to be under his government as a judge, he would not therefore deny them his instructions as a prophet. And they might be sure he would teach them no other than the *good and the right way:* and the right way is certainly the good way: the way of duty is the way of pleasure and profit.

4. He concludes with an earnest exhortation to practical religion and serious godliness, *v.* 24, 25. The great duty here pressed upon us is to *fear the Lord.* He had said (*v.* 20), *"Fear not* with a slavish fear," but here, "Fear the Lord, with a filial fear." As the fruit and evidence of this, serve him in the duties of religious worship and of a godly conversation, in truth and sincerity, and not in show and profession only, with your heart, and *with all your heart,* not dissembling, not dividing. And two things he urges by way of motive: — (1.) That they were bound in gratitude to serve God, considering *what great things he had done for them,* to engage them for ever to his service. (2.) That they were bound in interest to serve him, considering what great things he would do against them if they should still do wickedly: *"You shall be destroyed* by the judgments of God, *both you and your king* whom you are so proud of and expect so much from, and who will be a blessing to you if you keep in with God." Thus, as a faithful watchman, he gave them warning, and so delivered his own soul.

CHAPTER 13

Those that desired a king like all the nations fancied that, when they had one, they should look very great and considerable; but in this chapter we find it proved much otherwise. While Samuel was joined in commission with Saul things went well (11:7). But, now that Saul began to reign alone, all went to decay, and Samuel's words began to be fulfilled: "You shall be consumed, both you and your king;" for never was the state of Israel further gone in a consumption than in this chapter. I. Saul appears here a very silly prince. 1. Infatuated in his counsels (*v.* 1–3). 2. Invaded by his neighbours (*v.* 4, 5). 3. Deserted by his soldiers (*v.* 6, 7). 4. Disordered in his own spirit, and sacrificing in confusion (*v.* 8–10). 5. Chidden by Samuel (*v.* 11–13). 6. Rejected of God from being king (*v.* 14). II. The people appear hear a very miserable people. 1. Disheartened and dispersed (*v.* 6, 7). 2. Diminished (*v.* 15, 16). 3. Plundered (*v.* 17, 18). 4. Disarmed (*v.* 19–23). This they got by casting off God's government, and making themselves like the nations: all their glory departed from them.

Verses 1–7

We are not told wherein it was that the people of Israel offended God, so as to forfeit his presence and turn his hand against them, as Samuel had threatened (*ch.* 12:15); but doubtless they left God, else he would not have left them, as here it appears he did; for,

I.. Saul was very weak and impolitic, and did not order his affairs with discretion. *Saul was the son of one year* (so the first words are in the original), a phrase which we make to signify the date of his reign, but ordinarily it signifies the date of one's birth, and therefore some understand it figuratively — he was as innocent and good as a child of a year old; so the Chaldee paraphrase: he was *without fault, like the son of a year.* But, if we admit a figurative sense, it may as well intimate that he was ignorant and imprudent, and as unfit for business as a child of a year old: and the subsequent particulars make this more accordant with his character than the former. But we take it rather, as our own translation has it, *Saul reigned one year,* and nothing happened that was considerable, it was a year of no action; but in his second year he did as follows: — 1. he chose a band of 3000 men, of whom he himself commanded 2000, and his son Jonathan 1000, *v.* 2. The rest of the people he dismissed to their tents. If he intended these only for the guard of his person and his honorary attendants, it was impolitic to have so many, if for a standing army, in apprehension of danger from the Philistines, it was no less impolitic to have so few; and perhaps the confidence he put in this select number, and his disbanding the rest of that brave army with which he had lately beaten the Ammonites (*ch.* 11:8–11), was looked upon as an affront to the kingdom, excited general disgust, and was the reason he had so few at his call when he had occasion for them. The prince that relies on a particular party weakens his own interest in the whole community. 2. He ordered his son Jonathan to surprise and destroy the garrison of the Philistines that lay near him in Geba, *v.* 3. I wish there were no ground for supposing that this was a violation or infraction of some articles with the Philistines, and that it was done treacherously and perfidiously. The reason why I suspect it is because it is said that, for doing it, *Israel was had in abomination,* or, as the word is, *did stink with the Philistines* (*v.* 4), as men void of common honesty and whose word could not be relied on. If it was so, we will lay the blame, not on Jonathan who did it, but on Saul, his prince and father, who ordered him to do it, and perhaps kept him in ignorance of the truth of the matter. Nothing makes the name of Israel odious to those that are without so much as the fraud and dishonesty of those that are called by that worthy name. If professors of religion cheat and over-reach, break their word and betray their trust, religion suffers by it, and is *had in abomination with the Philistines.* Whom may one trust if not an Israelite, one that, it is expected, should be *without guile?* 3. When he had thus exasperated the Philistines, then he began to raise forces, which, if he had acted wisely, he would have done before. When the Philistines had a vast army ready to pour in upon him, to avenge the wrong he had done them, then was he *blowing the trumpet through the land,* among a careless, if not a disaffected people, saying, *Let the Hebrews hear* (*v.* 3), and so as many as thought fit came to Saul to Gilgal, *v.* 4. But now the generality, we may suppose, drew back (either in dislike of Saul's politics or in dread of the Philistines' power), who, if he had summoned them sooner, would have been as ready at his beck as they were when he marched against the Ammonites. We often find that after-wit would have done much better before and have prevented much inconvenience.

II. Never did the Philistines appear in such a formidable body as they did now, upon this provocation which Saul gave them. We may suppose they had great assistance from their allies, for (*v.* 5), besides 6000 horse, which in those times, when horses were not so much used in war as they are now, was a great body, they had an incredible number of chariots, 30,000 in all: most of them, we may suppose, were carriages for the bag and baggage of so vast an army, not chariots of war. But their foot was *innumerable as the sand of the sea-shore,* so jealous were they for the honour of their nation and so much enraged at the baseness of the Israelites in destroying their garrison. If Saul had asked counsel of God before he had given the Philistines this provocation, he and his people might the better have borne this threatening trouble which they had now brought on themselves by their own folly.

III. Never were the people of Israel so faint-hearted, so sneaking, so very cowardly, as they were now. Some considerable numbers, it may be, came to Saul to Gilgal; but, hearing of the Philistines' numbers and preparations, their spirits sunk within them, some think because they did not find Samuel there with Saul. Those that, awhile ago, were weary of him, and wished for a king, now had small joy of their king unless they could see him under Samuel's direction. Sooner or later, men will be made to see that God and his prophets are their best friends. Now that they saw the Philistines making war upon them, and Samuel not coming in to help them, they knew not what to do; *men's hearts failed them for fear.* And. 1. Some absconded. Rather than run upon death among the Philistines, they buried themselves alive in caves and thickets, *v.* 6. See what work sin makes; it exposes men to perils, and then robs them of their courage and dispirits them. A single person, by faith, can say, *I will not be afraid of* 10,000 (Ps. 3:6); but here thousands of degenerate Israelites tremble at the approach of a great crowd of Philistines. Guilt makes men cowards. 2. Others fled (*v.* 7): They *went over Jordan to the land of Gilead,* as far as they could from the danger, and to a place where they had lately been victorious over the Ammonites. Where they had triumphed they hoped to be sheltered. 3. Those that staid with Saul *followed him trembling,* expecting no other than to be cut off, and having their hands and hearts very much weakened by the desertion of so many of their troops. And perhaps Saul himself, though he had so much honour as to stand his ground, yet had no courage to spare wherewith to inspire his trembling soldiers.

Verses 8–14

Here is, I. Saul's offence in offering sacrifice before Samuel came. Samuel, when he anointed him, had ordered him to tarry for him seven days in Gilgal, promising that, at the end of those days, he would be sure to come to him, and both offer sacrifices for him and direct him what he should do. This we had *ch.* 10:8. Perhaps that order, though inserted there, was given him afterwards, or was given him as a general rule to be observed in every public congress at Gilgal, or, as is most probable, though not mentioned again, was lately repeated with reference to this particular occasion; for it is plain that Saul himself understood it as obliging him from God now to stay till Samuel came, else he would not have made so many excuses as he did for not staying, *v.* 11. This order Saul broke. He staid till the seventh day, yet had not patience to wait till the end of the seventh day. Perhaps he began to reproach Samuel as false to his word, careless of his country, and disrespectful of his prince, and thought it more fit that Samuel should wait for him than he for Samuel. However, 1. He presumed to offer sacrifice without Samuel, and nothing appears to the contrary but that he did it himself, though he was neither priest nor prophet, as if, because he was a king, he might do any thing, a piece of presumption which king Uzziah paid dearly for, 2 Chr. 26:16, etc. 2. He determined to engage the Philistines without Samuel's directions, though he had promised to *show him what he should do.* So self-sufficient Saul was that he thought it not worth while to stay for a prophet of the Lord, either to pray for him or to advise him. This was Saul's offence, and that which aggravated it was, (1.) That for aught that appears, he did not send any messenger to Samuel, to know his mind, to represent the case to him, and to receive fresh directions from him, though he had enough about him that were swift enough of foot at this time. (2.) That when Samuel came he rather seemed to boast of what he had done than to repent of it; for he *went forth to salute him,* as his brother-sacrificer, and seemed pleased with the opportunity he had of letting Samuel know that he needed him not, but could do well enough without him. He went out to *bless him,* so the word is, as if he now thought himself a complete priest, empowered to bless as well as sacrifice, whereas he should have gone out to be blessed by him. (3.) That he charged Samuel with breach of promise: *Thou camest not within the days appointed* (*v.* 11), and therefore if any thing was amiss Samuel must bear the blame, who was God's minister; whereas he did come according to his word, before the seven days had expired. Thus the *scoffers of the latter days* think the promise of Christ's coming is broken, because he does not come in their time, though it is certain he will come at the set time. (4.) That when he was charged with disobedience he justified himself in what he had done, and gave no sign at all of repentance for it. It is not sinning that ruins men, but sinning and not repenting, falling and not getting up again. See what excuses he made, *v.* 11, 12. He would have this act of disobedience pass, [1.] For an instance of his prudence. The people were most of them scattered from him, and he had no other way than this to keep those with him that remained and to prevent their deserting too. If Samuel neglected the public concerns, he would not. [2.] For an instance of his piety. He would be thought very devout, and in great care not to engage the Philistines till he had by prayer and sacrifice engaged God on his side: *"The Philistines,"* said he, *"will come down upon me, before I have made my supplication to the Lord,* and then I am undone. What! go to war before I have said my prayers!" Thus he covered his disobedience to God's command with a pretence of concern for God's favour. Hypocrites lay a great stress upon the external performances of religion, thinking thereby to excuse their neglect of the *weightier matters of the law.* And yet, lastly, He owns it went against his conscience to do it: *I forced myself and offered a burnt-offering,* perhaps boasting that he had broken through his convictions and got the better of them, or at least thinking this extenuated his fault, that he knew he should not have done as he did, but did it with reluctancy. Foolish man! to think that God would be well pleased with sacrifices offered in direct opposition both to his general and particular command.

II. The sentence passed upon Saul for this offence. Samuel found him standing by his burnt-offering, but, instead of an answer of peace, was sent to him with heavy tidings, and let him know that *the sacrifice of the wicked is abomination to the Lord,* much more when he brings it, as Saul did, *with a wicked mind.* 1. He shows him the aggravations of his crime, and says to this king, *Thou art wicked,* which it is not for any but a prophet of the Lord to say, Job 34:18. He charges him with being an enemy to himself and his interest — *Thou hast done foolishly,* and a rebel to God and his government — *"Thou hast not kept the commandment of the Lord thy God,* that commandment wherewith he intended to try thy obedience." Note, Those that disobey the commandments of God do foolishly for themselves. Sin is folly, and sinners are the greatest fools. 2. He reads his doom (*v.* 14): *"Thy kingdom shall not continue* long to thee or thy family; God has his eye upon another, *a man after his own heart,* and not like thee, that will have thy own will and way." The sentence is in effect the same with *Mene tekel,* only now there seems room left for Saul's repentance, upon which this sentence would have been reversed; but, upon the next act of disobedience, it was made irreversible, *ch.* 15:29. And now, better a thousand times he had continued in obscurity tending his asses than to be enthroned and so soon dethroned. But was not this hard, to pass so severe a sentence upon him and his house for a single error, an error that seemed so small, and in excuse for which he had so much to say? No, *The Lord is righteous in all his ways* and does no man any wrong, *will be justified when he speaks and clear when he judges.* By this, (1.) He shows that there is no sin little, because no little god to sin against; but that every sin is a forfeiture of the heavenly kingdom, for which we stood fair. (2.) He shows that disobedience to an express command, though in a small matter, is a great provocation, as in the case of our first parents. (3.) He warns us to *take heed of our spirits,* for that which to men may seem but a small offence, yet to him that knows from what principle and with what disposition of mind it is done, may appear a heinous crime. (4.) God, in rejecting Saul for an error seemingly little, sets off, as by a foil, the lustre of his mercy in forgiving such great sins as those of David, Manasseh, and others. (5.) We are taught hereby how necessary it is that we *wait on our God continually.* Saul lost his kingdom for want of two or three hours' patience.

Verses 15–23

Here, 1. Samuel departs in displeasure. Saul has set up for himself, and now he is left to himself: *Samuel gat him from Gilgal* (*v.* 15), and it does not appear that he either prayed with Saul or directed him. Yet in going up to Gibeah of Benjamin, which was Saul's city, he intimated that he had not quite abandoned him, but waited to do him a kindness another time. Or he went to the college of the prophets there, to pray for Saul when he did not think fit to pray with him. 2. Saul goes after him to Gibeah, and there musters his army, and finds his whole number to be but 600 men, *v.* 15, 16. Thus were they for their sin *diminished and brought low.* 3. The Philistines ravage the country, and put all the adjacent parts under contribution. The body of their army, or standing camp (as it is called in the margin, *v.* 23), lay in an advantageous pass at Michmash, but thence they sent out three separate parties or detachments that took several ways, to plunder the country, and bring in provisions for the army, *v.* 17, 18. By these the land of Israel was both terrified and impoverished, and the Philistines were animated and enriched. This the sin of Israel brought upon them, Isa. 42:24. 4. The Israelites that take the field with Saul are unarmed, having only slings and clubs, not a sword or spear among them all, except what Saul and Jonathan themselves have, *v.* 19, 22. See here, (1.) How politic the Philistines were, when they had power in their hands, and did what they pleased in Israel. They put down all the smiths' shops, transplanted the smiths into their own country, and forbade any Israelite, under severe penalties, to exercise the trade or mystery of working in brass or iron, though they had rich mines of both (Deu. 8:9) in such plenty that it was said of Asher, *his shoes shall be iron and brass,* Deu. 33:25. This was subtilely done of the Philistines, for hereby they not only prevented the people of Israel from making themselves weapons of war (by which they would be both disused to military exercises and unfurnished when there was occasion), but obliged them to a dependence upon them even for the instruments of husbandry; they must go to them, that is, to some or other of their garrisons, which were dispersed in the country, to have all their iron-work done, and no more might an Israelite do than use a file (*v.* 20, 21), and no doubt the Philistines' smiths brought the Israelites long bills for work done. (2.) How impolitic Saul was, that did not, in the beginning of his reign, set himself to redress this grievance. Samuel's not doing it was very excusable; he fought with other artillery; thunder and lightning, in answer to his prayer, were to him instead of sword and spear; but for Saul, that pretended to be a king like the kings of the nations, to leave his soldiers without swords and spears, and take no care to provide them, especially when he might have done it out of the spoils of the Ammonites whom he conquered in the beginning of his reign, was such a piece of negligence as could by no means be excused. (3.) How slothful and mean-spirited the Israelites were, that suffered the Philistines thus to impose upon them and had no thought nor spirit to help themselves. It was reckoned very bad with them when there was *not a shield or spear found among* 40,000 *in Israel* (Jdg. 5:8), and it was not better now, when there was never an Israelite with a sword by his side but the king and his son, never a soldier, never a gentleman; surely they were reduced to this, or began to be so, in Samuel's time, for we never find him with sword or spear in his hand. If they had not been dispirited, they could not have been disarmed, but it was sin that made them naked to their shame.

CHAPTER 14

We left the host of Israel in a very ill posture, in the close of the foregoing chapter; we saw in them no wisdom, nor strength, nor goodness, to give us ground to expect any other than that they should all be cut off by the army of the Philistines; yet here we find that infinite power which works without means, and that infinite goodness which gives without merit, glorified in a happy turn to their affairs, that still Samuel's words may be made good: "The Lord will not forsake his people, for his great name's sake," (12:22). In this chapter we have, I. The host of the Philistines trampled upon, and triumphed over, by the faith and courage of Jonathan, who unknown to his father (*v.* 1–3), with his armour-bearer only, made a brave attack upon them, encouraging himself in the Lord his God (*v.* 4–7). He challenged them (*v.* 8–12), and, upon their acceptance of the challenge, charged them with such fury, or rather such faith, that he put them to flight, and set them one against another (*v.* 13–15), which gave opportunity to Saul and his forces, with other Israelites, to follow the blow, and gain a victory (*v.* 16–23). II. The host of Israel troubled and perplexed by the rashness and folly of Saul, who adjured the people to eat no food till night, which 1. Brought Jonathan to a praemunire (*v.* 24–30). 2. Was a temptation to the people, when the time of their fast had expired, to eat with the blood, (*v.* 31–35). Jonathan's error, through ignorance, had like to have been his death, but the people rescued him (*v.* 36–46). III. In the close we have a general account of Saul's exploits (*v.* 47, 48) and of his family (*v.* 49–52).

Verses 1–15

We must here take notice,

I. Of the goodness of God in restraining the Philistines, who had a vast army of valiant men in the field, from falling upon that little handful of timorous trembling people that Saul had with him, whom they would easily have swallowed up at once. It is an invisible power that sets bounds to the malice of the church's enemies, and suffers them not to do that which we should think there is nothing to hinder them from.

II. Of the weakness of Saul, who seems here to have been quite at a loss, and unable to help himself. 1. He pitched his tent under a tree, and had but 600 men with him, *v.* 2. Where were now the 3000 men he had chosen, and put such a confidence in? *ch.* 13:2. Those whom he trusted too much to failed him when he most needed them. He durst not stay in Gibeah, but got into some obscure place, in the uttermost part of the city, under a pomegranate-tree, under *Rimmon* (so the word is), *Ha-Rimmon,* that Rimmon near Gibeah, in the caves of which those 600 Benjamites that escaped his themselves, Jdg. 20:47. Some think that there Saul took shelter, so mean and abject was his spirit, now that he had fallen under God's displeasure, every hour expecting the Philistines upon him, and thereby the accomplishment of Samuel's threatening, *ch.* 13:14. Those can never think themselves safe that see themselves cast out of God's protection. 2. Now he sent for a priest, and the ark, a priest from Shiloh, and the ark from Kirjath-jearim, *v.* 3, 18. Saul had once offended by offering sacrifice himself, *ch.* 13:9. Now he resolves never to fall into that error again, and therefore sends for a priest, and hopes to compromise the matter with God Almighty by a particular reformation, as many do whose hearts are unhumbled and unchanged. Samuel, the Lord's prophet, had forsaken him, but he thinks he can make up that loss by commanding Ahiah, the Lord's priest, to attend him, and *he* will not make him stay for him nor reprove him, as Samuel had done, but will do just as he bids him, *v.* 18, 19. Many love to have such ministers as will be what they would have them to be, and prophesy smooth things to them; and their caressing them because they are priests, they hope, will atone for their enmity to those ministers that deal faithfully and plainly with them. He will also have the ark brought, perhaps to upbraid Samuel, who in the days of his government, for aught that appears, had not made any public use of it; or in hopes that this would make up the deficiency of his forces; one would have supposed that they would never bring the ark into the camp again, since, the last time, it not only did not save them, but did itself fall into the Philistines' hands. But it is common for those that have lost the substance of religion to be most fond of the shadows of it, as here is a deserted prince courting a deserted priest.

III. Of the bravery and piety of Jonathan, the son of Saul, who was much fitter than the father to wear the crown. "A sweet imp (says bishop Hall) out of a crab-stock."

1. He resolved to go *incognito — unknown to any one,* into the camp of the Philistines; he did not acquaint his father with his design, for he knew he would forbid him; nor the people, for he knew they would all discourage him, and, because he resolved not to heed their objections, he resolved not to hear them, nor ask their advice, *v.* 1, 3. Nor had he so great an opinion of the priest as to consult him, but, being conscious of a divine impulse putting him upon it, he threw himself into the mouth of danger, in hope of doing service to his country. The way of access to the enemies' camp is described (*v.* 4, 5) as being peculiarly difficult, and their natural entrenchments impregnable, yet this does not discourage him; the strength and sharpness of the rocks do but harden and whet his resolutions. Great and generous souls are animated by opposition and take a pleasure in breaking through it.

2. He encouraged his armour-bearer, a young man that attended him, to go along with him in the daring enterprise, (*v.* 6): *"Come, and let us* put our lives in our hands, *and go over to the* enemies' *garrison,* and try what we can do to put them into confusion." See whence he draws his encouragements. (1.) "They are uncircumcised, and have not the seal of the covenant in their flesh, as we have. Fear not, we shall do well enough with them, for they are not under the protection of God's covenant as we are, cannot call him theirs as we can, by the sign of circumcision." If such as are enemies to us are also strangers to God, we need not fear them. (2.) "God is able to make us two victorious over their unnumbered regiments. *There is no restraint in the Lord,* no limitation to the holy One of Israel, but it is all one to him *to save by many or by few."* This is a true easily granted in general, that it is all alike to Omnipotence what the instruments are by which it works; and yet it is not so easy to apply it to a particular case; when we are but few and feeble then to believe that God can not only save us, but save by us, this is an instance of faith, which, wherever it is, shall obtain a good report. Let this strengthen the weak and encourage the timid: let it be pleaded with God for the enforcing of our petitions and with ourselves for the silencing of our fears: *It is nothing with God to help, whether with many or with those that have no power,* 2 Chr. 14:11. (3.) "Who knows but he that can use us for his glory will do it? *It may be the Lord will work for us,* work with us, work a sign or miracle for us." So the Chaldee. We may encourage ourselves with hope that God will appear for us, though we have not ground on which to build an assurance. An active faith will venture far in God's cause upon an *it may be.* Jonathan's armour-bearer, or esquire, as if he had learned to carry, not his arms only, but his heart, promised to stand by him and to follow him withersoever he went, *v.* 7. We have reason to think that Jonathan felt a divine impulse and impression putting him upon this bold adventure, in which he was encouraged by his servant's concurrence, otherwise the danger was so great which he ran upon that he would have tempted God rather than trusted him. And perhaps he had an actual regard to that word of Joshua (Jos. 23:10), *One man of you shall chase a thousand,* borrowed from Moses, Deu. 32:30.

3. How bold soever his resolution was, he resolved to follow Providence in the execution of it, which, he believed, would guide him *with its eye* (Ps. 32:8), and which therefore he would carefully attend and take hints of direction from. See how he put himself upon Providence, and resolved to be determined by it. "Come" (says he to his confidant), "we will discover ourselves to the enemy, as those that are not afraid to look them in the face (*v.* 8), and then, if they be so cautious as to bid us stand, we will advance no further, taking it for an intimation of Providence that God would have us act defensively, and we will prepare as well as we can to give them a warm reception (*v.* 9); but if they be so presumptuous as to challenge us, and the first sentinel we meet with bid us march on, we will push forward, and make as brisk an onset, assuredly gathering thence that it is the will of God we should act offensively, and then not doubting but he will *stand by us," v.* 10. And upon this issue he puts it, firmly believing, as we all should, (1.) That God has the governing of the hearts and tongues of all men, even of those that know him not, nor have any regard to him, and serves his own purposes by them, though they mean not so, neither do their hearts think so. Jonathan knew God could discover his mind to him if he pleased, and would do it, since he depended upon him, as surely by the mouth of a Philistine as by the mouth of a priest. (2.) That God will, some way or other, direct the steps of those that *acknowledge him in all their ways,* and seek unto him for direction, with full purpose of heart to follow it. Sometimes we find most comfort in that which is least our own doing, and into which we have been led by the unexpected, but well observed, turns of Providence.

4. Providence gave him the sign he expected, and he answered the signal. He and his armour-bearer did not surprise the Philistines when they were asleep, but discovered themselves to them by day-light, *v.* 11. The guards of the Philistines, (1.) Disdained them, upbraided them with the cowardice of many of their people, and looked upon them to be of the regiment of sneakers: *Behold, the Hebrews come forth out of their holes.* If some of Christ's soldiers play the coward, others that play the man may perhaps be upbraided with it. (2.) They defied them (*v.* 12): *Come, and we will show you a thing,* as if they came like children to gaze about them; but meaning, as Goliath (*ch.* 17:44), that they would *give them as meat to the fowls of the air.* They bantered them, not doubting but to make a prey of them. This greatly emboldened Jonathan. With it he encouraged his servant; he had spoken with uncertainty (*v.* 6): *It may be the Lord will work for us;* but now he speaks with assurance (*v.* 12): *The Lord has delivered them,* not into our hands (he sought not his own glory), but *into the hand of Israel,* for he aimed at nothing but the advantage of the public. His faith being thus strengthened, no difficulty can stand before him; he climbs up the rock upon all four (*v.* 13), though he has nothing to cover him, nor any but his own servant to second him, nor any human probability of any thing but death before him.

5. The wonderful success of this daring enterprise. The Philistines, instead of falling upon Jonathan, to slay him, or take him prisoner, fell before him (*v.* 13) unaccountably, upon the first blows he gave. They fell, that is, (1.) They were many of them slain by him and his armour-bearer, *v.* 14. Twenty Philistines fell presently. It was not so much the name of Jonathan that made them yield so tamely (though some think that this had become terrible to them, since he smote one of their garrisons, *ch.* 13:3), but it was God's right hand and his arm that got him this victory. (2.) The rest were put to flight, and fell foul upon one another (*v.* 15): *There was trembling in the host.* There was no visible cause for fear; they were so numerous, bold, and advantageously posted; the Israelites had fled before them; not an enemy made head against them, but one gentleman and his man; and yet they shook like an aspen-leaf. The consternation was general: they all trembled; even *the spoilers,* those that had been most bold and forward, shared in the common fright, the joints of their loins were loosed, and their knees smote one against another, and yet none of them could tell why or wherefore. It is called *a trembling of God* (so the original phrase is), signifying not only, as we render it, a very great trembling, which they could not resist nor reason themselves clear of, but that it was supernatural, and came immediately from the hand of God. He that made the heart knows how to make it tremble. To complete the confusion, even the earth quaked, and made them ready to fear that it would sink under them. Those that will not fear the eternal God, he can make afraid of a shadow. See Prov. 21:1; Isa. 33:14.

Verses 16–23

We have here the prosecution and improvement of the wonderful advantages which Jonathan and his armour-bearer gained against the Philistines.

I. The Philistines were, by the power of God, set against one another. They melted away like snow before the sun, and *went on beating down one another* (*v.* 16), for (*v.* 20) *every man's sword was against his fellow.* When they fled for fear, instead of turning back upon those that chased them, they reckoned those only their enemies that stood in their way, and treated them accordingly. The Philistines were very secure, because all the swords and spears were in their hands. Israel had none except what Saul and Jonathan had. But now God showed them the folly of that confidence, by making their own swords and spears the instruments of their own destruction, and more fatal in their own hands than if they had been in the hands of Israel. See the like done, Jdg. 7:22; 2 Chr. 20:23.

II. The Israelites were hereby animated against them.

1. Notice was soon taken of it by the watchmen of Saul, those that stood sentinel at Gibeah, *v.* 16. They were aware that the host of the enemy was in great confusion, and that a great slaughter was made among them, and yet, upon search, they found none of their own forces absent, but only Jonathan and his servant (*v.* 17), which no doubt greatly animated them, and assured them that it could be no other than the Lord's doing, when there was no more of man's doing than what those two could do against a great host.

2. Saul began to enquire of God, but soon desisted. His spirit had not come down so far as to allow him to consult Samuel, though, it is probable, he was near him; for we read (*ch.* 13:15) that he had come to Gibeah of Benjamin; but he called for the ark (*v.* 18), desiring to know whether it would be safe for him to attack the Philistines, upon the disorder they perceived them to be in. Many will consult God about their safety that would never consult him about their duty. But, perceiving by his scouts that the noise in the enemy's camp increased, he commanded the priest that officiated to break off abruptly: *"Withdraw thy hand* (*v.* 19), consult no more, wait no longer for an answer." He was very unwise indeed if (as some think) he forbade him to lift up his hands in prayer; for when Joshua was actually engaged with Amalek Moses continued still to lift up his hands. It is rather a prohibition to his enquiring of the Lord, either, (1.) Because now he thought he did not need an answer, the case was plain enough. And yet the more evident it was that God did all the more reason he had to enquire whether he would give him leave to do any thing. Or, (2.) Because now he would not stay for it; he was in such haste to fight a falling enemy that he would not stay to make and end of his devotions, nor hear what answer God would give him. A little thing will divert a vain and carnal mind from religious exercises. He that believeth will not make haste, such haste as this, nor reckon any business so urgent as not to allow time to take God along with him.

3. He, and all the little force he had, made a vigorous attack upon the enemy; and all the people *were cried together* (so the word is, *v.* 20), for want of the silver trumpets wherewith God appointed them to sound an alarm in the day of battle, Num. 10:9. They summoned them together by shouting, and their number was not so great but that they might soon be got together. And now they seem bold and brave when the work is done to their hands. Our Lord Jesus had conquered our spiritual enemies, routed and dispersed them, so that we are cowards indeed if we will not stand to our arms when it is only to pursue the victory and to divide the spoil.

4. Every Hebrew, even those from whom one would least have expected it, now turned his hand against the Philistines. (1.) Those that had deserted and gone over to the enemy, and were among them, now fought against them, *v.* 21. Some think, they were such as had been taken prisoners by them, and now they were goads in their sides. It rather seems that they went in to them voluntarily, but, now that they saw them falling, recovered the hearts of Israelites, and did valiantly for their country. (2.) Those that had fled their colours, and hid themselves in the mountains, returned to their posts, and joined in with the pursuers (*v.* 22), hoping by their great zeal and officiousness, now that the danger was over and the victory sure, to

atone for their former cowardice. It was not much to their praise to appear now, but it would have been more their reproach if they had not appeared. Those that are remiss and faint-hearted indeed that will not act in the cause of God when they see it victorious, as well as righteous. Thus all hands were at work against the Philistines, and every Israelite slew as many as he could, without sword or spear; yet it is said (*v.* 23), it *was the Lord that saved Israel that day.* He did it by them, for without him they could do nothing. *Salvation is of the Lord.*

Verses 24–35

We have here an account of the distress of the children of Israel, even in the day of their triumphs. Such alloys are all present joys subject to. And such obstructions does many a good cause meet with, even when it seems most prosperous, through the mismanagement of instruments.

I. Saul forbade the people, under the penalty of a curse, to taste any food that day, *v.* 24. Here we will suppose, 1. That as king he had power to put his soldiers under this interdict, and to bind it on with a curse; and therefore they submitted to it, and God so far owned it as to discover, by the lot, that Jonathan was the delinquent that had meddled with the accursed thing (though ignorantly), on which account God would not be at that time enquired of by them. 2. That he did it with a good intention, lest the people, who perhaps had been kept for some time at short allowance, when they found plenty of victuals in the deserted camp of the Philistines, should fall greedily upon that, and so lose time in pursing the enemy, and some of them, it may be, glut themselves to such a degree as not to be fit for any more service that day. To prevent this, he forbade them to taste any food, and laid himself, it is likely, under the same restraint. And yet his making this severe order was, (1.) Impolitic and very unwise; for, if it gained time, it lost strength, for the pursuit. (2.) It was imperious, and disobliging to the people, and worse than *muzzling the mouth of the ox when he treads out the corn.* To forbid them to feast would have been commendable, but to forbid them so much as to taste, though ever so hungry, was barbarous. (3.) It was impious to enforce the prohibition with a curse and an oath. Had he no penalty less than an anathema wherewith to support his military discipline? Death for such a crime would have been too much, but especially death with a curse. Though superiors may chide and correct, they may not curse their inferiors; our rule is, *Bless, and curse not.* When David speaks of an enemy he had that loved cursing perhaps he meant Saul, Ps. 109:17, 18.

II. The people observed his order, but it had many inconveniences attending it. 1. The soldiers were tantalized; for, in their pursuit of the enemy, it happened that they went through a wood so full of wild honey that it dropped from the trees upon the ground, the Philistines having perhaps, in their flight, broken in upon the honeycombs, for their own refreshment, and left them running. Canaan flowed with honey, and here is an instance of it. They sucked honey out of *the rock, the flinty rock* (Deu. 32:13); yet, for fear of the curse, they did not so much as taste the honey, *v.* 25, 26. Those are worthy of the name of Israelites that can deny themselves and their own appetites even when they are most craving, and the delights of sense most tempting, for fear of guilt and a curse, and the table becoming a snare. Let us never feed ourselves, much less feast ourselves, without fear. 2. Jonathan fell under the curse through ignorance. He heard not of the charge his father had given; for, having bravely forced the lines, he was then following the chase, and therefore might justly be looked upon as exempted from the charge and intended in it. But it seems it was taken for granted, and he himself did not object against it afterwards, that it extended to him, though absent upon so good an occasion. He, not knowing any peril in it, took up a piece of a honey-comb, upon the end of his staff, and sucked it (*v.* 27), and was sensibly refreshed by it: *His eyes were enlightened,* which began to grow dim through hunger and faintness; it made his countenance look pleasant and cheerful, for it was such as a stander-by might discern (*v.* 29): *See how my eyes have been enlightened.* He thought no harm, nor feared any, till one of the people acquainted him with the order, and then he found himself in a snare. Many a good son has been thus entangled and distressed, in more ways than one, by the rashness of an inconsiderate father. Jonathan, for his part, lost the crown he was heir to by his father's folly, which, it may be, this was an ill omen of. 3. The soldiers were faint, and grew feeble, in the pursuit of the Philistines. Jonathan foresaw this would be the effect of it; their spirits would flag, and their strength would fail, for want of sustenance. Such is the nature of our bodies that they soon grow unfit for service if they be not supplied with fresh recruits. Daily work cannot be done without daily bread, which our Father in heaven graciously gives us. It is *bread* that *strengthens man's heart;* therefore Jonathan reasoned very well, *If the people had eaten freely,* there would have been *a much greater slaughter* (*v.* 30); but, as it was, they were *very faint, too much fatigued* (so the Chaldee), and began to think more of their meat than of their work. 4. The worst effect of all was that at evening, when the restraint was taken off and they returned to their food again, they were so greedy and eager upon it that they ate the flesh with the blood, expressly contrary to the law of God, *v.* 32. Two hungry meals, we say, make the third a glutton; it was so here. They would not stay to have their meat either duly killed (for they slew the cattle upon the ground, and did not hang them up, as they used to do, that the blood might all run out of them) or duly dressed, but fell greedily upon it before it was half boiled or half roasted, *v.* 32. Saul, being informed of it, reproved them for the sin (*v.* 33): *You have transgressed;* but did not, as he should have done, reflect upon himself as having been accessory to it, and having *made the Lord's people to transgress.* To put a stop to this irregularity, Saul ordered them to set up a great stone before him, and let all that had cattle to kill, for their present use, bring them thither, and kill them under his eye upon that stone (*v.* 33), and the people did so (*v.* 34), so easily were they restrained and reformed when their prince took care to do his part. If magistrates would but use their power as they might, people would be made better than they are with more ease than is imagined.

III. On this occasion Saul built an altar (*v.* 35), that he might offer sacrifice, either by way of acknowledgment of the victory they had obtained or by the way of atonement for the sin they had been guilty of. *The same was the first altar that he built,* and perhaps the rolling of the great stone to kill the beasts on reminded him of converting it into an altar, else he would not have thought of it. Saul was turning aside from God, and yet now he began to build altars, being most zealous (as many are) for the form of godliness when he was denying the power of it. See Hos. 8:14, *Israel has forgotten his Maker, and buildeth temples.* Some read it, *He began to build that altar;* he laid the first stone, but was so hasty to pursue his victory that he could not stay to finish it.

Verses 36–46

Here is, I. Saul's boasting against the Philistines. He proposed, as soon as his soldiers had got their suppers, to pursue them all night, and *not leave a man of them, v.* 36. Here he showed much zeal, but little discretion; for his army, thus fatigued, could as ill spare a night's sleep as a meal's meat. But it is common for rash and foolish men to consider nobody but themselves, and, so that they might but have their humour, not to care what hardships they put upon those that are under them. However, the people were so obsequious to their king that they would by no means oppose the motion, but resolved to make the best of it, and, if he will go on, they will follow him: *Do whatsoever seemeth good to thee.* Only the priest thought it convenient to go on with the devotions that were broken off abruptly (*v.* 19), and to consult the oracle: *Let us draw near hither unto God.* Princes and great men have need of such about them as will thus be their remembrancers, wherever they go, to take God along with them. And, when the priest proposed it, Saul could not for shame reject the proposal, but *asked counsel of God* (*v.* 37): *"Shall I go down after the Philistines?* And shall I speed?"

II. His falling foul on his son Jonathan: and the rest of this paragraph is wholly concerning him: for, while he is prosecuted, the Philistines make their escape. We know not what mischief may ensue upon on rash resolve.

1. God, by giving an intimation of his displeasure, put Saul upon searching for an accursed thing. When, by the priest, he consulted the oracle, God *answered him not, v.* 37. Note, When God denies our prayers it concerns us to enquire what the sin is that has provoked him to do so. *Let us see where the sin is, v.* 38. For God's ear is not heavy that it cannot hear, but it is sin that separates between us and him. If God turns away our prayer, we have reason to suspect it is for some iniquity regarding our hearts, which we are concerned to find out, that we may put it away, may mortify it, and put it to death. Saul swears by his Maker that whoever was the Achan that troubled the camp, by eating the forbidden fruit, should certainly die, though it were Jonathan himself, that is, though ever so dear to himself and the people, little thinking that Jonathan was the man (*v.* 39): *He shall surely die,* the curse shall be executed upon him. But none of the people answered him, that is, none of those who knew Jonathan had broken the order would inform against him.

2. Jonathan was discovered by lot to be the offender. Saul would have lots cast between himself and Jonathan on the one side, and the people on the other, perhaps because he was as confident of Jonathan's innocency in this matter as of his own, *v.* 40. The people, seeing him in a heat, durst not gainsay any thing he proposed, but acquiesced: *Do as seemeth good unto thee.* Before he cast lots, he prayed that *God would give a perfect lot* (*v.* 41), that is, make a full discovery of this matter, or, as it is in the margin, that he would show the innocent. This was with an air of impartial justice. Judges should desire that truth may come out, whoever may suffer by it. Lots should be cast with prayer, because they are a solemn appeal to Providence, and by them we beg of God to direct and determine us (Acts 1:24), for which reason some have condemned games that depend purely upon lot or chance as making too bold with a sacred thing. Jonathan at length was taken (*v.* 42), Providence designing hereby to countenance and support a lawful authority, and to put an honour upon the administration of public justice in general, reserving another way to bring off one that had done nothing worthy of death.

3. Jonathan ingenuously confesses the fact, and Saul, with an angry curse, passes sentence upon him. Jonathan denies not the truth, nor goes about to conceal it, only he thinks it hard that he must *die for it, v.* 43. He might very fairly have pleaded his invincible ignorance of the law, or have insisted upon his merit, but he submitted to the necessity with a great and generous mind: "God's and my father's will be done:" thus he showed as much valour in receiving the messengers of death himself as in sending them among the Philistines. It is as brave to yield in some cases as it is in other cases to fight. Saul is not mollified by his filial submission nor the hardness of his case; but as one that affected to be thought firm to his word, and much more to his oath; even when it bound him hardest, with another imprecation he gives judgment upon Jonathan (*v.* 44): *"God do so and more also* to me if I do not execute the law upon thee, *for thou shalt surely die, Jonathan."* (1.) He passed this sentence too hastily, without consulting the oracle. Jonathan had a very good plea in arrest of the judgment. What he had done was not *malum in se — bad in itself;* and, as for the prohibition of it, he was ignorant of that, so that he could not be charged with rebellion or disobedience. (2.) He did it in fury. Had Jonathan been worthy to die, yet it would have become a judge, much more a father, to pass sentence with tenderness and compassion, and not with such an air of triumph, like a man perfectly divested of all humanity and natural affection. Justice is debased when it is administered with wrath and bitterness. (3.) He backed it with a curse upon himself if he did not see the sentence executed; and this curse did return upon his own head. Jonathan escaped, but God did so to Saul, and more also; for he was rejected of God and made anathema. Let none upon any occasion dare to use such imprecations as these, lest God say Amen to them, and *make their own tongues to fall upon them,* Ps. 64:8. This stone will return upon him that rolleth it. Yet we have reason to think that Saul's bowels yearned toward Jonathan, so that he really punished himself, and very justly, when he seemed so severe upon Jonathan. God made him feel the smart of his own rash edict, which might make him fear being again guilty of the like. By all these vexatious accidents God did likewise correct him for his presumption in offering sacrifice without Samuel. An expedition so ill begun could not end without some rebukes.

4. The people rescued Jonathan out of his father's hands, v. 45. Hitherto they had expressed themselves very observant of Saul. What seemed good to him they acquiesced in, v. 36, 40. But, when Jonathan is in danger, Saul's word is no longer a law to them, but with the utmost zeal they oppose the execution of his sentence: "*Shall Jonathan die* — that blessing, that darling, of his country? Shall that life be sacrificed to a punctilio of law and honour which was so bravely exposed for the public service, and to which we owe our lives and triumphs? No, we will never stand by and see him thus treated whom God delights to honour." It is good to see Israelites zealous for the protection of those whom God has made instruments of public good. Saul had sworn that Jonathan should die, but they oppose their oath to his, and swear he shall not die: "*As the Lord liveth there shall not* only not his head, but not *a hair of his head fall to the ground;"* they did not rescue him by violence, but by reason and resolution; and Josephus says they made their prayer to God that he might be loosed from the curse. They pleaded for him that *he has wrought with God this day;* that is, "he has owned God's cause, and God has owned his endeavours, and therefore his life is too precious to be thrown away upon a nicety." We may suppose Saul had not so perfectly forgotten the relation of a father but that he was willing enough to have Jonathan rescued, and well pleased to have that done which yet he would not do himself: and he that knows the heart of a father knows not how to blame him.

5. The design against the Philistines is quashed by this incident (v. 46): *Saul went up from following them,* and so an opportunity was lost of completing the victory. When Israel's shields are clashing with one another the public safety and service suffer by it.

Verses 47–52

Here is a general account of Saul's court and camp. 1. Of his court and family, the names of his sons and daughters (v. 49), and of his wife and his cousin-german that was general of his army, v. 50. There is mention of another wife of Saul's (2 Sa. 21:8), Rizpah, a secondary wife, and of the children he had by her. 2. Of his camp and military actions. (1.) How he levied his army: *When he saw any strong valiant man,* that was remarkably fit for service, *he took him unto him* (v. 52), as Samuel had told them the manner of the king would be (ch. 8:11); and, if he must have a standing army, it was his prudence to fill it up with the ablest men he could make choice of. (2.) How he employed his army. He guarded his country against the insults of its enemies on every side, and prevented their incursions, v. 47, 48. It is supposed that he acted only defensively against those that used to invade the borders of Israel; *and withersoever he turned himself,* as there was occasion, *he vexed them,* by checking and disappointing them. But the enemies he struggled most with were the Philistines, with whom he had *sore war all his days,* v. 52. He had little reason to be proud of his royal dignity, nor had any of his neighbours cause to envy him, for he had little enjoyment of himself after he took the kingdom. He could not vex his enemies without some vexation to himself, such thorns are crowns quilted with.

CHAPTER 15

In this chapter we have the final rejection of Saul from being king, for his disobedience to God's command in not utterly destroying the Amalekites. By his wars and victories he hoped to magnify and perpetuate his own name and honour, but, by his mismanagement of them, he ruined himself, and laid his honour in the dust. Here is, I. The commission God gave him to destroy the Amalekites, with a command to do it utterly (v. 1–3). II. Saul's preparation for this expedition (v. 4–6). III. His success, and partial execution of this commission (v. 7–9). IV. His examination before Samuel, and sentence passed upon him, notwithstanding the many frivolous pleas he made to excuse himself (v. 10–31). V. The slaying of Agag (v. 32, 33). VI. Samuel's final farewell to Saul (v. 34, 35).

Verses 1–9

Here, I. Samuel, in God's name, solemnly requires Saul to be obedient to the command of God, and plainly intimates that he was now about to put him upon a trial, in one particular instance, whether he would be obedient or no, v. 1. And the making of this so expressly the trial of his obedience did very much aggravate his disobedience. 1. He reminds him of what God had done for him: "*The Lord sent me to anoint thee to be a king.* God gave thee thy power, and therefore he expects thou shouldst use

thy power for him. He put honour upon thee, and now thou must study how to do him honour. He made thee king over Israel, and now thou must plead Israel's cause and avenge their quarrels. Thou art advanced to command Israel, but know that thou art a subject to the God of Israel and must be commanded by him." Men's preferment, instead of releasing them from their obedience to God, obliges them so much the more to it. Samuel had himself been employed to anoint Saul, and therefore was the fitter to be send with these orders to him. 2. He tells him, in general, that, in consideration of this, whatever God commanded him to do he was bound to do it: *Now therefore hearken to the voice of the Lord.* Note, God's favours to us lay strong obligations upon us to be obedient to him. This we must render, Ps. 116:12.

II. He appoints him a particular piece of service, in which he must now show his obedience to God more than in any thing he had done yet. Samuel premises God's authority to the command: *Thus says the Lord of hosts,* the Lord of all hosts, of Israel's hosts. He also gives him a reason for the command, that the severity he must use might not seem hard: *I remember that which Amalek did to Israel,* v. 2. God had an ancient quarrel with the Amalekites, for the injuries they did to his people Israel when he brought them out of Egypt. We have the story, Ex. 17:8, etc., and the crime is aggravated, Deu. 25:18. He basely smote the hindmost of them, and feared not God. God then swore that he would have *war with Amalek from generation to generation,* and that in process of time he *would utterly put out the remembrance of Amalek;* this is the work that Saul is now appointed to do (v. 3): "*Go and smite Amalek.* Israel is now strong, and the measure of the iniquity of Amalek is now full; now go and make a full riddance of that devoted nation." He is expressly commanded to kill and slay all before him, *man and woman, infant and suckling,* and not spare them out of pity; also *ox and sheep, camel and ass,* and not spare them out of covetousness. Note, 1. Injuries done to God's Israel will certainly be reckoned for sooner or later, especially the opposition given them when they are coming out of Egypt. 2. God often bears long with those that are marked for ruin. The sentence passed is not executed speedily. 3. Though he bear long, he will not bear always. The year of recompence for the controversy of Israel will come at last. Though divine justice strikes slowly it strikes surely. 4. The longer judgment is delayed many times the more severe it is when it comes. 5. God chooses out instruments to do his work that are fittest for it. This was bloody work, and therefore Saul who was a rough and severe man must do it.

III. Saul hereupon musters his forces, and makes a descent upon the country of Amalek. It was an immense army that he brought into the field (v. 4): 200,000 *footmen.* When he came to engage the Philistines, and the success was hazardous, he had but 600 attending him, ch. 13:15. But now that he was to attack the Amalekites by express order from heaven, in which he was sure of victory, he had thousands at his call. But, whatever it was at other times, it was not now for the honour of Judah that their forces were numbered by themselves, for their quota was scandalously short (whatever was the reason), but a twentieth part of the whole, for they were by 10,000, when the other ten tribes (for I except Levi) brought into the field 200,000. The day of Judah's honour drew near, but had not yet come. Saul numbered them in *Telaim,* which signifies *lambs.* He numbered then *like lambs* (so the vulgar Latin), numbered them *by the paschal lambs* (so the Chaldee), allowing ten to a lamb, a way of numbering used by the Jews in the later times of their nation. Saul drew all his forces to the *city of Amalek,* that city that was their metropolis (v. 5), that he might provoke them to give him battle.

IV. He gave friendly advice to the Kenites to separate themselves from the Amalekites among whom they dwelt, while this execution was in doing, v. 6. Herein he did prudently and piously, and, it is probable, according to the direction Samuel gave him. The Kenites were of the family and kindred of Jethro, Moses's father-in-law, a people that dwelt in tents, which made it easy for them, upon every occasion, to remove to other lands not appropriated. Many of them, at this time, dwelt among the Amalekites, where, though they dwelt in tents, they were fortified by nature, for *they put their nest in a rock,* being

hardy people that could live any where, and affected fastnesses, Num. 24:21. Balaam had foretold that they should be wasted, Num. 24:22. However, Saul must not waste them. But, 1. He acknowledges the kindness of their ancestors to Israel, when they came out of Egypt. Jethro and his family had been very helpful and serviceable to them in their passage through the wilderness, had been to them instead of eyes, and this is remembered to their posterity many ages after. Thus a good man leaves the divine blessing for an inheritance to his children's children; those that come after us may be reaping the benefit of our good works when we are in our graves. God is not unrighteous to forget the kindnesses shown to his people; but they shall be remembered another day, at furthest in the great day, *and recompensed in the resurrection of the just. I was hungry, and you gave me meat.* God's remembering the kindness of the Kenites' ancestors in favour to them, at the same time when he was punishing the injuries done by the ancestors of the Amalekites, helped to clear the righteousness of God in that dispensation. If he entail favours, why may he not entail frowns? He espouses his people's cause, so as to *bless those that bless them;* and therefore so as to *curse those that curse them,* Num. 24:9; Gen. 12:3. They cannot themselves requite the kindnesses nor avenge the injuries done them, but God will do both. 2. He desires them to remove their tents from among the Amalekites: *Go, depart, get you down from among them.* When destroying judgments are abroad God will take care to separate between the precious and the vile, and to hide the meek of the earth in the day of his anger. It is dangerous being found in the company of God's enemies, and it is our duty and interest to *come out from among them,* lest we share in their sins and plagues, Rev. 18:4. The Jews have a saying, *Woe to the wicked man and woe to his neighbour.*

V. Saul prevailed against the Amalekites, for it was rather an execution of condemned malefactors than a war with contending enemies. The issue could not be dubious when the cause was just and the call so clear: *He smote them* (v. 7), *utterly destroyed them,* v. 8. Now they paid dearly for the sin of their ancestors. God sometimes *lays up iniquity for the children.* They were idolaters, and were guilty of many other sins, for which they deserved to fall under the wrath of God; yet, when God would reckon with them, he fastened upon the sin of their ancestors in abusing his Israel as the ground of his quarrel. Lord, How unsearchable are thy judgments, yet how incontestable is thy righteousness!

VI. Yet he did his work by halves, v. 9. 1. He *spared Agag,* because he was a king like himself, and perhaps in hope to get a great ransom for him. 2. He spared the best of the cattle, and destroyed only the refuse, that was good for little. Many of the people, we may suppose, made their escape, and took their effects with them into other countries, and therefore we read of Amalekites after this; but that could not be helped. It was Saul's fault that he did not destroy such as came to his hands and were in his power. That which was now destroyed was in effect sacrificed to the justice of God, as the God to whom vengeance belongeth; and for Saul to think the torn and the sick, the lame and the lean, good enough for that, while he reserved for his own fields and his own table the firstlings and the fat, was really to honour himself more than God.

Verses 10–23

Saul is here called to account by Samuel concerning the execution of his commission against the Amalekites; and remarkable instances we are here furnished with of the strictness of the justice of God and the treachery and deceitfulness of the heart of man. We are here told,

I. What passed between God and Samuel, in secret, upon this occasion, v. 10, 11. 1. God determines Saul's rejection, and acquaints Samuel with it: *It repenteth me that I have set up Saul to be king.* Repentance in God is not, as it is in us, a change of his mind, but a change of his method or dispensation. He does not alter his will, but wills an alteration. The change was in Saul: *He has turned back from following me;* this construction God put upon the partiality of his obedience, and the prevalency of his covetousness. And hereby he did himself make God his enemy. God repented that he had given Saul the kingdom and the honour and power that belonged to it: but he never repented that he had given any man wisdom and grace, and his fear and love; these gifts and callings of God are without repentance. 2. Samuel laments and deprecates it. *It grieved Samuel* that Saul had forfeited God's favour, and that God had resolved to cast him off; and he *cried unto the Lord all night,* spent a whole night in interceding for him, that this decree might not go forth against him. When others were in their beds sleeping, he was upon his knees praying and wrestling with God. He did not thus deprecate his own exclusion from the government; nor was he secretly pleased, as many a one would have been, that Saul, who succeeded him, was so soon laid aside, but on the contrary prayed earnestly for his establishment, so far was he from desiring that woeful day. The rejection of sinners is the grief of good people; God delights not in their death, nor should we.

II. What passed between Samuel and Saul in public. Samuel, being sent of God to him with these heavy tidings, went, as Ezekiel, in *bitterness of soul,* to meet him, perhaps according to an appointment when Saul went forth on this expedition, for Saul had come to Gilgal (*v.* 12), the place where he was made king (*ch.* 11:15), and were now he would have been confirmed if he had approved himself well in the trial of his obedience. But Samuel was informed that Saul had set up a triumphal arch, or some monument of his victory, at Carmel, a city in the mountains of Judah, seeking his own honour more than the honour of God, for he set up this place (or *hand,* as the word is) for himself (he had more need to have been repenting of his sin and making his peace with God than boasting of his victory), and also that he had marched in great state to Gilgal, for this seems to be intimated in the manner of expression: *He has gone about, and passed on, and gone down,* with a great deal of pomp and parade. There Samuel gave him the meeting, and,

1. Saul makes his boast to Samuel of his obedience, because that was the thing by which he was now to signalize himself (*v.* 13): *"Blessed be thou of the Lord,* for thou sendest me upon a good errand, in which I have had great success, and *I have performed the commandment of the Lord."* It is very likely, if his conscience had now flown in his face at this time and charged him with disobedience, he would not have been so forward to proclaim his disobedience; for by this he hoped to prevent Samuel's reproving him. Thus sinners think, by justifying themselves, to escape being *judged of the Lord;* whereas the only way to do that is by *judging ourselves.* Those that boast most of their religion may be suspected of partiality and hypocrisy in it.

2. Samuel convicts him by a plain demonstration of his disobedience. "Hast thou performed the commandment of the Lord? *What means then the bleating of the sheep?" v.* 14. Saul would needs have it thought than God Almighty was wonderfully beholden to him for the good service he had done; but Samuel shows him that God was so far from being a debtor to him that he had just cause of action against him, and produces for evidence the *bleating of the sheep, and the lowing of the oxen,* which perhaps Saul appointed to bring up the rear of his triumph, but Samuel appears to them as witnesses against him. He needed not go far to disprove his professions. The noise the cattle made (like the *rust of silver,* Jam. 5:3) would be a *witness against him.* Note, It is no new thing for the plausible professions and protestations of hypocrites to be contradicted and disproved by the most plain and undeniable evidence. Many boast of their obedience to the command of God; but what mean then their indulgence of the flesh, their love of the world, their passion and uncharitableness, and their neglect of holy duties, which witness against them?

3. Saul insists upon his own justification against this charge, *v.* 15. The fact he cannot deny; the sheep and oxen were brought from the Amalekites. But, (1.) It was not his fault, for *the people spared them;* as if they durst have done it without the express orders of Saul, when they knew it was against the express orders of Samuel. Note, Those that are willing to justify themselves are commonly very forward to condemn others, and to lay the blame upon any rather than take it to themselves. Sin is a brat that nobody cares to have laid at his doors. It is the sorry subterfuge of an impenitent heart, that will not confess its guilt, to lay the blame on those that were tempters, or partners, or only followers in it. (2.) It was with a good intention: "It was *to sacrifice to the Lord thy God.* He is thy God, and thou wilt not be against any thing that is done, as this is, for his honour." This was a false plea, for both Saul and the people designed their own profit in sparing the cattle. But, if it had been true, it would still have been frivolous, for God hates robbery for burnt-offering. God appointed these cattle to be sacrificed to him in the field, and therefore will give those no thanks that bring them to be sacrificed at his altar; for he will be served in his own way, and according to the rule he himself has prescribed. Nor will a good intention justify a bad action.

4. Samuel overrules, or rather overlooks, his plea, and proceeds, in God's name, to give judgment against him. He premises his authority. What he was about to say was what the Lord had said to him (*v.* 16), otherwise he would have been far from passing so severe a censure upon him. Those who complain that their ministers are too harsh with them should remember that, while they keep to the word of God, they are but messengers, and must say as they are bidden, and therefore be willing, as Saul himself here was, that they should *say on.* Samuel delivers his message faithfully. (1.) He reminds Saul of the honour of God had done him in making him king (*v.* 17), *when he was little in his own sight.* God regarded the lowness of his state and rewarded the lowliness of his spirit. Note, Those that are advanced to honour and wealth ought often to remember their mean beginnings, that they may never think highly of themselves, but always study to do great things for the God that had advanced them. (2.) He lays before him the plainness of the orders he was to execute (*v.* 18): *The Lord sent thee on a journey;* so easy was the service, and so certain the success, that it was rather to be called a *journey* than a *war.* The work was honourable, to destroy the sworn enemies of God and Israel; and had he denied himself, and set aside the consideration of his own profit so far as to have destroyed all that belonged to Amalek, he would have been no loser by it at last, nor have gone this *warfare on his own charges.* God would no doubt have made it up to him, so that he should have no need of spoil. And therefore, (3.) He shows him how inexcusable he was in aiming to make a profit of this expedition, and to enrich himself by it (*v.* 19): *"Wherefore then didst thou fly upon the spoil,* and convert that to thy own use which was to have been destroyed for God's honour?" See what evil the love of money is the root of; but see what is the sinfulness of sin, and that in it which above any thing else makes it evil in the sight of the Lord. It is disobedience: *Thou didst not obey the voice of the Lord.*

5. Saul repeats his vindication of himself, as that which, in defiance of conviction, he resolved to abide by, *v.* 20, 21. He denies the charge (*v.* 20): *"Yea, I have obeyed,* I have done all I should do;" for he had done all which he thought he needed to do, so much wiser was he in his own eyes than God himself. God bade him kill all, and yet he puts in among the instances of his obedience that he brought Agag alive, which he thought was as good as if he had killed him. Thus carnal deceitful hearts think to excuse themselves from God's commandments with their own equivalents. He insists upon it that he has *utterly destroyed the Amalekites* themselves, which was the main thing intended; but, as to the spoil, he owns it should have been *utterly destroyed;* so that he knew his *Lord's will,* and was under no mistake about the command. But he thought that would be wilful waste; the cattle of the Midianites was taken for a prey in Moses's time (Num. 31:32, etc.), and why not the cattle of the Amalekites now? Better it should be prey to the Israelites than to the fowls of the air and the wild beasts; and therefore he connived at the people's carrying it away. But it was their doing and not his; and, besides, it was for *sacrifice to the Lord* here at Gilgal, whither they were now bringing them. See what a hard thing it is to convince the children of disobedience of their sin and to strip them of their fig-leaves.

6. Samuel gives a full answer to his apology, since he did insist upon it, *v.* 22, 23. He appeals to his own conscience: *Has the Lord as great delight in sacrifices as in obedience?* Though Saul was not a man of any great acquaintance with religion, yet he could not but know this, (1.) That nothing is so pleasing to God as obedience, no, not sacrifice and offering, and the fat of rams. See here what we should seek and aim at in all the exercises of religion, even acceptance with God, that he may delight in what we do. If God be well pleased with us and our services, we are happy, we have gained our point, but otherwise *to what purpose is it?* Isa. 1:11. Now here we are plainly told that humble, sincere, and conscientious obedience to the will of God, is more pleasing and acceptable to him than all *burnt-offerings and sacrifices.* A careful conformity to moral precepts recommends us to God more than all ceremonial observances, Mic. 6:6–8; Hos. 6:6. Obedience is enjoyed by the eternal law of nature, but sacrifice only by a positive law. Obedience was the law of innocency, but sacrifice supposes sin come into the world, and is but a feeble attempt to take that away which obedience would have prevented. God is more glorified and self more denied by obedience than by sacrifice. It is much easier to bring a bullock or lamb to be burnt upon the altar than to bring *every high thought into obedience* to God and the will subject to his will. Obedience is the glory of angels (Ps. 103:20), and it will be ours. (2.) That nothing is so provoking to God as disobedience, setting up our wills in competition with his. This is here called *rebellion* and *stubbornness,* and is said to be as bad as *witchcraft* and *idolatry, v.* 23. It is as bad to set up other gods as to live in disobedience to the true God. Those that are governed by their own corrupt inclinations, in opposition to the command of God, do, in effect, consult the *teraphim* (as the word here is for idolatry) or the diviners. It was disobedience that made us all sinners (Rom. 5:19), and this is the malignity of sin, that it is the *transgression of the law,* and consequently it is *enmity to God,* Rom. 8:7. Saul was a king, but if he disobey the command of God, his royal dignity and power will not excuse him from the guilt of rebellion and stubbornness. It is not the rebellion of the people against their prince, but of a prince against God, that this text speaks of.

7. He reads his doom: in short, *"Because thou has rejected the word of the Lord,* hast *despised it* (so the Chaldee), hast *made nothing of it* (so the Septuagint), hast cast off the government of it, therefore he has *rejected thee,* despised and made nothing of thee, but cast thee off *from being king.* He that made thee king has determined to unmake thee again." Those are unfit and unworthy to rule over men who are not willing that God should rule over them.

Verses 24–31

Saul is at length brought to put himself into the dress of the penitent; but it is too evident that he only acts the part of a penitent, and is not one indeed. Observe,

I. How poorly he expressed his repentance. It was with much ado that he was made sensible of his fault, and not till he was threatened with being deposed. This touched him in a tender part. Then he began to relent, and not till then. When Samuel told him he was *rejected from being king,* then he said, *I have sinned, v.* 24. His confession was not free nor ingenuous, but extorted by the rack, and forced from him. We observe here several bad signs of the hypocrisy of his repentance, and that it came short even of Ahab's. 1. He made his application to Samuel only, and seemed most solicitous to stand right in his opinion and to gain his favour. He makes a little god of him, only to preserve his reputation with the people, because they all knew Samuel to be a prophet, and the man that had been the instrument of his preferment. Thinking it would please Samuel, and be a sort of bribe to him, he puts it into his confession: *I have transgressed the commandment of the Lord and thy word;* as if he had been in God's stead, *v.* 24. David, though convinced by the ministry of Nathan, yet, in his confession, has his eye to God alone, not to Nathan. Ps. 51:4 *Against thee only have I sinned.* But Saul, ignorantly enough, confesses his sin as a transgression of Samuel's word; whereas his word was no other than a declaration of the *commandment of the Lord.* He also applies to Samuel for forgiveness (*v.* 25): *I pray thee, pardon my sin;* as if any could forgive sin but God only. Those wretchedly deceive themselves who, when they have fallen into scandalous sin, think it enough to make their peace with the church and their ministers, by the show and plausible profession of repentance, without taking care to make their peace with God by the sincerity of it. The most charitable construction we can put upon this of Saul is to suppose that he looked upon Samuel as a sort of mediator between him and God, and intended an address to God in his application to him. However, it was very weak. 2.

He excused his fault even in the confession of it, and that is never the fashion of a true penitent (*v.* 24): I did it *because I feared the people, and obeyed their voice.* We have reason enough to think that it was purely his own doing and not the people's; however, if they were forward to do it, it is plain, by what we have read before, that he knew how to keep up his authority among them and did not stand in any awe of them. So that the excuse was false and frivolous; whatever he pretended, he did not really fear the people. But it is common for sinners, in excusing their faults, to plead the thoughts and workings of their own minds, because those are things which, how groundless soever, no man can disprove; but they forget that God searchest the heart. 3. All his care was to save his credit, and preserve his interest in the people, lest they should revolt from him, or at least despise him. Therefore he courts Samuel with so much earnestness (*v.* 25) to turn again with him, and assist in a public thanksgiving for the victory. Very importunate he was in this matter when he laid hold on the skirt of his mantle to detain him (*v.* 27), not that he cared for Samuel, but he feared that if Samuel forsook him the people would do so too. Many seem zealously affected to good ministers and good people only for the sake of their own interest and reputation, while in heart they hate them. But his expression was very gross when he said (*v.* 30), *I have sinned, yet honour me, I pray thee, before my people.* Is this the language of a penitent? No, but the contrary: *"I have sinned,* shame me now, for to me belongs shame, and no man can loathe me so much as I loathe myself." Yet how often do we meet with the copies of this hypocrisy of Saul! It is very common for those who are convicted of sin to show themselves very solicitous to be honoured before the people. Whereas he that has lost the honour of an innocent can pretend to no other than that of a penitent, and it is the honour of a penitent to take shame to himself.

II. How little he got by these thin shows of repentance. What point did he gain by them? 1. Samuel repeated the sentence passed upon him, so far was he from giving any hopes of the repeal of it, *v.* 26, the same with *v.* 23. *He that covers his sins shall never prosper,* Prov. 28:13. Samuel refused to turn back with him, but *turned about to go away, v.* 27. As the thing appeared to him upon the first view, he thought it altogether unfit for him so far to countenance one whom God had rejected as to join with him in giving thanks to God for a victory which was made to serve rather Saul's covetousness than God's glory. Yet afterwards he did turn again with him (*v.* 31), upon further thoughts, and probably by divine direction, either to prevent a mutiny among the people or perhaps not to do honour to Saul (for, though Saul worshipped the Lord, *v.* 31, it is not said Samuel presided in that worship), but to do justice on Agag, *v.* 32. 2. He illustrated the sentence by a sign, which Saul himself, by his rudeness, gave occasion for. When Samuel was turning from him he tore his clothes to detain him (*v.* 27), so loth was he to part with the prophet; but Samuel put a construction upon this accident which none but a prophet could do. He made it to signify the *rending of the kingdom* from him (*v.* 28), and that, like this, was his own doing. "He hath rent it from thee, and *given it to a neighbour better than thou,"* namely, to David, who afterwards, upon occasion, cut off the skirt of Saul's robe (1 Sa. 24:4), upon which Saul said (1 Sa. 24:20), *I know that thou shalt surely be king,* perhaps remembering this sign, the tearing of the skirt of Samuel's mantle. 3. He ratified it by a solemn declaration of its being irreversible (*v.* 29): *The Strength of Israel will not lie.* The *Eternity* or *Victory of Israel,* so some read it; *the holy One,* so the Arabic; *the most noble One,* so the Syriac; the *triumphant King of Israel,* so bishop Patrick. "He is determined to depose thee, and he will not change his purpose. *He is not a man that should repent."* Men are fickle and alter their minds, feeble and cannot effect their purposes; something happens which they could not foresee, by which their measures are broken. But with God it is not so. God has sometimes repented of the evil which he thought to have done, repentance was hidden from Saul, and therefore hidden from God's eyes.

Verses 32–35

Samuel, as a prophet, is here set over kings, Jer. 1:10.

I. He destroys king Agag, doubtless by such special direction from heaven as none now can pretend to. He *hewed Agag in pieces.* Some think he only ordered it to be done; or perhaps he did it with his own hands, as a sacrifice to God's injured justice (*v.* 33), and sacrifices used to be cut in pieces. Now observe in this,

1. How Agag's present vain hopes were frustrated: He *came delicately,* in a stately manner, to show that he was a king, and therefore to be treated with respect, or in a soft effeminate manner, as one never used to hardship, that *could not set the sole of his foot to the ground for tenderness and delicacy* (Deu. 28:56), to move compassion: and he said, "Surely, now that the heat of the battle is over, *the bitterness of death is past, v.* 32. Having escaped the sword of Saul," that man of war, he thought he was in no danger from Samuel, and old prophet, a man of peace. Note, (1.) There is bitterness in death, it is terrible to nature. *Surely death is bitter,* so divers versions read those words of Agag; as the Septuagint read the former clause, *He came trembling.* Death will dismay the stoutest heart. (2.) Many think the bitterness of death is past when it is not so; they put that evil day far from them which is very near. True believers may, through grace, say this, upon good grounds, though death be not past, the bitterness of it is. *O death! where is thy sting?*

2. How his former wicked practices were now punished. Samuel calls him to account, not only for the sins of his ancestors, but his own sins: *Thy sword has made women childless, v.* 33. He trod in the steps of his ancestors' cruelty, and those under him, it is likely, did the same; justly therefore is all the righteous blood shed by Amalek required of this generation, Mt. 23:36. Agag, that was delicate and luxurious himself, was cruel and barbarous to others. It is commonly so: those who are indulgent in their appetites are not less indulgent of their passions. But blood will be reckoned for; even kings must account to the King of kings for the guiltless blood they shed or cause to be shed. It was that crime of king Manasseh which the Lord would not pardon, 2 Ki. 24:4. See Rev. 13:10.

II. He deserts king Saul, takes leave of him (*v.* 34), and *never came any more to see him* (*v.* 35), to advise or assist him in any of his affairs, because Saul did not desire his company nor would he be advised by him. He looked upon him as rejected of God, and therefore he forsook him. Though he might sometimes see him accidentally (as *ch.* 29:24), yet he never came to see him out of kindness or respect. Yet he *mourned for Saul,* thinking it a very lamentable thing that a man who stood so fair for great things should ruin himself so foolishly. He mourned for the bad state of the country, to which Saul was likely to have been so great a blessing, but now would prove a curse and a plague. He mourned for his everlasting state, having no hopes of bringing him to repentance. When he wept for him, it is likely, he made supplication, but the Lord had *repented that he had made Saul king,* and resolved to undo that work of his, so that Samuel's prayers prevailed not for him. Observe, We must mourn for the rejection of sinners, 1. Though we withdraw from them, and dare not converse familiarly with them. Thus the prophet determines to leave his people and go from them, and yet to *weep day and night for them,* Jer. 9:1, 2. 2. Though they do not mourn for themselves. Saul seems unconcerned at the tokens of God's displeasure which he lay under, and yet Samuel mourns day and night for him. Jerusalem was secure when Christ wept over it.

CHAPTER 16

At this chapter begins the story of David, one that makes as great a figure in the sacred story as almost any of the worthies of the Old Testament, one that both with his sword and with his pen served the honour of God and the interests of Israel as much as most ever did, and was as illustrious a type of Christ. Here I. Samuel is appointed and commissioned to anoint a king among the sons of Jesse at Bethlehem (*v.* 1–5). II. All his elder sons are passed by and David the youngest is pitched upon and anointed (*v.* 6–13). III. Saul growing melancholy, David is pitched upon to relieve him by music (*v.* 14–23). Thus small are the beginnings of that great man.

Verses 1–5

Samuel had retired to his own house in Ramah, with a resolution not to appear any more in public business, but to addict himself wholly to the instructing and training up of the sons of the prophets, over whom he presided, as we find, *ch.* 19:20. He promised himself more satisfaction in young prophets than in young princes; and we do not find that, to his dying day, God called him out to any public action relating to the state, but only here to anoint David.

I. God reproves him for continuing so long to mourn for the rejection of Saul. He does not blame him for mourning on that occasion, but for exceeding in his sorrow: *How long wilt thou mourn for Saul? v.* 1. We do not find here that he mourned at all for the setting aside of his own family and the deposing of his own sons; but for the rejecting of Saul and his seed he mourns without measure, for the former was done by the people's foolish discontent, this by the righteous wrath of God. Yet he must find time to recover himself, and not go mourning to his grave, 1. Because God has rejected him, and he ought to acquiesce in the divine justice, and forget his affection to Saul; if God will be glorified in his ruin, Samuel ought to be satisfied. Besides, to what purpose should he weep? The decree has gone forth, and all his prayers and tears cannot prevail for the reversing of it, 2 Sa. 12:22, 23. 2. Because Israel shall be no loser by it, and Samuel must prefer the public welfare before his own private affection to his friend. "Mourn not for Saul, for I *have provided me a king.* The people provided themselves a king and he proved bad, now I will provide myself one, *a man after my own heart."* See Ps. 89:20; Acts 13:22. "If Saul be rejected, yet Israel shall not be *as sheep having no shepherd.* I have another in store for them; let thy joy of him swallow up thy grief for the rejected prince."

II. He sends him to Bethlehem, to anoint one of the sons of Jesse, a person probably not unknown to Samuel. *Fill thy horn with oil.* Saul was anointed with a glass vial of oil, scanty and brittle, David with a horn of oil, which was more plentiful and durable; hence we read of a *horn of salvation in the house of his servant David,* Lu. 1:69.

III. Samuel objects the peril of going on this errand (*v.* 2): *If Saul hear it, he will kill me.* By this it appears. 1. That Saul had grown very wicked and outrageous since his rejection, else Samuel would not have mentioned this. What impiety would he not be guilty of who durst kill Samuel? 2. That Samuel's faith was not so strong as one would have expected, else he would not have thus feared the rage of Saul. Would not he that sent him protect him and bear him out? But the best men are not perfect in their faith, nor will fear be wholly cast out any where on this side heaven. But this may be understood as Samuel's desire of direction from heaven how to manage this matter prudently, so as not to expose himself, or any other, more than needed.

IV. God orders him to cover his design with a sacrifice: *Say, I have come to sacrifice;* and it was true he did, and it was proper that he should, when he came to anoint a king, *ch.* 11:15. As a prophet, he might sacrifice when and where God appointed him; and it was not all inconsistent with the laws of truth to say he came to sacrifice when really he did so, thought he had also a further end, which he thought fit to conceal. Let him give notice of a sacrifice, and invite Jesse (who, it is probable, was the principal man of the city) and his family to come to the feast upon the sacrifice; and, says God, *I will show thee what thou shalt do.* Those that go about God's work in God's way shall be directed step by step, wherever they are at a loss, to do it in the best manner.

V. Samuel went accordingly to Bethlehem, not in pomp, or with any retinue, only a servant to lead the heifer which he was to sacrifice; yet *the elders of Bethlehem trembled at his coming,* fearing it was an indication of God's displeasure against them and that he came to denounce some judgment for the iniquities of the place. Guilt causes fear. Yet indeed it becomes us to stand in awe of God's messengers, and to tremble at his word. Or they feared it might be an occasion of Saul's displeasure against them, for probably they knew how much he was exasperated at Samuel, and feared he would pick a quarrel with them for entertaining him. They asked him, *"Comest thou peaceably?* Art thou in peace thyself, and not flying from Saul? Art thou at peace with us, and not come with any message of wrath?" We should all covet earnestly to stand upon good terms with God's prophets, and dread having the word of God, or their prayers, against us. When the Son of David was born king of the Jews all Jerusalem was troubled, Mt. 2:3. Samuel kept at home, and it was a strange thing to see him so far from his own house: they therefore concluded it must needs be some extraordinary occasion that brought him, and feared the worst till he satisfied them (v. 5): "I come peaceably, for I come to sacrifice, not with a message of wrath against you, but with the methods of peace and reconciliation; and therefore you may bid me welcome and need not fear my coming; therefore sanctify yourselves, and prepare to join with me in the sacrifice, that you may have the benefit of it." Note, Before solemn ordinances there must be a solemn protestation. When we are to offer spiritual sacrifices it concerns us, by sequestering ourselves from the world and renewing the dedication of ourselves to God, to sanctify ourselves. When our Lord Jesus came into the world, though men had reason enough to tremble, fearing that his errand was to condemn the world, yet he gave full assurance that he came peaceably, for he came to sacrifice, and he brought his offering along with him: A body hast thou prepared me. Let us sanctify ourselves, that we may have an interest in his sacrifice. Note, Those that come to sacrifice should come peaceably; religious exercises must not be performed tumultuously.

VI. He had a particular regard to Jesse and his sons, for with them his private business lay, with which, it is likely, he acquainted Jesse at his first coming, and took up his lodging at his house. He spoke to all the elders to sanctify themselves, but he sanctified Jesse and his sons by praying with them and instructing them. Perhaps he had acquaintance with them before, and it appears (ch. 20:29, where we read of the sacrifices that family had) that it was a devout religious family. Samuel assisted them in their family preparations for the public sacrifice, and, it is probable, chose out David, and anointed him, at the family-solemnities, before the sacrifice was offered or the holy feast solemnized. Perhaps he offered private sacrifices, like Job, according to the number of them all (Job 1:5), and, under colour of that, called for them all to appear before him. When signal blessings are coming into a family they ought to sanctify themselves.

Verses 6–13

If the sons of Jesse were told that God would provide himself a king among them (as he had said, v. 1), we may well suppose they all made the best appearance they could, and each hoped he should be the man; but here we are told,

I. How all the elder sons, who stood fairest for the preferment, were passed by.

1. Eliab, the eldest, was privately presented first to Samuel, probably none being present but Jesse only, and Samuel thought he must needs be the man: Surely this is the Lord's anointed, v. 6. The prophets themselves, when they spoke from under the divine direction, were as liable to mistake as other men; as Nathan, 2 Sa. 7:3. But God rectified the prophet's mistake by a secret whisper to his mind: Look not on his countenance, v. 7. It was strange that Samuel, who had been so wretchedly disappointed in Saul, whose countenance and stature recommended him as much as any man's could, should be so forward to judge of a man by that rule. When God would please the people with a king he chose a comely man; but, when he would have one after his own heart, he should not be chosen by the outside. Men judge by the sight of the eyes, but God does not, Isa. 11:3. The Lord looks on the heart, that is, (1.) He knows it. We can tell how men look, but he can tell what they are. Man looks on the eyes (so the original word is), and is pleased with the liveliness and sprightliness that appear in them; but God looks on the heart, and sees the thoughts and intents of that. (2.) He judges of men by it. The good disposition of the heart, the holiness or goodness of that, recommends us to God, and is in his sight of great price (1 Pt. 3:4), not the majesty of the look, or the strength and stature of the body. Let us reckon that to be true beauty which is within, and judge of men, as far as we are capable, by their minds, not their mien.

2. When Eliab was set aside, Abinadab and Shammah, and, after them, four more of the sons of Jesse, seven in all, were presented to Samuel, as likely for his purpose; but Samuel, who not attended more carefully than he did at first to the divine direction, rejected them all: The Lord has not chosen these, v. 8, 10. Men dispose of their honours and estates to their sons according to their seniority of age and priority of birth, but God does not. The elder

shall serve the younger. Had it been left to Samuel, or Jesse, to make the choice, one of these would certainly have been chosen; but God will magnify his sovereignty in passing by some that were most promising as well as in fastening on others that were less so.

II. How David at length was pitched upon. He was the youngest of all the sons of Jesse; his name signifies beloved, for he was a type of the beloved Son. Observe, 1. How he was in the fields, keeping the sheep (v. 11), and was left there, though there was a sacrifice and a feast at his father's house. The youngest are commonly the fondlings of the family, but, it should seem, David was least set by of all the sons of Jesse; either they did not discern or did not duly value the excellent spirit he was of. Many a great genius lies buried in obscurity and contempt; and God often exalts those whom men despise and gives abundant honour to that part which lacked. The Son of David was he whom men despised, the stone which the builders refused, and yet he has a name above every name. David was taken from following ewes to feed Jacob (Ps. 78:71), as Moses from keeping the flock of Jethro, an instance of his humility and industry, both which God delights to put honour upon. We should think a military life, but God saw a pastoral life (which gives advantage for contemplation and communion with heaven), the best preparative for kingly power, at least for those graces of the Spirit which are necessary to the due discharge of that trust which attends it. David was keeping sheep, though it was a time of sacrifice; for there is mercy that takes precedence of sacrifice. 2. How earnest Samuel was to have him sent for: "We will not sit down to meat" (perhaps it was not the feast upon the sacrifice, but a common meal) "till he come hither; for, if all the rest be rejected, this must be he." He that designed not to sit at table at all is now waited for as the principal guest. If God will exalt those of low degree, who can hinder? 3. What appearance he made when he did come. No notice is taken of his clothing. No doubt that was according to his employment, mean and coarse, as shepherds' coats commonly are, and he did not change his clothes as Joseph did (Gen. 41:14), but he had a very honest look, not stately, as Saul's, but sweet and lovely: He was ruddy, of a beautiful countenance, and goodly to look to (v. 12), that is, he had a clear complexion, a good eye, and a lovely face; the features were extraordinary, and there was something in his looks that was very charming. Though he was so far from using any art to help his beauty that his employment exposed it to the sun and wind, yet nature kept its own, and, by the sweetness of his aspect, gave manifest indications of an amiable temper and disposition of mind. Perhaps his modest blush, when he was brought before Samuel, and received by him with surprising respect, made him look much the handsomer. 4. The anointing of him. The Lord told Samuel in his ear (as he had done, ch. 9:15) that this was he whom he must anoint, v. 12. Samuel objects not the meanness of his education, his youth, or the little respect he had in his own family, but, in obedience to the divine command, took his horn of oil and anointed him (v. 13), signifying thereby, (1.) A divine designation to the government, after the death of Saul, of which hereby he gave him a full assurance. Not that he was at present invested with the royal power, but it was entailed upon him, to come to him in due time. (2.) A divine communication of gifts and graces, to fit him for the government, and make him a type of him who was to be the Messiah, the anointed One, who received the Spirit, not by measure, but without measure. He is said to be anointed in the midst of his brethren, who yet, possibly, did not understand it as a designation to the government, and therefore did not envy David (as Joseph's brethren did him), because they saw no further marks of dignity put upon him, no, not so much as a coat of divers colours. But bishop Patrick reads it, He anointed him from the midst of his brethren, that is, he singled him out from the rest, and privately anointed him, but with a charge to keep his own counsel, and not to let his own brethren know it, as by what we find (ch. 17:28), it should seem, Eliab did not. It is computed that David now was about twenty years old; if so, his troubles by Saul lasted ten years, for he was thirty years old when Saul died. Dr. Lightfoot reckons that he was about twenty-five, and that his troubles lasted but five years. 5. The happy effects of this anointing: The Spirit of the Lord came upon David from that day forward, v. 13.

The anointing of him was not an empty ceremony, but a divine power went along with that instituted sign, and he found himself inwardly advanced in wisdom, and courage, and concern for the public, with all the qualifications of a prince, though not at all advanced in his outward circumstances. This would abundantly satisfy him that his election was of God. The best evidence of our being predestinated to the kingdom of glory is our being sealed with the Spirit of promise, and our experience of a work of grace in our own hearts. Some think that his courage, by which he slew the lion and the bear, and his extraordinary skill in music, were the effects and evidences of the Spirit's coming upon him. However, this made him the sweet psalmist of Israel, 2 Sa. 23:1. Samuel, having done this, went to Ramah in safety, and we never read of him again but once (ch. 19:18), till we read of his death; now he retired to die in peace, since his eyes had seen the salvation, even the sceptre brought into the tribe of Judah.

Verses 14–23

We have here Saul falling and David rising.

I. Here is Saul made a terror to himself (v. 14): The Spirit of the Lord departed from him. He having forsaken God and his duty, God, in a way of righteous judgment, withdrew from him those assistances of the good Spirit with which he was directed, animated, and encouraged in his government and wars. He lost all his good qualities. This was the effect of his rejecting God, and an evidence of his being rejected by him. Now God took his mercy from Saul (as it is expressed, 2 Sa. 7:15); for, when the Spirit of the Lord departs from us, all good goes. When men grieve and quench the Spirit, by wilful sin, he departs, and will not always strive. The consequence of this was that an evil spirit from God troubled him. Those that drive the good Spirit away from the do of course become prey to the evil spirit. If God and his grace do not rule us, sin and Satan will have possession of us. The devil, by the divine permission, troubled and terrified Saul, by means of the corrupt humours of his body and passions of his mind. He grew fretful, and peevish, and discontented, timorous and suspicious, ever and anon starting and trembling; he was sometimes, says Josephus, as if he had been choked or strangled, and a perfect demoniac by fits. This made him unfit for business, precipitate in his counsels, the contempt of his enemies, and a burden to all about him.

II. Here is David made a physician to Saul, and by this means brought to court, a physician that helped him against the worst of diseases, when none else could. David was newly appointed privately to the kingdom. It would be of use to him to go to court and see the world; and here his doing so is brought about for him without any contrivance of his own or his friends. Note, Those whom God designs for any service his providence shall concur with his grace to prepare and qualify for it. Saul is distempered; his servants have the honesty and courage to tell him what his distemper is (v. 15), an evil spirit, not by chance but from God and his providence, troubleth thee. Now, 1. The means they all advised him to for his relief was music (v. 16): "Let us have a cunning player on the harp to attend thee." How much better friends had they been to him if they had advised him, since the evil spirit was from the Lord, to give all diligence to make his peace with God by true repentance, to send for Samuel to pray with him and to intercede with God for him! then might he not only have had some present relief, but the good Spirit would have returned to him. But their project is to make him merry, and so cure him. Many whose consciences are convinced and startled are for ever ruined by such methods as these, which drown all care of the soul in the delights of sense. Yet Saul's servants did not amiss to send for music as a help to cheer up the spirits, if they had but withal sent for a prophet to give him good counsel. And (as bishop Hall observes) it was well they did not send for a witch or diviner, by his enchantments to cast out the evil spirit, which has been the abominably wicked practice of some that have worn the Christian name, who consult the devil in their distresses and make hell their refuge. It will be no less than a miracle of divine grace if those who thus agree with Satan ever break off from him again. 2. One of his servants recommended David to him, as a fit person to be employed in the use of these means, little imagining that he was the man whom Samuel meant when he told

Saul of a neighbour of his, better than he, who should have the kingdom, *ch.* 15:28. It is a very high character which the servant of Saul's here gives of David (*v.* 18), that he was not only fit for his purpose as a comely person and skilful in playing, but a man of courage and conduct, a mighty valiant man, and prudent in all matters, fit to be further preferred, and (which crowned his character) *the Lord is with him.* By this it appears that though David, after he was anointed, returned to his country business, and there remained on his head no marks of the oil, so careful was he to keep that secret, yet the workings of the Spirit signified by the oil could not be hid, but made him shine in obscurity, so that all his neighbours observed with wonder the great improvements of his mind on a sudden. David, even in his shepherd's garb, has become an oracle, a champion, and every thing that is great. His fame reached the court soon, for Saul was inquisitive after such young men, *ch.* 14:52. When the Spirit of God comes upon a man he will make his face to shine. 3. David is hereupon sent for to court. And it seems, (1.) His father was very willing to part with him, sent him very readily, and a present with him to Saul, *v.* 20. The present was, according to the usage of those times, bread and wine (compare, *ch.* 10:3, 4), therefore acceptable because expressive of the homage and allegiance of him that sent it. Probably Jesse, who knew what his son David was designed for, was aware that Providence was herein fitting him for it, and therefore he would not force Providence by sending him to court uncalled, yet he followed Providence very cheerfully when he saw it plainly putting him into the way of preferment. Some suggest that when Jesse received that message, *Send me David thy son,* he began to be afraid that Saul had got some intimation of his being anointed, and sent for him to do him a mischief, and therefore Jesse sent a present to pacify him; but it is probable that the person, whoever he was, that brought the message, gave him an account on what design he was sent for. (2.) Saul became very kind to him (*v.* 21), *loved him greatly,* and designed to *make him his armour-bearer,* and (contrary to the manner of the king, *ch.* 8:11) asked his father's leave to keep him in his service (*v.* 22): *Let David, I pray thee, stand before me.* And good reason he had to respect him, for he did him a great deal of service with his music, *v.* 23. Only his instrumental music with his harp is mentioned, but it should seem, by the account Josephus gives, that he added vocal music to it, and sung hymns, probably divine hymns, songs of praise, to his harp. David's music was Saul's physic. [1.] Music has a natural tendency to compose and exhilarate the mind, when it is disturbed and saddened. Elisha used it for the calming of his spirits, 2 Ki. 3:15. On some it has a greater influence and effect than on others, and, probably, Saul was one of those. Not that it charmed the evil spirit, but it made his spirit sedate, and allayed those tumults of the animal spirits by which the devil had advantage against him. The beams of the sun (it is the learned Bochart's comparison) cannot be cut with a sword, quenched with water, or blown out with wind, but, by closing the window-shutters, they may be kept out of the chamber. Music cannot work upon the devil, but it may shut up the passages by which he has access to the mind. [2.] David's music was extraordinary, and in mercy to him, that he might gain a reputation at court, as one that had the Lord with him. God made his performances in music more successful, in this case, than those of others would have been. Saul found, even after he had conceived an enmity to David, that no one else could do him the same service (*ch.* 19:9, 10), which was a great aggravation of his outrage against him. It is a pity that music, which may be so serviceable to the good temper of the mind, should ever be abused by any to the support of vanity and luxury, and made an occasion of drawing the heart away from God and serious things: if this be to any the effect of it, it drives away the good Spirit, not the evil spirit.

CHAPTER 17

David is the man whom God now delights to honour, for he is a man after his own heart. We read in the foregoing chapter how, after he was anointed, Providence made him famous in the court; we read in this chapter how Providence made him much more famous in the camp, and, by both, not only marked him for a great man, but fitted him for the throne for which he was designed. In the court he was only Saul's physician; but in the camp Israel's champion; there he fairly fought, and beat Goliath of Gath. In the story observe, I. What a noble figure Goliath made, and how daringly he challenged the armies of Israel (*v.* 1–11). II. What a mean figure David made, when Providence brought him to the army (*v.* 12–30). III. The unparalleled bravery wherewith David undertook to encounter this Philistine (*v.* 31–39). IV. The pious resolution with which he attacked him (*v.* 40–47). V. The glorious victory he obtained over him with a sling and a stone, and the advantage which the Israelites thereby gained against the Philistines (*v.* 48–54). VI. The great notice which was hereupon taken of David at court (*v.* 55–58).

Verses 1–11

It was not long ago that the Philistines were soundly beaten, and put to the worse, before Israel, and they would have been totally routed if Saul's rashness had not prevented; but here we have them making head again. Observe,

I. How they *defied Israel with their armies, v.* 1. They made a descent upon the Israelites' country, and possessed themselves, as it should seem, of some part of it, for they encamped in a place *which belonged to Judah.* Israel's ground would never have been footing for Philistine-armies if Israel had been faithful to their God. The Philistines (it is probable) had heard that Samuel had fallen out with Saul and forsaken him, and no longer assisted and advised him, and that Saul had grown melancholy and unfit for business, and this news encouraged them to make this attempt for the retrieving of the credit they had lately lost. The enemies of the church are watchful to take all advantages, and they never have greater advantages than when her protectors have provoked God's Spirit and prophets to leave them. Saul mustered his forces, and faced them, *v.* 2, 3. And here we must take notice, 1. That the evil spirit, for the present, had left Saul, *ch.* 16:23. David's harp having given him some relief, perhaps the alarms and affairs of the war prevented the return of the distemper. Business is a good antidote against melancholy. Let the mind have something without to fasten on and employ itself about, and it will be the less in danger of preying upon itself. God, in mercy to Israel, suspended the judgment for a while; for how distracted must the affairs of the public have been if at this juncture the prince had been distracted! 2. That David for the present had returned to Bethlehem, and had left the court, *v.* 15. When Saul had no further occasion to use him for the relief of his distemper, though, being anointed, he had a very good private reason, and, having a grant of the place of Saul's armour-bearer, he had a very plausible pretence to have continued his attendance, as a retainer to the court, yet he went home to Bethlehem, and returned to keep his father's sheep; this was a rare instance, in a young man that stood so fair for preferment, of humility and affection to his parents. He knew better than most do how to come down again after he had begun to rise, and strangely preferred the retirements of the pastoral life before all the pleasures and gaieties of the court. None more fit for honour than he, nor that deserved it better, and yet none more dead to it.

II. How they defied Israel with their champion Goliath, whom they were almost as proud of as he was of himself, hoping by him to recover their reputation and dominion. Perhaps the army of the Israelites was superior in number and strength to that of the Philistines, which made the Philistines decline a battle, and stand at bay with them, desiring rather to put the issue upon a single combat, in which, having such a champion, they hoped to gain the victory. Now concerning this champion observe,

1. His prodigious size. He was of the sons of Anak, who at Gath kept their ground in Joshua's time (Jos. 11:22), and kept up a race of giants there, of which Goliath was one, and, it is probable, one of the largest. He was in height *six cubits and a span, v.* 4. They learned bishop Cumberland has made it out that the scripture-cubit was above twenty-one inches (above three inches more than our half-yard) and a span was half a cubit, by which computation Goliath wanted but eight inches of four yard in height, eleven feet and four inches, a monstrous stature, and which made him very formidable, especially if he had strength and spirit proportionable.

2. His armour. Art, as well as nature, made him terrible. He was well furnished with defensive armour (*v.* 5, 6): *A helmet of brass on his head, a coat of mail,* made of brass plates laid over one another, like the scales of a fish; and, because his legs would lie most within the reach of an ordinary man, he wore brass boots, and had a large corselet of brass about his neck. The coat is said to weigh 5000 shekels, and a shekel was half an ounce avoirdupois, a vast weight for a man to carry, all the other parts of his armour being proportionable. But some think it should be translated, not the *weight* of the coat, but the *value* of it, was 5000 shekels; so much it cost. His offensive weapons were extraordinary, of which his spear only is here described, *v.* 7. It was like a weaver's beam. His arm could manage that which an ordinary man could scarcely heave. His shield only, which was the lightest of all his accoutrements, was carried before him by his esquire, probably for state; for he that was clad in brass little needed a shield.

3. His challenge. The Philistines having chosen him for their champion, to save themselves from the hazard of battle, he here throws down the gauntlet, and bids defiance to the armies of Israel, *v.* 8–10. He came into the valley that lay between the camps, and, his voice probably being as much stronger than other people's as his arm was, he cried so as to make them all hear him, *Give me a man, that we may fight together.* He looked upon himself with admiration, because he was so much taller and stronger than all about him; his heart (says bishop Hall) nothing but a lump of proud flesh. He looked upon Israel with disdain, because they had none among them of such a monstrous bulk, and defies them to find a man among them bold enough to enter the list with him. (1.) He upbraids them with their folly in drawing an army together: "*Why have you come to set the battle in array?* How dare you oppose the mighty Philistines?" Or, "Why should the two armies engage, when the controversy may be sooner decided, with only the expense of one life and the hazard of another?" (2.) He offers to put the war entirely upon the issue of the duel he proposes: "If your champion kill me, we will be your servants; if I kill him, you shall be ours." This, says bishop Patrick, was only a bravado, for no nation would be willing thus to venture its all upon the success of one man, nor is it justifiable; notwithstanding Goliath's stipulation here, when he was killed the Philistines did not stand to his word, nor submit themselves as servants to Israel. When he boasts, *I am a Philistine, and you are servants to Saul,* he would have it thought a great piece of condescension in him, who was a chief ruler, to enter the lists with an Israelite; for he looked on them as no better than slaves. The Chaldee paraphrase brings him in boasting that he was the man that had killed Hophni and Phinehas and taken the ark prisoner, but that the Philistines had never given him so much as the command of a regiment in recompence of his services, whereas Saul had been made king for his services: "Let him therefore take up the challenge."

4. The terror this struck upon Israel: *Saul and his army were greatly afraid, v.* 11. The people would not have been dismayed but that they observed Saul's courage failed him; and it is not to be expected that, if the leader be a coward, the followers should be bold. We found before, when the Spirit of the Lord came upon Saul (*ch.* 11:6), none could be more daring nor forward to answer the challenge of Nahash the Ammonite, but now that the *Spirit of the Lord had departed from him* even the big looks and big words of a single Philistine make him change colour. But where was Jonathan all this while? Why did not he accept the challenge, who, in the last war, had so bravely engaged a whole army of Philistines? Doubtless he did not feel himself stirred up of God to it, as he did in the former case. As the best, so the bravest men, are no more than what God makes them. Jonathan must now sit still, because the honour of engaging Goliath is reserved for David. In great and good actions, the wind of the Spirit blows when and where he listeth. Now the pious Israelites lament their king's breach with Samuel.

Verses 12–30

Forty days the two armies lay encamped facing one another, each advantageously posted, but neither forward to engage. Either they were parleying and treating of an accommodation or they were waiting for recruits; and perhaps there were frequent skirmishes between small detached parties. All this while, twice a day, morning and evening, did the insulting champion appear in the field and repeat his challenge, his own heart growing more and more proud for his not being answered and the people of Israel more and more timorous, while God designed hereby to ripen him for destruction and to make Israel's deliverance the more illustrious. All this while David is keeping his father's sheep, but at the end of forty days Providence brings him to the field to win and wear the laurel which no other Israelite dares venture for. We have in these verses,

I. The present state of his family. His father was old (*v.* 12): *He went among men for an old man,* was taken notice of for his great age, above what was usual at that time, and therefore was excused from pubic services, and went not in person to the wars, but sent his sons; he had the honours paid him that were due his age, his hoary head was a crown of glory to him. David's three elder brethren, who perhaps envied his place at the court, got their father to send for him home, and let them go to the camp, where they hoped to signalize themselves and eclipse him (*v.* 13, 14), while David himself was so far from being proud of the services he had done his prince, or ambitious of further preferment, that he not only returned from court to the obscurity of his father's house, but to care, and toil, and (as it proved, *v.* 34) the peril, of *keeping his father's sheep.* It was the praise of this humility that it came after he had the honour of a courtier, and the reward of it that it came before the honour of a conqueror. *Before honour is humility.* Now he had that opportunity of mediation and prayer, and other acts of devotion, which fitted him for what he was destined to more than all the military exercises of that inglorious camp could do.

II. The orders his father gave him to go and visit his brethren in the camp. He did not himself ask leave to go, to satisfy his curiosity, or to gain experience and make observations; but his father sent him on a mean and homely errand, on which any of his servants might have gone. He must carry some bread and cheese to his brethren, ten loaves with some parched corn for themselves (*v.* 17) and ten cheeses (which, it seems, he thought too good for them) for a present to their colonel, *v.* 18. David must still be the drudge of the family, though he was to be the greatest ornament of it. He had not so much as an ass at command to carry his load, but must take it on his back, and yet run to the camp. Jesse, we thought, was privy to his being anointed, and yet industriously kept him thus mean and obscure, probably to hide him from the eye of suspicion and envy, knowing that he was anointed to a crown in reversion. He must observe how his brethren fared, whether they were not reduced to short allowance, now that the encampment continued so long, that, if need were, he might send them more provisions. And he must take their pledge, that is, if they had pawned any thing, he must redeem it; *take notice of their company,* so some observe, whom they associate with, and what sort of life they lead. Perhaps David, like Joseph, had formerly brought to his father their evil report, and now he sends him to enquire concerning their manners. See the care the pious parents about their children when they are abroad from them, especially in places of temptation; they are solicitous how they conduct themselves, and particularly what company they keep. Let children think of this, and conduct themselves accordingly, remembering that, when they are from under their parents' eye, they are still under God's eye.

III. David's dutiful obedience to his father's command. His prudence and care made him be up early (*v.* 20), and yet not to leave his sheep without a keeper, so faithful was he in a few things and therefore the fitter to be made ruler over many things, and so well had he learnt to obey before he pretended to command. God's providence brought him to the camp very seasonably, when both sides had set the battle in array, and, as it should seem, were more likely to come to an engagement than they had yet been during all the forty days, *v.* 21. Both sides were now preparing to fight. Jesse little thought of sending his son to the army just at that critical juncture, but the wise God orders the time and all the circumstances of actions and affairs so as to serve his designs of securing the interests of Israel and advancing the men after his own heart. Now observe here,

1. How brisk and lively David was, *v.* 22. What articles he brought he honestly took care of, and left them with those that had the charge of the bag and baggage; but, though he had come a long journey with a great load, he *ran into the army,* to see what was doing there, and to pay his respects to his brethren. *Seest thou a man* thus *diligent in his business,* he is in the way of preferment, *he shall stand before kings.*

2. How bold and daring the Philistine was, *v.* 23. Now that the armies were drawn out into a line of battle he appeared first to renew his challenge, vainly imagining that he was in the eager chase of his own glory and triumph, whereas really he was but courting his own destruction.

3. How timorous and faint-hearted the men of Israel were. Though they had, for forty days together, been used to his haughty looks and threatening language, and, having seen no execution done by either, might have learned to despise both, yet, upon his approach, they *fled from him and were greatly afraid, v.* 24. One Philistine could never thus have chased 1000 Israelites, and put 10,000 to flight, unless their Rock, being treacherously forsaken by them, had justly *sold them, and shut them up,* Deu. 32:30.

4. How high Saul bid for a champion. Though he was the tallest of all the men of Israel, and, if he had not been so, while he kept close to God might himself have safely taken up the gauntlet which this insolent Philistine threw down, yet, the Spirit of the Lord having departed from him, he durst not do it, nor press Jonathan to do it; but whoever will do it shall have as good preferment as he can give him, *v.* 25. If the hope of wealth and honour will prevail with any man to expose himself so far, it is proclaimed that the bold adventurer, if he come off, shall marry the king's daughter and have a good portion with her; but, as it should seem, whether he come off or no, his *father's house shall be free in Israel,* from all toll, tribute, custom, and services to the crown, or shall be ennobled and advanced to the peerage.

5. How much concerned David was to assert the honour of God and Israel against the impudent challenges of this champion. He asked what reward was promised to him that should slay this Philistine (*v.* 26), though he knew already, not because he was ambitious of the honour, but because he would have it taken notice of, and reported to Saul, how much he resented the indignity hereby done to Israel and Israel's God. He might have presumed so far upon his acquaintance and interest at court as to go himself to Saul to offer his service; but his modesty would not let him do this. It was one of his own rules, before it was one of his son's proverbs, *Put not forth thyself in the presence of the king, and stand not in the place of great men* (Prov. 25:6); yet his zeal put him upon that method which he hoped would bring him into this great engagement. Two considerations, it seems, fired David with a holy indignation: — (1.) That the challenger was one that was uncircumcised, a stranger to God and out of covenant with him. (2.) That the challenged were the armies of the living God, devoted to him, employed by him and for him, so that the affronts offered to them reflected upon the living God himself, and *that* he could not bear. When therefore some had told him what was the reward proposed for killing the Philistine (*v.* 27) he asked others (*v.* 30), with the same resentment, which he expected would at length come to Saul's ear.

6. How he was brow-beaten and discouraged by his eldest brother Eliab, who, taking notice of his forwardness, fell into a passion upon it, and gave David very abusive language, *v.* 28. Consider this, (1.) As the fruit of Eliab's jealousy. He was the eldest brother, and David the youngest, and perhaps it had been customary with him (as it is with too many elder brothers) to trample upon him and take every occasion to chide him. But those who thus exalt themselves over their juniors may perhaps live to see themselves, by a righteous providence, abased, and those to whom they are abusive exalted. Time may come when the elder may serve the younger. But Eliab was now vexed that his younger brother should speak those bold words against the Philistine which he himself durst not say. He knew what honour David had already had in the court, and, if he should now get honour in the camp (from which he thought he had found means effectually to seclude him, *v.* 15), the glory of his elder brethren would be eclipsed and stained; and therefore (such is the nature of jealousy) he would rather that Goliath should triumph over Israel than that David should be the man that should triumph over him. *Wrath is cruel and anger is outrageous, but who can stand before envy,* especially the envy of a brother, the keenness of which Jacob, and Joseph, and David experienced? See Prov. 18:19. It is very ill-favoured language that Eliab here gives him; not only unjust and unkind, but, at this time, basely ungrateful; for David was now sent by his father, as Joseph by his, on a kind of visit to his brethren. Eliab intended, in what he said, not only to grieve and discourage David himself, and quench that noble fire which he perceived glowing in his breast, but to represent him to those about him as an idle proud lad, not fit to be taken notice of. He gives them to understand that his business was only to keep sheep, and falsely insinuates that he was a careless unfaithful shepherd; though he had left his charge in good hands (*v.* 20), yet he must tauntingly be asked, *With whom hast thou left those few sheep?* Though he came down now to the camp in disobedience to his father and kindness to his brethren, and Eliab knew this, yet his coming is turned to his reproach: "Thou hast come down, not to do any service, but to gratify thy own curiosity, and only to look about thee;" and thence he will infer *the pride and naughtiness of his heart,* and pretends to know it as certainly as if he were in his bosom. David could appeal to God concerning his humility and sincerity (Ps. 17:3; 131:1) and at this time gave proofs of both, and yet could not escape this hard character from his own brother. See the folly, absurdity, and wickedness, of a proud and envious passion; how groundless its jealousies are, how unjust its censures, how unfair its representations, how bitter its invectives, and how indecent its language. God, by his grace, keep us from such a spirit! (2.) As a trial of David's meekness, patience and constancy. A short trial it was, and he approved himself well in it; for, [1.] He bore the provocation with admirable temper (*v.* 29): *"What have I now done?* What fault have I committed, for which I should thus be chidden? *Is there not a cause* for my coming to the camp, when my father sent me? *Is there not a cause* for my resenting the injury done to Israel's honour by Goliath's challenges?" He had right and reason on his side, and knew it, and therefore did not render railing for railing, but with a soft answer turned away his brother's wrath. This conquest of his own passion was in some respects more honourable than his conquest of Goliath. *He that hath rule over his own spirit is better than the mighty.* It was no time for David to quarrel with his brother when the Philistines were upon them. The more threatening the church's enemies are the more forbearing her friends should be with one another. [2.] He broke through the discouragement with admirable resolution. He would not be driven off from his thoughts of engaging the Philistine by the ill-will of his brother. Those that undertake great and public services must not think it strange if they be discountenanced and opposed by those from whom they had reason to expect support and assistance; but must humbly go on with their work, in the face not only of their enemies' threats, but of their friends' slights and suspicions.

Verses 31–39

David is at length presented to Saul for his champion (*v.* 31) and he bravely undertakes to fight the Philistine (*v.* 32): *Let no man's heart fail because of him.* It would have reflected too much upon the valour of his prince if he had said, *Let not thy heart fail;* therefore he speaks generally: *Let no man's heart fail.* A little shepherd, come but this morning from keeping sheep, has more courage than all the mighty men of Israel, and encourages them. Thus does God often send good words to his Israel, and do great things for them, by the weak and foolish things of the world. David only desires a commission from Saul to go and fight with the Philistine, but says nothing to him of the reward he had proposed, because that was not the thing he was ambitious of, but only the honour of serving God and his country: nor would he seem to question Saul's generosity. Two things David had to do with Saul: —

I. To get clear of the objection Saul made against his undertaking. "Alas!" says Saul, "thou hast a good heart to it, but art by no means an equal match for this Philistine. To engage with him is to throw away a life which may better be reserved for more agreeable services. *Thou art but a youth,* rash and inconsiderate, weak and unversed in arms: he is a man that has the head and hands of a man, *a man of war,* trained up and inured to it *from his youth* (*v.* 33), and how canst thou expect but that he will be too hard for thee?" David, as he had answered his brother's passion with meekness, so he answered Saul's fear with faith, and *gives a reason of the hope* which was in him that he should conquer the Philistine, to the satisfaction of Saul. We have reason to fear that Saul had no great acquaintance with nor regard to the word of God, and therefore David, in reasoning with him, fetched not his arguments and encouragements thence, how much soever he had an eye to it in his own mind. But he argues from experience; though he was but a youth, and never in the wars, yet perhaps he had done as much as the killing of Goliath came to, for he had had, by divine assistance, spirit enough to encounter and strength enough to subdue a lion once and another time a bear that robbed him of his lambs, v. 34–36. To these he compares this uncircumcised Philistine, looks upon him to be as much a ravenous beast as either of them, and therefore doubts not but to deal as easily with him; and hereby he gives Saul to understand that he was not so inexperienced in hazardous combats as he took him to be.

1. He tells his story like a man of spirit. He is not ashamed to own that he kept his father's sheep, which his brother had just now upbraided him with. So far is he from concealing it that from his employment as a shepherd he fetches the experience that now animated him. But he lets those about him know that he was no ordinary shepherd. Whatever our profession or calling is, be it ever so mean, we should labour to excel in it, and do the business of it in the best manner. When David kept sheep, (1.) He approved himself very careful and tender of his flock, though it was not his own, but his father's. He could not see a lamb in distress but he would venture his life to rescue it. This temper made him fit to be a king, to whom the lives of subjects should be dear and their blood precious (Ps. 72:14), and fit to be a type of Christ, the good Shepherd, who *gathers the lambs in his arms and carries them in his bosom* (Isa. 40:11), and who not only ventured, but *laid down his life for his sheep.* Thus too was David fit to be an example to ministers with the utmost care and diligence to watch for souls, that they be not a prey to the roaring lion. (2.) He approved himself very bold and brave in the defence of his flock. This was that which he was now concerned to give proof of, and better evidence could not be demanded than this: "Thy servant not only rescued the lambs, but, to revenge the injury, *slew both the lion and the bear."*

2. He applies his story like a man of faith. He owns (v. 37) it was *the Lord that delivered him from the lion and the bear;* to him he gives the praise of that great achievement, and thence he infers, *He will deliver me out of the hand of this Philistine.* "The lion and the bear were enemies only to me and my sheep, and it was in defence of my own interest that I attacked them; but this Philistine is an enemy to God and Israel, *defies the armies of the living God,* and it is for their honour that I attack him." Note, (1.) Our experiences ought to be improved by us as our encouragements to trust in God and venture in the way of duty. He that has delivered does and will. (2.) By the care which common Providence takes of the inferior creatures, and the protection they are under, we may be encouraged to depend upon that special Providence which surrounds the Israel of God. He that sets bounds to the waves of the sea and the rage of wild beasts can and will restrain the wrath of wicked men. Paul seems to allude to this of David (2 Tim. 4:17, 18), *I was delivered out of the mouth of the lion,* and therefore, I trust, *the Lord shall deliver me.* And perhaps David here thought of the story of Samson, and encouraged himself with it; for his slaying a lion was a happy presage of his many illustrious victories over the Philistines in single combat. Thus David took off Saul's objection against his undertaking, and gained a commission to fight the Philistine, with which Saul gave him a hearty good wish; since he would not venture himself, he prayed for him that would: *Go, and the Lord be with thee,* a good word, if it was not spoken customarily, and in a formal manner, as too often it is. But David has somewhat to do likewise,

II. To get clear of the armour wherewith Saul would, by all means, have him dressed up when he went upon this great action (v. 38): *He armed David with his armour,* not that which he wore himself, the disproportion of his stature would not admit that, but some that he kept in his armoury, little thinking that he on whom he now put his helmet and coat of mail must shortly inherit his crown and robe. David, being not yet resolved which way to attack his enemy, *girded on his sword,* not knowing, as yet, but he should have occasion to make use of it; but he found the armour would but encumber him, and would be rath-

er his burden than his defence, and therefore he desires leave of Saul to put them off again: *I cannot go with these, for I have not proved them,* that is, "I have never been accustomed to such accoutrements as these." We may suppose Saul's armour was both very fine and very firm, but what good would it do David if it were not fit, or if he knew not how to manage himself in it? Those that aim at things above their education and usage, and covet the attire and armour of princes, forget that that is the best for us which we are fit for and accustomed to; if we had our desire, we should wish to be in our own coat again, and should say, "We cannot go with these;" we had therefore better go without them.

Verses 40–47

We are now coming near this famous combat, and have in these verses the preparations and remonstrances made on both sides.

I. The preparations made on both sides for the encounter. The Philistine was already fixed, as he had been daily for the last forty days. Well might he go with his armour, for he had sufficiently proved it. Only we are told (v. 41) that he *came on and drew near,* a signal, it is likely, being given that his challenge was accepted, and, as if he distrusted his helmet and coat of mail, a man went before him, *carrying his shield,* for his own hands were full with his sword and spear, v. 45. But what arms and ammunition is David furnished with? Truly none but what he brought with him as a shepherd; no breastplate, nor corselet, but his plain shepherd's coat; no spear, but his staff; no sword nor bow, but his sling; no quiver, but his scrip; nor any arrows, but, instead of them, five smooth stones picked up out of the brook, v. 40. By this it appeared that his confidence was purely in the power of God, and not in any sufficiency of his own, and that now at length he who put it into his heart to fight the Philistine put it into his head with what weapons to do it.

II. The conference which precedes the encounter, in which observe,

1. How very proud Goliath was, (1.) With what scorn he looked upon his adversary, v. 42. He looked about, expecting to meet some tall strong man, but, when he saw what a mean figure he made with whom he was to engage, he disdained him, thought it below him to enter the lists with him, fearing that the contemptibleness of the champion he contended with would lessen the glory of his victory. He took notice of his person, that he was but a youth, not come to his strength, *ruddy and of a fair countenance,* fitter to accompany the virgins of Israel in their dances (if mixed dancing was then in use) than to lead on the men of Israel in their battles. He took notice of his array with great indignation (v. 43): *"Am I a dog, that thou comest to me with staves?* Dost thou think to beat me as easily as thou dost thy shepherd's dog?"* (2.) With what confidence he presumed upon his success. He cursed David by his gods, imprecating the impotent vengeance of his idols against him, thinking these fire-balls thrown about him would secure his success: and therefore, in confidence of that, he darts his grimaces, as if threatening words would kill (v. 44): *"Come to me, and I will give thy flesh to the fowls of the air,* it will be a tender and delicate feast for them." Thus the security and presumption of fools destroy them.

2. How very pious David was. His speech savours nothing of ostentation, but God is all in all in it, v. 45–47. (1.) He derives his authority from God: *"I come to thee* by warrant and commission from heaven, *in the name of the Lord,* who has called me to and anointed me for this undertaking, who, by his universal providence, is the *Lord of hosts,* of all hosts, and therefore has power to do what he pleases, and, by the special grace of his covenant, is *the God of the armies of Israel,* and therefore has engaged and will employ his power for their protection, and against thee who hast impiously defied them." The name of God David relied on, as Goliath did on his sword and spear. See Ps. 20:7; 118:10, 11. (2.) He depends for success upon God, v. 46. David speaks with as much assurance as Goliath had done, but upon better ground; it is his faith that says, *"This day will the Lord deliver thee into my hand,* and not only thy carcase, but the carcases of the host of the Philistines, shall be given to the birds and beasts of prey." (3.) He devotes the praise and glory of all to God. He did not, like Goliath,

seek his own honour, but the honour of God, not doubting but by the success of this action, [1.] All the world should be made to know that there is a God, and that the God of Israel is the one only living and true God, and all other pretended deities are vanity and a lie. [2.] All Israel (whom he calls not this army, but *this assembly,* or church, because they were now religiously attending the *goings of their God and King,* as they used to do *in the sanctuary*) shall *know that the Lord saveth not with sword and spear* (v. 47), but can, when he pleases, save without either and against both, Ps. 46:9. David addresses himself to this combat rather as a priest that was going to offer a sacrifice to the justice of God than as a soldier that was going to engage an enemy of his country.

Verses 48–58

Here is 1. The engagement between the two champions, v. 48. To this engagement the Philistine advanced with a great deal of state and gravity; if he must encounter a pigmy, yet it shall be with the magnificence of a giant and a grandee. This is intimated in the manner of expression: He *arose, and came, and drew nigh,* like a stalking mountain, overlaid with brass and iron, *to meet David.* David advanced with no less activity and cheerfulness, as one that aimed more to do execution than to make a figure: He *hasted, and ran,* being lightly clad, to *meet the Philistine.* We may imagine with what tenderness and compassion the Israelites saw such a pleasing youth as this throwing himself into the mouth of destruction, but he knew whom he had believed and for whom he acted. 2. The fall of Goliath in this engagement. He was in no haste, because in no fear, but confident that he should soon at one stroke cleave his adversary's head; but, while he was preparing to do it solemnly, David did his business effectually, without any parade: he slang a stone which hit him in the forehead, and, in the twinkling of an eye, fetched him to the ground, v. 49. Goliath knew there were famous slingers in Israel (Jdg. 20:16), yet was either so forgetful or presumptuous as to go with the beaver of his helmet open, and thither, to the only part left exposed, not so much David's art as God's providence directed the stone, and brought it with such force that it sunk into his head, notwithstanding the impudence with which his forehead was brazened. See how frail and uncertain life is, even when it thinks itself best fortified, and how quickly, how easily, and with how small a matter, the passage may be opened for life to go out and death to enter. Goliath himself *has not power over the spirit to retain the spirit,* Eccl. 8:8. Let not the strong man glory in his strength, nor the armed man in his armour. See how God resists the proud and pours contempt upon those that bid defiance to him and his people. None ever hardened his heart against God and prospered. One of the Rabbin thinks that when Goliath said to David, *Come, and I will give thy flesh to the fowls of the air,* he threw up his head so hastily that his helmet fell off, and so left his broad forehead a fair mark for David. To complete the execution, David drew Goliath's own sword, a two-handed weapon for David, and with it *cut off his head,* v. 51. What need had David to take a sword of his own? his enemy's sword shall serve his purpose, when he has occasion for one. God is greatly glorified when his proud enemies are cut off with their own sword and he makes *their own tongues to fall upon them,* Ps. 64:8. David's victory over Goliath was typical of the triumphs of the son of David over Satan and all the powers of darkness, whom he *spoiled, and made a show of them openly* (Col. 2:15), and we through him are *more than conquerors.* 3. The defeat of the Philistines' army hereupon. They relied wholly upon the strength of their champion, and, therefore, when they saw him slain, they did not, as Goliath had offered, throw down their arms and surrender themselves servants to Israel (v. 9), but took to their heels, being wholly dispirited, and thinking it to no purpose to oppose one before whom such a mighty man had fallen: *They fled* (v. 51), and this put life into the Israelites, who *shouted and pursued them* (David, it is probable, leading them on in the pursuit) even to the gates of their own cities, v. 52. In their return from the chase they seized all the baggage, plundered the tents (v. 53), and enriched themselves with the spoil. 4. David's disposal of his trophies, v. 54. He brought the head of the Philistine to Jerusalem, to be a terror to the Jebusites, who held the strong-hold of Sion: it is probable that he carried it in triumph to other cities. *His armour he laid up in his tent;* only the sword was preserved behind the ephod in the tabernacle, as consecrated to God, and a memorial of the victory to his honour, *ch.* 21:9. 5. The notice that was taken of David. Though he had been at court formerly, yet, having been for some time absent (*v.* 15), Saul had forgotten him, being melancholy and mindless, and little thinking that his musician would have spirit enough to be his champion; and therefore, as if he had never seen him before, he asked whose son he was. Abner was a stranger to him, but brought him to Saul (*v.* 57), and he gave a modest account of himself, *v.* 58. And now he was introduced to the court with much greater advantages than before, in which he owned God's hand performing all things for him.

CHAPTER 18

In the course of the foregoing chapter we left David in triumph; now in this chapter we have, I. The improvement of his triumphs; he soon became, 1. Saul's constant attendant (*v.* 2). 2. Jonathan's covenant friend (*v.* 1, 3, 4). 3. The darling of his country (*v.* 5, 7, 16). II. The allays of his triumphs. This is the vanity that accompanies even a right work, that "for it a man is envied," Eccl. 4:4. So David was by Saul. 1. He hated him, and sought to kill him himself (*v.* 8–11). 2. He feared him, and contrived how he might have some mischief done him (*v.* 12–17). He proposed to marry his daughter to him; but, [1.] cheated him of the eldest to provoke him (*v.* 19), and, [2.] Gave him the younger, upon conditions which would endanger his life (*v.* 20–25). But David performed his conditions bravely (*v.* 26, 27), and grew to be more and more esteemed (*v.* 28–30). Still David is rising, but (as all that aim at the crown of life must expect) he had a great deal of difficulty and opposition to grapple with.

Verses 1–5

David was anointed to the crown to take it out of Saul's hand, and over Jonathan's head, and yet here we find,

I. That Saul, who was now in possession of the crown, reposed a confidence in him, God so ordering it, that he might by his preferment at court be prepared for future service. Saul now took David home with him, and would not suffer him to return again to his retirement, *v.* 2. And David having signalized himself above the men of war, in taking up the challenge which they declined, *Saul set him over the men of war* (*v.* 5), not that he made him general (Abner was in that post), but perhaps captain of the life-guard; or, though he was youngest, he ordered him to have the precedency, in recompence of his great services. He employed him in the affairs of government; *and David went out withersoever Saul sent him,* showing himself as dutiful as he was bold and courageous. Those that hope to rule must first learn to obey. He had approved himself a dutiful son to Jesse his father, and now a dutiful servant to Saul his master; those that are good in one relation it is to be hoped will be so in another.

II. That Jonathan, who was heir to the crown, entered into covenant with him, God so ordering it, that David's way might be the clearer when his rival was his friend. 1. Jonathan conceived an extraordinary kindness and affection for him (*v.* 1): *When he had made an end of speaking to Saul* he fell perfectly in love with him. Whether it refers to his conference with Saul before the battle (*ch.* 17:34, 37), or to that after (*v.* 51), in which it is probable much more was said than is there set down, is uncertain. But, in both, David expressed himself with so much prudence, modesty, and piety, such a felicity of expression, with so much boldness and yet so much sweetness, and all this so natural and unaffected, and the more surprising because of the disadvantages of his education and appearance, *that the soul of Jonathan was* immediately *knit* unto *the soul of David.* Jonathan had formerly set upon a Philistine army with the same faith and bravery with which David had now attacked a Philistine giant; so that there was between them a very near resemblance of affections, dispositions, and counsels, which made their spirits unite to easily, so quickly, so closely, that they seemed but as one soul in two bodies. None had so much reason to dislike David as Jonathan had, because he was to put him by the crown, yet none regards him more. Those that are governed in their love by principles of wisdom and grace will not suffer their affections to be alienated by any secular regards or considerations: the greater thoughts will swallow up and overrule the less. 2. He testified his love to David by a generous present he made him, *v.* 4. He was uneasy at seeing so great a soul, though lodged in so fair a body, yet disguised in the mean and despicable dress of a poor shepherd, and therefore takes care to put him speedily into the habit of a courtier (for he gave him a robe) and of a soldier, for he gave him, instead of his staff and sling, a sword and bow, and, instead of his shepherd's scrip, a girdle, either a belt or a sash; and, which made the present much more obliging, they were the same that he himself had worn, and (as a presage of what would follow) he stripped himself of them to dress David in them. Saul's would not fit him, but Jonathan's did. Their bodies were of a size, a circumstance which well agreed with the suitableness of their minds. When Saul put these marks of honour on David he put them off again, because he would first earn them and then wear them; but, now that he had given proofs of the spirit of a prince and a soldier, he was not ashamed to wear the habits of a prince and a soldier. David is seen in Jonathan's clothes, that all may take notice he is a Jonathan's second self. Our Lord Jesus has thus shown his love to us, that he stripped himself to clothe us, emptied himself to enrich us; nay, he did more than Jonathan, he clothed himself with our rags, whereas Jonathan did not put on David's. 3. He endeavored to perpetuate this friendship. So entirely satisfied were they in each other, even at the first interview, that they made a covenant with each other, *v.* 3. Their mutual affection was sincere; and he that bears an honest mind startles not at assurances. True love desires to be constant. Those who love Christ as their own souls will be willing to join themselves to him in an everlasting covenant.

III. That both court and country agree to bless him. It is but seldom that they agree in their favourites; yet David was *accepted in the sight of all the people, and also* (which was strange) *in the sight of Saul's servants, v.* 5. The former cordially loved him, the latter could not for shame but caress and compliment him. And it was certainly a great instance of the power of God's grace in David that he was able to bear all this respect and honour flowing in upon him on a sudden without being lifted up above measure. Those that climb so fast have need of good heads and good hearts. It is more difficult to know how to abound than how to be abased.

Verses 6–11

Now begin David's troubles, and they not only tread on the heels of his triumphs, but take rise from them, such is the vanity of that in this world which seems greatest.

I. He was too much magnified by the common people. Some time after the victory Saul went a triumphant progress through the cities of Israel that lay next him, to receive the congratulations of the country. And, when he made his public entry into any place, the women were most forward to show him respect, as was usual then in public triumphs (*v.* 6), and they had got a song, it seems, which they sang in their dances (made by some poet or other, that was a great admirer of David's bravery, and was more just than wise, in giving his achievements in the late action the preference before Saul's), the burden of which was, *Saul had slain his thousands, and David his ten thousands.* Such a difference as this Moses made between the numbers of Ephraim and Manasseh, Deu. 33:17.

II. This mightily displeased Saul, and made him envy David, *v.* 8, 9. He ought to have considered that they referred only to this late action, and intended not to diminish any of Saul's former exploits; and that in the action now celebrated it was undeniably true that David, in killing Goliath, did in effect slay all the Philistines that were slain that day and defeated the whole army; so that they did but give David his due. It may be, he that composed the song only used a poetic liberty, and intended not any invidious comparison between Saul and David; or, if he did, it was below the great mind of a prince to take notice of such a reflection upon his personal honour, when it appeared that the glory of the public was sincerely intended. But Saul was very wroth, and presently suspected some treasonable design at the bottom of it: *What can he have more but the kingdom?* This made him eye David as one he was jealous of and sought advantages against (*v.* 9): his countenance was not towards him as it had been. Proud men cannot endure to hear any praised but themselves, and think all their honour lost that goes by themselves. It is a sign that the Spirit of God has departed from men if they be peevish in their resentment of affronts, envious and suspicious of all about them, and ill-natured in their conduct; for the wisdom from above makes us quite otherwise.

III. In his fury he aimed to kill David, *v.* 10, 11. *Jealousy is the rage of a man;* it made Saul outrageous against David and impatient to get him out of the way. 1. His fits of frenzy returned upon him. The very next day after he conceived malice against David the evil spirit from God, that had formerly haunted him, seized him again. Those that indulge themselves in envy and uncharitableness *give place to the devil,* and prepare for the re-entry of the unclean spirit, with seven others more wicked. Where envy is there is confusion. Saul pretended a religious ecstasy: *He prophesied in the midst of the house,* that is, he had the gestures and motions of a prophet, and humoured the thing well enough to decoy David into a snare, and that he might be fearless of any danger and off his guard; and perhaps designing, if he could but kill him, to impute it to a divine impulse and to charge it upon the spirit of prophecy with which he seemed to be animated: but really it was a hellish fury that actuated him. 2. David, though advanced to a much higher post of honour, disdained not, for his master's service, to return to his harp: *He played with his hand as at other times.* Let not the highest think any thing below them whereby they may do good and be serviceable to those they are obliged to. 3. He took this opportunity to aim at the death of David. A sword in a madman's hand is a dangerous thing, especially such a madman as Saul was, that was mad with malice. Yet he had a javelin or dart in his hand, which he projected, endeavouring thereby to slay David, not in a sudden passion, but deliberately: *I will smite David to the wall with it,* with such a desperate force did he throw it. Justly does David complain of his enemies that they hated him with *a cruel hatred,* Ps. 25:19. No life is thought too precious to be sacrificed to malice. If a grateful sense of the great service David had done to the public could not assuage Saul's fury, yet one would think he should have allowed himself to consider the kindness David was now doing him, in relieving him, as no one else could, against the worst of troubles. Those are possessed with a devilish spirit indeed that render evil for good. Compare David, with his harp in his hand, aiming to serve Saul, and Saul, with his javelin in his hand, aiming to slay David; and observe the meekness and usefulness of God's persecuted people and the brutishness and barbarity of their persecutors. *The bloodthirsty hate the upright, but the just seek his soul,* Prov. 29:10. 4. David happily avoided the blow twice (namely, now, and afterwards, *ch.* 19:10); he did not throw the javelin at Saul again, but withdrew, not fighting but flying for his own preservation; though he had both strength and courage enough, and colour of right, to make resistance and revenge the injury, yet he did no more than secure himself, by getting out of the way of it. David, no doubt, had a watchful eye upon Saul's hand, and the javelin in it, and did as bravely in running from it as he did lately in running upon Goliath. Yet his safety must be ascribed to the watchful eye of God's providence upon him, saving his servant from the hurtful sword; and by this narrow escape it seemed he was designed for something extraordinary.

Verses 12–30

Saul had now, in effect, proclaimed war with David. He began in open hostility when he threw the javelin at him. Now we are here told how his enmity proceeded, and how David received the attacks of it.

I. See how Saul expressed his malice against David. 1. He was *afraid of him, v.* 12. Perhaps he pretended to be afraid that David would do himself mischief, to force his way to the crown. Those that design ill against others are commonly willing to have it thought that others design ill against them. But David's withdrawal (*v.* 11) was a plain evidence that he was far from such a thought. However, he really stood in awe of him, as Herod feared John, Mk. 6:20. Saul was sensible that he had lost the favourable presence of God himself, and that David had it, and for this reason he feared him. Note, Those are truly great and to be reverenced that have God with them. The more *wisely David behaved himself* the more *Saul feared him, v.* 15, and again *v.* 29. Men think the way to be feared is to hector and threaten, which makes them feared by fools only, but despised by the wise and good; whereas the way to be both feared and loved, feared by those to whom we would wish to be a terror and loved by those to whom we would wish to be a delight, is to *behave ourselves wisely.* Wisdom makes the face to shine and commands respect. 2. He removed him from court, and gave him a regiment in the country, *v.* 13. He made him captain over 1000, that he might be from under his eye, because he hated the sight of him; and that he might not secure the interest of the courtiers. Yet herein he did impolitely; for it gave David an opportunity of ingratiating himself with the people, who therefore *loved him* (*v.* 16) because he *went out and came in before them,* that is, he presided in the business of his country, civil as well as military, and have universal satisfaction. 3. He stirred him up to take all occasions of quarrelling with the Philistines and engaging them (*v.* 17), insinuating to him that hereby he would do good service to his prince *(be thou valiant for me),* and good service to his God *(fight the Lord's battles),* and a kindness to himself too, for hereby he would qualify himself for the honour he designed him, which was to marry his eldest daughter to him. This he had merited by killing Goliath, for it was promised by proclamation to him that should do that exploit (*ch.* 17:25); but David was so modest as not to demand it, and now, when Saul proposed it, it was with design of mischief to him, to make him venture upon hazardous attempts, saying in his heart, *Let the hand of the Philistines be upon him,* hoping that he would some time or other be the death of him; yet how could he expect this when he saw that God was with him? 4. He did what he could to provoke him to discontent and mutiny, by breaking his promise with him, and giving his daughter to another when the time came that she should have been given to him, *v.* 19. This was as great an affront as he could possibly put upon him, and touched him both in his honour and in his love. He therefore thought David's resentment of it would break out in some indecency or other, in word or deed, which might give him an advantage against him to take him off by the course of law. Thus evil men seek mischief. 5. When he was disappointed in his, he proffered him his other daughter (who it seems had a secret kindness for David, *v.* 20), but with this design, that she might be *a snare to him, v.* 21. (1.) Perhaps he hoped that she would, even after her marriage to David, take part with her father against her husband, and give him an opportunity of doing David an unkindness. However, (2.) The conditions of the marriage, he hoped, would be his destruction; for (so zealous will Saul seem against the Philistines) the conditions of the marriage must be that he killed 100 Philistines, and, as proofs that those he had slain were uncircumcised, he must bring in their foreskins cut off; this would be a just reproach upon the Philistines, who hated circumcision as it was an ordinance of God; and perhaps David, in doing this, would the more exasperate them against him, and make them seek to be revenged on him, which was the thing that Saul desired and designed, much more than to be avenged on the Philistines: *For Saul thought to make David fall by the Philistines, v.* 25. See here, [1.] What cheats bad men put upon themselves. Saul's conscience would not suffer him, except when the evil spirit was actually upon him, to aim at David's life himself, for even he could not but conceive a horror at the thought of murdering such an innocent and excellent person; but he thought that to expose him designedly to the Philistines had nothing bad in it *(Let not my hand be upon him, but the hand of the Philistines),* whereas that malicious design against him was as truly murder before God as if he had slain him with his own hands. [2.] What cheats they put upon the world. Saul pretended extraordinary kindness for David even when he aimed at his ruin, and was actually plotting it: *Thou shalt be my son-in-law,* says he (*v.* 21), notwithstanding he hated him implacably. Perhaps David refers to this when (Ps. 55:21) he speaks of his enemy as one whose words were *smoother than butter, but war was in his heart.* It is probable that Saul's employing his servants to persuade David to enter into a treaty of a match with his daughter Michal (*v.* 22) arose from an apprehension that either his having cheated him about his elder daughter (*v.* 19) or the hardness of the terms he intended now to propose would make him decline it.

II. See how David conducted himself when the tide of Saul's displeasure ran thus high against him.

1. *He behaved himself wisely in all his ways.* He per-

ceived Saul's jealousy of him, which made him very cautious and circumspect in every thing he said and did, and careful to give no offence. He did not complain of hard measure more make himself the head of a party, but managed all the affairs he was entrusted with as one that made it his business to do real service to his king and country, looking upon that to be the end of his preferment. And then *the Lord was with him* to give him success in all his undertakings. Though he procured Saul's ill-will by it, yet he obtained God's favour. Compare this with Ps. 101:2, where it is David's promise, *I will behave myself wisely;* and that promise he here performed; and it is his prayer, *O, when wilt thou come unto me?* And that prayer God here answered: *The Lord was with him.* However blind fortune may seem to favour fools, God will own and bless those that behave themselves wisely.

2. When it was proposed to him to be son-in-law to the king he once and again received the proposal with all possible modesty and humility. When Saul proposed his elder daughter to him (*v.* 18) he said, *Who am I, and what is my life?* When the courtier proposed the younger, he took no notice of the affront Saul had put upon him in disposing of the elder from him, but continued in the same mind (*v.* 23): *Seemeth it a light thing to you to be a king's son-in-law, seeing that I am a poor man and lightly esteemed?* He knew Michal loved him, and yet did not offer to improve his interest in her affections for the gaining of her without her father's consent, but waited till it was proposed to him. And then see, (1.) How highly he speaks of the honour offered him: *To be son-in-law to the king.* Though his king was but an upstart, in his original as mean as himself, in his management no better than he should be, yet, being a crowned head, he speaks of him and the royal family with all due respect. Note, Religion is so far from teaching us to be rude and unmannerly that it does not allow us to be so. We must *render honour to whom honour is due.* (2.) How humbly he speaks of himself: *Who am I?* This did not proceed from a mean, abject, sneaking spirit, for when there was occasion he made it appear that he had as high a sense of honour as most men; nor was it from his jealousy of Saul (though he had reason enough to fear a snake under the green grass), but from him true and deep humility: *Who am I, a poor man, and lightly esteemed?* David had as much reason as any man to value himself. He was of an ancient and honourable family of Judah, a comely person, a great statesman and soldier; his achievements were great, for he had won Goliath's head and Michal's heart. He knew himself destined by the divine counsels to the throne of Israel, and yet, *Whom am I, and what is my life?* Note, It well becomes us, however God has advanced us, always to have low thoughts of ourselves. *He that humbleth himself shall be exalted.* And, if David thus magnified the honour of being son-in-law to the king, how should we magnify the honour of being sons (not in law, but in gospel) to the King of kings! *Behold what manner of love the Father has bestowed upon us!* Who are we that we should be thus dignified?

3. When the slaying of 100 Philistines was made the condition of David's marrying Saul's daughter he readily closed with it (*v.* 26): *It pleased David well to be the king's son-in-law* upon those terms; and, before the time given him for the action had expired, he doubled the demand, and slew 200, *v.* 27. He would not seem to suspect that Saul designed his hurt by it (though he had reason enough), but would rather act as if Saul had meant to consult his honour, and therefore cheerfully undertook it, as became a brave soldier and a true lover, though we may suppose it uneasy to Michal. David hereby discovered likewise, (1.) A great confidence in the divine protection. He knew God was with him, and therefore, whatever Saul hoped, David did not fear falling by the Philistines, though he must needs expose himself much by such an undertaking as this. (2.) A great zeal for the good of his country, which he would not decline any occasion of doing service to, though with the hazard of his life. (3.) A right notion of honour, which consists not so much in being preferred as in deserving to be so. David was then pleased with the thoughts of being the king's son-in-law when he found the honour set at this high price, being more solicitous how to merit it than how to obtain it; nor could he wear it with satisfaction till he had won it.

4. Even after he was married he continued his good

services to Israel. When the princes of the Philistines began to move towards another war David was ready to oppose them, and *behaved himself more wisely than all the servants of Saul, v.* 30. The law dispensed with men from going to war the first year after they were married (Deu. 24:5), but David loved his country too well to make use of that dispensation. Many that have shown themselves forward to serve the public when they have been in pursuit of preferment have declined it when they have gained their point; but David acted from more generous principles.

III. Observe how God brought good to David out of Saul's project against him. 1. Saul gave him his daughter to be a snare to him, but in this respect that marriage was a kindness to him, that his being Saul's son-in-law made his succeeding him much the less invidious, especially when so many of his sons were slain with him, *ch.* 31:2. 2. Saul thought, by putting him upon dangerous services, to have him taken off, but that very thing confirmed his interest in the people; for the more he did against the Philistines the better they loved him, so that *his name was much set by* (*v.* 30), which would make his coming to the crown the more easy. Thus God makes even the wrath of man to praise him and serves his designs of kindness to his own people by it.

CHAPTER 19

Immediately after David's marriage, which one would have hoped would secure him Saul's affection, we find his troubles coming upon him faster than ever and Saul's enmity to him the cause of all. His death was vowed, and four fair escapes of his from the hurtful sword of Saul we have an account of in this chapter: the first by the prudent mediation of Jonathan (*v.* 1–7), the second by his own quickness (*v.* 8–10), the third by Michal's fidelity (*v.* 11–17), the fourth by Samuel's protection, and a change, for the present, wrought upon Saul (*v.* 18–24). Thus God has many ways of preserving his people. Providence is never at a loss.

Verses 1–7

Saul and Jonathan appear here in their different characters, with reference to David.

I. Never was enemy so unreasonably cruel as Saul. He spoke to his son and all his servants *that they should kill David, v.* 1. His projects to take him off had failed, and therefore he proclaims him an out-law, and charges all about him, upon their allegiance, to take the first opportunity to kill David. It is strange that he was not ashamed thus to avow his malice when he could give no reason for it, and that knowing all his servants loved David (for so he had said himself, *ch.* 18:22), he was not afraid of provoking them to rebel by this bloody order. Either malice was not then so politic, or justice was not so corrupted as it has been since, or else Saul would have had him indicted, and have suborned witnesses to swear treason against him, and so have had him taken off, as Naboth was, by colour of law. But there is least danger from this undisguised malice. It was strange that he who knew how well Jonathan loved him should expect him to kill him; but he thought that because he was heir to the crown he must needs be as envious at David as himself was. And Providence ordered it thus that he might befriend David's safety.

II. Never was friend so surprisingly kind as Jonathan. *A friend in need is a friend indeed.* Such a one Jonathan was to David. He not only continued to delight much in him, though David's glory eclipsed his, but bravely appeared for him now that the stream ran so strongly against him.

1. He took care for his present security by letting him know his danger (*v.* 2): *"Take heed to thyself, and keep out of harm's way."* Jonathan knew not but that some of the servants might be either so obsequious to Saul or so envious at David as to put the orders in execution which Saul had given, if they could light on David.

2. He took pains to pacify his father and reconcile him to David. The next morning he ventured to commune with him concerning David (*v.* 3), not that night, perhaps because he observed Saul to be drunk and not fit to be spoken to, or because he hoped that, when he had slept upon it, he would himself revoke the order, or because he could not have an opportunity of speaking to him till morning.

(1.) His intercession for David was very prudent. It was managed with a great deal of the meekness of wisdom; and he showed himself faithful to his friends by speaking good of him, though he was in danger of incurring his father's displeasure by it — a rare instance of valuable friendship! He pleads, [1.] The good services David had done to the public, and particularly to Saul: *His work has been to thee-ward very good, v.* 4. Witness the relief he had given him against his distemper with his harp, and his bold encounter with Goliath, that memorable action, which did, in effect, save Saul's life and kingdom. He appeals to himself concerning his: *Thou thyself sawest it, and didst rejoice.* In that and other instances it appeared that David was a favourite of heaven and a friend to Israel, as well as a good servant to Saul, for by him *the Lord wrought a great salvation for all Israel;* so that to order him to be slain was not only base ingratitude to so good a servant, but a great affront to God and a great injury to the public. [2.] He pleads his innocency. Though he had formerly done many good offices, yet, if he had now been chargeable with any crimes, it would have been another matter; but *he has not sinned against thee* (*v.* 1), his *blood is innocent* (*v.* 5), and, if he be slain, it is without cause. And Jonathan had therefore reason to protest against it because he could not entail any thing upon his family more pernicious than the guilt of innocent blood.

(2.) His intercession, being thus prudent, was prevalent. God inclined the heart of Saul to hearken to the voice of Jonathan. Note, We must be willing to hear reason, and to take all reproofs and good advice even from our inferiors, parents from their own children. How forcible are right words! Saul was, for the present, so far convinced of the unreasonableness of his enmity to David that, [1.] He recalled the bloody warrant for his execution (*v.* 6): *As the Lord liveth, he shall not be slain.* Whether Saul swore here with due solemnity or no does not appear; perhaps he did, and the matter was of such moment as to deserve it and of such uncertainty as to need it. But at other times Saul swore rashly and profanely, which made the sincerity of this oath justly questionable; for it may be feared that those who can so far jest with an oath as to make a by-word of it, and prostitute it to a trifle, have not such a due sense of the obligation of it but that, to serve a turn, they will prostitute it to a lie. Some suspect that Saul said and swore this with a malicious design to bring David within his reach again, intending to take the first opportunity to slay him. But, as bad as Saul was, we can scarcely think so ill of him; and therefore we suppose that he spoke as he thought for the present, but the convictions soon wore off and his corruptions prevailed and triumphed over them. [2.] He renewed the grant of his place at court. Jonathan brought him to Saul, and *he was in his presence as in times past* (*v.* 7), hoping that now the storm was over, and that his friend Jonathan would be instrumental to keep his father always in this good mind.

Verses 8–10

Here I. David continues his good services to his king and country. Though Saul had requited him evil for good, and even his usefulness was the very thing for which Saul envied him, yet he did not therefore retire in sullenness and decline public service. Those that are ill paid for doing good, yet must not be *weary of well doing,* remembering what a bountiful benefactor our heavenly Father is, even to the froward and unthankful. Notwithstanding the many affronts Saul had given to David, yet we find him, 1. As bold as ever in using his sword for the service of his country, *v.* 8. The war broke out again with the Philistines, which gave David occasion again to signalize himself. It was a great deal of bravery that he charged them; and he came off victorious, slaying many and putting the rest to flight. 2. As cheerful as ever in using his harp for the service of the prince. When Saul was disturbed with his former fits of melancholy *David played with his hand, v.* 9. He might have pleaded that this was a piece of service now below him; but a humble man will think nothing below him by which he may do good. He might have objected the danger he was in the last time he performed this service for Saul, *ch.* 18:10. But he had learned to render good for evil, and to trust God with his safety in the way of his duty. See how David was affected when his enemy was sick (Ps. 35:13, 14), which perhaps refers to Saul's sickness.

II. Saul continues his malice against David. He that but the other day had sworn by his Maker that David *should not be slain* now endeavors to slay him himself. So implacable, so incurable, is the enmity of the serpent against that of the woman, so deceitful and desperately wicked is the heart of man without the grace of God, Jer. 17:9. The fresh honours David had won in this last war with the Philistines, instead of extinguishing Saul's ill-will to him, and confirming his reconciliation, revived his envy and exasperated him yet more. And, when he indulged this wicked passion, no marvel that *the evil spirit came upon him* (*v.* 9), for when we *let the sun go down upon our wrath we give place to the devil* (Eph. 4:26, 27), we make room for him and invite him. Discomposures of mind, though helped forward by the agency of Satan, commonly owe their origin to men's own sins and follies. Saul's fear and jealousy made him a torment to himself, so that he could not sit in his house without a javelin in his hand, pretending it was for his preservation, but designing it for David's destruction; for he endeavored to nail him to the wall, running at him so violently that he struck the *javelin into the wall* (*v.* 10), so strong was the devil in him, so strong his own rage and passion. Perhaps he thought that, if he killed David now, he would be excusable before God and man, as being *non compos mentis — not in his right mind,* and that it would be imputed to his distraction. But God cannot be deceived by pretences, whatever men may be.

III. God continues his care of David and still watches over him for good. Saul missed his blow. David was too quick for him and fled, and by a kind providence escaped that night. To these preservations, among others, David often refers in his Psalms, when he speaks of God's being his shield and buckler, his rock and fortress, and delivering his *soul from death.*

Verses 11–17

Here is, I. Saul's further design of mischief to David. When David had escaped the javelin, supposing he went straight to his own house, as indeed he did, Saul sent some of his guards after him to lay wait at the door of his house, and to assassinate him in the morning as soon as he stirred out, *v.* 11. Josephus says the design was to seize him and to hurry him before a court of justice that was ordered to condemn him and put him to death as a traitor; but we are here told it was a shorter way they were to take with him: they were ordered to *slay him.* Well might David complain that his enemies were *bloody men,* as he did in the psalm which he penned at this time, and upon this occasion (Ps. 59), when Saul sent, and they watched the house to kill him. See *v.* 2, 3, and 7. He complains that *swords were in their lips.*

II. David's wonderful deliverance out of this danger. Michal was the instrument of it, whom Saul gave him to be a snare to him, but she proved to be his protector and helper. Often is the devil out-shot with his own bow. How Michal came to know the danger her husband was in does not appear; perhaps she had notice sent her from court, or rather was herself aware of the soldiers about the house, when they were going to bed, though they kept so still and silent that they said, *Who dost hear?* which David takes notice of, Ps. 59:7. She, knowing her father's great indignation at David, soon suspected the design, and bestirred herself for her husband's safety. 1. She got David out of the danger. She told him how imminent the peril was (*v.* 11): *To-morrow thou wilt be slain.* As Josephus paraphrases it, she told him that if the sun saw him there next morning it would never see him more; and then put him in a way of escape. David himself was better versed in the art of fighting than of flying, and had it been lawful it would have been easy for him to have cleared his house, by dint of sword, from those that haunted it; but *Michal let him down through a window* (*v.* 12), all the doors being guarded; and so he *fled and escaped.* And now it was that, either in his own closet before he went or in the hiding-place to which he fled, he penned that fifty-ninth Psalm, which shows that, in his fright and hurry, his mind was composed, and, in this great danger, his faith was strong and fixed on God; and, whereas the plot was to slay him *in the morning,* he speaks there with the greatest assurance (*v.* 16), *I will sing aloud of thy mercy in the morning.* 2. She practised a deception upon Saul and those whom he employed to be the instruments of his cruelty. When the doors of the house were opened in the morning, and David did not appear, the messengers would search the house for him, and did so. But Michal told them he was sick in bed (*v.* 14), and, if they would not believe her, they might see, for (*v.* 13) she had put a wooden image in the bed, and wrapped it up close and warm as if it had been David asleep, not in a condition to be spoken to; the goats' hair about the image was to resemble David's hair, the better to impose upon them. Michal can by no means be justified in telling a lie, and covering it thus with a cheat. God's truth needed not her lie. But she intended hereby to keep Saul in suspense for a while, that David might have some time to secure himself, not doubting but those messengers would pursue him if they found he had gone. The messengers had so much humanity as not to offer him any disturbance when they heard he was sick; for to those that are in this misery pity should be shown; but Saul, when he heard it, gave positive orders that he should be brought to him sick or well: *Bring him to me in the bed, that I may slay him, v.* 15. It was base and barbarous thus to triumph over a sick man; and to vow the death of one who for aught that he knew was dying by the hand of nature. So earnestly did he thirst after his blood, and so greedy was his revenge, that he could not be pleased to see him dead, unless he himself was the death of him; though awhile ago he had said, *Let not my hand be upon him.* Thus when men lay the reins on the neck of their passions they grow more and more outrageous. When the messengers were sent again, the cheat was discovered, *v.* 16. But by this time it was to be hoped that David was safe, and therefore Michal was not then much concerned at the discovery. Saul chid her for helping David to escape (*v.* 17): *Why hast thou deceived me so?* What a base spirit was Saul of, to expect that, because Michal was his daughter, she must therefore betray her own husband to him unjustly. Ought she not to forsake and forget her father and her father's house, to cleave to her husband? Those that themselves will be held by no bonds of reason or religion are ready to think that others should as easily break those bonds. In answer to Saul's chiding, Michal is not so careful of her husband's reputation as she had been of his person, when she makes this her excuse: *He said, Let me go, why should I kill thee?* As her insinuating that she would have hindered his flight was false (it was she that put him upon it and furthered it), so it was an unjust unworthy reflection upon him to suggest that he threatened to kill her if she would not let him go, and might confirm Saul in his rage against him. David was far from being so barbarous a man and so imperious a husband, so brutish in his resolves and so haughty in his menaces, as she here represented him. But David suffered both from friends and foes, and so did the son of David.

Verses 18–24

Here is, I. David's place of refuge. Having got away in the night from his own house, he fled not to Bethlehem to his relations, nor to any of the cities of Israel that had caressed and cried him up, to make an interest in them for his own preservation; but he ran straight to Samuel and *told him all that Saul had done to him, v.* 18. 1. Because Samuel was the man that had given him assurance of the crown, and his faith in that assurance now beginning to fail, and he being ready to say in his haste (or *in his flight,* as some read it, Ps. 116:11), *All men are liars* ("not only Saul that promised me my life, but Samuel himself that promised me the throne"), whither should he go but to Samuel, for such encouragements, in this day of distress, as would support his faith? In flying to Samuel he made God his refuge, trusting in the *shadow of his wings;* where else can a good man think himself safe? 2. Because Samuel, as a prophet, was best able to advise him what to do in this day of his distress. In the psalm he penned the night before he had lifted up his prayer to God, and now he takes the first opportunity of waiting upon Samuel to receive direction and instruction from God. If we expect answers of peace to our prayers, we must have our ears open to God's word. 3. Because with Samuel there was a college of prophets with whom he might join in praising God, and the pleasure of this exercise would be the greatest relief imaginable to him in his present distress. He met with little rest or satisfaction in Saul's court, and therefore went to seek it in Samuel's church. And, doubtless, what little pleasure is to be had in this world those have it that live a life of communion with God; to this David retired in the time of trouble, Ps. 27:4–6.

II. David's protection in this place: *He and Samuel went and dwelt* (or *lodged*) *in Naioth,* where the school of the prophets was, in Ramah, as in a privileged place, for the Philistines themselves would not disturb that meeting, *ch.* 10:10. But Saul, having notice of it by some of his spies (*v.* 19), sent officers to seize David, *v.* 20. When they did not bring him he sent more; when they returned not he sent the third time (*v.* 21), and, hearing no tidings of these, he went himself, *v.* 22. So impatient was he in his thirst after David's blood, so restless to compass his design against him, that, though baffled by one providence after another, he could not perceive that David was under the special protection of Heaven. It was below the king to go himself on such an errand as this; but persecutors will stoop to any thing, and stick at nothing, to gratify their malice. Saul lays aside all public business to hunt David. How was David delivered, now that he was just ready to fall (like his own lamb formerly) into the mouth of the lions? Not as he delivered his lamb, by slaying the lion, or, as Elijah was delivered, by consuming the messengers with *fire from heaven,* but by turning the lions for the present into lambs.

1. When the messengers came into the congregation where David was among the prophets *the Spirit of God* came upon them, and *they prophesied,* that is, they joined with the rest in praising God. Instead of seizing David, they themselves were seized. And thus, (1.) God secured David; for either they were put into such an ecstasy by the spirit of prophecy that they could not think of any thing else, and so forgot their errand and never minded David, or they were by it put, for the present, into so good a frame that they could not entertain the thought of doing so bad a thing. 2. He put an honour upon the sons of the prophets and the communion of saints, and showed how he can, when he pleases, strike an awe upon the worst of men, by the tokens of his presence in the assemblies of the faithful, and force them to acknowledge that *God is with them of a truth,* 1 Co. 14:24, 25. See also the benefit of religious societies, and what good impressions may be made by them on minds that seemed unapt to receive such impressions. And where may the influences of the Spirit be expected but in the congregations of the saints? (3.) He magnified his power over the spirits of men. He that made the heart and tongue can manage both to serve his own purposes. Balaam prophesied the happiness of Israel, whom he would have cursed; and some of the Jewish writers think these messengers prophesied the advancement of David to the throne of Israel.

2. Saul himself was likewise seized with the spirit of prophecy before he came to the place. One would have thought that so bad a man as he was in no danger of being turned into a prophet; yet, when God will take this way of protecting David, even Saul had no sooner come (as bishop Hall expresses it) within smell of the smoke of Naioth but he prophesies, as his messengers did, *v.* 23. He stripped off his royal robe and warlike habiliments, because they were either too fine or too heavy for this service, and fell into a trance as it should seem, or into a rapture, which continued all that day and night. The saints at Damascus were delivered from the range of the New-Testament Saul by a change wrought on his spirit, but of another nature from this. This was only amazing, but that sanctifying — this for a day, that for ever. Note, Many have great gifts and yet no grace, prophesy in Christ's name and yet are disowned by him, Mt. 7:22, 23. Now the proverb recurs, *Is Saul among the prophets?* See *ch.* 10:12. Then it was different from what it had been, but now *contrary.* He is rejected of God, and actuated by an evil spirit, and yet among the prophets.

CHAPTER 20

David, having several times narrowly escaped Saul's fury, begins to consider at last whether it may not be necessary for him to retire into the country and to take up arms in his own defence. But he will not do so daring a thing without consulting his faithful friend Jonathan; how he did this, and what passed between them, we have an account in this chapter, where we have as surprising instances of supernatural love as we had in the chapter before of unnatural hatred. I. David complains to Jonathan of his present distress, and engages him to be his friend (*v.* 1–8). II. Jonathan faithfully promises to get and give him intelligence how his father stood affected to him, and renews the covenant of friendship with him (*v.* 9–23). III. Jonathan, upon trial, finds, to his grief, that his father was implacably enraged against David (*v.* 24–34). IV. He gives David notice of this, according to the appointment between them (*v.* 35–42).

Verses 1–8

Here, I. David makes a representation to Jonathan of his present troubles. While Saul lay bound by his trance at Naioth David escaped to the court, and got to speak with Jonathan. And it was happy for him that he had such a friend at court, when he had such an enemy on the throne. If there be those that hate and despise us, let us not be disturbed at that, for there are those also that love and respect us. God hath set the one over against the other, and so must we. Jonathan was a friend that loved at all times, loved David as well now in his distress, and bade him as welcome into his arms, as he had done when he was in his triumph (*ch.* 18:1), and he was *a brother that was born for adversity,* Prov. 17:17. Now, 1. David appeals to Jonathan himself concerning his innocency, and he needed not say much to him for the proof of it, only he desired him that if he knew of any just offence he had given his father he would tell him, that he might humble himself and beg his pardon: *What have I done? v.* 1. 2. He endeavors to convince him that, notwithstanding his innocency, Saul sought his life. Jonathan, from a principal of filial respect to his father, was very loth to believe that he designed or would ever do so wicked a thing, *v.* 2. He the rather hoped so because he knew nothing of any such design, and he had usually been made privy to all his counsels. Jonathan, as became a dutiful son, endeavored to cover his father's shame, as far as was consistent with justice and fidelity to David. Charity is not forward to think evil of any, especially of a parent, 1 Co. 13:5. David therefore gives him the assurance of an oath concerning his own danger, swears the peace upon Saul, that he was in fear of his life by him: *"As the Lord liveth,* than which nothing more sure in itself, and as *thy soul liveth,* than which nothing more certain to thee, whatever thou thinkest, *there is but a step between me and death," v.* 3. And, as for Saul's concealing it from Jonathan, it was easy to account for that; he knew the friendship between him and David, and therefore, though in other things he advised with him, yet not in that. None more fit than Jonathan to serve him in every design that was just and honourable, but he knew him to be a man of more virtue than to be his confidant in so base a design as the murder of David.

II. Jonathan generously offers him his service (*v.* 4): *Whatsoever thou desirest,* he needed not insert the proviso of lawful and honest (for he knew David too well to think he would ask any thing that was otherwise), *I will even do it for thee.* This is true friendship. Thus Christ testifies his love to us: *Ask, and it shall be done for you;* and we must testify ours to him by keeping his commandments.

III. David only desires him to satisfy himself, and then to satisfy him whether Saul did really design his death or no. Perhaps David proposed this more for Jonathan's conviction than his own, for he himself was well satisfied. 1. The method of trial he proposed was very natural, and would certainly discover how Saul stood affected to him. The two next days Saul was to dine publicly, upon occasion of the solemnities of the new moon, when extraordinary sacrifices were offered and feasts made upon the sacrifices. Saul was rejected of God, and the Spirit of the Lord had departed from him, yet he kept up his observance of the holy feasts. There may be the remains of external devotion where there is nothing but the ruins of real virtue. At these solemn feasts Saul had either all his children to sit with him, and David had a seat as one of them, or all his great officers, and David had a seat as one of them. However it was, David resolved his seat should be empty (and that it never used to be at a sacred feast) those two days (*v.* 5), and he would abscond till the solemnity was over, and put it upon this issue: if Saul admitted an excuse for his absence, and dispensed with it, he would conclude he had changed his mind and was reconciled to him; but if he resented it, and was put into a passion by it, it was easy to conclude he designed him a mischief, since it was certain he did not love him so well as to desire his presence for any other end than that he might have an opportunity to do him a mischief, *v.* 7. 2. The excuse he desired Jonathan to make for his absence, we have reason to think, was true, that he was invited by his elder brother to Bethlehem, his own city, to celebrate this new moon with his relations there, because, besides the monthly solemnity in which they held communion with all Israel, they had now a yearly sacrifice, and a holy feast upon

it, for *all the family, v.* 6. They kept a day of thanksgiving in their family for the comforts they enjoyed, and of prayer for the continuance of them. By this it appears that the family David was of was a very religious family, a house that had a church in it. 3. The arguments he used with Jonathan to persuade him to do this kindness for him were very pressing, *v.* 8. (1.) That he had entered into a league of friendship with him, and it was Jonathan's own proposal: *Thou hast brought thy servant into a covenant of the Lord with thee.* (2.) That he would by no means urge him to espouse his cause if he was not sure that it was a righteous cause: *"If there be iniquity in me,* I am so far from desiring or expecting that the covenant between us should bind thee to be a confederate with me in that iniquity that I freely release thee from it, and wish that my hand may be first upon me: *Slay me thyself."* No honest man will urge his friend to do a dishonest thing for his sake.

Verses 9–23

Here, I. Jonathan protests his fidelity to David in his distress. Notwithstanding the strong confidence David had in Jonathan, yet, because he might have some reason to fear that his father's influence, and his own interest, should make him warp, or grow cool towards him, Jonathan thought it requisite solemnly to renew the professions of his friendship to him (*v.* 9): *"Far be it from thee* to think that I suspect thee of any crime for which I should either slay thee myself or deliver thee to my father; no, if thou hast any jealousy of that, *Come let us go into the field* (*v.* 11), and talk it over more fully." He did not challenge him to the field to fight him for an affront, but to fix him in his friendship. He faithfully promised him that he would let him know how, upon trial, he found his father affected towards him, and would make the matter neither better nor worse than it was. "If there be *good towards thee,* I will *show it thee,* that thou mayest be easy (*v.* 12), if evil, I will *send thee away,* that thou mayest be safe" (*v.* 13); and thus he would help to deliver him from the evil if it were real and from the fear of evil if it were but imaginary. For the confirmation of his promise he appeals to God, 1. As a witness (*v.* 12): *"O Lord God of Israel,* thou knowest I mean sincerely, and think as I speak." The strength of his passion made the manner of his speaking concise and abrupt. 2. As a judge: *"The Lord do so and much more to Jonathan* (*v.* 13), if I speak deceitfully, or break my word with my friend." He expressed himself thus solemnly that David might be abundantly assured of his sincerity. And thus God has confirmed his promises to us, that we might have *strong consolation,* Heb. 6:17, 18. Jonathan adds to his protestations his hearty prayers: *"The Lord be with thee,* to protect and prosper thee, *as he has been* formerly *with my father,* though now he has withdrawn." Thus he imitates his belief that David would be in his father's place, and his good wishes that he might prosper in it better than his father now did.

II. He provides for the entail of the covenant of friendship with David upon his posterity, *v.* 14–16. He engages David to be a friend to his family when he was gone (*v.* 15): *Thou shalt* promise that thou wilt *not cut off thy kindness from my house for ever.* This he spoke from a natural affection he had to his children, whom he desired it might go well with after his decease, and for whose future welfare he desired to improve his present interest. It also intimates his firm belief of David's advancement, and that it would be in the power of his hand to do a kindness or unkindness to his seed; for, in process of time, the *Lord would cut off his enemies,* Saul himself was not expected; then *"Do not thou cut off thy kindness from my house,* nor revenge my father's wrongs upon my children." The house of David must likewise be bound to the house of Jonathan from generation to generation; he *made a covenant* (*v.* 16) *with the house of David.* Note, True friends cannot but covet to transmit to theirs after them their mutual affections. *Thy own friend, and thy father's friend, forsake not.* This kindness, 1. He calls *the kindness of the Lord,* because it is such kindness as God shows to those he takes into covenant with himself; for he is a God to them and to their seed; they are *beloved for the fathers' sakes.* 2. He secures it by an imprecation (*v.* 16): *The Lord require it at the hand of David's seed* (for of David himself he had no suspicion) if they prove so far David's enemies as to deal wrongfully with the posterity of Jonathan, David's friend.

He feared lest David, or some of his, should hereafter be tempted, for the clearing and confirming of their title to the throne, to do by his seed as Abimelech had done by the sons of Gideon (Jdg. 9:5), and this he would effectually prevent; but the reason given (*v.* 17) why Jonathan was so earnest to have the friendship entailed is purely generous, and has nothing of self in it; it was because *he loved him as he loved his own soul,* and therefore desired that he and his might be beloved by him. David, though now in disgrace at court and in distress, was as amiable in the eyes of Jonathan as ever he had been, and he loved him never the less for his father's hating him, so pure were the principles on which his friendship was built. Having himself sworn to David, he caused David to swear to him, and (as we read it) *to swear again,* which David consented to (for he that bears an honest mind does not startle at assurances), to swear by his love to him, which he looked upon as a sacred thing. Jonathan's heart was so much upon it that, when they parted this time, he concluded with a solemn appeal to God: *The Lord be between me and thee for ever* (*v.* 23), that is, "God himself be judge between us and our families for ever, if on either side this league of friendship be violated." It was in remembrance of this covenant that David was kind to Mephibosheth, 2 Sa. 9:7; 21:7. It will be a kindness to ourselves and ours to secure an interest in those whom God favours and to make his friends ours.

III. He settles the method of intelligence, and by what signs and tokens he would give him notice how his father stood affected towards him. David would be missed the first day, or at least the second day, of the new moon, and would be enquired after, *v.* 18. On the third day, by which time he would have returned from Bethlehem, he must be at such a place (*v.* 19), and Jonathan would come towards that place with his bow and arrows to shoot for diversion (*v.* 20), would send his lad to fetch his arrows, and, if they were shot short of the lad, David must take it for a signal of safety, and not be afraid to show his head (*v.* 21); but, if he shot beyond the lad, it was a signal of danger, and he must shift for his safety, *v.* 22. This expedient he fixed lest he should not have the opportunity, which yet it proved he had, of talking with David, and making the report by word of mouth.

Verses 24–34

Jonathan is here effectually convinced of that which he was so loth to believe, that his father had an implacable enmity to David, and would certainly be the death of him if it were in his power; and he had like to have paid very dearly himself for the conviction.

I. David is missed from the feast on the first day, but nothing is said of him. *The king sat upon his seat,* to feast upon the peace-offerings *as at other times* (*v.* 25), and yet had his heart as full of envy and malice against David as it could hold. He should first have been reconciled to him, and then have come and offered his gift; but, instead of that, he hoped, at this feast, to drink the blood of David. What an abomination was that sacrifice which was brought with such a wicked mind as this! Prov. 21:27. When the king came to take his seat Jonathan arose, in reverence to him both as a father and as his sovereign; every one knew his place, but David's was empty. It did not use to be so. None more content than he in attending holy duties; nor had he been absent now but that he must have come at the peril of his life; self-preservation obliged him to withdraw. In imminent peril present opportunities may be waived, nay, we ought not to throw ourselves into the mouth of danger. Christ himself absconded often, till he knew that his hour had come. But that day Saul took no notice that he missed David, but said within himself, "*Surely he is not clean, v.* 26. Some ceremonial pollution has befallen him, which forbids him to eat of the holy things till he has *washed his clothes, and bathed his flesh in water, and been unclean until the evening.*" Saul knew what conscience David made of the law, and that he would rather keep away from the holy feast than come in his uncleanness. Blessed be God, no uncleanness is now a restraint upon us, but what we may by faith and repentance be washed from in the fountain opened, Ps. 26:6.

II. He is enquired for the second day, *v.* 27. Saul asked Jonathan, who he knew was his confidant, *Wherefore cometh not the son of Jesse to meat?* He was his own son by marriage, but he calls him in disdain, *the son of Jesse.* He asks for him as if he were not pleased that he should be absent from a religious feast; and so it should be example to masters of families to see to it that those under their charge be not absent from the worship of God, either in public or in the family. It is a bad thing for us, except in case of necessity, to omit an opportunity of statedly attending on God in solemn ordinances. Thomas lost a sight of Christ by being once absent from a meeting of the disciples. But that which displeased Saul was that hereby he missed the opportunity he expected of doing David a mischief.

III. Jonathan makes his excuse, *v.* 28, 29. 1. That he was absent upon a good occasion, keeping the feast in another place, though not here, sent for by his elder brother, who was now more respectful to him than he had been (*ch.* 17:28), and that he had gone to pay his respects to his relations, for the keeping up of brotherly love; and no master would deny a servant liberty to do that in due time. He pleads, 2. That he did not go without leave humbly asked and obtained from Jonathan, who, as his superior officer, was proper to be applied to for it. Thus he represents David as not wanting in any instance of respect and duty to the government.

IV. Saul hereupon breaks out into a most extravagant passion, and rages like a lion disappointed of his prey. David was out of his reach, but he falls upon Jonathan for his sake (*v.* 30, 31), gives him base language, not fit for a gentleman, a prince, to give to any man, especially his own son, heir apparent to his crown, a son that served him, the greatest stay and ornament of his family, before a great deal of company, at a feast, when all should be in good humour, at a sacred feast, by which all irregular passions should be mortified and subdued; yet he does in effect call him, 1. A bastard: *Thou son of the perverse rebellious woman;* that is, according to the foolish filthy language of men's brutish passion now a day, "Thou son of a whore." He tells him he was born *to the confusion of his mother,* that is, he had given the world cause to suspect that he was not the legitimate son of Saul, because he loved him whom Saul hated and supported him who would be the destruction of their family. 2. A traitor: *Thou son of a perverse rebellion* (so the word is), that is, "thou perverse rebel." At other times he reckoned no counsellor or commander that he had more trusty and well-beloved than Jonathan; yet now in this passion he represents him as dangerous to his crown and life. 3. A fool: *Thou hast chosen the son of Jesse* for thy friend *to thy own confusion,* for while he lives *thou shalt never be established.* Jonathan indeed did wisely and well for himself and family to secure an interest in David, whom Heaven had destined to the throne, yet, for this, he is branded as most impolitic. It is good taking God's people for our people and going with those that have him with them. It will prove to our advantage at last, however for the present it may be thought a disparagement, and a prejudice to our secular interest. It is probable Saul knew that David was anointed to the kingdom by the same hand that anointed him, and then not Jonathan, but himself, was the fool, to think to defeat the counsels of God. Yet nothing will serve him but David must die, and Jonathan must fetch him to execution. See how ill Saul's passion looks, and let it warn us against the indulgence of any thing like it in ourselves. Anger is madness, and *he that hates his brother is a murderer.*

V. Jonathan is sorely grieved and put into disorder by his father's barbarous passion, and the more because he had hoped better things, *v.* 2. He was troubled for his father, that he should be such a brute, troubled for his friend, whom he knew to be a friend of God, that he should be so basely abused; he was *grieved for David* (*v.* 34), and troubled for himself too, because *his father had done him shame,* and, though most unjustly, yet he must submit to it. One would pity Jonathan to see how he was put, 1. Into the peril of sin. Much ado that wise and good man had to keep his temper, upon such a provocation as this. His father's reflections upon himself made no return to; it becomes inferiors to bear with meekness and silence the contempts put upon them in wrath and passion. *When thou art the anvil lie thou still.* But his dooming David to die he could not bear: to that he replied with some heat (*v.* 32), *Wherefore shall he be slain? What has he done?* Generous spirits can much more easily bear to be abused themselves than to hear their friends abused. 2. Into the peril of death. Saul was now so outrageous that he threw his javelin at Jonathan, *v.* 33. He seemed to be in great care (*v.* 31) than Jonathan should be established in his kingdom, and yet now he himself aims at his life. What fools, what savage beasts and worse does anger make men! How necessary it is to put a hook in its nose and a bridle in its jaws! Jonathan was fully satisfied that evil was determined against David, which put him out of frame exceedingly: he *rose from table,* thinking it high time when his life was struck at, and *would eat no meat,* for they were not to eat of the holy things in their mourning. All the guests, we may suppose, were discomposed, and the mirth of the feast was spoiled. *He that is cruel troubles his own flesh,* Prov. 11:17.

Verses 35–42

Here is, 1. Jonathan's faithful performance of his promise to give David notice of the success of his dangerous experiment. He went at the time and to the place appointed (*v.* 35), within sight of which he knew David lay hid, sent his footboy to fetch his arrows, which he would shoot at random (*v.* 36), and gave David the fatal signal by shooting an arrow beyond the lad (*v.* 37): *Is not the arrow beyond thee?* That word [*beyond*] David knew the meaning of better than the lad. Jonathan dismissed the lad, who knew nothing of the matter, and, finding the coast clear and no danger of a discovery, he presumed upon one minute's personal conversation with David after he had bidden him flee for his life. 2. The most sorrowful parting of these two friends, who, for aught that appears, never came together again but once, and that was by stealth *in a wood, ch.* 23:16. (1.) David addressed himself to Jonathan with the reverence of a servant rather than the freedom of a friend: *He fell on his face to the ground, and bowed himself three times,* as one deeply sensible of his obligations to him for the good services he had done him. (2.) They took leave of each other with the greatest affection imaginable, with kisses and tears; they wept on each other's neck *till David exceeded, v.* 41. The separation of two such faithful friends was equally grievous to them both, but David's case was the more deplorable; for, when Jonathan was returning to his family and friends, David was leaving all his comforts, even those of God's sanctuary, and therefore his grief exceeded Jonathan's, or perhaps it was because his temper was more tender and his passions were stronger. (3.) They referred themselves to the covenant of friendship that was between them, both of them comforting themselves with this in this mournful separation: "*We have sworn both of us in the name of the Lord,* for ourselves and our heirs, that we and they will be faithful and kind to each other from generation to generation." Thus, while we are at home in the body and absent from the Lord, this is our comfort, that he has *made with us an everlasting covenant.*

CHAPTER 21

David has now quite taken leave both of Saul's court and of his camp, has bidden farewell to his alter idem — his other self, the beloved Jonathan; and henceforward to the end of this book he is looked upon and treated as an outlaw and proclaimed a traitor. We still find him shifting from place to place for his own safety, and Saul pursuing him. His troubles are very particularly related in this and the following chapters, not only to be a key to the Psalms, but that he might be, as other prophets, an example to the saints in all ages, "of suffering affliction, and of patience," and especially that he might be a type of Christ, who, being anointed to the kingdom, humbled himself, and was therefore highly exalted. But the example of the suffering Jesus was a copy without a blot, that of David was not so; witness the records of this chapter, where we find David in his flight, I. Imposing upon Abimelech the priest, to get from him both victuals and arms (*v.* 1–9). II. Imposing upon Achish, king of Gath, by feigning himself mad (*v.* 10–15). Justly are troubles called temptations, for many are by them drawn into sin.

Verses 1–9

Here, I. David, in distress, flies in the tabernacle of God, now pitched at Nob, supposed to be a city in the tribe of Benjamin. Since Shiloh was forsaken, the tabernacle was often removed, though the ark still remained at Kirjath-jearim. Hither David came in his flight from Saul's fury (*v.* 1), and applied to Ahimelech the priest. Samuel the prophet could not protect him, Jonathan the prince could not. He therefore has recourse next to Ahimelech the priest. He foresees he must now be an exile, and therefore comes to the tabernacle, 1. To take an affecting leave of it, for he knows not when he shall see it again, and nothing will be more afflictive to him in his banishment than his distance from the house of God, and his restraint from public ordinances, as appears by many of his psalms. He had given an affectionate farewell to his friend Jonathan, and cannot go till he has given the like to the tabernacle. 2. To enquire of the Lord there, and to beg direction from him in the way both of duty and safety, his case being difficult and dangerous. That this was his business appears *ch.* 22:10, where it is said that *Ahimelech enquired of the Lord for him,* as he had done formerly, *v.* 15. It is a great comfort to us in a day of trouble that we have a God to go to, to whom we may open our case, and from whom we may ask and expect direction.

II. Ahimelech the priest is surprised to see him in so poor an equipage; having heard that he had fallen into disgrace at court, he looked shy upon him, as most are apt to do upon their friends when the world frowns upon them. He was afraid of incurring Saul's displeasure by entertaining him, and took notice how mean a figure he now made to what he used to make: *Why art thou alone?* He had some with him (as appears Mk. 2:26), but they were only his own servants; he had none of the courtiers, no persons of quality with him, as he used to have at other times, when he came to enquire of the Lord. He says (Ps. 42:4) he was wont to *go with a multitude to the house of God;* and, having now but two or three with him, Ahimelech might well ask, *Why art thou alone?* He that was suddenly advanced from the solitude of a shepherd's life to the crowd and hurries of the camp is now as soon reduced to the desolate condition of an exile and is *alone like a sparrow on the housetop,* such charges are there in this world and so uncertain are its smiles! Those that are courted to-day may be deserted to-morrow.

III. David, under pretence of being sent by Saul upon public services, solicits Ahimelech to supply his present wants, *v.* 2, 3.

1. Here David did not behave like himself. He told Ahimelech a gross untruth, that Saul had ordered him business to despatch, that his attendants were dismissed to such a place, and that he was charged to observe secresy and therefore durst not communicate it, no, not to the priest himself. This was all false. What shall we say to this? The scripture does not conceal it, and we dare not justify it. It was ill done, and proved of bad consequence; for it *occasioned the death of the priests of the Lord,* as David reflected upon it afterwards with regret, *ch.* 22:22. It was needless for him thus to dissemble with the priest, for we may suppose that, if he had told him the truth, he would have sheltered and relieved him as readily as Samuel did, and would have known the better how to advise him and enquire of God for him. People should be free with their faithful ministers. David was a man of great faith and courage, and yet now both failed him, and he fell thus foully through fear and cowardice, and both owing to the weakness of his faith. Had he trusted God aright, he would not have used such a sorry sinful shift as this for his own preservation. It is written, not for our imitation, no, not in the greatest straits, but for our admonition. *Let him that thinks he stands take heed lest he fall;* and let us all pray daily, *Lord, lead us not into temptation.* Let us all take occasion from this to lament, (1.) The weakness and infirmity of good men; the best are not perfect on this side heaven. There may be true grace where yet there are many failings. (2.) The wickedness of bad times, which forces good men into such straits as prove temptations too strong for them. Oppression makes a wise man do foolishly.

2. Two things David begged of Ahimelech, *bread* and a *sword.*

(1.) He wanted bread: *five loaves, v.* 3. Travelling was then troublesome, when men generally carried their provisions with them in kind, having little money and no public houses, else David would not now have had to seek for bread. It seems David had known the *seed of the righteous begging bread* occasionally, but not constantly, Ps. 37:25. Now, [1.] The priest objected that he had none but hallowed bread, *show-bread,* which had stood a week on the golden table in the sanctuary, and was taken thence for the use of the priests and their families, *v.* 4. It seems the priest kept no good house, but wanted either a heart to be hospitable or provisions wherewithal to be so. Ahimelech thinks that the young men that attended David might not eat of this bread unless they had for some time abstained from women, even from their own wives; this was required at the *giving of the law* (Ex. 19:15), but otherwise we never find this made the matter of any ceremonial purity on the one side or pollution on the other, and therefore the priest here seems to be over-nice, not to say superstitious. [2.] David pleads that he and those that were with him, in this case of necessity, might lawfully eat of the hallowed bread, for they were not only able to answer his terms of keeping from women for three days past, but *the vessels* (that is, the bodies) *of the young men were holy,* being *possessed in sanctification and honour at all times* (1 Th. 4:4, 5), and therefore God would take particular care of them, that they wanted not necessary supports, and would have his priest to do so. Being thus holy, holy things were not forbidden them. Poor and pious Israelites were in effect priests to God, and, rather than be starved, might feed on the bread which was appropriated to the priests. Believers are spiritual priests, and the offerings of the Lord shall be their inheritance; they eat the bread of their God. He pleads that the bread is in a manner common, now that what was primarily the religious use of it is over; especially (as our margin reads it) *where there is other bread* (*hot, v.* 6) *sanctified that day in the vessel,* and put in the room of it upon the table. This was David's plea, and the Son of David approves it, and shows from it that mercy is to be preferred to sacrifice, that ritual observance must give way to moral duties, and that may be done in a case of an urgent providential necessity which may not otherwise be done. He brings it to justify his disciples in plucking the ears of corn on the sabbath day, for which the Pharisees censured them, Mt. 12:3, 4. [3.] Ahimelech hereupon supplies him: *He gave him hallowed bread* (*v.* 6), and some think it was about this that *he enquired of the Lord, ch.* 22:10. As a faithful servant he would not dispose of his master's provisions without his master's leave. This bread, we may suppose, was the more agreeable to David for its being hallowed, so precious were all sacred things to him. The show-bread was but twelve loaves in all, yet out of these he gave David five (*v.* 3), though they had no more in the house; but he trusted Providence.

(2.) He wanted a sword. Persons of quality, though officers of the army, did not then wear their swords so constantly as now they do, else surely David would not have been without one. It was a wonder that Jonathan did not furnish him with his, as he had before done, *ch.* 18:4. However, it happened that he had now no weapons with him, the reason of which he pretends to be because he came away in haste, *v.* 8. Those that are furnished with the sword of the Spirit and the shield of faith cannot be disarmed of them, nor need they, at any time, to be at a loss. But the priests, it seems, had no swords: the weapons of their warfare were not carnal. There was not a sword to be found about the tabernacle but the sword of Goliath, which was laid up behind the ephod, as a monument of the glorious victory David obtained over him. Probably David had an eye to that when he asked the priest to help him with a sword; for, that being mentioned, O! says he, *there is none like that, give it to me, v.* 9. He could not use Saul's armour, for he had not proved it; but this sword of Goliath he had made trial of and done execution with. By this it appears that he was now well grown in strength and stature, that he could wear and wield such a sword as that. God had *taught his hands to war,* so that he could do wonders, Ps. 18:34. Two things we may observe concerning this sword: — [1.] That God had graciously given it to him, as a pledge of his singular favour; so that whenever he drew it, nay, whenever he looked upon it, it would be a great support to his faith, by bringing to mind that great instance of the particular care and countenance of the divine providence respecting him. [2.] That he had gratefully given it back to God, dedicating it to him and to his honour as a token of his thankfulness; and now in his distress it stood him greatly in stead. Note, What we devote to God's praise, and serve him with, is most likely to redound, one way or other, to our own comfort and benefit. What we gave we have.

Thus was David well furnished with arms and victuals; but it fell out very unhappily that there was one of Saul's servants then attending before the Lord, *Doeg* by name, that proved a base traitor both to David and Ahimelech. He was by birth an Edomite (*v.* 7), and though proselyted to the Jewish religion, to get the preferment he now had under Saul, yet he retained the ancient and hereditary enmity of Edom to Israel. He was master of the herds, which perhaps was then a place of as much honour as master of the horse is now. Some occasion or other he had at this time to wait on the priest, either to be purified from some pollution or to pay some vow; but, whatever his business was, it is said, he was *detained before the Lord.* He must attend and could not help it, but he was sick of the service, *snuffed at it, and said, What a weariness is it!* Mal. 1:13. He would rather have been any where else than before the Lord, and therefore, instead of minding the business he came about, was plotting to do David a mischief and to be revenged on Ahimelech for detaining him. God's sanctuary could never secure such wolves in sheep's clothing. See Gal. 2:4.

Verses 10–15

David, though king elect, is here an exile — designed to be master of vast treasures, yet just now begging his bread — anointed to the crown, and yet here forced to flee from his country. Thus do God's providences sometimes seem to run counter to his promises, for the trial of his people's faith, and the glorifying of his name, in the accomplishment of his counsels, notwithstanding the difficulties that lay in the way. Here is, 1. David's flight into the land of the Philistines, where he hoped to be hid, and to remain undiscovered in the court or camp of Achish king of Gath, *v.* 10. Israel's darling is necessitated to quit the land of Israel, and he that was the Philistine's great enemy (upon I know not what inducements) goes to seek for shelter among them. It should seem that as, though the Israelites loved him, yet the king of Israel had a personal enmity to him, which obliged him to leave his own country, so, though the Philistines hated him, yet the king of Gath had a personal kindness for him, valuing his merit, and perhaps the more for his killing Goliath of Gath, who, it may be, had been no friend to Achish. To him David now went directly, as to one he could confide in, as afterwards (*ch.* 27:2, 3), and Achish would not have protected him but that he was afraid of disobliging his own people. God's persecuted people have often found better usage from Philistines than from Israelites, in the Gentile theatres than in the Jewish synagogues. The king of Judah imprisoned Jeremiah, and the king of Babylon set him at liberty. 2. The disgust which the servants of Achish took at his being there, and their complaint of it to Achish (*v.* 11): *"Is not this David?* Is not this he that has triumphed over the Philistines? witness that burden of the song which was so much talked of, *Saul has slain his thousands,* but *David,* this very man, *his ten thousands.* Nay, Is not this he that (if our intelligence from the land of Israel be true) is, or is to be, *king of the land?"* As such, "he must be an enemy to our country; and is it safe or honourable for us to protect or entertain such a man?" Achish perhaps had intimated to them that it would be policy to entertain David, because he was now an enemy to Saul, and he might be hereafter a friend to them. It is common for the outlaws of a nation to be sheltered by the enemies of that nation. But the servants of Achish objected to his politics, and thought it not at all fit that he should stay among them. 3. The fright which this put David into. Though he had some reason to put confidence in Achish, yet, when he perceived the servants of Achish jealous of him, he began to be afraid that Achish would be obliged to deliver him up to them, and he was *sorely afraid* (*v.* 12), and perhaps he was the more apprehensive of his own danger, when he was thus discovered, because he wore Goliath's sword, which, we may suppose, was well known in Gath, and with which he had reason to expect they would cut off his head, as he had cut off Goliath's with it. David now learned by experience what he has taught us (Ps. 118:9), *that it is better to trust in the Lord than to put confidence in princes.* Men of high degree are a lie, and, if we make them our hope, they may prove our fear. It was at this time that David penned Psalm 55 *(Michtam, a golden psalm), when the Philistines took him in Gath,* where having shown before God his distresses, he resolves (*v.* 3), *"What time I am afraid I will trust in thee;* and therefore (*v.* 11) *will not be afraid what man can do unto me,* no, not the sons of giants." 4. The course he took to get out of their hands: *He feigned himself mad, v.* 13. He used the gestures and fashions of a natural fool, or one that had gone out of his wits, supposing they would be ready enough to believe that the disgrace he had fallen into, and the troubles he was now in, had driven him distracted. This dissimulation of his cannot be justified (it was a mean thing thus to disparage himself, and inconsistent with truth thus to misrepresent himself, and therefore not becoming the honour and sincerity of such a man as David); yet it may in some degree be excused, for it was not a downright lie and it was like a stratagem in war, by which he imposed upon his enemies for the preservation of his own life. What David did here in pretence and for his own safety, which made it partly excusable, drunkards do really, and only to gratify a base lust: they made fools of themselves and change their behaviour; their words and actions commonly are either as silly and ridiculous as an idiot's or as furious and outrageous as a madman's, which has often made me wonder that ever men of sense and honour should allow themselves in it. 5. His escape by this means, *v.* 14, 15. I am apt to think Achish was aware that the delirium was but counterfeit, but, being desirous to protect David (as we find afterwards he was very kind to him, even when the lord of the Philistines favoured him not, *ch.* 28:1, 2; 29:6), he pretended to his servants that he really thought he was mad, and therefore had reason to question whether it was David or no; or, if it were, they need not fear him, what harm could he do them now that his reason had departed from him? They suspected that Achish was inclined to entertain him: "Not I," says he. "He is a madman. I'll have nothing to do with him. You need not fear that I should employ him, or give him any countenance." He humours the thing well enough when he asks, *"Have I need of madmen? Shall this fool come into my house?* I will show him no kindness, but then you shall do him no hurt, for, if he be a madmen, he is to be pitied." He therefore *drove him away,* as it is in the title of Ps. 34, which David penned upon this occasion, and an excellent psalm it is, and shows that he did not change his spirit when he changed his behaviour, but even in the greatest difficulties and hurries his *heart was fixed,* trusting in the Lord; and he concludes that psalm with this assurance, that *none of those that trust in God shall be desolate,* though they may be, as he now was, solitary and distressed, *persecuted, but not forsaken.*

CHAPTER 22

David, being driven from Achish, returns into the land of Israel to be hunted by Saul. I. David sets up his standard in the cave of Adullam, entertains his relations (*v.* 1), enlists soldiers (*v.* 2), but removes his aged parents to a more quiet settlement (*v.* 3, 4), and has the prophet Gad for his counsellor (*v.* 5). Saul resolves to pursue him and find him out, complains of his servants and Jonathan (*v.* 6–8), and, finding by Doeg's information that Ahimelech had been kind to David, he ordered him and all the priests that were with him, eighty-five in all, to be put to death, and all that belonged to them destroyed (*v.* 9–19) from the barbarous execution of which sentence Abiathar escaped to David (*v.* 20–23).

Verses 1–5

Here, I. David shelters himself in the cave of Adullam, *v.* 1. Whether it was a natural or artificial fastness does not appear; it is probable that the access to it was so difficult that David thought himself able, with Goliath's sword, to keep it against all the forces of Saul, and therefore buried himself alive in it, while he was waiting to see (and he says here, *v.* 3) what God would do with him. The promise of the kingdom implied a promise of preservation to it, and yet David used proper means for his own safety, otherwise he would have tempted God. He did not do any thing that aimed to destroy Saul, but only to secure himself. He that might have done great service to his country as a judge or general is here shut up in a cave, and thrown by as a vessel in which there was no pleasure. We must not think it strange if sometimes shining lights be thus eclipsed and hidden under a bushel. Perhaps the apostle refers to this instance of David, among others, when he speaks of some of the Old-Testament worthies that *wandered in deserts, in dens and caves of the earth,* Heb. 11:38. It was at this time that David penned Psalm 142, which is entitled, *A prayer when David was in the cave;* and there he complains that *no man would know him* and that refuge failed him, but hopes that shortly the *righteous would compass him about.*

II. Thither his relations flocked to him, *his brethren and all his father's house,* to be protected by him, to give assistance to him, and to take their lot with him. *A brother is born for adversity.* Now, Joab, and Abishai, and the rest of his relations, came to him, to suffer and venture with him, in hopes shortly to be advanced with him; and they were so. The first three of his worthies were those that first owed him when he was in the cave, 1 Chr. 11:15, etc.

III. Here he began to raise forces in his own defence, *v.* 2. He found by the late experiments he had made that he could not save himself by flight, and therefore was necessitated to do it by force, wherein he never acted offensively, never offered any violence to his prince nor gave any disturbance to the peace of the kingdom, but only used his forces as a guard to his own person. But, whatever defence his soldiers were to him, they did him no great credit, for the regiment he had was made up not of great men, nor rich men, nor stout men, no, nor good men, but men *in distress, in debt, and discontented,* men of broken fortunes and restless spirits, that were put to their shifts, and knew not well what to do with themselves. When David had fixed his headquarters in the cave of Adullam, they came and enlisted themselves under him to the number of about 400. See what weak instruments God sometimes makes use of, by which to bring about his own purposes. The Son of David is ready to receive distressed souls, that will appoint him their captain and be commanded by him.

IV. He took care to settle his parents in a place of safety. No such place could he find in all the land of Israel while Saul was so bitterly enraged against him and all that belonged to him for his sake; he therefore goes with them to the king of Moab, and puts them under his protection, *v.* 3, 4. Observe here, 1. With what a tender concern he provided for his aged parents. It was not fit they should be exposed either to the frights or to the fatigues which he must expect during his struggle with Saul (their age would by no means bear such exposure); therefore the first thing he does is to find them a quiet habitation, whatever became of himself. Let children learn from this to *show pity at home and requite their parents* (1 Tim. 5:4), in every thing consulting their ease and satisfaction. Though ever so highly preferred, and ever so much employed, let them not forget their aged parents. 2. With what a humble faith he expects the issue of his present distresses: *Till I know what God will do for me.* He expresses his hopes very modestly, as one that had entirely cast himself upon God and committed his way to him, expecting a good issue, not from his own arts, or arms, or merits, but from what the wisdom, power, and goodness of God would do for him. Now David's father and mother forsook him, but God did not, Ps. 27:10.

V. He had the advice and assistance of the prophet Gad, who probably was one of the sons of the prophets that were brought up under Samuel, and was by him recommended to David for his chaplain or spiritual guide. Being a prophet, he would pray for him and instruct him in the mind of God; and David, though he was himself a prophet, was glad of his assistance. He advised him to go into the land of Judah (*v.* 5), as one that was confident of his own innocency, and was well assured of the divine protection, and was desirous, even in his present hard circumstances, to do some service to his tribe and country. Let him not be ashamed to own his own cause nor decline the succours that would be offered him. Animated by this word, there he determined to appear publicly. Thus are *the steps of a good man ordered by the Lord.*

Verses 6–19

We have seen the progress of David's troubles; now here we have the progress of Saul's wickedness. He seems to have laid aside the thoughts of all other business and to have devoted himself wholly to the pursuit of David. He heard at length, by the common fame of the country, that David *was discovered* (that is, that he appeared publicly and enlisted men into his service); and hereupon he called all his servants about him, and sat down under a tree, or grove, in the high place at Gibeah, with his spear in his hand for a sceptre, intimating the force by which he designed to rule, and the present temper of his spirit, or its distemper rather, which was to kill all that stood in his way. In this bloody court of inquisition,

I. Saul seeks for information against David and Jonathan, *v.* 7, 8. Two things he was willing to suspect and desirous to see proved, that he might wreak his malice upon two of the best and most excellent men he had about him: — 1. That his servant David did *lie in wait* for him and seek his life, which was utterly false. He really sought David's life, and therefore pretended that David sought his life, though he could not charge him with any overt act that gave the least shadow of suspicion. 2. That his son Jonathan stirred him up to do so, and was confederate with him in compassing and imagining the death of the king. This also was notoriously false. A league of friendship there was between David and Jonathan, but no conspiracy in any evil thing; none of the articles of their covenant carried any mischief to Saul. If Jonathan had agreed, after the death of Saul, to resign to David, in compliance with the revealed will of God, what harm would that do to Saul? Yet thus the best friends to their prince and country have often been odiously represented as enemies to both; even Christ himself was so. Saul took it for granted that Jonathan and David were in a plot against him, his crown and dignity, and was displeased with his servants that they did not give him information of it, supposing that they could not but know it; whereas really there was no such thing. See the nature of a jealous malice, and its pitiful arts to extort discoveries of things that are not. He looked upon all about him as his enemies because they did not say just as he said; and told them, (1.) That they were very unwise, and acted against the interest both of their tribe (for they were Benjamites, and David, if he were advanced, would bring the honour into Judah which was now in Benjamin) and of their families; for David would never be able to give them such rewards as he had for them, of *fields and vineyards,* and such preferments, to be colonels and captains. (2.) That they were unfaithful: *You have conspired against me.* What a continual agitation and torment are those in that give way to a spirit of jealousy! *If a ruler hearken to lies, all his servants are wicked* (Prov. 29:12), that is, they seem to be so in his eyes. (3.) That they were very unkind. He thought to work upon their good nature with that word: *There is none of you that is* so much as *sorry for me,* or *solicitous for me,* as some read it. By these reasonings he stirred them up to act vigorously, as the instruments of his malice, that they might take away his suspicions of them.

II. Though he could not learn any thing from his servants against David or Jonathan, yet he got information from Doeg against Ahimelech the priest.

1. An indictment is brought against Ahimelech by Doeg, and he himself is evidence against him, *v.* 9, 10. Perhaps Doeg, as bad as he was, would not have given this information if Saul had not extorted it, for had he been very forward to it he would have done it sooner: but now he thinks they must be all deemed traitors if none of them be accusers, and therefore tells Saul what kindness Ahimelech had shown to David, which he himself happened to be an eye-witness of. He had *enquired of God for him* (which the priest used not to do but for public persons and about public affairs) and he had furnished him with *bread and a sword.* All this was true; but it was not the whole truth. He ought to have told Saul further that David had made Ahimelech believe he was then going upon the king's business; so that what service he did to David, however it proved, was designed in honour to Saul, and this would have cleared Ahimelech, whom Saul had in his power, and would have thrown all the blame upon David, who was out of his reach.

2. Ahimelech is seized, or summoned rather to appear before the king, and upon this indictment he is arraigned. The king sent for him and all the priests who then attended the sanctuary, whom he supposed to be aiding and abetting; and they, not being conscious of any guilt, and therefore not apprehensive of any danger, *came all of them to the king* (*v.* 11), and none of them attempted to make an escape, or to flee to David for shelter, as they would have done now that he had set up his standard if they had been as much in his interests as Saul suspected they were. Saul arraigns Ahimelech himself with the utmost disdain and indignation (*v.* 12): *Hear now, thou son of Ahitub;* not so much as calling him by his name, much less giving him his title of distinction. By this it appears that he had cast off the fear of God, that he showed no respect at all to his priests, but took a pleasure in affronting them and insulting them. Ahimelech holds up his hand at the bar in those words: *"Here I am, my lord,* ready to hear my charge,

knowing I have done no wrong." He does not object to the jurisdiction of Saul's court, nor insist upon an exemption as a priest, no, not though he is a high priest, to which office that of the judge, or chief magistrate, had not long since been annexed; but Saul having now the sovereignty vested in him, in things pertaining to the king, even the high priest sets himself on a level with common Israelites. *Let every soul be subject* (even clergymen) *to the higher powers.*

3. His indictment is read to him (*v.* 13), that he, as a false traitor, had joined himself with the son of Jesse in a plot to depose and murder the king. "His design" (says Saul) "was to *rise up against me,* and thou didst assist him with victuals and arms." See what bad constructions the most innocent actions are liable to, how unsafe those are that live under a tyrannical government, and what reason we have to be thankful for the happy constitution and administration of the government we are under.

4. To this indictment he pleads, Not guilty, *v.* 14, 15. He owns the fact, but denies that he did it traitorously or maliciously, or with any design against the king. He pleads that he was so far from knowing of any quarrel between Saul and David that he really took David to have been then as much in favour at court as ever he had been. Observe, He does not plead that David had told him an untruth, and with that had imposed upon him, though really it was so, because he would not proclaim the weakness of so good a man, no, not for his own vindication, especially to Saul, who sought all occasions against him; but he insists upon the settled reputation David had as the most faithful of all the servants of Saul, the honour the king had put upon him in marrying his daughter to him, the use the king had often made of him, and the trust he had reposed on him: "He *goes at thy bidding, and is honourable in thy house,* and therefore any one would think it a meritorious piece of service to the crown to show him respect, so far from apprehending it to be a crime." He pleads that he had been wont to *enquire of God for him* when he was sent by Saul upon any expedition, and did it now as innocently as ever he had done it. He protests his abhorrence of the thought of being in a plot against the king: *"Be it far from me.* I mind my own business, and meddle not with state matters." He begs the king's favour: *"Let him not impute* any crime to us;" and concludes with a declaration of his innocency: *Thy servant knew nothing of all this.* Could any man plead with more evidences of sincerity? Had he been tried by a jury of honest Israelites, he would certainly have been acquitted, for who can find any fault in him? But,

5. Saul himself gives judgment against him (*v.* 16): *Thou shalt surely die, Ahimelech,* as a rebel, *thou and all thy father's house.* What could be more unjust? *I saw under the sun the place of judgment, that wickedness was there,* Eccl. 3:16. (1.) It was unjust that Saul should himself, himself alone, give judgment in his own cause, without any appeal to judge or prophet, to his privy council, or to a council of war. (2.) That so fair a plea should be overruled and rejected without any reason given, or any attempt to disprove the allegations of it, but purely with a high hand. (3.) That sentence should be passed so hastily and with so much precipitation, the judge taking no time himself to consider of it, nor allowing the prisoner any time to move in arrest of judgment. (4.) That the sentence should be passed not only on Ahimelech, himself, who was the only person accused by Doeg, but on *all his father's house,* against whom nothing was alleged: must the children be put to death for the fathers? (5.) That the sentence should be pronounced in passion, not for the support of justice, but for the gratification of his brutish rage.

6. He issues out a warrant (a verbal warrant only) for the immediate execution of this bloody sentence.

(1.) He ordered his footmen to be the executioners of this sentence, but they refused, *v.* 17. Hereby he intended to put a further disgrace upon the priests; they may not die by the hands of the men of war (as 1 Ki. 2:29) or his usual ministers of justice, but his footmen must triumph over them, and wash their hands in their blood. [1.] Never was the command of a prince more barbarously given: *Turn and slay the priests of the Lord.* This is spoken with such an air of impiety as can scarcely be paralleled. Had he seemed to forget their sacred office or relation to God, and taken no notice of that, he would thereby have intimated some regret that men of that character should fall under his displeasure; but to call them *the priests of the Lord,* when he ordered his footmen to cut their throats, looked as if, upon that very account, he hated them. God having rejected him, and ordered another to be anointed in his room, he seems well pleased with this opportunity of being revenged on the priests of the Lord, since God himself was out of his reach. What wickedness will not the evil spirit hurry men to, when he gets the dominion! He alleged, in his order that which was utterly false and unproved to him, that they knew when David fled; whereas they knew nothing of the matter. But malice and murder are commonly supported with lies. [2.] Never was the command of a prince more honourably disobeyed. The footmen had more sense and grace than their master. Though they might expect to be turned out of their places, if not punished and put to death for their refusal, yet, come on them what would, they would not offer to fall upon the priests of the Lord, such a reverence had they for their office, and such a conviction of their innocence.

(2.) He ordered Doeg (the accuser) to be the executioner, and he obeyed. One would have thought that the footmen's refusal would awaken Saul's conscience, and that he would not insist upon the doing of a thing so barbarous as that his footmen startled at the thought of it. But his mind was blinded and his heart hardened, and, if they will not do it, the hands of the witness shall be upon the victims, Deu. 17:7. The most bloody tyrants have found out instruments of their cruelty as barbarous as themselves. Doeg is no sooner commanded to fall upon the priests than he does it willingly enough, and, meeting with no resistance, slays with his own hand (for aught that appears) on that same day eighty-five priests that were of the age of ministration, between twenty and fifty, for they *wore a linen ephod* (*v.* 18), and perhaps appeared at this time before Saul in their habits, and were slain in them. This (one would think) was enough to satiate the most bloodthirsty; but the horseleech of persecution still cries, "Give, give." Doeg, by Saul's order no doubt, having murdered the priests, went to their city Nob, and put all to the sword there (*v.* 19), *men, women, and children,* and the cattle too. Barbarous cruelty, and such as one cannot think of without horror! Strange that ever it should enter into the heart of man to be so impious, so inhuman! We may see in this, [1.] The desperate wickedness of Saul when the Spirit of the Lord had departed from him. Nothing so vile but those may be hurried to it who have provoked God to give them up to their hearts' lusts. He that was so compassionate as to spare Agag and the cattle of the Amalekites, in disobedience to the command of God, could now, with unrelenting bowels, see the priests of the Lord murdered, and nothing spared of all that belonged to them. For that sin God left him to this. [2.] The accomplishment of the threatenings long since pronounced against the house of Eli; for Ahimelech and his family were descendants from him. Though Saul was unrighteous in doing this, yet God was righteous in permitting it. Now God performed against Eli that at which the ears of those that heard it must needs tingle, as he had told him that he would *judge his house for ever ch.* 3:11–13. No word of God shall fall to the ground. [3.] This may be considered as a great judgment upon Israel, and the just punishment of their desiring a king before the time God intended them one. How deplorable was the state of religion at this time in Israel! Though the ark had long been in obscurity, yet it was some comfort to them that they had the altar, and priests to serve at it; but now to see their priests weltering in their own blood, and the heirs of the priesthood too, and the city of the priests made a desolation, so that the altar of God must needs be neglected for want of attendants, and this by the unjust and cruel order of their own king to satisfy his brutish rage — this could not but go to the heart of all pious Israelites, and make them wish a thousand times they had been satisfied with the government of Samuel and his sons. The worst enemies of their nation could not have done them a greater mischief.

Verses 20–23

Here is, 1. The escape of Abiathar, the son of Ahimelech, out of the desolations of the priests' city. Probably when his father went to appear, upon Saul's summons, he was left at home to attend the altar, by which means he escaped the first execution, and, before Doeg and his bloodhounds came to Nob, he had intelligence of the danger, and had time to shift for his own safety. And whither should he go but to David? *v.* 20. Let those that suffer for the Son of David *commit the keeping of their souls to him,* 1 Pt. 4:19. 2. David's resentment of the melancholy tidings he brought. He gave David an account of the bloody work Saul had made among the priests of the Lord (*v.* 21), as the disciples of John, when their master was beheaded, *went and told Jesus,* Mt. 14:12. And David greatly lamented the calamity itself, but especially his being accessory to it: *I have occasioned the death of all the persons of thy father's house, v.* 22. Note, It is a great trouble to a good man to find himself in any way an occasion of the calamities of the church and ministry. David knew Doeg's character so well that he feared he would do some such mischief as this when he saw him at the sanctuary: *I knew he would tell Saul.* He calls him *Doeg the Edomite,* because he retained the heart of an Edomite, though, by embracing the profession of the Jewish religion, he had put on the mask of an Israelite. 3. The protection he granted to Abiathar. He perceived him to be terrified, as he had reason to be, and therefore bade him not to fear, he would be as careful for him as for himself: *With me thou shalt be in safeguard, v.* 23. David, having now time to recollect himself, speaks with assurance of his own safety, and promises that Abiathar shall have the full benefit of his protection. It is promised to the Son of David that God will *hide him in the shadow of his hand* (Isa. 49:2), and, with him, all that are his may be sure that they shall be in safeguard, Ps. 91:1. David had now not only a prophet, but a priest, a high-priest, with him, to whom he was a blessing and they to him, and both a happy omen of his success. Yet it appears (by *ch.* 28:6) that Saul had a high priest too, for he had a urim to consult: it is supposed that he preferred Ahitub the father of Zadok, of the family of Eleazar (1 Chr. 6:8), for even those that hate the power of godliness yet will not be without the form. It must not be forgotten here that David at this time penned Psalm 52, as appears by the title of that psalm, wherein he represents Doeg not only as malicious and spiteful, but as false and deceitful, because though what he said was, for the substance of it, true, yet he put false colours upon it, with a design to do mischief. Yet even then, when the priesthood had become as a withered branch, he looks upon himself as a *green olive-tree in the house of God,* Ps. 52:8. In this great hurry and distraction that David was continually in, yet he found both time and a heart for communion with God, and found comfort in it.

CHAPTER 23

Saul, having made himself drunk with the blood of the priests of the Lord, is here, in this chapter, seeking David's life, who appears here doing good, and suffering ill, at the same time. Here is, I. The good service he did to his king and country, in rescuing the city of Keilah out of the hands of the Philistines (*v.* 1–6). II. The danger he was thereby brought into from the malice of the prince he served and the treachery of the city he saved, and his deliverance, by divine direction, from that danger (*v.* 7–13). III. David in a wood and his friend Jonathan visiting him there and encouraging him (*v.* 14–18). IV. The information which the Ziphites brought to Saul of David's haunts, and the expedition Saul made, in pursuit of him (*v.* 19–25). The narrow escape David had of falling into his hands (*v.* 26–29). "Many are the troubles of the righteous, but the Lord delivereth them out of them all."

Verses 1–6

Now we find why the prophet Gad (by divine direction, no doubt) ordered David to go into the land of Judah, *ch.* 22:5. It was that, since Saul neglected the public safety, he might take care of it, notwithstanding the ill treatment that was given him; for he must render good for evil, and therein be a type of him who not only ventured his life, but laid down his life, for those that were his enemies.

I. Tidings are brought to David, as to the patron and protector of his country's liberties, that the Philistines had made a descent upon the city of Keilah and plundered the country thereabouts, *v.* 1. Probably it was the departure both of God and David from Saul that encouraged the Philistines to make this incursion. When princes begin to persecute God's people and ministers, let them expect no other than vexation on all sides. The way for any country to be quiet is to let God's church be quiet in it. If Saul fight against David, the Philistines shall fight against his country.

II. David is forward enough to come in for their relief, but is willing to enquire of the Lord concerning it. Here is an instance, 1. Of David's generosity and public-spiritedness. Though his head and hands were full of his own business, and he had enough to do, with the little force he had, to secure himself, yet he was concerned for the safety of his country and could not sit still to see that ravaged: nay, though Saul, whose business it was to guard the borders of his land, hated him and sought his life, yet he was willing, to the utmost of his power, to serve him and his interests against the common enemy, and bravely abhorred the thought of sacrificing the common welfare to his private revenge. Those are unlike to David who sullenly decline to do good because they have not been so well considered as they deserved for the services they have done. 2. Of David's piety and regard to God. He enquired of the Lord by the prophet Gad; for it should seem (by *v.* 6) that Abiathar came not to him with the ephod till he was in Keilah. His enquiry is, *Shall I go and smite these Philistines?* He enquires both concerning the duty (whether he might lawfully take Saul's work out of his hand, and act without a commission from him) and concerning the event, whether he might safely venture against such a force as the Philistines had with such a handful of men at his feet, and such a dangerous enemy as Saul was at his back. It is our duty, and will be our case and comfort, whatever happens, to acknowledge God in all our ways and to seek direction from him.

III. God appointed him once and again to go against the Philistines, and promised him success: *Go, and smite the Philistines, v.* 2. His men opposed it, *v.* 3. No sooner did he begin to have soldiers of his own than he found it hard enough to manage them. They objected that they had enemies enough among their own countrymen, they needed not to make the Philistines their enemies. Their hearts failed them when they only apprehended themselves in danger from Saul's band of pursuers, much more when they came to engage the Philistine-armies. To satisfy them, therefore, he *enquired of the Lord again,* and now received, not only a full commission, which would warrant him to fight though he had no orders from Saul *(Arise, go down to Keilah),* but also a full assurance of victory: *I will deliver the Philistines into thy hand, v.* 4. This was enough to animate the greatest coward he had in his regiment.

IV. He went accordingly against the Philistines, routed them, and rescued Keilah, (*v.* 5), and it should seem he made a sally into the country of the Philistines, for he carried off their cattle by way of reprisal for the wrong they did to the men of Keilah in robbing their threshing-floors. Here notice is taken (*v.* 6) that it was while David remained in Keilah, after he had cleared it of the Philistines, that Abiathar came to him with the ephod in his hand, that is, the high priest's ephod, in which the urim and thummin were. It was a great comfort to David, in his banishment, that when he could not go to the house of God he had some of the choicest treasures of that house brought to him, the high priest and his breast-plate of judgment.

Verses 7–13

Here is, I. Saul contriving within himself the destruction of David (*v.* 7, 8): *He heard that he had come to Keilah;* and did he not hear what brought him thither? Was it not told him that he had bravely relieved Keilah and delivered it out of the hands of the Philistines? This, one would think, should have put Saul upon considering what honour and dignity should be done to David for this. But, instead of that, he catches at it as an opportunity of doing David a mischief. An ungrateful wretch he was, and for ever unworthy to have any service or kindness done him. Well might David complain of his enemies that they rewarded him *evil for good,* and that for his love they ere his adversaries, Ps. 35:12; 109:4. Christ was used thus basely, Jn. 10:32. Now observe, 1. How Saul abused the *God of Israel,* in making his providence to patronise and give countenance to his malicious designs, and thence promising himself success in them: *God hath delivered him into my hand;* as if he who was rejected of God were in this instance owned and favoured by him, and David infatuated. He vainly triumphs before the victory, forgetting how often he had had fairer advantages against David than he had now and had yet missed his aim. He impiously connects God with his cause, because he thought he had gained one point. Therefore David prays (Ps. 140:8), *Grant not, O Lord! the desires of the wicked; further not his wicked device, lest they exalt themselves.* We must not think that one smiling providence either justifies an unrighteous cause or secures its success. 2. How Saul abused the Israel of God, in making them the servants of his malice against David. He called all the people together to war, and they must with all speed march to Keilah, pretending to oppose the Philistines, but intending to besiege David and his men, though concealing that design; for it is said (*v.* 9) that he *secretly practised mischief against him.* Miserable is that people whose prince is a tyrant, for, while some are sufferers by his tyranny, others (which is worse) are made servants to it and instruments of it.

II. David consulting with God concerning his own preservation. He knew by the information bought him that Saul was plotting his ruin (*v.* 9) and therefore applied to his great protector for direction. No sooner is the ephod brought to him than he makes use of it: *Bring hither the ephod.* We have the scriptures, those lively oracles, in our hands; let us take advice from them in doubtful cases. "Bring hither the Bible."

1. David's address to God upon this occasion is, (1.) Very solemn and reverent. Twice he calls God the *Lord God of Israel,* and thrice calls himself his *servant, v.* 10, 11. Those that address God must know their distance, and who they are speaking to. (2.) Very particular and express. His representation of the case is so (*v.* 10): "Thy servant has certainly heard on good authority" (for he would not call for the ephod upon every idle rumour) "that Saul has a design upon Keilah;" he does not say, "to destroy me," but, "to destroy the city" (as he had lately done the city of Nob) "for my sake." He seems more solicitous for their safety than for his own, and will expose himself any where rather than they shall be brought into trouble by his being among them. Generous souls are thus minded. His queries upon the case are likewise very particular. God allows us to be so in our addresses to him: "Lord, direct me in this matter, about which I am now at a loss." He does indeed invert the due order of his queries, but God in his answer puts him into method. That question should have been put first, and was first answered, "Will Saul come down, as thy servant has heard?" "Yea," says the oracle, "he will come down; he has resolved it, is preparing for it, and will do it, unless he hear that thou hast quitted the town." "Well, but if he do come down will the men of Keilah stand by me in holding the city against him, or will they open to him the gates, and deliver me into his hand?" If he had asked the men (the magistrates or elders) of Keilah themselves what they would do in that case, they could not have told him, not knowing their own minds, nor what they should do when it came to the trial, much less which way the superior vote of their council would carry it; or they might have told him they would protect him, and yet afterwards have betrayed him; but God could tell him infallibly: "When Saul besieges their city, and demands of them that they surrender thee into his hands, how fond soever they now seem of thee, as their saviour, they will deliver thee up rather than stand the shock of Saul's fury." Note, [1.] God knows all men better than they know themselves, knows their length, their strength, what is in them, and what they will do if they come into such and such circumstances. [2.] He therefore knows not only what *will* be, but what *would* be if it were not prevented; and therefore knows how to deliver the godly out of temptation, and how to render to every man according to his works.

2. David, having thus far notice given him of his danger, quitted Keilah, *v.* 13. His followers had now increased in number to 600; with these he went out, not knowing whither he went, but resolving to follow Providence and put himself under its protection. This broke Saul's measures. He thought God had delivered David into his hand, but it proved that God delivered him out of his hand, as a bird out of the snare of the fowler. When *Saul heard that David had escaped from Keilah, he forbore to go forth* with the body of the army, as he intended (*v.* 8), and resolved to take only his own guards, and go in quest of his people's enemies and turn their counsels head-long.

Verses 14–18

Here is, I. David absconding. He abode in a *wilderness, in a mountain* (*v.* 14), *in a wood, v.* 15. We must here, 1. Commend his eminent virtues, his humility, modesty, fidelity to his prince, and patient attendance on the providence of his God, that he did not draw up his forces against Saul, fight him in the field, or surprise him by some stratagem or other, and so avenge his own quarrel and that of the Lord's priests upon him, and put an end to his own troubles and the calamities of the country under Saul's tyrannical government. No, he makes no such attempt; he keeps God's way, waits God's time, and is content to secure himself in woods and wildernesses, though with some it might seem a reproach to that courage for which he had been famous. But, 2. We must also lament his hard fate, that an innocent man should be thus terrified and put in fear of his life, that a man of honour should be thus disgraced, a man of merit thus recompensed for his services, and a man that delighted in the service both of God and his country should be debarred from both and wrapped up in obscurity. What shall we say to this? Let it make us think the worse of this world, which often gives such bad treatment to its best men; let it reconcile even great and active men to privacy and restraint, if Providence make these their lot, for they were David's; and let it make us long for that kingdom where goodness shall for ever be in glory and holiness in honour, and the righteous shall shine as the sun, which cannot be put under a bushel.

II. Saul hunting him, as his implacable enemy. He sought him every day, so restless was his malice, *v.* 14. He sought no less than his life, so cruel was his malice, *v.* 15. As it had been from the beginning, so it was now, and will be, *he that is born after the flesh persecuteth him that is born after the spirit,* Gal. 4:29.

III. God defending him, as his powerful protector. God delivered him not into Saul's hand, as Saul hoped (*v.* 7); and, unless God delivered him into his hand, he could not prevail against him, Jn. 19:11.

IV. Jonathan comforting him as his faithful and constant friend. True friends will find out means to get together. David, it is likely, appointed time and place for this interview, and Jonathan observed the appointment, though he exposed himself thereby to his father's displeasure, and, had it been discovered, it might have cost him his life. True friendship will not shrink from danger, but can easily venture, will not shrink from condescension, but can easily stoop, and exchange a palace for a wood, to serve a friend. The very sight of Jonathan was reviving to David; but, besides this, he said that to him which was very encouraging. 1. As a pious friend, he directed him to God, the foundation of his confidence and the fountain of his comfort: He *strengthened his hand in God.* David, though a strong believer, needed the help of his friends for the perfecting of what was lacking in his faith; and herein Jonathan was helpful to him, by reminding him of the promise of God, the holy oil wherewith he was anointed, the presence of God with him hitherto, and the many experiences he had had of God's goodness to him. Thus he strengthened his hands for action, by encouraging his heart, not in the creature, but in God. Jonathan was not in a capacity of doing any thing to strengthen him, but he assured him God would. 2. As a self-denying friend, he took a pleasure in the prospect of David's advancement to that honour which was his own birthright, *v.* 17. "Thou shalt live to be king, and I shall think it preferment enough to be next thee, near thee, though under thee, and will never pretend to be a rival with thee." This resignation which Jonathan made to David of his title would be a great satisfaction to him, and make his way much the more clear. This, he tells him, Saul knew very well, Jonathan having sometimes heard him say as much, whence it appears what a wicked man Saul was, to persecute one whom God favoured, and what a foolish man he was, in thinking to prevent that which God had determined and which would certainly come to pass. How could he disannul what God had purposed? 3. As a constant friend, he renewed his league of friendship with him. They made a covenant now, this third time, before the Lord, calling him to witness to it, *v.* 18. True love takes delight in repeating its engagements, giving and receiving fresh assurances of the firmness of the friendship. Our covenant with God should be often renewed, and therein our communion with him kept up. David and Jonathan now parted, and never came together again, that we find, in this world; for Jonathan said what he wished, not what he had ground to expect, when he promised himself that he should be next to David in his kingdom.

Verses 19–29

Here, 1. The Ziphites offer their service to Saul, to betray David to him, *v.* 19, 20. He was sheltering himself in the wilderness of Ziph (*v.* 14, 15), putting the more confidence in the people of that country because they were of his own tribe. They had reason to think themselves happy that they had an opportunity of serving one who was the ornament of their tribe and was likely to be much more so, who was so far from plundering the country, or giving it any disturbance with his troops, that he was ready to protect it and to them all the good offices that there was occasion for. But, to ingratiate themselves with Saul, they went to him, and not only informed him very particularly where David quartered (*v.* 19), but invited him to come with his forces into their country in pursuit of him, and promised to deliver him into his hand, *v.* 20. Saul had not sent to examine or threaten them, but of their own accord, and even without asking a reward (as Judas did — *What will you give me?*), they offered to betray David to him who, they knew, thirsted after his blood. 2. Saul thankfully receives their information, and gladly lays hold of the opportunity of hunting David in their wilderness, in hopes to make a prey of him at length. He intimates to them how kindly he took it (*v.* 21): *Blessed be you of the Lord* (so near is God to his mouth, though far from his heart), *for you have compassion on me.* It seems he looked upon himself as a miserable man and an object of pity; his own envy and ill-nature made him so, otherwise he might have been easy and have needed no man's compassion. He likewise insinuates the little concern that the generality of his people showed for him. "You have compassion on me, which others have not." Saul gives them instructions to search more particularly for his haunts (*v.* 22), "for" (says he) "I hear he deals very subtilely," representing him as a man crafty to do mischief, whereas all his subtlety was to secure himself. It was strange that Saul did not go down with them immediately, but he hoped by their means to set his game with the more certainty, and thus divine Providence gave David time to shift for himself. But the Ziphites had laid their spies upon all the places where he was likely to be discovered, and therefore Saul might come and seize him if he was in the land, *v.* 23. New he thought himself sure of his prey and pleased himself with the thoughts of devouring it. 3. The imminent peril that David was now brought into. Upon intelligence that the Ziphites had betrayed him, he retired from the hill of Hachilah to the wilderness of Maon (*v.* 24), and at this time he penned the 54th Psalm, as appears by the title, wherein he calls the Ziphites *strangers,* though they were Israelites, because they used him barbarously; but he puts himself under the divine protection: *"Behold, God is my helper,* and then all shall be well" Saul, having got intelligence of him, pursued him closely (*v.* 25), till he came so near him that there was but a mountain between them (*v.* 26), David and his men on one side of the mountain flying and Saul and his men on the other side pursuing, David in fear and Saul in hope. But this mountain was an emblem of the divine Providence coming between David and the destroyer, like the pillar of cloud between the Israelites and the Egyptians. David was concealed by this mountain and Saul confounded by it. David now flees *as a bird to his mountain* (Ps. 11:1) and finds God to him as the shadow of a great rock. Saul hoped with his numerous forces to enclose David, and compass him in and his men; but the ground did not prove convenient for his design, and so it failed. A new name was given to the place in remembrance of this (*v.* 28): *Selah-hammah-lekoth — the rock of division,* because it divided between Saul and David. 4. The deliverance of David out of this danger. Providence gave Saul a diversion, when he was just ready to lay hold of David; notice was brought him that the Philistines were *invading the land* (*v.* 27), probably that part of the land where his own estate lay, which would be seized, or at least spoiled, by the invaders; for the little notice he took of Keilah's distress and David's relief of it, in the beginning of this chapter, gives us cause to suspect that he would not now have left pursuing David, and gone to oppose the Philistines, if some private interests of his own had not been at stake. However it was, he found himself under a necessity of *going against the Philistines* (*v.* 28), and by this means David was delivered when he was on the brink of destruction. Saul was disappointed of his prey, and God was glorified as David's wonderful protector. When the Philistines invaded the land they were far from intending any kindness to David by it, yet the overruling providence of God, which orders all events and the times of them, made it very serviceable to him. The wisdom of God is never at a loss for ways and means to preserve his people. As this Saul was diverted, so another Saul was converted, just then when he was *breathing out threatenings and slaughter against the saints of the Lord,* Acts 9:1. 5. David, having thus escaped, took shelter in some natural fortresses, which he found in the wilderness of En-gedi, *v.* 29. And this Dr. Lightfoot thinks was the wilderness of Judah, in which David was when he penned Psalm 63, which breathes as much pious and devout affection as almost any of his psalms; for in all places and in all conditions he still kept up his communion with God.

CHAPTER 24

We have hitherto had Saul seeking an opportunity to destroy David, and, to his shame, he could never find it. In this chapter David had a fair opportunity to destroy Saul, and, to his honour, he did not make use of it; and his sparing Saul's life was as great an instance of God's grace in him as the preserving of his own life was of God's providence over him. Observe, I. How maliciously Saul sought David's life (*v.* 1, 2). II. How generously David saved Saul's life (when he had him at an advantage) and only cut off the skirt of his robe (*v.* 3–8). III. How pathetically he reasoned with Saul, upon this to bring him to a better temper towards him (*v.* 9–15). IV. The good impression this made upon Saul for the present (*v.* 16–22).

Verses 1–8

Here, I. Saul renews his pursuit of David, *v.* 1, 2. No sooner had he come home safely from chasing the Philistines, in which it should seem he had good success, than he enquired after David to do him a mischief, and resolved to have another thrust at him, *as if he had been delivered to do all these abominations,* Jer. 7:10. By the frequent incursions of the Philistines, he might have seen how necessary it was to recall David from his banishment and restore him to his place in the army again; but so far is he from doing this that now more than ever he is exasperated against him, and, hearing that he is *in the wilderness of En-gedi,* he draws out 3000 choice men, and goes with them at his feet in pursuit of him *upon the rocks of the wild goats,* where, one would think, David should not have been envied a habitation nor Saul desirous of disturbing him; for what harm could he fear from one who was no better accommodated? But it is not enough for Saul that David is thus cooped up; he cannot be easy while he is alive.

II. Providence brings Saul alone into the same cave wherein David and his men had hidden themselves, *v.* 3. In those countries there were very large caves in the sides of the rocks or mountains, partly natural, but probably much enlarged by art for the sheltering of sheep from the heat of the sun; hence we read of places where the flocks did rest at noon (Cant. 1:7), and this cave seems to be spoken of as one of the sheep-cotes. In the sides of this cave David and his men remained, perhaps not all his men, the whole 600, but only some few of his particular friends, the rest being disposed of in similar retirements. Saul, passing by, turned in himself alone, not in search of David (for, supposing him to be an aspiring ambitious man, he thought to find him rather climbing with the wild goats upon the rocks than retiring with the sheep into a cave), but thither he turned aside to *cover his feet,* that is, to sleep awhile, it being a cool and quiet place, and very refreshing in the heat of the day; probably he ordered his attendants to march before, reserving only a very few to wait for him at the mouth of the cave. Some by the covering of the feet understand the easing of nature, and think that this was Saul's errand into the cave: but the former interpretation is more probable.

III. David's servants stir him up to kill Saul now that he has so fair an opportunity to do it, *v.* 4. They reminded him that this was the day which he had long looked for, and of which God had spoken to him in general when he was anointed to the kingdom, which should put a period to his troubles and open the passage to his advancement. Saul now lay at his mercy, and it was easy to imagine how little mercy he would find with Saul and therefore what little reason he had to show mercy to him. "By all means" (say his servants) "give him the fatal blow now." See how apt we are to misunderstand, 1. The promises of God. God had assured David that he would deliver him from Saul, and his men interpret this as a warrant to destroy Saul. 2. The providences of God. Because it was now in his power to kill him, they concluded he might lawfully do it.

IV. David *cut off the skirt of his robe,* but soon repented that he had done this: *His heart smote him* for it (*v.* 5); though it did Saul no real hurt, and served David for a proof that it was in his power to have killed him (*v.* 11), yet, because it was an affront to Saul's royal dignity, he wished he had not done it. Note, It is a good thing to have a heart within us smiting us for sins that seem little; it is a sign that conscience is awake and tender, and will be the means of preventing greater sins.

V. He reasons strongly both with himself and with his servants against doing Saul any hurt. 1. He reasons with himself (*v.* 6): *The Lord forbid that I should do this thing.* Note, Sin is a thing which it becomes us to startle at, and to resist the temptations to, not only with resolution, but with a holy indignation. He considered Saul now, not as his enemy, and the only person that stood in the way of his preferment (for then he would be induced to hearken to the temptation), but as God's anointed (that is, the person whom God had appointed to reign as long as he lived, and who, as such, was under the particular protection of the divine law), and as his master, to whom he was obliged to be faithful. Let servants and subjects learn hence to be dutiful and loyal, whatever hardships are put upon them, 1 Pt. 2:18. 2. He reasons with his servants: *He suffered them not to rise against Saul, v.* 7. He would not only not do this evil thing himself, but he would not suffer those about him to do it. Thus did he render good for evil to him from whom he had received evil for good, and was herein both a type of Christ, who saved his persecutors, and an example to all Christians not to be *overcome of evil, but to overcome evil with good.*

VI. He followed Saul out of the cave, and, though he would not take the opportunity to slay him, yet he wisely took the opportunity, if possible, to slay his enmity, by convincing him that he was not such a man as he took him for. 1. Even in showing his head now he testified that he had an honourable opinion of Saul. He had too much reason to believe that, let him say what he would, Saul would immediately be the death of him as soon as he saw him, and yet he bravely lays aside that jealousy, and thinks Saul so much a man of sense as to hear his reasoning when he had so much to say in his own vindication and such fresh and sensible proofs to give of his own integrity. 2. His behaviour was very respectful: He *stooped with his face to the earth, and bowed himself,* giving honour to whom honour was due, and teaching us to order ourselves lowly and reverently to all our superiors, even to those that have been most injurious to us.

Verses 9–15

We have here David's warm and pathetic speech to Saul, wherein he endeavours to convince him that he did him a great deal of wrong in persecuting him thus and to persuade him therefore to be reconciled.

I. He calls him *father* (*v.* 11), for he was not only, as king, the father of his country, but he was, in particular, his father-in-law. From a father one may expect compassion and a favourable opinion. For a prince to seek the ruin of any of his good subjects is as unnatural as for a father to seek the ruin of his own children.

II. He lays the blame of his rage against him upon his evil counsellors: *Wherefore hearest thou men's words? v.* 9. It is a piece of respect due to crowned heads, if they do amiss, to charge it upon those about them, who either advised them to it or should have advised them against it. David had reason enough to think that Saul persecuted him purely from his own envy and malice, yet he courteously supposes that others put him on to do it, and made him believe that David was his enemy and sought his hurt. Satan, the great accuser of the brethren, has his agents in all places, and particularly in the courts of those princes that encourage them and give ear to them, who make it their business to represent the people of God as enemies to Caesar and hurtful to kings and provinces, that, being thus dressed up in bear-skins, they may "be baited."

III. He solemnly protests his own innocence, and that he is far from designing any hurt or mischief to Saul: *"There is neither evil nor transgression in my hand, v.* 11. I am not chargeable with any crime, nor conscious of any guilt, and, had I a window in my breast, thou mightest through it see the sincerity of my heart in this protestation: *I have not sinned against thee* (however I have sinned against God), *yet thou huntest my soul,*" that is, "my life." Perhaps it was about this time that David penned the seventh psalm, concerning the affair of Cush the Benjamite (that is, Saul, as some think), wherein he thus appeals to God (*v.* 3–5): *If there be iniquity in my hands, then let the enemy persecute my soul and take it,* putting in a parenthesis, with reference to the story of this chapter, *Yea, I have delivered him that without cause is my enemy.*

IV. He produces undeniable evidence to prove the falsehood of the suggestion upon which Saul's malice against him was grounded. David was charged with seeking Saul's hurt: "*See,*" says he, "*yea, see the skirt of thy robe, v.* 11. Let this be a witness for me, and an unexceptionable witness it is; had that been true of which I am accused, I should now have had thy head in my hand and not the skirt of thy robe, for I could as easily have cut off that as this." To corroborate this evidence he shows him, 1. That God's providence had given him opportunity to do it: *The lord delivered thee,* very surprisingly, *to day into my hand,* whence many a one would have gathered an intimation that it was the will of God he should now give the determining blow to him whose neck lay so fair for it. When Saul had but a very small advantage against David he cried out, *God has delivered him into my hand* (*ch.* 23:7), and resolved to make the best of that advantage; but David did not so. 2. That his counsellors and those about him had earnestly besought him to do it: *Some bade me kill thee.* He had blamed Saul for hearkening to men's words and justly; "for," says he, "if I had done so, thou wouldest not have been alive now." 3. That it was upon a good principle that he refused to do it; not because Saul's attendants were at hand, who, it may be, would have avenged his death; no, it was not by the fear of them, but by the fear of God, that he was restrained from it. "He is my lord, and the Lord's anointed, whom I ought to protect, and to whom I owe faith and allegiance, and therefore I said, I will not touch a hair of his head." Such a happy command he had of himself that his nature, in the midst of the greatest provocation, was not suffered to rebel against his principles.

V. He declares it to be his fixed resolution never to be his own avenger: "*The Lord avenge me of thee,* that is, deliver me out of thy hand; but, whatever comes of it, *my hand shall not be upon thee*" (*v.* 12), and again (*v.* 13), for *saith the proverb of the ancients, Wickedness proceedeth from the wicked.* The wisdom of the ancients is transmitted to posterity by their proverbial sayings. Many such we receive by tradition from our fathers; and the counsels of common persons are very much directed by this, "As the old saying is." Here is one that was in use in David's time: *Wickedness proceedeth from the wicked,* that is, 1. Men's own iniquity will ruin them at last, so some understand it. Forward furious men will cut their own throats with their own knives. Give them rope enough, and they will hang themselves. In this sense it comes in very fitly as a reason why *his hand should not be upon him.* 2. Bad men will do bad things; according as men's principles and dispositions are, so will their actions be. This also agrees very well with the connexion. If David had been a wicked man, as he was represented, he would have done this wicked thing; but he durst not, because of the fear of God. Or thus: Whatever injuries bad men do us (which we are not to wonder at; he that lies among thorns must expect to be scratched), yet we must not return them; never render railing for railing. Though *wickedness proceed from the wicked,* yet let it not therefore proceed from us by way of retaliation. Though the dog bark at the sheep, the sheep does not bark at the dog. See Isa. 32:6–8.

VI. He endeavours to convince Saul that as it was a bad thing, so it was a mean thing, for him to give chase to such an inconsiderable person as he was (*v.* 14): *Whom does the king of Israel pursue* with all this care and force? *A dead dog; a flea; one flea,* so it is in the Hebrew. It is below so great a king to enter the lists with one that is so unequal a match for him, one of his own servants, bred a poor shepherd, now an exile, neither able nor willing to make any resistance. To conquer him would not be to his honour, to attempt it was his disparagement. If Saul would consult his own reputation, he would slight such an enemy (supposing he were really his enemy) and would think himself in no danger from him. David was so far from aspiring that he was, in his own account, as a dead dog. Mephibosheth thus calls himself, 2 Sa. 9:8. This humble language would have wrought upon Saul if he had had any spark of generosity in him. *Satis est prostrâsse leoni — Enough for the lion that he has laid his victim low.* What credit would it be to Saul to trample upon a dead dog? What pleasure could it be to him to hunt a flea, a single flea, which (as some have observed), if it be sought, is not easily found, if it be found, is not easily caught, and, if it be caught, is a poor prize, especially for a prince. *Aquila non captat muscas — The eagle does not dart upon flies.* David thinks Saul had no more reason to fear him than to fear a flea-bite.

VII. He once and again appeals to God as the righteous Judge (*v.* 12 and *v.* 15): *The Lord judge between me and thee.* Note, The justice of God is the refuge and comfort of oppressed innocence. If men wrong us, God will right us, at furthest, in the judgment of the great day. With him David leaves his cause, and so rests satisfied, waiting his time to appear for him.

Verses 16–22

Here we have,

I. Saul's penitent reply to David's speech. It was strange that he had patience to hear him out, considering how outrageous he was against him, and how cutting David's discourse was. But God restrained him and his men; and we may suppose Saul struck with amazement at the singularity of the event, and much more when he found how much he had lain at David's mercy. His heart must have been harder than a stone if this had not affected him. 1. He melted into tears, and we will not suppose them to have been counterfeit but real expressions of his present concern at the sight of his own iniquity, so plainly proved upon him. He speaks as one quite overcome with David's kindness: *Is this thy voice, my son David?* And, as one that relented at the thought of his own folly and ingratitude, he *lifted up his voice and wept, v.* 16. Many mourn for their sins that do not truly repent of them, weep bitterly for them, and yet continue in love and league with them. 2. He ingenuously acknowledges David's integrity and his own iniquity (*v.* 17): *Thou art more righteous than I.* Now God made good to David that word on which he had caused him to hope, that he would *bring forth his righteousness as the light,* Ps. 37:6. Those who take care to keep a good conscience may leave it to God to secure them the credit of it. This fair confession was enough to prove David innocent (even his enemy himself being judge), but not enough to prove Saul himself a true penitent. He should have said, *Thou are righteous, but I am wicked;* but the utmost he will own is this: *Thou art more righteous than I.* Bad men will commonly go no further than this in their confessions; they will own they are not so good as some others are; there are those that are better than they, and more righteous. He now owns himself under a mistake concerning David (*v.* 18): "*Thou hast shown this day* that thou art so far from seeking my hurt *that thou hast dealt well with me.*" We are too apt to suspect others to be worse affected towards us then really they are, and than perhaps they are proved to be; and when, afterwards, our mistake is discovered, we should be forward to recall our suspicions, as Saul does here. 3. He prays God to recompense David for this his generous kindness to him. He owns that David's sparing him, when he had him in his power, was an uncommon and unparalleled instance of tenderness to an enemy; no man would have done the like; and therefore, either because he thought himself not able to give him a full recompence for so great a favour, or because he found himself not inclined to give him any recompence at all, he turns him over to God for his pay: *The Lord reward thee good, v.* 19. Poor beggars can do no less than pray for their benefactors, and Saul did no more. 4. He prophesies his advancement to the throne (*v.* 20): *I know well that thou shalt surely be king.* He knew it before, by the promise Samuel had made him of it compared with the excellent spirit that appeared in David, which highly aggravated his sin and folly in persecuting him as he did; he had as much reason to say concerning David as David concerning him, *How can I put forth my hand against the Lord's anointed?* But now he knew it by the interest he found David had in the people, the special providence of God in protecting him, and the generous kingly spirit he had now given a proof of in sparing his enemy. Now he knew it, that is, now that he was in a good temper he was willing to own that he knew it and to submit to the conviction of it. Note, Sooner or later, God will force even those that are of the synagogue of Satan to know and own those that he has loved, and to worship before their feet; for so is the promise, Rev. 3:9. This acknowledgement which Saul made of David's incontestable title to the crown was a great encouragement to David himself and a support to his faith and hope. 5. He binds David with an oath hereafter to show the same tenderness of his seed and of his name as he had now shown of his person, *v.* 21. David had more reason to oblige Saul by an oath that he would not destroy him, yet he insists not on that (if the laws of justice and honour would not bind him, an oath would not), but Saul knew David to be a conscientious man, and would think his interests safe if he could get them secured by his oath. Saul by his disobedience had ruined his own soul, and never took care by repentance to prevent that ruin, and yet is very solicitous that his name might not be destroyed nor his seed cut off. However, *David swore unto him, v.* 22. Though he might be tempted, not only in revenge, but in prudence, to extirpate Saul's family, yet he binds himself not to do it, knowing that God could and would establish the kingdom to him and his, without the use of such bloody methods. This oath he afterwards religiously observed; he supported Mephibosheth, and executed those as traitors that slew Ishbosheth. The hanging up of seven of Saul's posterity, to atone for the destruction of the Gibeonites, was God's appointment, not David's act, and therefore not the violation of this oath.

II. Their parting in peace. 1. Saul, for the present, desisted from the persecution. He went home convinced, but not converted; ashamed of his envy of David, yet retaining in his breast that root of bitterness; vexed that, when at last he had found David, he could not at that time find in his heart to destroy him, as he had designed. God has many ways to tie the hands of persecutors, when he does not turn their hearts. 2. David continued to shift for his own safety. He knew Saul too well to trust him, and therefore *got him up into the hold.* It is dangerous venturing upon the mercy of a reconciled enemy. We read of those who believed in Christ, and yet he *did not commit himself to them because he knew all men.* Those that like David are innocent as doves must thus like him be *wise as serpents.*

CHAPTER 25

We have here some intermission of David's troubles by Saul. Providence favoured him with a breathing time, and yet this chapter gives us instances of the troubles of David. If one vexation seems to be over, we must not be secure; a storm may arise from some other point, as here to David. I. Tidings of the death of Samuel could not but trouble him (*v.* 1). But, II. The abuse he received from Nabal is more largely recorded in this chapter. 1. The character of Nabal (*v.* 2, 3). 2. The humble request sent to him (*v.* 4–9). 3. His churlish answer (*v.* 10–12). 4. David's angry resentment of it (*v.* 13, 21, 22). 5. Abigail's prudent care to prevent the mischief it was likely to bring upon her family (*v.* 14–20). 6. Her address to David to pacify him (*v.* 23–31). 7. David's favourable reception of her (*v.* 32–35). 8. The death of Nabal (*v.* 36–38). 9. Abigail's marriage to David (*v.* 39–44).

Verse 1

We have here a short account of Samuel's death and burial. 1. Though he was a great man, and one that was admirably well qualified for public service, yet he spent the latter end of his days in retirement and obscurity, not because he was superannuated (for he knew how to preside in a college of the prophets, *ch.* 19:20), but because Israel had rejected him, for which God thus justly chastised them, and because his desire was to be quiet and to enjoy himself and his God in the exercises of devotion now in his advanced years, and in this desire God graciously indulged him. Let old people be willing to rest themselves, though it look like burying themselves alive. 2. Though he was a firm friend to David, for which Saul hated him, as also for dealing plainly with him, yet he died in peace even in the worst of the days of the tyranny of Saul, who, he sometimes feared, would kill him, *ch.* 16:2. Though Saul loved him not, yet he feared him, as Herod did John, and feared the people, for all knew him to be a prophet. Thus is Saul restrained from hurting him. 3. All Israel lamented him; and they had reason, for they had all a loss in him.

His personal merits commanded this honour to be done him at his death. His former services to the public, when he judged Israel, made this respect to his name and memory a just debt; it would have been very ungrateful to have withheld it. The sons of the prophets had lost the founder and president of their college, and whatever weakened them was a public loss. But that was not all: Samuel was a constant intercessor for Israel, prayed daily for them, *ch.* 12:23. If he go, they part with the best friend they have. The loss is the more grievous at this juncture when Saul has grown so outrageous and David is driven from his country; never more need of Samuel than now, yet now he is removed. We will hope that the Israelites lamented Samuel's death the more bitterly because they remembered against themselves their own sin and folly in rejecting him and desiring a king. Note, (1.) Those have hard hearts who can bury their faithful ministers with dry eyes, who are not sensible of the loss of those who have prayed for them and taught them the way of the Lord. (2.) When God's providence removes our relations and friends from us we ought to be humbled for our misconduct towards them while they were with us. 4. They buried him, not in the school of the prophets at Naioth, but in his own house (or perhaps in the garden pertaining to it) at Ramah, where he was born. 5. David, thereupon, went down to the wilderness of Paran, retiring perhaps to mourn the more solemnly for the death of Samuel. Or, rather, because now that he had lost so good a friend, who was (and he hoped would be) a great support to him, he apprehended his danger to be greater than ever, and therefore withdrew to a wilderness, out of the limits of the land of Israel; and now it was that he *dwelt in the tents of Kedar,* Ps. 120:5. In some parts of this wilderness of Paran Israel wandered when they came out of Egypt. The place would bring to mind God's care concerning them, and David might improve that for his own encouragement, now in his wilderness-state.

Verses 2–11

Here begins the story of Nabal.

I. A short account of him, who and what he was (*v.* 2, 3), a man wee should never have heard of if there had not happened some communication between him and David. Observe, 1. His name: *Nabal — a fool;* so it signifies. It was a wonder that his parents would give him that name and an ill omen of what proved to be this character. Yet indeed we all of us deserve to be so called when we come into the world, for *man is born like the wild ass's colt* and *foolishness is bound up in our hearts.* 2. His family: He was of the house of Caleb, but was indeed of another spirit. He inherited Caleb's estate; for Maon and Carmel lay near Hebron, which was given to Caleb (Jos. 15:54, 55; 14:14), but he was far from inheriting his virtues. He was a disgrace to his family, and then it was no honour to him. *Degeneranti genus opprobrium — A Good extraction is a reproach to him who degenerates from it.* The Septuagint, and some other ancient versions, read it appellatively, not, He was a Calebite, but He was a dogged man, of a currish disposition, surly and snappish, and always snarling. He was *anthrōpos kynikos — a man that was a cynic.* 3. His wealth: He was very great, that is, very rich (for riches make men look great in the eye of the world), otherwise, to one that takes his measures aright, he really looked very mean. Riches are common blessings, which God often gives to Nabals, to whom he gives neither wisdom nor grace. 4. His wife — Abigail, a woman of great understanding. Her name signifies, *the joy of her father;* yet he could not promise himself much joy of her when he married her to such a husband, enquiring more after his wealth than after his wisdom. Many a child is thrown away upon a great heap of the dirt of worldly wealth, married to that, and to nothing else that is desirable. Wisdom is good with an inheritance, but an inheritance is good for little without wisdom. Many an Abigail is tied to a Nabal; and if it be so, be her understanding, like Abigail's, ever so great, it will be little enough for her exercises. 5. His character. He had no sense either of honour or honesty; not of honour, for he was churlish, cross, and ill-humoured; not of honesty, for he was evil in his doings, hard and oppressive, and a man that cared not what fraud and violence he used in getting and saving, so he could but get and save. This is the character given of Nabal by him who knows what every man is.

II. David's humble request to him, that he would send him some victuals for himself and his men.

1. David, it seems, was in such distress that he would be glad to be beholden to him, and did in effect come a begging to his door. What little reason have we to value the wealth of this world when so great a churl as Nabal abounds and so great a saint as David suffers want! Once before we had David begging his bread, but then it was of Ahimelech the high priest, to whom one would not grudge to stoop. But to send a begging to Napal was what such a spirit as David had could not admit without some reluctancy; yet, if Providence bring him to these straits, he will not say that to beg he is ashamed. Yet see Ps. 37:25.

2. He chose a good time to send to Nabal, when he had many hands employed about him in shearing his sheep, for whom he was to make a plentiful entertainment, so that good cheer was stirring. Had he sent at another time, Nabal would have pretended he had nothing to spare, but now he could not have that excuse. It was usual to make feasts at their sheep-shearings, as appears by Absalom's feast on that occasion (2 Sa. 13:24), for wool was one of the staple commodities of Canaan.

3. David ordered his men to deliver their message to him with a great deal of courtesy and respect: *"Go to Nabal, and greet him in my name.* Tell him I sent you to present my service to him, and to enquire how he does and his family," *v.* 5. He puts words in their mouths (*v.* 6): *Thus shall you say to him that liveth;* our translators add, *in prosperity,* as if those live indeed that live as Nabal did, with abundance of the wealth of this world about them; whereas, in truth, those that *live in pleasure are dead while they live,* 1 Tim. *v.* 6. This was, methinks too high a compliment to pass upon Nabal, to call him *the man that liveth.* David knew better things, that in God's favour is life, not in the world's smiles; and by the rough answer he was well enough served, for this too smooth address to such a muckworm. Yet his good wishes were very commendable. *"Peace be to thee,* all good both to soul and body. *Peace be to thy house and to all that thou hast."* Tell him I am a hearty well-wisher to his health and prosperity. He bids them call him his *son David* (*v.* 8), intimating that, for his age and estate, David honoured him as a father, and therefore hoped to receive some fatherly kindness from him.

4. He pleaded the kindness which Nabal's shepherds had received from David and his men; and one good turn requires another. He appeals to Nabal's own servants, and shows that when David's soldiers were quartered among Nabal's shepherds, (1.) They did not hurt them themselves, did them no injury, gave them no disturbance, were not a terror to them, nor took any of the lambs out of the flock. Yet, considering the character of David's men, men in distress, and debt, and discontented, and the scarcity of provisions in his camp, it was not without a great deal of care and good management that they were kept from plundering. (2.) They protected them from being hurt by others. David himself does but *intimate* this, for he would not boast of his good offices: *Neither was there aught missing to them, v.* 7. But Nabal's servants, to whom he appealed, went further (*v.* 16): *They were a wall unto us, both by night and day.* David's soldiers were a guard to Nabal's shepherds when the bands of the *Philistines robbed the threshing-floors* (*ch.* 23:1) and would have robbed the sheepfolds. From those plunderers Nabal's flocks were protected by David's care, and therefore he says, *Let us find favour in thy eyes.* Those that have shown kindness may justly expect to receive kindness.

5. He was very modest in his request. Though David was anointed king, he insisted not upon royal dainties, but, "Give whatsoever comes to thy hand, and we will be thankful for it." Beggars must not be choosers. Those that deserved to have been served first will now be glad of what is left. They plead, *We come in a good day,* a festival, when not only the provision is more plentiful, but the heart and hand are usually more open and free than at other times, when much may be spared and yet not be missed. David demands not what he wanted as a debt, either by way of tribute as he was a king, or by way of contribution as he was a general, but asks it as a boon to a friend, that was his humble servant. David's servants delivered their message faithfully and very handsomely, not doubting but to go back well laden with provisions.

III. Nabal's churlish answer to this modest petition, *v.* 10, 11. One could not have imagined it possible that any man should be so very rude and ill-conditioned as Nabal was. David called himself his *son,* and asked bread and a fish, but, instead thereof, Nabal gave him a stone and a scorpion; not only denied him, but abused him. If he had not thought fit to send him any supplies for fear of Ahimelech's fate, who paid dearly for his kindness to David; yet he might have given a civil answer, and made the denial as modest as the request was. But, instead of that, he falls into a passion, as covetous men are apt to do when they are asked for any thing, thinking thus to cover one sin with another, and by abusing the poor to excuse themselves from relieving them. But God will not thus be mocked. 1. He speaks scornfully of David as an insignificant man, not worth taking notice of. The Philistines could say of him, *This is* David *the king of the land,* that *slew his ten thousands* (*ch.* 21:11), yet Nabal his near neighbour, and one of the same tribe, affects not to know him, or not to know him to be a man of any merit or distinction: *Who is David? And who is the son of Jesse?* He could not be ignorant how much the country was obliged to David for his public services, but his narrow soul thinks not of paying any part of that debt, nor so much as of acknowledging it; he speaks of David as an inconsiderable man, obscure, and not to be regarded. Think it not strange if great men and great merits be thus disgraced. 2. He upbraids him with his present distress, and takes occasion from it to represent him as a bad man, that was fitter to be set in the stocks for a vagrant than to have any kindness shown him. How naturally does he speak the churlish clownish language of those that hate to give alms! *There are many servants now-a-days* (as if there had been none such in former days) *that break every man from his master,* suggesting that David was one of them himself ("He might have kept his place with his master Saul, and then he needed not have sent to me for provisions"), and also that he entertained and harboured those that were fugitives like himself. It would make one's blood rise to hear so great and good a man as David thus vilified and reproached by such a base churl as Nabal. *But the vile person will speak villany,* Isa. 32:5–7. If men bring themselves into straits by their own folly, yet they are to be pitied and helped, and not trampled upon and starved. But David was reduced to this distress, not by any fault, no, nor any indiscretion, of his own, but purely by the good services he had done to his country and the honours which his God had put upon him; and yet he was represented as a fugitive and runagate. Let this help us to bear such reproaches and misrepresentations of us with patience and cheerfulness, and make us easy under them, that it has often been the lot of the excellent ones of the earth. Some of the best men that ever the world was blest with were counted as the *off-scouring of all things,* 1 Co. 4:13. 3. He insists much upon the property he had in the provisions of his table, and will by no means admit any body to share in them. "It is my bread and my flesh, yes, and my water too (though *usus communis aquarum — water is every one's property*), and it is prepared for my shearers," priding himself in it that it was all his own; and who denied it? Who offered to dispute his title? But this, he thinks, will justify him in keeping it all to himself, and giving David none; for may he not do what he will with his own? Whereas we mistake if we think we are absolute lords of what we have and may do what we please with it. No, we are but stewards, and must use it as we are directed, remembering it is not our own, but his that entrusted us with it. Riches are *ta allotria* (Lu. 16:12); they are *another's,* and we ought not to talk too much of their being our own.

Verses 12–17

Here is, I. The report made to David of the abuse Nabal had given to his messengers (*v.* 12): *They turned their way.* They showed their displeasure, as became them to do, by breaking off abruptly from such a churl, but prudently governed themselves so well as not to render railing for railing, not to call him as he deserved, much less to take by force what ought of right to have been given them, but came and told David that he might do as he thought fit. Christ's servants, when they are thus abused, must leave it to him to plead his own cause and wait till he appear in it. The servant showed his lord what affronts he had received, but did not return them, Lu. 14:21.

II. David's hasty resolution hereupon. He girded on his sword, and ordered his men to do so too, to the number of 400, *v.* 13. And what he said we are told, *v.* 21, 22. 1. He repented of the kindness he had done to Nabal, and looked upon it as thrown away upon him. He said, *"surely in vain have I kept all that this fellow hath in the wilderness.* I thought to oblige him and make him my friend, but I see it is to no purpose. He has no sense of gratitude, nor is he capable of receiving the impressions of a good turn, else he could not have used me thus. He hath *requited me evil for good."* But, when we are thus requited, we should not repent of the good we have done, nor be backward to do good another time. God is kind to the evil and unthankful, and why may not we? 2. He determined to destroy Nabal and all that belonged to him, *v.* 22. Here David did not act like himself. His resolution was bloody, to cut off all the males of Nabal's house, and spare none, man nor man-child. The ratification of his resolution was passionate: *So, and more also do to God* (he was going to say *to me,* but that would better become Saul's mouth, *ch.* 14:44, than David's, and therefore he decently turns it off) *to the enemies of David. Is this thy voice, O David?* Can the man after God's own heart speak thus unadvisedly with his lips? Has he been so long in the school of affliction, where he should have learned patience, and yet so passionate? Is this he who used to be dumb and deaf when he was reproached (Ps. 38:13), who but the other day spared him who sought his life, and yet now will not spare any thing that belongs to him who has only put an affront upon his messengers? He who at other times used to be calm and considerate is now put into such a heat by a few hard words that nothing will atone for them but the blood of a whole family. Lord, what is man! What are the best of men, when God leaves them to themselves, to try them, that they may know what is in their hearts? From Saul David expected injuries, and against those he was prepared and stood upon his guard, and so kept his temper; but from Nabal he expected kindness, and therefore the affront he gave him was a surprise to him, found him off his guard, and, by a sudden and unexpected attack, put him for the present into disorder. What need have we to pray, *Lord, lead us not into temptation!*

III. The account given of this matter to Abigail by one of the servants, who was more considerate than the rest, *v.* 14. Had this servant spoken to Nabal, and shown him the danger he had exposed himself to by his own rudeness, he would have said, "Servants are now-a-days so saucy, and so apt to prescribe, that there is no enduring them," and, it may be, would have turned him out of doors. But Abigail, being a woman of good understanding, took cognizance of the matter, even from her servant, who, 1. Did David justice in commending him and his men for their civility to Nabal's shepherds, *v.* 15, 16. "The men were very good to us, and, though they were themselves exposed, yet they protected us and were a wall unto us." Those who do that which is good shall, one way or other, have the praise of the same. Nabal's own servant will be a witness for David that he is a man of honour and conscience, whatever Nabal himself says of him. And, 2. He did Nabal no wrong in condemning him for his rudeness to David's messengers: *He railed on them* (*v.* 14), *he flew upon them* (so the word is) with an intolerable rage; "for," say they, "it is his usual practice, *v.* 17. He is such a son of Belial, so very morose and intractable, that a man cannot speak to him but he flies into a passion immediately." Abigail knew it too well herself. 3. He did Abigail and the whole family a kindness in making her sensible what was likely to be the consequence. He knew David so well that he had reason to think he would highly resent the affront, and perhaps had had information of David's orders to his men to march that way; for he is very positive *evil is determined against our master, and all his household,* himself among the rest, would be involved in it. Therefore he desires his mistress to consider what was to be done for their common safety. they could not resist the force David would bring down upon them, nor had they time to send to Saul to protect them; something therefore must be done to pacify David.

Verses 18–31

We have here an account of Abigail's prudent management for the preserving of her husband and family from the destruction that was just coming upon them; and we find that she did her part admirably well and fully answered her character. The passion of fools often makes those breaches in a little time which the wise, with all their wisdom, have much ado to make up again. It is hard to say whether Abigail was more miserable in such a husband or Nabal happy in such a wife. A *virtuous woman is a crown to her husband,* to protect as well as adorn, and will *do him good and not evil.* Wisdom in such a case as this was better than weapons of war. 1. It was her wisdom that what she did she did quickly, and without delay; she made haste, *v.* 18. It was no time to trifle or linger when all was in danger. Those that desire conditions of peace must send when the enemy is yet a great way off, Lu. 14:32. 2. It was her wisdom that what she did she did herself, because, being a woman of great prudence and very happy address, she knew better how to manage it than any servant she had. The virtuous woman will herself *look well to the ways of her household,* and not devolve this duty wholly upon others.

Abigail must endeavour to atone for Nabal's faults. Now he had been in two ways rude to David's messengers, and in them to David: He had denied them the provisions they asked for, and he had given them very provoking language. Now,

I. By a most generous present, Abigail atones for his denial of their request. If Nabal had given them what came next to hand, they would have gone away thankful; but Abigail prepares the very best the house afforded and abundance of it (*v.* 18), according to the usual entertainments of those times, not only *bread* and *flesh,* but *raisins* and *figs,* which were their dried sweet-meats. Nabal grudged them *water,* but she took *two bottles (casks* or *rundlets) of wine,* loaded her asses with these provisions, and sent them before; for *a gift pacifieth anger,* Prov. 21:14. Jacob thus pacified Esau. When the *instruments of the churl are evil, the liberal devises liberal things,* and loses nothing by it; for by *liberal things shall he stand,* Isa. 32:7, 8. Abigail not only lawfully, but laudably, disposed of all these goods of her husband's without his knowledge (even when she had reason to think that if he had known what she did he would not have consented to it), because it was not to gratify her own pride or vanity, but for the necessary defence of him and his family. which otherwise would have been inevitably ruined. Husbands and wives, for their common good and benefit, have a joint-interest in their worldly possessions; but if either waste, or unduly spend in any way, it is a robbing of the other.

II. By a most obliging demeanour, and charming speech, she atones for the abusive language which Nabal had given them. She met David upon the march, big with resentment, and meditating the destruction of Nabal (*v.* 20); but with all possible expressions of complaisance and respect she humbly begs his favour, and solicits him to pass by the offence. Her demeanour was very submissive: *She bowed herself to the ground before David* (*v.* 23) *and fell at his feet, v.* 24. Yielding pacifies great offences. She put herself into the place and posture of a penitent and of a petitioner, and was not ashamed to do it, when it was for the good of her house, in the sight both of her own servants and of David's soldiers. She humbly begs of David that he will give her the hearing: *Let thy handmaid speak in thy audience.* But she needed not thus to bespeak his attention and patience; what she said was sufficient to command it, for certainly nothing could be more fine nor more moving. No topic of argument is left untouched; every thing is well placed and well expressed, most pertinently and pathetically urged, and improved to the best advantage, with such a force of natural rhetoric as cannot easily be paralleled.

1. She speaks to him all along with the deference and respect due to so great and good a man, calls him *My lord,* over and over, to expiate her husband's crime in saying, "Who is David?" She does not upbraid him with the heat of his passion, though he deserved to be reproved for it; nor does she tell him how ill it became his character; but endeavours to soften him and bring him to a better temper, not doubting but that then his own conscience would upbraid him with it.

2. She takes the blame of the ill-treatment of his messengers upon herself: *"Upon me, my lord, upon me, let this iniquity be, v.* 24. If thou wilt be angry, be angry with me, rather than with my poor husband, and look upon it *as the trespass of thy handmaid," v.* 28. Sordid spirits care not how much others suffer for their faults, while generous spirits can be content to suffer for the faults of others. Abigail here discovered the sincerity and strength of her conjugal affection and concern for her family: whatever Nabal was, he was her husband.

3. She excuses her husband's fault by imputing it to his natural weakness and want of understanding (*v.* 25): *"Let not my lord* take notice of his rudeness and ill manners, for it is like him; it is not the first time that he has behaved so churlishly; he must be borne with, for it is for want of wit: *Nabal is his name"* (which signifies a *fool*), *"and folly is with him.* It was owing to his folly, not his malice. He is simple, but not spiteful. Forgive him, for he knows not what he does." What she said was too true, and she said it to excuse his fault and prevent his ruin, else she would not have done well to give such a bad character as this of her own husband, whom she ought to make the best of, and not to speak ill of.

4. She pleads her own ignorance of the matter: *"I saw not the young men,* else they should have had a better answer, and should not have gone without their errand," intimating hereby that though her husband was foolish, and unfit to manage his affairs himself, yet he had so much wisdom as to be ruled by her and take her advice.

5. She takes it for granted that she has gained her point already, perhaps perceiving, by David's countenance, that he began to change his mind (*v.* 26): *Seeing the Lord hath withholden thee.* She depends not upon her own reasonings, but God's grace, to mollify him, and doubts not but that grace would work powerfully upon him; and then, *"Let all thy enemies be as Nabal,* that is, if thou forbear to avenge thyself, no doubt God will avenge thee on him, as he will on all thy other enemies." Or it intimates that it was below him to take vengeance on so weak and impotent an enemy as Nabal was, who, as he would do him no kindness, so he could do him no hurt, for he needed to wish no more concerning his enemies than that they might be as unable to resist him as Nabal was. Perhaps she refers to his sparing Saul, when, but the other day, he had him at his mercy. "Didst thou forbear to avenge thyself on that lion that would devour thee, and wilt thou shed the blood of this dog that can but bark at thee?" The very mentioning of what he was about to do, to shed blood and to avenge himself, was enough to work upon such a tender gracious spirit as David had; and it should seem, by his replay (*v.* 33), that it affected him.

6. She makes a tender of the present she had brought, but speaks of it as unworthy of David's acceptance, and therefore desires it may be given to the *young men that followed him* (*v.* 27), and particularly to those ten that were his messengers to Nabal, and whom he had treated so rudely.

7. She applauds David for the good services he had done against the common enemies of his country, the glory of which great achievements, she hoped, he would not stain by any personal revenge: *"My lord fighteth the battles of the Lord* against the Philistines, and therefore he will leave it to God to fight his battles against those that affront him, *v.* 28. *Evil has not been found in thee all thy days.* Thou never yet didst wrong to any of thy countrymen (though persecuted as a traitor), and therefore thou wilt not begin now, nor do a thing which Saul will improve for the justifying of his malice against thee."

8. She foretels the glorious issue of his present troubles. "It is true *a man pursues thee* and *seeks thy life"* (she names not Saul, out of respect to his present character as king), "but thou needest not look with so sharp and jealous an eye upon every one that affronts thee;" for all these storms that now ruffle thee will be blown over shortly. She speaks it with assurance, (1.) That God would keep him safe: *The soul of my lord shall be bound in the bundle of life with the Lord thy God,* that is, God shall *hold thy soul in life* (as the expression is, Ps. 66:9) as we hold those things which are bundled up or which are precious to us, Ps. 116:15. *Thy soul shall be treasured up in the treasure of lives* (so the Chaldee), under lock and key as our treasure is. "Thou shalt abide under the special protection of the divine providence." The *bundle of life is with the Lord our God,* for in his hand our breath is, and our times. Those are safe, and may be easy, that have him for their protec-

tor. The Jews understand this not only of the *life that now is,* but of that *which is to come,* even the happiness of separate souls, and therefore use it commonly as an inscription on their gravestones. "Here we have laid the body, but trust that *the soul is bound up in the bundle of life, with the Lord our God.*" There it is safe, while the dust of the body is scattered. (2.) That God would make him victorious over his enemies. Their souls he shall *sling out, v.* 29. The stone is bound up in the sling, but it is in order to be thrown out again; so the souls of the godly shall be bundled as corn for the barn, but the souls of the wicked as tares for the fire. (3.) That God would settle him in wealth and power: *"The Lord will certainly make my lord a sure house,* and no enemy thou hast can hinder it; therefore *forgive this trespass,"* that is, "show mercy, as thou hopest to find mercy. God will make thee great, and it is the glory of great men to pass by offences."

9. She desires him to consider how much more comfortable it would be to him in the reflection to have forgiven this affront than to have revenged it, *v.* 30, 31. She reserves this argument for the last, as a very powerful one with so good a man, that the less he indulged his passion the more he consulted his peace and the repose of his own conscience, which every wise man will be tender of. (1.) She cannot but think that if he should avenge himself it would afterwards be a grief and an offence of heart to him, Many have done that in a heat which they have a thousand times wished undone again. The sweetness of revenge is soon turned into bitterness. (2.) She is confident that if he pass by the offence it will afterwards by no grief to him; but, on the contrary, it would yield him unspeakable satisfaction that his wisdom and grace had got the better of his passion. Note, When we are tempted to sin we should consider how it will appear in the reflection. Let us never do any thing for which our own consciences will afterwards have occasion to upbraid us, and which we shall look back upon with regret: *My heart shall not reproach me.*

10. She recommends herself to his favour: *When the Lord shall have dealt well with my lord, then remember thy handmaid,* as one that kept thee from doing that which would have disgraced thy honour, disquieted thy conscience, and made a blot in thy history. We have reason to remember those with respect and gratitude who have been instrumental to keep us from sin.

Verses 32–35

As an ear-ring of gold, and an ornament of fine gold, so is a wise reprover upon an obedient ear, Prov. 25:12. Abigail was a wise reprover of David's passion, and he gave an obedient ear to the reproof, according to his own principle (Ps. 141:5): *Let the righteous smite me, it shall be a kindness.* Never was such an admonition either better given or better taken.

I. David gives God thanks for sending him this happy check to a sinful way (*v.* 32): *Blessed be the Lord God of Israel, who sent thee this day to meet me.* Note, 1. God is to be acknowledged in all the kindnesses that our friends do us either for soul or body. Whoever meet us with counsel, direction, comfort, caution, or seasonable reproof, we must see God sending them. 2. We ought to be very thankful for those happy providences which are means of preventing sin.

II. He gives Abigail thanks for interposing so opportunely between him and the mischief he was about to do: *Blessed be thy advice, and blessed be thou, v.* 33. Most people think it enough if they take a reproof patiently, but we meet with few that will take it thankfully and will commend those that give it to them and accept it as a favour. Abigail did not rejoice more that she had been instrumental to save her husband and family from death than David did that Abigail had been instrumental to save him and his men from sin.

III. He seems very apprehensive of the great danger he was in, which magnified the mercy of his deliverance. 1. He speaks of the sin as very great. He was coming to shed blood, a sin of which when in his right mind he had a great horror, witness his prayer, *Deliver me from blood-guiltiness.* He was coming to *avenge himself with his own hand,* and that would be stepping into the throne of God, who has said, *Vengeance is mine; I will repay.* The more heinous any sin is the greater mercy it is to be kept from it. He seems to aggravate the evil of his design with this, that it would have been an injury to so wise and good a woman as Abigail: God has *kept me back from hurting thee, v.* 34. Or perhaps, at the first sight of Abigail, he was conscious of a thought to do her a mischief for offering to oppose him, and therefore reckons it a great mercy that God gave him patience to hear her speak. 2. He speaks of the danger of his falling into it as very imminent: *"Except thou hadst hasted,* the bloody execution had been done." The nearer we were to the commission of sin the greater was the mercy of a seasonable restraint — *Almost gone* (Ps. 73:2) and yet upheld.

IV. He dismissed her with an answer of peace, *v.* 35. He does, in effect, own himself overcome by her eloquence: *"I have hearkened to thy voice,* and will not prosecute the intended revenge, for I *have accepted thy person,* am well pleased with thee and what thou hast said." Note, 1. Wise and good men will hear reason, and let that rule them, though it come from those that are every way their inferiors, and though their passions are up and their spirits provoked. 2. Oaths cannot, bind us to that which is sinful. David had solemnly vowed the death of Nabal. He did evil to make such a vow, but he would have done worse if he had performed it. 3. A wise and faithful reproof is often better taken, and speeds better, than we expected, such is the hold God has of men's consciences. See Prov. 28:23.

Verses 36–44

We are now to attend Nabal's funeral and Abigail's wedding.

I. Nabal's funeral. The apostle speaks of some that were *twice dead,* Jude 12. We have hare Nabal *thrice* dead, though but just now wonderfully rescued from the sword of David and delivered from so great a death; for the preservations of wicked men are but reservations for some further sorer strokes of divine wrath. Here is,

1. *Nabal dead drunk, v.* 36. Abigail came home, and, it should seem, he had so many people and so much plenty about him that he neither missed her nor the provisions she took to David; but she found him in the midst of his jollity, little thinking how near he was to ruin by one whom he had foolishly made his enemy. Sinners are often most secure when they are most in danger and destruction is at the door. Observe, (1.) How extravagant he was in the entertainment of his company: *He held a feast like the feast of a king,* so magnificent and abundant, though his guests were but his sheep-shearers. This abundance might have been allowed if he had considered what God gave him his estate for, not to look great with, but to do good with. It is very common for those that are most niggardly in any act of piety or charity to be most profuse in gratifying a vain humour or a base lust. A mite is grudged to God and his poor; but, to make a *fair show in the flesh, gold is lavished out of the bag.* If Nabal had not answered to his name, he would never have been thus secure and jovial, till he had enquired whether he was safe from David's resentments; but (as bishop Hall observes) thus foolish are carnal men, that give themselves over to their pleasures before they have taken any care to make their peace with God. (2.) How sottish he was in the indulgence of his own brutish appetite: *He was very drunk,* a sign he was *Nabal, a fool,* that could not use his plenty without abusing it, could not be pleasant with his friends without making a beast of himself. There is not a surer sign that a man has but little wisdom, nor a surer way to ruin the little he has, than drinking to excess. Nabal, that never thought he could bestow too little in charity, never thought he could bestow too much in luxury. Abigail, finding him in this condition (and probably those about him little better, when the master of the feast set them so bad an example), had enough to do to set the disordered house to-rights a little, but told Nabal nothing of what she had done with reference to David, nothing of his folly in provoking David, of his danger or of his deliverance, for, being drunk, he was as incapable to hear reason as he was to speak it. To give good advice to those that are in drink is to *cast pearls before swine;* it is better to stay till they are sober.

2. Nabal again dead with melancholy, *v.* 37. Next morning, when he had come to himself a little, his wife told him how near to destruction he had brought himself and his family by his own rudeness, and with what difficulty she had interposed to prevent it; and, upon this, *his heart died within him and he became as a stone.* Some suggest that the expense of the satisfaction made to David, by the present Abigail brought him, broke his heart: it seems rather that the apprehension he now had of the danger he had narrowly escaped put him into a consternation, and seized his spirits so that he could not recover it. He grew sullen, and said little, ashamed of his own folly, put out of countenance by his wife's wisdom. How is he changed! His heart over-night merry with wine, next morning heavy as a stone; so deceitful are carnal pleasures, so transient the laughter of the fool. *The end of that mirth is heaviness.* Drunkards are sometimes sad when they reflect upon their own folly. Joy in God makes the heart always light. Abigail could never, by her wise reasonings, bring Nabal to repentance; but now, by her faithful reproof, she brings him to despair.

3. Nabal, at last, dead indeed: *About ten days after,* when he had been kept so long under this pressure and pain, *the Lord smote him that he died* (*v.* 38), and, it should seem, he never held up his head; it is just with God (says bishop Hall) that those who live without grace should die without comfort, nor can we expect better while we go on in our sins. Here is no lamentation made for Nabal. He departed without being lamented. Every one wished that the country might never sustain a greater loss. *David,* when he heard the news of his death, *gave God thanks* for it, *v.* 39. He blessed God, (1.) That he had kept him from killing him: *Blessed be the lord, who hath kept his servant from evil.* He rejoices that Nabal died a natural death and not by his hand. We should take all occasions to mention and magnify God's goodness to us in keeping us from sin. (2.) That he had taken the work into his own hands, and had vindicated David's honour, and not suffered him to go unpunished who had been abusive to him; hereby his interest would be confirmed, and all would stand in awe of him, as one for whom God fought. (3.) That he had thereby encouraged him and all others to commit their cause to God, when they are in any way injured, with an assurance that, in his own time, he will redress their wrongs if they sit still and leave the matter to him.

II. Abigail's wedding. David was so charmed with the beauty of her person, and the uncommon prudence of her conduct and address, that, as soon as was convenient, after he heard she was a widow, he informed her of his attachment to her (*v.* 39), not doubting but that she who approved herself so good a wife to so bad a husband as Nabal would much more make a good wife to him, and having taken notice of her respect to him and her confidence of his coming to the throne. 1. He courted by proxy, his affairs, perhaps, not permitting him to come himself. 2. She received the address with great modesty and humility (*v.* 41), reckoning herself unworthy of the honour, yet having such a respect for him that she would gladly be one of the poorest servants of his family, to wash the feet of the other servants. None so fit to be preferred as those that can thus humble themselves. 3. She agreed to the proposal, went with his messenger, took a retinue with her agreeable to her quality, and *she became his wife, v.* 42. She did not upbraid him with his present distresses, and ask him how he could maintain her, but valued him, (1.) Because she knew he was a very good man. (2.) Because she believed he would, in due time, be a very great man. She married him in faith, not questioning but that, though now he had not a house of his own that he durst bring her to, yet God's promise go him would at length be fulfilled. Thus those who join themselves to Christ must be willing now to suffer with him, believing that hereafter they shall reign with him.

Lastly, On this occasion we have some account of David's wives. 1. One that he had lost before he married Abigail, Michal, Saul's daughter, his first, and the wife of his youth, to whom he would have been constant if she would have been so to him, but Saul had given her to another (*v.* 44), in token of his displeasure against him and disclaiming the relation of a father-in-law to him. 2. Another that he married besides Abigail (*v.* 43), and, as should seem, before her, for she is named first, *ch.* 27:3. David was carried away by the corrupt custom of those times; but from the beginning it was not so, nor is it so now that Messias has come, and the times of reformation, Mt. 19:4, 5. Perhaps Saul's defrauding David of his only rightful wife was the occasion of his running into this irregularity; for, when the knot of conjugal affection is once loosed, it is scarcely ever tied fast again. When David could not keep his first wife he thought that would excuse him if he did not keep to his second. But we deceive ourselves if we think to make others' faults a cloak for our own.

CHAPTER 26

David's troubles from Saul here begin again; and the clouds return after the rain, when one would have hoped the storm had blown over, and the sky had cleared upon that side; but after Saul had owned his fault in persecuting David, and acknowledged David's title to the crown, yet here he revives the persecution, so perfectly lost was he to all sense of honour and virtue. I. The Ziphites informed him where David was (*v.* 1), and thereupon he marched out with a considerable force in quest of him (*v.* 2, 3). II. David gained intelligence of his motions (*v.* 4), and took a view of his camp (*v.* 5). III. He and one of his men ventured into his camp in the night and found him and all his guards fast asleep (*v.* 6, 7). IV. David, though much urged to it by his companions, would not take away Saul's life, but only carried off his spear and his cruse of water (*v.* 8–12). V. He produced these as a further witness for him that he did not design any ill to Saul, and reasoned with him upon his conduct (*v.* 13–20). VI. Saul was hereby convinced of his error, and once more desisted from persecuting David (*v.* 21–25). The story is much like that which we had (*ch.* 24). In both David is delivered out of Saul's hand, and Saul out of David's.

Verses 1–5

Here, 1. Saul gets information of David's movements and acts offensively. The Ziphites came to him and told him where David now was, in the same place where he was when they formerly betrayed him, *ch.* 23:19. Perhaps (though it is not mentioned) Saul had given them intimation, under-hand, that he continued his design against David, and would be glad of their assistance. If not, they were very officious to Saul, aware of what would please him, and very malicious against David, to whom they despaired of ever reconciling themselves, and therefore they stirred up Saul (who needed no such spur) against him, *v.* 1. For aught we know, Saul would have continued in the same good mind that he was in (*ch.* 24:17), and would not have given David this fresh trouble, if the Ziphites had not put him on. See what need we have to pray to God that, since we have so much of the tinner of corruption in our own hearts, the sparks of temptation may be kept far from us, lest, if they come together, we be set on fire of hell. Saul readily caught at the information, and went down with an army of 3000 men to the place where David hid himself, *v.* 2. How soon do unsanctified hearts lose the good impressions which their convictions have made upon them and return with the dog to their vomit!

2. David gets information of Saul's movements and acts defensively. He did not march out to meet and fight him; he sought only his own safety, not Saul's ruin; therefore he *abode in the wilderness* (*v.* 3), putting thereby a great force upon himself, and curbing the bravery of his own spirit by a silent retirement, showing more true valour than he could have done by an irregular resistance. (1.) He had spies who informed him of Saul's descent, *that he had come in very deed* (*v.* 4.); for he would not believe that Saul would deal so basely with him till he had the utmost evidence of it. (2.) He observed with his own eyes how Saul was encamped, *v.* 5. He came towards the place where Saul and his men had pitched their tents, so near as to be able, undiscovered, to take a view of their entrenchments, probably in the dusk of the evening.

Verses 6–12

Here is, I. David's bold adventure into Saul's camp in the night, accompanied only by his kinsman Abishai, the son of Zeruiah. He proposed it to him and to another of his confidants (*v.* 6), but the other either declined it as too dangerous an enterprise, or at least was content that Abishai, who was forward to it, should run the risk of it rather than himself. Whether David was prompted to do this by his own courage, or by an extraordinary impression upon his spirits, or by the oracle, does not appear; but, like Gideon, he ventured through the guards, with a special assurance of the divine protection.

II. The posture he found the camp in *Saul lay sleeping in the trench,* or, as some read it, *in his chariot, and in the midst of his carriages,* with *his spear stuck in the ground* by him, to be ready if his quarters should by beaten up (*v.* 7); and all the soldiers, even those that were appointed to stand sentinel, were *fast asleep, v.* 12. Thus were their eyes closed and their hands bound, *for a deep sleep from the Lord had fallen upon them;* something extraordinary there was in it that they should all be asleep together, and so fast asleep that David and Abishai walked and talked among them, and yet none of them stirred. Sleep, when God gives it to his beloved, is their rest and refreshment; but he can, when he pleases, make it to his enemies their imprisonment. Thus are the *stout-hearted spoiled; they have slept their sleep, and none of the men of might have found their hands, at thy rebuke, O God of Jacob!* Ps. 76:5, 6. *It was a deep sleep from the Lord,* who has the command of the powers of nature, and makes them to serve his purposes as he pleases. Whom God will disable, or destroy, he binds up with *a spirit of slumber,* Rom. 11:8. How helpless do Saul and all his forces lie, all, in effect, disarmed and chained! and yet nothing is done to them; they are only rocked asleep. How easily can God weaken the strongest, befool the wisest, and baffle the most watchful! Let all his friends therefore trust him and all his enemies fear him.

III. Abishai's request to David for a commission to dispatch Saul with the spear that stuck at his bolster, which (now that he lay so fair) he undertook to do at one blow, *v.* 8. He would not urge David to kill him himself, because he had declined doing this before when he had a similar opportunity; but he begged earnestly that David would give him leave to do it, pleading that he was his enemy, not only cruel and implacable, but false and perfidious, whom no reason would rule nor kindness work upon, and that *God had now delivered him into his hand,* and did in effect bid him strike. The last advantage he had of this kind was indeed but accidental, when Saul happened to be in the cave with him at the same time. But in this there was something extraordinary; the deep sleep that had fallen on Saul and all his guards was manifestly from the Lord, so that it was a special providence which gave him this opportunity; he ought not therefore to let it slip.

IV. David's generous refusal to suffer any harm to be done to Saul, and in it a resolute adherence to his principles of loyalty, *v.* 9. David charged Abishai not to destroy him, would not only not do it himself, but not permit another to do it. And he gave two reasons for it: — 1. It would be a sinful affront to God's ordinance. Saul was the Lord's anointed, king of Israel by the special appointment and nomination of the God of Israel, the power that was, and to resist him was to *resist the ordinance of God,* Rom. 13:2. No man could do it and be guiltless. The thing he feared was guilt and his concern respected his innocence more than his safety. 2. It would be a sinful anticipation of God's providence. God had sufficiently shown him, in Nabal's case, that, if he left it to him to avenge him, he would do it in due time. Encouraged therefore by his experience in that instance, he resolves to wait till God shall think fit to avenge him on Saul, and he will by no means *avenge himself* (*v.* 10): *"The Lord shall smite him,* as he did Nabal, with some sudden stroke, or he shall *die in battle* (as it proved he did soon after), or, if not, *his day shall come to die* a natural death, and I will contentedly wait till then, rather than force my way to the promised crown by any indirect methods." The temptation indeed was very strong; but, if he should yield, he would sin against God, and therefore he will resist the temptation with the utmost resolution (*v.* 11): *"The Lord forbid that I should stretch forth my hand against the Lord's anointed;* no, I will never do it, nor suffer it to be done." Thus bravely does he prefer his conscience to his interest and trusts God with the issue.

V. The improvement he made of this opportunity for the further evidence of his own integrity. He and Abishai carried away the spear and cruse of water which Saul had by his bed-side (*v.* 12), and, which was very strange, none of all the guards were aware of it. If a physician had given them the strongest opiate or stupifying dose, they could not have been faster locked up with sleep. Saul's spear which he had by him for defence, and his cup of water which he had for his refreshment, were both stolen from him while he slept. Thus do we lose our strength and our comfort when we are careless, and secure, and off our watch.

Verses 13–20

David having got safely from Saul's camp himself, and having brought with him proofs sufficient that he had been there, posts himself conveniently, so that they might hear him and yet not reach him (*v.* 13), and then begins to reason with them upon what had passed.

I. He reasons ironically with Abner, and keenly banters him. David knew well that it was from the mighty power of God that Abner and the rest of the guards were cast into so deep a sleep, and that God's immediate hand was in it; but he reproaches Abner as unworthy to be captain of the lifeguards, since he could sleep when the king his master lay so much exposed. By this it appears that the hand of God locked them up in this deep sleep that, as soon as ever David had got out of danger, a very little thing awakened them, even David's voice at a great distance roused them, *v.* 14. Abner got up (we may suppose it early in a summer's morning) and enquired who called, and disturbed the king's repose. "It is I," says David, and then he upbraids him with his sleeping when he should have been upon his guard. Perhaps Abner, looking upon David as a despicable enemy and one that there was no danger from, had neglected to set a watch; however, he himself ought to have been more wakeful. David, to put him into confusion, told him, 1. That he had lost his honour (*v.* 15): *"Art not thou a man?* (so the word is), a man in office, that art bound, by the duty of thy place, to inspect the soldiery? Art not thou in reputation for a valiant man? So thou wouldst be esteemed, a man of such courage and conduct that there is none like thee; but now thou art shamed for ever. Thou a general! Thou, a sluggard!" 2. That he deserved to lose his head (*v.* 16): *"You are all worthy to die,* by martial law, for being off your guard, when you had the king himself asleep in the midst of you. *Ecce signum — Behold this token.* See where the king's spear is, in the hand of him whom the king himself is pleased to count his enemy. Those that took away this might as easily and safely have taken away his life. Now see who are the king's best friends, you that neglected him and left him exposed or I that protected him when he was exposed. You pursue me as worthy to die, and irritate Saul against me; but who is worthy to die now?" Note, Sometimes those that unjustly condemn others are justly left to fall into condemnation themselves.

II. He reasons seriously and affectionately with Saul. By this time he was so well awake as to hear what was said, and to discern who said it (*v.* 17): *Is this thy voice, my son David?* In the same manner he had expressed his relentings, *ch.* 24:16. He had given his wife to another and yet calls him *son,* thirsted after his blood and yet is glad to hear his voice. Those are bad indeed that have never any convictions of good, nor ever sincerely utter good expressions. And now David has as fair an opportunity of reaching Saul's conscience as he had just now of taking away his life. This he lays hold on, though not of that, and enters into a close argument with him, concerning the trouble he still continued to give him, endeavouring to persuade him to let fall the prosecution and be reconciled.

1. He complains of the very melancholy condition he was brought into by the enmity of Saul against him. Two things he laments: — (1.) That he was driven from his master and from his business: *"My lord pursues after his servant, v.* 18. How gladly would I serve thee as formerly if my service might be accepted! but, instead of being owned as a servant, I am pursued as a rebel, and my lord is my enemy, and he whom I would follow with respect compels me to flee from him." (2.) That he was driven from his God and from his religion; and this was a much greater grievance than the former (*v.* 19): "They have *driven me out from the inheritance of the Lord,* have made Canaan too hot for me, at least the inhabited parts of it, have forced me into the deserts and mountains, and will, ere long, oblige me entirely to quit the country." And that which troubled him was not so much that he was driven out from his own inheritance as that he was driven out from the *inheritance of the Lord,* the holy land. It should be more comfortable to us to think of God's title to our estates and his interest in them then of our own, and that with them we may honour him then that with them we may maintain ourselves. Nor was it so much his trouble that he was constrained to live among strangers as that he was constrained to live among the worshippers of strange gods and was thereby thrust into temptation to join with them in their idolatrous worship. His enemies did, in effect, send him to *go and serve other gods,* and perhaps he had heard that some of them had spoken to that purport of him. Those that forbid our attendance on God's ordinances do what in them lies to estrange us from God and to make

us heathens. If David had not been a man of extraordinary grace, and firmness to his religion, the ill usage he met with from his own prince and people, who were Israelites and worshippers of the true God, would have prejudiced him against the religion they professed and have driven him to communicate with idolaters. "If these be Israelites," he might have said, "let me live and die with Philistines;" and no thanks to them that their conduct had not that effect. We are to reckon that the greatest injury that can be done us which exposes us to sin. Of those who thus led David into temptation he here says, *Cursed be they before the Lord.* Those fall under a curse that thrust out those whom God receives, and send those to the devil who are dear to God.

2. He insists upon his own innocency: *What have I done or what evil is in my hand? v.* 18. He had the testimony of his conscience for him that he had never done nor ever designed any mischief to the person, honour, or government, of his prince, nor to any of the interests of his country. He had lately had Saul's own testimony concerning him (*ch.* 24:17): *Thou art more righteous than I.* It was very unreasonable and wicked for Saul to pursue him as a criminal, when he could not charge him with any crime.

3. He endeavours to convince Saul that his pursuit of him is not only wrong, but mean, and much below him: "*The king of Israel,* whose dignity is great, and who has so much other work to do, *has come out to seek a flea, as when one doth hunt a partridge in the mountains," v.* 20 — a poor game for the king of Israel to pursue. He compares himself to a partridge, a vert innocent harmless bird, which, when attempts are made upon its life, flies if it can, but makes no resistance. And would Saul bring the flower of his army into the field only to hunt one poor partridge? What a disparagement was this to his honour! What a stain would it be on his memory to trample upon so weak and patient as well as so innocent an enemy! James *v.* 6, *You have killed the just, and he doth not resist you.*

4. He desires that the core of the controversy may be searched into and some proper method taken to bring it to an end, *v.* 19. Saul himself could not say that justice put him on thus to persecute David, or that he was obliged to do it for the public safety. David was not willing to say (though it was very true) that Saul's own envy and malice put him on to do it; and therefore he concludes it must be attributed either to the righteous judgment of God or to the unrighteous designs of evil men. Now, (1.) "*If the Lord have stirred thee up against me,* either in displeasure to me (taking this way to punish me for my sins against him, though, as to thee, I am guiltless) or in displeasure to thee, if it be the effect of that evil spirit from the Lord which troubles thee, *let him accept an offering* from us both — let us join in making our peace with God, reconciling ourselves to him, which may be done, by sacrifice; and then I hope the sin will be pardoned, whatever it is, and the trouble, which is so great a vexation both to thee and me, will come to an end." See the right method of peace-making; let us first make God our friend by Christ the great Sacrifice, and then all other enmities shall be slain, Eph. 2:16; Prov. 16:7. But, (2.) "If thou art incited to it by wicked men, that incense thee against me, *cursed be they before the Lord,*" that is, they are very wicked people, and it is fit that they should be abandoned as such, and excluded from the king's court and councils. He decently lays the blame upon the evil counsellors who advised the king to that which was dishonourable and dishonest, and insists upon it that they be removed from about him and forbidden his presence, as men cursed before the Lord, and then he hoped he should gain his petition, which is (*v.* 20), "*Let not my blood fall to the earth,* as thou threatenest, for it is *before the face of the Lord,* who will take cognizance of the wrong and avenge it." Thus pathetically does David plead with Saul for his life, and, in order to that, for his favourable opinion of him.

Verses 21–25

Here is, I. Saul's penitent confession of his fault and folly in persecuting David and his promise to do so no more. This second instance of David's respect to him wrought more upon him than the former, and extorted from him better acknowledgements, *v.* 21. 1. He owns himself melted and quite overcome by David's kindness to him: "*My soul was precious in thy eyes this day,* which, I thought,

had been odious!" 2. He acknowledges he has done very wrong to persecute him, that he has therein acted against God's law (*I have sinned*), and against his own interest (*I have played the fool*), in pursuing him as an enemy who would have been one of his best friends, if he could but have thought so. "Herein (says he) I have *erred exceedingly,* and wronged both thee and myself." Note, Those that sin play the fool and err exceedingly, those especially that hate and persecute God's people, Job 19:28. 3. He invites him to court again: *Return, my son David.* Those that have understanding will see it to be their interest to have those about them that *behave themselves wisely,* as David did, and have God with them. 4. He promises him that he will not persecute him as he has done, but protect him: *I will no more do thee harm.* We have reason to think, according to the mind he was now in, that he meant as he said, and yet neither his confession nor his promise of amendment came from a principle of true repentance.

II. David's improvement of Saul's convictions and confessions and the evidence he had to produce of his own sincerity. He desired that one of the footmen might fetch the spear (*v.* 22), and then (*v.* 23), 1. He appeals to God as judge of the controversy: *The Lord render to every man his righteousness.* David, by faith, is sure that he will do it because he infallibly knows the true characters of all persons and actions and is inflexibly just to render to every man according to his work, and, by prayer, he desires he would do it. Herein he does, in effect, pray against Saul, who had dealt unrighteously and unfaithfully with him (*Give them according to their deeds,* Ps. 28:4); but he principally intends it as a prayer for himself, that God would protect him in his righteousness and faithfulness, and also reward him, since Saul so ill requited him. 2. He reminds Saul again of the proof he had now given of his respect to him from a principle of loyalty: *I would not stretch forth my hand against the Lord's anointed,* intimating to Saul that the anointing oil was his protection, for which he was indebted to the Lord and ought to express his gratitude to him (had he been a common person David would not have been so tender of him), perhaps with this further implication, that Saul knew, or had reason to think, David was the Lord's anointed too, and therefore, by the same rule, Saul ought to be as tender of David's life as David had been of his. 3. Not relying much upon Saul's promises, he puts himself under God's protection and begs his favour (*v.* 24): "*Let my life be much set by in the eyes of the Lord,* how light soever thou makest of it." Thus, for his kindness to Saul, he takes God to be his paymaster, which those may with a holy confidence do that *do well and suffer for it.*

III. Saul's prediction of David's advancement. He commends him (*v.* 25): *Blessed be thou, my son David.* So strong was the conviction Saul was now under of David's honesty that he was not ashamed to condemn himself and applaud David, even in the hearing of his own soldiers, who could not but blush to think that they had come out so furiously against a man whom their master, when he meets him, caresses thus. He foretels his victories, and his elevation at last: *Thou shalt do great things.* Note, Those who make conscience of doing that which is truly good may come, by the divine assistance, to do that which is truly great. He adds, "*Thou shalt also still prevail,* more and more," he means against himself, but is loth to speak that out. The princely qualities which appeared in David — his generosity in sparing Saul, his military authority in reprimanding Abner for sleeping, his care of the public good, and the signal tokens of God's presence with him — convinced Saul that he would certainly be advanced to the throne at last, according to the prophecies concerning him.

Lastly, A palliative cure being thus made of the wound, they parted friends. Saul returned to Gibeah *re infectâ — without accomplishing his design,* and ashamed of the expedition he had made; but David could not take his word so far as to return with him. Those that have once been false are not easily trusted another time. Therefore *David went on his way.* And, after this parting, it does not appear that ever Saul and David saw one another again.

CHAPTER 27

David was a man after God's own heart, and yet he had his faults, which are recorded, not for our imitation, but for our admonition; witness the story of this chapter, in which, though, I. We find, to his praise, that he

prudently took care of his own safety and his family's (*v.* 2–4) and valiantly fought Israel's battles against the Canaanites (*v.* 8–9), yet, II. We find, to his dishonour, 1. That he began to despair of his deliverance (*v.* 1). 2. That he deserted his own country, and went to dwell in the land of the Philistines (*v.* 1, 5–7). 3. That he imposed upon Achish with an equivocation, if not a lie, concerning his expedition (*v.* 10–12).

Verses 1–7

Here is, I. The prevalency of David's fear, which was the effect of the weakness of his faith (*v.* 1): *He said to his heart* (so it may be read), in his communings with it concerning his present condition, *I shall now perish one day by the hand of Saul.* He represented to himself the restless rage and malice of Saul (who could not be wrought into a reconciliation) and the treachery of his own countrymen, witness that of the Ziphites, once and again; he looked upon his own forces, and observed how few they were, and that no recruits had come in to him for a great while, nor could he perceive that he got any ground; and hence, in a melancholy mood, he draws this dark conclusion: *I shall one day perish by the hand of Saul.* But, *O thou of little faith! wherefore dost thou doubt?* Was he not anointed to be king? Did not that imply an assurance that he should be preserved to the kingdom? Though he had no reason to trust Saul's promises, had he not all the reason in the world to trust the promises of God? His experience of the particular care Providence took of him ought to have encouraged him. He that has delivered does and will. But unbelief is a sin that easily besets even good men. When *without are fightings, within are fears,* and it is a hard matter to get over them. *Lord, increase our faith!*

II. The resolution he came to hereupon. Now that Saul had, for this time, returned to his place, he determined to take this opportunity of retiring into the Philistines' country. Consulting his own heart only, and not the ephod or the prophet, he concludes, *There is nothing better for me than that I should speedily escape into the land of the Philistines.* Long trials are in danger of tiring the faith and patience even of very good men. Now, 1. Saul was an enemy to himself and his kingdom in driving David to this extremity. He weakened his own interest when he expelled from his service, and forced into the service of his enemies, so great a general as David was, and so brave a regiment as he had the command of. 2. David was no friend to himself in taking this course. God had appointed him to set up his standard *in the land of Judah, ch.* 22:5. There God had wonderfully preserved him, and employed him sometimes for the good of his country; why then should he think of deserting his post? How could he expect the protection of the God of Israel if he went out of the borders of the land of Israel? Could he expect to be safe among the Philistines, out of whose hands he had lately escaped so narrowly by feigning himself mad? Would he receive obligations from those now whom he knew he must not return kindness to when he should come to be king, but be under an obligation to make war upon? Hereby he would gratify his enemies, who bade him go and serve other gods that they might have wherewith to reproach him, and very much weaken the hands of his friends, who would not have wherewith to answer that reproach. See what need we have to pray, *Lord, lead us not into temptation.*

III. The kind reception he had at Gath. Achish bade him welcome, partly out of generosity, being proud of entertaining so brave a man, partly out of policy, hoping to engage him for ever to his service, and that his example would invite many more to desert and come over to him. No doubt he gave David a solemn promise of protection, which he could rely upon when he could not trust Saul's promises. We may blush to think that the word of a Philistine should go further than the word of an Israelite, who, if an Israelite indeed, would be without guile, and that the city of Gath should be a place of refuge for a good man when the cities of Israel refuse him a safe abode. David, 1. Brought his men with him (*v.* 2) that they might guard him, and might themselves be safe where he was, and to recommend himself the more to Achish, who hoped to have service out of him. 2. He brought his family with him, his *wives* and *his household,* so did all *his men, v.* 2, 3. Masters of families ought to take care of those that are committed to them, to protect and provide for those of their own house, and to *dwell with them as men of knowledge.*

IV. Saul's desisting from the further prosecution of him

(*v.* 4): *He sought no more again for him;* this intimates that notwithstanding the professions of repentance he had lately made, if he had had David in his reach, he would have aimed another blow. But, because he dares not come where he is, he resolves to let him alone. Thus many seem to leave their sins, but really their sins leave them; they would persist in them if they could. Saul sought no more for him, contenting himself with his banishment, since he could not have his blood, and hoping, it may be (as he had done, *ch.* 18:25), that he would, some time or other, *fall by the hand of the Philistines;* and, though he would rather have the pleasure of destroying him himself, yet, if they do it, he will be satisfied, so that it be done effectually.

V. David's removal from Gath to Ziklag.

1. David's request for leave to remove was prudent and very modest, *v.* 5. (1.) It was really prudent. David knew what it was to be envied in the court of Saul, and had much more reason to fear in the court of Achish, and therefore declines preferment there, and wishes for a settlement in the country, where he might be private, more within himself, and less in other people's way. In a town of his own he might have the more free exercise of his religion, and keep his men better to it, and not have his righteous soul vexed, as it was at Gath, with the idolatries of the Philistines. (2.) As it was presented to Achish it was very modest. He does not prescribe to him what place he should assign him, only begs it may be in some town in the country, where he pleased (beggars must not be choosers); but he gives this for a reason, "*Why should thy servant dwell in the royal city,* to crowd thee, and disoblige those about thee?" Note, Those that would stand fast must not covet to stand high; and humble souls aim not to dwell in royal cities.

2. The grant which Achish made to him, upon that request, was very generous and kind (*v.* 6, 7): *Achish gave him Ziklag.* Hereby, (1.) Israel recovered their ancient right; for Ziklag was in the lot of the tribe of Judah (Jos. 15:31), and afterwards, out of that lot, was assigned, with some other cities, to Simeon, Jos. 19:5. But either it was never subdued, or the Philistines had, in some struggle with Israel, made themselves masters of it. Perhaps they had got it unjustly, and Achish, being a man of sense and honour, took this occasion to restore it. *The righteous God judgeth righteously.* (2.) David gained a commodious settlement, not only at a distance from Gath, but bordering upon Israel, where he might keep up a correspondence with his own countrymen, and whither they might resort to him at the revolution that was now approaching. Though we do not find that he augmented his forces at all while Saul lived (for, *ch.* 30:10, he had but his *six hundred men*), yet, immediately after Saul's death, that was the rendezvous of his friends. Nay, it should seem, while he kept himself close because of Saul, multitudes resorted to him, at least to assure him of their sincere intentions, 1 Chr. 12:1–22. And this further advantage David gained, that Ziklag was annexed to the crown, at least the royalty of it pertained to the kings of Judah, ever after, *v.* 6. Note, There is nothing lost by humility and modesty, and a willingness to retire. Real advantages follow those that flee from imaginary honours. Here David continued for some days, even *four months,* as it may very well be read (*v.* 7), or some days above four months: the Septuagint reads it, *some months;* so long he waited for the set time of his accession to the throne; for *he that believeth shall not make haste.*

Verses 8–12

Here is an account of David's actions while he was in the land of the Philistines, a fierce attack he made upon some remains of the devoted nations, his success in it, and the representation he gave of it to Achish. 1. We may acquit him of injustice and cruelty in this action because those people whom he cut off were such as heaven had long since doomed to destruction, and he that did it was one whom heaven had ordained to dominion; so that the thing was very fit to be done, and he was very fit to do it. It was not for him that was anointed to fight the Lord's battles to sit still in sloth, however he might think fit, in modesty, to retire. He desired to be safe from Saul only that he might expose himself for Israel. He avenged an old quarrel that God had with these nations, and at the same time fetched in provisions for himself and his army, for by their swords they must live. The Amalekites were to be all cut off. Probably the Geshurites and Gezrites were branches of Amalek. Saul was rejected for sparing them, David makes up the deficiency of his obedience before he succeeds him. He smote them, and *left none alive, v.* 8, 9. The service paid itself, for they carried off abundance of spoil, which served for the subsistence of David's forces. 2. Yet we cannot acquit him of dissimulation with Achish in the account he gave him of this expedition. (1.) David, it seems, was not willing that he should know the truth, and therefore spared none to carry tidings to Gath (*v.* 11), not because he was ashamed of what he had done as a bad thing, but because he was afraid, if the Philistines knew it, they would be apprehensive of danger to themselves or their allies by harbouring him among them and would expel him from their coasts. It would be easy to conclude, *If so he did, so will be his manner,* and therefore he industriously conceals it from them, which, it seems, he could do by putting them all to the sword, for none of their neighbours would inform against him, nor perhaps would soon come to the knowledge of what was done, intelligence not being so readily communicated then as now. (2.) He hid it from Achish with an equivocation not at all becoming his character. Being asked which way he had made his sally, he answered, *Against the south of Judah, v.* 13. It was true he had invaded those countries that lay south of Judah, but he made Achish believe he had invaded those that lay south in Judah, the Ziphites for example, that had once and again betrayed him; so Achish understood him, and thence inferred that he *had made his people Israel to abhor him,* and so riveted himself in the interest of Achish. The fidelity of Achish to him, his good opinion of him, and the confidence he put in him, aggravate his sin in deceiving him thus, which, with some other such instances, David seems penitently to reflect upon when he prays, *Remove from me the way of lying.*

CHAPTER 28

Preparations are herein making for that war which will put an end to the life and reign of Saul, and so make way for David to the throne. In this war, I. The Philistines are the aggressors and Achish their king makes David his confidant (*v.* 1, 2). II. The Israelites prepare to receive them, and Saul their king makes the devil his privy-counsellor, and thereby fills the measure of his iniquity. Observe, 1. The despairing condition which Saul was in (*v.* 3–6). 2. The application he made to a witch, to bring him up Samuel (*v.* 7–14). 3. His discourse with the apparition (*v.* 15–19). The damp it struck upon him (*v.* 20–25).

Verses 1–6

Here is, I. The design of the Philistines against Israel. They resolved to *fight them, v.* 1. If the Israelites had not forsaken God, there would have been no Philistines remaining to molest them; if Saul had not forsaken him, they would by this time have been put out of all danger by them. The Philistines took an opportunity to make this attempt when they had David among them, whom they feared more than Saul and all his forces.

II. The expectation Achish had of assistance from David in this war, and the encouragement David gave him to expect it: *"Thou shalt go with me to battle,"* says Achish. "If I protect thee, I may demand service from thee;" and he will think himself happy if he may have such a man as David on his side, who prospered whithersoever he went. David gave him an ambiguous answer: "We will see what will be done; it will be time enough to talk of that hereafter; but *surely thou shalt know what thy servant can do*" (*v.* 2), that is, "I will consider in what post I may be best able to serve thee, if thou wilt but give me leave to choose it." Thus he keeps himself free from a promise to serve him and yet keeps up his expectation of it; for Achish took it in no other sense than as an engagement to assist him, and promised him, thereupon, that he would make him captain of the guards, protector, or prime-minister of state.

III. The drawing of the armies, on both sides, into the field (*v.* 4): *The Philistines pitched in Shunem,* which was in the tribe of Issachar, a great way north from their country. The land of Israel, it seems, was ill-guarded, when the Philistines could march their army into the very heart of the country. Saul, while he pursued David, left his people naked and exposed. On some of the adjacent mountains of Gilboa Saul mustered his forces, and prepared to engage the Philistines, which he had little heart to do now that the *Spirit of the Lord had departed from him.*

IV. The terror Saul was in, and the loss he was at, upon this occasion: He *saw the host of the Philistines,* and by his own view of them, and the intelligence his spies brought him, he perceived they were more numerous, better armed, and in better heart, than his own were, which made him afraid, so that *his heart greatly trembled, v.* 5. Had he kept close to God, he needed not have been afraid at the sight of an army of Philistines; but now that he had provoked God to forsake him his interest failed, his armies dwindled and looked mean, and, which was worse, his spirits failed him, his heart sunk within him, a guilty conscience made him tremble at the shaking of a leaf. Now he remembered the guilty blood of the Amalekites which he had spared, and the innocent blood of the priests which he had spilt. His sins were set in order before his eyes, which put him into confusion, embarrassed all his counsels, robbed him of all his courage, and produced in him a certain fearful looking for of judgment and fiery indignation. Note, Troubles are terrors to the children of disobedience. In this distress *Saul enquired of the Lord, v.* 6. Need drives those to God who in the day of their prosperity slighted his oracles and altars. *Lord, in trouble have they visited thee,* Isa. 26:16. Did ever any seek the Lord and not find him? Yes, Saul did; *the Lord answered him not,* took no notice either of his petitions or of his enquiries; gave him no directions what to do, nor any encouragement to hope that he would be with him. *Should he be enquired of at all* by such a one as Saul? Eze. 14:3. No, he could not expect an answer of peace, for, 1. He enquired in such a manner that it was as if he had *not enquired at all.* Therefore it is said (1 Chr. 10:14), *He enquired not of the Lord;* for he did it faintly and coldly, and with a secret design, if God did not answer him, to consult the devil. He did not enquire in faith, but with a double unstable mind. 2. He enquired of the Lord when it was too late, when the days of his probation were over and he was finally rejected. *Seek the Lord while he may be found,* for there is a time when he will not be found. 3. He had forfeited the benefit of all the methods of enquiry. Could he that hated and persecuted Samuel and David, who were both prophets, expect to be answered by prophets? Could he that had slain the high priest, expect to be answered by Urim? Or could he that had sinned away the Spirit of grace, expect to be answered by dreams? No. *Be not deceived, God is not mocked.*

V. The mention of some things that had happened a good while ago, to introduce the following story, *v.* 3. 1. The death of Samuel. Samuel was dead, which made the Philistines the more bold and Saul the more afraid; for, had Samuel been alive, Saul probably thought that his presence and countenance, his good advice and good prayers, would have availed him in his distress. 2. Saul's edict against witchcraft. He had put the laws in execution against *those that had familiar spirits,* who must not be *suffered to live,* Ex. 22:18. Some think that he did this in the beginning of his reign, while he was under Samuel's influence; others think that it was lately done, for it is spoken of here (*v.* 9) as a late edict. Perhaps when Saul was himself troubled with an evil spirit he suspected that he was bewitched, and, for that reason, cut off all that had familiar spirits. Many seem zealous against sin, when they themselves are any way hurt by it (they will inform against swearers if they swear at them, or against drunkards if in their drink they abuse them), who otherwise have no concern for the glory of God, nor any dislike of sin as sin. However it was commendable in Saul thus to use his power for the terror and restraint of these evil-doers. Note, Many seem enemies to sin in others, while they indulge it in themselves. Saul will drive the devil out of his kingdom, and yet harbour him in his heart, by envy and malice.

Verses 7–14

Here, I. Saul seeks for a witch, *v.* 7. When God *answered him not,* if he had humbled himself by repentance and persevered in seeking God, who knows but that at length he might have been entreated for him? but, since he can discern no comfort either from heaven or earth (Isa. 8:21, 22), he resolves to knock at the gates of hell, and to see if any there will befriend him and give him advice: *Seek me a woman that has a familiar spirit, v.* 7. And his servants were too officious to serve him in this evil affair; they presently recommended one to him at Endor (a city not far off) who had escaped the execution of Saul's edict. To her he resolves to apply. Herein he is chargeable, 1. With contempt of the God of Israel; as if any creature could do him a kindness when God had left him and frowned upon him. 2. With contradiction to himself. He knew the heinousness of the sin of witchcraft, else he would not have cut off those that had familiar spirits; yet now he had recourse to that as an oracle which he had before condemned as an abomination. It is common for men to inveigh severely against those sins which they are in no temptation to, but afterwards to be themselves overcome by them. Had one told Saul, when he was destroying the witches, that he himself would, ere long, consult with one, he would have said, as Hazael did, *What? Is thy servant a dog?* But who knows what mischiefs those will run into that forsake God and are forsaken of him?

II. Hearing of one he hastens to her, but goes by night, and in disguise, only with two servants, and probably on foot, *v.* 8. See how those that are led captive by Satan are forced, 1. To disparage themselves. Never did Saul look so mean as when he went sneaking to a sorry witch to know his fortune. 2. To dissemble. Evil works are works of darkness, and they hate the light, neither care for coming to it. Saul went to the witch, not in his robes, but in the habit of a common soldier, not only lest the witch herself, if she had known him, should decline to serve him, either fearing he came to trepan her or resolving to be avenged on him for his edict against those of her profession, but lest his own people should know it and abhor him for it. Such is the power of natural conscience that even those who do evil blush and are ashamed to do it.

III. He tells her his errand and promises her impunity. 1. All he desires of her is to bring up one from the dead, whom he had a mind to discourse with. It was necromancy or divination by the dead, that he hoped to serve his purpose by. This was expressly forbidden by the law (Deu. 18:11), seeking *for the living to the dead,* Isa. 8:19. *Bring me up him whom I shall name, v.* 8. This supposes that it was generally taken for granted that souls exist after death, and that when men die there is not an end of them: it supposes too that great knowledge was attributed to separate souls. But to think that any good souls would come up at the beck of an evil spirit, or that God, who had denied a man the benefit of his own institutions, would suffer him to reap any real advantage by a cursed diabolical invention, was very absurd. 2. She signifies her fear of the law, and her suspicion that this stranger came to draw her into a snare (*v.* 9): *Thou knowest what Saul has done.* Providence ordered it so that Saul should be told to his face of his edict against witches, at this very time when he was consulting one, for the greater aggravation of his sin. She insists upon the peril of the law, perhaps to raise her price; for, though no mention is made of her fee, no doubt she demanded and had a large one. Observe how sensible she is of danger from the edict of Saul, and what care she is in to guard against it; but not at all apprehensive of the obligations off God's law and the terrors of his wrath. She considered what *Saul* had done, not what *God* had done, against such practices, and feared a snare laid for her life more than a snare laid for her soul. It is common for sinners to be more afraid of punishment from men than of God's righteous judgment. But, 3. Saul promises with an oath not to betray her, *v.* 10. It was his duty as a king to punish her and he knew it, yet he swears no to do it; as if he could by his own oath bind himself from doing that which, by the divine command, he was bound to do. But he promised more than he could perform when he said, *There shall no punishment happen to thee;* for he that could not secure himself could much less secure her from divine vengeance.

IV. Samuel, who was lately dead, is the person whom Saul desired to have some talk with; and the witch, with her enchantments, gratifies his desire, and brings them together. 1. As soon as Saul had given the witch the assurance she desired (that he would not discover her) she applied to her witchcrafts, and asked very confidently, *Whom shall I bring up to thee? v.* 11. Note, Hopes of impunity embolden sinners in their evil ways and harden their hearts. 2. Saul desires to speak with Samuel: *Bring me up Samuel.* Samuel had anointed him to the kingdom and had

formerly been his faithful friend and counsellor, and therefore with him he wished to advise. While Samuel was living at Ramah, not far from Gibeah of Saul, and presided there in the school of the prophets, we never read of Saul's going to him to consult him in any of the difficulties he was in (it would have been well for him if he had); then he slighted him, and perhaps hated him, looking upon him to be in David's interest. But now that he is dead, "O for Samuel again! By all means, *bring me up Samuel.*" Note, Many that despise and persecute God's saints and ministers when they are living would be glad to have them again when they are gone. *Send Lazarus to me,* and *send Lazarus to my father's house,* Lu. 16:24–27. The sepulchres of the righteous are garnished. 3. Here is a seeming defector chasm in the story. Saul said, *Bring me up Samuel,* and the very next words are, *When the woman saw Samuel,* (*v.* 12), whereas one would have expected to be told how she performed the operation, what spells and charms she used, or that some little intimation would be given of what she said or did; but the profound silence of the scripture concerning it forbids our coveting to *know the depths of Satan* (Rev. 2:24) or to have our curiosity gratified with an account of the mysteries of iniquity. It has been said of the books of some of the popish confessors that, by their descriptions of sin, they have taught men to commit it; but the scripture conceals sinful art, that we may be *simple concerning evil,* Rom. 16:19. 4. The witch, upon sight of the apparition, was aware that her client was Saul, her familiar spirit, it is likely, informing her of it (*v.* 12): "*Why hast thou deceived me* with a disguise; for thou art Saul, the very man that I am afraid of above any man?" Thus she gave Saul to understand the power of her art, in that she could discover him through his disguise; and yet she feared lest, hereafter, at least, he should take advantage against her for what she was now doing. Had she believed that it was really Samuel whom she saw, she would have had more reason to be afraid of him, who was a good prophet, than of Saul, who was a wicked king. But the wrath of earthly princes is feared by most more than the wrath of the King of kings. 5. Saul (who, we may suppose, was kept at a distance in the next room) bade her not to be afraid of him, but go on with the operation, and enquired *what she saw? v.* 13. O, says the woman, *I saw gods* (that is, a spirit) *ascending out of the earth;* they called angels *gods,* because spiritual beings. Poor gods that ascend *out of the earth!* But she speaks the language of the heathen, who had their infernal deities and had them in veneration. If Saul had thought it necessary to his conversation with Samuel that the body of Samuel should be called out of the grave, he would have taken the witch with him to Ramah, where his sepulchre was; but the design was wholly upon his soul, which yet, if it became visible, was expected to appear in the usual resemblance of the body; and God permitted the devil, to answer the design, to put on Samuel's shape, that those who would not *receive the love of the truth* might be *given up to strong delusions and believe a lie.* That it could not be the soul of Samuel himself they might easily apprehend when it *ascended out of the earth,* for the *spirit of a man,* much more of a good man, *goes upward,* Eccl. 3:21. But, if people will be deceived, it is just with God to say, "Let them be deceived." That the devil, by the divine permission, should be able to personate Samuel is not strange, since he can *transform himself into an angel of light!* nor is it strange that he should be permitted to do it upon this occasion, that Saul might be driven to despair, by enquiring of the devil, since he would not, in a right manner, enquire of the Lord, by which he might have had comfort. Saul, being told of gods ascending, was eager to know what was the form of this deity, and in what shape he appeared, so far was he from conceiving any horror at it, his heart being wretchedly *hardened by the deceitfulness of sin.* Saul, it seems, was not permitted to see any manner of similitude himself, but he must take the woman's word for it, that she saw *an old man covered with a mantle, or robe,* the habit of a judge, which Samuel had sometimes worn, and some think it was for the sake of that, and the majesty of its aspect, that she called this apparition *Elohim, a god or gods;* for so magistrates are styled, Ps. 82:1. 6. Saul, perceiving, by the woman's description, that it was Samuel, *stooped with his face to the ground,* either, as it is generally taken, in reverence to Samuel, though he saw him not, or perhaps to

listen to that soft and muttering voice which he now expected to hear (for those that had familiar spirits *peeped and muttered,* Isa. 8:19); and it should seem Saul bowed himself (probably by the witch's direction) that he might hear what was whispered and listen carefully to it; for the *voice of one that has a familiar spirit* is said to come *out of the ground, and whisper out of the dust,* Isa. 29:4. He would stoop to that who would not stoop to the word of God.

Verses 15–19

We have here the conference between Saul and Satan. Saul came in disguise (*v.* 8), but Satan soon discovered him, *v.* 12. Satan comes in disguise, in the disguise of Samuel's mantle, and Saul cannot discover him. Such is the disadvantage we labour under, in wrestling with *the rulers of the darkness of this world,* that they know us, while we are ignorant of their wiles and devices.

I. The spectre, or apparition, personating Samuel, asks why he is sent for (*v.* 15): *Why hast thou disquieted me to bring me up?* To us this discovers that it was an evil spirit that personated Samuel; for (as bishop Patrick observes) it is not in the power of witches to disturb the rest of good men and to bring them back into the world when they please; nor would the true Samuel have acknowledged such a power in magical arts: but to Saul this was a proper device of Satan's, to draw veneration from him, to possess him with an opinion of the power of divination, and so to rivet him in the devil's interests.

II. Saul makes his complaint to this counterfeit Samuel, mistaking him for the true; and a most doleful complaint it is: "*I am sorely distressed,* and know not what to do, *for the Philistines make war against me;* yet I should do well enough with them if I had but the tokens of God's presence with me; but, alas! God has departed from me.*" He complained not of God's withdrawings till he fell into trouble, till the *Philistines made war against him,* and then he began to lament God's departure. He that in his prosperity enquired not after God in his adversity thought it hard that God answered him not, nor took any notice of his enquiries, either by dreams or prophets, neither gave answers immediately himself nor sent them by any of his messengers. He does not, like a penitent, own the righteousness of God in this; but, like a man enraged, flies out against God as unkind and flies off from him: *Therefore I have called thee;* as if Samuel, a servant of God, would favour those whom God frowned upon, or as if a dead prophet could do him more service than the living ones. One would think, from this, that he really desired to meet with the devil, and expected no other (though under the covert of Samuel's name), for he desires advice otherwise than from God, therefore from the devil, who is a rival with God. "God denies me, *therefore I come to thee. Flectere si nequeo superos, Acheronta movebo." — If I fail with heaven, I will move hell.*

III. It is cold comfort which this evil spirit in Samuel's mantle gives to Saul, and is manifestly intended to drive him to despair and self-murder. Had it been the true Samuel, when Saul desired to be told what he should do he would have told him to repent and make his peace with God, and recall David from his banishment, and would then have told him that he might hope in this way to find mercy with God; but, instead of that, he represents his case as helpless and hopeless, serving him as he did Judas, to whom he was first a tempter and then a tormentor, persuading him first to sell his master and then to hang himself. 1. He upbraids him with his present distress (*v.* 16), tells him, not only that God had departed from him, but that he had become his enemy, and therefore he must expect no comfortable answer from him: "*Wherefore dost thou ask me?* How can I be thy friend when God is thy enemy, or thy counsellor when he has left thee?" 2. He upbraids him with the anointing of David to the kingdom, *v.* 17. He could not have touched upon a string that sounded more unpleasant in the ear of Saul than this. Nothing is said to reconcile him to David, but all tends rather to exasperate him against David and widen the breach. Yet, to make him believe that he was Samuel, the apparition affirmed that it was God who spoke by him. The devil knows how to speak with an air of religion, and can teach *false apostles to transform themselves into the apostles of Christ* and imitate their language. Those who use spells and charms, and plead, in defence of them, that they find nothing in them but what is good, may remember what good words the devil here spoke, and yet with what a malicious design. 3. He upbraids him with his disobedience to the command of God in not destroying the Amalekites, *v.* 18. Satan had helped him to palliate and excuse that sin when Samuel was dealing with him to bring him to repentance, but now he aggravates it, to make him despair of God's mercy. See what those get that hearken to Satan's temptations. He himself will be their accuser, and insult over them. And see whom those resemble that allure others to that which is evil and reproach them for it when they have done. 4. He foretels his approaching ruin, *v.* 19. (1.) That his army should be routed by the Philistines. This is twice mentioned: *The Lord shall deliver Israel into the hand of the Philistines.* This he might foresee, by considering the superior strength and number of the Philistines, the weakness of the armies of Israel, Saul's terror, and especially God's departure from them. Yet, to personate a prophet, he very gravely ascribes it once and again to God: *The Lord shall do it.* (2.) That he and his sons should be slain in the battle: *To-morrow,* that is, in a little time (and, supposing that it was now after midnight, I see not but it may be taken strictly for the very next day after that which had now begun), *thou and thy sons shall be with me,* that is, in the state of the dead, separate from the body. Had this been the true Samuel, he could not have foretold the event unless God had revealed it to him; and, though it were an evil spirit, God might by him foretel it; as we read of an evil spirit that foresaw Ahab's fall at Ramoth-Gilead and was instrumental in it (1 Ki. 22:20, etc.), as perhaps this evil spirit was, by the divine permission, in Saul's destruction. That evil spirit flattered Ahab, this frightened Saul, and both that they might fall; so miserable are those that are under the power of Satan; for, *whether he rage or laugh, there is no rest,* Prov. 29:9.

Verses 20–25

We are here told how Saul received this terrible message from the ghost he consulted. He desired to be told *what he should do* (*v.* 15), but was only told what he had not done and what should be done to him. Those that expect any good counsel or comfort otherwise than from God, and in the way of his institutions, will be as wretchedly disappointed as Saul here was. Observe,

I. How he sunk under the load, *v.* 20. He was indeed unfit to bear it, having *eaten nothing all the day* before, nor *that night.* He came fasting from the camp, and continued fasting; not for want of food, but for want of an appetite. The fear he was in of the power of the Philistines (*v.* 5) took away his appetite, or perhaps the struggle he had with his own conscience, after he had entertained the thought of consulting the witch, made him to nauseate even his necessary food, though ever so dainty. This made him an easy prey to this fresh terror that now came upon him like an armed man. *He fell all along on the earth,* as if the archers of the Philistines had already hit him, *and there was no strength in him* to bear up against these heavy tidings. Now he had enough of consulting witches, and found them miserable comforters. When God in his word speaks terror to sinners he opens to them, at the same time, a door of hope if they repent: but those that apply to the gates of hell for succour must there expect darkness without any glimpse of light.

II. With what difficulty he was persuaded to take so much relief as was necessary to carry him back to his post in the camp. The witch, it should seem, had left Saul alone with the spectre, to have his talk with him by himself; but perhaps hearing him fall and groan, and perceiving him to be in great agony, she came to him (*v.* 21), and was very importunate with him to take some refreshment, that he might be able to get clear from her house, fearing that if he should be ill, especially if he should die there, she should be punished for it as a traitor, though she had escaped punishment as a witch. This, it is probable, rather than any sentiment of kindness, made her solicitous to help him. But what a deplorable condition had he brought himself to when he needed so wretched a comforter! 1. She showed herself very importunate with him to take some refreshment. She pleaded (*v.* 21) that she had obeyed his voice to the endangering of her life, and why therefore should not he hearken to her voice for the relieving of his life? *v.* 22. She had a fat calf at hand (and the word signifies one that was made use of in treading out the corn, and therefore could the worse be spared); this she prepared for his entertainment, *v.* 24. Josephus is large in applauding the extraordinary courtesy and liberality of this woman, and recommending what she did as an example of compassion to the distressed, and readiness to communicate for their relief, though we have no prospect of being recompensed. 2. He showed himself very averse to it: *He refused, and said, I will not eat* (*v.* 23), choosing rather to die obscurely by famine than honourably by the sword. Had he laboured only under a defect of animal spirits, food might have helped him; but, alas! his case was out of the reach of such succours. What are dainty meats to a wounded conscience? *As vinegar upon nitre, so is he that sings songs to a heavy heart,* so disagreeable and unwelcome. 3. The woman at length, with the help of his servants, overpersuaded him, against his inclination and resolution, to take some refreshment. Not by force, but by friendly advice, they *compelled him* (*v.* 23), and of no other than such a rational and courteous compulsion are we to understand that in the parable, *Compel them to come in,* Lu. 14:23. *How forcible are right words,* when men are pressed by them to that which is for their own interest! Job 6:25. Saul was somewhat revived with this entertainment; so that he and his servants, when they had eaten, *rose up and went away* before it was light (*v.* 25), that they might hasten to their business and that they might not be seen to come out of such a scandalous house. Josephus here much admires the bravery and magnanimity of Saul, that, though he was assured he should lose both his life and honour, yet he would not desert his army, but resolutely returned to the camp, and stood ready for an engagement. I wonder more at the hardness of his heart, that he did not again apply to God by repentance and prayer, in hopes yet to obtain at least a reprieve; but he desperately ran headlong upon his own ruin. Perhaps, indeed, now that rage and envy possessed him to the uttermost, he was the better reconciled to his hard fate, being told that his sons, and Jonathan among the rest, whom he hated for his affection to David, should die with him. If he must fall, he cared not what desolations of his family and kingdom accompanied his fall, hoping it would be the worse for his successor. *Emou thanontos gaia michthetō pyri — I care not if, when I am dead, the world should be set on fire.* He begged not, as David, "Let thy hand be against me, but not against thy people."

CHAPTER 29

How Saul, who was forsaken of God, when he was in a strait was more and more perplexed and embarrassed with his own counsels, we read in the foregoing chapter. In this chapter we find how David, who kept close to God, when he was in a strait was extricated and brought off by the providence of God, without any contrivance of his own. We have him, I. Marching with the Philistines (*v.* 1, 2). II. Excepted against by the lords of the Philistines (*v.* 3–5). III. Happily dismissed by Achish from that service which did so ill become him, and which yet he knew not how to decline (*v.* 6–11).

Verses 1–5

Here is, I. The great strait that David was in, which we may suppose he himself was aware of, though we read not of his asking advice from God, nor of any project of his own to get clear of it. The two armies of the Philistines and the Israelites were encamped and ready to engage, *v.* 1. Achish, who had been kind to David, had obliged him to come himself and bring the forces he had into his service. David came accordingly, and, upon a review of the army, was found with Achish, in the post assigned him in the rear, *v.* 2. Now, 1. If, when the armies engaged, he should retire, and quit his post, he would fall under the indelible reproach, not only of cowardice and treachery, but of base ingratitude to Achish, who had been his protector and benefactor and had reposed a confidence in him, and from whom he had received a very honourable commission. Such an unprincipled thing as this he could by no means persuade himself to do. 2. If he should, as was expected from him, fight for the Philistines against Israel, he would incur the imputation of being an enemy to the Israel of God and a traitor to his country, would make his own people hate him, and unanimously oppose his coming to the crown, as unworthy the name of an Israelite, much more the honour and trust of a king of Israel, when he had fought against them under the banner of the uncircumcised. If Saul should be killed (as it proved he was) in this engagement, the fault would be laid at David's door, as if he had killed him. So that on each side there seemed to be both sin and scandal. This was the strait he was in; and a great strait it was to a good man, greater to see sin before him than to see trouble. Into this strait he brought himself by his own unadvisedness, in quitting the land of Judah, and going among the uncircumcised. It is strange if those that associate themselves with wicked people, and grow intimate with them, come off without guilt, or grief, or both. What he himself proposed to do does not appear. Perhaps he designed to act only as keeper to the king's head, the post assigned him (*ch.* 28:2) and not to do any thing offensively against Israel. But it would have been very hard to come so near the brink of sin and not to fall in. Therefore, though God might justly have left him in this difficulty, to chastise him for his folly, yet, because his heart was upright with him, he would *not suffer him to be tempted above what he was able, but with the temptation made a way for him to escape,* 1 Co. 10:13.

II. A door opened for his deliverance out of this strait. God inclined the hearts of the princes of the Philistines to oppose his being employed in the battle, and to insist upon his being dismissed. Thus their enmity befriended him, when no friend he had was capable of doing him such a kindness. 1. It was a proper question which they asked, upon the mustering of the forces, *"What do these Hebrews here? v.* 3. What confidence can we put in them, or what service can we expect from them?" A *Hebrew is out of his place,* and, if he has the spirit of a *Hebrew, is out of his element,* when he is in the camp of the Philistines, and deserves to be made uneasy there. David used to *hate the congregation of evil doers,* however he came now to be among them, Ps. 26:5. It was an honourable testimony which Achish, on this occasion, gave to David. He looked upon him as a refugee, that fled from a wrongful prosecution in his own country, and had put himself under his protection, whom therefore he was obliged, in justice, to take care of, and thought he might in prudence employ; "for (says he) he has been with me *these days,* or *these years,"* that is, a considerable time, many days at his court and a year or two in his country, and he never found any fault in him, nor saw any cause to distrust his fidelity, or to think any other than that he had heartily come over to him. By this it appears that David had conducted himself with a great deal of caution, and had prudently concealed the affection he still retained for his own people. We have need to *walk in wisdom towards those that are without, to keep our mouth when the wicked is before us,* and to be upon the reserve. 3. Yet the princes are peremptory in it, that he must be sent home; and they give good reasons for their insisting on it. (1.) Because he had been an old enemy to the Philistines; witness what was sung in honour of his triumphs over them: *Saul slew his thousands, and David his ten thousands, v.* 5. "It will be a reproach to us to harbour and trust so noted a destroyer of our people; nor can it be thought that he will now act heartily against Saul who then acted so vigorously with him and for him." Who would be fond of popular praise or applause when, even that may, another time, be turned against a man to his reproach? (2.) Because he might be a most dangerous enemy to them, and do them more mischief then all Saul's army could (*v.* 4): "He may *in the battle be an adversary to us,* and surprise us with an attack in the rear, while their army charges us in the front; and we have reason to think he will do so, that, by betraying us, he may reconcile himself to his master. Who can trust a man who, besides his affection to his country, will think it his interest to be false to us?" It is dangerous to put confidence in a reconciled enemy.

Verses 6–11

If the reasons Achish had to trust David were stronger than the reasons which the princes offered why they should distrust him (as I do not see that, in policy, they were, for the princes were certainly in the right), yet Achish was but one of five, though the chief, and the only one that had the title of king; accordingly, in a council of war held on this occasion, he was over-voted, and obliged to dismiss David, though he was extremely fond of him. Kings cannot always do as they would, nor have such as they would about them.

I. The discharge Achish gives him is very honourable, and not a final discharge, but only from the present service. 1. He signifies the great pleasure and satisfaction he had taken in him and in his conversation: *Thou art good in my sight as an angel of God, v.* 9. Wise and good men will gain respect, wherever they go, from all that know how to make a right estimate of persons and things, though of different professions in religion. What Achish says of David, God, by the prophet, says *of the house of David* (Zec. 12:8), that it shall be *as the angel of the Lord.* But the former is a court-compliment; the latter is a divine promise. 2. He gives him a testimonial of his good behaviour, *v.* 6. It is very full and in obliging terms: *"Thou hast been upright,* and thy whole conduct has been *good in my sight,* and *I have not found evil in thee."* Saul would not have given him such a testimonial, though he had done far more service to him than Achish. God's people should behave themselves always so inoffensively as if possible to get the good word of all they have dealings with; and it is a debt we owe to those who have acquitted themselves well to give them the praise of it. 3. He lays all the blame of his dismission upon the princes, who would by no means suffer him to continue in the camp. "The king loves thee entirely, and would venture his life in thy hand; *but the lords favour thee not,* and we must not disoblige them, nor can we oppose them; therefore *return and go in peace."* He had better part with his favourite than occasion a disgust among his generals and a mutiny in his army. Achish intimates a reason why they were uneasy. It was not so much for David's own sake as for the sake of his soldiers that attended him, whom he calls *his master's servants* (namely, Saul's), *v.* 10. They could trust him, but not them. (4.) He orders him to be gone early, as soon as it was light (*v.* 10), to prevent their further resentments, and the jealousies they would have been apt to conceive if he had lingered.

II. His reception of this discourse is very complimental; but, I fear, not without some degree of dissimulation. "What?" says David, "must I leave *my lord the king,* whom I am bound by office to protect, just now when he is going to expose himself in the field? Why may not I go and *fight against the enemies of my lord the king?" v.* 8. He seemed anxious to serve him when he was at this juncture really anxious to leave him, but he was not willing that Achish should know that he was. No one knows how strong the temptation is to compliment and dissemble which those are in that attend great men, and how hard it is to avoid it.

III. God's providence ordered it wisely and graciously for him. For, besides that the snare was broken and he was delivered out of the dilemma to which he was first reduced, it proved a happy hastening of him to the relief of his own city, which sorely wanted him, though he did not know it. Thus the disgrace which the lords of the Philistines put upon him prove, in more ways than one, an advantage to him. *The steps of a good man ore ordered by the Lord, and he delighteth in his way.* What he does with us we know not now, but we shall know hereafter, and shall see it was all for good.

CHAPTER 30

When David was dismissed from the army of the Philistines he did not go over to the camp of Israel, but, being expelled by Saul, observed an exact neutrality, and silently retired to his own city Ziklag, leaving the armies ready to engage. Now here we are told, I. What a melancholy posture he found the city in, all laid waste by the Amalekites, and what distress it occasioned him and his men (*v.* 1–6). II. What course he took to recover what he had lost. He enquired of God, and took out a commission from him (*v.* 7, 8), pursued the enemy (*v.* 9, 10), gained intelligence from a straggler (*v.* 11–15), attacked and routed the plunderers (*v.* 16, 17), and recovered all that they had carried off (*v.* 18–20). III. What method he observed in the distribution of the spoil (*v.* 21–31).

Verses 1–6

Here we have, I. The descent which the Amalekites made upon Ziklag in David's absence, and the desolations they made there. They surprised the city when it was left unguarded, plundered it, burnt it, and carried all the women and children captives, *v.* 1, 2. They intended, by this to revenge the like havoc that David had lately made of them and their country, *ch.* 27:8. He that had made so many enemies ought not to have left his own concerns so naked and defenceless. Those that make bold with others must expect that others will make as bold with them and provide accordingly. Now observe in this, 1. The cruelty of Saul's pity (as it proved) in sparing the Amalekites; if he had utterly destroyed them, as he ought to have done, these would not have been in being to do this mischief. 2. How David was corrected for being so forward to go with the Philistines against Israel. God showed him that he had better have staid at home and looked after his own business. When we go abroad in the way of our duty we may comfortably hope that God will take care of our families in our absence, but not otherwise. 3. How wonderfully God inclined the hearts of these Amalekites to carry the women and children away captives, and not to kill them. When David invaded them he put all to the sword (*ch.* 27:9), and no reason can be given why they did not retaliate upon this city, but that God restrained them; for he has all hearts in his hands, and says to the fury of the most cruel men, *Hitherto thou shalt come, and no further.* Whether they spared them to lead them in triumph, or to sell them, or to use them for slaves, God's hand must be acknowledged, who designed to make use of the Amalekites for the correction, not for the destruction, of the house of David.

II. The confusion and consternation that David and his men were in when they found their houses in ashes and their wives and children gone into captivity. Three days' march they had from the camp of the Philistines to Ziklag, and now that they came thither weary, but hoping to find rest in their houses and joy in their families, behold a black and dismal scene was presented to them (*v.* 3), which made them all weep (David himself not excepted), though they were men of war, *till they had no more power to weep, v.* 4. The mention of David's wives, *Ahinoam and Abigail,* and their being carried captive, intimates that this circumstance went nearer his heart than any thing else. Note, It is no disparagement to the boldest and bravest spirits to lament the calamities of relations and friends. Observe, 1. This trouble came upon them when they were absent. It was the ancient policy of Amalek to take Israel at an advantage. 2. It met them at their return, and, for aught that appears, their own eyes gave them the first intelligence of it. Note, When we go abroad we cannot foresee what evil tidings may meet us when we come home again. The going out may be very cheerful, and yet the coming in be very doleful. *Boast not thyself* therefore *of to-morrow,* nor of to-night either, *for thou knowest not what a day,* or a piece of a day, *may bring forth,* Prov. 27:1. If, when we come off a journey, we find our *tabernacles in peace,* and not laid waste as David here found his, let the Lord be praised for it.

III. The mutiny and murmuring of David's men against him (*v.* 6): *David was greatly distressed,* for, in the midst of all his losses, his own people spoke of stoning him, 1. Because they looked upon him as the occasion of their calamities, by the provocation he had given the Amalekites, and his indiscretion in leaving Ziklag without a garrison in it. Thus apt are we, when we are in trouble, to fly into a rage against those who are in any way the occasion of our trouble, while we overlook the divine providence, and have not that regard to the operations of God's hand in it which would silence our passions, and make us patient. 2. Because now they began to despair of that preferment which they had promised themselves in following David. They hoped ere this to have been all princes; and now to find themselves all beggars was such a disappointment to them as made them grow outrageous, and threaten the life of him on whom, under God, they had the greatest dependence. What absurdities will not ungoverned passions plunge men into? This was a sore trial to the man after God's own heart, and could not but go very near him. Saul had driven him from his country, the Philistines had driven him from their camp, the Amalekites had plundered his city, his wives were taken prisoners, and now, to complete his woe, his own familiar friends, in whom he trusted, whom he had sheltered, and who did eat of his bread, instead of sympathizing with him and offering him any relief, *lifted up the heel against him* and threatened to stone him. Great faith must expect such severe exercises. But it is observable that David was reduced to this extremity just before his accession to the throne. At this very time, perhaps, the stroke was struck which opened the door to his advancement. Things are sometimes at the worst with the church and people of God just before they begin to mend.

IV. David's pious dependence upon the divine providence and grace in this distress: *But David encouraged himself in the Lord his God.* His men fretted at their loss. *The soul of the people was bitter,* so the word is. Their own discontent and impatience added *wormwood and gall* to the affliction and misery, and made their case doubly grievous. But 1. David bore it better, though he had more reason than any of them to lament it; they gave liberty to their passions, but he set his graces on work, and by encouraging himself in God, while they dispirited each other, he kept his spirit calm and sedate. Or, 2. There may be a reference to the threatening words his men gave out against him. They *spoke of stoning him;* but he, not offering to avenge the affront, nor terrified by their menaces, *encouraged himself in the Lord his God,* believed, and considered with application to his present case, the power and providence of God, his justice and goodness, the method he commonly takes of bringing low and then raising up, his care of his people that serve him and trust in him, and the particular promises he had made to him of bringing him safely to the throne; with these considerations he supported himself, not doubting but the present trouble would end well. Note, Those that have taken the Lord for their God may take encouragement from their relation to him in the worst of times. It is the duty and interest of all good people, whatever happens, to encourage themselves in God as their Lord and their God, assuring themselves that he can and will bring light out of darkness, peace out of trouble, and good out of evil, to all that love him and are *the called according to his purpose,* Rom. 8:28. It was David's practice, and he had the comfort of it, *What time I am afraid I will trust in thee.* When he was at his wits' end he was not at his faith's end.

Verses 7–20

Solomon observes that *the righteous is delivered out of trouble* and *the wicked cometh in his stead,* that *the just falleth seven times a-day and riseth again;* so it was with David. Many were his troubles, but *the Lord delivered him out of them all,* and particularly out of this of which we have here an account.

I. He enquired of the Lord both concerning his duty — *Shall I pursue after this troop?* and concerning the event — *Shall I overtake them? v.* 8. It was a great advantage to David that he had the high priest with him and the breast-plate of judgment, which, as a public person, he might consult in all his affairs, Num. 27:21. We cannot think that he left Abiathar and the ephod at Ziklag, for then he and it would have been carried away by the Amalekites, unless we may suppose them hidden by a special providence, that they might be ready for David to consult at his return. If we conclude that David had his priest and ephod with him in the camp of the Philistines, it was certainly a great neglect in him that he did not enquire of the Lord by them concerning his engagement to Achish. Perhaps he was ashamed to own his religion so far among the uncircumcised; but now he begins to apprehend that this trouble is brought upon him to correct him for that oversight, and therefore the first thing he does is to call for the ephod. It is well if we get this good by our afflictions, to be reminded by them of neglected duties, and particularly to be quickened by them to enquire of the Lord. See 1 Chr. 15:13. David had no room to doubt but that his war against these Amalekites was just, and he had an inclination strong enough to set upon them when it was for the recovery of that which was dearest to him in this world; and yet he would not go about it without asking counsel of God, thereby owning his dependence upon God and submission to him. If we thus, in all our ways, acknowledge God, we may expect that he will direct our steps, as he did David's here, answering him above what he asked, with an assurance that he should recover all.

II. He went himself in person, and took with him all the force he had, in pursuit of the Amalekites, *v.* 9, 10. See how quickly, how easily, how effectually the mutiny among the soldiers was quelled by his patience and faith. When they *spoke of stoning him* (*v.* 6), if he had spoken of hanging them, or had ordered that the ringleaders of the faction should immediately have their heads struck off, though it would have been just, yet it might have been of pernicious consequence to his interest in this critical juncture; and, while he and his men were contending, the Amalekites would have clearly carried off their spoil. But when he, as a deaf man, heard not, smothered his resentments, and *encouraged himself in the Lord his God,* the tumult of the people was stilled by his gentleness and the power of God on their hearts; and, being thus mildly treated, they are now as ready to follow his foot as they were but a little before to fly in his face. Meekness is the security of any government. All his men were willing to go along with him in pursuit of the Amalekites, and he needed them all; but he was forced to drop a third part of them by the way; 200 out of 600 were so fatigued with their long march, and so sunk under the load of their grief, that they could not pass the brook Besor, but staid behind there. This was, 1. A great trial of David's faith, whether he could go on, in a dependence upon the word of God, when so many of his men failed him. When we are disappointed and discouraged in our expectations from second causes, then to go on with cheerfulness, confiding in the divine power, this is giving glory to God, by believing against hope, in hope. 2. A great instance of David's tenderness to his men, that he would by no means urge them beyond their strength, though the case itself was so very urgent. The Son of David thus considers the frame of his followers, who are not all alike strong and vigorous in their spiritual pursuits and conflicts; but, where we are weak, there he is kind; nay, more there he is strong, 2 Co. 12:9, 10.

III. Providence threw one in their way that gave them intelligence of the enemy's motions, and guided theirs; a poor Egyptian lad, scarcely alive, is made instrumental of a great deal of good to David. *God chooses the foolish things of the world,* with them *to confound the wise.* Observe, 1. His master's cruelty to him. He had got out of him all the service he could, and when the lad fell sick, probably being over-toiled with his work, he barbarously left him to perish in the field, when he was in no such haste but he might have put him into some of the carriages, and brought him home, or, at least, have left him wherewithal to support himself. That master has the spirit of an Amalekite, not of an Israelite, that can thus use a servant worse than one would use a beast. *The tender mercies of the wicked are cruel.* This Amalekite thought he should now have servants enough of the Israelite-captives, and therefore cared not what became of his Egyptian slave, but could willingly let him die in a ditch for want of necessaries, while he himself was *eating and drinking, v.* 16. Justly did Providence make this poor servant, that was thus basely abused, instrumental towards the destruction of a whole army of Amalekites and his master among the rest; for God hears the cry of oppressed servants. 2. David's compassion to him. Though he had reason to think he was one of those that had helped to destroy Ziklag, yet, finding him in distress, he generously relieved him, not only with *bread and water* (*v.* 11), but with *figs and raisins, v.* 12. Though the Israelites were in haste, and had no great plenty for themselves, yet they would not *forbear to deliver one that was drawn unto death,* nor say, *Behold, we knew it not,* Prov. 24:11, 12. Those are unworthy the name of Israelites who shut up the bowels of their compassion from persons in distress. It was also prudently done to relieve this Egyptian; for, though despicable, he was capable of doing them service: so it proved, though they were not certain of this when they relieved him. It is a good reason why we should neither do an injury nor deny a kindness to any man that we know not but, some time or other, it may be in his power to return either a kindness or an injury. 3. The intelligence David received from this poor Egyptian when he had come to himself. He gave him an account concerning his party. (1.) What they had done (*v.* 14): *We made an invasion,* etc. The countries which David had pretended to Achish to have made an incursion upon (*ch.* 27:10) they really had invaded and laid waste. What was then false now proved too true. (2.) Whither they had gone, *v.* 15. This he promised David to inform him of upon condition he would spare his life and protect him from his master, who, if he could hear of him again (he thought), would add cruelty to cruelty. Such an opinion this poor Egyptian had of the obligation of an oath that he desired no greater security for his life than this: *Swear unto me by God,* not by the gods of Egypt or Amalek, but by the one supreme God.

IV. David, being directed to the place where they lay, securely celebrating their triumphs, fell upon them, and, as he used to pray, *saw his desire upon his enemies.* 1. The spoilers were cut off. The Amalekites, finding the booty was rich, and having got with it (as they thought) out of the reach of danger, were making themselves very merry with it, *v.* 16. All thoughts of war were laid aside, nor were they in any haste to house their prey, but *spread themselves abroad on the earth* in the most careless manner that could be, and there they were found *eating, and drinking, and dancing,* probably in honour of their idol-gods, to whom they gave the praise of their success. In this posture David surprised them, which made the conquest of them, and the blow he gave them, the more easy to him and the more dismal to them. Then are sinners nearest to ruin when they cry, *Peace and safety,* and *put the evil day far from them.* Nor does any thing give our spiritual enemies more advantage against us than sensuality and the indulgence of the flesh. *Eating, and drinking, and dancing,* have been the soft and pleasant way in which many have gone down to the congregation of the dead. Finding them thus off their guard, and from their arms (many of them, it may be, drunk, and unable to make any resistance), he put them all to the sword, and only 400 escaped, *v.* 17. Thus is the triumphing of the wicked short, and wrath comes on them, as on Belshazzar, when they are in the midst of their jollity. 2. The spoil was recovered and brought off, and nothing was lost, but a great deal gotten. (1.) They retrieved all their own (*v.* 18, 19): *David rescued his two wives;* this is mentioned particularly, because this pleased David more than all the rest of his achievements. Providence had so ordered it that the Amalekites carefully preserved all that they had taken, concluding that they kept it for themselves, though really they preserved it for the right owners, so that there was nothing lacking to them; so it proved, when they concluded all was gone: so much better is God oftentimes to us than our own fears. Our Lord Jesus was indeed the Son of David and the Son of Abraham, in this resembling them both (Abraham, Gen. 14:16, and David here), that he *took the prey from the mighty, and led captivity captive.* But this was not all. (2.) They took all that belonged to the Amalekites besides (*v.* 20): *Flocks and herds,* either such as were taken from the Philistines and others, which David had the disposal of by the law of war; or perhaps he made a sally into the enemy's country, and fetched off these flocks and herds thence, as interest for his own. This drove was put in the van of the triumph, with this proclamation, *"This is David's spoil.* This we may thank him for." Those who lately spoke of stoning him now caressed him and cried him up, because they got by him more than they had then lost. Thus are the world and its sentiments governed by interest.

Verses 21–31

We have here an account of the distribution of the spoil which as taken from the Amalekites. When the Amalekites had carried away a rich booty from the land of Judah and the Philistines they spent it in sensuality, in eating, and drinking, and making merry with it; but David disposed of the spoil taken after another manner, as one that knew that justice and charity must govern us in the use we make of whatever we have in this world. What God gives us he designs we should do good with, not serve our lusts with. In the distribution of the spoil,

I. David was just and kind to those who abode by the stuff. They came forth to meet the conquerors, and to congratulate them on this success, though they could not contribute to it (*v.* 21); for we should rejoice in a good work done, though Providence had laid us aside and rendered us incapable of lending a hand to it. David received their address very kindly, and was so far from upbraiding them with their weakness that he showed himself solicitous concerning them. He saluted them; *he asked them of peace* (so the word is), enquired how they did, because he had left them faint and not well; or wished them peace, bade them be of good cheer, they should lose nothing by staying behind; for of this they seemed afraid, as perhaps David saw by their countenances.

1. There were those that opposed their coming in to share in the spoil; some of David's soldiers, probably the same that spoke of stoning him, spoke now of defrauding their brethren; they are called wicked men and *men of Belial, v.* 22. Let not the best of men think it strange if they have those attending them that are very bad and they cannot prevail to make them better. We may suppose that David had instructed his soldiers, and prayed with them, and yet there were many among them that were wicked men and men of Belial, often terrified with the apprehensions of death and yet wicked men still and men of Belial. These made a motion that the 200 men who abode by the stuff should only have their wives and children given them, but none of their goods. Well might they be called *wicked men;* for this bespeaks them, (1.) Very covetous themselves and greedy of gain; for hereby the more would fall to their share. Awhile ago they would gladly have given half their own to recover the other half, yet now that they have all their own they are not content unless they can have their brethren's too; so soon do men forget their low estate. All seek their own, and too often more than their own. (2.) Very barbarous to their brethren; for, to give them their wives and children, and not their estates, was to give them the mouths without the meat. What joy could they have of their families if they had nothing to maintain them with? Was this to do as they would be done by? Those are men of Belial indeed who delight in putting hardships upon their brethren, and care not who is starved, so they may be fed to the full.

2. David would by no means admit this, but ordered that those who tarried behind should come in for an equal share in the spoils with those that went to the battle, *v.* 23, 24. This he did, (1.) In gratitude to God. The spoil we have is that which God has given us; we have it from him, and therefore must use it under his direction as good stewards. Let this check us when we are tempted to misapply that which God has entrusted us with of this world's goods. "Nay, I must not do so with that which God has given me, not serve Satan and a base lust with those things which are not only the creatures of his power, but the gifts of his bounty. God has recompensed us by *delivering the company that came against us into our hand,* let not us then wrong our brethren. God has been kind to us in preserving us and giving us victory, let not us be unkind to them." God's mercy to us should make us merciful to one another. (2.) In justice to them. It was true they tarried behind; but, [1.] It was not for want of good-will to the cause or to their brethren, but because they had not strength to keep up with them. It was not their fault, but their infelicity; and therefore they ought not to suffer for it. [2.] Though they tarried behind now, they had formerly engaged many times in battle and done their part as well as the best of their brethren, and their former services must be considered now that there was something to enjoy. [3.] Even now they did good service, for they abode by the stuff, to guard that which somebody must take care of, else that might have fallen into the hands of some other enemy. Every post of service is not alike a post of honour, yet those that are in any way serviceable to the common interest, though in a meaner station, ought to share in the common advantages, as in the natural body every member has its use and therefore has its share of the nourishment. *First,* Thus David overruled the wicked men, and men of Belial, with reason, but with a great deal of mildness; for the force of reason is sufficient, without the force of passion. He calls them *his brethren, v.* 23. Superiors often lose their authority by haughtiness, but seldom by courtesy and condescension. *Secondly,* Thus he settled the matter for the time to come, made it a statute of his kingdom (a statute of distributions, *primo Davidis — in the first year of David's reign*), an ordinance of war (*v.* 25), that *as his part is that goes down to the battle,* and hazards his life in the high places of the field, so shall his be that guards the carriages. Abraham returned the spoils of Sodom to the right owners, and quitted his title to them *jure belli — derived from the laws of war.* If we help others to recover their right, we must not think that this alienates the property and makes it ours. God appointed that the spoil of Midian should be divided between the soldiers and the whole congregation, Num. 31:27. The case here was somewhat different, but governed by the same general rule — that we are members one of another. The disciples, at first, *had all things common,* and we should still be *ready to distribute, willing to communicate,* 1 Tim. 6:18. When *kings of armies did flee apace, she that tarried at home did divide the spoil,* Ps. 68:12.

II. David was generous and kind to all his friends. When he had given every one his own with interest there was a considerable overplus, which David, as general, had the disposal of; probably the spoil of the tents of the Amalekites consisted much in plate and jewels (Jdg. 8:24, 26), and these, because he thought they would but make his own soldiers proud and effeminate, he thought fit to make presents of to his friends, even the *elders of Judah, v.* 26. Several places are here named to which he sent of these presents, all of them in or near the tribe of Judah. The first place named is Bethel, which signifies *the house of God;* that place shall be first served for its name's sake; or perhaps it means not the city so called, but the place where the ark was, which was therefore *the house of God.* Thither David sent the first and best, to those that attended there, for his sake who is the first and best. *Hebron* is named last (*v.* 31), probably because thither he sent the residuum, which was the largest share, having an eye upon that place as fittest for his head-quarters, 2 Sa. 2:1. In David's sending these presents observe, 1. His generosity. He aimed not to enrich himself, but to serve his country; and therefore God afterwards enriched him, and set him to rule the country he had served. It becomes gracious souls to be generous. *There is that scatters, and yet increases.* 2. His gratitude. He sent presents to *all the places where he and his men were wont to haunt* (*v.* 31), that is, to all that he had received kindness from, that had sheltered him and sent him intelligence or provisions. Note, Honesty, as well as honour, obliges us to requite the favours that have been done us, or at least to make a real acknowledgment of them as far as is in the power of our hand. 3. His piety. He calls his present *a blessing;* for no present we give to our friends will be a comfort to them but as it is made so by the blessing of God: it intimates that his prayers for them accompanied his present. He also sent it out of *the spoil of the enemies of the Lord* (so he calls them, not *his* enemies), that they might rejoice in the victory for the Lord's sake, and might join with him in thanksgivings for it. 4. His policy. He sent these presents among his countrymen to engage them to be ready to appear for him upon his accession to the throne, which he now saw at hand. *A man's gift maketh room for him.* He was fit to be a king who thus showed the bounty and liberality of a king. Munificence recommends a man more than magnificence. The Ziphites had none of his presents, nor the men of Keilah; and thus he showed that, though he was such a saint as not to revenge affronts, yet he was not such a fool as not to take notice of them.

CHAPTER 31

In the foregoing chapter we had David conquering, yea, more than a conqueror. In this chapter we have Saul conquered and worse than a captive. Providence ordered it that both these things should be doing just at the same time. The very same day; perhaps, that David was triumphing over the Amalekites, were the Philistines triumphing over Saul. One is set over against the other, that men may see what comes of trusting in God and what comes of forsaking him. We left Saul ready to engage the Philistines, with a shaking hand and an aching heart, having had his doom read him from hell, which he would not regard when it was read him from heaven. Let us now see what becomes of him. Here is, I. His army routed (*v.* 1). II. His three sons slain (*v.* 2). III. Himself wounded (*v.* 3), and slain by his own hand (*v.* 4). The death of his armour-bearer (*v.* 5) and all his men (*v.* 6). IV. His country possessed by the Philistines (*v.* 7). His camp plundered, and his dead body deserted (*v.* 8). His fall triumphed in (*v.* 9). His body publicly exposed (*v.* 10) and with difficulty rescued by the men of Jabesh-Gilead (*v.* 11-13). Thus fell the man that was rejected of God.

Verses 1–7

The day of recompence has now come, in which Saul must account for the blood of the Amalekites which he had sinfully spared, and that of the priests which he had more sinfully spilt; that of David too, which he would have spilt, must come into the account. Now his day has come to fall, as David foresaw, when he should descend into battle and perish, *ch.* 26:10. Come and see the *righteous judgments of God.*

I. He sees his soldiers fall about him, *v.* 1. Whether the Philistines were more numerous, better posted, and better led on, or what other advantages they had, we are not told; but it seems they were more vigorous, for they made the onset; they fought against Israel, and the Israelites fled and fell. The best of the troops were put into disorder, and multitudes slain, probably those whom Saul had employed in pursuing David. Thus those who had followed him and served him in his sin went before him in his fall and shared with him in his plagues.

II. He sees his sons fall before him. The victorious Philistines pressed most forcibly upon the king of Israel and those about him. His three sons were next him, it is probable, and they were all three slain before his face, to his great grief (for they were the hopes of his family) and to his great terror, for they were now the guard of his person, and he could conclude no other than that his own turn would come next. His sons are named (*v.* 2), and it grieves us to find Jonathan among them: that wise, valiant, good man, who was as much David's friend as Saul was his enemy, yet falls with the rest. Duty to his father would not permit him to stay at home, or to retire when the armies engaged; and Providence so orders it that he falls in the common fate of his family, though he never involved himself in the guilt of it; so that the observation of Eliphaz does not hold (Job 4:7), *Who ever perished being innocent?* For here was one. What shall we say to it? 1. God would hereby complete the vexation of Saul in his dying moments, and the judgment that was to be executed upon his house. If the family must fall, Jonathan, that is one of it, must fall with it. 2. He would hereby make David's way to the crown the more clear and open. For, though Jonathan himself would have cheerfully resigned all his title and interest to him (we have no reason to suspect any other), yet it is very probable that many of the people would have made use of his name for the support of the house of Saul, or at least would have come in but slowly to David. If Ishbosheth (who was now left at home as one unfit for action, and so escaped) had so many friends, what would Jonathan have had, who had been the darling of the people and had never forfeited their favour? Those that were so anxious to have a king like the nations would be zealous for the right line, especially if that threw the crown upon such a head as Jonathan's. This would have embarrassed David; and, if Jonathan could have prevailed to bring in all his interest to David, then it would have been said that Jonathan had made him king, whereas God was to have all the glory. *This is the Lord's doing.* So that though the death of Jonathan would be a great affliction to David, yet, by making him mindful of his own frailty, as well as by facilitating his accession to the throne, it would be an advantage to him. 3. God would hereby show us that the difference between good and bad is to be made in the other world, not in this. *All things come alike to all.* We cannot judge of the spiritual or eternal state of any by the manner of their death; for in that *there is one event to the righteous and to the wicked.*

III. He himself is sorely wounded by the Philistines and then slain by his own hand. The archers hit him (*v.* 3), so that he could neither fight nor fly, and therefore must inevitably fall into their hands. Thus, to make him the more miserable, destruction comes gradually upon him, and he dies so as to feel himself die. To such an extremity was he now reduced that, 1. He was desirous to die by the hand of his own servant rather than by the hand of the Philistines, lest they should abuse him as they had abused Samson. Miserable man! He finds himself dying, and all his care is to keep his body out of the hands of the Philistines, instead of being solicitous to resign his soul into the hands of God who gave it, Eccl. 12:7. As he lived, so he died, proud and jealous, and a terror to himself and all about him. Those who rightly understand the matter think it of small account, in comparison, how it is with them in death, so it may but be well with them after death. Those are in a deplorable condition indeed who, being *bitter in soul, long for death, but it cometh not* (Job 3:20, 21), especially those who, despairing of the mercy of god, like Judas, leap into a hell before them, to escape a hell within them. 2. When he could not obtain that favour he became his own executioner, thinking hereby to avoid shame, but running upon a heinous sin, and with it entailing upon his own name a mark of perpetual infamy, as *felo de se — a self-murderer.* Jonathan, who received his death-wound from the hand of the Philistines and bravely yielded to the fate of war, died on the bed of honour; but Saul died as a fool dieth, as a coward dieth — a proud fool, a sneaking coward; he died as a man that had neither the fear of God nor hope in God, neither the reason of a man nor the religion of an Israelite, much less the dignity of a prince or the resolution of a soldier. Let us all pray, *Lord, lead us*

not into temptation, this temptation. His armour-bearer would not run him through, and he did well to refuse it; for no man's servant ought to be a slave to his master's lusts or passions of any kind. The reason given is that *he was sorely afraid,* not of death, for he himself ran wilfully upon that immediately; but, having a profound reverence for the king his master, he could not conquer that so far as to do him any hurt; or perhaps he feared lest his trembling hand should give him but half a blow, and so put him to the greater misery.

IV. His armour-bearer who refused to kill him refused not to die with him, but *fell likewise upon his sword, v.* 5. This was an aggravating circumstance of the death of Saul, that, by the example of his wickedness in murdering himself, he drew in his servant to be guilty of the same wickedness, and *perished not alone in his iniquity.* The Jews say that Saul's armour-bearer was Doeg, whom he preferred to that dignity for killing the priests, and, if so, justly does his *violent dealing return on his own head.* David had foretold concerning him that God would *destroy him for ever,* Ps. 52:5.

V. The country was put into such confusion by the rout of Saul's army that the inhabitants of the neighbouring cities (*on that side Jordan,* as it might be read) quitted them, and the Philistines, for a time, had possession of them, till things were settled in Israel (*v.* 7), to such a sad pass had Saul by his wickedness brought his country, which might have remained in the hands of the uncircumcised if David had not been raised up to repair the breaches of it. See what a king he proved for whom they rejected God and Samuel. They had still done wickedly (it is to be feared) as well as he, and therefore *were consumed both they and their king,* as the prophet had foretold concerning them, *ch.* 12:25. And to this reference is had long after. Hos. 13:10, 11, "Where are thy saviours in all thy cities, of whom thou saidst, Give me a king and princes? I gave thee a king in my anger, and took him away in my wrath;* that is, he was a plague to thee living and dying; thou couldst expect no other."

Verses 8–13

The scripture makes no mention of the souls of Saul and his sons, what became of them after they were dead (secret things belong not to us), but of their bodies only.

I. How they were basely abused by the Philistines. The day after the battle, when they had recovered their fatigue, they came to strip the slain, and, among the rest, found the bodies of Saul and his three sons, *v.* 8. Saul's armour-bearer perhaps intended to honour his master by following the example of his self-murder, and to show thereby how well he loved him; but, if he had consulted his reason more than his passions, he would have spared that foolish compliment, not only in justice to his own life, but in kindness to his master, to whom, by the opportunity of survivorship, he might have done all the service that could be done him by any man after he was dead; for he might, in the night, have conveyed away his body, and those of his sons, and buried them decently. But such false and foolish notions these vain men have (though they would be wise) of giving and receiving honour. Nay, it should seem, Saul might have saved himself the fatal thrust and have made his escape: for the pursuers (in fear of whom he slew himself) came not to the place where he was till the next day. But whom God will destroy he infatuates and utterly *consumes with his terrors.* See Job 18:5, etc. Finding Saul's body (which now that it lay extended on the bloody turf was distinguishable from the rest by its length, as it was, while erect, by its height, when he proudly overlooked the surrounding crowd), they will, in that, triumph over Israel's crown, and meanly gratify a barbarous and brutish revenge by insulting the deserted corpse, which, when alive, they had stood in awe of. 1. They cut off his head. Had they designed in this to revenge the cutting off of Goliath's head they would rather have cut off the head of David, who did that execution, when he was in their country. They intended it, in general, for a reproach to Israel, who promised themselves that a crowned and an anointed head would save them from the Philistines, and a particular reproach to Saul, who was taller by the head than other men (which perhaps he was wont to boast of), but was now shorter by the head. 2. They stripped him of his armour (*v.* 9), and sent that to be set up as a trophy of their victory, in the house of Ashtaroth their goddess (*v.* 10); and we are told, 1 Chr. 10:10 (though it is omitted here), that they fastened his head in the temple of Dagon. Thus did they ascribe the honour of their victory, not as they ought to have done to the real justice of the true God, but to the imaginary power of their false gods, and by this respect paid to pretended deities shame those who give not the praise of their achievements to the living God. Ashtaroth, the idol that Israel had many a time gone a whoring after, now triumphs over them. 3. They sent expresses throughout their country, and ordered public notice to be given in the houses of their gods of the victory they had obtained (*v.* 9), that public rejoicings might be made and thanks given to their gods. This David regretted sorely, 2 Sa. 1:20. *Tell it not in Gath.* 4. They fastened his body and the bodies of his sons (as appears, *v.* 12) to the wall of *Bethshan,* a city that lay not far from Gilboa and very near to the river Jordan. Hither the dead bodies were dragged and here hung up in chains, to be devoured by the birds of prey. Saul slew himself to avoid being abused by the Philistines, and never was royal corpse so abused as his was, perhaps the more if they understood that he slew himself for that reason. He that thinks to save his honour by sin will certainly lose it. See to what a height of insolence the Philistines had arrived just before David was raised up, who perfectly subdued them. Now that they had slain Saul and his sons they thought the land of Israel was their own for ever, but they soon found themselves deceived. When God has accomplished his whole work by them he will accomplish it upon them. See Isa. 10:6, 7.

II. How they were bravely rescued by the men of Jabesh-Gilead. Little more than the river Jordan lay between Beth-shan and Jabesh-Gilead, and Jordan was in that place passable by its fords; a bold adventure was therefore made by the valiant men of that city, who in the night passed the river, took down the dead bodies, and gave them decent burial, *v.* 11, 13. This they did, 1. Out of a common concern for the honour of Israel, or the land of Israel, which ought not to be defiled by the exposing of any dead bodies, and especially of the crown of Israel, which was thus profaned by the uncircumcised. 2. Out of a particular sense of gratitude to Saul, for his zeal and forwardness to rescue them from the Ammonites when he first came to the throne, *ch.* 11. It is an evidence of a generous spirit and an encouragement to beneficence when the remembrance of kindnesses is thus retained, and they are thus returned in an extremity. The men of Jabesh-Gilead would have done Saul better service if they had sent their valiant men to him sooner, to strengthen him against the Philistines. But his day had come to fall, and now this is all the service they can do him, in honour to his memory. We find not that any general mourning was made for the death of Saul, as was for the death of Samuel (*ch.* 25:1), only those Gileadites of Jabesh did him honour at his death; for, (1.) They made a burning for the bodies, to perfume them. So some understand the burning of them. They burnt spices over them, *v.* 12. And that it was usual thus to do honour to their deceased friends, at least their princes, appears by the account of Asa's funeral (2 Chr. 16:14), that *they made a very great burning for him.* Or (as some think) they burnt the flesh, because it began to putrefy. (2.) They buried the bodies, when, by burning over them, they had sweetened them (or, if they burnt them, they buried the bones and ashes), under a tree, which served for a grave-stone and monument. And, (3.) They *fasted seven days,* that is, each day of the seven they fasted till the evening; thus they lamented the death of Saul and the present distracted state of Israel, and perhaps joined prayers with their fasting for the re-establishment of their shattered state. Though, *when the wicked perish there is shouting* (that is, it is to be hoped a better state of things will ensue, which will be matter of joy), yet humanity obliges us to show a decent respect to dead bodies, especially those of princes.

This book began with the birth of Samuel, but now it ends with the burial of Saul, the comparing of which two together will teach us to prefer the honour that comes from God before any of the honours which this world pretends to have the disposal of.

AN EXPOSITION, WITH PRACTICAL OBSERVATIONS, OF

THE SECOND BOOK OF SAMUEL

This book is the history of the reign of king David. We had in the foregoing book an account of his designation to the government, and his struggles with Saul, which ended at length in the death of his persecutor. This book begins with his accession to the throne, and is entirely taken up with the affairs of the government during the forty years he reigned, and therefore is entitled by the Septuagint. *The Third Book of the Kings.* It gives us an account of David's triumphs and his troubles. I. His triumphs over the house of Saul (*ch.* 1–4), over the Jebusites and Philistines (*ch.* 5), at the bringing up of the ark (*ch.* 6 and 7), over the neighbouring nations that opposed him (*ch.* 8–10); and so far the history is agreeable to what we might expect from David's character and the choice made of him. But his cloud has a dark side. II. We have his troubles, the causes of them, his sin in the matter of Uriah (*ch.* 11 and 12), the troubles themselves from the sin of Amnon (*ch.* 13), the rebellion of Absalom (*ch.* 14–19) and of Sheba (*ch.* 20), and the plague in Israel for his numbering the people (*ch.* 24), besides the famine of the Gibeonites (*ch.* 21). His son we have (*ch.* 22), and his words and worthies (*ch.* 23). Many things in his history are very instructive; but for the hero who is the subject of it, though in many instances he appears here very great, and very good, and very much the favourite of heaven, yet it must be confessed that his honour shines brighter in his Psalms than in his Annals.

CHAPTER 1

In the close of the foregoing book (with which this is connected as a continuation of the same history) we had Saul's exit; he went down slain to the pit, though we was the terror of the mighty in the land of the living. We are now to look towards the rising sun, and to enquire where David is, and what he is doing. In this chapter we have, I. Tidings brought him to Ziklag of the death of Saul and Jonathan, by an Amalekite, who undertook to give him a particular narrative of it (*v.* 1–10). II. David's sorrowful reception of these tidings, (*v.* 11, 12). III. Justice done upon the messenger, who boasted that he had helped Saul to dispatch himself (*v.* 13–16). IV. An elegy which David penned upon this occasion (*v.* 17–27). And in all this David's breast appears very happily free from the sparks both of revenge and ambition, and he observes a very suitable demeanour.

Verses 1–10

Here is, I. David settling again in Ziklag, his own city, after he had rescued his family and friends out of the hands of the Amalekites (*v.* 1): He *abode in Ziklag.* Thence he was now sending presents to his friends (1 Sa. 30:26), and there he was ready to receive those that came into his interests; not men in distress and debt, as his first followers were, but persons of quality in their country, *mighty men, men of war,* and *captains of thousands* (as we find, 1 Chr. 12:1, 8, 20); such came day by day to him, God stirring up their hearts to do so, till he had a *great host, like the host of God,* as it is said, 1 Chr. 12:22. The secret springs of revolutions are unaccountable, and must be resolved into that Providence which turns all hearts as the rivers of water.

II. Intelligence brought him thither of the death of Saul. It was strange that he did not leave some spies about the camp, to bring him early notice of the issue of the engagement, a sign that he desired not Saul's woeful day, nor was impatient to come to the throne, but willing to wait till those tidings were brought to him which many a one would have sent more than half-way to meet. He that believes does not make haste, takes good news when it comes and is not uneasy while it is in the coming. 1. The messenger presents himself to David as an express, in the posture of a mourner for the deceased prince and a subject to the succeeding one. He came with his clothes rent, and made obeisance to David (*v.* 2), pleasing himself with the fancy that he had the honour to be the first that did him homage as his sovereign, but it proved he was the first that received from him sentence of death as his judge. He told David he came from the camp of Israel, and intimated the bad posture it was in when he said he had escaped out of it, having much ado to get away with his life, *v.* 3. 2. He gives him a general account of the issue of the battle. David was very desirous to know how the matter went, as one that had more reason than any to be concerned for the public; and he told him very distinctly that the army of Israel was routed, many slain, and, among the rest, Saul and Jonathan, *v.* 4. He named only Saul and Jonathan, because he knew David would be most solicitous to know their fate; for Saul was the man whom he most feared and Jonathan the man whom he most loved. 3. He gives him a more particular account of the death of Saul. It is probable that David had heard, by the report of others, what the issue of the war was, for multitudes resorted to him, it should seem, in consequence; but he was desirous to know the certainty of the report concerning Saul and Jonathan, either because he was not forward to believe it or because he would not proceed upon it to make his own claims till he was fully assured of it. He therefore asks, *How knowest thou that Saul and Jonathan are dead?* in answer to which the young man tells him a very ready story, putting it past doubt that Saul was dead, for he himself had been not only an eye-witness of his death, but an instrument of it, and therefore David might rely upon his testimony. He says nothing, in his narrative, of the death of Jonathan, knowing how ungrateful that would be to David, but accounts only for Saul, thinking (as David understood it well enough, *ch.* 4:10) that he should be welcome for that, and rewarded as one that brought good tidings. The account he gives of this matter is, (1.) Very particular. That he happened to go to the place where Saul was (*v.* 6) as a passenger, not as a soldier, and therefore an indifferent person, that he found Saul endeavouring to run himself through with his own spear, none of his attendants being willing to do it for him; and, it seems, he could not do it dexterously for himself: his hand and heart failed him. The miserable man had not courage enough either to live or die; he therefore called this stranger to him (*v.* 7), enquired what countryman he was, for, provided he was not a Philistine, he would gladly receive from his hand the *coup de grace* (as the French call it concerning those that are broken on the wheel) — *the merciful stroke,* that might dispatch him out of his pain. Understanding that he was an Amalekite (neither one of his subjects nor one of his enemies), he begs this favour from him (*v.* 9): *Stand upon me, and slay me.* He is now sick of his dignity and willing to be trampled upon, sick of his life and willing to be slain. Who then would be inordinately fond of life or honour? The case may he such, even with those that have no hope in their death, that yet they may *desire to die, and death flee from them,* Rev. 9:6. *Anguish has come upon me;* so we read it, as a complaint of the pain and terror his spirit was seized with. If his conscience now brought to mind the javelin he had cast at David, his pride, malice, and perfidiousness, and especially the murder of the priests, no marvel that anguish came upon him: moles (they say) open their eyes when they are dying. Sense of unpardoned guilt will make death indeed the king of terrors. Those that have baffled their convictions will perhaps, in their dying moments, be overpowered by them. The margin reads it as a complaint of the inconvenience of his clothes; that his coat of mail which he had for defence, or his embroidered coat which he had for ornament, hindered him, that he could not get the spear far enough into his body, or so straitened him, now that his body swelled with anguish, that he could not expire. Let no man's clothes be his pride, for it may so happen that they may be his burden and snare. "Hereupon," saith our young man, *"I stood upon him, and slew him"* (v. 10) at which word, perhaps, he observed David look upon him with some show of displeasure, and therefore he excuses himself in the next words: *"For I was sure he could not live;* his life was whole in him indeed, but he would certainly have fallen into the hands of the Philistines or given himself another thrust." (2.) It is doubtful whether this story be true. If it be, the righteousness of God is to be observed, that Saul, who spared the Amalekites in contempt of the divine command, received his death's wound from an Amalekite. But most interpreters think that it was false, and that, though he might happen to be present, yet he was not assisting in the death of Saul, but told David so in expectation that he would reward him for it, as having done him a piece of good service. Those who would rejoice at the fall of an enemy are apt to measure others by themselves, and to think that they will do so too. But a man after God's own heart is not to be judged of by common men. I am not clear whether this young man's story was true or no: it may consist with the narrative in the chapter before, and be an addition to it, as Peter's account of the death of Judas (Acts 1:18) is to the narrative, Mt. 27:5. What is there called *a sword* may here be called *a spear,* or when he fell upon his sword he leaned on his spear. (3.) However he produced that which was proof sufficient of the death of Saul, the crown that was upon his head and the bracelet that was on his arm. It should seem Saul was so foolishly fond of these as to wear them in the field of battle, which made him a fair mark for the archers, by distinguishing him from those about him; but as *pride* (we say) *feels no cold,* so it fears no danger, from that which gratifies it. These fell into the hands of this Amalekite. Saul spared the best of their spoil, and now the best of his came to one of that devoted nation. He brought them to David, as the rightful owner of them now that Saul was dead, not doubting but by his officiousness herein to recommend himself to the best preferments in his court or camp. The tradition of the Jews is that this Amalekite was the son of Doeg (for the Amalekites were descendants from Edom), and that Doeg, who they suppose was Saul's armourbearer, before he slew himself gave Saul's crown and bracelet (the ensigns of his royalty) to his son, and bade him carry them to David, to curry favour with him. But this is a groundless conceit. Doeg's son, it is likely, was so well known to Saul that he needed not ask him as he did this Amalekite (v. 8), *Who art thou?* David had been long waiting for the crown, and now it was brought to him by an Amalekite. See how God can serve his own purposes of kindness to his people, even by designing (ill-designing) men, who aim at nothing but to set up themselves.

Verses 11–16

Here is, I. David's reception of these tidings. So far was he from falling into a transport of joy, as the Amalekite expected, that he fell into a passion of weeping, *rent his clothes* (v. 11), *mourned and fasted* (v. 12), not only for his people Israel and Jonathan his friend but for Saul his enemy. This he did, not only as a man of honour, in observance of that decorum which forbids us to insult over those that are fallen, and requires us to attend our relations to the grave with respect, whatever we lost by their life or got by their death, but as a good man and a man of conscience, that had forgiven the injuries Saul had done him and bore him no malice. He knew it, before his son wrote it (Prov. 24:17, 18), that if we *rejoice when our enemy falls the Lord sees it, and it displeases him;* and that *he who is glad at calamities shall not go unpunished,* Prov. 17:5. By this it appears that those passages in David's psalms which express his desire of, and triumph in, the ruin of his enemies, proceeded not from a spirit of revenge, nor any irregular passion, but from a holy zeal for the glory of God and the public good; for by what he did here, when he heard of Saul's death, we may perceive that his natural temper was very tender, and that he was kindly affected even to those that hated him. He was very sincere, no question, in his mourning for Saul, and it was not pretended, or a copy of his countenance only. His passion was so strong, on this occasion, that it moved those about him; *all that were with him,* at least in complaisance to him, *rent their clothes,* and they *fasted till even,* in token of their sorrow; and probably it was a religious fast: they humbled

themselves under the hand of God, and prayed for the repairing of the breaches made upon Israel by this defeat.

II. The reward he gave to him that brought him the tidings. Instead of preferring him, he put him to death, judged him out of his own mouth, as a murderer of his prince, and ordered him to be forthwith executed for the same. What a surprise was this to the messenger, who thought he should have favour shown him for his pains. In vain did he plead that he had Saul's order for it, that it was a real kindness to him, that he must inevitably have died; all those pleas are overruled: *"Thy mouth has testified against thee, saying, I have slain the Lord's anointed* (v. 16), therefore thou must die." Now,

1. David herein did not do unjustly. For, (1.) The man was an Amalekite. This, lest he should have mistaken it in his narrative, he made him own a second time, v. 13. That nation, and all that belonged to it, were doomed to destruction, so that, in slaying him, David did what his predecessor should have done and was rejected for not doing. (2.) He did himself confess the crime, so that the evidence was, by the consent of all laws, sufficient to convict him; for every man is presumed to make the best of himself. If he did as he said, he deserved to die for treason (v. 14), doing that which, it is probable, he heard Saul's own armour-bearer refuse to do; if not, yet by boasting that he had done it he plainly showed that if there had been occasion he would have done it, and would have made nothing of it; and, by boasting of it to David, he showed what opinion he had of him, that he would rejoice in it, as one altogether like himself, which was an intolerable affront to him who had himself once and again refused to *stretch forth his hand against the Lord's anointed.* And his lying to David, if indeed it was a lie, was highly criminal, and proved, as sooner or later that sin will prove, lying against his own head.

2. He did honourably and well. Hereby he demonstrated the sincerity of his grief, discouraged all others from thinking by doing the like to ingratiate themselves with him, and did that which might probably oblige the house of Saul and win upon them, and recommend him to the people as one that was zealous for public justice, without regard to his own private interest. We may learn from it that to give assistance to any in murdering themselves, directly or indirectly, if done wittingly, incurs the guilt of blood, and that the lives of princes ought to be, in a special manner, precious to us.

Verses 17–27

When David had rent his clothes, mourned, and wept, and fasted, for the death of Saul, and done justice upon him who made himself guilty of it, one would think he had made full payment of the debt of honour he owed to his memory; yet this is not all: we have here a poem he wrote on that occasion; for he was a great master of his pen as well as of his sword. By this elegy he designed both to express his own sorrow for this great calamity and to impress the like on the minds of others, who ought to lay it to heart. The putting of lamentations into poems made them, 1. The more moving and affecting. The passion of the poet, or singer, is, by this way, wonderfully communicated to the readers and hearers. 2. The more lasting. Thus they were made, not only to spread far, but to continue long, from generation to generation. Those might gain information by poems that would not read history. Here we have,

I. The orders David gave with this elegy (v. 18): *He bade them teach the children of Judah* (his own tribe, whatever others did) *the use of the bow,* either. 1. The bow used in war. Not but that the children of Judah knew how to use the bow (it was so commonly used in war, long before this, that the sword and bow were put for all weapons of war, Gen. 48:22), but perhaps they had of late made more use of slings, as David in killing Goliath, because cheaper, and David would have them now to see the inconvenience of these (for it was the archers of the Philistines that bore so hard upon Saul, 1 Sa. 21:3), and to return more generally to the use of the bow, to exercise themselves in this weapon, that they might be in a capacity to avenge the death of their prince upon the Philistines, and to outdo them at their own weapon. It was a pity but those that had such good heads and hearts as the children of Judah should be well armed. David hereby showed his authority over and concern for the armies of Israel, and set himself to rectify the errors of the former reign. But we find that the companies which had now come to David to Ziklag were armed with bows (1 Chr. 12:2); therefore, 2.

Some understand it either of some musical instrument called *a bow* (to which he would have the mournful ditties sung) or of the elegy itself: *He bade them teach the children of Judah Kesheth, the bow,* that is, this song, which was so entitled for the sake of Jonathan's bow, the achievements of which are here celebrated. Moses commanded Israel to learn his song (Deu. 31:19), so David his. Probably he bade the Levites teach them. It is *written in the book of Jasher,* there it was kept upon record, and thence transcribed into this history. That book was probably a collection of state-poems; what is said to be written in that book (Jos. 10:13) is also poetical, a fragment of an historical poem. Even songs would be forgotten and lost if they were not committed to writing, that best conservatory of knowledge.

II. The elegy itself. It is not a divine hymn, nor given by inspiration of God to be used in divine service, nor is there any mention of God in it; but it is a human composition, and therefore was inserted, not in the book of Psalms (which, being of divine original, is preserved), but in the book of Jasher, which, being only a collection of common poems, is long since lost. This elegy proves David to have been,

1. A man of an excellent spirit, in four things: —

(1.) He was very generous to Saul, his sworn enemy. Saul was his father-in-law, his sovereign, and the anointed of the Lord; and therefore, though he had done him a great deal of wrong, David does not wreak his revenge upon his memory when he is in his grave; but like a good man, and a man of honour, [1.] He conceals his faults; and, though there was no preventing their appearance in his history, yet they should not appear in this elegy. Charity teaches us to make the best we can of every body and to say nothing of those of whom we can say no good, especially when they are gone. *De mortuis nil nisi bonum — Say nothing but good concerning the dead.* We ought to deny ourselves the satisfaction of making personal reflections upon those who have been injurious to us, much more drawing their character thence, as if every man must of necessity be a bad man that has done ill by us. Let the corrupt part of the memory be buried with the corrupt part of the man — earth to earth, ashes to ashes; let the blemish be hidden and a veil drawn over the deformity. [2.] He celebrates that which was praiseworthy in him. He does not commend him for that which he was not, says nothing of his piety or fidelity. Those funeral commendations which are gathered out of the spoils of truth are not at all to the praise of those on whom they are bestowed, but very much the dispraise of those who unjustly misplace them. But he has this to say in honour of Saul himself, *First,* That he was *anointed with oil* (v. 21), the sacred oil, which signified his elevation to, and qualification for, the government. Whatever he was otherwise, the *crown of the anointing oil of his God was upon him,* as is said of the high priest (Lev. 21:12), and on that account he was to be honoured, because God, the fountain of honour, had honoured him. *Secondly,* That he was a man of war, a *mighty man* (v. 19–21), that he had often been victorious over the enemies of Israel and *vexed them whithersoever he turned,* 1 Sa. 14:47. His *sword returned not empty,* but satiated with blood and spoil, v. 22. His disgrace and fall at last must not make his former successes and services to be forgotten. Though his sun set under a cloud, time was when it shone brightly. *Thirdly,* That take him with Jonathan he was a man of a very agreeable temper, that recommended himself to the affections of his subjects (v. 23): *Saul and Jonathan were lovely and pleasant.* Jonathan was always so, and Saul was so as long as he concurred with him. Take them together, and in the pursuit of the enemy, never were men more bold, more brave; they were *swifter than eagles and stronger than lions.* Observe, Those that were most fierce and fiery in the camp were no less sweet and lovely in the court, as amiable to the subject as they were formidable to the foe; a rare combination of softness and sharpness they had, which makes any man's temper very happy. It may be understood of the harmony and affection that for the most part subsisted between Saul and Jonathan: they were lovely and pleasant one to another, Jonathan a dutiful son, Saul an affectionate father; and therefore dear to each other in their lives, and *in their death they were not divided,* but kept close together in the stand they made against the Philistines, and fell together in the same cause. *Fourthly,* That he had enriched his country with the spoils of conquered nations, and introduced a more splendid attire. When they had a king like the nations, they must have clothes like the nations; and herein he was, in a particular manner, obliging to his female subjects, *v.* 24. The *daughters of Israel* he *clothed in scarlet,* which was their delight.

(2.) He was very grateful to Jonathan, his sworn friend. Besides the tears he shed over him, and the encomiums he gives of him in common with Saul, he mentions him with some marks of distinction (*v.* 25): *O Jonathan! thou wast slain in thy high places!* which (compared with *v.* 19) intimates that he meant him by *the beauty of Israel,* which, he there says, was slain upon the high places. He laments Jonathan as his particular friend (*v.* 26): *My brother, Jonathan;* not so much because of what he would have been to him if he had lived, very serviceable no doubt in his advancement to the throne and instrumental to prevent those long struggles which, for want of his assistance, he had with the house of Saul (had this been the only ground of his grief it would have been selfish), but he lamented him for what he had been: *"Very pleasant hast thou been unto me;* but that pleasantness is now over, and *I am distressed for thee."* He had reason to say that Jonathan's love to him was wonderful; surely never was the like, for a man to love one who he knew was to take the crown over his head, and to be so faithful to his rival: this far surpassed the highest degree of conjugal affection and constancy. See here, [1.] That nothing is more delightful in this world than a true friend, that is wise and good, that kindly receives and returns our affection, and is faithful to us in all our true interests. [2.] That nothing is more distressful than the loss of such a friend; it is parting with a piece of one's self. It is the vanity of this world that what is most pleasant to us we are most liable to be distressed in. The more we love the more we grieve.

(3.) He was deeply concerned for the honour of God; for this is what he has an eye to when he fears lest *the daughters of the uncircumcised,* that are out of covenant with God, should triumph over Israel, and the God of Israel, *v.* 20. Good men are touched in a very sensible part by the reproaches of those that reproach God.

(4.) He was deeply concerned for the public welfare. It was the beauty of Israel that was slain (*v.* 19) and the honour of the public that was disgraced: The *mighty have fallen* (this is three times lamented, *v.* 19, 25, 27), and so the strength of the people is weakened. Public losses are most laid to heart by men of public spirit. David hoped God would make him instrumental to repair those losses and yet laments them.

2. A man of a fine imagination, as well as a wise and holy man. The expressions are all excellent, and calculated to work upon the passions. (1.) The embargo he would fain lay upon Fame is elegant (*v.* 20): *Tell it not in Gath.* It grieved him to the heart to think that it would be proclaimed in the cities of the Philistines, and that they would insult over Israel upon it, and the more in remembrance of the triumphs of Israel over them formerly, when they sang, *Saul has slain his thousands;* for this would now be retorted. (2.) The curse he entails on the mountains of Gilboa, the theatre on which this tragedy was acted: *Let there be no dew upon you, nor fields of offerings, v.* 21. This is a poetical strain, like that of Job, *Let the day perish wherein I was born.* Not as if David wished that any part of the land of Israel might be barren, but, to express his sorrow for the thing, he speaks with a seeming indignation at the place. Observe, [1.] How the fruitfulness of the earth depends upon heaven. The worst thing he could wish to the mountains of Gilboa was barrenness and unprofitableness to man: those are miserable that are useless. It was the curse Christ pronounced on the fig-tree, *Never fruit grow on thee more,* and that took effect — the fig-tree withered away: this, on the mountains of Gilboa, did not. But, when he wished them barren, he wished there might be no rain upon them; and, if the heavens be brass, the earth will soon be iron. [2.] How the fruitfulness of the earth must therefore be devoted to heaven, which is intimated in his calling the fruitful fields *fields of offerings.* Those fruits of their land that were offered to God were the crown and glory of it: and therefore the failure of the offerings is the saddest consequent of the failure of the corn. See Joel 1:9. To want that wherewith we should honour God is worse than to want that wherewith we should sustain ourselves. This is the reproach David fastens upon the mountains of Gilboa, which, having been stained with royal blood, thereby forfeited celestial dews. In this elegy Saul had a more honourable interment than that which the men of Jabesh-Gilead gave him.

CHAPTER 2

David had paid due respect to the memory of Saul his prince and Jonathan his friend, and what he did was as much his praise as theirs; he is now considering what is to be done next. Saul is dead, now therefore David arise. I. By direction from God he went up to Hebron, and was there anointed king (*v.* 1–4). II. He returned thanks to the men of Jabesh-Gilead for burying Saul (*v.* 5–7). III. Ishbosheth, the son of Saul, is set up in opposition to him (*v.* 8–11). IV. A warm encounter happens between David's party and Ishbosheth's, in which, 1. Twelve of each side engaged hand to hand and were all slain (*v.* 12–16). 2. Saul's party was beaten (*v.* 17). 3. Asahel, on David's side, was slain by Abner (*v.* 18–23). 4. Joab, at Abner's request, sounds a retreat, (*v.* 24–28). 5. Abner makes the best of his way (*v.* 29), and the loss on both sides is computed (*v.* 30–32). So that here we have an account of a civil war in Israel, which, in process of time, ended in the complete settlement of David on the throne.

Verses 1–7

When Saul and Jonathan were dead, though David knew himself anointed to be king, and now saw his way very clear, yet he did not immediately send messengers through all the coasts of Israel to summon all people to come in and swear allegiance to him, upon pain of death, but proceeded leisurely; for he that believeth doth not make haste, but waits God's time for the accomplishment of God's promises. Many had come in to his assistance from several tribes while he continued at Ziklag, as we find (1 Chr. 12:1–22), and with such a force he might have come in by conquest. But he that will rule with meekness will not rise with violence. Observe here,

I. The direction he sought and had from God in this critical juncture, *v.* 1. He doubted not of success, yet he used proper means, both divine and human. Assurance of hope in God's promise will be so far from slackening that it will quicken pious endeavours. If I be elected to the crown of life, it does not follow, Then I will do nothing; but, Then I will do all that he directs me, and follow the guidance of him who chose me. This good use David made of his election, and so will all whom God has chosen. 1. David, according to the precept, *acknowledged God in his way.* He enquired of the Lord by the breast-plate of judgment, which Abiathar brought to him. We must apply to God not only when we are in distress, but even when the world smiles upon us and second causes work in favour of us. His enquiry was, *Shall I go up to any of the cities of Judah?* Shall I stir hence? Though Ziklag be in ruins, he will not quit it without direction from God. "If I stir hence, *Shall I go to one of the cities of Judah?"* not limiting God to them (if God should so direct him, he would go to any of the cities of Israel), but thus expressing his prudence (in the cities of Judah he would find most friends), and his modesty — he would look no further at present than his own tribe. In all our motions and removals it is comfortable to see God going before us; and we may, if by faith and prayer we set him before us. 2. God, according to the promise, directed his path, bade him go up, told him whither, unto Hebron, a priest's city, one of the cities of refuge, so it was to David, and an intimation that God himself would be to him a little sanctuary. The sepulchres of the patriarchs, adjoining to Hebron, would remind him of the ancient promise, on which God had caused him to hope. God sent him not to Bethlehem, his own city, because that was *little among the thousands of Judah* (Mic. 5:2), but to Hebron, a more considerable place, and which perhaps was then as the county-town of that tribe.

II. The care he took of his family and friends in his removal to Hebron. 1. He took his wives with him (*v.* 2), that, as they had been companions with him in tribulation, they might be so in the kingdom. It does not appear that as yet he had any children; his first was born in Hebron, *ch.* 3:2. 2. He took his friends and followers with him, *v.* 3. They had accompanied him in his wanderings, and therefore, when he gained a settlement, they settled with him. Thus, if we *suffer with Christ, we shall reign with him,* 2 Tim. 2:12. Nay, Christ does more for his good soldiers than David could do for his; David found lodging for them — *They dwelt in the cities of Hebron,* and adjacent towns; but to those who *continue with Christ in his temptations he appoints a kingdom,* and will *feast them at his own table,* Lu. 22:29, 30.

III. The honour done him by the men of Judah: They *anointed him king over the house of Judah, v.* 4. The tribe of Judah had often stood by itself more than any other of the tribes. In Saul's time it was numbered by itself as a distinct body (1 Sa. 15:4) and those of this tribe had been accustomed to act separately. They did so now; yet they did it for themselves only; they did not pretend to anoint him king *over all Israel* (as Jdg. 9:22), but only *over the house of Judah.* The rest of the tribes might do as they pleased, but, as for them and their house, they would be ruled by him whom God had chosen. See how David rose gradually; he was first anointed king *in reversion,* then *in possession* of one tribe only, and at last of all the tribes. Thus the kingdom of the Messiah, the Son of David, is set up by degrees; he is Lord of all by divine designation, but *we see not yet all things put under him,* Heb. 2:8. David's reigning at first over the house of Judah only was a tacit intimation of Providence that his kingdom would in a short time be reduced to that again, as it was when the ten tribes revolted from his grandson; and it would be an encouragement to the godly kings of Judah that David himself at first reigned over Judah only.

IV. The respectful message he sent to the men of Jabesh-Gilead, to return them thanks for their kindness to Saul. Still he studies to honour the memory of his predecessor, and thereby to show that he was far from aiming at the crown from any principle of ambition or enmity to Saul, but purely because he was called of God to it. It was told him that the men of Jabesh-Gilead buried Saul, perhaps by some that thought he would be displeased at them as over-officious. But he was far from that. 1. He commends them for it, *v.* 5. According as our obligations were to love and honour any while they lived, we ought to show respect to their remains (that is, their bodies, names, and families) when they are dead. "Saul was your lord," says David, "and therefore you did well to show him this kindness and do him this honour." 2. He prays to God to bless them for it, and to recompense it to them: *Blessed are you,* and blessed *may you be* of the Lord, who will deal kindly with those in a particular manner that *dealt kindly with the dead,* as it is in Ruth 1:8. Due respect and affection shown to the bodies, names, and families of those that are dead, in conscience towards God, is a piece of charity which shall in no wise lose its reward: *The Lord show kindness and truth to you* (*v.* 6), that is, kindness according to the promise. What kindness God shows is in truth, what one may trust to. 3. He promises to make them amends for it: *I also will requite you.* He does not turn them over to God for a recompense that he may excuse himself from rewarding them. Good wishes are good things, and instances of gratitude, but they are too cheap to be rested in where there is an ability to do more. 4. He prudently takes this opportunity to gain them to his interest, *v.* 7. They had paid their last respects to Saul, and he would have them to be the last: *"The house of Judah have anointed me king,* and it will be your wisdom to concur with them and in that to be valiant." We must not so dote on the dead, how much soever we have valued them, as to neglect or despise the blessings we have in those that survive, whom God has raised up to us in their stead.

Verses 8–17

Here is, I. A rivalship between two kings — David, whom God made king, and Ishbosheth, whom Abner made king. One would have thought, when Saul was slain, and all his sons that had sense and spirit enough to take the field with him, David would come to the throne without any opposition, since all Israel knew, not only how he had signalized himself, but how manifestly God had designated him to it; but such a spirit of contradiction is there, in the devices of men, to the counsels of God, that such a weak and silly thing as Ishbosheth, who was not thought fit to go with his father to the battle, shall yet be thought fit to succeed him in the government, rather than David shall come peaceably to it. Herein David's kingdom was typical of the Messiah's, against which *the heathens rage* and the *rulers take counsel,* Ps. 2:1, 2. 1. Abner was the person who set up Ishbosheth in competition with David, perhaps in his zeal for the lineal succession (since they must have a king like the nations, in *this* they must be like them, that the crown must descend from father to son), or rather in his affection to his own family and relations (for he was Saul's uncle), and because he had no other way to secure to himself the post of honour he was in, as captain of the host. See how much mischief the pride and ambition of one man may be the occasion of. Ishbosheth would never have set up himself if Abner had not set him up, and made a tool of him to serve his own purposes. 2. Mahanaim, the place where he first made his claim, was on the other side Jordan, where it was thought David had the least interest, and being at a distance from his forces they might have time to strengthen themselves. But having set up his standard there, the unthinking people of all the tribes of Israel (that is, the generality of them) submitted to him (*v.* 9), and Judah only was entirely for David. This was a further trial of the faith of David in the promise of God, and of his patience, whether he could wait God's time for the performance of that promise. 3. Some difficulty there is about the time of the continuance of this competition. David reigned about seven years over Judah only (*v.* 11), and yet (*v.* 10) Ishbosheth reigned over Israel but two years: before those two years, or after, or both, it was in general for the house of Saul (*ch.* 3:6), and not any particular person of that house, that Abner declared. Or these two years he reigned before the war broke out (*v.* 12), which continued long, even the remaining five years, *ch.* 3:1.

II. An encounter between their two armies.

1. It does not appear that either side brought their whole force into the field, for the slaughter was but small, *v.* 30, 31. We may wonder, (1.) That the men of Judah did not appear and act more vigorously for David, to reduce all the nation into obedience to him; but, it is likely, David would not suffer them to act offensively, choosing rather to wait till the thing would do itself or rather till God would do it for him, without the effusion of Israelitish blood; for to him, as a type of Christ, that was very precious, Ps. 72:14. Even those that were his adversaries he looked upon as his subjects, and would treat them accordingly. (2.) That the men of Israel could in a manner stand neuter, and sit down tamely under Ishbosheth, for so many years, especially considering what characters many of the tribes displayed at this time (as we find, 1 Chr. 12:23, etc.): *Wise men, mighty men, men of valour, expert in war,* and not of double heart, and yet for seven years together, for aught that appears, most of them seemed indifferent in whose hand the public administration was. Divine Providence serves its own purposes by the stupidity of men at some times and the activity of the same persons at other times; they are unlike themselves, and yet the motions of Providence are uniform.

2. In this battle Abner was the aggressor. David sat still to see how the matter would fall, but the house of Saul, and Abner at the head of it, gave the challenge, and they went by the worst. Therefore *go not forth hastily to strive,* nor be forward to begin quarrels, *lest thou know not what to do in the end thereof,* Prov. 25:8. A fool's lips and hands enter into contention.

3. The seat of the war was Gibeon. Abner chose it because it was in the lot of Benjamin, where Saul had the most friends; yet, since he offered battle, Joab, David's general, would not decline it, but there joined issue with him, and met him *by the pool of Gibeon, v.* 13. David's cause, being built upon God's promise, feared not the disadvantages of the ground. The pool between them gave both sides time to deliberate.

4. The engagement was at first proposed by Abner, and accepted by Joab, to be between twelve and twelve of a side. (1.) It should seem this trial of skill began in sport. Abner made the motion (*v.* 14): *Let the young men arise and play before us,* as gladiators. Perhaps Saul had used his men to these barbarous pastimes, like a tyrant indeed, and Abner had learnt of him to make a jest of wounds and death and divert himself with the scenes of blood and horror. He meant, "Let them *fight* before us," when he said, "Let them *play* before us." *Fools* thus *make a mock at sin.* but he is unworthy the name of a man that can be thus prodigal of human blood, that can thus *throw about firebrands, arrows, and death,* and say, *Am not I in sport?* Prov. 26:18, 19. Joab, having been bred up under David, had so much wisdom as not to make such a proposal, yet had not resolution enough to resist and gainsay it when another made it; for he stood upon a point of honour, and thought it a blemish to his reputation to refuse a challenge, and therefore said, *Let them arise;* not that he was fond of the sport, or expected that the duels would be decisive, but he would not be hectored by his antagonist. How many precious lives have thus been sacrificed to the caprices of proud men! Twelve of each side were accordingly called out as champions to enter the lists, a double jury of life and death, not of others', but their own; and the champions on Abner's side seem to have been most forward, for they took the field first (*v.* 15), having perhaps been bred up in a foolish ambition thus to serve the humour of their commander-in-chief. But, (2.) However it began, it ended in blood (*v.* 16): They thrust *every man his sword into his fellow's side* (spurred on by honour, not by enmity); so they *fell down together,* that is, all the twenty-four were slain, such an equal match were they for one another, and so resolute, that neither side would either beg or give quarter; they did as it were by agreement (says *Josephus*) dispatch one another with mutual wounds. Those that strike at other men's lives often throw away their own and death only conquers and rides in triumph. The wonderful obstinacy of both sides was remembered in the name given to the place: *Heldath-hazzurim — the field of rocky men,* men that were not only strong in body, but of firm and unshaken constancy, that stirred not at the sight of death. Yet *the stout-hearted were spoiled, and slept their sleep,* Ps. 76:5. Poor honour for men to purchase at so vast an expense! Those that lose their lives for Christ shall find them.

5. The whole army at length engaged, and Abner's forces were routed, *v.* 17. The former was a drawn battle, in which all were killed on both sides, and therefore they must put it upon another trial, in which (as it often happens) those that gave the challenge went away with loss. David had God on his side; his side therefore was victorious.

Verses 18–24

We have here the contest between Abner and Asahel. Asahel, the brother of Joab and cousin-german to David, was one of the principal commanders of David's forces, and was famous for swiftness in running: he was *as light of foot as a wild roe* (*v.* 18); this he got the name of by swift pursuing, not swift flying. Yet, we may suppose, he was not comparable to Abner as a skilful experienced soldier; we must therefore observe,

I. How rash he was in aiming to make Abner his prisoner. He pursued after him, and no other, *v.* 19. Proud of his relation to David and Joab, his own swiftness, and the success of his party, no less a trophy of victory would now serve the young warrior than Abner himself, either slain or bound, which he thought would put an end to the war and effectually open David's way to the throne. This made him very eager in the pursuit, and careless of the opportunities he had of seizing others in his way, on his right hand and on his left; his eye was on Abner only. The design was brave, had he been *par negotio — equal to its accomplishment:* but let not the swift man glory in his swiftness, any more than the strong man in his strength; *magnis excidit ausis — he perished in an attempt too vast for him.*

II. How generous Abner was in giving him notice of the danger he exposed himself to, and advising him not to *meddle to his own hurt,* 2 Chr. 25:19. 1. He bade him content himself with a less prey (*v.* 21): *"Lay hold of one of the young men,* plunder him and make him thy prisoner, meddle with thy match, but pretend not to one who is so much superior to thee." It is wisdom in all contests to compare our own strength with that of our adversaries, and to take heed of being partial to ourselves in making the comparison, lest we prove in the issue *enemies to ourselves,* Lu. 14:31. 2. He begged of him not to put him upon the necessity of slaying him in his own defence, which he was very loth to do, but must do rather than be slain by him, *v.* 22. Abner, it seems, either loved Joab or feared him; for he was very loth to incur his displeasure, which he would certainly do if he slew Asahel. It is commendable for enemies to be thus respectful one to another. Abner's care how he should lift up his face to Joab gives cause to suspect that he really believed David would have the kingdom at last, according to the divine designation, and then, in opposing him, he acted against his conscience.

III. How fatal Asahel's rashness was to him. He refused to turn aside, thinking that Abner spoke so courteously because he feared him; but what came of it? Abner, as soon as he came up to him, gave him his death's wound with a back stroke (*v.* 23): *He smote him with the hinder end of his spear,* from which he feared no danger. This was a pass which Asahel was not acquainted with, nor had learned to stand upon his guard against; but Abner, perhaps, had formerly used it, and done execution with it; and here it did effectual execution. Asahel died immediately of the wound. See here, 1. How death often comes upon us by ways that we least suspect. Who would fear the hand of a flying enemy or the butt-end of a spear? yet from these Asahel receives his death's wound. 2. How we are often betrayed by the accomplishments we are proud of. Asahel's swiftness, which he presumed so much upon, did him no kindness, but forwarded his fate, and with it he ran upon his death, instead of running from it. Asahel's fall was not only Abner's security from him, but put a full stop to the conqueror's pursuit and gave Abner time to rally again; for all that came to the place stood still, only Joab and Abishai, instead of being disheartened, were exasperated by it, pursued Abner with so much the more fury (*v.* 24), and overtook him at last about sunset, when the approaching night would oblige them to retire.

Verses 25–32

Here, I. Abner, being conquered, meanly begs for a cessation of arms. He rallied the remains of his forces on the top of a hill (*v.* 25), as if he would have made head again, but becomes a humble supplicant to Joab for a little breathing-time, *v.* 26. He that was most forward to fight was the first that had enough of it. He that made a jest of bloodshed *(Let the young men arise and play before us, v.* 14) is now shocked at it, when he finds himself on the losing side, and the sword he made so light of drawing threatening to touch himself. Observe how his note is changed. Then it was but playing with the sword; now, *Shall the sword devour for ever?* It had devoured but one day, yet to him it seemed forever, because it went against him; and very willing he is now that the sun should not go down upon the wrath. Now he can appeal to Joab himself concerning the miserable consequences of a civil war: *Knowest thou not that it will be bitterness in the latter end?* It will be reflected upon with regret when the account comes to be made up; for, whoever gets in a civil war, the community is sure to lose. Perhaps he refers to the bitterness that there was in the tribes of Israel, in the end of their war with Benjamin, when they wept sorely for the desolations which they themselves had made, Jdg. 21:2. Now he begs of Joab to sound a retreat, and pleads that they were brethren, who ought not thus to bite and devour one another. He that in the morning would have Joab bid the people fall upon their brethren now would have him bid them lay down their arms. See here, 1. How easy it is for men to use reason when it makes for them who would not use it if it made against them. If Abner had been the conqueror, we should not have had him complaining of the voraciousness of the sword and the miseries of a civil war, nor pleading that both sides were brethren; but, finding himself beaten, all these reasonings are mustered up and improved for the securing of his retreat and the saving of his scattered troops from being cut off. 2. How the issue of things alters men's minds. The same thing which looked pleasant in the morning at night looked dismal. Those that are forward to enter into contention will perhaps repent it before they have done with it, and therefore had better leave it off before it be meddled with, as Solomon advises. It is true of every sin (O that men would consider it in time!) that it will be *bitterness in the latter end. At the last it bites like a serpent* those on whom it fawned.

II. Joab, though a conqueror, generously grants it, and sounds a retreat, knowing very well his master's mind and how averse he was to the shedding of blood. He does indeed justly upbraid Abner with his forwardness to engage, and lays the blame upon him that there had been so much bloodshed as there was (*v.* 27): *"Unless thou hadst spoken,"* that is, "hadst given orders to fight, hadst bidden the young men arise and play before us, none of us would have struck a stroke, nor drawn a sword against our brethren. Thou complainest that the sword devours, but who first unsheathed it? Who began? Now thou wouldst have the people parted, but remember who set them on to fight. We should have retired in the morning if thou hadst not given the challenge." Those that are forward to make mischief are commonly the first to complain of it. This might have served to excuse Joab if he had pushed on his victory, and made a full end of Abner's forces; but like one that pitied the mistake of his adversaries, and scorned to make an army of Israelites pay dearly for the folly of their commander, he very honourably, by sound of trumpet, put a stop to the pursuit (*v.* 28) and suffered Abner to make an orderly retreat. It is good husbandry to be sparing of blood. As the soldiers were here very obsequious to the general's orders, so he, no doubt, observed the instructions of his prince, who sought the welfare of all Israel and therefore not the hurt of any.

III. The armies being separated, both retired to the places whence they came, and both marched in the night, Abner to Mahanaim, on the other side Jordan (*v.* 29), and Joab to Hebron, where David was, *v.* 32. The slain on both sides are computed. On David's side only nineteen men were missing, besides Asahel (*v.* 30), who was worth more than all; on Abner's side 360, *v.* 31. In civil wars formerly great slaughters had been made (as Jdg. 12:6, 20, 44), in comparison with which this was nothing. It is to be hoped that they had grown wiser and more moderate. Asahel's funeral is here mentioned; the rest they buried in the field of battle, but he was carried to Bethlehem, and buried in the sepulchre of his father, *v.* 32. Thus are distinctions made between the dust of some and that of others; but in the resurrection no other difference will be made but that between godly and ungodly, which will remain for ever.

CHAPTER 3

The battle between Joab and Abner did not end the controversy between the two houses of Saul and David, but it is in this chapter working towards a period. Here is, I. The gradual advance of David's interest (*v.* 1). II. The building up of his family (*v.* 2–5). III. Abner's quarrel with Ish-bosheth, and his treaty with David (*v.* 6–12). IV. The preliminaries settled (*v.* 13–16). V. Abner's undertaking and attempt to bring Israel over to David (*v.* 17–21). VI. The treacherous murder of Abner by Joab, when he was carrying on this matter (*v.* 22–27). VII. David's great concern and trouble for the death of Abner (*v.* 28–39).

Verses 1–6

Here is, I. The struggle that David had with the house of Saul before his settlement in the throne was completed, *v.* 1. 1. Both sides contested. Saul's house, though beheaded and diminished, would not fall tamely. It is not strange between them, but one would wonder it should be a long war, when David's house had right on its side, and therefore God on its side; but, though truth and equity will triumph at last, God made for wise and holy ends prolonged the conflict. The length of this war tried the faith and patience of David, and made his establishment at last the more welcome to him. 2. David's side got ground. The house of Saul waxed weaker and weaker, lost places, lost men, sunk in its reputation, grew less considerable, and was foiled in every engagement. But the house of David grew stronger and stronger. Many deserted the declining cause of Saul's house, and prudently came into David's interest, being convinced that he would certainly win the day. The contest between grace and corruption in the hearts of believers, who are sanctified but in part, may fitly be compared to this recorded here. There is a long war between them, the flesh lusted against the spirit and the spirit against the flesh; but, as the work of sanctification is carried on, corruption, like the house of Saul, grows weaker and weaker; while grace, like the house of David, grows stronger and stronger, till it come to a perfect man, and judgment be brought forth unto victory.

II. The increase of his own house. Here is an account of six sons he had by six several wives, in the seven years he reigned in Hebron. Perhaps this is here mentioned as that which strengthened David's interest. Every child, whose welfare was embarked in the common safety, was a fresh security given to the commonwealth for his care of it. He that has his quiver filled with these arrows shall *speak with his enemy in the gate,* Ps. 127:5. As the death of Saul's sons weakened his interest, so the birth of David's strengthened his. 1. It was David's fault thus to multiply wives, contrary to the law (Deu. 17:17), and it was a bad example to his successors. 2. It does not appear that in these seven years he had above one son by each of these wives; some have had as numerous a progeny, and with much more honour and comfort, by one wife. 3. We read not that any of these sons came to be famous (three of them were infamous, Amnon, Absalom, and Adonijah); we have therefore reason to rejoice with trembling in the building up of our families. 4. His son by Abigail is called *Chileab* (*v.* 3), whereas (1 Chr. 3:1) he is called *Daniel.* Bishop Patrick mentions the reason which the Hebrew doctors give for these names, that his first name was *Daniel — God has judged me* (namely, against Nabal), but David's enemies reproached him, and said, "It is Nabal's son, and not David's," to confute which calumny Providence so ordered it that, as he grew up, he became, in his countenance and features, extremely like David, and resembled him more than any of his children, upon which he gave him the name of *Chileab,* which signifies, *like his father,* or the father's picture. 5. Absalom's mother is said to be the daughter of Talmai king of Geshur, a heathen prince. Perhaps David thereby hoped to strengthen his interest, but the issue of the marriage was one that proved his grief and shame. 6. The last is called *David's wife,* which therefore, some think, was Michal, his first and most rightful wife, called here by another name; and, though she had no child after she mocked David, she might have had before.

Thus was David's house strengthened; but it was Abner that *made himself strong for the house of Saul,* which is mentioned (*v.* 6) to show that, if he failed them, they would fall of course.

Verses 7–21

Here, I. Abner breaks with Ish-bosheth, and deserts his interest, upon a little provocation which Ish-bosheth unadvisedly gave him. God can serve his own purposes by the sins and follies of men. 1. Ish-bosheth accused Abner of no less a crime than debauching one of his father's concubines, *v.* 7. Whether it was so or no does not appear, nor what ground he had for the suspicion: but, however it was, it would have been Ish-bosheth's prudence to be silent, considering how much it was his interest not to disoblige Abner. If the thing was false, and his jealousy groundless, it was very disingenuous and ungrateful to entertain unjust surmises of one who had ventured his all for him, and was certainly the best friend he had in the world. 2. Abner resented the charge very strongly. Whether he was guilty of the *fault concerning this woman* or no he does not say (*v.* 8), but we suspect he was guilty, for he does not expressly deny it; and, though he was, he lets Ish-bosheth know, (1.) That he scorned to be reproached with it by him, and would not take reproof at his hands. "What!" says Abner, *"Am I a dog's head,* a vile and contemptible animal, that thou exposest me thus? *v.* 8. Is this my recompence for the kindness I have shown to thee and thy father's house, and the good services I have done you?" He magnifies the service with this, that it was against Judah, the tribe on which the crown was settled, and which would certainly have it at last, so that, in supporting the house of Saul, he acted both against his conscience and against his interest, for which he deserved a better requital than this: and yet, perhaps, he would not have been so zealous for the house of Saul if he had not thereby gratified his own ambition and hoped to find his own account in it. Note, Proud men will not bear to be reproved, especially by those whom they think they have obliged. (2.) That he would certainly be revenged on him, *v.* 9, 10. With the utmost degree of arrogance and insolence he lets him know that, as he had raised him up, so he could pull him down again and would do it. He knew that God had sworn to David to give him the kingdom, and yet opposed it with all his might from a principle of ambition; but now he complies with it from a principle of revenge, under colour of some regard to the will of God, which was but a pretence. Those that are slaves to their lusts have many masters, which drive, some one way and some another, and, according as they make head, men are violently hurried into self-contradictions. Abner's ambition made him zealous for Ish-bosheth, and now his revenge made him as zealous for David. If he had sincerely regarded God's promise to David, and acted with an eye to that, he would have been steady and uniform in his counsels, and acted in consistency with himself. But, while Abner serves his own lusts, God by him serves his own purposes, makes even his wrath and revenge to praise him, and ordains strength to David by it. *Lastly,* See how Ish-bosheth was thunder-struck by Abner's insolence: He *could not answer him again, v.* 11. If Ish-bosheth had had the spirit of a man, especially of a prince, he might have answered him that his merits were the aggravation of his crimes, that he would not be served by so base a man, and doubted not but to do well enough without him. But he was conscious to himself of his own weakness, and therefore said not a word, lest he should make bad worse. His heart failed him, and he now became, as David had foretold concerning his enemies, like a bowing wall and a *tottering fence,* Ps. 62:3.

II. Abner treats with David. We must suppose that he began to grow weary of Ish-bosheth's cause, and sought an opportunity to desert it, or else, however he might threaten Ish-bosheth with it, for the quashing of the charge against himself, he would not have made good his angry words so soon as he did, *v.* 12. He *sent messengers to David,* to tell him that he was at his service. *"Whose is the land?* Is it not thine? For thou hast the best title to the government and the best interest in the people's affections." Note, God can find out ways to make those serviceable to the kingdom of Christ who yet have no sincere affection for it and who have vigorously set themselves against it. Enemies are sometimes made a footstool, not only to be trodden upon, but to ascend by. The earth helped the woman.

III. David enters into a treaty with Abner, but upon condition that he shall procure him the restitution of Michal his wife, *v.* 13. Hereby, 1. David showed the sincerity of his conjugal affection to his first and most rightful wife; neither her marrying another, nor his, had alienated him from her. Many waters could not quench that love. 2. He testified his respect to the house of Saul. So far was he from trampling upon it, now that it was fallen, that even in his elevation he valued himself not a little on his relation to it. He cannot be pleased with the honours of the throne unless he have Michal, Saul's daughter, to share with him in them, so far is he from bearing any malice to the family of his enemy. Abner sent him word that he must apply to Ish-bosheth, which he did (*v.* 14), pleading that he had purchased her at a dear rate, and she was wrongfully taken from him. Ish-bosheth durst not deny his demand, now that he had not Abner to stand by him, but took her from Phaltiel, to whom Saul had married her (*v.* 15), and Abner conducted her to David, not doubting but that then he should be doubly welcome when he brought him a wife in one hand and a crown in the other. Her latter husband was loth to part with her, and followed her *weeping* (*v.* 16), but there was no remedy: he must thank himself; for when he took her he knew that another had a right to her. Usurpers must expect to resign. Let no man therefore set his heart on that to which he is not entitled. If any disagreement has separated husband and wife, as they expect the blessing of God let them be reconciled, and come together again; let all former quarrels be forgotten, and let them live together in love, according to God's holy ordinance.

IV. Abner uses his interest with the elders of Israel to bring them over to David, knowing that whichever way they went the common people would follow of course. Now that it serves his own turn he can plead in David's behalf that he was, 1. Israel's choice (*v.* 17): *"You sought for him in times past to be king over you,* when he had signalized himself in so many engagements with the Philistines and done you so much good service; no man can pretend to greater personal merit than David nor to less than Ish-bosheth. You have tried them both, *Detur digniori — Give the crown to him that best deserves it.* Let David be your king." 2. God's choice (*v.* 18): *"The Lord hath spoken of David.* Compare *v.* 9. When God appointed Samuel to anoint him he did, in effect, promise that by his hand he would save Israel; for for that end he was made king. God having promised, by David's hand, to save Israel, it is both your duty, in compliance with God's will, and your interest, in order to your victories over your enemies, to submit to him; and it is the greatest folly in the world to oppose him." Who would have expected such reasonings as these out of Abner's mouth? But thus God will make the enemies of his people to know and own *that he has loved them,* Rev. 3:9. He particularly applied to the men of Benjamin, those of his own tribe, on whom he had the greatest influence, and whom he had drawn in to appear for the house of Saul. He was the man that had deceived them, and therefore he was concerned to undeceive them. Thus the multitude are as they are managed.

V. David concludes the treaty with Abner; and he did wisely and well therein; for, whatever induced Abner to it, it was a good work to put an end to the war, and to settle the Lord's anointed on the throne; and it was as lawful for David to make use of his agency as it is for a poor man to receive alms from a Pharisee, who gives it in pride and hypocrisy. Abner reported to David the sense of the people and the success of his communications with them, *v.* 19. He came now, not as at first privately, but with a retinue of twenty men, and David entertained them with *a feast* (*v.* 20) in token of reconciliation and joy and as a pledge of the agreement between them: it was a feast upon a covenant, like that, Gen. 26:30. *If thy enemy hunger, feed him;* but, if he submit, feast him. Abner, pleased with his entertainment, the prevention of his fall with Saul's house (which would have been inevitable if he had not taken this course), and much more with the prospect he had of preferment under David, undertakes in a little time to perfect the revolution, and to bring all Israel into obedience to David, *v.* 21. He tells David he shall *reign over all that his heart desired.* He knew David's elevation took rise from God's appointment, yet he insinuates that it sprang from his own ambition and desire of rule; thus (as bad men often do) he measured that good man by himself. However, David and he parted very good friends, and the affair between them was well settled. Thus it behoves all who fear God and keep his commandments to avoid strife, even with the wicked, to live at peace with all men, and to show the world that they are children of the light.

Verses 22–39

We have here an account of the murder of Abner by Joab, and David's deep resentment of it.

I. Joab very insolently fell foul upon David for treating with Abner. He happened to be abroad upon service when Abner was with David, pursuing a troop, either of Philistines or of Saul's party; but, upon his return, he was informed that Abner was just gone (*v.* 22, 23), and that a great many kind things had passed between David and him. He had all the reason in the world to be satisfied of David's prudence and to acquiesce in the measures he took, knowing him to be a wise and good man himself and under a divine conduct in all his affairs; and yet, as if he had the same sway in David's cause that Abner had in Ish-bosheth's, he chides David, and reproaches him to his face as impolitic (*v.* 24, 25): *What hast thou done?* As if David were accountable to him for what he did: "*Why hast thou sent him away,* when thou mightest have made him a prisoner? He came as a spy, and will certainly betray thee." I know not whether to wonder more that Joab had impudence enough to give such an affront to his prince or that David had patience enough to take it. He does, in effect, call David *a fool* when he tells him he knew Abner came to deceive him and yet he trusted him. We find no answer that David gave him, not because he feared him, as Ish-bosheth did Abner (*v.* 11), but because he despised him, or because Joab had not so much good manners as to stay for an answer.

II. He very treacherously sent for Abner back, and, under colour of a private conference with him, barbarously killed him with his own hand. That he made use of David's name, under pretence of giving him some further instructions, is intimated in that, *but David knew it not, v.* 26. Abner, designing no harm, feared none, but very innocently returned to Hebron, and, when he found Joab waiting for him at the gate, turned aside with him to speak with him privately, forgetting what he himself had said when he slew Asahel, *How shall I hold up my face to Joab thy brother?* (*ch.* 2:22), and there Joab murdered him (*v.* 27), and it is intimated (*v.* 30) that Abishai was privy to the design, and was aiding and abetting, and would have come in to his brother's assistance if there had been occasion; he is therefore charged as an accessary: *Joab and Abishai slew Abner,* though perhaps he only knew it who is privy to the thoughts and intents of men's hearts. Now in this, 1. It is certain that the Lord was righteous. Abner had maliciously, and against the convictions of his conscience, opposed David. He had now basely deserted Ish-bosheth, and betrayed him, under pretence of regard to God and Israel, but really from a principle of pride, and revenge, and impatience of control. God will not therefore use so bad a man, though David might, in so good a work as the uniting of Israel. Judgments are prepared for such scorners as Abner was. But, 2. It is as certain that Joab was unrighteous, and, in what he did, did wickedly. David was a man after God's own heart, but could not have those about him, no, not in places of the greatest trust, after his own heart. Many a good prince, and a good master, has been forced to employ bad men. (1.) Even the pretence for doing this was very unjust. Abner had indeed slain his brother Asahel, and Joab and Abishai pretended herein to be the avengers of his blood (*v.* 27, 30); but Abner slew Asahel in an open war, wherein Abner indeed had given the challenge, but Joab himself had accepted it and had slain many of Abner's friends. He did it likewise in his own defence, and not till he had given him fair warning (which he would not take), and he did it with reluctancy; but Joab here shed *the blood of war in peace,* 1 Ki. 2:5. (2.) That which we have reason to think was at the bottom of Joab's enmity to Abner made it much worse. Joab was now general of David's forces; but, if Abner should come into his interest, he would possibly be preferred before him, being a senior officer, and more experienced in the art of war. This Joab was jealous of, and could better bear the guilt of blood than the thoughts of a rival. (3.) He did it treacherously, and under pretence of speaking peaceably to him, Deu. 27:24. Had he challenged him, he would have done like a soldier; but to assassinate him was done villainously and like a coward. *His words were softer than oil, yet were they drawn swords,* Ps. 55:21. Thus he basely slew Amasa, *ch.* 20:9, 10. (4.) The doing of it was a great affront and injury to David, who was now in treaty with Abner, as Joab knew. Abner was now actually in his master's service, so that, through his side, he struck at David himself. (5.) It was a great aggravation of the murder that he did it in the gate, openly and avowedly, as one that was not ashamed, nor could blush. The gate was the place of judgment and the place of concourse, to that he did it in defiance of justice, both the just sentence of the magistrates and the just resentment of the crowd, as one that neither feared God nor regarded men, but thought himself above all control: and Hebron was a Levites' city and a city of refuge.

III. David laid deeply to heart and in many ways expressed his detestation of this execrable villany.

1. He washed his hands from the guilt of Abner's blood. Lest any should suspect that Joab had some secret intimation from David to do as he did (and the rather because he went so long unpunished), he here solemnly appeals to God concerning his innocency: *I and my kingdom are guiltless* (and my kingdom is so because I am so) *before the Lord for ever, v.* 28. It is a comfort to be able to say, when any bad thing is done, that we had no hand in it. *We have not shed this blood,* Deu. 21:7. However we may be censured or suspected, *our hearts shall not reproach us.*

2. He entailed the curse for it upon Joab and his family (*v.* 29): "*Let it rest on the head of Joab.* Let the blood cry against him, and let divine vengeance follow him. Let the iniquity be visited upon his children and children's children, in some hereditary disease or other. The longer the punishment is delayed, the longer let it last when it shall come. Let his posterity be stigmatized, blemished with an issue or a leprosy, which will shut them out from society; let them be beggars, or cripples, or come to some untimely end, that it may be said, He is one of Joab's race." This intimates that the guilt of blood brings a curse upon families; if men do not avenge it, God will, and will lay up the iniquity for the children. But methinks a resolute punishment of the murderer himself would better have become David than this passionate imprecation of God's judgments upon his posterity.

3. He called upon all about him, even Joab himself, to lament the death of Abner (*v.* 31): *Rend your clothes and mourn before Abner,* that is, before the hearse of Abner, as Abraham is said to mourn *before his dead* (Gen. 23:2, 3), and he gives a reason why they should attend his funeral with sincere and solemn mourning (*v.* 38), because there is *a prince and a great man fallen this day in Israel.* His alliance to Saul, his place as general, his interest, and the great services he had formerly done, were enough to denominate him *a prince and a great man.* When he could not call him a saint or a good man, he said nothing of that, but what was true he gave him the praise of, though he had been his enemy, that he was *a prince and a great man.* "Such a man has fallen in Israel, and fallen *this day,* just when he was doing the best deed he ever did in his life, *this day,* when he was likely to be so serviceable to the public peace and welfare and could so ill be spared." (1.) Let them all lament it. The humbling change death puts all men under is to be lamented, especially as affecting princes and great men. Alas! alas! (see Rev. 18:10) how mean, how little, are those made by death who made themselves the terror of the mighty in the land of the living! But we are especially obliged to lament the fall of useful men in the midst of their usefulness and when there is most need of them. A public loss must be every man's grief, for every man shares in it. Thus David took care that honour should be done to the memory of a man of merit, to animate others. (2.) Let Joab, in a particular manner, lament it, which he has less heart but more reason to do than any of them. If he could be brought to do it sincerely, it would be an expression of repentance for his sin in slaying him. If he did it in show only, as it is likely he did, yet it was a sort of penance imposed upon him, and a present commutation of the punishment. If he do not as yet expiate the murder with his blood, let him do something towards it with tears. This, perhaps, Joab submitted to with no great reluctancy, now he had gained his point. Now that he is on the bier, no matter in what pomp he lies. *Sit divus, modo non sit vivus — Let him be canonized, so that he be but killed.*

4. David himself followed the corpse as chief mourner, and made a funeral oration at the grave. He attended the bier (*v.* 31) *and wept at the grave, v.* 32. Though Abner had been his enemy, and might possibly have proved no very firm friend, yet because he had been a man of bravery in the field, and might have done great service in the public counsels at this critical juncture, all former quarrels are forgotten and David is a true mourner for his fall. What he said over the grave fetched fresh floods of tears from the eyes of all that were present, when they thought they had already paid the debt in full (*v.* 33, 34): *Died Abner as a fool dieth?* (1.) He speaks as one vexed that Abner was fooled out of his life, that so great a man as he, so famed for conduct and courage, should be imposed upon by a colour of friendship, slain by surprise, and so die as a fool dies. The wisest and stoutest of men have no fence against treachery. To see Abner, who thought himself the main hinge on which the great affairs of Israel turned, so considerable as himself to be able to turn the scale of a trembling government, his head full of great projects and great prospects, to see him made a fool of by a base rival, and falling on a sudden a sacrifice to his ambition and jealousy — this stains the pride of all glory, and should put one out of conceit with worldly grandeur. *Put not your trust in princes,* Ps. 146:3, 4. And let us therefore make that sure which we cannot be fooled out of. A man may have his life, and all that is dear to him, taken from him, and not be able to prevent it with all his wisdom, care, and integrity; but there is that which no thief can break through to steal. See here how much more we are beholden to God's providence than to our own prudence for the continuance of our lives and comforts. Were it not for the hold God has of the consciences of bad men, how soon would the weak and innocent become an easy prey to the strong and merciless and the wisest die as fools! Or, (2.) He speaks as one boasting that Abner did not fool himself out of his life: "*Died Abner as a fool dies?* No, he did not, not as a criminal, a traitor or felon, that forfeits his life into the hands of public justice; his hands were not pinioned, nor his feet fettered, as those of malefactors are: Abner falls not before just men, by a judicial sentence; but as *a man, an innocent man, falleth before wicked men,* thieves and robbers, so fellest thou." *Died Abner as Nabal died?* so the Septuagint reads it. Nabal died as he lived, like himself, like a sot; but Abner's fate was such as might have been the fate of the wisest and best man in the world. Abner did not throw away his life as Asahel did, who wilfully ran upon the spear, after fair warning, but he was struck by surprise. Note, It is a sad thing to die like a fool, as those do that in any way shorten their own days, and much more those that make no provision for another world.

5. He fasted all that day, and would by no means be persuaded to eat any thing till night, *v.* 35. It was then the custom of great mourners to refrain for the time from bodily refreshments, as *ch.* 1:12; 1 Sa. 31:13. How incongruous is it then to turn the house of mourning into a house of feasting! This respect which David paid to Abner was very pleasing to the people and satisfied them that he was not, in the least, accessory to the murder (*v.* 36, 37), of which he was solicitous to avoid the suspicion, lest Joab's villany should make him odious, as that of Simeon and Levi did Jacob, Gen. 34:30. On this occasion it is said, *Whatever the king did pleased all the people.* This intimates, (1.) His good affection to them. He studied to please them in every thing and carefully avoided what might be disobliging. (2.) Their good opinion of him. They thought every thing he did well done. Such a mutual willingness to please, and easiness to be pleased, will make every relation comfortable.

6. He bewailed it that he could not with safety do justice on the murderers, *v.* 30. He was weak, his kingdom was newly planted, and a little shake would overthrow it. Joab's family had a great interest, were bold and daring, and to make them his enemies now might be of bad consequence. These sons of Zeruiah were too hard for him, too big for the law to take hold of; and therefore, though by man, by the magistrate, the blood of a murderer *should be shed* (Gen. 9:6), David bears the sword in vain, and contents himself, as a private person, to leave them to the judgment of God: *The Lord shall reward the doer of evil according to his wickedness.* Now this is a diminution, (1.) To David's greatness. He is anointed king, and yet is kept in awe by his own subjects, and some of them are too hard for him. Who would be fond of power when a man may have the name of it, and must be accountable for it, and yet be hampered in the use of it? (2.) To David's goodness. He ought to have done his duty, and trusted God with the issue. *Fiat justitia, ruat coelum — Let justice be done, though the heavens should fall asunder.* If the law had had its course against Joab, perhaps the murder of Ishbosheth, Amnon, and others, would have been prevented. It was carnal policy and cruel pity that spared Joab. Righteousness supports the throne and will never shake it. Yet it was only a reprieve that David gave to Joab; on his death-bed he left

it to Solomon (who could the better wield the sword of justice because he had no occasion to draw the sword of war) to avenge the blood of Abner. Evil pursues sinners, and will overtake them at last. David preferred Abner's son Jaasiel, 1 Chr. 27:21.

CHAPTER 4

When Abner was slain David was at a loss for a friend to perfect the reduction of those tribes that were yet in Ish-bosheth's interest. Which way to adopt for the accomplishment of it he could not tell; but here Providence brings it about by the removal of Ish-bosheth. I. Two of his own servants slew him, and brought his head to David (*v.* 1–8). II. David, instead of rewarding them, put them to death for what they had done (*v.* 9–12).

Verses 1–8

Here is, I. The weakness of Saul's house. Still it grew weaker and weaker. 1. As for Ishbosheth, who was in possession of the throne, his hands were feeble, *v.* 1. All the strength they ever had was from Abner's support, and now that he was dead he had no spirit left in him. Though Abner had, in a passion, deserted his interest, yet he hoped, by his means, to make good terms with David; but now even this hope fails him, and he sees himself forsaken by his friends and at the mercy of his enemies. All the Israelites that adhered to him were troubled and at a loss what to do, whether to proceed in their treaty with David or no. 2. As for Mephibosheth, who in the right of his father Jonathan had a prior title, his feet were lame, and he was unfit for any service, *v.* 4. He was but five years old when his father and grandfather were killed. His nurse, hearing of the Philistines' victory, was apprehensive that, in pursuit of it, they would immediately send a party to Saul's house, to cut off all that pertained to it, and would especially aim at her young master, who was now next heir to the crown. Under the apprehension of this, she fled with the child in her arms, to secure it either in some secret place where he could not be found, or in some strong place where he could not be got at; and, making more haste than good speed, she fell with the child, and by the fall some bone was broken or put out, and not well set, so that he was lame of it as long as he lived, and unfit either for court or camp. See what sad accidents children are liable to in their infancy, the effect of which may be felt by them, to their great uneasiness, all their days. Even the children of princes and great men, the children of good men, for such a one Jonathan was, children that are well tended, and have nurses of their own to take care of them, yet are not always safe. What reason have we to be thankful to God for the preservation of our limbs and senses to us, through the many perils of the weak and helpless state of infancy, and to own his goodness in giving his angels a charge concerning us, to bear us up in their arms, out of which there is no danger of falling, Ps. 91:12.

II. The murder of Saul's son. We are here told,

1. Who were the murderers: *Baanah and Rechab, v.* 2, 3. They were own brothers, as Simeon and Levi, and partners in iniquity. They were or had been Ish-bosheth's own servants, employed under him, so much the more base and treacherous was it in them to do him a mischief. They were Benjamites, of his own tribe. They were of the city of Beeroth; for some reason which we cannot now account for care is here taken to let us know (in a parenthesis) that that city belonged to the lot of Benjamin, so we find (Jos. 18:25), but that the inhabitants, upon some occasion or other, perhaps upon the death of Saul, retired to Gittaim, another city which lay not far off in the same tribe, and was better fortified by nature, being situate (if we may depend upon Mr. Fuller's map) between the two rocks Bozez and Seneh. There the Beerothites were when this was written, and probably took root there, and never returned to Beeroth again, which made Beeroth, that had been one of the cities of the Gibeonites (Jos. 9:17), to be forgotten, and Gittaim to be famous long after, as we find, Neh. 11:33.

2. How the murder was committed, *v.* 5–7. See here, (1.) The slothfulness of Ish-bosheth. He lay upon his bed at noon. It does not appear that the country was at any time of the year so hot as to oblige the inhabitants to retire at noon, as we are told they do in Spain in the heat of summer; but Ish-bosheth was a sluggish man, loved his ease and hated business: and when he should have been, at this critical juncture, at the head of his forces in the field, or at the head of his counsels in a treaty with David, he was lying upon his bed and sleeping, for his hands were feeble (*v.* 1), and so were his head and heart. When those difficulties dispirit us which should rather invigorate us and sharpen our endeavours we betray both our crowns and lives. *Love not sleep, lest thou come to poverty and ruin.* The idle soul is an easy prey to the destroyer. (2.) The treachery of Baanah and Rechab. They came into the house, under pretence of fetching wheat for the victualling of their regiments; and such was the plainness of those times that the king's corn-chamber and his bed-chamber lay near together, which gave them an opportunity, when they were fetching wheat, to murder him as he lay on the bed. We know not when and where death will meet us. When we lie down to sleep we are not sure but that we may sleep the sleep of death before we awake; nor do we know from what unsuspected hand a fatal stroke may come. Ish-bosheth's own men, who should have protected his life, took it away.

3. The murderers triumphed in what they had done. As if they had performed some very glorious action, and the doing of it for David's advantage was enough not only to justify it, but to sanctify it, they made a present of Ish-bosheth's head to David (*v.* 8): *Behold the head of thy enemy,* than which they thought nothing could be more acceptable to him; yea, and they made themselves instruments of God's justice, ministers to bear his sword, though they had no commission: *The Lord hath avenged thee this day of Saul and of his seed.* Not that they had any regard either to God or to David's honour; they aimed at nothing but to make their own fortunes (as we say) and to get preferment in David's court; but, to ingratiate themselves with him, they pretended a concern for his life, a conviction of his title, and a zealous desire to see him in full possession of the throne. Jehu pretended *zeal for the Lord of hosts* when an ambition to set up himself and his own family was the spring of his actions.

Verses 9–12

We have here justice done upon the murderers of Ish-bosheth.

I. Sentence passed upon them. There needed no evidence, their own tongues witnessed against them; they were so far from denying the fact that they gloried in it. David therefore shows them the heinousness of the crime, and that blood called for blood from his hand, who was now the chief magistrate, and was by office the avenger of blood. And, perhaps, he was the more vigorous in the prosecution because for reasons of state he had spared Joab: *"Shall I not require the blood of the slain at the hand of the slayers,* and, since they cannot make restitution, take theirs instead of it?" Observe, 1. How he aggravates the crime, *v.* 11. Ish-bosheth was a righteous person, he had done them no wrong, nor designed them any. As to himself, David was satisfied that what opposition he gave him was not from malice, but mistake, from an idea he had of his own title to the crown, and the influence of others upon him, who urged him to put in for it. Note, Charity teaches us to make the best, not only of our friends, but of our enemies, and to think those may be righteous persons who yet, in some instances, do us wrong. I must not presently judge a man a bad man because I think him so to me. David owns Ish-bosheth an honest man, though he had created him a great deal of trouble unjustly. The manner of it much aggravated the crime. To slay him in his own house, which should have been his castle, and upon his bed, when he was in no capacity of making any opposition, this is treacherous and barbarous, and all that is base, and that which the heart of every man who is not perfectly lost to all honour and humanity will rise with indignation at the thought of. Assassinating is confessedly the most odious and villainous way of murdering. *Cursed is he that smiteth his neighbour secretly.* 2. He quotes a precedent (*v.* 10): he had put him to death who had brought him the tidings of the death of Saul, because he thought it would be good tidings to David. Nothing is here said of that Amalekite's helping Saul to kill himself, only of his bringing the tidings of his death, by which it should seem that the story he told was upon enquiry found to be false, and that he lied against his own head. "Now" (says David) "did I treat him as a criminal, and not a favourite" (as he expected), "who brought me Saul's crown, and shall those be held guiltless that bring me Ish-bosheth's head?" 3. He ratifies the sentence with an oath (*v.* 9): *As the Lord liveth, who hath redeemed my soul out of all adversity.* He expresses himself thus resolutely, to prevent the making of any intercession for the criminals by those about him, and thus piously to intimate that his dependence was upon God for the putting of him in possession of the promised throne, and that he would not be beholden to any man to help him to it by any indirect or unlawful practices. God had redeemed him from all adversity hitherto, helped him over many a difficulty and through many a danger, and therefore he would depend upon him to crown and complete his own work. He speaks of his redemption from all adversity as a thing done, though he had many a storm yet before him, because he knew that he who had delivered would deliver. 4. Hereupon he signs a warrant for the execution of these men, *v.* 12. This may seem severe, when they intended him a kindness in what they did; but, (1.) He would thus show his detestation of the villany. When he heard that *the Lord smote Nabal, he gave thanks* (1 Sa. 25:38, 39), *for he is the God to whom vengeance belongeth;* but, if wicked men smite Ish-bosheth, they deserve to die for taking God's work out of his hand. (2.) He would thus show his resentment of the great affront they put upon him in expecting that he should patronize and reward it; they could scarcely have done him a greater injury than thus to think him altogether such a one as themselves, one that cared not what blood he waded through to the crown.

II. Execution done. The murderers were put to death according to law, and their hands and feet were hung up; not their whole bodies, the law forbade that; but only their hands and feet, *in terrorem — to frighten others,* to be monuments of David's justice, and to make that to be taken notice of which would recommend him to the esteem of the people, as a man fit to rule, and that aimed not at his own preferment, nor had any enmity to the house of Saul, but only and sincerely designed the public welfare. But what a confusion was this to the two murderers! What a horrid disappointment! And such those will meet with who think to serve the interests of the Son of David by any immoral practices, by war and persecution, fraud and rapine, who, under colour of religion, murder princes, break solemn contracts, lay countries waste, *hate their brethren, and cast them out, and say, Let the Lord be glorified, kill them, and think they do God good service.* However men may canonize such methods of serving the church and the catholic cause, Christ will let them know, another day, that Christianity was not intended to destroy humanity; and those who thus think to merit heaven shall not escape the damnation of hell.

CHAPTER 5

How far Abner's deserting the house of Saul, his murder, and the murder of Ish-bosheth, might contribute to the perfecting of the revolution, and the establishing of David as king over all Israel, does not appear; but, it should seem, that happy change followed presently thereupon, which in this chapter we have an account of. Here is, I. David anointed king by all the tribes (*v.* 1–5). II. Making himself master of the strong-hold of Zion (*v.* 6–10). III. Building himself a house and strengthening himself in his kingdom (*v.* 11, 12). IV. His children that were born after this (*v.* 13–16). V. His victories over the Philistines (*v.* 17–25).

Verses 1–5

Here is, I. The humble address of all the tribes to David, beseeching him to take upon him the government (for they were now as sheep having no shepherd), and owning him for their king. Though David might by no means approve the murder of Ish-bosheth, yet he might improve the advantages he gained thereby, and accept the applications made to him thereupon. Judah had submitted to David as their king above seven years ago, and their ease and happiness, under his administration, encouraged the rest of the tribes to make their court to him. What numbers came from each tribe, with what zeal and sincerity they came, and how they were entertained for three days at Hebron, when they were all of one heart to make David king, we have a full account, 1 Chr. 12:23–40. Here we have only the heads of their address, containing the grounds they went upon in making David king. 1. Their relation to him was some inducement: *"We are thy bone and thy flesh* (*v.* 1), not only thou art our bone and our flesh, not a stranger, unqualified by the law to be king (Deu. 17:15), but we are thine," that is, "we know that thou considerest us as thy bone and thy flesh, and hast as tender a concern for us as a man has for his own body, which Saul and his house had not. *We are thy bone and thy flesh,* and therefore thou wilt be as glad as we shall be to put an end to this long civil war; and thou wilt take pity on us, protect us, and do thy utmost for our welfare." Those who take Christ for their king may thus plead with him: *"We are thy bone and thy flesh,* thou hast made thyself in all things *like unto thy brethren* (Heb. 2:17); therefore be thou our ruler, and let this ruin be under thy hand," Isa. 3:6. 2. His former good services to the public were a further inducement (*v.* 2): *"When Saul was king* he was but the cypher, thou wast the figure, *thou wast he that leddest out* Israel to battle, and broughtest them in in triumph; and therefore who so fit now to fill the vacant throne?" He that is faithful in a little deserves to be entrusted with more. Former good offices done for us should be gratefully remembered by us when there is occasion. 3. The divine appointment was the greatest inducement of all: *The Lord said, Thou shalt feed my people Israel,* that is, thou shalt rule them; for princes are to feed their people as shepherds, in every thing consulting the subjects' benefit, feeding them and not fleecing them. "And thou shalt be not only a king to govern in peace, but a captain to preside in war, and be exposed to all the toils and perils of the camp." Since God has said so, now at length, when need drives them to it, they are persuaded to say so too.

II. The public and solemn inauguration of David, *v.* 3. A convention of the states was called; all the elders of Israel came to him; the contract was settled, the *pacta conventa — covenants,* sworn to, and subscribed on both sides. He obliged himself to protect them as their judge in peace and captain in war; and they obliged themselves to obey him. He *made a league* with them to which God was a witness: it was *before the Lord.* Hereupon he was, for the third time, anointed king. His advances were gradual, that his faith might be tried and that he might gain experience. And thus his kingdom typified that of the Messiah, which was to come to its height by degrees; for *we see not yet all things put under him* (Heb. 2:8), but we shall see it, 1 Co. 15:25.

III. A general account of his reign and age. He was thirty years old when he began to reign, upon the death of Saul, *v.* 4. At that age the Levites were at first appointed to begin their administration, Num. 4:3. About that age the Son of David entered upon his public ministry, Lu. 3:23. Then men come to their full maturity of strength and judgment. He reigned, in all, forty years and six months, of which seven years and a half in Hebron and thirty-three years in Jerusalem, *v.* 5. Hebron had been famous, Jos. 14:15. It was a priest's city. But Jerusalem was to be more so, and to be the holy city. Great kings affected to raise cities of their own, Gen. 10:11, 36, 32–35. David did so, and Jerusalem was the city of David. It is a name famous to the end of the Bible (Rev. 21), where we read of a new Jerusalem.

Verses 6–10

If Salem, the place of which Melchizedec was king, was Jerusalem (as seems probable from Ps. 76:2), it was famous in Abraham's time. Joshua, in his time, found it the chief city of the south part of Canaan, Jos. 10:1–3. It fell to Benjamin's lot (Jos. 18:28), but joined close to Judah's, Jos. 15:8. The children of Judah had taken it (Jdg. 1:8), but the children of Benjamin suffered the Jebusites to dwell among them (Jdg. 1:21), and they grew so upon them that it became a *city of Jebusites,* Jdg. 19:11. Now the very first exploit David did, after he was anointed king over all Israel, was to gain Jerusalem out of the hand of the Jebusites, which, because it belonged to Benjamin, he could not well attempt till that tribe, which long adhered to Saul's house (1 Chr. 12:29), submitted to him. Here we have,

I. The Jebusites' defiance of David and his forces. They said, *Except thou take away the blind and the lame, thou shalt not come in hither, v.* 6. They sent David this provoking message, because, as it is said afterwards, on another occasion, they could not believe that *ever an enemy would enter into the gates of Jerusalem,* Lam. 4:12. They confided either, 1. In the protection of their gods, which David, in contempt, had called *the blind and the lame,* for *they have eyes and see not, feet and walk not.* "But," say they, "these are the guardians of our city, and except thou take these away (which thou canst never do) thou canst not come in hither." Some think they were constellated images of brass set up in the recess of the fort, and entrusted with the custody of the place. They called their idols their *Mauzzim,* or *strong-holds* (Dan. 11:38) and as such relied on them. *The name of the Lord is our strong tower,* and his arm is strong, his eyes are piercing. Or, 2. In the strength of their fortifications, which they thought were made so impregnable by nature or art, or both, that the blind and the lame were sufficient to defend them against the most powerful assailant. The strong-hold of Zion they especially depended on, as that which could not be forced. Probably they set blind and lame people, invalids or maimed soldiers, to make their appearance upon the walls, in scorn of David and his men, judging them an equal match for him. Though there remain but wounded men among them, yet they should serve to beat back the besiegers. Compare Jer. 37:10. Note, The enemies of God's people are often very confident of their own strength and most secure when their day to fall draws nigh.

II. David's success against the Jebusites. Their pride and insolence, instead of daunting him, animated him, and when he made a general assault he gave this order to his men: *"He that smiteth the Jebusites, let him also throw down into the ditch,* or gutter, *the lame and the blind,* which are set upon the wall to affront us and our God." It is probable they had themselves spoken blasphemous things, and were therefore hated of David's soul. Thus *v.* 8 may be read; we fetch our reading of it from 1 Chr. 11:6, which speaks only of smiting the Jebusites, but nothing of the blind and the lame. The Jebusites had said that if these images of theirs did not protect them *the blind and the lame should not come into the house,* that is, they would never again trust their palladium (so Mr. Gregory understands it) nor pay the respect they had paid to their images; and David, having gained the fort, said so too, that these images, which could not protect their worshippers, should never have any place there more.

III. His fixing his royal seat in Sion. He himself dwelt in the fort (the strength whereof, which had given him opposition, and was a terror to him, now contributed to his safety), and he built houses round about for his attendants and guards (*v.* 9) from Millo (the town-hall, or state-house) and inward. He proceeded and prospered in all he set his hand to, grew great in honour, strength, and wealth, more and more honourable in the eyes of his subjects and formidable in the eyes of his enemies; for *the Lord God of hosts was with him.* God has all creatures at his command, makes what use he pleases of them, and serves his own purposes by them; and he was with him, to direct, preserve, and prosper him, Those that have the Lord of hosts for them need not fear what hosts of men or devils can do against them. Those who grow great must ascribe their advancement to the presence of God with them, and give him the glory of it. The church is called *Sion,* and the *city of the living God.* The Jebusites, Christ's enemies, must first be conquered and dispossessed, the blind and the lame taken away, and then Christ divides the spoil, sets up his throne there, and makes it his residence by the Spirit.

Verses 11–16

Here is, I. David's house built, a royal palace, fit for the reception of the court he kept and the homage that was paid to him, *v.* 11. The Jews were husbandmen and shepherds, and did not much addict themselves either to merchandise or manufactures; and therefore Hiram, king of Tyre, a wealthy prince, when he sent to congratulate David on his accession to the throne, offered him workmen to build him a house. David thankfully accepted the offer, and Hiram's workmen built David a house to his mind. Many have excelled in arts and sciences who were strangers to the covenants of promise. Yet David's house was never the worse, nor the less fit to be dedicated to God, for being built by the sons of the stranger. It is prophesied of the gospel church, *The sons of the strangers shall build up thy walls, and their kings shall minister unto thee,* Isa. 60:10.

II. David's government settled and built up, *v.* 12. 1. His kingdom was established, there was nothing to shake it, none to disturb his possession or question his title. He that made him king established him, because he was to be a type of Christ, with whom God's hand should be established, and his *covenant stand fast,* Ps. 89:21–28. Saul was made king, but not established; so Adam in innocency. David was established king, so is the Son of David, with all who through him are made to our God *kings and priests.* 2. It was exalted in the eyes both of its friends and enemies. Never had the nation of Israel looked so great or made such a figure as it began now to do. Thus it is promised of Christ that he shall be *higher than the kings of the earth,* Ps. 89:27. God has *highly exalted him,* Phil. 2:9. 3. David perceived, by the wonderful concurrence of providences to his establishment and advancement, that God was with him. *By this I know that thou favourest me,* Ps. 41:11. Many have the favour of God and do not perceive it, and so want the comfort of it: but to be exalted to that and established in it, and to perceive it, is happiness enough. 4. He owned that it was for his people Israel's sake that God had done great things for him, that he might be a blessing to them and they might be happy under his administration. God did not make Israel his subjects for his sake, that he might be great, and rich, and absolute: but he made him their king for their sake, that he might lead, and guide, and protect them. Kings are *ministers of God to their people for good,* Rom. 13:4.

III. David's family multiplied and increased. All the sons that were born to him after he came to Jerusalem are here mentioned together, eleven in all, besides the six that were born to him before in Hebron, *ch.* 3:2, 5. *There* the mothers are mentioned, not *here;* only, in general, it is said that he *took more concubines and wives, v.* 13. Shall we praise him for this? We praise him not; we justify him not; nor can we scarcely excuse him. The bad example of the patriarchs might make him think there was no harm in it, and he might hope it would strengthen his interest, by multiplying his alliances, and increasing the royal family. *Happy is the man that has his quiver full of these arrows.* But one vine by the side of the house, with the blessing of God, may send boughs to the sea and branches to the rivers. Adam, by one wife, peopled the world, and Noah re-peopled it. David had many wives, and yet that did not keep him from coveting his neighbour's wife and defiling her; for men that have once broken the fence will wander endlessly. Of David's concubines, see 2 Sa. 15:16; 16:22; 19:5. Of his sons, see 1 Chr. 3:1–9.

Verses 17–25

The particular service for which David was raised up was to *save Israel out of the hand of the Philistines, ch.* 3:18. This therefore divine Providence, in the first place, gives him an opportunity of accomplishing. Two great victories obtained over the Philistines we have here an account of, by which David not only balanced the disgrace and retrieved the loss Israel had sustained in the battle wherein Saul was slain, but went far towards the total subduing of those vexatious neighbours, the last remains of the devoted nations.

I. In both these actions the Philistines were the aggressors, stirred first towards their own destruction, and pulled it on their own heads. 1. In the former they *came up to seek David* (*v.* 17), because they *heard that he was anointed king over Israel.* He that under Saul had slain his ten thousands, what would he do when he himself came to be king! They therefore thought it was time to look about them, and try to crush his government in its infancy, before it was well settled. Their success against Saul, some years ago, perhaps encouraged them to make this attack upon David; but they considered not that David had that presence of God with him which Saul had forfeited and lost. The kingdom of the Messiah, as soon as ever it was set up in the world, was thus vigorously attacked by the powers of darkness, who, with the combined force both of Jews and Gentiles, made head against it. The heathen raged, and the kings of the earth set themselves to oppose it; but all in vain, Ps. 2:1, etc. The destruction will turn, as this did, upon Satan's own kingdom. They took counsel together, but were *broken in pieces,* Isa. 8:9, 10. 2. In the latter they *came up yet again,* hoping to recover what they had lost in the former engagement, and their hearts being hardened to their destruction, *v.* 22. 3. In both they *spread themselves in the valley of Rephaim,* which lay very near Jerusalem. That city they hoped to make themselves masters of before David had completed the fortifications of it. Jerusalem, from its infancy, has been aimed at, and struck at, with a particular enmity. Their spreading themselves intimates that they were very numerous and that they made a very formidable appearance. We read of the church's enemies *going up on the breadth of the earth* (Rev. 20:9), but the further they spread themselves the fairer mark they are to God's arrows.

II. In both, David, though forward enough to go forth

against them (for as soon as he heard it he *went down to the hold,* to secure some important and advantageous post, *v.* 17), yet entered not upon action till he had *enquired of the Lord* by the breast-plate of judgment, *v.* 19, and again, *v.* 23. His enquiry was twofold: — 1. Concerning his duty: *"Shall I go up?* Shall I have a commission from heaven to engage them?" One would think he needed not doubt this; what was he made king for, but to fight the battles of the Lord and Israel? But a good man loves to see God going before him in every step he takes. "Shall I go up *now?"* It is to be done, but is it to be done at this time? *In all thy ways acknowledge him.* And besides, though the Philistines were public enemies, yet some of them had been his particular friends. Achish had been kind to him in his distress, and had protected him. "Now," says David, "ought not I, in remembrance of that, rather to make peace with them than to make war with them?" "No," says God, "they are Israel's enemies, and are doomed to destruction, and therefore scruple not, but *go up."* 2. Concerning his success. His conscience asked the former question, *Shall I go up?* His prudence asked this, *Wilt thou deliver them into my hand?* Hereby he owns his dependence on God for victory, that he could not conquer them unless God delivered them into his hand, and refers his cause to the good pleasure of God: *Wilt thou do it?* Yea, says God, *I will doubtless do it.* If God send us, he will bear us out and stand by us. The assurance God has given us of victory over our spiritual enemies, that he will tread Satan under our feet shortly, should animate us in our spiritual conflicts. We do not fight at uncertainty. David had now a great army at command and in good heart, yet he relied more on God's promise than his own force.

III. In the former of these engagements David routed the army of the Philistines by dint of sword (*v.* 20): He *smote them;* and when he had done, 1. He gave his God the glory; he said, *"The Lord has broken forth upon my enemies before me.* I could not have done it if he had not done it before me; he opened the breach like the breach of waters in a dam, which when once opened grows wider and wider." The principal part of the work was God's doing; nay, he did all; what David did was not worth speaking of; and therefore, *Not unto us, but unto the Lord, give glory.* He hoped likewise that this breach, like that of waters, was as the opening of the sluice, to let in a final desolation upon them; and, to perpetuate the remembrance of it, he called the place *Baal-perazim, the master of the breaches,* because, God having broken in upon their forces, he soon had the mastery of them. Let posterity take notice of it to God's honour. 2. He put their gods to shame. They brought the images of their gods into the field as their protectors, in imitation of the Israelites bringing the ark into their camp; but, being put to flight, they could not stay to carry off their images, for they were a *burden to the weary beasts* (Isa. 46:1), and therefore they left them to fall with the rest of their baggage into the hands of the conqueror. Their images failed them, and gave them no assistance, and therefore they left their images to shift for themselves. God can make men weary of those things that they have been most fond of, and compel them to desert what they dote upon, and cast even *the idols of silver and gold to the moles and the bats,* Isa. 2:20, 21. David and his men converted to their own use the rest of the plunder, but the images they burnt, as God had appointed (Deu. 7:5): *"You shall burn their graven images with fire,* in token of your detestation of idolatry, and lest they should be a snare." Bishop Patrick well observes here that when the ark fell into the Philistines' hands it consumed them, but, when these images fell into the hands of Israel, they could not save themselves from being consumed.

IV. In the latter of these engagements God gave David some sensible tokens of his presence with him, bade him not fall upon them directly, as he had done before, but *fetch a compass behind them, v.* 23. 1. God appoints him to draw back, as *Israel stood still to see the salvation of the Lord.* 2. He promised him to charge the enemy himself, by an invisible host of angels, *v.* 24. "Thou shalt hear the *sound of a going,* like the march of an army in the air, *upon the tops of the mulberry trees."* Angels tread light, and he that can walk upon the clouds can, when he pleases, walk on the tops of trees, or (as bishop Patrick understands it) at the head of the mulberry-trees, that is, of the wood, or hedge-row of those trees. "And, by that sign, thou shalt know that *the Lord goes out before thee;* though thou see him not, yet thou shalt hear him, and faith shall come and be confirmed by hearing. He goes forth *to smite the host of the Philistines."* When David had himself smitten them (*v.* 20), he ascribed it to God: *The Lord has broken forth upon my enemies,* to reward him for which thankful acknowledgment the next time God did it himself alone, without putting him to any toil or peril. Those that own God in what he has done for them will find him doing more. But observe, Though God promised to *go before him and smite the Philistines,* yet David, when he heard the sound of the going must bestir himself and be ready to pursue the victory. Note, God's grace must quicken our endeavours. If God work in us both to will and to do, it does not follow that we must sit still, as those that have nothing to do, but we must therefore, *work out our own salvation* with all possible care and diligence, Phil. 2:12, 13. The sound of the going was, (1.) A signal to David when to move; it is comfortable going out when God goes before us. And, (2.) Perhaps it was an alarm to the enemy, and put them into confusion. Hearing the march of an army against their front, they retreated with precipitation, and fell into David's army which lay behind them in their rear. Of those whom God fights against it is said (Lev. 26:36), *The sound of a shaken leaf shall chase them.* (3.) The success of this is briefly set down, *v.* 25. David observed his orders, waited till God moved, and stirred them, but not till then. Thus he was trained up in a dependence on God and his providence. God performed his promise, went before him, and routed all the enemies' force, and David failed not to improve his advantages; he smote the Philistines, even to the borders of their own country. When the kingdom of the Messiah was to be set up, the apostles that were to beat down the devil's kingdom must not attempt any thing till they received the promise of the Spirit, who *came with a sound from heaven as of a rushing mighty wind* (Acts 2:2), which was typified by this sound of the going on the tops of the mulberry trees; and, when they heard that, they must bestir themselves, and did so; they went forth conquering and to conquer.

CHAPTER 6

The obscurity of the ark, during the reign of Saul, had been as great a grievance to Israel as the insults of the Philistines. David, having humbled the Philistines and mortified them in gratitude for that favour, and in pursuance of his designs for the public welfare, is here bringing up the ark to his own city, that it might be near him, and be an ornament and strength to his new foundation. Here is, I. An attempt to do it, which failed and miscarried. The design was well laid (*v.* 1, 2). But, 1. They were guilty of an error in carrying it in a cart (*v.* 3–5). 2. They were punished for that error by the sudden death of Uzzah (*v.* 6, 7), which was a great terror to David (*v.* 8, 9) and put a stop to his proceedings (*v.* 10, 11). II. The great joy and satisfaction with which it was at last done (*v.* 12–15). And, 1. The good understanding between David and his people (*v.* 17–19). 2. The uneasiness between David and his wife upon that occasion (*v.* 16, 20–23). And, when we consider that the ark was both the token of God's presence and a type of Christ, we shall see that this story is very instructive.

Verses 1–5

We have not heard a word of the ark since it was lodged in Kirjath-jearim, immediately after its return out of its captivity among the Philistines (1 Sa. 7:1, 2), except that, once, Saul called for it, 1 Sa. 14:18. That which in former days had made so great a figure is now thrown aside, as a neglected thing, for many years. And, if now the ark was for so many years in a house, let it not seem strange that we find the church so long in the wilderness, Rev. 12:14. Perpetual visibility is no mark of the true church. God is graciously present with the souls of his people even when they want the external tokens of his presence. But now that David is settled in the throne the honour of the ark begins to revive, and *Israel's care of it to flourish again, wherein also,* no doubt, the good people among them *had been careful, but they lacked opportunity.* See Phil. 4:10.

I. Here is honourable mention made of the ark. Because it had not been spoken of a great while, now that it is spoken of observe how it is described (*v.* 2): it is *the ark of God whose name is called by the name of the Lord of hosts that dwelleth between the cherubim,* or *at which the name, even the name of the Lord of hosts, was called upon,* or *upon which the name of the Lord of hosts was called,* or *because of which the name is proclaimed, the name of the Lord of hosts* (that is, God was greatly magnified in the miracles done before the ark), or *the ark of God, who is called the name* (Lev. 24:11, 16), *the name of the Lord of hosts, sitting on the cherubim upon it.* Let us learn hence, 1. To think and speak highly of God. He is the name above every name, *the Lord of hosts,* that has all the creatures in heaven and earth at his command, and receives homage from them all, and yet is pleased to dwell between the cherubim, over the propitiatory or mercy-seat, graciously manifesting himself to his people, reconciled in a Mediator, and ready to do them good. 2. To think and speak honourably of holy ordinances, which are to us, as the ark was to Israel, the tokens of God's presence (Mt. 28:2), and the means of our communion with him, Ps. 27:4. It is the honour of the ark that it is the ark of God; he is jealous for it, is magnified in it, his name is called upon it. The divine institution puts a beauty and grandeur upon holy ordinances, which otherwise have no form nor comeliness. Christ is our ark. In and by him God manifests his favour and communicates his grace to us, and accepts our adoration and addresses.

II. Here is an honourable attendance given to the ark upon the removal of it. Now, at length, it is enquired after, David made the motion (1 Chr. 13:1–3), and the heads of the congregation agreed to it, *v.* 4. All the chosen men of Israel are called together to grace the solemnity, to pay their respect to the ark, and to testify their joy in its restoration. The nobility and gentry, elders and officers, came to the number of 30,000 (*v.* 1), and the generality of the common people besides (1 Chr. 13:5); for, some think, it was done at one of the three great festivals. This would make a noble cavalcade, and would help to inspire the young people of the nation, who perhaps had scarcely heard of the ark, with a great veneration for it, for this was certainly a treasure of inestimable value which the king himself and all the great men waited upon, and were a guard to.

III. Here are great expressions of joy upon the removal of the ark, *v.* 5. David himself, and all that were with him that were musically inclined, made use of such instruments as they had to excite and express their rejoicing upon this occasion. It might well put them into a transport of joy to see the ark rise out of obscurity and move towards a public station. It is better to have the ark in a house than not at all, better in a house than a captive in Dagon's temple; but it is very desirable to have it in a tent pitched on purpose for it, where the resort to it may be more free and open. As secret worship is better the more secret it is, so public worship is better the more public it is; and we have reason to rejoice when restraints are taken off, and the ark of God finds welcome in the city of David, and has not only the protection and support, but the countenance and encouragement, of the civil powers; for joy of this they *played before the Lord.* Note, Public joy must always be as *before the Lord,* with an eye to him and terminating in him, and must not degenerate into that which is carnal and sensual. Dr. Lightfoot supposes that, upon this occasion, David penned the 68th Psalm, because it begins with that ancient prayer of Moses at the removing of the ark, *Let God arise, and let his enemies be scattered;* and notice is taken there (*v.* 25) of the *singers and players on instruments* that attended, and (*v.* 27) of the princes of several of the tribes; and perhaps those words in the last verse, *O God, thou art terrible out of thy holy places,* were added upon occasion of the death of Uzzah.

IV. Here is an error that they were guilty of in this matter, that they carried the ark in a cart or carriage, whereas the priests should have carried it upon their shoulders, *v.* 3. The Kohathites that had the charge of the ark had no wagons assigned them, because *their service was to bear it upon their shoulders,* Num. 7:9. The ark was no such heavy burden but that they might, among them, have carried it as far as Mount Sion upon their shoulders, they needed not to put it in a cart like a common thing. It was no excuse for them that the Philistines had done so and were not punished for it; they knew no better, nor had they any priests or Levites with them to undertake the carrying of it; better carry it in a cart than that any of Dagon's priests should carry it. Philistines may cart the ark with impunity; but, if Israelites do so, they do it at their peril. And it mended the matter very little that it was a new cart; old or new, it was not what God had appointed. I wonder how so wise and good a man as David was, that conversed so much with the law of God, came to be guilty of such an oversight. We will charitably hope that it was because he was so extremely intent upon the substance of the service that he forgot to take care of this circumstance.

Verses 6–11

We have here Uzzah struck dead for touching the ark, when it was upon its journey towards the city of David, a sad providence, which damped their mirth, stopped the progress of the ark, and for the present, dispersed this great assembly, which had come together to attend it, and sent them home in a fright.

I. Uzzah's offence seems very small. He and his brother Ahio, the sons of Abinadab, in whose house the ark had long been lodged, having been used to attend it, to show their willingness to prefer the public benefit to their own private honour and advantage, undertook to drive the cart in which the ark was carried, this being perhaps the last service they were likely to do it; for others would be employed about it when it came to the city of David. Ahio went before, to clear the way, and, if need were, to lead the oxen. Uzzah followed close to the side of the cart. It happened that the oxen shook it, *v.* 6. The critics are not agreed about the signification of the original word: *They stumbled* (so our margin); *they kicked* (so some), perhaps against the goad with which Uzzah drove them; *they stuck in the mire,* by some. By some accident or other the ark was in danger of being overthrown. Uzzah thereupon laid hold of it, to save it from falling, we have reason to think with a very good intention, to preserve the reputation of the ark and to prevent a bad omen. Yet this was his crime. Uzzah was a Levite, but priests only might touch the ark. The law was express concerning the Kohathites, that, though they were to carry the ark by the staves, yet *they must not touch any holy thing, lest they die,* Num. 4:15. Uzzah's long familiarity with the ark, and the constant attendance he had given to it, might occasion his presumption, but would not excuse it.

II. His punishment for this offence seems very great (*v.* 7): *The anger of the Lord was kindled against him* (for in sacred things he is a jealous God) and he *smote him there for his rashness,* as the word is, and struck him dead upon the spot. There he sinned, and there he died, *by the ark of God;* even the mercy-seat would not save him. Why was God thus severe with him? 1. The touching of the ark was forbidden to the Levites expressly under pain of death — *lest they die;* and God, by this instance of severity, would show how he might justly have dealt with our first parents, when they had eaten that which was forbidden under the same penalty — *lest you die.* 2. God saw the presumption and irreverence of Uzzah's heart. Perhaps he affected to show, before this great assembly, how bold he could make with the ark, having been so long acquainted with it. Familiarity, even with that which is most awful, is apt to breed contempt. 3. David afterwards owned that Uzzah died for an error they were all guilty of, which was carrying the ark in a cart. Because it was not carried on the Levites' shoulders, *the Lord made that breach upon us,* 1 Chr. 15:13. But Uzzah was singled out to be made an example, perhaps because he had been most forward in advising that way of conveyance; however he had fallen into another error, which was occasioned by that. Perhaps the ark was not covered, as it should have been, with the covering of badgers' skins (Num. 4:6), and that was a further provocation. 4. God would hereby strike an awe upon the thousands of Israel, would convince them that the ark was never the less venerable for its having been so long in mean circumstances, and thus he would teach them to rejoice with trembling, and always to treat holy things with reverence and holy fear. 5. God would hereby teach us that a good intention will not justify a bad action; it will not suffice to say of that which is ill done that it was well meant. He will let us know that he can and will secure his ark, and needs not any man's sin to help him to do it. 6. If it was so great a crime for one to lay hold on the ark of the covenant that had no right to do so, what is it for those to lay claim to the privileges of the covenant that come not up to the terms of it? To the wicked God says, *What hast thou to do to take my covenant in thy mouth?* Ps. 50:16. *Friend, how camest thou in hither?* If the ark was so sacred, and not to be touched irreverently, what is the *blood of the covenant?* Heb. 10:29.

III. David's feelings on the infliction of this stroke were keen, and perhaps not altogether as they should have been. He should have humbled himself under God's hand, confessed his error, acknowledged God's righteousness, and deprecated the further tokens of his displeasure, and then have gone on with the good work he had in hand. But we find, 1. He was displeased. It is not said because Uzzah had affronted God, but because God had made a breach upon Uzzah (*v.* 8): *David's anger was kindled.* It is the same word that is used for God's displeasure, *v.* 7. Because God was angry, David was angry and out of humour. As if God might not assert the honour of his ark, and frown upon one that touched it rudely, without asking David leave. Shall mortal man pretend to be more just than God, arraign his proceedings, or charge him with iniquity? David did not now act like himself, like *a man after God's own heart.* It is not for us to be displeased at any thing that God does, how unpleasing soever it is to us. The death of Uzzah was indeed an eclipse to the glory of a solemnity which David valued himself upon more than any thing else, and might give birth to some speculations among those that were disaffected to him, as if God were departing from him too; but he ought nevertheless to have subscribed to the righteousness and wisdom of God in it, and not to have been displeased at it. When we lie under God's anger we must keep under our own. 2. He was afraid, *v.* 9. It should seem he was afraid with amazement; for he said, *How shall the ark of the Lord come to me?* As if God sought advantages against all that were about him, and was so extremely tender of his ark that there was no dealing with it; and therefore better for him to keep it at a distance. *Que procul a Jove, procul a fulmine — To retire from Jove is to retire from the thunder-bolt.* He should rather have said, "Let the ark come to me, and I will take warning by this to treat it with more reverence." *Provoke me not* (says God, Jer. 25:6) *and I will do you no hurt.* Or this may be looked upon as a good use which David made of this tremendous judgment. He did not say, "Surely Uzzah was a sinner above all men, because he suffered such things," but is concerned for himself, as one conscious, not only of his own unworthiness of God's favour, but his obnoxiousness to God's displeasure. "God might justly strike me dead as he did Uzzah. *My flesh trembles for fear of thee,"* Ps. 119:120. This God intends in his judgments, that others may hear and fear. David therefore will not bring the ark into his own city (*v.* 10) till he is better prepared for its reception. 3. He took care to perpetuate the remembrance of this stroke by a new name he gave to the place: *Perez-uzzah, the breach of Uzzah, v.* 8. He had been lately triumphing in the breach made upon his enemies, and called the place *Baal-perazim, a place of breaches.* But here is a breach upon his friends. When we see one breach, we should consider that we know not where the next will be. The memorial of this stroke would be a warning to posterity to take heed of all rashness and irreverence in dealing about holy things; for *God will be sanctified in those that come nigh unto him.* 4. He lodged the ark in a good house, the house of Obed-edom a Levite, which happened to be near the place where this disaster happened, and there, (1.) It was kindly entertained and welcomed, and continued there *three months, v.* 10, 11. Obed-edom knew what slaughter the ark had made among the Philistines that imprisoned it and the Bethshemites that looked into it. He saw Uzzah struck dead for touching it, and perceived that David himself was afraid of meddling with it; yet he cheerfully invites it to his own house, and opens his doors to it without fear, knowing it was a *savour of death unto death* only to those that treated it ill. "O the courage," says bishop Hall, "of an honest and faithful heart! nothing can make God otherwise than amiable to his own people: even his very justice is lovely." (2.) It paid well for its entertainment: *The Lord blessed Obed-edom and all his household.* The same hand that punished Uzzah's proud presumption rewarded Obed-edom's humble boldness, and made the ark to him a *savour of life unto life.* Let none think the worse of the gospel for the judgements inflicted on those that reject it, but set in opposition to them the blessings it brings to those that duly receive it. None ever had, nor ever shall have, reason to say that *it is in vain to serve God.* Let masters of families be encouraged to keep up religion in their families, and to serve God and the interests of his kingdom with their houses and estates, for that is the way to bring a blessing upon all they have. The ark is a guest which none shall lose by that bid it welcome. Josephus says that, whereas before Obed-edom was poor, on a sudden, in these three months, his estate increased, to the envy of his neighbours. Piety is the best friend to prosperity. In wisdom's left hand are riches and honour. His household shared in the blessing. It is good living in a family that entertains the ark, for all about it will fare the better for it.

Verses 12–19

We have here the second attempt to bring the ark home to the city of David; and this succeeded, though the former miscarried.

I. It should seem the blessing with which the house of Obed-edom was blessed for the ark's sake was a great inducement to David to bring it forward; for when that was told him (*v.* 12) he hastened to fetch it to him. For, 1. It was an evidence that God was reconciled to them, and his anger was turned away. As David could read God's frowns upon them all in Uzzah's stroke, so he could read God's favour to them all in Obed-edom's prosperity; and, if God be at peace with them, they can cheerfully go on with their design. 2. It was an evidence that the ark was not such a burdensome stone as it was taken to be, but, on the contrary, happy was the man that had it near him. Christ is indeed a *stone of stumbling, and a rock of offence,* to those that are disobedient; but to those who believe he is a *corner-stone, elect, precious,* 1 Pt. 2:6–8. When David heard that Obed-edom had such joy of the ark, then he would have it in his own city. Note, The experience others have had of the gains of godliness should encourage us to be religious. Is the ark a blessing to others' houses? let us bid it welcome to ours; we may have it, and the blessing of it, without fetching it from our neighbours.

II. Let us see how David managed the matter now. 1. He rectified the former error. He did not put the ark in a cart now, but ordered those whose business it was to carry it on their shoulders. This is implied here (*v.* 13) and expressed 1 Chr. 15:15. Then we make a good use of the judgments of God on ourselves and others when we are awakened by them to reform and amend whatever has been amiss. 2. At their first setting out he offered sacrifices to God (*v.* 13) by way of atonement for their former errors and in a thankful acknowledgment of the blessings bestowed on the house of Obed-edom. Then we are likely to speed in our enterprises when we begin with God and give diligence to make our peace with him, When we attend upon God in holy ordinances our eye must be to the great sacrifice, to which we owe it that we are taken into covenant and communion with God, Ps. 50:5. 3. He himself attended the solemnity with the highest expressions of joy that could be (*v.* 14): *He danced before the Lord with all his might;* he leaped for joy, as one transported with the occasion, and the more because of the disappointment he met with the last time. It is a pleasure to a good man to see his errors rectified and himself in the way of his duty. His dancing, I suppose, was not artificial, by any certain rule or measure, nor do we find that any danced with him; but it was a natural expression of his great joy and exultation of mind. He did it with all his might; so we should perform all our religious services, as those that are intent upon them and desire to do them in the best manner. All our might is little enough to be employed in holy duties: the work deserves it all. On this occasion David laid aside his imperial purple, and put on a plain linen ephod, which was light and convenient for dancing, and was used in religious exercises by those who were no priests, for Samuel wore one, 1 Sa. 2:18. That great prince thought it no disparagement to him to appear in the habit of a minister to the ark. 4. All the people triumphed in this advancement of the ark (*v.* 15): *They brought it up* into the royal city *with shouting,* and *with sound of trumpet,* so expressing their own joy in loud acclamations, and giving notice to all about them to rejoice with them. The public and free administration of ordinances, not only under the protection, but under the smiles, of the civil powers, is just matter of rejoicing to any people. 5. the ark was safely brought to, and honourably deposited in, the place prepared for it, *v.* 17. They set it in *the midst of the tabernacle,* or tent, *which David had pitched for it;* not the tabernacle which Moses reared, for that was at Gibeon (2 Chr. 1:13), and, we may suppose, being made of cloth, in so many hundred years it had gone to decay and was not fit to be removed; but this was a tent set up on purpose to receive the ark. He would not bring it into a private house, no, not his own, lest it should seem to be too much engrossed, and people's resort to it, to pray before it, should be less free; yet he would not build a house for it, lest that should supersede the building of a more stately temple in due time, and therefore, for the present, he placed it within curtains, under a canopy, in imitation of Moses's tabernacle. As soon as ever it was lodged, he offered burnt-offerings and peace-offerings, in thankfulness to God that the business was now done without any more errors or breaches, and in supplication to God for the continuance of his favour. Note, All our joys must be sanctified both with praises and prayers; *for with such sacrifices God is well pleased.* New, it should seem, he penned the 132nd Psalm. 6. The people were then dismissed with great satisfaction. He sent them away, (1.) With a gracious prayer: *He blessed them in the name of the Lord of hosts* (*v.* 18), having not only a particular interest in heaven as a prophet, but an authority over them as a prince; for *the less is blessed of the better,* Heb. 7:7. He prayed to God to bless them, and particularly to reward them for the honour and respect they had now shown to his ark, assuring them they should be no losers by their journey, but the blessing of God upon their affairs at home would more than bear their charges. He testified his desire for their welfare by this prayer for them, and let them know they had a king that loved them. (2.) With a generous treat; for so it was, rather than a distribution of alms. The great men, it is probable, he entertained at his own house, but to the *multitude of Israel, men* and *women* (and *children,* says Josephus), he dealt to every one a *cake of bread (a spice-cake,* so some), *a good piece of flesh — a handsome decent piece* (so some) — *a part of the peace-offerings* (so Josephus), that they might feast with him *upon the sacrifice,* and a *flagon,* or bottle, *of wine, v.* 19. Probably he ordered this provision to be made for them at their respective quarters, and this he did, [1.] In token of his joy and gratitude to God. When the heart is enlarged in cheerfulness the hand should be opened in liberality. The feast of Purim was observed with *sending portions one to another,* Esth. 9:22. As those to whom God is merciful ought to show mercy in forgiving, so those to whom God is bountiful ought to exercise bounty in giving. [2.] To recommend himself to the people, and confirm his interest in them; for *every one is a friend to him that giveth gifts.* Those that cared not for his prayers would love him for his generosity; and this would encourage them to attend him another time if he saw cause to call them together.

Verses 20–23

David, having dismissed the congregation with a blessing, *returned to bless his household* (*v.* 20), that is, to pray with them and for them, and to offer up his family thanksgiving for this national mercy. Ministers must not think that their public performances will excuse them from their family-worship; but when they have, with their instructions and prayers, blessed the solemn assemblies, they must return in the same manner to bless their households, for with them they are in a particular manner charged. David, though he had prophets, and priests, and Levites, about him, to be his chaplains, yet did not devolve the work upon them, but himself *blessed his household.* It is angels' work to worship God, and therefore surely that can be no disparagement to the greatest of men.

Never did David return to his house with so much pleasure and satisfaction as he did now that he had got the ark into his neighbourhood; and yet even this joyful day concluded with some uneasiness, occasioned by the pride and peevishness of his wife. Even the palaces of princes are not exempt from domestic troubles. David had pleased all the multitude of Israel, but Michal was not pleased with his dancing before the ark. For this, when he was at a distance, she scorned him, and when he came home she scolded him. She was not displeased at his generosity to the people, nor did she grudge the entertainment he gave them; but she thought he degraded himself too much in dancing before the ark. It was not her covetousness, but her pride, that made her fret.

I. When she saw David in the street dancing before the Lord she *despised him in her heart, v.* 16. She thought this mighty zeal of his for the ark of God, and the transport of joy he was in upon its coming home to him, was but a foolish thing, and unbecoming so great a soldier, and statesman, and monarch, as he was. It would have been enough for him to encourage the devotion of others, but she looked upon it as a thing below him to appear so very devout himself. "What a fool" (thinks she) "does my husband make of himself now! How fond is he of this ark, that might as well have lain still where it had lain for so many years! Much devotion has almost made him mad." Note, The exercises of religion appear very mean in the eyes of those that have little or no religion themselves.

II. When he came home in the very best disposition she began to upbraid him, and was so full of disdain and indignation that she could not contain till she had him in private, but went out to meet him with her reproaches. Observe,

1. How she taunted him (*v.* 20): *"How glorious was the king of Israel to-day!* What a figure didst thou make today in the midst of the mob! How unbecoming thy post and character!" Her contempt of him and his devotion began in the heart, but out of the abundance of that the mouth spoke. That which displeased her was his affection to the ark, which she wished he had no greater kindness for than she had: but she basely represents his conduct, in dancing before the ark, as lewd and immodest; and, while really she was displeased at it as a diminution to his honour, she pretended to dislike it as a reproach to his virtue, that he *uncovered himself in the eyes of the maid-servants,* as no man would have done but *one of the vain fellows* that cared not how much he shamed himself. We have no reason to think that this was true in fact. David, no doubt, observed decorum, and governed his zeal with discretion. But it is common for those that reproach religion thus to put false colours upon it and lay it under the most odious characters. To have abused any man thus for his pious zeal would have been very profane, but to abuse her own husband thus, whom she ought to have reverenced, and one whose prudence and virtue were above the reach of malice itself to disparage, one who had shown such affection for her that he would not accept a crown unless he might have her restored to him (*ch.* 3:13), was a most base and wicked thing, and showed her to have more of Saul's daughter in her than of David's wife or Jonathan's sister.

2. How he replied to her reproach. He did not upbraid her with her treacherous departure from him to embrace the bosom of a stranger. He had forgiven that, and therefore had forgotten it, though, it may be, his own conscience, on this occasion, upbraided him with his folly in receiving her again (for that is said to pollute the land, Jer. 3:1), but he justifies himself in what he did.

(1.) He designed thereby to honour God (*v.* 21): *It was before the Lord,* and with an eye to him. Whatever invidious construction she was pleased to put upon it, he had the testimony of his conscience for him that he sincerely aimed at the glory of God, for whom he thought he could never do enough. Here he reminds her indeed of the setting aside of her father's house, to make way for him to the throne, that she might not think herself the most proper judge of propriety: *"God chose me before thy father, and appointed me to be ruler over Israel,* and now I am the fountain of honour; and, if the expressions of a warm devotion to God were looked upon as mean and unfashionable in thy father's court, yet *I will play before the Lord,* and thereby bring them into reputation again. And, if this be to be vile (*v.* 22), *I will be yet more vile."* Note, [1.] We should be afraid of censuring the devotion of others though it may not agree with our sentiments, because, for aught that we know, the heart may be upright in it, and who are we that we should despise those whom God has accepted? [2.] If we can approve ourselves to God in what we do in religion, and do it as before the Lord, we need not value the censures and reproaches of men. If we appear right in God's eyes, no matter how mean we appear in the eyes of the world. [3.] The more we are vilified for well-doing the more resolute we should be in it, and hold our religion the faster, and bind it the closer to us, for the endeavours of Satan's agents to shake us and to shame us out of it. *I will be yet more vile.*

(2.) He designed thereby to humble himself: *"I will be base in my own sight,* and will think nothing too mean to stoop to for the honour of God." In the throne of judgment, and in the field of battle, none shall do more to support the grandeur and authority of a prince than David shall; but in acts of devotion he lays aside the thought of majesty, humbles himself to the dust before the Lord, joins in with the meanest services done in honour of the ark, and thinks all this no diminution to him. The greatest of men is less than the least of the ordinances of Jesus Christ.

(3.) He doubted not but even this would turn to his reputation among those whose reproach Michal pretended to fear: *Of the maid-servants shall I be had in honour.* The common people would be so far from thinking the worse of him for these pious condescensions that they would esteem and honour him so much the more. Those that are truly pious are sometimes *manifested in the consciences* even of those that speak ill of them, 2 Co. 5:11. Let us never be driven from our duty by the fear of reproach; for to be steady and resolute in it will perhaps turn to our reputation more than we think it will. Piety will have its praise. Let us not then be indifferent in it, nor afraid or ashamed to own it.

David was contented thus to justify himself, and did not any further animadvert upon Michal's insolence; but God punished her for it, writing her for ever childless from this time forward, *v.* 23. She unjustly reproached David for his devotion, and therefore God justly put her under the perpetual reproach of barrenness. *Those that honour God he will honour;* but those that despise him, and his servants and service, *shall be lightly esteemed.*

CHAPTER 7

Still the ark is David's care as well as his joy. In this chapter we have, I. His consultation with Nathan about building a house for it; he signifies his purpose to do it (*v.* 1, 2) and Nathan approves his purpose (*v.* 3). II. His communion with God about it. 1. A gracious message God sent him about it, accepting his purpose, countermanding the performance, and promising him an entail of blessings upon his family (*v.* 4–17). 2. A very humble prayer which David offered up to God in return to that gracious message, thankfully accepting God's promises to him, and earnestly praying for the performance of them (*v.* 18–29). And, in both these, there is an eye to the Messiah and his kingdom.

Verses 1–3

Here is, I. David at rest. *He sat in his house* (*v.* 1), quiet and undisturbed, having no occasion to take the field: *The Lord had given him rest round about,* from all those that were enemies to his settlement in the throne, and he set himself to enjoy that rest. Though he was a man of war, he was *for peace* (Ps. 120:7) and did not delight in war. He had not been long at rest, nor was it long before he was again engaged in war; but at present he enjoyed a calm, and he was in his element when he was sitting in his house, meditating in the law of God.

II. David's thought of building a temple for the honour of God. He had built a palace for himself and a city for his servants; and now he thinks of building a habitation for the ark. 1. Thus he would make a grateful return for the honours God put upon him. Note, When God, in his providence, has remarkably done much for us, it should put us upon contriving what we may do for him and his glory. *What shall I render unto the Lord?* 2. Thus he would improve the present calm, and make a good use of the rest God had given him. Now that he was not called out to serve God and Israel in the high places of the field, he would employ his thoughts, and time, and estate, in serving him another way, and not indulge himself in ease, much less in luxury. When God, in his providence, gives us rest, and finds us little to do of worldly business, we must do so much the more for God and our souls. How different were the thoughts of David when he sat in his palace from Nebuchadnezzar's when he *walked in his!* Dan. 4:29, 30. That proud man thought of nothing but the might of his own power, and the honour of his own majesty; this humble soul is full of contrivance how to glorify God, and give honour to him. And how God resisteth the proud, and giveth grace and glory to the humble, the event showed. David considered (*v.* 2) the stateliness of his own habitation *(I dwell in a house of cedar),* and compared with that the meanness of the habitation of the ark *(the ark dwells within curtains),* and thought this incongruous, that he should dwell in a palace and the ark in a tent. David had been uneasy till he found out *a place for the ark* (Ps. 132:4, 5), and now he is uneasy till he finds out a better place. Gracious grateful souls, (1.) Never think they can do enough for God, but, when they have done much, are still projecting to do more and devising liberal things. (2.) They cannot enjoy their own accommodations while they see the church of God in distress and under a cloud. David can take little pleasure in a house of cedar for himself, unless the ark have one. Those who *stretched themselves upon beds of ivory,* and were *not grieved for the affliction of Joseph,* though they had David's music, had not David's spirit (Amos 6:4, 6) nor those who dwelt in their ceiled houses while God's house lay waste.

III. His communicating this thought to Nathan the prophet. He told him, as a friend and confidant, whom he used to advise with. Could not David have gone about it himself? Was it not a good work? Was not he himself a prophet? Yes, but *in the multitude of counsellors there is safety.* David told him, that by him he might know the mind of God. It was certainly a good work, but it was uncertain whether it was the will of God that David should have the doing of it.

IV. Nathan's approbation of it: *Go, do all that is in thy heart; for the Lord is with thee, v.* 3. We do not find that David told him that he purposed to build a temple, only that it was a trouble to him that there was not one built, from which Nathan easily gathered what was in his heart, and bade him go on and prosper. Note, We ought to do all we can to encourage and promote the good purposes and designs of others, and put in a good word, as we have opportunity, to forward a good work. Nathan spoke this, not in God's name, but as from himself; not as a prophet, but as a wise and good man; it was agreeable to the revealed will of God, which requires that all in their places should lay out themselves for the advancement of religion and the service of God, though it seems his secret will was otherwise, that David should not do this. It was Christ's prerogative always to speak the mind of God, which he perfectly knew. Other prophets spoke it only when the spirit of prophecy was upon them; but, if in any thing they mistook (as Samuel, 1 Sa. 16:6, and Nathan here) God soon rectified the mistake.

Verses 4–17

We have here a full revelation of God's favour to David and the kind intentions of that favour, the notices and assurances of which God sent him by Nathan the prophet, whom he entrusted to deliver this long message to him. The design of it is to take him off from his purpose of building the temple and it was therefore sent, 1. By the same hand that had given him encouragement to do it, lest, if it had been sent by any other, Nathan should be despised and insulted and David should be perplexed, being encouraged by one prophet and discouraged by another. 2. The same night, that Nathan might not continue long in an error nor David have his head any further filled with thoughts of that which he must never bring to pass. God might have said this to David himself immediately, but he chose to send it by Nathan, to support the honour of his prophets, and to preserve in David a regard to them. Though he be the head, they must be the eyes by which he must see the visions of the Almighty, and the tongue by which he must hear the word of God. He that delivered this long message to Nathan assisted his memory to retain it, that he might deliver it fully (he being resolved to deliver it faithfully) as he received it of the Lord. Now in this message,

I. David's purpose to build God a house is superseded. God took notice of that purpose, for he knows what is in man; and he was well pleased with it, as appears 1 Ki. 8:18, *Thou didst well that it was in thy heart;* yet he forbade him to go on with his purpose (*v.* 5): *"Shalt thou build me a house?* No, *thou shalt not* (as it is explained in the parallel place, 1 Chr. 17:4); there is other work appointed for thee to do, which must be done first." David is a man of war, and he must enlarge the borders of Israel, by carrying on their conquests. David is a sweet psalmist, and he must prepare psalms for the use of the temple when it is built, and settle the courses of the Levites; but his son's genius will better suit for building the house, and he will have a better treasure to bear the charge of it, and therefore let it be reserved for him to do. *As every man hath received the gift, so let him minister.* The building of a temple was to be a work of time, and preparation made for it; but it was a thing that had never been spoken of till now. God tells him, 1. That hitherto he had never had a house built for him (*v.* 6), a tabernacle had served hitherto, and it might serve awhile longer. God regards not outward pomp in his service; his presence was as surely with his people when the ark was in a tent as when it was in a temple. David was uneasy that the ark was in curtains (a mean and movable habitation), but God never complained of it as any uneasiness to him. He did not dwell, but walk, and yet fainted not, nor was weary. Christ, like the ark, when here on earth walked in a tent or tabernacle, for he *went about doing good,* and dwelt not in any house of his own, till he ascended on high, to the mansions above, in his Father's house, and there he sat down. The church, like the ark, in this world is ambulatory, dwells in a tent, because its present state is both pastoral and military; its continuing city is to come. David, in his psalms, often calls the tabernacle a temple (as Ps. 5:7; 27:4; 29:9; 65:4; 138:2), because it answered the intention of a temple, though it was made but of curtains. Wise and good men value not the show, while they have the substance. David perhaps had more true devotion, and sweeter communion with God, in a house of curtains, than any of his successors in the house of cedar. 2. That he had never given any orders or directions, or the least intimation, to any of the sceptres of Israel, that is, to any of the judges, 1 Chr. 17:6 (for rulers are called *sceptres,* Eze. 19:14, the great Ruler is called so, Num. 24:17), concerning the building of the temple, *v.* 7. That worship only is acceptable which is instituted; why should David therefore design what God never ordained? Let him wait for a warrant, and then let him do it. Better a tent of God's appointing than a temple of his own inventing.

II. David is reminded of the great things God had done for him, to let him know that he was a favourite of heaven, though he had not the favour to be employed in this service, as also that God was not indebted to him for his good intentions, but, whatever he did for God's honour, God was beforehand with him, *v.* 8, 9. 1. He had raised him from a very mean and low condition: *He took him from the sheep-cote.* It is good for those who have come to great preferment to be often reminded of their small beginnings, that they may always be humble and thankful. 2. He had given him success and victory over his enemies (*v.* 9): *"I was with thee whithersoever thou wentest,* to protect thee when pursued, to prosper thee when pursuing. *I have cut off all thy enemies,* that stood in the way of thy advancement and settlement." 3. He had crowned him not only with power and dominion in Israel, but with honour and reputation among the nations about: *I have made thee a great name.* He had become famous for his courage, conduct, and great achievements, and was more talked of than any of the great men of his day. A great name is what those who have it have great reason to be thankful for and may improve to good purposes, but what those who have it not have no reason to be ambitious of: a good name is more desirable. A man may pass through the world very obscurely and yet very comfortably.

III. A happy establishment is promised to God's Israel, *v.* 10, 11. This comes in in a parenthesis, before the promises made to David himself, to let him understand that what God designed to do for him was for Israel's sake, that they might be happy under his administration, and to give him the satisfaction of foreseeing peace upon Israel, when it was promised him that he should *see his children's children,* Ps. 128:6. A good king cannot think himself happy unless his kingdom be so. The promises that follow relate to his family and posterity; these therefore, which speak of the settlement of Israel, intend the happiness of his own reign. Two things are promised: — 1. A quiet place: *I will appoint a place for my people Israel.* It was appointed long ago, yet they were disappointed, but now that appointment should be made good. Canaan should be clearly their own without any ejection or molestation. 2. A quiet enjoyment of that place: *The children of wickedness* (meaning especially the Philistines, who had been so long a plague to them) *shall not afflict them any more; but, as in the time that I caused judges to be over my people Israel, I will cause thee to rest from all thy enemies* (so *v.* 11 may be read), that is, "I will continue and complete that rest; the land shall rest from war, as it did under the judges."

IV. Blessings are entailed upon the family and posterity of David. David had purposed to build God a house, and, in requital, God promises to *build him a house, v.* 11. Whatever we do for God, or sincerely design to do though Providence prevents our doing it, we *shall in no wise lose our reward.* He had promised to make him a name (*v.* 9); here he promises to make him a house, which should bear up that name. It would be a great satisfaction to David, while he lived, to have the inviolable assurance of a divine promise that his family should flourish when he was dead. Next to the happiness of our souls, and the church of God, we should desire the happiness of our seed, that those who come of us may be praising God on earth when we are praising him in heaven.

1. Some of these promises relate to Solomon, his immediate successor, and to the royal line of Judah. (1.) That God would advance him to the throne. Those words, *when thy days be fulfilled, and thou shalt sleep with thy fathers,* intimate that David himself should come to his grave in peace; and then *I will set up thy seed.* This favour was so much the greater because it was more than God had done for Moses, or Joshua, or any of the judges whom he called to feed his people. David's government was the first that was entailed; for the promise made to Christ of the kingdom was to reach to his spiritual seed. *If children, then heirs.* (2.) That he would settle him in the throne: *I will establish his kingdom* (*v.* 12), *the throne of his kingdom, v.* 13. His title shall be clear and uncontested, his interest confirmed, and his administration steady. (3.) That he would employ him in that good work of building the temple, which David had only the satisfaction of designing: *He shall build a house for my name, v.* 13. The work shall be done, though David shall not have the doing of it. (4.) That he would take him into the covenant of adoption (*v.* 14, 15): *I will be his father, and he shall be my son.* We need no more to make us and ours happy than to have God to be a Father to us and them; and all those to whom God is a Father he by his grace makes his sons, by giving them the disposition of children. If he be a careful, tender, bountiful Father to us, we must be obedient, tractable, dutiful children to him. The promise here speaks *as unto sons.* [1.] That his Father would correct him when there was occasion; for *what son is he whom the Father chasteneth not?* Afflictions are an article of the covenant, and are not only consistent with, but flow from, God's fatherly love. *"If he commit iniquity,* as it proved he did (1 Ki. 11:1), *I will chasten him* to bring him to repentance, but it shall be *with the rod of men,* such a rod as men may wield — I will not *plead against him with the great power* of God," Job 23:6. Or rather such a rod as *men may bear* — "I will consider his frame, and correct him with all possible tenderness and compassion when there is need, and no more than there is need of; it shall be with *the stripes,* the *touches* (so the word is) *of the children of men;* not a stroke, or wound, but a gentle touch." [2.] That yet he would not disinherit him (*v.* 15): *My mercy* (and that is the inheritance of sons) *shall not depart from him.* The revolt of the ten tribes from the house of David was their correction for iniquity, but the constant adherence of the other two to that family, which was a competent support of the royal dignity, perpetuated the mercy of God to the seed of David, according to this promise; though that family was cut short, yet it was not cut off, as the house of Saul was. Never any other family swayed the sceptre of Judah than that of David. This is that covenant of royalty celebrated (Ps. 89:3, etc.) as typical of the covenant of redemption and grace.

2. Others of them relate to Christ, who is often called *David* and the *Son of David,* that Son of David to whom these promises pointed and in whom they had their full accomplishment. He was of the *seed of David,* Acts 13:23. To him God *gave the throne of his father David* (Lu. 1:32), all power both in heaven and earth, and authority to execute judgment. He was to build the gospel temple, a house for God's name, Zec. 6:12, 13. That promise, *I will be his Father, and he shall be my Son,* is expressly applied to Christ by the apostle, Heb. 1:5. But the establishing of his house, and his throne, and his *kingdom, for ever* (*v.* 13, and again, and a third time *v.* 16. *for ever*), can be applied to no other than Christ and his kingdom. David's house and kingdom have long since come to an end; it is only the Messiah's kingdom that is everlasting, and *of the increase of his government and peace there shall be no end.* The supposition of committing iniquity cannot indeed be applied to the Messiah himself, but it is applicable (and very comfortable) to his spiritual seed. True believers have their infirmities, for which they may expect to be corrected, but

they shall not be cast off. Every transgression in the covenant will not throw us out of covenant. Now, (1.) This message Nathan faithfully delivered to David (*v.* 17); though, in forbidding him to build the temple, he contradicted his own words, yet he was not backward to do it when he was better informed concerning the mind of God. (2.) These promises God faithfully performed to David and his seed in due time. Though David came short of making good his purpose to build God a house, yet God did not come short of making good his promise to build him a house. Such is the tenour of the covenant we are under; though there are many failures in our performances, there are none in God's.

Verses 18–29

We have here the solemn address David made to God, in answer to the gracious message God had sent him. We are not told what he said to Nathan; no doubt he received him very kindly and respectfully as God's messenger. But his answer to God he took himself, and did not send by Nathan. When ministers deliver God's message to us, it is not to them, but to God, that our hearts must reply; he understands the language of the heart, and to him we may come boldly. David had no sooner received the message than, while the impressions of it were fresh, he retired to return an answer. Observe,

I. The place he retired to: He *went in before the Lord,* that is, into the tabernacle where the ark was, which was the token of God's presence; before *that* he presented himself. God's will now is that men pray everywhere; but, wherever we pray, we must set ourselves as before the Lord and set him before us.

II. The posture he put himself into: He *sat before the Lord.* 1. It denotes the posture of his body. Kneeling or standing is certainly the most proper gesture to be used in prayer; but the Jews, from this instance, say, "It was allowed to the kings of the house of David to sit in the temple, and to no other." But this will by no means justify the ordinary use of that gesture in prayer, whatever may be allowed in a case of necessity. *David went in, and took his place before the Lord,* so it may be read; but, when he prayed, he stood up as the manner was. Or he *went in and continued before the Lord,* staid some time silently meditating, before he began his prayer, and then remained longer than usual in the tabernacle. Or, 2. It may denote the frame of his spirit at this time. He went in, and composed himself before the Lord; thus we should do in all our approaches to God. *O God, my heart is fixed, my heart is fixed.*

III. The prayer itself, which is full of the breathings of pious and devout affection towards God.

1. He speaks very humbly of himself and his own merits. So he begins as one astonished: *Who am I, O Lord God! and what is my house? v.* 18. God had reminded him of the meanness of his original (*v.* 8) and he subscribed to it; he had low thoughts, (1.) Of his personal merits: *Who am I?* He was upon all accounts a very considerable and valuable man. His endowments both of body and mind were extraordinary. His gifts and graces were eminent. He was a man of honour, success, and usefulness, the darling of his country and the dread of its enemies. Yet, when he comes to speak of himself before God, he says, *"Who am I?* A man not worth taking notice of." (2.) Of the merits of his family: *What is my house?* His house was of the royal tribe, and descended from the prince of that tribe; he was allied to the best families of the country, and yet, like Gideon, thinks his family poor in Judah and himself *the least in his father's house,* Jdg. 6:15. David thus humbled himself when Saul's daughter was proposed to him for a wife (1 Sa. 18:18), but now with much more reason. Note, It very well becomes the greatest and best of men, even in the midst of the highest advancements, to have low and mean thoughts of themselves; for the greatest of men are worms, the best are sinners, and those that are highest advanced have nothing but what they have received: *"What am I, that thou hast brought me hitherto,* brought me to the kingdom, and to a settlement in it, and rest from all my enemies?" It intimates that he could not have reached this himself by his own management, if God had not brought him to it. All our attainments must be looked upon as God's vouchsafements.

2. He speaks very highly and honourably of God's favours to him. (1.) In what he had done for him: *"Thou hast brought me hitherto,* to this great dignity and dominion. Hitherto thou hast helped me." Though we should be left at uncertainty concerning further mercy, we have great reason to be thankful for that which has been done for us hitherto, Acts 26:22. (2.) In what he had yet further promised him. God had done great things for him already, and yet, as if those had been nothing, he had promised to do much more, *v.* 19. Note, What God has laid out upon his people is much, but what he has laid up for them is infinitely more, Ps. 31:19. The present graces and comforts of the saints are invaluable gifts; and yet, as if these were too little for God to bestow upon his children, he has spoken concerning them for a great while to come, even as far as eternity itself reaches. Of this we must own, as David here, [1.] That it is far beyond what we could expect: *Is this the manner of men?* that is, *First,* Can man expect to be so dealt with by his Maker? *Is this the law of Adam?* Note, Considering what the character and condition of man are, it is very surprising and amazing that God should deal with him as he does. Man is a mean creature, and therefore under a law of distance — unprofitable to God, and therefore under a law of disesteem and disregard — guilty and obnoxious, and therefore under a law of death and damnation. But how unlike are God's dealings with man to this law of Adam! He is brought near to God, purchased at a high rate, taken into covenant and communion with God; could this ever have been thought of? *Secondly,* Do men usually deal thus with one another? No, the way of our God is far above the manner of men. Though he be high, he has respect to the lowly; and is this the manner of men? Though he is offended by us, he beseeches us to be reconciled, waits to be gracious, multiplies his pardons: and is this the manner of men? Some give another sense of this, reading it thus: *And this is the law of man, the Lord Jehovah,* that is, "This promise of one whose kingdom shall be established for ever must be understood of one that is a man and yet the Lord Jehovah, this must be the law of such a one. A Messiah from my loins must be man, but, reigning for ever, must be God." [2.] That beyond this there is nothing we can desire: *"And what can David say more unto thee? v.* 20. What can I ask or wish for more? *Thou, Lord, knowest thy servant,* knowest what will make me happy, and what thou hast promised is enough to do so." The promise of Christ includes all. If that man, the Lord God, be ours, what can we ask or think of more? Eph. 3:20. The promises of the covenant of grace are framed by him that knows us, and therefore knows how to adapt them to every branch of our necessity. He knows us better than we know ourselves; and therefore let us be satisfied with the provision he has made for us. What can we say more for ourselves in our prayers than he has said for us in his promises?

3. He ascribes all to the free grace of God (*v.* 21), both the great things he had done for him and the great things he had made known to him. All was, (1.) For his word's sake, that is, for the sake of Christ the eternal Word; it is all owing to his merit. Or, "That thou mayest magnify thy word of promise above all thy name, in making it the stay and store-house of thy people." (2.) According to thy own heart, thy gracious counsels and designs, *ex mero motu — of thy own good pleasure. Even so, Father, because it seemed good in thy eyes.* All that God does for his people in his providences, and secures to them in his promises, is for his pleasure and for his praise, the pleasure of his will and the praise of his word.

4. He adores the greatness and glory of God (*v.* 22): *Thou art great, O Lord God! for there is none like thee.* God's gracious condescension to him, and the honour he had put upon him, did not at all abate his awful veneration for the divine Majesty; for the nearer any are brought to God the more they see of his glory, and the dearer we are in his eyes the greater he should be in ours. And this we acknowledge concerning God, that there is no being like him, nor any God besides him, and that what we have seen with our eyes of his power and goodness is according to all that we have heard with our ears, and the one half not told us.

5. He expresses a great esteem for the Israel of God, *v.* 23, 24. As there was none among the gods to be compared with Jehovah, so none among the nations to be compared with Israel, considering,

(1.) The works he had done for them. He went to redeem them, applied himself to it as a great work, went about it with solemnity. *Elohim halecu, dii iveruni — Gods went,* as if there was the same consultation and concurrence of all the persons in the blessed Trinity about the work of redemption that there was about the work of creation, when God said, *Let us make man. Whom those that were sent of God went to redeem;* so the Chaldee, meaning, I suppose, Moses and Aaron. The redemption of Israel, as described here, was typical of our redemption by Christ in that, [1.] They were redeemed from the nations and their gods; so are we from all iniquity and all conformity to this present world. Christ came to save his people from their sins. [2.] They were redeemed to be a peculiar people unto God, purified and appropriated to himself, that he might make himself a great name and do for them great things. The honour of God, and the eternal happiness of the saints, are the two things aimed at in their redemption.

(2.) The covenant he had made with them, *v.* 24. It was, [1.] Mutual: "They to be a people to thee, and thou to be a God to them; all their interests consecrated to thee, and all thy attributes engaged for them." [2.] Immutable: "Thou hast confirmed them." He that makes the covenant makes it sure and will make it good.

6. He concludes with humble petitions to God. (1.) He grounds his petitions upon the message which God had sent him (*v.* 27): *Thou hast revealed this to thy servant,* that is, "Thou hast of thy own good will given me the promise that thou wilt build me a house, else I could never have found in my heart to pray such a prayer as this. I durst not have asked such great things if I had not been directed and encouraged by thy promise to ask them. They are indeed too great for me to beg, but not too great for thee to give. Thy servant has found in his heart to pray this prayer;" so it is in the original, and the Septuagint. Many, when they go to pray, have their hearts to seek, but David's heart was found, that is, it was fixed, gathered in from its wanderings, and entirely engaged to the duty and employed in it. That prayer which is found in the tongue only will not please God; it must be found in the heart; the heart must be lifted up and poured out before God. *My son, give God thy heart.* (2.) He builds his faith and hopes to speed upon the fidelity of God's promise (*v.* 25): *"Thou art that God* (thou art *he,* even *that God,* the *Lord of hosts,* and *God of Israel,* or *that God whose words are true,* that God whom one may depend upon); and *thou hast promised this goodness unto thy servant,* which I am therefore bold to pray for." (3.) Thence he fetches the matter of his prayer, and refers to that as the guide of his prayers. [1.] He prays for the performance of God's promise (*v.* 25): "Let the word be made good to me, *on which thou hast caused me to hope* (Ps. 119:49) *and do as thou hast said;* I desire no more, and I expect no less; so full is the promise, and so firm." Thus we must turn God's promises into prayers, and then they shall be turned into performances; for, with God, saying and doing are not two things, as they often are with men. God will do as he hath said. [2.] He prays for the glorifying of God's name (*v.* 26): *Let thy name be magnified for ever.* This ought to be the summary and centre of all our prayers, the Alpha and the Omega of them. Begin with *Hallowed be thy name,* and end with *Thine is the glory for ever.* "Whether I be magnified or no, *let thy name be magnified."* And he reckons that nothing magnifies God's name more than this, to say, with suitable affections, *The Lord of hosts is the God over Israel.* This bespeaks the *God of Israel gloriously great,* that he is the *Lord of hosts;* and this bespeaks the *Lord of hosts* gloriously good, that he is *God over Israel.* In both, *let his name be magnified for ever.* Let all the creatures and all the churches give him the glory of these two. David desired the performance of God's promise for the honour, not of his own name, but of God's. Thus the Son of David prayed, *Father, glorify thy name* (Jn. 12:28), and (Jn. 17:1), *Glorify thy Son, that thy Son may also glorify thee.* [3.] He prays for his house, for to that the promise has special reference, *First,* That it might be happy (*v.* 29): *Let it please thee to bless the house of thy servant;* and again, *with thy blessing.* "Let the house of thy servant be truly and eternally blessed. *Those whom thou blessest are blessed indeed."* The care of good men is very much concerning their families; and the best entail on their families is that of the blessing of God. The

repetition of this request is not a vain repetition, but expressive of the value he had of the divine blessing, and his earnest desire of it, as all in all to the happiness of his family. *Secondly,* That the happiness of it might remain: "Let it be *established before thee* (*v.* 26); let it *continue for ever before thee.*" *v.* 29. He prayed, 1. That the entail of the crown might not be cut off, but remain in his family, that none of his might ever forfeit it, but that they might walk before God, which would be their establishment. 2. That his kingdom might have its perfection and perpetuity in the kingdom of the Messiah. When Christ for ever sat down on the right hand of God (Heb. 10:12), and received all possible assurance that his seed and throne shall be as the days of heaven, this prayer of David the son of Jesse for his seed was abundantly answered, that it might *continue before God for ever.* See Ps. 72:17. The perpetuity of the Messiah's kingdom is the desire and faith of all good people.

CHAPTER 8

David having sought first the kingdom of God and the righteousness thereof, settling the ark as soon as he was himself well settled, we are here told how all other things were added to him. Here is an account, I. Of his conquests. He triumphed, 1. Over the Philistines (*v.* 1). 2. Over the Moabites (*v.* 2). 3. Over the king of Zobah (*v.* 3, 4). 4. Over the Syrians (*v.* 5–8, 13). 5. Over the Edomites (*v.* 14). II. Of the presents that were brought him and the wealth he got from the nations he subdued, which he dedicated to God (*v.* 9–12). III. Of his court, the administration of his government (*v.* 15), and his chief officers (*v.* 16–18). This gives us a general idea of the prosperity of David's reign.

Verses 1–8

God had given David rest from all his enemies that opposed him and made head against him; and he having made a good use of that rest, has now commission given him to make war upon them, and to act offensively for the avenging of Israel's quarrels and the recovery of their rights; for as yet they were not in full possession of that country to which by the promise of God they were entitled.

I. He quite subdued the Philistines, *v.* 1. They had attacked him when they thought him weak (*ch.* 5:17), and went by the worst then; but, when he found himself strong, he attacked them, and made himself master of their country. They had long been vexatious and oppressive to Israel. Saul got no ground against them; but David completed Israel's deliverance out of their hands, which Samson had begun long before, Jdg. 13:5. *Metheg-ammah* was *Gath* (the chief and royal city of the Philistines) and the towns belonging to it, among which there was a constant garrison kept by the Philistines on the hill Ammah (2 Sa. 2:24), which was *Metheg,* a *bridle* (so it signifies) or *curb* upon the people of Israel; this David took out of their hand and used it as a curb upon them. Thus, when the strong man is disarmed, the armour wherein he trusted is taken from him, and used against him, Lu. 11:22. And after the long and frequent struggles which the saints have had with the powers of darkness, like Israel with the Philistines, the Son of David shall tread them all under their feet and make the saints more than conquerors.

II. He smote the Moabites, and made them tributaries to Israel, *v.* 2. He divided the country into three parts, two of which he destroyed, casting down the strong-holds, and putting all to the sword; the third part he spared, to till the ground and be servants to Israel. Dr. Lightfoot says, "He laid them on the ground and measured them with a cord, who should be slain and who should live;" and this is called *meting out the valley of Succoth,* Ps. 60:6. The Jews say he used this severity with the Moabites because they had slain his parents and brethren, whom he put under the protection of the king of Moab during his exile, 1 Sa. 22:3, 4. He did it in justice, because they had been dangerous enemies to the Israel of God; and in policy, because, if left in their strength, they still would have been so. But observe, Though it was necessary that two-thirds should be cut off, yet the line that was to keep alive, though it was but one, is ordered to be a full line. Be sure to give that length enough; let the line of mercy be stretched to the utmost *in favorem vitae — so as to favour life.* Acts of indemnity must be construed so as to enlarge the favour. Now Balaam's prophecy was fulfilled, *A sceptre shall arise out of Israel, and shall smite the corners of Moab,* to the utmost of which the fatal line extended, Num. 24:17. The Moabites continued tributaries to Israel till after the death of Ahab, 2 Ki. 3:4, 5. Then they rebelled and were never reduced.

III. He smote the Syrians or Aramites. Of them there were two distinct kingdoms, as we find them spoken of in the title of the 60th Psalm: *Aram Naharaim, — Syria of the rivers,* whose head city was Damascus (famed for its rivers, 2 Ki. 5:12), and *Aram Zobah,* which joined to it, but extended to Euphrates. These were the two northern crowns. 1. David began with the Syrians of Zobah, *v.* 3, 4. As he went to settle his border at the river Euphrates (for so far the land conveyed by the divine grant to Abraham and his seed did extend, Gen. 15:18), the king of Zobah opposed him, being himself possessed of those countries which belonged to Israel; but David routed his forces, and took his chariots and horsemen. The horsemen are here said to be 700, but 1 Chr. 18:4 they are said to be 7000. If they divided their horse by ten in a company, as it is probable they did, the captains and companies were 700, but the horsemen were 7000. David houghed the horses, cut the sinews of their hams, and so lamed them, and made them unserviceable, at least in war, God having forbidden them to *multiply horses,* Deu. 17:16. David reserved only 100 chariots out of 1000 for his own use: for he placed his strength not in chariots nor horses, but in the living God (Ps. 20:7), and wrote it from his own observation that a *horse is a vain thing for safety,* Ps. 33:16, 17. 2. The Syrians of Damascus coming in to the relief of the king of Zobah fell with him. 22,000 were slain in the field, *v.* 5. So that it was easy for David to make himself master of the country, and garrison it for himself, *v.* 6. The enemies of God's church, that think to secure themselves, will prove, in the end, to ruin themselves, by their confederacies with each other. *Associate yourselves, and you shall be broken in pieces,* Isa. 8:9.

IV. In all these wars, 1. David was protected: *The Lord preserved him whithersoever he went.* It seems, he went in person, and, in the cause of God and Israel, jeoparded his own life in the high places of the field; but God covered his head in the day of battle, which he often speaks of, in his psalms, to the glory of God. 2. He was enriched. He took the shields of gold which the servants of Hadadezer had in their custody (*v.* 7) and much brass from several cities of Syria (*v.* 8), which he was entitled to, not only *jure belli — by the uncontrollable right of the longest sword* ("Get it, and take it"); but by commission from heaven, and the ancient entail of these countries on the seed of Abraham.

Verses 9–14

Here is, 1. The court made to David by the king of Hamath, who, it seems was at this time at war with the king of Zobah. He hearing of David's success against his enemy, sent his own son ambassador to him (*v.* 9, 10), to congratulate him on his victory, to return him thanks for the favour he had done him in breaking the power of one he was in fear of, and to beg his friendship. Thus he not only secured but strengthened himself. And David lost nothing by taking this little prince under his protection, any more than the old Romans did by the like policy; for the wealth he had from the countries he conquered by way of spoil he had from this by way of present or gratuity: *Vessels of silver and gold.* Better get by composition than by compulsion. 2. The offering David made to God of the spoils of the nations and all the rich things that were brought him. He dedicated all to the Lord. *v.* 11, 12. This crowned all his victories, and made them far to out-shine Alexander's or Caesar's, that they sought their own glory, but he aimed at the glory of God. All the precious things he was master of were dedicated things, that is, they were designed for the building of the temple; and a good omen it was of kindness to the Gentiles in the fulness of time, and of the making of God's house a house of prayer for all people, that the temple was built of the spoils and presents of Gentile nations, in allusion to which we find *the kings of the earth* bringing *their glory and honour into the new Jerusalem,* Rev. 21:24. Their gods of gold David burnt (2 Sa. 5:21), but their vessels of gold he dedicated. Thus in the conquest of a soul, by the grace of the Son of David, what stands in opposition to God must be destroyed, every lust mortified and crucified, but what may glorify him must be dedicated and the property of it altered. Even the merchandise and the hire must be *holiness to the Lord* (Isa. 23:18), the gain *consecrated to the Lord of the whole earth* (Mic. 4:13), and then it is truly our own and that most comfortably. 3. The reputation he got, in a particular manner, by his victory over the Syrians and their allies the Edomites, who acted in conjunction with them, as appears by comparing the title of the 60th Psalm, which was penned on this occasion, with *v.* 13. *He got himself a name* for all that conduct and courage which are the praise of a great and distinguished general. Something extraordinary, it is likely, there was in that action, which turned very much to his honour, yet he is careful to transfer the honour to God, as appears by the psalm he penned on this occasion, *v.* 12. It is through God that we do valiantly. 4. His success against the Edomites. They all became David's servants, *v.* 14. Now, and not till now, Isaac's blessing was accomplished, by which Jacob was made Esau's Lord (Gen. 27:37–40) and the Edomites continued long tributary to the kings of Judah, as the Moabites were to the kings of Israel, till, in Joram's time, they revolted (2 Chr. 21:8) as Isaac had there foretold that Esau should, in process of time, break the yoke from off his neck. Thus David by his conquests, (1.) Secured peace to his son, that he might have time to build the temple. And, (2.) Procured wealth for his son, that he might have wherewith to build it. God employs his servants variously, some in one employment, others in another, some in the spiritual battles, others in the spiritual buildings; and one prepares work for the other, that God may have the glory of all. All David's victories were typical of the success of the gospel against the kingdom of Satan, in which the Son of David rode forth, conquering and to conquer, and he shall reign till he has brought down all opposing rule, principality, and power: and he has, as David had (*v.* 2), a line to kill and a line to save; for the same gospel is to some a savour of life unto life, to others a savour of death unto death.

Verses 15–18

David was not so engaged in his wars abroad as to neglect the administration of the government at home.

I. His care extended itself to all the parts of his dominion: *He reigned over all Israel* (*v.* 15); not only he had a right to reign over all the tribes, but he did so; they were all safe under his protection, and shared in the fruits of his good government.

II. He did justice with an unbiased unshaken hand: *He executed judgment unto all his people,* neither did wrong nor denied or delayed right to any. This intimates, 1. His industry and close application to business, his easiness of access and readiness to admit all addresses and appeals made to him. All his people, even the meanest, and those too of the meanest tribes, were welcome to his council-board. 2. His impartiality and the equity of his proceedings, in administering justice. He never perverted justice through favour or affection, nor had respect of persons in judgment. Herein he was a type of Christ, who was faithful and true, and who doth *in righteousness both judge and make war,* Rev. 19:11. See Ps. 72:1, 2.

III. He kept good order and good officers in his court. David being the first king that had an established government (for Saul's reign was short and unsettled) he had the modelling of the administration. In Saul's time we read of no other great officer than Abner, that was captain of the host. But David appointed more officers: Joab that was general of the forces in the field, and Banaiah that was over the Cherethites and Pelethites, who were either the city train-bands *(archers and slingers,* so the Chaldee), or rather the life-guards, or standing force, that attended the king's person, the pretorian band, the militia. They were ready to do service at home, to assist in the administering of justice, and to preserve the public peace. We find them employed in proclaiming Solomon, 1 Ki. 1:38. 2. Two ecclesiastical officers: *Zadok and Ahimelech were priests,* that is, they were most employed in the priests' work under Abiathar, the high priest. 3. Two civil officers: one that was recorder, or remembrancer, to put the king in mind of business in its season (he was prime minister of state, yet not entrusted with the custody of the king's conscience, as they say of our lord chancellor, but only of the king's memory; let the king be put in mind of business and he would do it himself); another that was scribe, or secretary of state, that drew up public orders and despatches, and recorded judgments given. 4. David's sons, as they grew up to be fit for business, were made chief rulers; they had places of honour and trust assigned them, in the household, or in the camp, or in the courts of justice, according as their genius led them. They were chief about the king (so it is explained, 1 Chr. 18:17), employed near him, that they might be under his eye. Our Lord Jesus has appointed officers in his kingdom, for his honour and the good of the community; when he ascended on high *he gave these gifts* (Eph. 4:8–11), *to every man his work,* Mk. 13:34. David made his sons chief rulers; but all believers, Christ's spiritual seed, are better preferred, for they are *made to our God kings and priests,* Rev. 1:6.

CHAPTER 9

The only thing recorded in this chapter is the kindness David showed to Jonathan's seed for his sake. I. The kind enquiry he made after the remains of the house of Saul, and his discovery of Mephibosheth (*v.* 1–4). II. The kind reception he gave to Mephibosheth, when he was brought to him (*v.* 5–8). III. The kind provision he made for him and his (*v.* 9–13).

Verses 1–8

Here is, I. David's enquiry after the remains of the ruined house of Saul, *v.* 1. This was a great while after his accession to the throne, for it should seem that Mephibosheth, who was but five years old when Saul died, had now a son born, *v.* 12. David had too long forgotten his obligations to Jonathan, but now, at length, they are brought to his mind. It is good sometimes to bethink ourselves whether there be any promises or engagements that we have neglected to make good; better do it late than never. The compendium which Paul gives us of the life of David is this (Acts 13:36), that he *served his generation according to the will of God,* that is, he was a man that made it his business to do good; witness this instance, where we may observe,

1. That he sought an opportunity to do good. He might perhaps have satisfied his conscience with the performance of his promise to Jonathan if he had been only ready, upon request or application made to him by any of his seed, to help and succour them. But he does more, he enquires of those about him first (*v.* 1), and, when he met with a person that was likely to inform him, asked him particularly, *Is there any yet left of the house of Saul, that I may show him kindness? v.* 3. "Is there any, not only to whom I may do justice (Num. 5:8), but to whom I may show kindness?" Note, Good men should seek opportunities of doing good. *The liberal deviseth liberal things,* Isa. 32:8. For, the most proper objects of our kindness and charity are such as will not be frequently met with without enquiry. The most necessitous are the least clamorous.

2. Those he enquired after were the remains of the house of Saul, to whom he would show kindness for Jonathan's sake: *Is there any left of the house of Saul?* Saul had a very numerous family (1 Chr. 8:33), enough to replenish a country, and was yet so emptied that none of it appeared; but it was a matter of enquiry, *Is there any left?* See how the providence of God can empty full families; see how the sin of man will do it. Saul's was a bloody house, no marvel it was thus reduced, *ch.* 21:1. But, though God visited the iniquity of the father upon the children, David would not. "Is there any left that I can show kindness to, not for Saul's own sake, but for Jonathan's?" (1.) Saul was David's sworn enemy, and yet he would show kindness to his house with all his heart and was forward to do it. He does not say, "Is there any left of the house of Saul, that I may find some way to take them off, and prevent their giving disturbance to me or my successor?" It was against Abimelech's mind that any one was left of the house of Gideon (Jdg. 9:5), and against Athaliah's mind that any one was left of *the seed royal,* 2 Chr. 22:10, 11. Those were usurped governments. David's needed no such vile supports. He was desirous to show kindness to the house of Saul, not only because he trusted in God and feared not what they could do unto him, but because he was of a charitable disposition and forgave what they had done to him. Note, We must evince the sincerity of our forgiving those that have been any way unjust or injurious to us by being ready, as we have opportunity, to show kindness both to them and theirs. We must not only not avenge ourselves upon them, but we must love them, and *do them good* (Mt. 5:44), and not be backward to do any office of love and good-will to those that have done us many an injury. 1 Pt. 3:9, — *but, contrari-wise, blessing.*

This is the way to overcome evil, and to find mercy for ourselves and ours, when we or they need it. (2.) Jonathan was David's sworn friend, and therefore he would show kindness to his house. This teaches us, [1.] To be mindful of our covenant. The kindness we have promised we must conscientiously perform, though it should not be claimed. God is faithful to us; let us not be unfaithful to one another. [2.] To be mindful of our friendships, our old friendships. Note, Kindness to our friends, even to them and theirs, is one of the laws of our holy religion. *He that has friends must show himself friendly,* Prov. 18:24. If Providence has raised us, and our friends and their families are brought low, yet we must not forget former acquaintance, but rather look upon that as giving us so much the fairer opportunity of being kind to them: then our friends have most need of us and we are in the best capacity to help them. Though there be not a solemn league of friendship tying us to this constancy of love, yet there is a sacred law of friendship no less obliging, that to him that is in misery pity should be shown by his friend, Job 6:14. *A brother is born for adversity.* Friendship obliges us to take cognizance of the families and surviving relations of those we have loved, who, when they left us, left behind them their bodies, their names, and their posterity, to be kind to.

3. The kindness he promised to show them he calls the *kindness of God;* not only great kindness, but, (1.) Kindness in pursuance of the covenant that was between him and Jonathan, to which God was a witness. See 1 Sa. 20:42. (2.) Kindness after God's example; for we must be merciful as he is. He spares those whom he has advantage against, and so must we. Jonathan's request to David was (1 Sa. 20:14, 15), "*Show me the kindness of the Lord, that I die not,* and the same to my seed." The kindness of God is some greater instance of kindness than one can ordinarily expect from men. (3.) It is kindness done after a godly sort, and with an eye to God, and his honour and favour.

II. Information given him concerning Mephibosheth, the son of Jonathan. Ziba was an old retainer to Saul's family, and knew the state of it. He was sent for and examined, and informed the king that Jonathan's son was living, but *lame* (how he came to be so we read before, *ch.* 4:4), and that he lived in obscurity, probably among his mother's relations in Lo-debar in Gilead, on the other side Jordan, where he was *forgotten, as a dead man out of mind,* but bore this obscurity the more easily because he could remember little of the honour he fell from.

III. The bringing of him to court. The king sent (Ziba, it is likely) to bring him up to Jerusalem with all convenient speed, *v.* 5. Thus he eased Machir of his trouble, and perhaps recompensed him for what he had laid out on Mephibosheth's account. This Machir appears to have been a very generous free-hearted man, and to have entertained Mephibosheth, not out of any disaffection to David or his government, but in compassion to the reduced son of a prince, for afterwards we find him kind to David himself when he fled from Absalom. He is named (*ch.* 17:27) among those that furnished the king with what he wanted at Mahanaim, though David, when he sent for Mephibosheth from him, little thought that the time would come when he himself would gladly be beholden to him: and perhaps Machir was then the more ready to help David in recompence for his kindness to Mephibosheth. Therefore we should be forward to give, because we know not but we ourselves may some time be in want, Eccl. 11:2. *And he that watereth shall be watered also himself,* Prov. 11:25. Now,

1. Mephibosheth presented himself to David with all the respect that was due to his character. Lame as he was, *he fell on his face, and did homage, v.* 6. David had thus made his honours to Mephibosheth's father, Jonathan, when he was next to the throne (1 Sa. 20:41, *he bowed himself to him three times),* and now Mephibosheth, in like manner, addresses him, when affairs are so completely reversed. Those who, when they are in inferior relations, show respect, shall, when they come to be advanced, have respect shown to them.

2. David received him with all the kindness that could be. (1.) He spoke to him as one surprised, but pleased to see him. "Mephibosheth! Why, is there such a man living?" He remembered his name, for it is probable that he was born about the time of the intimacy between him and Jon-

athan. (2.) He bade him not be afraid: *Fear not, v.* 7. It is probable that the sight of David put him into some confusion, to free him from which he assures him that he sent for him, not out of any jealousy he had of him, nor with any bad design upon him, but to show him kindness. Great men should not take a pleasure in the timorous approaches of their inferiors (for the great God does not), but should encourage them. (3.) He gives him, by grant from the crown, *all the land of Saul his father,* that is, his paternal estate, which was forfeited by Ishbosheth's rebellion and added to his own revenue. This was a real favour, and more than giving him a kind word. True friendship will be generous. (4.) Though he had thus given him a good estate, sufficient to maintain him, yet for Jonathan's sake (whom perhaps he saw some resemblance of in Mephibosheth's face), he will take him to be a constant guest at his own table, where he will not only be comfortably fed, but have company and attendance suitable to his birth and quality. Though Mephibosheth was lame and unsightly, and does not appear to have had any great fitness for business, yet, for his good father's sake, David took him to be one of his family.

3. Mephibosheth accepts this kindness with great humility and self-abasement. He was not one of those that take every favour as a debt, and think every thing too little that their friends do for them; but, on the contrary, speaks as one amazed at the grants David made him (*v.* 8): *What is thy servant, that thou shouldst look upon such a dead dog as I am?* How does he vilify himself! Though the son of a prince, and the grandson of a king, yet his family being under guilt and wrath, and himself poor and lame, he calls himself *a dead dog* before David. Note, It is good to have the heart humble under humbling providences. If, when divine Providence brings our condition down, divine grace brings our spirits down with it, we shall be easy. And those who thus humble themselves shall be exalted. How does he magnify David's kindness! It would have been easy to lessen it if he had been so disposed. Had David restored him his father's estate? It was but giving him his own. Did he take him to his table? This was policy, that he might have an eye upon him. But Mephibosheth considered all that David said and did as very kind, and himself as less than the least of all his favours. See 1 Sa. 18:18.

Verses 9–13

The matter is here settled concerning Mephibosheth. 1. This grant of his father's estate is confirmed to him, and Ziba called to be a witness to it (*v.* 9); and, it should seem, Saul had a very good estate, for his father was a mighty man of substance (1 Sa. 9:1), and he had fields and vineyards to bestow, 1 Sa. 22:7. Be it ever so much, Mephibosheth is now master of it all. 2. The management of the estate is committed to Ziba, who knew what it was and how to make the most of it, in whom, having been his father's servant, he might confide, and who, having a numerous family of sons and servants, had hands sufficient to be employed about it, *v.* 10. Thus Mephibosheth is made very easy, having a good estate without care, and is in a fair way of being very rich, having much coming in and little occasion to spend, himself being kept at David's table. Yet he must have food to eat besides his own bread, provisions for his son and servants; and Ziba's sons and servants would come in for their share of his revenue, for which reason perhaps their number is here mentioned, *fifteen sons and twenty servants,* who would require nearly all there was; *for as goods are increased those are increased that eat them, and what good has the owner thereof save the beholding of them with his eyes? Eccl.* 5:11. *All that dwelt in the house of Ziba were servants to Mephibosheth* (*v.* 12), that is, they all lived upon him, and made a prey of his estate, under pretence of waiting on him and doing him service. The Jews have a saying, "He that multiplies servants multiplies thieves." Ziba is now pleased, for he loves wealth, and will have abundance. "As the king has *commanded, so will thy servant do, v.* 11. Let me alone with the estate: and *as for Mephibosheth*" (they seem to be Ziba's words), "if the king please, he need not trouble the court, *he shall eat at my table,* and be as well treated *as one of the king's sons.*" But David will have him at his own table, and Mephibosheth is as well pleased with his post as Ziba with his. How unfaithful Ziba was to him we shall find afterwards, *ch.* 16:3. Now because David was a type of Christ, his Lord and son, his root and offspring, let his kindness to Mephibosheth serve to illustrate the kindness and love of God our Saviour towards fallen man, which yet he was under no obligation to, as David was to Jonathan. Man was convicted of rebellion against God, and, like Saul's house, under a sentence of rejection from him, was not only brought low and impoverished, but lame and impotent, made so by the fall. The Son of God enquires after this degenerate race, that enquired not after him, comes to seek and save them. To those of them that humble themselves before him, and commit themselves to him, he restores the forfeited inheritance, he entitles them to a better paradise than that which Adam lost, and takes them into communion with himself, sets them with his children at his table, and feasts them with the dainties of heaven. *Lord, what is man, that thou shouldst thus magnify him!*

CHAPTER 10

This chapter gives us an account of a war David has with the Ammonites and the Syrians their allies, with the occasion and success of it. I. David sent a friendly embassy to Hanun king of the Ammonites (*v.* 1, 2). II. He, upon a base surmise that it was ill intended, abused David's ambassadors (*v.* 3, 4). III. David resenting it (*v.* 5), and the Ammonites prepared for war against him (*v.* 6). IV. David carried the war into their country, sent against them. Joab and Abishai, who addressed themselves to the battle with a great deal of conduct and bravery (*v.* 7–12). V. The Ammonites, and the Syrians their allies, were totally routed (*v.* 13, 14). VI. The forces of the Syrians, which rallied again, were a second time defeated (*v.* 15–19). Thus did David advance his own reputation for gratitude, in returning kindness, and for justice, in repaying injuries.

Verses 1–5

Here is, I. The great respect David paid to his neighbour, the king of the Ammonites, *v.* 1, 2. 1. The inducement to it was some kindness he had formerly received from Nahash the deceased king. He *showed kindness to me,* says David (*v.* 2), and therefore (having lately had satisfaction in showing kindness to Mephibosheth for his father's sake) he resolves to show kindness to his son, and to keep up a friendly correspondence with him. Thus the pleasure of doing one kind and generous action should excite us to another. Nahash had been an enemy to Israel, a cruel enemy (1 Sa. 11:2), and yet had shown kindness to David, perhaps only in contradiction to Saul, who was unkind to him: however, if David receives kindness, he is not nice in examining the grounds and principles of it, but resolves gratefully to return it. If a Pharisee give alms in pride, though God will not reward him, yet he that receives the alms ought to return thanks for it. God knows the heart, but we do not. 2. The particular instance of respect was sending an embassy to condole with him on his father's death, as is common among princes in alliance with each other: *David sent to comfort him.* Note, It is a comfort to children, when their parents are dead, to find that their parents' friends are theirs, and that they intend to keep up an acquaintance with them. It is a comfort to mourners to find that there are those who mourn with them, are sensible of their loss and share with them in it. It is a comfort to those who are honouring the memory of their deceased relations to find there are others who likewise honour it and who had a value for those whom they valued.

II. The great affront which Hanun the king of the Ammonites put upon David in his ambassadors. 1. He hearkened to the spiteful suggestions of his princes, who insinuated that David's ambassadors, under pretence of being comforters, were sent as spies, *v.* 3. False men are ready to think others as false as themselves; and those that bear ill-will to their neighbours are resolved not to believe that their neighbours bear any good-will to them. They would not thus have imagined that David dissembled but that they were conscious to themselves that they could have dissembled, to serve a turn. Unfounded suspicion argues a wicked mind. Bishop Patrick's note on this is that "there is nothing so well meant but it may be ill interpreted, and is wont to be so by men who love nobody but themselves." Men of the greatest honour and virtue must not think it strange if they be thus misrepresented. *Charity thinketh no evil.* 2. Entertaining this vile suggestion, he basely abused David's ambassadors, like a man of a sordid villainous spirit, that was fitter to rake a kennel than to wear a crown. If he had any reason to suspect that David's messengers came on a bad design, he would have done prudently enough to be upon the reserve with them, and to dismiss them as soon as he could; but it is plain he only sought an occasion to put the utmost disgrace he could upon them, out of an antipathy to their king and their country. They were themselves men of honour, and much more so as they represented the prince that sent them; they and their reputation were under the special protection of the law of nations; they put a confidence in the Ammonites, and came among them unarmed; yet Hanun used them like rogues and vagabonds, and worse, *shaved off the one half of their beards, and cut off their garments in the midst,* to expose them to the contempt and ridicule of his servants, that they might make sport with them and that these men might seem vile.

III. David's tender concern for his servants that were thus abused. He sent to meet them, and to let them know how much he interested himself in their quarrel and how soon he would avenge it, and directed them to stay at Jericho, a private place, where they would not have occasion to come into company, till that half of their beards which was shaved off had grown to such a length that the other half might be decently cut to it, *v.* 5. The Jews wore their beards long, reckoning it an honour to appear aged and grave; and therefore it was not fit that persons of their rank and figure should appear at court unlike their neighbours. Change of raiment, it is likely, they had with them, to put on, instead of that which was cut off; but the loss of their beards would not be so soon repaired; yet in time these would grow again, and all would be well. Let us learn not to lay too much to heart unjust reproaches; after awhile they will wear off of themselves, and turn only to the shame of their authors, while the injured reputation in a little time grows again, as these beards did. God will *bring forth thy righteousness as the light,* therefore *wait patiently for him,* Ps. 37:6, 7.

Some have thought that David, in the indignity he received from the king of Ammon, was but well enough served for courting and complimenting that pagan prince, whom he knew to be an inveterate enemy to Israel, and might now remember how, when he would have put out the right eyes of the men of Jabesh-Gilead, he designed that, as he did this, for a *reproach upon all Israel,* 1 Sam. 11:2. What better usage could he expect from such a spiteful family and people? Why should he covet the friendship of a people whom Israel must have so little to do with as that an Ammonite might not *enter into the congregation of the Lord, even to the tenth generation?* Deu. 23:3.

Verses 6–14

Here we have, I. The preparation which the Ammonites made for war, *v.* 6. They saw they had made themselves very odious to David and obnoxious to his just displeasure. This they might easily have foreseen when they abused his ambassadors, which was no other than a challenge to war, and a bold defiance of him. Yet, it seems, they had not considered how unable they were, with their thousands, to meet his; for now they found themselves an unequal match, and were forced to hire forces of other nations into their service. Thus sinners daringly provoke God, and expose themselves to his wrath, and never consider that he is *stronger than they,* 1 Co. 10:22. The Ammonites gave the affront first, and they were the first that raised forces to justify it. Had they humbled themselves, and begged David's pardon, probably an honorary satisfaction might have atoned for the offence. But, when they were thus desperately resolved to stand by what they had done, they courted their own ruin.

II. The speedy descent which David's forces made upon them, *v.* 7. When David heard of their military preparations, he sent Joab with a great army to attack them, *v.* 7. Those that are at war with the Son of David not only give the provocation, but begin the war; for he *waits to be gracious,* but they *strengthen themselves against him,* and therefore, *if they turn not, he will whet his sword,* Ps. 7:12. God has forces to send against those that set his wrath at defiance (Isa. 5:19), which will convince them, when it is too late, that *none ever hardened his heart against God and prospered.* It was David's prudence to carry the war into their country, and fight them at the entering in of the gate of their capital city, *Rabbah,* as some think, or *Medeba,* a city in their borders, before which they pitched to guard their coast, 1 Chr. 19:7. Such are the terrors and desolations of war that every good prince will, in love to his people, keep it as much as may be at a distance from them.

III. Preparations made on both sides for an engagement. 1. The enemy disposed themselves into two bodies, one of Ammonites, which, being their own, were posted at the gate of the city; the other of Syrians, whom they had taken into their pay, and who were therefore posted at a distance in the field, to charge the forces of Israel in the flank or rear, while the Ammonites charged them in the front, *v.* 8. 2. Joab, like a wise general, was soon aware of the design, and accordingly divided his forces: the choicest men he took under his own command, to fight the Syrians, whom probably he knew to be the better soldiers, and, being hired men, better versed in the arts of war, *v.* 9. The rest of the forces he put under the command of Abishai his brother, to engage the Ammonites, *v.* 10. It should seem, Joab found the enemy so well prepared to receive them that his conduct and courage were never so tried as now.

IV. Joab's speech before the battle, *v.* 11, 12. It is not long, but pertinent, and brave. 1. He prudently concerts the matter with Abishai his brother, that the dividing of the forces might not be the weakening of them, but that, which part soever was borne hard upon, the other should come in to its assistance. He supposes the worst, that one of them should be obliged to give back; and in that case, upon a signal given, the other should send a detachment to relieve it. Note, Mutual helpfulness is brotherly duty. If occasion be, *thou shalt help me, and I will help thee.* Christ's soldiers should thus strengthen one another's hands in their spiritual warfare. The strong must succour and help the weak. Those that through grace are conquerors over temptation must counsel, and comfort, and pray for, those that are tempted. *When thou art converted, strengthen thy brethren,* Lu. 22:32. The members of the natural body help one another, 1 Co. 12:21. 2. He bravely encourages himself, and his brother, and the rest of the officers and soldiers, to do their utmost. Great dangers put an edge upon true courage. When Joab saw the front of the battle was against him, both before and behind, instead of giving orders to make an honourable retreat, he animated his men to charge so much more furiously: *Be of good courage and let us play the men,* not for pay and preferment, for honour and fame, but *for our people, and for the cities of our God,* for the public safety and welfare, in which the glory of God is so much interested. *God and our country* was the word. "Let us be valiant, from a principle of love to Israel, that are our people, descended from the same stock, for whom we are employed, and in whose peace we shall have peace; and from a principle of love to God, for they are his cities that we are fighting in the defence of." The relation which any person or thing stands in to God should endear it to us, and engage us to do our utmost in its service. 3. He piously leaves the issue with God: "When we have done our part, according to the duty of our place, *let the Lord do that which seemeth to him good.*" Let nothing be wanting in us, whatever the success be; let God's work be done by us, and then God's will be done concerning us. When we make conscience of doing our duty we may, with the greatest satisfaction, leave the event with God, not thinking that our valour binds him to prosper us, but that still he may do as he pleases, yet hoping for his salvation in his own way and time.

V. The victory Joab obtained over the confederate forces of Syria and Ammon, *v.* 13, 14. He provided for the worst, and put the case that the Syrians and Ammonites might prove too strong for him (*v.* 11), but he proved too strong for them both. We do not hinder our success by preparing for disappointment. The Syrians were first routed by Joab, and then the Ammonites by Abishai; the Ammonites seem not to have fought at all, but, upon the retreat of the Syrians, to have fled into the city. It is a temptation to soldiers to fly when they have a city at their backs to fly to. It is one thing when men may either fight or fly and another thing when they must either fight or die.

Verses 15–19

Here is, 1. A new attempt of the Syrians to recover their lost honour and to check the progress of David's victorious arms. The forces that were lately dispersed rallied again, and *gathered themselves together,* *v.* 15. Even the baffled cause will make head as long as there is any life in it; the enemies of the Son of David do so, Matt, 22:34; Rev. 19:19. These, being conscious of their insufficiency, called in the aid of their allies and dependencies on the other side of *the river* (*v.* 16), and, being thus recruited, they hoped to make their part good against Israel, but *they knew not the thoughts of the Lord, for he gathered them as sheaves into the floor;* see Mic. 4:11–13. 2. The defeat of this attempt by the vigilance and valour of David, who, upon notice of their design, resolved not to stay till they attacked him, but went in person at the head of his army over Jordan (*v.* 17), and, in a pitched battle, routed the Syrians (*v.* 18), slew 7000 men, who belonged to 700 chariots, and 40,000 other soldiers, horse and foot, as appears by comparing 1 Chr. 19:18. Their general was killed in the battle, and David came home in triumph, no doubt. 3. The consequence of this victory over the Syrians. (1.) David gained several tributaries, *v.* 19. *The kings,* or petty princes, that had been subject to Hadarezer, when they saw how powerful David was, very wisely *made peace with Israel,* whom they found they could not make war with, *and served them,* since they were able to give them protection. Thus the promise made to Abraham (Gen. 15:18), and repeated to Joshua (*ch.* 1:4), that the borders of Israel should extend to the river Euphrates, was performed, at length. (2.) The Ammonites lost their old allies: *The Syrians feared to help the children of Ammon,* not because they had an unrighteous cause (justifying a crime which was a breach of the law of nations), but because they found it was an unsuccessful cause. It is dangerous helping those that have God against them; for, when they fall, their helpers will fall with them.

Jesus Christ, the Son of David, sent his ambassadors, his apostles and ministers, after all his servants the prophets, to the Jewish church and nation; but they treated them shamefully, as Hanun did David's ambassadors, mocked them, abused them, slew them; and it was this that filled the measure of their iniquity, and brought upon them ruin without remedy (Mt. 21:35, 41, 22:7; compare 2 Chr. 26:16); for Christ takes the affronts and injuries done to his ministers as done to himself and will avenge them accordingly.

CHAPTER 11

What David said of the mournful report of Saul's death may more fitly be applied to the sad story of this chapter, the adultery and murder David was guilty of. — "Tell it not in Gath, publish it not in the streets of Ashkelon." We wish we could draw a veil over it, and that it might never be known, might never be said, that David did such things as are here recorded of him. But it cannot, it must not, be concealed. The scripture is faithful in relating the faults even of those whom it most applauds, which is an instance of the sincerity of the penmen, and an evidence that it was not written to serve any party: and even such stories as these "were written for our learning," that "he that thinks he stands may take heed lest he fall," and that others' harms may be our warnings. Many, no doubt, have been emboldened to sin, and hardened in it, by this story, and to them it is a "savour of death unto death;" but many have by it been awakened to a holy jealousy over themselves, and constant watchfulness against sin, and to them it is a "savour of life unto life." Those are very great sins, and greatly aggravated, which here we find David guilty of. I. He committed adultery with Bath-sheba, the wife of Uriah (*v.* 1–5). II. He endeavoured to father the spurious brood upon Uriah (*v.* 6–13). III. When that project failed, he plotted the death of Uriah by the sword of the children of Ammon, and effected it (*v.* 14–25). IV. He married Bath-sheba (*v.* 26, 27). Is this David? Is this the man after God's own heart? How is his behaviour changed, worse than it was before Ahimelech! How has this gold become dim! Let him that readeth understand what the best of men are when God leaves them to themselves.

Verses 1–5

Here is, I. David's glory, in pursuing the war against the Ammonites, *v.* 1. We cannot take that pleasure in viewing this great action which hitherto we have taken in observing David's achievements, because the beauty of it was stained and sullied by sin; otherwise we might take notice of David's wisdom and bravery in following his blow. Having routed the army of the Ammonites in the field, as soon as ever the season of the year permitted he sent more forces to waste the country and further to avenge the quarrel of his ambassadors. Rabbah, their metropolis, made a stand, and held out a great while. To this city Joab laid close siege, and it was at the time of this siege that David fell into this sin.

II. David's shame, in being himself conquered, and led captive by his own lust. The sin he was guilty of was adultery, against the letter of the seventh commandment, and (in the judgment of the patriarchal age) a heinous crime, and *an iniquity to be punished by the judges* (Job 31:11), a sin which *takes away the heart,* and *gets a man a wound and dishonour,* more than any other, and the *reproach of which is not wiped away.*

1. Observe the occasions which led to this sin. (1.) Neglect of his business. When he should have been abroad with his army in the field, fighting the battles of the Lord, he devolved the care upon others, and he himself *tarried still at Jerusalem, v.* 1. To the war with the Syrians David went in person, *ch.* 10:17. Had he been now at his post at the head of his forces, he would have been out of the way of this temptation. When we are out of the way of our duty we are in the way of temptation. (2.) Love of ease, and the indulgence of a slothful temper: *He came off his bed at evening-tide, v.* 2. There he had dozed away the afternoon in idleness, which he should have spent in some exercise for his own improvement or the good of others. He used to pray, not only morning and evening, but at noon, in the day of his trouble: it is to be feared he had, this noon, omitted to do so. Idleness gives great advantage to the tempter. Standing waters gather filth. The bed of sloth often proves the bed of lust. (3.) A wandering eye: *He saw a woman washing herself,* probably from some ceremonial pollution, according to the law. The sin came in at the eye, as Eve's did. Perhaps he sought to see her, at least he did not practise according to his own prayer, *Turn away my eyes from beholding vanity,* and his son's caution in a like case, *Look not thou on the wine it is red.* Either he had not, like Job, *made a covenant with his eyes,* or, at this time, he had forgotten it.

2. The steps of the sin. When he saw her, lust immediately conceived, and, (1.) He enquired who she was (*v.* 3), perhaps intending only, if she were unmarried, to take her to wife, as he had taken several; but, if she were a wife, having no design upon her. (2.) The corrupt desire growing more violent, though he was told she was a wife, and whose wife she was, yet he sent messengers for her, and then, it may be, intended only to please himself with her company and conversation. But, (3.) When she came *he lay with her,* she too easily consenting, because he was a great man, and famed for his goodness too. Surely (thinks she) that can be no sin which such a man as David is the mover of. See how the way of sin is down-hill; when men begin to do evil they cannot soon stop themselves. *The beginning* of lust, as *of strife, is like the letting forth of water;* it is therefore wisdom to leave it off before it be meddled with. The foolish fly fires her wings, and fools away her life at last, by playing about the candle.

3. The aggravations of the sin. (1.) He was now in years, fifty at least, some think more, when those lusts which are more properly youthful, one would think, should not have been violent in him, (2.) He had many wives and concubines of his own; this is insisted on, *ch.* 12:8. (3.) Uriah, whom he wronged, was one of his own worthies, a person of honour and virtue, one that was now abroad in his service, hazarding his life in the high places of the field for the honour and safety of him and his kingdom, where he himself should have been. (4.) Bath-sheba, whom he debauched, was a lady of good reputation, and, till she was drawn by him and his influence into this wickedness, had no doubt preserved her purity. Little did she think that ever she could have done so bad a thing as to *forsake the guide of her youth, and forget the covenant of her God;* nor perhaps could any one in the world but David have prevailed against her. The adulterer not only wrongs and ruins his own soul, but, as much as he can, another's soul too. (5.) David was a king, whom God had entrusted with the sword of justice and the execution of the law upon other criminals, particularly upon adulterers, who were, by the law, to be put to death; for him therefore to be guilty of those crimes himself was to make himself a pattern, when he should have been a terror, to evil doers. With what face could he rebuke or punish that in others which he was conscious to himself of being guilty of? See Rom. 2:22. Much more might be said to aggravate the sin; and I can think but of one excuse for it, which is that it was done but once; it was far from being his practice; it was by the surprise of a temptation that he was drawn into it. He was not one of those of whom the prophet complains that *they were as fed horses, neighing every one after his neighbour's wife* (Jer. 5:8); but this once God left him to himself, as he did Hezekiah, *that he might know what was in his heart,* 2 Chr. 32:31. Had he been told of it before, he would have said, as Hazael, *What! is thy servant a dog?* But by this instance we are taught what need we have to pray every day, *Father, in heaven, lead us not into temptation,* and to watch, that we enter not into it.

Verses 6–13

Uriah, we may suppose, had now been absent from his wife some weeks, making the campaign in the country of the Ammonites, and not intending to return till the end of it. The situation of his wife would *bring to light the hidden works of darkness;* and when Uriah, at his return, should find how he had been abused, and by whom, it might well be expected, 1. That he would prosecute his wife, according to law, and have her stoned to death; for *jealousy is the rage of a man,* especially a man of honour, and he that is thus injured *will not spare in the day of vengeance,* Prov. 6:34. This Bath-sheba was apprehensive of when she sent to let David know she was with child, intimating that he was concerned to protect her, and, it is likely, if he had not promised her so to do (so wretchedly abusing his royal power), she would not have consented to him. Hope of impunity is a great encouragement to iniquity. 2. It might also be expected that since he could not prosecute David by law for an offence of this nature he would take his revenge another way, and raise a rebellion against him. There have been instances of kings who by provocations of this nature, given to some of their powerful subjects, have lost their crowns. To prevent this double mischief, David endeavours to father the child which should be born upon Uriah himself, and therefore sends for him home to stay a night or two with his wife. Observe,

I. How the plot was laid. Uriah must come home from the army under pretence of bringing David an account *how the war prospered,* and how they went on with the siege of Rabbah, *v.* 7. Thus does he pretend a more than ordinary concern for his army when that was the least thing in his thoughts; if he had not had another turn to serve, an express of much less figure than Uriah might have sufficed to bring him a report of the state of the war. David, having had as much conference with Uriah as he thought requisite to cover the design, sent him to his house, and, that he might be the more pleasant there with the wife of his youth, sent a dish of meat after him for their supper, *v.* 8. When that project failed the first night, and Uriah, being weary of his journey and more desirous of sleep than meat, lay all night in the guard-chamber, the next night *he made him drunk* (*v.* 13), or made him merry, tempted him to drink more than was fit, that he might forget his vow (*v.* 11), and might be disposed to go home to his own bed, to which perhaps, if David could have made him dead drunk, he would have ordered him to be carried. It is a very wicked thing, upon any design whatsoever, to make a person drunk. *Woe to him* that does so, Hab. 2:15, 16. God will put a cup of trembling into the hands of those who put into the hands of others the cup of drunkenness. Robbing a man of his reason is worse than robbing him of his money, and drawing him into sin worse than drawing him into any trouble whatsoever. Every good man, especially every magistrate, should endeavour to prevent this sin, by admonishing, restraining, and denying the glass to those whom they see falling into excess; but to further it is to do the devil's work, to officiate as factor for him.

II. How this plot was defeated by Uriah's firm resolution not to lie in his own bed. Both nights he slept with the life-guard, and *went not down to his house,* though, it is probable, his wife pressed him to do it as much as David, *v.* 9, 12. Now, 1. Some think he suspected what was done, being informed of his wife's attendance at court, and therefore he would not go near her. But if he had had any suspicion of that kind, surly he would have opened the letter that David sent by him to Joab. 2. Whether he suspected any thing or no, Providence put this resolution into his heart, and kept him to it, for the discovering of David's sin, and that the baffling of his design to conceal it might awaken David's conscience to confess it and repent of it. 3. The reason he gave to David for this strange instance of self-denial and mortification was very noble, *v.* 11. While the army was encamped in the field, he would not lie at ease in his own house. "The ark is in a tent," whether at home, in the tent David had pitched for it, or abroad, with

Joab in the camp, is not certain. "Joab, and all the mighty men of Israel, lie hard and uneasy, and much exposed to the weather and to the enemy; and shall I go and take my ease and pleasure at my own house?" No, he protests he will not do it. Now, (1.) This was in itself a generous resolution, and showed Uriah to be a man of a public spirit, bold and hardy, and mortified to the delights of sense. In times of public difficulty and danger it does not become us to repose ourselves in security, or roll ourselves in pleasure, or, with the king and Haman, to sit down to drink when the *city Shushan was perplexed,* Esth. 3:15. We should voluntarily endure hardness when the church of God is constrained to endure it. (2.) It might have been of use to awaken David's conscience, and make his heart to smite him for what he had done. [1.] That he had basely abused so brave a man as Uriah was, a man so heartily concerned for him and his kingdom, and that acted for him and it with so much vigour. [2.] That he was himself so unlike him. The consideration of the public hardships and hazards kept Uriah from lawful pleasures, yet could not keep David, though more nearly interested, from unlawful ones. Uriah's severity to himself should have shamed David for his indulgence of himself. The law was, *When the host goeth forth against the enemy then,* in a special manner, *keep thyself from every wicked thing,* Deu. 23:9. Uriah outdid that law, but David violated it.

Verses 14–27

When David's project of fathering the child upon Uriah himself failed, so that, in process of time, Uriah would certainly know the wrong that had been done him, to prevent the fruits of his revenge, the devil put it into David's heart to take him off, and then neither he nor Bath-sheba would be in any danger (what prosecution could there be when there was no prosecutor?), suggesting further that, when Uriah was out of the way, Bath-sheba might, if he pleased, be his own for ever. Adulteries have often occasioned murders, and one wickedness must be covered and secured with another. The beginnings of sin are therefore to be dreaded; for who knows where they will end? It is resolved in David's breast (which one would think could never possibly have harboured so vile a thought) that Uriah must die. That innocent, valiant, gallant man, who was ready to die for his prince's honour, must die by his prince's hand. David has sinned, and Bath-sheba has sinned, and both against him, and therefore he must die; David determines he must. Is this the man whose heart smote him because he had cut off Saul's skirt? *Quantum mutatus ab illo! — But ah, how changed!* Is this he that executed judgment and justice to all his people? How can he now do so unjust a thing? See how fleshly lusts war against the soul, and what devastations they make in that war; how they blink the eyes, harden the heart, sear the conscience, and deprive men of all sense of honour and justice. *Whoso committeth adultery with a woman lacketh understanding* and quite loses it; *he that doth it destroys his own soul,* Prov. 6:32. But, as the eye of the adulterer, so the hand of the murderer seeks concealment, Job 24:14, 15. Works of darkness hate the light. When David bravely slew Goliath it was done publicly, and he gloried in it; but, when he basely slew Uriah, it must be done clandestinely, for he is ashamed of it, and well he may. Who would do a thing that he dare not own? The devil, having as a poisonous serpent, put it into David's heart to murder Uriah, as a subtle serpent he puts it into his head how to do it. Not as Absalom slew Amnon, by commanding his servants to assassinate him, nor as Ahab slew Naboth by suborning witnesses to accuse him, but by exposing him to the enemy, a way of doing it which, perhaps, would not seem so odious to conscience and the world, because soldiers expose themselves of course. If Uriah had not been in that dangerous post, another must; he has (as we say) a chance for his life; if he fight stoutly, he may perhaps come off; and, if he die, it is in the field of honour, where a soldier would choose to die; and yet all this will not save it from being a wilful murder, of malice prepense.

I. Orders are sent to Joab to set Uriah in the front of the hottest battle, and then to desert him, and abandon him to the enemy, *v.* 14, 15. This was David's project to take off Uriah, and it succeeded, as he designed. Many were the aggravations of this murder. 1. It was deliberate. He took time to consider of it; and though he had time

to consider of it, for he wrote a letter about it, and though he had time to have countermanded the order afterwards before it could be put in execution, yet he persisted in it. 2. He sent the letter by Uriah himself, than which nothing could be more base and barbarous, to make him accessory to his own death. And what a paradox was it that he could bear such a malice against him in whom yet he could repose such a confidence as that he would carry letters which he must not know the purport of. 3. Advantage must be taken of Uriah's own courage and zeal for his king and country, which deserve the greatest praise and recompence, to betray him the more easily to his fate. If he had not been forward to expose himself, perhaps he was a man of such importance that Joab could not have exposed him; and that this noble fire should be designedly turned upon himself was a most detestable instance of ingratitude. 4. Many must be involved in the guilt. Joab, the general, to whom the blood of his soldiers, especially the worthies, ought to be precious, must do it; he, and all that retire from Uriah when they ought in conscience to support and second him, become guilty of his death. 5. Uriah cannot thus die alone: the party he commands is in danger of being cut off with him; and it proved so: some of the people, even the servants of David (so they are called, to aggravate David's sin in being so prodigal of their lives), fell with him, *v.* 17. Nay, this wilful misconduct by which Uriah must be betrayed might be of fatal consequence to the whole army, and might oblige them to raise the siege. 6. It will be the triumph and joy of the Ammonites, the sworn enemies of God and Israel; it will gratify them exceedingly. David prayed for himself, that he might not fall into the hands of man, nor flee from his enemies *(ch.* 24:13, 14); yet he sells his servant Uriah to the Ammonites, and not for any iniquity in his hand.

II. Joab executes these orders. In the next assault that is made upon the city Uriah has the most dangerous post assigned him, is encouraged to hope that if he be repulsed by the besieged he shall be relieved by Joab, in dependence on which he marches on with resolution, but, succours not coming on, the service proves too hot, and he is slain in it, *v.* 16, 17. It was strange that Joab would do such a thing merely upon a letter, without knowing the reason. But, 1. Perhaps he supposed Uriah had been guilty of some great crime, to enquire into which David had sent for him, and that, because he would not punish him openly, he took this course with him to put him to death. 2. Joab had been guilty of blood, and we may suppose it pleased him very well to see David himself falling into the same guilt, and he was willing enough to serve him in it, that he might continue to be favourable to him. It is common for those who have done ill themselves to desire to be countenanced therein by others doing ill likewise, especially by the sins of those that are eminent in the profession of religion. Or, perhaps, David knew that Joab had a pique against Uriah, and would gladly be avenged on him; otherwise Joab, when he saw cause, knew how to dispute the king's orders, as *ch.* 19:5; 24:3.

III. He sends an account of it to David. An express is despatched away immediately with a report of this last disgrace and loss which they had sustained, *v.* 18. And, to disguise the affair, 1. He supposes that David would appear to be angry at his bad conduct, would ask why they came so near the wall (*v.* 20), did they not know that Abimelech lost his life by doing do? *v.* 21. We had the story (Jdg. 9:53, which book, it is likely, was published as a part of the sacred history in Samuel's time; and (be it noted to their praise, and for imitation) even the soldiers were conversant with their bibles, and could readily quote the scripture-story, and make use of it for admonition to themselves not to run upon the same attempts which they found had been fatal. 2. He slyly orders the messenger to soothe it with telling him that Uriah the Hittite was dead also, which gave too broad an intimation to the messenger, and by him to others, that David would be secretly pleased to hear that; for murder will out. And, when men do such base things, they must expect to be bantered and upbraided with them, even by their inferiors. The messenger delivered his message agreeably to orders, *v.* 22–24. He makes the besieged to sally out first upon the besiegers *(they came out unto us into the field),* represents the besiegers as doing their part with great bravery *(we were upon them even to the entering of the gate* — we forced them to retire into the

city with precipitation), and so concludes with a slight mention of the slaughter made among them by some shot from the wall: *Some of the king's servants are dead,* and particularly *Uriah the Hittite,* an officer of note, stood first in the list of the slain.

IV. David receives the account with a secret satisfaction, *v.* 25. Let not Joab be displeased, for David is not. He blames not his conduct, nor thinks they did wrong in approaching so near the wall; all is well now that Uriah is put out of the way. This point being gained, he can make light of the loss, and turn it off easily with an excuse: *The sword devours one as well as another;* it was a chance of war, nothing more common. He orders Joab to make the battle more strong next time, while he, by his sin, was weakening it, and provoking God to blast the undertaking.

V. He marries the widow in a little time. She submitted to the ceremony of mourning for her husband as short a time as custom would admit (*v.* 26), and then David took her to his house as his wife, and she bore him a son. Uriah's revenge was prevented by his death, but the birth of the child so soon after the marriage published the crime. Sin will have shame. Yet that was not the worst of it: *The thing that David had done displeased the Lord.* The whole *matter of Uriah* (as it is called, 1 Ki. 15:5), the adultery, falsehood, murder, and this marriage at last, it was all displeasing to the Lord. He had pleased himself, but displeased God. Note, God sees and hates sin in his own people. Nay, the nearer any are to God in profession the more displeasing to him their sins are; for in them there is more ingratitude, treachery, and reproach, than in the sins of others. Let none therefore encourage themselves in sin by the example of David; for those that sin as he did will fall under the displeasure of God as he did. Let us therefore stand in awe and sin not, not sin after the similitude of his transgression.

CHAPTER 12

The foregoing chapter gave us the account of David's sin; this gives us the account of his repentance. Though he fell, he was not utterly cast down, but, by the grace of God, recovered himself, and found mercy with God. Here is, I. His conviction, by a message Nathan brought him from God, which was a parable that obliged him to condemn himself (*v.* 1–6), and the application of the parable, in which Nathan charged him with the sin (*v.* 7–9) and pronounced sentence upon him, *v.* 10–12). II. His repentance and remission, with a proviso (*v.* 13, 14). III. The sickness and death of the child, and his behaviour while it was sick and when it was dead (*v.* 15–23), in both which David gave evidence of his repentance. IV. The birth of Solomon, and God's gracious message concerning him, in which God gave an evidence of his reconciliation to David (*v.* 24, 25). V. The taking of Rabbah (*v.* 26–31), which is mentioned as a further instance that God did not deal with David according to his sins.

Verses 1–14

It seems to have been a great while after David had been guilty of adultery with Bath-sheba before he was brought to repentance for it. For, when Nathan was sent to him, the child was born (*v.* 14), so that it was about nine months that David lay under the guilt of that sin, and, for aught that appears, unrepented of. What shall we think of David's state all this while? Can we imagine that his heart never smote him for it, or that he never lamented it in secret before God? I would willingly hope that he did, and that Nathan was sent to him, immediately upon the birth of the child, when the thing by that means came to be publicly known and talked of, to draw from him an open confession of the sin, to the glory of God, the admonition of others, and that he might receive, by Nathan, absolution with certain limitations. But, during these nine months, we may well suppose his comforts and the exercises of his graces suspended, and his communion with God interrupted; during all that time, it is certain, he penned no psalms, his harp was out of tune, and his soul like a tree in winter, that has life in the root only. Therefore, after Nathan had been with him, he prays, *Restore unto me the joy of thy salvation, and open thou my lips,* Ps. 51:12, 15. Let us observe,

I. The messenger God sent to him. We were told by the last words of the foregoing chapter that the thing David had done displeased the Lord, upon which, one would think, it should have followed that the Lord sent enemies to invade him, terrors to take hold on him, and the messengers of death to arrest him. No, he sent a prophet to him — Nathan, his faithful friend and confidant, to instruct and counsel him, *v.* 1. David did not send for Nathan (though he had never had so much occasion as he had now for his confessor), but God sent Nathan to David. Note, Though God may suffer his people to fall into sin, he will not suffer them to lie still in it. *He went on frowardly in the way of his heart,* and if left to himself, would have wandered endlessly, but (saith God) *I have seen his ways, and will heal him,* Isa. 57:17, 18. He sends after us before we seek after him, else we should certainly be lost. Nathan was the prophet by whom God had sent him notice of his kind intentions towards him (*ch.* 7:4), and now, by the same hand, he sends him this message of wrath. God's word in the mouth of his ministers must be received, whether it speak terror or comfort. Nathan was obedient to the heavenly vision, and went on God's errand to David. He did not say, "David has sinned, I will not come near him." No; *count him not an enemy, but admonish him as a brother,* 2 Th. 3:15. He did not say, "David is a king, I dare not reprove him." No; if God sends him, he *sets his face like a flint,* Isa. 50:7.

II. The message Nathan delivered to him, in order to his conviction.

1. He fetched a compass with a parable, which seemed to David as a complaint made to him by Nathan against one of his subjects that had wronged his poor neighbour, in order to his redressing the injury and punishing the injurious. Nathan, it is likely, used to come to him upon such errands, which made this the less suspected. It becomes those who have interest in princes, and have free access to them, to intercede for those that are wronged, that they may have justice done them. (1.) Nathan represented to David a grievous injury which a rich man had done to an honest neighbour that was not able to contend with him: *The rich man had many flocks and herds* (*v.* 2); the poor man had one lamb only; so unequally is the world divided; and yet infinite wisdom, righteousness, and goodness, make the distribution, that the rich may learn charity and the poor contentment. This poor man had but one lamb, a ewe-lamb, a little ewe-lamb, having not wherewithal to buy or keep more. But it was a *cade*-lamb (as we call it); *it grew up with his children, v.* 3. He was fond of it, and it was familiar with him at all times. The rich man, having occasion for a lamb to entertain a friend with, took the poor man's lamb from him by violence and made use of that (*v.* 4), either out of covetousness, because he grudged to make use of his own, or rather out of luxury, because he fancied the lamb that was thus tenderly kept, and ate and drank like a child, must needs be more delicate food than any of his own and have a better relish. (2.) In this he showed him the evil of the sin he had been guilty of in defiling Bath-sheba. He had many wives and concubines, whom he kept at a distance, as rich men keep their flocks in their fields. Had he had but one, and had she been dear to him, as the ewe-lamb was to its owner, had she been dear to him *as the loving hind and the pleasant roe, her breasts would have satisfied him at all times,* and he would have looked no further, Prov. 5:19. Marriage is a remedy against fornication, but marrying many is not; for, when once the law of unity is transgressed, the indulged lust will hardly stint itself. Uriah, like the poor man, had only one wife, who was to him as his own soul, and always lay in his bosom, for he had no other, he desired no other, to lie there. The traveller or wayfaring man was, as bishop Patrick explains it from the Jewish writers, the evil imagination, disposition, or desire, which came into David's heart, which he might have satisfied with some of his own, yet nothing would serve but Uriah's darling. They observe that this evil disposition is called a traveller, for in the beginning it is only so, but, in time, it becomes a guest, and, in conclusion, is master of the house. For he that is called a traveller in the beginning of the verse is called *a man* (ish — a husband) in the close of it. Yet some observe that in David's breast lust was but as a wayfaring man that tarries only for a night; it did not constantly dwell and rule there. (3.) By this parable he drew from David a sentence against himself. For David supposing it to be a case in fact, and not doubting the truth of it when he had it from Nathan himself, gave judgment immediately against the offender, and confirmed it with an oath, *v.* 5, 6. [1.] That, for his injustice in taking away the lamb, he should restore four-fold, according to the law (Ex. 22:1), *four sheep for a sheep.* [2.] That for his tyranny and cruelty, and the pleasure he took in abusing a poor man, he should be put to death. If a poor man steal from a rich man, to satisfy his soul when he is hungry, he shall make restitution, though it cost him *all the substance of his house,* Prov. 6:30, 31 (and Solomon there compares the sin of adultery with that, *v.* 32); but if a rich man steal for stealing sake, not for want but wantonness, merely that he may be imperious and vexatious, he deserves to die for it, for to him the making of restitution is no punishment, or next to none. If the sentence be thought too severe, it must be imputed to the present roughness of David's temper, being under guilt, and not having himself as yet received mercy.

2. He closed in with him, at length, in the application of the parable. In beginning with a parable he showed his prudence, and great need there is of prudence in giving reproofs. It is well managed if, as here, the offender can be brought ere he is aware, to convict and condemn himself. But here, in his application, he shows his faithfulness, and deals as plainly and roundly with king David himself as if he had been a common person. In plain terms, *"Thou art the man* who hast done this wrong, and a much greater, to thy neighbour; and therefore, by thy own sentence, thou deservest to die, and shalt be judged out of thy own mouth. Did he deserve to die who took his neighbour's lamb? and dost not thou who hast taken thy neighbour's wife? Though he took the lamb, he did not cause the owner thereof to lose his life, as thou hast done, and therefore much more art thou worthy to die." Now he speaks immediately from God, and in his name. He begins with, *Thus saith the Lord God of Israel,* a name sacred and venerable to David, and which commanded his attention. Nathan now speaks, not as a petitioner for a poor man, but as an ambassador from the great God, with whom is no respect of persons.

(1.) God, by Nathan, reminds David of the great things he had done and designed for him, anointing him to be king, and preserving him to the kingdom (*v.* 7), giving him power over the house and household of his predecessor, and of others that had been his masters, Nabal for one. He had given him the house of Israel and Judah. The wealth of the kingdom was at his service and every body was willing to oblige him. Nay, he was ready to bestow any thing upon him to make him easy: *I would have given thee such and such things, v.* 8. See how liberal God is in his gifts; we are not straitened in him. Where he has given much, yet he gives more. And God's bounty to us is a great aggravation of our discontent and desire of forbidden fruit. It is ungrateful to covet what God has prohibited, while we have liberty to pray for what God has promised, and that is enough.

(2.) He charges him with a high contempt of the divine authority, in the sins he had been guilty of: *Wherefore hast thou* (presuming upon thy royal dignity and power) *despised the commandment of the Lord? v.* 9. This is the spring and this is the malignity of sin, that it is making light of the divine law and the law-maker; as if the obligation of it were weak, the precepts of it trifling, and the threats not at all formidable. Though no man ever wrote more honourably of the law of God than David did, yet, in this instance, he is justly charged with a contempt of it. His adultery with Bath-sheba, which began the mischief, is not mentioned, perhaps because he was already convinced of that, but, [1.] The murder of Uriah is twice mentioned: *"Thou hast killed Uriah with the sword,* though not with thy sword, yet, which is equally heinous, with thy pen, by ordering him to be set in the forefront of the battle." Those that contrive wickedness and command it are as truly guilty of it as those that execute it. It is repeated with an aggravation: *Thou hast slain him with the sword of the children of Ammon,* those uncircumcised enemies of God and Israel. [2.] The marrying of Bath-sheba is likewise twice mentioned, because he thought there was no harm in that (*v.* 9): *Thou hast taken his wife to be thy wife,* and again, *v.* 10. To marry her whom he had before defiled, and whose husband he had slain, was an affront upon the ordinance of marriage, making that not only to palliate, but in a manner to consecrate, such villanies. In all this he *despised the word of the Lord* (so it is in the Hebrew), not only his commandment in general which forbade such things, but the particular word of promise which God had, by Nathan, sent to him some time before, that he would build him a house. If he had had a due value and veneration for this sacred promise, he would not thus have polluted his house with lust and blood.

(3.) He threatens an entail of judgements upon his family for this sin (*v.* 10): *"The sword shall never depart from thy house,* not in thy time nor afterwards, but, for the most part, thou and thy posterity shall be engaged in war." Or it points at the slaughters that should be among his children, Amnon, Absalom, and Adonijah, all falling by the sword. God had promised that his mercy should not depart from him and his house (*ch.* 7:15), yet here threatens that the sword should not depart. Can the mercy and the sword consist with each other? Yes, those may lie under great and long afflictions who yet shall not be excluded from the grace of the covenant. The reason given is, *Because thou hast despised me.* Note, Those who despise the word and law of God despise God himself and shall be lightly esteemed. It is particularly threatened, [1.] That his children should be his grief: *I will raise up evil against thee out of thy own house.* Sin brings trouble into a family, and one sin is often made the punishment of another. [2.] That his wives should be his shame, that by an unparalleled piece of villany they should be publicly debauched before all Israel, *v.* 11, 12. It is not said that this should be done by his own son, lest the accomplishment should have been hindered by the prediction being too plain; but it was done by Absalom, at the counsel of Ahithophel, *ch.* 16:21, 22. *He that defiled his neighbour's wife should have his own defiled,* for thus that sin used to be punished, as appears by Job's imprecation, Job 31:10, *Then let my wife grind unto another,* and that threatening, Hos. 4:14. The sin was secret, and industriously concealed, but the punishment should be open, and industriously proclaimed, to the shame of David, whose sin in the matter of Uriah, though committed many years before, would then be called to mind and commonly talked of upon that occasion. As face answers to face in a glass, so does the punishment often answer to the sin; here is *blood for blood and uncleanness for uncleanness.* And thus God would show how much he hates sin, even in his own people, and that, wherever he find it, he will not let it go unpunished.

3. David's penitent confession of his sin hereupon. He says not a word to excuse himself or extenuate his sin, but freely owns it: *I have sinned against the Lord, v.* 13. It is probable that he said more to this purport; but this is enough to show that he was truly humbled by what Nathan said, and submitted to the conviction. He owns his guilt — *I have sinned,* and aggravates it — It was *against the Lord:* on this string he harps in the psalm he penned on this occasion. Ps. 51:1, *Against thee, thee only, have I sinned.*

4. His pardon declared, upon this penitent confession, but with a proviso. When David said *I have sinned,* and Nathan perceived that he was a true penitent,

(1.) He did, in God's name, assure him that his sin was forgiven: *"The Lord also has put away thy sin* out of the sight of his avenging eye; *thou shalt not die,"* that is, "not die eternally, nor be for ever put away from God, as thou wouldest have been if he had not put away the sin." The obligation to punishment is hereby cancelled and vacated. *He shall not come into condemnation:* that is the nature of forgiveness. "Thy iniquity shall not be thy everlasting ruin. *The sword shall not depart from thy house,* but, [1.] It shall not cut thee off, thou shalt come to thy grave in peace." David deserved to die as an adulterer and murderer, but God would not cut him off as he might justly have done. [2.] "Though thou shalt all thy days be *chastened of the Lord,* yet thou *shalt not be condemned with the world."* See how ready God is to forgive sin. To this instance, perhaps, David refers, Ps. 32:5, *I said, I will confess, and thou forgavest.* Let not great sinners despair of finding mercy with God if they truly repent; for who is a God like unto him, pardoning iniquity?

(2.) Yet he pronounces a sentence of death upon the child, *v.* 14. Behold the sovereignty of God! The guilty parent lives, and the guiltless infant dies; but all souls are his, and he may, in what way he pleases, glorify himself in his creatures. [1.] David had, by his sin, wronged God in his honour; he had *given occasion to the enemies of the Lord to blaspheme.* The wicked people of that generation, the infidels, idolaters, and profane, would triumph in David's fall, and speak ill of God and of his law, when they saw one guilty of such foul enormities that professed such an honour both for him and it. "These are your professors! This is he that prays and sings psalms, and is so very devout! What good can there be in such exercises, if they will not restrain men from adultery and murder?" They would say, "Was not Saul rejected for a less matter? why then must David live and reign still?" not considering that God *sees not as man sees, but searches the heart.* To this day there are those who reproach God, and are hardened in sin, through the example of David. Now, though it is true that none have any just reason to speak ill of God, or of his word and ways, for David's sake, and it is their sin that do so, yet he shall be reckoned with that laid the stumbling-block in their way, and gave, though not cause, yet colour, for the reproach. Note, There is this great evil in the scandalous sins of those that profess religion, and relation to God, that they furnish the enemies of God and religion with matter for reproach and blasphemy, Rom. 2:24. [2.] God will therefore vindicate his honour by showing his displeasure against David for this sin, and letting the world see that though he loves David he hates his sin; and he chooses to do it by the *death of the child.* The landlord may distrain on any part of the premises where he pleases. Perhaps the diseases and deaths of infants were not so common in those days as they are now, which might make this, as an unusual thing, the more evident token of God's displeasure; according to the word he had often said, that he would *visit the sins of the fathers upon the children.*

Verses 15–25

Nathan, having delivered his message, staid not at court, but went home, probably to pray for David, to whom he had been preaching. God, in making use of him as an instrument to bring David to repentance, and as the herald both of mercy and judgment, put an honour upon the ministry, *and magnified his word above all his name.* David named one of his sons by Bath-sheba *Nathan,* in honour of this prophet (1 Chr. 3:5), and it was that son of whom Christ, the great prophet, lineally descended, Lu. 3:31. When Nathan retired, David, it is probable, retired likewise, and penned the 51st Psalm, in which (though he had been assured that his sin was pardoned) he prays earnestly for pardon, and greatly laments his sin; for then will true penitents be ashamed of what they have done when God is *pacified towards them,* Eze. 16:63.

Here is, I. The child's illness: *The Lord struck* it, *and it was very sick,* perhaps with convulsions, or some other dreadful distemper, *v.* 15. The diseases and death of infants that have *not sinned after the similitude of Adam's transgression,* especially as they are sometimes sadly circumstanced, are sensible proofs of the original sin in which they are conceived.

II. David's humiliation under this token of God's displeasure, and the intercession he made with God for the life of the child (*v.* 16, 17): *He fasted, and lay all night upon the earth,* and would not suffer any of his attendants either to feed him or help him up. This was an evidence of the truth of his repentance. For, 1. Hereby it appeared that he was willing to bear the shame of his sin, to have it ever before him, and to be continually upbraided with it; for this child would be a continual memorandum of it, both to himself and others, if he lived: and therefore he was so far from desiring its death, as most in such circumstances do, that he prayed earnestly for its life. True penitents patiently *bear the reproach of their youth,* and of their youthful lusts, Jer. 31:19. 2. A very tender compassionate spirit appeared in this, and great humanity, above what is commonly found in men, especially men of war, towards little children, even their own; and this was another sign of a broken contrite spirit. Those that are penitent will be pitiful. 3. He discovered, in this, a great concern for another world, which is an evidence of repentance. Nathan had told him that certainly the child should die; yet, while it is in the reach of prayer, he earnestly intercedes with God for it, chiefly (as we may suppose) that its soul might be safe and happy in another world, and that his sin might not come against the child, and that it might not fare the worse for that in the future state. 4. He discovered, in this, a holy dread of God and of his displeasure. He deprecated the death of the child chiefly as it was a token of God's anger against him and his house, and was inflicted in performance of a threatening; therefore he prayed thus earnestly that, if it were the will of God, the child might live, because that would be to him a token of God's being reconciled to him. *Lord, chasten me not in thy hot displeasure.* Ps. 6:1.

III. The death of the child: It *died on the seventh day* (*v.* 18), when it was seven days old, and therefore not circumcised, which David might perhaps interpret as a further token of God's displeasure, that it died before it was brought under the seal of the covenant; yet he does not therefore doubt of its being happy for the benefits of the covenant do not depend upon the seals. David's servants, judging of him by themselves, were afraid to tell him that *the child was dead,* concluding that then he would disquiet himself most of all; so that he knew not till he asked, *v.* 19.

IV. David's wonderful calmness and composure of mind when he understood the child was dead. Observe,

1. What he did. (1.) He laid aside the expressions of his sorrow, washed and anointed himself, and called for clean linen, that he might decently appear before God in his house. (2.) *He went up to the tabernacle and worshipped,* like Job when he heard of the death of his children. He went to acknowledge the hand of God in the affliction, and to humble himself under it, and to submit to his holy will in it, to thank God that he himself was spared and his sin pardoned, and to pray that God would not proceed in his controversy with him, nor stir up all his wrath. *Is any afflicted? Let him pray.* Weeping must never hinder worshipping. (3.) *Then he went to his own house* and refreshed himself, as one who found benefit by his religion in the day of his affliction; for, having worshipped, *he did eat,* and his countenance was no more sad.

2. The reason he gave for what he did. His servants thought it strange that he should afflict himself so for the sickness of the child and yet take the death of it so easily, and asked him the reason of it (*v.* 21), in answer to which he gives this plain account of his conduct, (1.) That while the child was alive he thought it his duty to importune the divine favour towards it, *v.* 22. Nathan had indeed said the child should die, but, for aught that he knew, the threatening might be conditional, as that concerning Hezekiah: upon his great humiliation and earnest prayer, he that had so often *heard the voice of his weeping* might be pleased to reverse the sentence, and spare the child: *Who can tell whether God will yet be gracious to me?* God gives us leave to be earnest with him in prayer for particular blessings, from a confidence in his power and general mercy, though we have no particular promise to build upon: we cannot be sure, yet let us pray, *for who can tell but God will be gracious to us,* in this or that particular? When our relations and friends have fallen sick, the prayer of faith has prevailed much; while there is life there is hope, and, while there is hope, there is room for prayer. (2.) That now the child was dead he thought it as much his duty to be satisfied in the divine disposal concerning it (*v.* 23): *Now, wherefore should I fast?* Two things checked his grief: — [1.] *I cannot bring him back again;* and again, *He shall not return to me.* Those that are dead are out of the reach of prayer; nor can our tears profit them. We can neither weep nor pray them back to this life. Wherefore then should we fast? *To what purpose is this waste?* Yet David fasted and wept for Jonathan when he was dead, in honour to him. [2.] *I shall go to him. First,* To him to the grave. Note, The consideration of our own death should moderate our sorrow at the death of our relations. It is the common lot; instead of mourning for their death, we should think of our own: and, whatever loss we have of them now, we shall die shortly, and go to them. *Secondly,* To him to heaven, to a state of blessedness, which even the Old Testament saints had some expectation of. Godly parents have great reason to hope concerning their children that die in infancy that it is well with their souls in the other world; for *the promise is to us and to our seed,* which shall be performed to those that do not put a bar in their own door, as infants do not. *Favores sunt ampliandi — Favours received should produce the hope of more.* God calls those his children that are born unto him; and, if they be his, he will save them. This may comfort us when our children are removed from us by death, they are better provided for, both in work and wealth, than they could have been in this world. We shall be with them shortly, to part no more.

V. The birth of Solomon. Though David's marrying Bath-sheba had displeased the Lord, yet he was not therefore commanded to divorce her; so far from this that God gave him that son by her on whom the covenant of royalty should be entailed. Bath-sheba, no doubt, was greatly afflicted with the sense of her sin and the tokens of God's displeasure. But, God having restored to David the joys of his salvation, he comforted her with the same comforts with which he himself was comforted of God (*v.* 24): He *comforted Bath-sheba.* And both he and she had reason to be comforted in the tokens of God's reconciliation to them, 1. Inasmuch as, by his providence, he gave them a son, not as the former, who was given in anger and taken away in wrath, but a child graciously given, and written among the living in Jerusalem. They called him *Solomon — peaceful,* because his birth was a token of God's being at peace with them, because of the prosperity which was entailed upon him, and because he was to be a type of Christ, the prince of peace. God had removed one son from them, but now gave them another instead of him, like *Seth instead of Abel,* Gen. 4:25. Thus God often balances the griefs of his people with comforts in the same thing wherein he hath afflicted them, setting the one over-against the other. David had very patiently submitted to the will of God in the death of the other child, and now God made up the loss of that, abundantly to his advantage, in the birth of this. The way to have our creature-comforts either continued or restored, or the loss of them made up some other way, is cheerfully to resign them to God. 2. Inasmuch as, by his grace, he particularly owned and favoured that son: *The Lord loved him* (*v.* 24 and 25), ordered him, by the prophet Nathan, to be called *Jedidiah — Beloved of the Lord:* though a seed of evil-doers (for such David and Bath-sheba were), yet so well ordered was the covenant, and the crown entailed by it, that it took away all attainders and corruption of blood, signifying that those who were by nature children of wrath and disobedience should, by the covenant of grace, not only be reconciled, but made favourites. And, in this name, he typified Jesus Christ, that blessed Jedidiah, the son of God's love, concerning whom God declared again and again, *This is my beloved Son, in whom I am well pleased.*

Verses 26–31

We have here an account of the conquest of Rabbah, and other cities of the Ammonites. Though this comes in here after the birth of David's child, yet it is most probable that it was effected a good while before, and soon after the death of Uriah, perhaps during the days of Bath-sheba's mourning for him. Observe, 1. That God was very gracious in giving David this great success against his enemies, notwithstanding the sin he had been guilty of just at that time when he was engaged in this war, and the wicked use he had made of the sword of the children of Ammon in the murder of Uriah. Justly might he have made that sword, thenceforward, a plague to David and his kingdom; yet he breaks it, and makes David's sword victorious, even before he repents, that this *goodness of God might lead him to repentance.* Good reason had David to own that God *dealt not with him according to his sins,* Ps. 103:10. 2. That Joab acted very honestly and honourably; for when he had taken *the city of waters,* the royal city, where the palace was, and from which the rest of the city was supplied with water (and therefore, upon the cutting off of that, would be obliged speedily to surrender), he sent to David to come in person to complete this great action, that he might have the praise of it, *v.* 26–28. Herein he showed himself a faithful servant, that sought his master's honour, and his own only in subordination to his, and left an example to the servants of the Lord Jesus, in every thing they do, to consult his honour. *Not unto us, but to thy name, give glory.* 3. That David was both too haughty and too severe upon this occasion, and neither so humble nor so tender as he should have been. (1.) He seems to have been too fond of the crown of the king of Ammon, *v.* 30. Because it was of extraordinary value, by reason of the precious stones with which it was set, David would have it set upon his head, though it would have been better to have cast it at God's feet, and at this time to have put his own mouth in the dust, under guilt. The heart that is truly humbled for sin is dead to worldly glory and looks upon it with a holy contempt. (2.) He seems to have been too harsh with his prisoners of war, *v.* 31. Taking the city by storm, after it had obstinately held out against a long and expensive siege, if he had put all whom he found in arms to the sword in the heat of battle, it would have been severe enough; but to kill them afterwards in cold blood, and by cruel tortures, with saws and harrows, tearing them to pieces, did not become him who, when he entered upon the government, promised to sing of mercy as well as judgment, Ps. 101:1. Had he made examples of those only who had abused his ambassadors, or advised or assisted in it, that being a violation of the law of nations, it might have been looked upon as a piece of necessary justice for terror to other nations; but to be thus severe with all the cities of the children of Ammon (that is, the garrisons or soldiers of the cities) was extremely rigorous, and a sign that David's heart was not yet made soft by repentance, else the bowels of his compassion would not have been thus shut up — a sign that he had not yet found mercy, else he would have been more ready to show mercy.

CHAPTER 13

The righteous God had lately told David, by Nathan the prophet, that, to chastise him for his son in the matter of Uriah, he would "raise up evil against him out of his own house," (*ch.* 12:11). And here, in the very next chapter, we find the evil beginning to rise; henceforward he was followed with one trouble after another, which made the latter part of his reign less glorious and pleasant than the former part. Thus God chastened him with the rod of men, yet assured him that his "loving-kindness he would not utterly take away." Adultery and murder were David's sins, and those sins among his children (Amnon defiling his sister Tamar, and Absalom murdering his brother Amnon) were the beginnings of his punishment, and the more grievous because he had reason to fear that his bad example might help to bring them to these wickednesses. In this chapter we have, I. Amnon ravishing Tamar, assisted in his plot to do it by Jonadab his kinsman, and villainously executing it (*v.* 1–20). II. Absalom murdering Amnon for it (*v.* 21–39). Both were great griefs to David, and the more because he was unwittingly made accessory to both, by sending Tamar to Amnon and Amnon to Absalom.

Verses 1–20

We have here a particular account of the abominable wickedness of Amnon in ravishing his sister, a subject not fit to be enlarged upon nor indeed to be mentioned without blushing, that ever any man should be so vile, especially that a son of David should be so. Amnon's character, we have reason to think, was bad in other things; if he had not forsaken God, he would never have been given up to these vile affections. Godly parents have often been afflicted with wicked children; grace does not run in the blood, but corruption does. We do not find that David's children imitated him in his devotion; but his false steps they trod in, and in those did much worse, and repented not. Parents know not how fatal the consequences may be if in any instance they give their children bad examples. Observe the steps of Amnon's sin.

I. The devil, as an unclean spirit, put it into his heart to lust after his sister Tamar. Beauty is a snare to many; it was so to her. She was fair, and therefore Amnon coveted her, *v.* 1. Those that are peculiarly handsome have no reason, on that account, to be proud, but great reason to stand upon their watch. Amnon's lust was, 1. Unnatural in itself, to lust after his sister, which even natural conscience startles at and cannot think of without horror. Such a spirit of contradiction there is in man's corrupt nature that still it desires forbidden fruit, and the more strongly it is forbidden the more greedily it is desired. Can he entertain the thought of betraying that virtue and honour of which, as a brother, he ought to have been the protector? But what wickedness so vile as not to find admittance into an unsanctified unguarded heart, left to itself? 2. It was very uneasy to him. He was so vexed that he could not gain an opportunity to solicit her chastity (for innocent converse with her was not denied him) that he *fell sick, v.* 2. Fleshly lusts are their own punishment, and not only *war against the soul,* but against the body too, and are the *rottenness of the bones.* See what a hard master sinners serve, and how heavy his yoke is.

II. The devil, as a subtle serpent, put it into his head how to compass this wicked design. Amnon had a friend (so he called him, but he was really an enemy to him), a kinsman, that had in him more of David's blood (for he was his nephew) than of David's spirit, for he was a subtle man, cunning to carry on any bad design, especially an intrigue of this nature, *v.* 3.

1. He took notice that Amnon looked ill, and, being a subtle man, concluded that he was love-sick (*v.* 4), and asks him, *"Why art thou, being the king's son, lean from day to day?* Why dost thou pine, being the king's eldest son, and heir to the crown. *Being the king's son,"* (1.) "Thou hast the pleasures of the court to divert thee; take those pleasures then, and with them drive away the sorrow, whatever it is." Content and comfort are not always to be found in royal palaces. With much more reason may we ask dejected and disconsolate saints why they, who are the children of the King of kings and heirs of the crown of life, are thus *lean from day to day.* (2.) "Thou hast the power of a prince to command what thou wantest and wishest for; use that power therefore, and gratify thyself. Pine not away for that which, lawful or unlawful, thou, being the king's son, mayest have. *Quicquid libet licet — Your will is law.*" Thus Jezebel to Ahab in a like case (1 Ki. 21:7), *Dost not thou govern Israel?* The abuse of power is the most dangerous temptation of the great.

2. Amnon having the impudence to own his wicked lust, miscalling it *love (I love Tamar),* Jonadab put him in a way to compass his design, *v.* 5. Had he been what he pretended (Amnon's friend), he would have startled at the mention of such horrid wickedness, would have laid before him the evil of it, what an offence it was to God and what a wrong to his own soul to entertain such a vile thought, of what fatal consequence it would be to him to cherish and prosecute it; he would have used his subtlety to divert Amnon from it, by recommending some other person to him, whom he might lawfully marry. But he seems not at all surprised at it, objects not either the unlawfulness or the difficulty, the reproach or so much as his father's displeasure, but puts him in the way to get Tamar to his bed-side, and then he might do as he pleased. Note, The case of those is very miserable whose friends, instead of admonishing and reproving them, flatter them and forward them in their sinful ways, and are their counsellors and contrivers to do wickedly. Amnon is already sick, but goes about; he must take upon him to be so ill (and his thin looks will give colour enough to the pretence) as not to be able to get up, and to have no appetite to any thing but just that which pleases his fancy. Dainty meat is abhorred, Job 33:20. The best dish from the king's table cannot please him; but, if he can eat any thing, it must be from his sister Tamar's fair hand. This is what he is advised to.

3. Amnon followed these directions, and thus got Tamar within his reach: *He made himself sick, v.* 6. Thus he *lieth in wait secretly, as a lion in his den, to catch the poor,* and to *draw them into his net,* Ps. 10:8–10. David was always fond of his children, and concerned if any thing ailed them; he no sooner hears that Amnon is sick than he comes himself to visit him. Let parents learn hence to be tender of their children and compassionate towards them. The sick child commonly *the mother* comforteth (Isa. 66:13), but let not the *father* be unconcerned. We may suppose that when David came to see his sick son he gave him good counsel to make a right use of his affliction, and prayed with him, which yet did not alter his wicked purpose. At parting, the indulgent father asks, "Is there any thing thou hast a mind to, that I can procure for thee?" "Yes, Sir," says the dissembling son, "my stomach is weak, and I know not of any thing I can eat, unless it be a cake of my sister Tamar's making, and I cannot be satisfied that it is so unless I see her make it, and it will do me the more good if I eat it at her hand." David saw no reason to suspect any mischief intended. God hid his heart from understanding in this matter. He therefore immediately orders Tamar to go and attend her sick brother, *v.* 7. He does it very innocently, but afterwards, no doubt, reflected upon it with great regret. Tamar as innocently goes to her brother's chamber, neither dreading any abuse (why should she from a brother, a sick brother?) nor disdaining, in obedience to her father and love to her brother (though but her half-brother), to be his nurse, *v.* 8, 9. Though she was a king's daughter, a great beauty (*v.* 1), and well dressed (*v.* 18), yet she did not think it below her to knead cakes and bake them, nor would she have done this now if she had not been used to it. Good house-wifery is not a thing below the greatest ladies, nor ought they to think it a disparagement to them. The virtuous woman, whose husband sits among the elders, yet *works willingly with her hands,* Prov. 31:13. Modern ages have not been destitute of such instances, nor is it so unfashionable as some would make it. Preparing for the sick should be more the care and delight of the ladies than preparing for the nice, charity more than curiosity.

4. Having got her to him, he contrives to have her alone; for *the adulterer* (much more so vile an adulterer as this) is in care that *no eye see him,* Job 24:15. The meat is ready, but he cannot eat while he is looked at by those about him; they must all be turned out, *v.* 9. The sick must be humoured, and think they have a privilege to command. Tamar is willing to humour him; her chaste and virtuous soul has not the least thought of that which his polluted breast is full of; and therefore she makes no scruple of being alone with him *in the inner chamber, v.* 10. And now the mask is thrown off, the meat is thrown by, and the wicked wretch calls her *sister,* and yet impudently courts her to *come and lie with him, v.* 11. It was a base affront to her virtue to think it possible to persuade her to consent to such wickedness when he knew her behaviour to be always exemplarily modest and virtuous. But it is common for those that live in uncleanness to think others such as themselves, at least tinder to their sparks.

III. The devil, as a strong tempter, deafens his ear to all the reasonings with which she resisted his assaults and would have persuaded him to desist. We may well imagine what a surprise and terror it was to the young lady to be thus attacked, how she blushed and how she trembled; yet, in this great confusion, nothing could be said more pertinently, nor with greater strength of argument, than what she said to him. 1. She calls him *brother,* reminding him of the nearness of the relation, which made it unlawful for him to marry her, much more to debauch her. It was expressly forbidden (Lev. 18:9) under a severe penalty, Lev. 20:17. Great care must be taken lest the love that should be among relations degenerate into lust. 2. She entreats him not to force her, which intimates that she would never consent to it in any degree; and what satisfaction could he take in offering violence? 3. She lays before him the great wickedness of it. It is *folly;* all sin is so, especially uncleanness. It is wickedness of the worst kind. Such abominations ought not to be committed in Israel, among the professing people of God, that have better statutes than the heathen have. We are Israelites; if we do such things, we are more inexcusable than others, and our condemnation will be more intolerable, for we *reproach the Lord,* and *that worthy name by which we are called.* 4. She represents to him the shame of it, which perhaps might influence him more than the sin of it: "For my part, *whither shall I cause my shame to go?* If it should be concealed, yet I shall blush to think of it as long as I live; and, if ever it be known, how shall I be able to look any of my friends in the face? For thy part, *thou shalt be as one of the fools in Israel,"* that is, "Thou wilt be looked upon as an atrocious debauchee, the worst of men; thou wilt lose thy interest in the esteem of all that are wise and good, and so wilt be set aside as unfit to rule, though the first-born; for Israel will never submit to the government of such a fool." Prospect of shame, especially everlasting shame, should deter us from sin. 5. To divert him from his wicked purpose at this time, and (if possible) to get clear of him, she intimates to him that probably the king, rather than he should die for love of her, would dispense with the divine law and let him marry her: not as if she thought he had such a dispensing power, or would pretend to it; but she was confident that, upon notice given to the king by himself of this wicked desire, which he would scarcely have believed from any one else, he would take an effectual course to protect her from him. But all her arts and all her arguments availed not. His proud spirit cannot bear a denial; but her comfort, and honour, and all that was dear to her, must be sacrificed to his brutish and outrageous lust, *v.* 14. It is to be feared that Amnon, though young, had long lived a lewd life, which his father either knew not or punished not; for a man could not, of a sudden, arrive at such a pitch of wickedness as this. But is this his love to Tamar? Is this the recompence he gives her for her readiness to attend him in his sickness? Will he deal with his sister as with a harlot? Base villain! God deliver all that are modest and virtuous from such wicked and unreasonable men.

IV. The devil, as a tormentor and betrayer, immediately turns his love of her into hatred (*v.* 15): *He hated her with great hatred, greatly,* so it is in the margin, and grew as outrageous in his malice as he had been in his lust.

1. He basely turned her out of doors by force; nay, as if he now disdained to touch her with his own hands, he ordered his servant to *pull her out* and *bolt the door after her, v.* 17. Now, (1.) The innocent injured lady had reason to resent this as a great affront, and in some respects (as she says, *v.* 16) worse than the former; for nothing could have been done more barbarous and ill-natured, or more disgraceful to her. Had he taken care to conceal what was done, her honour would have been lost to herself only. Had he gone down on his knees and begged her pardon, it might have been some little reparation. Had he given her time to compose herself after the horrid confusion she was put into, she might have kept her countenance when she went out, and so have kept her counsel. But to dismiss her thus hurried, thus rudely, as if she had done some wicked thing, obliged her, in her own defence, to proclaim the wrong that had been done her. (2.) We may learn from it both the malignity of sin (unbridled passions are as bad as unbridled appetites) and the mischievous consequences of sin (at last, it bites like a serpent); for here we find, [1.] That sins, sweet in the commission, afterwards become odious and painful, and the sinner's own conscience makes them so to himself, Amnon hated Tamar because she would not consent to his wickedness, and so take part of the blame upon herself, but to the last resisted it, and reasoned against it, and so threw all the blame upon him. Had he hated the sin, and loathed himself for it, we might have hoped he was penitent. *Godly sorrow worketh indignation,* 2 Co. 7:11. But to hate the person he had abused showed that his conscience was terrified, but his heart not at all humbled. See what deceitful pleasures those of the flesh are, how soon they pass away, and turn into loathing; see Eze. 23:17. [2.] That sins, secret in the commission, afterwards become open and public, and the sinners themselves often make them so. Their own tongues fall upon them. The Jewish doctors say that, upon the occasion of this wickedness of Amnon, a law was made that a young man and a young woman should never be alone together; for, said they, if the king's daughter be so used, what will become of the children of private men?

2. We must now leave the criminal to the terrors of his own guilty conscience, and enquire what becomes of the poor victim. (1.) She bitterly lamented the injury she had received, as it was a stain to her honour, though no real blemish to her virtue. She tore her fine clothes in token of her grief, and put ashes upon her head, to deform herself, loathing her own beauty and ornaments, because they had occasioned Amnon's unlawful love; and she went on crying for another's sin, *v.* 19. (2.) She retired to her brother Absalom's house, because he was her own brother, and there she lived in solitude and sorrow, in token of her modesty and detestation of uncleanness. Absalom spoke kindly to her, bade her pass by the injury for the present, designing himself to revenge it, *v.* 20. It should seem by Absalom's question *(Has Amnon been with thee?)* that Amnon was notorious for such lewd practices, so that it was dangerous for a modest woman to be with him; this Absalom might know, and yet Tamar be wholly ignorant of it.

Verses 21–29

What Solomon says of the beginning of strife is as true of the beginning of all sin, it is as the letting forth of water; when once the flood-gates are plucked up, an inundation follows; one mischief begets another, and it is hard to say what shall be in the end thereof.

I. We are here told how David resented the tidings of Amnon's sin: *He was very wroth, v.* 21. So he had reason to be, that his own son should do such a wicked thing and draw him to be accessory to it. It would be a reproach to him for not giving him a better education; it would be a blot upon his family, the ruin of his daughter, a bad example to his kingdom, and a wrong to his son's soul. But was it enough for him to be angry? He ought to have punished his son for it, and have put him to open shame; both as a father and as a king he had power to do it. But the Septuagint here adds these words: *But he saddened not the spirit of his son Amnon, because he loved him, because he was his first-born.* He fell into Eli's error, whose sons *made themselves vile, and he frowned not on them.* If

Amnon was dear to him, his punishing him would have been so much the greater punishment to himself for his own uncleanness. But he cannot bear the shame those must submit to who correct that in others which they are conscious of in themselves, and therefore his anger must serve instead of his justice; and this hardens sinners, Eccl. 8:11.

II. How Absalom resented it. He resolves already to do the part of a judge in Israel; and, since his father will not punish Amnon, he will, from a principle, not of justice or zeal for virtue, but of revenge, because he reckons himself affronted in the abuse done to his sister. Their mother was daughter to a heathen prince (*ch.* 3:3), which perhaps they were upbraided with sometimes by their brethren, as children of a stranger. As such a one Absalom thought his sister was now treated; and, if Amnon thought her fit to be made his harlot, he would think him fit to be made his slave. This enraged him, and nothing less than the blood of Amnon will quench his rage. Here we have,

1. The design conceived: *Absalom hated Amnon* (*v.* 22), *and he that hateth his brother is a murderer* already, and, like *Cain, is of that wicked one,* 1 Jn. 3:12, 15. Absalom's hatred of his brother's crime would have been commendable, and he might justly have prosecuted him for it by a due course of law, for example to others, and the making of some compensation to his injured sister; but to hate his person, and design his death by assassination, was to put a great affront upon God, by offering to repair the breach of his seventh commandment by the violation of his sixth, as if they were not all alike sacred. *But he that said, Do not commit adultery, said also, Do not kill,* James 2:11.

2. The design concealed. He said nothing to Amnon of this matter, either good or bad, appeared as if he did not know it, and maintained towards him his usual civility, only waiting for a fair opportunity to do him a mischief. That malice is the worst, (1.) Which is hidden closely, and has no vent given to it. If Absalom had reasoned the matter with Amnon, he might have convinced him of his sin and brought him to repentance; but, saying nothing, Amnon's heart was hardened, and his own more and more embittered against him; therefore rebuking our neighbour is opposed to hating him in our hearts, Lev. 19:17. Let passion have vent and it will spend itself. (2.) Which is gilded over with a show of friendship; so Absalom's was, *his words smoother than butter but war in his heart.* See Prov. 26:26. (3.) Which is harboured long. Two full years Absalom nursed this root of bitterness, *v.* 24. It may be, at first, he did not intend to kill his brother (for, if he had, he might have had as fair an opportunity to do it as he had at last), and only waited for an occasion to disgrace him or do him some other mischief; but in time his hatred ripened to this, that he would be no less than the death of him. If the *sun going down* once *upon the wrath gives such place to the devil* (as is intimated, Eph. 4:26, 27), what would the sunsets of two full years do?

3. The design laid. (1.) Absalom has a feast at his house in the country, as Nabal had, on occasion of his sheepshearing, *v.* 23. Attentive as Absalom was to his person (*ch.* 14:26), and as high as he looked, he *knew the state of his flocks and looked well to his herds.* Those who have no other care about their estates in the country than how to spend them in the town take a ready way to see the end of them. When Absalom had sheep-shearers he would himself be with them. (2.) To this feast he invites the king his father, and all the princes of the blood (*v.* 24), not only that he might have this opportunity to pay his respects to them, but that he might make himself the more respected among his neighbours. Those that are akin to great folks are apt to value themselves too much on their kindred. (3.) The king would not go himself, because he would not put him to the expense of his entertainment, *v.* 25. It seems Absalom had an estate in his own hands, on which he lived like himself; the king had given it to him, but would have him to be a good husband of it: in both these he is an example to parents, when their children have grown up, to give them a competency to live upon, according to their rank, and then to take care that they do not live above it, especially that they be no way accessory to their doing so. It is prudent for young house-keepers to begin as they can hold out, and not to spend the wool upon the shearing of it. (4.) Absalom got leave for Amnon, and all the

rest of the king's sons, to come and grace his table in the country, *v.* 26, 27. Absalom had so effectually concealed his enmity to Amnon that David saw no reason to suspect any design upon him in that particular invitation: "Let my brother Amnon go;" but this would make the stroke more cutting to David that he was himself drawn in to consent to that which gave the opportunity for it, as before, *v.* 7. It seems, David's sons, though grown up, continued to pay such a deference to their father as not to go such a small journey as this without leave. Thus ought children, even when they have become men and women, to honour their parents, consult them, and do nothing material without their consent, much less against their mind.

4. The design executed, *v.* 28, 29. (1.) Absalom's entertainment was very plentiful; for he resolves that they shall all be merry with wine, at least concludes that Amnon will be so, for he knew that he was apt to drink to excess. But, (2.) The orders he gave to his servants concerning Amnon, that they should mingle his blood with his wine, were very barbarous. Had he challenged him, and, in reliance upon the goodness of his cause and the justice of God, fought him himself, though that would have been bad enough, yet it would have been more honourable and excusable (our ancient law, in some cases, allowed trial by battle); but to murder him, as he did, was to copy Cain's example, only that the reason made a difference: Abel was slain for his righteousness, Amnon for his wickedness. Observe the aggravations of this sin: — [1.] He would have Amnon slain *when his heart was merry with wine,* and he was consequently least apprehensive of danger, least able to resist it, and also least fit to go out of the world; as if his malice aimed to destroy both soul and body, not giving him time to say, *Lord, have mercy upon me.* What a dreadful surprise hath death been to many, whose hearts have been *overcharged with surfeiting and drunkenness!* [2.] His servants must be employed to do it, and so involved in the guilt. He was to give the word of command — *Smite Amnon;* and then they, in obedience to him, and, upon presumption that his authority would bear them out, must *kill him.* What an impious defiance does he bid to the divine law, when, though the command of God is express, *Thou shalt not kill,* he bids them kill Amnon, with this warrant, "*Have not I commanded you?* That is enough. *Be courageous,* and fear neither God nor man." Those servants are ill taught who obey their masters in contradiction to God, and those are wicked masters who have taught them to do so. Those are too obsequious that will damn their souls to please their masters, whose big words cannot secure them from God's wrath. Masters must always command their servants as those that know they also have a Master in heaven. [3.] He did it in the presence of *all the king's sons,* of whom it is said (*ch.* 8:18) that they were *chief rulers;* so that it was an affront to public justice which they had the administration of, and to the king his father whom they represented, and a contempt of that sword which should have been a terror to his evil deeds, while his evil deeds, on the contrary, were a terror to those that bore it. [4.] There is reason to suspect that Absalom did this, not only to revenge his sister's quarrel, but to make way for himself to the throne, which he was ambitious of, and which he would stand fair for if Amnon the eldest son was taken off. When the word of command was given Absalom's servants failed not to execute it, being buoyed up with an opinion that their master, being now next heir to the crown (for Chileab was dead, as bishop Patrick thinks), would save them from harm. Now the threatened sword is drawn in David's house which should not depart from it. *First,* His eldest son falls by it, himself being, by his wickedness, the cause of it, and his father, by his connivance, accessory to it. *Secondly,* All his sons flee from it, and come home in terror, not knowing how far their brother Absalom's bloody design might extend. See what mischief sin makes in families.

Verses 30–39

Here is, I. The fright that David was put into by a false report brought to Jerusalem that Absalom had *slain all the king's sons, v.* 30. It is common for fame to make bad worse; and the first news of such a thing as this represents it as more dreadful than afterwards it proves. Let us not therefore be afraid of evil tidings, while they want confirmation, but, when we hear the worst, hope the best, at least hope better. However, this false news gave as much affliction to David, for the present, as if it had been true; he *tore his garments, and lay on the earth,* while as yet it was only a flying story, *v.* 31. It was well that David had grace; he had need enough of it, for he had strong passions.

II. The rectifying of the mistake in two ways: — 1. By the sly suggestions of Jonadab, David's nephew, who could tell him, *Amnon only is dead,* and not all the king's sons (*v.* 32, 33), and could tell him too that it was done by the appointment of Absalom, and designed from the day Amnon forced his sister Tamar. What a wicked man was he, if he knew all this or had any cause to suspect it, that he did not make David acquainted with it sooner, that means might be used to make up the quarrel, or at least that David might not throw Amnon into the mouth of danger by letting him go to Absalom's house. If we do not our utmost to prevent mischief, we make ourselves accessory to it. *If we say, Behold, we knew it not; doth not he that pondereth the heart consider* whether we did or no? See Prov. 24:11, 12. It is well if Jonadab was not as guilty of Amnon's death as he was of his sin; such friends do those prove who are hearkened to as counsellors to do wickedly: he that would not be so kind as to prevent Amnon's sin would not be so kind as to prevent his ruin, when, it should seem, he might have done both. 2. By the safe return of all the king's sons except Amnon. They and their attendants were speedily discovered by the watch (*v.* 34, 35), and soon arrived, to show themselves alive, but to bring the certain sad news that Absalom had murdered their brother Amnon. The grief David had been in for that which was not made him the better able to bear that which was, by giving him a sensible occasion, when he was undeceived, to thank God that all his sons were not dead: yet that Amnon was dead, and slain by his own brother is such a treacherous barbarous manner, was enough to put the king and court, the king and kingdom, into real mourning. Sorrow is never more reasonable than when there is sin in the case.

III. Absalom's flight from justice: *Absalom* immediately *fled, v.* 34. He was now as much afraid of the king's sons as they were of him; they fled from his malice, he from their justice. No part of the land of Israel could shelter him. The cities of refuge gave no protection to a wilful murderer. Though David had let Amnon's incest go unpunished, Absalom could not promise himself his pardon for this murder; so express was the law in this case, and so well known David's justice, and his dread of blood-guiltiness. He therefore made the best of his way to his mother's relations, and was entertained by his grandfather *Talmai, king of Geshur* (*v.* 37), and there he was protected *three years* (*v.* 38), David not demanding him, and Talmai not thinking himself obliged to send him back unless he were demanded.

IV. David's uneasiness for his absence. He mourned for Amnon a good while (*v.* 37), but, he being past recall, time wore off that grief: he was *comforted concerning Amnon.* It also wore off too much his detestation of Absalom's sin; instead of loathing him as a murderer, he *longs to go forth to him, v.* 39. At first he could not find in his heart to do justice on him; now he can almost find in his heart to take him into his favour again. This was David's infirmity. Something God saw in his heart that made a difference, else we should have thought that he, as much as Eli, *honoured his sons more than God.*

CHAPTER 14

How Absalom threw himself out of his royal father's protection and favour we read in the foregoing chapter, which left him an exile, outlawed, and proscribed; in this chapter we have the arts that were used to bring him and his father together again, and how, at last, it was done, which is here recorded to show the folly of David in sparing him and indulging him in his wickedness, for which he was soon after severely corrected by his unnatural rebellion. I. Joab, by bringing a feigned issue (as the lawyers speak) to be tried before him, in the case of a poor widow of Tekoah, gains from him a judgment in general, That the case might be so as that the putting of a murderer to death ought to be dispensed with (*v.* 1–20). II. Upon the application of this, he gains from him an order to bring Absalom back to Jerusalem, while yet he was forbidden the court (*v.* 21–24). III. After an account of Absalom, his person, and family, we are told how at length he was introduced by Joab into the king's presence, and the king was thoroughly reconciled to him (*v.* 25–33).

Verses 1–20

Here is, I. Joab's design to get Absalom recalled out of banishment, his crime pardoned, and his attainder reversed, *v.* 1. Joab made himself very busy in this affair. 1. As a courtier that was studious, by all ways possible, to ingratiate himself with his prince and improve his interest in his favour: He *perceived that the king's heart was towards Absalom,* and that, the heat of his displeasure being over, he still retained his old affection for him, and only wanted a friend to court him to be reconciled, and to contrive for him how he might do it without impeaching the honour of his justice. Joab, finding how David stood affected, undertook this good office. 2. As a friend to Absalom, for whom perhaps he had a particular kindness, whom at least he looked upon as the rising sun, to whom it was his interest to recommend himself. He plainly foresaw that his father would at length be reconciled to him, and therefore thought he should make both his friends if he were instrumental to bring it about. 3. As a statesman, and one concerned for the public welfare. He knew how much Absalom was the darling of the people, and, if David should die while he was in banishment, it might occasion a civil war between those that were for him and those that were against him; for it is probable that though all Israel loved his person, yet they were much divided upon his case. 4. As one who was himself a delinquent, by the murder of Abner. He was conscious to himself of the guilt of blood, and that he was himself obnoxious to public justice, and therefore whatever favour he could procure to be shown to Absalom would corroborate his reprieve.

II. His contrivance to do it by laying somewhat of a parallel case before the king, which was done so dexterously by the person he employed that the king took it for a real case, and gave judgment upon it, as he had done upon Nathan's parable; and, the judgment being in favour of the criminal, the manager might, by that, discover his sentiments so far as to venture upon the application of it, and to show that it was the case of his own family, which, it is probable, she was instructed not to proceed to if the king's judgment upon her case should be severe.

1. The person he employed is not named, but she is said to be *a woman of Tekoah,* one whom he knew to be fit for such an undertaking: and it was requisite that the scene should be laid at a distance, that David might not think it strange that he had not heard of the case before. It is said, She was *a wise woman,* one that had a quicker wit and a readier tongue than most of her neighbours, *v.* 2. The truth of the story would be the less suspected when it came, as was supposed, from the person's own mouth.

2. The character she put on was that of a disconsolate widow, *v.* 2. Joab knew such a one would have an easy access to the king, who was always ready to comfort the mourners, especially the mourning widows, having himself mentioned it among the titles of God's honour that he is *a Judge of the widows,* Ps. 68:5. God's ear, no doubt, is more open to the cries of the afflicted, and his heart too, than that of the most merciful princes on earth can be.

3. It was a case of compassion which she had to represent to the king, and a case in which she could have no relief but from the chancery in the royal breast, the law (and consequently the judgment of all the inferior courts) being against her. She tells the king that she had buried her husband (*v.* 5), — that she had two sons that were the support and comfort of her widowed state, — that these two (as young men are apt to do) fell out and fought, and one of them unhappily killed the other (*v.* 6), — that, for her part, she was desirous to protect the manslayer (for, as Rebekah argued concerning her two sons, *Why should she be deprived of them both in one day?* Gen. 27:45), but though she, who was nearest of kin to the slain, was willing to let fall the demands of an avenger of blood, yet the other relations insisted upon it that the surviving brother should be put to death according to law, not out of any affection either to justice or to the memory of the slain brother, but that, by destroying the heir (which they had the impudence to own was the thing they aimed at), the inheritance might be theirs: and thus they would cut off, (1.) Her comfort: *"They shall quench my coal,* deprive me of the only support of my old age, and put a period to all my joy in this world, which is reduced to this one coal." (2.) Her husband's memory: "His family will be quite extinct, and they will *leave* him *neither name nor remainder," v.* 7.

4. The king promised her his favour and a protection for her son. Observe how she improved the king's compassionate concessions. (1.) Upon the representation of her case he promised to consider of it and to give orders about it, *v.* 8. This was encouraging, that he did not dismiss her petition with *"Currat lex — Let the law take its course;* blood calls for blood, and let it have what it calls for:" but he will take time to enquire whether the allegations of her petition be true. (2.) The woman was not content with this, but begged that he would immediately give judgment in her favour; and if the matter of fact were not as she represented it, and consequently a wrong judgment given upon it, let her bear the blame, and free *the king and his throne from guilt, v.* 9. Yet her saying this would not acquit the king if he should pass sentence without taking due cognizance of the case. (3.) Being thus pressed, he made a further promise that she should not be injured nor insulted by her adversaries, but he would protect her from all molestation, *v.* 10. Magistrates ought to be the patrons of oppressed widows. (4.) Yet this does not content her, unless she can get her son's pardon, and protection for him too. Parents are not easy, unless their children be safe, safe for both worlds: *"Let not the avenger of blood destroy my son* (*v.* 11), for I am undone if I lose him; as good take my life as his. *Therefore let the king remember the Lord thy God,"* that is, [1.] "Let him confirm this merciful sentence with an oath, making mention of the Lord our God, by way of appeal to him, that the sentence may be indisputable and irreversible; and then I shall be easy." See Heb. 6:17, 18. [2.] "Let him consider what good reason there is for this merciful sentence, and then he himself will be confirmed in it. *Remember* how gracious and merciful *the Lord thy God* is, how he bears long with sinners and does not deal with them according to their deserts, but is ready to forgive. *Remember* how *the Lord thy God* spared Cain, who slew his brother, and protected him from the avengers of blood, Gen. 4:15. *Remember* how *the Lord thy God* forgave thee the blood of Uriah, and let the king, that has found mercy, show mercy." Note, Nothing is more proper, nor more powerful, to engage us to every duty, especially to all acts of mercy and kindness, than to remember the Lord our God. (5.) This importunate widow, by pressing the matter thus closely, obtains at last a full pardon for her son, ratified with an oath as she desired: *As the Lord liveth, there shall not one hair of thy son fall to the earth,* that is, "I will undertake he shall come to no damage upon this account." The Son of David has assured all that put themselves under his protection that, though they should be put to death for his sake, *not a hair of their head shall perish* (Lu. 21:16–18), though they should lose for him, they shall not lose by him. Whether David did well this to undertake the protection of a murderer, whom the cities of refuge would not protect, I cannot say. But, as the matter of fact appeared to him, there was not only great reason for compassion to the mother, but room enough for a favourable judgment concerning the son: he had slain his brother, but he *hated him not in time past;* it was upon a sudden provocation, and, for aught that appeared, it might be done in his own defence. He pleaded not this himself, but the judge must be of counsel for the prisoner; and therefore, *Let mercy* at this time *rejoice against judgment.*

5. The case being thus adjudged in favour of her son, it is now time to apply it to the king's son, Absalom. The mask here begins to be thrown off, and another scene opened. The king is surprised, but not at all displeased, to find his humble petitioner, of a sudden, become his reprover, his privy-counsellor, an advocate for the prince his son, and the mouth of the people, undertaking to represent to him their sentiments. She begs his pardon, and his patience, for what she had further to say (*v.* 12), and has leave to say it, the king being very well pleased with her wit and humour. (1.) She supposes Absalom's case to be, in effect, the same with that which she had put as her son's; and therefore, if the king would protect her son, though he had slain his brother, much more ought he to protect his own, and to *fetch home his banished, v.* 13. *Mutato nomine, de te fabula narratur — Change but the name, to you the tale belongs.* She names not Absalom, nor needed she to name him. David longed so much after him, and had him so much in his thoughts, that he was soon aware whom she meant by his banished. And in those two words were two arguments which the king's tender spirit felt the force of: "He is banished, and has for three years undergone the disgrace and terror, and all the inconveniences,

of banishment. *Sufficient to such a one is this punishment.* But he is *thy* banished, thy own son, a piece of thyself, thy dear son, whom thou lovest." It is true, Absalom's case differed very much from that which she had put. Absalom did not slay his brother upon a hasty passion, but maliciously, and upon an old grudge; not in the field, where there were no witnesses, but at table, before all his guests. Absalom was not an only son, as hers was; David had many more, and one lately born, more likely to be his successor than Absalom, for he was called *Jedidiah,* because God loved him. But David was himself too well affected to the cause to be critical in his remarks upon the disparity of the cases, and was more desirous than she could be to bring that favourable judgment to his own son which he had given concerning hers. (2.) She reasons upon it with the king, to persuade him to recall Absalom out of banishment, give him his pardon, and take him into his favour again. [1.] She pleads the interest which the people of Israel had in him. "What is done against him is done *against the people of God,* who have their eye upon him as heir of the crown, at least have their eye upon the house of David in general, with which the covenant is made, and which therefore they cannot tamely see the diminution and decay of by the fall of so many of its branches in the flower of their age. Therefore *the king speaks as one that is faulty,* for he will provide that my husband's name and memory be not cut off, and yet takes no care though his own be in danger, which is of more value and importance than ten thousand of ours." [2.] She pleads man's mortality (*v.* 14): *"We must needs die.* Death is appointed for us; we cannot avoid the thing itself, nor defer it till another time. We are all under a fatal necessity of dying; and, when we are dead, we are past recall, as water spilt upon the ground; nay, even while we are alive, we are so, we have lost our immortality, past retrieve. Amnon must have died, some time, if Absalom had not killed him; and, if Absalom be now put to death for killing him, that will not bring him to life again." This was poor reasoning, and would serve against the punishment of any murderer: but, it should seem, Amnon was a man little regarded by the people and his death little lamented, and it was generally thought hard that so dear a life as Absalom's should go for one so little valued as Amnon's. [3.] She pleads God's mercy and his clemency towards poor guilty sinners: *"God does not take away the soul, or life, but devises means that his banished,* his children that have offended him, and are obnoxious to his justice, as Absalom is to thine, *be not* for ever *expelled from him," v.* 14. Here are two great instances of the mercy of God to sinners, properly urged as reasons for showing mercy: — *First,* The patience he exercises towards them. His law is broken, yet he does not immediately take away the life of those that break it, does not strike sinners dead, as justly he might, in the act of sin, but bears with them, and waits to be gracious. God's vengeance had suffered Absalom to live; why then should not David's justice suffer him? *Secondly,* The provision he has made for their restoration to his favour, that though by sin they have banished themselves from him, yet they might not be expelled, or cast off, for ever. Atonement might be made for sinners by sacrifice. Lepers, and others ceremonially unclean, were banished, but provision was made for their cleansing, that, though for a time excluded, they might not be finally expelled. The state of sinners is a state of banishment from God. Poor banished sinners are likely to be for ever expelled from God if some course be not taken to prevent it. It is against the mind of God that they should be so, for he is not willing that any should perish. Infinite wisdom has devised proper means to prevent it; so that it is the sinners' own fault if they be cast off. This instance of God's good-will toward us all should incline us to be merciful and compassionate one towards another, Mt. 18:32, 33.

6. She concludes her address with high compliments to the king, and strong expressions of her assurance that he would do what was just and kind both in the one case and in the other (*v.* 15–17); for, as if the case had been real, still she pleads for herself and her son, yet meaning Absalom. (1.) She would not have troubled the king thus but that the people made her afraid. Understanding it of her own case, all her neighbours made her apprehensive of the ruin she and her son were upon the brink of, from the avengers of blood, the terror of which made her thus bold in her application to the king himself. Understanding it of Absalom's case, she gives the king to understand, what he did not know before, that the nation was disgusted at his severity towards Absalom to such a degree that she was really afraid it would occasion a general mutiny or insurrection, for the preventing of which great mischief she ventured to speak to the king himself. The fright she was in must excuse her rudeness. (2.) She applied to him with a great confidence in his wisdom and clemency: "I said, *I will speak to the king* myself, and ask nobody to speak for me; for the king will hear reason, even from so mean a creature as I am, will hear the cries of the oppressed, and will not suffer the poorest of his subjects to be *destroyed out of the inheritance of God,"* that is, "driven out of the land of Israel, to seek for shelter among the uncircumcised, as Absalom is, whose case is so much the worse, that, being shut *out of the inheritance of God,* he wants God's law and ordinances, which might help to bring him to repentance, and is in danger of being infected with the idolatry of the heathen among whom he sojourns, and of bringing home the infection." To engage the king to grant her request, she expressed a confident hope that his answer would be comfortable, and such as angels bring (as bishop Patrick explains it), who are messengers of divine mercy. What this woman says by way of compliment the prophet says by way of promise (Zec. 12:8), that, when *the weak shall be as David, the house of David shall be as the angel of the Lord.* "And, in order to this, *the Lord thy God will be with thee,* to assist thee in this and every judgment thou givest." Great expectations are great engagements, especially to persons of honour, to do their utmost not to disappoint those that depend upon them.

7. The hand of Joab is suspected by the king, and acknowledged by the woman, to be in all this, *v.* 18–20. (1.) The king soon suspected it. For he could not think that such a woman as this would appeal to him, in a matter of such moment, of her own accord; and he knew none so likely to set her on as Joab, who was a politic man and a friend of Absalom. (2.) The woman very honestly owned it: *"Thy servant Joab bade me.* If it be well done, let him have the thanks; if ill, let him bear the blame." Though she found it very agreeable to the king, yet she would not take the praise of it to herself, but speaks the truth as it was, and gives us an example to do likewise, and never to tell a lie for the concealing of a well-managed scheme. *Dare to be true; nothing can need a lie.*

Verses 21–27

Observe here, I. Orders given for the bringing back of Absalom. The errand on which the woman came to David was so agreeable, and her management of it so very ingenious and surprising, that he was brought into a peculiarly kind humour: *Go* (says he to Joab), *bring the young man Absalom again, v.* 21. He was himself inclined to favour him, yet, for the honour of his justice, he would not do it but upon intercession made for him, which may illustrate the methods of divine grace. It is true God has thought of compassion towards poor sinners, not willing that any should perish, yet he is reconciled to them through a Mediator, who intercedes with him on their behalf, and to whom he has given these orders, *Go, bring them again. God was in Christ reconciling the world to himself,* and he came to this land of our banishment to bring us to God. Joab, having received these orders, 1. Returns thanks to the king for doing him the honour to employ him in an affair so universally grateful, *v.* 22. Joab took it as a kindness to himself, and (some think) as an indication that he would never call him to an account for the murder he had been guilty of. But, if he meant so, he was mistaken, as we shall find, 1 Ki. 2:5, 6. 2. Delays not to execute David's orders; he brought Absalom to Jerusalem, *v.* 23. I see not how David can be justified in suspending the execution of the ancient law (Gen. 9:6), *Whoso sheds man's blood, by man shall his blood be shed,* in which a righteous magistrate ought not to *acknowledge even his brethren, or know his own children.* God's laws were never designed to be like cobwebs, which catch the little flies, but suffer the great ones to break through. God justly made Absalom, whom his foolish pity spared, a scourge to him. But, though he allowed him to return to his own house, he forbade him the court, and would not see him himself, *v.* 24. He put him under this interdict, (1.) For his own honour, that he might not seem to countenance so great a criminal, nor to forgive him too easily. (2.) For Absalom's greater humiliation. Perhaps he had heard something of his conduct when Joab went to fetch him, which gave him too much reason to think that he was not truly penitent; he therefore put him under this mark of his displeasure, that he might be awakened to a sight of his sin and to sorrow for it, and might make his peace with God, upon the first notice of which, no doubt, David would be forward to receive him again into his favour.

II. Occasion taken hence to give an account of Absalom. Nothing is said of his wisdom and piety. Though he was the son of such a devout father, we read nothing of his devotion. Parents cannot give grace to their children, though they give them ever so good an education. All that is here said of him is, 1. That he was a very handsome man; there was not his equal in all Israel for beauty, (*v.* 25), a poor commendation for a man that had nothing else in him valuable. Handsome are those that handsome do. Many a polluted deformed soul dwells in a fair and comely body; witness Absalom's, that was polluted with blood, and deformed with unnatural disaffection to his father and prince. In his body there was no blemish, but in his mind nothing but wounds and bruises. Perhaps his comeliness was one reason why his father was so fond of him and protected him from justice. Those have reason to fear affliction in their children who are better pleased with their beauty than with their virtue. 2. That he had a very fine head of hair. Whether it was the length, or colour, or extraordinary softness of it, something there was which made it very valuable and very much an ornament to him, *v.* 26. This notice is taken of his hair, not as the hair of a Nazarite (he was far from that strictness), but as the hair of a beau. He let it grow till it was a burden to him, and was heavy on him, nor would he cut it as long as ever he could bear it; as pride feels no cold, so it feels no heat, and that which feeds and gratifies it is not complained of, though very uneasy. When he did poll it at certain times, for ostentation he had it weighed, that it might be seen how much it excelled other men's, and it weighed 200 shekels, which some reckon to be three pounds and two ounces of our weight; and with the oil and powder, especially if powdered (as Josephus says the fashion then was) with gold-dust, bishop Patrick thinks it is not at all incredible that it should weigh so much. This fine hair proved his halter, *ch.* 18:9. 3. That his family began to be built up. It is probable that it was a good while before he had a child; and then it was that, despairing of having one, he set up that pillar which is mentioned *ch.* 18:18, to bear up his name; but afterwards he had three sons and one daughter, *v.* 27. Or perhaps these sons, while he was hatching his rebellion, were all cut off by the righteous hand of God, and thereupon he set up that monument.

Verses 28–33

Three years Absalom had been an exile from his father-in-law, and now two years a prisoner at large in his own house, and, in both, better dealt with than he deserved; yet his spirit was still unhumbled, his pride unmortified, and, instead of being thankful that his life is spared, he thinks himself sorely wronged that he is not restored to all his places at court. Had he truly repented of his sin, his distance from the gaieties of the court, and his solitude and retirement in his own house, especially being in Jerusalem the holy city, would have been very agreeable to him. If a murderer must live, yet let him be for ever a recluse. But Absalom could not bear this just and gentle mortification. He longed to see the king's face, pretending it was because he loved him, but really because he wanted an opportunity to supplant him. He cannot do his father a mischief till he is reconciled to him; this therefore is the first branch of his plot; this snake cannot sting again till he be warmed in his father's bosom. He gained this point, not by pretended submissions and promises of reformation, but (would you think it?) by insults and injuries. 1. By his insolent carriage towards Joab, he brought him to mediate for him. Once and again he sent to Joab to come and speak with him, for he durst not go to him; but Joab would not come (*v.* 29), probably because Absalom had not owned the kindness he had done him in bringing him to Jerusalem so gratefully as he thought he should have done; proud men take every service done them for a debt. One would think that a person in Absalom's circumstances should have sent to Joab a kindly message, and offered him a large gratuity: courtiers expect noble presents. But, instead of this, he bids his servants set Joab's corn-fields on fire (*v.* 30), as spiteful a thing as he could do. Samson could not think of a greater injury to do the Philistines than this. Strange that Absalom should think, by doing Joab a mischief, to prevail with him to do him a kindness, or to recommend himself to the favour of his prince or people by showing himself so very malicious and ill-natured, and such an enemy to the public good, for the fire might spread to the corn of others. Yet by this means he brings Joab to him, *v.* 31. Thus God, by afflictions, brings those to him that kept at a distance from him. Absalom was obliged by the law to make restitution (Ex. 22:6), yet we do not find either that he offered it or that Joab demanded it. Joab (it might be) thought he could not justify his refusal to go and speak with him; and therefore Absalom thought he could justify his taking this way to fetch him. And now Joab (perhaps frightened at the surprising boldness and fury of Absalom, and apprehensive that he had made an interest in the people strong enough to bear him out in doing the most daring things, else he would never have done this) not only puts up with this injury, but goes on his errand to the king. See what some men can do by threats, and carrying things with a high hand. 2. By his insolent message (for I can call it no better) to the king, he recovered his place at court, to see the king's face, that is, to become a privy counsellor, Esth. 1:14. (1.) His message was haughty and imperious, and very unbecoming either a son or a subject, *v.* 32. He undervalued the favour that had been shown him in recalling him from banishment, and restoring him to his own house, and that in Jerusalem: *Wherefore have I come from Geshur?* He denies his own crimes, though most notorious, and will not own that there was any iniquity in him, insinuating that therefore he had been wronged in the rebuke he had been under. He defies the king's justice: "Let him kill me, if he can find in his heart," knowing he loved him too well to do it. (2.) Yet with this message he carried his point, *v.* 33. David's strong affection for him construed all this to be the language of a great respect to his father, and an earnest desire of his favour, when alas! it was far otherwise. See how easily wise and good men may be imposed upon by their own children that design ill, especially when they are blindly fond of them. Absalom, by the posture of his body, testified his submission to his father: *He bowed himself on his face to the ground;* and David, with a kiss, sealed his pardon. Did the bowels of a father prevail to reconcile him to an impenitent son, and shall penitent sinners question the compassion of him who is the Father of mercy? If Ephraim bemoan himself, God soon bemoans him, with all the kind expressions of a fatherly tenderness: *He is a dear son, a pleasant child,* Jer. 31:20.

CHAPTER 15

Absalom's name signifies "the peace of his father," yet he proves his greatest trouble; so often are we disappointed in our expectations from the creature. The sword entailed upon David's house had hitherto been among his children, but now it begins to be drawn against himself, with this aggravation, that he may thank himself for it, for, had he done justice upon the murderer, he would have prevented the traitor. The story of Absalom's rebellion begins with this chapter, but we must go over three or four more before we see the end of it. In this chapter we have, I. The arts Absalom used to insinuate himself into the people's affections (*v.* 1–6). II. His open avowal of his pretensions to the crown at Hebron, whither he went under colour of a vow, and the strong party that appeared for him there (*v.* 7–12). III. The notice brought of this to David, and his flight from Jerusalem thereupon (*v.* 13–18). In his flight we are told, 1. What passed between him and Ittai (*v.* 19–22). 2. The concern of the country for him (*v.* 23). 3. His conference with Zadok (*v.* 24–29). 4. His tears and prayers upon this occasion (*v.* 30–31). 5. Matters concerted by him with Hushai (*v.* 32–37). Now the word of God was fulfilled, that he would "raise up evil against him out of his own house.", 12:11.

Verses 1–6

Absalom is no sooner restored to his place at court than he aims to be in the throne. He that was unhumbled under his troubles became insufferably proud when they were over; and he cannot be content with the honour of being the king's son, and the prospect of being his successor, but he must be king now. His mother was a king's daughter; on that perhaps he valued himself, and despised his father, who was but the son of Jesse. She was the daughter of a heathen king, which made him the less concerned for the peace of Israel. David, in this unhappy issue of that marriage, smarted for his being unequally yoked with an unbeliever. When Absalom was restored to the king's favour, if he had had any sense of gratitude, he would have studied how to oblige his father, and make him easy; but, on the contrary, he meditates how to undermine him, by stealing the hearts of the people from him. Two things recommend a man to popular esteem — greatness and goodness.

I. Absalom looks great, *v.* 1. He had learned of the king of Geshur (what was not allowed to the kings of Israel) to multiply horses, which made him look desirable, while his father, on his mule, looked despicable. The people desired a king like the nations; and such a one Absalom will be, appearing in pomp and magnificence, above what had been seen in Jerusalem. Samuel had foretold that this would be *the manner of the king:* He shall *have chariots and horsemen, and some shall run before his chariots* (1 Sa. 8:11); and this is Absalom's manner. Fifty footmen (in rich liveries we may suppose) running before him, to give notice of his approach, would highly gratify his pride and the people's foolish fancy. David thinks that this parade is designed only to grace his court, and connives at it. Those parents know not what they do who indulge a proud humour in their children; for I have seen more young people ruined by pride than by any one lust whatsoever.

II. Absalom will seem very good too, but with a very bad design. Had he proved himself a good son and a good subject, and set himself to serve his father's interest, he would have done his present duty, and shown himself worthy of future honours, after his father's death. Those that know how to obey well know how to rule. But to show how good a judge and how good a king he will be is but to deceive himself and others. Those are good indeed that are good in their own place, not that pretend how good they would be in other people's places. But this is all the goodness we find in Absalom.

1. He wishes that he were a judge in Israel, *v.* 4. He had all the pomp and all the pleasure he could wish, lived as great and in as much ease as any man could; yet this will not content him, unless he have power too: *O that I were a judge in Israel!* He that should himself have been judged to death for murder has the impudence to aim at being a judge of others. We read not of Absalom's wisdom, virtue, or learning in the laws, nor had he given any proofs of his love to justice, but the contrary; yet he wishes he were judge. Note, Those are commonly most ambitious of preferment that are least fit for it; the best qualified are the most modest and self-diffident, while it is no better than the spirit of an Absalom that says, *O that I were a judge in Israel!*

2. He takes a very bad course for the accomplishing of his wish. Had he humbly petitioned his father to employ him in the administration of justice, and studied to qualify himself for it (according to the rule, Ex. 18:21), no doubt he would have been sure of the next judge's place that fell; but this is too mean a post for his proud spirit. It is below him to be subordinate, though to the king his father; he must be supreme or nothing. He wants to be such a judge that every man who has any cause shall come to him: in all causes, and over all persons, he must preside, little thinking what a fatigue this would be to have every man come to him. Moses himself could not bear it. Those know not what power is that grasp at so much, so very much. To gain the power he aims at, he endeavours to instil into the people's minds,

(1.) A bad opinion of the present administration, as if the affairs of the kingdom were altogether neglected, and no care taken about them. He got round him all he could that had business at the council-board, enquired what their business was; and, [1.] Upon a slight and general enquiry into their cause, he pronounced it good: *Thy matters are right.* A fit man indeed to be a judge, who would give judgment upon hearing one side only! For he has a bad cause indeed that cannot put a good colour upon it, when he himself has the telling of the story. But, [2.] He told them that it was to no purpose to appeal to the throne: *"There is no man deputed of the king to hear thee.* The king is himself old, and past business, or so taken up with his devotions that he never minds business; his sons are so addicted to their pleasures that, though they have the name of chief rulers, they take no care of the affairs committed to them." He further seems to insinuate what a great want there was of him while he was banished and confined, and how much the public suffered by his exile; what his father said truly in Saul's reign (Ps. 75:3) he says falsely: *The land and all the inhabitants of it are dissolved,* all will go to wreck and ruin, unless *I bear up the pillars of it.* Every appellant shall be made to believe that he will never have justice done him, unless Absalom be viceroy or lord-justice. It is the way of turbulent, factious, aspiring men, to reproach the government they are under. *Presumptuous are they, self-willed, and not afraid to speak evil of dignities,* 2 Pt. 2:10. Even David himself, the best of kings, and his administration, could not escape the worst of censures. Those that aim to usurp cry out of grievances, and pretend to design nothing but the redress of them: as Absalom here.

(2.) A good opinion of his own fitness to rule. That the people might say, "O that Absalom were a judge!" (and they are apt enough to desire changes), he recommends himself to them, [1.] As very diligent. He rose up early, and appeared in public before the rest of the king's sons were stirring, and he stood beside the way of the gate, where the courts of judgment sat, as one mightily concerned to see justice done and public business despatched. [2.] As very inquisitive and prying, and desirous to be acquainted with every one's case. He would know of what city every one was that came for judgment, that he might inform himself concerning every part of the kingdom and the state of it, *v.* 2. [3.] As very familiar and humble. If any Israelite offered to do obeisance to him he took him and embraced him as a friend. No man's conduct could be more condescending, while his heart was as proud as Lucifer's. Ambitious projects are often carried on by *a show of humility,* Col. 2:23. He knew what a grace it puts upon greatness to be affable and courteous, and how much it wins upon common people: had he been sincere in it, it would have been his praise; but to fawn upon the people that he might betray them was abominable hypocrisy. *He croucheth, and humbleth himself, to draw them into his net,* Ps. 10:9, 10.

Verses 7–12

We have here the breaking out of Absalom's rebellion, which he had long been contriving. It is said to be *after forty years, v.* 7. But whence it is to be dated we are not told; not from David's beginning his reign, for then it would fall in the last year of his life, which is not probable; but either from his first anointing by Samuel seven years before, or rather (I think) from the people's desiring a king, and the first change of the government into a monarchy, which might be about ten years before David began to reign; it is fitly dated thence, to show that the same restless spirit was still working, and still they were given to change: as fond now of a new man as then of a new model. So it fell about the thirtieth year of David's reign. Absalom's plot being now ripe for execution,

I. The place he chose for the rendezvous of his party was Hebron, the place where he was born and where his father began his reign and continued it several years, which would give some advantage to his pretensions. Every one knew Hebron to be a royal city; and it lay in the heart of Judah's lot, in which tribe, probably, he thought his interest strong.

II. The pretence he had both to go thither and to invite his friends to him there was to offer a sacrifice to God, in performance of a vow he had made during his banishment, *v.* 7, 8. We have cause enough to suspect that he had not made any such vow; it does not appear that he was so religiously inclined. But he that stuck not at murder and treason would not make conscience of a lie to serve his purpose. If he said he had made such a vow, nobody could disprove him. Under this pretence, 1. He got leave of his father to go to Hebron. David would be well pleased to hear that his son, in his exile, was so desirous to return to Jerusalem, not only his father's city, but the city of the living God, — that he looked up to God, to bring him back, — that he had vowed, if he were brought back, to serve the Lord, whose service he had hitherto neglected, — and that now, being brought back, he remembered his vow, and resolved to perform it. If he think fit to do it in Hebron, rather than in Sion or Gibeon, the good king is so well pleased with the thing itself that he will not object against his choice of the place. See how willing tender parents are to believe the best concerning their children, and, upon the least indication of good, to hope, even concerning those that have been untoward, that they will repent and reform. But how easy is it for children to take advantage of their good parents' credulity, and to impose upon them with the show of religion, while still they are what they were! David was overjoyed to hear that Absalom inclined to *serve the Lord*, and therefore readily gave him leave to go to Hebron, and to go thither with solemnity. 2. He got a good number of sober substantial citizens to go along with him, *v.* 11. There went 200 men, probably of the principal men of Jerusalem, whom he invited to join with him in his feast upon his sacrifice; and they went in their simplicity, not in the least suspecting that Absalom had any bad design in this journey. He knew that it was to no purpose to tempt them into his plot: they were inviolably firm to David. But he drew them in to accompany him, that the common people might think that they were in his interest, and that David was deserted by some of his best friends. Note, It is no new thing for very good men, and very good things, to be made use of by designing men to put a colour upon bad practices. When religion is made a stalking-horse, and sacrifice a shoeing-horn, to sedition and usurpation it is not to be wondered at if some that were well affected to religion, as these followers of Absalom here, are imposed upon by the fallacy, and drawn in to give countenance to that, with their names, which in their heart they abhor, not having known the depths of Satan.

III. The project he laid was to get himself proclaimed king throughout all the tribes of Israel upon a signal given, *v.* 10. Spies were sent abroad, to be ready in every country to receive the notice with satisfaction and acclamations of joy, and to make the people believe that the news was both very true and very good, and that they were all concerned to take up arms for their new king. Upon the sudden spreading of this proclamation, *"Absalom reigns in Hebron,"* some would conclude that David was dead, others that he had resigned: and thus those that were in the secret would draw in many to appear for Absalom, and to come into his assistance, who, if they had rightly understood the matter, would have abhorred the thought of it, but, being drawn in, would adhere to him. See what artifices ambitious men use for the compassing of their ends; and in matters of state, as well as in matters of religion, let us not be forward to believe every spirit, but try the spirits.

IV. The person he especially courted and relied upon in this affair was Ahithophel, a politic thinking man, and one that had a clear head and a great compass of thought, that had been David's counsellor, his guide and his acquaintance (Ps. 55:13), his *familiar friend, in whom he trusted, who did eat of his bread,* Ps. 41:9. But, upon some disgust of David's against him, or his against David, he was banished, or retired from public business, and lived privately in the country. How should a man of such good principles as David, and a man of such corrupt principles as Ahithophel, long agree? A fitter tool Absalom could not find in all the kingdom than one that was so great a statesman, and yet was disaffected to the present ministry. While Absalom was offering his sacrifices, in performance of his pretended vow, he sent for this man. So much was his heart on the projects of his ambition that he could not stay to make an end of his devotion, which showed what his eye was upon in all, and that it was but for a pretence that he made long offerings.

V. The party that joined with him proved at last very considerable. The people increased continually with Absalom, which made the conspiracy strong and formidable. Every one whom he had complimented and caressed (pronouncing his matters right and good, especially if afterwards the cause went against him) not only came himself, but made all the interest he could for him, so that he wanted not for numbers. The majority is no certain rule to judge of equity by. *All the world wondered after the beast.* Whether Absalom formed this design merely in the height of his ambition and fondness to rule, or whether there was not in it also malice against his father and revenge for his banishment and confinement, though this punishment was so much less than he deserved, does not appear. But, gen-

erally, that which aims at the crown aims at the head that wears it.

Verses 13–23

Here is, I. The notice brought to David of Absalom's rebellion, *v.* 13. The matter was bad enough, and yet it seems to have been made worse to him (as such things commonly are) than really it was; for he was told that *the hearts of the men of Israel* (that is, the generality of them, at least the leading men) were *after Absalom*. But David was the more apt to believe it because now he could call to mind the arts that Absalom had used to inveigle them, and perhaps reflected upon it with regret that he had not done more to counterwork him, and secure his own interest, which he had been too confident of. Note, It is the wisdom of princes to make sure of their subjects; for, if they have them, they have their purses, and arms, and all, at their service.

II. The alarm this gave to David, and the resolutions he came to thereupon. We may well imagine him in a manner thunderstruck, when he heard that the son he loved so dearly, and had been so indulgent to, was so unnaturally and ungratefully in arms against him. Well might he say with Caesar, *Kai sy teknon — What, thou my son?* Let not parents raise their hopes too high from their children, lest they be disappointed. David did not call a council, but, consulting only with God and his own heart, determined immediately to quit Jerusalem, *v.* 14. He took up this strange resolve, so disagreeable to his character as a man of courage, either, 1. As a penitent, submitting to the rod, and lying down under God's correcting hand. Conscience now reminded him of his sin in the matter of Uriah, and the sentence he was under for it, which was that *evil should arise against him out of his own house.* "Now," thinks he, "the word of God begins to be fulfilled, and it is not for me to contend with it or fight against it; God is righteous and I submit." Before unrighteous Absalom he could justify himself and stand it out; but before the righteous God he must condemn himself and yield to his judgments. Thus he *accepts the punishment of his iniquity.* Or, 2. As a politician. Jerusalem was a great city, but not tenable; it should seem, by David's prayer (Ps. 51:18), that the walls of it were not built up, much less was it regularly fortified. It was too large to be garrisoned by so small a force as David had now with him, He had reason to fear that the generality of the inhabitants were too well affected to Absalom to be true to him. Should he fortify himself here, he might lose the country, in which, especially among those that lay furthest from Absalom's tampering, he hoped to have the most friends. And he had such a kindness for Jerusalem that he was loth to make it the seat of war, and expose it to the calamities of a siege; he will rather quit it tamely to the rebels. Note, Good men, when they suffer themselves, care not how few are involved with them in suffering.

III. His hasty flight from Jerusalem. His servants agreed to the measures he took, faithfully adhered to him (*v.* 15), and assured him of their inviolable allegiance, whereupon, 1. He went out of Jerusalem himself on foot, while his son Absalom had chariots and horses. It is not always the best man, nor the best cause, that makes the best figure. See here, not only the servant, but the traitor, on horseback, while the prince, the rightful prince, *walks as a servant upon the earth,* Eccl. 10:7. Thus he chose to do, to abase himself so much the more under God's hand, and in condescension to his friends and followers, with whom he would walk, in token that he would live and die with them. 2. He took his household with him, his wives and children, that he might protect them in this day of danger, and that they might be a comfort to him in this day of grief. Masters of families, in their greatest frights, must not neglect their households. *Ten women,* that *were concubines,* he *left* behind, *to keep the house,* thinking that the weakness of their sex would secure them from murder, and their age and relation to him would secure them from rape; but God overruled this for the fulfilling of his word. 3. He took his life-guard with him, or band of pensioners, the Cherethites and Pelethites, who were under the command of Benaiah, and the Gittites, who were under the command of Ittai, *v.* 18. These Gittites seem to have been, by birth, Philistines of Gath, who came, a regiment of them, 600 in all, to enter themselves in David's service, having known

him at Gath, and being greatly in love with him for his virtue and piety, and having embraced the Jews' religion. David made them of his *garde du corps — his body-guard,* and they adhered to him in his distress. The Son of David *found not such great faith in Israel* as in a Roman centurion and a woman of Canaan. 4. As many as would, of the people of Jerusalem, he took with him, and made a halt at some distance from the city, to draw them up, *v.* 17. He compelled none. Those whose hearts were with Absalom, to Absalom let them go, and so shall their doom be: they will soon have enough of him. Christ enlists none but volunteers.

IV. His discourse with Ittai the Gittite, who commanded the Philistine-proselytes.

1. David dissuaded him from going along with him, *v.* 19, 20. Though he and his men might be greatly serviceable to him yet, (1.) He would try whether he was hearty for him, and not inclined to Absalom. He therefore bids him return to his post in Jerusalem, and serve the new king. If he was no more than a soldier of fortune (as we say), he would be for that side which would pay and prefer him best; and to that side let him go. (2.) If he was faithful to David, yet David would not have him exposed to the fatigues and perils he now counted upon. David's tender spirit cannot bear to think that a stranger and an exile, a proselyte and a new convert, who ought, by all means possible, to be encouraged and made easy, should, at his first coming, meet with such hard usage: "*Should I make thee go up and down with us?* No, return with thy brethren." Generous souls are more concerned at the share others have in their troubles than at their own. Ittai shall therefore be dismissed with a blessing: *Mercy and truth be with thee,* that is, God's mercy and truth, mercy according to promise, the promise made to those who renounce other gods and put themselves under the wings off the divine Majesty. This is a very proper pious farewell, when we part with a friend, "*Mercy and truth be with thee,* and then thou art safe, and mayest be easy, wherever thou art." David's dependence was upon the mercy and truth of God for comfort and happiness, both for himself and his friends; see Ps. 61:7.

2. Ittai bravely resolved not to leave him, *v.* 21. Where David is, *whether in life or death,* safe or in peril, there will this faithful friend of his be; and he confirms this resolution with an oath, that he might not be tempted to break it. Such a value has he for David, not for the sake of his wealth and greatness (for then he would have deserted him now that he saw him thus reduced), but for the sake of his wisdom and goodness, which were still the same, that, whatever comes of it, he will never leave him. Note, That is a friend indeed who loves at all times, and will adhere to us in adversity. Thus should we cleave to the Son of David with full purpose of heart that *neither life nor death shall separate us from his love.*

V. The common people's sympathy with David in his affliction. When he and his attendants *passed over the brook Kidron* (the very same brook that Christ passed over when he entered upon his sufferings, Jn. 18:1), *towards the way of the wilderness,* which lay between Jerusalem and Jericho, *all the country wept with a loud voice, v.* 23. Cause enough there was for weeping, 1. To see a prince thus reduced, one that had lived so great forced from his palace and in fear of his life, with a small retinue seeking shelter in a desert, to see the city of David, which he himself won, built, and fortified, made an unsafe abode for David himself. It would move the compassion even of strangers to see a man fallen thus low from such a height, and this by the wickedness of his own son; a piteous case it was. Parents that are abused and ruined by their own children merit the tender sympathy of their friends as much as any of the sons or daughters of affliction. Especially, 2. To see their own prince thus wronged, who had been so great a blessing to their land, and had not done any thing to forfeit the affections of his people; to see him in this distress, and themselves unable to help him, might well draw floods of tears from their eyes.

Verses 24–30

Here we have, I. The fidelity of the priests and Levites and their firm adherence to David and his interest. They knew David's great affection to them and their office, notwithstanding his failings. The method Absalom took to gain people's affections made no impression upon them; he had little religion in him, and therefore they steadily adhered to David. Zadok and Abiathar, and all the Levites, if he go, will accompany him, and take the ark with them, that, by it, they may ask counsel of God for him, *v.* 24. Note, Those that are friends to the ark in their prosperity will find it a friend to them in their adversity. Formerly David would not rest till he had found a resting-place for the ark; and now, if the priests may have their mind, the ark shall not rest till David return to his rest.

II. David's dismission of them back into the city, *v.* 25, 26. Abiathar was high priest (1 Ki. 2:35), but Zadok was his assistant, and attended the ark most closely, while Abiathar was active in public business, *v.* 24. Therefore David directs his speech to Zadok, and an excellent speech it is, and shows him to be in a very good frame under his affliction, and that still he holds fast his integrity. 1. He is very solicitous for the safety of the ark: "By all means *carry the ark back into the city,* let not that be unsettled and exposed with me, lodge that again in the tent pitched for it; surely Absalom, bad as he is, will do that no harm." David's heart, like Eli's trembles for the ark of God. Note, It argues a good principle to be more concerned for the church's prosperity than for our own, to *prefer Jerusalem* before our *chief joy* (Ps. 137:6), the success of the gospel, and the flourishing of the church, above our own wealth, credit, ease, and safety, even when they are most in hazard. 2. He is very desirous to return to the enjoyment of the privileges of God's house. He will reckon it the greatest instance of God's favour to him if he may but once more be brought back to see it and his habitation. This will be more his joy than to be brought back to his own palace and throne again. Note, Gracious souls measure their comforts and conveniences in this world by the opportunity they give them of communion with God. Hezekiah wished for the recovery of his health for this reason, that he might *go up to the house of the Lord,* Isa. 38:22. 3. He is very submissive to the holy will of God concerning the issue of this dark dispensation. He hopes the best (*v.* 25), and hopes for it from the favour of God, which he looks upon to be the fountain of all good: "If God favour me so far, I shall be settled again as formerly." But he provides for the worst: "If he deny me this favour — if he thus say, *I have no delight in thee* — I know I deserve the continuance of his displeasure; his holy will be done." See him here patiently awaiting the event: *"Behold, here am I,* as a servant expecting orders;" and see him willing to commit himself to God concerning it: *"Let him do to me as seemeth good to him.* I have nothing to object. All is well that God does." Observe with what satisfaction and holy complacency he speaks of the divine disposal: not only, "He can do what he will," subscribing to his power (Job 9:12), or, "He has a right to do what he will," subscribing to his sovereignty (Job 33:13), or, "He will do what he will," subscribing to his unchangeableness (Job 23:13, 15), but, *"Let him to what he will,"* subscribing to his wisdom and goodness. Note, It is our interest, as well as duty, cheerfully to acquiesce in the will of God, whatever befals us. That we may not complain of what is, let us see God's hand in all events; and, that we may not be afraid of what shall be, let us see all events in God's hand.

III. The confidence David put in the priests that they would serve his interest to the utmost of their power in his absence. He calls Zadok a *seer* (*v.* 27), that is, a wise man, a man that can see into business and discern time and judgment: "Thou hast thy *eyes in thy head* (Eccl. 2:14), and therefore art capable of doing me service, especially by sending me intelligence of the enemy's motions and resolutions." One friend that is a seer, in such an exigency as this, was worth twenty that were not so quick-sighted. For the settling of a private correspondence with the priests in his absence, he appoints, 1. Whom they should send to him — their two sons, Ahimaaz and Jonathan, whose coat, it might be hoped, would be their protection, and of whose prudence and faithfulness he had probably had experience. 2. Whither they should send. He would encamp *in the plain of the wilderness* till he heard from them (*v.* 28), and then would move according to the information and advice they should send him. Hereupon they returned to the city, to await the event. It was a pity that any disturbance should be given to a state so happy as this was, when the prince and the priests had such an entire affection for the confidence in each other.

IV. The melancholy posture that David and his men put themselves into, when, at the beginning of their march, they went up the *mount of Olives, v.* 30.

1. David himself, as a deep mourner, covered his head and face for shame and blushing, went bare-foot, as a prisoner or a slave, for mortification, and went weeping. Did it become a man of his reputation for courage and greatness of spirit thus to cry like a child, only for fear of an enemy at a distance, against whom he might easily have made head, and perhaps with one bold stroke have routed him? Yes, it did not ill become him, considering how much there was in this trouble, (1.) Of the unkindness of his son. He could not but weep to think that one who came out of his bowels, and had so often lain in his arms, should thus lift up the heel against him. God himself is said to be grieved with the rebellions of his own children (Ps. 95:10) and even *broken with their whorish heart,* Eze. 6:9. (2.) There was much of the displeasure of his God in it. This infused the wormwood and gall into the *affliction and misery,* Lam. 3:19. His sin was *ever before him* (Ps. 51:3), but never so plain nor ever appearing so black as now. He never wept thus when Saul hunted him: but a wounded conscience makes troubles lie heavily, Ps. 38:4.

2. When David wept all his company wept likewise, being much affected with his grief and willing to share in it. It is our duty to *weep with those that weep,* especially our superiors, and those that are better than we; for, *if this be done in the green tree, what will be done in the dry?* We must weep with those that weep for sin. When Hezekiah humbled himself for his sin all Jerusalem joined with him, 2 Chr. 32:26. To prevent suffering with sinners, let us sorrow with them.

Verses 31–37

Nothing, it seems, appeared to David more threatening in Absalom's plot than that Ahithophel was in it; for one good head, in such a design, is worth a thousand good hands. Absalom was himself no politician, but he had got one entirely in his interest that was, and would be the more dangerous because he had been all along acquainted with David's counsels and affairs; if therefore he can be baffled, Absalom is as good as routed and the head of the conspiracy cut off. This David endeavours to do.

I. By prayer. When he heard that Ahithophel was in the plot he lifted up his heart to God in this short prayer: *Lord, turn the counsel of Ahithophel into foolishness, v.* 31. He had not opportunity for a long prayer, but he was not one of those that thought he should be heard for his much speaking. It was a fervent prayer: *"Lord, I pray thee,* do this." God is well pleased with the importunity of those that come to him with their petitions. David is particular in this prayer; he names the person whose counsels he prays against. God gives us leave, in prayer, to be humbly and reverently free with him, and to mention the particular care, and fear, and grief, that lies heavily upon us. David prayed not against Ahithophel's person, but against his counsel, that God would *turn it into foolishness,* that, though he was a wise man, he might at this time give foolish counsel, or, if he gave wise counsel, that it might be rejected as foolish, or, if it were followed, that by some providence or other it might be defeated, and not attain the end. David prayed this in a firm belief that God has all hearts in his hand, and tongues too, that, when he pleases, he can *take away the understanding of the aged and make the judges fools,* (Job 12:17; Isa. 3:2, 3), and in hope that God would own and plead his just and injured cause. Note, We may pray in faith, and should pray with fervency, that God will turn that counsel into foolishness which is taken against his people.

II. By policy. We must second our prayer with our endeavours, else we tempt God. It is good service to countermine the policy of the church's enemies. When David came to the top of the mount, he *worshipped God, v.* 32. Note, Weeping must not hinder worshipping, but quicken it rather. Now he penned the third Psalm, as appears by the title; and some think that his singing this was the worship he now paid to God. Just now Providence brought Hushai to him. While he was yet speaking, God heard, and sent him the person that should be instrumental to befool Ahithophel. He came to condole with David on his present trouble, with his coat rent and earth upon his head; but David, having a great deal of confidence in his conduct and faithfulness, resolved to employ him as a spy upon Absalom. He would not take him with him (*v.* 33), for he had now more need of soldiers than counsellors, but sent him back to Jerusalem, to wait for Absalom's arrival, as a deserter from David, and to offer him his service, *v.* 34. Thus he might insinuate himself into his counsels, and defeat Ahithophel, either by dissuading Absalom from following his advice or by discovering it to David, that he might know where to stand upon his guard. How this gross dissimulation, which David put Hushai upon, can be justified, as a stratagem in war, I do not see. The best that can be made of it is that Absalom, if he rebel against his father, must stand upon his guard against all mankind, and, if he will be deceived, let him be deceived. David recommended Hushai to Zadok and Abiathar, as persons proper to be consulted with (*v.* 35), and to their two sons, as trusty men to be sent on errands to David, *v.* 36. Hushai, thus instructed, came to Jerusalem (*v.* 37), whither also Absalom soon after came with his forces. How soon do royal palaces and royal cities change their masters! But we look for a kingdom which cannot be thus shaken and in the possession of which we cannot be disturbed.

CHAPTER 16

In the close of the foregoing chapter we left David flying from Jerusalem, and Absalom entering into it; in this chapter, I. We are to follow David in his melancholy flight; and there we find him, 1. Cheated by Ziba (*v.* 1–4). 2. Cursed by Shimei, which he bears with wonderful patience (*v.* 5–14). II. We are to meet Absalom in his triumphant entry; and there we find him, 1. Cheated by Hushai (*v.* 15–19). 2. Counselled by Ahithophel to go in unto his father's concubines (*v.* 20–23).

Verses 1–4

We read before how kind David was to Mephibosheth the son of Jonathan, how he prudently entrusted his servant Ziba with the management of his estate, while he generously entertained him at his own table, *ch.* 9:10. This matter was well settled; but, it seems, Ziba is not content to be manager, he longs to be master, of Mephibosheth's estate. Now, he thinks, is his time to make himself so; if he can procure a grant of it from the crown, whether David or Absalom get the better it is all one to him, he hopes he shall secure his prey, which he promises himself by fishing in troubled waters. In order hereunto, 1. He made David a handsome present of provisions, which was the more welcome because it came seasonably (*v.* 1), and with this he designed to incline him to himself; for *a man's gift maketh room for him, and bringeth him before great men,* Prov. 18:16. Nay, *Whithersoever it turneth, it prospereth,* Prov. 17:8. David inferred from this that Ziba was a very discreet and generous man, and well affected to him, when, in all, he designed nothing but to make his own market and to get Mephibosheth's estate settled upon himself. Shall the prospect of advantage in this world make men generous to the rich? and shall not the belief of an abundant recompence in the resurrection of the just make us charitable to the poor? Lu. 14:14. Ziba was very considerate in the present he brought to David; it was what would do him some good in his present distress, *v.* 2. Observe, The wine was intended for those that were faint, not for the king's own drinking, or the courtiers; it seems, they did not commonly use it, but it was for cordials for those *that were ready to perish,* Prov. 31:6. Blessed art thou, O land! when thy princes use wine for strength, as David did, and not for drunkenness, as Absalom did, *ch.* 13:28. See Eccl. 10:17. Whatever Ziba intended in this present, God's providence sent it to David for his support very graciously. God makes use of bad men for good purposes to his people, and sends them meat by ravens. Having by his present insinuated himself into David's affection, and gained credit with him, the next thing he has to do for the compassing of his end is to incense him against Mephibosheth, which he does by a false accusation, representing him as ungratefully designing to raise himself by the present broils, and to recover the crown to his own head, now that David and his son were contending for it. David enquires for him as one of his family, which gives Ziba occasion to tell this false story of him, *v.* 3. What immense damages do masters often sustain by the lying tongues of their servants! David knew Mephibosheth not to be an ambitious man, but easy in his place, and well-affected to him and his government;

nor could he be so weak as to expect with his lame legs to climb the ladder of preferment; yet David gives credit to the calumny, and, without further enquiry or consideration, convicts Mephibosheth of treason, seizes his lands as forfeited, and grants them to Ziba: *Behold, thine are all that pertained to Mephibosheth* (*v.* 4), a rash judgment, and which afterwards he was ashamed of, when the truth came to light, *ch.* 19:29. Princes cannot help it, but they will be sometimes (as our law speaks) deceived in their grants; but they ought to use all means possible to discover the truth and to guard against malicious designing men, who would impose upon them, as Ziba did upon David. Having by his wiles gained his point, Ziba secretly laughed at the king's credulity, congratulated himself on his success, and departed, with a great compliment upon the king, that he valued his favour more than Mephibosheth's estate: "Let me *find grace in thy sight, O king!* and I have enough." Great men ought always to be jealous of flatterers, and remember that nature has given them two ears, that they may hear both sides.

Verses 5–14

We here find how David bore Shimei's curses much better than he had borne Ziba's flatteries. By the latter he was brought to pass a wrong judgment on another, by the former to pass a right judgment on himself. The world's smiles are more dangerous than its frowns. Observe here,

I. How insolent and furious Shimei was, and how his malice took occasion from David's present distress to be so much the more outrageous. David, in his flight, had come to Bahurim, a city of Benjamin in or near which this Shimei lived, who, being of the house of Saul (with the fall of which all his hopes of preferment fell), had an implacable enmity to David, unjustly looking upon him as the ruin of Saul and his family only because, by the divine appointment, he succeeded Saul. While David was in prosperity and power, Shimei hated him as much as he did now, but he durst not then say anything against him. God knows what is in the hearts of those that are disaffected to him and his government, but earthly princes do not. Now he came forth, and cursed David with all the bad words and wishes he could invent, *v.* 5. Observe,

1. Why he took this opportunity to give vent to his malice. (1.) Because now he thought he might do it safely; yet, if David had thought proper to resent the provocation, it would have cost Shimei his life. (2.) Because now it would be most grievous to David, would add affliction to his grief, and pour vinegar into his wounds. He complains of those as most barbarous who *talk to the grief of those whom God has wounded,* Ps. 69:26. So Shimei did, loading him with curses whom no generous eye could look upon without compassion. (3.) Because now he thought that Providence justified his reproaches, and that David's present afflictions proved him to be as bad a man as he was willing to represent him. Job's friends condemned him upon this false principle. Those that are under the rebukes of a gracious God must not think it strange if these bring upon them the reproaches of evil men. If once it be said, *God hath forsaken him,* presently it follows, *Persecute and take him,* Ps. 71:11. But it is the character of a base spirit thus to trample upon those that are down, and insult over them.

2. How his malice was expressed. See, (1.) What this wretched man did: *He cast stones at David* (*v.* 6), as if his king had been a dog, or the worst of criminals, whom all Israel must stone with stones till he die. Perhaps he kept at such a distance that the stones he threw could not reach David, nor any of his attendants, yet he showed what he would have done if it had been in his power. *He cast dust* (*v.* 13), which, probably, would blow into his own eyes, like the curses he threw, which, being causeless, would return upon his own head. Thus, while his malice made him odious, the impotency of it made him ridiculous and contemptible. Those that fight against God cannot hurt him, though they hate him. *If thou sinnest, what doest thou against him?* Job 35:6. It was an aggravation of his wickedness that David was attended with his mighty men on his right hand and on his left, so that he was not in so forlorn a condition as he thought *(persecuted but not forsaken),* and that he continued to do it, and did it the more passionately, for David's bearing it patiently. (2.) What he said. With the stones he shot his arrows, even bitter words (*v.* 7, 8), in contempt of that law, *Thou shalt not curse the gods,* Ex. 22:28. David was a man of honour and conscience, and in great reputation for every thing that was just and good; what could this foul mouth say against him? Why, truly, what was done long since to the house of Saul was the only thing which he could recollect, and with this he upbraided David because it was the thing that he himself was a loser by. See how apt we are to judge of men and their character by what they are to us, and to conclude that those are certainly evil men that have ever so justly been, or that we ever so unjustly think have been, instruments of evil to us. So partial are we to ourselves that no rule can be more fallacious than this. No man could be more innocent of the blood of the house of Saul than David was. Once and again he spared Saul's life, while Saul sought his. When Saul and his sons were slain by the Philistines, David and his men were many miles off; and, when they heard it, they lamented it. From the murder of Abner and Ish-bosheth he had sufficiently cleared himself; and yet all *the blood of the house of Saul* must be laid at his door. Innocency is no fence against malice and falsehood; nor are we to think it strange if we be charged with that from which we have been most careful to keep ourselves. It is well for us that men are not to be our judges, but he whose judgment is according to truth. The blood of the house of Saul is here most unjustly charged upon David, [1.] As that which gave him his character, and denominated him a bloody man and a man of Belial, *v.* 7. And, if a man of blood, no doubt a man of Belial, that is, a child of the devil, who is called *Belial* (2 Co. 6:15), and who was a murderer from the beginning. Bloody men are the worst of men. [2.] As that which brought the present trouble upon him: "Now that thou art dethroned, and driven out to the wilderness, *the Lord has returned upon thee the blood of the house of Saul.*" See how forward malicious men are to press God's judgments into the service of their own passion and revenge. If any who have, as they think, wronged them, should come into trouble, the injury done to them must be made the cause of the trouble. But we must take heed lest we wrong God by making his providence thus to patronise our foolish and unjust resentments. As the *wrath of man works not the righteousness of God,* so the righteousness of God serves not the wrath of man. [3.] As that which would now be his utter ruin; for he endeavours to make him despair of ever recovering his throne again. Now they said, *There is no help for him in God* (Ps. 3:2), *the Lord hath delivered the kingdom into the hand of Absalom* (not Mephibosheth — the house of Saul never dreamed of making *him* king, as Ziba suggested), *and thou art taken in thy mischief,* that is, "the mischief that will be thy destruction, and all because thou art a bloody man." Thus Shimei cursed.

II. See how patient and submissive David was under this abuse. The sons of Zeruiah, Abishai particularly, were forward to maintain David's honour with their swords; they resented the affront keenly, as well they might: *Why should this dead dog* be suffered to *curse the king? v.* 9. If David will but give them leave, they will put these lying cursing lips to silence, and take off his head; for his throwing stones at the king was an overt act, which abundantly proved that he compassed and imagined his death. But the king would by no means suffer it: *What have I to do with you? So let him curse.* Thus Christ rebuked the disciples, who, in zeal for his honour, would have commanded fire from heaven on the town that affronted him, Lu. 9:55. Let us see with what considerations David quieted himself. 1. The chief thing that silenced him was that he had deserved this affliction. This is not mentioned indeed; for a man may truly repent, and yet needs not, upon all occasions, proclaim his penitent reflections. Shimei unjustly upbraided him with the blood of Saul: from *that* his conscience acquitted him, but, at the same time, it charged him with the blood of Uriah. "The reproach is too true" (thinks David), "though false as he means it." Note, A humble tender spirit will turn reproaches into reproofs, and so get good by them, instead of being provoked by them. 2. He observes the hand of God in it: *The Lord hath said unto him, Curse David* (*v.* 10), and again, *So let him curse, for the Lord hath bidden him, v.* 11. As it was Shimei's sin, it was not from God, but from the devil and his own wicked heart, nor did God's hand in it excuse or extenuate it, much less justify it, any more than it did the sin of those who put Christ to death, Acts 2:23, 4:28. But, as it was David's affliction, it was from the Lord, one of the evils which he raised up against him. David looked above the instrument of his trouble to the supreme director, as Job, when the plunderers had stripped him, acknowledged, *The Lord hath taken away.* Nothing more proper to quiet a gracious soul under affliction than an eye to the hand of God in it. *I opened not my mouth, because thou didst it.* The scourge of the tongue is God's rod. 3. He quiets himself under the less affliction with the consideration of the greater (*v.* 11): *My son seeks my life, much more may this Benjamite.* Note, Tribulation works patience in those that are sanctified. The more we bear the better able we should be to bear still more; what tries our patience should improve it. The more we are inured to trouble the less we should be surprised at it, and not think it strange. Marvel not that enemies are injurious, when even friends are unkind; nor that friends are unkind, when even children are undutiful. 4. He comforts himself with hopes that God would, in some way or other, bring good to him out of his affliction, would balance the trouble itself, and recompense his patience under it: *"The Lord will requite me good for his cursing.* If God bid Shimei grieve me, it is that he himself may the more sensibly comfort me; surely he has mercy in store for me, which he is preparing me for by this trial." We may depend upon God as our pay-master, not only for our services, but for our sufferings. *Let them curse, but bless thou.* David, at length, is housed at Bahurim (*v.* 14), where he meets with refreshment, and is hidden from this strife of tongues.

Verses 15–23

Absalom had notice sent him speedily by some of his friends at Jerusalem that David had withdrawn, and with what a small retinue he had gone; so that the coasts were clear, Absalom might take possession of Jerusalem when he pleased. The gates were open, and there was none to oppose him. Accordingly he came without delay (*v.* 15), extremely elevated, no doubt, with this success at first, and that that in which, when he formed his design, he probably apprehended the greatest difficulty, was so easily and effectually done. Now that he is master of Jerusalem he concludes all his own, the country will follow of course. God suffers wicked men to prosper awhile in their wicked plots, even beyond their expectation, that their disappointment may be the more grievous and disgraceful. The most celebrated politicians of that age were Ahithophel and Hushai. The former Absalom brings with him to Jerusalem (*v.* 15), the other meets him there (*v.* 16), so that he cannot but think himself sure of success, when he has both these to be his counsellors; on them he relies, and consults not the ark, though he has that with him. But miserable counsellors were they both; for,

I. Hushai would never counsel him to do wisely. He was really his enemy, and designed to betray him, while he pretended to be in his interest; so that Absalom could not have a more dangerous man about him. 1. Hushai complimented him upon his accession to the throne, as if he had been abundantly satisfied in this title, and well pleased that he had come to the possession, *v.* 16. What arts of dissimulation are those tempted to use who govern themselves by fleshly wisdom! and how happy are those who have not known these depths of Satan, but have their conversation in the world with simplicity and godly sincerity! 2. Absalom was surprised to find *him* for him who was known to be David's intimate friend and confidant. He asks him, *Is this thy kindness to thy friend?* (*v.* 17), pleasing himself with this thought, that all would be his, since Hushai was. He doubts not of his sincerity, but easily believes what he wishes to be true, that David's best friends are so in love with himself as to take the first opportunity to declare for him, *though the pride of his heart deceived him,* Obad. 3. Hushai confirmed him in the belief that he was hearty for him. For, though David is his friend, yet he is for the king in *possession, v.* 18. Whom the people choose, and Providence smiles upon, he will be faithful to; and he is for the king in *succession* (*v.* 19), the rising sun. It was true, he loved his father; but he had had his day, and it was over; and why should he not love his successor as well? Thus he pretended to give reasons for a resolution he abhorred the thought of.

II. Ahithophel counselled him to do wickedly, and so did as effectually betray him as he did who was designedly false to him; for those that advise men to sin certainly advise them to their hurt; and that government which is founded in sin is founded in the sand.

1. It seems, Ahithophel was noted as a deep politician; his counsel was as if a man had enquired at the oracle of God, *v.* 23. Such reputation was he in for subtlety and sagacity in public affairs, such reaches had he beyond other privy-counselors, such reasons would he give for his advice, and such success generally his projects had, that all people, good and bad, both David and Absalom, had a profound regard for his sentiments, too much by far, when they regarded him *as an oracle of God;* shall the prudence of any mortal compare with him who only is wise? Let us observe from this account of Ahithophel's fame for policy, (1.) That many excel in worldly wisdom who are utterly destitute of heavenly grace, because those who set up for oracles themselves are apt to despise the oracles of God. *God has chosen the foolish things of the world;* and the greatest statesmen are seldom the greatest saints. (2.) That frequently the greatest politicians act most foolishly for themselves. Ahithophel was cried up for an oracle, and yet very unwisely took part with Absalom, who was not only a usurper, but a rash youth, never likely to come to good, whose fall, and the fall of all that adhered to him, any one, with the tenth part of the policy that Ahithophel pretended to, might foresee. Well, after all, honesty is the best policy, and will be found so in the long run. But,

2. His policy in this case defeated its own aim. Observe,

(1.) The wicked counsel Ahithophel gave to Absalom. Finding that David had left his concubines to keep the house, he advised him to *lie with them* (*v.* 21), a very wicked thing. The divine law had made it a capital crime, Lev. 20:11. The apostle speaks of it as a piece of villany *not so much as named among the Gentiles,* 1 Co. 5:1. Reuben lost his birthright for it. But Ahithophel advised Absalom to it as a public thing, because it would give assurance to all Israel, [1.] That he was in good earnest in his pretensions. No doubt he resolved to make himself master of all that belonged to his predecessor when he began with his concubines. [2.] That he was resolved never to make peace with his father upon any terms; for by this he would render himself so odious to his father that he would never be reconciled to him, which perhaps the people were jealous of and that they must be sacrificed to the reconciliation. Having drawn the sword, he did, by this provocation, throw away the scabbard, which would strengthen the hands of his party and keep them firmly to him. This was Ahithophel's cursed policy, which bespoke him rather *an oracle of devil than of God.*

(2.) Absalom's compliance with this counsel. It entirely suited his lewd and wicked mind, and he delayed not to put it in execution, *v.* 22. When an unnatural rebellion was the opera, what fitter prologue could there be to it than such unnatural lust? Thus was his wickedness all of a piece, and such as a conscience not quite seared could not entertain the thoughts of without the utmost horror. Nay, the client outdoes what his counsel advises. Ahithophel advised him to do it, that all Israel shall *see* it. A tent is accordingly spread on the top of the house for the purpose; so impudently does he declare his sin as Sodom. Yet, in this, the word of God was fulfilled in the letter of it: God had threatened, by Nathan, that, for defiling Bath-sheba, David should have his own wives publicly debauched (*ch.* 12:11, 12), and some think that Ahithophel, in advising it, designed to be revenged on David for the injury done to Bath-sheba, who was his grand-daughter: for she was the daughter of Eliam (*ch.* 11:3), who was the son of Ahithophel, *ch.* 23:34. Job speaks of this as the just punishment of adultery *(Let my wife grind to another,* Job 31:9, 10), and the prophet, Hos. 4:13, 14. What to think of these concubines, who submitted to this wickedness, I know not; but how unrighteous soever Absalom and they were, we must say, *The Lord is righteous:* nor shall any word of his fall to the ground.

CHAPTER 17

The contest between David and Absalom is now hasting towards a crisis. It must be determined by the sword, and preparation is made accordingly in this chapter. I. Absalom calls a council of war, in which Ahithophel urges despatch (*v.* 1–4), but Hushai recommends deliberation (*v.* 5–13); and Hushai's counsel is agreed to (*v.* 14), for vexation at which Ahithophel hangs himself (*v.* 23). II. Secret intelligence is sent to David (but with much difficulty) of their proceedings (*v.* 15–21). III. David marches to the other side Jordan (*v.* 22–24), and there his camp is victualled by some of his friends in that country (*v.* 27–29). IV. Absalom and his forces march after him into the land of Gilead on the other side Jordan (*v.* 25, 26). There we shall, in the next chapter, find the cause decided by a battle: hitherto, every thing has looked black upon poor David, but now the day of his deliverance begins to dawn.

Verses 1–14

Absalom is now in peaceable possession of Jerusalem; the palace-royal is his own, as are *the thrones of judgment, even the thrones of the house of David.* His good father reigned in Hebron, and only over the tribe of Judah, above seven years, and was not hasty to destroy his rival; his government was built upon a divine promise, the performance of which he was sure of in due time, and therefore he waited patiently in the mean time. But the young man, Absalom, not only hastens from Hebron to Jerusalem, but is impatient there till he has destroyed his father, cannot be content with his throne till he has his life; for his government is founded in iniquity, and therefore feels itself tottering and thinks itself obliged to do every thing with violence. That so profligate a wretch as Absalom should aim at the life of so good a father is not so strange (there are here and there monsters in nature); but that the body of the people of Israel, to whom David had been so great a blessing in all respects, should join with him in his attempt, is very amazing. But their fathers often mutinied against Moses. The best of parents, and the best of princes will not think it strange if they be made uneasy by those who should be their support and joy, when they consider what sons and what subjects David himself had.

David and all that adhered to him must be cut off. This was resolved, for aught that appears, *nemine contradicente — unanimously.* None durst mention his personal merits, and the great services done to his country, in opposition to this resolve, nor so much as ask, *"Why, what evil has he done* to forfeit his crown, much less his head?" None durst propose that his banishment should suffice, for the present, nor that agents should be sent to treat with him to resign the crown, which, having so tamely quitted the city, they might think he would easily be persuaded to do. It was not long since that Absalom himself fled for a crime, and David contented himself with his being an exile, though he deserved death, nay, he mourned and longed for him; but so perfectly void of all natural affection is this ungrateful Absalom that he eagerly thirsts after his own father's blood. It is past dispute that David must be destroyed; all the question is how he may be destroyed.

I. Ahithophel advises that he be pursued immediately, this very night, with a flying army (which he himself undertakes the command of), that the king only be smitten and his forces dispersed, and then the people that were now for him would fall in with Absalom of course, and there would not be such a long war as had been between the house of Saul and David: *The man whom thou seekest is as if all returned, v.* 1–3. By this it appears that Absalom had declared his design to be upon David's life, and Ahithophel concurs with him in it. *Smite the shepherd, and the sheep will be scattered,* and be an easy prey to the wolf. Thus he contrives to include the war in a little compass, by fighting neither with small nor great but the king of Israel only, and to conclude it in a little time, by falling upon him immediately. Nothing could be more fatal to David than the taking of these measures. It was too true that he was weary and weak-handed, that a little thing would make him afraid, else he would not have fled from his house upon the first alarm of Absalom's rebellion; it was probable enough that upon a fierce attack, especially in the night, the small force he had would be put into confusion and disorder, and it would bean easy thing to *smite the king only,* and then the business would be done, the whole nation would be reduced, of course, and *all the people,* says he, *shall be in peace.* See how a general ruin is called by usurpers a *general peace;* but thus the devil's palace is in peace, while he, as a strong man armed, keeps it. Compare with this the plot of Caiaphas (that second Ahithophel) against the Son of David, to crush his interest by destroying him. Let that *one man die for the people,* Jn. 11:50. *Kill the heir, and the inheritance shall be ours,* Mt. 21:38. But the counsel of them both was turned into foolishness. Yet the children of light may, in their generation, learn wisdom from the children of this world. What our hand finds to do let us do quickly, and with all our might. It is prudence to be vigorous and expeditious, and not to lose time, particularly in our spiritual warfare. If Satan flee from us, let us follow our blow. Those that have quarrelled with crowned heads have generally observed the decorum of declaring only against their evil counsellors, and calling them to an account *(The king himself can do no wrong,* it is they that do it); but Absalom's barefaced villany strikes at the king directly, nay, at the king only; for (would you think it?) this saying, *I will smite the king only,* pleased Absalom well (*v.* 4), nor had he so much sense of humor and virtue left him to pretend to startle at it or even to be reluctant in this barbarous and monstrous resolution. What good can stand before the heat of a furious ambition?

II. Hushai advises that they be not too hasty in pursuing David, but take time to draw up all their force against him, and to overpower him with numbers, as Ahithophel had advised to take him by surprise. Now Hushai, in giving this counsel, really intended to serve David and his interest, that he might have time to send him notice of his proceedings, and that David might gain time to gather an army and to remove into those countries beyond Jordan, in which, lying more remote, Absalom had probably least interest. Nothing would be of greater advantage to David in this juncture than time to turn himself in; that he may have this, Hushai counsels Absalom to do nothing rashly, but to proceed with caution and secure his success by securing his strength. Now,

1. Absalom gave Hushai a fair invitation to advise him. All the elders of Israel approved of Ahithophel's counsel, yet God overruled the heart of Absalom not to proceed upon it, till he had consulted Hushai (*v.* 5): *Let us hear what he saith.* Herein he thought he did wisely (two heads are better than one), but God taketh the wise in their own craftiness. See Mr. Poole's note on this.

2. Hushai gave very plausible reasons for what he said. (1.) He argued against Ahithophel's counsel, and undertook to show the danger of following his advice. It is with modesty, and all possible deference to Ahithophel's settled reputation, that he begs leave to differ from him, *v.* 7. He acknowledges that the counsel of Ahithophel is usually the best, and such as may be relied on; but, with submission to that noble peer, he is of opinion that his counsel is not good at this time, and that it is by no means safe to venture so great a cause as that in which they are now engaged upon so small a number, and such a hasty sally, as Ahithophel advises, remembering the defeat of Israel before Ai, Jos. 7:4. It has often proved of bad consequence to despise an enemy. See how plausibly Hushai reasoned. [1.] He insisted much upon it that David was a great soldier, a man of great conduct, courage, and experience; all knew and owned this, even Absalom himself: *"Thy father is a man of war* (*v.* 8), *a mighty man* (*v.* 10), and not so weary and weak-handed as Ahithophel imagines. His retiring from Jerusalem must be imputed, not to his cowardice, but his prudence." [2.] His attendants, though few, were mighty men (*v.* 8), valiant men (*v.* 10), men of celebrated bravery and versed in all the arts of war. Ahithophel, who perhaps had worn the gown more than the sword, would find himself an unequal match for them. *One of them would chase a thousand.* [3.] They were all exasperated against Absalom, who was the author of all this mischief, were chafed in their minds, and would fight with the utmost fury; so that, what with their courage, and what with their rage, there would be no standing before them, especially for such raw soldiers as Absalom's generally were. Thus did he represent them as formidable as Ahithophel had made them despicable. [4.] He suggested that probably David and some of his men would lie in ambush, in some pit, or other close place, and fall upon Absalom's soldiers before they were aware the terror of which would put them to flight; and the defeat, though but of a small party, would dispirit all the rest, especially their own consciences at the same time accusing them of treason against one that, they were sure, was not only God's anointed, *but a man after his own heart, v.* 9. "It will soon be given out that there is a slaughter among Absalom's men, and then they will all make the best of their way, and the heart of Ahithophel himself, though now it seems like the heart of a lion, will utterly melt. In short, he will not find it so

easy a matter to deal with David and his men as he thinks it is; and, if he be foiled, we shall all be routed."

(2.) He offered his own advice, and gave his reasons; and, [1.] He counselled that which he knew would gratify Absalom's proud vain-gloriuos humour, though it would not be really serviceable to his interest. *First,* He advised that all Israel should be gathered together, that is, the militia of all the tribes. His taking it for granted that they are all for him, and giving him an opportunity to see them all together under his command, would gratify him as much as any thing. *Secondly,* He advises that Absalom go to battle in his own person, as if he looked upon him to be a better soldier than Ahithophel, more fit to give command and have the honour of the victory, insinuating that Ahithophel had put a slight upon him in offering to go without him. See how easy it is to betray proud men, by applauding them, and feeding their pride. [2.] He counselled that which seemed to secure the success, at last, infallibly, without running any hazard. For, if they could raise such vast numbers as they promised themselves, wherever they found David they could not fail to crush him. *First,* If in the field, they should fall upon him, as the dew that covers the face of the ground, and cut off all his men with him, *v.* 12. Perhaps Absalom was better pleased with the design of cutting off all the men that were with him, having a particular antipathy to some of David's friends, than with Ahithophel's project of smiting the king only. Thus Hushai gained his point by humouring his revenge, as well as his pride. *Secondly,* If in a city, they need not fear conquering him, for they should have hands enough, if occasion were, to draw the city itself into its river with ropes, *v.* 13. This strange suggestion, how impracticable soever, being new, served for an amusement, and recommended itself by pleasing the fancy, for they would all smile at the humour of it.

(3.) By all these arts, Hushai gained not only Absalom's approbation of his advice, but the unanimous concurrence of this great counsel of war; they all agreed that the counsel of Hushai was better than the counsel of Ahithophel, *v.* 14. See here, [1.] How much the policy of man can do; If Hushai had not been there, Ahithophel's counsel would certainly have prevailed; and, though all had given their opinion, nothing could be really more for Absalom's interest than that which he advised; yet Hushai, with his management, brings them all over to his side, and none of them are aware that he says all this in favour of David and his interest, but all say as he says. See how the unthinking are imposed upon by the designing part of mankind; what tools, what fools, great men make of one another by their intrigues; and what tricks there are often in courts and councils, which those are happiest that are least conversant with. [2.] See how much more the providence of God can do. Hushai managed the plot with dexterity, yet the success is ascribed to God, and his agency on the minds of those concerned: *The Lord had appointed to defeat the good counsel of* Ahithophel. Be it observed, to the comfort of all that fear God, he turns all men's hearts as the rivers of water, though *they know not the thoughts of the Lord. He stands in the congregation of the mighty,* has an overruling hand in all counsels and a negative voice in all resolves, and laughs at men's projects against his anointed.

Verses 15–21

We must now leave David's enemies pleasing themselves with the thoughts of a sure victory by following Hushai's counsel, and sending a summons, no doubt, to all the tribes of Israel, to come to the general rendezvous at a place appointed, pursuant to that counsel; and we next find David's friends consulting how to get him notice of all this, that he might steer his course accordingly. Hushai tells the priests what had passed in council, *v.* 15. But, it should seem, he was not sure but that yet Ahithophel's counsel might be followed, and was therefore jealous lest, if he made not the best of his way, the king would be *swallowed up, and all the people that were with him, v.* 16. Perhaps, as he was called in to give advice (*v.* 5), so he was dismissed before they came to that resolve (*v.* 14) in favour of his advice, or he feared they might afterwards change their mind. However, it was good to provide against the worst, and therefore to hasten those valuable lives out of the reach of these destroyers. Such strict guards did Absalom set upon all the avenues to Jerusalem that they had much ado to get this necessary intelligence to David. 1. The young priests that were to be the messengers were forced to retire secretly out of the city, by *En-rogel,* which signifies, as some say, *the fountain of a spy.* Surely it went ill with Jerusalem when two such faithful priests as they were might not be seen to come into the city. 2. Instructions were sent to them by a poor simple young woman, who probably went to that well under pretence of fetching water, *v.* 17. If she carried the message by word of mouth, there was danger of her making some mistake or blunder in it; but Providence can make an ignorant girl a trusty messenger, and serve its wise counsels by the foolish things of the world. 3. Yet, by the vigilance of Absalom's spies, they were discovered, and information was brought to Absalom of their motions: *A lad saw them and told him, v.* 18. 4. They, being aware that they were discovered, sheltered themselves in a friend's house in Bahurim, where David had refreshed himself but just before, *ch.* 16:14. There they were happily hidden in a well, which now, in summer time, perhaps was dry, *v.* 18. The woman of the house very ingeniously covered the mouth of the well with a cloth, on which she spread corn to dry, so that the pursuers were not aware that there was a well; else they would have searched it, *v.* 19. Thus far the woman did well; but we know not how to justify her further concealing them with a lie, *v.* 20. We must not do evil that good may come of it. However, hereby the messengers were protected, and the pursuers were defeated and returned to Absalom without their prey. It was well that Absalom did not hereupon fall upon their two fathers, Zadok and Abiathar, as Saul on Ahimelech for his kindness to David: but God restrained him. Being thus preserved, they brought their intelligence very faithfully to David (*v.* 21), with this advice of his friends, that he should not delay to pass over Jordan, near to which, it seems, he now was. There, as some think, he penned the 42nd and 43rd Psalms, looking back upon *Jerusalem from the land of Jordan,* Ps. 42:6.

Verses 22–29

Here is, I. The transporting of David and his forces over Jordan, pursuant to the advice he had received from his friends at Jerusalem, *v.* 22. He, and all that were with him, went over in the night, whether in ferryboats, which probably always plied there, or through the fords, does not appear. But special notice is taken of this, that there lacked not one of them: none deserted him, though his distress was great, none staid behind sick or weary, nor were any lost or cast away in passing the river. Herein some make him a type of the Messiah, who said, in a difficult day, *Of all that thou hast given me have I lost none.* Having got over Jordan, he marched many miles forward to Mahanaim, a Levites' city in the tribe of Gad, in the utmost border of that tribe, and not far from Rabbah, the chief city of the Ammonites. This city, which Ishbosheth had made his royal city (*ch.* 2:8), David now made his head-quarters, *v.* 24. And now he had time to raise an army wherewith to oppose the rebels and give them a warm reception.

II. The death of Ahithophel, *v.* 23. He died by his own hands, *felo de se — a suicide.* He hanged himself for vexation that his counsel was not followed; for thereby, 1. He thought himself slighted, and an intolerable slur cast upon his reputation for wisdom. His judgment always used to sway at the counsel-board, but now another's opinion is thought wiser and better than his. His proud heart cannot bear the affront; it rises and swells, and the more he thinks of it the more violent his resentments grow, till they bring him at last to this desperate resolve not to live to see another preferred before him. All men think him a wise man, but he thinks himself the only wise man; and therefore to be avenged upon mankind for not thinking so too, he will die, that wisdom may die with him. The world is not worthy of such an oracle as he is, and therefore he will make them know the want of him. See what real enemies those are to themselves that think too well of themselves, and what mischiefs those run upon that are impatient of contempt. That will break a proud man's heart that will not break a humble man's sleep. 2. He thought himself endangered and his life exposed. He concluded that, because his counsel was not followed, Absalom's cause would certainly miscarry, and then, whoever would find David's mercy, he concluded that he, who was the greatest criminal, and had particularly advised him to lie with his father's concubines, must be sacrificed to justice. To prevent therefore the shame and terror of a public and solemn execution, he does justice upon himself, and, after his reputation for wisdom, by this last act puts a far greater disgrace upon himself than Absalom's privy-council had put upon him, and answers his name *Ahithophel,* which signifies, *the brother of a fool.* Nothing indicates so much folly as self-murder. Observe, How deliberately he did it, and of malice prepense against himself; not in a heat, but he went home to his city, to his house, to do it; and, which is strange, took time to consider of it, and yet did it. And, to prove himself *compos mentis — in his senses,* when he did it, he first put his household in order, made his will as a man of sane memory and understanding, settled his estate, balanced his accounts; yet he that had sense and prudence enough to do this had not consideration enough to revoke the sentence his pride and passion had passed upon his own neck, nor so much as to suspend the execution of it till he saw the event of Absalom's rebellion. Now herein we may see, (1.) Contempt poured upon the wisdom of man. He that was more renowned for policy than any man played the fool with himself more abundantly. *Let not the wise man glory in his wisdom,* when he sees him that was so great an oracle dying *as a fool dies.* (2.) Honour done to the justice of God. When the wicked are thus *snared in the work of their own hands, and sunk in a pit of their own digging, the Lord is known by the judgment which he executeth,* and we must say, *Higgaion, Selah;* it is a thing to be marked and meditated upon, Ps. 7:15, 16. (3.) Prayer answered, and an honest cause served even by its enemies. Now, as David had prayed, Ahithophel's counsel was *turned into foolishness to himself.* Dr. Lightfoot supposes that David penned the 55th Psalm upon occasion of Ahithophel's being in the plot against him, and that he is the man complained of (*v.* 13) that had been *his equal, his guide, and his acquaintance;* and, if so, this was an immediate answer to his prayer there (*v.* 15): *Let death seize upon them, and let them go down quickly into hell.* Ahithophel's death was an advantage to David's interest; for had he digested that affront (as those must resolve often to do that will live in this world), and continued his post at Absalom's elbow, he might have given him counsel afterwards that might have been of pernicious consequence to David. It is well that that breath is stopped and that head laid from which nothing could be expected but mischief. It seems, it was not then usual to disgrace the dead bodies of self-murderers, for Ahithophel was *buried,* we may suppose honourably buried, *in the sepulchre of his father,* though he deserved no better than the *burial of an ass.* See Eccl. 8:10.

III. Absalom's pursuit of his father. He had now got all the men of Israel with him, as Hushai advised, and he himself, at the head of them, *passed over Jordan, v.* 24. Not content that he had driven his good father to the utmost corner of his kingdom, he resolved to chase him out of the world. He *pitched in the land of Gilead* with all his forces, ready to give David battle, *v.* 26. Absalom made one Amasa his general (*v.* 25), whose father was by birth Jether, an Ishmaelite (1 Chr. 2:17), but by religion Ithra (as he is here called), an Israelite; probably he was not only proselyted, but, having married a near relation of David's, was, by some act of the state, naturalized, and is therefore called an Israelite. His wife, Amasa's mother, was Abigail, David's sister, whose other sister, Zeruiah, was Joab's mother (1 Chr. 2:16), so that Amasa was in the same relation to David that Joab was. In honour to his family, even while he was in arms against his father, Absalom made him commander-in-chief of all his forces. Jesse is here called *Nahash,* for many had two names; or perhaps this was his wife's name.

IV. The friends David met with in this distant country. Even Shobi, a younger brother of the royal family of the Ammonites, was kind to him, *v.* 27. It is probable that he had detested the indignity which his brother Hanun had done to David's ambassadors, and for that had received favours from David, which he now returned. Those that think their prosperity most confirmed know not but, some time or other, they may stand in need of the kindness of those that now lie at their mercy, and may be glad to be beholden to them, which is a reason why we should, as we have opportunity, *do good to all men,* for *he that wa-*

tereth shall be watered also himself, when there is occasion. Machir, the son of Ammiel, was he that maintained Mephibosheth (*ch.* 9:4), till David eased him of that charge, and is now repaid for it by that generous man, who, it seems, was the common patron of distressed princes. Barzillai we shall hear of again. These, compassionating David and his men, now that they were weary with a long march, brought him furniture for his house, *beds and basins,* and provision for his table, *wheat and barley,* etc., *v.* 28, 29. He did not put them under contribution, did not compel them to supply him, much less plunder them; but in token of their dutiful affection to him, and their sincere concern for him in his present straits, of their own good will they brought in plenty of all that which he had occasion for. Let us learn hence to be generous and open-handed, according as our ability is, to all in distress, especially great men, to whom it is most grievous, and good men, who deserve better treatment; and see how God sometimes makes up to his people that comfort from strangers which they are disappointed of in their own families.

CHAPTER 18

This chapter puts a period to Absalom's rebellion and life, and so makes way for David to his throne again, whither the next chapter brings him back in peace and triumph. We have here, I. David's preparations to engage the rebels (*v.* 1–5). II. The total defeat of Absalom's party and their dispersion (*v.* 6–8). III. The death of Absalom, and his burial (*v.* 9–18). IV. The bringing of the tidings to David, who tarried at Mahanaim (*v.* 19–32). V. His bitter lamentation for Absalom (*v.* 33).

Verses 1–8

Which way David raised an army here, and what reinforcements were sent him, we are not told; many, it is likely, from all the coasts of Israel, at least from the neighbouring tribes, came in to his assistance, so that, by degrees, he was able to make head against Absalom, as Ahithophel foresaw. Now here we have,

I. His army numbered and marshalled, *v.* 1, 2. He had, no doubt, committed his cause to God by prayer, for that was his relief in all his afflictions; and then he took an account of his forces. Josephus says they were, in all, but about 4000. These he divided into regiments and companies, to each of which he appointed proper officers, and then disposed them, as is usual, into the right wing, the left wing, and the centre, two of which he committed to his two old experienced generals, Joab and Abishai, and the third to his new friend Ittai. Good order and good conduct may sometimes be as serviceable in an army as great numbers. Wisdom teaches us to make the best of the strength we have, and let it reach to the utmost.

II. Himself over-persuaded not to go in person to the battle. He was Absalom's false friend that persuaded him to go, and served his pride more than his prudence; David's true friends would not let him go, remembering what they had been told of Ahithophels's design to *smite the king only.* David showed his affection to them by being willing to venture with them (*v.* 2), and they showed theirs to him by opposing it. We must never reckon it an affront to be gain-said for our good, and by those that therein consult our interest. 1. They would by no means have him to expose himself, for (say they) *thou art worth* 10,000 *of us.* Thus ought princes to be valued by their subjects, who, for their safety, must be willing to expose themselves. 2. They would not so far gratify the enemy, who would rejoice more in his fall than in the defeat of the whole army. 3. He might be more serviceable to them by tarrying in the city, with a reserve of his forces there, whence he might send them recruits. That may be a post of real service which yet is not a post of danger. The king acquiesced in their reasons, and changed his purpose (*v.* 4): *What seemeth to you best I will do.* It is no piece of wisdom to be stiff in our resolutions, but to be willing to hear reason, even from our inferiors, and to be overruled by their advice when it appears to be for our own good. Whether the people's prudence had an eye to it or no, God's providence wisely ordered it, that David should not be in the field of battle; for then his tenderness would certainly have interposed to save the life of Absalom, whom God had determined to destroy.

III. The charge he gave concerning Absalom, *v.* 5. When the army was drawn out, rank and file, Josephus says, he encouraged them, and prayed for them, but withal bade them all take heed of doing Absalom any hurt. How does he render good for evil! Absalom would have David only smitten. David would have Absalom only spared. What foils are these to each other! Never was unnatural hatred to a father more strong than in Absalom; nor was ever natural affection to a child more strong than in David. Each did his utmost, and showed what man is capable of doing, how bad it is possible for a child to be to the best of fathers and how good it is possible for a father to be to the worst of children; as if it were designed to be a resemblance of man's wickedness towards God and God's mercy towards man, of which it is hard to say which is more amazing. *"Deal gently,"* says David, "by all means, *with the young man, even with Absalom, for my sake;* he is a young man, rash and heady, and his age must excuse him; he is mine, whom I love; if you love me, be not severe with him." This charge supposes David's strong expectation of success. Having a good cause and a good God, he doubts not but Absalom would lie at their mercy, and therefore bids them deal gently with him, spare his life and reserve him for his judgment.

Bishop Hall thus descants on this: "What means this ill-placed love? This unjust mercy? Deal gently with a traitor? Of all traitors, with a son? Of all sons, with an Absalom? That graceless darling of so good a father? And all this, for thy sake, whose crown, whose blood, he hunts after? For whose sake must he be pursued, if forborne for thine? Must the cause of the quarrel be the motive of mercy? Even in the holiest parents, nature may be guilty of an injurious tenderness, of a bloody indulgence. But was not this done in type of that immeasurable mercy of the true King and Redeemer of Israel, who prayed for his persecutors, for his murderers, *Father, forgive them? Deal gently with them for my sake.*" When God sends and affliction to correct his children, it is with this charge, "Deal gently with them for my sake;" for he knows our frame.

IV. A complete victory gained over Absalom's forces. The battle was fought *in the wood of Ephraim* (*v.* 6), so called from some memorable action of the Ephraimites there, though it lay in the tribe of Gad. David thought fit to meet the enemy with his forces at some distance, before they came up to Mahanaim, lest he should bring that city into trouble which had so kindly sheltered him. The cause shall be decided by a pitched battle. Josephus represents the fight as very obstinate, but the rebels were at length totally routed and 20,000 of them slain, *v.* 7. Now they smarted justly for their treason against their lawful prince, their uneasiness under so good a government, and their base ingratitude to so good a governor; and they found what it was to take up arms for a usurper, who with his kisses and caresses had wheedled them into their own ruin. Now where are the rewards, the preferments, the golden days, they promised themselves from him? Now they see what it is to take counsel *against the Lord and his anointed,* and to think of *breaking his bands asunder.* And that they might see that God fought against them, 1. They are conquered by a few, an army, in all probability, much inferior to theirs in number. 2. By that flight with which they hoped to save themselves they destroyed themselves. *The wood,* which they sought to for shelter, *devoured more than the sword,* that they might see how, when they thought themselves safe from David's men, and said, *Surely the bitterness of death is past,* yet the justice of God pursued them and suffered them not to live. What refuge can rebels find from divine vengeance? The pits and bogs, the stumps and thickets, and, as the Chaldee paraphrase understands it, the wild beasts of the wood, were probably the death of multitudes of the dispersed distracted Israelites, besides the 20,000 that were slain with the sword. God herein fought for David, and yet fought against him; for all these that were slain were his own subjects, and the common interest of his kingdom was weakened by the slaughter. The Romans allowed no triumph for a victory in a civil war.

Verses 9–18

Here is Absalom quite at a loss, at his wit's end first, and then at his life's end. He that began the fight, big with the expectation of triumphing over David himself, with whom, if he had had him in his power, he would not have dealt gently, is now in the greatest consternation, when he *meets the servants of David, v.* 9. Though they were forbidden to meddle with him, he durst not look them in the face; but, finding they were near him, he clapped spurs to his mule and made the best of his way, through thick and thin, and so rode headlong upon his own destruction. Thus *he that fleeth from the fear shall fall into the pit, and he that getteth up out of the pit shall be taken in the snare,* Jer. 48:44. David is inclined to spare him, but divine justice passes sentence upon him as a traitor, and sees it executed — that he hang by the neck, be caught alive, be embowelled, and his body dispose of disgracefully.

I. He is hanged by the neck. Riding furiously, neck or nothing, *under the thick boughs of a great oak* which hung low and had never been cropped, either the twisted branches, or some one forked bough of the oak, caught hold of his head, either by his neck, or, as some think, by his long hair, which had been so much his pride, and was now justly made a halter for him, and there he hung, so astonished that he could not use his hands to help himself or so entangled that his hands could not help him, but the more he struggled the more he was embarrassed. This set him up for a fair mark to the servants of David, and he had the terror and shame of seeing himself thus exposed, while he could do nothing for his own relief, neither fight nor fly. Observe concerning this, 1. That his *mule went away* from *under him,* as if glad to get clear of such a burden, and resign it to the ignominious tree. Thus the whole creation groans under the burden of man's corruption, but shall shortly be delivered from its load, Rom. 8:21, 22. 2. The he hung *between heaven and earth,* as unworthy of either, as abandoned of both; earth would not keep him, heaven would not take him, hell therefore opens her mouth to receive him. 3. That this was a very surprising unusual thing. It was fit that it should be so, his crime being so monstrous: if, in his flight, his mule had thrown him, and left him half-dead upon the ground, till the servants of David had come up and dispatched him, the same thing would have been done as effectually; but that would have been too common a fate for so uncommon a criminal. God will here, as in the case of those other rebels, Dathan and Abiram, *create a new thing,* that it may be understood how much *this man has provoked the Lord,* Num. 16:29, 30. Absalom is here hung up, *in terrorem — to frighten* children from disobedience *to their parents.* See Prov. 30:17.

II. He is caught alive by one of the servants of David, who goes directly and tells Joab in what posture he found that archrebel, *v.* 10. Thus was he set up for a spectacle, as well as a mark, that the righteous might see him and *laugh at him* (ps. 52:6), while he had this further vexation in his breast, that of all the friends he had courted and confided in, and thought he had sure in his interest, though he hung long enough to have been relieved, yet he had none at hand to disentangle him. Joab chides the man for not dispatching him (*v.* 11), telling him, if he had given that bold stroke, he would have rewarded him with ten half-crowns and a girdle, that is, a captain's commission, which perhaps was signified by the delivery of a belt or girdle; see Isa. 22:21. But the man, though zealous enough against Absalom, justified himself in not doing it: "Dispatch him!" says he, "not for all the world: it would have cost my head: and thou thyself wast witness to the king's charge concerning him (*v.* 12), and, for all thy talk, wouldst have been my prosecutor if I had done it," *v.* 13. Those that love the treason hate the traitor. Joab could not deny this, nor blame the man for his caution, and therefore makes him no answer, but breaks off the discourse, under colour of haste (*v.* 14): *I may not tarry thus with thee.* Superiors should consider a reproof before they give it, lest they be ashamed of it afterwards, and find themselves unable to make it good.

III. He is (as I may say) embowelled and quartered, as traitors are, so pitifully mangled is he as he hangs there, and receives his death in such a manner as to see all its terrors and feel all its pain. 1. Joab throws three darts into his body, which put him, no doubt, to exquisite torment, while he is yet *alive in the midst of the oak, v.* 14. I know not whether Joab can be justified in this direct disobedience to the command of his sovereign; was this to *deal gently with the young man?* Would David have suffered him to do it if he had been upon the spot? Yet this may be said for him, that, while he broke the order of a too indulgent father, he did real service both to his king and country, and would have endangered welfare of both if he had not done it. *Salus populi suprema lex — The safety of the people is the supreme law.* 2. Joab's young men, ten of them, smite him, before he is dispatched, v. 15. They surrounded him, made a ring about him in triumph, and then *smote him and slew him.* So *let all they enemies perish, O Lord!* Joab hereupon sounds a retreat, v. 16. The danger is over, now that Absalom is slain; the people will soon return to their allegiance to David, and therefore no more blood shall be spilt; no prisoners are taken, to be tried as traitors and made examples; let every man return to his tent; they are all the king's subjects, all his good subjects again.

IV. His body is disposed of disgracefully (v. 17, 18): They *cast it into a great pit in the wood;* they would not bring it to his father (for that circumstance would but have added to his grief), nor would they preserve it to be buried, according to his order, but threw it into the next pit with indignation. Now where is the beauty he had been so proud of and for which he had been so much admired? Where are his aspiring projects, and the castles he had built in the air? His thoughts perish, and he with them. And, to signify how heavy *his iniquity lay upon his bones,* as the prophet speaks (Eze. 32:27), they raised a *great heap of stones upon him,* to be a monument of his villany, and to signify that he ought to have been stoned as a rebellious son, Deu. 21:21. Travelers say that the place is taken note of to this day, and that it is common for passengers to throw a stone to this heap, with words to this purport: *Cursed be the memory of rebellious Absalom, and cursed for ever be all wicked children that rise up in rebellion against their parents.* To aggravate the ignominy of Absalom's burial, the historian takes notice of a pillar he had erected in the valley of Kidron, near Jerusalem, to be a monument for himself, and keep his name in remembrance (v. 18), at the foot of which, it is probable, he designed to be buried. What foolish insignificant projects do proud men fill their heads with! And what care do many people take about the disposal of their bodies, when they are dead, that have no care at all what shall become of their precious souls! Absalom had three sons (ch. 14:27), but, it seems, now he had none; God had taken them away by death; and justly is a rebellious son written childless. To make up the want, he erects this pillar for a memorial; yet in this also Providence crosses him, and a rude heap of stones shall be his monument, instead of this marble pillar. Thus *those that exalt themselves shall be abased.* His care was to have his name kept in remembrance, and it is so, to his everlasting dishonour. He could not be content in the obscurity of the rest of David's sons, of whom nothing is recorded but their names, but would be famous, and is therefore justly made for ever infamous. The pillar shall bear his name, but not to his credit; it was designed for Absalom's glory, but proved Absalom's folly.

Verses 19–33

Absalom's business is done; and we are now told,

I. How David was informed of it. He staid behind at the city of Mahanaim, some miles from the wood where the battle was, and in the ·utmost border of the land. Absalom's scattered forces all made homeward toward Jordan, which was the contrary way from Mahanaim, so that his watchmen could not perceive how the battle went, till an express came on purpose to bring advice of the issue, which the king sat in the gate expecting to hear, v. 24.

1. Cushi was the man Joab ordered to carry the tidings (v. 21), an *Ethiopian,* so his name signifies, and some think that he was so by birth, a black that waited on Joab, probably one of the ten that had helped to dispatch Absalom (v. 15) as some think, though it was dangerous for one of those to bring the news to David, lest his fate should be the same with theirs that reported to him Saul's death, and Ish-bosheth's.

2. Ahimaaz, the young priest (one of those who brought David intelligence of Absalom's motions, *ch.* 17:17), was very forward to be the messenger of these tidings, so transported was he with joy that this cloud was blown over; let him go and tell the king that *the Lord hath avenged him of his enemies, v.* 19. This he desired, not so much in hope of a reward (he was above that) as that he might have the pleasure and satisfaction of bringing the king, whom he loved, this good news. Joab knew David better than Ahimaaz did, and that the tidings of Absalom's death, which must conclude the story, would spoil the acceptableness of all the rest; and he loves Ahimaaz too well to

let him be the messenger of those tidings (v. 20); they are fitter to be brought by a footman than by a priest. However, when Cushi was gone, Ahimaaz begged hard for leave to run after him, and with great importunity obtained it, v. 22, 23. One would wonder why he should be so fond of this office, when another was employed in it. (1.) Perhaps it was to show his swiftness; observing how heavily Cushi ran, and that he took the worse way, though the nearest, he had a mind to show how fast he could run, and that he could go the furthest way about and yet beat Cushi. No great praise for a priest to be swift of foot, yet perhaps Ahimaaz was proud of it. (2.) Perhaps it was in prudence and tenderness to the king that he desired it. He knew he could get before Cushi, and therefore was willing to prepare the king, by a vague and general report, for the plain truth which Cushi was ordered to tell him. If bad news must come, it is best that it come gradually, and will be the better borne.

3. They are both discovered by the watchman on the gate of Mahanaim, Ahimaaz first (v. 24), for, though Cushi had the lead, Ahimaaz soon outran him; but presently after Cushi appeared, v. 26. (1.) When the king hears of one running alone he concludes he is an express (v. 25): *If he be alone, there are tidings in his mouth;* for if they had been beaten, and were flying back from the enemy, there would have been many. (2.) When he hears it is Ahimaaz he concludes he brings good news, v. 27. Ahimaaz, it seems, was so famous for running that he was known by it at a distance, and so eminently good that it is taken for granted, if he be the messenger, the news must needs be good: *He is a good man,* zealously affected to the king's interest, and would not bring bad news. It is pity but the good tidings of the gospel should always be brought by good men; and how welcome should the messengers be to us for their message sake!

4. Ahimaaz is very forward to proclaim the victory (v. 28), cries at a distance, "Peace, there is peace;" peace after war, which is doubly welcome. *"All is well,* my lord O king! the danger is over, and we may return, when the king pleases, to Jerusalem." And, when he comes near, he tells him the news more particularly. "They are all cut off *that lifted up their hands against the king;"* and, as became a priest, while he gives the king the joy of it, he gives God the glory of it, the God of peace and war, the God of salvation and victory: *"Blessed be the Lord thy God,* that has done this for thee, as thy God, pursuant to the promises made to uphold thy throne," ch. 7:16. When he said this, *he fell down upon his face,* not only in reverence to the king, but in humble adoration of God, whose name he praised for this success. By directing David thus to give God thanks for his victory, he prepared him for the approaching news of its allay. The more our hearts are fixed and enlarged in thanksgiving to God for our mercies the better disposed we shall be to bear with patience the afflictions mixed with them. Poor David is so much a father that he forgets he is a king, and therefore cannot rejoice in the news of a victory, till he know whether the *young man Absalom be safe,* for whom his heart seems to tremble, almost as Eli's, in a similar case, for the ark of God. Ahimaaz soon discerned, what Joab intimated to him, that the death of the king's son would make the tidings of the day very unwelcome, and therefore in his report left that matter doubtful; and, though he gave occasion to suspect how it was, yet, that the thunderclap might not come too suddenly upon the poor perplexed king, he refers him to the next messenger, whom they saw coming, for a more particular account of it. "When Joab sent the king's servant (namely, *Cushi) and me thy servant,* to bring the news, *I saw a great tumult,* occasioned by something extraordinary, as you will hear by and by; but I have nothing to say about it. I have delivered that which was my message. Cushi is better able to inform you than I am. I will not be the messenger of evil tidings; nor will I pretend to know that which I cannot give a perfect account of." He is therefore told to stand by till Cushi come (v. 30), and, now, we may suppose, he gives the king a more particular account of the victory, which was the thing he came to bring the news of.

5. Cushi, the slow post, proves the sure one, and besides the confirmation of the news of the victory which Ahimaaz had brought — *The Lord has avenged thee of all those that rose up against thee* (v. 31) — he satisfied the

king's enquiry concerning Absalom, v. 32. *Is he safe?* says David. "Yes," says Cushi, "he is safe in his grave;" but he tells the news so discreetly that, how unwelcome soever the message is, the messenger can have no blame. He did not tell him plainly that Absalom was hanged, and run through and buried under a heap of stones; but only that his fate was what he desired might be the fate of all that were traitors against the king, his crown and dignity: *"The enemies of my lord the king,* whoever they are, *and all that rise against thee to do thee hurt, be as that young man is;* I need wish them no worse."

II. How David received the intelligence. He forgets all the joy of his deliverance, and is quite overwhelmed with the sorrowful tidings of Absalom's death, v. 33. As soon as he perceived by Cushi's reply that Absalom was dead, he asked no more questions, but fell into a passion of weeping, retired from company, and abandoned himself to sorrow; as he was going up to his chamber he was overheard to say *"O my son Absalom! my son, my son Absalom!* alas for thee! I lament thee. How hast thou fallen! *Would God I had died for thee,* and that thou hadst remained alive this day" (so the Chaldee adds) *"O Absalom! my son, my son!"* I wish I could see reason to think that this arose from a concern about Absalom's everlasting state, and that the reason why he wished he had *died for him* was because he had good hopes of his own salvation, and of Absalom's repentance if he had lived. It rather seems to have been spoken inconsiderately, and in a passion, and it was his infirmity. He is to be blamed, 1. For showing so great a fondness for a graceless son only because he was handsome and witty, while he was justly abandoned both of God and man. 2. For quarrelling, not only with divine providence, in the disposals of which he ought silently to have acquiesced, but with divine justice, the judgments of which he ought to have adored and subscribed to. See how Bildad argues (Job 8:3, 4), *If thy children have sinned against him, and he have cast them away in their transgression,* thou shouldst submit, *for doth God pervert judgment?* See Lev. 10:3. 3. For opposing the justice of the nation, which, as king, he was entrusted with the administration of, and which, with other public interests, he ought to have preferred before nay natural affection. 4. For despising the mercy of his deliverance, and the deliverance of his family and kingdom, from Absalom's wicked designs, as if this were no mercy, nor worth giving thanks for, because it cost the life of Absalom. 5. For indulging in a strong passion, and speaking unadvisedly with his lips. He now forgot his own reasonings upon the death of another child *(Can I bring him back again?)* and his own resolution to *keep his mouth as with a bridle* when *his heart was hot within him,* as well as his own practice at other times, when he *quieted himself as a child that was weaned from his mother.* The best men are not always in an equally good frame. What we over-loved we are apt to over-grieve for: in each affection, therefore, it is wisdom to have rule over our own spirits and to keep a strict guard upon ourselves when that is removed from us which was very dear to us. Losers think they may have leave to speak; but little said is soon amended. The penitent patient sufferer *sitteth alone and keepeth silence* (Lam. 3:28), or rather, with *Job,* says, *Blessed be the name of the Lord.*

CHAPTER 19

We left David's army in triumph and yet David himself in tears: now here we have, I. His return to himself, by the persuasion of Joab (v. 1–8). II. His return to his kingdom from his present banishment. 1. The men of Israel were forward of themselves to bring him back (v. 9, 10). 2. The men of Judah were dealt with by David's agents to do it (v. 11–14) and did it (v. 15). III. At the king's coming over Jordan, Shimei's treason is pardoned (v. 16–23), Mephibosheth's failure is excused (v. 24–30), and Barzillai's kindness is thankfully owned, and recompensed to his son (v. 31–39). IV. The men of Israel quarrelled with the men of Judah, for not calling them to the ceremony of the king's restoration, which occasioned a new rebellion, an account of which we have in the next chapter (v. 40–43).

Verses 1–8

Soon after the messengers had brought the news of the defeat and death of Absalom to the court of Mahanaim, Joab and his victorious army followed, to grace the king's triumphs and receive his further orders. Now here we are told,

I. What a damp and disappointment it was to them to find the king in tears for Absalom's death, which they construed as a token of displeasure against them for what they had done, whereas they expected him to have met them with joy and thanks for their good services: *It was told Joab, v.* 1 The report of it ran through the army (*v.* 2), *how the king was grieved for his son.* The people will take particular notice what their princes say and do. The more eyes we have upon us, and the greater our influence is, the more need we have to speak and act wisely and to govern our passions strictly. When they came to the city they found the king in close mourning, *v.* 4. He covered his face, and would not so much as look up, nor take any notice of the generals when they attended him. It could not but surprise them to find, 1. How the king proclaimed his passion, of which he ought to have been ashamed, and which he would have striven to smother and conceal if he had consulted either his reputation for courage, which was lessened by his mean submission to the tyranny of so absurd a passion, or his interest in the people, which would be prejudiced by his discountenancing what was done in zeal for his honour and the public safety. Yet see how he avows his grief: *He cries with a loud voice, O my son Absalom!* "My servants have all come home safe, but where is my son? He is dead; and, dying in sin, I fear he is lost for ever. I cannot now say, *I shall go to him,* for my soul shall not be gathered with such sinners; what shall be done for thee, *O Absalom! my son, my son!"* 2. How he prolonged his passion, even till the army had come up to him, which must be some time after he received the first intelligence. If he had contented himself with giving vent to his passion for an hour or two when he first heard the news, it would have been excusable, but to continue it thus for so bad a son as Absalom, like Jacob for so good a son as Joseph, with a resolution to go to the grave mourning and to stain his triumphs with his tears, was very unwise and very unworthy. Now see how ill this was taken by the people. They were loth to blame the king, for *whatever he did used to please them* (ch. 3:36), but they took it as a great mortification to them. *Their victory was turned into mourning, v.* 2. *They stole into the city as men ashamed, v.* 3. In compliment to their sovereign, they would not rejoice in that which they perceived so afflictive to him, and yet they could not but be uneasy that they were thus obliged to conceal their joy. Superiors ought not to put such hardships as these on their inferiors.

II. How plainly and vehemently Joab reproved David for this indiscreet management of himself in this critical juncture. David never more needed the hearts of his subjects than now, nor was ever more concerned to secure his interest in their affections; and therefore whatever tended to disoblige them now was the most impolitic thing he could do, and the greatest wrong imaginable to his friends that adhered to him. Joab therefore censures him, *v.* 5–7. He speaks a great deal of reason, but not with the respect and deference which he owed to his prince. *Is is fit to say to a king, Thou art wicked?* A plain case may be fairly pleaded with those that are above us, and they may be reproved for what they do amiss, but it must not be done with rudeness and insolence. David did indeed need to be roused and alarmed; and Joab thought it no time to dally with him. If superiors do that which is foolish, they must neither think it strange nor take it ill if their inferiors tell them of it, perhaps too bluntly. 1. Joab magnifies the services of David's soldiers: *"This day they have saved thy life,* and therefore deserve to be taken notice of, and have reason to resent it if they be not." It is implied that Absalom, whom he honoured with his tears, sought his ruin and the ruin of his family, while those whom by his tears he puts a slight upon were such as preserved from ruin him and all that was dear to him. Great mischiefs have arisen to princes from the contempt of great merits. 2. He aggravates the discouragement David had given them: *"Thou hast shamed their faces;* for, while they have shown such a value for thy life, thou hast shown no value for theirs, but preferrest a spoiled wicked youth, a false traitor to his king and country, whom we are happily rid of, before all thy wise counsellors, brave commanders, and loyal subjects. What can be more absurd than to love thy enemies and hate thy friends?" 3. He advises him to present himself immediately at the head of his troops, to smile upon them, welcome them home, congratulate their success, and return them thanks for their services. Even those that may be commanded yet expect to be thanked when they do well, and ought to be. 4. He threatens him with another

rebellion if he would not do this, intimating that rather than serve so ungrateful a prince he himself would head a revolt from him, and then (so confident is Joab of his own interest in the people) *"there will not tarry with thee one man.* If I go, they will go. Thou hast now nothing to mourn for: but, if thou persist, I will give thee something to mourn for (as Josephus expresses it) with a true and more bitter mourning."

III. How prudently and mildly David took the reproof and counsel given him, *v.* 8. He shook off his grief, anointed his head, and washed his face, that he might not appear unto men to mourn, and then made his appearance in public in the gate, which was as the guild-hall of the city. Hither the people flocked to him to congratulate his and their safety, and all was well. Note, When we are convinced of a fault, we must amend, though we are told of it by our inferiors, and indecently, or in heat and passion.

Verses 9–15

It is strange that David did not immediately upon the defeat and dispersion of Absalom's forces march with all expedition back to Jerusalem, to regain the possession of his capital city, while the rebels were in confusion and before they could rally again. What occasion was there to bring him back? Could not he himself go back with the victorious army he had with him in Gilead? He could, no doubt; but, 1. He would go back as a prince, with the consent and unanimous approbation of the people, and not as a conqueror forcing his way: he would restore their liberties, and not take occasion to seize them, or encroach upon them. 2. He would go back in peace and safety, and be sure that he should meet with no difficulty or opposition in his return, and therefore would be satisfied that the people were well-affected to have him before he would stir. 3. He would go back in honour, and like himself, and therefore would go back, not at the head of his forces, but in the arms of his subjects; for the prince that has wisdom and goodness enough to make himself his people's darling, without doubt, looks greater and makes a much better figure than the prince that has strength enough to make himself his people's terror. It is resolved therefore that David must be brought back to Jerusalem his own city, and his own house there, with some ceremony, and here we have that matter concerted.

I. The men of Israel (that is, the ten tribes) were the first that talked of it, *v.* 9, 10. The people were at strife about it; it was the great subject of discourse and dispute throughout all the country. Some perhaps opposed it: "Let him either come back himself or stay where he is;" others appeared zealous for it, and reasoned as follows here, to further the design, 1. That David had formerly helped them, had fought their battles, subdued their enemies, and done them much service, and therefore it was a shame that he should continue banished from their country who had been so great a benefactor to it. Note, Good services done to the public, though they may be forgotten for a while, yet will be remembered again when men come to their right minds. 2. That Absalom had now disappointed them. "We were foolishly sick of the cedar, and chose the branch to reign over us; but we have had enough of him: he is consumed, and we narrowly escaped being consumed with him. Let us therefore return to our allegiance, and think of bringing the king back." Perhaps this was all the strife among them, not a dispute whether the king should be brought back or no (all agreed it was to be done), but whose fault is was that it was not done. As is usual in such cases, every one justified himself and blamed his neighbour. The people laid the fault on the elders, and the elders on the people, and one tribe upon another. Mutual excitements to the doing of a good work are laudable, but not mutual accusations for the not doing of it; for usually when public services are neglected all sides must share in the blame; every one might do more than he does, in the reformation of manners, the healing of divisions, and the like.

II. The men of Judah, by David's contrivance, were the first that did it. It is strange that they, being David's own tribe, were not so forward as the rest. David had intelligence of the good disposition of all the rest towards him, but nothing from Judah, though he had always been particularly careful of them. But we do not always find the most kindness from those from whom we have most rea-

son to expect it. Yet David would not return till he knew the sense of his own tribe. *Judah was his lawgiver,* Ps. 60:7. That his way home might be the more clear, 1. He employed Zadok and Abiathar, the two chief priests, to treat with the elders of Judah, and to excite them to give the king an invitation back to his house, even to his house, which was the glory of their tribe, *v.* 11, 12. No men more proper to negociate this affair than the two priests, who were firm to David's interest, were prudent men, and had great influence with the people. Perhaps the men of Judah were remiss and careless, and did it not, because nobody put them on to do it, and then it was proper to stir them up to it. Many will follow in a good work who will not lead: it is a pity that they should continue idle for want of being spoken to. Or perhaps they were so sensible of the greatness of the provocation they had given to David, by joining with Absalom, that they were afraid to bring him back, despairing of his favour; he therefore warrants his agents to assure them of it, with this reason: *"You are my brethren, my bone and my flesh,* and therefore I cannot be severe with you." The Son of David has been pleased to call us *brethren, his bone and his flesh,* which encourages us to hope that we shall find favour with him. Or perhaps they were willing to see what the rest of the tribes would do before they stirred, with which they are here upbraided: "The speech of all Israel has come to the king to invite him back, and shall Judah be the last, that should have been the first? Where is now the celebrated bravery of that royal tribe? Where is its loyalty?" Note, We should be stirred up to that which is great and good by the examples both of our ancestors and of our neighbours, and by the consideration of our rank. Let not the first in dignity be last in duty. 2. He particularly courted into his interest Amasa, who had been Absalom's general, but was his own nephew as well as Joab, *v.* 13. He owns him for his kinsman, and promises him that, if he will appear for him now, he will make him captain-general of all his forces in the room of Joab, will not only pardon him (which, it may be, Amasa questioned), but prefer him. Sometimes there is nothing lost in purchasing the friendship of one that has been an enemy. Amasa's interest might do David good service at this juncture. But, if David did wisely for himself in designating Amasa for this post (Joab having now grown intolerably haughty), he did not do kindly by Amasa in letting his design be known, for it occasioned his death by Joab's hand, ch. 20:10. 3. The point was hereby gained. He bowed the heart of the men of Judah to pass a vote, *nemine contradicente — unanimously,* for the recall of the king, *v.* 14. God's providence, by the priests' persuasions and Amasa's interest, brought them to this resolve. David stirred not till he received this invitation, and then he came as far back as Jordan, at which river they were to meet him, *v.* 15. Our Lord Jesus will rule in those that invite him to the throne in their hearts and not till he be invited. He first bows the heart and makes it willing in the day of his power, and then *rules in the midst of his enemies,* Ps. 110:2, 3.

Verses 16–23

Perhaps Jordan was never passed with so much solemnity, nor with so many remarkable occurrences, as it was now, since Israel passed it under Joshua. David, in his afflictive flight, remembered God particularly *from the land of Jordan* (Ps. 42:6), and now that land, more than any other, was graced with the glories of his return. David's soldiers furnished themselves with accommodations for their passage over this river, but, for his own family, *a ferryboat* was sent on purpose, *v.* 18. *A fleet of boats,* say some; *a bridge of boats was made,* say others; the best convenience they had to serve him with. Two remarkable persons met him on the banks of Jordan, both of whom had abused him wretchedly when he was in his flight.

I. Ziba, who had abused him with his fair tongue, and by accusing his master, had obtained from the king a grant of his estate, ch. 16:4. A greater abuse he could not have done him, than, by imposing upon his credulity, to draw him in to do a thing so unkind to the son of his friend Jonathan. He comes now, with a retinue of sons and servants, to meet the king (*v.* 17), that he may obtain the king's favour, and so come off the better when Mephibosheth shall shortly undeceive him, and clear himself, *v.* 26.

II. Shimei, who had abused him with his foul tongue,

railed at him, and cursed him, *ch.* 16:5. If David had been defeated, no doubt he would have continued to trample upon him, and have gloried in what he had done; but now that he sees him coming home in triumph, and returning to his throne, he thinks it his interest to make his peace with him. Those who now slight and abuse the Son of David would be glad to make their peace too when he shall come in his glory; but it will be too late. Shimei, to recommend himself to the king, 1. Came with good company, with the men of Judah, as one in their interest. 2. He brought a regiment of the men of Benjamin with him, 1000, of which perhaps he was chiliarch, or commander-in-chief, offering his own and their service to the king; or perhaps they were volunteers, whom by his interest he had got together to meet the king, which was the more obliging because of all the tribes of Israel there were none, except these and Judah, that appeared to pay him this respect. 3. What he did he hastened to do; he lost no time. *Agree with thy adversary quickly, while thou art in the way.* Here is, (1.) The criminal's submission (*v.* 18–20): *He fell down before the king,* as a penitent, as a supplicant; and, that he might be thought sincere, he did it publicly before all David's servants, and his friends the men of Judah, yea, and before his own thousand. The offence was public, therefore the submission ought to be so. He owns his crime: *Thy servant doth know that I have sinned.* He aggravates it: *I did perversely.* He begs the king's pardon: *Let not the king impute iniquity to thy servant,* that is, deal with me as I deserve. He intimates that it was below the king's great and generous mind to *take it to his heart;* and pleads his early return to his allegiance, that he was *the first of all the house of Joseph* (that is, of Israel, who in the beginning of David's reign had distinguished themselves from Judah by their adherence to Ishbosheth, *ch.* 2:10) that came *to meet the king.* He came first, that by his example of duty the rest might be induced, and by his experience of the king's clemency the rest might be encouraged to follow. (2.) A motion made for judgment against him (*v.* 21): *"Shall not Shimei be put to death* as a traitor? Let him, of all men, be made an example." This motion was made by Abishai, who would have ventured his life to have been the death of Shimei when he was cursing, ch 16:9. David did not think fit to have it done then, because his judicial power was cut short; but, now that it was restored, why should not the law have its course? Abishai herein consulted what he supposed to be David's feelings more than his true interest. Princes have need to arm themselves against temptations to severity. (3.) His discharge by the king's order, *v.* 22, 23. He rejected Abishai's motion with displeasure: *What have I to do with you, you sons of Zeruiah?* The less we have to do with those who are of an angry revengeful spirit, and who put us upon doing what is harsh and rigorous, the better. He looks upon these prosecutors as adversaries to him, though they pretended friendship and zeal for his honour. Those who advise us to what is wrong are really *Satans,* adversaries to us. [1.] They were adversaries to his inclination, which was to clemency. He knew that he was *this day king in Israel,* restored to, and re-established in, his kingdom, and therefore his honour inclined him to forgive. It is the glory of kings to forgive those that humble and surrender themselves: *Satis est prostrasse leoni — it suffices the lion that he has laid his victim prostrate.* His joy inclined him to forgive. The pleasantness of his spirit on this great occasion forbade the entrance of any thing that was sour and peevish: joyful days should be forgiving days. Yet this was not all; his experience of God's mercy in restoring him to his kingdom, his exclusion from which he attributed to his sin, inclined him to show mercy to Shimei. Those that are forgiven must forgive. David had severely revenged the abuses done to his ambassadors by the Ammonites (*ch.* 12:31), but easily passes by the abuse done to himself by an Israelite. That was an affront to Israel in general, and touched the honour of his crown and kingdom; this was purely personal, and therefore (according to the usual disposition of good men) he could the more easily forgive it. [2.] They were adversaries to his interest. If he should put to death Shimei, who cursed him, those would expect the same fate who had taken up arms and actually levied war against him, which would drive them from him, while he was endeavouring to draw them to him. Acts of severity are seldom acts of policy. *The throne is established by mercy.* Shimei, hereupon, had his pardon signed and sealed with an oath, yet being bound, no doubt, to his good behaviour, and liable to be prosecuted if he afterwards misbehaved; and thus he was reserved to be, in due time, as much a monument of the justice of the government as he was now of its clemency, and in both of its prudence.

Verses 24–30

The day of David's return was a day of bringing to remembrance, a day of account, in which what had passed in his flight was called over again; among other things, after the case of Shimei, that of Mephibosheth comes to be enquired into, and he himself brings it on.

I. He went down in the crowd *to meet the king* (*v.* 24), and as a proof of the sincerity of his joy in the king's return, we are here told what a true mourner he was for the king's banishment. During that melancholy time, when one of the greatest glories of Israel had departed, Mephibosheth continued in a very melancholy state. He was never trimmed, nor put on clean linen, but wholly neglected himself, as one abandoned to grief for the king's affliction and the kingdom's misery. In times of public calamity we ought to abridge our enjoyments in the delights of sense, in conformity to the season. There are times when God calls to weeping and mourning, and we must comply with the call.

II. When the king came to Jerusalem (since he could not sooner have an opportunity) he made his appearance before him (*v.* 25); and when the king asked him why he, being one of his family, had staid behind, and not accompanied him in his exile, he opened his case fully to the king. 1. He complained of Ziba, his servant who should have been his friend, but had been in two ways his enemy; for, first, he had hindered him from going along with the king, by taking the ass himself which he was ordered to make ready for his master (*v.* 26), basely taking advantage of his lameness and his inability to help himself; and, secondly, he had accused him to David of a design to usurp the government, *v.* 27. How much mischief is it in the power of a wicked servant to do to the best master! 2. He gratefully acknowledged the king's great kindness to him when he and all his father's house lay at the king's mercy, *v.* 28. When he might justly have been dealt with as a rebel, he was treated as a friend, as a child: *Thou didst set thy servant among those that did eat at thy own table.* This shows that Ziba's suggestion was improbable; for could Mephibosheth be so foolish as to aim higher when he lived so easily, so happily as he did? And could he be so very disingenuous as to design any harm to David, of whose great kindness to him he was thus sensible? (3.) He referred his cause to the king's pleasure (*Do what is good in thy eyes* with me and my estate), depending on the king's wisdom, and his ability to discern between truth and falsehood *(My lord the king is as an angel from God),* and disclaiming all pretensions of his own merit: "So much kindness I have received above what I deserved, and *what right have I to cry any more unto the king?* Why should I trouble the king with my complaints when I have already been so troublesome to him? Why should I think any thing hard that is put upon me when I hitherto been so kindly treated?" We were all *as dead men before God;* yet he has not only spared us, *but taken us to sit at his table.* How little reason then have we to complain of any trouble we are in, and how much reason to take all well that God does!

III. David hereupon recalls the sequestration of Mephibosheth's estate; being deceived in his grant, he revokes it, and confirms his former settlement of it: *"I have said, Thou and Ziba divide the land* (*v.* 29), that is, Let it be as I first ordered it (*ch.* 9:10); the property shall still be vested in thee, but Ziba shall have occupancy: he shall till the land, paying thee a rent." Thus Mephibosheth is where he was; no harm is done, only Ziba goes away unpunished for his false and malicious information against his master. David either feared him too much, or loved him too well, to do justice upon him according to that law, Deu. 19:18, 19; and he was now in the humour of forgiving and resolved to make every body easy.

IV. Mephibosheth drowns all he cares about his estate in his joy for the king's return (*v.* 30): *"Yea, let him take all,* the presence and favour of the king shall be to me instead of all." A good man can contentedly bear his own private losses and disappointments, while he see Israel in peace, and the throne of the Son of David exalted and established. Let Ziba take all, so that David may be in peace.

Verses 31–39

David had already graced the triumphs of his restoration with the generous remission of the injuries that had been done to him; we have him here gracing them with a no less generous reward of the kindnesses that had been shown to him. Barzillai, the Gileadite, who had a noble seat at Rogelim, not far from Mahanaim, was the man who, of all the nobility and gentry of that country, had been most kind to David in his distress. If Absalom had prevailed, it is likely he would have suffered for his loyalty; but now he and his shall be no losers by it. Here is,

I. Barzillai's great respect to David, not only as a good man, but as his righteous sovereign: He *provided him with much sustenance,* for himself and his family, *while he lay at Mahanaim, v.* 32. God had given him a large estate, *for he was a very great man,* and, it seems, he had a large heart to do good with it: what else but that is a large estate good for? To reduced greatness generosity obliges us, and to oppressed goodness piety obliges us, to be in a particular manner kind, to the utmost of our power. Barzillai, to show that he was not weary of David, though he was so great a charge to him, attended him to Jordan, and went over with him, *v.* 31. Let subjects learn hence to render *tribute to whom tribute is due* and *honour to whom honour,* Rom. 13:7.

II. The kind invitation David gave to him to court (*v.* 33): *Come thou over with me.* He invited him, 1. That he might have the pleasure of his company and the benefit of his counsel; for we may suppose that he was very wise and good, as well as very rich, otherwise he would not have been called here *a very great man;* for it is what a man is, more than what he has, that renders him truly great. 2. That he might have an opportunity of returning his kindness: *"I will feed thee with me;* thou shalt fare as sumptuously as I fare, and this at Jerusalem, the royal and holy city." David did not take Barzillai's kindness to him as a debt (he was not one of those arbitrary princes who think that whatever their subjects have is theirs when they please), but accepted it and rewarded it as a favour. We must always study to be grateful to our friends, especially to those who have helped us in distress.

III. Barzillai's reply to this invitation, wherein,

1. He admires the king's generosity in making him this offer, lessening his service, and magnifying the king's return for it: *Why should the king recompense it with such a reward? v.* 36. Will the master thank that servant who only does what was his duty to do? He though he had done himself honour enough in doing the king any service. Thus, when the saints shall be called to inherit the kingdom in consideration of what they have done for Christ in this world, they will be amazed at the disproportion between the service and the recompence. Mt. 25:37, *Lord, when saw we thee hungry, and fed thee?*

2. He declines accepting the invitation. He begs his majesty's pardon for refusing so generous an offer: he should think himself very happy in being near the king, but, (1.) He is old, and unfit to remove at all, especially to court. He is old, and unfit for the *business* of the court: "Why *should I go up with the king to Jerusalem?* I can do him no service there, in the council, the camp, the treasury, or the courts of justice; for *how long have I to live? v.* 34. Shall I think of going into business, now that I am going out of this world?" He is old and unfit for the *diversions* of the court, which will be ill-bestowed, and even thrown away, upon one that can relish them so little, *v.* 35. As it was in Moses's time, so it was in barzillai's and it is not worse now, that, *if men be so strong that they come to fourscore years, their strength then is labour and sorrow,* Ps. 90:10. These were then, and are still, years of which men say they *have no pleasure in them,* Eccl. 12:1. Dainties are insipid when desire fails, and songs to the aged ear are little better than those sung to a heavy heart, very disagreeable: how should they be otherwise when the daughters of music are brought low? Let those that are old learn of Barzillai to be dead to the delights of sense; let grace second nature, and make a virtue of the necessity. Nay, Barzillai, being old, thinks he shall be *a burden to the king,* rather than any credit to him; and a good man would not go any where to be burdensome, or, if he must

be so, will rather be so to his own house than to another's. (2.) He is dying, and must begin to think of his long journey, his removal out of the world, *v.* 37. It is good for us all, but it especially becomes old people to think and speak much of dying. "Talk of going to court!" says Barzillai; "Let me go home and *die in my own city,* the place of my father's sepulchre; let me die *by the grave of my father,* that my bones may be quietly carried to the place of their rest. The grave is ready for me, let me go and get ready for it, go and die in my nest."

3. He desires the king to be kind to his son Chimham: *Let him go over with my lord the king,* and have preferment at court. What favour is done to him Barzillai will take as done to himself. Those that are old must not grudge young people those delights which they themselves are past the enjoyment of, nor confine them to their retirements. Barzillai will go back himself, but he will not make Chimham go back with him; though he could ill spare Chimham, yet, thinking it would gratify and advance him, he is willing to do it.

IV. David's farewell to Barzillai. 1. He sends him back into his country with a kiss and a blessing (*v.* 39), signifying that in gratitude for his kindnesses he would love him and pray for him, and with a promise that whatever request he should at any time make to him he would be ready to oblige him (*v.* 38): *Whatsoever thou shalt think of,* when thou comest home, to *ask of me,* that *will I do for thee.* What is the chief excellency of power but this, that it gives men a capacity of doing the more good? 2. He takes Chimham forward with him, and leaves it to Barzillai to choose him his preferment. I will *do to him what shall seem good to thee, v.* 38. And, it should seem, Barzillai, who had experienced the innocency and safety of retirement, begged a country seat for him near Jerusalem, but not in it; for, long after, we read of a place near Bethlehem, David's city, which is called *the habitation of Chimham,* allotted to him, probably, not out of the crown-lands or the forfeited estates, but out of David's paternal estate.

Verses 40–43

David came over Jordan attended and assisted only by the men of Judah; but when he had advanced as far as Gilgal, the first stage on this side Jordan, *half the people of Israel* (that is, of their elders and great men) had come to wait upon him, to kiss his hand, and congratulate him on his return, but found they came too late to witness the solemnity of his first entrance. This put them out of humour, and occasioned a quarrel between them and the men of Judah, which was a damp to the joy of the day, and the beginning of further mischief. Here is, 1. The complaint which the men of Israel brought to the king against the men of Judah (*v.* 41), that they had performed the ceremony of bringing the king over Jordan, and not given them notice, that they might have come to join in it. This reflected upon them, as if they were not so well affected to the king and his restoration as the men of Judah were, whereas the king himself knew that they had spoken of it before the men of Judah thought of it, *v.* 11. It seemed likewise as if they intended to monopolize the king's favours when he had come back, and to be looked upon as his only friends. See what mischief comes from pride and jealousy. 2. The excuse which the men of Judah made for themselves, *v.* 42. (1.) They plead relations to the king: *"He is near of kin to us,* and therefore in a matter of mere ceremony, as this was, we may claim precedency. It was into our country that he was to be brought, and therefore who so fit as we to bring him?" (2.) They deny the insinuated charge of self-seeking in what they had done: *"Have we eaten at all of the king's cost?* No, we have all borne our own charges. *Hath he given us any gift?* No, we have no design to engross the advantages of his return; you have come time enough to share in them." Too many that attend princes do so only for what they can get. 3. The men of Israel's vindication of their charge, *v.* 43. They pleaded, *"We have ten parts in the king"* (Judah having Simeon only, whose lot lay within his, to join with him), "and therefore it is a slight upon us that our advice was not asked about *bringing back the king."* See how uncertain the multitude is. They were lately striving against the king, to drive him out; now they are striving about him, which shall honour him most. A good man and a good cause will thus recover their credit and interest, though, for a time, they may seem to have lost them. See what is commonly the origin of strife, nothing so much as impatience of contempt or the least seeming slight. The men of Judah would have done better if they had taken their brethren's advice and assistance; but, since they did not, why should the men of Israel be so grievously offended? If a good work be done, and well done, let us not be displeased, nor the work disparaged, though we had no hand in it. 4. The scripture takes notice, by way of blame, which of the contending parties managed the cause with most passion: *The words of the men of Judah were fiercer than* those *of the men of Israel.* Though we have right and reason on our side, yet, if we express ourselves with fierceness, God takes notice of it and is much displeased with it.

CHAPTER 20

How do the clouds return after the rain! No sooner is one of David's troubles over than another arises, as it were out of the ashes of the former, wherein the threatening is fulfilled, that the sword should never depart from his house. I. Before he reaches Jerusalem a new rebellion is raised by Sheba (*v.* 1, 2). II. His first work, when he comes to Jerusalem, is to condemn his concubines to perpetual imprisonment (*v.* 3). III. Amass, whom he entrusts to raise an army against Sheba, is too slow in his motions, which puts him into a fright (*v.* 4–6). IV. One of his generals barbarously murders the other, when they are taking the field (*v.* 7–13). V. Sheba is at length shut up in the city of Abel (*v.* 14, 15), but the citizens deliver him up to Joab, and so his rebellion is crushed (*v.* 16–22). The chapter concludes with a short account of David's great officers (*v.* 23–26).

Verses 1–3

David, in the midst of his triumphs, has here the affliction to see his kingdom disturbed and his family disgraced.

I. His subjects revolting from him at the instigation of *a man of Belial,* whom they followed when they forsook the *man after God's own heart.* Observe, 1. That this happened immediately upon the crushing of Absalom's rebellion. We must not think it strange, while we are in this world, if the end of one trouble be the beginning of another: deep sometimes calls unto deep. 2. That the people were now just returning to their allegiance, when, of a sudden, they flew off from it. When a reconciliation is newly made, it ought to be handled with great tenderness and caution, lest the peace break again before it be settled. A broken bone, when it is set, must have time to knot. 3. That the ring-leader of this rebellion was Sheba, a Benjamite by birth (*v.* 1), who had his habitation in Mount Ephraim, *v.* 21. Shimei and he were both of Saul's tribe, and both retained the ancient grudge of that house. Against the kingdom of the Messiah there is an hereditary enmity in the serpent's seed, and a succession of attempts to overthrow it (Ps. 2:1, 2); but he that sits in heaven laughs at them all. 4. That the occasion of it was that foolish quarrel, which we read of in the close of the foregoing chapter, between the elders of Israel and the elders of Judah, about bringing the king back. It was a point of honour that was disputed between them, which had most interest in David. "We are more numerous," say the elders of Israel. "We are nearer akin to him," say the elders of Judah. Now one would think David very safe and happy when his subjects are striving which shall love him best, and be most forward to show him respect; yet even that strife proves the occasion of a rebellion. The men of Israel complained to David of the slight which the men of Judah had put upon them. If he had now countenanced their complaint, commended their zeal, and returned them thanks for it, he might have confirmed them in his interest; but he seemed partial to his own tribe: *Their words prevailed above the words of the men of Israel;* as some read the last words of the foregoing chapter. David inclined to justify them, and, when the men of Israel perceived this, they flew off with indignation. "If the king will suffer himself to be engrossed by the men of Judah, let him and them make their best of one another, and we will set up one for ourselves. We thought we had ten parts in David, but such an interest will not be allowed us; the men of Judah tell us, in effect, *we have no part in him,* and therefore we will have none, nor will we attend him any further in his return to Jerusalem, nor own him for our king." This was proclaimed by Sheba (*v.* 1), who probably was a man of note, and had been active in Absalom's rebellion; the disgusted Israelites took the hint, and *went up from after David to follow Sheba* (*v.* 2), that is, the generality of them did so, only the men of Judah adhered to him. Learn hence, (1.) That it is as impolitic for princes to be partial in their attentions to their subjects as it is for parents to be so to their children; both should carry it with an even hand. (2.) Those know not what they do that make light of the affections of their inferiors, by not countenancing and accepting it. Their hatred may be feared whose love is despised. (3.) *The beginning of strife is as the letting forth of water;* it is *therefore* wisdom to *leave it off before it be meddled with,* Prov. 17:14. How great a matter doth a little of this fire kindle! (4.) The perverting of words is the subverting of peace; and much mischief is made by forcing invidious constructions upon what is said and written and drawing consequences that were never intended. The men of Judah said, *The king is near of kin to us.* "By this," say the men of Israel, "you mean that *we have no part in him;"* whereas they meant no such thing. (5.) People are very apt to run into extremes. *We have ten parts in David,* said they; and, almost in the next breath, *We have no part in him.* Today *Hosanna,* to-morrow *Crucify.*

II. His concubines imprisoned for life, and he himself under a necessity of putting them in confinement, because they had been defiled by Absalom, *v.* 3. David had multiplied wives, contrary to the law and they proved a grief and shame to him. Those whom he had sinfully taken pleasure in he was now, 1. Obliged, in duty, to put away, they being rendered unclean to him by the vile uncleanness his son had committed with them. Those whom he had loved must now be loathed. 2. Obliged, in prudence, to shut up in privacy, not to be seen abroad for shame, lest the sight of them should give occasion to people to speak of what Absalom had done to them, which ought not to be so much as named, 1 Co. 5:1. That that villany might be buried in obscurity. 3. Obliged, in justice to shut up in prison, to punish them for their easy submission to Absalom's lust, despairing perhaps of David's return, and giving him up for gone. Let none expect to do ill and fare well.

Verses 4–13

We have here Amasa's fall just as he began to rise. He was nephew to David (*ch.* 17:25), had been Absalom's general and commander-in-chief of his rebellious army, but, that being routed, he came over into David's interest, upon a promise that he should be general of his forces instead of Joab. Sheba's rebellion gives David an occasion to fulfil his promise sooner than he could wish, but Joab's envy and emulation rendered its fulfillment of ill consequence both to him and David.

I. Amasa has a commission to raise forces for the suppressing of Sheba's rebellion, and is ordered to raise them with all possible expedition, *v.* 4. It seems, the men of Judah, though forward to attend the king's triumphs, were backward enough to fight his battles; else, when they were all in a body attending him to Jerusalem, they might immediately have pursued Sheba, and have crushed that cockatrice in the egg. But most love a loyalty, as well as a religion, that is cheap and easy. Many boast of their being akin to Christ that yet are very loth to venture for him. Amasa is sent to assemble the men of Judah within three days; but he finds them so backward and unready that he cannot do it within the time appointed (*v.* 5), though the promotion of Amasa, who had been their general under Absalom, was very obliging to them, and a proof of the clemency of David's government.

II. Upon Amasa's delay, Abishai, the brother of Joab, is ordered to take the guards and standing forces, and with them to pursue Sheba (*v.* 6, 7), for nothing could be of more dangerous consequence than to give him time. David gives these orders to Abishai, because he resolves to mortify Joab, and degrade him, not so much, I doubt, for the blood of Abner, which he had shed basely, as for the blood of Absalom, which he had shed justly and honourably. "Now (says bishop Hall) Joab smarteth for a loyal disobedience. How slippery are the stations of earthly honours and subject to continual mutability! Happy are those who are in favour with him in whom there is no shadow of change." Joab, without orders, though in disgrace, goes along with his brother, knowing he might be serviceable to the public, or perhaps now meditating the removal of his rival.

III. Joab, near Gibeon, meets with Amasa, and barbarously murders him, *v.* 8–10. It should seem, the great stone in Gibeon was the place appointed for the general rendezvous. There the rivals met; and Amasa, relying upon his commission, went before, as general both of the new-raised forces which he had got together, and of the veteran troops which Abishai had brought in; but Joab there took an opportunity to kill him with his own hand; and, 1. He did it subtilely, and with contrivance, and not upon a sudden provocation. He girded his coat about him, that it might not hang in his way, and girded his belt upon his coat, that his sword might be the readier to his hand; he also put his sword in a sheath too big for it, that, whenever he pleased, it might, upon a little shake, fall out, as if it fell by accident, and so he might take it into his hand, unsuspected, as if he were going to return it into the scabbard, when he designed to sheath it in the bowels of Amasa. The more there is of plot in a sin the worse it is. 2. He did it treacherously, and under pretence of friendship, that Amasa might not be upon his guard. He called him *brother,* for they were own cousins, enquired of his welfare *(Art thou in health?)* and *took him by the beard,* as one he was free with, to kiss him, while with the drawn sword in his other hand he was aiming at his heart. Was this done like a gentleman, like a soldier, like a general? No, but like a villain, like a base coward. Just thus he slew Abner, and went unpunished for it, which encouraged him to do the like again. 3. He did it impudently, not in a corner, but at the head of his troops, and in their sight, as one that was neither ashamed nor afraid to do it, that was so hardened in blood and murders that he could neither blush nor tremble. 4. He did it at one blow, gave the fatal push with a good-will, as we say, so that he needed not strike him again; with such a strong and steady hand he gave this one stroke that it was fatal. 5. He did it in contempt and defiance of David and the commission he had given to Amasa; for that commission was the only ground of his quarrel with him, so that David was struck at through the side of Amasa, and was, in effect, told to his face that Joab would be general, in spite of him. 6. He did it very unseasonably, when they were going against a common enemy and were concerned to be unanimous. This ill-timed quarrel might have scattered their forces, or engaged them one against another, and so have made them all an easy prey to Sheba. So contentedly could Joab sacrifice the interest both of king and kingdom to his personal revenge.

IV. Joab immediately resumes his general's place, and takes care to lead the army on in pursuit of Sheba, that, if possible, he might prevent any prejudice to the common cause by what he had done. 1. He leaves one of his men to make proclamation to the forces that were coming up that they were still engaged in David's cause, but under Joab's command, *v.* 11. He knew what an interest he had in the soldiery, and how many favoured him rather than Amasa, who had been a traitor, was now a turncoat, and had never been successful; on this he boldly relied, and called them all to follow him. What man of Judah would not be for his old king and his old general? But one would wonder with what face a murderer could pursue a traitor; and how, under such a heavy load of guilt, he had courage to enter upon danger. Surely his conscience was seared with a hot iron. 2. care is taken to remove the dead body out of the way, because at that they made a stand (as *ch.* 2:23), and to cover it with a cloth, *v.* 12, 13. Wicked men think themselves safe in their wickedness if they can but conceal it from the eye of the world: if it be hidden, it is with them as if it were never done. But the covering of blood with a cloth cannot stop its cry in God's ear for vengeance, or make it the less loud. However, since this was no time to arraign Joab for what he had done, and the common safety called for expedition, it was prudent to remove that which retarded the march of the army; and then they all went on after Joab, while David, who no doubt had notice soon brought him of this tragedy, could not but reflect upon it with regret that he had not formerly done justice upon Joab for the death of Abner, and that he now had exposed Amasa by preferring him. And perhaps his conscience reminded him of his employing Joab in the murder of Uriah, which had helped to harden him in cruelty.

Verses 14–22

We have here the conclusion of Sheba's attempt.

I. The rebel, when he had rambled over all the tribes of Israel, and found them not so willing, upon second thoughts, to follow him, as they had been upon a sudden provocation to desert David (having only picked up a few like himself, that sided with him), at length entered Abel-Beth-maacah, a strong city in the north, in the lot of Naphtali, where we find it placed, 2 Ki. 15:29. Here he took shelter, whether by force or with consent does not appear; but his adherents were most Berites, of Beeroth in Benjamin, *v.* 14. One bad man will find or make more.

II. Joab drew up all his force against the city, besieged it, battered the wall, and made it almost ready for a general storm, *v.* 15. Justly is that place attacked with all this fury which dares harbour a traitor; nor will that heart fare better which indulges those rebellious lusts that will not have Christ to reign over them.

III. A discreet good woman of the city of Abel brings this matter, by her prudent management, to a good issue, so as to satisfy Joab and yet save the city. Here is,

1. Her treaty with Joab, and her capitulation with him, by which he is engaged to raise the siege, upon condition that Sheba be delivered up. It seems, none of all the men of Abel, none of the elders or magistrates, offered to treat with Joab, no, not when they were reduced to the last extremity. They were stupid and unconcerned for the public safety, or they stood in awe of Sheba, or they despaired of gaining any good terms with Joab, or they had not sense enough to manage the treaty. But this one woman and her wisdom saved the city. Souls know no difference of sexes. Though the man be the head, it does not therefore follow that he has the monopoly of the brains, and therefore he ought not, by any salique law, to have the monopoly of the crown. Many a masculine heart, and more than masculine, has been found in a female breast; nor is the treasure of wisdom the less valuable for being lodged in the weaker vessel. In the treaty between this nameless heroine and Joab,

(1.) She gains his audience and attention, *v.* 16, 17. We may suppose it was the first time he had ever treated with a woman in martial affairs.

(2.) She reasons with him on behalf of her city, and very ingeniously. [1.] That it was a city famous for wisdom (*v.* 18), as we translate it. She pleads that this city had been long in such reputation for prudent knowing men that it was the common referee of the country, and all agreed to abide by the award of its elders. Their sentence was an oracle; let them be consulted and the matter is ended, all sides will acquiesce. Now shall such a city as this be laid in ashes and never treated with? [2.] That the inhabitants were generally peaceable and faithful in Israel, *v.* 19. She could speak, not for herself only, but for all those whose cause she pleaded, that they were not of turbulent and seditious spirits, but of known fidelity to their prince and peaceableness with their fellow-subjects; they were neither seditious nor litigious. [3.] That it was a mother in Israel, a guide and nurse to the towns and country about; and that it was a part of *the inheritance of the Lord,* a city of Israelites, not of heathen; and the destruction of it would lessen and weaken that nation which God had chosen for his heritage. [4.] That they expected him to offer them peace before he made an attack upon the, according to that known law of war, Deu. 20:10. So the margin reads (*v.* 18): *They plainly spoke in the beginning* (of the siege), *saying, Surely they will ask of Abel,* that is, "The besiegers will demand the traitor, and will ask us to surrender him; and if they do, we will soon come to an agreement, and so end the matter." Thus she tacitly upbraids Joab for not offering them peace, but hopes it is not too late to beg it.

(3.) Joab and Abel's advocate soon agree that Sheba's head shall be the ransom of the city. Joab, though in a personal quarrel he had lately swallowed up and destroyed Amasa, yet, when he acts as a general, will by no means bear the imputation of delighting in bloodshed: *"Far be it from me that I should* delight to *swallow up or destroy,* or design it but when it is necessary for the public safety, *v.* 20. The matter is not so. Our quarrel is not with your city; we would hazard our lives for its protection. Our quarrel is only with the traitor that is harboured among you; deliver him up, and we have done." A great deal of mischief would be prevented if contending parties would but understand one another. The city obstinately holds out, believing Joab aims at its ruin. Joab furiously attacks it, believing the citizens all confederates with Sheba. Whereas both were mistaken; let both sides be undeceived, and the matter is soon accommodated. The single condition of peace is the surrender of the traitor. It is so in God's dealing with the soul, when it is besieged by conviction and distress: sin is the traitor; the beloved lust is the rebel; part with that, cast away the transgression, and all shall be well. No peace on any other terms. Our wise woman immediately agrees to the proposal: *Behold, his head shall be thrown to thee presently.*

2. Her treaty with the citizens. She went to them in her wisdom (and perhaps she had as much need of it in dealing with them as in dealing with Joab) and persuaded them to cut off Sheba's head, probably by some public order of their government, and it was thrown over the wall to Joab. He knew the traitor's face, and therefore looked no further, intending not that any of his adherents should suffer. The public safety was secured, and he felt no wish to gratify the public revenge. Joab hereupon raised the siege, and marched back to Jerusalem, with the trophies rather of peace than victory.

Verses 23–26

Here is an account of the state of David's court after his restoration. Joab retained the office of general, being too great to be displaced. Benaiah, as before, was captain of the guards. Here is one new office erected, which we had not (*ch.* 8:16–18), that of *treasurer,* or one *over the tribute,* for it was not till towards the latter end of his time that David began to raise taxes. Adoram was long in this office, but it cost him his life at last, 1 Ki. 12:18.

CHAPTER 21

The date of the events of this chapter is uncertain. I incline to think that they happened as they are here placed, after Absalom's and Sheba's rebellion, and towards the latter end of David's reign. That the battles with the Philistines, mentioned here, were long after the Philistines were subdued, appears by comparing 1 Chr. 18:1 with 20:4. The numbering of the people was just before the fixing of the place of the temple (as appears 1 Chr. 22:1), and that was towards the close of David's life; and, it should seem, the people were numbered just after the three years' famine for the Gibeonites, for that which is threatened as "three" years' famine (1 Chr. 21:12) is called "seven" years (2 Sa. 24:12, 13), three more, with the year current, added to those three. We have here, I. The Gibeonites avenged, 1. By a famine in the land (*v.* 1). 2. By the putting of seven of Saul's posterity to death (*v.* 2–9), care, however, being taken of their dead bodies, and of the bones of Saul (*v.* 10–14). II. The giants of the Philistines slain in several battles (*v.* 15–22).

Verses 1–9

Here I. Were are told of the injury which Saul had, long before this, done to the Gibeonites, which we had no account of in the history of his reign, nor should we have heard of it here but that it came now to be reckoned for. The Gibeonites were of the remnant of the Amorites (*v.* 2), who by a stratagem had made peace with Israel, and had the public faith pledged to them by Joshua for their safety. We had the story Jos. 9, where it was agreed (*v.* 23) that they should have their lives secured, but be deprived of their lands and liberties, that they and theirs should be tenants in villanage to Israel. It does not appear that they had broken their part of the covenant, either by denying their service or attempting to recover their lands or liberties; nor was this pretended; but Saul, under colour of zeal for the honour of Israel, that it might not be said that they had any of the natives among them, aimed to root them out, and, in order to that, slew many of them. Thus he would seem wiser than his predecessors the judges, and more zealous for the public interest; and perhaps he designed it for an instance of his royal prerogative and the power which as king he assumed to rescind the former acts of government and to disannul the most solemn leagues. It may be, he designed, by this severity towards the Gibeonites, to atone for his clemency towards the Amalekites. Some conjecture that he sought to cut off the Gibeonites at the same time when he put away the witches (1 Sa. 28:3), or perhaps many of them were remarkably pious, and he sought to destroy them when he slew the priests their masters. That which made this an exceedingly sinful sin was that he not only shed innocent blood, but therein violated the solemn oath by which the nation was bound to protect them. See what brought ruin on Saul's house: it was a bloody house.

II. We find the nation of Israel chastised with a sore famine, long after, for this sin of Saul. Observe, 1. Even in the land of Israel, that fruitful land, and in the reign of David, that glorious reign, there was a famine, not extreme (for then notice would sooner have been taken of it and enquiry made into the cause of it), but great drought, and scarcity of provisions, the consequence of it, for three years together. If corn miss one year, commonly the next makes up the deficiency; but, if it miss three years successively, it will be a sore judgment; and the man of wisdom will by it hear God's voice crying to the country to repent of the abuse of plenty. 2. David enquired of God concerning it. Though he was himself a prophet, he must consult the oracle, and know God's mind in his own appointed way. Note, When we are under God's judgments we ought to enquire into the grounds of the controversy. *Lord, show me wherefore thou contendest with me.* It is strange that David did not sooner consult the oracle, not till the third year; but perhaps, till then, he apprehended it not to be an extraordinary judgment for some particular sin. Even good men are often slack and remiss in doing their duty. We continue in ignorance, and under mistake, because we delay to enquire. 3. God was ready in his answer, though David was slow in his enquiries: *It is for Saul.* Note, God's judgments often look a great way back, which obliges us to do so when we are under his rebukes. It is not for us to object against the people's smarting for the sin of their king (perhaps they were aiding and abetting), nor against this generation's suffering for the sin of the last God often *visiteth the sins of the fathers upon the children, and his judgments are a great deep.* He gives not account of any of his matters. Time does not wear out the guilt of sin; nor can we build hopes of impunity upon the delay of judgments. There is no statute of limitation to be pleaded against God's demands. *Nullum tempus occurrit Deo — God may punish when he pleases.*

III. We have vengeance taken upon the house of Saul for the turning away of God's wrath from the land, which, at present, smarted for his sin.

1. David, probably by divine direction, referred it to the Gibeonites themselves to prescribe what satisfaction should be given them for the wrong that had been done them, *v.* 3. They had many years remained silent, had not appealed to David, nor given the kingdom any disturbance with their complaints or demands; and now, at length, God speaks for them (*I heard not, for thou wilt hear,* Ps. 38:14, 15); and they are recompensed for their patience with this honour, that they are made judges in their own case, and have a blank given them to write their demands on: *What you shall say, that will I do* (*v.* 4), that atonement may be made, and that *you may bless the inheritance of the Lord, v.* 3. It is sad for any family or nation to have the prayers of oppressed innocency against them, and therefore the expense of a just restitution is well bestowed for the retrieving of *the blessing of those that were ready to perish,* Job 29:13. "My servant Job, whom you have wronged, shall pray for you," says God, "and then I will be reconciled to you, and not till then." Those understand not themselves that value not the prayers of the poor and despised.

2. They desired that seven of Saul's posterity might be put to death, and David granted their demand. (1.) They required no *silver, nor gold, v.* 4. Note, Money is no satisfaction for blood, see Num. 35:31–33. It is the ancient law that blood calls for blood (Gen. 9:6); and those over-value money and under-value life, that sell the blood of their relations for corruptible things, *such as silver and gold.* The Gibeonites had now a fair opportunity to get a discharge from their servitude, in compensation for the wrong done them, according to the equity of that law (Ex. 21:26), *If a man strike out his servant's eye, he shall let him go free for his eye's sake.* But they did not insist on this; though the covenant was broken on the other side, it should not be broken on theirs. They were *Nethinim,* given to God and his people Israel, and they would not seem weary of the service. (2.) They required no lives but of Saul's family. He had done them the wrong, and therefore his children must pay for it. We sue the heirs for the parents' debts. Men may not extend this principle so far as life, Deu. 24:16. *The children* in an ordinary course of law, *shall never be put to death for the parents.* But this case of the Gibeonites was altogether extraordinary. God had made himself an immediate party to the cause and no doubt put it into the heart of the Gibeonites to make this demand, for he owned what was done (*v.* 14), and his judgments are not subject to the rules which men's judgments must be subject to. Let parents take heed of sin, especially the sin of cruelty and oppression, for their poor children's sake, who may be smarting for it by the just hand of God when they themselves are in their graves. Guilt and a curse are a bad entail upon a family. It should seem, Saul's posterity trod in his steps, for it is called a *bloody house;* it was the spirit of the family, and therefore they are justly reckoned with for his sin, as well as for their own. (3.) They would not impose it upon David to do this execution: *Thou shalt not for us kill any man* (*v.* 4), but we will do it ourselves, *we will hang them up unto the Lord* (*v.* 6), that if there were any hardship in it, they might bear the blame, and not David or his house. By our old law, if a murderer had judgment given against him upon an appeal, the relations that appealed had the executing of him. (4.) They did not require this out of malice against Saul or his family (had they been revengeful, they would have moved it themselves long before), but out of love to the people of Israel, whom they saw plagued for the injury done to them: "*We will hang them up unto the Lord* (*v.* 6), to satisfy his justice, not to gratify any revenge of our own — for the good of the public, not for our own reputation." (5.) The nomination of the persons they left to David, who took care to secure Mephibosheth for Jonathan's sake, that, while he was avenging the breach of one oath, he might not himself break another (*v.* 7); but he delivered up two of Saul's sons whom he had by a concubine, and five of his grandsons, whom his daughter Merab bore to Adriel (1 Sa. 18:19), but his daughter Michal brought up, *v.* 8. Now Saul's treachery was punished, in giving Merab to Adriel, when he had promised her to David, with a design to provoke him. "It is a dangerous matter," says bishop Hall upon this, "to offer injury to any of God's faithful ones; if their meekness have easily remitted it, their God will not pass it over without a severe retribution, though it may be long first." (6.) The place, time, and manner, of their execution, all added to the solemnity of their being sacrificed to divine justice. [1.] They were hanged up, as anathemas, under a peculiar mark of God's displeasure; for the law had said, *He that is hanged is accursed of God,* Deu. 21:23; Gal. 3:13. Christ being made a curse for us, and dying to satisfy for our sins and to turn away the wrath of God, became obedient to this ignominious death. [2.] They were hanged up in Gibeah of Saul (*v.* 6), to show that it was for his sin that they died. They were hanged, as it were, before their own door, to expiate the guilt of the house of Saul; and thus God accomplished the ruin of that family, for the blood of the priests, and their families, which, doubtless, now came in remembrance before God, and inquisition was made for it, Ps. 9:12. Yet the blood of the *Gibeonites* only is mentioned, because that was shed in violation of a sacred oath, which, though sworn long before, though obtained by a wile, and the promise made to Canaanites, yet is thus severely reckoned for. The despising of the oath, and breaking of the covenant, will be recompensed on the head of those who thus profane God's sacred name, Eze. 17:18, 19. And thus God would show that with him rich and poor meet together. Even royal blood must go to atone for the blood of the Gibeonites, who were but the vassals for the congregation. [3.] They were put to death *in the days of harvest* (*v.* 9), *at the beginning of harvest* (*v.* 10), to show that they were thus sacrificed for the turning sway of that wrath of God which had withheld from them their harvest-mercies for some years past, and to obtain his favour in the present harvest. Thus there is no way of appeasing God's anger but by mortifying and crucifying our lusts and corruptions. In vain do we expect mercy from God, unless we do justice upon our sins. Those executions must not be complained of as cruel which have become necessary to the public welfare. Better that seven of Saul's bloody house be hanged than that all Israel be famished.

Verses 10–14

Here we have, I. Saul's sons not only hanged, but hanged in chains, their dead bodies left hanging, and exposed, till the judgment ceased, which their death was to turn away, by the sending of rain upon the land. They died as sacrifices, and thus they were, in a manner, offered up, not consumed all at once by fire, but gradually by the air. They died as anathemas, and by this ignominious usage they were represented as execrable, because iniquity was laid upon them. When our blessed Saviour was made sin for us he was made a curse for us. But how shall we reconcile this with the law which expressly required that those who were hanged should be buried on the same day? Deu. 21:23. One of the Jewish rabbin wishes this passage of story expunged, *that the name of God might be sanctified,* which, he thinks, is dishonoured by his acceptance of that which was a violation of his law: but this was an extraordinary case, and did not fall within that law; nay, the very reason for that law is a reason for this exception. he that is thus left hanged is accursed; therefore ordinary malefactors must not be so abused; but therefore these must, because they were sacrificed, not to the justice of the nation, but for the crime of the nation (no less a crime than the violation of the public faith) and for the deliverance of the nation from no less a judgment than a general famine. Being thus made as the *off-scouring of all things,* they were made a *spectacle to the world* (1 Co. 4:9, 13), God appointing, or at least allowing it.

II. Their dead bodies watched by Rizpah, the mother of two of them, *v.* 10. It was a great affliction to her, now in her old age, to see her two sons, who, we may suppose, had been a comfort to her, and were likely to be the support of her declining years, cut off in this dreadful manner. None know what sorrows they are reserved for. She may not see them decently interred, but they shall be decently attended. She attempts not to violate the sentence passed upon them, that they should hang there till God sent rain; she neither steals nor forces away their dead bodies, though the divine law might have been cited to bear her out; but she patiently submits, pitches a tent of sackcloth near the gibbets, where, with her servants and friends, she protects the dead bodies from birds and beasts of prey. Thus, 1. She indulged her grief, as mourners are too apt to do, to no good purpose. When sorrow, in such cases, is in danger of growing excessive, we should rather study how to divert and pacify it than how to humour and gratify it. Why should we thus harden ourselves in sorrow? 2. She testified her love. Thus she let the world know that her sons died, not for any sin of their own, not as stubborn and rebellious sons, *whose eye had despised to obey their mother;* if that had been the case, she would have suffered the *ravens of the valley to pick it out and the young eagles to eat it,* Prov. 30:17. But they died for their father's sin and therefore her mind could not be alienated from them by their hard fate. Though there is not remedy, but they must die, yet they shall die pitied and lamented.

III. The solemn interment of their dead bodies, with the bones of Saul and Jonathan, in the burying-place of their family. David was so far from being displeased at what Rizpah had done that he was himself stirred up by it to do honour to the house of Saul, and to these branches of it among the rest; thus it appeared that it was not out of any personal disgust to the family that he delivered them up, and that he had not desired the woeful day, but that he was obliged to do it for the public good. 1. He now bethought himself of removing the bodies of Saul and Jonathan from the place where the men of Jabesh-Gilead had decently, but privately and obscurely, interred them, *under a tree,* 1 Sa. 31:12, 13. Though the shield of Saul was vilely cast away, as if he had not been anointed with oil, yet let not royal dust be lost in the graves of the common people. Humanity obliges us to respect human bodies, especially of the great and good, in consideration both of what they have been and what they are to be. 2. With them he buried the bodies *of those that were hanged;* for, when God's anger was turned away, they were no longer to be looked upon as a curse, *v.* 13, 14. When *water dropped upon them out of heaven* (*v.* 10), that is, when God sent rain to water the earth (which perhaps was not many days after they were hung up), then they were taken down, for then it appeared *that God was entreated for the land.* When justice is done on earth vengeance from heaven ceases. Through Christ, who was hanged on a tree and so made a curse for us, to expiate our guilt (though he was himself guiltless), God is pacified, and is entreated for us: and it is said (Acts 13:29) that *when they had fulfilled all that was written of him,* in token of the completeness of the sacrifice and of God's acceptance of it, *they took him down from the tree and laid him in a sepulchre.*

Verses 15–22

We have here the story of some conflicts with the Philistines, which happened, as it should seem, in the latter end of David's reign. Though he had so subdued them that they could not bring any great numbers into the field, yet as long as they had any giants among them to be their champions, they would never be quiet, but took all occasions to disturb the peace of Israel, to challenge them, or make incursions upon them.

I. David himself was engaged with one of the giants. The Philistines began the war yet again, *v.* 15. The enemies of God's Israel are restless in their attempts against them. David, though old, desired not a writ of ease from the public service, but he *went down* in person to fight *against the Philistines (Senescit, non segnescit — He grows old, but not indolent),* a sign that he fought not for his own glory (at this age he was loaded with glory, and needed no more), but for the good of his kingdom. But in this engagement we find him, 1. In distress and danger. He thought he could bear the fatigues of war as well as he had done formerly; his will was good, and he hoped he could do as at other times. But he found himself deceived; age had cut his hair, and, after a little toil, he *waxed faint.* His body could not keep pace with his mind. The champion of the Philistines was soon aware of his advantage, perceived that David's strength failed him, and, being himself strong and well-armed, *he thought to slay David;* but God was not in his thoughts, and therefore in that very day they all perished. The enemies of God's people are often very strong, very subtle, and very sure of success, like Isbi-benob, but there is no strength, nor counsel, nor confidence against the Lord. 2. Wonderfully rescued by Abishai, who came seasonably in to his relief, *v.* 17. Herein we must own Abishai's courage and fidelity to his prince (to save whose life he bravely ventured his own), but much more the good providence of God, which brought him in to David's succour in the moment of his extremity. Such a cause and such a champion, though distressed, shall not be deserted. When *Abishai succoured him,* gave him a cordial, it may be, to relieve his fainting spirits, or appeared as his second, *he* (namely, David, so I understand it) *smote the Philistine and killed him;* for it is said (*v.* 22) that David had himself a hand in slaying the giants. David fainted, but he did not flee; though his strength failed him, he bravely kept his ground, and then God sent him this help in the time of need, which, though brought him by his junior and inferior, he thankfully accepted, and, with a little recruiting, gained his point, and came off a conqueror. Christ, in his agonies, was strengthened by an angel. In spiritual conflicts, even strong saints sometimes wax faint; then Satan attacks them furiously; but those that stand their ground and resist him shall be relieved, and made more than conquerors. 3. David's servants hereupon resolved that he should never expose himself thus any more. They had easily persuaded him not to fight against Absalom (*ch.* 18:3), but against the Philistines he would go, till, having had this narrow escape, it was resolved in council, and confirmed with an oath, that *the light of Israel* (its guide and glory, so David was) should never be put again into such hazard of being blown out. The lives of those who are as valuable to their country as David was ought to be preserved with a double care, both by themselves and others.

II. The rest of the giants fell by the hand of David's servants. 1. Saph was slain by Sibbechai, one of David's worthies, *v.* 18; 1 Chr. 11:29. 2. Another, who was brother to Goliath, was slain by Elhanan, who is mentioned *ch.* 23:24. 3. Another, who was of very unusual bulk, who had more fingers and toes than other people (*v.* 20), and such an unparalleled insolence that, though he had seen the fall of other giants, yet he defied Israel, was slain by *Jonathan the son of Shimea.* Shimea had one son named *Jonadab* (2 Sa. 13:3), whom I should have taken for the same with this Jonathan, but that the former was noted for subtlety, the latter for bravery. These giants were probably the remains of the sons of Anak, who, though long feared, fell at last. Now observe, (1.) It is folly for the strong man to *glory in his strength.* David's servants were no bigger nor stronger than other men; yet thus, by divine assistance, they mastered one giant after another. God chooses by the weak things to confound the mighty. (2.) It is common for those to go down slain to the pit who have been *the terror of the mighty in the land of the living,* Eze. 32:27. (3.) The most powerful enemies are often reserved for the last conflict. David began his glory with the conquest of one giant, and here concludes it with the conquest of four. Death is a Christian's last enemy, and a son of Anak; but, through him that triumphed for us, we hope to be more than conquerors at last, even over that enemy.

CHAPTER 22

This chapter is a psalm, a psalm of praise; we find it afterwards inserted among David's psalms (Ps. 18) with some little variation. We have it here as it was first composed for his own closed and his own harp; but there we have it as it was afterwards delivered to the chief musician for the service of the church, a second edition with some amendments; for, though it was calculated primarily for David's case, yet it might indifferently serve the devotion of others, in giving thanks for their deliverances; or it was intended that his people should thus join with him in his thanksgivings, because, being a public person, his deliverances were to be accounted public blessings and called for public acknowledgments. The inspired historian, having largely related David's deliverances in this and the foregoing book, and one particularly in the close of the foregoing chapter, thought fit to record this sacred poem as a memorial of all that had been before related. Some think that David penned this psalm when he was old, upon a general review of the mercies of his life and the many wonderful preservations God had blessed him with, from first to last. We should in our praises, look as far back as we can, and not suffer time to wear out the sense of God's favours. Others think that he penned it when he was young, upon occasion of some of his first deliverances, and kept it by him for his use afterwards, and that, upon every new deliverance, his practice was to sing this song. But the book of Psalms shows that he varied as there was occasion, and confined not himself to one form. Here is, I. The title of the psalm (*v.* 1). II. The psalm itself, in which, with a very warm devotion and very great fluency and copiousness of expression, 1. He gives glory to God. 2. He takes comfort in him; and he finds matter for both, (1.) In the experiences he had of God's former favours. (2.) In the expectations he had of his further favours. These are intermixed throughout the whole psalm.

Verse 1

Observe here, I. That it has often been the lot of God's people to have many enemies, and to be in imminent danger of falling into their hands. David was a man after God's heart, but not after men's heart: many were those that hated him, and sought his ruin; Saul is particularly named, either, 1. As distinguished from his enemies of the heathen nations. Saul hated David, but David did not hate Saul, and therefore would not reckon him among his enemies; or, rather, 2. As the chief of his enemies, who was more malicious and powerful than any of them. Let not those whom God loves marvel if the world hate them.

II. Those that trust God in the way of duty shall find him a present help to them in their greatest dangers. David did so. God delivered him out of the hand of Saul. He takes special notice of this. Remarkable preservations should be mentioned in our praises with a particular emphasis. He delivered him also *out of the hand of all his enemies,* one after another, sometimes in one way, sometimes in another; and David, from his own experience, has assured us *that, though many are the troubles of the righteous, yet the Lord delivers them out of them all,* Ps. 34:19. We shall never be delivered from all our enemies till we get to heaven; and to that heavenly kingdom God will preserve all that are his, 2 Tim. 4:18.

III. Those that have received many signal mercies from God ought to give him the glory of them. Every new mercy in our hand should put a new song into our mouth, even praises to our God. Where there is a grateful heart, out of the abundance of that the mouth will speak. David spoke, not only to himself, for his own pleasure, not merely to those about him, for their instruction, but *to the Lord,* for his honour, *the words of this song.* Then we sing with grace when we sing to the Lord. In distress he *cried with his voice* (Ps. 142:1), therefore with his voice he gave thanks. Thanksgiving to God is the sweetest vocal music.

IV. We ought to be speedy in our thankful returns to God: *In the day that God delivered him he sang this song.* While the mercy is fresh, and our devout affections are most excited by it, let the thank-offering be brought, that it may be kindled with the fire of those affections.

Verses 2–51

Let us observe, in this song of praise,

I. How David adores God, and gives him the glory of his infinite perfections. There is none like him, nor any to be compared with him (*v.* 32): *Who is God, save the Lord?* All others that are adored as deities are counterfeits and pretenders. None is to be relied on but he. *Who is a rock, save our God?* They are dead, but *the Lord liveth, v.* 47. They disappoint their worshippers when they most need them. But *as for God his way is perfect, v.* 31. Men begin in kindness, but end not — promise, but perform not; but God will finish his work, and his word is tried, and what we may trust.

II. How he triumphs in the interest he has in this God, and his relation to him, which he lays down as the foundation of all the benefits he has received from him: *He is my God;* as such he cries to him (*v.* 7), and cleaves to him (*v.* 22); "and, if *my God,* then *my rock*" (*v.* 2), that is, "my strength and my power (*v.* 33), the rock under which I take shelter (he who is to me as the shadow of a great rock in a weary land), the rock on which I build my hope," *v.* 3. Whatever is my strength and support, it is *the God of my rock that makes it so;* nay, he is *the God of the rock of my salvation* (*v.* 47): my saving strength is in him and from him. David often hid himself in a rock (1 Sa. 24:2), but God was his chief hiding-place. "He is my fortress, in which I am safe and think myself so — *my high tower,* or stronghold, in which I am out of the reach of real evils — the *tower of salvation* (*v.* 51), which can never be sealed nor battered, nor undermined. Salvation itself saves me. Am I in distress? he is my deliverer — struck at, shot at? he is my shield — pursued? he is my refuge — oppressed? he is my saviour, that rescues me out of the hand of those that seek my ruin. Nay, he is the *horn of my salvation,* by which I am strongly protected, and my enemies are strongly pushed." Christ is spoken of as the *horn of salvation* in the house of David, Lu. 1:69. "Am I burdened, and ready to sink? *The Lord is my stay* (*v.* 19), by whom I am supported. Am I in the dark, benighted, at a loss? *Thou art my lamp, O Lord!* to show me my way, and thou wilt dispel *my darkness,*" *v.* 29. If we sincerely take the Lord for our God, all this, and much more, he will be to us, all we need and can desire.

III. What improvement he makes of his interest in God. If he be mine, 1. *In him will I trust* (*v.* 3), that is, "I will resign myself to his direction, and then depend upon his power, and wisdom, and goodness, to conduct me well." 2. *On him I will call* (*v.* 4), *for he is worthy to be praised.* What we have found in God that is worthy to be praised should engage us to pray to him and give glory to him. 3. *To him will I give thanks* (*v.* 50), and that publicly. When he was among the heathen he would neither be afraid nor ashamed to own his obligations to the God of Israel.

IV. The full and large account he keeps for himself, and gives to others, of the great and kind things God had done for him. This takes up most of the song. He gives God the glory both of his deliverances and of his successes, showing both the perils he was delivered from and the power he was advanced to.

1. He magnifies the great salvations God had wrought for him. God sometimes brings his people into very great difficulties and dangers, that he may have the honour of saving them and they the comfort of being saved by him. He owns, *Thou hast saved me from violence* (*v.* 3), *from my enemies* (*v.* 4), *from my strong enemy,* meaning Saul, who, if God had not succoured him, would have been too hard for him, *v.* 18. Thou hast given me *the shield of thy salvation, v.* 36. To magnify the salvation, he observes,

(1.) That the danger was very great and threatening out of which he was delivered. Men *rose up against him* (*v.* 40, 49) that *hated him* (*v.* 41), *a violent man* (*v.* 49) namely, Saul, who was malicious in his designs against him and vigorous in his pursuit. This is expressed figuratively, *v.* 5, 6. He was surrounded with death on every side, threatened to be overwhelmed, and saw no way of escape. So violently did the waves of death beat upon him, so strongly did the cords and snares of death hold him, that he could not help himself, any more than a man in the grave can. The floods of Belial, the wicked one, and his wicked instruments, made him afraid; he trembled to see not only earth, but death and hell, in arms against him.

(2.) That his deliverance was an answer to prayer, *v.* 7. He has here left us a good example, when we are in distress, to cry unto God with importunity, as children in a fright cry to their parents; and great encouragement to do so, in that he found God ready to answer prayer out of his temple in heaven, where he is continually served and adored.

(3.) That God appeared in a singular and extraordinary manner for him and against his enemies. The expressions are borrowed from the descent of the divine Majesty upon Mount Sinai, *v.* 8, 9, etc. We do not find that in any of David's battles God fought for him with thunder (as in

Samuel's time), or with hail (as in Joshua's time), or with the stars in their courses (as in Deborah's time); but these lofty metaphors are used, [1.] To set forth the glory of God, which was manifested in his deliverance. God's wisdom and power, his goodness and faithfulness, his justice and holiness, and his sovereign dominion over all the creatures and all the counsels of men, which appeared in favour of David, were as clear and bright a discovery of God's glory to an eye of faith as such miraculous interpositions would have been to an eye of sense. [2.] To set forth God's displeasure against his enemies, God so espoused his cause that he showed himself an enemy to all his enemies; his anger is set forth by a *smoke out of his nostrils,* and *fire out of his mouth* (*v.* 9), *coals kindled* (*v.* 13), *arrows, v.* 15. Who knows the power and terror of his wrath? [3.] To set forth the extraordinary confusion which his enemies were put into, and the consternation that seized them; as if the earth had trembled and the *foundations of the world* had been discovered, *v.* 8, 16. Who can stand before God when he is angry? [4.] To show how ready God was to help him: *He rode upon a cherub and did fly, v.* 11. God hastened to his succour, and came to him with seasonable relief, though he had seemed at a distance; yet he was *a God hiding himself* (Isa. 14:15), for he made *darkness his pavilion* (*v.* 12), for the amazement of his enemies and the protection of his own people.

(4.) That God manifested his particular favour and kindness to him in these deliverances (*v.* 20): *He delivered me, because he delighted in me.* The deliverance came not from common providence, but covenant-love; he was herein treated as a favourite: so he perceived by the communications of divine grace and comfort to his soul with these deliverances, and the communion he had with God in them. Herein he was a type of Christ, whom God upheld because he *delighted in him,* Isa. 42:1, 2.

2. He magnifies the great successes God had crowned him with. He had not only preserved but prospered him. He was blessed, (1.) With liberty and enlargement. He was *brought into a large place* (*v.* 20), where he had room to thrive, and his *steps were enlarged under him,* so that he had room to stir (*v.* 37), being no longer straitened and confined. (2.) With military skill, and strength, and swiftness. Though he was bred up to the crook, he was well instructed in the arts of war and qualified for the toils and perils of it. God, having called him to fight his battles, qualified him for the service. He made him very ingenious (*He teacheth my hands to war, v.* 35. And this ingenuity was as good as strength, for it follows, "so *that a bow of steel is broken by my arms,*" not so much by main force as by dexterity), and very vigorous and valiant. (*Thou hast girded me with strength to battle, v.* 40. He gives God the glory of all his courage and ability for service), and very expeditious: *He maketh my feet swift like hinds feet* (*v.* 34), which is of great advantage both in charging and retreating. (3.) With victory over his enemies, not only Saul and Absalom, but the Philistines, Moabites, Ammonites, Syrians, and other neighbouring nations, whom he subdued and made tributaries to Israel. His wonderful victories are here described, *v.* 38–43. They were *speedy* victories (*I turned not again till I had consumed them, v.* 38) and *complete* victories. The enemies of Israel were *wounded, destroyed, consumed,* fell *under his feet,* trampled upon, and disabled to rise, and their necks lay at his mercy. They cried both to earth and heaven for help, but in vain. *There was none to save,* none that durst appear for them. God *answered them, not* for they were not on his side, nor did they cry unto him till they were brought to the last extremity. Being thus abandoned, they became an easy prey to David's righteous and victorious sword, so that he *beat them as small as the dust of the earth,* which is scattered by the wind and trodden on by every foot. (4.) With advancement to honour and power. To this he was anointed before his troubles began, and at length, *post tot discrimina rerum — after all his dangers and disasters,* he gained his point. God *made his way perfect* (*v.* 33), gave him success in all his undertakings, *set him upon his high places* (*v.* 34), denoting both safety and dignity. God's gentleness, his grace and tender mercy, *made him great* (*v.* 36), gave him great wealth, and great authority, and a name like that of the great men of the earth. He was *kept to be the head of the heathen* (*v.* 44); his signal preservations evinced that he was designed and reserved for something great — to rule over all Israel, notwithstanding the *strivings of the people,* and so that those whom *he had not known should serve him,* many of the nations that lay remote. Thus he was *lifted up on high,* as high as the throne, above those that *rose up against him, v.* 49.

V. The comfortable reflections he makes upon his own integrity, which God, by those wonderful deliverances, had graciously owned and witnessed to, *v.* 21–25. He means especially his integrity with reference to Saul and Ishbosheth, Absalom and Sheba, and those who either opposed his coming to the crown or endeavoured to dethrone him. They falsely accused him and misrepresented him, but he had the testimony of this conscience for him that he was not an ambitious aspiring man, a false and bloody man, as they called him, — that he had never taken any indirect unlawful courses to secure or raise himself, but in his whole conduct had kept in the way of his duty, — and that in the whole course of his conversation he had, for the main, made religion his business, so that he could take God's favours to him as the rewards of his righteousness, not of debt, but of grace. God had recompensed him, though not for his righteousness, as if that had merited any thing at the hand of God, yet according to his righteousness, which he was well pleased with, and had an eye to. His conscience witnessed for him, 1. That he had made the word of God his rule, and had kept to it, *v.* 23. Wherever he was, God's judgments were before him as his guide; whithersoever he went, he took his religion along with him, and though he was forced to depart from his country, and sent, as it were, to serve other gods, yet as for God's statutes, he did not depart from them, but kept the way of the Lord and walked in it. 2. That he had carefully avoided the bye-paths of sin. He had not wickedly departed from his God. He could not say but that he had taken some false steps, but he had not deserted God, nor forsaken his way. Sins of infirmity he could not acquit himself from, but the grace of God had kept him from presumptuous sins. Though he had sometimes *weakly* departed from his God. By this it appeared that he was *upright before God,* or *to God* (in his sight, and with an eye to him), that he *kept himself from his own iniquity,* not only from that particular sin of killing Saul when it was in the power of his hand to do it, but, in general, he was afraid of sin and watchful against it, and made conscience of what he said and did. The matter of Uriah is an exception (1 Ki. 15:5), like that in Hezekiah's character, 2 Chr. 32:31. Note, A careful abstaining from our own iniquity is one of the best evidences of our own integrity; and the testimony of our conscience for us that we have done so will be such a rejoicing as will not only lessen the griefs of an afflicted state, but increase the comforts of a prosperous state. David reflected with more comfort upon his victories over his own iniquity than upon his conquest of Goliath and all the hosts of the uncircumcised Philistines; and the witness of his own heart to his uprightness was sweeter though more silent music than theirs that sang, *David has slain his ten thousands.* If a great man be a good man, his goodness will be much more his satisfaction than his greatness. Let favour be shown to the upright and his uprightness will sweeten it, will double it.

VI. The comfortable prospects he has of God's further favour. As he looks back, so he looks forward, with pleasure, and assures himself of the kindness God has in store for all the saints, for himself, and also for his seed.

1. For all good people, *v.* 26–28. As God had dealt with him according to his uprightness, so he will with all others. He takes occasion here to lay down the established rules of God's procedure with the children of men: —

(1.) That he will do good to those that are upright in their hearts. As we are found towards God, he will be found towards us. [1.] God's mercy and grace will be the joy of those that are merciful and gracious. Even the merciful need mercy; and they shall obtain it. [2.] God's uprightness, his justice and faithfulness, will be the joy of those that are upright, just, and faithful, both towards God and man. [3.] God's purity and holiness will be the joy of those that are pure and holy, who therefore give thanks at the remembrance thereof. And, if any of these good people be *afflicted people, he will save* them, either out of their afflictions or by and after them. On the other hand,

(2.) That those who turn aside to crooked ways he will *lead forth with the workers of iniquity,* as he says in another psalm. *With the froward he will wrestle;* and those with whom God wrestles are sure to be foiled. *Woe unto him that strives with his Maker!* God will walk contrary to those that walk contrary to him and be displeased with those that are displeased with him. As for the haughty, his eyes are upon them, marking them out, as it were, to be brought down; for *he resists the proud.*

2. For himself. He foresaw that his conquests and kingdom would be yet further enlarged, *v.* 45, 46. Even the *sons of the stranger,* that would hear the report of his victories and the tokens of God's presence with him, would be possessed with a fear of him, would be forced to submit to him, though feignedly, and would be obedient to him. The successes which he had had he looked upon as earnests of more and means of more. Who durst oppose him by whom so many had been overcome? Thus the Son of David *goes on conquering and to conquer,* Rev. 6:2. His gospel, which has been victorious, shall be so more and more.

3. For his seed: He *showeth mercy to his Messiah* (*v.* 51), not only to David himself, but to that seed of his for evermore. David was himself anointed of God, not a usurper, but duly called to the government and qualified for it; therefore he doubted not but God would show mercy to him, that mercy which he had promised not to take from him nor from his posterity (*ch.* 7:15, 16); on that promise he depends, with an eye to Christ, who alone is his *seed for evermore,* whose throne and kingdom still continue, and will to the end, whereas the seed and lineage of David are long since extinct. See Ps. 89:28, 29. Thus all his joys and all his hopes terminate, as ours should, in the great Redeemer.

CHAPTER 23

The historian is now drawing towards a conclusion of David's reign, and therefore gives us an account here, I. Of some of his last words, which he spoke by inspiration, and which seem to have reference to his seed that was to be for evermore, spoken of in the close of the foregoing chapter (*v.* 1–7). II. Of the great men, especially the military men, that were employed under him, the first three (*v.* 8–17), two of the next three (*v.* 18–23), and then the thirty (*v.* 24–39).

Verses 1–7

We have here the last will and testament of king David, or a codicil annexed to it, after he had settled the crown upon Solomon and his treasures upon the temple which was to be built. The last words of great and good men are thought worthy to be in a special manner remarked and remembered. David would have those taken notice of, and added either to his Psalms (as they are here to that in the foregoing chapter) or to the chronicles of his reign. Those words especially in *v.* 5, though recorded before, we may suppose he often repeated for his own consolation, even to his last breath, and therefore they are called his *last words.* When we find death approaching we should endeavor both to honour God and to edify those about us with our last words. Let those that have had long experience of God's goodness and the pleasantness of wisdom, when they come to finish their course, leave a record of that experience and bear their testimony to the truth of the promise. We have upon record the last words of Jacob and Moses, and here of David, designed, as those, for a legacy to those that were left behind. We are here told,

I. Whose last will and testament this is. This is related either, or is usual, by the testator himself, or rather, by the historian, *v.* 1. He is described, 1. By the meanness of his original: He was *the son of Jesse.* It is good for those who are advanced to be corner-stones and top-stones to be reminded, and often to remind themselves, of *the rock out of which they were hewn.* 2. The height of his elevation: He *was raised up on high,* as one favoured of God, and designed for something great, raised up as a prince, to sit higher than his neighbours, and as a prophet, to see further; for, (1.) He was *the anointed of the God of Jacob,* and so was serviceable to the people of God in their civil interests, the protection of their country and the administration of justice among them. (2.) He was *the sweet psalmist of Israel,* and so was serviceable to them in their religious exercises. he penned the psalms, set the tunes, appointed both the singers and the instruments of music, by which the devotions of good people were much excited and enlarged. Note, The singing of psalms is a sweet ordinance, very agreeable to those that delight in praising

God. It is reckoned among the honours to which David was raised up that he was a psalmist: in that he was as truly great as in his being *the anointed of the God of Jacob.* Note, It is true preferment to be serviceable to the church in acts of devotion and instrumental to promote the blessed work of prayer and praise. Observe, Was David a prince? He was so for Jacob. Was he a psalmist? He was so for Israel. Note, the dispensation of the Spirit is given to every man to profit withal, and therefore, *as every man has received the gift, so let him minister the same.*

II. What the purport of it is. It is an account of his communion with God. Observe,

1. What God said to him both for his direction and for his encouragement as a king, and to be in like manner, of use to his successors. Pious persons take a pleasure in calling to mind what they have heard from God, in recollecting his word, and revolving it in their minds. Thus what God spoke once David heard twice, yea often. See here,

(1.) Who spoke: *The Spirit of the Lord, the God of Israel,* and *the Rock of Israel,* which some think is an intimation of the Trinity of persons in the Godhead — the Father *the God of Israel,* the Son *the Rock of Israel,* and *the Spirit* proceeding from the Father and the Son, *who spoke by the prophets,* and particularly by David, and whose word was not only in his heart, but in his tongue for the benefit of others. David here avows his divine inspiration, that in his psalms, and in this composition, *The Spirit of God spoke by him.* He, and other holy men, spoke and *wrote as they were moved by the Holy Ghost.* This puts an honour upon the book of Psalms, and recommends them to our use in our devotions, that they are words which the Holy Ghost teaches.

(2.) What was spoken. Here seems to be a distinction made between what the Spirit of God spoke *by* David, which includes all his psalms, and what the Rock of Israel spoke *to* David, which concerned himself and his family. Let ministers observe that those by whom God speaks to others are concerned to hear and heed what he speaks to themselves. Those whose office it is to teach others their duty must be sure to learn and do their own. Now that which is here said (*v.* 3, 4) may be considered, [1.] With application to David, and his royal family. And so here is, *First,* The duty of magistrates enjoined them. When a king was spoken to from God he was not to be complimented with the height of his dignity and the extent of his power, but to be told his duty. "Must is for the king," we say. Here is a *must* for the king: *He must be just, ruling in the fear of God;* and so must all inferior magistrates in their places. Let rulers remember that they rule over men — not over beasts which they may enslave and abuse at pleasure, but over reasonable creatures and of the same rank with themselves. They rule over men that have their follies and infirmities, and therefore must be borne with. They rule over men, but under God, and for him; and therefore, 1. They must be just, both to those over whom they rule, in allowing them their rights and properties, and between those over whom they rule, using their power to right the injured against the injurious; see Deu. 1:16, 17. It is not enough that they do no wrong, but they must not suffer wrong to be done. 2. They must rule in the fear of God, that is, they must themselves be possessed with a fear of God, by which they will be effectually restrained from all acts of injustice and oppression. Nehemiah was so (Neh. 5:15, *So did not I, because of the fear of God),* and Joseph, Gen. 43:18. They must also endeavor to promote the fear of God (that is, the practice of religion) among those over whom they rule. The magistrate is to be the keeper of both tables, and to protect both godliness and honesty. *Secondly,* Prosperity promised them if they do, this duty. *He that* rules *in the fear of God shall be as the light of the morning, v.* 4. Light is sweet and pleasant, and he that does his duty shall have the comfort of it; his rejoicing will be the testimony of his conscience. Light is bright, and a good prince is illustrious; his justice and piety will be his honour. Light is a blessing, nor are there any greater and more extensive blessings to the public than princes that *rule in the fear of God.* As *the light of the morning,* which is most welcome after the darkness of the night (so was David's government after Saul's, Ps. 75:3), which is increasing, shines more and more to the perfect day, such is the growing lustre of a good government. It is likewise compared to the tender grass, which the earth produces for the service of man; it brings with it a harvest of blessings. See Ps. 72:6, 16, which were also some of the last words of David, and seem to refer to those recorded here. [2.] With application to Christ, the Son of David, and then it must all be taken as a prophecy, and the original will bear it: *There shall be a rule among men,* or over men, that *shall be just,* and *shall rule in the fear of God,* that is, shall order the affairs of religion and divine worship according to his Father's will; and he shall be as *the light to the morning,* etc., for he is the light of the world, and *as the tender grass,* for he is the *branch of the Lord,* and the *fruit of the earth,* Isa. 11:1–5; 32:1, 2; Ps. 72:2. God, by the Spirit, gave David the foresight of this, to comfort him under the many calamities of his family and the melancholy prospects he had of the degeneracy of his seed.

2. What comfortable use he made of this which God spoke to him, and what were his devout meditations on it, by way of reply, *v.* 5. It is not unlike his meditation on occasion of such a message, 2 Sa. 7:18, etc. That which goes before the Rock of Israel spoke *to* him; this the Spirit of God spoke *by* him, and it is a most excellent confession of his faith and hope in the everlasting covenant. Here is,

(1.) Trouble supposed: *Although my house be not so with God,* and *although he make it not to grow.* David's family was not so with God as is described (*v.* 3, 4), and as he could wish, not so good, not so happy; it had not been so while he lived; he foresaw it would not be so when he was gone, that his house would be neither so pious nor so prosperous as one might have expected the offspring of such a father to be. [1.] *Not so with God.* Note, We and ours are that really which we are with God. This was what David's heart was upon concerning his children, that they might be right with God, faithful to him and zealous for him. But the children of godly parents are often neither so holy nor so happy as might be expected. We must be made to know that it is corruption, not grace, that runs in the blood, that the race is not to the swift, but that God gives his Spirit as a free-agent. [2.] *Not made to grow,* in number, in power; it is God that makes families to grow or not to grow, Ps. 107:41. Good men have often the melancholy prospect of a declining family. David's house was typical of the church of Christ, which is his house, Heb. 3:3. Suppose this be not so with God as we could wish, suppose it be diminished, distressed, disgraced, and weakened, by errors and corruptions, yea, almost extinct, yet God has made a covenant with the church's head, the Son of David, that he will preserve to him a seed, that the gates of hell shall never prevail against his house. This our Saviour comforted himself with in his sufferings, that the covenant with him stood firm, Isa. 53:10–12. (2.) Comfort ensured: *Yet he hath made with me an everlasting covenant.* Whatever trouble a child of God may have the prospect of, still he has some comfort or other to balance it with (2 Co. 4:8, 9), and there is none like this of the Psalmist, which may be understood, [1.] Of the covenant of royalty (in the type) which God made with David and his seed, touching the kingdom, Ps. 132:11, 12. But, [2.] It must look further, to the covenant of grace made with all believers, that God will be, in Christ, to them a God, which was signified by the covenant of royalty, and therefore the promises of the covenant are called *the sure mercies of David,* Isa. 55:3. It is this only that is the everlasting covenant, and it cannot be imagined that David, who, in so many of his psalms, speaks so clearly concerning Christ and the grace of the gospel, should forget it in his last words. God has made a covenant of grace with us in Jesus Christ, and we are here told, *First,* That it is an *everlasting* covenant, from everlasting in the contrivance and counsel of it, and to everlasting in the continuance and consequences of it. *Secondly,* That it is *ordered,* well ordered in all things, admirably well, to advance the glory of God and the honour of the Mediator, together with the holiness and comfort of believers. It is herein well ordered, that whatever is required in the covenant is promised, and that every transgression in the covenant does not throw us out of covenant, and that it puts our salvation, not in our own keeping, but in the keeping of a Mediator. *Thirdly,* That it is *sure,* and *therefore* sure because well ordered; the general offer of it is sure; the promised mercies are sure on the performance of the conditions. The particular application of it to true believers is sure; it is sure to all the seed. *Fourthly,* That it is *all our salvation.* Nothing but this will save us, and this is sufficient: it is this only upon which our salvation depends. *Fifthly,* That therefore it must be *all our desire.* Let me have an interest in this covenant and the promises of it, and I have enough, I desire no more.

3. Here is the doom of the sons of Belial read, *v.* 6, 7. (1.) They shall be thrust away as thorns — rejected, abandoned. They are like thorns, not to be touched with hands, so passionate and furious that they cannot be managed or dealt with by a wise and faithful reproof, but must be restrained by law and the sword of justice (Ps. 32:9); and therefore, like thorns, (2.) They shall, at length, be utterly burnt with fire in the same place, Heb. 6:8. Now this is intended, [1.] As a direction to magistrates to use their power for the punishing and suppressing of wickedness. Let them *thrust away the sons of Belial;* see Ps. 101:8. Or, [2.] As a caution to magistrates, and particularly to David's sons and successors, to see that they be not themselves sons of Belial (as too many of them were), for then neither the dignity of their place nor their relation to David would secure them from being thrust away by the righteous judgments of God. Though men could not deal with them, God would. Or, [3.] As a prediction of the ruin of all the implacable enemies of Christ's kingdom. There are enemies without, that openly oppose it and fight against it, and enemies within, that secretly betray it and are false to it; both are sons of Belial, children of the wicked one, of the serpent's seed; both are as thorns, grievous and vexatious: but both shall be so thrust away as that Christ will set up his kingdom in despite of their enmity, will *go through them* (Isa. 27:4), and will, in due time, bless his church with such peace that there shall be *no pricking brier nor grieving thorn.* And those that will not repent, to give glory to God, shall, in the judgment-day (to which the Chaldee paraphrast refers this), be burnt with unquenchable fire. See Lu. 19:27.

Verses 8–39

I. The catalogue which the historian has here left upon record of the great soldiers that were in David's time is intended, 1. For the honour of David, who trained them up in the arts of exercises of war, and set them an example of conduct and courage. It is the reputation as well as the advantage of a prince to be attended and served by such brave men as are here described. 2. For the honour of those worthies themselves, who were instrumental to bring David to the crown, settle and protect him in the throne, and enlarge his conquests. Note, Those that in public stations venture themselves, and lay out themselves, to serve the interests of their country, are worthy of double honour, both to be respected by those of their own age and to be remembered by posterity. 3. To excite those that come after to a generous emulation. 4. To show how much religion contributes to the inspiring of men with true courage. David, both by his psalms and by his offerings for the service of the temple, greatly promoted piety among the grandees of the kingdom (1 Chr. 29:6), and, when they became famous for piety, they became famous for bravery.

II. Now these mighty men are here divided into three ranks: —

1. The first three, who had done the greatest exploits and thereby gained the greatest reputation — Adino (*v.* 8), Eleazar (*v.* 9, 10), and Shammah, *v.* 11, 12. I do not remember that we read of any of these, or of their actions, any where in all the story of David but here and in the parallel place, 1 Chr. 11. Many great and remarkable events are passed by in the annals, which relate rather the blemishes than the glories of David's reign, especially after his sin in the matter Uriah; so that we may conclude his reign to have been really more illustrious than it has appeared to us while reading the records of it. The exploits of this brave triumvirate are here recorded. They signalized themselves in the wars of Israel against their enemies, especially the Philistines. (1.) Adino slew 800 at once with his spear. (2.) Eleazar defied the Philistines, as they by Goliath, had defied Israel, but with better success and greater bravery; for when the men of Israel had gone away, he not only kept his ground, but *arose, and smote the Philistines,* on whom God struck a terror equal to the courage with which this great hero was inspired. His hand was weary, and yet it clave to his sword; as long as he had any strength remaining he held his weapon and followed his blow. Thus, in the service of God, we should keep up the

willingness and resolution of the spirit, notwithstanding the weakness and weariness of the flesh — faint, yet pursuing (Jdg. 8:4), the hand weary, yet not quitting the sword. Now that Eleazar had beaten the enemy, the men of Israel, who had gone away from the battle (*v.* 9), returned to spoil, *v.* 10. It is common for those who quit the field, when any thing is to be done to hasten to it when any thing is to be gotten. (3.) Shammah met with a party of the enemy, that were foraging, and routed them, *v.* 11, 12. But observe, both concerning this exploit and the former, it is here said, *The Lord wrought a great victory.* Note, How great soever the bravery of the instruments is, the praise of the achievement must be given to God. These fought the battles, but God wrought the victory. Let not the strong man then glory in his strength, nor in any of his military operations, but *let him that glories glory in the Lord.*

2. The next three were distinguished from, and dignified above, the thirty, but attained not to the first three, *v.* 23. All great men are not of the same size. Many a bright and benign star there is which is not of the first magnitude, and many a good ship not of the first rate. Of this second triumvirate two only are named, Abishai and Benaiah, whom we have often met with in the story of David, and who seem to have been not inferior in serviceableness, though they were in dignity, to the first three. Here is,

(1.) A brave action of these three in conjunction. They attended David in his troubles, when he absconded, in the cave of Adullam (*v.* 13), suffered with him, and therefore were afterwards preferred by him. When David and his brave men who attended him, who had acted so vigorously against the Philistines, were, by the iniquity of the times, in Saul's reign, driven to shelter themselves from his rage in caves and strong holds, no marvel that the Philistines pitched in the valley of Rephaim, and put a garrison even in Bethlehem itself, *v.* 13, 14. If the church's guides are so misled as to persecute some of her best friends and champions, the common enemy will, no doubt, get advantage by it. If David had had his liberty, Bethlehem would not have been now in the Philistines' hands. But, being so, we are here told, [1.] How earnestly David longed for the water of the well of Bethlehem. Some make it a public-spirited wish, and that he meant, "O that we could drive the garrison of the Philistines out of Bethlehem, and make that beloved city of mine our own again!" the well being put for the city, as the river often signifies the country it passes through. But if he meant so, those about him did not understand him; therefore it seems rather to be an instance of his weakness. It was harvest-time; the weather was hot; he was thirsty; perhaps good water was scarce, and therefore he earnestly wished, "O that I could but have one draught of the water of the well of Bethlehem!" With the water of that well he had often refreshed himself when he was a youth, and nothing now will serve him but that, though it is almost impossible to come at it. He strangely indulged a humour which he could give no reason for. Other water might quench his thirst as well, but he had a fancy for that above any. It is folly to entertain such fancies and greater folly to insist upon the gratification of them. We ought to check our appetites when they go out inordinately towards those things that really are more pleasant and grateful than other things *(Be not desirous of dainties),* much more when they are thus set upon such things as only please a humour. [2.] How bravely his three mighty men, Abishai, Benaiah, and another not named, ventured through the camp of the Philistines, upon the very mouth of danger, and fetched water from the well of Bethlehem, without David's knowledge, *v.* 16. When he wished for it he was far from desiring that any of his men should venture their lives for it; but those three did, to show, *First,* How much they valued their prince, and with what pleasure they could run the greatest hardships in his service. David, though anointed king, was as yet an exile, a poor prince that had no external advantages to recommend him to the affection and esteem of his attendants, nor was he in any capacity to prefer or reward them; yet those three were thus zealous for his satisfaction, firmly believing the time of recompence would come. Let us be willing to venture in the cause of Christ, even when it is a suffering cause, as those who are assured that it will prevail and that we shall not lose by it at last. Were they so forward to expose themselves upon the least hint of their prince's mind and so ambitious to please him? And shall not we covet to approve ourselves to our Lord Jesus by a ready compliance with every intimation of his will given us by his word, Spirit and providence? *Secondly,* How little they feared the Philistines. They were glad of an occasion to defy them. Whether they broke through the host clandestinely, and with such art that the Philistines did not discover them, or openly, and with such terror in their looks that the Philistines durst not oppose them, is not certain; it should seem, they forced their way, sword in hand. But see, [3.] How self-denyingly David, when he had this far-fetched dear-bought water, *poured it out before the Lord, v.* 17. *First,* Thus he would show the tender regard he had to the lives of his soldiers, and how far he was from being prodigal of their blood, Ps. 72:14. In God's sight the death of his saints is precious. *Secondly,* Thus he would testify his sorrow for speaking that foolish word which occasioned those men to put their lives in their hands. Great men should take heed what they say, lest any bad use be made of it by those about them. *Thirdly,* Thus he would prevent the like rashness in any of his men for the future. *Fourthly,* Thus he would cross his own foolish fancy, and punish himself for entertaining and indulging it, and show that he had sober thoughts to correct his rash ones, and knew how to deny himself even in that which he was most fond of. Such generous mortifications become the wise, the great, and the good. *Fifthly,* Thus he would honour God and give glory to him. The water purchased at this rate he thought too precious for his own drinking and fit only to be poured out to God as a drink-offering. If it was the blood of these men, it was God's due, for the blood was always his. *Sixthly,* Bishop Patrick speaks of some who think that David hereby showed that it was not material water he longed for, but the Messiah, who had the water of life, who, he knew, should be born at Bethlehem, which the Philistines therefore should not be able to destroy. *Seventhly,* Did David look upon that water as very precious which was got at the hazard of these men's blood, and shall not we much more value those benefits for the purchasing of which our blessed Saviour shed his blood? Let us not undervalue the blood of the covenant, as those do that undervalue the blessings of the covenant.

(2.) The brave actions of two of them on other occasions. Abishai slew 300 men at once, *v.* 18, 19. Benaiah did many great things. [1.] He slew two Moabites that were lion-like men, so bold and strong, so fierce and furious. [2.] He slew an Egyptian, on what occasion it is not said; he was well armed but Benaiah attacked him with no other weapon than a walking staff, dexterously wrested his spear out of his hand, and slew him with it, *v.* 21. For these and similar exploits David preferred him to be captain of the life-guard or standing forces, *v.* 23.

3. Inferior to the second three, but of great note, were the thirty-one here mentioned by name, *v.* 24, etc. Asahel is the first, who was slain by Abner in the beginning of David's reign, but lost not his place in this catalogue. Elhanan is the next, brother to Eleazar, one of the first three, *v.* 9. The surnames here given them are taken, as it should seem, from the places of their birth or habitation, as many surnames with us originally were. From all parts of the nation, the most wise and valiant were picked up to serve the king. Several of those who are named we find captains of the twelve courses which David appointed, one for each month in the year, 1 Chr. 27. Those that did worthily were preferred according to their merits. One of them was the son of Ahithophel (*v.* 34), the son famous in the camp as the father at the council-board. But to find Uriah the Hittite bringing up the rear of these worthies, as it revives the remembrance of David's sin, so it aggravates it, that a man who deserved so well of his king and country should be so ill treated. Joab is not mentioned among all these, either, (1.) to be mentioned; the first, of the first three sat chief among the captains, but Joab was over them as general. Or, (2.) Because he was so bad that he did not deserve to be mentioned; for though he was confessedly a great soldier, and one that had so much religion in him as to dedicate of his spoils to the house of God (1 Chr. 26:28), yet he lost as much honour by slaying two of David's friends as ever he got by slaying his enemies.

Christ, the Son of David, has his worthies too, who like David's, are influenced by his example, fight his battles against the spiritual enemies of his kingdom, and in his strength are more than conquerors. Christ's apostles were his immediate attendants, did and suffered great things for him, and at length came to reign with him. They are mentioned with honour in the New Testament, as these in the Old, especially, Rev. 21:14. Nay, all the good soldiers of Jesus Christ have their names better preserved than even these worthies have; for they are written in heaven. This honour have all his saints.

CHAPTER 24

The last words of David, which we read in the chapter before, were admirably good, but in this chapter we read of some of his last works, which were none of the best; yet he repented, and did his first works again, and so he finished well. We have here, I. His sin, which was numbering the people in the pride of his heart (*v.* 1–9). II. His conviction of the sin, and repentance for it (*v.* 10). III. The judgment inflicted upon him for it (*v.* 11–15). IV. The staying of the judgment (*v.* 16, 17). V. The erecting of an altar in token of God's reconciliation to him and his people (*v.* 18–25).

Verses 1–9

Here we have,

I. The orders which David gave to Joab to number the people of Israel and Judah, *v.* 1, 2. Two things here seem strange: — 1. The sinfulness of this. What harm was there in it? Did not Moses twice number the people without any crime? Does not political arithmetic come in among the other policies of a prince? Should not the shepherd know the number of his sheep? Does not the Son of David know all his own by name? Might not he make good use of this calculation? What evil has he done, if he do this? *Answer,* It is certain that it was a sin, and a great sin; but where the evil of it lay is not so certain. (1.) Some think the fault was that he numbered those that were under twenty years old if they were but of stature and strength able to bear arms, and that this was the reason why this account was not enrolled, because it was illegal, 1 Chr. 27:23, 24. (2.) Others think the fault was that he did not require the half-shekel, which was to be paid for the service of the sanctuary whenever the people were numbered, as a *ransom for their souls,* Ex. 30:12. (3.) Others think that he did it with a design to impose a tribute upon them for himself, to be put into his treasury, and this by way of poll, so that when he knew their numbers he could tell what it would amount to. But nothing of this appears, nor was David ever a raiser of taxes. (4.) This was the fault, that he had no orders from God to do it, nor was there any occasion for the doing of it. It was a needless trouble both to himself and to his people. (5.) Some think that it was an affront to the ancient promise which God made to Abraham, that his seed should be innumerable as the dust of the earth; it savoured of distrust of that promise, or a design to show that it was not fulfilled in the letter of it. He would number those of whom God had said that they could not be numbered. Those know not what they do that go about to disprove the word of God. (6.) That which was the worst thing in numbering the people was that David did it in the pride of his heart, which was Hezekiah's sin in showing his treasures to the ambassadors. [1.] It was a proud conceit of his own greatness in having the command of so numerous a people, as if their increase, which was to be ascribed purely to the blessing of God, had been owing to any conduct of his own. [2.] It was a proud confidence in his own strength. By publishing among the nations the number of his people, he thought to appear the more formidable, and doubted not that, if he should have any war, he should overpower his enemies with the multitude of his forces, trusting in God only. God judges not of sin as we do. What appears to us harmless, or at least but a small offence, may be a great sin in the eye of God, who sees men's principles, and is a discerner of the thoughts and intents of the heart. But his judgment, we are sure, is according to truth.

2. The spring from which it is here said to arise is yet more strange, *v.* 1. It is not strange that *the anger of the Lord should be kindled against Israel.* There was cause enough for it. They were unthankful for the blessings of David's government, and strangely drawn in to take part with Absalom first and afterwards with Sheba. We have reason to think that their peace and plenty made them secure and sensual, and that God was therefore displeased with them. But that, in this displeasure, he should move David to number the people is very strange. We are sure that God is not the author of sin; he tempts no man: we

are told (1 Chr. 21:1) that *Satan provoked David to number Israel.* Satan, as an enemy, suggested it for a sin, as he put it into the heart of Judas to betray Christ. God, as righteous Judge, permitted it, with a design, from this sin of David, to take an occasion to punish Israel for other sins, for which he might justly have punished them without this. But, as before he brought a famine upon them for the sin of Saul, so now a pestilence for the sin of David, that princes may from these instances learn, when the judgments of God are abroad, to suspect that their sins are the ground of the controversy, and may therefore repent and reform themselves, which should have a great influence upon national repentance and reformation, and that people may learn to pray for those in authority, that God would keep them from sin, because, if they sin, the kingdom smarts.

II. The opposition which Joab made to these orders. Even he was aware of David's folly and vain-glory in this design. He observed that David gave no reason for it, only, *Number the people, that I may know the number of the people;* and therefore he endeavored to divert his pride, and in a much more respectful manner than he had before endeavoured to divert his passion upon the death of Absalom; then he spoke rudely and insolently (*ch.* 19:5–7), but now as became him: *Now the Lord thy God add unto the people a hundred fold, v.* 3. There was no occasion to tax them, nor to enlist them, nor to make any distribution of them. They were all easy and happy; and Joab wished both that their number might increase and that the king, though old, might live to see their increase, and have the satisfaction of it. *"But why doth my lord the king delight in this thing?* What need is there of doing it?" *Pauperis est numerare pecus — Leave it to the poor to count their flocks.* Especially why should David, who speaks so much of delighting in God and the exercises of devotion, and who, being old, one would think, should have put away childish things, take a pleasure (so he calls it modestly, but he means taking pride) in a thing of this nature? Note, Many things, not in themselves sinful, turn into sin to us by our inordinately delighting in them. Joab was aware of David's vanity herein, but he himself was not. It would be good for us to have a friend that would faithfully admonish us when we say or do any thing proud or vain-glorious, for we often do so and are not ourselves aware of it.

III. The orders executed notwithstanding. *The king's word prevailed, v.* 4. He would have it done; Joab must not gainsay it, lest he be thought to grudge his time and pains in the king's service. It is an unhappiness to great men to have those about them that will aid them and serve them in that which is evil. Joab, according to order, applied himself with some reluctancy to this unpleasing task, and took the captains of the host to help him. They began in the most distant places, in the east first, on the other side Jordan (*v.* 5), then they went towards Dan in the north (*v.* 6), so to Tyre on the east, and thence to Beersheba in the south, *v.* 7. Above nine months were spent in taking this account, a great deal of trouble and amazement were occasioned by it in the country (*v.* 8), and the sum total was, at length, brought to the king at Jerusalem, *v.* 9. Whether the numbers answered David's expectation or no we are not told, nor whether the account fed his pride or mortified it. The people were very many, but, it may be, not so many as he thought they were. They had not increased in Canaan as they had in Egypt, nor were much more than double to what they were when they came into Canaan under Joshua, about 400 years before; yet it is an evidence that Canaan was a very fruitful land that so many thousands were maintained within so narrow a compass.

Verses 10–17

We have here David repenting of the sin and yet punished for it, God repenting of the judgment and David thereby made more penitent.

I. Here is David's penitent reflection upon and confession of his sin in numbering the people. While the thing was in doing, during all those nine months, we do not find that David was sensible of his sin, for had he been so he would have countermanded the orders he had given; but, when the account was finished and laid before him, that very night his conscience was awakened, and he felt the pain of it just then when he promised himself the pleasure of it. When he was about to feast on the satisfaction of the number of his people, it was turned into the gall of asps within him; sense of the sin cast a damp upon the joy, *v.* 10. 1. He was convinced of his sin: *His heart smote him* before the prophet came to him (I think it should not be read *for, v.* 11, but *and, when David was up,* so it is in the original), his conscience showed him the evil of what he had done; now that appeared sin, and exceedingly sinful, which before he saw no harm in. He reflected upon it with great regret and his heart reproached him for it. Note, It is a good thing, when a man has sinned, to have a heart within him to smite him for it; it is a good sign of a principle of grace in the heart, and a good step towards repentance and reformation. 2. He confessed it to God and begged earnestly for the forgiveness of it. (1.) He owned that he had sinned, sinned greatly, though to others it might seem no sin at all, or a very little one. True penitents, whose consciences are tender and well informed, see that evil in sin which others do not see. (2.) He owned that he had *done foolishly, very foolishly,* because he had done it in the pride of his heart; and it was folly for him to be proud of the numbers of his people, when they were God's people, not his, and, as many as they were, God could soon make them fewer. (3.) He cried to God for pardon: *I beseech thee, O Lord! take away the iniquity of thy servant. If we confess our sins,* we may pray in faith that God *will forgive them,* and take away, by pardoning mercy, that iniquity which we cast away by sincere repentance.

II. The just and necessary correction which he suffered for this sin. David had been full of tossings to and fro all night under the sense of his sin, having no rest in his bones because of it, *and he arose in the morning* expecting to hear of God's displeasure against him for what he had done, or designing to speak with Gad his seer concerning it. Gad is called his *seer* because he had him always at hand to advise with in the things of God, and made use of him as his confessor and counsellor; but God prevented him, and directed the prophet Gad what to say to him (*v.* 11), and,

1. Three things are taken for granted, (1.) That David must be corrected for his fault. It is too great a crime, and reflects too much dishonour upon God, to go unpunished, even in David himself. Of the seven things that God hates, pride is the first, Prov. 6:17. Note, Those who truly repent of their sins, and have them pardoned are yet often made to smart for them in this world. (2.) The punishment must answer to the sin. He was proud of the judgment he must be chastised with for this sin must be such as will make them fewer. Note, What we make the matter of our pride it is just with God to take from us, or embitter to us, and, some way or other, to make the matter of our punishment. (3.) It must be such a punishment as the people must have a large share in, *for God's anger was kindled against Israel, v.* 1. Though it was David's sin that immediately opened the sluice, the sins of the people all contributed to the deluge.

2. As to the punishment that must be inflicted,

(1.) David is told to choose what rod he will be beaten with, *v.* 12, 13. His heavenly Father must correct him, but, to show that he does not do it willingly, he gives David leave to make choice whether it shall be by war, famine, or pestilence, three sore judgments, which greatly weaken and diminish a people. God, by putting him thus to his choice, designed, [1.] To humble him the more for his sin, which we would see to be exceedingly sinful when he came to consider each of these judgments as exceedingly dreadful. Or, [2.] To upbraid him with the proud conceit he had of his own sovereignty over Israel. He that is so great a prince begins to think he may have what he will. "Come then," says God, "which wilt thou have of these three things?" Compare Jer. 34:17, *I proclaim a liberty for you,* but it is such a liberty as this of David's *to the sword, to the pestilence, and to the famine;* and Jer. 15:2, *Such as are for death to death.* Or [3.] To give him some encouragement under the correction, letting him know that God did not cast him out of communion with himself, but that still his secret was with him, and in afflicting him he considered his frame and what he could best bear. Or [4.] That he might the more patiently bear the rod when it was a rod of his own choosing. The prophet bids him advise with himself, and then tell him what answer he should *return to him that sent him.* Note, Ministers are sent of God to us, and they must give an account of the success of their embassy. It concerns us therefore to consider what answer they shall return from us, that they may give up their account of us with joy.

(2.) He objects only against the judgments of the sword, and, for the other two, he refers the matter to God, but intimates his choice of the pestilence rather (*v.* 14): *I am in a great strait;* and well he might be *when fear, and the pit, and the snare, were before him,* and if he escape one, he must inevitably fall into the other, Jer. 48:43, 44. Note, Sin brings men into straits; wise and good men often distress themselves by their own folly. [1.] He begs that he may *not fall into the hand of man.* "Whatever comes, *let us not flee three months before our enemies;"* this would sully all the glory of David's triumphs and give occasion to the enemies of God and Israel to *behave themselves proudly.* See Deu. 32:26, 27. "Their tender mercies are cruel; and in three months they will do that damage to the nation which many years will not repair." But, [2.] He casts himself upon God: *Let us fall now into the hand of the Lord, for his mercies are great.* Men are *God's hand* (so they are called, Ps. 17:14, the sword of his sending), yet there are some judgments which come more immediately from his hand than others, as famine and pestilence, and David refers it to God which of these shall be the scourge, and God chooses the shortest, that he may the sooner testify his being reconciled. But some think that David, by these words, intimates his choice of the pestilence. The land had not yet recovered the famine under which it smarted three years upon the Gibeonites' account, and therefore, "Let us not be corrected with that rod, for that also will be the triumph of our neighbours," hence we read of *the reproach of famine* (Eze. 36:30); "but if Israel must be diminished, let it be by the pestilence, for that is *falling into the hands of the Lord,"* who usually inflicted that judgment by the hand of his own immediate servants, the angels, as in the death of the first-born of Egypt. That is a judgment to which David himself, and his own family, lie as open as the meanest subject, but not so either to famine or sword, and therefore David, tenderly conscious of his guilt, chooses that. Sword and famine will devour one as well as another, but, it may be thought, the destroying angel will draw his sword against those who are known to God to be most guilty. This will be of the shortest continuance, and he dreads the thought of lying long under the tokens of God's displeasure. *It is a dreadful thing,* the apostle says, *to fall into the hands of the living God* (Heb. 10:31), a fearful thing indeed for sinners that have, by their impenitency, shut themselves out from all hope of his mercy. But David, a penitent, dares cast himself into God's hand, knowing he shall find that *his mercies are great.* Good men, even when they are under God's frowns, yet will entertain no other than good thoughts of him. *Though he slay me, yet will I trust in him.*

(3.) A pestilence is accordingly sent (*v.* 15), which, for the extent of it, spread from Dan to Beersheba, from one end of the kingdom to the other, which showed it to come immediately from God's hand and not from any natural causes. David has his choice; he suffers by miracle, and not by ordinary means. For the continuance of it, it lasted from morning (this very morning on which it was put to David's choice) to the time appointed that is, to the third day (so Mr. Poole), or only to the evening of the first day, the time appointed for the evening sacrifice, so bishop Patrick and others, who reckon that the pestilence lasted but nine hours, and that, in compassion to David, God shortened the time he had first mentioned. The execution the pestilence did was very severe. *There died* 70,000 *men,* that were all well, and sick, and dead, in a few hours. What a great cry, may we suppose, was there now throughout all the land of Israel, as there was in Egypt when the first-born were slain! but that was at midnight, this in the day-time, Ps. 91:6. See the power of the angels, when God gives them commission, either to save or to destroy. Joab is nine months in passing with his pen, the angel but nine hours in passing with his sword, through all the coasts and corners of the land of Israel. See how easily God can bring down the proudest sinners, and how much we owe daily to the divine patience. David's adultery is punished, for the present, only with the death of one infant, his pride with the death of all those thousands, so much does God hate pride. The number slain amounted to almost half a decimation, 70,000 being about one in twenty. Now, we may suppose, David's flesh *trembled for fear of God and he was afraid of his judgments,* Ps. 119:120.

III. God's gracious relaxation of the judgment, when it began to be inflicted upon Jerusalem (*v.* 16): *The angel stretched out his hand upon Jerusalem,* as if he intended to do greater execution there than any where else, even *to destroy it.* The country had drunk of the bitter cup, but Jerusalem must drink the dregs. It should seem that was last numbered, and therefore was reserved to be last plagued; perhaps there was more wickedness, especially more pride (and that was the sin now chastised), in Jerusalem than elsewhere, therefore the hand of the destroyer is stretched out upon that; but then *the Lord repented him of the evil,* changed not his mind, but his way; and said to the destroying angel, *It is enough; stay now thy hand,* and *let mercy rejoice against judgment.* Jerusalem shall be spared for the ark's sake, for it is the place God hath chosen to put his name there. See here how ready God is to forgive and how little pleasure he takes in punishing; and let it encourage us to meet him by repentance in the way of his judgments. This was on Mount Moriah. Dr. Lightfoot observes that in the very place where Abraham, by a countermand from heaven, was stayed from slaying his son, this angel, by a like countermand, was stayed from destroying Jerusalem. It is for the sake of the great sacrifice that our forfeited lives are preserved from the destroying angel.

IV. David's renewed repentance for his sin upon this occasion, *v.* 17. He saw the angel (God opening his eyes for that purpose), saw his sword stretched out to destroy, a flaming sword, saw him ready to sheath it upon the orders given him to stay proceedings; seeing all this, he spoke, not to the angel (he knew better than to address himself to the servant in the presence of the Master, or to give that honour to the creature which is the Creator's due), but *to the Lord, and said, Lo, I have sinned.* Note, True penitents, the more they perceive of God's sparing pardoning mercy the more humbled they are for sin and the more resolved against it. They shall be ashamed *when I am pacified towards them,* Eze. 16:63. Observe, 1. How he criminates himself, as if he could never speak ill enough of his own fault: *"I have sinned, and I have done wickedly;* mine is the crime, and therefore on me be the cross. *Let thy hand be against me, and my father's house.* I am the sinner, let me be the sufferer;" so willing was he to accept the punishment of his iniquity, though he was worth 10,000 of them. 2. How he intercedes for the people, whose bitter lamentations made his heart to ache, and his ears to tin-

gle: *These sheep, what have they done?* Done! Why they had done much amiss; it was their sin that provoked God to leave David to himself to do as he did; yet, as becomes a penitent, he is severe upon his own faults, while he extenuates theirs. Most people, when God's judgments are abroad, charge others with being the cause of them, and care not who falls by them, so they can escape. But David's penitent and public spirit was otherwise affected. Let this remind us of the grace of our Lord Jesus, who gave himself for our sins and was willing that God's hand should be against him, that we might escape. The shepherd was smitten that the sheep might be spared.

Verses 18–25

Here is, I. A command sent to David to erect an altar in the place where he saw the angel, *v.* 18. This was to intimate to David, 1. That, upon his repeated submission and humiliation, God was now thoroughly reconciled to him; *for, if the Lord had been pleased to kill him, he would not have accepted an offering,* and therefore would not have ordered him to *build an altar.* God's encouraging us to offer to him spiritual sacrifices is a comfortable evidence of his reconciling us to himself. 2. That peace is made between God and sinners by sacrifice, and not otherwise, even by Christ the great propitiation, of whom all the legal sacrifices were types. It is for his sake that the destroying angel is told to stay his hand. 3. That when God's judgments are graciously stayed we ought to acknowledge it with thankfulness to his praise. This altar was to be for thank-offerings. See Isa. 12:1.

II. The purchase which David made of the ground in order hereunto. It seems the owner was a Jebusite, Araunah by name, proselyted no doubt to the Jewish religion, though by birth a Gentile, and therefore allowed, not only to dwell among the Israelites, but to have a possession of his own in a city, Lev. 25:29, 30. The piece of ground was a threshing-floor, a mean place, *yet* thus dignified — a place of labour, *therefore* thus dignified. Now,

1. David went in person to the owner, to treat with him. See his justice, that he would not so much as use this place in the present exigence, though the proprietor was an alien, though he himself was a king, and though he had express orders from God to rear an altar there, till he had bought it and paid for it. God *hates robbery for burnt-offering.* See his humility, how far he was from taking state; though a king, he was now a penitent, and therefore, in token of his self-abasement, he neither sent for Araunah to come to him nor sent another to deal with him, but went himself (*v.* 19), and, though it looked like a dimin-

ution of himself, he lost no honour by it. Araunah, when he saw him, went and *bowed himself to the ground before him v.* 20. Great men will never be the less respected for their humility, but the more.

2. Araunah, when he understood his business (*v.* 21), generously offered him, not only the ground to build his altar on, but *oxen for sacrifices,* and other things that might be of use to him in the service (*v.* 22), and all this *gratis,* and a good prayer into the bargain: *The Lord thy God accept thee!* This he did, (1.) Because he had a generous spirit with a great estate. *He gave as a king* (*v.* 23); though an ordinary subject, he had the spirit of a prince. In the Hebrew it is, *He gave, even the king to the king,* whence it is supposed that Araunah had been king of the Jebusites in that place, or was descended from their royal family, though now a tributary to David. (2.) Because he highly esteemed David, though his conqueror, upon the score of his personal merits, and never thought he could do too much to oblige him. (3.) Because he had an affection for Israel, and earnestly desired that *the plague might be stayed;* and the honour of its being stayed at *his threshing-floor,* he would account a valuable consideration for all he now tendered to David. 3. David resolved to pay the full value of it, and did so, *v.* 24. Here were two generous souls well met. Araunah is very willing to give; but David is determined to buy, and for a good reason: he will not offer that to God which costs him nothing. He would not take advantage of the pious Jebusite's generosity. He thanked him, no doubt, for his kind offer, but paid him *fifty shekels of silver* for the floor and the oxen for the present service, and afterwards 600 shekels of gold for the ground adjoining, to build the temple on. Note, Those know not what religion is whose chief care it is to make it cheap and easy to themselves, and who are best pleased with that which costs them least pains or money. What have we our substance for but to honour God with it? and how can it be better bestowed?

III. The building of the altar, and the offering of the proper sacrifices upon it (*v.* 25), burnt-offerings to the glory of God's justice in the execution that had been done, and peace-offerings to the glory of his mercy in the seasonable staying of the process. Hereupon God showed (it is supposed by fire from heaven consuming the sacrifices) that *he was entreated for the land,* and that it was in mercy that the plague was removed and in token of God's being reconciled both to prince and people. Christ is our altar, our sacrifice; in him alone we may expect to find favour with God, to escape his wrath, and the sword, the flaming sword, of the cherubim who *keep the way of the tree of life.*

AN EXPOSITION, WITH PRACTICAL OBSERVATIONS, OF

THE FIRST BOOK OF KINGS

Many histories are books of kings and their reigns, to which the affairs of their kingdoms are reduced; this is a piece of honour that has commonly been paid to crowned heads. The holy Scripture is the history of the kingdom of God among men, under the several administrations of it; but there the King is one and his name one. The particular history now before us accounts for the affairs of the kingdoms of Judah and Israel, yet with special regard to the kingdom of God among them; for still it is a sacred history, much more instructive and not less entertaining than any of the histories of the kings of the earth, to which (those of them that are of any certainty) it is prior in time; for though there were kings in Edom before there was any king in Israel, Gen. 36:31 (foreigners, in that point of state, got the precedency), yet the history of the kings of Israel lives, and will live, in holy Writ, to the end of the world, whereas that of the kings of Edom is long since buried in oblivion; for the honour that comes from God is durable, while the honour of the world is like a mushroom, which comes up in a night and perishes in a night. — The Bible began with the story of patriarchs, and prophets, and judges, men whose converse with heaven was more immediate, the record of which strengthens our faith, but is not so easily accommodated to our case, now that we expect not visions, as the subsequent history of affairs like ours under the direction of common providence; and here also we find, though not many types and figures of the Messiah, yet great expectations of him; for not only prophets, but kings, desired to see the great mysteries of the gospel, Lu. 10:24 — The two books of Samuel are introductions to the books of the Kings, as they relate the origin of the royal government in Saul and of the royal family in David. These two books give us an account of David's successor, Solomon, the division of his kingdom, and the suc-

cession of the several kings both of Judah and Israel, with an abstract of their history down to the captivity. And as from the book of Genesis we may collect excellent rules of economics, for the good governing of families, so from these books we may collect rules of politics, for the directing of public affairs. There is in these books special regard had to the house and lineage of David, from which Christ came. Some of his sons trod in his steps, and others did not. The characters of the kings of Judah may be thus briefly given: — David the devout, Solomon the wise, Rehoboam the simple, Abijah the valiant, Asa the upright, Jehoshaphat the religious, Jehoram the wicked, Ahaziah the profane, Joash the backslider, Amaziah the rash, Uzziah the mighty, Jotham the peaceable, Ahaz the idolater, Hezekiah the reformer, Manasseh the penitent, Amon the obscure, Josiah the tender-hearted, Jehoahaz, Jehoiakim, Jehoiachin, and Zedekiah, all wicked, and such as brought ruin quickly on themselves and their kingdom. The number of the good and bad is nearly equal, but the reigns of the good were generally long and those of the bad short, the consideration of which will make the state of Israel not altogether so bad in this period as at first it seems. In this first book we have, I. The death of David, *ch.* 1 and 2. II. The glorious reign of Solomon, and his building the temple (*ch.* 3–10), but the cloud his sun set under, *ch.* 11. III. The division of the kingdoms in Rehoboam, and his reign and Jeroboam's, *ch.* 12–14. IV. The reigns of Abijah and Asa over Judah, Baasha and Omri over Israel, *ch.* 15 and 16. V. Elijah's miracles, *ch.* 17–19. VI. Ahab's success against Benhadad, his wickedness and fall, *ch.* 20–22. And in all this history it appears that kings, though gods to us, are men to God, mortal and accountable.

CHAPTER 1

In this chapter we have, I. David declining in his health (*v.* 1–4). II. Adonijah aspiring to the kingdom, and treating his party, in order to it (*v.* 5–10). III. Nathan and Bathsheba contriving to secure the succession to Solomon, and prevailing for an order from David for the purpose (*v.* 11–31). IV. The anointing of Solomon accordingly, and the people's joy therein (*v.* 32–40). V. The effectual stop this put to Adonijah's usurpation, and the dispersion of his party thereupon (*v.* 41–49). VI. Solomon's dismission of Adonijah upon his good behaviour (*v.* 50–53).

Verses 1–4

David, as recorded in the foregoing chapter, had, by the great mercy of God, escaped the sword of the destroying angel. But our deliverances from or through diseases and dangers are but reprieves; if the candle be not blown out, it will burn out of itself. We have David here sinking under the infirmities of old age, and brought by them to the gates of the grave. He that *cometh up out of the pit shall fall into the snare;* and, one way or other, *we must needs die.* 1. It would have troubled one to see David so infirm. He as old, and his natural heat so wasted that no clothes could keep him warm, *v.* 1. David had been a valiant active man and a man of business, and very vehement had the flame always been in his breast; and yet now his blood is chilled and stagnated, he is confined to his bed, and there can get no heat. He was now seventy years old. Many, at that age, are as lively and fit for business as ever; but David was now chastised for his former sins, especially that in the matter of Uriah, and felt from his former toils and the hardships he had gone through in his youth, which then he made nothing of, but was now the worse for. *Let not the strong man glory in his strength,* which may soon be weakened by sickness, or at last will be weakened by old age. Let young people *remember their Creator in the days of their youth,* before these evil days come. What our hand finds to do for God, and our souls, and our generation, let us do with all our might, because the night comes, the night of old age, in which no man can work; and, when our strength has gone, it will be a comfort to remember that we used it well. 2. It would have troubled one to see his physicians so weak and unskilful that they knew no other way of relieving him than by outward applications. No cordials, no spirits, but, (1.) *They covered him with clothes,* which, where there is any inward heat, will keep it in, and so increase it; but, where it is not, they have none to communicate, no, not royal clothing. Elihu makes it a difficulty to understand *how our garments are warm upon us* (Job 37:17); but, if God deny his blessing, men *clothe themselves, and there is none warm* (Hag. 1:6), David here was not. (2.) They foolishly prescribed nuptials to one that should rather have been preparing for his funeral (*v.* 2–4); but they knew what would gratify their own corruptions, and perhaps were too willing to gratify his, under colour of consulting his health. His prophets should have been consulted as well as his physicians in an affair of this nature. However, this might be excused then, when even good men ignorantly allowed themselves to have many wives. We now have not so learned of Christ, but are taught that one man must have but one wife (Mt. 19:5), and further that *it is good for a man not to touch a woman,* 1 Co. 7:1. That Abishag was married to David before she lay with him, and was his secondary wife, appears from its being imputed as a great crime to Adonijah that he desired to marry her (*ch.* 2:22) after his father's death.

Verses 5–10

David had much affliction in his children. Amnon and Absalom had both been his grief; the one his first-born, the other his third, 2 Sa. 3:2, 3. His second, whom he had by Abigail, we will suppose he had comfort in; his fourth was Adonijah (2 Sa. 3:4); he was one of those that were born in Hebron; we have heard nothing of him till now, and here we are told that he was a comely person, and that he was next in age, and (as it proved) next in temper to Absalom, *v.* 6. And, further, that in his father's eyes he had been a jewel, but was now a thorn.

I. His father had made a fondling of him, *v.* 6. He had not displeased him at any time. It is not said that he never displeased his father; it is probably that he had done so frequently, and his father was secretly troubled at his misconduct and lamented it before God. But his father had not displeased him, by crossing him in his humours, denying him any thing he had a mind to, or by calling him to an account as to what he had done and where he had been, or by keeping him to his book or his business, or reproving him for what he saw or heard of that he did amiss; he never said to him, *Why hast thou done so?* because he saw it was uneasy to him, and he could not bear it without fretting. It was the son's fault that he was displeased at reproof and took it for affront, whereby he lost the benefit of it; and it was the father's fault that, because he saw it displeased him, he did not reprove him; and now he justly smarted for indulging him. Those who honour their sons more than God, as those do who keep them not under good discipline, thereby forfeit the honour they might expect from their sons.

II. He, in return, made a fool of his father. Because he was old, and confined to his bed, he thought no notice was to be taken of him, and therefore *exalted himself,* and said, *I will be king, v.* 5. Children that are indulged learn to be proud and ambitious, which is the ruin of a great many young people. The way to keep them humble is to keep them under. Observe Adonijah's insolence. 1. He looked upon the days of mourning for his father to be at hand, and therefore he prepared to succeed him, though he knew that by the designation both of God and David Solomon was to be the man; for public notice had been given of it by David himself, and the succession settled, as it were by act of parliament, in pursuance of God's appointment, 1 Chr. 22:9; 23:1. This entail Adonijah attempted by force to cut off, in contempt both of God and his father. Thus is the kingdom of Christ opposed, and there are those that say, "We will not have him to reign over us." 2. He looked upon his father as superannuated and good for nothing, and therefore he entered immediately upon the possession of the throne. He cannot wait till his father's head be laid low, but it must now be said, *Adonijah reigns* (*v.* 18), and, *God save king Adonijah, v.* 25. His father is not fit to govern, for he is old and past ruling, nor Solomon, for he is young, and not yet able to rule; and therefore Adonijah will take the government upon him. It argues a very base and wicked mind for children to insult over their parents because of the infirmities of their age. 3. In pursuance of this ambitious project, (1.) He got a great retinue (*v.* 5), *chariots and horsemen,* both for state and strength, to wait on him, and to fight for him. (2.) He made great interest with no less than Joab, the general of the army, and Abiathar the high priest, *v.* 7. That he should make his court to those who by their influence in church and camp were capable of doing him great service is not strange; but we may well wonder by what arts they could be drawn to follow him and help him. They were old men, who had been faithful to David in the most difficult and troublesome of his times, men of sense and experience, who, one would think, would not easily be wheedled. They could not propose any advantage to themselves by supporting Adonijah, for they were both at the top of their preferment and stood fast in it. They could not be ignorant of the entail of the crown upon Solomon, which it was not in their power to cut off, and therefore it was their interest to oblige him. But God, in this matter, left them to themselves, perhaps to correct them for some former misconduct with a scourge of their own making. We are told (*v.* 8) who those were that were of such approved fidelity to David that Adonijah had not the confidence so much as to propose his project to them — Zadok, Benaiah, and Nathan. A man that has given proofs of his resolute adherence to that which is good shall not be asked to do a bad thing. (3.) He prepared a great entertainment (*v.* 9) at En-rogel, not far from Jerusalem; his guests were the king's sons, and the king's servants, whom he feasted and caressed to bring them over to his party; but Solomon was not invited, either because he despised him or because he despaired of him, *v.* 10. Such as serve their own belly, and will be in the interest of those that will feast them what side soever they are of, are an easy prey to seducers, Rom. 16:18. Some think that Adonijah slew these sheep and oxen, even fat ones, for sacrifice, and that it was a religious feast he made, beginning his usurpation with a show of devotion, as Absalom under the colour of a vow (2 Sa. 15:7), which he might do the more plausibly when he had the high priest himself on his side. It is a pity that any occasion should ever be given to say, *In nomine Domini incipit omne malam — In the name of the Lord begins all evil,* and that all religious exercises should be made to patronise all religious practices.

Verses 11–31

We have here the effectual endeavours that were used by Nathan and Bathsheba to obtain from David a ratification of Solomon's succession, for the crushing of Adonijah's usurpation. 1. David himself knew not what was doing. Disobedient children think that they are well enough off if they can but keep their good old parents ignorant of their bad courses; but a *bird of the air will carry the voice.* 2. Bathsheba lived retired, and knew nothing of it either, till Nathan informed her. Many get very comfortably through this world that know little how the world goes. 3. Solomon, it is likely, knew of it, but was as a deaf man that heard not. Though he had years, and wisdom above his years, yet we do not find that he stirred to oppose Adonijah, but quietly composed himself and left it to God and his friends to order the matter. Hence David, in his Psalm for Solomon, observes that while men, in pursuit of the world, in vain *rise early and sit up late, God giveth his beloved* (his *Jedidiahs*) *sleep,* in giving them to be easy, and to gain their point without agitation, Ps. 127:1, 2. How then is the design brought about?

I. Nathan the prophet alarms Bathsheba by acquainting her with the case, and puts her in a way to get an order from the king for the confirming of Solomon's title. He was concerned, because he knew God's mind, and David's and Israel's interest; it was by him that God had named Solomon *Jedidiah* (2 Sa. 12:25), and therefore he could not sit still and see the throne usurped, which he knew was Solomon's right by the will of him from whom promotion cometh. When crowns were disposed of by immediate direction from heaven, no marvel that prophets were so much interested and employed in that matter; but now that common providence rules the affairs of the kingdom of men (Dan. 4:32) the subordinate agency must be left to common persons, and let not prophets intermeddle in them, but keep to the affairs of the kingdom of God among men. Nathan applied to Bathsheba, as one that had the greatest concern for Solomon, and could have the freest access to David. He informed her of Adonijah's attempt (*v.* 11), and that it was not with David's consent or knowledge. He suggested to her that not only Solomon was in danger of losing the crown, but that he and she too were in danger of losing their lives if Adonijah prevailed. A humble spirit may be indifferent to a crown, and may be content, notwithstanding the prospect of it, to sit down short of the possession of it. But the law of self-preservation, and the sixth commandment, obliges us to use all possible endeavours to secure our own life and the life of others. Now, says Nathan, let me *give thee counsel how to save thy own life and the life of thy son, v.* 12. Such as this is the counsel that Christ's ministers give us in his name, to give all diligence, not only *that no man take our crown* (Rev. 3:11), but that we *save our lives,* even the lives of our souls. He directs her (*v.* 13) to go to the king, to remind him of his word and oath, that Solomon should be his successor; and to ask him in the most humble manner, *Why doth Adonijah reign?* He thought David was not so cold but this would warm him. Conscience, as well as a sense of honour, would put life into him upon such an occasion as this; and he promised (*v.* 24) that, while she was reasoning with the king in this matter, he would come in and second her, as if he came accidentally, which perhaps the king might look upon as a special providence (and he was one that took notice of such evidences, 1 Sa. 25:32, 33), or, at least, it would help to awaken him so much the more.

II. Bathsheba, according to Nathan's advice and direction, loses no time, but immediately makes her application to the king, on the same errand on which Esther came to king Ahasuerus, to intercede for her life. She needed not wait for a call as Esther did, she knew she should be welcome at any time; but it is remarked that when she visited the king Abishag was ministering to him (*v.* 15), and Bathsheba took no displeasure either at him or her for it, also that she *bowed and did obeisance to the king* (*v.* 16), in token of her respect to him both as her prince and as her husband; such a genuine daughter was she of Sarah, who obeyed Abraham, calling him *lord.* Those that would find favour with superiors mush show them reverence, and be dutiful to those whom they expect to be kind to them.

Her address to the king, on this occasion, is very discreet. 1. She reminded him of his promise made to her and confirmed with a solemn oath, that Solomon should succeed him, v. 17. She knew how fast this would hold such a conscientious man as David was. 2. She informed him of Adonijah's attempt, which he was ignorant of (v. 18): "Adonijah reigns, in competition with thee for the present and in contradiction to thy promise for the future. The fault is not thine, for thou knewest it not; but now that thou knowest it thou wilt, in pursuance of thy promise, take care to suppress this usurpation." She told him who were Adonijah's guests, and who were in his interest, and added, but "*Solomon thy servant has he not called*, which plainly shows he looks upon him as his rival, and aims to undermine him, v. 19. It is not an oversight, but a contempt of the act of settlement, that Solomon is neglected." 3. She pleads that it is very much in his power to obviate this mischief (v. 20): *The eyes of all Israel are upon thee*, not only as a *king*, for we cannot suppose it the prerogative of any prince to bequeath his subjects by will (as if they were his goods and chattels) to whom he pleases, but as a *prophet*. All Israel knew that David was not only himself *the anointed of the God of Jacob*, but that the *Spirit of the Lord spoke by him* (2 Sa. 23:1, 2), and therefore waiting for and depending upon a divine designation, in a matter of such importance, David's word would be an oracle and a law to them; this therefore (says Bathsheba) they expect, and it will end the controversy and effectually quash all Adonijah's pretensions. *A divine sentence is in the lips of the king*. Note, Whatever power, interest or influence, men have, they ought to improve it to the utmost for the preserving and advancing of the kingdom of the Messiah, of which Solomon's kingdom was a type. 4. She suggested the imminent peril which she and her son would be in if this matter was not settled in David's life-time, v. 21. "If Adonijah prevail, as he is likely to do (having Joab the general and Abiathar the priest on his side) unless speedily suppressed, Solomon and all his friends will be looked upon as traitors and dealt with accordingly." Usurpers are most cruel. If Adonijah had got into the throne, he would not have dealt so fairly with Solomon as Solomon did with him. Those hazard everything who stand in the way of such as against right force their entrance.

III. Nathan the prophet, according to his promise, seasonably stepped in, and seconded her, while she was speaking, before the king had given his answer, lest. if he had heard Bathsheba's representation only, his answer should be dilatory and only that he would consider of it: but out of the mouth of two witnesses, two such witnesses, the word would be established, and he would immediately give positive orders. The king is told that Nathan the prophet has come, and he is sure to be always welcome to the king, especially when either he is not well or has any great affair upon his thoughts; for, in either case, a prophet will be, in a particular manner, serviceable to him. Nathan knows he must render honour to whom honour is due, and therefore pays the king the same respect now that he finds him sick in bed as he would have done if he had found him in his throne: He *bowed himself with his face to the ground*, v. 23. He deals a little more plainly with the king than Bathsheba had done. In this his character would support him, and the present languor of the king's spirits made it necessary that they should be roused. 1. He makes the same representation of Adonijah's attempt as Bathsheba had made (v. 25, 26), adding that his party had already got to such a height of assurance as to shout, *God save king Adonijah*, as if king David were already dead, taking notice also that they had not invited him to their feast (*Me thy servant has he not called*), thereby intimating that they resolved not to consult either God or David in the matter, for Nathan was *secretioribus consiliis* — intimately acquainted with the mind of both. 2. He makes David sensible how much he was concerned to clear himself from having a hand in it: *Hast thou said, Adonijah shall reign after me?* (v. 24), and again (v. 27), "*Is this thing done by my lord the king?* If it be, he is not so faithful either to God's word or to his own as we all took him to be; if it be not, it is high time that we witness against the usurpation, and declare Solomon his successor. If it be, why is not Nathan made acquainted with it, who is not only in general, the king's confidant, but is particularly concerned in this matter, having been employed to notify to

David the mind of God concerning the succession; but, if my lord the king knows nothing of the matter (as certainly he does not), what daring insolence are Adonijah and his party guilty of!" Thus he endeavoured to incense David against them, that he might act the more vigorously for the support of Solomon's interest. Note, Good men would do their duty if they were reminded of it, and put upon it, and told what occasion there is for them to appear; and those who thus are their remembrancers do them a real kindness, as Nathan here did to David.

IV. David, hereupon, made a solemn declaration of his firm adherence to his former resolution, that Solomon should be his successor. Bathsheba is called in (v. 28), and to her, as acting for and on behalf of her son, the king gives these fresh assurances. 1. He repeats his former promise and oath, owns that he had *sworn unto her by the Lord God of Israel that Solomon would reign after him*, v. 30. Though he is old, and his memory begins to fail him, yet he remembers this. Note, An oath is so sacred a thing that the obligations of it cannot be broken, and so solemn a thing that the impressions of it, one would think, cannot be forgotten. 2. He ratifies it with another, because the occasion called for it: *As the Lord liveth, that hath redeemed my soul out of all distress, even so will I certainly do this day*, without dispute, without delay. His form of swearing seems to be what he commonly used on solemn occasions, for we find it, 2 Sa. 4:9. And it carries in it a grateful acknowledgment of the goodness of God to him, in bringing him safely through the many difficulties and hardships which had lain in his way, and which he now makes mention of to the glory of God (as Jacob, when he lay a dying, Gen. 48:16), thus setting to his seal, from his own experience, that that was true which the Spirit of the Lord spoke by him. Ps. 34:22, *The Lord redeemeth the soul of his servants*. Dying saints ought to be witnesses for God, and speak of him as they have found. Perhaps he speaks thus, on this occasion, for the encouragement of his son and successor to trust in God in the distresses he also might meet with.

V. Bathsheba receives these assurances (v. 31), 1. With great complaisance to the king's person; she did reverence to him; while Adonijah and his party affronted him. 2. With hearty good wishes for the king's health; *Let him live*. So far was she from thinking that he lived too long that she prayed he might live for ever, if it were possible, to adorn the crown he wore and to be a blessing to his people. We should earnestly desire the prolonging of useful lives, however it may be the postponing of any advantages of our own.

Verses 32–40

We have here the effectual care David took both to secure Solomon's right and to preserve the public peace, by crushing Adonijah's project in the bud. Observe,

I. The express orders he gave for the proclaiming of Solomon. The persons he entrusted with this great affair were Zadok, Nathan, and Benaiah, men of power and interest whom David had always reposed a confidence in and found faithful to him, and whom Adonijah had passed by in his invitation, v. 10. David orders them forthwith, with all possible solemnity, to proclaim Solomon. They must take with them *the servants of their lord*, the lifeguards, and all the servants of the household. They must set Solomon on the mule the king used to ride, for he kept not such stables of horses as his son afterwards did. He appoints them whither to go (v. 33 and v. 34, 35), and what to do. 1. Zadok and Nathan, the two ecclesiastical persons, must, in God's name, anoint him king; for though he was not the first of his family, as Saul and David were, yet he was a younger son, was made king by divine appointment, and his title was contested, which made it necessary that hereby it should be settled. This unction was typical of the designation and qualification of the Messiah, or Christ, the anointed one, on whom the Spirit, that oil of gladness, was poured without measure, Heb. 1:9, Ps. 89:20. And all Christians, being *heirs of the kingdom* (Jam. 2:5), do from him *receive the anointing*, 1 Jn. 2:27. 2. The great officers, civil and military, are ordered to give public notice of this, and to express the public joy upon this occasion by sound of trumpet, by which the law of Moses directed the gracing of great solemnities; to this must be added the acclamations of the people: "*Let king Solomon*

live, let him prosper, let his kingdom be established and perpetuated, and let him long continue in the enjoyment of it;" so it had been promised concerning him. Ps. 72:15, *He shall live*. 3. They must then bring him in state to the city of David, and he must sit upon the throne of his father, as his substitute now, or viceroy, to despatch public business during his weakness and be his successor after his death: *He shall be king in my stead*. It would be a great satisfaction to David himself, and to all parties concerned, to have this done immediately, that upon the demise of the king there might be no dispute, or agitation, in the public affairs. David was far from grudging his successor the honour of appearing such in his life-time, and yet perhaps was so taken up with his devotions on his sick-bed that, if he had not been put in mind of it by others, this great good work, which was so necessary to the public repose, would have been left undone.

II. The great satisfaction which Benaiah, in the name of the rest, professed in these orders. The king said, "Solomon shall reign for me, and reign after me." "Amen" (says Benaiah heartily); "as the king says, so say we; we are entirely satisfied in the nomination, and concur in the choice, we give our vote for Solomon, *nemine contradicente — unanimously*, and since we can bring nothing to pass, much less establish it, without the concurrence of a propitious providence, *The Lord God of my lord the king say so too!*" v. 36. This is the language of his faith in that promise of God on which Solomon's government was founded. If we say as God says in his word, we may hope that he will say as we say by his providence. To this he adds a prayer for Solomon (v. 37), that God would be with him as he had been with David, and make his throne greater. He knew David was not one of those that envy their children's greatness, and that therefore he would not be disquieted at this prayer, nor take it as an affront, but would heartily say Amen to it. The wisest and best man in the world desires his children may be wiser and better than he, for he himself desires to be wiser and better than he is; and wisdom and goodness are true greatness.

III. The immediate execution of these orders, v. 38–40. No time was lost, but Solomon was brought in state to the place appointed, and there Zadok (who, though he was not as yet high priest, was, we may suppose, the suffragan, the Jews called him the *sagan*, or second priest) anointed him by the direction of Nathan the prophet and David the king, v. 39. In the tabernacle, where the ark was now lodged, was kept among other sacred things, the holy oil for many religious services thence Zadok took a *horn of oil*, which denotes both power and plenty, and therewith anointed Solomon. We do not find that Abiathar pretended to anoint Adonijah: he was made king by a feast, not by an unction. Whom God calls, he will qualify, which was signified by the anointing; usurpers had it not. *Christ* signifies *anointed*, and he is the king whom God hath *set upon his holy hill of Sion*, according to decree, Ps. 2:6, 7. Christians also are *made to our God* (and *by* him) *kings*, and they have an *unction from the Holy One*, 1 Jn. 2:20. The people, hereupon, express their great joy and satisfaction in the elevation of Solomon, surround him with their Hosannas — *God save king Solomon*, and attend him with their music and shouts of joy, v. 40. Hereby they declared their concurrence in the choice, and that he was not forced upon them, but cheerfully accepted by them. The power of a prince can be little satisfaction to himself, unless he knows it to be a satisfaction to his people. Every Israelite indeed rejoices in the exaltation of the Son of David.

Verses 41–53

We have here,

I. The tidings of Solomon's inauguration brought to Adonijah and his party, in the midst of their jollity: *They had made an end of eating*, and, it should seem, it was a great while before they made an end, for all the affair of Solomon's anointing was ordered and finished while they were at dinner, glutting themselves. Thus those who *serve not our Lord Christ*, but oppose him, are commonly such as *serve their own belly* (Rom. 16:18) and made *a god of it*, Phil. 3:19. Their long feast intimates likewise that they were very secure and confident of their interest, else they would not have lost so much time. The old world and Sodom were *eating and drinking*, secure and sensual, when their destruction came, Lu. 17:26, etc. When *they made an end of eating,* and were preparing themselves to proclaim their king, and bring him in triumph into the city, they *heard the sound of the trumpet* (*v.* 41), and a *dreadful sound it was in their ears,* Job 15:21. Joab was an old man, and was alarmed at it, apprehending the city to be in an uproar; but Adonijah was very confident that the messenger, being a *worthy man, brought good tidings, v.* 42. Usurpers flatter themselves with the hopes of success, and those are commonly least timorous whose condition is most dangerous. But how can those who do evil deeds expect to have good tidings? No, the worthiest man will bring them the worst news, as the priest's son did here to Adonijah, *v.* 43. "*Verily,* the best tidings I have to bring you is that *Solomon is made king,* so that your pretensions are all quashed." He relates to them very particularly, 1. With what great solemnity *Solomon was made king* (*v.* 44, 45), and that he was now *sitting on the throne of the kingdom, v.* 46. Adonijah thought to have stepped into the throne before him, but Solomon was too quick for him. 2. With what general satisfaction Solomon was made king, so that that which was done was not likely to be undone again. (1.) The people were pleased, witness their joyful acclamations, *v.* 45. (2.) The courtiers were pleased: *The kings servants* attended him with an address of congratulation upon this occasion, *v.* 47. We have here the heads of their address: They *blessed king David,* applauded his prudent care for the public welfare, acknowledged their happiness under his government, and prayed heartily for his recovery. They also prayed for Solomon, that God would make his name better than his father's, which it might well be when he had his father's foundation to build upon. A child, on a giant's shoulders, is higher than the giant himself. (3.) The king himself was pleased: He *bowed himself upon the bed,* not only to signify his acceptance of his servants' address, but to offer up his own address to God (*v.* 48): "*Blessed be the Lord God of Israel,* who, as Israel's God, for Israel's good, has brought this matter to such a happy issue, *my eyes even seeing it.*" Note, It is a great satisfaction to good men, when they are going out of the world, to see the affairs of their families in a good posture, their children rising up in their stead to serve God and their generation, and especially to see peace upon Israel and the establishment of it.

II. The effectual crush which this gave to Adonijah's attempt. It spoiled the sport of his party, dispersed the company, and obliged every man to shift for his own safety. *The triumphing of the wicked is short.* They were building a castle in the air, which, having no foundation, would soon fall and crush them. They were afraid of being taken in the fact, while they were together hatching their treason, and therefore each one made the best of his way.

III. The terror Adonijah himself was in, and the course he took to secure himself. he was now as much depressed as he had been elevated, *v.* 42, 50. He had despised Solomon as not worthy to be his guest (*v.* 10), but now he dreads him as his judge: He *feared because of Solomon.* Thus those who oppose Christ and his kingdom will shortly be made to tremble before him, and call in vain to rocks and mountains to shelter them from his wrath. He *took hold on the horns of the altar,* which was always looked upon as a sanctuary, or place of refuge (Ex. 21:14), intimating hereby that he durst not stand a trial, but threw himself upon the mercy of his prince, in suing for which he relied upon no other plea than the mercy of God, which was manifested in the institution and acceptance of the sacrifices that were offered on that altar and the remission of sin thereupon. Perhaps Adonijah had formerly slighted the service of the altar, yet now he courts the protection of it. Many who in the day of their security neglect the great salvation, under the arrests of the terrors of the Lord would gladly be beholden to Christ and his merit, and, when it is too late, will *catch hold of the horns of the altar.*

IV. His humble address to Solomon for mercy. By those who brought Solomon tidings where he was, he sent a request for his life (*v.* 51): *Let king Solomon swear to me that he will not slay his servant.* He owns Solomon for his prince, and himself his servant, dares not justify himself, but *makes supplication to his judge.* It was a great change with him. He that in the morning was grasping at a crown is before night begging for his life. Then Adonijah reigned, now Adonijah trembles, and cannot think himself safe unless Solomon promise, with an oath, not to put him to death.

V. The orders Solomon gave concerning him. He discharges him upon his good behaviour, *v.* 52, 53. He considered that Adonijah was his brother, and that it was the first offence. Perhaps, being so soon made sensible of his error and then not persisting in his rebellion, he might prove not only a peaceable, but a serviceable subject, and therefore, if he will conduct himself well for the future, what is past shall be pardoned: but if he be fond disaffected, turbulent, and aspiring, this offence shall be remembered against him, he shall be called up upon his former conviction (as our law speaks), and execution shall be awarded against him. Thus the Son of David receives those to mercy that have been rebellious: if they will return to their allegiance, and be faithful to their Sovereign, their former crimes shall not be mentioned against them; but, if still they continue in the interests of the world and the flesh, this will be their ruin. Adonijah is sent for, and told upon what terms he stands, which he signifies his grateful submission to, and then is told to go to his house and live retired there. Solomon not only gave him his life, but his estate, thus *establishing his throne by mercy.*

CHAPTER 2

In this chapter we have David setting and Solomon at the same time rising. I. The conclusion of David's reign with his life. 1. The charge he gives to Solomon upon his death-bed, in general, to serve God (*v.* 1–4), in particular, concerning Joab, Barzillai, and Shimei (*v.* 5–9). 2. His death and burial, and the years of his reign (*v.* 10, 11). II. The beginning of Solomon's reign (*v.* 12). Though he was to be a prince of peace, he began his reign with some remarkable acts of justice, 1. Upon Adonijah, whom he put to death for his aspiring pretensions (*v.* 13–25). 2. Upon Abiathar, whom he deposed from the high priesthood for siding with Adonijah (*v.* 26, 27). 3. Upon Joab, who he put to death for his late treasons and former murders (*v.* 28–35). 4. Upon Shimei, whom, for cursing David, he confined to Jerusalem (*v.* 36–38), and three years after, for transgressing the rules, put to death (*v.* 39–46).

Verses 1–11

David, that great and good man, is here a dying man (*v.* 1), and a dead man, *v.* 10. It is well there is another life after this, for death stains all the glory of this, and lays it in the dust. We have here,

I. The charge and instructions which David, when he was dying, gave to Solomon, his son and declared successor. He feels himself declining, and is not backward to own it, nor afraid to hear or speak of dying: *I go the way of all the earth, v.* 2. Heb. *I am walking in it.* Note, Death is a way; not only a period of this life, but a passage to a better. It is *the way of all the earth,* of all mankind who dwell on earth, and are themselves earth, and therefore must return to their earth. Even the sons and heirs of heaven must *go the way of all the earth,* they must needs die; but they walk with pleasure in this way, *through the valley of the shadow of death,* Ps. 23:4. Prophets, and even kings, must go this way to brighter light and honour than prophecy or sovereignty. David is going this way, and therefore gives Solomon directions what to do.

1. He charges him, in general, to keep God's commandments and to make conscience of his duty, *v.* 2–4. He prescribes to him, (1.) A good rule to act by — the divine will: "Govern thyself by that." David's charge to him is to *keep the charge of the Lord* his *God.* The authority of a dying father is much, but nothing to that of a living God. There are great trusts which we are charged with by the Lord our God — let us keep them carefully, as those that must give account; and excellent statutes, which we must be ruled by — let us also keep them. The written word is our rule. Solomon must himself do *as was written in the law of Moses.* (2.) A good spirit to act with: Be *strong and show thyself a man,* though in years but a child. Those that would keep the charge of the Lord their God must put on resolution. (3.) Good reasons for all this. This would effectually conduce, [1.] To the prosperity of his kingdom. It is the way to *prosper in all thou doest,* and to succeed with honour and satisfaction in every undertaking. [2.] To the perpetuity of it: *That the Lord may continue* and so confirm *his word which he spoke concerning me.* Those that rightly value the treasure of the promise, that sacred *depositum,* cannot but be solicitous to preserve the entail of it, and very desirous that those who come after them may do nothing to cut it off. Let each, in his own age, successively, keep God's charge, and then God will be sure to continue his word. We never let fall the promise till we let fall the precept. God had promised David that the Messiah should come from his loins, and that promise was absolute: but the promise that there should not fail him *a man on the throne of Israel* was conditional — if his seed behave themselves as they should. If Solomon, in his day, fulfil the condition, he does his part towards the perpetuating of the promise. The condition is that he walk before God in all his institutions, in sincerity, with zeal and resolution; and, in order hereunto, that he *take heed to his way.* In order to our constancy in religion, nothing is more necessary than caution and circumspection.

2. He gives him directions concerning some particular persons, what to do with them, that he might make up his deficiencies in justice to some and kindness to others. (1.) Concerning Joab, *v.* 5 David was now conscious to himself that he had not done well to spare him, when he had made himself once again obnoxious to the law, but the murder of Abner first and afterwards of Amasa, both of them great men, *captains of the hosts of Israel.* He slew them treacherously *(shed the blood of war in peace),* and injuriously to David: *Thou knowest what* he *did to me* therein. The murder of a subject is a wrong to the prince, it is a loss to him, and is against the peace of our sovereign lord the king. These murders were particularly against David, reflecting upon his reputation, he being, at that time, in treaty with the victims, and hazarded his interest, which they were very capable of serving. Magistrates are the avengers of the blood of those they have the charge of. It aggravated Joab's crime that he was neither ashamed of the sin nor afraid of the punishment, but daringly wore the girdle and shoes that were stained with innocent blood, in defiance of the justice both of God and the king. David refers him to Solomon's wisdom (*v.* 6), with an intimation that he left him to his justice. Say not, "He has a hoary head; it is a pity it should be cut off, for it will shortly fall of itself." No, let it not *go down to the grave in peace.* Though he has been long reprieved, he shall be reckoned with at last; time does not wear out the guilt of any sin, particularly that of murder. (2.) Concerning Barzillai's family, to whom he orders him to be kind for Barzillai's sake, who, we may suppose, by this time, was dead, *v.* 7. When David, upon his death-bed, was remembering the injuries that had been done, he could not forget the kindnesses that had been shown, but leaves it as a charge upon his son to return them. Note, the kindnesses we have received from our friends must not be buried either in their graves or ours, but our children must return them to theirs. Hence, perhaps, Solomon fetched that rule (Prov. 27:10), *Thy own friend, and thy father's friend, forsake not.* Paul prays for the house of Onesiphorus, who had often refreshed him. (3.) Concerning Shimei, *v.* 8, 9. [1.] His crime is remembered: *He cursed me with a grievous curse;* the more grievous because he insulted him when he was in misery and poured vinegar into his wounds. The Jews say that one thing which made this a grievous curse was that, besides all that is mentioned (2 Sa. 16), Shimei upbraided him with his descent from Ruth the Moabitess. [2.] His pardon is not forgotten. David owned he had sworn to him that he would not himself put him to death, because he seasonably submitted, and cried *Peccavi — I have sinned,* and he was not willing, especially at that juncture, to use the sword of public justice for the avenging of wrongs done to himself. But, [3.] His case, as it now stands, is left with Solomon, as one that knew what was fit to be done and would do as he found occasion. David intimates to him that his pardon was not designed to be perpetual, but only a reprieve for David's life: "*Hold him not guiltless;* do not think him any true friend to thee or thy government, nor fit to be trusted. He has no less malice than he had then, though he has more sense to conceal it. He is still a debtor to the public justice for what he did then; and, though I promised him that I would not put him to death, I never promised that my successor should not. His turbulent spirit will soon give thee an occasion, which thou shouldst not fail to take, for the bringing of his *hoary head to the grave with blood.*" This proceeded not from personal revenge, but a prudent zeal for the honour of the government and the covenant God had made with his family, the contempt of which ought not to go unpunished. Even a hoary head, if a guilty and forfeited head, ought not to

be any man's protection from justice. *The sinner, being a hundred years old, shall be accursed,* Isa. 65:20.

II. David's death and burial (*v.* 10): He *was buried in the city of David,* not in the burying place of his father, as Saul was, but in his own city, which he was the founder of. There were set the thrones, and there the tombs, of the house of David. Now *David, after he had served his own generation, by the will of God, fell asleep, and was laid to his fathers, and saw corruption,* Acts 13:36, and see Acts 2:29. His epitaph may be taken from 2 Sa. 23:1. Here lies *David the son of Jesse, the man who was raised up on high, the anointed of the God of Jacob, and the sweet psalmist of Israel,* adding his own words (Ps. 16:9), *My flesh also shall rest in hope.* Josephus says that, besides the usual magnificence with which his son Solomon buried him, he put into his sepulchre a vast deal of money; and that 1300 years after (so he reckons) it was opened by Hircanus the high priest, in the time of Antiochus, and 3000 talents were taken out for the public service. The years of his reign are here computed (*v.* 11) to be forty years; the odd six months which he reigned above seven years in Hebron are not reckoned, but the even sum only.

Verses 12–25

Here is, I. Solomon's accession to the throne, *v.* 12. He came to it much more easily and peaceably than David did, and much sooner saw his government established. It is happy for a kingdom when the end of one good reign is the beginning of another, as it was here.

II. His just and necessary removal of Adonijah his rival, in order to the establishment of his throne. Adonijah had made some bold pretensions to the crown, but was soon obliged to let them fail and throw himself upon Solomon's mercy, who dismissed him upon his good behaviour, and, had he been easy, he might have been safe. But here we have him betraying himself into the hands of Solomon's justice, and falling by it, the righteous God leaving him to himself, that he might be punished for his former treason and that Solomon's throne might be established. Many thus ruin themselves, because they know not when they are well off, or well done to; and sinners, by presuming on God's patience, treasure up wrath to themselves. Now observe,

1. Adonijah's treasonable project, which was to marry Abishag, David's concubine, not because he was in love with her, but because, by her, he hoped to renew his claim to the crown, which might stand him in stead, or because it was then looked upon as a branch of the government to have *the wives of the predecessor,* 2 Sa. 12:8. Absalom thought his pretensions much supported by lying with his father's concubines. Adonijah flatters himself that if he may succeed him in his bed, especially with the best of his wives, he may by that means step up to succeed him in his throne. Restless and turbulent spirits reach high. It was but a small game to play at, as it should seem, yet he hoped to make it an after-game for the kingdom, and now to gain that by a wife which he could not gain by force.

2. The means he used to compass this. he durst not make suit to Abishag immediately (he knew she was at Solomon's disposal, and he would justly resent it if his consent were not first obtained, as even Ishbosheth did, in a like case, 2 Sa. 3:7), nor durst he himself apply immediately to Solomon, knowing that he lay under his displeasure; but he engaged Bathsheba to be his friend in this matter, who would be forward to believe it a matter of love, and not apt to suspect it a matter of policy. Bathsheba was surprised to see Adonijah in her apartment, and asked him if he did not come with a design to do her a mischief, because she had been instrumental to crush his late attempt. "No," says he, "I come *peaceably* (*v.* 13), and to beg a favour" (*v.* 14), that she would use the great interest she had in her son to gain his consent, that he might marry Abishag (*v.* 16, 17), and, if he may but obtain this, he will thankfully accept it, (1.) As a compensation for his loss of the kingdom. He insinuates (*v.* 15), "Thou knowest the kingdom was mine, as my father's eldest son, living at the time of his death, *and all Israel set their faces on me."* This was false; they were but a few that he had on his side; yet thus he would represent himself as an object of compassion, that had been deprived of a crown, and therefore might well be gratified in a wife. If he may not inherit his father's throne, yet let him have something valuable that was his father's, to keep for his sake, and let it be Abishag. (2.) As his reward for his acquiescence in that loss. He owns Solomon's right to the kingdom: *"It was his from the Lord.* I was foolish in offering to contest it; and now that it is turned about to him I am satisfied." Thus he pretends to be well pleased with Solomon's accession to the throne, when he is doing all he can to give him disturbance. *His words were smoother than butter, but war was in his heart.*

3. Bathsheba's address to Solomon on his behalf. She promised to speak to the king for him (*v.* 18) and did so, *v.* 19. Solomon received her with all the respect that was due to a mother, though he himself was a king: He *rose up to meet her, bowed himself to her,* and caused her *to sit on his right hand,* according to the law of the fifth commandment. Children, not only when grown up, but when grown great, must give honour to their parents, and behave dutifully and respectfully towards them. *Despise not thy mother when she is old.* As a further instance of the deference he paid to his mother's wisdom and authority, when he understood she had a petition to present to him, he promised not to say her nay, a promise which both he and she understood with this necessary limitation, provided it be just and reasonable and fit to be granted; but, if it were otherwise, he was sure he should convince her that it was so, and that then she would withdraw it. She tells him her errand at last (*v.* 21): *Let Abishag be given to Adonijah thy brother.* It was strange that she did not suspect the treason, but more strange that she did not abhor the incest, that was in the proposal. But either she did not take Abishag to be David's wife, because the marriage was not consummated, or she thought it might be dispensed with to gratify Adonijah, in consideration of his tame submission to Solomon. This was her weakness and folly: it was well that she was not regent. Note, Those that have the ear of princes and great men, as it is their wisdom not to be too prodigal of their interest, so it is their duty never to use it for the assistance of sin or the furtherance of any wicked design. Let not princes be asked that which they ought not to grant. It ill becomes a good man to prefer a bad request or appear in a bad cause.

4. Solomon's just and judicious rejection of the request. Though his mother herself was the advocate, and called it *a small petition,* and perhaps it was the first she had troubled him with since he was king, yet he denied it, without violation of the general promise he had made, *v.* 20. If Herod had not had a mind to cut off John Baptist's head, he would not have thought himself obliged to do it by a general promise, like this, made to Herodias. The best friend we have in the world must not have such an interest in us as to bring us to do a wrong thing, either unjust or unwise. (1.) Solomon convinces his mother of the unreasonableness of the request, and shows her the tendency of it, which, before, she was not aware of. His reply is somewhat sharp: *"Ask for him the kingdom also, v.* 22. To ask that he may succeed the king in his bed is, in effect, to ask that he may succeed him in his throne; for that is it he aims at." Probably he had information, or cause for a strong suspicion, that Adonijah was plotting with Joab and Abiathar to give him disturbance, which warranted him to put this construction upon Adonijah's request. (2.) He convicts and condemns Adonijah for his pretensions, and both with an oath. He convicts him out of his own mouth, *v.* 23. His own tongue shall fall upon him; and a heavier load a man needs not fall under. Bathsheba may be imposed upon, but Solomon cannot; he plainly sees what Adonijah aims at, and concludes, "He has *spoken this word against his own life;* he is snared in the words of his own lips; now he shows what he would be at." He condemns him to die immediately: *He shall be put to death this day, v.* 24. God had himself declared with an oath that he would establish David's throne (Ps. 89:35), and therefore Solomon pledges the same assurance to secure that establishment, by cutting off the enemies of it. "As God liveth, that establisheth the government, Adonijah shall die, that would unsettle it." Thus the ruin of the enemies of Christ's kingdom is as sure as the stability of his kingdom, and both are as sure as the being and life of God, the founder of it. The warrant is immediately signed for his execution, and no less a man than Benaiah, the son of Jehoiada, general of the army, is ordered to be the executioner, *v.* 25. It is strange that Adonijah may not be heard to speak for himself: but Solomon's wisdom did not see it needful to examine the matter any further; it was plain enough that Adonijah aimed at the crown, and Solomon could not be safe while he lived. Ambitious turbulent spirits commonly prepare for themselves the instruments of death. Many a head has been lost by catching at a crown.

Verses 26–34

Abiathar and Joab were both aiding and abetting in Adonijah's rebellious attempt, and it is probable were at the bottom of this new motion made of Adonijah for Abishag, and it should seem Solomon knew it, *v.* 22. This was, in both, an intolerable affront both to God and to the government, and the worse because of their high station and the great influence their examples might have upon many. They therefore come next to be reckoned with. They are both equally guilty of the treason, but, in the judgment passed upon them, a difference is made and with good reason.

I. Abiathar, in consideration of his old services, is only degraded, *v.* 26, 27. 1. Solomon convicts him, and by his great wisdom finds him guilty: *"Thou art worthy of death,* for joining with Adonijah, when thou knewest on whose head God intended to set the crown." 2. He calls to mind the respect he had formerly shown to David his father, and that he had both ministered to him in holy things *(had borne before him the ark of the Lord),* and also had tenderly sympathized with him in his afflictions and been afflicted in them all, particularly when he was in exile and distress both by Saul's persecution and Absalom's rebellion. Note, Those that show kindness to God's people shall have it remembered to their advantage one time or other. 3. For this reason he spares Abiathar's life, but deposes him from his offices, and confines him to his country seat at Anathoth, forbids him the court, the city, the tabernacle, the altar, and all inter-meddling in public business, with an intimation likewise that he was upon his good behaviour, and that though Solomon did not put him to death at this time he might another time, if he did not conduct himself well. But, for the present, he was only thrust out from being priest, as rendered unworthy that high station by the opposition he had given to that which he knew to be the will of God. Saul, for a supposed crime, had barbarously slain Abiathar's father, and eighty-five priests, their families, and city. Solomon spares Abiathar himself, though guilty of a real crime. Thus was Saul's government ruined and Solomon's established. As men are to God's ministers, they will find him to them. 4. The depriving of Abiathar was the fulfilling of the threatening against the house of Eli (1 Sa. 2:30), for he was the last high priest of that family. It was now above eighty years since the ruin was threatened; but God's judgments, though not executed speedily, will be executed surely.

II. Joab, in consideration of his old sins, is put to death.

1. His guilty conscience sent him to the horns of the altar. He heard that Adonijah was executed and Abiathar deposed, and therefore, fearing his turn would be next, he fled for refuge to the altar. Many that, in the day of their security, care not for the service of the altar, will be glad of the protection of it in the day of their distress. Some think Joab designed thereby to devote himself for the future to a constant attendance upon the altar, hoping thereby to obtain his pardon, as some that have lived a dissolute life all their days have thought to atone for their crimes by retiring into a monastery when they are old, leaving the world when it has left them and no thanks to them.

2. Solomon ordered him to be put to death there for the murder of Abner and Amasa; for these were the crimes upon which he thought fit to ground the sentence, rather than upon his treasonable adherence to Adonijah. Joab was indeed worthy of death for turning after Adonijah, in contempt of Solomon and his designation to the throne, *though he had not turned after Absalom, v.* 28. Former fidelity will not serve to excuse any after treachery; yet, besides that, Joab had merited well of the house of David, to which and to his country he had done a great deal of good service in his day, in consideration of which, it is probable, Solomon would have pardoned him his offence against him (for clemency gives great reputation and establishment to an infant government), and would have only displaced him as he did Abiathar; but he must die for the murders he had formerly been guilty of, which his father had charged Solomon to call him to an account for. The

debt he owed to the innocent blood that was shed, by answering its cries with the blood of him that shed, he could not pay himself, but left it to his son to pay it, who, having power wherewithal, failed not to do it. On this he grounds the sentence, aggravating the crime (*v.* 32), that he *fell upon two men more righteous and better than he,* that had done him no wrong nor meant him any, and, had they lived, might probably have done David better service (if the blood shed be not only innocent, but excellent, the life more valuable that common lives, the crime is the more heinous), that David knew not of it, and yet the case was such that he would be suspected as privy to it; so that Joab endangered his prince's reputation in taking away the life of his rivals, which was a further aggravation. For these crimes, (1.) He must die, and die by the sword of public justice. *By man must his blood be shed,* and it lies upon his own head (*v.* 32), as theirs does whom he had murdered, *v.* 33. Woe to the head that lies under the guilt of blood! Vengeance for murder was long in coming upon Joab; but, when it did come, it remained the longer, being here entailed *upon the head of his seed for ever* (*v.* 33), who, instead of deriving honour, as otherwise they might have done, from his heroic actions, derived guilt, and shame, and a curse, from his villainous actions, on account of which they fared the worse in this world. The seed of such evil doers shall never be renowned. (2.) He must die at the altar, rather than escape. Joab resolved not to stir from the altar (*v.* 30), hoping thereby either to secure himself or else to render Solomon odious to the people, as a profaner of the holy place, if he should put him to death there. Benaiah made a scruple of either killing him there or dragging him thence; but Solomon knew the law, that the altar of God should give no protection to wilful murderers. Ex. 21:14, *Thou shalt take him from my altar that he may die,* may die a sacrifice. In case of such sins as the blood of beasts would atone for the altar was a refuge, but not in Joab's case. He therefore orders him to be executed there, if he could not be got thence, to show that he feared not the censure of the people in doing his duty, but would rectify their mistake, and let them know that the administration of justice is better than sacrifice, and that the holiness of any place should never countenance the wickedness of any person. Those who, by a lively faith, take hold on Christ and his righteousness, with a resolution, if they perish, to perish there, shall find in him a more powerful protection than Joab found at the horns of the altar. Benaiah slew him (*v.* 34), with the solemnity, no doubt, of a public execution. The law being thus satisfied, he was *buried in his own house in the wilderness,* privately, like a criminal, not pompously, like a soldier; yet no indignity was done to his dead body. It is not for man to lay the iniquity upon the bones, whatever God does.

3. Solomon pleased himself with this act of justice, not as it gratified any personal revenge, but as it was the fulfilling of his father's orders and a real kindness to himself and his own government. (1.) Guilt was hereby removed, *v.* 31. By returning the innocent blood that had been shed upon the head of him that shed it, it was taken away from him and from the house of his father, which implies that the blood which is not required from the murderer will be required from the magistrate, at least there is danger lest it should. Those that would have their houses safe and built up must put away iniquity far from them. (2.) Peace was hereby secured (*v.* 33) upon David. He does not mean his person, but, as he explains himself in the next words, Upon *his seed, his house, and his throne,* shall there be *peace for ever from the Lord;* thus he expresses his desire that it may be so and his hope that it shall be so. "Now that justice is done, and the cry of blood is satisfied, the government will prosper." Thus *righteousness and peace kiss each other.* Now that such a turbulent man as Joab is removed there shall be peace. *Take away the wicked from before the king, and his throne shall be established in righteousness,* Prov. 25:5. Solomon, in this blessing of peace upon his house and throne, piously looks upward to God as the author of it. "It shall be peace from the Lord, and peace for ever from the Lord." The Lord of peace himself give us that peace which is everlasting.

Verses 35–46

Here is, I. The preferment of Benaiah and Zadok, two faithful friends to Solomon and his government, *v.* 35. Joab being put to death, Benaiah was advanced to be general of the forces in his room, and, Abiathar being deposed, Zadok was made high priest in his room, and therein was fulfilled the word of God, when he threatened to cut off the house of Eli (1 Sa. 2:35), *I will raise me up a faithful priest, and will build him a sure house.* Though sacred offices may be disgraced, they shall not be destroyed, by the mal-administration of those that are entrusted with them, nor shall God's work ever stand still for want of hands to carry it on. No wonder that he who was a king so immediately of God's making was empowered to make whom he though fit high priest; and he exercised this power with equity, for the ancient right was in Zadok, he being of the family of Eleazar, whereas Eli and his house were of Ithamar.

II. The course that was taken with Shimei. He is sent for, by a messenger, from his house at Bahurim, expecting perhaps no better than Adonijah's doom, being conscious of his enmity to the house of David; but Solomon knows how to make a difference of crimes and criminals. David had promised Shimei his life for his time. Solomon is not bound by that promise, yet he will not go directly contrary to it. 1. He confines him to Jerusalem, and forbids him, upon any pretence whatsoever, to go out of the city any further than the brook Kidron, *v.* 36, 37. He would suffer him to continue at his country seat lest he should make mischief among his neighbours, but took him to Jerusalem, where he kept him prisoner at large. This might make Shimei's confinement easy to himself, for Jerusalem was beautiful for situation, *the joy of the whole earth,* the royal city, the holy city (he had no reason to complain of being shut up in such a paradise); it would also make it the more safe for Solomon, for there he would have him under his eye and be able to watch his motions; and he plainly tells him that if he ever go out of the rules he shall certainly die for it. This was a fair trial of his obedience, and such a test of his loyalty as he had no reason to complain of. He has his life upon easy terms: he shall live if he will but be content to live at Jerusalem. 2. Shimei submits to the confinement, and thankfully takes his life upon those terms. He enters into recognizance (*v.* 38), under the penalty of death, not to stir out of Jerusalem, and owns that the saying is good. Even those that perish cannot but own the conditions of pardon and life unexceptionable, so that their blood, like Shimei's, must rest upon their own heads. Shimei promised, with an oath, to keep within his bounds, *v.* 42. 3. Shimei forfeits his recognizance, which was the thing Solomon expected; and God was righteous in suffering him to do it, that he might now suffer for his old sins. Two of his servants (it seems, though he was a prisoner, he lived like himself, well attended) ran from him to the land of the Philistines, *v.* 39. Thither he pursued them, and thence brought them back to Jerusalem, *v.* 40. For the keeping of it private he *saddled his ass* himself, probably went in the night, and came home he thought undiscovered. "Seeking his servants," says bishop Hall, "he lost himself; those earthly things either are, or should be, our servants. How commonly do we see men run out of the bounds set by God's law, to hunt after them, till their souls incur a fearful judgment!" 4. Solomon takes the forfeiture. Information is given him that Shimei has transgressed, *v.* 41. The king sends for him, and, (1.) charges him with the present crime (*v.* 42, 43), that he had put a great contempt upon the authority and wrath both of God and the king, that he had broken *the oath of the Lord* and disobeyed the commandment of his prince, and by this it appeared what manner of spirit he was of, that he would not be held by the bonds of gratitude or conscience. Had he represented to Solomon the urgency of the occasion, and begged leave to go, perhaps Solomon might have given him leave; but to presume either upon his ignorance or his connivance was to affront him in the highest degree. (2.) He condemns him for his former crime, cursing David, and throwing stones at him in the day of his affliction: *The wickedness which thy heart is privy to, v.* 44. There was no need to examine witnesses for the proof of the fact, his own conscience was instead of a thousand witnesses. That wickedness which men's *own hearts* alone *are privy to* is enough, if duly considered, to fill them with confusion, in expectation of its return upon *their own heads;* for if the heart be privy to it, God is greater than the heart and knoweth all things. Others knew of Shimei's cursing David, but Shimei himself knew of the wicked principles of hatred and malice against David which he displayed in cursing him and that his submission was but feigned and forced. (3.) He blessed himself and his government (*v.* 45.): *King Solomon shall be blessed,* notwithstanding Shimei's impotent curses, which perhaps, in fury and despair, he now vented freely: *Let them curse, but bless thou.* And *the throne of David shall be established,* by taking away those that would undermine it. It is a comfort, in reference to the enmity of the church's enemies, that, how much soever they rage, it is a vain thing they imagine. Christ's throne is established, and they cannot shake it. (4.) He gives orders for the execution of Shimei immediately, *v.* 46. All judgment is committed to the Lord Jesus, and, though he be King of peace, he will be found a King of righteousness; and this will shortly be his word of command concerning all his enemies, that would not have him to reign over them: *Bring them forth, and slay them before me;* the reproaches of those that blasphemed him will fall on themselves, to their eternal condemnation.

CHAPTER 3

Solomon's reign looked bloody in the foregoing chapter, but the necessary acts of justice must not be called cruelty; in this chapter it appears with another face. We must not think the worse of God's mercy to his subjects for his judgments on rebels. We have here, I. Solomon's marriage to Pharaoh's daughter (*v.* 1). II. A general view of his religion (*v.* 2–4). III. A particular account of his prayer to God for wisdom, and the answer to that prayer (*v.* 5–15). IV. A particular instance of his wisdom in deciding the controversy between the two harlots (*v.* 16–28). And very great he looks here, both at the altar and on the bench, and therefore on the bench because at the altar.

Verses 1–4

We are here told concerning Solomon,

I. Something that was unquestionably good, for which he is to be praised and in which he is to be imitated. 1. He *loved the Lord, v.* 3. Particular notice was taken of God's love to him, 2 Sa. 12:24. He had his name from it: *Jedidiah — beloved of the Lord.* And here we find he returned that love, as John, the beloved disciple, was most full of love. Solomon was a wise man, a rich man; yet the brightest encomium of him is that which is the character of all the saints, even the poorest, He *loved the Lord,* so the Chaldee; all that love God love his worship, love to hear from him and speak to him, and so to have communion with him. 2. He *walked in the statutes of David his father,* that is, in the statutes that David gave him, *ch.* 2:2, 3; 1 Chr. 28:9, 10 (his dying father's charge was sacred, and as a law to him), or in God's statutes, which David his father walked in before him; he kept close to God's ordinances, carefully observed them and diligently attended them. Those that truly *love God* will make conscience of *walking in his statutes.* 3. He was very free and generous in what he did for the honour of God. When he offered sacrifice he offered like a king, in some proportion to his great wealth, a *thousand burnt-offerings, v.* 4. Where God sows plentifully he expects to reap accordingly; and those that truly love God and his worship will not grudge the expenses of their religion. We may be tempted to say, *To what purpose is this waste?* Might not these cattle have been given to the poor? But we must never think that wasted which is laid out in the service of God. It seems strange how so many beasts should be burnt upon one altar in one feast, though it continued seven days; but the fire on the altar is supposed to be more quick and devouring than common fire, for it represented that fierce and mighty wrath of God which fell upon the sacrifices, that the offerers might escape. *Our God is a consuming fire.* Bishop Patrick quotes it as a tradition of the Jews that the smoke of the sacrifices ascended directly in a straight pillar, and was not scattered, otherwise it would have choked those that attended, when so many sacrifices were offered as were here.

II. Here is something concerning which it may be doubted whether it was good or no. 1. His marrying Pharaoh's daughter, *v.* 1. We will suppose she was proselyted, otherwise the marriage would not have been lawful; yet, if so, surely it was not advisable. He that *loved the Lord* should, for his sake, have fixed his love upon one of the Lord's people. Unequal matches of the sons of God with the daughters of men have often been of pernicious consequence; yet some think that he did this with the advice of his friends, that she was a sincere convert (for the gods of the Egyptians are not reckoned among the strange gods which his strange wives drew him in to the worship of, *ch.* 11:5, 6), and that the book of Canticles and the 45th Psalm were penned on this occasion, by which these nuptials were made typical of the mystical espousals of the church to Christ, especially the Gentile church. 2. His worshipping in the high places, and thereby tempting the people to do so too, *v.* 2, 3. Abraham built his altars on mountains (Gen. 12:8; 22:2), and worshipped in a grove, Gen. 21:33. Thence the custom was derived, and was proper, till the divine law confined them to one place, Deu. 12:5, 6. David kept to the ark, and did not care for the high places, but Solomon, though in other things he *walked in the statutes of his father*, in this came short of him. He showed thereby a great zeal for sacrificing, but to obey would have been better. This was an irregularity. Though there was as yet no house built, there was a tent pitched, to the name of the Lord, and the ark ought to have been the centre of their unity. It was so by divine institution; from it the high places separated; yet while they worshipped God only, and in other things according to the rule, he graciously overlooked their weakness, and accepted their services; and it is owned that *Solomon loved the Lord*, though he *burnt incense in the high places*, and let not men be more severe than God is.

Verses 5–15

We have here an account of a gracious visit which God paid to Solomon, and the communion he had with God in it, which put a greater honour upon Solomon than all the wealth and power of his kingdom did.

I. The circumstances of this visit, *v.* 5. 1. The place. It was in Gibeon; that was the great high place, and should have been the only one, because there the tabernacle and the brazen altar were, 2 Chr. 1:3. There Solomon offered his great sacrifices, and there God owned him more than in any other of the high places. The nearer we come to the rule in our worship the more reason we have to expect the tokens of God's presence. Where God records his name, there he will meet us and bless us. 2. The time. It was by night, the night after he had offered that generous sacrifice, *v.* 4. The more we abound in God's work the more comfort we may expect in him; if the day has been busy for him, the night will be easy in him. Silence and retirement befriend our communion with God. His kindest visits are often in the night, Ps. 17:3. 3. The manner. It was in a dream, when he was asleep, his senses locked up, that God's access to his mind might be the more free and immediate. In this way God used to speak to the prophets (Num. 12:6) and to private persons, for their own benefit, Job 33:15, 16. These divine dreams, no doubt, were plainly distinguishable from those in which there are divers vanities, Eccl. 5:7.

II. The gracious offer God made him of the favour he should choose, whatever it might be, *v.* 5. He saw the glory of God shine about him, and heard a voice saying, *Ask what I shall give thee.* Not that God was indebted to him for his sacrifices, but thus he would testify his acceptance of them, and signify to him what great mercy he had in store for him, if he were not wanting to himself. Thus he would try his inclinations and put an honour upon the prayer of faith. God, in like manner, condescends to us, and puts us in the ready way to be happy by assuring us that we shall have what we will for the asking, Jn. 16:23; 1 Jn. 5:14. What would we more? *Ask, and it shall be given you.*

III. The pious request Solomon hereupon made to God. He readily laid hold of this offer. Why do we neglect the like offer made to us, like Ahaz, who said, *I will not ask?* Isa. 7:12. Solomon prayed in his sleep, God's grace assisting him; yet it was a lively prayer. What we are most in care about, and which makes the greatest impression upon us when we are awake, commonly affects us when we are asleep; and by our dreams, sometimes, we may know what our hearts are upon and how our pulse beats. Plutarch makes virtuous dreams one evidence of increase in virtue. Yet this must be attributed to a higher source. Solomon's making such an intelligent choice as this when he was asleep, and the powers of reason were least active, showed that it came purely from the grace of God, which wrought in him these gracious desires. If his *reins* thus in-

struct him in the night season, he must *bless the Lord* who *gave him counsel*, Ps. 16:7. Now, in this prayer,

1. He acknowledges God's great goodness to his father David, *v.* 6. He speaks honourably of his father's piety, that he had *walked before God in uprightness of heart*, drawing a veil over his faults. It is to be hoped that those who praise their godly parents will imitate them. But he speaks more honourably of God's goodness to his father, the mercy he had shown to him while he lived, in giving him to be sincerely religious and then recompensing his sincerity and the great kindness he had kept for him, to be bestowed on the family when he was gone, in *giving him a son to sit on his throne.* Children should give God thanks for his mercies to their parents, for the sure mercies of David. God's favours are doubly sweet when we observe them transmitted to us through the hands of those that have gone before us. The way to get the entail perpetuated is to bless God that it has hitherto been preserved.

2. He owns his own insufficiency for the discharge of that great trust to which he is called, *v.* 7, 8. And here is a double plea to enforce his petition for wisdom: — (1.) That his place required it, as he was successor to David ("*Thou hast made me king instead of David,* who was a very wise and good man: Lord, give me wisdom, that I may keep up what he wrought, and carry on what he began") and as he was ruler over Israel: "Lord, give me wisdom to rule well; for they are a numerous people, that will not be managed without much care, and they are thy people, whom thou hast chosen, and therefore to be ruled for thee, and the more wisely they are ruled the more glory thou wilt have from them." (2.) That he wanted it. As one that had a humble sense of his own deficiency, he pleads, "*Lord, I am but a little child* (so he calls himself, a child in understanding, though his father called him *a wise man, ch.* 2:9); *I know not how to go out or come in* as I should, nor to do so much as the common daily business of the government, much less what to do in a critical juncture." Note, Those who are employed in public stations ought to be very sensible of the weight and importance of their work and their own insufficiency for it, and then they are qualified for receiving divine instruction. Paul's question *(Who is sufficient for these things?)* is much like Solomon's here, *Who is able to judge this thy so great a people? v.* 9. Absalom, who was a wise man, trembles at the undertaking and suspects his own fitness for it. The more knowing and considerate men are the better acquainted they are with their own weakness and the more jealous of themselves.

3. He begs of God to give him wisdom (*v.* 9); *Give therefore thy servant an understanding heart.* He calls himself *God's servant*, pleased with that relation to God (Ps. 116:16) and pleading it with him: "I am devoted to thee, and employed for thee; give me that which is requisite to the services in which I am employed." Thus his good father prayed, and thus he pleaded, Ps. 119:125, *I am thy servant, give me understanding.* An understanding heart is God's gift, Prov. 2:6. We must pray for it (James 1:5), and pray for it with application to our particular calling and the various occasions we have for it; as Solomon, *Give me an understanding*, not to please my own curiosity with, or puzzle my neighbours, but *to judge thy people.* That is the best knowledge which will be serviceable to us in doing our duty; and such that knowledge is which enables us to *discern between good and bad*, right and wrong, sin and duty, truth and falsehood, so as not to be imposed upon by false colours in judging either of others' actions or of our own.

4. The favourable answer God gave to his request. It was a pleasing prayer (*v.* 10): *The speech pleased the Lord.* God is well pleased with his own work in his people, the desires of his own kindling, the prayers of his Spirit's inditing. By this choice Solomon made it appear that he desired to be good more than great, and to serve God's honour more than to advance his own. Those are accepted of God who prefer spiritual blessings to temporal, and are more solicitous to be found in the way of their duty than in the way to preferment. But that was not all; it was a prevailing prayer, and prevailed for more than he asked. (1.) God gave him wisdom, *v.* 12. He fitted him for all that great work to which he had called him, gave him such a right understanding of the law which he was to judge by, and the cases he was to judge of, that he was unequalled for a clear head, a solid judgment, and a piercing eye. Such

an insight, and such a foresight, never was prince so blessed with. (2.) He gave him riches and honour over and above into the bargain (*v.* 13), and it was promised that in these he should as much exceed his predecessors, his successors, and all his neighbours, as in wisdom. These also are God's gift, and, as far as is good for them, are promised to all that *seek first the kingdom of God and the righteousness thereof*, Mt. 6:33. Let young people learn to prefer grace to gold in all that they choose, because *godliness has the promise of the life that now is*, but *the life that now is* has not *the promise of godliness.* How completely blessed was Solomon, that had both wisdom and wealth! He that has wealth and power without wisdom and grace is in danger of doing hurt with them; he that has wisdom and grace without wealth and power is not capable of doing so much good with them as he that has both. Wisdom is good, is so much the better, with an inheritance, Eccles. 7:11. But, if we make sure of wisdom and grace, these will either bring outward prosperity with them or sweeten the want of it. God promised Solomon riches and honour absolutely, but long life upon condition (*v.* 14). *If thou wilt walk in my ways, as David did, then I will lengthen thy days.* He failed in the condition; and therefore, though he had riches and honour, he did not live so long to enjoy them as in the course of nature he might have done. Length of days is wisdom's right-hand blessing, typical of eternal life; but it is in her left hand that riches and honour are, Prov. 3:16. Let us see here, [1.] That the way to obtain spiritual blessings is to be importunate for them, to wrestle with God in prayer for them, as Solomon did for wisdom, asking that only, as the *one thing needful.* [2.] That the way to obtain temporal blessings is to be indifferent to them and to refer ourselves to God concerning them. Solomon had wisdom given him because he did ask it and wealth because he did not ask it.

5. The grateful return Solomon made for the visit God was pleased to pay him, *v.* 15. He awoke, we may suppose in a transport of joy, awoke, and *his sleep was sweet to him*, as the prophet speaks (Jer. 31:26); being satisfied of God's favour, he was satisfied with it, and he began to think *what he should render to the Lord.* He had made his prayer at the high place at Gibeon, and there God had graciously met him; but he comes to Jerusalem to give thanks *before the ark of the covenant*, blaming himself, as it were, that he had not prayed there, the ark being the token of God's presence, and wondering that God had met him any where else. God's passing by our mistakes should persuade us to amend them. There he, (1.) Offered a great sacrifice to God. We must give God praise for his gifts in the promise, though not yet fully performed. David used to *praise God's word*, as well as his *works* (Ps. 56:10, and particularly, 2 Sa. 7:18), and Solomon trod in his steps. (2.) He made a great feast upon the sacrifice, that those about him might rejoice with him in the grace of God.

Verses 16–28

An instance is here given of Solomon's wisdom, to show that the grant lately made him had a real effect upon him. The proof is fetched, not from the mysteries of state and the policies of the council-board, though there no doubt he excelled, but from the trial and determination of a cause between party and party, which princes, though they devolve them upon their judges, must not think it below them to take cognizance of. Observe,

I. The case opened, not by lawyers, but by the parties themselves, though they were women, which made it the easier to such a piercing eye as Solomon had to discern between right and wrong by their own showing. These two women were harlots, kept a public house, and their children, some think, were born of fornication, because here is no mention of their husbands. It is probable the cause had been heard in the inferior courts, before it was brought before Solomon, and had been found special, the judges being unable to determine it, that Solomon's wisdom in deciding it at last might be the more taken notice of. These two women, who lived in a house together, were each of them delivered of a son within three days of one another, *v.* 17, 18. They were so poor that they had no servant or nurse to be with them, so slighted, because harlots, that they had no friend or relation to accompany them. One of them overlaid her child, and, in the night, exchanged it with the other (*v.* 19, 20), who was soon aware of the cheat put upon her, and appealed to public justice to be righted, *v.* 21. See, 1. What anxiety is caused by little children, how uncertain their lives are, and to how many dangers they are continually exposed. The age of infancy is the valley of the shadow of death; and the lamp of life, when first lighted, is easily blown out. It is a wonder of mercy that so few perish in the perils of nursing. 2. How much better it was in those times with children born in fornication than commonly it is now. harlots then loved their children, nursed them, and were loth to part with them; whereas now they are often sent to a distance, abandoned, or killed. But thus is was foretold that *in the last days perilous times should come,* when people should be without natural affection, 2 Tim. 3:1, 3.

II. The difficulty of the case. The question was, Who was the mother of this living child, which was brought into court, to be finally adjudged either to the one or to the other? Both mothers were vehement in their claim, and showed a deep concern about it. Both were peremptory in their asseverations: "It is mine," says one. "Nay, it is mine," says the other. Neither will own the dead child, though it would be cheaper to bury that than to maintain the other: but it is the living one they strive for. The living child is therefore the parent's joy because it is their hope; and may not the dead children be so? See Jer. 31:17. Now the difficulty of the case was that there was no evidence on either side. The neighbours, though it is probable that some of them were present at the birth and circumcision of the children, yet had not taken so much notice of them as to be able to distinguish them. To put the parties to the rack would have been barbarous; not she who had justice on her side, but she who was most hardy, would have had the judgment in her favour. Little stress is to be laid on extorted evidence. Judges and juries have need of wisdom to find out truth when it thus lies hid.

III. The determination of it. Solomon, having patiently heard what both sides had to say, sums up the evidence, *v.* 23. And now the whole court is in expectation what course Solomon's wisdom will take to find out the truth. One knows not what to say to it; another, perhaps, would determine it by lot. Solomon calls for a sword, and gives orders to divide the living child between the two contenders. Now, 1. This seemed a ridiculous decision of the case, and a brutal cutting of the knot which he could not untie. "Is this," think the sages of the law, "the wisdom of Solomon?" little dreaming what he aimed at in it. *The hearts of kings,* such kings, *are unsearchable,* Prov. 25:3. There was a law concerning the dividing of a living ox and a dead one. (Ex. 21:35), but that did not reach this case. But, 2. It proved an effectual discovery of the truth. Some think that Solomon did himself discern it, before he made this experiment, by the countenances of the women and their way of speaking: but by this he gave satisfaction to all the company, and silenced the pretender. To find out the true mother, he could not try which the child loved best, and must therefore try which loved the child best; both pretended to a motherly affection, but their sincerity will be tried when the child is in danger. (1.) She that knew the child was not her own, but in contending for it stood upon a point of honour, was well content to have it divided. She that had overlaid her own child cared not what became of this, so that the true mother might not have it: *Let it be neither mine nor thine, but divide it.* By this it appeared that she knew her own title to be bad, and feared Solomon would find it so, though she little suspected she was betraying herself, but thought Solomon in good earnest. If she had been the true mother she would not have forfeited her interest in the child by agreeing so readily to this bloody decision. But, (2.) She that knew the child was her own, rather than the child should be butchered, gives it up to her adversary. How feelingly does she cry out, *O, my lord! give her the living child, v.* 26. "Let me see it hers, rather than not see it at all." By this tenderness towards the child it appeared that she was not the careless mother that had overlaid the dead child, but was the true mother of the living one, that could not endure to see its death, having compassion on the son of her womb. "The case is plain," says Solomon; "what need of witnesses? *Give her the living child;* for you all see, by this undissembled compassion, *she is the mother of it.*" Let parents show their love to their children by taking care of them, especially by taking care of their souls, and, with a holy violence, snatching them as brands out of the burning. Those are most likely to have the comfort of children that do their duty to them. Satan pretends to the heart of man, but by this it appears that he is only a pretender, that he would be content to divide with God, whereas the rightful sovereign of the heart will have all or none.

IV. We are told what a great reputation Solomon got among his people by this and other instances of his wisdom, which would have a great influence upon the ease of his government: *They feared the king* (*v.* 28), highly reverenced him, durst not in any thing oppose him, and were afraid of doing an unjust thing; for they knew, if ever it came before him, he would certainly discover it, *for they saw that the wisdom of God was in him,* that is, that wisdom with which God had promised to endue him. This *made his face to shine,* Eccl. 8:1. This *strengthened him,* Eccl. 7:19. This was better to him *than weapons of war,* Eccl. 9:18. For this he was both feared and loved.

CHAPTER 4

An instance of the wisdom God granted to Solomon we had in the close of the foregoing chapter. In this we have an account of his wealth and prosperity, the other branch of the promise there made him. We have here, I. The magnificence of his court, his ministers of state (*v.* 1–6), and the purveyors of his household (*v.* 7–19), and their office (*v.* 27, 28). II. The provisions for his table (*v.* 22, 23). III. The extent of his dominion (*v.* 21–24). IV. The numbers, case, and peace, of his subjects (*v.* 20–25). V. His stables (*v.* 26). VI. His great reputation for wisdom and learning (*v.* 29–34). Thus great was Solomon, but our Lord Jesus was greater than he (Mt. 12:42), though he took upon him the form of a servant; for divinity, in its lowest humiliation, infinitely transcends royalty in its highest elevation.

Verses 1–19

Here we have,

I. Solomon upon his throne (*v.* 1): *So king Solomon was king,* that is, he was confirmed and established king *over all Israel,* and not, as his successors, only over two tribes. He was a king, that is, he did the work and duty of a king, with the wisdom God had given him. Those preserve the name and honour of their place that mind the business of it and make conscience of it.

II. The great officers of his court, in the choice of whom, no doubt, his wisdom much appeared. It is observable, 1. That several of them are the same that were in his father's time. Zadok and Abiathar were then priests (2 Sa. 20:25), so they were now; only then Abiathar had the precedency, now Zadok. Jehoshaphat was then recorder, or keeper of the great seal, so he was now. Benaiah, in his father's time, was a principal man in military affairs, and so he was now. Shisha was his father's scribe, and his sons were his, *v.* 3. Solomon, though a wise man, would not affect to be wiser than his father in this matter. When sons come to inherit their father's wealth, honour, and power, it is a piece of respect to their memory, *caeteris paribus — where it can properly be done,* to employ those whom they employed, and trust those whom they trusted. Many pride themselves in being the reverse of their good parents. 2. The rest were priests' sons. His prime-minister of state was *Azariah the son of Zadok the priest.* Two others of the first rank were the sons of Nathan the prophet, *v.* 5. In preferring them he testified the grateful respect he had for their good father, whom he loved *in the name of a prophet.*

III. The purveyors for his household, whose business it was to send in provisions from several parts of the country, for the king's tables and cellars (*v.* 7) and for his stables (*v.* 27, 28), that thus, 1. His house might always be well furnished at the best hand. Let great men learn hence good house-keeping, to be generous in spending according to their ability, but prudent in providing. It is the character of the virtuous woman that she *bringeth her food from afar* (Prov. 31:14), not far-fetched and dear-bought, but the contrary, every thing bought where it is cheapest. 2. That thus he himself, and those who immediately attended him, might be eased of a great deal of care, and the more closely apply themselves to the business of the state, not troubled about much serving, provision for that being got ready to their hand. 3. That thus all the parts of the kingdom might be equally benefited by the taking off of the commodities that were the productions of their country and the circulating of the coin. Industry would hereby be encouraged, and consequently wealth increased, even in those tribes that lay most remote from the court. The providence of God extends itself to all *places of his dominions* (Ps. 103:22); so should the prudence and care of princes. 4. The dividing of this trust into so many hands was prudent, that no man might be continually burdened with the care of it nor grow exorbitantly rich with the profit of it, but that Solomon might have those, in every district, who, having a dependence upon the court, would be serviceable to him and his interest as there was occasion. These commissioners of the victualling-office, not for the army or navy (Solomon was engaged in no war), but for the household, are here named, several of them only by their surnames, as great men commonly call their servants: *Ben-hur, Ben-dekar, etc.,* though several of them have also their proper names prefixed. Two of them married Solomon's daughters, Ben-Abinadab (*v.* 11) and Ahimaaz (*v.* 15), and no disparagement to them to marry men of business. Better match with the officers of their father's court that were Israelites than with the sons of princes that were *strangers to the covenant of promise.* The son of Geber was in Ramoth-Gilead (*v.* 19), and Geber himself was in the country of Sihon and Og, which included that and Mahanaim, *v.* 14. He is therefore said to be *the only officer in that land,* because the other two, mentioned *v.* 13, 14, depended on him, and were subordinate to him.

Verses 20–28

Such a kingdom, and such a court, surely never any prince had, as Solomon's are here described to be.

I. Such a kingdom. Never did the crown of Israel shine so brightly as it did when Solomon wore it, never in his father's days, never in the days of any of his successors; nor was that kingdom ever so glorious a type of the kingdom of the Messiah as it was then. The account here given of it is such as fully answers the prophecies which we have concerning it in Ps. 72, which is a psalm for Solomon, but with reference to Christ. 1. The territories of his kingdom were large and its tributaries many; so it was foretold that he should *have dominion from sea to sea,* Ps. 72:8–11. Solomon reigned not only over all Israel, who were his subjects by choice, but over all the neighbouring kingdoms, who were his subjects by constraint. All the princes from the river Euphrates, north-east to the border of Egypt south-west, not only added to his honour by doing him homage and holding their crowns from him, but added to his wealth by serving him, and bringing him presents, *v.* 21. David, by his successful wars, compelled them to this subjection, and Solomon, by his admirable wisdom, made it easy and reasonable; for it is fit that the fool should be *servant to the wise in heart.* If they gave him presents, he gave them instructions, and still *taught the people knowledge,* not only his own people, but those of other nations: and *wisdom is better than gold.* He had *peace on all sides, v.* 24. None of all the nations that were subject to him offered to shake off his yoke, or to give him any disturbance, but rather thought themselves happy in their dependence upon him. Herein his kingdom typified the Messiah's; for to him it is promised that he shall have the *heathen for his inheritance* and that *princes shall worship him,* Isa. 49:6, 7; 53:12. 2. The subjects of his kingdom and its inhabitants, were many and cheerful. (1.) They were numerous and country was exceedingly populous (*v.* 20): *Judah and Israel were many,* and that good land was sufficient to maintain them all. *They were as the sand of the sea in multitude.* Now was fulfilled the promise made to Abraham concerning the increase of his seed (Gen. 22:17), as well as that concerning the extent of their dominion, Gen. 15:18. This was their strength and beauty, the honour of their prince, the terror of their enemies, and an advancement of the wealth of the nation. If they grew so numerous that the place was any where too strait for them, they might remove with advantage into the countries that were subject to them. God's spiritual Israel are many, at least they will be so when they come all together, Rev. 7:9. (2.) They were easy, they dwelt safely, or with confidence and assurance (*v.* 25), not jealous of their king or of his officers, not disaffected either to him or one to another, nor under any apprehension or danger from enemies foreign or domestic. They were happy and knew it, safe and willing to think themselves so. They dwelt every man under *his vine and fig-tree.* Solomon invaded no man's property, took not to himself their vineyards and olive-yards, as sometimes was the manner of the king (1 Sa. 8:14), but what they had they could call their own: he protected every man in the possession and enjoyment of his property. Those that had vines and fig-trees ate the fruit of them themselves; and so great was the peace of the country that they might, if they pleased, dwell as safely under the shadow of them as within the walls of a city. Or, because it was usual to have *vines by the sides of their houses* (Ps. 128:3), they are said to *dwell under their vines.* (3.) They were cheerful in the use of their plenty, *eating and drinking, and making merry, v.* 20. Solomon did not only keep a good table himself, but enabled all his subjects, according to their rank, to do so too, and taught them that God gave them their abundance that they might use it soberly and pleasantly, not that they might hoard it up. *There is nothing better* than for a man to *eat the labour of his hands* (Eccl. 2:24), and that *with a merry heart,* Eccl. 9:7. His father, in the Psalms, had led his people into the comforts of communion with God, and now he led them into the comfortable use of the good things of this life. This pleasant posture of Israel's affairs extended, in place, from Dan to Beersheba — no part of the country was exposed nor upon any account uneasy; and it continued a long time, *all the days of Solomon,* without any material interruption. Go where you would, you might see all the marks of plenty, peace, and satisfaction. The spiritual peace, and joy, and holy security, of all the faithful subjects of the Lord Jesus were typified by this. *The kingdom of God is not,* as Solomon's was, *meat and drink,* but, what is infinitely better, *righteousness, and peace, and joy in the Holy Ghost.*

II. Such a court Solomon kept as can scarcely be paralleled. We may guess at the vast number of his attendants, and the great resort there was to him, by the provision that was made daily for his table. Of bread there were so many measures of flour and meal as, it is computed, would richly serve 3000 men (Carellus computes above 4800 men), and the provision of flesh (*v.* 23) was rather more in proportion. What vast quantities were here of beef, mutton, and venison, and the choicest of all *fatted things,* as some read that which we translate *fatted fowl!* Ahasuerus, once in his reign, made a *great feast,* to *show the riches of his kingdom,* Esth. 1:3, 4. But it was much more the honour of Solomon that he kept a constant table and a very noble one, not of dainties or deceitful meats (he himself witnessed against them, Prov. 23:3), but substantial food, for the entertainment of those who came to hear his wisdom. Thus Christ fed those whom he taught, 5000 at a time, more than ever Solomon's table would entertain at once: and all believers have in him a continual feast. Herein he far outdoes Solomon, that he feeds all his subjects, not with the bread that perishes, but *with that which endures to eternal life.* It added much both to the strength and glory of Solomon's kingdom that he had such abundance of horses, 40,000 for chariots and 12,000 for his troops, 1000 horse, perhaps, in every tribe, for the preserving of the public peace, *v.* 26. God had commanded that their king should not multiply horses (Deu. 17:16), nor, according to the account here given, considering the extent and wealth of Solomon's kingdom, did he multiply horses in proportion to his neighbours; for we find even the Philistines bringing into the field 30,000 chariots (1 Sa. 13:5) and the Syrians at least 40,000 horse, 2 Sa. 10:18. The same officers that provided for his house provided also for his stable, *v.* 27, 28. Every one knew his place, and work, and time; and so this great court was kept without confusion. Solomon, that had vast incomes, lived at a vast expense, and perhaps wrote that with application to himself, Eccl. 5:11. *When goods increase those are increased that eat them; and what good is there to the owners thereof, saving the beholding of them with their eyes,* unless withal they have the satisfaction of doing good with them?

Verses 29–34

Solomon's wisdom was more his glory than his wealth, and here we have a general account of it.

I. The fountain of his wisdom: *God gave it him, v.* 29. He owns it himself. Prov. 2:6, *The Lord giveth wisdom.* He gives the powers of reason (Job 38:36), preserves and improves them. The ordinary advances of them are owing to his providence, the sanctification of them to his grace, and this extraordinary pitch at which they arrived in Solomon to a special grant of his favour to him in answer to prayer.

II. The fulness of it: *He had wisdom and understanding, exceeding much,* great knowledge of distant countries and the histories of former times, a quickness of thought, strength of memory, and clearness of judgment, such as never any man had. It is called *largeness of heart;* for the heart is often put for the intellectual powers. He had a vast compass of knowledge, could take things entire, and had an admirable faculty of laying things together. Some, by his *largeness of heart,* understand his courage and boldness, and that great assurance with which he delivered his dictates and determinations. Or it may be meant of his disposition to do good with his knowledge. He was very free and communicative, had the gift of utterance as well as wisdom, was as free of his learning as he was of his meat, and grudged neither to any that were about him. Note, It is very desirable that those who have large gifts of any kind should have large hearts to use them for the good of others; and this is *from the hand of God,* Eccl. 2:24. He shall *enlarge the heart,* Ps. 119:32. The greatness of Solomon's wisdom is illustrated by comparison. Chaldea and Egypt were nations famous for learning; thence the Greeks borrowed theirs; but the greatest scholars of these nations came short of Solomon, *v.* 30. If nature excels art, much more does grace. The knowledge which God gives by special favour goes beyond that which man gets by his own labour. Some wise men there were in Solomon's time, who were in great repute, particularly Heman, and others who were Levites, and employed by David in the temple-music, 1 Chr. 15:19. Heman was *his seer in the word of God,* 1 Chr. 25:5. Chalcol and Darda were own brothers, and they also were noted for learning and wisdom. But *Solomon excelled them all* (*v.* 30), he out-did them and confounded them; his counsel was much more valuable.

III. The fame of it. It was talked of *in all nations round about.* His great wealth and glory made his wisdom much more illustrious, and have him those opportunities of showing it which those cannot have that live in poverty and obscurity. The jewel of wisdom may receive great advantage by the setting of it.

IV. The fruits of it; by these the tree is known: he did not bury his talent, but showed his wisdom,

1. In his compositions. Those in divinity, written by divine inspiration, are not mentioned here, for they are extant, and will remain to the world's end monuments of his wisdom, and are, as other parts of scripture, of use to make us *wise unto salvation.* But, besides these, it appears by what he spoke, or dictated to be written from him, (1.) That he was a moralist, and a man of great prudence, for he spoke 3000 *proverbs,* wise sayings, apophthegms, of admirable use for the conduct of human life. The world is much governed by proverbs, and was never better furnished with useful ones than by Solomon. Whether those proverbs of Solomon that we have were any part of the 3000 is uncertain. (2.) That he was a poet and a man of great wit: *His songs were* 1005, of which one only is extant, because that only was divinely inspired, which is therefore called his *Song of songs.* His wise instructions were communicated by proverbs, that they might be familiar to those whom he designed to teach and ready on all occasions, and by *songs,* that they might be pleasant and move the affections. (3.) That he was a natural philosopher, and a man of great learning and insight into the mysteries of nature. From his own and others' observations and experience, he wrote both of plants and animals (*v.* 33), descriptions of their natures and qualities, and (some think) of the medicinal use of them.

2. In his conversation. There came persons from all parts, who were more inquisitive after knowledge than their neighbours, to *hear the wisdom of Solomon, v.* 34. Kings that had heard of it sent their ambassadors to hear it and to bring them instructions from it. Solomon's court was the staple of learning, and the rendezvous of philosophers, that is, the lovers of wisdom, who all came to light their candle at his lamp and to borrow from him. Let those who magnify the modern learning above that of the ancients produce such a treasure of knowledge any where in these latter ages as that was which Solomon was master of; yet this puts an honour upon human learning, that Solomon was praised for it, and recommends it to the great men of the earth, as well worthy their diligent search. But,

Lastly, Solomon was, herein, a type of Christ, *in whom are hidden all the treasures of wisdom and knowledge,* and hidden for use; for he is *made of God to us wisdom.*

CHAPTER 5

The great work which Solomon was raised up to do was the building of the temple; his wealth and wisdom were given him to qualify him for that. In this, especially, he was to be a type of Christ, for "he shall build the temple of the Lord," Zec. 6:12. In this chapter we have an account of the preparations he made for that and his other buildings. Gold and silver his good father had prepared in abundance, but timber and stones he must get ready; and about these we have him treating with Hiram king of Tyre. I. Hiram congratulated him on his accession to the throne (*v.* 1). II. Solomon signified to him his design to build the temple and desired him to furnish him with workmen (*v.* 2–6). III. Hiram agreed to do it (*v.* 7–9). IV. Solomon's work was accordingly well done and Hiram's workmen were well paid (*v.* 10–18).

Verses 1–9

We have here an account of the amicable correspondence between Solomon and Hiram. Tyre was a famous trading city, that lay close upon the sea, in the border of Israel; its inhabitants (as should seem) were none of the devoted nations, nor ever at enmity with Israel, and therefore David never offered to destroy them, but lived in friendship with them. It is here said of Hiram their king that he was *ever a lover of David;* and we have reason to think he was a worshipper of the true God, and had himself renounced, though he could not reform, the idolatry of his city. David's character will win the affections even of those that are without. Here is,

I. Hiram's embassy of compliment to Solomon, *v.* 1. He sent, as is usual among princes, to condole with him on the death of David, and to renew his alliances with him upon his succession to the government. It is good keeping up friendship and communion with the families in which religion is uppermost.

II. Solomon's embassy of business to Hiram, sent, it is likely, by messengers of his own. In wealth, honour, and power, Hiram was very much inferior to Solomon, yet Solomon had occasion to be beholden to him and begged his favour. Let us never look with disdain on those below us, because we know not how soon we may need them. Solomon, in his letter to Hiram, acquaints him,

1. With his design to build a temple to the honour of God. Some think that temples among the heathen took their first rise and copy from the tabernacle which Moses erected in the wilderness, and that there were none before that; however there were many houses built in honour of the false gods before this was built in honour of the God of Israel, so little is external splendour a mark of the true church. Solomon tells Hiram, who was himself no stranger to the affair, (1.) That David's wars were an obstruction to him, that he could not build this temple, though he designed it, *v.* 3. They took up much of his time, and thoughts, and cares, were a constant expense to him and a constant employment of his subjects; so that he could not do it so well as it must be done, and therefore, it not being essential to religion, he must leave it to be done by his successor. See what need we have to pray that God will *give peace in our time,* because, in time or war, the building of the gospel temple commonly goes on slowly. (2.) That peace gave him an opportunity to build it, and therefore he resolved to set about it immediately: *God has given me rest* both at home and abroad, and there is no adversary (*v.* 4), no *Satan* (so the word is), no instrument of Satan to oppose it, or to divert us from it. Satan does all he can to hinder temple work (1 Th. 2:18; Zec. 3:1), but when he is bound (Rev. 20:2) we should be busy. When there is *no evil occurrent,* then let us be vigorous and zealous in that which is good and get it forward. When the churches have rest let them be edified, Acts 9:31. Days of peace and prosperity present us with a fair gale, which we must account for if we improve not. As God's providence excited Solomon to think of building the temple, by giving him wealth and leisure, so his promise encouraged him. God had told David that his *son should build him a house, v.* 5. He will take it as a pleasure to be thus employed, and will not lose the honour designed him by that promise. It may stir us up much to good undertakings to be assured of good success in them. Let God's promise quicken our endeavours.

2. With his desire that Hiram would assist him herein. Lebanon was the place whence timber must be had, a noble forest in the north of Canaan, particularly expressed in the grant of that land to Israel — *all Lebanon,* Jos. 13:5. So that Solomon was proprietor of all its productions. The *cedars of Lebanon* are spoken of as, in a special manner,

the *planting of the Lord* (Ps. 109:16), being designed for Israel's use and particularly for temple service. But Solomon owned that though the trees were his the Israelites had not *skill to hew timber* like the Sidonians, who were Hiram's subjects. Canaan was *a land of wheat and barley* (Deu. 8:8), which employed Israel in the affairs of husbandry, so that they were not at all versed in manufactures: in them the Sidonians excelled. Israel, in the things of God, are a *wise and understanding people;* and yet, in curious arts, inferior to their neighbours. True piety is a much more valuable gift of heaven than the highest degree of ingenuity. Better be an Israelite skilful in the law than a Sidonian skilful to hew timber. But, the case being thus, Solomon courts Hiram to send him workmen, and promises (*v.* 6) both to *assist* them *(my servants shall be with thy servants,* to work under them), and to *pay* them *(unto thee will I give hire for thy servants);* for the labourer, even in church-work, though it be indeed its own wages, *is worthy of his hire,* The evangelical prophet, foretelling the glory of the church in the days of the Messiah, seems to allude to this story, Isa. 60, where he prophesies, (1.) That the *sons of strangers* (such were the Tyrians and Sidonians) shall *build up the wall* of the gospel temple, *v.* 10. Ministers were raised up among the Gentiles for the edifying of the body of Christ. (2.) That *the glory of Lebanon* shall be brought to it to *beautify it, v.* 13. All external endowments and advantages shall be made serviceable to the interests of Christ's kingdom.

3. Hiram's reception of, and return to, this message. (1.) He received it with great satisfaction to himself: He *rejoiced greatly* (*v.* 7) that Solomon trod in his father's steps, and carried on his designs, and was likely to be so great a blessing to his kingdom. In this Hiram's generous spirit rejoiced, and not merely in the prospect he had of making an advantage to himself by Solomon's employing him. What he had the pleasure of he gave God the praise of: *Blessed be the Lord, who has given to David* (who was himself a wise man) *a wise son* to rule *over this great people.* See here, [1.] With what pleasure Hiram speaks of Solomon's wisdom and the extent of his dominion. Let us learn not to envy others either those secular advantages or those endowments of the mind wherein they excel us. What a great comfort it is to those that wish well to the Israel of God to see religion and wisdom kept up in families from one generation to another, especially in great families and those that have great influence on others! where it is so, God must have the glory of it. If to godly parents be given a godly seed (Mal. 2:15), it is a token for good, and a happy indication that the entail of the blessing shall not be cut off.

(2.) He answered it with great satisfaction to Solomon, granting him what he desired, and showing himself very forward to assist him in this great and good work to which he was laying his hand. We have here his articles of agreement with Solomon concerning this affair, in which we may observe Hiram's prudence. [1.] He deliberated upon the proposal, before he returned an answer (*v.* 8): *I have considered the things.* It is common for those that make bargains rashly afterwards to wish them unmade again. The virtuous woman *considers a field* and then *buys it,* Prov. 31:16. Those do not lose time who take time to consider. [2.] He descended to particulars in the articles, that there might be no misunderstanding afterwards, to occasion a quarrel. Solomon had spoken of hewing the trees (*v.* 6), and Hiram agrees to what he desired concerning that (*v.* 8); but nothing had been said concerning carriage, and this matter therefore must be settled. Land-carriage would be very troublesome and chargeable; he therefore undertakes to bring all the timber down from Lebanon by sea, a coasting voyage. Conveyance by water is a great convenience to trade, for which God is to have praise, who taught man that discretion. Observe what a definite bargain Hiram made. Solomon must appoint the place where the timber shall be delivered, and thither Hiram will undertake to bring it and be responsible for its safety. As the Sidonians excelled the Israelites in timber-work, so they did in sailing; for Tyre and Sidon were *situate at the entry of the sea* (Eze. 27:3): they therefore were fittest to take care of the water-carriage. *Tractant fabrilia fabri — Every artist has his trade assigned.* And, [3.] If Hiram undertake for the work, and *do all Solomon's desire concerning the timber* (*v.* 8), he justly expects that Solomon shall undertake for the wages: *"Thou shalt accomplish my desire in giving food for my household* (*v.* 9), not only for the workmen, but for my own family." If Tyre supply Israel with craftsmen, Israel will supply Tyre with corn, Eze. 27:17. Thus, by the wise disposal of Providence, one country has need of another and is benefited by another, that there may be mutual correspondence and dependence, to the glory of God our common parent.

Verses 10–18

Here is, I. The performance of the agreement between Solomon and Hiram. Each of the parties made good his engagement. 1. Hiram delivered Solomon the timber, according to his bargain, *v.* 10. The trees were Solomon's, but perhaps — *Materiam superabat opus — The workmanship was of more value than the article.* Hiram is therefore said to deliver the trees. 2. Solomon conveyed to Hiram the corn which he had promised him, *v.* 11. Thus let justice be followed (as the expression is, Deu. 16:20), justice on both sides, in every bargain.

II. The confirmation of the friendship that was between them hereby. *God gave Solomon wisdom* (*v.* 12), which was more and better than any thing Hiram did or could give him; but this made Hiram love him, and enabled Solomon to improve his kindness, so that they were both willing to ripen their mutual love into a mutual league, that it might be lasting. It is wisdom to strengthen our friendship with those whom we find to be honest and fair, lest new friends prove not so firm and so kind as old ones.

III. The labourers whom Solomon employed in preparing materials for the temple. 1. Some were Israelites, who were employed in the more easy and honourable part of the work, felling trees and helping to square them, in conjunction with Hiram's servants; for this he appointed 30,000, but employed only 10,000 at a time, so that for one month's work they had two months' vacation, both for rest and for the despatch of their own affairs at home, *v.* 13, 14. It was temple service, yet Solomon takes care that they shall not be over-worked. Great men ought to consider that their servants must rest as well as they. 2. Others were captives of other nations, who were to bear burdens and to hew stone (*v.* 15), and we read not that these had their resting times as the other had, for they were doomed to servitude. 3. There were some employed as directors and overseers (*v.* 16), 3300 that ruled over the people, and they were as necessary and useful in their place as the labourers in theirs; here were many hands and many eyes employed, for preparation was now to be made, not only for the temple, but for all the rest of Solomon's buildings, at Jerusalem, and here in the forest of Lebanon, and in other places of his dominion, of which see *ch.* 9:17–19. He speaks of the vastness of his undertakings (Eccl. 2:4, *I made me great works*), which required this vast number of workmen.

IV. The laying of the foundation of the temple; for that is the building his heart is chiefly upon, and therefore he begins with that, *v.* 17, 18. It should seem, Solomon was himself present, and president, at the founding of the temple, and that the first stone (as has been usual in famous buildings) was laid with some solemnity. *Solomon commanded and they brought costly stones* for the foundation; he would do every thing like himself, generously, and therefore would have some of the costliest stones laid, or buried rather, in the foundation, though, being out of sight, worse might have served. Christ, who is laid for a foundation, is an elect and precious stone (Isa. 28:16), and the foundations of the church are said to be *laid with sapphires,* Isa. 54:11, compare Rev. 21:19. That sincerity which is our gospel perfection obliges us to lay our foundation firm and to bestow most pains on that part of our religion which lies out of the sight of men.

CHAPTER 6

Great and long preparation had been making for the building of the temple, and here, at length, comes an account of the building of it; a noble piece of work it was, one of the wonders of the world, and taking in its spiritual significancy, one of the glories of the church. Here is, I. The time when it was built (*v.* 1), and how long it was in the building (*v.* 37, 38). II. The silence with which it was build (*v.* 7). III. The dimensions of it (*v.* 2, 3). IV. The message God sent to Solomon, when it was in the building (*v.* 11–13). V. The particulars: windows (*v.* 4), chambers (*v.* 5, 6, 8–10), the walls and flooring (*v.* 15–18), the oracle (*v.* 19–22), the cherubim (*v.* 23–30), the doors (*v.* 31–35), and the inner court (*v.* 36). Many learned men have well bestowed their pains in expounding the description here given of the temple according to the rules of architecture, and solving the difficulties which, upon search, they find in it; but in that matter, having nothing new to offer, we will not be particular or curious; it was then well understood, and every man's eyes that saw this glorious structure furnished him with the best critical exposition of this chapter.

Verses 1–10

Here, I. The temple is called *the house of the Lord* (*v.* 1), because it was, 1. Directed and modelled by him. Infinite Wisdom was the architect, and gave David the plan or pattern by the Spirit, not by word of mouth only, but, for the greater certainty and exactness, in writing (1 Chr. 28:11, 12), as he had given to Moses in the mouth a draught of the tabernacle. 2. Dedicated and devoted to him and to his honour, to be employed in his service, so his as never any other house was, for he manifested his glory in it (so as never in any other) in a way agreeable to that dispensation; for, when there were carnal ordinances, there was a *worldly sanctuary,* Heb. 9:1, 10. This gave it its *beauty of holiness,* that it was *the house of the Lord,* which far transcended all its other beauties.

II. The time when it began to be built is exactly set down. 1. It was just 480 years after the bringing of the children of Israel out of Egypt. Allowing forty years to Moses, seventeen to Joshua, 299 to the Judges, forty to Eli, forty to Samuel and Saul, forty to David, and four to Solomon before he began the work, we have just the sum of 480. So long it was after that holy state was founded before that holy house was built, which, in less than 430 years, was burnt by Nebuchadnezzar. It was thus deferred because Israel had, by their sins, rendered themselves unworthy of this honour, and because God would show how little he values external pomp and splendour in his service: he was in no haste for a temple. David's tent, which was clean and convenient, though it was neither stately nor rich, nor, for aught that appears, ever consecrated, is called the *house of the Lord* (2 Sa. 12:20), and served as well as Solomon's temple; yet, when God gave Solomon great wealth, he put it into his heart thus to employ it, and graciously accepted him, chiefly because it was to be a shadow of good things to come, Heb. 9:9. 2. It was in the fourth year of Solomon's reign, the first three years being taken up in settling the affairs of his kingdom, that he might not find any embarrassment from them in this work. It is not time lost which is spent in composing ourselves for the work of God, and disentangling ourselves from every thing which might distract or divert us. During this time he was adding to the preparations which his father had made (1 Chr. 22:14), hewing the stone, squaring the timber, and getting every thing ready, so that he is not to be blamed for slackness in deferring it so long. We are truly serving God when we are preparing for his service and furnishing ourselves for it.

III. The materials are brought in, ready for their place (*v.* 7), so ready that there was *neither hammer nor ax heard in the house while it was in building.* In all building Solomon prescribes it as a rule of prudence to *prepare the work in the field,* and *afterwards build,* Prov. 24:27. But here, it seems, the preparation was more than ordinarily full and exact, to such a degree that, when the several parts came to be put together, there was nothing defective to be added, nothing amiss to be amended. It was to be the temple of God of peace, and therefore no iron tool must be heard in it. Quietness and silence both become and befriend religious exercises: God's work should be done with as much care and as little noise as may be. The temple was thrown down with axes and hammers, and those that threw it down roared *in the midst of the congregation* (Ps. 74:4, 6); but it was built up in silence. Clamour and violence often hinder the work of God, but never further it.

IV. The dimensions are laid down (*v.* 2, 3) according to the rules of proportion. Some observe that the length and breadth were just double to that of the tabernacle. Now that Israel had grown more numerous the place of their meeting needed to be enlarged (Isa. 54:1, 2), and now that they had grown richer they were the better able to enlarge it. Where God sows plentifully he expects to reap so.

V. An account of the windows (*v.* 4): They were *broad within, and narrow without, Marg.* Such should the eyes of our mind be, reflecting nearer on ourselves than on other people, looking much within, to judge ourselves, but little without, to censure our brethren. The narrowness of the lights intimated the darkness of that dispensation, in comparison with the gospel day.

VI. The chambers are described (*v.* 5, 6), which served as vestries, in which the utensils of the tabernacle were carefully laid up, and where the priests dressed and undressed themselves and left the clothes in which they ministered: probably in some of these chambers they feasted upon the holy things. Solomon was not so intent upon the magnificence of the house as to neglect the conveniences that were requisite for the offices thereof, that every thing might be done decently and in order. Care was taken that the beams should not be fastened in the walls to weaken them, *v.* 6. Let not the church's strength be impaired under pretence of adding to its beauty or convenience.

Verses 11–14

Here is, I. The word God sent to Solomon, when he was engaged in building the temple. God let him know that he took notice of what he was doing, *the house he was now building, v.* 12. None employ themselves for God without having his eye upon them. *"I know thy works,* thy good works." He assured him that if he would proceed and persevere in obedience to the divine law, and keep in the way of duty and the true worship of God, the divine loving-kindness should be drawn out both to himself *(I will perform my word with thee)* and to his kingdom: "Israel shall be ever owned as my people; I will *dwell among them,* and *not forsake them."* This word God sent him probably by a prophet, 1. That by the promise he might be encouraged and comforted in his work. Perhaps sometimes the great care, expense, and fatigue of it, made him ready to wish he had never begun it; but this would help him through the difficulties of it, that the promised establishment of his family and kingdom would abundantly recompense all his pains. An eye to the promise will carry us cheerfully through our work; and those who wish well to the public will think nothing too much that they can do to secure and perpetuate to it the tokens of God's presence. 2. That, by the condition annexed, he might be awakened to consider that though he built the temple ever so strong the glory of it would soon depart, unless he and his people continued *to walk in God's statutes.* God plainly let him know that all this charge which he and his people were at, in erecting this temple, would neither excuse them from obedience to the law of God nor shelter them from his judgments in case of disobedience. Keeping God's commandments is better, and more pleasing to him, than building churches.

II. The work Solomon did for God: *So he built the house* (*v.* 14), *so* animated by the message God had sent him, *so* admonished not to expect that God should own his building unless he were obedient to his laws: "Lord, I proceed upon these terms, being firmly resolved to walk in thy statutes." The strictness of God's government will never drive a good man from his service, but quicken him in it. Solomon built and finished, he went on with the work, and God went along with him till it was completed. It is spoken both to God's praise and his: he grew not weary of the work, met not with any obstructions (as Ezra 4:24), did not out-build his property, nor do it by halves, but, having begun to build, was both able and willing to finish; for he was a wise builder.

Verses 15–38

Here, I. We have a particular account of the details of the building.

1. The wainscot of the temple. It was of cedar (*v.* 15), which was strong and durable, and of a very sweet smell. The wainscot was curiously carved with knops (like eggs or apples) and flowers, no doubt as the fashion then was, *v.* 18.

2. The gilding. It was not like ours, washed over, but *the whole house,* all the inside of the temple (*v.* 22), even the floor (*v.* 30), he *overlaid with gold,* and the most holy place with *pure gold, v.* 21. Solomon would spare no expense necessary to make it every way sumptuous. Gold was under foot there, as it should be in all the living temples: the abundance of it lessened its worth.

3. The oracle, or *speaking-place* (for so the word signifies), *the holy of holies,* so called because thence God spoke to Moses, and perhaps to the high priest, when he consulted with the breast-plate of judgment. In this place *the ark of the covenant was to be set, v.* 19. Solomon made every thing new, and more magnificent than it had been, except the ark, which was still the same that Moses made, with its mercy-seat and cherubim; that was the token of God's presence, which is always the same with his people whether they meet in tent or temple, and changes not with their condition.

4. The cherubim. Besides those at the ends of the mercy-seat, which covered the ark, (1.) Solomon set up two more, very large ones, images of young men (as some think), with wings made of olive-wood, and all overlaid with gold, *v.* 23, etc. This most holy place was much larger than that in the tabernacle, and therefore the ark would have seemed lost in it, and the dead wall would have been unsightly, if it had not been thus adorned. (2.) He carved cherubim upon all the walls of the house, *v.* 29. The heathen set up images of their gods and worshipped them; but these were designed to represent the servants and attendants of the God of Israel, the holy angels, not to be themselves worshipped *(see thou do it not),* but to show how great he is whom we are to worship.

5. The doors. The folding doors that led into the oracle were but a fifth part of the wall (*v.* 31), those into the temple were a fourth part (*v.* 33); but both were beautified with cherubim engraven on them, *v.* 32, 35.

6. The inner court, in which the brazen altar was at which the priests ministered. This was separated from the court where the people were by a low wall, three rows of hewn stone tipped with a cornice of cedar (*v.* 36), that over it the people might see what was done and hear what the priests said to them; for, even under that dispensation, they were not kept wholly either in the dark or at a distance.

7. The time spent in this building. It was but seven years and a half from the founding to the finishing of it, *v.* 38. Considering the vastness and elegance of the building, and the many appurtenances to it which were necessary to fit it for use, it was soon done. Solomon was in earnest in it, had money enough, had nothing to divert him from it, and many hands made quick work. He finished it (as the margin reads it) with all the appurtenances thereof, and with all the ordinances thereof, not only built the place, but set forward the work for which it was built.

II. Let us now see what was typified by this temple. 1. Christ is the true temple; he himself spoke of the temple of his body, Jn. 2:21. God himself prepared him his body, Heb. 10:5. *In him dwelt the fulness of the Godhead,* as the *Shechinah* in the temple. In him meet all God's spiritual Israel. Through him we have access with confidence to God. All the angels of God, those blessed cherubim, have a charge to worship him. 2. Every believer is a living temple, in whom the Spirit of God dwells, 1 Co. 3:16. Even the body is such by virtue of its union with the soul, 1 Co. 6:19. We are not only wonderfully made by the divine providence, but more wonderfully made anew by the divine grace. This living temple is built upon Christ as its foundation and will be perfected in due time. 3. The gospel church is the mystical temple; it grows to a *holy temple in the Lord* (Eph. 2:21), enriched and beautified with the gifts and graces of the Spirit, as Solomon's temple with gold and precious stones. Only Jews built the tabernacle, but Gentiles joined with them in building the temple. Even strangers and foreigners are built up *a habitation of God,* Eph. 2:19, 22. The temple was divided into the holy place and the most holy, the courts of it into the outer and inner; so there are the visible and the invisible church. The door into the temple was wider than that into the oracle. Many enter into profession that come short of salvation. This temple is built firm, upon a rock, not to be taken down as the tabernacle of the Old Testament was. The temple was long in preparing, but was built at last. The top-stone of the gospel church will, at length, be brought forth with shoutings, and it is a pity that there should be the clashing of axes and hammers in the building of it. Angels are ministering spirits, attending the church on all sides and all the members of it. 4. Heaven is the everlasting temple. There the church will be fixed, and no longer movable. The streets of the new Jerusalem, in allusion to the flooring of the temple, are said to be *of pure gold,* Rev. 21:21. The cherubim there always attend the throne of glory. The temple was uniform, and in heaven there is the perfection of beauty and harmony. In Solomon's temple there was no noise of axes and hammers. Every thing is quiet and serene in heaven; all that shall be stones in that building must in the present sate of probation and preparation be fitted and made ready for it, must be hewn and squared by divine grace, and so made meet for a place there.

CHAPTER 7

As, in the story of David, one chapter of wars and victories follows another, so, in the story of Solomon, one chapter concerning his buildings follows another. In this chapter we have, I. His fitting up several buildings for himself and his own use (*v.* 1–12). II. His furnishing the temple which he had built for God, 1. With two pillars (*v.* 13–22). 2. With a molten sea (*v.* 23–26). 3. With ten basins of brass (*v.* 27–37), and ten layers upon them (*v.* 38, 39). 4. With all the other utensils of the temple (*v.* 40–50). 5. With the things that his father had dedicated (*v.* 51). The particular description of these things was not needless when it was written, nor is it now useless.

Verses 1–12

Never had any man so much of the spirit of building as Solomon had, nor to better purpose; he began with the temple, built for God first, and then all his other buildings were comfortable. The surest foundations of lasting prosperity are those which are laid in an early piety, Mt. 6:33. 1. He built a house for himself (*v.* 1), *where he dwelt, v.* 8. His father had built a good house; but it was no reflection upon his father for him to build a better, in proportion to the estate wherewith God had blessed him. Much of the comfort of this life is connected with an agreeable house. He was thirteen years building this house, whereas he built the temple in little more than seven years; not that he was more exact, but less eager and intent, in building his own house than in building God's. He was in no haste for his own palace, but impatient till the temple was finished and fit for use. Thus we ought to prefer God's honour before our own ease and satisfaction. 2. He built *the house of the forest at Lebanon* (*v.* 2), supposed to be a country seat near Jerusalem, so called from the pleasantness of its situation and the trees that encompassed it. I rather incline to think that it was a house built in the forest of Lebanon itself, whither (though far distant from Jerusalem) Solomon (having so many chariots and horses, and those dispersed into chariot-cities, which probably were his stages) might frequently retire with ease. It does not appear that his throne (mentioned *v.* 7) was at the house of the forest of Lebanon, and it was not at all improper to put his shields there as in a magazine. Express notice is taken of his buildings, not only in Jerusalem, but in Lebanon (*ch.* 9:19), and we read of the tower of Lebanon, which looks towards Damascus (Cant. 7:4), which probably was part of this house. A particular account is given of this house, that being built in Lebanon, a place famed for cedars, the pillars, and beams, and roof, were all cedar (*v.* 2, 3), and, being designed for pleasant prospects, there were three tiers of windows on each side, *light against light* (*v.* 4, 5), or, as it may be read, *prospect against prospect.* Those whose lost i cast in the country may be well reconciled to a country life by this, that some of the greatest princes have thought those the most pleasant of their days which they have spent in their country retirements. 3. He built piazzas before one of his houses, either that at Jerusalem or that in Lebanon, which were very famous — a porch of pillars (*v.* 6), perhaps for an exchange or a guard-house, or for those to walk in that attended him about business till they could have audience, or for state and magnificence. He himself speaks of Wisdom's building her house, and *hewing out her seven pillars* (Prov. 9:1), for the shelter of those that, three verses before (*ch.* 8:34), are said to *watch daily at her gates and to wait at the posts of her doors.* 4. At his house where he dwelt in Jerusalem he built a great hall, or porch of judgment, where was set the throne, or king's bench, for the trial of causes, in which he himself was appealed to *(placita coram ipso rege tenenda — causes were to be adjusted in the king's presence),* and this was richly wainscoted with cedar, from the floor to the roof, *v.* 7. He had there also *another court within the porch,* nearer his house, of similar work, for his attendants to walk in, *v.* 8. 5. He built a house for his wife, where she kept her court, *v.* 8. It is said to be *like the porch,* because built of cedar like it, though not in the same form; this, no doubt, was nearer adjoining to his own palace, yet perhaps if it had been as near as it ought to have been Solomon would not have multiplied wives as he did.

The wonderful magnificence of all these buildings is

taken notice of, *v.* 9, etc. All the materials were the best of their kind. The foundation-stones were costly for their size, four or five yards square, or at least so many yards long (*v.* 10), and the stones of the building were costly for the workmanship, hewn and sawn, and in all respects finely wrought, *v.* 9, 11. The court of his own house was like that of the temple (*v.* 12, compare *ch.* 6:36); so well did he like the model of God's courts that he made his own by it.

Verses 13–47

We have here an account of the brass-work about the temple. There was no iron about the temple, though we find David preparing for the temple *iron for things of iron,* 1 Chr. 29:2. What those things were we are not told, but some of the things of brass are here described and the rest mentioned.

I. The brasier whom Solomon employed to preside in this part of the work was Hiram, or Huram (2 Chr. 4:11), who was by his mother's side an Israelite, of the tribe of Naphtali, by his father's side a man of Tyre, *v.* 14. If he had the ingenuity of a Tyrian, and the affection of an Israelite to the house of God (the head of a Tyrian and the heart of an Israelite), it was happy that the blood of the two nations mixed in him, for thereby he was qualified for the work to which he was designed. As the tabernacle was built with the wealth of Egypt, so the temple with the wit of Tyre. God will serve himself by the common gifts of the children of men.

II. The brass he made use of was the best he could get. All the brazen vessels were of *bright brass* (*v.* 45), *good* brass, so the Chaldee, that which was strongest and looked finest. God, who is the best, must be served and honoured with the best.

III. The place where all the brazen vessels were cast was the plain of Jordan, because the ground there was stiff and clayey, fit to make moulds of for the casting of the brass (*v.* 46), and Solomon would not have this dirty smoky work done in or near Jerusalem.

IV. The quantity was not accounted for. The vessels were *unnumbered* (so it may be read, *v.* 47, as well as *unweighed*), *because they were exceedingly numerous,* and it would have been an endless thing to keep the account of them; *neither was the weight of the brass,* when it was delivered to the workmen, searched or enquired into; so honest were the workmen, and such great plenty of brass they had, that there was no danger of wanting. We must ascribe it to Solomon's care that he provided so much, not to his carelessness that he kept no account of it.

V. Some particulars of the brass-work are described.

1. Two brazen pillars, which were set up *in the porch of the temple* (*v.* 21), whether under the cover of the porch or in the open air is not certain; it was between the temple and the court of the priests. These pillars were neither to hang gates upon nor to rest any building upon, but purely for ornament and significancy. (1.) What an ornament they were we may gather from the account here given of the curious work that was about them, chequer-work, chain-work, net-work, lily-work, and pomegranates in rows, and all of bright brass, and framed no doubt according to the best rules of proportion, to please the eye. (2.) Their significancy is intimated in the names given them (*v.* 21): *Jachin — he will establish;* and *Boaz — in him is strength.* Some think they were intended for memorials of the pillar of cloud and fire which led Israel through the wilderness: I rather think them designed for memorandums to the priests and others that came to worship at God's door, [1.] To depend upon God only, and not upon any sufficiency of their own, for strength and establishment in all their religious exercises. When we come to wait upon God, and find our hearts wandering and unfixed, then by faith let us fetch in help from heaven: *Jachin — God will fix this roving mind. It is a good thing that the heart be established with grace.* We find ourselves weak and unable for holy duties, but this is our encouragement: *Boaz — in him is our strength,* who works in us both to will and to do. *I will go in the strength of the Lord God.* Spiritual strength and stability are to be had at the door of God's temple, where we must wait for the gifts of grace in the use of the means of grace. [2.] It was a memorandum to them of the strength and establishment of the temple of God among them. Let them keep close to God and duty, and they should never lose their dignities and privileges, but the grant should be confirmed and perpetuated to them. The gospel church is what God will establish, what he will strengthen, and what the gates of hell can never prevail against. But, with respect to this temple, when it was destroyed particular notice was taken of the destroying of these pillars (2 Ki. 25:13, 17), which had been the tokens of its establishment, and would have been so if they had not forsaken God.

2. A brazen sea, a very large vessel, above five yards in diameter, and which contained above 500 barrels of water for the priests' use, in washing themselves and the sacrifices, and keeping the courts of the temple clean, *v.* 23, etc. It stood raised upon the figures of twelve oxen in brass, so high that either they must have stairs to climb up to it or cocks at the bottom to draw water from it. The Gibeonites, or Nethinim, who were to draw water for the house of God, had the care of filling it. Some think Solomon made the images of oxen to support this great cistern in contempt of the golden calf which Israel had worshipped, that (as bishop Patrick expresses it) the people might see there was nothing worthy of adoration in those figures; they were fitter to make posts of than to make gods of. Yet this prevailed not to prevent Jerusalem's setting up the calves for deities. In the court of the tabernacle there was only a laver of brass provided to wash in, but in the court of the temple a sea of brass, intimating that by the gospel of Christ much fuller preparation is made for our cleansing than was by the law of Moses. That had a laver, this has a sea, *a fountain opened,* Zec. 13:1.

3. Ten bases, or stands, or settles, of brass, on which were put ten lavers, to be filled with water for the service of the temple, because there would not be room at the molten sea for all that had occasion to wash there. The bases on which the lavers were fixed are very largely described here, *v.* 27, etc. They were curiously adorned and set upon wheels, that the lavers might be removed as there was occasion; but ordinarily they stood in two rows, five on one side of the court and five on the other, *v.* 39. Each laver contained forty baths, that is, about ten barrels, *v.* 38. Those must be very *clean that bear the vessels of the Lord.* Spiritual priests and spiritual sacrifices must be washed in the laver of Christ's blood and of regeneration. We must wash often, for we daily contract pollution, must cleanse our hands and purify our hearts. Plentiful provision is made for our cleansing; so that if we have our lot for ever among the unclean it will be our own fault.

4. Besides these, there was a vast number of brass pots made to boil the flesh of the peace-offerings in, which the priests and offerers were to feast upon before the Lord (see 1 Sa. 2:14); also shovels, wherewith they took out the ashes of the altar. Some think the word signifies *flesh-hooks,* with which they took meat out of the pot. The basins also were made of brass, to receive the blood of the sacrifices. These are put for all the utensils of the brazen altar, Ex. 38:3. While they were about it they made abundance of them, that they might have a good stock by them when those that were first in use wore out and went to decay. Thus Solomon, having wherewithal to do so, provided for posterity.

Verses 48–51

Here is, 1. The making of the gold work of the temple, which it seems was done last, for with it the work of the house of God ended. All within doors was gold, and all made new (except the ark, with its mercy-seat and cherubim), the old being either melted down or laid by — the golden altar, table, and candlestick, with all their appurtenances. The altar of incense was still *one,* for Christ and his intercession are so: but he made ten golden tables, 2 Chr. 4:8 (though here mention is made of that one only *on which the show-bread was, v.* 48, which we may suppose was larger than the rest and to which the rest were as side-boards), and *ten golden candlesticks* (*v.* 49), intimating the much greater plenty both of spiritual food and heavenly light which the gospel blesses us with than the law of Moses did our could afford. Even the hinges of the door were of gold (*v.* 50), that every thing might be alike magnificent, and bespeak Solomon's generosity. Some suggest that every thing was made thus splendid in God's temple to keep the people from idolatry, for none of the idol-temples were so rich and fine as this: but how little the expedient availed the event showed. 2. The bringing in of the dedicated things, which David had devoted to the honour of God, *v.* 51. What was not expended in the building and furniture was laid up in the treasury, for repairs, exigencies, and the constant charge of the temple-service. What the parents have dedicated to God the children ought by no means to alienate or recall, but should cheerfully devote what was intended for pious and charitable uses, that they may, with their estates, inherit the blessing.

CHAPTER 8

The building and furniture of the temple were very glorious, but the dedication of it exceeds in glory as much as prayer and praise, the work of saints, exceed the casting of metal and the graving of stones, the work of the craftsman. The temple was designed for the keeping up of the correspondence between God and his people; and here we have an account of the solemnity of their first meeting there. I. The representatives of all Israel were called together (*v.* 1, 2), to keep a feast to the honour of God, for fourteen days (*v.* 65). II. The priests brought the ark into the most holy place, and fixed it there (*v.* 3–9). III. God took possession of it by a cloud (*v.* 10, 11). IV. Solomon, with thankful acknowledgments to God, informed the people touching the occasion of their meeting (*v.* 12–21). V. In a long prayer he recommended to God's gracious acceptance all the prayers that should be made in or towards this place (*v.* 22–53). VI. He dismissed the assembly with a blessing and an exhortation (*v.* 54–61). VII. He offered abundance of sacrifices, on which he and his people feasted, and so parted, with great satisfaction (*v.* 62–66). These were Israel's golden days, days of the Son of man in type.

Verses 1–11

The temple, though richly beautified, yet while it was without the ark was like a body without a soul, or a candlestick without a candle, or (to speak more properly) a house without an inhabitant. All the cost and pains bestowed on this stately structure are lost if God do not accept them; and, unless he please to own it as the place where he will record his name, it is after all but a ruinous heap. When therefore *all the work* is ended (*ch.* 7:51), the *one thing needful* is yet behind, and that is the bringing in of the ark. This therefore is the end which must crown the work, and which here we have an account of the doing of with great solemnity.

I. Solomon presides in this service, as David did in the bringing up of the ark to Jerusalem; and neither of them thought it below him to follow the ark nor to lead the people in their attendance on it. Solomon glories in the title of the *preacher* (Eccl. 1:1), and the *master of assemblies,* Eccl. 12:11. This great assembly he summons (*v.* 1), and he is the centre of it, for to him they all assembled (*v.* 2) *at the feast in the seventh month,* namely, the feast of tabernacles, which was appointed on the fifteenth day of that month, Lev. 23:34. David, like a very *good* man, brings the ark to a *convenient* place, near him; Solomon, like a very *great* man, brings it to a *magnificent* place. As every man has received the gift, so let him minister; and let children proceed in God's service where their parents left off.

II. All Israel attend the service, their judges and the chief of their tribes and families, all their officers, civil and military, and (as they speak in the north) the heads of their clans. A convention of these might well be called *an assembly of all Israel.* These came together, on this occasion, 1. To do honour to Solomon, and to return him the thanks of the nation for all the good offices he had done in kindness to them. 2. To do honour to the ark, to pay respect to it, and testify their universal joy and satisfaction in its settlement. The advancement of the ark in external splendour, though it has often proved too strong a temptation to its hypocritical followers, yet, because it may prove an advantage to its true interests, is to be rejoiced in (with trembling) by all that wish well to it. Public mercies call for public acknowledgments. Those that appeared before the Lord did not appear empty, for they all sacrificed sheep and oxen innumerable, *v.* 5. The people in Solomon's time were very rich, very easy, and very cheerful, and therefore it was fit that, on this occasion, they should consecrate not only their cheerfulness, but a part of their wealth, to God and his honour.

III. The priests do their part of the service. In the wilderness, the Levites were to carry the ark, because then there were not priests enough to do it; but here (it being the last time that the ark was to be carried) the priests themselves did it, as they were ordered to do when it surrounded Jericho. We are here told, 1. What was in the ark, nothing but the two tables of stone (*v.* 9), a treasure far exceeding all the dedicated things both of David and Solomon. The pot of manna and Aaron's rod were *by* the ark, but not *in* it. 2. What was brought up with the ark (*v.* 4): *The tabernacle of the congregation.* It is probable that both that which Moses set up in the wilderness, which was in Gibeon, and that which David pitched in Zion, were brought to the temple, to which they did, as it were, surrender all their holiness, merging it in that of the temple, which must henceforward be the place where God must be sought unto. Thus will all the church's holy things on earth, that are so much its joy and glory, be swallowed up in the perfection of holiness above. 3. Where it was fixed in its place, the place appointed for its rest after all its wanderings (*v.* 6): *In the oracle of the house,* whence they expected God to speak to them, even in the most holy place, which was made so by the presence of the ark, *under the wings of the* great *cherubim* which Solomon set up (*ch.* 6:27), signifying the special protection of angels, under which God's ordinances and the assemblies of his people are taken. The staves of the ark were drawn out, so as to be seen from under the wings of the cherubim, to direct the high priest to the mercy-seat, over the ark, when he went in, once a year, to sprinkle the blood there; so that still they continued of some use, though there was no longer occasion for them to carry it by.

IV. God graciously owns what is done and testifies his acceptance of it, *v.* 10, 11. The priests might come into the most holy place till God manifested his glory there; but, thenceforward, none might, at their peril, approach the ark, except the high priest, on the day of atonement. Therefore it was not till the priests had come out of the oracle that the *Shechinah* took possession of it, in a cloud, which filled not only the most holy place, but the temple, so that the priests who burnt incense at the golden altar could not bear it. By this visible emanation of the divine glory, 1. God put an honour upon the ark, and owned it as a token of his presence. The glory of it had been long diminished and eclipsed by its frequent removes, the meanness of its lodging, and its being exposed too much to common view; but God will now show that it is as dear to him as ever, and he will have it looked upon with as much veneration as it was when Moses first brought it into his tabernacle. 2. He testified his acceptance of the building and furnishing of the temple as good service done to his name and his kingdom among men. 3. He struck an awe upon this great assembly; and, by what they saw, confirmed their belief of what they read in the books of Moses concerning the glory of God's appearance to their fathers, that hereby they might be kept close to the service of the God of Israel and fortified against temptations to idolatry. 4. He showed himself ready to hear the prayer Solomon was now about to make; and not only so, but took up his residence in this house, that all his praying people might there be encouraged to make their applications to him. But the glory of God appeared in a cloud, a dark cloud, to signify, (1.) The darkness of that dispensation in comparison with the light of the gospel, by which, *with open face, we behold, as in a glass, the glory of the Lord.* (2.) The darkness of our present state in comparison with the vision of God, which will be the happiness of heaven, where the divine glory is unveiled. Now we can only say what he is not, but then we shall see him as he is.

Verses 12–21

Here, I. Solomon encourages the priests, who came out of the temple from their ministration, much astonished at the dark cloud that overshadowed them. The disciples of Christ *feared when they entered into the cloud,* though it was a *bright cloud* (Lu. 9:34), so did the priests when they found themselves wrapped in a thick cloud. To silence their fears, 1. He reminds them of that which they could not but know, that this was a token of God's presence (*v.* 12): *The Lord said he would dwell in the thick darkness.* It is so far from being a token of his displeasure that it is an indication of his favour; for he had said, *I will appear in a cloud,* Lev. 16:2. Note, Nothing is more effectual to reconcile us to dark dispensations than to consider what God hath said, and to compare his word and works together; as Lev. 10:3, *This is that which the Lord hath said.* God is light (1 Jn. 1:5), and he dwells in light (1 Tim. 6:16), but he dwells with men *in the thick darkness,* makes that his pavilion, because they could not bear the dazzling brightness of his glory. *Verily thou art a God that hidest thyself.* Thus our holy faith is exercised and our holy fear is increased. Where God dwells in light faith is swallowed up in vision and fear in love. 2. He himself bids it welcome, as worthy of all acceptation; and since God, by this cloud, came down to take possession, he does, in a few words, solemnly give him possession (*v.* 13): *"Surely I come,"* says God. *"Amen,"* says Solomon, *"Even so, come, Lord,*. The house is thy own, entirely thy own, *I have surely built it for thee,* and furnished it for thee; it is for ever thy own, *a settled place for thee to abide in for ever;* it shall never be alienated nor converted to any other use; the ark shall never be removed from it, never unsettled again." It is Solomon's joy that God has taken possession; and it is his desire that he would keep possession. Let not the priests therefore dread that in which Solomon so much triumphs.

II. He instructs the people, and gives them a plain account concerning this house, which they now saw God take possession of. He spoke briefly to the priests, to satisfy them (a word to the wise), but *turned his face about* (*v.* 14) from them *to the congregation* that stood in the outer court, and addressed himself to them largely.

1. He blessed them. When they saw the dark cloud enter the temple they blessed themselves, being astonished at it and afraid lest the thick darkness should be utter darkness to them. The amazing sight, such as they had never seen in their days, we may suppose, drove every man to his prayers, and the vainest minds were made serious by it. Solomon therefore set in with their prayers, and blessed them all, as one having authority (for *the less is blessed of the better);* in God's name, he spoke peace to them, and a blessing, like that with which the angel blessed Gideon when he was in a fright, upon a similar occasion. Jdg. 6:22, 23, *Peace be unto thee. Fear not; thou shalt not die.* Solomon *blessed them,* that is, he pacified them, and freed them from the consternation they were in. To receive this blessing, they all stood up, in token of reverence and readiness to hear and accept it. It is a proper posture to be in when the blessing is pronounced.

2. He informed them concerning this house which he had built and was now dedicating.

(1.) He began his account with a thankful acknowledgment of the good hand of his God upon him hitherto: *Blessed be the Lord God of Israel, v.* 15. What we have the pleasure of God must have the praise of. He thus engaged the congregation to lift up their hearts in thanksgivings to God, which would help to still the tumult of spirit which, probably, they were in. "Come," says he, "let God's awful appearances not drive us from him, but draw us to him; *let us bless the Lord God of Israel."* Thus Job, under a dark scene, *blessed the name of the Lord.* Solomon here blessed God, [1.] For his promise which he *spoke with his mouth to David.* [2.] For the performance, that he had now *fulfilled it with his hand.* We have then the best sense of God's mercies, and most grateful both to ourselves and to our God, when we run up those streams to the fountain of the covenant, and compare what God does with what he has said.

(2.) Solomon is now making a solemn surrender or dedication of this house unto God, delivering it to God by his own act and deed. Grants and conveyances commonly begin with recitals of what has been before done, leading to what is now done: accordingly, here is a recital of the special causes and considerations moving Solomon to build this house. [1.] He recites the want of such a place. It was necessary that this should be premised; for, according to the dispensation they were under, there must be but one place in which they must expect God to record his name. If, therefore, there were any other chosen, this would be a usurpation. But he shows, from what God himself had said, that there was no other (*v.* 16): *I chose no city to build a house in for my name;* therefore there is occasion for the building of this. [2.] He recites David's purpose to build such a place. God chose the person first that should rule his people *(I chose David, v.* 16) and then put it into *his heart to build a house* for God's name, *v.* 17. It was not a project of his own, for the magnifying of himself; but his good father, of blessed memory, laid the first design of it, though he lived not to lay the first stone. [3.] He recites God's promise concerning himself. God approved his father's purpose (*v.* 18): *Thou didst well, that it was in thy heart.* Note, Sincere intentions to do good shall be graciously approved and accepted of God, though Providence prevent our putting them in execution. *The desire of a man is his kindness.* See 2 Co. 8:12. God accepted David's good will, yet would not permit him to do the good work, but reserved the honour of it for his son (*v.* 19): *He shall build the house to my name;* so that what he had done was not of his own head, nor for his own glory, but the work itself was according to his father's design and his doing it was according to God's designation. [4.] He recites what he himself had done, and with what intention: *I have built a house,* not for my own name, but *for the name of the Lord God of Israel* (*v.* 20), and *set there a place for the ark, v.* 21. Thus all the right, title, interest, claim, and demand, whatsoever, which he or his had or might have in or to this house, or any of its appurtenances, he resigns, surrenders, and gives up, to God for ever. It is for his name, and his ark. In this, says he, *the Lord hath performed his word that he spoke.* Note, Whatever good we do, we must look upon it as the performance of God's promise to us, rather than the performance of our promises to him. The more we do for God the more we are indebted to him; for our sufficiency is of him, and not of ourselves.

Verses 22–53

Solomon having made a general surrender of this house to God, which God had signified his acceptance of by taking possession, next follows Solomon's prayer, in which he makes a more particular declaration of the uses of that surrender, with all humility and reverence, desiring that God would agree thereto. In short, it is his request that this temple may be deemed and taken, not only for a house of sacrifice (no mention is made of that in all this prayer, that was taken for granted), but a *house of prayer for all people;* and herein it was a type of the gospel church; see Isa. 56:7, compared with Mt. 21:13. Therefore Solomon opened this house, not only with an extraordinary sacrifice, but with an extraordinary prayer.

I. The person that prayed this prayer was great. Solomon did not appoint one of the priests to do it, nor one of the prophets, but did it himself, *in the presence of all the congregation of Israel, v.* 22. 1. It was well that he was able to do it, a sign that he had made a good improvement of the pious education which his parents gave him. With all his learning, it seems, he learnt to pray well, and knew how to express himself to God in a suitable manner, *pro re nata — on the spur of the occasion,* without a prescribed form. In the crowd of his philosophical transactions, his proverbs, and songs, he did not forget his devotions. He was a gainer by prayer (*ch.* 3:11, etc.), and, we may suppose, gave himself much to it, so that he excelled, as we find here, in praying gifts. 2. It was well that he was willing to do it, and not shy of performing divine service before so great a congregation. He was far from thinking it any disparagement to him to be his own chaplain and the mouth of the assembly to God; and shall any think themselves too great to do this office for their own families? Solomon, in all his other glory, even on his ivory throne, looked not so great as he did now. Great men should thus support the reputation of religious exercises and so honour God with their greatness. Solomon was herein a type of Christ, the great intercessor for all over whom he rules.

II. The posture in which he prayed was very reverent, and expressive of humility, seriousness, and fervency in prayer. He *stood before the altar of the Lord,* intimating that he expected the success of his prayer in virtue of that sacrifice which should be offered up in the fulness of time, typified by the sacrifices offered at that altar. But when he addressed himself to prayer, 1. He *kneeled down,* as appears, *v.* 54, where he is said to *rise from his knees;* compare 2 Chr. 6:13. Kneeling is the most proper posture for prayer, Eph. 3:14. The greatest of men must not think it below them to *kneel before the Lord their Maker.* Mr. Herbert says, "Kneeling never spoiled silk stocking." 2. *He spread forth his hands towards heaven,* and (as it should seem by *v.* 54) continued so to the end of the prayer, hereby expressing his desire towards, and expectations from, God, as a *Father in heaven.* He spread forth his hands, as it were to offer up the prayer from an open enlarged heart and to present it to heaven, and also to receive thence, with both arms, the mercy which he prayed for. Such outward expressions of the fixedness and fervour of devotion ought not to be despised or ridiculed.

III. The prayer itself was very long, and perhaps much

longer than is here recorded. At the throne of grace we have liberty of speech, and should use our liberty. It is not making long prayers, but making them for a pretence, that Christ condemns. In this excellent prayer Solomon does, as we should in every prayer,

1. Give glory to God. This he begins with, as the most proper act of adoration. He addresses himself to God as the *Lord God of Israel,* a God in covenant with them And, (1.) He gives him the praise of what he is, in general, the best of beings in himself ("*There is no God like thee,* none of the powers in heaven or earth to be compared with thee"), and the best of masters to his people: "*Who keepest covenant and mercy with thy servants;* not only as good as thy word in keeping covenant, but better than thy word in keeping mercy, doing that for them of which thou hast not given them an express promise, provided they *walk before thee with all their heart,* are zealous for thee, with an eye to thee." (2.) He gives him thanks for what he had done, in particular, for his family (*v.* 24): "*Thou hast kept with thy servant David,* as with thy other servants, *that which thou promisedst him.*" The promise was a great favour to him, his support and joy, and now performance is the crown of it: *Thou hast fulfilled it, as it is this day.* Fresh experiences of the truth of God's promises call for enlarged praises.

2. He sues for grace and favour from God.

(1.) That God would perform to him and his the mercy which he had promised, *v.* 25, 26. Observe how this comes in. He thankfully acknowledges the performance of the promise in part; hitherto God had been faithful to his word: "*Thou hast kept with thy servant David that which thou promisedst him,* so far that his son fills his throne and has built the intended temple; *therefore now keep with thy servant David that which thou hast* further *promised him,* and which yet remains to be fulfilled in its season." Note, The experiences we have had of God's performing his promises should encourage us to depend upon them and plead them with God: and those who expect further mercies must be thankful for former mercies. Hitherto God has helped, 2 Co. 1:10. Solomon repeats the promise (*v.* 25): *There shall not fail thee a man to sit on the throne,* not omitting the condition, *so that thy children take heed to their way;* for we cannot expect God's performance of the promise but upon our performance of the condition. And then he humbly begs this entail (*v.* 26): *Now, O God of Israel! let thy word be verified.* God's promises (as we have often observed) must be both the guide of our desires and the ground of our hopes and expectations in prayer. David had prayed (2 Sa. 7:25): *Lord, do as thou hast said.* Note, Children should learn of their godly parents how to pray, and plead in prayer.

(2.) That God would have respect to this temple which he had now taken possession of, and that his eyes might be *continually open towards it* (*v.* 29), that he would graciously own it, and so put an honour upon it. To this purpose,

[1.] He premises, *First,* A humble admiration of God's gracious condescension (*v.* 27): "*But will God indeed dwell on the earth?* Can we imagine that a Being infinitely high, and holy, and happy, will stoop so low as to let it be said of him that he *dwells upon the earth* and blesses the worms of the earth with his presence — the earth, that is corrupt, and overspread with sin — cursed, and reserved to fire? *Lord, how is it?*" *Secondly,* A humble acknowledgment of the incapacity of the house he had built, though very capacious, to contain God: "*The heaven of heavens cannot contain thee,* for no place can include him who is present in all places; even this house is too little, too mean to be the residence of him that is infinite in being and glory." Note, When we have done the most we can for God we must acknowledge the infinite distance and disproportion between us and him, between our services and his perfections.

[2.] This premised, he prays in general, *First,* That God would graciously hear and answer the prayer he was now praying, *v.* 28. It was a humble prayer *(the prayer of thy servant),* an earnest prayer (such a prayer as is a *cry*), a prayer made in faith (*before thee,* as the Lord, and my God): "Lord, *hearken to it, have respect to it,* not as the prayer of Israel's king (no man's dignity in the world, or titles of honour, will recommend him to God), but as the prayer of thy servant." *Secondly,* That God would in like manner hear and answer all the prayers that should, at any time hereafter, be made in or towards this house which he had now built, and of which God had said, *My name shall be there* (*v.* 29), his own prayers *(Hearken to the prayers which thy servant shall make),* and the prayers of all Israel, and of every particular Israelite (*v.* 30): "*Hear it in heaven, that* is indeed *thy dwelling-place,* of which this is but a figure; and, *when thou hearest, forgive* the sin that separates between them and God, even the *iniquity of their holy things.*" *a.* He supposes that God's people will ever be a prayer people; he resolves to adhere to that duty himself. *b.* He directs them to have an eye, in their prayers, to that place where God was pleased to manifest his glory as he did not any where else on earth. None but priests might come into that place; but, when they worshipped in the courts of the temple, it must be with an eye towards it, not as the object of their worship (that were idolatry), but as an instituted medium of their worship, helping the weakness of their faith, and typifying the mediation of Jesus Christ, who is the true temple, to whom we must have an eye in every thing wherein we have to do with God. Those that were at a distance looked towards Jerusalem, for the sake of the temple, even when it was in ruins, Dan. 6:10. *c.* He begs that God will *hear the prayers,* and *forgive the sins,* of all that look this way in their prayers. Not as if he thought all the devout prayers offered up to God by those who had no knowledge of this house, or regard to it, were therefore rejected; but he desired that the sensible tokens of the divine presence with which this house was blessed might always give sensible encouragement and comfort to believing petitioners.

[3.] More particularly, he here puts divers cases in which he supposed application would be made to God by prayer in or towards this house of prayer.

First, If God were appealed to by an oath for the determining of any controverted right between man and man, and the oath were taken before this altar, he prayed that God would, in some way or other, discover the truth, and judge between the contending parties, *v.* 31, 32. He prayed that, in difficult matters, this throne of grace might be a throne of judgment, from which God would right the injured that believingly appealed to it, and punish the injurious that presumptuously appealed to it. It was usual to swear by the temple and altar (Mt. 23:16, 18), which corruption perhaps took its rise from this supposition of an oath taken, not *by* the temple or altar, but *at* or *near* them, for the greater solemnity.

Secondly, If the people of Israel were groaning under any national calamity, or any particular Israelite under any personal calamity, he desired that the prayers they should make in or towards this house might be heard and answered.

a. In case of public judgments, war (*v.* 33), want of rain (*v.* 35), famine, or pestilence (*v.* 37), and he ends with an *et cetera* — any plague or sickness; for no calamity befals other people which may not befal God's Israel. Now he supposes, (*a.*) That the cause of the judgment would be sin, and nothing else. "If they be *smitten before the enemy,* if there be no rain, it is *because they have sinned against thee.*" It is sin that makes all the mischief. (*b.*) That the consequence of the judgment would be that they would cry to God, and make supplication to him in or towards that house. Those that slighted him before would solicit him then. *Lord, in trouble have they visited thee. In their afflictions they will seek me early* and earnestly. (*c.*) That the condition of the removal of the judgment was something more than barely praying for it. He could not, he would not, ask that their prayer might be answered unless they did also *turn from their sin* (*v.* 35) and *turn again to God* (*v.* 33), that is, unless they did truly repent and reform. On no other terms may we look for salvation in this world or the other. But, if they did thus qualify themselves for mercy, he prays, [*a.*] That God would hear from heaven, his holy temple above, to which they must look, through *this* temple. [*b.*] That he would forgive their sin; for then only are judgments removed in mercy when sin is pardoned. [*c.*] That he would *teach them the good way wherein they should walk,* by his Spirit, with his word and prophets; and thus they might be both profited by their trouble (for *blessed is the man whom God chastens and teaches*), and prepared for deliverance, which then comes in love when it finds us brought back to the good way of God and duty. [*d.*] That he would then remove the judgment, and redress the grievance, whatever it might be — not only accept the prayer, but give in the mercy prayed for.

b. In case of personal afflictions, *v.* 38–40. "If any man of Israel has an errand to thee, here let him find thee, here let him find favour with thee." He does not mention particulars, so numerous, so various, are the grievances of the children of men. (*a.*) He supposes that the complainants themselves would very sensibly feel their own burden, and would open that case to God which otherwise they kept to themselves and did not make any man acquainted with: They *shall know every man the plague of his own heart,* what it is that pains him, and (as we say) where the shoe pinches, and shall spread their hands, that is, spread their case, as Hezekiah spread the letter, in prayer, towards this house; whether the trouble be of body or mind, they shall represent it before God. Inward burdens seem especially meant. Sin is the plague of our own heart; our indwelling corruptions are our spiritual diseases. Every Israelite indeed endeavours to know these, that he may mortify them and watch against the risings of them. These he complains of. This is the burden he groans under: *O wretched man that I am!* These drive him to his knees, drive him to the sanctuary. Lamenting these, *he spreads forth his hands* in prayer. (*b.*) He refers all cases of this kind, that should be brought hither, to God. [*a.*] To his omniscience: "*Thou, even thou only, knowest the hearts of all the children of men,* not only the plagues of their hearts, their several wants and burdens" (these he knows, but he will know them from us), "but the desire and intent of the heart, the sincerity or hypocrisy of it. Thou knowest which prayer comes from the heart, and which from the lips only." The hearts of kings are not unsearchable to God. [*b.*] To his justice: *Give to every man according to his ways;* and he will not fail to do so, by the rules of grace, not the law, for then we should all be undone. [*c.*] To his mercy: *Hear, and forgive, and do* (*v.* 39), *that they may fear thee all their days, v.* 40. This use we should make of the mercy of God to us in hearing our prayers and forgiving our sins, we should thereby be engaged to fear him while we live. *Fear the Lord and his goodness. There is forgiveness with him, that he may be feared.*

c. The case of the stranger that is not an Israelite is next mentioned, a proselyte that comes to the temple to pray to the God of Israel, being convinced of the folly and wickedness of worshipping the gods of his country. (*a.*) He supposed that there would be many such (*v.* 41, 42), that the fame of God's great works which he had wrought for Israel, by which he proved himself to be above all gods, nay, to be God alone, would reach to distant countries: "Those that live remote *shall hear of thy strong hand, and thy stretched-out arm;* and this will bring all thinking considerate people to pray towards this house, that they may obtain the favour of a God that is able to do them a real kindness." (*b.*) He begged that God would accept and answer the proselyte's prayer (*v.* 43): *Do according to all that the stranger calleth to thee for.* Thus early, thus ancient, were the indications of favour towards the *sinners of the Gentiles:* as there was then *one law for the native and for the stranger* (Ex. 12:49), so there was one gospel for both. (*c.*) Herein he aimed at the glory of God and the propagating of the knowledge of him: "O let the stranger, in a special manner, speed well in his addresses, that he may carry away with him to his own country a good report of the God of Israel, *that all people may know thee and fear thee* (and, if they know thee aright, they will fear thee) *as do thy people Israel.*" So far was Solomon from monopolizing the knowledge and service of God, and wishing to have them confined to Israel only (which was the envious desire of the Jews in the days of Christ and his apostles), that he prayed that *all people might fear God as Israel did.* Would to God that all the children of men might receive the adoption, and be made God's children! *Father,* thus *glorify thy name.*

d. The case of an army going forth to battle is next recommended by Solomon to the divine favour. It is supposed that the army is encamped at a distance, somewhere a great way off, sent by divine order *against the enemy, v.* 44. "When they are ready to engage, and consider the perils and doubtful issues of battle, and put up a prayer to God for protection and success, with their eye *towards this city and temple,* then *hear their prayer,* encourage their hearts, strengthen their hands, cover their heads, and so maintain their cause and give them victory." Soldiers in the field must not think it enough that those who tarry at home pray for them, but must pray for themselves, and they are here encouraged to hope fore a gracious answer. Praying should always go along with fighting.

e. The case of poor captives is the last that is here mentioned as a proper object of divine compassion. (*a.*) He supposes that Israel will sin. He knew them, and himself, and the nature of man, too well to think this a foreign supposition; *for there is no man that sinneth not,* that does not enough to justify God in the severest rebukes of his providence, no man but what is in danger of falling into gross sin, and will if God leave him to himself. (*b.*) He supposes, what may well be expected, that, if Israel revolt from God, God will be *angry with them,* and *deliver them into the hand of their enemies,* to be carried captive into a strange country, *v.* 46. (*c.*) He then supposes that they will bethink themselves, will consider their ways (for afflictions put men upon consideration), and, when once they are brought to consider, they will repent and pray, will confess their sins, and humble themselves, saying, *We have sinned and have done perversely* (*v.* 47), and *in the land of their enemies will return to God,* whom they had forsaken in their own land. (*d.*) He supposes that in their prayers they will look towards their own land, the holy land, Jerusalem, the holy city, and the temple, the holy house, and directs them so to do (*v.* 48), for his sake who gave them that land, chose that city, and to whose honour that house was built. (*e.*) He prays that then God would *hear their prayers, forgive their sins, plead their cause,* and incline their enemies to *have compassion on them, v.* 49. 50. God has all hearts in his hand, and can, when he pleases, turn the strongest stream the contrary way, and make those to pity his people who have been their most cruel persecutors. See this prayer answered, Ps. 106:46. He *made them to be pitied of those that carried them captive,* which, if it did not release them, yet eased their captivity. (*f.*) He pleads their relation to God, and his interest in them: "They are thy people, whom thou hast taken into thy covenant and under thy care and conduct, thy inheritance, from which, more than from any other nation, thy rent and tribute of glory issue and arise (*v.* 51), *separated from among all people* to be so and by distinguishing favours appropriated to thee," *v.* 53.

Lastly, After all these particulars, he concludes with this general request, that God would hearken to all his praying people *in all that they call unto him for, v.* 52. No place now, under the gospel, can be imagined to add any acceptableness to the prayers made in or towards it, as the temple then did. That was a shadow: the substance is Christ; whatever we ask in his name, it shall be given us.

Verses 54–61

Solomon, after his sermon in Ecclesiastes, gives us the conclusion of the whole matter; so he does here, after this long prayer; it is called his *blessing the people, v.* 55. He pronounced it standing, that he might be the better heard, and because he blessed as one having authority. Never were words more fitly spoken, nor more pertinently. Never was congregation dismissed with that which was more likely to affect them and abide with them.

I. He gives God the glory of the great and kind things he had done for Israel, *v.* 56. He stood up to *bless the congregation* (*v.* 55), but began with blessing God; for we must in *every thing give thanks.* Do we expect God should do well for us and ours? let us take all occasion to speak well of him and his. He blesses God who has given, he does not say wealth, and honour, and power, and victory, to Israel, but *rest,* as if that were a blessing more valuable than any of those. Let not those who have rest under-value that blessing, though they want some others. He compares the blessings God had bestowed upon them with the promises he had given them, that God might have the honour of his faithfulness and the truth of that word of his which he has *magnified above all his name.* 1. He refers to the *promises given by the hand of Moses,* as he did (*v.* 15, 24) to those which were made to David. There were promises given by Moses, as well as precepts. It was long ere God gave Israel the promised rest, but they had it at last, after many trials. The day will come when God's spiritual Israel will *rest from all their labours.* 2. He does, as it were, write a receipt in full on the back of these bonds: *There has not failed one word of all his good promises.* This discharge he gives in the name of all Israel, to the everlasting honour of the divine faithfulness, and the everlasting encouragement of all those that build upon the divine promises.

II. He blesses himself and the congregation, expressing his earnest desire and hope of these four things: — 1. The presence of God with them, which is all in all to the happiness of a church and nation and of every particular person. This great congregation was now shortly to be scattered, and it was not likely that they would ever be all together again in this world. Solomon therefore dismisses them with this blessing: *"The Lord be present with us,* and that will be comfort enough when we are absent from each other. *The Lord our God be with us, as he was with our fathers* (*v.* 57); *let him not leave us,* let him be to us to day, and to ours for ever, what he was to those that went before us." 2. The power of his grace upon them: *"Let him be with us,* and continue with us, not that he may enlarge our coasts and increase our wealth, but *that he may incline our hearts to himself, to walk in all his ways and to keep his commandments," v.* 58. Spiritual blessings are the best blessings, with which we should covet earnestly to be blessed. Our hearts are naturally averse to our duty, and apt to decline from God; it is his grace that inclines them, grace that must be obtained by prayer. 3. An answer to the prayer he had now made: *"Let these my words be nigh unto the Lord our God day and night, v.* 59. Let a gracious return be made to every prayer that shall be made here, and that will be a continual answer to this prayer." What Solomon asks here for his prayer is still granted in the intercession of Christ, of which his supplication was a type; that powerful prevailing intercession *is before the Lord our God day and night,* for our great Advocate attends continually to this very thing, and we may depend upon him to maintain our cause (against the adversary that accuses us *day* and *night,* Rev. 12:10) *and the* common *cause of his people Israel, at all times,* upon all occasions, as the matter shall require, so as to speak for us *the word of the day in its day,* as the original here reads it, from which we shall receive grace sufficient, suitable, and seasonable, *in every time of need.* 4. The glorifying of God in the enlargement of his kingdom among men. Let Israel be thus blessed, thus favoured; not that all people may become tributaries to us (Solomon sees his kingdom as great as he desires), but *that all people may know that the Lord is God,* and he only, and may come and worship him, *v.* 60. With this Solomon's prayers, like *the prayers of his father David, the son of Jesse, are ended* (Ps. 72:19, 20): *Let the whole earth be filled with his glory.* We cannot close our prayers with a better summary than this, *Father, glorify thy name.*

III. He solemnly charges his people to continue and persevere in their duty to God. Having spoken to God for them, he here speaks from God to them, and those only would fare the better for his prayers that were made better by his preaching. His admonition, at parting, is, *"Let your heart be perfect with the Lord our God, v.* 61. Let your obedience be universal, without dividing — upright, without dissembling — constant, without declining;" this is evangelical perfection.

Verses 62–66

We read before that Judah and Israel were eating and drinking, and very cheerful under their own vines and fig-trees; here we have them so in God's courts. Now they found Solomon's words true concerning Wisdom's ways, that they are ways of pleasantness.

I. They had abundant joy and satisfaction while they attended at God's house, for there, 1. Solomon offered a great sacrifice, 22,000 oxen and 120,000 sheep, enough to have drained the country of cattle if it had not been a very fruitful land. The heathen thought themselves very generous when they offered sacrifices by *hundreds (hecatombs* they called them), but Solomon out-did them: he offered them by *thousands.* When Moses dedicated his altar, the peace-offerings were twenty-four *bullocks, and of rams, goats, and lambs,* 180 (Num. 7:88); then the people were poor, but now that they had increased in wealth more was expected from them. Where God sows plentifully he must reap accordingly. All these sacrifices could not be offered in one day, but in the several days of the feast. Thirty oxen a day served Solomon's table, but thousands shall go to God's altar. Few are thus minded, to spend more on their souls than on their bodies. The flesh of the peace-offerings, which belonged to the offerer, it is likely, Solomon treated the people with. Christ fed those who attended him. The brazen altar was not large enough to receive all these sacrifices, so that, to serve the present occasion, they were forced to offer many of them *in the middle of the court,* (*v.* 64), some think on altars, altars of earth or stone, erected for the purpose and taken down when the solemnity was over, others think on the bare ground. Those that will be generous in serving God need not stint themselves for want of room and occasion to be so. 2. He kept a feast, the feast of tabernacles, as it should seem, after the feast of dedication, and both together lasted fourteen days (*v.* 65), yet they said not, *Behold, what a weariness is this!*

II. They carried this joy and satisfaction with them to their own houses. When they were dismissed they blessed the king (*v.* 66), applauded him, admired him, and returned him the thanks of the congregation, and then *went to their tents joyful and glad of heart,* all easy and pleased. God's goodness was the matter of their joy, so it should be of ours at all times. They rejoiced in God's blessing both on the royal family and on the kingdom; thus should we go home rejoicing from holy ordinances, and go on our way rejoicing for God's goodness to our Lord Jesus (of whom David his servant was a type, in the advancement and establishment of his throne, pursuant to the covenant of redemption), and to all believers, his spiritual Israel, in their sanctification and consolation, pursuant to the covenant of grace. If we rejoice not herein always it is our own fault.

CHAPTER 9

In this chapter we have, I. The answer which God, in a vision, gave to Solomon's prayer, and the terms he settled with him (*v.* 1–9). II. The interchanging of grateful kindnesses between Solomon and Hiram (*v.* 10–14). III. His workmen and buildings (*v.* 15–24). IV. His devotion (*v.* 25). V. His trading navy (*v.* 26–28).

Verses 1–9

God had given a real answer to Solomon's prayer, and tokens of his acceptance of it, immediately, by the *fire from heaven* which consumed the sacrifices (as we find 2 Chr. 7:1); but here we have a more express and distinct answer to it. Observe,

I. In what way God gave him this answer. He appeared to him, as he had done at Gibeon, in the beginning of his reign, in a dream or vision, *v.* 2. The comparing of it with that intimates that it was the very night after he had finished the solemnities of his festival, for so that was, 2 Chr. 1:6, 7. And then *v.* 1, speaking of Solomon's finishing all his buildings, which was not till many years after the dedication of the temple, must be read thus, *Solomon finished* (as it is 2 Chr. 7:11), and *v.* 2 must be read, *and the Lord had appeared.*

II. The purport of this answer. 1. He assures him of his special presence in the temple he had built, in answer to the prayer he had made (*v.* 3): *I have hallowed this house.* Solomon had dedicated it, but it was God's prerogative to hallow it — to sanctify or consecrate it. Men cannot make a place holy, yet what we, in sincerity, devote to God, we may hope he will graciously accept as his; and *his eyes and his heart shall be upon it.* Apply it to persons, the living temples. Those whom God hallows or sanctifies, whom he sets apart for himself, have his eye, his heart, his love and care, and this perpetually. 2. He shows him that he and his people were for the future *upon their good behaviour.* Let them not be secure now, as if they might live as they please now that they have the *temple of the Lord* among them, Jer. 7:4. No, this house was designed to protect them in their allegiance to God, but not in their rebellion or disobedience. God deals plainly with us, sets before us good and evil, the blessing and the curse, and lets us know what we must trust to. God here tells Solomon, (1.) That the establishment of his kingdom depended upon the constancy of his obedience (*v.* 4, 5): *"If thou wilt walk before me as David did,* who left thee a good example and encouragement enough to follow it (and advantage thou wilt be accountable for if thou do not improve it), *if thou wilt walk as he did, in integrity of heart and uprightness"* (for that is the main matter — no religion without sincerity), *"then I will establish the throne of thy kingdom,* and not otherwise," for on that condition the promise was made, Ps. 132:12. If we perform our part of the covenant, God will not fail to perform his; if we improve the grace God has given us, he will confirm us to the end. Let not the children of godly parents expect the entail of the blessing, unless they tread in the steps of those that have gone before them to heaven, and keep up the virtue and piety of their ancestors. (2.) That the ruin of his kingdom would be the certain consequence of his or his children's apostasy from God (*v.* 6): "But know thou, and let thy family and kingdom know it, and be admonished by it, that *if you shall altogether turn from following me*" (so it is thought it should be read), "if you forsake my service, desert my altar, and go and serve other gods" (for that was the covenant-breaking sin), "if you or your children break off from me, this house will not save you. But, [1.] Israel, though a holy nation, will be cut off (*v.* 7), by one judgment after another, till they become a proverb and a by-word, and the most despicable people under the sun, though now the most honourable." This supposes the destruction of the royal family, though it is not particularly threatened; the king is, of course, undone, if the kingdom be. [2.] "The temple, though a holy house, which God himself has *hallowed for his name,* shall be abandoned and laid desolate (*v.* 8, 9): *This house which is high."* They prided themselves in the stateliness and magnificence of the structure, but let them know that it is not so high as to be out of the reach of God's judgments, if they vilify it so as to exchange it for groves and idol-temples, and yet, at the same time, magnify it so as to think it will secure the favour of God to them though they ever so much corrupt themselves. *This house which is high.* Those that *now pass by it are astonished* at the bulk and beauty of it; the richness, contrivance, and workmanship, are admired by all spectators, and it is called a stupendous fabric; but, if you forsake God, its height will make its fall the more amazing, and those that pass by will be as much astonished at its ruins, while the guilty, self-convicted, self-condemned, Israelites, will be forced to acknowledge, with shame, that they themselves were the ruin of it; for when it shall be asked, *Why hath the Lord done thus to his house?* they cannot but answer, It was *because they forsook the Lord their God.* See Deu. 29:24, 25. Their sin will be read in their punishment. They deserted the temple, and therefore God deserted it; they profaned it with their sins and laid it common, and therefore God profaned it with his judgments and laid it waste. God gave Solomon fair warning of this, now that he had newly built and dedicated it, that he and his people might not be high-minded, but fear.

Verses 10–14

What agreement was made between Solomon and Hiram, when the building-work was to be begun, we read before, *ch.* 5. Here we have an account of their fair and friendly parting when the work was done. 1. Hiram made good his bargain to the utmost. He had furnished Solomon with materials for his buildings, according to all his desire (*v.* 11), and with gold, *v.* 15. So far was he from envying Solomon's growing greatness and reputation, and being jealous of him, that he helped to magnify him. Solomon's power, with Solomon's wisdom, needs not be dreaded by any of his neighbours. God honours him; therefore Hiram will. 2. Solomon, no doubt, made good his bargain, and gave Hiram *food for his household,* as was agreed, *ch.* 5:9. But here we are told that, over and above that, he gave him twenty cities (small ones we may suppose, like those mentioned here, *v.* 19) *in the land of Galilee, v.* 11. It should seem, these were not allotted to any of the tribes of Israel (for the border of Asher came up to them, Jos. 19:27, which intimates that it did not include them), but continued in the hands of the natives till Solomon made himself master of them, and then made a present of them to Hiram. It becomes those that are great and good to be generous. Hiram came to see these cities, and did not like them (*v.* 12): *They pleased him not.* He called the country the land of *Cabul,* a Phoenician word (says Josephus) which signifies *displeasing, v.* 13. He therefore returned them to Solomon (as we find, 2 Chr. 8:2), who repaired them, and then *caused the children of Israel to inhabit them,* which intimates that before they did not; but, when Solomon received back what he had given, no doubt he honourably gave Hiram an equivalent in something else. But what shall we think of this? Did Solomon act meanly in giving Hiram what was not worth his acceptance? Or was Hiram humoursome and hard to please? I am willing to believe it was neither the one nor the other. The country was truly valuable, and so were the cities in it, but not agreeable to Hiram's genius. The Tyrians were merchants, trading men, that lived in fine houses, and became rich by navigation, but knew not how to value a country that was fit for corn and pasture (that was business that lay out of their way); and therefore Hiram desired Solomon to take them again, he knew not what to do with them, and, if he would please to gratify him, let it be in his own element, by becoming his partner in trade, as we find he did, *v.* 27. Hiram, who was used to the clean streets of Tyre, could by no means agree with the miry lanes in the land of Cabul, whereas the best lands have commonly the worst roads through them. See how the providence of God suits both the accommodation of this earth to the various dispositions of men and the dispositions of men to the various accommodations of the earth, and all for the good of mankind in general. Some take delight in husbandry, and wonder what pleasure sailors can take on a rough sea; others take as much delight in navigation, and wonder what pleasure husbandmen can take in a dirty country, like the land of Cabul. It is so in many other instances, in which we may observe the wisdom of him whose all souls are and all lands.

Verses 15–28

We have here a further account of Solomon's greatness. I. His buildings. He raised a great levy both of men and money, because he projected a great deal of building, which would both employ many hands and put him to a vast expense, *v.* 15. And he was a wise builder, who sat down first, and counted the cost, and would not begin to build till he found himself able to finish. Perhaps there was some complaint of the heaviness of the taxes, which the historian excuses from the greatness of his undertakings. He raised it, not for war (as other princes), which would spend the blood of his subjects, but for building, which would require only their labour and purses. Perhaps David observed Solomon's genius to lie towards building, and foresaw he would have his head and hands full of it, when he penned that song of degrees for Solomon, which begins, *Except the Lord build the house, those labour in vain that build it* (Ps. 127:1), directing him to acknowledge God in all his ways, and, by prayer and faith in his providence, to take him along with him in all his designs of this kind. And Solomon verily began his work at the right end, for he built God's house first, and finished that before he began his own; and then God blessed him, and he prospered in all his other buildings. If we begin with God, he will go on with us. Let the first-fruits be his, and the after-fruits will the more comfortably be ours, Mt. 6:33. Solomon built a church first and then he was enabled to build houses, and cities, and walls. Those consult not their own interest that defer to the last what they design for pious uses. The further order in Solomon's buildings is observable. God's house first for religion, then his own for his own convenience, then a house for his wife, to which she removed as soon as it was ready for her (*v.* 24), then Millo, the town-house or guild-hall, then the wall of Jerusalem, the royal city, then some cities of note and strength in the country, which were decayed and unfortified, Hazor, Megiddo, etc. As he rebuilt these at his own charge, the inhabitants would be not only his subjects, but his tenants, which would increase the revenues of the crown for the benefit of his successors. Among the rest, he built Gezer, which Pharaoh took out of the hands of the Canaanites, and made a present of to his daughter, Solomon's wife, *v.* 16. See how God *maketh the earth to help the woman.* Solomon was not himself a warlike prince, but the king of Egypt, who was, took cities for him to build. Then he built cities for convenience, for store, for his chariots, and for his horsemen, *v.* 19. And, *lastly,* he built for pleasure in Lebanon, for his hunting perhaps, or other diversions there. Let piety begin, and profit proceed, and leave pleasure to the last.

II. His workmen and servants. In doing such great works, he must needs employ abundance of workmen. The honour of great men is borrowed from their inferiors, who do that which they have the credit of. 1. Solomon employed those who remained of the conquered and devoted nations in all the slavish work, *v.* 20, 21. We may suppose that they renounced their idolatry and submitted to Solomon's government, so that he could not, in honour, utterly destroy them, and they were so poor that he could not levy money on them; therefore he served himself of their labour. Herein he observed God's law (Lev. 25:44, *Thy bondmen shall be of the heathen),* and fulfilled Noah's curse upon Canaan, *A servant of servants shall he be unto his brethren,* Gen. 9:25. 2. He employed Israelites in the more creditable services (*v.* 22, 23): *Of them he made no bondmen,* for they were God's freemen, but he made them soldiers and courtiers, and gave them offices, as he saw them qualified, among his chariots and horsemen, appointing some to support the service of the inferior labourers. Thus he preserved the dignity and liberty of Israel and honoured their relation to God as a kingdom of priests.

III. His piety and devotion (*v.* 25): *Three times in a year* he offered burnt-offerings extraordinary (namely, at the three yearly feasts, the passover, pentecost, and feast of tabernacles) in honour of the divine institution, besides what he offered at other times, both statedly and upon special occasions. With his sacrifices he burnt incense, not himself (that was king Uzziah's crime), but the priest for him, at his charge, and for his particular use. It is said, He offered *on the altar which he* himself *built.* He took care to build it, and then, 1. He himself made use of it. Many will assist the devotions of others that neglect their own. Solomon did not think his building an altar would excuse him from sacrificing, but rather engage him the more to it. 2. He himself had the benefit and comfort of it. Whatever pains we take, for the support of religion, to the glory of God and the edification of others, we ourselves are likely to have the advantage of it.

IV. His merchandise. He built a fleet of trading ships at Ezion-geber (*v.* 26), a port on the coast of the Red Sea, the furthest stage of the Israelites when they wandered in the wilderness, Num. 33:35. Probably that wilderness now began to be peopled by the Edomites, which it was not then. To them this port had belonged, but, David having subdued the Edomites, it now pertained to the crown of Judah. The fleet traded to Ophir in the East Indies, supposed to be that which is now called *Ceylon.* Gold was the commodity traded for, substantial wealth. It should seem, Solomon had before been Hiram's partner, or put a venture into his ships, which made him a rich return of 120 talents (*v.* 14), which encouraged him to build a fleet of his own. The success of others in any employment should quicken our industry; for *in all labour there is profit.* Solomon sent his own servants as factors, and merchants, and super-cargoes, but hired Tyrians for sailors, for they had *knowledge of the sea, v.* 27. Thus one nation needs another, Providence so ordering it that there may be mutual commerce and assistance; for not only as Christians, but as men, we are members one of another. The fleet brought home to Solomon 420 *talents of gold, v.* 28. Canaan, the holy land, the glory of all lands, had no gold in it, which teaches us that that part of the wealth of this world which is for hoarding and trading is not the best part of it, but that which is more immediately for the present support and comfort of life, our own and others'; such were the productions of Canaan. Solomon got much by his merchandise, but, it should seem, David got much more by his conquests. What were Solomon's 420 *talents* to David's 100,000 *talents of gold?* 1 Chr. 22:14; 29:4. Solomon got much by his merchandise, and yet has directed us to a better trade, within reach of the poorest, having assured us from his own experience of both that the *merchandise of wisdom is better than the merchandise of silver and the gain thereof than fine gold,* Prov. 3:14.

CHAPTER 10

Still Solomon looks great, and every thing in this chapter adds to his magnificence. We read nothing indeed of his charity, of no hospitals he built, or alms-houses; he made his kingdom so rich that it did not need them; yet, no question, many poor were relieved from the abundance of his table. A church he had built, never to be equalled; schools or colleges he need not build any, his own palace is an academy, and his court a rendezvous of wise and learned men, as well as the centre of all the circulating riches of that part of the world. I. What abundance of wisdom there was there appears from the application the queen of Sheba made to him, and the great satisfaction she had in her entertainment there (*v.* 1–13), and others likewise (*v.* 24). II. What abundance of wealth there was there appears here by the gold imported, with other things, yearly (*v.* 14, 15), and in a triennial return (*v.* 22). Gold presented (*v.* 25), and gold used in targets and shields (*v.* 16, 17), and vessels (*v.* 21). A stately throne made (*v.* 18–20). His chariots and horsemen (*v.* 26). His trade with Egypt (*v.* 28, 29). And the great plenty of silver and cedars among his people (v. 27). So that, putting all together, it must be owned, as it is here said (v. 23), that "king Solomon exceeded all the kings of the earth for riches, and for wisdom." Yet what was he to the King of kings? Where Christ is, by his word and Spirit, "Behold, a greater than Solomon is there."

Verses 1–13

We have here an account of the visit which the queen of Sheba made to Solomon, no doubt when he was in the height of his piety and prosperity. Our Saviour calls her *the queen of the south*, for Sheba lay south of Canaan. The common opinion is that it was in Africa; and the Christians in Ethiopia, to this day, are confident that she came from their country, and that Candace was her successor, who is mentioned Acts 8:27. But it is more probable that she came from the south part of Arabia the happy. It should seem she was a queen regent, sovereign of her country. Many a kingdom would have been deprived of its greatest blessings if a Salique law had been admitted into its constitution. Observe,

I. On what errand the queen of Sheba came — not to treat of trade or commerce, to adjust the limits of their dominions, to court his alliance for their mutual strength or his assistance against some common enemy, which are the common occasions of the congress of crowned heads and their interviews, but she came, 1. To satisfy her curiosity; for she had heard of his fame, especially for wisdom, and she came to prove him, whether he was so great a man as he was reported to be, v. 1. Solomon's fleet sailed near the coast of her country, and probably might put in there for fresh water; perhaps it was thus that *she heard of the fame of Solomon*, that he excelled in wisdom all the children of the east, and nothing would serve her but she would go herself and know the truth of the report. 2. To receive instruction from him. She came to *hear his wisdom*, and thereby to improve her own (Mt. 12:42), that she might be the better able to govern her own kingdom by his maxims of policy. Those whom God has called to any public employment, particularly in the magistracy and ministry, should, by all means possible, be still improving themselves in that knowledge which will more and more qualify them for it, and enable them to discharge their trust well. But, it should seem, that which she chiefly aimed at was to be instructed in the things of God. She was religiously inclined, and had heard not only of the fame of Solomon, but *concerning the name of the Lord* (v. 1), the great name of that God whom Solomon worshipped and from whom he received his wisdom, and with this God she desired to be better acquainted. Therefore does our Saviour mention her enquiries after God, by Solomon, as an aggravation of the stupidity of those who enquire not after God by our Lord Jesus Christ, though he, having lain in his bosom, was much better able to instruct them.

II. With what equipage she came, with a very great retinue, agreeable to her rank, intending to try Solomon's wealth and generosity, as well as his wisdom, what entertainment he could and would give to a royal visitant, v. 2. Yet she came not as one begging, but brought enough to bear her charges, and abundantly to recompense Solomon for his attention to her, nothing mean or common, but gold, and precious stones, and spices, because she came to trade for wisdom, which she would purchase at any rate.

III. What entertainment Solomon gave her. He despised not the weakness of her sex, blamed her not for leaving her own business at home to come so long a journey, and put herself and him to so much trouble and expense merely to satisfy her curiosity; but he made her welcome and all her train, gave her liberty to put all her questions, though some perhaps were frivolous, some captious, and some over-curious; he allowed her to *commune with him of all that was in her heart* (v. 2) and gave her a satisfactory answer to *all her questions* (v. 3), whether natural, moral, political, or divine. Were they designed to try him? he gave them such turns as abundantly satisfied her of his uncommon knowledge. Were they designed for her own instruction? (as we suppose most of them were), she received abundant instruction from him, and he made things surprisingly easy which she apprehended insuperably difficult, and satisfied her that there was *a divine sentence in the lips of* this *king*. But he informed her no doubt, with particular care, concerning God, and his law and instituted worship. He had taken it for granted (ch. 8:42) that *strangers would hear of his great name*, and would come

thither to enquire after him; and now that so great a stranger came we may be sure he was not wanting to assist and encourage her enquiries, and give her a description of the temple, and the officers and services of it, that she might be persuaded to serve the Lord whom she now sought.

IV. How she was affected with what she saw and heard in Solomon's court. Divers things are here mentioned which she admired, the buildings and furniture of his palace, the provision that was made very day for his table (when she saw that perhaps she wondered where there were mouths for all that meat, but when she saw the multitude of his attendants and guests she was as ready to wonder where was the meat for all those mouths), the orderly sitting of his servants, every one in his place, and the ready attendance of his ministers, without any confusion, their rich liveries, and the propriety with which his cup-bearers waited at his table. These things she admired, as adding much to his magnificence. But, above all these, the first thing mentioned (which contained all) is his wisdom (v. 4), of the transcendency of which she now had incontestable proofs: and the last thing mentioned, which crowned all, is his piety, the *ascent by which he went up to the house of the Lord*, with what gravity and seriousness, and an air of devotion in his countenance, he appeared, when he went to the temple to worship God, with as much humility then as majesty at other times. Many of the ancient versions read it, The *burnt-offerings which he offered in the house of the Lord;* she observed with what a generous bounty he brought his sacrifices, and with what a pious fervour he attended the offering of them; never did she see so much goodness with so much greatness. Every thing was so surprising that there was no more spirit in her, but she stood amazed; she had never seen the like.

V. How she expressed herself upon this occasion. 1. She owned her expectation far out-done, though it was highly raised by the report she heard, v. 6, 7. She is far from repenting her journey or calling herself a *fool* for undertaking it, but acknowledges it was well worth her while to come so far for the sight of that which she could not believe the report of. Usually things are represented to us, both by common fame and by our own imagination, much greater than we find them when we come to examine them; but here the truth exceeded both fame and fancy. Those who, through grace, are brought to experience the delights of communion with God will say that the one-half was not told them of the pleasures of Wisdom's ways and the advantages of her gates. Glorified saints, much more, will say that it was a true report which they heard of the happiness of heaven, but that the thousandth part was not told them, 1 Co. 2:9. 2. She pronounced those happy that constantly attended him, and waited on him at table: "*Happy are thy men, happy are these thy servants* (v. 8); they may improve their own wisdom by hearing thine." She was tempted to envy them and to which herself one of them. Note, It is a great advantage to be in good families, and to have opportunity of frequent converse with those that are wise, and good, and communicative. Many have this happiness who know not how to value it. With much more reason may we say this of Christ's servants, *Blessed are those that dwell in his house, they will be still praising him.* 3. She blessed God, the giver of Solomon's wisdom and wealth, and the author of his advancement, who had made him king, (1.) In kindness to him, that he might have the larger opportunity of doing good with his wisdom: He *delighted in thee, to set thee on the throne of Israel*, v. 9. Solomon's preferment began in the prophet's calling him *Jedidiah, because the Lord loved him*, 2 Sa. 12:25. It more than doubles our comforts if we have reason to hope they come from God's delight in us. *It was his pleasure concerning thee* (so it may be read) to *set thee on the throne*, not for thy merit's sake, but because it so seemed good unto him. (2.) In kindness to the people, *because the Lord loved Israel for ever*, designed them a lasting bliss, long to survive him that laid the foundations of it. "He has made thee king, not that thou mayest live in pomp and pleasure, and do what thou wilt, but *to do judgment and justice.*" This she kindly reminded Solomon of, and no doubt he took it kindly. Both magistrates and ministers must be more solicitous to do the duty of their places than to secure the honours and profits of them. To this she attributes his prosperity, not to his wisdom, for bread is not always *to the wise* (Eccl. 9:11), but whoso *doeth judg-*

ment and justice, it shall be *well with him*, Jer. 22:15. Thus *giving of thanks* must be *made for kings*, for good kings, for such kings; they are what God makes them to be.

VI. How they parted. 1. She made a noble present to Solomon of *gold and spices*, v. 10. David had foretold concerning Solomon that *to him should be given of the gold of Sheba*, Ps. 72:15. The present of gold and spices which the wise men of the east brought to Christ was signified by this, Mt. 2:11. Thus she paid for the wisdom she had learned and did not think she bought it dearly. Let those that are taught of God give him their hearts, and the present will be more acceptable than this of gold and spices. Mention is made of the great abundance Solomon had of his own, notwithstanding she presented and he accepted this gold. What we present to Christ he needs not, but will have us so to express our gratitude. The almug-trees are here spoken of (v. 11, 12) as extraordinary, because perhaps much admired by the queen of Sheba. 2. Solomon was not behind-hand with her: He *gave her whatsoever, she asked*, patterns, we may suppose, of those things that were curious, by which she might make the like; or perhaps he gave her his precepts of wisdom and piety in writing, *besides that which he gave her of his royal bounty*, v. 13. Thus those who apply to our Lord Jesus will find him not only greater than Solomon, and wiser, but more kind; whatsoever we ask, it shall be done for us; nay, he will, out of his divine bounty, which infinitely exceeds royal bounty, even Solomon's, do for us *more than we are able to ask or think*.

Verses 14–29

We have here a further account of Solomon's prosperity.

I. How he increased his wealth. Though he had much, he still coveted to have more, being willing to try the utmost the things of this world could do to make men happy. 1. Besides the gold that came from Ophir (ch. 9:28), he brought so much into his country from other places that the whole amounted, every year, to 666 *talents* (v. 14), an ominous number, compare Rev. 13:18, and Ezra 2:13. 2. He received a great deal in customs from the merchants, and in land-taxes from the countries his father had conquered and made tributaries to Israel, v. 15. 3. He was Hiram's partner in a Tharshish fleet, of and for Tyre, which imported once in three years, not only gold, and silver, and ivory, substantial goods and serviceable, but apes to play with and peacocks to please the eye with their feathers, v. 22. I wish this may not be an evidence that Solomon and his people, being overcharged with prosperity, by this time grew childish and wanton. 4. He had presents made him, every year, from the neighbouring princes and great men, to engage the continuance of his friendship, not so much because they feared him or were jealous of him as because they loved him and admired his wisdom, had often occasion to consult him as an oracle, and sent him these presents by way of recompence for his advice in politics, and (whether it became his grandeur and generosity or no we will not enquire) he took all that came, even garments and spices, horses and mules, v. 24, 25. 5. He traded to Egypt for horses and linen-yarn (or, as some read it, *linen-cloth),* the staple commodities of that country, and had his own merchants or factors whom he employed in this traffic and who were accountable to him, v. 28, 28. The custom to be paid to the king of Egypt for exported chariots and horses out of Egypt was very high, but (as bishop Patrick understands it) Solomon, having married his daughter, got him to compound for the customs, so that he could bring them up cheaper than his neighbours, which obliged them to buy them of him, which he was wise enough no doubt to make his advantage of. This puts an honour upon the trading part of a nation, and sets a tradesman not so much below a gentleman as some place him, that Solomon, one of the greatest men that ever was, thought it no disparagement to him to deal in trade. In all labour there is profit.

II. What use he made of his wealth. He did not hoard it up in his coffers, that he might have it to look upon and leave behind him. He has, in his Ecclesiastes, so much exposed the folly of hoarding that we cannot suppose he would himself be guilty of it. No, God that had given him riches, and wealth, and honour, gave him also power to eat thereof, and to take his portion, Eccles. 5:19.

1. He laid out his gold in fine things for himself, which

he might the better be allowed to do when he had before laid out so much in fine things for the house of God. (1.) He made 200 targets, and 300 shields, of beaten gold (*v.* 16, 17), not for service, but for state, to be carried before him when he appeared in pomp. With us, magistrates have *swords* and *maces* carried before them, as the Romans had their *rods* and *axes*, in token of their power to correct and punish the bad, to whom they are to be a terror. But Solomon had *shields* and *targets* carried before him, to signify that he took more pleasure in using his power for the defence and protection of the good, to whom he would be a praise. Magistrates are *shields of the earth.* (2.) He made a stately throne, on which he sat, to give laws to his subjects, audience to ambassadors, and judgment upon appeals, *v.* 18–20. It was made of ivory, or elephants' teeth, which was very rich; and yet, as if he had so much gold that he knew not what to do with it, he *overlaid that with gold,* the best gold. Yet some think he did not cover the ivory all over, but here and there. He rolled it, flowered it, or inlaid it, with gold. The stays or arms of this stately chair were supported by the images of lions in gold; so were the steps and paces by which he went up to it, to be a memorandum to him of that courage and resolution wherewith he ought to execute judgment, not fearing the face of man. *The righteous,* in that post, *is bold as a lion.* (3.) He made all his drinking vessels, and all the furniture of his table, even at his country seat, of pure gold, *v.* 21. He did not grudge himself what he had, but took the credit and comfort of it, such as it was. That is good that does us good.

2. He made it circulate among his subjects, so that the kingdom was as rich as the king; for he had no separate interests of his own to consult, but sought the welfare of his people. Those princes are not governed by Solomon's maxims who think it policy to keep their subjects poor. Solomon was herein a type of Christ, who is not only rich himself, but enriches all that are his. Solomon was instrumental to bring so much gold into the country, and disperse it, that *silver was nothing accounted of, v.* 21. There was such plenty of it in Jerusalem that it was as the stones; and cedars, that used to be great rarities, were as common *as sycamore trees, v.* 27. Such is the nature of worldly wealth, plenty of it makes it the less valuable; much more should the enjoyment of spiritual riches lessen our esteem of all earthly possessions. If *gold in abundance* would make silver to seem so despicable, shall not wisdom, and grace, and the foretastes of heaven, which are far better than gold, make earthly wealth seem much more despicable?

Lastly, Well, thus rich, thus great, was Solomon, and thus did he *exceed all the kings of the earth, v.* 23. Now let us remember, 1. That this was he who, when he was *setting out in the world,* did not ask for the wealth and honour of it, but asked for *a wise and understanding heart.* The more moderate our desires are towards earthly things the better qualified we are for the enjoyment of them and the more likely to have them. See, in Solomon's greatness, the performance of God's promise (*ch.* 3:13), and let it encourage us to *seek first the righteousness of God's kingdom.* 2. That this was he who, having tasted all these enjoyments, wrote a whole book to show the vanity of all worldly things and the vexation of spirit that attends them, their insufficiency to make us happy and the folly of setting our hearts upon them, and to recommend to us the practice of serious godliness, as that which is the whole of man, and will do infinitely more towards the making of us easy and happy than all the wealth and power that he was master of, and which, through the grace of God, is within our reach, when the thousandth part of Solomon's greatness is a thousand times more than we can ever be so vain as to promise ourselves in this world.

CHAPTER 11

This chapter begins with as melancholy a "but" as almost any we find in all the Bible. Hitherto we have read nothing of Solomon but what was great and good; but the lustre both of his goodness and of his greatness is here sullied and eclipsed, and his sun sets under a cloud. I. The glory of his piety is stained by his departure from God and his duty, in his latter days, marrying strange wives and worshipping strange gods (*v.* 4–8). II. The glory of his prosperity is stained by God's displeasure against him and the fruits of that displeasure. 1. He sent him an angry message (*v.* 9–13). 2. He stirred up enemies, who gave him disturbance, Hadad (*v.* 14–22), Rezon (*v.* 23–25). 3. He gave away ten tribes of his twelve, from his posterity after

him, to Jeroboam, whom therefore he sought in vain to slay (*v.* 26–40), and this is all that remains here to be told concerning Solomon, except his death and burial (*v.* 41–43), for there is nothing perfect under the sun, but all is so above the sun.

Verses 1–8

This is a sad story, and very surprising, of Solomon's defection and degeneracy.

I. Let us enquire into the occasions and particulars of it. Shall Solomon fall, that was the beauty of Israel, and so great a blessing of his generation? Yes, it is too true, and the scripture is faithful in relating it, and repeating it, and referring to it long after, Neh. 13:26. *There was no king like Solomon who was beloved of his God, yet even him did outlandish women cause to sin.* There is the summary of his apostasy; it was the woman that *deceived him,* and was *first in the transgression.*

1. He doted on strange women, *many strange women.* Here his revolt began. (1.) He gave himself to women, which his mother had particularly cautioned him against. Prov. 31:3, *Give not thy strength unto women* (perhaps alluding to Samson, who lost his strength by giving information of it to a woman), for it is that which, as much as any thing, destroys kings. His father David's fall began with the lusts of the flesh, which he should have taken warning by. The love of women has *cast down many wounded* (Prov. 7:26) and *many* (says bishop Hall) *have had their head broken by their own rib.* (2.) He took many women, so many that, at last, they amounted to 700 wives and 300 concubines, 1000 in all, and not one good one among them, as he himself owns in his penitential sermon (Eccl. 7:28), for no woman of established virtue would be one of such a set. God had, by his law, particularly forbidden the kings to multiply either horses or wives, Deu. 17:16, 17. How he broke the former law, in multiplying horses, and having them *out of Egypt* too (which was expressly prohibited in that law) we read *ch.* 10:29, and here we are told how he broke the latter (which proved of more fatal consequence) in multiplying wives. Note, Less sins, made gold with, open the door to greater. David had multiplied wives too much, and perhaps that made Solomon presume it lawful. Note, If those that are in reputation for religion in any thing set a bad example, they know not what a deal of mischief they may do by it, particularly to their own children. One bad act of a good man may be of more pernicious consequence to others than twenty of a wicked man. Probably Solomon, when he began to multiply wives, intended not to exceed his father's number. But the way of sin is down-hill; those that have got into it cannot easily stop themselves. Divine wisdom has appointed one woman for one man, did so at first; and those who do not think one enough will not think two or three enough. Unbridled lust will be unbounded, and the loosened hind will wander endlessly. But this was not all: (3.) They were strange women, Moabites, Ammonites, etc., of the nations which God had particularly forbidden them to intermarry with, *v.* 2. Some think it was in policy that he married these foreigners, by them to get intelligence of the state of those countries. I rather fear it was because the daughters of Israel were too grave and modest for him, and those foreigners pleased him with the looseness and wantonness of their dress, and air, and conversation. Or, perhaps, it was looked upon as a piece of state to have his seraglio, as his other treasures, replenished with that which was far-fetched; as if that were too great an honour for the best of his subjects which would really have been a disgrace to the meanest of them — to be his mistresses. And, (4.) To complete the mischief, *Solomon clave unto these in love, v.* 2. He not only kept them, but was extravagantly fond of them, set his heart upon them, spent his time among them, thought every thing well they said and did, and despised Pharaoh's daughter, his rightful wife, who had been dear to him, and all the ladies of Israel, in comparison of them. Solomon was master of a great deal of knowledge, but to what purpose, when he had no better a government of his appetites?

2. He was drawn by them to the worship of strange gods, as Israel to Baal-peor by the daughters of Moab. This was the bad consequence of his multiplying wives. We have reason to think it impaired his health, and hastened upon him the decays of age; it exhausted his treasure, which, though vast indeed, would be found little enough to main-

tain the pride and vanity of all these women; perhaps it occasioned him, in his latter end, to neglect his business, by which he lost his supplies from abroad, and was forced, for the keeping up of his grandeur, to burden his subjects with those taxes which they complained of, *ch.* 12:4. But none of these consequences were so bad as this: *His wives turned away his heart after other gods, v.* 3, 4. (1.) He grew cool and indifferent in his own religion and remiss in the service of the God of Israel: *His heart was not perfect with the Lord his God* (*v.* 4), nor did he *follow him fully* (*v.* 6), like David. We cannot suppose that he quite cast off the worship of God, much less that he restrained or hindered it (the temple-service went on as usual); but he grew less frequent, and less serious, in *his ascent to the house of the Lord* and his attendance on his altar. He left his first love, lost his zeal for God, and did not persevere to the end as he had begun; therefore it is said *he was not perfect,* because he was not *constant;* and he followed not God fully, because he turned from following him, and did not continue to the end. His father David had many faults, but he never neglected the worship of God, nor grew remiss in that, as Solomon did (his wives using all their arts to divert him from it), and *there* began his apostasy. (2.) He tolerated and maintained his wives in their idolatry and made no scruple of joining with them in it. Pharaoh's daughter was proselyted (as is supposed) to the Jews' religion, but, when he began to grow careless in the worship of God himself, he used no means to convert his other wives to it; in complaisance to them, he built chapels for their gods (*v.* 7, 8), maintained their priests, and occasionally did himself attend their altars, making a jest of it, asking, "What harm is there in it? Are not all religions alike?" which (says bishop Patrick) has been the *disease of some great wits.* When he humoured one thus, the rest would take it ill if he did not, in like manner, gratify them, so that he did it for all his wives (*v.* 8), and at last came to such a degree of impiety that he set up a high place for *Chemosh in the hill that is before Jerusalem,* the *mount of Olives,* as if to confront the temple which he himself had built. These high places continued here, not utterly demolished, till Josiah's time, 2 Ki. 23:13. This is the account here given of Solomon's apostasy.

II. Let us now pause awhile, and lament Solomon's fall; and we may justly stand and wonder at it. *How has the gold become dim! How has the most fine gold changed! Be astonished, O heavens! at this, and be horribly afraid,* as the prophet exclaims in a like case, Jer. 2:12.

1. How strange, (1.) That Solomon, in his old age, should be ensnared with fleshly lusts, youthful lusts. As we must never presume upon the strength of our resolutions, so neither upon the weakness of our corruptions, so as to be secure and off our guard. (2.) That so wise a man as Solomon was, so famed for a quick understanding and sound judgment, should suffer himself to be made such a fool of by these foolish women. (3.) That one who had so often and so plainly warned others of the danger of the love of women should himself be so wretchedly bewitched with it; it is easier to see a mischief, and to show it to others, than to shun it ourselves. (4.) That so good a man, so zealous for the worship of God, who had been so conversant with divine things, and who prayed that excellent prayer at the dedication of the temple, should do these sinful things. Is this Solomon? Have all his wisdom and devotion come to this at last? Never was gallant ship so wrecked; never was crown so profaned.

2. What shall we say to all this? Why God permitted it it is not for us to enquire; his way is in the sea and his path in the great waters; he knew how to bring glory to himself out of it. God foresaw it when he said concerning him that should build the temple, *If he commit iniquity,* etc., 2 Sa. 7:14. But it concerns us to enquire what good use we may make of it. (1.) Let him that thinks he stands take heed lest he fall. We see how weak we are of ourselves, without the grace of God; let us therefore live in a constant dependence on that grace. (2.) See the danger of a prosperous condition, and how hard it is to overcome the temptations of it. Solomon, like Jeshurun, waxed fat and then kicked. The food convenient, which Agur prayed for, is safer and better than the food abundant, which Solomon was even surfeited with. (3.) See what need those have to stand upon their guard who have made a great profession of religion, and shown themselves forward and

zealous in devotion, because the devil will set upon them most violently, and, if they misbehave, the reproach is the greater. It is the evening that commends the day; let us therefore fear, lest, having run well, we seem to come short.

Verses 9–13

Here is, I. God's anger against Solomon for his sin. The thing he did *displeased the Lord.* Time was then the Lord *loved Solomon* (2 Sa. 12:24) and delighted in him (*ch.* 10:9), but now *the Lord was angry with Solomon* (*v.* 9), for there was in his sin, 1. The most base ingratitude that could be. He turned from the Lord *who had appeared unto him twice,* once before he began to build the temple (*ch.* 3:5) and once after he had dedicated it, *ch.* 9:2. God keeps account of the gracious visits he makes us, whether we do or no, knows how often he has appeared *to* us and *for* us, and will remember it against us if we *turn from him.* God's appearing to Solomon was such a sensible confirmation of his faith as should have for ever prevented his worshipping *any other god;* it was also such a distinguishing favour, and put such an honour upon him, as he ought never to have forgotten, especially considering what God said to him in both these appearances. 2. The most wilful disobedience. This was the very thing concerning which *God had commanded him — that he should not go after other gods,* yet he was not restrained by such an express admonition, *v.* 10. Those who have dominion over men are apt to forget God's dominion over them; and, while they demand obedience from their inferiors, to deny it to him who is the Supreme.

II. The message he sent him hereupon (*v.* 11): *The Lord said unto Solomon* (it is likely by a prophet) that he must expect to smart for his apostasy. And here, 1. The sentence is just, that, since he had revolted from God, part of his kingdom should revolt from his family; he had given God's glory to the creature, and therefore God would give his crown to his servant: *"I will rend the kingdom from thee,* in thy posterity, and will *give it to thy servant,* who shall bear rule over much of that for which thou hast laboured." This was a great mortification to Solomon, who pleased himself no doubt with the prospect of the entail of his rich kingdom upon his heirs for ever. Sin brings ruin upon families, cuts off entails, alienates estates, and lays men's honour in the dust. 2. Yet the mitigations of it are very kind, for David's sake (*v.* 12, 13), that is, for the sake of the promise made to David. Thus all the favour God shows to man is for *Christ's sake,* and for the sake of the covenant made with him. The kingdom shall be rent from Solomon's house, but, (1.) Not immediately. Solomon shall not live to see it done, but it shall be rent *out of the hand of his son,* a son that was born to him by one of his strange wives, for his mother was an Ammonitess (1 Ki. 14:31) and probably had been a promoter of idolatry. What comfort can a man take in leaving children and an estate behind him if he do not leave a blessing behind him? Yet, if judgments be coming, it is a favour to us if they come not in our days, as 2 Ki. 20:19. (2.) Not wholly. One tribe, that of Judah, the strongest and most numerous, shall remain to the house of David (*v.* 13), for Jerusalem's sake, which David built, and for the sake of the temple there, which Solomon built; these shall not go into other hands. Solomon did not quickly nor wholly turn away from God; therefore God did not quickly nor wholly take the kingdom from him.

Upon this message which God graciously sent to Solomon, to awaken his conscience and bring him to repentance, we have reason to hope that he humbled himself before God, confessed his sin, begged pardon, and returned to his duty, that he then published his repentance in the book of Ecclesiastes, where he bitterly laments his own folly and madness (*ch.* 7:25, 26), and warns others to take heed of the like evil courses, and to *fear God* and *keep his commandments,* in consideration of *the judgment to come,* which, it is likely, had made him tremble, as it did Felix. That penitential sermon was as true an indication of a heart broken for sin and turned from it as David's penitential psalms were, though of another nature. God's grace in his people works variously. Thus, though Solomon fell, *he was not utterly cast down;* what God had said to David concerning him was fulfilled: *I will chasten him with the rod of men, but my mercy shall not depart from him,* 2 Sa. 7:14, 15. Though God may suffer those whom he loves to fall into sin, he will not suffer them to lie still in it. Solomon's defection, though it was much his reproach and a great blemish to his personal character, yet did not so far break in upon the character of his reign but that it was afterwards made the pattern of a good reign, 2 Chr. 11:17, where the kings are said to have done well, while *they walked in the way of David and Solomon.* But, though we have all this reason to hope he repented and found mercy, yet the Holy Ghost did not think fit expressly to record his recovery, but left it doubtful, for warning to others not to sin upon presumption of repenting, for it is but a peradventure whether *God will give them repentance,* or, if he do, whether he will give the evidence of it to themselves or others. Great sinners may recover themselves and have the benefit of their repentance, and yet be denied both the comfort and credit of it; the guilt may be taken away, and yet not the reproach.

Verses 14–25

While Solomon kept closely to God and to his duty there was *no adversary nor evil occurrent* (*ch.* 5:4), nothing to create him any disturbance or uneasiness in the least; but here we have an account of two adversaries that appeared against him, inconsiderable, and that could not have done any thing worth taking notice of if Solomon had not first made God his enemy. What hurt could Hadad or Rezon have done to so great and powerful a king as Solomon was if he had not, by sin, made himself mean and weak? And then those little people menace and insult him. If God be on our side, we need not fear the greatest adversary; but, if he be against us, he can made us fear the least, and the very grasshopper shall be a burden. Observe,

I. Both these adversaries God stirred up, *v.* 14, 23. Though they themselves were moved by principles of ambition or revenge, God made use of them to serve his design of correcting Solomon. The principal judgment threatened was deferred, namely, the rending of the kingdom from him, but he himself was made to fee the smart of the rod, for his greater humiliation. Note, Whoever are, in any way, adversaries to us, we must take notice of the hand of God stirring them up to be so, as he bade Shimei curse David; we must look through the instruments of our trouble to the author of it and hear the Lord's controversy in it.

II. Both these adversaries had the origin of their enmity to Solomon and Israel laid in David's time, and in his conquests of their respective countries, *v.* 15, 24. Solomon had the benefit and advantage of his father's successes both in the enlargement of his dominion and the increase of his treasure, and would never have known any thing but the benefit of them if he had kept closely to God; but now he finds evils to balance the advantages, and that David had made himself enemies, who were thorns in his sides. Those that are too free in giving provocation ought to consider that perhaps it may be remembered in time to come and returned with interest to theirs after them; having so few friends in this world, it is our wisdom not to make ourselves more enemies than we needs must.

1. Hadad, an Edomite, was an adversary to Solomon. We are not told what he did against him, nor which way he gave him disturbance, only, in general, that he was an adversary to him: but we are told, (1.) What induced him to bear Solomon a grudge. David had conquered Edom, 2 Sa. 8:14. Joab put all the males to the sword, *v.* 15, 16. A terrible execution he made, avenging on Edom their old enmity to Israel, yet perhaps with too great a severity. From this general slaughter, while Joab was burying the slain (for he left not any alive of their own people to bury them, and buried they must be, or they would be an annoyance to the country, Eze. 39:12), Hadad, a branch of the royal family, then a little child, was taken and preserved by some of the king's servants, and conveyed to Egypt, *v.* 17. They halted by the way, in Midian first, and then in Paran, where they furnished themselves with men, not to fight for them or force their passage, but to attend them, that their young master might go into Egypt with an equipage agreeable to his quality. There he was kindly sheltered and entertained by Pharaoh, as a distressed prince, as well provided for, and so recommended himself that, in process of time, he married the queen's sister (*v.* 19), and by her had a child, which the queen herself conceived such a kindness for that she brought him up in Pharaoh's house, among the king's children. (2.) What enabled him to do Solomon a mischief. Upon the death of David and Joab, he returned to his own country, in which, it should seem, he settled and remained quiet while Solomon continued wise and watchful for the public good, but from which he had opportunity of making inroads upon Israel when Solomon, having sinned away his wisdom as Samson did his strength (and in the same way), grew careless of public affairs, was off his guard himself, and had forfeited the divine protection. What vexation Hadad gave to Solomon we are not here told, but only how loth Pharaoh was to part with him and how earnestly he solicited his stay (*v.* 22): *What hast thou lacked with me?* "Nothing," says Hadad; "but let me go to my own country, my native air, my native soil." Peter Martyr has a pious reflection upon this: "Heaven is our home, and we ought to keep up a holy affection to that, and desire towards it, even when the world, the place of our banishment, smiles most upon us." Does it ask, What have you lacked, that you are so willing to be gone? We may answer, "Nothing that the world can do for us; but still let us go thither, where our hope, and honour, and treasure are."

2. Rezon, a Syrian, was another adversary to Solomon. When David conquered the Syrians, he headed the remains, lived at large by spoil and rapine, till Solomon grew careless, and then he got possession of Damascus, reigned there (*v.* 24) and over the country about (*v.* 25), and he created troubles to Israel, probably in conjunction with Hadad, all the days of Solomon (namely, after his apostasy), or he was an enemy to Israel during all Solomon's reign, and upon all occasions vented his then impotent malice against them, but till Solomon's revolt, when his defence had departed from him, he could not do them any mischief. It is said of him that *he abhorred Israel.* Other princes loved and admired Israel and Solomon, and courted their friendship, but here was one that abhorred them. The greatest and best of princes and people, however much they may in general be respected, will yet perhaps be hated and abhorred by some.

Verses 26–40

We have here the first mention of that infamous name *Jeroboam the son of Nebat, that made Israel to sin;* he is here brought upon the stage as an adversary to Solomon, whom God had expressly told (*v.* 11) that he would give the greatest part of his kingdom to his servant, and Jeroboam was the man. We have here an account,

I. Of his extraction, *v.* 26. He was of the tribe of Ephraim, he next in honour to Judah. His mother was a widow, to whom Providence had made up the loss of a husband in a son that was active and ingenious, and (we may suppose) a great support and comfort to her.

II. Of his elevation. It was Solomon's wisdom, when he had work to do, to employ proper persons in it. He observed Jeroboam to be a very industrious young man, one that minded his business, took a pleasure in it, and did it with all his might, and therefore he gradually advanced him, till at length he made him receiver-general for the two tribes of Ephraim and Manasseh, or perhaps put him into an office equivalent to that of lord-lieutenant of those two counties, for he was ruler of the burden, or tribute, that is, either of the taxes or of the militia of the house of Joseph. Note, Industry is the way to preferment. *Seest thou a man diligent in his business,* that will take care and pains, and go through with it? he shall *stand before kings,* and not always be on the level with mean men. Observe a difference between David, and both his predecessor and his successor: when Saul saw a *valiant man he took him to himself* (1 Sa. 14:52); when Solomon saw an *industrious* man he preferred him; but David's *eyes were upon the faithful in the land,* that they might *dwell with him:* if he saw a godly man, he preferred him, for he was a man after God's own heart, whose *countenance beholds the upright.*

III. Of his designation to the government of the ten tribes after the death of Solomon. Some think he was himself plotting against Solomon, and contriving to rise to the throne, that he was turbulent and aspiring. The Jews say that when he was employed by Solomon in building Millo he took opportunities of reflecting upon Solomon as oppressive to his people, and suggesting that which would alienate them from his government. It is not indeed probable that he should say much to that purport, for Solomon would have got notice of it, and it would have hindered his preferment; but it is plainly intimated that he had it in his thoughts, for the prophet tells him (*v.* 37), *Thou shalt reign according to all that thy soul desireth.* But this was the *cause,* or rather this was the *story,* of the lifting up of his hand against the king: Solomon made him ruler over the tribes of Joseph, and, as he was going to take possession of his government, he was told by a prophet in God's name that he should be king, which emboldened him to aim high, and in some instances to oppose the king and give him vexation. 1. The prophet by whom this message was sent was *Ahijah of Shiloh;* we shall read of him again, *ch.* 14:2. It seems, Shiloh was not so perfectly forsaken and forgotten of God but that, in remembrance of the former days, it was blessed with a prophet. He delivered his message to Jeroboam in the way, his servants being probably ordered to retire, as in a like case (1 Sa. 9:27), when Samuel delivered his message to Saul. God's word was not the less sacred and sure for being delivered to him thus obscurely, under a hedge it may be. 2. The sign by which it was represented to him was the rending of a garment into twelve pieces, and giving him ten, *v.* 30, 31. It is not certain whether the garment was Jeroboam's, as is commonly taken for granted, or Ahijah's, which is more probable: *He* (that is, the prophet) *had clad himself with a new garment,* on purpose that he might with it give him a sign. The rending of the kingdom from Saul was signified by the rending of Samuel's mantle, not Saul's, 1 Sa. 15:27, 28. And it was more significant to give Jeroboam ten pieces of that which was not his own before than of that which was. The prophets, both true and false, used such signs, even in the New Testament, as Agabus, Acts 21:10, 11. 3. The message itself, which is very particular, (1.) He assures him that he shall be king over ten of the twelve tribes of Israel, *v.* 31. The meanness of his extraction and employment shall be no hindrance to his advancement, when the God of Israel says (by whom kings reign), *I will give ten tribes unto thee.* (2.) He tells him the reason; not for his good character or deserts, but for the chastising of Solomon's apostasy: "Because he, and his family, and many of his people with him, *have forsaken me, and worshipped other gods,*" *v.* 33. It was because they had done ill, not because he was likely to do much better. Thus Israel must know that it is not *for their righteousness* that they are made masters of Canaan, but for the wickedness of the Canaanites, Deu. 9:4. Jeroboam did not deserve so good a post, but Israel deserved so bad a prince. In telling him that the reason why he rent the kingdom from the house of Solomon was because they had forsaken God, he warns him to take heed of sinning away his preferment in like manner. (3.) He limits his expectations to the ten tribes only, and to them in reversion after the death of Solomon, lest he should aim at the whole and give immediate disturbance to Solomon's government. He is here told, [1.] That two tribes (called here *one tribe,* because little Benjamin was in a manner lost in the thousands of Judah) should remain sure to the house of David, and he must never make any attempt upon them: *He shall have one tribe* (*v.* 32), and again (*v.* 36), *That David may have a lamp,* that is, a shining name and memory (Ps. 132:17), and his family, as a royal family, may not be extinct. He must not think that David was rejected, as Saul was. No, God would not take his loving-kindness from him, as he did from Saul. The house of David must be supported and kept in reputation, for all this, because out of it the Messiah must arise. *Destroy it not,* for that *blessing is in it.* [2.] That Solomon must keep possession during his life, *v.* 34, 35. Jeroboam therefore must not offer to dethrone him, but wait with patience till his day shall come to fall. Solomon shall be *prince, all the days of his life,* not for his own sake (he had forfeited his crown to the justice of God), but for *David my servant's sake, because he kept my commandments.* Children that do not tread in their parents' steps yet often fare the better in this world for their good parents' piety. (4.) He gives him to understand that he will be upon his good behaviour. The grant of the crown must run *quamdiu se bene gesserit — during good behaviour.* "If thou wilt *do what is right in my sight, I will build thee a sure house,* and not otherwise" (*v.* 38), intimating that, if he forsook God, even his advancement to the throne would in time lay his family in the dust; whereas the seed of David, though afflicted, should not be afflicted for ever (*v.* 39), but should flourish again, as it did in many of the illustrious kings of Judah, who reigned in glory when Jeroboam's family was extirpated.

IV. Jeroboam's flight into Egypt, *v.* 40. In some way or other Solomon came to know of all this, probably from Jeroboam's own talk of it; he could not conceal it as Saul did, nor keep his own counsel; if he had, he might have staid in his country, and been preparing there for his future advancement; but letting it be known, 1. Solomon foolishly sought to kill his successor. Had not he taught others that, whatever devices are in men's hearts, *the counsel of the Lord shall stand?* And yet does he himself think to defeat that counsel? 2. Jeroboam prudently withdrew into Egypt. Though God's promise would have secured him any where, yet he would use means for his own preservation, and was content to live in exile and obscurity for a while, being sure of a kingdom at last. And shall not we be so, who have a better kingdom in reserve?

Verses 41–43

We have here the conclusion of Solomon's story, and in it, 1. Reference is had to another history then extant, but (not being divinely inspired) since lost, *the Book of the Acts of Solomon, v.* 41. Probably this book was written by a chronologer or historiographer, whom Solomon employed to write his annals, out of which the sacred writer extracted what God saw fit to transmit to the church. 2. A summary of the years of his reign (*v.* 42): *He reigned in Jerusalem* (not, as his father, part of his time in Hebron and part in Jerusalem), *over all Israel* (not as his son, and his father in the beginning of his time, over Judah only), *forty years.* His reign was as long as his father's, but not his life. Sin shortened his days. 3. His death and burial, and his successor, *v.* 43. (1.) He followed his fathers to the grave, slept with them, and was buried in David's burying-place, with honour no doubt. (2.) His son followed him in the throne. Thus the graves are filling with the generations that go off, and houses are filling with those that are growing up. As the grave cries, "Give, give," so land is never lost for want of an heir.

CHAPTER 12

The glory of the kingdom of Israel was in its height and perfection in Solomon; it was long in coming to it, but it soon declined, and began to sink and wither in the very next reign, as we find in this chapter, where we have the kingdom divided, and thereby weakened and made little in comparison with what it had been. Here is, I. Rehoboam's accession to the throne and Jeroboam's return out of Egypt (*v.* 1, 2). II. The people's petition to Rehoboam for the redress of grievances, and the rough answer he gave, by the advice of his young counsellors, to that petition (*v.* 3–15). III. The revolt of the ten tribes thereupon, and their setting up Jeroboam (*v.* 16–20). IV. Rehoboam's attempt to reduce them and the prohibition God gave to that attempt (*v.* 21–24). V. Jeroboam's establishment of his government upon idolatry (*v.* 25–33). Thus did Judah become weak, being deserted by their brethren, and Israel, by deserting the house of the Lord.

Verses 1–15

Solomon had 1000 wives and concubines, yet we read but of one son he had to bear up his name, and he a fool. It is said (Hos. 4:10), *They shall commit whoredom, and shall not increase.* Sin is a bad way of building up a family. Rehoboam was the son of the wisest of men, yet did not inherit his father's wisdom, and then it stood him in little stead to inherit his father's throne. Neither wisdom nor grace runs in the blood. Solomon came to the crown very young, yet he was then a wise man. Rehoboam came to the crown at forty years old, when men will be wise if ever they will, yet he was then foolish. Wisdom does not go by age, nor is it the multitude of years nor the advantage of education that reaches it. Solomon's court was a mart of wisdom and the rendezvous of learned men, and Rehoboam was the darling of the court; and yet all was not sufficient to make him a wise man. *The race is not to the swift, nor the battle to the strong.* No dispute is made of Rehoboam's succession; upon the death of his father, he was immediately proclaimed. But,

I. The people desired a treaty with him at Shechem, and he condescended to meet them there. 1. Their pretence was to make him king, but the design was to unmake him. They would give him a public inauguration in another place than the city of David, that he might not seem to be king of Judah only. They had ten parts in him, and would have him among themselves for once, that they might recognize his title. 2. The place was ominous: at *Shechem,* where Abimelech set up himself (Jdg. 9); yet it had been famous for the convention of the states there, Jos. 24:1. Rehoboam, we may suppose, knew of the threatening, that the kingdom should be rent from him, and hoped by going to Shechem, and treating there with the ten tribes, to prevent it: yet it proved the most impolitic thing he could do, and hastened the rupture.

II. The representatives of the tribes addressed him, praying to be eased of the taxes they were burdened with. The meeting being appointed, they sent for Jeroboam out of Egypt to come and be their speaker. This they needed not to have done: he knew what God had designed him for, and would have come though he had not been sent for, for now was his time to expect the possession of the promised crown. In their address, 1. They complain of the last reign: *Thy father made our yoke grievous, v.* 4. They complain not of his father's idolatry and revolt from God; that which was the greatest grievance of all was none to them, so careless and indifferent were they in the matters of religion, as if God or Moloch were all one, so they might but live at ease and pay no taxes. Yet the complaint was groundless and unjust. Never did people live more at ease than they did, nor in great plenty. Did they pay taxes? It was to advance the strength and magnificence of their kingdom. If Solomon's buildings cost them money, they cost them no blood, as war would do. Were many servile hands employed about them? They were not the hands of the Israelites. Were the taxes a burden? How could that be, when Solomon imported bullion in such plenty that silver was, in a manner, as common as the stones? So that they did but render to Solomon the things that were Solomon's. Nay, suppose there was some hardship put upon them, were they not told before that this would be the manner of the king and yet they would have one? The best government cannot secure itself from reproach and censure, no, not Solomon's. Factious spirits will never want something to complain of. I know nothing in Solomon's administration that could make the people's yoke grievous, unless perhaps the women whom in his latter days he doted on were connived at in oppressing them. 2. They demand relief from him, and on this condition will continue in their allegiance to the house of David. They asked not to be wholly free from paying taxes, but to have the burden made lighter; this was all their care, to save their money, whether their religion was supported and the government protected or no. All seek their own.

III. Rehoboam consulted with those about him concerning the answer he should give to this address. It was prudent to take advice, especially having so weak a head of his own; yet, upon this occasion, it was impolitic to take time himself to consider, for thereby he gave time to the disaffected people to ripen things for a revolt, and his deliberating in so plain a case would be improved as an indication of the little concern he had for the people's ease. They saw what they must expect, and prepared accordingly. Now, 1. The grave experienced men of his council advised him by all means to give the petitioners a kind answer, to give them good words, to promise them fair, and this day, this critical day, to serve them, that is, to tell them that he was their servant, and that he would redress all their grievances and make it his business to please them and make them easy. "Deny thyself (say they) so far as to do this for this once, and they will be *thy servants for ever.* When the present heat is allayed with a soft answer, and the assembly dismissed, their cooler thoughts will reconcile and fix them to Solomon's family still." Note, The way to rule is to serve, to do good, and stoop to do it, to become all things to all men and so win their hearts. Those who are in power really sit highest, and easiest, and safest, when they take this method. 2. The young men of his council were hot and haughty, and they advised him to return a severe and threatening answer to the people's demands. It was an instance of Rehoboam's weakness, (1.) That he did not prefer aged counsellors, but had a better opinion of the young men that had grown up with him and with whom he was familiar, *v.* 8. Days should speak. It was a folly for him to think that, because they had been his agreeable companions in the sports and pleasures of his youth, they were therefore fit to have the management of the affairs of his kingdom. Great wits have not always the most wisdom; nor are those to be relied on as our best friends that know how to make us merry, for that will not make us happy. It is of great consequence to young people, that are setting out in the world, whom they associate with, accommodate themselves to, and depend upon for advice. If they reckon those that feed their pride, gratify their vanity, and further them in their pleasures, their best friends, they are already marked for ruin. (2.) That he did not prefer moderate counsels, but was pleased with those that put him upon harsh and rigorous methods, and advised him to double the taxes, whether there was occasion for so doing or no, and to tell them in plain terms that he would do so, *v.* 10, 11. These young counsellors thought the old men expressed themselves but dully, *v.* 7. They affect to be witty in their advice, and value themselves on that. The old men did not undertake to put words into Rehoboam's mouth, only counselled him to speak good words; but the young men will furnish him with very quaint and pretty phrases, with pointed and pert similitudes: *My little finger shall be thicker than my father's loins,* etc. That is not always the best sense that is best worded.

IV. He answered the people according to the counsel of the young men, *v.* 14, 15. He affected to be haughty and imperious, and fancied he could carry all before him with a high hand, and therefore would rather run the risk of losing them than deny himself so far as to give them good words. Note, Many ruin themselves by consulting their humour more than their interest. See,

1. How Rehoboam was infatuated in his counsels. He could not have acted more foolishly and impoliticly. (1.) He owned their reflections upon his father's government to be true: *My father made your yoke heavy;* and therein he was unjust to his father's memory, which he might easily have vindicated from the imputation. (2.) He fancied himself better able to manage them, and impose upon them, than his father was, not considering that he was vastly inferior to him in capacity. Could he think to support the blemishes of his father's reign who could never pretend to come near the glories of it? (3.) He threatened not only to squeeze them by taxes, but to chastise them by cruel laws and severe executions of them, which should be not as whips only, but as scorpions, whips with rowels in them, that will fetch blood at every lash. In short, he would use them as brute beasts, load them and beat them at his pleasure: not caring whether they loved him or no, he would make them fear him. (4.) He gave this provocation to a people that by long ease and prosperity were made wealthy, and strong, and proud, and would not be trampled upon (as a poor cowed dispirited people may), to a people that were now disposed to revolt, and had one ready to head them. Never, surely, was man so blinded by pride and affectation of arbitrary power, than which nothing is more fatal.

2. How God's counsels were hereby fulfilled. It was *from the Lord, v.* 15. He left Rehoboam to his own folly, and *hid from his eyes* the *things which belonged to his peace,* that the kingdom might be rent from him. Note, God serves his own wise and righteous purposes by the imprudences and iniquities of men, and snares sinners in the work of their own hands. Those that lose the kingdom of heaven throw it away, as Rehoboam did his, by their own wilfulness and folly.

Verses 16–24

We have here the rending of the kingdom of the ten tribes from the house of David, to effect which,

I. The people were hold and resolute in their revolt. They highly resented the provocation that Rehoboam had given them, were incensed at his menaces, concluded that that government would in the progress of it be intolerably grievous which in the beginning of it was so very haughty, and therefore immediately came to this resolve, one and all: *What portion have we in David? v.* 16. They speak here very unbecomingly of David, that great benefactor of their nation, calling him *the son of Jesse,* no greater a man than his neighbours. How soon are good men, and their good services to the public, forgotten! The rashness of their resolution was also much to be blamed. In time, and with prudent management, they might have settled the original contract with Rehoboam to mutual satisfaction. Had they enquired who gave Rehoboam this advice, and taken a course to remove those evil counsellors from about him, the rupture might have been prevented: otherwise their jealousy for their liberty and property well became that free people. *Israel is not a servant, is not a homeborn slave; why should he be spoiled?* Jer. 2:14. They are willing to be ruled, but not to be ridden. Protection draws allegiance, but destruction cannot. No marvel that *Israel falls away from the house of David* (*v.* 19) if the house of David fall away from the great ends of their advancement, which was to be *ministers of God to them for good.* But thus to rebel against the seed of David, whom God had advanced to the kingdom (entailing it on his seed), and to set up another king in opposition to that family, was a great sin; see 2 Chr. 13:5–8. To this God refers, Hos. 8:4. *They have set up kings, but not by me.* And it is here mentioned to the praise of the tribe of Judah that they *followed the house of David* (*v.* 17, 20), and, for aught that appears, they found Rehoboam better than his word, nor did he rule with the rigour which at first he threatened.

II. Rehoboam was imprudent in the further management of this affair, and more and more infatuated. Having foolishly thrown himself into a quick-sand, he sunk the further in with plunging to get out. 1. He was very unadvised in sending Adoram, who was *over the tribute,* to treat with them, *v.* 18. The tribute was the thing, and, for the sake of that, Adoram was the person, they most complained of. The very sight of him, whose name was odious among them, exasperated them, and made them outrageous. He was one to whom they could not so much as give a patient hearing, but *stoned him to death* in a popular tumult. Rehoboam was now as unhappy in the choice of his ambassador as before of his counsellors. 2. Some think he was also unadvised in quitting his ground, and making so much haste to Jerusalem, for thereby he deserted his friends and gave advantage to his enemies, who had gone to their tents indeed (*v.* 16) in disgust, but did not offer to make Jeroboam king till Rehoboam had gone, *v.* 20. See how soon this foolish prince went from one extreme to the other. He hectored and talked big when he thought all was his own, but sneaked and looked very mean when he saw himself in danger. It is common for those that are most haughty in their prosperity to be most abject in adversity.

III. God forbade his attempt to recover by the sword what he had lost. What was done was of God, who would not suffer that it should be undone again (as it would be if Rehoboam got the better and reduced the ten tribes), nor that more should be done to the prejudice of the house of David, as would be if Jeroboam got the better and conquered the two tribes. The thing must rest as it is, and therefore God forbids the battle. 1. It was brave in Rehoboam to design the reducing of the revolters by force. His courage came to him when he had come to Jerusalem, *v.* 21. There he thought himself among his firm friends, who generously adhered to him and appeared for him. Judah and Benjamin (who feared the Lord and the king, and meddled not with those that were given to change) presently raised an army of 180,000 men, for the recovery of their king's right to the ten tribes, and were resolved to stand by him (as we say) with their lives and fortunes, having either not such cause, or rather not such a disposition, to complain, as the rest had. 2. It as more brave in Rehoboam to desist when God, by a prophet, ordered him to lay down his arms. He would not lose a kingdom tamely, for then he would have been unworthy the title of a prince; and yet he would not contend for it in opposition to God, for then he would have been unworthy the title of an Israelite. To proceed in this war would be not only to *fight against their brethren* (*v.* 24), whom they ought to love, but to fight against their God, to whom they ought to submit: *This thing is from me.* These two considerations should reconcile us to our losses and troubles, that God is the author of them and our brethren are the instruments of them; let us not therefore meditate revenge. Rehoboam and his people *hearkened to the word of the Lord,* disbanded the army, and acquiesced. Though, in human probability, they had a fair prospect of success (for their army was numerous and resolute, Jeroboam's party weak and unsettled), though it would turn to their reproach among their neighbours to lose so much of their strength and never have one push for it, to make a flourish and do nothing, yet, (1.) They regarded the command of God though sent by a poor prophet. When we know God's mind we must submit to it, how much soever it crosses our own mind. (2.) They consulted their own interest, concluding that though they had all the advantages, even that of right, on their side, yet they could not prosper if they fought in disobedience to God; and it was better to sit still than to rise up and fall. In the next reign God allowed them to fight, and gave them victory (2 Chr. 13), but not now.

Verses 25–33

We have here the beginning of the reign of Jeroboam. He built Shechem first and then Penuel — beautified and fortified them, and probably had a palace in each of them for himself (*v.* 25), the former in Ephraim, the latter in Gad, on the other side Jordan. This might be proper; but he formed another project for the establishing of his kingdom which was fatal to the interests of religion in it.

I. That which he designed was by some effectual means to secure those to himself who had now chosen him for their king, and to prevent their return to the house of David, *v.* 26, 27. It seems, 1. He was jealous of the people, afraid that, some time or other, they would kill him and go again to Rehoboam. Many that have been advanced in one tumult have been hurled down in another. Jeroboam could not put any confidence in the affections of his people, though now they seemed extremely fond of him; for what is got by wrong and usurpation cannot be enjoyed nor kept with any security or satisfaction. 2. He was distrustful of the promise of God, could not take his word that, if he would keep close to his duty, *God would build him a sure house* (*ch.* 11:38); but he would contrive ways and means, and sinful ones too, for his own safety. A practical disbelief of God's all-sufficiency is at the bottom of all our treacherous departures from him.

II. The way he took to do this was by keeping the people from going up to Jerusalem to worship. That was the place God had chosen, to put his name there. Solomon's temple was there, which God had, in the sight of all Israel, and in the memory of many now living, taken solemn possession of in a cloud of glory. At the altar there the priest of the Lord attended, there all Israel were to keep the feasts, and thither they were to bring their sacrifices. Now,

1. Jeroboam apprehended that, if the people continued to do this, they would in time return to the house of David, allured by the magnificence both of the court and of the temple. If they cleave to their old religion, they will go back to their old king. We may suppose, if he had treated with Rehoboam for the safe conduct of himself and his people to and from Jerusalem at the times appointed for their solemn feasts, it would not have been denied him; therefore he fears not their being driven back by force, but their going back voluntarily to Rehoboam.

2. He therefore dissuaded them from going up to Jerusalem, pretending to consult their ease: *"It is too much for you* to go so far to worship God, *v.* 28. It is a heavy yoke, and it is time to shake it off; *you have gone long enough to Jerusalem"* (so some read it); "the temple, now that you are used to it, does not appear so glorious and sacred as it did at first" (sensible glories wither by degrees in men's estimation); "you have greed yourselves from other burdens, free yourselves from this: why should we now be tied to one place any more than in Samuel's time?"

3. He provided for the assistance of their devotion at home. Upon consultation with some of his politicians, he came to this resolve, to set up two golden calves, as tokens or signs of the divine presence, and persuade the people that they might as well stay at home and offer sacrifice to those as go to Jerusalem to worship before the ark: and some are so charitable as to think they were made to represent the mercy-seat and the cherubim over the ark; but more probably he adopted the idolatry of the Egyptians, in whose land he had sojourned for some time and who worshipped their god Apis under the similitude of a bull or calf. (1.) He would not be at the charge of building a golden temple, as Solomon had done; two golden calves are the most that he can afford. (2.) He intended, no doubt, by these to represent, or rather make present, not any false god, as Moloch or Chemosh, but the true God only, the God of Israel, the God that brought them up out of the land of Egypt, as he declares, *v.* 28. So that it was no violation of the first commandment, but the second. And he chose thus to engage the people's devotion because he knew there were many among them so in love with images that for the sake of the calves they would willingly quit God's temple, where all images were forbidden. (3.) He set up two, by degrees to break people off from the

belief of the unity of the godhead, which would pave the way to the polytheism of the Pagans. He set up these two at Dan and Beth-el (one the utmost border of his country northward), the other southward, as if they were the guardians and protectors of the kingdom. Beth-el lay close to Judah. He set up one there, to tempt those of Rehoboam's subjects over to him who were inclined to image-worship, in lieu of those of his subjects that would continue to go to Jerusalem. He set up the other at Dan, for the convenience of those that lay most remote, and because Micah's images had been set up there, and great veneration paid to them for many ages, Jdg. 18:30, 31. *Beth-el* signifies *the house of God,* which gave some colour to the superstition; but the prophet called it *Beth-aven, the house of vanity,* or iniquity.

4. The people complied with him herein, and were fond enough of the novelty: They *went to worship before the one, even unto Dan* (*v.* 30), to that at Dan first because it was first set up, or *even* to that at Dan, though it lay such a great way off. Those that thought it much to go to Jerusalem, to worship God according to his institution, made no difficulty of going twice as far, to Dan, to worship him according to their own inventions. Or they are said to go to one of the calves at Dan because Abijah, king of Judah, within twenty years, recovered Beth-el (2 Chr. 13:19), and it is likely removed the golden calf, or forbade the use of it, and then they had only that at Dan to go to. *This became a sin;* and a great sin it was, against the express letter of the second commandment. God had sometimes dispensed with the law concerning worshipping in one place, but never allowed the worship of him by images. Hereby they justified their fathers in making the calf at Horeb, though God had so fully shown his displeasure against them for it and threatened to visit for it in the day of visitation (Ex. 32:34), so that it was as great a contempt of God's wrath as it was of his law; and thus they added sin to sin. Bishop Patrick quotes a saying of the Jews, That till Jeroboam's time the Israelites sucked but one calf, but from that time they sucked two.

5. Having set up the gods, he fitted up accommodations for them; and wherein he varied from the divine appointment we are here told, which intimates that in other things he imitated what was done in Judah (*v.* 32) as well as he could. See how one error multiplied into many. (1.) He made a house of high-places, or of altars, one temple at Dan, we may suppose, and another at Beth-el (*v.* 31), and in each many altars, probably complaining of it as an inconvenience that in the temple at Jerusalem there was but one. The multiplying of altars passed with some for a piece of devotion, but God, by the prophet, puts another construction upon it, Hos. 8:11. *Ephraim has made many altars to sin.* (2.) He made priests of the lowest of the people; and the lowest of the people were good enough to be priests to his calves, and too good. He made priests *from the extremest parts of the people,* that is, some out of every corner of the country, whom he ordered to reside among their neighbours, to instruct them in his appointments and reconcile them to them. Thus were they dispersed as the Levites, but *were not of the sons of Levi.* But the priests of the high-laces, or altars, he ordered to reside in Beth-el, as the priests at Jerusalem (*v.* 32), to attend the public service. (3.) The feast of tabernacles, which God had appointed on the fifteenth day of the seventh month, he adjourned to the fifteenth day of the eighth month (*v.* 32), *the month which he devised of his own heart,* to show his power in ecclesiastical matters, *v.* 33. The passover and pentecost he observed in their proper season, or did not observe them at all, or with little solemnity in comparison with this. (4.) He himself assuming a power to make priests, no marvel if he undertook to do the priests' work with his own hands: *He offered upon the altar.* This is twice mentioned (*v.* 32, 33), as also that he burnt incense. This was connived at in him because it was of a piece with the rest of his irregularities; but in king Uzziah it was immediately punished with the plague of leprosy. He did it himself, to make himself look great among the people and to get the reputation of a devout man, also to grace the solemnity of his new festival, with which, it is likely, at this time he joined the feast of the dedication of his altar. And thus, [1.] Jeroboam sinned himself, yet perhaps excused himself to the world and his own conscience with this, that he did not do so ill as Solomon did, who worshipped other gods. [2.] He *made Israel to sin,* drew them off from the worship of God and entailed idolatry upon their seed. And hereby they were punished for deserting the thrones *of the house of David.* The learned Mr. Whiston, in his chronology, for the adjusting of the annals of the two kingdoms of Judah and Israel, supposes that Jeroboam changed the calculation of the year and made it to contain but eleven months, and that by those years the reigns of the kings of Israel are measured till Jehu's revolution and no longer, so that during this interval eleven years of the annals of Judah answer to twelve in those of Israel.

CHAPTER 13

In the close of the foregoing chapter we left Jeroboam attending his altar at Beth-el, and there we find him in the beginning of this, when he received a testimony from God against his idolatry and apostasy. This was sent to him by a prophet, a man of God that lived in Judah, who is the principal subject of the story of this chapter, where we are told, I. What passed between him and the new king. 1. The prophet threatened Jeroboam's altar (*v.* 1, 2), and gave him a sign (*v.* 3), which immediately came to pass (*v.* 5). 2. The king threatened the prophet, and was himself made another sign, by the withering of his hand (*v.* 4), and the restoring of it upon his submission and the prophet's intercession (*v.* 6). 3. The prophet refused the kindness offered him thereupon (*v.* 7–10). II. What passed between him and the old prophet. 1. The old prophet fetched him back by a lie, and gave him entertainment (*v.* 11–19). 2. He, for accepting it, in disobedience to the divine command, is threatened with death (*v.* 20–22). And, 3. The threatening is executed, for he is slain by a lion (*v.* 23, 24), and buried at Beth-el (*v.* 25–32). 4. Jeroboam is hardened in his idolatry (*v.* 33, 34). "Thy judgments, Lord, are a great deep."

Verses 1–10

Here is, I. A messenger sent to Jeroboam, to signify to him God's displeasure against his idolatry, *v.* 1. The army of Judah that aimed to ruin him was countermanded, and might not draw a sword against him (*ch.* 12:24); but a prophet of Judah is, instead thereof, sent to reclaim him from his evil way, and is sent in time, while he is but dedicating his altar, before his heart is hardened by the deceitfulness of his sin; for God delights not in the death of sinners, but would rather they would burn and live. How bold was the messenger that durst attack the king in his pride and interrupt the solemnity he was proud of! Those that go on God's errand must not fear the face of man; they know who will bear them out. How kind was he that sent him to warn Jeroboam of the wrath of God *revealed from heaven* against his *ungodliness* and *unrighteousness!*

II. The message delivered in God's name, not whispered, but cried with a loud voice, denoting both the prophet's courage, that he was neither afraid nor ashamed to own it, and his earnestness, that he desired to be heard and heeded by all that were present, who were not a few, on this great occasion. It was directed, not to Jeroboam nor to the people, but to the altar, the stones of which would sooner hear and yield than those who were mad upon their idols and deaf to divine calls. Yet, in threatening the altar, God threatened the founder and worshippers, to whom it was as dear as their own souls, and who might conclude, "If God's wrath fasten upon the lifeless guiltless altar, how shall we escape?" That which was foretold concerning the altar (*v.* 2) was that, in process of time, a prince of the house of David, Josiah by name, should pollute this altar by sacrificing the idolatrous priests themselves upon it, and burning the bones of dead men. Let Jeroboam know and be sure, 1. That the altar he now consecrated should be desecrated. Idolatrous worship will not continue, but the word of the Lord will endure for ever. 2. That the *priests of the high places* he now made should themselves be made sacrifices to the justice of God, and the first and only sacrifices upon this altar that would be pleasing to him. If the offering be such as is an abomination to God, it will follow, of course, that the offerers must themselves fall under his wrath, which will abide upon them, since it is not otherwise transmitted. 3. That this should be done by a branch *of the house of David.* That family which he and his kingdom had despised and treacherously deserted should recover so much power as to demolish that altar which he thought to establish; so that right and truth should at length prevail, both in civil and sacred matters, notwithstanding the present triumphs of those that were given to change the fear both *of God and the king.* It was about 356 years ere this prediction was fulfilled, yet it was spoken of as sure and nigh at hand, for a thousand years with God are but as one day. Nothing more contingent and arbitrary than the giving of names to persons, yet Josiah was here named above 300 years before he was born. Nothing future is hidden from God. There are *names in the book* of the divine prescience (Phil. 4:3), names *written in heaven.*

III. A sign is given for the confirming of the truth of this prediction, that the altar should be shaken to pieces by an invisible power and the ashes of the sacrifice scattered (*v.* 3), which came to pass immediately, *v.* 5. This was, 1. A proof that the prophet was sent of God, *who confirmed the word with this sign following,* Mk. 16:20. 2. A present indication of God's displeasure against these idolatrous sacrifices. How could the gift be acceptable when the altar that should sanctify it was an abomination? 3. It was a reproach to the people, whose hearts were harder than these stones and rent not under the word of the Lord. 4. It was a specimen of what should be done to it in the accomplishment of this prophecy by Josiah; it was now rent, in token of its being then ruined.

IV. Jeroboam's hand withered, which he stretched out to seize or smite the man of God, *v.* 4. Instead of trembling at the message, as he might well have done, he assaulted him that brought it, in defiance of the wrath of which he was warned and contempt of that grace which sent him the warning. *Rebuke a sinner* and *he will hate thee,* and do thee a mischief if he can; yet God's prophets must rather expose themselves than betray their trust: he that employs them will protect them, and restrain the wrath of man, as he did Jeroboam's here by withering his hand, so that he could neither hurt the prophet nor draw it in to help himself. When his hand was stretched out to burn incense to his calves it was not withered; but, when it is stretched out against a prophet, he shall have no use of it till he humble himself. Of all the wickedness of the wicked there is none more provoking to God than their malicious attempts against his prophets, of whom he has said, *Touch them not, do them no harm.* As this was a punishment of Jeroboam, and answering to the sin, so it was the deliverance of the prophet. God has many ways of disabling the enemies of his church from executing their mischievous purposes. Jeroboam's inability to pull in his hand made him a spectacle to all about him, that they might see and fear. If God, in justice, harden the hearts of sinners, so that the hand they have stretched out in sin they cannot pull in again by repentance, that is a spiritual judgment, represented by this, and much more dreadful.

V. The sudden healing of the hand that was suddenly dried up, upon his submission, *v.* 6. That word of God which should have touched his conscience humbled him not, but this which *touched his bone and his flesh* brings down his proud spirit. He looks for help now, 1. Not from his calves, but from God only, from his power and his favour. He wounded, and no hand but his can make whole. 2. Not by his own sacrifice or incense, but by the prayer and intercession of the prophet, whom he had just now threatened and aimed to destroy. The time may come when those that hate the preaching would be glad of the prayers of faithful ministers. "Pray to the Lord thy God," says Jeroboam; "thou hast an interest in him; improve it for me." But observe, He did not desire the prophet to pray that his sin might be pardoned, and his heart changed, only that *his hand might be restored;* thus Pharaoh would have Moses to pray that God would *take away this death* only (Ex. 10:17), not this *sin.* The prophet, as became a man of God, renders good for evil, upbraids not Jeroboam with his impotent malice, nor triumphs in his submission, but immediately addresses himself to God for him. Those only are entitled to the blessing Christ pronounced on the persecuted that learn of him to pray for their persecutors, Mt. 5:10, 44. When the prophet thus honoured God, by showing himself of a forgiving spirit, God put this further honour upon him, that at his word he recalled the judgment and by another miracle healed the withered hand, that by the goodness of God Jeroboam might be led to repentance, and, if he were not broken by the judgment, yet might be melted by the mercy. With both he seemed affected for the present, but the impressions wore off.

VI. The prophet's refusal of Jeroboam's kind invitation, in which observe, 1. That God forbade his messenger to eat or drink in Beth-el (*v.* 9), to show his detestation of their execrable idolatry and apostasy from God, and to teach us not to have fellowship with the works of darkness, lest we have infection from them or give encouragement to them. He must not *turn back the same way,* but deliver his message, as it were, *in transitu — as he passes along.* He shall not seem to be sent on purpose (they were unworthy such a favour), but as if he only called by the way, his spirit being stirred, like Paul's at Athens, as he *passed and saw their devotions.* God would, by this command, try his prophet, as he did Ezekiel, whether he would not be *rebellious, like that rebellious house,* Eze. 2:8. 2. That Jeroboam was so affected with the cure of his hand that though we read not of his thanksgivings to God for the mercy, or of his sending an offering to the altar at Jerusalem in acknowledgment of it, yet he was willing to express his gratitude to the prophet and pay him for his prayers, *v.* 7. Favours to the body will make even graceless men seem grateful to good ministers. 3. That the prophet, though hungry and weary, and perhaps poor, in obedience to the divine command refused both the entertainment and the reward proffered him. He might have supposed his acceptance of it would give him an opportunity of discoursing further with the king, in order to his effectual reformation, now that he was convinced; yet he will not think himself wiser than God, but, like a faithful careful messenger, hastens home when he has done his errand. Those have little learned the lessons of self-denial that cannot forbear one forbidden meal.

Verses 11–22

The man of God had honestly and resolutely refused the king's invitation, though he promised him a reward; yet he was over-persuaded by an old prophet to come back with him, and dine in Beth-el, contrary to the command given him. Here we find how dearly his dinner cost him. Observe with wonder,

I. The old prophet's wickedness. I cannot but call him a false prophet and a bad man, it being much easier to believe that from one of such a bad character should be extorted a confirmation of what the man of God said (as we find, *v.* 32) than that a true prophet, and a good man, should tell such a deliberate lie as he did, and father it upon God. *A good tree could never bring forth such corrupt fruit.* Perhaps he was trained up among the sons of the prophets, in one of Samuel's colleges not far off, whence he retained the name of a prophet, but, growing worldly and profane, the spirit of prophecy had departed from him. If he had been a good prophet he would have reproved Jeroboam's idolatry, and not have suffered his sons to attend his altars, as, it should seem, they did. Now, 1. Whether he had any good design in fetching back the man of God is not certain. One may hope that he did it in compassion to him, concluding he wanted refreshment, and out of a desire to be better acquainted with him and more fully to understand his errand than he could from the report of his sons; yet his sons having told him all that passed, and particularly that the prophet was forbidden to eat or drink there, which he had openly told Jeroboam, I suppose it was done with a bad design, to draw him into a snare, and so to expose him; for false prophets have ever been the worst enemies to the true prophets, usually aiming to destroy them, but sometimes, as here, to debauch them and draw them from their duty. Thus they *gave the Nazarites wine to drink* (Amos 2:12), that they might glory in their fall. But, 2. It is certain that he took a very bad method to bring him back. When the man of God had told him, "I may not, and therefore I will not, return to eat bread with thee" (his resolutions concurring with the divine command, *v.* 16, 17), he wickedly pretended that he had an order from heaven to fetch him back. He imposed upon him by asserting his quondam character as a prophet: *I am a prophet also as thou art;* he pretended he had a vision of an angel that sent him on this errand. But it was all a lie; it was a banter upon prophecy, and profane in the highest degree. When this old prophet is spoken of (2 Ki. 23:18) he is called *the prophet that came out of Samaria,* whereas there was no such place as Samaria till long after, *ch.* 16:24. Therefore I take it he is so called there, though he was of Beth-el, because he was like those who were afterwards *the prophets of Samaria,* who *caused God's people Israel to err,* Jer. 23:13.

II. The good prophet's weakness, in suffering himself to be thus imposed upon: *He went back with him, v.* 19. He that had resolution enough to refuse the invitation of the king, who promised him a reward, could not resist the insinuations of one that pretended to be a prophet. God's people are more in danger of being drawn from their duty by the plausible pretences of divinity and sanctity than by external inducements; we have therefore need to *beware of false prophets,* and not *believe every spirit.*

III. The proceedings of divine justice hereupon; and here we may well wonder that the wicked prophet, who told the lie and did the mischief, went unpunished, while the holy man of God, that was drawn by him into sin, was suddenly and severely punished for it. What shall we make of this! The judgments of God are unfathomable. *The deceived and the deceiver are his,* and he *giveth not account of any of his matters.* Certainly there must be a judgment to come, when these things will be called over again, and when those that sinned most and suffered least, in this world, will receive according to their works. 1. The message delivered to the man of God was strange. His crime is recited, *v.* 21, 22. It was, in one word, disobedience to an express command. Judgment is given upon it: *Thy carcase shall not come to the sepulchre of thy fathers,* that is, "Thou shalt never reach thy own house, but shalt be a carcase quickly, nor shall thy dead body be brought to *the place of thy fathers' sepulchres,* to be interred." 2. Yet it was more strange that the old prophet himself should be the messenger. Of this we can give no account but that God would have it so, as he spoke to Balaam by his ass and read Saul his doom by the devil in Samuel's likeness. We may think God designed hereby, (1.) To startle the lying prophet, and make him sensible of his sin. The message could not but affect him the more when he himself had the delivering of it, and had so strong an impression made upon his spirit by it that he cried out, as one in an agony, *v.* 21. He had reason to think, if he must die for his disobedience in a small matter who sinned by surprise, of how much sorer punishment he should be thought worthy who had belied an angel of God and cheated a man of God by a deliberate forgery. *If this were done to the green tree, what shall be done to the dry?* Perhaps it had a good effect upon him. Those who preach God's wrath to others have hard hearts indeed if they fear it not themselves. (2.) To put the greater mortification upon the prophet that was deceived, and to show what those must expect who hearken to the great deceiver. Those that yield to him as a tempter will be terrified by him as a tormentor; whom he now fawns upon he will afterwards fly upon, and whom he now draws into sin he will do what he can to drive to despair.

Verses 23–34

Here is, I. The death of the deceived disobedient prophet. The old prophet that had deluded him, as if he would make him some amends for the wrong he had done him or help to prevent the mischief threatened him, furnished him with an ass to ride home on; but by the way a lion set upon him, and killed him, *v.* 23, 24. He did but return back to refresh himself when he was hungry, and behold he must die for it; see 1 Sa. 14:43. But we must consider, 1. That his offence was great, and it would by no means justify him that he was drawn into it by a lie; he could not be so certain of the countermand sent by another as he was of the command given to himself, nor had he any ground to think that the command would be recalled, when the reason of it remained in force, which was that he might testify his detestation of the wickedness of that place. He had great reason to suspect the honesty of this old prophet, who did not himself bear his testimony, nor did God think fit to make use of him as a witness against the idolatry of the city he lived in. However, he should have taken time to beg direction from God, and not have complied so soon. Did he think this old prophet's house safer to eat in than other houses at Beth-el, when God had forbidden him to eat in any? That was to refine upon the command, and make himself wiser than God. Did he think to excuse himself that he was hungry? Had he never read that *man lives not by bread alone?* 2. That his death was for the glory of God; for by this it appeared, (1.) That nothing is more provoking to him than disobedience to an express command, though in a small matter, which makes his proceedings against our first parents, for eating the forbidden fruit, the easier to be accounted for. (2.) That God is displeased at the sins of his own people, and no man shall be protected in disobedience by the sanctity of his profession, the dignity of his office, his nearness to God, or any good services he has done for him. Perhaps God by this intended, in a way of righteous judgment, to harden Jeroboam's heart, since he was not reformed by the withering of his hand; for he would be apt to make a bad use of it, and to say that the prophet was well enough served for meddling with his altar, he had better have staid at home; any, he would say that Providence had punished him for his insolence, and the lion had done that which his withered hand might not do. However, by this God intended to warn all those whom he employs strictly to observe their orders, at their peril.

II. The wonderful preservation of his dead body, which was a token of God's mercy remembered in the midst of wrath. The lion that gently strangled him, or tore him, did not devour his dead body, nor so much as tear the ass, *v.* 24, 25, 26. Nay, what was more, he did not set upon the travellers that passed by and saw it, nor upon the old prophet (who had reason enough to fear it) when he came to take up the corpse. His commission was to kill the prophet; hitherto he should go, but no further. Thus God showed that, though he was angry with him, his anger was turned away, and the punishment went *no further than death.*

III. The care which the old prophet took of his burial. When he heard of this unusual accident, he concluded it was *the man of God, who was disobedient* to his Master (and whose fault was that?), *therefore the Lord has delivered him to the lion, v.* 26. It would well have become him to ask why the lion was not sent against him and his house, rather than against the good man whom he had cheated. He *took up the corpse, v.* 29. If there by any truth in the vulgar opinion, surely the corpse bled afresh when he touched it, for he was in effect the murderer, and it was but a poor reparation for the injury to inter the dead body. Perhaps when he cheated him into his ruin he intended to laugh at him; yet now his conscience so far relents that he weeps over him, and, like Joab at Abner's funeral, is compelled to be a mourner for him whom he had been the death of. They said, *Alas! my brother, v.* 30. The case was indeed very lamentable that so good a man, a prophet so faithful, and so bold in God's cause, should, for one offence, die as a criminal, while an old lying prophet lives at ease and an idolatrous prince in pomp and power. *Thy way, O God! is in the sea, and thy path in the great waters.* We cannot judge of men by their sufferings, nor of sins by their present punishments; with some the flesh is destroyed that the spirit may be saved, while with others the flesh is pampered that the soul may ripen for hell.

IV. The charge which the old prophet gave his sons concerning his own burial, that they should be sure to bury him in the same grave where the man of God was buried (*v.* 3): *"Lay my bones beside his bones,* close by them, as near as may be, so that my dust may mingle with his." Though he was a lying prophet, yet he desired to *die the death of a* true prophet. "Gather not my soul with the sinners of Beth-el, but with the man of God." The reason he gives is because *what he cried against the altar of Beth-el,* that men's bones should be burnt upon it, *shall surely come to pass, v.* 32. Thus, 1. He ratifies the prediction, that *out of the mouth of two witnesses* (and one of them such a one as St. Paul quotes, Titus 1:12, *one of themselves, even a prophet of their own)*— the *word might be established,* if possible to convince and reclaim Jeroboam. 2. He does honour to the deceased prophet, as one whose *word* would not fall to the ground, though *he* did. Ministers die, die prematurely it may be; but the word of the Lord endures for ever, and does not die with them. 3. He consults his own interest. It was foretold that men's bones should be burnt upon Jeroboam's altar: "Lay mine (says he) close to his, and then they will not be disturbed;" and it was, accordingly, their security, as we find, 2 Ki. 23:18. Sleeping and waking, living and dying, it is safe being in good company. No mention is made here of the inscription on the prophet's tomb; but it is spoken of 2 Ki. 23:17, where Josiah asks, *What title is that?* and is told, *It is the sepulchre of the man of God that came from Judah, who proclaimed these things which thou hast done;* so that the epitaph upon the prophet's grave preserved the remembrance of his prophecy, and was a standing testimony against the idolatries of Beth-el, which it would not have been so remarkably if he had died and been buried elsewhere. The cities of Israel are here called *cities of Samaria,* though that name was not yet known; for, however the old prophet spoke, the inspired historian wrote in the language of his own time.

V. The obstinacy of Jeroboam in his idolatry (*v.* 33): *He returned not from his evil way;* some hand was found that durst repair the altar God had rent, and then Jeroboam offered sacrifice on it again, and the more boldly because the prophet who disturbed him before was in his grave (Rev. 11:10) and because the prophecy was for a great while to come. Various methods had been used to reclaim him, but neither threats nor signs, neither judgments nor mercies, wrought upon him, so strangely was he wedded to his calves. He did not reform, no, not his priesthood, but whoever would, he filled his hand, and made him priest, though ever so illiterate or immoral, and of what tribe soever; *and this became sin,* that is, a snare first, and then a ruin, to Jeroboam's house, to *cut if off, v.* 34. Note, The diminution, disquiet, and desolation of families, are the fruit of sin; he promised himself that the calves would secure the crown to his family, but it proved they lost it, and sunk his family. Those betray themselves that think by any sin to support themselves.

CHAPTER 14

The kingdom being divided into that of Judah and that of Israel, we must henceforward, in these books of Kings, expect and attend their separate history, the succession of their kings, and the affairs of their kingdoms, accounted for distinctly. In this chapter we have, I. The prophecy of the destruction of Jeroboam's house (*v.* 7–16). The sickness of his child was the occasion of it (*v.* 1–6), and the death of his child the earnest of it (*v.* 17, 18), together with the conclusion of his reign (*v.* 19, 20). II. The history of the declension and diminution of Rehoboam's house and kingdom (*v.* 21–28) and the conclusion of his reign (*v.* 29–31). In both we may read the mischievous consequences of sin and the calamities it brings on kingdoms and families.

Verses 1–6

How Jeroboam persisted in his contempt of God and religion we read in the close of the foregoing chapter. Here we are told how God proceeded in his controversy with him; for when God judges he will overcome, and sinners shall either bend or break before him.

I. His child fell sick, *v.* 1. It is probable that he was his eldest son, and heir-apparent to the crown; for at his death all the kingdom went into mourning for him, *ch.* 13. His dignity as a prince, his age as a young prince, and his interest in heaven as a pious prince, could not exempt him from sickness, dangerous sickness. Let none be secure of the continuance of their health, but improve it, while it continues, for the best purposes. Lord, *behold, he whom thou lovest,* thy favourite, he whom Israel loves, their darling, *is sick. At that time,* when Jeroboam prostituted the profaned the priesthood (*ch.* 13:33), his child sickened. When sickness comes into our families we should enquire whether there be not some particular sin harboured in our houses, which the affliction is sent to convince us of and reclaim us from.

II. He sent his wife in disguise to enquire of Ahijah the prophet *what should become of the child, v.* 2, 3. The sickness of his child touched him in a tender part. The withering of this branch of the family would, perhaps, be as sore an affliction to him as the withering of that branch of his body, *ch.* 13:4. Such is the force of natural affection; our children are ourselves but once removed. Now,

1. Jeroboam's great desire, under this affliction, is to know *what shall become of the child,* whether he will live or die. (1.) It would have been more prudent if he had desired to know what means they should use for the recovery of the child, what they should give him, and what they should do to him; but by this instance, and those of Ahaziah (2 Ki. 1:2) and Benhadad (2 Ki. 8:8), it should seem they had then such a foolish notion of fatality as took them off from all use of means; for, if they were sure the patient would live, they thought means needless; if he would die, they thought them useless; not considering that duty is ours, events are God's, and that he that ordained the end ordained the means. Why should a prophet be desired to show that which a little time will show? (2.) It would have been more pious if he had desired to know wherefore God contended with him, had begged the prophet's prayers, and cast away his idols from him; then the child might have been restored to him, as his hand was. But most people would rather be told their fortune than their faults or their duty.

2. That he might know the child's doom, he sent to Ahijah the prophet, who lived obscurely and neglected in Shiloh, blind through age, yet still blest with the visions of the Almighty, which need not bodily eyes, but are rather favoured by the want of them, the eyes of the mind being then most intent and least diverted. Jeroboam sent not to him for advice about the setting up of his calves, or the consecrating of his priests, but had recourse to him in his distress, when the gods he served could give him no relief. *Lord, in trouble have those visited thee* who before slighted thee. Some have by sickness been reminded of their forgotten ministers and praying friends. He sent to Ahijah, because he had *told him he should be king, v.* 2. "He was once the messenger of good tidings, surely he will be so again." Those that by sin disqualify themselves for comfort, and yet expect their ministers, because they are good men, should speak peace and comfort to them, greatly wrong both themselves and their ministers.

3. He sent his wife to enquire of the prophet, because she could best put the question without naming names, or making any other description than this, "Sir, I have a son ill; will he recover or not?" The heart of her husband safely trusted in her that she would be faithful both in delivering the message and bringing him the answer; and it seems there were none of all his counsellors in whom he could repose such a confidence; otherwise the sick child could very ill spare her, for mothers are the best nurses, and it would have been much fitter for her to have staid at home to tend him than go to Shiloh to enquire what would become of him. If she go, she must be *incognito — in disguise,* must change her dress, cover her face, and go by another name, not only to conceal herself from her own court and the country through which she passed (as if it were below her quality to go upon such an errand, and what she had reason to be ashamed of, as Nicodemus that came to Jesus by night, whereas it is no disparagement to the greatest to attend God's prophets), but also to conceal herself from the prophet himself, that he might only answer her question concerning her son, and not enter upon the unpleasing subject of her husband's defection. Thus some people love to prescribe to their ministers, limit them to smooth things, and care not for having the *whole counsel of God declared* to them, lest it prove to prophesy *no good concerning them, but evil.* But what a strange notion had Jeroboam of God's prophet when he believed that he could and would certainly tell what would *become of the child,* and yet either could not or would not discover who was the mother! Could he see into the thick darkness of futurity, and yet not see through the thin veil of this disguise? Did Jeroboam think the God of Israel like his calves, just what he pleased? *Be not deceived, God is not mocked.*

III. God gave Ahijah notice of the approach of Jeroboam's wife, and that she came in disguise, and full instructions what to say to her (*v.* 5), which enabled him, as she came in at the door, to call her by her name, to her great surprise, and so to discover to all about him who she was (*v.* 6): *Come in, thou wife of Jeroboam, why feignest thou thyself to be another?* He had no regard, 1. To her rank. She was a queen, but what was that to him, who had a message to deliver to her immediately from God, before whom all the children of men stand upon the same level? Nor, 2. To her present. It was usual for those who consulted prophets to bring them tokens of respect, which they accepted, and yet were no hirelings. She brought him a handsome country present (*v.* 3), but he did not think himself obliged by that to give her any finer language than the nature of her message required. Nor, 3. To her industrious concealment of herself. It is a piece of civility not to take notice of those who desire not to be taken notice of; but the prophet was no courtier, nor gave flattering titles; plain dealing is best, and she shall know, at the first word, what she has to trust to: *I am sent to thee with heavy tidings.* Note, Those who think by their disguises to hide themselves from God will be wretchedly confounded when they find themselves disappointed in the day of discovery. Sinners now appear in the garb of saints, and are taken to be such; but how will they blush and tremble when they find themselves stripped of their false colours, and are called by their own name: "Go out, thou treacherous false-hearted hypocrite. *I never knew thee. Why feignest thou thyself to be another?*" Tidings of a portion with hypocrites will be heavy tidings. God will judge men according to what they are, not according to what they seem.

Verses 7–20

When those that set up idols, and keep them up, go to enquire of the Lord, he determines to answer them, not according to the pretensions of their enquiry, but *according to the multitude of their idols,* Eze. 14:4. So Jeroboam is answered here.

I. The prophet anticipates the enquiry concerning the child, and foretels the ruin of Jeroboam's house for the wickedness of it. No one else durst have carried such a message: a servant would have smothered it, but his own wife cannot be suspected of ill-will to him.

1. God calls himself the *Lord God of Israel.* Though Israel had forsaken God, God had not cast them off, nor given them a bill of divorce for their whoredoms. He is Israel's God, and therefore will take vengeance on him who did them the greatest mischief he could do them, debauched them and drew them away from God.

2. He upbraids Jeroboam with the great favour he had bestowed upon him, in making him king, exalting him from among the people, the common people, to be prince over God's chosen Israel, and taking the kingdom *from the house of David,* to bestow it upon him. Whether we keep an account of God's mercies to us or no, he does, and will set even them in order before us, if we be ungrateful, to our greater confusion; otherwise he gives and upbraids not.

3. He charges him with his impiety and apostasy, and his idolatry particularly: *Thou hast done evil above all that were before thee, v.* 9. Saul, that was rejected, never worshipped idols; Solomon did it but occasionally, in his dotage, and never made Israel to sin. Jeroboam's calves, though pretended to be set up in honour of the God of Israel, that brought *them up out of Egypt,* yet are here called *other gods,* or *strange gods,* because in them he worshipped God as the heathen worshipped their strange gods, because by them he *changed the truth of God into a lie* and represented him as altogether different from what he is, and because many of the ignorant worshippers terminated their devotion in the image, and did not at all regard the God of Israel. Though they were calves of gold, the richness of the metal was so far from making them acceptable to God that they *provoked him to anger,* designedly affronted him, under colour of pleasing him. In doing this, (1.) He had not set David before him (*v.* 8): *Thou hast not been as my servant David,* who, though he had his faults and some bad ones, yet never forsook the worship of God nor grew loose nor cold to that; his faithful adherence to that gained him this honourable character, that he *followed God with all his heart,* and herein he was proposed for an example to all his successors. Those did not do well that did not do like David. (2.) He had not *set God before him,* but (*v.* 9), *"Thou hast cast me behind thy back,* my law, my fear; thou hast neglected me, forgotten me, and preferred thy policies before my precepts."

4. He foretels the utter ruin of Jeroboam's house, *v.* 10, 11. He thought, by his idolatry, to establish his government, and by that he not only lost it, but brought destruction upon his family, the universal destruction of all the males, whether shut up or left, married or unmarried. (1.) Shameful destruction. They shall be taken away as dung, which is loathsome and which men are glad to be rid of. He worshipped dunghill-deities, and God removed his family as a great dunghill. Noble and royal families, if wicked, are no better in God's account. (2.) Unusual destruction. Their very dead bodies should be meat for the dogs in the street, or the birds of prey in the field, *v.* 11. Thus evil pursues sinners. See this fulfilled, *ch.* 15:29.

5. He foretels the immediate death of the sick child, *v.* 12, 13.

(1.) In mercy to him, lest, if he live, he be infected with the sin, and so involved in the ruin, of his father's house. Observe the character given of him: *In him was found some good thing towards the Lord God of Israel, in the house of Jeroboam.* He had an affection for the true worship of God and disliked the worship of the calves. Note, [1.] Those are good *in whom are good things towards the Lord God of Israel,* good inclinations, good intentions, good desires, towards him. [2.] Where there is but *some* good thing of that kind it will be found: God, who seeks it, sees it be it ever so little and is pleased with it. [3.] A little grace goes a great way with great people. It is so rare to find princes well affected to religion that, when they are so, they are worthy of double honour. [4.] Pious dispositions are in a peculiar manner amiable and acceptable when they are found in those that are young. The divine image in miniature has a peculiar beauty and lustre in it. [5.] Those that are good in bad times and places shine very brightly in the eyes of God. A good child *in the house of Jeroboam* is a miracle of divine grace: to be there untainted is like being in the fiery furnace unhurt, unsinged. Observe the care taken of him: he only, of all Jeroboam's family, shall die in honour, shall be buried, and shall be lamented as one that lived desired. Note, Those that are distinguished by divine grace shall be distinguished by divine providence. This hopeful child dies first of all the family, for God often *takes those soonest whom he loves best.* Heaven is the fittest place for them; this earth is not worthy of them.

(2.) In wrath to the family. [1.] It was a sign the family would be ruined when *he* was taken by whom it might have been reformed. The righteous are removed from the evil to come in this world, to the good to come in a better world. It is a bad omen to a family when the best in it are buried out of it; when what was valuable is picked out the rest is for the fire. [2.] It was likewise a present affliction to the family and kingdom, by which both ought to have been bettered; and this aggravated the affliction to the poor mother that she should not reach home time enough to see her son alive: *When thy feet enter into the city,* just then *the child shall die.* This was to be a sign to her of the accomplishment of the rest of the threatenings, as 1 Sa. 2:34.

6. He foretels the setting up of another family to rule over Israel, *v.* 14. This was fulfilled in Baasha of Issachar, who conspired against Nadab the son of Jeroboam, in the second year of his reign, murdered him and all his family. *"But what? Even now.* Why do I speak of it as a thing at a distance? It is at the door. It shall be done *even now."* Sometimes God makes quick work with sinners; he did so with the house of Jeroboam. It was not twenty-four years from his first elevation to the final extirpation of his family.

7. He foretels the judgments which should come upon the people of Israel for conforming to the worship which Jeroboam had established. *If the blind lead the blind,* both the blind leaders and the blind followers shall *fall into the ditch.* It is here foretold, *v.* 15, (1.) That they should never be easy, nor rightly settled in their land, but continually *shaken like a reed in the water.* After they left the house of David, the government never continued long in one family, but one undermined and destroyed another, which must needs occasion great disorders and disturbances among the people. (2.) That they should, ere long, be totally expelled out of their land, that good land, and given up to ruin, *v.* 16. This was fulfilled in the captivity of the ten tribes by the king of Assyria. Families and kingdoms are ruined by sin, ruined by the wickedness of the heads of them. *Jeroboam did sin, and made Israel to sin.* If great men do wickedly, they involve many others both in the guilt and in the snare; multitudes *follow their pernicious ways.* They go to hell with a long train, and their condemnation will be the more intolerable, for they must answer, not only for their own sins, but for the sins which others have been drawn into and kept in by their influence.

II. Jeroboam's wife has nothing to say against the word of the Lord, but she goes home with a heavy heart to their house in *Tirzah,* a *sweet delightful place,* so the name signifies, famed for its beauty, Cant. 6:4. But death, which will stain its beauty and embitter all its delights, cannot be shut out from it. Hither she came, and here we leave her attending the funeral of her son, and expecting the fate of her family. 1. *The child died* (*v.* 17), and justly did all Israel mourn, not only for the loss of so hopeful a prince, whom they were not worthy of, but because his death plucked up the flood-gates, and made a breach, at which an inundation of judgments broke in. 2. Jeroboam himself died soon after, *v.* 20. It is said (2 Chr. 13:20), *The Lord struck him* with some sore disease, so that he died miserably, when he had reigned twenty-two years, and left his crown to a son who lost it, and his life too, and all the lives of his family, within two years after. For a further account of him the reader is referred to the annals of his reign, drawn up by his own secretaries, or to the public records, like those in the Tower, called here, *The Book* or register, *of the Chronicles of the Kings of Israel,* to which recourse might then be had; but, not being divinely inspired, these records are long since lost.

Verses 21–31

Judah's story and Israel's are intermixed in this book. Jeroboam out-lived Rehoboam, four or five years, yet his history is despatched first, that the account of Rehoboam's reign may be laid together; and a sad account it is.

I. Here is no good said of the king. All the account we have of him here is, 1. That he was forty-one years old when he began to reign, by which reckoning he was born in the last year of David, and had his education, and the forming of his mind, in the best days of Solomon; yet he lived not up to these advantages. Solomon's defection at last did more to corrupt him than his wisdom and devotion had done to give him good principles. 2. That he reigned seventeen years in Jerusalem, *the city where God put his name,* where he had opportunity enough to know his duty, if he had but had a heart to do it. 3. That his mother was Naamah, an Ammonitess; this is twice mentioned, *v.* 21, 31. It was strange that David would marry his son Solomon to an Ammonitess (for it was done while he lived), but it is probable that Solomon was in love with her, because she was *Naamah,* a *beauty* (so it signifies), and his father was loth to cross him, but it proved to have a very bad influence upon posterity. Probably she was daughter to Shobi the Ammonite, who was kind to David (2 Sa. 17:27), and David was too willing to requite him by matching his son into his family. None can imagine how lasting and how fatal the consequences may be of being unequally yoked with unbelievers. 4. That he had continual war with Jeroboam (*v.* 30), which could not but be a perpetual uneasiness to him. 5. That when he had reigned but seventeen years he died, and left his throne to his son. His father, and grandfather, and grandson, that reigned well, reigned long, forty years apiece. But sin often shortens men's lives and comforts.

II. Here is much evil said of the subjects, both as to their character and their condition.

1. See here how wicked and profane they were. It is a most sad account that is here given of their apostasy from God, *v.* 22–24. Judah, the only professing people God had in the world, *did evil in his sight,* in contempt and defiance of him and the tokens of his special presence with them; *they provoked him to jealousy,* as the adulterous wife provokes her husband by breaking the marriage-covenant. Their fathers had been bad enough, especially in the times of the judges, but they did abominable things, *above all that their fathers had done.* The magnificence of their temple, the pomp of their priesthood, and all the secular advantages with which their religion was attended, could not prevail to keep them to it. Nothing less than the *pouring out of the Spirit from on high* will keep God's Israel in their allegiance to him. The account here given of the wickedness of the Jews agrees with that which the apostle gives of the wickedness of the Gentile world (Rom. 1:21, 24), so that both *Jew and Gentile are* alike *under sin,* Rom. 3:9. (1.) They became *vain in their imaginations* concerning God, and *changed his glory into an image,* for they built themselves *high places, images, and groves* (*v.* 23), profaning God's name by affixing to it their images, and God's ordinances by serving their idols with them. They foolishly fancies that they exalted God when they worshipped him on high hills and pleased him when they worshipped him under the pleasant shadow of green trees. (2.) They were given up to vile affections (as those idolaters Rom. 1:26, 27), for there were *sodomites in the land* (*v.* 24), *men with men working that which is unseemly,* and not to be thought of, much less mentioned, without abhorrence and indignation. They dishonoured God by one sin and then God left them to dishonour themselves by another. They profaned the privileges of a holy nation, therefore God gave them up to their own hearts' lusts, to imitate the abominations of the accursed Canaanites; and herein the Lord was righteous. And, when they did *like those that were cast out,* how could they expect any other than to be cast out like them?

2. See here how weak and poor they were; and this was the consequence of the former. Sin exposes, impoverishes, and weakens any people. Shishak, king of Egypt, came against them, and so far, either by force or surrender, made himself master of Jerusalem itself that he took away the treasures both of the temple and of the exchequer, of the house of the Lord and of the king's house, which David and Solomon had amassed, *v.* 25, 26. These, it is likely, tempted him to make his descent; and, to save the rest, Rehoboam perhaps tamely surrendered them, as Ahab, *ch.* 20:4. He also took away the golden shields that were made but in his father's time, *v.* 26. These the king of Egypt carried off as trophies of his victory; and, instead of them, Rehoboam made brazen shields, which the lifeguard carried before him when he went to church in state, *v.* 27, 28. This was an emblem of the diminution of his glory. Sin makes the gold become dim, changes the most fine gold, and turns it into brass. We commend Rehoboam for going to *the house of the Lord,* perhaps the oftener for the rebuke he had been under, and do not condemn him for going in pomp. Great men should honour God with their honour, and then they are themselves most honoured by it.

CHAPTER 15

In this chapter we have an abstract of the history, I. Of two of the kings of Judah, Abijam, the days of whose reign were few and evil (*v.* 1–8), and Asa, who reigned well and long (*v.* 9–24). II. Of two of the kings of Israel, Nadab the son of Jeroboam, and Baasha the destroyer of Jeroboam's house (*v.* 25–34).

Verses 1–8

We have here a short account of the short reign of Abijam the son of Rehoboam king of Judah. He makes a better figure, 2 Chr. 13, where we have an account of his war with Jeroboam, the speech which he made before the armies engaged, and the wonderful victory he obtained by the help of God. There he is called *Abijah — My father is the Lord,* because no wickedness is there laid to his charge. But here, where we are told of his faults, *Jah,* the name of God, is, in disgrace to him, taken away from his name, and he is called *Abijam.* See Jer. 22:24.

I. Few particulars are related concerning him. 1. Here began his reign in the beginning of Jeroboam's eighteenth year; for Rehoboam reigned but seventeen, *ch.* 14:21. Jeroboam indeed survived Rehoboam, but Rehoboam's Abijah lived to succeed him and to be a terror to Jeroboam, while Jeroboam's Abijah (whom we read of *ch.* 14:1) died before him. 2. He reigned scarcely three years, for he died before the end of Jeroboam's twentieth year, *v.* 9. Being made proud and secure by his great victory over Jeroboam (2 Chr. 13:21), God cut him off, to make way for his son Asa, who would be a better man. 3. *His mother's name was Maachah, the daughter of Abishalom,* that is, Absalom, David's son, as I am the rather inclined to think because two other of Rehoboam's wives were his near relations (2 Chr. 11:18), one the daughter of Jerimoth, David's son, and another the daughter of Eliab, David's brother. He took warning by his father not to marry strangers; yet thought it below him to marry his subjects, except they were of the royal family. 4. He carried on his father's wars with Jeroboam. As there was continual war between Rehoboam and Jeroboam, not set battles (these were forbidden, *ch.* 12:24), but frequent encounters, especially upon the borders, one making incursions and reprisals on the other, so there was between Abijam and Jeroboam (*v.* 7), till Jeroboam, with a great army, invaded him, and then Abijam, not being forbidden to act in his own defence, routed him, and weakened him, so that he compelled him to be quiet during the rest of his reign, 2 Chr. 13:20.

II. But, in general, we are told, 1. That he was not like David, had no hearty affection for the ordinances of God, though, to serve his purpose against Jeroboam, he pleaded his possession of the temple and priesthood, as that upon which he valued himself, 2 Chr. 13:10–12. Many boast of their profession of godliness who are strangers to the power of it, and plead the truth of their religion who yet are not true to it. *His heart was not perfect with the Lord his God.* He seemed to have zeal, but he wanted sincerity; he began pretty well, but he fell off, and *walked in all the sins of his father,* followed his bad example, though he had seen the bad consequences of it. He that was all his days in war ought to have been so wise as to make and keep his peace with God, and not to make him his enemy, especially having found him so good a friend in his war with Jeroboam, 2 Chr. 13:18. *Let favour be shown to the wicked, yet will he not learn righteousness,* Isa. 26:10. 2. That yet it was for David's sake that he was advanced, and continued upon the throne; it was *for his sake* (v. 4, 5) that God thus *set up his son after him;* not for his own sake, nor for the sake of his father, in whose steps he trod, *but for the sake of David,* whose example he would not follow. Note, it aggravates the sin of a degenerate seed that they fare the better for the piety of their ancestors and owe their blessings to it, and yet will not imitate it. They stand upon that ground, and yet despise it, and trample upon it, and unreasonably ridicule and oppose that which they enjoy the benefit of. The kingdom of Judah was supported, (1.) That David might have a lamp, pursuant to the divine ordination of *a lamp for his anointed,* Ps. 132:17. (2.) That Jerusalem might be established, not only that the honours put upon it in David's and Solomon's time might be preserved to it, but that it might be reserved to the honours designed for it in after-times. The character here given of David is very great — *that he did that which was right in the eyes of the Lord;* but the exception is very remarkable — *save only in the matter of Uriah,* including both his murder and the debauching of his wife. That was a bad matter; it was a remaining blot upon his name, a bar in his escutcheon, and the reproach of it was not wiped away, though the guilt was. David was guilty of other faults, but they were nothing in comparison of that; yet even that being repented of, though it be mentioned for warning to others, did not prevail to throw him out of the covenant, nor to cut off the entail of the promise upon his seed.

Verses 9–24

We have here a short account of the reign of Asa; we shall find a more copious history of it 2 Chr. 14, 15, and 16. Here is,

I. The length of it: *He reigned forty-one years in Jerusalem, v.* 10. In the account we have of the kings of Judah we find the number of the good kings and the bad ones nearly equal; but then we may observe, to our comfort, that the reign of the good kings was generally long, but that of the bad kings short, the consideration of which will make the state of God's church not altogether so bad within that period as it appears at first sight. Length of days is in Wisdom's right hand. *Honour thy father,* much more thy heavenly Father, *that thy days may be long.*

II. The general good character of it (v. 11): *Asa did that which was right in the eyes of the Lord,* and that is right indeed which is so in God's eyes; those are approved whom he commends. He did *as did David his father,* kept close to God, and to his instituted worship, was hearty and zealous for that, which gave him this honourable character, that he was like David, though he was not a prophet, or psalmist, as David was. If we come up to the graces of those that have gone before us it will be our praise with God, though we come short of their gifts. Asa was like David, though he was neither such a conqueror nor such an author; for *his heart was perfect with the Lord all his days* (v. 14), that is, he was both cordial and constant in his religion. What he did for God he was sincere in, steady and uniform, and did it from a good principle, with a single eye to the glory of God.

III. The particular instances of Asa's piety. His times were times of reformation. For,

1. He removed that which was evil. There reformation begins; and a great deal of work of that kind his hand found to do. For, though it was but twenty years after the death of Solomon that he began to reign, yet very gross corruption had spread far and taken deep root. Immorality he first struck at: *He took away the sodomites out of the land,* suppressed the brothels; for how can either prince or people prosper while those cages of unclean and filthy birds, more dangerous than pest-houses, are suffered to remain? Then he proceeded against idolatry: *He removed all the idols,* even those *that his father had made, v.* 12. His father having made them, he was the more concerned to remove them, that he might cut off the entail of the curse, and prevent the visiting of that iniquity upon him and his. Nay (which redounds much to his honour, and shows his heart was perfect with God), when he found idolatry in the court, he rooted it out thence, *v.* 13. When it appeared that Maachah his mother, or rather his grandmother (but called his *mother* because she had the educating of him in his childhood), had an idol in a grove, though she was his mother, his grandmother, — though,

it is likely, she had a particular fondness for it, — though, being old, she could not live long to patronise it, — though she kept it for her own use only, yet he would by no means connive at her idolatry. Reformation must begin at home. Bad practices will never be suppressed in the country while they are supported in the court. Asa, in every thing else, will honour and respect his mother; he loves her well, but he loves God better, and (like the Levite, Deu. 33:9) readily forgets the relation when it comes in competition with his duty. If she be an idolater, (1.) Her idol shall be destroyed, publicly exposed to contempt, defaced, and burnt to ashes *by the brook Kidron,* on which, it is probable, he strewed the ashes, in imitation of Moses (Ex. 32:20) and in token of his detestation of idolatry and his indignation at it wherever he found it. Let no remains of a court-idol appear. (2.) She shall be deposed, He removed her from being queen, or from the queen, that is, from conversing with his wife; he banished her from the court, and confined her to an obscure and private life. Those that have power are happy when thus they have hearts to use it well.

2. He re-established that which was good (v. 15): He *brought into the house of God the dedicated things* which he himself had vowed out of the spoils of the Ethiopians he had conquered, and which his father had vowed, but lived not to bring in pursuant to his vow. We must not only cease to do evil, but learn to do well, not only cast away the idols of our iniquity, but dedicate ourselves and our all to God's honour and glory. When those who, in their infancy, were by baptism devoted to God, make it their own act and deed to join themselves to him and vigorously employ themselves in his service, this is bringing in the dedicated things which they and their fathers have dedicated: it is necessary justice — rendering to God the things that are his.

VI. The policy of his reign. He built cities himself, to encourage the increase of his people (v. 23) and to invite others to him by the conveniences of habitation; and he was very zealous to hinder Baasha from building Ramah, because he designed it for the cutting off of communication between his people and Jerusalem and to hinder those who in obedience to God would come to worship there. An enemy must by no means be suffered to fortify a frontier town.

V. The faults of his reign. In both the things for which he was praised he was found defective. The fairest characters are not without some *but* or other in them. 1. Did he take away the idols? That was well; *but the high places were not removed* (v. 14); therein his reformation fell short. He removed all images which were rivals with the true God or false representations of him; but the altars which were set up in high places, and to which those sacrifices were brought which should have been offered on the altar in the temple, those he suffered to stand, thinking there was no great harm in them, they having been used by good men before the temple was built, and being loth to disoblige the people, who had a kindness to them and were wedded to them both by custom and convenience; whereas in Judah and Benjamin, the only tribes under Asa's government which lay so near Jerusalem and the altars there, there was less pretence for them than in those tribes which lay more remote. They were against the law, which obliged them to worship *at one place,* Deu. 12:11. They lessened men's esteem of the temple and the altars there, and were an open gap for idolatry to enter in at, while the people were so much addicted to it. It was not well that Asa, when his hand was in, did not remove these. *Nevertheless his heart was perfect with the Lord.* This affords us a comfortable note, That those may be found honest and upright with God, and be accepted of him, who yet, in some instances, come short of doing the good they might and should do. The perfection which is made the indispensable condition of the new covenant is not to be understood of sinlessness (then we were all undone), but sincerity. 2. Did he bring in the dedicated things? That was well; but he afterwards alienated the dedicated things, when he took the gold and silver out of the house of God and sent them as a bribe to Benhadad, to hire him to break his league with Baasha, and, by making an inroad upon his country, to give him a diversion from the building of Ramah, *v.* 18, 19. Here he sinned, (1.) In tempting Benhadad to break his league, and so to violate the public faith. If he did wrong in doing it, as certainly he did, Asa did

wrong in persuading him to do it. (2.) In that he could not trust God, who had done so much for him, to free him out of this strait, without using such indirect means to help himself. (3.) In taking the gold out of the treasury of the temple, which was not to be made use of but on extraordinary occasions. The project succeeded. Benhadad made a descent upon the land of Israel, which obliged Baasha to retire with his whole force from Ramah (v. 20, 21), which gave Asa a fair opportunity to demolish his works there, and the timber and stones served him for the building of some cities of his own, v. 22. But, though the design prospered, we find it was displeasing to God; and though Asa valued himself upon the policy of it, and promised himself that it would effectually secure his peace, he was told by the prophet that he had done foolishly, and that *thenceforth he should have wars;* see 2 Chr. 16:7–9.

VI. The troubles of his reign. For the most part he prospered; but, 1. Baasha king of Israel was a very troublesome neighbour to him. He reigned twenty-four years, and all his days had war, more or less, with Asa, v. 16. This was the effect of the division of the kingdoms, that they were continually vexing one another, and so weakened one another, which made them both an easier prey to the common enemy. 2. In his old age he was himself afflicted with the gout: He was *diseased in his feet,* which made him less fit for business and peevish towards those about him.

VII. The conclusion of his reign. The acts of it were more largely recorded in the common history (to which reference is here had, *v.* 23) than in this sacred one. He reigned long, but finished at last with honour, and left his throne to a successor no way inferior to him.

Verses 25–34

We are now to take a view of the miserable state of Israel, while the kingdom of Judah was happy under Asa's good government. It was threatened that they should be as *a reed shaken in the water* (ch. 14:15), and so they were, when, during the single reign of Asa, the government of their kingdom was in six or seven different hands, as we find in this and the following chapter. Jeroboam was upon the throne in the beginning of his reign and Ahab at the end of it, and between them were Nadab, Baasha, Elah, Zimri, Tibni, and Omri, undermining and destroying one another. This they got by deserting the house both of God and of David. Here we have, 1. The ruin and extirpation of the family of Jeroboam, according to the word of the Lord by Ahijah. His son Nadab succeeded him. If the death of his brother Abijah had had a due influence upon him to make him religious, and the honour done him at his death had engaged him to follow his good example, his reign might have been long and glorious; but he *walked in the way of his father* (v. 26), kept up the worship of his calves, and forbade his subjects to go up to Jerusalem to worship, *sinned and made Israel to sin,* and therefore God brought ruin upon him quickly, in the second year of his reign. He was besieging Gibbethon, a city which the Philistines had taken from the Danites, and was endeavouring to re-take it; and there, in the midst of his army, did Baasha, with others, conspire against him and kill him, (v. 27), and so little interest had he in the affections of his people that his army did not only not avenge his death, but chose his murderer for his successor. Whether Baasha did it upon a personal pique against Nadab, or to be avenged on the house of Jeroboam for some affront received from them, or whether under pretence of freeing his country from the tyranny of a bad prince, or whether merely from a principle of ambition, to make way for himself to the throne, does not appear; but he *slew him and reigned in his stead,* v. 28. And the first thing he did when he came to the crown was to *cut off all the house of Jeroboam,* that he might the better secure himself and his own usurped government. He thought it not enough to imprison or banish them, but he destroyed them, left not only no males (as was foretold, *ch.* 14:10), but none that breathed. Herein he was barbarous, but God was righteous. Jeroboam's sin was punished (v. 30); for those that provoke God do it *to their own confusion;* see Jer. 7:19. Ahijah's prophecy was accomplished (v. 29); for no word of God shall fall to the ground. Divine threatenings are not bugbears. 2. The elevation of Baasha. He shall be tried awhile, as Jeroboam was. Twenty-four years he reigned (v. 33), but showed that it was not from any dislike to

Jeroboam's sin that he destroyed his family, but from malice and ambition; for, when he had rooted out the sinner, he himself clave to the sin, and *walked in the way of Jeroboam* (*v.* 34), though he had seen the end of that way; so strangely was his heart hardened with the deceitfulness of sin.

CHAPTER 16

This chapter relates wholly to the kingdom of Israel, and the revolutions of that kingdom — many in a little time. The utter ruin of Jeroboam's family, after it had been twenty-four years a royal family, we read of in the foregoing chapter. In this chapter we have, I. The ruin of Baasha's family, after it had been but twenty-six years a royal family, foretold by a prophet (*v.* 1–7), and executed by Zimri, one of his captains (*v.* 8–14). II. The seven days' reign of Zimri, and his sudden fall (*v.* 15–20). III. The struggle between Omri and Tibni, and Omri's prevalency, and his reign (*v.* 21–28). IV. The beginning of the reign of Ahab, of whom we shall afterwards read much (*v.* 29–33). V. The rebuilding of Jericho (*v.* 34). All this while, in Judah, things went well.

Verses 1–14

Here is, I. The ruin of the family of Baasha foretold. He was a man likely enough to have raised and established his family — active, politic, and daring; but he was an idolater, and this brought destruction upon his family.

1. God sent him warning of it before. (1.) That, if he were thereby wrought upon to repent and reform, the ruin might be prevented; for God threatens, that he may not strike, as one that desires not the death of sinners. (2.) That, if not, it might appear that the destruction when it did come, whoever might be instruments of it, was the act of God's justice and the punishment of sin.

2. The warning was sent by *Jehu the son of Hanani.* The father was a seer, or prophet, at the same time (2 Chr. 16:7), and was sent to Asa king of Judah; but the son, who was young and more active, was sent on this longer and more dangerous expedition to Baasha king of Israel. *Juniores ad labores — Toil and adventure are for the young.* This Jehu was a prophet and the son of a prophet. Prophecy, thus happily entailed, was worthy of so much the more honour. This Jehu continued long in his usefulness, for we find him reproving Jehoshaphat (2 Chr. 19:2) above forty years after, and writing the annals of that prince, 2 Chr. 20:34. The message which this prophet brought to Baasha is much the same with that which Ahijah sent to Jeroboam by his wife.

(1.) He reminds Baasha of the great things God had done for him (*v.* 2): *I exalted thee out of the dust* to the *throne of glory,* a great instance of the divine sovereignty and power, 1 Sa. 2:8. Baasha seemed to have raised himself by his own treachery and cruelty, yet there was a hand of Providence in it, to bring about God's counsel, concerning Jeroboam's house; and God's owning his advancement as his act and deed does by no means amount to the patronising of his ambition and treachery. It is God that puts power into bad men's hands, which he makes to serve his good purposes, notwithstanding the bad use they make of it. *I made thee prince over my people.* God calls Israel his people still, though wretchedly corrupted, because they retained the covenant of circumcision, and there were many good people among them; it was not till long after that they were called *Loammi, not a people,* Hos. 1:9.

(2.) He charges him with high crimes and misdemeanours, [1.] That he had caused *Israel to sin,* had seduced God's subjects from their allegiance and brought them to pay to dunghill-deities the homage due to him only, and herein he had *walked in the way of Jeroboam* (*v.* 2), and been *like his house, v.* 7. [2.] That he had himself *provoked God to anger with the work of his hands,* that is, by worshipping images, the *work of men's hands;* though perhaps others made them, yet he served them and thereby avowed the making of them, and they are therefore called the *work of his hands.* [3.] That he had *destroyed the house of Jeroboam* (*v.* 7), *because he killed him,* namely, Jeroboam's son and all his: if he had done that with an eye to God, to his will and glory, and from a holy indignation against the sins of Jeroboam and his house, he would have been accepted and applauded as a minister of God's justice; but, as he did it, he was only the tool of God's justice, but a servant to his own lusts, and is justly punished for the malice and ambition which actuated and governed him in all he did. Note, Those who are in any way employed in denouncing or executing the justice of God (magistrates or ministers) are concerned to do it from a good principle and in a holy manner, lest it turn into sin to them and they make themselves obnoxious by it.

(3.) He foretels the same destruction to come upon his family which he himself had been employed to bring upon the family of Jeroboam, *v.* 3, 4. Note, Those who resemble others in their sins may expect to resemble them in their plagues, especially those who seem zealous against such sins in others as they allow themselves in; the house of Jehu was reckoned with for the blood of the house of Ahab, Hos. 1:4.

II. A reprieve granted for some time, so long that Baasha himself dies in peace, and is buried with honour in his own royal city (*v.* 6), so far is he from being a prey either to the dogs or to the fowls, which yet was threatened to his house, *v.* 4. He lives not either to see or feel the punishment threatened, yet he was himself the greatest delinquent. Certainly there must be a future state, in which impenitent sinners will suffer in their own persons, and not escape, as often they do in this world. Baasha died under no visible stroke of divine vengeance for aught that appears, but *God laid up his iniquity for his children,* as Job speaks, *ch.* 21:19. Thus he often visits sin. Observe, Baasha is punished by the destruction of his children after his death, and his children are punished by the abuse of their bodies after their death; that is the only thing which the threatening specifies (*v.* 4), that the dogs and the fowls of the air should eat them, as if herein were designed a tacit intimation that there are punishments after death, when death has done its worst, which will be the sorest punishments and are most to be dreaded; these judgments on the body and posterity signified judgments on the soul when separated from the body, by him who, *after he has killed, has power to cast into hell.*

III. Execution done at last. Baasha's son Elah, like Jeroboam's son Nadab, reigned two years, and then was slain by Zimri, one of his own soldiers, as Nadab was by Baasha; so like was his house made to that of Jeroboam, as was threatened, *v.* 3. Because his idolatry was like his, and one of the sins for which God contended with him being the destruction of Jeroboam's family, the more the destruction of his own resembled that, the nearer did the punishment resemble the sin, as face answers to face in a glass.

1. As then, so now, the king himself was first slain, but Elah fell more ingloriously than Nadab. Nadab was slain in the field of action and honour, he and his army then besieging Gibbethon (*ch.* 15:27); but the siege being then raised upon that disaster, and the city remaining still in the Philistines' hands, the army of Israel was now renewing the attempt (*v.* 15) and Elah should have been with them to command in chief, but he loved his own ease and safety better than his honour or duty, or the public good, and therefore staid behind to take his pleasure; and, when he was *drinking himself drunk in his servant's house,* Zimri killed him, *v.* 9, 10. Let it be a warning to drunkards, especially to those who designedly drink themselves drunk, that they know not but death may surprise them in that condition. (1.) Death comes easily upon men when they are drunk. Besides the chronic diseases which men frequently bring themselves into by hard drinking, and which cut them off in the midst of their days, men in that condition are more easily overcome by an enemy, as Amnon by Absalom, and are liable to more bad accidents, being unable to help themselves, (2.) Death comes terribly upon men in that condition. Finding them in the act of sin, and incapacitated for any act of devotion, that day *comes upon them unawares* (Lu. 21:34), like a thief.

2. As then, so now, the whole family was cut off, and rooted out. The traitor was the successor, to whom the unthinking people tamely submitted, as if it were all one to them what kind they had, so that they had one. The first thing Zimri did was to *slay all the house of Baasha;* thus he held by cruelty what he got by treason. His cruelty seems to have extended further than Baasha's did against the house of Jeroboam, for he left to Elah *none of his kinsfolks or friends* (*v.* 11), *none of his avengers* (so the word is), none that were likely to avenge his death; yet divine justice soon avenged it so remarkably that it was used as a proverb long after, *Had Zimri peace who slew his master?* 2 Ki. 9:31. In this, (1.) The word of God was fulfilled, *v.* 12. (2.) The sins of Baasha and Elah were reckoned for, with which they *provoked God by their vanities, v.* 13. Their idols are called their *vanities,* for they cannot profit nor help. Miserable are those whose deities are vanities.

Verses 15–28

Solomon observes (Prov. 28:2) that *for the transgression of a land many were the princes thereof* (so it was here in Israel), *but by a man of understanding the state thereof shall be prolonged* — so it was with Judah at the same time under Asa. When men forsake God they are out of the way of rest and establishment. Zimri, and Tibni, and Omri, are here striving for the crown. Proud aspiring men ruin one another, and involve others in the ruin. These confusions end in the settlement of Omri; we must therefore take him along with us through this part of the story.

I. How he was chosen, as the Roman emperors often were, by the army in the field, now encamped before Gibbethon. Notice was soon brought thither that Zimri had slain their king (*v.* 16) and set up himself in Tirzah, the royal city, whereupon they chose Omri king in the camp, that they might without delay avenge the death of Elah upon Zimri. Though he was idle and intemperate, yet he was their king, and they would not tamely submit to his murderer, nor let the treason go unpunished. They did not attempt to avenge the death of Nadab upon Baasha, perhaps because the house of Baasha had ruled with more gentleness than the house of Jeroboam; but Zimri shall feel the resentments of the provoked army. The siege of Gibbethon is quitted (Philistines are sure to gain when Israelites quarrel) and Zimri is prosecuted.

II. How he conquered Zimri, who is said to have reigned seven days (*v.* 15), so long before Omri was proclaimed king and himself proclaimed traitor; but we may suppose it was a longer time before he died, for he continued long enough to show his inclination to the way of Jeroboam, and to make himself obnoxious to the justice of God by supporting his idolatry, *v.* 19. Tirzah was a beautiful city, but not fortified, so that Omri soon made himself master of it (*v.* 17), forced Zimri into the palace, which being unable to defend, and yet unwilling to surrender, he burnt, and himself in it, *v.* 18. Unwilling that his rival should ever enjoy that sumptuous palace, he burnt it; and fearing that if he fell into the hands of the army, either alive or dead, he should be ignominiously treated, he burnt himself in it. See what desperate practices men's wickedness sometimes brings them to, and how it hurries them into their own ruin; see the disposition of incendiaries, who set palaces and kingdoms on fire, though they are themselves in danger of perishing in the flame.

III. How he struggled with Tibni, and at length got clear of him: *Half of the people followed this Tibni* (*v.* 21), probably those who were in Zimri's interest, with whom others joined, who would not have a king chosen in the camp (lest he should rule by the sword and a standing army), but in a convention of the states. The contest between these two lasted some years, and, it is likely, cost a great deal of blood on both sides, for it was in the twenty-seventh year of Asa that Omri was first elected (*v.* 15) and thence the twelve years of his reign are to be dated; but it was not till the thirty-first year of Asa that he began to reign without a rival; then Tibni died, it is likely in battle, *and Omri reigned, v.* 22. Sir Walter Raleigh, in his History of the World (2.19.6), enquires here why it was that in all these confusions and revolutions of the kingdom of Israel they never thought of returning to the house of David, and uniting themselves again to Judah, *for then it was better with them than now;* and he thinks the reason was because the kings of Judah assumed a more absolute, arbitrary, and despotic power than the kings of Israel. It was the heaviness of the yoke that they complained of when they first revolted from the house of David, and the dread of that made them ever after averse to it, and attached to kings of their own, who ruled more by law and the rules of a limited monarchy.

IV. How he reigned when he was at length settled on the throne. 1. He made himself famous by building Samaria, which, ever after, was the royal city of the kings of Israel (the palace at Tirzah being burnt), and in process of time grew so considerable that it gave name to the middle part of Canaan (which lay between Galilee on the north and Judea on the south) and to the inhabitants of that country, who were called *Samaritans.* He bought the ground for *two talents of silver,* somewhat more than 700*l.* of our money, for a talent was 353*l.* 11*s.* 10½*d.* Perhaps Shemer, who sold him the ground, let him have it considerably the cheaper upon condition that the city should be called after his name, for otherwise it would have borne the name of the purchaser; it was called *Samaria,* or *Shemeren* (as it is in the Hebrew), from Shemer, the former owner, *v.* 24. The kings of Israel changed their royal seats, Shechem first, then Tirzah, now Samaria; but the kings of Judah were constant to Jerusalem, the city of God. Those that cleave to the Lord fix, but those that leave him ever wander. 2. He made himself infamous by his wickedness; for *he did worse than all that were before him, v.* 25. Though he was brought to the throne with much difficulty, and Providence had remarkably favoured him in his advancement, yet he was more profane, or more superstitious, and a greater persecutor, than either of the houses of Jeroboam or Baasha. He went further than they had done in *establishing iniquity by a law,* and forcing his subjects to comply with him in it; for we read of the statutes of Omri, the keeping of which made *Israel a desolation,* Mic. 6:16. Jeroboam caused Israel to sin by temptation, example, and allurement; but Omri did it by compulsion.

V. How he ended his reign, *v.* 27, 28. He was in some repute for the might which he showed. Many a bad man has been a stout man. He died in his bed, as did Jeroboam and Baasha themselves; but, like them, left it to his posterity to fill up the measure, and then pay off the scores, of his iniquity.

Verses 29–34

We have here the beginning of the reign of Ahab, of whom we have more particulars recorded than of any of the kings of Israel. We have here only a general idea given us of him, as the worst of all the kings, that we may expect what the particulars will be. He reigned twenty-two years, long enough to do a great deal of mischief.

I. He exceeded all his predecessors in wickedness, *did evil above all that were before him* (*v.* 30), and, as if it were done with a particular enmity both to God and Israel, to affront him and ruin them, it is said, *He did more* purposely *to provoke the Lord God of Israel to anger,* and, consequently, to send judgments on his land, *than all the kings of Israel that were before him, v.* 33. It was bad with the people when every successive king was worse than his predecessor. What would they come to at last? He had seen the ruin of other wicked kings and their families; yet, instead of taking warning, his heart was hardened and enraged against God by it. He thought it *a light thing to walk in the sins of Jeroboam, v.* 31. It was nothing to break the second commandment by image-worship, he would set aside the first also by introducing other gods; his little finger should fall heavier upon God's ordinances than Jeroboam's loins. Making light of less sins makes way for greater, and those that endeavour to extenuate other people's sins will but aggravate their own.

II. He married a wicked woman, who he knew would bring in the worship of Baal, and seemed to marry her with that design. *As if it had been a light thing to walk in the sins of Jeroboam, he took to wife Jezebel* (*v.* 31), a zealous idolater, extremely imperious and malicious in her natural temper, addicted to witchcrafts and whoredoms (2 Ki. 9:22), and every way vicious. The false prophetess spoken of Rev. 2:20 is there called *Jezebel,* for a wicked woman could not be called by a worse name than hers; what mischiefs she did, and what mischief at last befel her (2 Ki. 9:33), we shall find in the following story; this one strange wife debauched Israel more than all the strange wives of Solomon.

III. He set up the worship of Baal, forsook the God of Israel and served the god of the Sidonians, Jupiter instead of Jehovah, the sun (so some think), a deified hero of the Phoenicians (so others): he was weary of the golden calves, and thought they had been worshipped long enough; such vanities were they that those who had been fondest of them at length grew sick of them, and, like adulterers, much have variety. In honour of this mock deity, whom they called *Baal — lord,* and for the convenience of his worship, 1. Ahab built a temple in Samaria, the royal city, because the temple of God was in Jerusalem, the royal city of the other kingdom. He would have Baal's temple near him, that he might the better frequent it, protect it, and put honour upon it. 2. He reared an altar in that temple, on which to offer sacrifice to Baal, by which they acknowledged their dependence upon him and sought his favour. O the stupidity of idolaters, who are at a great expense to make one their friend whom they might have chosen whether they would make a god of or no! 3. He made a grove about his temple, either a natural one, by planting shady trees there, or, if those would be too long in growing, an artificial one in imitation of it; for it is not said he *planted,* but he *made* a grove, something that answered the intention, which was to conceal and so countenance the abominable impurities that were committed in the filthy worship of Baal. *Lucus, à lucendo, quia non lucet — He that doeth evil hateth the light.*

IV. One of his subjects, in imitation of his presumption, ventured to build Jericho, in defiance of the curse Joshua had long since pronounced on him that should attempt it, *v.* 34. It comes in as an instance of the height of impiety to which men had arrived, especially at Bethel, where one of the calves was, for of that city this daring sinner was. Observe, 1. How ill he did. Like Achan he meddled with the accursed thing, turned that to his own use which was devoted to God's honour. He began to build, in defiance of the curse well known in Israel, jesting with it perhaps as a bugbear, or fancying its force worn out by length of time, for it was above 500 years since it was pronounced, Jos. 6:26. He went on to build, in defiance of the execution of the curse in part; for, though his eldest son died when he began, yet he would proceed in contempt of God and his wrath revealed from heaven against his ungodliness. 2. How ill he sped. He built for his children, but God wrote him childless; his eldest son died when he began, the youngest when he finished, and all the rest (it is supposed) between. Note, Those whom God curses are cursed indeed; none ever hardened his heart against God and prospered. God keep us back from presumptuous sins, those great transgressions!

CHAPTER 17

So sad was the character both of the princes and people of Israel, as described in the foregoing chapter, that one might have expected God would cast off a people that had so cast him off; but, as an evidence to the contrary, never was Israel so blessed with a good prophet as when it was so plagued with a bad king. Never was king so bold to sin as Ahab; never was prophet so bold to reprove and threaten as Elijah, whose story begins in this chapter and is full of wonders. Scarcely any part of the Old-Testament history shines brighter than this history of the spirit and power of Elias; he only, of all the prophets, had the honour of Enoch, the first prophet, to be translated, that he should not see death, and the honour of Moses, the great prophet, to attend our Saviour in his transfiguration. Other prophets prophesied and wrote, he prophesied and acted, but wrote nothing; but his actions cast more lustre on his name than their writings did on theirs. In this chapter we have, I. His prediction of a famine in Israel, through the want of rain (*v.* 1). II. The provision made for him in that famine, 1. By the ravens at the brook Cherith (*v.* 2–7). 2. When that failed, by the widow at Zarephath, who received him in the name of a prophet and had a prophet's reward; for (1.) He multiplied her meal and her oil (*v.* 8–16). (2.) He raised her dead son to life (*v.* 17–24). Thus his story begins with judgments and miracles, designed to awaken that stupid generation that had to deeply corrupted themselves.

Verses 1–7

The history of Elijah begins somewhat abruptly. Usually, when a prophet enters, we have some account of his parentage, are told whose son he was and of what tribe; but Elijah drops (so to speak) out of the clouds, as if, like Melchisedek, he were without father, without mother, and without descent, which made some of the Jews fancy that he was an angel sent from heaven; but the apostle has assured us that *he was a man subject to like passions as we are* (James 5:17), which perhaps intimates, not only that he was liable to the common infirmities of human nature, but that, by his natural temper, he was a man of strong passions, more hot and eager than most men, and therefore the more fit to deal with the daring sinners of the age he lived in: so wonderfully does God suit men to the work he designs them for. Rough spirits are called to rough services. The reformation needed such a man as Luther to break the ice. Observe, 1. The prophet's name: *Elijahu — "My God Jehovah is he"* (so it signifies), "is he who sends me and will own me and bear me out, is he to whom I would bring Israel back and who alone can effect that great work." 2. His country: He was *of the inhabitants of Gilead,* on the other side Jordan, either of the tribe of Gad or the half of Manasseh, for Gilead was divided between them; but whether a native of either of those tribes is uncertain. The obscurity of his parentage was no prejudice to his eminency afterwards. We need not enquire whence men are, but what they are: if it be a good thing, no matter though it come out of Nazareth. Israel was sorely wounded when God sent them this balm from Gilead and this physician thence. He is called a *Tishbite* from Thisbe, a town in that country. Two things we have an account of here in the beginning of his story: —

I. How he foretold a famine, a long and grievous famine, with which Israel should be punished for their sins. That fruitful land, for want of rain, should be turned into barrenness, for the iniquity of those that dwelt therein. He went and told Ahab this; did not whisper it to the people, to make them disaffected to the government, but proclaimed it to the king, in whose power it was to reform the land, and so to prevent the judgment. It is probable that he reproved Ahab for his idolatry and other wickedness, and told him that unless he repented and reformed this judgment would be brought upon his land. There should be *neither dew nor rain for some years,* none but *according to my word,* that is, "Expect none till you hear from me again." The apostle teaches us to understand this, not only of the word of prophecy, but the word of prayer, which turned the key of the clouds, James 5:17, 18. He prayed earnestly (in a holy indignation at Israel's apostasy, and a holy zeal for the glory of God, whose judgments were defied) *that it might not rain;* and, according to his prayers, the heavens became as brass, till he *prayed again that it might rain.* In allusion to this story it is said of God's witnesses (Rev. 11:6), *These have power to shut heaven, that it rain not in the days of their prophecy.* Elijah lets Ahab know, 1. That *the Lord Jehovah* is the *God of Israel,* whom he had forsaken. 2. That he is a *living God,* and not like the gods he worshipped, which were dead dumb idols. 3. That he himself was God's servant in office, and a messenger sent from him: "It is he *before whom I stand,* to minister to him," or "whom IO now represent, in whose stead I stand, and in whose name I speak, in defiance of the prophets of Baal and the groves." 4. That, notwithstanding the present peace and prosperity of the kingdom of Israel, God was displeased with them for their idolatry and would chastise them for it by the want of rain (which, when he withheld it, it was not in the power of the gods they served to bestow; for *are there any of the vanities of the heathen that can give rain?* Jer. 14:22), which would effectually prove their impotency, and the folly of those who left the living God, to make their court to such as could do neither good nor evil; and this he confirms with a solemn oath — *As the Lord God of Israel liveth,* that Ahab might stand the more in awe of the threatening, the divine life being engaged for the accomplishment of it. 5. He lets Ahab know what interest he had in heaven: It shall be *according to my word.* With what dignity does he speak when he speaks in God's name, as one who well understood that commission of a prophet (Jer. 1:10), *I have set thee over the nations and over the kingdoms.* See the power of prayer and the truth of God's word; for he performeth the counsel of his messengers.

II. How he was himself taken care of in that famine. 1. How he was hidden. God bade him *go and hide himself by the brook Cherith, v.* 3. This was intended, not so much for his preservation, for it does not appear that Ahab immediately sought his life, but as a judgment to the people, to whom, if he had publicly appeared, he might have been a blessing both by his instructions and his intercession, and so have shortened the days of their calamity; but God had determined it should last three years and a half, and therefore, so long, appointed Elijah to abscond, that he might not be solicited to revoke the sentence, the execution of which he had said should be *according to his word.* When God *speaks concerning a nation, to pluck up and destroy,* he finds some way or other to remove those that would stand in the gap to turn away his wrath. It bodes ill to a people when good men and good ministers are ordered to hide themselves. When God intended to *send rain upon the earth* then he bade Elijah go and *show himself to Ahab, ch.* 18:1. For the present, in obedience to the divine command, he went and dwelt all alone in some obscure unfrequented place, where he was not discovered, probably among the reeds of the brook. If Providence calls us to solitude and retirement, it becomes us to acquiesce; when we cannot be useful we must be patient, and when we cannot work for God we must sit still quietly for him. 2.

How he was fed. Though he could not work there, having nothing to do but to meditate and pray (which would help to prepare him for his usefulness afterwards), yet he shall eat, for he is in the way of his duty, and *verily he shall be fed, in the day of famine he shall be satisfied.* When the woman, the church, is *driven into the wilderness,* care it taken that she be fed and nourished there, time, times, and half a time, that is, three years and a half, which was just the time of Elijah's concealment. See Rev. 12:6, 14. Elijah must drink of the brook, and the ravens were appointed to *bring him meat* (*v.* 4) and did so, *v.* 6. Here, (1.) The provision was plentiful, and good, and constant, bread and flesh twice a day, daily bread and food convenient. We may suppose that he fared not so sumptuously as the prophets of the groves, who *did eat at Jezebel's table* (*ch.* 18:19), and yet better than the rest of the Lord's prophets, whom Obadiah fed with bread and water, *ch.* 18:4. It ill becomes God's servants, especially his servants the prophets, to be nice and curious about their food and to affect dainties and varieties; if nature be sustained, no matter though the palate be not pleased; instead of envying those who have daintier fare, we should think how many there are, better than we, who live comfortably upon coarser fare and would be glad of our leavings. Elijah had but one meal brought him at a time, every morning and every evening, to teach him not to take thought for the morrow. Let those who have but from hand to mouth learn to live upon Providence, and trust it for *the bread of the day in the day;* thank God for bread this day, and let to-morrow bring bread with it. (2.) The caterers were very unlikely; the *ravens* brought it to him. Obadiah, and others in Israel that had not bowed the knee to Baal, would gladly have entertained Elijah; but he was a man by himself, and must be red in an extraordinary way. He was a figure of John the baptist, whose meat was locusts and wild honey. God could have sent angels to minister to him, as he did afterwards (*ch.* 19:5) and as he did to our Saviour (Mt. 4:11), but he chose to send by winged messengers of another nature, to show that when he pleases he can serve his own purposes by the meanest creatures as effectually as by the mightiest. If it be asked whence the ravens had this provision, how and where it was cooked, and whether they came honestly by it, we must answer, as Jacob did (Gen. 27:20), *The Lord our God brought it to them,* whose the earth is and the fulness thereof, the world and those that dwell therein. But why ravens? [1.] They are birds of prey, ravenous devouring creatures, more likely to have taken his meat from him, or to have picked out his eyes (Prov. 30:17); but thus Samson's riddle is again unriddled, *Out of the eater comes forth meat.* [2.] They are unclean creatures.*Every raven after his kind* was, by the law, forbidden to be eaten (Lev. 11:15), yet Elijah did not think the meat they brought ever the worse for that, but ate and gave thanks, asking no question for conscience' sake. Noah's dove was to him a more faithful messenger than his raven; yet here the ravens are faithful and constant to Elijah. [3.] Ravens feed on insects and carrion themselves, yet they brought the prophet man's meat and wholesome food. It is a pity that those who bring the bread of life to others should themselves take up with *that which is not bread.* [4.] Ravens could bring but a little, and broken meat, yet Elijah was content with such things as he had, and thankful that the was fed, though not feasted. [5.] Ravens neglect their own young ones, and do not feed them; yet when God pleases they shall feed his prophet. Young lions and young ravens may lack, and suffer hunger, but not those that fear the Lord, Ps. 34:10. [6.] Ravens are themselves fed by special providence (Job 38:41; Ps. 147:9), and now they fed the prophet. Have we experienced God's special goodness to us and ours? Let us reckon ourselves obliged thereby to be kind to those that are his, for his sake. Let us learn hence, *First,* To acknowledge the sovereignty and power of God over all the creatures; he can make what use he pleases of them, either for judgment or mercy. *Secondly,* To encourage ourselves in God in the greatest straits, and never to distrust him. He that could furnish a table in the wilderness, and make ravens purveyors, cooks, and servitors to his prophet, is able to supply all our need according to his riches in glory.

Thus does Elijah, for a great while, *eat his morsels alone,* and his provision of water, which he has in an ordinary way from the brook, fails him before that which he has by miracle. The powers of nature are limited, but not the powers of the God of nature. Elijah's brook dried up (*v.* 7) *because there was no rain.* If the heavens fail, earth fails of course; such are all our creature-comforts; we lose them when we most need them, like the brooks in summer, Job 6:15. But there is *a river which makes glad the city of God* and which never runs dry (Ps. 46:4), *a well of water that springs up to eternal life.* Lord, give us that living water!

Verses 8–16

We have here an account of the further protection Elijah was taken under, and the further provision made for him in his retirement. *At destruction and famine he shall laugh* that has God for his friend to guard and maintain him. The brook Cherith is dried up, but God's care of his people, and kindness to them, never slacken, never fail, but are still the same, are still continued and drawn out to those that know him, Ps. 36:10. When the brook was dried up Jordan was not; why did not God send him thither? Surely because he would show that he has a variety of ways to provide for his people and is not tied to any one. God will now provide for him where he shall have some company and opportunity of usefulness, and not be, as he had been, buried alive. Observe,

I. The place he is sent to, to *Zarephath,* or *Sarepta,* a city of Sidon, out of the borders of the land of Israel, *v.* 9. Our Saviour takes notice of this as an early and ancient indication of the favour of God designed for the poor Gentiles, in the fulness of time, Lu. 4:25, 26. *Many widows were in Israel in the days of Elias,* and some, it is likely, that would have bidden him welcome to their houses; yet he is sent to honour and bless with his presence a city of Sidon, a Gentile city, and so becomes (says Dr. Lightfoot) *the first prophet of the Gentiles.* Israel had corrupted themselves with the idolatries of the nations and become worse than they; justly therefore is *the casting off of them the riches of the world.* Elijah was hated and driven out by his countrymen; therefore, lo, he turns to the Gentiles, as the apostles were afterwards ordered to do, Acts 18:6. But why to a city of Sidon? Perhaps because the worship of Baal, which was now the crying sin of Israel, came lately thence with Jezebel, who was a Sidonian (*ch.* 16:31); therefore thither he shall go, that thence may be fetched the destroyer of that idolatry, "Even out of Sidon have I called my prophet, my reformer." Jezebel was Elijah's greatest enemy; yet, to show her the impotency of her malice, God will find a hiding-place for him even in her country. Christ never went among the Gentiles except once *into the coast of Sidon,* Mt. 15:21.

II. The person that is appointed to entertain him, not one of the rich merchants or great men, of Sidon, not such a one as Obadiah, that was governor of Ahab's house and fed the prophets; but a poor widow woman, destitute and desolate, is commanded (that is, is made both able and willing) to sustain him. It is God's way, and it is his glory, to make use of the *weak and foolish things of the world* and put honour upon them. He is, in a special manner, the widows' God, and feeds them, and therefore they must study what they shall render to him.

III. The provision made for him there. Providence brought the widow woman to meet him very opportunely at the gate of the city (*v.* 10), and, by what is here related of what passed between Elijah and her, we find,

1. Her case and character; and it appears, (1.) That she was very poor and necessitous. She had nothing to live upon but a handful of meal and a little oil, needy at the best, and now, by the general scarcity, reduced to the last extremity. When she has eaten the little she has, for aught she yet sees, she must die for want, she and her son, *v.* 12. She had no fuel but the sticks she gathered in the streets, and, having no servant, she must gather them herself (*v.* 10), being thus more in a condition to receive alms than give entertainment. To her Elijah was sent, that he might still live upon Providence as much as he did when the ravens fed him. It was in compassion to the low estate of his handmaiden that God sent the prophet to her, not to beg of her, but to board with her, and he would pay well for his table. (2.) That she was very humble and industrious. He found her gathering sticks, and preparing to bake her own bread, *v.* 10, 12. Her mind was brought to her condition, and she complained not of the hardship she was brought to, nor quarrelled with the divine Providence for withholding rain, but accommodated herself to it as well as she could. Such as are of this temper in a day of trouble are best prepared for honour and relief from God. (3.) That she was very charitable and generous. When this stranger desired her to go and fetch him some water to drink, she readily went, at the first word, *v.* 10, 11. She objected not to the present scarcity of it, nor asked him what he would give her for a draught of water (for now it was worth money), nor hinted that he was a stranger, an Israelite, with whom perhaps the Sidonians cared not for having any dealings, any more than the Samaritans, Jn. 4:9. She did not excuse herself on account of her weakness through famine, or the urgency of her own affairs, did not tell him she had something else to do than to go on his errands, but left off gathering the sticks for herself to fetch water for him, which perhaps she did the more willingly, being moved with the gravity of his aspect. We should be ready to do any office of kindness even to strangers; if we have not wherewith to give to the distressed, we must be the more ready to work for them. A cup of cold water, though it cost us no more than the labour of fetching, shall in no wise lose its reward. (4.) That she had a great confidence in the word of God. It was a great trial for her faith and obedience when, having gold the prophet how low her stock of meal and oil was and that she had but just enough for herself and her son, he bade her *make a cake for him,* and make *his* first, and then *prepare for herself and her son.* If we consider, it will appear as great a trial as could be in so small a matter. "Let the children first be served" (might she have said); "charity begins at home. I cannot be expected to give, having but little, and not knowing, when that is gone, where to obtain more." She had much more reason than Nabal to ask, "Shall I take my meat and my oil and *give it to one that I know not whence he is?"* Elijah, it is true, made mention of *the God of Israel* (*v.* 14), but what was that to a Sidonian? Or if she had a veneration for the name *Jehovah,* and valued the God of Israel as the true God, yet what assurance had she that this stranger was his prophet or had any warrant to speak in his name? It was easy for a hungry vagrant to impose upon her. But she gets over all these objections, and obeys the precept in dependence upon the promise: She *went and did according to the saying of Elijah, v.* 15. *O woman! great was thy faith;* one has not found the like, *no, not in Israel:* all things considered, it exceeded that of the widow who, when she had but two mites, cast them into the treasury. She took the prophet's word, that she should not lose by it, but it should be repaid with interest. Those that can venture upon the promise of God will make no difficulty of exposing and emptying themselves in his service, by giving him his dues out of a little and giving him his part first. Those that deal with God must deal upon trust; seek first his kingdom, and then other things shall be added. By the law, the first-fruits were God's, the tithe was taken out first, and the heave-offering of their dough was first offered, Num. 15:20, 21. But surely the increase of this widow's faith, to such a degree as to enable her thus to deny herself and to depend upon the divine promise, was as great a miracle in the kingdom of grace as the increase of her oil was in the kingdom of providence. Happy are those who can thus, against hope, believe and obey in hope.

2. The care God took of her guest: *The barrel of meal wasted not, nor did the cruse of oil fail,* but still as they took from them more was added to them by the divine power, *v.* 16. Never did corn or olive so increase in the growing (says bishop Hall) as these did in the using; but the *multiplying of the seed sown* (2 Co. 9:10) in the common course of providence is an instance of the power and goodness of God not to be overlooked because common. The meal and the oil multiplied, not in the hoarding, but in the spending; for *there is that scattereth and yet increaseth.* When God blesses a little, it will go a great way, even beyond expectation; as, on the contrary, though there be abundance, if he blow upon it, it comes to little, Hag. 1:9; 2:16. (1.) This was a maintenance for the prophet. Still miracles shall be his daily bread. Hitherto he had been fed with bread and flesh, now he was fed with bread and oil, which they used as we do butter. Manna was both, for the *taste of it was as the taste of fresh oil,* Num. 11:8. This Elijah was thankful for, though he had been used to flesh twice a day and now had none at all. Those that cannot

live without flesh, once a day at least, because they have been used to it, could not have boarded contentedly with Elijah, no, not to live upon a miracle. (2.) It was a maintenance for *the poor widow and her son,* and a recompence to her for entertaining the prophet. There is nothing lost by being kind to God's people and ministers; she that received a prophet had a prophet's reward; she gave him house-room, and he repaid her with food for her household. Christ has promised to those who open their doors to him that he will come in to them, and *sup with them,* and *they with him,* Rev. 3:20. Like Elijah here, he brings to those who bid him welcome, not only his own entertainment, but theirs too. See how the reward answered the service. She generously made one cake for the prophet, and was repaid with many for herself and her son. When Abraham offers his only son to God he is told he shall be the father of multitudes. What is laid out in piety or charity is let out to the best interest, upon the best securities. One poor meal's meat this poor widow gave the prophet, and, in recompence of it, *she and her son did eat many days* (*v.* 15), above two years, in a time of general scarcity; and to have their food from God's special favour, and to eat it in such good company as Elijah's, made it more than doubly sweet. It is promised to those that trust in God that they *shall not be ashamed in the evil time, but in the days of famine they shall be satisfied,* Ps. 37:19.

Verses 17–24

We have here a further recompence made to the widow for her kindness to the prophet; as if it were a small thing to be kept alive, her son, when dead, is restored to life, and so restored to her. Observe,

I. The sickness and death of the child. For aught that appears he was her only son, the comfort of her widowed estate. He was fed miraculously, and yet that did not secure him from sickness and death. *Your fathers did eat manna, and are dead,* but *there is bread of which a man may eat and not die,* which was given for the life of the world, Jn. 6:49, 50. The affliction was to this widow as a thorn in the flesh, lest she should be lifted up above measure with the favours that were done her and the honours that were put upon her. 1. She was nurse to a great prophet, was employed to sustain him, and had strong reason to think the Lord would do her good; yet now she loses her child. Note, We must not think it strange if we meet with very sharp afflictions, even when we are in the way of duty, and of eminent service to God. 2. She was herself nursed by miracle, and kept a good house without charge or care, by a distinguishing blessing from heaven; and in the midst of all this satisfaction she was thus afflicted. Note, When we have the clearest manifestations of God's favour and good-will towards us, even then we must prepare for the rebukes of Providence. Our mountain never stands so strong but it may be moved, and therefore, in this world, we must always rejoice with trembling.

II. Her pathetic complaint to the prophet of this affliction. It should seem, the child died suddenly, else she would have applied to Elijah, while he was sick, for the cure of him; but being dead, dead in her bosom, she expostulates with the prophet upon it, rather to give vent to her sorrow than in any hope of relief, *v.* 18. 1. She expresses herself passionately: *What have I to do with thee, O thou man of God?* How calmly had she spoken of her own and her child's death when she expected to die for want (*v.* 12) — *that we may eat, and die!* Yet now that her child dies, and not so miserably as by famine, she is extremely disturbed at it. We may speak lightly of an affliction at a distance, but when it *toucheth us we are troubled,* Job 4:5. Then she spoke deliberately, now in haste; the death of her child was now a surprise to her, and it is hard to keep our spirits composed when troubles come upon us suddenly and unexpectedly, and in the midst of our peace and prosperity. She calls him *a man of God,* and yet quarrels with him as if he had occasioned the death of her child, and is ready to which she had never seen him, forgetting past mercies and miracles: "What have I done against thee?" (so some understand it), "Wherein have I offended thee, or been wanting in my duty? *Show me wherefore thou contendest with me.*" 2. Yet she expresses herself penitently: *"Hast thou come to call my sin to* thy *remembrance,* as the cause of the affliction, and so to call it to *my* remembrance, as the effect of the affliction?" Perhaps she knew of Elijah's intercession against Israel, and, being conscious to herself of sin, perhaps her former worshipping of Baal the god of the Sidonians, she apprehends he had made intercession against her. Note, (1.) When God removes our comforts from use he remembers our sins against us, perhaps the iniquities of our youth, though long since past, Job 13:26. Our sins are the death of our children. (2.) When God thus remembers our sins against us he designs thereby to make us remember them against ourselves and repent of them.

III. The prophet's address to God upon this occasion. He gave no answer to her expostulation, but brought it to God, and laid the case before him, not knowing what to say to it himself. He took the dead child from the mother's bosom to his own bed, *v.* 19. Probably he had taken a particular kindness to the child, and found the affliction his own more than by sympathy. He retired to his chamber, and, 1. He humbly reasons with God concerning the death of the child, *v.* 20. He sees death striking by commission from God: *Thou hast brought this evil* for is there any evil of this kind in the city, in the family, and the Lord has not done it? He pleads the greatness of the affliction to the poor mother: "It is *evil upon the widow;* thou art the widow's God, and dost not usually bring evil upon widows; it is affliction added to the afflicted." He pleads his own concern: "It is the widow *with whom I sojourn;* wilt thou, that art my God, bring evil upon one of the best of my benefactors? I shall be reflected upon, and others will be afraid of entertaining me, if I bring death into the house where I come." 2. He earnestly begs of God to restore the child to life again, *v.* 21. We do not read before this of any that were raised to life; yet Elijah, by a divine impulse, prays for the resurrection of this child, which yet will not warrant us to do the like. David expected not, by fasting and prayer, to bring his child back to life (2 Sa. 12:23), but Elijah had a power to work miracles, which David had not. He *stretched himself upon the child,* to affect himself with the case and to show how much he was affected with it and how desirous he was of the restoration of the child — he would if he could put life into him by his own breath and warmth; also to give a sign of what God would do by his power, and what he does by his grace, in raising dead souls to a spiritual life; the Holy Ghost comes upon them, overshadows them, and puts life into them. He is very particular in his prayer: *I pray thee let this child's soul come into him again,* which plainly supposes the existence of the soul in a state of separation from the body, and consequently its immortality, which Grotius thinks God designed by this miracle to give intimation and evidence of, for the encouragement of his suffering people.

IV. The resurrection of the child, and the great satisfaction it gave to the mother: the child revived, *v.* 22. See the power of prayer and the power of him that hears prayer, who *kills and makes alive.* Elijah brought him to his mother, who, we may suppose, could scarcely believe her own eyes, and therefore Elijah assures her it is her own: "It is *thy son that liveth;* see it is thy own, and not another," *v.* 23. The good woman hereupon cries out, *Now I know that thou art a man of God;* though she knew it before, by the increase of her meal, yet the death of her child she took so unkindly that she began to question it (a good man surely would not serve her so); but now she was abundantly satisfied that he had both the power and goodness of a man of God, and will never doubt of it again, but give up herself to the direction of his word and the worship of the God of Israel. Thus the death of the child (like that of Lazarus, Jn. 11:4) was for the glory of God and the honour of his prophet.

CHAPTER 18

We left the prophet Elijah wrapt up in obscurity. It does not appear that either the increase of the provision or the raising of the child had caused him to be taken notice of at Zarephath, for then Ahab would have discovered him; he would rather do good than be known to do it. But in this chapter his appearance was as public as before his retirement was close; the days appointed for his concealment (which was part of the judgment upon Israel) being finished, he is not commanded to show himself to Ahab, and to expect rain upon the earth (*v.* 1). Pursuant to this order we have here, I. His interview with Obadiah, one of Ahab's servants, by whom he sends notice to Ahab of his coming (*v.* 2–16). II. His interview with Ahab himself (*v.* 17–20). III. His interview with all Israel upon Mount Carmel, in order to a public trial of titles between the Lord and Baal; a most distinguished solemnity it was, in which, 1. Baal and his prophets were confounded. 2. God and Elijah were honoured (*v.* 21–39). IV. The execution he did upon the prophets of Baal (*v.* 40). V. The return of the mercy of rain, at the word of Elijah (*v.* 41–46). It is a chapter in which are many things very observable.

Verses 1–16

In these verses we find,

I. The sad state of Israel at this time, upon two accounts:—

1. *Jezebel cut off the prophets of the Lord* (*v.* 4), *slew them, v.* 13. Being an idolater, she was a persecutor, and made Ahab one. Even in those bad times, when the calves were worshipped and the temple at Jerusalem deserted, yet there were some good people that feared God and served him, and some good prophets that instructed them in the knowledge of him and assisted them in their devotions. The priests and the Levites had all gone to Judah and Jerusalem (2 Chr. 11:13, 14), but, instead of them, God raised up these prophets, who read and expounded the law in private meetings, or in the families that retained their integrity, for we read not of any synagogues at this time; they had not the spirit of prophecy as Elijah, nor did they offer sacrifice, or burn incense, but taught people to live well, and keep close to the God of Israel. These Jezebel aimed to extirpate, and put many of them to death, which was as much a public calamity as a public iniquity, and threatened the utter ruin of religion's poor remains in Israel. Those few that escaped the sword were forced to abscond, and hide themselves in caves, where they were buried alive and cut off, though not from life, yet from usefulness, which is the end and comfort of life; and, when the prophets were persecuted and driven into corners, no doubt their friends, those few good people that were in the land, were treated in like manner. Yet, bad as things were,

(1.) There was one very good man, who was a great man at court, *Obadiah,* who answered his name — *a servant of the Lord,* one who feared God and was faithful to him, and yet was steward of the household to Ahab. Observe his character: He *feared the Lord greatly* (*v.* 3), was not only a good man, but zealously and eminently good; his great place put a lustre upon his goodness, and gave him great opportunities of doing good; and he *feared the Lord from his youth* (*v.* 12), he began betimes to be religious and had continued long. Note, Early piety, it is to be hoped, will be eminent piety; those that are good betimes are likely to be very good; he that feared God from his youth came to fear him greatly. He that will thrive must rise betimes. But it is strange to find such an eminently good man governor of Ahab's house, an office of great honour, power, and trust. [1.] It was strange that so wicked a man as Ahab would prefer him to it and continue him in it; certainly it was because he was a man of celebrated honesty, industry, and ingenuity, and one in whom he could repose a confidence, whose eyes he could trust as much as his own, as appears here, *v.* 5. Joseph and Daniel were preferred because there were none so fit as they for the places they were preferred to. Note, Those who profess religion should study to recommend themselves to the esteem even of those that are without by their integrity, fidelity, and application to business. [2.] It was strange that so good a man as Obadiah would accept of preferment in a court so addicted to idolatry and all manner of wickedness. We may be sure it was not made necessary to qualify him for preferment that he should be of the king's religion, that he should conform to the *statues of Omri, or the law of the house of Ahab.* Obadiah would not have accepted the place if he could not have had it without bowing the knee to Baal, nor was Ahab so impolitic as to exclude those from offices that were fit to serve him, merely because they would not join with him in his devotions. That man that is true to his God will be faithful to his prince. Obadiah therefore could with a good conscience enjoy the place, and therefore would not decline it, nor give it up, though he foresaw he could not do the good he desired to do in it. Those that fear God need not go out of the world, bad as it is. [3.] It was strange that either he did not reform Ahab or Ahab corrupt him; but it seems they were both fixed; he that was filthy would be filthy still, and he that was holy would be holy still. Those fear God greatly that keep up the fear of him in bad times and places; thus Obadiah did. God has his remnant among all sorts, high and low; there were saints in Nero's household, and in Ahab's.

(2.) This great good man used his power for the protection of God's prophets. He hid 100 of them in two caves, when the persecution was hot, and *fed them with bread and water, v.* 4. He did not think it enough to fear God himself, but, having wealth and power wherewith to do it, he thought himself obliged to assist and countenance others that feared God; nor did he think his being kind to them would excuse him from being good himself, but he did both, he both feared God greatly himself and patronised those that feared him likewise. See how wonderfully God raises up friends for his ministers and people, for their shelter in difficult times, even where one would least expect them. Bread and water were now scarce commodities, yet Obadiah will find a competence of both for God's prophets, to keep them alive for service hereafter, though now they were laid aside.

2. When Jezebel cut off God's prophets God cut off the necessary provisions by the extremity of the drought. Perhaps Jezebel persecuted God's prophets under pretence that they were the cause of the judgment, because Elijah had foretold it. *Christianos ad leones — Away with Christians to the lions.* But God made them know the contrary, for the famine continued till Baal's prophets were sacrificed, and so great a scarcity of water there was that the king himself and Obadiah went in person throughout the land to seek for grass for the cattle, *v.* 5, 6. Providence ordered it so, that Ahab might, with his own eyes, see how bad the consequences of this judgment were, that so he might be the better inclined to hearken to Elijah, who would direct him into the only way to put an end to it. Ahab's care was not to *lose all the beasts,* many being already lost; but he took no care about his soul, not to lose that; he took a deal of pains to seek grass, but none to seek the favour of God, fencing against the effect, but not enquiring how to remove the cause. The land of Judah lay close to the land of Israel, yet we find no complaint there of the want of rain; for *Judah yet ruled with God, and was faithful with the saints* and prophets (Hos. 11:12), by which distinction Israel might plainly have seen the ground of God's controversy, when God *caused it to rain upon one city and not upon another* (Amos 4:7, 8); but they blinded their eyes, and hardened their hearts, and would not see.

II. The steps taken towards redressing the grievance, by Elijah's appearing again upon the stage, to act as a *Tishbite,* a *converter* or *reformer* of Israel, for so (some think) that title of his signifies. Turn them again to the Lord God of hosts, from whom they have revolted, and all will be well quickly; this must be Elijah's doing. See Lu. 1:16, 17.

1. Ahab had made diligent search for him (*v.* 10), had offered rewards to any one that would discover him, sent spies *into every tribe and lordship* of his own dominions, as some understand it, or, as others, into all the neighbouring nations and kingdoms that were in alliance with him; and, when they denied that they knew any thing of him, he would not believe them unless they swore it, and, as should seem, promised likewise upon oath that, if ever they found him among them, they would discover him and deliver him up. It should seem, he made this diligent search for him, not so much that he might punish him for what he had done in denouncing the judgment as that he might oblige him to undo it again, by recalling the sentence, because he had said it should be *according to his word,* having such an opinion of him as men foolishly conceive of witches (that, if they can but compel them to bless that which they have bewitched, it will be well again), or such as the king of Moab had of Balaam. I incline to this because we find, when they came together, Elijah, knowing what Ahab wanted him for, appointed him to meet him on Mount Carmel, and Ahab complied with the appointment, though Elijah took such a way to revoke the sentence and bless the land as perhaps he little thought of.

2. God, at length, ordered Elijah to present himself to Ahab, because the time had now come when he would *send rain upon the earth* (*v.* 1), or rather *upon the land.* Above two years he had lain hid with the widow at Zarephath, after he had been concealed one year by the brook Cherith; so that the third year of his sojourning there, here spoken of (*v.* 1), was the fourth of the famine, which lasted in all three years and six months, as we find, Lu. 4:25; James 5:17. Such was Elijah's zeal, no doubt, against the

idolatry of Baal, and such his compassion to his people, that he thought it long to be thus confined to a corner; yet he appeared not till God bade him: *"Go and show thyself to Ahab,* for now thy hour has come, even *the time to favour Israel."* Note, It bodes well to any people when God calls his ministers out of their corners, and bids them show themselves — a sign that he will *give rain on the earth;* at least we may the better be content with the bread of affliction while *our eyes see our teachers,* Isa. 30:20, 21.

3. Elijah first surrendered, or rather discovered, himself to Obadiah. He knew, by the Spirit, where to meet him, and we are here told what passed between them.

(1.) Obadiah saluted him with great respect, fell on his face, and humbly asked, *Art thou that my lord Elijah? v.* 7. As he had shown the tenderness of a father to the sons of the prophets, so he showed the reverence of a son to this father of the prophets; and by this made it appear that he did indeed *fear God greatly,* that he did honour to one that was his extraordinary ambassador and had a great interest in heaven.

(2.) Elijah, in answer to him, [1.] Transfers the title of honour he gave him to Ahab: "Call him thy lord, not me;" that is a fitter title for a prince than for a prophet, *who seeks not honour from men.* Prophets should be called *seers,* and *shepherds,* and *watchmen,* and *ministers,* rather than *lords,* as those that mind duty more than dominion. [2.] He bids Obadiah go and tell the king that he is there to speak with him: *Tell thy lord, Behold, Elijah* is forth-coming, *v.* 8. He would have the king know before, that it might not be a surprise to him and that he might be sure it was the prophet's own act to present himself to him.

(3.) Obadiah begs to be excused from carrying this message to Ahab, for it might prove as much as his life was worth. [1.] He tells Elijah what great search Ahab had made for him and how much his heart was upon it to find him out, *v.* 10. [2.] He takes it for granted that Elijah would again withdraw (*v.* 12): *The Spirit of the Lord shall carry thee* (as it is likely he had done sometimes, when Ahab thought he had been sure of him) *whither I know not.* See 2 Ki. 2:16. He thought Elijah was not in good earnest when he bade him tell Ahab where he was, but intended only to expose the impotency of his malice; for he knew Ahab was not worthy to receive any kindness from the prophet and it was not fit that the prophet should receive any mischief from him. [3.] He is sure Ahab would be so enraged at the disappointment that he would put him to death for making a fool of him, or for not laying hands on Elijah himself, when he had him in his reach, *v.* 12. Tyrants and persecutors, in their passion, are often unreasonably outrageous, even towards their friends and confidants. [4.] He pleads that he did not deserve to be thus exposed, and put in peril of his life: *What have I said amiss? v.* 9. Nay (*v.* 13), *Was it not told my lord how I hid the prophets?* He mentions this, not in pride or ostentation, but to convince Elijah that though he was Ahab's servant he was not in his interest, and therefore deserved not to be bantered as one of the tools of his persecution. He that had protected so many prophets, he hoped, should not have his own life hazarded by so great a prophet.

(4.) Elijah satisfied him that he might with safety deliver this message to Ahab, by assuring him, with an oath, that he would, this very day, present himself to Ahab, *v.* 15. Let but Obadiah know that he spoke seriously and really intended it, and he will make no scruple to carry the message to Ahab. Elijah swears by *the Lord of hosts,* who has all power in his hands, and is therefore able to protect his servants against all the powers of hell and earth.

(5.) Notice is hereby soon brought to Ahab that Elijah had sent him a challenge to meet him immediately at such a place, and Ahab accepts the challenge: *He went to meet Elijah, v.* 16. We may suppose it was a great surprise to Ahab to hear that Elijah, whom he had so long sought and not found, was now found without seeking. He went in quest of grass, and found him from whose word, at God's mouth, he must expect rain. Yet his guilty conscience gave him little reason to hope for it, but, rather, to fear some other more dreadful judgment. Had he, by his spies, surprised Elijah, he would have triumphed over him; but, now that he was thus surprised by him, we may suppose he even trembled to look him in the face, hated him, and yet feared him, as Herod did John.

Verses 17–20

We have here the meeting between Ahab and Elijah, as bad a king as ever the world was plagued with and as good a prophet as ever the church was blessed with. 1. Ahab, like himself, basely accused Elijah. He durst not strike him, remembering that Jeroboam's hand withered when it was stretched out against a prophet, but gave him bad language, which was no less an affront to him that sent him. It was a very coarse compliment with which he accosted him at the first word: *Art thou he that troubleth Israel? v.* 17. How unlike was this to that with which his servant Obadiah saluted him (*v.* 7): *Art thou that my lord Elijah?* Obadiah feared God greatly; Ahab had sold himself to work wickedness; and both discovered their character by the manner of their address to the prophet. One may guess how people stand affected to God by observing how they stand affected to his people and ministers. Elijah now came to bring blessings to Israel, tidings of the return of the rain; yet he was thus affronted. Had it been true that he was the *troubler of Israel,* Ahab, as king, would have been bound to animadvert upon him. There are those who trouble Israel by their wickedness, whom the conservators of the public peace are concerned to enquire after. But it was utterly false concerning Elijah; so far was he from being an enemy to Israel's welfare that he as the stay of it, *the chariots and horsemen of Israel.* Note, It has been the lot of the best and most useful men to be called and counted *the troublers of the land,* and to be run down as public grievances. Even Christ and his apostles were thus misrepresented, Acts 17:6. 2. Elijah, like himself, boldly returned the charge upon the king, and proved it upon him, that he was *the troubler of Israel, v.* 18. Elijah is not the Achan: *"I have not troubled Israel,* have neither done them any wrong nor designed them any hurt." Those that procure God's judgments do the mischief, not he that merely foretels them and gives warning of them, that the nation may repent and prevent them. *I would have healed Israel, but they would not be healed.* Ahab is the Achan, the troubler, who follows Baalim, those accursed things. Nothing creates more trouble to a land than the impiety and profaneness of princes and their families. 3. As one having authority immediately from the King of kings, he ordered a convention of the states to be forthwith summoned to meet at Mount Carmel, where there had been an altar built to God, *v.* 30. Probably on that mountain they had an eminent high place, where formerly the pure worship of God had been kept up as well as it could be any where but at Jerusalem. Thither all Israel must come, to give Elijah the meeting; and the prophets of Baal who were dispersed all the country over, with those of the groves who were Jezebel's domestic chaplains, must there make their personal appearance. 4. Ahab issued out writs accordingly, for the convening of this great assembly (*v.* 20), either because he feared Elijah and durst not oppose him (Saul stood in awe of Samuel more than of God), or because he hoped Elijah would bless the land, and speak the word that they might have rain, and upon those terms they would be all at his beck. Those that slighted and hated his counsels would gladly be beholden to him for his prayers. Now God *made those who said they were Jews and were not, but were of the synagogue of Satan, to come, and, in effect, to worship at his feet, and to know that God had loved him,* Rev. 3:9.

Verses 21–40

Ahab and the people expected that Elijah would, in this solemn assembly, *bless the land,* and pray for rain; but he had other work to do first. The people must be brought to repent and reform, and then they may look for the removal of the judgment, but not till then. This is the right method. God will first *prepare our heart,* and then *cause his ear to hear,* will first *turn us to him,* and then *turn to us,* Ps. 10:17; 80:3. Deserters must not look for God's favour till they return to their allegiance. Elijah might have looked for rain seventy times seven times, and not have seen it, if he had not thus begun his work at the right end. Three years and a half's famine would not bring them back to God. Elijah would endeavour to convince their judgments, and no doubt it was by special warrant and direction from heaven that he put the controversy between God and Baal upon a public trial. It was great condescension in God that he would suffer so plain a case to be disputed, and would permit Baal to be a competitor with him; but thus God would have every mouth to be stopped and all flesh to become silent before him. God's cause is so incontestably just that it needs not fear to have the evidences of its equity searched into and weighed.

I. Elijah reproved the people for mixing the worship of God and the worship of Baal together. Not only some Israelites worshipped God and others Baal, but the same Israelites sometimes worshipped one and sometimes the other. This he calls (*v.* 21) *halting between two opinions,* or *thoughts.* They worshipped God to please the prophets, but worshipped Baal to please Jezebel and curry favour at court. They thought to trim the matter, and play on both sides, as the Samaritans, 2 Ki. 17:33. Now Elijah shows them the absurdity of this. He does not insist upon their relation to Jehovah — "Is he not yours, and the God of your fathers, while Baal is the god of the Sidonians? And *will a nation change their god?"* Jer. 2:11. No, he waives the prescription, and enters upon the merits of the cause: — "There can be but one God, but one infinite and but one supreme: there needs but one God, one omnipotent, one all-sufficient. What occasion for addition to that which is perfect? Now if, upon trial, it appears that Baal is that one infinite omnipotent Being, that one supreme Lord and all-sufficient benefactor, you ought to renounce Jehovah and cleave to Baal only: but, if Jehovah be that one God, Baal is a cheat, and you must have no more to do with him." Note, 1. It is a very bad thing to *halt between God and Baal.* "In reconcilable differences (says bishop Hall) nothing more safe than indifferency both of practice and opinion; but, in cases of such necessary hostility as betwixt God and Baal, *he that is not with God is against him."* Compare Mk. 9:38, 39, with Mt. 21:30. The service of God and the service of sin, the dominion of Christ and the dominion of our lusts, these are the two thoughts which it is dangerous halting between. Those halt between them that are unresolved under their convictions, unstable and unsteady in their purposes, promise fair, but do not perform, begin well, but do not hold on, that are inconsistent with themselves, or indifferent and lukewarm in that which is good. *Their heart is divided* (Hos. 10:2), whereas God will have all or none. 2. We are fairly put to our choice *whom we will serve,* Jos. 24:15. If we can find one that has more right to us, or will be a better master to us, than God, we may take him at our peril. God demands no more from us than he can make out a title to. To this fair proposal of the case, which Elijah here makes, the people knew not what to say: *They answered him not a word.* They could say nothing to justify themselves, and they would say nothing to condemn themselves, but, as people confounded, let him say what he would.

II. He proposed to bring the matter to a fair trial; and it was so much the fairer because Baal had all the external advantages on his side. The king and court were all for Baal; so was the body of the people. The managers of Baal's cause were 450 men, fat and well fed (*v.* 22), besides 400 more, their supporters or seconds, *v.* 19. The manager of God's cause was but one man, lately a poor exile, hardly kept from starving; so that God's cause has nothing to support it but its own right. However, it is put to this experiment, "Let each side prepare a sacrifice, and pray to its God, and *the God that answereth by fire, let him be God;* if neither shall thus answer, let the people turn Atheists; if both, let them continue to *halt between two."* Elijah, doubtless, had a special commission from God to put it to this test, otherwise he would have tempted God and affronted religion; but the case was extraordinary, and the judgment upon it would be of use, not only then, but in all ages. It is an instance of the courage of Elijah that he durst stand alone in the cause of God against such powers and numbers; and the issue encourages all God's witnesses and advocates never to fear the face of man. Elijah does not say, "The God that answers by *water"* (though that was the thing the country needed), but "that *answers by fire, let him be God;"* because the atonement was to be made by sacrifice, before the judgment could be removed in mercy. The God therefore that has power to pardon sin, and to signify it by consuming the sin-offering, must needs be the God that can relieve us against the calamity. He that can give fire can give rain; see Mt. 9:2, 6.

III. The people join issue with him: *It is well spoken, v.* 24. They allow the proposal to be fair and unexceptionable "God has often answered by fire; if Baal cannot do so, let him be cast out for a usurper." They were very desirous to see the experiment tried, and seemed resolved to abide by the issue, whatever it should be. Those that were firm for God doubted not but it would end to his honour; those that were indifferent were willing to be determined; and Ahab and the prophets of Baal durst not oppose for fear of the people, and hoped that either *they* could obtain fire from heaven (though they never had yet), and the rather because, as some think, they worshipped the sun in Baal, or that *Elijah* could not, because not at the temple, where God was wont thus to manifest his glory. If, in this trial, they could but bring it to a drawn battle, their other advantages would give them the victory. Let it go on therefore to a trial.

IV. The prophets of Baal try first, but in vain, with their god. They covet the precedency, not only for the honour of it, but that, if they can but in the least seem to gain their point, Elijah may not be admitted to make the trial. Elijah allows it to them (*v.* 25), gives them the lead for their greater confusion; only, knowing that the working of Satan is with lying wonders, he takes care to prevent a fraud: Be sure to *put no fire under.* Now in their experiment observe,

1. How importunate and noisy the prophets of Baal were in their applications to him. They got their sacrifices ready; and we may well imagine what a noise 450 men made, when they cried as one man, and with all their might, *O Baal! hear us, O Baal! answer us;* as it is in the margin: and this for some hours together, longer than Diana's worshippers made their cry, *Great is Diana of the Ephesians,* Acts 19:34. How senseless, how brutish, were they in their addresses to Baal! (1.) Like fools, *they leaped upon the altar,* as if they would themselves become sacrifices with their bullock; or thus they expressed their great earnestness of mind. *They leaped up and down,* or danced about the altar (so some): they hoped, by their dancing, to please their deity, as Herodias did Herod, and so to obtain their request. (2.) Like madmen they *cut themselves in pieces with knives and lancets* (*v.* 28) for vexation that they were not answered, or in a sort of prophetic fury, hoping to obtain the favour of their god by offering to him their own blood, when they could not obtain it with the blood of their bullock. God never required his worshippers thus to honour him; but the service of the devil, though in some instances it pleases and pampers the body, yet in other things it is really cruel to it, as in envy and drunkenness. It seems, this was the manner of the worshippers of Baal. God expressly forbade his worshippers to cut themselves, Deu. 14:1. He insists upon it that we mortify our lusts and corruptions; but corporeal penances and severities, such as the Papists use, which have no tendency to that, are no pleasure to him. *Who has required these things at your hands?*

2. How sharp Elijah was upon them, *v.* 27. He stood by them, and patiently heard them for so many hours praying to an idol, yet with secret indignation and disdain; and at noon, when the sun was at the hottest, and they too expecting fire (then if ever), he upbraided them with their folly; and notwithstanding the gravity of his office, and the seriousness of the work he had before him, bantered them: *"Cry aloud, for he is a god,* a goodly god that cannot be made to hear without all this clamour. Surely you think he is talking or meditating (as the word is) or he is pursuing some deep thoughts, (in a brown study, as we say), thinking of somewhat else and not minding his own matter, when not your credit only, but all his honour lies at stake, and his interest in Israel. His new conquest will be lost if he do not look about him quickly." Note, The worship of idols is a most ridiculous thing, and it is but justice to represent it so and expose it to scorn. This will, by no means, justify those who ridicule the worshippers of God in Christ because the worship is not performed just in their way. Baal's prophets were so far from being convinced and put to shame by the just reproach Elijah cast upon them that it made them the more violent and led them to act more ridiculously. *A deceived heart had turned them aside,* they *could not deliver their souls* by saying, *Is there not a lie in our right hand?*

3. How deaf Baal was to them. Elijah did not interrupt them, but let them go on till they were tired, and quite despaired of success, which was not *till the time of the evening sacrifice, v.* 29. During all that time some of them prayed, while others of them prophesied, sang hymns, perhaps to the praise of Baal, or rather encouraged those that were praying to proceed, telling them that Baal would answer them at last; but there was *no answer, nor any that regarded.* Idols could do neither good nor evil. The prince of the power of the air, if God has permitted him, could have caused *fire to come down from heaven* on this occasion, and gladly would have done it for the support of his Baal. We find that the beast which deceived the world does it. *He maketh fire come down from heaven in the sight of men and so deceiveth them,* Rev. 13:13, 14. But God would not suffer the devil to do it now, because the trial of his title was put on that issue by consent of parties.

V. Elijah soon obtains from his God an answer by fire. The Baalites are forced to give up their cause, and now it is Elijah's turn to produce his. Let us see if he speed better.

1. He fitted up an altar. He would not make use of theirs, which had been polluted with their prayers to Baal, but, finding the ruins of an altar there, which had formerly been used in the service of the Lord, he chose to repair that (*v.* 30), to intimate to them that he was not about to introduce any new religion, but to revive the faith and worship of their fathers' God, and reduce them to their first love, their first works. He could not bring them to the altar at Jerusalem unless he could unite the two kingdoms again (which, for correction to both, God designed should not now be done), therefore, by his prophetic authority, he builds an altar on Mount Carmel, and so owns that which had formerly been built there. When we cannot carry a reformation so far as we would we must do what we can, and rather comply with some corruptions than not do our utmost towards the extirpation of Baal. He repaired this altar with *twelve stones, according to the number of the twelve tribes, v.* 31. Though ten of the tribes had revolted to Baal, he would look upon them as belonging to God still, by virtue of the ancient covenant with their fathers: and, though those ten were unhappily divided from the other two in civil interest, yet in the worship of the God of Israel they had communion with each other, and they twelve were one. Mention is made of God's calling their father Jacob by the name of *Israel, a prince with God* (*v.* 31), to shame his degenerate seed, who worshipped a god which they saw could not hear nor answer them, and to encourage the prophet who was now to wrestle with God as Jacob did; he also shall be a prince with God. Ps. 24:6, *Thy face, O Jacob!* Hos. 12:4. *There he spoke with us.*

2. Having built his altar *in the name of the Lord* (*v.* 32), by direction from him and with an eye to him, and not for his own honour, he prepared his sacrifice, *v.* 33. *Behold the bullock and the wood; but where is the fire?* Gen. 22:7, 8. *God will provide himself fire.* If we, in sincerity, offer our hearts to God, he will, by his grace, kindle a holy fire in them. Elijah was no priest, nor were his attendants Levites. Carmel had neither tabernacle nor temple; it was a great way distant from the ark of the testimony and the place God had chosen; this was not the altar that sanctified the gift; yet never was any sacrifice more acceptable to God than this. The particular Levitical institutions were so often dispensed with (as in the time of the Judges, Samuel's time, and now) that one would be tempted to think they were more designed for types to be fulfilled in the evangelical anti-types than for laws to be fulfilled in the strict observance of them. Their perishing thus is the using, as the apostle speaks of them (Col. 2:22), was to intimate the utter abolition of them after a little while, Heb. 8:13.

3. He ordered abundance of water to be poured upon his altar, which he had prepared a trench for the reception of (*v.* 32), and, some think, made the altar hollow. Twelve barrels of water (probably sea-water, for the sea was near, and so much fresh water in this time of drought was too precious for him to be so prodigal of it), thrice four, he poured upon his sacrifice, to prevent the suspicion of any fire under (for, if there had been any, this would have put it out), and to make the expected miracle the more illustrious.

4. He then solemnly addressed himself to God by prayer before his altar, humbly beseeching him to *turn to ashes his burnt-offering* (as the phrase is, Ps. 20:3), and to testify his acceptance of it. His prayer was not long, for he used no vain repetitions, nor thought he should be *heard for*

his much speaking; but it was very grave and composed, and showed his mind to be calm and sedate, and far from the heats and disorders that Baal's prophets were in, *v.* 36, 37. Though he was not at the *place* appointed, he chose the appointed *time of the offering of the evening sacrifice*, thereby to testify his communion with the altar at Jerusalem. Though he expected an answer by fire, yet he came near to the altar with boldness, and feared not that fire. He addressed himself to God as *the God of Abraham, Isaac, and Israel*, acting faith on God's ancient covenant, and reminding people too (for prayer may prevail) of their relation both to God and to the patriarchs. Two things he pleads here: — (1.) The glory of God: "Lord, hear me, and answer me, *that it may be known* (for it is now by the most denied or forgotten) *that thou art God in Israel*, to whom alone the homage and devotion of Israel are due, and *that I am thy servant*, and do all that I have done, am doing, and shall do, as thy agent, *at thy word*, and not to gratify any humour or passion of my own. Thou employest me; Lord, make it appear that thou dost so;" see Num. 16:28, 29. Elijah sought not his own glory but in subserviency to God's, and for his own necessary vindication. (2.) The edification of the people: *"That they may know that thou art the Lord*, and may experience thy grace, *turning their heart*, by this miracle, as a means, *back again to thee*, in order to thy return in a way of mercy to them."

5. God immediately answered him by fire, *v.* 38. Elijah's God was neither talking nor pursuing, needed not to be either awakened or quickened; while he was yet speaking, *the fire of the Lord fell*, and not only, as at other times (Lev. 9:24; 1 Chr. 21:26; 2 Chr. 7:1) *consumed the sacrifice and the wood*, in token of God's acceptance of the offering, but *licked up all the water in the trench*, exhaling that, and drawing it up as a vapour, in order to the intended rain, which was to be the fruit of this sacrifice and prayer, more than the product of natural causes. Compare Ps. 135:7. *He causeth vapours to ascend, and maketh lightnings for the rain;* for this rain he did both. As for those who fall as victims to the fire of God's wrath, no water can shelter them from it, any more than briers or thorns, Isa. 27:4, 5. But this was not all; to complete the miracle, the fire consumed the *stones of the altar, and* the very *dust*, to show that it was no ordinary fire, and perhaps to intimate that, though God accepted this occasional sacrifice from this altar, yet for the future they ought to demolish all the altars on their high places, and, for their constant sacrifices, make use of that at Jerusalem only. Moses's altar and Solomon's were consecrated by the fire from heaven; but this was destroyed, because no more to be used. We may well imagine what a terror the fire struck on guilty Ahab and all the worshippers of Baal, and how they fled from it as far and as fast as they could, saying, *Lest it consume us also*, alluding to Num. 16:34.

VI. What was the result of this fair trial. The prophets of Baal had failed in their proof, and could give no evidence at all to make out their pretensions on behalf of their god, but were perfectly non-suited Elijah had, by the most convincing and undeniable evidence, proved his claims on behalf of the God of Israel. And now, 1. The people, as the jury, gave in their verdict upon the trial, and they are all agreed in it; the case is so plain that they need not go from the bar to consider of their verdict or consult about it: *They fell on their faces*, and all, as one man, said, "Jehovah, he is the God, and not Baal; we are convinced and satisfied of it: *Jehovah, he is the God"* (*v.* 39), whence, one would think, they should have inferred, "If he be the God, he shall be our God, and we will serve him only," as Jos. 24:24. Some, we hope, had their hearts thus turned back, but the generality of them were convinced only, not converted, yielded to the truth of God, that he is the God, but consented not to his covenant, that he should be theirs. Blessed are those that have not seen what *they* saw and yet have believed and been wrought upon by it more than those that saw it. Let it for ever be looked upon as a point adjudged against all pretenders (for it was carried, upon a full hearing, against one of the most daring and threatening competitors that ever the God of Israel was affronted by) that *Jehovah, he is God*, God alone. 2. The prophets of Baal, as criminals, are seized, condemned, and executed, according to law, *v.* 40. If Jehovah be the true God, Baal is a false God, to whom these Israelites had revolted, and seduced others to the worship of him; and therefore,

by the express law of God, they were to be put to death, Deu. 13:1–11. There needed no proof of the fact; all Israel were witnesses of it: and therefore Elijah (acting still by an extraordinary commission, which is not to be drawn into a precedent) orders them all to be slain immediately as the troublers of the land, and Ahab himself is so terrified, for the present, with the fire from heaven, that he dares not oppose it. These were the 450 prophets of Baal; the 400 prophets of the groves (who, some think, were Sidonians), though summoned (*v.* 19), yet, as it should seem, did not attend, and so escaped this execution, which fair escape perhaps Ahab and Jezebel thought themselves happy in; but it proved they were reserved to be the instruments of Ahab's destruction, some time after, by encouraging him to go up to Ramoth-Gilead, *ch.* 22:6.

Verses 41–46

Israel being thus far reformed that they had acknowledged the Lord to be God, and had consented to the execution of Baal's prophets, that they might not seduce them any more, though this was far short of a thorough reformation, yet it was so far accepted that God thereupon opened the bottles of heaven, and poured out blessings upon his land, that very evening (as it should seem) on which they did this good work, which should have confirmed them in their reformation; see Hag. 2:18, 19.

I. Elijah sent Ahab to *eat and drink*, for joy that God *had now accepted his works*, and that rain was coming; see Eccl. 9:7. Ahab had continued fasting all day, either religiously, it being a day of prayer, or for want of leisure, it being a day of great expectation; but now let him *eat and rink* for, though others perceive no sign of it, Elijah, by faith, hears *the sound of abundance of rain, v.* 41. God reveals his secrets to his servants the prophets; and yet, without a revelation, we may foresee that when man's judgments run down like a river God's mercy will. Rain is *the river of God*, Ps. 65:9.

II. He himself retired to pray (for though God had promised rain, he must ask it, Zec. 10:1), and to give thanks for God's answer by fire, now hoping for an answer by water. What he said we are not told; but, 1. He withdrew to a strange place, to the *top of Carmel*, which was very high and very private. Hence we read of those that *hide themselves in the top of Carmel*, Amos 9:3. There he would be alone. Those who are called to appear and act in public for God must yet find time to be private with him and keep up their converse with him in solitude. There he set himself, as it were, *upon his watch-tower*, like the prophet, Hab. 2:1. 2. He put himself into a strange posture. He cast himself down on his knees upon the earth, in token of humility, reverence, and importunity, and *put his face between his knees* (that is, bowed his head so low that it touched his knees), thus abasing himself in the sense of his own meanness now that God had thus honoured him.

III. He ordered his servant to bring him notice as soon as he discerned a cloud arising out of the sea, the Mediterranean Sea, which he had a large prospect of from the top of Carmel. The sailors at this day call it *Cape Carmel*. Six times his servant goes to the point of the hill and sees nothing, brings no good news to his master; yet Elijah continues praying, will not be diverted so far as to go and see with his own eyes, but still sends his servant to see if he can discover any hopeful cloud, while he keeps his mind close and intent in prayer, and abides by it, as one that has taken up his father Jacob's resolution, *I will not let thee go except thou bless me.* Note, Though the answer of our fervent and believing supplications may not come quickly, yet we must continue instant in prayer, and not faint nor desist; for *at the end it shall speak and not lie.*

IV. A little cloud at length appeared, no bigger than a man's hand, which presently overspread the heavens and watered the earth, *v.* 44, 45. Great blessings often arise from small beginnings, and showers of plenty from a cloud of a span long. Let us therefore never *despise the day of small things*, but hope and wait for great things from it. This was not as a morning cloud, which passes away (though Israel's goodness was so), but one that produced a plentiful rain (Ps. 68:9), and an earnest of more.

V. Elijah hereupon hastened Ahab home, and attended him himself. Ahab rode in his chariot, at ease and in state, *v.* 45. Elijah ran on foot before him. If Ahab had paid the respect to Elijah that he deserved he would have taken

him into his chariot, as the eunuch did Philip, that he might honour him before the elders of Israel, and confer with him further about the reformation of the kingdom. But his corruptions got the better of his convictions, and he was glad to get clear of him, as Felix of Paul, when he dismissed him, and adjourned his conference with him to a more convenient season. But, since Ahab invites him not to ride with him, he will *run before him* (*v.* 46) as one of his footmen, that he may not seem to be lifted up with the great honour God had put upon him or to abate in his civil respect to his prince, though he reproved him faithfully. God's ministers should make it appear that, how great soever they look when they deliver God's message, yet they are far from affecting worldly grandeur: let them leave that to the kings of the earth.

CHAPTER 19

We left Elijah at the entrance of Jezreel, still appearing publicly, and all the people's eyes upon him. In this chapter we have him again absconding, and driven into obscurity, at a time when he could ill be spared; but we are to look upon it as a punishment to Israel for the insincerity and inconstancy of their reformation. When people will not learn it is just with God to remove their teachers into corners. Now observe, I. How he was driven into banishment by the malice of Jezebel his sworn enemy (*v.* 1–3). II. How he was met, in his banishment, by the favour of God, his covenant-friend. 1. How God fed him (*v.* 4–8). 2. How he conversed with him, and manifested himself to him (*v.* 9, 11–13), heard his complaint (*v.* 10–14), directed him what to do (*v.* 15–17), and encouraged him (*v.* 18). III. How his hands were strengthened, at his return out of banishment, by the joining of Elisha with him (*v.* 19–21).

Verses 1–8

One would have expected, after such a public and sensible manifestation of the glory of God and such a clear decision of the controversy depending between him and Baal, to the honour of Elijah, the confusion of Baal's prophets, and the universal satisfaction of the people — after they had seen both fire and water come from heaven at the prayer of Elijah, and both in mercy to them, the one as it signified the acceptance of their offering, the other as it *refreshed their inheritance, which was weary* — that now they would all, as one man, return to the worship of the God of Israel and take Elijah for their guide and oracle, that he would thenceforward be prime-minister of state, and his directions would be as laws both to king and kingdom. But it is quite otherwise; he is neglected whom God honoured; no respect is paid to him, nor care taken of him, nor any use made of him, but, on the contrary, the land of Israel, to which he had been, and might have been, so great a blessing, is now made too hot for him. 1. Ahab incensed Jezebel against him. That queen-consort, it seems, was in effect queen-regent, as she was afterwards when she was queen-dowager, an imperious woman that managed king and kingdom and did what she would. Ahab's conscience would not let him persecute Elijah (some remains he had in him of the blood and spirit of an Israelite, which tied his hands), but he told Jezebel all that Elijah had done (*v.* 1), not ton convince, but to exasperate her. It is not said he told her what *God* had done, but what *Elijah* had done, as if he, by some spell or charm, had brought fire from heaven, and the hand of the Lord had not been in it. Especially he represented to her, as that which would make her outrageous against him, that he had slain the prophets; the prophets of Baal he calls *the prophets*, as if none but they were worthy of the name. His heart was set upon them, and he aggravated the slaying of them as Elijah's crime, without taking notice that it was a just reprisal upon Jezebel for killing God's prophets, *ch.* 18:4. Those who, when they cannot for shame or fear do mischief themselves, yet stir up others to do it, will have it laid to their charge as if they had themselves done it. 2. Jezebel sent him a threatening message (*v.* 2), that she had vowed and sworn to be the death of him within twenty-four hours. Something prevents her from doing it just now, but she resolves it shall not be long undone. Note, Carnal hearts are hardened and enraged against God by that which should convince and conquer them and bring them into subjection to him. She swears by her gods, and, raging like one distracted, curseth herself if she slay not him, without any proviso of a divine permission. Cruelty and confidence often meet in persecutors. *I will pursue, I will overtake*, Ex. 15:9. But how came she to send him word of her design, and so to give him an opportunity of making his escape? Did she think him so daring that he would not flee, or herself so formidable that she could prevent him? Or was there a special providence in it, that she should be thus infatuated by her own fury? I am apt to think that though she desired nothing more than his blood, yet, at this time, she durst not meddle with him *for fear of the people, all counting him a prophet,* a great prophet, and therefore sent this message to him merely to frighten him and get him out of the way. for the present, that he might not carry on what he had begun. The backing of her threats with an oath and imprecation does not at all prove that she really intended to slay him, but only that she intended to make him believe so. The gods she swore by could do her no harm. 3. Elijah, hereupon, in a great fright, fled for his life, it is likely by night, and came to Beer-sheba, *v.* 3. Shall we praise him for this? We praise him not. Where was the courage with which he had lately confronted Ahab and all the prophets of Baal? Nay, which kept him by his sacrifice when the fire of God fell upon it? He that stood undaunted in the midst of the terrors both of heaven and earth trembles at the impotent menaces of a proud passionate woman. *Lord, what is man!* Great faith is not always alike strong. He could not but know that he might be very serviceable to Israel at this juncture, and had all the reason in the world to depend upon God's protection while he was doing God's work; yet he fled. In his former danger God had bidden him hide himself (*ch.* 17:3), therefore he supposed he might do so now. 4. From Beer-sheba he went forward into the wilderness, that vast howling wilderness in which the Israelites wandered. Beer-sheba was so far distant from Jezreel, and within the dominion of so good a king as Jehoshaphat, that he could not but be safe there; yet, as if his fears haunted him even when he was out of the reach of danger, he could not rest there, but went a day's journey into the desert. Yet perhaps he retired thither not so much for his safety as that he might be wholly retired from the world, in order to a more free and intimate communion with God. *He left his servant at Beer-sheba* that he might be private in the wilderness, as Abraham left his servants at the bottom of the hill when he went up into the mount to worship God, and as Christ in the garden was *withdrawn from his disciples,* or perhaps it was because he would not expose his servant, who was young and tender, to the hardships of the wilderness, which would have been putting new wine into old bottles. We ought thus to consider the frame of those who are under our charge, for God considers ours. 5. Being wearied with his journey, he grew cross (like children when they are sleepy) and *wished he might die, v.* 4. He *requested for his life* (so it is ion the margin), *that he might die;* for death is life to a good man; the death of the body is the life of the soul. Yet that was not the reason why he wished to die; it was not the deliberate desire of grace, as Paul's, to *depart and be with Christ,* but the passionate wish of his corruption, as Job's. Those that are, in this manner, forward to die are not in the fittest frame for dying. Jezebel has sworn his death, and therefore he, in a fret, prays for it, runs from death to death, yet with this difference, he wishes to die by the hand of the Lord, whose tender mercies are great, and not to fall into the hands of man, whose tender mercies are cruel. He would rather die in the wilderness than as Baal's prophet died, according to Jezebel's threatening (*v.* 2), lest the worshippers of Baal should triumph and blaspheme the God of Israel, whom they will think themselves too hard for, if they can run down his advocate. He pleads, "It is enough. I have done enough, and suffered enough. I am weary of living." Those that have secured a happiness in the other world will soon have enough of this world. He pleads, *"I am not better than my fathers,* not better able to bear those fatigues, and therefore why should I be longer burdened with them than they were?" But is this *that my lord Elijah?* Can that great and gallant spirit shrink thus? God thus left him to himself, to show that when he was bold and strong it was *in the Lord and the power of his might,* but of himself he was *no better than his fathers* or brethren. 6. God, by an angel, fed him in that wilderness, into the wants and perils of which he had wilfully thrown himself, and in which, if God had not graciously succoured him, he would have perished. How much better does God deal with his froward children than they deserve! Elijah, in a pet, wished to die; God needed him not, yet he designed further to employ and honour him, and therefore sent an angel to *keep him alive.* Our case would be bad sometimes if God should take us at our word and grant us our foolish passionate requests. Having prayed that he might die, he *laid down and slept* (*v.* 5), wishing it may be to die in his sleep, and not to awake again; but he is awakened out of his sleep, and finds himself not only well provided for with bread and water (*v.* 6), but, which was more, attended by an angle, who guarded him when he slept, and twice called him to his food when it was ready for him, *v.* 5, 7. He needed not to complain of the unkindness of men when it was thus made up by the ministration of angels. Thus provided for, he had reason to think he had fared better than the *prophets of the groves,* that *did eat at Jezebel's table.* Wherever God's children are, as they are still upon their Father's ground, so they are still under their Father's eye and care. They may lose themselves in a wilderness, but God has not lost them; there they may *look at him that lives and sees them, as Hagar,* Gen. 16:13. 7. He was carried, in the strength of this meat, to Horeb, *the mount of God, v.* 8. Thither the Spirit of the Lord led him, probably beyond his own intention, that he might have communion with God in the same place where Moses had, the law that was given by Moses being revived by him. The angel bade him eat the second time, because of the greatness *of the journey* that was *before him, v.* 7. Note God knows what he designs us for, though we do not, what service, what trials, and will take care for us when we, for want of foresight, cannot for ourselves, that we be furnished for them with *grace sufficient.* He that appoints what the voyage shall be will victual the ship accordingly. See how many different ways God took to keep Elijah alive; he fed him by ravens, with multiplied meals — then by an angel — and now, to show that *man lives not by bread alone,* he kept him alive forty days without meat, not resting and sleeping, which might make him the less to crave sustenance, but continually traversing the mazes of the desert, a day for a year of Israel's wanderings; yet he neither needs food nor desires it. The place, no doubt, reminds him of the manna, and encourages him to hope that God will sustain him here, and in due time bring him hence, as he did Israel, though, like him, fretful and distrustful.

Verses 9–18

Here is, I. Elijah housed in a cave at Mount Horeb, which is called *the mount of God,* because on it God had formerly manifested his glory. And perhaps this was the same cave, or cleft of a rock, in which Moses was hidden when the Lord *passed by before him and proclaimed his name,* Ex. 33:22. What Elijah proposed to himself in coming to lodge here, I cannot conceive, unless it was to indulge his melancholy, or to satisfy his curiosity and assist his faith and devotion with the sight of that famous place where the law was given and where so many great things were done, and hoping to meet with God himself there, where Moses met with him, or in token of his abandoning his people Israel, who hated to be reformed (in the latter case, it agrees with Jeremiah's wish, Jer. 9:2, *O that I had in the wilderness a lodging place of wayfaring men, that I might leave my people, and go from them, for they are all adulterers)* and so it was a bad omen of God's forsaking them; or it was because the thought he could not be safe any where else, and to this instance of the hardships this good man was reduced to the apostle refers, Heb. 11:38. *They wandered in deserts and in mountains, and in dens and caves of the earth.*

II. The visit God paid to him there and the enquiry he made concerning him: *The word of the Lord came to him.* We cannot go any where to be out of the reach of God's eye, his arm, and his word. *Whither can I flee from thy Spirit?* Ps. 139:7, etc. God will take care of his out-casts; and those who, for his sake, are driven out from among men, he will find, and own, and gather with everlasting loving-kindnesses. John saw the visions of the Almighty when he was in banishment in the isle of Patmos, Rev. 1:9. The question God puts to the prophet it, *What doest* thou *here, Elijah? v.* 9, and again *v.* 13. This is a reproof, 1. For his fleeing hither. "What brings thee so far from home? Dost thou flee from Jezebel? Couldst thou not depend upon almighty power for thy protection?" Lay the emphasis upon the pronoun *thou.* "What *thou!* So great a man, so great a prophet, so famed for resolution — dost thou flee thy country, forsake thy colours thus?" This cowardice would have been more excusable in another, and not so bad an example. *Should such a man as I flee?* Neh. 6:11. *Howl, fir-trees, if the cedars be* thus *shaken.* 2. For his fixing here. "What doest thou here, in this cave? Is this a place for a prophet of the Lord to lodge in? Is this a time for such men to retreat, when the public has such need of them?" In the retirement to which God sent Elijah (*ch.* 17) he was a blessing to a poor widow at Sarepta, but here he had no opportunity of doing good. Note, It concerns us often to enquire whether we be in our place and in the way of our duty. "Am I where I should be, whither God calls me, where my business lies, and where I may be useful?"

III. The account he gives of himself, in answer to the question put to him (*v.* 10), and repeated, in answer to the same question, *v.* 14.

1. He excuses his retreat, and desires it may not be imputed to his want of zeal for reformation, but to his despair of success. For God knew, and his own conscience witnessed for him, that as long as there was any hope of doing good he had been *very jealous for the Lord God of Hosts;* but now that he had *laboured in vain,* and all his endeavours were to no purpose, he thought it was time to give up the cause, and mourn for what he could not mend. *Abi in cellam, et dic, Miserere mei — "Away to thy cell, and cry, Have compassion on me."*

2. He complains of the people, their obstinacy in sin, and the height of impiety to which they had arrived: *"The children of Israel have forsaken thy covenant,* and that is the reason I have forsaken them; who can stay among them, to see every thing that is sacred ruined and run down?" This the apostle calls his *making intercession against Israel,* Rom. 11:2, 3. He had often been, of choice, their advocate, but now he is necessitated to be their accuser, before God. Thus Jn. 5:45, *There is one that accuseth you, even Moses, whom you trust.* Those are truly miserable that have the testimony and prayers of God's prophets against them. (1.) He charges them with having forsaken God's covenant; though they retained circumcision, that sign and seal of it, yet they had quitted his worship and service, which was the intention of it. Those who neglect God's ordinances, and let fall their communion with him, do really forsake his covenant, and break their league with him. (2.) With having *thrown down his altars,* not only deserted them and suffered them to go to decay, but, in their zeal for the worship of Baal, wilfully demolished them. This alludes to the private altars which the prophets of the Lord had, and which good people attended, who could not go up to Jerusalem and would not worship the calves nor Baal. These separate altars, though breaking in upon the unity of the church, yet, being erected and attended by those that sincerely aimed at the glory of God and served him faithfully, the seeming schism was excused. God owned them for his altars, as well as that at Jerusalem, and the putting of them down is charged upon Israel as a crying sin. But this was not all. (3.) *They have slain thy prophets with the sword,* who, it is probable, ministered at those altars. Jezebel, a foreigner, slew them (*ch.* 18:4), but the crime is charged upon the body of the people because the generality of them were *consenting to their death,* and pleased with it.

3. He gives the reasons why he retired into this desert and took up his residence in this cave. (1.) It was because he could not appear to any purpose: *"I only am left,* and have none to second or support me in any good design. They all said, *The Lord he is God,* but none of them would stand by me nor offer to shelter me. That point then gained was presently lost again, and Jezebel can do more to debauch them than I can to reform them. What can one do against thousands?" Despair of success hinders many a good enterprise. No one is willing to venture alone, forgetting that those are not alone who have God with them. (2.) It was because he could not appear with any safety: *"They seek my life to take it away;* and I had better spend my life in a useless solitude than lose my life in a fruitless endeavour to reform those that hate to be reformed."

IV. God's manifestation of himself to him. Did he come hither to meet with God? He shall find that God will not fail to give him the meeting. Moses was put into the cave when God's glory passed before him; but Elijah was called out of it: *Stand upon the mount before the Lord, v.* 11. He *saw no manner of similitude,* any more than Israel did when God *talked to them in Horeb.* But, 1. He heard a strong wind, and saw the terrible effects of it, for it rent the mountains and tore the rocks. Thus was the trumpet sounded before the Judge of heaven and earth, by his angels, whom he makes *spirits,* or *winds* (Ps. 104:4), sounded so loud that the earth not only rang, but rent again. 2. He felt the shock of an earthquake. 3. He saw an eruption of fire, *v.* 12. These were to usher in the designed manifestation of the divine glory, angels being employed in them, whom he *maketh a flame of fire,* and who, as his ministers, march before him, to *prepare in this desert a highway for our God.* But, 4. At last he perceived a *still small voice,* in which *the Lord was,* that is, by which he spoke to him, and not out of the wind, or the earthquake, or the fire. Those struck an awe upon him, awakened his attention, and inspired humility and reverence; but God chose to make known his mind to him in whispers soft, not in those dreadful sounds. When he perceived this, (1.) *He wrapped hi face in his mantle,* as one afraid to look upon the glory of God, and apprehensive that it would dazzle his eyes and overcome him. The angels *cover their faces* before God in token of reverence, Isa. 6:2. Elijah hid his face in token of shame for having been such a coward as to flee from his duty when he had such a God of power to stand by him in it. The wind, and earthquake, and fire, did not make him cover his face, but the still voice did. Gracious souls are more affected by the tender mercies of the Lord than by his terrors. (2.) He stood at the entrance of the cave, ready to hear what God had to say to him. This method of God's manifesting himself here at Mount Horeb seems to refer to the discoveries God formerly made of himself at this place to Moses. [1.] Then there was a tempest, an earthquake, and fire (Heb. 12:18); but, when God would show Moses his glory, he *proclaimed his goodness;* and so here: *He was, the Word* was, in the *still small voice.* [2.] Then the law was thus given to Israel, with the appearances of terror first and then with a voice of words; and Elijah being now called to revive that law, especially the first two commandments of it, is here taught how to manage it; he must not only awaken and terrify the people with amazing signs, like the earthquake and fire, but he must endeavour, with a still small voice, to convince and persuade them, and not forsake them when he should be addressing them. Faith comes by hearing the word of God; miracles do but make way for it. [3.] Then God spoke to his people with terror; but in the gospel of Christ, which was to be introduced by the spirit and power of Elias, he would speak by a still small voice, the dread of which should not make us afraid; see Heb. 12:18, etc.

V. The orders God gives him to execute. He repeats the question he had put to him before, *"What dost thou here?* This is not a place for thee now." Elijah gives the same answer (*v.* 14), complaining of Israel's apostasy from God and the ruin of religion among them. To this God gives him a reply. When he wished *he might die* (*v.* 4) God answered him not according to his folly, but was so far from letting him die that he not only kept him alive then but provided that he should never die, but be translated. But when he complained of his discouragement (and whither should God's prophets go with their complaints of that kind but to their Master?) God gave him an answer. He sends him back with directions to appoint Hazael king of Syria (*v.* 15), Jehu king of Israel, and Elisha his successor in the eminency of the prophetical office (*v.* 16), which is intended as a prediction that by these God would chastise the degenerate Israelites, plead his own cause among them, and *avenge the quarrel of his covenant, v.* 17. Elijah complained that the wickedness of Israel was unpunished. The judgment of famine was too gentle, and had not reclaimed them; it was removed before they were reformed: *"I have been jealous,"* says he, "for God's name, but he himself has not appeared jealous for it." "Well," says God, "be content; it is all in good time; *judgments are prepared for those scorners,* though they are not yet inflicted; the persons are pitched upon, and shall now be nominated, for they are now in being, who shall do the business." 1. "When Hazael comes to be king of Syria, he shall make bloody work among the people (2 Ki. 8:12) and so correct them for their idolatry." 2. "When Jehu comes to be king of Israel he shall make bloody work with the royal family, and shall utterly destroy the house of Ahab, that set up and maintained idolatry." 3. "Elisha, while thou art on earth, shall strengthen thy hands; and, when thou art gone, shall carry on thy work, and be a remaining witness against the apostasy of Israel, and even he shall slay the children of Bethel, that idolatrous city." Note, The wicked are reserved to judgment. *Evil pursues sinners,* and there is no escaping it; to attempt an escape is but to run from one sword's point upon another. See Jer. 48:44, *He that flees from the fear shall fall into the pit; and he that gets up out of the pit shall be taken in the snare.* Elisha, with the *sword of the Spirit,* shall terrify and wound the consciences of those who escape Hazael's sword of war and Jehu's sword of justice. *With the breath of his lips shall he slay the wicked,* Isa. 11:4; 2 Th. 2:8; Hos. 6:5. It is a great comfort to good men and good ministers to think that God will never want instruments to do his work in his time, but, when they are gone, others shall be raised up to carry it on.

VI. The comfortable information God gives him of the number of Israelites who retained their integrity, though he thought he was left alone (*v.* 18): *I have left 7000 in Israel* (besides Judea) *who have not bowed the knee to Baal.* Note, 1. In times of the greatest degeneracy and apostasy God has always had, and will have, a remnant faithful to him, some that keep their integrity and do not go down the stream. The apostle mentions this answer of God to Elijah (Rom. 11:4) and applies it to his own day, when the Jews generally rejected the gospel. *Yet,* says he, *at this time also there is a remnant, v.* 5. 2. It is God's work to preserve that remnant, and distinguish them from the rest, for without his grace they could not have distinguished themselves: *I have left me;* it is therefore said to be a remnant *according to the election of grace.* 3. It is but a little remnant, in comparison with the degenerate race; what are 7000 to the thousands of Israel? Yet, when those of every age come together, they will be found many more, 12,000 *sealed out of each tribe,* Rev. 7:4. 4. God's faithful ones are often his hidden ones (Ps. 83:3), and the visible church is scarcely visible, the wheat lost in the chaff and the gold in the dross, till the sifting, refining, separating day comes. 5. *The Lord knows those that are his,* though we do not; he sees in secret. 6. There are more good people in the world than some wise and holy men think there are. Their jealousy of themselves, and for God, makes them think the corruption is universal; but God sees not as they do. When we come to heaven, as we shall miss a great many whom we thought to meet there, so we shall meet a great many whom we little thought to find there. God's love often proves larger than man's charity and more extensive.

Verses 19–21

Elisha was named last in the orders God gave to Elijah, but he was first called, for by him the other two were to be called. He must come in Elijah's room; yet Elijah is forward to raise him, and is far from being jealous of his successor, but rejoices to think that he shall leave the work of God in such good hands. Concerning the call of Elisha observe, 1. That it was an unexpected surprising call. Elijah found him by divine direction, or perhaps he was before acquainted with him and knew where to find him. He found him, not in the schools of the prophets, but *in the field,* not reading, nor praying, nor sacrificing, but *ploughing, v.* 19. Though a great man (as appears by his feast, *v.* 21), master of the ground, and oxen, and servants, yet he did not think it any disparagement to him to follow his business himself, and not only to inspect his servants, but himself to lay his hand to the plough. Idleness is no man's honour, nor is husbandry any man's disgrace. An honest calling in the world does not at all put us out of the way of our heavenly calling, any more than it did Elisha, who was taken from following the plough the feed Israel and to sow the *seed of the word,* as the apostles were taken from fishing to catch men. Elisha enquired not after Elijah, but was anticipated with this call. We love God, and choose him, because he chose us, and loved us, first. 2. That it was a powerful call. Elijah did but *cast his mantle upon him.* (*v.* 19), in token of friendship, that he would take him under his care and tuition as he did under his mantle, and to be one with him in the same clothes, or in token of his being clothed with the spirit of Elijah (now he put some of his honour upon him, as Moses on Joshua, Num. 27:20); but, when Elijah went to heaven, he had the mantle entire, 2 Ki. 2:13. And immediately he *left the oxen* to go as they would, and *ran after Elijah,* and assured him that he would follow him presently, *v.* 20. An invisible hand touched his heart, and unaccountably inclined him by a secret power, without any external persuasions, to quit his husbandry and give himself to the ministry. It is in a day of power that Christ's subjects are made willing (Ps. 110:3), nor would any come to Christ unless they were thus drawn. Elisha came to a resolution presently, but begged a little time, not to *ask* leave, but only to *take* leave, of his parents. This was not an excuse for delay, like his (Lu. 9:61) that desired he might *bid those farewell that were at home,* but only a reservation of the respect and duty he owed to his father and mother. Elijah bade him to back and do it, he would not hinder him; nay, if he would, he might go back, and not return, for any thing he had done to him. He will not force him, nor take him against his will; let him sit down and count the cost, and make it his own act. The efficacy of God's grace preserves the native liberty of man's will, so that those who are good are good of choice and not by constraint, not pressed men, but volunteers. 3. That it was a pleasant and acceptable call to him, which appears by the farewell-feast he made for his family (*v.* 21), though he not only quitted all the comforts of his father's house, but exposed himself to the malignity of Jezebel and her party. It was a discouraging time for prophets to set out in. A man that had consulted with flesh and blood would not be fond of Elijah's mantle, nor willing to wear his coat; yet Elisha cheerfully, and with a great deal of satisfaction, leaves all to accompany him. Thus Matthew made a great fast when he left the receipt of custom to follow Christ. 4. That it was an effectual call. Elijah did not stay for him, lest he should seem to compel him, but left him to his own choice, and he soon arose, went after him, and not only associated with him, but *ministered to him* as his servitor, *poured water on his hands,* 2 Ki. 3:11. It is of great advantage to young ministers to spend some time under the direction of those that are aged and experienced, whose years teach wisdom, and not to think much, if occasion be, to minister to them. Those that would be fit to teach must have time to learn; and those that hope hereafter to rise and rule must be willing at first to stoop and serve.

CHAPTER 20

This chapter is the history of a war between Ben-hadad king of Syria and Ahab king of Israel, in which Ahab was, once and again, victorious. We read nothing of Elijah or Elishain all this story; Jezebel's rage, it is probable, had abated, and the persecution of the prophets began to cool, which gleam of peace Elijah improved. He appeared not at court, but, being told how many thousands of good people there were in Israel more than he thought of, employed himself, as we may suppose, in founding religious houses, schools, or colleges of prophets, in several parts of the country, to be nurseries of religion, that they might help to reform the nation when the throne and court would not be reformed. While he was thus busied, God favoured the nation with the successes we here read of, which were the more remarkable because obtained against Ben-hadad king of Syria, whose successor, Hazael, was ordained to be a scourge to Israel. They must shortly suffer by the Syrians, and yet now triumphed over them, that, if possible, they might be led to repentance by the goodness of God. Here is, I. Ben-hadad's descent upon Israel, and his insolent demand (*v.* 1–11). II. The defeat Ahab gave him, encouraged and directed by a prophet (*v.* 12–21). III. The Syrians rallying again, and the second defeat Ahab gave them (*v.* 22–30). IV. The covenant of peace Ahab made with Ben-hadad, when he had him at his mercy (*v.* 31–34), for which he is reproved and threatened by a prophet (*v.* 35–43).

Verses 1–11

Here is, I. The threatening descent which Ben-hadad made upon Ahab's kingdom, and the siege he laid to Samaria, his royal city, *v.* 1. What the ground of the quarrel was we are not told; covetousness and ambition were the principle, which would never want some pretence or other. David in his time had quite subdued the Syrians and made them tributaries to Israel, but Israel's apostasy from God makes them formidable again. Asa had tempted the Syrians to invade Israel once (*ch.* 15:18–20), and now they did it of their own accord. It is dangerous bringing a foreign force into the country: posterity may pay dearly for it. Ben-hadad had with him thirty-two kings, who were either tributaries to him, and bound in duty to attend him, or confederates with him, and bound in interest to assist him. How little did the title of king look when all these poor petty governors pretended to it!

II. The treaty between these two kings. Surely Israel's defence had departed from them, or else the Syrians could not have marched so readily, and with so little opposition, to Samaria, the head and heart of the country, a city lately built, and therefore, we may suppose, not well fortified, but likely to fall quickly into the hands of the invaders; both sides are aware of this, and therefore,

1. Ben-hadad's proud spirit sends Ahab a very insolent demand, *v.* 2, 3. A parley is sounded, and a trumpeter (we may suppose) is sent into the city, to let Ahab know that he will raise the siege upon condition that Ahab become his vassal (Nay, his *villain),* and not only pay him a tribute out of what he has, but make over his title to Ben-hadad, and hold all at his will, even his wives and children, the godliest of them. The manner of expression is designed to gall them; "All shall be mine, without exception."

2. Ahab's poor spirit sends Ben-hadad a very disgraceful submission. It is general indeed (he cannot mention particulars in his surrender with so much pleasure as Ben-hadad did in his demand), but it is effectual: *I am thine, and all that I have, v.* 4. See the effect of sin. (1.) If he had not by sin provoked God to depart from him, Ben-hadad could not have made such a demand. Sin brings men into such straits, by putting them out of divine protection. If God may not rule us, our enemies shall. A rebel to God is a slave to all besides. Ahab had prepared his silver and gold for Baal, Hos. 2:8. Justly therefore is it taken from him; such an alienating amounts to a forfeiture. (2.) If he had not by sin wronged his own conscience, and set that against him, he could not have made such a mean surrender. Guilt dispirits men, and makes them cowards. He knew Baal could not help, and had no reason to think that God would, and therefore was content to buy his life upon any terms. Skin for skin, and all that is dear to him, he will give for it; he will rather live a beggar than not die a prince.

3. Ben-hadad's proud spirit rises upon his submission, and becomes yet more insolent and imperious, *v.* 5, 6. Ahab had laid his all at his feet, at his mercy, expecting that one king would use another generously, that this acknowledgment of Ben-hadad's sovereignty would content him, the honour was sufficient for the present, and he might hereafter make use of it if he saw cause *(Satis est prostrasse leoni — It suffices the lion to have laid his victim prostrate);* but this will not serve. (1.) Ben-hadad is as covetous as he is proud, and cannot go away unless he have the possession as well as the dominion. He thinks it not enough to call it his, unless he have it in his hands. He will not so much as lend Ahab the use of his own goods above a day longer. (2.) He is as spiteful as he is haughty. Had he come himself to select what he had a mind for, it would have shown some respect to a crowned head; but he will send his servants to insult the prince, and hector over him, to rifle the palace, and strip it of all its ornaments; nay, to give Ahab the more vexation, they shall be ordered, not only to take what they please, but, if they can learn which are the persons or things that Ahab is in a particular manner fond of, to take those: *Whatsoever is pleasant in thy eyes they shall take away.* We are often crossed in that which we most dote upon; and that proves least safe which is most dear. (3.) He is as unreasonable as he is unjust, and will construe the surrender Ahab made for himself as made for all his subjects too, and will have them also to lie at his mercy: "They shall search, not only thy house, but *the houses of thy servants* too, and plunder them at discretion." Blessed be God for peace and property, and that what we have we can call our own.

4. Ahab's poor spirit begins to rise too, upon this growing insolence; and, if it becomes not bold, yet it becomes desperate, and he will rather hazard his life than give up all thus. (1.) How he takes advice of his privy-council, who encourage him to stand it out. He speaks but poorly (*v.* 7), appeals to them whether Ben-hadad be not an unreasonable enemy, and do not seek mischief. What else could he expect from one who, without any provocation given him, had invaded his country and besieged his capital city? He owns to them how he had truckled to him before, and will have them advise him what he should do in this strait; and they speak bravely (*Hearken not to him, nor consent, v.* 8), promising no doubt to stand by him in the refusal. (2.) Yet he expresses himself very modestly in his denial, *v.* 9. He owns Ben-hadad's dominion over him: *"Tell my lord the king* I have no design to affront him, nor to receded from the surrender I have already made; what I offered at first I will stand to, *but this thing I may not do;* I must not give what is none of my own." It was a mortification to Ben-hadad that even such an abject spirit as Ahab's durst deny him; yet it should seem, by his manner of expressing himself, that he durst not have done it if his people had not animated him.

5. Ben-hadad proudly swears the ruin of Samaria. The threatening waves of his wrath, meeting with this check, rage and foam, and make a noise. In his fury, he imprecates the impotent revenge of his gods, *if the dust of Samaria serve for handfuls for his army* (*v.* 10), so numerous, so resolute, an army will be bring into the field against Samaria, and so confident is he of their success; it will be done as easily as the taking up of a handful of dust; all shall be carried away, even the ground on which the city stands. Thus confident is his pride, thus cruel is his malice; this prepares him to be ruined, though such a prince and such a people are unworthy of the satisfaction of seeing him ruined.

6. Ahab sends him a decent rebuke to his assurance, dares not defy his menaces, only reminds him of the uncertain turns of war (*v.* 11): "Let not him that begins a war, and is girding on his sword, his armour, his harness, boast of victory, or think himself sure of it, *as if he had put it off,* and had come home a conqueror." This was one of the wisest words that ever Ahab spoke, and is a good item or momento to us all; it is folly to boast beforehand of any day, since we know not what it may bring forth (Prov. 27:1), but especially to boast of a day of battle, which may prove as much against us as we promise ourselves it will be for us. It is impolitic to despise an enemy, and to be too sure of victory is the way to be beaten. Apply it to our spiritual conflicts. Peter fell by his confidence. While we are here we are but girding on the harness, and therefore must never boast as though we had put it off. *Happy is the man that feareth always,* and is never off his watch.

Verses 12–21

The treaty between the besiegers and the besieged being broken off abruptly, we have here an account of the battle that ensued immediately.

I. The Syrians, the besiegers, had their directions from a drunken king, who gave orders over his cups, as he was *drinking* (*v.* 12), *drinking himself drunk* (*v.* 16) *with the kings in the pavilions,* and this at noon. Drunkenness is a sin which armies and their officers have of old been addicted to. Say not thou then that the former days were, in this respect, better than these, though these are bad enough. Had he not been very secure he would not have sat to drink; and, had he not be intoxicated, he would not have been so very secure. Security and sensuality went together in the old world, and Sodom, Lu. 17:26, etc. Ben-hadad's drunkenness was the forerunner of his fall, as Belshazzar's was, Dan. 5. How could he prosper that preferred his pleasure before his business, and kept his kings to drink with him when they should have been at their respective posts to fight for him? In his drink, 1. He orders the town to be invested, the engines fixed, and every thing got ready for the making of a general attack (*v.* 12), but stirs not from his drunken club to see it done. *Woe unto thee, O land! when thy king is* such *a child.* 2. When the besieged made a sally (and, by that time, he was far gone) he gave orders to take them alive (*v.* 18), not to kill them, which might have been done more easily and safely, but to seize them, which gave them an opportunity of killing the aggressors; so imprudent was he in the orders he gave, as well as unjust, in ordering them to be taken prisoners though they came for peace and to renew the treaty. Thus, as is usual, he drinks, and forgets the law, both the policies and the justice of war.

II. The Israelites, the besieged, had their directions from an inspired prophet, one of the prophets of the Lord, whom Ahab had hated and persecuted: *And behold a prophet, even one, drew near to the king of Israel;* so it may be read, *v.* 13.

1. Behold, and wonder, that God should send a prophet with a kind and gracious message to so wicked a prince as Ahab was; but he did it, (1.) For his people Israel's sake, who, though wickedly degenerated, were the seed of Abraham his friend and Jacob his chosen, the children of the covenant, and not yet cast off. (2.) That he might magnify his mercy, in doing good to one so evil and unthankful, might either bring him to repentance or leave him the more inexcusable. (3.) That he might mortify the pride of Ben-hadad and check his insolence. Ahab's idolatry shall be punished hereafter, but Ben-hadad's haughtiness shall be chastised now; for God resists the proud, and is pleased to say that *he fears the wrath of the enemy,* Deu. 32:26, 27. There was but one prophet perhaps to be had in Samaria, and he drew near with this message, intimating that he had been forced to keep at a distance. Ahab, in his prosperity, would not have borne the sight of him, but now he bids him welcome, when none of the prophets of the groves can give him any assistance. He enquired not for a prophet of the Lord, but God sent one to him unasked, for he waits to be gracious.

2. Two things the prophet does: — (1.) He animates Ahab with an assurance of victory, which was more than all the elders of Israel could give him (*v.* 8), though they promised to stand by him. This prophet, who is not named (for he *spoke in God's name),* tells him from God that this very day the siege shall be raised, and the army of the Syrians routed, *v.* 13. When the prophet said, *Thus saith the Lord,* we may suppose Ahab began to tremble, expecting a message of wrath; but he is revived when it proves a gracious one. He is informed what use he ought to make of this blessed turn of affairs: *"Thou shalt know that I am Jehovah,* the sovereign Lord of all." God's foretelling a thing that was so very unlikely proved that it was his own doing. (2.) He instructs him what to do for the gaining of this victory. [1.] He must not stay till the enemy attacked him, but must sally out upon them and surprise them in their trenches. [2.] The persons employed must be the *young men of the princes of the provinces,* the pages, the footmen, who were few in number, only 232, utterly unacquainted with war, and the unlikeliest men that could be thought of for such a bold attempt; yet these must do it, these weak and foolish things must be instruments of confounding the wise and strong, that, while Ben-hadad's boasting is punished, Ahab's may be prevented and precluded, and the *excellency of the power may appear to be of God.* [3.] Ahab must himself so far testify his confidence in the word of God as to command in person, though, in the eye of reason, he exposed himself to the utmost danger by it. But it is fit that those who have the benefit of God's promises should enter upon them. Yet, [4.] He is allowed to make use of what other forces he has at hand, to follow the blow, when these young men have broken the ice. All he had in Samaria, or within call, were but 7000 men, *v.* 15. It is observable that it is the same number with theirs that he not *bowed the knee to Baal* (*ch.* 19:18), though, it is likely, not the same men.

III. The issue was accordingly. The proud Syrians were beaten, and the poor despised Israelites were more than conquerors. The young men gave an alarm to the Syrians just at noon, at high dinner-time, supported by what little force they had, *v.* 16. Ben-hadad despised them at first (*v.* 18), but when they had, with unparalleled bravery and dexterity, *slain every one his man,* and so put the army into disorder, that proud man durst not face them, but mounted immediately, drunk as he was, and made the best of his way, *v.* 20. See how God *takes away the spirit of princes,* and makes himself *terrible to the kings of the earth.* Now where are the silver and gold he demanded of Ahab? Where are the handfuls of Samaria's dust? Those that are most secure are commonly least courageous. Ahab failed not to improve this advantage, but *slew the Syrians with a great slaughter, v.* 21. Note, God oftentimes makes one wicked man a scourge to another.

Verses 22–30

We have here an account of another successful campaign which Ahab, by divine aid, made against the Syrians, in which he gave them a greater defeat than in the former. Strange! Ahab idolatrous and yet victorious, a persecutor and yet a conqueror! God has wise and holy ends in suffering wicked men to prosper, and glorifies his own name thereby.

I. Ahab is admonished by a prophet to prepare for another war, *v.* 22. It should seem, he was now secure, and looked but a little way before him. Those that are careless of their souls are often as careless of their outwards affairs; but the prophet (to whom God made known the following counsels of the Syrians) told him they would renew their attempt at the return of the year, hoping to retrieve the honour they had lost and be avenged for the blow they had received. He therefore bade him strengthen himself, put himself into a posture of defence, and be ready to give them a warm reception. God had decreed the end, but Ahab must use the means, else he tempts God: "Help thyself, strengthen thyself, and God will help and strengthen thee." The enemies of God's Israel are restless in their malice, and, though they may take some breathing-time for themselves, yet they are still *breathing out threatenings and slaughter* against the church. It concerns us always to expect assaults from our spiritual enemies, and therefore to mark and see what we do.

II. Ben-hadad is advised by those about him concerning the operations of the next campaign. 1. They advised him to *change his ground, v.* 23. They took it for granted that it was not Israel, but Israel's gods, that beat them (so great a regard was then universally had to invisible powers); but they speak very ignorantly of Jehovah — that he was *many,* whereas he is one and his name one, — that he was *their* God only, a local deity, peculiar to that nation, whereas he is the Creator and ruler of all the world, — and that he was a God *of the hills* only, because David their great prophet had said, *I will lift up my eyes to the hills whence cometh my help* (Ps. 121:1), and that *his foundation was in the holy mountain* (Ps. 87:1; 78:54), and much was said of his *holy hill* (Ps. 15:1; 24:3); supposing him altogether such a one as their imaginary deities, they fancied he was confined to his hills, and could not or would not come down from them, and therefore an army in the valley would be below his cognizance and from under his protection. Thus vain were the *Gentiles in their imaginations* concerning God, so wretchedly were *their foolish hearts darkened,* and, *professing themselves to be wise, they became fools.* 2. They advised him to change his officers (*v.* 24, 25), not to employ the kings, who were commanders by birth, but captains rather, who were commanders by merit, who were inured to war, would not affect to make a show like the kings, but would go through with business. Let every man be employed in that which he is brought up to and used to, and preferred to that which he is fit for. Syria, it seems, was rich and populous, when it could furnish recruits sufficient, after so great a defeat, *horse for horse, chariot for chariot.*

III. Both armies take the field. Ben-hadad, with his Syrians, encamps near Aphek, in the tribe of Asher. It is probable that Asher was a city in his own possession, one of those which his father had won (*v.* 34), and the country about it was flat and level, and fit for his purpose, *v.* 26. Ahab, with his forces, posted himself at some distance over against them, *v.* 27. The disproportion of numbers was very remarkable. *The children of Israel,* who were cantoned in two battalions, looked like *two little flocks of kids,* their numbers small, their equipage mean, and the figure they made contemptible; *but the Syrians filled the country* with their numbers, their noise, their chariots, their carriages, and their baggage.

IV. Ahab is encouraged to fight the Syrians, notwithstanding their advantages and confidence. A man of God is sent to him, to tell him that this numerous army shall *all be delivered into his hand* (*v.* 28), but not for his sake; be it known to him, he is utterly unworthy for whom God will do this. God would not do it because Ahab had praised God or prayed to him (we do not read that he did either), but because the Syrians had blasphemed God, and had said, He is *the God of the hills and not of the valleys;* therefore God will do it in his own vindication, and to preserve the honour of his own name. If the Syrians had said, "Ahab and his people have forgotten their God, and so put themselves out of his protection, and therefore we may venture to attack them," God would probably have delivered Israel into their hands; but when they go upon a presumption so very injurious to the divine omnipotence, and the honour of him who is Lord of all hosts, not only in hills and valleys, but in heaven and earth, which they are willingly ignorant of, they shall be undeceived, at the expense of that vast army which is so much their pride and confidence.

V. After the armies had faced one another seven days (the Syrians, it is likely, boasting, and the Israelites trembling), they engaged, and the Syrians were totally routed, 100,000 men slain by the sword of Israel in the field of battle (*v.* 29), and 27,000 men, that thought themselves safe *under the walls of Aphek,* a fortified city (from the walls of which the shooters might annoy the enemy if they pursued them, 2 Sa. 11:24), found their bane where they hoped for protection: the wall fell upon them, probably overthrown by an earthquake, and, the cities of Canaan being walled up to heaven, it reached a great way, and they were all killed, or hurt, or overwhelmed with dismay. Ben-hadad, who thought his city Aphek would hold out against the conquerors, finding it thus unwalled, and the remnant of his forces dispirited and dispersed, had nothing but secresy to rely upon for safety, and therefore hid himself in *a chamber within a chamber,* lest the pursuers should seize him. See how the greatest confidence often ends in the greatest cowardice. "Now is the God of Israel the *God of the valleys* or no?" He shall know now that he is forced *into an inner chamber to hide himself,* see *ch.* 22:25.

Verses 31–43

Here is an account of what followed upon the victory which Israel obtained over the Syrians.

I. Ben-hadad's tame and mean submission. Even in his inner chamber he feared, and would, if he could, flee further, though none pursued. His servants, seeing him and themselves reduced to the last extremity, advised that they should surrender at discretion, and make themselves prisoners and petitioners to Ahab for their lives, *v.* 31. The servants will put their lives in their hands, and venture first, and their master will act according as they speed. Their inducement to take this course is the great reputation the kings of Israel had for clemency above any of their neighbours: "We have heard that they are merciful kings, not oppressive to their subjects that are under their power" (as governments then went, that of Israel was one of the most easy and gentle), "and therefore not cruel to their enemies when they lie at their mercy." Perhaps they had this notion of the kings of Israel because they had heard that the God of Israel proclaimed his name *gracious and merciful,* and they concluded their kings would make their God their pattern. It was an honour to the kings of Israel to be thus represented, as indeed every Israelite is then dressed as becomes him when he *puts on bowels of mercies.* "They are merciful kings, therefore we may hope to find mercy upon our submission." This encouragement poor sinners have to repent and humble themselves before God. "Have we not heard that the God of Israel is a merciful God? Have we not found him so? Let us therefore rend our hearts and return to him." Joel 2:13. That is evangelical repentance which flows from an apprehension of the mercy of God in Christ; *there is forgiveness with him.* Two things Ben-hadad's servants undertake to represent to Ahab: — 1. Their master a penitent; for they *girded sackcloth on their loins,* as mourners, and *put ropes on their heads,* as condemned criminals going to execution, pretending to be sorry that they had invaded his country and disturbed his repose, and owning that they deserved to be hanged for it. Here they are ready to do penance for it, and throw themselves at the feet of him whom they had injured. Many pretend to repent of their wrong-doing, when it does not succeed, who, if they had prospered in it, would have justified it and gloried in it. 2. Their master a beggar, a beggar for his life: *Thy servant Ben-hadad saith, "I pray thee, let me live, v.* 32. Though I live a perpetual exile from my own country, and captive in this, yet, upon any terms, *let me live."* What a great change is here, (1.) In his condition! How has he fallen from the height of power and prosperity to the depths of disgrace and distress, and all the miseries of poverty and slavery! See the uncertainty of human affairs; such turns are they subject to that the spoke which was uppermost may soon come to be undermost. (2.) In his temper — in the beginning of the chapter hectoring, swearing, and threatening, and none more high in his demands, but here crouching and whining and none more low in his requests! How meanly does he beg hi life at the hand of him upon whom he had there been trampling! The most haughty in prosperity are commonly most abject in adversity: an even spirit will be the same in both conditions. See how God glorified himself when he *looks upon proud men and abases them, and hides them in the dust together,* Job 40:11–13.

II. Ahab's foolish acceptance of his submission, and the league he suddenly made with him upon it. He was proud to be thus courted by him whom he had feared, and enquired for him with great tenderness: *Is he yet alive? He is my brother,* brother-king, though not brother-Israelite: and Ahab valued himself more upon his royalty than on his religion, and others accordingly. *"Is he thy brother, Ahab?* Did he use thee like a brother when he sent thee that barbarous message? *v.* 5, 6. Would he have called thee brother if he had been the conqueror? Would he now have called himself *thy servant* if he had not been reduced to the utmost strait? Canst thou suffer thyself to be thus imposed upon by a forced and counterfeit submission?" This word *brother* they caught at (*v.* 33), and were thereby encouraged to go and fetch him to the king. He that calls him *brother* will let him live. Let poor penitents hear God, in his word, calling them *children* (Jer. 31:20), catch at it, echo to it, and call him *Father.* Ben-hadad, upon his submission, shall not only be honourably conveyed (he *took him up into the chariot),* but treated with as an ally (*v.* 34): he *made a covenant with him,* not consulting God's prophets, or the elders of the land, or himself, concerning what was fit to be insisted on, but, as if Ben-hadad had been conqueror, he shall make his own terms. He might now have demanded some of Ben-hadad's cities, when all of them lay at the mercy of his victorious army; but was content with the restitution of his own. He might now have demanded the stores, and treasures, and magazines of Damascus, to augment the wealth and strength of his own kingdom, but was content with a poor liberty, at his own expense, to build streets there, a point of honour and no advantage, or no more than what the kings of Syria had had in Samaria, though they had never had so much power as he had now to support the demand of it. With this covenant he sent him away, without so much as reproving him for his blasphemous reflections upon the God of Israel, for whose honour Ahab had no concern. Note, There are those on whom success is ill bestowed; they know not how to serve God, or their generation, or even their own true interests, with their prosperity. *Let favour be shown to the wicked, yet will he not learn righteousness.*

III. The reproof given to Ahab for his clemency to Ben-hadad and his covenant with him. It was given him by a prophet, in the name of the Lord, the Jews say by Micaiah, and not unlikely, for Ahab complains of him (*ch.* 22:8) that he used to *prophesy evil concerning him.* This prophet designed to reprove Ahab by a parable, that he might oblige him to condemn himself, as Nathan and the woman of Tekoa did David. To make his parable the more plausible, he finds it necessary to put himself into the posture of a wounded soldier. 1. With some difficulty he gets himself wounded, for he would not wound himself with his own hands. He commanded one of his brother prophets, his *neighbour,* or *companion* (for so the word signifies), to smite him, and this in God's name (*v.* 35), but finds him not so willing to give the blow as he is to receive it; he refused to smite him: others, he thought, were forward enough to smite prophets, they need not smite one another. We cannot but think it was from a good principle he declined it. "If it must be done, let another do it, not I; I cannot find it in my heart to strike my friend." Good men can much more easily receive a wrongful blow than give one; yet because he disobeyed an express command of God (which was so much the worse if he was himself a prophet), like that other disobedient prophet (*ch.* 13:24), he was presently *slain by a lion, v.* 36. This was intended, not only to show, in general, how provoking disobedience is (Col. 3:6), but to intimate to Ahab (who no doubt was told the story) that if a good prophet were thus punished for sparing his friend and God's, when God said, *Smite,* of much sorer punishment should a wicked king be thought worthy, who spared his enemy and God's, when God said, *Smite. Shall mortal man* pretend to *be more just than God, more pure* or more compassionate *than his Maker?* We must be merciful as he is merciful, and not otherwise. The next he met with made no difficulty of smiting him *(Volenti non fit injuria — He that asks for an injury is not wronged by it)* and did it so that he *wounded him, v.* 37. He fetched blood with the blow, probably in his face. 2. Wounded as he was, and disguised with ashes that he might not be known to be a prophet, he made his application to the king in a story wherein he charged himself with such a crime as the king was now guilty of in sparing Ben-hadad, and waited for the king's judgment upon it. The case in short is this — A prisoner taken in the battle was committed to his custody by a man (we may suppose one that had authority over him as his superior officer) with this charge, *If he be missing, thy life shall be for his life, v.* 39. The prisoner has made his escape through his carelessness. Can the chancery in the king's breast relieve him against his captain, who demands his life in lieu of the prisoner's? "By no means," says the king, "thou shouldst either not have undertaken the trust or been more careful and faithful to it; there is no remedy *(Currat lex — Let the law take its course),* thou hast forfeited thy bond, and execution must go out upon it: *So shall thy doom be, thou thyself hast decided it."* Now the prophet has what he would have, puts off his disguise, and is known by Ahab himself to be a prophet (*v.* 41) and plainly tells him, *"Thou art the man.* Is it *my* doom? No, it is *thine; thou thyself hast decided it.* Out of thy own mouth art thou judged. God, thy superior and commander-in-chief, delivered into thy hands one plainly marked for destruction both by his own pride and God's providence, and thou hast not carelessly lost him, but wittingly and willingly dismissed him, and so hast been false to thy trust, and lost the end of thy victory; expect therefore no other than that *thy life shall go for his life,* which thou hast spared" (and so it did, *ch.* 22:35), "and thy *people for his people,* whom likewise thou hast spared," and so they did afterwards, 2 Ki. 10:32, 33. When their other sins brought them low, this came into the account. There is a time when *keeping back the sword from blood* is *doing the work of the Lord deceitfully,* Jer. 48:10. Foolish pity spoils the city. 3. We are told how Ahab resented this reproof. He *went to his house heavy and displeased* (*v.* 43), not truly penitent, or seeking to undo what he had done amiss, but enraged at the prophet, exasperated against God (as if he had been too severe in the sentence passed upon him), and yet vexed at himself, every way out of humour, notwithstanding his victory. He who by his providence had mortified the pride of one king, by his word cast a damp upon the triumphs of another. *Be wise therefore, O you kings! and be instructed to serve the Lord with fear and rejoice with trembling,* Ps. 2:10, 11.

CHAPTER 21

Ahab is still the unhappy subject of the sacred history; from the great affairs of his camp and kingdom this chapter leads us into his garden, and gives us an account of some ill things (and ill indeed they proved to him) relating to his domestic affairs. I. Ahab is sick for Naboth's vineyard (*v.* 1–4). II. Naboth dies by Jezebel's plot, that the vineyard may escheat to Ahab (*v.* 5–14). III. Ahab goes to take possession (*v.* 15–16). IV. Elijah meets him, and denounces the judgments of God against him for his injustice (*v.* 17–24). V. Upon his humiliation a reprieve is granted (*v.* 25–29).

Verses 1–4

Here is, 1. Ahab coveting his neighbour's vineyard, which unhappily lay near his palace and conveniently for a kitchen-garden. Perhaps Naboth had been pleased that he had a vineyard which lay so advantageously for a prospect of the royal gardens, or the vending of its productions to the royal family; but the situation of it proved fatal to him. If he had had no vineyard, or it had lain obscure in some remote place, he would have preserved his life. But many a man's possessions have been his snare, and his neighbourhood to greatness has been of pernicious consequence. Ahab sets his eye and heart on this vineyard, *v.* 2. It will be a pretty addition to his demesne, a convenient out-let to his palace; and nothing will serve him but it must be his own. He is welcome to the fruits of it, welcome to walk in it; Naboth perhaps would have made him a lease of it for his life, to please him; but nothing will please him unless he have an absolute property in it, he and his heirs for ever. Yet he is not such a tyrant as to take it by force, but fairly proposes either to give Naboth the full value of it in money or a better vineyard in exchange. He had tamely quitted the great advantages God had given him of enlarging his dominion for the honour of his kingdom, by his victory over the Syrians, and now is eager to enlarge his garden, only for the convenience of his house, as if to be penny wise would atone for being pound foolish. To desire a convenience to his estate was not evil (there would be no buying if there were no desire of what is bought; the virtuous woman *considers a field and buys it);* but to desire any thing inordinately, though we would compass it by lawful means, is a fruit of selfishness, as if we must engross all the conveniences, and none must live, or live comfortably, by us, contrary to the law of contentment, and the letter of the tenth commandment, *Thou shalt not covet thy neighbour's house.* 2. The repulse he met with in this desire. Naboth would by no means part with it (*v.* 3): *The Lord forbid it me;* and the Lord did forbid it, else he would not have been so rude and uncivil to his prince as not to gratify him in so small a matter. Canaan was in a peculiar manner God's land; the Israelites were his tenants; and this was one of the conditions of their leases, that they should not alienate (no, not to one another) any part of that which fell to their lot, unless in case of extreme necessity, and then only till the year of jubilee, Lev. 25:28. Now Naboth foresaw that, if his vineyard were sold to the crown, it would never return to his heirs, no, not in the jubilee. He would gladly oblige the king, but he must obey God rather than men, and therefore in this matter desires to be excused. Ahab knew the law, or should have known it, and therefore did ill to ask that which his subject could not grant without sin. Some conceive that Naboth looked upon his earthly inheritance as an earnest of his lot in the heavenly Canaan, and therefore would not part with the former, lest it should amount to a forfeiture of the latter. He seems to have been a conscientious man, who would rather hazard the king's displeasure than offend God, and probably was one of the 7000 that had not bowed the knee to Baal, for which, it may be, Ahab owed him a grudge. 3. Ahab's great discontent and uneasiness hereupon. He was as before (*ch.* 20:43) *heavy and displeased* (*v.* 4), grew melancholy upon it, threw himself upon his bed, would not eat nor admit company to come to him. He could by no means digest the affront. His proud spirit aggravated the indignity Naboth did him in denying him, as a thing not to be suffered. He cursed the squeamishness of Naboth's conscience, which he pretended to consult the peace of, and secretly meditated revenge. Nor could he bear the disappointment; it cut him to the heart to be crossed in his desires, and he was perfectly sick for vexation. Note, (1.) Discontent is a sin that is its own punishment and makes men torment themselves; it makes the spirit sad, the body sick, and all the enjoyments sour; it is the heaviness of the heart and the rottenness of the bones. (2.) It is a sin that is its own parent. It arises not from the condition, but from the mind. As we find Paul contented in a prison, so Ahab discontent in a palace. He had all the delights of Canaan, that pleasant land, at command the wealth of a kingdom, the pleasures of a court, and the honours and powers of a throne; and *yet all this avails him nothing* without Naboth's vineyard. Inordinate desires expose men to continual vexations, and those that are disposed to fret, be they ever so happy, will always find something or other to fret at.

Verses 5–16

Nothing but mischief is to be expected when Jezebel enters into the story — *that cursed woman,* 2 Ki. 9:34.

I. Under pretence of comforting her afflicted husband, she feeds his pride and passion, and blows the coals of his corruptions. It became her to take notice of his grief and to enquire into the cause of it, *v.* 5. Those have forgotten both the duty and affection of the conjugal relation that interest not themselves in each other's troubles. He told her what troubled him (*v.* 6), yet invidiously concealed Naboth's reason for his refusal, representing it as peevish, when it was conscientious — *I will not give it thee,* whereas he said, *I may not.* What! says Jezebel (*v.* 7), *Dost thou govern Israel? Arise, and eat bread.* She does well to persuade him to shake off his melancholy, and not to sink under his burden, to be easy and cheerful; whatever was his grief, grieving would not redress it, but pleasantness would alleviate it. Her plea is, *Dost thou now govern Israel?* This is capable of a good sense: "Does it become so great a prince as thou art to cast thyself down for so small a matter? Thou shamest thyself, and profanest thy crown; it is below thee to take notice of so inconsiderable a thing. Art thou fit to govern Israel, who hast no better a government of thy own passions? Or hast thou so rich a kingdom at command and canst not thou be without this one vineyard?" We should learn to quiet ourselves, under our crosses, with the thoughts of the mercies we enjoy, especially our hopes of the kingdom. But she meant it in a bad sense: *"Dost thou govern Israel,* and shall any subject thou hast deny thee any thing thou hast a mind to? Art thou a king? It is below thee to buy and pay, much more to beg and pray; use thy prerogative, and take by force what thou canst not compass by fair means; instead of resenting the affront thus, revenge it. If thou knowest not how to support the dignity of a king, let me alone to do it; give me but leave to make use of thy name, and I will soon *give thee the vineyard of Naboth;* right or wrong, it shall be thy own shortly, and cost thee nothing." Unhappy princes those are, and hurried apace towards their ruin, who have those about them that stir them up to acts of tyranny and teach them how to abuse their power.

II. In order to gratify him, she projects and compasses the death of Naboth. No less than his blood will serve to atone for the affront he has given to Ahab, which she thirsts after the more greedily because of his adherence to the law of the God of Israel.

1. Had she aimed only at his land, her false witnesses might have sworn him out of that by a forged deed (she could not have set up so weak a title but the elders of Jezreel would have adjudged it good); but *the adulteress will hunt for the precious life,* Prov. 6:26. Revenge is sweet. Naboth must die, and die as a malefactor, to gratify it.

(1.) Never were more wicked orders given by any prince than those which Jezebel sent to the magistrates of Jezreel, *v.* 8–10. She borrows the privy-seal, but the king shall not know what she will do with it. It is probable this was not the first time he had lent it to her, but that with it she had signed warrants for the slaying of the prophets. She makes use of the king's name, knowing the thing would please him when it was done, yet fearing he might scruple at the manner of doing it; in short, she commands them, upon their allegiance, to put Naboth to death, without giving them any reason for so doing. Had she sent witnesses to inform against him, the judges (who must go *secundum allegata et probata — according to allegations and proofs*) might have been imposed upon, and their sentence might have been rather their unhappiness than their crime; but to oblige them to find the witnesses, sons of Belial, to suborn them themselves, and then to give judgment upon a testimony which they knew to be false, was such an impudent defiance to every thing that is just and sacred as we hope cannot be paralleled in any story. She must have looked upon the elders of Jezreel as men perfectly lost to every thing that is honest and honourable when she expected these orders should be obeyed. But she will put them in a way how to do it, having as much of the serpent's subtlety as she had of his poison. [1.] It must be done under colour of religion: *"Proclaim a fast;* signify to your city that you are apprehensive of some dreadful judgment coming upon you, which you must endeavour to avert, not only by prayer, but by finding out and by putting away the accursed thing; pretend to be afraid that there is some great offender among you undiscovered, for whose sake God is angry with your city; charge the people, if they know of any such, on that solemn occasion to inform against him, as they regard the welfare of the city; and at last let Naboth be fastened upon as the suspected person, probably because he does not join with his neighbours in their worship. This may serve for a pretence to *set him on high among the people,* to call him to the bar. Let proclamation be made that, if any one can inform the court against the prisoner, and prove him to be the Achan, they shall be heard; and then let the witnesses appear to give evidence against him." Note, There is no wickedness so vile, so horrid, but religion has sometimes been made a cloak and cover for it. We must not think at all the worse of fasting and praying for their having been sometimes thus abused, but much the worse of those wicked designs that have at any time been carried on under the shelter of them. [2.] It must be done *under colour of justice* too, and with the formalities of a legal process. Had she sent to them to hire some of their danbitti, some desperate suffirans, to assassinate him, to stab him as he went along the streets in the night, the deed would have been bad enough; but to destroy him by a course of law, to use that power for the murdering of the innocent which ought to be their protection, was such a *violent perversion of justice and judgment* as was truly monstrous, yet such as we are directed *not to marvel at,* Eccl. 5:8. The crime they must lay to his charge was *blaspheming God and the king* — a complicated blasphemy. Surely she could not think to put a blasphemous sense upon the answer he had given to Ahab, as if denying him his vineyard were blaspheming the king, and giving the divine law for the reason were blaspheming God. No, she pretends not any ground at all for the charge: though there was no colour of truth in it, the witnesses must swear it, and Naboth must not be permitted to speak for himself, or cross-examine the witnesses, but immediately, under pretence of a universal detestation of the crime, they must *carry him out and stone him.* His blaspheming God would be the forfeiture of his life, but not of his estate, and therefore he is also charged with treason, in *blaspheming the king,* for which his estate was to be confiscated, that so Ahab might have his vineyard.

(2.) Never were wicked orders more wickedly obeyed than these were by the magistrates of Jezreel. They did not so much as dispute the command nor make any objections against it, though so palpably unjust, but punctually observed all the particulars of it, either because they feared Jezebel's cruelty or because they hated Naboth's piety, or both: They did *as it was written in the letters* (*v.* 11, 12), neither made any difficulty of it, nor met with any difficulty in it, but cleverly carried on the villany. They stoned Naboth to death (*v.* 13), and, as it should seem, his sons with him, or after him; for, when God came to make inquisition for blood, we find this article in the account (2 Ki. 9:26), *I have seen the blood of Naboth and the blood of his sons.* Perhaps they were secretly murdered, that they might not claim their father's estate nor complain of the wrong done him.

2. Let us take occasion from this sad story, (1.) To stand amazed at the wickedness of the wicked, and the power of Satan in the children of disobedience. What a holy indignation may we be filled with to see *wickedness in the place of judgment!* Eccl. 3:16. (2.) To lament the hard case of oppressed innocency, and to mingle our tears with *the tears of the oppressed that have no comforter,* while *on the side of the oppressors there is power,* Eccl. 4:1. (3.) To commit the keeping of our lives and comforts to God, for innocency itself will not always be our security. (4.) To rejoice in the belief of a judgment to come, in which such wrong judgments as these will be called over. Now we see that *there are just men to whom it happens according to the work of the wicked* (Eccl. 8:14), but all will be set to rights in the great day.

III. Naboth being taken off, Ahab takes possession of his vineyard. 1. The elders of Jezreel sent notice to Jezebel very unconcernedly, sent it to her as a piece of agreeable news, *Naboth is stoned and is dead, v.* 14. Here let us observe that, as obsequious as the elders of Jezreel were to Jezebel's orders which she sent from Samaria for the murder of Naboth, so obsequious were the elders of Samaria afterwards to Jehu's orders which he sent from Jezreel for the murder of Ahab's seventy sons, only that was not done by course of law, 2 Ki. 10:6, 7. Those tyrants that by their wicked orders debauch the consciences of their inferior magistrates may perhaps find at last the wheel return upon them, and that those who will not stick to do one cruel thing for them will be as ready to do another cruel thing against them. 2. Jezebel, jocund enough that her plot succeeded so well, brings notice to Ahab that *Naboth is not alive, but dead;* therefore, says she, *Arise, take possession of his vineyard, v.* 15. He might have taken possession by one of his officers, but so pleased is he with this accession to his estate that he will make a journey to Jezreel himself to enter upon it; and it should seem he went in state too, as if he had obtained some mighty victory, for Jehu remembers long after that he and Bidkar attended him at this time, 2 Ki. 9:25. If Naboth's sons were all put to death, Ahab thought himself entitled to the estate, *ob defectum sanguinis — in default of heirs* (as our law expresses it); if not, yet, Naboth dying as a criminal, he claimed it *ob delictum criminis — as forfeited by his crime.* Or, if neither would make him a good title, the absolute power of Jezebel would give it to him, and who would dare to oppose her will? Might often prevails against right, and wonderful is the divine patience that suffers it to do so. God is certainly *of purer eyes than to behold iniquity,* and yet for a time *keeps silence when the wicked devours the man that is more righteous than he,* Hab. 1:13.

Verses 17–29

In these verses we may observe,

I. The very bad character that is given of Ahab (*v.* 25, 26), which comes in here to justify God in the heavy sentence passed upon him, and to show that though it was passed upon occasion of his sin in the matter of Naboth (which David's sin in the matter of Uriah did too much resemble), yet God would not have punished him so severely if he had not been guilty of many other sins, especially idolatry; whereas David, except in that one matter, *did that which was right.* But, as to Ahab, there was *none like him,* so ingenious and industrious in sin, and that made a trade of it. He *sold himself to work wickedness,* that is, he made himself a perfect slave to his lusts, and was as much at their beck and command as ever any servant was at his master's. He was wholly given up to sin, and, upon condition he might have the pleasures of it, he would take the wages of it, which is death, Rom. 6:23. Blessed Paul complained that he was *sold under sin* (Rom. 7:14), as a poor captive against his will; but Ahab was voluntary: he *sold himself to sin;* of choice, and as his own act and deed, he submitted to the dominion of sin. It was no excuse of his crimes that *Jezebel his wife stirred him up* to do wickedly, and made him, in many respects, worse than otherwise he would have been. To what a pitch of impiety did he arrive who had such tinder of corruption in his heart and such a temper in his bosom to strike fire into it! In many things he did ill, but he did *most abominably in following idols,* like the Canaanites; his immoralities were very provoking to God, but his idolatries were especially so. Israel's case was sad when a prince of such a character as this reigned over them.

II. The message with which Elijah was sent to him, when he went to take possession of Naboth's vineyard, *v.* 17–19.

1. Hitherto God kept silence, did not intercept Jezebel's letters, nor stay the process of the elders of Jezreel; but now Ahab is reproved and his *sin set in order before his eyes.* (1.) The person sent is Elijah. A prophet of lower rank was sent with messages of kindness to him, *ch.* 20:13. But the father of the prophets is sent to try him, and condemn him, for his murder. (2.) The place is Naboth's vineyard and the time just when he is taking possession of it; then, and there, must his doom be read him. By taking possession, he avowed all that was done, and made himself guilty *ex post facto — as an accessary after the fact.* There he was taken in the commission of the errors, and therefore the conviction would come upon him with so much the more force. "What hast thou to do in this vineyard? What good canst thou expect from it when it is *purchased with blood* (Hab. 2:12) and thou hast *caused the owner thereof to lose his life?"* Job 31:39. Now that he is pleasing himself with his ill-gotten wealth, and giving direction for the turning of this vineyard into a flower-garden, his *meat in his bowels is turned. He shall not feel quietness. When he is about to fill his belly, God shall cast the fury of his wrath upon him,* Job 20:14, 20, 23.

2. Let us see what passed between him and the prophet.

(1.) Ahab vented his wrath against Elijah, fell into a passion at the sight of him, and, instead of humbling himself before the prophet, as he ought to have done (2 Chr. 36:12), was ready to fly in his face. *Hast thou found me, O my enemy? v.* 20. This shows, [1.] That he hated him. The last time we found them together they parted very good friends, *ch.* 18:46. Then Ahab had countenanced the reformation, and therefore then all was well between him and the prophet; but now he had relapsed, and was worse than ever. His conscience told him he had made God his enemy, and therefore he could not expect Elijah should be his friend. Note, That man's condition is very miserable that has made the word of God his enemy, and his condition is very desperate that reckons the ministers of that word his enemies because they *tell him the truth,* Gal. 4:16. Ahab, having sold himself to sin, was resolved to stand to his bargain, and could not endure him that would have helped him to recover himself, [2.] That he feared him: *Hast thou found me?* intimating that he shunned him all he could, and it was now a terror to him to see him. The sight of him was like that of the handwriting upon the wall to Belshazzar; it made his *countenance change, the joints of his loins were loosed, and his knees smote one against another.* Never was poor debtor or criminal so confounded at the sight of the officer that came to arrest him. Men may thank themselves if they make God and his word a terror to them.

(2.) Elijah denounced God's wrath against Ahab: *I have found thee* (says he, *v.* 20), *because thou hast sold thyself to work evil.* Note, Those that give up themselves to sin will certainly be found out, sooner or later, to their unspeakable horror and amazement. Ahab is now set to the bar, as Naboth was, and trembles more than he did. [1.] Elijah finds the indictment against him, and convicts him upon the notorious evidence of the fact (*v.* 19): *Hast thou killed, and also taken possession?* He was thus charged with the murder of Naboth, and it would not serve him to say the law killed him (perverted justice is the highest injustice), nor that, if he was unjustly prosecuted, it was not his doing — he knew nothing of it; for it was to please him that it was done, and he had shown himself pleased with it, and so had made himself guilty of all that was done in the unjust prosecution of Naboth. He killed, for he took possession. If he takes the garden, he takes the guilt with it. *Terra transit cum onere — The land with the incumbrance.* [2.] He passes judgment upon him. He told him from God that his family should be ruined and rooted out (*v.* 21) and all his posterity cut off, — that his house should be made like the houses of his wicked predecessors, Jeroboam and Baasha (*v.* 22), particularly that those who died in the city should be meat for dogs and those who died in the field meat for birds (*v.* 24), which had been foretold of Jeroboam's house (*ch.* 14:11), and of Baasha's (*ch.* 16:4), — that Jezebel, particularly, should be devoured by dogs (*v.* 23), which was fulfilled (2 Ki. 9:36), — and, as for Ahab himself, that the dogs should *lick his blood* in the very same place where they licked Naboth's (*v.* 19 — *"Thy blood, even thine,* though it be royal blood, though it swell thy veins with pride and boil in thy heart with anger, shall ere long be an entertainment for the dogs"), which was fulfilled, *ch.* 22:38. This intimates that he should die a violent death, should come to his grave with blood, and that disgrace should attend him, the foresight of which must needs be a great mortification to such a proud man. Punishments after death are here most insisted on, which, though such as affected the body only, were perhaps designed as figures of the soul's misery after death.

III. Ahab's humiliation under the sentence passed upon him, and the favourable message sent him thereupon. 1. Ahab was a kind of penitent. The message Elijah delivered to him in God's name put him into a fright for the present, so that he *rent his clothes* and *put on sackcloth, v.* 27. He was still a proud hardened sinner, and yet thus reduced. Note, God can make the stoutest heart to tremble and the proudest to humble itself. His word is quick and powerful, and is, when the pleases to make it so, like a *fire and a hammer,* Jer. 23:29. It made Felix tremble. Ahab put on the garb and guise of a penitent, and yet his heart was unhumbled and unchanged. After this, we find, he hated a faithful prophet, *ch.* 22:8. Note, It is no new thing to find the show and profession of repentance where yet the truth and substance of it are wanting. Ahab's repentance was only what might be seen of men: *Seest thou* (says God to Elijah) *how Ahab humbles himself;* it was external only, the garments rent, but not the heart. A hypocrite may go very far in the outward performance of holy duties and yet come short. 2. He obtained hereby a reprieve, which I may call a kind of pardon. Though it was but an outside repentance (lamenting the judgment only, and not the sin), though he did not leave his idols, nor restore the vineyard to Naboth's heirs, yet, because he did hereby give some glory to God, God took notice of it, and bade Elijah take notice of it: *Seest thou how Ahab humbles himself? v.* 29. In consideration of this the threatened ruin of his house, which had not been fixed to any time, should be *adjourned to his son's days.* The sentence should not be revoked, but the execution suspended. Now, (1.) This discovers the great goodness of God, and his readiness to show mercy, which here *rejoices against judgment.* Favour was shown to this wicked man that God might magnify his goodness (says bishop Sanderson) even to the hazard of his other divine perfections; as if (says he) God would be thought unholy, or untrue, or unjust (though he be none of these), or any thing, rather than unmerciful. (2.) This teaches us to take notice of that which is good even in those who are not so good as they should be: let it be commended as far as it goes. (3.) This gives a reason why wicked people sometimes prosper long; God is rewarding their external services with external mercies. (4.) This encourages all those that truly repent and unfeignedly believe the holy gospel. If a pretending partial penitent shall go to his house reprieved, doubtless a sincere penitent shall *go to his house justified.*

CHAPTER 22

This chapter finishes the history of Ahab's reign. It was promised in the close of the foregoing chapter that the ruin of his house should not come in his days, but his days were soon at an end. His war with the Syrians at Ramoth-Gilead is that which we have an account of in this chapter. I. His preparations for that war. He consulted, 1. His privy-council (*v.* 1–3). 2. Jehoshaphat (*v.* 4). 3. His prophets. (1.) His own, who encouraged him to go on this expedition (*v.* 5, 6), Zedekiah particularly (*v.* 11, 12). (2.) A prophet of the Lord, Micaiah, who was desired to come by Jehoshaphat (*v.* 7, 8), sent for (*v.* 9, 10–13, 14), upbraided Ahab with his confidence in the false prophets (*v.* 15), but foretold his fall in this expedition (*v.* 16–18), and gave him an account how he came to be thus imposed upon by his prophets (*v.* 19–23). He is abused by Zedekiah (*v.* 24, 25), and imprisoned by Ahab (*v.* 26–28). II. The battle itself, in which, 1. Jehoshaphat is exposed. But, 2. Ahab is slain (*v.* 29–40). In the close of the chapter we have a short account, (1.) Of the good reign of Jehoshaphat king of Judah (*v.* 41–50). (2.) Of the wicked reign of Ahaziah king of Israel (*v.* 51–53).

Verses 1–14

Though Ahab continued under guilt and wrath, and the dominion of the lusts to which he had sold himself, yet, as a reward for his professions of repentance and humiliation, though the time drew near when he should descend into battle and perish, yet we have him blessed with a three years' peace (*v.* 1) and an honourable visit made him by Jehoshaphat king of Judah, *v.* 2. The Jews have a fabulous conceit, that when Ahab humbled himself for his sin, and lay in sackcloth, he sent for Jehoshaphat to come to him, to chastise him; and that he staid with him for some time, and gave him so many stripes every day. This is a groundless tradition. He came now, it is probable, to consult him about the affairs of their kingdoms. It is strange that so great a man as Jehoshaphat would pay so much respect to a kingdom revolted from the house of David, and that so good a man should show so much kindness to a king revolted from the worship of God. But, though he was a godly man, his temper was too easy, which betrayed him into snares and inconveniences. The Syrians durst not give Ahab any disturbance. But,

I. Ahab here meditates a war against the Syrians, and advises concerning it with those about him, *v.* 3. The king of Syria gave him the provocation; when he lay at his mercy, he promised to restore him his cities (*ch.* 20:34), and Ahab foolishly took his word, when he ought not to have dismissed him till the cities were put into his possession. But now he knows by experience, what he ought before to have considered, that as the kisses, so the promises, *of an enemy are deceitful,* and there is no confidence to be put in leagues extorted by distress. Benhadad is one of those princes that think themselves bound by their word no further and no longer than it is for their interest. Whether any other cities were restored we do not find, but Ramoth-Gilead was not, a considerable city in the tribe of Gad, on the other side Jordan, a Levites' city, and one of the cities of refuge. Ahab blames himself, and his people, that they did not bestir themselves to recover it out of the hands of the Syrians, and to chastise Ben-hadad's violation of his league; and resolves to let that ungrateful perfidious prince know that as he had given him peace he could give him trouble. Ahab has a good cause, yet succeeds not. Equity is not to be judged of by prosperity.

II. He engages Jehoshaphat, and draws him in, to join with him in this expedition, for the recovery of Ramoth-Gilead, *v.* 4. And here I do not wonder that Ahab should desire the assistance of so pious and prosperous a neighbour. Even bad men have often coveted the friendship of the good. It is desirable to have an interest in those that have an interest in heaven, and to have those with us that have God with them. But it is strange that Jehoshaphat will go so entirely into Ahab's interests as to say, *I am as thou art, and my people as thy people.* I hope not; Jehoshaphat and his people are not so wicked and corrupt as Ahab and his people. Too great a complaisance to evildoers has brought many good people, through unwariness, into a dangerous fellowship with *the unfruitful works of darkness.* Jehoshaphat had like to have paid dearly for his compliment when, in battle, he was taken for Ahab. Yet some observe that in joining with Israel against Syria he atoned for his father's fault in joining with Syria against Israel, *ch.* 15:19, 20.

III. At the special instance and request of Jehoshaphat, he asks counsel of the prophets concerning this expedition. Ahab thought it enough to consult with his statesmen, but Jehoshaphat moves that they should *enquire of the word of the Lord, v.* 5. Note, 1. Whithersoever a good man goes he desires to take God along with him, and will acknowledge him in all his ways, ask leave of him, and look up to him for success. 2. Whithersoever a good man goes he ought to take his religion along with him, and not be ashamed to own it, no, not when he is with those who have no kindness for it. Jehoshaphat has not left behind him, at Jerusalem, his affection, his veneration, for *the word of the Lord,* but both avows it and endeavours to introduce it into Ahab's court. If Ahab drew him into his wars, he will draw Ahab into his devotions.

IV. Ahab's 400 prophets, the standing regiment he had of them (*prophets of the groves* they called them), agreed to encourage him in this expedition and to assure him of success, *v.* 6. He put the question to them with a seeming fairness: *Shall I go or shall I forbear?* But they knew which way his inclination was and designed only to humour the two kings. To please Jehoshaphat, they made use of the name *Jehovah:* He shall *deliver it into the hand of the king;* they stole the word from the true prophets (Jer. 23:30) and spoke their language. To please Ahab they said, *Go up.* They had indeed probabilities on their side: Ahab had, not long since, beaten the Syrians twice; he had now a good cause, and was much strengthened by his alliance with Jehoshaphat. But they pretended to speak by prophecy, not by rational conjecture, by divine, not human, foresight: "Thou shalt certainly recover Ramoth-Gilead." Zedekiah, a leading man among these prophets, in imitation of the true prophets, illustrated his false prophecy with a sign, *v.* 11. He made himself a pair of iron horns, representing the two kings, and their honour and power (both of which were signified by horns, exaltation and force), and with these the Syrians must be pushed. All the prophets agreed, as one man, that Ahab should return from this expedition a conqueror, *v.* 12. Unity is not always the mark of a true church and a true ministry. Here were 400 men that prophesied with one mind and one mouth, and yet all in an error.

V. Jehoshaphat cannot relish this sort of preaching; it is not like what he was used to. The false prophets cannot so mimic the true but that he who had spiritual senses exercised could discern the fallacy, and therefore he enquired for a *prophet of the Lord besides, v.* 7. He is too much of a courtier to say any thing by way of reflection on the king's chaplains, but he waits to see a *prophet of the Lord,* intimating that he could not look upon these to be so. They *seemed to be somewhat* (whatever they were, it made no matter to him), but, in conference, they *added nothing to him,* they gave him no satisfaction, Gal. 2:6. One faithful prophet of the Lord was worth them all.

VI. Ahab has another, but one he hates, Micaiah by name, and, to please Jehoshaphat, he is willing to have him sent for, *v.* 8–10. Ahab owned that they might *enquire of the Lord by him,* that he was a true prophet, and one that knew God's mind. And yet, 1. He hated him, and was not ashamed to own to the king of Judah that he did so, and to give this for a reason. He *doth not prophesy good concerning me, but evil.* And whose fault was that? If Ahab had done well, he would have heard nothing but good from heaven; if he do ill, he may thank himself for all the uneasiness which the reproofs and threats of God's word gave him. Note, Those are wretchedly hardened in sin, and are ripening apace for ruin, who hate God's ministers because they deal plainly with them and faithfully warn them of their misery and danger by reason of sin, and reckon those their enemies that *tell them the truth.* 2. He had (it should seem) imprisoned him; for, when he committed him (*v.* 26), he bade the officer carry him back, namely, to the place whence he came. We may suppose that this was he that reproved him for his clemency to Ben-hadad (*ch.* 20:38, etc.) and for so doing was cast into prison, where he had lain these three years. This was the reason why Ahab knew where to find him so readily, *v.* 9. But his imprisonment had not excluded him for divine visits: the spirit of prophecy continued with him there. He was bound, but *the word of the Lord was not.* Nor did it in the lease abate his courage, nor make him less confident or faithful in delivering his message. Jehoshaphat gave too gentle a reproof to Ahab for expressing his indignation against a faithful prophet: *Let not the king say so, v.* 8. He should have said, "Thou art unjust to the prophet, unkind to thyself, and puttest an affront upon his Lord and thine, in saying so." Such sinners as Ahab must be rebuked sharply. However he so far yielded to the reproof for that, for fear of provoking Jehoshaphat to break off from his alliance with him, he orders Micaiah to be sent for with all speed, *v.* 9. The two kings sat each in their robes and chairs of state, in the gate of Samaria, ready to receive this poor prophet, and to hear what he had to say; for many will give God's word the hearing that will not lend it an obedient ear. They were attended with a crowd of flattering prophets, that could not think of prophesying any thing but what was very sweet and very smooth to two such glorious princes now in confederacy. Those that love to be flattered shall not want flatterers.

VII. Micaiah is pressed by the officer that fetches him to follow the cry, *v.* 13. That officer was unworthy the name of an Israelite who pretended to prescribe to a prophet; but he thought him altogether such a one as the rest, who studied to please men and not God. He told Micaiah how unanimous the other prophets were in foretelling the king's good success, how agreeable it was to the king, intimating that it was his interest to say as they said — he might thereby gain, not only enlargement, but preferment. Those that dote upon worldly things themselves think every body else should do so too, and true or false, right or wrong, speak and act for their secular interest only. He intimated likewise that it would be to no purpose to contradict such a numerous and unanimous vote; he would be ridiculed, as affecting a foolish singularity, if he should. But Micaiah, who knows better things, protests, and backs his protestation with an oath, that he will deliver his message from God with all faithfulness, whether it be pleasing or displeasing to his prince (*v.* 14): *"What the Lord saith to me, that will I speak,* without addition, diminution, or alteration." This was nobly resolved, and as became one who had his eye to a greater King than either of these, arrayed with brighter robes, and sitting on a higher throne.

Verses 15–28

Here Micaiah does well, but, as is common, suffers ill for so doing.

I. We are told how faithfully he delivered his message, as one that was more solicitous to please God than to humour either the great or the many. In three ways he delivers his message, and all displeasing to Ahab: —

1. He spoke as the rest of the prophets had spoken, but ironically: *Go, and prosper, v.* 15. Ahab put the same question to him that he had put to his own prophets *(Shall we go, or shall we forbear?)* seeming desirous to know God's mind, when, like Balaam, he was strongly bent to do his own, which Micaiah plainly took notice of when he bade him go, but with such an air and pronunciation as plainly showed he spoke it by way of derision; as if he had said, "I know you are determined to go, and I hear your own prophets are unanimous in assuring you of success; go then and take what follows. They say, *The Lord shall deliver it into the hand of the king;* but I do not tell thee that *thus saith the Lord;* no, he saith otherwise." Note, Those deserve to be bantered that love to be flattered; and it is just with God to give up those to their own counsels that give up themselves to their own lusts. Eccl. 11:9. In answer to this Ahab adjured him to tell him the truth, and not to jest with him (*v.* 16), as if he sincerely desired to know both what God would have him to do and what he would do with him, yet intending to represent the prophet as a perverse ill-humoured man, that would not tell him the truth till he was thus put to his oath, or adjured to do it.

2. Being thus pressed, he plainly foretold that the king would be cut off in this expedition, and his army scattered, *v.* 17. He saw them in a vision, or in a dream, dispersed upon the mountains, as sheep that had no one to guide them. *Smite the shepherd, and the sheep will be scattered,* Zec. 13:7. This intimates, (1.) That Israel should be deprived of their king, who was their shepherd. God took notice of it, *These have no master.* (2.) That they would be obliged to retire *re infecta — without accomplishing their object.* He does not foresee any great slaughter in the army, but that they should make a dishonorable retreat. *Let them return every man to his house in peace,* put into disorder indeed for the present, but no great losers by the death of their king; he shall fall in war, but they shall go home

in peace. Thus Micaiah, in his prophecy, testified what he had seen and heard (let them take it how they pleased), while the others prophesied merely *out of their own hearts;* see Jer. 23:28. "The prophet that has a dream let him tell that, and so quote his authority; *and he that has my word, let him speak my word faithfully,* and not his own; for *what is the chaff to the wheat?*" Now Ahab finds himself aggrieved, turns to Jehoshaphat, and appeals to him whether Micaiah had not manifestly a spite against him, *v.* 18. Those that bear malice to others are generally willing to believe that others bear malice to them, though they have no cause for it, and therefore to put the worst constructions upon all they say. What evil did Micaiah prophesy to Ahab in telling him that, if he proceeded in this expedition, it would be fatal to him, while he might choose whether he would proceed in it or no? The greatest kindness we can do to one that is going a dangerous way is to tell him of his danger.

3. He informed the king how it was that all his prophets encouraged him to proceed, that God permitted Satan by them to deceive him into his ruin, and he by vision knew of it; it was represented to him, and he represented it to Ahab, that the God of heaven had determined he should fall at Ramoth-Gilead (*v.* 19, 20), that the favour he had wickedly shown to Ben-hadad might be punished by him and his Syrians, and that he being in some doubt whether he should go to Ramoth-Gilead or no, and resolving to be advised by his prophets, they should persuade him to it and prevail (*v.* 21, 22); and hence it was that they encouraged him with so much assurance (*v.* 23); it was a lie from the father of lies, but by divine permission. This matter is here represented after the manner of men. We are not to imagine that God is ever put upon new counsels, or is ever at a loss for means whereby to effect his purposes, nor that he needs to consult with angels, or any creature, about the methods he should take, nor that he is the author of sin or the cause of any man's either telling or believing a lie; but, besides what was intended by this with reference to Ahab himself, it is to teach us, (1.) That God is a great king above all kings, and has a throne above all the thrones of earthly princes. "You have your thrones," said Micaiah to these two kings, "and you think you may do what you will, and we must all say as you would have us; but *I saw the Lord sitting upon his throne,* and every man's judgment proceeding from him, and therefore I must say as he says; he is not a man, as you are." (2.) That he is continually attended and served by an innumerable company of angels, those heavenly hosts, who stand by him, ready to go where he sends them and to do what he bids them, messengers of mercy *on his right hand,* of wrath *on his left hand.* (3.) That he not only takes cognizance of, but presides over, all the affairs of this lower world, and overrules them *according to the counsel of his own will.* The rise and fall of princes, the issues of war, and all the great affairs of state, which are the subject of the consultations of wise and great men, are no more above God's direction than the meanest concerns of the poorest cottages are below his notice. (4.) That God has many ways of bringing about his own counsels, particularly concerning the fall of sinners when they are ripe for ruin; he can do it either in this manner or in that manner. (5.) That there are malicious and lying spirits which go about continually seeking to devour, and, in order to that, seeking to deceive, and especially to put lies into the mouths of prophets, by them to entice many to their destruction. (6.) It is not without the divine permission that the devil deceives men, and even thereby God serves his own purposes. *With him are strength and wisdom, the deceived and the deceivers are his,* Job 12:16. When he pleases, for the punishment of those who receive not the truth in the love of it, he not only *lets Satan loose to deceive them* (Rev. 20:7, 8), but *gives men up to strong delusions to believe* him, 2 Th. 2:11, 12. (7.) Those are manifestly marked for ruin that are thus given up. God has certainly *spoken evil concerning those* whom he had given up to be imposed upon by lying prophets. Thus Micaiah gave Ahab fair warning, not only of the danger of proceeding in this war, but of the danger of believing those that encouraged him to proceed. Thus we are warned to *beware of false prophets,* and to try the spirits; the lying spirit never deceives so fatally as *in the mouth of prophets.*

II. We are told how he was abused for delivering his message thus faithfully, thus plainly, in a way so very proper both to convince and to affect. 1. Zedekiah, a wicked prophet, impudently insulted him in the face of the court, *smote him on the cheek,* to reproach him, to silence him and stop his mouth, and to express his indignation at him (thus was our blessed Saviour abused, Mt. 26:67, that Judge of Israel, Mic. 5:1); and as if he not only had the spirit of the Lord, but the monopoly of this Spirit, that he might not go without his leave, he asks, *Which way went the Spirit of the Lord from me to speak to thee? v.* 24. The false prophets were always the worst enemies the true prophets had, and not only stirred up the government against them, but were themselves abusive to them, as Zedekiah here. To strike within the verge of the court, especially in the king's presence, is looked upon by our law as a high misdemeanour; yet this wicked prophet gives this abuse to a prophet of the Lord, and is not reprimanded nor bound to his good behaviour for it. Ahab was pleased with it, and Jehoshaphat had not courage to appear for the injured prophet, pretending it was out of his jurisdiction; but Micaiah, though he returns not his blow (God's prophets are not strikers nor persecutors, dare not avenge themselves, render blow for blow, or be in any way accessory to the breach of the peace), yet, since he boasted so much of the Spirit, as those commonly do that know least of his operations, he leaves him to be convinced of his error by the event: *Thou shalt know when thou hidest thyself in an inner chamber, v.* 25. It is likely Zedekiah went with Ahab to the battle, and took his horns of iron with him to encourage the soldiers, to see with pleasure the accomplishment of his prophecy, and return in triumph with the king; but, the army being routed, he fled among the rest from the sword of the enemy, sheltered himself as Ben-hadad had done in *a chamber within a chamber* (*ch.* 20:30), lest he should perish, as he knew he deserved to do, with those whom he had deluded, as Balaam did (Num. 31:8), and lest the blind prophet should *fall into the ditch* with the blinded prince whom he had misled. Note, Those that will not have their mistakes rectified in time by the word of God will be undeceived, when it is too late, by the judgments of God. 2. Ahab, that wicked king, committed him to prison (*v.* 27), not only ordered him to be taken into custody, or remitted to the prison whence he came, but to be fed with bread and water, coarse bread and puddle-water, till he should return, not doubting but that he should return a conqueror, and then he would put him to death for a false prophet (*v.* 27) — hard usage for one that would have prevented his ruin! But by this it appeared that God had *determined to destroy him,* as 2 Chr. 25:16. How confident is Ahab of success. He doubts not but he shall return in peace, forgetting what he himself had reminded Ben-hadad of, *Let not him that girdeth on the harness boast;* but there was little likelihood of his coming home in peace when he left one of God's prophets behind him in prison. Micaiah put it upon the issue, and called all the people to be witnesses that he did so: *"If thou return in peace, the Lord has not spoken by me, v.* 28. Let me incur the reproach and punishment of a false prophet, if the king come home alive." He ran no hazard by this appeal, for he knew whom he had believed; he that is terrible to the kings of the earth, and treads upon princes as mortar, will rather let thousands of them fall to the ground than one jot or tittle of his own word; he will not fail to *confirm the word of his servants,* Isa. 44:26.

Verses 29–40

The matter in contest between God's prophet and Ahab's prophets is here soon determined, and it is made to appear which was in the right. Here,

I. The two kings march with their forces to Ramoth-Gilead, *v.* 29. That the king of Israel, who hated God's prophet, should so far disbelieve his admonition as to persist in his resolution, notwithstanding, is not strange; but that Jehoshaphat, that pious prince, who had desired to enquire by a *prophet of the Lord,* as disrelishing and discrediting Ahab's prophets, should yet proceed, after so fair a warning, is matter of astonishment. But by the easiness of his temper he was carried away with the delusion (as Barnabas was with the dissimulation, Gal. 2:113) of his friends. He gave too much heed to Ahab's prophets, because they pretended to speak from God too, and in his country he had never been imposed upon by such cheats. He was ready to give his opinion with the majority, and to conclude that it was 400 to one but they should succeed. Micaiah had not forbidden them to go; nay, at first, he said, *Go, and prosper.* If it came to the worst, it was only Ahab's fall that was foretold, and therefore Jehoshaphat hoped he might safely venture.

II. Ahab adopts a contrivance by which he hopes to secure himself and expose his friend (*v.* 30): *"I will disguise myself,* and go in the habit of a common soldier, but let *Jehoshaphat put on his robes,* to appear in the dress of a general." He pretended thereby to do honour to Jehoshaphat, and to compliment him with the sole command of the army in this action. He shall direct and give orders, and Ahab will serve as a soldier under him. But he intended, 1. To make a liar of a good prophet. Thus he hoped to elude the danger, and so to defeat the threatening, as if, by disguising himself, he could escape the divine cognizance and the judgments that pursued him. 2. To make a fool of a good king, whom he did not cordially love, because he was one that adhered to God and so condemned his apostasy. He knew that if any perished it must be the shepherd (so Micaiah had foretold); and perhaps he had intimation of the charge the enemy had to fight chiefly *against the king of Israel,* and therefore basely intended to betray Jehoshaphat to the danger, that he might secure himself. Ahab was marked for ruin; one would not have been in his coat for a great sum; yet he will over-persuade this godly king to muster for him. See what those get that join in affinity with vicious men, whose consciences are debauched, and who are lost to every thing that is honourable. How can it be expected that he should be true to his friend that has been false to his God?

III. Jehoshaphat, having more piety than policy, put himself into the post of honour, though it was the post of danger, and was thereby brought into the peril of his life, but God graciously delivered him. The king of Syria charged his captains to level their force, not against the king of Judah, for with him he had no quarrel, but against the king of Israel only (*v.* 31), to aim at his person, as if against him he had a particular enmity. Now Ahab was justly repaid for sparing Ben-hadad, who, as the seed of the serpent commonly do, stung the bosom in which he was fostered and saved from perishing. Some think that he designed only to have him taken prisoner, that he might now give him as honourable a treatment as he had formerly received from him. Whatever was the reason, this charge the officers received, and endeavoured to oblige their prince in this matter; for, seeing Jehoshaphat in his royal habit, they took him for the king of Israel, and surrounded him. Now, 1. By his danger God let him know that he was displeased with him for joining in confederacy with Ahab. Jehoshaphat had said, in compliment to Ahab (*v.* 4), *I am as thou art;* and now he was indeed taken for him. Those that associate with evil doers are in danger of sharing in their plagues. 2. By his deliverance God let him know that, though he was displeased with him, yet he had not deserted him. Some of the captains that knew him perceived their mistake, and so retired from the pursuit of him; but it is said (2 Chr. 18:31) that *God moved them* (for he has all hearts in his hand) *to depart from him.* To him he cried out, not in cowardice, but devotion, and from him his relief came: Ahab was in no care to succour him. God is a friend that will not fail us when other friends do.

IV. Ahab receives his mortal wound in the battle, notwithstanding his endeavours to secure himself in the habit of a private sentinel. Let no man think to hide himself from God's judgment, no, not in masquerade. *Thy hand shall find out all thy enemies,* whatever disguise they are in, *v.* 34. The Syrian that shot him little thought of doing such a piece of service to God and his king; for he *drew a bow at a venture,* not aiming particularly at any man, yet God so directed the arrow that, 1. He hit the right person, the man that was marked for destruction, whom, if they had taken alive, as was designed, perhaps Ben-hadad would have spared. Those cannot escape with life whom God hath doomed to death. 2. He hit him in the right place, *between the joints of the harness,* the only place about him where this arrow of death could find entrance. No armour is of proof against the darts of divine vengeance. Case the criminal in steel, and it is all one, *he that made him can make his sword to approach him.* That which to us seems altogether casual is done by the determinate counsel and fore-knowledge of God.

V. The army is dispersed by the enemy and sent home by the king. Either Jehoshaphat or Ahab ordered the retreat of the sheep, when the shepherd was smitten: *Every man to his city,* for it is to no purpose to attempt any thing more, *v.* 36. Ahab himself lived long enough to see that part of Micaiah's prophecy accomplished that all Israel should be scattered *upon the mountains of Gilead* (*v.* 17), and perhaps with his dying lips did himself give orders for it; for though he would be carried out of the army, to have his wounds dressed (*v.* 34), yet he would be *held up in his chariot,* to see if his army were victorious. But, when he saw the battle increase against them, his spirits sunk, and he died, but his death was so lingering that he had time to feel himself die; and we may well imagine with what horror he now reflected upon the wickedness he had committed, the warnings he had slighted, Baal's altars, Naboth's vineyard, Micaiah's imprisonment. Now he sees himself flattered into his own ruin, and Zedekiah's horns of iron pushing, not the Syrians, but himself, into destruction. Thus is he *brought to the king of terrors* without *hope in his death.*

VI. The royal corpse is brought to Samaria and buried there (*v.* 37), and hither are brought the bloody chariot and bloody armour in which he died, *v.* 38. One particular circumstance is taken notice of, because there was in it the accomplishment of a prophecy, that when they brought the chariot to the pool of Samaria, to be washed, the dogs (and swine, says the Septuagint) gathered about it, and, as is usual, *licked the blood,* or, as some think, the water in which it was washed, with which the blood was mingled: the dogs made no difference between royal blood and other blood. Now Naboth's blood was avenged (*ch.* 21:19), and that word of David, as well as Elijah's word, was fulfilled (Ps. 68:23), *That thy foot may be dipped in the blood of thy enemies, and the tongue of thy dogs in the same.* The dogs licking the guilty blood was perhaps designed to represent the terrors that prey upon the guilty soul after death.

Lastly, The story of Ahab is here concluded in the usual form, *v.* 39, 40. Among his works mention is made of an ivory house which he built, so called because many parts of it were inlaid with ivory; perhaps it was intended to vie with the stately palace of the kings of Judah, which Solomon built.

Verses 41–53

Here is, I. A short account of the reign of Jehoshaphat king of Judah, of which we shall have a much fuller narrative in the book of Chronicles, and of the greatness and goodness of that prince, neither of which was lessened or sullied by any thing but his intimacy with the house of Ahab, which, upon several accounts, was a diminution to him. His confederacy with Ahab in war we have already found dangerous to him, and his confederacy with Ahaziah his son in trade sped no better. He offered to go partner with him in a fleet of merchant-ships, that should fetch gold from Ophir, as Solomon's navy did, *v.* 49. See 2 Chr. 20:35, 36. But, while they were preparing to set sail, they were exceedingly damaged and disabled by a storm *(broken at Ezion-geber),* which a prophet gave Jehoshaphat to understand was a rebuke to him for his league with wicked Ahaziah (2 Chr. 20:37); and therefore, as we are told here (*v.* 49), when Ahaziah desired a second time to be a partner with him, or, if that could not be obtained, that he might but send his servants with some effects of board Jehoshaphat's ships, he refused: *Jehoshaphat would not.* The rod of God, expounded by the word of God, had effectually broken him off from his confederacy with that ungodly unhappy prince. Better buy wisdom dear than be without it; but experience is therefore said to be the mistress of fools because those are fools that will not learn till they are taught by experience, and particularly till they are taught the danger of associating with wicked people. Now Jehoshaphat's reign appears here to have been none of the longest, but one of the best. 1. It was none of the longest, for he reigned but twenty-five years (*v.* 42), but then it was in the prime of his time, between thirty-five and sixty, and these twenty-five, added to his father's happy forty-one, give us a grateful idea of the flourishing condition of the kingdom of Judah, and of religion in it, for a great while, even when things were very bad, upon all accounts, in the kingdom of Israel. If Jehoshaphat reigned not so long as his father, to balance this he had not those blemishes on the latter end of his reign that his father had (2 Chr. 16:9, 10, 12), and it is better for a man that has been in reputation for wisdom and honour to die in the midst of it than to outlive it. 2. Yet is was one of the best, both in respect of piety and prosperity. (1.) He did well: He *did that which was right in the eyes of the Lord* (*v.* 43), observed the commands of his God, and trod in the steps of his good father; and he persevered therein: He *turned not aside from it.* Yet every man's character has some *but* or other, so had his; the *high places were not taken away,* no not out of Judah and Benjamin, though those tribes lay so near Jerusalem that they might easily bring their offerings and incense to the altar there, and could not pretend, as some other of the tribes, the inconveniency of lying remote. But old corruptions are with difficulty rooted out, especially when they have formerly had the patronage of those that were good, as the high places had of Samuel, Solomon, and some others. (2.) His affairs did well. He prevented the mischiefs which had attended their wars with the kingdom of Israel, establishing a lasting peace (*v.* 44), which would have been a greater blessing if he had contented himself with a peace, and not carried it on to an affinity with Israel; he ut a deputy, or viceroy, in Edom, so that the kingdom was tributary to him (*v.* 47), and therein the prophecy concerning Esau and Jacob was fulfilled, that *the elder should serve the younger.* And, in general, mention is made of his might and his wars, *v.* 45. He pleased God, and God blessed him with strength and success. His death is spoken of (*v.* 50), to shut up his story, yet, in the history of the kings of Israel, we find mention of him afterwards, 2 Ki. 3:7.

II. The beginning of the story of Ahaziah the son of Ahab, *v.* 51–53. His reign was very short, not two years. Some sinners God makes quick work with. It is a very bad character that is here given him. He not only kept up Jeroboam's idolatry, but the worship of Baal likewise; though he had heard of the ruin of Jeroboam's family, and had seen his own father drawn into destruction by the prophets of Baal, who had often been proved false prophets, yet he received no instruction, took no warning, but followed the example of his wicked father and the counsel of his more wicked mother Jezebel, who was still living. Miserable are the children that not only derive a stock of corruption from their parents, but are thus taught by them to trade with it; and unhappy, most unhappy parents, are those that help to damn their children's souls.

AN EXPOSITION, WITH PRACTICAL OBSERVATIONS, OF
THE SECOND BOOK OF KINGS

This second book of the Kings (which the Septuagint, numbering from Samuel, called the *fourth)* is a continuation of the former book; and, some think, might better have been made to begin with the fifty-first verse of the foregoing chapter, where the reign of Ahaziah begins. The former book had an illustrious beginning, in the glories of the kingdom of Israel, when it was entire; this has a melancholy conclusion, in the desolations of the kingdoms of Israel first, and then of Judah, after they had been long broken into two: for a kingdom divided against itself cometh to destruction. But, as Elijah's mighty works were very much the glory of the former book, towards the latter end of it, so were Elisha's the glory of this, towards the beginning of it. These prophets out-shone their princes; and therefore, as far as they go, the history shall be accounted for in them. Here is, I. Elijah fetching fire from heaven and ascending in fire to heaven, *ch.* 1 and 2. II. Elisha working many miracles, both for prince and people, Israelites and foreigners, *ch.* 3–7. III. Hazael and Jehu anointed, the former for the correction of Israel, the latter for the destruction of the house of Ahab and the worship of Baal, *ch.* 8–10. IV. The reign of several of the kings, both of Judah and Israel, *ch.* 11–16. V. The captivity of the ten tribes, *ch.* 17. VI. The good and glorious reign of Hezekiah, *ch.* 18–20. VII. Manassah's wicked reign, and Josiah's good one, *ch.* 21–23. VIII. The destruction of Jerusalem by the king of Babylon, *ch.* 24 and 25. This history, in the several passages of it, confirms that observation of Solomon, *That righteousness exalts a nation, but sin is the reproach of any people.*

CHAPTER 1

We here find Ahaziah, the genuine son and successor of Ahab, on the throne of Israel. His reign continued not two years; he died by a fall in his own house, of which, after the mention of the revolt of Moab (*v.* 1), we have here an account. I. The message which, on that occasion, he sent to the god of Ekron (*v.* 2). II. The message he received from the God of Israel (*v.* 3–8). III. The destruction of the messengers he sent to seize the prophet, once and again (*v.* 9–12). IV. His compassion to, and compliance with, the third messenger, upon his submission, and the delivery of the message to the king himself (*v.* 13–16). IV. The death of Ahaziah (*v.* 17, 18). In the story we may observe how great the prophet looks and how little the prince.

Verses 1–8

We have here Ahaziah, the wicked king of Israel, under God's rebukes both by his providence and by his prophet, by his rod and by his word.

I. He is crossed in his affairs. How can those expect to prosper that *do evil in the sight of the Lord,* and *provoke him to anger?* When he rebelled against God, and revolted from his allegiance to him, Moab rebelled against Israel, and revolted from the subjection that had long paid to the kings of Israel, *v.* 1. The Edomites that bordered on Judah, and were tributaries to the kings of Judah, still continued so, as we find in the chapter before (*v.* 47), till, in the wicked reign of Joram, they broke that yoke (*ch.* 8:22) as the Moabites did now. If men break their covenants with us, and neglect their duty, we must reflect upon our breach of covenant with God, and the neglect of our duty to him. Sin weakens and impoverishes us. We shall hear of the Moabites, *ch.* 3:5.

II. He is seized with sickness in body, not from any inward cause, but by a severe accident. *He fell down through a lattice,* and was much bruised with the fall; perhaps it threw him into a fever, *v.* 2. Whatever we go, there is but a step between us and death. A man's house is his castle, but not to secure him against the judgments of God. The cracked lattice is a fatal to the son, when God pleases to make it so, as the bow drawn at a venture was to the father. Ahaziah would not attempt to reduce the Moabites, lest he should perish in the field of battle: but he is not safe, though he tarry at home. Royal palaces do not always yield firm footing. The snare is laid for the sinner in the ground where he thinks least of it, Job 18:9, 10. The whole creation, which groans under the man's sin, will at length sink and break under the weight, like this lattice. He is never safe that has God for his enemy.

III. In his distress he sends messengers to enquire of the god Ekron whether he should recover or no, *v.* 2. And here, 1. His enquiry was very foolish: *Shall I recover?* Even nature itself would rather have asked, "What means may I use that I may recover?" But as one solicitous only to know his fortune, not to know his duty, his question is only this, *Shall I recover?* to which a little time would give an answer. We should be more thoughtful what will become of us after death than how, or when, or where, we shall die, and more desirous to be told how we may conduct ourselves well in our sickness, and get good to our souls by it, than whether we shall recover from it. 2. His sending to Baal-zebub was very wicked; to make a dead and dumb idol, perhaps newly erected (for idolaters were fond of new gods), his oracle, was not less a reproach to his reason than to his religion. Baal-zebub, which signifies *the lord of a fly,* was one of their Baals that perhaps gave his answers either by the power of the demons or the craft of the priests, with a humming noise, like that of a great fly, or that had (as they fancied) rid their country of the swarms of flies wherewith it was infested, or of some pestilential disease brought among them by flies. Perhaps this dunghill-diety was as famous then as the oracle of Delphos was, long afterwards, in Greece. In the New Testament *the prince of the devils* is called *Beelzebub* (Mt. 12:24), for the gods of the Gentiles were devils, and this perhaps grew to be one of the most famous.

IV. Elijah, by direction from God, meets the messengers, and turns them back with an answer that shall save them the labour of going to Ekron. Had Ahaziah sent for Elijah, humbled himself, and begged his prayers, he might have had an answer of peace; but if he send to the god of Ekron, instead of the God of Israel, this, like Saul's consulting the witch, shall fill the measure of his iniquity, and bring upon him a sentence of death. Those that will not enquire of the word of God for their comfort shall be made to hear it, whether they will or not, to their amazement.

1. He faithfully reproves his sin (*v.* 3): *Is it not because there is not* (that is, because you think there is not) a God in Israel (*because there is no God, none in Israel,* so it may be read), *that you go to enquire of Baal-zebub, the god of Ekron,* a despicable town of the Philistines (Zec. 9:7), long since vanquished by Israel? Here, (1.) The sin was bad enough, giving that honour to the devil which is due to God alone, which was done as much by their enquiries as by their sacrifices. Note, It is a very wicked thing, upon any occasion or pretence whatsoever, to consult with the devil. This wickedness reigned in the heathen world (Isa. 47:12, 13) and remains too much even in the Christian world, and the devil's kingdom is supported by it. (2.) The construction which Elijah, in God's name, puts upon it, makes it much worse: "It is because you think not only that the God of Israel is not able to tell you, but that there is no God at all in Israel, else you would not send so far for a divine answer." Note, A practical and constructive atheism is the cause and malignity of our departures from God. Surely we think there is *no God in Israel* when we live at large, make flesh our arm, and seek a portion in the things of this world.

2. He plainly reads his doom: Go, tell him *he shall surely die, v.* 4. "Since he is so anxious to know his fate, this is it; let him make the best of it." The certain fearful looking for of judgment and indignation which this message must needs cause cannot but cut him to the heart.

V. The message being delivered to him by his servants, he enquires of them by whom it was sent to him, and concludes, by their description of him, that it must be Elijah, *v.* 7, 8. For, 1. His dress was the same that he had seen him in, in his father's court. He was clad in a hairy garment, and had a leathern girdle about him, was plain and homely in his garb. John Baptist, the Elias of the New Testament, herein resembled him, for his clothes were made of hair cloth, and he was girt with a leathern girdle, Mt. 3:4. He that was clothed with the Spirit despised all rich and gay clothing. 2. His message was such as he used to deliver to his father, to whom he never prophesied good, but evil. Elijah is one of those witnesses that still torment the inhabitants of the earth, Rev. 11:10. He that was a thorn in Ahab's eyes will be so in the eyes of his son while he treads in the steps of his father's wickedness; and he is ready to cry out, as his father did, *Hast thou found me, O my enemy?* Let sinners consider that the word which *took hold of their fathers* is still as quick and powerful as ever. See Zec. 1:6; Heb. 4:12.

Verses 9–18

Here, I. The king issues out a warrant for the apprehending of Elijah. If the God of Ekron had told him he should die, it is probable he would have taken it quietly; but now that a prophet of the Lord tells him so, reproving him for his sin and reminding him of the God of Israel, he cannot bear it. So far is he from making any good improvement of the warning given him that he is enraged against the prophet; neither his sickness, nor the thoughts of death, made any good impressions upon him, nor possessed him with any fear of God. No external alarms will startle and soften secure sinners, but rather exasperate them. Did the king think Elijah a prophet, a true prophet? Why then durst he persecute him? Did he think him a common person? What occasion was there to send such a force, in order to seize him? Thus a band of men must take our Lord Jesus.

II. The captain that was sent with his fifty soldiers found Elijah on the top of a hill (some think Carmel), and commanded him, in the king's name, to surrender himself, *v.* 9. Elijah was now so far from absconding, as formerly, into the close recesses of a cave, that he makes a bold appearance on the top of a hill; experience of God's protection makes him more bold. The captain calls him *a man of God,* not that he believed him to be so, or reverenced him a such a one, but because he was commonly called so. Had he really looked upon him as a prophet, he would not have attempted to make him his prisoner; and, had he thought him entrusted with the word of God, he would not have pretended to command him with the word of a king.

III. Elijah calls for fire from heaven, to consume this haughty daring sinner, not to secure himself (he could have done that some other way), nor to avenge himself (for it was not his own cause that he appeared and acted in), but to prove his mission, and to *reveal the wrath of God* from *heaven against the ungodliness and unrighteousness of men.* This captain had, in scorn, called him *a man of God:* "If I be so," says Elijah, "thou shalt pay dearly for making a jest of it." He valued himself upon his commission (the king has said, *Come down),* but Elijah will let him know that the God of Israel is superior to the king of Israel and has a greater power to enforce his commands. It was not long since Elijah had fetched fire from heaven, to consume the sacrifice (1 Ki. 17:38), in token of God's acceptance of that sacrifice as an atonement for the sins of the people; but, they having slighted that, now the fire falls, not on the sacrifice, but on the sinners themselves, *v.* 10. See here, 1. What an interest the prophets had in heaven; what the Spirit of God in them demanded the power of God effected. Elijah did but speak, and it was done. He that formerly had fetched water from heaven now fetches fire. O the power of prayer! *Concerning the work of my hands, command you me,* Isa. 14:11. 2. What an interest heaven had in the prophets! God was always ready to plead their cause, and avenge the injuries done to them; kings shall still be *rebuked for their sakes,* and charged to do *his prophets no harm;* one Elijah is more to God than 10,000 captains and their fifties. Doubtless Elijah did this by a divine impulse, and yet our Saviour would not allow the disciples to draw it into a precedent, Lu. 9:54. They were now not far from the place where Elias did this act of justice upon provoking Israelites, and would needs, in like manner, call for fire upon those provoking Samaritans. "No," says Christ, "by no means, *you know not what manner of spirit you are of,*" that is, (1.) "You do not consider *what manner of spirit,* as disciples, you are called to, and how different from that of the Old-Testament dispensation; it was agreeable enough to that dispensation of terror, and of the letter, for Elias to call for fire, but the dispensation of the Spirit and of grace will by no means allow it." (2.) "You are not aware what manner of spirit you are, upon this occasion, actuated by, and how different from that of Elias: he did it in holy zeal, you in passion; he was concerned for God's glory, you for your own reputation only." God judges men's practices by their principles, and his judgment is according to truth.

IV. This is repeated a second time; would one think it? 1. Ahaziah sends, a second time, to apprehend Elijah (*v.* 11), as if he were resolved not to be baffled by omnipotence itself. Obstinate sinners must be convinced and conquered, at last, by the fire of hell, for fire from heaven, it seems, will not subdue them. 2. Another captain is ready with his fifty, who, in his blind rage against the prophet, and his blind obedience to the king, dares engage in that service which had been fatal to the last undertakers. This is as impudent and imperious as the last, and more in haste; not only, *"Come down quietly,* and do not struggle," but without taking any notice of what had been done, he says, *"Come down quickly,* and do not trifle, the king's business requires haste; come down, or I will fetch thee down." 3. Elijah relents not, but calls for another flash of lightning, which instantly lays this captain and his fifty dead upon the spot. Those that will sin like others must expect to suffer like them; God is inflexibly just.

V. The third captain humbled himself and cast himself upon the mercy of God and Elijah. It does not appear that Ahaziah ordered him to do so (his stubborn heart is as hard as ever; so regardless is he of the terrors of the Lord, so little affected with the manifestations of his wrath, and withal so prodigal of the lives of his subjects, that he sends a third with the same provoking message to Elijah), but he took warning by the fate of his predecessors, who, perhaps, lay dead before his eyes; and, instead of summoning the prophet down, fell down before him, and begged for his life and the lives of his soldiers, acknowledging their own evil deserts and the prophet's power (*v.* 13, 14): *Let my life be precious in thy sight.* Note, There is nothing to be got by contending with God: if we would prevail with him, it must be by supplication; if we would not fall before God, we must bow before him; and those are wise for themselves who learn submission from the fatal consequences of the obstinacy of others.

VI. Elijah does more than grant the request of this third captain. God is not so severe with those that stand it out against him but he is as ready to show mercy to those that repent and submit to him; never any found it in vain to cast themselves upon the mercy of God. This captain, not only has his life spared, but is permitted to carry his point: Elijah, being so commanded by the angel, *goes down with him to the king, v.* 15. Thus he shows that he before refused to come, not because he feared the king or court, but because he would not be imperiously compelled, which would lessen the honour of his master; he *magnifies his office.* He comes boldly to the king, and tells him to his face (let him take it as he may) what he had before sent to him (*v.* 16), that he shall surely and shortly die; he mitigates not the sentence, either for fear of the king's displeasure or in pity to his misery. The God of Israel has condemned him, let him send to see whether the god of Ekron can deliver him. So thunder-struck is Ahaziah with this message, when it comes from the prophet's own mouth, that neither he nor any of those about him durst offer him any violence, nor so much as give him an affront; but out of that den of lions he comes unhurt, like Daniel. Who can harm those whom God will shelter?

Lastly, The prediction is accomplished in a few days. Ahaziah died (*v.* 17), and, dying childless, left his kingdom to his brother Jehoram. His father reigned wickedly twenty-two years, he not two. Sometimes the *wicked live, become old, yea, are mighty in power;* but those who therefore promise themselves prosperity in impiety may perhaps find themselves deceived; for (as bishop Hall observes here), "Some sinners live long, to aggravate their judgment, others die soon, to hasten it;" but it is certain that evil pursues sinners, and, sooner or later, it will overtake them; nor will any thing fill the measure sooner than that complicated iniquity of Ahaziah — honouring the devil's oracles and hating God's oracles.

CHAPTER 2

In this chapter we have, I. That extraordinary event, the translation of Elijah. In the close of the foregoing chapter we had a wicked king leaving the world in disgrace, here we have a holy prophet leaving it in honour; the departure of the former was his greatest misery, of the latter his greatest bliss: men are as their end is. Here is, 1. Elijah taking leave of his friends, the sons of the prophets, and especially Elisha, who kept close to him, and walked with him through Jordan (*v.* 1–10). 2. Elijah taken into heaven by the ministry of angels (*v.* 11), and Elisha's lamentation of the loss this earth has of him (*v.* 12). II. The manifestation of Elisha, as a prophet in his room. 1. By the dividing of Jordan (*v.* 13, 14). 2. By the respect which the sons of the prophets paid him (*v.* 15–18). 3. By the healing of the unwholesome waters of Jericho (*v.* 19–22). 4. By the destruction of the children of Bethel that mocked him (*v.* 23–25). This revolution in prophecy makes a greater figure than the revolution of a kingdom.

Verses 1–8

Elijah's times, and the events concerning him, are as little dated as those of any great man in scripture; we are not told of his age, nor in what year of Ahab's reign he first appeared, nor in what year of Joram's he disappeared, and therefore cannot conjecture how long he flourished; it is supposed about twenty years in all. Here we are told,

I. That God had determined to take him up into heaven by a whirlwind, *v.* 1. He would do it, and it is probable let him know of his purpose some time before, that he would shortly take him from the world, not by death, but translate him body and soul to heaven, as Enoch was, only causing him to undergo such a change as would be necessary to the qualifying of him to be an inhabitant in that world of spirits, and such as those shall undergo who will be found alive at Christ's coming. It is not for us to say why God would put such a peculiar honour upon Elijah above any other of the prophets; he was a man *subject to like passions as we are,* knew sin, and yet never tasted death. Wherefore is he thus dignified, thus distinguished, as a man whom the Kings of kings did delight to honour? We may suppose that herein, 1. God looked back upon his past services, which were eminent and extraordinary, and intended a recompence for those and an encouragement to the sons of the prophets to tread in the steps of his zeal and faithfulness, and, whatever it cost them, to witness against the corruptions of the age they lived in. 2. He looked down upon the present dark and degenerate state of the church, and would thus give a very sensible proof of another life after this, and draw the hearts of the faithful few upward towards himself, and that other life. 3. He looked forward to the evangelical dispensation, and, in the translation of Elijah, gave a type and figure of the ascension of Christ and the *opening of the kingdom of heaven to all believers.* Elijah had, by faith and prayer, conversed much with heaven, and now he is taken thither, to assure us that if we have our conversation in heaven, while we are here on earth, we shall be there shortly, the soul shall (and that is the man) be happy there, there for ever.

II. That Elisha had determined, as long as he continued on earth to cleave to him, and not to leave him. Elijah seemed desirous to shake him off, would have had him stay behind at Gilgal, at Bethel, at Jericho, *v.* 2, 4, 6. Some think out of humility; he knew what glory God designed for him, but would not seem to glory in it, nor desired it should be seen of men (God's favourites covet not to have it proclaimed before them that they are so, as the favourites of earthly princes do), or rather it was to try him, and make his constant adherence to him the more commendable, like Naomi's persuading Ruth to go back. In vain does Elijah entreat him to tarry here and tarry there; he resolves to tarry nowhere behind his master, till he goes to heaven, and leaves him behind on this earth. "Whatever comes of it, *I will not leave thee;*" and why so? Not only because he loved him, but, 1. Because he desired to be edified by his holy heavenly converse as long as he staid on earth; it had always been profitable, but, we may suppose, was now more so than ever. We should do all the spiritual good we can one to another, and get all we can one by another, while we are together, because we are to be *together but a little while.* 2. Because he desired to be satisfied concerning his departure, and to see him when he was taken up, that his faith might be confirmed and his acquaintance with the invisible world increased. He had long followed Elijah, and he would not leave him now when he hoped for the parting blessing. Let not those that follow Christ come short by tiring at last.

III. That Elijah, before his departure, visited the schools of the prophets and took leave of them. It seems that there were such schools in many of the cities of Israel, probably even in Samaria itself. Here we find *sons of the prophets,* and considerable numbers of them, even at Bethel, where one of the calves was set up, and at Jericho, which was lately built in defiance of a divine curse. At Jerusalem, and in the kingdom of Judah, they had priests and Levites, and the temple-service, the want of which, in the kingdom of Israel, God graciously made up by those colleges, where men were trained up and employed in the exercises of religion and devotion, and whither good people resorted to solemnize the appointed feasts with praying and hearing, when they had not conveniences for sacrifice or incense, and thus religion was kept up in a time of general apostasy. Much of God was among these prophets, and *more were the children of the desolate* than the *children of the married wife.* None of all the high priests were comparable to those two great men Elijah and Elisha, who, for aught we know, never attended in the temple at Jerusalem. These seminaries of religion and virtue, which Elijah, it is probable, had been instrumental to found, he now visits, before his departure, to instruct, encourage, and bless them. Note, Those that are going to heaven themselves ought to be concerned for those they leave behind them on earth, and to leave with them their experiences, testimonies, counsels, and prayers, 2 Pt. 1:15. When Christ said, with triumph, *Now I am no more in the world,* he added, with tenderness, *But these are. Father, keep them.*

IV. That the sons of the prophets had intelligence (either from Elijah himself, or by the spirit of prophecy in some of their own society), or suspected by the solemnity of Elijah's farewell, that he was now shortly to be removed; and, 1. They told Elisha of it, both at Bethel (*v.* 3) and at Jericho (*v.* 5): *Knowest thou that the Lord will take away thy master from thy head to day?* This they said, not as upbraiding him with his loss, or expecting that when his master was gone he would be upon the level with them, but to show how full they were of the thoughts of this matter and big with expectation of the event, and to admonish Elisha to prepare for the loss. Know we not that our nearest relations, and dearest friends, must shortly be taken from us? *The Lord will* take them; we lose them not till he calls for them whose they are, and who *taketh away and none can hinder him.* He takes away superiors from our head, inferiors from our feet, equals from our arms; let us therefore carefully do the duty of every relation, that we may reflect upon it with comfort when it comes to be dissolved. Elisha knew it too well, and *sorrow had filled his heart* upon this account (as the disciples in a like case, Jn. 16:6), and therefore he did not need to be told of it, did not care for hearing of it, and would not be interrupted in his contemplations on this great concern, or in the least diverted from his attendance upon his master. *I know it; hold you your peace.* He speaks not this peevishly, or in contempt of the sons of the prophets, but as one that was himself and would have them composed and sedate, and with an awful silence expecting the event: *I know it; be silent,* Zec. 2:13. 2. They went themselves to be witnesses of it at a distance, though they might not closely attend (*v.* 7): *Fifty of them stood to view afar off,* intending to satisfy their curiosity, but God so ordered it that they might be eye-witnesses of the honour heaven did to that prophet, who was *despised and rejected of men.* God's works are well worthy our notice; when a *door is opened in heaven* the call is, *Come up hither, come and see.*

V. That the miraculous dividing of the river Jordan was the preface to Elijah's translation into the heavenly Canaan, as it had been to the entrance of Israel into the earthly Canaan, *v.* 8. He must go on to the other side Jordan to be translated, because it was his native country, and that he might be near the place where Moses died, and that thus honour might be put on that part of the country which was most despised. he and Elisha might have gone over Jordan by a ferry, as other passengers did, but God would magnify Elijah in his exit, as he did Joshua in his entrance, by the dividing of this river, Jos. 3:7. As Moses with his rod divided the sea, so Elijah with his mantle divided Jordan, both being the *insignia — the badges* of their office. These waters of old yielded to the ark, now to the prophet's mantle, which, to those that wanted the ark was an equivalent token of God's presence. When God will take up his faithful ones to heaven death is the Jordan which, immediately before their translation, they must pass through, and they find a way through it, as safe and comfortable way; the death of Christ has divided those waters, that the ransomed of the Lord may pass over. *O death! where is thy sting,* thy hurt, thy terror?

Verses 9–12

Here, I. Elijah makes his will, and leaves Elisha his heir, now anointing him to be prophet in his room, more than when he *cast his mantle upon him,* 1 Ki. 19:19.

1. Elijah, being greatly pleased with the constancy of Elisha's affection and attendance, bade him ask what he should do for him, what blessing he should leave him at parting; he does not say (as bishop Hall observes), *"Ask of me when I am gone,* in heaven I shall be better able to befriend thee," but, "Ask before I go." Our friends on earth may be spoken to, and can give us an answer, but we know not that we can have access to any friend in heaven but Christ, and God in him. *Abraham is ignorant of us.*

2. Elisha, having this fair opportunity to enrich himself with the best riches, prays for a *double portion of his spirit.* He asks not for wealth, nor honour, nor exemption from trouble, but to be qualified for the service of God and his generation, he asks, (1.) For the Spirit, not that the gifts and graces of the Spirit were in Elijah's power to give, therefore he says not, "Give me the Spirit" (he knew very well it was God's gift), but *"Let it be upon me,* intercede with God for this for me." Christ bade his disciples ask what they would, not one, but all, and promised to send the Spirit, with much more authority and assurance than Elijah could. (2.) For *his* spirit, because he was to be a prophet in his room, to carry on his work, to father the sons of the prophets and face their enemies, because he had the same perverse generation to deal with that he had, so that, if he have not his spirit, he has not *strength according to the day.* (3.) For a *double portion of his spirit;* he does not mean double to what Elijah had, but double to what the rest of the prophets had, from whom so much would not be expected as from Elisha, who had been brought up under Elijah. It is a holy ambition to *covet earnestly the best gifts,* and those which will render us most serviceable to God and our brethren. Note, We all ought, both ministers and people, to set before us the example of our predecessors, to labour after their spirit, and to be earnest with God for that grace which carried them through their work and enabled them to finish well.

3. Elijah promised him that which he asked, but under two provisos, *v.* 10. (1.) Provided he put a due value upon it and esteem it highly: this he teaches him to do by calling it *a hard thing,* not too hard for God to do, but too great for him to expect. Those are best prepared for spiritual blessings that are most sensible of their worth and their own unworthiness to receive them. (2.) Provided he kept close to his master, even to the last, and was observant of him: *If thou see me when I am taken from thee, it shall be* so, otherwise not. A diligent attendance upon his master's instructions, and a careful observance of his example, particularly now in his last scene, were the condition and would be a proper means of obtaining much of his spirit. Taking strict notice of the manner of his ascension would likewise be of great use to him. The comforts of departing saints, and their experiences, will mightily help both to gild our comforts and to steel our resolutions. Or, perhaps, this was intended only as a sign: "If God favour thee so far as to give thee a sight of me when I ascend, take that for a token that he will do this for thee, and depend upon it." Christ's disciples saw him ascend, and were thereupon assured that they should, in a little time, be filled with his Spirit, Acts 1:8. Elisha, we may suppose, hereupon prayed earnestly, *Lord, show me this token for good.*

II. Elijah is carried up to heaven in a fiery chariot, *v.* 11. Like Enoch, he was translated, *that he should not see death;* and was (as Mr. Cowley expresses it) *the second man that leaped the ditch where all the rest of mankind fell, and went not downward to the sky.* Many curious questions might be asked about this matter, which could not be answered. Let it suffice that we are here told,

1. What his Lord, when he came, found him doing. He was talking with Elisha, instructing and encouraging him, directing him in his work, and quickening him to it, for the good of those whom he left behind. He was not meditating nor praying, as one wholly taken up with the world he was going to, but engaged in edifying discourse, as one concerned about the kingdom of God among men. We mistake if we think our preparation for heaven is carried on only by contemplation and the acts of devotion. Usefulness to others will pass as well in our account as any thing. Thinking of divine things is good, but talking of them (if it come from the heart) is better, because for edification, 1 Co. 14:4. Christ ascended as he was blessing his disciples.

2. What convoy his Lord sent for him — *a chariot of fire and horses of fire,* which appeared either descending upon them from the clouds or (as bishop Patrick thinks) running towards them upon the ground: in this form the angels appeared. The souls of all the faithful are carried by an invisible guard of angels into the bosom of Abraham; but, Elijah being to carry his body with him, this heavenly guard was visible, not in a human shape, as usual, though they might so have borne him up in their arms, or carried him as on eagles' wings, but that would have been to carry him like a child, like a lamp (Isa. 40:11, 31); they appear in the form of a chariot and horses, that he may ride in state, may ride in triumph, like a prince, like a conqueror, yea, *more than a conqueror.* The angels are called in scripture *cherubim* and *seraphim,* and their appearance here, though it may seem below their dignity, answers to both those names; for (1.) *Seraphim* signifies *fiery,* and God is said to make them *a flame of fire,* Ps. 104:4. (2.) *Cherubim* (as many think) signifies *chariots,* and they are called *the chariots of God* (Ps. 68:17), and he is said to *ride upon a cherub* (Ps. 18:10), to which perhaps there is an allusion in Ezekiel's vision of four living creatures, and wheels, like horses and chariots; in Zechariah's vision, they are so represented, Zec. 1:8; 6:1. Compare Rev. 6:2, etc. See the readiness of the angels to do the will go God, even in the meanest services, for the good of those that shall be heirs of salvation. Elijah must remove to the world of angels, and therefore, to show how desirous they were of his company, some of them would come to fetch him. The chariot and horses appeared like fire, not for burning, but brightness, not to torture or consume him, but to render his ascension conspicuous and illustrious in the eyes of those that stood afar off to view it. Elijah had burned with holy zeal

for God and his honour, and now with a heavenly fire he was refined and translated.

3. How he was separated from Elisha. This chariot parted them both asunder. Note, The dearest friends must part. Elisha had protested he would not leave him, yet now is left behind by him.

4. Whither he was carried. He *went up by a whirlwind into heaven.* The fire tends upward; the whirlwind helped to carry him through the atmosphere, out of the reach of the magnetic virtue of this earth, and then how swiftly he ascended through the pure ether to the world of holy and blessed spirits we cannot conceive.

"But where he stopped will ne'er be known,
'Till Phenix-nature, aged grown,
To a better being shall aspire,
Mounting herself, like him, to eternity in fire."
— Cowley

Elijah had once, in a passion, wished he might die; yet God was so gracious to him as not only not to take him at his word then, but to honour him with this singular privilege, that he should never see death; and by this instance, and that of Enoch, (1.) God showed how men should have left the world if they had not sinned, not by death, but by a translation. (2.) He gave a glimpse of that life and immortality which are brought to light by the gospel, of the glory reserved for the bodies of the saints, and the *opening of the kingdom of heaven to all believers,* as then to Elijah. It was also a figure of Christ's ascension.

III. Elisha pathetically laments the loss of that great prophet, but attends him with an ecomium, *v.* 12. 1. He saw it; thus he received the sign by which he was assured of the grant of his request for a double portion of Elijah's spirit. He looked stedfastly towards heaven, whence he was to expect that gift, as the disciples did, Acts 1:10. he saw it awhile, but the vision was presently out of his sight; and *he saw him no more.* 2. He rent his own clothes, in token of the sense he had of his own and the public loss. Though Elijah had gone triumphantly to heaven, yet this world could ill spare him, and therefore his removal ought to be much regretted by the survivors. Surely their hearts are hard whose eyes are dry when God, by taking away faithful useful men, calls for weeping and mourning. Though Elijah's departure made way for Elisha's eminency, especially since he was now sure of a double portion of his spirit, yet he lamented the loss of him, for he loved him, and could have served him for ever. 3. He gave him a very honourable character, as the reason why he thus lamented the loss of him. (1.) He himself had lost the guide of his youth: *My father, my father.* He saw his own condition like that of a fatherless child thrown upon the world, and lamented it accordingly. Christ, when he left his disciples, did not leave them orphans (Jn. 14:15), but Elijah must. (2.) The public had lost its best guard; he was *the chariot of Israel, and the horsemen thereof.* He would have brought them all to heaven, as in this chariot, if it had not been their own fault; they used not chariots and horses in their wars, but Elijah was to them, by his counsels, reproofs, and prayers, better than the strongest force of chariot and horse, and kept off the judgments of God. His departure was like the routing of an army, an irreparable loss. "Better have lost all our men of war than this man of God."

Verses 13–18

We have here an account of what followed immediately after the translation of Elijah.

I. The tokens of God's presence with Elisha, and the marks of his elevation into Elijah's room, to be, as he had been, a father to the sons of the prophets, and the chariots and horsemen of Israel.

1. He was possessed of Elijah's mantle, the badge of his office, which, we may suppose, he put on and wore for his master's sake, *v.* 13. When Elijah went to heaven, though he did not let fall his body as others do, he let fall his mantle instead of it; for he was unclothed, that he might be clothed upon with immortality: he was going to a world where he needed not the mantle to adorn him, nor to shelter him from the weather, nor to wrap his face in, as 1 Ki. 19:13. He left his mantle as a legacy to Elisha, and, though in itself it was of small value, yet as it was a token of the descent of the Spirit upon him, it was more than if he had bequeathed to him thousands of gold and silver. Elisha took it up, not as a sacred relic to be worshipped, but as a significant garment to be worn, and a recompence to him for his own garments which he had rent. he loved this cloak ever since it was first cast over him, 1 Ki. 19:19. He that then so cheerfully obeyed the summons of it, and became Elihah's servant, is now dignified with it, and becomes his successor. There are remains of great and good men, which, like this mantle, ought to be gathered up and preserved by the survivors, their sayings, their writings, their examples, that, as their works follow them in the reward of them, they may stay behind in the benefit of them.

2. He was possessed of Elijah's power to divide Jordan, *v.* 14. Having parted with his father, he returns to his sons in the schools of the prophets. Jordan was between him and them; it had been divided to make way for Elijah to his glory; he will try whether it will divide to make way for him to his business, and by that he will know that God is with him, and that he has the double portion of Elijah's spirit. Elijah's last miracle shall be Elisha's first; thus he begins where Elijah left off and there is no vacancy. In dividing the waters, (1.) He made use of Elijah's mantle, as Elijah himself had done (*v.* 8), to signify that he designed to keep to his master's methods and would not introduce any thing new, as those affect to do that think themselves wiser than their predecessors. (2.) He applied to Elijah's God: *Where is the Lord God of Elijah?* He does not ask, "Where is Elijah?" as poring upon the loss of him, as if he could not be easy now that he was gone, — or as doubting of his happy state, as if, like the sons of the prophets here, he knew not what had become of him, — or as curiously enquiring concerning him, and the particular of that state he was removed to (no, that is a hidden life, it does not yet appear what we shall be), — nor as expecting help from him; no, Elijah is happy, but is neither omniscient nor omnipotent; but he asks, *Where is the Lord God of Elijah?* Now that Elijah was taken to heaven God had abundantly proved himself the God of Elijah; if he had not prepared for him that city, and done better for him there than ever he did for him in this world, he *would have been ashamed to be called his God,* Heb. 11:16; Mt. 27:31, 32. Now that Elijah was taken to heaven Elisha enquired, [1.] After God. When our creature-comforts are removed, we have a God to go to, that lives for ever. [2.] After *The God of Elijah,* the God that Elijah served, and honoured, and pleaded for, and adhered to when all Israel had deserted him. This honour is done to those who cleave to God in times of general apostasy, that God will be, in a peculiar manner, their God. "The God that owned, and protected, and provided for Elijah, and many ways honoured him, especially now at last, where is he? Lord, am not I promised Elijah's spirit? Make good that promise." The words which next follow in the original, *Aph-his — even he,* which we join to the following clause, *when he also had smitten the waters,* some make an answer to this question, *Where is Elijah's God? Etiam ille adhuc superest* — "*He is in being still,* and nigh at hand. We have lost Elijah, but we have not lost Elijah's God. He *has not forsaken the earth;* it is even he that is still with me." Note, *First,* It is the duty and interest of the saints on earth to enquire after God, and apply to him as the Lord God of the saints that have gone before to heaven, *the God of our fathers. Secondly,* It is very comfortable to those who enquire of him; it is *even he* that *is in his holy temple* (Ps. 11:4) and *nigh to all who call upon him,* Ps. 145:18. *Thirdly,* Those that walk in the spirit and steps of their godly faithful predecessors shall certainly experience the same grace that they experienced; Elijah's God will be Elisha's too. The Lord God of the holy prophets is the same yesterday, to-day, and for ever; and what will it avail us to have the mantles of those that are gone, their places, their books, if we have not their spirit, their God?

3. He was possessed of Elijah's interest in the sons of the prophets, *v.* 15. Some of the fellows of the college at Jericho, who had placed themselves conveniently near Jordan, to see what passed, were surprised to see Jordan divided before Elisha in his return, and took that as a convincing evidence that *the spirit of Elijah did rest upon him,* and that therefore they ought to pay the same respect and deference to him that they had paid to Elijah. Accordingly they went to meet him, to congratulate him on his safe passage through fire and water, and the honour God had put upon him; and they *bowed themselves to the ground before him.* They were trained up in the schools; Elisha was taken from the plough; yet when they perceived that God was with him, and that this was *the man whom he delighted to honour,* they readily submitted to him as their head and father, as the people to Joshua when Moses was dead, Jos. 1:17. Those that appear to have God's Spirit and presence with them ought to have our esteem and best affections, notwithstanding the meanness of their extraction and education. This ready submission of the sons of the prophets, no doubt, was a great encouragement to Elisha, and helped to clear his call.

II. The needless search which the sons of the prophets made for Elijah. 1. They suggested that possibly he was dropped, either alive or dead, upon some mountain, or in some valley; and it would be a satisfaction to them if they sent some strong men, whom they had at command, in quest of him, *v.* 16. Some of them perhaps started this as a demurrer to the choice of Elisha: "Let us first be sure that Elijah has quite gone. Can we think Elijah thus neglected by heaven, that chosen vessel thus cast away as a vessel in which was no pleasure?" 2. Elisha consented not to their motion till they overcame him with importunity, *v.* 17. They urged him till he was ashamed to oppose it any further lest he should be thought wanting in his respect to his old master or loth to resign the mantle again. Wise men may yield to that, for the sake of peace and the good opinion of others, which yet their judgment is against as needless and fruitless. 3. The issue made them as much ashamed of their proposal as they, by their importunity, had made Elisha ashamed of his opposing it. Their messengers, after they had tired themselves with fruitless search, returned with a *non est inventus — he is not to be found,* and gave Elisha an opportunity of upbraiding his friends with their folly: *Did I not say unto you, Go not? v.* 18. This would make them the more willing to acquiesce in his judgment another time. Traversing hills and valleys will never bring us to Elijah, but the imitation of his holy faith and zeal will, in due time.

Verses 19–25

Elisha had, in this respect, a double portion of Elijah's spirit, that he wrought more miracles than Elijah. Some reckon them in number just double. Two are recorded in these verses — a miracle of mercy to Jericho and a miracle of judgment to Bethel, Ps. 101:1.

I. Here is a blessing upon the waters of Jericho, which was effectual to heal them. Jericho was built in disobedience to a command, in defiance to a threatening, and at the expense of the lives of all the builder's children; yet, when it was built, it was not ordered to be demolished again, nor were God's prophets or people forbidden to dwell in it, but even within those walls that were built by iniquity we find a nursery of piety. Fools, they say, build houses for wise men to dwell in. Here the wealth of the sinner provided a habitation for the just. We find Christ at Jericho, Lu. 19:1. Hither Elisha came, to confirm the souls of the disciples with a more particular account of Elijah's translation than their spies, who saw at a distance, could give them. Here he staid while the fifty men were searching for him. And, 1. The men of Jericho represented to him their grievance, *v.* 19. God's faithful prophets love to be employed; it is wisdom to make use of them during the little while that their light is with us. They had not applied to Elijah concerning the matter, perhaps because he was not so easy of access as Elisha was; but now, we may hope, by the influence of the divinity-school in their city, they were reformed. The situation was pleasant and afforded a good prospect; but they had neither wholesome water to drink nor fruitful soil to yield them food, and what pleasure could they take in their prospect? Water is a common mercy, which we should estimate by the greatness of the calamity which the want or unwholesomeness of it would be. Some think that it was not all the ground about Jericho that was barren and had bad water, but some one part only, and *that* where the sons of the prophets had their lodgings, who are here called *the men of the city.* 2. He soon redressed their grievance. Prophets should endeavour to make every place they come to, some way or other, the better for them, endeavouring to sweeten bitter spirits, and to make barren souls fruitful, by the due application of the word of God. Elisha will heal their waters; but, (1.) They must furnish him with salt in a new cruse, *v.* 20. If salt had been proper to season the water, yet what could so small a quantity do towards it and what the better for being in a new cruse? But thus those that would be helped must be employed and have their faith and obedience tried. God's works of grace are wrought, not by any operations of ours, but in observance of his institutions. (2.) He cast the salt *into the spring of the waters,* and so healed the streams and the ground they watered. Thus the way to reform men's lives is to renew their hearts; let those be seasoned with the salt of grace; for *out of them are the issues of life. Make the tree good and the fruit will be good.* Purify the heart and that will cleanse the hands. (3.) He did not pretend to do this by his own power, but in God's name: *Thus saith the Lord, I have healed these waters.* He is but the instrument, the channel through which God is pleased to convey this healing virtue. By doing them this kindness with a *Thus saith the Lord,* they would be made the more willing hereafter, to receive from him a reproof, admonition, or command, with the same preface. If, in God's name, he can help them, in God's name let him teach and rule them. *Thus saith the Lord,* out of Elisha's mouth, must, ever after, be of mighty force with them. (4.) The cure was lasting, and not for the present only: *The waters were healed unto this day, v.* 22. What God does *shall be for ever,* Eccl. 3:14. When he, by his Spirit, *heals a soul,* there shall be *no more death nor barrenness;* the property is altered: what was useless and offensive becomes grateful and serviceable.

II. Here is a curse upon the children of Bethel, which was effectual to destroy them; for it was not a curse causeless. At Bethel there was another school of prophets. Thither Elisha went next, in this his primary visitation, and the scholars there no doubt welcomed him with all possible respect, but the townsmen were abusive to him. One of Jeroboam's calves was at Bethel; this they were proud of, and fond of, and hated those that reproved them. The law did not empower them to suppress this pious academy, but we may suppose it was their usual practice to jeer the prophets as they went along the streets, to call them by some nickname or other, that they might expose them to contempt, prejudice their youth against them, and, if possible, drive them out of their town. Had the abuse done to Elisha been the first offence of that kind, it is probable that it would not have been so severely punished. But *mocking the messengers of the Lord,* and *misusing the prophets,* was one of the *crying sins of Israel,* as we find, 2 Chr. 36:16. Now here we have, 1. An instance of that sin. The little *children of Bethel,* the boys and girls that were playing in the streets (notice, it is likely, having come to the town of his approach), went out to meet him, not with their hosannas, as they ought to have done, but with their scoffs; they gathered about him and mocked him, as if he had been a fool, or one fit to make sport with. Among other things that they used to jeer the prophets with, they had this particular taunt for him, *Go up, thou bald head, go up, thou bald head.* It is a wicked thing to reproach persons for their natural infirmities or deformities; it is adding affliction to the afflicted; and, if they are as God made them, the reproach reflects upon him. But this was such a thing as scarcely deserved to be called a blemish, and would never have been turned to his reproach if they had had any thing else to reproach him with. It was his character as a prophet that they designed to abuse. The honour God had crowned him with should have been sufficient to cover his bald head and protect him from their scoffs. They bade him *go up,* perhaps reflecting on the assumption of Elijah: "Thy master," they say, "has gone up; why dost not thou go up after him? Where is the fiery chariot? When shall we be rid of thee too?" These children said as they were taught; they had learned of their idolatrous parents to call foul names and give bad language, especially to prophets. These young cocks, as we say, crowed after the old ones. Perhaps their parents did at this time send them out and set them on, that, if possible, they might keep the prophet out of their town. 2. A specimen of that ruin which came down upon Israel at last, for misusing God's prophets, and of which this was intended to give them fair warning. Elisha heard their taunts, a good while, with patience; but at length the fire of holy zeal for God was kindled in his breast by the continued provocation, and he *turned and looked upon them,* to try if a grave and severe look would put them out of countenance and oblige them to retire, to see if he could discern in their faces any marks of ingenuousness; but they *were not ashamed, neither could they blush;* and therefore he *cursed them in the name of the Lord,* both imprecated and denounced the following judgment, not in personal revenge for the indignity done to himself, but as the mouth of divine justice to punish the dishonour done to God. His summons was immediately obeyed. two she-bears (bears perhaps robbed of their whelps) came out of an adjacent wood, and presently killed forty-two children, *v.* 24. Now in this, (1.) The prophet must be justified, for he did it by divine impulse. Had the curse come from any bad principle God would not have said *Amen* to it. We may think it would have been better to have called for two rods for the correction of these children than two bears for the destruction of them. But Elisha knew, by the Spirit, the bad character of these children. He knew what a generation of vipers those were, and what mischievous enemies they would be to God's prophets if they should live to be men, who began so early to be abusive to them. He intended hereby to punish the parents and to make them afraid of God's judgments. (2.) God must be glorified as a righteous God, that hates sin, and will reckon for it, even in little children. Let the wicked wretched brood make our flesh tremble for fear of God. Let little children be afraid of speaking wicked words, for God notices what they say,. Let them not mock any for their defects in mind or body, but pity them rather; especially let them know that it is at their peril if they jeer God's people or ministers, and scoff at any for well-doing. Let parents, that would have comfort in their children, train them up well, and do their utmost betimes to drive out the foolishness that is bound up in their hearts; for, as bishop Hall says, "In vain do we look for good from those children whose education we have neglected; and in vain do we grieve for those miscarriages which our care might have prevented." Elisha comes to Bethel and fears not the revenges of the bereaved parents; God, who bade him do what he did, he knew would bear him out. Thence he goes to Mount Carmel (*v.* 25), where it is probable there was a religious house fit for retirement and contemplation. Thence he returned to Samaria, where, being a public place, this father of the prophets might be most serviceable. Bishop Hall observes here, "That he can never be a profitable seer who is either always or never alone."

CHAPTER 3

We are now called to attend the public affairs of Israel, in which we shall find Elisha concerned. Here is, I. The general character of Jehoram, king of Israel (*v.* 1–3). II. A war with Moab, in which Jehoram and his allies were engaged (*v.* 4–8). III. The straits which the confederate army were reduced to in their expedition against Moab, and their consulting Elisha in that distress, with the answer of peace he gave them (*v.* 9–19). IV. The glorious issue of this campaign (*v.* 20–25) and the barbarous method the king of Moab took to oblige the confederate army to retire (*v.* 26, 27). The house of Ahab is doomed to destruction; and, though in this chapter we have both its character and its condition better than before, yet the threatened ruin is not far off.

Verses 1–5

Jehoram, the son of Ahab, and brother of Ahaziah, is here upon the throne of Israel; and, though he was but a bad man, yet two commendable things are here recorded of him: —

I. That he removed his father's idols. He did evil in many things, but not like his father Ahab or his mother Jezebel, *v.* 2. Bad he was, but not so bad, so *overmuch wicked,* as Solomon speaks, Eccl. 7:17. Perhaps Jehoshaphat, though by his alliance with the house of Ahab he made his own family worse, did something towards making Ahab's better. Jehoram saw his father and brother cut off for worshipping Baal, and wisely took warning by God's judgments on them, and *put away the image of Baal,* resolving to worship the God of Israel only, and consult none but his prophets. So far was well, yet it did not prevent the destruction of Ahab's family, nay, that destruction came *in his days,* and fell immediately *upon him* (*ch.* 9:24), though he was one of the best of the family, for then the measure of its iniquity was full. Jehoram's reformation was next to none; for, 1. He only put away the image of Baal *which his father had made,* and this probably in compliment to Jehoshaphat, who otherwise would not have come into confederacy with him, any more than with his brother, 1 Ki. 22:49. But he did not destroy the worship of Baal among the people, for Jehu found it prevalent, *ch.* 10:19. It was well to reform his family, but it was not enough; he ought to have used his power for the reforming of his kingdom. 2. When he put away the image of Baal, he adhered to the worship of the calves, that politic sin of Jeroboam, *v.* 3. *He departed not therefrom,* because that was the state engine by which the division between the two tribes was supported. Those do not truly, nor acceptably, repent or reform, who only part with the sins that they lose by, but continue their affection to the sins that they get by. 3. He only *put away* the image of Baal, he did not break it in pieces, as he ought to have done. He laid it aside for the present, yet not knowing but he might have occasion for it another time; and Jezebel, for reasons of state, was content to worship her Baal in private.

II. That he did what he could to recover his brother's losses. As he had something more of the religion of an Israelite than his father, so he had something more of the spirit of a king than his brother. Moab rebelled against Israel, immediately upon the death of Ahab, *ch.* 1:1. And we do not find that Ahaziah made any attempt to chastise or reduce them, but tamely let go his interest in them, rather than entertain the cares, undergo the fatigues, and run the hazards, of a war with them. His folly and pusillanimity herein, and his indifference to the public good, were the more aggravated because the tribute which the king of Moab paid was a very considerable branch of the revenue of the crown of Israel: 100,000 *lambs, and* 100,000 *wethers, v.* 4. The riches of kings then lay more in cattle than coin, and they thought it not below them to *know the state of their flocks and herds* themselves, because, as Solomon observes, *the crown doth not endure to every generation,* Prov. 27:23, 24. Taxes were then paid not so much in money as in the commodities of the country, which was an ease to the subject, whether it was an advantage to the prince or no. The revolt of Moab was a great loss to Israel, yet Ahaziah sat still in sloth and ease. But an upper chamber in his house proved as fatal to him as the high places of the field could have been (*ch.* 1:2), and the breaking of his lattice let into his throne a man of the more active genius, that would not lose the dominion of Moab without making at least one push for its preservation.

Verses 6–19

Jehoram has no sooner got the sceptre into his hand than he takes the sword into his hand, to reduce Moab. Crowns bring great cares and perils to the heads that wear them; no sooner in honour than in war. Now here we have,

I. The concerting of this expedition between Jehoram king of Israel and Jehoshaphat king of Judah. Jehoram levied an army (*v.* 6), and such an opinion he had of the godly king of Judah that, 1. He courted him to be his confederate: *Wilt thou go with me against Moab?* And he gained him. Jehoshaphat said, *I will go up. I am as thou art, v.* 7. Judah and Israel, though unhappily divided from each other, yet can unite against Moab a common enemy. Jehoshaphat upbraids them not with their revolt from the house of David, nor makes it an article of their alliance that they shall return to their allegiance, though he had good reason to insist upon it, but treats with Israel as a sister-kingdom. Those are no friends to their own peace and strength who can never find in their hearts to forgive and forget an old injury, and unite with those that have formerly broken in upon their rights. *Quod initio non vulvit, tractu temporis invalescit — That which was originally destitute of authority in the progress of time acquires it.* 2. He consulted him as his confidant, *v.* 8. He took advice of Jehoshaphat, who had more wisdom and experience than himself, which way they should make their descent upon the country of Moab; and he advised that they should not march against them the nearest way, over Jordan, but go round *through the wilderness of Edom,* that they might take the king of Edom (who was tributary to him) and his forces along with them If two be better than one, much more will not a *threefold cord be easily broken.* Jehoshaphat had like to have paid dearly for joining with Ahab, yet he joined with his son, and this expedition also had like to have been fatal to him. There is nothing got by being yoked with unbelievers.

II. The great straits that the army of the confederates was reduced to in this expedition. Before they saw the face of an enemy they were all in danger of perishing for want of water, *v.* 9. This ought to have been considered before they ventured a march through the wilderness, the same wilderness (or very near it) where their ancestors wanted water, Num. 20:2. God suffers his people, by their own improvidence, to bring themselves into distress, that the wisdom, power, and goodness of his providence may be glorified in their relief. What is more cheap and common than water? It is *drink to every beast of the field,* Ps. 104:11. Yet the want of it will soon humble and ruin kings and armies. The king of Israel sadly lamented the present distress, and the imminent danger it put them in of falling into the hands of their enemies the Moabites, to whom, when weakened by thirst, they would be an easy prey, *v.* 10. it was he that had *called these kings together;* yet he charges it upon Providence, and reflects upon that as unkind: The Lord has *called them together.* Thus *the foolishness of man perverteth his way,* and then *his heart fretteth against the Lord,* Prov. 19:3.

III. Jehoshaphat's good motion to ask counsel of God in this exigency, *v.* 11. The place they were now in could not but remind them of the *wonders of which their fathers told them,* the waters fetched out of the rock for Israel's seasonable supply. The thought of this, we may suppose, encouraged Jehoshaphat to ask, *Is there not here a prophet of the Lord,* like unto Moses? He was the more concerned because it was by his advice that they fetched this compass through the wilderness, *v.* 8. It was well that Jehoshaphat enquired of the Lord now, but it would have been much better if he had done it sooner, before he engaged in this war, or steered this course; so the distress might have been prevented. Good men are sometimes remiss and forgetful, and neglect their duty till necessity and affliction drive them to it.

IV. Elisha recommended as a proper person for them to consult with *v.* 11. And here we may wonder, 1. That Elisha should follow the camp, especially in such a tedious march as this, as a volunteer, unasked, unobserved, and in no post of honour at all; not in the office of *priest of the war* (Deu. 20:2) or president of the council of war, but in such obscurity that none of the kings knew they had such a jewel in the treasures of their camp, nor so good a friend in their retinue. We may suppose it was by special direction from heaven that Elisha attended the war, as *the chariot of Israel and the horsemen thereof.* Thus does God anticipate his people with the blessings of his goodness and provide his oracles for those that provide them not for themselves. It would often be bad with us if God did not take more care of us, both for soul and body, than we take for ourselves. 2. That a servant of the king of Israel knew of his being there when the king himself did not. Probably it was such a servant as Obadiah was to his father Ahab, one that *feared the Lord;* to such a one Elisha made himself known, not to the kings. The account he gives of him is that it was he that *poured water on the hands of Elijah,* that is, he was his servant, and particularly attended him when he washed his hands. He that will be great, let him learn to minister: he that will rise high, let him begin low.

V. The application which the kings made to Elisha. They went down to him to his quarters, *v.* 12. Jehoshaphat had such an esteem for a prophet with whom the word of the Lord was that he would condescend to visit him in his own person and not send for him up to him. The other two were moved by the straits they were in to make their court to the prophet. He that humbled himself was thus exalted, and looked great, when three kings came to knock at his door, and beg his assistance; see Rev. 3:9.

VI. The entertainment which Elisha gave them. 1. He was very plain with the wicked king of Israel (*v.* 13): *"What have I to do with thee?* How canst thou expect an answer of peace from me? *Get thee to the prophets of thy father and mother,* whom thou hast countenanced and maintained in thy prosperity, and let them help thee now in thy distress." Elisha was not imposed upon, as Jehoshaphat was, by his partial and hypocritical reformation; he knew that, though he had put away the image of Baal, Baal's prophets were still dear to him, and perhaps some of the were now in his camp. "Go," said he, *"go to them. Get you to the gods whom you have served,* Jdg. 10:14. The world and the flesh have ruled you, let them help you; why should God be *enquired of by* you?" Eze. 14:3. Elisha tells him to his face, in a holy indignation at his wickedness, that he can scarcely find in his heart to *look towards him* or to *see him, v.* 14. Jehoram is to be respected as a prince, but as a wicked man he is a vile person, and is to be condemned, Ps. 15:4. Elisha, as a subject, will honour him, but as a prophet he will cause him to know his iniquity. For those that had such an extraordinary commission it was fit (though not for a common person) to say to a king, *Thou art wicked,* Job 34:18. Jehoram has so much self-command as to take this plain dealing patiently; he cares not now for hearing of the prophets of Baal, but is a humble suitor to the God of Israel and his prophet, representing the present case as very deplorable and humbly recommending it to the prophet's compassionate consideration. In effect, he owns himself unworthy, but let not the other kings be ruined for his sake. 2. Elisha showed a great respect to the godly king of Judah, *regarded his presence,* and, for his sake, would *enquire of the Lord* for them all. It is good being with those that have God's favour and his prophet's love. Wicked people often fare the better for the friendship and society of those that are godly. 3. He composed himself to receive instructions from God. His mind was somewhat ruffled and disturbed at the sight of Jehoram; though he was not put into a sinful heat or passion, nor had spoken unadvisedly, yet his zeal for the present indisposed him for prayer and the operations of the Spirit, which required a mind very calm and sedate. He therefore called for a musician (*v.* 15), a devout musician, one accustomed to play upon his harp and sign psalms to it. To hear God's praises sweetly sung, as David had appointed, would cheer his spirits, and settle his mind, and help to put him into a right frame both to speak to him and to hear from him. We find a company of prophets prophesying with *a psaltery and a tabret before them,* 1 Sa. 10:5. Those that desire communion with God must keep their spirits quiet and serene. Elisha being refreshed, and having the tumult of his spirits laid by this divine music, *the hand of the Lord came upon him,* and his visit did him more honour than that of three kings. 4. God, by him, gave them assurance that the issue of the present distress would be comfortable and glorious. (1.) They should speedily be supplied with water, *v.* 16, 17. To try their faith and obedience, he bids them *make the valley full of ditches* to receive the water. Those that expect God's blessings must prepare room for them, *dig the pools* for the rain to fill, as they did in the valley of Baca, and so made even that a well, Ps. 84:6. To raise the wonder, he tells them they shall have water enough, and yet there shall be *neither wind nor rain.* Elijah, by prayer, obtained water out of the clouds, but Elisha fetches it nobody knows whence. The spring of these waters shall be as secret as the head of the Nile. God is not tied to second causes. Ordinarily it is by a plentiful rain that God *confirms his inheritance* (Ps. 68:9), but here it is done without rain, at least without rain in that place. Some of the *fountains of the great deep,* it is likely, *were broken up* on this occasion; and, to increase the miracle, *that valley* only (as it should seem) *was filled with water,* and no other place had any share of it. (2.) That supply should be an earnest of victory (*v.* 18): *"This is but a light thing in the sight of the Lord;* you shall not only be saved from perishing, but shall return in triumph." As God gives freely to the unworthy, so he gives richly, like himself, more than we are *able to ask or think.* His grants out-do our requests and expectations. Those that sincerely seek for the dew of God's grace shall have it, and by it be made *more than conquerors.* It is promised that they shall be masters of the rebellious country, and they are permitted to lay it waste and ruin it, *v.* 19. The law forbade them to fell fruit-trees to be employed in their sieges (Deu. 20:19), but not when it was intended, in justice, for the starving of a country that had forfeited its fruits, by denying *tribute to those to whom tribute was due.*

Verses 20–27

I. We have here the divine gift of both those things which God had promised by Elisha — water and victory, and the former not only a pledge of the latter, but a means of it. God, who created, and commands, all the waters, both above and beneath the firmament, sent them an abundance of water on a sudden, which did them double service.

1. It relieved their armies, which were ready to perish, *v.* 20. And, which was very observable, this relief came just at the time of the *offering of the morning sacrifice* upon the altar at Jerusalem, a certain time, and universally known. That time Elisha chose for his *hour of prayer* (it is likely *looking towards the temple,* for so there were to do in their prayers when they were *going out to battle* and encamped at a distance, 1 Ki. 8:44), in token of his communion with the temple-service, and his expectation of success by virtue of the great sacrifice. We now cannot pitch upon any hour more acceptable than another, because our high priest is always appearing for us, to present and plead his sacrifice. That time God chose for the hour of mercy to put an honour upon the daily sacrifice, which had been despised. God answered Daniel's prayer just at the *time of the evening sacrifice* (Dan. 9:21); for he will acknowledge his own institutions.

2. It deceived their enemies, who were ready to triumph, into the destruction. Notice was given to the Moabites of the advances of the confederate army, to oppose which *all that were able to put on armour* were posted upon the frontiers, where they were ready to give the Israelites a warm reception (*v.* 21), promising themselves that it would be easy dealing with an army fatigued by so long a march through the wilderness of Edom. But see here,

(1.) How easily they were drawn into their own delusions. Observe the steps of their self-deceit. [1.] They saw the water in the valley where the army of Israel encamped, and conceited it was blood (*v.* 22), because they knew the valley to be dry, and (there having been no rain) they could not imagine it should be water. The sun shone upon it, and probably *the sky was red and lowering,* a presage of *foul weather that day* (Mt. 16:3), and so it proved to them. But, this making the water look red, their own fancies, which made them willing to believe what made for them, suggested, *This is blood,* God permitting them thus to impose upon themselves. [2.] If their camp was thus full of blood, they conclude, "Certainly the kings have fallen out (as confederates of different interests are apt to do) and they have *slain one another* (*v.* 23), for who else should slay them?" And, [3.] "If the armies have slain one another, we have nothing to do but to divide the prey. *Now therefore, Moab, to the spoil."* These were the gradual suggestions of some sanguine spirits among them, that thought themselves wiser and happier in their conjectures than their neighbours; and the rest, being desirous it should be so, were forward to believe it was so. *Quod volumus facile credimus — What we wish we readily believe.* Thus those that are to be destroyed are first deceived (Rev. 20:8), and none are so effectually deceived as those that deceive themselves.

(2.) How fatally they thereby ran upon their own destruction. They rushed carelessly into the camp of Israel, to plunder it, but were undeceived when it was too late. The Israelites, animated by the assurances Elisha had given them of victory, fell upon them with the utmost fury, routed them, and pursued them into their own country (*v.* 24), which they laid waste (*v.* 25), destroyed the cities, marred the ground, stopped up the wells, felled the timber, and left only the royal city standing, in the walls of which they made great breaches with their battering engines. This they got by rebelling against Israel. Who ever *hardened his heart against God and prospered?*

II. In the close of the chapter we are told what the king of Moab did when he found himself reduced to the last extremity by the besiegers, and that his capital city was likely to fall into their hands. 1. He attempted that which was bold and brave. he got together 700 choice men, and with them sallied out upon the intrenchments of the king of Edom, who, being but a mercenary in this expedition, would not, he hoped, make any great resistance if vigorously attacked, and so he might make his escape that way. But it would not do; even the king of Edom proved too hard for him, and obliged him to retire, *v.* 26. 2. This failing, he did that which was brutish and barbarous; he took his own son, his eldest son, that was to succeed him, than whom nothing could be more dear to himself and his people, and *offered him for a burnt-offering upon the wall, v.* 27. He designed by this, (1.) To obtain the favour of Chemosh his god, which, being a devil, delighted in blood and murder, and the destruction of mankind. The dearer any thing was to them the more acceptable those idolaters thought it must needs be if offered in sacrifice to their gods, and therefore burnt their children in the fire to their honour. (2.) To terrify the besiegers, and oblige them to retire. Therefore he did it *upon the wall,* in their sight, that they might see what desperate courses he resolved to take rather than surrender, and how dearly he would sell his city and life. He intended hereby to render them odious, and to exasperate and enrage his own subjects against them. This effect it had: *There was great indignation against Israel* for driving him to this extremity, whereupon they raised the siege and returned. Tender and generous spirits will not do that, though just, which will drive any man distracted, or make him desperate.

CHAPTER 4

Great service Elisha had done, in he foregoing chapter, for the three kings: to his prayers and prophecies they owed their lives and triumphs. One would have expected that the next chapter would tell us what honours and what dignities were conferred on Elisha for this, that he should immediately be preferred at court, and made prime-minister of state, that Jehoshaphat should take him home with him, and advance him in his kingdom. No, the wise man delivered the army, but no man remembered the wise man, Eccl. 9:15. Or, if he had preferment offered him, he declined it: he preferred the honour of doing good in the schools of the prophets before that of being great in the courts of princes. God magnified him, and that sufficed him — magnified him indeed, for we have him here employed in working no fewer than five miracles. I. He multiplied the poor widow's oil (*v.* 1–7). II. He obtained for the good Shunammite the blessing of a son in her old age (*v.* 8–17). III. He raised that child to life when it was dead (*v.* 18–27). IV. He healed the deadly pottage (*v.* 38–41). V. He fed 100 men with twenty small loaves (*v.* 42–44).

Verses 1–7

Elisha's miracles were for use, not for show; this recorded here was an act of real charity. Such also were the miracles of Christ, not only great wonders, but great favours to those for whom they were wrought. God magnifies his goodness with his power.

I. Elisha readily receives a poor widow's complaint. She was a prophet's widow; to whom therefore should she apply, but to him that was a father to the sons of the prophets, and concerned himself in the welfare of their families? It seems, the prophets had wives as well as the priests, though prophecy went not by entail, as the priesthood did. Marriage is honourable in all, and not inconsistent with the most sacred professions. Now, by the complaint of this poor woman (v. 1), we are given to understand, 1. That her husband, being *one of the sons of the prophets*, was well know to Elisha. Ministers of eminent gifts and stations should make themselves familiar with those that are every way their inferiors, and know their character and state. 2. That he had the reputation of a godly man. Elisha knew him to be one that feared the Lord, else he would have been unworthy of the honour and unfit for the work of a prophet. He was one that kept his integrity in a time of general apostasy, one of the 7000 that had not bowed the knee to Baal. 3. That he was dead, though a good man, a good minister. The prophets — do they live for ever? Those that were clothed with the Spirit of prophecy were not thereby armed against the stroke of death. 4. That he died poor, and in debt more than he was worth. He did not contract his debts by prodigality, and luxury, and riotous living, for he was one that feared the Lord, and therefore durst not allow himself in such courses: nay, religion obliges men not to live above what they have, nor to spend more than what God gives them, no, not in expenses otherwise lawful; for thereby, of necessity, they must disable themselves, at last, to give every one his own, and so prove guilty of a continued act of injustice all along. Yet it may be the lot of those that fear God to be in debt, and insolvent, through afflictive providences, losses by sea, or bad debts, or their own imprudence, for the *children of light* are not always *wise for this world*. Perhaps this prophet was impoverished by persecution: when Jezebel ruled, prophets had much ado to live, and especially if they had families. 5. That the creditors were very severe with her Two sons she had to be the support of her widowed state, and their labour is reckoned *assets* in her hand; that must go therefore, and they must be bondmen for seven years (Ex. 21:2) to work out this debt. Those that leave their families under a load of debt disproportionable to their estates know not what trouble they entail. In this distress the poor widow goes to Elisha, in dependence upon the promise that the seed of the righteous shall not be forsaken. The generation of the upright may expect help from God's providence and countenance from his prophets.

II. He effectually relieves this poor widow's distress, and puts her in a way both to pay her debt and to maintain herself and her family. He did not say, *Be warmed, be filled*, but gave her real help. He did not give her some small matter for her present provision, but set her up in the world to sell oil, and put a stock into her hand to begin with. This was done by miracle, but it is an indication to us what is the best method of charity, and the greatest kindness one can do to poor people, which is, if possible, to help them into a way of improving what little they have by their own industry and ingenuity.

1. He directed her what to do, considered her case: *What shall I do for thee?* The sons of the prophets were poor, and it would signify little to make a collection for her among them: but the God of the holy prophets is able to supply all her need; and, if she has a little committed to her management, her need must be supplied by his blessing and increasing that little. Elisha therefore enquired what she had to make money of, and found she had nothing to sell but one pot of oil, v. 2. If she had had any plate or furniture, he would have bidden her part with it, to enable her to be just to her creditors. We cannot reckon any thing really, nor comfortably, our own, but what is so when all our debts are paid. If she had not had this pot of oil, the divine power could have supplied her; but, having this, it will work upon this, and so teach us to make the best of what we have. The prophet, knowing her to have credit among her neighbours, bids her borrow of them *empty vessels* (v. 3), for, it seems, she had sold her own, towards the satisfying of her creditors. He directs her to shut the door upon herself and her sons, while she filled all those vessels out of that one. She must shut the door, to prevent interruptions from the creditors, and others while it was in the doing, that they might not seem proudly to boast

of this miraculous supply, and that they might have opportunity for prayer and praise to God upon this extraordinary occasion. Observe, (1.) The oil was to be multiplied in the pouring, as the other widow's meal in the spending. The way to increase what we have is to use it; to him that so hath shall be given. It is not hoarding the talents, but trading with them, that doubles them. (2.) It must be poured out by herself, not by Elisha nor by any of the sons of the prophets, to intimate that it is in connexion with our own careful and diligent endeavours that we may expect the blessing of God to enrich us both for this world and the other. What we have will increase best in our own hand.

2. She did it accordingly. She did not tell the prophet he designed to make a fool of her; but firmly believing the divine power and goodness, and in pure obedience to the prophet, she borrowed vessels large and many of her neighbours, and poured out her oil into them. One of her sons was employed to bring her empty vessels, and the other carefully to set aside those that were full, while they were all amazed to find their pot, like a fountain of living water, always flowing, and yet always full. They saw not the spring that supplied it, but believed it to be in him *in whom all our springs are.* Job's metaphor was now verified in the letter (Job 29:6), *The rock poured me out rivers of oil.* Perhaps this was in the tribe of Asher, part of whose blessing it was that he should *dip his foot in oil*, Deu. 33:24.

3. The oil continued flowing as long as she had any empty vessels to receive it; when every vessel was full the oil stayed (v. 6), for it was not fit that this precious liquor should run over, and be as water spilt on the ground, which cannot be gathered up again. Note, We are never straitened in God, in his power and bounty, and the riches of his grace; all our straitness is in ourselves. It is our faith that fails, not his promise. He gives above what we ask: were there more vessels, there is enough in God to fill them — enough for all, enough for each. Was not this pot of oil exhausted as long as there were any vessels to be filled from it? And shall we fear lest the golden oil which flows from the very root and fatness of the good olive should fail, as long as there are any lamps to be supplied from it? Zec. 4:12.

4. The prophet directed her what to do with the oil she had, v. 7. She must not keep it for her own use, to *make her face to shine.* Those whom Providence has made poor must be content with poor accommodations for themselves (this is *knowing how to want*), and must not think, when they get a little of that which is better than ordinary, to feed their own luxury: no, (1.) She must sell the oil to those that were rich, and could afford to bestow it on themselves. We may suppose, being produced by miracle, it was the best of its kind, like the wine (Jn. 2:10), so that she might have both a good price and a good market for it. Probably the merchants bought it to export, for oil was one of the commodities that Israel traded in, Eze. 27:17. (2.) She must pay her debt with the money she received for her oil. Though her creditors were too rigorous with her, yet they must not therefore lose their debt. Her first care, now that she has wherewithal to do so, must be to discharge that, even before she makes any provision for her children. It is one of the fundamental laws of our religion that we render to all their due, pay every just debt, give every one his own, though we leave ever so little for ourselves; and this, not of constraint but willingly and without grudging; not only for wrath, to avoid being sued, but also for conscience' sake. Those that possess an honest mind cannot with pleasure eat their daily bread, unless it be their own bread. (3.) The rest must not be laid up, but she and her children must live upon it, not upon the oil, but upon the money received from it, with which they must put themselves into a capacity of getting an honest livelihood. No doubt she did as the man of God directed; and hence, [1.] Let those that are poor and in distress be encouraged to trust God for supply in the way of duty. *Verily thou shalt be fed*, though not feasted. It is true we cannot now expect miracles, yet we may expect mercies, if we wait on God and seek to him. Let widows particularly, and prophets' widows in a special manner, depend upon him to preserve them and their fatherless children alive, for to them he will be a husband, a father. [2.] Let those whom God has blessed with plenty use it for the glory of God and under the direction of his word: let them do justly with it, as this widow did, and serve God cheerfully in the use of it, and as Elisha, be ready to do good to those that need them, be eyes to the blind, and feet to the lame.

Verses 8–17

The giving of a son to such as were old, and had been long childless, was an ancient instance of the divine power and favour, in the case of Abraham, and Isaac, and Manoah, and Elkanah; we find it here among the wonders wrought by Elisha. This was wrought in recompence for the kind entertainment which a good woman gave him, as the promise of a son was given to Abraham when he entertained angels. Observe here,

I. The kindness of the Shunammite woman to Elisha. Things are bad enough in Israel, yet not so bad but that God's prophet finds friends, wherever he goes. Shunem was a city in the tribe of Issachar, that lay in the road between Samaria and Carmel, a road that Elisha often travelled, as we find *ch.* 2:25. *There* lived *a great woman*, who kept a good house, and was very hospitable, her husband having a good estate, and his heart safely trusting in her, and in her discreet management, Prov. 31:11. So famous a man as Elisha could not pass and repass unobserved. Probably he had been accustomed to take some private obscure lodgings in the town; but this pious matron, having notice once of his being there, pressed him with great importunity, and, with much difficulty, constrained him to dine with her, v. 8. He was modest and loth to be troublesome, humble and affected not to associate with those of the first rank; so that it was not without some difficulty that he was first drawn into an acquaintance there; but afterwards, whenever he went that way in his circuit, he constantly called there. So well pleased was she with her guest, and so desirous of his company, that she would not only bid him welcome to her table, but provide a lodging-room for him in her house, that he might make the longer stay, not doubting but her house would be blessed for his sake, and all under her roof edified by his pious instructions and example — a good design, yet she would not do it without acquainting her husband, would neither lay out his money nor invite strangers to his house without his consent asked and obtained, v. 9, 10. She suggests to him, 1. That the stranger she would invite was a *holy man of God*, who therefore would do good to their family, and God would recompense the kindness done to him; perhaps she had heard how well paid the widow of Sarepta was for entertaining Elijah. 2. That the kindness she intended him would be no great charge to them; she would build him only a little chamber. Perhaps she had no spare room in the house, or none private and retired enough for him, who spent much of his time in contemplation, and cared not for being disturbed with the noise of the family. The furniture shall be very plain; no costly hangings, no stands, no couches, no looking-glasses, but a bed, and a table, a stool, and a candlestick, all that was needful for his convenience, not only for his repose, but for his study, his reading and writing. Elisha seemed highly pleased with these accommodations, for he turned in and lay there (v. 11) and, as it should seem, his man in the same chamber, for he was far from taking state.

II. Elisha's gratitude for this kindness. Being exceedingly pleased with the quietness of his apartment, and the friendliness of his entertainment, he began to consider with himself what recompence he should make her. Those that receive courtesies should study to return them; it ill becomes men of God to be ungrateful, or to sponge upon those that are generous. 1. He offered to use his interest for her in the king's court (v. 13): *Thou hast been careful for us with all this care* (thus did he magnify the kindness he received, as those that are humble are accustomed to do, though in the purse of one so rich, and in the breast of one so free, it was as nothing); now *what shall be done for thee?* As the liberal devise liberal things, so the grateful devise grateful things. "*Wouldst thou be spoken for to the king, or the captain of the host,* for an office for thy husband, civil or military? Hast thou any complaint to make, any petition to present, any suit at law depending, that needs the countenance of the high powers? Wherein can I serve thee?" It seems Elisha had got such an interest by his late services that, though he chose not to prefer himself by it, yet he was capable of preferring his friends. A good man can take as much pleasure in serving others as in raising himself. But she needs not any good offices of this kind to be done for her: *I dwell* (says she) *among my own people*, that is, "We are well off as we are, and do not aim at preferment." It is a happiness to *dwell among our own people*, that love and respect us, and to whom we are in a capacity of doing good; and a greater happiness to be content to do so, to be easy, and to know when we are well off. Why should those that live comfortably among their own people covet to live delicately in kings' palaces? It would be well with many if they did but know when they were well off. Some years after this we find this Shunammite had occasion to be spoken for to the king, though now she needed it not, *ch.* 8:3, 4. Those that dwell among their own people must not think their mountain stands so strong as that it cannot be moved; they may be driven, as this good woman was, to sojourn among strangers. Our continuing city is above. 2. He did use his interest for her in the court of heaven, which was far better. Elisha consulted with his servant what kindness he should do for her, to such a freedom did this great prophet admit even his servant. Gehazi reminded him that she was childless, had a great estate, but no son to leave it to, and was past hopes of having any, her husband being old. If Elisha could obtain this favour from God for her, it would be the removal of that which at present was her only grievance. Those are the most welcome kindnesses which are most suited to our necessities. He sent for her immediately. She very humbly and respectfully *stood in the door* (*v.* 15), according to her accustomed modesty, and then he assured her that within a year she should bring forth a son, *v.* 16. She had received this prophet *in the name of a prophet,* and now she had not a courtier's reward, in being spoken for to the king, but a prophet's reward, a signal mercy given by prophets and in answer to prayer: the promise was a surprise to her, and she begged that she might not be flattered by it: *"Nay, my lord, thou* are *a man of God,* and therefore I hope speakest seriously, and doth not jest with me, nor lie unto thy handmaid." The event, within the time limited, confirmed the truth of the promise: *She bore a son* at the season that Elisha spoke of, *v.* 17. God built up her house, in reward to her kindness in building the prophet a chamber. We may well imagine what joy this brought to the family. *Sing, O barren! thou that didst not bear.*

Verses 18–37

We may well suppose that, after the birth of this son, the prophet was doubly welcome to the good Shunammite. He had thought himself indebted to her, but henceforth, as long as she lives, she will think herself in his debt, and that she can never do too much for him. We may also suppose that the child was very dear to the prophet, as the son of his prayers, and very dear to the parents, as the son of their old age. But here is,

I. The sudden death of the child, though so much a darling. he was so far past the perils of infancy that he was able to go to the field to his father, who no doubt was pleased with his engaging talk, and his joy of his son was greater than the joy of his harvest; but either the cold or the heat of the open field overcame the child, who was bred tenderly, and he complained to his father that his head ached, *v.* 19. Whither should we go with our complaints, but to our heavenly Father? Thither the Spirit of adoption brings believers with all their grievances, all their desires, teaching them to cry, with groanings that cannot be uttered, *"My head, my head;* my heart, my heart." The father sent him to his mother's arms, his mother's lap, little suspecting any danger in his indisposition, but hoping he would drop asleep in his mother's bosom and awake well; but the sickness proved fatal; he slept the sleep of death (*v.* 20), was well in the morning and dead by noon: all the mother's care and tenderness could not keep him alive. A child of promise, a child of prayer, and given in love, yet taken away. Little children lie open to the arrests of sickness and death. But how admirably does the prudent pious mother guard her lips under this surprising affliction! Not one peevish murmuring word comes from her. She has a strong belief that the child will be raised to life again: like a genuine daughter of Abraham's faith, as well as loins, she accounts that God is able to raise him from the dead, for thence at first she *received him in a figure,* Heb. 11:19. She had heard of the raising of the widow's son of Sarepta, and that the spirit of Elijah rested on Elisha; and such confidence had she of God's goodness that she was very ready to believe that he who so soon took away what he had given would restore what he had now taken away. By this faith *women received their dead raised to life,* Heb. 11:35. In this faith she makes no preparation for the burial of her dead child, but for its resurrection; for she *lays him on the prophet's bed* (*v.* 21), expecting that he will stand her friend. *O woman! great is thy faith.* he that wrought it would not frustrate it.

II. The sorrowful mother's application to the prophet on this sad occasion; for it happened very opportunely that he was now at the college upon Mount Carmel, not far off.

1. She begged leave of her husband to go to the prophet, yet not acquainting him with her errand, lest he should not have faith enough to let her go, *v.* 22. He objected, *It is neither new moon nor sabbath* (*v.* 23), which intimates that on those feasts of the Lord she used to go to the assembly in which he presided, with other good people, to hear the word, and to join with him in prayers and praises. She did not think it enough to have his help sometimes in her own family, but, though a great woman, attended on public worship, for which this was none of the times appointed; *therefore,* said the husband, "why wilt thou go to day? What is the matter?" "No harm," said she, *"It shall be well,* so you will say yourself hereafter." See how this husband and wife vied with each other in showing mutual regard; she was so dutiful to him that she would not go till she had acquainted him with her journey, and he so kind to her that he would not oppose it, though she did not think fit to acquaint him with her business. 2. She made all the haste she could to the prophet (*v.* 24), and he, seeing her at a distance, sent his servant to enquire whether any thing was amiss, *v.* 25, 26. The questions were particular: *Is it well with thee? Is it well with thy husband? Is it well with the child?* Note, It well becomes the men of God, with tenderness and concern, to enquire about the welfare of their friends and their families. The answer was general *It is well.* Gehazi was not the man that she came to complain to, and therefore she put him off with this; she said little, and little said is soon amended (Ps. 39:1, 2), but what she did say was very patient: "It is well with me, with my husband, with the child" — all well, and yet the child dead in the house. Note, When God calls away our dearest relations by death it becomes us quietly to say, "It is well both with us and them;" it is well, for all is well that God does; all is well with those that are gone if they have gone to heaven, and all well with us that stay behind if by the affliction we are furthered in our way thither. 3. When she came to the prophet she humbly reasoned with him concerning her present affliction. She threw herself at his feet, as one troubled and in grief, which she never showed till she came to him who, she believed, could help her, *v.* 27. When her passion would do her service she knew how to discover it, as well as how to conceal it when it would do her disservice. Gehazi knew his master would not be pleased to see her lie at his feet, and therefore would have raised her up; but Elisha waited to hear from her, since he might not know immediately from God, what was the cause of her trouble. God discovered things to his prophets as he saw fit, not always as they desired; God did not show this to the prophet, because he might know it from the good woman herself. What she said was very pathetic. She appealed to the prophet, (1.) Concerning her indifference to this mercy which was now taken from her: *"Did I desire a son of my lord?* No, thou knowest I did not; it was thy own proposal, not mine; I did not fret for the want of a son, as Hannah, nor beg, as Rachel, *Give me children or else I die."* Note, When any creature-comfort is taken from us, it is well if we can say, through grace, that we did not set our hearts inordinately upon it; for, if we did, we have reason to fear it was given in anger and taken away in wrath. (2.) Concerning her entire dependence upon the prophet's word: *Did I not say, Do not deceive me?* Yes, she did say so (*v.* 16), and this reflection upon it may be considered either, [1.] As quarrelling with the prophet for deceiving her. She was ready to think herself mocked with the mercy when it was so soon removed, and that it would have been better she had never had this child than to be deprived of him when she began to have comfort in him. Note, The loss of a mercy should not make us undervalue the gift of it. Or, [2.] As pleading with the prophet for the raising of the child to life again: *"I said, Do not deceive me,* and I know thou wilt not." Note, However the providence of God may disappoint us, we may be sure the promise of God never did, nor ever will, deceive us: hope in that will not make us ashamed.

III. The raising of the child to life again. We may suppose that the woman gave Elisha a more express account of the child's death, and he gave her a more express promise of his resurrection, than is here related, where we are briefly told,

1. That Elisha sent Gehazi to go in all haste to the dead child, gave him his staff, and bade him lay that on the face of the child, *v.* 29. I know not what to make of this. Elisha knew that Elijah raised the dead child with a very close application, stretching himself upon the child, and praying again and again, and could he think to raise this child by so slight a ceremony as this, especially when nothing hindered him from coming himself? Shall such a power as this be delegated, and to no better man that Gehazi? Bishop Hall suggests that it was done out of human conceit, and not by divine instinct, and therefore it failed of the effect; God will not have such great favours made too cheap, nor shall they be too easily come by, lest they be undervalued.

2. The woman resolved not to go back without the prophet himself (*v.* 30): *I will not leave thee.* She had no great expectation from the staff, she would have the hand, and she was in the right of it. Perhaps God intended hereby to teach us not to put that confidence in creatures, that are servants, which the power of the Creator, their Master and ours, will alone bear the weight of. Gehazi returns *re infecta — without success,* without the tidings of any sign of life in the child (*v.* 31): *The child is not awaked,* intimating, to the comfort of the mother, that its death was but a sleep, and that he expected that it would shortly be awaked. In the raising of dead souls to spiritual life ministers can do no more by their own power than Gehazi here could; they lay the word, like the prophet's staff, before their faces, but there is neither voice nor hearing, till Christ, by his Spirit, comes himself. The letter alone kills; it is the Spirit that gives life. It is not prophesying upon dry bones that will put life into them, breath must come from heaven and breathe upon those slain.

3. The prophet, by earnest prayer, obtained from God the restoring of this dead child to life again. He found the child dead upon his own bed (*v.* 32), *and shut the door upon them twain, v.* 33. Even the dead child is spoken of as a person, one of the twain, for it was still in being and not lost. He shut out all company, that he might not seem to glory in the power God had given him, or to use it for ostentation and to be seen of men. Observe,

(1.) How closely the prophet applied himself to this great operation, perhaps being sensible that he had tempted God too much in thinking to effect it by the staff in Gehazi's hand, for which he thought himself rebuked by the disappointment. He now found it a harder task than he then thought, and therefore addressed himself to it with great solemnity. [1.] He *prayed unto the Lord* (*v.* 33), probably as Elijah had done, *Let this child's soul come into him again.* Christ raised the dead to life as one having authority *— Damsel, arise — young man, I say unto thee, Arise — Lazarus, come forth* (for he was powerful and faithful as a Son, the Lord of life), but Elijah and Elisha did it by petition, as servants. [2.] He *lay upon the child* (*v.* 34), as if he would communicate to him some of his vital heat or spirits. Thus he expressed the earnestness of his desire, and gave a sign of that divine power which he depended upon for the accomplishment of this great work. He first *put his mouth to the child's mouth,* as if, in God's name, he would breathe into him the breath of life; then *his eyes to the child's eyes,* to open them again to the light of life; then *his hands to the child's hands,* to put strength into them. He then *returned, and walked in the house,* as one full of care and concern, and wholly intent upon what he was about. Then he went up stairs again, and the second time, *stretched himself upon the child, v.* 35. Those that would be instrumental in conveying spiritual life to dead souls must thus affect themselves with their case, and accommodate themselves to it, and labour fervently in prayer for them.

(2.) How gradually the operation was performed. At the first application, *the flesh of the child waxed warm* (*v.* 34), which gave the prophet encouragement to continue instant in prayer. After a while, *the child sneezed seven times,* which was an indication, not only of life, but liveliness. Some have reported it as an ancient tradition that when God breathed into Adam the breath of life the first evidence of his being alive was sneezing, which gave rise to the usage of paying respect to those that sneeze. Some observe here that sneezing clears the head, and there lay the child's distemper.

(3.) How joyfully the child was restored alive to his mother (*v.* 36, 37), and all parties concerned *were not a little comforted,* Acts 20:12. See the power of God, who kills and makes alive again. See the power of prayer; as it has the key of the clouds, so it has the key of death. See the power of faith; that fixed law of nature (that death is a way whence there is no returning) shall rather be dispensed with than this believing Shunammite shall be disappointed.

Verses 38–44

We have here Elisha in his place, in his element, among the sons of the prophets, teaching them, and, as a father, providing for them; and happy it was for them that they had one over them who naturally cared for their state, under whom they were well fed and well taught. There was a dearth in the land, for the wickedness of those that dwelt therein, the same that we read of, *ch.* 8:1. It continued seven years, just as long again as that in Elijah's time. A famine of bread there was, but not of hearing the word of God, for Elisha had the sons of the prophets sitting before him, to hear his wisdom, who were taught, that they might teach others. Two instances we have here of the care he took about their meat. Christ twice fed those to whom he preached. Elisha was in the more care about it now because of the dearth, that the sons of the prophets might not be ashamed in this evil time, but, even in *the days of famine, might be satisfied,* Ps. 37:19.

I. He made hurtful food to become safe and wholesome. 1. On the lecture-day, the sons of the prophets being all to attend, he ordered his servant to provide food for their bodies, while he was breaking to them the bread of life for their souls. Whether there was any flesh-meat for them does not appear; he orders only that pottage should be seethed for them of herbs, *v.* 38. The sons of the prophets should be examples of temperance and mortification, not desirous of dainties, but content with plain food. If they have neither savoury meats nor sweet meats, nay, if a mess of pottage be all the dinner, let them remember that this great prophet entertained himself and his guests no better. 2. One of the servitors, who was sent to gather herbs (which, it should seem, must serve instead of flesh for the pottage), by mistake brought in that which was noxious, or at least very nauseous, and shred it into the pottage: *wild gourds* they are called, *v.* 39. Some think it was *coloquintida,* a herb strongly cathartic, and, if not qualified, dangerous. The sons of the prophets, it seems, were better skilled in divinity than in natural philosophy, and read their Bibles more than their herbals. If any of the fruits of the earth be hurtful, we must look upon it as an effect of the curse *(thorns and thistles shall it bring forth unto thee),* for the original blessing made all good. 3. The guests complained to Elisha of the unwholesomeness of their food. Nature has given man the sense of tasting, not only that wholesome food may be pleasant, but that that which is unwholesome may be discovered before it comes to the stomach; the mouth tries meat by tasting it, Job 12:11. This pottage was soon found by the taste of it to be dangerous, so that they cried out, *There is death in the pot, v.* 40. The table often becomes a snare, and that which should be for our welfare proves a trap, which is a good reason why we should not feed ourselves without fear; when we are receiving the supports and comforts of life we must keep up an expectation of death and a fear of sin. 4. Elisha immediately cured the bad taste and prevented the bad consequences of this unwholesome pottage; as before he had healed the bitter waters with salt, so now the bitter broth with meal, *v.* 41. It is probable that there was meal in it before, but that was put in by a common hand, only to thicken the pottage; this was the same thing, but cast in by Elisha's hand, and with intent to heal the pottage, by which it appears that the change was not owing to the meal (that was the sign only, not the means), but to the divine power. Now all was well, not only no death, but no harm in the pot. We must acknowledge God's goodness in making our food wholesome and nourishing. *I am the Lord that healeth thee.*

II. He made a little food to go a great way. 1. Elisha had a present brought him of twenty barley-loaves and some ears of corn (*v.* 42), a present which, in those ages, would not be despicable at any time, but now in a special manner valuable, when there was a dearth in the land. It is said to be of *the first-fruits,* which was God's due out of their increase; and when the priests and Levites were all at Jerusalem, out of their reach, the religious people among them, with good reason, looked upon the prophets as God's receivers, and brought their first-fruits to them, which helped to maintain their schools. 2. Having freely received, he freely gave, ordering it all to be set before the sons of the prophets, reserving none for himself, none for the hereafter. *"Let the morrow take thought for the things of itself,* give it all to the people that they may eat." It well becomes the men of God to be generous and open-handed, and the fathers of the prophets to be liberal to the sons of the prophets. 3. Though the loaves were little, it is likely no more than what one man would ordinarily eat at a meal, yet with twenty of them he satisfied 100 men, *v.* 43, 44. his servant thought that to set so little meat before so many men was but to tantalize them, and shame his master for making so great an invitation to such short commons; but he in God's name, pronounced it a full meal for them, and so it proved; they did eat, and left thereof, not because their stomachs failed them, but because the bread increased in the eating. God has promised his church (Ps. 132:15) *that he will abundantly bless her provision, and satisfy her poor with bread;* for whom he feeds he fills, and what he blesses comes to much, as what he blows upon comes to little, Hag. 1:9. Christ's feeding his hearers was a miracle far beyond this; but both teach us that those who wait upon God in the way of duty may hope to be both protected and supplied by a particular care of divine Providence.

CHAPTER 5

Two more of Elisha's miracles are recorded in this chapter. I. The cleansing of Naaman, a Syrian, a stranger, from his leprosy, and there, 1. The badness of his case (*v.* 1). 2. The providence that brought him to Elisha, the intelligence given him by a captive maid (*v.* 2–4). A letter from the king of Syria to the king of Israel, to introduce him (*v.* 5–7). And the invitation Elisha sent him (*v.* 8). 3. The method prescribed for his cure, his submission, with much ado, to that method, and his cure thereby (*v.* 9–14). 4. The grateful acknowledgments he made to Elisha hereupon (*v.* 15–19). II. The smiting of Gehazi, his own servant, with that leprosy. 1. Gehazi's sins, which were belying his master to Naaman (*v.* 20–24), and lying to his master when he examined him (*v.* 25). 2. His punishment for these sins. Naaman's leprosy was entailed on his family (*v.* 26, 27). And, if Naaman's cure was typical of the calling of the Gentiles, as our Saviour seems to make it (Lu. 4:27), Gehazi's stroke may be looked upon as typical of the blinding and rejecting of the Jews, who envied God's grace to the Gentiles, as Gehazi envied Elisha's favour to Naaman.

Verses 1–8

Our saviour's miracles were intended for the lost sheep of the house of Israel, yet one, like a crumb, fell from the table to a woman of Canaan; so this one miracle Elisha wrought for Naaman, a Syrian; for God does good to all, and will have all men to be saved. Here is,

I. The great affliction Naaman was under, in the midst of all his honours, *v.* 1. He was a great man, in a great place; not only rich and raised, but particularly happy for two things: — 1. That he had been very serviceable to his country. God made him so: *By him the Lord had* often *given deliverance to Syria,* success in their wars even with Israel. The preservation and prosperity even of those that do not know God and serve him must be ascribed to him, for *he is the Saviour of all men,* but *especially of those that believe.* Let Israel know that when the Syrians prevailed it was from the Lord. 2. That he was very acceptable to his prince, was his favourite, and prime-minister of state; so great was he, so high, so honourable, and a mighty man of valour; but he was a leper, was under that loathsome disease, which made him a burden to himself. Note, (1.) No man's greatness, or honour, or interest, or valour, or victory, can set him out of the reach of the sorest calamities of human life; there is many a sickly crazy body under rich and gay clothing. (2.) Every man has some *but* or other in his character, something that blemishes and diminishes him, some allay to his grandeur, some damp to his joy; he may be very happy, very good, yet, in something or other, not so good as he should be nor so happy as he would be. Naaman was a great as the world could make him, and yet (as bishop Hall expresses it) the basest slave in Syria would not change skins with him.

II. The notice that was given him of Elisha's power, by a little maid that waited on his lady, *v.* 2, 3. This maid was, by birth, an Israelite, providentially carried captive into Syria, and there preferred into Naaman's family, where she published Elisha's fame to the honour of Israel and Israel's God. The unhappy dispersing of the people of God has sometimes proved the happy occasion of the diffusion of the knowledge of God, Acts 8:4. This little maid, 1. As became a true-born Israelite, consulted the honour of her country, and could give an account, though but a girl, of the famous prophet they had among them. Children should betimes acquaint themselves with the wondrous works of God, that, wherever they go, they may have them to talk of. See Ps. 8:2. 2. As became a good servant, she desired the health and welfare of her master, though she was a captive, a servant by force; much more should servants of choice seek their masters' good. The Jews in Babylon were to seek the peace of the land of their captivity. Jer. 29:7. *Elisha* had *not cleansed any leper in Israel* (Lu. 4:27), yet this little maid, from the other miracles he had wrought, inferred that he *could* cure her master, and from his common beneficence inferred that he *would* do it, though he was a Syrian. Servants may be blessings to the families where they are, by telling what they know of the glory of God and the honour of his prophets.

III. The application which the king of Syria hereupon made to the king of Israel on Naaman's behalf. Naaman took notice of the intelligence, though given by a simple maid, and did not despise it for the sake of her meanness, when it tended to his bodily health. he did not say, "The girl talks like a fool; how can any prophet of Israel do that for me which all the physicians of Syria have attempted in vain?" Though he neither loved nor honoured the Jewish nation, yet, if one of that nation can but cure him of his leprosy, he will thankfully acknowledge the obligation. O that those who are spiritually diseased would hearken thus readily to the tidings brought them of the great Physician! See what Naaman did upon this little hint. 1. He would not send for the prophet to come to him, but such honour would he pay to one that had so much of a divine power with him as to be able to cure diseases that he would go to him himself, though he himself was sickly, unfit for society, the journey long, and the country an enemy's; princes, he thinks, must stoop to prophets when they need them. 2. He would not go *incognito — in disguise,* though his errand proclaimed his loathsome disease, but went in state, and with a great retinue, to do the more honour to the prophet. 3. He would not go empty-handed, but took with him gold, silver, and raiment, to present to his physician. Those that have wealth, and want health show which they reckon the more valuable blessing; what will they not give for ease, and strength, and soundness of body? 4. He would not go without a letter to the king of Israel from the king his master, who did himself earnestly desire his recovery. He knows not where in Samaria to find this wonder-working prophet, but takes it for granted the king knows where to find him; and, to engage the prophet to do his utmost for Naaman, he will go to him supported with the interest of two kings. If the king of Syria must entreat his help, he hopes the king of Israel, being his liege-lord, may command it. The gifts of the subject must all be (he thinks) for the service and honour of the prince, and therefore he desires the king that he would *recover the leper* (*v.* 6), taking it for granted that there was a greater intimacy between the king and the prophet than really there was.

IV. The alarm this gave to the king of Israel, *v.* 7. He apprehended there was in this letter, 1. A great affront upon God, and therefore he rent his clothes, according to the custom of the Jews when they heard or read that which they thought blasphemous; and what less could it be than to attribute to him a divine power? *"Am I a God, to kill* whom I will, and *make alive* whom I will? No, I pretend not to such an authority." Nebuchadnezzar did, as we find, Dan. 5:19. *"Am I a God, to kill* with a word, *and make alive* with a word? No, I pretend not to such a power;" thus this great man, this bad man, is made to own that he is but a man. Why did he not, with this consideration, correct himself for his idolatry, and reason thus: — Shall I worship those as gods that can neither kill nor make alive, can *do neither good nor evil?* 2. A bad design upon himself. He appeals to those about him for this: *"See how he seeketh a quarrel against me;* he requires me to recover the leper, and if I do not, though I cannot, he will make that a pretence to wage war with me," which he suspects the rather because Naaman is his general. had he rightly understood the meaning of the letter, that when the king wrote to him to recover the leper he meant that he would take care he might be recovered, he would not have been in this fright. Note, We often create a great deal of uneasiness to ourselves by misinterpreting the words and actions of others that are well intended: it is charity to ourselves to think no evil. If he had bethought himself of Elisha, and his power, he would easily have understood the letter, and have known what he had to do; but he is put into this confusion by making himself a stranger to the prophet: the captive maid had him more in her thoughts than the king had.

V. The proffer which Elisha made of his services. He was willing to do any thing to make his prince easy, though he was neglected and his former good services were forgotten by him. Hearing on which occasion the king had rent his clothes, he sent to him to let him know that if his patient would come to him he should not lose his labour (*v.* 8): *He shall know that there is a prophet in Israel* (and it were sad with Israel if there were not), that there is a prophet in Israel who can do that which the king of Israel dares not attempt, which the prophets of Syria cannot pretend to. It was not for his own honour, but for the honour of God, that he coveted to make them all know *that there was a prophet in Israel,* though obscure and overlooked.

Verses 9–14

We have here the cure of Naaman's leprosy.

I. The short and plain direction which the prophet gave him, with assurance of success. Naaman designed to do honour to Elisha when he came in his chariot, and with all his retinue, to Elisha's door, *v.* 9. Those that showed little respect to prophets at other times were very complaisant to them when they needed them. He attended at Elisha's door as a beggar for an alms. Those that would be cleansed from the spiritual leprosy must wait at *Wisdom's gate, and watch at the posts of her doors.* Naaman expected to have his compliment returned, but Elisha gave him his answer without any formality, would not go to the door to him, lest he should seem too much pleased with the honour done him, but sent a messenger to him, saying, *Go wash in Jordan seven times,* and promising him that if he did so his disease should be cured. The promise was express: *Thou shalt be clean.* The method prescribed was plain: *Go wash in Jordan.* This was not intended as any means of the cure; for, though cold bathing is recommended by many as a very wholesome thing, yet some think that in the case of a leprosy it was rather hurtful. But it was intended as a sign of the cure, and a trial of his obedience. Those that will be helped of God must do as they are bidden. But why did Elisha send a messenger to him with these directions? 1. Because he had retired, at this time, for devotion, was intent upon his prayers for the cure, and would not be diverted; or, 2. Because he knew Naaman to be a proud man, and he would let him know that before the great God all men stand upon the same level.

II. Naaman's disgust at the method prescribed, because it was not what he expected. Two things disgusted him: —

1. That Elisha, as he thought, put a slight upon his person, in sending him orders by a servant, and not coming to him himself, *v.* 11. Being big with the expectation of a cure, he had been fancying how this cure would be wrought, and the scheme he had laid was this: *"He will surely come out to me,* that is the least he can do to me, a peer of Syria, to me that have come to him in all this state, to me that have so often been victorious over Israel. *He will stand,* and *call on the name of his God,* and name me in his prayer, and then he will *wave his hand over the place,* and so effect the cure." And, because the thing was not done just thus, he fell into a passion, forgetting, (1.) That he was a leper, and the law of Moses, which Elisha would religiously observe, shut lepers out from society — a leper, and therefore he ought not to insist upon the punctilios of honor. Note, Many have hearts unhumbled under humbling providences; see Num. 12:14. (2.) That he was a petitioner, suing for a favour which he could not demand; and beggars must not be choosers, patients must not prescribe to their physicians. See in Naaman the folly of pride. A cure will not content him unless he be cured with ceremony, with a great deal of pomp and parade; he scorns to be healed, unless he be humoured.

2. That Elisha, as he thought, put a slight upon his country. He took it hard that he must be sent to wash in Jordan, a river of Israel, when he thought *Abana and Pharpar, rivers of Damascus, better than all the waters of Israel.* How magnificently does he speak of these two rivers that watered Damascus, which soon after fell into one, called by geographers *Chrysoroas — the golden stream!* How scornfully does he speak of all the waters of Israel, though God had called the land of Israel *the glory of all lands,* and particularly for its *brooks of water!* Deu. 8:7. So common it is for God and man to differ in their judgments. How slightly does he speak of the prophet's directions! *May I not wash in them and be clean?* He might wash in them and be clean from dirt, but not wash in them and be clean from leprosy. He was angry that the prophet bade him wash and be clean; he thought that the prophet must do all and was not pleased that he was bidden to do any thing, — or he thought this too cheap, too plain, too common a thing for so great a man to be cured by, — or he did not believe it would at all effect the cure, or, if it would, what medicinal virtue was there in Jordan more than in the rivers of Damascus? But he did not consider, (1.) That Jordan belonged to Israel's God, from whom he was to expect the cure, and not from the gods of Damascus; it watered the Lord's land, the holy land, and, in a miraculous cure, relation to God was much more considerable than the depth of the channel or the beauty of the stream. (2.) That Jordan had more than once before this obeyed the commands of omnipotence. It had of old yielded a passage to Israel, and of late to Elijah and Elisha, and therefore was fitter for such a purpose than those rivers which had only observed the common law of their creation, and had never been thus distinguished; but, above all, (3.) Jordan was the river appointed, and, if he expected a cure from the divine power, he ought to acquiesce in the divine will, without asking why or wherefore. Note, It is common for those that are wise in their own conceit to look with contempt on the dictates and prescriptions of divine wisdom and to prefer their own fancies before them; those that are for *establishing their own righteousness* will not *submit to the righteousness of God,* Rom. 10:3. Naaman talked himself into such a heat (as passionate men usually do) that he turned away from the prophet's door in a rage, ready to swear he would never have any thing more to say to Elisha; and who then would be the loser? Note, *Those that observe lying vanities forsake their own mercies.* Jonah 2:8. Proud men are the worst enemies to themselves and forego their own redemption.

III. The modest advice which his servants gave him, to observe the prophet's prescriptions, with a tacit reproof of his resentments, *v.* 13. Though at other times they kept their distance, and now saw him in a passion, yet, knowing him to be a man that would hear reason at any time, and from any body (a good character of great men, and a very rare one), they drew near, and made bold to argue the matter a little with him. They had conceived a great opinion of the prophet (having, perhaps, heard more of him from the common people, whom they had conversed with, than Naaman had heard from the king and courtiers, whom he had conversed with), and therefore begged of him to consider: *"If the prophet had bidden thee to do some great thing,* had ordered thee into a tedious course of physic, or to submit to some painful operation, blistering, or cupping, or salivating, *Wouldst thou not have done it?* No doubt thou wouldst. And wilt thou not submit to so easy a method as this, *Wash and be clean?"* Observe, 1. His own servants gave him this reproof and counsel, which was no more disparagement to him than that he had intelligence of one that could cure him from his wife's maid, *v.* 3. Note, It is a great mercy to have those about us that will be free with us, and faithfully tell us of our faults and follies, though they be our inferiors. Masters must be willing to hear reason from their servants, Job 31:13, 14. As we should be deaf to the counsel of the ungodly, though given by the greatest and most venerable names, so we should have our ear open to good advice, though brought us by those who are much below us: no matter who speaks, if the thing be well said. 2. The reproof was very modest and respectful. They call him *Father;* for servants must honour and obey their masters with a kind of filial affection. In giving reproof or counsel we must make it appear that it comes from love and true honour, and that we intend, not reproach, but reformation. 3. It was very rational and considerate. If the rude and unthinking servants had stirred up their master's angry resentment, and offered to avenge his quarrel upon the prophet, who (he thought) affronted him, how mischievous would the consequences have been! Fire from heaven, probably, upon them all! But they, to our great surprise, took the prophet's part. Elisha, though it is likely he perceived that what he had said had put Naaman out of humour, did not care to pacify him: it was at his peril if he persisted in his wrath. But his servants were made use of by Providence to reduce him to temper. They reasoned with him, (1.) From his earnest desire of a cure: *Wouldst thou not do* any thing? Note, When diseased sinners come to this, that they are content to do any thing, to submit to any thing, to part with any thing, for a cure, then, and not till then, there begin to be some hopes of them. Then they will take Christ on his own terms when they are made willing to have Christ upon any terms. (2.) From the easiness of the method prescribed: "It is but, *Wash and be clean.* It is but trying; the experiment is cheap and easy, it can do no hurt, but may do good." Note, the methods prescribed for the healing of the leprosy of sin are so plain that we are utterly inexcusable if we do not observe them. It is but, "Believe, and be saved" — "Repent, and be pardoned" — "Wash, and be clean."

IV. The cure effected, in the use of the means prescribed, *v.* 14. Naaman, upon second thoughts, yielded to make the experiment, yet, it should seem, with no great faith and resolution; for, whereas the prophet bade him wash in Jordan seven times, he did but dip himself so many times, as lightly as he could. However God was pleased so far to honour himself and his word as to make that effectual. *His flesh came again, like the flesh of a child.* to his great surprise and joy. This men get by yielding to the will of God, by attending to his institutions. His being cleansed by washing put an honour on the law for cleansing lepers. God will magnify his word above all his name.

Verses 15–19

Of the ten lepers that our Saviour cleansed, the only one that *returned to give thanks* was a *Samaritan,* Lu. 17:16. This Syrian did so, and here expresses himself.

I. Convinced of the power of the God of Israel, not only that he is God, but that he is God alone, and that indeed *there is no God in all the earth but in Israel* (*v.* 15) — a noble confession, but such as intimates the misery of the Gentile world; for the nations that had many gods really had no God, but were without God in the world. He had formerly thought the gods of Syria gods indeed, but now experience had rectified his mistake, and he knew Israel's God was God alone, the sovereign Lord of all. Had he seen other lepers cleansed, perhaps the sight would not have convinced him, but the mercy of the cure affected him more than the miracle of it. Those are best able to speak of the power of divine grace who have themselves experienced it.

II. Grateful to Elisha the prophet: "Therefore, for his sake whose servant thou art, I have a present for thee, silver, and gold, and raiment, whatever thou wilt please to accept." He valued the cure, not by the easiness of it to the prophet, but the acceptableness of it to himself, and would gladly pay for it accordingly. But Elisha generously refused the fee, though urged to accept it; and, to prevent further importunity, backed his refusal with an oath: *As the Lord liveth, I will receive none* (*v.* 16), not because he did not need it, for he was poor enough, and knew what to do with it, and how to bestow it among the sons of the prophets, nor because he thought it unlawful, for he received presents from others; but he would not be beholden to this Syrian, nor should *he* say, *I have made Elisha rich,* Gen. 14:23. It would be much for the honour of God to show this new convert that the servants of the God of Israel were taught to look upon the wealth of this world with a holy contempt, which would confirm him in his belief that *there was no God but in Israel.* See 1 Co. 9:18; 2 Co. 11:9.

III. Proselyted to the worship of the God of Israel. He will not only offer a sacrifice to the Lord, in thanks for his present cure, but he resolves he will never offer sacrifice to any other gods, *v.* 17. It was a happy cure of his leprosy which cured him of his idolatry, a more dangerous disease. But here are two instances of his weakness and infirmity in his conversion: — 1. In one instance he over-did it, that he would not only worship the God of Israel, but he would have clods of earth out of the prophet's garden, or at least of the prophet's ordering, to *make an altar of, v.* 17. He that awhile ago had spoken very slightly of the waters of Israel (*v.* 12) now is in another extreme, and over-values the earth of Israel, supposing (since God has appointed *altars of earth,* Ex. 20:24) that an altar of that earth would be most acceptable to him, not considering that all *the earth is the Lord's and the fulness thereof.* Or perhaps the transport of his affection and veneration for the prophet, not only upon the account of his power, but of his virtue and generosity, made him, as we say, love the very ground he went upon and desire to have some of it home with him. The modern compliment equivalent to this would be, "Pray, sir, let me have your picture." 2. In another instance he under-did it, that he reserved to himself a liberty to bow in the house of Rimmon, in complaisance to the king his master, and according to the duty of his place at court (*v.* 18), *in this thing* he must be excused. He owns he ought not to do it, but that he cannot otherwise not do it, but that he cannot otherwise keep his place, — protests that his bowing is not, nor ever shall be, as it had been, in honour to the idol, but only in honour to the king, — and therefore he hopes God will forgive him. Perhaps, all things considered, this might admit of some apology, though it was not justifiable. But, as to us, I am sure, (1.) If, in covenanting with God, we make a reservation for any known sin, which we will continue to indulge ourselves in, that reservation is a defeasance of his covenant. We must cast away all our transgressions and not except any house of Rimmon. (2.) Though we are encouraged to pray for the remission of the sins we have committed, yet, if we ask for a dispensation to go on in any sin for the future, we mock God, and deceive ourselves. (3.) Those that know not how to quit a place at court when they cannot keep it without sinning against God, and wronging their consciences, do not rightly value the divine favour. (4.) Those that truly hate evil will make conscience of abstaining from all appearances of evil. Though Naaman's dissembling his religion cannot be approved, yet because his promise to offer no sacrifice to any god but the God of Israel only was a great point gained with a Syrian, and because, by asking pardon in this matter, he showed such a degree of conviction and ingenuousness as gave hopes of improvement, the prophet took fair leave of him, and bade him *Go in peace, v.* 19. Young converts must be tenderly dealt with.

Verses 20–27

Naaman, a Syrian, a courtier, a soldier, had many servants, and we read how wise and good they were, *v.* 13. Elisha, a holy prophet, a man of God, has but one servant, and he proves a base, lying, naughty fellow. Those that heard of Elisha at a distance honoured him, and got good by what they heard; but he that stood continually before him, to hear his wisdom, had no good impressions made upon him either by his doctrine or miracles. One would have expected that Elisha's servant should be a saint (even Ahab's servant, Obadiah, was), but even Christ himself had a Judas among his followers. The means of grace cannot give grace. The best men, the best ministers have often had those about them that have been their grief and shame. The nearer the church the further from God. *Many come from the east and west to sit down with Abraham when the children of the kingdom shall be cast out.* Here is,

I. Gehazi's sin. It was a complicated sin. 1. The love of money, that root of all evil, was at the bottom of it. His master contemned Naaman's treasures, but he coveted them, *v.* 20. His heart (says bishop Hall) was packed up in Naaman's chests, and he must run after him to fetch it. Multitudes, by coveting worldly wealth, have *erred from the faith* and *pierced themselves with many sorrows.* 2. He blamed his master for refusing Naaman's present, condemned him as foolish in not taking gold when he might have it, envied and grudged his kindness and generosity to this stranger, though it was for the good of his soul. In short, he thought himself wiser than his master. 3. When Naaman, like a person of accomplished manners, alighted from his chariot to meet him (*v.* 21), he told him a deliberate lie, that his master sent him to him, and so he received that courtesy to himself that Naaman intended to his master. 4. He abused his master, and basely misrepresented him to Naaman as one that had soon repented of his generosity, that was fickle, and did not know his own mind, that would say and unsay, swear and unswear, that would not do an honourable thing but he must presently undo it again. His story of the two sons of the prophets was as silly as it was false; if he would have begged a token for two young scholars, surely less than a talent of silver might serve them. 5. There was danger of his alienating Naaman from that holy religion which he had espoused,

and lessening his good opinion of it. he would be ready to say, as Paul's enemies suggested concerning him (2 Co. 12:16, 17), that, though Elisha himself did not burden him, yet being crafty he caught him with guile, sending those that made a gain of him. We hope that he understood afterwards that Elisha's hand was not in it, and that Gehazi was forced to restore what he had unjustly got, else it might have driven him to his idols again. 6. His seeking to conceal what he had unjustly got added much to his sin. (1.) He hid it, as Achan did his gain, by sacrilege, in the tower, a secret place, a strong place, till he should have an opportunity of laying it out, *v.* 24. Now he thought himself sure of it, and applauded his own management of a fraud by which he had imposed, not only upon the prudence of Naaman, but upon Elisha's spirit of discerning, as Ananias and Sapphira upon the apostles. (2.) He denied it: He *went in, and stood before his master,* ready to receive his orders. None looked more observant of his master, though really none more injurious to him; he thought, as Ephraim, *I have become rich, but they shall find no iniquity in me,* Hos. 12:8. His master asked him where he had been, "Nowhere, sir" (said he), "out of the house." Note, One lie commonly begets another: the way of that sin is down-hill; therefore dare to be true.

II. The punishment of this sin. Elisha immediately called him to an account for it; and observe,

1. How he was convicted. he thought to impose upon the prophet, but was soon given to understand that the Spirit of prophecy could not be deceived, and that it was in vain to lie to the Holy Ghost. Elisha could tell him, (1.) What he had done, though he had denied it. "Thou sayest thou wentest nowhere, but *went not my heart with thee?" v.* 26. Had Gehazi yet to learn that prophets had spiritual eyes? or could he think to hide any thing from a seer, from him with whom the secret of the Lord was? Note, It is folly to presume upon sin in hopes of secresy. When thou goest aside into any by-path does not thy own conscience go with thee? Does not the eye of God go with thee? *He that covers his sin shall not prosper,* particularly *a lying tongue is but for a moment,* Prov. 12:19. Truth will transpire, and often comes to light strangely, to the confusion of those that make lies their refuge. (2.) What he designed, though he kept that in his own breast. He could tell him the very thoughts and intents of his heart, that he was projecting, now that he had got these two talents, to purchase ground and cattle, to leave Elisha's service, and to set up for himself. Note, All the foolish hopes and contrivances of carnal worldlings are open before God. And he tells him also the evil of it: *"Is it a time to receive money?* Is this an opportunity of enriching thyself? Couldst thou find no better way of getting money than by belying thy master and laying a stumbling-block before a young convert?" Note, Those that are for getting wealth at any time, and by any ways and means whatsoever, right or wrong, lay themselves open to a great deal of temptation. Those that will be rich (*per fas, per nefas; rem, rem, quocunque modo rem — by fair means, by foul means; careless of principle, intent only on money) drown themselves in destruction and perdition,* 1 Tim. 6:9. War, and fire, and plague, and shipwreck, are not, as many make them, things to get money by. It is not a time to increase our wealth when we cannot do it but in such ways as are dishonourable to God and religion or injurious to our brethren or the public.

2. How he was punished for it: *The leprosy of Naaman shall cleave to thee, v.* 27. If he will have his money, he shall take his disease with it, *Transit cum onere — It passes with this incumbrance.* He was contriving to entail lands upon his posterity; but, instead of them, he entails a loathsome disease on the heirs of his body, from generation to generation. The sentence was immediately executed on himself; no sooner said than done: He *went out from his presence a leper as white as snow.* Thus he is stigmatized and made infamous, and carries the mark of his shame wherever he goes: thus he loads himself and family with a curse, which shall not only for the present proclaim his villany, but for ever perpetuate the remembrance of it. Note, *The getting of treasures by a lying tongue is a vanity tossed to and fro of those that seek death,* Prov. 21:6. Those who get wealth by fraud and injustice cannot expect either the comfort or the continuance of it. What was Gehazi profited, though he gained his two talents, when thereby he lost his health, his honour, his peace, his service,

and, if repentance prevented not, his soul for ever? See Job 20:12, etc.

CHAPTER 6

In this chapter we have, I. A further account of the wondrous works of Elisha. 1. His making iron to swim (*v.* 1–7). 2. His disclosing to the king of Israel the secret counsels of the king of Syria (*v.* 8–12). 3. His saving himself out of the hands of those who were sent to apprehend him (*v.* 13–23). II. The besieging of Samaria by the Syrians and the great distress the city was reduced to (*v.* 24–33). The relief of it is another of the wonders wrought by Elisha's word, which we shall have the story of in the next chapter. Elisha is still a great blessing both to church and state, both to the sons of the prophets and to his prince.

Verses 1–7

Several things may be observed here,

I. Concerning the sons of the prophets, and their condition and character. The college here spoken of seems to be that at Gilgal, for there Elisha was (*ch.* 4:38), and it was near Jordan; and, probably, wherever Elisha resided as many as could of the sons of the prophets flocked to him for the advantage of his instructions, counsels, and prayers. Every one would covet to dwell with him and be near him. Those that would be teachers should lay out themselves to get the best advantages for learning. Now observe,

1. Their number increased so that they wanted room: *The place is too strait for us* (*v.* 1) — a good hearing, for it is a sign many are added to them. Elisha's miracles doubtless drew in many. Perhaps they increased the more now that Gehazi was cashiered, and, it is likely, an honester man put in his room, to take care of their provisions; for it should seem (by that instance, *ch.* 4:43) that Naaman's case was not the only one in which he grudged his master's generosity.

2. They were humble men and did not affect that which was gay or great. When they wanted room they did not speak of sending for cedars, and marble stones, and curious artificers, but only of getting every man a beam, to run up a plain hut or cottage with. It becomes the sons of the prophets, who profess to look for great things in the other world, to be content with mean things in this.

3. They were poor men, and men that had no interest in great ones It was a sign that Joram was king, and Jezebel ruled too, or the sons of the prophets, when they wanted room, would have needed only to apply to the government, not to consult among themselves about the enlargement of their buildings. God's prophets have seldom been the world's favourites. Nay, so poor were they that they had not wherewithal to hire workmen (but must leave their studies, and work for themselves), no, nor to buy tools, but must borrow of their neighbours. Poverty then is no bar to prophecy.

4. They were industrious men, and willing to take pains. They desired not to live, like idle drones (idle *monks,* I might have said), upon the labours of others, but only desired leave of their president to work for themselves. As the sons of the prophets must not be so taken up with contemplation as to render themselves unfit for action, so much less must they so indulge themselves in their ease as to be averse to labour. He that must eat or die must work or starve, 2 Th. 3:8, 10. Let no man think an honest employment either a burden or disparagement.

5. They were men that had a great value and veneration for Elisha; though they were themselves prophets, they paid much deference to him. (1.) They would not go about to build at all without his leave, *v.* 2. It is good for us all to be suspicious of our own judgment, even when we think we have most reason for it, and to be desirous of the advice of those who are wiser and more experienced; and it is especially commendable in the sons of the prophets to take their fathers along with them, and to act in all things of moment under their direction, *permissu superiorum — by permission of their superiors.* (2.) They would not willingly go to fell timber without his company: "*Go with thy servants* (*v.* 3), not only to advise us in any exigence, but to keep good order among us, that, being under they eye, we may behave as becomes us." Good disciples desire to be always under good discipline.

6. They were honest men, and men that were in care to give all men their own. When one of them, accidentally fetching too fierce a stroke (as those that work seldom are apt to be violent), threw off his axe-head into the

water, he did not say, "It was a mischance, and who can help it? It was the fault of the helve, and the owner deserved to stand to the loss." No, he cries out with deep concern, *Alas, master! For it was borrowed, v.* 5. Had the axe been his own, it would only have troubled him that he could not be further serviceable to his brethren; but now, besides that, it troubles him that he cannot be just to the owner, to whom he ought to be not only just but grateful. Note, We ought to be as careful of that which is borrowed as of that which is our own, that it receives no damage, because we must love our neighbour as ourselves and do as we would be done by. It is likely this prophet was poor, and had not wherewithal to pay for the axe, which made the loss of it so much the greater trouble. To those that have an honest mind the sorest grievance of poverty is not so much their own want or disgrace as their being by it rendered unable to pay their just debts.

II. Concerning the father of the prophets, Elisha. 1. That he was a man of great condescension and compassion; he went with the sons of the prophets to the woods, when they desired his company, *v.* 3. Let no man, especially no minister, think himself to great to stoop to do good, but be tender to all. 2. That he was a man of great power; he could make iron to swim, contrary to its nature (*v.* 6), for the God of nature is not tied up to its laws. He did not throw the helve after the hatchet, but cut down a new stick, and cast it into the river. We need not double the miracle by supposing that the stick sunk to fetch up the iron, it was enough that it was a signal of the divine summons to the iron to rise. God's grace can thus raise the stony iron heart which has sunk into the mud of this world, and raise up affections naturally earthly, to things above.

Verses 8–12

Here we have Elisha, with his spirit of prophecy, serving the king, as before helping the sons of the prophets; for that, as other gifts, is given to every man to profit withal; and, whatever abilities any man has of doing good, he is by them made a debtor both to the wise and unwise. Observe here,

I. How the king of Israel was informed by Elisha of all the designs and motions of his enemy, the king of Syria, more effectually than he could have been by the most vigilant and faithful spies. If the king of Syria, in a secret council of war, determined in which place to make an inroad upon the coasts of Israel, where he thought it would be the greatest surprise and they would be least able to make resistance, before his forces could receive his orders the king of Israel had notice of them from Elisha, and so had opportunity of preventing the mischief; and many a time, *v.* 8–10. See here, 1. That the enemies of God's Israel are politic in their devices, and restless in their attempts, against him. *They shall not know, nor see, till we come in the midst among them, and slay them,* Neh. 4:11. 2. All those devices are known to God, even those that are deepest laid. He knows not only what men do, but what they design, and has many ways of countermining them. 3. It is a great advantage to us to be warned of our danger, that we may stand upon our guard against it. The work of God's prophets is to give us warning; if, being warned, we do not save ourselves, it is our own fault, and our blood will be upon our own head. The king of Israel would regard the warnings Elisha gave him of his danger by the Syrians, but not the warnings he gave him of his danger by his sins. Such warnings are little heeded by the most; they will save themselves from death, but not from hell.

II. How the king of Syria resented this. He suspected treachery among his senators, and that his counsels were betrayed, *v.* 11. But one of his servants, that had heard, by Naaman and others, of Elisha's wondrous works, concludes it must needs be he that gave this intelligence to the king of Israel, *v.* 12. What could not he discover who could tell Gehazi his thoughts? Here a confession of the boundless knowledge, as before of the boundless power, of Israel's God, is extorted from Syrians. Nothing done, said, thought, by any person, in any place, at any time, is out of the reach of God's cognizance.

Verses 13–23

Here is, 1. The great force which the king of Syria sent to seize Elisha. He found out where he was, at Dothan (*v.* 13), which was not far from Samaria; thither he sent a great host, who were to come upon him by night, and to bring him dead or alive, *v.* 14. Perhaps he had heard that when only one captain and his fifty men were sent to take Elijah they were baffled in the attempt, and therefore he sent an *army* against Elisha, as if the fire from heaven that consumed fifty men could not as easily consume 50,000. Naaman could tell him that Elisha dwelt not in any stronghold, nor was attended with any guards, nor had any such great interest in the people that he needed to fear a tumult among them; what occasion then was there for this great force? But thus he hoped to make sure of him, especially coming upon him by surprise. Foolish man! Did he believe that Elisha had informed the king of Israel of his secret counsels or not? If not, what quarrel had he with him? If he did, could he be so weak as to imagine that Elisha would not discover the designs laid against himself, and that, having interest enough in heaven to discover them, he would not have interest enough to defeat them? Those that fight against God, his people, and prophet, know not what they do.

II. The grievous fright which the prophet's servant was in, when he perceived the city surrounded by the Syrians, and the effectual course which the prophet took to pacify him and free him from his fears. It seems, Elisha accustomed his servant to rise early, that is the way to bring something to pass, and to do the work of a day in its day. Being up, we may suppose he heard the noise of soldiers, and thereupon looked out, and was aware of an army compassing the city (*v.* 15), with great assurance no doubt of success, and that they should have this troublesome prophet in their hands presently. Now observe, 1. What a consternation he was in. He ran straight to Elisha, to bring him an account of it: *"Alas, master!"* (said he) *"what shall we do?* We are undone, it is to no purpose to think either of fighting or flying, but we must unavoidably fall into their hands." Had he but studied David's Psalms, which were then extant, he might have learnt *not to be afraid of* 10,000 of people (Ps. 3:6), no, not of *a host encamped against him,* Ps. 27:3. Had he considered that he was embarked with his master, by whom God had done great things, and whom he would not now leave to *fall into the hands of the uncircumcised,* and who, having saved others, would no doubt save himself, he would not have been thus at a loss. If he had only said, *What shall I do?* it would have been like that of the disciples: *Lord, save us, we perish;* but he needed not to include his master as being in distress, nor to say, *What shall we do?* 2. How his master quieted him, (1.) By word. What he said to him (*v.* 16) is spoken to all the faithful servants of God, when *without are fightings and within are fears: "Fear not* with that fear which has torment and amazement, *for those that are with us,* to protect us, *are more than those that are against us,* to destroy us — angels unspeakably more numerous — God infinitely more powerful." When we are magnifying the causes of our fear we ought to possess ourselves with clear, and great, and high thoughts of God and the invisible world. *If God be for us,* we know what follows, Rom. 8:31. (2.) By vision, *v.* 17. [1.] It seems Elisha was much concerned for the satisfaction of his servant. Good men desire, not only to be easy themselves, but to have those about them easy. Elisha had lately parted with his old man, and this, having newly come into his service, had not the advantage of experience; his master was therefore desirous to give him other convincing evidence of that omnipotence which employed him and was therefore employed for him. Note, Those whose faith is strong ought tenderly to consider and compassionate those who are weak and of a timorous spirit, and to do what they can to strengthen their hands. [2.] He saw himself safe, and wished no more than that his servant might see what he saw, a guard of angels round about him; such as were his master's convoy to the gates of heaven were his protectors against the gates of hell — *chariots of fire, and horses of fire.* Fire is both dreadful and devouring; that power which was engaged for Elisha's protection could both terrify and consume the assailants. As angels are God's messengers, so they are his soldiers, his hosts (Gen. 32:2), his legions, or regiments, (Mt. 26:53), for the good of his people. [3.] For the satisfaction of his servant there needed no more than the opening of his eyes; *that* therefore he prayed for, and obtained for him: *Lord, open his eyes that he may see.* The eyes of his body were open, and with them he saw the danger. "Lord, open the eyes of his faith, that with them he may see the protection we are under." Note, *First,* The greatest kindness we can do for those that are fearful and faint-hearted is to pray for them, and so to recommend them to the mighty grace of God. *Secondly,* The opening of our eyes will be the silencing of our fears. In the dark we are most apt to be frightened. The clearer sight we have of the sovereignty and power of heaven the less we shall fear the calamities of this earth.

III. The shameful defeat which Elisha gave to the host of Syrians who came to seize him. They thought to make a prey of him, but he made fools of them, perfectly played with them, so far was he from fearing them or any damage by them. 1. He prayed to God to smite them with blindness, and they were all struck blind immediately, not stone-blind, nor so as to be themselves aware that they were blind, for they could see the light, but their sight was so altered that they could not know the persons and places they were before acquainted with, *v.* 18. They were so confounded that those among them whom they depended upon for information did not know this place to be Dothan nor this person to be Elisha, but *groped at noon day as in the night* (Isa. 59:10; Job 12:24, 25); their memory failed them, and their distinguishing faculty. See the power of God over the minds and understanding of men, both ways; he enlightened the eyes of Elisha's friend, and darkened the eyes of his foes, that they might see indeed, but not perceive, Isa. 6:9 *For this* twofold judgment Christ came into this world, *that those who see not might see, and that those who see might be made blind* (Jn. 9:39), a savour of life to some, of death to others.

2. When they were thus bewildered and confounded he led them to Samaria (*v.* 19), promising that he would show them the man whom they sought, and he did so. He did not lie to them when he told them, *This is not the way, nor is this the city* where Elisha is; for he had now come out of the city; and if they would see him, they must go to another city to which he would direct them. Those that fight against God and his prophets deceive themselves, and are justly given up to delusions. 3. When he had brought them to Samaria he prayed to God so to open their eyes and restore them their memories that they might see where they were (*v.* 20), *and behold,* to their great terror, *they were in the midst of Samaria,* where, it is probable, there was a standing force sufficient to cut them all off, or make them prisoners of war. Satan, the god of this world, blinds men's eyes, and so deludes them into their own ruin; but, when God enlightens their eyes, they then see themselves in the midst of their enemies, captives to Satan and in danger of hell, though before they thought their condition good. The enemies of God and his church, when they fancy themselves ready to triumph, will find themselves conquered and triumphed over. 4. When he had them at his mercy he made it appear that he was influenced by a divine goodness as well as a divine power. (1.) He took care to protect them from the danger into which he had brought them, and was content to show them what he could have done; he needed not the sword of an angel to avenge his cause, the sword of the king of Israel is at his service if he please (*v.* 21): *My father* (so, respectfully does the king now speak to him, though, soon after, he swore his death), *shall I smite them?* And, again, as if he longed for the assault, *Shall I smite them?* Perhaps, he remembered how God was displeased at his father for *letting go out of his hands* those whom he had put it in his power to destroy, and he would not offend in like manner; yet such a reverence has he for the prophet that he will not strike a stroke without his commission. But the prophet would by no means suffer him to meddle with them; they were brought hither to be convinced and shamed, not to be killed, *v.* 22. Had they been *his* prisoners, taken captive by his sword and bow, when they asked quarter it would have been barbarous to deny, and, when he had given it to them, it would have been perfidious to do them any hurt, and against the laws of arms to kill men in cool blood. But they were not his prisoners; they were God's prisoners and the prophet's, and therefore he must do them no harm. Those that humble themselves under God's hand take the best course to secure themselves. (2.) He took care to provide for them; he ordered the king to treat them handsomely and then dismiss them fairly, which he did, *v.* 23. [1.] It was the king's praise that he was so

obsequious to the prophet, contrary to his inclination, and, as it seemed, to his interest, 1 Sa. 24:19. Nay, so willing was he to oblige Elisha that, whereas he was ordered openly to set *bread and water* before them (which are good fare for captives), he *prepared great provision* for them, for the credit of his court and country and of Elisha. [2.] It was the prophet's praise that he was so generous to his enemies, who, though they came to take him, could not but go away admiring him, as both the mightiest and kindest man they ever met with. The great duty of loving enemies, and doing good to those that hate us, was both commanded in the Old Testament (Prov. 25:21, 22, *If thy enemy hunger, feed him,* Ex. 23:4, 5) and practised, as here by Elisha. His predecessor had given a specimen of divine justice when he called for flames of fire on the heads of his persecutors to consume them, but he have a specimen of divine mercy in heaping coals of fire on the heads of his persecutors to melt them. Let not us then be *overcome of evil, but overcome evil with good.*

IV. The good effect this had, for the present, upon the Syrians. They *came no more into the land of Israel* (*v.* 23), namely, upon this errand, to take Elisha; they saw it was to no purpose to attempt that, nor would any of their bands be persuaded to make an assault on so great and good a man. The most glorious victory over an enemy is to turn him into a friend.

Verses 24–33

This last paragraph of this chapter should, of right, have been the first of the next chapter, for it begins a new story, which is there continued and concluded. Here is,

I. The siege which the king of Syria laid to Samaria and the great distress which the city was reduced to thereby. The Syrians had soon forgotten the kindnesses they had lately received in Samaria, and very ungratefully, for aught that appears without any provocation, sought the destruction of it, *v.* 24. There are base spirits that can never feel obliged. The country, we may suppose, was plundered and laid waste when this capital city was brought to the last extremity, *v.* 25. The dearth which had of late been in the land was probably the occasion of the emptiness of their stores, or the siege was so sudden that they had not time to lay in provisions; so that, while the sword devoured without, the famine within was more grievous (Lam. 4:9): for, it should seem, the Syrians designed not to storm the city, but to starve it. So great was the scarcity that an ass's head, that has but little flesh on it and that unsavoury, unwholesome, and ceremonially unclean, was sold for five pounds, and a small quantity of fitches, or lentiles, or some such coarse corn, then called *dove's dung,* no more of it than the quantity of six eggs, for five pieces of silver, about twelve or fifteen shillings. Learn to value plenty, and to be thankful for it; see how contemptible money is, when, in time of famine, it is so freely parted with for anything that is eatable.

II. The sad complaint which a poor woman had to make to the king, in the extremity of the famine. He was *passing by upon the wall* to give orders for the mounting of the guard, the posting of the archers, the repair of the breaches, and the like, when a woman of the city cried to him, *Help, my lord, O king! v.* 26. Whither should the subject, in distress, go for help but to the prince, who is, by office, the protector of right and the avenger of wrong? He returns but a melancholy answer (*v.* 27): *If the Lord do not help thee, whence shall I?* Some think it was a *quarrelling* word, and the language of his fretfulness: "Why dost thou expect anything from me, when God himself deals thus hardly with us?" Because he could not help her as he would, out of the floor or the wine-press, he would not help her at all. We must take heed of being made cross by afflictive providences. It rather seems to be a *quieting* word: "Let us be content, and make the best of our affliction, looking up to God, for, till he help us, I cannot help thee." 1. He laments the emptiness of the floor and the wine-press. These were not as they had been; even the king's failed. We read (*v.* 23) of great provisions which he had a command, sufficient for the entertainment of an army, yet now he has not wherewithal to relieve one poor woman. Scarcity sometimes follows upon great plenty; we cannot be sure that *to-morrow shall be as this day,* Isa. 56:12; Ps. 30:6. 2. He acknowledges himself thereby disabled to help, unless God would help them. Note, Creatures are helpless things without God, for every creature is that, all that, and only that, which he makes it to be. However, though he cannot help her, he is willing to hear her (*v.* 28): "*What ails thee?* Is there anything singular in thy case, or dost thou fare worse than thy neighbours?" Truly yes; she and one of her neighbours had made a barbarous agreement, that, all provisions failing, they should boil and eat her son first and then her neighbour's; hers was eaten (who can think of it without horror?) and now her neighbour hid hers, *v.* 28, 29. See an instance of the dominion which the flesh has got above the spirit, when the most natural affections of the mind may be thus overpowered by the natural appetites of the body. See the word of God fulfilled; among the threatenings of God's judgments upon Israel for their sins this was one (Deu. 28:53–57), that they should eat the flesh of their own children, which one would think incredible, yet it came to pass.

III. The king's indignation against Elisha upon this occasion. He lamented the calamity, *rent his clothes, and had sackcloth upon his flesh* (*v.* 30), as one heartily concerned for the misery of his people, and that it was not in his power to help them; but he did not lament his own iniquity, nor the iniquity of his people, which was the procuring cause of the calamity; he was not sensible that his *ways and his doings had procured this to himself; this is his wickedness, for it is bitter. The foolishness of man perverteth his way,* and then *his heart fretteth against the Lord.* Instead of vowing to pull down the calves at Dan and Bethel, or letting the law have its course against the prophets of Baal and of the groves, he swears *the death of Elisha, v.* 31. Why, what is the matter? What had Elisha done? his head is the most innocent and valuable in all Israel, and yet that must be devoted, and made an anathema. Thus in the days of the persecuting emperors, when the empire groaned under any extraordinary calamity, the fault was laid on the Christians, and they were doomed to destruction. *Christianos ad leones — Away with the Christians to the lions.* Perhaps Jehoram was in this heat against Elisha because he had foretold this judgment, or had persuaded him to hold out, and not surrender, or rather because he did not, by his prayers, raise the siege, and relieve the city, which he though he could do but would not; whereas till they repented and reformed, and were ready for deliverance, they had no reason to expect that the prophet should pray for it.

IV. The foresight Elisha had of the king's design against him, *v.* 32. He sat in his house well composed, and the elders with him, well employed no doubt, while the king was like a wild bull in a net, or like the troubled sea when it cannot rest; he told the elders there was an officer coming from the king to cut off his head, and bade them stop him at the door, and not let him in, for the king his master was just following him, to revoke the order, as we may suppose. The same spirit of prophecy that enabled Elisha to tell him what was done at a distance authorized him to call the king *the son of a murderer,* which, unless we could produce such an extraordinary commission, it is not for us to initiate; far be it from us to despise dominion and to speak evil of dignities. He appealed to the elders whether he had deserved so ill at the king's hands: "See whether in this he be not the son of a murderer?" For *what evil had Elisha done?* He *had not desired the woeful day,* Jer. 17:16.

V. The king's passionate speech, when he came to prevent the execution of his edict for the beheading of Elisha. He seems to have been in a struggle between his convictions and his corruptions, knew not what to say, but, seeing things brought to the last extremity, he even abandoned himself to despair (*v.* 33): *This evil is of the Lord.* Therein his notions were right and well applied; it is a general truth that all penal evil is of the Lord, as the first cause, and sovereign judge (Amos 3:6), and this we ought to apply to particular cases: if all evil, then this evil, whatever it is we are now groaning under, whoever are the instruments, God is the principal agent of it. But his inference from this truth was foolish and wicked: *What should I wait for the Lord any longer?* When Eli, and David, and Job, said, *It is of the Lord,* they grew patient upon it, but this bad man grew outrageous upon it: "I will neither fear worse nor expect better, for worse cannot come and better never will come: we are all undone, and there is no remedy." It is an unreasonable thing to be weary of waiting for God, for he is a God of judgment, and blessed are all those that wait for him.

CHAPTER 7

Relief is here brought to Samaria and her king, when the case is, in a manner, desperate, and the king despairing. I. It is foretold by Elisha, and an unbelieving lord shut out from the benefit of it (*v.* 1, 2). II. It is brought about, 1. By an unaccountable fright into which God put the Syrians (*v.* 6), which caused them to retire precipitately (*v.* 7). 2. By the seasonable discovery which four lepers made of this (*v.* 3–5), and the account which they gave of it to the court (*v.* 8–11). 3. By the cautious trial which the king made of the truth of it (*v.* 12–15). III. The event answered the prediction both in the sudden plenty (*v.* 16), and the death of the unbelieving lord (*v.* 17–20); for no word of God shall fall to the ground.

Verses 1–2

Here, I. Elisha foretels that, notwithstanding the great straits to which the city of Samaria is reduced, yet within twenty-four hours they shall have plenty, *v.* 1. The king of Israel despaired of it and grew weary of waiting: then Elisha foretold it, when things were at the worst. Man's extremity is God's opportunity of magnifying his own power; his time to appear for his people is when *their strength is gone,* Deu. 32:36. When they had given over expecting help it came. *When the son of man comes shall he find faith on the earth?* Lu. 18:8. The king said, *What shall I wait for the Lord any longer?* And perhaps some of the elders were ready to say the same: "Well," said Elisha, "you hear what these say; *now hear you the word of the Lord,* hear what he says, hear it and heed it and believe it: tomorrow corn shall be sold at the usual rate in the gate of Samaria;" that is, the siege shall be raised, for the gate of the city shall be opened, and the market shall be held there as formerly. The return of peace is thus expressed (Jdg. *v.* 11), *Then shall the people of the Lord go down to the gates,* to buy and sell there. 2. The consequence of that shall be great plenty. This would, in time, follow of course, but that corn should be thus cheap in so short a time was quite beyond what could be thought of. Though the king of Israel had just now threatened Elisha's life, God promises to save his life and the life of his people; for *where sin abounded grace doth much more abound.*

II. A peer of Israel that happened to be present openly declared his disbelief of this prediction, *v.* 2. He was a courtier whom the king had an affection for, as the man of his right hand, on whom he leaned, that is, on whose prudence he much relied, and in whom he reposed much confidence. He thought it impossible, unless God should rain corn out of the clouds, as once he did manna; no less than the repetition of Moses's miracle will serve him, though that of Elijah might have served to answer this intention, the increasing of the meal in the barrel.

III. The just doom passed upon him for his infidelity, that he should see this great plenty for this conviction, and yet not eat of it to his comfort. Note, Unbelief is a sin by which men greatly dishonour and displease God, and deprive themselves of the favours he designed for them. The murmuring Israelites saw Canaan, but could not enter in because of unbelief. Such (says bishop Patrick) will be the portion of those that believe not the promise of eternal life; they shall see it at a distance — Abraham afar off, but shall never taste of it; for they forfeit the benefit of the promise if they cannot find in their heart to take God's word.

Verses 3–11

We are here told,

I. How the siege of Samaria was raised in the evening, at the edge of night (*v.* 6, 7), not by might or power, but by the Spirit of the Lord of hosts, striking terror upon the spirits of the besiegers. Here was not a sword drawn against them, not a drop of blood shed, it was not by thunder or hailstones that they were discomfited, nor were they slain, as Sennacherib's army before Jerusalem, by a destroying angel; but, 1. *The Lord made them to hear a noise of chariots and horses.* The Syrians that besieged Dothan had their *sight* imposed upon, *ch.* 6:18. These had their *hearing* imposed upon. For God knows how to work upon every sense, pursuant to his own counsels as *he makes the hearing ear and the seeing eye,* so he makes *the deaf and the blind,* Ex. 4:11. Whether the noise was really made in the air by the ministry of angels, or whether it was only a sound in their ears, is not certain; which soever it was, it was from God, who both *brings the wind out of his treas-*

ures, and *forms the spirit of man within him.* The sight of horses and chariots had encouraged the prophet's servant, *ch.* 6:17. The noise of horses and chariots terrified the hosts of Syria. For notices from the invisible world are either very comfortable or very dreadful, according as men are at peace with God or at war with him. 2. Hearing this noise, they concluded the king of Israel had certainly procured assistance from some foreign power: *He has hired against us the kings of the Hittites and the kings of the Egyptians.* There was, for aught we know but one king of Egypt, and what kings there were of the Hittites nobody can imagine; but, as they were imposed upon by that dreadful sound in their ears, so they imposed upon themselves by the interpretation they made of it. Had they supposed the king of Judah to have come with his forces, there would have been more of probability in their apprehensions than to dream of the *kings of the Hittites and the Egyptians.* If the fancies of any of them raised this spectre, yet their reasons might soon have laid it: how could the king of Israel, who was closely besieged, hold intelligence with those distant princes? What had he to hire them with? It was impossible but some notice would come, before, of the motions of so great a host; but *there were they in great fear where no fear was.* 3. Hereupon they all fled with incredible precipitation, as for their lives, left their camp as it was: even their horses, that might have hastened their flight, they could not stay to take with them, *v.* 7. None of them had so much sense as to send out scouts to discover the supposed enemy, much less courage enough to face the enemy, though fatigued with a long march. *The wicked flee when none pursues.* God can, when he pleases, dispirit the boldest and most brave, and make the stoutest heart to tremble. Those that will not fear God he can make to fear at the shaking of a leaf.

II. How the Syrians' flight was discovered by four leprous men. Samaria was delivered, and did not know it. The watchmen on the walls were not aware of the retreat of the enemy, so silently did they steal away. But Providence employed four lepers to be the intelligencers, who had their lodging without the gate, being excluded from the city, as ceremonially unclean: the Jews say they were Gehazi and his three sons; perhaps Gehazi might be one of them, which might cause him to be taken notice of afterwards by the king, *ch.* 8:4. See here, 1. How these lepers reasoned themselves into a resolution to make a visit in the night to the camp of the Syrians, *v.* 3, 4. They were ready to perish for hunger; none passed through the gate to relieve them. Should they go into the city, there was nothing to be had there, they mist die in the streets; should they sit still, they must pine to death in their cottage. They therefore determine to go over to the enemy, and throw themselves upon their mercy: if they killed them, better die by the sword than by famine, one death than a thousand; but perhaps they would save them alive, as objects of compassion. Common prudence will put us upon that method which may better our condition, but cannot make it worse. The prodigal son resolves to return to his father, whose displeasure he had reason to fear, rather than perish with hunger in the far country. These lepers conclude, "If they kill us, we shall but die;" and happy they who, in another sense, can thus speak of dying. "We shall but die, that is the worst of it, not die and be damned, not be hurt of the second death." According to this resolution, they went, in the beginning of the night, to the camp of the Syrians, and, to their great surprise, found it wholly deserted, not a man to be seen or heard in it, *v.* 5. Providence ordered it, that these lepers came as soon as ever the Syrians had fled, for they fled in the twilight, the evening twilight (*v.* 7), and in the twilight the lepers came (*v.* 5), and so no time was lost. 2. How they reasoned themselves into a resolution to bring tidings of this to the city. They feasted in the first tent they came to (*v.* 8) and then began to think of enriching themselves with the plunder; but they corrected themselves (*v.* 9): "*We do not well* to conceal these good tidings from the community we are members of, under colour of being avenged upon them for excluding us from their society; it was the law that did it, not they, and therefore let us bring them the news. Though it awake them from sleep, it will be *life from the dead* to them." Their own consciences told them that some mischief would befal them if they acted separately, and sought themselves only. Selfish narrow-spirited people cannot ex-

pect to prosper; the most comfortable advantage is that which our brethren share with us in. According to this resolution, they returned to the gate, and acquainted the sentinel with what they had discovered (*v.* 10), who straightway brought the intelligence to court (*v.* 11), and it was not the less acceptable for being first brought by lepers.

Verses 12–20

Here we have,

I. The king's jealousy of a stratagem in the Syrian's retreat, *v.* 12. He feared that they had withdrawn into an ambush, to draw out the besieged, that they might fall on them with more advantage. he knew he had no reason to expect that God should appear thus wonderfully for him, having forfeited his favour by his unbelief and impatience. He knew no reason the Syrians had to fly, for it does not appear that he or any of this attendants heard the noise of the chariots which the Syrians were frightened at. Let not those who, like him, are *unstable in all their ways, think to receive any thing from God;* nay, a guilty conscience fears the worst and makes men suspicious.

II. The course they took for their satisfaction, and to prevent their falling into a snare. They sent out spies to see what had become of the Syrians, and found they had all fled indeed, commanders as well a common soldiers. They could track them by the garments which they threw off, and left by the way, for their greater expedition, *v.* 15. He that gave this advice seems to have been very sensible of the deplorable condition the people were in (*v.* 13); for speaking of the horses, many of which were dead and the rest ready to perish for hunger, he says, and repeats it, *"They are as all the multitude of Israel.* Israel used to glory in their multitude, but now they are diminished and brought low." He advised to send five horsemen, but, it should seem, there were only two horses fit to be sent, and those chariot-horses, *v.* 14. Now the Lord repented himself concerning his servants, when he saw that their strength was gone, Deu. 32:36.

III. The plenty that was in Samaria, from the plunder of the camp of the Syrians, *v.* 16. Had the Syrians been governed by the modern policies of war, when they could not take their baggage and their tents with them they would rather have burnt them (as it is common to do with the forage of a country) than let them fall into their enemies' hands; but God determined that the besieging of Samaria, which was intended for its ruin, should turn to its advantage, and that Israel should now be enriched with the spoil of the Syrians as of old with that of the Egyptians. here see, 1. The *wealth of the sinner laid up for the just* (Job 27:16, 17) and the spoilers spoiled, Isa. 33:1. 2. The wants of Israel supplied in a way that they little thought of, which should encourage us to depend upon the power and goodness of God in our greatest straits. 3. The word of Elisha fulfilled to a tittle: *A measure of fine flour was sold for a shekel;* those that spoiled the camp had not only enough to supply themselves with, but an overplus to sell at an easy rate for the benefit of others, and so even *those that tarried at home did divide the spoil,* Ps. 68:12; Isa. 33:23. God's promise may be safely relied on, for no word of his shall fall to the ground.

IV. The death of the unbelieving courtier, that questioned the truth of Elisha's word. Divine threatenings will as surely be accomplished as divine promises. *He that believeth not shall be damned* stands as firm as *He that believeth shall be saved.* This lord, 1. Was preferred by the king to the *charge of the gate* (*v.* 17), to keep the peace, and to see that there was no tumult or disorder in dividing and disposing of the spoil. So much trust did the king repose in him, in his prudence and gravity, and so much did he delight to honour him. He that will be great, let him serve the public. 2. Was trodden to death by the people in the gate, either by accident, the crowd being exceedingly great, and he in the thickest of it, or perhaps designedly, because he abused his power, and was imperious in restraining the people from satisfying their hunger. However it was, God's justice was glorified, and the word of Elisha was fulfilled. He saw the plenty, for the silencing and shaming of his unbelief, corn cheap without *opening windows in heaven,* and therein saw his own folly in prescribing to God; but he did not eat of the plenty he saw. *When he was about to fill his belly* God *cast the fury of his wrath upon him* (Job 20:23) and it came be-

tween the cup and the lip. Justly are those thus tantalized with the world's promises that think themselves tantalized with the promises of God. If believing shall not be seeing, seeing shall not be enjoying. This matter is repeated, and the event very particularly compared with the prediction (*v.* 18–20), that we might take special notice of it, and might learn, (1.) How deeply God resents out distrust of him, of his power, providence, and promise. When Israel said, *Can God furnish a table? the Lord heard it and was wroth.* Infinite wisdom will not be limited by our folly. God never promises the end without knowing where to provide the means. (2.) How uncertain life and the enjoyments of it are. Honour and power cannot secure men from sudden and inglorious deaths. He whom the king leaned upon the people trod upon; he who fancied himself the stay and support of the government was trampled under foot as the mire in the streets. Thus hath the pride of men's glory been often stained. (3.) How certain God's threatenings are, and how sure to alight on the guilty and obnoxious heads. Let all men fear before the great God, who *treads upon princes as mortar* and is *terrible to the kings of the earth.*

CHAPTER 8

The passages of story recorded in this chapter oblige us to look back. I. We read before of a Shuuammite woman that was a kind benefactor to Elisha; now here we are told how she fared the better for it, afterwards, in the advice Elisha gave her, and the favour the king showed her for his sake (*v.* 1–6). II. We read before of the designation of Hazael to be king of Syria (1 Ki. 19:15), and here we have an account of his elevation to that throne and the way he forced for himself to it, by killing his master (*v.* 7–15). III. We read before of Jehoram's reigning over Judah in the room of his father Jehoshaphat (1 Ki. 22:50), now here we have a short and sad history of his short and wicked reign (*v.* 16–24), and the beginning of the history of the reign of his son Ahaziah (*v.* 25–29).

Verses 1–6

Here we have,

I. The wickedness of Israel punished with a long famine, one of God's sore judgments often threatened in the law. *Canaan,* that fruitful land, *was turned into barrenness,* for the *iniquity of those that dwelt therein.* The famine in Samaria was soon relieved by the raising of that siege, but neither that judgment nor that mercy had a due influence upon them, and therefore *the Lord called for another famine;* for when he judgeth he will overcome. If less judgments do not prevail to bring men to repentance, he will send greater and longer; they are at his beck, and will come when he calls for them. He does, by his ministers, call for reformation and obedience, and, if those calls be not regarded, we may expect he will call for some plague or other, for he will be heard. This famine continued seven years, as long again as that in Elijah's time; for if men will walk contrary to him, he will heat the furnace yet hotter.

II. The kindness of the good Shunammite to the prophet rewarded by the care that was taken of her in that famine; she was not indeed fed by miracle, as the widow of Sarepta was, but, 1. She had notice given her of this famine before it came, that she might provide accordingly, and was directed to remove to some other country; any where but in Israel she would find plenty. It was a great advantage to Egypt in Joseph's time that they had notice of the famine before it came, so it was to this Shunammite; others would be forced to remove at last, after they had long borne the grievances of the famine, and had wasted their substance, and could not settle elsewhere upon such good terms as she might that went early, before the crowd, and took her stock with her unbroken. It is our happiness to foresee an evil, and our wisdom, when we foresee an evil, and our wisdom, when we foresee it, to hide ourselves. 2. Providence gave her a comfortable settlement in *the land of the Philistines,* who, though subdued by David, yet were not wholly rooted out. It seems the famine was peculiar to the land of Israel, and other countries that joined close to them had plenty at the same time, which plainly showed the immediate hand of God in it (as in the plagues of Egypt, when they distinguished between the Israelites and the Egyptians) and that the sins of Israel, against whom this judgment was directly levelled, were more provoking to God than the sins of their neighbours, because of their profession of relation to God. *You only have I known, therefore will I punish you,* Amos 3:2. Other countries had rain when they had none, were free from locusts and caterpillars when they were eaten up with them; for some think this was the famine spoken of, Joel 1:3, 4. It is strange that when there was plenty in the neighbouring countries there were not those that made it their business to import corn into the land of Israel, which might have prevented the inhabitants from removing; but, as they were befooled with their idolatries, so they were infatuated even in the matters of their civil interest.

III. Her petition to the king at her return, favoured by the seasonableness of her application to him. 1. When the famine was over she *returned out of the land of the Philistines;* that was no proper place for an Israelite to dwell any longer than there was a necessity for so doing, for there she could not keep her new moons and her sabbaths as she used to do in her own country, among the schools of the prophets, *ch.* 4:23. 2. At her return she found herself kept out of the possession of her own estate, it being either confiscated to the exchequer, seized by the lord, or usurped in her absence by some of the neighbours; or perhaps the person she had entrusted with the management of it proved false, and would neither resign it to her nor come to an account with her for the profits: so hard is it to find a person that one can put a confidence in *in a time of trouble,* Prov. 25:19; Mic. 7:5. 3. She made her application to the king himself for redress; for, it seems (be it observed to his praise), he was easy of access, and did himself take cognizance of the complaint of his injured subjects. Time was when she dwelt so securely among her own people that she had no occasion to be *spoken for to the king, or to the captain of the host* (*ch.* 4:13); but now her own familiar friends, in whom she trusted, proved so unjust and unkind that she was glad to appeal to the king against them. Such uncertainty there is in the creature that that may fail us which we most depend upon and that befriend us which we think we shall never need. 4. She found the king talking with Gehazi about Elisha's miracles, *v.* 4. It was his shame that he needed now to be informed concerning them, when he might have acquainted himself with them as they were done from Elisha himself, if he had not been wiling to shut his eyes against the convincing evidence of his mission; yet it was his praise that he was now better disposed, and would rather talk with a leper that was capable of giving a good account of them than continue ignorant of them. The law did not forbid all conversation with lepers, but only dwelling with them. There being then no priests in Israel, perhaps the king, or some one appointed by him, had the inspection of lepers, and passed the judgment upon them, which might bring him acquainted with Behazi. 5. This happy coincidence befriended both Behazi's narrative and her petition. Providence is to be acknowledged in ordering the circumstances of events, for sometimes those that are minute in themselves prove of great consequence, as this did, for, (1.) It made the king ready to believe Gehazi's narrative when it was thus confirmed by the persons most nearly concerned: *"This is the woman, and this her son;* let them speak for themselves," *v.* 5. Thus did God even force him to believe what he might have had some colour to question if he had only had Gehazi's word for it, because he was branded for a liar, witness his leprosy. (2.) It made him ready to grant her request; for who would not be ready to favour one whom heaven had thus favoured, and to support a life which was given once and again by miracle? In consideration of this the king gave orders that her land should be restored to her and all the profits that were made of it in her absence. If it was to himself that the land and profits had escheated, it was generous and kind to make so full a restitution; he would not (as Pharaoh did in Joseph's time) enrich the crown by the calamities of his subjects. If it was by some other person that her property was invaded, it was an act of justice in the king, and part of the duty of his place, to give her redress, Ps. 82:3, 4; Prov. 31:9. It is not enough for those in authority that they do no wrong themselves, but they must support the right of those that are wronged.

Verses 7–15

Here, I. We may enquire what brought Elisha to Damascus, the chief city of Syria. Was he sent to any but the *lost sheep of the house of Israel?* It seems he was. Perhaps he went to pay a visit to Naaman his convert, and to confirm him in his choice of the true religion, which was the more needful now because, it should seem, he was not out of his place (for Hazael is supposed to be captain of that host); either he resigned it or was turned out of it, because he would not bow, or not bow heartily, in the house of Rimmon. Some think he went to Damascus upon account of the famine, or rather he went thither in obedience to the orders God gave Elijah, 1 Ki. 19:15, *"Go to Damascus to anoint Hazael,* thou, or thy successor."

II. We may observe that Ben-hadad, a great king, rich and mighty, lay sick. No honour, wealth, or power, will secure men from the common diseases and disasters of human life; palaces and thrones lie as open to the arrests of sickness and death as the meanest cottage.

III. We may wonder that the king of Syria, in his sickness, should make Elisha his oracle.

1. Notice was soon brought him that *the man of God* (for by that title he was well known in Syria since he cured Naaman) had come to Damascus, *v.* 7. "Never in better time," says Ben-hadad. *"Go, and enquire of the Lord by him."* In his health he *bowed in the house of Rimmon,* but now that he is sick he distrusts his idol, and sends to enquire of the God of Israel. Affliction brings those to God who in their prosperity had made light of him; sometimes sickness opens men's eyes and rectifies their mistakes. This is the more observable, (1.) Because it was not long since a king of Israel had, in his sickness, sent to enquire of the god of Ekron (*ch.* 1:2), as if there had been no God in Israel. Note, God sometimes fetches to himself that honour from strangers which is denied him and alienated from him by his own professing people. (2.) Because it was not long since this Ben-hadad had sent a great force to treat Elisha as an enemy (*ch.* 6:14), yet now he courts him as a prophet. Note, Among other instances of the change of men's minds by sickness and affliction, this is one, that it often gives them other thoughts of God's ministers, and teaches them to value the counsels and prayers of those whom they had hated and despised.

2. To put an honour upon the prophet, (1.) He sends *to* him, and does not send *for* him, as if, with the centurion, he thought himself not worthy that the man of God should come under his roof. (2.) He sends to him by Hazael, his prime-minister of state, and not by a common messenger. It is no disparagement to the greatest of men to attend the prophets of the Lord. Hazael must go and meet him at a place where he had appointed a meeting with his friends. (3.) He sends him a noble present, *of every good thing of Damascus,* as much as loaded forty camels (*v.* 9), testifying hereby his affection to the prophet, bidding him welcome to Damascus, and providing for his sustenance while he sojourned there. It is probable that Elisha accepted it (why should he not?), though he refused Naaman's. (4.) He orders Hazael to call him *his son Ben-hadad,* conforming to the language of Israel, who called the prophets *fathers.* (5.) He puts an honour upon him as one acquainted with the secrets of heaven, when he enquires of him, *Shall I recover?* It is natural to us to desire to know things to come in time, while things to come in eternity are little thought of or enquired after.

IV. What passed between Hazael and Elisha is especially remarkable.

1. Elisha answered his enquiry concerning the king, that he might recover, the disease was not mortal, but that he should die another way (*v.* 10), not a natural but a violent death. There are many ways out of the world, and sometimes, while men think to avoid one, they fall by another.

2. He looked Hazael in the face with an unusual concern, till he made Hazael blush and himself weep, *v.* 11. The man of God could outface the man of war. It was not in Hazael's countenance that Elisha read what he would do, but God did, at this time, reveal it to him, and it fetched tears from his eyes. The more foresight men have the more grief they are liable to.

3. When Hazael asked him why he wept he told him what a great deal of mischief he foresaw he would do to the Israel of God (*v.* 12), what desolations he would make of their strong-holds, and barbarous destruction of their men, women, and children. The sins of Israel provoked God to give them up into the hands of their cruel enemies, yet Elisha wept to think that ever Israelites should be thus abused; for, though he foretold, he did not desire the woeful day. See what havock war makes, what havock sin makes, and how the nature of man is changed by the fall, and stripped even of humanity itself.

4. Hazael was greatly surprised at this prediction (*v.* 13): *What,* says he, *Is thy servant a dog, that he should do this great thing?* This great thing he looks upon to be, (1.) An act of great power, not to be done but by a crowned head. "It must be some mighty potentate that can think to prevail thus against Israel, and therefore not I." Many are raised to that dominion which they never thought of and it often proves *to their own hurt,* Eccl. 8:9. (2.) An act of great barbarity, which could not be done but by one lost to all honour and virtue: "Therefore," says he, "it is what I shall never find in my heart to be guilty of: *Is thy servant a dog,* to rend, and tear, and devour? Unless I were a dog, I could not do it." See here, [1.] What a bad opinion he had of the sin; he looked upon it to be great wickedness, fitter for a brute, for a beast of prey, to do than a man. Note, It is possible for a wicked man, under the convictions and restraints of natural conscience, to express great abhorrence of a sin, and yet afterwards to be well reconciled to it. [2.] What a good opinion he had of himself, how much better than he deserved; he thought it impossible he should do such barbarous things as the prophet foresaw. Note, We are apt to think ourselves sufficiently armed against those sins which yet we are afterwards overcome by, as Peter, Mt. 26:35.

5. In answer to this Elisha only told him *he should be king over Syria;* then he would have power to do it, and then he would find in his heart to do it. *Honours change men's tempers and manners,* and seldom for the better: "Thou knowest not what thou wilt do when thou comest to be king, but I tell thee this thou wilt do." Those that are little and low in the world cannot imagine how strong the temptations of power and prosperity are, and, if ever they arrive at them, they will find how deceitful their hearts were and how much worse than they suspected.

V. What mischief Hazael did to his master hereupon. If he took any occasion to do it from what Elisha had said the fault was in him, not in the word. 1. He basely cheated his master, and belied the prophet (*v.* 14): *He told me thou shouldst certainly recover.* This was abominably false; he told him he should die (*v.* 10), but he unfairly and unfaithfully concealed that, either because he was loth to put the king out of humour with bad news or because hereby he might the more effectually carry on that bloody design which he conceived when he was told he should be his successor. The devil ruins men by telling them they shall certainly recover and do well, so rocking them asleep in security, than which nothing is more fatal. This was an injury to the king, who lost the benefit of this warning to prepare for death, and an injury to Elisha, who would be counted a false prophet. 2. He barbarously murdered his master, and so made good the prophet's word, *v.* 15. He dipped a thick cloth in cold water, and spread it upon his face, under pretence of cooling and refreshing him, but so that it stopped his breath, and stifled him presently, he being weak (and not able to help himself) or perhaps asleep: such a bubble is the life of the greatest of men, and so much exposed are princes to violence. Hazael, who was Ben-hadad's confidant, was his murderer, and some think, was not suspected, nor did the truth ever come out but by the pen of this inspired historian. We found this haughty monarch (1 Ki. 20) *the terror of the mighty in the land of the living,* but he *goes down slain to the pit* with *his iniquity upon his bones,* Eze. 32:27.

Verses 16–24

We have here a brief account of the life and reign of Jehoram (or Joram), one of the worst of the kings of Judah, but the son and successor of Jehoshaphat, one of the best. Note, 1. Parents cannot give grace to their children. Many that have themselves been godly have had the grief and shame of seeing those that came forth out of their bowels wicked and vile. Let not the families that are thus afflicted think it strange. 2. If the children of good parents prove wicked, commonly they are worse than others. The unclean spirit brings in seven others more wicked than himself, Lu. 11:26. 3. A nation is sometimes justly punished with the miseries of a bad reign for not improving the blessings and advantages of a good one.

Concerning this Jehoram observe,

I. The general idea here given of his wickedness (*v.* 18): *He did as the house of Ahab,* and worse he could not do. His character is taken from the bad example he followed, for men are according to the company they converse with and the copies they write after. No mistake is more fatal to young people than a mistake in the choice of those whom they would recommend themselves to and take their measures from, and whose good opinion they value themselves by. Jehoram chose the house of Ahab for his pattern rather than his father's house, and this choice was his ruin. We have a particular account of his wickedness (2 Chr. 21), murder, idolatry, persecution, everything that was bad.

II. The occasions of his wickedness. His father was a very good man, and no doubt took care to have him taught the good knowledge of the Lord, but, 1. It is certain he did ill to marry him to the daughter of Ahab; no good could come of an alliance with an idolatrous family, but all mischief with such a daughter of such a mother as Athaliah the daughter of Jezebel. The degeneracy of the old world took rise from the unequal yoking of professors with profane. Those that are ill-matched are already half-ruined. 2. I doubt he did not do well to make him king in his own life-time. It is said here (*v.* 16) that he *began to reign, Jehoshaphat being then king;* hereby he gratified his pride (than which nothing is more pernicious to young people), indulged him in his ambition, in hopes to reform him by humouring him, and so brought a curse upon his family, as Eli did, *whose sons made themselves vile and he restrained them not.* Jehoshaphat had made this wicked son of his viceroy once when he went with Ahab to Ramoth-Gilead, from which Jehoshaphat's seventeenth year (1 Ki. 22:51) is made Jehoram's second (2 Ki. 1:17), but afterwards, in his twenty-second year, he made him partner in his government, and thence Joram's eight years are to be dated, three years before his father's death. It has been hurtful to many young men to come too soon to their estates. Samuel got nothing by *making his sons judges.*

III. The rebukes of Providence which he was under for his wickedness. 1. The Edomites revolted, who had been under the government of the kings of Judah ever since David's time, about 150 years, *v.* 20. He attempted to reduce them, and gave them a defeat (*v.* 21), but he could not improve the advantage he had got, so as to recover his dominion over them: *Yet Edom revolted* (*v.* 22), and the Edomites were, after this, bitter enemies to the Jews, as appears by the prophecy of Obadiah and Ps. 137:7. Now Isaac's prophecy was fulfilled, that this Esau the elder should serve Jacob the younger; yet, in process of time, he should *break that yoke from off his neck,* Gen. 27:40. 2. Libnah revolted. This was a city in Judah, in the heart of his country, a priests' city; the inhabitants of this city shook off his government *because he had forsaken God,* and would have compelled them to do so too, 2 Chr. 21:10, 11. In order that they might preserve their religion they set up for a free state. Perhaps other cities did the same. 3. His reign was short. God cut him off in the midst of his days, when he was but forty years old, and had reigned but eight years. *Bloody and deceitful men shall not live out half their days.*

IV. The gracious care of Providence for the keeping up of the kingdom of Judah, and the house of David, notwithstanding the apostasies and calamities of Jehoram's reign (*v.* 19): *Yet the Lord would not destroy Judah.* He could easily have done it; he might justly have done it; it would have been no loss to him to have done it; yet he would not do it, for David's sake, not for the sake of any merit of his which could challenge this favour to his family as a debt, but for the sake of a promise made to him that he should always have a lamp (that is, a succession of kings from one generation to another, by which his name should be kept bright and illustrious, as a lamp is kept burning by a constant fresh supply of oil), that his family should never be extinct till it terminated in the Messiah, that Son of David on whom was to be *hung all the glory of his Father's house* and in whose everlasting kingdom that promise to David is fulfilled (Ps. 132:17), *I have ordained a lamp for my anointed.*

V. The conclusion of this impious and inglorious reign, *v.* 23, 24. Nothing peculiar is here said of him; but we are told (2 Chr. 21:19, 20) that he *died of sore diseases* and *died without being desired.*

Verses 25–29

As among common persons there are some that we call *little men,* who make no figure, are little regarded, as less valued, so among kings there are some whom, in comparison with others, we may call *little kings.* This Ahaziah was one of these; he looks mean in the history, and in God's account vile, because wicked. It is too plain an evidence of the affinity between Jehoshaphat and Ahab that they had the same names in their families at the same time, in which, we may suppose, they designed to compliment one another. Ahab had two sons, Ahaziah and Jehoram, who reigned successively; Jehoshaphat had a son and grandson names Jehoshaphat had a son and grandson names Jehoram and Ahaziah, who, in like manner, reigned successively. Names indeed do not make natures, but it was a bad omen to Jehoshaphat's family to borrow names from Ahab's; or, if he lent the names to that wretched family, he could not communicate with them the devotion of their significations, *Ahaziah — Taking hold of the Lord,* and *Jehoram — The Lord exalted.* Ahaziah king of Israel had reigned but two years, Ahaziah king of Judah reigned but one. We are here told that his relation to Ahab's family was the occasion, 1. Of his wickedness (*v.* 27): *He walked in the way of the house of Ahab,* that idolatrous bloody house; for his mother was Ahab's daughter (*v.* 26), so that he sucked in wickedness with his milk. *Partus sequitur ventrem — The child may be expected to resemble the mother.* When men choose wives for themselves they must remember they are choosing mothers for their children, and are concerned to choose accordingly. 2. Of his fall. Joram, his mother's brother, courted him to join with him for the recovery of Ramoth-Gilead, an attempt fatal to Ahab; so it was to Joram his son, for in that expedition he was wounded (*v.* 28), and returned to Jezreel to be cured, leaving his army there in possession of the place. Ahaziah likewise returned, but went to Jezreel to see how Jehoram did, *v.* 29. Providence so ordered it, that he who had been debauched by the house of Ahab might be cut off with them, when the measure of their iniquity was full, as we shall find in the next chapter. Those who partake with sinners in their sins must expect to partake with them in their plagues.

CHAPTER 9

Hazael and Jehu were the men that were designed to be the instruments of God's justice in punishing and destroying the house of Ahab. Elijah was told to appoint them to this service; but, upon Ahab's humiliation, a reprieve was granted, and so it was left to Elisha to appoint them. Hazael's elevation to the throne of Syria we read of in the foregoing chapter; and we must now attend Jehu to the throne of Israel; for him that escapeth the sword of Hazael, as Joram and Ahaziah did, Jehu must slay, of which this chapter gives us an account. I. A commission is sent to Jehu by the hand of one of the prophets, to take upon him the government, and destroy the house of Ahab (*v.* 1–10). II. Here is his speedy execution of this commission. 1. He communicates it to his captains (*v.* 11–15). 2. He marches directly to Jezreel (*v.* 16–20), and there dispatches (1.) Joram king of Israel (*v.* 21–26). (2.) Ahaziah king of Judah (*v.* 27–29). (3.) Jezebel (*v.* 30–37).

Verses 1–10

We have here the anointing of Jehu to be king, who was, at this time, a commander (probably commander-in-chief) of the forces employed at Ramoth-Gilead, *v.* 14. There he was fighting for the king his master, but received orders from a higher king to fight against him. It does not appear that Jehu aimed at the government, or that he ever thought of it, but the commission given him was a perfect surprise to him. Some think that he had been anointed before by Elijah, whom God ordered to do it, but privately, and with an intimation that he must not act till further orders, as Samuel anointed David long before he was to come to the throne: but that it not at all probable, for then we must suppose Elijah had anointed Hazael too. No, when God bade him do these things he bade him anoint Elisha to *be prophet in his room,* to do them when he was gone, as God should direct him. Here is,

I. The commission sent.

1. Elisha did not go himself to anoint Jehu, because he was old and unfit for such a journey and so well known that he could not do it privately, could not go and come without observation; therefore he sends *one of the sons of the prophets* to do it, *v.* 1. They not only reverences him as their father (*ch.* 2:15), but observed and obeyed him as their father. This service of anointing Jehu, (1.) Had danger in it (1 Sa. 16:2), and therefore it was not fit that Elisha should expose himself, but one of the sons of the prophets, whose life was of less value, and who could do it with less danger. (2.) It required labour and was therefore fitter for a young man in his full strength. Let youth work and age direct. (3.) Yet it was an honourable piece of service, to anoint a king, and he that did it might hope to be preferred for it afterwards, and therefore, for the encouragement of the young prophets, Elisha employed one of them: he would not engross all the honours to himself, nor grudge the young prophets a share in them.

2. When he sent him, (1.) He put the oil into his hand with which he must anoint Jehu: *Take this box of oil* Solomon was anointed with *oil out of the tabernacle,* 1 Ki. 1:39. That could not now be had, but oil from a prophet's hand was equivalent to oil out of God's house. Probably it was not the constant practice to anoint kings, but upon the disturbance of the succession, as in the case of Solomon, or the interruption of it, as in the case of Joash (*ch.* 11:12), or the translation of the government to a new family, as here and in the case of David; yet it might be used generally, though the scripture does not mention it. (2.) He put *the words into his mouth* which he must say (*v.* 3) — *I have anointed thee king,* and, no doubt, told him all the rest that he said, *v.* 7–10. Those whom God sends on his errands shall not go without full instructions. (3.) He also ordered him, [1.] To do it privately, to single out Jehu from the rest of the captains and anoint him *in an inner chamber* (*v.* 2), that Jehu's confidence in his commission might be tried, when he had no witness to attest it. His being suddenly animated for the service would be proof sufficient of his being anointed to it. There needed no other proof. The thing signified was the best evidence of the sign. [2.] To do it expeditiously. When he went about it he must *gird up his loins;* when he had done it he must *flee and not tarry* for a fee, or a treat, or to see what Jehu would do. It becomes the sons of the prophets to be quick and lively at their work, to go about it and go through it as men that hate sauntering and trifling. They should be as angels that fly swiftly.

II. The commission delivered. The young prophet did his business with despatch, was at Ramoth-Gilead presently, *v.* 4. There he found the general officers sitting together, either at dinner or in a council of war, *v.* 5. With the assurance that became a messenger from God, notwithstanding the meanness of his appearance, he called Jehu out from the rest, not waiting his leisure, or begging his pardon for disturbing him, but as one having authority: *I have an errand to thee, O captain.* Perhaps Jehu had some intimation of his business; and therefore, that he might not seem too forward to catch at the honour, he asked, *To which of all us?* that it might not be said afterwards he got it by speaking first, but they might all be satisfied he was indeed the person designed. When the prophet had him alone he anointed him, *v.* 6. The anointing of the Spirit is a hidden thing, that new name which none knows but those that have it. Herewith,

1. He invests him with the royal dignity: *Thus saith the Lord God of Israel,* whose messenger I am, in his name *I have anointed thee king over the people of the Lord.* He gives him an incontestable title, but reminds him that he was made king, (1.) *By the God of Israel;* from him he must see his power derived (for by him kings reign), for he must use it, and to him he must be accountable. Magistrates are the ministers of God, and must therefore act in dependence upon him and with an entire devotedness to him and to his glory. (2.) *Over the Israel of God.* Though the people of Israel were wretchedly corrupted, and had forfeited all the honour of relationship to God, yet they are here called the *people of the Lord,* for he had a right to them and had not yet given them a bill of divorce. Jehu must look upon the people he was made king of as the *people of the Lord,* not as his vassals, but God's freemen, his sons, his first-born, not to be abused or tyrannized over, *God's people,* and therefore to be ruled for him, and according to his laws.

2. He instructs him in his present service, which was to destroy all the house of Ahab (*v.* 7), not that he might clear his own way to the throne, and secure to himself the possession of it, but that he might execute the judgments of God upon that guilty and obnoxious family. He calls Ahab his *master,* that the relation might be no objection. "He was thy master, and to lift up thy hand against his son and successor would be not only base ingratitude, but treason, rebellion, and all that is bad, if thou hadst not an immediate command from God to do it. But thou art under

higher obligations to thy Master in heaven than to thy master Ahab. He has determined that *the whole house of Ahab shall perish,* and *by thy hand;* fear not: has not he commanded thee? Fear not sin; his command will justify thee and bear thee out: fear not danger; his command will secure and prosper thee." That he might intelligently, and in a right manner, do this great execution on the house of Ahab, he tells him, (1.) What was their crime, what the ground of the controversy, and wherefore God had quarrel with them, that he might have an eye to that which God had an eye to, and that was *the blood of God's servants, the prophets* and others, faithful worshippers, which they had shed, and which must now be required at the hand of Jezebel. That they were idolaters was bad enough, and merited all that was brought upon them; yet that is not mentioned here, but the controversy God has with them is for their being persecutors, not so much their *throwing down God's altars* as their *slaying his prophets with the sword.* Nothing fills the measure of the iniquity of any prince or people as this does nor brings a surer or a sorer ruin. This was the sin that brought on Jerusalem its first destruction (2 Chr. 36:16) and its final one, Mt. 23:37, 38. Jezebel's whoredoms and witchcrafts were not so provoking as her persecuting the prophets, killing some and driving the rest into corners and caves, 1 Ki. 18:4. (2.) What was their doom. They were sentenced to utter destruction; not to be corrected, but to be cut off and rooted out. This Jehu must know, that his eye might not spare for pity, favour, or affection. All that belonged to Ahab must be slain, *v.* 8. A pattern is given him of the destruction intended, in the destruction of the families of Jeroboam and Baasha (*v.* 9), and he is particularly directed to throw Jezebel to the dogs, *v.* 10. The whole stock of royal blood was little enough, and too little, to atone for the blood of the prophets, the saints and martyrs, which, in God's account, is of great price.

The prophet, having done this errand, made the best of his way home again, and left Jehu alone to consider what he had to do and beg direction from God.

Verses 11–15

Jehu, after some pause, returned to his place at the board, taking no notice of what had passed, but, as it should seem, designing, for the present, to keep it to himself, if they had not urged him to disclose it. Let us therefore see what passed between him and the captains.

I. With what contempt the captains speak of the young prophet (*v.* 11): *"Wherefore came this mad fellow to thee?* What business had he with thee? And why wouldst thou humour him so far as to retire for conversation with him? Are prophets company for captains?" They are called him *a mad fellow,* because he was one of those that would not *run with them to an excess of riot* (1 Pt. 4:4), but lived a life of self-denial, mortification, and contempt of the world, and spent their time in devotion; for these things they thought the prophets were fools and the *spiritual men were mad,* Hos. 9:7. Note, Those that have no religion commonly speak with disdain of those that are religious, and look upon them as mad. They said of our Saviour, *He is beside himself,* of John Baptist, *He has a devil* (is a poor melancholy man), of St. Paul, *Much learning has made him mad.* The highest wisdom is thus represented as folly, and those that best understand themselves are looked upon as beside themselves. Perhaps Jehu intended it for a rebuke to his friends when he said, *"You know the man* to be a prophet, why then do you call him a mad fellow? You know the way of his communication to be not from madness, but inspiration." Or, "Being a prophet, you may guess what his business is, to tell me of my faults, and to teach me my duty; I need not inform you concerning it." Thus he thought to put them off, but they urged him to tell them. "It is false," say they, "we cannot conjecture what was his errand, and therefore tell us." Being thus pressed to it, he told them that the prophet had *anointed him king,* and it is probable showed them the oil upon his head, *v.* 12. He knew not but some of them either out of loyalty to Joram or envy of him, might oppose him, and go near to crush his interest in its infancy; but he relied on the divine appointment, and was not afraid to own it, knowing whom he had trusted: he that raised him would stand by him.

II. With what respect they compliment the new king upon the first notice of his advancement, *v.* 13. How meanly soever they thought of the prophet that anointed him, and of his office, they expressed a grat veneration for the royal dignity of him that was anointed, and were very forward to proclaim him and sound of trumpet. In token of their subjection and allegiance to him, their affection to his person and government, and their desire to see him high and easy in it, they put their garments under him, that he might stand or sit upon them *on the top of the stairs,* in sight of the soldiers, who, upon the first intimation, came together to grace the solemnity. God put it into their hearts thus readily to own him, for he turns the hearts of people as well as kings, like the rivers of water, into what channel he pleases. Perhaps they were disquieted at Joram's government or had a particular affection for Jehu; or, however this might be, things it seems were ripe for the revolution, and they all came into Jehu's interest and *conspired against Joram, v.* 14.

III. With what caution Jehu proceeded. He had advantages against Joram, and he knew how to improve them. He had the army with him. Joram had left it, and had gone home badly wounded. Jehu's good conduct appears in two things: — 1. That he complimented the captains, and would do nothing without their advice and consent ("If it be your minds, we will do so and so, else not"), thereby intimating the deference he paid to their judgment and the confidence he had in their fidelity, both which tended to please and fix them. It is the wisdom of those that would rise fast, and stand firm, to take their friends along with them. 2. That he contrived to surprise Joram; and, in order thereto, to come upon him with speed, and to prevent his having notice of what was now done: *"Let none go forth to tell it in Jezereel,* that, as a snare, the ruin may come on him and his house." The suddenness of an attack sometimes turns to as good an account as the force of it.

Verses 16–29

From Ramoth-Gilead to Jezreel was more than one day's march; about the mid-way between them the river Jordan must be crossed. We may suppose Jehu to have marched with all possible expedition, and to have taken the utmost precaution to prevent the tidings from getting to Jezreel before him; and, at length, we have him within sight first, and then within reach, of the devoted king.

I. Joram's watchman discovers him first at a distance, him and his retinue, and gives notice to the king of the approach of a company, whether of friends or foes he cannot tell. But the king (impatient to know what is the matter, and perhaps jealous that the Syrians, who had wounded him, had traced him by the blood to his own palace, and were coming to seize him) sent first one messenger, and then another, to bring him intelligence, *v.* 17–19. He had scarcely recovered from the fright he was put into in the battle, and his guilty conscience put him into a continual terror. Each messenger asked the same question: *"Is it peace?* are you for us or for our adversaries? Do you bring good tidings or bad?" Each had the same answer: *What hast thou to do with peace? Turn thee behind me, v.* 18. 19. As if he had said, "It is not to thee, but to him that sent thee, that I will give answer; for thy part, if thou consult thy own safety, *turn thee behind me,* and enlist thyself among my followers." The watchman gave notice that the messengers were taken prisoners, and at length observed that the leader of this troop drove like Jehu, who it seems was noted for driving furiously, thereby discovering himself to be a man of a hot eager spirit, intent upon his business, and pushing forward with all his might. A man of such a violent temper was fittest for the service to which Jehu was designated. The wisdom of God is seen in the choice of proper instruments to be employed in his work. But it is not much for any man's reputation to be known by his fury. He that has rule over his own spirit is better than the mighty. The Chaldee paraphrase gives this a contrary sense: *The leading is like that of Jehu, for he leads quietly.* And, it should seem, he did not come up very fast, for then there would not have been time for all this that passed. And some think he chose to march slowly, that he might give Joram time to come out to him, and so dispatch him before he entered the city.

II. Joram himself goes out to meet him, and takes Ahaziah king of Judah along with him, neither of them equipped for war, as not expecting an enemy, but in haste to have their curiosity satisfied. How strangely has Providence sometimes ordered it, that men have been in haste to meet their ruin when their day has come to fall.

1. The place where Joram met Jehu was ominous: *In the portion of Naboth the Jezreelite, v.* 21. The very sight of that ground was enough to make Joram tremble and Jehu triumph; for Joram had the guilt of Naboth's blood fighting against him and Jehu had the force of Elijah's curse fighting for him. The circumstances of events are sometimes so ordered by divine Providence as to make the punishment answer to the sin as face answers to face in a glass.

2. Joram's demand was still the same: *"Is it peace, Jehu?* Is all well? Dost thou come home thus flying from the Syrians or more than a conqueror over them?" It seems, he looked for peace, and could not entertain any other thought. Note, It is very common for great sinners, even when they are upon the brink of ruin, to flatter themselves with an opinion that all is well with them, and to cry peace to themselves.

3. Jehu's reply was very startling. He answered him with a question: *What peace* canst thou expect, *so long as the whoredoms of thy mother Jezebel* (who, though queen dowager, was in effect queen regent) *and her witchcrafts are so many?* See how plainly Jehu deals with him. Formerly he durst not do so, but now he had another spirit. Note, Sinners will not always be flattered; one time or other, they will have their own given them, Ps. 36:2. Observe, (1.) He charges upon him his mother's wickedness, because he had at first learned it and then with his kingly power protected it. She stands impeached for whoredom, corporal and spiritual (serving idols and serving them with the very acts of lewdness), for witchcraft likewise, enchantments and divinations, used in honour of her idols; and these multiplied, the whoredoms and the witchcrafts many; for those that abandon themselves to wicked courses know not where they will stop. One sin begets another. (2.) Upon that account he throws him off from all pretensions to peace: "What peace can come to that house in which there is so much wickedness unrepented of?" Note, The way of sin can never be the way of peace, Isa. 57:21. What peace can sinners have with God, what peace with their own consciences, what good, what comfort, can they expect in life, in death, or after death, who go on still in their trespasses? No peace so long as sin is persisted in; but, as soon as it is repented of and forsaken, there is peace.

4. The execution was done immediately. When Joram heard of his mother's crimes his heart failed him; he presently concluded the long-threatened day of reckoning had now come, and cried out, *"There is treachery, O Ahaziah!* Jehu is our enemy, and it is time for us to shift for our safety." Both fled, and, (1.) Joram king of Israel was slain presently, *v.* 24. Jehu dispatched him with his own hands. The bow was not drawn at a venture, as that which sent the fatal arrow through the joints of his father's harness, but Jehu directed the arrow between his shoulders as he fled (it was one of God's arrows which he *has ordained against the persecutor,* Ps. 7:13), and it reached to his heart, so that he died upon the spot. He was now the top branch of Ahab's house, and therefore was first cut off. He died a criminal, under the sentence of the law, which Jehu, the executioner, pursues in the disposal of the dead body. Naboth's vineyard was hard by, which put him in mind of that circumstance of the doom Elijah passed upon Ahab, *"I will requite thee in this plat, said the Lord* (*v.* 25, 26), *for the blood of Naboth* himself, and *for the blood of his sons,"* who were either put to death with him as partners in his crime, or secretly murdered afterwards, lest they should bring an appeal, or find some way to avenge their father's death, or break their hearts for the loss of him, or (his whole estate being confiscated, as well as his vineyard) lose their livelihoods, which was in effect to lose their lives. For this the house of Ahab must be reckoned with; and that very piece of ground which he, with so much pride and pleasure, had made himself master of at the expense of the guilt of innocent blood, now became the theatre on which his son's dead body lay exposed a spectacle to the world. Thus *the Lord is known by the judgment which he executeth. Higgaion. Selah.* (2.) Ahaziah king of Judah was pursued, and slain in a little time, and not far off, *v.* 27, 28. [1.] Though he was now in Joram's company, he would not have been slain but that he was joined with the house of Ahab both in affinity and in iniquity. He was one of them (so he had made himself by his sins) and there-

fore he must fare as they fared. Jehu justly construed his commission as extending to them. Yet, [2.] Perhaps he would not at this time have fallen with them if he had not been found in company with them. It is a dangerous thing to associate with evil-doers; we may be entangled both in guilt and misery by it.

Verses 30–37

The greatest delinquent in the house of Ahab was Jezebel: it was she that introduced Baal, slew the Lord's prophets, contrived the murder of Naboth, stirred up her husband first, and then her sons, to do wickedly; a *cursed woman* she is here called (*v.* 34), a curse to the country, and whom all that wished well to their country had a curse for. Three reigns her reign had lasted, but now, at length, her day had come to fall. We read of a false prophetess in the church of Thyatira that is compared to Jezebel, and called by her name (Rev. 2:20), her wickedness the same, seducing God's servants to idolatry, a long *space given her to repent* (*v.* 21) as to Jezebel, and a fearful ruin brought upon her at last (*v.* 22, 23), as here upon Jezebel. So that Jezebel's destruction may be looked upon as typical of the destruction of idolaters and persecutors, especially that great whore, that mother of harlots, that hath made herself *drunk with the blood of saints* and the nations *drunk with the wine of her fornications,* when God shall put it into the heart of the kings of the earth to hate her, Rev. 17:5, 6. 16. Now here we have,

I. Jezebel daring the judgment. She heard that Jehu had slain her son, and slain him for her whoredoms and witchcrafts, and thrown his dead body into the portion of Naboth, according to the word of the Lord, and that he was now coming to Jezreel, where she could not but expect herself to fall next a sacrifice to his revenging sword. Now see how she meets her fate; she posted herself in a window at the entering of the gate, to affront Jehu and set him at defiance. 1. Instead of hiding herself, as one afraid of divine vengeance, she exposed herself to it and scorned to flee, mocked at fear and was not affrighted. See how a heart hardened against God will brave it out to the last, *run upon him, even upon his neck,* Job 15:26. But never did any thus harden their hearts against him and prosper. 2. Instead of humbling herself, and putting herself into close mourning for her son, she *painted her face, and tired her head,* that she might appear like herself, that is (as she thought), great and majestic, hoping thereby to daunt Jehu, to put him out of countenance, and to stop his career. *The Lord God called to baldness and girding with sackcloth,* but behold painting and dressing, walking contrary to God, Isa. 22:12, 13. There is not a surer presage of ruin than an unhumbled heart under humbling providences. Let painted faces look in Jezebel's glass, and see how they like themselves. 3. Instead of trembling before Jehu, the instrument of God's vengeance, she thought to make him tremble with that threatening question, *Had Zimri peace, who slew his master?* Observe, (1.) She took no notice of the hand of God gone out against her family, but flew in the face of him that was only the sword in his hand. We are very apt, when we are in trouble, to break out into a passion against the instruments of our trouble, when we ought to be submissive to God and angry at ourselves only. (2.) She pleased herself with the thought that what Jehu was now doing would certainly end in his own ruin, and that he would not have peace in it. He had cut her off from all pretensions to peace (*v.* 22), and now she thought to cut him off likewise. Note, It is no new thing for those that are doing God's work to be looked upon as out of the way of peace. Active reformers, faithful reprovers, are threatened with trouble; but let them be in nothing terrified, Phil. 1:28. (3.) She quoted a precedent, to deter him from the prosecution of this enterprise: *"Had Zimri peace?* No, he had not; he came to the throne by blood and treachery, and within seven days was constrained to burn the palace over his head and himself in it: and canst thou expect to fare any better?" Had the case been parallel, it would have been proper enough to give him this memorandum; for the judgments of God upon those that have gone before us in any sinful way should be warnings to us to take heed of treading in their steps. But the instance of Zimri was misapplied to Jehu. Zimri had no warrant for what he did, but was incited to it merely by his own ambition and cruelty; whereas Jehu was anointed by one of the sons of the prophets, and did this by order from heaven, which would bear him out. In comparing persons and things we must carefully distinguish between the precious and the vile, and take heed lest from the fate of sinful men we read the doom of useful men.

II. Jehu demanding aid against her. He looked up to the window, not daunted at the menaces of her impudent but impotent rage, and cried, *Who is on my side? Who?* *v.* 32. He was called out to do God's work, in reforming the land and punishing those that had debauched it; and here he calls out for assistance in the doing of it, looked as if there were any to help, any to uphold, Isa. 63:5. He lifts up a standard, and makes proclamation, as Moses (Ex. 32:26), *Who is on the Lord's side?* And the Psalmist (Ps. 94:16), *Who will rise up for me against the evil-doers?* Note, When reformation-work is set on foot, it is time to ask, "Who sides with it?"

III. Her own attendants delivering her up to his just revenge. Two or three chamberlains looked out to Jehu with such a countenance as encouraged him to believe they were on his side, and to them he called not to seize or secure her till further orders, but immediately to throw her down, which was one way of stoning malefactors, casting them headlong from some steep place. Thus was vengeance taken on her for the stoning of Naboth. They threw her down, *v.* 33. If God's command would justify Jehu, his command would justify them. Perhaps they had a secret dislike of Jezebel's wickedness, and hated her, though they served her; or, it may be, she was barbarous and injurious to those about her, and they were pleased with this opportunity of being avenged on her; or, observing Jehu's success, they hoped thus to ingratiate themselves with him, and keep their places in his court. However it was, thus she was most shamefully put to death, dashed against the wall and the pavement, and then trodden on by the horses, which were all besmeared with her blood and brains. See the end of pride and cruelty, and say, *The Lord is righteous.*

IV. The very dogs completing her shame and ruin, according to the prophecy. When Jehu had taken some refreshment in the palace, he bethought himself of showing so much respect to Jezebel's sex and quality as to bury her. As bad as she was, she was a daughter, a king's daughter, a king's wife, a king's mother: *Go and bury her, v.* 34. But, though he had forgotten what the prophet said (*v.* 10, *Dogs shall eat Jezebel*), God had not forgotten it. While he was eating and drinking, the dogs had devoured her dead body, the dogs that *went about the city* (Ps. 59:6) and fed upon the carrion, so that there was nothing left but her bare skull (the painted face gone) and her feet and hands. The hungry dogs had no respect to the dignity of her extraction; a king's daughter was no more to them than a common person. When we pamper our bodies, and use them deliciously, let us think how vile they are, and that shortly they will be either a feast for worms under ground or beasts above ground. When notice was brought of this to Jehu, he remembered the threatening (1 Ki. 21:23), *The dogs shall eat Jezebel by the wall of Jezreel.* Nothing should remain of her but the monuments of her infamy. She had been used to appear on public days in great state, and the cry was, "This is Jezebel. What a majestic port and figure! How great she looks!" But now it shall be said no more. We have often seen the wicked buried (Eccl. 8:10), yet sometimes, as here, they have no burial, Eccl. 6:3. Jezebel's name nowhere remained, but as stigmatized in sacred writ: they could not so much as say, "This is Jezebel's dust, This is Jezebel's grave," or "This is Jezebel's seed." Thus the name of the wicked shall rot — rot above ground.

CHAPTER 10

We have in this chapter, I. A further account of Jehu's execution of his commission. He cut off, 1. All Ahab's sons (*v.* 1–10). 2. All Ahab's kindred (*v.* 11–14, 17). 3. Ahab's idolatry: his zeal against this he took Jonadab to be witness to (*v.* 15, 16), summoned all the worshippers of Baal to attend (*v.* 18–23) and slew them all (*v.* 24, 25), and then abolished that idolatry (*v.* 26–28). II. A short account of the administration of his government. 1. The old idolatry of Israel, the worship of the calves, was retained (*v.* 29–31). 2. This brought God's judgments upon them by Hazael, with which his reign concludes (*v.* 32–36).

Verses 1–14

We left Jehu in quiet possession of Jezreel, triumphing over Joram and Jezebel; and we must now attend his further motions. He knew the whole house of Ahab must be cut off, and therefore proceeded in this bloody work, and did not do it deceitfully, or by halves, Jer. 48:10.

I. He got the heads of all the sons of Ahab cut off by their own guardians at Samaria. Seventy sons (or grandsons) Ahab had, Gideon's number, Jdg. 8:30. In such a number that bore his name his family was likely to be perpetuated, and yet it is extirpated all at once. Such a quiver full of arrows could not protect his house from divine vengeance. Numerous families, if vicious, must not expect to be long prosperous. These sons of Ahab were now at Samaria, a strong city, perhaps brought thither upon occasion of the war with Syria, as a place of safety, or upon notice of Jehu's insurrection; with them were the rulers of Jezreel, that is, the great officers of the court, who went to Samaria to secure themselves or to consult what was to be done. Those of them that were yet under tuition had their tutors with them, who were entrusted with their education in learning, agreeable to their birth and quality, but, it is to be feared, brought them up in the idolatries of their father's house and made them all worshippers of Baal. Jehu did not think fit to bring his forces to Samaria to destroy them, but, that the hand of God might appear the more remarkably in it, made their guardians their murderers. 1. He sent a challenge to their friends to stand by them, *v.* 2, 3. "You that are hearty well-wishers to the house of Ahab, and entirely in its interests, now is your time to appear for it. Samaria is a strong city; you are in possession of it; you have forces at command; you may choose out the likeliest person of all the royal family to head you; you know you are not tied to the eldest, unless he be *the best and meetest of your master's sons.* If you have any spirit in you, show it, and set one of them on his father's throne, and stand by him with your lives and fortunes." Not that he desired they should do this, or expected they would, but thus he upbraided them with their cowardice and utter inability to contest with the divine counsels. "Do if you dare, and see what will come of it." Those that have forsaken their religion have often, with it, lost both their sense and their courage, and deserve to be upbraided with it. 2. Hereby he gained from them a submission. They prudently reasoned with themselves: *"Behold, two kings stood not before him,* but fell as sacrifices to his rage; *how then shall we stand?" v.* 4. Therefore they sent him a surrender of themselves: *"We are thy servants,* thy subjects, and *will do all that thou shalt bid us,* right or wrong, and will set up nobody in competition with thee." They saw it was to no purpose to contend with him, and therefore it was their interest to submit to him. With much more reason may we thus argue ourselves into a subjection to the great God. Many kings and great men have fallen before his wrath, for their wickedness; and how then shall we stand? *Do we provoke the Lord to jealousy? Are we stronger than he?* No, we must either bend or break. 3. This was improved so far as to make them the executioners of those whom they had the tuition of (*v.* 6): *If you be mine, bring me the heads of your master's sons by to-morrow at this time.* Though he knew it must be done, and was loth to do it himself, one would think he could not expect they should do it. Could they betray such a trust? Could they be cruel to their master's sons? It seems, so low did they stoop in their adoration to the rising sun that they did it; they cut off the heads of those seventy princes, and sent them in baskets a present to Jehu, *v.* 7. Learn hence not to trust in a friend nor to put confidence in a guide not governed by conscience. One can scarcely expect that he who has been false to his God should ever be faithful to his prince. But observe God's righteousness in their unrighteousness. These elders of Jezreel had been wickedly obsequious to Jezebel's order for the murder of Naboth, 1 Ki. 21:11. She gloried, it is likely, in the power she had over them; and now the same base spirit makes them as pliable to Jehu and as ready to obey his orders for the murder of Ahab's sons. Let none aim at arbitrary power, lest they be found rolling a stone which, some time or other, will return upon them. Princes that make their people slaves take the readiest way to make them rebels; and by forcing men's consciences, as Jezebel did, they lose their hold of them. When the separated heads were presented to Jehu, he slyly upbraided those that were the executioners of this vengeance. The heads were laid in two heaps at the gate, the proper place of judgment. There he acquitted the people before God and the world (*v.* 9, *You are righteous*), and, by what the rulers of Samaria had now done, comparatively acquitted himself: "I slew but one; they have slain all these: I did it by conspiracy and with design; they have done this merely in compliance and with an implicit obedience. Let not the people of Samaria, nor any of the friends of the house of Ahab, ever reproach me for what I have done, when their own elders, and the very guardians of the orphans, have done this." It is common for those who have done something base to attempt the mitigation of their own reproach by drawing others in to do something worse. But, (2.) He resolves all into the righteous judgment of God (*v.* 10): *The Lord hath done that which he spoke by Elijah.* God is not the author of any man's sin, but even by that which men do from bad principles God serves his own purposes and glorifies his own name; and he is righteous in that wherein men are unrighteous. When the Assyrian is made the *rod of God's anger,* and the instrument of his justice, *he meaneth not so, neither does his heart think so,* Isa. 10:7.

II. He proceeded to destroy all that remained of the house of Ahab, not only those that descended from him, but those that were in any relation to him, all the officers of his household, ministers of state, and those in command under him, called here his *great men* (*v.* 11), all his kinsfolks and acquaintance, who had been partners with him in his wickedness, and his priests, or domestic chaplains, whom he employed in his idolatrous services and who strengthened his hand that he should not turn from his evil way. Having done this in Jezreel, he did the same in Samaria (*v.* 17), *slew all that remained to Ahab in Samaria.* This was bloody work, and is not now, in any case, to be drawn into a precedent. Let the guilty suffer, but not the guiltless for their sakes. Perhaps such terrible destructions as these were intended as types of the final destruction of all the ungodly. God has a sword, bathed in heaven, which will come down upon the people of his curse, and *be filled with blood.* Isa. 34:5, 6. Then *his eye will not spare, neither will he pity.*

III. Providence bringing the brethren of Ahaziah in his way, as he was going on with this execution, he slew them likewise, *v.* 12–14. The brethren of Ahaziah were slain by the Arabians (2 Chr. 22:1), but these were the sons of his brethren, as it is there explained (*v.* 8), and they are said to be princes of Judah, and to minister to Ahaziah. Several things concurred to make them obnoxious to the vengeance Jehu was now executing. 1. They were branches of Ahab's house, being descended from Athaliah, and therefore fell within his commission. 2. They were tainted with the wickedness of the house of Ahab. 3. They were now going to make their court to the princes of the house of Ahab, to *salute the children of the king and the queen,* Joram and Jezebel, which showed that they were linked to them in affection as well as in affinity. These princes, forty-two in number, being appointed as sheep for the sacrifice, were slain with solemnity, *at the pit of the shearing-house. The Lord is known by these judgments which he executeth.*

Verses 15–28

Jehu, pushing on his work, is here,

I. Courting the friendship of a good man, *Jehonadab the son of Rechab, v.* 15, 16. This Jehonadab, though mortified to the world and meddling little with the business of it (as appears by his charge to his posterity, which they religiously observed 300 years after, not to drink wine nor dwell in cities, Jer. 35:6, etc.), yet, upon this occasion, went to meet Jehu, that he might encourage him in the work to which God had called him. The countenance of good men is a thing which great men, if they be wise, will value, and value themselves by. David prayed, *Let those that fear thee turn to me,* Ps. 119:79. This Jehonadab, though no prophet, priest, or Levite, no prince or ruler, was, we may suppose, very eminent for prudence and piety, and generally respected for that life of self-denial and devotion which he lived: Jehu, though a soldier, knew him and honoured him. He did not indeed think of sending for him, but when he met him (though it is likely he drove now as furiously as ever) he stopped to speak to him; and we are here told what passed between them. 1. Jehu saluted him; he *blessed him* (so the word is), paid him the respect and showed him the good-will that were due to so great an example of serious godliness. 2. Jehonadab assured him that he was sincerely in his interest and a hearty well-wisher to his cause. Jehu professed that *his heart was right with him,* that he had a true affection for his person and a veneration for the crown of his Nazariteship, and desired to know whether he had the same affection for him and satisfaction in that crown of royal dignity which God had put upon his head: *Is thy heart right?* a question we should often put to ourselves. "I make a plausible profession, have gained a reputation among men, but *is my heart right?* Am I sincere and inward with God?" Jehonadab gave him his word *(It is),* and gave him his hand as a pledge of his heart, *yielded to him* (so giving the hand is rendered, 2 Chr. 30:8), concurred and covenanted with him, and owned him in the work both of revenge and of reformation he was now about. 3. Jehu took him up into his chariot and took him along with him to Samaria. He put some honour upon him, by taking him into the chariot with him (Jehonadab was not accustomed to ride in a chariot, much less with a king); but he received more honour from him, and from the countenance he gave to his present work. All sober people would think the better of Jehu when they saw Jehonadab in the chariot with him. This was not the only time in which the piety of some has been made to serve the policy of others, and designing men have strengthened themselves by drawing good men into their interests. Jehonadab is a stranger to the arts of fleshly wisdom, and has his *conversation in simplicity and godly sincerity;* and therefore, if Jehu be a servant of God and an enemy to Ball, he will be his faithful friend. "Come then" (says Jehu), "come with me, *and see my zeal for the Lord;* and then thou wilt see reason to espouse my cause." This is commonly taken as not well said by Jehu, and as giving cause to suspect that his heart was not right with God in what he did, and that the zeal he pretended for the Lord was really zeal for himself and his own advancement. For, (1.) He boasted of it, and spoke as if God and man were mightily indebted to him for it. (2.) He desired it might be seen and taken notice of, like the Pharisees, who did all to be seen of men. An upright heart approves itself to God and covets no more than his acceptance. If we aim at the applause of men, and make their praise our highest end, we are upon a false bottom. Whether Jehu looked any further we cannot judge; however Jehonadab went with him, and, it is likely, animated and assisted him in the further execution of his commission (*v.* 17), destroying all Ahab's friends in Samaria. A man may hate cruelty and yet love justice, may be far from thirsting after blood and yet may *wash his feet in the blood of the wicked,* Ps. 58:10.

II. Contriving the destruction of all the worshippers of Baal. The service of Baal was the crying sin of the house of Ahab: that root of this idolatry was plucked up, but multitudes yet remained that were infected with it, and would be in danger of infecting others. The law of God was express, that they were to be put to death; but they were so numerous, and so dispersed throughout all parts of the kingdom, and perhaps so alarmed with Jehu's beginnings, that it would be a hard matter to find them all out and an endless task to prosecute and execute them one by one. Jehu's project therefore is to cut them all off together. 1. By a wile, by a fraud, he brought them together to the temple of Baal. He pretended he would worship Baal more than ever Ahab had done, *v.* 18. Perhaps he spoke this ironically, or to try the body of the people whether they would oppose such a resolution as this, and would resent his threatening to increase his predecessor's exactions, and say, "If it be so, we have no part in Jehu, nor inheritance in the son of Nimshi." But it rather seems to have been spoken purposely to deceive the worshippers of Baal, and then it cannot be justified. The truth of God needs not any man's lie. He issued a proclamation, requiring the attendance of all the worshippers of Baal to join with him in a sacrifice to Baal (*v.* 19, 20), not only the prophets and priests, but all, throughout the kingdom, who worshipped Baal, who were not nearly so many as they had been in Elijah's time. Jehu's friends, we may suppose, were aware of what he designed, and were not offended at it; but the bigoted besotted Baalites began to think themselves very happy, and that now they should see golden days again. *Joram had put away the image of Baal, ch.* 3:2. If Jehu will restore it, they have what they would have, and come up to Samaria with joy from all parts to celebrate the solemnity; and they are pleased to see the house of Baal crowded (*v.* 21), to see his priests in their vestments (*v.* 22), and themselves perhaps with some badges or other to notify their relation to Baal, for there were vestments for all his worshippers. 2. He took care that none of the servants of the Lord should be among them, *v.* 23. This they took as a provision to preserve the worship of Baal from being profaned by strangers; but it was a wonder that they did not, by this, see themselves brought into a snare and discern a design upon them. No marvel if those that suffer themselves to be deceived by Baal (as all idolaters were by their idols), are deceived by Jehu to their destruction. 3. He gave order for the cutting of them all off, and Jehonadab joined with him therein, *v.* 23. When a strict search was made lest any of the servants of God should, either for company or curiosity, have got among them — lest any wheat should be mixed with those tares, and when eighty men were set to stand guard at all the avenues to Baal's temple, that none might escape (*v.* 24), then the guards were sent in to put them all to the sword and to *mingle their blood with their sacrifices,* in a way of just revenge, as they themselves had sometimes done, when, in their blind devotion, they *cut themselves with knives and lancets till the blood gushed out,* 1 Ki. 18:28. This was accordingly done, and the doing of it, though seemingly barbarous, was, considering the nature of their crime, really righteous. *The Lord, whose name is jealous, is a jealous God.* 4. The idolaters being thus destroyed, the idolatry itself was utterly abolished. The buildings about the house of Baal (which were so many and so stately that they are here called a *city*), where Baal's priests and their families lived, were destroyed; all the little images, statues, pictures, or shrines, which beautified Baal's temple, with the great image of Baal himself, were brought out and burnt (*v.* 26, 27), and the temple of Baal was broken down, and made a dunghill, the common sink, or sewer, of the city, that the remembrance of it might be blotted out or made infamous. Thus was the worship of Baal quite destroyed, at least for the present, out of Israel, though it had once prevailed so far that there were but 7000 of all the thousands of Israel that had not bowed the knee to Baal, and those concealed. Thus will God destroy all the gods of the heathen, and, sooner or later, triumph over them all.

Verses 29–36

Here is all the account of the reign of Jehu, though it continued twenty-eight years. The progress of it answered not to the glory of its beginning. We have here,

I. God's approbation of what Jehu had done. Many, it is probable, censured him as treacherous and barbarous — called him a rebel, a usurper, a murderer, and prognosticated ill concerning him, that a family thus raised would soon be ruined; but God said, *Well done* (*v.* 30), and then it signified little who said otherwise. 1. God pronounced that to be right which he had done. It is justly questionable whether he did it from a good principle and whether he did not take some false steps in the doing of it; and yet (says God), *Thou hast done well in executing that which is right in my eyes.* The extirpating of idolaters and idolatry was a thing right in God's eyes, for it is an iniquity he visits as surely and severely as any: it was *according to all that was in his heart,* all he desired, all he designed. Jehu went through with his work. 2. God promised him a reward, that his children of the fourth generation from him should *sit upon the throne of Israel.* This was more than what took place in any of the dignities or royal families of that kingdom; of the house of Ahab there were indeed four kings, Omri, Ahab, Ahaziah, and Joram, but the last two were brothers, so that it reached but to the third generation, and that whole family continued but about forty-five years in all, whereas Jehu's continued in four, besides himself, and in all about 120 years. Note, No services done for God shall go unrewarded.

II. Jehu's carelessness in what he was further to do. By this it appeared that his heart was not right with God, that he was partial in his reformation. 1. He did not put away all the evil. He departed from the sins of Ahab, but not from the sins of Jeroboam — discarded Baal, but adhered to the calves. The worship of Baal was indeed the greater evil, and more heinous in the sight of God, but the worship of the calves was a great evil, and true conversion is not only from gross sin, but from all sin — not only from false gods, but from false worships. The worship of Baal weakened and diminished Israel, and made them beholden to the Sidonians, and therefore he could easily part with that; but the worship of the calves was a politic idolatry, was begun and kept up for reasons of state, to prevent the return of the ten tribes to the house of David, and therefore Jehu clave to that. True conversion is not only from wasteful sins, but from gainful sins — not only from those sins that are destructive to the secular interest, but from those that support and befriend it, in forsaking which is the great trial whether we can deny ourselves and trust God. 2. He put away evil, but he did not mind that which was good (*v.* 31): *He took no heed to walk in the law of the Lord God of Israel.* He abolished the worship of Baal, but did not keep up the worship of God, nor walk in his law. He had shown great care and zeal for the rooting out of a false religion; but in the true religion, (1.) He showed no care, took no heed, lived at large, was not at all solicitous to please God and to do his duty, took no heed to the scriptures, to the prophets, to his own conscience, but walked at all adventures. Those that are heedless, it is to be feared, are graceless; for, where there is a good principle in the heart, it will make men cautious and circumspect, desirous to please God and jealous of doing any thing to offend him. (2.) He showed no zeal; what he did in religion he did not do with his heart, with all his heart, but did it as if he did it not, without any liveliness or concern. It seems, he was a man that had little religion himself, and yet God made use of him as an instrument of reformation in Israel. It is a pity but that those that do good to others should always be good themselves.

III. The judgment that came upon Israel in his reign. We have reason to fear that when Jehu took no heed himself to walk in God's law the people were generally as careless as he, both in their devotions and in their conversations. There was a general decay of piety and increase of profaneness; and therefore it is not strange that the next news we hear is, *In those days the Lord began to cut Israel short, v.* 32. Their neighbours encroached upon them on every side; they were short in their duty to God, and therefore God cut them short in their extent, wealth, and power. Hazael king of Syria was, above any other, vexatious and mischievous to them, *smote them in all the coasts of Israel,* particularly the countries on the other side Jordan, which lay next him, and most exposed; on these he made continual inroads, and laid them waste. Now the Reubenites and Gadites smarted for the choice which their ancestors made of an inheritance on that side Jordan, which Moses reproved them for, Num. 32. Now Hazael did what Elisha foresaw and foretold he would do. Yet, for doing it, God had a quarrel with him and with his kingdom, as we may find, Amos 1:3, 4. Because those of Damascus have *threshed Gilead with threshing instruments of iron,* therefore (says God) *I will send a fire into the house of Hazael, which shall devour the palaces of Benhadad.*

Lastly, The conclusion of Jehu's reign, *v.* 34–36. Notice is taken, in general, of his might; but, because he took no heed to serve God, the memorials of his mighty enterprises and achievements are justly buried in oblivion.

CHAPTER 11

The revolution in the kingdom of Israel was soon perfected in Jehu's settlement; we must now enquire into the affairs of the kingdom of Judah, which lost its head (such as it was) at the same time, and by the same hand, as Israel lost its head; but things continued longer there in distraction than in Israel, yet, after some years, they were brought into a good posture, as we find in this chapter. I. Athaliah usurps the government and destroys all the seed-royal (*v.* 1). II. Joash, a child of a year old, is wonderfully preserved (*v.* 2, 3). III. At six years' end he is produced, and, by the agency of Jehoiada, made king (*v.* 4–12). IV. Athaliah is slain (*v.* 13–16). V. Both the civil and religious interests of the kingdom are well settled in the hands of Joash (*v.* 17–21). And thus, after some interruption, things returned with advantage into the old channel.

Verses 1–3

God had assured David of the continuance of his family, which is called his *ordaining a lamp for his anointed;* and this cannot but appear a great thing, now that we have read of the utter extirpation of so many royal families, one after another. Now here we have David's promised lamp almost extinguished and yet wonderfully preserved.

I. It was almost extinguished by the barbarous malice of Athaliah, the queen-mother, who, when she heard that her son Ahaziah was slain by Jehu, *arose and destroyed all the seed-royal* (*v.* 1), all that she knew to be akin to the crown. Her husband Jehoram had slain all his brethren the sons of Jehoshaphat, 2 Chr. 21:4. The Arabians had slain all Jehoram's sons except Ahaziah, 2 Chr. 22:1. Jehu had slain all their sons (2 Chr. 22:8) and Ahaziah himself. Surely never was royal blood so profusely shed. Happy the men of inferior birth, who live below envy and emulation! But, as if all this were but a small matter, Athaliah destroyed all that were left of the seed-royal. It was strange that one of the tender sex could be so barbarous, that one who had been herself a king's daughter, a king's wife, and a king's mother, could be so barbarous to a royal family, and a family into which she was herself ingrafted; but she did it, 1. From a spirit of ambition. She thirsted after rule, and thought she could not get to it any other way. That none might reign with her, she slew even the infants and sucklings that might have reigned after her. For fear of a competitor, not any must be reserved for a successor. 2. From a spirit of revenge and rage against God. The house of Ahab being utterly destroyed, and her son Ahaziah among the rest, because he was akin to it, she resolved, as it were, by way of reprisal, to destroy the house of David, and cut off his line, in defiance of God's promise to perpetuate it — a foolish attempt and fruitless, for who can disannul what God hath purposed? Grandmothers have been thought more fond of their grandchildren than they were of their own; yet Ahaziah's own mother is the wilful murderer of Ahazaiah's own sons, and in their infancy too, when she was obliged, above any other, to nurse them and take care of them. Well might she be called *Athaliah, that wicked woman* (2 Chr. 24:7), Jezebel's own daughter; yet herein God was righteous, and visited the iniquity of Joram and Ahaziah, those degenerate branches of David's house, upon their children.

II. It was wonderfully preserved by the pious care of one of Joram's daughters (who was wife to Jehoiada the priest), who stole away one of the king's sons, Joash by name, and hid him, *v.* 2, 3. This was a brand plucked out of the fire; what number were slain we are not told, but, it seems, this being a child in the nurse's arms was not missed, or not enquired after, or at least no found. The person that delivered him was his own aunt, the daughter of wicked Joram; for God will raise up protectors for those whom he will have protected. The place of his safety was the house of the Lord, one of the chambers belonging to the temple, a place Athaliah seldom troubled. His aunt, by bringing him hither, put him under God's special protection, and so hid him by faith, as Moses was hidden. Now were David's words made good to one of his seed (Ps. 27:5), *In the secret of his tabernacle shall he hide me.* With good reason did this Joash, when he grew up, set himself to repair the house of the Lord, for it had been a sanctuary to him. Now was the promise made to David bound up in one life, and yet it did not fail. Thus to the son of David will God, according to his promise, secure a spiritual seed, which, though sometimes reduced to a small number, brought very low, and seemingly lost, will be perpetuated to the end of time, hidden sometimes and unseen, but hidden in God's pavilion and unhurt. It was a special providence that Joram, though a king, a wicked king, married his daughter to Jehoiada a priest, a godly priest. Some perhaps thought it a disparagement to the royal family to marry a daughter to a clergyman, but it proved a happy marriage, and the saving of the royal family from ruin; for Jehoiada's interest in the temple gave *her* an opportunity to preserve the child, and her interest in the royal family gave *him* an opportunity to set him on the throne. See the wisdom and care of Providence, and how it prepares for what it designs; and see what blessings those lay up in store for their families that marry their children to those that are wise and good.

Verses 4–12

Six years Athaliah tyrannised. We have not a particular account of her reign; no doubt it was of a piece with the beginning. While Jehu was extirpating the worship of Baal in Israel, she was establishing it in Judah, as appears, 2 Chr. 24:7. The court and kingdom of Judah had been debauched by their alliance with the house of Ahab, and now one of that house is a curse and a plague to both: sinful friendships speed no better. All this while, Joash lay hid, entitled to a crown and intended for it, and yet buried alive in obscurity. Though the sons and heirs of heaven are now hidden, *the world knows them not* (1 Jn. 3:1), yet the time is fixed when they shall appear in glory, as Joash in his seventh year; by that time he was ready to be shown, not a babe, but, having served his first apprenticeship to life and arrived at his first climacterical year, he had taken a good step towards manhood; by that time the people had grown weary of Athaliah's tyranny and ripe for a revolution. How that revolution was effected we are here told.

I. The manager of this great affair was Jehoiada the priest, probably the high priest, or at least the *sagan* (as the Jews called him) or suffragan to the high priest. By his birth and office he was a man in authority, whom the people were bound by the law to observe and obey, especially when there was no rightful king upon the throne, Deu. 17:12. By marriage he was allied to the royal family, and, if all the seed-royal were destroyed, his wife, as daughter to Joram, had a better title to the crown than Athaliah had. By his eminent gifts and graces he was fitted to serve his country, and better service he could not do it than to free it from Athaliah's usurpation; and we have reason to think he did not make this attempt till he had first asked counsel of God and known his mind, either by prophets or Urim, perhaps by both.

II. The management was very discreet and as became so wise and good a man as Jehoiada was.

1. He concerted the matter with the *rulers of hundreds and the captains,* the men in office, ecclesiastical, civil, and military; he got them to him to the temple, consulted with them, laid before them the grievances they at present laboured under, gave them an oath of secresy, and, finding them free and forward to join with him, *showed them the king's son* (*v.* 4), and so well satisfied were they with his fidelity that they saw no reason to suspect an imposition. We may well think what a pleasing surprise it was to the good people among them, who feared that the house and lineage of David were quite cut off, to find such a spark as this in the embers.

2. He posted the priests and Levites, who were more immediately under his direction, in the several avenues to the temple, to keep the guard, putting them under the command of the *rulers of hundreds, v.* 9. David had divided the priests into courses, which waited by turns. Every sabbath-day morning a new company came into waiting, but the company of the foregoing week did not go out of waiting till the sabbath evening, so that on the sabbath day, when double service was to be done, there was a double number to do it, both those that were to come in and those that were to go out. These Jehoiada employed to attend on this great occasion; he armed them out of the magazines of the temple with David's spears and shields, either his own or those he had taken from his enemies, which he devoted to God's honour, *v.* 10. If they were old and unfashionable, yet those that used them might, by their being David's, be reminded of God's covenant with him, which they were now acting in the defence of. Two things they were ordered to do: — (1.) To protect the young king from being insulted; they must *keep the watch of the king's house* (*v.* 5), *compass the king, and be with him* (*v.* 8), to guard him from Athaliah's partizans, for still there were those that thirsted after royal blood. (2.) To preserve the holy temple from being profaned by the concourse of people that would come together on this occasion (*v.* 6): *Keep the watch of the house, that it be* neither broken through nor broken down, and so strangers should crowd in, or such as were unclean. He was not so zealous for the projected revolution as to forget his religion. In times of the greatest hurry care must be taken, *Ne detrimentum capiat ecclesia — That the holy things of God be not trenched upon.* It is observable that Jehoiada appointed to each his place as well as his work (*v.* 6, 7), for good order contributes very much to the expediting and accomplishing of any great enterprise. Let every man know, and keep, and make good, his post, and then the work will be done quickly.

3. When the guards were fixed, then the king was brought forth, *v.* 12. *Rejoice greatly, O daughter of Sion!* for even in thy holy mountain thy king appears, a child indeed, but not such a one as brings a woe upon the land, for he is the son of nobles, the son of David (Eccl. 10:17) — a child indeed, but he had a good guardian, and, which was better, a good God, to go to. Jehoiada, without delay,

proceeded to the coronation of this young king; for, though he was not yet capable of despatching business, he would be growing up towards it by degrees. This was done with great solemnity, *v.* 12. (1.) In token of his being invested with kingly power, he *put the crown upon him,* though it was yet too large and heavy for his head. The regalia, it is probable, were kept in the temple, and so the crown was ready at hand. (2.) In token of his obligation to govern by law, and to make the word of God his rule, he gave him the testimony, put into his hand a Bible, in which he must *read all the days of his life,* Deu. 17:18, 19. (3.) In token of his receiving the Spirit, to qualify him for this great work to which he before was called, he anointed him. Though notice is taken of the anointing of the kings only in case of interruption, as here, and in Solomon's case, yet I know not but the ceremony might be used for all their kings, at least those of the house of David, because their royalty was typical of Christ's, who was to be anointed above his fellows, above all the sons of David. (4.) In token of the people's acceptance of him and subjection to his government, they clapped their hands for joy, and expressed their hearty good wishes to him: *Let the king live;* and thus they made him king, made him their king, consented to, and concurred with, the divine appointment. They had reason to rejoice in the period now put to Athaliah's tyranny, and the prospect they had of the restoration and establishment of religion by a king under the tuition of so good a man as Jehoiada. They had reason to bid him welcome to the crown whose right it was, and to pray, *Let him live,* concerning him who came to them as life from the dead and in whom the house of David was to live. With such acclamations of joy and satisfaction must the kingdom of Christ be welcomed into our hearts when his throne is set up there and Satan the usurper is deposed. *Hosanna, blessed is he that comes:* clap hands, and say, "Let King Jesus live, for ever live and reign, in my soul, and in all the world;" it is promised (Ps. 72:15), *He shall live, and prayer shall be made for him,* and his kingdom, *continually.*

Verses 13–16

We may suppose it was designed when they had finished the solemnity of the king's inauguration, to pay a visit to Athaliah, and call her to an account for her murders, usurpation, and tyranny; but, like her mother Jezebel, she saved them the labour, went out to meet them, and hastened her own destruction. 1. Hearing the noise, she came in a fright to see what was the matter, *v.* 13. Jehoiada and his friends began in silence, but now that they found their strength, they proclaimed what they were doing. It seems, Athaliah was little regarded, else she would have had intelligence brought her of this daring attempt before with her own ears she heard the noise; had the design been discovered before it was perfected, it might have been quashed, but now it was too late. When she heard the noise it was strange that she was so ill advised as to come herself, and, for aught that appears, to come alone. Surely she was not so neglected as to have none to go for her, or none to go with her, but she was wretchedly infatuated by the transport both of fear and indignation she was in. Whom God will destroy he befools. 2. Seeing what was done she cried out for help. She saw the king's place by the pillar possessed by one to whom the princes and people did homage (*v.* 14) and had reason to conclude her power at an end, which she knew was usurped; this made her rend her clothes, like one distracted, and cry, "Treason! treason! Come and help against the traitors." Josephus adds that she cried to have him killed that possessed the king's place. What was now doing was the highest justice, yet it was branded as the highest crime; she herself was the greatest traitor, and yet was first and loudest in crying Treason! treason! Those that are themselves most guilty are commonly most forward to reproach others. 3. Jehoiada gave orders to put her to death as an idolater, a usurper, and an enemy to the public peace. Care was taken, (1.) That she should not be killed in the temple, or any of the courts of it, in reverence to that holy place, which must not be stained with the blood of any human sacrifice, though ever so justly offered. (2.) That whoever appeared for her should die with her: "Him that follows her, to protect or rescue her, any of her attendants that resolve to adhere to her and will not come into the interests of their rightful sovereign, *kill with the sword,* but not unless they follow her now," *v.* 15. According to these orders, she endeavouring to make her escape the back way to the palace, through the stalls, they pursued her, and there killed her, *v.* 16. *So let thy enemies perish, O Lord!* thus give the bloody harlot blood to drink, for she is worthy.

Verses 17–21

Jehoiada had now got over the harlot part of his work, when, by the death of Athaliah, the young prince had his way to the throne cleared of all opposition. He had now to improve his advantages for the perfecting of the revolution and the settling of the government. Two things we have an account of here: —

I. The good foundations he laid, by an original contract, *v.* 17. Now that prince and people were together in God's house, as it should seem before they stirred, Jehoiada took care that they should jointly covenant with God, and mutually covenant with each other, that they might rightly understand their duty both to God and to one another, and be firmly bound to it. 1. He endeavoured to settle and secure the interests of religion among them, by a covenant between them and God. King and people would then cleave most firmly to each other when both had joined themselves to the Lord. God had already, on his part, promised to be their God (Jehoiada could show them that in the book of the testimony); now the king and people on their part must covenant and agree that *they will be the Lord's people:* in this covenant, the king stands upon the same level with his subjects and is as much bound as any of them to serve the Lord. By this engagement they renounced Baal, whom many of them had worshipped, and resigned themselves to God's government. It is well with a people when all the changes that pass over them help to revive, strengthen, and advance the interests of religion among them. And those are likely to prosper who set out in the world under fresh and sensible obligations to God and their duty. By our bonds to God the bonds of every relation are strengthened. They *first gave themselves to the Lord,* and then *to us,* 2 Co. 8:5. 2. He then settled both the coronation-oath and the oath of allegiance, the *pacta conventa — covenant,* between the king and the people, by which the king was obliged to govern according to law and to protect his subjects, and they were obliged, while he did so, to obey him and to bear faith and true allegiance to him. Covenants are of use both to remind us of and to bind us to those duties which are already binding on us. It is good, in all relations, for the parties to understand one another fully, particularly in that between prince and subject, that the one may understand the limits of his power and prerogative, the other those of his liberty and property; and never may the ancient landmarks which our fathers have set before them be removed.

II. The good beginnings he raised on those foundations. 1. Pursuant to their covenant with God they immediately abolished idolatry, which the preceding kings, in compliance with the house of Ahab, had introduced (*v.* 18): *All the people of the land,* the mob, got together, to show their zeal against idolatry; and every one, now that they were so well headed, would lend a hand to pull down Baal's temple, his altars, and his images. All his worshippers, it should seem, deserted him; only his priest Mattan stuck to his altar. Though all men forsook Baal, he would not, and there he was slain, the best sacrifice that ever was offered upon that altar. Having destroyed Baal's temple, they appointed *officers over the house of God,* to see that the service of God was regularly performed by the proper persons, in due time, and according to the institutional manner. 2. Pursuant to their covenant with one another they expressed a mutual readiness to and satisfaction in each other. (1.) The king was brought in state to the royal palace, and sat there on the throne of judgment, *the thrones of the house of David* (*v.* 19), ready to receive petitions and appeals, which he would refer it to Jehoiada to give answers to and to give judgment upon. (2.) The people rejoiced, and Jerusalem was in quiet (*v.* 20), and Josephus says they kept a feast of joy many days, making good Solomon's observation (Prov. 11:10), *When it goes well with the righteous the city rejoices, and when the wicked perish there is shouting.*

CHAPTER 12

This chapter gives us the history of the reign of Joash, which does not answer to that glorious beginning of it which we had an account of in the foregoing chapter; he was not so illustrious at forty years old as he was at seven, yet his reign is to be reckoned one of the better sort, and appears much worse in Chronicles (2 Chr. 24) than it does here, for there we find the blood of one of God's prophets laid at his door; here we are only told, I. That he did well while Jehoiada lived (*v.* 1–3). II. That he was careful and active to repair the temple (*v.* 4–16). III. That after a mean compact with Hazael (*v.* 17, 18) he died ingloriously (*v.* 19–21).

Verses 1–3

The general account here given of Joash is, 1. That he reigned forty years. As he began his reign when he was very young, he might, in the course of nature, have continued much longer, for he was cut off when he was but forty-seven years old, *v.* 1. 2. That he did that which was right as long as Jehoiada lived to instruct him, *v.* 2. Many young men have come too soon to an estate — have had wealth, and power, and liberty, before they knew how to use them — and it has been of bad consequence to them; but against this danger Joash was well guarded by having such a good director as Jehoiada was, so wise, and experienced, and faithful to him, and by having so much wisdom as to hearken to him and be directed by him, even when he was grown up. Note, It is a great mercy to young people, and especially to young princes, and all young men of consequence, to be under good direction, and to have those about them that will instruct them to do *that which is right in the sight of the Lord;* and they then do wisely and well for themselves when they are willing to be counselled and ruled by such. *A child left to himself brings his mother to shame,* but a child left to such a tuition may bring himself to honour and comfort. 3. That the *high places were not taken away, v.* 3. Up and down the country they had altars both for sacrifice and incense, to the honour of the God of Israel only, but in competition with, and at least in tacit contempt of, his altar at Jerusalem. These private altars, perhaps, had been more used in the late bad reigns than formerly, because it was not safe to go up to Jerusalem, nor was the temple-service performed as it should have been; and, it may be, Jehoiada connived at them, because some well-meaning people were glad of them when they could not have better, and he hoped that the reforming of the temple, and putting things into a good posture there, would by degrees draw people from their high places and they would dwindle of themselves; or perhaps neither the king nor the priest had zeal enough to carry on their reformation so far, nor courage and strength enough to encounter such an inveterate usage.

Verses 4–16

We have here an account of the repairing of the temple in the reign of Joash.

I. It seems, the temple had gone out of repair. Though Solomon built it very strong, of the best materials and in the best manner, yet in time it went to decay, and there were *breaches found in it* (*v.* 5), in the roofs, or walls, or floors, the ceiling, or wainscoting, or windows, or the partitions of the courts. Even temples themselves are the worse for the wearing; but the heavenly temple will never wax old. Yet it was not only the teeth of time that made these breaches, the sons of Athaliah had *broken up the house of God* (2 Chr. 24:7), and, out of enmity to the service of the temple, had damaged the buildings of it, and the priests had not taken care to repair the breaches in time, so that they went worse and worse. Unworthy were those husbandmen to have this valuable vineyard let out to them upon such easy terms who could not afford to keep the winepress in due and tenantable repair, Mt. 21:33. Justly did their great Lord sue them for this permissive waste, and by his judgments recover *locum vastatum — for dilapidations* (as the law speaks), when this neglected temple was laid even with the ground.

II. The king himself was (as it should seem) the first and forwardest man that took care for the repair of it. We do not find that the priests complained of it or that Jehoiada himself was active in it, but the king was zealous in the matter, 1. Because he was king, and God expects and requires from those who have power that they use it for the maintenance and support of religion, the redress of grievances, and reparation of decays, for the exciting and engaging of ministers to do their part and people theirs. 2. Because the temple had been both his nursery and his sanctuary when he was a child, in a grateful remembrance of which he now appeared zealous for the honour of it. Those who have experienced the comfort and benefit of religious assemblies will make the reproach of them their burden (Zep. 3:18), the support of them their care, and the prosperity of them their chief joy.

III. The priests were ordered to collect money for these repairs, and to take care that the work was done. The king had the affairs of his kingdom to mind, and could not himself inspect this affair, but he employed the priests to manage it, the fittest persons, and most likely, one would think, to be hearty in it. 1. He gave them orders for the levying of the money of the dedicated things. They must not stay till it was paid in, but they must call for it where they knew it was due, in their respective districts, as redemption-money (by virtue of the law, Lev. 27:2, 3), or as a free-will offering, *v.* 4. This they were to gather every man of his acquaintance, and it was supposed that there was no man but had acquaintance with some or other of the priests. Note, We should take the opportunity that God gives us of exciting those we have a particular acquaintance with to that which is good. 2. He gave them orders for laying out the money they had levied in *repairing the breaches of the house, v.* 5.

IV. This method did not answer the intention, *v.* 6. Little money was raised. Either the priests were careless, and did not call on the people to pay in their dues, or the people had so little confidence in the priests' management that they were backward to pay money into their hands; if they were distrusted without cause, it was the people's shame; if with, it was more theirs. But what money was raised was not applied to the proper use: *The breaches of the house were not repaired;* the priests thought it might serve as well as it had done, and therefore put off repairing from time to time. Church work is usually slow work, but it is a pity that churchmen, of all men, should be slow at it. Perhaps what little money they raised they thought it necessary to use for the maintenance of the priests, which must needs fall much short when ten tribes had wholly revolted and the other two were wretchedly corrupted.

V. Another method was therefore taken. The king had his heart much set upon having the *breaches of the house repaired, v.* 7. His apostasy, at last, gives us cause to question whether he had as good an affection for the service of the temple as he had for the structure. Many have been zealous for building and beautifying churches, and for other forms of godliness, who yet have been strangers to the power of it. However, we commend his zeal, and blame him not for reproving even his tutor Jehoiada himself when he saw him remiss; and so convincing was his reproof that the priests owned themselves unworthy to be any longer employed, and consented to the taking of some other measures, and the giving up of the money they had received into other hands, *v.* 8. It was honestly done, when they found they had not spirit to do it themselves, not to hinder other people from doing it. Another course was taken,

1. For raising money, *v.* 9, 10. The money was not paid into private hands, but put into a public chest, and then people brought it in readily and in great abundance, not only their dues, but their free-will offerings for so good a work. The high priest and the secretary of state counted the money out of the chest, and laid it by *in specie* for the use to which it was appropriated. When public distributions are made faithfully public contributions will be made cheerfully. The money that was given, (1.) Was dropped into the chest through a hole in the lid, past recall, to intimate that what has been once resigned to God must never be resumed. *Every man, as he purposeth in his heart, so let him give.* (2.) The chest was put on the right hand as they went in, which, some think, is alluded to in that rule of charity which our Saviour gives, *Let not thy left hand know what thy right hand doeth.* But, while they were getting all they could for the repair of the temple, they did not break in upon that which was the stated maintenance of the priests, *v.* 16. The trespass-money and the sin-money (which were given to them by that law, Lev. 5:15, 16) were reserved to them. Let not the servants of the temple be starved under colour of repairing the breaches of it.

2. For laying out the money that was raised.

(1.) They did not put it into the hands of the priests, who were not versed in affairs of this nature, having other work to mind, but *into the hands of those that did the work,* or at least *had the oversight of it, v.* 11. Those were fittest to be entrusted with this business whose employment lay that way. *Tractant fabrilia fabri — Every artist has his trade assigned;* but let not those who are called to war the holy warfare entangle themselves in the affairs of this life. Those that were thus entrusted did the business, [1.] Carefully, purchasing materials and paying workmen, *v.* 12. Business is done with expedition when those are employed in it that understand it and know which way to go about it. [2.] Faithfully; such a reputation they got for honesty that there was no occasion to examine their bills or audit their accounts. Let all that are entrusted with public money, or public work, learn hence to deal faithfully, as those that know God will reckon with them, whether men do or no. Those that think it is no sin to cheat the government, cheat the country, or cheat the church, will be of another mind when God shall set their sins in order before them.

(2.) They did not lay it out in ornaments for the temple, in vessels of gold or silver, but in necessary repairs first (*v.* 13), whence we may learn, in all our expenses to give that the preference which is most needful, and, in dealing for the public, to deal as we would for ourselves. After the repairs were finished we find the overplus turned into plate for the service of the temple, 2 Chr. 24:14.

Verses 17–21

When Joash had revolted from God and become both an idolater and a persecutor the hand of the Lord went out against him, and his *last state was worse than his first.*

I. His wealth and honour became an easy prey to his neighbours. Hazael, when he had chastised Israel (*ch.* 10:32), threatened Judah and Jerusalem likewise, took Gath, a strong city (*v.* 17), and thence intended to march with his forces against Jerusalem, the royal city, the holy city, but whose defence, on account of its sinfulness, had departed. Joash had neither spirit nor strength to make head against him, but gave him all the hallowed things, and all the gold that was found both in his exchequer and in the treasures of the temple (*v.* 18), to bribe him to march another way. If it were lawful to do this for the public safety, better part with the gold of the temple than expose the temple itself; yet, 1. If he had not forsaken God, and forfeited his protection, his affairs would not have been brought to this extremity, but he might have forced Hazael to retire. 2. He diminished himself, and made himself very mean, lost the honour of a prince and a soldier, and of an Israelite too, in alienating the dedicated things. 3. He impoverished himself and his kingdom. And, 4. He tempted Hazael to come again, when he could carry home so rich a booty without striking a stroke. And it had this effect, for the next year the host of Syria came up against Jerusalem, destroyed the prince, and plundered the city, 2 Chr. 24:23, 24.

II. His life became an easy prey to his own servants. They conspired against him and slew him (*v.* 20, 21), not aiming at his kingdom, for they opposed not his son's succeeding him, but to be avenged on him for some crime he had committed; and we are told in Chronicles that his murdering the prophet, Jehoiada's son, was the provocation. In this, how unrighteous soever they were (vengeance was not theirs, nor did it belong to them to repay), God was righteous; and this was not the only time that he let even kings know that it was at their peril if they touched his anointed and did his prophets any harm, and that, when he comes to make inquisition for blood, the blood of prophets will run the account very high. Thus fell Joash, who began in the spirit and ended in the flesh. God usually sets marks of his displeasure upon apostates, even in this life; for they, of all sinners, do most *reproach the Lord.*

CHAPTER 13

This chapter brings us again to the history of the kings of Israel, and particularly of the family of Jehu. We have here an account of the reign, I. Of his son Jehoahaz, which continued seventeen years. 1. His bad character in general (*v.* 1, 2), the trouble he was brought into (*v.* 3), and the low ebb of his affairs (*v.* 7). 2. His humiliation before God, and God's compassion towards him (*v.* 4, 5, and 23). 3. His continuance in his idolatry notwithstanding (*v.* 6). 4. His death (*v.* 8, 9). II. Of his grandson Joash, which continued sixteen years. Here is a general account of his reign in the usual

form (*v.* 10–13), but a particular account of the death of Elisha in his time. 1. The kind visit the king made him (*v.* 14), the encouragement he gave the king in his wars with Syria (*v.* 15–19). 2. His death and burial (*v.* 20), and a miracle wrought by his bones (*v.* 21). And, lastly, the advantages Joash gained against the Syrians, according to his predictions (*v.* 24, 25).

Verses 1–9

This general account of the reign of Jehoahaz, and of the state of Israel during his seventeen years, though short, is long enough to let us see two things which are very affecting and instructive: —

I. The glory of Israel raked up in the ashes, buried and lost, and turned into shame. How unlike does Israel appear here to what it had been and might have been! How is its crown profaned and its honour laid in the dust! 1. It was the honour of Israel that they worshipped the only living and true God, who is a Spirit, an eternal mind, and had rules by which to worship him of his own appointment; but by *changing the glory of their incorruptible God into the similitude of an ox, the truth of God into a lie,* they lost this honour, and levelled themselves with the nations that worshipped the work of their own hands. We find here that the king *followed the sins of Jeroboam* (*v.* 2), and the people departed *not from them, but walked therein, v.* 6. There could not be a greater reproach than these two idolized calves were to a people that were instructed in the service of God and entrusted with the lively oracles. In all the history of the ten tribes we never find the least shock given to that idolatry, but, in every reign, still the calf was their god, and they separated themselves to that shame. 2. It was the honour of Israel that they were taken under the special protection of heaven; God himself was their defence, the shield of their help and the sword of their excellency. Happy wast thou, O Israel! upon this account. But here, as often before, we find them stripped of this glory, and exposed to the insults of all their neighbours. They by their sins provoked God to anger, and then he *delivered them into the hands of Hazael and Benhadad, v.* 3. *Hazael oppressed Israel v.* 22. Surely never was any nation so often plucked and pillaged by their neighbours as Israel was. This the people brought upon themselves by sin; when they had provoked God to pluck up their hedge, the goodness of their land did but tempt their neighbours to prey upon them. So low was Israel brought in this reign, by the many depravations which the Syrians made upon them, that the militia of the kingdom and all the force they could bring into the field were but *fifty horsemen, ten chariots, and 10,000 footmen,* a despicable muster, *v.* 7. Have the thousands of Israel come to this? *How has the gold become dim!* The debauching of a nation will certainly be the debasing of it.

II. Some sparks of Israel's ancient honour appearing in these ashes. It is not quite forgotten, notwithstanding all these quarrels, that this people is the Israel of God and he is the God of Israel. For, 1. It was the ancient honour of Israel that they were a praying people: and here we find somewhat of that honour revived; for Jehoahaz their king, in his distress, *besought the Lord* (*v.* 4), applied for help, not to the calves (what help could they give him?) but to the Lord. It becomes kings to be beggars at God's door, and the greatest of men to be humble petitioners at the footstool of his throne. Need will drive them to it. 2. It was the ancient honour of Israel that they had *God nigh unto them in all that which they called upon him for* (Deu. 4:7), and so he was here. Though he might justly have rejected the prayer as an abomination to him, yet *the Lord hearkened unto Jehoahaz,* and to his prayer for himself and for his people (*v.* 4), and, *he gave Israel a saviour v.* 5) not Jehoahaz himself, for all his days Hazael oppressed Israel (*v.* 22), but his son, to whom, in answer to his father's prayers, God gave success against the Syrians, so that he recovered the cities which they had taken from his father, *v.* 25. This gracious answer God gave to the prayer of Jehoahaz, not for his sake, or the sake of that unworthy people, but in remembrance of his covenant with Abraham (*v.* 23), which, in such exigencies as these, he had long since promised to have respect to, Lev. 26:42. See swift God is to show mercy, how ready to hear prayers, how willing to find out a reason to be gracious, else he would not look so far back as that ancient covenant which Israel had so often broken and forfeited all the benefit of. Let this invite and engage us for ever to him, and encourage even those that have forsaken him to return and repent; for *there is forgiveness with him, that he may be feared.*

Verses 10–19

We have here Jehoash, or Joash, the son of Jehoahaz and grandson of Jehu, upon the throne of Israel. Probably the house of Jehu intended some respect to the house of David when they gave this heir-apparent to the crown the same name with him that was then king of Judah.

I. The general account here given of him and his reign is much the same with what we have already met with, and has little in it remarkable, *v.* 10–13. He was none of the worst, and yet, because he kept up that ancient and politic idolatry of the house of Jeroboam, it is said, *He did that which was evil in the sight of the Lord.* That one evil was enough to leave an indelible mark of infamy upon his name; for, how little evil soever men saw in it, it was, *in the sight of the Lord,* a very wicked thing; and we are sure that his judgment is according to truth. It is observable how lightly the inspired penman passes over his acts, and his might wherewith he warred, leaving it to the common historians to record them, while he takes notice only of the respect he showed to Elisha. One good action shall make a better figure in God's book than twenty great ones; and, in his account, it gains a man a much better reputation to honour a prophet than to conquer a king and his army.

II. The particular account of what passed between him and Elisha has several things in it remarkable.

1. Elisha fell sick, *v.* 14. Observe, (1.) He lived long; for it was now about sixty years since he was first called to be a prophet. It was a great mercy to Israel, and especially to the sons of the prophets, that he was continued so long a burning and shining light. Elijah finished his testimony in a fourth part of that time. God's prophets have their day set them, some longer, others shorter, as Infinite Wisdom sees fit. (2.) All the latter part of his time, from the anointing of Jehu, which was forty-five years before Joash began his reign, we find no mention made of him, or of any thing he did, till we find him here upon his deathbed. He might be useful to the last, and yet not so famous as he had sometimes been. The time of his flourishing was less than the time of his living. Let not old people complain of obscurity, but rather be well pleased with retirement. (3.) The spirit of Elijah rested on Elisha, and yet he was not sent for to heaven in a fiery chariot, as Elijah was, but went the common road out of the world, and was *visited with the visitation of all men.* If God honour some above others, who yet are not inferior to them in gifts or graces, who shall find fault? *May he not do what he will with his own?*

2. King Joash visited him in his sickness, and *wept over him, v.* 14. This was an evidence of some good in him, that he had a value and affection for a faithful prophet; so far was he from hating and persecuting him as a troubler of Israel that he loved and honoured him as one of the greatest blessings of his kingdom, and lamented the loss of him. There have been those who would not be obedient to the word of God, and yet have the faithful ministers of it so manifested in their consciences that they could not but have an honour for them. Observe here, (1.) When the king heard of Elisha's sickness he came to visit him, and to receive his dying counsel and blessing; and it was no disparagement to him, though a king, thus to honour one whom God honoured. Note, It may turn much to our spiritual advantage to attend the sick-beds and death-beds of good ministers and other good men, that we may learn to die, and may be encouraged in religion by the living comforts they have from it in a dying hour. (2.) Though Elisha was very old, had been a great while useful, and, in the course of nature, could not continue long, yet the king, when he saw him sick and likely to die, wept over him. The aged are most experienced and therefore can worst be spared. In many causes, one old witness is worth ten young ones. (3.) He lamented him in the same words with which Elisha had himself lamented the removal of Elijah: *My father, my father.* It is probable he had heard or read them in that famous story. Note, Those that give just honours to the generation that goes before them are often recompensed with the like from the generation that comes after them. He that watereth, that watereth with tears, shall be watered, shall be so watered, also himself, when it comes to his own turn, Prov. 11:25. (4.) This king was herein selfish; he lamented the loss of Elisha because he was as the chariot and horsemen of Israel, and therefore could be ill spared when Israel was so poor in chariots and horsemen, as we find they were (*v.* 7), when they had in all but fifty horsemen and ten chariots. Those who consider how much good men contribute to the defence of a nation, and the keeping off of God's judgments, will see cause to lament the removal of them.

3. Elisha gave the king great assurances of his success against the Syrians, Israel's present oppressors, and encouraged him to prosecute the war against them with vigour. Elisha was aware that therefore he was loth to part with him because he looked upon him as the great bulwark of the kingdom against that common enemy, and depended much upon his blessings and prayers in his designs against them. "Well," says Elisha, "if that be the cause of your grief, let not that trouble thee, for thou shalt be victorious over the Syrians when I am in my grave. *I die, but God will surely visit you.* He has the residue of the Spirit, and can raise up other prophets to pray for you." God's grace is not tied to one hand. He can bury his workmen and yet carry on his work. To animate the king against the Syrians he gives him a sign, orders him to *take bow and arrows* (*v.* 15), to intimate to him that, in order to the deliverance of his kingdom from the Syrians, he must put himself into a military posture and resolve to undergo the perils and fatigues of war. God would be the agent, but he must be the instrument. And that he should be successful he gives him a token, by directing him,

(1.) To shoot an arrow towards Syria, *v.* 16, 17. The king, no doubt, knew how to manage a bow better than the prophet did, and yet, because the arrow now to be shot was to have its significancy from the divine institution, as if he were now to be disciplined, he received the words of command from the prophet: *Put thy hand upon the bow — Open the window — Shoot.* Nay, as if he had been a child that never drew a bow before, *Elisha put his hands upon the king's hands,* to signify that in all his expeditions against the Syrians he must look up to God for direction and strength, must reckon his own hands not sufficient for him, but go on in a dependence upon divine aid. *He teacheth my hands to war,* Ps. 18:34; 144:1. The trembling hands of a dying prophet, as they signified the concurrence and communication of the power of God, gave this arrow more force than the hands of the king in his full strength. The Syrians had made themselves masters of the country that lay eastward, *ch.* 10:33. Thitherward therefore the arrow was directed, and such an interpretation given by the prophet of the shooting of this arrow, though shot in one respect at random, as made it, [1.] A commission to the king to attack the Syrians, notwithstanding their power and possession. [2.] A promise of success therein. It is the *arrow of the Lord's deliverance, even the arrow of deliverance from Syria.* It is God that commands deliverance; and, when he will effect it, who can hinder? The arrow of deliverance is his. He shoots out his arrows, and the work is done, Ps. 18:14. *"Thou shalt smite the Syrians in Aphek,* where they are now encamped, or where they are to have a general rendezvous of their forces, *till thou have consumed* those of them that are vexatious and oppressive to thee and thy kingdom."

(2.) To *strike with the arrows, v.* 18, 19. The prophet having in God's name assured him of victory over the Syrians, he will now try him and see what improvement he will make of his victories, whether he will push them on with more zeal than Ahab did when Benhadad lay at his mercy. For the trial of this he bids him *smite with the arrows on the ground:* "Believe them brought to the ground by the *arrow of the Lord's deliverance,* and laid at thy feet; and now show me what thou wilt do to them when thou hast them down, whether thou wilt do as David did when God *gave him the necks of his enemies, beat them small as the dust before the wind,"* Ps. 18:40, 42. The king showed not that eagerness and flame which one might have expected upon this occasion, but smote thrice, and no more. Either out of foolish tenderness to the Syrians, he smote as if he were afraid of hurting them, at least of ruining them, willing to show mercy to those that never did, nor ever would, show mercy to him or his people. Or, perhaps, he smote thrice, and very coldly, because he thought it but a silly thing, that it looked idle and childish for a king to beat the floor with his arrows; and thrice was often enough for him to play the fool merely to please the prophet. But, by contemning the sign, he lost the thing signified, sorely to the grief of the dying prophet, who was angry with him, and told him he should have smitten five or six times. Not being straitened in the power and promise of God, why should he be straitened in his own expectations and endeavours? Note, It cannot but be a trouble to good men to see those they wish well to stand in their own light and forsake their own mercies, to see them lose their advantages against their spiritual enemies, and to give them advantage.

Verses 20–25

We must here attend,

I. The sepulchre of Elisha: he died in a good old age, and they buried him; and what follows shows, 1. What power there was in his life to keep off judgments; for, as soon as he was dead, the bands of the Moabites invaded the land — not great armies to face them in the field, but roving skulking bands, that murdered and plundered by surprise. God has many ways to chastise a provoking people. The king was apprehensive of danger only from the Syrians, but, behold, the Moabites invade him. Trouble comes sometimes from that point whence we least feared it. The mentioning of this immediately upon the death of Elisha intimates that the removal of God's faithful prophets is a presage of judgments coming. When ambassadors are recalled heralds may be expected. 2. What power there was in his dead body: it communicated life to another dead body, *v.* 21. This great miracle, though very briefly related, was a decided proof of his mission and a confirmation of all his prophecies. It was also a plain indication of another life after this. When Elisha died, there was not an end of him, for then he could not have done this. From operation we may infer existence. By this it appeared that the Lord was still the God of Elisha; therefore Elisha still lived, for *God is not the God of the dead, but of the living.* And it may, perhaps, have a reference to Christ, by whose death and burial the grave is made to all believers a safe and happy passage to life. It likewise intimated that though Elisha was dead, yet, in virtue of the promises made by him, Israel's interests, though they seemed quite sunk and lost, should revive and flourish again. The neighbours were carrying the dead body of a man to the grave, and, fearing to fall into the hands of the Moabites, a party of whom they saw at a distance near the place where the body was to be interred, they laid the corpse in the next convenient place, which proved to be Elisha's sepulchre. The dead man, upon touching Elisha's bones, revived, and, it is likely, went home again with his friends. Josephus relates the story otherwise, That some thieves, having robbed and murdered an honest traveller, threw his dead body into Elisha's grave, and it immediately revived. Elijah was honoured *in* his departure. Elisha was honoured *after* his departure. God thus dispenses honours as he pleases, but, one way or other, the rest of all the saints will be glorious, Isa. 11:10. It is good being near the saints and having our lot with them both in life and death.

II. The sword of Joash king of Israel; and we find it successful against the Syrians. 1. The cause of his success was God's favour (*v.* 23): *The Lord was gracious to them, had compassion on them* in their miseries and *respect unto them.* The several expressions here of the same import call upon us to observe and admire the triumphs of divine goodness in the deliverance of such a provoking people. It was of the Lord's mercies that they were not consumed, because he would not destroy them as yet. He foresaw they would destroy themselves at last, but as yet he would reprieve them, and give them space to repent. The slowness of God's processes against sinners must be construed to the honour of his mercy, not the impeachment of his justice. 2. The effect of his success was Israel's benefit. He recovered out of the hands of Benhadad the cities of Israel which the Syrians were possessed of, *v.* 25. This was a great kindness to the cities themselves, which were hereby brought from under the yoke of oppression, and to the whole kingdom, which was much strengthened by the reduction of those cities. Thrice Joash beat the Syrians, just as often as he had struck the ground with the arrows, and then a full stop was put to the course of his victories. Many have repented, when it was too late, of their distrusts and the straitness of their desires.

CHAPTER 14

This chapter continues the history of the succession in the kingdoms both of Judah and Israel. I. In the kingdom of Judah here is, 1. The entire history (as much as is recorded in this book) of Amaziah's reign (1.) His good character (v. 1–4). (2.) The justice he executed on the murderers of his father (v. 5, 6). (3.) His victory over the Edomites (v. 7). (4.) His war with Joash, and his defeat in that war (v. 8–14). (5.) His fall, as last, by a conspiracy against him (v. 17–20). 2. The beginning of the history of Azariah (v. 21, 22). II. In the kingdom of Israel, the conclusion of the reign of Joash (v. 15, 16), and the entire history of Jeroboam his son, the second of that name (v. 23–29). How many great men are made to stand in a little compass in God's book!

Verses 1–7

Amaziah, the son and successor of Joash, is the king whom here we have an account of. Let us take a view of him,

I. In the temple; and there he acted, in some measure, well, like Joash, but not like David, v. 3. He began well, but did not persevere: He *did that which was right in the sight of the Lord*, kept up his attendance on God's altars and his attention to God's word, yet not like David. It is not enough to do that which our pious predecessors did, merely to keep up the usage, but we must do it *as they* did it, from the same principle of faith and devotion and with the same sincerity and resolution. It is here taken notice of, as before, that *the high places were not taken away, v.* 4. It is hard to get clear of those corruptions which, by long usage, have gained both prescription and a favourable opinion.

II. On the bench; and there we have him doing justice on the traitors that murdered his father, not as soon as ever he came to the crown, lest it should occasion some disturbance, but he prudently deferred it till *the kingdom was confirmed in his hand, v.* 5. To weaken a factious party gradually, when it is not safe to provoke, often proves the way to ruin it effectually. Justice strikes surely by striking slowly, and is often executed most prudently when it is not executed presently. Wisdom here is profitable to direct. Amaziah did thus, 1. According to the rule of the law, that ancient rule, that *he that sheds man's blood by man shall his blood be shed.* Never let traitors or murderers expect to come to their graves like other men. *Let them flee to the pit, and let no man stay them.* 2. Under the limitation of the law: *The children of the murderers he slew not*, because the law of Moses had expressly provided that *the children should not be put to death for the fathers, v.* 6. It is probable that this is taken notice of because there were those about him that advised him to that rigour, both in revenge (because the crime was extraordinary — the murder of a king) and in policy, that the children might not plot against him, in revenge of their father's death. But against these insinuations he opposed the express law of God (Deu. 24:16), which he was to judge by, and which he resolved to adhere to and trust God with the issue. God visits the iniquity of the fathers upon the children, because every man is guilty before him and owes him a death; so that, if he require the life for the father's sin, he does not wrong, the sinner having forfeited it already by his own. But he does not allow earthly princes to do thus: the children, before them, are innocent, and therefore must not suffer as guilty.

III. In the field; and there we find him triumphing over the Edomites, v. 7. Edom had *revolted from under the hand of Judah* in Joram's time, *ch.* 8:22. Now he makes war upon them to bring them back to their allegiance, kills 10,000 and takes the chief city of Arabia the stony (called *Selah — a rock*), and gave it a new name. We shall find a larger account of this expedition, 2 Chr. 25:5, etc.

Verses 8–14

For several successions after the division of the kingdoms that of Judah suffered much by the *enmity* of Israel. After Asa's time, for several successions, it suffered more by the *friendship* of Israel, and by the alliance and affinity made with them. But now we meet with hostility between them again, which had not been for some ages before.

I. Amaziah, upon no provocation, and without showing any cause of quarrel, challenged Joash into the field (v. 8): "*Come, let us look one another in the face;* let us try our strength in battle." Had he challenged him to a personal duel only, the error would have remained with himself, but each must bring all their forces into the field, and thousands of lives on both sides must be sacrificed to his capricious humour. Hereby he showed himself proud, presumptuous, and prodigal of blood. Some think that he intended to avenge the injury which the dismissed disgusted Israelites had lately done to his country, in their return (2 Chr. 25:13), and that he had also the vanity to think of subduing the kingdom of Israel, and reuniting it to Judah. A *fool's lips thus enter into contention, and his mouth calleth for strokes.* Those that challenge are chargeable with that beginning of strife, which is as the letting forth of water. He that is eager either to fight or to go to law may perhaps have enough of it quickly, and be the first that repents it.

II. Joash sent him a grave rebuke for his challenge, with advice to withdraw it, v. 9, 10. 1. He mortifies his pride, by comparing himself to a cedar, a stately tree, and Amaziah to a thistle, a sorry weed, telling him he was so far from fearing him that he despised him, and scorned as much to have any thing to do with him, or make any alliance with him, as the cedar would to match his daughter to a thistle. The ancient house of David he thinks not worthy to be named the same day with the house of Jehu, though an upstart. How may a humble man smile to hear two proud and scornful men set their wits on work to vilify and undervalue one another! 2. He foretels his fall: *A wild beast trode down the thistle,* and so put an end to his treaty with the cedar; so easily does Joash think his forces can crush Amaziah, and so unable does he think him to make any resistance. 3. He shows him the folly of his challenge: "*Thou hast indeed smitten Edom,* a weak, unarmed, undisciplined body of men, and therefore thinkest thou canst carry all before thee and subdue the regular forces of Israel with as much ease. *Thy heart has lifted thee up.*" See where the root of all sin lies; it is in the heart, thence it flows, and that must bear the blame. It is not Providence, the event, the occasion (whatever it is), that makes men proud, or secure, or discontented, or the like, but it is their own heart that does it. "Thou art proud of the blow thou hast given to Edom, as if that had made thee formidable to all mankind." Those wretchedly deceive themselves that magnify their own performances, and, because they have been blessed with some little success and reputation, conclude themselves fit for any thing and no less sure of it. 4. He counsels him to be content with the honour he has won, and not to hazard that, by grasping at more that was out of his reach: *Why shouldst thou meddle to thy hurt,* as fools often do, that will be meddling? Prov. 20:3. Many would have had wealth and honour enough if they had but known when they had enough. He warns him of the consequence, that it would be fatal not to himself only, but to his kingdom, which he ought to protect.

III. Amaziah persisted in his resolution, and the issue was bad; he had better have tarried at home, for Joash gave him such a look in the face as put him to confusion. Challengers commonly prove to be on the losing side. 1. His army was routed and dispersed, v. 12. Josephus says, When they were to engage they were struck with such terror that they did not strike a stroke, but every one made the best of his way. 2. He himself was taken prisoner by the king of Israel, and then had enough of *looking him in the face.* Amaziah's pedigree comes in here somewhat abruptly *(the son of Joash, the son of Ahaziah)*, because perhaps he had gloried in the dignity of his ancestors, or because he now smarted for their iniquity. 3. The conqueror entered Jerusalem, which tamely opened to him, and yet he broke down their wall (and, as Josephus says, drove his chariot in triumph through the breach), in reproach to them, and that he might, when he pleased, take possession of the royal city. 4. He plundered Jerusalem, took away all that was valuable, and returned to Samaria, laden with spoils, v. 14. It was said of Joash that he did that which was *evil in the sight of the Lord*, and of Amaziah that he did *that which was right;* and yet Joash triumphs thus over Amaziah, and why so? Because God would show, in Amaziah's fate, that he resists the proud, or because, whatever they were otherwise, Joash had lately been respectful to one of God's prophets (*ch.* 13:14), but Amaziah had been abusive to another (2 Chr. 25:16), and God will honour those who honour him in his prophets, but those who despise them, and him in them, shall be lightly esteemed.

Verses 15–22

Here are three kings brought to their graves in these few verses: — 1. Joash king of Israel, v. 15, 16. We attended his funeral once before, ch. 13:12, 13. But, because the historian had occasion to give a further account of his life and actions, he again mentions his death and burial. 2. Amaziah king of Judah. Fifteen years he survived his conqueror the king of Israel, v. 17. A man may live a great while after he has been shamed, may be thoroughly mortified (as Amaziah no doubt was) and yet not dead. His acts are said to be found written in his annals (v. 18), but not his might; for his cruelty when he was a conqueror over the Edomites, and his insolence when he challenged the king of Israel, showed him void of true courage. He was slain by his own subjects, who hated him for his maladministration (v. 19) and made Jerusalem too hot for him, the ignominious breach made in their walls being occasioned by his folly and presumption. He fled to Lachish. How long he continued concealed or sheltered there we are not told, but, at last, he was there murdered, v. 19. No further did the rage of the rebels extend, for they brought him in a chariot to Jerusalem, and buried him there among his ancestors. 3. Azariah succeeded Amaziah, but not till twelve years after his father's death, for Amaziah died in the fifteenth year of Jeroboam (as appears by comparing v. 23 with v. 2), but Azariah did not begin his reign till the twenty-seventh of Jeroboam (ch. 15:1), for he was but four years old at the death of his father, so that, for twelve years, till he came to be sixteen, the government was in the hands of protectors. He reigned very long (ch. 15:2) and yet the account of his reign is here industriously huddled up, and broken off abruptly (v. 22): He built Elath (which had belonged to the Edomites, but, it is probable, was recovered by his father, v. 7), *after that the king slept with his fathers,* as if that had been all he did that was worth mentioning, or rather it is meant of king Amaziah: he built it soon after Amaziah died.

Verses 23–29

Here is an account of the reign of Jeroboam the second. I doubt it is an indication of the affection and adherence of the house of Jehu to the sins of *Jeroboam the son of Nebat, who made Israel to sin,* that they called an heir-apparent to the crown by his name, thinking that an honourable name which in the book of God is infamous and stigmatized as much as any.

I. His reign was long, the longest of all the reigns of the kings of Israel: *He reigned forty-one years;* yet his contemporary Azariah, the king of Judah, reigned longer, even fifty-two years. This Jeroboam reigned just as long as Asa had done (1 Ki. 15:10), yet one did that which was good and the other that which was evil. We cannot measure men's characters by the length of their lives or by their outward prosperity. *There is one event to the righteous and to the wicked.*

II. His character was the same with that of the rest of those kings: *He did that which was evil* (v. 24), for *he departed not from the sins of Jeroboam;* he kept up the worship of the calves, and never left that, thinking there was no harm in it, because it had been the way of all his ancestors and predecessors. But a sin is never the less evil in God's sight, whatever it is in ours, for its being an ancient usage; and a frivolous plea it will be against doing good, that we have been accustomed to do evil.

III. Yet he prospered more than most of them, for though, in that one thing, he did evil in the sight of the Lord, yet it is likely, in other respects, there was some good found in him and therefore God owned him, 1. By prophecy. He raised up Jonah the son of Amittai, a Galilean (so much were those mistaken that said, *Out of Galilee ariseth no prophet,* Jn. 7:52), and by him intimated the purposes of his favour to Israel, notwithstanding their provocations, encouraged him and his kingdom to take up arms for the recovery of their ancient possessions, and (which would contribute not a little to their success) assured them of victory. It is a sign that God has not cast off his people if he continue faithful ministers among them; when Elisha, who strengthened the hands of Joash, was removed, Jonah was sent to encourage his son. Happy is the land that has a succession of prophets running parallel with a succession of princes, that the word of the Lord may endure for ever. Of this Jonah we read much in that little book of scripture that bears his name. It is probable that it was when he was a young man, and fit for such an expedition, that God sent him to Nineveh, and that it was when he had yet been but a little conversant with the visions of God that he flew off and fretted as he did; and, if so, this is an undoubted evidence of the forgiveness of his faults and follies, that he was afterwards employed as a messenger of mercy to Israel. A commission amounts to a pardon, and he that had himself found mercy, notwithstanding his provocations, could the better encourage them with the hope of mercy notwithstanding theirs. Some that have been foolish and passionate, and have gone about their work very awkwardly at first, yet afterwards have proved useful and eminent. Men must not be thrown away for every fault. 2. By providence. The event was *according to the word of the Lord:* his arms were successful; he *restored the coast of Israel,* recovered those frontier-towns and countries that lay from Hamath in the north to the sea of the plain, (that is, the sea of Sodom) in the south, all which the Syrians had possessed themselves of, *v.* 25. Two reasons are here given why God blessed them with those victories: — (1.) Because their distress was very great, which made them the objects of his compassion, *v.* 26. Though he saw not any signs of their repentance and formation, yet *he saw their affliction, that it was very bitter.* Those that lived in those countries which the enemies were masters of were miserably oppressed and enslaved, and could call nothing their own; the rest, we may suppose, were much impoverished by the frequent incursions the enemy made upon them to plunder them, and continually terrified by their threatenings, so that *there was none shut up or left,* both towns and countries were laid waste and stripped of their wealth, and no helper appeared. To this extremity were they reduced, in many parts of the country, in the beginning of Jeroboam's reign, when God, in mere pity to them, heard the cry of their affliction (for no mention is made here of the cry of their prayers), and wrought this deliverance for them by the hand of Jeroboam. Let those whose case is pitiable take comfort from the divine pity; we read of God's bowels of mercy (Isa. 63:15; Jer. 31:20) and that he is full of compassion, Ps. 86:15. (2.) Because the decree had not yet gone forth for their utter destruction; he had not as yet said *he would blot out the name of Israel* (*v.* 27), and because he had not said it he would not do it. If this be understood of the dispersion of the ten tribes, he did say it and do it, for that name still remains under heaven in the *gospel Israel,* and will to the end of time; and because they, at present, bore that name which was to have this lasting honour, he showed them this favour, as well as for the sake of the ancient honour of that name, *ch.* 13:23.

IV. Here is the conclusion of Jeroboam's reign. We read (*v.* 28) of his might, and how he warred, but (*v.* 29) he *slept with his fathers;* for the mightiest must yield to death, and there is no discharge in that war. Many prophets there had been in Israel, a constant succession of them in every age, but none of the prophets had left any of their prophecies in writing till those of this age began to do it, and their prophecies are part of the canon of scripture. It was in the reign of this Jeroboam that *Hosea* (who continued very long a prophet) began to prophesy, and he was the first that wrote his prophecies; therefore the word of the Lord by him is called *the beginning of the word of the Lord,* Hos. 1:2. Then *that part of the word of the Lord* began to be written. At the same time *Amos* prophesied, and wrote his prophecy, soon afterwards *Micah,* and then *Isaiah,* in the days of Ahaz and Hezekiah. Thus God never left himself without witness, but, in the darkest and most degenerate ages of the church, raised up some to be burning and shining lights in it to their own age by their preaching and living, and a few by their writings to reflect light upon us on whom the ends of the world have come.

CHAPTER 15

In this chapter, I. The history of two of the kings of Judah is briefly recorded: — 1. Of Azariah, or Uzziah (*v.* 1-7). 2. Of Jotham his son (*v.* 32-38). II. The history of many of the kings of Israel that reigned at the same time is given us in short, five in succession, all of whom, except one, went down slain to the pit, and their murders were their successors. 1. Zachariah, the last of the house of Jehu, reigned six months, and then was slain and succeeded by Shallum (*v.* 8-12). 2. Shallum reigned one month, and then was slain and succeeded by Menahem (*v.* 13-15). 3. Menahem reigned ten years, or tyrannised rather, such were his barbarous cruelties (*v.* 16) and

unreasonable exactions (*v.* 20), and then died in his bed, and left his son to succeed him first, and then suffer for him (*v.* 16-22). 4. Pekahiah reigned two years, and then was slain and succeeded by Pekah (*v.* 23-26). 5. Pekah reigned twenty years, and then was slain and succeeded by Hoshea, the last of all the kings of Israel (*v.* 27-31) for things were now working and hastening apace towards the final destruction of that kingdom.

Verses 1-7

This is a short account of the reign of Azariah. 1. Most of it is general, and the same that has been given of others; he began young and reigned long (*v.* 2), did, for the most part, that which was right, *v.* 3 (it was happy for the kingdom that a good reign was a long one), only he had not zeal and courage enough to take away the high places, *v.* 4. 2. That which is peculiar, *v.* 5 (that God smote him with a leprosy) is more largely related, with the occasion of it, 2 Chr. 26:16, etc., where we have also a fuller account of the glories of the former part of his reign, as well as of the disgraces of the latter part of it. He did that which was right, as Amaziah had done; like him, he began well, but failed before he finished. Here we are told, (1.) That he was a leper. The greatest of men are not only subject to the common calamities, but also to the common infirmities, of human nature; and, if they be guilty of any heinous sin, they lie as open as the meanest to the most grievous strokes of divine vengeance. (2.) God smote him with this leprosy, to chastise him for his presumptuous invasion of the priests' office. If great men be proud men, some way or other God will humble them, and make them know he is both above them and against them, for he resisteth the proud. (3.) That he was a leper *to the day of his death.* Though we have reason to think he repented and the sin was pardoned, yet, for warning to others, he was continued under this mark of God's displeasure as long as he lived, and perhaps it was for the good of his soul that he was so. (4.) That he *dwelt in a separate house,* as being made ceremonially unclean by the law, to the discipline of which, though a king, he must submit. He that presumptuously intruded into God's temple, and pretended to be a priest, was justly shut out from his own palace, and shut up as a prisoner or recluse, ever after. We suppose that his *separate house* was made as convenient and agreeable as might be. Some translate it a *free house,* where he had liberty to take his pleasure. However, it was a great mortification to one that had been so much a man of honour, and a man of business, as he had been, to be cut off from society and dwell always in a *separate house:* it would almost make life itself a burden, even to kings, though they have never any to converse with but their inferiors; the most contemplative men would soon be weary of it. (5.) That his son was his viceroy in the affairs both of his court (for *he was over the house*) and of his kingdom (for he was *judging the people of the land*); and it was both a comfort to him and a blessing to his kingdom that he had such a son to fill up his room.

Verses 8-31

The best days of the kingdom of Israel were while the government was in Jehu's family. In his reign, and the next three reigns, though there were many abominable corruptions and miserable grievances in Israel, yet the crown went in succession, the kings died in their beds, and some care was taken of public affairs; but, now that those days are at an end, the history which we have in these verses of about thirty-three years represents the affairs of that kingdom in the utmost confusion imaginable. Woe to those that were with child (*v.* 16) and to those that gave suck in those days, for then must needs be great tribulations, when, for *the transgression of the land, many were the princes thereof.*

I. Let us observe something, in general, concerning these unhappy revolutions and the calamities which must needs attend them — these bad times, as they may truly be called. 1. God had tried the people of Israel both with judgments and mercies, explained and enforced by his servants the prophets, and yet they continued impenitent and unreformed, and therefore God justly brought these miseries upon them, as Moses had warned them. If you will yet *walk contrary to me, I will punish you yet seven times more,* Lev. 26:21, etc. 2. God made good his promise to Jehu, that his sons to the fourth generation after him should sit upon the throne of Israel, which was a greater favour than was shown to any of the royal families either

before or after his. God had said it should be so (*ch.* 10:30) and we are told in this chapter (*v.* 12) that so it came to pass. See how punctual God is to his promises. These calamities God long designed for Israel, and they deserved them, yet they were not inflicted till that word had taken effect to the full. Thus God rewarded Jehu for his zeal in destroying the worship of Baal and the house of Ahab; and yet, when the measure of the sins of the house of Jehu was full, God avenged upon it the blood then shed, called *the blood of Jezreel,* Hos. 1:4. 3. All these kings did that which was *evil in the sight of the Lord,* for *they walked in the sins of Jeroboam the son of Nebat.* Though at variance with one another, yet in this they agreed, to keep up idolatry, and the people loved to have it so; though they were emptied from vessel to vessel, that *taste remained in them,* and *that scent was not changed.* It was sad indeed when their government was so often altered, yet never for the better — that among all those contending interests none of them should think it as much their interest to destroy the calves as others had done to support them. 4. Each of these (except one) conspired against his predecessor, and slew him — *Shallum, Menahem, Pekah,* and *Hoshea,* all traitors and murderers, and yet all kings awhile, one of them ten, another twenty, and another nine years; for God may suffer wickedness to prosper and to carry away the wealth and honours awhile, but, sooner or later, blood shall have blood, and he that dealt treacherously shalt be dealt treacherously with. One wicked man is often made a scourge to another, and every wicked man, at length, a ruin to himself. 5. The ambition of the great men made the nation miserable. Here is Tiphsah, a city of Israel, barbarously destroyed, with all the coasts thereof, by one of these pretenders (*v.* 16), and no doubt it was through blood that each of them waded to the throne, nor could any of these kings perish alone. No land can have greater pests, nor Israel worse troubles, than such men as care not how much the welfare and repose of their country are sacrificed to their revenge and affectation of dominion. 6. While the nation was thus shattered by divisions at home the kings of Assyria, first one (*v.* 19) and then another (*v.* 29), came against it and did what they pleased. Nothing does more towards the making of a nation an easy prey to a common enemy than intestine broils and contests for the sovereignty. Happy the land where that is settled. 7. This was the condition of Israel just before they were quite ruined and carried away captive, for that was in the ninth year of Hoshea, the last of these usurpers. If they had, in these days of confusion and perplexity, humbled themselves before God and sought his face, that final destruction might have been prevented; but when God judgeth he will overcome. These factions, the fruit of an evil spirit sent among them, hastened that captivity, for a kingdom thus divided against itself will soon come to desolation.

II. Let us take a short view of the particular reigns.

1. Zachariah, the son of Jeroboam, began to reign in the thirty-eighth year of Azariah, or Uzziah, king of Judah, *v.* 8. Some of the most critical chronologers reckon that between Jeroboam and his son Zachariah the throne was vacant twenty-two years, others eleven years, through the disturbances and dissensions that were in the kingdom; and then it was not strange that Zachariah was deposed before he was well seated on the throne: he reigned but six months, and then Shallum *slew him before the people,* perhaps as Caesar was slain in the senate, or he put him to death publicly as a criminal, with the approbation of the people, to whom he had, some way or other, made himself odious; so ended the line of Jehu.

2. But had Shallum peace, who slew his master? No, he had not (*v.* 13), one month of days measured his reign and then he was cut off; perhaps to this the prophet, who then lived, refers (Hos. 5:7), *Now shall a month devour them with their portions.* That dominion seldom lasts long which is founded in blood and falsehood. Menahem, either provoked by his crime or animated by his example, soon served him as he had served his master — *slew him and reigned in his stead, v.* 14. Probably he was general in the army, which then lay encamped at Tirzah, and, hearing of Shallum's treason and usurpation, hastened to punish it, as Omri did that of Zimri in a like case, 1 Ki. 16:17.

3. Menahem held the kingdom ten years, *v.* 17. But, whereas we have heard that the *kings of the house of Is-*

rael were merciful kings (1 Ki. 20:31), this Menahem (the scandal of his country) was so prodigiously cruel to those of his own nation who hesitated a little at submitting to him that he not only ruined a city, and the coasts thereof, but, forgetting that he himself was born of a woman, *ripped up all the women with child, v.* 16. We may well wonder that ever it should enter into the heart of any man to be so barbarous, and to be so perfectly lost to humanity itself. By these cruel methods he hoped to strengthen himself and to frighten all others into his interests; but it seems he did not gain his point, for when the king of Assyria came against him, (1.) So little confidence had he in his people that he durst not meet him as an enemy, but was obliged, at a vast expense, to purchase a peace with him. (2.) Such need had he of help *to confirm the kingdom in his hand* that he made it part of his bargain with him (a bargain which, no doubt, the king of Assyria knew how to make a good hand of another time) that he should assist him against his own subjects that were disaffected to him. The money wherewith he purchased his friendship was a vast sum, no less than 1000 talents of silver (*v.* 19), which Menahem exacted, it is probable, by military execution, *of all the mighty men of wealth,* very considerately sparing the poor, and laying the burden (as was fit) on those that were best able to bear it; being raised, it was given *to the king of Assyria,* as pay for his army, fifty shekels of silver for each man in it. Thus he got clear of the king of Assyria for this time; he staid not to quarter in the land (*v.* 20), but his army now got so rich a booty with so little trouble that it encouraged them to come again, not long after, when they laid all waste. Thus was *he* the betrayer of his country that should have been the protector of it.

4. Pekahiah, the son of Menahem, succeeded his father, but reigned only two years, and then was treacherously slain by Pekah, falling under the load both of his own and of his father's wickedness. It is repeated concerning him as before that he *departed not from the sins of Jeroboam.* Still this is mentioned, to show that God was righteous in bringing that destruction upon them which came not long after, because they hated to be reformed, *v.* 24. Pekah, it seems, had some persons of figure in his interest, two of whom are here named (*v.* 25), and with their help he compassed his design.

5. Pekah, though he got the kingdom by treason, kept it twenty years (*v.* 27), so long it was before his violent dealing returned upon his own head, but it returned at last. This Pekah, son of Remaliah, (1.) Made himself more considerable abroad than any of these usurpers, for he was, even in the latter end of his time (in the reign of Ahaz, which began in his seventeenth year), a great terror to the kingdom of Judah, as we find, Isa. 7:1, etc. (2.) He lost a great part of his kingdom to the king of Assyria. Several cities are here named (*v.* 29) which were taken from him, all the land of Gilead on the other side Jordan, and Galilee in the north containing the tribes of Naphtali and Zebulon, were seized, and the inhabitants carried captive into Assyria. By this judgment God punished him for his attempt upon Judah and Jerusalem. It was then foretold that within two or three years after he made that attempt, before a child, then born, should be able to cry *My father and my mother,* the riches of Samaria should be *taken away before the king of Assyria* (Isa. 8:4), and here we have the accomplishment of that prediction. (3.) Soon after this he forfeited his life to the resentments of his countrymen, who, it is probable, were disgusted at him for leaving them exposed to a foreign enemy, while he was invading Judah, of which Hoshea took advantage and, to gain his crown, seized his life, *slew him, and reigned in his stead.* Surely he was fond of a crown indeed who, at this time, would run such a hazard as a traitor did; for the crown of Israel, now that it had lost the choicest of its flowers and jewels, was lined more than ever with thorns, had of late been fatal to all the heads that had worn it, was forfeited to divine justice, and now ready to be laid in the dust — a crown which a wise man would not have taken up in the street, yet Hoshea not only ventured *upon* it but ventured *for* it, and it cost him dear.

Verses 32–38

We have here a short account of the reign of Jotham king of Judah, of whom we are told, 1. That he reigned very well, *did that which was right in the sight of the Lord, v.* 34. Josephus gives him a very high character, stating that he was pious towards God, just towards men, and laid out himself for the public good, — that, whatever was amiss, he took care to have it rectified, — and, in short, wanted no virtue that became a good prince. Though the high places were not taken away, yet to draw people from them, and keep them close to God's holy place, he showed great respect to the temple, and built the higher gate which he went through to the temple. If magistrates cannot do all they would for the suppressing of vice and profaneness, let them do so much the more for the support and advancement of piety and virtue, and the bringing of them into reputation. If they cannot pull down the high places of sin, yet let them build and beautify the high gate of God's house. 2. That he died in the midst of his days, *v.* 33. Of most of the kings of Judah we are told how old they were when they began their reign, and by that may compute how old they were when they died; but no account is kept of the *age* of any of the kings of Israel that I remember, only of the years of their *reigns.* This honour God would put upon the kings of the house of David above those of other families. And by these accounts it appears that there was none of all the kings of Judah that reached David's age, seventy, the common age of man. Asa's age I do not find. Uzziah lived to be sixty-eight, Manasseh sixty-seven, and Jehoshaphat sixty; and these were the three oldest; many of those that were of note did not reach fifty. This Jotham died at forty-one. He was too great a blessing to be continued long to such an unworthy people. His death was a judgment, especially considering the character of his son and successor. 3. That in his days the confederacy was formed against Judah by Rezin and Remaliah's son, the king of Syria and the king of Israel, which appeared so very formidable in the beginning of the reign of Ahaz that, upon notice of it, the heart of that prince was moved and *the heart of the people, as the trees of the wood are moved with the wind,* Isa. 7:2. The confederates were unjust in the attempt, yet it is here said (*v.* 37), *The Lord began to send them against Judah,* as he bade Shimei curse David, and took away from Job what the Sabeans robbed him of. Men are God's hand — the sword, the rod in his hand — which he makes use of as he pleases to serve his own righteous counsels, though men be unrighteous in their intentions. This storm gathered in the reign of pious Jotham, but he came to his grave in peace and it fell upon his degenerate son.

CHAPTER 16

This chapter is wholly taken up with the reign of Ahaz; and we have quite enough of it, unless it were better. He had a good father, and a better son, and yet was himself one of the worst of the kings of Judah. I. He was a notorious idolater (*v.* 1–4). II. With the treasures of the temple, as well as his own, he hired the king of Assyria to invade Syria and Israel (*v.* 5–9). III. He took pattern from an idol's altar which he saw at Damascus for a new altar in God's temple (*v.* 10–16). IV. He abused and embezzled the furniture of the temple (*v.* 17, 18). And so his story ends (*v.* 19, 20).

Verses 1–4

We have here a general character of the reign of Ahaz. Few and evil were his days — few, for he died at thirty-six — evil, for we are here told, 1. That he *did not that which was right like David* (*v.* 2), that is, he had none of that concern and affection for the instituted service and worship of God for which David was celebrated. He had no love for the temple, made no conscience of his duty to God, nor had any regard to his law. Herein he was unlike David; it was his honour that he was of the house and lineage of David, and it was owing to God's ancient covenant with David that he was now upon the throne, which aggravated his wickedness; for he was a reproach to that honourable name and family, which therefore was really a reproach to him *(Degeneranti genus opprobrium — A good extraction is a disgrace to him who degenerates from it),* and though he enjoyed the benefit of David's piety he did not tread in the steps of it. 2. That he walked *in the way of the kings of Israel* (*v.* 3), who all worshipped the calves. He was not joined in any affinity with them, as Jehoram and Ahaziah were with the house of Ahab, but, *ex mero motu — without any instigation,* walked in their way. The kings of Israel pleaded policy and reasons of state for their idolatry, but Ahaz had no such pretence: in him it was the most unreasonable impolitic thing that could be. They were his enemies, and had proved enemies to themselves too by their idolatry; yet he walked in their way. 3. That he *made his sons to pass through the fire,* to the honour of his dunghill-deities. He burnt them, so it is expressly said of him (2 Chr. 28:3), burnt some of them, and perhaps made others of them (Hezekiah himself not excepted, though afterwards he was never the worse for it) to pass between two fires, or to be drawn through a flame, in token of their dedication to the idol. 4. That he did *according to the abominations of the heathen whom the Lord had cast out.* it was an instance of his great folly that he would be guided in his religion by those whom he saw fallen into the ditch before his eyes, and follow them; and it was an instance of his great impiety that he would conform to those usages which God had declared to be abominable to him, and set himself to write after the copy of those whom God had cast out, thus walking directly contrary to God. 5. That he *sacrificed in the high places, v.* 4. If his father had but had zeal enough to take them away, the debauching of his sons might have been prevented; but those that connive at sin know not what dangerous snares they lay for those that come after them. He forsook God's house, was weary of that place where, in his father's time, he had often been detained before the Lord, and performed his devotions on high hills, where he had a better prospect, and under green trees, where he had a more pleasant shade. It was a religion little worth, which was guided by fancy, not by faith.

Verses 5–9

Here is, 1. The attempt of his confederate neighbours, the kings of Syria and Israel, upon him. They thought to make themselves masters of Jerusalem, and to set a king of their own in it, Isa. 7:6. In this they fell short, but the king of Syria recovered Elath, a considerable port upon the Red Sea, which Amaziah had taken from the Syrians, *ch.* 14:22. What can those keep that have lost their religion? Let them expect, thenceforward, to be always on the losing hand. 2. His project to get clear of them. Having forsaken God, he had neither courage nor strength to make head against his enemies, nor could he, with any boldness, ask help of God; but he made his court to the king of Assyria, and got him to come in for his relief. Those whose hearts condemn them will go any where in a day of distress rather than to God. Was it because there was not a God in Israel that he sent to the Assyrian for help? Was the rock of ages removed out of its place, that he stayed himself on this broken reed? The sin itself was its own punishment; for, though it is true that he gained his point (the king of Assyria hearkened to him, and, to serve his own turn, made a descent upon Damascus, whereby he gave a powerful diversion to the king of Syria, *v.* 9, and obliged him to let fall his design against Ahaz, carrying the Syrians captive to Kir, as Amos had expressly foretold, *ch.* 1:5), yet, considering all, he made but a bad bargain; for, to compass this, (1.) He enslaved himself (*v.* 7): *I am thy servant and thy son,* that is, "I will be as dutiful and obedient to thee as to a master or father, if thou wilt but do me this good turn." Had he thus humbled himself to God, and implored his favour, he might have been delivered upon easier terms; he might have saved his money, and needed only to have parted with his sins. But, if the prodigal forsake his father's house, he soon becomes a slave to the worst of masters, Lu. 15:15. (2.) He impoverished himself; for he took the silver and gold that were laid up in the treasury both of the temple and of the kingdom, and sent it to the king of Assyria, *v.* 8. Both church and state must be squeezed and exhausted, to gratify this his new patron and guardian. I know not what authority he had thus to dispose of the public stock; but it is common for those that have brought themselves into straits by one sin to help themselves out by another; and those that have alienated themselves from God will make no difficulty of alienating any of his rights.

Verses 10–16

Though Ahaz had himself sacrificed in high places, on hills, and under every green tree (*v.* 4), yet God's altar had hitherto continued in its place and in use, and the *king's burnt-offering and his meat-offering* (*v.* 15) had been offered upon it by the priests that attended it; but here we have it taken away by wicked Ahaz, and another altar, an idolatrous one, put in the room of it — a bolder stroke than the worst of the kings had yet given to religion. We have here,

I. The model of this new altar, taken from one at Damascus, by the king himself, *v.* 10. The king of Assyria having taken Damascus, thither Ahaz went, to congratulate him on his success, to return him thanks for the kindness he had done him by this expedition, and, as his servant and son, to receive his commands. Had he been faithful to his God, he would not have needed to crouch thus meanly to a foreign power. At Damascus, either while viewing the rarities of the place, or rather while joining with them in their devotions (for, when he was there, he thought it no harm to do as they did), he saw an altar that pleased his fancy extremely, not such a plain old-fashioned one as that which he had been trained up in attendance upon at Jerusalem, but curiously carved, it is likely, and adorned with image-work; there were many pretty things about it which he thought significant, surprising, very charming, and calculated to excite his devotion. Solomon had but a dull fancy, he thought, compared with the ingenious artist that made this altar. Nothing will serve him but he must have an altar just like this: a pattern of it must be taken immediately; he cannot stay till he returns himself, but sends it before him in all haste, with orders to Urijah the priest to get one made exactly according to this model and have it ready against he came home. The pattern God showed to Moses in the mount or to David by the Spirit was not comparable to this pattern sent from Damascus. The hearts of idolaters walked after their eyes, which are therefore said to *go a whoring after their idols;* but the true worshippers worship the true God by faith.

II. The making of it by Urijah the priests, *v.* 11. This Urijah, it is likely, was the chief priest who at this time presided in the temple-service. To him Ahaz sent an intimation of his mind (for we read not of any express orders he gave him), to get an altar made by this pattern. And, without any dispute or objection, he put it in hand immediately, being perhaps as fond of it as the king was, at least being very willing to humour the king and desirous to curry favour with him. Perhaps he might have this excuse for gratifying the king herein, that, by this means, he might keep him to the temple at Jerusalem and prevent his totally deserting it for the high places and the groves. "Let us oblige him in this," thinks Urijah, "and then he will bring all his sacrifices to us; for by this craft we get our living." But, whatever pretence he had, it was a most base wicked thing for him that was a priest, a chief priest, to make this altar, in compliance with an idolatrous prince, for hereby, 1. He prostituted his authority and profaned the crown of his priesthood, making himself a servant to the lusts of men. There is not a greater disgrace to the ministry than obsequiousness to such wicked commands as this was. 2. He betrayed his trust. As priest, he was bound to maintain and defend God's institutions, and to oppose and witness against all innovations; and, for him to assist and serve the king in setting up an altar to confront the altar which by divine appointment he was consecrated to minister at, was such a piece of treachery and perfidiousness as may justly render him infamous to all posterity. Had he only connived at the doing of it, — had he been frightened into it by menaces, — had he endeavoured to dissuade the king from it, or but delayed the doing of it till he came home, that he might first talk with him about it, — it would not have been so bad; but so willingly to walk after his commandment, as if he were glad of the opportunity to oblige him, was such an affront to the God he served as was utterly inexcusable.

III. The dedicating of it. Urijah, perceiving that the king's heart was much upon it, took care to have it ready against he came down, and set it near the brazen altar, but somewhat lower and further from the door of the temple. The king was exceedingly pleased with it, approached it with all possible veneration, and offered thereon his burnt-offering, etc., *v.* 12, 13. His sacrifices were not offered to the God of Israel, but to the gods of Damascus (as we find 2 Chr. 28:23), and, when he borrowed the Syrians' altar, no marvel that he borrowed their gods. Naaman, the Syrian, embraced the God of Israel when he got earth from the land of Israel to make an altar of.

IV. The removal of God's altar, to make room for it. Urijah was so modest that he put this altar at the lower end of the court, and left God's altar in its place, *between this and the house of the Lord, v.* 14. But that would not satisfy Ahaz; he removed God's altar to an obscure corner in the north side of the court, and put his own before the sanctuary, in the place of it. He thinks his new altar is much more stately, and much more sightly, and disgraces that; and therefore "let that be laid aside as a vessel in which there is no pleasure." His superstitious invention, at first, jostled *with* God's sacred institution, but at length jostled it *out.* Note, Those will soon come to make nothing of God that will not be content to make him their all. Ahaz durst not (perhaps for fear of the people) quite demolish the brazen altar and knock it to pieces; but, while he ordered all the sacrifices to be offered upon this new altar (*v.* 15), *The brazen altar* (says he) *shall be for me to enquire by.* Having thrust it out from the use for which it was instituted, which was to sanctify the gifts offered upon it, he pretends to advance it above its institution, which it is common for superstitious people to do. The altar was never designed for an oracle, yet Ahaz will have it for that use. The Romish church seemingly magnifies Christ's sacraments, yet wretchedly corrupts them. But some give another sense of Ahaz's purpose: "As for the brazen altar, I will consider what to do with it, and give order about it." The Jews say that, afterwards, of the brass of it he made that famous dial which was called *the dial of Ahaz, ch.* 20:11. The base compliance of the poor-spirited priest with the presumptuous usurpations of an ill-spirited king is again taken notice of (*v.* 16): *Urijah the priest did according to all that king Ahaz commanded.* Miserable is the case of great men when those that should reprove them for their sins strengthen and serve them in their sins.

Verses 17–20

Here is, I. Ahaz abusing the temple, not the building itself, but some of the furniture of it. 1. He defaced the bases on which the lavers were set (1 Ki. 7:28, 29) and took down the molten sea, *v.* 17. These the priests used for washing; against them therefore he seems to have had a particular spite. It is one of the greatest prejudices that can be done to religion to obstruct the purifying of the priests, the Lord's ministers. 2. He removed *the covert for the sabbath,* erected either in honour of the sabbath or for the conveniency of the priests, when, on the sabbath, they officiated in greater numbers than on other days. Whatever it was, it should seem that in removing it he intended to put a contempt upon the sabbath, and so to open as wide an inlet as any to all manner of impiety. 3. The king's entry, which led to the house of the Lord, for the convenience of the royal family (perhaps that ascent which Solomon had made, and which the queen of Sheba admired, 1 Ki. 10:5), he turned another way, to show that he did not intend to frequent the house of the Lord any more. This he did for the king of Assyria, to oblige him, who perhaps returned his visit, and found fault with this entry, as an inconvenience and disparagement to his palace. When those that have had a ready passage to the house of the Lord, to please their neighbours, turn it another way, they are going down the hill apace towards their ruin.

II. Ahaz resigning his life in the midst of his days, at thirty-six years of age (*v.* 19) and leaving his kingdom to a better man, Hezekiah his son (*v.* 20), who proved as much a friend to the temple as he had been an enemy to it. Perhaps this very son he had made to pass through the fire, and thereby dedicated him to Moloch; but God, by his grace, snatched him as a brand out of the burning.

CHAPTER 17

This chapter gives us an account of the captivity of the ten tribes, and so finishes the history of that kingdom, after it had continued about 265 years, from the setting up of Jeroboam the son of Nebat. In it we have, I. A short narrative of this destruction (*v.* 1–6). II. Remarks upon it, and the causes of it, for the justifying of God in it and for warning to others (*v.* 7–23). III. An account of the nations which succeeded them in the possession of their land, and the mongrel religion set up among them (*v.* 24–41).

Verses 1–6

We have here the reign and ruin of Hoshea, the last of the kings of Israel, concerning whom observe,

I. That, though he forced his way to the crown by treason and murder (as we read *ch.* 15:30), yet he gained not the possession of it till seven or eight years after; for it was in the fourth year of Ahaz that he slew Pekah, but did not himself begin to reign till the twelfth year of Ahaz, *v.* 1. Whether by the king of Assyria, or by the king of Judah, or by some of his own people, does not appear, but it seems so long he was kept out of the throne he aimed at. Justly were his bad practices thus chastised, and the word of the prophet was thus fulfilled (Hos. 10:3), *Now they shall say We have no king, because we feared not the Lord.*

II. That, though he was bad, yet not so bad as the kings of Israel had been before him (*v.* 2), not so devoted to the calves as they had been. One of them (that at Dan), the Jews say, had been, before this, carried away by the king of Assyria in the expedition recorded *ch.* 15:29, (to which perhaps the prophet refers, Hos. 8:5, *Thy calf, O Samaria! has cast thee off*), which made him put the less confidence in the other. And some say that this Hoshea took off the embargo which the former kings had put their subjects under, forbidding them to go up to Jerusalem to worship, which he permitted those to do that had a mind to it. But what shall we think of this dispensation of providence, that the destruction of the kingdom of Israel should come in the reign of one of the best of its kings? *Thy judgments,* O God! *are a great deep.* God would hereby show that in bringing this ruin upon them he designed to punish, 1. Not only the sins of that generation, but of the foregoing ages, and to reckon for the iniquities of their fathers, who had been long in filing the measure and treasuring up wrath against this day of wrath. 2. Not only the sins of their kings, but the sins of the people. If Hoshea was not so bad as the former kings, yet the people were as bad as those that went before them, and it was an aggravation of their badness, and brought ruin the sooner, that their king did not set them so bad an example as the former kings had done, nor hinder them from reforming; he gave them leave to do better, but they did as bad as ever, which laid the blame of their sin and ruin wholly upon themselves.

III. That the destruction came gradually. They were for some time made tributaries before they were made captives to the king of Assyria (*v.* 3), and, if that less judgment had prevailed to humble and reform them, the greater would have been prevented.

IV. That they brought it upon themselves by the indirect course they took to shake off the yoke of the king of Assyria, *v.* 4. Had the king and people of Israel applied to God, made their peace with him and their prayers to him, they might have recovered their liberty, ease, and honour; but they withheld their tribute, and trusted to the king of Egypt to assist them in their revolt, which, if it had taken effect, would have been but to change their oppressors. But Egypt became to them the staff of a broken reed. This provoked the king of Assyria to proceed against them with the more severity. Men get nothing by struggling with the net, but entangle themselves the more.

V. That it was an utter destruction that came upon them. 1. The king of Israel was made a prisoner; he was shut up and bound, being, it is probable, taken by surprise, before Samaria was besieged. 2. The land of Israel was made a prey. The army of the king of Assyria came up throughout all the land, made themselves master of it (*v.* 5), and treated the people as traitors to be punished with the sword of justice rather than as fair enemies. 3. The royal city of Israel was besieged, and at length taken. Three years it held out after the country was conquered, and no doubt a great deal of misery was endured at that time which is not particularly recorded; but the brevity of the story, and the passing of this matter over lightly, methinks, intimate that they were abandoned of God and he did not now regard the affliction of Israel, as sometimes as he had done. 4. The people of Israel were carried captives into Assyria, *v.* 6. The generality of the people, those that were of any note, were forced away into the conqueror's country, to be slaves and beggars there. (1.) Thus he was pleased to exercise a dominion over them, and to show that they were entirely at his disposal. (2.) By depriving them of their possessions and estates, real and personal, and exposing them to all the hardships and reproaches of a removal to a strange country, under the power of an imperious army, he chastised them for their rebellion and their endeavour to shake off his yoke. (3.) Thus he effectually prevented all such attempts for the future and secured their country to himself. (4.) Thus he got the benefit of their service in his own country, as Pharaoh did that of their fathers; and so this unworthy people were lost as they were found, and ended as they began, in servitude and under oppression. (5.) Thus he made room for those of his own country that had little, and little to do, at home, to settle in a good land, a land flowing with milk and honey. In all these several ways he served himself by this captivity of the ten tribes. We are here told in what places of his kingdom he disposed of them — in *Halah* and *Habor,* in places, we may suppose, far distant from each other, lest they should keep up a correspondence, incorporate again, and become formidable. There, we have reason to think, after some time they were so mingled with the nations that they were lost, and *the name of Israel was no more in remembrance.* Those that forgot God were themselves forgotten; those that studied to be like the nations were buried among them; and those that would not serve God in their own land were made to serve their enemies in a strange land. It is probable that they were the men of honour and estates who were carried captive, and that many of the meaner sort of people were left behind, many of every tribe, who either went over to Judah or became subject to the Assyrian colonies, and their posterity were *Galileans* or *Samaritans.* But thus ended Israel as a nation; now they became *Lo-ammi — not a people,* and *Lo-ruhamah — unpitied.* Now Canaan spued them out. When we read of their entry under Hoshea the son of Nun who would have thought that such as this should be their exit under Hoshea the son of Elah? Thus Rome's glory in Augustus sunk, many ages after, in Augustulus. Providence so ordered the eclipsing of the honour of the ten tribes that the honour of Judah (the royal tribe) and Levi (the holy tribe), which yet remained, might shine the brighter. Yet we find a number sealed of every one of the twelve tribes (Rev. 7) except Dan. James writes to the twelve tribes scattered abroad (Jam. 1:1) and Paul speaks of the twelve tribes which *instantly served God day and night* (Acts 26:7); so that though we never read of those that were carried captive, nor have any reason to credit the conjecture of some (that they yet remain a distinct body in some remote corner of the world), yet a remnant of them did escape, to keep up the name of Israel, till it came to be worn by the gospel church, the spiritual Israel, in which it will ever remain, Gal. 6:16.

Verses 7–23

Though the destruction of the kingdom of the ten tribes was but briefly related, it is in these verses largely commented upon by our historian, and the reasons of it assigned, not taken from the second causes — the weakness of Israel, their impolitic management, and the strength and growing greatness of the Assyrian monarch (these things are overlooked) — but only from the First Cause. Observe, 1. It was *the Lord that removed Israel out of his sight;* whoever were the instruments, he was the author of this calamity. It was *destruction from the Almighty;* the Assyrian was but the *rod of his anger,* Isa. 10:5. It was *the Lord that rejected the seed of Israel,* else their enemies could not have seized upon them, *v.* 20. *Who gave Jacob for a spoil, and Israel to the robbers? Did not the Lord?* Isa. 43:24. We lose the benefit of national judgments if we do not eye the hand of God in them, and the fulfilling of the scripture, for that also is taken notice of here (*v.* 23): *The Lord removed Israel* out of his favour, and out of their own land, *as he had said by all his servants the prophets.* Rather shall heaven and earth pass than one tittle of God's word fall to the ground. When God's word and his works are compared, it will be found not only that they agree, but that they illustrate each other. But why would God ruin a people that were raised and incorporated, as Israel was, by miracles and oracles? Why would he undo that which he himself had done at so vast an expense? Was it purely an act of sovereignty? No, it was an act of necessary justice. For, 2. They provoked him to do this by their wickedness. Was it God's doing? Nay, it was their own; by their *way and their doings* they *procured all this to themselves,* and it was their own wickedness that did correct them. This the sacred historian shows here at large, that it might appear that God did them no wrong and that others might hear and fear. Come and see what it was that did all this mischief, that broke their power and laid their honour in the dust; it was sin; that, and nothing else, separated between them and God. This is here very movingly laid open as the cause of all the desolations of Israel. He here shows,

I. What God had done for Israel, to engage them to serve him. 1. He gave them their liberty (*v.* 7): He *brought them from under the hand of Pharaoh* who oppressed them, asserted their freedom *(Israel is my son),* and effected their freedom with a high hand. Thus they were bound in duty and gratitude to be his servants, for he had loosed their bonds; nor would he that rescued them out of the hand of the king of Egypt have contradicted himself so far as to deliver them into the hand of the king of Assyria, as he did, if they had not, by their iniquity, betrayed their liberty and sold themselves. 2. He gave them their law, and was himself their king. They were immediately under a divine regimen. They could not plead ignorance of good and evil, sin and duty, for God had particularly charged them against those very things which here he charges them with (*v.* 15), *That they should not do like the heathen.* Nor could they be in any doubt concerning their obligation to observe the laws which they are here charged with rejecting, for they were *the commandments and statutes* of the Lord their God (*v.* 13), so that no room was left to dispute whether they should keep them or no. He had not *dealt so with other nations,* Ps. 147:19, 20. 3. He gave them *their land,* for he *cast out the heathen from before them* (*v.* 8), to make room for them; and the casting out of them for their idolatries was as fair a warning as could be given to Israel not to do like them.

II. What they had done against God, notwithstanding these engagements which he had laid upon them. 1. In general. They *sinned against the Lord their God* (*v.* 7), they *did those things that were not right* (*v.* 9), but *secretly.* So wedded were they to their evil practices that when they could not do them publicly, could not for shame or could not for fear, they would do them secretly — an evidence of their atheism, that they thought what was done in secret was from under the eye of God himself and would not be required. Again, they wrought wicked things in such a direct contradiction to the divine law that they seemed as if they were done on purpose to *provoke the Lord to anger* (*v.* 11), in contempt of his authority and defiance of his justice. They *rejected God's statutes and his covenant* (*v.* 15), would not be bound up either by his command or the consent they themselves had given to the covenant, but threw off the obligations of both, and therefore God justly rejected them, *v.* 20. See Hos. 4:6. They *left all the commandments of the Lord their God* (*v.* 16), left the way, left the work, which those commandments prescribed them and directed them in. Nay, lastly, they *sold themselves to do evil in the sight of the Lord,* that is, they wholly addicted themselves to sin, as slaves to the service of those to whom they are sold, and, by their obstinately persisting in sin, so hardened their own hearts that at length it had become morally impossible for them to recover themselves, as one that has sold himself has put his liberty past recall. 2. In particular. Though they were guilty (no doubt) of many immoralities, and violated all the commands of the second table, yet nothing is here specified, but their idolatry. *This* was the sin that did most easily beset them; this was, of all sins, most provoking to God: it was the spiritual adultery that broke the marriage-covenant, and was the inlet of all other wickedness. Hence it is again and again mentioned here as the sin that ruined them. (1.) They feared other gods (*v.* 7), that is, worshipped them and paid their homage to them, as if they feared their displeasure. (2.) They *walked in the statutes of the heathen,* which were contrary to God's statutes (*v.* 8), did *as did the heathen* (*v.* 11), *went after the heathen that were round about them* (*v.* 15), so prostituting the honour of their peculiarity, and defeating God's design concerning them, which was that they should be distinguished from the heathen. Must those that were taught of God go to school to the heathen — those that were appropriated to God take their measures from the nations that were abandoned by him? (3.) They *walked in the statutes of the* idolatrous *kings of Israel* (*v.* 8), *in all the sins of Jeroboam, v.* 22. When their kings assumed a power to alter and add to the divine institutions they submitted to them, and thought the command of their kings would bear them out in disobedience to the command of their God. (4.) They *built themselves high places in all their cities, v.* 9. If in any place there was but the tower of the watchmen (a country tower that had no walls, but only a tower to shelter the watch in time of danger), or but a lodge for shepherds, it must be honoured with a high place, and that with an altar. If there was a fenced city, it must be further fortified with a high place. Having forsaken God's only place, they knew no end of high places, in which every man followed his own fancy and directed his devotion to what god he pleased. Sacred things were hereby profaned and laid common, when their altars were *as heaps in the furrows of the field,* Hos. 12:11. (5.) They *set them up images and groves — Asherim* (even *wooden images,* so some think the term, which we translate *groves,* should be rendered) or *Ashtaroth* (so others) — directed contrary to the second commandment, *v.* 10. They served idols (*v.* 12), the works of their own hands and creatures of their own fancy, though God had warned them particularly not to do this thing. (6.) They *burnt incense in all the high places,* to the honour of strange gods, for it was to the dishonour of the true God, *v.* 11. (7.) They followed vanity. Idols are called so, because they could do neither good nor evil, but were the most insignificant things that could be; those that worshipped them were like unto them, and so they became vain and good for nothing (*v.* 16), vain in their devotions, which were brutish and ridiculous, and so became vain in their whole conversation. (8.) Besides the molten images, even the two calves, they *worshipped all the host of heaven —* the sun, moon, and stars: for it is not meant of the heavenly host of angels; they could not rise so far above sensible things as to think of them. And, withal, they served Baal, the deified heroes of the Gentiles, *v.* 16. (9.) *They caused their children to pass through the fire,* in token of their dedicating them to their idols. (10.) They used divinations and enchantments, that they might receive directions from the gods to whom they paid their devotions.

III. What means God used with them, to bring them off from their idolatries, and to how little purpose. He testified against them, showed them their sins and warned them of the fatal consequences of them by all the prophets and all the *seers* (for so the prophets had been formerly called), and pressed them to *turn from their evil ways, v.* 13. We have read of prophets, more or less, in every reign. Though they had forsaken God's family of priests, he did not leave them without a succession of prophets, who made it their business to teach them the good knowledge of the Lord, but all in vain (*v.* 14); they would not hear, but hardened their necks, persisted in their idolatries, and were like their fathers, that would not bow their necks to God's yoke, because they *did not believe in him,* did not receive his truths, nor would venture upon his promises: it seems to refer to their fathers in the wilderness; the same sin that kept them out of Canaan turned these out, and that was unbelief.

IV. How God punished them for their sins. He *was very angry with them* (*v.* 18); for, in the matter of his worship, he is a jealous God, and resents nothing more deeply than giving that honour to any creature which is due to himself only. He afflicted them (*v.* 20) and *delivered them into the hand of spoilers,* in the days of the judges and of Saul, and afterwards in the days of most of their kings, to see if they would be awakened by the judgments of God to consider and amend their ways; but, when all these corrections did not prevail to drive out the folly, God first *rent Israel from the house of David,* under which they might have been happy. As Judah was hereby weakened, so Israel was hereby corrupted; for they made a man king who *drove them from following the Lord and caused them to sin a great sin, v.* 21. This was a national judgment, and the punishment of their former idolatries; and, at length, he *removed them quite out of his sight* (*v.* 18, 23), without giving them any hopes of a return out of their captivity.

Lastly, Here is a complaint against Judah in the midst of all (*v.* 19): *Also Judah kept not the commandments of God;* though they were not as yet quite so bad as Israel, yet they *walked in the statutes of Israel;* and this aggravated the sin of Israel, that they communicated the infection of it to Judah; see Eze. 23:11. Those that bring sin into a country or family bring a plague into it and will have to answer for all the mischief that follows.

Verses 24–41

Never was land lost, we say, for want of an heir. When the children of Israel were dispossessed, and turned out of Canaan, the king of Assyria soon transplanted thither the supernumeraries of his own country, such as it could well spare, who should be servants to him and masters to the Israelites that remained; and here we have an account of these new inhabitants, whose story is related here that we may take our leave of Samaria, as also of the Israelites that were carried captive into Assyria.

I. Concerning the Assyrians that were brought into the land of Israel we are here told, 1. That they possessed Samaria and *dwelt in the cities thereof, v.* 24. It is common for lands to change their owners, but sad that the holy land should become a heathen land again. See what work sin makes. 2. That at their first coming God *sent lions among them.* They were probably insufficient to people the country, which occasioned *the beasts of the field to multiply against them* (Ex. 23:29); yet, besides the natural cause, there was a manifest hand of God in it, who is Lord of hosts, of all the creatures, and can serve his own purposes by which he pleases, small or great, lice or lions. God ordered them this rough welcome to check their pride and insolence, and to let them know that though they had conquered Israel the God of Israel had power enough to deal with them — that he could have prevented their settling here, by ordering lions into the service of Israel, and that he permitted it, not for their righteousness, but the wickedness of his own people — and that they were now under his visitation. They had lived without God in their own land, and were not plagued with lions; but, if they do so in this land, it is at their peril. 3. That they sent a remonstrance of this grievance to the king their master, setting forth, it is likely, the loss their infant colony had sustained by the lions and the continual fear they were in of them, and stating that they looked upon it to be a judgment upon them for not worshipping the God of the land, which they could not, because they knew not how, *v.* 26. The God of Israel was the God of the whole world, but they ignorantly call him the *God of the land,* apprehending themselves therefore within his reach, and concerned to be upon good terms with him. Herein they shamed the Israelites, who were not so ready to hear the voice of God's judgments as they were, and who had not served the *God of that land,* though he was the God of their fathers and their great benefactor, and though they were well instructed in the manner of his worship. Assyrians begged to be taught that which Israelites hated to be taught. 4. That the king of Assyria took care to have them taught *the manner of the God of the land* (*v.* 27, 28), not out of any affection to that God, but to save his subjects from the lions. On this errand he sent back one of the priests whom he had carried away captive. A prophet would have done them more good, for this was but one of the priests of the calves, and therefore chose to dwell at Bethel for old acquaintance' sake, and, though he might teach them to do better than they did, he was not likely to teach them to do well, unless he had taught his own people better. However, he came and dwelt among them, to teach them how they should *fear the Lord.* Whether he taught them out of the book of the law, or only by word of mouth, is uncertain. 5. That, being thus taught, they made a mongrel religion of it, worshipped the God of Israel for fear and their own idols for love (*v.* 33): *They feared the Lord,* but they *served their own gods.* They all agreed to worship the God of the land according to the manner, to serve the Jewish festivals and rites of sacrificing, but every nation made gods of their own besides, not only for their private use in their own families, but to be put *in the houses of their high places, v.* 92. The idols of each country are here named, *v.* 30, 31. The learned are at a loss for the signification of several of these names, and cannot agree by what representations these gods were worshipped. If we may credit the traditions of the Jewish doctors, they tell us that Succoth-Benoth was worshipped in a hen and chickens, Nergal in a cock, Ashima in a smooth goat, Nibhaz in a dog, Tartak in an ass, Adrammelech in a peacock, Anammelech in a pheasant. Our own tell us, more probably, that Succoth-Benoth (signifying *the tents of the daughters*) was Venus. Nergal, being worshipped by the Cuthites, or Persians, was *the fire,* Adrammelech and Anammelech were only distinctions of Moloch. See how vain idolaters were in their imaginations, and wonder at their sottishness. Our very ignorance concerning these idols teaches us the accomplishment of that word which God has spoken, that these false gods should all perish (Jer. 10:11); they are all buried in oblivion, while the name of the true God shall continue for ever. 6. This medley superstition is here said to *continue unto this day* (*v.* 41), till the time when this book was written and long after, above 300 years in all, till the time of Alexander the Great, when Manasse, brother to Jaddus the high priest of the Jews, having married the daughter of Sanballat, governor of the Samaritans, went over to them, got leave of Alexander to build a temple in Mount Gerizim, drew over many of the Jews to him, and prevailed with the Samaritans to cast away all their idols and to worship the God of Israel only; yet their worship was mixed with so much superstition that our Saviour told them they knew not what they worshipped, Jn. 4:22.

II. Concerning the Israelites that were carried into the land of Assyria. This historian has occasion to speak of them (*v.* 22), showing that their successors in the land did as they had done *(after the manner of the nations whom they carried away),* they worshipped both the God of Israel and those other gods; but what did the captives do in the land of their affliction? Were they reformed, and brought to repentance, by their troubles? No, they did after the former manner, *v.* 34. When the two tribes were afterwards carried into Babylon, they were cured by it of their idolatry, and therefore, after seventy years, they were brought back with joy; but the ten tribes were hardened in the furnace, and therefore were justly lost in it and left to perish. This obstinacy of theirs is here aggravated by the consideration, 1. Of the honour God had put upon them, as the seed of Jacob, *whom he named Israel,* and from him they were so named, but were a reproach to *that worthy name by which they were called.* 2. Of the covenant he made with them, and the charge he gave them upon that covenant, which is here very fully recited, that they should *fear and serve the Lord Jehovah* only, who had *brought them up out of Egypt* (*v.* 36), that, having received his statutes and ordinances in writing, they should *observe to do them for evermore* (*v.* 37), and never forget that covenant which God had made with them, the promises and conditions of that covenant, especially that great article of it which is here thrice repeated, because it had been so often inculcated and so much insisted on, that they *should not fear other gods.* He had told them that, if they kept close to him, he would *deliver them out of the hand of all their enemies* (*v.* 39); yet when they were in the hand of their enemies, and stood in need of deliverance, they were so stupid, and had so little sense of their own interest, that they did after the former manner (*v.* 40), they served both the true God and false gods, as if they knew no difference. *Ephraim is joined to idols, let him alone.* So they did, and so did the nations that succeeded them. Well might the apostle ask, *What then, Are we better than they? No, in no wise, for both Jews and Gentiles are all under sin,* Rom. 3:9.

CHAPTER 18

When the prophet had condemned Ephriam for lies and deceit he comforted himself with this, that Judah yet "ruled with God, and was faithful with the Most Holy," Hos. 11:12. It was a very melancholy view which the last chapter gave us of the desolations of Israel; but this chapter shows us the affairs of Judah in a good posture at the same time, that it may appear God has not quite cast off the seed of Abraham, Rom. 11:1. Hezekiah is here upon the throne, I. Reforming his kingdom (*v.* 1–6). II. Prospering in all his undertakings (*v.* 7, 8), and this at the same time when the ten tribes were led captive (*v.* 9–12). III. Yet invaded by Sennacherib, the king of Assyria (*v.* 13). 1. His country put under contribution (*v.* 14–16). 2. Jerusalem besieged (*v.* 17). 3. God blasphemed, himself reviled, and his people solicited to revolt, in a virulent speech made by Rabshakeh (*v.* 18–37). But how well it ended, and how much to the honour and comfort of our great reformer, we shall find in the next chapter.

Verses 1–8

We have here a general account of the reign of Hezekiah. It appears, by comparing his age with his father's, that he was born when his father was about eleven or twelve years old, divine Providence so ordering that he might be of full age, and fit for business, when the measure of his father's iniquity should be full. Here is,

I. His great piety, which was the more wonderful because his father was very wicked and vile, one of the worst of the kings, yet he was one of the best, which may intimate to us that what good there is in any is not of nature, but of grace, free grace, sovereign grace, which, contrary to nature, grafts into the good olive that which was wild by nature (Rom. 11:24), and also that grace gets over the greatest difficulties and disadvantages: Ahaz, it is likely, gave his son a bad education as well as a bad example; Urijah his priest perhaps had the tuition of him; his attendants and companions, we may suppose, were such as were addicted to idolatry; and yet Hezekiah became eminently good. When God's grace will work what can hinder it?

1. He was a genuine son of David, who had a great many degenerate ones (*v.* 3): *He did that which was right, according to all that David his father did,* with whom the covenant was made, and therefore he was entitled to the benefit of it. We have read of some of them who did that which was right, *but not like David, ch.* 14:3. They did not love God's ordinances, nor cleave to them, as he did; but Hezekiah was a second David, had such a love for God's word, and God's house, as he had. Let us not be frightened with an apprehension of the continual decay of virtue, as if, when times and men are bad, they must needs, of course, grow worse and worse; that does not follow, for, after many bad kings, God raised up one that was like David himself.

2. He was a zealous reformer of his kingdom, and as we find (2 Chr. 29:3) he began betimes to be so, fell to work as soon as ever he came to the crown, and lost no time. He found his kingdom very corrupt, the people in all things too superstitious. They had always been so, but in the last reign worse than ever. By the influence of his wicked father, a deluge of idolatry had overspread the land; his spirit was stirred against this idolatry, we may suppose (as Paul's at Athens), while his father lived, and therefore, as soon as ever he had power in his hands, he set himself to abolish it (*v.* 4), though, considering how the people were wedded to it, he might think it could not be done without opposition. (1.) The images and the groves were downright idolatrous and of heathenish original. These he broke and destroyed. Though his own father had set them up, and shown an affection for them, yet he would not protect them. We must never dishonour God in honour to our earthly parents. (2.) The high places, though they had sometimes been used by the prophets upon special occasions and had been hitherto connived at by the good kings, were nevertheless an affront to the temple and a breach of the law which required them to worship there only, and, being from under the inspection of the priests, gave opportunity for the introducing of idolatrous usages. Hezekiah therefore, who made God's word his rule, not the example of his predecessors, removed them, made a law for the removal of them, the demolishing of the chapels, tabernacles, and altars there erected, and the suppressing of the use of them, which law was put in execution with vigour; and, it is probable, the terrible judgments which the kingdom of Israel was now under for their idolatry made Hezekiah the more zealous and the people the more willing to comply with him. It is well when our neighbours' harms are our warnings. (3.) The brazen serpent was originally of divine institution, and yet, because it had been abused to idolatry, he broke it to pieces. The children of Israel had brought that with them to Canaan; where they set it up we are not told, but, it seems, it had been carefully preserved, as a memorial of God's goodness to their fathers in the wilderness and a traditional evidence of the truth of that story, Num. 21:9, for the encouragement of the sick to apply to God for a cure and of penitent sinners to apply to him for mercy. But in process of time, when they began to worship the creature more than the Creator, those that would not worship images borrowed from the heathen, as some of their neighbours did, were drawn in by the tempter to burn incense to the brazen serpent, because that was made by order from God himself and had been an instrument of good to them. But Hezekiah, in his pious zeal for God's honour, not only forbade the people to worship it, but, that it might never be so abused any more, he showed the people that it was *Nehushtan,* nothing else but *a piece of brass,* and that therefore it was an idle wicked thing to burn incense to it; he then broke it to pieces, that is, as bishop Patrick expounds it, ground it to powder, which he scattered in the air, that no fragment of it might remain. If any think that the just honour of the brazen serpent was hereby diminished they will find it abundantly made up again, Jn. 3:14, where our Saviour makes it a type of himself. Good things, when idolized, are better parted with than kept.

3. Herein he was a nonesuch, *v.* 5. None of all the kings of Judah were like him, *either before or after him.* Two

things he was eminent for in his reformation: — (1.) Courage and confidence in God. In abolishing idolatry, there was danger of disobliging his subjects, and provoking them to rebel; but *he trusted in the Lord God of Israel* to bear him out in what he did and save him from harm. A firm belief of God's all-sufficiency to protect and reward us will conduce much to make us sincere, bold, and vigorous, in the way of our duty, like Hezekiah. When he came to the crown he found his kingdom compassed with enemies, but he did not seek for succour to foreign aids, as his father did, but trusted in the God of Israel to be the keeper of Israel. (2.) Constancy and perseverance in his duty. For this there was none like him, that he clave to the Lord with a fixed resolution and never *departed from following him*, *v.* 6. Some of his predecessors that began well fell off: but he, like Caleb, followed the Lord *fully.* He not only abolished all idolatrous usages, but kept God's commandments, and in every thing made conscience of his duty.

II. His great prosperity, *v.* 7, 8. He was with God, and then God was with him, and, having the special presence of God with him, *he prospered whithersoever he went,* had wonderful success in all his enterprises, in his wars, his buildings, and especially his reformation, for that good work was carried on with less difficulty than he could have expected. Those that do God's work with an eye to his glory, and with confidence in his strength, may expect to prosper in it. Great is the truth and will prevail. Finding himself successful, 1. He threw off the yoke of the king of Assyria, which his father had basely submitted to. This is called *rebelling against him,* because so the king of Assyria called it; but it was really an asserting of the just rights of his crown, which it was not in the power of Ahaz to alienate. If it was imprudent to make this bold struggle so soon, yet I see not that it was, as some think, unjust; when he had thrown out the idolatry of the nations he might well throw off the yoke of their oppression. The surest way to liberty is to serve God. 2. He made a vigorous attack upon the Philistines, and smote them even unto Gaza, both the country villages and the fortified town, *the tower of the watchmen and the fenced cities,* reducing those places which they had made themselves masters of in his father's time, 2 Chr. 28:18. When he had purged out the corruptions his father had brought in he might expect to recover the possessions his father had lost. Of his victories over the Philistines Isaiah prophesied, Isa. 14:28, etc.

Verses 9–16

The kingdom of Assyria had now grown considerable, though we never read of it till the last reign. Such changes there are in the affairs of nations and families: those that have been despicable become formidable, and those, on the contrary, are brought low that have made a great noise and figure. We have here an account,

I. Of the success of Shalmaneser, king of Assyria, against Israel, his besieging Samaria (*v.* 9), taking it (*v.* 10), and carrying the people into captivity (*v.* 11), with the reason why God brought this judgment upon them (*v.* 12): *Because they obeyed not the voice of the Lord their God.* This was related more largely in the foregoing chapter, but it is here repeated, 1. As that which stirred up Hezekiah and his people to purge out idolatry with so much zeal, because they saw the ruin which it brought upon Israel. When their neighbour's house was on fire, and their own in danger, it was time to cast away the accursed thing. 2. As that which Hezekiah much lamented, but had not strength to prevent. Though the ten tribes had revolted from, and often been vexatious to, the house of David, no longer ago than in his father's reign, yet being of the seed of Israel he could not be glad at their calamities. 3. As that which laid Hezekiah and his kingdom open to the king of Assyria, and made it much more easy for him to invade the land. It is said of the ten tribes here that they would neither *hear* God's commandments nor *do* them, *v.* 12. Many will be content to give God the hearing that will give him no more (Eze. 33:31), but these, being resolved not to do their duty, did not care to hear of it.

II. Of the attempt of Sennacherib, the succeeding king of Assyria, against Judah, in which he was encouraged by his predecessor's success against Israel, whose honours he would vie with and whose victories he would push forward. The descent he made upon Judah was a great calamity to that kingdom, by which God would try the faith of Hezekiah and chastise the people, who are called *a hypocritical nation* (Isa. 10:6), because they did not comply with Hezekiah's reformation, nor willingly part with their idols, but kept them up in their hearts, and perhaps in their houses, though their high places were removed. Even times of reformation may prove troublesome times, made so by those that oppose it, and then the blame is laid upon the reformers. This calamity will appear great upon Hezekiah if we consider, 1. How much he lost of his country, *v.* 13. The king of Assyria took all or most of the fenced cities of Judah, the frontier-towns and the garrisons, and then all the rest fell into his hands of course. The confusion which the country was put into by this invasion is described by the prophet, Isa. 10:28–31. 2. How dearly he paid for his peace. He saw Jerusalem itself in danger of falling into the enemies' hand, as Samaria had done, and was willing to purchase its safety at the expense, (1.) Of a mean submission: *"I have offended* in denying the usual tribute, and am ready to make satisfaction as shall be demanded," *v.* 14. Where was Hezekiah's courage? Where his confidence in God? Why did he not advise with Isaiah before he sent this crouching message? (2.) Of a vast sum of money — 300 talents of silver and thirty of gold (above 200,000*l.*), not to be paid annually, but as a present ransom. To raise this sum, he was forced not only to empty the public treasures (*v.* 15), but to take the golden plates off from the doors of the temple, and from the pillars, *v.* 16. Though *the temple sanctified the gold* which he had dedicated, yet, the necessity being urgent, he thought he might make as bold with that as his father David (whom he took for his pattern) did with the show-bread, and that it was neither impious nor imprudent to give a part for the preservation of the whole. His father Ahaz had plundered the temple in contempt of it, 2 Chr. 28:24. He had repaid with interest what his father took; and now, with all due reverence, he only begged leave to borrow it again in an exigency and for a greater good, with a resolution to restore it in full as soon as he should be in a capacity to do so.

Verses 17–37

Here is, I. Jerusalem besieged by Sennacherib's army, *v.* 17. He sent three of his great generals with a great host against Jerusalem. Is this the great king, the king of Assyria? No, never call him so; he is a base, false, perfidious man, and worthy to be made infamous to all ages; let him never be named with honour that could do such a dishonourable thing as this, to take Hezekiah's money, which he gave him upon condition he should withdraw his army, and then, instead of quitting his country according to the agreement, to advance against his capital city, and not send him his money again either. Those are wicked men indeed, and, let them be ever so great, we will call them so, whose principle it is not to make their promises binding any further than is for their interest. Now Hezekiah had too much reason to repent his treaty with Sennacherib, which made him much the poorer and never the safer.

II. Hezekiah, and his princes and people, railed upon by Rabshakeh, the chief speaker of the three generals, and one that had the most satirical genius. He was no doubt instructed what to say by Sennacherib, who intended hereby to pick a new quarrel with Hezekiah. He had promised, upon the receipt of Hezekiah's money, to withdraw his army, and therefore could not for shame make a forcible attack upon Jerusalem immediately; but he sent Rabshakeh to persuade Hezekiah to surrender it, and, if he should refuse, the refusal would serve him for a pretence (and a very poor one) to besiege it, and, if it hold out, to take it by storm. Rabshakeh had the impudence to desire audience of the king himself at the conduit of the upper pool, without the walls; but Hezekiah had the prudence to decline a personal treaty, and sent three commissioners (the prime ministers of state) to hear what he had to say, but with a charge to them not to answer that fool *according to his folly* (*v.* 36), for they could not convince him, but would certainly provoke him, and Hezekiah had learned of his father David to believe that God would hear when he, *as a deaf man, heard not,* Ps. 38:13–15. One interruption they gave him in his discourse, which was only to desire that he would speak to them now in the Syrian language, and they would consider what he said and report it to the king, and, if they did not give him a satisfactory answer, then he might appeal to the people, by speaking *in the Jews' language, v.* 26. This was a reasonable request, and agreeable to the custom of treaties, which is that the plenipotentiaries should settle matters between themselves before any thing be made public; but Hilkiah did not consider what an unreasonable man he had to deal with, else he would not have made this request, for it did but exasperate Rabshakeh, and make him the more rude and boisterous, *v.* 27. Against all the rules of decency and honour, instead of treating with the commissioners, he menaces the soldiery, persuades them to desert or mutiny, threatens if they hold out to reduce the to the last extremities of famine, and then goes on with his discourse, the scope of which is to persuade Hezekiah, and his princes and people, to surrender the city. Observe how, in order to do this,

1. He magnifies his master the king of Assyria. Once and again he calls him *That great king, the king of Assyria, v.* 19, 28. What an idol did he make of that prince whose creature he was! God is the great King, but Sennacherib was in his eye a little god, and he would possess them with the same veneration for him that he had, and thereby frighten them into a submission to him. But to those who by faith see the King of kings in his power and glory even the king of Assyria looks mean and little. What are the greatest of men when either they come to compare with God or God comes to contend with them? Ps. 82:6, 7.

2. He endeavours to make them believe that it will be much for their advantage to surrender. If they held out, they must expect no other than to eat their own dung, by reason of the want of provisions, which would be entirely cut off from them by the besiegers; but if they would capitulate, seek his favour with a present and cast themselves upon his mercy, he would give them very good treatment, *v.* 31. I wonder with what face Rabshakeh could speak of making an agreement with a present when his master had so lately broken the agreement Hezekiah made with him with that great present, *v.* 14. Can those expect to be trusted that have been so grossly perfidious? But, *Ad populum phaleras — Gild the chain and the vulgar will let you bind them.* He thought to soothe up all with a promise that if they would surrender upon discretion, though they must expect to be prisoners and captives, yet it would really be happy for them to be so. One would wonder he should ever think to prevail by such gross suggestions as these, but that the devil does thus impose upon sinners every day by his temptations. He will needs persuade them, (1.) That their imprisonment would be to their advantage, for they should *eat every man of his own vine* (*v.* 31); though the property of their estates would be vested in the conquerors, yet they should have the free use of them. But he does not explain it now to them as he would afterwards, that it must be understood just as much, and just as long, as the conqueror pleases. (2.) That their captivity would be much more to their advantage: *I will take you away to a land like your own land;* and what the better would they be for that, when they must have nothing in it to call their own?

3. That which he aims at especially is to convince them that it is to no purpose for them to stand it out: *What confidence is this wherein thou trustest?* So he insults over Hezekiah, *v.* 19. To the people he says (*v.* 29), *"Let not Hezekiah deceive you* into your own ruin, for *he shall not be able to deliver you;* you must either bend or break." It were well if sinners would submit to the force of this argument, in making their peace with God — That it is *therefore* our wisdom to yield to him, because it is in vain to contend with him: what confidence is that which those trust in who stand it out against him? *Are we stronger than he?* Or what shall we get by setting briars and thorns before a consuming fire? But Hezekiah was not so helpless and defenceless as Rabshakeh would here represent him. Three things he supposes Hezekiah might trust to, and he endeavours to make out the insufficiency of these: — (1.) His own military preparations: *Thou sayest, I have counsel and strength for the war;* and we find that so he had, 2 Chr. 32:3. But this Rabshakeh turns off with a slight: *"They are but vain words;* thou art an unequal match for us," *v.* 20. With the greatest haughtiness and disdain imaginable, he challenges him to produce 2000 men of all his people that know how to manage a horse, and will venture to give him 2000

horses if he can. He falsely insinuates that Hezekiah has no men, or none fit to be soldiers, *v.* 23. Thus he thinks to run him down with confidence and banter, and will lay him any wager that one captain of the least of his master's servants is able to baffle him and all his forces. (2.) His alliance with Egypt. He supposes that Hezekiah trusts to Egypt for chariots and horsemen (*v.* 24), because the king of Israel had done so, and of this confidence he truly says, It is *a broken reed* (*v.* 21), it will not only fail a man when he leans on it and expects it to bear his weight, but *it will run into his hand and pierce it,* and rend his shoulder, as the prophet further illustrates this similitude, with application to Egypt, Eze. 29:6, 7. So is the king of Egypt, says he; and truly so had the king of Assyria been to Ahaz, who trusted in him, but he *distressed him, and strengthened him not,* 2 Chr. 28:20. Those that trust to any arm of flesh will find it no better than a broken reed; but God is the rock of ages. (3.) His interest in God and relation to him. This was indeed the confidence in which Hezekiah trusts, *v.* 22. He supported himself by depending on the power and promise of God; with this he encouraged himself and his people (*v.* 30): *The Lord will surely deliver us,* and again *v.* 32. This Rabshakeh was sensible was their great stay, and therefore he was most large in his endeavours to shake this, as David's enemies, who used all the arts they had to drive him from his confidence in God (Ps. 3:2; 11:1), and thus did Christ's enemies, Mt. 27:43. Three things Rabshakeh suggested to discourage their confidence in God, and they were all false: — [1.] That Hezekiah had forfeited God's protection, and thrown himself out of it, by *destroying the high places and the altars, v.* 22. Here he measures the God of Israel by the gods of the heathen, who delighted in the multitude of altars and temples, and concludes that Hezekiah has given a great offence to the God of Israel, in confining his people to one altar: thus is one of the best deeds he ever did in his life misconstrued as impious and profane, by one that did not, or would not, know the law of the God of Israel. If that be represented by ignorant and malicious men as evil and a provocation to God which is really good and pleasing to him, we must not think it strange. If this was to be sacrilegious, Hezekiah would ever be so. [2.] That God had given orders for the destruction of Jerusalem at this time (*v.* 25): *Have I now come up without the Lord?* This is all banter and rhodomontade. He did not himself think he had any commission from God to do what he did (by whom should he have it?) but he made this pretence to amuse and terrify the *people that were on the wall.* If he had any colour at all for what he said, it might be taken from the notice which perhaps he had had, by the writings of the prophets, of the hand of God in the destruction of the ten tribes, and he thought he had as good a warrant for the seizing of Jerusalem as of Samaria. Many that have fought against God have pretended commissions from him. [3.] That if Jehovah, the God of Israel, should undertake to protect them from the king of Assyria, yet he was notable to do it. With this blasphemy he concluded his speech (*v.* 33–35), comparing the God of Israel with the gods of the nations whom he had conquered and putting him upon the level with them, and concluding that because they could not defend and deliver their worshippers the God of Israel could not defend and deliver his. See here, *First,* His pride. When he conquered a city he reckoned himself to have conquered its gods, and valued himself mightily upon it. His high opinion of the idols made him have a high opinion of himself as too hard for them. *Secondly,* His profaneness. The God of Israel was not a local deity, but the God of the whole earth, the only living and true God, the ancient of days, and had often proved himself to be above all gods; yet he makes no more of him than of the upstart fictitious gods of Hamath and Arpad, unfairly arguing that the gods (as some now say the priests) of all religions are the same, and himself above them all. The tradition of the Jews is that Rabshakeh was an apostate Jew, which made him so ready in the Jews' language; if so, his ignorance of the God of Israel was the less excusable and his enmity the less strange, for apostates are commonly the most bitter and spiteful enemies, witness Julian. A great deal of art and management, it must be owned, there were in this speech of Rabshakeh, but, withal, a great deal of pride, malice, falsehood, and blasphemy. One grain of sincerity would have been worth all this wit and rhetoric.

Lastly, We are told what the commissioners on Hezekiah's part did. 1. They held their peace, not for want of something to say both on God's behalf and Hezekiah's: they might easily and justly have upbraided him with his master's treachery and breach of faith, and have asked him, What religion encourages you to hope that such conduct will prosper? At least they might have given that grave hint which Ahab gave to Benhadad's like insolent demands — *Let not him that girdeth on the harness boast as though he had put it off.* But the king had commanded them not to answer him, and they observed their instructions. There is a time to keep silence, as well as a time to speak, and there are those to whom to offer any thing religious or rational is to cast pearls before swine. What can be said to a madman? It is probable that their silence made Rabshakeh yet more proud and secure, and so his heart was lifted up and hardened to his destruction. 2. They rent their clothes in detestation of his blasphemy and in grief for the despised afflicted condition of Jerusalem, the reproach of which was a burden to them. 3. They faithfully reported the matter to the king, their master, and *told him the words of Rabshakeh,* that he might consider what was to be done, what course they should take and what answer they should return to Rabshakeh's summons.

CHAPTER 19

Jerusalem's great distress we read of in the foregoing chapter, and left it besieged, insulted, threatened, terrified, and just ready to be swallowed up by the Assyrian army. But in this chapter we have an account of its glorious deliverance, not by sword or bow, but by prayer and prophecy, and by the hand of an angel. I. Hezekiah, in great concern, sent to the prophet Isaiah, to desire his prayers (*v.* 1–5) and received from him an answer of peace (*v.* 6, 7). II. Sennacherib sent a letter to Hezekiah to fright him into a surrender (*v.* 8–13). III. Hezekiah thereupon, by a very solemn prayer, recommended his case to God, the righteous Judge, and begged help from him (*v.* 14–19). IV. God, by Isaiah, sent him a very comfortable message, assuring him of deliverance (*v.* 20–34). V. The army of the Assyrians was all cut off by an angel and Sennacherib himself slain by his own sons (*v.* 35–37). And so God glorified himself and saved his people.

Verses 1–7

The contents of Rabshakeh's speech being brought to Hezekiah, one would have expected (and it is likely Rabshakeh did expect) that he would call a council of war and it would be debated whether it was best to capitulate or no. Before the siege, he had *taken counsel with his princes and his mighty men,* 2 Chr. 32:3. But that would not do now; his greatest relief is that he has a God to go to, and what passed between him and his God on this occasion we have here an account of.

I. Hezekiah discovered a deep concern at the dishonour done to God by Rabshakeh's blasphemy. When he heard it, though at second hand, he *rent his clothes and covered himself with sackcloth, v.* 1. Good men were wont to do so when they heard of any reproach cast on God's name; and great men must not think it any disparagement to them to sympathize with the injured honour of the great God. Royal robes are not too good to be rent, nor royal flesh too good to be clothed with sackcloth, in humiliation for indignities done to God and for the perils and terrors of his Jerusalem. To this God now called, and was displeased with those who were not thus affected. Isa. 22:12–14, *Behold joy and gladness, slaying oxen and killing sheep,* though it was a *day of trouble and perplexity in the valley of vision* (*v.* 5), which refers to this very event. The king was in sackcloth, but many of his subjects were in soft clothing.

II. He *went up to the house of the Lord,* according to the example of the psalmist, who, when he was grieved at the pride and prosperity of the wicked, *went into the sanctuary of God* and there *understood their end,* Ps. 73:17. He went to the house of God, to meditate and pray, and get his spirit into a sedate composed frame, after this agitation. He was not considering what answer to return to Rabshakeh, but refers the matter to God. *"Thou shalt answer, Lord, for me."* — Herbert. In the house of the Lord he found a place both of rest and refuge, a treasury, a magazine, a council-chamber, and all he needed, all in God. Note, When the church's enemies are very daring and threatening it is the wisdom and duty of the church's friends to apply to God, appeal to him, and leave their cause with him.

III. He sent to the prophet Isaiah, by honourable messengers, in token of the great respect he had for him, to desire his prayers, *v.* 2–4. Eliakim and Shebna were two of those that had heard the words of Rabshakeh and were the better able both to acquaint and to affect Isaiah with the case. The elders of the priests were themselves to pray for the people in time of trouble (Joel 2:17); but they must go to engage Isaiah's prayers, because he could pray better and had a better interest in heaven. The messengers were to go in sackcloth, because they were to represent the king, who was so clothed.

1. Their errand to Isaiah was, *"Lift up thy prayer for the remnant that is left,* that is, for Judah, which is but a remnant now that the ten tribes are gone — for Jerusalem, which is but a remnant now that the defenced cities of Judah are taken." Note, (1.) It is very desirable, and what we should be desirous of when we are in trouble, to have the prayers of our friends for us. In begging to have them we honour God, we honour prayer, and we honour our brethren. (2.) When we desire the prayers of others for us we must not think we are excused from praying for ourselves. When Hezekiah sent to Isaiah to pray for him he himself *went into the house of the Lord* to offer up his own prayers. (3.) Those who speak from God to us we should in a particular manner desire to speak to God for us. *He is a prophet, and he shall pray for thee,* Gen. 20:7. The great prophet is the great intercessor. (4.) Those are likely to prevail with God that *lift up* their prayers, that is, that lift up their hearts in prayer. (5.) When the interests of God's church are brought very low, so that there is but a remnant left, few friends, and those weak and at a loss, then it is time to *lift up our prayer for that remnant.*

2. Two things are urged to Isaiah, to engage his prayers for them: — (1.) Their fears of the enemy (*v.* 3): "He is insolent and haughty; it is *a day of rebuke and blasphemy.* We are despised. God is dishonoured. Upon this account it is a day of trouble. Never were such a king and kingdom so trampled on and abused as we are: *our soul is exceedingly filled with the contempt of the proud,* and it is *a sword in our bones* to hear them reproach our confidence in God, and say, Where is now your God? and, which is worst of all, we see not which way we can help ourselves and get clear of the reproach. Our cause is good, our people are faithful; but we are quite overpowered with numbers. The children are brought to the birth; now is the time, the critical moment, when, if ever, we must be relieved. One successful blow given to the enemy would accomplish our wishes. But, alas! we are not able to give it: *There is not strength to bring forth.* Our case is as deplorable, and calls for as speedy help, as that of a woman in travail, that is quite spent with her throes, so that she has not strength to bear the child. Compare with this Hos. 13:13. We are ready to perish; *if thou canst do any thing, have compassion upon us and help us."* (2.) Their hopes in God. To him they look, on him they depend, to appear for them. One word from him will turn the scale, and save the sinking remnant. If he but reprove the words of Rabshakeh (that is, disprove them, *v.* 4) — if he undertake to convince and confound the blasphemer — all will be well. And this they trust he will do, not for their merit's sake, but for his own honour's sake, because he has *reproached the living God,* by levelling him with deaf and dumb idols. They have reason to think the issue will be good, for they can interest God in the quarrel. Ps. 74:22, *Arise O God! plead thy own cause.* "He is the Lord thy God," say they to Isaiah — *"thine,* whose glory thou art concerned for, and whose favour thou art interested in. He has heard and known the blasphemous words of Rabshakeh, and therefore, it may be, he will hear and rebuke them. We hope he will. Help us with thy prayers to bring the cause before him, and then we are content to leave it with him."

IV. God, by Isaiah, sent to Hezekiah, to assure him that he would glorify himself in the ruin of the Assyrians. Hezekiah sent to Isaiah, not to enquire concerning the event, as many did that sent to the prophets (*Shall I recover?* or the like), but to desire his assistance in his duty. It was this that he was solicitous about; and therefore God let him know what the event should be, in recompence of his care to do his duty, *v.* 6, 7. 1. God interested himself in the cause: *They have blasphemed me.* 2. He encouraged Hezekiah, who was much dismayed: *Be not afraid of the words which thou hast heard;* they are but words (though swelling and fiery words), and words are but wind. 3. He promised to frighten the king of Assyria worse than Rabshakeh had frightened him: *"I will send a blast upon him* (that pestilential breath which killed his army), upon which terrors shall seize him and drive him into his own country, where death shall meet him." This short threatening from the mouth of God would do execution, when all the impotent menaces that came from Rabshakeh's mouth would vanish into air.

Verses 8–19

Rabshakeh, having delivered his message and received no answer (whether he took this silence for a consent or a slight does not appear), left his army before Jerusalem, under the command of the other generals, and went himself to attend the king his master for further orders. He found him besieging Libnah, a city that had revolted from Judah, *ch.* 8:22. Whether he had taken Lachish or no is not certain; some think he departed from it because he found the taking of it impracticable, *v.* 8. However, he was now alarmed with the rumour that the king of the Cushites, who bordered upon the Arabians, was coming out against him with a great army, *v.* 9. This made him very desirous to gain Jerusalem with all speed. To take it by force would cost him more time and men than he could well spare, and therefore he renewed his attack upon Hezekiah to persuade him tamely to surrender it. Having found him an easy man once (*ch.* 18:14), when he said, *That which thou puttest on me I will bear,* he hoped again to frighten him into a submission, but in vain. Here,

I. Sennacherib sent a letter to Hezekiah, a railing letter, a blaspheming letter, to persuade him to surrender Jerusalem, because it would be to no purpose for him to think of standing it out. His letter is to the same purport with Rabshakeh's speech; there is nothing new offered in it. Rabshakeh had said to the people, *Let not Hezekiah deceive you, ch.* 18:29. Sennacherib writes to Hezekiah, *Let not thy God deceive thee, v.* 10. Those that have the God of *Jacob for their help, and whose hope is in the Lord their God,* need not fear being deceived by him, as the heathen were by their gods. To terrify Hezekiah, and drive him from his anchor, he magnifies himself and his own achievements. See how proudly he boasts, 1. Of the lands he had conquered (*v.* 11): *All lands,* and destroyed utterly! How are the mole-hills of his victories swelled to mountains! So far was he from destroying all lands that at this time the land of Cush, and Tirhakah its king, were a terror to him. What vast hyperboles may one expect in proud men's praises of themselves! 2. Of the gods he had conquered, *v.* 12. "Each vanquished nation and its gods, which were so far from being able to deliver them that they fell with them: and shall thy God deliver thee?" 3. Of the kings he had conquered (*v.* 13), the *king of Hamath and the king of Arpad.* Whether he means the prince or the idol, he means to make himself appear greater than either, and therefore very formidable, and the *terror of the mighty in the land of the living.*

II. Hezekiah encloses this in another letter, a praying letter, a believing letter, and sends it to the King of kings, who judges among the gods. Hezekiah was not so haughty as not to receive the letter, though we may suppose the superscription did not give him his due titles; when he had received it he was not so careless as not to read it; when he had read it he was not in such a passion as to write an answer to it in the same provoking language; but he immediately went up to the temple, presented himself, and then *spread the letter before the Lord* (*v.* 14), not as if God needed to have the letter shown to him (he knew what was in it before Hezekiah did), but hereby he signified that he acknowledged God in all his ways, — that he desired not to aggravate the injuries his enemies did him nor to make them appear worse than they were, but desired they might be set in a true light, — and that he referred himself to God, and his righteous judgment, upon the whole matter. Hereby likewise he would affect himself in the prayer he came to the temple to make; and we have need of all possible helps to quicken us in that duty. In the prayer which Hezekiah prayed over this letter, 1. He adores the God whom Sennacherib had blasphemed (*v.* 15), calls him *the God of Israel,* because Israel was his peculiar people, and *the God that dwelt between the cherubim,* because there was the peculiar residence of his glory upon earth; but he gives glory to him as *the God of the whole earth,* and not, as Sennacherib fancied him to be, *the God of Israel only,* and confined to the temple. "Let them say what they will, thou art sovereign Lord, for thou art the God, the God of gods, sole Lord, even thou alone, universal Lord *of all the kingdoms of the earth,* and rightful Lord, *for thou hast made heaven and earth.* Being Creator of all, by an incontestable title thou art owner and ruler of all." 2. He appeals to God concerning the insolence and profaneness of Sennacherib (*v.* 16): *"Lord, hear; Lord, see.* Here it is under his own hand; here it is in black and white." Had Hezekiah only been abused, he would have passed it by; but it is God, the living God, that is reproached, the jealous God. *Lord, what wilt thou do for thy great name?* 3. He owns Sennacherib's triumphs over the gods of the heathen, but distinguishes between them and the God of Israel (*v.* 17, 18): He has indeed *cast their gods into the fire;* for *they were no gods,* unable to help either themselves or their worshipers, and therefore no wonder that he has destroyed them; and, in destroying them, though he knew it not, he really served the justice and jealousy of the God of Israel, who has determined to extirpate all the gods of the heathen. But those are deceived who think they can therefore be too hard for him. He is none of the gods whom men's hands have made, but he has himself made all things, Ps. 115:3, 4. 4. He prays that God will now glorify himself in the defeat of Sennacherib and the deliverance of Jerusalem out of his hands (*v.* 19): *"Now therefore save us;* for if we be conquered, as other lands are, they will say that thou art conquered, as the gods of those lands were: but, Lord, distinguish thyself, by distinguishing us, and let all the world know, and be made to confess, that *thou art the Lord God,* the self-existent sovereign God, *even thou only,* and that all pretenders are vanity and a lie." Note, The best pleas in prayer are those which are taken from God's honour; and therefore the Lord's prayer begins with *Hallowed be thy name,* and concludes with *Thine is the glory.*

Verses 20–34

We have here the gracious copious answer which God gave to Hezekiah's prayer. The message which he sent him by the same hand (*v.* 6, 7), one would think, was an answer sufficient to his prayer; but, that he might have strong consolation, he was encouraged by two immutable things, *in which it was impossible for God to lie,* Heb. 6:18. In general, God assured him that his prayer was heard, his prayer against Sennacherib, *v.* 20. Note, The case of those that have the prayers of God's people against them is miserable. For, if the oppressed cry to God against the oppressor, *he will hear,* Ex. 22:23. God hears and answers, hears *with the saving strength of his right hand,* Ps. 20:6.

This message bespeaks two things: —

I. Confusion and shame to Sennacherib and his forces. It is here foretold that he should be humbled and broken. The prophet elegantly directs his speech to him, as he does, Isa. 10:5. *O Assyrian! the rod of my anger.* Not that this message was sent to him, but what is here said to him he was made to know by the event. Providence spoke it to him with a witness; and perhaps his own heart was made to whisper this to him: for God has more ways than one of speaking to sinners in his wrath, so as to *vex them in his sore displeasure,* Ps. 2:5. Sennacherib is here represented,

1. As the scorn of Jerusalem, *v.* 21. He thought himself the terror of the daughter of Zion, that chaste and beautiful virgin, and that by his threats he could force her to submit to him: "But, being a virgin in her Father's house and under his protection, she defies thee, despises thee, laughs thee to scorn. Thy impotent malice is ridiculous; he that sits in heaven laughs at thee, and therefore so do those that abide under his shadow." By this word God intended to silence the fears of Hezekiah and his people. Though to an eye of sense the enemy looked formidable, to an eye of faith he looked despicable.

2. As an enemy to God; and that was enough to make him miserable. Hezekiah pleaded this: "Lord, he has reproached thee," *v.* 16. "He has," saith God, "and I take it as against myself (*v.* 22): *Whom hast thou reproached?* Is it not the Holy One of Israel, whose honour is dear to him, and who has power to vindicate it, which the gods of the heathen have not?" *Meno me impune lacesset — No one shall provoke me with impunity.*

3. As a proud vainglorious fool, that spoke *great swelling words of vanity,* and *boasted of a false gift,* by his boasts, as well as by his threats, reproaching the Lord. For, (1.) He magnified his own achievements out of measure and quite above what really they were (*v.* 23, 24): *Thou hast said* so and so. This was not in the letter he wrote, but God let Hezekiah know that he not only saw what was written there, but heard what he said elsewhere, probably in the speeches he made to his councils or armies. Note, God takes notice of the boasts of proud men, and will call them to an account, that he *may look upon them and abuse them,* Job 40:11. What a mighty figure does Sennacherib think he makes! Driving his chariots to the tops of the highest mountains, forcing his way through woods and rivers, breaking through all difficulties, making himself master of all he had a mind to. Nothing could stand before him or be withheld from him; no hills too high for him to climb, no trees too strong for him to fell, no waters too deep for him to dry up; as if he had the power of a God, to speak and it is done. (2.) He took to himself the glory of doing these great things, whereas they were all *the Lord's doing, v.* 25, 26. Sennacherib, in his letter, had appealed to what Hezekiah had heard (*v.* 11): *Thou hast heard what the kings of Assyria have done;* but, in answer to that, he is reminded of what God has done for Israel of old, drying up the Red Sea, leading them through the wilderness, planting them in Canaan. "What are all thy doings to these? And as for the desolations thou hast made in the earth, and particularly in Judah, thou art but the instrument in God's hand, a mere tool: it is *I that have brought it to pass.* I gave thee thy power, gave thee thy success, and made thee what thou art, raised thee up to lay waste fenced cities and so to punish them for their wickedness, and *therefore their inhabitants were of small power.*" What a foolish insolent thing was it for him to exalt himself above God, and against God, upon that which he had done by him and under him. Sennacherib's boasts here are expounded in Isa. 10:13, 14, *By the strength of my hand I have done it, and by my wisdom,* etc.; and they are answered (*v.* 15), *Shall the axe boast itself against him that heweth therewith?* It is surely absurd for the fly upon the wheel to say, What a dust do I make! or for the sword in the hand to say, What execution I do! If God be the principal agent in all that is done, boasting is for ever excluded.

4. As under the check and rebuke of that God whom he blasphemed. All his motions were, (1.) Under the divine cognizance (*v.* 27): *"I have thy abode,* and what thou dost secretly devise and design, *thy going out and coming in,* marches and counter-marches, and *thy rage against me* and my people, the tumult of thy passions, the tumult of thy preparations, the noise and bluster thou makest: I know it all." That was more than Hezekiah did, who wished for intelligence of the enemy's motions; but what need was there for this when the eye of God was a constant spy upon him? 2 Chr. 16:9. (2.) Under the divine control (*v.* 28): *"I will put my hook in thy nose,* thou great Leviathan (Job 41:1, 2), *my bridle in thy jaws,* thou great Behemoth. I will restrain thee, manage thee, turn thee where I please, send thee home like a fool as thou camest, *re infecta — disappointed of thy aim.*" Note, It is a great comfort to all the church's friends that God has a hook in the nose and a bridle in the jaws of all her enemies, can make even their wrath to serve and praise him and then restrain the remainder of it. *Here shall its proud waves be stayed.*

II. Salvation and joy to Hezekiah and his people. This shall be a sign to them of God's favour, and that he is reconciled to them, and *his anger is turned away* (Isa. 12:1), a wonder in their eyes (for so a sign sometimes signifies), a token for good, and an earnest of the further mercy God has in store for them, that a good issue shall be put to their present distress in every respect.

1. Provisions were scarce and dear; and what should they do for food? The fruits of the earth were devoured by the Assyrian army, Isa. 32:9, 10, etc. Why, they shall not only dwell in the land, but *verily they shall be fed.* If God save them, he will not starve them, nor let them die by famine, when they have escaped the sword: *"Eat you this year that which groweth of itself,* and you shall find enough of that. Did the Assyrians reap what you sowed? You shall reap what you did not sow." But the next year was the sabbatical year, when the land was to rest, and they must neither sow nor reap. What must they do that year? Why, *Jehovah-jireh — The Lord will provide.* God's

blessing shall save them seed and labour, and, that year too, the voluntary productions of the earth shall serve to maintain them, to remind them that the earth brought forth before there was a man to till it, Gen. 1:11. And then, the third year, their husbandry should return into its former channel, and they should sow and reap as they used to do. 2. The country was laid waste, families were broken up and scattered, and all was in confusion; how should it be otherwise when it was over-run by such an army? As to this, it is promised that *the remnant that has escaped of the house of Judah* (that is, of the country people) shall yet again be planted in their own habitations, upon their own estates, shall take root there, shall increase and grow rich, *v.* 30. See how their prosperity is described: it is *taking root downwards,* and *bearing fruit upwards,* being well fixed and well provided for themselves, and then doing good to others. Such is the prosperity of the soul: it is taking root downwards by faith in Christ, and then being fruitful in fruits of righteousness. 3. The city was shut up, none went out or came in; but now the remnant in Jerusalem and Zion shall go forth freely, and there shall be none to hinder them, or make them afraid, *v.* 31. Great destruction had been made both in city and country, bit in both there was a remnant that escaped, which typified the saved remnant of Israelites indeed (as appears by comparing Isa. 10:22, 23, which speaks of this very event, with Rom. 9:27, 28), and they shall go forth into the glorious liberty of the children of God. 4. The Assyrians were advancing towards Jerusalem, and would in a little time besiege it in form, and it was in great danger of falling into their hands. But it is here promised that the siege they feared should be prevented, — that, though the enemy had now (as it should seem) encamped before the city, yet they should never *come into the city,* no, nor so much as *shoot an arrow* into it (*v.* 32, 33), — that he should be forced to retire with shame, and a thousand times to repent his undertaking. God himself undertakes to defend the city (*v.* 34), and that person, that place, cannot but be safe, the protection of which he undertakes. 5. The honour and truth of God are engaged for the doing of all this. These are great things, but how will they be effected? Why, *the zeal of the Lord of hosts shall do this, v.* 31. He is Lord of hosts, has all creatures at his beck, therefore he is able to do it; he is *jealous for Jerusalem with great jealousy* (Zec. 1:14); having espoused her a chaste virgin to himself, he will not suffer he to be abused, *v.* 21. "You have reason to think yourselves unworthy that such great things should be done for you; but God's own zeal will do it." His zeal, (1.) For his own honour (*v.* 34): "I will do it for my own sake, to make myself an everlasting name." God's reasons of mercy are fetched from within himself. (2.) For his own truth: "I will do it for my servant David's sake; not for the sake of his merit, but the promise made to him and the covenant made with him, those sure mercies of David." Thus all the deliverances of the church are wrought for the sake of Christ, the Son of David.

Verses 35–37

Sometimes it was long ere prophecies were accomplished and promises performed; but here the word was no sooner spoken than the work was done.

I. The army of Assyria was entirely routed. That night which immediately followed the sending of this message to Hezekiah, when the enemy had just set down before the city and were preparing (as we now say) to open the trenches, that night was the main body of their army slain upon the spot by an angel, *v.* 35. Hezekiah had not force sufficient to sally out upon them and attack their camp, nor would God do it by sword or bow; but he sent his angel, a destroying angel, in the dead of the night, to make an assault upon them, which their sentinels, though ever so wakeful, could neither discover nor resist. It was *not by the sword of a mighty man or of a mean man,* that is, not of any man at all, but of an angel, that the Assyrians army was to fall (Isa. 31:8), such an angel as slew the first-born of Egypt. Josephus says it was done by a pestilential disease, which was instant death to them. The number slain was very great, 185,000 men, and Rabshakeh, it is likely, among the rest. When the besieged *arose, early in the morning, behold they were all dead corpses,* scarcely a living man among them. Some think the 76th Psalm was penned on this occasion, where we read that the *stout-hearted were spoiled and slept their sleep,* their last, their long sleep, *v.* 5. See how great, in power and might, the holy angels are, when one angel, in one night, could make so great a slaughter. See how weak the mightiest of men are before almighty God: who ever hardened himself against him and prospered? The pride and blasphemy of the king are punished by the destruction of his army. All these lives are sacrificed to God's glory and Zion's safety. The prophet shows that *therefore* God suffered this vast rendezvous to be made, *that they might be gathered as sheaves into the floor,* Mic. 4:12, 13.

II. The king of Assyria was hereby put into the utmost confusion. Ashamed to see himself, after all his proud boasts, thus defeated and disabled to pursue his conquests and secure what he had (for this, we may suppose, was the flower of his army), and continually afraid of falling under the like stroke himself, *He departed, and went, and returned;* the manner of the expression intimates the great disorder and distraction of mind he was in, *v.* 36. And it was not long before God cut him off too, by the hands of *two of his own sons, v.* 37. 1. Those that did it were very wicked, to kill their own father (whom they were bound to protect) and in the act of his devotion; monstrous villany! But, 2. God was righteous in it. Justly are the sons suffered to rebel against their father that begat them, when he was in rebellion against the God that made him. Those whose children are undutiful to them ought to consider whether they have not been so to their Father in heaven. The God of Israel had done enough to convince him that he was the only true God, whom therefore he ought to worship; yet he persists in his idolatry, and seeks to his false god for protection against a God of irresistible power. Justly is his blood mingled with his sacrifices, since he will not be convinced by such a plain and dear-bought demonstration of his folly in worshipping idols. His sons that murdered him were suffered to escape, and no pursuit was made after them, his subjects perhaps being weary of the government of so proud a man and thinking themselves well rid of him. And his sons would be looked upon as the more excusable in what they had done if it be true (as bishop Patrick suggested) that he was now vowing to sacrifice them to his god, so that it was for their own preservation that they sacrificed him. His successor was another son, *Esarhaddon,* who (as it should seem) did not aim, like his father, to enlarge his conquests, but rather to improve them; for he it was that first sent colonies of Assyrians to inhabit the country of Samaria, though it is mentioned before (*ch.* 17:24), as appears, Ezra 4:2, where the Samaritans say it was *Esarhaddon that brought them thither.*

CHAPER 20

In this chapter we have, I. Hezekiah's sickness, and his recovery from that, in answer to prayer, in performance of a promise, in the use of means, and confirmed with a sign (*v.* 1–11). II. Hezekiah's sin, and his recovery from that (*v.* 12–19). In both of these, Isaiah was God's messenger to him. III. The conclusion of his reign (*v.* 20, 21).

Verses 1–11

The historian, having shown us blaspheming Sennacherib destroyed in the midst of the prospects of life, here shows us praying Hezekiah delivered in the midst of the prospects of death — the days of the former shortened, of the latter prolonged.

I. Here is Hezekiah's sickness. *In those days,* that is, in the same year in which the king of Assyria besieged Jerusalem; for he reigning *reigned?* in all twenty-nine years, and surviving this fifteen years, this must be in his fourteenth year, and so was that, *ch.* 18:13. Some think it was at the time that the Assyrian army was besieging the city or preparing for it, because God promises (*v.* 6): *I will defend the city,* which promise was afterwards repeated, when the danger came to be most imminent, *ch.* 19:34. Others think it was soon after the defeat of Sennacherib; and then it shows us the uncertainty of all our comforts in this world. Hezekiah, in the midst of his triumphs in the favour of God, and over the forces of his enemies, is seized with sickness, and under the arrest of death. We must therefore always rejoice with trembling. It should seem he was sick of the plague, for we read of the boil or plague-sore, *v.* 7. The same disease which was killing to the Assyrians was trying to him; God took it from him, and put it upon his enemies. Neither greatness nor goodness can exempt us from sickness, from sore and mortal sicknesses. Hezekiah, lately favoured of heaven above most men, yet is sick unto death — in the midst of his days (under forty) and yet sick and dying; and perhaps he was the more apprehensive of its being fatal to him because his father died when he was about his age, two or three years younger. "In the midst of life we are in death."

II. Warning brought him to prepare for death. It is brought by Isaiah, who had been twice, as stated in the former chapter, a messenger of good tidings to him. We cannot expect to receive from God's prophets any other than what they have received from the Lord, and we must welcome that, be it pleasing or unpleasing. The prophet tells him, 1. That his disease is mortal, and, if he be not recovered by a miracle of mercy, will certainly be fatal: *Thou shalt die, and not live.* 2. That therefore he must, with all speed, get ready for death: *Set thy house in order.* This we should feel highly concerned to do when we are in health, but are most loudly called to do when we come to be sick. Set the heart in order by renewed acts of repentance, and faith, and resignation to God, with cheerful farewells to this world and welcomes to another; and, if not done before (which is the best and wisest course), set the house in order, make thy will, settle thy estate, put thy affairs in the best posture thou canst, for the ease of those that shall come after thee. Isaiah speaks not to Hezekiah of his *kingdom,* only of his *house.* David, being a prophet, had authority to appoint who should reign after him, but other kings did not pretend to bequeath their crowns as part of their goods and chattels.

III. His prayer hereupon: *He prayed unto the Lord, v.* 2. Is any sick? Let him be prayed for, let him be prayed with, and let him pray. Hezekiah had found, as recorded in the foregoing chapter, that it was not in vain to wait upon God, but that the prayers of faith bring in answers of peace; therefore will he *call upon God as long as he lives.* Happy experiences of the prevalency of prayer are engagements and encouragements to continue instant in prayer. He had now received the sentence of death within himself, and, if it was reversible, it must be reversed by prayer. When God purposes mercy he will, *for this, be enquired of,* Eze. 36:37. We have not if we ask not, or ask amiss. If the sentence was irreversible, yet prayer is one of the best preparations for death, because by it we fetch in strength and grace from God to enable us to finish well. Observe,

1. The circumstances of this prayer. (1.) He *turned his face to the wall,* probably as he lay in his bed. This he did perhaps for privacy; he could not retire to his closet as he used to do, but he retired as well as he could, turned from the company that were about him, to converse with God. When we cannot be so private as we would be in our devotions, nor perform them with the usual outward expressions of reverence and solemnity, yet we must not therefore omit them, but compose ourselves to them as well as we can. Or, as some think, he turned his face towards the temple, to show how willingly he would have gone up thither, to pray this prayer (as he did, *ch.* 19:1, 14), if he had been able, and remembering what encouragements were given to all the prayers that should be made in or towards that house. Christ is our temple; to him we must have an eye in all our prayers, for no man, no service, *comes to the Father but by him.* (2.) He *wept sorely.* Some gather from this that he was unwilling to die. It is in the nature of man to have some dread of the separation of soul and body, and it was not strange if the Old-Testament saints, to whom another world was but darkly revealed, were not so willing to leave this as Paul and other New-Testament saints were. There was also something peculiar in Hezekiah's case: he was now in the midst of his usefulness, had begun a good work of reformation, which he feared would, through the corruption of the people, fall to the ground, if he should die. If this was before the defeat of the Assyrian army, as some think, he might therefore be loth to die, because his kingdom was in imminent danger of being ruined. However, it does not appear that he had now any son: Manasseh, that succeeded him, was not born till three years after; and, if he should die childless, both the peace of his kingdom and the promise to David would be in danger. But perhaps these were only tears of importunity, and expressions of a lively affection in prayer. Jacob wept and made supplication; and our blessed Saviour, though most willing to die, yet offered

up strong cries, with tears, to him whom he knew to be *able to save him,* Heb. 5:7. Let Hezekiah's prayer interpret his tears, and in *that* we find nothing that intimates him to have been under any of that fear of death which has either bondage or torment.

2. The prayer itself: *"Remember now, O Lord! how I have walked before thee in truth;* and either spare me to live, that I may continue thus to walk, if, if my work be done, receive me to that glory which thou hast prepared for those that have thus walked." Observe here, (1.) The description of Hezekiah's piety. He had had his conversation in the world with right intentions ("I have walked before thee, as under thy eye and with an eye ever towards thee"), from a right principle *("in truth, and with an upright heart"),* and by a right rule — *"I have done that which is good in thy sight."* (2.) The comfort he now had in reflecting upon it; it made his sick-bed easy. Note, The testimony of conscience for us that we have walked with God in our integrity will be much our support and rejoicing when we come to look death in the face, 2 Co. 1:12. (3.) The humble mention he makes of it to God. *Lord, remember it now;* not as if God needed to be put in mind of any thing by us (he is greater than our hearts, and knows all things), or as if the reward were of debt, and might be demanded as due (it is Christ's righteousness only that is the purchase of mercy and grace); but our own sincerity may be pleaded as the condition of the covenant which God has wrought in us: "It is the work of thy own hands. Lord, own it." Hezekiah does not pray, "Lord, spare me," or, "Lord, take me; God's will be done;" but, *Lord, remember me; whether I live or die, let me be thine.*

IV. The answer which God immediately gave to this prayer of Hezekiah. The prophet had got but to the middle court when he was sent back with another message to Hezekiah (*v.* 4, 5), to tell him that he should recover; not that there is with God yea and nay, or that he ever says and unsays; but upon Hezekiah's prayer, which he foresaw and which his Spirit inclined him to, God did that for him which otherwise he would not have done. God here calls Hezekiah *the captain of his people,* to intimate that he would reprieve him for his people's sake, because, in this time of war, they could ill spare such a captain: he calls himself *the God of David,* to intimate that he would reprieve him out of a regard to the covenant made with David and the promise that he would always ordain a lamp for him. In this answer, 1. God honours his prayers by the notice he takes of them and the reference he has to them in this message: *I have heard thy prayers, I have seen thy tears.* Prayers that have much life and affection in them are in a special manner pleasing to God. 2. God exceeds his prayers; he only begged that God would remember his integrity, but God here promises (1.) To restore him from his illness: *I will heal thee.* Diseases are his servants; as they go where he sends them, so they come when he remands them. Mt. 8:8, 9. *I am the Lord that healeth thee,* Ex. 15:26. (2.) To restore him to such a degree of health that *on the third day he should go up to the house of the Lord,* to return thanks. God knew Hezekiah's heart, how dearly he loved the habitation of God's house and the place where his honour dwelt, and that as soon as he was well he would go to attend on public ordinances; thitherward he turned his face when he was sick, and thitherward he would turn his feet when he was recovered; and therefore, because nothing would please him better, he promises him this, *Let my soul live, and it shall praise thee.* The man whom Christ healed was soon after *found in the temple,* Jn. 5:14. (3.) To add fifteen years to his life. This would not bring him to be an old man; it would reach but to fifty-four or fifty-five; yet that was longer than he had lately expected to live. His lease was renewed, which he thought was expiring. We have not the instance of any other that was told before-hand just how long he should live; that good man no doubt made a good use of it; but God has wisely kept us at uncertainties, that we may be always ready. (4.) To deliver Jerusalem from the king of Assyria, *v.* 6. This was the thing which Hezekiah's heart was upon a much as his own recovery, and therefore the promise of this is here repeated. If this was after the raising of the siege, yet there was cause to fear Sennacherib's rallying again. "No," says God, *"I will defend this city."*

V. The means which were to be used for his recovery, *v.* 7. Isaiah was his physician. He ordered an outward application, a very cheap and common thing: "Lay a *lump of figs to the boil,* to ripen it and bring it to a head, that the matter of the disease may be discharged that way." This might contribute something to the cure, and yet, considering to what a height the disease had come, and how suddenly it was checked, the cure was no less than miraculous. Note, 1. It is our duty, when we are sick, to make use of such means as are proper to help nature, else we do not trust God, but tempt him. 2. Plain and ordinary medicines must not be despised, for many such God has graciously made serviceable to man, in consideration of the poor. 3. What God appoints he will bless and make effectual.

VI. The sign which was given for the encouragement of his faith. 1. He begged it, not in any distrust of the power or promise of God, or as if he staggered at that, but because he looked upon the things promised to be very great things and worthy to be so confirmed, and because it had been usual with God thus to glorify himself and favour his people; and he remembered how much Gos was displeased with his father for refusing to ask a sign, Isa. 7:10–12. Observe, Hezekiah asked *What is the sign,* not that I shall go up to the thrones of judgment or up to the gate, but *up to the house of the Lord?* He desired to recover that he might glorify God *in the gates of the daughter of Zion.* It is not worth while to live for any other purpose than to serve God. 2. It was put to his choice whether the sun should go back or go forward; for it was equal to Omnipotence, and it would be the more likely to confirm his faith if he chose that which he thought the more difficult of the two. Perhaps to this that of this prophet may refer (Isa. 45:11), *Ask me of things to come concerning my sons, and concerning the work of my hands command you me.* It is supposed that the degrees were half hours, and that it was just noon when the proposal was made, and the question is, "Shall the sun go back to its place at seven in the morning or forward to its place at five in the evening?" 3. He humbly desired the sun might go back ten degrees, because, though either would be a great miracle, yet, it being the natural course of the sun to go forward, its going back would seem more strange, and would be more significant of Hezekiah's *returning to the days of his youth* (Job 33:25) and the lengthening out of the day of his life. It was accordingly done, upon the prayer of Isaiah (*v.* 11): He *cried unto the Lord* by special warrant and direction, and God brought the sun back ten degrees, which appeared to Hezekiah (for the sign was intended for him) by the going back of the shadow upon the dial of Ahaz, which, it is likely, he could see through his chamber-window; and the same was observed upon all other dials, even in Babylon, 2 Chr. 32:31. Whether this retrograde motion of the sun was gradual or *per saltum — suddenly —* whether it went back at the same pace that it used to go forward, which would make the day ten hours longer than usual — or whether it darted back on a sudden, and, after continuing a little while, was restored again to its usual place, so that no change was made in the state of the heavenly bodies (as the learned bishop Patrick thinks) — we are not told; but this work of wonder shows the power of God in heaven as well as on earth, the great notice he takes of prayer, and the great favour he bears to his chosen. The most plausible idolatry of the heathen was theirs that worshipped the sun; yet that was hereby convicted of the most egregious folly and absurdity, for by this it appeared that their god was under the check of the God of Israel. Dr. Lightfoot suggests that the fifteen songs of degrees (Ps. 120, etc.) might perhaps be so called because selected by Hezekiah to be sung to his stringed instruments (Isa. 38:20) in remembrance of the degrees on the dial which the sun went back and the fifteen years added to his life; and he observes how much of these psalms is applicable to Jerusalem's distress and deliverance and Hezekiah's sickness and recovery.

Verses 12–21

Here is, I. An embassy sent to Hezekiah by the king of Babylon, to congratulate him on his recovery, *v.* 12. The kings of Babylon had hitherto been only deputies and tributaries to the kings of Assyria, and Nineveh was the royal city. We find Babylon subject to the king of Assyria, *ch.* 17:24. But this king of Babylon began to set up for himself, and by degrees things were so changed that Assyria became subject to the kings of Babylon. This king of Babylon sent to compliment Hezekiah, and ingratiate himself with him upon a double account. 1. Upon the account of religion. The Babylonians worshipped the sun, and, perceiving what honour their god had done to Hezekiah, in going back for his sake, they thought themselves obliged to do honour to him likewise. It is good having those our friends whom we perceive to be the favourites of heaven. 2. Upon the account of civil interest. If the king of Babylon was now mediating a revolt from the king of Assyria, it was policy to get Hezekiah into his interest, in answer to whose prayers, and for whose protection, heaven had given that fatal blow to the king of Assyria. He found himself obliged to Hezekiah, and his God, for the weakening of the Assyrian forces, and had reason to think he could not have a more powerful and valuable ally than one that had so good an interest in the upper world. He therefore made his court to him with all possible respect by ambassadors, letters, and a present.

II. The kind entertainment Hezekiah gave to these ambassadors, *v.* 13. It was his duty to be civil to them, and receive them with the respect due to ambassadors; but he exceeded, and was courteous to a fault. 1. He was too fond of them. He *hearkened unto them.* Though they were idolaters, yet he became intimate with them, was forward to come into a confederacy with the king their master, and granted them all they came for. He was more open and free than he should have been, and stood not so much upon his guard. What reason had he that was in covenant with God so eagerly to catch at an alliance with a heathen prince, or to value himself at all upon his respectful notice? What honour could this embassy add to one whom God had so highly favoured, that he should please himself so much with it? 2. He was too fond of showing them his palace, his treasures, and his magazines, that they might see, and might report to their master, what a great king he was, and how well worthy of the honour their master did him. It is not said that he showed them the temple, the book of the law, and the manner of his worship, that he might proselyte them to the true religion, which he had now a fair opportunity of doing; but in compliment to them, lest he should affront them, he waived that, and showed them the rich furniture of his closet, that house of his precious things, the wealth he had heaped up since the king of Assyria had emptied his coffers, his *silver, and gold, and spices.* All the valuable things he had he showed them, either himself or by his officers. And what harm was there in this? What is more commonly, and (as we think) more innocently, done, than to show strangers the riches and rarities of a country — to show our friends our houses and their furniture, our gardens, stables, and libraries? But if we do this in the pride of our hearts, as Hezekiah did, to gain applause from men, and not giving praise to God, it turns into sin to us, as it did to him.

III. The examination of Hezekiah concerning this matter, *v.* 14, 15. Isaiah, who had often been his comforter, is now his reprover. The blessed Spirit is both, Jn. 16:7, 8. Ministers must be both, as there is occasion. Isaiah spoke in God's name, and therefore called him to account as one having authority: "Who are these? Whence come they? What is their business? What have they seen?" Hezekiah not only submitted to the examination (did not ask him, "Why should you concern yourself and question me about this affair?"), but made an ingenuous confession: *There is nothing among my treasures that I have not shown them.* Why then did he not bring them to Isaiah, and show him to them who was without doubt the best treasure he had in his dominions, and who by his prayers and prophecies had been instrumental in all those wonders which these ambassadors came to enquire into? I hope Hezekiah had the same value for Isaiah now that he had in his distress; but it would have become him to show it by bringing these ambassadors to him in the first place, which might have prevented the false step he took.

IV. The sentence passed upon him for his pride and vanity, and the too great relish he had of the things of the world, after that intimate acquaintance he had so lately been admitted into with divine things. The sentence is (*v.* 17, 18), 1. That the treasures he was so proud of should hereafter become a prey, and his family should be robbed of them all. It is just with God to take that from us which we make the matter of our pride and in which we put our confidence. 2. That the king of Babylon, with whom he was so fond of an alliance, should be the enemy that should make a prey of them. Not that it was for this sin that that judgment should be brought upon them: the sins of Manasseh, his idolatries and murders, were the cause of that calamity; but it is now foretold to Hezekiah, to convince him of the folly of his pride and of the value he had for the king of Babylon, and to make him ashamed of it. Hezekiah was fond of assisting the king of Babylon to rise, and to reduce the exorbitant power of the kings of Assyria; but he is told that the snake he is cherishing will ere long sting the bosom that cherishes it, and that his royal seed shall become the king of Babylon's slave (which was fulfilled, Dan. 1:1, etc.), than which there could not be any thing more mortifying to Hezekiah to think of. Babylon will be the ruin of those that are fond of Babylon. Wise therefore and happy are those that *come out from her,* Rev. 18:4.

V. Hezekiah's humble and patient submission to this sentence, *v.* 19. Observe how he argues himself into this submission. 1. He lays it down for a truth that *"good is the word of the Lord,* even this word, though a threatening; for every word of his is so. It is not only just, but good; for, as he does no wrong to any, so he means no hurt to good men. It is good; for he will bring good out of it, and do me good by the foresight of it." We should believe this concerning every providence, that it is good, is working for good. 2. He takes notice of that in this word which was good, that he should not live to see this evil, much less to share in it. He makes the best of the bad: "Is it not good? Yes, certainly it is, and better than I deserve." Note, (1.) True penitents, when they are under divine rebukes, call them not only just, but good; not only submit to the punishment of their iniquity, but accept of it. So Hezekiah did, and by this it appeared that he was indeed *humbled for the pride of his heart.* (2.) When at any time we are under dark dispensations, or have dark prospects, public or personal, we must take notice of what is *for* us as well as what is *against* us, that we may by thanksgiving honour God, and may in our patience possess our own souls. (3.) As to public affairs, it is good, and we are bound to think it *so, if peace and truth be in our days.* That is, [1.] Whatever else we want, it is good if we have peace and truth, if we have the true religion professed and protected, Bibles and ministers, and enjoy these in peace, not terrified with the alarms of war or persecution. [2.] Whatever trouble may come when we are gone, it is good if all be well in our days. Not that we should be unconcerned for posterity; it is a grief to foresee evils: but we should own that the deferring of judgments is a great favour in general, and to have them deferred so long as what we may die in peace is a particular favour to us, for charity begins at home. We know not how we shall bear the trial, and therefore have reason to think it well if we may but get safely to heaven before it comes.

Lastly, Here is the conclusion of Hezekiah's life and story, *v.* 20, 21. In 2 Chr. *ch.* 29–32 much more is recorded of Hezekiah's work of reformation than in this book of Kings; and it seems that in the civil chronicles, not now extant, there were many things recorded of his might and the good offices he did for Jerusalem, particularly his bringing water by pipes into the city. To have water in plenty, without striving for it and without being terrified with the noise of archers in the drawing of it, to have it at hand and convenient for us, is to be reckoned a great mercy; for the want of water would be a great calamity. But here this historian leaves him *asleep with his fathers,* and a son in his throne that proved very untoward; for parents cannot give grace to their children. Wicked Ahaz was the son of a godly father and the father of a godly son; holy Hezekiah was the son of a wicked father and the father of a wicked son. When the land was not reformed, as it should have been, by a good reign, it was plagued and ripened for ruin by a bad one; yet then tried again with a good one, that it might appear how loth God was to cut off his people.

CHAPTER 21

In this chapter we have a short but sad account of the reigns of two of the kings of Judah, Manasseh and Amon. I. Concerning Manasseh, all the account we have of him here is, 1. That he devoted himself to sin, to all manner of wickedness, idolatry, and murder (*v.* 1–9 and 16). 2. That therefore God devoted him, and Jerusalem for his sake, to ruin (*v.* 10–18). In the book of Chronicles we have an account of his troubles, and his repentance. II. Concerning Amon we are only told that he lived in sin (*v.* 19–22), died quickly by the sword, and left good Josiah his successor (*v.* 23–26). By these two reigns Jerusalem was much debauched and much weakened, and so hastened apace towards its destruction, which slumbered not.

Verses 1–9

How delightful were our meditations on the last reign! How many pleasing views had we of Sion in its glory (that is, in its purity and in its triumphs), of the king in his beauty! (for Isa. 33:17 refers to Hezekiah), and (as it follows there, *v.* 20) Jerusalem was *a quiet habitation* because *a city of righteousness,* Isa. 1:26. But now we have melancholy work upon our hands, unpleasant ground to travel, and cannot but drive heavily. *How has the gold become dim and the most fine gold changed!* The beauty of Jerusalem is stained, and all her glory, all her joy, sunk and gone. These verses give such an account of this reign as make it, in all respects, the reverse of the last, and, in a manner, the ruin of it.

I. Manasseh began young. He was but *twelve years old when he began to reign* (*v.* 1), born when his father was about forty-two years old, three years after his sickness. If he had sons before, either they were dead, or set by as unpromising. As yet they knew of nothing bad in *him,* and they hoped he would prove good; but he proved very bad, and perhaps his coming to the crown so young might help to make it so, which yet will by no means excuse him, for his grandson Josiah came to it younger than he and yet acted well. But being young, 1. He was puffed up with his honour and proud of it; and thinking himself very wise, because he was very great, valued himself upon his undoing what his father had done. It is too common for novices to be lifted up with pride, and so to *fall into the condemnation of the devil.* 2. He was easily wrought upon and drawn aside by seducers, that lay in wait to deceive. Those that were enemies to Hezekiah's reformation, and retained an affection for the old idolatries, flattered him, and so gained his ear, and used his power at their pleasure. Many have been undone by coming too soon to their honours and estates.

II. He reigned long, longest of any of the kings of Judah, fifty-five years. This was the only very bad reign that was a long one; Joram's was but eight years, and Ahaz's sixteen; as for Manasseh's, we hope that in the beginning of his reign for some time affairs continued to move in the course that his father left them in, and that in the latter end of his reign, after his repentance, religion got head again; and, no doubt, when things were at the worst God had his remnant that kept their integrity. Though he reigned long, yet some of this time he was a prisoner in Babylon, which may well be looked upon as a drawback from these years, though they are reckoned in the number because then he repented and began to reform.

III. He reigned very ill.

1. In general, (1.) *He did that which was evil in the sight of the Lord,* and which, having been well educated, he could not but know was so (*v.* 2): *He wrought much wickedness in the sight of the Lord,* as if on purpose to provoke him to anger, *v.* 6. (2.) *He did after the abominations of the heathen* (*v.* 2) and as did Ahab (*v.* 3), not taking warning by the destruction both of the nations of Canaan and the house of Ahab for their idolatry; nay (*v.* 9), he *did more evil than did the nations whom the Lord destroyed.* When the holy seed degenerate, they are commonly worse than the worst of the profane.

2. More particularly, (1.) He *rebuilt the high places which his father had destroyed, v.* 3. Thus did he trample upon the dust, and affront the memory, of his worthy father, though he knew how much he was favoured of God and honoured of men. He concurred, it is probable, with Rabshakeh's sentiments (*ch.* 18:22), that Hezekiah had done ill in destroying those high places, and pretended the honour of God, and the edification and convenience of the people, in rebuilding them. This he began with, but proceeded to that which was much worse; for, (2.) He set up other gods, *Baal* and *Ashtaroth* (which we translate *a grove*), and all the host of heaven, the sun and moon, the other planets, and the constellations; these he worshipped and served (*v.* 3), gave their names to the images he made, and then did homage to them and prayed for help from them. To these he built altars (*v.* 5), and offered sacrifices, no doubt, on these altars. (3.) He *made his son pass through the fire,* by which he dedicated him a votary to Moloch, in contempt of the seal of circumcision by which he had been dedicated to God. (4.) He made the devil his oracle, and, in contempt both of urim and prophecy, he *used enchantments and dealt with familiar spirits* (*v.* 6) like Saul. Conjurers and fortune-tellers (who pretended, by the stars or the clouds, lucky and unlucky days, good and bad omens, the flight of birds, or the entrails of beasts, to foretel things to come) were great men with him, his intimates, his confidants; their arts pleased his fancy, and gained his belief, and his counsels were under their direction. (5.) We find afterwards (*v.* 16) that he shed innocent blood very much in gratification of his own passion and revenge; some perhaps were secretly murdered, others taken off by colour of law. Probably much of the blood he shed was theirs that opposed idolatry and witnessed against it, that would not bow the knee to Baal. The *blood of the prophets* is, in a particular manner, charged upon Jerusalem, and it is probable that he put to death many of them. The tradition of the Jews is that he caused the prophet Isaiah to be sawn asunder; and many think the apostle refers to this in Heb. 11:37, where he speaks of those that had so suffered.

3. Three things are here mentioned as aggravations of Manasseh's idolatry: — (1.) That he set up his images and altars *in the house of the Lord* (*v.* 4), in the two courts of the temple (*v.* 5), in the very house of which God had said to Solomon, *Here will I put my name, v.* 7. Thus he defied God to his face, and impudently affronted him with his rivals immediately under his eye, as one that was neither afraid of God's wrath nor ashamed of his own folly and wickedness. Thus he desecrated what had been consecrated to God, and did, in effect, turn God out of his own house and put the rebels in possession of it. Thus, when the faithful worshippers of God came to the place he had appointed for the performance of their duty to him, they found, to their great grief and terror, other gods ready to receive their offerings. God had said that here he would record his name, here he would put it for ever, and here it was accordingly preserved, while the idolatrous altars were kept at a distance; but Manasseh, by bringing them into God's house, did what he could to alter the property, and to make the name of the God of Israel to be no more in remembrance. (2.) That hereby he put a great slight upon the word of God, and his covenant with Israel. Observe the favour he had shown to that people in putting his name among them, — the kindness he intended them, never to *make them move out of that good land,* — and the reasonableness of his expectations from them, *only if they will observe to do according to all that I have commanded them, v.* 7, 8. Upon these good terms did Israel stand with God, and had as fair a prospect of being happy as any people could have; but *they hearkened not, v.* 9. They would not be kept close to God either by his precepts or by his promises; both were cast behind their back. (3.) That hereby he seduced the people of God, debauched them, and drew them into idolatry, *v.* 9. He caused Judah to sin (*v.* 11), as Jeroboam had caused *Israel to sin.* His very example was enough to corrupt the generality of unthinking people, who would do as their king did, right or wrong. All that aimed at preferment would do as the court did; and others thought it safest to comply, for fear of making their king their enemy. Thus, one way or other, the holy city became a harlot, and Manasseh made her so. Those will have a great deal to answer for that not only are wicked themselves, but help to make others so.

Verses 10–18

Here is the doom of Judah and Jerusalem read, and it is heavy doom. The prophets were sent, in the first place, to teach them the knowledge of God, to remind them of their duty and direct them in it. If they succeeded not in that, their next work was to reprove them for their sins, and to set them in view before them, that they might repent and reform, and return to their duty. If in this they prevailed not, but sinners went on frowardly, their next work was to foretel the judgments of God, that the terror of them might awaken those to repentance who would not be made sensible of the obligations of his love, or else that the execution of them, in their season, might be a demonstration of the divine mission of the prophets that foretold them. The prophets were deputed judges to those that would not hear and receive them as teachers. We have here,

I. A recital of the crime. The indictment is read upon which the judgment is grounded, *v.* 11. Manasseh had done wickedly himself, though he knew better things, had even justified the Amorites, whose copy he wrote after, by outdoing them in impieties, and debauched the people of God, whom he had taught to sin and forced to sin; and besides that (though that was bad enough) *he had filled Jerusalem with innocent blood* (*v.* 16), had multiplied his murders in every corner of the city, and filled the measure of Jerusalem's blood-guiltiness (Mt. 23:32) up to the brim, and all this against the crown and dignity of the King of kings, the peace of his kingdom, and the statutes in these cases made and provided.

II. A prediction of the judgment God would bring upon them for this: *They have done that which was evil,* and therefore *I am bringing evil upon them* (*v.* 12); it will come and it is not far off. The judgment should be, 1. Very terrible and amazing; the very report of it should *make men's ears to tingle* (*v.* 12), that is, their hearts to tremble. It should make a great noise in the world and occasion many speculations. 2. It should be copied out (as the sins of Jerusalem had been) from Samaria and the house of Ahab, *v.* 13. When God lays righteousness to the line it shall be the line of Samaria, measuring out to Jerusalem that which had been the lot of Samaria; when he lays judgment to the plummet it shall be *the plummet of the house of Ahab,* marking out for the same ruin to which that wretched family was devoted. See Isa. 28:17. Note, Those who resemble and imitate others in their sins must expect to fare as they fared. 3. That it should be an utter destruction: *I will wipe it as a man wipes a dish.* This intimates, (1.) That every thing should be put into disorder, and their state subverted; they should be turned upside down, and all their foundations put out of course. (2.) That the city should be emptied of its inhabitants, which had been the filth of it, as a dish is emptied when it is wiped: "They shall all be carried captive, the *land shall enjoy her sabbaths,* and be laid by as a dish when it is wiped." See the comparison of the boiled pot, not much unlike this, Eze. 24:1–14. (3.) That yet this should be in order to the purifying, not the destroying, of Jerusalem. The dish shall not be dropped, not broken to pieces, or melted down, but only wiped. This shall be the fruit, the taking away of the sinners first, and then of the sin. 4. That *therefore* they should be destroyed, because they should be deserted (*v.* 14): *I will forsake the remnant of my inheritance.* Justly are those that forsake God forsaken of him; nor does he ever leave any till they have first left him: but, when God has forsaken a people, their defence has departed, and they become a prey, an easy prey, to all their enemies. Sin is spoken of here as the alpha and omega of their miseries. (1.) Old guilt came in remembrance, as that which began to fill the measure (*v.* 15): *"They have provoked me to anger* from their conception and birth as a people, *since the day their fathers came out of Egypt."* The men of this generation, treading in their fathers' steps, are justly reckoned with for their fathers' sins. (2.) The guilt of blood was that which filled the measure, *v.* 16. Nothing has a louder cry, nor brings a sorer vengeance, than that.

This is all we have here of Manasseh; he stands convicted and condemned; but we hope in the book of Chronicles to hear of his repentance, and acceptance with God. Meantime, we must be content, in this place, to have only one intimation of his repentance (for so we are willing to take it), that he was buried, it is likely by his own order, *in the garden of his own house* (*v.* 18); for, being truly humbled for his sins, he judged himself *no more worthy to be called a son,* a son of David, and therefore not worthy to have even his dead body buried *in the sepulchres of his fathers.* True penitents take shame to themselves, not honour; yet, having lost the credit of an innocent, the credit of a penitent was the next best he was capable of. And better it is, and more honourable, for a sinner to die repenting, and be buried in a garden, than to die impenitent, and be buried in the abbey.

Verses 19–26

Here is a short account of the short and inglorious reign of Amon, the son of Manasseh. Whether Manasseh, in his blind and brutish zeal for his idols, had sacrificed his other sons — or whether, having been dedicated to his idols, they were refused by the people — so it was that his successor was a son not born till he was forty-five years old. And of him we are here told, 1. That his reign was very wicked: *He forsook the God of his fathers* (*v.* 22), disobeyed the commands given to his fathers, and disclaimed the covenant made with his fathers, *and walked not in the way of the Lord,* but *in all the way which his father walked in, v.* 20, 21. He trod in the steps of his father's idolatry, and revived that which he, in the latter end of his days, had put down. Note, Those who set bad examples, though they may repent themselves, yet cannot be sure that those whom they have drawn into sin by their example will repent; it is often otherwise. 2. That his end was very tragical. He having rebelled against God, his own servants *conspired against him and slew him,* probably upon some personal disgust, when he had reigned but two years, *v.* 23. His servants, who should have guarded him, murdered him; his own house, that should have been his castle of defence, was the place of his execution. He had profaned God's house with his idols, and now God suffered his own house to be polluted with his blood. How unrighteous soever those were that did it, God was righteous who suffered it to be done. Two things the people of the land did, by their representatives, hereupon: — (1.) They did justice on the traitors that had slain the king, and put them to death; for, though he was a *bad* king, he was *their* king, and it was a part of their allegiance to him to avenge his death. Thus they cleared themselves from having any hand in the crime, and did what was incumbent on them to deter others from the like villainous practices. (2.) They did a kindness to themselves in *making Josiah his son king in his stead,* whom probably the conspirators had a design to put by, but the people stood by him and settled him in the throne, encouraged, it may be, by the indications he gave, even in his early days, of a good disposition. Now they made a happy change from one of the worst to one of the best of all the kings of Judah. "Once more," says God, "they shall be tried with a reformation; and, if that succeed, well; if not, then after that I will cut them down." Amon was buried in the same garden where his father was, *v.* 26. If his father put himself under that humiliation, the people will put him under it.

CHAPTER 22

This chapter begins the story of the reign of good king Josiah, whose goodness shines the brighter because it came just after so much wickedness, which he had the honour to reform, and just before so great a destruction, which yet he had not the honour to prevent. Here, after his general character (*v.* 1, 2), we have a particular account of the respect he paid I. To God's house, which he repaired (*v.* 3–7). II. To God's book, which he was much affected with the reading of (*v.* 8–11). III. To God's messengers, whom he thereupon consulted (*v.* 12–14). And by whom he received from God an answer threatening Jerusalem's destruction (*v.* 15–17), but promising favour to him (*v.* 18–20), upon which he set about that glorious work of reformation which we have an account of in the next chapter.

Verses 1–10

Concerning Josiah we are here told,

I. That he was very young when he began to reign (*v.* 1), only eight years old. Solomon says, *Woe unto thee, O land! when thy king is a child;* but happy art thou, O land! when thy king is *such* a child. Our English Israel had once a king that was such a child, Edward VI. Josiah, being young, had not received any bad impressions from the example of his father and grandfather, but soon saw their errors, and God gave his grace to take warning by them. See Eze. 18:14, etc.

II. That he *did that which was right in the sight of the Lord, v.* 2. See the sovereignty of divine grace — the father passed by and left to perish in his sin, the son a chosen vessel. See the triumphs of that grace — Josiah born of a wicked father, no good education nor good example given him, but many about him who no doubt advised him to tread in his father's steps and few that gave him any good counsel, and yet the grace of God made him an eminent saint, *cut him off from the wild olive* and *grafted him into the good olive,* Rom. 11:24. Nothing is too hard for that grace to do. He walked in a good way, and turned not aside (as some of his predecessors had done who began well) *to the right hand nor to the left.* There are errors on both hands, but God kept him in the right way; he fell neither into superstition nor profaneness.

III. That he took care for the repair of the temple. This he did in the eighteenth year of his reign, *v.* 3. Compare 2 Chr. 34:8. He began much sooner to *seek the Lord* (as appears, 2 Chr. 34:3), but it is to be feared the work of reformation went slowly on and met with much opposition, so that he could not effect what he desired and designed, till his power was thoroughly confirmed. The consideration of the time we unavoidably lost in our minority should quicken us, when we have come to years, to act with so much the more vigour in the service of God. Having begun late we have need work hard. He sent Shaphan, the secretary of state, to Hilkiah the high priest, to take an account of the money that was collected for this use by the door-keepers (*v.* 4); for, it seems, they took much the same way of raising the money that Joash took, *ch.* 12:9. When people gave by a little at a time the burden was insensible, and, the contribution being voluntary, it was not complained of. This money, so collected, he ordered him to lay out for the repair of the temple, *v.* 5, 6. And now, it seems, the workmen (as in the days of Joash) acquitted themselves so well that *there was no reckoning made with them* (*v.* 7), which is certainly mentioned to the praise of the workmen, that they gained such a reputation for honesty, but whether to the praise of those that employed them I know not; a man should count money (we say) after his own father; it would not have been amiss to have *reckoned with the workmen,* that others also might be satisfied of their honesty.

IV. That, in repairing the temple, *the book of the law* was happily found and brought to the king, *v.* 8, 10. Some think this book was the autograph, or original manuscript, of the five books of Moses, under his own hand; others think it was only an ancient and authentic copy. Most likely it was that which, by the command of Moses, was laid up in the most holy place, Deu. 31:24, etc. 1. It seems, this book of the law was lost or missing. Perhaps it was carelessly mislaid and neglected, thrown by into a corner (as some throw their Bibles), by those that knew not the value of it, and forgotten there; or it was maliciously concealed by some of the idolatrous kings, or their agents, who were restrained by the providence of God or their own consciences from burning and destroying it, but buried it, in hopes it would never see the light again; or, as some think, it was carefully laid up by some of its friends, lest it should fall into the hands of its enemies. Whoever were the instruments of its preservation, we ought to acknowledge the hand of God in it. If this was the only authentic copy of the Pentateuch then in being, which had (as I may say) so narrow a turn for its life and was so near perishing, I wonder the hearts of all good people did not tremble for that sacred treasure, as Eli's for the ark, and I am sure we now have reason to thank God, upon our knees, for that happy providence by which Hilkiah found this book at this time, found it when *he sought it not,* Isa. 65:1. If the holy scriptures had not been of God, they would not have been in being at this day; God's care of the Bible is a plain indication of his interest in it. 2. Whether this was the only authentic copy in being or no, it seems the things contained in it were new both to the king himself and to the high priest; for the king, upon the reading of it, rent his clothes. We have reason to think that neither the command for the king's writing a copy of the law, nor that for the public reading of the law every seventh year (Deu. 17:18; 31:10, 11), had been observed for a long time; and when the instituted means of keeping up religion are neglected religion itself will soon go to decay. Yet, on the other hand, if the book of the law was lost, it seems difficult to determine what rule Josiah went by in doing that which was *right in the sight of the Lord,* and how the priests and people kept up the rites of their religion. I am apt to think that the people generally took up with abstracts of the law, like our abridgements of the statutes, which the priests, to save themselves the trouble of writing and the people of reading the book at large, had furnished them with — a sort of ritual, directing them in the observances of their religion, but leaving out what they thought fit, and particularly the promises and threatenings (Lev. 26 and Deu. 28, etc.), for I observe that these were the portions of the law which Josiah was so much affected with (*v.* 13), for these were new to him. No summaries, extracts, or collections, out of the Bible (though they may have their use) can be effectual to convey and preserve the knowledge of God and his will like the Bible itself. It was no marvel that the people were so corrupt when the book of the law was such a scarce thing among them; where that vision is not the people perish. Those that endeavoured to debauch them no doubt used all the arts they could to get that book out of their hands. The church of Rome could not keep up the use of images but by forbidding the use of the scripture. 3. It was a great instance of God's favour, and a token for good to Josiah and his people, that the book of the law was thus seasonably brought to light, to direct and quicken that blessed reformation which Josiah had begun. It is a sign that God has mercy in store for a people when he magnifies his law among them and makes that honourable, and furnishes them with means for the increase of scripture-knowledge. The translating of the scriptures into vulgar tongues was the glory, strength, and joy of the Reformation from Popery. It is observable that they were about a good work, repairing the temple, when they found the book of the law. Those that do their duty according to their knowledge shall have their knowledge increased. To him that hath shall be given. The book of the law was an abundant recompence for all their care and cost about the repair of the temple. 4. Hilkiah the priest was exceedingly well pleased with the discovery. "O," says he to Shaphan, "rejoice with me, for *I have found the book of the law, heurēka, heurēka, — I have found, I have found,* that jewel of inestimable value. Here, carry it to the king; it is the richest jewel of his crown. Read it before him. He walks in *the way of David his father,* and, if he be like him, he will love the book of the law and bid that welcome; that will be his delight and his counsellor."

Verses 11—20

We hear no more of the repairing of the temple: no doubt that good work went on well; but the book of the law that was found in it occupies us now, and well it may. It is not laid up in the king's cabinet as a piece of antiquity, a rarity to be admired, but it is read before the king. Those put the truest honour upon their Bibles that study them and converse with them daily, feed on that bread and walk by that light. Men of honour and business must look upon an acquaintance with God's word to be their best business and honour. Now here we have,

I. The impressions which the reading of the law made upon Josiah. He rent his clothes, as one ashamed of the sin of his people and afraid of the wrath of God; he had long thought the case of his kingdom bad, by reason of the idolatries and impieties that had been found among them, but he never thought it so bad as he perceived it to be by the book of the law now read to him. The rending of his clothes signified the rending of his heart for the dishonour done to God, and the ruin he saw coming upon his people.

II. The application he made to God hereupon: *Go, enquire of the Lord for me, v.* 13.

1. Two things we may suppose he desired to know: — "Enquire, (1.) What we shall do; what course we shall take to turn away God's wrath and prevent the judgments which our sins have deserved." Convictions of sin and wrath should put us upon this enquiry, *What shall we do to be saved? Wherewithal shall we come before the Lord?* If you will thus enquire, enquire quickly, before it be too late. (2.) "What we may expect and must provide for." He acknowledges, *"Our fathers have not hearkened to the words of this book;* if this be the rule of right, certainly our fathers have been much in the wrong." Now that *the commandment came sin revived,* and appeared sin; in the glass of the law, he saw the sins of his people more numerous and more heinous than he had before seen them, and more exceedingly sinful. He infers hence, "Certainly *great is the wrath that is kindled against us;* if this be the word of God, as no doubt it is, and he will be true to his word, as no doubt he will be, we are all undone. I never thought the threatenings of the law so severe, and the curses of the covenant so terrible, as now I find them to be; it is time to look about us if these be in force against us." Note, Those who are truly apprehensive of the weight of God's wrath cannot but be very solicitous to obtain his favour, and inquisitive how they may make their peace with him. Magistrates should enquire for their people, and study how to prevent the judgments of God that they see hanging over them.

2. This enquiry Josiah sent, (1.) By some of his great men, who are named *v.* 12, and again *v.* 14. Thus he put

an honour upon the oracle, by employing those of the first rank to attend it. (2.) To Huldah the prophetess, *v.* 14. The spirit of prophecy, that inestimable treasure, was sometimes put not only into *earthen* vessels, but into the *weaker* vessels, *that the excellency of the power might be of God.* Miriam helped to lead Israel out of Egypt (Mic. 6:4), Deborah judged them, and now Huldah instructed them in the mind of God, and her being a wife was no prejudice at all to her being a prophetess; *marriage is honourable in all.* It was a mercy to Jerusalem that when Bibles were scarce they had prophets, as afterwards, when prophecy ceased, that they had more Bibles; for God never leaves himself without witness, because he will leave sinners without excuse. Jeremiah and Zephaniah prophesied at this time, yet the king's messengers made Huldah their oracle, probably because her husband having a place at court (for he was keeper of the wardrobe) they had had more and longer acquaintance with her and greater assurances of her commission than of any other; they had, it is likely, consulted her upon other occasions, and had found that the word of God in her mouth was truth. She was near, for she dwelt at Jerusalem, in a place called *Mishneh,* the second rank of buildings from the royal palace. The Jews say that she prophesied among the women, the court ladies, being herself one of them, who it is probable had their apartments in that place. Happy the court that had a prophetess within the verge of it, and knew how to value her.

III. The answer he received from God to his enquiry. Huldah returned it not in the language of a courtier — "Pray give my humble service to his Majesty, and let him know that this is the message I have for him from the God of Israel;" but in the dialect of a prophetess, speaking from him before whom all stand upon the same level — *Tell the man that sent you to me, v.* 15. Even kings, though gods to us, are men to God, and shall so be dealt with; for *with him there is no respect of persons.*

1. She let him know what judgments God had in store for Judah and Jerusalem (*v.* 16, 17): *My wrath shall be kindled against this place;* and what is hell itself but the fire of God's wrath kindled against sinners? Observe, (1.) The degree and duration of it. It is so kindled that *it shall not be quenched;* the decree has gone forth; it is too late now to think of preventing it; the iniquity of Jerusalem shall not be purged with sacrifice or offering. Hell is unquenchable fire. (2.) The reference it has, [1.] To their sins: "They have committed them, as it were, with design, and on purpose to provoke me to anger. It is a fire of their own kindling; they would provoke me, and at length I am provoked." [2.] To God's threatenings: "The evil I bring is according to the words of the book which the king of Judah has read; the scripture is fulfilled in it. Those that would not be bound by the precept shall be bound by the penalty." God will be found no less terrible to impenitent sinners than his word makes him to be.

2. She let him know what mercy God had in store for him. (1.) Notice is taken of his great tenderness and concern for the glory of God and the welfare of his kingdom (*v.* 19): *Thy heart was tender.* Note, God will distinguish those that distinguish themselves. The generality of the people were hardened and their hearts unhumbled, so were the wicked kings his predecessors, but Josiah's heart was tender. He received the impressions of God's word, trembled at it and yielded to it; he was exceedingly grieved for the dishonour done to God by the sins of his fathers and of his people; he was afraid of the judgments of God, which he saw coming upon Jerusalem, and earnestly deprecated them. This is tenderness of heart, and thus he *humbled himself before the Lord,* and expressed these pious affections by rending his clothes and weeping before God, probably in his closet; but he that sees in secret says it was *before him,* and he heard it, and put every tear of tenderness into his bottle. Note, Those that most fear God's wrath are least likely to feel it. It should seem that those words (Lev. 26:32) much affected Josiah, *I will bring the land into desolation;* for when he heard of the *desolation and of the curse,* that is, that God would forsake them and *separate them to evil* (for till it came to that they were neither desolate nor accursed), then he rent his clothes: the threatening went to his heart. (2.) A reprieve is granted till after his death (*v.* 20): *I will gather thee to thy fathers.* The saints then, no doubt, had a comfortable prospect of happiness on the other side death, else being gathered to

their fathers would not have been so often made the matter of a promise as we find it was. Josiah could not prevail to prevent the judgment itself, but God promised him he should not live to see it, which (especially considering that he died in the midst of his days, before he was forty years old) would have been but a small reward for his eminent piety if there had not been another world in which he should be abundantly recompensed, Heb. 11:16. When the righteous is *taken away from the evil to come he enters into peace,* Isa. 57:1, 2. This is promised to Josiah here: *Thou shalt go to thy grave in peace,* which refers not to the manner of his death (for he was killed in a battle), but to the time of it; it was a little before the captivity in Babylon, that great trouble, in comparison with which the rest were as nothing, so that he might be truly said to die in peace that did not live to share in that. He died in the love and favour of God, which secure such a peace as no circumstances of dying, no, not dying in the field of war, could alter the nature of, or break in upon.

CHAPTER 23

We have here, I. The happy continuance of the goodness of Josiah's reign, and the progress of the reformation he began, reading the law (v. 1, 2), renewing the covenant (v. 3), cleansing the temple (v. 4), and rooting out idols and idolatry, with all the relics thereof, in all places, as far as his power reached (v. 5–20), keeping a solemn passover (v. 21–23), and clearing the country of witches (v. 24), and in all this acting with extraordinary vigour (v. 25). II. The unhappy conclusion of it in his untimely death, as a token of the continuance of God's wrath against Jerusalem (v. 26–30). III. The more unhappy consequences of his death, in the bad reigns of his two sons Jehoahaz and Jehoiakim, that came after him (v. 31–37).

Verses 1–3

Josiah had received a message from God that there was no preventing the ruin of Jerusalem, but that he should deliver only his own soul; yet he did not therefore sit down in despair, and resolve to do nothing for his country because he could not do all he would. No, he would do his duty, and then leave the event to God. A public reformation was the thing resolved on; if any thing could prevent the threatened ruin it must be that; and here we have the preparations for that reformation. 1. He summoned a general assembly of the states, the elders, the magistrates or representatives of Judah and Jerusalem, to meet him *in the house of the Lord,* with the priests and prophets, the ordinary and extraordinary ministers, that, they all joining in it, it might become a national act and so be the more likely to prevent national judgments; they were all called to attend (*v.* 1, 2), that the business might be done with the more solemnity, that they might all advise and assist in it, and that those who were against it might be discouraged from making any opposition. Parliaments are no diminution at all to the honour and power of good princes, but a great support to them. 2. Instead of making a speech to this convention, he ordered the book of the law to be read to them; nay, it should seem, he read it himself (*v.* 2), as one much affected with it and desirous that they should be so too. Josiah thinks it not below him to be a reader, any more than Solomon did to be a preacher, nay, and David himself to be a door-keeper in the house of God. Besides the convention of the great men, he had a congregation of the *men of Judah and the inhabitants of Jerusalem* to hear the law read. It is really the interest of princes to promote the knowledge of the scriptures in their dominions. If the people be but as stedfastly resolved to obey by law as he is to govern by law, the kingdom will be happy. All people are concerned to know the scripture, and all in authority to spread the knowledge of it. 3. Instead of proposing laws for the confirming of them in their duty, he proposed an association by which they should all jointly engage themselves to God, *v.* 3. The book of the law was the book of the covenant, that, if they would be to God a people, he would be to them a God; they here engage themselves to do their part, not doubting but that then God would do his. (1.) The covenant was that they should walk after the Lord, in compliance with his will, in his ordinances and his providences, should answer all his calls and attend all his motions — that they should make conscience of all his commandments, moral, ceremonial, and judicial, and should carefully observe them *with all their heart and all their soul,* with all possible care and caution, sincerity, vigour, courage, and resolution, and so fulfil the conditions of this covenant, in dependence upon the promises of it. (2.) The covenanters were, in the first place, the king himself, who stood by his pillar (*ch.* 11:14) and publicly declared his consent to this covenant, to set them an example, and to assure them not only of his protection but of his presidency and all the furtherance his power could give them in their obedience. It is no abridgment of the liberty even of princes themselves to be in bonds to God. *All the people* likewise *stood to the covenant,* that is, they signified their consent to it and promised to abide by it. It is of good use to oblige ourselves to our duty with all possible solemnity, and this is especially seasonable after notorious backslidings to sin and decays in that which is good. He that bears an honest mind does not shrink from positive engagements: fast bind, fast find.

Verses 4–24

We have here an account of such a reformation as we have not met with in all the history of the kings of Judah, such thorough riddance made of all the abominable things and such foundations laid of a glorious good work; and here I cannot but wonder at two things: — 1. That so many wicked things should have got in, and kept standing so long, as we find here removed. 2. That notwithstanding the removal of these wicked things, and the hopeful prospects here given of a happy settlement, yet within a few years Jerusalem was utterly destroyed, and even this did not save it; for the generality of the people, after all, hated to be reformed. *The founder melteth in vain,* and therefore *reprobate silver shall men call them,* Jer. 6:29, 30. Let us here observe,

I. What abundance of wickedness there was, and had been, in Judah and Jerusalem. One would not have believed it possible that in Judah, where God was known — in Israel, where his name was great — in Salem, in Sion, where his dwelling place was, such abominations should be found as here we have an account of. Josiah had now reigned eighteen years, and had himself set the people a good example, and kept up religion according to law; and yet, when he came to make inquisition for idolatry, the depth and extent of the dunghill he had to carry away appeared almost incredible. 1. Even in the house of the Lord, that sacred temple which Solomon built, and dedicated to the honour and for the worship of the God of Israel, there were found vessels, all manner of utensils, for the worship of Baal, *and of the grove* (or *Ashtaroth*), and *of all the host of heaven, v.* 4. Though Josiah had suppressed the worship of idols, yet the utensils made for that worship were all carefully preserved, even in the temple itself, to be used again whenever the present restraint should be taken off; nay, even the grove itself, the image of it, was yet standing in the temple (*v.* 6); some make it the image of Venus, the same with Ashtaroth. 2. Just *at the entering in of the house of the Lord* was a stable for horses kept (would you think it?) for a religious use; they were holy horses, *given to the sun* (*v.* 11), as if he needed them who *rejoiceth as a strong man to run a race* (Ps. 19:5), or rather they would thus represent to themselves the swiftness of his motion, which they much admired, making their religion to conform to the poetical fictions of the chariot of the sun, the follies of which even a little philosophy, without any divinity, would have exposed and made them ashamed of. Some say that those horses were to be led forth in pomp every morning to meet the rising sun, others that the worshippers of the sun rode out upon them to adore the rising sun; it should seem that they drew the chariots of the sun, which the people worshipped. Strange that ever men who had the written word of God among them should be thus *vain in their imaginations!* 3. Hard *by the house of the Lord* there were *houses of the Sodomites,* where all manner of lewdness and filthiness, even that which was most unnatural, was practised, and under pretence of religion too, in honour of their impure deities. Corporal and spiritual whoredom went together, and the vile affections to which the people were given up were the punishment of their vain imaginations. Those that dishonoured their God were justly left thus to dishonour themselves, Rom. 1:24, etc. There were women that *wove hangings for the grove* (*v.* 7), tents which encompassed the image of Venus, where the worshippers committed all manner of lewdness, and this *in the house of the Lord.* Those did ill that made our Father's house a house of merchandise; those did worse that made it a den of thieves; but those did worst of all that made it *(Horrendum dictu! — Horrible to relate!)* a brothel, in an impudent defiance of the holiness of God and of his temple. Well might the apostle call them *abominable idolatries.* 4. There were many idolatrous altars found (*v.* 12), some in the palace, *on the top of the upper chamber of Ahaz.* The roofs of their houses being flat, they made them their high places, and set up altars upon them (Jer. 19:13; Zep. 1:5), domestic altars. The kings of Judah did so: and, though Josiah never used them, yet to this time they remained there. Manasseh had built altars for his idols in the house of the Lord. When he repented he removed them, and *cast them out of the city* (2 Chr. 33:15), but, not destroying them, his son Amon, it seems, had brought them again into the courts of the temple; there Josiah found them, and thence he *broke them down, v.* 12. 5. There was *Tophet, in the valley of the son of Hinnom,* very near Jerusalem, where the image of Moloch (that god of unnatural cruelty, as others were of unnatural uncleanness) was kept, to which some sacrificed their children, burning them in the fire, others dedicated them, making them to pass through the fire (*v.* 10), *labouring in the very fire,* Hab. 2:13. It is supposed to have been called *Tophet* from *toph,* a drum, because they beat drums at the burning of the children, that their shrieks might not be heard. 6. There were *high places before Jerusalem,* which *Solomon had built, v.* 13. The altars and images on those high places, we may suppose, had been taken away by some of the preceding godly kings, or perhaps Solomon himself had removed them when he became a penitent; but the buildings, or some parts of them, remained, with other high places, till Josiah's time. Those that introduce corruptions into religion know not how far they will reach nor how long they will last. Antiquity is no certain proof of verity. There were also high places all the kingdom over, from *Geba to Beer-sheba* (*v.* 8), and *high places of the gates, in the entering in of the gate of the governor.* In these high places (bishop Patrick thinks) they burnt incense to those tutelar gods to whom their idolatrous kings had committed the protection of their city; and probably the governor of the city had a private altar for his *penates — his household-gods.* 7. There were idolatrous priests, that officiated at all those idolatrous altars (*v.* 5), chemarim, black men, or that wore black. See Zep. 1:4. Those that sacrificed to Osiris, or that wept for Tammuz (Eze. 8:14), or that worshipped the infernal deities, put on black garments as mourners. These idolatrous priests the kings of *Judah had ordained to burn incense in the high places;* they were, it should seem, priests of the house of Aaron, who thus profaned their dignity, and there were others also who had no right at all to the priesthood, who burnt incense to Baal. 8. There were conjurers and wizards, and such as *dealt with familiar spirits, v.* 24. When they worshipped the devil as their god no marvel that they consulted him as their oracle.

II. What a full destruction good Josiah made of all those relics of idolatry. Such is his zeal for the Lord of hosts, and his holy indignation against all that is displeasing to him, that nothing shall stand before him. The law was that the monuments of the Canaanites' idolatry must be all destroyed (Deu. 7:5), much more those of the idolatry of the Israelites, in whom it was much more impious, profane, and perfidious. 1. He ordered Hilkiah, and the other priests, to clear the temple. This was their province, *v.* 4. Away with all the vessels that were made for Baal. They must never be employed in the service of God, no, nor reserved for any common use; they must all be burnt, and the ashes of them carried to Bethel. That place had been the common source of idolatry, for there was set up one of the calves, and, that lying next to Judah, the infection had thence spread into that kingdom, and therefore Josiah made it the lay-stall of idolatry, the dunghill to which he carried the filth and offscouring of all things, that, if possible, it might be made loathsome to those that had been fond of it. 2. The idolatrous priests were all put down. Those of them that were not of the house of Aaron, or had sacrificed to Baal or other false gods, he put to death, according to the law, *v.* 20. He *slew them upon their own altars,* the most acceptable sacrifice that ever had been offered upon them, a sacrifice to the justice of God. Those that were descendants from Aaron, and yet had burnt incense in the high places, but to the true God only, he forbade ever to approach the altar of the Lord; they had forfeited that honour (*v.* 9): He *brought them out of the cities of Judah* (*v.* 8), that they might not do mischief in the country by secretly keeping up their old idolatrous usages; but he allowed them to *eat of the unleavened bread* (the bread of the meat-offering, Lev. 2:4, 5) *among their brethren,* with whom they were to reside, that being under their eye they might be kept from doing hurt and taught to do well; that bread, that unleavened bread (heavy and unpleasant as it was), was better than they deserved, and that would serve to keep them alive. But whether they were permitted to eat of all the sacrifices, as blemished priests were (Lev. 21:22), which is called, in general, *the bread of their God,* may be justly questioned. 3. All the images were broken to pieces and burnt. The image of the grove (*v.* 6), some goddess or other, was reduced to ashes, and the *ashes cast upon the graves of the common people* (*v.* 6), the common burying-place of the city. By the law a ceremonial uncleanness was contracted by the touch of a grave, so that in casting them here he declared them most impure, and none could touch them without thereby making themselves unclean. *He cast it into the graves* (so the Chaldee), intimating that he would have all idolatry buried out of his sight, as a loathsome thing, and forgotten, as dead men are out of mind, *v.* 14. He *filled the places of the groves with the bones of men;* as he carried the ashes of the images to the graves, to mingle them with dead men's bones, so he carried dead men's bones to the places where the images had been, and put them in the room of them, that, both ways, idolatry might be rendered loathsome, and the people kept both from the dust of the images and from the ruins of the places where they had been worshipped. Dead men and dead gods were much alike and fittest to go together. 4. All the wicked houses were suppressed, those nests of impiety that harboured idolaters, the houses of the Sodomites, *v.* 7. "Down with them, down with them, rase them to the foundations." The high places were in like manner broken down and levelled with the ground (*v.* 8), even that which belonged to the governor of the city; for no man's greatness or power may protect him in idolatry or profaneness. Let governors be obliged, in the first place, to reform, and then the governed will be the sooner influenced. He defiled the high places (*v.* 8 and again *v.* 13), did all he could to render them abominable, and put the people out of conceit with them, as Jehu did when he made the house of Baal a draught-house, 2 Ki. 10:27. Tophet, which, contrary to other places of idolatry, was in a valley, whereas they were on hills or high places, was likewise defiled (*v.* 10), was made the burying-place of the city. Concerning this we have a whole sermon, Jer. 19:1, 2, etc., where it is said, *They shall bury in Tophet,* and the whole city is threatened to be made like Tophet. 5. The horses that had been given to the sun were taken away and put to common use, and so were delivered from the vanity to which they were made subject; and the chariots of the sun (what a pity was it that those horses and chariots should be kept as the chariots and horsemen of Israel!) he burnt with fire; and, if the sun be a flame, they never resembled him so much as they did when they were chariots of fire. 6. The workers with familiar spirits and the wizards were put away, *v.* 24. Those of them that were convicted of witchcraft, it is likely, he put to death, and so deterred others from those diabolical practices. In all this he had a sincere regard to *the words of the law which were written in the book* lately found, *v.* 24. He made that law his rule and kept that in his eye throughout this reformation.

III. How his zeal extended itself to the cities of Israel that were within his reach. The ten tribes were carried captive and the Assyrian colonies did not fully people the country, so that, it is likely, many cities had put themselves under the protection of the kings of Judah, 2 Chr. 30:1; 34:6. These he here visits, to carry on his reformation. As far as our influence goes our endeavours should go to do good and bring the wickedness of the wicked to an end.

1. He defiled and demolished Jeroboam's altar at Bethel, with the high place and the grove that belonged to it, *v.* 15, 16. The golden calf, it should seem, was gone *(thy calf, O Samaria! has cast thee off),* but the altar was there, which those that were wedded to their old idolatries made use of still. This was, (1.) Defiled, *v.* 16. Josiah, in his pious zeal, was ransacking the old seats of idolatry, and spied the sepulchres in the mount, in which probably the idolatrous priests were buried, not far from the altar at which

they had officiated, and which they were so fond of that they were desirous to lay their bones by it; these he opened, took out the bones, and *burnt them upon the altar,* to show that thus he would have done by the priests themselves if they had been alive, as he did by those whom he found alive, *v.* 20. Thus he polluted the altar, desecrated it, and made it odious. It is threatened against idolaters (Jer. 8:1, 2) that *their bones shall be spread before the sun;* that which is there threatened and this which is here executed (bespeaking their *iniquity to be upon their bones,* Eze. 32:27) are an intimation of a punishment after death, reserved for those that live and die impenitent in that or any other sin; the burning of the bones, if that were all, is a small matter, but, if it signify the torment of the soul in a worse flame (Lu. 16:24), it is very dreadful. This, as it was Josiah's act, seems to have been the result of a very sudden resolve; he would not have done it but that he happened to turn himself, and spy the sepulchres; and yet it was foretold above 350 years before, when this altar was first built by Jeroboam, 1 Ki. 13:2. God always foresees, and has sometimes foretold as certain, that which yet to us seems most contingent. *The king's heart is in the hand of the Lord;* king Josiah's was so, and he turned it (or ever he himself was aware, Cant. 6:12) to do this. No work of God shall fall to the ground. (2.) It was demolished. He broke down the altar and all its appurtenances (*v.* 15), burnt what was combustible, and, since an idol is nothing in the world, he went as far towards the annihilating of it as he could; for he *stamped it small to powder* and made it *as dust before the wind.*

2. He destroyed all the houses of the high places, all those synagogues of Satan that were *in the cities of Samaria, v.* 19. These the kings of Israel built, and God raised up this king of Judah to pull them down, for the honour of the ancient house of David, from which the ten tribes had revolted; the priests he justly made sacrifices *upon their own altars, v.* 20.

3. He carefully preserved the sepulchre of that man of God who came from Judah to foretel this, which now a king who came from Judah executed. This was that good prophet who *proclaimed these things against the altar of Bethel,* and yet was himself slain by a lion for disobeying the word of the Lord; but to show that God's displeasure against him went no further than his death, but ended there, God so ordered it that when all the graves about his were disturbed his was safe (*v.* 17, 18) and no man moved his bones. He had entered into peace, and therefore should rest in his bed, Isa. 57:2. The old lying prophet, who desired to be buried as near him as might be, it should seem, knew what he did; for his dust also, being mingled with that of the good prophet, was preserved for his sake; see Num. 23:10.

IV. We are here told what a solemn passover Josiah and his people kept after all this. When they had cleared the country of the old leaven they then applied themselves to the keeping of the feast. When Jehu had destroyed the worship of Baal, yet he took no heed to walk in the commandments and ordinances of God; but Josiah considered that we must learn to do well, and no *only* cease to do evil, and that the way to keep out all abominable customs is to keep up all instituted ordinances (see Lev. 18:30), and therefore he commanded all the people to keep the passover, which was not only a memorial of their deliverance out of Egypt, but a token of their dedication to him that brought them out and their communion with him. This he found written in the *book of the law,* here called *the book of the covenant;* for, though the divine authority may deal with us in a way of absolute command, divine grace condescends to federal transactions, and therefore he observed it. We have not such a particular account of this passover as of that in Hezekiah's time, 2 Chr. 30. But, in general, we are told that *there was not holden such a passover* in any of the foregoing reigns, no, not *from the days of the judges* (*v.* 22), which, by the way, intimates that, though the account which the book of Judges gives of the state of Israel under that dynasty looks but melancholy, yet there were then some golden days. This passover, it seems, was extraordinary for the number and devotion of the communicants, their sacrifices and offerings, and their exact observance of the laws of the feast; and it was not now as in Hezekiah's passover, when many communicated that were not cleansed according to the purification of

the sanctuary, and the Levites were permitted to do the priests' work. We have reason to think that during all the remainder of Josiah's reign religion flourished and the feasts of the Lord were very carefully observed; but in this passover the satisfaction they took in the covenant lately renewed, the reformation in pursuance of it, and the revival of an ordinance of which they had lately found the divine original in the book of the law, and which had long been neglected or carelessly kept, put them into great transports of holy joy; and God was pleased to recompense their zeal in destroying idolatry with uncommon tokens of his presence and favour. All this concurred to make it a distinguished passover.

Verses 25–30

Upon the reading of these verses we must say, Lord, though *thy righteousness* be *as the great mountains* — evident, conspicuous, and past dispute, yet *thy judgments are a great deep,* unfathomable and past finding out, Ps. 36:6. What shall we say to this?

I. It is here owned that Josiah was one of the best kings that ever sat upon the throne of David, *v.* 25. As Hezekiah was a non-such for faith and dependence upon God in straits (*ch.* 18:5), so Josiah was a non-such for sincerity and zeal in carrying on a work of reformation. For this there was none like him, 1. That he *turned to the Lord* from whom his fathers had revolted. It is true religion to turn to God as one we have chosen and love. He did what he could to turn his kingdom also to the Lord. 2. That he did this *with his heart and soul;* his affections and aims were right in what he did. Those make nothing of their religion that do not make heart-work of it. 3. That he did it with *all his heart,* and *all his soul,* and *all his might* — with vigour, and courage, and resolution: he could not otherwise have broken through the difficulties he had to grapple with. What great things may we bring to pass in the service of God if we be but lively and hearty in it! 4. That he did this *according to all the law of Moses,* in an exact observance of that law and with an actual regard to it. His zeal did not transport him into any irregularities, but, in all he did, he walked by rule.

II. Notwithstanding this he was cut off by a violent death in the midst of his days, and his kingdom was ruined within a few years after. Consequent upon such a reformation as this, one would have expected nothing but the prosperity and glory both of king and kingdom; but, quite contrary, we find both under a cloud. 1. Even the reformed kingdom continues marked for ruin. For all this (*v.* 26) *the Lord turned not from the fierceness of his great wrath.* That is certainly true, which God spoke by the prophet (Jer. 18:7, 8), that if a nation, doomed to destruction, *turn from the evil* of sin, God will *repent of the evil* of punishment; and therefore we must conclude that Josiah's people, though they submitted to Josiah's power, did not heartily imbibe Josiah's principles. They were turned by force, and did not voluntarily *turn from their evil way,* but still continued their affection for their idols; and therefore he that knows men's hearts would not recall the sentence, which was, That Judah should be removed, as Israel had been, and Jerusalem itself cast off, *v.* 27. Yet even this destruction was intended to be their effectual reformation; so that we must say, not only that the criminals had filled their measure and were ripe for ruin, but also that the disease had come to a crisis, and was ready for a cure; and this shall be all the fruit, even the taking away of sin. 2. As an evidence of this, even the reforming king is cut off in the midst of his usefulness — in mercy to him, that he might not see the evil which was coming upon his kingdom, but in wrath to his people, for his death was an inlet to their desolations. The king of Egypt waged war, it seems, with the king of Assyria: so the king of Babylon is now called. Josiah's kingdom lay between them. He therefore thought himself concerned to oppose the king of Egypt, and check the growing, threatening, greatness of his power; for though, at this time, he protested that he had no design against Josiah, yet, if he should prevail to unite the river of Egypt and the river Euphrates, the land of Judah would soon be overflowed between them. Therefore *Josiah went against him,* and was killed in the first engagement, *v.* 29, 30. Here, (1.) We cannot justify Josiah's conduct. He had no clear call to engage in this war, nor do we find that he asked counsel of God by urim or prophets concerning it. What

had he to do to appear and act as a friend and ally to the king of Assyria? *Should he help the ungodly and love those that hate the Lord?* If the kings of Egypt and Assyria quarrelled, he had reason to think God would bring good out of it to him and his people, by making them instrumental to weaken one another. Some understand the promise made to him that he should *come to his grave in peace* in a sense in which it was not performed because, by his miscarriage in this matter, he forfeited the benefit of it. God has promised to keep us *in all our ways;* but, if we go out of our way, we throw ourselves out of his protection. I understand the promise so as that I believe it was fulfilled, for he *died in peace* with God and his own conscience, and saw not, nor had any immediate prospect of, the destruction of Judah and Jerusalem by the Chaldeans; yet I understand the providence to be a rebuke to him for his rashness. (2.) We must adore God's righteousness in taking away such a jewel from an unthankful people that knew not how to value it. They greatly lamented his death (2 Chr. 35:25), urged to it by Jeremiah, who told them the meaning of it, and what a threatening omen it was; but they had not made a due improvement of the mercies they enjoyed by his life, of which God taught them the worth by the want.

Verses 31–37

Jerusalem saw not a good day after Josiah was laid in his grave, but one trouble came after another, till within twenty-two years it was quite destroyed. Of the reign of two of his sons here is a short account; the former we find here a prisoner and the latter a tributary to the king of Egypt, and both so in the very beginning of their reign. This king of Egypt having slain Josiah, though he had not had any design upon Judah, yet, being provoked by the opposition which Josiah gave him, now, it should seem, he bent all his force against his family and kingdom. If Josiah's sons had trodden in his steps, they would have fared the better for his piety; but, deviating from them, they fared the worse for his rashness.

I. Jehoahaz, a younger son, was first made king by *the people of the land,* probably because he was observed to be of a more active warlike genius than his elder brother, and likely to make head against the king of Egypt and to avenge his father's death, which perhaps the people were more solicitous about, in point of honour, than the keeping up and carrying on of his father's reformation; and the issue was accordingly. 1. He did ill, *v.* 32. Though he had a good education and a good example given him, and many a good prayer, we may suppose, put up for him, yet he *did that which was evil in the sight of the Lord,* and, it is to be feared, began to do so in his father's lifetime, for his reign was so short that he could not, in that, show much of his character. He did *according to all that his* wicked *fathers had done.* Though he had not time to do much, yet he had chosen his patterns, and showed whom he intended to follow and whose steps he resolved to tread in; and, having done this, he is here reckoned to have done according to all the evil which those did whom he proposed to imitate. It is of great consequence to young people whom they choose to take for their patterns and whom they emulate. An error in this choice is fatal. Phil. 3:17, 18. 2. Doing ill, no wonder that he fared ill. He was but three months a prince, and was then made a prisoner, and lived and died so. The king of Egypt seized him, and put him in bands (*v.* 33), fearing lest he should give him disturbance, and carried him to Egypt, where he died soon after, *v.* 34. This Jehoahaz is that young lion whom Ezekiel speaks of in his *lamentation for the princes of Israel,* that learnt to *catch the prey and devour men* (that was the evil which he did in the sight of the Lord); but *the nations heard of him, he was taken in their pit, and they brought him with chains into the land of Egypt,* Eze. 19:1–4. See Jer. 22:10–12.

II. Eliakim, another son of Josiah, was made king by the king of Egypt, it is not said *in the room of Jehoahaz* (his reign was so short that it was scarcely worth taking notice of), but *in the room of Josiah.* The crown of Judah had hitherto always descended from a father to a son, and never, till now, from one brother to another; once the succession had so happened in the house of Ahab, but never, till now, in the house of David. The king of Egypt, having used his power in making him king, further showed it in changing his name; he called him *Jehoiakim,* a name that has reference to Jehovah, for he had no design to make him renounce or forget the religion of his country. "All people will walk in the name of their God, and let him do so." The king of Babylon did not do so by those whose names he changed, Dan. 1:7. Of this Jehoiakim we are here told, 1. That the king of Egypt made him poor, exacted from him a vast tribute of 100 *talents of silver and a talent of gold* (*v.* 33), which, with much difficulty, he squeezed out of his subjects and gave to Pharaoh, *v.* 35. Formerly the Israelites had spoiled the Egyptians; now the Egyptians spoil Israel. See what woeful changes sin makes. 2. That which made him poor, yet did not make him good. Notwithstanding the rebukes of Providence he was under, by which he should have been convinced, humbled, and reformed, he *did that which was evil in the sight of the Lord* (*v.* 37), and so prepared against himself greater judgments; for such God will send if less do not do the work for which they are sent.

CHAPTER 24

Things are here ripening for, and hastening towards, the utter destruction of Jerusalem. We left Jehoiakim on the throne, placed there by the king of Egypt: now here we have, I. The troubles of his reign, how he was brought into subjection by the king of Babylon, and severely chastised for attempting to shake off the yoke (*v.* 1–6), and how Egypt also was conquered by Nebuchadnezzar (*v.* 7). II. The desolations of his son's reign, which continued but three months; and then he and all his great men, being forced to surrender at discretion, were carried captives to Babylon (*v.* 8–16). III. The preparatives of the next reign (which was the last of all) for the utter ruin of Jerusalem, which the next chapter will give us an account of (*v.* 17–20).

Verses 1–7

We have here the first mention of a name which makes a great figure both in the histories and in the prophecies of the Old Testament; it is that of *Nebuchadnezzar,* king of Babylon (*v.* 1), that head of gold. He was a potent prince, and one that was the terror of the mighty in the land of the living; and yet his name would not have been known in sacred writ if he had not been employed in the destruction of Jerusalem and the captivity of the Jews.

I. He made Jehoiakim his tributary and kept him in subjection three years, *v.* 1. Nebuchadnezzar began his reign in the fourth year of Jehoiakim. In his eighth year he made him his prisoner, but restored him upon his promise of faithfulness to him. That promise he kept about three years, but then rebelled, probably in hopes of assistance from the king of Egypt. If Jehoiakim had served his God as he should have done, he would not have been servant to the king of Babylon; but God would thus make him know the difference between his service and *the service of the kings of the countries,* 2 Chr. 12:8. If he had been content with his servitude, and true to his word, his condition would have been no worse; but, rebelling against the king of Babylon, he plunged himself into more trouble.

II. When he rebelled Nebuchadnezzar sent his forces against him to destroy his country, bands of Chaldeans, Syrians, Moabites, Ammonites, who were all now in the service and pay of the king of Babylon (*v.* 2), and withal retained, and now showed, their ancient enmity to the Israel of God. Yet no mention is here made of their commission from the king of Babylon, but only of that from the King of kings: *The Lord sent against him* all these bands; and again (*v.* 3), *Surely at the commandment of the Lord came this upon Judah,* else the commandment of Nebuchadnezzar could not have brought it. Many are serving God's purposes who are not aware of it. Two things God intended in suffering Judah to be thus harassed: — 1. The punishment of the sins of Manasseh, which God now visited upon *the third and fourth generation.* So long he waited before he visited them, to see if the nation would repent; but they continued impenitent, notwithstanding Josiah's endeavours to reform them, and ready to relapse, upon the first turn, into their former idolatries. Now that the old bond was put in suit they were called up upon the former judgment; that was revived which God had *laid up in store,* and *sealed among his treasures* (Deu. 32:34; Job 14:17), and in remembrance of that he removed Judah out of his sight, and let the world know that *time will not wear out the guilt of sin* and that reprieves are not pardons. All that Manasseh did was called to mind, but especially the *innocent blood that he shed,* much of which, we may suppose, was the blood of God's witnesses and worshippers, *which the Lord would not pardon.* Is there then any unpardonable sin but the blasphemy against the Holy Ghost? This is meant of the remitting of the temporal punishment. Though Manasseh repented, and we have reason to think even the persecutions and murders he was guilty of were pardoned, so that he was delivered from the wrath to come; yet, as they were national sins, they lay still charged upon the land, crying for national judgments. Perhaps some were now living who were aiding and abetting; and the present king was guilty of innocent blood, as appears Jer. 22:17. See what a provoking sin murder is, how loud it cries, and how long. See what need nations have to lament the sins of their fathers, lest they smart for them. God intended hereby the accomplishment of the prophecies; it was *according to the word of the Lord, which he spoke by his servants the prophets.* Rather shall Judah be *removed out of his sight,* nay, rather shall *heaven and earth pass away,* than any word of God fall to the ground. Threatenings will be fulfilled as certainly as promises, if the sinner's repentance prevent not.

III. The king of Egypt was likewise subdued by the king of Babylon, and a great part of his country taken from him, *v.* 7. It was but lately that he had oppressed Israel, *ch.* 23:33. Now he is himself brought down and disabled to attempt any thing for the recovery of his losses or the assistance of his allies. He dares not *come any more out of his land.* Afterwards he attempted to give Zedekiah some relief, but was obliged to retire, Jer. 37:7.

IV. Jehoiakim, seeing his country laid waste and himself ready to fall into the enemy's hand, as it should seem, died of a broken heart, in the midst of his days (*v.* 6). So *Jehoiakim slept with his fathers;* but it is not said that he was *buried with them,* for no doubt the prophecy of Jeremiah was fulfilled, that he should not be lamented, as his father was, but *buried with the burial of an ass* (Jer. 22:18, 19), and his dead body cast out, Jer. 36:30.

Verses 8–20

This should have been the history of king Jehoiachin's *reign,* but, alas! it is only the history of king Jehoiachin's *captivity,* as it is called, Eze. 1:2. He came to the crown, not to have the honour of wearing it, but the shame of losing it. *Ideo tantum venerat, ut exiret — He came in only to go out.*

I. His reign was short and inconsiderable. He reigned but three months, and then was removed and carried captive to Babylon, as his father, it is likely, would have been if he had lived but so much longer. What an unhappy young prince was this, that was thrust into a falling house, a sinking throne! What an unnatural father had he, who begat him to suffer for him, and by his own sin and folly had left himself nothing to bequeath to his son but his own miseries! Yet this young prince reigned long enough to show that he justly smarted for his fathers' sins, for he trod in their steps (*v.* 9): *He did that which was evil in the sight of the Lord,* as they had done; he did nothing to cut off the entail of the curse, to discharge the incumbrances of his crown, and therefore *(transit cum onere — the incumbrance descends with the crown)* with his own iniquity that of his fathers shall come into the account.

II. The calamities that came upon him, and his family, and people, in the very beginning of his reign, were very grievous. 1. Jerusalem was besieged by the king of Babylon, *v.* 10, 11. He had sent his forces to ravage the country, *v.* 2. Now he came himself, and laid siege to the city. Now the word of God was fulfilled (Deu. 28:49, etc.), *The Lord shall bring a nation against thee from far, of fierce countenance,* that shall first *eat of the fruit of thy land* and then *besiege thee in all thy gates.* 2. Jehoiachin immediately surrendered at discretion. As soon as he heard the king of Babylon had come in person against the city, his name having at this time become very formidable, he beat a parley and went out to him, *v.* 12. Had he made his peace with God, and taken the method that Hezekiah did in the like case, he needed not to have feared the king of Babylon, but might have held out with courage, honour, and success (one should have chased a thousand); but, wanting the faith and piety of an Israelite, he had not the resolution of a man, of a soldier, of a prince. He and his royal family, his mother and wives, his servants and princes, delivered themselves up prisoners of war; this was the consequence of their being servants of sin. 3. Nebuchadnezzar rifled the treasuries both of the church and of the state, and carried away the silver and gold of both, *v.* 13. Now the word of God by Isaiah was fulfilled (*ch.* 20:17), *All that is in thy house shall be carried to Babylon.* Even the vessels of the temple which Solomon had made, and laid up in store to be used as the old ones were worn out, he cut off from the temple, and began to cut them in pieces, but, upon second thoughts, reserved them for his own use, for we find Belshazzar drinking wine in them, Dan. 5:2, 3. 4. He carried away a great part of Jerusalem into captivity, to weaken it, that he might effectually secure to himself the dominion of it and prevent its revolt, and to enrich himself with the wealth or service of those he took away. There had been some carried away eight years before this, in the first year of Nebuchadnezzar and the third of Jehoiakim, among whom were Daniel and his fellows. See Dan. 1:1, 6. They had approved themselves so well that this politic prince coveted more of them. Now he carried off, (1.) The young king himself and his family (*v.* 15), and we find (*ch.* 25:27–29) that for thirty-seven years he continued a close prisoner. (2.) All the great men, the princes and officers, whose riches were *kept for the owners thereof to their hurt* (Eccl. 5:13), tempting the enemies to make a prey of them first. (3.) All the military men, the *mighty men of valour* (*v.* 14), *the mighty of the land* (*v.* 15), *the men of might, even all that were strong and apt for war, v.* 16. These could not defend themselves, and the conqueror would not leave them to defend their country, but took them away, to be employed in his service. (4.) All the craftsmen and smiths who made weapons of war; in taking them he did, in effect, disarm the city, according to the Philistines' policy, 1 Sa. 13:19. In this captivity Ezekiel the prophet was carried away (Eze. 1:1, 2) and Mordecai, Esth. 2:6. This Jehoiachin was also called *Jeconiah* (1 Chr. 3:16), and in contempt (Jer. 22:24, where his captivity is foretold) *Coniah.*

III. The successor whom the king of Babylon appointed in the room of Jehoiachin. God had written him childless (Jer. 22:30) and therefore his uncle was entrusted with the government. The king of Babylon made Mattaniah king, the son of Josiah; and to remind him, and let all the world know, that he was his creature, he changed his name and called him *Zedekiah, v.* 17. God had sometimes charged it upon his people, *They have set up kings, but not by me* (Hos. 8:4), and now, to punish them for that, the king of Babylon shall have the setting up of their kings. Those are justly deprived of their liberty that use it, and insist upon it, against God's authority. This Zedekiah was the last of the kings of Judah. The name which the king of Babylon gave him signifies *The justice of the Lord,* and was a presage of the glorifying of God's justice in his ruin. 1. See how impious this Zedekiah was. Though the judgments of God upon his three immediate predecessors might have been a warning to him not to tread in their steps, yet *he did that which was evil,* like all the rest, *v.* 19. 2. See how impolitic he was. As his predecessor lost his courage, so he his wisdom, with his religion, for he *rebelled against the king of Babylon* (*v.* 20), whose tributary he was, and so provoked him whom he was utterly unable to contend with, and who, if he had continued true to him, would have protected him. This was the most foolish thing he could do, and hastened the ruin of his kingdom. This came to pass *through the anger of the Lord, that he might cast them out from his presence.* Note, When those that are entrusted with the counsels of a nation act unwisely, and against their true interest, we ought to take notice of the displeasure of God in it. It is for the sins of a people that God *removes the speech of the trusty and takes away the understanding of the aged,* and *hides from their eyes the things that belong to* the public *peace.* Whom God will destroy he infatuates.

CHAPTER 25

Ever since David's time Jerusalem had been a celebrated place, beautiful for situation and the joy of the whole earth: while the book of psalms lasts that name will sound great. In the New Testament we read much of it, when it was, as here, ripening again for its ruin. In the close of the Bible we read of a new Jerusalem. Every thing therefore that concerns Jerusalem is worthy our regard. In this chapter we have, I. The utter destruction of Jerusalem by the Chaldeans, the city besieged and taken (*v.* 1–4), the houses burnt (*v.* 8, 9), and wall broken down (*v.* 10), and the inhabitants carried away into captivity (*v.* 11, 12). The glory of Jerusalem was, 1. That it was the royal city, where were set "the thrones of the house of David;" but that glory has now departed, for the prince is made a most miserable prisoner, the seed royal is destroyed (*v.* 5–7), and the principal officers are put to death (*v.* 18–21). 2. That it was the holy city, where was the testimony of Israel; but that glory has departed, for Solomon's temple is burnt to the ground (*v.* 9) and the sacred vessels that remained are carried away to Babylon (*v.* 13–17). Thus has Jerusalem become as a widow, Lam. 1:1. Ichabod — Where is the glory? II. The distraction and dispersion of the remnant that was left in Judah under Gedaliah (*v.* 22–26). III. The countenance which, after thirty-seven years' imprisonment, was given to Jehoiachin the captive king of Judah (*v.* 27–30).

Verses 1–7

We left king Zedekiah in rebellion against the king of Babylon (*ch.* 24:20), contriving and endeavouring to shake off his yoke, when he was no way able to do it, nor took the right method by making God his friend first. Now here we have an account of the fatal consequences of that attempt.

I. The king of Babylon's army laid siege to Jerusalem, *v.* 1. What should hinder them when the country was already in their possession? *ch.* 24:2. They *built forts against the city round about,* whence, by such arts of war as they then had, they battered it, sent into it instruments of death, and kept out of it the necessary supports of life. Formerly Jerusalem had been compassed with the favour of God as with a shield, but now their defence had departed from them and their enemies surrounded them on every side. Those that by sin have provoked God to leave them will find that *innumerable evils will compass them about.* Two years this siege lasted; at first the army retired, for fear of the king of Egypt (Jer. 37:11), but, finding him not so powerful as they thought, they soon returned, with a resolution not to quit the city till they had made themselves masters of it.

II. During this siege the famine prevailed (*v.* 3), so that for a long time they *ate their bread by weight and with care,* Eze. 4:16. Thus they were punished for their gluttony and excess, their *fulness of bread* and *feeding themselves without fear.* At length *there was no bread for the people of the land,* that is, the common people, the soldiers, whereby they were weakened and rendered unfit for service. Now they ate their own children for want of food. See this foretold by one prophet (Eze. 5:10) and bewailed by another, Lam. 4:3, etc. Jeremiah earnestly persuaded the king to surrender (Jer. 38:17), but his heart was hardened to his destruction.

III. At length the city was taken by storm: it was *broken up, v.* 4. The besiegers made a breach in the wall, at which they forced their way into it. The besieged, unable any longer to defend it, endeavoured to quit it, and make the best of their way; and many, no doubt, were put to the sword, the victorious army being much exasperated by their obstinacy.

IV. The king, his family, and all his great men, made their escape in the night, by some secret passages which the besiegers either had not discovered or did not keep their eye upon, *v.* 4. But those as much deceive themselves who think to escape God's judgments as those who think to brave them; the feet of him that flees from them will as surely fail as the hands of him that fights against them. When God judges he will overcome. Intelligence was given to the Chaldeans of the king's flight, and which way he had gone, so that they soon overtook him, *v.* 5. His guards were scattered from him, every man shifting for his own safety. Had he put himself under God's protection, that would not have failed him now. He presently fell into the enemies' hands, and here we are told what they did with him. 1. He was brought to the king of Babylon, and tried by a council of war for rebelling against him who set him up, and to whom he had sworn fidelity. God and man had a quarrel with him for this; see Eze. 17:16, etc. The king of Babylon now lay at Riblah (which lay between Judea and Babylon), that he might be ready to give orders both to his court at home and his army abroad. 2. His *sons were slain before his eyes,* though children, that this doleful spectacle, the last his eyes were to behold, might leave an impression of grief and horror upon his spirit as long as he lived. In slaying his sons, they showed their indignation at his falsehood, and in effect declared that neither he nor any of his were fit to be trusted, and therefore that they were not fit to live. 3. His eyes were put out, by which he was deprived of that common comfort of human life which is given even to *those that are in misery, and to the bitter in soul,* the light of the sun, by which he was also disabled for any service. He dreaded being mocked, and therefore would not be persuaded to yield (Jer. 38:19), but that which he feared came upon him with a witness, and no doubt added much to his misery; for, as those that are deaf suspect that every body talks of them, so those that are blind suspect that every body laughs at them. By this two prophecies that seemed to contradict one another were both fulfilled. Jeremiah prophesied that Zedekiah should be brought to Babylon, Jer. 32:5; 34:3. Ezekiel prophesied that he should not see Babylon, Eze. 12:13. He was brought thither, but, his eyes being put out, he did not see it. Thus he ended his days, before he ended his life. 4. He was *bound in fetters of brass* and so *carried to Babylon.* He that was blind needed not be bound (his blindness fettered him), but, for his greater disgrace, they led him bound; only, whereas common malefactors are laid in irons (Ps. 105:18; 107:10), he, being a prince, was bound with fetters of brass; but that the metal was somewhat nobler and lighter was little comfort, while still he was in fetters. Let it not seem strange if those that have been held in the cords of iniquity come to be thus *held in the cords of affliction,* Job 36:8.

Verses 8–21

Though we have reason to think that the army of the Chaldeans were much enraged against the city for holding out with so much stubbornness, yet they did not therefore put all to fire and sword as soon as they had taken the city (which is too commonly done in such cases), but about a month after (compare *v.* 8 with *v.* 3) Nebuzar-adan was sent with orders to complete the destruction of Jerusalem. This space God gave them to repent, after all the foregoing days of his patience, but in vain; their hearts (for aught that appears) were still hardened, and therefore execution is awarded to the utmost. 1. The city and temple are burnt, *v.* 9. It does not appear that the king of Babylon designed to send any colonies to people Jerusalem and therefore he ordered it to be laid in ashes, as a nest of rebels. At the burning of the king's house and *the houses of the great men* one cannot so much wonder (the inhabitants had, by their sins, made them combustible), but that the *house of the Lord* should perish in these flames, that that holy and beautiful house should be burnt with fire (Isa. 64:11), is very strange. That house which David prepared for, and which Solomon built at such a vast expense — that house which had the eye and heart of God perpetually upon it (1 Ki. 9:3) — might not that have been snatched as a brand out of this burning? No, it must not be fire-proof against God's judgments. This stately structure must be turned into ashes, and it is probable the ark in it, for the enemies, having heard how dearly the Philistines paid for the abusing of it, durst not seize that, nor did any of its friends take care to preserve it, for then we should have heard of it again in the second temple. One of the apocryphal writers does indeed tell us that the prophet Jeremiah got it out of the temple, and conveyed it to a cave in Mount Nebo on the other side Jordan, and hid it there (2 Macc. 2:4, 5), but that could not be, for Jeremiah was a close prisoner at that time. By the burning of the temple God would show how little cares for the external pomp of his worship when the life and power of religion are neglected. The people trusted to the temple, as if that would protect them in their sins (Jer. 7:4), but God, by this, let them know that when they had profaned it they would find it but a refuge of lies. This temple had stood about 420, some say 430 years. The people having forfeited the promises made concerning it, those promises must be understood of the gospel-temple, which is God's rest for ever. It is observable that the second temple was burnt by the Romans the same month, and the same day of the month, that the first temple was burnt by the Chaldeans, which, Josephus says, was the tenth of August. 2. The walls of Jerusalem are demolished (*v.* 10), as if the victorious army would be revenged on them for having kept them out so long, or at least prevent the like opposition another time. Sin unwalls a people and takes away their defence. These walls were never repaired till Nehemiah's time. 3. The residue of the people are carried away captive to Babylon, *v.* 11. Most of the inhabitants had perished by sword or famine, or had made their escape when the king did (for it is said, *v.* 5, *His army was scattered from him*), so that there were very few left, who with the deserters, making in all but 832 persons (as appears, Jer. 52:29), were carried away into captivity; only *the poor of the land were left behind* (*v.* 12), to till the ground and dress the vineyards for the Chaldeans. Sometimes poverty is a protection; for those that have nothing have nothing to lose. When the rich Jews, who had been oppressive to the poor, were made strangers, nay, prisoners, in an enemy's country, the poor whom they had despised and oppressed had liberty and peace in their own country. Thus Providence sometimes remarkably humbles the proud and favours those of low degree. 4. The brazen vessels, and other appurtenances of the temple, are carried away, those of silver and gold being most of them gone before. Those two famous columns of brass, *Jachin* and *Boaz,* which signified the strength and stability of the house of God, were broken to pieces and the brass of them was carried to Babylon, *v.* 13. When the things signified were sinned away what should the signs stand there for? Ahaz had profanely *cut off the borders of the bases,* and put *the brazen sea upon a pavement of stones* (2 Ki. 16:17); justly therefore are the brass themselves, and the brazen sea, delivered into the enemy's hand. It is just with God to take away his ordinances from those that profane and abuse them, that curtail and depress them. Some things remained of gold and silver (*v.* 15) which were now carried off; but most of this plunder was brass, such a vast quantity of it that it is said to be *without weight, v.* 16. The carrying away of *the vessels wherewith they ministered* (*v.* 14) put an end to the ministration. It was a righteous thing with God to deprive those of the benefit of his worship who had slighted it so long and preferred false worships before it. Those that would have many altars shall now have none. 5. Several of the great men are slain in cold blood — Seraiah the chief priest (who was the father of Ezra as appears, Ezra 7:1), the second priest (who, when there was occasion, officiated for him), and three door-keepers of the temple (*v.* 18), the general of the army, five privy-counsellors (afterwards they made them up seven, Jer. 52:25), the secretary of war, or pay-master of the army, and sixty country gentlemen who had concealed themselves in the city. These, being persons of some rank, were brought to the king of Babylon (*v.* 19, 20), who ordered them to be all put to death (*v.* 21), when, in reason, they might have hoped that surely the bitterness of death was past. These the king of Babylon's revenge looked upon as most active in opposing him; but divine justice, we may suppose, looked upon them as ringleaders in that idolatry and impiety which were punished by these desolations. This completed the calamity: *So Judah was carried away out of their land,* about 860 years after they were put in possession of it by Joshua. Now the scripture was fulfilled, *The Lord shall bring thee, and the king which thou shalt set over thee, into a nation which thou hast not known,* Deu. 28:36. Sin kept their fathers forty years out of Canaan, and now turned *them* out. The Lord is known by those judgments which he executes, and makes good that word which he has spoken, Amos 3:2. *You only have I known of all the families of the earth, therefore I will punish you for all your iniquities.*

Verses 22–30

In these verses we have,

I. The dispersion of the remaining people. The city of Jerusalem was quite laid waste. Some people there were in the land of Judah (*v.* 22) that had weathered the storm, and (which was no small favour at this time, Jer. 45:5) had *their lives given them for a prey.* Now see, 1. What a good posture they were put into. The king of Babylon appointed Gedaliah, one of themselves, to be their governor and protector under him, a very good man, and one that would make the best of the bad, *v.* 22. His father Ahikam was one that countenanced and protected Jeremiah when the princes had vowed his death, Jer. 26:24. It is probable that this Gedaliah, by the advice of Jeremiah, had gone over the Chaldeans, and had conducted himself so well that the king of Babylon entrusted him with the government. He resided not at Jerusalem, but at Mizpah, in the land of Benjamin, a place famous in Samuel's time. Thither those came who had fled from Zedekiah (*v.* 4) and put themselves under his protection (*v.* 23), which he assured them of if they would be patient and peaceable under the government of the king of Babylon, *v.* 24. Gedaliah, though he had not the pomp and power of a sovereign prince, yet might have been a greater blessing to them than many of their kings had been, especially having such a privy-council as Jeremiah, who was now with them, and interested himself in their affairs, Jer. 40:5, 6. 2. What a fatal breach was made upon them, soon afterwards, by the death of Gedaliah, within two months after he entered upon his government. The utter extirpation of the Jews, for the present, was determined, and therefore it was in vain for them to think of taking root again: the whole land must be plucked up, Jer. 45:4. Yet this hopeful settlement is dashed to pieces, not by the Chaldeans, but by some of themselves. The things of their peace were so hidden from their eyes that they knew not when they were well off, nor would believe when they were told. (1.) They had a good governor of their own, and him they slew, out of spite to the Chaldeans, because he was appointed by Nebuchadnezzar, v. 25. Ishmael, who was of the royal family, envying Gedaliah's advancement and the happy settlement of the people under him, though he could not propose to set up himself, resolved to ruin him, and basely slew him and all his friends, both Jews and Chaldeans. Nebuchadnezzar would not, could not, have been a more mischievous enemy to their peace than this degenerate branch of the house of David was. (2.) They were as yet in their own good land, but they forsook it, and went to Egypt, for fear of the Chaldeans, v. 26. The Chaldeans had reason enough to be offended at the murder of Gedaliah; but if those that remained had humbly remonstrated, alleging that it was only the act of Ishmael and his party, we may suppose that those who were innocent of it, nay, who suffered greatly by it, would not have been punished for it: but, under pretence of this apprehension, contrary to the counsel of Jeremiah, they all went to Egypt, where, it is probable, they mixed with the Egyptians by degrees, and were never heard of more as Israelites. Thus was there a full end made of them by their own folly and disobedience, and Egypt had the last of them, that the last verse of that chapter of threatenings might be fulfilled, after all the rest, Deu. 28:68, *The Lord shall bring thee into Egypt again.* These events are more largely related by the prophet Jeremiah, *ch.* 40 to *ch.* 45. *Quaeque ipse miserrima vidit, et quorum pars magna fuit — Which scenes he was doomed to behold, and in which he bore a melancholy part.*

II. The reviving of the captive prince. Of Zedekiah we hear no more after he was carried blind to Babylon; it is probable that he did not live long, but that when he died he was buried with some marks of honour, Jer. 34:5. Of Jehoiachin, or Jeconiah, who surrendered himself (*ch.* 24:12), we are here told that as soon as Evil-merodach came to the crown, upon the death of his father Nebuchadnezzar, he released him out of prison (where he had lain thirty-seven years, and was now fifty-five years old), *spoke kindly to him,* paid more respect to him than to any other of the kings his father had left in captivity (v. 28), gave him princely clothing instead of his prison-garments, maintained him in his own palace (v. 29), and allowed him a pension for himself and his family in some measure corresponding to his rank, *a daily rate for every day as long as he lived.* Consider this, 1. As a very happy change of Jehoiachin's condition. To have honour and liberty after he had been so long in confinement and disgrace, the plenty and pleasure of a court after he had been so long accustomed to the straits and miseries of a prison, was like the return of the morning after a very dark and tedious night. Let none say that they shall never see good again because they have long seen little but evil; the most miserable know not what blessed turn Providence may yet give to their affairs, nor what comforts they are reserved for, *according to the days wherein they have been afflicted,* Ps. 110:15. However the death of afflicted saints is to them such a change as this was to Jehoiachin: it will release them out of their prison, shake off the body, that prison-garment, and open the way to their advancement; it will send them to the throne, to the table, of the King of kings, the glorious liberty of God's children. 2. As a very generous act of Evil-merodach's. He thought his father made the yoke of his captives too heavy, and therefore, with the tenderness of a man and the honour of a prince, made it lighter. It should seem all the kings he had in his power were favoured, but Jehoiachin above them all, some think for the sake of the antiquity of his family and the honour of his renowned ancestors, David and Solomon. None of the kings of the nations, it is likely, had descended from so long a race of kings in a direct lineal succession, and by a male line, as the king of Judah. The Jews say that this Evil-merodach had been himself imprisoned by his own father, when he returned from his madness, for some mismanagement at that time, and that in prison he contracted a friendship with Jehoiachin, in consequence of which, as soon as he had it in his power, he showed him this kindness as a sufferer, as a fellow-sufferer. Some suggest that Evil-merodach had learned from Daniel and his fellows the principles of the true religion, and was well affected to them, and upon that account favoured Jehoiachin. 3. As a kind dispensation of Providence, for the encouragement of the Jews in captivity, and the support of their faith and hope concerning their enlargement in due time. This happened just about the midnight of their captivity. Thirty-six of the seventy years were now past, and almost as many were yet behind, and now to see their king thus advanced would be a comfortable earnest to them of their own release in due time, in the set time. *Unto the upright there* thus *ariseth light in the darkness,* to encourage them to hope, even in the *cloudy and dark day,* that at *evening time it shall be light;* when therefore we are perplexed, let us not be in despair.

AN EXPOSITION, WITH PRACTICAL OBSERVATIONS, OF
THE FIRST BOOK OF CHRONICLES

In common things repetition is thought needless and nauseous; but, in sacred things, *precept must be upon precept and line upon line. To me,* says the apostle, *to write the same things is not grievous, but for you it is safe,* Phil. 3:1. These books of Chronicles are in a great measure repetition; so are much of the second and third of the four evangelists: and yet there are no tautologies either here or there no *vain repetitions.* We may be ready to think that of all the books of holy scripture we could best spare these two books of Chronicles. Perhaps we might, and yet we could ill spare them: for there are many most excellent useful things in them, which we find not elsewhere. And as for what we find here which we have already met with, 1. It might be of great use to those who lived when these books were first published, before the canon of the Old Testament was completed and the particles of it put together; for it would remind them of what was more fully related in the other books. Abstracts, abridgments, and references, are of use in divinity as well as law. That, perhaps, may not be said in vain which yet has been said before. 2. It is still of use, that *out of the mouth of two witnesses every word may be established,* and, being inculcated, may be remembered. The penman of these books is supposed to be Ezra, that *ready scribe in the law of the Lord,* Ezra 7:6. It is a groundless story of that apocryphal writer (2 Esdr. 14:21, etc.) that, all the law being burnt, Ezra was divinely inspired to write it all over again, which yet might take rise from the books of Chronicles, where we find, though not all the same story repeated, yet the names of all those who

were the subjects of that story. These books are called in the Hebrew *words of days* — journals or annals, because, by divine direction, collected out of some public and authentic records. The collection was made after the captivity, and yet the language of the originals, written before, it sometimes retained, as 2 Chr. 5:9, *there it is unto this day,* which must have been written before the destruction of the temple. The Septuagint calls it a book *Paraleipomenōn* — of *things left,* or overlooked, by the preceding historians; and several such things there are in it. It is the rereward, the gathering host, of this sacred camp, which gathers up what remained, that nothing might be lost. In this first book we have, I. A collection of sacred genealogies, from Adam to David: and they are none of those which the apostle calls *endless genealogies,* but have their use and end in Christ, *ch.* 1–9. Divers little passages of history are here inserted which we had not before. II. A repetition of the history of the translation of the kingdom from Saul to David, and of the triumph of David's reign, with large additions, *ch.* 10–21. III. An original account of the settlement David made of the ecclesiastical affairs, and the preparation he made for the building of the temple, *ch.* 22–29. These are *words of days,* of the oldest days, of the best days, of the Old-Testament church. The reigns of kings and dates of kingdoms, as well as the lives of common persons, are reckoned by *days;* for a little time often gives a great turn, and yet all time is nothing to eternity.

CHAPTER 1

This chapter and many that follow it repeat the genealogies we have hitherto met with in the sacred history, and put them all together, with considerable additions. We may be tempted, it may be, to think it would have been well if they had not been written, because, when they come to be compared with other parallel places, there are differences found, which we can scarcely accommodate to our satisfaction; yet we must not therefore stumble at the word, but bless God that the things necessary to salvation are plain enough. And since the wise God has thought fit to write these things to us, we should not pass them over unread. All scripture is profitable, though not all alike profitable; and we may take occasion for good thoughts and meditations even from those parts of scripture that do not furnish so much matter for profitable remarks as some other parts. These genealogies, 1. Were then of great use, when they were here preserved, and put into the hands of the Jews after their return from Babylon; for the captivity, like the deluge, had put all into confusion, and they, in that dispersion and despair, would be in danger of losing the distinctions of their tribes and families. This therefore revives the ancient landmarks even of some of the tribes that were carried captive into Assyria. Perhaps it might invite the Jews to study the sacred writings which had been neglected, to find the names of their ancestors, and the rise of their families in them. 2. They are still of some use for the illustrating of the scripture-story, and especially for the clearing of the pedigrees of the Messiah, that it might appear that our blessed Saviour was, according to the prophecies which went before of him, the son of David, the son of Judah, the son of Abraham, the son of Adam. And, now that he has come for whose sake these registers were preserved, the Jews since have so lost all their genealogies that even that of the priests, the most sacred of all, is forgotten, and they know not of any one man in the world that can prove himself of the house of Aaron. When the building is reared the scaffolds are removed. When the promised Seed has come the line that was to lead to him is broken off. In this chapter we have an abstract of all the genealogies in the book of Genesis, till we come to Jacob. I. The descents from Adam to Noah and his sons, out of Gen. 5, (v. 1–4). II. The posterity of Noah's sons, by which the earth was repeopled, out of Gen. 10, (v. 5–23). III. The descents from Shem to Abraham, out of Gen. 11, (v. 24–28). IV. The posterity of Ishmael, and of Abraham's sons by Keturah, out of Gen. 25, (v. 29–35). V. The posterity of Esau, out of Gen. 36, (v. 36–54). These, it is likely, were passed over lightly in Genesis; and therefore, according to the law of the school, we are made to go over that lesson again which we did not learn well.

Verses 1–27

This paragraph has *Adam* for its first word and *Abraham* for its last. Between the creation of the former and the birth of the latter were 2000 years, almost the one-half of which time Adam himself lived. Adam was the common father of our flesh, Abraham the common father of the faithful. By the breach which the former made of the covenant of innocency, we were all made miserable; by the covenant of grace made with the latter, we all are, or may be, made happy. We all are, by nature, the seed of Adam, branches of that wild olive. Let us see to it that, by faith, we become the seed of Abraham (Rom. 4:11, 12), that we be grafted into the good olive and partake of its root and fatness.

I. The first four verses of this paragraph, and the last four, which are linked together by Shem (v. 4, 24), contain the sacred line of Christ from Adam to Abraham, and are inserted in his pedigree, Lu. 3:34–38, the order ascending as here it descends. This genealogy proves the falsehood of that reproach, *As for this man, we know not whence* he is. Bishop Patrick well observes here that, a genealogy being to be drawn of the families of the Jews, this appears as the peculiar glory of the Jewish nation, that they alone were able to derive their pedigree from the first man that God created, which no other nation pretended to, but abused themselves and their posterity with fabulous accounts of their originals, the Arcadians fancying that they were before the moon, the people of Thessaly that they sprang from stones, the Athenians that they grew out of the earth, much like the vain imaginations which some of the philosophers had of the origin of the universe. The account which the holy scripture gives both of the creation of the world and of the rise of nations carries with it as clear evidences of its own truth as those idle traditions do of their own vanity and falsehood.

II. All the verses between repeat the account of the replenishing of the earth by the sons of Noah after the flood. 1. The historian begins with those who were strangers to the church, the sons of Japhet, who were planted in the isles of the Gentiles, those western parts of the world, the countries of Europe. Of these he gives a short account (*v.* 5–7), because with these the Jews had hitherto had little or no dealings. 2. He proceeds to those who had many of them been enemies to the church, the sons of Ham, who moved southward towards Africa and those parts of Asia which lay that way. Nimrod the son of Cush began to be an oppressor, probably to the people of God in his time. But Mizraim, from whom came the Egyptians, and Canaan, from whom came the Canaanites, are both of them names of great note in the Jewish story; for with their descendants the Israel of God had severe struggles to get out of the land of Egypt and into the land of Canaan; and therefore the branches of Mizraim are particularly recorded (*v.* 11, 12), and of Canaan, *v.* 13–16. See at what a rate God valued Israel when he gave *Egypt for their ransom* (Isa. 43:3), and cast out all these nations before them, Ps. 70:8. 3. He then gives an account of those that were the ancestors and allies of the church, the posterity of Shem, *v.* 17–23. These peopled Asia, and spread themselves eastward. The Assyrians, Syrians, Chaldeans, Persians, and Arabians, descended from these. At first the originals of the respective nations were known; but at this day, we have reason to think, the nations are so mingled with one another, by the enlargement of commerce and dominion, the transplanting of colonies, the carrying away of captives, and many other circumstances, that no one nation, no, nor the greatest part of any, is descended entire from any one of these fountains. Only this we are sure of, that God has *created of one blood all nations of men;* they have all descended from one Adam, one Noah. *Have we not all one father? Has not one God created us?* Mal. 2:10. Our register hastens to the line of Abraham, breaking off abruptly from all the other families of the sons of Noah but that of Arphaxad, from whom Christ was to come. The great promise of the Messiah (says bishop Patrick) was translated from Adam to Seth, from him to Shem, from him to Eber, and so to the Hebrew nation, who were entrusted, above all nations, with that sacred treasure, till the promise was performed and the Messiah had come, and then that nation was made *not a people.*

Verses 28–54

All nations but the seed of Abraham are already shaken off from this genealogy: they have no part nor lot in this matter. *The Lord's portion is his people.* Of them he keeps an account, knows them by name; but those who are strangers to him he beholds afar off. Not that we are to conclude that therefore no particular persons of any other nation but the seed of Abraham found favour with God. It was a truth, before Peter perceived it, *that in every nation he that feared God and wrought righteousness was accepted of him.* Multitudes will be brought to heaven out of *all nations* (Rev. 7:9), and we are willing to hope there were many, very many, good people in the world, that lay out of the pale of God's covenant of peculiarity with Abraham, whose names were in the book of life, though not descended from any of the following families written in this book. *The Lord knows those that are his.* But Israel was a chosen nation, elect in type; and no other nation, in its national capacity, was so dignified and privileged as the Jewish nation was. That is the holy nation which is the subject of the sacred story; and therefore we are next to shake off all the seed of Abraham but the posterity of Jacob only, which were all incorporated into one nation and joined to the Lord, while the other descendants

from Abraham, for aught that appears, were estranged both from God and from one another.

I. We shall have little to say of the *Ishmaelites.* They were the sons of the bondwoman, that were to be cast out and not to be heirs with the child of the promise; and their case was to represent that of the unbelieving Jews, who were rejected (Gal. 4:22, etc.), and therefore there is little notice taken of that nation. Ishmael's twelve sons are just named here (*v.* 29–31), to show the performance of the promise God made to Abraham, in answer to his prayer for him, that, for Abraham's sake, he should become a great nation, and particularly that he should beget twelve princes, Gen. 17:20.

II. We shall have little to say of the *Midianites,* who descended from Abraham's children by Keturah. They were *children of the east* (probably Job was one of them), and were separated from Isaac, the heir of the promise (Gen. 25:6), and therefore they are only named here, *v.* 32. The sons of Jokshan, the son of Keturah, are named also, and the sons of Midian (*v.* 32, 33), who became most eminent, and perhaps gave denomination to all these families, as Judah to the Jews.

III. We shall not have much to say of the *Edomites.* They had an inveterate enmity to God's Israel; yet because they descended from Esau, the son of Isaac, we have here an account of their families, and the names of some of their famous men, *v.* 35 to the end. Some slight differences there are between some of the names here, and as we had them in Gen. 36, whence this whole account is taken. Three of four names that were written with a *Vau* there are written with a *Jod* here, probably the pronunciation being altered, as is usual in other languages. we now write many words very differently from what they were written but 200 years ago. Let us take occasion, from the reading of these genealogies, to think, 1. Of the multitudes that have gone through this world, have acted their part in it, and then quitted it. Job, even in his early day, saw not only *every man drawing after him,* but *innumerable before him,* Job 21:33. All these, and all theirs, had their day; many of them made a mighty noise and figure in the world; but their day came to fall, and their place knew them no more. The paths of death are trodden paths, but *vestigia nulla retrorsum — none can retrace their steps.* 2. Of the providence of God, which keeps up the generations of men, and so preserves that degenerate race, though guilty and obnoxious, in being upon earth. How easily could he cut it off without either a deluge or a conflagration! Write but all the children of men childless, as some are, and in a few years the earth will be eased of the burden under which it groans; but the divine patience lets the trees that cumber the ground not only grow, but propagate. As one generation, even of sinful men, passes away, another comes (Eccl. 1:4; Num. 32:14), and will do so while the earth remains. *Destroy it not, for a blessing is in it.*

CHAPTER 2

We have now come to what was principally intended, the register of the children of Israel, that distinguished people, that were to "dwell alone, and not be reckoned among the nations." Here we have, I. The names of the twelve sons of Israel (*v.* 1, 2). II. An account of the tribe of Judah, which has the precedency, not so much for the sake of David as for the sake of the Son of David, our Lord, who sprang out of Judah, Heb. 7:14. 1. The first descendants from Judah, down to Jesse (*v.* 3–12). 2. The children of Jesse (*v.* 13–17). 3. The posterity of Hezron, not only through Ram, from whom David came, but through Caleb (*v.* 18–20), Segub (*v.* 21–24), Jerahmeel (*v.* 25–33, and so to *v.* 41), and more by Caleb (*v.* 42–49), with the family of Caleb the son of Hur (*v.* 50–55). The best exposition we can have of this and the following chapters, and which will give the clearest view of them, is found in those genealogical tables which were published with some of the first impressions of the last English Bible about 100 years ago, and continued for some time; and it is a pity but they were revived in some of our later editions, for they are of great use to those who diligently search the scriptures. They are said to be drawn up by that great master in scripture-learning, Mr. Hugh Broughton. We meet with them sometimes in old Bibles.

Verses 1–17

Here is, I. The family of Jacob. His twelve sons are here named, that illustrious number so often celebrated almost throughout the whole Bible, from the first to the last book of it. At every turn we meet with the twelve tribes that descended from these twelve patriarchs. The personal character of several of them was none of the best (the first four were much blemished), and yet the covenant was entailed on their seed; for it was of grace, free grace, that it was said, *Jacob have I loved — not of works, lest any man should boast.*

II. The family of Judah. That tribe was most praised, most increased, and most dignified, of any of the tribes, and there-

fore the genealogy of it is the first and largest of them all. In the account here given of the first branches of that illustrious tree, of which Christ was to be the top branch, we meet, 1. With some that were very bad. Here is Er, Judah's eldest son, that was *evil in the sight of the Lord,* and was cut off, in the beginning of his days, by a stroke of divine vengeance: The *Lord slew him, v.* 3. His next brother, Onan, was no better, and fared no better. Here is Tamar, with whom Judah, her father-in-law, committed incest, *v.* 4. And here is Achan, called *Achar — a troubler,* that troubled Israel by taking of the accursed thing, *v.* 7. Note, The best and most honourable families may have those belonging to them that are blemishes. 2. With some that were very wise and good, as Heman and Ethan, Calcol and Dara, who were not perhaps the immediate sons of Zerah, but descendants from him, and are named because they were the glory of their father's house; for, when the Holy Ghost would magnify the wisdom of Solomon, he declares him wiser than these four men, who, though the sons of Mahol, are called Ezrahites, from Zerah, 1 Ki. 4:31. That four brothers should be eminent for wisdom and grace was a rare thing. 3. With some that were very great, as Nahshon, who was prince of the tribe of Judah when the camp of Israel was formed in the wilderness, and so led the van in that glorious march, and Salman, or Salmon, who was in that post of honour when they entered into Canaan, *v.* 10, 11. III. The family of Jesse, of which a particularly account is kept for the sake of David, and the Son of David, who is *a rod out of the stem of Jesse,* Isa. 11:1. Hence it appears that David was a seventh son, and that his three great commanders, Joab, Abishai, and Asahel, were the sons of one of his sisters, and Amasa of another. Three of the four went down slain to the pit, though they were the terror of the mighty.

Verses 18–55

The persons mentioned in the former paragraph are most of them such as we read of, and most of them such as we read much of, in other scriptures; but very few of those to whom this paragraph relates are mentioned any where else. It should seem, the tribe of Judah were more full and exact in their genealogies than any other of the tribes, in which we must acknowledge a special providence, for the clearing of the genealogy of Christ. 1. Here we find Bezaleel, who was head-workman in building the tabernacle, Ex. 31:2. 2. Hezron, who was the son of Pharez (*v.* 5), was the father of all this progeny, his sons, Caleb and Jerahmeel, being very fruitful, and he himself likewise, even in his old age, for he left his wife pregnant when he died, *v.* 24. This Hezron was one of the seventy that went down with Jacob into Egypt, Gen. 46:12. There his family thus increased, as other oppressed families there did. We cannot but suppose that he died during the Israelites' bondage in Egypt; and yet it is here said he died in Caleb-Ephratah (that is, Bethlehem), in the land of Canaan, *v.* 24. Perhaps, though the body of the people continued in Egypt, yet some that were more active than the rest, at least before their bondage came to be extreme, visited Canaan sometimes and got footing there, though afterwards they lost it. The achievements of Jair, here mentioned (*v.* 22, 23), we had an account of in Num. 32:41; and, it is supposed, they were long after the conquest of Canaan. The Jews say, Hezron married his third wife when he was sixty years old (*v.* 21), and another afterwards (*v.* 24), because he had a great desire of posterity in the family of Pharez, from whom the Messiah was to descend. 3. Here is mention of one that *died without children* (*v.* 30), and another (*v.* 32), and of one that *had no sons, but daughters, v.* 34. Let those that are in any of these ways afflicted not think their case new or singular. Providence orders these affairs of families by an incontestable sovereignty, as pleaseth him, giving children, or withholding them, or giving all of one sex. He is not bound to please us, but we are bound to acquiesce in his good pleasure. To those that love him he will himself be better than ten sons, and give them in his house a place and a name better than of sons and daughters. Let not those therefore that are written childless envy the families that are built up and replenished. Shall our eye be evil because God's is good? 4. Here is mention of one who had an only daughter, and married her to his servant an Egyptian, *v.* 34, 35. If it be mentioned to his praise, we must suppose that this Egyptian was proselyted to the Jewish religion and that he was very eminent for wisdom and virtue, otherwise it would not have become a true-born Israelite to match a daughter to him, especially an only daughter. If Egyptians become converts, and servants do worthily, neither their parentage nor their servitude should be a bar to their preferment. Such a one this Egyptian servant might be that she who married him might live as happily with him as if she had married one of the rulers of her tribe. 5. The pedigree of several of these terminates, not in a person, but in a place or country, as one is said to be *the father of Kirjath-jearim* (*v.* 50), another of Bethlehem (*v.* 51), which was afterwards David's city, because these places fell to their lot in the division of the land. 6. here are some that are said to be *families of scribes* (*v.* 55), such as kept up learning in their family, especially scripture-learning, and taught the people the good knowledge of God. Among all these great families we are glad to find some that were *families of scribes. Would to God that all the Lord's people were prophets* — all the families of Israel families of scribes, well instructed to the kingdom of heaven, and able to bring out of their treasury things new and old!

CHAPTER 3

Of all the families of Israel none was so illustrious as the family of David. That is the family which was mentioned in the foregoing chapter (*v.* 15). Here we have a full account of it. I. David's sons (*v.* 1–9). II. His successors in the throne as long as the kingdom continued (*v.* 10–16). III. The remains of his family in and after the captivity (*v.* 17–24). From this family, "as concerning the flesh, Christ came."

Verses 1–9

We had an account of David's sons, 2 Sa. 3:2, etc., and 5:14, etc. 1. He had many sons; and no doubt wrote as he thought, Ps. 127:5. *Happy is the man that hath his quiver full of* these arrows. 2. Some of them were a grief to him, as Amnon, Absalom, and Adonijah; and we do not read of any of them that imitated his piety or devotion except Solomon, and he came far short of it. 3. One of them, which Bathsheba bore to him, he called Nathan, probably in honour of Nathan the prophet, who reproved him for his sin in that matter and was instrumental to bring him to repentance. It seems he loved him the better for it as long as he lived. It is wisdom to esteem those our best friends that deal faithfully with us. From this son of David our Lord Jesus descended, as appears Lu. 3:31. 4. Here are two Elishamas, and two Eliphelets, *v.* 6, 8. Probably the two former were dead, and therefore David called two more by their names, which he would not have done if there had been any ill omen in this practice as some fancy. 5. David had many concubines; but their children are not named, as not worthy of the honour (*v.* 9), the rather because the concubines had dealt treacherously with David in the affair of Absalom. 6. Of all David's sons Solomon was chosen to succeed him, perhaps not for any personal merits (his wisdom was God's gift), but so, *Father, because it seemed good unto thee.*

Verses 10–24

David having nineteen sons, we may suppose them to have raised many noble families in Israel whom we never hear of in the history. But the scripture gives us an account only of the descendants of Solomon here, and of Nathan, Lu. 3. The rest had the honour to be the sons of David; but these only had the honour to be related to the Messiah. The sons of Nathan were his fathers as man, the sons of Solomon his predecessors as king. We have here, 1. The great and celebrated names by which the line of David is drawn down to the captivity, the kings of Judah in a lineal succession, the history of whom we have had at large in the two books of Kings and shall meet with again in the second book of Chronicles. Seldom has a crown gone in a direct line from father to son for seventeen descents together, as here. This was the recompence of David's piety. About the time of the captivity the lineal descent was interrupted, and the crown went from one brother to another and from a nephew to an uncle, which was a presage of the eclipsing of the glory of that house. 2. The less famous, and most of them very obscure, names, in which the house of David subsisted after the captivity. The only famous man of that house that we meet with at their return from captivity was Zerubbabel, elsewhere called *the son of Salathiel,* but appearing here to be his grandson (*v.* 17–19), which is usual in scripture. Belshazzar is called *Nebuchadnezzar's son,* but was his grandson. Salathiel is said to be *the son* of Jeconiah because adopted by him, and because, as some think, he succeeded him in the dignity to which he was restored by Evil-merodach. Otherwise Jeconiah was written childless: he was *the signet God plucked from his right hand* (Jer. 22:24), and in his room Zerubbabel was placed, and therefore God saith to him (Hag. 2:23), *I will make thee as a signet.* The posterity of Zerubbabel here bear not the same names that they do in the genealogies (Mt. 1, or Lu. 3), but those no doubt were taken from the then herald's office, the public registers which the priests kept of all the families of Judah, especially that of David. The last person named in this chapter is Anani, of whom bishop Patrick says that the Targum adds these words, *He is the king Messiah, who is to be revealed,* and some of the Jewish writers give this reason, because it is said (Dan. 7:13), the son of man came *gnim gnanani — with the clouds of heaven.* The reason indeed is very foreign and far-fetched; but that learned man thinks it may be made use of as an evidence that their minds were always full of the thoughts of the Messiah and that they expected it would not be very long after the days of Zerubbabel before the set time of his approach would come.

CHAPTER 4

In this chapter we have, I. A further account of the genealogies of the tribe of Judah, the most numerous and most famous of all the tribes. The posterity of Shobal the son of Hur (*v.* 1–4), of Ashur the posthumous son of Hezron (who was mentioned, 2:24), with something particular concerning Jabez (*v.* 5–10), of Chelub and others (*v.* 11–20), of Shelah (*v.* 21–23). II. An account of the posterity and cities of Simeon, their conquest of Gedon, and of the Amalekites in Mount Seir (*v.* 24–43).

Verses 1–10

One reason, no doubt, why Ezra is here most particular in the register of the tribe of Judah is because it was that tribe which, with its appendages, Simeon, Benjamin, and Levi, made up the kingdom of Judah, which not only long survived the other tribes in Canaan, but in process of time, now when this was written, returned out of captivity, when the generality of the other tribes were lost in the kingdom of Assyria. The most remarkable person in this paragraph is Jabez. It is not said whose son he was, nor does it appear in what age he lived; but, it should seem, he was the founder of one of the families of Aharhel, mentioned *v.* 8. Here is,

I. The reason of his name: his mother gave him the name with this reason, *Because I bore him with sorrow, v.* 9. All children are borne with sorrow (for the sentence upon the woman is, *In sorrow shalt thou bring forth children*), but some with much more sorrow than others. Usually the sorrow in bearing is afterwards forgotten *for joy that the child is born;* but here it seems it was so extraordinary that it was remembered when the child came to be circumcised, and care was taken to perpetuate the remembrance of it while he lived. Perhaps the mother called Habez, as Rachel called her son Benoni, when she was dying of the sorrow. Or, if she recovered it, yet thus she recorded it, 1. That it might be a continual memorandum to herself, to be thankful to God as long as she lived for supporting her under and bringing her through that sorrow. It may be of use to be often reminded of our sorrows, that we may always have such thoughts of things as we had in the day of our affliction, and may learn to rejoice with trembling. 2. That it might likewise be a memorandum to him what this world is into which she bore him, a vale of tears, in which he must expect *few days and full of trouble.* The sorrow he carried in his name might help to put a seriousness upon his spirit. It might also remind him to love and honour his mother, and labour, in every thing, to be a comfort to her who brought him into the world with so much sorrow. It is piety in children thus to requite their parents, 1 Tim. 5:4.

II. The eminence of his character: *He was more honourable than his brethren,* qualified above them by the divine grace and dignified above them by the divine providence; they did virtuously, but he excelled them all. Now the sorrow with which his mother bore him was abundantly recompensed. That son which of all her children cost her most dear she was most happy in, and was made glad in proportion to the affliction, Ps. 110:15. We are not told upon what account he was *more honourable than his brethren,* whether because he raised a greater estate, or was preferred to the magistracy, or signalized himself in war; we have most reason to think it was upon the account of his learning and piety, not only because these, above any thing, put honour upon a man, but because we have reason to think that in these Jabez was eminent. 1. In learning, because we find that *the families of the scribes dwelt at Jabez* (*ch.* 2:55), a city which, it is likely, took its name from him. The Jews say that he was a famous doctor of the law and left many disciples behind him. And it should seem, by the mentioning of him so abruptly here, that his name was well known when Ezra wrote this. 2. In piety, because we find here that he was a praying man. His inclination to devotion made him truly honourable, and by prayer he obtained those blessings from God which added much to his honour. The way to be truly great is to be truly good and to pray much.

III. The prayer he made, probably like Solomon's prayer for wisdom, just when he was setting out in the world. He set himself to acknowledge God in all his ways, put himself under the divine blessing and protection, and prospered accordingly. Perhaps these were the heads on which he enlarged in his daily prayers; for this purpose it was his constant practice to pray alone, and with his family, as Daniel. Some think that it was upon some particular occasion, when he was straitened and threatened by his enemies, that he prayed this prayer. Observe,

1. To whom he prayed, not to any of the gods of the Gentiles; no, he *called on the God of Israel,* the living and true God, who alone can hear and answer prayer, and in prayer had an eye to him as the God of Israel, a God in covenant with his people, the God with whom Jacob wrestled and prevailed and was thence called Israel.

2. What was the nature of his prayer. (1.) As the *margin* reads it, it was a solemn vow — *If thou wilt bless me indeed, etc.* and then the sense is imperfect, but may easily be filled up from Jacob's vow, or some such like — *then thou shalt be my God.* He did not express his promise, but left it to be understood, either because he was afraid to promise in his own strength or because he resolved to devote himself entirely to God. He does, as it were, give God a blank paper, let him write what he pleases: "Lord, if thou wilt bless me and keep me, do what thou wilt with me, I will be at thy command and disposal for ever." (2.) As the *text* reads it, it was the language of a most ardent and affectionate desire: *O that thou wouldst bless me!*

3. What was the matter of his prayer. Four things he prayed for: — (1.) That God would bless him indeed: "That, *blessing, thou wilt bless me,* bless me greatly with manifold and abundant blessings." Perhaps he had an eye to the promise God made to Abraham (Gen. 22:17), *In blessing, I will bless thee.* "Let that blessing of Abraham come upon me." Spiritual blessings are the best blessings, and those are blessed indeed who are blessed with them. God's blessings are real things and produce real effects. We can but wish a blessing: he commands it. Those whom he blesses are blessed indeed. (2.) That he would enlarge his coast, that he would prosper his endeavours for the increase of what fell to his lot either by work or war. That God would enlarge our hearts, and so enlarge our portion in himself and in the heavenly Canaan, ought to be our desire and prayer. (3.) That God's hand might be with him. The prayer of Moses for this tribe of Judah was, That his own *hands might be sufficient for him,* Deu. 33:7; but Jabez expects not that this can be the case, unless he have *God's* hand with him and the presence of his power. God's hand with us, to lead us, protect us, strengthen us, and to work all our works in us and for us, is indeed a hand sufficient for us, all-sufficient. (4.) That he would keep him from evil, the evil of sin, the evil of trouble, all the evil designs of his enemies, that they might not hurt him, nor grieve him, nor make him a *Jabez* indeed, *a man of sorrow:* in the original there is an allusion to his name. *Father in heaven, deliver me from evil.*

4. What was the success of his prayer: *God granted him that which he requested,* prospered him remarkably, and gave him success in his undertakings, in his studies, in his worldly business, in his conflicts with the Canaanites, and so he became *more honourable than his brethren.* God was of old always ready to hear prayer, and *his ear is not yet heavy.*

Verses 11–23

We may observe in these verses, 1. That here is a whole family of craftsmen, handicraft tradesmen, that applied themselves to all sorts of manufactures, in which they were ingenious and industrious above their neighbours, *v.* 14. There was a valley where they lived which was, from them, called *the valley of craftsmen.* Those that are craftsmen are not therefore to be looked upon as mean men. These craftsmen, though two of a trade often disagree, yet chose to live together, for the improving of arts by comparing notes, and that they might support one another's reputation. 2. That one of these married the daughter of Pharaoh (*v.* 18), which was the common name of the kings of Egypt. If an Israelite in Egypt before the bondage began, while Joseph's merits were yet fresh in mind, was preferred to be the king's son-in-law, it is not to be thought strange: few Israelites could, like Moses, refuse an alliance with the court. 3. That another is said to be the *father of the house of those that wrought fine linen, v.* 21. It is inserted in their genealogy as their honour that they were the best weavers in the kingdom, and they brought up their children, from one generation to another, to the same business, not aiming to make them gentlemen. This Laadah is said to be the *father of those that wrought fine linen,* as before the flood Jubal is said to be *the father of musicians* and Jabal of *shepherds,* etc. His posterity inhabited the city of Mareshah, the manufacture or staple commodity of which place was linen-cloth, with which their kings and priests were clothed. 4. That another family had had *dominion in Moab,* but were now in *servitude in Babylon, v.* 22, 23. (1.) It was found among the *ancient things* that they had the *dominion in Moab.* Probably in David's time, when that country was conquered, they transplanted themselves thither, and were put in places of power there, which they held for several generations; but this was a great while ago, time out of mind. (2.) Their posterity were now potters and gardeners, as is supposed in Babylon, where they *dwelt with the king for his work,* got a good livelihood by their industry, and therefore cared not for returning with their brethren to their own land, after the years of captivity had expired. Those that now have dominion know not what their posterity may be reduced to, nor what mean employments they may be glad to take up with. But those were unworthy the name of *Israelites* that would dwell among *plants and hedges* rather than be at the pains to return to Canaan.

Verses 24–43

We have here some of the genealogies of the tribe of Simeon (though it was not a tribe of great note), especially the princes of that tribe, *v.* 38. Of this tribe it is said that they *increased greatly,* but *not like the children of Judah, v.* 27. Those whom God increases ought to be thankful, though they see others that are more increased. Here observe, 1. The cities allotted them (*v.* 28), of which see Joshua 19:1, etc. When it is said that they were theirs *unto the reign of David* (*v.* 31) intimation is given that when the ten tribes revolted from the house of David many of the Simeonites quitted these cities, because they lay within Judah, and seated themselves elsewhere. 2. The ground they got elsewhere. When those of this tribe that revolted from the house of David were carried captive with the rest into Assyria those that adhered to Judah were remarkably owned of God and prospered in their endeavours to enlarge their coasts. It was in the days of Hezekiah that a generation of Simeonites, whose tribe had long crouched and truckled, was animated to make these bold efforts. (1.) Some of them attacked a place in Arabia, as it should seem, called *the entrance of Gedor,* inhabited by the posterity of accursed Ham (*v.* 40), made themselves masters of it, and dwelt there. This adds to the glory of Hezekiah's pious reign, that, as his kingdom in general prospered, so did particular families. It is said that they found fat pastures, and yet *the land was quiet;* even when the kings of Assyria were giving disturbance to all their neighbours this land escaped their alarms. The inhabitants being shepherds, who molested none, were not themselves molested, till the Simeonites came and drove them out and succeeded them, not only in the plenty, but in the peace, of their land. Those who dwell (as we do) in a fruitful country, and whose land is wide, and quiet, and peaceable, have reason to own themselves indebted to that God who *appoints the bounds of our habitation.* (2.) Others of them, to the number of 500, under the command of four brethren here named, made a descent upon Mount Seir, and smote the remainder of the devoted Amalekites, and took possession of their country, *v.* 42, 43. Now the curses on Ham and Amalek had a further accomplishment, when they seemed dormant, if not dead; as had also the curse on Simeon, that he should be divided and scattered (Gen. 49:7): yet to him it was turned into a blessing, for the families of Simeon, which thus transplanted themselves into those distant countries, are said to *dwell there unto this day* (*v.* 43), by which it should seem they escaped the calamities of the captivity. Providence sometimes sends those out of trouble that are designed for preservation.

CHAPTER 5

This chapter gives us some account of the two tribes and a half that were seated on the other side Jordan. I. Of Reuben (*v.* 1–10). II. Of Gad (*v.* 11–17). III. Of the half-tribe of Manasseh (*v.* 23, 24). IV. Concerning all three acting in conjunction we are told, 1. How they conquered the Hagarites (*v.* 18–22). 2. How they were, at length, themselves conquered, and made captives, by the king of Assyria, because they had forsaken God (*v.* 25, 26).

Verses 1–17

We have here an extract out of the genealogies,

I. Of the tribe of Reuben, where we have,

1. The reason why this tribe is thus postponed. It is confessed that Reuben was the first-born of Israel, and, upon that account, might challenge the precedency; but he forfeited his birthright by defiling his father's concubine, and was, for that, sentenced *not to excel,* Gen. 49:4. Sin lessens men, thrusts them down from their excellency. Seventh-commandment sins especially leave an indelible stain upon men's names and families, a reproach which time will not wipe away. Reuben's seed, to the last, bear the disgrace of Reuben's sin. Yet, though that tribe was degraded, it was not discarded or disinherited. The sullying of the honour of an Israelite is not the losing of his happiness. Reuben loses his birthright, yet it does not devolve upon Simeon the next in order; for it was typical, and therefore must attend, not the course of nature, but the choice of grace. The advantages of the birthright were dominion and a double portion. Reuben having forfeited these, it was thought too much that both should be transferred to any one, and therefore they were divided. (1.) Joseph had the double portion; for two tribes descended from him, Ephraim and Manasseh, each of whom had a child's part (for so Jacob by faith blessed them, Heb. 11:21; Gen. 48:15, 22), and each of those tribes was as considerable, and made as good a figure, as any one of the twelve, except Judah. But, (2.) Judah had the dominion; on him the dying patriarch entailed the sceptre, Gen. 49:10 Of him came the chief ruler, David first, and, in the fulness of time, Messiah the Prince, Mic. 5:2. This honour was secured to Judah, though the birthright was Joseph's; and, having this, he needed not envy Joseph the double portion.

2. The genealogy of the princes of this tribe, the chief family of it (many, no doubt, being omitted), to Beerah, who was head of this clan when the king of Assyria carried them captive, *v.* 4–6. Perhaps he is mentioned as prince of the Reubenites at that time because he did not do his part to prevent the captivity.

3. The enlargement of the coasts of this tribe. They increasing, and their cattle being multiplied, they crowded out their neighbours the Hagarites, and extended their conquests, though not to the river Euphrates, yet to the wilderness which abutted upon that river, *v.* 9, 10. Thus God did for his people as he promised them: he cast out the enemy from before them by little and little, and gave them their land as they had occasion for it, Ex. 23:30.

II. Of the tribe of Gad. Some great families of that tribe are here named (*v.* 12), seven that were the children of Abihail, whose pedigree is carried upwards from the son to the father (*v.* 14, 15), as that *v.* 4, 5, is brought downwards from father to son. These genealogies were perfected in the days of Jotham king of Judah, but were begun some years before, in the reign of Jeroboam II, king of Israel. What particular reason there was for taking these accounts then does not appear; but it was just before they were carried away captive by the Assyrians, as appears 2 Ki. 15:29, 31. When the judgments of God were ready to break out against them for their wretched degeneracy and apostasy then were they priding themselves in their genealogies, that they were the children of the covenant; as the Jews, in our Saviour's time, who, when they were ripe for ruin, boasted, *We have Abraham to our father.* Or there might be a special providence in it, and a favourable intimation that though they were, for the present, cast out, they were not cast off for ever. What we design to call for hereafter we keep an inventory of.

Verses 18–26

The heads of the half-tribe of Manasseh, that were seated on the other side Jordan, are named here, *v.* 23, 24. Their lot, at first, was Bashan only; but afterwards they increased so much in wealth and power that they spread far north, even unto Hermon. Two things only are here recorded concerning these tribes on the other side Jordan, in which they were all concerned. They all shared,

I. In a glorious victory over the Hagarites, so the Ishmaelites were now called, to remind them that they were *the sons of the bond-woman,* that was *cast out.* We are not told when this victory was obtained: whether it be the same with that of the Reubenites (which is said *v.* 10 to be *in the days of Saul*), or whether that success of one of these tribes animated and excited the other two to join with them in another expedition, is not certain. It seems, though in Saul's time the common interests of the kingdom were weak and low, some of the tribes that acted separately did well for themselves. We are here told,

1. What a brave army these frontier-tribes brought into the field against the Hagarites, 44,000 men and upwards, all strong, and brave, and skilful in war, so many effective men, that knew how to manage their weapons, *v.* 18. How much more considerable might Israel have been than they were in the time of the judges if all the tribes had acted in conjunction!

2. What course they took to engage God for them: They *cried to God,* and *put their trust in him, v.* 20. Now they acted as Israelites indeed. (1.) As the seed of believing Abraham, they *put their trust in God.* Though they had a powerful army, they relied not on that, but on the divine power. They depended on the commission they had from God to wage war with their neighbours for the enlarging of their coasts, if there was occasion, even with those that were very far off, besides the devoted nations. See Deu. 20:15. They depended on God's providence to give them success. (2.) As the seed of praying Jacob, *they cried unto God,* especially *in the battle,* when perhaps, at first, they were in danger of being overpowered. See the like done, 2 Chr. 13:14. In distress, God expects we should cry to him; he distrains upon us for this tribute, this rent. In our spiritual conflicts, we must look up to heaven for strength; and it is the believing prayer that will be the prevailing prayer.

3. We are told what success they had: *God was entreated of them,* though need drove them to him; so ready is he to hear and answer prayer. They were helped against their enemies; for God never yet failed any that trusted in him. And then they routed the enemy's army, though far superior in number to theirs, slew many (*v.* 22), took 100,000 prisoners, enriched themselves greatly with the spoil, and settled themselves in their country (*v.* 21, 22), and all this *because the war was of God,* undertaken in his fear and carried on in a dependence upon him. If the battle be the Lord's, there is reason to hope it will be successful. Then we may expect to prosper in any enterprise, and then only, when we take God along with us.

II. They shared, at length, in an inglorious captivity. Had they kept close to God and their duty, they would have continued to enjoy both their ancient lot and their new conquests; but they *transgressed against the God of their fathers, v.* 25. They lay upon the borders, and conversed most with the neighbouring nations, by which means they learned their idolatrous usages and transmitted the infection to the other tribes; for this God had a controversy with them. He was *a husband to them,* and no marvel that his jealousy burnt like fire when they *went a whoring after other gods.* Justly is a bill of divorce given to the adulteress. *God stirred up the spirit of the kings of Assyria,* first one and then another, against them, served his own purposes by the designs of those ambitious monarchs, employed them to chastise these revolters first, and, when that humbled them not, then wholly to *root them out, v.* 26. These tribes were first placed, and they were first displaced. They would have the best land, not considering that it lay most exposed. But those who are governed more by sense than by reason or faith in their choices may expect to fare accordingly.

CHAPTER 6

Though Joseph and Judah shared between them the forfeited honours of the birthright, yet Levi was first of all the tribes, dignified and distinguished with an honour more valuable than either the precedency or the double portion, and that was the priesthood. That tribe God set apart for himself; it was Moses's tribe, and perhaps for his sake was thus favoured. Of that tribe we have an account in this chapter. I. Their pedigree, the first fathers of the tribe (*v.* 1–3), the line of the priests, from Aaron to the captivity (*v.* 4–15), and of some other of their families (*v.* 16–30). II. Their work, the work of the Levites (*v.* 31–48), of the priests (*v.* 49–53). III. The cities appointed them in the land of Canaan (*v.* 54–81).

Verses 1–30

The priests and Levites were more concerned than any other Israelites to preserve their pedigree clear and to be able to prove it, because all the honours and privileges of their office depended upon their descent. And we read of those who, though perhaps they really were children of the priests, yet, because they could not find the register of their genealogies, nor make out their descent by any authentic record, were, *as polluted, put from the priesthood,* and forbidden to eat of the holy things, Ezra 2:62, 63. It is but very little that is here recorded of the genealogies of this sacred tribe. I. The first fathers of it are here named twice, *v.* 1, 16. Gershom, Kohath, and Merari, are three names which we were very conversant with in the book of Numbers, when the families of the Levites were marshalled and had their work assigned to them. Aaron, and Moses, and Miriam, we have known much more of than their names, and cannot pass them over here without remembering that this was that Moses and Aaron whom God honoured in making them instruments of Israel's deliverance and settlement and *figures of him that was to come,* Moses as a prophet and Aaron as a priest. And the mention of Nadab and Abihu (though, having no children, there was no occasion to bring them into the genealogy) cannot but remind us of the terrors of that divine justice which they were made monuments of for offering strange fire, that we may always fear before him. 2. The line of Eleazar, the successor of Aaron, is here drawn down to the time of the captivity, *v.* 4–15. It begins with Eleazar, who came out of the house of bondage in Egypt, and ends with Jehozadak, who went into the house of bondage in Babylon. Thus, for their sins, they were left as they were found, which might also intimate that the Levitical priesthood did not make anything perfect, but this was to be done by the *bringing in of a better hope.* All these here named were not high priests; for, in the time of the judges, that dignity was, upon some occasion or other, brought into the family of Ithamar, of which Eli was; but in Zadok it returned again to the right line. Of Azariah it is here said (*v.* 10), *He it is that executed the priest's office in the temple that Solomon built.* It is supposed that this was that Azariah who bravely opposed the presumption of king Uzziah when he invaded the priest's office (2 Chr. 26:17, 18), though he ventured his neck by so doing. This was done like a priest, like one that was truly zealous for his God. He that thus boldly maintained and defended the priest's office, and made good its barriers against such a daring insult, might well be said to *execute it;* and this honour is put upon him for it; while Urijah, one of his successors, for a base compliance with King Ahaz, in building him an idolatrous altar, has the disgrace put upon him of being left out of this genealogy, as perhaps some others are. But some think that this remark upon this Azariah should have been added to his grandfather of the same name (*v.* 9), who was the son of Ahimaaz, and that he was the priest who first officiated in Solomon's temple. 3. Some other of the families of the Levites are here accounted for. One of the families of Gershom (that of Libni) is here drawn down as far as Samuel, who had the honour of a prophet added to that of a Levite. One of the families of Merari (that of Mahli) is likewise drawn down for several descents, *v.* 29, 30.

Verses 31–53

When the Levites were first ordained in the wilderness much of the work then appointed them lay in carrying and taking care of the tabernacle and the utensils of it, while they were in their march through the wilderness. In David's time their number was increased; and, though the greater part of them was dispersed all the nation over, to teach the people the good knowledge of the Lord, yet those that attended the house of God were so numerous that there was not constant work for them all; and therefore David, by special commission and direction from God, new-modelled the Levites, as we shall find in the latter part of this book. Here we are told what the work was which he assigned them.

I. Singing-work, *v.* 31. David was raised up on high to be the sweet psalmist of Israel (2 Sa. 23:1), not only to pen psalms, but to appoint the singing of them in the house of the Lord (not so much because he was musical as because he was devout), and this he did *after that the ark had rest.* While that was in captivity, obscure, and unsettled, the harps were hung upon the willow-trees: singing was then thought unseasonable (when the bridegroom is taken away they shall fast); but the harps being resumed, and the songs revived, at the bringing up of the ark, they were continued afterwards. For we should rejoice as much in the prolonging of our spiritual privileges as in the restoring of them. When the service of the ark was much superseded by its rest they had other work cut out for them (for Levites should never be idle) and were employed in the service of song. Thus when the people of God come to the rest which remains for them above they shall take leave of all their burdens and be employed in everlasting songs. These singers kept up that service in the tabernacle till the temple was built, and then they *waited on their office* there, *v.* 32. When they came to that stately magnificent house they kept as close both to their office and to their order as they had done in the tabernacle. It is a pity that the preferment of the Levites should ever make them remiss in their business. We have here an account of the three great masters who were employed in the service of the sacred song, with their respective families; for they *waited with their children,* that is, such as descended from them or were allied to them, *v.* 33. Heman, Asaph, and Ethan, were the three that were appointed to this service, one of each of the three houses of the Levites, that there might be an equality in the distribution of this work and honour, and that every one might know his post, such an admirable order was there in this choir service. 1. Of the house of Kohath was Heman with his family (*v.* 33), a man of a sorrowful spirit, if it be the same Heman that penned the 88th psalm, and yet a singer. He was the grandson of Samuel the prophet, the son of Joel, of whom it is said that *he walked not in the ways of Samuel* (1 Sa. 8:2, 3); but it seems, though the son did not, the grandson did. Thus does the blessing entailed on the seed of the upright sometimes pass over one generation and fasten upon the next. And this Heman, though the grandson of that mighty prince, did not think it below him to be a precentor in the house of God. David himself was willing to be a door-keeper. Rather we may look upon this preferment of the grandson in the church as a recompense for the humble modest resignation which the grandfather made of his authority in the state. Many such ways God has of making up his people's losses and balancing their disgraces. Perhaps David, in making Heman the chief, had some respect to his old friend Samuel. 2. Of the house of Gershom was Asaph, called *his brother,* because in the same office and of the same tribe, though of another family. He was posted on Heman's right hand in the choir, *v.* 39. Several of the psalms bear his name, being either penned by him or tuned by him as the chief musician. It is plain that he was the penman of some psalms; for we read of those that praised the Lord in the words of David and of Asaph. He was a seer as well as a singer, 2 Chr. 29:30. His pedigree is traced up here, through names utterly unknown, as high as Levi, *v.* 39–43. 3. Of the house of Merari was Ethan (*v.* 44), who was appointed to Heman's left hand. His pedigree is also traced up to Levi, *v.* 47. If these were the Heman and Ethan that penned the 88th and 89th psalms, there appears no reason here why they should be called *Ezrahites* (see the titles of those psalms), as there does why those should be called so who are mentioned *ch.* 2:6, and who were the sons of Zerah.

II. There was serving-work, abundance of service to be done *in the tabernacle of the house of God* (*v.* 48), to provide water and fuel, — to wash and sweep, and carry out ashes, — to kill, and flay, and boil the sacrifices; and to all such services there were Levites appointed, those of other families, or perhaps those that were not fit to be singers, that had either no good voice or no good ear. *As every one has received the gift, so let him minister.* Those that could not sing must not therefore be laid aside as good for nothing; though they were not fit for that service, there was other service they might be useful in.

III. There was sacrificing-work, and that was to be done by the priests only, *v.* 49. They only were to sprinkle the blood and burn the incense; as for *the work of the most holy place,* that was to be done by the high priest only. Each had his work, and they both needed one another and both helped one another in it. Concerning the work of the priests we are here told, 1. What was the end they were to have in their eye. They were to *make an atonement for Israel,* to mediate between the people and God; not to magnify and enrich themselves, but to serve the public. They were *ordained for men.* 2. What was the rule they were to have in their eye. They presided in God's house, yet must do as they were bidden, according to all that God commanded. That law the highest are subject to.

Verses 54–81

We have here an account of the Levites' cities. They are here called their *castles* (*v.* 54), not only because walled and fortified, and well guarded by the country (for it is the interest of every nation to protect its ministers), but because they and their possessions were, in a particular manner, the care of the divine providence: as God was their portion, so God was their protection; and a cottage will be a castle to those that abide under the shadow of the Almighty. This account is much the same with that which we had, Jos. 21. We need not be critical in comparing them (what good will it do us?) nor will it do any hurt to the credit of the holy scripture if the names of some of the places be not spelt just the same here as they were there. We know it is common for cities to have several names. *Sarum* and *Salisbury, Salop* and *Shrewsbury,* are more unlike than *Hilen* (*v.* 58) and *Holon* (Jos. 21:15), *Ashan* (*v.* 59) and *Ain* (Jos. 21:16), *Alemeth* (*v.* 60) and *Almon* (Jos. 21:18); and time changes names. We are only to observe that in this appointment of cities for the Levites God took care, 1. For the accomplishment of dying Jacob's prediction concerning this tribe, that it should be *scattered in Israel,* Gen. 49:7. 2. For the diffusing of the knowledge of himself and his law to all parts of the land of Israel. Every tribe had Levites' cities in it; and so every room was furnished with a candle, so that none could be ignorant of his duty but it was either his own fault or the Levites'. 3. For a comfortable maintenance for those that ministered in holy things. Besides their tithes and offerings, they had glebe-lands and cities of their own to dwell in. Some of the most considerable cities of Israel fell to the Levites' lot. Every tribe had benefit by the Levites, and therefore every tribe must contribute to their support. *Let him that is taught in the word communicate to him that teacheth,* and do it cheerfully.

CHAPTER 7

In this chapter we have some account of the genealogies, I. Of Issachar (*v.* 1–5). II. Of Benjamin (*v.* 6–12). III. Of Naphtali (*v.* 13). IV. Of Manasseh (*v.* 14–19). V. Of Ephraim (*v.* 20–29). VI. Of Asher (*v.* 30–40). Here is no account either of Zebulun or Dan. Why they only should be omitted we can assign no reason; only it is the disgrace of the tribe of Dan that idolatry began in that colony of the Danites which fixed in Laish, and called Dan, and there one of the golden calves was set up by Jeroboam. Dan is omitted, Rev. 7.

Verses 1–19

We have here a short view given us,

I. Of the tribe of Issachar, whom Jacob had compared to a *strong ass, couching between two burdens* (Gen. 49:14), an industrious tribe, that minded their country business very closely and *rejoiced in their tents,* Deu. 33:18. And here it appears, 1. That they were a numerous tribe; for they had many wives. So fruitful their country was that they saw no danger of over-stocking the pasture, and so ingenious the people were that they could find work for all hands. Let no people complain of their numbers, provided they suffer none to be idle. 2. That they were a valiant tribe, *men of might* (*v.* 2, 5), *chief men, v.* 3. Those that were inured to labour and business were of all men the fittest to serve their country when there was occasion, The number of the respective families, as taken in the days of David, is here set down, amounting in the whole to above 145,000 men fit for war. The account, some think, was taken when Joab numbered the people, 2 Sa. 24. But I rather think it refers to some other computation that was made, perhaps among themselves, because it is said (1 Chr. 27:24) that that account was not inserted in the chronicles of king David, it having offended God.

II. Of the tribe of Benjamin. Some account is here given of this tribe, but much larger in the next chapter. The militia of this tribe scarcely reached to 60,000; but they are said to be *mighty men of valour, v.* 7, 9, 11. *Benjamin shall ravin as a wolf,* Gen. 49:27. It was the honour of this tribe that it produced Saul the first king, and more its honour that it adhered to the rightful kings of the house of David when the other tribes revolted. Here is mention (*v.* 12) of Hushim the sons of Aher. The sons of Dan are said to be *Hushim* (Gen. 46:23), and therefore some read Aher appellatively, *Hushim* — the *sons of another* (that is, another of Jacob's sons) or the sons of a stranger, which Israelites should not be, but such the Danites were when they set up Micah's graven and molten image among them.

III. Of the tribe of Naphtali, *v.* 13. The first fathers only of that tribe are named, the very same that we shall find, Gen. 46:24, only that *Shillem* there is *Shallum* here. None of their descendents are named, perhaps because their genealogies were lost.

IV. Of the tribe of Manasseh, that part of it which was seated within Jordan; for of the other part we had some account before, *ch.* 5:23, etc. Of this tribe observe, 1. That one of them married an Aramitess, that is, a Syrian, *v.* 14. This was during their bondage in Egypt, so early did they begin to mingle with the nations. 2. That, though the father married a Syrian, Machir, the son of that marriage, perhaps seeing the inconvenience of it in his father's house, took to wife a daughter of Benjamin, *v.* 15. It is good for the children to take warning by their father's mistakes and not stumble at the same stone. 3. Here is mention of Bedan (v, 17), who perhaps is the same with that Bedan who is mentioned as one of Israel's deliverers, 1 Sa. 12:11. Jair perhaps, who was of Manasseh (Jdg. 10:3), was the man.

Verses 20–40

We have here an account,

I. Of the tribe of Ephraim. Great things we read of that tribe when it came to maturity. Here we have an account of the disasters of its infancy, while it was in Egypt as it should seem; for Ephraim himself was alive when those things were done, which yet is hard to imagine if it were, as is here computed, seven generations off. Therefore I am apt to think that either it was another Ephraim or that those who were slain were the immediate sons of that Ephraim that was the son of Joseph. In this passage, which is related here only, we have, 1. The great breach that was made upon the family of Ephraim. The men of Gath, Philistines, giants, slew many of the sons of that family, *because they came down to take away their cattle, v.* 21. It is uncertain who were the aggressors here. Some make the men of Gath the aggressors, men *born in the land of Egypt,* but now resident in Gath, supposing that they came down into the land of Goshen, to drive away the Ephraimites' cattle, and slew the owners, because they stood up in the defence of them. Many a man's life has been exposed and betrayed by his wealth; so far is it from being a strong city. Others think that the Ephraimites made a descent upon the men of Gath to plunder them, presuming that the time had come when they should be put in possession of Canaan; but they paid dearly for their rashness and precipitation. Those that will not wait God's time cannot expect God's blessing. I rather think that the men of Gath came down upon the Ephraimites, because the Israelites in Egypt were shepherds, not soldiers, abounded in cattle of their own, and therefore were not likely to venture their lives for their neighbours' cattle: and the words may be read, *The men of Gath slew them, for they came down to take away their cattle.* Zabad the son of Ephraim, and Shuthelah, and Ezer, and Elead (his grandchildren), were, as Dr. Lightfoot thinks, the men that were slain. Jacob had foretold that the seed of Ephraim should become a *multitude of nations* (Gen. 48:19), and yet that plant is thus nipped in the bud. God's providences often seem to contradict his promises; but, when they do so, they really magnify the promise, and make the performance of it, notwithstanding, so much more illustrious. The Ephraimites were the posterity of Joseph, and yet his power could not protect them, though some think he was yet living. The sword devours one as well as another. 2. The great grief which oppressed the father of the family hereupon: *Ephraim mourned many days.* Nothing brings the aged to the grave with more sorrow than their following the young that descend from them to the grave first, especially if in blood. It is often the burden of those that live to be old that they see those go before them of whom they said, *These same shall comfort us.* It was a brotherly friendly office which his brethren did, when *they came to comfort him* under this great affliction, to express their sympathy with him and concern for him, and to suggest that to him which would support and quiet him under this sad providence. Probably they reminded him of the promise of increase which Jacob had blessed him when he laid his right hand upon his head. Although his house was not so with God as he hoped, but a house of mourning, a shattered family, yet that promise was sure, 2 Sa. 23:5. 3. The repair of this breach, in some measure, by addition of another son to his family in his old age (*v.* 23), like Seth, *another seed instead of that of Abel whom Cain slew,* Gen. 4:25. When God thus restores comfort to his mourners, *makes glad according to the days wherein he afflicted,* setting the mercies over against the crosses, we ought therein to take notice of the kindness and tenderness of divine Providence; it is as if *it repented God concerning his servants,* Ps. 90:13, 15. Yet joy that a man was born into his family could not make him forget his grief; for he gives a melancholy name to his son, *Beriah — in trouble,* for he was born when the family was in mourning, when *it went evil with his house.* It is good to have in remembrance the affliction and the misery, the wormwood and the gall, that our souls may be *humbled within us,* Lam. 3:19, 20. What name more proper for *man that is born of a woman* than *Beriah,* because born into a troublesome world? It is added, as a further honour to the house of Ephraim, (1.) That a daughter of that tribe, *Sherah* by name, at the time of Israel's setting in Canaan, built some cities, either at her own charge or by her own care; one of them bore her name, *Uzzen-sherah, v.* 24. A virtuous woman may be as great an honour and blessing to a family as a mighty man. (2.) That a son of that tribe was employed in the conquest of Canaan, *Joshua the son of Nun, v.* 27. In this also the breach made on Ephraim's family was further repaired; and perhaps the resentment of this injury formerly done by the Canaanites to the Ephraimites might make him more vigorous in the war.

II. Of the tribe of Asher. Some men of note of that tribe are here named. Their militia was not numerous in comparison with some other tribes, only 26,000 men in all; but their princes were *choice and mighty men of valour, chief of the princes* (*v.* 40), and perhaps it was their wisdom that they coveted not to make their trained bands numerous, but rather to have a few, and those apt to the war and serviceable men.

CHAPTER 8

We had some account given us of Benjamin in the foregoing chapter; here we have a larger catalogue of the great men of that tribe. 1. Because of that tribe Saul came, the first king of Israel, to the story of whom the sacred writer is hastening, 10:1. 2. Because that tribe clave to Judah, inhabited much of Jerusalem, was one of the two tribes that went into captivity, and returned back; and that story also he has an eye to, 9:1. Here is, I. Some of the heads of that tribe named (*v.* 1–32). II. A more particular account of the family of Saul (*v.* 33–40).

Verses 1–32

There is little or nothing of history in all these verses; we have not therefore much to observe. 1. As to the difficulties that occur in this and the foregoing genealogies we need not perplex ourselves. I presume Ezra took them as he found them *in the books of the kings of Israel and Judah* (*ch.* 9:1), according as they were given in by the several tribes, each observing what method they thought fit. Hence some *as*cend, others *de*secnd; some have *numbers* affixed, others *places;* some have historical remarks intermixed, others have not; some are shorter, others longer; some agree with other records, others differ; some, it is likely, were torn, erased, and blotted, others more legible. Those of Dan and Reuben were entirely lost. This holy man wrote as he was moved by the Holy Ghost; but there was no necessity for the making up of the defects, no, nor for the rectifying of the mistakes, of these genealogies by inspiration. It was sufficient that he copied them out as they came into his hand, or so much of them as was requisite to the present purpose, which was the directing of the returned captives to settle as nearly as they could with those of their own family, and in the places of their former residence. We may suppose that many things in these genealogies which to us seem intricate, abrupt, and perplexed, were plain and easy to them then (who knew how to fill up the deficiencies) and abundantly answered the intention of the publishing of them. 2. Many great and mighty nations there were now in being upon earth, and many illustrious men in them, whose names are buried in perpetual oblivion, while the names of multitudes of the Israel of God are here carefully preserved in everlasting remembrance. They are *Jasher, Jeshurun — just ones,* and *the memory of the just is blessed.* Many of these we have reason to fear, came short of everlasting honour (for even the wicked kings of Judah come into the genealogy), yet the perpetuating of their names here was a figure of the writing of the names of all God's spiritual Israel in the Lamb's book of life. 3. This tribe of Benjamin was once brought to a very low ebb, in the time of the judges, upon the occasion of the iniquity of Gibeah, when only 600 men escaped the sword of justice; and yet, in these genealogies, it makes as good a figure as almost any of the tribes: for it is the honour of God to help the weakest and raise up those that are most diminished and abased. 4. Here is mention of one Ehud (*v.* 6), in the preceding verse of one Gera (*v.* 5) and (*v.* 8) of one that descended from him, that *begat children in the country of Moab,* which inclines me to think it was that Ehud who was the second of the judges of Israel; for he is said to be *the son of Gera* and *a Benjamite* (Jdg. 3:15), and he delivered Israel from the oppression of the Moabites by killing the king of Moab, which might give him a greater sway in the country of Moab than we find evidence of in his history and might occasion some of his posterity to settle there. 5. Here is mention of some of the Benjamites that *drove away the inhabitants of Gath* (*v.* 13), perhaps those that had slain the Ephraimites (*ch.* 7:21) or their posterity, by way of reprisal: and one of those that did this piece of justice was named *Beriah* too, that name in which the memorial of that injury was preserved. 6. Particular notice is taken of those that *dwelt in Jerusalem* (*v.* 28 and again *v.* 32), that those whose ancestors had had their residence there might thereby be induced, at their return from captivity, to settle there too, which, for aught that appears, few were willing to do, because it was the post of danger: and therefore we find (Neh. 11:2) *the people blessed those that willingly offered themselves to dwell at Jerusalem,* the greater part being inclined to prefer the cities of Judah. Those whose godly parents had their conversation in the new Jerusalem should thereby be engaged to set their faces thitherward and pursue the way thither, whatever it cost them.

Verses 33–40

It is observable that among all the genealogies of the tribes there is no mention of any of the kings of Israel after the defection from the house of David, much less of their families; not a word of Jeroboam's house or Baasha's, of Umri's or Jehu's; for they were all idolaters. But of the family of Saul, which was the royal family before the elevation of David, we have here a particular account. 1. Before Saul, Kish and Ner only are named, his father and grandfather, *v.* 33. His pedigree is carried higher 1 Sa. 9:1, only there Kish is said to be *the son of Abiel,* here *of Ner.* He was in truth the son of Ner but the grandson of Abiel, as appears by 1 Sa. 14:51, where it is said that *Ner was the son of Abiel,* and that Abner, who was the son of Ner, was Saul's uncle (that is, his father's brother); therefore his father was also the son of Ner. It is common in all languages to put sons for grandsons and other descendents, much more in the scanty language of the Hebrews. 2. After Saul, divers of his sons are named, but the posterity of none of them, save Jonathan only, who was blessed with numerous issue and those honoured with a place in the sacred genealogies for the sake of his sincere kindness to David. The line of Jonathan is drawn down here for about ten generations. Perhaps David was, in a particular manner, careful to preserve that, and assigned it a page by itself, because of the covenant made between his seed and Jonathan's seed forever, 1 Sa. 20:15, 23, 42. This genealogy ends in Ulam, whose family became famous in the tribe of Benjamin for the number of its valiant men. Of that one man's posterity there were, as it should seem, at one time, 150 archers brought into the field of battle, that were *mighty men of valour, v.* 40. That is taken notice of concerning them which is more a man's praise than his pomp or wealth is, that they were qualified to serve their country.

CHAPTER 9

This chapter intimates to us that one end of recording all these genealogies was to direct the Jews, now that they had returned out of captivity, with whom to incorporate and where to reside; for here we have an account of those who first took possession of Jerusalem after their return from Babylon, and began the rebuilding of it upon the old foundation. I. The Israelites (*v.* 2–9). II. The priests (*v.* 10–13). III. The Levites and other Nethinim (*v.* 14–26). IV. Here is the particular charge of some of the priests and Levites (*v.* 27–34). V. A repetition of the genealogy of king Saul (*v.* 35–44).

Verses 1–13

The first verse looks back upon the foregoing genealogies, and tells us they were gathered out of *the books of the kings of Israel and Judah,* not that which we have in the canon of scripture, but another civil record, which was authentic, as the king's books with us. Mentioning Israel and Judah, the historian takes notice of their being *carried away to Babylon for their transgression.* Let that judgment never be forgotten, but ever be remembered, for warning to posterity to take heed of those sins that brought it upon them. Whenever we speak of any calamity that has befallen us, it is good to add this, "it was for my transgression," that God may be justified and clear when he judges. Then follows an account of the first inhabitants, after their return from captivity, that dwelt in their cities, especially in Jerusalem. 1. The Israelites. That general name is used (*v.* 2) because with those of Judah and Benjamin there were many of Ephraim and Manasseh, and the other ten tribes (*v.* 3), such as had escaped to Judah when the body of the ten tribes were carried captive or returned to Judah upon the revolutions in Assyria, and so went into captivity with them, or met them when they were in Babylon, associated with them, and so shared in the benefit of their enlargement. It was foretold that the *children of Judah and of Israel* should be *gathered together and come up out of the land* (Hos. 1:11), and that they should be one nation again, Eze. 37:22. Trouble drives those together that have been at variance; and the pieces of metal that had been separated will run together again when melted in the same crucible. Many both of Judah and Israel staid behind in captivity; but some of both, whose spirit God stirred up, enquired the way to Zion again. Divers are here named, and many more numbered, who were *chief of the fathers* (*v.* 9), who ought to be remembered with honour, as Israelites indeed. 2. The priests, *v.* 10. It was their praise that they came with the first. Who should lead in a good work if the priests, the Lord's ministers, do not? It was the people's praise that they would not come without them; for who but the priests should keep knowledge? Who but the priests should bless them in the name of the Lord? (1.) It is said of one of them that he was *the ruler of the house of God* (*v.* 11) not the chief ruler, for Joshua was then the high priest, but the sagan, and the next under him, his deputy, who perhaps applied more diligently to the business than the high priest himself. In the house of God it is requisite that there be rulers, not to make new laws, but to take care that the laws of God be duly observed by priests as well as people. (2.) It is said of many of them that they were *very able men for the service of the house of God, v.* 13. In the house of God there is service to be done, constant service; and it is well for the church when those are employed in that service who are qualified for it, *able ministers of the New Testament,* 2 Co. 3:6. The service of the temple was such as required at all times, especially in this critical juncture, when they had newly come out of Babylon, great courage and vigour of mind, as well as strength of body; and therefore they are praised as *mighty men of valour.*

Verses 14–34

We have here a further account of the good posture which the affairs of religion were put into immediately upon the return of the people out of Babylon. They had smarted for their former neglect of ordinances and under the late want of ordinances. Both these considerations made them very zealous and forward in setting up the worship of God among them; so they began their worship of God at the right end. Instances hereof we have here.

I. Before the house of the Lord was built they had the house of the tabernacle, a plain and movable tent, which they made use of in the mean time. Those that cannot yet reach to have a temple must not be without a tabernacle, but be thankful for that and make the best of it. Never let God's work be left undone for want of a place to do it in.

II. In allotting to the priests and Levites their respective employments, they had an eye to the model that was drawn up by David, and Samuel the seer, *v.* 22. Samuel, in his time, had drawn the scheme of it, and laid the foundation, though the ark was then in obscurity, and David afterwards finished it, and both acted by immediate direction from God. Or David, as soon as he was anointed had this matter in his mind and consulted Samuel about it, though he was then in his troubles, and the plan was formed in concert between them. This perhaps had been little regarded for many ages; but now, after a long interruption, it was revived. In dividing the work, they observed these ancient land-marks.

III. The most of them dwelt at Jerusalem (*v.* 34), yet there were some that dwelt in the villages (*v.* 16, 22), because, it may be, there was not yet room for them in Jerusalem. However they were employed in the service of the tabernacle (*v.* 25): *They were to come after seven days from time to time.* They had their week's attendance in their turns.

IV. Many of the Levites were employed as porters at the gates of the house of God, four chief porters (*v.* 26), and, under them, others, to the number of 212, *v.* 22. They had the oversight of the gates (*v.* 23), were keepers of the *thresholds,* as in the margin (*v.* 19), and keepers of the entry. This seemed a mean office; and yet David would rather have it than *dwell in the tents of wickedness,* Ps. 84:10. Their office was, 1. To open the doors of God's house every morning (*v.* 27) and shut them at night. 2. To keep off the unclean, and hinder those from thrusting in that were forbidden by the law. 3. To direct and introduce into the courts of the Lord those that came thither to worship, and to show them where to go and what to do, that they might not incur punishment. This required care, and diligence, and constant attendance. Ministers have work to do of this kind.

V. Here is one Phinehas, a son of Eleazar, that is said to be a *ruler over them in time past* (*v.* 20), not the famous high priest of that name, but (as is supposed) an eminent Levite, of whom it is here said that *the Lord was with him,* or (as the Chaldee reads it) *the Word of the Lord was his helper* — the eternal Word, who is *Jehovah, the mighty one on whom help is laid.*

VI. It is said of some of them that, because the charge was upon them, *they lodged round about the house of God, v.* 27. It is good for ministers to be near their work, that they may give themselves wholly to it. The Levites pitched about the tabernacle when they marched through the wilderness. Then they were porters in one sense, bearing the burdens of the sanctuary, now porters in another sense, attending the gates and the doors — in both instances keeping the charge of the sanctuary.

VII. Every one knew his charge. Some were entrusted with the plate, the ministering vessels, to bring them in and out by tale, *v.* 28. Others were appointed to prepare the fine flour, wine, oil, etc., *v.* 29. Others, that were priests, made up the holy anointing oil, *v.* 30. Others took care of the meat-offerings, *v.* 31. Others of the show-bread, *v.* 32. As in other great houses, so in God's house, the work is likely to be done well when every one knows the duty of his place and makes a business of it. God is the God of order: but that which is every body's work will be nobody's work.

VIII. The singers *were employed in that work day and night, v.* 33. They were the *chief fathers of the Levites* that made a business of it, not mean singing-men, that made a trade of it. They remained in the chambers of the temple, that they might closely and constantly attend it, and were therefore excused from all other services. It should seem, some companies were continually singing, at least at stated hours, both day and night. Thus was God continually praised, as it is fit he should be who is continually doing good. Thus devout people might, at any hour, have assistance in their devotion. Thus was the temple a figure of the heavenly one, where they *rest not day nor night* from praising God, Rev. 4:8. *Blessed are those that dwell in thy house; they will be still praising thee.*

Verses 35–44

These verses are the very same with *ch.* 8:29–38, giving an account of the ancestors of Saul and the posterity of Jonathan. *There* it is the conclusion of the genealogy of Benjamin; *here* it is an introduction to the story of Saul. We take the repetition as we find it; but if we admit that there are in the originals, especially in these books, some errors of the transcribers, I should be tempted to think this repetition arose from a blunder. Some one, in copying out these genealogies, having written those words, *v.* 34 *(These dwelt in Jerusalem),* cast his eye on the same words, *ch.* 8:28 *(These dwelt in Jerusalem),* and so went on with what followed there, instead of going on with what followed here; and, when he perceived his mistake, was loth to make a blot in his book, and so let it stand. We have a rule in our law, *Redundans non nocet — Redundancies do no harm.*

CHAPTER 10

The design of Ezra, in these books of the Chronicles, was to preserve the records of the house of David, which, though much sunk and lessened in a common eye by the captivity, yet grew more and more illustrious in the eyes of those that lived by faith by the nearer approach of the Son of David. And therefore he repeats, not the history of Saul's reign, but only of his death, by which way was made for David to the throne. In this chapter we have, I. The fatal rout which the Philistines gave to Saul's army, and the fatal stroke which he gave himself (*v.* 1–7). II. The Philistines' triumph therein (*v.* 8–10). III. The respect which the men of Jabesh-Gilead showed the royal corpse (*v.* 11, 12). IV. The reason of Saul's rejection (*v.* 13, 14).

Verses 1–7

This account of Saul's death is the same with that which we had, 1 Sa. 31:1, etc. We need not repeat the exposition of it. Only let us observe, 1. Princes sin and the people suffer for it. It was a bad time with Israel when they *fled before the Philistines* and *fell down slain* (*v.* 1), when they quitted their cities, and *the Philistines came and dwelt in them, v.* 7. We do not find that they were at this time guilty of idolatry, as they had been before, in the days of the judges, and were afterwards, in the days of the kings. Samuel had reformed them, and they were reformed: and yet they are thus *given to the spoil and to the robbers.* No doubt there was enough in them to deserve this judgment; but that which divine Justice had chiefly an eye to was the sin of Saul. Note, Princes and great men should in a special manner take heed of provoking God's wrath; for, if they kindle that fire, they know not how many may be consumed by it for their sakes. 2. Parents sin and the children suffer for it. When the measure of Saul's iniquity was full, and his day came to fall (which David foresaw, 1 Sa. 26:10), he not only descended into battle and perished himself, but his sons (all but Ishbosheth) perished with him, and Jonathan among the rest, that gracious, generous man; for *all things come alike to all.* Thus was the iniquity of the fathers visited upon the children, and they fell as parts of the condemned father. Note, Those that love their seed must leave their sins, lest they perish not alone in their iniquity, but bring ruin on their families with themselves, or entail a curse upon them when they are gone. 3. Sinners sin and at length suffer for it themselves, though they be long reprieved; for, although sentence be not executed speedily, it will be executed. It was so upon Saul; and the manner of his fall was such as, in various particulars, answered to his sin. (1.) He had thrown a javelin more than once at David, and missed him; but the archers hit him, and he was wounded of the archers. (2.) He had commanded Doeg to slay the priests of the Lord; and now, in despair, he commands his armour-bearer to *draw his sword and thrust him through.* (3.) He had disobeyed the command of God in not destroying the Amalekites, and his armour-bearer disobeys him in not destroying him. (4.) He that was the murderer of the priests is justly left to himself to be his own murderer; and his family is cut off who cut off the city of the priests. See, and say, *The Lord is righteous.*

Verses 8–14

Here, I. From the triumph of the Philistines over the body of Saul we may learn, 1. That the greater dignity men are advanced to the greater disgrace they are in danger of falling into. Saul's dead body, because he was king, was abused more than any other of the slain. Advancement makes men a mark for malice. 2. That, if we give not to God the glory of our successes, even the Philistines will rise up in judgment against us and condemn us; for, when they had obtained a victory over Saul, they *sent tidings to their idols* — poor idols, that knew not what was done a few miles off till the tidings were brought to them, nor then either! They also put Saul's armour *in the house of their gods, v.* 10. Shall Dagon have so honourable a share in their triumphs and the true and living God be forgotten in ours?

II. From the triumph of the men of Jabesh-Gilead in the rescue of the bodies of Saul and his sons we learn that there is a respect due to the remains of the deceased, especially of deceased princes. We are not to enquire concerning the eternal state; that must be left to God: but we must treat the dead body as those who remember it has been united to an immortal soul and must be so again.

III. From the triumphs of divine Justice in the ruin of Saul we may learn, 1. That the sin of sinners will certainly find them out, sooner or later: *Saul died for his transgression.* 2. That no man's greatness can exempt him from the judgments of God. 3. Disobedience is a killing thing. Saul died for *not keeping the word of the Lord,* by which he was ordered to destroy the Amalekites. 4. Consulting with witches is a sin that fills the measure of iniquity as soon as any thing. Saul enquired of one that *had a familiar spirit,* and *enquired not of the Lord, therefore he slew him, v.* 13, 14. Saul slew himself, and yet it is said, *God slew him.* What is done by wicked hands is yet done *by the determinate counsel and foreknowledge of God.* Those that abandon themselves to the devil shall be abandoned to him; so shall their doom be. It is said (1 Sa. 28:6) that Saul did *enquire of the Lord* and he *answered him not:* but here it is said, *Saul did not enquire of God;* for he did not till he was brought to the last extremity, and then it was too late.

CHAPTER 11

In this chapter is repeated, I. The elevation of David to the throne, immediately upon the death of Saul, by common consent (*v.* 1–3). II. His gaining the castle of Zion out of the hands of the Jebusites (*v.* 4–9). III. The catalogue of the worthies and great men of his kingdom (*v.* 10–47).

Verses 1–9

David is here brought to the possession.

I. Of the throne of Israel, after he had reigned seven years in Hebron, over Judah only. In consideration of his relation to them (*v.* 1), his former good services, and especially the divine designation (*v.* 2), they anointed him their king: he covenanted to protect them, and they to bear faith and true allegiance to him, *v.* 3. Observe, 1. God's counsels will be fulfilled at last, whatever difficulties lie in the way. If God had said, *David shall rule,* it is in vain to oppose it. 2. Men that have long stood in their own light, when they have long wearied themselves with their lying vanities, it is to be hoped, will understand the things that belong to their peace and return to *their own mercies.* 3. Between prince and people there is an original contract, which both ought religiously to observe. If ever any prince might have claimed an absolute despotic power, David might, and might as safely as any have been entrusted with it; and yet he made a covenant with the people, took the coronation-oath, to rule by law.

II. Of the strong-hold of Zion, which was held by the Jebusites till David's time. Whether David had a particular eye upon it as a place fit to make a royal city, or whether he had a promise of it from God, it seems that one of his first exploits was to make himself master of that fort; and, when he had it, he called it the *city of David, v.* 7. To this reference is had, Ps. 2:6. *I have set my king upon my holy hill of Zion.* See here what quickens and engages resolution in great undertakings. 1. Opposition. When the Jebusites set David at defiance, and said, *Thou shalt not come hither.* he resolved to force it, whatever it cost him. 2. Prospect of preferment. When David proposed to give the general's place to him that would lead the attack upon the castle of Zion, Joab was fired with the proposal, and he *went up first, and was chief.* It has been said, "Take away honour out of the soldier's eye and you cut off the spurs from his heels."

Verses 10–47

We have here an account of David's worthies, the great men of his time that served him and were preferred by him. The first edition of this catalogue we had, 2 Sa. 23:8, etc. This is much the same, only that those named here from *v.* 41 to the end are added. Observe,

I. The connexion of this catalogue with that which is said concerning David, *v.* 9. 1. *David waxed greater and greater,* and these were his mighty men. Much of the strength and honour of great men is borrowed from their servants and depends upon them, which cannot but somewhat diminish pomp and power in the opinion of those that are wise. David is great because he has great men about him; take these away, and he is where he was. 2. *The Lord of hosts was with him, and these were the mighty men which he had.* God was with him and wrought for him, but by men and means and the use of second causes. By *this* it appeared that God was with him, that he inclined the hearts of those to come over to him that were able to serve his interest. As, if God be for us none can be against us, so, if God be for us, all shall be for us that we have occasion for. Yet David ascribed his success and increase, not to the hosts he had, but to the *Lord of hosts,* not to the mighty men that were with him, but to the mighty God whose presence with us is all in all.

II. The title of this catalogue (*v.* 10): *These are the men who strengthened themselves with him.* In strengthening him they strengthened themselves and their own interest; for his advancement was theirs. What we do in our places for the support of the kingdom of the Son of David we shall be gainers by. In strengthening it we strengthen ourselves. It may be read, *They held strongly with him and with all Israel.* Note, When God has work to do he will not want fit instruments to do it with. If it be work that requires mighty men, mighty men shall either be found or made to effect it, *according to the word of the Lord.*

III. That which made all these men honourable was the good service that they did to their king and country; they helped to make David king (*v.* 10) — a good work. They slew the Philistines, and other public enemies, and were instrumental to save Israel. Note, The way to be great is to do good. Nor did they gain this honour without labour and the hazard of their lives. The honours of Christ's kingdom are prepared for those that *fight the good fight of faith,* that labour and suffer, and are willing to venture all, even life itself, for Christ and a good conscience. It is by a patient continuance in well-doing that we must seek for glory, and honour, and immortality; and those that are faithful to the Son of David shall find their names registered and enrolled much more to their honour than these are in the records of fame.

IV. Among all the great exploits of David's mighty men, here is nothing great mentioned concerning David himself but his *pouring out water before the Lord* which he had *longed for, v.* 18, 19. Four very honourable dispositions of David appeared in that action, which, for aught I know, made it as great as any of the achievements of those worthies. 1. Repentance for his own weakness. It is really an honour to a man, when he is made sensible that he has said or done any thing unadvisedly, to unsay it and undo it again by repentance, as it is a shame to a man when he has said or done amiss to stand to it. 2. Denial of his own appetite. He longed for the water of the well of Bethlehem; but, when he had it, he would not drink it, because he would not so far humour himself and gratify a foolish fancy. He that has such a rule as this *over his own spirit is better than the mighty.* It is an honour to a man to have the command of himself; but he that will command himself must sometimes cross himself. 3. Devotion towards God. That water which he thought too good, too precious, for his own drinking, he *poured out to the Lord* for a *drink offering.* If we have any thing better than another, let God be honoured with it, who is the best, and should have the best. 4. Tenderness of his servants. It put him into the greatest confusion imaginable to think that three brave men should hazard their lives to fetch water for him. In his account it turns the water into blood. It is the honour of great men not to be prodigal of the blood of those they employ, but, in all the commands they give them, to put their own souls into their souls' stead.

V. In the wonderful achievements of these heroes the power of God must be acknowledged. How could one slay 300 and another the same number (*v.* 11, 20), another two lion-like men (*v.* 22), and another an Egyptian giant (*v.* 23), if they had not had the extraordinary presence of God with them, according to that promise, Jos. 23:10, *One man of you shall chase a thousand, for the Lord your God fighteth for you?*

VI. One of these worthies is said to be *an Ammonite* (*v.* 39), another *a Moabite* (*v.* 46), and yet the law was that an *Ammonite* and *a Moabite should not enter into the congregation of the Lord,* Deu. 23:3. These, it is likely, had approved themselves so hearty for the interest of Israel that in their case it was thought fit to dispense with that law, and the rather because it was an indication that the Son of David would have worthies among the Gentiles: with him there is neither Greek nor Jew.

CHAPTER 12

What the mighty men did towards making David king we read in the foregoing chapter. Here we are told what the many did towards it. It was not all at once, but gradually, that David ascended the throne. His kingdom was to last; and therefore, like fruits that keep longest, it ripened slowly. After he had long waited for the vacancy of the throne, it was at two steps and those above seven years distant, that he ascended it. Now we are here told, I. What help came in to him to Ziklag, to make him king of Judah (*v.* 1–22). II. What help came in to him in Hebron, to make him king over all Israel, above seven years after (*v.* 23–40).

Verses 1–22

We have here an account of those that appeared and acted as David's friends, upon the death of Saul, to bring about the revolution. All the forces he had, while he was persecuted, was but 600 men, who served for his guards; but, when the time had come that he must begin to act offensively, Providence brought in more to his assistance. Even while he *kept himself close, because of Saul* (*v.* 1), while he did not appear, to invite or encourage his friends and well-wishers to come in to him (not foreseeing that the death of Saul was so near), God was inclining and preparing them to come over to him with seasonable succours. Those that trust God to do his work for them in his own way and time shall find his providence outdoing all their forecast and contrivance. The war was God's, and he found out helpers of the war, whose forwardness to act for the man God designed for the government is here recorded to their honour.

I. Some, even of Saul's brethren, of the tribe of Benjamin, and a-kin to him, came over to David, *v.* 2. What moved them to it we are not told. Probably a generous indignation at the base treatment which Saul, one of their tribe, gave him, animated them to appear the more vigorously for him, that the guilt and reproach of it might not lie upon them. These Benjamites are described to be men of great dexterity, that were trained up in shooting and slinging, and used both hands alike — ingenious active men; a few of these might do David a great deal of service. Several of the leading men of them are here named. See Jdg. 20:16.

II. Some of the tribe of Gad, though seated on the other side Jordan, had such a conviction of David's title to the government, and fitness for it, that they *separated themselves from their brethren* (a laudable separation it was) to go to David, though he was *in the hold in the wilderness* (*v.* 8), probably some of his strong holds in the wilderness of Engedi. They were but few, eleven in all, here named, but they added much to David's strength. Those that had hitherto come in to his assistance were most of them men of broken fortunes, distressed, discontented, and soldiers of fortune, that came to him rather for protection than to do him any service, 1 Sa. 22:2. But these Gadites were brave men, *men of war, and fit for the battle, v.* 8. For, 1. They were *able-bodied men,* men of incredible swiftness, not to fly from, but to fly upon, the enemy, and to pursue the scattered forces. In this they were *as swift as the roes upon the mountains,* so that no man could escape from them; and yet they had *faces like the faces of lions,* so that no man could out-fight them. 2. They were disciplined men, trained up to military exercises; they could handle shield and buckler, use both offensive and defensive weapons. 3. They were officers of the militia in their own tribe (*v.* 14), so that though they did not bring soldiers with them they had them at command, hundreds, thousands. 4. They were daring men, that could break through the greatest difficulties. Upon some expedition or other, perhaps this to David, they swam over the Jordan, when it *overflowed all its banks, v.* 15. Those are fit to be employed in the cause of God that can venture thus in a dependence upon the divine protection. 5. They were men that would go through with the business they engaged in. What enemies those were that they met with in the valleys, when they had passed Jordan, does not appear; but they put them to flight with their lion-like faces, and pursued them with matchless fury, both *towards the east and towards the west;* which way soever they turned, they followed their blow, and did not do their work by halves.

III. Some of Judah and Benjamin came to him, *v.* 16. Their leader was Amasai, whether the same with that Amasa that afterwards sided with Absalom (2 Sa. 17:25) or no does not appear. Now here we have,

1. David's prudent treaty with them, *v.* 17. He was surprised to see them, and could not but conceive some jealousy of the intentions of their coming, having been so often in danger by the treachery of the men of Ziph and the men of Keilah, who yet were all men of Judah. He might well be timorous whose life was so much struck at; he might well be suspicious who had been deceived in so many that he said, in his haste, *All men are liars.* No marvel that he meets these men of Judah with caution. Observe,

(1.) How he puts the matter to themselves, how fairly he deals with them. As they are, they shall find him; so shall all that deal with the Son of David. [1.] If they be faithful and honourable, he will be their rewarder: *"If you have come peaceably unto me, to help me,* though you have come late and have left me exposed a great while, though you bring no great strength with you to turn the scale for me, yet I will thankfully accept your good-will, and *my heart shall be knit unto you;* I will love you and honour you, and do you all the kindness I can." Affection, respect, and service, that are cordial and sincere, will find favour with a good man, as they do with a good God, though clogged with infirmities, and turning to no great account. But, [2.] If they be false, and come to betray him into the hands of Saul, under colour of friendship, he leaves them to God to be their avenger, as he is, and will be, of every thing that is treacherous and perfidious. Never was man more violently run upon, and run down, than David was (except the Son of David himself), and yet he had the testimony of his conscience that there was no wrong in his hands. He meant no harm to any man, which was his rejoicing in the day of evil, and enabled him, when he feared treachery, to commit his cause to him that judges righteously. He will not be judge in his own cause, though a wise man, nor avenge himself, though a man of valour; but let the righteous God, who hath said, *Vengeance is mine,* do both. *The God of our fathers look thereon and rebuke it.*

(2.) In this appeal observe, [1.] He calls God the *God of our fathers,* both his fathers and theirs. Thus he reminded them not to deal ill with him; for they were both descendants from the same patriarchs, and both dependents on the same God. Thus he encouraged himself to believe that God would right him if he should be abused; for he was the *God of his fathers* and therefore a blessing was entailed on him, and a God to all Israel and therefore not only a Judge to all the earth, but particularly concerned in determining controversies between contesting Israelites. [2.] He does not imprecate any fearful judgement upon them, though they should deal treacherously, but very modestly refers his cause to the divine wisdom and justice: The Lord *look thereon,* and judge as he sees (for he sees men's hearts), and *rebuke it.* It becomes those that appeal to God to express themselves with great temper and moderation; for the wrath of man *works not the righteousness of God.*

2. Their hearty closure with him, *v.* 18. Amasai was their spokesman, on whom the *Spirit of the Lord came,* not a spirit of prophecy, but a spirit of wisdom and resolution, according to the occasion, putting words into his mouth, unpremeditated, which were proper both to give David satisfaction and to animate those that accompanied him. Nothing could be said finer, more lively, or more pertinent to the occasion. For himself and all his associates, (1.) He professed a very cordial adherence to David, and his interest, against all that opposed him, and a resolution to stand by him with the hazard of all that was dear to him: *Thine are we, David, and on thy side, thou son of Jesse.* In calling him *son of Jesse* they reminded themselves that he was lineally descended from Nahshon and Salmon, who in their days were princes of the tribe of Judah. Saul called him so in disdain (1 Sa. 20:27; 22:7), but they looked upon it as his honour. They were convinced that God was on his side; and therefore, *Thine are we, David, and on thy side.* It is good, if we must side, to side with those that side with God and have God with them. (2.) He wished prosperity to David and his cause, not drinking a health, but praying for peace to him and all his friends and well-wishers: *"Peace, peace, be unto thee,* all the good thy heart desires, and *peace be to thy helpers,* among whom we desire to be reckoned, that peace may be on us." (3.) He assured him of help from heaven: *"For thy God helpeth thee;* therefore we wish peace may be, and therefore we doubt not but peace shall be, to thee and thy helpers. God is thy God, and those that have him for their God no doubt have him for their helper in every time of need and danger." From these expressions of Amasai we may take instruction how to testify our affection and allegiance to the Lord Jesus. His we must be without reservation or power of revocation. On his side we must be forward to appear and act. To his interest we must be hearty well-wishers: "Hosanna! prosperity to his gospel and kingdom;" for his God helpeth him, and will till he shall have put down all opposing rule, principality, and power.

3. David's cheerful acceptance of them into his interest and friendship. Charity and honour teach us to let fall our jealousies as soon as satisfaction is given us: *David received them,* and preferred them to be *captains of the band.*

IV. Some of Manasseh likewise joined with him, *v.* 19. Providence gave them a fair opportunity to do so when he and his men marched through their country upon this occasion. Achish took David with him when he went out to fight with Saul; but the lords of the Philistines obliged him to withdraw. We have the story, 1 Sa. 29:4, etc. In his return some great men of Manasseh, who had no heart to join with Saul against the Philistines struck in with David, and very seasonably, to help him *against the band of Amelekites* who plundered Ziklag; they were not many, but they were all mighty men and did David good service upon that occasion, 1 Sa. 30. See how Providence provides. David's interest grew strangely just when he had occasion to make use of it, *v.* 22. Auxiliary forces flocked in daily, *till he had a great host.* When the promise comes to the birth, leave it to God to find strength to bring forth.

Verses 23–40

We have here an account of those who were active in perfecting the settlement of David upon the throne, after the death of Ishbosheth. We read (*ch.* 11:1, and before 2 Sa. 5:1) that *all the tribes of Israel came,* either themselves or by their representatives, to Hebron, to make David king; now here we have an account of the quota which every tribe brought in *ready armed to the war,* in case there should be any opposition, *v.* 23. We may observe here,

I. That those tribes that lived nearest brought the fewest — Judah but 6800 (*v.* 24), Simeon but 7100 (*v.* 25); whereas Zebulun, that lay remote, brought 50,000, Asher 40,000, and the two tribes and a half on the other side Jordan 120,000. Not as if the next adjacent tribes were cold in the cause; but they showed as much of their prudence in bringing few, since all the rest lay so near within call, as the others did of their zeal in bringing so many. The men of Judah had enough to do to entertain those that came from afar.

II. The Levites themselves, and the priests (called here the *Aaronites),* appeared very hearty in this cause, and were ready, if there were occasion, to fight for David, as well as pray for him, because they knew he was called of God to the government, *v.* 26–28.

III. Even some of the kindred of Saul came over to David (*v.* 29), not so many as of the other tribes, because a foolish affection for their own tribe, and a jealousy for the honour of it, kept many of them long in the sinking interest of Saul's family. Kindred should never over-rule conscience. Call no man *Father* to this extent, but God only.

IV. It is said of most of these that they were *mighty men of valour* (*v.* 25, 28, 30), of others that they were *expert in war* (*v.* 35, 36), and of them all that they *could keep rank, v.* 38. They had a great deal of martial fire, and yet were governable and subject to the rules of order — warm hearts but cool heads.

V. Some were so considerate as to bring with them arms, and all instruments for war (*v.* 24, 33, 37), for how could they think that David should be able to furnish them?

VI. The men of Issachar were the fewest af all, only 200, and yet as serviceable to David's interest as those that brought in the greatest numbers, these few being in effect the whole tribe. For, 1. They were men of great skill above any of their neighbours, men that *had understanding of the times, to know what Israel ought to do.* They understood the natural times, could *discern the face of the sky,* were weather-wise, could advise their neighbours in the proper times for ploughing, sowing reaping, etc. Or the ceremonial times, the times appointed for the solemn feasts; therefore they are said to *call the people to the mountain* (Deu. 33:19), for almanacs were not then so common as now. Or, rather, the political times; they understood public affairs, the temper of the nation, and the tendencies of the present events. It is the periphrasis of statesmen that they *know the times,* Esth. 1. 13. Those of that tribe were greatly intent on public affairs, had good intelligence from abroad and made a good use of it. They knew *what Israel ought to do:* from their observation and experience they learned both their own and others' duty and interest. In this critical juncture they knew Israel ought to make David king. It was not only expedient, but necessary; the present posture of affairs called for it. The men of Issachar dealt mostly in country business, and did not much intermeddle in public affairs, which gave them an opportunity of observing others and conversing with themselves. A stander-by sees sometimes more than a gamester. 2. They were men of great interests; for *all their brethren were at their commandment.* The commonality of that tribe having *bowed their shoulder to bear* (Gen. 49:15), the great men had them at their beck. Hence we read of *the princes of Issachar,* Jdg. 5:15. They knew how to rule, and the rest knew how to obey. It is happy indeed when those that should lead are intelligent and judicious, and those who are to follow are modest and obsequious.

VII. It is said of them all that they engaged in this enterprise *with a perfect heart* (*v.* 38), and particularly of the men of Zebulun that they were *not of double heart, v.* 33. They were, in this matter, *Israelites indeed, in whom was no guile.* And this was their perfection, that they were of one heart, *v.* 38. None had any separate interests, but all for the public good.

VIII. The men of Judah, and others of the adjacent tribes, prepared for the victualling of their respective camps when they came to Hebron, *v.* 39, 40. Those that were at the least pains in travelling to this convention, or congress of states, thought themselves obliged to be at so much the more charge in entertaining the rest, that there might be something of an equality. A noble feast was made (was *made for laughter,* Eccl. 10:19) upon this occasion, for there was *joy in Israel, v.* 40. And good reason; for *when the righteous* bear *rule the city rejoices.* Thus, when the throne of Christ is set up in a soul, there is, or ought to be, great joy in that soul: and provision is made for the feasting of it, not as here for two or three days, but for the whole life, nay, for eternity.

CHAPTER 13

In the foregoing chapter we have David made king, by which the civil government was happily settled. In this chapter care is taken about religion. I. David consults with the representatives of the people about bringing up the ark out of its obscurity into a public place; and it is resolved on (*v.* 1–4). II. With a great deal of solemnity and joy, it is carried from Kirjathjearim (*v.* 5–8). III. Uzza is struck dead for touching it, which, for the present, spoils the solemnity and stops the proceedings (*v.* 9–14).

Verses 1–8

Here is, I. David's pious proposal to bring up the ark of God to Jerusalem, that the royal city might be the holy city, *v.* 1–3. This part of the story we had not in Samuel. We may observe in this proposal,

1. That as soon as David was well seated on his throne he had thoughts concerning the ark of God: *Let us bring the ark to us, v.* 3. Two things he aimed at herein: — (1.) To do honour to God, by showing respect to his ark, the token of his presence. As soon as he had power in his hand he would use it for the advancement and encouragement of religion. Note, It ought to be the first and great care of those that are enriched and preferred to honour God with their honours, and to serve him, and the interests of his kingdom among men, with their wealth and power. David said not, "What pompous thing shall I do now?" or, "What pleasant thing?" but, "What pious thing?" (2.) To have the comfort and benefit of that sacred oracle. "Let us bring it to us, not only that we may be a credit to it, but that it may be a blessing to us." Those that honour God profit themselves. Note, It is the wisdom of those who are setting out in the world to take God's ark with them, to make his oracles their counsellors and his laws their rule. Those are likely to proceed in the favour of God who thus begin in the fear of God.

2. That he consulted with the leaders of the people about it, *v.* 1. Though it was without doubt a very good work, and being king, he had the authority to command the doing of it, yet he chose rather to do it by consultation, (1.) That he might show respect to the great men of the kingdom and put honour upon them. Though they made him king, yet he would not rule with a high hand. He did not say, "We will and command, and it is our royal pleasure, that you do so and so; and we will be obeyed," but, *"If it seem good to you,* and you think that the motion comes from the Lord our God, let us send out orders for this purpose." No prince that is wise will covet to be absolute. The people's allegiance is best secured by taking their concurrence in their representatives. Happy then art thou, O Britain! (2.). That he might be advised by them in the manner of doing it, whether just now, whether publicly. David was a very intelligent man himself, and yet consulted with his captains; *for in the multitude of counsellors there is safety.* It is wisdom to make use of the wisdom of others. (3.) That, they joining in it, it might pass the better for a national act and so might procure a national blessing.

3. That he would have all the people summoned to attend on this occasion, both for the honour of the ark and for the people's satisfaction and edification, *v.* 2. Observe, (1.) He calls the common people *brethren,* which bespeaks his humility and condescension (notwithstanding his advancement), and the tender concern he had for them. Thus our Lord Jesus is not ashamed to call his people brethren, Heb. 2:11. (2.) He speaks of the people as a remnant that had escaped: *Our brethren that are left in all the land of Israel.* They had been under scattering providences. Their wars with the Philistines, and with the house of Saul, had wasted the country and cut off many. We now hope to see an end of these troubles. Let those that are left be quickened by late judgments, and present mercies, to seek unto God. (3.) He takes care that the priests and Levites espe-

cially should be summoned to attend the ark; for it was their province in a particular manner. Thus Christian magistrates should stir up ministers to do their duty when they see them remiss.

4. That all this is upon supposition that it is *of the Lord their God.* "Though it should *seem good to you* and me, yet if it be not *of the Lord our God,* we will not do it." What ever we undertake, this must be our enquiry, "Is it of the Lord? Is it agreeable to his mind? Can we approve ourselves to him in it? May we expect that he will own us?"

5. That thus it was requisite they should amend what has been amiss in the last reign, and, as it were, atone for their neglect: "For *we enquired not at it in the days of Saul,* and this was the reason why things went so ill with us: let that original error be amended, and then we may hope to see our affairs in a better posture." Observe, David makes no peevish reflections upon Saul. He does not say, "Saul never cared for the ark, at least in the latter end of this reign;" but, in general, *We enquired not at it,* making himself with others guilty of this neglect. It better becomes us to judge ourselves than others. Humble good men lament their own share in national guilt, and take shame to themselves, Dan. 9:5, etc.

II. The people's ready agreement to this proposal (*v.* 4): *The thing* was *right in the eyes of all the people.* Nobody could say to the contrary, but that it was a very good work and very seasonable; so that it was resolved, *nemine contradicente — unanimously,* that they would do so. Those that prudently proposed a good work, and lead in it, will perhaps find a more ready concurrence in it than they expected. Great men know not what a great deal of good they are capable of doing by their influence on others.

III. The solemnity of bringing up the ark, *v.* 5, etc., which we read before, 2 Sa. 6:1, etc. Here therefore we shall only observe, 1. That it is worth while to travel far to attend the ark of God. They came out of all parts of the country, from the *river of Egypt,* the utmost part south, to the entering of Hemath, which lay furthest north, (*v.* 5), to grace this solemnity. 2. That we have reason greatly to rejoice in the revival of neglected ordinances and the return of the tokens of God's presence. When the light of religion shines out of obscurity, when it is openly and freely professed, is brought into reputation, and countenanced by princes and great ones, it is such a happy omen to a people as is worthy to be welcomed with all possible expressions of joy. 3. When, after long disuse, ordinances come to be revived, it is too common for even wise and good men to make some mistakes. Who would have thought that David would commit such an error as this, to carry the ark upon a cart? *v.* 7. because the Philistines so carried it, and a special providence drove the cart (1 Sa. 6:12), he thought they might do so too. But we must walk by rule, not by example when it varies from the rule, no, not even by those examples which Providence has owned.

Verses 9–14

This breach upon Uzza, which caused all the joy to cease, we had an account of, 2 Sa. 6:6, etc. 1. Let the sin of Uzza warn us all to take heed of presumption, rashness, and irreverence, in dealing about holy things (*v.* 9), and not to think that a good intention will justify a bad action. In our communion with God we must carefully watch over our own hearts, lest familiarity breed contempt, and we think God is in any way beholden to us. 2. Let the punishment of Uzza convince us that the God with whom we have to do is a jealous God. His death, like that of Nadab and Abihu, proclaims aloud that God will be *sanctified in those that come nigh unto him* (Lev. 10:3), and that the nearer any are to him the more displeased he is with their presumptions. Let us not dare to trifle with God in our approaches to him; and yet let us, through Christ, *come boldly to the throne of grace;* for we are under the dispensation of liberty and grace, not of bondage and terror. 3. Let the damp this gave to the joy of Israel be a memorandum to us always to rejoice with trembling, and to *serve the Lord with fear,* even when we *serve him with gladness.* 4. Let David's displeasure upon this occasion caution us to take heed to our spirits when we are under divine rebukes, lest, instead of submitting to God, we quarrel with him. If God be angry with us, shall we dare to be angry with him? 5. Let the stop thus put to the solemnity caution us not to be driven off from our duty by those providences which are only intended to drive us from our sins. David should have gone on with the work notwithstanding the breach made upon Uzza; so might the breach have been made up. 6. Let the blessing which the ark brought with it to the house of Obed-edom encourage us to welcome God's ordinances into our houses, as those that believe the ark is a guest that nobody shall lose by; not let it be less precious to us for its being to some a stone of stumbling and a rock of offence. If the gospel be to some a savour of death unto death, as the ark was to Uzza, yet let us receive it in the love of it and it will be to us a saviour of life unto life.

CHAPTER 14

In this chapter we have, I. David's kingdom established (*v.* 1, 2). II. His family built up (*v.* 3–7). III. His enemies, the Philistines, routed in two campaigns (*v.* 8–17). This is repeated here from 2 Sa. 5:11, etc.

Verses 1–7

We may observe here, 1. There is no man that has such a sufficiency in himself but he has need of his neighbours and has reason to be thankful for their help: David had a very large kingdom, Hiram a very little one; yet David could not build himself a house to his mind unless Hiram furnished him with both workmen and materials, *v.* 1. This is a reason why we should despise none, but, as we have opportunity, be obliging to all. 2. It is a great satisfaction to a wise man to be settled, and to a good man to see the special providences of God in his settlement. The people had made David king; but he could not be easy, nor think himself happy, till he perceived that *the Lord had confirmed him king over Israel, v.* 2. "Who shall unfix me if God hath fixed me?" 3. We must look upon all our advancements as designed for our usefulness. *David's kingdom was lifted up on high,* not for his own sake, that he might look great, but *because of his people Israel,* that he might be a guide and protector to them. We are blessed in order that we may be blessings. See Gen. 12:2. We are not born, nor do we live, for ourselves. 4. It is difficult to thrive without growing secure and indulgent to the flesh. It was David's infirmity that when he settled in his kingdom *he took more wives* (*v.* 3), yet the numerous issue he had added to his honour and strength. Lo, *children are a heritage of the Lord.* We had an account of David's children, not only in Samuel, but in this book (*ch.* 3:1, etc.) and now here again; for it was their honour to have such a father.

Verses 8–17

This narrative of David's triumph over the Philistines is much the same with that, 2 Sa. 5:17, etc. 1. Let the attack which the Philistines made upon David forbid us to be secure in any settlement or advancement, and engage us to expect molestation in this world. When we are most easy something or other may come to be a terror or vexation to us. Christ's kingdom will thus be insulted by the serpent's seed, especially when it makes any advances. 2. Let David's enquiry of God, once and again, upon occasion of the Philistines' invading him, direct us in all our ways to acknowledge God — in distress to fly to him, when we are wronged to appeal to him, and, when we know not what to do, to ask counsel at his oracles, to put ourselves under his direction, and to beg of him to show us the right way. 3. Let David's success encourage us to resist our spiritual enemies, in observance of divine directions and dependence on divine strength. Resist the devil, and he shall flee as the Philistines did before David. 4. Let the sound of the going in the tops of the mulberry trees direct us to attend God's motions both in his providence and in the influences of his Spirit. When we perceive God to go before us let us gird up our loins, gird on our armour, and follow him. 5. Let David's burning the gods of the Philistines, when they fell into his hands, teach us a holy indignation against idolatry and all the remains of it. 6. Let David's thankful acknowledgment of the hand of God in his successes direct us to bring all our sacrifices of praise to God's altar. *Not unto us, O Lord! not unto us, but to thy name give glory.* 7. Let the reputation which David obtained, not only in his kingdom, but among his neighbours, be looked upon as a type and figure of the exalted honour of the Son of David (*v.* 17): *The fame of David went out into all lands;* he was generally talked of, and admired by all people, and *the Lord brought the fear of him upon all nations.* All looked upon him as a formidable enemy and a desirable ally. Thus has God highly exalted our Redeemer, and given him a name above every name.

CHAPTER 15

The bringing in of the ark to the city of David was a very good work; it was resolved upon (13:4), and attempted, but not perfected; it lay by the way in the house of Obed-edom. Now this chapter gives us an account of the completing of that good work. I. How it was done more regularly than before. 1. A place was prepared for it (*v.* 1). 2. The priests were ordered to carry it (*v.* 2–15). 3. The Levites had their offices assigned them in attending on it (*v.* 16–24). II. How it was done more successfully than before (*v.* 25). 1. The Levites made no mistake in their work (*v.* 26). 2. David and the people met with no damp upon their joy (*v.* 27, 28). As for Michal's despising David, it was nothing (*v.* 29).

Verses 1–24

Preparation is here made for the bringing of the ark home to the city of David from the house of Obed-edom. It is here owned that in the former attempt, though it was a very good work and in it they *sought God,* yet they *sought him, not after the due order, v.* 13. "We did not go about our work considerately; and therefore we sped so ill." Note, It is not enough that we do that which is good, but we must do it well — not enough that we seek God in a due ordinance, but we must seek after him, in a due order. Note, also, When we have suffered for our irregularities we must learn thereby to be more regular; then we answer the end of chastisement. Let us see how the matter was mended. 1. David now prepared a place for the reception of the ark, before he brought it to him; and thus he sought in the due order. He had not time to *build a house,* but he *pitched a tent* for it (*v.* 1), probably according to the pattern shown to Moses in the mount, or as near it as might be, of curtains and boards. Observe, When he made houses for himself in the city of David he prepared a place for the ark. Note, Wherever we build for ourselves, we must be sure to make room for God's ark, for a church in the house. 2. David now ordered that the Levites or priests should carry the ark upon their shoulders. Now he bethought himself of that which he could not but know before, that, *none ought to carry the ark but the Levites, v.* 2. The Kohathites carried it in their ordinary marches, and therefore had no wagons allotted them, because their work was to *bear upon their shoulders,* Num. 7:9. But upon extraordinary occasions, as when they passed Jordan and compassed Jericho, the priests carried it. This rule was express, and yet David himself forgot it, and put the ark upon a cart. Note, Even those that are very knowing in the word of God, yet have it not always so ready to them as were to be wished when they have occasion to use it. Wise and good men may be guilty of an oversight, which, as soon as they are aware of, they will correct. David did not go about to justify what had been done amiss, nor to lay the blame on others, but owned himself guilty, with others, of not seeking God in a due order, and now took care not only to summon the Levites to the solemnity, as he did all Israel (*v.* 3), and had done before (*ch.* 13:2), but to see that they assembled (*v.* 4), especially the sons of Aaron, *v.* 11. To them he gives the solemn charge (*v.* 12): *You are the chief of the fathers of the Levites,* therefore do you *bring up the ark of the Lord.* It is expected that those who are advanced above others in dignity should go before others in duty. "You are the chief, and therefore more is expected from you than from others, both by way of service yourselves and influence on the rest. You did it not at first, neither did your duty yourselves nor took care to instruct us, and we smarted for it: *The Lord made a breach upon us;* we have all smarted for your neglect; *this has been by your means* (see Mal. 1:9): therefore *sanctify yourselves,* and mind your business." When those that have suffered for doing ill thus learn to do better the correction is well bestowed. 3. The Levites and priests sanctified themselves (*v.* 14) and were ready to carry the ark on their shoulders, according to the law, *v.* 15. Note, Many that are very remiss in their duty, if they were but faithfully told of it, would reform and do better. The breach upon Uzza made the priests more careful to sanctify themselves, that is, to cleanse themselves from all ceremonial pollution and to compose themselves for the solemn service of God, so as to strike a reverence upon the people. Some are made examples, that others may be made exemplary and very cautious. 4. Officers were appointed to be ready to bid the ark welcome, with every possible expression of joy, *v.* 16. David ordered the chief of the Levites to nominate those that they knew to be proficients for this service. Heman, Asaph, and Ethan, were now first appointed, *v.* 17. They undertook to sound with symbols (*v.* 19), others with psalteries (*v.* 20), others with harps, on the *Sheminith,* or *eighth,* eight notes higher or lower than the rest, according to the rules of the concert, *v.* 21. Some that were priests blew with the trumpet (*v.* 24), as was usual at the removal of the ark (Num. 10:8) and at solemn feasts, Ps. 81:3. And one was appointed for song (*v.* 22), for he was skilful in it, could sing well himself and instruct others. Note, As every man has *received the gift,* so he ought to *minister the same,* 1 Pt. 4:10. And those that excel in any endowment should not only use it for the common good themselves, but teach others also, and not grudge to make others as wise as themselves. This way of praising God by musical instruments had not hitherto been in use. But David, being a prophet, instituted it by divine direction, and added it to the other *carnal ordinances* of that dispensation, as the apostle calls them, Heb. 9:10. The New Testament keeps up singing of psalms, but has not appointed church-music. Some were appointed to be porters (*v.* 18), others door-keepers for the ark (*v.* 23, 24), and one of these was Obed-edom, who reckoned it no doubt a place of honour, and accepted it as recompence for the entertainment he had given to the ark. He had been for three months housekeeper to the ark, and indeed its landlord. But, when he might not be so any longer, such an affection had he for it that he was glad to be its door-keeper.

Verses 25–29

All things being got ready for the carrying of the ark to the city of David, and its reception there, we have here an account of the solemnity of this conveyance thither from the house of Obed-edom.

I. God helped the Levites that carried it. The ark was no very great burden, that those who carried it needed any extraordinary help. But, 1. It is good to take notice of the assistance of the divine providence even in those things that fall within the compass of our natural powers: if God did not help us, we could not stir a step. 2. In all our religious exercises we must particularly derive help from heaven. See Acts 26:22. All our sufficiency for holy duties is from God. 3. The Levites, remembering the breach upon Uzza, were probably ready to tremble when they took up the ark; but God helped them, that is, he encouraged them to it, silenced their fears, and strengthened their faith. 4. God helped them to do it decently and well, and without making any mistake. If we perform any religious duties so as to escape a breach, and come off with our lives, we must own it is God that helps us; for, if left to ourselves, we should be guilty of some fatal miscarriages. God's ministers that bear the vessels of the Lord have special need of divine help in their ministrations, that God in them may be glorified and his church edified. And, if God help the Levites, the people have the benefit of it.

II. When they experienced the tokens of God's presence with them they offered sacrifices of praise to him, *v.* 26. This also he helped them to do. They offered these bullocks and rams perhaps by way of atonement for the former error, that it might not now be remembered against them, as well as by way of acknowledgment for the help now received.

III. There were great expressions of rejoicing used: the sacred music was played, David danced, the singers sang, and the common people shouted, *v.* 27, 28. This we had before, 2 Sa. 6:14, 15. Learn hence, 1. That we serve a good master, who delights to have his servants sing at their work. 2. That times of public reformation are, and should be, times of public rejoicing. Those are unworthy of the ark that are not glad of it. 3. It is not any disparagement to the greatest of men to show themselves zealous in the acts of devotion. Michal indeed despised David (*v.* 29); but *her* despising him did not make him at all despicable; he did not regard it himself, nor did any that were wise and good (and why should we covet the esteem of any but such?) think the worse of him.

CHAPTER 16

This chapter concludes that great affair of the settlement of the ark in the royal city, and with it the settlement of the public worship of God during the reign of David. Here is, I. The solemnity with which the ark was fixed (*v.* 1–6). II. The psalm David gave to be sung on this occasion (*v.* 7–36). III. The settling of the stated public worship of God in order thenceforward (*v.* 37–43).

Verses 1–6

It was a glorious day when the ark of God was safely lodged in the tent David had pitched for it. That good man had his heart much upon it, could not sleep contentedly till it was done, Ps. 132:4, 5.

I. The circumstances of the ark were now, 1. Better than what they had been. It had been obscure in a country town, in the fields of the wood; now it was removed to a public place, to the royal city, where all might resort to it. It had been neglected, as a despised broken vessel; now it was attended with veneration, and God was enquired of by it. It had borrowed a room in a private house, which it enjoyed by courtesy; now it had a habitation of its own entirely to itself, was set in the midst of it, and not crowded into a corner. Note, Though God's word and ordinances may be clouded and eclipsed for a time, they shall at length shine out of obscurity. Yet, 2. They were much short of what was intended in the next reign, when the temple was to be built. This was but a tent, a poor mean dwelling; yet this was the tabernacle, the temple which David in his psalms often speaks of with so much affection. David, who pitched a tent for the ark and continued steadfast to it, did far better than Solomon, who built a temple for it and yet in his latter end turned his back upon it. The church's poorest times were its purest.

II. Now David was easy in his mind, the ark was fixed, and fixed near him. Now see how he takes care, 1. That God shall have the glory of it. Two ways he gives him honour upon this occasion: — (1.) By sacrifices (*v.* 1), burnt-offerings in adoration of his perfections, peace-offerings in acknowledgment of his favours. (2.) By songs: he appointed Levites to record this story in a song for the benefit of others, or to celebrate it themselves by *thanking and praising the God of Israel, v.* 4. All our rejoicings must express themselves in thanksgivings to him from whom all our comforts are received. 2. That the people shall have the joy of it. They shall fare the better for this day's solemnity; for he gives them all what is worth coming for, not only a royal treat in honour of the day (*v.* 3), in which David showed himself generous to his subjects, as he had found God gracious to him (those whose hearts are enlarged with holy joy should show it by being open-handed); but (which is far better) he gives them also a *blessing in the name of the Lord,* as a father, as a prophet, *v.* 2. He prayed to God for them, and commended them to his grace. *In the name of the Word of the Lord* (so the Targum), the essential eternal Word, who is Jehovah, and through whom all blessings come to us.

Verses 7–36

We have here the thanksgiving psalm which David, by the Spirit, composed, and delivered to the chief musician, to be sung upon occasion of the public entry the ark made into the tent prepared for it. Some think he appointed this hymn to be daily used in the temple service, as duly as the day came; whatever other psalms they sung, they must not omit this. David had penned many psalms before this, some in the time of his trouble by Saul. This was composed before, but was now first delivered into the hand of Asaph, for the use of the church. It is gathered out of several psalms (from the beginning to *v.* 23 is taken from Ps. 105:1, etc.; and then *v.* 23 to *v.* 34 is the whole 96th psalm, with little variation; *v.* 34 is taken from Ps. 136:1 and divers others; and then the last two verses are taken from the close of Ps. 106), which some think warrants us to do likewise, and make up hymns out of David's psalms, a part of one and a part of another put together so as may be most proper to express and excite the devotion of Christians. These psalms will be best expounded in their proper places (if the Lord will); here we take them as they are put together, with a design to *thank the Lord* (*v.* 7), a great duty, to which we need to be excited and in which we need to be assisted. 1. Let God be glorified in our praises; let his honour be the centre in which all the lines meet. Let us glorify him by our thanksgivings *(Give thanks to the Lord),* by our prayers (*Call on his name, v.* 8), by our songs *(Sing psalms unto him),* by our discourse — *Talk of all his wondrous works, v.* 9. Let us glorify him as *a great God, and greatly to be praised* (*v.* 25), as supreme God (above all gods), as sole God, for all others are idols, *v.* 26. Let us glorify him as most bright and blessed in himself (*Glory and honour are in his presence, v.* 27), as creator *(The Lord made the heavens),* as the ruler of the whole creation (*His judgments are in all the earth, v.* 14), and as ours — *He is the Lord our God.* Thus must we *give unto the Lord the glory due to his name* (*v.* 28, 29), and own it, and much more, his due. 2. Let other be edified and instructed: *Make known his deeds among the people* (*v.* 8), *declare his glory among the heathen* (*v.* 24), that those who are strangers to him may be led into acquaintance with him, allegiance to him, and the adoration of him. Thus must we serve the interests of his kingdom among men, that all the earth may *fear before him, v.* 30. 3. Let us be ourselves encouraged to triumph and trust in God. Those that give glory to God's name are allowed to *glory in it* (*v.* 10), to value themselves upon their relation to God and venture themselves upon his promise to them. *Let the heart of those rejoice that seek the Lord,* much more of those that have found him. *Seek him, and his strength, and his face:* that is, seek him by the ark of his strength, in which he manifests himself. 4. Let the everlasting covenant be the great matter of our joy and praise (*v.* 15): *Be mindful of his covenant.* In the parallel place it is, *He will be ever mindful of it,* Ps. 105:8. Seeing God never will forget it, we never must. The covenant is said to be *commanded,* because God has obliged us to obey the conditions of it, and because he has both authority to make the promise and ability to make it good. This covenant was ancient, yet never to be forgotten. It was made with Abraham, Isaac, and Jacob, who were long since dead (*v.* 16–18), yet still sure to the spiritual seed, and the promises of it pleadable. 5. Let God's former mercies to his people of old, to our ancestors and our predecessors in profession, be commemorated by us now with thankfulness to his praise. Let it be remembered how God protected the patriarchs in their unsettled condition. When they came strangers to Canaan and were sojourners in it, when they were few and might easily have been swallowed up, when they were continually upon the remove and so exposed, when there were many that bore them ill-will and sought to do them mischief, yet no man was suffered to do them wrong — not the Canaanites, Philistines, Egyptians. Kings were reproved and plagued for their sakes. Pharaoh was so, and Abimelech. They were the *anointed of the Lord,* sanctified by his grace, sanctified by his glory, and had received the unction of the Spirit. They were his prophets, instructed in the things of God themselves and commissioned to instruct others (and prophets are said to be *anointed,* 1 Ki. 19:16; Isa. 61:1); therefore, if any touch them, they touch the apple of God's eye; if any harm them, it is at their peril, *v.* 19–22. 6. Let the great salvation of the Lord be especially the subject of our praises (*v.* 23): *Show forth from day to day his salvation,* that is (says bishop Patrick), his promised salvation by Christ. We have reason to celebrate that from day to day; for we daily receive the benefits of it, and it is a subject that can never be exhausted. 7. Let God be praised by a due and constant attendance upon him in the ordinances he has appointed: *Bring an offering,* then the fruit of the *ground,* now the fruit of the *lips,* of the *heart* (Heb. 13:15), and *worship him in the beauty of holiness,* in the holy places and in a holy manner, *v.* 29. Holiness is the beauty of the Lord, the beauty of all sanctified souls and all religious performances. 8. Let God's universal monarchy be the fear and joy of all people. Let us reverence it: *Fear before him, all the earth.* And let us rejoice in it: *Let the heavens be glad and rejoice,* because *the Lord reigns,* and by his providence establishes the world, so that, though it be moved, it cannot be removed, nor the measures broken which Infinite Wisdom has taken in the government of it, *v.* 30, 31. 9. Let the prospect of the judgment to come inspire us with an awful pleasure, Let earth and sea, fields and woods, though in the great day of the Lord they will all be consumed, yet rejoice that he will come, doth come, to *judge the earth, v.* 32, 33. 10. In the midst of our praises we must not forget to pray for the succour and relief of those saints and servants of God that are in distress (*v.* 35): *Save us, gather us, deliver us from the heathen,* those of us that are scattered and oppressed. When we are rejoicing in God's favours to us we must remember our afflicted brethren, and pray for their salvation and deliverance as our own. We are members one of another; and therefore when we mean, "Lord, save *them,*" it is not improper to say, "Lord, save *us.*" *Lastly,* Let us make God the Alpha and Omega of our praises. David begins with (*v.* 8), *Give thanks to the Lord;* he concludes (*v.* 36), *Blessed be the Lord.* And whereas in the place whence this doxology is taken (Ps. 106:48) it is added, *Let all the people say, Amen, Hallelujah,* here we find they did according to that directory: *All the people said, Amen, and praised the Lord.* When the Levites had finished this psalm or prayer and praise, then, and not till then, the people that attended signified their consent and concurrence by saying, *Amen,* And so they praised the Lord, much affected no doubt with this newly instituted way of devotion, which had been hitherto used in the schools of the prophets only, 1 Sa. 10:5. And, if this way of praising God *please the Lord better than an ox or a bullock that has horns and hoofs, the humble shall see it and be glad,* Ps. 69:31, 32.

Verses 37–43

The worship of God is not only to be the work of a solemn day now and then, brought in to grace a triumph; but it ought to be the work of every day. David therefore settles it here for a constancy, puts it into a method, which he obliged those that officiated to observe in their respective posts. In the tabernacle of Moses, and afterwards in the temple of Solomon, the ark and the altar were together; but, ever since Eli's time, they had been separated, and still continued so till the temple was built. I cannot conceive what reason there was why David, who knew the law and was zealous for it, did not either bring the ark to Gibeon, where the tabernacle and the altar were, or bring them to Mount Zion, where the ark was. Perhaps the curtains and hangings of Moses's tabernacle were so worn with time and weather that they were not fit to be removed, nor fit to be a shelter for the ark; and yet he would not make all new, but only a tent for the ark, because the time was at hand when the temple should be built. Whatever was the reason, all David's time they were asunder, but he took care that neither of them should be neglected. 1. At Jerusalem, where the ark was, Asaph and his brethren were appointed to attend, to *minister before the ark continually,* with songs of praise, *as every day's work required, v.* 37. No sacrifices were offered there, nor incense burnt, because the altars were not there: but David's prayers were *directed as incense, and the lifting up of his hands as the evening sacrifice* (Ps. 141:2), so early did spiritual worship take place of ceremonial. 2. Yet the ceremonial worship, being of divine institution, must by no means be omitted; and therefore at Gibeon were the altars where the priests attended, for their work was to sacrifice and burn incense, which they did *continually, morning and evening, according to the law of Moses, v.* 39, 40. These must be kept up because, however in their own nature they were inferior to the moral services of prayer and praise, yet, as they were types of the mediation of Christ, they had a great deal of honour put upon them, and the observance of them was of great consequence. Here Zadok attended, to preside in the service of the altar; as (it is probable) Abiathar settled at Jerusalem, to attend the ark, because he had the breast-plate of judgment, which must be consulted before the ark: this is the reason why we read in David's time both Zadok and Abiathar were the priests (2 Sa. 8:17; 20:25), one where the altar was and the other where the ark was. At Gibeon, where the altars were, David also appointed *singers to give thanks to the Lord,* and the burden of all their songs must be, *For his mercy endureth for ever, v.* 41. They did it *with musical instruments of God,* such instruments as were appointed and appropriated to this service, not such as they used on other occasions. Between common mirth and holy joy there is a vast difference, and the limits and distances between them must be carefully observed and kept up. Matters being thus settled, and the affairs of religion put into a happy channel, (1.) The people were satisfied, and went home pleased. (2.) David returned to bless his house, resolving to keep up family worship still, which public worship must not supersede.

CHAPTER 17

This excellent chapter is the same with 2 Sa. 7. It will be worth while to look back upon what was there said upon it. Two things in general we have in it: — I. God's gracious acceptance of David's purpose to build him a house, and the promise he made thereupon (*v.* 1–15). II. David's gracious acceptance of God's good promise to build him a house, and the prayer he made thereupon (*v.* 16–27).

Verses 1–15

Let us observe here,

I. How desirous and solicitous good people should be to serve the interests of God's kingdom in the world, to the utmost of their capacity. David could not be easy in a house of cedar while the ark was lodged within curtains, *v.* 1. The concerns of the public should always be near our hearts. What pleasure can we take in our own prosperity if we see not the good of Jerusalem? When David is advanced to wealth and power see what his cares and projects are. Not, "What shall I do for my children to get portions for them? What shall I do to fill my coffers and enlarge my dominions?" But, "What shall I do for God, to serve and honour him?" Those that are contriving where to bestow their fruits and their good would do well to enquire what condition the ark is in, and whether some may not be well bestowed upon it.

II. How ready God's prophets should be to encourage every good purpose. Nathan was no sooner aware of David's good design than he bade him *go and do all that was within his heart* (*v.* 2), for he had no reason to doubt but that God was with him in it. Ministers should stir up the gifts and graces that are in others as well as in themselves.

III. How little God affects external pomp and splendour in his service. His ark was content with a tabernacle (*v.* 5) and he never so much as mentioned the building of a house for it; no, not when he had fixed his people in great and goodly cities which they builded not, Deu. 6:10. He commanded the judges to *feed his people,* but never bade them *build him a house, v.* 6. We may well be content awhile with mean accommodations; God's ark was so.

IV. How graciously God accepts his people's good purposes, yea, though he himself prevents the performance of them. David must not *build this house, v.* 4. He must prepare for it, but not do it; as Moses must bring Israel within sight of Canaan, but must them leave it to Joshua to put them in possession of it. It is the prerogative of Christ to be both the author and finisher of his work. Yet David must not think that, because he was not permitted to build the temple, 1. His preferment was in vain; no, *"I took thee from the sheep-cote,* though not to be a builder of the temple, yet to be *ruler over my people Israel;* that is honour enough for thee; leave the other to one that shall come after thee," *v.* 7. Why should one man think to engross all the business and to bring every good work to perfection? Let something be left for those that succeed. God had given him victories, and made him a name (*v.* 8), and, further, intended by him to establish his people Israel and secure them against their enemies, *v.* 9. That must be *his* work, who is a man of war and fit for it, and he must let the building of churches be left to one that was never cut out for a soldier. Nor, 2. Must he think that his good purpose was in vain, and that he should lose the reward of it; no, it being God's act to prevent the execution of it, he shall be as fully recompensed as if he had done it; *"The Lord will build thee a house,* and annex the crown of Israel to it," *v.* 10. If there be a willing mind, it shall not only be accepted, but thus rewarded. Nor, 3. Must he think that because *he* might not do this good work therefore it would never be done, and that it was in vain to think of it; no, *I will raise up thy seed, and he shall build me a house, v.* 11, 12. God's temple shall be built in the time appointed, though we may not have the honour of helping to build it or the satisfaction of seeing it built. Nor, 4. Must he confine his thoughts to the temporal prosperity of his family, but must entertain himself with the prospect of the kingdom of the Messiah, who should descend from his loins, and whose throne should be *established for evermore, v.* 14. Solomon was not himself so settled in God's house as he should have been, nor was his family settled in the kingdom: "But there shall one descend from thee whom I will settle in my house and in my kingdom," which intimates that he should be both a high priest over the house of God and should have the sole administration of the affairs of God's kingdom among men, all power both in heaven and in earth, in the house and in the kingdom, in the church and in the world. He shall be *a priest upon his throne,* and *the counsel of peace shall be between them both,* and *he shall build the temple of the Lord,* Zec. 6:12, 13.

Verses 16–27

We have here David's solemn address to God, in answer to the gracious message he had now received from him. By faith he receives the promises, embraces them, and is persuaded of them, as the patriarchs, Heb, 11:13. How humbly does he here abase himself, and acknowledge his own unworthiness! How highly does he advance the name of God and admire his condescending grace and favour! With what devout affections does he magnify the God of Israel and what a value has he for the Israel of God! With what assurance does he build upon the promise, and with what a lively faith does he put it in suit! What an example is this to us of humble, believing, fervent prayer! The Lord enable us all thus to seek him! These things were largely observed, 2 Sa. 7. We shall therefore here observe only those few expressions in which the prayer, as we find it here, differs from the record of it there, and has something added to it.

I. That which is there expressed by way of question *(Is this the manner of men, O Lord God?)* is here an acknowledgment: *"Thou hast regarded me according to the estate of a man of high degree.* Thou hast made me a great man, and then treated me accordingly." God, by the covenant-relations into which he admits believers, the titles he gives them, the favours he bestows on them, and the preparations he has made for them, regards them according to the estate of men of high degree, though they are mean and vile. Having himself distinguished them, he treats them as persons of distinction, according to the quality he has been pleased to put upon them. Some give these words here another reading: *"Thou hast looked upon me in the form of a man who art in the highest, the Lord God;* or, *Thou hast made me to see according to the form of a man the majesty of the Lord God."* And so it points at the Messiah; for, as Abraham, so David, saw his day and was glad, saw it by faith, saw it in *fashion as a man, the Word made flesh,* and yet saw his *glory as* that *of the only-begotten of the Father.* And this was that which God spoke concerning his house for a great while to come, the foresight of which affected him more than any thing. And let it not be thought strange that David should speak so plainly of the two natures of Christ who in spirit called him *Lord,* though he knew he was to be his *Son* (Ps. 110:1), and foresaw him *lower than the angels* for a little while, but afterwards *crowned with glory and honour,* Heb. 2:6, 7.

II. After the words *What can David say more unto thee,* it is here added, *for the honour of they servant? v.* 18. Note, The honour God puts upon his servants, by taking them into covenant and communion with himself, is so great that they need not, they cannot, desire to be more highly honoured. Were they to sit down and wish, they could not speak more for their own honour than the word of God has spoken.

III. It is very observable that what in Samuel is said to be *for thy word's sake* is here said to be *for thy servant's sake, v.* 19. Jesus Christ is both *the Word of God* (Rev. 19:13) and *the servant of God* (Isa. 42:1), and it is for his sake, upon the score of his meditation, that the promises are both made and made good to all believers; it is in him that they are *yea and amen.* For his sake is all kindness done, for his sake it is made known; to him we owe all this greatness and from him we are to expect all these great things; they are *the unsearchable riches of Christ,* which, if by faith we see in themselves and see in the hand of the Lord Jesus, we cannot but magnify as great things, the only true greatness, and speak honourably of accordingly.

IV. In Samuel, the Lord of hosts is said to be the *God over Israel;* here he is said to be *the God of Israel, even a God to Israel, v.* 24. His being the God *of* Israel bespeaks his having the name of *their God* and so calling himself; his being a God *to* Israel bespeaks his answering to the name, his filling up the relation, and doing all that to them which might be expected from him. There were those that were called *gods* of such and such nations, gods of Assyria and Egypt, gods of Hamad and Arpad; but they were no gods to them, for they stood them in no stead at all, were mere ciphers, nothing but a name. But *the God of Israel* is a *God to Israel;* all his attributes and perfections redound to their real benefit and advantage. *Happy therefore, thrice happy, is the people whose God is Jehovah;* for he will be a God to them, a God all-sufficient.

V. The closing words in Samuel are, *With thy blessing let the house of thy servant be blessed forever.* That is the language of a holy desire. But the closing words here are the language of a most holy faith: *For thou blessest, O Lord! and it shall be blessed for ever, v.* 27. 1. He was encouraged to beg a blessing because God had intimated to him that he had blessings in store for him and his family: *"Thou blessest, O Lord!* and therefore unto thee shall all flesh come for a blessing; unto thee do I come for the blessing promised to me." Promises are intended to direct and excite prayer. Has God said, *I will bless?* Let our hearts answer, *Lord, bless me,* 2. He was earnest for the blessing because he believed that those whom God blesses are truly and eternally blessed: *Thou blessest, and it shall be blessed.* Men can but *beg* the blessing; it is God that *commands* it. What he designs he effects; what he promises he performs; saying and doing are not two things with him. Nay, *it shall be blessed for ever.* His blessings shall not be revoked, cannot be opposed, and the benefits conferred by them are such as will survive time and days. David's prayer concludes as God's promise did (*v.* 14) with that which is *for ever.* God's word looks at things eternal, and so should our desires and hopes.

CHAPTER 18

David's piety and his prayer we had an account of in the foregoing chapter; here follows immediately that which one might reasonably expect, an account of his prosperity; for those that seek first the kingdom of God and the righteousness thereof, as David did, shall have other things added to them as far as God sees good for them. Here is, I. His prosperity abroad. He conquered the Philistines (*v.* 1), the Moabites (*v.* 2), the king of Zobah (*v.* 3, 4), the Syrians (*v.* 5–8), made the king of Hamath his tributary (*v.* 9–11), and the Edomites (*v.* 12, 13). II. His prosperity at home. His court and kingdom flourished (*v.* 14–17). All this we had an account of before, 2 Sa. 8.

Verses 1–8

After this, it is said (*v.* 1), David did those great exploits. After the sweet communion he had had with God by the word and prayer, as mentioned in the foregoing chapter, he went on his work with extraordinary vigour and courage, *conquering and to conquer.* Thus Jacob, after his vision, lifted up his feet, Gen. 29:1.

We have taken a view of these victories before, and shall now only observe, 1. Those that have been long enemies to the Israel of God will be brought down at last. The Philistines had, for several generations, been vexatious to Israel, but now *David subdued them, v.* 1. Thus shall all opposing *rule, principality, and power,* be, at the end of time, put down by the Son of David, and the most inveterate enemies shall fall before him. 2. Such is the uncertainty of this world that frequently men lose their wealth and power when they think to confirm it. Hadarezer was smitten *as he went to establish his dominion, v.* 3. 3. *A horse is a vain thing for safety,* so David said (Ps. 33:17), and it seems he believed what he said, for he *houghed the chariot-horses, v.* 4. Being resolved not to trust to them (Ps. 20:7), he would not use them. 4. The enemies of God's church are often made to ruin themselves by helping one another, *v.* 5. The Syrians of Damascus were smitten when they came to help Hadarezer. When hand thus joins in hand they shall not only not go unpunished, but thereby they shall be gathered *as the sheaves into the floor,* Mic. 4:11, 12. 5. The *wealth of the sinner* sometimes proves to have been *laid up for the just.* The *Syrians brought gifts, v.* 6. Their shields of gold and their brass were brought to Jerusalem, *v.* 7, 8. As the tabernacle was built of the spoils of the Egyptians, so the temple of the spoils of other Gentile nations, a happy presage of the interest the Gentiles should have in the gospel church.

Verses 9–17

Here let us learn, 1. That it is our interest to make those our friends who have the presence of God with them. The king of Hamath, hearing of David's great success, sent to congratulate him and to court his favour with a noble present, *v.* 9, 10. It is in vain to contend with the Son of David. *Kiss the Son,* therefore, *lest he be angry;* let the kings and judges of the earth, and all inferior people too, be thus wise, thus instructed. The presents we are to bring him are not *vessels of gold and silver,* as here (those shall be welcomed to him who have no such presents to bring), but our hearts and sincere affections, our whole selves, we must present to him as living sacrifices. 2. That what God blesses us with we must honour him with. The presents of his friends, as well as the spoils of his enemies, *David dedicated unto the Lord* (*v.* 11), that is, he laid them up towards the building and enriching of the temple. That is most truly and most comfortably our own which we have consecrated unto the Lord, and which we use for his glory. Let our *merchandise and our hire be holiness to the Lord,* Isa. 23:18. 3. That those who take God along with them whithersoever they go may expect to prosper, and be preserved, whithersoever they go. It was said before (*v.* 6) and here it is repeated (*v.* 13) that *the Lord preserved David whithersoever he went.* Those are always under the eye of God that have God always in their eye. 4. God gives men power, not that they may look great with it, but that they may do good with it. When David reigned over all Israel he *executed judgment and justice among all his people,* and so answered the end of his elevation. He was not so intent on his conquests abroad as to neglect the administration of justice at home. Herein he served the purposes of the kingdom of providence, and of that God who *sits in the throne judging right;* and he was an eminent type of the Messiah, the *sceptre of whose kingdom is a right sceptre.*

CHAPTER 19

The story is here repeated of David's war with the Ammonites and the Syrians their allies, and the victories he obtained over them, which we read just as it is here related, 2 Sa. 10. Here is, I. David's civility to the king of Ammon, in sending an embassy of condolence to him on occasion of his father's death (*v.* 1, 2). II. His great incivility to David, in the base usage he gave to his ambassadors (*v.* 3, 4). III. David's just resentment of it, and the war which broke out thereupon, in which the Ammonites acted with policy in bringing the Syrians to their assistance (*v.* 6, 7), Joab did bravely (*v.* 8–13), and Israel was once and again victorious (*v.* 14–19).

Verses 1–5

Let us here observe, 1. That is becomes good people to be neighbourly, and especially to be grateful. David will pay respect to Hanun because he is his neighbour; and religion teaches us to be civil and obliging to all, to honour all men, and to be ready to do all offices of kindness to those we live among; nor must difference in religion be any obstruction to this. But, besides this, David remembered the kindness which his father showed to him. Those that have received kindness must return it as they have ability and opportunity: those that have received it from the parents must return it to the children when they are gone. 2. That, as saith the proverb of the ancients, *Wickedness proceedeth from the wicked,* 1 Sa. 24:13. The vile person will speak villany, and the instruments of the churl will be evil, to *destroy those with lying words that speak right,* Isa. 32:6, 7. Those that are base, and design ill themselves, are apt to be jealous and to suspect ill of others without cause. Hanun's servant suggested that David's ambassadors came as spies, as if so great and mighty a man as David needed to do so mean a thing (if he had any design upon the Ammonites, he could effect it by open force, and had no occasion for any fraudulent practices), or as if a man of such virtue and honour would do so base a thing. Yet Hanun hearkened to the suggestion, and, against the law of nations, treated David's ambassadors villainously. 3. Masters ought to protect their servants, and with the greatest tenderness to concern themselves for them if they come by any loss or damage in their service. David did so for his ambassadors, *v.* 5. Christ will do so for his ministers; and let all masters thus *give unto their servants that which is just and equal.*

Verses 6–19

We may see here, 1. How the hearts of sinners that are marked for ruin are hardened to their destruction. The children of Ammon saw that *they had made themselves odious to David* (*v.* 6), and then it would have been their wisdom to desire conditions of peace, to humble themselves and offer any satisfaction for the injury they had done him, the rather because they had made themselves not only odious to David, but obnoxious to the justice of God, who is *King of nations,* and will assert the injured rights and maintain the violated laws of nations. But, instead of this, they prepared for war, and so brought upon themselves, by David's hand, those desolations which he never intended them. 2. How the courage of brave men is heightened and invigorated by difficulties. When Joab saw that the battle was set against him before and behind (*v.* 10), instead of meditating a retreat, he doubled his resolution; and, though he could not double, he divided his army, and not only spoke, but acted, like a gallant man, that had great presence of mind when he saw himself surrounded. He engaged with his brother for mutual assistance (*v.* 12), excited himself and the rest of the officers to act vigorously in their respective posts, with an eye to God's glory and their country's good, not to any honour and advantage of their own, and then left the issue to God: *Let the Lord do that which is right in his sight.* 3. How vain the greatest art and strength are against justice and equity. The Ammonites did their utmost to make the best of their position: they brought as good a force into the field, and disposed it with as much policy as possible; yet, having a bad cause, and acting in defence of wrong, it would not do; they were put to the worst. Right will prevail and triumph at last. 4. To how little purpose it is for those to rally again, and reinforce themselves, that have not God on their side. The Syrians, though in no way concerned in the merits of the cause, but serving only as mercenaries to the Ammonites, when they were beaten, thought themselves concerned to retrieve their honour, and therefore called in the assistance of the Syrians on the other side Euphrates; but to no purpose, for still they *fled before Israel* (*v.* 18); they lost 7000 men, who are said to be the men of 700 chariots, 2 Sa. 10:18. For, as now in a man of war for sea-service they allot ten men to a gun, so then, in land-service, ten men to a chariot. 5. those who have *meddled with strife that belongs not to them,* and have found that they *meddled to their own heart,* do well to learn wit at length and meddle no further. The Syrians, finding that Israel was the conquering side, not only broke off their alliance with the Ammonites and would help them no more (*v.* 19), *but made peace with David and became his servants.* Let those who have in vain stood it out against God be thus wise for themselves, and *agree with him quickly, while they are in the way.* Let them become his servants; for they cannot but see themselves undone if they be his enemies.

CHAPTER 20

Here is a repetition of the story of David's wars, I. With the Ammonites, and the taking of Rabbah (*v.* 1–3). II. With the giants of the Philistines (*v.* 4–8).

Verses 1–3

How the army of the Ammonites and their allies was routed in the field we read in the foregoing chapters. Here we have the destruction of Rabbah, the metropolis of their kingdom (*v.* 1), the putting of their king's crown upon David's head (*v.* 2), and the great severity that was used towards the people, *v.* 3. Of this we had a more full account in 2 Sa. 11, 12, and cannot but remember it by this sad token, that while Joab was besieging Rabbah David fell into that great sin in the matter of Uriah. But it is observable that, though the rest of the story is repeated, that is not: a hint only is given of it, in those words which lie here in a parenthesis — *But David tarried at Jerusalem.* If he had been abroad with his army, he would have been out of the way of that temptation; but, indulging his ease, he fell into uncleanness. Now, as the relating of the sin David fell into is an instance of the impartiality and fidelity of the sacred writers, so the avoiding of the repetition of it here, when there was a fair occasion given to speak of it again, is designed to teach us that, though there may be a just occasion to speak of the faults and miscarriages of others, yet we should not take delight in the repetition of them. That should always be looked upon as an unpleasing subject which, though sometimes one cannot help falling upon, yet one would not choose to dwell upon, any more than we should love to rake in a dunghill. The persons, or actions, we can say no good of, we had best say nothing of.

Verses 4–8

The Philistines were nearly subdued (*ch.* 18:1); but, as in the destruction of the Canaanites by Joshua the sons of Anak were last subdued (Jos. 11:21), so here in the conquest of the Philistines the giants of Gath were last brought down. In the conflicts between grace and corruption there are some sins which, like these giants, keep their ground a great while and are not mastered without much difficulty and a long struggle: but judgment will be brought forth unto victory at last. Observe, 1. We never read of giants among the Israelites as we do of the giants among the Philistines — giants of Gath, but not giants of Jerusalem. The growth of God's plants is in usefulness, not in bulk. Those who covet to have *cubits added to their stature* do not consider that it will but make then more unwieldy. In the balance of the sanctuary David far outweighs Goliath. 2. The servants of David, though men of ordinary stature, were too hard for the giants of Gath in every encounter, because they had God on their side, who takes pleasure in abasing lofty looks, and mortifying the giants that are in the earth, as he did of old by the deluge, though they were men of renown. Never let the church's friends be disheartened by the power and pride of the church's enemies. We need not fear great men against us while we have the great God for us. What will a finger more on each hand do, or a toe more on each foot, in contest with Omnipotence? 3. These giants *defied Israel* (*v.* 7) and were thus made to pay for their insolence. None are more visibly marked for ruin that those who reproach God and his Israel. God will do great things rather than suffer the enemy to *behave themselves proudly,* Deu. 32:27. The victories of the Son of David, like those of David himself, are gradual. *We see not yet all things put under him;* but it will be seen shortly: and death itself, the last enemy, like these giants, will be triumphed over.

CHAPTER 21

As this rehearsal makes no mention of David's sin in the matter of Uriah, so neither of the troubles of his family that followed upon it; not a word of Absalom's rebellion, or Sheba's. But David's sin, in numbering the people, is here related, because, in the atonement made for that sin, an intimation was given of the spot of ground on which the temple should be built. Here is, I. David's sin, in forcing Joab to number the people (*v.* 1–6). II. David's sorrow for what he had done, as soon as he perceived the sinfulness of it (*v.* 7, 8). III. The sad dilemma (or trilemma rather) he was brought to, when it was put to him to choose how he would be punished for this sin, and what rod he would be beaten with (*v.* 9–13). IV. The woeful havoc which was made by the pestilence in the country, and the narrow escape which Jerusalem had from being laid waste by it (*v.* 14–17). V. David's repentance, and sacrifice, upon this occasion, and the staying of the plaque thereupon (*v.* 18–30). This awful story we met with, and meditated upon, 2 Sa. 24.

Verses 1–6

Numbering the people, one would think, was no bad thing. Why should not the shepherd know the number of his flock? But God sees not as man sees. It is plain it was wrong in David to do it, and a great provocation to God, because he did it in the pride of his heart; and there is no sin that has in it more of contradiction and therefore more of offence to God than pride. The sin was David's; he alone must bear the blame of it. But here we are told,

I. How active the tempter was in it (*v.* 1): *Satan stood up against Israel, and provoked David* to do it. Is is said (2 Sa. 24:1) that *the anger of the Lord was kindled against Israel, and he moved David* to do it. The righteous judgments of God are to be observed and acknowledged even in the sins and unrighteousness of men. We are sure that God is not the author of sin — he *tempts no man;* and therefore, when it is said that he moved David to do it, it must be explained by what is intimated here, that, for wise and holy ends, he permitted the devil to do it. Here we trace this foul stream to its foundation. That Satan, the enemy of God and all good, should *stand up against Israel,* is not strange; it is what he aims at, to weaken the strength, diminish the numbers, and eclipse the glory of God's Israel, to whom he is *Satan,* a sworn *adversary.* But that he should influence David, the man of God's own heart to do a wrong thing, may well be wondered at. One would think him one of those whom the wicked one touches not. No, even the best saints, till they come to heaven, must never think themselves out of the reach of Satan's temptations. Now, when Satan meant to do Israel a mischief, what course did he take? He did not *move God against them to destroy them* (as Job, ch 2:3), but he provoked David, the best friend they had, to number them, and so to offend God, and set him against them. Note, 1. The devil does us more mischief by tempting us to sin against our God than he does by accusing us before our God. He destroys none but by their own hands, 2. The greatest spite he can do to the church of God is to tempt the rulers of the church to pride; for none can conceive the fatal consequences of that sin in all, especially in church-rulers. *You shall not be so,* Lu. 22:26.

II. How passive the instrument was. Joab, the person whom David employed, was an active man in public business; but to this he was perfectly forced, and did it with the greatest reluctance imaginable.

1. He put in a remonstrance against it before he began it. No man more forward that he in any thing that really tended to the honour of the king or the welfare of the kingdom; but in this matter he would gladly be excused. For, (1.) It was a needless thing. there was not occasion at all for it. God had promised to multiply them, and he needed not question the accomplishment of that promise. They were all his servants, and he needed not doubt of their loyalty and affection to him. Their number was as much his strength as he could desire. (2.) It was a dangerous thing. In doing it he might be a cause of trespass to Israel, and might provoke God against them. This Joab apprehended, and yet David himself did not. The most learned in the laws of God are not always the most quick-sighted in the application of those laws.

2. He was quite weary of it before he had done it; for *the king's word was abominable to Joab, v.* 6. Time was when whatever king David did *pleased all the people,* 2 Sa. 3:36. But now there was a general disgust at these orders, which confirmed Joab in his dislike of them. so that, though the produce of this muster was really very great, yet he had no heart to perfect it, but left two tribes unnumbered (*v.* 5, 6), two considerable ones, Levi and Benjamin, and perhaps was not very exact in numbering the rest, because he did not do it with any pleasure, which might be one occasion of the difference between the sums here and 2 Sa. 24:9.

Verses 7–17

David is here under the rod for numbering the people, that rod of correction which drives out the foolishness that is bound up in the heart, the foolishness of pride. Let us briefly observe,

I. How he was corrected. If God's dearest children do amiss, they must expect to smart for it. 1. He is given to understand that God is displeased; and that it is no small uneasiness to so good a man as David, *v.* 7. God takes notice of, and is displeased with, the sins of his people; and no sin is more displeasing to him than pride of heart: nor is anything more humbling, and grieving, and mortifying to a gracious soul, than to see itself under God's displeasure. 2. He is put to his choice whether he will be punished by war, famine, or pestilence; for punished he must be, and by one of these. Thus, for his further humiliation, he is put into a strait, a great strait, and has the terror of all the three judgments impressed upon his mind, no doubt to his great amazement, while he is considering which he shall choose. 3. He hears of 70,000 of his subjects who in a few hours were struck dead by the pestilence, *v.* 14. He was proud of the multitude of his people, but divine Justice took a course to make them fewer. Justly is that taken from us, weakened, or embittered to us, which we are proud of. David must have the people numbered: *Bring me the number of them,* says he, *that I may know it.* But now God numbers them after another manner, *numbers to the sword,* Isa. 65:12. And David had another number of them brought, more to his confusion than was to his satisfaction, namely, the number of the slain — a black bill of mortality, which is a drawback to his muster-roll. 4. He sees the destroying angel, with his sword drawn against Jerusalem, *v.* 16. This could not but be very terrible to him, as it was a visible indication of the anger of Heaven, and threatened the utter destruction of that beloved city. Pestilences make the greatest devastations in the most populous places. The sight of an angel, though coming peaceably and on a friendly errand, has made even mighty men to tremble; how dreadful then must this sight be of an angel with a drawn sword in his hand, a flaming sword, like that of the cherubim, which turned every way to keep the way of the tree of life! While we lie under the wrath of God the holy angels are armed against us, though we see them not as David did.

II. How he bore the correction. 1. He made a very penitent confession of his sin, and prayed earnestly for the pardon of it, *v.* 8. Now he owned that he had sinned, had sinned greatly, had done foolishly, very foolishly; and he entreated that, however he might be corrected for it, the iniquity of it might be done away. 2. He accepted the punishment of his iniquity: "Let thy hand be *on me, and on my father's house, v.* 17. I submit to the rod, only let me be the sufferer, for I am the sinner; mine is the guilty head at which the sword should be pointed." 3. He cast himself upon the mercy of God (though he knew he was angry with him) and did not entertain any hard thoughts of him. However it be, *Let us fall into the hands of the Lord, for his mercies are great, v.* 13. Good men, even when God frowns upon them, think well of him. *Though he slay me, yet will I trust in him.* 4. He expressed a very tender concern for the people, and it went to his heart to see them plagued for his transgression: *These sheep, what have they done?*

Verses 18–30

We have here the controversy concluded, and, upon David's repentance, his peace made with God. *Though thou wast angry with me, thy anger is turned away.* 1. A stop was put to the progress of the execution, *v.* 15. When David repented of the sin God repented of the judgment, and ordered the destroying angel to *stay his hand* and *sheath his sword, v.* 27. 2. Direction was given to David to rear an altar in the threshing-floor of Ornan, *v.* 18. The angel commanded the prophet Gad to bring David this direction. The same angel that had, in God's name, carried on the war, is here forward to set on foot the treaty of peace; for angels do not desire the woeful day. The angel could have given this order to David himself; but he chose to do it by his seer, that he might put an honour upon the prophetic office. Thus the revelation of Jesus Christ was notified by the angel to John, and by him to the churches. The commanding of David to build an altar was a blessed token of reconciliation; for, if God had been pleased to kill him, he would not have appointed, because he would not have accepted, a sacrifice at his hands. 3. David immediately made a bargain with Ornan for the threshing-floor; for he would not serve God at other people's charge. Ornan generously offered it to him gratis, not only in complaisance to the king, but because he had himself *seen the angel* (*v.* 20), which so terrified him that he and his four sons hid themselves, as unable to bear the brightness of his glory and afraid of his drawn sword. Under these apprehensions he was willing to do anything towards making the atonement. Those that are duly sensible of the terrors of the Lord will do all they can, in their places, to promote religion, and encourage all the methods of reconciliation for the turning away of God's wrath. 4. God testified his acceptance of David's offerings on this altar; He *answered him from heaven by fire, v.* 26. To signify that God's anger was turned away from him, the fire that might justly have fastened upon the sinner fastened upon the sacrifice and consumed that; and, upon this, the destroying sword was returned into its sheath. Thus Christ was made sin and a curse for us, and it pleased the Lord to bruise him, that through him God might be to us, not a consuming fire, but a reconciled Father. 5. He continued to offer his sacrifices upon this altar. The brazen altar which Moses made was at Gibeon (*v.* 29), and there all the sacrifices of Israel were offered; but David was so terrified at the sight of the sword of the angel that he *could not go thither, v.* 30. The business required haste, when the plague was begun. Aaron must go quickly, nay, he must *run,* to make atonement, Num. 16:46, 47. And the case here was no less urgent; so that David had not time to go to Gibeon: nor durst he leave the angel with his sword drawn over Jerusalem, lest the fatal stroke should be given before he came back. And therefore God, in tenderness to him, bade him build an altar in that place, dispensing with his own law concerning one altar because of the present distress, and accepting the sacrifices offered on this new altar, which was not set up in opposition to that, but in concurrence with it. The symbols of unity were not so much insisted on as unity itself. Nay, when the present distress was over (as it should seem), David, as long as he lived, sacrificed there, though the altar at Gibeon was still kept up; for God had owned the sacrifices that were here offered and had testified his acceptance of them, *v.* 28. On those administrations in which we have experienced the tokens of God's presence, and have found that he is with us of a truth, it is good to continue our attendance. "Here God had graciously met me, and therefore I will still expect to meet with him."

CHAPTER 22

"Out of the eater comes forth meat." It was upon occasion of the terrible judgment inflicted on Israel for the sin of David that God gave intimation of the setting up of another altar, and of the place where he would have the temple to be built, upon which David was excited with great vigour to make preparation for that great work, wherein, though he had long since designed it, it should seem, he had, of late, grown remiss, till awakened by the alarm of that judgment. The tokens of God's favour he received after those of his displeasure, I. Directed him to the place (*v.* 1). II. Encouraged and quickened him to the work. 1. He set himself to prepare for the building (*v.* 2–5). 2. He instructed Solomon, and gave him a charge concerning this work (*v.* 6–16). 3. He commanded the princes to assist him in it (*v.* 17–19). There is a great deal of difference between the frame of David's spirit in the beginning of the former chapter and in the beginning of this. There, in the pride of his heart, he was numbering the people; here, in his humility, preparing for the service of God. There corruption was uppermost (but the well of living water in the soul, though it may be muddied, will work itself clear again); grace here has recovered the upper hand.

Verses 1–5

Here is, I. The place fixed for the building of the temple (*v.* 1): *Then David said,* by inspiration of God, and as a declaration of his mind, *This is the house of the Lord God.* If a temple must be built for God, it is fit that it be left to him to choose the ground, for all the earth is his; and this is the ground he makes choice of — ground that pertained to a Jebusite, and perhaps there was not a spot of ground besides, in or about Jerusalem, that did so — a happy presage of the setting up of the gospel temple among the Gentiles. See Acts 15:16, 17. The ground was a threshing-floor; for the church of the living God is his floor, his threshing, and *the corn of his floor,* Isa. 21:10. Christ's fan is in his hand, thoroughly to purge his floor. This is to be the house because this is the altar. The temple was built for the sake of the altar. There were altars long before there were temples.

II. Preparation made for that building. David must not build it, but he would do all he could towards it: He *prepared abundantly before his death, v.* 5. This intimates that the consideration of his age and growing infirmities, which showed him his death approaching, quickened him, towards his latter end, to be very diligent in making this preparation. What our hands find to do for God, and our souls, and our generation, let us do it with all our might before our death, because, after death, there is no device nor working. Now we are here told,

1. What induced him to make such preparation. Two things he considered: — (1.) That Solomon was young and tender, and not likely to apply with any great vigour to this business at first; so that, unless he found the wheels set a-going, he would be in danger of losing a great deal of time at first, the rather because, being young, he would be tempted to put it off; whereas, if he found the materials got ready to his hand, the most difficult part of the work would be over, and this would excite and encourage him to go about it in the beginnings of his reign. Note, Those that are aged and experienced should consider those that are young and tender, and provide them what help they can, that they may make the work of God as easy to them as possible. (2.) That the house must be exceedingly magnificent, very stately and sumptuous, strong and beautiful, every thing about it the best in its kind, and for a good reason, since it was intended for the honour of the great God, the Lord of the whole earth, and was to be a type of Christ, in whom all fulness dwells and in whom are hid all treasures. Men were then to be taught by sensible methods. The grandeur of the house would help to affect the worshippers with a holy awe and reverence of God, and would invite strangers to come to see it, and the wonder of the world, who thereby would be brought acquainted with the true God. Therefore it is here designed to be of fame and glory throughout all countries. David foretold this good effect of its being magnificent, Ps. 68:29 *Because of thy temple at Jerusalem shall kings bring presents unto thee.*

2. What preparation he made. In general, he prepared abundantly, as we shall find afterwards; cedar and stones,

iron and brass, are here specified, *v.* 2–4. Cedar he had from the Tyrians and the Zidonians. *The daughter of Tyre shall be there with a gift,* Ps. 45:12. He also got workmen together, *the strangers that were in the land of Israel.* Some think that he employed them because they were generally better artists, and more ingenious in manual operations, than the Israelites; or, rather, because he would not employ the free-born Israelites in any thing that looked mean and servile. They were delivered from the bondage of making bricks in Egypt, and must not return to hew stone. These strangers were proselytes to the Jewish religion, but, though not enslaved, they were not of equal dignity with Israelites.

Verses 6–16

Though Solomon was young and tender, he was capable of receiving instructions, which his father accordingly gave him, concerning the work for which he was designed. When David came to the throne he had many things to do, for the foundations were all out of course; but Solomon had only one thing in charge, and that was *to build a house for the Lord God of Israel, v.* 6. Now,

I. David tells him why he did not do it himself. It was in his mind to do it (*v.* 7), but God forbade him, because *he had shed much blood, v.* 8. Some think this refers to the blood of Uriah, which fastened such a reproach upon him as rendered him unworthy the honour of building the temple: but that honour was forbidden him before he had shed that blood; therefore it must be meant, as it is here explained, of the blood he shed in his wars (for he had been a man of war from his youth), which, though shed very justly and honourably in the service of God and Israel, yet made him unfit to be employed in this service, or rather less fit than another that had never been called to such bloody work. God, by assigning this as the reason of laying David aside from this work, showed how precious human life is to him, and intended a type of him who should build the gospel temple, not by *destroying men's lives,* but *by saving them,* Lu. 9:56.

II. He gives him the reason why he imposed this task upon him. 1. Because God had designed him for it, nominated him as the man that should do it: *A son shall be born to thee,* that shall be called *Solomon,* and *he shall build a house for my name, v.* 9, 10. Nothing is more powerful to engage us to any service for God, and encourage us in it, than to know that hereunto we are appointed. 2. Because he would have leisure and opportunity to do it. He should be a man of rest, and therefore should not have his time, or thoughts, or wealth, diverted from this business. He should have rest from his enemies abroad (none of them should invade or threaten him, or give him provocation), and he should have peace and quietness at home; and therefore let him build the house. Note, Where God gives rest he expects work. 3. Because God had promised to establish his kingdom. Let this encourage him to honour God, that God had honour in store for him; let him build up God's house, and God will build up his throne. Note, God's gracious promises should quicken and invigorate our religious service.

III. He delivers him an account of the vast preparations he had made for this building (*v.* 14), not in a way of pride and vain glory (he speaks of it as a poor thing — *I have, in my poverty, prepared,* margin), but as an encouragement to Solomon to engage cheerfully in the work, for which so solid a foundation was laid. The treasure here mentioned of the 100,000 talents of gold, and 1,000,000 talents of silver, amounts to such an incredible sum that most interpreters either allow an error in the copy or think the talent here signifies no more than a plate or piece: *ingots* we call them. I am inclined to suppose that a certain number is here put for an uncertain, because it is said (*v.* 16) that of the gold and silver, as well as of the brass and iron, there was no number, and that David here includes all the dedicated things (*ch.* 18:11) which he designed *for the house of the Lord,* that is, not only for the building of it, but for the treasure of it; and putting all together, it might come pretty near what is here spoken of. Hundreds and thousands are numbers which we often use to express that which is very much, when yet we would not be understood strictly.

IV. He charges them to keep God's commandments and to take heed to his duty in every thing, *v.* 13. He must not

think by building the temple to purchase a dispensation to sin; no, on the contrary, his doing that would not be accepted, nor accounted of, if he did not *take heed to fulfil the statutes which the Lord charged Moses with, v.* 13. Though he was to be king of Israel, he must always remember that he was a subject to the God of Israel.

V. He encourages him to go about this great work, and to go on in it (*v.* 13): "*Be strong, and of good courage,* Though it is a vast undertaking, thou needest not fear coming under the reproach of the foolish builder, who began to build and was not able to finish it; it is God's work, and it shall come to perfection. *Dread not, nor be dismayed."* In our spiritual work, as well as in our spiritual warfare, we have need of courage and resolution.

VI. He quickens him not to rest in the preparations he had made, but to add thereto, *v.* 14. Those that enter into the labours of others, and build upon their advantages, must still be improving.

VII. He prays for him: *The Lord give thee wisdom and understanding, and give thee charge concerning Israel, v.* 12. Whatever charge we have, if we see God giving us the charge and calling us to it, we may hope he will give us wisdom for the discharge of it. Perhaps Solomon had an eye to this prayer of his father for him, in the prayer he offered for himself: Lord, *give me a wise and understanding heart.* He concludes (*v.* 16), Up, *and be doing, and the Lord be with thee.* Hope of God's presence must not slacken our endeavours. Though the Lord be with us, we must *rise and be doing,* and, if we do this, we have reason to believe he is and will be with us. Work out your salvation, and God will work in you.

Verses 17–19

David here engages the princes of Israel to assist Solomon in the great work he had to do, and every one to lend him a hand towards the carrying of it on. Those that are in the throne cannot do the good they would, unless those about the throne set in with them. David would therefore have the princes to advise Solomon and quicken him, and make the work as easy to him as they could, by promoting it every one in his place. 1. He shows them what obligations they lay under to be zealous in this matter, in gratitude to God for the great things he had done for them. He had given them victory, and rest, and a good land for an inheritance, *v.* 18. The more God has done for us the more we should study to do for him. 2. He presses that upon them which should make them zealous in it (*v.* 19): "*Set your heart and soul to seek God,* place your happiness in his favour, and keep your eye upon his glory. Seek him as your chief good and highest end, and this *with your heart and soul.* Make religion your choice and business; and then you will grudge no pains nor cost to promote the building of his sanctuary." Let but the heart be sincerely engaged for God, and the head and hand, the estate and interest, and all will be cheerfully employed for him.

CHAPTER 23

David, having given charge concerning the building of the temple, in this and the following chapters settles the method of the temple-service and puts into order the offices and officers of it. In the late irregular times, and during the wars in the beginning of his reign, we may suppose that, though the Levitical ordinances were kept up, yet it was not in the order, nor with the beauty and exactness, that were desirable. Now David, being a prophet, as well as a prince, by divine warrant and direction, "set in order the things that were wanting." In this chapter we are informed, I. He declared Solomon to be his successor, (*v.* 1). II. He numbered the Levites, and appointed them to their respective offices (*v.* 2–5). III. He took an account of the several families of the Levites (*v.* 6–23). IV. He made a new reckoning of them from twenty years old, and appointed them their work (*v.* 24–32). And in this he prepared for the temple as truly as when he laid up gold and silver for it; for the place is of small account in comparison with the work.

Verses 1–23

Here we have, I. The crown entailed, according to the divine appointment, *v.* 1. David made Solomon king, not to reign with him, or reign under him, but only to reign after him. This he did, 1. When he was old and full of days. He was but seventy years old when he died, and yet he was full of days, *satur dierum — satisfied with living* in this world. When he found himself going off, he made provision for the welfare of the kingdom after his decease, and pleased himself with the hopeful prospect of a happy settlement both in church and state. 2. He did it in parliament, in a solemn assembly of all the princes of Israel, which made Adonijah's attempt to break in upon Solomon's title and set it aside, notwithstanding this public recognition and establishment of it, the more impudent, impious, and ridiculous. Note, The settling or securing of the crown in the interests of the temple is a great blessing to the people and a great satisfaction to those who are themselves leaving the world.

II. The Levites numbered, according to the rule in Moses's time, from thirty years old to fifty, Num. 4:2, 3. Their number in Moses's time. by this rule, was 8580 (Num. 4:47, 48), but now it had increased above four-fold, much more in proportion than the rest of the tribes; for the serviceable men of Levi's tribe were now 38,000, unless we suppose that here those were reckoned who were above fifty, which was not the case there. Joab had not numbered the Levites (*ch.* 21:6), but David now did, not in pride, but for a good purpose, and then he needed not fear wrath for it.

III. The Levites distributed to their respective posts (*v.* 4, 5), that every hand might be employed (for, of all men, an idle Levite makes the worst figure), and that every part of the work might be carefully done. Now it was for the honour of God that so great a number of servants attended his house and the business of it. Much of the state of great men consists in the greatness of their retinue. When God kept house in Israel see what a great household he had, and all well fed and well taught. But what were these to the attendants of his throne above, and the innumerable company of angels? It was the happiness of Israel that they had among them such a considerable body of men who were obliged by their office to promote and keep up religion among them. If the worship of God go to decay in Israel, let it not be said that it was for want of due provision for the support of it, but that those who should have done it were careless and false. The work assigned the Levites was four-fold: — 1. Some, and indeed far the greater number, were to set forward the work of the house of the Lord: 24,000, almost two-thirds, were appointed for this service, to attend the priests in killing the sacrifices, flaying them, washing them, cutting them up, burning them, to have the meat-offerings and drink-offerings ready, to carry out dirt, and keep all the vessels and utensils of the temple clean, and every thing in its place, that the service might be performed both with expedition and with exactness. These served 1000 a-week, and so went round in twenty-four courses. Perhaps while the temple was in building some of these were employed to set forward that work, to assist the builders, at least to quicken them, and keep good order among them, and the decorum which became temple-work. 2. Others were officers and judges, not in the affairs of the temple, and in the controversies that arose there (for there, we may suppose, the priests presided), but in the country. They were magistrates, to give the laws of God in charge, to resolves difficulties, and to determine controversies that arose upon them. Of these there were 6000, in the several parts of the kingdom, that assisted the princes and elders of every tribe in the administration of justice. 3. Others were porters, to guard all the avenues of the house of God, to examine those that desired entrance, and to resist those that would force an entrance. These were the life-guards of the temple, and probably were armed accordingly. 4. Others were singers and players on instruments, whose business it was to keep up that part of the service; this was a new-erected office.

IV. The Levites mustered, and disposed of into their respective families and kindreds, that an account of them might the better be kept, and those that neglected their duty might be the more easily discovered, by calling over the roll, and obliging them to answer to their names, which each family might do for itself. When those of the same family were employed together it would engage them to love and assist one another. When Christ sent forth his disciples two and two he put together those that were brethren. Two families were here joined in one (*v.* 11) because they had not many sons. Those that are weak and little, separately, may be put together and appear considerable. That which is most observable in this account of the families of the Levites is that the posterity of Moses (that great man) stood upon the level with common Levites, and had no dignities or privileges at all peculiar to them; whilst the posterity of Aaron were advanced to the priest's office, to *sanctify the most holy things, v.* 13. It is said indeed of the grandson of Moses, Rehabiah, that *his sons were highly multiplied, v.* 17, *margin.* When God proposed to him that, if he would let fall his intercession for Israel, he would make of him a great nation, he generously refused it, in recompence for which his family is here greatly increased, and makes up in number what it wants in figure, in the tribe of Levi. Now, 1. The levelling of Moses' family with the rest is an evidence of his self-denial. Such an interest had he both with God and man that if he had aimed to raise his own family, to dignify and enrich that, he might easily have done so; but he was no self-seeking man, as appears from his leaving to his children no marks of distinction, which was a sign that he had the spirit of God and not the spirit of the world. 2. The elevation of Aaron's family above the rest was a recompence for his self-denial. When Moses (his younger brother) was made a god to Pharaoh, and he only his prophet or spokesman, to observe his orders and do as he was bidden, Aaron never disputed it, nor insisted upon his seniority, but readily took the inferior post God put him in, submitted to Moses, and, upon occasion, called him *his lord;* and because he thus submitted himself, in his own person, to his junior, in compliance with the will of God, God highly exalted his family, even above that of Moses himself. Those that are content to stoop are in the fairest way to rise. Before honour is humility.

Verses 24–32

Here is, I. An alteration made in the computation of the effective men of the Levites — that whereas, in Moses's time, they were not enlisted, or taken into service, till they were thirty-years old, nor admitted as probationers till twenty-five (Num. 8:24), David ordered, by direction from God, that they should be numbered *for the service of the house of the Lord,* from the age of twenty years and upwards, *v.* 24. This order he confirmed by his last words, *v.* 27. When he put his last hand to the draught of this establishment he expressly appointed this to be done for ever after; yet not he; but the Lord. 1. Perhaps the young Levites, having no work appointed them till twenty-five years old, had many of them got a habit of idleness, or grew addicted to their pleasures, which proved both a blemish to their reputation and a hindrance to their usefulness afterwards, to prevent which inconvenience they are set to work, and brought under discipline, at twenty-years old. Those that will be eminent must learn to take care and take care betimes. 2. When the work of the Levites was to carry burdens, heavy burdens, the tabernacle and the furniture of it, God would not call any to it till they had come to their full strength; for he considers our frame, and, in service as well as sufferings, will lay no more upon us than we are able to bear. But now God had given rest to his people, and made Jerusalem his dwelling-place for ever, so that there was no more occasion to carry the tabernacle and the vessels thereof, the service was much easier, and what would not over-work them nor over-load them if they entered upon it at twenty-years old. 3. Now the people of Israel were multiplied, and there was a more general resort to Jerusalem, and would be when the temple was built, than had ever been at Shiloh, or Nob, or Gibeon; it was therefore requisite there should be more hands employed in the temple-service, that every Israelite who brought an offering might find a Levite ready to assist him. When more work is to be done it is a pity but there should be more workmen fetched in for the doing of it. When the harvest is plenteous why should the labourers be few?

II. A further account of the Levites' work. What the work of the priests was we are told (*v.* 13): *To sanctify the most holy things, to burn incense before the Lord,* and to *bless in his name;* that work the Levites were not to meddle with, and yet they had work enough, and good work, according to that to which they were appointed, *v.* 4, 5. 1. Those of them that were to *set forward the work of the house of God* (*v.* 4) were therein to *wait on the sons of Aaron* (*v.* 28), were to do the drudgery-work (if any work for God is to be called *drudgery*) of the house of God, to keep the courts and chambers clean, set things in their places, and have them ready when there was occasion to use them. They were to prepare the show-bread which the priests were to set on the table, to provide the flour and cakes for the meat-offerings, that the priests might have every thing ready to their hands. 2. Those of them that were judges and officers had an eye particularly upon all *measure and size, v.* 29. The standards of all weights and measures were kept in the sanctuary; and the Levites had the care of them, to see that they were exact, and to try other weights and measures by them when they were appealed to. 3. The work of the singers was to *thank and praise the Lord* (*v.* 30), at the offering of the morning and evening sacrifices, and other oblations on the sabbaths, new moons, etc., *v.* 31. Moses appointed that they should blow with trumpets over their burnt offerings and other sacrifices, and on their solemn days, Num. 10:10. The sound of the trumpet was awful, and might be affecting to the worshippers, but was not articulate, nor such a reasonable service as this which David appointed, of singing psalms on those occasions. As the Jewish church grew up from its infancy, it grew more and more intelligent in its devotions, till it came at length, in the gospel, to *put away childish things,* 1 Co. 13:11; Gal. 4:3, 9. 4. The work of the porters (*v.* 5) was to keep *the charge of the tabernacle and of the holy place,* that none might come nigh but such as were allowed, and those no nearer than was allowed them, *v.* 32. They were likewise to keep the charge of the sons of Aaron, to be at their beck and go on their errands, who are yet called *their brethren,* to be a memorandum to the priests that, though they were advanced to a high station, yet they were *hewn out of the same rock* with common Levites, and therefore must not lord it over them, but in all instances treat them as brethren.

CHAPTER 24

This chapter gives us a more particular account of the distribution of the priests and Levites into their respective classes, for the more regular discharge of the duties of their offices, according to their families. I. Of the priests (*v.* 1–19). II. Of the Levites (*v.* 20–31).

Verses 1–19

The particular account of these establishments is of little use to us now; but, when Ezra published it, it was of great use to direct their church affairs after their return from captivity into the old channel again. The title of this record we have *v.* 1 — *These are the divisions of the sons of Aaron,* not by which they divided one from another, or were at variance one with another (it is a pity there should ever be any such divisions among the sons of Israel, but especially among the sons of Aaron), but the distribution of them in order to the dividing of their work among themselves; it was a division which God made, and was made for him. 1. This distribution was made for the more regular discharge of the duties of their office. God was, and still is, the God of order, and not of confusion, particularly in the things of his worship. Number without order is but a clog and an occasion of tumult; but when every one has, and knows, and keeps, his place and work, the more the better. In the mystical body, every member has its use, for the good of the whole, Rom. 12:4, 5; 1 Co. 12:12. 2. It was made by lot, that the disposal thereof might be of the Lord, and so all quarrels and contentions might be prevented, and no man could be charged with partiality, nor could any say that they had wrong done them. As God is the God or order, so he is the God of peace. Solomon says of the lot that it *causeth contention to cease.* 3. The lot was cast publicly, and with great solemnity, in the presence of the king, princes, and priests, that there might be no room for any fraudulent practices or the suspicion of them. The lot is an appeal to God, and ought to be managed with corresponding reverence and sincerity. Matthias was chosen to the apostleship by lot, with prayer (Acts 1:24, 26), and I know not but it might be still used in faith in parallel cases, as an instituted ordinance. We have here the name of the public notary that was employed in writing the names, and drawing the lots, (*v.* 6): *Shemaiah, one of the Levites.* 4. What those priests were chosen to was to preside in the affairs of the sanctuary (*v.* 5), in their several courses and turns. That which was to be determined by the lot was only the precedency, not who should serve (for they chose all the chief men), but who should serve first, and who next, that every one might know his course, and attend in it. Of the twenty-four chief men of the priests sixteen were of the house of Eleazar and eight of Ithamar; for the house of Ithamar may well be supposed to have dwindled since the sentence passed on the family of

Eli, who was of that house. The method of drawing the lots is intimated (*v.* 6), one chief household being taken for Eleazar, and one for Ithamar. The sixteen chief names of Eleazar were put in one urn, the eight for Ithamar in another, and they drew out of them alternately, as long as those for Ithamar lasted, and then out of those only for Eleazar, or two for Eleazar, and then one for Ithamar, throughout. 5. Among these twenty-four courses the eighth is that of Abijah or Abia (*v.* 10), which is mentioned (Lu. 1:5) as the course which Zechariah was of, the father of John the Baptist, by which it appears that these courses which David now settled, though interrupted perhaps in the bad reigns and long broken off by the captivity, yet continued in succession till the destruction of the second temple by the Romans. And each course was called by the name of him in whom it was first founded, as the high priest is here called *Aaron* (*v.* 19), because succeeding in his dignity and power, though we read not of any of them that bore that name. Whoever was high priest must be reverenced and observed by the inferior priests as their father, as Aaron their father. Christ is high priest over the house of God, to whom all believers, being made priests, are to be in subjection.

Verses 20–31

Most of the Levites here named were mentioned before, *ch.* 23:16, etc. They were of those who were to attend the priests in the service of the house of God. But they are here mentioned again as heads of the twenty-four courses of Levites (and about so many are here named), who were to attend the twenty-four courses of the priests: they are therefore said to *cast lots over against their brethren* (so they are called, not their *lords*), *the sons of Aaron,* who were not to lord it over God's *clergy,* as the original word is, 1 Pt. 5:3. And, that the whole disposal of the affair might be of the Lord, the principal fathers cast lots over against their younger brethren; that is, those that were of the elder house came upon he level with those of the younger families, and took their place, not by seniority, but as God by the lot directed. Note, In Christ no difference is made between bond and free, elder and younger. The younger brethren, if they be faithful and sincere, shall be no less acceptable to Christ than the principal fathers.

CHAPTER 25

David, having settled the courses of these Levites that were to attend the priests in their ministrations, proceeds, in this chapter, to put those into a method that were appointed to be singers and musicians in the temple. Here is, I. The persons that were to be employed, Asaph, Heman, and Jeduthun (*v.* 1), their sons (*v.* 2–6), and other skilful persons (*v.* 7). II. The order in which they were to attend determined by lot (*v.* 8–31).

Verses 1–7

Observe, I. Singing the praises of God is here called *prophesying* (*v.* 1–3), not that all those who were employed in this service were honoured with the visions of God, or could foretel things to come. Heman indeed is said to be the *king's seer in the words of God* (*v.* 5); but the psalms they sang were composed by the prophets, and many of them were prophetical; and the edification of the church was intended in it, as well as the glory of God. In Samuel's time singing the praises of God went by the name of *prophesying* (1 Sa. 10:5; 19:20), and perhaps that is intended in what St. Paul calls *prophesying,* 1 Co. 11:4; 14:24.

II. This is here called a *service,* and the persons employed in it *workmen, v.* 1. Not but that it is the greatest liberty and pleasure to be employed in praising God: what is heaven bu that? But it intimates that it is our duty to make a business of it, and stir up all that is within us to it; and that, in our present state of corruption and infirmity, it will not be done as it should be done without labour and struggle. We must take pains with our hearts to bring them, and keep them, to this work, and to engage all that is within us.

III. Here were, in compliance with the temper of that dispensation, a great variety of musical instruments used, *harps, psalteries, cymbals* (*v.* 1, 6), and here was one that *lifted up the horn* (*v.* 5), that is, used wind-music. The bringing of such concerts of music into the worship of God now is what none pretend to. But those who use such concerts for their own entertainment should feel themselves obliged to preserve them always free from any thing that savours of immorality or profaneness, by this consideration, that time was when they were sacred; and then *those* were justly condemned who brought them into common use, Amos 6:5. *They invented to themselves instruments of music like David.*

IV. The glory and honour of God were principally intended in all this temple-music, whether vocal or instrumental. It was *to give thanks, and praise the Lord,* that the singers were employed, *v.* 3. It was *in the songs of the Lord that they were instructed* (*v.* 7), that is, *for songs in the house of the Lord, v.* 6. This agrees with the intention of the perpetuating of psalmody in the gospel-church, which is *to make melody with the heart,* in conjunction with the voice, *unto the Lord,* Eph. 5:19.

V. The order of the king is likewise taken notice of, *v.* 2 and again *v.* 6. In those matters indeed David acted as a prophet; but his taking care for the due and regular observance of divine institutions, both ancient and modern, is an example to all in authority to use their power for the promoting of religion, and the enforcing of the laws of Christ. Let them thus be *ministers of God for good.*

VI. The fathers presided in this service, Asaph, Heman, and Jeduthun (*v.* 1), and the children were *under the hands of their father, v.* 2, 3, 6. This gives a good example to parents to train up their children, and indeed to all seniors to instruct their juniors in the service of God, and particularly in praising him, than which there is no part of our work more necessary or more worthy to be transmitted to the succeeding generations. It gives also an example to the younger to *submit themselves to the elder* (whose experience and observation fit them for direction), and, as far as may be, to do what they do *under their hand.* It is probable that Heman, Asaph, and Jeduthun, were bred up under Samuel, and had their education in the schools of the prophets which he was the founder and president of; then they were pupils, now they came to be masters. Those that would be eminent must begin early, and take time to prepare themselves. This good work of singing God's praises Samuel revived, and set on foot, but lived not to see it brought to the perfection it appears in here. Solomon perfects what David began, so David perfects what Samuel began. Let all, in their day, do what they can for God and his church, though they cannot carry it so far as they would; when they are gone God can out of stones raise up others who shall build upon their foundation and bring forth the top-stone.

VII. There were others also, besides the sons of these three great men, who are called their *brethren* (probably because they had been wont to join with them in their private concerts), who were *instructed in the songs of the Lord,* and were cunning or well skilled therein, *v.* 7. They were all Levites and were in number 288. Now, 1. These were a good number, and a competent number to keep up the service in the house of God; for they were all skilful in the work to which they were called. When David the king was so much addicted to divine poesy and music many others, all that had a genius for it, applied their studies and endeavours that way. Those do religion a great deal of good service that bring the exercises of devotion into reputation. 2. Yet these were but a small number in comparison with the 4000 whom David appointed thus to *praise the Lord, ch.* 23:5. Where were all the rest when only 288, and those but by twelve in a course, were separated to this service? It is probable that all the rest were divided into as many courses, and were to follow as these led. Or, perhaps, these were *for songs in the house of the Lord* (*v.* 6), with whom any that worshipped in the courts of that house might join; and the rest were disposed of, all the kingdom over, to preside in the country congregations, in this good work: for, though the sacrifices instituted by the hand of Moses might be offered but at one place, the psalms penned by David might be sung every where, 1 Tim. 2:8.

Verses 8–31

Twenty-four persons are named in the beginning of this chapter as sons of those three great men, Asaph, Heman, and Jeduthun. Ethan was the third (*ch.* 6:44), but probably he was dead before the establishment was perfected and Jeduthun came in his room. [Or perhaps Ethan and Jeduthun were two names for the same person.] Of these three Providence so ordered it that Asaph had four sons, Jeduthun six [only five are mentioned *v.* 3; Shimei, mentioned *v.* 17, is supposed to have been the sixth], and Heman fourteen, in all twenty-four (who were named, *v.* 2–4), who were all qualified for the service and called to it. But the question was, In what order must they serve? This was determined by lot, to prevent strife for precedency, a sin which most easily besets many that otherwise are good people.

I. The lot was thrown impartially. They were placed in twenty-four companies, twelve in a company, in two rows, twelve companies in a row, and so they cast lots, *ward against ward,* putting them all upon a level, small and great, teacher and scholar. They did not go according to their age, or according to their standing, or the degrees they had taken in the music-schools; but it was referred to God, *v.* 8. Small and great, teachers and scholars, stand alike before God, who goes not according to our rules of distinction and precedency. See Mt. 20:23.

II. God determined it as he pleased, taking account, it is probable, of the respective merits of the persons, which are of much more importance than seniority of age or priority of birth. Let us compare them with the preceding catalogue and we shall find that, 1. Josephus was the second son of Asaph. 2. Gedaliah the eldest son of Jeduthun. 3. Zaccur the eldest of Asaph. 4. Izri the second of Jeduthun. 5. Nethaniah the third of Asaph. 6. Bukkiah the eldest of Heman. 7. Jesharelah the youngest of Asaph. 8. Jeshaiah the third of Jeduthun. 9. Mattaniah the second of Heman. 10. Shimei the youngest of Jeduthun. 11. Azareel the third of Heman. 12. Hashabiah the fourth of Jeduthun. 13. Shubael the fourth of Heman. 14. Mattithiah the fifth of Jeduthun. 15. Jeremoth the fifth of Heman. 16. Hananiah the sixth of Heman. 17. Joshbekashah the eleventh of Heman. 18. Hanani the seventh of Heman. 19. Mallothi the twelfth of Heman. 20. Eliathah the eighth of Heman. 21. Hothir the thirteenth of Heman. 22. Giddalti the ninth of Heman. 23. Mehazioth the fourteenth of Heman. And, *lastly,* Romamti-ezer, the tenth of Heman. See how God increased some and preferred the younger before the elder.

III. Each of these had in his chorus the number of twelve, called *their sons and their brethren,* because they observed them as sons, and concurred with them as brethren. Probably twelve, some for the voice and others for the instrument, made up the concert. Let us learn with one mind and one mouth to glorify God, and that will be the best concert.

CHAPTER 26

We have here an account of the business of the Levites. That tribe had made but a very small figure all the time of the judges, till Eli and Samuel appeared. But when David revived religion the Levites were, of all men, in the greatest reputation. And happy it was that they had Levites who were men of sense, fit to support the honour of their tribe. We have here an account, I. Of the Levites that were appointed to be porters (*v.* 1–19). II. Of those that were appointed to be treasurers and storekeepers (*v.* 20–28). III. Of those that were officers and judges in the country, and were entrusted with the administration of public affairs (*v.* 29–32).

Verses 1–19

Observe, I. There were porters appointed to attend the temple, who guarded all the avenues that let to it, opened and shut all the outer gates and attended at them, not only for the state, but for service, to direct and instruct those who were going to worship in the courts of the sanctuary in the decorum they were to observe, to encourage those that were timorous, to send back the strangers and unclean, and to guard against thieves and others that were enemies to the house of God. In allusion to this office, ministers are said to have *the keys to the kingdom of heaven* committed to them (Mt. 16:19), that they may admit, and exclude, according to the law of Christ.

II. Of several of those that were called to this service, it is taken notice of that they were *mighty men of valour* (*v.* 6), *strong men* (*v.* 7), *able men* (*v.* 8), and one of them that he was a *wise counsellor* (*v.* 14), who probably, when he had *used this office of a deacon well* and given proofs of more than ordinary wisdom, *purchased to himself a good degree,* and was preferred from the gate to the council-board, 1 Tim. 3:13. As for those that excelled in strength of body, and courage and resolution of mind, they were thereby qualified for the post assigned them; for whatever service God calls men to he either finds them fit or makes them so.

III. The sons of Obed-edom were employed in this office, sixty-two of that family. This was he that entertained the ark with reverence and cheerfulness; and see how he was rewarded for it. 1. He had eight *sons* (*v.* 5), *for God blessed him.* The increase and building up of families are owing to the divine blessing; and a great blessing it is to a family to have many children, when like these they are able for, and eminent in, the service of God. 2. His sons were preferred to places of trust in the sanctuary. They had faithfully attended the ark in their own house, and now were called to attend it in God's house. He that is trusty in little shall be trusted with more. He that keeps God's ordinances in his own tent is fit to have the custody of them in God's tabernacle, 1 Tim. 3:4, 5. *I have kept thy law,* says David, and *this I had because I kept thy precepts,* Ps. 119:55, 56.

IV. It is said of one here that *though he was not the first-born his father made him the chief* (*v.* 10), either because he was very excellent, or because the elder son was very weak. He was made chief, perhaps not in inheriting the estate (for that was forbidden by the law, Deu. 21:16, 17), but in this service, which required personal qualifications.

V. The porters, as the singers, had their post assigned them by lot, so many at such a gate, and so many at such a one, that every one might know his post and make it good, *v.* 13. It is not said that they were cast into twenty-four courses, as before; but here are the names of about twenty-four (*v.* 1–11), and the posts assigned are twenty-four, *v.* 17, 18. We have therefore reason to think they were distributed into as many companies. Happy are those who dwell in God's house: for, as they are well fed, well taught, and well employed, so they are well guarded. Men attended at the gates of the temple, but angels attend at the gates of the New Jerusalem, Rev. 21:12.

Verses 20–28

Observe, 1. There were *treasures of the house of God.* A great house cannot be well kept without stores of all manner of provisions. Much was expended daily upon the altar — flour, wine, oil, salt, fuel, besides the lamps; quantities of these were to be kept beforehand, besides the sacred vestments and utensils. These were the *treasures of the house of God.* And, because money answers all things, doubtless they had an abundance of it, which was received from the people's offerings, wherewith they bought in what they had occasion for. And perhaps much was laid up for an exigence. These treasures typified the plenty there is in our heavenly Father's house, enough and to spare. In Christ, the true temple, are hid *treasures of wisdom and knowledge,* and *unsearchable riches.* 2. There were *treasures of dedicated things,* dedicated mostly *out of the spoils won in battle* (*v.* 27), as a grateful acknowledgment of the divine protection. Abraham gave Melchisedec the *tenth of the spoils* Heb. 7:4. In Moses's time the officers of the army, when they returned victorious, brought of their spoils an *oblation to the Lord,* Num. 31:50. Of late this pious custom had been revived; and not only Samuel and David, but Saul, and Abner, and Joab, had dedicated of their spoils to the honour and support of the house of God, *v.* 28. Note, The more God bestows upon us the more he expects from us in works of piety and charity. Great successes call for proportionable returns. When we look over our estates we should consider, "Here are convenient things, rich things, it may be, and fine things; but where are the dedicated things?" Men of war must honour God with their spoils. 3. These treasures had treasurers, those that were over them (*v.* 20, 26), whose business it was to keep them, that neither *moth nor rust* might *corrupt them,* nor *thieves break through and steal,* to give out as there was occasion and to see that they were not wasted, embezzled, or alienated to the common use; and it is probable that they kept accounts of all that was brought in and how it was laid out.

Verses 29–32

All the offices of the house of God being well provided with Levites, we have here an account of those that were employed as officers and judges in the outward business, which must not be neglected, no, not for the temple itself. The magistracy is an ordinance of God for the good of the church as truly as the ministry is. And here we are told, 1. That the Levites were employed in the administration of justice in concurrence with the princes and elders of the several tribes, who could not be supposed to understand the law so well as the Levites, who made it their business to study it. None of those Levites who were employed in the service of the sanctuary, none of the singers or porters, were concerned in this outward business; either one was enough to engage the whole man or it was presumption to undertake both. 2. Their charge was both *in all business of the Lord,* and *in the service of the kings, v.* 30 and again *v.* 32. They managed the affairs of the country, as well ecclesiastical as civil, took care both of God's tithes and the king's taxes, punished offences committed immediately against God and his honour and those against the government and the public peace, guarded both against idolatry and against injustice, and took care to put the laws in execution against both. Some, it is likely, applied themselves to the affairs of religion, others to secular affairs; and so, between both, God and the king were well served. It is happy with a kingdom when its civil and sacred interests are thus interwoven and jointly minded and advanced. 3. There were more Levites employed as judges with the two tribes and a half on the other side of Jordan than with all the rest of the tribes; there were 2700; whereas as the west side of Jordan there were 1700, *v.* 30, 32. Either those remote tribes were not so well furnished as the rest with judges of their own, or because they, lying furthest from Jerusalem and on the borders of the neighbouring nations, were most in danger of being infected with idolatry, and most needed the help of Levites to prevent it. The frontiers must be well guarded. 4. This is said to be done (as were all the foregoing settlements) in the fortieth year of the reign of David (*v.* 31), that is, the last year of his reign. We should be so much the more industrious to do good *as we can see the day approaching.* If we live to enjoy the fruit of our labours, grudge it not to those that shall come after us.

CHAPTER 27

In this chapter we have the civil list, including the military, I. The twelve captains for every separate month of the year (*v.* 1–15). II. The princes of the several tribes (*v.* 16–24). III. The officers of the court (*v.* 25–34).

Verses 1–15

We have here an account of the regulation of the militia of the kingdom. David was himself a man of war, and had done great things with the sword; he had brought into the field great armies. Now here we are told how he marshalled them when God had given him rest from all his enemies. He did not keep them all together, for that would have been a hardship on them and the country; yet he did not disband and disperse them all, for then he would have left his kingdom naked, and his people would have forgotten the arts of war, wherein they had been instructed. He therefore contrived to keep up a constant force, and yet not a standing army. The model is very prudent. 1. He kept up 24,000 constantly in arms, I suppose in a body, and disciplined, in one part or other of the kingdom, the freeholders carrying their own arms and bearing their own charges while they were up. This was a sufficient strength for the securing of the public peace and safety. Those that are Israelites indeed must learn war; for we have enemies to grapple with, whom we are concerned constantly to stand upon our guard against. 2. He changed them every month; so that the whole number of the militia amounted to 288,000, perhaps about a fifth part of the able men of the kingdom. By being thus distributed into twelve courses, they were all instructed in, and accustomed to, military exercises; and yet none were compelled to be in service, and at expenses, above one month in the year (which they might very well afford), unless upon extraordinary occasions, and then they might all be got together quickly. It is the wisdom of governors, and much their praise, while they provide for the public safety, to contrive how to make it effectual and yet easy, and as little as possible burdensome to the people. 3. Every course had a commander in chief over it. Besides the subaltern officers that were rulers over thousands and hundreds, and fifties, there was one general officer to each course or legion. All these twelve great commanders are mentioned among David's worthies and champions, 2 Sa. 23 and 1 Chr. 11. They had first signalized themselves by their great actions and then they were advanced to those great preferments. It is well with a kingdom when honour thus attends merit. Bena-

iah is here called *a chief priest, v.* 5. But, *cohen* signifying both a *priest* and a *prince,* it might better be translated here *a chief ruler,* or (as in the margin) *a principal officer.* Dodai had Mikloth (*v.* 4) either for his substitute when he was absent or infirm, or for his successor when he was dead. Benaiah had his son under him, *v.* 6. Asahel had his son after him (*v.* 7), and by this it seems that this plan of the militia was laid in the beginning of David's reign; for Asahel was killed by Abner while David reigned in Hebron. When his wars were over he revived this method, and left the military affairs in this posture, for the peaceable reign of his son Solomon. When we think ourselves most safe, yet, while we are here in the body, we must keep in a readiness for spiritual conflicts. *Let not him that girdeth on the harness boast as he that puts it off.*

Verses 16–34

We have here an account,

I. Of the princes of the tribes. Something of the ancient order instituted by Moses in the wilderness was still kept up, that every tribe should have its prince or chief. It is probable that it was kept up all along, either by election or by succession, in the same family; and those are here named who were found in that office when this account was taken. Elihu, or Eliab, who was prince of Judah, was the eldest son of Jesse, and descended in a right line from Nahshon and Salmon, the princes of this tribe in Moses's time. Whether these princes were of the nature of lord-lieutenants that guided them in their military affairs, or chief-justices that presided in their courts of judgment, does not appear. Their power, we may suppose, was much less now that all the tribes were united under one king than it had been when, for the most part, they acted separately. Our religion obliges us to be subject, not only to the *king as supreme, but unto governors under him* (1 Pt. 2:13, 14), the princes that decree justice. Of Benjamin was Jaaziel the son of Abner, *v.* 21. Though Abner was David's enemy, and opposed his coming to the throne, yet David would not oppose the preferment of his son, but perhaps nominated him to this post of honour, which teaches us to render good for evil.

II. Of the numbering of the people, *v.* 23, 24. It is here said, 1. That when David ordered the people to be numbered he forbade the numbering of those under twenty years old, thinking thereby to save the reflection which what he did might otherwise cast upon the promise that they should be innumerable; yet it was but a poor salvo, for it had never been customary to number those under twenty, and the promise of their numbers chiefly respected the effective men. 2. That the account which David took of the people, in the pride of his heart, turned to no good account; for it was never perfected, nor done with exactness, nor was it ever recorded as an authentic account. Joab was disgusted with it, and did it by halves; David was ashamed of it, and willing it should be forgotten, because there fell wrath for it against Israel. A good man cannot, in the reflection, please himself with that which he knows God is displeased with, cannot make use of that, nor take comfort in that, which is obtained by sin.

III. Of the officers of the court. 1. The *rulers of the king's substance* (as they are called, *v.* 31), such as had the oversight and charge of the king's tillage, his vineyards, his olive-yards, his herds, his camels, his asses, his flocks. Here are no officers for state, none for sport, no master of the wardrobe, no master of the ceremonies, no master of the horse, no master of the hounds, but all for service, agreeable to the simplicity and plainness of those times. David was a great soldier, a great scholar, and a great prince, and yet a great husband of his estate, kept a great deal of ground in his own hand, and stocked it, not for pleasure, but for profit; for the king himself is *served of the field,* Eccles. 5:9. Those magistrates that would have their subjects industrious must themselves be examples of industry and application to business. We find, however, that afterwards the poor of the land were thought good enough to be vine-dressers and husbandmen, 2 Ki. 25:12. Now David put his great men to preside in these employments. 2. The attendants on the king's person. They were such as were eminent for wisdom, being designed for conversation. His uncle, who was a wise man and a scribe, not only well skilled in politics, but well read in the scriptures, was his counsellor, *v.* 32. Another, who no doubt excelled in learning and prudence, was tutor to his children. Ahithophel, a very cunning man, was his counsellor: but Hushai, an honest man, was his companion and confidant. It does not appear that he had many counsellors; but those he had were men of great abilities. Much of the wisdom of princes is seen in the choice of their ministry. But David, though he had all these trusty and well-beloved cousins and counsellors about him, preferred his Bible before them all. Ps. 119:24, *Thy testimonies are my delight and my counsellors.*

CHAPTER 28

The account we have of David's exit, in the beginning of the first book of Kings, does not make his sun nearly so bright as that given in this and the following chapter, where we have his solemn farewell both to his son and his subjects, and must own that he finished well. In this chapter we have, I. A general convention of the states summoned to meet (*v.* 1). II. A solemn declaration of the divine entail both of the crown and of the honour of building the temple upon Solomon (*v.* 2–7). III. An exhortation both to the people and to Solomon to make religion their business (*v.* 8–10). IV. The model and materials delivered to Solomon for the building of the temple (*v.* 11–19). V. Encouragement given him to undertake it and proceed in it (*v.* 20, 21).

Verses 1–10

A great deal of service David had done in his day, had *served his generation according to the will of God,* Acts 13:36. But now the time draws night that he must die, and, as a type of the Son of David, the nearer he comes to his end the more busy he is, and does his work with all his might. He is now a little recovered from the indisposition mentioned 1 Ki. 1:1, when they covered him with clothes, and he got no heat: but was cure is there for old age? He therefore improves his recovery, as giving him an opportunity of doing God and his country a little more service.

I. He summoned all the great men to attend him, that he might take leave of them all together, *v.* 1. Thus Moses did (Deu. 31:28), and Joshua, *ch.* 23:2; 24:1. David would not declare the settlement of the crown but in the presence, and to the satisfaction, of those that were the representatives of the people.

II. He addressed them with a great deal of respect and tenderness. He not only exerted himself to rise from his bed, to give them the meeting (the occasion putting new spirits into him), but he rose out of his chair, and *stood up upon his feet* (*v.* 2), in reverence to God whose will he was to declare, and in reverence to this solemn assembly of the Israel of God, as if he looked upon himself, though *major singulis — greater than any individual among them,* yet *minor universis — less than the whole of them together.* His age and infirmities, as well as his dignity, might well have allowed him to keep his seat; but he would show that he was indeed humbled for the pride of his heart both in the numbers of his people and his dominion over them. It had been too much his pleasure that they were all his *servants* (*ch.* 21:3), but now he calls them his *brethren,* whom he loved, his people, whom he took care of, not his servants, whom he had command of: *Hear me, my brethren, and my people.* It becomes superiors thus to speak with affection and condescension even to their inferiors; they will not be the less honoured for it, but the more beloved. Thus he engages their attention to what he was about to say.

III. He declared the purpose he had formed to build a temple for God, and God's disallowing that purpose, *v.* 2, 3. This he had signified to Solomon before, *ch.* 22:7, 8. *A house of rest for the ark* is here said to be *a house of rest for the footstool of our God;* for heaven is his throne of glory; the earth, and the most magnificent temples that can be built upon it, are but his footstool: so much difference is there between the manifestations of the divine glory in the upper and lower world. Angels surround his throne, Isa. 6:1. We poor worms do but *worship at his footstool* Ps. 99:5; 132:7. As an evidence of the sincerity of his purpose to build the temple, he tells them that he had made ready for it, but that God would not suffer him to proceed because he had appointed other work for him to do, which was enough for one man, namely, the managing of the wars of Israel. He must serve the public with the sword; another must do it with the line and plummet. Times of rest are building times, Acts 9:31.

IV. He produced his own title first, and then Solomon's, to the crown; both were undoubtedly *jure divino — divine.* They could make out such a title as no monarch on earth can; the Lord God of Israel chose them both immediately, by prophecy, not providence, *v.* 4, 5. No right of primogeniture is pretended. *Detur digniori, non seniori — It went by worth, not by age.* 1. Judah was not the eldest son of Jacob, yet God chose that tribe to be the ruling tribe; Jacob entailed the sceptre upon it, Gen. 49:10. 2. It does not appear that the family of Jesse was the senior house of that tribe; from Judah it is certain that it was not, for Shelah was before Pharez; whether from Nahshon and Salmon is not certain. Ram, the father of Nahshon, had a elder brother, 1 Chr. 2:9. Perhaps so had Boaz, Obed, and Jesse. Yet *"God chose the house of my father."* 3. David was the youngest son of Jesse, yet God liked him to make him king; so it seemed good unto him. God takes whom he likes, and likes whom he makes like himself, as he did David, a man after his own heart. 4. Solomon was one of the youngest sons of David, and yet God chose him to sit upon the throne, because he was the likeliest of them all to build the temple, the wisest and best inclined.

V. He opened to them God's gracious purposes concerning Solomon (*v.* 6, 7): *I have chosen him to be my son.* Thus he declares the decree, that the Lord had said to Solomon, as a type of Christ, *Thou art my son* (Ps. 2:7), the son of my love; for he was called *Jedidiah,* because the Lord loved him, and Christ is his beloved Son. Of him God said, as a figure of him that was to come, 1. *He shall build my house.* Christ is both the founder and the foundation of the gospel temple. 2. *I will establish his kingdom for ever.* This must have its accomplishment in the kingdom of the Messiah, which shall continue in his hands through all the ages of time (Isa. 9:7; Lu. 1:33) and shall then be delivered up to God, even the Father, yet perhaps to be delivered back to the Redeemer for ever. As to Solomon, this promise of the establishment of his kingdom is here made conditional: *If he be constant to do my commandments, as at this day.* Solomon was now very towardly and good: "If he continue so, his kingdom shall continue, otherwise not." Note, If we be constant to our duty, then, and not otherwise, we may expect the continuance of God's favour. Let those that are well taught, and begin well, take notice of this — if they be constant, they are happy; perseverance wears the crown, though it wins it not.

VI. He charged them to adhere stedfastly to God and their duty, *v.* 8. Observe, 1. The matter for this charge: *Keep, and seek for all the commandments of the Lord your God.* The Lord was their God; his commandments must be their rule; they must have respect to them all, must make conscience of keeping them, and, in order thereunto, must seek for them, that is, must be inquisitive concerning their duty, search the scriptures, take advice, seek the law at the mouth of those whose lips were to keep this knowledge, and pray to God to teach and direct them. God's commandments will not be kept without great care. 2. The solemnity of it. He charged them in the sight of all Israel, who would all have notice of this public charge, and in the audience of their God. "God is witness, and this congregation is witness, that they have good counsel given them, and fair warning; if they do not take it, it is their fault, and God and man will be witnesses against them." See 1 Tim. 5:21; 2 Tim. 4:1. Those that profess religion, as they tender the favour of God and their reputation with men, must be faithful to their profession. 3. The motive to observe this charge. It was the way to be happy, to have the peaceable possession of this good land themselves and to preserve the entail of it upon their children.

VII. He concluded with a charge to Solomon himself, *v.* 9, 10. He was much concerned that Solomon should be religious. He was to be a great man, but he must not think religion below him — a wise man, and this would be his wisdom. Observe,

1. The charge he gives him. He must look upon God and the God of his father, his good father, who had devoted him to God and educated him for God. He was born in God's house and therefore bound in duty to be his, brought up in his house and therefore bound in gratitude. *Thy own friend, and thy father's friend, forsake not.* He must know God and serve him. We cannot serve God aright if we do not know him; and in vain do we know him if we do not serve him, serve him with heart and mind. We make nothing of religion if we do not mind it, and make heart-work of it. Serve him with a perfect, that is, an upright heart (for sincerity is our gospel perfection), and with a willing mind, from a principle of love, and as a willing people, cheerfully and with pleasure.

2. The arguments to enforce this charge.

(1.) Two arguments of general inducement: — [1.] That the secrets of our souls are open before God; he searches all hearts, even the hearts of kings, which to men are unsearchable, Prov. 25:3. We must *therefore* be sincere, because, if we deal deceitfully, God sees it, and cannot be imposed upon; we must *therefore* employ our thoughts, and engage them in God's service, because he fully understands all the imaginations of them, both good and bad. [2.] That we are happy or miserable here, and for ever, according as we do, or do not, serve God. *If we seek him diligently, he will be found of us,* and that is enough to make us happy, Heb. 11:6. If we forsake him, desert his service and turn from following him, he will cast us off for ever, and that is enough to make us miserable. Note, God never casts any off till they have first cast him off. Here is,

(2.) One argument peculiar to Solomon (*v.* 10): *"Thou art to build a house for the sanctuary;* therefore seek and serve God, that that work may be done from a good principle, in a right manner, and may be accepted."

3. The means prescribed in order hereunto, and they are prescribed to us all. (1.) Caution: *Take heed;* beware of every thing that looks like, or leads to, that which is evil. (2.) Courage: *Be strong, and do it.* We cannot do our work as we should unless we put on resolution, and fetch in strength from divine grace.

Verses 11–21

As for the general charge that David gave his son to seek God and serve him, the book of the law was, in that, his only rule, and there needed no other; but, in building the temple, David was now to give him three things: — 1. A model of the building, because it was to be such a building as neither he nor his architects ever saw. Moses had a pattern of the tabernacle shown him in the mount (Heb. 8:5), so had David of the temple, by the immediate hand of God upon him, *v.* 19. It was given him in writing, probably by the ministry of an angel, or as clearly and exactly represented to his mind as if it had been in writing. But it is said (*v.* 12), *He had this pattern by the Spirit.* The contrivance either of David's devotion or of Solomon's wisdom must not be trusted to in an affair of this nature. The temple must be a sacred thing and a type of Christ; there must be in it not only convenience and decency, but significancy: it was a kind of sacrament, and therefore it must not be left to man's art or invention to contrive it, but must be framed by divine institution. Christ the true temple, the church the gospel temple, and heaven the everlasting temple, are all framed according to the divine councils, and the plan laid in the divine wisdom, ordained before the world for God's glory and ours. This pattern David gave to Solomon, that he might know what to provide and might go by a certain rule. When Christ left with his disciples a charge to build his gospel church he gave them an exact model of it, ordering them to observe that, and that only, which he commanded. The particular models are here mentioned, of the porch, which was higher than the rest, like a steeple, — then the houses, both the holy place and the most holy, with the rooms adjoining, which were for treasuries, chambers, and parlours, — especially *the place of the mercy-seat* (*v.* 11), — of the courts likewise, and the chambers about them, in which the dedicated things were laid up. Bishop Patrick supposes that, among other things, the tabernacle which Moses reared and all the utensils of it, which there was now no further occasion for, were laid up here, signifying that in the fulness of time all the Mosaic economy, all the rites and ceremonies of that dispensation, should be respectfully laid aside, and something better come in their room. He gave him a table of the courses of the priests, patterns of the vessels of service (*v.* 13), and a pattern of the chariot of the cherubim, *v.* 18. Besides the two cherubim over the mercy-seat, there were two much larger, whose wings reached from wall to wall (1 Ki. 6:23, etc.), and of these David here gave Solomon the pattern, called a *chariot;* for the angels are the chariots of God, Ps. 68:17. 2. Materials for the most costly of the utensils of the temple. That they might not be made any less than the patterns, he weighed out the exact quantity for each vessel both of gold and silver, *v.* 14. In the tabernacle there was but one golden candlestick; in the temple there were ten (1 Ki. 7:49), besides silver ones, which, it is supposed, were hand-candlesticks, *v.* 15. In the tabernacle there was but one table; but in the temple, besides that on which the show-bread was set, there were ten others for other uses (2 Chr. 4:8), besides silver tables; for, this house being much larger than that, it would look bare if it had not furniture proportionable. The gold for the altar of incense is particularly said to be *refined gold* (*v.* 18), purer than any of the rest; for that was typical of the intercession of Christ, than which nothing is more pure and perfect. 3. Directions which way to look for help in this great undertaking. "Fear not opposition; fear not the charge, care, and trouble; fear not miscarrying in it, as in the case of Uzza; fear not the reproach of the foolish builder, that began to build and was not able to finish. Be not dismayed. (1.) God will help thee, and thou must look up to him in the first place (*v.* 20): *The Lord God, even my God,* whom I have chosen and served, who has all along been present with me and prospered me, and to whom, from my own experience of his power and goodness, I recommend thee, he will be with thee, to direct, strengthen, and prosper thee; he will not fail thee nor forsake thee." Note, We may be sure that God, who owned our fathers and carried them through the services of their day, will, in like manner, if we be faithful to him, go along with us in our day, and will never leave us, while he has any work to do in us or by us. The same that was Joshua's encouragement (Jos. 1:5), and Solomon's, is given to all believers, Heb. 13:5. *He will never leave thee, nor forsake thee.* God never leaves any unless they first leave him. (2.) "Good men will help thee, *v.* 21. The priests and Levites will advise thee, and thou mayest consult them. Thou hast good workmen, who are both willing and skilful;" and these are two very good properties in a workman, especially in those that work at the temple. And, *lastly,* "The princes and the people will be so far from opposing or retarding the work that they will be wholly at thy command, every one in his place ready to further it." Then good work is likely to go on when all parties concerned are hearty in it, and none secretly clog it, but all drive on heartily in it.

CHAPTER 29

David has said what he had to say to Solomon. But he had something more to say to the congregation before he parted with them. I. He pressed them to contribute, according to their ability, towards the building and furnishing of the temple (*v.* 1–5). II. They made their presents accordingly with great generosity (*v.* 6–9). III. David offered up solemn prayers and praises to God upon that occasion (*v.* 10–20), with sacrifices (*v.* 21, 22). IV. Solomon was hereupon enthroned, with great joy and magnificence (*v.* 23–25). V. David, soon after this finished his course (*v.* 26–30). And it is hard to say which shines brighter here, the setting sun or the rising sun.

Verses 1–9

We may here observe,

I. How handsomely David spoke to the great men of Israel, to engage them to contribute towards the building of the temple. It is our duty to *provoke one another to love and to good works,* not only to do good ourselves, but to draw in others to do good too as much as we can. There were many very rich men in Israel; they were all to share in the benefit of the temple, and of those peaceable days which were to befriend the building of it; and therefore, though David would not impose on them, as a tax, what they should give towards it, he would recommend the present as a fair occasion for a free-will offering, because what is done in works of piety and charity should be done willingly and not by constraint; for God loves a cheerful giver. 1. He would have them consider that Solomon was young and tender, and needed help; but that he was the person whom God had chosen to do this work, and therefore was well worthy their assistance. It is good service to encourage those in the work of God that are as yet young and tender. 2. That the world was great, and all hands should contribute to the carrying of it on. The palace to be built was not for man, but for the Lord God; and the more was contributed towards the building the more magnificent it would be, and therefore the better would it answer the intention. 3. He tells them what great preparations had been made for this work. He did not intend to throw all the burden upon them, nor that it should be built wholly by contributions, but that they should show their good will, by adding to what was done (*v.* 2): *I have prepared with all my might,* that is, "I have made it my business." Work for God must be done with all our might, or we shall bring nothing to pass in it. 4. He sets them a good example. Besides what was dedicated to this service out of the spoils and presents of the neighbouring nations, which was for the building of the house (of which before, *ch.* 22:14), he had, out of his own share, offered largely for the beautifying and enriching of it, 3000 talents of gold and 7000 talents of silver (*v.* 4, 5), and this because he had set his affection on the house of his God. He gave all this, not as Papists build churches, in commutation of penance, or to make atonement for sin, nor as Pharisees give alms, to be seen of men; but purely because he loved the habitation of God's house; so he professed (Ps. 26:8) and here he proved it. Those who set their affection upon the service of God will think no pains nor cost too much to bestow upon it; and then our offerings are pleasing to God when they come from love. Those that set their affection on things above will set their affection on the house of God, through which our way to heaven lies. Now this he gives them an account of, to stir them up to do likewise. Note, Those who would draw others to do that which is good must themselves lead. Those especially who are advanced above others in place and dignity should particularly contrive how to make their light shine before men, because the influence of their example is more powerful and extensive than that of other people. 5. He stirs them up to do as he had done (*v.* 5): *And who then is willing to concentrate his service this day unto the Lord?* (1.) We must each of us, in our several places, serve the Lord, and consecrate our service to him, separate it from other things that are foreign and interfere with it, and direct and design it for the honour and glory of God. (2.) We must make the service of God our business, must *fill our hands to the Lord,* so the Hebrew phrase is. Those who engage themselves in the service of God will have their hands full; there is work enough for the whole man in that service. The filling of our hands with the service of God intimates that we must serve him only, serve him liberally, and serve him in the strength of grace derived from him. (3.) We must be free herein, do it willingly and speedily, do it this day, when we are in a good mind. *Who is willing?* Now let him show it.

II. How handsomely they all contributed towards the building of the temple when they were thus stirred up to it. Though they were persuaded to it, yet it is said, *They offered willingly, v.* 6. So he said who knew their hearts. Nay, they offered *with a perfect heart,* from a good principle and with a sincere respect to the glory of God, *v.* 9. How generous they were appears by the sum total of the contributions, *v.* 7, 8. They gave like themselves, like princes, like princes of Israel. And a pleasant day's work it was; for, 1. *The people rejoiced,* which may be meant of the people themselves that offered: they were glad of the opportunity of honouring God thus with their substance, and glad of the prospect of bringing this good work to perfection. Or the common people rejoiced in the generosity of their princes, that they had such rulers over them as were forward to this good work. Every Israelite is glad to see temple work carried on with vigour. 2. *David rejoiced with great joy* to see the good effects of his psalms and the other helps of devotion he had furnished them with, rejoiced that his son and successor would have those about him that were so well affected to the house of God, and that this work, upon which his heart was so much set, was likely to go on. Note, It is a great reviving to good men, when they are leaving the world, to see those they leave behind zealous for religion and likely to keep it up. *Lord, now let thou thy servant depart in peace.*

Verses 10–22

We have here,

I. The solemn address which David made to God upon occasion of the noble subscriptions of the princes towards the building of the temple (*v.* 10): *Wherefore David blessed the Lord,* not only alone in his closet, but *before all the congregation.* This I expected when we read (*v.* 9) that *David rejoiced with great joy;* for such a devout man as he would no doubt make that the matter of his thanksgiving which was so much the matter of his rejoicing. He that looked round with comfort would certainly look up with praise. David was now old and looked upon himself as near his end; and it well becomes aged saints, and dying saints, to have their hearts much enlarged in praise and thanksgiving. This will silence their complaints of their bodily infirmities, and help to make the prospect of death itself less gloomy. David's psalms, toward the latter end of the book, are most of them psalms of praise. The nearer we come to the world of everlasting praise the more we should speak the language and do the work of that world. In this address,

1. He adores God, and ascribes glory to him as the God of Israel, *blessed for ever and ever.* Our Lord's prayer ends with a doxology much like this which David here begins with — *for thine is the kingdom, the power, and the glory.* This is properly praising God — with holy awe and reverence, and agreeable affection, acknowledging, (1.) His infinite perfections; not only that he is great, powerful, glorious, etc., but that his is the greatness, power, and glory, that is, he has them in and of himself, *v.* 11. He is the fountain and centre of every thing that is bright and blessed. All that we can, in our most exalted praises, attribute to him he has an unquestionable title to. His is the *greatness;* his greatness is immense and incomprehensible; and all others are little, are nothing, in comparison of him. His is the *power,* and it is almighty and irresistible; power belongs to him, and all the power of all the creatures is derived from him and depends upon him. His is the *glory;* for his glory is his own end and the end of the whole creation. All the glory we can give him with our hearts, lips, and lives, comes infinitely short of what is his due. His is the *victory;* he transcends and surpasses all, and is able to conquer and subdue all things to himself; and his victories are incontestable and uncontrollable. And his is the *majesty,* real and personal; with him is terrible majesty, inexpressible and inconceivable. (2.) His sovereign dominion, as rightful owner and possessor of all: *"All that is in the heaven, and in the earth, is thine,* and at thy disposal, by the indisputable right of creation, and as supreme ruler and commander of all: *thine is the kingdom,* and all kings are thy subjects; for thou art head, and art to be exalted and worshipped as head above all." (3.) His universal influence and agency. All that are rich and honourable among the children of men have their riches and honours from God. This acknowledgment he would have the princes take notice of and join in, that they might not think they had merited any thing of God by their generosity; for from God they had their riches and honour, and what they had returned to him was but a small part of what they had received from him. Whoever are great among men, it is God's hand that makes them so; and, whatever strength we have, it is God that gives it to us, as the *God of Israel our father, v.* 10. Ps. 68:35.

2. He acknowledges with thankfulness the grace of God enabling them to contribute so cheerfully towards the building of the temple (*v.* 13, 14): *Now therefore, our God, we thank thee.* Note, The more we do for God the more we are indebted to him for the honour of being employed in his service, and for grace enabling us, in any measure, to serve him. *Does he* therefore *thank that servant?* Lu. 17:9. No: but that servant has a great deal of reason to thank him. He thanks God that they were *able to offer so willingly.* Note, (1.) It is a great instance of the power of God's grace in us to be able to do the work of God willingly. He works *both to will and to do;* and it is in the day of his power that his people are made willing, Ps. 110:3. (2.) We must give God all the glory of all the good that is at any time done by ourselves or others. Our own good works must not be the matter of our pride, nor the good works of others the matter of our flattery, but both the matter of our praise; for certainly it is the greatest honour and pleasure in the world faithfully to serve God.

3. He speaks very humbly of himself, and his people, and the offerings they had now presented to God. (1.) For himself, and those that joined with him, though they were princes, he wondered that God should take such notice of them and do so much for them (*v.* 14): *Who am I, and what is my people?* David was the most honourable person, and Israel the most honourable person, then in the world; yet thus does he speak of himself and them, as unworthy the divine cognizance and favour. David now looks very great, presiding in an august assembly, appointing his successor, and making a noble present to the honour of God; and yet he is little and low in his own eyes: *Who am I, O Lord?* for (*v.* 15) *we are strangers before thee, and sojourners,* poor

despicable creatures. Angels in heaven are at home there; saints on earth are but strangers here: *Our days on the earth are as a shadow.* David's days had as much of substance in them as most men's; for he was a great man, a good man, a useful man, and now an old man, one that lived long and lived to good purpose: and yet he puts himself not only into the number, but in the front, of those who must acknowledge that their *days on the earth are as a shadow,* which intimates that our life is a vain life, a dark life, a transient life, and a life that will have its periods either in perfect light or perfect darkness. The next words explain it: *There is no abiding,* Heb. *no expectation.* We cannot expect any great matters from it, nor can we expect any long continuance of it. This is mentioned here as that which forbids us to boast of the service we do to God. Alas! it is confined to a scantling of time, it is the service of a frail and short life, and therefore what can we pretend to merit by it? (2.) As to their offerings, *Lord,* says he, *of thy own have we given thee* (*v.* 14), and again (*v.* 16), *It cometh of thy hand, and is all thy own.* "We have it from thee as a free gift, and therefore are bound to use it for thee; and what we present to thee is but rent or interest from thy own." "In like manner" (says bishop Patrick) "we ought to acknowledge God in all spiritual things, referring every good thought, good purpose, good work, to his grace, from whom we receive it." *Let him that glories* therefore *glory in the Lord.*

4. He appeals to God concerning his own sincerity in what he did, *v.* 17. It is a great satisfaction to a good man to think that God *tries the heart* and *has pleasure in uprightness,* that, whoever may misinterpret or contemn it, he is acquainted with and approves of the *way of the righteous.* It was David's comfort that God knew with what pleasure he both offered his own and saw the people's offering. He was neither proud of his own good work nor envious of the good works of others.

5. He prays to God both for the people and for Solomon, that both might hold on as they began. In this prayer he addresses God as *the God of Abraham, Isaac, and Jacob,* a God in covenant with them and with us for their sakes. Lord, give us grace to make good our part of the covenant, that we may not forfeit the benefit of it. Or thus: they were kept in their integrity by the grace of God establishing their way; let the same grace that was sufficient for them be so for us. (1.) For the people he prays (*v.* 18) that what good God had put into their minds he would always keep there, that they might never be worse than they were now, might never lose the convictions they were now under, nor cool in their affections to the house of God, but always have the same thoughts of things as they now seemed to have. Great consequences depend upon what is innermost, and what uppermost, in the imagination of the thoughts of our heart, what we aim at and what we love to think of. If any good have got possession of our hearts, or the hearts of our friends, it is good by prayer to commit the custody of it to the grace of God: "Lord, keep it there, keep it for ever there. David has prepared materials for the temple; but, Lord, do thou prepare their hearts for such a privilege;" *establish* their hearts, so the *margin.* "Confirm their resolutions. They are in a good mind; keep them so when I am gone, them and theirs for ever." (2.) For Solomon he prays (*v.* 19), *Give him a perfect heart.* He had charged him (*ch.* 28:9) to serve God *with a perfect heart;* now here he prays to God to give him such a heart. He does not pray, "Lord, make him a rich man, a great man, a learned man;" but, "Lord, make him an honest man;" for that is better than all. "Lord, *give him a perfect heart,* not only in general *to keep thy commandments,* but in particular *to build the palace,* that he may do that service with a single eye." Yet his building the house would not prove him to have a perfect heart unless he made conscience of keeping God's commandments. It is not helping to build churches that will save us if we live in disobedience to God's law.

II. The cheerful concurrence of this great assembly in this great solemnity. 1. They joined with David in the adoration of God. When he had done his prayer he called to them to testify their concurrence (*Now bless the Lord your God, v.* 20), which accordingly they did, by *bowing down their heads,* a gesture of adoration. Whoever is the mouth of the congregation, those only have the benefit who join with him, not by *bowing down the head* so much as by *lifting up the soul.* 2. They paid their respects to the king, looking upon him as an instrument in God's hand of much good to them; and, in honouring him, they honoured God. 3. The next day they offered abundance of sacrifices to God (*v.* 21), both burnt-offerings, which were wholly consumed, and peace-offerings, which the offerer had the greatest part of to himself. Hereby they testified a generous gratitude to God for the good posture their public affairs were in, though David was going the way of all the earth. 4. They feasted and rejoiced before God, *v.* 22. In token of their joy in God, and communion with him, they feasted upon their peace-offerings in a religious manner before the Lord. What had been offered to God they feasted upon, by which was intimated to them that they should be never the poorer for their late liberal contributions to the service of the temple; they themselves should feast upon the comfort of it. 5. They made Solomon king the second time. He having been before anointed in haste, upon occasion of Adonijah's rebellion, it was thought fit to repeat the ceremony, for the greater satisfaction of the people. They *anointed him to the Lord.* Magistrates must look upon themselves as set apart for God, to be his ministers, and must rule accordingly in the fear of God. Zadok also was anointed to be priest in the room of Abiathar, who had lately forfeited his honour. Happy art thou, O Israel! under such a prince and such a pontiff.

Verses 23–30

These verses bring king Solomon to his throne and king David to his grave. Thus the rising generation thrusts out that which went before, and says, "Make room for us." Every one has his day.

I. Here is Solomon rising (*v.* 23): *Solomon sat on the throne of the Lord.* Not his throne which he prepared in the heavens, but the throne of Israel is called *the throne of the Lord* because not only is he King of all nations, and all kings rule under him, but he was in a peculiar manner King of Israel, 1 Sa. 12:12. He had the founding, he had the filling, of their throne, by immediate direction. The municipal laws of their kingdom were divine. Urim and prophets were the privy counsellors of their princes; therefore is their throne called *the throne of the Lord.* Solomon's kingdom typified the kingdom of the Messiah, and his is indeed *the throne of the Lord;* for the Father judgeth no man, but hath committed all judgment to him; hence he calls him *his King,* Ps. 2:6. Being set on the *throne of the Lord,* the throne to which God called him, he prospered. Those that follow the divine guidance may expect success by the divine blessing. Solomon prospered; for, 1. His people paid honour to him, as one to whom honour is due: *All Israel obeyed him,* that is, were ready to swear allegiance to him (*v.* 23), the *princes and mighty men,* and even *the sons of David,* though by seniority their title to the crown was prior to his, and they might think themselves wronged by his advancement. God thought fit to make him king, and made him fit to be so, and therefore they all *submitted themselves to him.* God inclined their hearts to do so, that his reign might, from the first, be peaceable. His father was a better man than he, and yet came to the crown with much difficulty, after long delay, and by many and slow steps. David had more faith, and therefore had it more tried. *They submitted themselves* (Heb. *They gave the hand under Solomon*), that is, bound themselves by oath to be true to him (putting the hand under the thigh was a ceremony anciently used in swearing); or they were so entirely devoted that they would put their hand under his feet to serve him. 2. God put honour upon him; for those that honour him he will honour: *The Lord magnified Solomon exceedingly, v.* 25. His very countenance and presence, I am apt to think, had something in them very great and awful. All he said and all he did commanded respect. None of all the judges or kings of Israel, his predecessors, made such a figure as he did nor lived in such splendour.

II. Here is David's setting, that great man going off the stage. The historian here brings him to the end of his day, leaves him asleep, and draws the curtains about him.

1. He gives a summary account of the years of his reign, *v.* 26, 27. He reigned forty years, as did Moses, Othniel, Deborah, Gideon, Eli, Samuel, and Saul, who were before him, and Solomon after him.

2. He gives a short account of his death (*v.* 28), that he died *full of days, riches, and honour;* that is, (1.) Loaded with them. He was very old, and very rich, and very much honoured both of God and man. He had been a man of war from his youth, and, as such, had his soul continually in his hand; yet he was not cut off in the midst of his days, but was preserved through all dangers of a military life, lived to a good old age, and died in peace, died in his bed, and yet in the bed of honour. (2.) Satiated with them. He was *full of days, riches, and honour;* that is, he had enough of this world and of the riches and honours of it, and knew when he had enough, for he was very willing to die and leave it, having said (Ps. 49:15), *God shall receive me,* and (Ps. 23:4), *Thou art with me.* A good man will soon be full of days, riches, and honour, but will never be satisfied with them; no satisfaction but in God's loving kindness.

3. For a fuller account of David's life and reign he refers to the histories or records of those times, which were written by Samuel while he lived, and continued, after his death, by Nathan and Gad, *v.* 29. *There* was related what was observable in his government at home and his wars abroad, *the times,* that is, the events of *the times, that went over him, v.* 29, 30. These registers were then in being, but are now lost. Note, Good use may be made of those histories of the church which are authentic though not sacred or of divine inspiration.

AN EXPOSITION, WITH PRACTICAL OBSERVATIONS, OF

THE SECOND BOOK OF CHRONICLES

This book begins with the reign of Solomon and the building of the temple, and continues the history of the kings of Judah thenceforward to the captivity and so concludes with the fall of that illustrious monarchy and the destruction of the temple. That monarchy of the house of David, as it was prior in time, so it was superior in worth and dignity to all those four celebrated ones of which Nebuchadnezzar dreamed. The Babylonian monarchy I reckon to begin in Nebuchadnezzar himself — *Thou art that head of gold,* and that lasted but about seventy years; The Persian monarchy, in several families, about 130; the Grecian, in their several branches, about 300; and 300 more went far with the Roman. But as I reckon David a greater hero than any of the founders of those monarchies, and Solomon a more magnificent prince than any of those that were the glories of them, so the succession was kept up in a lineal descent throughout the whole monarchy, which continued considerable between 400 and 500 years, and, after a long eclipse, shone forth again in the kingdom of the Messiah, *of the increase of whose government and peace there shall be no end.* This history of the Jewish monarchy, as it is more authentic, so it is more entertaining and more instructive, than the histories of any of those monarchies. We had the story of the house of David before, in the first and second books of Kings, intermixed with that of the kings of Israel, which *there* took more room than that of Judah; but here we have it entire. Much is repeated here which we had before, yet many of the passages of the story are enlarged upon, and divers added, which we had not before, especially relating to the affairs of religion; for it is a church-history, and it is written for our learning, to let nations and families know that then, and then only, they can expect to prosper, when they keep in the way of their duty to God: for all along the good kings prospered and the wicked kings suffered. The peaceable reign of Solomon we have (*ch.* 1–9), the blemished reign of Rehoboam (*ch.* 10–12), the short but busy reign of Abijah (*ch.* 13), the long and happy reign of Asa (*ch.* 14–16), the pious and prosperous reign of Jehoshaphat (*ch.* 17–20), the impious and infamous reigns of Jehoram and Ahaziah (*ch.* 21–22), the unsteady reigns of Joash and Amaziah (*ch.* 24, 25), the long and prosperous reign of Uzziah (*ch.* 26), the regular reign of Jotham (*ch.* 27), the profane and wicked reign of Ahaz (*ch.* 28), the gracious glorious reign of Hezekiah (*ch.* 29–32), the wicked reigns of Manasseh and Amon (*ch.* 33), the reforming reign of Josiah (*ch.* 34, 35), the ruining reigns of his sons (*ch.* 36). Put all these together, and the truth of that word of God will appear, *Those that honour me I will honour, but those that despise me shall be lightly esteemed.* The learned Mr. Whiston, in his chronology, suggests that the historical books which were written after the captivity (namely, the two books of Chronicles, Ezra, and Nehemiah) have more mistakes in names and numbers than all the books of the Old Testament besides, through the carelessness of transcribers: but, though that should be allowed, the things are so very minute that we may be confident *the foundation of God stands sure* notwithstanding.

CHAPTER 1

In the close of the foregoing book we read how God magnified Solomon and Israel obeyed him; God and Israel concurred to honour him. Now here we have an account, I. How he honoured God by sacrifice (*v.* 1–6) and by prayer (*v.* 7–12). II. How he honoured Israel by increasing their strength, wealth, and trade (*v.* 13–17).

Verses 1–12

Here is, I. Solomon's great prosperity, *v.* 1. Though he had a contested title, yet, God being with him, he was *strengthened in his kingdom;* his heart and hands were strengthened, and his interest in the people. God's presence will be our strength.

II. His great piety and devotion. His father was a prophet, a psalmist, and kept mostly to the ark; but Solomon, having read much in his Bible concerning the tabernacle which Moses built and the altars there, paid more respect to them than, it should seem, David had done. Both did well, and let neither be censured. If the zeal of one be carried out most to one instance of religion, and of another to some other instance, let them not judge nor despise each other.

1. All his great men must thus far be good men that they must join with him in worshipping God. He spoke to the captains and judges, the governors and chief of the fathers, to go with him to Gibeon, *v.* 2, 3. Authority and interest are well bestowed on those that will thus use them for the glory of God, and the promoting of religion. It is our duty to engage all with whom we have influence in the solemnities of religion, and it is very desirable to have many join with us in those solemnities — the more the better; it is the more like heaven. Solomon began his reign with this public pious visit to God's altar, and it was a very good omen. Magistrates are then likely to do well for themselves and their people when they thus take God along with them at their setting out.

2. He offered abundance of sacrifices to God there (*v.* 6): 1000 *burnt-offerings,* and perhaps a greater number of peace-offerings, on which he and his company *feasted before the Lord.* Where God sows plentifully he expects to reap accordingly. His father David had left him flocks and herds in abundance (1 Chr. 27:29, 31), and thus he gave God his dues out of them. The ark was at Jerusalem (*v.* 4), but the altar was at Gibeon (*v.* 5), and thither he brought his sacrifices; for *it is the altar that sanctifieth every gift.*

3. He prayed a good prayer to God: this, with the answer to it, we had before, 1 Ki. 3:5, etc. (1.) God bade him ask what he would; not only that he might put him in the right way of obtaining the favours that were intended him *(Ask, and you shall receive, that your joy may be full),* but that he might try him, how he stood affected, and might discover what was in his heart. Men's characters appear in their choices and desires. What wouldst thou *have?* tries a man as much as, What wouldst thou *do?* Thus God tried whether Solomon was one of the *children of this world,* that say, *Who will show us any good,* or of the children of light, that say, *Lord, lift up the light of thy countenance upon us.* As we choose we shall have, and that is likely to be our portion to which we give the preference, whether the wealth and pleasure of this world or spiritual riches or delights. (2.) Like a genuine son of David, he chose spiritual blessings rather than temporal. His petition here is, *Give me wisdom and knowledge.* He owns those to be desirable gifts, and God to be the giver of them, Prov. 2:6. God gave the faculty of understanding, and to him we must apply for the furniture of it. Two things are here pleaded which we had not in Kings: — [1.] *Thou hast made me reign in my father's stead, v.* 8. "Lord, thou hast put me into this place, and therefore I can in faith ask of thee grace to enable me to do the duty of it." What service we have reason to believe God calls us to we have reason to hope he will qualify us for. But that is not all. "Lord, thou hast put me into this place in the stead of David, the great and good man that filled it up so well; therefore give me wisdom, that Israel may not suffer damage by the change. Must I reign in my father's stead? Lord, give me my father's spirit." Note, The eminency of those that went before us, and the obligation that lies upon us to keep up and carry on the good work they were engaged in, should provoke us to a gracious emulation, and quicken our prayers to God for wisdom and grace, that we may do the work of God in our day as faithfully and well as they did in theirs. [2.] *Let thy promise to David my father be established, v.* 9. He means the promise of concerning his successor. "In performance of that promise, *Lord, give me wisdom.*" We do not find that wisdom was any of the things promised, but it was necessary in order to the accomplishment of what was promised, 2 Sa. 7:13–15. The promise was, *He shall build a house for my name, I will establish his throne, he shall be my son,* and *my mercy shall not depart from him.* "Now, Lord, unless thou give me wisdom, thy house will not be built, nor my throne established; I shall behave in a manner unbecoming my relation to thee as a Father, shall forfeit thy mercy, and fool it away; therefore, *Lord, give me wisdom.*" Note, *First,* God's promises are our best pleas in prayer. *Remember thy word unto thy servant. Secondly,* Children may take the comfort of the promises of that covenant which their parents, in their baptism, laid claim to, and took hold of, for them. *Thirdly,* The best way to obtain the benefit of the promises and privileges of the covenant is to be earnest in prayer with God for wisdom and grace to do the duties of it.

4. He received a gracious answer to this prayer, *v.* 11, 12. (1.) God gave him the wisdom that he asked for because he asked for it. Wisdom is a gift that God gives as freely and liberally as any gift to those that value it, and wrestle for it; and will resolve to make use of it; and he upbraids not the poor petitioners with their folly, James 1:5. God's grace shall never be wanting to those who sincerely desire to know and do their duty. (2.) God gave him the wealth and honour which he did not ask for because he asked not for them. Those that pursue present things most earnestly are most likely to miss of them; while those that refer themselves to the providence of God, if they have not the most of those things, have the most comfort in them. Those that make this world their end come short of the other and are disappointed in this too; but those that make the other world their end shall not only obtain that, and full satisfaction in it, but shall enjoy as much as is convenient of this world in their way.

Verses 13–17

Here is, 1. Solomon's entrance upon the government (*v.* 13): He came *from before the tabernacle, and reigned over Israel.* He would not do any acts of government till he had done his acts of devotion, would not take honour to himself till he had given honour to God — first the tabernacle, and then the throne. But, when he had obtained wisdom from God, he did not bury his talent, but as he received the gift ministered the same, did not give up himself to ease and pleasure, but minded business: he reigned over Israel. 2. The magnificence of his court (*v.* 14): *He gathered chariots and horsemen.* Shall we praise him for this? We praise him not; for the king was forbidden to multiply horses, Deu. 17:16. I do not remember that ever we find his good father in a chariot or on horseback; a mule was the highest he mounted. We should endeavor to excel those that went before us in goodness rather than in grandeur. 3. The wealth and trade of his kingdom. He made silver and gold very cheap and common, *v.* 15. The increase of gold lowers the value of it; but the increase of grace advances its price; the more men have of that the more they value it. *How much better* therefore *is it to get wisdom than gold!* He opened also a trade with Egypt, whence he imported horses and linen-yarn, which he exported again to the kings of Syria, with great advantage no doubt, *v.* 16, 17. This we had before, 1 Ki. 10:28, 29. It is the wisdom of princes to promote industry and encourage trade in their dominions. Perhaps Solomon took the hint of setting up the linen-manufacture, bringing linen-yarn out of Egypt, working it into cloth, and then sending that to other nations, from what his mother taught when she specified this as one of the characteristics of the virtuous woman, *She maketh fine linen, and selleth it, and delivereth girdles* of it *to the merchant,* Prov. 31:24. *In all labour there is profit.*

CHAPTER 2

Solomon's trading, which we read of in the close of the foregoing chapter, and the encouragement he gave both to merchandise and manufacturers, were very commendable. But building was the work he was designed for, and to that business he is here applying himself. Here is, I. Solomon's determination to build the temple and a royal palace, and his appointing labourers to be employed herein (*v.* 1, 2, 17, 18). II. His request to Huram king of Tyre to furnish him both with artists and materials (*v.* 3–10). III. Huram's obliging answer to, and compliance with, his request (*v.* 11–16).

Verses 1–10

Solomon's wisdom was given him, not merely for speculation, to entertain himself (though it is indeed a princely entertainment), nor merely for conversation, to entertain his friends, but for action; and therefore to action he immediately applies himself. Observe,

I. His resolution within himself concerning his business (*v.* 1): *He determined to build,* in the first place, a *house for the name of the Lord.* It is fit that he who is the first should be served — first a temple and then a palace, a house not so much for himself, or his own convenience and magnitude, as for the kingdom, for the honour of it among its neighbours and for the decent reception of the people whenever they had occasion to apply to their prince; so that in both he aimed at the public good. Those are the wisest men that lay out themselves most for the honour of the name of the Lord and the welfare of communities. We are not born for ourselves, but for God and our country.

II. His embassy to Huram, king of Tyre, to engage his assistance in the prosecution of his designs. The purport of his errand to him is much the same here as we had it 1 Ki. 5:2, etc., only here it is more largely set forth.

1. The reasons why he makes this application to Huram are here more fully represented, for information to Huram as well as for inducement. (1.) He pleads his father's interest in Huram, and the kindness he had received from him (*v.* 3): *As thou didst deal with David, so deal with me.* As we must show kindness to, so we may expect kindness from, our fathers' friends, and with them should cultivate a correspondence. (2.) He represents his design in building the temple: he intended it for a place of religious worship (*v.* 4), that all the offerings which God had appointed for the honour of his name might be offered up there. The house was built that it might be dedicated to God and used in his service. This we should aim at in all our business, that our havings and doings may be all to the glory of God. He mentions various particular services that were there to be performed, for the instruction of Huram. The mysteries of the true religion, unlike those of the Gentile superstition, coveted not concealment. (3.) He endeavors to inspire Huram with very great and high thoughts of the God of Israel, by expressing the mighty veneration he had for his holy name: *Great is our God above all gods,* above all idols, above all princes. Idols are nothing, princes are little, and both under the control of the God of Israel; and therefore, [1.] "The house must be great; not in proportion to the greatness of that God to whom it is to be dedicated (for between finite and infinite there can be no proportion), but in some proportion to the great value and esteem we have for this God." [2.] "Yet, be it ever so great,

it cannot be a habitation for the great God. Let not Huram think that the God of Israel, like the gods of the nations, *dwells in temples made with hands,* Acts 17:24. No, the *heaven of heavens cannot contain him.* It is intended only for the convenience of his priests and worshippers, that they may have a fit place wherein to burn sacrifice before him." [3.] He looked upon himself, though a mighty prince, as unworthy the honour of being employed in this great work: *Who am I that I should build him a house?* It becomes us to go about every work for God with a due sense of our utter insufficiency for it and our incapacity to do any thing adequate to the divine perfections. It is part of the wisdom wherein we ought to walk towards those that are without carefully to guard against all misapprehension which any thing we say or do may occasion concerning God; so Solomon does here in his treaty with Huram.

2. The requests he makes to him are more particularly set down here. (1.) He desired Huram would furnish him with a good hand to work (*v.* 7): *Send me a man.* He had *cunning men* with him in Jerusalem and Judah, whom David provided, 1 Chr. 22:15. Let them not think but that Jews had some among them that were artists. But *"send me a man* to direct them. There are ingenious men in Jerusalem, but not such engravers as are in Tyre; and therefore, since temple-work must be the best in its kind, let me have the best workmen that can be got." (2.) With good materials to work on (*v.* 8), cedar and other timber in abundance (*v.* 8, 9); for the house must be *wonderfully great,* that is, very stately and magnificent, no cost must be spared, nor any contrivance wanting in it.

3. Here is Solomon's engagement to maintain the workmen (*v.* 10), to give them so much wheat and barley, so much wine and oil. He did not feed his workmen with bread and water, but with plenty, and every thing of the best. Those that employ labourers ought to take care they be not only well paid, but well provided for with sufficient of that which is wholesome and fit for them. Let the rich masters do for their poor workmen as they would be done by if the tables were turned.

Verses 11–18

Here we have, I. The return which Huram made to Solomon's embassy, in which he shows a great respect for Solomon and a readiness to serve him. Meaner people may learn of these great ones to be neighbourly and complaisant. 1. He congratulates Israel on having such a king as Solomon was (*v.* 11): *Because the Lord loved his people, he has made thee king.* Note, A wise and good government is a great blessing to a people, and may well be accounted a singular token of God's favour. He does not say, *Because he loved* thee (though that was true, 2 Sa. 12:24) *he made thee king,* but because he *loved his people.* Princes must look upon themselves as preferred for the public good, not for their own personal satisfaction, and should rule so as to prove that they were given in love and not in anger. 2. He blesses God for raising up such a successor to David, *v.* 12. It should seem that Huram was not only very well affected to the Jewish nation, and well pleased with their prosperity, but that he was proselyted to the Jewish religion, and worshipped Jehovah, *the God of Israel* (who was now known by that name to the neighbouring nations), as *the God that made heaven and earth,* and as the fountain of power as well as being; for he sets up kings. Now that the people of Israel kept close to the law and worship of God, and so preserved their honour, the neighbouring nations were as willing to be instructed by them in the true religion as Israel had been, in the days of their apostasy, to be infected with the idolatries and superstitions of their neighbours. This made them high, that they lent to many nations and did not borrow, lent truth to them, and did not borrow error from them; as when they did the contrary it was their shame. 3. He sent him a very ingenious curious workman, that would not fail to answer his expectations in every thing, one that had both Jewish and Gentile blood meeting in him; for his mother was an Israelite (Huram though she was of the tribe of Dan, and therefore says so here, *v.* 14, but it seems she was of the tribe of Naphtali, 1 Ki. 7:14), but his father was a Tyrian — a good omen of uniting Jew and Gentile in the gospel temple, as it was afterwards when the building of the second temple was greatly furthered by Darius (Ezra 6), who is supposed to have been the son of Esther — an Israelite by the mother's side. 4. He engaged for the timber, as much as he would have occasion for, and undertook to deliver it at Joppa, and withal signified his dependence upon Solomon for the maintenance of the workmen as he had promised, *v.* 15, 16. This agreement we had, 1 Ki. 5:8, 9.

II. The orders which Solomon gave about the workmen. He would not employ the free-born Israelites in the drudgery work of the temple itself, not so much as to be overseers of it. In this he employed the strangers who were proselyted to the Jewish religion, who had not lands of inheritance in Canaan as the Israelites had, and therefore applied to trades, and got their living by their ingenuity and industry. There were, at this time, vast numbers of them in the land (*v.* 17), who, if they were of any of the devoted nations, perhaps fell within the case, and therefore fell under the law, of the Gibeonites, to be hewers of wood for the congregation: if not, yet being in many respects well provided for by the law of Moses, and put upon an equal footing with the native Israelites, they were bound in gratitude to do what they could for the service of the temple. Yet, no doubt, they were well paid in money or money's worth: the law was, *Thou shalt not oppress a stranger.* The distribution of them we have here (*v.* 2, and again *v.* 18), in all 150,000. Canaan was a fruitful land, that found meat for so many mouths more than the numerous natives; and the temple was a vast building, that found work for so many bands. Mr. Fuller suggests that the expedient peculiar to this structure, of framing all beforehand, must needs increase the work. I think it rather left so much the more room for this vast multitude of hands to be employed in it; for in the forest of Lebanon they might all be at work together, without crowding one another, which they could not have been upon Mount Sion. And, if there had not been such vast numbers employed, so large and curious a fabric, which was begun and ended in seven years, might, for aught I know, have been as long in building as St. Paul's.

CHAPTER 3

It was a much larger and more particular account of the building of the temple which we had in the book of Kings than is here in this book of Chronicles. In this chapter we have, I. The place and time of building the temple (*v.* 1, 2). II. The dimensions and rich ornaments of it (*v.* 3–9). III. The cherubim in the most holy place (*v.* 10–13). IV. The veil (*v.* 14). V. The two pillars (*v.* 15–17). Of all this we have already and an account, 1 Ki. 6, 7.

Verses 1–9

Here is, I. The place where the temple was built. Solomon was neither at liberty to choose nor at a loss to fix the place. It was before determined (1 Chr. 22:1), which was an ease to his mind. 1. It must be at Jerusalem; for that was the place where God had chosen to put his name there. The royal city must be the holy city. *There* must be *the testimony of Israel; for there are set the thrones of judgment,* Ps. 122:4, 5. 2. It must be on Mount Moriah, which, some think, was that very place in the land of Moriah where Abraham offered Isaac, Gen. 22:2. So the Targum says expressly, adding, *But he was delivered by the word of the Lord, and a ram provided in his place.* That was typical of Christ's sacrifice of himself; therefore fitly was the temple, which was likewise a type of him, built there. 3. It must be *where the Lord appeared to David,* and *answered him by fire,* 1 Chr. 21:18, 26. There atonement was made once; and therefore, in remembrance of that, there atonement was made once; and therefore, in remembrance of that, there atonement must still be made. Where God has met with me it is to be hoped that he will still manifest himself. 4. It must be in the place which David has prepared, not only which he had purchased with his money, but which he had purchased with his money, but which he had pitched upon divine direction. It was Solomon's wisdom not to enquire out a more convenient place, but to acquiesce in the appointment of God, whatever might be objected against it. 5. It must be in the threshold floor of Ornan, which, if (as a Jebusite) it gives encouragement to the Gentiles, obliges us to look upon temple-work as that which requires the labour of the mind, no less than threshing-work dos that of the body.

II. The time when it was begun; not till the fourth year of Solomon's reign, *v.* 2. Not that the first three years were trifled away, or spent in deliberating whether they should build the temple or no; but they were employed in the necessary preparations for it, wherein three years would be soon gone, considering how many hands were to be got together and set to work. Some conjecture that this was a sabbatical year, or year of release and rest to the land, when the people, being discharged from their husbandry, might more easily lend a hand to the beginning of this work; and then the year in which it was finished would fall out to be another sabbatical year, when they would likewise have leisure to attend the solemnity of the dedication of it.

III. The dimensions of it, in which Solomon was instructed (*v.* 3), as he was in other things, by his father. *This was the foundation* (so it may be read) *which Solomon laid for the building of the house.* This was the rule he went by, so many cubits the length and breadth, *after the first measure,* that is, according to the measure first fixed, which there was no reason to make any alteration of when the work came to be done; for the dimensions were given by divine wisdom, and *what God does shall be for ever; nothing can be put to it, or taken from it,* Eccl. 3:14. His first measure will be the last.

IV. The ornaments of the temple. The timber-work was very fine, and yet, within, it was *overlaid with pure gold* (*v.* 4), with *fine gold* (*v.* 5). and that embossed with *palm-trees and chains.* It was gold of *Parvaim* (*v.* 6), the best gold. The *beams* and *posts,* the *walls* and *doors,* were *overlaid with gold, v.* 7. The most holy place, which was ten yards square, was all *overlaid with fine gold* (*v.* 8), even the *upper chambers,* or rather the *upper floor or roof* — top, bottom, and sides, were all overlaid with gold. Every nail, or screw, or pin, with which the golden plates were fastened to the walls that were overlaid with them, weighed fifty shekels, or was worth so much, workmanship and all. A great many precious stones were dedicated to God (1 Chr. 29:2, 8), and these were set here and there, where they would show to the best advantage. The finest houses now pretend to no better garnishing than good paint on the roof and walls; but the ornaments of the temple were most substantially rich. It was set with *precious stones,* because it was a type of the new Jerusalem, which has no temple in it because it is all temple, and the walls, gates, and foundations of which are said to be of *precious stones and pearls,* Rev. 21:18, 19, 21.

Verses 10–17

Here is an account of 1. The two cherubim, which were set up in the holy of holies. There were two already over the ark, which covered the mercy-seat with their wings; these were small ones. Now that the most holy place was enlarged, though these were continued (being appurtenances to the ark, which was not to be made new, as all the other utensils of the tabernacle were), yet those two large ones were added, doubtless by divine appointment, to fill up the holy place, which otherwise would have looked bare, like a room unfurnished. These cherubim are said to be of *image-work* (*v.* 10), designed, it is likely, to represent the angels who attend the divine Majesty. Each wing extended five cubits, so that the whole was twenty cubits (*v.* 12, 13), which was just the breadth of the most holy place, *v.* 8. They stood on their feet, as servants, their faces inward toward the ark (*v.* 13), that it might appear they were not set there to be adored (for then they would have been made sitting, as on a throne, and their faces towards their worshippers), but rather as themselves attendants on the invisible God. We must not worship angels, but we must worship *with* angels; for we have come into communion with them (Heb. 12:22), and must do the will of God as the angels do it. The thought that we are worshipping him before whom the angels cover their faces will help to inspire us with reverence in all our approaches to God. Compare 1 Co. 11:10 with Isa. 6:2. 2. The veil that parted between the temple and the most holy place, *v.* 14. This denoted the darkness of that dispensation, and the distance which the worshippers were kept at; but, at the death of Christ, this veil was rent; for through him we are made nigh, and have boldness not only to look, but to enter, into the holiest. On this he was wrought cherubim. Heb. *he caused them to ascend,* that is, they were made in raised work, embossed. Or he made them on the wing in an ascending posture, as the other two that stood on their feet in an attending posture, to remind the worshippers to lift up their hearts, and to soar upwards in their devotions. 3. The two pillars which were set up before the temple. Both together were somewhat above thirty-five cubits in length (*v.* 15), about eighteen cubits high a-piece. See 1 Ki. 7:15, etc., where we took a view of those pillars, *Jachin* and *Boaz, establishment* and *strength* in temple-work and by it.

CHAPTER 4

We have here a further account of the furniture of God's house. I. Those things that were of brass. The altar for burnt-offerings (*v.* 1), the sea and lavers to hold water (*v.* 2–6), the plates with which the doors of the court were overlaid (*v.* 9), the vessels of the altar, and other things (*v.* 10–18). II. Those that were of gold. The candlesticks and tables (*v.* 7, 8), the altar of incense (*v.* 19), and the appurtenances of each of these (*v.* 20–22). All these, except the brazen altar (*v.* 1), were accounted for more largely, 1 Ki. 7:23, etc.

Verses 1–10

David often speaks with much affection both of the *house of the Lord* and of the *courts of our God.* Both without doors and within there was that which typified the grace of the gospel and *shadowed* out *good things to come,* of which the substance is Christ.

I. There were those things in the open court, in the view of all the people, which were very significant.

1. There was the *brazen altar, v.* 1. The making of this was not mentioned in the Kings. On this all the sacrifices were offered, and it sanctified the gift. This altar was much larger than that which Moses made in the tabernacle; that was five cubits square, this was twenty cubits square. Now that Israel had become both numerous and more rich, and it was to be hoped more devout (for every age should aim to be wiser and better than that which went before it), it was expected that there would be a greater abundance of offerings brought to God's altar than had been. It was therefore made such a capacious scaffold that it might hold them all, and none might excuse themselves from bringing those temptations of their devotion by alleging that there was not room to receive them. God had greatly enlarged their borders; it was therefore fit that they should enlarge his altars. Our returns should bear some proportion to our receivings. It was ten cubits high, so that the people who worshipped in the courts might see the sacrifice burnt, and their eye might affect their heart with sorrow for sin: "It is of the Lord's mercies that I am not thus consumed, and that this is accepted as an expiation of my guilt." They might thus be led to consider the great sacrifice which should be offered in the fulness of time to take away sin and abolish death, which the blood of bulls and goats could not possibly do. And with the smoke of the sacrifices their hearts might ascend to heaven in holy desires towards God and his favour. In all our devotions we must keep the eye of faith fixed upon Christ, the great propitiation. How they went up to this altar, and carried the sacrifices up to it, we are not told; some think by a plain ascent like a hill: if by steps, doubtless they were so contrived as that the end of the law (mentioned Ex. 20:26) might be answered.

2. There was the molten sea, a very large brass pan, in which they put water for the priests to wash in. *v.* 2, 6. It was put just at the entrance into the court of the priests, like the font at the church door. If it were filled to the brim, it would hold 3000 baths (as here, *v.* 5), but ordinarily there were only 2000 baths in it, 1 Ki. 7:26. The Holy Ghost by this signified, (1.) Our great gospel privilege, that *the blood of Christ cleanseth from all sin,* 1 Jn. 1:7. To us there is a *fountain opened* for all believers (who are spiritual priests, Rev. 1:5, 6), nay, for *all the inhabitants of Jerusalem to wash in,* from sin, which is uncleanness. There is a fulness of merit in Jesus Christ for all those that by faith apply to him for the purifying of their consciences, that they might serve the *living God,* Heb. 9:14. (2.) Our great gospel duty, which is to cleanse ourselves by true repentance from all the pollutions of the flesh and the corruption that is in the world. Our hearts must be sanctified, or we cannot sanctify the name of God. Those that draw nigh to God must *cleanse their hands, and purify their hearts,* Jam. 4:8. *If I was thee not, thou hast no part with me;* and he that *is washed* still needs *to wash his feet,* to renew his repentance, whenever he *goes in to minister,* Jn. 13:10.

3. There were *ten lavers* of brass, in which *they washed such things as they offered for the burnt-offerings, v.* 6. As the priests must be washed, so must the sacrifices. We must

not only purify ourselves in preparation for our religious performances, but carefully put away all those vain thoughts and corrupt aims which cleave to our performances themselves and pollute them.

4. The doors of the court were overlaid with brass (*v.* 9), both for strength and beauty, and that they might not be rotted with the weather, to which they were exposed. *Gates of brass* we read of, Ps. 107:16.

II. There were those things in *the house of the Lord* (into which the priests alone went to minister) that were very significant. All was gold there. The nearer we come to God the purer we must be, the purer we shall be. 1. There were ten *golden candlesticks,* according to the form of that one which was in the tabernacle, *v.* 7. The written word is a lamp and a light, shining in a dark place. In Moses's time they had but one candlestick, the Pentateuch; but the additions which, in process of time, were to be made of other books of scripture might be signified by this increase of the number of the candlesticks. Light was growing. The candlesticks are the churches, Rev. 1:20. Moses set up but one, the church of the Jews; but, in the gospel temple, not only believers, but churches, are multiplied. 2. There were ten *golden tables* (*v.* 8), *tables whereon the show-bread was set, v.* 19. Perhaps every one of the tables had twelve loaves of show-bread on it. As the house was enlarged, the housekeeping was. *In my father's house there is bread enough for the whole family.* To those tables belonged 100 golden basins, or dishes; for God's table is well furnished. 3. There was a *golden altar* (*v.* 19), on which they burnt incense. It is probable that this was enlarged in proportion to the brazen altar. Christ, who once for all made atonement for sin, ever lives, making intercession, in virtue of that atonement.

Verses 11–22

We have here such a summary both of the brass-work and the gold-work of the temple as we had before (1 Ki. 7:13, etc.), in which we have nothing more to observe than, 1. That Huram the workman was very punctual: *He finished all that he was to make* (*v.* 11), and left no part of his work undone. *Huram, his father,* he is called, *v.* 16. Probably it was a sort of nickname by which he was commonly known, *Father Huram;* for the king of Tyre called him *Huram Abi, my father,* in compliance with whom Solomon called him his, he being a great artist and *father of the artificers* in brass and iron. He acquitted himself well both for ingenuity and industry. 2. Solomon was very generous. He made *all the vessels in great abundance* (*v.* 18), many of a sort, that many hands might be employed, and so the work might go on with expedition, or that some might be laid up for use when others were worn out. Freely he has received, and he will freely give. When he had made vessels enough for the present he could not convert the remainder of the brass to his own use; it is devoted to God, and it shall be used for him.

CHAPTER 5

The temple being built and furnished for God, we have here, I. Possession given to him, by bringing in the dedicated things (*v.* 1), but especially the ark, the token of his presence (*v.* 2–10). II. Possession taken by him, in a cloud (*v.* 11–14). For if any man open the door of his heart to God he will come in, Rev. 3:20.

Verses 1–10

This agrees with what we had 1 Ki. 8:2, etc., where an account was given of the solemn introduction of the ark into the new-erected temple. 1. There needed no great solemnity for the bringing in of the dedicated things, *v.* 1. They added to the wealth, and perhaps were so disposed as to add to the beauty of it; but they could not add to the holiness, for it was the *temple that sanctified the gold,* Mt. 23:17. See how just Solomon was both to God and to his father. Whatever David had dedicated to God, however much he might have liked it himself, he would by no means alienate it, but put it among the treasures of the temple. Those children that would inherit their godly parents' blessing must religiously pursue their pious intentions and not defeat them. When Solomon had made all the vessels of the temple in abundance (*ch.* 4:18), many of the materials were left, which he would not convert to any other use, but laid up in the treasury for a time of need. Dedicated things must not be alienated. It is sacrilege to do it. 2. But it was fit that the ark should be brought in

with great solemnity; and so it was. All the other vessels were made new, and larger, in proportion to the house, than they had been in the tabernacle. But the ark, with the mercy-seat and the cherubim, was the same; for the presence and the grace of God are the same in little assemblies that they are in large ones, in the poor condition of the church that they are in its prosperous estate. Wherever two or three are gathered together in Christ's name there is he as truly present with them as if there were 2000 or 3000. The ark was brought in attended by a very great assembly of the elders of Israel, who came to grace and solemnity; and a very sumptuous appearance no doubt they made, *v.* 2–4. It was carried by the priests (*v.* 7), brought into the most holy place, and put under the wings of the great cherubim which Solomon had set up there, *v.* 7, 8. *There they are unto this day* (*v.* 9), not the day when this book was written after the captivity, but when that was written out of which this story was transcribed. Or they were there (so it might be read) unto this day, the day of Jerusalem's desolations, that fatal day, Ps. 137:7. The ark was a type of Christ, and, as such, a token of the presence of God. That gracious promise, *Lo, I am with you always, even unto the end of the world,* does in effect bring the ark into our religious assemblies if we by faith and prayer put that promise in suit; and this we should be most solicitous and earnest for. *Lord, if thy presence go not up with us,* wherefore should we go up? The temple itself, if Christ leave it, is a desolate place, Mt. 23:38. 3. With the ark they brought up the tabernacle and all the *holy vessels that were in the tabernacle, v.* 5. Those were not alienated, because they had been dedicated to God, were not altered or melted down for the new work, though there was no need of them; but they were carefully laid up as monuments of antiquity, and probably as many of the vessels as were fit for use were still used. 4. This was done with great joy. They kept a holy feast upon the occasion (*v.* 3), and *sacrificed sheep and oxen without number, v.* 6. Note, (1.) The establishment of the public worship of God according to his institution, and with the tokens of his presence, is, and ought to be, matter of great joy to any people. (2.) When Christ is formed in a soul, the law written in the heart, the ark of the covenant settled there, so that it becomes the temple of the Holy Ghost, there is true satisfaction in that soul. (3.) Whatever we have the comfort of we must, by the sacrifice of praise, give God the glory of, and not be straitened therein; *for with such sacrifices God is well pleased.* If God favour us with his presence, we must honour him with our services, the best we have.

Verses 11–14

Solomon, and the elders of Israel, had done what they could to grace the solemnity of the introduction of the ark; but God, by testifying his acceptance of what they did, put the greatest honour upon it. The cloud of glory that filled the house beautified it more than all the gold with which it was overlaid or the precious stones with which it was garnished; and yet that was no glory in comparison with the glory of the gospel dispensation, 2 Co. 3:8–10. Observe,

I. How God took possession of the temple: He *filled it with a cloud, v.* 13. 1. Thus he signified his acceptance of this temple to be the same to him that the tabernacle of Moses was, and assured them that he would be the same in it; for it was by a cloud that he made his public entry into that, Ex. 40:34. 2. Thus he considered the weakness and infirmity of those to whom he manifested himself, who could not bear the dazzling lustre of the divine light: it would have overpowered them; he therefore *spread his cloud upon it,* Job 26:9. Christ revealed things unto his disciples as they were able to bear them, and in parables, which wrapped up divine things as in a cloud. 3. Thus he would affect all that worshipped in his courts with holy reverence and fear. Christ's disciples were afraid when they entered into a cloud, Lu. 9:34. 4. Thus he would intimate the darkness of that dispensation, by reason of which they could not stedfastly look to the end of those things which were now abolished, 2 Co. 3:13.

II. When he took possession of it. 1. *When the priests had come out of the holy place, v.* 11. This is the way of giving possession. All must come out, that the rightful owner may come in. Would we have God dwell in our hearts? We must leave room for him; let every thing else give way. We are here told that upon this occasion the whole family of the priests attended, and not any one particular course: *All the priests that were present were sanctified* (*v.* 11), because there was work enough for them all, when such a multitude of sacrifices were to be offered, and because it was fit that they should all be eye-witnesses of this solemnity and receive the impressions of it. 2. When the singers and musicians praised God, then the house was filled with a cloud. This is very observable; it was not when they *offered sacrifices,* but when they *sang the praises of God,* that God gave them this token of his favour; for the sacrifice of praise *pleaseth the Lord* better than that of *an ox or bullock,* Ps. 69:31. All the singers and musicians were employed, those of all the three families; and, to complete the concert, 120 priests, with their trumpets, joined with them, all standing at the east end of the altar, on that side of the court which lay outmost towards the people, *v.* 12. And, when this part of the service began, the glory of God appeared. Observe, (1.) It was when they were unanimous, when they were as one, to make one sound. The Holy God descended on the apostles when they met with one accord, Acts 2:1–4. Where unity is the Lord commands the blessing. (2.) It was when they were lively and hearty, and *lifted up their voice to praise the Lord.* Then we serve God acceptably when we are fervent in spirit serving him. (3.) It was when they were, in their praises, celebrating the everlasting mercy and goodness of God. As there is one saying oftener repeated in scripture than this, *his mercy endureth for ever* (twenty-six times in one psalm, Ps. 136, and often elsewhere), so there is none more signally owned from heaven; for it was not the expression of some rapturous flights that the priests were singing when the glory of God appeared, but this plain song, *He is good, and his mercy endureth for ever.* God's goodness is his glory, and he is pleased when we give him the glory of it.

III. What was the effect of it. The *priests themselves could not stand to minister, by reason of the cloud* (*v.* 14), which, as it was an evidence that the law made men priests that had infirmity, so (as bishop Patrick observes) it was a plain intimation that the Levitical priesthood should cease, and stand no longer to minister, when the Messiah should come, in whom *the fulness of the godhead should dwell bodily.* In him the glory of God dwelt among us, but covered with a cloud. The Word was made flesh; and when he comes to his temple, like a refiner's fire, *who may abide the day of his coming?* And *who shall stand when he appeareth?* Mal. 3:1, 2.

CHAPTER 6

The glory of the Lord, in the vehicle of a thick cloud, having filled the house which Solomon built, by which God manifested his presence there, he immediately improves the opportunity, and addresses God, as a God now, in a peculiar manner, nigh at hand. I. He makes a solemn declaration of his intention in building this house, to the satisfaction of the people and the honour of God, both of whom he blessed (*v.* 1–11). II. He makes a solemn prayer to God that he would please graciously to accept and answer all the prayers that should be made in, or towards, that house (*v.* 12–42). This whole chapter we had before, with very little variation (1 Ki. 8:12–53), to which it may not be amiss here to look back.

Verses 1–11

It is of great consequence, in all our religious actions, that we design well, and that our eye be single. If Solomon had built this temple in the pride of his heart, as Ahasuerus made his feast, only to *show the riches of his kingdom and the honour of his majesty,* it would not have turned at all to his account. But here he declares upon what inducements he undertook it, and they are such as not only justify, but magnify, the undertaking. 1. He did it for the glory and honour of God; this was his highest and ultimate end in it. It was *for the name of the Lord God of Israel* (*v.* 10), to be *a house of habitation for him, v.* 2. He has indeed, as to us, *made darkness his pavilion* (*v.* 1), but let this house be the residence of that darkness; for it is in the upper world that he dwells in light, such as no eye can approach. 2. He did it in compliance with the choice God had been pleased to make of Jerusalem, to be the city in which he would record his name (*v.* 6): *I have chosen Jerusalem.* A great many stately buildings there were in Jerusalem for the king, his princes, and the royal family. If God chooses that place, it is fit that there be a building for him which may excel all the rest. If men were thus honoured there, let God be thus honoured. 3. He did it in pursuance of his father's good intentions, which he never had an opportunity to put into execution: *"It was in the heart of David my father to build a house for God;"* the project was his, be it known, to his honour (*v.* 7), and God approved of it, though he permitted him not to put it in execution (*v.* 8), *Thou didst well that it was in thy heart.* Temple-work is often thus done; one sows and another reaps (Jn. 4:37, 38), one age begins that which the next brings to perfection. And let not the wisest of men think it any disparagement to them to pursue the good designs which those that went before them have laid, and to build upon their foundation. Every good piece is not an original. 4. He did it in performance of the word which God had spoken. God had said, *Thy son shall build the house for my name;* and now he had done it, *v.* 9, 10. The service was appointed him, and the honour of it designed him, by the divine promise; so that he did not do it of his own head, but was called of God to do it. It is fit that he who appoints the work should have the appointing of the workmen; and those may go on in their work with great satisfaction who see their call to it clear.

Verses 12–42

Solomon had, in the foregoing verses, signed and sealed, as it were, the deed of dedication, by which the temple was appropriated to the honour and service of God. Now here he prays the consecration-prayer, by which it was made a figure of Christ, the great Mediator, through whom we are to offer all our prayers, and to expect all God's favours, and to whom we are to have an eye in every thing where we have to do with God. We have opened the particulars of this prayer (1 Ki. 8) and therefore shall now only glean up some few passages in it which may be the proper subjects of our meditation.

I. Here are some doctrinal truths occasionally laid down. As, 1. That the God of Israel is a being of incomparable perfection. We cannot describe him; but this we know, there is *none like him in heaven or in earth, v.* 14. All the creatures have their fellow-creatures, but the Creator has not his peer. He is infinitely above all, and *over all, God blessed for ever.* 2. That he is, and will be, true to every word that he has spoken; and all that serve him in sincerity shall certainly find him both faithful and kind. Those that set God always before them, and *walk before him with all their hearts,* shall find him as good as his word and better; he will both keep covenant with them and show mercy to them, *v.* 14. 3. That he is a being infinite and immense, whom the heaven, and heaven of heavens, cannot contain, and to whose felicity nothing is added by the utmost we can do in his service, *v.* 18. He is infinitely beyond the bounds of the creation and infinitely above the praises of all intelligent creatures. 4. That he, and *he only, knows the hearts of the children of men, v.* 30. All men's thoughts, aims, and affections, are naked and open before him; and, however the imaginations and intents of our hearts may be concealed from men, angels, and devils, they cannot be hidden from God, who knows not only what is in the heart, but the heart itself and all the beatings of it. 5. That there is no such thing as a sinless perfection to be found in this life (*v.* 36): *There is no man who sinneth not;* nay, who *doeth good and sinneth not;* so he writes, agreeable to what he here says, Eccl. 7:20.

II. Here are some suppositions or cases put which are to be taken notice of. 1. He supposed that if doubts and controversies arose between man and man both sides would agree to appeal to God, and lay an oath upon the person whose testimony must decide the matter, *v.* 22. The religious reverence of an oath, as it was ancient, so, it may be presumed, it will continue as long as there are any remains of conscience and right reason among men. 2. He supposed that, though Israel enjoyed a profound peace and tranquillity, yet troublesome times would come. He did not think the mountain of their prosperity stood so strong but that it might be moved; nay, he expected sin would move it. 3. He supposed that those who had not called upon God at other times, yet, in their affliction, would seek him early and earnestly. "When they are in distress they will confess their sins, and confess thy name, and make supplication to thee." Trouble will drive those to God who have said to him, Depart, *v.* 24, 26, 28. 4. He supposed that strangers would come from afar to worship the God of Israel and to pay homage to him; and this also might reasonably be expected, considering what worthless things the gods of the nations were, and what proofs the God of Israel had given of his being Lord of the whole earth.

III. Here are petitions very pertinent. 1. That God would own this house, and have an eye to it, as the place of which he had said that he would put his name there, *v.* 20. He could not, in faith, have asked God to show such peculiar favour to this house above any other if he himself had not said that it should be his rest for ever. The prayer that will speed must be warranted by the word. We may with humble confidence pray to God to be well pleased with us in Jesus Christ, because he had declared himself well pleased in him — *This is my beloved Son;* but he says not now of any house, "This is my beloved place." 2. That God would hear and accept the prayers which should be made in or towards that place, *v.* 21. He asked not that God should help them whether they prayed for themselves or no, but that God would help them in answer to their prayers. Even Christ's intercessions do not supersede but encourage our supplications. He prayed that God would hear from his dwelling-place, even from heaven. Heaven in his dwelling-place still, not this temple; and thence help must come. *When thou hearest forgive.* Note, The forgiveness of our sins is that which makes way for all the other answers to our prayers, *Removendo prohibens — The evil which it drives away it keeps away.* 3. That God would give judgment according to equity upon all the appeals that should be made to him, *v.* 23, 30. This we may, in faith, pray for, for we are sure it shall be done. God sitteth on the throne judging right. 4. That God would return in mercy to his people when they repented, and reformed, and sought unto him, *v.* 25, 27, 38, 39. This we also may, in faith, pray for, building upon the repeated declarations God has made of his readiness to accepts penitents. 5. That God would bid the strangers welcome to this house, and answer their prayers (*v.* 33); for, if there be in duty, why should there not be in privilege one law for the stranger and for one born in the land? Lev. 24:22. 6. That God would, upon all occasions, own and plead the cause of his people Israel, against all the opposers of it (*v.* 35): *Maintain their cause;* and again, *v.* 39. If they be the Israel of God, their cause is the cause of God, and he would espouse it. 7. He concludes this prayer with some expressions which he had learned of his good father, and borrowed from one of his psalms. We had then not in the Kings, but here we have them, *v.* 41, 42. The whole word of God is of use to direct us in prayer; and how can we express ourselves in better language to God than that of his own Spirit? But these words were of use, in a special manner, to direct Solomon, because they had reference to this very work that he was now doing. We have them, Ps. 132:8–10. He prayer (*v.* 41), (1.) That God would take possession of the temple, and keep possession, that he would make it his resting-place: *Thou and the ark;* what will the ark do without the God of the ark — ordinances without the God of the ordinances? (2.) That he would make the ministers of the temple public blessings: *Clothe them with salvation,* that is, not only save them, but make them instrumental to save others, by offering the sacrifices of righteousness. (3.) That the service of the temple might turn abundantly to the joy and satisfaction of all the Lord's people: *Let thy saints rejoice in goodness,* that is, in the *goodness of thy house,* Ps. 65:4. "Let all that come hither to worship, like the eunuch, go away rejoicing." He pleads two things, *v.* 42. [1.] His own relation to God: *"Turn not away the face of thy anointed.* Lord, thou hast appointed me to be king, and wilt not thou own me?" [2.] God's covenant with his father: *Remember thy mercies of David thy servant* — the *piety* of David towards God (so some understand it and so the word sometimes signifies), his pious care of the ark, and concern for it (see Ps. 132:1, 2, etc.), or the *promises* of God to David, which were mercies to him, his great support and comforts in all his troubles. We may plead, as Solomon does here, with an eye to Christ: — "We deserve that God should turn away our face, that he should reject us and our prayers; but we come in the name of the Lord Jesus, *thy anointed, thy Messiah* (so the word is), *thy Christ,* so the LXX. Him thou hearest always, and wilt never *turn away his face.* We have no righteousness of our own to plead, but, Lord, *remember the mercies of David thy servant."* Christ is God's servant (Isa. 42:1), and is called *David,* Hos. 3:5. "Lord, remember his mercies, and accept us on the account of them. Remember his tender concern for his Father's honour and man's salvation, and what he did and suffered from that principle. Remember the promises of the everlasting covenant, which free grace has made to us in Christ, and which are called *the sure mercies of David*," Isa. 55:3 and Acts 13:34. This must be all our desire and all our hope, all our prayer and all our plea; for it is all our salvation.

CHAPTER 7

In this chapter we have God's answer to Solomon's prayer. I. His public answer by fire from heaven, which consumed the sacrifices (*v.* 1), with which the priests and people were much affected (*v.* 2, 3). By that token of God's acceptance they were encouraged to continue the solemnities of the feast for fourteen days, and Solomon was encouraged to pursue all his designs for the honour of God (*v.* 4–11). II. His private answer by word of mouth, in a dream or vision of the night (*v.* 12–22). Most of these things we had before, 1 Ki. 8 and 9.

Verses 1–11

Here is, I. The gracious answer which God immediately made to Solomon's prayer: The *fire came down from heaven and consumed the sacrifice, v.* 1. In this way God testified his acceptance of Moses (Lev. 9:24), of Gideon (Jdg. 6:21), of David (1 Chr. 21:26), of Elijah (1 Ki. 18:38); and, in general, to accept the burnt-sacrifice is, in the Hebrew phrase, to turn it to ashes, Ps. 20:3. The fire came down here, not upon the killing of the sacrifices, but the praying of the prayer.

1. This fire intimated that God was, (1.) Glorious in himself; for *our God is a consuming fire,* terrible even in his holy places. This fire, breaking forth (as it is probable) out of the thick darkness, made it the more terrible, as on Mount Sinai, Ex. 24:16, 17. *The sinners in Sion* had reason to be *afraid* at that sight, and to say, *Who among us shall dwell near this devouring fire?* Isa. 33:14. And yet, (2.) Gracious to Israel; for this fire, which might justly have consumed them, fastened upon the sacrifice which was offered in their stead, and consumed that, by which God signified to them that he accepted their offerings and that his anger was turned away from them.

2. Let us apply this, (1.) To the suffering of Christ. When it pleased the Lord to bruise him, and put him to grief, in that he showed his good-will to men, having laid on him the iniquity of us all. His death was our life, and he was made sin and a curse that we might inherit righteousness and a blessing. That sacrifice was consumed that we might escape. *Here am I, let these go their way.* (2.) To the sanctification of the Spirit, who descends like fire, burning up our lusts and corruptions, those beasts that must be sacrificed or we are undone, and kindling in our souls a holy fire of pious and devout affections, always to be kept burning on the altar of the heart. The surest evidence of God's acceptance of our prayers is the descent of the holy fire upon us. *Did not our hearts burn within us?* Lu. 24:32. As a further evidence that God accepted Solomon's prayer, still *the glory of the Lord filled the house.* The heart that is thus filled with a holy awe and reverence of the divine glory, the heart to which God manifests himself in his greatness, and (which is no less his glory) in his goodness, is thereby owned as a living temple.

II. The grateful return made to God for this gracious token of his favour.

1. The people *worshipped and praised God, v.* 3. When they saw the fire of God come down from heaven thus they did not run away affrighted, but kept their ground in the courts of the Lord, and took occasion from it, (1.) With reverence to adore the glory of God: *They bowed their faces to the ground and worshipped,* thus expressing their awful dread of the divine majesty, their cheerful submission to the divine authority, and the sense they had of their unworthiness to come into God's presence and their inability to stand before the power of his wrath. (2.) With thankfulness to acknowledge the goodness of God; even when the fire of the Lord came down they praised him, saying, *He is good, for his mercy endureth for ever.* This is a song never out of season, and for which our hearts and tongues should be never out of tune. However it be, yet God is good. When he manifests himself as a consuming fire to sinners, his people can rejoice in him as their light. Nay, they had reason to say that in this God was good. "*It is of the Lord's mercies that we are not consumed,* but the sacrifice in our stead, for which we are bound to be very thankful."

2. The king and all the people offered sacrifices in abundance, *v.* 4, 5. With these they feasted this holy fire, and bade it welcome to the altar. They had offered sacrifices before, but now they increased them. Note, The tokens of God's favour to us should enlarge our hearts in his service, and make us to abound therein more and more. The king's example stirred up the people. Good work is then likely to go on when the leaders of a people lead in it. The sacrifices were so numerous that the altar could not contain them all; but, rather than any of them should be turned back (though we may suppose the blood of them all was sprinkled upon the altar), the flesh of the burnt-offerings and the fat of the peace-offerings were burnt *in the midst of the court* (*v.* 7), which Solomon either hallowed for that service or hallowed by it. In case of necessity the pavement might be an altar.

3. The priests did their part; they waited on their offices, and the singers and musicians on theirs (*v.* 6), with the instruments that David made, and the *hymn that David had put into their hand,* as some think it may be read (meaning that 1 Chr. 16:7), or, as we read it, *when David praised by their ministry.* He employed, directed, and encouraged them in this work of praising God; and therefore their performances were accepted as his act, and he is said *to praise by their ministry.*

4. The whole congregation expressed the greatest joy and satisfaction imaginable. They kept the feast of the dedication of the altar seven days, from the second to the ninth; the tenth day was the day of atonement, when they were to afflict their souls for sin, and that was not unseasonable in the midst of their rejoicings; on the fifteenth day began the feast of tabernacles, which continued to the twenty-second, and they did not separate till the twenty-third. We must never grudge the time that we spend in the worship of God and communion with him, nor think it long, or grow weary of it.

5. Solomon went on in his work, and prosperously effected all he designed for the adorning both of God's house and his own, *v.* 11. Those that begin with the service of God are likely to go on successfully in their own affairs. It was Solomon's praise that what he undertook he went through with, and it was by the grace of God that he prospered in it.

Verses 12–22

That God accepted Solomon's prayer appeared by the fire from heaven. But a prayer may be accepted and yet not answered in the letter of it; and therefore God appeared to him in the night, as he did once before (*ch.* 1:7), and after a day of sacrifice too, as then, and gave him a peculiar answer to his prayer. We had the substance of it before, 1 Ki. 9:2–9.

I. He promised to own this house for *a house of sacrifice to Israel* and a *house of prayer for all people* (Isa. 56:7): *My name shall be there for ever* (*v.* 12, 16), that is, "There will I make myself known, and there will I be called upon."

II. He promised to answer the prayers of his people that should at any time be made in that place, *v.* 13–15. National judgments are here supposed (*v.* 13), famine, and pestilence, and perhaps war, for by the locusts devouring the land meant enemies as greedy as locusts, and laying all waste. 2. National repentance, prayer, and reformation, are required, *v.* 14. God expects that his people who are called by his name, if they have dishonoured his name by their iniquity, should honour it by accepting the punishment of their iniquity. They must be humble themselves under his hand, must pray for the removal of the judgment, must seek the face and favour of God; and yet all this will not do unless they turn from their wicked ways, and return to the God from whom they have revolted. 3. National mercy is then promised, that God will forgive their sin, which brought the judgment upon them, and then heal their land, redress all their grievances. Pardoning mercy makes ways for healing mercy, Ps. 103:3; Mt. 9:2.

III. He promised to perpetuate Solomon's kingdom, upon condition that he persevered in his duty, *v.* 17, 18. If he hoped for the benefit of God's covenant with David, he must imitate the example of David. But he set before him death as well as life, the curse as well as the blessing. 1. He supposed it possible that though they had this temple built to the honour of God, yet they might be drawn aside to worship other gods, *v.* 19. He knew their proneness to backslide into that sin. 2. He threatened it as certain that, if they did so, it would certainly be the ruin of both church and state. (1.) It would be the ruin of their state, *v.* 20. "Though they have taken deep root, and taken root long, in this good land, yet I will pluck them up by the roots, extirpate the whole nation, pluck them up as men pluck up weeds out of their garden, which are thrown to the dunghill." (2.) It would be the ruin of their church. This sanctuary would be no sanctuary to them, to protect them from the judgment of God, as they imagined, saying, *The temple of the Lord are we,* Jer. 7:4. "This house which is high, not only for the magnificence of its structure, but for the designed ends and uses of it, shall be an astonishment, it shall come down wonderfully (Lam. 1:9), to the amazement of all the neighbours."

CHAPTER 8

In this chapter we are told, I. What cities Solomon built (*v.* 1–6). II. What workmen Solomon employed (*v.* 7–10). III. What care he took about a proper settlement for his wife (*v.* 11). IV. What a good method he put the temple-service into (*v.* 12–16). V. What trading he had with foreign countries (*v.* 17, 18).

Verses 1–11

This we had 1 Ki. 9:10–24, and therefore shall only observe here,

I. Though Solomon was a man of great learning and knowledge, yet he spent his days, not in contemplation, but in action, not in his study, but in his country, in building cities and fortifying them, in a time of peace preparing for a time of war, which is as much a man's business as it is in summer to provide food for winter.

II. As he was a man of business himself, and did not consult his own ease, so he employed a great many hands, kept abundance of people to work. It is the interest of a state by all means possible to promote and encourage industry, and to keep its subjects from idleness. A great many strangers there were in Israel, many that remained of the Canaanites; and they were welcome to live there, but not to live and do nothing. The men of Laish, who had no business, were an easy prey to the invaders, Jdg. 18:7.

III. When Solomon had begun with building the house of God, and made good work and quick work of that, he prospered in all his undertakings, so that *he built all that he desired to build, v.* 6. Those who have a genius for building find that one project draws on another, and the latter must amend and improve the former. Now observe, 1. How the divine providence gratified even Solomon's humour, and gave him success, not only in all that he needed to build and that it was for his advantage to build, but in all that he had a mind to build. So indulgent a Father God is sometimes to the innocent desires of his children that serve him. Thus he pleased Jacob with that promise, *Joseph shall put his hand on thy eyes.* 2. Solomon knew how to set bounds to his desires. He was not one of those that enlarge them endlessly, and can never be satisfied, but knew when to draw in; for he finished all he desired, and then he desired no more. He did not sit down and fret that he had not more cities to build, as Alexander did that he had not more worlds to conquer, Hab. 2:5.

IV. That one reason why Solomon built a palace on purpose for the queen, and removed her and her court to it, was because he thought it by no means proper that she should *dwell in the house of David* (*v.* 11), considering that that had been a place of great piety, and perhaps her house was a place of great vanity. She was proselyted, it is likely, to the Jewish religion; but it is a question whether all her servants were. Perhaps they had among them the idols of Egypt, and a great deal of profaneness and debauchery. Now, though Solomon had not zeal and courage enough to suppress and punish what was amiss there, yet he so far consulted the honour of his father's memory that he would not suffer that place to be thus profaned where the ark of God had been and where holy David had prayed many a good prayer and sung many a sweet psalm. Not that all the places where the ark had been were so holy as never to be put to a common use; for then the houses of Abinadab and Obed-edom must have been so. But the place where it had been so long, and had been so publicly attended on, was so venerable that it was not fit to be the place of so much gaiety, not to say iniquity, as was to be found, I fear, in the court that Pharaoh's daughter kept. Note, Between things sacred and things common the ancient landmarks ought to be kept up. It was an outer-court of the temple that was the *court of the women.*

Verses 12–18

Here is, I. Solomon's devotion. The building of the temple was in order to the service of the temple. Whatever cost he was at in rearing the structure, if he had neglected the worship that was to be performed there, it would all have been to no purpose. Assisting the devotion of others will not atone for our own neglects. When Solomon had built the temple, 1. He kept up the holy sacrifices there, according to the law of Moses, *v.* 12, 13. In vain had the altar been built, and in vain had fire come down from heaven, if sacrifices had not been constantly brought as the food of the altar and the fuel of that fire. There were daily sacrifices, *a certain rate every day,* as duly as the day came, weekly sacrifices on the sabbath, double to what was offered on other days, monthly sacrifices *on the new moons,* and yearly sacrifices at the three solemn feasts. Those are spiritual sacrifices that are now required of us, which we are to bring daily and weekly; and it is good to be in a settled method of devotion. 2. He kept up the holy songs there, according to the *law of David,* who is here called the *man of God,* as Moses was, because he was both instructed and authorised of God to make these establishments; and Solomon took care to see them observed *as the duty of every day required, v.* 14. Solomon, though a wise and great man and the builder of the temple, did not attempt to amend, alter, or add to what the man of God had, in God's name, commanded, but closely adhered to that, and used his authority to have that duly observed; and then *none departed from the commandment of the king concerning any matter, v.* 15. He observed God's laws, and then all obeyed his orders. When the service of the temple was put into this good order, then it is said, *The house of the Lord was perfected, v.* 16. The work was the main matter, not the place; the temple was unfinished till all this was done.

II. Solomon's merchandise. He did himself in person visit the sea-port towns of Eloth and Ezion-geber; for those that deal much in the world will find it their interest, as far as they can, to inspect their affairs themselves and to see with their own eyes, *v.* 17. Canaan was a rich country, and yet must send to Ophir for gold; the Israelites were a wise and understanding people, and yet must be beholden to the king of Tyre for *men that had knowledge of the seas, v.* 18. Yet Canaan was God's peculiar land, and Israel God's peculiar people. This teaches us that grace, and not gold, is the best riches, and acquaintance with God and his law, not with arts and sciences, the best knowledge.

CHAPTER 9

Solomon here continues to appear great both at home and abroad. We had this account of his grandeur, 1 Ki. 10. Nothing is here added; but his defection towards his latter end, which we have there (*ch.* 11), is here omitted, and the close of this chapter brings him to the grave with an unstained reputation. Perhaps none of the chapters in the Chronicles agree so much with a chapter in the Kings as this does with 1 Ki. 10 verse for verse, only that the first two verses there are put into one here, and verse 25 here is taken from 1 Ki. 4:26, and the last three verses here from 1 Ki. 11:41–43. Here is, I. The honour which the queen of Sheba did to Solomon, in the visit she made him to hear his wisdom (*v.* 1–12). II. Many instances given of the riches and splendour of Solomon's court (*v.* 13–28). III. The conclusion of his reign (*v.* 29–31).

Verses 1–12

This passage of story had been largely considered in the Kings; yet, because our Saviour has proposed it as an example to us in our enquiries after him (Mt. 12:42), we must not pass it over without observing briefly, 1. *Those who honour God he will honour,* 1 Sa. 2:30. Solomon had greatly honoured God, in building, beautifying, and dedicating the temple; all his wisdom and all his wealth were employed for the making of that a consummate piece: and now God made his wisdom and wealth to redound greatly to his reputation. The way to have both the credit and comfort of all our endowments and all our enjoyments is to consecrate them to God and use them for him. 2. Those who know the worth of true wisdom will grudge no pains nor cost to obtain it. The queen of Sheba put herself to a great deal of trouble and expense to hear the wisdom of Solomon; and yet, learning from him to serve God and do her duty, she thought herself well paid for her pains. Heavenly wisdom is that *pearl of great price* which is a good bargain to purchase by parting with all that we have. 3. As every man has received the gift so he ought to minister the same for the edification of others, as he has opportunity. Solomon was communicative of his wisdom and willing to teach others what he knew himself. Being taught of God, freely he had received, and freely he gave. Let those that are rich in wisdom, as well as wealth, learn *to do good* and *be ready to distribute. Give to every one that asketh.* 4. Good order in a family, a great family, especially in the things of God, and a regular discharge of the duties of religious worship, are highly expedient, and to be much admired wherever found. The queen of Sheba was exceedingly affected to see the propriety with which Solomon's servants attended him and with which both he and they attended in the house of God. David's ascent to the house of the Lord was also pleasant and interesting, Ps. 42:4. 5. Those are happy who have the opportunity of a constant converse with such as are knowing, wise, and good. The queen of Sheba thought Solomon's servants happy who continually *heard his wisdom;* for, it seems, even to them he was communicative. And it is observable that the posterity of those who had places in his court were willing to have the names of their ancestors forgotten, and thought themselves sufficiently distinguished and dignified when they were called the *children of Solomon's servants* (Ezra 2:55; Neh. 7:57); so eminent were they that it was honour enough to be named from them. 6. We ought to rejoice and give God thanks for the gifts, graces, and usefulness, of others. The queen of Sheba blessed God for the honour he put upon Solomon, and the favour he did to Israel, in advancing him to the throne, *v.* 8. By giving God the praise of the prosperity of others, we share in the comfort of it; whereas, by envying the prosperity of others, we lose the comfort even of our own. The happiness of both king and kingdom she traces up to the fountain of all bliss, the divine favour: it was because *thy God delighted in thee* and because he *loved Israel.* Those mercies are doubly sweet in which we can taste the kindness and good will of God as our God. 7. It becomes those that are wise and good to be generous according to their place and power. The queen of Sheba was so to Solomon, Solomon was so to her, *v.* 9, 12. They both knew how to value wisdom, and therefore were neither of them covetous of their money, but cultivated the acquaintance and confirmed the friendship they had contracted by mutual presents. Our Lord Jesus has promised to give us all our desire: *Ask, and it shall be given you.* Let us study what we shall render to him, and not think any thing too much to do, or suffer, or part with, for him.

Verses 13–31

We have here Solomon in his throne, and Solomon in his grave; for the throne would not secure him from the grave. *Mors sceptra ligonibus aequat — Death wrenches from the hand the sceptre as well as the spade.*

I. Here is Solomon reigning in wealth and power, in ease and fulness, such as, for aught I know, could never since be paralleled by any king whatsoever. In cannot pretend to be critical in comparing the grandeur of Solomon with that of some of the great princes of the earth. But I may observe that the most illustrious of them were famed for their wars, whereas Solomon reigned forty years in profound peace. Some of those that might be thought to vie with Solomon affected retirement, kept people in awe by keeping them at a great distance; nobody must see them, or come near him, upon pain of death: but Solomon went much abroad, and appeared in public business. So that, all things considered, the promise was fulfilled, that God would give him riches, and wealth, and honour, such as no kings *have had, or shall have, ch.* 1:12. 1. Never any prince appeared in public with great splendour than Solomon did, which to those that judge by the sight of the eye, as most people do, would very much recommend him. He had 200 targets and 300 shields, all of beaten gold, carried before him (*v.* 15, 16), and sat upon a most stately throne, *v.* 17–19. *There was not the like in any kingdom.* The lustre wherein he appeared was typical of the spiritual glory of the kingdom of the Messiah and but a faint representation of his throne, which is above every throne. Solomon's pomp was all artificial; and therefore our Saviour prefers the natural beauty of the *lilies of the field* before it. Mt. 6:29, *Solomon, in all his glory, was not arrayed like one of these.* 2. Never any prince had greater plenty of gold and silver, though there were no gold or silver mines in his own kingdom. Either he made himself master of the mines in other countries, and, having a populous country, sent hands to dig out those rich metals, or, having a fruitful country, he exported the commodities of it and with them fetched home all this gold that is here spoken of, *v.* 13, 14–21. 3. Never any prince had such presents brought him by all his neighbours as Solomon had: *All the kings of Arabia, and governors of the country, brought him gold and silver* (*v.* 14), not as tribute which he extorted from them, but as freewill offerings to procure his favour, or in a way of exchange for some of the productions of his husbandry, corn or cattle. All the kings of the earth brought him presents, that is, all in those parts of the world (*v.* 24, 28), because they coveted his acquaintance and friendship. Herein he was a type of Christ, to whom, as soon as he was born, the wise men of the east brought presents, *gold, frankincense, and myrrh* (Mt. 2:11), and to whom all that are about him must bring presents, Ps. 76:11; Rom. 12:1. 4. Never any prince was so renowned for wisdom, so courted, so consulted, so admired (*v.* 23): *The kings of the earth* (for it was too great a favour for common persons to pretend to) *sought to hear his wisdom* — his natural philosophy, or his skill in physic, or his state policy, or his rules of prudence for the conduct of human life, or perhaps the principles of his religion, and the reasons of it. The application which they then made to Solomon to hear his wisdom will aggravate, shame, and condemn, men's general contempt of Christ and his gospel. Though in them are *hidden all the treasures of wisdom and knowledge, yet none of the princes of this world* desire to know them, for they are foolishness to them, 1 Co. 2:8, 14.

II. Here is Solomon dying, stripped of his pomp, and leaving all his wealth and power, not to one concerning whom he knew not *whether he would be a wise man or a fool* (Eccles. 2:19), but who he knew would be a fool. This was not only vanity but vexation of spirit, *v.* 29–31. It is very observable that no mention is here made of Solomon's departure from God in his latter days, not the least hint given of it, 1. Because the Holy Ghost would teach us not to take delight in repeating the faults and follies of others. If those that have been in reputation for wisdom and honour misbehave, though it may be of use to take notice of their misconduct for warning to ourselves and others, yet we must not be forward to mention it, once the speaking of it is enough; why should that unpleasing string be again struck upon? Why can we not do as the sacred historian here does, speak largely of that in others which is praise-worthy, without saying any thing of their blemishes, yea, though they have been gross and obvious? This is but doing as we would be done by. 2. Because, though he fell, yet he was not utterly cast down. His sin is not again recorded, because it was repented of, and pardoned, and became as if it had never been. Scripture-silence sometimes speaks. I am willing to believe that its silence here concerning the sin of Solomon is an intimation that none of the sins he committed were mentioned against him, Eze. 33:16. When God pardons sin he *casts it behind his back and remembers it no more.*

CHAPTER 10

This chapter is copied almost verbatim from 1 Ki. 12:1–19, where it was opened at large. Solomon's defection from God was not repeated, but the defection of the ten tribes from his family is, in this chapter, where we find, I. How foolish Rehoboam was in his treating with them (*v.* 1, 5–14). II. How wicked the people were in complaining of Solomon (*v.* 2–4). and forsaking Rehoboam (v 16–19). III. How just and righteous God was in all this (*v.* 15). His counsel was thereby fulfilled. With him are strength and wisdom; both the deceived and the deceiver (the fool and the knave) are his (Job 12:16), that is, are made use of by him to suit his purposes.

Verses 1–11

We may observe here, 1. The wisest and best cannot give every body content. Solomon enriched and advanced his kingdom, did all (one would think) that could be done to make then happy and easy; and yet either he was indiscreet in burdening them with the imposition of taxes and services, or at least there was some colour of reason to think him so. No man is perfectly wise. It is probable that it was when Solomon had declined from God and his duty that his wisdom failed him, and God left him to himself to act in this impolitic manner. Even Solomon's treasures were exhausted by his love of women; and probably it was to maintain them, and their pride, luxury, and idolatry, that he burdened his subjects. 2. Turbulent and ungrateful spirits will find fault with the government, and complain of grievances, when they have very little reason to do so. Had they not peace in Solomon's time? They were never plundered by invaders, as formerly, never put in fear by the alarms of war, nor obliged to hazard their lives in the high places of the field. Had they not plenty — meat enough, and money enough? What would they more? *O fortunatos nimium, sua si bona norint! — O happy, if they knew their happy state!* And yet they complain that Solomon made their yoke grievous. If any complain thus of the yoke of Christ, that they might have a pretence to break his bands in sunder and cast away his cords from them, we are sure that he never gave them any cause at all for the complaint, whatever Solomon did. *His yoke is easy, and his burden is light.* He never *made us serve with an offering, nor wearied us with incense.* 3. Many ruin themselves and their interests by trampling upon and provoking their inferiors. Rehoboam thought that because he was king he might assume as much authority as his father had done, might have what he would, and do what he would, and carry all before him. But, though he wore his father's crown, he wanted his father's brains, and ought to have considered that, being quite a different man from what his father was, he ought to take other measures. Such a wise man as Solomon may do as we will, but such a fool as Rehoboam must do as he can. The high-mettled horse may be kicked and spurred by him that has the art of managing him; but, if an unskilful horseman do it, it is at his peril. Rehoboam paid dearly for threatening, and talking big, and thinking to carry matters with a high hand. It was Job's wisdom, as well as his virtue, that he *despised not the cause of his man-servant or maid-servant,* when they argued with him (Job 31:13), but heard them patiently, considered their reasons, and gave them a soft answer. And a similar tender consideration of those in subjection, and a forwardness to make them easy, will be the comfort and praise of all in authority, in the church, in the state, and in families. 4. Moderate counsels are generally wisest and best. Gentleness will do what violence will not do. Most people love to be accosted mildly. Rehoboam's old experienced counsellors directed him to this method (*v.* 7): *"Be kind to this people, and please them, and speak good words to them,* and thou art sure of them for ever." Good words cost nothing but a little self-denial, and yet they purchase good things. 5. God often fulfils the counsels of his own wisdom by infatuating men, and giving them up to the counsels of their own folly. No more needs to be done to ruin men than to leave them to themselves, and their own pride and passion.

Verses 12–19

We may learn here, 1. That when public affairs are in a ferment violent proceedings do but make bad worse. Rough answers (such as Rehoboam here gave) do but stir up anger and bring oil to the flames. The pilot has need to steer steadily in a storm. Many have been driven to the mischief they did not intend by being too severely dealt with for what they did intend. 2. That, whatever the devices and designs of men are, God is, by all, doing his own work, and fulfilling the word which he has spoken, no iota or tittle of which shall fall to the ground. The cause of the king's obstinacy and thoughtlessness was *of God, that he might perform the word which he spoke by Ahijah, v.* 15. This does not at all excuse Rehoboam's folly, nor lessen the guilt of his haughtiness and passion, that God was pleased to serve his own ends by them. 3. That worldly wealth, honour, and dominion, are very uncertain things. *Solomon reigned over all Israel,* and, one would think, had done enough to secure the monarchy entire to his family for many ages; and yet he is scarcely cold in his grave before ten of the twelve tribes finally revolt from his son. All the good services he had done for Israel were now forgotten: *What portion have we in David?* Thus is the government of Christ cast off by many, notwithstanding all he has done to bind the children of men for ever to himself; they say, *We will not have this man to reign over us.* But this rebellion will certainly be their ruin. 4. That God often visits the iniquities of the fathers upon the children. Solomon forsakes God, and therefore not he, but his son after him, is forsaken by the greatest part of his people. Thus God, by making the penal consequences of sin to last long and visibly to continue after the sinner's death, would give an indication of its malignity, and perhaps some intimation of the perpetuity of its punishment. He that sins against God not only wrongs his soul, but perhaps wrongs his seed more than he thinks of. 5. That, when God is fulfilling his threatenings, he will take care of that, at the same time, promises do not fall to the ground. When Solomon's iniquity is remembered, and for it his son loses ten tribes, David's piety is not forgotten, nor the promise made to him; but for the sake of that his grandson had two tribes preserved to him. The failings of the saints shall not frustrate any promise made to Christ their Head. They shall be chastised, but the covenant not broken, Ps. 89:31–34.

CHAPTER 11

We are here going on with the history of Rehoboam. I. His attempt to recover the ten tribes he has lost, and the letting fall of that attempt in obedience to the divine command (*v.* 1–4). II. His successful endeavours to preserve the two tribes that remained (*v.* 5–12). III. The resort of the priests and Levites to him (*v.* 13–17). IV. An account of his wives and children (*v.* 18–23).

Verses 1–12

How the ten tribes deserted the house of David we read in the foregoing chapter. They had formerly sat loose to that family (2 Sa. 20:1, 2), and now they quite threw it off, not considering how much it would weaken the common interest and take Israel down from that pitch of glory at which it had arrived in the last reign. But thus the *kingdom* must be corrected as well as the *house* of David. 1. Rehoboam at length, like a bold man, raises an army, with a design to reduce the revolters, *v.* 1. Judah and Benjamin were not only resolved to continue their allegiance to him, but ready to give him the best assistance they could for the recovery of his right. Judah was his own tribe, that owned him some years before the rest did; Benjamin was the tribe in which Jerusalem, or the greatest part of it, stood, which perhaps was one reason why that tribe clave to him. 2. Yet, like a conscientious man, when God forbade him to prosecute this design, in obedience to him he let it fall, either because he reverenced the divine authority or because he knew that he should not prosper if he should go contrary to God's command, but instead of retrieving what was lost would be in danger of losing what he had. It is dangerous undertaking any thing, but especially undertaking a war, contrary to the will of God. God calls him (*v.* 3), *Rehoboam the son of Solomon,* to intimate that this was determined for the sin of Solomon, and it would be to no purpose to oppose a decree that had gone forth. They *obeyed the words of the Lord;* and though it looked mean, and would turn to their reproach among their neighbours, yet, because God would have it so, they laid down their arms. 3. Like a discreet man, he fortified his own country. He saw it was to no purpose to think of reducing those that had revolted. A few good words might have prevented their defection, but now all the forces of his kingdom cannot bring them back. The think is done, and so it must rest; it is his wisdom to make the best of it. Perhaps the same young counsellors that had advised him to answer them roughly urged him to fight them, notwithstanding the divine inhibition; but he had paid dearly enough for being advised by them, and therefore now, we may suppose, his aged and experienced counsellors were hearkened to, and they advised him to submit to the will of God concerning what was lost, and to make it his business to keep what he had. It was probably by their advice that, (1.) He fortified his frontiers, and many of the principal cities of his kingdom, which, in Solomon's peaceable reign, no care had been taken for the defence of. (2.) He furnished them with good stores of victuals and arms, *v.* 11, 12. Because God forbade him to fight, he did not therefore sit down sullenly, and say that he would do nothing for the public safety if he might not do that, but prudently provided against an attack. Those that may not be conquerors, yet may be builders.

Verses 13–23

See here,

I. How Rehoboam was strengthened by the accession of the priests and Levites, and all the devout and pious Israelites, to him, even all that were true to their God and their religion.

1. Jeroboam cast them off, that is, he set up such a way of worship as he knew they could not in conscience comply with, which obliged them to withdraw from his altar, and at the same time he would not allow them to go up to Jerusalem to worship at the altar there; so that he totally *cast them off from executing the priest's office, v.* 14. And very willing he was that they should turn themselves out of their places, that room might be made for those mean and scandalous persons whom he *ordained priests for the high places, v.* 15. Compare 1 Ki. 12:31. No marvel if he that cast off God cast off his ministers; they were not for his purpose, would not do whatever he might bid them do, would not *serve his gods, nor worship the golden image which he had set up.*

2. They thereupon *left their suburbs and possessions, v.* 14. Out of the lot of each tribe the Levites had cities allowed them, where they were comfortable provided for and had opportunity of doing much good. But now they were driven out of all their cities except those in Judah and Benjamin. One would think their maintenance well settled, and yet they lost it. It was a comfort to them that the law so often reminded them that the *Lord was their inheritance,* and so they should find him when they were turned out of their house and possessions. But why did they leave their possessions? (1.) Because they saw they could do no good among their neighbours, in whom (now that Jeroboam set up his calves) the old proneness to idolatry revived. (2.) Because they themselves would be in continual temptation to some base compliances, and in danger of being drawn insensibly to that which was evil. If we pray, in sincerity, not to be led into temptation, we shall get and keep as far as we can out of the way of it. (3.) Because, if they retained their integrity, they had reason to expect persecution from Jeroboam and his sons. The priests they made for the devils would not let the Lord's priests be long among them. No secular advantages whatsoever should draw us thither, or detain us there, where we are in danger of making shipwreck of faith and a good conscience.

3. They *came to Judah and Jerusalem* (*v.* 14) and *presented themselves to Rehoboam, v.* 13, *margin.* Where should God's priests and Levites be, but where his altar was? Thither they came because it was their business to attend at the times appointed. (1.) It was a mercy to them that they had a place of refuge to flee to, and that when Jeroboam cast them off there were those so near that would entertain them, and bid them welcome, and they were not forced into the lands of the heathen. (2.) It was an evidence that they loved their work better than their maintenance, in that they *left their suburbs and possessions in the country* (where they might have lived at ease upon their own), because they were restrained from serving God there, and cast themselves upon God's providence and the charity of their brethren in coming to a place where they might have the free enjoyment of God's ordinances, according to his institution. Poverty in the way of duty is to be chosen rather than plenty in the way of sin. Better live upon alms, or die in a prison, with a good conscience, than roll in wealth and pleasure with a prostituted one. (3.) It was the wisdom and praise of Rehoboam and his people that they bade them welcome, though they crowded themselves perhaps to make room for them. Conscientious refugees will bring a blessing along with them to the countries that entertain them, as they leave a curse behind them with those that expel them. *Open the gates, that the righteous nation, which keepeth truth, may enter in;* it will be good policy. See Isa. 26:1, 2.

4. When the priests and Levites came to Jerusalem all the devout pious Israelites of every tribe followed them. Such as *set their hearts to seek the Lord God of Israel,* that made conscience of their duty to God and were sincere and resolute in it, left the inheritance of their fathers and went and took houses in Jerusalem, that they might have free access to the altar of God and be out of the temptation to worship the calves, *v.* 16. Note, (1.) That is best for us which is best for our souls; and, in all our choices, advantages for religion must take place of all outward conveniences. (2.) Where God's faithful priests are his faithful people should be. If Jeroboam cast off God's ministers,

every true-born Israelite will think himself obliged to own them and stand by them. *Forsake not the Levite,* the outcast Levite, *as long as thou livest.* When *the ark removes do you remove and go after it,* Jos. 3:3.

5. They *strengthened the kingdom of Judah* (*v.* 17), not only by the addition of so many persons to it, who, it is likely, brought what they could of their effects with them, but by their piety and their prayers they procured a blessing upon the kingdom which was a sanctuary to them. See Zec. 12:5. It is the interest of a nation to protect and encourage religion and religious people, and adds more than any thing to its strength. They made him and his people *strong three years;* for so long they *walked in the way of David and Solomon,* their *good* way. But when they forsook that, and so threw themselves out of God's favour and protection, the best friends they had could no longer help to strengthen them. We retain our strength while we cleave to God and our duty, and no longer.

II. How Rehoboam was weakened by indulging himself in his pleasures. He *desired many wives,* as his father did (*v.* 23), yet, 1. In *this* he was more wise than his father, that he does not appear to have married strange wives. The wives mentioned here were not only daughters of Israel, but of the family of David; one was a descendant from Eliab, David's brother (*v.* 18), another from Absalom, probably that Absalom who was David's son (*v.* 20), another from Jerimoth, David's son. 2. In *this* he was more happy than his father, that he had many sons and daughters; whereas we read not of more than one son that his father had. One can scarcely imagine that he had no more; but, if he had, they were not worth mentioning; whereas several of Rehoboam's sons are here named (*v.* 19, 20) as men of note, and such active men that he thought it his wisdom to *disperse them throughout the countries of Judah and Benjamin* (*v.* 23), either, (1.) That they might not be rivals with his son Abijah, whom he designed for his successor, or rather, (2.) Because he could repose a confidence in them for the preserving of the public peace and safety, could trust them with fenced cities, which he took care to have well victualled, that they might stand him in stead in case of an invasion. After-wisdom is better than none at all; nay, they say, "Wit is never good till it is bought;" though he was dearly bought with the loss of a kingdom.

CHAPTER 12

This chapter gives us a more full account of the reign of Rehoboam than we had before in Kings and it is a very melancholy account. Methinks we are in the book of Judges again; for, I. Rehoboam and his people did evil in the sight of the Lord (*v.* 1). II. God thereupon sold them into the hands of Shishak, king of Egypt, who greatly oppressed them (*v.* 2–4) III. God sent a prophet to them, to expound to them the judgment and to call them to repentance (*v.* 5). IV. They thereupon humbled themselves (*v.* 6). V. God, upon their repentance, turned from his anger (*v.* 7, 12) and yet left them under the marks of his displeasure (*v.* 8–11). Lastly, Here is a general character of Rehoboam and his reign, with the conclusion of it (*v.* 13–16).

Verses 1–12

Israel was very much disgraced and weakened by being divided into two kingdoms; yet the kingdom of Judah, having both the temple and the royal city, both the house of David and the house of Aaron, might have done very well if they had continued in the way of their duty; but here we have all out of order there.

I. Rehoboam and his people left God: He *forsook the law of the Lord,* and so in effect forsook God, and *all Israel with him, v.* 1. He had his happy triennium, when he walked in the way of David and Solomon (*ch.* 11:17), but it expired, and he grew remiss in the worship of God; in what instances we are not told, but he fell off, and Judah with him, here called *Israel,* because they walked in the evil ways into which Jeroboam had drawn the kingdom of Israel. Thus he did *when he had established the kingdom and strengthened himself.* As long as he thought his throne tottered he kept to his duty, that he might make God his friend; but, when he found it stood pretty firmly, he thought he had no more occasion for religion; he was safe enough without it. Thus *the prosperity of fools destroys them. Jeshurun waxed fat and kicked.* When men prosper, and are in no apprehension of troubles, they are ready to say to God, *Depart from us.*

II. God quickly brought troubles upon them, to awaken them, and recover them to repentance, before their hearts were hardened. It was but in the fourth year of Rehoboam that they began to corrupt themselves, and in the fifth year the king of Egypt came up against them with a vast army, took *the fenced cities of Judah, and came against Jerusalem, v.* 2, 3, 4. This great calamity coming upon them so soon after they began to desert the worship of God, by a hand they had little reason to suspect (having had a great deal of friendly correspondence with Egypt in the last reign), and coming with so much violence that all the *fenced cities of Judah,* which Rehoboam had lately fortified and garrisoned and on which he relied much for the safety of his kingdom, fell immediately into the hands of the enemy, without making any resistance, plainly showed that it was from the Lord, because they had transgressed against him.

III. Lest they should not readily or not rightly understand the meaning of this providence, God by the word explains the rod, *v.* 5. When the princes of Judah had all met at Jerusalem, probably in a great council of war, to concert measures for their own safety in this critical juncture, he sent a prophet to them, the same that had brought them an injunction from God not to fight against the ten tribes (*ch.* 11:2), Shemaiah by name; he told them plainly that the reason why Shishak prevailed against them was not because they had been impolitic in the management of their affairs (which perhaps the princes in this congress were at this time scrutinizing), but because they had forsaken God. God never leaves any till they first leave him.

IV. The rebukes both of the word and of the rod being thus joined, the king and princes humbled themselves before God for their iniquity, penitently acknowledged the sin, and patiently accepted the punishment of it, saying, *The Lord is righteous, v.* 6. "We have none to blame but ourselves; let God be clear when he judgeth." Thus it becomes us, when we are under the rebukes of Providence, to justify God and judge ourselves. Even kings and princes must either bend or break before God, either be humbled or be ruined.

V. Upon the profession they made of repentance God showed them some favour, saved them from ruin, and yet left them under some remaining fears of the judgment, to prevent their revolt again.

1. God, in mercy, prevented the destruction they were now upon the brink of. Such a vast and now victorious army as Shishak had, having made themselves masters of all the fenced cities, what could be expected but that the whole country, and even Jerusalem itself, would in a little time be theirs? But when God saith, *Here shall the proud waves be stayed,* the most threatening force strangely dwindles and becomes impotent. Here again the destroying angel, when he comes to Jerusalem, is forbidden to destroy it: *"My wrath shall not be poured out upon Jerusalem;* not at this time, not by this hand, not utterly to destroy it," *v.* 7, 12. Note, Those that acknowledge God righteous in afflicting them shall find him gracious. Those that humble themselves before him shall find favour with him. So ready is the God of mercy to take the first occasion to show mercy. If we have humbled hearts under humbling providences, the affliction has done its work, and it shall either be removed or the property of it altered.

2. He granted them some deliverance, not complete, but in part; he gave them some advantages against the enemy, so that they recruited a little; he *gave them deliverance for a little while,* so some. They reformed but partially, and for a little while, soon relapsing again; and, as their reformation was, so was their deliverance. Yet it is said (*v.* 12), *in Judah things went well,* and began to look with a better face. (1.) In respect of piety. *There were good things in Judah* (so it is in the margin), good ministers, good people, good families, who were made better by the calamities of their country. Note, In times of great corruption and degeneracy it is some comfort if there be a remnant among whom good things ar found; this is a ground of hope in Israel. (2.) In respect of prosperity. In Judah things went ill when all the fenced cities were taken (*v.* 4), but when they repented the posture of their affairs altered, and things went well. Note, If things do not go so well as we could wish, yet we have reason to take notice of it with thankfulness if they go better than was to have been expected, better than formerly, and better than we deserved. We should own God's goodness if he do but grant us some deliverance.

3. Yet he left them to smart sorely by the hand of Shishak, both in their liberty and in their wealth.

(1.) In their liberty (*v.* 8): *They shall be his servants* (that is, they shall lie much at his mercy and be put under contribution by him, and some of them perhaps be taken prisoners and held in captivity by him), *that they may know my service, and the service of the kingdoms of the countries.* They complained, it may be, of the strictness of their religion, and *forsook the law of the Lord* (*v.* 1) because they thought it a yoke to hard, too heavy, upon them. "Well," saith God, "let them better themselves if they can; let the neighbouring princes rule them awhile, since they are not willing that I should rule them, and let them try how they like that. They might have *served God with joyfulness and gladness of heart,* and would not; let them *serve their enemies then in hunger and thirst* (Deu. 28:47, 48), till they think of returning to *their first Master, for then it was better with them,"* Hos. 2:7. This, some think, is the meaning of Eze. 20:24, 25. *Because they despised my statutes, I gave them statutes that were not good.* Note, [1.] The more God's service is compared with other services the more reasonable and easy it will appear. [2.] Whatever difficulties or hardships we may imagine there are in the way of obedience, it is better a thousand times to go through them than to expose ourselves to the punishment of disobedience. Are the laws of temperance thought hard? The effects of intemperance will be much harder. The service of virtue is perfect liberty; the service of lust is perfect slavery.

(2.) In their wealth. The king of Egypt plundered both the temple and the exchequer, the treasuries of both which Solomon left very full; but he *took them away;* yea, he *took all,* all he could lay his hands on, *v.* 9. This was what he came for. David and Solomon, who walked in the way of God, filled the treasuries, one by war and the other by merchandise; but Rehoboam, who forsook the law of God, emptied them. The taking away of the golden shields, and the substituting of brazen ones in their place (*v.* 9–11), we had an account of before, 1 Ki. 14:25–28.

Verses 13–16

The story of Rehoboam's reign is here concluded, much as the story of the other reigns concludes. Two things especially are observable here: — 1. That he was at length pretty well *fixed in his kingdom, v.* 13. His fenced cities in Judah did not answer his expectation, so he now *strengthened himself in Jerusalem,* which he made it his business to fortify, and there he reigned seventeen years, in *the city which the Lord had chosen to put his name there.* This intimates his honour and privilege, that he had his royal seat in the holy city, which yet was but an aggravation of his impiety — near the temple, but far from God. Frequent skirmishes there were between his subjects and Jeroboam's, such as amounted to *continual wars,* (*v.* 15), but he held his own, and reigned, and, as it should seem, did not so grossly *forsake the law of God* as he had done (*v.* 1) in his fourth year. 2. That he was never rightly fixed in his religion, *v.* 14. He never quite cast off God; and yet in this he did evil, that he *prepared not, he engaged not, his heart to seek the Lord.* See what the fault is laid upon. (1.) He did not serve the Lord because he did not seek the Lord. He did not pray, as Solomon did, for wisdom and grace. If we prayed better, we should be every way better. Or he did not consult the word of God, did not seek to that as his oracle, nor take directions from it. (2.) He made nothing of his religion because he did not set his heart to it, never minded it with any closeness of application, and never any hearty disposition to it, nor ever came up to a steady resolution in it. What little goodness he had was transient and passed away like the morning cloud. He did evil because he was never determined for that which is good. Those are easily drawn by Satan to any evil who are wavering and inconstant in that which is good and are never persuaded to make religion their business.

999

CHAPTER 13

We have here a much fuller account of the reign of Abijah, the son of Rehoboam, than we had in the Kings. There we found that his character was no better than his father's — he "walked in the sins of his father, and his heart was not right with God," 1 Ki. 25:2, 3. But here we find him more brave and successful in war than his father was. He reigned but three years, and was chiefly famous for a glorious victory he obtained over the forces of Jeroboam. Here we have, I. The armies brought into the field on both sides (*v.* 3). The remonstrance which Abijah made before the battle, setting forth the justice of his cause (v. 4–12). III. The distress which Judah was brought into by the policy of Jeroboam (v. 13, 14). IV. The victory they obtained notwithstanding, by the power of God (v. 15–20). V. The conclusion of Abijah's reign (v. 21, 22).

Verses 1–12

Abijah's mother was called *Maachah,* the daughter of Absalom, *ch.* 11:20; here she is called *Michaiah,* the daughter of Uriel. It is most probable that she was a granddaughter of Absalom, by his daughter Tamar (2 Sa. 14:27), and that her immediate father was this Uriel. But we are here to attend Abijah into the field of battle with Jeroboam king of Israel.

I. God gave him leave to engage with Jeroboam, and owned him in the conflict, though he would not permit Rehoboam to do it, *ch.* 11:4. 1. Jeroboam, it is probable, was now the aggressor, and what Abijah did was in his own necessary defence. Jeroboam, it may be, happening to survive Rehoboam, claimed the crown of Judah be survivorship, at least hoped to get it from this young king, upon his accession to the throne. Against these impudent pretensions it was brave in Abijah to take up arms, and God stood by him. 2. When Rehoboam attempted to recover his ten tribes Jeroboam was upon his good behaviour, and there must be some trial of him; but now that he had discovered what manner of man he was, by setting up the calves and casting off the priests, Abijah is allowed to chastise him, and it does not appear that he intended any more; whereas Rehoboam aimed at no less than the utter reduction of the ten tribes, which was contrary to the counsel of God.

II. Jeroboam's army was double in number to that of Abijah (v. 3), for he had ten tribes to raise an army out of, while Abijah had but two. Of the army on both sides it is said, they were *mighty men, chosen men,* and *valiant;* but the army of Judah consisted only of 400,000, while Jeroboam's army amounted to 800,000. The inferior number however proved victorious; for the battle is not always to the strong nor the cause to the majority.

III. Abijah, before he fought them, reasoned with them, to persuade them, though not to return to the house of David (that matter was settled by the divine determination and he acquiesced), yet to desist from fighting against the house of David. He would not have them *withstand the kingdom of the Lord in the hands of the sons of David* (v. 8), but at least to be content with what they had. Note, It is good to try reason before we use force. If the point may be gained by dint of argument, better so than by dint of sword. We must never fly to violent methods till all the arts of persuasion have been tried in vain. War must be the *ultima ratio regum — the last resort of kings.* Fair reasoning may do a great deal of good and prevent a good deal of mischief. *How forcible are right words!* Abijah had got with his army into the heart of their country; for he made this speech upon a hill in Mount Ephraim, where he might be heard by Jeroboam and the principal officers, with whom it is probable he desired to have a treaty, to which they consented. It has been usual for great generals to make speeches to their soldiers to animate them, and this speech of Abijah had some tendency to do this, but was directed to Jeroboam and all Israel. Two things Abijah undertakes to make out, for the satisfaction of his own men and the conviction of the enemy: —

1. That he had right on his side, a *jus divinum — a divine right:* "You know, or ought to know, that *God gave the kingdom to David and his sons for ever"* (v. 5), not by common providence, his usual way of disposing of kingdoms, but by a covenant of salt, a lasting covenant, a covenant made by sacrifice, which was always salted; so bishop Patrick. All Israel had owned that David was a king of God's making, and that God had entailed the crown upon his family; so that Jeroboam's taking the crown of Israel at first was not justifiable: yet it is not certain that Abijah referred chiefly to that, for he knew that Jeroboam had a grant from God of the ten tribes. His attempt, however, to disturb the peace and possession of the king of Judah was by no means excusable; for when the ten tribes were given to him two were reserved for the house of David. Abijah shows, (1.) That there was a great deal of dishonesty and disingenuousness in Jeroboam's first setting himself up: He *rebelled against his lord* (v. 6) who had preferred

him (1 Ki. 11:28), and basely took advantage of Rehoboam's weakness in a critical juncture, when, in gratitude to his old master and in justice to his title, he ought rather to have stood by him, and helped to secure the people in their allegiance to him, than to head a party against him and make a prey of him, which was unworthily done and what he could not expect to prosper in. Those that supported him are here called *vain men* (a character perhaps borrowed from Jdg. 11:3), men that did not act from any steady principle, but were given to change, and men of Belial, that were for shaking off the yoke of government and setting those over them that would do just as they would have them do. (2.) That there was a great deal of impiety in his present attempt; for, in fighting against the house of David, he fought *against the kingdom of the Lord.* Those who oppose right oppose the righteous God who sits in the throne judging right, and cannot promise themselves success in so doing. Right may indeed go by the worst for a time, but it will prevail at last.

2. That he had God on his side. This he insisted much upon, that the religion of Jeroboam and his army was false and idolatrous, but that he and his people, the men of Judah, had the pure worship of the true and living God among them. It appears from the character given of Abijah (1 Ki. 15:3) that he was not himself in this war chiefly from the religion of his kingdom. For, (1.) Whatever he was otherwise, it should seem that he was no idolator, or, if he connived at the high places and images (*ch.* 14:3, 5), yet he constantly kept up the temple-service. (2.) Whatever corruptions there were in the kingdom of Judah, the state of religion among them was better than in the kingdom of Israel, with which they were now contending. (3.) It is common for those that deny the power of godliness to boast of the form of it. (4.) It was the cause of his kingdom that he was pleading; and, though he was not himself so good as he should have been, yet he hoped that, for the sake of the good men and good things that were in Judah, God would now appear for them. Many that have little religion themselves yet have so much sense and grace as to value it in others. See how he describes, [1.] The apostasy of Israel from God. *"You are a great multitude,"* said he, "far superior to us in number; but we need not fear you, for you have that among yourselves which is enough to ruin you. For," *First,* "You have calves for your gods (v. 8), that are unable to protect and help you and will certainly cause the true and living God to oppose you. Those will be Achans, troublers of your camp." *Secondly,* "You have base men for your priests, v. 9. You have cast off the tribes of Levi, and the house of Aaron, whom God appointed to minister in holy things; and, in conformity to the custom of the idolatrous nations, make any man a priest that has a mind to the office and will be at the charge of the consecration, though ever so much a scandal to the office." Yet such, though very unfit to be priests, were fittest of all to be *their* priests; for what more agreeable to gods that were no gods than priests that were no priests? Like to like, both pretenders and usurpers. [2.] The adherence of Judah to God: *"But as for us* (v. 10) *we have not forsaken God.* Jehovah is our God, the God of our fathers, the God of Israel, who is able to protect us, and give us success. He is with us, for we are with him." *First,* "At home in his temple: We *keep his charge, v.* 10, 11. We worship no images, have no priests but what he has ordained, no rites of worship but what he has prescribed. Both the temple service and the temple furniture are of his appointing. His appointment we abide by, and neither add nor diminish. These we have the comfort of, these we now stand up in the defence of: so that upon a religious as well as a civil account we have the better cause. *Secondly,* Here in the camp; he is our captain, and we may therefore be sure that he is with us, because we are with him, v. 12. And, as a token of his presence, we have here with us his priests, sounding his trumpets according to the law, as a testimony against you, and an assurance to us that in the day of battle we shall be *remembered before the Lord our God and saved from our enemies;"* for so this sacred signal is explained, Num. 10:9. Nothing is more effectual to embolden men, and put spirit into them, than to be sure that God is with them and fights for them. He concludes with fair warning to his enemies. *"Fight not against the God of your fathers.* It is folly to fight against the God of almighty power; but it is treachery and base ingratitude to

fight against your fathers' God, and you cannot expect to prosper."

Verses 13–22

We do not find that Jeroboam offered to make any answer at all to Abijah's speech. Though it was much to the purpose, he resolved not to heed it, and therefore he heard it as though he heard it not. He came to fight, not to dispute. The longest sword, he thought, would determine the matter, not the better cause. Let us therefore see the issue, whether right and religion carried the day or no.

I. Jeroboam, who trusted to his politics, was beaten. He was so far from fair reasoning that he was not for fair fighting. We may suppose that he felt a sovereign contempt for Abijah's harangue. "One stratagem," thinks he, "is worth twenty such speeches; we will soon give him an answer to all his arguments; he shall soon find himself overpowered with numbers, surrounded on every side with the instruments of death, and then let him boast of his religion and his title to the crown." A parley, it is probable, was agreed on, yet Jeroboam basely takes the advantage of it, and, while he was treating, *laid his ambushment behind Judah,* against all the laws of arms. What honour could be expected in a *servant when he reigned?* Abijah was *for peace,* but, *when he spoke, they were for war,* Ps. 120:7.

II. Abijah and his people, who trusted in their God, came off conquerors, notwithstanding the disproportion of their strength and numbers.

1. They were brought into a great strait, put into a great fright, for *the battle was before and behind.* A good cause, and one which is designed to be victorious, may for a season be involved in embarrassment and distress. It was David's case. *They compassed me about like bees,* Ps. 118:10–12.

2. In their distress, when danger was on every side, which way should they look but upwards for deliverance? It is an unspeakable comfort that no enemy (not the most powerful or politic), no stratagem or ambushment, can cut off our communication with heaven; our way thitherward is always open. (1.) *They cried unto the Lord, v.* 14. We hope they did this before they engaged in this war, but the distress they were in made them renew their prayers and quickened them to be importunate. God brings his people into straits, that he may teach them to *cry unto him.* Earnest praying is crying. (2.) They *relied on the God of their fathers,* depended upon his power to help them and committed themselves to him, v. 18. The prayer of faith is the prevailing prayer, and this is that by which we overcome the world, *even our faith,* 1 Jn. 5:4. (3.) The *priests sounded the trumpets* to animate them by giving them an assurance of God's presence with them. It was not only a martial but a sacred sound, and put life into their faith. (4.) They shouted in confidence of victory: "The day is our own, for God is with us." To the cry of the prayer they added the shout of faith, and so became more than conquerors.

3. Thus they obtained a complete victory: As the men of Judah *shouted* for joy in God's salvation, *God smote Jeroboam* and his army with such terror and amazement that they could not strike a stroke, but fled with the greatest precipitation imaginable, and the conquerors gave no quarter, so that they put to the sword 500,000 chosen men (v. 17), more, it is said, than ever we read of in any history to have been killed in one battle; but the battle was the Lord's, who would thus chastise the idolatry of Israel and own the house of David. But see the sad effect of division: it was the blood of Israelites that was thus shed like water by Israelites, while the heathen, their neighbours, to whom the name of Israel had formerly been a terror, cried, *Aha! so would we have it.*

4. The consequence of this was that the children of Israel, though they were not brought back to the house of David (which by so great a blow surely they would have been had not the determinate counsel of God been otherwise), yet, for that time, were *brought under, v.* 18. Many cities were taken, and remained in the possession of the kings of Judah; as Bethel particularly, v. 19. What became of the golden calf there, when it came into the hands of the king of Judah, we are not told; perhaps it was removed to some place of greater safety, and at length to Samaria (Hos. 8:5); yet in Jehu's time we find it at Bethel, 2 Ki. 10:29. Perhaps Abijah, when it was in his power to demolish it,

suffered it to stand, for *his heart was not perfect* with God; and, not improving what he had got for the honour of God, he soon lost it all again.

Lastly, The death of both of the conquered and of the conqueror, not long after. 1. Jeroboam never looked up after this defeat, though he survived it two or three years. He could not recover *strength again, v.* 20. The Lord struck him either with some bodily disease, of which he languished, or with melancholy and trouble of mind; his heart was broken, and vexation at his loss brought his head, probably by this time a hoary head, with sorrow to the grave. He escaped the sword of Abijah, but God struck him: and there is no escaping his sword. 2. Abijah waxed mighty upon it. What number of wives and children he had before does not appear; but now he multiplied his wives to fourteen in all, by whom he had thirty-eight children, *v.* 21. Happy is the man that hath his quiver full of those arrows. It seems, he had ways peculiar to himself, and sayings of his own, which were recorded with his acts in the history of those times, *v.* 22. But the number of his months was cut off in the midst, and, soon after his triumphs, death conquered the conqueror. Perhaps he was too much lifted up with his victories, and therefore God would not let him live long to enjoy the honour of them.

CHAPTER 14

In this and the two following chapters we have the history of the reign of Asa, a good reign and a long one. In this chapter we have, I. His piety (*v.* 1–5). II. His policy (*v.* 6–8). III. His prosperity, and particularly a glorious victory he obtained over a great army of Ethiopians that came out against him (*v.* 9–15).

Verses 1–8

Here is, I. Asa's general character (*v.* 2): He did *that which was good and right in the eyes of the Lord his God.* 1. He aimed at pleasing God, studied to approve himself to him. Happy are those that walk by this rule, to do that which is right, not in their own eyes, or in the eye of the world, but in the eyes of God. 2. He saw God's eye always upon him, and that helped much to keep him to what was good and right. 3. God graciously accepted him in what he did, and approved his conduct as good and right.

II. A blessed work of reformation which he set on foot immediately upon his accession to the crown. 1. He removed and abolished idolatry. Since Solomon admitted idolatry, in the latter end of his reign, nothing had been done to suppress it, and so, we presume, it had got ground. Strange gods were worshipped and had their altars, images, and groves; and the temple service, though kept up by the priests (*ch.* 13:10), was neglected by many of the people. Asa, as soon as he had power in his hands, made it his business to destroy all those idolatrous altars and images (*v.* 3, 5), they being a great provocation to a jealous God and a great temptation to a careless unthinking people. He hoped by destroying the idols to reform the idolaters, which he aimed at, rather than to ruin them. 2. He revived and established the pure worship of God; and, since the priests did their part in attending God's altars, he obliged the people to do theirs (*v.* 4): *He commanded Judah to seek the Lord God of their fathers,* and not the gods of the heathen, and *to do the law and the commandments,* that is, to observe all divine institutions, which many had utterly neglected. In doing this, *the land was quiet before him, v.* 5. Though they were much in love with their idols, and very loth to leave them, yet the convictions of their consciences sided with the commands of Asa, and they could not, for shame, refuse to comply with them. Note, Those that have power in their hands, and will use it vigorously for the suppression of profaneness and the reformation of manners, will not meet with so much difficulty and opposition therein as perhaps they feared. Vice is a sneaking thing, and virtue has reason enough on its side to make *all iniquity stop her mouth,* Ps. 107:42.

III. The tranquillity of his kingdom, after constant alarms of war during the last two reigns: *In his days the land was quiet ten years* (*v.* 1), no war with the kingdom of Israel, who did not recover the blow given them in the last reign for a great while. Abijah's victory, which was owing, under God, to his courage and bravery, laid a foundation for Asa's peace, which was the reward of his piety and reformation. Though Abijah had little religion himself, he was instrumental to prepare the way for one that had much. If Abijah had not done what he did to quiet the land, Asa could not have done what he did to reform it; for *inter arma silent leges — amidst the din of arms the voice of law is unheard.*

IV. The prudent improvement he made of that tranquillity: *The land had rest, for the Lord had given him rest.* Note, *If God give quietness, who then can make trouble?* Job 34:29. Those have rest indeed to whom God gives rest, peace indeed to whom Christ gives peace, *not as the world giveth,* Jn. 14:27. Now, 1. Asa takes notice of the rest they had as the gift of God (*He hath given us rest on every side.* Note, God must be acknowledged with thankfulness in the rest we are blessed with, of body and mind, family and country), and as the reward of the reformation begun: *Because we have sought the Lord our God, he has given us rest.* Note, As the frowns and rebukes of Providence should be observed for a check to us in an evil way, so the smiles of Providence should be taken notice of for our encouragement in that which is good. See Hag. 2:18, 19; Mal. 3:10. We find by experience that it is good to *seek the Lord;* it *gives us rest.* While we pursue the world we meet with nothing but vexation. 2. He consults with his people, by their representatives, how to make a good use of the present gleams of peace they enjoyed, and concludes with them, (1.) That they must not be idle, but busy. Times of rest from war should be employed in work, for we must always find ourselves something to do. In the years when he had no war he said, "Let us build; still let us be doing." When the *churches had rest* they were *built up,* Acts 9:31. When the sword is sheathed take up the trowel. (2.) That they must not be secure, but prepare for wars. In times of peace we must be getting ready for trouble, expect it and lay up in store for it. [1.] He fortified his principle cities with *walls, towers, gates, and bars, v.* 7. "This let us do," says he, *"while the land is yet before us,"* that is, "while we have opportunity and advantage for it and have nothing to hinder us." He speaks as if he expected that, some way or other, trouble would arise, when it would be too late to fortify, and when they would wish they had done it. *So they built and prospered.* [2.] He had a good army ready to bring into the field (*v.* 8), not a standing army, but the militia or trained-bands of the country. Judah and Benjamin were mustered severally; and Benjamin (which not long ago was called *little Benjamin,* Ps. 68:27) had almost as many soldiers as Judah, came as near as 28 to 30, so strangely had that tribe increased of late. The blessing of God can make a *little one to become a thousand.* It should seem, these two tribes were differently armed, both offensively and defensively. The men of Judah guarded themselves with targets, the men of Benjamin with shields, the former of which were much larger than the latter, 1 Ki. 10:16, 17. The men of Judah fought with spears when they closed in with the enemy; the men of Benjamin drew bows, to reach the enemy at a distance. Both did good service, and neither could say to the other, I have *no need of thee.* Different gifts and employments are for the common good.

Verses 9–15

Here is, I. Disturbance given to the peace of Asa's kingdom by a formidable army of Ethiopians that invaded them, *v.* 9, 10. Though still they sought God, yet this fear came upon them, that their faith in God might be tried, and that God might have an opportunity of doing great things for them. It was a vast number that the Ethiopians brought against him: 1,000,000 *men;* and now he found the benefit of having an army ready raised against such a time of need. That provision which we thought needless may soon appear to be of great advantage.

II. The application Asa made to God on occasion of the threatening cloud which now hung over his head, *v.* 11. He that sought God in the day of his peace and prosperity could with holy boldness cry to God in the day of his trouble, and call him *his God.* His prayer is short, but has much in it. 1. He gives to God the glory of his infinite power and sovereignty: *It is nothing with thee to help* and save by many or few, by those that are mighty or by *those that have no power.* See 1 Sa. 14:6. God works in his own strength, not in the strength of instruments (Ps. 21:13), nay, it is his glory to *help the weakest* and to *perfect strength out of the mouth of babes and sucklings.* "We do not say, Lord, take our part, for we have a good army for thee to work by; but, take our part, for without thee we have no power." 2. He takes hold of their covenant-relation to God as theirs. *O Lord, our God!* and again, *"Thou art our God,* whom we have chosen and cleave to as ours, and who hast promised to be ours." 3. He pleads their dependence upon God, and the eye they had to him in this expedition. he was well prepared for it, yet trusted not to his preparations; but, "Lord, *we rest on thee, and in thy name we go against this multitude,* by warrant from thee, aiming at thy glory, and trusting to thy strength." 4. He interests God in their cause: *"Let not man" (mortal man,* so the word is) *"prevail against thee.* If he prevail against us, it will be said that he prevails against thee, because thou art our God, and we rest on thee and go forth in thy name, which thou hast encouraged us to do. The enemy is a mortal man; make it to appear what an unequal match he is for an immortal God. Lord, maintain thy own honour; *hallowed by thy name."*

III. The glorious victory God gave him over his enemies. 1. God defeated the enemy, and put their forces into disorder (*v.* 12): *The Lord smote the Ethiopians,* smote them with terror, and an unaccountable consternation, so that they fled, and knew neither why nor whither. 2. Asa and his soldiers took the advantage God gave them against the enemy. (1.) They destroyed them. They fell *before the Lord* (for who can stand before him?) and before his host, either an invisible host of angels that were employed to destroy them or the host of Israel, called *God's host* because owned by him. (2.) They took the plunder of their camp, *carried away very much spoil* from the slain and from the baggage. (3.) They *smote the cities* that were in league with them, to which they fled for shelter, and carried off the spoil of them (*v.* 14); and they were not able to make any resistance, *for the fear of the Lord came upon them,* that is, a fear which God struck them with to such a degree that they had no heart to withstand the conquerors. (4.) They fetched away the cattle out of the enemy's country, in vast numbers, *v.* 15. Thus the wealth of the sinner is laid up for the just.

CHAPTER 15

Asa and his army were now returning in triumph from the battle, laden with spoils and adorned with the trophies of victory, the pious prince, we may now suppose, studying what he should render to God for this great favour. He knew that the work of reformation, which he had begun in his kingdom, was not perfected; his enemies abroad were subdued, but there were more dangerous enemies at home that were yet unconquered — idols in Judah and Benjamin: his victory over the former emboldened him vigorously to renew his attack upon the latter. Now here we have, I. The message which God sent to him, by a prophet, to engage him to, and encourage him in, the prosecution of his reformation (*v.* 1–7). II. The life which this message put into that good cause, and their proceedings in pursuance of it. Idols removed (*v.* 8). The spoil dedicated to God (*v.* 9–11). A covenant made with God, and a law for the punishing of idolaters (*v.* 12–15). A reformation at court (*v.* 16). Dedicated things brought into the house of God (*v.* 18). All well, but that the high places were permitted (*v.* 17). And the effect of this was great peace (*v.* 19).

Verses 1–7

It was a great happiness to Israel that they had prophets among them; yet, while they were thus blessed, they were strangely addicted to idolatry, whereas, when the spirit of prophecy had ceased under the second temple, and the canon of the Old Temple was completed (which was constantly read in their synagogues), they were pure from idolatry; for the scriptures are of all other the *most sure word of prophecy,* and most effectual, and the church could not be so easily imposed upon by a counterfeit Bible as by a counterfeit prophet. Here was a prophet sent to Asa and his army, when they returned victorious from the war with the Ethiopians, not to compliment them and congratulate them on their success, but to quicken them to their duty; this is the proper business of God's ministers, even with princes and the greatest men. The *Spirit of God came* upon the prophet (*v.* 1), both to instruct him what he should say and to enable him to say it with clearness and boldness.

I. He told them plainly upon what terms they stood with God. Let them not think that, having obtained this victory, all was their own for ever; no, he must let them know they were upon their good behaviour. Let them do well, and it will be well with them, otherwise not. 1. *The Lord is with you while you are with him.* This is both a word of comfort, that those who keep close to God shall always have his presence with them, and also a word of caution: "He is *with you, while you are with him,* but no longer; you have now a signal token of his favourable presence with you, but the continuance of it depends upon your perseverance in the way of your duty." 2. *"If you seek him, he will be found of you.* Sincerely desire his favour, and aim at it, and you shall obtain it. Pray, and you shall prevail. He never said, nor ever will, *Seek you me in vain."* See Heb. 11:6. But, 3. "If you forsake him and his ordinances, he is not tied to you, but will certainly forsake you, and then you are undone, your present triumphs will be no security to you; woe to you when God departs."

II. He set before them the dangerous consequence of forsaking God and his ordinances, and that there was no way of having grievances redressed, but by repenting, and returning unto God. When Israel forsook their duty they were over-run with a deluge of atheism, impiety, irreligion, and all irregularity (*v.* 3), and were continually embarrassed with vexatious and destroying wars, foreign and domestic, *v.* 5, 6. But when their troubles drove them to God they found it not in vain to seek him, *v.* 4. But the question is, What time does this refer to? 1. Some think it looks as far back as the days of the Judges. *A long season* ago Israel was *without the true God,* for they worshipped false gods; it was a time of ignorance, for, though they had priests, they had no teaching priests, though they had elders, yet no law to any purpose, *v.* 3. These were sad times, when they were frequently oppressed by one enemy or other and grievously harassed by Moabites, Midianites, Ammonites, and other nations. They were *vexed with all adversity* (*v.* 6), yet when, in their perplexity, they turned to God by repentance, prayer, and reformation, he raised up deliverers for them. Then was that maxim often verified, that God is with us while we are with him. Whatsoever things of this kind were written aforetime were written for our admonition. 2. Others think it describes the state of the ten tribes (who were now properly called *Israel*) in the days of Asa. *"Now,* since Jeroboam set up the calves, though he pretended to honour the God that brought them out of Egypt, yet his idolatry has brought them to downright infidelity; they are *without the true God,"* and no marvel when they were without teaching priests. Jeroboam's priests were not teachers, and thus they came to be without law. It is next to impossible that any thing of religion should be kept up without a preaching ministry. In those times there was no peace, *v.* 5. Their war with Judah gave them frequent alarms; so did the late insurrection of Baasha and other occasions not mentioned. They provoked God with all iniquity, and then he *vexed them with all adversity;* yet, *when they turned to God,* he was entreated for them. Let Judah take notice of this; let their neighbours' harms be their warnings. Give no countenance to graven images for you see what mischiefs they produce. 3. Others think the whole passage may be read in the future tense, and that it looks forward: Hereafter *Israel will be without the true God and a teaching priest,* and they will be destroyed by one judgment after another till they *return to God* and *seek him.* See Hos. 3:4.

III. Upon this he grounded his exhortation to prosecute the work of reformation with vigour (*v.* 7): *Be strong, for your work shall be rewarded.* Note, 1. God's work should be done with diligence and cheerfulness, but will not be done without resolution. 2. This should quicken us to the work of religion, that we shall be sure not to lose by it ultimately. It will not go unrewarded. How should it, when the work is its own reward?

Verses 8–19

We are here told what good effect the foregoing sermon had upon Asa.

I. He grew more bold for God than he had been. His victory would inspire him with some new degrees of resolution, but this message from God with much more. Now he took courage. he saw how necessary a further reformation was, and what assurance he had of God's presence with him in it; and this made him daring, and helped him over the difficulties which had before deterred him and driven him off from the undertaking. Now he ventured to destroy all the abominable idols (and all idolatries are abominable, 1 Pt. 4:3) as far as ever his power went. Away with them all. He also *renewed the altar of the Lord,* which, it seems, had gone out of repair, though it was not above thirty-five years since Solomon's head was laid, who erected it. So soon did these ceremonial institutions begin to wax old, as things which, in the fulness of time, must *vanish away,* Heb. 8:13.

II. He extended his influence further than before, *v.* 9. He summoned a solemn assembly, and particularly brought the strangers to it, who had come over to him from the ten tribes. 1. Their coming was a great encouragement to him; for the reason of their coming was because *they saw that the Lord his God was with him.* It is good to be with those that have God with them, to come into relation to, and contract acquaintance and friendship with, those that live in the fear and favour of God. *We will go with you, for we have heard that God is with you,* Zec. 8:23. 2. The cognizance he took of them, and the invitation he gave them to the general assembly, were a great encouragement to them. All strangers are to be helped, but those that cast themselves upon God's good providence, purely to keep a good conscience, are worthy of double honour. Asa gave orders for the gathering of them together (*v.* 9), yet it is said (*v.* 10) that they *gathered themselves together,* made it their own act, so forward were they to obey the king's orders. This meeting was held in the third month, probably at the feast of Pentecost, which was in that month.

III. He and his people offered sacrifices to God, as his share of the spoil they had got, *v.* 11. Their offering here was nothing to Solomon's (*ch.* 7:5), which was owing to the diminution either of their zeal or of their wealth, or of both. These sacrifices were intended by way of thanksgiving for the favours they had received, and supplication for further favours. Prayers and praises are now our spiritual sacrifices. And, as he took care that the altar should have its gift, so he took care that the temple should have its gold: *He brought into the house of God all the dedicated things, v.* 18. It is honesty to render to God the things that are his. What has been long designed for him, and long laid by for him, as it should seem these dedicated things had been, should at length be laid out for him. Will a man rob God, or make slow payment to him, who is always ready to do us good?

IV. *They entered into covenant with God,* repenting that they had violated their engagements to him and resolving to do better for the future. It is proper for penitents, for converts, to renew their covenants. It should seem, the motion came not from Asa, but from the people themselves. Let every man be a volunteer that covenants with God. *Thy people shall be willing,* Ps. 110:3. Observe,

1. What was the matter of this covenant. Nothing but what they were before obliged to; and, though no vow or promise of theirs could lay any higher obligation upon them than they were already under from the divine precept, yet it would help to increase their sense of the obligation, to arm them against temptations, and would be a testimony to the equity and goodness of the precept. And, by joining all together in this covenant, they strengthened the hands one of another. Two things they engaged themselves to: — (1.) That they would diligently seek God themselves, seek his precepts, seek his favour. What is religion but seeking God, enquiring after him, applying to him, upon all occasions? We shall not enjoy him till we come to heaven; while we are here we must continue seeking. They would seek God as the *God of their fathers,* in the way that their fathers sought him and in dependence upon the promise made to their fathers; and they would do it *with all their heart* and *with all their soul,* for those only seek God acceptably and successfully that are inward with him, intent upon him, and entire for him, in their seeking him. We make nothing of our religion if we do not make heart-work of it. God will have all the heart or none; and, when a jewel of such inestimable value as the divine favour is to be found, it is worth while to seek it *with all our soul.* (2.) That they would, to the utmost of their power, oblige others to seek him, *v.* 13. They agreed that *whosoever would not seek the Lord God of Israel* (that is, would either worship other gods or refuse to join with them in the worship of the true God, that was either an obstinate idolater or an obstinate atheist) he should be put to death. This was no new law of their own making, but an order to put in execution that law of God to this purport, Deu. 17:2, etc. If this law had been duly executed, there would not have been so many abominable idols found in Judah and Benjamin, *v.* 8. Whether men may now, under the gospel, be compelled by such methods as these to seek the Lord is justly questioned; for the weapons of our warfare are not carnal, and yet mighty.

2. In what manner they made this covenant. (1.) With great cheerfulness, and all possible expressions of joy: *The swore unto the Lord;* not secretly, as if they were either ashamed of what they did or afraid of binding themselves too fast to him, but with a loud voice, to express their own zeal and to animate one another; and they all rejoiced at the oath, *v.* 14, 15. They did not swear to God with reluctancy (as the poor debtor confesses a judgment to his creditor), but with all the pleasure and satisfaction imaginable, as the bridegroom plights his troth to the bride in the marriage covenant. Every honest Israelite was pleased with his own engagements to God, and they were all pleased with one another's. They rejoiced in it as a hopeful expedient to prevent their apostasy from God and a happy indication of God's presence with them. Note, The times of renewing our covenant with God should be times of rejoicing, and national reformation cannot but give general satisfaction to all that are good. It is an honour and happiness to be in bonds to God. (2.) They did it with great sincerity, zeal and resolution: *They swore to God with all their hearts,* and *sought him with their whole desire.* The Israelites were now in an extraordinarily good frame. O that there had always been such a heart in them! This comes in as the reason why they rejoiced so much in what they did: it was because they were hearty in it. Note, Those only experience the pleasure and comfort of religion that are sincere and upright in it. What is done in hypocrisy is a mere drudgery. But, if God has the heart, we have the joy.

V. We are told what was the effect of this their solemn covenanting with God. 1. God did well for them: *He was found of them, and gave them rest round about* (*v.* 15), so that there was no war for a long time after (*v.* 19), no open general war, though there were constant bickerings between Judah and Israel upon the frontiers, 1 Ki. 15:16. National piety procures national blessings. 2. They did, on the whole, well for him. They carried on the reformation so far that Maachah the queen-mother was deposed for idolatry and her idol destroyed, *v.* 16. This was bravely done of Asa, that he would not connive at idolatry in those that were nearest to him, like Levi, that *said to his father and mother, I have not seen him,* Deu. 33:9. Asa knows he must honour God more than his grandmother, and dares not leave an idol in an apartment of his palace while he is destroying idols in the cities of his kingdom. We may suppose this Maachah was so far convinced of her sin that she was willing to subscribe the association mentioned (*v.* 12, 13), binding herself to seek the Lord, and therefore was not put to death as those were that refused to sign it, great as well as small, women as well as men: probably it was with an eye to her that *women* were specified. But because she had been an idolater Asa thought fit to divest her of the dignity and authority she had, and probably he banished her the court and confined her to privacy, lest she should influence and infect others. But the reformation was not complete; the high places were not all taken away, though many of them were, *ch.* 14:3, 5. Those in the cities were removed, but not those in the cities of Judah, but not those in the cities of Israel which were reduced to the house of David; or those that were used in the service of false gods, but not those that were used in the service of the God of Israel. These he connived at, and yet his heart was perfect. There may be defects in some particular duties where yet the heart, in the man, is upright with God. Sincerity is something less than sinless perfection.

CHAPTER 16

This chapter concludes the history of the reign of Asa, but does not furnish so pleasing an account of his latter end as we had of his beginning. I. Here is a foolish treaty with Benhadad king of Syria (*v.* 1–6). II. The reproof which God sent him for it by a prophet (*v.* 7–9). III. Asa's displeasure against the prophet for his faithfulness (*v.* 10). IV. The sickness, death, and burial of Asa (*v.* 11–14).

Verses 1–6

How to reconcile the date of this event with the history of the kings I am quite at a loss. Baasha died in the twenty-sixth year of Asa, 1 Ki. 16:8. How then could this be done in his thirty-sixth year, when Baasha's family was quite cut off, and Omri was upon the throne? It is generally said to be meant of the thirty-sixth year of the kingdom of Asa, namely, that of Judah, beginning from the first of Rehoboam, and so it coincides with the sixteenth of Asa's reign; but then *ch.* 15:19 must be so understood; and how could it be spoken of as a great thing that there was no more war till the fifteenth year of Asa, when that passage immediately before was in his fifteenth year? (*ch.* 15:10), and after this miscarriage of his, here recorded, he had wars, *v.* 9. Josephus places it in his twenty-sixth year, and then we must suppose a mistake in the transcriber here and *ch.* 15:19, the admission of which renders the computation easy. This passage we had before (1 Ki. 15:17, etc.) and Asa was in several ways faulty in it. 1. He did not do well to make a league with Benhadad, a heathen king, and to value himself so much upon it as he seems to have done, *v.* 3. Had he relied more upon his covenant, and his father's, with God, he would not have boasted so much of his league, and his father's, with the royal family of Syria. 2. If he had had a due regard to the honour of Israel in general, he would have found some other expedient to give Baasha a diversion than by calling in a foreign force, and inviting into the country a common enemy, who, in process of time, might be a plague to Judah too. 3. It was doubtless a sin in Benhadad to break his league with Baasha upon no provocation, but merely through the influence of a bribe; and, if so, certainly it was a sin in Asa to move him to it, especially to hire him to do it. The public faith of kings and kingdoms must not be made so cheap a thing. 4. To take silver and gold out of the house of the Lord for this purpose was a great aggravation of the sin, *v.* 2. Must the temple be plundered to serve his carnal politics? He had better have brought gifts and offerings with prayers and supplications, to the house of the Lord, that he might have engaged God on his side and made him his friend; then he would not have needed to be at this expense to make Benhadad his friend. 5. It was well if Asa had not to answer for all the mischief that the army of Benhadad did unjustly to the cities of Israel, all the blood they shed and all the spoil they made, *v.* 4. Perhaps Asa intended not that they should carry the matter so far. But those that draw others to sin know not what they do, nor where it will end. The beginning of sin is as the letting forth of water. However the project succeeded. Benhadad gave Baasha a powerful diversion, obliged him to leave off building Ramah and betake himself to the defence of his own country northward, which gave Asa an opportunity, not only to demolish his fortifications, but to seize the materials and convert them to his own use.

Verses 7–14

Here is, I. A plain and faithful reproof given to Asa by a prophet of the Lord, for making this league with Baasha. The reprover was Hanani the seer, the father of Jehu, another prophet, whom we read of 1 Ki. 16:1; 2 Chr. 19:2. We observed several things amiss in Asa's treaty with Benhadad. But that which the prophet here charges upon him as the greatest fault he was guilty of in that matter is his *relying on the king of Syria and not on the Lord his God, v.* 7. He thought that, though God was on his side, this would not stand him in stead unless he had Benhadad on his side, that God either could not or would not help him, but he must take this indirect course to help himself. Note, God is much displeased when he is distrusted and when an arm of flesh is relied on more than his power and goodness. By putting our confidence in God we give honour to him, and therefore he thinks himself affronted if we give that honour to another. He plainly tells the king that herein he had done foolishly, *v.* 9. It is a foolish thing to lean on a broken reed, when we have the rock of ages to rely upon. To convince him of his folly he shows him,

1. That he acted against his experience, *v.* 8. He, of all men, had no reason to distrust God, who had found him such a present powerful helper, by whom he had been made to triumph over a threatening enemy, as his father before him, *because he relied upon the Lord his God, ch.* 13:18; 14:11. "*What!*" said the prophet, "Were not the Ethiopians and the Lubim a huge host, enough to swallow up a kingdom? And yet, *because thou didst rely on the Lord, he delivered them into thy hand;* and was not he sufficient to help thee against Baasha?" Note, The many experiences we have had of the goodness of God to us aggravate our distrust of him. Has he not helped us in six troubles? And have we any reason to suspect him in the seventh? But see how deceitful our hearts are! We trust in God when we have nothing else to trust to, when need drives us to him; but, when we have other things to stay on, we are apt to stay too much on them and to lean on our own understanding as long as that has any thing to offer; but a believing confidence will be in God only, when a smiling world courts it most.

2. That he acted against his knowledge of God and his providence, *v.* 9. Asa could not be ignorant that *the eyes of the Lord run to and fro through the earth, strongly to hold with those* (so it may be read) *whose heart is perfect towards him;* that is, (1.) That God governs the world in infinite wisdom, and the creatures, and all their actions, are continually under his eye. The eye of Providence is quick-sighted — it *runs;* it is intent — it runs *to and fro;* it reaches far — *through the whole earth,* no corner of which is from under it, not the most dark or distant; and his eye directs his hand, and the arm of his power; for he shows himself strong. Does Satan walk to and fro in the earth? Providence *runs* to and fro, is never out of the way, never to seek, never at a loss. (2.) That God governs the world for the good of his people, does all in pursuance of the counsels of his love concerning their salvation, all *for Jacob his servant's sake, and Israel his elect,* Isa. 45:4. *Christ is head over all things to his church,* Eph. 1:22. (3.) That those whose hearts are upright with him may be sure of his protection and have all the reason in the world to depend upon it. He is able to protect them in the way of their duty (for wisdom and might are his), and he actually intends their protection. A practical disbelief of this is at the bottom of all our departures from God and double-dealing with him. Asa could not trust God and therefore made court to Benhadad.

3. That he acted against his interest. (1.) He had lost an opportunity of checking the growing greatness of the king of Syria, (*v.* 7): His *host has escaped out of thy hand,* which otherwise would have joined with Baasha's and fallen with it. (2.) He had incurred God's displeasure and henceforth must expect no peace, but the constant alarms of war, *v.* 9. Those that cannot find in their hearts to trust God forfeit his protection and throw themselves out of it.

II. Asa's displeasure at this reproof. Though it came from God by one that was known to be his messenger, though the reproof was just and the reasoning fair, and all intended for his good, yet he was wroth with the seer for telling him of his folly; nay, *he was in a rage with him, v.* 10. Is this Asa? Is this he whose heart was perfect with the Lord all his days? Well, let him that thinks he stands take heed lest he fall. A wise man, and yet in a rage! An Israelite, and yet in a rage with a prophet! A good man, and yet impatient of reproof, and that cannot bear to be told of his faults! Lord, what is man, when God leaves him to himself? Those that idolize their own conduct cannot bear contradiction; and those that indulge a peevish passionate temper may be transported by it into impieties as well as into indecencies, and will, some time or other, fly in the face of God himself. See what gall and wormwood this root of bitterness bore. 1. In his rage he committed the prophet to the jail, *put him in a prison-house,* as a malefactor, *in the stocks* (so some read it,) or into *little-ease.* God's prophets meet with many that cannot bear reproof, but take it much amiss, yet they must do their duty. 2. Having proceeded thus far, *he oppressed some of the people,* probably such as owned the prophet in his sufferings, or were known to be his particular friends. He that abused his power for the persecuting of God's prophet was left to himself further to abuse it for the crushing of his own subjects, whereby he weakened himself and lost his interest. Most persecutors have been tyrants.

III. His sickness. Two years before he died *he was diseased in his feet* (*v.* 12), afflicted with the gout in a high degree. He had put the prophet in the stocks, and now God put him in the stocks; so his punishment answered his sin. *His disease was exceedingly great;* it came to the height (so some); it flew up to his head (so others), and then it was mortal. This was his affliction; but his sin was that in his disease, instead of seeking to the Lord for relief, he *sought to the physicians.* His making use of physicians was his duty; but trusting to them, and expecting that from them which was to be had from God only, were his sin and folly. The help of creatures must always be used with an eye to the Creator, and in dependence upon him, who makes every creature that to us which it is, and without whom the most skilful and faithful are physicians of no value. Some think that these physicians were strangers to the commonwealth of Israel, and were a sort of conjurers, to whom he applied as if there were not a God in Israel.

IV. His death and burial. His funeral had something of extraordinary solemnity in it, *v.* 14. They made a very magnificent *burying for him.* I am loth to think (as some do) that he himself ordered this funeral pomp, and that it was an instance of his vanity, that he would be buried like the Gentiles, and not after the way of the Jews. It is said indeed, *He digged the sepulchre for himself,* as one mindful of his grave; but I am willing to believe that this funeral pomp was rather an expression of the great respect his people retained for him, notwithstanding the failings and infirmities of his latter days. It was agreed to do him honour at his death. Note, The eminent piety and usefulness of good men ought to be remembered to their praise, though they have had their blemishes. Let their faults be buried in their graves, while their services are remembered over their graves. He that said, *There is not a just man that doeth good and sinneth not, yet* said also, *The memory of the just is blessed;* and let it be so.

CHAPTER 17

Here begin the life and reign of Jehoshaphat, who was one of the first three among the royal worthies, one of the best that ever swayed the sceptre of Judah since David's head was laid. He was the good son of a good father, so that, as this time, grace ran in the blood, even in the blood-royal. Happy the son that had such a father, to lay a good foundation in him and for him. Happy the father that had such a son, to build so wall upon the foundation he had laid! Happy the kingdom that was blessed with two such kings, two such reigns, together! In this chapter we have, I. His accession to and establishment in the throne (*v.* 1, 2, 5). II. His persona piety (*v.* 3, 4, 6). III. The course he took to promote religion in his kingdom (*v.* 7–9). IV. The mighty sway he bore among the neighbours (*v.* 10, 11). V. The great strength of his kingdom, both in garrisons and standing forces (*v.* 12–19). Thus was his prosperity the reward of his piety and his piety the brightest grace and ornament of his prosperity.

Verses 1–9

Here we find concerning Jehoshaphat,

I. What a wise man he was. As soon as he came to the crown he *strengthened himself against Israel, v.* 1. Ahab, an active warlike prince, had now been three years upon the throne of Israel, the vigour of his beginning falling in with the decay of Asa's conclusion. It is probable that the kingdom of Israel had, of late, got ground of the kingdom of Judah and began to grow formidable to it; so that the first thing Jehoshaphat had to do was to make his part good on that side, and to check the growing greatness of the king of Israel, which he did so effectually, and without bloodshed, that Ahab soon courted his alliance, so far was he from giving him any disturbance, and proved more dangerous as a friend than he could have been as an enemy. Jehoshaphat strengthened himself not to act offensively against Israel or invade them, but only to maintain his own, which he did by fortifying the cities that were on his frontiers, and putting garrisons, stronger than had been, in the cities of Ephraim, which he was master of, *v.* 2. He did not strengthen himself, as his father did, by a league with the king of Syria, but by fair and regular methods, on which he might expect the blessing of God and in which he trusted God.

II. What a good man he was. It is an excellent character that is here given him. 1. He *walked in the ways of his father David.* In the characters of the kings, David's ways are often made the standard, as 1 Ki. 15:3, 11; 2 Ki. 14:3; 16:2; 18:3. But the distinction is nowhere so strongly marked as here between his first ways and his last ways; for the last were not so good as the first. his ways, before he fell so foully in the matter of Uriah (which is mentioned long afterwards as the bar in his escutcheon, 1 Ki. 15:5), were good ways, and, though he happily recovered from that fall, yet perhaps he never, while he lived, fully retrieved the spiritual strength and comfort he lost by it. Jehoshaphat followed David as far as he followed God and no further. Paul himself thus limits our imitation of him (1 Co. 11:1): *Follow me, as I follow Christ,* and not otherwise. Many good people have had their first ways, which were their best ways, their first love, which was their strongest love; and in every copy we propose to write after, as we must single out that only which is good, so that chiefly which is best. The words here will admit another reading; they run thus: *He walked in the ways of David his father (Hareshonim), those first ways,* or those *ancient ways.* He proposed to himself, for his example, the primitive times of the royal family, those purest times, before the corruptions of the late reigns came in. See Jer. 6:16. The Septuagint leaves out David, and so refers it to Asa: *He walked in the first ways of his father,* and did not imitate him in what was amiss in him, towards the latter end of his time. It is good to be cautious in following the best men, lest we step aside after them. 2. He *sought not to Baalim, but sought to the Lord God of his father, v.* 3, 4. The neighbouring nations had their Baalim, one had one Baal and another had another; but he abhorred them all, had nothing to do with them. he *worshipped the Lord God of his father* and him only, prayed to him only and enquired of him only; both are included in seeking him. 3. That he *walked in God's commandments,* not only worshipped the true God, but worshipped him according to his own institution, *and not after the doings of Israel, v.* 4. Though the king of Israel was his neighbour and ally, yet he did not learn his way. Whatever dealings he had with him in civil matters, he would not have communion with him, nor comply with him in his religion. In this he kept close to the rule. 4. *His heart was lifted up in the ways of the Lord (v.* 6), or *he lifted up his heart.* He brought his heart to his work, and lifted up his heart in it; that is, he had a sincere regard to God in it. *Unto thee, O Lord! do I lift up my soul.* His heart was enlarged in that which is good, Ps. 119:32. He never thought he could do enough for God. He was lively and affectionate in his religion, *fervent in spirit, serving the Lord,* cheerful and pleasant in it; he went on in his work with alacrity, as Jacob, who, after his vision of God at Bethel, *lifted up his feet,* Gen. 29:1, *margin.* He was bold and resolute in the ways of God and went on with courage. His heart was lifted up above the consideration of the difficulties that were in the way of his duty; he easily got over them all, and was not frightened with *winds and clouds* from *sowing and reaping,* Eccl. 11:4. Let us walk in the same spirit.

III. What a useful man he was, not only a good man, but a good king. He not only was good himself, but did good in his generation, did a great deal of good. 1. He took away the teachers of lies, so images are called (Hab. 2:18), the *high places* and *the groves, v.* 6. It is meant of those in which idols were worshipped; for those that were dedicated to the true God only were not taken away, *ch.* 20:33. It was only idolatry that he abolished. Nothing debauched the nation more than those idolatrous groves or images which he took away. 2. He sent forth teachers of truth. When he enquired into the state of religion in his kingdom he found his people generally very ignorant: they *knew not that they did evil.* Even in the last good reign there had been little care taken to instruct them in their duty; and therefore Jehoshaphat resolves to begin his work at the right end, deals with them as reasonable creatures, will not lead them blindfold, no, not into a reformation, but endeavours to have them well taught, knowing that that was the way to have them well cured. In this good work he employed, (1.) His princes. Those about him he sent forth; those in the country he sent *to teach in the cities of Judah, v.* 7. He ordered them, in the administration of justice, not only to correct the people when they did ill, but to teach them how to do better, and to give a reason for what they did, that the people might be informed of the difference between good and evil. The princes or judges upon the bench have a great opportunity of teaching people their duty to God and man, and it is not out of their province, for the laws of God are to be looked upon as laws of the land. (2.) The *Levites* and *priests* went *with the princes,* and *taught in Judah, having the book of the law with them, v.* 8,9. They were teachers by office, Deu. 33:10. Teaching was part of the work for which they had their maintenance. The priests and the Levites had little else to do. But, it seems, they had neglected it, pretending perhaps that they could not get the people to hear them. "Well," says Jehoshaphat, "you shall go along with the princes, and they with their authority shall oblige the people to come and hear you; and then, if they be not well instructed, it is your fault." What an abundance of good may be done when Moses and Aaron thus go hand in hand in the doing of it, when princes with their power, and priests and Levites with their scripture learning, agree to

teach the people the good knowledge of God and their duty! These itinerant judges and itinerant preachers together were instrumental to diffuse a blessed light throughout the cities of Judah. But it is said, *They had the book of the law of the Lord with them.* [1.] For their own direction, that thence they might fetch all the instructions they gave to the people, and not *teach for doctrines the commandments of men.* [2.] For the conviction of the people, that they might see that they had a divine warrant for what they said and delivered to them that only which they received from the Lord. Note, Ministers, when they go to teach the people, should have their Bibles with them.

IV. What a happy man he was. 1. How happy he was in the favour of his God, who signally owned and blessed him: *The Lord was with him (v.* 3); the word of the Lord was his helper (so the Chaldee paraphrase); *the Lord established the kingdom in his hand, v.* 5. Those stand firmly that have the presence of God with them. If the *beauty of the Lord our God be upon us,* that will *establish the work of our hands* and establish us in our integrity. 2. How happy he was in the affections of his people *(v.* 5): *All Judah brought him presents,* in acknowledgment of his kindness in sending preachers among them. The more there is of true religion among a people the more there will be of conscientious loyalty. A government that answers the end of government will be supported. The effect of the favour both of God and his kingdom was that he had *riches and honour in abundance.* It is undoubtedly true, though few will believe it, that religion and piety are the best friends to outward prosperity. And, observe, it follows immediately, *His heart was lifted up in the ways of the Lord.* Riches and honour in abundance prove to many a clog and a hindrance in the ways of the Lord, an occasion of pride, security, and sensuality; but they had a quite contrary effect upon Jehoshaphat: his abundance was oil to the wheels of his obedience, and the more he had of the wealth of this world the more was his heart *lifted up in the ways of the Lord.*

Verses 10—19

We have here a further account of Jehoshaphat's great prosperity and the flourishing state of his kingdom.

I. He had good interest in the neighbouring princes and nations. Though he was not perhaps so great a soldier as David (which might have made him their terror), nor so great a scholar as Solomon (which might have made him their oracle), yet *the fear of the Lord fell so upon them* (that is, God so influenced and governed their spirits) that they had all a reverence for him, *v.* 10. And, 1. *None of them made war against him.* God's good providence so ordered it that, while the princes and priests were instructing and reforming the country, none of his neighbours gave him any molestations, to take him off from that good work. Thus when Jacob and his sons were going to worship at Bethel the terror of God was upon the neighbouring cities, that they *did not pursue after them,* Gen. 35:5, and see Ex. 34:24. 2. Many of them brought presents to him *(v.* 11), to secure his friendship. Perhaps these were a tribute imposed upon them by Asa, who made himself master of the cities of the Philistines, and the tents of the Arabians, *ch.* 14:14, 15. With the 7700 rams, and the same number of he-goats, which the Arabians brought, there was probably a proportionable number of ewes and lambs, she-goats and kids.

II. He had a very considerable stores laid up in the cities of Judah. He pulled down his barns, and built larger *(v.* 12), *castles and cities of store,* for arms and victuals. He was a man of business, and aimed at the public good in all his undertakings, either to preserve the peace or prepare for war.

III. He had the militia in good order. It was never in better since David modelled it. Five *lord-lieutenants* (if I may so call them) are here named, with the numbers of those under their command (the serviceable men, that were fit for war in their respective districts), three in Judah, and two in Benjamin. It is said of one of these great commanders, *Amasiah,* that *he willingly offered himself unto the Lord (v.* 16), not only to the king, to serve him in this post, but to the Lord, to glorify him in it. He was the most eminent among them for religion, he accepted the place, not for the honour, or power, or profit of it, but for conscience' sake towards God, that he might serve his coun-

try,. It was usual for great generals then to offer of their spoils to the Lord, 1 Chr. 26:26. But this good man offered himself first to the Lord, and then his dedicated things. The number of the soldiers under these five generals amounts to 1,160,000 men, a vast number for so small a compass of ground as Judah's and Benjamin's lot to furnish out and maintain. Abijah could bring into the field but 400,000 *(ch.* 13:3), Asa not 600,000 *(ch.* 14:8), yet Jehoshaphat has at command almost 1,200,000. But it must be considered, 1. That God had promised to make the seed of Abraham like the sand of the sea for number. 2. There had now been a long peace. 3. We may suppose that the city of Jerusalem was very much enlarged. 4. Many had come over to them from the kingdom of Israel *(ch.* 15:19), which would increase the numbers of the people. 5. Jehoshaphat was under a special blessing of God, which made his affairs to prosper greatly. The armies, we may suppose, were dispersed all the country over, and each man resided for the most part on his own estate; but they appeared often, to be mustered and trained, and were ready at call whenever there was occasion. The commanders waited on the king *(v.* 19) as officers of his court, privy-counsellors, and ministers of state.

But, *lastly,* observe, It was not this formidable army that struck a terror upon the neighbouring nations, that restrained them from attempting any thing against Israel, or obliged them to pay tribute, but the fear of God which fell upon them when Jehoshaphat reformed his country and set up a preaching ministry in it, *v.* 10. The ordinances of God are more the strength and safety of a kingdom than its military force — its men of God more than its men of war.

CHAPTER 18

The story of this chapter we had just as it is here related in the story of the reign of Ahab king of Israel, 1 Ki. 22. There it looks more creditable to Ahab than any thing else recorded of him that he was in league with so good a man as Jehoshaphat; here it is a great blemish in the reign of Jehoshaphat that he thus connected himself with so bad a man as Ahab. Here is, I. The alliance he contracted himself with Ahab *(v.* 1). II. His consent to join with him in his expedition for the recovery of Remoth-Gilead out of the hands of the Syrians *(v.* 2, 3). III. Their consulting with the prophets, false and true, before they went *(v.* 4—27). IV. The success of their expedition. Jehoshaphat hardly escaped *(v.* 28—32) and Ahab received his death's wound *(v.* 33, 34).

Verses 1—3

Here is, I. Jehoshaphat growing greater. It was said before *(ch.* 17:5) that he had *riches and honour in abundance;* and here it is said again that his wealth and honour increased upon him by piety and good management.

II. Not growing wiser, else he would not have joined with Ahab, that degenerate Israelite, who had sold himself to work wickedness. What good could he get by a man that was so bad? What good could he do to a man that was so obstinately wicked — an idolater, a persecutor? With him he joined in affinity, that is, married his son Jehoram to Ahab's daughter Athaliah.

1. This was the worst match that ever was made by any of the house of David. I wonder what Jehoshaphat could promise himself by it. (1.) Perhaps pride made the match, as it does many a one, which speeds accordingly. His religion forbade him to marry his son to a daughter of any of the heathen princes that were about him — *Thou shalt not take their daughters to thy sons;* and, having riches and honour in abundance, he thought it a disparagement to marry him to a subject. A king's daughter it must be, and therefore Ahab's, little considering that Jezebel was her mother. (2.) Some think he did it in policy, hoping by this expedient to unite the kingdoms in his son, Ahab perhaps flattering him with hopes that he would make him his heir, when he intended no such thing.

2. This match drew Jehoshaphat, (1.) Into an intimate familiarity with Ahab. He paid him a visit at Samaria, and Ahab, proud of the honour which Jehoshaphat did him, gave him a very splendid entertainment, according to the splendour of those times: He *killed sheep and oxen for him,* plain meat, *in abundance, v.* 2. In this Jehoshaphat did not walk so closely as he should have done in the ways of his father David, who *hated the congregation of evil-doers and would not sit with the wicked* (Ps. 26:5), nor desired to *eat of their dainties,* Ps. 141:4. (2.) Into a league with Ahab against the Syrians. Ahab persuaded him to join forces with him in an expedition for the recovery of Ramoth-Gilead,

a city in the tribe of Gad, on the other side Jordan. Did not Ahab know that that, and all the other cities of Israel, did of right belong to Jehoshaphat, as heir of the house of David? With what face then could he ask Jehoshaphat to assist him in recovering it for himself, whose title to the crown was usurped and precarious? Yet Jehoshaphat, an easy man, yields to go with him: *I am as thou art, v.* 3. Some men's kindnesses are dangerous, as well as their society infectious. The feast Ahab made for Jehoshaphat was designed only to wheedle him into the expedition. The *kisses of an enemy are deceitful.*

Verses 4–27

This is almost word for word the same with what we had, 1 Ki. 22. We will not repeat what was there said, nor have we much to add, but may take occasion to think, 1. Of the great duty of acknowledging God in all our ways *and enquiring at his word,* whatever we undertake. Jehoshaphat was not willing to proceed till he had done this, *v.* 4. By particular believing prayer, by an unbiased consultation of the scripture and our own consciences, and by an observant regard to the hints of providence, we may make such enquiries and very much to our satisfaction. 2. Of the great danger of bad company even to good men. Those that have more wisdom, grace, and resolution, cannot be sure that they can converse familiarly with wicked people and get no hurt by them. Jehoshaphat here, in complaisance to Ahab, sits in his robes, patiently hearing the false prophets speaking lies in the name of the Lord (*v.* 9), can scarcely find in his heart to give him a too mild and gentle reproof for hating a prophet of the Lord (*v.* 7), and dares not rebuke that false prophet who basely abused the faithful seer nor oppose Ahab who committed him to prison. Those who venture among the seats of the scornful cannot come off without a great deal of the guilt attaching to at least the omission of their duty, unless they have such measures of wisdom and courage as few can pretend to. 3. Of the unhappiness of those who are surrounded with flatterers, especially flattering prophets, who cry peace to them and prophesy nothing but smooth things. Thus was Ahab cheated into his ruin, and justly; for he hearkened to such, and preferred those that humoured him before a good prophet that gave him fair warning of his danger. Those do best for themselves that give their friends leave, and particularly their ministers, to deal plainly and faithfully with them, and take their reproofs not only patiently, but kindly. That counsel is not always best for us that is most pleasing to us. 4. Of the power of Satan, by the divine permission, *in the children of disobedience.* One lying spirit can make 400 lying prophets and make use of them to deceive Ahab, *v.* 21. The devil becomes a murderer by being a liar and destroys men by deceiving them. 5. Of the justice of God in giving those up to strong delusions, to believe a lie, who will not receive the love of the truth, but rebel against it, *v.* 21. Let the *lying spirit prevail* to entice those to their ruin that will not be persuaded to their duty and happiness. 6. Of the hard case of faithful ministers, whose lot it has often been to be hated, and persecuted, and ill-treated, for being true to their God and just and kind to the souls of men. Micaiah, for discharging a good conscience, was buffeted, imprisoned, and condemned to the bread and water of affliction. But he could with assurance appeal to the issue, as all those may do who are persecuted for their faithfulness, *v.* 27. The day will declare who is in the right and who in the wrong, when Christ will appear, to the unspeakable consolation of his persecuted people and the everlasting confusion of their persecutors, who will be made *to see in that day* (*v.* 24) what they will not now believe.

Verses 28–34

We have here, 1. Good Jehoshaphat exposing himself in his robes, thereby endangered, and yet delivered. We have reason to think that Ahab, while he pretended friendship, really aimed at Jehoshaphat's life, to take him off, that he might have the management of his successor, who was his son-in-law, else he would never have advised him to enter into the battle with his robes on, which was but to make himself an easy mark to the enemy: and, if really he intended that, it was as unprincipled a piece of treachery as ever man was guilty of, and justly was he himself taken in the pit he digged for his friend. The enemy had soon an eye upon the robes, and vigorously attacked the unwary prince who now, when it was too late, wished himself in the habit of the poorest soldier, rather than in his princely raiment. he cried out, either to his friends to relieve him (but Ahab took no care of that), or to his enemies, to rectify their mistake, and let them know that he was not the king of Israel. Or perhaps he cried to God for succour and deliverance (to whom else should he cry?) and he found it was not in vain: *The Lord helped him out* of his distress, by *moving the captains to depart from him, v.* 31. God has all men's hearts in his hand, and turns them as he pleases, contrary to their own first intentions, to serve his purposes. Many are moved unaccountably both to themselves and others, but an invisible power moves them. 2. Wicked Ahab disguising himself, arming himself thereby as he thought securing himself, and yet slain, *v.* 33. No art, no arms, can save those whom God has appointed to ruin. What can hurt those whom God will protect? And what can shelter those whom God will destroy? Jehoshaphat is safe in his robes, Ahab killed in his armour; for the race is not to the swift nor the battle to the strong.

CHAPTER 19

We have here a further account of the good reign of Jehoshaphat, I. His return in peace to Jerusalem (*v.* 1). II. The reproof given him for his league with Ahab, and his acting in conjunction with him (*v.* 2, 3). III. The great care he took thereupon to reform his kingdom (*v.* 4). IV. The instructions he gave to his judges, both those in the country towns that kept the inferior courts (*v.* 5–7), and those in Jerusalem that sat in the supreme judicature of the kingdom (*v.* 8–11).

Verses 1–4

Here is, I. The great favour God showed to Jehoshaphat,

1. In bringing him back in safety from his dangerous expedition with Ahab, which had like to have cost him dearly (*v.* 1): *He returned to his house in peace.* Notice is taken of this to intimate, (1.) That he fared better than he had expected. He had been in imminent peril, and yet came home in peace. Whenever we return in peace to our houses we ought to acknowledge God's providence in preserving our going out and our coming in. But, if we have been kept through more than ordinary dangers, we are in a special manner bound to be thankful. There was but a step perhaps between us and death, and yet we are alive. (2.) That he fared better than he deserved. He was out of the way of his duty, had been out upon an expedition which he could not well account for to God and his conscience, and yet he returned in peace; for God is not extreme to mark what we do amiss, nor does he withdraw his protection every time we forfeit it. (3.) That he fared better than Ahab king of Israel did, who was brought home slain. Though Jehoshaphat had said to Ahab, *I am as thou art,* God distinguished him; for he knows and owns *the way of the righteous,* but *the way of the ungodly shall perish.* Distinguishing mercies are very obliging. here were two kings in the field together, *one taken and the other left,* one brought home in blood, the other in peace.

2. In sending him a reproof for his affinity with Ahab. It is a great mercy to be made sensible of our faults, and to be told in time wherein we have erred, that we may repent and amend the error before it be too late. The prophet by whom the reproof is sent is Jehu the son of Hanani. The father was an eminent prophet in the last reign, as appeared by Asa's putting him in the stocks for his plain dealing; yet the son was not afraid to reprove another king. Paul would have his son Timothy not only discouraged, but animated by his sufferings, 2 Tim. 3:11, 14. (1.) The prophet told him plainly that he had done very ill in joining with Ahab: *"Shouldst thou,* a godly man, *help the ungodly,* give them a hand of fellowship, and lend them a hand of assistance?" Or, *"Shouldst thou love those that hate the Lord;* wilt thou lay those in thy bosom whom God beholds afar off?" It is the black character of wicked people that they are *haters of God,* Rom. 1:30. Idolaters are so reputed in the second commandment; and therefore it is not for those that love God to take delight in them or contract an intimacy with them. *Do I not hate those,* says David, *that hate thee?* Ps. 139:21, 11. Those whom the grace of God has dignified ought not to debase themselves. Let God's people be of God's mind. (2.) That God was displeased with him for doing this: *"There is wrath upon thee from before the Lord,* and thou must, by repentance, make thy peace with him, or it will be the worse for thee." He did so, and God's anger was turned away. Yet his trouble, as recorded in the next chapter, was a rebuke to him for meddling with strife that belonged not to him. If he be so fond of war, he shall have enough of it. And the great mischief which his seed after him fell into by the house of Ahab was the just punishment of his affinity with that house. (3.) Yet he took notice of that which was praiseworthy, as it is proper for us to do when we give a reproof (*v.* 3): *"There are good things found in thee;* and therefore, though God be displeased with thee, he does not, he will not, cast thee off." His abolishing idolatry with a heart fixed for God and engaged to seek him was a good thing, which God accepted and would have him go on with, notwithstanding the displeasure he had now incurred.

II. The return of duty which Jehoshaphat made to God for this favour. he took the reproof well, was not wroth with the seer as his father was, but submitted. *Let the righteous smite me, it shall be a kindness.* See what effect the reproof had upon him. 1. He *dwelt at Jerusalem* (*v.* 4), minded his own business at home, and would not expose himself by paying any more such visits to Ahab. *Rebuke a wise man, and he will be yet wiser,* and will take warning, Prov. 9:8, 9. 2. To atone (as I may say) for the visit he had paid to Ahab, he made a pious profitable visitation of his own kingdom: He *went out through the people* in his own person from Beersheba in the south to Mount Ephriam in the north, and *brought them back to the Lord God of their fathers,* that is, did all he could towards recovering them. (1.) By what the prophet said he perceived that his former attempts for reformation were well pleasing to God, and therefore he revived them, and did what was then left undone. It is good when commendations thus quicken us to our duty, and when the more we are praised for doing well the more vigorous we are in well-doing. (2.) Perhaps he found that his late affinity with the idolatrous house of Ahab and kingdom of Israel had had a bad influence upon his own kingdom. Many, we may suppose, were emboldened to revolt to idolatry when they saw even their reforming king so intimate with idolaters; and therefore he thought himself doubly obliged to do all he could to restore them. If we truly repent of our sin, we shall do our utmost to repair the damage we have any way done by it to religion or the souls of others. We are particularly concerned to recover those that have fallen into sin, or been hardened in it, by our example.

Verses 5–11

Jehoshaphat, having done what he could to make his people good, is here providing, if possible, to keep them so by the influence of a settled magistracy. He had sent preachers among them, to instruct them (*ch.* 17:7–9), and that provision did well; but now he saw it further requisite to send judges among them, to see the laws put in execution, and to be a terror to evil-doers. It is probable that there were judges up and down the country before, but either they neglected their business or the people slighted them, so that the end of the institution was not answered; and therefore it was necessary it should be newmodelled, new men employed, and a new charge given them. That is it which is here done.

I. He erected inferior courts of justice in the several cities of the kingdom, *v.* 5. The judges of these courts were to keep the people in the worship of God, to punish the violations of the law, and to decide controversies between man and man. Here is the charge he gave them (*v.* 6), in which we have,

1. The means he prescribes to them for the keeping of them closely to their duty; and these are two: — (1.) Great caution and circumspection: *Take heed what you do, v.* 6. And again, *"Take heed and do it, v.* 7. Mind your business; take heed of making any mistakes; be afraid of misunderstanding any point of law, or the matter of fact." Judges, of all men, have need to be cautious, because so much depends upon the correctness of their judgment. (2.) Great piety and religion: *"Let the fear of God be upon you,* and that will be a restraint upon you to keep you from doing wrong (Neh. *v.* 15; Gen. 42:18) and an engagement to you to be active in doing the duty of your place." Let destruction from God be a terror to them, as Job speaks (Job 31:23), and then they will be a terror to none but evil-doers.

2. The motives he would have them consider, to en-

gage them to faithfulness. These are three, all taken from God: — (1.) That from him they had their commission; his ministers they were. The powers that be are ordained by him and for him: *"You judge not for man, but for the Lord;* your business is to glorify him, and serve the interests of his kingdom among men." (2.) That his eye was upon them: "He is *with you in the judgment,* to take notice what you do and call you to an account if you do amiss." (3.) That he is the great example of justice to all magistrates: *There is no iniquity with him,* no bribery, nor respect of persons. Magistrates are called gods, and therefore must endeavour to resemble him.

II. He erected a supreme court at Jerusalem, which was advised with, and appealed to, in all the difficult causes that occurred in the inferior courts, and which gave judgment upon demurrers (to speak in the language of our own law), special verdicts, and writs of error. This court sat in Jerusalem; for *there were set the thrones of judgment:* there they would be under the inspection of the king himself. Observe,

1. The causes cognizable in this court; and they were of two kinds, as with us: — (1.) Pleas of the crown, called here *the judgment of the Lord,* because the law of God was the law of the realm. All criminals were charged with the breach of some part of his law and were said to offend against his peace, his crown and dignity. (2.) Common pleas, between party and party, called here *controversies* (*v.* 8) and *causes of their brethren* (*v.* 10), differences *between blood and blood* (this refers to Deu. 17:8), between the blood of the person slain and the blood of the manslayer. Since the revolt of the ten tribes all the cities of refuge, except Hebron, belonged to the kingdom of Israel; and therefore, we may suppose, the courts of the temple, or the horns of the altar, were chiefly used as sanctuaries in that case, and hence the trial of homicides was reserved for the court at Jerusalem. If the inferior judges did not agree about the sense of any law or commandment, any statute or judgment, this court must determine the controversy.

2. The judges of this court were some of *the Levites and priests* that were most learned in the law, eminent for wisdom, and of approved integrity, and some of *the chief of the fathers of Israel, peers of the realm,* as I may call them, or persons of age and experience, that had been men of business, who would be the most competent judges of matters of fact, as the priests and Levites were of the sense of the law.

3. The two chiefs, or presidents, of this court. Amariah, the high priest, was to preside in ecclesiastical causes, to direct the court and be the mouth of it, or perhaps to be last consulted in cases which the judges themselves doubted of. Zebadiah, the prime-minister of that state, was to preside in all civil causes, *v.* 11. Thus there are diversities of gifts and operations, but all from the same Spirit, and for the good of the body. Some best understand *the matters of the Lord,* others *the king's matters;* neither can say to the other, *I have no need of thee,* for God's Israel has need of both; and, as every one has received the gift, so let him minister the same. Blessed be God both for magistrates and ministers, scribes and statesmen, men of books and men of business.

4. The inferior officers of the court. "Some of *the Levites* (such as had not abilities to qualify them for judges) *shall be officers before you," v.* 11. They were to bring causes into the court, and to see the sentence of the judges executed. And these hands and feet were as necessary in their places as the eyes and heads (the judges) in theirs.

5. The charge which the king gave them. (1.) They must see to it that they acted from a good principle; they must do all in the *fear of the Lord,* setting him always before them, and then they would act faithfully, conscientiously, and *with a perfect upright heart, v.* 9. (2.) They must make it their great and constant care to prevent sin, *to warn the people that they trespass not against the Lord,* inspire them with a dread of sin, not only as hurtful to themselves and the public peace, but as an offence to God, and that which would bring wrath upon the people if they committed it and upon the magistrates if they did not punish it. *"This do, and you shall not trespass;"* this implies that those who have power in their hands contract the guilt of sin themselves if they do not use their power for the preventing and restraining of sin in others. "You trespass if you do not keep them from trespassing." (3.) They must act with resolution. "Deal courageously, and fear not the face of man; be bold and daring in the discharge of your duty, and, whoever is against you, God will protect you: *The Lord shall be with the good."* Wherever he finds a good man, a good magistrate, he will be found a good God.

CHAPTER 20

We have here, I. The great danger and distress that Jehoshaphat and his kingdom were in from a foreign invasion (*v.* 1, 2). II. The pious course he took for their safety, by fasting, and praying, and seeking God (*v.* 3–13). III. The assurance which God, by a prophet, immediately gave them of victory (*v.* 14–17). IV. Their thankful believing reception of those assurances (*v.* 18–21). V. The defeat which God gave to their enemies thereupon (*v.* 22–25). VI. A solemn thanksgiving which they kept for their victory, and for a happy consequences of it (*v.* 26–30). VII. The conclusion of the reign of Jehoshaphat, not without some blemishes (*v.* 31–37).

Verses 1–13

We left Jehoshaphat, in the foregoing chapter, well employed in reforming his kingdom and providing for the due administration of justice and support of religion in it, and expected nothing but to hear of the peace and prosperity of his reign; but here we have him in distress, which distress, however, was followed by such a glorious deliverance as was an abundant recompence for his piety. If we meet with trouble in the way of duty, we may believe it is that God may have an opportunity of showing us so much the more of his marvellous loving-kindness. We have here,

I. A formidable invasion of Jehoshaphat's kingdom by the Moabites, and Ammonites, and their auxiliaries, *v.* 1. Jehoshaphat was surprised with the intelligence of it when the enemy had already entered his country, *v.* 2. What pretence they had to quarrel with Jehoshaphat does not appear; they are said to come *from beyond the sea,* meaning *the Dead Sea,* where Sodom had stood. It should seem, they marched through those of the ten tribes that lay beyond Jordan, and they gave them passage through their borders; so ungrateful were they to Jehoshaphat, who had lately put his hand to help them in recovering Ramoth-Gilead. Several nations joined in this confederacy, but especially *the children of Lot,* whom the rest helped, Ps. 83:6–8. The neighbouring nations had feared Jehoshaphat (*ch.* 17:10), but perhaps his affinity with Ahab had lessened him in their esteem, and they had some intimation that his God was displeased with him for it, which they fancied would give them an opportunity to make a prey of his kingdom.

II. The preparation Jehoshaphat made against the invaders. No mention is made of his mustering his forces, which yet it is most probable he did, for God must be trusted in the use of means. But his great care was to obtain the favour of God, and secure him on his side, which perhaps he was the more solicitous about because he had been lately told that there was *wrath upon him from before the Lord, ch.* 19:2. But he is of the mind of his father David. If we must be corrected, yet *let us not fall into the hands of man.* 1. He feared. Consciousness of guilt made him fear. Those that have least sin are the most sensible of it. The surprise added to the fright. Holy fear is a spur to prayer and preparation, Heb. 11:7. 2. *He set himself to seek the Lord,* and, in the first place, to make him his friend. Those that would seek the Lord so as to find him, and to find favour with him, must *set* themselves to seek him, must do it with fixedness of thought, with sincerity of intention, and with the utmost vigour and resolution to continue seeking him. 3. He *proclaimed a fast throughout all Judah,* appointed a day of humiliation and prayer, that they might join together in confessing their sins and *asking help of the Lord.* Fasting from bodily refreshments, upon such extraordinary occasions, is a token of self-judging for the sins we have committed (we own ourselves unworthy of the bread we eat, and that God might justly withhold it from us), and of self-denial for the future; fasting *for* sin implies a resolution to fast *from* it, though it has been to us as a sweet morsel. Magistrates are to call their people to the duty of fasting and prayer upon such occasions, that it may be a national act, and so may obtain national mercies. 4. The people readily assembled out of all the cities of Judah in the court of the temple to join in prayer (*v.* 4), and they *stood before the Lord,* as beggars at his door, with their wives and children; they and their families were in danger, and therefore they bring their families with them to seek the Lord. "Lord, we are indeed a provoking people, that deserve to be abandoned to ruin; but here are little ones that are innocent, let not them perish in the storm." Nineveh was spared for the sake of the little ones, Jonah 4:11. The place they met in was the *house of the Lord,* before *the new court,* which was perhaps lately added to the former courts (that, as some think, which was called the *court of the women*); thus they came within reach of that gracious promise which God had made, in answer to Solomon's prayer, *ch.* 7:15. *My ears shall be attentive to the prayer that is made in this place.* 5. Jehoshaphat himself was the mouth of the congregation to God, and did not devolve the work upon his chaplains. Though the kings were forbidden to burn incense, they were allowed to pray and preach; as Solomon and Jehoshaphat here. The prayer Jehoshaphat prayed, upon this occasion, is here recorded, or part of it; and an excellent prayer it is. (1.) He acknowledges the sovereign dominion of the divine Providence, gives to God the glory of it and takes to himself the comfort of it (*v.* 6): *"Art not thou God in heaven?* No doubt thou art, which none of the gods of the heathen are; make it to appear then. Is not thy dominion, supreme over kingdoms themselves, and universal, over all kingdoms, even those of the heathen that know thee not? Control these heathen then; set bounds to their daring threatening insults. Is there not *in thy hand* the *power and might* which *none is able to withstand?* Lord, exert it on our behalf. Glorify thy own omnipotence." (2.) He lays hold on their covenant-relation to God and interest in him. "Thou that art *God in heaven* art the *God of our fathers* (*v.* 6) and *our God, v.* 7. Whom should we seek to, whom should we trust to, for relief, but to the God we have chosen and served?" (3.) He shows the title they had to this good land they were now in possession of; an indisputable title it was: *"Thou gavest it to the seed of Abraham thy friend.* He was thy friend (this is referred to, James 2:23, to show the honour of Abraham, that *he was called the friend of God*); we are *his seed,* and hope to be *beloved for the father's sake,"* Rom. 11:28; Deu. 7:8, 9. "We hold this land by grant from thee. Lord, maintain thy own grant, and warrant it against all unjust claims. Suffer us not to be *cast out of they possession.* We are tenants; thou art our landlord; wilt thou not hold thy own?" *v.* 11. Those that use what they have for God may comfortably hope that he will secure it to them. (4.) He makes mention of the sanctuary, the temple they had built for God's name (*v.* 8), not as if that merited any thing at God's hand, for *of his own they gave him,* but it was such a token of God's favourable presence with them that they had promised themselves he would hear and help them when, in their distress, they cried to him before that house, *v.* 8, 9. "Lord, when it was built it was intended for the encouragement of our faith at such a time as this. Here thy name is; here we are. Lord, help us, for the glory of thy name." (5.) He pleads the ingratitude and injustice of his enemies: "We are such as it will be thy glory to appear *for;* they are such as it will be thy glory to appear *against;* for, [1.] They ill requite our ancient kindnesses. Thou *wouldst not let Israel invade them,* nor give them any disturbance." Deu. 2:5, 9, 19, *Meddle not with the Edomites, distress not the Moabites, come not nigh the children of Ammon,* no not though they provoke you. "Yet now see how they invade us." We may comfortably appear to God against those that render us evil for good. [2.] "They break in upon our ancient rights. They come *to cast us out of our possessions,* and seize our land for themselves. *O! our God, wilt thou not judge them? v.* 12. Wilt thou not give sentence against them, and execute it upon them?" The justice of God is the refuge of those that are wronged. (6.) He professes his entire dependence upon God for deliverance. Though he had a great army on foot, and well disciplined; yet he said, *"We have no might against this great company,* none without thee, none that we can expect any thing from without thy special presence and blessing, none to boast of, none to trust to; but *our eyes are upon thee.* We rely upon thee, and from thee is all our expectation. The disease seems desperate: *we know not what to do,* are quite at a loss, in a great strait. But this is a sovereign remedy, *our eyes are upon thee,* an eye of acknowledgment and humble submission, an eye of faith and entire dependence, an eye of desire and hearty prayer, an eye of hope and patient expectation. *In thee, O God! do we put our trust; our souls wait on thee."*

Verses 14–19

We have here God's gracious answer to Jehoshaphat's prayer; and it was a speedy answer. *While he was yet speaking God heard:* before the congregation was dismissed they had assurance given them that they should be victorious; for it is never in vain to seek God. 1. The spirit of prophecy came upon a Levite that was present, not in any place of eminency, but *in the midst of the congregation, v.* 14. The Spirit, like the wind, *blows where* and on whom *he listeth.* He was of the sons of Asaph, and therefore one of the singers; on that office God would put an honour. Whether he was a prophet before this or no is uncertain, most probably he was, which would make him the more regarded. There needed no sign, the thing itself was to be performed the very next day, and that would be confirmation enough to his prophecy. 2. He encouraged them to trust in God, though the danger was very threatening (*v.* 15): "*Be not afraid;* you have admitted fear enough to bring you to God, do not now admit that which will drive you to God, do not now admit that which will drive you from him again. *The battle is not yours;* it is not in your own strength, not for your own cause, that you engage; the *battle is God's:* he does and will, as you have desired, interest himself in the cause." 3. He gives them intelligence of the motions of the enemy, and orders them to march towards them, with particular directions where they should find them. *To-morrow* (the day after the fast) *go you down against them, v.* 16, 17. It is fit that he who commands the deliverance should command those for whom the deliverance is to be wrought, and give the necessary orders, both for time and place. 4. He assures them that they should be, not the glorious instruments, but the joyful spectators, of the total defeat of the enemy: "You shall not need to strike a stroke; the work shall be done to your hands; only stand still and see it," *v.* 17. As Moses said to Israel at the Red Sea (Ex. 14:13), "*God is with you,* who is able to do his work himself, and will do it. If the battle be his, the victory shall be his too." Let but the Christian soldier go out against his spiritual enemies, and the God of peace will *tread them under his feet* and make *him more than a conqueror.* 5. Jehoshaphat and his people received these assurances with faith, reverence, and thankfulness. (1.) They *bowed their heads,* Jehoshaphat first, and then all the people, *fell before the Lord, and worshipped,* receiving with a holy awe and fear of God this token of his favour, and saying with faith, *Be it unto us according to thy word.* (2.) They lifted up their voices in praise to God, *v.* 19. An active faith can give thanks for a promise though it be not yet performed, knowing that God's bonds are as good as ready money. *God hath spoken in his holiness; I will rejoice,* Ps. 60:5.

Verses 20–30

We have here the foregoing prayer answered and the foregoing promise performed, in the total overthrow of the enemies' forces and the triumph (for so it was rather than a victory) of Jehoshaphat's forces over them.

I. Never was army drawn out to the field of battle as Jehoshaphat's was. He had soldiers *ready prepared for war* (*ch.* 17:18), but here is no notice taken of their military equipment, their swords or spears, their shields or bows. But Jehoshaphat took care, 1. That faith should be their armour. As they went forth, instead of calling them to handle their arms, and stand to them, to keep ranks, observe orders, and fight valiantly, he bade them *believe in the Lord God* and give credit to his word in the mouth of his prophets, and assured them that they should *prosper* and *be established, v.* 20. That is true courage which faith inspires a man with; nor will any thing contribute more to the establishing of the heart in shaking times than a firm belief of the power, and mercy, and promise of God. The heart is *fixed* that thus *trusteth in the Lord,* and is kept in perfect peace. In our spiritual conflicts, this is the victory, this is the prosperity, even our faith. 2. That praise and thanksgiving should be their vanguard, *v.* 21. Jehoshaphat called a council of war, and it was resolved to appoint *singers to go out before the army,* to charge in the front, who had nothing else to do but to praise God, to praise his holiness, which is his beauty, to praise him as they did in the temple (that beauty of holiness) with that ancient and good doxology which eternity itself will not wear thread-bare, *Praise the Lord; for his mercy endureth for ever.* By this strange advance towards the field of battle, Jehoshaphat intended to express his firm reliance upon the word of God (which enabled him to triumph before the battle), to animate his own soldiers, to confound the enemy, and to engage God on their side; for praise pleases God better than all *burnt offering and sacrifice.*

II. Never was army so unaccountably destroyed as that of the enemy; not by thunder, or hail, or the sword of an angel, not by dint of sword, or strength of arm, or any surprising alarm, like that which Gideon gave the Midianites; but the Lord set ambushments against them, either hosts of angels, or, as bishop Patrick thinks, their own ambushments, whom God struck with such confusion that they fell upon their own friends as if they had been enemies, and *every one helped to destroy another,* so that *none escaped.* This God did *when his people began to sing and to praise* (*v.* 22), for he delights to furnish those with *matter* for praise that have *hearts* for it. We read of his being *angry at the prayers of his people* (Ps. 80:4), but never at their *praises.* When they did but begin the work of praise God perfected the work of their deliverance. What ground there was for their jealousies one of another does not appear, perhaps there was none; but so it was that the Ammonites and the Moabites fell foul upon the Edomites and cut them off, and then they fell out with one another and cut one another off, *v.* 23. Thus God often makes wicked people instruments of destruction to one another; and what alliances can be so firm as to keep those together whom God designs to dash in pieces one against another? See the mischievous consequences of divisions which neither of the contending parties can give any good account of the reason of. Those are wretchedly infatuated, to their ruin, that fall foul upon their friends as if they were enemies.

III. Never was spoil so cheerfully divided, for Jehoshaphat's army had nothing to do besides; the rest was done for them. When they came to the view of this vast army, instead of finding living men to fight with, they found them all dead men, and their carcases spread as dung upon the face of the earth, *v.* 24. See how rich God is in mercy to those that call upon him in truth, and how often he outdoes him in truth, and how often he out-does the prayers and expectations of his people. Jehoshaphat and his people prayed to be delivered from being spoiled by the enemy; and God not only delivered them, but enriched them with the spoil of the enemy. The plunder of the field was very great and very rich. They found precious jewels with the dead bodies, which yet could not save them from being loathsome carcases. The spoil *was more than they could carry away* at once, and they were *three days in gathering it, v.* 25. Now it appeared what was God's end in bringing this great army against Judah; it was to humble them and prove them, that he might *do them good in their latter end.* It seemed at first a disturbance to their reformation, but it proved a recompence of it.

IV. Never was victory celebrated with more solemn and enlarged thanksgivings. 1. They kept a day of praise in the camp, before they drew their forces out of the field. Many thanksgivings, no doubt, were offered up to God immediately; but on the fourth day they assembled in a valley, where they blessed God with so much zeal and fervency that that day's work gave a name to the place, the valley of *Berachah,* that is, *of blessing, v.* 26. The remembrance of this work of wonder was hereby perpetuated, for the encouragement of succeeding generations to trust in God. 2. Yet they did not think this enough, but came in solemn procession, all in a body, and Jehoshaphat at the head of them, to Jerusalem, that the country, as they passed along, might join with them in their praises, and that they might give thanks for the mercy where they had by prayer obtained it, *in the house of the Lord, v.* 27, 28. Praising God must not be the work of a day only; but our praises, when we have received mercy, must be often repeated, as our prayers were when we were in the pursuit of it. Every day we must bless God; as long as we live, and while we have any being, we must praise him, spending our time in that work in which we hope to spend our eternity. Public mercies call for public acknowledgments *in the courts of the Lord's house,* Ps. 116:19.

V. Never did victory turn to a better account than this; for, 1. Jehoshaphat's kingdom was hereby made to look very great and considerable abroad, *v.* 29. When they heard that God fought thus for Israel, they could not but say, *There is none like unto the God of Jeshurun,* and *Happy art thou, O Israel!* It begat in the neighbours a reverence of God and a cautious fear of doing any injury to his people. It is dangerous fighting against those who have God with them. 2. It was made very easy and quiet at home, *v.* 30. (1.) They were quiet among themselves. Those that were displeased at the destroying of the images and groves were now satisfied, and obliged to own that since the God of Israel could deliver after this sort he only is to be worshipped, in that way only which he himself has appointed. (2.) They were quiet from the fear of insults from their neighbours, God having given them rest round about. And, if he give rest, who can give disturbance?

Verses 31–37

We are now drawing towards the close of the history of Jehoshaphat's reign, for a further account of which those who lived when this book was published were referred to an authentic history of it, written by Jehu the prophet (*ch.* 19:2), which was then extant, *v.* 34. This was the general character of his reign, that he did that which was right in the sight of the Lord, kept close to the worship of God himself and did what he could to keep his people close to it. But two things are here to be lamented: — 1. The people still retained a partiality for the high places, *v.* 33. Those that were erected to the honour of strange gods were taken away (*ch.* 17:6); but those where the true God was worshipped, being less culpable, were thought allowable, and Jehoshaphat was loth to disoblige the people so far as to take them away, for as yet they had not prepared their hearts to serve the God of their fathers. They complied with Jehoshaphat's reformation because they could not for shame do otherwise, but they were not hearty in it, did not direct their hearts to God in it, did not act in it from any good principle nor with any zeal or resolution: and the best magistrates cannot bring to pass what they would, in reformation, when the people are cool in it. 2. Jehoshaphat himself still retained a partiality for the house of Ahab, because he had married his son to a daughter of that family, though he had been plainly reproved for it and had like to have smarted for it. He saw and knew that Ahaziah, the son of Ahab, did very wickedly, and therefore could not expect to prosper; yet he joined himself with him, not in war, as with his father, but in trade, became his partner in an East India fleet bound for Ophir, *v.* 35, 36. There is an emphasis laid upon the time — *after this,* after God had done such great things for him, without any such scandalous and pernicious confederacies, given him not only victory, but wealth, yet after this to go and join himself with a wicked king was very ungrateful. *After God had given him such a deliverance as this should he again break God's commandments, and join in affinity with the people of these abominations?* What could he expect but that *God should be angry with him?* Ezra 9:13, 14. Yet he sends to him, to show him his error and bring him to repentance, (1.) By a prophet, who foretold the blasting of his project, *v.* 37. And, (2.) By a storm, which broke the ships in the port before they set sail, by which he was warned to break off his alliance with Ahaziah; and it seems he took the warning, for, when Ahaziah afterwards pressed him to join with him, he *would not,* 1 Ki. 22:49. See how pernicious a thing it is to join in friendship and society with evil-doers. It is a hard matter to break off from it. A man may much better keep himself from being taken in the snare than recover himself out of it.

CHAPTER 21

Never surely did any kingdom change its king so much for the worse as Judah did, when Jehoram, one of the vilest, succeeded Jehoshaphat, one of the best. Thus were they punished for not making a better use of Jehoshaphat's good government, and their disaffectedness (or coldness at least) to his reformation, 20:33. Those that knew not now to value a good king are justly plagued with a bad one. Here is, I. Jehoram's elevation to the throne (*v.* 1–3). II. The wicked course he took to establish himself in it, by the murder of his brethren (*v.* 4). III. The idolatries and other wickedness he was guilty of (*v.* 5, 6, 11). IV. The prophecy of Elijah against him (*v.* 12–15). V. The judgments of God upon him, in the revolt of his subjects from him (*v.* 8–10) and the success of his enemies against him (*v.* 16, 17). VI. His miserable sickness and inglorious exit (*v.* 18–20). VII. The preservation of the house of David notwithstanding (*v.* 7).

Verses 1–11

We find here,

I. That Jehoshaphat was a very careful indulgent father to Jehoram. He had many sons, who are here named (*v.* 2), and it is said (*v.* 13) that they were better than Jehoram, had a great deal more wisdom and virtue, and lived up to their education, which he went counter to. They were very hopeful, and any of them more fit for the crown than he; and yet, because he was the first-born (*v.* 3), his father secured the kingdom to him, and portioned his brethren and disposed of them so as that they would be easy and give him no disturbance; as Abraham, when he made Isaac his heir, dismissed his other children with gifts. Herein Jehoshaphat was very kind and fair to his son, which might have obliged him to be respectful to him, and tread in the steps of so good a father. But it is no new thing for the children that have been most indulged by their parents to be least dutiful to them. Whether in doing this he acted wisely and well for his people, and was just to them, I cannot say. His birthright entitled him to a double portion of his father's estate, Deu. 21:17. But if he appeared utterly unfit for government (the end of which is the good of the people), and likely to undo all that his father had done, it would have been better perhaps to have set him aside, and taken the next that was hopeful, and not inclined as he was to idolatry. Power is a sacred thing, with which men may either do much good or much hurt; and therefore *Detur digniori — Let him that deserves it have it. Salus populi suprema lex — The security of the people is the first consideration.*

II. That Jehoram was a most barbarous brother to his father's sons. As soon as he had settled himself in the throne he slew all his brethren with the sword, either by false accusation, under colour of law, or rather by assassination. By some wicked hand or other he got them all murdered, pretending (it is likely) that he could not think himself safe in the government till they were taken out of the way. Those that mean ill themselves are commonly, without cause, jealous of those about them. The wicked fear where no fear is, or pretend to do so, in order to conceal their malice. Jehoram, it is likely, hated his brethren and slew them for the same reason that Cain hated Abel and slew him, because their piety condemned his impiety and won them that esteem with the people which he had lost. With them he slew divers of the princes of Israel, who adhered to them, or were likely to avenge their death. The princes of Judah, those who had taught the good knowledge of the Lord (*ch.* 17:7), are here called princes of Israel, as before *fathers of Israel* (*ch.* 19:8), because they were Israelites indeed, men of integrity. The sword which the good father had put into their hands this wicked son sheathed in their bowels. Woe unto him that thus *foundeth a kingdom in blood* (Hab. 2:12); it will prove a foundation that will sink the superstructure.

III. That Jehoram was a most wicked king, who corrupted and debauched his kingdom, and ruined the reformation that his good father and grandfather had carried on: He *walked in the way of the house of Ahab* (*v.* 6), made high places, which the people were of themselves too forward to make, and did his utmost to set up idolatry again, *v.* 11. 1. As for the inhabitants of Jerusalem, where he kept his court, he easily drew them into his spiritual whoredom: He *caused them to commit fornication,* seducing them *to eat things sacrificed to idols,* Rev. 2:20. 2. The country people seem to have been brought to it with more difficulty; but those that would not be corrupted by flatteries were driven by force to partake in his abominable idolatries: He *compelled Judah thereto.* He used that power for the destruction of the church which was given him for the edification of it.

IV. That when he forsook God and his worship his subjects withdrew from their allegiance to him. 1. Some of the provinces abroad that were tributaries to him did so. The Edomites revolted (*v.* 8), and, though he chastised them (*v.* 9), yet he could not reduce them, *v.* 10. 2. One of the cities of his own kingdom did so. Libnah revolted (*v.* 10) and set up for a free state, as of old it had a king of its own, Jos. 12:15. And the reason is here given, not only why God permitted it, but why they did it; they shook off his government because he had forsaken the Lord God of his fathers, had become an idolater and a worshipper of false gods, and they could not continue subject to him without some danger of being themselves also drawn away from God and their duty. While he adhered to God they adhered to him; but, when he cast God off, they cast him off. Whether this reason will justify them in their revolt of no, it will justify God's providence which ordered it so.

V. That yet God was tender of his covenant with the house of David, and therefore would not destroy the royal family, though it was so wretchedly corrupted and degenerated, *v.* 7. These things we had before, 2 Ki. 8:19–22. The tenour of the covenant was that David's seed should be visited for their transgressions, but the covenant should never be broken, Ps. 89:30, etc.

Verses 12–20

Here we have, I. A warning from God sent to Jehoram by a writing from Elijah the prophet. By this it appears that Jehoram came to the throne, and showed himself what he was before Elijah's translation. It is true we find Elisha attending Jehoshaphat, and described as pouring water on the hands of Elijah, after the story of Elijah's translation (2 Ki. 3:11); but that might be, and that description might be given of him, while Elijah was yet on earth: and it is certain that that history is put out of its proper place, for we read of Jehoshaphat's death, and Jehoram's coming to the crown, before we read of Elijah's translation, 1 Ki. 22:50. We will suppose that the time of his departure was at hand, so that he could not go in person to Jehoram; but that, hearing of his great wickedness in murdering his brethren, he left this writing it is probable with Elisha, to be sent him by the first opportunity, that it might either be a means to reclaim him or a witness against him that he was fairly told what would be in the end hereof. The message is sent him in the name of *the Lord God of David his father* (*v.* 12), upbraiding him with his relation to David as that which, though it was his honour, was an aggravation of his degeneracy. 1. His crimes are plainly charged upon him — his departure from the good ways of God, in which he had been educated, and which he had been directed and encouraged to walk in by the example of his good father and grandfather, who lived and died in peace and honour (*v.* 12) — his conformity to the ways of the house of Ahab, that impious scandalous family — his setting up and enforcing idolatry in his kingdom — and his murdering his brethren because they were better than himself, *v.* 13. These are the heads of the indictment against him. 2. Judgment is given against him for these crimes; he is plainly told that his sin should certainly be the ruin, (1.) Of his kingdom and family (*v.* 14): "With a heavy stroke, even that of war and captivity, *will the Lord smite thy people and thy children,*" etc. Bad men bring God's judgments upon all about them. His people justly suffer because they had complied with his idolatry, and his wives because they had drawn him to it. (2.) Of his health and life: "Thou shalt have great sickness, very painful and tedious, and at last mortal," *v.* 15. This he is warned of before, that his blood might be upon his own head, the watchman having delivered his soul; and that when these things so particularly foretold, came to pass, it might appear that they did not come by chance, but as the punishment of his sins, and were so intended. And now if, as he had learned of Ahab to do wickedly, he had but learned even of Ahab to humble himself upon the receipt of this threatening message from Elijah — if, like (1 Ki. 21:27), he had *rent his clothes, put on sackcloth, and fasted* — who knows but, like him, he might have obtained at least a reprieve? But it does not appear that he took any notice of it; he threw it by as waste-paper; Elijah seemed to him *as one that mocked.* But those that will not believe shall feel.

II. The threatened judgments brought upon him because he slighted the warning. No marvel that hardened sinners are not frightened from sin and to repentance by the threatenings of misery in another world, which is future and out of sight, when the certain prospect of misery in this world, the sinking of their estates and the ruin of their healths, will not restrain them from vicious courses.

1. See Jehoram here stripped of all his comforts. God *stirred up the spirit of his neighbours* against him, who had loved and feared Jehoshaphat, but hated and despised him, looking upon it as a scandalous thing for a nation to change their gods. Some occasion or other they took to quarrel with him, invaded his country, but, as it should seem, fought neither against small nor great, but the king's house only; they made directly to that, and *carried away all the substance that was found in it.* No mention is made of their carrying any away captive but the *king's wives* and *his sons, v.* 17. Thus God made it evident that the controversy was with him and his house. Here it is only said, They *carried away* his sons; but we find (*ch.* 22:1) that they *slew them all.* Blood for blood. He had slain all his brethren, to strengthen himself; and now all his sons are slain but one, and so he is weakened. If he had not been of the house of David, that one would not have escaped. When Jeroboam's house, and Baasha's, and Ahab's, were destroyed, there was none left; but David's house must not be wholly extirpated, though sometimes wretchedly degenerated, because a blessing was in it, no less a blessing than that of the Messiah.

2. See him tormented with *sore diseases and of long continuance,* such as were threatened in the law against those that would not *fear the Lord their God,* Deu. 28:58, 59. His disease was very grievous. It lay in his bowels, producing a continual griping, and with this there was a complication of other sore diseases. The affliction was moreover very tedious. Two years he continued ill, and could get no relief; for the disease was incurable, though he was in the prime of life, not forty years old. Asa, whose heart was perfect with God though in some instances he stepped aside, was diseased only in his feet; but Jehoram, whose heart was wicked, was struck in his inwards, and he that had no bowels of compassion towards his brethren was so plagued in his bowels that they fell out. Even good men, and those who are very dear to God, may be afflicted with diseases of this kind; but to them they are fatherly chastisements, and by the support of divine consolations the soul may dwell at ease even then when the body lies in pain. These sore diseases seized him just after his house was plundered and his wives and children were carried away. (1.) Perhaps his grief and anguish of mind for that calamity might occasion his sickness, or at least contribute to the heightening of it. (2.) By this sickness he was disabled to do any thing for the recovery of them or the revenge of the injury done him. (3.) It added, no doubt, very much to his grief, in his sickness, that he was deprived of the society of his wives and children and that all the substance of his house was carried away. To be sick and poor, sick and solitary, but especially to be sick and in sin, sick and under the curse of God, sick and destitute of grace to bear the affliction, and of comfort to counterbalance it — is a most deplorable case.

3. See him buried in disgrace. He reigned but eight years, and then *departed without being desired, v.* 20. Nobody valued him while he lived, none lamented him when he died, but all wished that no greater loss might ever come to Jerusalem. To show what little affection or respect they had for him, they would not *bury him in the sepulchres of the kings,* as thinking him unworthy to be numbered among them who had governed so ill. The excluding of his body from the sepulchres of his fathers might be ordered by Providence as an intimation of the everlasting separation of the souls of the wicked after death, from the spirits of just men. This further disgrace they put upon him, that they *made no burning for him, like the burning of his fathers, v.* 19. His memory was far from being sweet and precious to them, and therefore they did not honour it with any sweet odours or precious spices, though we may suppose that his dead body, after so long and loathsome a disease, needed something to perfume it. The generality of the people, though prone to idolatry, yet had no true kindness for their idolatrous kings. Wickedness and profaneness make men despicable even in the eyes of those who have but little religion themselves, while natural conscience itself often gives honour to those who are truly pious. Those that *despise God shall be lightly esteemed,* as Jehoram was.

CHAPTER 22

We read, in the foregoing chapter, of the carrying away of Jehoram's sons and his wives; but here we find one of his sons and one of his wives left, his son Ahaziah and his wife Athaliah, both reserved to be the shame and plague of his family. I. Ahaziah was the shame of it as a partaker, 1. In the sin, and, 2. In the destruction, of the house of Ahab (*v.* 1–9). II. Athaliah was the plague of it, for she destroyed all the seed-royal, and usurped the throne (*v.* 10–12).

Verses 1–9

We have here an account of the reign of Ahaziah, a short reign (of one year only), yet long enough, unless it had been better. He was called *Jeho-ahaz* (*ch.* 21:17); here he is called *Ahaz-iah,* which is the same name and of the same signification, only the words of which it is compounded are transposed. He is here said to be forty-two years old when he began to reign (*v.* 2), which could not be, for his father, his immediate predecessor, was but forty when he died, and it is said (2 Ki. 8:26) that he was twenty-two years old when *he began to reign.* Some make this forty-two to be the age of his mother Athaliah, for in the original it is, *he was the son of forty-two years,* that is, the son of a mother that was of that age; and justly is her age put for his, in reproach to him, because she managed him, and did what she would — she, in effect, reigned, and he had little more than the title of king. Many good expositors are ready to allow that this, with some few more such difficulties, arise from the mistake of some transcriber, who put forty-two for twenty-two, and the copies by which the error should have been corrected might be lost. Many ancient translations read it here twenty-two. Few books are now printed without some *errata,* yet the authors do not therefore disown them, nor are the errors of the press imputed to the author, but the candid reader amends them by the sense, or by comparing them with some other part of the work, as we may easily do this.

The history of Ahaziah's reign is briefly summed up in two clauses, *v.* 3, 4. His mother and her relations were his counselors to do wickedly, and it was to his destruction.

I. He did wickedly. Though by a special providence of God he was preserved alive, when all his brethren were slain, and reserved for the crown, notwithstanding he was the youngest of them — though *the inhabitants of Jerusalem,* when they had buried his father ingloriously, made him king, in hopes he would take warning by that not to tread in his steps, but would do better for himself and his kingdom — yet he was not influenced by the favours either of God or man, but *walked in the way of the house of Ahab, did evil in the sight of the Lord* like them (*v.* 3, 4), that is, he worshipped, Baalim and Ashtaroth, supposing (as the learned bishop Patrick thinks) that by these demons, as mediators, they might have easier access to the supreme *Numen,* the God of Israel, or that *these they might resort to at all times* and *for all matters,* as being *nearer at hand,* and *not of so high a dignity,* but of a *middle nature* between the immortal God and mortal men — deified heroes; so they worshipped them as the church of Rome does saints and angels. That was sufficiently bad; but I wish there was no reason to suspect worse. I am apprehensive that they looked upon Jehovah, the God of their fathers, to be altogether such a one as these Baalim, and them to be as great and as good as he, nay, upon one account, more eligible inasmuch as these Baalim encouraged in their worshippers all manner of lewdness and sensuality, which the God of Israel strictly forbade.

II. He was counselled by his mother and her relations to do so. *She was his counsellor* (*v.* 3) and so were *they, after the death of his father, v.* 4. While his father lived *he* took care to keep him to idolatry; but, when he was dead, the house of Ahab feared lest his father's miserable end should deter him from it, and therefore they were very industrious to keep him closely to it, and to make him *seven times* more a *child of hell than themselves.* The counsel of the ungodly is the ruin of many young persons when they are setting out in the world. This young prince might have had better advice if he had pleased from the princes and the judges, the priests and the Levites, that had been famous in his good grandfather's time for teaching in the knowledge of God; but the house of Ahab humoured him, and *he walked after their counsel,* gave himself up to be led by them, and did just as they would have him. Thus do those debase and destroy themselves that forsake the divine guidance.

III. He was counselled by them to his destruction. So it proved. Those that counsel us to do wickedly counsel us to our destruction; while they fawn, and flatter, and pretend friendship, they are really our worst enemies. Those that debauch young men destroy them. It was bad enough that they exposed him to the sword of the Syrians, drawing him in to join with Joram king of Israel in an expedition to Ramoth-Gilead, where Joram was wounded, an expedition that was not for his honour. Those that give us bad counsel in the affairs of religion, if regarded by us, may justly be made of God our counsellors to do foolishly in our own affairs. But that was not all: by engaging him in an intimacy with Joram king of Israel, they involved him in the common ruin of the house of Ahab. He came on a visit to Joram (*v.* 6) just at the time that Jehu was executing the judgment of God upon that idolatrous family, and so was cut off with them, *v.* 7–9. Here, 1. See and dread the mischief of bad company — of joining in with sinners. If not the infection, yet let the destruction be feared. *Come out from Babylon,* that falling house, Rev. 18:4. 2. See and acknowledge the justice of God. His providence brought Ahaziah, just at this fatal juncture, to see Joram, that he might fall with him and be taken as in a snare. This we had an account of before, 2 Ki. 9:27, 28. It is here added that he was decently buried (not as Jehoram, whose dead body was cast into Naboth's vineyard, 2 Ki. 9:26), and the reason given is because he was the son (that is, the grandson) of good Jehoshaphat, *who sought the Lord with his heart.* Thus is *he* remembered with honour long after his death, and some respect shown even to his degenerate unworthy seed for his sake. *The memory of the just is blessed, but the name of the wicked shall rot.*

Verses 10–12

We have here what we had before, 2 Ki. 11:1, etc. 1. A wicked woman endeavouring to destroy the house of David, that she might set up a throne for herself upon the ruins of it. Athaliah barbarously cut off all the seed-royal (*v.* 10), perhaps intending to transmit the crown of Judah after herself to some of her own relations, that though her family was cut off in Israel by Jehu it might be planted in Judah. 2. A good woman effectually preserving it from being wholly extirpated. One of the late king's sons, a child of a year old, was rescued from among the dead, and saved alive by the care of Jehoiada's wife (*v.* 11, 12), that a *lamp might be ordained for God's anointed;* for no word of God shall fall to the ground.

CHAPTER 23

Six years bloody Athaliah had tyrannised; in this chapter we have her deposed and slain, and Joash, the rightful heir, enthroned. We had the story before nearly as it is here related, 2 Ki. 11:4, etc. I. Jehoiada prepared the people for the king, acquainted them with his design, armed them, and appointed them their posts (*v.* 1–10). II. He produced the king to the people, crowned him, and anointed him (*v.* 11). III. He slew the usurper (*v.* 12–15). IV. He reformed the kingdom, re-established religion, and restored the civil government (*v.* 16–21).

Verses 1–11

We may well imagine the bad posture of affairs in Jerusalem during Athaliah's six years' usurpation, and may wonder that God permitted it and his people bore it so long; but after such a dark and tedious night the returning day in this revolution was the brighter and the more welcome. The continuance of David's seed and throne was what God had sworn by his holiness (Ps. 89:35), and an interruption was no defeasance; the stream of government here runs again in the right channel. The instrument and chief manager of the restoration is Jehoiada, who appears to have been, 1. A man of great prudence, who reserved the young prince for so many years till he was fit to appear in public, and till the nation had grown weary of the usurper, who prepared his work beforehand, and then effected it with admirable secresy and expedition. When God has work to do he will qualify and animate men for it. 2. A man of great interest. The captains joined with him, *v.* 1. The Levites and the chief of the fathers of Israel came at his call to Jerusalem (*v.* 2) and were there ready to receive his orders. See what a command wisdom and virtue will give men. *The Levites and all Judah did as Jehoiada commanded* (*v.* 8), and, which is strange, all that were entrusted with the secret kept their own counsel till it was executed. Thus *the words of the wise are heard in quiet,* Eccl. 9:17. 3. A man of great faith. It was not only common equity (much less his wife's relation to the royal family) that put him upon this undertaking, but a regard to the word of God, and the divine entail of the crown (*v.* 3): *The king's son shall reign,* must reign, *as the Lord hath said.* His eye to the promise, and dependence upon that, added a great deal of glory to this undertaking. 4. A man of great religion. This matter was to be done in the temple, which might occasion some breach of rule, and the necessity of the case might be thought to excuse it; but he gave special order that none of the people should come into the house of the Lord, but the priests and Levites only, who were holy, upon pain of death, *v.* 6, 7. Never let sacred things be profaned, no, not for the support of civil rights. 5. A man of great resolution. When he had undertaken this business he went through with it, *brought out the king, crowned him, and gave him the testimony, v.* 11. He ventured his head, but it was in a good cause, and therefore he went on boldly. It is here said that his sons joined with him in anointing the young king. One of them, it is likely, was that Zechariah whom Joash afterwards put to death for reproving him (*ch.* 24:20), which was so much the more ungrateful because he bore a willing part in anointing him.

Verses 12–21

Here we have, I. The people pleased, *v.* 12, 13. When the king stood at his pillar, whose right it was to stand there, *all the people of the land rejoiced to see a rod sprung out of the stem of Jesse,* Isa. 11:1. When it seemed a withered root in a dry ground, to see what they despaired of ever seeing — a king of the house of David, what a pleasing surprise was it to them! They ran in transports of joy to see this sight, praised the king, and praised God, for they had with them such as *taught to sing praise.*

II. Athaliah slain. She ran upon the point of the sword of justice; for, imagining her interest much better than it was, she ventured *into the house of the Lord* at that time, and cried, *Treason, treason!* But nobody seconded her, or sided with her. The pride of her heart deceived her. She thought all her own, whereas none were cordially so. Jehoiada, as protector in the king's minority, ordered her to be slain (*v.* 14), which was done immediately (*v.* 15), only care was taken that she should not be *slain in the house of the Lord,* that sacred place must not be so far disgraced, nor that wicked woman so far honoured.

III. The original contract agreed to, *v.* 16. In the *Kings* it is said that Jehoiada made a covenant between the *Lord,* the people, and the king, 2 Ki. 11:17. Here it is said to be between *himself,* the people, and the king; for he, as God's priest, was his representative in this transaction, or a sort of mediator, as Moses was. The indenture was tripartite, but the true intent and meaning of the whole was that *they should be the Lord's people.* God covenanted by Jehoiada to take them for his people; the king and people covenanted with him to be his; and then the king covenanted with the people to govern them *as the people of God,* and the people with the king to be subject to him *as the Lord's people,* in his fear and for his sake. Let us look upon ourselves and one another as *the Lord's people,* and this will have a powerful influence upon us in the discharge of all our duty both to God and man.

IV. Baal destroyed, *v.* 17. They would not have done half their work if they had only destroyed the usurper of the *king's* right, and not the usurper of *God's* right — if they had asserted the honour of the throne, and not that of the altar. The greatest grievance of Athaliah's reign was the bringing in of the worship of Baal, and supporting of that; therefore that must be abolished in the first place. Down with Baal's house, his altars, his images; down with them all, and let the blood of his priests be mingled with his sacrifices; for God had commanded that seducers to idolatry should be put to death, Deu. 13:5, 6.

V. The temple service revived, *v.* 18, 19. This had been neglected in the last reigns, the priest and people wanting either power or zeal to keep it up when they had princes that were disaffected to it. But Jehoiada restored *the offices of the house of the Lord,* which in the late times had been disturbed and invaded, to the proper course and proper hands. 1. He appointed the priests to their courses, for the due offering of sacrifices, according to the law of Moses. 2. The singers to theirs, according to the appointment of David. The sacrifices (it should seem) were *offered with rejoicing and singing,* and with good reason. We *joy in God* when we *receive the atonement,* Rom. 11. 3. The porters were put in their respective posts as David ordered (*v.* 19), and their office was to take care that none who were upon any account ceremonially unclean should be admitted into the courts of the temple.

VI. The civil government re-established, *v.* 20. They brought the king in state to his own palace, and set him *upon the throne of the kingdom,* to give law, and give judgment, either in his own person or by Jehoiada his tutor.

Thus was this happy revolution perfected. The generality of the people rejoiced in it, and the rest were quiet and made no opposition, *v.* 21. When the Son of David is enthroned in the soul all is quiet and springs of joy are opened.

CHAPTER 24

We have here the history of the reign of Joash, the progress of which, and especially its termination, were not of a piece with its beginning, nor shone with so much lustre. How wonderfully he was preserved for the throne, and placed in it, we read before; now here we are told how he began in the spirit, but ended in the flesh. I. In the beginning of his time, while Jehoiada lived, he did well; particularly, he took care to put the temple in good repair (*v.* 1–14). II. In the latter end of his time, after Jehoiada's death, he apostatized from God, and his apostasy was his ruin. 1. He set up the worship of Baal again (*v.* 15–18), though warned to the contrary (*v.* 19). 2. He put Zechariah the prophet to death because he reproved him for what he had done (*v.* 20–22). 3. The judgments of God came upon him for it. The Syrians invaded him (*v.* 23, 24). He was struck with sore diseases; his own servants conspired against him and slew him; and, as a mark of infamy upon him, he was not buried in the burying-place of the kings (*v.* 25–27).

Verses 1–14

This account of Joash's good beginnings we had as it stands here 2 Ki. 12:1, etc., though the latter part of this chapter, concerning his apostasy, we had little of there. What is good in men we should take all occasions to speak of and often repeat it; what is evil we should make mention of but sparingly, and no more than is needful. We shall here only observe, 1. That it is a happy thing for young people, when they are setting out in the world, to be under the direction of those that are wise and good and faithful to them, as Joash was under the influence of Jehoiada, during whose time he *did that which was right.* Let those that are young reckon it a blessing to them, and not a burden and check upon them, to have those with them that will caution them against that which is evil and advise and quicken them to that which is good; and let them reckon it not a mark of weakness and subjection, but of wisdom and discretion, to hearken to such. He that will not be counselled cannot be helped. It is especially prudent for young people to take advice in their marriages, as Joash did, who left it to his guardian to choose him his wives, because Jezebel and Athaliah had been such plagues, *v.* 3. This is a turn of life which often proves either the making or marring of young people, and therefore should be attended to with great care. 2. Men may go far in the external performances of religion, and keep long to them, merely by the power of their education and the influence of their friends, who yet have no hearty affection for divine things nor any inward relish of them. Foreign inducements may push men on to that which is good who are not actuated by a living principle of grace in their hearts. 3. In the outward expressions of devotion it is possible that those who have only the form of godliness may out-strip those who have the power of it. Joash is more solicitous and more zealous about the repair of the temple than Jehoiada himself, whom he reproves for his remissness in that matter, *v.* 6. It is easier to build temples than to be temples to God. 4. The repairing of churches is a good work, which all in their places should promote, for the decency and conveniency of religious assemblies. The learned tell us that in the Christian church, anciently, part of the tithes were applied that way. 5. Many a good work would be done that now lies undone if there were but a few active men to stir in it and to put it forward. When Joash found the money did not come in as he expected in one way he tried another way, and that answered the intention. Many have honesty enough to follow that have not zeal enough to lead in that which is good. The throwing of money into a chest, through a hole in the lid of it, was a way that had not been used before, and perhaps the very novelty of the thing made it a successful expedient for the raising of money; a great deal was thrown in and with a great deal of cheerfulness: they all rejoiced, *v.* 10. An invention to please people's humour may sometimes bring them to their duty. Wisdom herein is profitable to direct. 6. Faithfulness is the greatest praise and will be the greatest comfort of those that are entrusted with public treasure or employed in public business. The king and Jehoiada faithfully paid the money to the workmen, who faithfully did the work, *v.* 12, 13.

Verses 15–27

We have here a sad account of the degeneracy and apostasy of Joash. God had done great things for him; he had done something for God; but now he proved ungrateful to his God and false to the engagements he had laid himself under to him. *How has the gold become dim, and the most fine gold changed!* Here we find,

I. The occasions of his apostasy. When he did that which was right it was *not with a perfect heart.* He never was sincere, never acted from principle, but in compliance to Jehoiada, who had helped him to the crown, and because he had been protected in the temple and rose upon the ruins of idolatry; and therefore, when the wind turned, he turned with it. 1. His good counsellor left him, and was by death removed from him. It was a mercy to him and his kingdom that Jehoiada lived so long — 130 years (*v.* 15), by which it appears that he was born in Solomon's time, and had lived six entire reigns before this. It was an encouragement to him to go on in that good way which Jehoiada had trained him up in to see what honour was done to Jehoiada at his death: *They buried him among the kings,* with this honourable encomium (perhaps it was part of the inscription on his grave-stone), that *he had done good in Israel.* Judah is called *Israel,* because, the other tribes having revolted from God, they only were Israelites indeed. Note, It is the greatest honour to do good in our generations, and those who *do that which is good shall have praise of the same.* He had done good towards God; not that any man's goodness can extend unto him, but he had done good towards his house, in reviving the temple service, *ch.* 23:8. Note, Those do the greatest good to their country that lay out themselves in their places to promote religion. Well, Jehoiada finished his course with honour; but the little religion that Joash had was all buried in his grave, and, after his death, both king and kingdom miserably degenerated. See how much one head may sustain, and what a great judgment to any prince or people the death of godly, zealous, useful men is. See how necessary it is that, as our Saviour speaks, we *have salt in ourselves,* that we act in religion from an inward principle, which will carry us on through all changes. Then the loss of a parent, a minister, a friend, will not involve the loss of our religion. 2. Bad counsellors got about him, insinuated themselves into his affections, wheedled him, flattered him, *made obeisance* to him, and, instead of condoling, congratulated him upon the death of his old tutor, as his release from the discipline he had been so long under, unworthy a man, a king. They tell him he must be priest-ridden no longer, he is now discharged from *grave lessons and restraints,* he may do as he pleases: and (would you think it?) the princes of Judah were the men that were so industrious to debauch him, *v.* 17. His father and grandfather were corrupted by the house of Ahab, from whom no better could be expected. But that the princes of Judah should be seducers to their king was very sad. But those that incline to the *counsels of the ungodly* will never want ungodly counsellors. They *made obeisance to the king,* flattered him into an opinion of his absolute power, promised to stand by him in making his royal will and pleasure pass for a law, any divine precept or institution to the contrary in any wise notwithstanding. And he hearkened to them: their discourse pleased him, and was more agreeable than Jehoiada's dictates used to be. Princes and inferior people have been many a time thus flattered into their ruin by those who have promised them liberty and dignity, but who have really brought them into the greatest servitude and disgrace.

II. The apostasy itself: *They left the house of God, and served groves and idols, v.* 18. The princes, it is likely, had a request to the king, which they tell him they durst not offer while Jehoiada lived; but now they hope it will give no offence: it is that they may set up the groves and idols again which were thrown down in the beginning of his reign, for they hate to be always confined to the dull old-fashioned service of the temple. And he not only gave them leave to do it themselves, but he joined with them. The king and princes, who, a little while ago, were repairing the temple, now forsook the temple; those who had pulled down groves and idols now themselves served them. So inconstant a thing is man and so little confidence is to be put in him!

III. The aggravations of this apostasy and the additions of guilt to it. God *sent prophets to them* (*v.* 19) to reprove them for their wickedness, and to tell them what would be in the end thereof, and so *to bring them again unto the Lord.* It is the work of ministers to bring people, not to themselves, but to God — to bring those again to him who have gone a whoring from him. In the most degenerate times God *left not himself without witness;* though they had dealt very disingenuously with God, yet he sent prophets to them to convince and instruct them, and to assure them that they should find favour with him if yet they would return; for he would rather sinners should *turn and live* than *go on and die,* and those that perish shall be left inexcusable. The prophets did their part: *they testified against them;* but, few or none *received their testimony.*

1. They slighted all the prophets; they would not give ear, were so strangely wedded to their idols that no reproofs, warnings, threatenings, nor any of the various methods which the prophets took to convince them would reclaim them. Few would hear them, fewer would heed them, but fewest of all would believe them or be governed by them.

2. They slew one of the most eminent, *Zechariah the son of Jehoiada,* and perhaps others. Concerning him observe,

(1.) The message which he delivered to them in the name of God, *v.* 20. The people were assembled in the court of the temple (for they had not quite left it), probably on occasion of some solemn feast, when this Zechariah, being filled with the spirit of prophecy, and known (it is likely) to be a prophet, stood up in some of the desks that were in the court of the priests, and very plainly, but without any provoking language, told the people of their sin and what would be the consequences of it. He did not impeach any particular persons, nor predict any particular judgments, as sometimes the prophets did, but as inoffensively as possible reminded them of what was written in the law. Let them but look into their Bibles, and there they would find, [1.] The precept they broke: "*You transgress the commandments of the Lord,* you know you do so, in serving groves and idols: and why will you so offend God and wrong yourselves?" [2.] The penalty they incurred: "You know, if the word of God be true, you cannot prosper in this evil way; never expect to do ill and fare well. Nay, you find already that *because you have forsaken the Lord he hath forsaken you,* as he told you he would," Deu. 29:25; 31:16,17. This is the work of ministers, by the word of God, as a lamp and a light, to expose the sin of men and expound the providences of God.

(2.) The barbarous treatment they gave him for his kindness and faithfulness in delivering this message to them, *v.* 21. By the conspiracy of the princes, or some of their party, and *by the commandment of the king,* who thought himself affronted by this fair warning, they stoned him to death immediately, not under colour of law, accusing him as a blasphemer, a traitor, or a false prophet, but in a popular tumult, *in the court of the house of the Lord* — as horrid a piece of wickedness as perhaps any we read of in all the history of the kings. The *person* was sacred — a priest, the *place* sacred — the court of the temple (the inner court, *between the porch and the altar),* the *message* yet more sacred, and we have reason to think that they knew it came from the spirit of prophecy. The reproof was just, the warning fair, both backed with scripture, and the delivery very gentle and tender; and yet so impudently and daringly do they defy God himself that nothing less than the blood of the prophet can satisfy their indignation at the prophecy. *Be astonished, O heavens! at this,* and *tremble, O earth!* that ever such villany should be committed by men, by Israelites, in contempt and violation of every thing that is just, honourable, and sacred — that a king, in covenant with God, should command the murder of one whom it was his office to protect and countenance! The Jews say there were seven transgressions in this; for they killed a priest, a prophet, a judge, they shed innocent blood, and polluted the court of the temple, the sabbath, and the day of expiation: for on that day, their tradition says, this happened.

(3.) The aggravation of this sin, that this Zechariah, who suffered martyrdom for his faithfulness to God and his country, was the son of Jehoiada, who had done so much good in Israel, and particularly had been as a father to

Joash, *v.* 22. The affront done by it to God, and the contempt put on religion, are not so particularly taken notice of as the ingratitude there was in it to the memory of Jehoiada. He remembered not the kindness of the father, but slew the son for doing his duty, and what the father would have done if he had been there. Call a man ungrateful, and you can call him no worse.

(4.) The dying martyr's prophetic imprecation of vengeance upon his murderers: *The Lord look upon it, and require it!* This came not from a spirit of revenge, but a spirit of prophecy: *He will require it.* This would be the continual cry of the blood they shed, as Abel's blood cried against Cain: "Let the God to whom vengeance belongs demand blood for blood. He will do it, for he is righteous." This precious blood was quickly reckoned for in the judgments that came upon this apostate prince; it came into the account afterwards in the destruction of Jerusalem by the Chaldeans — their misusing the prophets was that which brought upon them ruin without remedy (*ch.* 36:16); nay, our Saviour makes the persecutors of him and his gospel answerable for the blood of this Zechariah; so loud, so long, does the blood of the martyrs cry. See Mt. 23:35. Such as this is the cry of the souls under the altar (Rev. 6:10), *How long ere thou avenge our blood?* For it shall not always go unrevenged.

IV. The judgments of God which came upon Joash for this aggravated wickedness of his. 1. A small army of Syrians made themselves masters of Jerusalem, destroyed the princes, plundered the city, and sent the spoil of it to Damascus, *v.* 23, 24. God's people, while they kept in with God, had often been conquerors when the enemy had the advantage of the greater number; but now, on the contrary, an inconsiderable handful of Syrians routed a *very great host of Israelites, because they had forsaken the Lord God of their fathers,* and then they were not only put upon the level with their enemies, but opposed them with the utmost disadvantage; for their God not only departed from them, but *turned to be their enemy and fought against them.* The Syrians were employed as instruments in God's hand to *execute judgments against Joash,* though they little thought so, Isa. 10:6, 7, and see Deu. 32:30. 2. God smote him with great diseases, of body, or mind, or both, either like his grandfather (*ch.* 21:18), or, like Saul, an evil spirit from God troubling him. While he was plagued with the Syrians he thought that, if he could but get clear of them, he should do well enough. But, before they departed from him, God smote him with diseases. If vengeance pursue men, the end of one trouble will but be the beginning of another. 3. His own servants conspired against him. Perhaps he began to hope his disease would be cured — he was but a middle-aged man and might recover it; but *he that cometh up out of the pit shall fall into the snare.* When he thought he should escape death by sickness he met it by the sword. They slew him in his bed *for the blood of the sons of Jehoiada,* by which it should seem that he did not only slay Zechariah, but others of the sons of Jehoiada for his sake. Perhaps those that slew him *intended* to take vengeance for that blood; but, whether they did or not, this was what God intended in permitting them to slay him. Those that drink the blood of the saints shall have their own blood given them to drink, for they are worthy. The regicides are here named (*v.* 26), and it is observable that the mothers of them both were foreigners, one an Ammonitess and the other a Moabitess. The idolatrous kings, it is likely, countenanced those marriages which the law prohibited for the prevention of idolatry; and see how they resulted in their own destruction. 4. His people would not bury him in the sepulchres of the kings because he had stained his honour by his mal-administration. *Let him not be written with the righteous,* Ps. 69:28. These judgments are called the *burdens laid upon him* (*v.* 27), for the wrath of God is a heavy burden, too heavy for any man to bear. Or it may be meant of the threatenings denounced against him by the prophets, for those are called *burdens.* Usually God sets some special marks of his displeasure upon apostates in this life, for warning to all to *remember Lot's wife.*

CHAPTER 25

Amaziah's reign, recorded in this chapter, was not one of the worse and yet far from good. Most of the passages in this chapter we had before more briefly related, 2 Ki. 14. Here we find Amaziah, I. A just revenger of his father's death (*v.* 1–4). II. An obedient observer of the command of God (*v.* 5–10). III. A cruel conqueror of the Edomites (*v.* 11–13). IV. a foolish worshipper of the gods of Edom and impatient of reproof for it (*v.* 14–16). V. Rashly challenging the king of Israel, and smarting for his rashness (*v.* 17–24). And, lastly, ending his days ingloriously (*v.* 25–28).

Verses 1–13

Here is, I. The general character of Amaziah: *He did that which was right in the eyes of the Lord,* worshipped the true God, kept the temple service a going, and countenanced religion in his kingdom; but he did not do it *with a perfect heart* (*v.* 2), that is, he was not a man of serious piety or devotion himself, nor had he any zeal for the exercises of religion. He was no enemy to it, but a cool and indifferent friend. Such is the character of too many in this Laodicean age: they do that which is good, but not with the heart, not with a perfect heart.

II. A necessary piece of justice which he did upon the traitors that murdered his father: he put them to death, *v.* 3. Though we should suppose they intended to avenge on their king the death of the prophet (as was intimated, *ch.* 24:25), yet this would by no means justify their wickedness; for *they* were not the avengers, but presumptuously took God's work out of his hands: and therefore Amaziah did what became him in calling them to an account for it, but forbade the putting of the children to death for the parents' sin, *v.* 4.

III. An expedition of his against the Edomites, who, some time ago, had revolted from under the dominion of Judah, to which he attempted to reduce them. Observe,

1. The great preparation he made for this expedition. (1.) He mustered his own forces, and marshalled them (*v.* 5), and found Judah and Benjamin in all but 300,000 men that were fit for war, whereas, in Jehoshaphat's time, fifty or sixty years before, they were four times as many. Sin weakens a people, diminishes them, dispirits them, and lessens their number and figure. (2.) He hired auxiliary troops out of the kingdom of Israel, *v.* 6. Finding his own kingdom defective in men, he thought to make up the deficiency with his money, and therefore took into his pay 100,000 Israelites. If he had advised with any of his prophets before he did this, or had but considered how little any of his ancestors got by their alliances with Israel, he would not have had this to undo again. But rashness makes work for repentance.

2. The command which God sent him by a prophet to dismiss out of his service the forces of Israel, *v.* 7, 8. He would not have him call in any assistance at all: it looked like distrust of God. If he made sure of God's presence, the army he had of his own was sufficient. But particularly he must not take in *their* assistance: *For the Lord is not with the children of Ephraim, because they are not with him,* but worship the calves. This was a good reason why he should not make use of them, because he could not depend upon them to do him any service. What good could be expected from those that had not God with them, nor his blessings upon their undertakings? It is comfortable to employ those who, we have reason to hope, have an interest in heaven, and dangerous to associate with those from whom the Lord has departed. The prophet assured him that if he persisted in his resolution to take these idolatrous apostate Israelites with him, in hopes thereby to make himself strong for the battle, it was at his peril; they would prove a dead weight to his army, would sink and betray it: *"God shall make thee fall before the enemy,* and these Israelites will be the ruin of thy cause; for God has power to help thee without them, and to cast thee down though thou hast them with thee."

3. The objection which Amaziah made against this command, and the satisfactory answer which the prophet gave to that objection, *v.* 9. The king had remitted 100 talents to the men of Israel for advance-money. "Now," says he, "if I send them back, I shall lose that: *But what shall we do for the 100 talents?"* This is an objection men often make against their duty: they are afraid of losing by it. "Regard not that," says the prophet: *"The Lord is able to give thee much more than this;* and, thou mayest depend upon it, he will not see thee lose by him. What are 100 talents between thee and him? He has ways enough to make up the loss to thee; it is below thee to speak of it." Note, A firm belief of God's all-sufficiency to bear us out in our duty, and to make up all the loss and damage we sustain in his service abundantly to our advantage, will make his yoke very easy and his burden very light. What is it to trust in God, but to be willing to venture the loss of any thing for him, in confidence of the goodness of the security he gives us that we shall not lose by him, but that whatever we part with for his sake shall be made up to us in kind or kindness. When we grudge to part with any thing for God and our religion, this should satisfy us, that God is able to give us much more than this. He is just, and he is good, and he is solvent. The king lost 100 talents by his obedience; and we find just that sum given to his grandson Jotham as a present (*ch.* 27:5); then the principal was repaid, and, for interest, 10,000 measures of wheat and as many of barley.

4. His obedience to the command of God, which is upon record to his honour. He would rather lose his money, disoblige his allies, and dismiss a fourth part of his army just as they were going to take the field, than offend God: *He separated the army of Ephraim, to go home again, v.* 10. And they went home in great anger, taking it as a great affront thus to be made fools of, and to be cashiered as men not fit to be employed, and being perhaps disappointed of the advantages they promised themselves in spoil and plunder by joining with Judah against Edom. Men are apt to resent that which touches them in their profit or reputation, though it frees them from trouble.

5. His triumphs over the Edomites, *v.* 11, 12. He left dead upon the spot, in the field of battle, 10,000 men; 10,000 more he took prisoners, and barbarously killed them all by throwing them down some steep and craggy precipice. What provocation he had to exercise this cruelty towards them we are not told; but it was certainly very severe.

6. The mischief which the disbanded soldiers of Israel did to the cities of Judah, either in their return or soon after, *v.* 13. They were so enraged at being sent home that, if they might not go to share with Judah in the spoil of Edom, they would make a prey of Judah. Several cities that lay upon the borders they plundered, killing 3000 men that made resistance. But why should God suffer this to be done? Was it not in obedience to him that they were sent home, and yet shall the country thus suffer by it? Surely God's way is in the sea! Did not the prophet say that God was not with the children of Ephraim, and yet they are suffered to prevail against Judah? Doubtless God intended hereby to chastise those cities of Judah for their idolatries, which were found most in those parts that lay next to Israel. The men of Israel had corrupted them, and now they were made a plague to them. Satan both tempts and torments.

Verses 14–16

Here is, I. The revolt of Amaziah from the God of Israel to the gods of the Edomites. Egregious folly! Ahaz worshipped the gods of those that had conquered him, for which he had some little colour, *ch.* 28:23. But to worship the gods of those whom he had conquered, who could not protect their own worshippers, was the greatest absurdity that could be. What did he see in the gods of the children of Seir that could tempt him to set them up for *his gods* and *bow himself down before them? v.* 14. If he had cast the idols down from the rock and broken them to pieces, instead of the prisoners, he would have manifested more of the piety as well as more of the pity of an Israelite; but perhaps for that barbarous inhumanity he was given up to this ridiculous idolatry.

II. The reproof which God sent to him, by a prophet, for this sin. *The anger of the Lord was kindled against him,* and justly; yet, before he sent to destroy him, he sent to convince and reclaim him, and so to prevent his destruction. The prophet reasoned with him very fairly and very mildly: *Why hast thou sought* the favour of those gods *which could not deliver their own people? v.* 15. If men would but duly consider the inability of all those things to help them to which they have recourse when they forsake God, they would not be such enemies to themselves.

III. The check he gave to the reprover, *v.* 16. He could say nothing in excuse of his own folly; the reproof was too just to be answered. But he fell into a passion with the reprover. 1. He taunted him as saucy and impertinent, and meddling with that which did not belong to him: *Art thou made of the king's counsel?* Could not a man speak reasonably to him, but he must be upbraided as usurping the place of a privy-counsellor? But, as a prophet, he really was made of the king's counsel by the King of kings, in duty to whom the king was bound not only to hear, but to ask and take his counsel. 2. He silenced him, bade him forbear and say not a word more to him. He *said to the seer, See not,* Isa. 30:10. Men would gladly have their prophets thus under their girdles, as we say, to speak just when and what they would have them speak, and not otherwise. 3. He threatened him: "*Why shouldst thou be smitten?* It is at thy peril if thou sayest a word more of this matter." He seems to remind him of Zechariah's fate in the last reign, who was put to death for making bold with the king; and bids him take warning by him. Thus he justifies the killing of that prophet by menacing this, and so, in effect, makes himself guilty of the blood of both. He had hearkened to the prophet who ordered him to send back the army of Israel, and was ruled by him, though he contradicted his politics and lost him 100 talents, *v.* 10. But this prophet, who dissuaded him from worshipping the gods of the Edomites, he ran upon with an unaccountable rage, which must be attributed to the witchcraft of idolatry. He was easily persuaded to part with his talents of silver, but by no means with his gods of silver.

IV. The doom which the prophet passed upon him for this. He had more to say to him by way of instruction and advice; but, finding him obstinate in his iniquity, he forbore. He is *joined to idols; let him alone,* Hos. 4:17. Miserable is the condition of that man with whom the blessed Spirit, by ministers and conscience, *forbears to strive,* Gen. 6:3. And both the reprovers in the gate and that in the bosom, if long brow-beaten and baffled, will at length forbear. So I *gave them up to their own hearts' lusts.* The secure sinner perhaps values himself upon it as a noble and happy achievement to have silenced his reprovers and monitors, and to get clear of them; but what comes of it? "*I know that God has determined to destroy thee;* it is a plain indication that thou art marked for ruin *that thou hast done this, and hast not hearkened to my counsel.*" Those that are deaf to reproof are ripening apace for destruction, Prov. 29:1.

Verses 17–28

We have here this degenerate prince mortified by his neighbour and murdered by his own subjects.

I. Never was proud prince more thoroughly mortified than Amaziah was by Joash king of Israel.

1. This part of the story (which was as fully related 2 Ki. 14:8, etc., as it is here) — embracing the foolish challenge which Amaziah sent to Joash (*v.* 17), his haughty scornful answer to it (*v.* 18), with the friendly advice he gave him to sit still and know when he was well off, (*v.* 19), — his wilfully persisting in his challenge (*v.* 20, 21), the defeat that was given him (*v.* 22), and the calamity he brought upon himself and his city thereby (*v.* 23, 24), — verifies two of Solomon's proverbs: — (1.) That *a man's pride will bring him low,* Prov. 29:23. It goes before his destruction; not only procures it meritoriously, but is often the immediate occasion of it. *He that exalteth himself shall be abased.* (2.) That he that *goes forth hastily to strive* will probably not know what to do in the end thereof, *when his neighbour has put him to shame,* Prov. 25:8. He that is fond of contention may have enough of it sooner than he thinks of.

2. But there are two passages in this story which we had not before in the *Kings.* (1.) That *Amaziah took advice* before he challenged the king of Israel, *v.* 17. But of whom? Not of the prophet — he was *not made of the king's counsel;* but of his statesmen that would flatter him and bid him go up and prosper. It is good to take advice, but then it must be of those that are fit to advise us. Those that will not take advice from the word of God, which would guide them aright, will justly be left to the bad advice of those that will counsel them to their destruction. Let those be made fools that will not be made wise. (2.) Amaziah's imprudence is here made the punishment of his impiety (*v.* 20): *It was of the Lord;* he left him to himself to act thus foolishly, that he and his people might be *delivered into the hands of their enemies, because* they had forsaken God and *sought after the gods of Edom.* Those that will not persuaded to do well for their souls will justly be given up to their own counsels to do ill for themselves even in their outward affairs.

II. Never was poor prince more violently pursued by his own subjects. *From the time* that he departed from the Lord (so it may be read, *v.* 27) the hearts of his subjects departed from him, and they began to form a design against him in Jerusalem. It is probable they were exasperated against him more for his rashly engaging in a war against Israel than for his worshipping the gods of Edom. But at length the ferment grew so high, and he perceived the plot to be laid so deeply, that he thought fit to quit his royal city and flee to Lachish, either as a private place where he might be hid or as a strong place where he might be guarded; but they sent after him thither, and slew him there. By this the putting of him to death seems to have been done deliberately, and to have been the act, not of a disgusted servant or two, but of a considerable body that durst avow it. How unrighteous soever they were herein, God was righteous.

CHAPTER 26

This chapter gives us an account of the reign of Uzziah (Azariah he was called in the Kings) more fully than we had it before, though it was long, and in some respects illustrious, yet it was very briefly related, 2 Ki. 14:21; 15:1, etc. Here is, I. His good character in general (*v.* 1–5) II. His great prosperity in his wars, his buildings, and all the affairs of his kingdom (*v.* 6–15). III. His presumption in invading the priests' office, for which he was struck with a leprosy, and confined by it (*v.* 16–21) even to his death (*v.* 22, 23).

Verses 1–15

We have here an account of two things concerning Uzziah: —

I. His piety. In this he was not very eminent or zealous; yet *he did that which was right in the sight of the Lord.* He kept up the pure worship of the true God *as his father* did, and was better than his father, inasmuch as we have no reason to think he ever worshipped idols as his father did, no, not in his latter days, when *his heart was lifted up.* It is said (*v.* 5), He *sought God in the days of Zechariah,* who, some think, was the son of the Zechariah whom his grandfather Joash slew. This Zechariah was one that *had understanding in the visions of God,* either the visions which he himself was favoured with or the visions of the preceding prophets. He was well versed in prophecy, and conversed much with the upper world, was an intelligent, devout, good man; and, it seems, had great influence with Uzziah. Happy are the great men who have such about them and are willing to be advised by them; but unhappy those who seek God only while they have such with them and have not a principle in themselves to bear them out to the end.

II. His prosperity.

1. In general, *as long as he sought the Lord,* and minded religion, *God made him to prosper.* Note, (1.) Those only prosper whom *God makes to prosper;* for prosperity is his gift. (2.) Religion and piety are very friendly to outward prosperity. Many have found and owned this, that as long as they sought the Lord and kept close to their duty they prospered; but since they forsook God every thing has gone cross.

2. Here are several particular instances of his prosperity: — (1.) His success in his wars: *God helped him* (*v.* 7), and then he triumphed over the Philistines (those old enemies of God's people), demolished the fortifications of their cities, and put garrisons of his own among them, *v.* 6. He obliged the Ammonites to pay him tribute, *v.* 8. He made all quiet about him, and kept them in awe. (2.) The greatness of his fame and reputation. His name was celebrated throughout all the neighbouring countries (*v.* 8) and it was a good name, a name for good things with God and good people. This is true fame, and makes a man truly honourable. (3.) His buildings. While he acted offensively abroad, he did not neglect the defence of his kingdom at home, but *built towers in Jerusalem* and fortified them, *v.* 9. Much of the wall of Jerusalem was in his father's time broken down, particularly at *the corner gate.* But his best fortification of Jerusalem was his close adherence to the worship of God: if his father had not forsaken this the wall of Jerusalem would not have been broken down. While he fortified the city, he did not forget the country, but *built towers in the desert* too (*v.* 10), to protect the country people from the inroads of the plunderers, bands of whom sometimes alarmed them and plundered them, as *ch.* 21:16. (4.) His husbandry. He dealt much in cattle and corn, employed many hands, and got much wealth by his dealing; for he took a pleasure in it: he *loved husbandry* (*v.* 10), and probably did himself inspect his affairs in the country, which was no disparagement to him, but an advantage, as it encouraged industry among his subjects. It is an honour to the husbandman's calling that one of the most illustrious princes of the house of David followed it and loved it. He was not one of those that delight in war, nor did he addict himself to sport and pleasure, but delighted in the innocent and quiet employments of the husbandman. (5.) His standing armies. He had, as it should seem, two military establishments. [1.] A *host of fighting men* that were to make excursions abroad. These *went out to war by bands, v.* 11. They fetched in spoil from the neighbouring countries by way of reprisal for the depredations they had so often made upon Judah, [2.] Another army for *guards and garrisons,* that were ready to defend the country in case it should be invaded, *v.* 12, 13. So great were their number and valour that they *made war with mighty power;* no enemy durst face them, or, at least, could stand before them. Men unarmed can do little in war. Uzziah therefore furnished himself with a great armoury, whence his soldiers were supplied with arms offensive and defensive (*v.* 14), spears, bows, and slings, shields, helmets, and habergeons: swords are not mentioned, because it is probable that every man had a sword of his own, which he wore constantly. Engines were invented, in his time, for annoying besiegers with darts and stones shot from the towers and bulwarks, *v.* 15. What a pity it is that the wars and fightings which come from men's lusts have made it necessary for cunning men to employ their skill in inventing instruments of death.

Verses 16–23

Here is the only blot we find on the name of king Uzziah, and it is such a one as lies not on any other of the kings. Whoredom, murder, oppression, persecution, and especially idolatry, gave characters to the bad kings and some of them blemishes to the good ones, David himself not excepted, witness the matter of Uriah. But we find not Uzziah charged with any of these; and yet he *transgressed against the Lord his God,* and fell under the marks of his displeasure in consequence, not, as other kings, in vexatious wars or rebellions, but an incurable disease.

I. His sin was invading the priest's office. The good way is one; by-paths are many. The transgression of his predecessors was forsaking the temple of the Lord, flying off from it (*ch.* 24:18), and burning incense upon idolatrous altars, *ch.* 25:14. *His* was intruding *into the temple of the Lord* further than was allowed him, and attempting him to *burn incense upon the altar* of God, for which, it is likely, he pretended an extraordinary zeal and affection. See how hard it is to avoid one extreme and not run into another.

1. That which was at the bottom of his sin was pride of heart, a lust that ruins more than any other whatsoever (*v.* 16): *When he was strong* (and he was marvellously helped by the good providence of God *till he was so, v.* 15), when he had grown very great and considerable in wealth, interest, and power, instead of lifting up the name of God in gratitude to him who had done so much for him, his *heart was lifted up to his destruction.* Thus the prosperity of fools, by puffing them up with pride, destroys them. Now that he had done so much business, and won so much honour, he began to think no business, no honour, too great or too good for him, no, not that of the priesthood Men's pretending to forbidden knowledge, and exercising themselves in things too high for them, are owing to the pride of their heart, and the fleshly mind they are *vainly puffed up with.*

2. His sin was *going into the temple of the Lord to burn incense,* probably on some solemn feast day, or when he himself had some special occasion for supplicating the divine favour. What could move him to this piece of presumption, or put it into his head, I cannot conjecture. None of all his predecessors, not the best, not the worst, attempted it. The law, he knew, was express against him, and there was no usage or precedent for him. He could not pretend any necessity, as there was for David's eating the showbread. (1.) Perhaps he fancied the priests did not do their office so dexterously, decently, and devoutly, as they ought, and he could do it better. Or, (2.) He observed that the idolatrous kings did themselves burn incense at the altars of their gods; his father did so, and Jeroboam (1 Ki. 13:1), an ambition of which honour was perhaps one thing that

tempted them from the house of God, where it was not permitted them; and he, being resolved to cleave to God's altar, would try to break through this restraint and come as near it as the idolatrous kings did to their altars. But it is called a *transgression against the Lord his God*. He was not content with the honours God had put upon him, but would usurp those that were forbidden him, like our first parents.

3. He was opposed in this attempt by the chief priest and other priests that attended and assisted him, *v.* 17, 18. They were ready to burn incense for the king, according to the duty of their place; but, when he offered to do it himself, they plainly let him know that he meddled with that which did not belong to him, and that it was at his peril. They did not resist him by laying violent hands on him, though they were valiant men, but by reasoning with him and showing him, (1.) That it was not lawful for him to burn incense: *"It appertaineth not to thee, O Uzziah! but to the priests,* whose birthright it is, as sons of Aaron, and who are consecrated to the service." Aaron and his sons were appointed by the law to burn incense, Ex. 30:7. See Deu. 33:10; 1 Chr. 23:13. David had blessed the people and Solomon and Jehoshaphat had prayed with them and preached to them. Uzziah might have done this, and it would have been to his praise; but as for burning incense, that service was to be performed by the priests only. The kingly and priestly offices were separated by the law of Moses, not to be united again but in the person of the Messiah. If Uzziah did intend to honour God, and gain acceptance with him, in what he did, he was quite out in his aim; for, being a service purely of divine institution, he could not expect it should be accepted unless it were done in the way and by the hands that God had appointed. (2.) That it was not safe. It shall not be *for thy honour from the Lord God*. More is implied: "It will be thy disgrace, and it is at thy peril." The law runs expressly against all strangers that came nigh (Num. 3:10, 18:7), that is, all that were not priests. Korah and his accomplices, though Levites, paid dearly for offering to burn incense, which was the work of the priests only, Num. 16:35. The incense of our prayers must be by faith put into the hands of our Lord Jesus, the great high priest of our profession, else we cannot expect it should be accepted by God, Rev. 8:3.

4. He fell into a passion with the priests that reproved him, and would push forward to do what he intended notwithstanding (*v.* 19): *Uzziah was wroth,* and would not part with the censer out of his hand. He took it ill to be checked, and would not bear interference. *Nitimur in vetitum — We are prone to do what is forbidden.*

II. His punishment was an incurable leprosy, which rose up in his forehead while he was contending with the priests. If he had submitted to the priests' admonition, acknowledged his error, and gone back, all would have been well; but *when he was wroth with the priests,* and fell foul upon them, then God was wroth with him and smote him with a plague of leprosy. Josephus says that he threatened the priests with death if they opposed him, and that then the earth shook, the roof of the temple opened, and through the cleft a beam of the sun darted directly upon the king's face, wherein immediately the leprosy appeared. And some conjecture that that was the earthquake in the days of Uzziah which we read of Amos 1:1 and Zec. 14:5. Now this sudden stroke, 1. Ended the controversy between him and the priests; for, when the leprosy appeared, they were emboldened to thrust him out of the temple; nay, he himself *hasted to go out, because the Lord had smitten him* with a disease which was in a particular manner a token of his displeasure, and which he knew secluded him from common converse with men, much more from the altar of God. He would not be convinced by what the priests said, but God took an effectual course to convince him. If presumptuous men will not be made to see their error by the judgments of God's mouth, they shall be made to see it by the judgments of his hand. It evinced some religious fear of God in the heart of this king, even in the midst of his transgression, that, as soon as he found God was angry with him, he not only let fall his attempt, but retired with the utmost precipitation. Though he strove with the priests, he would not strive with his Maker. 2. It remained a lasting punishment of his transgression; for he continued a *leper to the day of his death,* shut up in confinement, and shut out from society, and forced to leave

it to his son to manage all his business, *v.* 21. Thus God gave an instance of his resisting the proud and of his jealousy for the purity and honour of his own institutions; thus he gave fair warning even to great and good men to know and keep their distance, and not to intrude into those things which they have not seen; and thus he gave Uzziah a loud and constant call to repentance, and a long space to repent, which we have reason to hope he improved. He had been a man of much business in the world; but being taken off from that, and confined to a *separate house,* he had leisure to think of another world and prepare for it. By this judgment upon the king God intended to possess the people with a great veneration for the temple, the priesthood, and other sacred things, which they had been apt to think meanly of. While the king was a leper, he was as good as dead, dead while he lived, and buried alive; and so the law was, in effect, answered, that the stranger who cometh nigh shall be put to death. The disgrace survived him; for, when he was dead, they would not bury him in the *sepulchres of the kings* because he was a leper, which stained all his other glory. 3. It was a punishment that answered the sin as face does face in a glass. (1.) Pride was at the bottom of his transgression, and thus God humbled him and put dishonour upon him. (2.) He invaded the office of the priests in contempt of them, and God struck him with a disease which in a particular manner made him subject to the inspection and sentence of the priests; for to them pertained the *judgment of the leprosy,* Deu. 24:8. (3.) He thrust himself into the temple of God, whither the priests only had admission, and for that was thrust out of the very courts of the temple, into which the meanest of his subjects that was ceremonially clean had free access. (4.) He confronted the priests that faced him and opposed his presumption, and for that the leprosy *rose in his forehead,* which, in Miriam's case, is compared to her father's *spitting in her face,* Num. 12:14. (5.) He invaded the dignity of the priesthood, which he had no right to, and for that he was deprived even of his royal dignity, which he had a right to. Those that covet forbidden honours forfeit allowed ones. Adam, by catching at the tree of knowledge of which he might not eat, debarred himself from the tree of life, of which he might have eaten. Let all that read it say, *The Lord is righteous.*

CHAPTER 27

Here is a very short account of the reign of Jotham, a pious prosperous prince, of whom one would wish to have known more: but we may better dispense with the brevity of his story because that which lengthened the history of the last three kings was their degeneracy in their latter end, of which we have had a faithful account; but there was no occasion for such a melancholy conclusion of the history of this reign, which is only an account, I. Of the date and continuance of this reign (*v.* 1, 8). II. The general good character of it (*v.* 2, 6). III. The prosperity of it (*v.* 3–5). IV. The period of it (*v.* 7, 9).

Verses 1–9

There is not much more related here concerning Jotham than we had before, 2 Ki. 15:32, etc.

I. He reigned well. He *did that which was right in the sight of the Lord;* the course of his reign was good, and pleasing to God, whose favour he made his end, and his word his rule, and, (which shows that he acted from a good principle) he *prepared his ways before the Lord his God* (*v.* 6), that is, he walked circumspectly and with much caution, contrived how to shun that which was evil and compass that which was good. He looked before him, and cast his affairs into such a posture and method as made the regular management of them the more easy. Or he established or fixed his ways before the Lord, that is, he walked steadily and constantly in the way of his duty, was uniform and resolute in it: not like some of those that went before him, who, though they had some good in them, lost their credit by their inconstancy and inconsistency with themselves. They had run well, but something hindered them. It was not so with Jotham. Two things are observed here in his character: — 1. What was amiss in his father he amended in himself (*v.* 2): He did *according to all that his father did* well and wisely; howbeit he would not imitate him in which he did amiss; for he *entered not into the temple of the Lord* to burn incense as his father did, but took warning by his fate not to dare so presumptuous a thing. Note, We must not imitate the best men, and those we have the greatest veneration for, any further than they

did well; but, on the contrary, their falls, and the injurious consequences of them, must be warnings to us to walk the more circumspectly, that we stumble not at the same stone that they stumbled at. 2. What was amiss in his people he could not prevail to amend: *The people did yet corruptly.* Perhaps it reflects some blame upon him, that he was wanting in his part towards the reformation of the land. Men may be very good themselves, and yet not have courage and zeal to do what they might do towards the reforming of others. however it certainly reflects a great deal of blame upon the people, that they did not do what they might have done to improve the advantages of so good a reign: they had good instructions given them and a good example set before them, but they would not be reformed; so that even in the reign of their good kings, as well as in that of the bad ones, they were *treasuring up wrath against the day of wrath;* for they still did corruptly, and the founder melted in vain.

II. He prospered, and became truly reputable. 1. He built. He began with *the gate of the house of the Lord,* which he repaired, beautified, and raised. He then *fortified the wall of Ophel, and built cities in the mountains of Judah* (*v.* 3, 4), took all possible care for the fortifying of his country and the replenishing of it. 2. He conquered. He prevailed against the Ammonites, who had invaded Judah in Jehoshaphat's time, *ch.* 20:1. He triumphed over them, and exacted great contributions from them, *v.* 5. He *became mighty* (*v.* 6) in wealth and power, and influence upon the neighbouring nations, who courted his friendship and feared his displeasure; and this he got by *preparing his ways before the Lord his God.* The more stedfast we are in religion the more mighty we are both for the resistance of that which is evil and for the performance of that which is good.

III. He finished his course too soon, but finished it with honour. He had the unhappiness to die in the midst of his days; but, to balance that, the happiness not to out-live his reputation, as the last three of his predecessors did. He died when he was but forty-one years of age (*v.* 8); but *his wars and his ways,* his wars abroad and his ways at home, were so glorious that they were recorded in the book of the kings of Israel, as well as of the kings of Judah, *v.* 7. The last words of the chapter are the most melancholy, as they inform us that *Ahaz his son,* whose character, in all respects, was the reverse of his, *reigned in his stead.* When the wealth and power with which wise men have done good devolve upon fools, that will do hurt with them, it is a lamentation, and shall be for a lamentation.

CHAPTER 28

This chapter is the history of the reign of Ahaz the son of Jotham; a bad reign it was, and which helped to augment the fierce anger of the Lord. We have here, I. His great wickedness (*v.* 1–4). II. The trouble he brought himself into by it (*v.* 5–8). III. The reproof which God sent by a prophet to the army of Israel for trampling upon their brethren of Judah, and the obedient ear they gave to that reproof (*v.* 9–15). IV. The many calamities that followed to Ahaz and his people (*v.* 16–21). V. The continuance of his idolatry notwithstanding (*v.* 22–25), and so his story ends (*v.* 26, 27).

Verses 1–5

Never surely had a man greater opportunity of doing well than Ahaz had, finding things in a good posture, the kingdom rich and strong and religion established; and yet here we have him in these few verses, 1. Wretchedly corrupted and debauched. He had had a good education given him and a good example set him: but parents cannot give grace to their children. All the instructions he had were lost upon him: *He did not that which was right in the sight of the Lord* (*v.* 1), nay, he did a great deal that was wrong, a wrong to God, to his own soul, and to his people; he walked in the way of the revolted Israelites and the devoted Canaanites, made molten images and worshipped them, contrary to the second commandment; nay, he made them for Baalim, contrary to the first commandment. he forsook the temple of the Lord and sacrificed and burnt incense on the hills, as if they would place him nearer heaven, and under every green tree, as if they would signify the protection and influence of heaven by their shade and dropping. To complete his wickedness, as one perfectly divested of all natural affection as well as religion and perfectly devoted to the service and interest of the great enemy of mankind, he *burnt his children in the fire to Moloch* (*v.* 3), not thinking it enough to dedicate them to that infernal fiend by causing them to pass through the fire. See what an absolute sway the prince of the power of the air bears among the children of disobedience. 2. Wretchedly spoiled and made a prey of. When he forsook God, and at a vast expense put himself under the protection of false gods, God, who of right was his God, delivered him into the hands of his enemies, *v.* 5. (1.) The Syrians insulted him and triumphed over him, beat him in the field and carried away a great many of his people into captivity. (2.) The king of Israel, though an idolater too, was made a scourge to him, and *smote him with a great slaughter.* The people suffered by these judgments: their blood was shed, their country wasted, their families ruined; for when they had a good king, though *they did corruptly* (*ch.* 27:2), yet then his goodness sheltered them; but now that they had a bad one all the defence had departed from them and an inundation of judgments broke in upon them. Those that knew not their happiness in the foregoing reign were taught to value it by the miseries of this reign.

Verses 6–15

We have here,

I. Treacherous Judah under the rebukes of God's providence, and they are very severe. Never was such bloody work made among them since they were a kingdom, and by Israelites too. Ahaz walked in the ways of the kings of Israel, and the king of Israel was the instrument God made use of for his punishment. It is just with God to make those our plagues whom we make our patterns or make ourselves partners with in sin. A war broke out between Judah and Israel, in which Judah was worsted. For, 1. There was a great slaughter of men in the field of battle. Vast numbers (120,000 men, and valiant men too at other times) were slain (*v.* 6) and some of the first rank, the king's son for one. He had sacrificed some of this sons to Moloch; justly therefore is this sacrificed to the divine vengeance. Here is another that was *next the king,* his friend, the prime-minister of state, or perhaps next him in the battle, so that the king himself had a narrow escape, *v.* 7. The kingdom of Israel was not strong at this time, and yet strong enough to bring this great destruction upon Judah. But certainly so many men, great men, stout men, could not have been cut off in one day if they had not been strangely dispirited both by the consciousness of their own guilt and by the righteous hand of God upon them. Even valiant men were numbered *as sheep for the slaughter,* and became an easy prey to the enemy *because they had forsaken the Lord God of their fathers,* and he had therefore forsaken them. 2. There was a great captivity of *women and children, v.* 8. When the army in the field was routed, the cities, and towns, and country villages, were all easily stripped, the inhabitants taken for slaves, and their wealth for a prey.

II. Even victorious Israel under the rebuke of God's word for the bad principle they had gone upon in making war with Judah and the bad use they had made of their success, and the good effect of this rebuke. Here is,

1. The message which God sent them by a prophet, who went out to meet them, not to applaud their valour or congratulate them on their victory, though they returned laden with spoils and triumphs, but in God's name to tell them of their faults and warn them of the judgments of God.

(1.) He told them how they came by this victory of which they were so proud. It was not because God favoured them, or that they had merited it at his hand, but *because he was wroth with Judah,* and made them the rod of his indignation. *Not for your righteousness,* be it known to you, but *for their wickedness* (Deu. 9:5) *they are broken off; therefore be not you high-minded, but fear lest God also spare not you,* Rom. 11:20, 21.

(2.) He charged them with the abuse of the power God had given them over their brethren. Those understand not what victory is who think it gives them authority to do what they will, and that the longest sword is the clearest claim to lives and estates *(Jusque datum sceleri — might is right);* no, as it is impolitic not to use a victory, so it is impious to abuse it. The conquerors are here reproved, [1.] For the cruelty of the slaughter they had made in the field. They had indeed *shed the blood of war in war;* we suppose that to be lawful, but it turned into sin to them, because they did it from a bad principle of enmity to their

brethren and after a bad manner, with a barbarous fury, *a rage reaching up to heaven,* that is, that cried to God for vengeance against such bloody men, that delighted in military execution. Those that serve God's justice, if they do it with rage and a spirit of revenge, make themselves obnoxious to it, and forfeit the honour of acting for him; *for the wrath of man worketh not the righteousness of God.* [2.] For the imperious treatment they gave their prisoners. *"You now purpose to keep them under,* to use them or sell them as slaves, though they are your brethren and freeborn Israelites." God takes notice of what men purpose, as well as of what they say and do.

(3.) He reminded them of their own sins, by which they also were obnoxious to the wrath of God: *Are there not with you, even with you, sins against the Lord your God? v.* 10. He appeals to their own consciences, and to the notorious evidence of the thing. "Though you are now made the instruments of correcting Judah for sin, yet do not think that you are therefore innocent yourselves; no, you also are guilty before God." This is intended as a check, [1.] To their triumph in their success. "You are sinners, and it ill becomes sinners to be proud; you have carried the day now, but be not secure, the wheel may ere long return upon yourselves, for, if judgment begin thus with those that have *the house of God* among them, what shall be the end of such as worship the calves?" [2.] To their severity towards their brethren. "You have now got them under, but you ought to show mercy to them, for you yourselves are undone if you do not find mercy with God. It ill becomes sinners to be cruel. You have transgressions enough to answer for already, and need not add this to the rest."

(4.) He commanded them to release the prisoners, and to send them home again carefully (*v.* 11); "for you having sinned, *the fierce wrath of God is upon you,* and there is no other way of escaping it than by showing mercy."

2. The resolution of the princes thereupon not to detain the prisoners. They *stood up against those that came from the war,* though flushed with victory, and told them plainly that they should not bring their captives into Samaria, *v.* 12, 13. They had sin enough already to answer for, and would have nothing done to add to their trespass. In this they discovered an obedient regard to the word of God by his prophet and a tender compassion towards their brethren, which was wrought in them by the tender mercy of God; for he regarded the affliction of this poor people, and hears their cry, and *made them to be pitied of all those that carried them captive,* Ps. 106:44, 46.

3. The compliance of the soldiers with the resolutions of the princes in this matter, and the dismission of the captives thereupon. (1.) The armed men, though being armed they might be force have maintained their title to what they got by the sword, acquiesced, and left their captives and the spoil to the disposal of *the princes* (*v.* 14), and herein they showed more truly heroic bravery than they did in taking them. It is a great honour for any man to yield to the authority of reason and religion against his interest. (2.) The princes very generously sent home the poor captives well accommodated, *v.* 15. Those that hope to find mercy with God must learn hence with what tenderness to carry themselves towards those that lie at their mercy. It is strange that these princes, who in this instance discovered such a deference to the word of God, and such an influence upon the people, had not so much grace as, in obedience to the calls of God by so many prophets, to root idolatry out of their kingdom, which, soon after this, was the ruin of it.

Verses 16–27

Here is, I. The great distress which the kingdom of Ahaz was reduced to for his sin. In general, 1. *The Lord brought Judah low, v.* 19. They had lately been very high in wealth and power; but God found means to bring them down, and make them as despicable as they had been formidable. Those that will not humble themselves under the word of God will justly be humbled by his judgments. Iniquity brings men low, Ps. 106:43. 2. Ahaz made Judah naked. As his sin debased them, so it exposed them. It made them naked to their shame; for it exposed them to contempt, as a man unclothed. It made them naked to their danger; for it exposed them to assaults, as a man unarmed, Ex. 32:25. Sin strips men. In particular, the Edomites, to be revenged for Amaziah's cruel treatment of them (*ch.* 25:12),

smote Judah, and carried off many captives, *v.* 17. The Philistines also insulted them, took and kept possession of several cities and villages that lay near them (*v.* 18), and so they were revenged for the incursions which Uzziah had made upon them, *ch.* 26:6. And, to show that it was purely the sin of Ahaz that brought the Philistines upon his country, in the very year that he died the prophet Isaiah foretold the destruction of the Philistines by his son, Isa. 14:28, 29.

II. The addition which Ahaz made both to the national distress and the national guilt.

1. He added to the distress, by making court to strange kings, in hopes they would relieve him. When the Edomites and Philistines were vexatious to him, *he sent to the kings of Assyria to help him* (*v.* 16); for he found his own kingdom weakened and made naked, and he could not put any confidence in God, and therefore was at a vast expense to get an interest in the king of Assyria. He pillaged the house of God, and the king's house, and squeezed the princes for money to hire these foreign forces into his service, *v.* 21. Though he had conformed to the idolatry of the heathen nations, his neighbours, they did not value him for that, nor love him the better, nor did his compliance, by which he lost God, gain them, nor could he make any interest in them, but with his money. It is often found that wicked men themselves have no real affection for those that revolt to them, nor do they care to do them a kindness. A degenerate branch is looked upon, on all sides, as *an abominable branch,* Isa. 14:19. But what did Ahaz get by the king of Assyria? Why, he *came to him,* but he *distressed him,* and *strengthened him not* (*v.* 20), *helped him not, v.* 21. The forces of the Assyrian quartered upon his country, and so impoverished and weakened it; they grew insolent and imperious, and created him a great deal of vexation, like a broken reed, which not only fails, but pierces the hand.

2. He added to the guilt, by making court to strange gods, in hopes they would relieve him. In his distress, instead of repenting of his idolatry, which he had reason enough to see the folly of, *he trespassed yet more* (*v.* 22), was more mad than ever upon his idols. A brand of infamy is here set upon him for it: *This is that king Ahaz,* that wretched man, who was the scandal of the house of David and the curse and plague of his generation. Note, Those are wicked and vile indeed that are made worse by their afflictions, instead of being made better by them, who *in their distress trespass yet more,* have their corruptions exasperated by that which should mollify them, and their hearts more *fully set in them to do evil.* Let us see what his trespass was. (1.) He abused the house of God; for he *cut in pieces the vessels* of it, that the priests might not perform the service of the temple, or not as it should be performed, for want of vessels; and, at length, he *shut up the doors,* that the people might not attend it, *v.* 24. This was worse than the worst of the kings before him had done. (2.) He confronted the altar of God, for he *made himself altars in every corner of Jerusalem;* so that, as the prophet speaks, they were like *heaps in the furrows of the fields,* Hos. 12:11. And in the cities of Judah, either by his power or by his purse, perhaps by both, he erected high places for the people to burn incense to what idols they pleased, as if on purpose to *provoke the God of his fathers, v.* 25. (3.) He cast off God himself; for he *sacrificed to the gods of Damascus* (*v.* 23), not because he loved them, for he thought they smote him; but because he feared them, thinking that they helped his enemies, and that, if he could bring them into his interest, they would help him. Foolish man! It was his own God that smote him and strengthened the Syrians against him, not the gods of Damascus; had he sacrificed to him, and to him only, he would have helped him. But no marvel that men's affections and devotions are misplaced when they mistake the author of their trouble and their help. And what comes of it? The gods of Syria befriend Ahaz no more than the kings of Assyria did; they were the *ruin of him and of all Israel.* This sin provoked God to bring judgments upon them, to cut him off in the midst of his days, when he was but thirty-six years old; and it debauched the people so that the reformation of the next reign could not prevail to cure them of their inclination to idolatry, but they retained that root of bitterness till the captivity in Babylon plucked it up.

The chapter concludes with the conclusion of the reign

of Ahaz, *v.* 26, 27. For aught that appears, he died impenitent, and therefore died inglorious; for he was not buried *in the sepulchres of the kings.* Justly was he thought unworthy to be laid among them who was so unlike them — to be buried with kings who had used his kingly power for the destruction of the church and not for its protection or edification.

CHAPTER 29

We are here entering upon a pleasant scene, the good and glorious reign of Hezekiah, in which we shall find more of God and religion than perhaps in any of the good reigns we have yet met with; for he was a very zealous, devout, good man, none like him. In this chapter we have an account of the work of reformation which he set about with vigour immediately after his accession to the crown. Here is, I. His exhortation to the priests and Levites, when he put them in possession of the house of God again (*v.* 1–11). II. The care and pains which the Levites took to cleanse the temple, and put things in order there (*v.* 12–19). III. A solemn revival of God's ordinances that had been neglected, in which atonement was made for the sins of the last reign, and the wheels were set a-going again, to the great satisfaction of king and people (*v.* 20–36).

Verses 1–11

Here is, I. Hezekiah's age when he came to the crown. He was *twenty-five years old.* Joash, who came to the crown after two bad reigns, was but seven years old; Josiah, who came after two bad reigns, was but eight, which occasioned the delay of the reformation; but Hezekiah had come to years, and so applied himself immediately to it. We may well think with what a sorrowful heart he beheld his father's idolatry and profaneness, how it troubled him to see the doors of the temple shut, though, while his father lived, he durst not open them. His soul no doubt wept in secret for it, and he vowed that when he should receive the congregation he would redress these grievances, which made him do it with more readiness and resolution.

II. His general character. He *did that which was right like David, v.* 2. Of several of his predecessors it had been said that they did that which was right, *but not like David,* not with David's integrity and zeal. But here was one that had as hearty an affection for the ark and law of God as ever David had.

III. His speedy application to the great work of restoring religion. The first thing he did was to *open the doors of the house of the Lord, v.* 3. We are willing to hope his father had not quite suppressed the temple service; for then the holy fire on the altar must have gone out, and we do not read of the re-kindling of it; but he had hindered the people from attending it, and the priests, except such of them as were of his own party, 2 Ki. 16:15. But Hezekiah immediately threw the church doors open, and *brought in the priests and Levites.* He found Judah low and naked, yet did not make it his first business to revive the civil interests of his kingdom, but to restore religion to its good posture again. Those that begin with God begin at the right end of their work, and it will prosper accordingly.

IV. His speech to the priests and Levites. It was well known, no doubt, that he had a real kindness for religion and was disaffected to the corruptions of the last reign; yet we do not find the priests and Levites making application to him for the restoration of the temple service but he calls upon them, which, I doubt, bespeaks their coldness as much as his zeal; and perhaps, if they had done their part with vigour, things would not have been brought into so very bad a posture as Hezekiah found them in. Hezekiah's exhortation to the Levites is very pathetic.

1. He laid before them the desolations of religion and the deplorable state to which it was brought among them (*v.* 6, 7): *Our fathers have trespassed.* He said not *"My* father," because it became him, as a son, to be as tender as might be of his father's name, and because his father would not have done all this if their fathers had not neglected their duty. Urijah the priest had joined with Ahaz in setting up an idolatrous altar. He complained, (1.) That the house of God had been deserted: *They have forsaken God, and turned their backs upon his habitation.* Note, Those that turn their backs upon God's ordinances may truly be said to forsake God himself. (2.) That the instituted worship of God there had been let fall. The lamps were not lighted, and incense was not burnt. There are still such neglects as these, and they are no less culpable, when the word is not duly read and opened (for that was signified by the *lighting of the lamps*) and when prayers and praises are not duly offered up, for that was signified by *the burning of incense.*

2. He showed the sad consequences of the neglect and decay of religion among them, *v.* 8. 9. This was the cause of all the calamities they had lain under. God had in anger delivered them to trouble, to the sword, and to captivity. When we are under the rebukes of God's providence it is good for us to enquire whether we have not neglected God's ordinances and whether the controversy he has with us may not be traced to this neglect.

3. He declared his own full purpose and resolution to revive religion and make it his business to promote it (*v.* 10): *"It is in my heart* (that is, I am fully resolved) *to make a covenant with the Lord God of Israel* (that is, to worship him only, and in that way which he has appointed); for I am sure that, otherwise, his fierce anger will not turn away from us." This covenant he would not only make himself, but bring his people into the bond of.

4. He engaged and excited the Levites and priests to do their duty on this occasion. This he begins with (*v.* 5); this he ends with, *v.* 11. He called them *Levites* to remind them of their obligation to God, called them his *sons* to remind them of the relation to himself, that he expected that, *as a son with the father, they should serve with him* in the reformation of the land. (1.) he told them what was their duty, to sanctify *themselves* first (by repenting of their neglects, reforming their own hearts and lives, and renewing their covenants with God to do their duty better for the time to come), and then to *sanctify the house of God,* as his servants, to make it clean from every thing that was disagreeable, either through the disuse or the profanation of it, and to set it up for the purposes for which it was made. (2.) He stirred them up to do it (*v.* 11): *"Be not now negligent,* or remiss, in your duty. Let not this good work be retarded through your carelessness." *Be not deceived,* so the *margin.* Note, Those that by their negligence in the service of God think to mock God, and put a cheat upon him, do but deceive themselves, and put a damning cheat upon their own souls. *Be not secure* (so some), as if there were no urgent call to do it or no danger in not doing it. Note, Men's negligence in religion is owing to their carnal security. The consideration he quickens them with is derived from their office. God had herein put honour upon them: He has *chosen you to stand before him.* God therefore expected work from them. They were not chosen to be idle, to enjoy the dignity and leave the duty to be done by others, but to serve him and to minister to him. They must therefore be ashamed of their late remissness, and, now that the doors of the temple were opened again, must set about their work with double diligence.

Verses 12–19

We have here busy work, good work, and needful work, the cleansing of the house of the Lord.

I. The persons employed in this work were the priests and Levites, who should have kept the temple clean, but, not having done that, were concerned to make it clean. Several of the Levites are here named, two of each of the three principal houses, Kohath, Gershon, and Merari (*v.* 12), and two of each of the three families of singers, Asaph, Heman, and Jeduthun, *v.* 13, 14. We cannot think these are named merely because they were chief in place (for then surely the high priest, or some of the heads of the courses of the priests, would have been mentioned), but because they were more zealous and active than the rest. When God has work to do he will raise up leading men to preside in it. And it is not always that the first in place and rank are most fit for service or most forward to it. These Levites not only bestirred themselves, but *gathered their brethren,* and quickened them to do *according to the commandment of the king by the word of the Lord.* Observe, They did according to the king's command, but with an eye to God's word. The king commanded them what was already their duty by the word of God, and, in doing it, they regarded God's word as a rule to them and the king's commandment as a spur to them.

II. The work was *cleansing the house of God,* 1. From the common dirt it had contracted while it was shut up — dust, and cobwebs, and the rust of the vessels. 2. From the idols and idolatrous altars that were set up in it, which, though kept ever so neat, were a greater pollution to it than if it had been made the common sewer of the city. The priests were none of them mentioned as leading men in this work, yet none but they durst go *into the inner part of the house, no, not to cleanse it,* which they did, and perhaps the high priest into the holy of holies, to cleanse that. And, though the Levites had the honour to be the leaders in the work, they did not disdain to be servitors to the priests according to their office; for what filth the priests brought into the court the Levites carried to the brook Kidron. Let not men's usefulness, be it ever so eminent, make them forget their place.

III. The expedition with which they did this work was very remarkable. They began on the first day of the first month, a happy beginning of the new-year, and one that promised a good year. Thus should every year begin with the reformation of what is amiss, and the purging away, by true repentance, of all the defilements contracted the foregoing year. In eight days they cleared and cleansed the temple, and in eight days more the *courts* of the temple, *v.* 17. Let those that do good work learn to rid work and get it done. Let what is amiss be amended quickly.

IV. The report they made of it to Hezekiah was very agreeable, *v.* 18, 19. They gave him an account of what they had done, because it was he that set them on work, boasted not of their own care and pains, nor did they come to him to be paid, but to let him know that all things that had been profaned were now sanctified according to law, and were ready to be used again whenever he pleased. They knew the good king had set his heart upon God's altar, and longed to be attending that, and therefore they insisted most upon the readiness they had put that into — that the vessels for the altar were scoured and brightened. Those vessels which Ahaz, in his *transgression, had cast away* as vessels in which there was no pleasure, they gathered together, sanctified them, and laid them in their place *before the altar.* Though the vessels of the sanctuary may be profaned for a while, God will find a time and a way to sanctify them. Neither his ordinances nor his people shall be suffered to fail for ever.

Verses 20–36

The temple being cleansed, we have here an account of the good use that was immediately made of it. A solemn assembly was called to meet the king at the temple, the very next day (*v.* 20); and very glad, no doubt, all the good people in Jerusalem were, when it was said, *Let us go up to the house of the Lord,* Ps. 122:1. As soon as Hezekiah heard that the temple was ready for him he lost no time, but made it appear that he was ready for it. He rose early to go up to the house of the Lord, earlier on that day than on other days, to show that his heart was upon his work there. Now this day's work was to look two ways: —

I. Atonement must be made for the sins of the last reign. They thought it not enough to lament and forsake those sins, but they brought a sin-offering. Even our repentance and reformation will not obtain pardon but in and through Christ, who was made *sin* (that is, a sin-offering) for us. No peace but through his blood, no, not for penitents. Observe, 1. The sin-offering was *for the kingdom, for the sanctuary,* and *for Judah* (*v.* 21), that is, to make atonement for the sins of princes, priests, and people, for they had all corrupted their way. The law of Moses appointed sacrifices to make atonement for the sins of the whole congregation (Lev. 4:13, 14; Num. 15:24, 25), that the national judgments which their national sins deserved might be turned away. For this purpose we must now have an eye to Christ the great propitiation, as well as for the remission and salvation of particular persons. 2. The law appointed only one goat for a sin-offering, as on the day of atonement (Lev. 16:15) and on such extraordinary occasions as this, Num. 15:24. But they here offered seven (*v.* 21), because the sins of the congregation had been very great and long continued in. Seven is a number of perfection. Our great sin-offering is but one, yet that one *perfects* for ever *those that are sanctified.* 3. The king and the *congregation* (that is, the representatives of the congregation) *laid their hands on the heads of the goats* that were for the *sin-offering* (*v.* 23), thereby owning themselves guilty before God and expressing their desire that the guilt of the sinner might be transferred to the sacrifice. By faith we lay our hands on the Lord Jesus, and so *receive the atonement,* Rom. 5:11. 4. Burnt-offerings were offered with the sin-offerings, *seven bullocks, seven rams*, and *seven lambs*. The intention of the burnt-offerings was to give glory to the God of Israel, whom they owned as the only true God, which it was proper to do at the same time that they were by the sin-offering making atonement for their offences. The blood of those, as well as of the sin-offering, was *sprinkled upon the altar* (*v.* 22), to make reconciliation *for all Israel* (*v.* 24), and not for Judah only. Christ is a propitiation, not for the sins of Israel only, but *of the whole world*, 1 Jn. 2:1, 2. 5. While the offerings were burning upon the altar the *Levites* sang *the song of the Lord* (*v.* 27), the Psalms composed by David and Asaph (*v.* 30), accompanied by the musical instruments which God by his prophets had commanded the use of (*v.* 25), and which had been long neglected. Even sorrow for sin must not put us out of tune for praising God. By faith we must rejoice in Christ Jesus as our righteousness; and our prayers and praises must ascend with his offering, to be accepted only in virtue of it. 6. The king and all the congregation testified their consent to and concurrence in all that was done, by *bowing their heads* and *worshipping*, expressing an awful veneration of the divine Majesty, by postures of adoration. This is taken notice of, *v.* 28–30. It is not enough for us to be where God is worshipped, if we do not ourselves worship him, and that not with bodily exercise only, which profits little, but with the heart.

II. The solemnities of this day did likewise look forward. The temple service was to be set up again, that it might be continually kept up; and this Hezekiah calls them to, *v.* 31. "Now that you have *consecrated yourselves to the Lord* — have both made an atonement and made a covenant by sacrifice, are solemnly reconciled and engaged to him — now *come near, and bring sacrifices*." Note, Our covenant with God must be pursued and improved in communion with him. Having consecrated ourselves, in the first place, to the Lord, we must bring the sacrifices of prayer, and praise, and alms, to his house. Now, in this work, it was found.

1. That the people were free. Being called to it by the king, they brought in their offerings, though not in such abundance as in the glorious days of Solomon (for Judah was now diminished, impoverished, and brought low), but according to what they had, and as much as one could expect considering their poverty and the great decay of piety among them. (1.) Some were so generous as to bring burnt-offerings, which were wholly consumed to the honour of God, and of which the offerer had no part. Of this sort there were seventy bullocks, 100 rams, and 200 lambs, *v.* 32. (2.) Others brought peace-offerings and thank-offerings, the fat of which was burnt upon the altar, and the flesh divided between the priests and the offerers, *v.* 35. Of this sort there were 600 oxen and 3000 sheep, *v.* 33. Perhaps the remembrance of their sin in sacrificing on the high places made them more willing to bring their sacrifices now to God's altar.

2. That *the priests were few*, too few for the service, *v.* 34. Many of them, it is likely, were suspended and laid aside as polluted and uncanonical, for having sacrificed to idols in the last reign, and the rest had not the zeal that one might have expected upon such an occasion. They thought that the king needed not to be so forward, that there was no necessity for such haste in opening the doors of the temple, and therefore they took no care to sanctify themselves, and being unsanctified, and so unqualified, they made that their excuse for being absent from the service; as if their offence would be their defence. It is recorded here, to the perpetual shame of the priests, that, though they were so well provided for out of the offerings of the Lord made by fire, yet they did not mind their business. Here was work to do, and there wanted proper hands to do it.

3. That the Levites were forward. They had been *more upright in heart to sanctify themselves than the priests* (*v.* 34), were better affected to the work and better prepared and qualified for it. This was their praise, and, in recompence for it, they had the honour to be employed in that which was the priests' work: they *helped them to flay the offerings*. This was not according to the law (Lev. 1:5, 6), but the irregularity was dispensed with in cases of necessity, and thus encouragement was given to the faithful zealous Levites and a just disgrace put upon the careless priests. What the Levites wanted in the ceremonial ad-

vantages of their birth and consecration was abundantly made up in their eminent qualifications of skill and will to do the work.

4. That all were pleased. The king and all the people rejoiced in this blessed turn of affairs and the new face of religion which the kingdom had put on, *v.* 36. Two things in this matter pleased them: — (1.) That it was soon brought about: *The thing was done suddenly*, in a little time, with a great deal of ease, and without any opposition. Those that go about the work of God in faith and with resolution will find that there is not that difficulty in it which they sometimes imagine, but it will be a pleasing surprise to them to see how soon it is done. (2.) That the hand of God was plainly in it: *God had prepared the people* by the secret influences of his grace, so that many of those who had in the last reign doted on the idolatrous altars were now as much in love with God's altar. This change, which God wrought on their minds, did very much expedite and facilitate the work. Let magistrates and ministers do their part towards the reforming of a land, and ascribe to him the glory of what is done, especially when it is done suddenly and is a pleasing surprise. *This is the Lord's doing, and it is marvellous.*

CHAPTER 30

In this chapter we have an account of the solemn passover which Hezekiah kept in the first year of his reign. I. The consultation about it, and the resolution he and his people came to for the observance of it (*v.* 2–5). II. The invitation he sent to Judah and Israel to come and keep it (*v.* 1, 6–12). III. The joyful celebration of it (*v.* 13–27). By this the reformation, set on foot in the foregoing chapter, was greatly advanced and established, and that nail in God's holy place clenched.

Verses 1–12

Here is, I. A passover resolved upon. That annual feast was instituted as a memorial of the bringing of the children of Israel out of Egypt. It happened that the reviving of the temple service fell within the appointed days of that feast, the seventeenth day of the first month: this brought that forgotten solemnity to mind. "What shall we do," says Hezekiah, "about the passover? It is a very comfortable ordinance, and has been long neglected. How shall we revive it? The time has elapsed for this year; we cannot go about it immediately; the congregation is thin, the people have not notice, the priests are not prepared, *v.* 3. Must we defer it till another year?" Many, it is likely, were for deferring it; but Hezekiah considered that by that time twelve-month the good affections of the people would cool, and it would be too long to want the benefit of the ordinance; and therefore, finding a proviso in the law of Moses that particular persons who were unclean in the first month might keep the passover the fourteenth day of the second month and be accepted (Num. 9:11), he doubted not but that it might be extended to the congregation. Whereupon they resolved to keep the passover *in the second month*. Let the circumstance give way to the substance, and let not the thing itself be lost upon a nicety about the time. It is good striking while the iron is hot, and taking people when they are in a good mind. Delays are dangerous.

II. A proclamation issued out to give notice of this passover and to summon the people to it.

1. An invitation was sent to the ten revolted tribes to stir them up to come and attend this solemnity. Letters were written to Ephraim and Manasseh to invite them to Jerusalem to keep this passover (*v.* 1), not with any political design, to bring them back to the house of David, but with a pious design to bring them back to the Lord God of Israel. "Let them take whom they will for their king," says Hezekiah, "so they will but take him for their God." The matters in difference between Judah and Israel, either upon a civil or sacred account, shall not hinder but that if the people of Israel will sincerely return to the Lord their God Hezekiah will bid them as welcome to the passover as any of his own subjects. Expresses are sent post throughout all the tribes of Israel with memorials earnestly pressing the people to take this opportunity of returning to the God from whom they had revolted. Now here we have,

(1.) The contents of the circular letters that were despatched upon the occasion, in which Hezekiah discovers a great concern both for the honour of God and for the welfare of the neighbouring kingdom, the prosperity of

which he seems passionately desirous of, though he not only received no toll, tribute, or custom, from it, but it had often, and not long since, been vexatious to his kingdom. This is rendering good for evil. Observe,

[1.] What it is which he presses them to (*v.* 8): "*Yield yourselves unto the Lord*. Before you can come into communion with him you must come into covenant with him." *Give the hand to the Lord* (so the word is), that is, "Consent to take him for your God." A bargain is confirmed by giving the hand. "Strike this bargain. Join yourselves to him in an everlasting covenant. *Subscribe with the hand* to be his, Isa. 44:5. Give him your hand, in token of giving him your heart. Lay your hand to his plough. Devote yourselves to his service, to work for him. *Yield to him*," that is, "Come up to his terms, come under his government, stand it not out any longer against him." "*Yield to him*, to be absolutely and universally at his command, at his disposal, to be, and do, and have, and suffer, whatever he pleases. In order to this, be not *stiff-necked as your fathers were;* let not your corrupt and wicked wills rise up in resistance of and rebellion against the will of God. Say not that you will do what you please, but resolve to do what he pleases." There is in the carnal mind a stiffness, an obstinacy, an unaptness to comply with God. We have it from our fathers; it is bred in the bone with us. This must be conquered; and the will that had in it a spirit of contradiction must be melted into the will of God; and to his yoke the neck that was an iron sinew must be bowed and fitted. In pursuance of this resignation to God, he presses them *to enter into his sanctuary*, that is, to attend upon him in that place which he had chosen, to put his name there, and serve him in the ordinances which he had appointed. "The doors of the sanctuary are now opened, and you have liberty to enter; the temple service is now revived, and you are welcome to join in it." The king says, *Come;* the princes and priests say, *Come; whosoever will, let him come.* This he calls (*v.* 6) *turning to the Lord God;* for they had forsaken him, and worshipped other gods. *Repent now, and be converted.* Thus those who through grace have turned to God themselves should do all they can to bring others back to him.

[2.] What arguments he uses to persuade them to do this. *First*, "You are children of Israel, and therefore stand related, stand obliged, to the God of Israel, from whom you have revolted." *Secondly*, "The God you are called to return to is the God of Abraham, Isaac, and Jacob, a God in covenant with your first fathers, who served him and yielded themselves to him; and it was their honour and happiness that they did so." *Thirdly*, "Your late fathers that forsook him and trespassed against him have been given up to desolation; their apostasy and idolatry have been their ruin, as you see (*v.* 7); let their harms be your warnings." *Fourthly*, "You yourselves are but a *remnant* narrowly *escaped out of the hands of the kings of Assyria* (*v.* 6), and therefore are concerned to put yourselves under the protection of the God of your fathers, that you be not quite swallowed up." *Fifthly*, "This is the only way of *turning away the fierceness of God's anger from you* (*v.* 8), which will certainly consume you if you continue stiff-necked." *Lastly*, "If you return to God in a way of duty, he will return to you in a way of mercy." This he begins with (*v.* 6) and concludes with, *v.* 9. In general, "You will find him *gracious and merciful*, and one that *will not turn away his face from you*, if you seek him, notwithstanding the provocations you have given him." Particularly, "You may hope that he will turn again the captivity of your brethren that are carried away, and bring them back to their own land." Could any thing be expressed more pathetically, more movingly? Could there be a better cause, or could it be better pleaded?

(2.) The entertainment which Hezekiah's messengers and message met with. It does not appear that Hoshea, who was now king of Israel, took any umbrage from, or gave any opposition to, the dispersing of these proclamations through his kingdom, nor that he forbade his subjects to accept the invitation. He seems to have left them entirely to their liberty. They might go to Jerusalem to worship if they pleased; for, though he did evil, yet *not like the kings of Israel that were before him*, 2 Ki. 17:2. He saw ruin coming upon his kingdom, and, if any of his subjects would try this expedient to prevent it, they had his full permission. But, for the people, [1.] The generality of them slighted the call and turned a deaf ear to it. The messengers went from city to city, some to one and some to another, and used pressing entreaties with the people to come up to Jerusalem to keep the passover; but they were so far from complying with the message that they abused those that brought it, *laughed them to scorn, and mocked them* (v. 10), not only refused, but refused with disdain. Tell them of the God of Abraham! they knew him not, they had other gods to serve, Baal and Ashtaroth. Tell them of the sanctuary! their high places were as good. Tell them of God's mercy and wrath! they neither dreaded the one nor desired the other. No marvel that the king's messengers were thus despitefully used by this apostate race when God's messengers were so, his servants the prophets, who produced credentials from him. The destruction of the kingdom of the ten tribes was now at hand. It was but two or three years after this that the king of Assyria laid siege to Samaria, which ended in the captivity of those tribes. Just before this they had not only a king of their own that permitted them to return to God's sanctuary, but a king of Judah that earnestly invited them to do it. Had they generally accepted this invitation, it might have prevented their ruin; but their contempt of it hastened and aggravated it, and left them inexcusable. [2.] Yet there were some few that accepted the invitation. The message, though to some it was a *savour of death unto death*, was to others a *savour of life unto life*, v. 11. In the worst of times God has had a remnant; so he had here, many of Asher, Manasseh, and Zebulun (here is no mention of any out of Ephraim, though some of that tribe are mentioned, v. 18), *humbled themselves, and came to Jerusalem*, that is, were sorry for their sins and submitted to God. Pride keeps men from yielding themselves to the Lord; when that is brought down, the work is done.

2. A command was given to the men of Judah to attend this solemnity; and they universally obeyed it, v. 12. They did it with one heart, were all of a mind in it, and *the hand of God gave* them that *one heart*; for it is in the day of power that Christ's subjects are made willing. It is God that works both *to will* and *to do*. When people, at any time, manifest an unexpected forwardness to do that which is good, we must acknowledge that hand of God in it.

Verses 13–20

The time appointed for the passover having arrived, a very great congregation came together upon the occasion, v. 13. Now here we have,

I. The preparation they made for the passover, and good preparation it was: *They took away* all *the idolatrous altars* that were found, not only in the temple, but *in Jerusalem*, v. 14. Before they kept the feast, they cast out this old leaven. The best preparation we can make for the gospel passover is to cast away our iniquities, our spiritual idolatries.

II. The celebration of the passover. In this the people were so forward and zealous that the priests and Levites blushed to see themselves out-done by the commonalty, to see them more ready to bring sacrifices than they were to offer them. This put them upon sanctifying themselves (v. 15), that the work might not stand still for want of hands to carry it on. The notice we take of the zeal of others should make us ashamed of our own coldness, and quicken us not only to do our duty, but to do it well, and to sanctify ourselves to it. They did according to the duty of their place (v. 16), sprinkling *the blood upon the altar*, which was a type of Christ our passover sacrificed for us.

III. The irregularities they were guilty of in this solemnity. The substance was well managed, and with a great deal of devotion; but, besides that it was a month out of time, 1. The *Levites killed the passover*, which should have been done by the priests only, v. 17. They also assisted more than the law ordinarily allowed in offering the other sacrifices, particularly those that were for the purifying of the unclean, many of which there was now occasion for. Some think that it was the offerers' work, not the priests', that the Levites had here the charge of. Ordinarily every man killed his lamb, but now for those that were under any ceremonial pollution the Levites killed it. 2. Many were permitted to eat the passover who were not purified according to the strictness of the law, v. 18. This was the second month, and there was not warrant to put

them off further to the third month, as, if it had been the first month, the law would have permitted them to eat it the second. And they were loth to forbid them communicating at all, lest they should discourage new converts, and send those away complaining whom they desired to send away rejoicing. Grotius observes from this that ritual institutions must give way, not only to a public necessity, but to a public benefit and advantage.

IV. Hezekiah's prayer to God for the forgiveness of this irregularity. It was his zeal that had called them together in such haste, and he would not that any should fare the worse for being straitened of time in their preparation. He therefore thought himself concerned to be an intercessor for those that *ate the passover otherwise than it was written*, that there might not be wrath upon them from the Lord. His prayer was,

1. A short prayer, but to the purpose: *The good Lord pardon every one* in the congregation that has fixed, engaged, or *prepared, his heart* to those services, though the ceremonial preparation be wanting. Note, (1.) The great thing required in our attendance upon God in solemn ordinances is that we *prepare our hearts to seek him*, that we be sincere and upright in all we do, that the inward man be engaged and employed in it, and that we make heart-work of it; it is all nothing without this. *Behold, thou desirest truth in the inward part.* Hezekiah does not pray that this might be dispensed with, nor that the want of other things might be pardoned where there was not this. For *this* is the *one thing needful*, that we *seek God*, his favour, his honour, and that we set our hearts to do it. (2.) Where this sincerity and fixedness of heart are there may still be many defects and infirmities, both the frame of the spirit and the performance of the service may be short of *the purification of the sanctuary*. Corruptions may not be so fully conquered, thoughts not so closely fixed, affections not so lively, faith not so operative, as they should be. Here is a defect in sanctuary purification. There is nothing perfect under the sun, nor *a just man that doeth good, and sinneth not*. (3.) These defects need pardoning healing grace; for omissions in duty are sins as well as omissions of duty. If God should deal with us in strict justice according to the best of our performances, we should be undone. (4.) The way to obtain pardon for our deficiencies in duty, and all the iniquities of our holy things, is to seek it of God by prayer; it is not so a pardon of course but that it must be obtained by petition through the blood of Christ. (5.) In this prayer we must take encouragement from the goodness of God: *The good Lord pardon;* for, when he proclaimed his goodness, he insisted most upon this branch of it, *forgiving iniquity, transgression, and sin.* (6.) It is the duty of those that have the charge of others, not only to look to themselves, but to those also that are under their charge, to see wherein they are wanting, and to pray for them, as Hezekiah here. See Job 1:5.

2. A successful prayer: *The Lord hearkened to Hezekiah*, was well pleased with his pious concern for the congregation, and, in answer to his prayer, *healed the people* (v. 20), not only did not lay their sin to their charge, but graciously accepted their services notwithstanding; for healing denotes not only forgiveness (Isa. 6:10; Ps. 103:3), but comfort and peace, Isa. 57:18; Mal. 4:2.

Verses 21–27

After the passover followed the feast of unleavened bread, which continued seven days. How that was observed we are here told, and every thing in this account looks pleasant and lively. 1. Abundance of sacrifices were offered to God in peace-offerings, by which they both acknowledged and implored the favour of God, and on part of which the offerers feasted with their friends during these seven days (v. 22), in token of their communion with God and the comfort they took in his favour and their reconciliation to him. To keep up this part of the service, that God's altar might be abundantly regaled with the fat and blood and his priests and people with the flesh of the peace-offerings, Hezekiah gave out of his own stock 1000 bullocks and 7000 sheep, and the princes, excited by his pious example, gave the same number of bullocks and a greater number of sheep, and all for peace-offerings, v. 24. By this God was honoured, the joy of the festival was kept up, and the strangers were encouraged to come again to

Jerusalem. It was generously done of the king and the princes thus plentifully to entertain the whole congregation; but what is a great estate good for but that it puts men into a capacity of doing so much the more good? Christ feasted those that followed him. I believe neither Hezekiah nor his princes were the poorer at the year's end for this their pious liberality. 2. Many good prayers were put up to God with the peace-offerings, v. 22. They *made confession to the Lord God of their fathers*, in which the intent and meaning of the peace-offerings were directed and explained. When the priests sprinkled the blood and burnt the fat they made confession, so did the people when they feasted on their part. They made a religious confession of their relation to God and dependence upon him, a penitent confession of their sins and infirmities, a thankful confession of God's mercies to them, and a supplicatory confession of their wants and desires; and, in all these, they had an eye to God as *the God of their fathers*, a God in covenant with them. 3. There was a great deal of good preaching. The Levites (whose office it was, Deu. 33:10) *taught the people the good knowledge of the Lord*, read and opened the scriptures, and instructed the congregation concerning God and their duty to him; and great need there was of this, after so long a famine of the word as there had been in the last reign. Hezekiah did not himself preach, but he *spoke comfortably to the Levites* that did, attended their preaching, commended their diligence, and assured them of his protection and countenance. Hereby he encouraged them to study hard and take pains, and put a reputation upon them, that the people might respect and regard them the more. Princes and magistrates, by owning and encouraging faithful and laborious preachers, greatly serve the interest of God's kingdom among men. 4. They sang psalms every day (v. 21): *The Levites and priests praised the Lord day by day*, both with songs and musical instruments, thus expressing their own and exciting one another's joy in God and thankfulness to him. Praising God should be much of our work in our religious assemblies. 5. Having kept the seven days of the feast in this religious manner, they had so much comfort in the service that they *kept other seven days*, v. 23. They did not institute any new modes of worship, but repeated and continued the old. The case was extraordinary: they had been long without the ordinance; guilt had been contracted by the neglect of it; they had now got a very great congregation together, and were in a devout serious frame; they knew not when they might have such another opportunity, and therefore could not now find in their hearts to separate till they had doubled the time. Many of them were a great way from home, and had business in the country to look after, for, this being the second month, they were in the midst of their harvest; yet they were in no haste to return: the zeal of God's house made them forget their secular affairs. How unlike those who snuffed at God's service, and said, *What a weariness is it!* Or those who asked, *When will the sabbath be gone?* The servants of God should abound in his work. 6. All this they did *with gladness* (v. 23); they all rejoiced, and particularly *the strangers*, v. 25. *So there was great joy in Jerusalem*, v. 26. Never was the like since the dedication of the temple in Solomon's time. Note, Holy duties should be performed with holy gladness; we should be forward to them, and take pleasure in them, relish the sweetness of communion with God, and look upon it as matter of unspeakable joy and comfort that we are thus favoured and have such earnests of everlasting joy. 7. The congregation was at length dismissed with a solemn blessing, v. 27. (1.) The priests pronounced it; for it was part of their office to *bless the people* (Num. 6:22, 23), in which they were both the people's mouth to God by way of prayer and God's mouth to the people by way of promise; for their blessing included both. In it they testified both their desire of the people's welfare and their dependence upon God and that word of his grace to which they commended them. What a comfort is it to a congregation to be sent home thus crowned! (2.) God said *Amen* to it. The voice of the priests, when they *blessed the people, was heard in heaven* and came up to the *habitation of God's holiness*. When they pronounced the blessing God commanded it, and perhaps gave some sensible token of the ratification of it. The prayer that comes up to heaven in a cloud of incense will come down again to this earth in showers of blessings.

CHAPTER 31

We have here a further account of that blessed reformation of which Hezekiah was a glorious instrument, and of the happy advances he made in it. I. All the remnants of idolatry were destroyed and abolished (*v.* 1). II. The priests and Levites were set to work again, every man in his place (*v.* 2). III. Care was taken for their maintenance. 1. The royal bounty to the clergy, and for the support of the temple service, was duly paid (*v.* 3). 2. Orders were given for the raising of the people's quota (*v.* 4). 3. The people, thereupon, brought in their dues abundantly (*v.* 5–10). 4. Commissioners were appointed for the due distribution of what was brought in (*v.* 11–19). Lastly, Here is the general praise of Hezekiah's sincerity in all his undertakings (*v.* 20, 21).

Verses 1–10

We have here an account of what was done after the passover. What was wanting in the solemnities of preparation for it before was made up in that which is better, a due improvement of it after. When the religious exercises of a Lord's day or a communion are finished we must not think that then the work is done. No, then the hardest part of our work begins, which is to exemplify the impressions of the ordinance upon our minds in all the instances of a holy conversation. So it was here; when all this was finished there was more to be done.

I. They applied themselves with vigour to destroy all the monuments of idolatry, *v.* 1. The king had done what he could of this kind (2 Ki. 18:4), but the people could discover those profane relics which escaped the eye of the king's officers, and therefore they went out to see what they could do, *v.* 1. This was done immediately after the passover. Note, The comfort of communion with God should kindle in us a holy zeal and indignation against sin, against every thing that is offensive to God. If our hearts have been made to burn within us at an ordinance, that spirit of burning will consume the dross of corruption. *What have I* now *to do any more with idols?* Their zeal here in destroying the *images and groves, the high places and altars,* appeared, 1. In that they did this, not only in the cities of Judah and Benjamin, but in those of Ephraim and Manasseh. Some think that those cities are meant which had come under the protection and the jurisdiction of the kings of Judah. Others think that, Hoshea king of Israel not forbidding it, their zeal carried them out to the destruction of idolatry even in many parts of his kingdom. At least those that came out of Ephraim and Manasseh to keep the passover (as many did, *ch.* 30:18) destroyed all their own images and groves, and did the like for as many more as they had influence upon or could make interest in for leave to do it. We should not only reform ourselves, but do all we can to reform others too. 2. They destroyed all: they *utterly destroyed all;* they spared none through favour or affection either to the images or to their worshippers; though ever so ancient, ever so costly, ever so beautiful, and ever so well patronised, yet they must all be destroyed. Note, Those that sincerely set themselves against sin will set themselves against all sin. 3. They would not return to their houses, though they had been long absent, till this was done. They could not be easy, nor think themselves safe, in their cities, as long as the images and groves, those betrayers and destroyers of their country, were left standing. Perhaps the prophet Isaiah pointed to this when, a little before, he spoke of a day in which men should cast away the very idols that they themselves had made. So surprising was this blessed change, Isa. 2:20; 31:6, 7.

II. Hezekiah revived and restored the courses of the priests and Levites, which David had appointed and which had of late been put out of course, *v.* 2. The temple service was put into its proper method again, to run in the old channel. Every man was made to know his work, his place, his time, and what was expected from him. Note, Good order contributes much to the carrying on of a good work. The priests were appointed in their courses for *burnt-offerings and peace-offerings;* the Levites in their courses were some to minister to the priests, others to *give thanks and praise.* See 1 Chr. 23:4, 5. And all this in the *gates* or *courts* of *the tents of the Lord.* The temple is here called a tent because the temple privileges are movable things and this temple was shortly to be removed.

III. He appropriated a branch of the revenue of his crown to the maintenance and support of the altar. Though the people were to be at the charge of the daily offerings, and those on the sabbaths, new moons, and feasts, yet, rather than they should be burdened with the expense, he allowed out of his own estate, or out of his exchequer, for all those offerings, *v.* 3. It was a generous act of piety, wherein he consulted both God's honour and his people's ease, as a faithful servant to him and a tender father to them. Let princes and great men reckon that well bestowed, and set out to the best interest, which they give for the support and encouragement of religion in their country.

IV. He issued out an order to the inhabitants of Jerusalem first, *v.* 4 (that those who were nearest the temple, and both saved and got by being so, might give a good example to others), but which was afterwards extended to, or at least admitted by, the *cities of Judah,* that they should carefully pay in their dues, according to the law, to the priests and Levites. This had been long neglected, which made the work to be neglected (for a scandalous maintenance makes a scandalous ministry); but Hezekiah, having himself been liberal, might with a good grace require his subjects to be just to the temple service. And observe the end he aims at in recovering and restoring to the priests and Levites their portion, that they *might be encouraged in the law of the Lord,* in the study of it, and in doing their duty according to it. Observe here, 1. It is fit that ministers should be not only maintained, but encouraged, that they should not only be kept to do their work, but that they should also have wherewith to live comfortably, that they may do it with cheerfulness. 2. Yet they are to be maintained, not in idleness, pride, and luxury, but in *the law of the Lord,* in their observance of it themselves and in teaching others the good knowledge of it.

V. The people thereupon brought in their tithes very readily. They wanted nothing but to be called upon; and therefore, *as soon as the commandment came abroad,* the first-fruits and all the holy things were duly brought in, *v.* 5, 6. What the priests had occasion for, for themselves and their families, they made use of, and the overplus was *laid in heaps, v.* 6. All harvest-time they were increasing these heaps, as the fruits of the earth were gathered in; for God was to have his dues out of them all. Though a prescription may be pleaded for a *modus decimandi — tenth proportion,* yet it cannot be pleaded *pro non decminado — for the omission of the tenth.* When harvest ended they finished their heaps, *v.* 7. Now here we have, 1. The account given to Hezekiah concerning those heaps. He *questioned the priests and Levites* concerning them, why they did not use what was paid in, but hoarded it up thus, (*v.* 9), to which it was answered that they had made use of all they had occasion for, for the maintenance of themselves and their families and for their winter store, and that this was that which was left over and above, *v.* 10. They did not hoard these heaps for covetousness, but to show what plentiful provision God by his law had made for them, if they could but have it collected and brought in, and that those who conscientiously give God his dues out of their estates bring a blessing upon all they have: *Since they began to bring in the offerings the Lord has blessed his people.* See for this Hag. 2:19. "Try me," says God, "if you will not otherwise trust me, whether, upon your bringing the tithes into the store-house, you have not a blessing poured out upon you," Mal. 3:10, 11; Eze. 44:30. 2. The acknowledgment which the king and princes made of it, *v.* 8. They gave thanks to God for his good providence, which gave them something to bring, and his good grace, which gave them hearts to bring it. And they also *blessed the people,* that is, commended them for their doing well now, without reproaching them for their former neglects. It is observable that after they had tasted the sweetness of God's ordinance, in the late comfortable passover, they were thus free in maintaining the temple service. Those that experience the benefit of a settled ministry will not grudge the expense of it.

Verses 11–21

Here we have,

I. Two particular instances of the care of Hezekiah concerning church matters, having put them into good order, to keep them so. The tithes and other holy things being brought in, he provided, 1. That they should be carefully laid up, and not left exposed in loose heaps, liable to be wasted and embezzled. He ordered chambers to be made ready in some of the courts of the temple for store-chambers (*v.* 11), and into them the offerings were brought and there kept under lock and key, *v.* 12, 13. Treasures or store-keepers were appointed, who had the oversight of them, to see that *moth and rust* did not *corrupt* them nor *thieves break through to steal.* This wisdom of laying up the surplus in days of plenty we may learn from the ant, who *provideth meat in summer.* The laying up in store what was brought in was an encouragement to people to pay in their contributions. That will be given cheerfully by the public which appears to be well husbanded. 2. That they should be faithfully laid out, according to the uses they were intended for. Church treasures are not to be hoarded any longer than till there is occasion for them, lest even the rust should be a witness against those who hoard them. Officers were appointed, men (no doubt) of approved wisdom and faithfulness, to *distribute the oblations of the Lord and the most holy things* among the priests (*v.* 14), and to see that they all had a competent maintenance for themselves and their families. The law provided sufficient for them all, and therefore, if some had too little, it must be because others had too much; to prevent such inequality these officers were to go by some certain rule of proportion in the disposal of the incomes of the temple. It is said of the priests here (*v.* 18) *that in their set office they sanctified themselves; in faith* they sanctified themselves (so the word is), that is, as bishop Patrick explains it, they attended their ministry at the house of God, not doubting but they should be provided with all things necessary. Now, because they served God in that confidence, care was taken that they should not be made ashamed of their hope. Note, Those that sanctify themselves to God and his service in faith, believing that he will see them want for nothing that is good for them, *shall* certainly *be fed.* Out of the offerings of the Lord distribution was made, (1.) To the priests in the cities (*v.* 15), who staid at home while their brethren went to Jerusalem, and did good there in *teaching the good knowledge of the Lord.* The preaching priests were maintained as well as the sacrificing priests, and those that abode by the stuff as well as those that warred the warfare. (2.) To those that *entered into the house of the Lord,* all the *males from three years old and upwards;* for the male children even at that tender age, it seems, were allowed to come into the temple with their parents, and shared with them in this distribution, *v.* 16. (3.) Even the Levites from twenty years old and upwards had their share, *v.* 17. (4.) The wives and children of the priests and Levites had a comfortable maintenance out of those offerings, *v.* 18. In maintaining ministers, regard must be had to their families, that not they only, but theirs, may have food convenient. In some countries where ministers have their salary paid them by the state an addition is made to it upon the birth of a child. (5.) The priests in the country, that lived *in the fields of the suburbs,* were not overlooked in this ministration, *v.* 19. Those also had their share who were *inhabitants of the villages,* though they might be supposed to live at a less expense.

II. A general character of Hezekiah's services for the support of religion, *v.* 20, 21. 1. His pious zeal reached to all the parts of his kingdom: *Thus he did throughout all Judah;* every part of the country, and not those only that lay next him, shared in the good fruits of his government. 2. He sincerely designed to please God, and approved himself to him in all he did: He *wrought that which was good before the Lord his God;* all his care was to do that which should be accepted of God, which was *right* (that is, agreeable to natural equity), *and truth* (that is, agreeable to divine revelation and his covenant with God), *before the Lord;* to do according to that law which is holy, just, and good. 3. What he began he went through with, prosecuted it with vigour, and *did it with all his heart.* 4. All his good intentions were brought to a good issue; whatever he did in the service of the house of God, and in the government of his kingdom, he prospered in it. Note, What is undertaken with a sincere regard to the glory of God will succeed to our own honour and comfort at last.

CHAPTER 32

This chapter continues and concludes the history of the reign of Hezekiah. I. The descent which Sennacherib made upon him, and the care he took to fortify himself, his city, and the minds of his people, against that enemy (*v.* 1–8). II. The insolent blasphemous letters and messages which

Sennacherib sent him (*v.* 9–19). III. The real answer God gave to Sennacherib's blasphemies, and to Hezekiah's prayers, in the total rout of the Assyrian army, to the shame of Sennacherib and the honour of Hezekiah (*v.* 20–23). IV. Hezekiah's sickness and his recovery from that, his sin and his recovery from that, with the honours that attended him living and dead (*v.* 24–33).

Verses 1–8

Here is, I. The formidable design of Sennacherib against Hezekiah's kingdom, and the vigorous attempt he made upon it. This Sennacherib was now, as Nebuchadnezzar was afterwards, the terror and scourge and great oppressor of that part of the world. He aimed to raise a boundless monarchy for himself upon the ruins of all his neighbours. His predecessor Shalmaneser had lately made himself master of the kingdom of Israel, and carried the ten tribes captives. Sennacherib thought, in like manner, to win Judah for himself. Pride and ambition put men upon grasping at universal dominion. It is observable that, just about this time, Rome, a city which afterwards came to reign more than any other had done *over the kings of the earth,* was built by Romulus. Sennacherib invaded Judah immediately after the reformation of it and the re-establishment of religion in it: *After these things he entered into Judah, v.* 1. 1. It was well ordered by the divine Providence that he did not give them this disturbance before the reformation was finished and established, as it might then have put a stop to it. 2. Perhaps he intended to chastise Hezekiah for destroying that idolatry to which he himself was devoted. He looked upon Hezekiah as profane in what he had done, and as having thrown himself out of the divine protection. He accordingly considered him as one who might easily be made a prey of. 3. God ordered it at this time that he might have an opportunity of showing himself strong on the behalf of this returning reforming people. He brought this trouble upon them that he might have the honour, and might put on them the honour, of their deliverance. *After these things, and the establishment thereof,* one would have expected to hear of nothing but perfect peace, and that none durst meddle with a people thus qualified for the divine favour; yet the next news we hear is that a threatening destroying army enters the country, and is ready to lay all waste. We may be in the way of our duty and yet meet with trouble and danger. God orders it so for the trial of our confidence in him and the manifestation of his care concerning us. The little opposition which Sennacherib met with in entering Judah induced him to imagine that all was his own. He thought to *win all the fenced cities* (*v.* 1), and purposed to *fight against Jerusalem, v.* 2. See 2 Ki. 18:7, 13.

II. The preparation which Hezekiah prudently made against this storm that threatened him: *He took counsel with his princes* what he should do, what measures he should take, *v.* 3. With their advice he provided, 1. That the country should give him a cold reception, for he took care that he should find no water in it (and then his army must perish for thirst), or at least that there should be a scarcity of water, by which his army would be weakened and unfitted for service. A powerful army, if it want water but a few days, will be but a heap of dry dust. All hands were set immediately to work to *stop up the fountains,* and *the brook that ran through the midst of the land,* turning that (it is probable) into the city by pipes under-ground. Such as this is the policy commonly practised now-a-days of destroying the forage before an invading army. 2. That the city should give him a warm reception. In order to this he repaired the wall, raised towers, and made darts (or, as it is in the margin, *swords* or *weapons)* and shields in abundance (*v.* 5), and appointed captains, *v.* 6. Note, Those that trust God with their safety must yet use proper means for their safety, otherwise they tempt him, and do not trust him. *God will provide,* but so must we also.

III. The encouragement which he gave to his people to depend upon God in this distress. He gathered them together in a broad open street, and *spoke comfortably to them, v.* 6. He was himself undaunted, being confident the invasion would issue well. He was not like his father, who had much guilt to terrify him and no faith to encourage him, so that, in a time of public danger, *his heart was moved, as the trees of the wood are moved with the wind,* and then no marvel that *the heart of his people was so too,* Isa. 7:2. With what he said he put life into his people, his captains especially, and *spoke to their heart,* as the word is. 1. He endeavoured to keep down their fears: *"Be strong and courageous;* do not think of surrendering the city or capitulating, but resolve to hold it out to the last man; do not think of losing the city, nor of falling into the enemy's hand; there is no danger. Let the soldiers be bold and brave, make good their posts, stand to their arms, and fight manfully, and let the citizens encourage them to do so: *Be not afraid nor dismayed for the king of Assyria."* The prophet had thus encouraged them from God (Isa. 10:24): *Be not afraid of the Assyrians;* and here the king from him. Now it was that *the sinners in Zion were afraid* (Isa. 33:14), but the righteous *dwelt on high* (Isa. 33:15, 16) and *meditated on terror* so as to conquer it. See Isa. 33:18, which refers to what is recorded here. 2. He endeavoured to keep up their faith, in order to the silencing and suppressing of their fears. "Sennacherib has a *multitude with him,* and yet there are *more with us than with him;* for we have God with us, and how many do you reckon him for? With our enemy is an arm of flesh, which he trusts to; but *with us is the Lord,* whose power is irresistible, our God, whose promise is inviolable, a God in covenant with us, *to help us, and to fight our battles,* not only to help us to fight them, but to fight them for us if he please:" and so he did here. Note, A believing confidence in God will raise us above the prevailing fear of man. He that *feareth the fury of the oppressor forgetteth the Lord his Maker,* Isa. 51:12, 13. It is probable that Hezekiah said more to this purport, and that the people rested themselves upon what he said, not merely upon his word, but on the things he said concerning the presence of God with them and his power to relieve them, the belief of which made them easy. Let the good subjects and soldiers of Jesus Christ rest thus upon his word, and boldly say, *Since God is for us, who can be against us?*

Verses 9–23

This story of the rage and blasphemy of Sennacherib, Hezekiah's prayer, and the deliverance of Jerusalem by the destruction of the Assyrian army, we had more at large in the book of Kings, 2 Ki. 18 and 19. It is contracted here, yet large enough to show these three things: —

I. The impiety and malice of the church's enemies. Sennacherib has his hands full in besieging Lachish (*v.* 9), but hears that Hezekiah is fortifying Jerusalem and encouraging his people to stand it out; and therefore, before he come in person to besiege it, he sends messengers to make speeches, and he himself writes letters to frighten Hezekiah and his people into a surrender of the city. See, 1. His great malice against the king of Judah, in endeavouring to withdraw his subjects from their allegiance to him. He did not treat with Hezekiah as a man of honour would have done, nor propose fair terms to him, but used mean and base artifices, unbecoming a crowned head, to terrify the common people and persuade them to desert him. he represented Hezekiah as one who designed to deceive his subjects into their ruin and betray them *to famine and thirst* (*v.* 11), as one who had done them great wrong and exposed them already to the divine displeasure by taking away the high places and altars (*v.* 12), and who, against the common interest of his people, held out against a force that would certainly be their ruin, *v.* 15. 2. His great impiety against the God of Israel, *the God of Jerusalem* he is called (*v.* 19), because that was the place he had chosen to put his name there, and because that was the place which was now threatened by the enemy and which the divine Providence had under its special protection. This proud blasphemer compared the great Jehovah, the Maker of heaven and earth, with the dunghill gods of the nations, the work of men's hands, and thought him no more able to deliver his worshippers than they were to deliver theirs (*v.* 19), as if an infinite and eternal Spirit had no more wisdom and power than a stone or the stock of a tree. He boasted of his triumphs over the gods of the nations, that they could none of them protect their people (*v.* 13–15), and thence inferred not only, *How shall your God deliver you?* (*v.* 14), but, as if he were inferior to them all, *How much less shall your God deliver you?* as if he were less able to help than any of them. Thus did they rail, rail in writing (which, being more deliberate, is so much the worse), *on the Lord God of Israel,* as if he were a cipher and an empty name, like all the rest, *v.* 17. Sennacherib, in the instructions he gave, said more than enough; but, as if his blasphemies had been too little, his servants, who learned insolence from their master, spoke yet more than he bade them *against the Lord God and his servant Hezekiah, v.* 16. And God resents what is said against his servants, and will reckon for it, as well as what is said against himself. All this was intended to frighten the people from their hope in God, which David's enemies sought to take him off from (Ps. 11:1; 42:10), saying, *There is no help for him in God,* Ps. 3:2; 71:11. Thus they hoped to take the city by weakening the hands of those that should defend it. Satan, in his temptations, aims to destroy our faith in God's all-sufficiency, knowing that he shall gain his point if he can do that; as we keep our ground if our *faith fail not,* Lu. 22:32.

II. The duty as well as the interest of the church's friends, and that is in the day of distress to pray and cry to Heaven. So Hezekiah did, and the prophet Isaiah, *v.* 20. It was a happy time when the king and the prophet joined thus in prayer. Is any troubled? Is any terrified? Let him pray. So we engage God for us; so we encourage ourselves in him. Praying to God is here called *crying to Heaven,* because we are, in prayer, to eye him as our Father in heaven, whence he beholds the children of men, and where he has prepared his throne.

III. The power and goodness of the church's God. He is able both to control his enemies, be they ever so high, and to relieve his friends, be they ever so low.

1. As the blasphemies of his enemies engage him against them (Deu. 32:27), so the prayers of his people engage him for them. They did so here. (1.) The army of the Assyrians was cut off by the sword of an angel, which triumphed particularly in the slaughter of the mighty men of valour, and the leaders and captains, who defied the sword of any man. God delights to abase the proud and secure. The Targum says, The Word of the Lord (the eternal Word) sent Gabriel to do this execution, and that it was done with lightning, and in the passover night: that was the night in which the angel destroyed the first-born of Egypt. But that was not all. (2.) The king of the Assyrians, having received this disgrace, was cut off by the sword of his own sons. Those that *came forth of his own bowels slew him, v.* 21. Thus was he mortified first, and then murdered — shamed first, and then slain. Evil pursues sinners; and, when they escape one mischief, they run upon another unseen.

2. By this work of wonder, (1.) God was glorified, as the protector of his people. Thus he saved Jerusalem, not only from the hand of Sennacherib, but from the hand *of all others, v.* 22; for such a deliverance as this was an earnest of much mercy in store; and he *guided them,* that is, he guarded them, on every side. God defends his people by directing them, shows them what they should do, and so saves them from what is designed or done against them. For this *many brought gifts unto the Lord,* when they saw the great power of God in the defence of his people. Strangers were thereby induced to supplicate his favour and enemies to deprecate his wrath, and both brought gifts to his temple, in token of their care and desire. (2.) Hezekiah was magnified as the favourite and particular care of Heaven. Many *brought presents to him* (*v.* 22, 23), in token of the honour they had for him, and to make an interest in him. By the favour of God enemies are lost and friends gained.

Verses 24–33

Here we conclude the story of Hezekiah with an account of three things concerning him: —

I. His sickness and his recovery from it, *v.* 24. The account of his sickness is but briefly mentioned here; we had a large narrative of it, 2 Ki. 20. His disease seemed likely to be mortal. In the extremity of it he prayed. God answered him, and gave him a sign that he should recover, the going back of the sun ten degrees.

II. His sin and his repentance for it, which were also more largely related, 2 Ki. 20:12, etc. Yet several things are here observed concerning his sin which we had not there. 1. The occasion of it was the king of Babylon's sending an honourable embassy to him to congratulate him on his recovery. But here it is added that they came to enquire of *the wonder that was done in the land* (*v.* 31), either the destruction of the Assyrian army or the going back of the sun. The Assyrians were their enemies; they came to enquire concerning their fall, that they might triumph in it.

The sun was their god; they came to enquire concerning the favour he had shown to Hezekiah, that they might honour him whom their god honoured, *v.* 31. These miracles were wrought to alarm and awaken a stupid careless world, and turn them from dumb and lame idols to the living God; and men were startled by them, but not converted till a greater wonder was done in that land, in the appearing of Jesus Christ, Mt. 2:1, 2. 2. God left him to himself in it, to try him, *v.* 31. God, by the power of his almighty grace, could have prevented the sin; but he permitted it for wise and holy ends, that, by this trial and his weakness in it, he might know, that is, it might be known (a usual Hebraism), what was in his heart, that he was not so perfect in grace as he thought he was, but had his follies and infirmities as other men. God left him to himself to be proud of his wealth, to keep him from being proud of his holiness. It is good for us to know ourselves, and our own weakness and sinfulness, that we may not be conceited or self-confident, but may always think meanly of ourselves and live in a dependence upon divine grace. We know not the corruption of our own hearts, nor what we shall do if God leave us to ourselves. *Lord, lead us not into temptation.* 3. His sin was the *his heart was lifted up, v.* 25. He was proud of the honour God had put upon him in so many instances, the honour his neighbours did him in bringing him presents, and now that the king of Babylon should send an embassy to him to caress and court him: this exalted him above measure. When Hezekiah had destroyed other idolatries he began to idolize himself. O what need have great men, and good men, and useful men, to study their own infirmities and follies, and their obligations to free grace, that they may never think highly of themselves, and to beg earnestly of God that he will hide pride from them and always keep them humble! 4. The aggravation of his sin was the he made so bad a return to God for his favours to him, making even those favours the food and fuel of his pride (*v.* 25): *He rendered not again according to the benefit done unto him.* Note, It is justly expected that those who have received mercy from God should study to make some suitable returns for the mercies they have received; and, if they do not, their ingratitude will certainly be charged upon them. Though we cannot render an equivalent, or the payment of a debt, we must render the acknowledgment of a favour. *What shall I render* that may be so accepted? Ps. 116:12. 5. The divine displeasure he was under for this sin; though it was but a heart-sin, and the overt-act seemed not only innocent but civil (the showing of his treasures to a friend), yet wrath came upon him and his kingdom for it, *v.* 25. Note, Pride is a sin that God hates as much as any, and particularly in his own people. Those that exalt themselves must expect to be abased, and put under humbling providences. Wrath came on David for his pride in numbering the people. 6. His repentance for this sin: *He humbled himself for the pride of his heart.* Note, (1.) Though God may, for wise and holy ends, suffer his people to fall into sin, yet he will not suffer them to lie still in it; they *shall not be utterly cast down.* (2.) Heart-sins are to be repented of, though they go no further. (3.) Self-humiliation is a necessary branch of repentance. (4.) Pride of heart, by which we have lifted up ourselves, is a sin for which we ought in a special manner to humble ourselves. (5.) People ought to mourn for the sins of their rulers. The inhabitants of Jerusalem humbled themselves with Hezekiah, because they either knew that they also had been guilty of the same sin, or at least feared that they might share in the punishment. When David, in his pride, numbered the people, they all smarted for his sin. 7. The reprieve granted thereupon. The wrath came not in his days. While he lived the country had peace and truth prevailed; so much does repentance avail to put by, or at least to put off, the tokens of God's anger.

III. Here is the honour done to Hezekiah, 1. By the providence of God while he lived. He had *exceeding much riches and honour* (*v.* 27), replenished his stores, victualled his campus, fortified his city, and did all he wished to do; for God *had given him very much substance, v.* 29. Among his great performances, his turning the water-course of Gihon is mentioned (*v.* 30), which was done upon occasion of Sennacherib's invasion, *v.* 3, 4. The water had come into that which is called the *old pool* (Isa. 22:11) and the *upper pool* (Isa. 7:3); but he gathered the waters into a new place, for the greater convenience of the city, called the *lower pool,* Isa. 22:9. And, in general, he *prospered in all his works,* for they were good works. 2. By the respect paid to his memory when he was dead. (1.) The prophet Isaiah wrote his life and reign (*v.* 32), his acts and his goodness or piety, or which it is part of the honour to be recorded and remembered, for examples to others. (2.) The people *did him honour at his death* (*v.* 33), buried him in the chief of the sepulchres, made as great a burning for him as for Asa, or, which is a much greater honour, made great lamentation for him, as for Josiah. See how the honour of serious godliness is manifested in the consciences of men. Though it is to be feared that the generality of the people did not heartily comply with the reforming kings, yet they could not but praise their endeavours for reformation, and the memory of those kings was blessed among them. It is a debt we owe to those who have been eminently useful in their day to do them honour at their death, when they are out of the reach of flattery and we have seen the end of their conversation. The due payment of this debt will be an encouragement to others to do likewise.

CHAPTER 33

In this chapter we have the history of the reign, I. Of Manasseh, who reigned long. 1. His wretched apostasy from God, and revolt to idolatry and all wickedness (*v.* 1–10). 2. His happy return to God in his affliction; his repentance (*v.* 11–13), his reformation (*v.* 15–17), and prosperity (*v.* 14), with the conclusion of his reign (*v.* 18–20). II. Of Amon, who reigned very wickedly (*v.* 21–23), and soon ended his days unhappily (*v.* 24, 25).

Verses 1–10

We have here an account of the great wickedness of Manasseh. It is the same almost word for word with that which we had 2 Ki. 21:1–9, and took a melancholy view of. It is no such pleasing subject that we should delight to dwell upon it again. This foolish young prince, in contradiction to the good example and good education his father gave him, abandoned himself to all impiety, transcribed the abominations of the heathen (*v.* 2), ruined the established religion, unravelled his father's glorious reformation (*v.* 3), profaned the house of God with his idolatry (*v.* 4, 5), dedicated his children to Moloch, and made the devil's lying oracles his guides and his counsellors, *v.* 6. In contempt of the choice God had made of Sion to be his rest for ever and Israel to be his covenant-people (*v.* 8), and the fair terms he stood upon with God, he embraced other gods, profaned God's chosen temple, and debauched his chosen people. He *made them to err,* and *do worse than the heathen* (*v.* 9); for, if the unclean spirit returns, he brings with him *seven other spirits more wicked than himself.* That which aggravated the sin of Manasseh was that God *spoke to him and his people* by the prophets, *but they would not hearken, v.* 10. We may here admire the grace of God in speaking to them, and their obstinacy in turning a deaf ear to him, that either their badness did not quite turn away his goodness, but still he waited to be gracious, or that his goodness did not turn them from their badness, but still they hated to be reformed. Now from this let us learn, 1. That it is no new thing, but a very sad thing, for the children of godly parents to turn aside from that good way of God in which they have been trained. Parents may give many good things to their children, but they cannot give them grace. 2. Corruptions in worship are such diseases of the church as it is very apt to relapse into again even when they seem to be cured. 3. The god of this world has strangely blinded men's minds, and has a wonderful power over those that are led captive by him; else he could not draw them from God, their best friend, to depend upon their sworn enemy.

Verses 11–20

We have seen Manasseh by his wickedness undoing the good that his father had done; here we have him by repentance undoing the evil that he himself had done. It is strange that this was not so much as mentioned in the book of *Kings,* nor does any thing appear there to the contrary but that he persisted and perished in his son. But perhaps the reason was because the design of that history was to show the wickedness of the nation which brought destruction upon them; and this repentance of Manasseh and the benefit of it, being personal only and not national, is overlooked there; yet here it is fully related, and a memorable instance it is of the riches of God's pardoning mercy and the power of his renewing grace. Here is,

I. The occasion of Manasseh's repentance, and that was his affliction. In his distress he did not (like king Ahaz) *trespass yet more against God,* but humbled himself and returned to God. Sanctified afflictions often prove happy means of conversion. What his distress was we are told, *v.* 11. God brought a foreign enemy upon him; the king of Babylon, that courted his father who faithfully served God, invaded him now that he had treacherously departed from God. He is here called *king of Assyria,* because he had made himself master of Assyria, which he would the more easily do for the defeat of Sennacherib's army, and its destruction before Jerusalem. He aimed at the treasures which the ambassadors had seen, and all those precious things; but God sent him to chastise a sinful people, and subdue a straying prince. The captain took *Manasseh among the thorns,* in some bush or other, perhaps in his garden, where he had hid himself. Or it is spoken figuratively: he was perplexed in his counsels and embarrassed in his affairs. He was, as we say, in the briers, and knew not which way to extricate himself, and so became an easy prey to the Assyrian captains, who no doubt plundered his house and took away what they pleased, as Isaiah had foretold, 2 Ki. 20:17, 18. What was Hezekiah's pride was their prey. They bound Manasseh, who had been held before with the cords of his own iniquity, and carried him prisoner to Babylon. About what time of his reign this was we are not told; the Jews say it was in his twenty-second year.

II. The expressions of his repentance (*v.* 12, 13): *When he was in affliction* he had time to bethink himself and reason enough too. He saw what he had brought himself to by his sin. He found the gods he had served unable to help him. He knew that repentance was the only way of restoring his affairs; and therefore to him he returned from whom he had revolted. 1. He was convinced the Jehovah is the only living and true God: *Then he knew* (that is, he believed and considered) that the *Lord he was God.* He might have known it at a less expense if he would have given due attention and credit to the word written and preached: but it was better to pay thus dearly for the knowledge of God than to perish in ignorance and unbelief. Had he been a prince in the palace of Babylon, it is probable he would have been confirmed in his idolatry; but, being a captive in the prisons of Babylon, he was convinced of it and reclaimed from it. 2. He applied to him as *his* God now, renouncing all others, and resolving to cleave to him only, the God of his fathers, and a God on covenant with him. 3. He humbled himself greatly before him, was truly sorry for his sins, ashamed of them, and afraid of the wrath of God. It becomes sinners to humble themselves before the face of that God whom they have offended. It becomes sufferers to humble themselves under the hand of that God who corrects them, and to accept the punishment of their iniquity. Our hearts should be humbled under humbling providences; then we accommodate ourselves to them, and answer God's end in them. 4. He prayed to him for the pardon of sin and the return of his favour. Prayer is the relief of penitents, the relief of the afflicted. That is a good prayer, and very pertinent in this case, which we find among the apocryphal books, entitled, *The prayer of Manasses, king of Judah, when he was holden captive in Babylon.* Whether it was his or no is uncertain; if it was, in it he *gives glory to God* as the *God of their fathers* and *their righteous seed,* as the Creator of the world, a God whose *anger is insupportable,* and yet *his merciful promise unmeasurable.* He pleads that God has *promised repentance and forgiveness to those that have sinned,* and has *appointed repentance unto sinners, that they may be saved,* not *unto the just,* as to *Abraham, Isaac, and Jacob,* but *to me* (says he) *that am a sinner; for I have sinned above the number of the sands of the sea:* so he confesses his sin largely, and aggravates it. He prays, *Forgive me, O Lord! forgive me, and destroy me not;* he pleads, *Thou art the God of those that repent,* etc., and concludes, *Therefore I will praise thee for ever,* etc.

III. God's gracious acceptance of his repentance: *God was entreated of him, and heard his supplication.* Though affliction drive us to God, he will not therefore reject us if in sincerity we seek him, for afflictions are sent on purpose to bring us to him. As a token of God's favour to him, he made a way for his escape. Afflictions are continued no longer than till they have done their work. When Manasseh is brought back to his God and to his duty he shall soon be *brought back to his kingdom.* See how ready God is to accept and welcome returning sinners, and how *swift to show mercy.* Let not great sinners despair, when Manasseh himself, upon his repentance, found favour with God; in him God *showed forth a pattern of long-suffering,* as 1 Tim. 1:16; Isa. 1:18.

IV. The *fruits meet for repentance* which he brought forth after his return to his own land, *v.* 15, 16. 1. He turned from his sins. He *took away the strange gods,* the images of them, and that idol (whatever it was) which he had set up with so much solemnity *in the house of the Lord,* as if it had been master of that house. He cast out all the idolatrous altars that were *in the mount of the house* and in Jerusalem, as detestable things. Now (we hope) he loathed them as much as ever he had loved them, and said to them, *Get you hence,* Isa. 30:22. "*What have I to do any more with idols?* I have had enough of them." 2. He returned to his duty; for he *repaired the altar of the Lord,* which had either been abused and broken down by some of the idolatrous priests, or, at least, neglected and gone out of repair. He sacrificed thereon peace-offerings to implore God's favour, and thank-offerings to praise him for his deliverance. Nay, he now used his power to reform his people, as before he had abused it to corrupt them: *He commanded Judah to serve the Lord God of Israel.* Note, Those that truly repent of their sins will not only return to God themselves, but will do all they can to recover those that have by their example been seduced and drawn away from God; else they do not thoroughly (as they ought) undo what they have done amiss, nor make the plaster as wide as the wound. We find that he prevailed to bring them off from their *false gods,* but not from their *high places, v.* 17. They still sacrificed in them, *yet to the Lord their God only;* Manasseh could not carry the reformation so far as he had carried the corruption. It is an easy thing to debauch men's manners, but not so easy to reform them again.

V. His prosperity, in some measure, after his repentance. He might plainly see it was sin that ruined him; for, when he returned to God in a way of duty, God returned to him in a way of mercy: and then he *built a wall about the city of David* (*v.* 14), for by sin he had unwalled it and exposed it to the enemy. He also put captains of war in the fenced cities for the security of his country. Josephus says that all the rest of his time he was so changed for the better that he was looked upon as a very happy man.

Lastly, Here is the conclusion of his history. The heads of those things for a full narrative of which we are referred to the other writings that were then extant are more than of any of the kings, *v.* 18, 19. A particular account, it seems, was kept, 1. Of *all his sin, and his trespass,* the *high places* he built, *the groves and images he set up, before he was humbled.* Probably this was taken from his own confession which he made of his sin when God gave him repentance, and which he left upon record, in a book entitled, *The words of the seers.* To those seers that *spoke to him* (*v.* 18) to reprove him for his sin he sent his confession when he repented, to be inserted in their memoirs, as a token of his gratitude to them for their kindness in reproving him. Thus it becomes penitents to take shame to themselves, to give thanks to their reprovers, and warning to others. 2. Of *the words of the seers that spoke to him in the name of the Lord* (*v.* 10, 18), the reproofs they gave him for his sin and their exhortations to repentance. Note, Sinners ought to consider, that, how little notice soever they take of them, an account is kept of the words of the seers that speak to them from God to admonish them of their sins, warn them of their danger, and call them to their duty, which will be produced against them in the great day. 3. Of his *prayer to God* (this is twice mentioned as a remarkable thing) *and how God was entreated of him.* This was *written for the generations to come, that the people that should be created might praise the Lord* for his readiness to receive returning prodigals. Notice is taken of the place of his burial, not in *the sepulchres of the kings,* but *in his own house;* he was buried privately, and nothing of that honour was done him at his death that was done to his father. Penitents may recover their comfort sooner than their credit.

Verses 21–25

We have little recorded concerning Amon, but enough unless it were better. Here is,

I. His great wickedness. He did as *Manasseh had done* in the days of his apostasy, *v.* 22. Those who think this an evidence that Manasseh did not truly repent forget how many good kings had wicked sons. Only it should seem that Manasseh was in *this* defective, that, when he *cast out the images,* he did not utterly deface and destroy them, according to the law which required Israel to *burn the images with fire,* Deu. 7:2. How necessary that law was this instance shows; for the *carved images* being only thrown by, and not burnt, Amon knew where to find them, soon set them up, and sacrificed to them. It is added, to represent him exceedingly sinful and to justify God in cutting him off so soon, 1. That he out-did his father in sinning: *He trespassed more and more, v.* 23. His father did ill, but he did worse. Those that were joined to idols grew more and more mad upon them. 2. That he came short of his father in repenting: He *humbled not himself before the Lord, as his father had humbled himself.* He fell like him, but did not get up again like him. It is not so much sin as impenitence in sin that ruins men, not so much that they offend as that they do not humble themselves for their offences, not the disease, but the neglect of the remedy.

II. His speedy destruction. He reigned but two years and then his servants *conspired against him* and *slew him, v.* 24. Perhaps when Amon sinned as his father did in the beginning of his days he promised himself that he should repent as his father did in the latter end of his days. But his case shows what a madness it is to presume upon that. If he hoped to repent when he was old, he was wretchedly disappointed; for he was cut off when he was young. He rebelled against God, and his own servants rebelled against him. Herein God was righteous, but they were wicked, and justly did the *people of the land* put them to death as traitors. The lives of kings are particularly under the protection of Providence and the laws both of God and man.

CHAPTER 34

Before we see Judah and Jerusalem ruined we shall yet see some glorious years, while good Josiah sits at the helm. By his pious endeavours for reformation God tried them yet once more; if they had known in this their day, the day of their visitation, the things that belonged to their peace and improved them, their ruin might have been prevented. But after this reign they were hidden from their eyes, and the next reigns brought an utter desolation upon them. In this chapter we have, I. A general account of Josiah's character (*v.* 1, 2). II. His zeal to root out idolatry (*v.* 3–7). III. His care to repair the temple (*v.* 8–13). IV. The finding of the book of the law and the good use made of it (*v.* 14–28). V. The public reading of the law to the people and their renewing their covenant with God thereupon (*v.* 29–33). Much of this we had 2 Ki. 22.

Verses 1–7

Concerning Josiah we are here told, 1. That he came to the crown when he was very young, only eight years old (yet his infancy did not debar him from his right), and he reigned *thirty-one years* (*v.* 1), a considerable time. I fear, however, that in the beginning of his reign things went much as they had done in his father's time, because, being a child, he must have left the management of them to others; so that it was not till his twelfth year, which goes far in the number of his years, that the reformation began, *v.* 3. He could not, as Hezekiah did, fall about it immediately. 2. That he reigned very well (*v.* 2), approved himself to God, trod in the steps of David, and did not decline either *to the right hand of to the left:* for there are errors on both hands. 3. That while he was young, about sixteen years old, he *began to seek after God, v.* 3. We have reason to think he had not so good an education as Manasseh had (it is well if those about him did not endeavour to corrupt and debauch him); yet he thus sought God when he was young. It is the duty and interest of young people, and will particularly be the honour of young gentlemen, as soon as they come to years of understanding, to *begin to seek God;* for those that seek him early shall find him. 4. That in the twelfth year of his reign, when it is probable he took the administration of the government entirely into his own hands, he *began to purge his kingdom from the remains of idolatry;* he destroyed the high places, groves, images, altars, all the utensils of idolatry, *v.* 3, 4. He not only cast them out as Manasseh did, but broke them to pieces, and made dust of them. This destruction of idolatry is here said to be in his twelfth year, but it was said (2 Ki. 23:23) to be in his eighteenth year. Something was probably done towards it in his twelfth year; then he began to purge out idolatry, but that good work met with opposition, so that it was not thoroughly done till they had found the book of the law six years afterwards. But here the whole work is laid together briefly which was much more largely and particularly related in the *Kings.* His zeal carried him out to do this, not only in Judah and Jerusalem, but in the cities of Israel too, as far as he had any influence upon them.

Verses 8–13

Here, 1. Orders are given by the king for the repair of the temple, *v.* 8. When he had purged the house of the corruptions of it he began to fit it up for the services that were to be performed in it. Thus we must do by the spiritual temple of the heart, get it cleansed from the pollutions of sin, and then renewed, so as to be transformed into the image of God. Josiah, in this order, calls God *the Lord his God.* Those that truly love God will *love the habitation of his house.* 2. Care is taken about it, effectual care. The Levites went about the country and gathered money towards it, which was returned to the three trustees mentioned, *v.* 8. They brought it to Hilkiah the high priest (*v.* 9), and he and they put it into the hands of workmen, both overseers and labourers, who undertook to do it by the great, as we say, or *in the gross, v.* 10, 11. It is observed that the workmen were industrious and honest: They *did the work faithfully* (*v.* 12); and workmen are not completely faithful if they are not both careful and diligent, for a confidence is reposed in them that they will be so. It is also intimated that the overseers were ingenious; for it is said that all those were employed to inspect this work who were skilful in *instruments of music;* not that their skill in music could be of any use in architecture, but it was an evidence that they were men of sense and ingenuity, and particularly that their genius lay towards the mathematics, which qualified them very much for this trust. Witty men are then wise men when they employ their wit in doing good, in helping their friends, and, as they have opportunity, in serving the public. Observe, in this work, how God dispenses his gifts variously; here were some that were *bearers of burdens,* cut out for bodily labour and fit to work. Here were others (made *meliori luto — of finer materials*) that had skill in music, and they were *overseers of those that laboured,* and scribes and officers. The former were the hands: these were the heads. They had need of one another, and the work needed both. Let not the overseers of the work despise the bearers of burdens, nor let those that work in the service grudge at those whose office it is to direct; but let each esteem and serve the other in love, and let God have the glory and the church the benefit of the different gifts and dispositions of both.

Verses 14–28

This whole paragraph we had, just as it is here related, 2 Ki. 22:8–20, and have nothing to add here to what was there observed. But, 1. We may hence take occasion to bless God that we have plenty of Bibles, and that they are, or may be, in all hands, — that the book of the law and gospel is not lost, is not scarce, — that, in this sense, the *word of the Lord* is not *precious.* Bibles are jewels, but, thanks be to God, they are not rarities. The fountain of the waters of life is not a spring shut up or a fountain sealed, but the streams of it, in all places, *make glad the city of our God. Usus communis aquarum — These waters flow for general use.* What a great deal shall we have to answer for if the great things of God's law, being thus made common, should be accounted by us as strange things! 2. We may hence learn, whenever we read or hear the word of God, to affect our hearts with it, and to get them possessed with a holy fear of that wrath of God which is there revealed against all ungodliness and unrighteousness of men, as Josiah's tender heart was. When he heard the words of the law he *rent his clothes* (*v.* 19), and God was well pleased with his doing so, *v.* 27. Were the things contained in the scripture new to us, as they were here to Josiah, surely they would make deeper impressions upon us than commonly they do; but they are not the less weighty, and therefore should not be the less considered by us, for their being well known. Rend the heart therefore, not the garments. 3. We are here directed when we are under convictions of sin, and apprehensions of divine wrath, to enquire of the Lord; so Josiah did, v. 21. It concerns us to ask (as they did, Acts 2:37), *Men and brethren, what shall we do?* and more particularly (as the jailor), *What must I do to be saved?* Acts 16:30. *If you will* thus *enquire, enquire* (Isa. 21:12); and, blessed be God, we have the lively oracles to which to apply with these enquiries. 4. We are here warned of the ruin that sin brings upon nations and kingdoms. Those that forsake God bring evil upon themselves (v. 24, 25), and kindle a fire *which shall not be quenched.* Such will the fire of God's wrath be when the decree has gone forth against those that obstinately and impenitently persist in their wicked ways. 5. We are here encouraged to humble ourselves before God and seek unto him, as Josiah did. If we cannot prevail thereby to turn away God's wrath from our land, yet we shall deliver our own souls, v. 27, 28. And good people are here taught to be so far from fearing death as to welcome it rather when it *takes them away from the evil to come.* See how the property of it is altered by making it the matter of a promise: *Thou shalt be gathered to thy grave in peace*, housed in that ark, as Noah, when a deluge is coming.

Verses 29–33

We have here an account of the further advances which Josiah made towards the reformation of his kingdom upon the hearing of the law read and the receipt of the message God sent him by the prophetess. Happy the people that had such a king; for here we find that, 1. They were well taught. He did not go about to force them to do their duty, till he had first instructed them in it. He called all the people together, great and small, young and old, rich and poor, high and low. *He that hath ears to hear, let him hear* the words of *the book of the covenant;* for they are all concerned in those words. To put an honour upon the service, and to engage attention the more, though there were priests and Levites present, the king himself read the book to the people (v. 30), and he read it, no doubt, in such a manner as to show that he was himself affected with it, which would be a means of affecting the hearers. 2. They were well fixed. The articles of agreement between God and Israel being read, that they might intelligently covenant with God, both king and people with great solemnity did as it were subscribe the articles. The king in his place covenanted to keep God's commandments with all his heart and soul, according to what was *written in the book* (v. 31), and urged the people to declare their consent likewise to this covenant, and solemnly to promise that they would faithfully perform, fulfil, and keep, all and every thing that was on their part to be done, according to this covenant: this they did; they could not for shame do otherwise. He caused *all that were present to stand to it* (v. 32), and made them all *to serve, even to serve the Lord their God* (v. 33), to do it and to *make a business* of it. he did all he could to bring them to it — *to serve, even to serve;* the repetition denotes that this was the only thing his heart was set on; he aimed at nothing else in what he did but to engage them to God and their duty. 3. They were well tended, were honest with good looking to. *All his days they departed not from following the Lord;* he kept them, with much ado, from running into idolatry again. *All his days* were days of restraint upon them; but this intimated that there was in them a *bent to backslide*, a strong inclination to idolatry. Many of them wanted nothing but to have him out of the way, and then they would have their high places and their images up again. And therefore we find that *in the days of Josiah* (Jer. 3:6) God charged it upon treacherous Judah that she *had not returned to him with all her heart, but feignedly* (v. 10), nay, had *played the harlot* (v. 8) and thereby had even *justified backsliding Israel*, v. 11. In the twenty-third year of this reign, four or five years after this, they had *gone on to provoke God to anger with the works of their hands* (Jer. 25:3–7); and, which is very observable, it is from the beginning of Josiah's reformation, his twelfth or thirteenth year, that *the iniquity of the house of Judah*, which brought ruin upon them, and which the prophet was to bear lying on his right side, was dated (Eze. 4:6); for thence to the destruction of Jerusalem was just forty years. Josiah was sincere in what he did, but the generality of the people were averse to it and hankered after their idols still; so that the reformation, though well

designed and well prosecuted by the prince, had little or no effect upon the people. It was with reluctancy that they parted with their idols; still they were in heart joined to them, and wished for them again. This God saw, and therefore from that time, when one would have thought the foundations had been laid for a perpetual security and peace, from that very time did the decree go forth for their destruction. Nothing hastens the ruin of a people nor ripens them for it more than the baffling of hopeful attempts for reformation and a hypocritical return to God. *Be not deceived, God is not mocked.*

CHAPTER 35

We are here to attend Josiah, I. To the temple, where we see his religious care for the due observance of the ordinance of the passover, according to the law (v. 1–19). II. To the field of battle, where we see his rashness in engaging with the king of Egypt, and how dearly it cost him (v. 20–23). III. To the grave, where we see him bitterly lamented (v. 24–27). And so we must take our leave of Josiah.

Verses 1–19

The destruction which Josiah made of idols and idolatry was more largely related in the *Kings*, but just mentioned here in the foregoing chapter (v. 33); but his solemnizing the passover, which was touched upon there (2 Ki. 23:21), is very particularly related here. Many were the feasts of the Lord, appointed by the ceremonial law, but the passover was the chief. It *began them all* in the night wherein Israel came out of Egypt; it *concluded them all* in the night wherein Christ was betrayed; and in the celebration of it Hezekiah and Josiah, those two great reformers, revived religion in their day. The ordinance of the Lord's supper resembles the passover more than it does any of the Jewish festivals; and the due observance of that ordinance, according to the rule, is an instance and means both of the growing purity and beauty of churches and of the growing piety and devotion of particular Christians. Religion cannot flourish where that passover is either wholly neglected or not duly observed; return to that, revive that, make a solemn business of that affecting binding ordinance, and then, it is to be hoped, there will be a reformation in other instances also.

In the account we had of Hezekiah's passover the great zeal of the people was observable, and the transport of devout affection that they were in; but little of the same spirit appears here. It was more in compliance with the king that they all kept the passover (v. 17, 18) than from any great inclination they had to it themselves. Some pride they took in this form of godliness, but little pleasure in the power of it. But, whatever defect there was among the people in the spirit of the duty, both the magistrates and the ministers did their part and took care that the external part of the service should be performed with due solemnity.

I. The king exhorted and directed, quickened and encouraged, the priests and Levites to do their office in this solemnity. Perhaps he saw them remiss and indifferent, unwilling to go out of their road or mend their pace. If ministers are so, it is not amiss for any, but most proper for magistrates, to stir them up to their business. Say to Archippus, *Take heed to thy ministry*, Col. 4:17. Let us see how this good king managed his clergy upon this occasion. 1. He reduced them to the office they were appointed to by the law of Moses (v. 6) and the order they were put into by David and Solomon, v. 4. *He set them in their charge*, v. 2. He did not cut them out new work, nor put them into any new method, but called them back to their institution. Their courses were settled in writing; let them have recourse to that writing, and marshal themselves according to the *divisions of their families*, v. 5. Our rule is settled in the written word; let magistrates take care that ministers walk according to that rule and they do their duty. 2. He ordered the ark to be put in its place. It should seem, it had of late been displaced, either by the wicked kings, to make room for their idols in the most holy place, or by Hezekiah, to make room for the workmen that repaired the temple. However it was, Josiah bids the *Levites put the ark in the house* (v. 3), and not carry it about from place to place, as perhaps of late they had done, justifying themselves therein by the practice before the temple was built. Now that the priests were discharged from this burden of the ark they must be careful in other services about it. 3. He charged them to *serve God and his people Israel*, v. 3.

Ministers must look upon themselves as servants both to Christ and to his church for his sake, 2 Co. 4:5. They must take care, and take pains, and lay out themselves to the utmost, (1.) For the glory and honour of God, and to advance the interests of his kingdom among men. Paul, *a servant of God*, Tit. 1:1. (2.) For the welfare and benefit of his people, not as having dominion over their faith, but as helpers of their holiness and joy; and there will be no difficulty, in the strength of God, in honestly serving these two masters. 4. He charged them to *sanctify themselves*, and *prepare their brethren*, v. 6. Ministers' work must begin at home, and they must sanctify themselves in the first place, purify themselves from sin, sequester themselves from the world, and devote themselves to God. But it must not end there; they must do what they can to *prepare their brethren* by admonishing, instructing, exhorting, quickening, and comforting, them. *The preparation of the heart* is indeed *from the Lord;* but ministers must be instruments in his hand. 5. He *encouraged them to the service*, v. 2. He spoke comfortably to them, as Hezekiah did, *ch.* 30:22. He promised them his countenance. Note, Those whom we charge we should encourage. Most people love to be commended, and will be wrought upon by encouragements more than by threats.

II. The king and the princes, influenced by his example, gave liberally for the bearing of the charges of this passover. The ceremonial services were expensive, which perhaps was one reason why they had been neglected. People had not zeal enough to be at the charge of them; nor were they now very fond of them, for that reason, and therefore, 1. Josiah, at his own proper cost, furnished the congregation with paschal lambs, and other sacrifices, to be offered during the seven days of the feast. He allowed out of his own estate 30,000 *lambs* for *passover offerings*, which the offerers were to feast upon, and 3000 bullocks (v. 7) to be offered during the following seven days. Note, Those who are serious in religion should, when they persuade others to do that which is good, make it as cheap and easy to them as may be. And where God sows plentifully he expects to reap accordingly. It is to be feared that the congregation generally had not come provided; so that, if Josiah had not furnished them, the work of God must have stood still. 2. The chief of the priests, who were men of great estates, contributed towards the priests' charges, as Josiah did towards the people's. *The princes* (v. 8), that is, the chief of the priests, the princes of the holy tribe, *rulers of the house of God*, bore the priests' charges. And some of the rich and great men of the Levites furnished them also with cattle, both great and small, for offerings, v. 9. For, as to those that sincerely desire to be found in the way of their duty, Providence sometimes raises up friends to bear them out in it, beyond what they could have expected.

III. The priests and Levites performed their office very readily, v. 10. They killed the paschal lambs in the court of the temple, the priests sprinkled the blood upon the altar, the Levites flayed them, and then gave the flesh to the people according to their families (v. 11, 12), not fewer than ten, nor more than twenty, to a lamb. They took it to their several apartments, roasted it, and ate it *according to the ordinance*, v. 13. As for the other sacrifices that were eucharistical, the flesh of them was boiled according to the law of the peace-offerings and was *divided speedily among the people*, that they might feast upon it as a token of their joy in the atonement made and their reconciliation to God thereby. And, *lastly*, The priests and Levites took care to honour God by *eating of the passover* themselves, v. 14. Let not ministers think that the care they take for the souls of others will excuse their neglect of their own, or that being employed so much in public worship will supersede the religious exercises of their closets and families. The Levites here mace ready for themselves and for the priests, because the priests were wholly taken up all day in the service of the altar; therefore, that they might not have their lamb to dress when they should eat it, the Levites got it ready for them against supper time. Let ministers learn hence to help one another, and to forward one another's work, as brethren, and fellow-servants of the same Master.

IV. The singers and porters attended in their places, and did their office, v. 15. The singers with their sacred songs and music expressed and excited the joy of the congregation, and made the service very pleasant to them; and the porters at the gates took care that there should be no breaking in of any thing to defile or disquiet the assembly, nor going out of any from it, that none should steal away till the service was done. While they were thus employed their brethren the Levites prepared paschal lambs for them.

V. The whole solemnity was performed with great exactness, according to the law (*v.* 16, 17), and, upon that account, there was none like it since Samuel's time (*v.* 18), for in Hezekiah's passover there were several irregularities. And bishop Patrick observes that in this also it exceeded the other passovers which the preceding kings had kept, that though Josiah was by no means so rich as David, and Solomon, and Jehoshaphat, yet he furnished the whole congregation with beasts for sacrifice, both paschal and eucharistical, at his own proper cost and charge, which was more than any king ever did before him.

Verses 20–27

It was thirteen years from Josiah's famous passover to his death. During this time, we may hope, thing went well in his kingdom, that he prospered, and religion flourished; yet we are not entertained with the pleasing account of those years, but they are passed over in silence, because the people, for all this, were not turned from the love of their sins nor God from the fierceness of his anger. The next news therefore we hear of Josiah is that he is cut off in the midst of his days and usefulness, before he is full forty years old. We had this sad story, 2 Ki. 23:29, 30. Here it is somewhat more largely related. That appears here, more than did there, which reflects such blame on Josiah and such praise on the people as one would not have expected.

I. Josiah was a very good prince, yet he was much to be blamed for his rashness and presumption in going out to war against the king of Egypt without cause or call. It was bad enough, as it appeared in the *Kings,* that he meddled with strife which belonged not to him. But here it looks worse; for, it seems, the king of Egypt sent ambassadors to him, to warn him against this enterprise, *v.* 21.

1. The king of Egypt argued with Josiah, (1.) From principles of justice. He professed that he had no desire to do him any hurt, and therefore it was unfair, against common equity and the law of nations, for Josiah to take up arms against him. If even a *righteous man* engage in an *unrighteous cause,* let him not expect to prosper. *God is no respecter of persons.* See Prov. 3:30; 25:8. (2.) From principles of religion: *"God is with me;* nay, *He commanded me to make haste,* and therefore, if thou retard my motions, thou meddlest with God." It cannot be that the king of Egypt only pretended this (as Sennacherib did in a like case, 2 Ki. 18:25), hoping thereby to make Josiah desist, because he knew he had a veneration for the word of God; for it is said here (*v.* 22) that the words of Necho were from the mouth of God. We must therefore suppose that either by a dream, or by a strong impulse upon his spirit which he had reason to think was from God, or by Jeremiah or some other prophet, he had ordered him to make war upon the king of Assyria. (3.) From principles of policy: *"That he destroy thee not;* it is at thy peril if thou engage against one that has not only a better army and a better cause, but God on his side."

2. It was not in wrath to Josiah, whose heart was upright with the Lord his God, but in wrath to a hypocritical nation, who were unworthy of so good a king, that he was so far infatuated as not to hearken to these fair reasonings and desist from his enterprise. He *would not turn his face from him,* but went in person and fought the Egyptian army in the *valley of Megiddo, v.* 22. If perhaps he could not believe that the king of Egypt had a command from God to do what he did, yet, upon his pleading such a command, he ought to have consulted the oracles of God before he went out against him. His not doing that was his great fault, and of fatal consequence. In this matter he walked not in the ways of David his father; for, had it been his case, he would have enquired of the Lord, *Shall I go up? Wilt thou deliver them into my hands?* How can we think to prosper in our ways if we do not acknowledge God in them?

II. The people were a very wicked people, yet they were much to be commended for lamenting the death of Josiah as they did. That Jeremiah lamented him I do not wonder; he was the weeping prophet, and plainly foresaw the utter ruin of his country following upon the death of this good king. But it is strange to find that all Judah and Jerusalem, that stupid senseless people, *mourned for him* (*v.* 24), contrived how to have their mourning excited by singing men and singing women, how to have it spread through the kingdom (they made an ordinance in Israel that the mournful ditties penned on this sad occasion should be learned and sung by all sorts of people), and also how to have the remembrance of it perpetuated: these elegies were inserted in the collections of state poems; they are written in the Lamentations. Hereby it appeared, 1. That they had some respect to their good prince, and that, though they did not cordially comply with him in all his good designs, they could not but greatly honour him. Pious useful men will be manifested in the consciences even of those that will not be influenced by their example; and many that will not submit to the rules of serious godliness themselves yet cannot but give it their good word and esteem it in others. Perhaps those lamented Josiah when he was dead that were not thankful to God for him while he lived. The Israelites murmured at Moses and Aaron while they were with them and spoke sometimes of stoning them, and yet, when they died, they mourned for them many days. We are often taught to value mercies by the loss of them which, when we enjoyed them, we did not prize as we ought. 2. That they had some sense of their own danger now that he was gone. Jeremiah told them, it is likely, of the evil they might now expect to come upon them, from which he was taken away; and so far they credited what he said that they lamented the death of him that was their defence. Note, Many will more easily be persuaded to lament the miseries that are coming upon them than to take the proper way by universal reformation to prevent them, will shed tears for their troubles, but will not be prevailed upon to part with their sins. But godly sorrow worketh repentance and that repentance will be to salvation.

CHAPTER 36

We have here, I. A short but sad account of the utter ruin of Judah and Jerusalem within a few years after Josiah's death. 1. The history of it in the unhappy reigns of Jehoahaz for three months (*v.* 1–4), Jehoiakim (*v.* 5–8) for eleven years, Jehoiachin three months (*v.* 9, 10), and Zedekiah eleven years (*v.* 11). Additions were made to the national guilt, and advances towards the national destruction, in each of those reigns. The destruction was, at length, completed in the slaughter of multitudes (*v.* 17), the plundering and burning of the temple and all the palaces, the desolation of the city (*v.* 18, 19), and the captivity of the people that remained (*v.* 20). 2. Some remarks upon it — that herein sin was punished, Zedekiah's wickedness (*v.* 12, 13), the idolatry the people were guilty of (*v.* 14), and their abuse of God's prophets (*v.* 15, 16). The word of God was herein fulfilled (*v.* 21). II. The dawning of the day of their deliverance in Cyrus's proclamation (*v.* 22, 23).

Verses 1–10

The destruction of Judah and Jerusalem is here coming on by degrees. God so ordered it to show that he has no pleasure in the ruin of sinners, but had rather they would turn and live, and therefore gives them both time and inducement to repent and waits to be gracious. The history of these reigns was more largely recorded in the last three chapters of the second of *Kings.* 1. Jehoahaz was set up by the people (*v.* 1), but in one quarter of a year was deposed by Pharaoh-necho, and carried a prisoner to Egypt, and the land fined for setting him up, *v.* 2–4. Of this young prince we hear no more. Had he trodden in the steps of his father's piety he might have reigned long and prospered; but we are told in the *Kings* that *he did evil in the sight of the Lord,* and therefore his triumphing was short and his joy but for a moment. 2. Jehoiakim was set up by the king of Egypt, an old enemy to their land, gave what king he pleased to the kingdom and what name he pleased to the king! *v.* 4. He made Eliakim king, and called him *Jehoiakim,* in token of his authority over him. *Jehoiakim did that which was evil* (*v.* 5), nay, we read of the *abominations which he did* (*v.* 8); he was very wild and wicked. Idolatries generally go under the name of abominations. We hear no more of the king of Egypt, but the king of Babylon came up against him (*v.* 6), seized him, and bound him with a design to carry him to Babylon; but, it seems, he either changed his mind, and suffered him to reign as his vassal, or death released the prisoner before he was carried away. However the best and most valuable vessels of the temple were now carried away and made use of in Nebuchadnezzar's temple in Babylon (*v.* 7); for, we may suppose, no temple in the world was so richly furnished as that of Jerusalem. The sin of Judah was that they had brought the idols of the heathen into God's temple; and now their punishment was that the vessels of the temple were carried away to the service of the gods of the nations. If men will profane God's institutions by their sins, it is just with God to suffer them to be profaned by their enemies. These were the vessels which the false prophets flattered the people with hopes of the return of, Jer. 27:16. But Jeremiah told them that the rest should go after them (Jer. 27:21, 22), and they did so. But, as the carrying away of these vessels to Babylon began the calamity of Jerusalem, so Belshazzar's daring profanation of them there filled the measure of the iniquity of Babylon; for, when he drank wine in them to the honour of his gods, the handwriting on the wall presented him with his doom, Dan. 5:3, etc. In the reference to the book of the *Kings* concerning this Jehoiakim mention is made of *that which was found in him* (*v.* 8), which seems to be meant of the treachery that was found in him towards the king of Babylon; but some of the Jewish writers understand it of certain private marks or signatures found in his dead body, in honour of his idol, such cuttings as God had forbidden, Lev. 19:28. 3. Jehoiachin, or Jeconiah, the son of Jehoiakim, attempted to reign in his stead, and reigned long enough to show his evil inclination; but, after three months and ten days, the king of Babylon sent and fetched him away captive, with more of the goodly vessels of the temple. He is here said to be eight years old, but in *Kings* he is said to be eighteen when he began to reign, so that this seems to be a mistake of the transcriber, unless we suppose that his father took him at eight years old to join with him in the government, as some think.

Verses 11–21

We have here an account of the destruction of the kingdom of Judah and the city of Jerusalem by the Chaldeans. Abraham, God's friend, was called out of that country, from Ur of the Chaldees, when God took him into covenant and communion with himself; and now his degenerate seed were carried into that country again, to signify that they had forfeited all that kindness wherewith they had been regarded for the father's sake, and the benefit of that covenant into which he was called; all was now undone again. Here we have,

I. The sins that brought this desolation.

1. Zedekiah, the king in whose days it came, brought it upon himself by his own folly; for he conducted himself very ill both towards God and towards the king of Babylon. (1.) If he had but made God his friend, that would have prevented the ruin. Jeremiah brought him messages from God, which, if he had given due regard to them, might have secured a lengthening of his tranquillity; but it is here charged upon him that he *humbled not himself before Jeremiah, v.* 12. It was expected that this mighty prince, high as he was, should humble himself before a poor prophet, when *he spoke from the mouth of the Lord,* should submit to his admonitions and be amended by them, to his counsels and be ruled by them, should lay himself under the commanding power of the word of God in his mouth; and, because he would not thus make himself a servant to God, he was made a slave to his enemies. God will find some way or other to humble those that will not humble themselves. Jeremiah, as a prophet, was set *over the nations and kingdoms* (Jer. 1:10), and, as mean a figure as he made, whoever would not humble themselves before him found that it was at their peril. (2.) If he had but been true to his covenant with the king of Babylon, that would have prevented his ruin; but he *rebelled against him,* though he had sworn to be his faithful tributary, and perfidiously violated his engagements to him, *v.* 13. It was this that provoked the king of Babylon to deal so severely with him as he did. All nations looked upon an oath as a sacred thing, and on those that durst break through the obligations of it as the worst of men, abandoned of God and to be abhorred by all mankind. If therefore Zedekiah falsify his oath, *when, lo, he has given his hand,* he *shall not escape,* Eze. 17:18. Though Nebuchadnezzar was a heathen, an enemy, yet if, having sworn to him, he be false to him, he shall know *there is a God to whom vengeance be-*

longs. The thing that ruined Zedekiah was not only that he *turned not to the Lord God of Israel,* but that he *stiffened his neck and hardened his heart from turning to him,* that is, he as obstinately resolved not to return to him, would not lay his neck under God's yoke nor his heart under the impressions of his word, and so, in effect, he *would not be healed,* he *would not live.*

2. The great sin that brought this destruction was idolatry. The priests and people went after *the abominations of the heathen,* forsook the pure worship of God for the lewd and filthy rites of the Pagan superstition, and so *polluted the house of the Lord, v.* 14. The priests, the chief of the priests, who should have opposed idolatry, were ringleaders in it. That place is not far from ruin in which religion is already ruined.

3. The great aggravation of their sin, and that which filled the measure of it, was the abuse they gave to God's prophets, who were sent to call them to repentance, *v.* 15, 16. Here we have, (1.) God's tender compassion towards them in sending prophets to them. Because he was the *God of their fathers,* in covenant with them, and whom they worshipped (though this degenerate race forsook him), therefore he *sent to them by his messengers,* to convince them of their sin and warn them of the ruin they would bring upon themselves by it, *rising up betimes and sending,* which denotes not only that he did it with the greatest care and concern imaginable, as men rise betimes to set their servants to work when their heart is upon their business, but that, upon their first deviation from God to idols, if they took but one step that way, God immediately sent to them by his messengers to reprove them for it. He gave them early timely notice both of their duty and danger. Let this quicken us to seek God early, that he rises betimes to send to us. The prophets that were sent rose betimes to speak to them, were diligent and faithful in their office, lost no time, slipped no opportunity of dealing with them; and therefore God is said to rise betimes. The more pains ministers take in their work the more will the people have to answer for if it be all in vain. The reason given why God by his prophets did thus strive with them is because *he had compassion on his people and on his dwelling-lace,* and would by these means have prevented their ruin. Note, The methods God takes to reclaim sinners by his word, by ministers, by conscience, by providences, are all instances of his compassion towards them and his unwillingness *that any should perish.* (2.) Their base and disingenuous carriage towards God (*v.* 16): *They mocked the messengers of God* (which was a high affront to him that sent them), *despised his word* in their mouths, and not only so, but *misused the prophets,* treating them as their enemies. The ill usage they gave Jeremiah who lived at this time, and which we read much of in the book of his prophecy, is an instance of this. This was an evidence of an implacable enmity to God, and an invincible resolution to go on in their sins. This brought wrath upon them without remedy, for it was sinning against the remedy. Nothing is more provoking to God than abuses given to his faithful ministers; for what is done against them he takes as done against himself. *Saul, Saul, why persecutest thou me?* Persecution was the sin that brought upon Jerusalem its final destruction by the Romans. See Mt. 23:34–37. Those that mock at God's faithful ministers, and do all they can to render them despicable or odious, that vex and misuse them, to discourage them and to keep others from hearkening to them, should be reminded that a wrong done to an ambassador is construed as done to the prince that sends him, and that the day is coming when they will find it would have been better for them if they had been thrown *into the sea* with a mill-stone about their necks; for hell is deeper and more dreadful.

II. The desolation itself, and some few of the particular so fit, which we had more largely 2 Ki. 25:1. Multitudes were put to the sword, even *in the house of their sanctuary* (*v.* 17), whither they fled for refuge, hoping that the holiness of the place would be their protection. But how could they expect to find it so when they themselves had polluted it with their abominations? *v.* 14. Those that cast off the dominion of their religion forfeit all the benefit and comfort of it. The Chaldeans not only paid no reverence to the sanctuary, but showed no natural pity either to the tender sex or to venerable age. They forsook God, who had compassion on them (*v.* 15), and would have none of him; justly therefore are they given up into the hands of cruel men, for they *had no compassion on young man or maiden.* 2. All the remaining vessels of the temple, great and small, and all the treasures, sacred and secular, the treasures of God's house and of the king and his princes, were seized, and brought to Babylon, *v.* 18. 3. The temple was burnt, the walls of Jerusalem were demolished, the houses (called here the *palaces,* as Ps. 48:3, so stately, rich, and sumptuous were they) laid in ashes, and all the furniture, called here *the goodly vessels thereof,* destroyed, *v.* 19. Let us see where what woeful havock sin makes, and, as we value the comfort and continuance of our estates, keep that worm from the root of them. 4. The remainder of the people that escaped the sword were carried captives to Babylon (*v.* 20), impoverished, enslaved, insulted, and exposed to all the miseries, not only of a strange and barbarous land, but of an enemy's land, where those that hated them bore rule over them. They were servants to those monarchs, and no doubt were ruled with rigour so long as that monarchy lasted. Now they sat down by the rivers of Babylon, with the streams of which they mingled their tears, Ps. 137:1. And though there, it should seem, they were cured of idolatry, yet, as appears by the prophet Ezekiel, they were not cured of mocking the prophets. 5. The land lay desolate while they were captives in Babylon, *v.* 21. That fruitful land, the glory of all lands, was now turned into a desert, not tilled, nor husbanded. The pastures were not clothed as they used to be with flocks, nor the valleys with corn, but all lay neglected. Now this may be considered, (1.) As the just punishment of their former abuse of it. They had served Baal with its fruits; *cursed* therefore *is the ground for their sakes.* Now the land *enjoyed her sabbaths;* (*v.* 21), as God had threatened by Moses, Lev. 26:34, and the reason there given (*v.* 35) is, "Because *it did not rest on your sabbaths;* you profaned the sabbath-day, did not observe the sabbatical year." They many a time ploughed and sowed their land in the seventh year, when it should have rested, and now it lay unploughed and unsown for ten times seven years. Note, God will be no loser in his glory at last by the disobedience of men: if the tribute be not paid, he will distrain and recover it, as he speaks, Hos. 2:9. If they would not let the land rest, God would make it rest whether they would or no. Some think they had neglected the observance of seventy sabbatical years in all, and just so many, by way of reprisal, the land now enjoyed; or, if those that had been neglected were fewer, it was fit that the law should be satisfied with interest. We find that one of the quarrels God had with them at this time was for not observing another law which related to the seventh year, and that was the release of servants; see Jer. 34:13, etc. (2.) Yet we may consider it as giving some encouragement to their hopes that they should, in due time, return to it again. Had others come and taken possession of it, they might have despaired of ever recovering it; but, while it lay desolate, it did, as it were, lie waiting for them again, and refuse to acknowledge any other owners.

Verses 22–23

These last two verses of this book have a double aspect. 1. They look back to the prophecy of Jeremiah, and show how that was accomplished, *v.* 22. God had, by him, promised the restoring of the captives and the rebuilding of Jerusalem, at the end of seventy years; and that time to favour Sion, that set time, came at last. After a long and dark night the day-spring from on high visited them. God will be found true to every word he has spoken. 2. They look forward to the history of Ezra, which begins with the repetition of these last two verses. They are there the introduction to a pleasant story; here they are the conclusion of a very melancholy one; and so we learn from them that, though God's church be cast down, it is not cast off, though his people be corrected, they are not abandoned, though thrown into the furnace, yet not lost there, nor left there any longer than till the dross be separated. Though God contend long, he will not contend always. The Israel of God shall be fetched out of Babylon in due time, and even the dry bones made to live. It may be long first; but the vision is for an appointed time, and at the end it shall speak and not lie; therefore, though it tarry, wait for it.

AN EXPOSITION, WITH PRACTICAL OBSERVATIONS, OF

THE BOOK OF EZRA

The Jewish church puts on quite another face in this book from what it had appeared with; its state much better, and more pleasant, than it was of late in Babylon, and yet far inferior to what it had been formerly. The dry bones here live again, but *in the form of a servant;* the yoke of their captivity is taken off, but the marks of it in their galled necks remain. Kings we hear no more of; *the crown has fallen from their heads.* Prophets they are blessed with, to direct them in their re-establishment, but, after a while, prophecy ceases among them, till the great prophet appears, and his fore-runner. The history of this book is the accomplishment of Jeremiah's prophecy concerning the return of the Jews out of Babylon at the end of seventy years, and a type of the accomplishment of the prophecies of the Apocalypse concerning the deliverance of the gospel church out of the New-Testament Babylon. Ezra preserved the records of that great revolution and transmitted them to the church in this book. His name signifies a helper; and so he was to that people. A particular account concerning him we shall meet with, *ch.* 7, where he himself enters upon the stage of action. The book gives us an account, I. Of the Jews' return out of their captivity, *ch.* 1, 2. II. Of the building of the temple, the opposition it met with, and yet the perfecting of it at last, *ch.* 3–6. III. Of Ezra's coming to Jerusalem, *ch.* 7, 8. IV. Of the good service he did there, in obliging those that had married strange wives to put them away, *ch.* 9, 10. This beginning again of the Jewish nation was small, yet its latter end greatly increased.

CHAPTER 1

In this chapter we have, I. The proclamation which Cyrus, king of Persia, issued out for the release of all the Jews that he found captives in Babylon, and the building of their temple in Jerusalem (*v.* 1–4). II. The return of many thereupon (*v.* 5, 6). III. Orders given for the restoring of the vessels of the temple (*v.* 7–11). And this is the dawning of the day of their deliverance.

Verses 1–4

It will be proper for us here to consider, 1. What was the state of the captive Jews in Babylon. It was upon many accounts very deplorable; they were under the power of those that hated them, had nothing they could call their own; they had no temple, no altar; if they sang psalms, their enemies ridiculed them; and yet they had prophets among them. Ezekiel and Daniel were kept distinct from the heathen. Some of them were preferred at court, others had comfortable settlements in the country, and they were all borne up with hope that, in due time, they should return to their own land again, in expectation of which they preserved among them the distinction of their families, the knowledge of their religion, and an aversion to idolatry. 2. What was the state of the government under which they were. Nebuchadnezzar carried many of them into captivity in the first year of his reign, which was the fourth of Jehoiakim; he reigned forty-five years, his son Evil-merodach twenty-three, and his grandson Belshazzar three years, which make up the seventy years. So Dr. Lightfoot, It is charged upon Nebuchadnezzar that he *opened not the house of his prisoners*, Isa. 14:17. And, if he had shown mercy to the poor Jews, Daniel told him it would have been the *lengthening of his tranquillity,* Dan. 4:27. But the measure of the sins of Babylon was at length full, and then destruction was brought upon them by Darius the Mede and Cyrus the Persian, which we read of, Dan. 5. Darius, being old, left the government to Cyrus, and he was employed as the instrument of the Jews' deliverance, which he gave orders for as soon as ever he was master of the kingdom of Babylon, perhaps in contradiction to Nebuchadnezzar, whose family he had cut off, and because he took a pleasure in undoing what he had done, or in policy, to recommend his newly-acquired dominion as merciful and gentle, or (as some think) in a pious regard to the prophecy of Isaiah, which had been published, and well known, above 150 years before, where he was expressly named as the man that should do this for God, and for whom God would do great things (Isa. 44:28; 45:1, etc.), and which perhaps was shown to him by those about him. His name (some say) in the Persian language signifies the *sun,* for he brought light and healing to the church of God, and was an eminent type of Christ the *Sun of righteousness.* Some was that his name signifies a *father,* and Christ is the everlasting Father. Now here we are told,

I. Whence this proclamation took its rise. *The Lord stirred up the spirit of Cyrus.* Note, The hearts of kings are in the hand of the Lord, and, like the rivulets of water, he turneth them which way soever he will. It is said of Cyrus that he knew not God, nor how to serve him; but God knew him, and how to serve himself by him, Isa. 45:4. God governs the world by his influence on the spirits of men, and, whatever good is done at any time, it is God that stirs up the spirit to do it, puts thoughts into the mind, gives to the understanding to form a right judgment, and directs the will which way he pleases. Whatever good offices therefore are, at any time, done for the church of God, he must have the glory of them.

II. The reference it had to the prophecy of Jeremiah, by whom God had not only promised that they should return, but had fixed the time, which set time to favour Sion had now come. Seventy years were determined (Jer. 25:12; 29:10); and he that kept the promise made concerning Israel's deliverance out of *Egypt to a day* (Ex. 12:41) was doubtless as punctual to this. What Cyrus now did was long since said to be the *confirming of the word of God's servants,* Isa. 44:26. Jeremiah, while he lived, was hated and despised; yet thus did Providence honour him long after, that a mighty monarch was influenced to act in pursuance of the word of the Lord by his mouth.

III. The date of this proclamation. It was in his first year, not the first of his reign over Persia, the kingdom he was born to, but the first of his reign over Babylon, the kingdom he had conquered. Those are much honoured whose spirits are stirred up to begin with God and to serve him in their first years.

IV. The publication of it, both by word of mouth (he *caused a voice to pass throughout all his kingdom,* like a jubilee-trumpet, a joyful sabbatical year after many melancholy ones, proclaiming liberty to the captives), and also in black and white: he put it in writing, that it might be the more satisfactory, and might be sent to those distant provinces where the ten tribes were scattered in Assyria and Media, 2 Ki. 17:6.

V. The purport of this proclamation of liberty.

1. The preamble shows the causes and considerations by which he was influenced, *v.* 2. It should seem, his mind was enlightened with the knowledge of *Jehovah* (for so he calls him), the God of Israel, as the only *living and true God,* the *God of heaven,* who is the sovereign Lord and disposer of all *the kingdoms of the earth;* of him he says (*v.* 3), *He is the God,* God alone, God above all. Though he had not known God by education, God made him so far to know him now as that he did this service with an eye to him. He professes that he does it, (1.) In gratitude to God for the favours he had bestowed upon him: *The God of heaven has given me all the kingdoms of the earth.* This sounds a little vain-glorious, for there were *many kingdoms of the earth* which he had nothing to do with; but he means that God had given him all that was given to Nebuchadnezzar, whose dominion, Daniel says, was *to the end of the earth,* Dan. 4:22; 5:19. Note, God is the fountain of power; the kingdoms of the earth are at his disposal; whatever share any have of them they have from him: and those whom God has entrusted with great power and large possessions should look upon themselves as obliged thereby to do much for him. (2.) In obedience to God. He hat *charged me to build him a house at Jerusalem;* probably by a dream or vision of the night, confirmed by comparing it with the prophecy of Isaiah, where his doing it was foretold. Israel's disobedience to God's charge, which they were often told of, is aggravated by the obedience of this heathen king.

2. He gives free leave to all the Jews that were in his dominions to go up to Jerusalem, and to *build the temple of the Lord* there, *v.* 3. His regard to God made him overlook, (1.) The secular interest of his government. It would have been his policy to keep so great a number of serviceable men in his dominions, and seemed impolitic to let them go and take root again in their own land; but piety is the best policy. (2.) The honour of the religion of his country. Why did he not order them to build a temple to the gods of Babylon or Persia? He believed the God of Israel to be the *God of heaven,* and therefore obliged his Israel to worship him only. Let them *walk in the name of the Lord their God.*

3. He subjoins a brief for a collection to bear the charges of such as were poor and not able to bear their own, *v.* 4. "Whosoever remaineth, because he has not the means to bear his charges to Jerusalem, *let the men of his place help him.*" Some take it as an order to the king's officers to supply them out of his revenue, as *ch.* 6:8. But it may mean a warrant to the captives to ask and receive the alms and charitable contributions of all the king's loving subjects. And we may suppose the Jews had conducted themselves so well among their neighbours that they would be as forward to accommodate them because they loved them as the Egyptians were because they were weary of them. At least many would be kind to them because they saw the government would take it well. Cyrus not only gave his good wishes with those that went (*Their God be with them, v.* 3), but took care also to furnish them with such things as they needed. He took it for granted that those among them who were of ability would offer their *free-will offerings for the house of God,* to promote the rebuilding of it. But, besides that, he would have them supplied out of his kingdom. Well-wishers to the temple should be well-doers for it.

Verses 5–11

We are here told,

I. How Cyrus's proclamation succeeded with others. 1. He having given leave to the Jews to go up to Jerusalem, many of them went up accordingly, *v.* 5. The leaders herein were the *chief of the fathers* of Judah and Benjamin, eminent and experienced men, from whom it might justly be expected that, as they were above their brethren in dignity, so they should go before them in duty. The priests and Levites were (as became them) with the first that set their faces again towards Zion. If any good work is to be done, let ministers lead in it. Those that accompanied them were such as God had inclined to go up. The same God that had raised up the spirit of Cyrus to proclaim this liberty raised up their spirits to take the benefit of it; for it was done, *not by might, nor by power, but by the Spirit of the Lord of hosts,* Zec. 4:6. The temptation perhaps was strong to some of them to stay in Babylon. They had convenient settlements there, had contracted an agreeable acquaintance with the neighbours, and were ready to say, *It is good to be here.* The discouragements of their return were many and great, the journey long, their wives and children unfit for travelling, their own land was to them a strange land, the road to it an unknown road. Go up to Jerusalem! And what should they do there? It was all in ruins, and in the midst of enemies to whom they would be an easy prey. Many were wrought upon by these considerations to stay in Babylon, at least not to go with the first. But there were some that got over these difficulties, that ventured to break the ice, and feared not the lion in the way, the lion in the streets; and they were those whose spirits God raised. He, by his Spirit and grace, filled them with a generous ambition of liberty, a gracious affection to their own land, and a desire of the free and public exercise of their religion. Had God left them to themselves, and to the counsels of flesh and blood, they would have staid in Babylon; but he put it into their hearts to set their faces Zionward, and, as strangers, to ask the way thither (Jer. 50:5); for they, being a new generation, went out like their father Abraham from this land of the Chaldees, not knowing whither they went, Heb. 11:8. Note, Whatever good we do, it is owing purely to the grace of God, and he raises up our spirits to the doing of it, *works in us both to will and to do.* Our spirits naturally incline to this earth and to the things of it. If they move upwards, in any good affections or good actions, it is God that raises them. The call and offer of the gospel are like Cyrus's proclamation. *Deliverance is preached to the captives,* Lu. 4:18. Those that are bound under the unrighteous dominion of sin, and bound over to the righteous judgment of God, may be made free by Jesus Christ. Whoever will, by repentance and faith, return to God, his duty to God, his happiness in God, Jesus Christ has opened the way for him, and let him go up out of the slavery of sin into the *glorious liberty of the children of God.* The offer is general to all. Christ makes it, in pursuance of the grant which the Father has made him of *all power both in heaven and in earth* (a much greater dominion than that given to Cyrus, *v.* 2) and of the charge given him to *build God a house,* to set him up a church in the world, a kingdom among men. Many that hear this joyful sound choose to sit still in Babylon, are in love with their sins and will not venture upon the difficulties of a holy life; but some there are that break through the discouragements, and resolve to *build the house of God,* to make heaven of their religion, whatever it cost them, and they are those *whose spirit God has raised* above the world and the flesh and whom he has made *willing in the day of his power,* Ps. 110:3. Thus will the heavenly Canaan be replenished, though many perish in Babylon; and the gospel-offer will not be made in vain. 2. Cyrus having given order that their neighbours should help them, they did so, *v.* 6. All those that were about them furnished them with plate and goods to bear the charges of their journey, and to help them in building and furnishing both their own houses and God's temple. As the tabernacle was made of the spoils of Egypt, and the first temple built by the labours of the strangers, so the second by the contributions of the Chaldeans, all intimating the admission of the Gentiles into the church in due time. God can, where he pleases, incline the hearts of strangers to be kind to his people, and make those to strengthen their hands that have weakened them. *The earth helped the woman. Besides what was willingly offered* by the Jews themselves who staid behind, from a principle of love to God and his house, much was offered, as one may say, unwillingly by the Babylonians, who were influenced to do it by a divine power on their minds of which they themselves could give no account.

How this proclamation was seconded by Cyrus himself. To give proof of the sincerity of his affection to the house of God, he not only released the people of God, but restored the vessels of the temple, *v.* 7, 8. Observe here, 1. How careful Providence was of the vessels of the temple, that they were not lost, melted down, or so mixed with other vessels that they could not be known, but that they were all now forthcoming. Such care God has of the living *vessels of mercy, vessels of honour,* of whom it is said (2 Tim. 2:19, 20), *The Lord knows those that are his,* and they shall *none of them perish.* 2. Though they had been put into an idol's temple, and probably used in the service of idols, yet they were given back, to be used for God. God will recover his own; and the spoil of the strong man armed shall be converted to the use of the conqueror. 3. Judah had a prince, even in captivity. Sheshbazzar, supposed to be the same with Zerubbabel, is here called *prince of Judah;* the Chaldeans called him *Sheshbazzar,* which signifies *joy in tribulation;* but among his own people he went by the name of *Zerubbabel — a stronger in Babylon;* so he looked upon himself, and considered Jerusalem his home, though, as Josephus says, he was captain of the lifeguard to the king of Babylon. He took care of the affairs of the Jews, and had some authority over them, probably from the death of Jehoiachin, or Jeconiah, who made him his heir, he being of the house of David. 4. To him the sacred vessels were numbered out (*v.* 8), and he took care for their safe conveyance to Jerusalem, *v.* 11. It would encourage them to build the temple that they had so much rich furniture ready to put into it when it was built. Though God's ordinances, like the vessels of the sanctuary, may be corrupted and profaned by the New-Testament Babylon, they shall, in due time, be restored to their primitive use and intention; for not one jot or tittle of divine institution shall fall to the ground.

CHAPTER 2

That many returned out of Babylon upon Cyrus's proclamation we were told in the foregoing chapter; we have here a catalogue of the several families that returned (*v.* 1). I. The leaders (*v.* 2). II. The people (*v.* 3–35). III. The priests, Levites, and retainers to the temple (*v.* 35–63). IV. The sum total, with an account of their retinue (*v.* 64–67). V. Their offerings to the service of the temple (*v.* 68–70).

Verses 1–35

We may observe here, 1. That an account was kept in writing of the families that came up out of captivity, and the numbers of each family. This was done for their honour, as part of their recompence for their faith and courage, their confidence in God and their affection to their own land, and to stir up others to follow their good example. Those that honour God he will thus honour. The names of all those Israelites indeed that accept the offer of deliverance by Christ shall be found, to their honour, in a more sacred record than this, even in *the Lamb's book of life.* The account that was kept of the families that came up from the captivity was intended also for the benefit of posterity, that they might know from whom they descended and to whom they were allied. 2. That they are called *children of the province.* Judah, which had been an illustrious kingdom, to which other kingdoms had been made provinces, subject to it and dependent on it, was now itself made a province, to receive laws and commissions from the king of Persia and to be accountable to him. See how sin diminishes and debases a nation, which righteousness would exalt. But by thus being made servants (as the patriarchs by being sojourners in a country which was theirs by promise) they were reminded of the *better country, that is, the heavenly* (Heb. 11:16), a *kingdom which cannot be moved,* or changed into a province. 3. That they are said to come *every one to his city,* that is, the city appointed them, in which appointment an eye, no doubt, was had to their former settlement by Joshua; and to that, as near as might be, they returned: for it does not appear that any others, at least any that were able to oppose them, had possessed them in their absence. 4. That the leaders are first mentioned, *v.* 2. Zerubbabel and Jeshua were their Moses and Aaron, the former their chief prince, the latter their chief priest. Nehemiah and Mordecai are mentioned here; some think not the same with the famous men we afterwards meet with of those names: probably they were the same, but afterwards returned to court for the service of their country. 5. Some of these several families are named from the persons that were their ancestors, others from the places in which they had formerly resided; as with us many surnames are the proper names of persons, others of places. 6. Some little difference there is between the numbers of some of the families here and in Neh. 7, where this catalogue is repeated, which might arise from this, that some who had given in their names at first to come afterwards drew back — said, *I go, Sir, but went not,* which would lessen the number of the families they belonged to; others that declined, at first, *afterwards repented and went,* and so increased the number. 7. Here are two families that are called *the children of Elam* (one *v.* 7, another *v.* 31), and, which is strange, the number of both is the same, 1254. 8. The children of Adonikam, which signifies *a high lord,* were 666, just the *number of the beast* (Rev. 13:18), which is there said to be *the number of a man,* which, Mr. Hugh Broughton thinks, has reference to this man. 9. The children of Bethlehem (*v.* 21) were but 123, though it was David's city; for Bethlehem was *little among the thousands of Judah,* yet there must the Messiah arise, Mic. 5:2. 10. Anathoth had been a famous place in the tribe of Benjamin and yet here it numbered but 128 (*v.* 23), which is to be imputed to the divine curse which the men of Anathoth brought upon themselves by persecuting Jeremi-

ah, who was of their city. Jer. 11:21, 23, *There shall be no remnant of them, for I will bring evil upon the men of Anathoth.* And see Isa. 10:30, *O poor Anathoth!* Nothing brings ruin on a people sooner than persecution.

Verses 36–63

Here is an account, I. Of the priests that returned, and they were a considerable number, about a tenth part of the whole company: for the whole were above 42,000 (*v.* 64), and four families of priests made up above 4200 (*v.* 36–39); thus was the tenth God's part — a blessed decimation. Three of the fathers of the priests here named were heads of courses, 1 Chr. 24:7, 8, 14. The fourth was Pashur, *v.* 38. If these were of the posterity of that Pashur that abused Jeremiah (Jer. 20:1), it is strange that so bad a man should have so good a seed, and so numerous. II. Of the Levites. I cannot but wonder at the small number of them, for, taking in both the singers and the porters (*v.* 40–42), they did not make 350. Time was when the Levites were more forward to their duty than the priests (2 Chr. 29:34), but they were not so now. If one place, one family, has the reputation for pious zeal now, another may have it another time. *The wind blows where it listeth,* and shifts its points. III. Of the Nethinim, who, it is supposed, were the Gibeonites, *given* (so their name signifies) by Joshua first (Jos. 9:27), and again by David (Ezra 8:20), when Saul had expelled them, to be employed by the Levites in the work of God's house as hewers of wood and drawers of water; and, with them, of the children of Solomon's servants, whom he gave for the like use (whether they were Jews or Gentiles does not appear) and who were here taken notice of among the retainers of the temple and numbered with the Nethinim, *v.* 55, 58. Note, It is an honour to belong to God's house, though in the meanest office there. IV. Of some that were looked upon as Israelites by birth, and others as priests, and yet could not make out a clear title to the honour. 1. There were some that could not prove themselves Israelites (*v.* 59, 60), a considerable number, who presumed they were of the seed of Jacob, but could not produce their pedigrees, and yet would go up to Jerusalem, having an affection to the house and people of God. These shamed those who were true-born Israelites, and yet were not called Israelites indeed, *who came out of the waters of Judah* (Isa. 48:1), but had lost the relish of those waters. 2. There were others that could not prove themselves priests, and yet were supposed to be of the seed of Aaron. What is not preserved in black and white will, in all likelihood, be forgotten in a little time. Now we are here told, (1.) How they lost their evidence. One of their ancestors married a daughter of Barzillai, that great man whom we read of in David's time; he gloried in an alliance to that honourable family, and, preferring that before the dignity of his priesthood, would have his children called after Barzillai's family, and their pedigree preserved in the registers of that house, not of the house of Aaron, and so they lost it. In Babylon there was nothing to be got by the priesthood, and therefore they cared not for being akin to it. Those who think their ministry, or their relation to ministers, a diminution or disparagement to them, forget who it was that said, *I magnify my office.* (2.) What they lost with it. It could not be taken for granted that they were priests when they could not produce their proofs, but they were, *as polluted, put from the priesthood.* Now that the priests had recovered their rights, and had the altar to live upon again, they would gladly be looked upon as priests. But they had sold their birthright for the honour of being gentlemen, and therefore were justly degraded, and forbidden to *eat of the most holy things.* Note, Christ will be ashamed of those that are ashamed of him and his service. It was the tirshatha, or governor, that put them under this sequestration, which some understand of Zerubbabel the present governor, others of Nehemiah (who is so called, Neh. 8:9, 10:1, and who gave this order when he came some years after); but the prohibition was not absolute, it was only a suspension, till there should be a high priest *with Urim and Thummin,* by whom they might know God's mind in this matter. This, it seems, was expected and desired, but it does not appear that ever they were blessed with it under the second temple. They had the canon of the Old Testament complete, which was better than Urim; and, by the want of that oracle, they were taught to ex-

pect the Messiah the great Oracle, which the Urim and Thummim was but a type of. Nor does it appear that the second temple had the ark in it, either the old one or a new one. Those shadows by degrees vanished, as the substance approached; and God, by the prophet, intimates to his people that they should sustain no damage by the want of the ark, Jer. 3:16, 17. *In those days,* when *they shall call Jerusalem the throne of the Lord,* and *all the nations shall be gathered* to it, they shall *say no more, The ark of the covenant of the Lord, neither shall it come to mind,* for they shall do very well without it.

Verses 64–70

Here is, I. The sum total of the company that returned out of Babylon. The particular sums before mentioned amount not quite to 30,000 (29, 818), so that there were above 12,000 that come out into any of those accounts, who, it is probable, were of the rest of the tribes of Israel, besides Judah and Benjamin, that could not tell of what particular family or city they were, but that they were Israelites, and of what tribe. Now, 1. This was more than double the number that were carried captive into Babylon by Nebuchadnezzar, so that, as in Egypt, the time of their affliction was the time of their increase. 2. These were but few to begin a nation with, and yet, by virtue of the old promise made to their fathers, they multiplied so as before their last destruction by the Romans, about 500 years after, to be a very numerous people. When God says, "Increase and multiply," *a little one shall become a thousand.*

II. Their retinue. They were themselves little better than servants, and therefore no wonder that their servants were comparatively but few (*v.* 65) and their beasts of burden about as many, *v.* 66, 67. It was not with them now as in days past. But notice is taken of 200 *singing-men and women* whom they had among them, who, we will suppose, were intended (as those 2 Chr. 35:25) to excite *their mourning,* for it was foretold that they should, upon this occasion, *go weeping* (Jer. 50:4), with ditties of lamentation.

III. Their oblations. It is said (*v.* 68, 69), 1. That they *came to the house of the Lord at Jerusalem;* and yet that house, that holy and beautiful house, was now in ruins, a heap of rubbish. But, like their father Abraham, when the altar was gone they came with devotion to *the place of the altar* (Gen. 13:4); and it is the character of the genuine sons of Zion that they favour even *the dust thereof,* Ps. 102:14. 2. That they offered freely towards the *setting of it up in its place.* That, it seems, was the first house they talked of setting up; and though they came off a journey, and were beginning the world (two chargeable things), yet they offered, and offered freely, towards the building of the temple. Let none complain of the necessary expenses of their religion, but believe that when they come to balance the account they will find that it clears the cost. Their offering was nothing in comparison with the offerings of the princes in David's time; then they offered by talents (1 Chr. 29:7), now by drams, yet these drams, being after their ability, were as acceptable to God as those talents, like the widow's two mites. The 61,000 drams of gold amount, by Cumberland's calculation, to so many pounds of our money and so many groats. Every maneh, or pound of silver, he reckons to be sixty shekels (that is, thirty ounces), which we may reckon 7*l.* 10*s.* of our money, so that this 5000 pounds of silver will be above 37,000*l.* of our money. It seems, God had blessed them with an increase of their wealth, as well as of their numbers, in Babylon; and, as God had prospered them, they gave cheerfully to the service of his house. 3. That they *dwelt in their cities, v.* 70. Though their cities were out of repair, yet, because they were their cities, such as God had assigned them, they were content to dwell in them, and were thankful for liberty and property, though they had little of pomp, plenty, or power. Their poverty was a bad cause, but their unity and unanimity were a good effect of it. Here was room enough for them all and all their substance, so that there was no strife among them, but perfect harmony, a blessed presage of their settlement, as their discords in the latter times of that state were of their ruin.

CHAPTER 3

In the close of the foregoing chapter we left Israel in their cities, but we may well imagine what a bad posture their affairs were in, the ground untilled, the cities in ruins, all out of order; but here we have an account of the early care they took about the re-establishment of religion among them. Thus did they lay the foundation well, and begin their work at the right end. I. They set up an altar, and offered sacrifices upon it, kept the feasts, and contributed towards the rebuilding of the temple (*v.* 1–7). II. They laid the foundation of the temple with a mixture of joy and sorrow (*v.* 8–13). This was the day of small things, which was not to be despised, Zec. 4:10.

Verses 1–7

Here is, I. A general assembly of the returned Israelites at Jerusalem, in the *seventh month, v.* 1. We may suppose that they came from Babylon in the spring, and must allow at least four months for the journey, for so long Ezra and his company were in coming, *ch.* 7:9. The seventh month therefore soon came, in which many of the feasts of the Lord were to be solemnized; and then they gathered themselves together by agreement among themselves, rather than by the command of authority, to Jerusalem. Though they had newly come to their cities, and had their hands full of business there, to provide necessaries for themselves and their families, which might have excused them from attending on God's altar till the hurry was a little over, as many foolishly put off their coming to the communion till they are settled in the world, yet such was their zeal for religion, now that they had newly come from under correction for their irreligion, that they left all their business in the country, to attend God's altar; and (which is strange) in this pious zeal they were all of a mind, they came *as one man.* Let worldly business be postponed to the business of religion and it will prosper the better.

II. The care which their leading men took to have an altar ready for them to attend upon.

1. Joshua and his brethren the priests, Zerubbabel and his brethren the princes, built *the altar of the God of Israel* (*v.* 2), in the same place (it is likely) where it had stood, upon the same bases, *v.* 3. Bishop Patrick, observing that before the temple was built there seems to have been a tabernacle pitched for the divine service, as was in David's time, not on Mount Moriah, but Mount Sion (1 Chr. 9:23), supposes that this altar was erected there, to be sued while the temple was in building. Let us learn hence, (1.) To *begin with God.* The more difficult and necessitous our case is the more concerned we are to take him along with us in all our ways. If we expect to be directed by his oracles, let him be honoured by our offerings. (2.) To *do what we can* in the worship of God when *we cannot do what we would.* They could not immediately have a temple, but they would not be without an altar. Abraham, wherever he came, *built an altar;* and wherever we come, though we may perhaps want the benefit of the candlestick of preaching, and the showbread of the eucharist, yet, if we bring not the sacrifices of prayer and praise, we are wanting in our duty, for we have an altar that sanctifies the gift ever ready.

2. Observe the reason here given why they hastened to set up the altar: *Fear was upon them, because of the people of the land.* They were in the midst of enemies that bore ill will to them and their religion, for whom they were an unequal match. And, (1.) *Though* they were so, yet they built the altar (so some read it); they would not be frightened from their religion by the opposition they were likely to meet with in it. Never let the fear of man bring us into this snare. (2.) *Because* they were so, therefore they set up the altar. Apprehension of danger should stir us up to our duty. Have we many enemies? Then it is good to have God our friend and to keep up our correspondence with him. This good use we should make of our fears, we should be driven by them to our knees. Even Saul would think himself undone if the enemy should come upon him before he had made his supplication to God, 1 Sa. 13:12.

III. The sacrifices they offered upon the altar. The altar was reared to be used, and they used it accordingly. Let not those that have an altar starve it.

1. They began *on the first day of the seventh month, v.* 6. It does not appear that they had any fire from heaven to begin with, as Moses and Solomon had, but common fire served them, as it did the patriarchs.

2. Having begun, they kept up the *continual burnt-offering* (*v.* 5), *morning and evening, v.* 3. They had known by sad experience what it was to want the comfort of the daily sacrifice to plead in their daily prayers, and now that it was revived they resolved not to let it fall again. The daily lamb typified the Lamb of God, whose righteousness must be our confidence in all our prayers.

3. They observed all the *set feasts of the Lord,* and offered the sacrifices appointed for each, and particularly *the feast of tabernacles, v.* 4, 5. Now that they had received such great mercy from God that joyful feast was in a special manner seasonable. And now that they were beginning to settle in their cities it might serve well to remind them of their fathers dwelling in tents in the wilderness. That feast also which had a peculiar reference to gospel times (as appears, Zec. 14:18) was brought, in a special manner, into reputation, now that those times drew on. Of the services of this feast, which continued seven days and had peculiar sacrifices appointed, it is said that they did *as the duty of every day required* (see Num. 29:13, 17, etc.), *Verbum die in die suo — the word, or matter, of the day in its day* (so it is in the original) — a phrase that has become proverbial with those that have used themselves to scripture-language. If the feast of tabernacles was a figure of a gospel conversation, in respect of continual weanedness from the world and joy in God, we may infer that it concerns us all to do the *work of the day in its day, according as the duty of the day requires,* that is, (1.) We must improve time, by finding some business to do every day that will turn to a good account. (2.) We must improve opportunity, by accommodating ourselves to that which is the proper business of the present day. Every thing is beautiful in its season. The tenth day of this month was the day of atonement, a solemn day, and very seasonable now: it is very probable that they observed it, yet it is not mentioned, nor indeed in all the Old Testament do I remember the least mention of the observance of that day; as if it were enough that we have the law of it in Lev. 16, and the gospel of it, which was the chief intention of it, in the New Testament.

4. They offered *every man's free-will offering, v.* 5. The law required much, but they brought more; for, though they had little wealth to support the expense of their sacrifices, they had much zeal, and, we may suppose, spared at their own tables that they might plentifully supply God's altar. Happy are those that bring with them out of the furnace of affliction such a holy heat as this.

IV. The preparation they made for the building of the temple, *v.* 7. This they applied themselves immediately to; for, while we do what we can, we must still be aiming to do more and better. Tyre and Sidon must now, as of old, furnish them with workmen, and Lebanon with timber, orders for both which they had from Cyrus. What God calls us to we may depend upon his providence to furnish us for.

Verses 8–13

There was no dispute among the returned Jews whether they should build the temple or no; that was immediately resolved on, and that it should be done with all speed; what comfort could they take in their own land if they had not that token of God's presence with them and the record of his name among them? We have here therefore an account of the beginning of that good work. Observe,

I. When it was begun — in the second month of the second year, as soon as ever the season of the year would permit (*v.* 8), and when they had ended the solemnities of the passover. They took little more than half a year for making preparation of the ground and materials; so much were their hearts upon it. Note, When any good work is to be done it will be our wisdom to set about it quickly, and not to lose time, yea, though we foresee difficulty and opposition in it. Thus we engage ourselves to it, and engage God for us. Well begun (we say) is half ended.

II. Who began it — Zerubbabel, and Jeshua, and their brethren. Then the work of God is likely to go on well when magistrates, ministers, and people, are hearty for it, and agree in their places to promote it. It was God that gave them one heart for this service, and it boded well.

III. Who were employed to further it. They appointed the *Levites to set forward the work* (*v.* 8), and they did it by *setting forward the workmen* (*v.* 9), and strengthening their hands with good and comfortable words. Note, Those that do not work themselves may yet do good service by quickening and encouraging those that do work.

IV. How God was praised at the laying of the foundation of the temple (*v.* 10, 11); the priests with the trumpets appointed by Moses, and the Levites with the cymbals appointed by David, made up a concert of music, not to please the ear, but to assist the singing of that everlasting hymn which will never be out of date, and to which our tongues should never be out of tune, *God is good, and his mercy endureth for ever,* the burden of Ps. 136. Let all the streams of mercy be traced up to the fountain. Whatever our condition is, how many soever our griefs and fears, let it be owned that God is good; and, whatever fails, that his mercy fails not. Let this be sung with application, as here; not only his mercy endures for ever, but it endures for ever towards Israel, Israel when captives in a strange land and strangers in their own land. However it be, yet *God is good to Israel* (Ps. 73:1), good to us. Let the reviving of the church's interests, when they seemed dead, be ascribed to the continuance of God's mercy for ever, for therefore the church continues.

V. How the people were affected. A remarkable mixture of various affections there was upon this occasion. Different sentiments there were among the people of God, and each expressed himself according to his sentiments, and yet there was no disagreement among them, their minds were not alienated from each other nor the common concern retarded by it. 1. Those that only knew the misery of having no temple at all praised the Lord with shouts of joy when they saw but the foundation of one laid, *v.* 11. To them even this foundation seemed great, and was as life from the dead; to their hungry souls even this was sweet. They shouted, so that *the noise was heard afar off.* Note, We ought to be thankful for the beginnings of mercy, though we have not yet come to the perfection of it; and the foundations of a temple, after long desolations, cannot but be fountains of joy to every faithful Israelite. 2. Those that remembered the glory of the first temple which Solomon built, and considered how far this was likely to be inferior to that, perhaps in dimensions, certainly in magnificence and sumptuousness, *wept with a loud voice, v.* 12. If we date the captivity with the first, from the fourth of Jehoiakim, it was about fifty-two years since the temple was burnt; if from Jeconiah's captivity, it was but fifty-nine. So that many now alive might remember it standing; and a great mercy it was to the captives that they had the lives of so many of their priests and Levites lengthened out, who could tell them what they themselves remembered of the glory of Jerusalem, to quicken them in their return. These lamented the disproportion between this temple and the former. And, (1.) There was some reason for it; and if they turned their tears into the right channel, and bewailed the sin that was the cause of this melancholy change, they did well. Sin sullies the glory of any church or people, and, when they find themselves diminished and brought low, that must bear the blame. (2.) Yet it was their infirmity to mingle those tears with the common joys and so to cast a damp upon them. They *despised the day of small things,* and were unthankful for the good they enjoyed, because it was not so much as their ancestors had, though it was much more than they deserved. In the harmony of public joys, let not us be jarring strings. It was an aggravation of the discouragement they hereby gave to the people that they were priests and Levites, who should have known and taught others how to be duly affected under various providences, and not to let the remembrance of former afflictions drown the sense of present mercies. This mixture of sorrow and joy here is a representation of this world. Some are bathing in rivers of joy, while others are drowned in floods of tears. In heaven all are singing, and none sighing; in hell all are weeping and wailing, and none rejoicing; but here on earth we can scarcely *discern the shouts of joy from the noise of the weeping.* Let us learn to *rejoice with those that do rejoice* and *weep with those that weep,* and ourselves to rejoice as though we rejoiced not, and weep as though we wept not.

CHAPTER 4

The good work of rebuilding the temple was no sooner begun than it met with opposition from those that bore ill will to it; the Samaritans were enemies to the Jews and their religion, and they set themselves to obstruct it. I. They offered to be partners in the building of it, that they might have it in their power to retard it; but they were refused (*v.* 1–3). II. They discouraged them in it, and dissuaded them from it (*v.* 4, 5). III. They basely misrepresented the undertaking, and the undertakers, to the king of Persia, by a memorial they sent him (*v.* 6–16). IV. They obtained from him an order to stop the building (*v.* 17–22), which they immediately put in execution (*v.* 23, 24).

Verses 1–5

We have here an instance of the old enmity that was put between the seed of the woman and the seed of the serpent. God's temple cannot be built, but Satan will rage, and the *gates of hell* will *fight against it.* The gospel kingdom was, in like manner, to be set up with much struggling and contention. In this respect the glory of the latter house was greater than the glory of the former, and it was more a figure of the temple of Christ's church, in that Solomon built his temple when there was *no adversary nor evil occurrent,* (1 Ki. 5:4); but this second temple was built notwithstanding great opposition, in the removing and conquering of which, and the bringing of the work to perfection at last in spite of it, the wisdom, power, and goodness of God were much glorified, and the church was encouraged to trust in him.

I. The undertakers are here called the *children of the captivity* (v. 1), which makes them look very little. They had newly come out of captivity, were born in captivity, had still the marks of their captivity upon them; though they were not now captives, they were under the control of those whose captives they had lately been. Israel was God's son, his first-born; but by their iniquity the people sold and enslaved themselves, and so became children of the captivity. But, it should seem, the thought of their being so quickened them to this work, for it was by their neglect of the temple that they lost their freedom.

II. The opposers of the undertaking are here said to be *the adversaries of Judah and Benjamin,* not the Chaldeans or Persians (they gave them no disturbance — "let them build and welcome"), but the relics of the ten tribes, and the foreigners that had joined themselves to them, and patched up that mongrel religion we had an account of, 2 Ki. 17:33. *They feared the Lord, and served their own gods too.* They are called *the people of the land, v.* 4. The worst enemies Judah and Benjamin had were those that *said they were Jews and were not,* Rev. 3:9.

III. The opposition they gave had in it much of the subtlety of the old serpent. When they heard that the temple was in building they were immediately aware that it would be a fatal blow to their superstition, and set themselves to oppose it. They had not power to do it forcibly, but they tried all the ways they could to do it effectually.

1. They offered their service to build with the Israelites only that thereby they might get an opportunity to retard the work, while they pretended to further it. Now, (1.) Their offer was plausible enough, and looked kind: *"We will build with you,* will help you to contrive, and will contribute towards the expense; *for we seek your God as you do," v.* 2. This was false, for, though they sought the same God, they did not seek him only, nor seek him in the way he appointed, and therefore did not seek him as they did. Herein they designed, if it were possible, to hinder the building of it, at least to hinder their comfortable enjoyment of it; as good almost not have it as not have it to themselves, for the pure worship of the true God and him only. Thus are the *kisses of an enemy deceitful;* his words are smoother than butter when war is in his heart. But, (2.) The refusal of their proffered service was very just, v. 3. *The chief of the fathers of Israel* were soon aware that they meant them no kindness, whatever they pretended, but really designed to do them a mischief, and therefore (though they had need enough of help if it had been such as they could confide in) told them plainly, *"You have nothing to do with us,* have no part nor lot in this matter, are not true-born Israelites nor faithful worshippers of God; *you worship you know not what,* Jn. 4:22. You are none of those with whom we dare hold communion, and therefore we ourselves will build it." They plead not to them the law of their God, which forbade them to mingle with strangers (though that especially they had an eye to), but that which they would take more notice of, the king's commission, which was directed to them only: "The king of Persia has commanded us to build this house, and we shall distrust and affront him if we call in foreign aid." Note, In doing good there is need of the *wisdom of the serpent,* as well as the *innocency of the dove,* and we have need, as it follows there, to *beware of men,* Mt. 10:16, 17. We should carefully consider with whom we are associated and on whose hand we lean. While we trust God with a pious confidence we must trust men with a prudent jealousy and caution.

2. When this plot failed they did what they could to divert them from the work and discourage them in it. They weakened their hands by telling them it was in vain to attempt it, calling them *foolish builders,* who began what they were not able to finish, and by their insinuations troubled them, and made them drive heavily in the work. All were not alike zealous in it. Those that were cool and indifferent were by these artifices drawn off from the work, which wanted their help, v. 4. And because what they themselves said the Jews would suspect to be ill meant, and not be influenced by, they, underhand, *hired counsellors against them,* who, pretending to advise them for the best, should dissuade them from proceeding, and so *frustrate their purpose (v.* 5), or dissuade the men of Tyre and Sidon from furnishing them with the timber they had bargained for (ch. 3:7); or whatever business they had at the Persian court, to solicit for any particular grants or favours, pursuant to the general edict for their liberty, there were those that were hired and lay ready to appear of counsel against them. Wonder not at the restlessness of the church's enemies in their attempts against the building of God's temple. He whom they serve, and whose work they are doing, is *unwearied* in *walking to and fro through the earth* to do mischief. And let those who discourage a good work, and weaken the hands of those that are employed in it, see whose pattern they follow.

Verses 6–16

Cyrus stedfastly adhered to the Jews' interest, and supported his own grant. It was to no purpose to offer any thing to him in prejudice of it. What he did was from a good principle, and in the fear of God, and therefore he adhered to it. But, though his reign in all was thirty years, yet after the conquest of Babylon, and his decree for the release of the Jews, some think that he reigned but three years, others seven, and then either died or gave up that part of his government, in which his successor was Ahasuerus (v. 6), called also *Artaxerxes (v.* 7), supposed to be the same that in heathen authors is called *Cambyses,* who had never taken such cognizance of the despised Jews as to concern himself for them, nor had he that knowledge of the God of Israel which his predecessor had. To him these Samaritans applied by letter for an order to stop the building of the temple; and they did it in the beginning of his reign, being resolved to lose no time when they thought they had a king for their purpose. See how watchful the church's enemies are to take the first opportunity of doing it a mischief; let not its friends be less careful to do it a kindness. Here is,

I. The general purport of the letter which they sent to the king, to inform him of this matter. It is called (v. 6) *an accusation against the inhabitants of Judah and Jerusalem.* The devil is the *accuser of the brethren* (Rev. 12:10), and he carries on his malicious designs against them, not only by accusing them himself before God, as he did Job, but by acting as a lying spirit in the mouths of his instruments, whom he employs to accuse them before magistrates and kings and to make them odious to the many and obnoxious to the mighty. Marvel not if the same arts be still used to depreciate serious godliness.

II. The persons concerned in writing this letter. The contrivers are named (v. 7) that plotted the thing, the writers (v. 8) that put it into form, and the subscribers (v. 9) that concurred in it and joined with them in this representation, this misrepresentation I should call it. Now see here, 1. How the *rulers take counsel together against the Lord* and his temple, with their companions. The building of the temple would do them no harm, yet they appear against it with the utmost concern and virulence, perhaps because the prophets of the God of Israel had foretold the *famishing* and *perishing* of all the *gods of the heathen,* Zep. 2:11; Jer. 10:11. 2. How the people concurred with them in imagining this vain thing. They followed the cry, though ignorant of the merits of the cause. All the several colonies of that plantation (nine are here mentioned), who had their denomination from the cities or countries of Assyria, Chaldea, Persia, etc., whence they came, set their hands, by their representatives, to this letter. Perhaps they were incensed against these returned Jews because many of the ten tribes were among them, whose estates they had got into their possession, and of whom they were therefore jealous, lest they should attempt the recovery of them hereafter.

III. A copy of the letter itself, which Ezra inserts here out of the records of the kingdom of Persia, into which it had been entered; and it is well we have it, that we may see whence the like methods, still taken to expose good people and baffle good designs, are copied.

1. They represent themselves as very loyal to the government, and greatly concerned for the honour and interest of it, and would have it thought that the king had no such loving faithful subjects in all his dominions as they were, none so sensible of their obligations to him, v. 14. *Because we are salted with the salt of the palace* (so it is in the margin), "we have our salary from the court, and could no more live without it than flesh could be preserved without salt;" or, as some think, their pay or pension was sent them in salt; or "Because we had our education in the palace, and were brought up at the king's table," as we find, Dan. 1:5. These were those whom he intended to prefer; they did *eat their portion of the king's meat.* "Now, in consideration of this, *it is not meet for us to see the king's dishonour;"* and therefore they urge him to stop the building of the temple, which would certainly be the king's dishonour more than any thing else. Note, A secret enmity to Christ and his gospel is often gilded over with a pretended affection to Caesar and his power. The Jews hated the Roman government, and yet, to serve a turn, could cry, *We have no king but Caesar.* But (to allude to this), if those that lived upon the crown thought themselves bound in gratitude thus to support the interest of it, much more reason have we thus to argue ourselves into a pious concern for God's honour; *we have our maintenance from the God of heaven* and are *salted with his salt,* live upon his bounty and are the care of his providence; and therefore it is not *meet for us to see his dishonour* without resenting it and doing what we can to prevent it.

2. They represent the Jews as disloyal, and dangerous to the government, that Jerusalem was *the rebellious and bad city* (v. 12), *hurtful to kings and provinces, v.* 15. See how Jerusalem, *the joy of the whole earth* (Ps. 48:2), is here reproached as the scandal of the whole earth. The enemies of the church could not do the bad things they design against it if they did not first give it a bad name. Jerusalem had been a loyal city to its rightful princes, and its present inhabitants were as well affected to the king and his government as any of his provinces whatsoever. Daniel, who was a Jew, had lately approved himself so faithful to his prince that his worst enemies could find no fault in his management, Dan. 6:4. But thus was Elijah most unjustly charged with troubling Israel, the apostles with *turning the world upside down,* and Christ himself with *perverting the nation* and *forbidding to give tribute to Caesar;* and we must not think it strange if the same game be still played. Now here,

(1.) Their history of what was past was invidious, that *within this city sedition had been moved of old time,* and, for *that cause, it was destroyed, v.* 15. It cannot be denied but that there was some colour given for this suggestion by the attempts of Jehoiakim and Zedekiah to shake off the yoke of the king of Babylon, which, if they had kept close to their religion and the temple they were now rebuilding, they would never have come under. But it must be considered, [1.] That they were themselves, and their ancestors, sovereign princes, and their efforts to recover their rights, if there had not been in them the violation of an oath, for aught I know, would have been justifiable, and successful too, had they taken the right method and made their peace with God first. [2.] Though these Jews, and their princes, had been guilty of rebellion, yet it was unjust therefore to fasten this as an indelible brand upon this city, as if that must for ever after go under the name of *the rebellious and bad city.* The Jews, in their captivity, had given such specimens of good behaviour as were sufficient, with any reasonable men, to roll away that one reproach; for they were instructed (and we have reason to hope that they observed their instructions) to *seek the peace of the city where* they were *captives* and *pray to the Lord for it,* Jer. 29:7. It was therefore very unfair, though not uncommon, thus to impute the iniquity of the fathers to the children.

(2.) Their information concerning what was now doing was grossly false in matter of fact. Very careful they were to inform the king that the Jews had *set up the walls of this city,* nay, had *finished* them (so it is in the *margin)* and *joined the foundations* (*v.* 12), when this was far from being the case. They had only begun to build the temple, which Cyrus commanded them to do, but, as for the walls, there was nothing done nor designed towards the repair of them, as appears by the condition they were in many years after (Neh. 1:3), all in ruins. *What shall be given,* and what *done, to these false tongues,* nay, which is worse, these false pens? *sharp arrows,* doubtless, *of the mighty,* and *coals of juniper,* Ps. 120:3, 4. If they had not been perfectly lost to all virtue and honour they would not, and if they had not been very secure of the king's countenance they durst not, have written that to the king which all their neighbours knew to be a notorious lie. See Prov. 29:12.

(3.) Their prognostics of the consequences were altogether groundless and absurd. They were very confident, and would have the king believe it upon their word, that if this city should be built, not only the Jews would *pay no toll, tribute, or custom* (*v.* 13), but (since a great lie is as soon spoken as a little one) that the king would have no portion at all on this side the river (*v.* 16), that all the countries on this side Euphrates would instantly revolt, drawn in to do so by their example; and, if the prince in possession should connive at this, he would wrong, not only himself, but his successors: *Thou shalt endamage the revenue of the kings.* See how every line in this letter breathes both the subtlety and malice of the old serpent.

Verses 17–24

Here we have,

I. The orders which the king of Persia gave, in answer to the information sent him by the Samaritans against the Jews. He suffered himself to be imposed upon by their fraud and falsehood, took no care to examine the allegations of their petition concerning that which the Jews were now doing, but took it for granted that the charge was true, and was very willing to gratify them with an order of council to stay proceedings. 1. He consulted the records concerning Jerusalem, and found that it had indeed rebelled against the king of Babylon, and therefore that it was, as they called it, a *bad city* (*v.* 19), and withal that in times past kings had reigned there, to whom all the countries on that side the river had been tributaries (*v.* 20), and that therefore there was danger that if ever they were able (which they were never likely to be) they would claim them again. Thus he says as they said, and pretends to give a reason for so doing. See the hard fate of princes, who must see and hear with other men's eyes and ears, and give judgment upon things as they are represented to them, though often represented falsely. God's judgment is always just because he sees things as they are, and it is according to truth. 2. He appointed these Samaritans to stop the building of the city immediately, till further orders should be given about it, *v.* 21, 22. Neither they, in their letter, nor he, in his order, make any mention of the temple, and the building of that, because both they and he knew that they had not only a permission, but a command, from Cyrus to rebuild that, which even these Samaritans had not the confidence to move for the repeal of. They spoke only of the *city:* "Let not *that* be built," that is, as a city with walls and gates; "whatever you do, prevent *that, lest damage grow to the hurt of the kings:*" he would not that the crown should lose by his wearing it.

II. The use which the enemies of the Jews made of these orders, so fraudulently obtained; upon the receipt of them they went up *in haste to Jerusalem, v.* 23. *Their feet ran to evil,* Prov. 1:16. They were impatient till the builders were served with this prohibition, which they produced as their warrant to *make them cease by force and power.* As they abused the king in obtaining this order by their misinformations, so they abused him in the execution of it; for the order was only to prevent the walling of the *city,* but, having force and power on their side, they construed it as relating to the *temple,* for it was that to which they had an ill will, and which they only wanted some colour to hinder the building of. There was indeed a general clause in the order, to *cause these men to cease,* which had reference to their complaint about building the walls; but they applied it to the building of the temple. See what need we have to pray, not only for kings, but for all in authority under them, and *the governors sent by them,* because the *quietness* and *peaceableness* of our lives, *in all godliness and honesty,* depend very much upon the integrity and wisdom of inferior magistrates, as well as the supreme. The consequence was that *the work of the house of God ceased* for a time, through the power and insolence of its enemies; and so, through the coldness and indifference of its friends, it stood still till the second year of Darius Hystaspes, for to me it seems clear by the thread of this sacred history that it was that Darius, *v.* 24. Though now a stop was put to it by the violence of the Samaritans, yet that they might soon after have gone on by connivance, if they had had a due affection to the work, appears by this, that before they had that express warrant from the king for doing it (*ch.* 6) they were reproved by the prophets for not doing it, *ch.* 5:1,, compared with Hag. 1:1, etc. If they had taken due care to inform Cambyses of the truth of this case, perhaps he would have recalled his order; but, for aught I know, some of the builders were almost as willing it should cease as the adversaries themselves were. At some periods the church has suffered more by the coldness of its friends than by the heat of its enemies; but both together commonly make church-work slow work.

CHAPTER 5

We left the temple-work at a full stop; but, being God's work, it shall be revived, and here we have an account of the reviving of it. It was hindered by might and power, but it was set a-going again "by the Spirit of the Lord of hosts." Now here we are told how that blessed Spirit, I. Warmed its cool-hearted friends and excited them to built (*v.* 1, 2). II. Cooled its hot-headed enemies, and brought them to better tempers; for, though they secretly disliked the work as much as those in the foregoing chapter, yet, 1. They were more mild towards the builders (*v.* 3–5). 2. They were more fair in their representation of the matter to the king, of which we have here an account (*v.* 6–17).

Verses 1–2

Some reckon that the building of the temple was suspended for only nine years; I am willing to believe that fifteen years were the utmost. During this time they had an altar and a tabernacle, which no doubt they made use of. When we cannot do what we would we must do what we can in the service of God, and be sorry we can do no better. But the counsellors that were hired to hinder the work (*ch.* 4:5) told them, and perhaps with a pretence to inspiration, that the time had not come for the building of the temple (Hag. 1:2), urging that it was long ere the time came for the building of Solomon's temple; and thus the people were made easy in their own *ceiled houses,* while *God's house lay waste.* Now here we are told how life was put into that good cause which seemed to lie dead.

I. They had two good ministers, who, in God's name, earnestly persuaded them to put the wheel of business in motion again. Observe,

1. Who these ministers were, namely, the prophets Haggai and Zechariah, who both began to prophesy in the second year of Darius, as appears, Hag. 1:1; Zec. 1:1. Note, (1.) The temple of God among men is to be built by prophecy, not by secular force (that often hinders it, but seldom furthers it), but by *the word of God.* As the *weapons of our warfare,* so the instruments of our building, *are not carnal,* but *spiritual,* and they are the ministers of the gospel that are the master-builders. (2.) It is the business of God's prophets to stir up God's people to that which is good, and to help them in it, to strengthen their hands, and, by suitable considerations fetched from the word of God, to quicken them to their duty and encourage them in it. (3.) It is a sign that God has mercy in store for a people when he raises up prophets among them to be their helpers in the way and work of God, their guides, overseers, and rulers.

2. To whom they were sent. They prophesied unto the *Jews* (for, as to them pertained the giving of the law, so also the gift of prophecy, and therefore they are called *the children of the prophets,* Acts 3:25, because they were educated under their tuition and instruction), *even unto them, upon them,* even *upon them* (so it is in the original), as Ezekiel prophesied *upon the dry bones,* that they might live, Eze. 37:4. They prophesied *against* them (so bishop Patrick), for they reproved them because they did not build the temple. The word of God, if it be not received now as a testimony to us, will be received now as a testimony to us, will be received another day as a testimony against us, and will judge us.

3. Who sent them. They prophesied in the name, or (as some read it) *in the cause,* or for the sake, *of the God of Israel;* they spoke by commission from him, and argued from his authority over them, his interest in them, and the concern of his glory among them.

II. They had two good magistrates, who were forward and active in this work. Zerubbabel their chief prince, and Jeshua their chief priest, *v.* 2. Those that are in places of dignity and power ought with their dignity to put honour upon and with their power to put life into every good work: thus it becomes those that preceded, and those that preside, with an exemplary care and zeal to *fulfil all righteousness* and to *go before in a good work.* These great men thought it no disparagement to them, but a happiness, to be taught and prescribed to by the prophets of the Lord, and were glad of their help in reviving this good work. Read the first chapter of the prophecy of Haggai here (for that is the best comment on these two verses) and see what great things God does by his word, which he magnifies above all his name, and by his Spirit working with it.

Verses 3–17

We have here, I. The cognizance which their neighbours soon took of the reviving of this good work. A jealous eye, it seems, they had upon them, and no sooner did the Spirit of God stir up the friends of the temple to appear for it than the evil spirit stirred up its enemies to appear against it. While the people built and ceiled their own houses their enemies gave them no molestation (Hag. 1:4), though the king's order was to put a stop to the building of the city (*ch.* 4:21); but when they fell to work again at the temple then the alarm was taken, and all heads were at work to hinder them, *v.* 3, 4. The adversaries are here named: *Tatnai* and *Shethar-boznai.* The governors we read of (*ch.* 4) were, it is probable, displaced at the beginning of this reign, as is usual. It is the policy of princes often to change their deputies, proconsuls, and rulers of provinces. These, though real enemies to the building of the temple, were men of better temper than the other, and made some conscience of telling truth. If *all men have not faith* (2 Th. 3:2), it is well some have, and a sense of honour. The church's enemies are not all equally wicked and unreasonable. The historian begins to relate what passed between the builders and those inquisitors (*v.* 3, 4), but breaks off his account, and refers to the ensuing copy of the letter they sent to the king, where the same appears more fully and at large, which he began to abridge (*v.* 4), or make an extract out of, though, upon second thoughts, he inserted the whole.

II. The care which the divine Providence took of this good work (*v.* 5): *The eye of their God was upon the elders of the Jews,* who were active in the work, so that their enemies could not cause them to cease, as they would have done, till the matter came to Darius. They desired they would only cease till they had instructions from the king about it. But they would not so much as yield them that, for *the eye of God was upon them,* even their God. And, 1. That baffled their enemies, infatuated and enfeebled them, and protected the builders from their malicious designs. While we are employed in God's work we are taken under his special protection; his eye is upon us for good, seven eyes upon one stone in his temple; see Zec. 3:9; 4:10. 2. That quickened them. The elders of the Jews saw *the eye of God upon them,* to observe what they did and own them in what they did well, and then they had courage enough to face their enemies and to go on vigorously with their work, notwithstanding all the opposition they met with. our eye upon God, observing his eye upon us, will keep us to our duty and encourage us in it when the difficulties are ever so discouraging.

III. The account they sent to the king of this matter, in which we may observe,

1. How fully the elders of the Jews gave the Samaritans an account of their proceedings. They, finding them both busy and prosperous, that all hands were at work to run up this building and that it went on rapidly, put these questions to them: — "By what authority do you do these things, and who gave you that authority? Who set you to work? Have you that which will bear you out?" To this they answered that they had sufficient warrant to do what they did; for, (1.) "*We are the servants of the God of heaven and earth.* The God we worship is not a local deity, and therefore we cannot be charged with making a faction, or setting up a sect, in building this temple to his honour: but

we pay our homage to a God on whom the whole creation depends, and therefore ought to be protected and assisted by all and hindered by none." It is the wisdom as well as duty of kings to countenance the servants of the *God of heaven.* (2.) "We have a prescription to this house; it was built for the honour of our God by Solomon many ages ago. It is no novel invention of our own; we are but *raising the foundations of many generations,"* Isa. 58:12. (3.) "It was to punish us for our sins that we were, for a time, put out of the possession of this house; not because the gods of the nations had prevailed against our God, but because we had provoked him (*v.* 12), for which he delivered us and our temple into the hands of the king of Babylon, but never intended thereby to put a final period to our religion. We were only suspended for a time, not deprived for ever." (4.) "We have the royal decree of Cyrus to justify us and bear us out in what we do. He not only permitted and allowed us, but charged and commanded us to build this house (*v.* 13), and to build it in its place (*v.* 15), the same place where it had stood before." He ordered this, not only in compassion to the Jews, but in veneration of their God, saying, *He is the God.* He also delivered the vessels of the temple to one whom he entrusted to see them restored to their ancient place and use, *v.* 14. And they had these to show in confirmation of what they alleged. (5.) "The building was begun according to this order as soon as ever we had returned, so that we have not forfeited the benefit of the order for want of pursuing it in time; still it has been in building, but, because we have met with opposition, it is not finished." But, observe, they mention not the falsehood and malice of the former governors, nor make any complaint of them, though they had cause enough, to teach us not to render bitterness for bitterness, nor the most just reproach for that which is most unjust, but to think it enough if we can obtain fair treatment for the future, without an invidious reference to former injuries, *v.* 16. This is the account they give of their proceedings, not asking what authority they had to examine them, nor upbraiding them with their idolatry, and superstitions, and medley religion. Let us learn hence with meekness and fear to *give a reason of the hope that is in us* (1 Pt. 3:15), rightly to understand, and then readily to declare, what we do in God's service and why we do it.

2. How fairly the Samaritans represented this to the king. (1.) They called the temple at Jerusalem the *house of the great God* (*v.* 8); for though the Samaritans, as it should seem, had yet gods many and lords many, they owned the God of Israel to be the *great God,* who is above all gods. "It is the house of the *great God,* and therefore we dare not oppose the building of it without orders from thee." (2.) They told him truly what was done, not stating, as their predecessors did, that they were fortifying the city as if they intended war, but only that they were rearing the temple as those that intended worship, *v.* 8. (3.) They fully represented their plea, told him what they had to say for themselves, and were willing that the cause should be set in a true light. (4.) They left it to the king to consult the records whether Cyrus had indeed made such a decree, and then to give directions as he should think fit, *v.* 17. We have reason to think that if Artaxerxes, in the foregoing chapter, had had the Jews' cause as fairly represented to him as it was here to Darius, he would not have ordered the work to be hindered. God's people could not be persecuted if they were not belied, could not be baited if they were not dressed up in bears' skins. Let but the cause of God and truth be fairly stated, and fairly heard, and it will keep its ground.

CHAPTER 6

How solemnly the foundation of the temple was laid we read in *ch.* 3. How slowly the building went on, and with how much difficulty, we found in *ch.* 4 and 5. But how gloriously the topstone was at length brought forth with shoutings we find in this chapter; and even we, at this distance of time, when we read of it, may cry, "Grace, grace to it." As for God, his work is perfect; it may be slow work, but it will be sure work. We have here, I. A recital of the decree of Cyrus for the building of the temple (*v.* 1–5). II. The enforcing of that decree by a new order from Darius for the perfecting of that work (*v.* 6–12). III. The finishing of it thereupon (*v.* 13–15). IV. The solemn dedication of it when it was built (*v.* 16–18), and the handselling of it (as I may say) with the celebration of the passover (*v.* 19–22). And now we may say that in Judah and Jerusalem things went well, very well.

Verses 1–12

We have here, I. The decree of Cyrus for the building of the temple repeated. To this the Samaritans referred because the Jews pleaded it, and perhaps hoped it would not be found, and then their plea would be over-ruled and a stop put to their work. Search was ordered to be made for it among the records; for, it seems, the tribes had not taken care to provide themselves with an authentic copy of it, which might have stood them in good stead, but they must appeal to the original. It was looked for in Babylon (*v.* 1), where Cyrus was when he signed it. But, when it was not found there, Darius did not make that a pretence to conclude that therefore there was no such decree, and thereupon to give judgment against the Jews; but it is probable, having himself heard that such a decree was certainly made, he ordered the rolls in other places to be searched, and at length it was found at Achmetha, in the province of the Medes, *v.* 2. Perhaps some that durst not destroy it, yet hid it there, out of ill will to the Jews, that they might lose the benefit of it. But Providence so ordered that it came to light; and it is here inserted, *v.* 3–5. 1. Here is a warrant for the building of the temple: *Let the house of God at Jerusalem,* yea, *let that house be built* (so it may be read), within such and such dimensions, and with such and such materials. 2. A warrant for the taking of the expenses of the building out of the king's revenue, *v.* 4. We do not find that they had received what was here ordered them, the face of things at court being soon changed. 3. A warrant for the restoring of the vessels and utensils of the temple, which Nebuchadnezzar had taken away (*v.* 5), with an order that the priests, the Lord's ministers, should return them all to their places in the house of God.

II. The confirmation of it by a decree of Darius, grounded upon it and in pursuance of it.

1. The decree of Darius is very explicit and satisfactory. (1.) He forbids his officers to do any thing in opposition to the building of the temple. The manner of expression intimates that he knew they had a mind to hinder it: *Be you far hence* (*v.* 6); *let the work of this house of God alone, v.* 7. Thus was the wrath of the enemy *made to praise God* and the remainder thereof did he restrain.

(2.) He orders them out of his own revenue to assist the builders with money, [1.] For carrying on the building, *v.* 8. Herein he pursues the example of Cyrus, *v.* 4. [2.] For maintaining the sacrifices there when it was built, *v.* 9. He ordered that they should be supplied with every thing they wanted both for burnt-offerings and meat-offerings. He was content it should be a rent-charge upon his revenue, and ordered it to be paid every day, and this without fail, that they might offer sacrifices and prayers with them (for the patriarchs, when they offered sacrifice, *called on the name of the Lord,* so did Samuel, Elijah, and others) for the life (that is, the happiness and prosperity) of the king and his sons, *v.* 10. See here how he gives honour, *First,* To Israel's God, whom he calls once and again the *God of heaven. Secondly,* To his ministers, in ordering his commissioners to give out supplies for the temple service at the appointment of the priests. Those that thought to control them must now be, in this matter, at their command. It was a new thing for God's priests to have such an interest in the public money. *Thirdly,* To prayer: *That they may pray for the life of the king.* He knew they were a praying people, and had heard that God was nigh to them in all that which they called upon him for. He was sensible he needed their prayers and might receive benefit by them, and was kind to them in order that he might have an interest in their prayers. It is the duty of God's people to pray for those that are in authority over them, not only for the good and gentle, but also for the forward; but they are particularly bound in gratitude to pray for their protectors and benefactors; and it is the wisdom of princes to desire their prayers, and to engage them. Let not the greatest princes despise the prayers of the meanest saints; it is desirable to have them for us, and dreadful to have them against us.

(3.) He enforces his decree with a penalty (*v.* 11): "Let none either oppose the work and service of the temple or withhold the supports granted to it by the crown upon pain of death. If any alter this decree, let him be (*hanged before his own door* as we say), hanged upon a beam of his own house, and, as an execrable man, *let his house be made a dunghill."*

(4.) He entails a divine curse upon all those kings and people that should ever have any hand in the destruction of this house, *v.* 12. What he would not do himself for the protection of the temple he desired that God, *to whom vengeance belongs,* would do. This bespeaks him zealous in the cause; and though this temple was, at length, most justly destroyed by the righteous hand of God, yet perhaps the Romans, who were the instruments of that destruction, felt the effects of this curse, for that empire sensibly declined ever after.

2. From all this we learn, (1.) That the heart of kings is in the hand of God, and he turns it which way soever he pleases; what they are he makes them to be, for he is *King of kings.* (2.) That when God's time has come for the accomplishing of his gracious purposes concerning his church he will raise up instruments to promote them from whom such good service was not expected. *The earth sometimes helps the woman* (Rev. 12:16), and those are made use of for the defence of religion who have little religion themselves. (3.) That what is intended for the prejudice of the church has often, by the overruling providence of God, been made serviceable to it, Phil. 1:12. The enemies of the Jews, in appealing to Darius, hoped to get an order to suppress them, but, instead of that, they got an order to supply them. Thus *out of the eater comes forth meat.* The apocryphal Esdras (or Ezra), Book 1 *ch.* 3 and 4, gives another account of this decree in favour of the Jews, that Darius had vowed that if ever he came to the kingdom he would build the temple at Jerusalem, and that Zerubbabel, who was one of his attendants (whereas it is plain here that he was now at Jerusalem), for making an ingenious discourse before him on that subject *(Great is the truth and will prevail),* was told to ask what recompence he would, and asked only for this order, in pursuance of the king's vow.

Verses 13–22

Here we have, I. The Jews' enemies made their friends. When they received this order from the king they came with as much haste to encourage and assist the work as their predecessors had done to put a stop to it, *ch.* 4:23. What the king ordered they did, and, because they would not be thought to do it with reluctance, they *did it speedily, v.* 13. The king's moderation made them, contrary to their own inclination, moderate too.

II. The building of the temple carried on, and finished in a little time, *v.* 14, 15. Now the *elders of the Jews built* with cheerfulness. For aught I know, the elders themselves laboured at it *with their own hands;* and, if they did, it was no disparagement to their eldership, but an encouragement to the other workmen. 1. They found themselves bound to it *by the commandment of the God of Israel,* who had given them power that they might use it in his service. 2. They found themselves shamed into it by the commandment of the heathen kings, Cyrus formerly, Darius now, and Artaxerxes some time after. Can the elders of the Jews be remiss in this good work when these foreign princes appear so warm in it? Shall native Israelites grudge their pains and care about this building when strangers grudge not to be at the expense of it? 3. They found themselves encouraged in it by the prophesying of Haggai and Zechariah, who, it is likely, represented to them (as bishop Patrick suggests) the wonderful goodness of God in inclining the heart of the king of Persia to favour them thus. And now the work went on so prosperously that, in four hears' time, it was brought to perfection. *As for God, his work is perfect.* The gospel church, that spiritual temple, is long in the building, but it will be finished at last, when the mystical body is completed. Every believer is a *living temple, building up himself in his most holy faith.* Much opposition is given to this work by Satan and our own corruptions. We trifle, and proceed in it with many stops and pauses; but he that has *begun the good work* will see it performed, and will *bring forth judgment unto victory. Spirits of just men* will be *made perfect.*

III. The dedication of the temple. When it was built, being designed only for sacred uses, *they showed by an example how it should be used,* which (says bishop Patrick) is the proper sense of the word *dedicate.* They entered upon it with solemnity and probably with a public declaration of the separating of it from common uses and the surrender of it to the honour of God, to be employed in his worship. 1. The persons employed in this service were not only *the priests and Levites* who officiated, but *the children of Israel,* some of each of the *twelve tribes,* though Judah and Benjamin were the chief, and *the rest of the children of the captivity* or *transportation,* which intimates that there were many besides the children of Israel, of other nations, who transported themselves with them, and became proselytes to their religion, unless we read it, *even the remnant of the children of the captivity,* and then, we may suppose, notice is hereby taken of their mean and afflicted condition, because the consideration of that helped to make them devout and serious in this and other religious exercises. A sad change! The *children of Israel* have become *children of the captivity,* and there appears but a remnant of *them,* according to that prediction (Isa. 7:3), *Shear-jashub — The remnant shall return.* 2. The sacrifices that were offered upon this occasion were *bullocks, rams, and lambs* (*v.* 17), for burnt-offerings and peace-offerings; not to be compared, in number, with what had been offered at the dedication of Solomon's temple, but, being according to their present ability, they were accepted, for, *after a great trial of affliction, the abundance of their joy, and their deep poverty, abounded to the riches of their liberality,* 2 Co. 8:2. These hundreds were more to them than Solomon's thousands were to him. But, besides these, they offered twelve he-goats for sin-offerings, one for every tribe, to make atonement for their sins, which they looked upon as necessary in order to the acceptance of their services. Thus, by getting iniquity taken away, they would free themselves from that which had been the sting of their late troubles, and which, if not removed, would be a worm at the root of their present comforts. 3. This service was performed with joy. They were all glad to see the temple built and the concerns of it in so good a posture. Let us learn to welcome holy ordinances with joy and attend on them with pleasure. Let us serve the Lord with gladness. Whatever we dedicate to God, let it be done with joy that he will please to accept of it. 4. When they dedicated the house they settled the household. Small comfort could they have in the temple without the temple service, and therefore they *set the priests in their divisions* and *the Levites in their courses, v.* 18. Having set up the worship of God in this dedication, they took care to keep it up, and made *the book of Moses* their rule, to which they had an eye in this establishment. Though the temple service could not now be performed with so much pomp and plenty as formerly, because of their poverty, yet perhaps it was performed with as much purity and close adherence to the divine institution as ever, which was the true glory of it. No beauty like the beauty of holiness.

IV. The celebration of the passover in the newly-erected temple. Now that they were newly delivered out of their bondage in Babylon it was seasonable to commemorate their deliverance out of their bondage in Egypt. Fresh mercies should put us in mind of former mercies. We may suppose that they had kept the passover, after a sort, every year since their return, for they had an altar and a tabernacle. But they were liable to frequent disturbances from their enemies, were straitened for room, and had not conveniences about them, so that they could not do it with due solemnity till the temple was built; and now they made a joyful festival of it, it falling out in the next month after the temple was finished and dedicated, *v.* 19. Notice is here taken, 1. Of the purity of the priests and Levites that *killed the passover, v.* 20. In Hezekiah's time the priests were many of them under blame for not purifying themselves. But now it is observed, to their praise, that *they were purified together, as one man* (so the word is); they were unanimous both in their resolutions and in their endeavours to make and keep themselves ceremonially clean for this solemnity; they joined together in their preparations, that they might help one another, so that all of them were pure, to a man. The purity of ministers adds much to the beauty of their ministrations; so does their unity. 2. Of the proselytes that communicated with them in this ordinance: *All such as had separated themselves unto them,* had left their country and the superstitions of it and cast in their lot with the Israel of God, and had *turned from the filthiness of the heathen of the land,* both their idolatries and immoralities, *to seek the Lord God of Israel* as their God, did eat the passover. See how the proselytes, the converts, are described. They separated themselves from the filthiness of sin and fellowship with sinners, joined themselves with the Israel of God in conformity and communion, and set themselves to seek the God of Israel; and those that do so in sincerity, though strangers and foreigners, are welcome to eat of the gospel feast, as *fellow-citizens with the saints and of the household of God.* 3. Of the great pleasure and satisfaction wherewith they *kept the feast of unleavened bread, v.* 22. *The Lord had made them joyful,* had given them both cause to rejoice and hearts to rejoice. It was now about twenty years since the foundation of this temple was laid, and we may suppose the old men that then wept at the remembrance of the first temple were most of them dead by this time, so that now there were no tears mingled with their joys. Those that are, upon good grounds, joyful, have therefore reason to be thankful, because it is God that *makes them to rejoice.* He is the fountain whence all the streams of our joy flow. God has promised to all those who take hold of his covenant that *he will make them joyful in his house of prayer.* The particular occasion they had for joy at this time was that God had *turned the heart* of the emperor to them, to *strengthen their hands.* If those that have been, or who we feared would have been, against us, prove to be for us, we may rejoice in it as a token for good, that *our ways please the Lord* (Prov. 16:7), and he must have the glory of it.

CHAPTER 7

Ezra's precious name saluted us, at first, in the title of the book, but in the history we have not met with it till this chapter introduces him into public action in another reign, that of Artaxerxes. Zerubbabel and Jeshua we will suppose, by this time, to have grown old, if not gone off; nor do we hear any more of Haggai and Zechariah; they have finished their testimony. What shall become of the cause of God and Israel when these useful instruments are laid aside? Trust God, who has the residue of the Spirit, to raise up others in their room. Ezra here, and Nehemiah in the next book, are as serviceable in their days as those were in theirs. Here is, I. An account, in general, of Ezra himself, and of his expedition to Jerusalem for the public good (*v.* 1–10). II. A copy of the commission which Artaxerxes gave him (*v.* 11–26). III. His thankfulness to God for it (*v.* 27, 28). The next chapter will give us a more particular narrative of his associates, his journey, and his arrival at Jerusalem.

Verses 1–10

Here is, I. Ezra's pedigree. He was one of the sons of Aaron, a priest. Him God chose to be an instrument of good to Israel, that he might put honour upon the priesthood, the glory of which had been much eclipsed by the captivity. He is said to be *the son of Seraiah,* that Seraiah, as is supposed, whom the king of Babylon put to death when he sacked Jerusalem, 2 Ki. 25:18, 21. If we take the shortest computation, it was seventy-five years since Seraiah died; many reckon it much longer, and, because they suppose Ezra called out in the prime of his time to public service, do therefore think that Seraiah was not his immediate parent, but his grandfather or great-grandfather, but that he was the first eminent person that occurred in his genealogy upwards, which is carried up here as high as Aaron, yet leaving out many for brevity-sake, which may be supplied from 1 Chr. 6:4, etc. He was a younger brother, or his father was Jozadak, the father of Jeshua, so that he was not high priest, but nearly allied to the high priest.

II. His character. Though of the younger house, his personal qualifications made him very eminent. 1. He was a man of great learning, a scribe, a *ready scribe, in the law of Moses, v.* 6. He was very much conversant with the scriptures, especially the writings of Moses, had the words ready and was well acquainted with the sense and meaning of them. It is to be feared that learning ran low among the Jews in Babylon; but Ezra was instrumental to revive it. The Jews say that he collected and collated all the copies of the law he could find out, and published an accurate edition of it, with all the prophetical books, historical and poetical, that were given by divine inspiration, and so made up the canon of the Old Testament, with the addition of the prophecies and histories of his own time. If he was raised up of God, and qualified and inclined to do this, all generations have reason to call him blessed, and to bless God for him. God sent to the Jews *prophets and scribes,* Mt. 23:34. Ezra went under the latter denomination. Now that prophecy was about to cease it was time to promote scripture-knowledge, pursuant to the counsel of God by the last of the prophets, Mal. 4:4. *Remember the law of Moses.* Gospel ministers are called *scribes instructed to the kingdom of heaven* (Mt. 13:52), New-Testament scribes. It was a pity that such a worthy name as this should be worn, as it was in the degenerate ages of the Jewish church, by men who were professed enemies to Christ and his gospel *(Woe unto you, scribes and Pharisees),* who were learned in the letter of the law, but strangers to the spirit of it. 2. He was a man of great piety and holy zeal (*v.* 10): *He had prepared his heart to seek the law of the Lord,* etc. (1.) That which he chose for his study was *the law of the Lord.* The Chaldeans, among whom he was born and bred, were famed for literature, especially the study of the stars, to which, being a studious man, we may suppose that Ezra was tempted to apply himself. But he got over the temptation; the law of his God was more to him than all the writings of their magicians and astrologers, which he knew enough of with good reason to despise them. (2.) He *sought the law of the Lord,* that is, he made it his business to enquire into it, searched the scriptures, and sought the knowledge of God, of his mind and will, in the scriptures, which is to be found there, but not without seeking. (3.) He made conscience of doing according to it; he set it before him as his rule, formed his sentiments and temper by it, and managed himself in his whole conversation according to it. This use we must make of our knowledge of the scriptures; for happy are we if we do what we know of the will of God. (4.) He set himself *to teach Israel the statutes and judgments* of that law. What he knew he was willing to communicate for the good of others; for *the ministration of the Spirit is given to every man to profit withal.* But observe the method: he first learned and then taught, sought the law of the Lord and so laid up a good treasure, and then instructed others and laid out what he had laid up. He also first did and then taught, practised the commandments himself and then directed others in the practice of them; thus his example confirmed his doctrine. (5.) He *prepared his heart* to do all this, or he fixed his heart. He took pains in his studies, and thoroughly furnished himself for what he designed, and then put on resolution to proceed and persevere in them, and thus he became a ready scribe. Moses in Egypt, Ezra in Babylon, and both in captivity, were wonderfully fitted for eminent services to the church.

III. His expedition to Jerusalem for the good of his country: *He went up from Babylon* (*v.* 6), and, in four months' time, came to Jerusalem, *v.* 8. It was strange that such a man as he staid so long in Babylon after his brethren had gone up; but God sent him not thither till he had work for him to do there; and none went but those *whose spirits God raised* to go up. Some think that this Artaxerxes was the same with that Darius whose decree we had (*ch.* 6), and that Ezra came the very year after the temple was finished: that was the sixth year, this the seventh (*v.* 8), so Dr. Lightfoot. My worthy and learned friend, lately deceased, Mr. Talents, in his chronological tables, places it about fifty-seven years after the finishing of the temple; others further on. I have only to observe, 1. How kind the king was to him. He *granted him all his request,* whatever he desired to put him into a capacity to serve his country. 2. How kind his people were to him. When he went many more went with him, because they desired not to stay in Babylon when he had gone thence, and because they would venture to dwell in Jerusalem when he had gone thither. 3. How kind his God was to him. He obtained this favour from his king and country by *the good hand of the Lord that was upon him, v.* 6, 9. Note, Every creature is that to us which God makes it to be, and from him our judgment proceeds. As we must see the events that *shall* occur in the hand of God, so we must see the hand of God in the events that *do* occur, and acknowledge him with thankfulness when we have reason to call it his *good hand.*

Verses 11–26

We have here the commission which the Persian emperor granted to Ezra, giving him authority to act for the good of the Jews; and it is very ample and full, and beyond what could have been expected. The commission runs, we suppose, in the usual form: *Artaxerxes, King of kings.* This however is too high a title for any mortal man to assume; he was indeed king of some kings, but to speak as if he were king of all kings was to usurp *his* prerogative who hath *all power both in heaven and in earth.* He sends greeting to his trusty and well-beloved Ezra, whom he calls a *scribe of the law of the God of heaven* (*v.* 12), a title which (it seems by this) Ezra valued himself by, and desired no other, no, not when he was advanced to the proconsular dignity. He reckoned it more his honour to be a *scribe of God's law* than to be a peer or prince of the empire. Let us observe the articles of this commission.

I. He gives Ezra leave to go up to Jerusalem, and as many of his countrymen as pleased to go up with him, *v.* 13. He and they were captives, and therefore they would not quit his dominions without his royal license.

II. He gives him authority to enquire into the affairs of Judah and Jerusalem, *v.* 14. The rule of his enquiry was to be *the law of his God, which was in his hand.* He must enquire whether the Jews, in their religion, had and did according to that law — whether the temple was built, the priesthood was settled, and the sacrifices were offered conformably to the divine appointment. If, upon enquiry, he found any thing amiss, he must see to get it amended, and, like Titus in Crete, must *set in order the things that were wanting,* Tit. 1:5. Thus is God's law magnified and made honourable, and thus are the Jews restored to their ancient privilege of governing themselves by that law, and are no longer under *the statutes that were not good,* the statutes of their oppressors, Eze. 20:25.

III. He entrusts him with the money that was freely given by the king himself and his counsellors, and collected among his subjects, for the service of the house of God, *v.* 15, 16.

1. Let this be taken notice of, (1.) To the honour of God, as the one only living and true God;' for even those that worshipped other gods were so convinced of the sovereignty of the God of Israel that they were willing to incur expenses in order to recommend themselves to his favour. See Ps. 45:12; 68:26. (2.) To the praise of this heathen king, that he honoured the God of Israel though his worshippers were a despicable handful of poor men, who were not able to bear the charges of their own religion and were now his vassals, and that, though he was not wrought upon to quit his own superstitions, yet he protected and encouraged the Jews in their religion, and did not only say, *Be you warmed, and be you filled,* but gave them such things as they needed. (3.) To the reproach of the memory of the wicked kings of Judah. Those that had been trained up in the knowledge and worship of the *God of Israel,* and had his law and his prophets, often plundered and impoverished the temple; but here a heathen prince enriched it. Thus afterwards the gospel was rejected by the Jews, but welcomed by the Gentiles. See Rom. 11:11, *Through their fall salvation has come to the Gentiles.* Acts 13:46.

2. We are here told that Ezra was entrusted, (1.) To receive this money and to carry it to Jerusalem; for he was a man of known integrity, whom they could confide in, that he would not convert to his own use the least part of that which was given to the public. We find Paul going to Jerusalem upon such an errand, *to bring alms to his nation and offerings,* Acts 24:17. (2.) To lay out this money in the best manner, in sacrifices to be offered upon the altar of God (*v.* 17), and in whatever else he or his brethren thought fit (*v.* 18), with this limitation only that it should be *after the will of their God,* which they were better acquainted with than the king was. Let the *will of our God* be always our rule in our expenses, and particularly in what we lay out for his service. God's work must always be done according to his will. Besides money, he had vessels also given him for the service of the temple, *v.* 19. Cyrus restored what of right belonged to the temple, but these were given over and above: thus it *receiveth its own with usury.* These he must *deliver before the God of Jerusalem,* as intended for his honour, there where he had *put his name.*

IV. He draws him a bill, or warrant rather, upon the *treasurers on that side the river,* requiring them to furnish him with what he had occasion for out of the king's revenues, and to place it to the king's account, *v.* 20, 22. This was considerately done; for Ezra, having yet to enquire into the sate of things, knew not what he should have occasion for and was modest in his demand. It was also kindly done, and evinced a great affection to the temple and a great confidence in Ezra. It is the interest of princes and great men to use their wealth and power for the support and encouragement of religion. What else are great revenues good for but that they enable men to do much good of this kind if they have but hearts to do it?

V. He charges him to let nothing be wanting that was requisite to be done in or about the temple for the hon-

our of the God of Israel. Observe, in this charge (*v.* 23), 1. How honourably he speaks of God. He had called him before *the God of Jerusalem;* but here, lest it should be thought that he looked upon him as a local deity, he calls him twice, with great veneration, the *God of heaven.* 2. How strictly he eyes the word and law of God, which, it is likely, he had read and admired: "Whatsoever is *commanded by your God"* (whose institutions, though he wrote himself *King of kings,* he would not presume in the least iota or tittle to alter or add to) "let it be done, let it be diligently done, with care and speed." And, 3. How solicitously he deprecates the wrath of God: *Why should there be wrath against the realm?* The neglect and contempt of religion bring the judgments of God upon kings and kingdoms; and the likeliest expedient to turn away his wrath, when it is ready to break out against a people, is to support and encourage religion. Would we secure our peace and prosperity? Let us take care that the cause of God be not starved.

VI. He exempts all the ministers of the temple from paying taxes to the government. From the greatest of the priests to the least of the Nethinim, *it shall not be lawful for the king's officers to impose that toll, tribute, or custom upon them,* which the rest of the king's subjects paid, *v.* 24. This put a great honour upon them as free denizens of the empire, and would gain them respect as favourites of the crown; and it gave them liberty to attend their ministry with more cheerfulness and freedom. We suppose it was only what they needed for themselves and their families, and the maintenance of their ministry, that was hereby allowed to come to them custom-free. If any of them should take occasion from this privilege to meddle in trade and merchandise, they justly lost the benefit of it.

VII. He empowers Ezra to nominate and appoint judges and magistrates for all the Jews on that side the river, *v.* 25, 26. It was a great favour to the Jews to have such nobles of themselves, and especially to have them of Ezra's nomination. 1. All that *knew the laws of Ezra's God* (that is, all that professed the Jewish religion) were to be under the jurisdiction of these judges, which intimates that they were exempted from the jurisdiction of the heathen magistrates. 2. These judges were allowed and encouraged to make proselytes: Let them *teach the laws of God* to *those that do not know them.* Though he would not turn Jew himself, he cared not how many of his subjects did. 3. They were authorized to enforce the judgments they gave, and the orders they made, conformable to the *law of God* (which was hereby made the *law of the king),* with severe penalties — imprisonment, banishment, fine, or death, according as their law directed. They were not allowed to make new laws, but must see the laws of God duly executed; and they were entrusted with the sword in order that they might be *a terror to evil doers.* What could Jehoshaphat, or Hezekiah, or David himself, as king, have done more for the honour of God and the furtherance of religion?

Verses 27–28

Ezra cannot proceed in his story without inserting his thankful acknowledgement of the goodness of God to him and his people in this matter. As soon as he has concluded the king's commission, instead of subjoining, *God save the king* (though that would have been proper enough), he adds, *Blessed be the Lord;* for we must *in every thing give thanks,* and, whatever occurrences please us, we must own God's hand in them, and praise his name. Two things Ezra blessed God for: — 1. For his commission. We suppose he kissed the king's hand for it, but that was not all: *Blessed be God* (says he) *that put such a thing as this into the king's heart.* God can put things into men's hearts which would not arise there of themselves, and into their heads too, both by his providence and by his grace, in things *pertaining both to life and godliness.* If any good appear to be in our own hearts, or in the hearts of others, we must own it was God that put it there, and bless him for it; for it is he that *worketh in us both to will and to do* that which is good. When princes and magistrates act for the suppression of vice, and the encouragement of religion, we must thank God that *put it into their hearts* to do so, as much as if they had granted us some particular favour. When God's house was built Ezra rejoiced in what was done to beautify it. We read not of any orders given to

paint or gild it, or to garnish it with precious stones, but to be sure that the ordinances of God were administered there constantly, and carefully, and exactly according to the institution; and that was indeed the beautifying of the temple. 2. For the encouragement he had to act in pursuance of his commission (*v.* 28): *He has extended mercy to me.* The king, in the honour he did him, we may suppose, had an eye to his merit, and preferred him because he looked upon him to be a very sensible ingenious man; but he himself ascribes his preferment purely to God's mercy. It was this that recommended him to the favour of his prince. Ezra himself was a man of courage, yet he attributed his encouragement not to his own heart, but to God's hand: "I was strengthened to undertake the services, *as the hand of the Lord my God was upon me* to direct and support me." If God gives us his hand, we are bold and cheerful; if he withdraws it, we are weak as water. Whatever service we are enabled to do for God and our generation, God must have all the glory of it. Strength for it is derived from him, and therefore the praise of it must be given to him.

CHAPTER 8

This chapter gives us a more particular narrative of Ezra's journey to Jerusalem, of which we had a general account in the foregoing chapter. I. The company that went up with him (*v.* 1–20). II. The solemn fast which he kept with his company, to implore God's presence with them in this journey (*v.* 21–23). III. The care he took of the treasure he had with him, and the charge he gave concerning it to the priests, to whose custody he committed it (*v.* 24–30). IV. The care God took of him and his company in the way (*v.* 31). V. Their safe arrival at Jerusalem, where they delivered their treasure to the priests (*v.* 32–34), their commissions to the kings lieutenants (*v.* 36), offered sacrifices to God (*v.* 35), and then applied to their business.

Verses 1–20

Ezra, having received his commission from the king, beats up for volunteers, as it were, sets up an ensign to assemble the outcasts of Israel and the dispersed of Judah, Isa. 11:12. "Whoever of the sons of Sion, that *swell with the daughters of Babylon,* is disposed to go to Jerusalem, now that the temple there is finished and the temple-service set a-going, now is their time." Now one would think that under such a leader, with such encouragements, all the Jews should at length have *shaken themselves from their dust,* and *loosed the bands of their neck,* according to that call, Isa. 52:1, 2, etc. I wonder how any of them could read that chapter and yet stay behind. But multitudes did. They loved their ease better than their religion, thought themselves well off where they were, and either believed not that Jerusalem would better their condition or durst not go thither through any difficulties. But here we are told,

I. That some offered themselves willingly to go with Ezra. The heads of the several families are here named, for their honour, and the numbers of the males that each brought in, amounting in all to 1496. Two priests are named (*v.* 2) and one of the sons of David; but, it should seem, they came without their families, probably intending to see how they liked Jerusalem and then either to send for their families or return to them as they saw cause. Several of their families, or clans, here named, we had before, *ch.* 2. Some went up from them at that time, more went up now, as God inclined their hearts; some were called into the vineyard at the third hour, others not till the eleventh, yet even those were not rejected. But here we read of *the last sons of Adonikam* (*v.* 13), which some understand to their dispraise, that they were the last that enlisted themselves under Ezra; I rather understand it to their honour, that now all the sons of that family returned and none staid behind.

II. That the Levites who went in this company were in a manner pressed into the service. Ezra appointed a general rendezvous of all his company at a certain place upon new-year's day, the first day of the first month. *ch.* 7:9. Then and there he took a view of them, and mustered them, and (which was strange) *found there none of the sons of Levi,* *v.* 15. Some priests there were, but no others that were Levites. Where was the spirit of that sacred tribe? Ezra, a priest, like Moses proclaims, *Who is on the Lord's side?* They, unlike to Levi, shrink, and desire to *abide among the sheep-folds to hear the bleatings of the flock.* Synagogues we suppose they had in Babylon, in which they prayed, and preached, and kept sabbaths (and, when they could not have better, they had reason to be thankful for them); but now that the temple at Jerusalem was opened, to the service of which they were ordained, they ought to have preferred the gates of Zion before all those synagogues. It is upon record here, to their reproach; but *tell it not in Gath.* Ezra, when he observed that he had no Levites in his retinue, was much at a loss. He had money enough for the service of the temple, but wanted men. The king and princes had more than done their part, but the sons of Levi had not half done theirs. Eleven men, chief men, and men of understanding, he chooses out of his company, to be employed for the filling up of this lamentable vacancy; and here we are informed, 1. Of their being sent. Ezra sent them to a proper place, where there as a college of Levites, *the place Casiphia,* probably a street or square in Babylon allowed for that purpose — *Silver Street* one may call it, for *ceseph* signifies *silver.* He sent them to a proper person, to Iddo, the chief president of the college, not to urge him to come himself (we will suppose him to be old and unfit for such a remove), but to send some of the juniors, *ministers for the house of our God, v.* 17. The furnishing of God's house with good ministers is a good work, which will redound to the comfort and credit of all that have a hand in it. 2. Of their success. They did not return without their errand, but, though the warning was short, they brought about forty Levites to attend Ezra, Sherebiah, noted as a very intelligent man, and eighteen with him (*v.* 18). Hashabiah, and Jeshaiah, and twenty with them. *v.* 19. By this it appears that they were not averse to go, but were slothful and inattentive, and only wanted to be called upon and excited to go. What a pity it is that good men should omit a good work, merely for want of being spoken to! What a pity that they should need it, but, if they do, what a pity that they should be left without it! Of the Nethinim, the servitors of the sacred college, the *species infima — the lowest order* of the temple ministers, more appeared forward to go than of the Levites themselves. Of them 220, upon this hasty summons, enlisted themselves, and had the honour to be expressed by name in Ezra's muster-roll, *v.* 20. "Thus," says Ezra, "were we furnished with Levites, *by the good hand of our God upon us.*" If, where ministers have been wanting, the vacancies are well supplied, let God have the glory, and his good hand be acknowledged as qualifying them for the service, inclining them to it, and then opening a door of opportunity for them.

Verses 21–23

Ezra has procured Levites to go along with him; but what will that avail, unless he have God with him? That is therefore his chief care. In all our ways we must acknowledge God, and in those particularly wherein we are endeavouring to serve the interest of his kingdom among men. Ezra does so here. Observe,

I. The stedfast confidence he had in God and in his gracious protection. He told the king (*v.* 22) what principles he went upon, that those who seek God are safe under the shadow of his wings, even in their greats dangers, but that those who forsake him are continually exposed, even when they are most secure. God's servants have his power engaged for them; his enemies have it engaged against them. This Ezra believed with his heart, and with his mouth made confession of it before the king; and therefore he was ashamed to ask of the king a convoy, lest thereby he should give occasion to the king, and those about him, to suspect either God's power to help his people or Ezra's confidence in that power. Those that trust in God, and triumph in him, will be ashamed of seeking to the creature for protection, especially of using any sorry shifts for their own safety, because thereby they contradict themselves and their own confidence. Not but that those who depend upon God must use proper means for their preservation, and they need not be ashamed to do so; but, when the honour of God is concerned, one would rather expose one's-self than do any thing to the prejudice of that, which ought to be dearer to us than our lives.

II. The solemn application he made to God in that confidence: He *proclaimed a fast, v.* 21. No doubt he had himself begged of God direction in this affair from the first time he had it in his thoughts; but for public mercies public prayers must be made, that all who are to share in the comfort of them may join in the request for them. Their fasting was, 1. To express their humiliation. This he declares to be the intent and meaning of it. *"that we might afflict ourselves before our God* for our sins, and so be qualified for the pardon of them." When we are entering upon any new condition of life our care should be to bring none of the guilt of the sins of our former condition into it. When we are in any imminent peril let us be sure to make our peace with God, and then we are safe: nothing can do us any real hurt. 2. To excite their supplications. Prayer was always joined with religious fasting. Their errand to the throne of grace was *to seek of God the right way,* that is, to commit themselves to the guidance of the divine Providence, to put themselves under the divine protection, and to beg of God to guide and keep them in their journey and bring them safely to their journey's end. They were strangers in the road, were to march through their enemies' countries, and had not a pillar of cloud and fire to lead them, as their fathers had; but they believed that the power and favour of God, and the ministration of his angels, would be to them instead of that, and hoped by prayer to obtain divine assistance. Note, All our concerns about ourselves, our families, and our estates, it is our wisdom and duty by prayer to commit to God, and leave the care of with him, Phil. 4:6.

III. The good success of their doing so (*v.* 23): *We besought our God* by joint-prayer, *and he was entreated of us.* They had some comfortable assurance in their own minds that their prayers were answered, and the event declared it; for never any that sought God in earnest sought him in vain.

Verses 24–30

We have here an account of the particular care which Ezra took of the treasure he had with him, that belonged to God's sanctuary, Observe, 1. Having committed the keeping of it to God, he committed the keeping of it to proper men, whose business it was to watch it, though without God they would have waked in vain. Note, Our prayers must always be seconded with our endeavours; the care of Christ's gospel, his church, and ordinances, must not be so left with him but that it must also be *committed to faithful men,* 2 Tim. 2:2. 2. Having prayed to God to preserve all the substance they had with them, he shows himself especially solicitous for that part of it which belonged to the house of God and was an offering to him. Do we expect that God should, by his providence, keep that which belongs to us? Let us, by his grace, keep that which belongs to him. Let God's honour and interest be our care; and then we may expect that our lives and comforts will be his. Observe, (1.) The persons to whom he delivered the offerings of the house of God. Twelve chief priests, and as many Levites, he appointed to this trust (*v.* 24, 30), who were bound by their office to take care of the things of God, and were in a particular manner to have the benefit of these sacred treasures. Ezra tells them why he put those things into their hands (*v.* 28): *You are holy unto the Lord, the vessels are holy also;* and who so fit to take care of holy things as holy persons? Those that have the dignity and honour of the priesthood must take along with them the trust and duty of it. The prophet is foretelling the return of God's people and ministers out of Babylon, when he gives the solemn charge (Isa. 52:11), *Be you clean that bear the vessels of the Lord.* (2.) The great exactness with which he lodged this trust in their hands: He *weighed to them the silver, the gold, and the vessels* (*v.* 25), because he expected to have it from them again by weight. In all trust, but especially sacred ones, we ought to be punctual, and preserve a right understanding on both sides. In Zerubbabel's time the vessels were delivered by number, here by weight, that all might be forth-coming and it might easily appear if any were missing, to intimate that such as are entrusted with holy things (as all the stewards of the mysteries of God are) are concerned to remember, both in receiving their trust and in discharging it, that they must shortly give a very particular account of it, that they may be faithful to it and so give up their account with joy. (3.) The charge he have them with these treasures (*v.* 29): *"Watch you, and keep them,* that they be not lost, nor embezzled, nor mingled with the other articles. Keep them together; keep them by themselves; keep them safely, till you weigh them in the temple, before the great men there," hereby intimating how much it was their concern to be careful and faithful and how much it would be their honour to be found so. Thus when Paul charges Timothy with the gospel treasure he bids him keep it *until the appearing of Jesus Christ,* and his appearing before him to give account of his trust, when his fidelity would be his crown.

Verses 31–36

We are now to attend Ezra to Jerusalem, a journey of about four months in all; but his multitude made his marches slow and his stages short. Now here we are told,

I. That his God was good, and he acknowledged his goodness: *The hand of our God was upon us,* to animate us for our undertaking. To him they owed it, 1. That they were preserved in their journey, and not all cut off; for there were enemies that *laid wait for them by the way* to do them a mischief, or at least, like Amalek, to *smite the hindmost of them,* but God protected them, *v.* 31. Even the common perils of journeys are such as oblige us to sanctify our going out with prayer and our returns in peace with praise and thanksgiving; much more ought God to be thus eyed in such a dangerous expedition as this was. 2. That they were brought in safety to their journey's end, *v.* 32. Let those that have stedfastly set their faces towards the new Jerusalem proceed and persevere to the end *till they appear before God in Zion,* and they shall find that he *who has begun the good work will perform it.*

II. That his treasurers were faithful. When they had come to Jerusalem they were impatient to be discharged of their trust, and therefore applied to the great men of the temple, who received it from them and gave them an acquittance in full, *v.* 33, 34. It is a great ease to one's mind to be discharged from a trust, and a great honour to one's name to be able to make it appear that it has been faithfully discharged.

III. That his companions were devout. As soon as they came to be near the altar they thought themselves obliged to offer sacrifice, whatever they had done in Babylon, *v.* 35. That will be dispensed with when we want opportunity which when the door is opened again will be expected from us. It is observable, 1. That among their sacrifices they had a sin-offering; for it is the atonement that sweetens and secures every mercy to us, which will not be truly comfortable unless *iniquity be taken away* and our peace made with God. 2. That the number of their offerings related to the number of the tribes, twelve bullocks, twelve he-goats, and ninety-six rams (that is, eight times twelve), intimating the union of the two kingdoms, according to what was foretold, Eze. 37:22. They did not any longer go two tribes one way and ten another, but all the twelve met by their representatives at the same altar.

IV. That even the enemies of the Jews became their friends, bowed to Ezra's commission, and, instead of hindering the people of God, furthered them (*v.* 36), purely in complaisance to the king: when he appeared moderate they all coveted to appear so too. *Then had the churches rest.*

CHAPTER 9

The affairs of the church were in a very good posture, we may well suppose, now that Ezra presided in them. Look without; the government was kind to them. We hear no complaints of persecution and oppression; their enemies had either their hearts turned or at least their hands tied; their neighbours were civil, and we hear of no wars nor rumours of wars; there were none to make them afraid; all was as well as could be, considering that they were few, and poor, and subjects to a foreign prince. Look at home; we hear nothing of Baal, or Ashtaroth, nor Moloch, no images, nor groves, nor golden calves, no, nor so much as high places (not only no idolatrous altars, but no separate ones), but the temple was duly respected and the temple service carefully kept up. Yet all was not well either. The purest ages of the church have had some corruptions, and it will never be presented "without spot or wrinkle" till it is "a glorious church," a church "triumphant," Eph. 5:27. We have here, I. A complaint brought to Ezra of the many marriages that had been made with strange wives (*v.* 1, 2). II. The great trouble which he, and others influenced by his example, were in upon this information (*v.* 3, 4). III. The solemn confession which he made of this sin to God, with godly sorrow, and shame (*v.* 5–15).

Verses 1–4

Ezra, like Barnabas when he came to Jerusalem and *saw the grace of God* to his brethren there, no doubt *was glad, and exhorted them all that with purpose of heart they would cleave to the Lord,* Acts 11:23. He saw nothing amiss (many corruptions lurk out of the view of the most vigilant rulers); but here is a damp upon his joys: information is brought him that many of the people, yea, and some of the rulers, had married wives out of heathen families, and joined themselves in affinity with strangers. Observe,

I. What the sin was that they were guilty of: it was *mingling with the people of those lands* (*v.* 2), associating with them both in trade and in conversation, making themselves familiar with them, and, to complete the affinity, taking *their daughters in marriages* to their sons. We are willing to hope that they did not worship their gods, but that their captivity had cured them of their idolatry: it is said indeed that they *did according to their abominations;* but that (says bishop Patrick) signifies here only the imitation of the heathen in promiscuous marriages with any nation whatsoever, which by degrees would lead them to idolatry. Herein, 1. They disobeyed the express command of God, which forbade all intimacy with the heathen, and particularly in matrimonial contracts, Deu. 7:3. 2. They profaned the crown of their peculiarity, and set themselves upon a level with those above whom God had by singular marks of his favour, of late as well as formerly, dignified them. 3. They distrusted the power of God to protect and advance them, and were led by carnal policy, hoping to strengthen themselves and make an interest among their neighbours by these alliances. A practical disbelief of God's all-sufficiency is at the bottom of all the sorry shifts we make to help ourselves. 4. They exposed themselves, and much more their children, to the peril of idolatry, the very sin, and introduced by this very way, that had cone been the ruin of their church and nation.

II. Who were the persons that were guilty of this sin, not only some of the unthinking people of Israel, that knew no better, but *many of the priests and Levites,* whose office it was to teach the law, and this law among the rest, and in whom, by reason of their elevation above common Israelites, it was a greater crime. It was a diminution to the sons of that tribe to match into any other tribe, and they seldom did except into the royal tribe; but for them to match with heathen, with Canaanites, and Hittites, and I know not whom, was such a disparagement as, if they had had any sense, though not of duty, yet of honour, one would think, they would never have been guilty of. Yet this was not the worst: *The hand of the princes and rulers,* who by their power should have prevented or reformed this high misdemeanour, *was chief in this trespass.* If princes be in a trespass, they will be charged as chief in it, because of the influence their examples will have upon others. *Many will follow their pernicious ways.* But miserable is the case of that people whose leaders debauch them and cause them to err.

III. The information that was given of this to Ezra. It was given by the persons that were most proper to complain, the princes, those of them that had kept their integrity and with it their dignity; they could not have accused others if they themselves had not been free from blame. It was given to the person who had power to mend the matter, who, as a *ready scribe in the law of God,* could argue with them, and, as king's commissioner, could awe them. It is probable that these princes had often endeavoured to redress this grievance and could not; but now they applied to Ezra, hoping that his wisdom, authority, and interest, would prevail to do it. Those that cannot of themselves reform public abuses may yet do good service by giving information to those that can.

IV. The impression this made upon Ezra (*v.* 3): *He rent his clothes, plucked off his hair,* and *sat down astonished.* Thus he expressed the deep sense he had, 1. Of the dishonour hereby done to God. It grieved him to the heart to think that a people called by his name should so grossly violate his law, should be so little benefited by his correction, and make such bad returns for his favours. 2. Of the mischief the people had hereby done to themselves and the danger they were in of the wrath of God breaking out against them. Note, (1.) The sins of others should be our sorrow, and the injury done by them to God's honour and the souls of men is what we should lay to heart. (2.) Sorrow for sin must be great sorrow; such Ezra's was, *as for an only son or a first-born.* (3.) The scandalous sins of professors are what we have reason to be astonished at. We may stand amazed to see men contradict, disparage, prejudice, ruin, themselves. Strange that men should act so inconsiderately and so inconsistently with themselves! Upright men are astonished at it.

V. The influence which Ezra's grief for this had upon others. We may suppose that he *went up to the house of the Lord,* there to humble himself, because he had an eye to God in his grief and that was the proper place for deprecating his displeasure. Public notice was soon taken of it, and all the devout serious people that were at hand assembled themselves to him, it should seem of their own accord, for nothing is said of their being sent, to, *v.* 4. Note, 1. It is the character of good people that they *tremble at God's word;* they stand in awe of the authority of its precepts and the severity and justice of its threatenings, and to those that do so *will God look,* Isa. 66:2. 2. Those that tremble *at the word of God* cannot but tremble *at the sins of men,* by which the law of God is broken and his wrath and curse are incurred. 3. The pious zeal of one against sin may perhaps provoke very many to the like, as the apostle speaks in another case, 2 Co. 9:2. Many will follow who have not consideration, talent, and courage, enough to lead in a good work. 4. All good people ought to own those that appear and act in the cause of God against vice and profaneness, to stand by them, and do what they can to strengthen their hands.

Verses 5–15

What the meditations of Ezra's heart were, while for some hours he sat down astonished, we may guess by the words of his mouth when at length he *spoke with his tongue;* and a most pathetic address he here makes to Heaven upon this occasion. Observe,

I. The time when he made this address — *at the evening sacrifice, v.* 5. Then (it is likely) devout people used to come into the courts of the temple, to grace the solemnity of the sacrifice and to offer up their own prayers to God in concurrence with it. In their hearing Ezra chose to make this confession, that they might be made duly sensible of the sins of their people, which hitherto they had either not taken notice of or had made light of. Prayer may preach. The sacrifice, and especially the evening sacrifice, was a type of the great propitiation, that *blessed Lamb of God* which in the evening of the world was to *take away sin by the sacrifice of himself,* to which we may suppose Ezra had an eye of faith in this penitential address to God; he makes confession with his hand, as it were, upon the head of that great sacrifice, through which *we receive the atonement.* Certainly Ezra was no stranger to the message which the angel Gabriel had some years ago delivered to Daniel, at the time of the evening sacrifice, and as it were in explication of it, concerning Messiah the Prince (Dan. 9:21, 24); and perhaps he had regard to that in choosing this time.

II. His preparation for this address. 1. He *rose up from his heaviness,* and so far shook off the burden of his grief as was necessary to the lifting up of his heart to God. He recovered from his astonishment, got the tumult of his troubled spirits somewhat stilled and his spirit composed for communion with God. 2. He *fell upon his knees,* put himself into the posture of a penitent humbling himself and a petitioner suing for mercy, in both representing the people for whom he was now an intercessor. 3. He *spread out his hands,* as one affected with what he was going to say, offering it up unto God, waiting, and reaching out, as it were, with an earnest expectation, to receive a gracious answer. In this he had an eye to God as the Lord, and as his God, a God of power, but a God of grace.

III. The address itself. It is not properly to be called a prayer, for there is not a word of petition in it; but, if we give prayer its full latitude, it is the offering up of pious and devout affections to God, and very devout, very pious, are the affections which Ezra here expresses. His address is a penitent confession of sin, not his own (from a conscience burdened with its own guilt and apprehensive of his own danger), but the sin of his people, from a gracious concern for the honour of God and the welfare of Israel. Here is a lively picture of ingenuous repentance. Observe in this address,

1. The confession he makes of the sin and the aggravations of it, which he insists upon, to affect his own heart and theirs that joined with him with holy sorrow and shame and fear, in the consideration of it, that they might be deeply humbled for it. And it is observable that, though he himself was wholly clear from this guilt, yet he puts himself into the number of the sinners, because he was a member of the same community — *our sins and our trespass.* Perhaps he now remembered it against himself, as his fault, that he had staid so long after his brethren in Babylon, and had not separated himself so soon as he might have done from the people of those lands. When we are lamenting the wickedness of the wicked, it may be, if we duly reflect upon ourselves and give our own hearts leave to deal faithfully with us, we may find something of the same nature, though in a lower degree, that we also have been guilty of. However, he speaks that which was, or should have been, the general complaint.

(1.) He owns their sins to have been very great: *"Our iniquities are increased over our heads* (*v.* 6); we are ready to perish in them as in keep waters;" so general was the prevalency of them, so violent the power of them, and so threatening were they of the most pernicious consequences. "Iniquity has grown up to such a height among us that it reaches to the heavens, so very impudent that it dares heaven, so very provoking that, like the sin of Sodom, it cries to heaven for vengeance." But let this be the comfort of true penitents that though their sins reach to the heavens God's mercy is *in the heavens,* Ps. 36:5. *Where sin abounds grace will much more abound.*

(2.) Their sin had been long persisted in (*v.* 7): *Since the days of our fathers have we been in a great trespass.* The example of those that had gone before them he thought so far from excusing their fault that it aggravated it. "We should have taken warning not to stumble at the same stone. The corruption is so much the worse that it has taken deep root and begins to plead prescription, but by this means we have reason to fear that the measure of the iniquity is nearly full."

(3.) The great and sore judgments which God had brought upon them for their sins did very much aggravate them: *"For our iniquities we have been delivered to the sword and to captivity* (*v.* 7), and yet not reformed, yet not reclaimed — brayed in the mortar, and yet the *folly not gone* (Prov. 27:22) — corrected, but not reclaimed."

(4.) The late mercies God had bestowed upon them did likewise very much aggravate their sins. This he insists largely upon, *v.* 8, 9. Observe, [1.] The time of mercy: *Now for a little space,* that is, "It is but a little while since we had our liberty, and it is not likely to continue long." This greatly aggravated their sin, that they were so lately in the furnace and that they knew not how soon they might return to it again; and could they yet be secure? [2.] The fountain of mercy: *Grace has been shown us from the Lord.* The kings of Persia were the instruments of their enlargement; but he ascribes it to God and to his grace, his free grace, without any merit of theirs. [3.] The streams of mercy, — that they were *not forsaken in their bondage,* but even in Babylon had the tokens of God's presence, — that they were a remnant of Israelites left, a few out of many, and those narrowly escaped out of the hands of their enemies, by the favour of the kings of Persia, — and especially that they had *a nail in his holy place,* that is (as it is explained, *v.* 9), that they had set up the *house of God.* They had their religion settled and the service of the temple in a constant method. We are to reckon it a great comfort and advantage to have stated opportunities of worshipping God. *Blessed are those that dwell in God's house,* like Anna that departed not from the temple. *This is my rest for ever,* says the gracious soul. [4.] The effects of all this. It enlightened their eyes, and it revived their hearts; that is, it was very comfortable to them, and the more sensibly so because it was in their bondage: it was life from the dead to them. Though but *a little reviving,* it was a great favour, considering that they deserved none and the day of small things was an earnest of greater. "Now," says Ezra, "how ungrateful are we to offend a God that has been so kind to us! how disingenuous to mingle in sin with those nations from whom we have been, in wonderful mercy, delivered! how unwise to expose ourselves to God's displeasure when we are tried with the returns of his favour and are upon our good behaviour for the continuance of it!"

(5.) It was a great aggravation of the sin that it was against an express command: *We have forsaken thy commandments, v.* 10. It seems to have been an ancient law of the house of Jacob not to match with the families of the uncircumcised, Gen. 34:14. But, besides that, God had strictly forbidden it. He recites the command, *v.* 11, 12. For sin appears sin, appears exceedingly sinful, when we compare it with the law which is broken by it. Nothing could be more express: *Give not your daughters to their sons, nor take their daughters to your sons.* The reason given is because, if they mingled with those nations, they would pollute themselves. It was an unclean land, and they were a holy people; but if they kept themselves distinct from them it would be their honour and safety, and the perpetuating of their prosperity. Now to violate a command so express, backed with such reasons, and a fundamental law of their constitution, was very provoking to the God of heaven.

(6.) That in the judgments by which they had already smarted for their sins God had *punished them less than their iniquities deserved,* so that he looked upon them to be still in debt upon the old account. "What! and yet shall we run up a new score? Has God dealt so gently with us in correcting us, and shall we thus abuse his favour and turn his grace into wantonness?" God, in his grace and mercy, had said concerning Sion's captivity, *She hath received of the Lord's hand double for all her sins* (Isa. 40:2); but Ezra, in a penitential sense of the great malignity that was in their sin, acknowledged that, though the punishment was very great, it was less than they deserved.

2. The devout affections that were working in him, in making this confession. Speaking of sin,

(1.) He speaks as one much ashamed. With this he begins (*v.* 6), *O my God! I am ashamed and blush, O my God!* (so the words are placed) *to lift up my face unto thee.* Note, [1.] Sin is a shameful thing; as soon as ever our first parents had eaten forbidden fruit they were ashamed of themselves. [2.] Holy shame is as necessary an ingredient in true and ingenuous repentance as holy sorrow. [3.] The sins of others should be our shame, and we should blush for those who do not blush for themselves. We may well be ashamed that we are any thing akin to those who are so ungrateful to God and unwise for themselves. This is *clearing ourselves,* 2 Co. 7:11. [4.] Penitent sinners never see so much reason to blush and be ashamed as when they come to *lift up their faces before God.* A natural sense of our own honour which we have injured will make us ashamed, when we have done a wrong thing, to look men in the face; but a gracious concern for God's honour will make us much more ashamed to look him in the face. The publican, when he went to the temple to pray, hung down his head more than ever, as one ashamed, Lu. 18:13. [5.] An eye to God as our God will be of great use to us in the exercise of repentance. Ezra begins, *O my God!* and again in the same breath, *My God.* The consideration of our covenant-relation to God as ours will help to humble us, and break our hearts for sin, that we should violate both his precepts to us and our promises to him; it will also encourage us to hope for pardon upon repentance. "He is my God, notwithstanding this;" and every transgression in the covenant does not throw us out of covenant.

(2.) He speaks as one much amazed (*v.* 10) *"What shall we say after this?* For my part I know not what to say: if God do not help us, we are undone." The discoveries of guilt excite amazement: the more we think of sin the worse it looks. The difficulty of the case excites amazement. How shall we recover ourselves? Which way shall we make our peace with God? [1.] True penitents are at a loss what to say. Shall we say, We have *not sinned,* or, *God will not require it?* If we do, *we deceive ourselves, and the truth is not in us.* Shall we say, Have patience with us and we will pay thee all, with *thousands of rams, or our first-born for our transgression?* God will not thus be mocked: he knows we are insolvent. Shall we say, *There is no hope,* and *let come on us what will?* That is but to make bad worse. [2.] True penitents will consider what to say, and should, as Ezra, beg of God to teach them. What shall we say? Say, "I have sinned; I have done foolishly; God be merciful to me a sinner;" and the like. See Hos. 14:2.

(3.) He speaks as one much afraid, *v.* 13, 14. "After all the judgments that have come upon us to reclaim us from sin, and all the deliverances that have been wrought for us to engage us to God and duty, *if we should again break God's commandments, by joining in affinity with the children of disobedience* and learning their ways, what else could we expect but that God should be *angry with us till he had consumed us,* and there should not be so much as a remnant left, nor any to escape the destruction?" There is not a surer nor sadder presage of ruin to any peo-

ple than revolting to sin, to the same sins again, after great judgments and great deliverances. Those that will be wrought upon neither by the one nor by the other are fit to be rejected, as reprobate silver, for the *founder melteth in vain.*

(4.) He speaks as one much assured of the righteousness of God, and resolved to acquiesce in that and to leave the matter with him whose judgment is *according to truth* (*v.* 15): *"Thou art righteous,* wise, just, and good; thou wilt neither do us wrong nor be hard upon us; and therefore behold *we are before thee,* we lie at thy feet, waiting our doom; *we cannot stand before thee,* insisting upon any righteousness of our own, having no plea to support us or bring us off, and therefore we fall down before thee, in our trespass, and cast ourselves on thy mercy. *Do unto us whatsoever seemeth good unto thee,* Jdg. 10:15. We have nothing to say, nothing to do, but to *make supplication to our Judge,"* Job 9:15. Thus does this good man lay his grief before God and then leave it with him.

CHAPTER 10

In this chapter we have that grievance redressed which was complained of and lamented in the foregoing chapter. Observe, I. How the people's hearts were prepared for the redress of it by their deep humiliation for the sin (*v.* 1). II. How it was proposed to Ezra by Shechaniah (*v.* 2–4). III. How the proposal was put in execution. 1. The great men were sworn to stand to it (*v.* 5). 2. Ezra appeared first in it (*v.* 6). 3. A general assembly was called (*v.* 7–9). 4. They all, in compliance with Ezra's exhortation, agreed to the reformation (*v.* 10–14). 5. Commissioners were appointed to sit "de die in diem" — day after day, to enquire who had married strange wives and to oblige them to put them away, which was done accordingly (*v.* 15–17). and a last of the names of those that were found guilty given in (*v.* 18–44).

Verses 1–5

We are here told,

I. What good impressions were made upon the people by Ezra's humiliation and confession of sin. No sooner was it noised in the city that their new governor, in whom they rejoiced, was himself in grief, and to so great a degree, for them and their sin, than presently there *assembled to him a very great congregation,* to see what the matter was and to mingle their tears with his, *v.* 1. Our weeping for other people's sins may perhaps set those a weeping for them themselves who otherwise would continue senseless and remorseless. See what a happy influence the good examples of great ones may have upon their inferiors. When Ezra, a scribe, a scholar, a man in authority under the king, so deeply lamented the public corruptions, they concluded that they were indeed very grievous, else he would not thus have grieved for them; and this drew tears from every eye: *men, women, and children, wept very sore,* when he wept thus.

II. What a good motion Shechaniah made upon this occasion. The place was *Bochim* — a place of *weepers;* but, for aught that appears, there was a profound silence among them, as among Job's friends, who *spoke not a word to him, because they saw that his grief was very great,* till Shechaniah (one of Ezra's companions from Babylon, *ch.* 8:3, 5) stood up, and made a speech addressed to Ezra, in which,

1. He owns the national guilt, sums up all Ezra's confession in one word, and sets to his seal that it is true: *"We have trespassed against our God, and have taken strange wives, v.* 2. The matter is too plain to be denied and too bad to be excused." It does not appear that Shechaniah was himself culpable in this matter (if he had had the beam in his own eye, he could not have seen so clearly to pluck it out of his brother's eye), but his father was guilty, and several of his father's house (as appears *v.* 26), and therefore he reckons himself among the trespassers; nor does he seek to excuse or palliate the sin, though some of his own relations were guilty of it, but, in the cause of God, *says to his father, I have not known him,* as Levi, Deu. 33:9. Perhaps the strange wife that his father had married had been an unjust unkind step-mother to him, and had made mischief in the family, and he supposed that others had done the like, which made him the more forward to appear against this corruption; if so, this was not the only time that private resentments have been over ruled by the providence of God to serve the public good.

2. He encourages himself and others to hope that though the matter was bad it might be amended: *Yet now*

there is hope in Israel (where else should there be hope but in Israel? those that are strangers to that commonwealth are said to have *no hope,* Eph. 2:12) even *concerning this thing.* The case is sad, but it is not desperate; the disease is threatening, but not incurable. There is hope that the people may be reformed, the guilty reclaimed, a stop put to the spreading of the contagion; and so the judgments which the sin deserves may be prevented and all will be well. *Now there is hope;* now that the disease is discovered it is half-cured. Now that the alarm is taken the people begin to be sensible of the mischief, and to lament it, a spirit of repentance seems to be poured out upon them, and they are all thus humbling themselves before God for it, *now there is hope* that God will forgive, and have mercy. The *valley of Achor* (that is, of *trouble*) is the *door of hope* (Hos. 2:15); for the sin that truly troubles us shall not ruin us. There is hope now that Israel has such a prudent, pious, zealous governor as Ezra to manage this affair. Note, (1.) In melancholy times we must see and observe what makes for us, as well as what makes against us. (2.) There may be good hopes through grace, even when there is the sense of great guilt before God. (3.) Where sin is seen and lamented, and good steps are taken towards a reformation, even sinners ought to be encouraged. (4.) Even great saints must thankfully receive seasonable counsel and comfort from those that are much their inferiors, as Ezra from Shechaniah.

3. He advises that a speedy and effectual course should be taken for the divorcing of the strange wives. The case is plain; what has been done amiss must be undone again as far as possible; nothing less than this is true repentance. *Let us put away all the wives, and such as are born of them, v.* 3. Ezra, though he knew this was the only way of redressing the grievance, yet perhaps did not think it feasible, and despaired of ever bringing the people to it, which put him into that confusion in which we left him in the foregoing chapter; but Shechaniah, who conversed more with the people than he did, assured him the thing was practicable if they went wisely to work. As to us now, it is certain that sin must be put away, a bill of divorce must be given it, with a resolution never to have any thing more to do with it, though it be dear as the wife of thy bosom, nay, as a right eye or a right hand, otherwise there is no pardon, no peace. What has been unjustly got cannot be justly kept, but must be restored; but, as to the case of being *unequally yoked with unbelievers,* Shechaniah's counsel, which he was then so clear in, will not hold now; such marriages, it is certain, are sinful, and ought not to be made, but they are not null. *Quod fieri non debuit, factum valet — That which ought not to have been done must, when done, abide.* Our rule, under the gospel, is, *If a brother has a wife that believeth not,* and *she be pleased to dwell with him, let him not put her away,* 1 Co. 7:12, 13.

4. He puts them in a good method for the effecting of this reformation, and shows them not only that it must be done, but how. (1.) "Let Ezra, and all those that are present in this assembly, agree in a resolution that this must be done (pass a vote immediately to this effect: it will now pass *nemine contradicente* — unanimously), that it may be said to be done *according to the counsel of my lord,* the president of the assembly, with the unanimous concurrence of those that *tremble at the commandment of our God,* which is the description of those that were gathered to him, *ch.* 9:4. Declare it to be the sense of all the sober serious people among us, which cannot but have a great sway among Israelites." (2.) "Let the command of God in this matter, which Ezra recited in his prayer, be laid before the people, and let them see that it is *done according to the law;* we have that to warrant us, nay, that binds us to what we do; it is not an addition of our own to the divine law, but the necessary execution of it." (3.) "While we are in a good mind, let us bind ourselves by a solemn vow and covenant that we will do it, lest, when the present impressions are worn off, the thing be left undone. Let us covenant, not only that, if we have strange wives ourselves, we will put them away, but that, if we have not, we will do what we can in our places to oblige others to put away theirs." (4.) "Let Ezra himself preside in this matter, who is authorized by the king's commission to enquire whether the law of God be duly observed in Judah and Jerusalem (*ch.* 7:14), and let us all resolve to stand by him in it (*v.* 4): *Arise, be of good courage.* Weeping, in this case, is good, but re-

forming is better." See what God said to Joshua in a like case, Jos. 7:10, 11.

III. What a good resolution they came to upon this good motion, *v.* 5. They not only agreed that it should be done, but bound themselves with an oath that they would do according to this word. Fast bind, fast find.

Verses 6–14

We have here an account of the proceedings upon the resolutions lately taken up concerning the strange wives; no time was lost; they struck when the iron was hot, and soon set the wheels of reformation a-going. 1. Ezra went to the council-chamber where, it is probable, the priests used to meet upon public business; *and till he came thither* (so bishop Patrick thinks it should be read), till he saw something done, and more likely to be done, for the redress of this grievance, *he did neither eat nor drink,* but continued mourning. Sorrow for sin should be abiding sorrow; be sure to let it continue till the sin be put away. 2. He sent orders to all the children of the captivity to attend him at Jerusalem *within three days* (*v.* 7, 8); and, being authorized by the king to enforce his orders with penalties annexed (*ch.* 7:26), he threatened that whosoever refused to obey the summons should forfeit his estate and be outlawed. The doom of him that would not attend on this religious occasion should be that his substance should, in his stead, be for ever after appropriated to the service of their religion, and he himself, for his contempt, should for ever after be excluded from the honours and privileges of their religion; he should be excommunicated. 3. Within the time limited the generality of the people met at Jerusalem and made their appearance *in the street of the house of God, v.* 9. Those that had no zeal for the work they were called to, nay, perhaps had a dislike to it, being themselves delinquents, yet paid such a deference to Ezra's authority, and were so awed by the penalty, that they durst not stay away. 4. God gave them a token of his displeasure in the great rain that happened at that time (*v.* 9 and again *v.* 13), which perhaps kept some away, and was very grievous to those that met in the open street. When they wept the heavens wept too, signifying that, though God was angry with them for their sin, yet he was well pleased with their repentance, and (as it is said, Jdg. 10:16) *his soul was grieved for the misery of Israel;* it was also an indication of the good fruits of their repentance, for the rain makes the earth fruitful. 5. Ezra gave the charge at this great assize. He told them upon what account he called them together now, that it was because he found that since their return out of captivity they had *increased the trespass of Israel* by *marrying strange wives,* had added to their former sins this new transgression, which would certainly be a means of again introducing idolatry, the very sin they had smarted for and which he hoped they had been cured of in their captivity; and he called them together that they might *confess their sin to God,* and, having done that, might declare themselves ready and willing to do his pleasure, as it should be made known to them (which all those will do that truly repent of what they have done to incur his displeasure), and particularly that they might separate themselves from all idolaters, especially idolatrous wives, *v.* 10, 11. On these heads, we may suppose, he enlarged, and probably made such another confession of the sin now as he made *ch.* 9, to which he required them to say *Amen.* 6. The people submitted not only to Ezra's jurisdiction in general, but to his inquisition and determination in this matter: *"As thou hast said, so must we do, v.* 12. We have sinned in mingling with the heathen, and have thereby been in danger, not only of being corrupted by them, for we are frail, but of being lost among them, for we are few; we are therefore convinced that there is an absolute necessity of our separating from them again." There is hope concerning people when they are convinced, not only that it is good to part with their sins, but that it is indispensably necessary: we must do it, or we are undone. 7. It was agreed that this affair should be carried on, not in a popular assembly, nor that they should think to go through with it all on a sudden, but that a court of delegates should be appointed to receive complaints and to hear and determine upon them. It could not be done at this time, for it was not put into a method, nor could the people stand out because of the rain. The delinquents were many, and it would require time to discover and examine them. Nice cases would arise, which could not be adjudged without debate and deliberation, *v.* 13. "And therefore let the crowd be dismissed, and the rulers stand to receive informations; let them proceed city by city, and let the offenders be convicted before them in the presence of the judges and elders of their own city; and let them be entrusted to see the orders executed. Thus *take time and we shall have done the sooner;* whereas, if we do it in a hurry, we shall do it by halves, *v.* 14. If, in this method, a thorough reformation be made, the *fierce wrath of God* will be *turned from us,* which, we are sensible, is ready to break forth against us for this transgression." Ezra was willing that his zeal should be guided by the people's prudence, and put the matter into this method; he was not ashamed to own that the advice came from them, any more than he was to comply with it.

Verses 15–44

The method of proceeding in this matter being concluded on, and the congregation dismissed, that each in his respective place might gain and give intelligence to facilitate the matter, we are here told, 1. Who were the persons that undertook to manage the matter and bring the causes regularly before the commissioners — *Jonathan* and *Jahaziah,* two active men, whether of the priests or of the people does not appear; probably they were the men that made that proposal (*v.* 13, 14) and were therefore the fittest to see it pursued; two honest Levites were joined with them, and *helped them, v.* 15. Dr. Lightfoot gives a contrary sense of this: *only* (or *nevertheless) Jonathan and Jahaziah stood against this matter* (which reading the original will very well bear), and these two *Levites helped them* in opposing it, either the thing itself or this method of proceeding. It was strange if a work of this kind was carried on and met with no opposition. 2. Who were the commissioners that sat upon this matter. Ezra was president, and with him *certain chief* men *of the fathers* who were qualified with wisdom and zeal above others for this service, *v.* 16. It was happy for them that they had such a man as Ezra to head them; they could not have done it well without his direction, yet he would not do it without their concurrence. 3. How long they were about it. They began *the first day of the tenth month to examine the matter* (*v.* 16), which was but ten days after this method was proposed (*v.* 9), and they finished in three months, *v.* 17. They sat closely and minded their business, otherwise they could not have despatched so many causes as they had before them in so little time; for we may suppose that all who were impeached were fairly asked what cause they could show why they should not be parted, and, if we may judge by other cases, provided the wife were proselyted to the Jewish religion she was not to be put away, the trial of which would require great care. 4. Who the persons were that were found guilty of this crime. Their names are here recorded to their perpetual reproach; many of the priests, nay, of the family of Jeshua, the high priest, were found guilty (*v.* 18), though the law had particularly provided, for the preserving of their honour in their marriages, that being holy themselves they should not marry such as were profane, Lev. 21:7. Those that should have taught others the law broke it themselves and by their example emboldened others to do likewise. But, having lost their innocency in this matter, they did well to recant and give an example of repentance; for they promised *under their hand* to put away their strange wives (some think that they made oath to do so with their *hands lifted up),* and they took the appointed way of obtaining pardon, bringing the ram which was appointed by the law *for a trespass offering* (Lev. 6:6), so owning their guilt and the desert of it, and humbly suing for forgiveness. About 113 in all are here named who had married strange wives, and some of them, it is said (*v.* 44), had children by them, which implies that not many of them had, God not crowning those marriages with the blessing of increase. Whether the children were turned off with the mothers, as Shechaniah proposed, does not appear; it should seem not: however it is probable that the wives which were put away were well provided for, according to their rank. One would think this grievance was now thoroughly redressed, yet we meet with it again (Neh. 13:23 and Mal. 2:11), for such corruptions are easily and insensibly brought in, but not without great difficulty purged out again. The best reformers can but do their endeavour, but, when the Redeemer himself shall *come to Sion,* he shall effectually *turn away ungodliness from Jacob.*

AN EXPOSITION, WITH PRACTICAL OBSERVATIONS, OF

THE BOOK OF NEHEMIAH

This book continues the history of the *children of the captivity,* the poor Jews, that had lately returned out of Babylon to their own land. At this time not only the Persian monarchy flourished in great pomp and power, but Greece and Rome began to be very great and to make a figure. Of the affairs of those high and mighty states we have authentic accounts extant; but the sacred and inspired history takes cognizance only of the state of the Jews, and makes no mention of other nations but as the Israel of God had dealings with them: for the Lord's portion is his people; they are his peculiar treasure, and, in comparison with them, the rest of the world is but as lumber. In my esteem, Ezra the scribe and Nehemiah the tirshatha, though neither of them ever wore a crown, commanded an army, conquered any country, or was famed for philosophy or oratory, yet both of them, being pious praying men, and very serviceable in their day to the church of God and the interests of religion, were really greater men and more honourable, not only than any of the Roman consuls or dictators, but than Xenophon, or Demosthenes, or Plato himself, who lived at the same time, the bright ornaments of Greece. Nehemiah's agency for the advancing of the settlement of Israel we have a full account of in this book of his own commentaries or memoirs, wherein he records not only the works of his hands, but the workings of his heart, in the management of public affairs, inserting in the story many devout reflections and ejaculations, which discover in his mind a very deep tincture of serious piety and are peculiar to his writing. Twelve years, from his twentieth year (*ch.* 1:1) to his thirty-second year (*ch.* 13:6), he was governor of Judea, under Artaxerxes king of Persia, whom Dr. Lightfoot supposes to be the same Artaxerxes as Ezra has his commission from. This book relates, I. Nehemiah's concern for Jerusalem and the commission he obtained from the king to go thither, *ch.* 1, 2. II. His building the wall of Jerusalem notwithstanding the opposition he met with, *ch.* 3, 4. III. His redressing the grievances of the people, *ch.* 5. IV. His finishing the wall, *ch.* 6. V. The account he took of the people, *ch.* 7. VI. The religious solemnities of reading the law, fasting, and praying, and renewing their covenants, to which he called the people (*ch.* 8–10). VII. The care he took for the replenishing of the holy city and the settling of the holy tribe, *ch.* 11, 12. VIII. His zeal in reforming various abuses, *ch.* 13. Some call this *the second book of Ezra,* not because he was the penman of it, but because it is a continuation of the history of the foregoing book, with which it is connected (*v.* 1). This was the last *historical* book that was written, as Malachi was the last *prophetical* book, of the Old Testament.

CHAPTER 1

Here we first meet with Nehemiah at the Persian court, where we find him, I. Inquisitive concerning the state of the Jews and Jerusalem (*v.* 1, 2). II. Informed of their deplorable condition (*v.* 3). III. Fasting and praying thereupon (*v.* 4), with a particular account of his prayer (*v.* 5–11). Such is the rise of this great man, by piety, not by policy.

Verses 1–4

What a tribe Nehemiah was of does nowhere appear; but, if it be true (which we are told by the author of the Maccabees, 2 Mac. 1:18) that he offered sacrifice, we must conclude him to have been a priest. Observe,

I. Nehemiah's station at the court of Persia. We are here told that he was *in Shushan the palace,* or royal city, of the king of Persia, where the court was ordinarily kept (*v.* 1), and (*v.* 11) that he was *the king's cup-bearer.* Kings and great men probably looked upon it as a piece of state to be attended by those of other nations. By this place at court he would be the better qualified for the service of his country in that post for which God had designed him, as Moses was the fitter to govern for being bred up in Pharaoh's court, and David in Saul's. He would also have the fairer opportunity of serving his country by his interest in the king and those about him. Observe, He is not forward to tell us what great preferment he had at court; it is not till the end of the chapter that he tells us he was *the king's cup-bearer* (a place of great trust, as well as of honour and profit), when he could not avoid the mentioning of it because of the following story; but at first he only said, *I was in Shushan the palace.* We may hence learn to be humble and modest, and slow to speak of our own advancements. But in the providences of God concerning him we may observe, to our comfort, 1. That when God has work to do he will never want instruments to do it with. 2. That those whom God designs to employ in his service he will find out proper ways both to fit for it and to call to it. 3. That God has his remnant in all places; we read of Obadiah in the house of Ahab, saints in Caesar's household, and a devout Nehemiah in Shushan the palace. 4. That God can make the courts of princes sometimes nurseries and sometimes sanctuaries to the friends and patrons of the church's cause.

II. Nehemiah's tender and compassionate enquiry concerning the state of the Jews in their own land, *v.* 2. It happened that a friend and relation of his came to the court, with some other company, by whom he had an opportunity of informing himself fully how it went with the children of the captivity and what posture Jerusalem, the beloved city, was in. Nehemiah lived at ease, in honour and fulness, himself, but could not forget that he was an Israelite, nor shake off the thoughts of his brethren in distress, but in spirit (like Moses, Acts 7:23) he *visited them and looked upon their burdens.* As distance of place did not alienate his affections from them (though they were out of sight, yet not out of mind), so neither did, 1. The dignity to which he was advanced. Though he was a great man, and probably rising higher, yet he did not think it below him to take cognizance of his brethren that were low and despised, nor was he ashamed to own his relation to them and concern for them. 2. The diversity of their sentiments from his, and the difference of their practice accordingly. Though he did not go to settle at Jerusalem himself (as we think he ought to have done now that liberty was proclaimed), but conformed to the court, and staid there, yet he did not therefore judge nor despise those that had returned, nor upbraid them as impolitic, but kindly concerned himself for them, was ready to do them all the good offices he could, and, that he might know which way to do them a kindness, *asked concerning them.* Note, It is lawful and good to enquire, "What news?" We should enquire especially concerning the state of the church and religion, and how it fares with the people of God; and the design of our enquiry must be, not that, like the Athenians, we may have something to talk of, but that we may know how to direct our prayers and our praises.

III. The melancholy account which is here given him of the present state of the Jews and Jerusalem, *v.* 3. Hanani, the person he enquired of, has this character given of him (*ch.* 7:2), that he *feared God above many,* and therefore would not only speak truly, but, when he spoke of the desolations of Jerusalem, would speak tenderly. It is probable that his errand to court at this time was to solicit some favour, some relief or other, that they stood in need of. Now the account he gives is, 1. That the holy seed was miserably trampled on and abused, *in great affliction and reproach,* insulted upon all occasions by their neighbours, and *filled with the scorning of those that were at ease.* 2. That the holy city was exposed and in ruins. *The wall of Jerusalem was* still *broken down, and the gates* were, as the Chaldeans left them, in ruins. This made the condition of the inhabitants both very despicable under the abiding marks of poverty and slavery, and very dangerous, for their enemies might when they pleased make an easy prey of them. The temple was built, the government settled, and a work of reformation brought to some head, but here was one good work yet undone; this was still wanting. Every Jerusalem, on this side the heavenly one, will have some defect or other in it, for the making up of which it will required the help and service of its friends.

IV. The great affliction this gave to Nehemiah and the deep concern it put him into, *v.* 4. 1. He *wept and mourned.* It was not only just when he heard the news that he fell into a passion of weeping, but his sorrow continued *certain days.* Note, The desolations and distresses of the church ought to be the matter of our grief, how much soever we live at ease. 2. He *fasted and prayed;* not in public (he had no opportunity of doing that), but *before the God of heaven,* who sees in secret, and will reward openly. By his fasting and praying, (1.) He consecrated his sorrows, and directed his tears aright, *sorrowed after a godly sort,* with an eye to God, because his name was reproached in the contempt cast on his people, whose cause therefore he thus commits to him. (2.) He eased his sorrows, and unburdened his spirit, by pouring out his complaint before God and leaving it with him. (3.) He took the right method of fetching in relief for his people and direction for himself in what way to serve them. Let those who are forming any good designs for the service of the public take God along with them for the first conception of them, and utter all their projects before him; this is the way to prosper in them.

Verses 5–11

We have here Nehemiah's prayer, a prayer that has reference to all the prayers which he had for some time before been putting up to God day and night, while he continued his sorrows for the desolations of Jerusalem, and withal to the petition he was now intending to present to the king his master for his favour to Jerusalem. We may observe in this prayer,

I. His humble and reverent address to God, in which he prostrates himself before him, and gives unto him the glory due unto his name, *v.* 5. It is much the same with that of Daniel, *ch.* 9:4. It teaches us to draw near to God, 1. With a holy awe of his majesty and glory, remembering that he is the God of heaven, infinitely above us, and sovereign Lord over us, and that he is *the great and terrible God,* infinitely excelling all the principalities and powers both of the upper and of the lower world, angels and kings; and he is a God to be worshipped with fear by all his people, and whose powerful wrath all his enemies have reason to be afraid of. Even the terrors of the Lord are improvable for the comfort and encouragement of those that trust in him. 2. With a holy confidence in his grace and truth, for he *keepeth covenant and mercy for those that love him,* not only the mercy that is promised, but even more than he promised: nothing shall be thought too much to be done for those that *love him and keep his commandments.*

II. His general request for the audience and acceptance of all the prayers and confessions he now made to God (*v.* 6): *"Let thy ear be attentive to the prayer,* not which I *say* (barely *saying* prayer will not serve), but which I *pray* before thee (then we are likely to speed in praying when we pray in praying), and let *they eyes be open* upon the heart from which the prayer comes, and the case which is in prayer laid before thee." God *formed the eye* and *planted the ear;* and therefore shall he not see clearly? shall not he hear attentively?

III. His penitent confession of sin; not only Israel has sinned (it was no great mortification to him to own that), but *I and my father's house have sinned, v.* 6. Thus does he humble himself, and take shame to himself, in this confession. *We have* (I and my family among the rest) *dealt very corruptly against thee, v.* 7. In the confession of sin, let these two things be owned as the malignity of it — that it is a corruption of ourselves and an affront to God; it is *dealing corruptly against God,* setting up the corruptions of our own hearts in opposition to the commands of God.

IV. The pleas he urges for mercy for his people Israel.

1. He pleads what God had of old said to them, the rule he had settled of his proceedings towards them, which might be the rule of their expectations from him, *v.* 8, 9. He had said indeed that, if they broke covenant with him, he would *scatter them among the nations,* and that threatening was fulfilled in their captivity: never was people so widely dispersed as Israel was at this time, though at first so closely incorporated; but he had said withal that if they *turned to him* (as now they began to do, having renounced idolatry and kept to the temple service) he would *gather them again.* This he quotes from Deu. 30:1–5, and begs leave to put God in mind of it (though the Eternal Mind needs no remembrancer) as that which he guided his desires by, and grounded his faith and hope upon, in praying this prayer: *Remember, I beseech thee, that word;* for thou hast said, *Put me in remembrance.* He had owned (*v.* 7), *We have not kept the judgments which thou commandedst thy servant Moses;* yet he begs (*v.* 8), Lord, *remember the word which thou commandedst thy servant Moses;* for the covenant is often said to be commanded. If God were not more mindful of his promises than we are of his precepts we should be undone. Our best pleas therefore in prayer are those that are taken from the promise of God, the *word on which he has caused us to hope,* Ps. 119:49.

2. He pleads the relation wherein of old they stood to God: "These are *thy servants and thy people* (*v.* 10), whom thou hast set apart for thyself, and taken into covenant with thee. Wilt thou suffer thy sworn enemies to trample upon and oppress thy sworn servants? If thou wilt not appear for thy people, whom wilt thou appear for?" See Isa. 63:19. As an evidence of their being God's servants he gives them this character (*v.* 11): *"They desire to fear thy name;* they are not only called by thy name, but really have a reverence for thy name; they now worship thee, and thee only, according to thy will, and have an awe of all the discoveries thou art pleased to make of thyself; this they have a desire to do," which denotes, (1.) Their good will to it. "It is their constant care and endeavour to be found in the way of their duty, and they aim at it, though in many instances they come short." (2.) Their complacency in it. "They take pleasure to fear thy name (so it may be read), not only do their duty, but do it with delight." Those shall graciously be accepted of God that truly desire to fear his name; for such a desire is his own work.

3. He pleads the great things God had formerly done for them (*v.* 10): *"Whom thou hast redeemed by thy great power,* in the days of old. Thy power is still the same; wilt thou not therefore still redeem them and perfect their redemption? Let not those be overpowered by the enemy that have a God of infinite power on their side."

Lastly, He concludes with a particular petition, that God would prosper him in his undertaking, and give him favour with the king: *this man* he calls him, for the greatest of men are but men before God; they must know themselves to be so (Ps. 9:20), and others must know them to be so. *Who art thou that thou shouldst be afraid of a man? Mercy in the sight of this man* is what he prays for, meaning not the king's mercy, but mercy from God in his address to the king. Favour with men is then comfortable when we can see it springing from the mercy of God.

CHAPTER 2

How Nehemiah wrestled with God and prevailed we read in the foregoing chapter; now here we are told how, like Jacob, he prevailed with men also, and so found that his prayers were heard and answered. I. He prevailed with the king to send him to Jerusalem with a commission to build a wall about it, and grant him what was necessary for it (*v.* 1–8). II. He prevailed against the enemies that would have obstructed him in his journey (*v.* 9–11) and laughed him out of his undertaking (*v.* 19, 20). III. He prevailed upon his own people to join with him in this good work, viewing the desolations of the walls (*v.* 12–16) and then gaining them to lend every one a hand towards the rebuilding of them (*v.* 17, 18). Thus did God own him in the work to which he called him.

Verses 1–8

When Nehemiah had prayed for the relief of his countrymen, and perhaps in David's words (Ps. 51:18, *Build thou the walls of Jerusalem),* he did not sit still and say, "Let

God now do his own work, for I have no more to do," but set himself to forecast what he could do towards it. our prayers must be seconded with our serious endeavours, else we mock God. Nearly four months passed, from Chisleu to Nisan (from November to March), before Nehemiah made his application to the king for leave to go to Jerusalem, either because the winter was not a proper time for such a journey, and he would not make the motion till he could pursue it, or because it was so long before his month of waiting came, and there was no coming into the king's presence uncalled, Esth. 4:11. Now that he attended the king's table he hoped to have his ear. We are not thus limited to certain moments in our addresses to the King of kings, but have liberty of access to him at all times; to the throne of grace we never come unseasonably. Now here is,

I. The occasion which he gave the king to enquire into his cares and griefs, by appearing sad in his presence. Those that speak to such great men must not fall abruptly upon their business, but fetch a compass. Nehemiah would try whether he was in a good humour before he ventured to tell him his errand, and this method he took to try him. He took up the wine and gave it to the king when he called for it, expecting that then he would look him in the face. He had not used to be sad in the king's presence, but conformed to the rules of the court (as courtiers must do), which would admit no sorrows, Esth. 4:2. Though he was a stranger, a captive, he was easy and pleasant. Good men should do what they can by their cheerfulness to convince the world of the pleasantness of religious ways and to roll away the reproach cast upon them as melancholy; but there is a time for all things, Eccl. 3:4. Nehemiah now saw cause both to be sad and to appear so. The miseries of Jerusalem gave him cause to be sad, and his showing his grief would give occasion to the king to enquire into the cause. He did not dissemble sadness, for he was really in grief for the afflictions of Joseph, and was not like the hypocrites who *disfigure their faces;* yet he could have concealed his grief if it had been necessary (the heart knows its own bitterness, and in the midst of laughter is often sad), but it would now serve his purpose to discover his sadness. Though he had wine before him, and probably, according to the office of the cup-bearer, did himself drink of it before he gave it to the king, yet it would not *make his heart glad,* while God's Israel was in distress.

II. The kind notice which the king took of his sadness and the enquiry he made into the cause of it (*v.* 2): *Why is thy countenance sad, seeing thou art not sick?* Note, 1. We ought, from a principle of Christian sympathy, to concern ourselves in the sorrows and sadnesses of others, even of our inferiors, and not say, What is it to us? Let not masters despise their servants' griefs, but desire to make them easy. The great God is not pleased with the dejections and disquietments of his people, but would have them both *serve him with gladness* and *eat their bread with joy.* 2. It is not strange if those that are sick have sad countenances, because of what is felt and what is feared; sickness will make those grave that were most airy and gay: yet a good man, even in sickness, may be of good cheer if he knows that his sins are forgiven. 3. Freedom from sickness is so great a mercy that while we have that we ought not to be inordinately dejected under any outward burden; yet sorrow for our own sins, the sins of others, and the calamities of God's church, may well sadden the countenance, without sickness.

III. The account which Nehemiah gave the king of the cause of his sadness, which he gave with meekness and fear. 1. With fear. He owned that now (though it appears by the following story that he was a man of courage) *he was sorely afraid,* perhaps of the king's wrath (for those eastern monarchs assumed an absolute power of life and death, Dan. 2:12, 13; 5:19) or of misplacing a word, and losing his request by the mismanagement of it. Though he was a wise man, he was jealous of himself, lest he should say any thing imprudently; it becomes us to be so. A good assurance is indeed a good accomplishment, yet a humble self-diffidence is not man's dispraise. 2. With meekness. Without reflection upon any man, and with all the respect, deference, and good-will, imaginable to the king his master, he says, *"Let the king live for ever;* he is wise and good, and the fittest man in the world to rule." He modestly asked, *"Why should not my countenance be sad* as it is *when* (though I myself am well and at east) *the city"* (the king knew what city he meant), *"the place of my fathers' sepulchres, lieth waste?"* Many are melancholy and sad but can give no reason for being so, cannot tell why nor wherefore; such should chide themselves for, and chide themselves out of, their unjust and unreasonable griefs and fears. But Nehemiah could give so good a reason for his sadness as to appeal to the king himself concerning it. Observe, (1.) He calls Jerusalem *the place of his fathers' sepulchres,* the place where his ancestors were buried. It is good for us to think often of our fathers' sepulchres; we are apt to dwell in our thoughts upon their honours and titles, their houses and estates, but let us think also of their sepulchres, and consider that those who have gone before us in the world have also gone before us out of the world, and their monuments are momentos to us. There is also a great respect owing to the memory of our fathers, which we should not be willing to see injured. All nations, even those that have had no expectation of the resurrection of the dead, have looked upon the sepulchres of their ancestors as in some degree sacred and not to be violated. (2.) He justifies himself in his grief: "I do well to be sad. Why should I not be so?" There is a time even for pious and prosperous men to be sad and to show their grief. The best men must not think to antedate heaven by banishing all sorrowful thoughts; it is a vale of tears we pass through, and we must submit to the temper of the climate. (3.) He assigns the ruins of Jerusalem as the true cause of his grief. Note, All the grievances of the church, but especially its desolations, are, and ought to be, matter of grief and sadness to all good people, to all that have a concern for God's honour and that are living members of Christ's mystical body, and are of a public spirit; they favour even Zion's dust, Ps. 102:14.

IV. The encouragement which the king gave him to tell his mind, and the application he thereupon made in his heart to God, *v.* 4. The king had an affection for him, and was not pleased to see him melancholy. It is also probable that he had a kindness for the Jews' religion; he had discovered it before in the commission he gave to Ezra, who was a churchman, and now again in the power he put Nehemiah into, who was a statesman. Wanting therefore only to know how he might be serviceable to Jerusalem, he asks this its anxious friend, *"For what dost thou make request?* Something thou wouldst have; what is it?" He was afraid to speak (*v.* 2), but this gave him boldness; much more may the invitation Christ has given us to pray, and the promise that we shall speed, enable us to come boldly to the throne of grace. Nehemiah immediately *prayed to the God of heaven* that he would give him wisdom to ask properly and incline the king's heart to grant him his request. Those that would find favour with kings must secure the favour of the King of kings. He prayed to the God of heaven as infinitely above even this mighty monarch. It was not a solemn prayer (he had not opportunity for that), but a secret sudden ejaculation; he lifted up his heart to that God who understands the language of his heart: *Lord, give me a mouth and wisdom; Lord, give me favour in the sight of this man.* Note, It is good to be much in pious ejaculations, especially upon particular occasions. Wherever we are we have a way open heaven-ward. This will not hinder any business, but further it rather; therefore let no business hinder this, but give rise to it rather. Nehemiah had prayed very solemnly with reference to this very occasion (*ch.* 1:11), yet, when it comes to the push, he prays again. Ejaculations and solemn prayers must not jostle out one another, but each have its place.

V. His humble petition to the king. When he had this encouragement he presented his petition very modestly and with submission to the king's wisdom (*v.* 5), but very explicitly. He asked for a commission to go as governor to Judah, to build the wall of Jerusalem, and to stay there for a certain time, so many months, we may suppose; and then either he had his commission renewed or went back and was sent again, so that he presided there twelve years at least, *ch.* 5:14. He also asked for a convoy (*v.* 7), and an order upon the governors, not only to permit and suffer him to pass through their respective provinces, but to supply him with what he had occasion for, with another order upon the keeper of the forest of Lebanon to give him timber for the work that he designed.

VI. The king's great favour to him in asking him *when he would return, v.* 6. He intimated that he was unwilling to lose him, or to be long without him, yet to gratify him, and to do a real office of kindness to his people, he would spare him awhile, and let him have what clauses he pleased inserted in his commission, *v.* 8. Here was an immediate answer to his prayer; for the seed of Jacob never sought the God of Jacob in vain. In the account he gives of the success of his petition he takes notice, 1. Of the presence of the queen; she sat by (*v.* 6), which (they say) was not usual in the Persian court, Esth. 1:11. Whether the queen was his back friend, that would have hindered him, and he observes it to the praise of God's powerful providence that though she was by yet he succeeded, or whether she was his true friend, and it is observed to the praise of God's kind providence that she was present to help forward his request, is not certain. 2. Of the power and grace of God. He gained his point, not according to his merit, his interest in the king, or his good management, but *according to the good hand of his God upon him.* Gracious souls take notice of God's hand, his good hand, in all events which turn in favour of them. *This is the Lord's doing,* and therefore doubly acceptable.

Verses 9–20

We are here told,

I. Now Nehemiah was dismissed by the court he was sent from. The king appointed *captains of the army* and *horsemen* to go *with him* (*v.* 9), both for his guard and to show that he was a man whom *the king did delight to honour,* that all the king's servants might respect him accordingly. Those whom the King of kings sends he thus protects, he thus dignifies with a host of angels to attend them.

II. How he was received by the country he was sent to.

1. By the Jews and their friends at Jerusalem. We are told,

(1.) That while he concealed his errand they took little notice of him. He was at *Jerusalem three days* (*v.* 11), and it does not appear that any of the great men of the city waited on him to congratulate him on his arrival, but he remained unknown. The king sent horsemen to attend him, but the Jews sent none to meet him; he had no beast with him, but that which he himself rode on, *v.* 12. Wise men, and those who are worthy of double honour, yet covet not to come with observation, to make a show, or make a noise, no, not when they come with the greatest blessings. Those that shortly are to have *the dominion in the morning* the world now knows not, but they lie hid, 1 Jn. 3:1.

(2.) That though they took little notice of him he took great notice of them and their state. He arose in the night, and viewed the ruins of the walls, probably by moon-light (*v.* 13), that he might see what was to be done and in what method they must go about it, whether the old foundation would serve, and what there was of the old materials that would be of use. Note, [1.] Good work is likely to be well done when it is first well considered. [2.] It is the wisdom of those who are engaged in public business, as much as may be, to *see with their own eyes,* and not to proceed altogether upon the reports and representations of others, and yet to do this without noise, and if possible unobserved. [3.] Those that would build up the church's walls must first take notice of the ruins of those walls. Those that would know how to amend must enquire what is amiss, what needs reformation, and what may serve as it is.

(3.) That when he disclosed his design to the rulers and people they cheerfully concurred with him in it. He did not tell them, at first, what he came about (*v.* 16), because he would not seem to do it for ostentation, and because, if he found it impracticable, he might retreat the more honourably. Upright humble men will not sound a trumpet before their alms or any other of their good offices. But when he had viewed and considered the thing, and probably felt the pulse of the rulers and people, he told them *what God had put into his heart* (*v.* 12), even to *build up the wall of Jerusalem, v.* 17. Observe, [1.] How fairly he proposed the undertaking to them: *"You see the distress we are in,* how we lie exposed to the enemies that are round about us, how justly they reproach us as foolish and despicable, how easily they may make a prey of us whenever they have a mind; *come, therefore, and let us build up the wall."* He did not undertake to do the work without them (it could not be the work of one man), nor did he charge or command imperiously, though he had the king's commission; but in a friendly brotherly way he exhorted and excited them to join with him in this work. To encourage them hereto, he speaks of the design, *First,* As that which owed it origin to the special grace of God. He takes not the praise of it to himself, as a good thought of his own, but acknowledges that God *put it into his heart,* and therefore they all ought to countenance it (whatever is of God must be promoted), and might hope to prosper in it, for what God puts men upon he will own them in. *Secondly,* As that which owed its progress hitherto to the special providence of God. He produced the king's commission, told them how readily it was granted and how forward the king was to favour his design, in which he saw the hand of his God *good upon him.* It would encourage both him and them to proceed in an undertaking which God had so remarkably smiled upon. Thus he proposed it to them; and, [2.] They presently came to a resolution, one and all, to concur with him: *Let us rise up and build.* They are ashamed that they have sat still so long without so much as attempting this needful work, and now resolve to rise up out of their slothfulness, to bestir themselves, and to stir up one another. *"Let us rise up,"* that is, "let us do it with vigour, and diligence, and resolution, as those that are determined to go through with it." *So they strengthened their hands,* their own and one another's, *for this good work.* Note, *First,* Many a good work would find hands enough to be laid to it if there were but one good head to lead in it. They all saw the desolations of Jerusalem, yet none proposed the repair of them; but, when Nehemiah proposed it, they all consented to it. It is a pity that a good motion should be lost purely for want of one to move it and to break the ice in it. *Secondly,* By stirring up ourselves and one another to that which is good, we strengthen ourselves and one another for it; for the great reason why we are weak in our duty is because we are cold to it, indifferent and unresolved. Let us now see how Nehemiah was received,

2. By those that wished ill to the Jews. Those whom God and his Israel blessed they cursed. (1.) When he did but show his face it vexed them, *v.* 10. Sanballat and Tobiah, two of the Samaritans, but by birth the former a Moabite, the latter an Ammonite, when they saw one come armed with a commission from the king to do service to Israel, *were exceedingly grieved* that all their little paltry arts to weaken Israel were thus baffled and frustrated by a fair, and noble, and generous project to strengthen them. Nothing is a greater vexation to the enemies of good people, who have misrepresented them to princes as turbulent, and factious, and not fit to live, than to see them stand right in the opinion of their rulers, their innocency cleared and their reproach rolled away, and that they are thought not only fit to live, but fit to be trusted. When they saw a man come in that manner, who professedly *sought the welfare of the children of Israel,* it vexed them to the heart. *The wicked shall see it, and be grieved.* (2.) When he began to act they set themselves to hinder him, but in vain, *v.* 19, 20. [1.] See here with what little reason the enemies attempted to discourage him. They represented the undertaking as a silly thing: *They laughed us to scorn and despised us* as foolish builders, that could not finish what we began. They represented the undertaking also as a wicked thing, no better than treason: *Will you rebel against the king?* Because this was the old invidious charge, though now they had a commission from the king and were taken under his protection, yet still they must be called rebels. [2.] See also with what good reason the Jews slighted these discouragements. They bore up themselves with this that they were the *servants of the God of heaven,* the only true and living God, that they were acting for him in what they did, and that therefore he would bear them out and prosper them, though the heathen raged, Ps. 2:1. They considered also that the reason why these enemies did so malign them was because they had no right in Jerusalem, but envied them their right in it. Thus may the impotent menaces of the church's enemies be easily despised by the church's friends.

CHAPTER 3

Saying and doing are often two things: many are ready to say, "Let us rise up and build," who sit still and do nothing, like that fair-spoken son who said,"I go, Sir, but went not." The undertakers here were none of those. As soon as they had resolved to build the wall about Jerusalem they lost no time, but set about it presently, as we find in this chapter. Let it never be said that we left that good work to be done to-morrow which we might as well have done to-day. This chapter gives an account of two things: — I. The names of the builders, which are recorded here to their honour, for they were such as herein discovered a great zeal for God and their country, both a pious and a public spirit, a great degree both of industry and courage; and what they did was fit to be thus largely registered, both for their praise and for the encouragement of others to follow their example. II. The order of the building; they took it before them, and ended where they began. They repaired, 1. From the sheep-gate to the fish-gate (*v.* 1, 2). 2. Thence to the old-gate (*v.* 3–5). 3. Thence to the valley-gate (*v.* 6–12). 4. Thence to the dung-gate (*v.* 13, 14). 5. Thence to the gate of the fountain (*v.* 15). 6. Thence to the water-gate (*v.* 16–26). 7. Thence by the horse-gate to the sheep-gate again, where they began (*v.* 27–32), and so they brought their work quite round the city.

Verses 1–32

The best way to know how to divide this chapter is to observe how the work was divided among the undertakers, that every one might know what he had to do, and mind it accordingly with a holy emulation, and desire to excel, yet without any contention, animosity, or separate interest. No strife appears among them but which should do most for the public good. Several things are observable in the account here given of the building of the wall about Jerusalem: —

I. That Eliashib the high priest, with his brethren the priests, led the van in this troop of builders, *v.* 1. Ministers should be foremost in every good work; for their office obliges them to teach and quicken by their example, as well as by their doctrine. If there be labour in it, who so fit as they to work? if danger, who so fit as they to venture? The dignity of the high priest was very great, and obliged him to signalize himself in this service. The priests repaired the *sheep-gate,* so called because through it were brought the sheep that were to be sacrificed in the temple; and therefore the priests undertook the repair of it because *the offerings of the Lord made by fire were* their inheritance. And of this gate only it is said that *they sanctified it* with the word and prayer, and perhaps with sacrifices perhaps, 1. Because it led to the temple; or, 2. Because with this the building of the wall began, and it is probable (though they were at work in all parts of the wall at the same time) that this was first finished, and therefore at this gate they solemnly committed their city and the walls of it to the divine protection; or, 3. Because the priests were the builders of it; and it becomes ministers above others, being themselves in a peculiar manner sanctified to God, to sanctify to him all their performances, and to do even their common actions *after a godly sort.*

II. That the undertakers were very many, who each took his share, some more and some less, in this work, according as their ability was. Note, What is to be done for the public good every one should assist in, and further, to the utmost of his place and power. United force will conquer that which no individual dares venture on. Many hands will make light work.

III. That many were active in this work who were not themselves inhabitants of Jerusalem, and therefore consulted purely the public welfare and not any private interest or advantage of their own. Here are the men of Jericho with the first (*v.* 2), the men of Gibeon and Mizpah (*v.* 7), and Zanoah, *v.* 13. Every Israelite should lend a hand towards the building up of Jerusalem.

IV. That several rulers, both of Jerusalem and of other cities, were active in this work, thinking themselves bound in honour to do the utmost that their wealth and power enabled them to do for the furtherance of this good work. But it is observable that they are called rulers of *part,* or the *half part,* of their respective cities. One was *ruler of the half part of Jerusalem* (*v.* 12), another of part of Beth-haccerem (*v.* 14), another of part of Mizpah (*v.* 15), another of *the half part of Beth-zur* (*v.* 16), one was ruler of *one half part,* and another of *the other half part, of Keilah, v.* 17, 18. Perhaps the Persian government would not entrust any one with a strong city, but appointed two to be a watch upon each other. Rome had two consuls.

V. Here is a just reproach fastened upon the nobles of Tekoa, that they *put not their necks to the work of their Lord* (*v.* 5), that is, they would not come under the yoke of an obligation to this service; as if the dignity and liberty of their peerage were their discharge from serving God and doing good, which are indeed the highest honour and the truest freedom. Let not nobles think any thing below them by which they may advance the interests of their country; for what else is their nobility good for but that it puts them in a higher and larger sphere of usefulness than that in which inferior persons move?

VI. Two persons joined in repairing *the old gate* (*v.* 6), and so were co-founders, and shared the honour of it between them. The good work which we cannot compass ourselves we must be thankful to those that will go partners with us in. Some think that this is called the *old gate* because it belonged to the ancient Salem, which was said to be first built by Melchizedek.

VII. Several good honest tradesmen, as well as priests and rulers, were active in this work — *goldsmiths, apothecaries, merchants, v.* 8, 32. They did not think their callings excused them, nor plead that they could not leave their shops to attend the public business, knowing that what they lost would certainly be made up to them by the blessing of God upon their callings.

VIII. Some ladies are spoken of as helping forward this work — *Shallum and his daughters* (*v.* 12), who, though not capable of personal service, yet having their portions in their own hands, or being rich widows, contributed money for buying materials and paying workmen. St. Paul speaks of some good women that *laboured with him in the gospel,* Phil. 4:3.

IX. Of some it is said that they repaired *over against their houses* (*v.* 10, 23, 28, 29), and of one (who, it is likely, was only a lodger) that he repaired *over against his chamber, v.* 30. When a general good work is to be done each should apply himself to that part of it that falls nearest to him and is within his reach. If every one will sweep before his own door, the street will be clean; if every one will mend one, we shall be all mended. If he that has but a chamber will repair before that, he does his part.

X. Of one it is said that he *earnestly* repaired that which fell to his share (*v.* 20) — he did it with an inflamed zeal; not that others were cold or indifferent, but he was the most vigorous of any of them and consequently made himself remarkable. It is good to be thus *zealously affected in a good thin;* and it is probable that this good man's zeal provoked very many to take the more pains and make the more haste.

XI. Of one of these builders it is observed that he was *the sixth son* of his father, *v.* 30. His five elder brethren, it seems, laid not their hand to this work, but he did. In doing that which is good we need not stay to see our elders go before us; if they decline it, it does not therefore follow that we must. Thus the younger brother, if he be the better man, and does God and his generation better service, is indeed the better gentleman; those are most honourable that are most useful.

XII. Some of those that had *first done helped their fellows,* and undertook another share where they saw there was most need. Meremoth repaired, *v.* 4. and again, *v.* 21. And the Tekoites, besides the piece they repaired (*v.* 5), undertook another piece (*v.* 27), which is the more remarkable because their nobles set them a bad example by withdrawing from the service, which, instead of serving them for an excuse to sit still, perhaps made them the more forward to do double work, that by their zeal they might either shame or atone for the covetousness and carelessness of their nobles.

Lastly, Here is no mention of any particular share that Nehemiah himself had in this work. A name-sake of his is mentioned, *v.* 16. But did he do nothing? Yes, though he undertook not any particular piece of the wall, yet he did more than any of them, for he had the oversight of them all; half of his servants worked where there was most need, and the other half stood sentinel, as we find afterwards (*ch.* 4:16), while he himself in his own person walked the rounds, directed and encouraged the builders, set his hand to the work where he saw occasion, and kept a watchful eye upon the motions of the enemy, as we shall find in the next chapter. The pilot needs not haul at a rope: it is enough for him to steer.

CHAPTER 4

We left all hands at work for the building of the wall about Jerusalem. But such good work is not wont to be carried on without opposition; now here we are told what opposition was given to it, and what methods Nehemiah took to forward the work, notwithstanding that opposition. I. Their enemies reproached and ridiculed their undertaking, but their scoffs they answered with prayers: they heeded them not, but went on with their work notwithstanding (*v.* 1–6). II. They formed a bloody design against them, to hinder them by force of arms (*v.* 7, 8, 10–12). To guard against this Nehemiah prayed (*v.* 9), set guards (*v.* 13), and encouraged them to fight (*v.* 14), by which the design was broken (*v.* 15), and so the work was carried on with all needful precaution against a surprise (*v.* 16–23). In all this Nehemiah approved himself a man of great wisdom and courage, as well as great piety.

Verses 1–6

Here is, I. The spiteful scornful reflection which Sanballat and Tobiah cast upon the Jews for their attempt to build the wall about Jerusalem. The country rang of it presently; intelligence was brought of it to Samaria, that nest of enemies to the Jews and their prosperity; and here we are told how they received the tidings. 1. In heart. They were very angry at the undertaking, and had *great indignation, v.* 1. It vexed them that Nehemiah came to seek the welfare of the children of Israel (*ch.* 2:10); but, when they heard of this great undertaking for their good, they were out of all patience. They had hitherto pleased themselves with the thought that while Jerusalem was unwalled they could swallow it up and make themselves masters of it when they pleased; but, if it be walled, it will not only be fenced against them, but by degrees become formidable to them. The strength and safety of the church are the grief and vexation of its enemies. 2. In word. They despised it, and made it the subject of their ridicule. In this they sufficiently displayed their malice; but good was brought out of it; for, looking upon it as a foolish undertaking that would sink under its own weight, they did not go about to obstruct it till it was too late. Let us see with what pride and malice they set themselves publicly to banter it. (1.) Sanballat speaks with scorn of the workmen: *"These feeble Jews"* (*v.* 2), "what will they do for materials? *Will they revive the stones out of the rubbish?* And what mean they by being so hasty? Do they think to make the walling of a city but one day's work, and to keep the feast of dedication with sacrifice the next day? Poor silly people! See how ridiculous they make themselves!" (2.) Tobiah speaks with no less scorn of the work itself. He has his jest too, and must show his wit, *v.* 3. Profane scoffers sharpen one another. "Sorry work," says he, "they are likely to make of it; they themselves will be ashamed of it: *If a fox go up,* not with his subtlety, but with his weight, he *will break down their stone wall.*" Many a good work has been thus looked upon with contempt by the *proud and haughty scorners.*

II. Nehemiah's humble and devout address to God when he heard of these reflections. He had notice brought him of what they said. It is probable that they themselves sent him a message to this purport, to discourage him, hoping to jeer him out of his attempt; but he did not answer these fools according to their folly; he did not upbraid them with their weakness, but looked up to God by prayer.

1. He begs of God to take notice of the indignities that were done them (*v.* 4), and in this we are to imitate him: *Hear, O our God! for we are despised.* Note, (1.) God's people have often been a despised people, and loaded with contempt. (2.) God does, and will, hear all the slights that are put upon his people, and it is their comfort that he does so and a good reason why they should be as though they were deaf, Ps. 38:13, 15. "Thou art our God to whom we appeal; our cause needs no more than a fair hearing."

2. He begs of God to avenge their cause and turn the reproach upon the enemies themselves (*v.* 4, 5); and this was spoken rather by a spirit of prophecy than by a spirit of prayer, and is not to be imitated by us who are taught of Christ to *pray for* those that *despitefully use and persecute us.* Christ himself prayed for those that reproached him: *Father, forgive them.* Nehemiah here prays, *Cover not their iniquity.* Note, (1.) Those that cast contempt on God's people do but prepare everlasting shame for themselves. (2.) It is a sin from which sinners are seldom recovered. Doubtless Nehemiah had reason to think the hearts of those sinners were desperately hardened, so that they would never repent of it, else he would not have prayed that it might *never be blotted out.* The reason he gives is not, *They have abused us,* but, *They have provoked thee,* and that *before the builders,* to whom, it is likely, they sent a spiteful message. Note, We should be angry at the malice of persecutors, not because it is abusive to us, but because it is offensive to God; and on that we may ground an expectation that God will appear against it, Ps. 74:18, 22.

III. The vigour of the builders, notwithstanding these reflections, *v.* 6. They made such good speed that in a little time they had run up the wall to half its height, for *the people had a mind to work;* their hearts were upon it, and they would have it forwarded. Note, 1. Good work goes on well when people have a mind to it. 2. The reproaches of enemies should rather quicken us to our duty than drive us from it.

Verses 7–15

We have here,

I. The conspiracy which the Jews' enemies formed against them, to stay the building by slaying the builders. The conspirators were not only Sanballat and Tobiah, but other neighbouring people whom they had drawn into the plot. They flattered themselves with a fancy that the work would soon stand still of itself; but, when they heard that it went on a prospered, they were angry at the Jews for being so hasty to push the work forward and angry at themselves for being so slow in opposing it (*v.* 7): *They were very wroth. Cursed be their anger, for it was fierce, and their wrath, for it was cruel.* Nothing would serve but they would *fight against Jerusalem, v.* 8. Why, what quarrel had they with the Jews? Had they done them any wrong? Or did they design them any? No, they lived peaceably by them; but it was merely out of envy and malice; they hated the Jews' piety, and were therefore vexed at their prosperity and sought their ruin. Observe, 1. How unanimous they were: *They conspired all of them together,* though of different interests among themselves, yet one in their opposition to the work of God. 2. How close they were; they said, *"They shall not know, neither see,* till we have them at our mercy." Thus they took crafty counsel, and digged deep to hide it from the Lord, and promised themselves security and success from the secresy of their management. 3. How cruel they were: *We will come and slay them.* If nothing less than the murder of the workmen will put a stop to the work, they will not stick at that; nay, it is their blood they thirst for, and they are glad of any pretence to glut themselves with it. 4. What the design was and how confident they were of success: it was to *cause the work to cease* (*v.* 11), and this they were confident that they should effect. The hindering of good work is that which bad men aim at and promise themselves; but good work is God's work, and it shall prosper.

II. The discouragements which the builders themselves laboured under. At the very time when the adversaries said, Let us *cause the work to cease,* Judah said, "Let us even let it fall, for we are not able to go forward with it," *v.* 10. They represent the labourers as tired, and the remaining difficulties, even of that first part of their work, the removing of the rubbish, as insuperable, and therefore they think it advisable to desist for the present. Can Judah, that warlike valiant tribe, sneak thus? Active leading men have many times as much ado to grapple with the fears of their friends as with the terrors of their enemies.

III. The information that was brought to Nehemiah of the enemies' designs, *v.* 12. There were *Jews that dwelt by them,* in the country, who, though they had not zeal enough to bring them to Jerusalem to help their brethren in building the wall, yet, having by their situation opportunity to discover the enemies' motions, had so much honesty and affection to the cause as to give intelligence of them; nay, that their intelligence might be the more credited, they came themselves to give it, and they said it ten times, repeating it as men in earnest, and under a concern, and the report was confirmed by many witnesses. The intelligence they gave is expressed abruptly, and finds work for the critics to make out the sense of it, which perhaps is designed to intimate that they gave this intelligence as men out of breath and in confusion, whose very looks would make up the deficiencies of their words. I think it may be read, without supplying any thing: *"Whatever place you turn to, they are against us,* so that you have need to be upon your guard on all sides." Note, God has many ways of bringing to light, and so bringing to nought, the devices and designs of his and his church's enemies. Even the cold and feeble Jews that contentedly dwell by them shall be made to serve as spies upon them; nay, rather than fail, *a bird of the air shall carry their voice.*

IV. The pious and prudent methods which Nehemiah, hereupon, took to baffle the design, and to secure his work and workmen.

1. It is said (*v.* 14) he *looked.* (1.) He looked up, engaged God for him, and put himself and his cause under the divine protection (*v.* 9): *We made our prayer unto our God.* That was the way of this good man, and should be our way; all his cares, all his griefs, all his fears, he spread before God, and thereby made himself easy. This was the first thing he did; before he used any means, he made his prayer to God, for with him we must always begin. (2.) He looked about him. Having prayed, he *set a watch against them.* The instructions Christ has given us in our spiritual warfare agree with this example, Mt. 26:41. *Watch and pray.* If we think to secure ourselves by prayer only, without watchfulness, we are slothful and tempt God; if by watchfulness, without prayer, we are proud and slight God; and, either way, we forfeit his protection.

2. Observe, (1.) How he posted the guards, *v.* 13. *In the lower places* he set them *behind the wall,* that they might annoy the enemy over it, as a breast-work; but *in the higher places,* where the wall was raised to its full height, he set them upon it, that from the top of it they might throw down stones or darts upon the heads of the assailants: he set them *after their families,* that mutual relation might engage them to mutual assistance. (2.) How he animated and encouraged the people, *v.* 14. He observed even the nobles and rulers themselves, as well as the rest of the people, to be in a great consternation upon the intelligence that was brought them, and ready to conclude that they were all undone, by which their hands were weakened both for work and war, and therefore, he endeavours to silence their fears. "Come," says he, *"be not afraid of them,* but behave yourselves valiantly, considering, [1.] Whom you fight under. You cannot have a better captain: *Remember the Lord, who is great and terrible;* you think your enemies *great and terrible,* but what are they in comparison with God, especially in opposition to him? He is great above them to control them, and will be terrible to them when he comes to reckon with them." Those that with an eye of faith see the church's God to be great and terrible will see the church's enemies to be mean and despicable. The reigning fear of God is the best antidote against the ensnaring fear of man. He that is afraid of *a man that shall die forgets the Lord his Maker,* Isa. 51:12, 13. [2.] "Whom you fight for. You cannot have a better cause; you fight for *your brethren* (Ps. 122:8), *your sons, and your daughters.* All that is dear to you in their world lies at stake; therefore *behave yourselves valiantly.*"

V. The happy disappointment which this gave to the enemies, *v.* 15. When they found that their design was discovered, and that the Jews were upon their guard, they concluded that it was to no purpose to attempt any thing, but that *God had brought their counsel to nought.* They knew they could not gain their point but by surprise, and, if their plot was known, it was quashed. The Jews hereupon *returned every one to his work,* with so much the more cheerfulness because they saw plainly that God owned it and owned them in the doing of it. Note, God's care of our safety should engage and encourage us to go on with vigour in our duty. As soon as ever a danger is over let us *return to our work,* and trust God another time.

Verses 16–23

When the builders had so far reason to think the design of the enemies broken *as to return to their work,* yet they were not so secure as to lay down their arms, knowing how restless and unwearied they were in their attempts, and that, if one design failed, they would be hatching another. Thus must we watch always against our spiritual enemies, and not expect that our warfare will be accomplished till our work is. See what course Nehemiah took, that the people might hold themselves in a readiness, in case there should be an attack. 1. While one half were at work, the other half were under their arms, holding *spears, and shields, and bows,* not only for themselves but for the labourers too, who would immediately quit their work, and betake themselves to their weapons, upon the first alarm, *v.* 16. It is probable that they changed services at stated hours, which would relieve the fatigue of both, and particularly would be an ease to the *bearers of burdens,* whose *strength* had *decayed* (*v.* 10); while they held the weapons, they were eased and yet not idle. Thus dividing their time between the trowels and the spears, they are said to *work with one hand* and hold their weapons *with the other* (*v.* 17), which cannot be understood literally, for the work would require both hands; but it intimates that they were equally employed in both. Thus must we work out our salvation with the weapons of our warfare in our hand; for in every duty we must expect to meet with opposition from our spiritual enemies, against whom we must still be *fighting the good fight of faith.* 2. Every builder had a sword by his side (*v.* 18), which he could carry without hindering his labour. The word of God is the sword of the Spirit, which we ought to have always at hand and never to seek, both in our labours and in our conflicts as Christians. 3. Care was taken both to get and give early notice of the approach of the enemy, in case they should endeavour to surprise them. Nehemiah kept a trumpeter always by him to sound an alarm, upon the first intimation of danger. The work was large, and the builders were dispersed; for in all parts of the wall they were labouring at the same time. Nehemiah continually walked round to oversee the work and encourage the workmen, and so would have speedy intelligence if the enemy made an attack, of which, by sound of trumpet, he would soon give notice to all, and they must immediately repair to him with a full assurance that their *God* would *fight for them, v.* 18–20. When they acted as workmen, it was requisite they should be dispersed wherever there was work to do; but when as soldiers it was requisite they should come into close order, and be found in a body. Thus should the labourers in Christ's building be ready to unite against a common foe. 4. The inhabitants of the villages were ordered to lodge within Jerusalem, with their servants, not only that they might be the nearer to their work in the morning, but that they might be ready to help in case of an attack in the night, *v.* 22. The strength of a city lies more in its hands than in its walls; secure them, and God's blessing upon them, and be secure. 5. Nehemiah himself, and all his men, kept closely to their business. The spears were held up, with the sight of them to terrify the enemy, not only from sun to sun, but from twilight to twilight every day, *v.* 21. Thus ought we to be always upon our guard against our spiritual enemies, not only (as here) while *it is light,* but when *it is dark,* for they are the *rulers of the darkness of this world.* Nay, so very intent was Nehemiah upon his work, and so fast did he hold his servants to it, that while the heat of the business lasted neither he himself nor his attendants went into bed, but every night lay and slept in their clothes (*v.* 23), except that they shifted them now and then, either for cleanliness or in a case of ceremonial pollution. It was a sign that their heart was upon their work when they could not find time to dress and undress, but resolved they would be at all times ready for service. Good work is likely to go on successfully when those that labour in it thus make a business of it.

CHAPTER 5

How bravely Nehemiah, as a wise and faithful governor, stood upon his guard against the attacks of enemies abroad, we read in the foregoing chapter. Here we have him no less bold and active to redress grievances at home, and, having kept them from being destroyed by their enemies, to keep them from destroying one another. Here is, I. The complaint which the poor made to him of the great hardships which the rich (of whom they were forced to borrow money) put upon them, *v.* 1–5). II. The effectual course which Nehemiah took both to reform the oppressors and to relieve the oppressed (*v.* 6–13). III. The good example which he himself, as governor, set them of compassion and tenderness (*v.* 14–19).

Verses 1–5

We have here the tears of the oppressed, which Solomon considered, Eccl. 4:1. Let us consider them as here they are dropped before Nehemiah, whose office it was, as governor, to *deliver the poor and needy, and rid them out of the hand of the wicked* oppressors, Ps. 82:4. Hard times and hard hearts made the poor miserable.

I. The times they lived in were hard. There was a dearth of corn (*v.* 3), probably for want of rain, with which God had chastised their neglect of his house (Hag. 1:9–11) and the non-payment of their church-dues, Mal. 3:9, 10. Thus foolish sinful men bring God's judgments upon themselves, and then fret and complain of them. When the markets are high, and provisions scarce and dear, the poor soon feel from it, and are pinched by it. Blessed be God for the mercy, and God deliver us from the sin, of *fulness of bread,* Eze. 16:49. That which made the scarcity here complained of the more grievous was that their *sons and their daughters were many, v.* 2. The families that were most necessitous were most numerous; here were the mouths, but where was the meat? Some have estates and no children to inherit them; others have children and no estates to leave them. Those who have both have reason to be thankful; those who have neither may the more easily be content. Those who have great families and little substance must learn to live by faith in God's providence and promise; and those who have little families and great substance must *make their abundance a supply for the wants of others.* But this was not all: as corn was dear, so the taxes were high; the king's tribute must be paid, *v.* 4. This mark of their captivity still remained upon them. Perhaps it was a poll-money that was required, and then, their sons and their daughters being many, it rose the higher. The more they had to maintain (a hard case!) the more they had to pay. Now, it seems, they had not wherewithal of their own to buy corn and pay taxes, but were necessitated to borrow. Their families came poor out of Babylon; they had been at great expense in building them houses, and had not yet got up their strength when these new burdens came upon them. The straits of poor housekeepers who make hard shift to get an honest livelihood, and sometimes want what is fitting for them and their families, are well worthy the compassionate consideration of those who either with their wealth or with their power are in a capacity to help them.

II. The persons they dealt with were hard. Money must be had, but it must be borrowed; and those that lent them money, taking advantage of their necessity, were very hard upon them and made a prey of them. 1. They exacted interest from them at twelve per cent, the hundredth part every month, *v.* 11. If men borrow large sums to trade with, to increase their stocks, or to purchase land, there is no reason why the lender should not share with the borrower in his profit; or if to spend upon their lusts, or repair what they have so spent, why should they not pay for their extravagances? But if the poor borrow to maintain their families, and we be able to help them, it is certain we ought either to lend freely what they have occasion for, or (if they be not likely to repay it) to give freely something towards it. Nay, 2. They forced them to mortgage to them their lands and houses for the securing of the money (*v.* 3), and not only so, but took the profits of them for interest (*v.* 5, compare *v.* 11), that by degrees they might make themselves masters of all they had. Yet this was not the worst. 3. They took their children for bond-servants, to be enslaved or sold at pleasure, *v.* 5. This they complain of most sensibly, as that which touched them in a tender part, and they aggravate it with this: *"Our children are as their children,* as dear to us as theirs are to them; not only of the same human nature, and entitled to the honours and liberties of that (Mal. 2:10; Job 31:15), but of the same holy nation, free-born Israelites, and dignified with the same privileges. Our flesh carries in it the sacred seal of the covenant of circumcision, as well *as the flesh of our brethren;* yet our heirs must be their slaves, and *it is not in our power to redeem them."* This they made a humble remonstrance of to Nehemiah, not only because they saw he was a great man that could relieve them, but a good man that would. Whither should the injured poor flee for succour but *to the shields of the earth?* Whither but to the chancery, to the charity, in the royal breast, and those deputed by it for relief against the *summum jus — the extremity of the law?*

Lastly, We will leave Nehemiah hearing the complaint, and enquiring into the truth of the complainants' allegations (for the clamours of the poor are not always just), while we sit down and look, (1.) With a gracious compassion upon the oppressed, and lament the hardships which many in the world are groaning under; putting our souls into their souls' stead, and remembering in our prayers and succours those that are burdened, as burdened with them. (2.) With a gracious indignation at the oppressors, and abhorrence of their pride and cruelty, who drink the tears, the blood, of those they have under their feet. But let those who show no mercy expect *judgment without mercy.* It was an aggravation of the sin of these oppressing Jews that they were themselves so lately delivered out of the house of bondage, which obliged them in gratitude to *undo the heavy burdens,* Isa. 58:6.

Verses 6–13

It should seem the foregoing complaint was made to Nehemiah at the time when he had his head and hands as full as possible of the public business about building the wall; yet, perceiving it to be just, he did not reject it because it was unseasonable; he did not chide the petitioners, nor fall into a passion with them, for disturbing him when they saw how much he had to do, a fault which men of business are too often guilty of; nor did he so much as adjourn the hearing of the cause or proceedings upon it till he had more leisure. The case called for speedy interposition, and therefore he applied himself immediately to the consideration of it, knowing that, let him build Jerusalem's walls ever so high, so thick, so strong, the city could not be safe while such abuses as these were tolerated. Now observe, What method he took for the redress of this grievance which was so threatening to the public.

I. He *was very angry* (*v.* 6); he expressed a great displeasure at it, as a very bad thing. Note, It well becomes rulers to show themselves angry at sin, that by the anger itself they may be excited to their duty, and by the expressions of it others may be deterred from evil.

II. He *consulted with himself, v.* 7. By this it appears that his anger was not excessive, but kept within bounds, that, though his spirit was provoked, he did not say or do any thing unadvisedly. Before he rebuked the nobles, he consulted with himself what to say, and when, and how. Note, Reproofs must be given with great consideration, that what is well meant may not come short of its end for want of being well managed. It is the *reproof of instruction* that *giveth life.* Even wise men lose the benefit of their wisdom sometimes for want of consulting with themselves and taking time to deliberate.

III. He *rebuked the nobles and rulers,* who were the monied men, and whose power perhaps made them the more bold to oppress. Note, Even nobles and rulers, if they do that which is evil, ought to be told of it by proper persons. Let no man imagine that his dignity sets him above reproof.

IV. He set a great assembly against them. He called the people together to be witnesses of what he said, and to bear their testimony (which the people will generally be forward to do) against the oppressions and extortions their rulers were guilty of, *v.* 12. Ezra and Nehemiah were both of them very wise, good, useful men, yet, in cases not unlike, there was a great deal of difference between their management: when Ezra was told of the sin of the rulers in marrying strange wives he rent his clothes, and wept, and prayed, and was hardly persuaded to attempt a reformation, fearing it to be impracticable, for he was a man of a mild tender spirit; when Nehemiah was told of as bad a thing he kindled immediately, reproached the delinquents, incensed the people against them, and never rested till, by all the rough methods he could use, he forced them to reform; for he was a man of a hot and eager spirit. Note, 1. Very holy men may differ much from each other in their natural temper and in other things that result from it. 2. God's work may be done, well done, and successfully, and yet different methods taken in the doing of it, which is a good reason why we should neither arraign the management of others nor make our own a standard. There are diversities of operation, but the same Spirit.

V. He fairly reasoned the case with them, and showed them the evil of what they did. The regular way of reforming men's lives is to endeavour, in the first place, to convince their consciences. Several things he offered to their consideration, which are so pertinent and just that it appeared he had consulted with himself. He lays it before them, 1. That those whom they oppressed were their brethren: *You exact every one of his brother.* It was bad enough to oppress strangers, but much worse to oppress their poor brethren, from whom the divine law did not allow them to *take any usury,* Deu. 23:19, 20. 2. That they were but lately redeemed *out of the hand of the heathen.* The body of the people were so by the wonderful providence of God; some particular persons among them were so, who, besides their share in the general captivity, were in servitude to heathen masters, and ransomed at the charge of Nehemiah and other pious and well-disposed persons. "Now," says he, "have we taken all this pains to get their liberty out of the hands of the heathen, and shall their own rulers enslave them? What an absurd thing is this! Must we be at the same trouble and expense to redeem them from you as we were to redeem them from Babylon?" *v.* 8. Those whom God by his grace has made free ought not to be again brought under *a yoke of bondage,* Gal. 5:1; 1 Co. 7:23. 3. That it was a great sin thus to oppress the poor (*v.* 9): *"It is not good that you do;* though you get money by it, you contract guilt by it, and *ought you not to walk in the fear of God?* Certainly you ought, for you profess religion, and relation to him; and, if you do walk in the fear of God, you will not be either covetous of worldly gain or cruel towards your brethren." Those that walk in the fear of God will not dare to do a wicked thing, Job 31:13, 14, 23. 4. That it was a great scandal, and a reproach to their profession. "Consider *the reproach of the heathen our enemies,* enemies to us, to our God, and to our holy religion. They will be glad of any occasion to speak against us, and this will give them great occasion; they will say, These Jews, that profess so much devotion to God, see how barbarous they are one to another." Note, (1.) All that profess religion should be very careful that they do nothing to expose themselves to the reproach of those that are without, lest religion be wounded through their sides. (2.) Nothing exposes religion more to the reproach of its enemies than the worldliness and hard-heartedness of the professors of it. 5. That he himself had set them a better example (*v.* 10), which he enlarges upon afterwards, *v.* 14, etc. Those that rigorously insist upon their right themselves will with a very ill grace persuade others to recede from theirs.

VI. He earnestly pressed them not only not to make their poor neighbours any more such hard bargains, but to restore that which they had got into their hands, *v.* 11. See how familiarly he speaks to them: *Let us leave off this usury,* putting himself in, as becomes reprovers, though far from being any way guilty of the crime. See how earnestly, and yet humbly, he persuades them: *I pray you* leave off; and *I pray you* restore. Though he had authority to command, yet, *for love's sake, he rather beseeches.* See how particularly he presses them to be kind to the poor, to give them up their mortgages, put them again in possession of their estates, remit the interest, and give them time to pay in the principal. He urged them to their loss, yet, urging them to their duty, it would be, at length, to their advantage. What we charitably forgive will be remembered and recompensed, as well as what we charitably give.

VII. He laid them under all the obligations possible to do what he pressed them to. 1. He got a promise from them (*v.* 12): *We will restore them.* 2. He sent for the priests to give them their oath that they would perform this promise; now that their convictions were strong, and they seemed resolved, he would keep them to it. 3. He bound them by a solemn curse or execration, hoping that would strike some awe upon them: *So let God shake out every man that performeth not this promise, v.* 13. This was a threatening that he would certainly do so, to which the people said *Amen,* as to those curses at Mount Ebal (Deu. 27), that their throats might be cut with their own tongues if they should falsify their engagement, and that by the dread of that they might be kept to their promise. With this *Amen* the people *praised the Lord;* so far were they from promising with regret that they promised with all possible expressions of joy and thankfulness. Thus David, when he took God's vows upon him, *sang and gave praise,* Ps. 56:12. This cheerfulness in promising was well, but that which follows was better: *They did according to this promise,* and adhered to what they had done, not as their ancestors in a like case, who re-enslaved those whom a little before they had released, Jer. 34:10, 11. Good promises are good things, but good performances are all in all.

Verses 14–19

Nehemiah had mentioned his own practice, as an inducement to the nobles not to burden the poor, no, not with just demands; here he relates more particularly what his practice was, not inn pride or vain-glory, nor to pass a compliment upon himself, but as an inducement both to his successors and to the inferior magistrates to be as tender as might be of the people's ease.

I. He intimates what had been the way of his predecessors, *v.* 15. He does not name them, because what he had to say of them was not to their honour, and in such a case it is good to spare names; but the people knew how chargeable they had been, and how dearly the country paid for all the benefit of their government. The government allowed them *forty shekels of silver,* which was nearly five pounds (so much a day, it is probable); but, besides that, they obliged the people to furnish them with *bread and wine,* which they claimed as perquisites of their office; and not only so, but they suffered their servants to squeeze the people, and to get all they could out of them. Note, 1. It is no new thing for those who are in public places to seek themselves more than the public welfare, any, and to serve themselves by the public loss. 2. Masters must be accountable for all the acts of fraud and injustice, violence and oppression, which they connive at in their servants.

II. He tells us what had been his own way.

1. In general, he had not done as the former governors did; he would not, he durst not, *because of the fear of God.* He had an awe of God's majesty and a dread of his wrath. And, (1.) The fear of God restrained him from oppressing the people. Those that truly fear God will not dare to do any thing cruel or unjust. (2.) It was purely that which restrained him. He was thus generous, not that he might have praise of men, or serve a turn by his interest in the people, but purely for conscience' sake, because of the fear of God. This will not only be a powerful, but an acceptable principle both of justice and charity. What a good hand his predecessors made of their place appeared by the estates they raised; but Nehemiah, for his part, got nothing, except the satisfaction of doing good: *Neither bought we any land, v.* 16. Say not then that he was a bad husband, but that he was a good governor, who aimed not to feather his own nest. Let us *remember the words of the Lord,* how he said, *It is more blessed to give than to receive,* Acts 20:35.

2. More particularly, observe here, (1.) How little Nehemiah received of what he might have required. He did the work of the governor, but he did not *eat the bread of the governor* (*v.* 14), did not require it, *v.* 18. So far was he from extorting more than his due that he never demanded that, but lived upon what he had got in the king of Persia's court and his own estate in Judea: the reason he gives for this piece of self-denial is, *Because the bondage was heavy upon the people.* He might have used the common excuse for rigour in such cases, that it would be a wrong to his successors not to demand his dues; but let them look to themselves: he considered the afflicted state of the Jews, and, while they groaned under so much hardship, he could not find it in his heart to add to their burden, but would rather lessen his own estate than ruin them. note, In our demands we must consider not only the justice of them, but the ability of those on whom we make them; where there is nothing to be had we know who loses his right. (2.) How much he gave which he might have withheld. [1.] His servants' work, *v.* 16. The servants of princes think themselves excused from labour; but Nehemiah's servants, by his order no doubt, were *all gathered to the work.* Those that have many servants should contrive how they may do good with them and keep them well employed. [2.] His own meat, *v.* 17, 18. He kept a very good table, not on certain days, but constantly; he had many honourable guests, at least 150 of his own countrymen, persons of the first rank, besides strangers that came to him upon business; and he had plentiful provisions for his guests, beef, and mutton, and fowl, and all sorts of wine. Let those in public places remember that they were preferred to do good, not to enrich themselves; and let people in humbler stations learn to *use hospitality one to another without grudging,* 1 Pt. 4:9.

III. He concludes with a prayer (*v.* 19): *Think upon me, my God, for good.* 1. Nehemiah here mentions what he had *done for this people,* not in pride, as boasting of himself, nor in passion, as upbraiding them, nor does it appear that he had occasion to do it in his own vindication, as Paul had to relate his like self-denying tenderness towards the Corinthians, but to shame the rulers out of their oppressions; let them learn of him to be neither greedy in their demands nor paltry in their expenses, and then they would have the credit and comfort of their liberality, as he had. 2. He mentions it to God in prayer, not as if he thought he had hereby merited any favour from God, as a debt, but to show that he looked not for any recompence of his generosity from men, but depended upon God only to make up to him what he had lost and laid out for his honour; and he reckoned the favour of God reward enough. "If God do but *think upon me for good,* I have enough." His thoughts to us-ward are our happiness, Ps. 40:5. He refers it to God to recompense him in such a manner as he pleased. "If men forget me, let my God think on me, and I desire no more."

CHAPTER 6

The cries of oppressed poverty being stilled, we are now to enquire how the building of the wall goes forward, and in this chapter we find it carried on with vigour and finished with joy, notwithstanding the restless attempts of the gates of hell to hinder it. How the Jews' enemies were baffled in their design to put a stop to it by force we read before, *ch.* 4. Here we find how their endeavours to drive Nehemiah off from it were frustrated. I. When they courted him to an interview, with design to do him a mischief, he would not stir (*v.* 1–4). II. When they would have made him believe his undertaking was represented as seditious and treasonable, he regarded not the insinuation (*v.* 5–9). III. When they hired pretended prophets to advise him to retire into the temple for his own safety, still he kept his ground (*v.* 10–14). IV. Notwithstanding the secret correspondence that was kept up between them and some false and treacherous Jews, the work was finished in a short time (*v.* 15–19). Such as these were the struggles between the church and its enemies. But great is God's cause and it will be prosperous and victorious.

Verses 1–9

Two plots upon Nehemiah we have here an account of, how cunningly they were laid by his enemies and how happily frustrated by God's good providence and his prudence.

I. A plot to trepan him into a snare. The enemies had an account of the good forwardness the work was in, that all the breaches of the wall were made up, so that they considered it as good as done, though at that time the *doors of the gates* were off the hinges (*v.* 1); they must therefore now or never, by one bold stroke, take off Nehemiah. They heard how well guarded he was, so that there was no attacking him upon the spot; they will therefore try by all the arts of wheedling to get him among them. Observe, 1. With what hellish subtlety they courted him to meet them, not in any city, lest that should excite a suspicion that they intended to secure him, but in a village in the lot of Benjamin: *"Come, let us meet together* to consult about the common interests of our provinces." Or they would have him think that they coveted his friendship, and would be glad to be better acquainted with him, in order to a good understanding between them and the settling of a good correspondence. *But they thought to do him a mischief.* It is probable that he had some secret intelligence given him that they designed to imprison or murder him; or he knew them so well that, without breach of charity, he concluded they aimed at his life, and therefore, when they *spoke fair, he believed them not.* 2. See with what heavenly wisdom he declined the motion. His *God did instruct him* to give them that prudent answer by messengers of his own: *"I am doing a great work,* am very busy, and am loth to let the work stand still while I leave it to *come down to you," v.* 3. His care was that the work might not cease; he knew it would if he left it ever so little; and *why should it cease while I come down to you?* He says nothing of his jealousies, nor reproaches them for their treacherous design, but gives them a good reason and one of the true reasons why he would not come. Compliment must always give way to business. Let those that are tempted to idle merry meetings by their vain companions thus answer the temptation, "We have work to do, and must not neglect it." Four times they attacked him with the same solicitation, and he as often returned the same answer, which, we may suppose, was very vexatious to them; for really it was the ceasing of the work that they aimed at, and it would make them despair of breaking the undertaking to see the undertaker so intent upon it. *I answered them* (says he) *after the same manner, v.* 4. Note, We must never suffer ourselves to be overcome by the greatest importunity to do any thing sinful or imprudent; but, when we are attacked with the same temptation, must still resist it with the same reason and resolution.

II. A plot to terrify him from his work. Could they but drive him off, the work would cease of course. This therefore Sanballat attempts, but in vain. 1. he endeavours to possess Nehemiah with an apprehension that his undertaking to build the walls of Jerusalem was generally represented as factious and seditious, and would be resented accordingly at court, *v.* 5–7. The best men, even in their most innocent and excellent performances, have lain under this imputation. This is written to him in *an open letter,* as a thing generally known and talked of, that it was reported among the nations, and Gashmu will aver it for truth, that Nehemiah was aiming to make himself king and to shake off the Persian yoke. Note, It is common for that which is the sense only of the malicious to be falsely represented by them as the sense of the many. Now Sanballat pretends to inform Nehemiah of this as a friend, that he might hasten to court to clear himself, or stay his proceedings, for fear they should be thus misconstrued; at least, upon this surmise, he urges him to give him the meeting — *"Let us take counsel together* how to quell the report," hoping by this means either to take him off, or at least to take him off from his business. Thus were his words *softer than oil,* and yet *war was in his heart,* and he hoped, like Judas, to kiss and kill. But surely in vain is the net spread in the sight of any bird. Nehemiah was soon aware what they aimed at, to *weaken their hands from the work* (*v.* 9), and therefore not only denied that such things were true, but that they were reported; he was better known than to be thus suspected. 2. Thus he escaped the snare and kept his ground, nor would he be frightened by winds and clouds from sowing and reaping. Suppose it was thus reported, we must never omit known duty merely for fear it should be misconstrued; but, while we keep a good conscience, let us trust God with our good name. But indeed it was not thus reported. God's people, though sufficiently loaded with reproach, yet are not really so low in reputation as some would have them thought to be.

In the midst of his complaint of their malice, in endeavouring to frighten him, and so weaken his hands, he lifts up his heart to Heaven in this short prayer: *Now therefore, O God! strengthen my hands.* It is the great support and relief of good people that in all their straits and difficulties they have a good God to go to, from whom, by faith and prayer, they may fetch in grace to silence their fears and *strengthen their hands* when their enemies are endeavouring to fill them with fears and weaken their hands. When, in our Christian work and warfare, we are entering upon any particular services or conflicts, this is a good prayer for us to put up: "I have such a duty to do, such a temptation to grapple with; *now therefore, O God! strengthen my hands."* Some read it, not as a prayer, but as a holy resolution (for *O God* is supplied in our translation): *Now therefore I will strengthen my hands.* Note, Christian fortitude will be sharpened by opposition. Every temptation to draw us from duty should quicken us so much the more to duty.

Verses 10–14

The Jews' enemies leave no stone unturned, no way untried, to take Nehemiah off from building the wall about Jerusalem. In order to this they had tried to fetch him into the country to them, but in vain; now they try to drive him into the temple for his own safety; let him be any where but at his work. Observing him to be a cautious man, they will endeavour to gain their point by making him cowardly. Observe,

I. How basely the enemies managed this temptation.

1. That which they designed was to bring Nehemiah to do a foolish thing, that they might laugh at him, and insult over him for doing it, and so lessen his interest and influence (*v.* 13): *That I should be afraid,* and so they might have *matter for an evil report,* and *might reproach me.* This was indeed doing the devil's work, who is men's tempter that he may be their accuser, draws men to sin that he may glory in their shame. The greatest mischief our enemies can do us is to frighten us from our duty and bring us to do what is sinful.

2. The tools they made use of were a pretended prophet and prophetess, whom they hired to persuade Nehemiah to quit his work and retire for his own safety. The pretended prophet was Shemaiah, of whom it is said that he was *shut up* in his own house, either under pretence of retirement for meditation and to consult the mind of God or to give Nehemiah a sign in like manner to make himself a recluse. It should seem, Nehemiah had a value for him, for he went to his house to consult him, *v.* 10. Other prophets there were, and one prophetess, Noadiah (*v.* 14), that were in the interest of the Jews' enemies, pensioners to them and traitors to their country. Whether they pretended to inspiration does not appear; they do not say, *Thus saith the Lord,* as the false prophets of old did; if not so, yet they would be thought to excel in divine knowledge, and human prudence, and to have uncommon measures of insight and foresight, and were therefore consulted in difficult cases, as prophets had been. These the enemies feed to be of counsel for them. Let us hence take occasion to lament, (1.) The wickedness of such bad men as these prophets, that ever any should be so perfidious as to betray the cause of God and their country even under the pretence of communion with God and concern for their country. (2.) The unhappiness of such good men as Nehemiah, who are in danger of being imposed upon by such cheats, and to whom no temptation comes with more force than that which comes under a colour of religion, of revelation and devotion, and is brought by the hand of prophets.

3. The pretence was plausible. These prophets suggested to Nehemiah that the enemies would come and slay him, *in the night* they would slay him, which he had reason enough to believe was true; they would, if they could, if they durst. They pretended to be much concerned for his safety. The people would be all undone if any harm should come to him; and therefore they very gravely advised him to hide himself in the temple till the danger was over; that was a strong and sacred place, where he would be under the special protection of Heaven, Ps. 27:5. If Nehemiah had been prevailed upon to do this, immediately the people would both have left off their work and thrown down their arms, and every one would have shifted for his own safety; and then the enemies might easily, and without opposition, have demolished the works, broken down the wall again, and so gained their point. Though self-preservation is a fundamental principle of the law of nature, yet that is not always the best and wisest counsel which pretends to go upon that principle.

II. See how bravely Nehemiah vanquished this temptation, and came off a conqueror.

1. He immediately resolved not to yield to it, *v.* 11. See here, (1.) What his reasonings are: *"Should such a man as I flee?* Shall I desert God's work, or discourage my own workmen whom I have employed and encouraged? Shall I be over-credulous of report, and over-solicitous about my own life? I that am the governor, on whom so many eyes are, both of friends and foes? Another might flee, but not I. *Who is there that being as I am,* in my post of honour, and power, and trust, would go into the temple, and lurk there, when business is to be done, yea, though it were to save his life?" Note, When we are tempted to sin we should remember who and what we are, that we may not do any thing unbecoming us, and the profession we make. *It is not for kings, O Lemuel!* Prov. 31:4. (2.) What was the result of his reasonings. He is at a point: "I will not go in. I will rather die at my work than live in an inglorious retreat from it." Note, Holy courage and magnanimity will engage us, whatever it cost us, never to *decline a good work,* nor ever to *do a bad one.*

2. He was immediately aware of what was the rise of it (*v.* 12): *"I perceived that God had not sent him,* that he gave this advice, not by any divine direction, ordinary or extraordinary, but with a design against me." The wickedness of such mercenary wretches will sooner or later be brought to light. Two things Nehemiah says he dreaded in that which he was advised to: — (1.) Offending God: *That I should be afraid, and do so, and sin.* Note, Sin is that which above any thing we should dread; and a good preservative it is against sin to be afraid of nothing but sin. (2.) Shaming himself: *That they might reproach me.* Note, Next to the sinfulness of sin we should dread the scandalousness of it.

3. He humbly begs of God to reckon with them for their base designs upon him (*v.* 14): *My God, think thou upon Tobiah,* and the rest of them, *according to their works.* As, when he had mentioned his own good services, he did not covetously or ambitiously prescribe to God what reward he should give him, but modestly prayed, *Think upon me, my God* (*ch.* 5:19), so here he does not revengefully imprecate any particular judgment upon his enemies, but refers the matter to God. "Thou knowest their hearts, and art the avenger of falsehood and wrong; take cognizance of this cause; judge between me and them, and take what way and time thou mayest please to call them to an account for it." Note, Whatever injuries are done us we must not avenge ourselves, but commit our cause to him that judgeth righteously.

Verses 15–19

Nehemiah is here finishing the wall of Jerusalem, and yet still has trouble created him by his enemies.

I. Tobiah, and the other adversaries of the Jews, had the mortification to see the wall built up, notwithstanding all their attempts to hinder it. The wall was begun and finished *in fifty-two days,* and yet we have reason to believe they rested on the sabbaths, *v.* 15. Many were employed, and there was room for them; what they did they did cheerfully, and minded their business because they loved it. The threats of their enemies, which were intended to weaken them, it is likely, quickened them to go on with their work the more vigorously, that they might get it done before the enemy came. Thus *out of the eater came forth meat.* See what a great deal of work may be done in a little time if we would set about it in earnest and keep close to it. When the enemies heard that the wall was finished before they thought it was well begun, and, when they doubted not but to put a stop to it, they were *much cast down in their own eyes, v.* 16. 1. They were ashamed of their own confidence that they should *cause the work to cease;* they were crest-fallen upon the disappointment. 2. They envied the prosperity and success of the Jews, grieved to see the walls of Jerusalem built, while, it may be, the kings of Persia had not permitted them thus to fortify the cities of Samaria. When Cain envied his brother his *countenance fell,* Gen. 4:5. 3. They despaired of ever doing them the mischief they designed them, of bringing them down and making a prey of them; and well they might, for they perceived, by the wonderful success, *that the work was wrought of God.* Even these heathens had so much sense as, [1.] To see a special providence of God conversant about the affairs of the church when they did remarkably prosper. They *said among the heathen, The Lord has done great things for them;* it is his doing, Ps. 126:2. God fighteth for Israel and worketh with them. [2.] To believe that God's work would be perfect. When the perceived that the *work was of God* they expected no other than that it would go on and prosper. [3.] To conclude that, if it were of God, it was to no purpose to think of opposing it; it would certainly prevail and be victorious.

II. Nehemiah had the vexation, notwithstanding this, to see some of his own people treacherously corresponding with Tobiah and serving his interest; and a great grief and discouragement, no doubt, it was to him. 1. Even of the nobles of Judah there were those who had so little sense of honour and their country's good as to communicate with Tobiah by letter, *v.* 17. They wrote with all the freedom and familiarity of friends to him, and welcomed his letters to them. Could nobles do a thing so mean? Nobles of Judah so wicked a thing? It seems great men are not always wise, not always honest. 2. Many in Judah were in a strict but secret confederacy with him to advance the interest of his country, though it would certainly be the ruin of their own. They were *sworn unto him,* not as their prince, but as their friend and ally, because both he and his son had married daughters of Israel, *v.* 18. See the mischief of marrying with strangers; for one heathen that was converted by it ten Jews were perverted. When once they became akin to Tobiah they soon became sworn to him. A sinful love leads to a sinful league. 3. They had the impudence to court Nehemiah himself into a friendship with him: *"They reported his good deeds before me,* represented him as an intelligent gentleman and well worthy my acquaintance, an honest gentleman and one that I might confide in." We are indeed required to *speak ill of no man,* but never to speak well of bad men. *Those that forsake the law praise the wicked,* Prov. 28:4. 4. They were so false as to betray Nehemiah's counsels to him; they uttered Nehemiah's words to him, perverting them, no doubt, and putting false constructions upon them, which furnished Tobiah with matter for letters to put him in fear and so drive him from his work and discourage him in it. Thus were all their thoughts against him for evil, yet God thought upon him for good.

CHAPTER 7

The success of one good design for God and our generation should encourage us to proceed and form some other; Nehemiah did so, having fortified Jerusalem with gates and walls, his next care is, I. To see the city well kept (*v.* 1–4). II. To see it well peopled, in order to which he here reviews and calls over the register of the children of the captivity, the families that returned at first, and records it (*v.* 5–73). It is the same, in effect, with that which we had, Ezra 2. What use he made of it we shall find afterwards, when he brought one of ten to live in Jerusalem, 11:1.

Verses 1–4

God saith concerning his church (Isa. 62:6), *I have set watchmen upon thy walls, O Jerusalem!* This is Nehemiah's care here; for dead walls, without living watchmen, are but a poor defence to a city.

I. He appointed *the porters, singers, and Levites,* in their places to their work. This is meant of their work in general, which was to attend the temple service; it had been neglected in some degree, but now was revived. God's worship is the defence of a place, and his ministers, when they mind their duty, are watchmen on the walls. Or, in particular, he ordered them to be ready against the wall was to be dedicated, that they might perform that service in an orderly and solemn manner; and the dedication of it was its strength. That is likely to be beneficial to us which is devoted to God.

II. He appointed two governors or consuls, to whom he committed the care of the city, and gave them in charge to provide for the public peace and safety. Hanani, his brother, who came to him with the tidings of the desolations of Jerusalem, was one, a man of approved integrity and affection to his country; the other was Hananiah, who had been ruler of the palace: for he that has approved himself faithful in less shall be entrusted with more. Of this Hananiah it is said that he was a *faithful man and one that feared God above many, v.* 2. Note, 1. Among those who fear God truly there are some who fear him greatly, and excel others in the expressions and instances of that fear; and they are worthy a double portion of that honour which is due to those that *fear the Lord,* Ps. 15:4. There were many in Jerusalem that feared God, but this good man was more eminent for religion and serious godliness than any. 2. Those that fear God must evidence it by their being faithful to all men and universally conscientious. 3. God's Jerusalem is then likely to flourish when those rule in it, and have charge of it, who excel in virtue, and are eminent both for godliness and honesty. It is supposed, by some, that Nehemiah was now about to return to the Persian court to have his commission renewed, and that he left these two worthy men in charge with the affairs of the city in his absence. Good governors, when and where they cannot act themselves, must be very careful whom they depute.

III. He gave orders about the shutting of the gates and the guarding of the walls, *v.* 3, 4. See here, 1. What the present state of Jerusalem was. The city, in compass, was large and great. The walls enclosed the same ground as formerly; but much of it lay waste, for the houses were not built, few at least in comparison with what had been; so that Nehemiah walled the city in faith, and with an eye to that promise of the replenishing of it which God had lately made by the prophet, Zec. 8:3, etc. Though the people were now few, he believed they would be multiplied, and therefore built the walls so as to make room for them; had he not depended upon this he might have thought walls without a city as great a reproach as a city without walls. 2. What was the care of Nehemiah for it. He ordered the rulers of the city themselves, (1.) To stand by, and see the city-gates shut up and barred every night; for in vain had they a wall if they were careless of their gates. (2.) To take care that they should not be opened in the morning till they could see that all was clear and quiet. (3.) To set sentinels upon the walls, or elsewhere, at convenient distances, who should, in case of the approach of the enemy, give timely notice to the city of the danger; and, as it came to their turn to watch, they must post themselves *over against their own houses,* because of them, it might be presumed, they would be in a particular manner careful. The public safety depends upon every one's particular care to guard himself and his own family against sin, that common enemy. It is every one's interest to watch, but many understand not their own interest; it is therefore incumbent upon magistrates to appoint watches. And as this people had lately found God with them in their building (else they would have built in vain), so now that the wall was built, no doubt, they were made sensible that *except the Lord kept the city the watchman waked but in vain,* Ps. 127:1.

Verses 5–73

We have here another good project of Nehemiah's; for wise and zealous men will be always contriving something or other for the glory of God and the edification of his church. He knew very well that the safety of a city, under God, depends more upon the number and valour of the inhabitants than upon the height or strength of its walls; and therefore, observing that the people were few that dwelt in it, he thought fit to take an account of the people, that he might find what families had formerly had their settlement in Jerusalem, but were now removed into the country, that he might bring them back, and what families could in any other way be influenced by their religion, or by their business, to come and rebuild the houses in Jerusalem and dwell in them. So little reason have we to wish that we may be placed alone in the earth, or in Jerusalem itself, that much of our safety and comfort depends upon our neighbours and friends; the more the stronger, the more the merrier. It is the wisdom of the governors of a nation to keep the balance even between the city and country, that the metropolis be not so extravagantly large as to drain and impoverish the country, nor yet so weak as not to be able to protect it. Now observe,

I. Whence this good design of Nehemiah's came. He owns, *My God put it into my heart, v.* 5. Note, Whatever good motion is in our minds, either prudent or pious, we must acknowledge it to come from God. It was he that *put it into our hearts;* for every good gift and every good work are from above. He gives knowledge; he gives grace; all is of him, and therefore all must be to him. What is done by human prudence must be ascribed to the direction of divine Providence; he that teaches the husbandman his discretion (Isa. 28:26) teaches the statesman his.

II. What method he took in prosecution of it.

1. He called the rulers together, and the people, that he might have an account of the present state of their families — their number and strength, and where they were settled. It is probable that when he summoned them to come together he ordered them to bring such an account along with them out of their several districts. And I doubt they were not so many but that it might be soon done.

2. He reviewed the old *register of the genealogy of those who came up at the first,* and compared the present accounts with that; and here we have the repetition of that out of Ezra 2. The title is the same here (*v.* 6, 7) as there (*v.* 1, 2): *These are the children of the province,* etc. Two things are here repeated and recorded a second time from thence — the names and numbers of their several families, and their oblations to the service of the temple. The repetition of these accounts may intimate to us the delight which the great God is pleased to take in the persons, families, and services of his spiritual Israel, and the particular notice he takes of them. He knows those that are his, knows them all, knows them by name, has his eye on the register of those children of the captivity, and does all according to the ancient counsel of his will concerning them.

(1.) Here is an account of the heads of the several families that first came up, *v.* 6–69. As to this, [1.] Though it seem of little use to us now, yet then it was of great use, to compare what they had been with what they now were. We may suppose they were much increased by this time; but it would do well for them to remember their small beginnings, that they might acknowledge God in multiplying their families and building them up. By this means likewise their genealogies would be preserved, and the distinction of their families kept up, till the Messiah should come, and then an end be put to all their genealogies, which were preserved for his sake, but afterwards were endless. But, [2.] There are many differences in the numbers between this catalogue and that in Ezra. Most of them indeed are exactly the same, and some others within a very few under or over (one or two perhaps); and therefore I cannot think, as some do, that that was the number of these families at their first coming and this as they were now, which was at least forty years after (some make it much more); for we cannot suppose so many families to be not at all, or but little, altered in their numbers in all that time; therefore what differences there are we may suppose to arise either from the mistakes of transcribers, which easily happen in numbers, or from the diversity of the copies from which they were taken. Or perhaps one was the account of them when they set out from Babylon with Zerubbabel, the other when they came to Jerusalem. The sum totals are all just the same there and here, except of the singing-men and singing-women, which there are 200, here 245. These were not of such importance as that they should keep any strict account of them.

(2.) Here is an account of the offerings which were given towards the work of God, *v.* 70, etc. This differs much from that in Ezra 2:68, 69, and it may be questioned whether it refers to the same contribution; here the tirshatha, or chief governor, who there was not mentioned, begins the offering; and the single sum mentioned there exceeds all those here put together; yet it is probable that it was the same, but that followed one copy of the lists, this another; for the last verse is the same here that it was Ezra 2:70, adding *ch.* 3:1. Blessed be God that our faith and hope are not built upon the niceties of names and numbers, genealogy and chronology, but on the great things of the law and gospel. Whatever is given to the work of God, he is not unrighteous to forget it; nor shall even a cup of cold water, wherewith he is honoured, go without its reward.

CHAPTER 8

Ezra came up out of Babylon thirteen years before Nehemiah came, yet we have here a piece of good work which he did, that might have been done before, but was not done till Nehemiah came, who, though he was not such a scholar nor such a divine as Ezra, nor such a scribe in the law of his God, yet was a man of a more lively active spirit. His zeal set Ezra's learning on work, and then great things were done, as we find here, where we have, I. The public and solemn reading and expounding of the law (*v.* 1–8). II. The joy which the people were ordered to express upon that occasion (*v.* 9–12). III. The solemn keeping of the feast of tabernacles according to the law (*v.* 13–18).

Verses 1–8

We have here an account of a solemn religious assembly, and the good work that was done in that assembly, to the honour of God and the edification of the church.

I. The time of it was the *first day of the seventh month, v.* 2. That was the day of the *feast of trumpets,* which is called a *sabbath,* and on which they were to have a *holy convocation,* Lev. 23:24; Num. 29:1. But that was not all: it was one that day that the altar was set up, and they began to offer their burnt-offerings after their return out of captivity, a recent mercy in the memory of many then living; in a thankful remembrance of that, it is likely, they had kept this feast ever since with more than ordinary solemnity. Divine favours which are fresh in mind, and which we ourselves have been witnesses of, should be, and usually are, most affecting.

II. The place was in the *street that was before the watergate* (*v.* 1), a spacious broad street, able to contain so great a multitude, which the court of the temple was not; for probably it was not now built nearly so large as it had been in Solomon's time. Sacrifices were to be offered only at the door of the temple, but praying, and praising, and preaching, were, and are, services of religion as acceptably performed in one place as in another. When this congregation thus met in the street of the city no doubt God was with them.

III. The persons that met were all the people, who were not compelled to come, but voluntarily gathered themselves together by common agreement, as one man: not only men came, but women and children, even as many as were capable of understanding what they heard. Masters of families should bring their families with them to the public worship of God. Women and children have souls to save, and are therefore concerned to acquaint themselves with the word of God and attend on the means of knowledge and grace. Little ones, as they come to the exercise of reason, must be trained up in the exercises of religion.

IV. The master of this assembly was Ezra the priest; he presided in this service. None so fit to expound and preach as he who was such a ready scribe in the law of his God. 1. His call to the service was very clear; for being in office as a priest, and qualified as a scribe, the *people spoke to him to bring the book of the law* and read it to them, *v.* 1. God gave him ability and authority, and then the people gave him opportunity and invitation. Knowledge is spiritual alms, which those that are able should give to every one that needs, to every one that asks. 2. His post was very convenient. He stood in a pulpit or tower of wood, *which they made for the word* (so it is in the original), *for the preaching of the word,* that what he said might be the more gracefully delivered and the better heard, and that the eyes of the hearers might be upon him, which would engage their attention, as Lu. 4:20. 3. He had several assistants. Some of these stood with him (*v.* 4), six on his right hand and seven on his left: either his pulpit was so contrived as to hold them all in a row, as in a gallery (but then it would scarcely have been called a *tower*), or they had desks a degree lower. Some think, that he appointed them to read when he was weary; at least his taking them as assessors with him put an honour upon them before the people, in order to their being employed in the same service another time. Others who are mentioned (*v.* 7) seem to have been employed at the same time in other places near at hand, to read and expound to those who could not come within hearing of Ezra. Of these also there were thirteen priests, whose lips were to keep knowledge, Mal. 2:7. It is a great mercy to a people thus to be furnished with ministers that are apt to teach. Happy was Ezra in having such assistants as these, and happy were they in having such a guide as Ezra.

V. The religious exercises performed in this assembly were not ceremonial, but moral, praying and preaching. Ezra, as president of the assembly, was, 1. The people's mouth to God, and they affectionately joined with him, *v.* 6. He blessed the Lord as the great God, gave honour to him by praising his perfections and praying for his favour; and the people, in token of their concurrence with him both in prayers and praises, said, *Amen, Amen, lifted up their hands* in token of their desire being towards God and all their expectations from him, and *bowed their heads* in token of their reverence of him and subjection to him. Thus must we adore God, and address ourselves to him, when we are going to read and hear the word of God, as those that see God in his word very great and very good. 2. God's mouth to the people, and they attentively hearkened to him. This was the chief business of the solemnity, and observe, (1.) *Ezra brought the law before the congregation, v.* 2. He had taken care to provide himself with the best and most correct copies of the law; and what he had laid up for his own use and satisfaction he here brought forth, as a good householder out of his treasury, for the benefit of the church. Observe, [1.] The book of the law is not to be confined to the scribes' studies, but to be brought before the congregation and read to them in their own language. [2.] Ministers, when they go to the pulpit, should take their Bibles with them; Ezra did so; thence they must fetch their knowledge, and according to that rule they must speak and must show that they do so. See 2 Chr. 17:9. (2.) He opened the book with great reverence and solemnity, *in the sight of all the people, v.* 5. He brought it forth with a sense of the great mercy of God to them in giving them that book; he opened it with a sense of his mercy to them in giving them leave to read it, that it was not a spring shut up and a fountain sealed. The *taking of the books, and the opening of the seals,* we find celebrated with joy and praise, Rev. 5:9. Let us learn to address ourselves to the services of religion with solemn stops and pauses, and not to go about them rashly; let us consider what we are doing when we take God's book into our hands, and open it, and so also when we bow our knees in prayer; and what we do let us do deliberately, Eccl. 5:1. (3.) He and others read in the book of the law, *from morning till noon* (*v.* 3), and they read *distinctly, v.* 8. Reading the scriptures in religious assemblies is an ordinance of God, whereby he is honoured and his church edified. And, upon special occasions, we must be willing to attend for many hours together on the reading and expounding of the word of God: those mentioned here were thus employed for six hours. Let those that read and preach the word learn also to deliver themselves distinctly, as those who understand what they say and are affected with it themselves, and who desire that those they speak to may understand it, retain it, and be affected with it likewise. *It is a snare for a man to devour that which is holy.* (4.)

What they read they expounded, showed the intent and meaning of it, and what use was to be made of it; they gave the sense in other words, that they might *cause the people to understand the reading, v.* 7, 8. Note, [1.] It is requisite that those who hear the word should understand it, else it is to them but an empty sound of words, Mt. 24:15. [2.] It is therefore required of those who are teachers by office that they explain the word and give the sense of it. *Understandest thou what thou readest?* and, *Have you understood all these things?* are good questions to be put to the hearers; but, *How should we except someone guide us?* is as proper a question for them to put to their teachers, Acts 8:30, 31. Reading is good, and preaching good, but expounding brings the reading and the preaching together, and thus makes the reading the more intelligible and the preaching the more convincing. (5.) The people conducted themselves very properly when the word was read and opened to them. [1.] With great reverence. When Ezra opened the book *all the people stood up* (*v.* 5), thereby showing respect both to Ezra and to the word he was about to read. It becomes servants to stand when their master speaks to them, in honour to their master and to show a readiness to do as they are bidden. [2.] With great fixedness and composedness. They *stood in their place* (*v.* 7); several ministers were reading and expounding at some distance from each other, and every one of the people kept his post, did not go to hear first one and then another, to make remarks upon them, but stood in his place, that he might neither give disturbance to another nor receive any disturbance himself. [3.] With great attention and a close application of mind: *The ears of all the people were unto the book of the law* (*v.* 3), were even chained to it; they heard readily, and minded every word. The word of God commands attention and deserves it. If through carelessness we let much slip in hearing, there is danger that through forgetfulness we shall let all slip after hearing.

Verses 9–12

We may here observe,

I. How the people were wounded with the words of the law that were read to them. The law works death, and speaks terror, shows men their sins, and their misery and danger because of sin, and thunders a curse against every one that continues not in every part of his duty. Therefore when they heard it they *all wept* (*v.* 9): it was a good sign that their hearts were tender, like Josiah's when he heard the words of the law. They wept to think how they had offended God, and exposed themselves, by their many violations of the law; when some wept all wept, for they all saw themselves guilty before God.

II. How they were healed and comforted with the words of peace that were spoken to them. It was well that they were so much affected with the word of God, and received the impressions of it; but they must not yield unduly to their mourning, especially at this time, because the day was holy to the Lord; it was one of the solemn feasts, on which it was their duty to rejoice; and even sorrow for sin must not hinder our joy in God, but rather lead us to it and prepare us for it.

1. The masters of the assembly endeavoured to pacify them and encourage them. Now Nehemiah is brought in, and not before, in this chapter; he took notice of the people's weeping. Ezra was pleased to see them so affected with the word, but Nehemiah observed to him, and Ezra concurred in the thought, that it was now unseasonable. This day was holy (it is called a *sabbath,* Lev. 23:24), and therefore was to be celebrated with joy and praise, not as if it were *a day to afflict their souls.* (1.) They forbade the people to *mourn and weep* (*v.* 9): *Be not sorry* (*v.* 10); *hold your peace, neither be you grieved, v.* 11. Every thing is beautiful in its season; as we must not be merry when God calls to mourning, so we must not frighten and afflict ourselves when God gives us occasion to rejoice. Even sorrow for sin must not grow so excessive as to hinder our joy in God and our cheerfulness in his service. (2.) They commanded them to testify their joy, to put *on the garments of praise instead of the spirit of heaviness.* They allowed them, in token of their joy, to feast themselves, to eat and drink better than on other days, *to eat the fat and drink the sweet;* but then it must be, [1.] With charity to the poor: "*Send portions to those for whom nothing is prepared* that your abundance may supply their want, that

they may rejoice with you and their loins may bless you." Christ directs those that make feasts to invite their poor neighbours, Lu. 14:13. But it is especially the duty of a religious feast, as well as of a religious fast, to *draw out the soul to the hungry,* Isa. 58:7, 10. God's bounty should make us bountiful. Many will eat the fat and drink the sweet themselves, even to excess, that will never allow portions, nor scarcely crumbs, to the poor, who may read their own doom in the parable of the rich man, Lu. 16:19, etc. But such know not, or consider not, what God gave them their estates for. Observe, We must not only give to those that offer themselves, but send to those that are out of sight. *The liberal devises liberal things,* and seeks objects of charity. [2.] It must be with piety and devotion: *The joy of the Lord is your strength.* Let it not be a carnal sensual joy, but holy and spiritual, the *joy of the Lord,* joy in the goodness of God, under the direction and government of the grace of God, joy arising from our interest in the love and favour of God and the tokens of his favour. "This joy will be your strength, therefore encourage it; it will be your strength, *First,* For the performance of the other duties of the feast." The more cheerful we are in our religious exercises the more we shall abound in them. *Secondly,* "For all that which you have to do in conformity to the law of God which has been read to you." Holy joy will be oil to the wheels of our obedience. *Thirdly,* "For the resisting of your enemies that are plotting against you." The joy of the Lord will arm us against the assaults of our spiritual enemies, and put our mouths out of taste for those pleasures with which the tempter baits his hooks.

2. The assembly complied with the directions that were given them. Their weeping was *stilled* (*v.* 11) and they *made great mirth, v.* 12. Note, We ought always to have such a command of every passion as that, however it may break out, it may soon be restrained and called in again when we are convinced that it is either unreasonable or unseasonable. *He that has such a rule as this over his own spirit is better than the mighty.* Observe, (1.) After they had wept they rejoiced. Holy mourning makes way for holy mirth; those that *sow in tears shall reap in joy;* those that tremble at the convictions of the word may triumph in the consolations of it. (2.) The ground of their joy was very good. They made mirth, not because they had the fat to eat and the sweet to drink, and a great deal of good company, but because they had *understood the words that were declared to them.* note, [1.] To have the holy scriptures with us, and helps to understand them, is a very great mercy, which we have abundant reason to rejoice in. Bibles and ministers are the joy of God's Israel. [2.] The better we understand the word of God the more comfort we shall find in it; for the darkness of trouble arises from the darkness of ignorance and mistake. When the words were first declared to them they wept; but, when they understood them, they rejoiced, finding at length precious promises made to those who repented and reformed and that therefore there was hope in Israel.

Verses 13–18

We have here,

I. The people's renewed attendance upon the word. They had spent the greatest part of one day in praying and hearing, and yet were so far from being weary of that new moon and sabbath that the next day after, though it was no festival, the chief of them came together again to hear Ezra expound (*v.* 13), which they found more delightful and gainful than any worldly pleasure or profit whatsoever. Note, The more we converse with the word of God, if we rightly understand it and be affected with it, the more we shall covet to converse with it, and to increase in our acquaintance with it, saying, *How sweet are thy words unto my mouth!* Those that understand the scriptures well will still be desirous to understand them better. Now the priests and the Levites themselves came with *the chief of the people to Ezra,* that prince of expositors, *to understand the words of the law,* or, as it is in the margin, *that they might instruct in the words of the law;* they came to be taught themselves, that they might be qualified to teach others. Observe, 1. Though, on the first day, Ezra's humility had set them *on his right hand and on his left, as teachers with him* (*v.* 4, 7), yet now, they being by trial made more sensible than ever of their own deficiencies and his excellencies, on the second day their humility set them at Ezra's feet, as learners of him. 2. Those that would teach others must themselves receive instructions. Priests and Levites must be taught first and then teach.

II. The people's ready obedience to the word, in one particular instance, as soon as they were made sensible of their duty therein. It is probable that Ezra, *after the wisdom of his God that was in his hand* (Ezra 7:25), when they applied to him for instruction out of the law on the second day of the seventh month, read to them those laws which concerned the feasts of that month, and, among the rest, that of the feast of tabernacles, Lev. 23:34; Deu. 16:13. Ministers should preach not only that which is true and good, but that which is seasonable, directing to the *work of the day in its day.* Here is, 1. The divine appointment of the feast of tabernacles reviewed, *v.* 14, 14. *They found written in the law* a commandment concerning it. Those that diligently search the scriptures will find those things written there which they had forgotten or not duly considered. This feast of tabernacles was a memorial of their dwelling in tents in the wilderness, a representation of our tabernacle state in this world, and a type of the holy joy of the gospel church. The conversion of the nations to the faith of Christ is foretold under the figure of this feast (Zec. 14:16); they shall come to *keep the feast of tabernacles,* as having here no continuing city. This feast was to be proclaimed in all their cities. The people were themselves to fetch boughs of trees (they of Jerusalem fetched them from the mount of Olives) and to make booths, or arbours, of them, in which they were to lodge (as much as the weather would permit) and to make merry during the feast. 2. This appointment religiously observed, *v.* 16, 17. Then we read and hear the word acceptably and profitably when we do according to what is written therein, when what appears to be our duty is revived after it has been neglected. (1.) They observed the ceremony: *They sat in booths,* which the priests and Levites set up in the courts of the temple; those that had houses of their own set up booths on the roofs of them, or in their courts; and those that had not such conveniences set them up in the streets. This feast had usually been observed (2 Chr. 5:3; Ezra 3:4), but never with such solemnity as now since Joshua's time, when they were newly settled, as they were now newly re-settled in Canaan. That man loves his house too well that cannot find in his heart to quit it, awhile, in compliance either with an ordinance or with a providence of God. (2.) They minded the substance, else the ceremony, how significant soever, would have been insignificant. [1.] They did it with gladness, with *very great gladness,* rejoicing in God and his goodness to them. All their holy feasts, but this especially, were to be celebrated with joy, which would be much for the honour of God, and their own encouragement in his service. [2.] They attended the reading and expounding of the word of God during all the days of the feast, *v.* 18. They improved their leisure for this good work. Spare hours cannot be better spent than in studying the scriptures and conversing with them. At this feast of tabernacles God appointed the law to be read once in seven years. Whether this was that year of release in which that service was to be performed (Deu. 31:10, 11) does not appear; however they spent all the days of the feast in that good work, and on the eighth day was a solemn assembly, as God had appointed, in which they finished the solemnity the twenty-second day of the month, yet did not separate, for the twenty-fourth day was appointed to be spent in fasting and prayer. Holy joy just not indispose us for godly sorrow any more than godly sorrow for holy joy.

CHAPTER 9

The tenth day of the seventh month between the feast of trumpets (*ch.* 8:2) and the feast of tabernacles (*v.* 14) was appointed to be the day of atonement; we have no reason to think but that it was religiously observed, though it is not mentioned. But here we have an account of an occasional fast that was kept a fortnight after that, with reference to the present posture of their affairs, and it was, as that, a day of humiliation. There is a time to weep as well as a time to laugh. We have here an account. I. How this fast was observed (*v.* 1–3). II. What were the heads of the prayer that was made to God on that occasion, wherein they made a thankful acknowledgment of God's mercies, a penitent confession of sin, and a humble submission to the righteous hand of God in the judgments that were brought upon them, concluding with a solemn resolution of new obedience (*v.* 4–38).

Verses 1–3

We have here a general account of a public fast which the children of Israel kept, probably by order from Nehemiah, by and with the advice and consent of the chief of the fathers. It was a fast that men appointed, but such *a fast as God had chosen;* for, 1. It was a day *to afflict the soul,* Isa. 58:5. Probably they assembled in the courts of the temple, and they there appeared in sackcloth and in the posture of mourners, with earth on their heads, *v.* 1. By these outward expressions of sorrow and humiliation they gave glory to God, took shame to themselves, and stirred up one another to repentance. They were restrained from *weeping, ch.* 8:9, but now they were directed to weep. The joy of our holy feasts must give way to the sorrow of our solemn fasts when they come. Every thing is beautiful in its season. 2. It was a day *to loose the bands of wickedness,* and that is the fast that God has chosen, Isa. 58:6. Without this, spreading sackcloth and ashes under us is but a jest. The seed of Israel, because they were a holy seed, appropriated to God and more excellent than their neighbours, *separated themselves from all strangers* with whom they had mingled and joined in affinity, *v.* 2. Ezra had separated them from their strange wives some years before, but they had relapsed into the same sin, and had either made marriages or at least made friendships with them, and contracted such an intimacy as was a snare to them. But now they separated themselves from the strange children as well as from the strange wives. Those that intend by prayers and covenants to join themselves to God must separate themselves from sin and sinners; for *what communion hath light with darkness?* 3. It was a day of communion with God. *They fasted to him, even to him* (Zec. 7:5); for, (1.) They spoke to him in prayer, offered their pious and devout affections to him in the confession of sin and the adoration of him as the Lord and their God. Fasting without prayer is a body without a soul, a worthless carcase. (2.) They heard him speaking to them by his word; for they read in the book of the law, which is very proper on fasting days, that, in the glass of the law, we may see our deformities and defilements, and know what to acknowledge and what to amend. The word will direct and quicken prayer, for by it the Spirit helps our praying infirmities. Observe how the time was equally divided between these two. Three hours (for that is the fourth part of a day) they spent in reading, expounding, and applying the scriptures, and three hours in confessing sin and praying; so that they staid together six hours, and spent all the time in the solemn acts of religion, without saying, *Behold, what a weariness is it!* The varying of the exercises made it the less tedious, and, as the word they read would furnish them with matter for prayer, so prayer would make the word the more profitable. Bishop Patrick thinks that they spent the whole twelve hours of the day in devotion, that from six o'clock in the morning till nine they read, and then from nine to twelve they prayed, from twelve to three they read again, and from three till six at night they prayed again. The word of a fast day is good work, and therefore we should endeavour to make a day's work, a good day's work, of it.

Verses 4–38

We have here an account how the work of this fast-day was carried on. 1. The names of the ministers that were employed. They are twice named (*v.* 4, 5), only with some variation of the names. Either they prayed successively, according to that rule which the apostle gives (1 Co. 14:31, *You may all prophesy one by one),* or, as some think, there were eight several congregations at some distance from each other, and each had a Levite to preside in it. 2. The work itself in which they employed themselves. (1.) They prayed to God, cried to him with a loud voice (*v.* 4), for the pardon of the sins of Israel and God's favour to them. They cried aloud, not that God might the better hear them, as Baal's worshippers, but that the people might, and to excite their fervency. (2.) They praised God; for the work of praise is not unseasonable on a fast-day; in all acts of devotion we must aim at this, to *give unto God the glory due to his name.* The summary of their prayers we have here upon record; whether drawn up before, as a directory to the Levites what to enlarge on, or recollected after, as the heads of what they had in prayer enlarged upon, is uncertain. Much more no doubt was said than is here recorded, else confessing and worshipping God would not have taken up a fourth part of the day, much less two-fourths.

In this solemn address to God we have,

I. An awful adoration of God, as a perfect and glorious Being, and the fountain of all beings, *v.* 5, 6. The congregation is called upon to signify their concurrence herewith by standing up; and so the minister directs himself to God, *Blessed be thy glorious name.* God is here adored, 1. As the only living and true God: *Thou art Jehovah alone,* self-existent and independent; there is no God besides thee. 2. As the Creator of all things: *Thou hast made heaven, earth, and seas,* and all that is in them. The first article of our creed is fitly made the first article of our praises. 3. As the great Protector of the whole creation: "Thou preservest in being all the creatures thou hast given being to." God's providence extends itself to the highest beings, for they need it, and to the meanest, for they are not slighted by it. What God has made he will preserve; what he does is done effectually, Eccl. 3:14. 4. As the object of the creatures' praises: *"The host of heaven,* the world of holy angels, *worshippeth thee, v.* 6. But thy *name is exalted above all blessing and praise;* it needs not the praises of the creatures, nor is any addition made to its glory by those praises." The best performances in the praising of God's name, even those of the angels themselves, fall infinitely short of what it deserves. It is not only exalted above our blessing, but above all blessing. Put all the praises of heaven and earth together, and the thousandth part is not said of what might and should be said of the glory of God. *Our goodness extendeth not to him.*

II. A thankful acknowledgment of God's favours to Israel.

1. Many of these are here reckoned up in order before him, and very much to the purpose, for, (1.) We must take all occasions to mention the loving kindness of the Lord, and *in every prayer give thanks.* (2.) When we are confessing our sins it is good to take notice of the mercies of God as the aggravations of our sins, that we may be the more humbled and ashamed, and call ourselves by the scandalous name of ungrateful. (3.) When we are seeking to God for mercy and relief in the time of distress it is an encouragement to our faith and hope to look back upon our own and our fathers' experiences: "Lord, thou hast done well for us formerly; shall it be all undone again? Art not thou the same God still?"

2. Let us briefly observe the particular instances of God's goodness to Israel here recounted. (1.) The call of Abraham, *v.* 7. God's favour to him was distinguishing: "Thou didst choose him." His grace in him was powerful to bring him out of Ur of the Chaldees, and, in giving him the name of Abraham, he put honour upon him as his own and assured him that he should be the *father of many nations. Look unto Abraham your father* (Isa. 51:2) and see free grace glorified in him. (2.) The covenant God made with him to give the land of Canaan to him and his seed, a type of the better country, *v.* 8. And this covenant was sure, for God found Abraham's heart faithful before God, and found it so because he made it so (for faith is not of ourselves, it is the gift of God), and therefore performed his words; *for with the upright he will show himself upright,* and wherever he finds a faithful heart he will be found a faithful God. (3.) The deliverance of Israel out of Egypt, *v.* 9–11. It was seasonable to remember this now that they were interceding for the perfecting of their deliverance out of Babylon. They were then delivered, in compassion to their affliction, in answer to their cry, and in resistance of the pride and insolence of their persecutors. Wherein they dealt proudly, God showed himself *above them* (Ex. 18:11), and so got himself *a name;* for he said, *I will get me honour upon Pharaoh.* Even to this day the name of God is glorified for that wonderful work. It was done miraculously: signs and wonders were shown for the effecting of it; their deliverance was the destruction of their enemies; they were *thrown into the deeps,* as irrecoverably *as a stone into the mighty waters.* (4.) The conducting of them through the wilderness, by the pillar of cloud and fire, which showed them which way they should go, when they should remove, and when and where they should rest, directed all their stages and all their steps, *v.* 12. It was also a visible token of God's presence with them, to guide and guard them. They mention this again (*v.* 19), observing that though they had by their sins provoked God to withdraw

from them, and leave them to wander and perish in the by-paths of the wilderness, yet in his manifold mercy he continued to lead them, and took not away the *pillar of cloud and fire, v.* 19. When mercies, though forfeited, are continued, we are bound to be doubly thankful. (5.) The plentiful provision made for them in the wilderness, that they might not perish for hunger: Thou *gavest them bread from heaven,* and *water out of the rock* (*v.* 15), and, to hold up their hearts, a promise that they should go in and possess the land of Canaan. They had meat and drink, food convenient in the way, and the good land at their journey's end; what would they more? This also is repeated (*v.* 20, 21) as that which was continued, notwithstanding their provocations: *Forty years didst thou sustain them.* Never was people so long nursed and so tenderly; they were wonderfully provided for, and, in so long a time, *their clothes waxed not old,* and, though the way was rough and tedious, *their feet swelled not;* for they were *carried as upon eagles' wings.* (6.) The giving of the law upon Mount Sinai. This was the greatest favour of all that was done them and the greatest honour that was put upon them. The Law-giver was very glorious, *v.* 13. "Thou didst not only send, but camest down thyself, and *didst speak with them,*" Deu. 4:33. The law given was very good. No nation under the sun had such *right judgments, true laws,* and *good statutes,* Deu. 4:8. The moral and judicial precepts were true and right, founded upon natural equity and the eternal reasons of good and evil; and even the ceremonial institutions were good, tokens of God's goodness to them and types of gospel grace. Particular notice is taken of the law of the fourth commandment as a great favour to them: *Thou madest known unto them thy holy sabbath,* which was a token of God's particular favour to them, distinguishing them from the nations who had revolted from God and quite lost that ancient part of revealed religion, and was likewise a means of keeping up their communion with him. And, with *the law* and *the sabbath,* he *gave his good Spirit to instruct them, v.* 20. Besides the law given on Mount Sinai, the five books of Moses, which he wrote *as he was moved by the Holy Ghost,* were constant instructions to them, particularly the book of Deuteronomy, in which God's Spirit by Moses instructed them fully. Bezaleel was filled *with the Spirit of God* (Ex. 31:3), so was Joshua (Num. 27:18), and Caleb had another spirit. (7.) The putting of them in possession of Canaan, that good land, *kingdoms and nations, v.* 22. They were made so numerous as to replenish it (*v.* 23) and so victorious as to be masters of it (*v.* 24); the natives were given into their hands, *that they might do with them as they would,* set their feet, if they pleased, on the necks of their kings. Thus they gained a happy *settlement, v.* 25. Look upon their cities, and you see them strong and well fortified. Look into their houses, and you find them fine and well furnished, filled with all sorts of rich goods. Take a view of the country, and you will say that you never saw such a fat land, so well stored with *vineyards and oliveyards.* All these they found made ready to their hands; so they delighted themselves in the gifts of God's great goodness. They could not wish to be more easy or happy than they were, or might have been, in Canaan, had it not been their own fault. (8.) God's great readiness to pardon their sins, and work deliverance for them, when they had by their provocations brought his judgments upon themselves. When they were in the wilderness they found him *a God ready to pardon* (*v.* 17), a *God of pardons* (so the margin reads it), who had proclaimed his name as a God *forgiving iniquity, transgression, and sin,* who has power to forgive sin, is willing to forgive, and glories in forgiving. Though they forsook him, he did not forsake them, as justly he might have done, but continued his care of them and favour to them. Afterwards, when they were settled in Canaan and sold themselves by their sins into the hands of their enemies, upon their submission and humble request he *gave them saviours* (*v.* 27), the judges, by whom God wrought many a great deliverance for them when they were on the brink of ruin. This he did, not for any merit of theirs, for their deserved nothing but ill, but according to his mercies, his manifold mercies. (9.) The admonitions and fair warnings he gave them by his servants the prophets. When he delivered them from their troubles he *testified against their sins* (*v.* 28, 29), that they might not misconstrue their deliverances as connivances at their wickedness. That which was designed in all the testimonies which the prophets bore against them was to bring them again to God's law, to lay their necks under its yoke, and walk by its rule. The end of our ministry is to bring people to God by bringing them to his law, not to bring them to ourselves by bringing them under any law of ours. This we have again (*v.* 30): *Thou testifiedst against them by thy Spirit in thy prophets.* The testimony of the prophets was the testimony of the Spirit in the prophets, and it was the Spirit of Christ in them, 1 Pt. 1:10, 11. They *spoke as they were moved by the Holy Ghost,* and what they said is to be received accordingly. God gave them *his Spirit to instruct them* (*v.* 20), but, they not receiving that instruction, he did by his Spirit testify against them. If we will not suffer God's word to teach and rule us, it will accuse and judge us. God sends prophets, in compassion to his people (2 Chr. 36:15), that he may not send judgments. (10.) The lengthening out of his patience and the moderating of his rebukes: *Many years did he forbear them* (*v.* 30), as loth to punish them, and waiting to see if they would repent; and, when he did punish them, he did not *utterly consume them nor forsake them, v.* 31. Had he forsaken them they would have been utterly consumed; but he did not stir up all his wrath, for he designed their reformation, not their destruction. Thus do they multiply, thus do they magnify, the instances of God's goodness to Israel, and we should do in like manner, that the goodness of God, duly considered by us, may lead us to repentance, and overcome our badness. The more thankful we are for God's mercies the more humbled we shall be for our own sins.

III. Here is a penitent confession of sin, their own sins, and the sins of their fathers. The mention of these is interwoven with the memorials of God's favours, that God's goodness, notwithstanding their provocations, might appear the more illustrious, and their sins, notwithstanding his favours, might appear the more heinous. Many passages in this acknowledgment of sins and mercies are taken from Eze. 20:5–26, as will appear by comparing those verses with these; for the word of God is of use to direct us in prayer, and by what he says to us we may learn what to say to him.

1. They begin with the sins of Israel in the wilderness: *They, even our fathers* (so it might better be read), *dealt proudly* (though, considering what they were, and how lately they had come out of slavery, they had no reason to be proud), *and hardened their necks, v.* 16. Pride is at the bottom of men's obstinacy and disobedience; they think it below them to bow their necks to God's yoke, and a piece of state to set up their own will in opposition to the will of God himself. (1.) There were two things which they did not duly give heed to, else they would not have done as they did: — The word of God they heard, but they did not hearken to God's commandments; and the works of God they saw, but they were not mindful of his wonders: had they duly considered them as miracles, they would have obeyed from a principle of faith and holy fear; had they duly considered them as mercies, they would have obeyed from a principle of gratitude and holy love. But, when men make no right use either of God's ordinances or of his providences, what can be expected from them? (2.) Two great sins are here specified; which they were guilty of in the wilderness — meditating a return, [1.] To Egyptian slavery, which, for the sake of the garlick and onions, they preferred before the glorious liberty of the Israel of God attended with some difficulty and inconvenience. *In their rebellion they appointed a captain to return to their bondage,* in distrust of God's power and contempt of his holy promise, *v.* 17. [2.] To Egyptian idolatry: *They made a molten calf,* and were so sottish as to say, *This is thy God.*

2. They next bewail the provocations of their fathers after they were put in possession of Canaan. Though they were *delighted themselves in God's great goodness,* yet that would not prevail to keep them closely to him; for, *nevertheless, they were disobedient* (*v.* 26) *and wrought great provocations.* For, (1.) They abused God's prophets, *slew them* because they *testified against them to turn them to God* (*v.* 26), so returning the greatest injury for the greatest kindness. (2.) They abused his favours: *After they had rest,* they *did evil again, v.* 28. They were not wrought upon either by their troubles or their deliverances out of trouble. Neither fear nor love would hold them to their duty.

3. They at length come nearer to their own day, and lament the sins which had brought those judgments upon them which they had long been groaning under and were now but in part delivered from: *We have done wickedly* (*v.* 33): *our kings, our princes, our priests, and our fathers,* have all been guilty, and we in them, *v.* 34. Two things they charge upon themselves and their fathers, as the cause of their troubles: — (1.) A contempt of the good law God had given them: They *sinned against thy judgments,* the dictates of divine wisdom, and the demands of divine sovereignty. Though they were told how much it would be for their own advantage to govern themselves by them, for, *if a man do them, he shall live in them* (*v.* 29), yet they would not do them, and so, in effect, said that they *would not live.* They *forsook their own mercies.* This abridgment of the covenant, *Do this and live,* is taken from Eze. 20:13, and is quoted, Gal. 3:12, to prove that *the law is not of faith;* it was not them as it is now, *Believe and live,* yet *they gave a withdrawing shoulder,* so it is in the margin. They pretended to lay their shoulders under the burden of God's law, and put their shoulders to the work, but they proved withdrawing shoulders; they soon flew off, would not keep to it, would not abide by it. When it came, as we say, to the setting to, they shrunk back, and would not hear. They had a backsliding heart; and, though God by his prophets called them to return, they *would not give ear, v.* 30. He *stretched out his hands, but no man regarded.* (2.) A contempt of the good land god had given them (*v.* 35): "Our kings have *not served thee in their kingdom,* have not used their power for the support of religion; our people have not served thee in the use of the gifts of thy great goodness, and in that large and fat land which thou not only gavest them by thy grant, but gavest before them by the expulsion of the natives and the complete victories they obtained over them." Those that would not serve God in their own land were made to serve their enemies in a strange land, as was threatened, Deu. 28:47, 48. It is a pity that a good land should have bad inhabitants, but so it was with Sodom. Fatness and fulness often make men proud and sensual.

IV. Here is a humble representation of the judgments of God, which they had been and were now under.

1. Former judgments are remembered as aggravations of their sins, that they had not taken warning. In the days of the judges their *enemies vexed them* (*v.* 27); and, when they did evil again, God did again *leave them in the hand of their enemies,* who could not have touched them if God had not given them up; but, when God left them, they got and kept dominion over them.

2. Their present calamitous state is laid before the Lord (*v.* 36, 37): *We are servants this day.* Free-born Israelites are enslaved, and the land which they had long held by a much more honourable tenure than grand sergeantry itself, even by immediate grant from the crown of heaven to them as a peculiar people above all people on the earth, they now held by as base a tenure as villenage itself, by, from, and under, the kings of Persia, whose vassals they were. A sad change! But see what work sin makes! They were bound to personal service: They have *dominion over our bodies;* they held all they had precariously, were tenants at will, and the land-tax that they paid was so great that it amounted even to a rack-rent; so that all the rents, issues, and profits, of their land did in effect accrue to the king, and it was as much as they could do to get a bare subsistence for themselves and their families out of it. This, they honestly own, was for their sins. Poverty and slavery are the fruits of sin; it is sin that brings us into all our distresses.

V. Here is their address to God under these calamities. 1. By way of request, that their trouble might not *seem little, v.* 32. It is the only petition in all this prayer. The trouble was universal; it had come on their *kings, princes, priests, prophets, fathers, and all their people;* they had all shared in the sin (*v.* 34), and now all shared in the judgment. It was of long continuance: *From the time of the kings of Assyria,* who carried the ten tribes captive, *unto this day.* "Lord, let it not all seem little and not worthy to be regarded, or not needing to be relieved." They do not prescribe to God what he shall do for them, but leave it to him, only desiring he would please to take cognizance of it, remembering that when he saw the affliction of his people in Egypt to be great he came down to deliver them, Ex. 3:7, 8. In this request they have an eye to God as one that is to be feared (for he is *the great, the mighty, and the terrible, God),* and as one that is to be trusted, for he is *our God* in covenant, and a God that *keeps covenant and mercy.* 2. By way of acknowledgment, notwithstanding, that really it was less than they deserved, *v.* 33. They own the justice of God in all their troubles, that he had done them no wrong. "We have done wickedly in breaking thy laws, and therefore thou hast done right in bringing all these miseries upon us." Note, It becomes us, when we are under the rebukes of divine Providence, though ever so sharp and ever so long, to justify God and to judge ourselves; for he will be *clear when he judgeth.* Ps. 51:4.

VI. Here is the result and conclusion of this whole matter. After this long remonstrance of their case was made they came at last to this resolution, that they would return to God and to their duty, and oblige themselves never to forsake God, but always to continue in their duty. "Because of all this, we make a sure covenant with God; in consideration of our frequent departures from God, we will now more firmly than ever bind ourselves to him. Because we have smarted so much for sin, we will now stedfastly resolve against it, that we may not any more withdraw the shoulder." Observe, 1. This covenant was made with serious consideration. It is the result of a chain of suitable thoughts, and so is a reasonable service. 2. With great solemnity. It was written, *in perpetuam rei memoriam — that it might remain a memorial for all ages;* it was sealed and left upon record, that it might be a witness against them if they dealt deceitfully. 3. With join consent: *"We make* it; we are all agreed in making it, and do it unanimously, that we may strengthen the hands one of another." 4. With fixed resolution: "It is *a sure covenant,* without reserving a power of revocation. It is what we will live and die by, and never go back from." A certain number of the princes, priests, and Levites, were chosen as the representatives of the congregation, to subscribe and seal it for and in the name of the rest. Now was fulfilled that promise concerning the Jews, that, when they returned out of captivity, they should *join themselves to the Lord in a perpetual covenant* (Jer. 50:5), and that in Isa. 44:5, that they should *subscribe with their hand unto the Lord.* He that bears an honest mind will not startle at assurances; nor will those that know the deceitfulness of their own hearts think them needless.

CHAPTER 10

We have in this chapter a particular account of the covenant which in the close of the foregoing chapter was resolved upon; they struck while the iron was not, and immediately put that good resolve in execution, when they were in a good frame, lest, if it should be delayed, it might be dropped. Here we have, I. The names of those that set their hands and seals to it (*v.* 1–27). II. An account of those who signified their consent and concurrence (*v.* 28, 29). III. The covenant itself, and the articles of it in general, that they would "keep God's commandments" (*v.* 29); in particular, that they would not marry with the heathen (*v.* 30), nor profane the sabbath, nor be rigorous with their debtors (*v.* 31), and that they would carefully pay their church-dues, for the maintenance of the temple service, which they promise faithfully to adhere to (*v.* 32–39).

Verses 1–31

When Israel was first brought into covenant with God it was done by sacrifice and the sprinkling of blood, Ex. 24. But here it was done by the more natural and common way of sealing and subscribing the written articles of the covenant, which bound them to no more than was already their duty. Now here we have,

I. The names of those public persons who, as the representatives and heads of the congregation, set their hands and seals to this covenant, because it would have been an endless piece of work for every particular person to do it; and, if these leading men did their part in pursuance of this covenant, their example would have a good influence upon all the people. Now observe, 1. Nehemiah, who was the governor, signed first, to show his forwardness in this work and to set others a good example, *v.* 1. Those that are above others in dignity and power should go before them in the way of God. 2. Next to him subscribed twenty-two priests, among whom I wonder we do not find Ezra, who was an active man in the solemnity (*ch.* 8:2) which was but the first day of the same month, and therefore we cannot think he was absent; but he, having before done his part as a scribe, now left it to others to do theirs. 3. Next to the priests, seventeen Levites subscribed this covenant, among whom we find all or most of those who were the mouth of the congregation in prayer, *ch.* 9:4, 5. This showed that they themselves were affected with what they had said, and would not bind those burdens on others which they themselves declined to touch. Those that lead in prayer should lead in every other good work. 4. Next to the Levites, forty-four of the chief of the people gave it under their hands for themselves and all the rest, chiefly those whom they had influence upon, that they would keep God's commandments. Their names are left upon record here, to their honour, as men that were forward and active in reviving and endeavouring to perpetuate religion in their country. The memory of such shall be blessed. It is observable that most of those who were mentioned, *ch.* 7:8, etc., as heads of houses or clans, are here mentioned among the first of the chief of the people that subscribed, whoever was the present head bearing the name of him that was head when they came out of Babylon, and these were fittest to subscribe for all those of their father's house. Here are *Parosh, Pahathmoab, Elam, Zatthu, Bani* (*v.* 14), *Azgad, Bebai, Bigvai, Adin, Ater, Hashum, Bezai, Hariph, Anathoth,* and some others in the following verses, that are all found in that catalogue. Those that have interest must use it for God.

II. The concurrence of the rest of the people with them, and the rest of the priests and Levites, who signified their consent to what their chiefs did. With them joined, 1. Their wives and children; for they had transgressed, and they must reform. Every one that had knowledge and understanding must covenant with God. As soon as young people grow up to be capable of distinguishing between good and evil, and of acting intelligently, they ought to make it their own act and deed to *join themselves to the Lord.* 2. The proselytes of other nations, *all that had separated themselves from the people of the lands,* their gods and their worship, *unto the law of God,* and the observance of that law. See what conversion it; it is separating ourselves from the course and custom of this world, and devoting ourselves to the conduce of the word of God. And, as there is one law, so there is one covenant, one baptism, for the stranger and for him that is born in the land. Observe how the concurrence of the people is expressed, *v.* 29. (1.) *They clave to their brethren* one and all. Here those whom the court blessed the country blessed too! The commonalty agreed with their nobles in this good work. Great men never look so great as when they encourage religion, and are examples of it; and they would by that, as much as any thing, secure an interest in the most valuable of their inferiors. Let but the nobles cordially espouse religious causes, and perhaps they will find people cleave to them therein closer than they can imagine. Observe, Their nobles are called their *brethren;* for, in the things of God, rich and poor, high and low, meet together. (2.) They *entered into a curse and an oath.* As the nobles confirmed the covenant with their hands and seals, so the people with a curse and an oath, solemnly appealing to God concerning their sincerity, and imprecating his just revenge if they dealt deceitfully. Every oath has in it a conditional curse upon the soul, which makes it a strong bond upon the soul; for our own tongues, if false and lying tongues, will fall, and fall heavily, upon ourselves.

III. The general purport of this covenant. They laid upon themselves no other burden than this necessary thing, which they were already obliged to by all other engagements of duty, interest, and gratitude — *to walk in God's law, and to do all his commandments, v.* 29. Thus David swore that he would *keep God's righteous judgments,* Ps. 119:106. Our own covenant binds us to this, if not more strongly, yet more sensibly, than we were before bound, and therefore we must not think it needless thus to bind ourselves. Observe, When we bind ourselves to do the commandments of God we bind ourselves to do *all* his commandments, and therein to have an eye to him as the Lord and our Lord.

IV. Some of the particular articles of this covenant, such as were adapted to their present temptations. 1. That they would not intermarry with the heathen, *v.* 30. Many of them had been guilty of this, Ezra 9:1. In our covenants with God we should engage particularly against those sins that we have been most frequently overtaken in and damaged by. Those that resolve to *keep the commandments of God must say to evil doers, Depart,* Ps. 119:115. 2. That they would keep no markets on the sabbath day, or any other day of which the law had said, *You shall do no work therein.* They would not only not sell goods themselves for gain on that day, but they would not encourage the heathen to sell on that day by buying of them, no not victuals, under pretence of necessity; but would buy in their provisions for their families the day before, *v.* 31. Note, Those that covenant to keep all God's commandments must particularly covenant to keep sabbaths well; for the profanation of them is an inlet to other instances of profaneness. The sabbath is a market day for our souls, but not for our bodies. 3. That they would not be severe in exacting their debts, but would observe the seventh year as a year of release, according to the law, *v.* 31. In this matter they had been faulty (*ch.* 5), and here therefore they promise to reform. This was the acceptable fast, to *undo the heavy burden,* and to *let the oppressed go free,* Isa. 58:6. It was in the close of the day of expiation that the jubilee trumpet sounded. It was for the neglect of observing the seventh year as a year of rest for the land that God had made it enjoy its sabbaths seventy years (Lev. 26:35), and therefore they covenanted to observe that law. Those are stubborn children indeed that will not amend the fault for which they have been particularly corrected.

Verses 32–39

Having covenanted against the sins they had been guilty of, they proceed in obliging themselves to revive and observe the duties they had neglected. We must not only *cease to do evil,* but *learn to do well.*

I. It was resolved, in general, that the temple service should be carefully kept up, that the work of the house of their God should be done in its season, according to the law, *v.* 33. Let not any people expect the blessing of God unless they make conscience of observing his ordinances and keeping up the public worship of him. Then it is likely to go well with our houses when care is taken that the work of God's house go on well. It was likewise resolved that they would never *forsake the house of their God* (*v.* 39), as they and their fathers had done, would not forsake it for the house of any other god, or for the high places, as idolaters did, nor forsake it for their farms and merchandises, as those did that were atheistical and profane. Those that forsake the worship of God forsake God.

II. It was resolved, in pursuance of this, that they would liberally maintain the temple service, and not starve it. The priests were ready to do their part in all the work of God's house, if the people would do theirs, which was to find them with materials to work upon. Now here it was agreed and concluded, 1. That a stock should be raised for the furnishing of God's table and altar plentifully. Formerly there were treasures in the house of the Lord for this purpose, but these were gone, and there was no settled fund to supply the want of them. It was a constant charge to provide show-bread for the table, two lambs for the daily offerings, four for the sabbaths, and more, and more costly, sacrifices for other festivals, occasional sin-offerings, and meat-offerings, and drink-offerings for them all. They had no rich king to provide these, as Hezekiah did; the priests could not afford to provide them, their maintenance was so small; the people therefore agreed to contribute yearly, every one of them, the third part of a shekel, about ten pence a-piece for the bearing of this expense. When every one will act, and every one will give, though but little, towards a good work, the whole amount will be considerable. The tirshatha did not impose this tax, but the people made it an ordinance for themselves, and charged themselves with it, *v.* 32, 33. 2. That particular care should be taken to provide wood for the altar, to keep the fire always burning upon it, and wherewith to boil the peace-offerings. All of them, priests and Levites as well as people, agreed to bring in their quota, and cast lots in what order they should bring it in, which family first and which next, that there might be a constant supply, and not a scarcity at one time and an overplus at another, *v.* 34. Thus they provided the fire and the wood, as well as the lambs for the burnt-offerings. 3. That all those things which the divine law had appointed for the maintenance of the priests and Levites should be duly paid in, for their encouragement to mind their business, and that they might not be under any temptation to neglect it for the making of necessary provision for their families. Then the work of the house of God is likely to go on when those that serve at the altar live, and live comfortably, upon the altar. First-fruits and tenths were then the principal branches of the ministers' revenues; and they here resolved, (1.) To bring in the first-fruits justly, the first-fruits of their ground and trees (Ex. 23:19; Lev. 19:23), the first-born of their children (even the money wherewith they were to be redeemed) and of their cattle, Ex. 13:2, 11, 12 (this was given to the priests, Num. 18:15, 16), also the first-fruits of their dough (Num. 15:21), concerning which there is a particular order given in the prophecy concerning the second temple, Eze. 44:30. (2.) To bring in their tenths likewise, which were due to the Levites (*v.* 37), and a tenth out of those tenths to the priest, *v.* 38. This was the law (Num. 18:21–28); but these dues had been withheld, in consequence of which God, by the prophet, charges them with *robbing him* (Mal. 3:8, 9), at the same time encouraging them to be more just to him and his receivers, with a promise that, if they brought the *tithes into the store-house,* he would *pour out blessings upon them, v.* 10. This therefore they resolved to do, that there might be meat in God's house, and plenty in the store-chambers of the temple, where the vessels of the sanctuary were, *v.* 39. "We will do it (say they) *in all the cities of our tillage," v.* 37. *In all the cities of our servitude,* so the Septuagint, for they were servants in their own land, *ch.* 9:36. But (as Mr. Poole well observes), though they paid great taxes to the kings of Persia, and had much hardship put upon them, they would not make that an excuse for not paying their tithes, but would render to God the things that were his, as well as to Caesar the things that were his. We must do what we can in works of piety and charity notwithstanding the taxes we pay to the government, and cheerfully perform our duty to God in our servitude, which will be the surest way to ease and liberty in God's due time.

CHAPTER 11

Jerusalem was walled round, but it was not as yet fully inhabited, and therefore was weak and despicable. Nehemiah's next care is to bring people into it; of that we have here an account. I. The methods taken to replenish it (*v.* 1, 2). II. The principal persons that resided there, of Judah and Benjamin (*v.* 3–9), of the priests and Levites (*v.* 10–19). III. The several cities and villages of Judah and Benjamin that were peopled by the rest of their families (*v.* 20–36).

Verses 1–19

Jerusalem is called here *the holy city* (*v.* 1), because there the temple was, and that was the place God had chosen to put his name there; upon this account, one would think, the holy seed should all have chosen to dwell there and have striven for a habitation there; but, on the contrary, it seems they declined dwelling there, 1. Because a greater strictness of conversation was expected from the inhabitants of Jerusalem than from others, which they were not willing to come up to. Those who care not for being holy themselves are shy of dwelling in a holy city; they would not dwell in the *New Jerusalem* itself for that reason, but would wish to have a continuing city here upon earth. Or, 2. Because Jerusalem, of all places, was most hated by the heathen their neighbours, and against it their malicious designs were levelled, which made that the post of danger (as the post of honour usually is) and therefore they were not willing to expose themselves there. Fear of persecution and reproach, and of running themselves into trouble, keeps many out of the holy city, and makes them backward to appear for God and religion, not considering that, as Jerusalem is with a special malice threatened and insulted by its enemies, so it is with a special care protected by its God and made a *quiet habitation,* Isa. 33:20; Ps. 46:4, 5. Or, 3. Because it was more for their worldly advantage to dwell in the country. Jerusalem was no trading city, and therefore there was no money to be got there by merchandise, as there was in the country by corn and cattle. Note, *All seek their own, not the things that are Jesus Christ's,* Phil. 2:21. It is a general and just complaint that most people prefer their own wealth, credit, pleasure, ease, and safety, before the glory of God and the public good. People being thus backward to dwell at Jerusalem, now that it was poor, we are here told,

I. By what means it was replenished. 1. The rulers dwelt there, *v.* 1. That was the proper place for them to reside in, because *there were set the thrones of judgment* (Ps. 122:5), and thither, in all difficult matters, the people resorted with their last appeals. And if it were an instance of eminent affection to the house of God, zeal for the public good, and of faith, and holy courage, and self-denial, to dwell there at this time, the rulers would be examples of these to their inferiors. Their dwelling there would invite and encourage others to dwell there too. *Magnates magnetes — the mighty are magnetic.* When great men choose the holy city for their habitation their example brings holiness into reputation, and their zeal will provoke very many. 2. There were some that willingly offered themselves to dwell at Jerusalem, nobly foregoing their own secular interest for the public welfare, *v.* 2. It is upon record, to their honour, that when others were shy of venturing upon difficulty, loss, and danger, they *sought the good of Jerusalem, because of the house of the Lord their God. Those shall prosper that thus love Zion,* Ps. 122:6, 9. It is said, *The people blessed them.* They praised them; they prayed for them; they praised God for them. Many that do not appear forward themselves for the public good will yet give a good word to those that do. God and man will bless those that are public blessings, which should encourage us to be zealous in doing good. 3. They, finding that *yet there was room,* concluded upon a review of their whole body to bring one in ten to dwell in Jerusalem; who they should be was determined by lot, the disposal whereof, all knew, was of the Lord. This would prevent strife, and would be a great satisfaction to those on whom the lot fell to dwell at Jerusalem, that they plainly saw God appointing the bounds of their habitation. They observed the proportion of one in ten, as we may suppose, to bring the balance between the city and country to a just and equal poise; so it seems to refer to the ancient rule of giving the tenth to God; and what is given to the holy city he reckons given to himself.

II. By what persons it was replenished. A general account is here given of the inhabitants of Jerusalem because the *governors of Judah* looked upon them as *their strength in the Lord of hosts their God,* and valued them accordingly, Zec. 12:5. 1. Many of the children of Judah and Benjamin dwelt there; for, originally, part of the city law in the lot of one of those tribes and part in that of the other; but the greater part was in the lot of Benjamin, and therefore here we find of the children of Judah only 468 families in Jerusalem (*v.* 6), but of Benjamin 928, *v.* 7, 8. Thus small were its beginnings, but afterwards, before our Saviour's time, it grew much more populous. Those of Judah all descended from Perez, or Pharez, that son of Judah of whom, as concerning the flesh, Christ came. And, though the Benjamites were more in number, yet of the men of Judah it is said (*v.* 6) that they were valiant men, fit for service, and able to defend the city in case of an attack. Judah has not lost its ancient character of a lion's whelp, bold and daring. Of the Benjamites that dwelt in Jerusalem we are here told who was *overseer,* and who was second, *v.* 9. For it is as necessary for a people to have good order kept up among themselves as to be fortified against the attacks of their enemies from abroad, to have good magistrates as to have good soldiers. 2. The priests and Levites did many of them settle at Jerusalem; where else should men that were holy to God dwell, but in the holy city? (1.) Most of the priests, we may suppose, dwelt there, for their business lay where the temple was. Of those that did the work of the house in their courses here were 822 of one family, 242 of another, and 128 of another, *v.* 12–14. It was well that those labourers were not few. It is said of some of them that they were *mighty men of valour* (*v.* 14); it was necessary that they should be so, for the priesthood was not only a work, which required might, but a warfare, which required valour, especially now. Of one of these priests it is said that he was *the son of one of the great men.* It was no disparagement to the greatest man they had to have his son in the priesthood; he might magnify his office, for his office did not in the least diminish him. (2.) Some of the Levites also came and dwelt at Jerusalem, yet but few in comparison, 284 in all (*v.* 18), with 172 porters (*v.* 19), for much of their work was to *teach the good knowledge of God* up and down the country, for which purpose they were to be scattered in Israel. As many as there was occasion for attended at Jerusalem; the rest were doing good elsewhere. [1.] It is said of one of the Levites that he had *the oversight of the outward business of the house of God, v.* 16. The priests were chief managers of the business within the temple gates; but this Levite was entrusted with the secular concerns of God's house, that were *in ordine ad spiritualia — subservient to its spiritual concerns,* the collecting of the contributions, the providing of materials for the temple service, and the like, which it was necessary to oversee, else the inward business would have been starved and have stood still. Those who take care of the *ta exō — the outward concerns* of the church, the serving of its tables, are as necessary in their place as those who take care of its *ta esō — its inward concerns,* who give themselves to the word and prayer. [2.] It is said of another that he was *the principal to begin the thanksgiving in prayer.* Probably he had a good ear and a good voice, and was a scientific singer, and therefore was chosen to lead the psalm. He was precentor in the temple. Observe, Thanksgiving is necessary in prayer; they should go together; giving thanks for former mercies is a becoming way of begging further mercies. And care should be taken in public service that every thing be done in the best manner, *decently and in good order* — in prayer, that one speak and the rest join — in singing, that one begin and the rest follow.

Verses 20–36

Having given an account of the principal persons that dwelt in Jerusalem (a larger account of whom he had before, 1 Chr. 9:2, etc.), Nehemiah, in these verses, gives us some account of the other cities, in which dwelt *the residue of Israel, v.* 20. It was requisite that Jerusalem should be replenished, yet not so as to drain the country. *The king himself is served of the field,* which will do little service if there be not hands to manage it. Let there therefore be no strife, no envy, no contempt, no ill will, between the inhabitants of the cities and those of the villages; both are needful, both useful, and neither can be spared. 1. The Nethinims, the posterity of the Gibeonites, dwelt in Ophel, which was upon the wall of Jerusalem (*ch.* 3:26), because they were to do the servile work of the temple, which therefore they must be posted near to, that they might be ready to attend, *v.* 21. 2. Though the Levites were dispersed through the cities of Judah, yet they had an overseer who resided in Jerusalem, superior of their order and their provincial, to whom they applied for direction, who took care of their affairs and took cognizance of their conduct, whether they did their duty, *v.* 22. 3. Some of the singers were appointed to look after the necessary repairs of the temple, being ingenious men, and having leisure between their hours of service; they were *over the business of the house of God, v.* 22. And, it seems, the king of Persia had such a kindness for their office that he allotted a particular maintenance for them, besides what belonged to them as Levites, *v.* 23. 4. Here is one that was the king's commissioner at Jerusalem. He was of the posterity of Zerah (*v.* 24); for of *that* family of Judah there were some new settled in Jerusalem, and not all of Pharez, as appears by that other catalogue, 1 Chr. 9:6. He is said to be *at the king's hand,* or *on the king's part,* in *all matters concerning the people,* to determine controversies that arose between the king's officers and his subjects, to see that what was due to the king from the people was duly paid in and what was allowed by the king for the temple service was duly paid out, and happy it was for the Jews that one of themselves was in this post. 5. Here is an account of the villages, or country towns, which were inhabited by the residue of Israel — the towns in which the children of Judah dwelt (*v.* 25–30), those that were inhabited by the children of Benjamin (*v.* 31–35), and divisions for the Levites among both, *v.* 36. We will now suppose them safe and easy, though few and poor, but by the blessing of God they were likely to increase in wealth and power, and they would have been more likely if there had not been that general profaneness among them, and lukewarmness in religion, with which they were charged in God's name by the prophet Malachi, who, it is supposed, prophesied about this time, and in whom prophecy ceased for some ages, till it revived in the great prophet and his forerunner.

CHAPTER 12

In this chapter are preserved upon record, I. The names of the chief of the priests and the Levites that came up with Zerubbabel (*v.* 1–9). II. The succession of the high priests (*v.* 10, 11). III. The names of the next generation of the other chief priests (*v.* 12–21). IV. The eminent Levites that were in Nehemiah's time (*v.* 22–26). V. The solemnity of dedicating the wall of Jerusalem (*v.* 27–43). VI. The settling of the offices of the priests and Levites in the temple (*v.* 44–47).

Verses 1–26

We have here the names, and little more than the names, of a great many priests and Levites, that were eminent in their day among the returned Jews. Why this register should be here inserted by Nehemiah does not appear, perhaps to keep in remembrance those good men, that posterity might know to whom they were beholden, under God, for the happy revival and re-establishment of their religion among them. Thus must we contribute towards the performance of that promise, Ps. 112:6, *The righteous shall be in everlasting remembrance.* Let the memory of the just be blessed, be perpetuated. It is a debt we still owe to faithful ministers to *remember our guides,* who have *spoken to us the word of God,* Heb. 13:7. Perhaps it is intended to stir up their posterity, who succeeded them in the priest's office and inherited their dignities and preferments, to imitate their courage and fidelity. It is good to know what our godly ancestors and predecessors were, that we may learn thereby what we should be. We have here, 1. The names of the priests and Levites that came up with the first out of Babylon, when Jeshua was high priest. Jeremiah and Ezra are mentioned with the first (*v.* 1), but, it is supposed, not Jeremiah the prophet nor Ezra the scribe; the fame of the one was long before and that of the other some time after, though both of them were priests. Of one of the Levites it is said (*v.* 8) that he was *over the thanksgiving,* that is, he was entrusted to see that the psalms, the thanksgiving psalms, were constantly sung in the temple in due time and manner. The Levites kept their turns in their watches, reliving one another as becomes brethren, fellow-labourers, and fellow-soldiers. 2. The succession of high priests during the Persian monarchy, from Jeshua (or Jesus), who was high priest at the time of the restoration, to Jaddua (or Jaddus), who was high priest when Alexander the Great, after the conquest of Tyre, came to Jerusalem, and paid great respect to this Jaddus, who met him in his pontifical habit, and showed him the prophecy of Daniel, which foretold his conquests. 3. The next generation of priests, who were chief men, and active in the days of Joiakim, sons of the first set. Note, We have reason to acknowledge God's favour to his church, and care of it, in that, as one generation of ministers passes away, another comes. All those who are mentioned *v.* 1, etc., as eminent in their generation, are again mentioned, though with some variation in several of the names, *v.* 12, etc., except two, as having sons that were likewise eminent in their generation — a rare instance, that twenty good fathers should leave behind them twenty good sons (for so many here are) that filled up their places. 4. The next generation of Levites, or rather a latter generation; for those priests who are mentioned flourished in the days of Joiakim the high priest, these Levites in the days of Eliashib, *v.* 22. Perhaps *then* the forementioned families of the priests began to degenerate, and the third generation of them came short of the first two; but the work of God shall never fail for want of instruments. Then a generation of Levites was *raised up,* who were *recorded chief of the fathers* (*v.* 22), and were eminently serviceable to the interests of the church, and their service not the less acceptable either to God or to his people for their being Levites only, of the lower rank of ministers. Eliashib the high priest being allied to Tobiah (*ch.* 13:4), the other priests grew remiss; but then the Levites appeared the more zealous, as appears by this, that those who were now employed in expounding (*ch.* 8:7) and in praying (*ch.* 9:4, 5) were all Levites, not priests, regard being had to their personal qualifications more than to their order. These Levites were some of them singers (*v.* 24), *to praise and give thanks,* others of them porters (*v.* 25), *keeping the ward at the thresholds of the gates, and both according to the command of David.*

Verses 27–43

We have read of the building of the wall of Jerusalem with a great deal of fear and trembling; we have here an account of the dedicating of it with a great deal of joy and triumph. *Those that sow in tears shall* thus *reap.*

I. We must enquire what was the meaning of this dedication of the wall; we will suppose it to include the dedication of the city too *(continens pro contento — the thing containing for the thing contained),* and therefore it was not done till the city was pretty well replenished, *ch.* 11:1. It was a solemn thanksgiving to God for his great mercy to them in the perfecting of this undertaking, of which they were the more sensible because of the difficulty and opposition they had met with in it. 2. They hereby devoted the city in a peculiar manner to God and to his honour, and took possession of it for him and in his name. All our cities, all our houses, must have holiness to the Lord written upon them; but this city was (so as never any other was) a *holy city,* the *city of the great King* (Ps. 48:2 and Mt. 5:35): it had been so ever since God chose it to put his name there, and as such, it being now refitted, it was afresh dedicated to God by the builders and inhabitants, in token of their acknowledgment that they were his tenants, and their desire that it might still be is and that the property of it might never be altered. Whatever is done for their safety, ease, and comfort, must be designed for God's honour and glory. 3. They hereby put the city and its walls under the divine protection, owning that *unless the Lord kept the city* the walls were *built in vain.* When this city was in possession of the Jebusites, they committed the guardianship of it to their gods, though they were blind and lame ones, 2 Sa. 5:6. With much more reason do the people of God commit it to his keeping who is allwise and almighty. The superstitious founders of cities had an eye to the lucky position of the heavens (see Mr. Gregory's works, p. 29, etc.); but these pious founders had an eye to God only, to his providence, and not to fortune.

II. We must observe with what solemnity it was performed, under the direction of Nehemiah. 1. The Levites from all parts of the country were summoned to attend. The city must be dedicated to God, and therefore his ministers must be employed in the dedicating of it, and the surrender must pass through their hands. When those solemn feasts were over (*ch.* 8 and 9) they went home to their respective posts, to mind their cures in the country; but now their presence and assistance were again called for. 2. Pursuant to this summons, there was a general rendezvous of all the Levites, *v.* 28, 29. Observe in what method they proceeded. (1.) They *purified themselves, v.* 30. We are concerned to *cleanse our hands,* and *purify our hearts,* when any work for God is to pass through them. They purified themselves and then the people. Those that would be instrumental to sanctify others must sanctify themselves, and set themselves apart for God, with purity of mind and sincerity of intention. Then they purified *the gates and the wall.* Then may we expect comfort when we are prepared to receive it. *To the pure all things are pure* (Tit. 1:15); and, to those who are sanctified, houses and tables, and all their creature comforts and enjoyments, are sanctified, 1 Tim. 4:4, 5. This purification was performed, it is probable, by sprinkling the *water of purifying* (or of *separation,* as it is called, Num. 19:9) on *themselves* and the *people,* the walls and the gates — a type of the blood of Christ, with which our consciences being *purged from dead works,* we become fit to *serve the living God* (Heb. 9:14) and to be his care. (2.) The princes, priests, and Levites, walked round upon the wall in two companies, with musical instruments, to signify the dedication of it all to God, the whole circuit of it (*v.* 36); so that it is likely they sung psalms as they went along, to the praise and glory of God. This procession is here largely described. They had a rendezvous at one certain lace, where they divided themselves into two companies. Half of the princes, with several priests and Levites, went on the right hand, Ezra leading their van, *v.* 36. The other half of the princes and priests, who gave thanks likewise, went to the left hand, Nehemiah bringing up the rear, *v.* 38. At length both companies met in the temple, where they joined their thanksgivings, *v.* 40. The crowd of people, it is likely, walked on the ground, some within the wall and others without, one end of this ceremony being to affect them with the mercy they were giving thanks for, and to perpetuate the remembrance of it among them. Processions, for such purposes, have their use. (3.) The people *greatly rejoiced, v.* 43. While the princes, priests, and Levites, testified their joy and thankfulness by *great sacrifices, sound of trumpet, musical instruments, and songs of praise,* the common people testified theirs by loud shouts, which were heard afar off, further than the more harmonious sound of their songs and music: and these shouts, coming from a sincere and hearty joy, are here taken notice of; for God overlooks not, but graciously accepts, the honest zealous services of mean people, though there is in them little of art and they are far from being fine. It is observed that *the women and children rejoiced;* and their hosannas were not despised, but recorded to their praise. All that share in public mercies ought to join in public thanksgivings. The reason given is that *God had made them rejoice with great joy.* He had given them both matter for joy and hearts to rejoice; his providence had made them safe and easy, and then his grace made them cheerful and thankful. The baffled opposition of their enemies, no doubt, added to their joy and mixed triumph with it. Great mercies call for the most solemn returns of praise, *in the courts of the Lord's house, in the midst of thee, O Jerusalem!*

Verses 44–47

We have here an account of the remaining good effects of the universal joy that was at the dedication of the wall. When the solemnities of a thanksgiving day leave such impressions on ministers and people as that both are more careful and cheerful in doing their duty afterwards, then they are indeed acceptable to God and turn to a good account. So it was here. 1. The ministers were more careful than they had been of their work; the respect the people paid them upon this occasion encouraged them to diligence and watchfulness, *v.* 45. *The singers kept the ward of their God,* attending in due time to the duty of their office; the *porters,* too, *kept the ward of the purification,* that is, they took care to preserve the purity of the temple by denying admission to those that were ceremonially unclean. When the joy of the Lord thus engages us to our duty, and enlarges us in it, it is then an earnest of that joy which, in concurrence with the perfection of holiness, will be our everlasting bliss. 2. The people were more careful than they had been of the maintenance of their ministers. The people, at the dedication of the wall, among other things which they made matter of their joy, rejoiced *for the priests and for the Levites that waited, v.* 44. They had a great deal of comfort in their ministers, and were glad of them. When they observed how diligently they waited, and what pains they took in their work, they rejoiced in them. Note, The surest way for ministers to recommend themselves to their people, and gain an interest in their affections, is *to wait on their ministry* (Rom. 12:7), to be humble and industrious, and to mind their business. When these did so the people thought nothing too much to do for them, to encourage them. The law had provided then *their portions* (*v.* 44), but what the better were they for that provision if what the law appointed them either was not duly collected or not justly paid to them? Now, (1.) Care is here taken for the collecting of their dues. They were modest, and would rather lose their right than call for it themselves. The people were many of them careless and would not bring their dues unless they were called upon; and therefore *some were appointed* whose office it should be to gather into the treasuries, *out of the fields of the cities, the portions of the law for the priests and Levites* (*v.* 44), that their portion might not be lost for want of being demanded. This is a piece of good service both to ministers and people, that the one may not come short of their maintenance nor the other of their duty. (2.) Care is taken that, being *gathered in,* they might be duly *paid out, v.* 47. They gave the singers and porters their daily portion, over and above what was due to them as Levites; for we may suppose that when David and Solomon appointed them their work (*v.* 45, 46), above what was required from them as Levites, they settled a fund for their further encouragement. Let those that labour more abundantly in the word and doctrine be counted worthy of this double honour. As for the other Levites, the tithes, here called *the holy things,* were duly set apart for them, out of which they paid the priests their tithe according to the law. Both are said to be *sanctified;* when what is contributed, either voluntarily or by law, for the support of religion and the maintenance of the ministry, is given with an eye to God and his honour, it is sanctified, and shall be accepted of him accordingly, and it will *cause the blessing to rest on the house* and all that is in it, Eze. 44:30.

CHAPTER 13

Nehemiah, having finished what he undertook for the fencing and filling of the holy city, returned to the king his master, who was not willing to be long without him, as appears (*v.* 6). But, after some time, he obtained leave to come back again to Jerusalem, to redress grievances, and purge out some corruptions which had crept in in his absence; and very active he was in reforming several abuses, which here we have an account of. I. He turned out from Israel the mixed multitude, the Moabites and Ammonites especially (v. 1–3). With a particular indignation, he expelled Tobiah out of the lodgings he had got in the court of the temple (v. 4–9). II. He secured the maintenance of the priests and Levites to them more firmly than it had been (v. 10–14). III. He restrained the profanation of the sabbath day, and provided for the due sanctification of it (v. 15–22). IV. He checked the growing mischief of marrying strange wives (v. 23–31).

Verses 1–9

It was the honour of Israel, and the greatest preservation of their holiness, that they were a peculiar people, and were so to keep themselves, and not to mingle with the nations, nor suffer any of them to incorporate with them. Now here we have,

I. The law to this purport, which happened to be read *on that day, in the audience of the people* (v. 1), on the day of the dedication of the wall, as it should seem, for with their prayers and praises they joined the reading of the word; and though it was long after that the other grievances, here mentioned, were redressed by Nehemiah's power, yet this of the mixed multitude might be redressed then by the people's own act, for so it seems to be, v. 3. Or, perhaps, it was on the anniversary commemoration of that day, some years after, and therefore said to be *on that day.* They found a law, that the Ammonites and Moabites should not be naturalized, should not settle among them, nor unite with them, v. 1. The reason given is because they had been injurious and ill-natured to the Israel of God (v. 2), had not shown them common civility, but sought their ruin, though they not only did them no harm, but were expressly forbidden to do them any. This law we have, with this reason, Deu. 23:3–5.

II. The people's ready compliance with this law, v. 3. See the benefit of the public reading of the word of God; when it is duly attended to it discovers to us sin and duty, good and evil, and shows us wherein we have erred. Then we profit by the discovery when by it we are wrought upon to separate ourselves from all that evil to which we had addicted ourselves. They *separated from Israel all the mixed multitude,* which had of old been a snare to them, for the *mixed multitude fell a lusting,* Num. 11:4. These inmates they expelled, as usurpers and dangerous.

III. The particular case of Tobiah, who was an Ammonite, and to whom, it is likely, the historian had an eye in the recital of the law (v. 1), and the reason of it, v. 2. For he had the same enmity to Israel that his ancestors had, the spirit of an Ammonite, witness his indignation at Nehemiah (ch. 2:10) and the opposition he had given to his undertakings, ch. 4:7, 8. Observe,

1. How basely Eliashib the chief priest took this Tobiah in to be a lodger even in the courts of the temple. (1.) He was allied to Tobiah (v. 4), by marriage first and then by friendship. His grandson had married Sanballat's daughter, v. 28. Probably some other of his family had married Tobiah's, and (would you think it?) the high priest thought the alliance an honour to his family, and was very proud of it, though really it was his greatest disgrace, and what he had reason to be ashamed of. It was expressly provided by the law that the high priest should marry *one of his own people,* else he *profanes his seed among his people,* Lev. 21:14, 15. And for Eliashib to contract an alliance with an Ammonite, a *servant* (for so he is called) and to value himself upon it, probably because he has a wit and a beau, and cried up for a fine gentleman (ch. 6:19), was such a contempt of the crown of his consecration as one would not wish should be told in Gath or published in the streets of Ashkelon. (2.) Being allied to him, he must be acquainted with him. Tobiah, being a man of business, has often occasion to be at Jerusalem, I doubt upon no good design. Eliashib is fond of his new kinsman, pleased with his company, and must have him as near him as he can. He has not a room for him stately enough in his own apartment, in the courts of the temple; therefore, out of several little chambers which had been used for store-chambers, by taking down the partitions, he contrived to make one great chamber, a state-room for Tobiah, v. 5. A wretched thing it was, [1.] That Tobiah the Ammonite should be entertained with respect in Israel, and have a magnificent reception. [2.] That the high priest, who should have taught the people the law and set them a good example, should, contrary to the law, give him entertain-

ment, and make use of the power he had, as overseer of the chambers of the temple, for that purpose. [3.] That he should lodge him in the courts of God's house, as if to confront God himself; this was next to setting up an idol there, as the wicked kings of old had done. An Ammonite must not *come into the congregation;* and shall one of the worst and vilest of the Ammonites be courted into the temple itself, and caressed there? [4.] That he should throw out the stores of the temple, to make room for him, and so expose them to be lost, wasted, and embezzled, though they were the *portions of the priests,* merely to gratify Tobiah. Thus did he *corrupt the covenant of Levi,* as Malachi complained at this time, ch. 2:8. Well might Nehemiah add (v. 6), *But all this time was not I at Jerusalem.* If he had been there, the high priest durst not have done such a thing. The envious one, who sows tares in God's field, knows how to take an opportunity to do it when the *servants sleep* or are absent, Mt. 13:25. The golden calf was made when Moses was in the mount.

2. How bravely Nehemiah, the chief governor, threw him out, and all that belonged to him, and restored the chambers to their proper use. When he came to Jerusalem, and was informed by the good people who were troubled at it what an intimacy had grown between their chief priest and their chief enemy, it *grieve him sorely* (v. 7, 8) that God's house should be so profaned, his enemies so caressed and trusted, and his cause betrayed by him that should have been its protector and patron. Nothing grieves a good man, a good magistrate, more than to see the ministers of God's house do any wicked thing. Nehemiah has power and he will use it for God. (1.) Tobiah shall be expelled. He fears not disobliging him, fears not his resentments, or Eliashib's, nor excuses himself from interposing in an affair that lay within the jurisdiction of the high priest; but, like one zealously affected in a good thing, he expels the intruder, by casting forth all his household stuff. He did not seize it for his own use, but cast it out, that Tobiah, who it is probable was now absent, when he came again, might have no conveniences for his reception there. Our Saviour thus *cleansed the temple,* that the *house of prayer* might not be a *den of thieves.* And thus those that would expel sin out of their hearts, those living temples, must throw out its household stuff and all the provision made for it, strip it, starve it, and take away all those things that are the food and fuel of lust; this is, in effect, to mortify it. (2.) The temple stores shall be brought in again, and the *vessels of the house of God put in their places;* but the chambers must first be sprinkled with the water of purification, and so cleansed, because they had been profaned. Thus, when sin is cast out of the heart by repentance, let the blood of Christ be applied to it by faith, and then let it be furnished with the graces of God's Spirit for every good work.

Verses 10–14

Here is another grievance redressed by Nehemiah.

I. The Levites had been wronged. This was the grievance: their *portions had not been given them,* v. 10. Perhaps Tobiah, when he took possession of the store-chambers, seized the stores too, and, by the connivance of Eliashib, converted them to his own use. The complaint is not that they were not collected from the people, but that they were not given to the Levites, and the Levites were so modest as not to sue for them; *for the Levites and singers fled every one to his field.* This comes in as a reason either, (1.) Why their payments were withheld. The Levites were non-residents: when they should have been doing their work about the temple, they were at their farms in the country; and therefore the people were little inclined to give them their maintenance. If ministers have not the encouragement they should have, let them consider whether they themselves be not accessory to the contempt they are under, by the neglect of their business. Or rather, (2.) It is the reason why Nehemiah soon perceived that their dues had been denied them, because he missed them from their posts. "Where are the singers" (said Nehemiah); "why do not they attend according to their office, to praise God?" "Why, truly, they have gone every one to his country seat, to get a livelihood for themselves and their families out of their grounds; for their profession would not maintain them." A scandalous maintenance makes a scandalous ministry. The work is neglected because the workmen are. It

was not long since the payment of the salaries appointed for the singers was put into a very good method (ch. 12:47); and yet how soon did it fail for want of being looked after!

II. Nehemiah laid the fault upon the rulers, who should have taken care that the Levites minded their business and had all due encouragement therein. This is required from Christian magistrates, that they use their power to oblige ministers to do their duty, and people to do theirs. Nehemiah began with the rulers, and called them to an account: *"Why is the house of God forsaken? v.* 11. Why are the Levites starved out of it? Why did not you take notice of this and prevent it?" The people *forsook the Levites,* which was expressly forbidden (Deu. 12:19; 14:27); and then the Levites forsook their post in the house of God. Both ministers and people who forsake religion and the services of it, and magistrates too who do not what they can to keep them to it, will have a great deal to answer for.

III. He delayed not to bring the dispersed Levites to *their places* again, and set them in *their stations* (as the word is), v. 11. A Levite in his field *(clericus in foro — a minister keeping the market)* is out of his station. God's house is his place, and there let him be found. Many that are careless would do much better than they do if they were but called upon. *Say to Archippus, Take heed to thy ministry.*

IV. He obliged the people to bring in their tithes, v. 12. His zeal provoked theirs; and, when they saw the Levites at their work, they could not for shame withhold their wages any longer, but honestly and cheerfully brought them in. The better church-work is done the better will church-dues be paid.

V. He provided that just and prompt payment should be made of the Levites' stipends. Commissioners were appointed to see to this (v. 13), and they were such as *were accounted faithful,* that is, had approved themselves so in other trusts committed to them, and so had *purchased to themselves this good degree,* 1 Tim. 3:13. Let men be tried first and then trusted, tried in the less and then trusted with more. Their office was to receive and pay, to distribute to their brethren in due season and due proportions.

VI. Having no recompence (it is a question whether he had thanks) from those for whom he did these good services, he looks up to God as his paymaster (v. 14): *Remember me, O my God! concerning this.* Nehemiah was a man much in pious ejaculations; on every occasion he looked up to God, and committed himself and his affairs to him. 1. He here reflects with comfort and much satisfaction upon what he had done for the house of God and the offices thereof; it pleased him to think that he had been any way instrumental to revive and support religion in his country and to reform what was amiss. What kindness any show to God's ministers, thus shall it be returned into their own bosoms, in the secret joy they shall have there, not only in having done well, but in having done good, good to many, good to souls. 2. He here refers it to God to consider him for it, not in pride, or as boasting of what he had done, much less depending upon it as his righteousness, or as if he thought he had made God a debtor to him, but in a humble appeal to him concerning his integrity and honest intention in what he had done, and a believing expectation that he would not be unrighteous to *forget his work and labour of love,* Heb. 6:10. Observe how modest he is in his requests. He only prays, Remember me, not *Reward me — Wipe not out my good deeds,* not *Publish them, Record them.* Yet he was rewarded and his good deeds were recorded; for God does more than we are able to ask. Note, Deeds done *for the house of God and the offices of it,* for the support of religion and the encouragement of it, are good deeds. There is both righteousness and godliness in them, and God will certainly remember them, and not wipe them out; they shall in no wise lose their reward.

Verses 15–22

Here is another instance of that blessed reformation in which Nehemiah was so active. He revived sabbath-sanctification, and maintained the authority of the fourth commandment; and a very good deed this was for the house of God and the offices thereof, for, where holy time is over-looked and made nothing of, it is not strange if all holy duties be neglected. Here is,

I. A remonstrance of the abuse. The law of the sabbath was very strict and much insisted one, and with good reason, for religion is never in the throne while sabbaths are trodden under foot. But Nehemiah discovered even in Judah, among those to whom sabbaths were given for a sign, this law wretchedly violated. His own eyes were his informers. Magistrates who are in care to discharge their duty aright will as much as may be *see with their own eyes,* and *accomplish a diligent search* to find out that which is evil. To his great grief it appeared that there was a general profanation of the sabbath, that holy day, even in Jerusalem, that holy city, which was so lately dedicated to God. 1. The husbandmen trod their wine-presses and brought home their corn on that day (*v.* 15), through there was an express command that *in earing-time, and in harvest-time, they should rest* on the sabbaths (Ex. 34:21), because then they might be tempted to take a greater liberty, and to fancy that God would indulge them in it. 2. The carriers *loaded their asses with all manner of burdens,* and made no scruple of it, though there was a particular proviso in the law for the cattle resting (Deu. 5:14) and that they should *bear no burden on the sabbath day,* Jer. 17:21. 3. The hawkers, and pedlars, and petty chapmen, that were men of Tyre, that famous trading city, *sold all manner of wares* on the sabbath day (*v.* 16); and the children of Judah and Jerusalem had so little grace as to buy of them, and so encourage them in making our Father's day a day of merchandise, contrary to the law of the fourth commandment, which forbids the *doing any manner of work.* No wonder there was a general decay of religion and corruption of manners among this people when they *forsook the sanctuary* and *profaned the sabbath.*

II. The reformation of it. Those that are jealous for the honour of God cannot bear to see his sabbath profaned. Observe in what method this good man proceeded in his zeal for the sabbath.

1. *He testified against those* who profaned it, *v.* 15, and again *v.* 21. He not only expressed his own dislike of it, but endeavoured to convince them that it was a great sin, and showed them the testimony of the word of God against it. He would not punish it till he had laid open the evil of it.

2. He reasoned with the rulers concerning it, took the nobles of Judah to task, and contended with them, *v.* 17. The greatest of men are not too high to be told of their faults by those whose proper office it is to reprove them; nay, great men should be, as here, contended with in the first place, because of the influence they have upon others.

(1.) He charges them with it: *You do it.* They did not carry corn, nor sell fish, but, [1.] They connived at those that did, and did not use their power to restrain them, and so made themselves guilty, as those magistrates do who bear the sword in vain. [2.] They set a bad example in other things. If the nobles allowed themselves in sports and recreations, in idle visits and idle talk, on the sabbath day, the men of business, both in city and country, would profane it by their worldly employments, as more justifiable. We must be responsible for the sins which others are led to commit by our example.

(2.) He charges it upon them as an evil thing, for so it is, proceeding from a great contempt of God and our own souls.

(3.) He reasons the case with them (*v.* 18), and shows them that sabbath breaking was one of the sins for which God had brought judgments upon them, and that if they did not take warning, but returned to the same sins again, they had reason to expect further judgments: *You bring more wrath upon Israel by profaning the sabbath.* Thus Ezra concluded, *If we again break thy commandments, wilt not thou be angry with us till thou hast consumed us?* Ezra 9:14.

3. He took care to prevent the profanation of the sabbath, as one that aimed only at reformation. If he could reform them, he would not punish them, and, if he should punish them, it was but that he might reform them. This is an example to magistrates to be heirs of restraint, and prudently to use the bit and bridle, that there may be no occasion for the lash. (1.) He ordered the gates of Jerusalem to be kept shut from the evening before the sabbath to the morning after, and set his own servants (whose care, courage and honesty, he could confide in) to watch them, that no burdens should be brought in on the sabbath day, nor late the night before, nor early in the morning after, lest sabbath time should be encroached upon, *v.* 19. Those that came in to worship in the courts of the temple were no doubt admitted to pass and repass, but none that came to sell goods; *they* were forced to *lodge without the city* (*v.* 20), where no doubt they wished the sabbath were gone, that they might sell corn. (2.) He threatened those who came with goods to the gates, who pressed hard for entrance, telling them that, if they came again, he would certainly lay hands on them (*v.* 21), and this deterred them from coming any more. Note, If reformers will but put on resolution, more may be done towards the breaking of bad customs than they can imagine. Vice connived at is indeed a daring thing, and will bid defiance to counsel and reproof; but it may be made cowardly, and will be so when magistrates make themselves a terror to it. *The king that sits on the throne of judgment scatters away all evil with his eyes.* (3.) He charged the Levites to take care about the due sanctifying of the sabbath, that they should cleanse themselves in the first place, and so give a good example to the people, and *that they should* some of them *come and keep the gates, v.* 22. Because he and his servants must shortly return to court, he would leave this charge with some that might abide by it, that not only when he was present, but in his absence, the sabbath might be sanctified. Then there is likely to be a reformation, in this and other respects, when magistrates and ministers join their forces. The courage, zeal, and prudence of Nehemiah in this matter, are here recorded for our imitation; and we have reason to think that the cure he wrought was lasting; for, in our Saviour's time, we find the Jews in the other extreme, over-scrupulous in the ceremonial part of sabbath-sanctification.

4. He concludes this passage with a prayer (*v.* 22), in which observe, (1.) The petitions: *Remember me* (as the thief on the cross, *Lord, remember me);* that is enough. God's thoughts to us ward are very precious, Ps. 40:5. He adds, *Spare me.* So far is he from thinking that what he had done did properly merit a reward in strict justice that he cries earnestly to God to *spare him,* as Jeremiah (*ch.* 15:15), *Take me not away in thy long-suffering* (*ch.* 10:24), *Correct me not in anger,* and (*ch.* 17:17), *Be not a terror to me.* Note, The best saints, even when they do the best actions, stand in need of *sparing mercy;* for *there is not a just man that doeth good and sinneth not.* (2.) The plea: *According to the greatness* (or multitude) *of thy mercies.* Note, God's mercy is what we must depend upon, and not any merit of our own, when we appear before God.

Verses 23–31

We have here one instance more of Nehemiah's pious zeal for the purifying of his countrymen as a peculiar people to God; that was the thing he aimed at in the use of his power, not the enriching of himself. See here,

I. How they had corrupted themselves by marrying strange wives. This was complained of in Ezra's time, and much done towards a reformation, Ezra 9 and 10. But, when the unclean spirit is cast out, if a watchful eye be not kept upon him, he will re-enter; so he did here. Though in Ezra's time those that had married strange wives were forced to put them away, which could not but occasion trouble and confusion in families, yet others would not take warning. *Nitimur in vetitum — we still lean towards what is forbidden.* Nehemiah, like a good governor, enquired into the state of the families of those that were under his charge, that he might reform what was amiss in them, and so heal the streams by healing the springs. 1. He enquired whence they had their wives, and found that many of the Jews had *married wives of Ashdod, of Ammon, and of Moab* (*v.* 23), either because they were fond of what was far-fetched or because they hoped by these alliances to strengthen and enrich themselves. See how God by the prophet reproves this, Mal. 2:11. *Judah has dealt treacherously,* and broken covenant with God, the covenant made in Ezra's time with reference to this very thing; he has *profaned the holiness of the Lord* by *marrying the daughter* (that is, the worshipper) *of a strange god.* 2. He talked with the children, and found they were *children of strangers,* for their *speech betrayed them.* The children were bred up with their mothers, and learned of them and their nurses and servants to speak, so that they could not speak the Jews' language, could not speak it at all, or not readily, or not purely, but *half in the speech of Ashdod,* or Ammon, or Moab, according as the country was which the mother was a native of. Observe, (1.) Children, in their childhood, learn much of their mothers. *Partus sequitur ventrem — they are prone to imitate their mothers.* (2.) If either side be bad, the corrupt nature will incline the children to take after that, which is a good reason why Christians should not be unequally yoked. (3.) In the education of children great care should be taken about the government of their tongues, that they learn not the language of Ashdod, any impious or impure talk, any corrupt communication.

II. What course Nehemiah took to purge out this corruption, when he discovered how much it had prevailed.

1. He showed them the evil of it, and the obligation he lay under to witness against it. He did not seek an occasion against them, but this was an iniquity to be punished by the judge, and which he must by no means connive at (*v.* 27): "*Shall we hearken to you,* who endeavour to palliate and excuse it? No, it is an evil, a great evil, it is a *transgression against our God, to marry strange wives,* and we must do our utmost to put a stop to it. You beg that they may not be divorced from you, but we cannot hearken to you, for there is no other remedy to clear us from the guilt and prevent infection." (1.) He quotes a precept, to prove that it was in itself a great sin; and makes them swear to that precept: *You shall not give your daughters unto their sons,* etc., which is taken from Deu. 7:3. When we would reclaim people from sin we must show them the sinfulness of it in the glass of the commandment. (2.) He quotes a precedent, to show the pernicious consequences of it, which made it necessary to be animadverted upon by the government (*v.* 26): *Did not Solomon king of Israel sin by these things?* The falls of great and good men are recorded in order that we may take warning by them to shun the temptations which they were overcome by. Solomon was famous for wisdom; there was no king like him for it; yet, when he married strange wives, his wisdom could not secure him from their snares, nay, it departed from him, and he did very foolishly. He was beloved of God, but his marrying strange wives threw him out of God's favour, and went near to extinguish the holy fire of grace in his soul: he was king over all Israel; but his doing this occasioned the loss of ten of his twelve tribes. You plead that you can marry strange wives and yet retain the purity of Israelites; but Solomon himself could not; even *him did outlandish women cause to sin.* Therefore let him that *thinks he stands take heed lest he fall* when he runs upon such a precipice.

2. He showed himself highly displeased at it, that he might awaken them to a due sense of the evil of it: *He contended with them, v.* 25. They offered to justify themselves in what they did, but he showed them how frivolous their excuses were, and argued it warmly with them. When he had silenced them he *cursed them,* that is, he denounced the judgments of God against them, and showed them what their sin deserved. He then picked out some of them that were more obstinate than the rest, and fit to be made examples, and *smote them* (that is, ordered them to be beaten by the proper officers according to the law, Deu. 25:2, 3), to which he added this further mark of infamy that he *plucked off their hair,* or cut or shaved it off; for it may so be understood. Perhaps they had prided themselves in their hair, and therefore he took it off to deform and humble them, and put them to shame; it was, in effect, to stigmatize them, at least for a time. Ezra, in this case, had plucked off his own hair, in holy sorrow for the sin; Nehemiah plucked off their hair, in a holy indignation at the sinners. See the different tempers of wise, and good, and useful men, and the divers graces, as well as divers gifts, of the same Spirit.

3. He obliged them not to take any more such wives, and separated those whom they had taken: *He cleansed them from all strangers,* both men and women (*v.* 30), and made them promise with an oath that they would never do so again, *v.* 25. Thus did he try all ways and means to put a stop to this mischief and to prevent another relapse into this disease.

4. He took particular care of the priests' families, that they might not lie under this stain, this guilt. He found, upon enquiry, that a branch of the high priest's own family, one of his grandsons, had married a daughter of Sanballat, that notorious enemy of the Jews (*ch.* 2:10; 4:1), and so had, in effect, twisted interests with the Samaritans, *v.* 28. How little love had that man either to God or his country who could make himself in duty and interest a

friend to him that was a sworn enemy to both. It seems this young priest would not put away his wife, and therefore Nehemiah *chased him from him,* deprived him, degraded him, and made him for ever incapable of the priesthood. Josephus says that this expelled priest was Manasseh, and that when Nehemiah drove him away he went to his father-in-law Sanballat, who built him a temple upon Mount Gerazim, like that at Jerusalem, and promised him he should be high priest in it, and that then was laid the foundation of the Samaritans' pretensions, which continued warm to our Saviour's time. Jn. 4:20, *Our fathers worshipped in this mountain.* When Nehemiah had thus expelled one that had forfeited the honour of the priesthood he again posted the *priests and Levites every one in his business, v.* 30. It was no loss to them to part with one that was the scandal of their cloth; the work would be done better without him. When Judas had gone out Christ said, *Now is the Son of Man glorified,* Jn. 13:30, 31. Here are Nehemiah's prayers on this occasion. (1.) He prays, *Remember them, O my God! v.* 29. "Lord, convince and convert them; put them in mind of what they should be and do, that they may come to themselves." Or, "Remember them to reckon with them for their sin; remember it against them." If we take it so, this prayer is a prophecy that God would remember it against them. Those that defile the priesthood despise God, and shall be lightly esteemed. Perhaps they were too many and too great for him to deal with. "Lord" (says he), "deal thou with them; take the work into thy own hands." (2.) He prays, *Remember me, O my God! v.* 31. The best services done to the public have sometimes been forgotten by those for whom they were done (Eccl. 9:15); therefore Nehemiah refers it to God to recompense him, takes him for his paymaster, and then doubts not but he shall be well paid. This may well be the summary of our petitions; we need no more to make us happy than this: *Remember me, O my God! for good.*

AN EXPOSITION, WITH PRACTICAL OBSERVATIONS, OF

THE BOOK OF ESTHER

How the providence of God watched over the Jews that had returned out of captivity to their own land, and what great and kind things were done for them, we read in the two foregoing books; but there were many who staid behind, having not zeal enough for God's house, and the holy land and city, to carry them through the difficulties of a removal thither. These, one would think, should have been excluded the special protection of Providence, as unworthy the name of Israelites; but our God deals not with us according to our folly and weakness. We find in this book that even those Jews who were scattered in the provinces of the heathen were taken care of, as well as those who were gathered in the land of Judea, and were wonderfully preserved, when doomed to destruction and appointed as sheep for the slaughter. Who drew up this story is uncertain. Mordecai was as able as any man to relate, on his own knowledge, the several passages of it; *quorum pars magna fuit — for he bore a conspicuous part in it;* and that he wrote such an account of them as was necessary to inform his people of the grounds of their observing the feast of Purim we are told (*ch.* 9:20, *Mordecai wrote these things,* and sent them enclosed in letters to all the Jews), and therefore we have reason to think he was the penman of the whole book. It is the narrative of a plot laid against the Jews to cut them all off, and which was wonderfully disappointed by a concurrence of providences. The most compendious exposition of it will be to read it deliberately all together at one time, for the latter events expound the former and show what providence intended in them. The name of God is not found in this book; but the apocryphal addition to it (which is not in the Hebrew, nor was ever received by the Jews into the can on), containing six chapters, begins thus, *Then Mordecai said, God has done these things.* But, though the name of God be not in it, the finger of God is, directing many minute events for the bringing about of his people's deliverance. The particulars are not only surprising and very entertaining, but edifying and very encouraging to the faith and hope of God's people in the most difficult and dangerous times. We cannot now expect such miracles to be wrought for us as were for Israel when they were brought out of Egypt, but we may expect that in such ways as God here took to defeat Haman's plot he will still protect his people. We are told, I. How Esther came to be queen and Mordecai to be great at court, who were to be the instruments of the intended deliverance, *ch.* 1, 2. II. Upon what provocation, and by what arts, Haman the Amalekite obtained an order for the destruction of all the Jews, *ch.* 3. III. The great distress the Jews, and their patriots especially, were in thereupon, *ch.* 4. IV. The defeating of Haman's particular plot against Mordecai's life, *ch.* 5–7. V. The defeating of his general plot against the Jews, *ch.* 8. VI. The care that was taken to perpetuate the remembrance of this, *ch.* 9, 10. The whole story confirms the Psalmist's observation (Ps. 37:12, 13), *The wicked plotteth against the just, and gnasheth upon him with his teeth. The Lord shall laugh at him; he sees that his day is coming.*

CHAPTER 1

Several things in this chapter itself are very instructive and of great use; but the design of recording the story of it is to show how way was made for Esther to the crown, in order to her being instrumental to defeat Haman's plot, and this long before the plot was laid, that we may observe and admire the foresight and vast reaches of Providence. "Known unto God are all his works" before-hand. Ahasuerus the king, I. In his height feasts all his great men (*v.* 1–9). II. In his heat he divorces his queen, because she would not come to him when he sent for her (*v.* 10–22). This shows how God serves his own purposes even by the sins and follies of men, which he would not permit if he know not how to bring good out of them.

Verses 1–9

Which of the kings of Persia this Ahasuerus was the learned are not agreed. Mordecai is said to have been one of those that were *carried* captive from *Jerusalem* (*ch.* 2:5, 6), whence it should seem that this Ahasuerus was one of the first kings of that empire. Dr. Lightfoot thinks that he was that Artaxerxes who hindered the building of the temple, who is called also *Ahasuerus* (Ezra 4:6, 7), after his great-grandfather of the Medes, Dan. 9:1. We have here an account,

I. Of the vast extent of his dominion. In the time of Darius and Cyrus there were but 120 princes (Dan. 6:1); now there were 127, *from India to Ethiopia, v.* 1. It had become an over-grown kingdom, which in time would sink with its own weight, and, as usual, would lose its provinces as fast as it got them. If such vast power be put into a bad hand, it is able to do so much the more mischief; but, if into a good hand, it is able to do so much the more good. Christ's kingdom is, or shall be, far larger than this, when the kingdoms of the world shall all become his; and it shall be everlasting.

II. Of the great pomp and magnificence of his court. When he found himself fixed in his throne, the pride of his heart rising with the grandeur of his kingdom, he made a most extravagant feast, wherein he put himself to vast expense and trouble only *to show the riches of his glorious kingdom and the honour of his excellent majesty, v.* 4. This was vain glory, an affection of pomp to no purpose at all; for none questioned the riches of his kingdom, nor offered to vie with him for honour. If he had shown the riches of his kingdom and the honour of his majesty, as some of his successors did, in contributing largely towards the building of the temple and the maintaining of the temple service (Ezra 6:8, 7:22), it would have turned to a much better account. Two feasts Ahasuerus made: — 1. One for his nobles and princes, which lasted *a hundred and eighty days, v.* 3, 4. Not that he feasted the same persons every day for all that time, but perhaps the nobles and princes of one province one day, of another province another day, while thus he and his constant attendants fared sumptuously every day. The Chaldee paraphrast (who is very bold in his additions to the story of this book) says that there had been a rebellion among his subjects and that this feast was kept for joy of the quashing of it. 2. Another was made for *all the people, both great and small,* which lasted *seven days,* some one day and some another; and, because no house would hold them, they were entertained *in the court of the garden, v.* 5. The hangings with which the several apartments were divided or the tents which were there pitched for the company, were very fine and rich; so were the beds or benches on which they sat, and the pavement under their feet, *v.* 6. Better is a dinner of herbs with quietness, and the enjoyment of one's self and a friend, than this banquet of wine with all the noise and tumult that must needs attend it.

III. Of the good order which in some respects was kept there notwithstanding. We do not find this like Belshazzar's feast, in which dunghill-gods were praised and the vessels of the sanctuary profaned, Dan. 5:3, 4. Yet the Chaldee paraphrase says that the vessels of the sanctuary were used in this feast, to the great grief of the pious Jews. It was not like Herod's feast, which reserved a prophet's head for the last dish. Two things which are laudable we may gather from the account here given of this feast: — 1. That there was no forcing of healths, nor urging of them: *The drinking was according to the law,* probably some law lately made; *none did compel,* no, not by continual proposing of it (as Josephus explains it); they did not send the glass about, but every man drank as he pleased (*v.* 8), so that if there were any that drank to excess it was their own fault, a fault which few would commit when the king's order put an honour upon sobriety. This caution of a heathen prince, even when he would show his generosity, may shame many who are called Christians, who think they do not sufficiently show their good housekeeping, nor bid their friends welcome, unless they make them drunk, and, under pretence of sending the health round, send the sin round, and death with it. There is a woe to those that do so; let them read it and tremble, Hab. 2:15, 16. It is robbing men of their reason, their richest jewel, and making them fools, the greatest wrong that can be. 2. That there was no mixed dancing; for the gentlemen and ladies were entertained asunder, not as in the feast of Belshazzar, whose wives and concubines drank with him (Dan. 5:2), or that of Herod, whose daughter *danced before him.* Vashti feasted the women in her own apartment; not openly in the court of the garden, but *in the royal house, v.* 9. Thus, while the king showed the honour of his majesty, she and her ladies showed the honour of their modesty, which is truly the majesty of the fair sex.

Verses 10–22

We have here a damp to all the mirth of Ahasuerus's feast; it ended in heaviness, not as Job's children's feast by a wind from the wilderness, not as Belshazzar's by a handwriting on the wall, but by is own folly. An unhappy falling out there was, at the end of the feast, between the king and queen, which broke of the feast abruptly, and sent the guests away silent and ashamed.

I. It was certainly the king's weakness to send for Vashti into his presence when he was drunk, and in company with abundance of gentlemen, many of whom, it is likely, were in the same condition. *When his heart was merry with wine* nothing would serve him but Vashti must come, well dressed as she was, with *the crown on her head,* that the princes and people might see what a handsome woman she was, *v.* 10, 11. Hereby, 1. He dishonoured himself as a husband, who ought to protect, but by no means expose, the modesty of his wife, who ought to be to her *a covering of the eyes* (Gen. 20:16), not to uncover them. 2. He diminished himself as a king, in commanding that from his wife which she might refuse, much to the honour of her virtue. It was against the custom of the Persians for the women to appear in public, and he put a great hardship upon her when he did not court, but command her to do so uncouth a thing, and make her a show. If he had not been put out of the possession of himself by drinking to excess, he would not have done such a thing, but would have been angry at any one that should have mentioned it. When the wine is in the wit is out, and men's reason departs from them.

II. However, perhaps it was not her wisdom to deny him. *She refused to come* (*v.* 12); though he sent his command by seven honourable messengers, and publicly, and Josephus says sent again and again, yet she persisted in her denial. Had she come, while it was evident that she did it in pure obedience, it would have been no reflection upon her modesty, nor a bad example. The thing was not in itself sinful, and therefore to obey would have been more her honour than to be so precise. Perhaps she refused in a haughty manner, and then it was certainly evil; she *scorned to come at the king's commandment.* What a mortification was this to him! While he was showing the glory of his kingdom he showed the reproach of his family, that he had a wife that would do as she pleased. Strifes between yoke-fellows are bad enough at any time, but before company they are very scandalous, and occasion blushing and uneasiness.

III. The king thereupon grew outrageous. He that had rule over 127 provinces had no rule over his own spirit, but his *anger burned in him, v.* 12. He would have consulted his own comfort and credit more if he had stifled his resentment, had passed by the affront his wife gave him, and turned it off with a jest.

IV. Though he was very angry, he would not do any thing in this matter till he advised with his privy-counsellors; as he had seven chamberlains to execute his orders, who are named (*v.* 10), so he had seven counsellors to direct his orders. The greater power a man has the greater need he has of advice, that he may not abuse his power. Of these counsellors it is said that they were learned men, for they *knew law* and *judgment,* — that they were wise men, for they *knew the times,* — and that the king put great confidence in them and honour upon them, for they *saw the king's face and sat first in the kingdom, v.* 13, 14. In the multitude of such counsellors there is safety. Now here is,

1. The question proposed to this cabinet-council (*v.* 15): *What shall we do to the queen Vashti according to the law?* Observe, (1.) Though it was the queen that was guilty, the law must have its course. (2.) Though the king was very angry, yet he would do nothing but what he was advised was according to law.

2. The proposal which Memucan made, that Vashti should be divorced for her disobedience. Some suggest that he gave this severe advice, and the rest agreed to it, because they knew it would please the king, would gratify both his passion now and his appetite afterwards. But Josephus says that, on the contrary, he had a strong affection for Vashti, and would not have put her away for this offence if he could legally have passed it by; and then we must suppose Memucan, in his advice, to have had a sincere regard to justice and the public good. (1.) He shows what would be the bad consequences of the queen's disobedience to her husband, if it were passed by and not animadverted upon, that it would embolden other wives both to disobey their husbands and to domineer over them. Had this unhappy falling out between the king and his wife, wherein she was conqueror, been private, the error would have remained with themselves and the quarrel might have been settled privately between themselves; but it happening to be public, and perhaps the ladies that were now feasting with the queen having shown themselves pleased with her refusal, her bad example would be likely to have a bad influence upon all the families of the kingdom. If the queen must have her humour, and the king must submit to it (since the houses of private persons commonly take their measures from the courts of princes), the wives would be haughty and imperious and would scorn to obey their husbands, and the poor despised husbands might fret at it, but could not help themselves; for the *contentions of a wife are a continual dropping,* Prov. 19:13; 27:15; and see Prov. 21:9; 25:24. When wives *despise their husbands,* whom they ought to *reverence* (Eph. 5:33), and contend for *dominion* over those to whom they ought to be in *subjection* (1 Pt. 3:1), there cannot but be continual guilt and grief, confusion and every evil work. And great ones must take heed of setting copies of this kind, *v.* 16–18. (2.) He shows what would be the good consequence of a decree against Vashti that she should be divorced. We may suppose that before they proceeded to this extremity they sent to Vashti to know if she would yet submit, cry *Peccavi — I have done wrong,* and ask the king's pardon, and that, if she had done so, the mischief of her example would have been effectually prevented, and process would have been stayed; but it is likely she continued obstinate, and insisted upon it as her prerogative to do as she pleased, whether it pleased the king or no, and therefore they gave this judgment against her, that she *come no more before the king,* and this judgment so ratified as never to be reversed, *v.* 19. The consequence of this, it was hoped, would be that *the wives would give to their husbands honour,* even the wives of the *great,* notwithstanding their own greatness, and the wives of the *small,* notwithstanding the husband's meanness (*v.* 20); and thus every man would bear rule in his own house, as he ought to do, and, the wives being subject, the children and servants would be so too. It is the interest of states and kingdoms to provide that good order be kept in private families.

3. The edict that passed according to this proposal, signifying that the queen was divorced for contumacy, according to the law, and that, if other wives were in like manner undutiful to their husbands, they must expect to be in like manner disgraced (*v.* 21, 22): were they better than the queen? Whether it was the passion or the policy of the king that was served by this edict, God's providence served its own purpose by it, which was to make way for Esther to the crown.

CHAPTER 2

Two things are recorded in this chapter, which were working towards the deliverance of the Jews from Haman's conspiracy: — I. The advancement of Esther to be queen instead of Vashti. Many others were candidates for the honour (*v.* 1–4); but Esther, an orphan, a captive-Jewess (*v.* 5–7), recommended herself to the king's chamberlain first (*v.* 8–11) and then to the king (*v.* 12–17), who made her queen (*v.* 18–20). II. The good service that Mordecai did to the king in discovering a plot against his life (*v.* 21–23).

Verses 1–20

How God put down one that was high and mighty from her seat we read in the chapter before, and are now to be told how he exalted one of low degree, as the virgin Mary observes in her song (Lu. 1:52) and Hannah before her, 1 Sa. 2:4–8. Vashti being humbled for her height, Esther is advanced for her humility. Observe,

I. The extravagant course that was taken to please the king with another wife instead of Vashti. Josephus says that when his anger was over he was exceedingly grieved that the matter was carried so far, and would have been reconciled to Vashti but that, by the constitution of the government, the judgment was irrevocable — that therefore, to make him forget her, they contrived how to entertain him first with a great variety of concubines, and then to fix him to the most agreeable of them all for a wife instead of Vashti. The marriages of princes are commonly made by policy and interest, for the enlarging of their dominions and the strengthening of their alliances; but this must be made partly by the agreeableness of the person to the king's fancy, whether she was rich or poor, noble or ignoble. What pains were taken to humour the king! As if his power and wealth were given him for no other end than that he might have all the delights of the sense wound up to the height of pleasurableness, and exquisitely refined, though at the best they are but dross and dregs in comparison with divine and spiritual pleasures. 1. All the provinces of his kingdom must be searched for fair young virgins, and officers appointed to choose them, *v.* 3. 2. A house (a seraglio) was prepared on purpose for them, and a person appointed to have the charge of them, to see that they were well provided for. 3. No less than twelve months was allowed them for their purification, some of them at least who were brought out of the country, that they might be very clean, and perfumed, *v.* 12. Even those who were the masterpieces of nature must yet have all this help from art to recommend them to a vain and carnal mind. 4. After the king had once taken them to his bed, they were made recluses ever after, except the king pleased at any time to send for them (*v.* 14); they were looked upon as secondary wives, were maintained by the king accordingly, and might not marry. We may see, by this instance, to what absurd practices those came who were destitute of divine revelation, and who, as a punishment for their idolatry, were given up to vile affections. Having broken through that law of creation which resulted from God's making man, they broke through another law, which was founded upon his making one man and one woman. See what need there was of the gospel of Christ to purify men from the lusts of the flesh and to reduce them to the original institution. Those that have *learned Christ* will think it *a shame even to speak of such things as* these which *were done of them,* not only *in secret,* but avowedly, Eph. 5:12.

II. The overruling providence of God thus brining Esther to be queen. Had she been recommended to Ahasuerus for a wife, he would have rejected the motion with disdain; but when she came in her turn, after several others, and it was found that though many of them were ingenious and discreet, graceful and agreeable, yet Esther excelled them all, way was made for her, even by her rivals, into the king's affections and the honours consequent thereupon. It is certain, as bishop Patrick says, that those who suggest that she committed a great sin to come at this dignity do not consider the custom of those times and countries. Every one that the king took to his bed was married to him, and was his wife of a lower rank, as Hagar was Abraham's; so that, if Esther had not been made queen, the sons of Jacob need not say that he *dealt with their sister as with a harlot.* Concerning Esther we must observe,

1. Her original and character. (1.) She was one of the *children of the captivity,* a Jewess and a sharer with her people in their bondage. Daniel and his fellows were advanced in the land where they were captives; for they were of those whom God sent thither *for their good,* Jer. 24:5. (2.) She was an orphan; her father and mother were both dead (*v.* 7), but, when they had forsaken here, then the Lord took her up, Ps. 27:10. When those whose unhappiness it is to be thus deprived of their parents in their childhood yet afterwards come to be eminently pious and prosperous, we ought to take notice of it to the glory of that God, and his grace and providence, who has taken it among the titles of his honour to be a *Father of the fatherless.* (3.) She was a beauty, *fair of form, good of countenance;* so it is in the margin, *v.* 7. Her wisdom and virtue were her greatest beauty, but it is an advantage to be a diamond to be well set. (4.) Mordecai, her cousin-german, was her guardian, *brought her up, and took her for his own daughter.* The Septuagint says that he designed to make her his wife; if that were so, he was to be praised that he opposed not her better preferment. let God be acknowledged in raising up friends for the fatherless and motherless; let it be an encouragement to that pious instance of charity that many who have taken care of the education of orphans have lived to see the good fruit of their care and pains, abundantly to their comfort. Dr. Lightfoot thinks that this Mordecai is the same with that mentioned in Ezra 2:2, who went up to Jerusalem with the first, and helped forward the settlement of his people until the building of the temple was stopped, and then went back to the Persian court, to see what service he could do them there. Mordecai being Esther's guardian or pro-parent, we are told, [1.] How tender he was of her, as if she had been his own child (*v.* 11): he walked before her door every day, to know how she did, and what interest she had. Let those whose relations are thus cast upon them by divine Providence be thus kindly affectioned to them and solicitous for them. [2.] How respectful she was to him. Though in relation she was his equal, yet, being in age and dependence his inferior, she honoured him as her father — *did his commandment, v.* 20. This is an example to orphans; if they fall into the hands of those who love them and take care of them, let them make suitable returns of duty and affection. The less obliged their guardians were in duty to provide for them the more obliged they are in gratitude to honour and obey their guardians. Here is an instance of Esther's obsequiousness t Mordecai, that she did not *show her people of her kindred,* because Mordecai had charged her that she should not, *v.* 10. he did not bid her deny her country, nor tell a lie to conceal her parentage; if he had told her to do so, she must not have done it. But

he only told her not to proclaim her country. All truths are not to be spoken at all times, though an untruth is not to be spoken at any time. She being born in Shushan, and her parents being dead, all took her to be of Persian extraction, and she was not bound to undeceive them.

2. Her preferment. Who would have thought that a Jewess, a captive, and orphan, was born to be a queen, an empress! Yet so it proved. Providence sometimes *raiseth up the poor out of the dust, to set them among princes,* 1 Sa. 2:8. (1.) The king's chamberlain honoured her (*v.* 9), and was ready to serve her. Wisdom and virtue will gain respect. Those that make sure of God's favour shall find favour with man too as far as it is good for them. All that looked upon Esther admired her (*v.* 15) and concluded that she was the lady that would win the prize, and she did win it. (2.) The king himself fell in love with her. She was not solicitous, as the rest of the maidens were, to set herself off with artificial beauty; she *required nothing* but just what was *appointed* for her (*v.* 15) and yet she was most acceptable. The more natural beauty is the more agreeable. *The king loved Esther above all the women, v.* 17. Now he needed not to make any further trials, or take time to deliberate; he is soon determined to *set the royal crown upon her head, and make her queen, v.* 17. This was done in his seventh year (*v.* 16) and Vashti was divorced in his third year (*ch.* 1:3); so that he was four years without a queen. Notice is taken, [1.] Of the honours the king put upon Esther. He graced the solemnity of her coronation with a *royal feast* (*v.* 18), at which perhaps Esther, in compliance with the king, made a public appearance, which Vashti had refused to do, that she might have the praise of obedience in the same instance in which the other incurred the blot of disobedience. He also granted a *release to the provinces,* either a remittance of the taxes in arrear or an act of grace for criminals; as Pilate, at the feast, released a prisoner. This was to add t the joy. [2.] Of the deference Esther continued to pay to her former guardian. She still *did the commandment of Mordecai, as when she was brought up with him, v.* 20. Mordecai say *in the king's gate;* that was the height of his preferment: he was one of the porters or door-keepers of the court. Whether he had this place before, or whether Esther obtained it for him, we are not told; but there he sat contentedly, and aimed no higher; and yet Esther who was advanced to the throne was observant of him. This was an evidence of a humble and grateful disposition, that she had a sense of his former kindnesses and his continued wisdom. It is a great ornament to those that are advanced, and much to their praise, to remember their benefactors, to retain the impressions of their good education, to be diffident of themselves, willing to take advice, and thankful for it.

Verses 21–23

This good service which Mordecai did to the government, in discovering a plot against the life of the king, is here recorded, because the mention of it will again occur to his advantage. No step is yet taken towards Haman's design of the Jews' destruction, but several steps are taken towards God's design of their deliverance, and this for one. God now gives Mordecai an opportunity of doing the king a good turn, that he might have the fairer opportunity afterwards of doing the Jews a good turn. 1. A design was laid against the king by two of his own servants, who sought *to lay hands on him,* not only to make him a prisoner, but to take away his life, *v.* 21. Probably they resented some affront which they thought he had given them, or some injury which he had done them. Who would be great, to be so much the object of envy? Who would be arbitrary, to be so much the object of ill-will? Princes, above any mortals, have their souls continually in their hands, and often go down *slain to the pit,* especially those who *caused terror in the land of the living.* 2. Mordecai got notice of their treason, and, by Esther's means, discovered it to the king, hereby confirming her in and recommending himself to the king's favour. How he came to the knowledge of it does not appear. Whether he overheard their discourse, or whether they offered to draw him in with them, so it was that *the thing was known* to him. This ought to be a warning against all traitorous and seditious practices: though men presume upon secresy, *a bird of the air shall carry the voice.* Mordecai, as soon as he knew it, caused it to be made known to the king, which ought to be an instruction and example to all that would be found good subjects not to conceal any bad design they know of against the prince or the public peace, for it is making a confederacy with public enemies. 3. The traitors were hanged, as they deserved, but not till their treason was, upon search, fully proved against them (*v.* 23), and the whole matter was recorded in the king's journals, with a particular remark that Mordecai was the man who discovered the treason. He was not rewarded presently, but a book of remembrance was written. Thus with respect to those who serve Christ, though their recompence is adjourned till the resurrection of the just, yet an account is kept of their *work of faith and labour of love,* which *God is not unrighteous to forget,* Heb. 6:10.

CHAPTER 3

A very black and mournful scene here opens, and which threatens the ruin of all the people of God. Were there not some such dark nights, the light of the morning would not be so welcome. I. Haman is made the king's favourite (*v.* 1). II. Mordecai refuses to give him the honour he demands (*v.* 2–4). III. Haman, for his sake, vows to be revenged upon all the Jews (*v.* 5, 6). IV. He, upon a malicious suggestion, obtains an order from the king to have the all massacred upon a certain day (*v.* 7–13). V. This order is dispersed through the kingdom (*v.* 14, 15).

Verses 1–6

Here we have,

I. Haman advanced by the prince, and adored thereupon by the people. Ahasuerus had lately laid Esther in his bosom, but she had no such interest in him as to get her friends preferred, or to prevent the preferring of one who she knew was an enemy to her people. When those that are good become great they still find that they cannot do good, nor prevent mischief, as they would. This Haman was an Agagite (an Amalekite, says Josephus), probably of the descendants of Agag, a common name of the princes of Amalek, as appears, Num. 24:7. Some think that he was by birth a prince, as Jehoiakim was, whose seat was set above the rest of the captive kings (2 Ki. 25:28), as Haman's here was, *v.* 1. The king took a fancy to him (princes are not bound to give reasons for their favours), made him his favourite, his confidant, his prime-minister of state. Such a commanding influence the court then had that (contrary to the proverb) those whom it blessed the country blessed too; for all men adored this rising sun, and the king's servants were particularly commanded *to bow before him and to do him reverence* (*v.* 2), and they did so. I wonder what the king saw in Haman that was commendable or meritorious; it is plain that he was not a man of honour or justice, of any true courage or steady conduct, but proud, and passionate, and revengeful; yet was he promoted, and caressed, and there was none so great as he. Princes' darlings are not always worthies.

II. Mordecai adhering to his principles with a bold and daring resolution, and therefore refusing to reverence Haman as the rest of the king's servants did, *v.* 2. He was urged to it by his friends, who reminded him of the king's commandment, and consequently of the danger he incurred if he refused to comply with it; it was as much as his life was worth, especially considering Haman's insolence, *v.* 3. They *spoke daily to him* (*v.* 4), to persuade him to conform, but all in vain: he hearkened not to them, but told them plainly that he was a Jew, and could not in conscience do it. Doubtless his refusal, when it came to be taken notice of and made the subject of discourse, was commonly attributed to pride and envy, that he would not pay respect to Haman because, on the score of his alliance to Esther, he was not himself as much promoted, or to a factious seditious spirit and a disaffection to the king and his government; those that would make the best of it looked upon it as his weakness, or his want of breeding, called it a humour, and a piece of affected singularity. It does not appear that any one scrupled at conforming to it except Mordecai; and yet his refusal was pious, conscientious, and pleasing to God, for the religion of a Jew forbade him, 1. To give such extravagant honours as were required to any mortal man, especially so wicked a man as Haman was. In the apocryphal chapters of this book (*ch.* 13:12–14) Mordecai is brought in thus appealing to God in this matter: *Thou knowest, Lord, that it was neither in contempt nor pride, nor for any desire of glory, that I did not bow down to proud Haman, for I could have been content with good will, for the salvation of Israel, to kiss the soles of his feet; but I did this that I might not prefer the glory of man above the glory of God, neither will I worship any but thee.* 2. He especially thought it a piece of injustice to his nation to give such honour to an Amalekite, one of that devoted nation with which God had sworn that he would have perpetual war (Ex. 17:16) and concerning which he had given that solemn charge (Deu. 25:17), *Remember what Amalek did.* Though religion does by no means destroy good manners, but teaches us to render *honour to whom honour* is due, yet it is the character of a citizen of Zion that not only in his heart, but *in his eyes,* such a *vile person as Haman was is contemned,* Ps. 15:4. Let those who are governed by principles of conscience be steady and resolute, however censured or threatened, as Mordecai was.

III. Haman meditating revenge. Some that hoped thereby to curry favour with Haman took notice to him of Mordecai's rudeness, waiting to see whether he would bend or break, *v.* 4. Haman then observed it himself, and was *full of wrath, v.* 5. A meek and humble man would have slighted the affront, and have said, "Let him have his humour; what am I the worse for it?" But it makes Haman's proud spirit rage, and fret, and boil, within him, so that he becomes uneasy to himself and all about him. It is soon resolved that Mordecai must die. The head must come off that will not bow to Haman; if he cannot have his honours, he will have his blood. It is as penal in this court not to worship Haman as it was in Nebuchadnezzar's not to worship the golden image which he had set up. Mordecai is a person of quality, in a post of honour, and own cousin to the queen; and yet Haman thinks his life nothing towards a satisfaction for the affront: thousands of innocent and valuable lives must be sacrificed to his indignation; and therefore he vows the destruction of all the people of Mordecai, for his sake, because his being a Jew was the reason he gave why he did not reverence Haman. Herein appear Haman's intolerable pride, insatiable cruelty, and the ancient antipathy of an Amalekite to the Israel of God. Saul the son of Kish, a Benjamite, spared Agag, but Mordecai the son of Kish, a Benjamite (*ch.* 2:5), shall find no mercy with this Agagite, whose design is to *destroy all the Jews throughout the whole kingdom of Ahasuerus* (*v.* 6), which, I suppose, would include those that had returned to their own land, for that was now a province of his kingdom. *Come and let us cut them off from being a nation,* Ps. 83:4. Nero's barbarous wish is his, that they had all but one neck.

Verses 7–15

Haman values himself upon that bold and daring thought, which he fancied well became his great spirit, of destroying all the Jews — an undertaking worthy of its author, and which he promised himself would perpetuate his memory. He doubts not but to find desperate and bloody hands enough to cut all their throats if the king will but give him leave. How he obtained leave, and commission to do it, we are here told. He had the king's ear, let him alone to manage him.

I. He makes a false and malicious representation of Jews, and their character, to the king, *v.* 8. The enemies of God's people could not give them such bad treatment as they do if they did not first give them a bad name. He would have the king believe, 1. That the Jews were a despicable people, and that it was not for his credit to harbour them:*"A certain people there is,"* without name, as if nobody knew whence they came and what they were; "they are not incorporated, *but scattered abroad and dispersed in all the provinces* as fugitives and vagabonds on the earth, and inmates in all countries, the burden and scandal of the places where they live." 2. That they were a dangerous people, and that it was not safe to harbour them. "They have laws and usages of their own, and conform not to the statutes of the kingdom and the customs of the country; and therefore they may be looked upon as disaffected to the government and likely to infect others with their singularities, which may end in a rebellion." It is no new thing for the best of men to have such invidious characters as these given of them; if it be no sin to kill them, it is no sin to belie them.

II. He bids high for leave to destroy them all, *v.* 9. He knew there were many that hated the Jews, and would willingly fall upon them if they might but have a commission:

Let it be written therefore *that they may be destroyed.* Give but orders for a general massacre of all the Jews, and Haman will undertake it shall be easily done. If the king will gratify him in this matter, he will make him a present of *ten thousand talents,* which shall be *paid into the king's treasuries.* This, he thought, would be a powerful inducement to the king to consent, and would obviate the strongest objection against him, which was that the government must needs sustain loss in its revenues by the destruction of so many of its subjects; so great a sum, he hoped, would be equivalent for that. Proud and malicious men will not stick at the expenses of their revenge, nor spare any cost to gratify it. Yet no doubt Haman knew how to re-imburse himself out of the spoil of the Jews, which his janizaries were to seize for him (*v.* 13), and so to make them bear the charges of their own ruin; while he himself hoped to be not only a saver but a gainer by the bargain.

III. He obtains what he desired, a full commission to do what he would with the Jews, *v.* 10, 11. The king was so inattentive to business, and so bewitched with Haman, that he took no time to examine the truth of his allegations, but was as willing as Haman could wish to believe the worst concerning the Jews, and therefore he gave them up into his hands, as lambs to the lion: *The people are thine, do with them as it seemeth good unto thee.* He does not say, "Kill them, slay them" (hoping Haman's own cooler thoughts would abate the rigour of that sentence and induce him to sell them for slaves); but "Do what thou wilt with them." And so little did he consider how much he should lose in his tribute, and how much Haman would gain in the spoil, that he gave him withal the ten thousand talents: *The silver is thine.* Such an implicit confidence likewise he had in Haman, and so perfectly had he abandoned all care of his kingdom, that he gave Haman his ring, his privy-seal, or sign-manual, wherewith to confirm whatever edict he pleased to draw up for this purpose. Miserable is the kingdom that is at the disposal of such a head as this, which has one ear only, and a nose to be led by, but neither eyes nor brains, nor scarcely a tongue of its own.

IV. He then consults with his soothsayers to find out a lucky day for the designed massacre, *v.* 7. The resolve was taken up in the first month, in the twelfth year of the king, when Esther had been his wife about five years. Some day or other in that year must be pitched upon; and, as if he doubted not but that Heaven would favour his design and further it, he refers it to *the lot,* that is, to the divine Providence, to choose the day for him; but that, in the decision, proved a better friend to the Jews than to him, for the lot fell upon *the twelfth month,* so that Mordecai and Esther had eleven months to turn themselves in for the defeating of the design, or, if they could not defeat it, space would be left for the Jews to make their escape and shift for their safety. Haman, though eager to have the Jews cut off, yet will submit to the laws of his superstition, and not anticipate the supposed fortunate day, no, not to gratify his impatient revenge. Probably he was in some fear lest the Jews should prove too hard for their enemies, and therefore durst not venture on such a hazardous enterprise but under the smiles of a good omen. This may shame us, who often acquiesce not in the directions and disposals of Providence when they cross our desires and intentions. He that believeth the lot, much more that believeth the promise, will not make haste. But see how God's wisdom serves its own purposes by men's folly. Haman has appealed to the lot, and to the lot he shall go, which, by adjourning the execution, gives judgment against him and breaks the neck of the plot.

V. The bloody edict is hereupon drawn up, signed, and published, giving orders to the militia of every province to be ready against *the thirteenth day of the twelfth month,* and, on that day, to murder all the Jews, men, women, and children, and seize their effects, *v.* 12–14. Had the decree been to banish all the Jews and expel them out of the king's dominions, it would have been severe enough; but surely never any act of cruelty appeared so barefaced as this, to *destroy, to kill, and to cause to perish, all the Jews,* appointing them *as sheep for the slaughter* without showing any cause for so doing. No crime is laid to their charge; it is not pretended that they were obnoxious to the public justice, nor is any condition offered, upon performance of which they might have their lives spared; but die they must, without mercy. Thus have the church's enemies thirsted after blood, the *blood of the saints and the martyrs of* Jesus, and drunk of it till they have been perfectly intoxicated (Rev. 17:6); yet still, like *the horse-leech,* they cry, *Give, give.* This cruel offer is ratified with the king's seal, directed to the king's lieutenants, and drawn up in the king's name, and yet the king knows not what he does. Posts are sent out, with all expedition, to carry copies of the decree to the respective provinces, *v.* 15. See how restless the malice of the church's enemies is: it will spare no pains; it will lose no time.

VI. The different temper of the court and city hereupon. 1. The court was very merry upon it: *The king and Haman sat down to drink,* perhaps to drink "Confusion to all the Jews." Haman was afraid lest the king's conscience should smite him for what he had done and he should begin to wish it undone again, to prevent which he engrossed him to himself, and kept him drinking. This cursed method many take to drown their convictions, and harden their own hearts and the hearts of others in sin. 2. The city was very sad upon it (and the other cities of the kingdom, no doubt, when they had notice of it): *The city Shushan was perplexed,* not only the Jews themselves, but all their neighbours that had any principles of justice and compassion. It grieved them to see their king so abused, to see *wickedness in the place of judgment* (Eccl. 3:16), to see men that lived peaceably treated so barbarously; and what would be the consequences of it to themselves they knew not. But the king and Haman cared for none of these things. Note, It is an absurd and impious thing to indulge ourselves in mirth and pleasure when the church is in distress and the public are perplexed.

CHAPTER 4

We left God's Isaac bound upon the altar and ready to be sacrificed, and the enemies triumphing in the prospect of it; but things here begin to work towards a deliverance, and they begin at the right end. I. The Jews' friends lay to heart the danger and lament it (*v.* 1–4). II. Matters are concerted between Mordecai and Esther for the preventing of it. 1. Esther enquires into this case, and receives a particular account of it (*v.* 5–7). 2. Mordecai urges her to intercede with the king for a revocation of the edict (*v.* 8, 9). III. Esther objects the danger of addressing the king uncalled (*v.* 10–12). IV. Mordecai presses her to venture (*v.* 13, 14). V. Esther, after a religious fast of three days, promises to do so (*v.* 15–17), and we shall find that she sped well.

Verses 1–4

Here we have an account of the general sorrow that there was among the Jews upon the publishing of Haman's bloody edict against them. It was a sad time with the church. 1. Mordecai cried bitterly, *rent his clothes, and put on sackcloth, v.* 1, 2. He not only thus vented his grief, but proclaimed it, that all might take notice of it that he was not ashamed to own himself a friend to the Jews, and a fellow-sufferer with them, their brother and companion in tribulation, how despicable and how odious soever they were now represented by Haman's faction. It was nobly done thus publicly to espouse what he knew to be a righteous cause, and the cause of God, even when it seemed a desperate and a sinking cause. Mordecai laid the danger to heart more than any because he knew that Haman's spite was against him primarily, and that it was for his sake that the rest of the Jews were struck at; and therefore, though he did not repent of what some would call his obstinacy, for he persisted in it (*ch.* 5:9), yet it troubled him greatly that his people should suffer for his scruples, which perhaps occasioned some of them to reflect upon him as too precise. But, being able to appeal to God that what he did he did from a principle of conscience, he could with comfort commit his own cause and that of his people to him that judgeth righteously. God will keep those that are exposed by the tenderness of their consciences. Notice is here taken of a law that *none might enter into the king's gate clothed with sackcloth;* though the arbitrary power of their kings often, as now, set many a mourning, yet none must come near the king in a mourning dress, because he was not willing to hear the complaints of such. Nothing but what was gay and pleasant must appear at court, and every thing that was melancholy must be banished thence; all in king's palaces *wear soft clothing* (Mt. 11:8), not sackcloth. But thus to keep out the badges of sorrow, unless they could withal have kept out the causes of sorrow — to forbid sackcloth to enter, unless they could have forbidden sickness, and trouble, and death to enter — was jest. However this obliged Mordecai to keep his distance, and only to come before the gate, not to take his place in the gate. 2. All the Jews in every province laid it much to heart, *v.* 3. They denied themselves the comfort of their tables (for they fasted and mingled tears with their meat and drink), and the comfort of their beds at night, for *they lay in sackcloth and ashes.* Those who for want of confidence in God, and affection to their own land, has staid in the land of their captivity, when Cyrus gave them liberty to be gone, now perhaps repented of their folly, and wished, when it was too late, that they had complied with the call of God. 3. Esther the queen, upon a general intimation of the trouble Mordecai was in, *was exceedingly grieved, v.* 4. Mordecai's grief was hers, such a respect did she still retain for him; and the Jews' danger was her distress; for, though a queen, she forgot not her relation to them. Let not the greatest think it below them to *grieve for the affliction of Joseph,* though they themselves be *anointed with the chief ointments,* Amos 6:6. Esther sent change of raiment to Mordecai, the *oil of joy for mourning and the garments of praise for the spirit of heaviness;* but because he would make her sensible of the greatness of his grief, and consequently of the cause of it, *he received it not,* but was as one that refused to be comforted.

Verses 5–17

So strictly did the laws of Persia confine the wives, especially the king's wives, that it was not possible for Mordecai to have a conference with Esther about this important affair, but divers messages are here carried between them by Hatach, whom the king had appointed to attend her, and it seems he was one she could confide in.

I. She sent to Mordecai to know more particularly and fully what the trouble was which he was now lamenting (*v.* 5) and why it was that he would not put off his sackcloth. To enquire thus after news, that we may know the better how to direct our griefs and joys, our prayers and praises, well becomes all that love Sion. If we must weep with those that weep, we must know why they weep.

II. Mordecai sent her an authentic account of the whole matter, with a charge to her to intercede with the king in this matter: *Mordecai told him all that had happened unto him* (*v.* 7), what a pique Haman had against him for now bowing to him, and by what arts he had procured this edict; he sent her also a true copy of the edict, that she might see what imminent danger she and her people were in, and charged her, if she had any respect for him or any kindness for the Jewish nation, that she should appear now on their behalf, rectify the misinformations with which the king was imposed upon, and set the matter in a true light, not doubting but that then he would vacate the decree.

III. She sent her case to Mordecai, that she could not, without peril of her life, address the king, and that therefore he put a great hardship upon her in urging her to it. Gladly would she wait, gladly would she stoop, to do the Jews a kindness; but, if she must run the hazard of being put to death as a malefactor, she might well say, *I pray thee have me excused,* and find out some other intercessor.

1. The law was express, and all knew it, that whosoever came to the king uncalled should be put to death, unless he was pleased to *hold out the golden sceptre to them,* and it was extremely doubtful whether she should find him in so good a humour, *v.* 11. This law was made, not so much in prudence, for the greater safety of the king's person, as in pride, that being seldom seen, and not without great difficulty, he might be adored as a little god. A foolish law it was; for, (1.) It made the kings themselves unhappy, confining them to their retirements for fear they should be seen. This made the royal palace little better than a royal prison, and the kings themselves could not but become morose, and perhaps melancholy, and so a terror to others and a burden to themselves. Many have their lives made miserable by their own haughtiness and ill nature. (2.) It was bad for the subjects; for what good had they of a king that they might never have liberty to apply to for the redress of grievances and appeal to from the inferior judges? It is not thus in the court of the King of kings; to the footstool of his throne of grace we may at any time *come boldly,* and may be sure of an answer of peace to the prayer of faith. We are welcome, not only into the inner court, but even into the holiest, through the blood of Jesus. (3.) It was particularly very uncomfortable

for their wives (for there was not a proviso in the law to except them), who were *bone of their bone* and *flesh of their flesh.* But perhaps it was wickedly intended as much against them as any other, that the kings might the more freely enjoy their concubines, and Esther knew it. Miserable was the kingdom when the princes framed their laws to serve their lusts.

2. Her case was at present very discouraging. Providence so ordered it that, just at this juncture, she was under a cloud, and the king's affections cooled towards her, for she had been *kept from his presence thirty days,* that her faith and courage might be the more tried, and that God's goodness in the favour she now found with the king notwithstanding might shine the brighter. It is probable that Haman endeavoured by women, as well as wine, to divert the king from thinking of what he had done, and then Esther was neglected, from whom no doubt he did what he could to alienate the king, knowing her to be averse to him.

IV. Mordecai still insisted upon it that, whatever hazard she might run, she must apply to the king in this great affair, *v.* 13, 14. No excuse will serve, but she must appear an advocate in this cause; he suggested to her, 1. That it was her own cause, for that the decree to *destroy all the Jews* did not except here: *"Think not* therefore that *thou shalt escape in the king's house,* that the palace will be thy protection, and the crown save thy head: no, thou art a Jewess, and, if the rest be cut off, thou wilt be cut off too." It was certainly her wisdom rather to expose herself to a conditional death from her husband than to a certain death from her enemy. 2. That it was a cause which, one way or other, would certainly be carried, and which therefore she might safely venture in. "If thou shouldst decline the service, *enlargement and deliverance will arise to the Jews from another place."* This was the language of a strong faith, which *staggered not at the promise* when the danger was most threatening, but *against hope believed in hope.* Instruments may fail, but God's covenant will not. 3. That if she deserted her friends now, through cowardice and unbelief, she would have reason to fear that some judgment from heaven would be the ruin of her and her family: *"Thou and thy father's house shall be destroyed,* when the rest of the families of the Jews shall be preserved." He that by sinful shifts will save his life, and cannot find in his heart to trust God with it in the way of duty, shall lose it in the way of sin. 4. That divine Providence had an eye to this in bringing her to be queen: *"Who knows whether thou hast come to the kingdom for such a time as this?"* and therefore, (1.) "Thou art bound in gratitude to do this service for God and his church, else thou dost not answer the end of thy elevation." (2.) "Thou needest not fear miscarrying in the enterprise; if God designed thee for it, he will bear thee out and give thee success." Now, [1.] It appeared, by the event, that she did come to the kingdom that she might be an instrument of the Jews' deliverance, so that Mordecai was right in the conjecture. *Because the Lord loved his people,* therefore he made Esther queen. There is a wise counsel and design in all the providences of God, which is unknown to us till it is accomplished, but it will prove, in the issue, that they are all intended for, and centre in, the good of the church. [2.] The probability of this was a good reason why she should now bestir herself, and do her utmost for her people. We should every one of us consider for what end God has put us in the place where we are, and study to answer that end; and, when any particular opportunity of serving God and our generation offers itself, we must take care that we do not let it slip; for we were entrusted with it that we might improve it. These things Mordecai urges to Esther; and some of the Jewish writers, who are fruitful in invention, add another thing which had *happened to him* (*v.* 7) which he desired she might be told, "that going home, the night before, in great heaviness, upon the notice of Haman's plot, he met three Jewish children coming from school, of whom he enquired what they had learned that day; one of them told him his lesson was, Prov. 3:25, 26, *Be not afraid of sudden fear;* the second told him his was, Isa. 8:10, *Take counsel together, and it shall come to nought;* the third told him his was Isa. 46:4, *I have made, and I will bear, even I will carry and will deliver you.* 'O the goodness of God,' says Mordecai, 'who out of the mouth of babes and sucklings ordains strength!'"

V. Esther hereupon resolved, whatever it might cost her, to apply to the king, but not till she and her friends had first applied to God. Let them first by fasting and prayer obtain God's favour, and then she should hope to find favour with the king, *v.* 15, 16. She speaks here,

1. With the piety and devotion that became an Israelite. She had here eye up unto God, in whose hands the hearts of kings are, and on whom she depended to incline this king's heart towards her. She went in peril of her life, but would think herself safe, and would be easy, when she had committed the keeping of her soul to God and had put herself under his protection. She believed that God's favour was to be obtained by prayer, that his people are a praying people, and he a prayer-hearing God. She knew it was the practice of good people, in extraordinary cases, to join fasting with prayer, and many of them to join together in both. She therefore, (1.) Desired that Mordecai would direct the Jews that were in Shushan to *sanctify a fast* and *call a solemn assembly,* to meet in the respective synagogues to which they belonged, and to pray for her, and to keep a solemn fast, abstaining from all set meals and all pleasant food for three days, and as much as possible from all food, in token of their humiliation for sin and in a sense of their unworthiness of God's mercy. Those know not how to value the divine favours who grudge thus much labour and self-denial in the pursuit of it. (2.) She promised that she and her family would sanctify this fast in her apartment of the palace, for she might not come to their assemblies; her maids were either Jewesses or so far proselytes that they joined with her in her fasting and praying. Here is a good example of a mistress praying with her maids, and it is worthy to be imitated. Observe also, Those who are confined to privacy may join their prayers with those of the solemn assemblies of God's people; those that are absent in body may be present in spirit. Those who desire, and have, the prayers of others for them, must not think that this will excuse them from praying for themselves.

2. With the courage and resolution that became a queen. "When we have sought God in this matter, *I will go unto the king* to intercede for my people. *I know it is not according to the king's law,* but it is according to God's law; and therefore, whatever comes of it, I will venture, and not count my life dear to me, so that I may serve God and his church, and, *if I perish, I perish.* I cannot lose my life in a better cause. Better do my duty and die for my people than shrink from my duty and die with them." She reasons as the lepers (2 Ki. 7:4): *"If I sit still, I die;* if I venture, I may live, and be the life of my people: if the worst come to the worst," as we say, *"I shall but die."* Nothing venture, nothing win. She said not this in despair or passion, but in a holy resolution to do her duty and trust God with the issue; welcome his holy will. In the apocryphal part of this book (*ch.* 13 and 14) we have Mordecai's prayer and Esther's upon this occasion, and both of them very particular and pertinent. In the sequel of the story we shall find that God said not to this seed of Jacob, *Seek you me in vain.*

CHAPTER 5

The last news we had of Haman left him in his cups, 3:15. Our last news of queen Esther left her in tears, fasting and praying. Now this chapter brings in, I. Esther in her joys, smiled upon by the king and honoured with his company at her banquet of wine (*v.* 1–8). II. Haman upon the fret, because he had not Mordecai's cap and knee, and with great indignation setting up a gallows for him (*v.* 9–14). Thus those that sow in tears shall reap in joy, but the triumphing of the wicked is short.

Verses 1–8

Here is, I. Esther's bold approach to the king, *v.* 1. When the time appointed for their fast was finished she lost no time, but on the third day, when the impression of her devotions were fresh upon her spirit, she addressed the king. When the heart is enlarged in communion with God it will be emboldened in doing and suffering for him. Some think that the three days' fast was only one whole day and two whole nights, in all which time they did not take any food at all, and that this is called *three days,* as Christ's lying in the grave so long is. This exposition is favoured by the consideration that on the third day the queen made her appearance at court. Resolutions which have difficulties and dangers to break though should be pursued without delay, lest they cool and slacken. *What thou doest,* which must be done boldly, *do it quickly.* Now she *put on her royal apparel,* that she might the better recommend herself to the king, and laid aside her fast-day clothes. She put on her fine clothes, not to please herself, but her husband; in her prayer, as we find in the Apocrypha (Esther 14:16), she thus appeals to God: *Thou knowest, Lord, I abhor the sign of my high estate which is upon my head, in the days wherein I show myself, etc.* Let hose whose rank obliges them to wear rich clothes learn hence to be dead to them, and not make them their adorning. She stood *in the inner court over against the king,* expecting her doom, between hope and fear.

II. The favourable reception which the king gave her. When he *saw her* she *obtained favour in his sight.* The apocryphal author and Josephus say that she took two maids with her, on one of whom she leaned, while the other bore up her train, — that her countenance was cheerful and very amiable, but her heart was in anguish, — that the king, lifting up his countenance that shone with majesty, at first looked very fiercely upon here, whereupon she grew pale, and fainted, and bowed herself on the head of the maid that went by her; but then God changed the spirit of the king, and, in a fear, he leaped from his throne, took her in his arms till she came to herself, and comforted her with loving words. Here we are only told,

1. That he protected her from the law, and assured her of safety, by *holding out to her the golden sceptre* (*v.* 2), which she thankfully *touched the top of,* thereby presenting herself to him as a humble petitioner. Thus having had power with God and prevailed, like Jacob, she had power with men too. *He that will lose his life* for God shall *save it,* or find it in a better life.

2. That he encouraged her address (*v.* 3): *What wilt thou, queen Esther, and what is thy request?* So far was he from counting her an offender that he seemed glad to see her, and desirous to oblige her. He that had divorced one wife for not coming when she was sent for would not be severe to another for coming when she was not sent for. God can turn the hearts of men, of great men, of those that act most arbitrarily, which way he pleases towards us. Esther feared that she should perish, but was promised that she should have what she might ask for, though it were *the half of the kingdom.* Note, God in his providence often prevents the fears, and outdoes the hopes, of his people, especially when they venture in his cause. Let us from this story infer, as our Saviour does from the parable of the unjust judge, an encouragement to *pray always* to our God, *and not faint,* Lu. 18:6–8. Hear what this haughty king says *(What is thy petition, and what is thy request? It shall be granted thee),* and say *shall not God* hear and answer the prayers of *his own elect, that cry day and night to him?* Esther came to a proud imperious man; we come to the God of love and grace. She was not called; we are: the Spirit says, *Come,* and the bride says, *Come.* She had a law against her; we have a promise, many a promise, in favour of us: *Ask, and it shall be given you.* She had no friend to introduce her, or intercede for her, while on the contrary he that was then the king's favourite was her enemy; but we have an advocate with the Father, in whom he is well pleased. *Let us therefore come boldly to the throne of grace.*

3. That all the request she had to make to him, at this time, was that he would please to come to a banquet which she had prepared for him, and bring Haman along with him, *v.* 4, 5. Hereby, (1.) She would intimate to him how much she valued his favour and company. Whatever she had to ask, she desired his favour above any thing, and would purchase it at any rate. (2.) She would try how he stood affected to her; for, if he should refuse this, it would be to no purpose as yet to present her other request. (3.) She would endeavour to bring him into a pleasant humour, and soften his spirit, that he might with the more tenderness receive the impressions of the complaint she had to make to him. (4.) She would please him, by making court to Haman his favourite, and inviting him to come whose company she knew he loved and whom she desired to have present when she made her complaint; for she would say nothing of him but what she durst say to his face. (5.) She hoped at the banquet of wine to have a fairer and more favourable opportunity of presenting her petition. Wisdom is profitable to direct how to manage

some men that are hard to deal with, and to take them by the right handle.

4. That he readily came, and ordered Haman to come along with him (*v.* 5), which was an indication of the kindness he still retained for her; if he really designed the destruction of her and her people, he would not have accepted her banquet. There he renewed his kind enquiry *(What is thy petition?)* and his generous promise, that it should be granted, *even to the half of the kingdom* (*v.* 6), a proverbial expression, by which he assured her that he would deny her nothing in reason. Herod used it, Mk. 6:23.

5. That then Esther thought fit to ask no more than a promise that he would please to accept of another treat, the next day, in her apartment, and Haman with him (*v.* 7, 8), intimating to him that then she would let him know what her business was. This adjourning of the main petition may be attributed, (1.) To Esther's prudence; thus she hoped yet further to win upon him and ingratiate herself with him. Perhaps her heart failed her now when she was going to make her request, and she desired to take some further time for prayer, that God would give her *a mouth and wisdom.* The putting of it off thus, it is likely, she knew would be well taken as an expression of the great reverence she had for the king, and her unwillingness to be too pressing upon him. What is hastily asked is often as hastily denied; but what is asked with a pause deserves to be considered. (2.) To God's providence putting it into Esther's heart to delay her petition a day longer, she knew not why, but God did, that what was to happen in the night intervening between this and to-morrow might further her design and make way for her success, that Haman might arrive at the highest pitch of malice against Mordecai and might begin to *fall before him.* The Jews perhaps blamed Ester as dilatory, and some of them began to suspect her sincerity, or at least her zeal; but the event disproved their jealousy, and all was for the best.

Verses 9–14

This account here given of Haman is a comment upon that of Solomon, Prov. 21:24. *Proud and haughty scorner is his name that deals in proud wrath.* Never did any man more answer that name than Haman, in whom pride and wrath had so much the ascendant. See him,

I. Puffed up with the honour of being invited to Esther's feast. He was *joyful and glad of heart* at it, *v.* 9. Observe with what a high gust he speaks of it (*v.* 12), how he values himself upon it, and how near he thinks it brings him to the perfection of felicity, that Esther the queen did let no man come with the king to the banquet but his mighty self, and he thought it was because she was exceedingly charmed with his conversation that the next day she had invited him also to come with the king; none so fit as he to bear the king company. Note, Self-admirers and self-flatterers are really self-deceivers. Haman pleased himself with the fancy that the queen, by this repeated invitation, designed to honour him, whereas really she designed to accuse him, and, in calling him to the banquet, did but call him to the bar. What magnifying glasses do proud men look at their faces in! And how does the *pride of their heart deceive them!* Obad. 3.

II. Vexing and fretting at the slight that Mordecai put upon him, and thereby made uneasy to himself and to all about him. 1. Mordecai was as determined as ever: *He stood not up, nor moved for him, v.* 9. What he did was from a principle of conscience, and therefore he persevered in it, and would not cringe to Haman, no, not when he had reason to fear him and Esther herself complimented him. He knew God could and would deliver him and his people from the rage of Haman, without any such mean and sneaking expedients to mollify him. Those that walk in holy sincerity may walk in holy security, and go on in their work, not fearing what man can do unto them. *He that walks uprightly walks surely.* 2. Haman can as ill bear it as ever; nay, the higher he is lifted up, the more impatient is her of contempt and the more enraged at it. (1.) It made his own spirit restless, and put him into a grievous agitation. He was *full of indignation* (*v.* 9) and yet *refrained himself, v.* 10. Gladly would he have drawn his sword and run Mordecai through for affronting him thus; but he hoped shortly to see him fall with all the Jews, and therefore with much ado prevailed with himself to forbear stabbing him. What a struggle had he in his own bosom between his anger, which required Mordecai's death immediately (*O that I had of his flesh! I cannot be satisfied!* Job 31:31), and his malice, which had determined to wait for the general massacre! Thus *thorns and snares are in the way of the froward.* (2.) It made all his enjoyments sapless. This little affront which he received from Mordecai was the dead fly which spoiled all his pot of precious ointment; he himself owned in the presence of his wife and friends, to the everlasting reproach of a proud and discontented mind, that he had no comfort in his estate, preferment, and family, as long as Mordecai lived and had a place *in the king's gate, v.* 10–13. He took notice of his own riches and honours, the numerousness of his family, and the high posts to which he was advanced, that he was the darling of the prince and the idol of the court; and *yet all this avails him nothing* as long as Mordecai is unhanged. Those that are disposed to be uneasy will never want something or other to be uneasy at; and proud men, though they have *much* to their mind, yet, if they have not *all* to their mind, it is as nothing to them. The thousandth part of what Haman had would serve to make a humble modest man as much of a happiness as he expects from this world; and yet Haman complained as passionately as if he had been sunk into the lowest degree of poverty and disgrace.

III. Meditating revenge, and assisted therein by his wife and his friends, *v.* 14. They saw how gladly he would dispense with his own resolution of deferring the slaughter till the time determined by the lot, and therefore advised him to take an earnest and foretaste of the satisfaction he then expected in the speedy execution of Mordecai; let him have that to please him at the moment; and having, as he thought, made sure the destruction of all the Jews, at the time appointed, he will not think scorn, for the present, to lay hands on Mordecai alone. 1. For the pleasing of his fancy they advise him to get *a gallows ready,* and have it set up before his own door, that, as soon as ever he could get the warrant signed, there might be no delay of the execution; he would not need so much as to stay the making of the gallows. This is very agreeable to Haman, who has the gallows made and fixed immediately; it must be fifty cubits high, or as near that as might be, for the greater disgrace of Mordecai and to make him a spectacle to every one that passed by; and it must be before Haman's door, that all men might take notice it was to the idol of his revenge that Mordecai was sacrificed and that he might feed his eyes with the sight. 2. For the gaining of his point they advise him to go early in the morning to the king, and get an order from him for the hanging of Mordecai, which, they doubted not, would be readily granted to one who was so much the king's favourite and who had so easily obtained an edict for the destruction of the whole nation of the Jews. There needed no feigned suggestion; it was enough if he let the king know that Mordecai, in contempt of the king's command, refused to reverence him. And now we leave Haman to go to bed, pleased with the thoughts of seeing Mordecai hanged the next day, and then going merrily to the banquet, and not dreaming of handselling his own gallows.

CHAPTER 6

It is a very surprising scene that opens in this chapter. Haman, when he hoped to be Mordecai's judge, was made his page, to his great confusion and mortification; and thus way was made for the defeat of Haman's plot and the deliverance of the Jews. I. The providence of God recommends Mordecai in the night to the king's favour (*v.* 1–3). II. Haman, who came to incense the king against him, is employed as an instrument of the king's favour to him (*v.* 4–11). III. From this his friends read him his doom, which is executed in the next chapter (*v.* 12–14). And now it appears that Esther's intercession for her people was happily adjourned, "De die in diem" — from day to day.

Verses 1–3

Now Satan put it into the heart of Haman to contrive Mordecai's death we read in the foregoing chapter; how God put it into the heart of the king to contrive Mordecai's honour we are here told. Now, if the king's word will prevail above Haman's (for, though Haman be a great man, the king in the throne must be above him), much more will the *counsel of God stand,* whatever *devices there are in men's hearts.* It is to no purpose therefore for Haman to oppose it, when both God and the king will have Mordecai honoured, and in this juncture too, when his preferment, and Haman's disappointment, would help to ripen the great affair of the Jewish deliverance for the effort that Esther was to make towards it the next day. Sometimes delay may prove to have been good conduct. Stay awhile, and we may have done the sooner. *Cunctando restituit rem — He conquered by delay.* Let us trace the steps which Providence took towards the advancement of Mordecai.

I. *On that night could not the king sleep.* His *sleep fled away* (so the word is); and perhaps, like a shadow, the more carefully he pursued it the further it went from him. Sometimes we cannot sleep because we fain would sleep. Even after a banquet of wine he could not sleep when Providence had a design to serve in keeping him waking. We read of no bodily indisposition he was under, that might break his sleep; but God, *whose gift sleep is,* withheld it from him. Those that are ever so much resolved to cast away care cannot always do it; they find it in their pillows when they neither expect nor welcome it. He that commanded 127 provinces could not command one hour's sleep. Perhaps the charms of Esther's conversation the day before gave occasion to his heart to reproach him for neglecting her, and banishing her from his presence, though she was the wife of his bosom, for above thirty days; and that might keep him waking. An offended conscience can find a time to speak when it will be heard.

II. When he could not sleep he called to have the book of records, the Journals of his reign, read to him, *v.* 1. Surely he did not design that that should lull him asleep; it would rather fill his head with cares, and drive away sleep. But God put it into his heart to call for it, rather than for music or songs, which the Persian kings used to be attended with (Dan. 6:18) and which would have been more likely to compose him to rest. When men do that which is unaccountable we know not what God intends by it. Perhaps he would have this book of business read to him that he might improve time and be forming some useful projects. Had it been king David's case, he would have found some other entertainment for his thoughts; when he could not sleep he would have remembered God and meditated upon him (Ps. 64:6), and, if he would have had any book read to him, it would have been his Bible; for *in that law did he meditate day and night.*

III. The servant that read to him either lighted first on that article which concerned Mordecai, or, reading long, came to it at length. Among other things it was found written that Mordecai had discovered a plot against the life of the king which prevented the execution of it, *v.* 2. Mordecai was not in such favour at court that the reader should designedly pitch upon that place; but Providence directed him to it; nay, if we may believe the Jews' tradition (as bishop Patrick relates it), opening the book at this place he turned over the leaves, and would have read another part of the book, but the leaves flew back again to the same place where he opened it; so that he was forced to read that paragraph. How Mordecai's good service was recorded we read *ch.* 2:23, and here it is found upon record.

IV. The king enquired *what honour and dignity had been done to Mordecai* for this, suspecting that this good service had gone unrewarded, and, like Pharaoh's butler, remembering it as *his fault this day,* Gen. 41:9. Note, The law of gratitude is a law of nature. We ought particularly to be grateful to our inferiors, and not to think all their services such debts to us but that they make us indebted to them. Two rules of gratitude may be gathered from the king's enquiry here: — 1. Better honour than nothing. If we cannot, or need not, make recompence to those who have been kind to us, yet let us do them honour by acknowledging their kindnesses and owning our obligations to them. 2. Better late than never. If we have long neglected to make grateful returns for good offices done us, let us at length bethink ourselves of our debts.

V. The servants informed him that nothing had been done to Mordecai for that eminent service; in the king's gate he sat before, and there he still sat. Note, 1. It is common for great men to take little notice of their inferiors. The king knew not whether Mordecai was preferred or no till his servants informed him. High spirits take a pride in being careless and unconcerned about those that are below them and ignorant of their state. The great God takes cognizance of the meanest of his servants, knows what dignity is done them and what disgrace. 2. Humility, modesty, and self-denial, though in God's account of great price, yet commonly hinder men's preferment in the world. Mordecai rises no higher than the king's gate, while proud ambitious Haman gets the king's ear and heart; but, though the aspiring rise fast, the humble stand fast. Honour makes proud men giddy, but *upholds the humble in spirit,* Prov. 29:23. 3. Honour and dignity are rated high in the king's books. He does not ask, What reward has been given Mordecai? what money? what estate? but only, What honour? — a poor thing, and which, if he had not wherewith to support it, would be but a burden. 4. The greatest merits and the best services are often overlooked and go unrewarded among men. Little honour is done to those who best deserve it, and fittest for it, and would do most good with it. See Eccl. 9:14–16. The acquisition of wealth and honour is usually a perfect lottery, in which those that venture least commonly carry off the best prize. Nay, 5. Good services are sometimes so far from being a man's preferment that they will not be his protection. Mordecai is at this time, by the king's edict, doomed to destruction, with all the Jews, though it is owned that he deserved dignity. Those that faithfully serve God need not fear being thus ill paid.

Verses 4–11

It is now morning, and people begin to stir.

I. Haman is so impatient to get Mordecai hanged that he comes early to court, to be ready at the king's levee, before any other business is brought before him, to get a warrant for his execution (*v.* 4), which he makes sure that he shall have at the first word. The king would gratify him in a greater thing than that; and he could tell the king that he was so confident of the justice of his request, and the king's favour to him in it, that he had got the gallows ready: one word from the king would complete his satisfaction.

II. The king is so impatient to have Mordecai honoured that he sends to know who is in the court that is fit to be employed in it. Word is brought him that Haman is in the court, *v.* 5. *Let him come in,* says the king, the fittest man to be made use of both in directing and in dispensing the king's favour; and the king knew nothing of any quarrel he had with Mordecai. Haman is brought in immediately, proud of the honour done him in being admitted into the king's bed-chamber, as it should seem, *before he was up;* for let the king but give orders for the dignifying of Mordecai, and he will be easy in his mind and try to sleep. Now Haman thinks he has the fairest opportunity he can wish for to solicit against Mordecai; but the king's heart is as full as his, and it is fit he should speak first.

III. The king asks Haman how he should express his favour to one whom he had marked for a favourite: *What shall be done to the man whom the king delights to honour? v.* 6. Note, It is a good property in kings, and other superiors, to delight in bestowing rewards and not to delight in punishing. Parents and masters should take a pleasure in commending and encouraging that which is good in those under their charge.

IV. Haman concludes that he himself is the favourite intended, and therefore prescribes the highest expressions of honour that could, for once, be bestowed upon a subject. His proud heart presently suggested, "To whom will the king delight to do honour more than to myself? No one deserves it so well as I," thinks Haman, "nor stands so fair for it." See how men's pride deceives them. 1. Haman had a better opinion of his merits than there was cause for: he thought none so worthy of honour as himself. It is a foolish thing for us thus to think ourselves the only deserving persons, or more deserving than any other. The deceitfulness of our own hearts appears in nothing so much as in the good conceit we have of ourselves and our own performances, against which we should therefore constantly watch and pray. 2. He had a better opinion of his interest than there was reason for. He thought the king loved and valued no one but himself, but he was deceived. We should suspect that the esteem which others profess for us is not so great as it seems to be or as we are sometimes willing to believe it is, that we may not think too well of ourselves nor place too much confidence in others. Now Haman thinks he is carving out honour for himself, and therefore does it very liberally, *v.* 8, 9. Nay, he does it presumptuously, prescribing honours too great to be conferred upon any subject, that he must be dressed in the royal robes, wear the royal crown, and ride on the king's own horse; in short, he must appear in all the pomp and grandeur of the king himself, only he must not carry the

sceptre, the emblem of power. He must be attended by one of *the king's most noble princes,* who must be his lacquey, and all the people must be made to take notice of him and do him reverence; for he must ride in state through the streets, and it must be *proclaimed before him,* for his honour, and the encouragement of all to seek the ruler's favour, *Thus shall it be done to the man whom the king delights to honour,* which had the same intention with that which was proclaimed before Joseph, *Bow the knee;* for every good subject will honour those whom the king delights to honour. And shall not every good Christian then honour those whom the King of kings delights to honour and call the *saints that are on the earth the excellent ones?*

V. The king confounds him with a positive order that he should immediately go himself and put all this honour upon Mordecai the Jew, *v.* 10. If the king had but said, as Haman expected, *Thou art the man,* what a fair opportunity would he have had to do the errand he came on, and to desire that, to grace the solemnity of his triumphs, Mordecai, his sworn enemy, might be hanged at the same time! But how is he thunderstruck when the king bids him not to order all this to be done, but to do it himself to Mordecai the Jew, the very man he hated above all men and whose ruin he was now designing! Now, it is to no purpose to think of moving any thing to the king against Mordecai when he is *the man whom the king delights to honour.* Solomon says, *The heart of the king is unsearchable* (Prov. 25:3), but it is not unchangeable.

VI. Haman dares not dispute nor so much as seem to dislike the king's order, but, with the greatest regret and reluctance imaginable, brings it to Mordecai, who I suppose did no more cringe to Haman now than he had done, valuing his counterfeit respect no more than he had valued his concealed malice. The apparel is brought, Mordecai is dressed up, and rides in state through the city, recognized as the king's favourite, *v.* 11. It is hard to say which of the two put a greater force upon himself, proud Haman in putting this honour upon Mordecai, or humble Mordecai in accepting it: the king would have it so, and both must submit. Upon *this* account it was agreeable to Mordecai as it was an indication of the king's favour, and gave hope that Esther would prevail for the reversing of the edict against the Jews.

Verses 12–14

We may here observe,

I. How little Mordecai was puffed up with his advancement. he *came again to the king's gate* (*v.* 12); he returned to his place and the duty of it immediately, and minded his business as closely as he had done before. Honour is well bestowed on those that are not made proud and idle by it, and will not think themselves above their business.

II. How much Haman was cast down with his disappointment. he could not bear it. To wait upon any man, especially Mordecai, and at this time, when he hoped to have seen him hanged, was enough to break such a proud heart as he had. He *hasted to his house mourning, and having his head covered,* as one that looked upon himself as sunk and in a manner condemned. What harm had it done him to stoop thus to Mordecai? Was he ever the worse for it? Was it not what he himself proposed to be done by *one of the king's most noble princes?* Why then should he grudge to do it himself? But that will break a proud man's heart which would not break a humble man's sleep.

III. How his doom was, out of this event, read to him by his wife and his friends: "If Mordecai be, as they say he is, *of the seed of the Jews, before whom thou hast begun to fall,* though but in a point of honour, never expect to *prevail against him;* for thou *shalt surely fall before him," v.* 13. Miserable comforters were they all; they did not advise him to repent, and ask Mordecai's pardon for his bad design against him, but foretold his destiny as fatal and unavoidable. Two things they foresaw: — 1. That Haman would be disappointed in his enterprise against the Jews: *"Thou shalt not prevail to root out that people.* Heaven plainly fights against thee." 2. That he himself would be destroyed: *Thou shalt surely fall before him.* The contest between Michael and the dragon will not be a drawn battle; no, Haman must fall before Mordecai. Two things they grounded their prognostications upon: — (1.) This Mordecai was *of the seed of the Jews; feeble Jews* their enemies sometimes called them, but formidable Jews they

sometimes found them. They are a holy seed, a praying seed, in covenant with God, and a seed that the Lord hath all along blessed, and therefore let not their enemies expect to triumph over them. (2.) Haman had begun to fall, and therefore he was certainly a gone man. It has been observed of great court-favourites that when once they have been frowned upon they have fallen utterly, as fast as they rose; it is true of the church's enemies that when God begins with them he will make an end. As for God his work is perfect.

IV. How seasonably he was now sent for to the banquet that Esther had prepared, *v.* 14. He thought it seasonable, in hopes it would revive his drooping spirits and save his sinking honour. But really it was seasonable because, his spirits being broken by this sore disappointment, he might the more easily be run down by Esther's complaint against him. The wisdom of God is seen in timing the means of his church's deliverance so as to manifest his own glory.

CHAPTER 7

We are now to attend the second banquet to which the king and Haman were invited: and there, I. Esther presents her petition to the king for her life and the life of her people (*v.* 1–4). II. She plainly tells the king that Haman is the man who designed her ruin and the ruin of all her friends (*v.* 5, 6). III. The king thereupon gave orders for the hanging of Haman upon the gallows that he had prepared for Mordecai, which was done accordingly (*v.* 7–10). And thus, by the destruction of the plotter, a good step was taken towards the defeating of the plot.

Verses 1–6

The king in humour, and Haman out of humour, meet at Esther's table. Now,

I. The king urged Esther, a third time, to tell him what her request was, for he longed to know, and repeated his promise that it should be granted, *v.* 2. If the king had now forgotten that Esther had an errand to him, and had not again asked what it was, she could scarcely have known how to renew it herself; but he was mindful of it, and now was bound with the threefold cord of a promise thrice made to favour her.

II. Esther, at length, surprises the king with a petition, not for wealth or honour, or the preferment of some of her friends to some high post, which the king expected, but for the preservation of herself and her countrymen from death and destruction, *v.* 3, 4.

1. Even a stranger, a criminal, shall be permitted to petition for his life; but that a friend, a wife, should have occasion to present such a petition was very affecting: *Let my life be given me at my petition, and my people at my request.* Two things bespeak lives to be very precious, and fit to be saved, if innocent, at any expense: — (1.) Majesty. If it be a crowned head that is struck at, it is time to stir. Esther's was such: *"Let my life be given me.* If thou hast any affection for the wife of thy bosom, now is the time to show it; for that is the life that lies at stake." (2.) Multitude. If they be many lives, very many, and those no way forfeited, that are aimed at, no time should be lost nor pains spared to prevent the mischief. "It is not a friend or two, but *my people,* a whole nation, and a nation dear to me, for the saving of which I now intercede."

2. To move the king the more she suggests, (1.) That she and her people were bought and sold. They had not sold themselves by any offence against the government, but were sold to gratify the pride and revenge of one man. (2.) That it was not their liberty only, but their lives that were sold. "Had we been sold" (she says) "into slavery, I would not have complained; for in time we might have recovered our liberty, thought eh king would have made but a bad bargain of it, and not have increased his wealth by our price. Whatever had been paid for us, the loss of so many industrious hands out of his kingdom would have been more damage to the treasury than the price would countervail." To persecute good people is as impolitic as it is impious, and a manifest wrong to the interests of princes and states; they are weakened and impoverished by it. But this was not the case. *We are sold* (says she) *to be destroyed, to be slain, and to perish;* and then it is time to speak. She refers to the words of the decree (*ch.* 3:13), which aimed at nothing short of their destruction; this would touch in a tender part if there were any such in the king's heart, and would bring him to relent.

III. The king stands amazed at the remonstrance, and

asks (*v.* 5) *"Who is he, and where is he, that durst presume in his heart to do so?* What! contrive the murder of the queen and all her friends? Is there such a man, such a monster rather, in nature? *Who is he, and where is he, whose heart has filled him to do so?"* Or, Who hath *filled his heart.* He wonders, 1. That any one should be so bad as to think such a thing; Satan certainly filled his heart. 2. That any one should be so bold as to do such a thing, should have his heart so fully set in him to do wickedly, should be so very daring. Note, (1.) It is hard to imagine that there should be such horrid wickedness committed in the world as really there is. Who, where is he, that dares, presumes, to question the being of God and his providence, to banter his oracles, profane his name, persecute his people, and yet bid defiance to his wrath? Such there are, to think of whom is enough to make *horror take hold of us,* Ps. 119:53. (2.) We sometimes startle at the mention of that evil which yet we ourselves are chargeable with. Ahasuerus is amazed at that wickedness which he himself is guilty of; for he consented to that bloody edict against the Jews. *Thou art the man,* might Esther too truly have said.

IV. Esther plainly charged Haman with it before his face: "Here he is, let him speak for himself, for therefore he is invited: *The adversary and enemy is this wicked Haman* (*v.* 6); it is he that has designed our murder, and, which is worse, has basely drawn the king in to be *particeps criminis — a partaker of his crime,* ignorantly agreeing to it."

V. Haman is soon apprehensive of his danger: *He was afraid before the king and queen;* and it was time for him to fear when the queen was his prosecutor, the king his judge, and his own conscience a witness against him; and the surprising operations of Providence against him that same morning could not but increase his fear. Now he has little joy of his being invited to the banquet of wine, but finds himself in straits when he thought himself *in the fulness of his sufficiency. He is cast into a net by his own feet.*

Verses 7–10

Here, I. The king retires in anger. He rose from table in a great passion, and *went into the palace garden* to cool himself and to consider what was to be done, *v.* 7. He sent not for his *seven wise counsellors who knew the times,* being ashamed to consult them about the undoing of that which he had rashly done without their knowledge or advice; but he went to walk in the garden awhile, to compare in his thoughts what Esther had now informed him of with what had formerly passed between him and Haman. And we may suppose him, 1. Vexed at himself, that he should be such a fool as to doom a guiltless nation to destruction, and his own queen among the rest, upon the base suggestions of a self-seeking man, without examining the truth of his allegations. Those that do things with self-will reflect upon them afterwards with self-reproach. 2. Vexed at Haman whom he had laid in his bosom, that he should be such a villain as to abuse his interest in him to draw him to consent to so wicked a measure. When he saw himself betrayed by one he had caressed he was full of indignation at him; yet he would say nothing till he had taken time for second thoughts, to see whether they would make the matter better or worse than it first appeared, that he might proceed accordingly. When we are angry we should pause awhile before we come to any resolution, as those that have *a rule over our own spirits* and are governed by reason.

II. Haman becomes a humble petitioner to the queen for his life. He might easily perceived by the king's hastily flying out of the room that *there was evil determined against him.* For *the wrath of a king,* such a king, *is as the roaring of a lion* and as *messengers of death;* and now see, 1. How mean Haman looks, when he stands up first and then falls down at Esther's feet, to beg she would save his life and take all he had. Those that are most haughty, insolent, and imperious, when they are in power and prosperity, are commonly the most abject and poor-spirited when the wheel turns upon them. Cowards, they say, are most cruel, and then consciousness of their cruelty makes them the more cowardly. 2. How great Esther looks, who of late had been neglected and doomed to the slaughter *tanquam ovis — as a sheep;* now her sworn enemy owns that he lies at her mercy, a d begs his life at her hand. Thus did God *regard the low estate of his handmaiden* and *scatter the proud in the imagination of their hearts,* Lu. 1:48, 51. Compare with this that promise made to the Philadelphian church (Rev. 3:9), *I will make those of the synagogue of Satan to come and to worship before thy feet and to know that I have loved thee.* The day is coming when those that hate and persecute God's chosen ones would gladly be beholden to them. *Give us of your oil. Father Abraham, send Lazarus. The upright shall have dominion in the morning.*

III. The king returns yet more exasperated against Haman. The more he thinks of him the worse he thinks of him and of what he had done. It was but lately that every thing Haman said and did, even that which was most criminal, was taken well and construed to his advantage; now, on the contrary, what Haman did that was not only innocent, but a sign of repentance, is ill taken, and, without colour of reason, construed to his disadvantage. He lay in terror at Esther's feet, to beg for his life. What! (says the king) *will he force the queen also before me in the house?* Not that he thought he had any such intention, but having been musing on Haman's design to slay the queen, and finding him in this posture, he takes occasion from it thus to vent his passion against Haman, as a man that would not scruple at the greatest and most impudent piece of wickedness. "He designed to slay the queen, and to slay her *wish me in the house;* will he in like manner force her? What! ravish her first and then murder her? He that had a design upon her life may well be suspected to have a design upon her chastity."

IV. Those about him were ready to be the instruments of his wrath. The courtiers that adored Haman when he was the rising sun set themselves as much against him now that he is a falling star, and are even glad of an occasion to run him down: so little sure can proud men be of the interest they think they have. 1. As soon as the king spoke an angry word *they covered Haman's face,* as a condemned man, not worthy any more either to see the king or to be seen by him; they marked him for execution. Those that are hanged commonly have their faces covered. See how ready the servants were to take the first hint of the king's mind in this matter. *Turba Romae sequitur fortunam, et semper et odit damnatos — The Roman populace change as the aspects f fortune do, and always oppress the fallen.* If Haman be going down, they all cry, "Down with him." 2. One of those that had been lately sent to Haman's house, to fetch him to the banquet, informed the king of the gallows which Haman had prepared for Mordecai, *v.* 9. Now that Mordecai is the favourite the chamberlain applauds him — he *spoke good for the king;* and, Haman being in disgrace, every thing is taken notice of that might make against him, incense the king against him, and fill up the measure of his iniquity.

V. The king gave orders that he should be hanged upon his own gallows, which was done accordingly, nor was he so much as asked what he had to say why this judgment should not be passed upon him and execution awarded. The sentence is short — *Hang him thereon;* and the execution speedy — *So they hanged Haman on the gallows, v.* 10. See here, 1. Pride brought down. He that expected every one to do him homage is now made an ignominious spectacle to the world, and he himself sacrificed to his revenge. God resists the proud; and those whom he resists will find him irresistible. 2. Persecution punished. Haman was upon many accounts a wicked man, but his enmity to God's church was his most provoking crime, and for *that* the God to whom vengeance belongs here reckons with him, and, though his plot was defeated, gives him *according to the wickedness of his endeavours,* Ps. 28:4. 3. Mischief returned upon the person himself that contrived it, the *wicked snared in the work of his own hands,* Ps. 7:15, 16; 9:15, 16. Haman was justly hanged on the very gallows he had unjustly prepared for Mordecai. If he had not set up that gallows, perhaps the king would not have thought of ordering him to be hanged; but, if he rear a gallows for *the man whom the king delights to honour,* the thought is very natural that he should be ordered to try it himself, and see how it fits him, see how he likes it. The enemies of God's church have often been thus taken in their own craftiness. In the morning Haman was designing himself for the robes and Mordecai for the gallows; but the tables are turned: Mordecai has the crown, Haman the cross. *The Lord is known by such judgments.* See Prov. 11:8; 21:18.

Lastly, The satisfaction which the king had in this execution. *Then was the king's wrath pacified,* and not till then. He was as well pleased in ordering Haman to be hanged as in ordering Mordecai to be honoured. Thus shall it be done to the man whom the king delights to take vengeance on. God saith of wicked men (Eze. 5:13), *I will cause my fury to rest upon them, and I will be comforted.*

CHAPTER 8

We left the plotter hanging, and are now to see what becomes of his plot. I. His plot was to raise an estate for himself; and all his estate, being confiscated for treason, is given to Esther and Mordecai (*v.* 1, 2). II. His plot was to ruin the Jews; and as to that, 1. Esther earnestly intercedes for the reversing of the edict against them (*v.* 3–6). 2. It is in effect done by another edict, here published, empowering the Jews to stand up in their own defence against their enemies (*v.* 7–14). III. This occasions great joy to the Jews and all their friends (*v.* 15–17).

Verses 1–2

It was but lately that we had Esther and Mordecai in tears and in fears, but fasting and praying; now let us see how to them there arose light in darkness. Here is, 1. Esther enriched. Haman was hanged as a traitor, therefore his estate was forfeited to the crown, and the king gave it all to Esther, in recompence for the fright that wicked man had put her into and the vexation he had created her, *v.* 1. His houses and lands, good sand chattels, and all the money he had heaped up which he was prime-minister of state (which, we may suppose, was no little), are given to Esther; they are all her own, added to the allowance she already had. Thus is *the wealth of the sinner laid up for the just,* and the *innocent divides the silver,* Prov. 13:22; Job 27:17, 18. What Haman would have done mischief with Esther will do good with; and estates are to be valued as they are used. 2. Mordecai advanced. His pompous procession, this morning, through the streets of the city, was but a sudden flash or blaze of honour; but here we have the more durable and gainful preferments to which he was raised, which yet the other happily made way for. (1.) He is now owned as the queen's cousin, which till now, though Esther had been four years queen, for aught that appears, the king did not know. So humble, so modest, a man was Mordecai, and so far from being ambitious of a place at court, that he concealed his relation to the queen and her obligations to him as her guardian, and never made us of her interest for any advantage of his own. Who but Mordecai could have taken so little notice of so great an honour? But now he was brought *before the king,* introduced, as we say, to kiss his hand; for now, at length, *Esther had told what he was to her,* not only near a-kin to her, but the best friend she had in the world, who took care of her when she was an orphan, and one whom she still respected as a father. Now the king finds himself, for his wife's sake, more obliged than he thought he had been to delight in doing honour to Mordecai. How great were the merits of that man to whom both king and queen did in effect owe their lives! Being brought before the king, to him no doubt he bowed, and did reverence, though he would not to Haman an Amalekite. (2.) The king makes his lord privy-seal in the room of Haman. All the trust he had reposed in Haman, and all the power he had given him, are here transferred to Mordecai; for the ring which he had taken from Haman he gave to Mordecai, and made this trusty humble man as much his favourite, his confidant, and his agent, as ever that proud perfidious wretch was; a happy change he made of his bosom-friends, and so, no doubt, he and his people soon found it. (3.) The queen makes him here steward, for the management of Haman's estate, and for getting and keeping possession of it: *She set Mordecai over the house of Haman.* See the vanity of laying up treasure upon earth; he that *heapeth up riches knoweth not who shall gather them* (Ps. 39:6), not only *whether he shall be a wise man or a fool* (Eccl. 2:19), but whether he shall be a friend or an enemy. With what little pleasure, nay, with what constant vexation, would Haman have looked upon his estate if he could have foreseen that Mordecai, the man he hated above all men in the world, should have *rule over all that wherein he had laboured,* and thought that he showed himself wise! It is our interest, therefore, to make sure those riches which will not be left behind, but will go with us to another world.

Verses 3–14

Haman, the chief enemy of the Jews, was hanged, Mordecai and Esther, their chief friends, were sufficiently protected; but many others there were in the king's dominions that hated the Jews and desired their ruin, and to their rage and malice all the rest of that people lay exposed; for the edict against them was still in force, and, in pursuance of it, their enemies would on the day appointed fall upon them, and they would be deemed as rebels against the king and his government if they should offer to resist and take up arms in their own defence. For the preventing of this,

I. The queen here makes intercession with much affection and importunity. She came, a second time, uncalled into the king's presence (*v.* 3), and was as before encouraged to present her petition, by the king's holding out the golden sceptre to her, *v.* 4. Her petition is that the king, having put away Haman, would put away the mischief of Haman and his device against the Jews, that that might not take place now that he was taken off. Many a man's mischief survives him, and the wickedness he devised operates when he is gone. What men project and write may, after their death, be either very profitable or very pernicious. It was therefore requisite in this case that, for the defeating of Haman's plot, they should apply to the king for a further act of grace, that by another edict he would reverse the letters devised by Haman, and which he wrote (she does not say which the king *consented to and confirmed with his own seal;* she leaves it to his own conscience to say that), by which he took an effectual course to *destroy the Jews in all the king's provinces, v.* 5. If the king were indeed, as he seemed to be, troubled that such a decree was made, he could not do less than revoke it; for what is repentance, but undoing, to the utmost of our power, what we have done amiss? 1. This petition Esther presents with much affection: She *fell down at the king's feet and besought him with tears* (*v.* 3), every tear as precious as any of the pearls with which she was adorned. It was time to be earnest when the church of God lay at stake. Let none be so great as to be unwilling to stoop, none so merry as to be unwilling to weep, when thereby they may do any service to God's church and people. Esther, though safe herself, fell down, and begged with tears for the deliverance of her people. 2. She expresses it with great submission, and a profound deference to the king and his wisdom and will (*v.* 5): *If it please the king and if I have found favour in his sight* — and again, "If the thing itself seem right and reasonable before the king, and if I that ask it *be pleasing in his eyes,* let the decree be reversed." Even when we have the utmost reason and justice on our side, and have the clearest cause to plead, yet it becomes us to speak to our superiors with humility and modesty, and all possible expressions of respect, and not to talk like demandants when we are supplicants. There is nothing lost be decency and good breeding. As *soft answers turn away wrath,* so soft askings obtain favour. 3. She enforces her petition with a pathetic plea: *"For how can I endure to see the evil that shall come upon my people?* Little comfort can I have of my own life if I cannot prevail for theirs: as good share in the evil myself as see it come upon them; for *how can I endure to see the destruction of my kindred,* that are dear to me?" Esther, a queen, owns her poor kindred, and speaks of them with a very tender concern. Now it was that she mingled her tears with her words, that *she wept and made supplication;* we read of no tears when she begged for her own life, but, now that she was sure of that, she wept for her people. Tears of pity and tenderness are the most Christ-like. Those that are truly concerned for the public would rather die in the last ditch than live to see the desolations of the church of God and the ruin of their country. Tender spirits cannot bear to think of the destruction of their people and kindred, and therefore dare not omit any opportunity of giving them relief.

II. The king here takes a course for the preventing of the mischief that Haman had designed. 1. The king knew, and informed the queen, that, according to the constitution of the Persian government, the former edict could not be revoked (*v.* 8): What is *written in the king's name, and sealed with the king's ring,* may not, under any pretence whatsoever, be reversed. This was a fundamental article of their *magna charta,* that no law or decree, when once it had passed the royal assent, could be repealed or recalled, no judgment vacated, no attainder reversed, Dan. 6:15. This is so far from bespeaking the wisdom and honour of the Medes and Persians that really it bespeaks their pride and folly, and consequently their shame. It is ridiculous in itself for any man, or company of men, to pretend to such an infallibility of wisdom as to foresee all the consequences of what they decree; and therefore it is unjust, and injurious to mankind, to claim such a supremacy of power as to make their decrees irrevocable, whether the consequences prove good or bad. This savours of that old presumption which ruined us all: *We will be as gods.* Much more prudent is that proviso of our constitution, that no law can, by any words or sanctions whatsoever, be made unrepealable, any more than any estate unalienable. *Cujus est instruere, ejus est destruere — the right to enact implies the right to repeal.* It is God's prerogative not to repent, and to say what can never be altered or unsaid. 2. Yet he found an expedient to undo the devices of Haman, and defeat his design, by signing and publishing another decree to authorize the Jews to stand upon their defence, *vim vi repellere, et invasorem occidere — to oppose force to force, and destroy the assailant.* This would be their effectual security. The king shows them that he had done enough already to convince them that he had a concern for the Jewish nation, for he had ordered his favourite to be hanged *because he laid his hand upon the Jews* (*v.* 7), and he therefore would d the utmost he could to protect them; and he leaves it as fully with Esther and Mordecai to use his name and power for their deliverance as before he had left it with Haman to use his name and power for their destruction: *"Write for the Jews as it liketh you* (*v.* 8), saving only the honour of our constitution. Let the mischief be put away as effectually as may be without reversing the letters." The secretaries of state were ordered to attend to draw up this edict on the twenty-third day of the third month (*v.* 9), about two months after the promulgation of the former, but nine months before the time set for its execution: it was to be drawn up and published in the respective languages of all the provinces. Shall the subjects of an earthly prince have his decrees in a language they understand? and shall God's oracles and laws be locked up from his servants in an unknown tongue? It was to be directed to the proper officers of every province, both to the justices of peace and to the deputy-lieutenants. It was to be carefully dispersed throughout all the king's dominions, and true copies sent by expresses to all the provinces. The purport of this decree was to commission the Jews, upon the day which was appointed for their destruction, to draw together in a body for their own defence. And, (1.) To stand for their life, that, whoever assaulted them, it might be at their peril. (2.) They might not only act defensively, but might *destroy, and slay, and cause to perish, all the power of the people that would assault them, men, women, and children* (*v.* 11), and thus *to avenge themselves on their enemies* (*v.* 13), and, if they pleased, to enrich themselves by their enemies, for they were empowered to take the spoil of them for a prey. Now, [1.] This showed his kindness to the Jews, and sufficiently provided for their safety; for he latter decree would be looked upon as a tacit revocation of the former, though not in expression. But, [2.] It shows the absurdity of that branch of their constitution that none of the king's edicts might be repealed; for it laid the king here under a necessity of enacting a civil war in his own dominions, between the Jews and their enemies, so that both sides took up arms *by* his authority, and yet *against* his authority. No better could come of men's pretending to be wise above what is given them. Great expedition was used in dispersing this decree, the king himself being in pain lest it should come too late and any mischief should be done to the Jews by virtue of the former decree before the notice of this arrived. It was therefore *by the king's commandment,* as well as Mordecai's, that the messengers were *hastened and pressed on* (*v.* 14), and had swift beasts provided them, *v.* 10. It was not a time to trifle when so many lives were in danger.

Verses 15–17

It was but a few days ago that we had Mordecai in sackcloth and all the Jews in sorrow; but here is a blessed change, Mordecai in purple and all the Jews in joy. See Ps. 30:5, 11, 12. 1. Mordecai in purple, *v.* 15. Having obtained an order for the relief of all the Jews, he was easy, he parted with his mourning weeds, and put on the *royal apparel,* which either belonged to his place or which the king appointed him as a favourite. His robes were rich, *blue and white, of fine linen and purple;* so was his coronet: it was *of gold.* These are things not worth taking notice of, but as they were marks of the king's favour, and *that* the fruit of God's favour to his church. It is well with a land when the ensigns of dignity are made the ornaments of serious piety. The *city Shushan* was sensible of its advantage in the preferment of Mordecai, and therefore *rejoiced and was glad,* not only pleased in general with the advancement of virtue, but promising itself, in particular, better times, now that so good a man was entrusted with power. Haman was hanged; *and, when the wicked perish, there is shouting,* Prov. 11:10. Mordecai was preferred; and, *when the righteous are in authority, the people rejoice.* 2. The Jews in joy, *v.* 16, 17. The Jews, who awhile ago were under a dark cloud, dejected and disgraced, now had *light and gladness, joy and honour, a feast and a good lay.* If they had not been threatened and in distress they would not have had occasion for this extraordinary joy. Thus are God's people sometimes made *to sow in tears* that they may *reap in* so much the more *joy.* The suddenness and strangeness of the turn of affairs in their favour added much to their joy. They were *like those that dream; then was their mouth filled with laughter,* Ps. 126:1, 2. One good effect of this deliverance was that *many of the people of the land,* that were considerate, sober, and well inclined, became Jews, were proselyted to the Jewish religion, renounced idolatry, and worshipped the true God only. Haman thought to extirpate the Jews, but it proves, in the issue, that their numbers are greatly increased and many added to the church. Observe, When *the Jews had joy and gladness* then *many of the people of the land became Jews.* The holy cheerfulness of those that profess religion is a great ornament to their profession, and will invite and encourage others to be religious. The reason here given why so many became Jews at this time is because *the fear of the Jews fell upon them.* When they observed how wonderfully divine Providence had owned them and wrought for them in this critical juncture, (1.) They thought them great, and considered those happy that were among them; and therefore they came over to them, as was foretold, Zec. 8:23. *We will go with you, for we have heard,* we have seen, *that God is with you, the shield of your help, and the sword of your excellency,* Deu. 33:29. When the church prospers, and is smiled upon, many will come into it that will be shy of it when it is in trouble. (2.) They thought them formidable, and considered those miserable that were against them. They plainly saw in Haman's fate that, if any offered injury to the Jews, it was at their peril; and therefore, for their own security, they joined themselves to them. It is folly to think of contending with the God of Israel, and therefore it is wisdom to think of submitting to him.

CHAPTER 9

We left two royal edicts in force, both given at the court of Shushan, one bearing date the thirteenth day of the first month, appointing that on the thirteenth day of the twelfth month then next ensuing all the Jews should be killed; another bearing date the twenty-third day of the third month, empowering the Jews, on the day appointed for their slaughter, to draw the sword in their own defence and make their part good against their enemies as well as they could. Great expectation there was, no doubt, of this day, and the issue of it. The Jews' cause was to be tried by battle and the day was fixed for the combat by authority. Their enemies resolved not to lose the advantages given them by the first edict, in hope to overpower them by numbers; the Jews relied on the goodness of their God and the justice of their cause, and resolved to make their utmost efforts against their enemies. The day comes at length; and here we are told, I. What a glorious day it was, that year, to the Jews, and the two days following — a day of victory and triumph, both in the city Shushan and in all the rest of the king's provinces (*v.* 1–19). II. What a memorable day it was made to posterity, by an annual feast, in commemoration of this great deliverance, called "the feast of Purim," (*v.* 20–32).

Verses 1–19

We have here a decisive battle fought between the Jews and their enemies, in which the Jews were victorious. Neither side was surprised; for both had notice of it long enough before, so that it was a fair trial of skill between them. Nor could either side call the other *rebels,* for they were both supported by the royal authority.

I. The enemies of the Jews were the aggressors. They

hoped, notwithstanding the latter edict, *to have power over them*, by virtue of the former (*v.* 1), and made assaults upon them accordingly; they formed themselves into bodies, and joined in confederacy against them, to *seek their hurt, v.* 2. The Chaldee paraphrase says that none appeared against the Jews but Amalekites only, who were infatuated, and had their hearts hardened, as Pharaoh's against Israel, to take up arms to their own destruction. Some had such an inveterate implacable malice against the Jews that Haman's fall and Mordecai's advancement, instead of convincing them, did but exasperate them, and make them the more outrageous and resolute to cut all their throats. The sons of Haman, particularly, vowed to avenge their father's death, and pursue his designs, which they call *noble and brave*, whatever hazards they run; and a strong party they had formed both in Shushan and in the provinces in order hereunto. Fight they would, though they plainly saw Providence fight against them; and thus they were infatuated to their own destruction. If they would have sat still, and attempted nothing against the people of God, not a hair of their head would have fallen to the ground: but they cannot persuade themselves to do that; they must be meddling, though it prove to their own ruin, and roll a burdensome stone, which will return upon them.

II. But the Jews were the conquerors. That very day when the king's decree for their destruction was to be put in execution, and which the enemies thought would have been *their* day, proved *God's* day, Ps. 37:13. It was *turned to the contrary* of what was expected, and *the Jews had rule over those that hated them, v.* 1. We are here told,

1. What the Jews did for themselves (*v.* 2): *They gathered themselves together in their cities*, embodied, and stood upon their defence, offering violence to none, but bidding defiance to all. If they had not had an edict to warrant them, they durst not have done it, but, being so supported, they strove lawfully. Had they acted separately, each family apart, they would have been an easy prey to their enemies; but acting in concert, and gathering together in their cities, they strengthened one another, and durst face their enemies. *Vis unita fortior — forces act most powerfully when combined*. Those that write of the state of the Jews at this day give this as a reason why, though they are very numerous in many parts, and very rich, they are yet so despicable, because they are generally so selfish that they cannot incorporate, and, being under the curse of dispersion, they cannot unite, nor (as here) *gather together*, for, if they could, they might with their numbers and wealth threaten the most potent states.

2. What the rulers of the provinces did for them, under the influence of Mordecai. All the officers of the king, who, by the bloody edict, were ordered to help forward their destruction (*ch.* 3:12, 13), conformed to the latter edict (which, being an estopel against an estopel, had set the matter at large, and left them at liberty to observe which they pleased) and *helped the Jews*, which turned the scale on their side, *v.* 3. The provinces would generally do as the rulers of the provinces inclined, and therefore their favouring the Jews would greatly further them. But why did they help them? Not because they had any kindness for them, but because *the fear of Mordecai fell upon them*, he having manifestly the countenance both of God and the king. They all saw it their interest to help Mordecai's friends because he was not only great in the king's house, and caressed by the courtiers (as many are who have no intrinsic worth to support their reputation), but *his fame* for wisdom and virtue *went out* thence *throughout all the provinces:* in all places he was extolled as a great man. He was looked upon also as a thriving man, and one that *waxed greater and greater* (*v.* 4), and therefore for fear of him all the king's officers helped the Jews. Great men may, by their influence, do a great deal of good; many that fear not God will stand in awe of them.

3. What God did for them: he struck *all people* with a *fear of them* (*v.* 2), as the Canaanites were made afraid of Israel (Jos. 2:9, 5:1), so that, though they had so much hardiness as to assault them, yet they had not courage to prosecute the assault. Their hearts failed them when they came to engage, and *none of the men of might could find their hands.*

4. What execution they did hereupon: *No man could withstand them* (*v.* 2), but *they did what they would to those that hated them, v.* 5. So strangely were the Jews strength-

ened and animated, and their enemies weakened and dispirited, that none of those who had marked themselves for their destruction escaped, but they *smote them with the stroke of the sword*. Particularly, (1.) On the thirteenth day of the month Adar they slew in the city Shushan 500 men (*v.* 6) and the ten sons of *Haman, v.* 10. The Jews, when on the feast of Purim they read this book of Esther, oblige themselves to read the names of Haman's ten sons all in one breath, without any pause, because they say that they were all killed together, and all gave up the ghost just in the same moment. — *Buxt. Synag. Jud.* c. 24. The Chaldee paraphrase says that, when these ten were slain, Zeresh, with seventy more of his children, escaped, and afterwards begged their bread from door to door. (2.) On the fourteenth day they slew in Shushan 300 more, who had escaped the sword on the former day of execution, *v.* 15. This Esther obtained leave of the king for them to do, for the greater terror of their enemies, and the utter crushing of that malignant party of men. The king had taken account of the numbers that were put to the sword the first day (*v.* 11), and told Esther (*v.* 12), and asked her what more she desired. "Nothing," says she, "but commission to do such another day's work." Esther surely was none of the blood-thirsty, none of those that delight in slaughter, but she had some very good reasons that moved her to make this request. She also desired that the dead bodies of Haman's ten sons might be hanged up on the gallows on which their father was hanged, for the greater disgrace of the family and terror of the party (*v.* 13), and it was done accordingly, *v.* 14. It is supposed that they were hanged in chains and left hanging for some time. (3.) The Jews in the country kept to their orders, and slew no more of their enemies than what were slain the thirteenth day, which were in all, among all the provinces, 75,000, *v.* 16. If all these were Amalekites (as the Jews say), surely now it was that the remembrance of Amalek was *utterly put out*, Ex. 17:14. However, that which justifies them in the execution of so many is that they did it in their own just and necessary defence; they *stood for their lives*, authorized to do so by the law of self-preservation, as well as by the king's decree. (4.) In these several executions it is taken notice of that on the prey they laid not their hand, *v.* 10, 15, 16. The king's commission had warranted them to *take the spoil* of their enemies *for a prey* (*ch.* 8:11), and a fair opportunity they had of enriching themselves with it; if Haman's party had prevailed, no doubt, they would have made use of their authority to seize the goods and estates of the Jews, *ch.* 3:13. But the Jews would not do so by them, [1.] That they might, to the honour of their religion, evidence a holy and generous contempt of worldly wealth, in imitation of their father Abraham, who scorned to enrich himself with the spoils of Sodom. [2.] That they might make it appear that they aimed at nothing but their own preservation, and used their interest at court for the saving of their lives, not for the raising of their estates. [3.] Their commission empowered them to destroy the families of their enemies, even the *little ones* and *the women, ch.* 8:11. But their humanity forbade them to do that, though that was designed against them. They slew none but those they found in arms; and therefore they did not take the spoil, but left it to the women and little ones, whom they spared, for their subsistence; otherwise as good slay them as starve them, take away their lives as take away their livelihoods. Herein they acted with a consideration and compassion well worthy of imitation.

5. What a satisfaction they had in their deliverance. The Jews in the country cleared themselves of their enemies on the thirteenth day of the month, and they rested on the fourteenth day (*v.* 17), and made that a thanksgiving day, *v.* 19. The Jews in Shushan, the royal city, took two days for their military execution, so that they rested on the fifteenth day, and made that their thanksgiving-day, *v.* 18. Both of them celebrated their festival the very day after they had finished their work and gained their point. When we have received signal mercies from God we ought to be quick and speedy in making our thankful returns to him, while the mercy is fresh and the impressions of it are most sensible.

Verses 20–32

We may well imagine how much affected Mordecai and Esther were with the triumphs of the Jews over their en-

emies, and how they saw the issue of that decisive day with a satisfaction proportionable to the care and concern with which they expected it. How were their hearts enlarged with joy in God and his salvation, and what new songs of praise were put into their mouths! But here we are told what course they took to spread the knowledge of it among their people, and to perpetuate the remembrance of it to posterity, for the honour of God and the encouragement of his people to trust in him at all times.

I. The history was written, and copies of it were dispersed among all the Jews in all the provinces of the empire, *both nigh and far, v.* 20. They all knew something of the story, being nearly concerned in it — were by the first edict made sensible of their danger and by the second of their deliverance; but how this amazing turn was given they could not tell. Mordecai therefore *wrote all these things*. And if this book be the same that he wrote, as many think it is, I cannot but observe what a difference there is between Mordecai's style and Nehemiah's. Nehemiah, at every turn, takes notice of divine Providence and the *good hand of his God* upon him, which is very proper to stir up devout affections in the minds of his readers; but Mordecai never so much as mentions the name of God in the whole story. Nehemiah wrote his book at Jerusalem, where religion was in fashion and an air of it appeared in men's common conversation; Mordecai wrote his at Shushan the palace, where policy reigned more then piety, and he wrote according to the genius of the place. Even those that have the root of the matter in them are apt to lose the savour of religion, and let their leaf wither, when they converse wholly with those that have little religion. Commend me to Nehemiah's way of writing; *that* I would imitate, and yet learn from Mordecai's that men may be truly devout though they do not abound in the shows and expressions of devotion, and therefore that we must not judge nor despise our brethren. But, because there is so little of the language of Canaan in this book, many think it was not written by Mordecai, but was an extract out of the journals of the kings of Persia, giving an account of the matter of fact, which the Jews themselves knew how to comment upon.

II. A festival was instituted, to be observed yearly from generation to generation by the Jews, in remembrance of this wonderful work which God wrought for them, that *the children who should be born* might know it, and *declare it to their children, that they might set their hope in God*, Ps. 78:6, 7. It would be for the honour of God as the protector of his people, and the honour of Israel as the care of Heaven, a confirmation of the fidelity of God's covenant, an invitation to strangers to come into the bonds of it, and an encouragement to God's own people cheerfully to depend upon his wisdom, power, and goodness, in the greatest straits. Posterity would reap the benefit of this deliverance, and therefore ought to celebrate the memorial of it. Now concerning this festival we are here told,

1. When it was observed — every year on *the fourteenth and fifteenth days of the twelfth month*, just a month before the passover, *v.* 21. Thus the first month and the last month of the year kept in remembrance the months that were past, even *the days when God preserved them*. They kept two days together as thanksgiving days, and did not think them too much to spend in praising God. Let us not be niggardly in our returns of praise to him who bestows his favours so liberally upon us. Observe, They did not keep the day when they fought, but the days when they rested, and on the fifteenth those in Shushan, and both those days they kept. The sabbath was appointed not on the day that God finished his work, but on the day that he *rested from it*. The modern Jews observe the thirteenth day, the day appointed for their destruction, as a fasting-day, grounding the practice on *v.* 31, *the matters of their fastings and cry*. But that refers to what was in the day of their distress (*ch.* 4:3, 16), which was not to be continued when God had turned their fasts into *joy and gladness*, Zec. 8:19.

2. How it was called — *The feast of Purim* (*v.* 26), from *Pur*, a Persian word which signified *a lot*, because Haman had by lot determined this to be the time of the Jews' destruction, but the Lord, at whose disposal the lot is, had determined it to be the time of their triumph. The name of this festival would remind them of the sovereign dominion of the God of Israel, who served his own purposes by the foolish superstitions of the heathen, and outwitted

the *monthly prognosticators* in their own craft (Isa. 47:13), *frustrating the tokens of the liars and making the diviners mad,* Isa. 44:25, 26.

3. By whom it was instituted and enacted. It was not a divine institution, and therefore it is not called a *holy day,* but a human appointment, by which it was made a *good day, v.* 19, 22. (1.) The Jews ordained it, and took it upon themselves (*v.* 27), voluntarily *undertook to do as they had begun. v.* 23. They bound themselves to this by common consent. (2.) Mordecai and Esther confirmed their resolve, that it might be the more binding on posterity, and might come well recommended by those great names. They *wrote,* [1.] *With all authority* (*v.* 29), as well they might, Esther being queen and Mordecai prime-minister of state. It is well when those who are in authority use their authority to authorize that which is good. [2.] *With words of peace and truth..* Though they wrote with authority, they wrote with tenderness, not imperious, not imposing, but in such language as the council at Jerusalem use in their decree (Acts 15:29): "If you do so and so, *you shall do well. Fare you well.*" Such was the style of these letters, or such the salutation or valediction of them: *Peace and truth be with you.*

4. By whom it was to be observed — by *all the Jews,* and by *their seed,* and by all such as *joined themselves to them, v.* 27. The observance of this feast was to be both universal and perpetual; the proselytes must observe it, in token of their sincere affection to the Jewish nation and their having united interests with them. A concurrence in joys and praises is one branch of the communion of saints.

5. Why it was to be observed — that the memorial of the great things God had done for his church might never *perish from their seed, v.* 28. God does not work wonders for a day, but to be had in everlasting remembrance. *What he does shall be for ever,* and therefore should for ever be had in mind, Eccl. 3:14. In this affair they would remember, (1.) Haman's bad practices against the church, to his perpetual reproach (*v.* 24): *Because he had devised against the Jews to destroy them.* Let this be kept in mind, that God's people may never be secure, while they have such malicious enemies, on whom they ought to have a jealous eye. Their enemies aim at no less then their destruction; on God therefore let them depend for salvation. (2.) Esther's good services to the church, to her immortal honour. When Esther, in peril of her life, *came before the king,* he repealed the edict, *v.* 25. This also must be remembered, that wherever this feast should be kept, and this history read in explication of it, this which she did might be *told for a memorial of her.* Good deeds done for the Israel of God ought to be remembered, for the encouragement of others to do the like. God will not forget them, and therefore we must not. (3.) Their own prayers, and the answers given to them (*v.* 31): *The matters of their fastings and their cry.* The more cries we have offered up in our trouble, and the more prayers for deliverance, the more we are obliged to be thankful to God for deliverance. *Call upon me in the time of trouble,* and then *offer to God thanksgiving.*

6. How it was to be observed. And of this let us see, (1.) What was here enjoined, which was very good, that they should make it, [1.] A day of cheerfulness, *a day of feasting and joy* (*v.* 22), and *a feast was made for laughter,* Eccl. 10:19. When God gives us cause to rejoice why should we not express our joy? [2.] A day of generosity, *sending portions one to another,* in token of their pleasantness and mutual respect, and their being knit by this and other public common dangers and deliverances so much the closer to each other in love. Friends have their goods in common. [3.] A day of charity, sending *gifts to the poor.* It is not to our kinsmen and rich neighbours only that we are to send tokens, but to *the poor and the maimed,* Lu. 14:12, 13. Those that have received mercy must, in token of their gratitude, show mercy; and there never wants occasion, for the poor we have always with us. Thanksgiving and almsgiving should go together, that, when we are rejoicing and blessing God, the heart of the poor may rejoice with us and their loins may bless us.

(2.) What was added to this, which was much better. They always, at the feast, read the whole story over in the synagogue each day, and put up three prayers to God, in the first of which they praise God for counting them worthy to attend this divine service; in the second they thank him for the miraculous preservation of their ancestors; in the third they praise him that they have lived to observe another festival in memory of it. So bishop Patrick.

(3.) What it has since degenerated to, which is much worse. Their own writers acknowledge that this feast is commonly celebrated among them with gluttony, and drunkenness, and excess of riot. Their Talmud says expressly that, in the feast of Purim, a man should drink till he knows not the difference between *Cursed be Haman,* and *Blessed be Mordecai.* See what the corrupt and wicked nature of man often brings that to which was at first well intended: here is a religious feast turned into a carnival, a perfect revel, as wakes are among us. Nothing more purifies the heart and adorns religion than holy joy; nothing more pollutes the heart and reproaches religion than carnal mirth and sensual pleasure. *Corruptio optimi est pessima — What is best becomes when corrupted the worst.*

CHAPTER 10

This is but a part of a chapter; the rest of it, beginning at *v.* 4, with six chapters more, being found only in the Greek, is rejected as apocryphal. In these three verses we have only some short hints, I. Concerning Ahasuerus in the throne, what a mighty prince he was (*v.* 1, 2). II. Concerning Mordecai his favourite, what a distinguished blessing he was to his people (*v.* 2, 3).

Verses 1–3

We are here told,

I. How great and powerful king Ahasuerus was. He had a vast dominion, both in the continent and among the islands, from which he raised a vast revenue. Besides the usual customs which the kings of Persia exacted (Ezra 4:13), he laid an additional tribute upon his subjects, to serve for some great occasion he had for money (*v.* 1): *The king laid a tribute.* Happy is our island, that pays no tribute but what is laid upon it by its representatives, and those of its own choosing, and is not squeezed or oppressed by an arbitrary power, as some of the neighbouring nations are. Besides this instance of the grandeur of Ahasuerus, many more might be given, that were *acts of his power and of his might.* These however are not thought fit to be recorded here in the sacred story, which is confined to the Jews, and relates the affairs of other nations only as they fell in with their affairs; but they are *written in the Persian chronicles* (*v.* 2), which are long since lost and buried in oblivion, while the sacred writings live, live in honour, and will live till time shall be no more. When the *kingdoms of men,* monarchs and monarchies, are destroyed, and *their memorial has perished with them* (Ps. 9:6), the kingdom of God among men, and the records of that kingdom, shall remain and be *as the days of heaven,* Dan. 2:44.

II. How great and good Mordecai was.

1. He was great; and it does one good to see virtue and piety thus in honour. (1.) He was great with the king, next to him, as one he most delighted and confided in. Long had Mordecai sat contentedly in the king's gate, and now at length he is advanced to the head of his council-board. Men of merit may for a time seem buried alive; but often, by some means or other, they are discovered and preferred at last. The declaration of the greatness to which the king advanced Mordecai was *written in the chronicles of the kingdom,* as very memorable, and contributing to the great achievements of the king. He never did such acts of power as he did when Mordecai was his right hand. (2.) He was *great among the Jews* (*v.* 3), not only great above them, more honourable than any of them, but great with them, dear to them, familiar with them, and much respected by them. So far were they from envying his preferment that they rejoiced in it, and added to it by giving him a commanding interest among them and submitting all their affairs to his direction.

2. He was good, very good, for he did good. This goodness made him truly great, and then his greatness gave him an opportunity of doing so much the more good. When the king advanced him, (1.) He did not disown his people the Jews, nor was he ashamed of his relation to them, though they were strangers and captives, dispersed and despised. Still he wrote himself *Mordecai the Jew,* and therefore no doubt adhered to the Jews' religion, by the observances of which he distinguished himself, and yet it was no hindrance to his preferment, nor looked upon as a blemish to him. (2.) He did not seek his own wealth, or the raising of an estate for himself and his family, which is the chief thing most aim at when they get into great places at court; but he consulted the welfare of his people, and made it his business to advance that. His power, his wealth, and all his interest in the king and queen, he improved for the public good. (3.) He not only did good, but he did it in a humble condescending way, was easy of access, courteous and affable in his behaviour, and spoke peace to all that made their application to him. Doing good works is the best and chief thing expected from those that have wealth and power; but giving good words is also commendable, and makes the good deed the more acceptable. (4.) He did not side with any one party of his people against another, nor make some his favourites, while the rest were neglected and crushed; but, whatever differences there were among them, he was a common father to them all, recommended himself to *the multitude of his brethren,* not despising the crowd, and spoke peace *to all their seed,* without distinction. Thus making himself acceptable by humility and beneficence, he was universally accepted, and gained the good word of all his brethren. Thanks be to God, such a government as this we are blessed with, which *seeks the welfare of our people, speaking peace to all their seed.* God continue it long, very long, and grant us, under the happy protection and influence of it, to *live quiet and peaceable lives, in godliness, honesty,* and charity!

AN EXPOSITION, WITH PRACTICAL OBSERVATIONS, OF

THE BOOK OF JOB

This book of Job stands by itself, is not connected with any other, and is therefore to be considered alone. Many copies of the Hebrew Bible place it after the book of Psalms, and some after the Proverbs, which perhaps has given occasion to some learned men to imagine it to have been written by Isaiah or some of the later prophets. But, as the subject appears to have been much more ancient, so we have no reason to think but that the composition of the book was, and that therefore it is most fitly placed first in this collection of divine morals: also, being doctrinal, it is proper to precede and introduce the book of Psalms, which is devotional, and the book of Proverbs, which is practical; for how shall we worship or obey a God whom we know not? As to this book,

I. We are sure that it is given by inspiration of God, though we are not certain who was the penman of it. The Jews, though no friends to Job, because he was a stranger to the commonwealth of Israel, yet, as faithful conservators of *the oracles of God* committed to them, always retained this book in their sacred canon. The history is referred to by one apostle (James 5:11) and one passage (*ch.* 5:13) is quoted by another apostle, with the usual form of quoting scripture, *It is written,* 1 Co. 3:19. It is the opinion of many of the ancients that this history was written by Moses himself in Midian, and delivered to his suffering brethren in Egypt, for their support and comfort under their burdens, and the encouragement of their hope that God would in due time deliver and enrich them, as he did this patient sufferer. Some conjecture that it was written originally in Arabic, and afterwards translated into Hebrew, for the use of the Jewish church, by Solomon (so Monsieur Jurieu) or some other inspired writer. It seems most probable to me that Elihu was the penman of it, at least of the discourses, because (*ch.* 32:15, 16) he mingles the words of a historian with those of a disputant: but Moses perhaps wrote the first two chapters and the last, to give light to the discourses; for in them God is frequently called *Jehovah,* but not once in all the discourses, except *ch.* 12:9. That name was but little known to the patriarchs before Moses, Ex. 6:3. If Job wrote it himself, some of the Jewish writers themselves own him a *prophet among the Gentiles;* if Elihu, we find he had a spirit of prophecy which *filled him with matter and constrained him, ch.* 32:18.

II. We are sure that it is, for the substance of it, a true history, and not a romance, though the dialogues are poetical. No doubt there was such a man as Job; the prophet Ezekiel names him with Noah and Daniel, Eze. 14:14. The narrative we have here of his prosperity and piety, his strange afflictions and exemplary patience, the substance of his conferences with his friends, and God's discourse with him out of the whirlwind, with his return at length to a very prosperous condition, no doubt is exactly true, though the inspired penman is allowed the usual liberty of putting the matter of which Job and his friends discoursed into his own words.

III. We are sure that it is very ancient, though we cannot fix the precise time either when Job lived or when the book was written. So many, so evident, are its hoary hairs, the marks of its antiquity, that we have reason to think it of equal date with the book of Genesis itself, and that holy Job was contemporary with Isaac and Jacob; though not coheir with them of the promise of the earthly Canaan, yet a joint-expectant with them of the *better country,* that is, *the heavenly.* Probably he was of the posterity of Nahor, Abraham's brother, whose first-born was *Uz* (Gen. 22:21), and in whose family religion was for some ages kept up, as appears, Gen. 31:53, where God is called, not only *the God of Abraham,* but *the God of Nahor.* He lived before the age of man was shortened to seventy or eighty, as it was in Moses's time, before sacrifices were confined to one altar, before the general apostasy of the nations from the knowledge and worship of the true God, and while yet there was no other idolatry known than the worship of the sun and moon, and that punished by the Judges, *ch.* 31:26–28. He lived while God was known by the name of *God Almighty* more than by the name of *Jehovah;* for he is called *Shaddai — the Almighty,* above thirty times in this book. He lived while divine knowledge was conveyed, not by writing, but by tradition; for to that appeals are here made, *ch.* 8:8; 21:29; 15:18; 5:1. And we have therefore reason to think that he lived before Moses, because here is no mention at all of the deliverance of Israel out of Egypt, or the giving of the law. There is indeed one passage which might be made to allude to the drowning of Pharaoh (*ch.* 26:12): *He divideth the sea with his power, and by his understanding he smiteth through Rahab,* which name Egypt is frequently called by in scripture, as Ps. 87:4; 89:10; Isa. 51:9. But that may as well refer to the proud waves of the sea. We conclude therefore that we are here got back to the patriarchal age, and, besides its authority, we receive this book with veneration for its antiquity.

IV. We are sure that it is of great use to the church, and to every good Christian, though there are many passages in it dark and hard to be understood. We cannot perhaps be confident of the true meaning of every Arabic word and phrase we meet with in it. It is a book that finds a great deal of work for the critics; but enough is plain to make the whole profitable, and it was all written for our learning.

1. This noble poem presents to us, in very clear and lively characters, these five things among others: — (1.) *A monument of primitive theology.* The first and great principles of the light of nature, on which natural religion is founded, are here, in a warm, and long, and learned dispute, not only taken for granted on all sides and not the least doubt made of them, but by common consent plainly laid down as eternal truths, illustrated and urged as affecting commanding truths. Were ever the being of God, his glorious attributes and perfections, his unsearchable wisdom, his irresistible power, his inconceivable glory, his inflexible justice, and his incontestable sovereignty, discoursed of with more clearness, fulness, reverence, and divine eloquence, than in this book? The creation of the world, and the government of it, are here admirably described, not as matters of nice speculation, but as laying most powerful obligations upon us to fear and serve, to submit to and trust in, our Creator, owner, Lord, and ruler. Moral good and evil, virtue and vice, were never drawn more to the life (the beauty of the one and the deformity of the other) than in this book; nor the inviolable rule of God's judgment more plainly laid down, That *happy are the righteous, it shall be well with them;* and *Woe to the wicked, it shall be ill with them.* These are not questions of the schools to keep the learned world in action, nor engines of state to keep the unlearned world in awe; no, it appears by this book that they are sacred truths of undoubted certainty, and which all the wise and sober part of mankind have in every age subscribed and submitted to. (2.) It presents us with *a specimen of Gentile piety.* This great saint descended probably not from Abraham, but Nahor; or, if from Abraham, not from Isaac, but from one of the sons of the concubines that were sent into the east-country (Gen. 25:6); or, if from Isaac, yet not from Jacob, but Esau; so that he was out of the pale of the covenant of peculiarity, no Israelite, no proselyte, and yet none like him for religion, nor such a favourite of heaven upon this earth. It was a truth therefore, before St. Peter perceived it, that *in every nation he that fears God and works righteousness is accepted of him,* Acts 10:35. There were *children of God scattered abroad* (Jn. 11:52) besides the incorporated *children of the kingdom,* Mt. 8:11, 12. (3.) It presents us with *an exposition of the book of Providence,* and a clear and satisfactory solution of many of the difficult and obscure passages of it. The prosperity of the wicked and the afflictions of the righteous have always been reckoned two as hard chapters as any in that book; but they are here expounded, and reconciled with the divine wisdom, purity, and goodness, by the *end of these things.* (4.) It presents us with *a great example of patience* and close adherence to God in the midst of the sorest calamities. Sir Richard Blackmore's most ingenious pen, in his excellent preface to his paraphrase on this book, makes Job a hero proper for an epic poem; for, says he, "He appears brave in distress and valiant in affliction, maintains his virtue, and with that his character, under the most exasperating provocations that the malice of hell could invent, and thereby gives a most noble example of passive fortitude, a character no way inferior to that of the active hero," etc. (5.) It presents us with *an illustrious type of Christ,* the particulars of which we shall endeavour to take notice of as we go along. In general, Job was a great sufferer, was emptied and humbled, but in order to his greater glory. So Christ abased himself, that we might be exalted. The learned bishop Patrick quotes St. Jerome ore than once speaking of Job as a type of Christ, who *for the job that was set before him endured the cross,* who was persecuted, for a time, by men and devils, and seemed forsaken of God too, but was raised to be an intercessor even for his friends and had added affliction to his misery. When the apostle speaks of the *patience of Job* he immediately takes notice of *the end of the Lord,* that is, of the Lord Jesus (as some understand it), typified by Job, James 5:11.

2. In this book we have, (1.) The history of Job's sufferings, and his patience under them (*ch.* 1, 2, not without a mixture of human frailty, *ch.* 3. (2.) A dispute between him and his friends upon them, in which, [1.] The opponents were Eliphaz, Bildad, and Zophar. [2.] The respondent was Job. [3.] The moderators were, *First,* Elihu, *ch.* 32–37. *Secondly,* God himself, *ch.* 38–41. (3.) The issue of all in Job's honour and prosperity, *ch.* 42. Upon the whole, we learn that *many are the afflictions of the righteous, but* that when the Lord *delivers them out of them all* the *trial of their faith will be found to praise, and honour, and glory.*

CHAPTER 1

The history of Job begins here with an account, I. Of his great piety in general (*v.* 1), and in a particular instance (*v.* 5). II. Of his great prosperity (*v.* 2–4). III. Of the malice of Satan against him, and the permission he obtained to try his constancy (*v.* 6–12). IV. Of the surprising troubles that befel him, the ruin of his estate (*v.* 13–17), and the death of his children (*v.* 18, 19). V. Of his exemplary patience and piety under these troubles (*v.* 20–22). In all this he is set forth for an example of suffering affliction, from which no prosperity can secure us, but through which integrity and uprightness will preserve us.

Verses 1–3

Concerning Job we are here told,

I. That he was a man; therefore subject to like passions as we are. He was *Ish,* a worthy man, a man of note and eminency, a magistrate, a man in authority. The country he lived in was the land of Uz, in the eastern part of Arabia, which lay towards Chaldea, near Euphrates, probably not far from Ur of the Chaldees, whence Abraham was called. When God called one good man out of that country, yet he *left not himself without witness,* but raised up another in it to be a *preacher of righteousness.* God has his remnant in all places, sealed ones out of every nation, as well as out of every tribe of Israel, Rev. 7:9. It was the privilege of the land of Uz to have so good a man as Job in it; now it was *Arabia the Happy* indeed: and it was the praise of Job that he was eminently good in so bad a place; the worse others were round about him the better he was. His name *Job,* or *Jjob,* some say, signifies *one hated* and counted as an enemy. Others make it to signify one that grieves or groans; thus the sorrow he carried in his name might be a check to his joy in his prosperity. Dr. Cave derives it from *Jaab — to love,* or *desire,* intimating how welcome his birth was to his parents, and how much he was *the desire of their eyes;* and yet there was a time when he cursed the day of his birth. Who can tell what the day may prove which yet begins with a bright morning?

II. That he was a very good man, eminently pious, and better than his neighbours: *He was perfect and upright.* This is intended to show us, not only what reputation he had among men (that he was generally taken for an honest man), but what was really his character; for it is the judgment of God concerning him, and we are sure that is according to truth. 1. Job was a religious man, *one that feared God,* that is, worshipped him according to his will, and governed himself by the rules of the divine law in every thing. 2. He was sincere in his religion: He was *perfect;* not sinless, as he himself owns (*ch.* 9:20): *If I say I am perfect, I shall be proved perverse.* But, having a respect to all God's commandments, aiming at perfection, he was really as good as he seemed to be, and did not dissemble in his profession of piety; his heart was sound and his eye single. Sincerity is gospel perfection. I know no religion without it. 3. He was upright in his dealings both with God and man, was faithful to his promises, steady in his counsels, true to every trust reposed in him, and made conscience of all he said and did. See Isa. 33:15. Though he was not *of* Israel, he was indeed an *Israelite without guile.* 4. The fear of God reigning in his heart was the principle that governed his whole conversation. This made him perfect and upright, inward and entire for God, universal and uniform in religion; this kept him close and constant to his duty. He *feared God,* had a reverence for his majesty, a regard to his authority, and a dread of his wrath. 5. He dreaded the thought of doing what was wrong; with the utmost abhorrence and detestation, and with a constant care and watchfulness, he *eschewed evil,* avoided all appearances of sin and approaches to it, and this *because of the fear of God,* Neh. 5:15. *The fear of the Lord is to hate evil* (Prov. 8:13) and then *by the fear of the Lord men depart from evil,* Prov. 16:6.

III. That he was a man who prospered greatly in this world, and made a considerable figure in his country. He was prosperous and yet pious. Though it is hard and rare, it is not impossible, for *a rich man to enter into the kingdom of heaven.* With God even this is possible, and by his grace the temptations of worldly wealth are not insuperable. He was pious, and his piety was a friend to his prosperity; for godliness has the promise of the life that now is. He was prosperous, and his prosperity put a lustre upon his piety, and gave him who was so good so much greater opportunity of doing good. The acts of his piety were grateful returns to God for the instances of his prosperity; and, in the abundance of the good things God gave him, he served God the more cheerfully. 1. He had a numerous family. He was eminent for religion, and yet not a hermit, not a recluse, but the father and master of a family. It was an instance of his prosperity that his house was filled with children, which are a *heritage of the Lord,* and his *reward,* Ps. 127:3. he had *seven sons and three daughters, v.* 2. Some of each sex, and more of the more noble sex, in which the family is built up. Children must be looked upon as blessings, for so they are, especially to good people, that will give them good instructions, and set them good examples, and put up good prayers for them. Job had many children, and yet he was neither oppressive nor uncharitable, but very liberal to the poor, *ch.* 31:17, etc. Those that have great families to provide for ought to consider that what is prudently given in alms is set out to the best interest and put into the best fund for their children's benefit. 2. He had a good estate for the support of his family; his *substance* was considerable, *v.* 3. Riches are called *substance,* in conformity to the common form of speaking; otherwise, to the soul and another world, they are but shadows, *things that are not,* Prov. 23:5. It is only in heavenly wisdom that we *inherit substance,* Prov. 8:21. In those days, when the earth was not fully peopled, it was as now in some of the plantations, men might have land enough upon easy terms if they had but wherewithal to stock it; and therefore Job's substance is described, not by the acres of land he was lord of, but, (1.) By his cattle — *sheep and camels, oxen and asses.* The numbers of each are here set down, probably not the exact number, but thereabout, a very few under or over. The sheep are put first, because of most use in the family, as Solomon observes (Prov. 27:23, 26, 27): *Lambs for thy clothing, and milk for the food of thy household.* Job, it is likely, had silver and gold as well as Abraham (Gen. 13:2); but then men valued their own and their neighbours' estates by that which was for service and present use more than by that which was for show and state, and fit only to be hoarded. As soon as God had made man, and provided for his maintenance by the herbs and fruits, he made him rich and great by giving him *dominion over the creatures,* Gen. 1:28. That therefore being still continued to man, notwithstanding his defection (Gen. 9:2), is still to be reckoned one of the most considerable instances of men's wealth, honour, and power, Ps. 8:6. (2.) By his servants. He had a very good household or husbandry, many that were employed for him and maintained by him; and thus he both had honour and did good; yet thus he was involved in a great deal of care and put to a great deal of charge. See the vanity of this world; as goods are increased those must be increased that tend them and occupy them, and *those will be increased that eat them; and what good has the owner thereof save the beholding of them with his eyes?* Eccles. 5:11. In a word, *Job was the greatest of all the men of the east;* and they were the richest in the world: those were rich indeed who were *replenished more than the east,* Isa. 2:6. Margin. Job's wealth, with his wisdom, entitled him to the honour and power he had in his country, which he describes (*ch.* 29), and made him sit chief. Job was upright and honest, and yet grew rich, nay, *therefore* grew rich; for honesty is the best policy, and piety and charity are ordinarily the surest ways of thriving. He had a great household and much business, and yet kept up the fear and worship of God; and he and his house served the Lord. The account of Job's piety and prosperity comes before the history of his great afflictions, to show that neither will secure us from the common, no, nor from the uncommon calamities of human life. Piety will not secure us, as Job's mistaken friends thought, for *all things come alike to all;* prosperity will not, as a careless world thinks, Isa. 47:8. I sit *as a queen* and therefore shall *see no sorrow.*

Verses 4–5

We have here a further account of Job's prosperity and his piety.

I. His great comfort in his children is taken notice of as an instance of his prosperity; for our temporal comforts are borrowed, depend upon others, and are as those about us are. Job himself mentions it as one of the greatest joys of his prosperous estate that his *children were about him, ch.* 29:5. They kept a circular feast at some certain times (*v.* 4); they *went and feasted in their houses.* It was a comfort to this good man, 1. To see his children grown up and settled in the world. All his sons were in houses of their own, probably married, and to each of them he had given a competent portion to set up with. Those that had been olive-plants round his table were removed to tables of their own. 2. To see them thrive in their affairs, and able to feast one another, as well as to feed themselves. Good parents desire, promote, and rejoice in, their children's wealth and prosperity as their own. 3. To see them in health, no sickness in their houses, for that would have spoiled their feasting and turned it into mourning. 4. Especially to see them live in love, and unity, and mutual good affection, no jars or quarrels among them, no strangeness, no shyness one of another, no strait-handedness, but, though every one knew his own, they lived with as much freedom as if they had had all in common. It is comfortable to the hearts of parents, and comely in the eyes of all, to see brethren thus knit together. *Behold, how good and how pleasant it is!* Ps. 133:1. 5. It added to his comfort to see the brothers so kind to their sisters, that they sent for them to feast with them; for they were so modest that they would not have gone if they had not been sent for. Those brothers that slight their sisters, care not for their company, and have no concern for their comfort, are ill-bred, ill-natured, and very unlike Job's sons. It seems their feast was so sober and decent that their sisters were good company for them at it. 6. They feasted in their own houses, not in public houses, where they would be more exposed to temptations, and which were not so creditable. We do not find that Job himself feasted with them. Doubtless they invited him, and he would have been the most welcome guest at any of their tables; nor was it from any sourness or moroseness of temper, or for want of natural affection, that he kept away, but he was old and dead to these things, like Barzillai (2 Sa. 19:35), and considered that the young people would be more free and pleasant if there were none but themselves. Yet he would not restrain his children from that diversion which he denied himself. Young people may be allowed a youthful liberty, provided they flee youthful lusts.

II. His great care about his children is taken notice of as an instance of his piety: for that we are really which we are relatively. Those that are good will be good to their children, and especially do what they can for the good of their souls. Observe (*v.* 5) Job's pious concern for the spiritual welfare of his children,

1. He was jealous over them with a godly jealousy; and so we ought to be over ourselves and those that are dearest to us, as far as is necessary to our care and endeavour for their good. Job had given his children a good education, had comfort in them and good hope concerning them; and yet he said, *"It may be, my sons have sinned* in the days of their feasting more than at other times, have been too merry, have taken too great a liberty in eating and drinking, and have *cursed God in their hearts,"* that is, "have entertained atheistical or profane thoughts in their minds, unworthy notions of God and his providence, and the exercises of religion." When they were *full* they were ready to *deny God, and to say, Who is the Lord?* (Prov. 30:9), ready to *forget* God and to say, The *power of our hand* has *gotten us this wealth,* Deu. 8:12, etc. Nothing alienates the mind more from God than the indulgence of the flesh.

2. As soon as the days of their feasting were over he called them to the solemn exercises of religion. Not while their feasting lasted (let them take their time for that; there is a time for all things), but when it was over, their good father reminded them that they must know when to desist, and not think to fare sumptuously every day; though they had their days of feasting the *week* round, they must not think to have them the *year* round; they had something else to do. Note, Those that are merry must find a time to be serious.

3. He sent to them to prepare for solemn ordinances, *sent and sanctified them,* ordered them to examine their own consciences and repent of what they had done amiss in their feasting, to lay aside their vanity and compose themselves for religious exercises. Thus he kept his authority over them for their good, and they submitted to it, though they had got into houses of their own. Still he was the priest of the family, and at his altar they all attended, valuing their share in his prayers more than their share in his estate. Parents cannot give grace to their children (it is God that sanctifies), but they ought by seasonable admonitions and counsels to further their sanctification. In their baptism they were sanctified to God; let it be our desire and endeavour that they may be sanctified for him.

4. He offered sacrifice for them, both to atone for the sins he feared they had been guilty of in the days of their feasting and to implore for them mercy to pardon and grace to prevent the debauching of their minds and corrupting of their manners by the liberty they had taken, and to preserve their piety and purity.

> For he with mournful eyes had often spied,
> Scattered on Pleasure's smooth but treacherous tide,
> The spoils of virtue overpowered by sense,
> And floating wrecks of ruined innocence.
> — Sir R. Blackmore.

Job, like Abraham, had an altar for his family, on which, it is likely, he offered sacrifice daily; but, on this extraordinary occasion, he offered more sacrifices than usual, and with more solemnity, *according to the number of them all,* one for each child. Parents should be particular in their addresses to God for the several branches of their family. "For this child I prayed, according to its particular temper, genius, and condition," to which the prayers, as well as the endeavours, must be accommodated. When these sacrifices were to be offered, (1.) He rose early, as one in care that his children might not lie long under guilt and as one whose heart was upon his work and his desire towards it. (2.) He required his children to attend the sacrifice, that they might join with him in the prayers he offered with the sacrifice, that the sight of the killing of the sacrifice might humble them much for their sins, for which they deserved to die, and the sight of the offering of it up might lead them to a Mediator. This serious work would help to make them serious again after the days of their gaiety.

5. Thus he did *continually,* and not merely whenever an occasion of this kind recurred; for *he that is washed needs to wash his feet,* Jn. 13:10. The acts of repentance and faith must be often renewed, because we often repeat our transgressions. All days, every day, he offered up his sacrifices, was constant to his devotions, and did not omit them any day. The occasional exercises of religion will not excuse us from those that are stated. He that serves God uprightly will serve him continually.

Verses 6–12

Job was not only so rich and great, but withal so wise and good, and had such an interest both in heaven and earth, that one would think the mountain of his prosperity stood so strong that it could not be moved; but here we have a thick cloud gathering over his head, pregnant with a horrible tempest. We must never think ourselves secure from storms while we are in this lower region. Before we are told how his troubles surprised and seized him here in this visible world, we are here told how they were concerted in the world of spirits, that the devil, having a great enmity to Job for his eminent piety, begged and obtained leave to torment him. It does not at all derogate from the credibility of Job's story in general to allow that this discourse between God and Satan, in these verses, is parabolical, like that of Micaiah (1 Ki. 22:19, etc.), and an allegory designed to represent the malice of the devil against good men and the divine check and restraint which that malice is under; only thus much further is intimated, that the affairs of this earth are very much the subject of the counsels of the unseen world. That world is dark to us, but we lie very open to it. Now here we have,

I. Satan among the sons of God (*v.* 6), an *adversary* (so *Satan* signifies) to God, to men, to all good: he thrust himself into an assembly of the *sons of God* that came to *present themselves before the Lord.* This means either, 1. A meeting of the saints on earth. Professors of religion, in the patriarchal age, were called *sons of God* (Gen. 6:2); they had then religious assemblies and stated times for them. The King came in to see his guests; the eye of God was on all present. But there was a serpent in paradise, a Satan among the sons of God; when they come together he is among them, to distract and disturb them, stands at their right hand to resist them. *The Lord rebuke thee, Satan!* Or, 2. A meeting of the angels in heaven. They are *the sons of God, ch.* 38:7. They came to give an account of their negotiations on earth and to receive new instructions. Satan was one of them originally; but *how hast thou fallen, O Lucifer!* He shall no more stand in that congregation, yet he is here represented, as coming among them, either summoned to appear as a criminal or connived at, for the present, though an intruder.

II. His examination, how he came thither (*v.* 7): *The Lord said unto Satan, Whence comest thou?* He knew very well whence he came, and with what design he came thither, that as the good angels came to do good he came for a permission to do hurt; but he would, by calling him to an account, show him that he was under check and control. *Whence comest thou?* He asks this, 1. As wondering what brought him thither. *Is Saul among the prophets?* Satan among the sons of God? Yes, for he *transforms himself into an angel of light* (2 Co. 11:13, 14), and would seem one of them. Note, It is possible that a man may be a child of the devil and yet be found in the assemblies of the sons of God in this world, and *there* may pass undiscovered by men, and yet be challenged by the all-seeing God. *Friend, how camest thou in hither?* Or, 2. As enquiring what he had been doing before he came thither. The same question was perhaps put to the rest of those that presented themselves before the Lord, "Whence came you?" We are accountable to God for all our haunts and all the ways we traverse.

III. The account he gives of himself and of the tour he had made. I come (says he) *from going to and fro on the earth.* 1. He could not pretend he had been doing any good, could give no such account of himself as the sons of God could, who *presented themselves before the Lord,* who came from executing his orders, serving the interest of his kingdom, and ministering to the heirs of salvation. 2. He would not own he had been doing any hurt, that he had been drawing men from the allegiance to God, deceiving and destroying souls; no. *I have done no wickedness,* Prov. 30:20. *Thy servant went nowhere.* In saying that he had *walked to and fro through the earth,* he intimates that he had kept himself within the bounds allotted him, and had not transgressed his bounds; for *the dragon is cast out into the earth* (Rev. 12:9) and not yet confined to his place of torment. While we are on this earth we are within his reach, and with so much subtlety, swiftness, and industry, does he penetrate into all the corners of it, that we cannot be in any place secure from his temptations. 3. He yet seems to give some representation of his own character. (1.) Perhaps it is spoken proudly, and with an air of haughtiness, as if he were indeed the *prince of this world,* as if *the kingdoms of the world and the glory of them* were his (Lu. 4:6), and he had now been walking in circuit through his own territories. (2.) Perhaps it is spoken fretfully, and with discontent. He had been walking to and fro, and could find no rest, but was as much a fugitive and a vagabond as Cain in the land of Nod. (3.) Perhaps it is spoken carefully: "I have been hard at work, going to and fro," or (as some read it) "searching about in the earth," really in quest of an opportunity to do mischief. He walks abut seeking whom he may devour. It concerns us therefore to be sober and vigilant.

IV. The question God puts to him concerning Job (*v.* 8): *Hast thou considered my servant Job?* As when we meet with one that has been in a distant place, where we have a friend we dearly love, we are ready to ask, "You have been in such a place; pray did you see my friend there?" Observe, 1. How honourably God speaks of Job: He is *my servant.* Good men are God's servants, and he is pleased to reckon himself honoured in their services, and they are to him for *a name and a praise* (Jer. 13:11) *and a crown of glory,* Isa. 62:3. "Yonder is *my servant Job;* there is *none like him,* none I value like him, of all the princes and potentates of the earth; one such saint as he is worth them all: *none like him* for uprightness and serious piety; many do well, but *he excelleth them all;* there is not to be found *such great faith, no, not in Israel.*" Thus Christ, long after, commended the centurion and the woman of Canaan, who were both of them, like Job, strangers to that commonwealth. The saints glory in God — *Who is like thee among the gods?* and he is pleased to glory in them — *Who is like Israel among the people?* So here, *none like Job,* none in earth, that state of imperfection. Those in heaven do indeed far outshine him; those who are least in that kingdom are greater than he; but *on earth there is not his like.* There is none like him in that land; so some good men are the glory of their country. 2. How closely he gives to Satan this good character of Job: *Hast thou set thy heart to my servant Job?* designing hereby, (1.) To aggravate the apostasy and misery of that wicked spirit: "How unlike him are thou!" Note, The holiness and happiness of the saints are the shame and torment of the devil and the devil's children. (2.) To answer the devil's seeming boast of the interest he had in this earth. "I have been walking to and fro in it," says he, "and it is all my own; all flesh have corrupted their way; they all sit still, and are at rest in their sins," Zec. 1:10, 11. "Nay, hold," saith God, "Job is my faithful servant." Satan may boast, but he shall not triumph. (3.) To anticipate his accusations, as if he had said, "Satan, I know thy errand; thou hast come to inform against Job; but *hast thou considered him?* Does not his unquestionable character give thee the lie?" Note, God knows all the malice of the devil and his instruments against his ser-

vants; and we have an advocate ready to appear for us, even before we are accused.

V. The devil's base insinuation against Job, in answer to God's encomium of him. He could not deny but that Job feared God, but suggested that he was a mercenary in his religion, and therefore a hypocrite (*v.* 9): *Doth Job fear God for nought?* Observe, 1. How impatient the devil was of hearing Job praised, though it was God himself that praised him. Those are like the devil who cannot endure that any body should be praised but themselves, but grudge the just share of reputation others have, as Saul (1 Sa. 18:5, etc.) and the Pharisees, Mt. 21:15. 2. How much at a loss he was for something to object against him; he could not accuse him of any thing that was bad, and therefore charged him with by-ends in doing good. Had the one half of that been true which his angry friends, in the heat of dispute, charged him with (*ch.* 15:4, 22:5), Satan would no doubt have brought against him now; but no such thing could be alleged, and therefore, 3. See how slyly he censured him as a hypocrite, not asserting that he was so, but only asking, "Is he not so?" This is the common way of slanderers, whisperers, backbiters, to suggest that by way of query which yet they have no reason to think is true. Note, It is not strange if those that are approved and accepted of God be unjustly censured by the devil and his instruments; if they are otherwise unexceptionable, it is easy to charge them with hypocrisy, as Satan charged Job, and they have no way to clear themselves, but patiently to wait for the judgment of God. As there is nothing we should dread more than being hypocrites, so there is nothing we need dread less that being called and counted so without cause. 4. How unjustly he accused him as mercenary, to prove him a hypocrite. It was a great truth that Job did not fear God for nought; he got much by it, for godliness is great gain: but it was a falsehood that he would not have feared God if he had not got this by it, as the event proved. Job's friends charged him with hypocrisy because he was greatly afflicted, Satan because he greatly prospered. It is no hard matter for those to calumniate that seek an occasion. It is not mercenary to look at the eternal recompence in our obedience; but to aim at temporal advantages in our religion, and to make it subservient to them, is spiritual idolatry, worshipping the creature more than the Creator, and is likely to end in a fatal apostasy. Men cannot long *serve God and mammon.*

VI. The complaint Satan made of Job's prosperity, *v.* 10. Observe, 1. What God had done for Job. He had protected him, made a hedge about him, for the defence of his person, his family, and all his possessions. Note, God's peculiar people are taken under his special protection, they and all that belong to them; divine grace makes a hedge about their spiritual life, and divine providence about their natural life, so they are safe and easy. He had prospered him, not in idleness or injustice (the devil could not accuse him of them), but in the way of honest diligence: *Thou hast blessed the work of his hands.* Without that blessing, be the hands ever so strong, ever so skilful, the work will not prosper; but, with that, *his substance has wonderfully increased in the land.* The blessing of the Lord makes rich: Satan himself owns it. 2. What notice the devil took of it, and how he improved it against him. The devil speaks of it with vexation. "I see thou hast *made a hedge about him, round about;*" as if he had walked it round, to see if he could spy a single gap in it, for him to enter in at, to do him a mischief; but he was disappointed: it was a complete hedge. *The wicked* one *saw it and was grieved,* and argued against Job that the only reason why he served God was because God prospered him. "No thanks to him to be true to the government that prefers him, and to serve a Master that pays him so well."

VII. The proof Satan undertakes to give of the hypocrisy and mercenariness of Job's religion, if he might but have leave to strip him of his wealth. "Let it be put to this issue," says he (*v.* 11); "make him poor, frown upon him, turn thy hand against him, and then see where his religion will be; touch what he has and it will appear what he is. *If he curse thee not to thy face,* let me never be believed, but posted for a liar and false accuser. Let me perish if he curse thee not;" so some supply the imprecation, which the devil himself modestly concealed, but the profane swearers of our age impudently and daringly speak out. Observe, 1. How slightly he speaks of the affliction

he desired that Job might be tried with: "Do but touch all that he has, do but begin with him, do but threaten to make him poor; a little cross will change his tone." 2. How spitefully he speaks of the impression it would make upon Job: "He will not only let fall his devotion, but turn it into an open defiance — not only think hardly of thee, but *even curse thee to thy face.*" The word translated curse is *barac,* the same that ordinarily, and originally, signifies to *bless;* but cursing God is so impious a thing that the holy language would not admit the name: but that where the sense requires it it must be so understood is plain form 1 Ki. 21:10–13, where the word is used concerning the crime charged on Naboth, that he did blaspheme God and the king. Now, (1.) It is likely that Satan did think that Job, if impoverished, would renounce his religion and so disprove his profession, and if so (as a learned gentleman has observed in his *Mount of Spirits*) Satan would have made out his own universal empire among the children of men. God declared Job the best man then living: now, if Satan can prove him a hypocrite, it will follow that God had not one faithful servant among men and that there was no such thing as true and sincere piety in the world, but religion was all a sham, and Satan was king *de facto — in fact,* over all mankind. But it appeared that *the Lord knows those that are his* and is not deceived in any. (2.) However, if Job should retain his religion, Satan would have the satisfaction to see him sorely afflicted. He hates good men, and delights in their griefs, as God has *pleasure in their prosperity.*

VIII. The permission God gave to Satan to afflict Job for the trial of his sincerity. Satan desired God to do it: *Put forth thy hand now.* God allowed him to do it (*v.* 12): "*All that he has is in thy hand;* make the trial as sharp as thou canst; do thy worst at him." Now, 1. It is a matter of wonder that God should give Satan such a permission as this, should *deliver the soul of his turtle-dove* into the hand of the adversary, such a lamb to such a lion; but he did it for his own glory, the honour of Job, the explanation of Providence, and the encouragement of his afflicted people in all ages, to make a case which, being adjudged, might be a useful precedent. He suffered Job to be tried, as he suffered Peter to be sifted, but took care that *his faith should not fail* (Lu. 22:32) and then the trial of it was *found unto praise, and honour, and glory,* 1 Pt. 1:7. But, 2. It is a matter of comfort that God has the devil *in a chain,* in a great chain, Rev. 20:1. He could not afflict Job without leave from God first asked and obtained, and then no further than he had leave: "*Only upon himself put not forth thy hand;* meddle not with his body, but only with his estate." It is a limited power that the devil has; he has no power to debauch men but what they give him themselves, nor power to afflict men but what is *given him from above.*

IX. Satan's departure from this meeting of the sons of God. Before they broke up, Satan went forth (as Cain, Gen. 4:16) *from the presence of the Lord;* no longer detained before him (as Doeg was, 1 Sa. 21:7) than till he had accomplished his malicious purpose. He went forth, 1. Glad that he had gained his point, proud of the permission he had to do mischief to a good man; and, 2. Resolved to lose no time, but speedily to put his project in execution. He went forth now, not to go to and fro, rambling through the earth, but with a direct course, to fall upon poor Job, who is carefully going on in the way of his duty, and knows nothing of the matter. What passes between good and bad spirits concerning us we are not aware of.

Verses 13–19

We have here a particular account of Job's troubles.

I. Satan brought them upon him on the very day that his children began their course of feasting, at their *eldest brother's house* (*v.* 13), where, he having (we may suppose) the double portion, the entertainment was the richest and most plentiful. The whole family, no doubt, was in perfect repose, and all were easy and under no apprehension of the trouble, now when they revived this custom; and this time Satan chose, that the trouble, coming now, might be the more grievous. *The night of my pleasure has he turned into fear,* Isa. 21:4.

II. They all come upon him at once; while one messenger of evil tidings was speaking another came, and, before he had told his story, a third, and a fourth, followed immediately. Thus Satan, by the divine permission, ordered it, 1. That there might appear a more than ordinary displeasure of God against him in his troubles, and by that he might be exasperated against divine Providence, as if it were resolved, right or wrong, to ruin him, and not give him time to speak for himself. 2. That he might not have leisure to consider and recollect himself, and reason himself into a gracious submission, but might be overwhelmed and overpowered by a complication of calamities. If he have not room to pause a little, he will be apt to speak in haste, and then, if ever, he will curse his God. Note, The children of God are often in heaviness through manifold temptations; deep calls to deep; waves and billows come one upon the neck of another. Let one affliction therefore quicken and help us to prepare for another; for, how deep soever we have drunk of the bitter cup, as long as we are in this world we cannot be sure that we have drunk our share and that it will finally pass from us.

III. They took from him all that he had, and made a full end of his enjoyments. The detail of his losses answers to the foregoing inventory of his possessions.

1. He had 500 *yoke of oxen,* and 500 *she-asses,* and a competent number of servants to attend them; and all these he lost at once, *v.* 14, 15. The account he has of this lets him know, (1.) That it was not through any carelessness of his servants; for then his resentment might have spent itself upon them: *The oxen were ploughing,* not playing, and the asses not suffered to stray and so taken up as waifs, but *feeding beside them,* under the servant's eye, each in their place; and those that passed by, we may suppose, blessed them, and said, *God speed the plough.* Note, All our prudence, care, and diligence, cannot secure us from affliction, no, not from those afflictions which are commonly owing to imprudence and negligence. *Except the Lord keep the city, the watchman,* though ever so wakeful, *wakes but in vain.* Yet it is some comfort under a trouble if it found us in the way of our duty, and not in any by-path. (2.) That is was through the wickedness of his neighbours the Sabeans, probably a sort of robbers that lived by spoil and plunder. They carried off the oxen and asses, and slew the servants that faithfully and bravely did their best to defend them, and *one only escaped,* not in kindness to him or his master, but that Job might have the certain intelligence of it by an eye-witness before he heard it by a flying report, which would have brought it upon him gradually. We have no reason to suspect that either Job or his servants had given any provocation to the Sabeans to make this inroad, but Satan put it into their hearts to do it, to do it now, and so gained a double point, for he made both Job to suffer and them to sin. Note, When Satan has God's permission to do mischief he will not want mischievous men to be his instruments in doing it, for he is a *spirit that works in the children of disobedience.*

2. He had 7000 *sheep,* and shepherds that kept them; and all those he lost at the same time by lightning, *v.* 16. Job was perhaps, in his own mind, ready to reproach the Sabeans, and fly out against them for their injustice and cruelty, when the next news immediately directs him to look upwards: *The fire of God has fallen from heaven.* As thunder is his voice, so lightning is his fire: but this was such an extraordinary lightning, and levelled so directly against Job, that all his sheep and shepherds were not only killed, but consumed by it at once, and one shepherd only was left alive to carry the news to poor Job. The devil, aiming to make him curse God and renounce his religion, managed this part of the trial very artfully, in order thereto. (1.) His sheep, with which especially he used to honour God in sacrifice, were all taken from him, as if God were angry at his offerings and would punish him in those very things which he had employed in his service. Having misrepresented Job to God as a false servant, in pursuance of his old design to set Heaven and earth at variance, he here misrepresented God to Jacob as a hard Master, who would not protect those flocks out of which he had so many burnt-offerings. This would tempt Job to say, *It is in vain to serve God.* (2.) The messenger called the lightning the *fire of God* (and innocently enough), but perhaps Satan thereby designed to strike into his mind this thought, that God had *turned to be his enemy and fought against him,* which was much more grievous to him than all the insults of the Sabeans. He owned (*ch.* 31:23) that *destruction from God was a terror to him.* How terrible then were the tidings of this destruction, which came immediately from

the hand of God! Had the fire from heaven consumed the sheep upon the altar, he might have construed it into a token of God's favour; but, the fire consuming them in the pasture, he could not but look upon it as a token of God's displeasure. There have not been the like since Sodom was burned.

3. He had 3000 *camels,* and servants tending them; and he lost them all at the same time by the Chaldeans, who came in three bands, and drove them away, and slew the servants, *v.* 17. If the fire of God, which fell upon Job's honest servants, who were in the way of their duty, had fallen upon the Sabean and Chaldean robbers who were doing mischief, God's judgments therein would have been like the great mountains, evident and conspicuous; but when the way of the wicked prospers, and they carry off their booty, while just and good men are suddenly cut off, God's righteousness is like the great deep, the bottom of which we cannot find, Ps. 36:6.

4. His dearest and most valuable possessions were his ten children; and, to conclude the tragedy, news if brought him, at the same time, that they were killed and buried in the ruins of the house in which they were feasting, and all the servants that waited on them, except one that came express with the tidings of it, *v.* 18, 19. This was the greatest of Job's losses, and which could not but go nearest him; and therefore the devil reserved it for the last, that, if the other provocations failed, this might make him curse God. Our children are pieces of ourselves; it is very hard to part with them, and touches a good man in as tender a part as any. But to part with them all at once, and for them to be all cut off in a moment, who had been so many years his cares and hopes, went to the quick indeed. (1.) They all died together, and not one of them was left alive. David, though a wise and good man, was very much discomposed by the death of one son. How hard then did it bear upon poor Job who lost them all, and, in one moment, was written childless! (2.) They died suddenly. Had they been taken away by some lingering disease, he would have had notice to expect their death, and prepare for the breach; but this came upon him without giving him any warning. (3.) They died when they were feasting and making merry. Had they died suddenly when they were praying, he might the better have borne it. He would have hoped that death had found them in a good frame if their blood had been mingled with their feast, where he himself used to be jealous of them that they had *sinned, and cursed God in their hearts* — to have that day come upon them unawares, like a thief in the night, when perhaps their heads were overcharged with surfeiting and drunkenness — this could not but add much to his grief, considering what a tender concern he always had for his children's souls, and that they were now out of the reach of the sacrifices he used to offer *according to the number of them all.* See how all things come alike to all. Job's children were constantly prayed for by their father, and lived in love one with another, and yet came to this untimely end. (4.) They died by a wind of the devil's raising, who is *the prince of the power of the air* (Eph. 2:2), but it was looked upon to be an immediate hand of God, and a token of his wrath. So Bildad construed it (*ch.* 8:4): *Thy children have sinned against him, and he has cast them away in their transgression.* (5.) They were taken away when he had most need of them to comfort him under all his other losses. Such miserable comforters are all creatures. In God only we have a present help at all times.

Verses 20–22

The devil had done all he desired leave to do against Job, to provoke him to curse God. He had touched all he had, touched it with a witness; he whom the rising sun saw the richest of all the men in the east was before night poor to a proverb. If his riches had been, as Satan insinuated, the only principle of his religion now that he had lost his riches he would certainly have lost his religion; but the account we have, in these verses, of his pious deportment under his affliction, sufficiently proved the devil a liar and Job an honest man.

I. He conducted himself like a man under his afflictions, not stupid and senseless, like a stock or stone, not unnatural and unaffected at the death of his children and servants; no (*v.* 20), he *arose, and rent his mantle, and shaved his head,* which were the usual expressions of great sor-

row, to show that he was sensible of the hand of the Lord that had gone out against him; yet he did not break out into any indecencies, nor discover any extravagant passion. He did not faint away, but arose, as a champion to the combat; he did not, in a heat, throw off his clothes, but very gravely, in conformity to the custom of the country, rent his mantle, his cloak, or outer garment; he did not passionately tear his hair, but deliberately shaved his head. By all this it appeared that he kept his temper, and bravely maintained the possession and repose of his own soul, in the midst of all these provocations. The time when he began to show his feelings is observable; it was not till he heard of the death of his children, and then he arose, then he rent his mantle. A worldly unbelieving heart would have said, "Now that the meat is gone it is well that the mouths are gone too; now that there are no portions it is well that there are no children:" but Job knew better, and would have been thankful if Providence had spared his children, though he had little of nothing for them, for *Jehovah-jireh — the Lord will provide.* Some expositors, remembering that it was usual with the Jews to rend their clothes when they heard blasphemy, conjecture that Job rent his clothes in a holy indignation at the blasphemous thoughts which Satan now cast into his mind, tempting him to curse God.

II. He conducted himself like a wise and good man under his affliction, like a *perfect and upright man,* and *one that feared God* and *eschewed* the *evil* of sin more than that of outward trouble.

1. He humbled himself under the hand of God, and accommodated himself to the providences he was under, as one that knew how to want as well as how to abound. When God called to weeping and mourning he wept and mourned, *rent his mantle and shaved his head;* and, as one that abased himself even to the dust before God, he *fell down upon the ground,* in a penitent sense of sin and a patient submission to the will of God, *accepting the punishment of his iniquity.* Hereby he showed his sincerity; for *hypocrites cry not when God binds them,* ch. 36:13. Hereby he prepared himself to get good by the affliction; for how can we improve the grief which we will not feel?

2. He composed himself with quieting considerations, that he might not be disturbed and put out of the possession of his own soul by these events. He reasons from the common state of human life, which he describes with application to himself: *Naked came I* (as others do) *out of my mother's womb, and naked shall I return thither,* into the lap of our common mother — the earth, as the child, when it is sick or weary, lays its head in its mother's bosom. *Dust we were* in our original, and *to dust we return* in our exit (Gen. 3:19), *to the earth as we were* (Eccl. 12:7), *naked shall we return thither,* whence we were taken, namely, to the clay, *ch.* 33:6. St. Paul refers to this of Job, 1 Tim. 6:7. *We brought nothing* of this world's goods *into the world,* but have them from others; and *it is certain that we can carry nothing out,* but must leave them to others. We come into the world naked, not only unarmed, but unclothed, helpless, shiftless, not so well covered and fenced as other creatures. The sin we are born in makes us naked, to our shame, in the eyes of the holy God. We go out of the world naked; the body does, though the sanctified soul goes clothed, 2 Co. 5:3. Death strips us of all our enjoyments; clothing can neither warm nor adorn a dead body. This consideration silenced Job under all his losses. (1.) He is but where he was at first. He looks upon himself only as naked, not maimed, not wounded; he was himself still his own man, when nothing else was his own, and therefore but reduced to his first condition. *Nemo tam pauper potest esse quam natus est — no one can be so poor as he was when born. — Min. Felix.* If we are impoverished, we are not wronged, nor much hurt, for we are but as we were born. (2.) He is but where he must have been at last, and is only unclothed, or unloaded rather, a little sooner than he expected. If we put off our clothes before we go to bed, it is some inconvenience, but it may be the better borne when it is near bed-time.

3. He gave glory to God, and expressed himself upon this occasion with a great veneration for the divine Providence, and a meek submission to its disposals. We may well rejoice to find Job in this good frame, because this was the very thing upon which the trial of his integrity was put, though he did not know it. The devil said that

he would, under his affliction, curse God; but he blessed him, and so proved himself an honest man.

(1.) He acknowledged the hand of God both in the mercies he had formerly enjoyed and in the afflictions he was now exercised with: *The Lord gave, and the Lord has taken away.* We must own the divine Providence, [1.] In all our comforts. God gave us our being, *made us, and not we ourselves,* gave us our wealth; it was not our own ingenuity or industry that enriched us, but God's blessing on our cares and endeavours. He gave us power to get wealth, not only made the creatures for us, but bestowed upon us our share. [2.] In all our crosses. The same that gave hath taken away; and may he not do what he will with his own? See how Job looks above instruments, and keeps his eye upon the first Cause. He does not say, "The Lord gave, and the Sabeans and Chaldeans have taken away; God made me rich, and the devil has made me poor;" but, "He that gave has taken;" and for that reason he is dumb, and has nothing to say, because God did it. He that gave all may take what, and when, and how much he pleases. Seneca could argue thus, *Abstulit, sed et dedit — he took away, but he also gave;* and Epictetus excellently (cap. 15), "When thou art deprived of any comfort, suppose a child taken away by death, or a part of thy estate lost, say not *apōlesa auto — I have lost it;* but *apedōka — I have restored it to the right owner;* but thou wilt object (says he), *kakos ho aphelomenos — he is a bad man that has robbed me;* to which he answers, *ti de soi melei — What is it to thee by what hand he that gives remands what he gave?"*

(2.) He adored God in both. When all was gone he fell down and worshipped. Note, Afflictions must not divert us from, but quicken us to, the exercises of religion. Weeping must not hinder sowing, nor hinder worshipping. He eyed not only the hand of God, but the name of God, in his afflictions, and gave glory to that: *Blessed be the name of the Lord.* He has still the same great and good thoughts of God that ever he had, and is as forward as ever to speak them forth to his praise; he can find in his heart to bless God even when he takes away as well as when he gives. Thus must we *sing both of mercy and judgment,* Ps. 101:i. [1.] He blesses God for what was given, though now it was taken away. When our comforts are removed from us we must thank God that ever we had them and had them so much longer than we deserved. Nay, [2.] He adores God even in taking away, and gives him honour by a willing submission; nay, he gives him thanks for good designed him by his afflictions, for gracious supports under his afflictions, and the believing hopes he had of a happy issue at last.

Lastly, Here is the honourable testimony which the Holy Ghost gives to Job's constancy and good conduct under his afflictions. He passed his trials with applause, *v.* 22. In all this Job did not act amiss, for he did not attribute folly to God, nor in the least reflect upon his wisdom in what he had done. Discontent and impatience do in effect charge God with folly. Against the workings of these therefore Job carefully watched; and so must we, acknowledging that as God has done right, but we have done wickedly, so God has done wisely, but we have done foolishly, very foolishly. Those who not only keep their temper under crosses and provocations, but keep up good thoughts of God and sweet communion with him, whether their praise be of men or no, it will be of God, as Job's here was.

CHAPTER 2

We left Job honourably acquitted upon a fair trial between God and Satan concerning him. Satan had leave to touch, to touch and take, all he had, and was confident that he would then curse God to his face; but, on the contrary, he blessed him, and so he was proved an honest man and Satan a false accuser. Now, one would have thought, this would be conclusive, and that Job would never have his reputation called in question again; but Job is known to be armour of proof, and therefore is here set up for a mark, and brought upon his trial, a second time. I. Satan moves for another trial, which should touch his bone and his flesh (*v.* 1–5). II. God, for holy ends, permits it (*v.* 6). III. Satan smites him with a very painful and loathsome disease (*v.* 7, 8). IV. His wife tempts him to curse God, but he resists the temptation (*v.* 9, 10). V. His friends come to condole with him and to comfort him (*v.* 11–13). And in this that good man is set forth for an example of suffering affliction and of patience.

Verses 1–6

Satan, that sworn enemy to God and all good men, is here pushing forward his malicious prosecution of Job, whom he hated because God loved him, and did all he could to separate between him and his God, to sow discord and make mischief between them, urging God to afflict him and then urging him to blaspheme God. One would have thought that he had enough of his former attempt upon Job, in which he was so shamefully baffled and disappointed; but malice is restless: the devil and his instruments are so. Those that calumniate good people, and accuse them falsely, will have their saying, though the evidence to the contrary be ever so plain and full and they have been cast in the issue which they themselves have put it upon. Satan will have Job's cause called over again. The malicious, unreasonable, importunity of that great persecutor of the saints is represented (Rev. 12:10) by his accusing them before our God day and night, still repeating and urging that against them which has been many a time answered: so did Satan here accuse Job day after day. Here is,

I. The court set, and the prosecutor, or accuser, making his appearance (*v.* 1, 2), as before, *ch.* 1:6, 7. The angels attended God's throne and Satan among them. One would have expected him to come and confess his malice against Job and his mistake concerning him, to cry, *Pecavi — I have done wrong,* for belying one whom God spoke well of, and to beg pardon; but, instead of that, he comes with a further design against Job. He is asked the same question as before, *Whence comest thou?* and answers as before, *From going to and fro in the earth;* as if he had been doing no harm, though he had been abusing that good man.

II. The judge himself of counsel for the accused, and pleading for him (*v.* 3): *"Hast thou considered my servant Job* better than thou didst, and art thou now at length convinced that he is a faithful servant of mine, *a perfect and an upright man;* for thou seest he *still holds fast his integrity?"* This is now added to his character, as a further achievement; instead of letting go his religion, and cursing God, he holds it faster than ever, as that which he has now more than ordinary occasion for. He is the same in adversity that he was in prosperity, and rather better, and more hearty and lively in blessing God than ever he was, and takes root the faster for being thus shaken. See, 1. How Satan is condemned for his allegations against Job: *"Thou movedst me against him,* as an accuser, *to destroy him without cause."* Or, "Thou in vain movedst me to destroy him, for I will never do that." Good men, when they are *cast down,* are *not destroyed,* 2 Co. 4:9. How well is it for us that neither men nor devils are to be our judges, for perhaps they would destroy us, right or wrong; but our judgment proceeds from the Lord, whose judgment never errs nor is biassed. 2. How Job is commended for his constancy notwithstanding the attacks made upon him: "Still he holds fast his integrity, as his weapon, and thou canst not disarm him — as his treasure, and thou canst not rob him of that; nay, thy endeavours to do it make him hold it the faster; instead of losing ground by the temptation, he gets ground." God speaks of it with wonder, and pleasure, and something of triumph in the power of his own grace; *Still he holds fast his integrity.* Thus the trial of Job's faith was found to his *praise and honour,* 1 Pt. 1:7. Constancy crowns integrity.

III. The accusation further prosecuted, *v.* 4. What excuse can Satan make for the failure of his former attempt? What can he say to palliate it, when he had been so very confident that he should gain his point? Why, truly, he has this to say, *Skin for skin, and all that a man has, will he give for his life.* Something of truth there is in this, that self-love and self-preservation are very powerful commanding principles in the hearts of men. Men love themselves better than their nearest relations, even their children, that are parts of themselves, will not only venture, but give, their estates to save their lives. All account life sweet and precious, and, while they are themselves in health and at ease, they can keep trouble from their hearts, whatever they lose. We ought to make a good use of this consideration, and, while God continues to us our life and health and the use of our limbs and senses, we should the more patiently bear the loss of other comforts. See Mt. 6:25. But Satan grounds upon this an accusation of Job, slyly representing him, 1. As unnatural to those about him, and one that laid not to heart the death of his children and servants, nor cared how many of them had their skins (as I may say) stripped over their ears, so long as he slept in a whole skin himself; as if he that was so tender of his children's souls could be careless of their bodies, and, like the ostrich, hardened against his young ones, as though they were not his. 2. As wholly selfish, and minding nothing but his own ease and safety; as if his religion made him sour, and morose, and ill-natured. Thus are the ways and people of God often misrepresented by the devil and his agents.

IV. A challenge given to make a further trial of Job's integrity (*v.* 5): *"Put forth thy hand now* (for I find my hand too short to reach him, and too weak to hurt him) *and touch his bone and his flesh* (that is with him the only tender part, *make him sick with smiting him,* Mic. 6:13), and then, I dare say, *he will curse thee to thy face,* and let go his integrity." Satan knew it, and we find it by experience, that nothing is more likely to ruffle the thoughts and put the mind into disorder than acute pain and distemper of body. There is no disputing against sense. St. Paul himself had much ado to bear a thorn in the flesh, nor could he have borne it without special grace from Christ, 2 Co. 12:7, 9.

V. A permission granted to Satan to make this trial, *v.* 6. Satan would have had God put forth his hand and do it; but he *afflicts not willingly,* nor takes any pleasure in *grieving the children of men,* much less his own children (Lam. 3:33), and therefore, if it must be done, let Satan do it, who delights in such work: *"He is in thy hand,* do thy worst with him; but with a proviso and limitation, *only save his life,* or his soul. Afflict him, but not to death." Satan hunted for the precious life, would have taken that if he might, in hopes that dying agonies would force Job to curse his God; but God had mercy in store for Job after this trial, and therefore he must survive it, and, however he is afflicted, must have his life given him for a prey. If God did not chain up the roaring lion, how soon would he devour us! As far as he permits the wrath of Satan and wicked men to proceed against his people he will make it turn to his praise and theirs, and *the remainder thereof he will restrain,* Ps. 76:10. "Save his soul," that is, "his reason" (so some), "preserve to him the use of that, for otherwise it will be no fair trial; if, in his delirium, he should curse God, that will be no disproof of his integrity. It would be the language not of his heart, but of his distemper." Job, in being thus maligned by Satan, was a type of Christ, the first prophecy of whom was that Satan should *bruise his heel* (Gen. 3:15), and so he was foiled, as in Job's case. Satan tempted him to let go his integrity, his adoption (Mt. 4:6): *If thou be the Son of God.* He entered into the heart of Judas who betrayed Christ, and (some think) with his terrors put Christ into his agony in the garden. He had permission to touch his bone and his flesh without exception of his life, because by dying he was to do that which Job could not do — *destroy him that had the power of death, that is, the devil.*

Verses 7–10

The devil, having got leave to tear and worry poor Job, presently fell to work with him, as a tormentor first and then as a tempter. His own children he tempts first, and draws them to sin, and afterwards torments, when thereby he has brought them to ruin; but this child of God he tormented with an affliction, and then tempted to make a bad use of his affliction. That which he aimed at was to make Job curse God; now here we are told what course he took both to move him to it and move it to him, both to give him the provocation, else he would not have thought of it: thus artfully in the temptation managed with all the subtlety of the old serpent, who is here playing the same game against Job that he played against our first parents (Gen. 3), aiming to seduce him from his allegiance to his God and to rob him of his integrity.

I. He provokes him to curse God by smiting him with sore boils, and so making him a burden to himself, *v.* 7, 8. The former attack was extremely violent, but Job kept his ground, bravely made good the pass and carried the day. Yet he is still but girding on the harness; there is worse behind. The clouds return after the rain. Satan, by the divine permission, follows his blow, and now *deep calls unto deep.*

1. The disease with which Job was seized was very grievous: Satan *smote him with boils, sore boils,* all over him, from head to foot, with *an evil inflammation* (so some

render it), an erysipelas, perhaps, in a higher degree. One boil, when it is gathering, is torment enough, and gives a man abundance of pain and uneasiness. What a condition was Job then in, that had boils all over him, and no part free, and those as of raging a heat as the devil could make them, and, as it were, *set on fire of hell!* The small-pox is a very grievous and painful disease, and would be much more terrible than it is but that we know the extremity of it ordinarily lasts but a few days; how grievous then was the disease of Job, who was smitten all over with sore boils or grievous ulcers, which made him sick at heart, put him to exquisite torture, and so spread themselves over him that he could lie down no way for any ease. If at any time we be exercised with sore and grievous distempers, let us not think ourselves dealt with any otherwise than as God has sometimes dealt with the best of his saints and servants. We know not how much Satan may have a hand (by divine permission) in the diseases with which the children of men, and especially the children of God, are afflicted, what infections that prince of the air may spread, what inflammations may come from that fiery serpent. We read of one whom Satan had bound many years, Lu. 13:16. Should God suffer that roaring lion to have his will against any of us, how miserable would he soon make us!

2. His management of himself, in this distemper, was very strange, *v.* 8.

(1.) Instead of healing salves, *he took a potsherd,* a piece of a broken pitcher, *to scrape himself withal.* A very sad pass this poor man had come to. When a man is sick and sore he may bear it the better if he be well tended and carefully looked after. Many rich people have with a soft and tender hand charitably ministered to the poor in such a condition as this; even Lazarus had some ease from the tongues of the dogs that came and *licked his sores;* but poor Job has no help afforded him. [1.] Nothing is done to his sore but what he does himself, with his own hands. His children and servants are all dead, his wife unkind, *ch.* 19:17. He has not wherewithal to fee a physician or surgeon; and, which is most sad of all, none of those he had formerly been kind to had so much sense of honour and gratitude as to minister to him in his distress, and lend him a hand to dress or wipe his running sores, either because the disease was loathsome and noisome or because they apprehended it to be infectious. Thus it was in the former days, as it will be in the last days, men were *lovers of their own selves, unthankful, and without natural affection.* [2.] All that he does to his sores is to *scrape them;* they are not bound up with soft rags, not mollified with ointment, not washed or kept clean, no healing plasters laid on them, no opiates, no anodynes, ministered to the poor patient, to alleviate the pain and compose him to rest, nor any cordials to support his spirits; all the operation is the scraping of the ulcers, which, when they had come to a head and began to die, made his body all over like a scurf, as is usual in the end of the small-pox. It would have been an endless thing to dress his boils one by one; he therefore resolves thus to do it by wholesale — a remedy which one would think as bad as the disease. [3.] He has nothing to do this with but a *potsherd,* no surgeon's instrument proper for the purpose, but that which would rather rake into his wounds, and add to his pain, than give him any ease. People that are sick and sore have need to be under the discipline and direction of others, for they are often but bad managers of themselves.

(2.) Instead of reposing in a soft and warm bed, he *sat down among the ashes.* Probably he had a bed left him (for, though his fields were stripped, we do not find that his house was burnt or plundered), but he chose to sit in the ashes, either because he was weary of his bed or because he would put himself into the place and posture of a penitent, who, in token of his self-abhorrence, lay in dust and ashes, *ch.* 42:6; Isa. 58:5; Jonah 3:6. Thus did he humble himself under the mighty hand of God, and bring his mind to the meanness and poverty of his condition. He complains (*ch.* 7:5) that his flesh was *clothed with worms* and *clods of dust;* and therefore *dust to dust, ashes to ashes.* If God lay him among the ashes, there he will contentedly sit down. A low spirit becomes low circumstances, and will help to reconcile us to them. The Septuagint reads it, He sat *down upon a dunghill without the city* (which is commonly said, in mentioning this story); but the original says no more than that he sat *in the midst of the ashes,* which he might do in his own house.

II. He urges him, by the persuasions of his own wife, to curse God, *v.* 9. The Jews (who covet much to be wise above what is written) say that Job's wife was Dinah, Jacob's daughter: so the Chaldee paraphrase. It is not likely that she was; but, whoever it was, she was to him like Michal to David, a scoffer at his piety. She was spared to him, when the rest of his comforts were taken away, for this purpose, to be a troubler and tempter to him. If Satan leaves any thing that he has permission to take away, it is with a design of mischief. It is his policy to send his temptations by the hand of those that are dear to us, as he tempted Adam by Eve and Christ by Peter. We must therefore carefully watch that we be not drawn to say or do a wrong thing by the influence, interest, or entreaty, of any, no, not those for whose opinion and favour we have ever so great a value. Observe how strong this temptation was. 1. She banters Job for his constancy in his religion: *"Dost thou still retain thy integrity?* Art thou so very obstinate in thy religion that nothing will cure thee of it? so tame and sheepish as thus to truckle to a God who is so far from rewarding thy services with marks of his favour that he seems to take a pleasure in making thee miserable, strips thee, and scourges thee, without any provocation given? Is this a God to be still loved, and blessed, and served?"

> Dost thou not see that thy devotion's vain?
> What have thy prayers procured but woe and pain?
> Hast thou not yet thy int'rest understood?
> Perversely righteous, and absurdly good?
> Those painful sores, and all thy losses, show
> How Heaven regards the foolish saint below.
> Incorrigibly pious! Can't thy God
> Reform thy stupid virtue with his rod?
>
> — Sir R. Blackmore

Thus Satan still endeavours to draw men from God, as he did our first parents, by suggesting hard thoughts of him, as one that envies the happiness and delights in the misery of his creatures, than which nothing is more false. Another artifice he uses is to drive men from their religion by loading them with scoffs and reproaches for their adherence to it. We have reason to expect it, but we are fools if we heed it. Our Master himself has undergone it, we shall be abundantly recompensed for it, and with much more reason may we retort it upon the scoffers, "Are you such fools as still to retain your impiety, when you might *bless God and live?"* 2. She urges him to renounce his religion, to blaspheme God, set him at defiance, and dare him to do his worst: *"Curse God and die;* live no longer in dependence upon God, wait not for relief from him, but be thy own deliverer by being thy own executioner; end thy troubles by ending thy life; better die once than be always dying thus; thou mayest now despair of having any help from thy God, even curse him, and hang thyself." These are two of the blackest and most horrid of all Satan's temptations, and yet such as good men have sometimes been violently assaulted with. Nothing is more contrary to natural conscience than blaspheming God, nor to natural sense than self-murder; therefore the suggestion of either of these may well be suspected to come immediately from Satan. Lord, *lead us not into temptation,* not into such, not into any temptation, but *deliver us from the evil one.*

III. He bravely resists and overcomes the temptation, *v.* 10. He soon gave her an answer (for Satan spared him the use of his tongue, in hopes he would curse God with it), which showed his constant resolution to cleave to God, to keep his good thoughts of him, and not to let go his integrity. See,

1. How he resented the temptation. He was very indignant at having such a thing mentioned to him: "What! Curse God? I abhor the thought of it. *Get thee behind me, Satan."* In other cases Job reasoned with his wife with a great deal of mildness, even when she was unkind to him (*ch.* 19:17): *I entreated her for the children's sake of my own body.* But, when she persuaded him to curse God, he was much displeased: *Thou speakest as one of the foolish women speaketh.* He does not call her *a fool* and *an atheist,* nor does he break out into any indecent expressions of his displeasure, as those who ar sick and sore are apt to do, and think they may be excused; but he shows her the evil of what she said, and she spoke the language of the infidels and idolaters, who, when they are *hardly bestead, fret themselves, and curse their king and their God,* Isa. 8:21. We have reason to suppose that in such a pious household as Job had his wife was one that had been well affected to religion, but that now, when all their estate and comfort were gone, she could not bear the loss with that temper of mind that Job had; but that she should go about to infect his mind with her wretched distemper was a great provocation to him, and he could not forbear thus showing his resentment. Note, (1.) Those are angry and sin not who are angry only at sin and take a temptation as the greatest affront, who *cannot bear those that are evil,* Rev. 2:2. When Peter was a Satan to Christ he told him plainly, *Thou art an offence to me.* (2.) If those whom we think wise and good at any time speak that which is foolish and bad, we ought to reprove them faithfully for it and show them the evil of what they say, that we suffer not sin upon them. (3.) Temptations to curse God ought to be rejected with the greatest abhorrence, and not so much as to be parleyed with. Whoever persuades us to that must be looked upon as our enemy, to whom if we yield it is at our peril Job did not curse God and then think to come off with Adam's excuse: *"The woman whom thou gavest to be with me* persuaded me to do it" (Gen. 3:12), which had in it a tacit reflection on God, his ordinance and providence. No; if thou scornest, if thou cursest, thou alone shalt bear it.

2. How he reasoned against the temptation: *Shall we receive good at the hand of God, and shall we not receive evil also?* Those whom we reprove we must endeavour to convince; and it is no hard matter to give a reason why we should still hold fast our integrity even when we are stripped of every thing else. He considers that, though good and evil are contraries, yet they do not come from contrary causes, but both from the hand of God (Isa. 45:7, Lam. 3:38), and therefore that in both we must have our eye up unto him, with thankfulness for the good he sends and without fretfulness at the evil. Observe the force of his argument.

(1.) What he argues for, not only the bearing, but the receiving of evil: *Shall we not receive evil,* that is, [1.] "Shall we not expect to receive it? If God give us so many good things, shall we be surprised, or think it strange, if he sometimes afflict us, when he has told us that prosperity and adversity are set the one over against the other?" 1 Pt. 4:12. [2.] "Shall we not set ourselves to receive it aright?" The word signifies to receive as a gift, and denotes a pious affection and disposition of soul under our afflictions, neither despising them nor fainting under them, accounting them gifts (Phil. 1:29), accepting them as punishments of our iniquity (Lev. 26:41), acquiescing in the will of God in them ("Let him do with me as seemeth him good"), and accommodating ourselves to them, as those that know how to want as well as how to abound, Phil. 4:12. When the heart is humbled and weaned, by humbling weaning providence, then we *receive correction* (Zep. 3:2) and take up our cross.

(2.) What he argues from: "Shall we receive so much good as has come to us from the hand of God during all those years of peace and prosperity that we have lived, and shall we not now receive evil, when God thinks fit to lay it on us?" Note, The consideration of the mercies we receive from God, both past and present, should make us receive our afflictions with a suitable disposition of spirit. If we receive our share of the common good in the seven years of plenty, shall we not receive our share of the common evil in the years of famine? *Qui sentit commodum, sentire debet et onus — he who feels the privilege, should prepare for the privation.* If we have so much that pleases us, why should we not be content with that which pleases God? If we receive so many comforts, shall we not receive some afflictions, which will serve as foils to our comforts, to make them the more valuable (we are taught the worth of mercies by being made to want them sometimes), and as allays to our comforts, to make them the less dangerous, to keep the balance even, and to prevent our being *lifted up above measure?* 2 Co. 12:7. If we receive so much good for the body, shall we not receive some good for the soul; that is, some afflictions, by which we partake of God's holiness (Heb. 12:10), something which, by saddening the countenance, makes the heart better? Let murmuring therefore, as well as boasting, be for ever excluded.

IV. Thus, in a good measure, Job still held fast his integrity, and Satan's design against him was defeated: *In all* this did not Job sin with his lips; he not only said this well, but all he said at this time was under the government of religion and right reason. In the midst of all these grievances he did not speak a word amiss; and we have no reason to think but that he also preserved a good temper of mind, so that, though there might be some stirrings and risings of corruption in his heart, yet grace got the upper hand and he took care that the root of bitterness might not spring up to trouble him, Heb. 12:15. The *abundance of his heart* was for God, produced good things, and suppressed the evil that was there, which was out-voted by the better side. If he did think any evil, yet he *laid his hand upon his mouth* (Prov. 30:32), stifled the evil thought and let it go no further, by which it appeared, not only that he had true grace, but that it was strong and victorious: in short, that he had not forfeited the character of a *perfect and upright man;* for so *he* appears to be who, in the midst of such temptations, *offends not in word,* Jam. 3:2; Ps. 17:3.

Verses 11–13

We have here an account of the kind visit which Job's three friends paid him in his affliction. The news of his extraordinary troubles spread into all parts, he being an eminent man both for greatness and goodness, and the circumstances of his troubles being very uncommon. Some, who were his enemies, triumphed in his calamities, *ch.* 16:10; 19:18; 30:1, etc. Perhaps they made ballads on him. But his friends concerned themselves for him, and endeavoured to comfort him. *A friend loveth at all times, and a brother is born for adversity.* Three of them are here named (*v.* 11), Eliphaz, Bildad, and Zophar. We shall afterwards meet with a fourth, who it should seem was present at the whole conference, namely, Elihu. Whether he came as a friend of Job or only as an auditor does not appear. These three are said to be his *friends,* his intimate acquaintance, as David and Solomon had each of them one in their court that was called *the king's friend.* These three were eminently wise and good men, as appears by their discourses. They were old men, very old, had a great reputation for knowledge, and much deference was paid to their judgment, *ch.* 32:6. It is probable that they were men of figure in their country — princes, or heads of houses. Now observe,

I. That Job, in his prosperity, had contracted a friendship with them. If they were his equals, yet he had not that jealousy of them — if his inferiors, yet he had not that disdain of them, which was any hindrance to an intimate converse and correspondence with them. to have such friends added more to his happiness in the day of his prosperity than all the head of cattle he was master of. Much of the comfort of this life lies in acquaintance and friendship with those that are prudent and virtuous; and he that has a few such friends ought to value them highly. Job's three friends are supposed to have been all of them of the posterity of Abraham, which, for some descents, even in the families that were shut out from the covenant of peculiarity, retained some good fruits of that pious education which the father of the faithful gave to those under his charge. Eliphaz descended from Teman, the grandson of Esau (Gen. 36:11), Bildad (it is probable) from Shuah, Abraham's son by Keturah, Gen. 25:2. Zophar is thought by some to be the same with Zepho, a descendant from Esau, Gen. 26:11. The preserving of so much wisdom and piety among those that were strangers to the covenants of promise was a happy presage of God's grace to the Gentiles, when the partition-wall should in the latter days be taken down. Esau was rejected; yet many that came from him inherited some of the best blessings.

II. That they continued their friendship with Job in his adversity, when most of his friends had forsaken him, *ch.* 19:14. In two ways they showed their friendship: —

1. By the kind visit they paid him in his affliction, to mourn with him and to comfort him, *v.* 11. Probably they had been wont to visit him in his prosperity, not to hunt or hawk with him, not to dance or play at cards with him, but to entertain and edify themselves with his learned and pious converse; and now that he was in adversity they come to share with him in his griefs, as formerly they had come to share with him in his comforts. These were wise men, whose *heart was in the house of mourning,* Eccl. 7:4. Visiting the afflicted, sick or sore,

fatherless or childless, in their sorrow, is made a branch of *pure religion and undefiled* (Jam. 1:27), and, if done from a good principle, will be abundantly recompensed shortly, Mt. 25:36.

(1.) By visiting the sons and daughters of affliction we may contribute to the improvement, [1.] Of our own graces; for many a good lesson is to be learned from the troubles of others; we may look upon them and receive instruction, and be made wise and serious. [2.] Of their comforts. By putting a respect upon them we encourage them, and some good word may be spoken to them which may help to make them easy. Job's friends came, not to satisfy their curiosity with an account of his troubles and the strangeness of the circumstances of them, much less, as David's false friends, to make invidious remarks upon him (Ps. 41:6-8), but to mourn with him, to mingle their tears with his, and so to comfort him. It is much more pleasant to visit those in affliction to whom comfort belongs than those to whom we must first speak conviction.

(2.) Concerning these visitants observe, [1.] That they were not sent for, but came of their own accord (*ch.* 6:22), whence Mr. Caryl observes that *it is good manners to be an unbidden guest at the house of mourning,* and, in comforting our friends, to anticipate their invitations. [2.] That they made an appointment to come. Note, Good people should make appointments among themselves for doing good, so exciting and binding one another to it, and assisting and encouraging one another in it. For the carrying on of any pious design let hand join in hand. [3.] That they came with a design (and we have reason to think it was a sincere design) to comfort him, and yet proved miserable comforters, through their unskilful management of his case. Many that aim well do, by mistake, come short of their aim.

2. By their tender sympathy with him and concern for him in his affliction. When they saw him at some distance he was so disfigured and deformed with his sores that *they knew him not, v.* 12. His face was *foul with weeping* (*ch.* 16:16), like Jerusalem's Nazarites, which had been *ruddy as the rubies,* but were now *blacker than a coal,* Lam. 4:7, 8. What a change will a sore disease, or, without that, oppressing care and grief, make in the countenance, in a little time! *Is this Naomi?* Ruth 1:19. So, *Is this Job?* How hast thou fallen! How is thy glory stained and sullied, and all thy honour laid in the dust! God fits us for such changes! Observing him thus miserably altered, they did not leave him, in a fright or loathing, but expressed so much the more tenderness towards him. (1.) Coming to mourn with him, they vented their undissembled grief in all the then usual expressions of that passion. *They wept* aloud; the sight of them (as is usual) revived Job's grief, and set him a weeping afresh, which fetched floods of tears from their eyes. *They rent their clothes, and sprinkled dust upon their heads,* as men that would strip themselves, and abase themselves, with their friend that was stripped and abased. (2.) Coming to comfort him, *they sat down with him upon the ground,* for so he received visits; and they, not in compliment to him, but in true compassion, put themselves into the same humble and uneasy place and posture. They had many a time, it is likely, sat with him on his couches and at his table, in his prosperity, and were therefore willing to share with him in his grief and poverty because they had shared with him in his joy and plenty. It was not a modish short visit that they made him, just to look upon him and be gone; but, as those that could have had no enjoyment of themselves if they had returned to their place while their friend was in so much misery, they resolved to stay with him till they saw him mend or end, and therefore took lodgings near him, though he was not now able to entertain them as he had done, and they must therefore bear their own charges. Every day, for seven days together, at the house in which he admitted company, they came and sat with him, as his companions in tribulation, and exceptions from that rule, *Nullus ad amissas ibit amicus opes — Those who have lost their wealth are not to expect the visits of their friends.* They sat with him, but *none spoke a word* to him, only they all attended to the particular narratives he gave of his troubles. They were silent, as men astonished and amazed. *Curae leves loquuntur, ingentes stupent — Our lighter griefs have a voice; those which are more oppressive are mute.*

So long a time they held their peace, to show
A reverence due to such prodigious woe.
— Sir R. Blackmore

They spoke not a word to him, whatever they said one to another, by way of instruction, for the improvement of the present providence. They said nothing to that purport to which afterwards they said much — nothing to grieve him (*ch.* 4:2), because they saw his grief was very great already, and they were loth at first to add affliction to the afflicted. There is a *time to keep silence,* when either the *wicked is before us,* and by speaking we may harden them (Ps. 39:1), or when by speaking we may *offend the generation of God's children,* Ps. 73:15. Their not entering upon the following solemn discourses till the seventh day may perhaps intimate that it was the sabbath day, which doubtless was observed in the patriarchal age, and to that day they adjourned the intended conference, because probably then company resorted, as usual, to Job's house, to join with him in his devotions, who might be edified by the discourse. Or, rather, by their silence so long they would intimate that what they afterwards said was well considered and digested and the result of many thoughts. *The heart of the wise studies to answer.* We should think twice before we speak once, especially in such a case as this, think long, and we shall be the better able to speak short and to the purpose.

CHAPTER 3

"You have heard of the patience of Job," says the apostle, Jam. 5:11. So we have, and of his impatience too. We wondered that a man should be so patient as he was (*ch.* 1 and 2), but we wonder also that a good man should be so impatient as he is in this chapter, where we find him cursing his day, and, in passion, I. Complaining that he was born (*v.* 1–10). II. Complaining that he did not die as soon as he was born (*v.* 11–19). III. Complaining that his life was now continued when he was in misery (*v.* 20–26). In this it must be owned that Job sinned with his lips, and it is written, not for our imitation, but our admonition, that he who things he stands may take heed lest he fall.

Verses 1–10

Long was Job's heart hot within him; and, while he was musing, the fire burned, and the more for being stifled and suppressed. At length he spoke with his tongue, but not such a good word as David spoke after a long pause: *Lord, make me to know my end,* Ps. 39:3, 4. Seven days the prophet Ezekiel sat down astonished with the captives, and then (probably on the sabbath day) *the word of the Lord came to him,* Eze. 3:15, 16. So long Job and his friends sat thinking, but said nothing; *they* were afraid of speaking what they thought, lest they should grieve him, and *he* durst not give vent to his thoughts, lest he should offend them. They came to comfort him, but, finding his afflictions very extraordinary, they began to think comfort did not belong to him, suspecting him to be a hypocrite, and therefore they said nothing. But losers think they may have leave to speak, and therefore Job first gives vent to his thoughts. Unless they had been better, it would however have been well if he had kept them to himself. In short, he cursed his day, the day of his birth, wished he had never been born, could not think or speak of his own birth without regret and vexation. Whereas men usually observe the annual return of their birth-day with rejoicing, he looked upon it as the unhappiest day of the year, because the unhappiest of his life, being the inlet into all his woe. Now,

I. This was bad enough. The extremity of his trouble and the discomposure of his spirits may excuse it in part, but he can by no means be justified in it. Now he has forgotten the good he was born to, the lean kine have eaten up the fat ones, and he is filled with thoughts of the evil only, and wishes he had never been born. The prophet Jeremiah himself expressed his painful sense of his calamities in language not much unlike this: *Woe is me, my mother, that thou hast borne me!* Jer. 15:10. *Cursed be the day wherein I was born,* Jer. 20:14, etc. We may suppose that Job in his prosperity had many a time blessed God for the day of his birth, and reckoned it a happy day; yet now he brands it with all possible marks of infamy. When we consider the iniquity in which we were conceived and born we have reason enough to reflect with sorrow and shame upon the day of our birth, and to say that the *day of our death,* by which we are *freed from sin* (Rom. 6:7), is far *better.* Eccl. 7:1. But to curse the day of our birth because then we entered upon the calamitous scene of life is to quarrel with the God of nature, to despise the dignity of our being, and to indulge a passion which our own calm and sober thoughts will make us ashamed of. Certainly there is no condition of life a man can be in in this world but he may in it (if it be not his own fault) so honour God, and work out his own salvation, and make sure a happiness for himself in a better world, that he will have no reason at all to wish he had never been born, but a great deal of reason to say that he had his being to good purpose. Yet it must be owned, if there were not another life after this, and divine consolations to support us in the prospect of it, so many are the sorrows and troubles of this that we might sometimes be tempted to say that we were *made in vain* (Ps. 89:47), and to wish we had never been. There are those in hell who with good reason wish they had never been born, as Judas, Mt. 26:24. But, on this side hell, there can be no reason for so vain and ungrateful a wish. It was Job's folly and weakness to curse his day. We must say of it, This was his infirmity; but good men have sometimes failed in the exercise of those graces which they have been most eminent for, that we may understand that when they are said to be *perfect* it is meant that they were upright, not that they were sinless. *Lastly,* Let us observe it, to the honour of the spiritual life above the natural, that though many have cursed the day of their first birth, never any cursed the day of their new-birth, nor wished they never had had grace, and the Spirit of grace, given them. Those are the most excellent gifts, above life and being itself, and which will never be a burden.

II. Yet it was not so bad as Satan promised himself. Job cursed his day, but he did not curse his God — was weary of his life, and would gladly have parted with that, but not weary of his religion; he resolutely cleaves to that, and will never let it go. The dispute between God and Satan concerning Job was not whether Job had his infirmities, and whether he was subject to like passions as we are (that was granted), but whether he was a hypocrite, who secretly hated God, and if he were provoked, would show his hatred; and, upon trial, it proved that he was no such man. Nay, all this may consist with his being a pattern of patience; for, though he did thus speak unadvisedly with his lips, yet both before and after he expressed great submission and resignation to the holy will of God and repented of his impatience; he condemned himself for it, and therefore God did not condemn him, nor must we, but watch the more carefully over ourselves, lest we sin after the similitude of this transgression.

1. The particular expressions which Job used in cursing his day are full of poetical fancy, flame, and rapture, and create as much difficulty to the critics as the thing itself does to the divines: we need not be particular in our observations upon them. When he would express his passionate wish that he had never been, he falls foul upon the day, and wishes,

(1.) That earth might forget it: *Let it perish* (v. 3); *let it not be joined to the days of the year, v.* 6. "Let it be not only not inserted in the calendar in red letters, as the day of the king's nativity useth to be" (and Job was a king, *ch.* 29:25), "but let it be erased and blotted out, and buried in oblivion. Let not the world know that ever such a man as I was born into it, and lived in it, who am made such a spectacle of misery."

(2.) That Heaven might frown upon it: *Let not God regard it from above, v.* 4. "Every thing is indeed as it is with God; that day is honourable on which he puts honour, and which he distinguishes and crowns with his favour and blessing, as he did the seventh day of the week; but let my birthday never be so honoured; let it be *nigro carbone notandus* — marked as with a black coal for an evil day by him that determines the times before appointed. The father and fountain of light appointed the greater light to rule the day and the less lights to rule the night; but let that want the benefit of both." [1.] *Let that day be darkness* (v. 4); and, if the light of the day be darkness, *how great is that darkness!* how terrible! because then we look for light. Let the gloominess of the day represent Job's condition, whose sun went down at noon. [2.] As for that night too, let it want the benefit of moon and stars, and *let darkness seize upon it,* thick darkness, darkness that may be felt, which will not befriend the repose of the night by its silence, but rather disturb it with its terrors.

(3.) That all joy might forsake it: "Let it be a melan-

choly night, solitary, and not a merry night of music and dancing. *Let no joyful voice come therein* (v. 7); let it be a long night, and not *see the eye-lids of the morning* (v. 9), which bring joy with them."

(4.) That all curses might follow it (v. 8): "Let none ever desire to see it, or bid it welcome when it comes, but, on the contrary, *let those curse it that curse the day.* Whatever day any are tempted to curse, let them at the same time bestow one curse upon my birth-day, particularly those that make it their trade to raise up mourning at funerals with their ditties of lamentation. Let those that curse the day of the death of others in the same breath curse the day of my birth." Or those who are so fierce and daring as to be ready to raise up the *Leviathan* (for that is the word here), who, being about to strike the whale or crocodile, curse it with the bitterest curse they can invent, hoping by their incantations to weaken it, and so to make themselves master of it. Probably some such custom might there be used, to which our divine poet alludes. "Let it be as odious as *the day wherein men bewail the greatest misfortune,* or the time *wherein they see the most dreadful apparition;"* so bishop Patrick, I suppose taking the Leviathan here to signify the devil, as others do, who understand it of the curses used by conjurors and magicians in raising the devil, or when they have raised a devil that they cannot lay.

2. But what is the ground of Job's quarrel with the day and night of his birth? It is *because it shut not up the doors of his mother's womb, v.* 10. See the folly and madness of a passionate discontent, and how absurdly and extravagantly it talks when the reins are laid on the neck of it. Is this Job, who was so much admired for his wisdom that *unto him men gave ear, and kept silence at his counsel,* and *after his words they spoke not again? ch.* 29:21, 11. Surely his wisdom failed him, (1.) When he took so much pains to express his desire that he had never been born, which, at the best was a vain wish, for it is impossible to make that which has been not to have been. (2.) When he was so liberal of his curses upon a day and a night that could not be hurt, or made any the worse for his curses. (3.) When he wished a thing so very barbarous to his own mother as that she had not brought him forth when her full time had come, which must inevitably have been her death, and a miserable death. (4.) When he despised the goodness of God to him in giving him a being (such a being, so noble and excellent a life, such a life, so far above that of any other creature in this lower world), and undervalued the gift, as not worth the acceptance, only because *transit cum onere — it was clogged with a proviso of trouble,* which now at length came upon him, after many years' enjoyment of its pleasures. What a foolish thing it was to wish that his eyes had never seen the light, that so they might not have seen sorrow, which yet he might hope to see through, and beyond which he might see joy! Did Job believe and hope that he should *in his flesh see God at the latter day* (ch. 19:26), and yet would he wish he had never had a being capable of such a bliss, only because, for the present, he had sorrow in the flesh? God by his grace arm us against this foolish and hurtful lust of impatience.

Verses 11–19

Job, perhaps reflecting upon himself for his folly in wishing he had never been born, follows it, and thinks to mend it, with another, little better, that he had died as soon as he was born, which he enlarges upon in these verses. When our Saviour would set forth a very calamitous state of things he seems to allow such a saying as this, *Blessed are the barren, and the wombs that never bore, and the paps which never gave suck* (Lu. 23:29); but blessing the barren womb is one thing and cursing the fruitful womb is another! It is good to make the best of afflictions, but it is not good to make the worst of mercies. Our rule is, *Bless, and curse not.* Life is often put for all good, and death for all evil; yet Job here very absurdly complains of life and its supports as a curse and plague to him, and covets death and the grave as the greatest and most desirable bliss. Surely Satan was deceived in Job when he applied that maxim to him, *All that a man hath will he give for his life;* for never any man valued life at a lower rate than he did.

I. He ungratefully quarrels with life, and is angry that

it was not taken from him as soon as it was given him (v. 11, 12): *Why died not I from the womb?* See here, 1. What a weak and helpless creature man is when he comes into the world, and how slender the thread of life is when it is first drawn. We are ready to die from the womb, and to breathe our last as soon as we begin to breathe at all. We can do nothing for ourselves, as other creatures can, but should drop into the grave if the knees did not prevent us; and the lamp of life, when first lighted, would go out of itself if the breasts given us, that we should suck, did not supply it with fresh oil. 2. What a merciful and tender care divine Providence took of us at our entrance into the world. It was owing to this that we *died not from the womb* and did not *give up the ghost when we came out of the belly.* Why were we not cut off as soon as we were born? Not because we did not deserve it. Justly might such weeds have been plucked up as soon as they appeared; justly might such cockatrices have been crushed in the egg. Nor was it because we did, or could, take any care of ourselves and our own safety: no creature comes into the world so shiftless as man. It was not our might, or the power of our hand, that preserved us these beings, but God's power and providence upheld our frail lives, and his pity and patience spared our forfeited lives. It was owing to this that the knees prevented us. Natural affection is put into parents' hearts by the hand of the God of nature: and hence it was that the blessings of the breast attended those of the womb. 3. What a great deal of vanity and vexation of spirit attends human life. If we had not a God to serve in this world, and better things to hope for in another world, considering the faculties we are endued with and the troubles we are surrounded with, we should be strongly tempted to wish that we had *died from the womb,* which would have prevented a great deal both of sin and misery.

> He that is born to-day, and dies to-morrow,
> Loses some hours of joy, but months of sorrow.

4. The evil of impatience, fretfulness, and discontent. When they thus prevail they are unreasonable and absurd, impious and ungrateful. To indulge them is a slighting and undervaluing of God's favour. How much soever life is embittered, we must say, "It was of the Lord's mercies that we died not from the womb, that we were not consumed." Hatred of life is a contradiction to the common sense and sentiments of mankind, and to our own at any other time. Let discontented people declaim ever so much against life, they will be loth to part with it when it comes to the point. When the old man in the fable, being tired with his burden, threw it down with discontent and called for Death, and Death came to him and asked him what he would have with him, he then answered, "Nothing, but to help me up with my burden."

II. He passionately applauds death and the grave, and seems quite in love with them. To desire to die that we may be with Christ, that we may be free from sin, and that we may be *clothed upon with our house which is from heaven,* is the effect and evidence of grace; but to desire to die only that we may be quiet in the grave, and delivered from the troubles of this life, savours of corruption. Job's considerations here may be of good use to reconcile us to death when it comes, and to make us easy under the arrest of it; but they ought not to be made use of as a pretence to quarrel with life while it is continued, or to make us uneasy under the burdens of it. It is our wisdom and duty to make the best of that which is, be it living or dying, and so to *live to the Lord* and *die to the Lord,* and to be his in both, Rom. 14:8. Job here frets himself with thinking that if he had but died as soon as he was born, and been carried from the womb to the grave, 1. His condition would have been as good as that of the best: I would have been (says he, v. 14) *with kings and counsellors of the earth,* whose pomp, power, and policy, cannot set them out of the reach of death, nor secure them from the grave, nor distinguish theirs from common dust in the grave. Even princes, who had gold in abundance, could not with it bribe Death to overlook them when he came with commission; and, though they filled their houses with silver, yet they were forced to leave it all behind them, no more to return to it. Some, by the *desolate places* which the kings and counsellors are here said *to build for themselves,* understand the sepulchres or monuments they prepared for themselves in their life-time; as Shebna (Isa. 22:16) *hewed himself out a sepulchre;* and by the gold which the princes had, and the silver with which they filled their houses, they understand the treasures which, they say, it was usual to deposit in the graves of great men. Such arts have been used to preserve their dignity, if possible, on the other side death, and to keep themselves from lying even with those of inferior rank; but it will not do: death is, and will be, an irresistible leveller. *Mors sceptra ligonibus aequat — Death mingles sceptres with spades. Rich and poor meet together* in the grave; and there a *hidden untimely birth* (*v.* 16), a child that either never saw light or but just opened its eyes and peeped into the world, and, not liking it, closed them again and hastened out of it, lies as soft and easy, lies as high and safe, as kings and counsellors, and princes, that had gold. "And therefore," says Job, "would I had lain there in the dust, rather than to lie here in the ashes!" 2. His condition would have been much better than now it was (*v.* 13): *"Then should I have lain still, and been quiet,* which now I cannot do, I cannot be, but am still tossing and unquiet; then *I should have slept,* whereas now sleep departeth from my eyes; *then had I been at rest,* whereas now I am restless." Now that life and immortality are brought to a much clearer light by the gospel than before they were placed in good Christians can give a better account than this of the gain of death: "Then should I have been present with the Lord; then should I have seen his glory face to face, and no longer through a glass darkly." But all that poor Job dreamed of was rest and quietness in the grave out of the fear of evil tidings and out of the feeling of sore boils. *Then should I have been quiet;* and had he kept his temper, his even easy temper still, which he was in as recorded in the two foregoing chapters, entirely resigned to the holy will of God and acquiescing in it, he might have been quiet now; his soul, at least, might have dwelt at ease, even when his body lay in pain, Ps. 25:13. Observe how finely he describes the repose of the grave, which (provided the soul also be at rest in God) may much assist our triumphs over it. (1.) Those that now are troubled will there be out of the reach of trouble (*v.* 17): *There the wicked cease from troubling.* When persecutors die they can no longer persecute; their *hatred and envy* will then *perish.* Herod had vexed the church, but, when he became a prey for worms, he ceased from troubling. When the persecuted die they are out of the danger of being any further troubled. Had Job been at rest in his grave, he would have had no disturbance from the Sabeans and Chaldeans, none of all his enemies would have created him any trouble. (2.) Those that are now toiled will there see the period of their toils. *There the weary are at rest.* Heaven is more than a rest to the souls of the saints, but the grave is a rest to their bodies. Their pilgrimage is a weary pilgrimage; sin and the world they are weary of; their services, sufferings, and expectations, they are wearied with; but in the grave they *rest from all their labours,* Rev. 14:13; Isa. 57:23. They are easy there, and make no complaints; there believers sleep in Jesus. (3.) Those that were here enslaved are there at liberty. Death is the prisoner's discharge, the relief of the oppressed, and the servant's manumission (*v.* 18): *There the prisoners,* though they walk not at large, yet they *rest together,* and are not put to work, to grind in that prison-house. They are no more insulted and trampled upon, menaced and terrified, by their cruel task-masters: *They hear not the voice of the oppressor.* Those that were here doomed to perpetual servitude, that could call nothing their own, no, not their own bodies, are there no longer under command or control: *There the servant is free from his master,* which is a good reason why those that have power should use it moderately, and those that are in subjection should bear it patiently, yet a little while. (4.) Those that were at a vast distance from others are there upon a level (*v.* 19): *The small and great are there,* there the same, there all one, all alike free among the dead. The tedious pomp and state which attend the great are at an end there. All the inconveniences of a poor and low condition are likewise over; death and the grave know no difference.

> Levelled by death, the conqueror and the slave,
> The wise and foolish, cowards and the brave,
> Lie mixed and undistinguished in the grave.
> — Sir R. Blackmore

Verses 20–26

Job, finding it to no purpose to wish either that he had not been born or had died as soon as he was born, here complains that his life was now continued and not cut off. When men are set on quarrelling there is no end of it; the corrupt heart will carry on the humour. Having cursed the day of his birth, here he courts the day of his death. The beginning of this strife and impatience is as the letting forth of water.

I. He thinks it hard, in general, that miserable lives should be prolonged (*v.* 20–22): *Wherefore is light in life given to those that are bitter in soul?* Bitterness of soul, through spiritual grievances, makes life itself bitter. *Why doth he give light?* (so it is in the original): he means *God,* yet does not name him, though the devil had said, "He will curse thee to thy face;" but he tacitly reflects on the divine Providence as unjust and unkind in continuing life when the comforts of life are removed. Life is called *light,* because pleasant and serviceable for walking and working. It is candle-light; the longer it burns the shorter it is, and the nearer to the socket. This light is said to be given us; for, if it were not daily renewed to us by a fresh gift, it would be lost. But Job reckons that to those who are in misery it is *dōron adōron — gift and no gift,* a gift that they had better be without, while the light only serves them to see their own misery by. Such is the vanity of human life that it sometimes becomes a vexation of spirit; and so alterable is the property of death that, though dreadful to nature, it may become desirable even to nature itself. He here speaks of those, 1. Who long for death, when they have out-lived their comforts and usefulness, are burdened with age and infirmities, with pain or sickness, poverty or disgrace, and yet it comes not; while, at the same time, it comes to many who dread it and would put it far from them. The continuance and period of life must be according to God's will, not according to ours. It is not fit that we should be consulted how long we would live and when we would die; our times are in a better hand than our own. 2. Who *dig for it as for hidden treasures,* that is, would give any thing for a fair dismission out of this world, which supposes that *then* the thought of men's being their own executioners was not so much as entertained or suggested, else those who longed for it needed not take much pains for it, they might soon come at it (as Seneca tells them) if they are pleased. 3. Who bid it welcome, and *are glad* when they can find the grave and see themselves stepping into it. If the miseries of this life can prevail, contrary to nature, to make death itself desirable, shall not much more the hopes and prospects of a better life, to which death is our passage, make it so, and set us quite above the fear of it? It may be a sin to long for death, but I am sure it is no sin to long for heaven.

II. He thinks himself, in particular, hardly dealt with, that he might not be eased of his pain and misery by death when he could not get ease in any other way. To be thus impatient of life for the sake of the troubles we meet with is not only unnatural in itself, but ungrateful to the giver of life, and argues a sinful indulgence of our own passion and a sinful inconsideration of our future state. Let it be our great and constant care to get ready for another world, and then let us leave it to God to order the circumstances of our removal thither as he thinks fit: "Lord, when and how thou pleasest;" and this with such an indifference that, if he should refer it to us, we would refer it to him again. Grace teaches us, in the midst of life's greatest comforts, to be willing to die, and, in the midst of its greatest crosses, to be willing to live. Job, to excuse himself in this earnest desire which he had to die, pleads the little comfort and satisfaction he had in life.

1. In his present afflicted state troubles were continually felt, and were likely to be so. He thought he had cause enough to be weary of living, for, (1.) He had no comfort of his life: *My sighing comes before I eat, v.* 24. The sorrows of life prevented and anticipated the supports of life; nay, they took away his appetite for his necessary food. His griefs returned as duly as his meals, and affliction was his daily bread. Nay, so great was the extremity of his pain and anguish that he did not only sigh, but roar, and his *roarings were poured out like the waters* in a full and constant stream. Our Master was acquainted with grief, and we must expect to be so too. (2.) He had no prospect of bettering his condition: *His way was hidden,* and God had *hedged him in, v.* 23. He saw no way open of deliverance, nor knew he what course to take; his way was *hedged up with thorns,* that he could not find his path. See *ch.* 23:8; Lam. 3:7.

2. Even in his former prosperous state troubles were continually feared; so that *then* he was never easy, *v.* 25, 26. He knew so much of the vanity of the world, and the troubles to which, of course, he was born, that he was *not in safety, neither had he rest* then. That which made his grief now the more grievous was that he was not conscious to himself of any great degree either of negligence or security in the day of his prosperity, which might provoke God thus to chastise him. (1.) He had not been negligent and unmindful of his affairs, but kept up such a fear of trouble as was necessary to the maintaining of his guard. He was afraid for his children when they were feasting, lest they should offend God (*ch.* 1:5), afraid for his servants lest they should offend his neighbours; he took all the care he could of his own health, and managed himself and his affairs with all possible precaution; yet all would not do. (2.) He had not been secure, nor indulged himself in ease and softness, had not trusted in his wealth, nor flattered himself with the hopes of the perpetuity of his mirth; yet trouble came, to convince and remind him of the vanity of the world, which yet he had not forgotten when he lived at ease. Thus his way was hidden, for he knew not wherefore God contended with him. Now this consideration, instead of aggravating his grief, might rather serve to alleviate it. Nothing will make trouble easy so much as the testimony of our consciences for us, that, in some measure, we did our duty in a day of prosperity; and an expectation of trouble will make it sit the lighter when it comes. The less it is a surprise the less it is a terror.

CHAPTER 4

Job having warmly given vent to his passion, and so broken the ice, his friends here come gravely to give vent to their judgment upon his case, which perhaps they had communicated to one another apart, compared notes upon it and talked it over among themselves, and found they were all agreed in their verdict, that Job's afflictions certainly proved him to be a hypocrite; but they did not attack Job with this high charge till by the expressions of his discontent and impatience, in which they thought he reflected on God himself, he had confirmed them in the bad opinion they had before conceived of him and his character. Now they set upon him with great fear. The dispute begins, and it soon becomes fierce. The opponents are Job's three friends. Job himself is respondent. Elihu appears, first, as moderator, and at length God himself gives judgment upon the controversy and the management of it. The question in dispute is whether Job was an honest man or no, the same question that was in dispute between God and Satan in the first two chapters. Satan had yielded it, and durst not pretend that his cursing his day was a constructive cursing of his God; no, he cannot deny but that Job still holds fast his integrity; but Job's friends will needs have it that, if Job were an honest man, he would not have been thus sorely and thus tediously afflicted, and therefore urge him to confess himself a hypocrite in the profession he had made of religion: "No," says Job, "that I will never do; I have offended God, but my heart, notwithstanding, has been upright with him;" and still he holds fast the comfort of his integrity. Eliphaz, who, it is likely, was the senior, or of the best quality, begins with him in this chapter, in which, I. He bespeaks a patient hearing (*v.* 2). II. He compliments Job with an acknowledgment of the eminence and usefulness of the profession he had made of religion (*v.* 3, 4). III. He charges him with hypocrisy in his profession, grounding his charge upon his present troubles and his conduct under them (*v.* 5, 6). IV. To make good the inference, he maintains that man's wickedness is that which always brings God's judgments (*v.* 7–11). V. He corroborates his assertion by a vision which he had, in which he was reminded of the incontestable purity and justice of God, and the meanness, weakness, and sinfulness of man (*v.* 12–21). By all this he aims to bring down Job's spirit and to make him both penitent and patient under his afflictions.

Verses 1–6

In these verses,

I. Eliphaz excuses the trouble he is now about to give to Job by his discourse (*v.* 2): *"If we assay a word with thee,* offer a word of reproof and counsel, wilt thou be grieved and take it ill?" We have reason to fear thou wilt; but there is no remedy: *"Who can refrain from words?"* Observe, 1. With what modesty he speaks of himself and his own attempt. He will not undertake the management of the cause alone, but very humbly joins his friends with him: "We will commune with thee." Those that plead God's cause must be glad of help, lest it suffer through their weakness. He will not promise much, but begs leave to assay or attempt, and try if he could propose any thing that might be pertinent, and suit Job's case. In difficult matters it becomes us to pretend no further, but only to try what may be said or done. Many excellent discourses have gone under the modest title of *Essays.* 2. With what tenderness he speaks of Job, and his present afflicted condition: "If we tell thee our mind, *wilt thou be grieved?* Wilt thou take it ill? Wilt thou lay it to thy own heart as thy affliction or to our charge as our fault? Shall we be reckoned unkind and cruel if we deal plainly and faithfully with thee? We desire we may not; we hope we shall not, and should be sorry if that should be ill resented which is well intended." Note, We ought to be afraid of grieving any, especially those that are already in grief, lest we add affliction to the afflicted, as David's enemies, Ps. 69:26. We should show ourselves backward to say that which we foresee will be grievous, though ever so necessary. God himself, though he afflicts justly, does not afflict willingly, Lam. 3:33. 3. With what assurance he speaks of the truth and pertinency of what he was about to say: *Who can withhold himself from speaking?* Surely it was a pious zeal for God's honour, and the spiritual welfare of Job, that laid him under this necessity of speaking. "Who can forbear speaking in vindication of God's honour, which we hear reproved, in love to thy soul, which we see endangered?" Note, It is foolish pity not to reprove our friends, even our friends in affliction, for what they say or do amiss, only for fear of offending them. Whether men take it well or ill, we must with wisdom and meekness do our duty and discharge a good conscience.

II. He exhibits a twofold charge against Job.

1. As to his particular conduct under this affliction. He charges him with weakness and faint-heartedness, and this article of his charge there was too much ground for, *v.* 3–5. And here,

(1.) He takes notice of Job's former serviceableness to the comfort of others. He owns that Job had instructed many, not only his own children and servants, but many others, his neighbours and friends, as many as fell within the sphere of his activity. He did not only encourage those who were teachers by office, and countenance them, and pay for the teaching of those who were poor, but he did himself instruct many. Though a great man, he did not think it below him (king Solomon was a preacher); though a man of business, he found time to do it, went among his neighbours, talked to them about their souls, and gave them good counsel. O that this example of Job were imitated by our great men! If he met with those who were ready to fall into sin, or sink under their troubles, his words upheld them: a wonderful dexterity he had in offering that which was proper to fortify persons against temptations, to support them under their burdens, and to comfort afflicted consciences. He had, and used, the tongue of the learned, knew how to speak a word in season to those that were weary, and employed himself much in that good work. With suitable counsels and comforts he *strengthened the weak hands* for work and service and the spiritual warfare, and the feeble knees for bearing up the man in his journey and under his load. It is not only our duty to *lift up our own hands that hang down,* by quickening and encouraging ourselves in the way of duty (Heb. 12:12), but we must also strengthen the weak hands of others, as there is occasion, and do what we can to confirm their feeble knees, by saying *to those that are of a fearful heart, Be strong,* Isa. 35:3, 4. The expressions seem to be borrowed thence. Note, Those should abound in spiritual charity. A good word, well and wisely spoken, may do more good than perhaps we think of. But why does Eliphaz mention this here? [1.] Perhaps he praises him thus for the good he had done that he might make the intended reproof the more passable with him. Just commendation is a good preface to a just reprehension, will help to remove prejudices, and will show that the reproof comes not from ill will. Paul praised the Corinthians before he chided them, 1 Co. 11:2. [2.] He remembers how Job had comforted others as a reason why he might justly expect to be himself comforted; and yet, if conviction was necessary in order to comfort, they must be excused if they applied themselves to that first. The *Comforter shall reprove,* Jn. 16:8. [3.] He speaks this, perhaps, in a way of pity, lamenting that through the extremity of his affliction he could not apply those comforts to himself which he had formerly administered to others. It is easier to give good counsel than to take it, to preach meekness and patience than to practise them. *Facile omnes, cum valemus, rectum consilium aegrotis damus — We all find it easy, when in health, to give good advice to the sick. — Terent.* [4.] Most think that he mentions it as an aggravation of his present discontent, upbraiding him with his knowledge, and the good offices he had done for others, as if he had said, "Thou that hast taught others, why dost thou not teach thyself? Is not this an evidence of thy hypocrisy, that thou hast prescribed that medicine to others which thou wilt not now take thyself, and so contradictest thyself, and actest against thy own know principles? Thou that teachest another to faint, dost thou faint? Rom. 2:21. Physician, heal thyself." Those who have rebuked others must expect to hear of it if they themselves become obnoxious to rebuke.

(2.) He upbraids him with his present low-spiritedness, *v.* 5. "*Now* that *it has come upon thee,* now that it is thy turn to be afflicted, and the bitter cup that goes round is put into thy hand, now that *it touches thee, thou faintest, thou art troubled.*" Here, [1.] He makes too light of Job's afflictions: "It *touches* thee." The very word that Satan himself had used, *ch.* 1:11, 2:5. Had Eliphaz felt but the one-half of Job's affliction, he would have said, "It smites me, it wounds me;" but, speaking of Job's afflictions, he makes a mere trifle of it: "It touches thee and thou canst not bear to be touched." *Noli me tangere — Touch me not.* [2.] He makes too much of Job's resentments, and aggravates them: "Thou faintest, or thou art beside thyself; thou ravest, and knowest not what thou sayest." Men in deep distress must have grains of allowance, and a favourable construction put upon what they say; when we make the worst of every word we do not as we would be done by.

2. As to his general character before this affliction. he charges him with wickedness and false-heartedness, and this article of his charge was utterly groundless and unjust. How unkindly does he banter him, and upbraid him with the great profession of religion he had made, as if it had all now come to nothing and proved a sham (*v.* 6): "*Is not this thy fear, thy confidence, thy hope, and the uprightness of thy ways?* Does it not all appear now to be a mere pretence? For, hadst thou been sincere in it, God would not thus have afflicted thee, nor wouldst thou have behaved thus under the affliction." This was the very thing Satan aimed at, to prove Job a hypocrite, and disprove the character God had given of him. When he could not himself do this to God, but he still saw and said, *Job is perfect and upright,* then he endeavoured, by his friends, to do it to Job himself, and to persuade him to confess himself a hypocrite. Could he have gained that point he would have triumphed. *Habes confitentem reum — Out of thy own mouth will I condemn thee.* But, by the grace of God, Job was enabled to hold fast his integrity, and would not bear false witness against himself. Note, Those that pass rash and uncharitable censures upon their brethren, and condemn them as hypocrites, do Satan's work, and serve his interest, more than they are aware of. I know not how it comes to pass that this verse is differently read in several editions of our common English Bibles; the original, and all the ancient versions, put *thy hope* before *the uprightness of thy ways.* So does the Geneva, and most of the editions of the last translation; but I find one of the first, in 1612, has it, *Is not this thy fear, thy confidence, the uprightness of thy ways, and thy hope?* Both the Assembly's Annotations and Mr. Pool's have that reading: and an edition in 1660 reads it, "*Is not thy fear thy confidence, and the uprightness of thy ways thy hope?* Does it not appear now that all the religion both of thy devotion and of thy conversation was only in hope and confidence that thou shouldst grow rich by it? Was it not all mercenary?" The very thing that Satan suggested. *Is not thy religion thy hope, and are not thy ways thy confidence?* so Mr. Broughton. Or, "Was it not? Didst thou not think that that would be thy protection? But thou art deceived." Or, "Would it not have been so? If it had been sincere, would it not have kept thee from this despair?" It is true, *if thou faint in the day of adversity, thy strength,* thy grace, *is small* (Prov. 24:10); but it does not therefore follow that thou hast no grace, no strength at all. A man's character is not to be taken from a single act.

Verses 7–11

Eliphaz here advances another argument to prove Job a hypocrite, and will have not only his impatience under his afflictions to be evidence against him but even his afflictions themselves, being so very great and extraordinary, and there being no prospect at all of his deliverance out of them. To strengthen his argument he here lays down these two principles, which seem plausible enough: —

I. That good men were never thus ruined. For the proof of this he appeals to Job's own observation (*v.* 7): "*Remember, I pray thee;* recollect all that thou hast seen, heard, or read, and give me an instance of any one that was innocent and righteous, and yet perished as thou dost, and was cut off as thou art." If we understand it of a final and eternal destruction, his principle is true. None that are innocent and righteous perish for ever: it is only a *man of sin* that is a *son of perdition,* 2 Th. 2:3. But then it is ill applied to Job; he did not thus perish, nor was he cut off: a man is never undone till he is in hell. But, if we understand it of any temporal calamity, his principle is not true. *The righteous perish* (Isa. 57:1): *there is one event both to the righteous and to the wicked* (Eccl. 9:2), both in life and death; the great and certain difference is after death. Even before Job's time (as early as it was) there were instances sufficient to contradict this principle. Did not righteous Abel *perish being innocent?* and was he not cut off in the beginning of his days? Was not righteous Lot burnt out of house and harbour, and forced to retire to a melancholy cave? Was not righteous Jacob *a Syrian ready to perish?* Deu. 26:5. Other such instances, no doubt, there were, which are not on record.

II. That wicked men were often thus ruined. For the proof of this he vouches his own observation (*v.* 8): "*Even as I have seen,* many a time, *those that plough iniquity, and sow wickedness, reap accordingly; by the blast of God they perish, v.* 9. We have daily instances of that; and therefore, since thou dost thus perish and art consumed, we have reason to think that, whatever profession of religion thou hast made, thou hast but ploughed iniquity and sown wickedness. Even as I have seen in others, so do I see in thee."

1. He speaks of sinners in general, politic busy sinners, that take pains in sin, for they plough iniquity; and expect gain by sin, for they sow wickedness. Those that plough plough in hope, but what is the issue? *They reap the same.* They shall of the *flesh reap corruption* and ruin, Gal. 6:7, 8. The harvest will be *a heap in the day of grief and desperate sorrow,* Isa. 17:11. He shall reap *the same,* that is, the proper product of that seedness. That which the sinner sows, he *sows not that body that shall be,* but God will give it a body, a body of death, *the end of those things,* Rom. 6:21. Some, by iniquity and wickedness, understand wrong and injury done to others. Those who plough and sow them shall reap the same, that is, they shall be paid in their own coin. Those who are troublesome shall be troubled, 2 Th. 1:6; Jos. 7:25. The *spoilers shall be spoiled* (Isa. 33:1), and those that led captive shall *go captive,* Rev. 13:10. He further describes their destruction (*v.* 9): *By the blast of God they perish.* The projects they take so much pains in are defeated; God cuts asunder the cords of those ploughers, Ps. 129:3, 4. They themselves are destroyed, which is the just punishment of their iniquity. *They perish,* that is, they are destroyed utterly; *they are consumed,* that is, they are destroyed gradually; and this by the blast and breath of God, that is, (1.) By his wrath. His anger is the ruin of sinners, who are therefore called *vessels of wrath,* and his breath is said to *kindle Tophet,* Isa. 30:33. *Who knows the power of his anger?* Ps. 90:11. (2.) By his word. He speaks and it is done, easily and effectually. The Spirit of God, in the word, consumes sinners; with that he slays them, Hos. 6:5. Saying and doing are not two things with God. The man of sin is said to be consumed with the *breath of Christ's mouth,* 2 Th. 2:8. Compare Isa. 11:4; Rev. 19:21. Some think that in attributing the destruction of sinners to the blast of God, and *the breath of his nostrils,* he refers to the wind which blew the house down upon Job's children, as if they were therefore *sinners above all men because they suffered such things.* Lu. 13:2.

2. He speaks particularly of tyrants and cruel oppressors, under the similitude of lions, *v.* 10, 11. Observe, (1.) How he describes their cruelty and oppression. The Hebrew tongue has five several names for lions, and they are all here used to set forth the terrible tearing power, fierceness, and cruelty, of proud oppressors. They roar, and rend, and prey upon all about them, and bring up their young ones to do so too, Eze. 19:3. The devil is a roaring lion; and they partake of his nature, and do his lusts. They are strong as lions, and subtle (Ps. 10:9; 17:12); and, as far as they prevail, they lay all desolate about them. (2.) How he describes their destruction, the destruction both of their power and of their persons. They shall be restrained from

doing further hurt and reckoned with for the hurt they have done. An effectual course shall be taken, [1.] That they shall not terrify. The voice of their roaring shall be stopped. [2.] That they shall not tear. God will disarm them, will take away their power to do hurt: *The teeth of the young lions are broken.* See Ps. 3:7. Thus shall the remainder of wrath be restrained. [3.] That they shall not enrich themselves with the spoil of their neighbours. Even *the old lion is famished, and perishes for lack of prey.* Those that have surfeited on spoil and rapine are perhaps reduced to such straits as to die of hunger at last. [4.] That they shall not, as they promise themselves, leave a succession: *The stout lion's whelps are scattered abroad,* to seek for food themselves, which the old ones used to bring in for them, Nah. 2:12. *The lion did tear in pieces for his whelps,* but now they must shift for themselves. Perhaps Eliphaz intended, in this, to reflect upon Job, as if he, being *the greatest of all the men of the east,* had got his estate by spoil and used his power in oppressing his neighbours, but now his power and estate were gone, and his family was scattered: if so, it was a pity that a man whom God praised should be thus abused.

Verses 12–21

Eliphaz, having undertaken to convince Job of the sin and folly of his discontent and impatience, here vouches a vision he had been favoured with, which he relates to Job for his conviction. What comes immediately from God all men will pay a particular deference to, and Job, no doubt, as much as any. Some think Eliphaz had this vision now *lately,* since he came to Job, putting words into his mouth wherewith to reason with him; and it would have been well if he had kept to the purport of this vision, which would serve for a ground on which to reprove Job for his murmuring, but not to condemn him as a hypocrite. Others think he had it *formerly;* for God did, in this way, often communicate his mind to the children of men in those first ages of the world, ch. 33:15. Probably God had sent Eliphaz this messenger and message some time or other, when he was himself in an unquiet discontented frame, to calm and pacify him. Note, As we should comfort others with that wherewith we have been comforted (2 Co. 1:4), so we should endeavour to convince others with that which has been powerful to convince us. The people of God had not then any written word to quote, and therefore God sometimes notified to them even common truths by the extraordinary ways of revelation. We that have Bibles have there (thanks be to God) a more sure word to depend upon than even visions and voices, 2 Pt. 1:19. Observe,

I. The manner in which this message was sent to Eliphaz, and the circumstances of the conveyance of it to him. 1. It was *brought to him secretly,* or by stealth. Some of the sweetest communion gracious souls have with God is in secret, where no eye sees but that of him who is all eye. God has ways of bringing conviction, counsel, and comfort, to his people, unobserved by the world, by private whispers, as powerfully and effectually as by the public ministry. *His secret is with them,* Ps. 25:14. As the evil spirit often steals good words out of the heart (Mt. 13:19), so the good Spirit sometimes steals good words into the heart, or ever we are aware. 2. *He received a little thereof, v.* 12. And it is but a little of divine knowledge that the best receive in this world. We know little in comparison with what is to be known, and with what we shall know when we come to heaven. *How little a portion is heard of God! ch.* 26:14. *We know but in part,* 1 Co. 13:12. See his humility and modesty. He pretends not to have understood it fully, but something of it he perceived. 3. It was brought to him in the *visions of the night* (*v.* 13), when he had retired from the world and the hurry of it, and all about him was composed and quiet. Note, The more we are withdrawn from the world and the things of it the fitter we are for communion with God. When we are *communing with our own hearts, and are still* (Ps. 4:4), then is a proper time for the Holy Spirit to commune with us. When others were asleep Eliphaz was ready to receive this visit from Heaven, and probably, like David, was *meditating upon God in the night-watches;* in the midst of those good thoughts this thing was brought to him. We should hear more from God if we thought more of him; yet some are surprised with convictions in the night, ch. 33:14, 15. 4.

It was prefaced with terrors: *Fear came upon him, and trembling, v.* 14. It should seem, before he either heard or saw any thing, he was seized with this trembling, which shook his bones, and perhaps the bed under him. A holy awe and reverence of God and his majesty being struck upon his spirit, he was thereby prepared for a divine visit. Whom God intends to honour he first humbles and lays low, and will have us all to serve him with holy fear, and to rejoice with trembling.

II. The messenger by whom it was sent — *a spirit,* one of the good angels, who are employed not only as the ministers of God's providence, but sometimes as the ministers of his word. Concerning this apparition which Eliphaz saw we are here told (*v.* 15, 16), 1. That it was real, and not a dream, not a fancy. *An image* was before his eyes; he plainly saw it; at first it passed and repassed before his face, moved up and down, but at length it *stood still* to speak to him. If some have been so knavish as to impose false visions on others, and some so foolish as to be themselves imposed upon, it does not therefore follow but that there may have been apparitions of spirits, both good and bad. 2. That it was indistinct, and somewhat confused. He *could not discern the form thereof,* so as to frame any exact idea of it in his own mind, much less to give a description of it. His conscience was to be awakened and informed, not his curiosity gratified. We know little of spirits; we are not capable of knowing much of them, nor is it fit that we should: all in good time; we must shortly remove to the world of spirits, and shall then be better acquainted with them. 3. That it puts him into a great consternation, so that his hair stood on end. Ever since man sinned it has been terrible to him to receive an express from heaven, as conscious to himself that he can expect no good tidings thence; apparitions therefore, even of good spirits, have always made deep impressions of fear, even upon good men. How well it is for us that God sends us his messages, not by spirits, but by men like ourselves, *whose terror shall not make us afraid!* See Dan. 7:28; 10:8, 9.

III. The message itself. Before it was delivered *there was silence,* profound silence, *v.* 16. When we are to speak either from God or to him it becomes us to address ourselves to it with a solemn pause, and so to set bounds about the mount on which God is to come down, and not be hasty to utter any thing. It was in a still small voice that the message was delivered, and this was it (*v.* 17): "*Shall mortal man be more just than God, the immortal God? Shall a man be* thought to be, or pretend to be, *more pure than his Maker?* Away with such a thought!" 1. Some think that Eliphaz aims hereby to prove that Job's great afflictions were a certain evidence of his being a wicked man. A mortal man would be thought unjust and very impure if he should thus correct and punish a servant or subject, unless he had been guilty of some very great crime: "If therefore there were not some great crimes for which God thus punishes thee, man would be more just than God, which is not to be imagined." 2. I rather think it is only a reproof of Job's murmuring and discontent: "Shall a man pretend to be more just and pure than God? more truly to understand, and more strictly to observe, the rules and laws of equity than God? Shall *Enosh,* mortal and miserable man, be so insolent; nay, shall *Geber,* the strongest and most eminent man, man at his best estate, pretend to compare with God, or stand in competition with him?" Note, It is most impious and absurd to think either others or ourselves more just and pure than God. Those that quarrel and find fault with the directions of the divine law, the dispensations of the divine grace, or the disposals of the divine providence, make themselves more just and pure than God; and those who thus *reprove God, let them answer it.* What! sinful man! (for he would not have been mortal if he had not been sinful) short-sighted man! Shall he pretend to be more just, more pure, than God, who, being his Maker, is his Lord and owner? Shall the clay contend with the potter? What justice and purity there is in man, God is the author of it, and therefore is himself more just and pure. See Ps. 94:9, 10.

IV. The comment which Eliphaz makes upon this, for so it seems to be; yet some take all the following verses to be spoken in vision. It comes all to one.

1. He shows how little the angels themselves are in comparison with God, *v.* 18. Angels are God's servants, waiting servants, working servants; they are his ministers (Ps.

104:4); bright and blessed beings they are, but God neither needs them nor is benefited by them and is himself infinitely above them, and therefore, (1.) He puts no trust in them, did not repose a confidence in them, as we do in those we cannot live without. There is no service in which he employs them but, if he pleased, he could have it done as well without them. he never made them his confidants, or of his cabinet-council, Mt. 24:36. He does not leave his business wholly to them, but *his own eyes run to and fro through the earth,* 2 Chr. 16:9. See this phrase, *ch.* 39:11. Some give this sense of it: "So mutable is even the angelical nature that God would not trust angels with their own integrity; if he had, they would all have done as some did, left their first estate; but he saw it necessary to give them supernatural grace to confirm them." (2.) He charges them with folly, vanity, weakness, infirmity, and imperfection, in comparison with himself. If the world were left to the government of the angels, and they were trusted with the sole management of affairs, they would take false steps, and everything would not be done for the best, as now it is. Angels are intelligences, but finite ones. Though not chargeable with iniquity, yet with imprudence. This last clause is variously rendered by the critics. I think it would bear this reading, repeating the negation, which is very common: *He will put no trust in his saints; nor will he glory in his angels (in angelis suis non ponet gloriationem) or make his boast* of them, as if their praises, or services, added any thing to him: it is his glory that he is infinitely happy without them.

2. Thence he infers how much less man is, how much less to be trusted in or gloried in. If there is such a distance between God and angels, what is there between God and man! See how man is represented here in his meanness.

(1.) Look upon man in his life, and he is very mean, *v.* 19. Take man in his best estate, and he is a very despicable creature in comparison with the holy angels, though honourable if compared with the brutes. It is true, angels are spirits, and the souls of men are spirits; but, [1.] Angels are pure spirits; the souls of men *dwell in houses of clay:* such the bodies of men are. Angels are free; human souls are housed, and the body is a cloud, a clog, to it; it is its cage; it is its prison. It is a house of clay, mean and mouldering; an earthen vessel, soon broken, as it was first formed, according to the good pleasure of the potter. It is a cottage, not a house of cedar or a house of ivory, but of clay, which would soon be in ruins if not kept in constant repair. [2.] Angels are fixed, but the very *foundation* of that house of clay in which man dwells *is in the dust.* A house of clay, if built upon a rock, might stand long; but, if founded in the dust, the uncertainty of the foundation will hasten its fall, and it will sink with its own weight. As man was made out of the earth, so he is maintained and supported by that which cometh out of the earth. Take away that, and his body returns to its earth. We stand but upon the dust; some have a higher heap of dust to stand upon than others, but still it is the earth that stays us up and will shortly swallow us up. [3.] Angels are immortal, but man is soon crushed; the *earthly house of his tabernacle is dissolved; he dies and wastes away, is crushed like a moth* between one's fingers, as easily, as quickly; one may almost as soon kill a man as kill a moth. A little thing will destroy his life. He is *crushed before the face of the moth,* so the word is. If some lingering distemper, which consumes like a moth, be commissioned to destroy him, he can no more resist it than he can resist an acute distemper, which comes roaring upon him like a lion. See Hos. 5:12–14. Is such a creature as this to be trusted in, or can any service be expected from him by that God who puts no trust in angels themselves?

(2.) Look upon him in his death, and he appears yet more despicable, and unfit to be trusted. Men are mortal and dying, *v.* 20, 21. [1.] In death *they are destroyed, and perish for ever,* as to this world; it is the final period of their lives, and all the employments and enjoyments here; their place will know them no more. [2.] They are dying daily, and continually wasting: *Destroyed from morning to evening.* Death is still working in us, like a mole digging our grave at each remove, and we so continually lie exposed that we are killed all the day long. [3.] Their life is short, and in a little time they are cut off. It lasts perhaps but from morning to evening. It is but a day (so some understand it); their birth and death are but the sun-rise and sun-set of the same day. [4.] In death all their excellency passes away; beauty, strength, learning, not only cannot secure them from death, but must die with them, nor shall their pomp, their wealth, or power, descend after them. [5.] Their wisdom cannot save them from death: *They die without wisdom,* die for want of wisdom, by their own foolish management of themselves, digging their graves with their own teeth. [6.] It is so common a thing that nobody heeds it, nor takes any notice of it: *They perish without any regarding it,* or laying it to heart. The deaths of others are much the subject of common talk, but little the subject of serious thought. Some think the eternal damnation of sinners is here spoken of, as well as their temporal death: *They are destroyed, or broken to pieces, by death, from morning to evening; and, if they repent not, they perish for ever* (so some read it), *v.* 20. They perish for ever because they regard not God and their duty; they *consider not their latter end,* Lam. 1:9. They have no excellency but that which death takes away, and they die, they die the second death, for want of wisdom to lay hold on eternal life. Shall such a mean, weak, foolish, sinful, dying creature as this pretend to be *more just than God and more pure than his Maker?* No, instead of quarrelling with his afflictions, let him wonder that he is out of hell.

CHAPTER 5

Eliphaz, in the foregoing chapter, for the making good of his charge against Job, had vouched a word from heaven, sent him in a vision. In this chapter he appeals to those that bear record on earth, to the saints, the faithful witnesses of God's truth in all ages (*v.* 1). They will testify, I. That the sin of sinners is their ruin (*v.* 2–5). II. That yet affliction is the common lot of mankind (*v.* 6, 7). III. That when we are in affliction it is our wisdom and duty to apply to God, for he is able and ready to help us (*v.* 8–16). IV. That the afflictions which are borne well will end well; and Job particularly, if he would come to a better temper, might assure himself that God had great mercy in store for him (*v.* 17–27). So that he concludes his discourse in somewhat a better humour than he began it.

Verses 1–5

A very warm dispute being begun between Job and his friends, Eliphaz here makes a fair motion to put the matter to a reference. In all debates perhaps the sooner this is done the better if the contenders cannot end it between themselves. So well assured is Eliphaz of the goodness of his own cause that he moves Job himself to choose the arbitrators (*v.* 1): *Call now, if there be any that will answer thee;* that is, 1. "If there be any that suffer as thou sufferest. Canst thou produce an instance of any one that was really a saint that was reduced to such an extremity as thou art now reduced to? God never dealt with any that love his name as he deals with thee, and therefore surely thou art none of them." 2. "If there be any that say as thou sayest. Did ever any good man curse his day as thou dost? Or will any of the saints justify thee in these heats or passions, or say that these are the spots of God's children? Thou wilt find none of the saints that will be either thy advocates or my antagonists. *To which of the saints wilt thou turn?* Turn to which thou wilt, and thou wilt find they are all of my mind. I have the *communis sensus fidelium — the unanimous vote of the faithful* on my side; they will all subscribe to what I am going to say." Observe, (1.) Good people are called *saints* even in the Old Testament; and therefore I know not why we should, in common speaking (unless because we must *loqui cum vulgo — speak as our neighbours*), appropriate the title to those of the New Testament, and not say St. Abraham, St. Moses, and St. Isaiah, as well as St. Matthew and St. Mark; and St. David the psalmist, as well as St. David the British bishop. Aaron is expressly called *the saint of the Lord.* (2.) All that are themselves saints will turn to those that are so, will choose them for their friends and converse with them, will choose them for their judges and consult them. See Ps. 119:79. The saints shall *judge the world,* 1 Co. 6:1, 2. *Walk in the way of good men* (Prov. 2:20), *the old way, the footsteps of the flock.* Every one chooses some sort of people or other to whom he studies to recommend himself, and whose sentiments are to him the test of honour and dishonour. Now all true saints endeavour to recommend themselves to those that are such, and to stand right in their opinion. (3.) There are some truths so plain, and so universally known and believed, that one may venture to appeal to any of the saints concerning them. However there are some things about which they unhappily differ, there are many more, and more considerable, in which they are agreed; as the evil of sin, the vanity of the world, the worth of the soul, the necessity of a holy life, and the like. Though they do not all live up, as they should, to their belief of these truths, yet they are all ready to bear their testimony to them.

Now there are two things which Eliphaz here maintains, and in which he doubts not but all the saints concur with him: —

I. That the sin of sinners directly tends to their own ruin (*v.* 2): *Wrath kills the foolish man,* his own wrath, and therefore he is foolish for indulging it; it is a fire in his bones, in his blood, enough to put him into a fever. *Envy* is the rottenness of the bones, and so *slays the silly one* that frets himself with it. "So it is with thee," says Eliphaz, "while thou quarrellest with God thou doest thyself the greatest mischief; thy anger at thy own troubles, and thy envy at our prosperity, do but add to thy pain and misery: turn to the saints, and thou wilt find they understand their interest better." Job had told his wife she spoke as the foolish women; now Eliphaz tells him he acted as the foolish men, the silly ones. Or it may be meant thus: "If men are ruined and undone, it is always their own folly that ruins and undoes them. They kill themselves by some lust or other; therefore, no doubt, Job, thou hast done some foolish thing, by which thou hast brought thyself into this calamitous condition." Many understand it of God's wrath and jealousy. Job needed not be uneasy at the prosperity of the wicked, for the world's smiles can never shelter them from God's frowns; they are foolish and silly if they think they will. God's anger will be the death, the eternal death, of those on whom it fastens. What is hell but God's anger without mixture or period?

II. That their prosperity is short and their destruction certain, *v.* 3–5. He seems here to parallel Job's case with that which is commonly the case of wicked people. 1. Job had prospered for a time, seemed confirmed, and was secure in his prosperity; and it is common for foolish wicked men to do so: *I have seen them taking root* — planted, and, in their own and others' apprehension, fixed, and likely to continue. See Jer. 12:2; Ps. 37:35, 36. We see worldly men taking root in the earth; on earthly things they fix the standing of their hopes, and from them they draw the sap of their comforts. The outward estate may be flourishing, but the soul cannot prosper that takes root in the earth. 2. Job's prosperity was now at an end, and so has the prosperity of other wicked people quickly been. (1.) Eliphaz foresaw their ruin with an eye of faith. Those who looked only at present things blessed their habitation, and thought them happy, blessed it long, and wished themselves in their condition. But Eliphaz cursed it, suddenly cursed it, as soon as he saw them begin to take root, that is, he plainly foresaw and foretold their ruin; not that he prayed for it *(I have not desired the woeful day),* but he prognosticated it. *He went into the sanctuary,* and there *understood their end* and heard their doom read (Ps. 73:17, 18), that the *prosperity of fools will destroy them,* Prov. 1:32. Those who believe the word of God can see a *curse in the house of the wicked* (Prov. 3:33), though it be ever so finely and firmly built, and ever so full of all good things; and they can foresee that the curse will, in time, infallibly consume it with the timber thereof, and the stones thereof, Zec. 5:4. (2.) He saw, at length, what he had foreseen. He was not disappointed in his expectation concerning him; the event answered it; his family was undone, and his estate ruined. In these particulars he plainly and very invidiously reflects on Job's calamities. [1.] His children were crushed, *v.* 4. They thought themselves safe in their eldest brother's house, but were *far from safety,* for they were *crushed in the gate.* Perhaps the door or gate of the house was highest built, and fell heaviest upon them, *and there was none to deliver them* from perishing in the ruins. This is commonly understood of the destruction of the families of wicked men, by the execution of justice upon them, to oblige them to restore what they have ill-gotten. They leave it to their children; but the descent shall not bar the entry of the rightful owners, who will crush their children, and cast them by due course of law (and there shall be none to help them), or perhaps by oppression, Ps. 109:9, etc. [2.] His estate was plundered, *v.* 5. Job's was so. The hungry robbers, the Sabeans and Chaldeans, ran away with it, and swallowed it; and this, says he, I have often observed in others. What has been got by spoil and rapine has been lost in the same way. The careful owner hedged it about with thorns, and then thought it safe; but the fence proved insignificant against the greediness of the spoilers (if hunger will break through the stone walls, much more through thorn hedges), and against the divine curse, which will go through the thorns and briers, and *burn them together,* Isa. 27:4.

Verses 6–16

Eliphaz, having touched Job in a very tender part, in mentioning both the loss of his estate and the death of his children as the just punishment of his sin, that he might not drive him to despair, here begins to encourage him, and puts him in a way to make himself easy. Now he very much changes his voice (Gal. 4:20), and speaks in the accents of kindness, as if he would atone for the hard words he had given him.

I. He reminds him that no affliction comes by chance, nor is to be attributed to second causes: It *doth not come forth of the dust,* nor *spring out of the ground,* as the grass doth, *v.* 6. It doth not come of course, at certain seasons of the year, as natural productions do, by a chain of second causes. The proportion between prosperity and adversity is not so exactly observed by Providence as that between day and night, summer and winter, but according to the will and counsel of God, when and as he thinks fit. Some read it, *Sin comes not forth out of the dust, nor iniquity of the ground.* If men be bad, they must not lay the blame upon the soil, the climate, or the stars, but on themselves. *If thou scornest, thou alone shalt bear it.* We must not attribute our afflictions to fortune, for they are from God, nor our sins to fate, for they are from ourselves; so that, whatever trouble we are in, we must own that God sends it upon us and we procure it to ourselves: the former is a reason why we should be very patient, the latter why we should be very penitent, when we are afflicted.

II. He reminds him that trouble and affliction are what we have all reason to expect in this world: *Man is brought to trouble* (*v.* 7), not as man (had he kept his innocency he would have been born to pleasure), but as sinful man, as *born of a woman* (*ch.* 14:1), who was in the transgression. Man is born in sin, and therefore born to trouble. Even those that are born to honour and estate are yet born to trouble in the flesh. In our fallen state it has become natural to us to sin, and the natural consequence of that is affliction, Rom. 5:12. There is nothing in this world we are born to, and can truly call our own, but sin and trouble; both are as the sparks that fly upwards. Actual transgressions are the sparks that fly out of the furnace of original corruption; and, being called *transgressors from the womb,* no wonder that we *deal very treacherously,* Isa. 48:8. Such too is the frailty of our bodies, and the vanity of all our enjoyments, that our troubles also thence arise as naturally *as the sparks fly upwards* — so many are they, so thick and so fast does one follow another. Why then should we be surprised at our afflictions as strange, or quarrel with them as hard, when they are but what we are born to? Man is born to *labour* (so it is in the margin), is sentenced to eat his bread in the sweat of his face, which should inure him to hardness, and make him bear his afflictions the better.

III. He directs him how to behave himself under his affliction (*v.* 8): *I would seek unto God; surely I would:* so it is in the original. Here is, 1. A tacit reproof to Job for not seeking to God, but quarrelling with him: "Job, if I had been in thy case, I would not have been so peevish and passionate as thou art. I would have acquiesced in the will of God." It is easy to say what we would do if we were in such a one's case; but when it comes to the trial, perhaps it will be found not so easy to do as we say. 2. Very good and seasonable advice to him, which Eliphaz transfers to himself in a figure: "For my part, the best way I should think I could take, if I were in thy condition, would be to apply to God." Note, We should give our friends no other counsel than what we would take ourselves if we were in their case, that we may be easy under our afflictions, may get good by them, and may see a good issue of them. (1.) We must by prayer fetch in mercy and grace from God, seek to him as a Father and friend, though he contend with us, as one who is alone able to support and succour us. His favour we must seek when we have lost all we have in the world; to him we must address ourselves as the fountain and Father of all good, all consolation. *Is any afflicted? let him pray.* It is heart's-ease, a salve for every sore. (2.) We must by patience refer ourselves and our cause to him: *To God would I commit my cause;* having spread it before him, I would leave it with him; having laid it at his feet, I would lodge it in his hand. *"Here I am, let the Lord do with me as seemeth him good."* If our cause be indeed a good cause, we need not fear committing it to God, for he is both just and kind. Those that would seek so as to speed must refer themselves to God.

IV. He encourages him thus to seek to God, and commit his cause to him. It will not be in vain to do so, for he is one in whom we shall find effectual help.

1. He recommends to his consideration God's almighty power and sovereign dominion. In general, he *doeth great things* (*v.* 9), great indeed, for he can do any thing, he doth do every thing, and all according to the counsel of his own will — great indeed, for the operations of his power are, (1.) *Unsearchable,* and such as can never be fathomed, can never be found out *from the beginning to the end,* Eccl. 3:11. The works of nature are mysterious; the most curious searches come far short of full discoveries and the wisest philosophers have owned themselves at a loss. The designs of Providence ar much more deep and unaccountable, Rom. 11:33. (2.) *Numerous,* and such as can never be reckoned up. He doeth great *things without number;* his power is never exhausted, nor will all his purposes ever be fulfilled till the end of time. (3.) They are *marvellous,* and such as never can be sufficiently admired; eternity itself will be short enough to be spent in the admiration of them. Now, by the consideration of this, Eliphaz intends, [1.] To convince Job of his fault and folly in quarrelling with God. We must not pretend to pass a judgment upon his works, for they are unsearchable and above our enquiries; nor must we strive with our Maker, for he will certainly be too hard for us, and is able to crush us in a moment. [2.] To encourage Job to seek unto God, and to refer his cause to him. What more encouraging than to see that he is one to whom power belongs? He can do great things and marvellous for our relief, when we are brought ever so low.

2. He gives some instances of God's dominion and power.

(1.) God doeth great things in the kingdom of nature: *He gives rain upon the earth* (*v.* 10), put here for all the gifts of common providence, all the *fruitful seasons* by which he *filleth our hearts with food and gladness,* Acts 14:17. Observe, When he would show what great things God does he speaks of his giving rain, which, because it is a common thing, we are apt to look upon as a little thing, but, if we duly consider both how it is produced and what is produced by it, we shall see it to be a great work both of power and goodness.

(2.) He doeth great things in the affairs of the children of men, not only enriches the poor and comforts the needy, by the rain he sends (*v.* 10), but, in order to the advancing of those that are low, he *disappoints the devices of the crafty;* for *v.* 11 is to be joined to *v.* 12. Compare with Lu. 1:51–53. He hath *scattered the proud in the imagination of their hearts,* and so hath *exalted those of low degree,* and *filled the heart with good things.* See,

[1.] How he frustrates the counsels of the proud and politic, *v.* 12–14. There is a supreme power that manages and overrules men who think themselves free and absolute, and fulfils its own purposes in spite of their projects. Observe, *First,* The froward, that walk contrary to God and the interests of his kingdom, are often very crafty; for they are the seed of the old serpent that was noted for his subtlety. They think themselves wise, but, at the end, will be fools. *Secondly,* The Froward enemies of God's kingdom have their devices, their enterprises, and their counsels, against it, and against the loyal faithful subjects of it. They are restless and unwearied in their designs, close in their consultations, high in their hopes, deep in their politics, and fast-linked in their confederacies, Ps. 2:1, 2. *Thirdly,* God easily can, and (as far as is for his glory) certainly will, blast and defeat all the designs of his and his people's enemies. How were the plots of Ahithophel, Sanbállat, and Haman baffled! How were the confederacies of Syria and Ephraim against Judah, of Gebal, and Ammon, and Amalek, against God's Israel, the kings of the earth and the princes against the Lord and against his anointed, broken! The hands that have been stretched out against God and his church have not performed their enterprise, nor have the weapons formed against Sion prospered. *Fourthly,* That which enemies have designed for the ruin of the church has often turned to their own ruin (*v.* 13): *He takes the wise in their own craftiness,* and *snares them in the work of their own hands,* Ps. 7:15, 16; 9:15, 16. This is quoted by the apostle (1 Co. 3:19) to show how the learned men of the heathen were befooled by their own vain philosophy. *Fifthly,* When God infatuates men they are perplexed, and at a loss, even in those things that seem most plain and easy (*v.* 14): *They meet with darkness* even *in the day-time:* nay (as in the margin), *They run themselves into darkness* by the violence and precipitation of their own counsels. See *ch.* 12:20, 24, 25.

[2.] How he favours the cause of the poor and humble, and espouses that. *First,* He exalts the humble, *v.* 11. Those whom proud men contrive to crush he raises from under their feet, and sets them in safety, Ps. 12:5. The lowly in heart, and those that mourn, he advances, comforts, and makes to *dwell on high,* in the *munitions of rocks,* Isa. 33:16. Sion's mourners are the sealed ones, marked for safety, Eze. 9:4. *Secondly,* He delivers the oppressed, *v.* 15. The designs of the crafty are to ruin the poor. Tongue, and hand, and sword, and all, are at work in order to this; but God takes under his special protection those who, being poor and unable to help themselves, being his poor and devoted to his praise, have committed themselves to him. He saves them from the mouth that speaks hard things against them and the hand that does hard things against them; for he can, when he pleases, tie the tongue and wither the hand. The effect of this is (*v.* 16), 1. That weak and timorous saints are comforted: *So the poor,* who began to despair, *has hope.* The experiences of some are encouragement to others to hope the best in the worst of times; for it is the glory of God to send help to the helpless and hope to the hopeless. 2. That daring threatening sinners are confounded: *Iniquity stops her mouth,* being surprised at the strangeness of the deliverance, ashamed of its enmity against those who appear to be the favourites of Heaven, mortified at the disappointment, and compelled to acknowledge the justice of God's proceedings, having nothing to object against them. Those that domineered over God's poor, that frightened them, menaced them, and falsely accused them, will not have a word to say against them when God appears for them. See Ps. 76:8, 9; Isa. 26:11; Mic. 7:16.

Verses 17–27

Eliphaz, in this concluding paragraph of his discourse, gives Job (what he himself knew not how to take) a comfortable prospect of the issue of his afflictions, if he did but recover his temper and accommodate himself to them. Observe,

I. The seasonable word of caution and exhortation that he gives him (*v.* 17): *"Despise not thou the chastening of the Almighty.* Call it a chastening, which comes from the father's love and is designed for the child's good. Call it the chastening of the Almighty, with whom it is madness to contend, to whom it is wisdom and duty to submit, and who will be a God all-sufficient (for so the word signifies) to all those that trust in him. Do not *despise* it;" it is a copious word in the original. 1. "Be not averse to it. Let grace conquer the antipathy which nature has to suffering, and reconcile thyself to the will of God in it." We need the rod and we deserve it; and therefore we ought not to think it either strange or hard if we feel the smart of it. Let not the heart rise against a bitter pill or potion, when it is prescribed for our good. 2. "Do not think ill of it; do not put it from thee (as that which is either hurtful or at least not useful, which there is not occasion for nor advantage by) only because for the present it is not joyous, but grievous." We must never scorn to stoop to God, nor think it a thing below us to come under his discipline, but reckon, on the contrary, that God really magnifies man when he thus *visits and tries him, ch.* 7:17, 18. 3. "Do not overlook and disregard it, as if it were only a chance, and the production of second causes, but take great notice of it as the voice of God and a messenger from heaven." More is implied than is expressed: *"Reverence the chastening of the Lord;* have a humble awful regard to this correcting hand, and tremble when the lion roars, Amos 3:8. Submit to the chastening, and study to answer the call, to answer the end of it, and then you reverence it." When God by an affliction draws upon us for some of the effects he has entrusted us with we must honour his bill by accepting it, and subscribing it, resigning him his own when he calls for it.

II. The comfortable words of encouragement which he gives him thus to accommodate himself to his condition, and (as he himself had expressed it) to receive evil at the hand of God, and not despise it as a gift not worth the accepting.

1. If his affliction was thus borne, (1.) The nature and property of it would be altered. Though it looked like a man's misery, it would really be his bliss: *Happy is the man whom God correcteth* if he make but a due improvement of the correction. A good man is happy though he be afflicted, for, whatever he has lost, he has not lost his enjoyment of God nor his title to heaven. Nay, he is happy because he is afflicted; correction is an evidence of his sonship and a means of his sanctification; it mortifies his corruptions, weans his heart from the world, draws him nearer to God, brings him to his Bible, brings him to his knees, works him for, and so is working for him, a far more exceeding and eternal weight of glory. *Happy* therefore *is the man whom God correcteth,* Jam. 1:12. (2.) The issue and consequence of it would be very good, *v.* 18. [1.] Though *he makes sore* the body with sore boils, the mind with sad thoughts, yet he *binds up* at the same time, as the skilful tender surgeon binds up the wounds he had occasion to make with his incision-knife. When God makes sores by the rebukes of his providence he binds up by the consolations of his Spirit, which oftentimes abound most as afflictions do abound, and counterbalance them, to the unspeakable satisfaction of the patient sufferers. [2.] Though *he wounds,* yet *his hands make whole* in due time; as he supports his people, and makes them easy under their afflictions, so in due time he delivers them, and makes a way for them to escape. All is well again; and he comforts them *according to the time wherein he afflicted them.* God's usual method is first to wound and then to heal, first to convince and then to comfort, first to humble and then to exalt; and (as Mr. Caryl observes) he never makes a wound too great, too deep, for his own cure. *Una eademque manus vulnus opemque tulit — The hand that inflicts the wound applies the cure.* God tears the wicked and goes away; let those heal that will, if they can (Hos. 5:14); but the humble and penitent may say, *He has torn and he will heal us,* Hos. 6:1. This is general, but,

2. In the following verses Eliphaz addresses himself directly to Job, and gives him many precious promises of great and kind things which God would do for him if he did but humble himself under his hand. Though then they had no Bibles that we know of, yet Eliphaz had sufficient warrant to give Job these assurances, from the general discoveries God had made of his good will to his people. And, though in every thing which Job's friends said they were not directed by the Spirit of God (for they spoke both of God and Job some things that were not right), yet the general doctrines they laid down expressed the pious sense of the patriarchal age, and as St. Paul quoted *v.* 13 for canonical scripture, and as the command *v.* 17 is no doubt binding on us, so these promises here may be, and must be, received and applied as divine promises, and we may *through patience and comfort of this* part of *scripture have hope.* Let us therefore give diligence to make sure our interest in these promises, and then view the particulars of them and take the comfort of them.

(1.) It is here promised that as afflictions and troubles recur supports and deliverances shall be graciously repeated, be it ever so often: *In six troubles he shall* be ready to *deliver thee; yea, and in seven, v.* 19. This intimates that, as long as we are here in this world, we must expect a succession of troubles, that the clouds will return after the rain. After six troubles may come a seventh; after many, look for more; but out of them all will God deliver those that are his, 2 Tim. 3:11; Ps. 34:19. Former deliverances are not, as among men, excuses from further deliverances, but earnests of them, Prov. 19:19.

(2.) That, whatever troubles good men may be in, *there shall no evil touch them;* they shall do them no real harm; the malignity of them, the sting, shall be taken out; they may hiss, but they cannot hurt, Ps. 91:10. The *evil one* toucheth not God's children, 1 Jn. 5:18. Being kept from sin, they are kept from the evil of every trouble.

(3.) That, when desolating judgments are abroad, they shall be taken under special protection, v. 20. Do many perish about them for want of the necessary supports of life? They shall be supplied. *"In famine he shall redeem thee from death;* whatever becomes of others, thou shalt be *kept alive,* Ps. 33:19. *Verily, thou shalt be fed,* nay, even *in the days of famine thou shalt be satisfied,* Ps. 37:3, 19. *In* time of *war,* when thousands fall on the right and left hand, he shall redeem thee *from the power of the sword.* If God please, it shall not touch thee; or if it wound thee, if it kill thee, it shall not hurt thee; it can but kill the body, nor has it power to do that unless it be given from above."

(4.) That, whatever is maliciously said against them, it shall not affect them to do them any hurt, v. 21. *"Thou shalt* not only be protected from the killing sword of war, but shalt *be hidden from the scourge of the* tongue, which, like a scourge, is vexing and painful, though not mortal." The best men, and the most inoffensive, cannot, even in their innocency, secure themselves from calumny, reproach, and false accusation. From these a man cannot hide himself, but God can hide him, so that the most malicious slanders shall be so little heeded by him as not to disturb his peace, and so little heeded by others as not to blemish his reputation: and the remainder of wrath God can and does restrain, for it is owing to the hold he has of the consciences of bad men that the scourge of the tongue is not the ruin of all the comforts of good men in this world.

(5.) That they shall have a holy security and serenity of mind, arising from their hope and confidence in God, even in the worst of times. When dangers are most threatening they shall be easy, believing themselves safe; and they *shall not be afraid of destruction,* no, not when they see it coming (v. 21), nor *of the beasts of the field* when they set upon them, nor of men as cruel as beasts; nay, *at destruction and famine thou shalt laugh* (v. 22), not so as to despise any of God's chastenings or make a jest of his judgments, but so as to triumph in God, in his power and goodness, and therein to triumph over the world and all its grievances, to be not only easy, but cheerful and joyful, in tribulation. Blessed Paul laughed at destruction when he said, *O death! where is thy sting?* when, in the name of all the saints, he defied all the calamities of this present time to *separate us from the love of God,* concluding that *in all these things we are more than conquerors,* Rom. 8:35, etc. See Isa. 37:22.

(6.) That, being at peace with God, there shall be a covenant of friendship between them and the whole creation, v. 23. "When thou walkest over thy grounds thou shalt not need to fear stumbling, for *thou shalt be at league with the stones of the field,* not to dash thy foot against any of them, nor shalt thou be in danger from the *beasts of the field,* for they shall all be at peace with thee;" compare Hos. 2:18, *I will make a covenant for them with the beasts of the field.* This implies that while man is at enmity with his Maker the inferior creatures are at war with him; but *tranquillus Deus tranquillat omnia — a reconciled God reconciles all things.* Our covenant with God is a covenant with all the creatures that they shall do us no hurt but be ready to serve us and do us good.

(7.) That their houses and families shall be comfortable to them, v. 24. Peace and piety in the family will make it so. *"Thou shalt know* and be assured *that thy tabernacle* is and *shall be in peace;* thou mayest be confident both of its present and its future prosperity." *That peace is thy tabernacle* (so the word is); peace is the house in which those dwell who dwell in God, and are at home in him. *"Thou shalt visit"* (that is, enquire into the affairs of) *"thy habitation,* and take a review of them, *and shalt not sin."* [1.] God will provide a settlement for his people, mean perhaps and movable, a cottage, a tabernacle, but a fixed and quiet habitation. "Thou shalt not sin," or *wander;* that is, as some understand it, "thou shalt not be a fugitive and a vagabond" (Cain's curse), "but shalt dwell in the land, and verily, not uncertainly as vagrants, shalt thou be fed." [2.] Their families shall be taken under the special protection of the divine Providence, and shall prosper as far as is for their good. [3.] They shall be assured of peace, and of the continuance and entail of it. "Thou shalt know, to thy unspeakable satisfaction, that peace is sure to thee and thine, having the word of God for it." Providence may

change, but the promise cannot. [4.] They shall have wisdom to govern their families aright, to order their affairs with discretion, and to look well to the ways of their household, which is here called *visiting their habitation.* Masters of families must not be strangers at home, but must have a watchful eye over what they have and what their servants do. [5.] They shall have grace to manage the concerns of their families after a godly sort, and not to sin in the management of them. They shall call their servants to account without passion, pride, covetousness, worldliness, or the like; they shall look into their affairs without discontent at what is or distrust of what shall be. Family piety crowns family peace and prosperity. The greatest blessing, both in our employments and in our enjoyments, is to be kept from sin in them. When we are abroad it is comfortable to hear that our tabernacle is in peace; and when we return home it is comfortable to visit our habitation with satisfaction in our success, that we have not failed in our business, and with a good conscience, that we have not offended God.

(8.) That their posterity shall be numerous and prosperous. Job had lost all his children; "but," says Eliphaz, "if thou return to God, he will again build up thy family, and thy seed shall be many and as great as ever, and thy offspring increasing and flourishing *as the grass of the earth* (v. 25), and thou shalt know it." God has blessings in store for the seed of the faithful, which they shall have if they do not stand in their own light and forfeit them by their folly. It is a comfort to parents to see the prosperity, especially the spiritual prosperity, of their children; if they are truly good, they are truly great, how small a figure soever they may make in the world.

(9.) That their death shall be seasonable, and they shall finish their course, at length, with joy and honour, v. 26. It is a great mercy, [1.] To live to a full age, and not to have the number of our months cut off in the midst. If the providence of God do not give us long life, yet, if the grace of God give us to be satisfied with the time allotted us, we may be said to come to a full age. That man lives long enough that has done his work and is fit for another world. [2.] To be willing to die, to come cheerfully to the grave, and not to be forced thither, as he whose soul was required of him. [3.] To die seasonably, as the corn is cut and housed when it is fully ripe; not till then, but then not suffered to stand a day longer, lest it shed. Our times are in God's hand; it is well they are so, for he will take care that those who are his shall die in the best time: however their death may seem to us untimely, it will be found not unseasonable.

3. In the last verse he recommends these promises to Job, (1.) As faithful sayings, which he might be confident of the truth of: *"Lo, this we have searched, and so it is.* We have indeed received these things by tradition from our fathers, but we have not taken them upon trust; we have carefully searched them, have compared spiritual things with spiritual, have diligently studied them, and been confirmed in our belief of them from our own observation and experience; and we are all of a mind that so it is." Truth is a treasure that is well worth digging for, diving for; and then we shall know both how to value it ourselves and how to communicate it to others when we have taken pains in searching for it. (2.) As well worthy of all acceptation, which he might improve to his great advantage: *Hear it, and know thou it for thy good.* It is not enough to hear and know the truth, but we must improve it, and be made wiser and better by it, receive the impressions of it, and submit to the commanding power of it. *Know it for thyself* (so the word is), with application to thyself, and thy own case; not only "This is true," but "this is true concerning me." That which we thus hear and know for ourselves we hear and know for our good, as we are nourished by the meat which we digest. That is indeed a good sermon to us which does us good.

CHAPTER 6

Eliphaz concluded his discourse with an air of assurance; very confident he was that what he had said was so plain and so pertinent that nothing could be objected in answer to it. But, though he that is first in his own cause seems just, yet his neighbour comes and searches him. Job is not convinced by all he had said, but still justifies himself in his complaints and condemns him for the weakness of his arguing. I. He shows that he had just cause to complain as he did of his troubles, and so it would appear to any impartial judge (v. 2–7). II. He continues his passionate wish that he might speedily be cut off by the stroke of death, and so be eased

of all his miseries (v. 8–13). III. He reproves his friends for their uncharitable censures of him and their unkind treatment (v. 14–30). It must be owned that Job, in all this, spoke much that was reasonable, but with a mixture of passion and human infirmity. And in this contest, as indeed in most contests, there was fault on both sides.

Verses 1-7

Eliphaz, in the beginning of his discourse, had been very sharp upon Job, and yet it does not appear that Job gave him any interruption, but heard him patiently till he had said all he had to say. Those that would make an impartial judgment of a discourse must hear it out, and take it entire. But, when he had concluded, he makes his reply, in which he speaks very feelingly.

I. He represents his calamity, in general, as much heavier than either he had expressed it or they had apprehended it, v. 2, 3. He could not fully describe it; they would not fully apprehend it, or at least would not own that they did; and therefore he would gladly appeal to a third person, who had just weights and just balances with which to weigh his grief and calamity, and would do it with an impartial hand. He wished that they would set his grief and all the expressions of it in one scale, his calamity and all the particulars of it in the other, and (though he would not altogether justify himself in his grief) they would find (as he says, ch. 23:2) that *his stroke was heavier than his groaning;* for, whatever his grief was, his calamity was *heavier than the sand of the sea:* it was complicated, it was aggravated, every grievance weighty, and all together numerous as the sand. "Therefore (says he) *my words are swallowed up;"* that is, "Therefore you must excuse both the brokenness and the bitterness of my expressions. Do not think it strange if my speech be not so fine and polite as that of an eloquent orator, or so grave and regular as that of a morose philosopher: no, in these circumstances I can pretend neither to the one nor to the other; my words are, as I am, quite swallowed up." Now, 1. He hereby complains of it as his unhappiness that his friends undertook to administer spiritual physic to him before they thoroughly understood his case and knew the worst of it. It is seldom that those who are at ease themselves rightly weigh the afflictions of the afflicted. Every one feels most from his own burden; few feel from other people's. 2. He excuses the passionate expressions he had used when he cursed his day. Though he could not himself justify all he had said, yet he thought his friends should not thus violently condemn it, for really the case was extraordinary, and that might be connived at in such a man of sorrows as he now was which in any common grief would by no means be allowed. 3. He bespeaks the charitable and compassionate sympathy of his friends with him, and hopes, by representing the greatness of his calamity, to bring them to a better temper towards him. To those that are pained it is some ease to be pitied.

II. He complains of the trouble and terror of mind he was in as the sorest part of his calamity, v. 4. Herein he was a type of Christ, who, in his sufferings, complained most of the sufferings of his soul. *Now is my soul troubled,* Jn. 12:27. *My soul is exceedingly sorrowful,* Mt. 26:38. *My God, my God, why hast thou forsaken me?* Mt. 27:46. Poor Job sadly complains here, 1. Of what he felt *The arrows of the Almighty are within me.* It was not so much the troubles themselves he was under that put him into this confusion, his poverty, disgrace, and bodily pain; but that which cut him to the heart and put him into this agitation, was to think that the God he loved and served had brought all this upon him and laid him under these marks of his displeasure. Note, Trouble of mind is the sorest trouble. *A wounded spirit who can bear!* Whatever burden of affliction, in body or estate, God is pleased to lay upon us, we may well afford to submit to it as long as he continues to the use of our reason and the peace of our consciences; but, if in either of these we be disturbed, our case is sad indeed and very pitiable. The way to prevent God's fiery darts of trouble is with the shield of faith to quench Satan's fiery darts of temptation. Observe, He calls them the *arrows of the Almighty;* for it is an instance of the power of God above that of any man that he can with his arrows reach the soul. He that made the soul can make his sword to approach to it. The poison or heat of these arrows is said to drink up his spirit, because it disturbed his reason, shook his resolution, exhausted his vigour, and threatened his life; and therefore his passionate expressions, though they could not be justified, might be excused. 2. Of what he feared. He saw himself charged by *the terrors of God,* as by an army set in battle-array, and surrounded by them. God, by his terrors, fought against him. As he had no comfort when he retired inward into his own bosom, so he had none when he looked upward towards Heaven. He that used to be encouraged with the consolations of God not only wanted those, but was amazed with the terrors of God.

III. He reflects upon his friends for their severe censures of his complaints and their unskilful management of his case. 1. Their reproofs were causeless. He complained, it is true, now that he was in this affliction, but he never used to complain, as those do who are of a fretful unquiet spirit, when he was in prosperity: he did not *bray when he had grass,* nor *low over his fodder, v.* 5. But, now that he was utterly deprived of all his comforts, he must be a stock or a stone, and not have the sense of an ox or a wild ass, if he did not give some vent to his grief. He was forced to eat unsavoury meats, and was so poor that he had not a grain of salt wherewith to season them, nor to give a little taste to the white of an egg, which was now the choicest dish he had at his table, *v.* 6. Even that food which once he would have scorned to touch he was now glad of, and it was his *sorrowful meat, v.* 7. Note, It is wisdom not to use ourselves or our children to be nice and dainty about meat and drink, because we know not how we or they may be reduced, nor how that which we now disdain may be made acceptable by necessity. 2. Their comforts were sapless and insipid; so some understand *v.* 6, 7. He complains he had nothing now offered to him for his relief that was proper for him, no cordial, nothing to revive and cheer his spirits; what they had afforded was in itself as tasteless as the white of an egg, and, when applied to him, as loathsome and burdensome as the most sorrowful meat. I am sorry he should say thus of what Eliphaz had excellently well said, *ch.* 5:8, etc. But peevish spirits are too apt thus to abuse their comforters.

Verses 8–13

Ungoverned passion often grows more violent when it meets with some rebuke and check. The troubled sea rages most when it dashes against a rock. Job had been courting death, as that which would be the happy period of his miseries, *ch.* 3. For this Eliphaz had gravely reproved him, but he, instead of unsaying what he had said, says it here again with more vehemence than before; and it is as ill said as almost any thing we meet with in all his discourses, and is recorded for our admonition, not our imitation.

I. He is still most passionately desirous to die, as if it were not possible that he should ever see good days again in this world, or that, by the exercise of grace and devotion, he might make even these days of affliction good days. He could see no end of his trouble but death, and had not patience to wait the time appointed for that. He has a request to make; there is a thing he longs for (*v.* 8); and what is that? One would think it should be, "That it would please God to deliver me, and restore me to my prosperity again;" no, *That it would please God to destroy me, v.* 9. "As once he let loose his hand to make me poor, and then to make me sick, let him loose it once more to put an end to my life. Let him give the fatal stroke; it shall be to me the *coup de grace — the stroke of favour,*" as, in France, they call the last blow which dispatches those that are broken on the wheel. There was a time when *destruction from the Almighty was a terror* to Job (*ch.* 31:23), yet now he courts the destruction of the flesh, but in hopes that the spirit should be saved in the day of the Lord Jesus. Observe, Though Job was extremely desirous of death, and very angry at its delays, yet he did not offer to destroy himself, nor to take away his own life, only he begged *that it would please God to destroy him.* Seneca's morals, which recommend self-murder as the lawful redress of insupportable grievances, were not then known, nor will ever be entertained by any that have the least regard to the law of God and nature. How uneasy soever the soul's confinement in the body may be, it must by no means break prison, but wait for a fair discharge.

II. He puts this desire into a prayer, that God would grant him this request, that it would please God to do this for him. It was his sin so passionately to desire the hastening of his own death, and offering up that desire to God made it no better; nay, what looked ill in his wish looked worse in his prayer, for we ought not to ask any thing of God but what we can ask in faith, and we cannot ask any thing in faith but what is agreeable to the will of God. Passionate prayers are the worst of passionate expressions, for we should *lift up pure hands without wrath.*

III. He promises himself effectual relief, and the redress of all his grievances, by the stroke of death (*v.* 10): *"Then should I yet have comfort,* which now I have not, nor ever expect till then." See, 1. The vanity of human life; so uncertain a good is it that it often proves men's greatest burden and nothing is so desirable as to get clear of it. Let grace make us willing to part with it whenever God calls; for it may so happen that even sense may make us desirous to part with it before he calls. 2. The hope which the righteous have in their death. If Job had not had a good conscience, he could not have spoken with this assurance of comfort on the other side death, which turns the tables between the rich man and Lazarus. *Now he is comforted, and thou art tormented.*

IV. He challenges death to do its worst. If he could not die without the dreadful prefaces of bitter pains and agonies, and strong convulsions, if he must be racked before he be executed, yet, in prospect of dying at last, he would make nothing of dying pangs: *"I would harden myself in sorrow,* would open my breast to receive death's darts, and not shrink from them. *Let him not spare;* I desire no mitigation of that pain which will put a happy period to all my pains. Rather than not die, let me die so as to feel myself die." These are passionate words, which might better have been spared. We should soften ourselves in sorrow, that we may receive the good impressions of it, and by the sadness of the countenance our hearts, being made tender, may be made better; but, if we harden ourselves, we provoke God to proceed in his controversy; *for when he judgeth he will overcome.* It is great presumption to dare the Almighty, and to say, *Let him not spare;* for *are we stronger than he?* 1 Co. 10:22. We are much indebted to sparing mercy; it is bad indeed with us when we are weary of that. Let us rather say with David, *O spare me a little.*

V. He grounds his comfort upon the testimony of his conscience for him that he had been faithful and firm to his profession of religion, and in some degree useful and serviceable to the glory of God in his generation: *I have not concealed the words of the Holy One.* Observe, 1. Job had the words of the Holy One committed to him. The people of God were at that time blessed with divine revelation. 2. It was his comfort that he had not concealed them, had not received the grace of God therein in vain. (1.) He had not kept them from himself, but had given them full scope to operate upon him, and in every thing to guide and govern him. He had not stifled his convictions, *imprisoned the truth in unrighteousness,* nor done any thing to hinder the digestion of this spiritual food and the operation of this spiritual physic. Let us never conceal God's word from ourselves, but always receive it in the light of it. (2.) He had not kept them to himself, but had been ready, on all occasions, to communicate his knowledge for the good of others, was never ashamed nor afraid to own the word of God to be his rule, nor remiss in his endeavours to bring others into an acquaintance with it. Note Those, and those only, may promise themselves comfort in death who are good, and do good, while they live.

VI. He justifies himself, in this extreme desire of death, from the deplorable condition he was now in, *v.* 11, 12. Eliphaz, in the close of his discourse, had put him in hopes that he should yet see a good issue of his troubles; but poor Job puts these cordials away from him, refuses to be comforted, abandons himself to despair, and very ingeniously, yet perversely, argues against the encouragements that were given him. Disconsolate spirits will reason strangely against themselves. In answer to the pleasing prospects Eliphaz had flattered him with, he here intimates, 1. That he had no reason to expect any such thing: *"What is my strength, that I should hope?* You see how I am weakened and brought low, how unable I am to grapple with my distempers, and therefore what reason have I to hope that I should out-live them, and see better days? *Is my strength the strength of stones?* Are my muscles brass and my sinews steel? No, they are not, and therefore I cannot hold out always in this pain and misery, but must needs sink under the load. Had I strength to grapple with my distemper, I might hope to look through it; but, alas! I have not. The *weakening of my strength in the way* will certainly be the *shortening of my days,"* Ps. 102:23. Note, All things considered, we have no reason to reckon upon the long continuance of life in this world. *What is our strength?* It is depending strength. We have no more strength than God gives us; for in him we live and move. It is decaying strength; we are daily spending the stock, and by degrees it will be exhausted. It is disproportionable to the encounters we may meet with; what is our strength to be depended upon, when two or three days' sickness will make us weak as water? Instead of expecting a long life, we have reason to wonder that we have lived hitherto and to feel that we are hastening off apace. 2. That he had no reason to desire any such thing: *"What is my end, that I should desire to prolong my life?* What comfort can I promise myself in life, comparable to the comfort I promise myself in death?" Note, Those who, through grace, are ready for another world, cannot see much to invite their stay in this world, or to make them fond of it. That, if it be God's will, we may do him more service and may get to be fitter and riper for heaven, is an end for which we may wish the prolonging of life, in subservience to our chief end; but, otherwise, what can we propose to ourselves in desiring to tarry here? The longer life is the more grievous will its burdens be (Eccl. 12:1), and the longer life is the less pleasant will be its delights, 2 Sa. 19:34, 35. We have already seen the best of this world, but we are not sure that we have seen the worst of it.

VII. He obviates the suspicion of his being delirious (*v.* 13): *Is not my help in me?* that is, "Have I not the use of my reason, with which, I thank God, I can help myself, though you do not help me? Do you think wisdom is driven quite from me, and that I am gone distracted? No, I am not mad, most noble Eliphaz, but *speak the words of truth and soberness."* Note, Those who have grace in them, who have the evidence of it and have it in exercise, have wisdom in them, which will be their help in the worst of times. *Sat lucis intus — They have light within.*

Verses 14–21

Eliphaz had been very severe in his censures of Job; and his companions, though as yet they had said little, yet had intimated their concurrence with him. Their unkindness therein poor Job here complains of, as an aggravation of his calamity and a further excuse of his desire to die; for what satisfaction could he ever expect in this world when those that should have been his comforters thus proved his tormentors?

I. He shows what reason he had to expect kindness from them. His expectation was grounded upon the common principles of humanity (*v.* 14): *"To him that is afflicted,* and that is wasting and melting under his affliction, *pity should be shown from his friend;* and he that does not show that pity *forsakes the fear of the Almighty."* Note, 1. Compassion is a debt owing to those that are in affliction. The least which those that are at ease can do for those that are pained and in anguish is to pity them, — to manifest the sincerity of a tender concern for them, and to sympathize with them, — to take cognizance of their case, enquire into their grievances, hear their complaints, and mingle their tears with theirs, — to comfort them, and to do all they can to help and relieve them: this well becomes the members of the same body, who should feel for the grievances of their fellow-members, not knowing how soon the same may be their own. 2. Inhumanity is impiety and irreligion. *He that withholds compassion from his friend forsakes the fear of the Almighty.* So the Chaldee. *How dwells the love of God in that man?* 1 Jn. 3:17. Surely those have no fear of the rod of God upon themselves who have no compassion for those that feel the smart of it. See Jam. 1:27. 3. Troubles are the trials of friendship. When a man is afflicted he will see who are his friends indeed and who are but pretenders; for *a brother is born for adversity,* Prov. 17:17; 18:24.

II. He shows how wretchedly he was disappointed in his expectations from them (*v.* 15): *"My brethren,* who should have helped me, *have dealt deceitfully as a brook."* They came by appointment, with a great deal of ceremony, to mourn with him and to comfort him (*ch.* 2:11); and some extraordinary things were expected from such wise, learned, knowing men, and Job's particular friends. None questioned but that the drift of their discourses would be to comfort Job with the remembrance of his former piety, the assurance of God's favour to him, and the prospect of a glorious issue; but, instead of this, they most barbarously fall upon him with their reproaches and censures, condemn him as a hypocrite, insult over his calamities, and pour vinegar, instead of oil, into his wounds, and thus they deal deceitfully with him. Note, It is fraud and deceit not only to violate our engagements to our friends, but to frustrate their just expectations from us, especially the expectations we have raised. Note, further, It is our wisdom to cease from man. We cannot expect too little from the creature nor too much from the Creator. It is no new thing even for brethren to *deal deceitfully* (Jer. 9:4, 5; Mic. 7:5); let us therefore put our confidence in the rock of ages, not in broken reeds — in the fountain of life, not in broken cisterns. God will out-do our hopes as much as men come short of them. This disappointment which Job met with he here illustrates by the failing of brooks in summer.

1. The similitude is very elegant, *v.* 15–20. (1.) Their pretensions are fitly compared to the great show which the brooks make when they are swollen with the waters of a land flood, by the melting of the ice and snow, which make them blackish or muddy, *v.* 16. (2.) His expectations from them, which their coming so solemnly to comfort him had raised, he compares to the expectation which the weary thirsty travellers have of finding water in the summer where they have often seen it in great abundance in the winter, *v.* 19. *The troops of Tema and Sheba,* the caravans of the merchants of those countries, whose road lay through the deserts of Arabia, looked and waited for supply of water from those brooks. "Hard by here," says one, "A little further," says another, "when I last travelled this way, there was water enough; we shall have that to refresh us." Where we have met with relief or comfort we are apt to expect it again; and yet it does not follow; for, (3.) The disappointment of his expectation is here compared to the confusion which seizes the poor travellers when they find heaps of sand where they expected floods of water. In the winter, when they were not thirsty, there was water enough. Every one will applaud and admire those that are full and in prosperity. But in the heat of summer, when they needed water, then it failed them; it was consumed (*v.* 17); it was turned aside, *v.* 18. When those who are rich and high are sunk and impoverished, and stand in need of comfort, then those who before gathered about them stand aloof from them, those who before commended them are forward to run them down. Thus those who raise their expectations high from the creature will find it fail them when it should help them; whereas those who make God their confidence have help *in the time of need,* Heb. 4:16. Those who make gold their hope will sooner or later be ashamed of it, and of their confidence in it (Eze. 7:19); and the greater their confidence was the greater their shame will be: *They were confounded because they had hoped, v.* 20. We prepare confusion for ourselves by our vain hopes: the reeds break under us because we lean upon them. If we build a house upon the sand, we shall certainly be confounded, for it will fall in the storm, and we must thank ourselves for being such fools as to expect it would stand. We are not deceived unless we deceive ourselves.

2. The application is very close (*v.* 21): *For now you are nothing.* They seemed to be somewhat, but in conference they added nothing to him. Allude to Gal. 2:6. He was never the wiser, never the better, for the visit they made him. Note, Whatever complacency we may take, or whatever confidence we may put, in creatures, how great soever they may seem and how dear soever they may be to us, one time or other we shall say of them, *Now you are nothing.* When Job was in prosperity his friends were something to him, he took complacency in them and their society; but *"Now you are nothing,* now I can find no comfort but in God." It were well for us if we had always such convictions of the vanity of the creature, and its insufficiency to make us happy, as we have sometimes had, or shall have on a sick-bed, a death-bed, or in trouble of conscience: *"Now you are nothing.* You are not what you have been, what you should be, what you pretend to be, what I thought you would have been; *for you see my casting down and are afraid.* When you saw me in my elevation you caressed me; but now that you see me in my dejection you are shy of me, are afraid of showing yourselves kind, lest I should thereby be emboldened to beg something of you, or to borrow" (compare *v.* 22); "you are afraid lest, if you own me, you should be obliged to keep me." Perhaps they were afraid of catching his distemper or of coming within smell of the noisomeness of it. It is not good, either out of pride or niceness, for love of our purses or of our bodies, to be shy of those who are in distress and afraid of coming near them. Their case may soon be our own.

Verses 22–30

Poor Job goes on here to upbraid his friends with their unkindness and the hard usage they gave him. He here appeals to themselves concerning several things which tended both to justify him and to condemn them. If they would but think impartially, and speak as they thought, they could not but own,

I. That, though he was necessitous, yet he was not craving, nor burdensome to his friends. Those that are so, whose troubles serve them to beg by, are commonly less pitied than the silent poor. Job would be glad to see his friends, but he did not say, *Bring unto me* (*v.* 22), or, *Deliver me, v.* 23. He did not desire to put them to any expense, did not urge his friends either, 1. To make a collection for him, to set him up again in the world. Though he could plead that his losses came upon him by the hand of God and not by any fault or folly of his own, — that he was utterly ruined and impoverished, — that he had lived in good condition, and that when he had wherewithal he was charitable and ready to help those that were in distress, — that his friends were rich, and able to help him, yet he did not say, *Give me of your substance.* Note, A good man, when troubled himself, is afraid of being troublesome to his friends. Or, 2. To raise the country for him, to help him to recover his cattle out of the hands of the Sabeans and Chaldeans, or to make reprisals upon them: "Did I send for you to *deliver me out of the hand of the mighty?* No, I never expected you should either expose yourselves to any danger or put yourselves to any charge upon my account. I will rather sit down content under my affliction, and make the best of it, than sponge upon my friends." St. Paul worked with his hands, that he might not be burdensome to any. Job's not asking their help did not excuse them from offering it when he needed it and it was in the power of their hands to give it; but it much aggravated their unkindness when he desired no more from them than a good look, and a good word, and yet could not obtain them. It often happens that from man, even when we expect little, we have less, but from God, even when we expect much, we have more, Eph. 3:20.

II. That, though he differed in opinion from them, yet he was not obstinate, but ready to yield to conviction, and to strike sail to truth as soon as ever it was made to appear to him that he was in an error (*v.* 24, 25): "If, instead of invidious reflections and uncharitable insinuations, you will give me plain instructions and solid arguments, which shall carry their own evidence along with them, I am ready to acknowledge my error and own myself in a fault: *Teach me, and I will hold my tongue;* for I have often found, with pleasure and wonder, *how forcible right words are.* But the method you take will never make proselytes: *What doth your arguing reprove?* Your hypothesis is false, your surmises are groundless, your management is weak, and your application peevish and uncharitable." Note, 1. Fair reasoning has a commanding power, and it is a wonder if men are not conquered by it; but railing and foul language are impotent and foolish, and it is no wonder if men are exasperated and hardened by them. 2. It is the undoubted character of every honest man that he is truly desirous to have his mistakes rectified, and to be made to understand wherein he has erred; and he will acknowledge that right words, when they appear to him to be so, though contrary to his former sentiments, are both forcible and acceptable.

III. That, though he had been indeed in a fault, yet they ought not to have given him such hard usage (*v.* 26, 27): *"Do you imagine,* or contrive with a great deal of art" (for so the word signifies), *"to reprove words,* some passionate expressions of mine in this desperate condition, as if they were certain indications of reigning impiety and atheism? A little candour and charity would have served to excuse them, and to put a better construction upon them. Shall a man's spiritual state be judged of by some rash and hasty words, which a surprising trouble extorts from him? Is it fair, is it kind, is it just, to criticize in such a case? Would you yourselves be served thus?" Two things aggravated their unkind treatment of him: — 1. That they took advantage of his weakness and the helpless condition he was in: *You overwhelm the fatherless,* a proverbial expression, denoting that which is most barbarous and inhuman. "The fatherless cannot secure themselves from insults, which emboldens men of base and sordid spirits to insult them and trample upon them; and you do so by me." Job, being a childless father, thought himself as much exposed to injury as a fatherless child (Ps. 127:5) and had reason to be offended with those who therefore triumphed over him. Let those who overwhelm and overpower such as upon any account may be looked upon as fatherless know that therein they not only put off the compassions of man, but fight against the compassions of God, who is, and will be, a Father of the fatherless and a helper of the helpless. 2. That they made a pretence of kindness: *"You dig a pit for your friend;* not only you are unkind to me, who am your friend, but, under colour of friendship, you ensnare me." When they came to see and sit with him he thought he might speak his mind freely to them, and that the more bitter his complaints to them were the more they would endeavour to comfort him. This made him take a greater liberty than otherwise he would have done. David, though he smothered his resentments when the wicked were before him, would probably have given vent to them if none had been by but friends, Ps. 39:1. But this freedom of speech, which their professions of concern for him made him use, had exposed him to their censures, and so they might be said to dig a pit for him. Thus, when our hearts are hot within us, what is ill done we are apt to misrepresent as if done designedly.

IV. That, though he had let fall some passionate expressions, yet in the main he was in the right, and that his afflictions, though very extraordinary, did not prove him to be a hypocrite or a wicked man. His righteousness he holds fast, and will not let it go. For the evincing of it he here appeals, 1. To what they saw in him (*v.* 28): *"Be content,* and *look upon me;* what do you see in me that bespeaks me either a madman or a wicked man? Nay, look in my face, and you may discern there the indications of a patient and submissive spirit, for all this. Let the show of my countenance witness for me that, though I have cursed my day, I do not curse my God." Or rather, "Look upon my ulcers and sore boils, and by them it will be evident to you that I do not lie," that is, "that I do not complain without cause. Let your own eyes convince you that my condition is very sad, and that I do not quarrel with God by making it worse than it is." 2. To what they heard from him, *v.* 30. "You hear what I have to say: *Is there iniquity in my tongue?* that iniquity that you charge me with? Have I blasphemed God or renounced him? Are not my present arguings right? Do not you perceive, by what I say, that I can discern perverse things? I can discover your fallacies and mistakes, and, if I were myself in an error, I could perceive it. Whatever you think of me, I know what I say." 3. To their own second and sober thoughts (*v.* 29): *"Return, I pray you,* consider the thing over again without prejudice and partiality, and let not the result be iniquity, let it not be an unrighteous sentence; and you will find *my righteousness is in it,"* that is, "I am in the right in this matter; and, though I cannot keep my temper as I should, I keep my integrity, and have not said, nor done, nor suffered, any thing which will prove me other than an honest man." A just cause desires nothing more than a just hearing, and if need be a re-hearing.

CHAPTER 7

Job, in this chapter, goes on to express the bitter sense he had of his calamities and to justify himself in his desire of death. I. He complains to himself and his friends of his troubles, and the constant agitation he was in (*v.* 1–6). II. He turns to God, and expostulates with him (*v.* 7, to the end), in which, 1. He pleads the final period which death puts to our present state (*v.* 7–10). 2. He passionately complains of the miserable condition he was now in (*v.* 11–16). 3. He wonders that God will thus contend with him, and begs for the pardon of his sins and a speedy release out of his miseries (*v.* 17–21). It is hard to methodize the speeches of one who owned himself almost desperate, *ch.* 6:26.

Verses 1–6

Job is here excusing what he could not justify, even his inordinate desire of death. Why should he not wish for the termination of life, which would be the termination of his miseries? To enforce this reason he argues,

I. From the general condition of man upon earth (*v.* 1): "He *is of few days, and full of trouble.* Every man must die shortly, and every man has some reason (more or less) to desire to die shortly; and therefore why should you impute it to me as so heinous a crime that I wish to die shortly?" Or thus: "Pray mistake not my desires of death, as if I thought the time appointed of God could be anticipated: no, I know very well that that is fixed; only in such language as this I take the liberty to express my present uneasiness: *Is there not an appointed time (a warfare,* so the word is) to *man upon earth?* and *are not his days* here *like the days of a hireling?"* Observe, 1. Man's present place. He is upon earth, which God *has given to the children of men,* Ps. 115:16. This bespeaks man's meanness and inferiority. How much below the inhabitants of yonder elevated and refined regions is he situated! It also bespeaks God's mercy to him. He is yet upon the earth, not under it; on earth, not in hell. Our time on earth is limited and short, according to the narrow bounds of this earth; but heaven cannot be measured, nor the days of heaven numbered. 2. His continuance in that place. Is there not a time appointed for his abode here? Yes, certainly there is, and it is easy to say by whom the appointment is made, even by him that made us and set us here. We are not to be on this earth always, nor long, but for a certain time, which is determined by him in whose hand our times are. We are not to think that we are governed by the blind fortune of the Epicureans, but by the wise, holy, and sovereign counsel of God. 3. His condition during that continuance. Man's life is *a warfare,* and *as the days of a hireling.* We are every one of us to look upon ourselves in this world, (1.) As soldiers, exposed to hardship and in the midst of enemies; we must serve and be under command; and, when our warfare is accomplished, we must be disbanded, dismissed with either shame or honour, according to what we have done in the body. (2.) As day-labourers, that have the work of the day to do in its day and must make up their account at night.

II. From his own condition at this time. He had as much reason, he thought, to wish for death, as a poor servant or hireling that is tired with his work has to wish for the shadows of the evening, when he shall receive his penny and go to rest, *v.* 2. The darkness of the night is as welcome to the labourer as the light of the morning is to the watchman, Ps. 130:6. The God of nature has provided for the repose of labourers, and no wonder that they desire it. *The sleep of the labouring man is sweet,* Eccl. 5:12. No pleasure more grateful, more relishing, to the luxurious than rest to the laborious; nor can any rich man take so much satisfaction in the return of his rent-days as the hireling in his day's wages. The comparison is plain, the application is concise and somewhat obscure, but we must supply a word or two, and then it is easy: exactness of language is not to be expected from one in Job's condition. *"As a servant earnestly desires the shadow, so* and for the same reason I earnestly desire death; for *I am made to possess,* etc." Hear his complaint.

1. His days were useless, and had been so a great while. He was wholly taken off from business, and utterly unfit for it. Every day was a burden to him, because he was in no capacity of doing good, or of spending it to any purpose. *Et vitae partem non attigit ullam — He could not fill up his time with any thing that would turn to account.* This he calls *possessing months of vanity, v.* 3. It very much increases the affliction of sickness and age, to a good man, that he is thereby forced from his usefulness. He insists not so much upon it that they are days in which he has no pleasure as that they are days in which he does not good; on that account they are months of vanity. But when we are disabled to work for God, if we will but sit still quietly for him, it is all one; we shall be accepted.

2. His nights were restless, *v.* 3, 4. The night relieves the toil and fatigue of the day, not only to the labourers, but to the sufferers: if a sick man can but get a little sleep in the night, it helps nature, and it is hoped that he will do well, Jn. 11:12. However, be the trouble what it will, sleep gives some intermission to the cares, and pains, and griefs, that afflict us; it is the parenthesis of our sorrows. But poor Job could not gain this relief. (1.) His nights were wearisome, and, instead of taking any rest, he did but tire himself more with tossing to and fro until morning. Those that are in great uneasiness, through pain of body or anguish of mind, think by changing sides, changing places, changing postures, to get some ease; but, while the cause is the same within, it is all to no purpose; it is but a resemblance of a fretful discontented spirit, that is ever shifting, but never easy. This made him dread the night as much as the servant desires it, and, when he lay down, to say, *When will the night be gone?* (2.) These *wearisome nights* were *appointed* to him. God, who determines the times before appointed, had allotted him such nights as these. Whatever is at any time grievous to us, it is good to see it appointed for us, that we may acquiesce in the event, not only as unavoidable because appointed, but as therefore designed for some holy end. When we have comfortable nights we must see them also appointed to us and be thankful for them; many better than we have wearisome nights.

3. His body was noisome, *v.* 5. His sores bred worms, the scabs were like clods of dust, and his skin was broken; so evil was the disease which cleaved fast to him. See what vile bodies we have, and what little reason we have to pamper them or be proud of them; they have in themselves the principles of their own corruption: as fond as we are of them now, the time may come when we may loathe them and long to get rid of them.

4. His life was hastening apace towards a period, *v.* 6. He thought he had no reason to expect a long life, for he found himself declining fast (*v.* 6): *My days are swifter than a weaver's shuttle,* that is, "My time is now but short, and there are but a few sands more in my glass, which will speedily run out." Natural motions are more swift near the centre. Job thought his days ran swiftly because he thought he should soon be at his journey's end; he looked upon them as good as spent already, and he was therefore without hope of being restored to his former prosperity. It is applicable to man's life in general. Our days are like a weaver's shuttle, thrown from one side of the web to the other in the twinkling of an eye, and then back again, to and fro, until at length it is quite exhausted of the thread it carried, and then we *cut off, like a weaver, our life,* Isa. 38:12. Time hastens on apace; the motion of it cannot be stopped, and, when it is past, it cannot be recalled. While we are living, as we are sowing (Gal. 6:8), so we are weaving. Every day, like the shuttle, leaves a thread behind it. Many weave the spider's web, which will fail them, *ch.* 8:14. If we are weaving to ourselves holy garments and robes of righteousness, we shall have the benefit of them when our work comes to be reviewed and every man shall reap as he sowed and wear as he wove.

Verses 7–16

Job, observing perhaps that his friends, though they would not interrupt him in his discourse, yet began to grow weary, and not to heed much what he said, here turns to God, and speaks to him. If men will not hear us, God will; if men cannot help us, he can; for his arm is not shortened, neither is his ear heavy. Yet we must not go to school to Job here to learn how to speak to God; for, it must be confessed, there is a great mixture of passion and corruption in what he here says. But, if God be not extreme to mark what his people say amiss, let us also make the best of it. Job is here begging of God either to ease him or to end him. He here represents himself to God,

I. As a dying man, surely and speedily dying. It is good for us, when we are sick, to think and speak of death, for sickness is sent on purpose to put us in mind of it; and, if we be duly mindful of it ourselves, we may in faith put God in mind of it, as Job does here (*v.* 7): *O remember that my life is wind.* He recommends himself to God as an object of his pity and compassion, with this consideration, that he was a very weak frail creature, his abode in this world short and uncertain, his removal out of it sure and speedy, and his return to it again impossible and never to be expected — that his life was wind, as the lives of all men are, noisy perhaps and blustering, like the wind, but vain and empty, soon gone, and, when gone, past recall. God had compassion on Israel, *remembering that they were but flesh, a wind that passeth away and cometh not again,* Ps. 78:38, 39. Observe,

1. The pious reflections Job makes upon his own life and death. Such plain truths as these concerning the shortness and vanity of life, the unavoidableness and irrecoverableness of death, *then* do us good when we think and speak of them with application to ourselves. Let us consider then, (1.) That we must shortly take our leave of all the things that are seen, that are temporal. The eye of the body must be closed, and shall no more see good, the good which most men set their hearts upon; for their cry is, *Who will make us to see good?* Ps. 4:6. If we be such fools as to place our happiness in visible good things, what will become of us when they shall be for ever hidden from our eyes, and we shall no more see good? Let us therefore live by that faith which is the substance and evidence of things not seen. (2.) That we must then remove to an invisible world: *The eye of him that hath* here *seen me shall see me no more* there. It is *hadēs — an unseen state, v.* 8. Death removes our lovers and friends into darkness (Ps. 88:18), and will shortly remove us out of their sight; when we *go hence we shall be seen no more* (Ps. 39:13), but go to converse with the things that are not seen, that are eternal. (3.) That God can easily, and in a moment, put an end to our lives, and send us to another world (*v.* 8): *"Thy eyes are upon me and I am not;* thou canst look me into eternity, frown me into the grave, when thou pleasest."

> Shouldst thou, displeased, give me a frowning look,
> I sink, I die, as if with lightning struck.
> — Sir R. Blackmore

He takes away our breath, and we die; nay, he but *looks on the earth* and it *trembles,* Ps. 14:29, 30. (4.) That, when we are once removed to another world, we must never return to this. There is constant passing from this world to the other, but *vestigia nulla retrorsum — there is no repassing.* "Therefore, Lord, kindly ease me by death, for that will be a perpetual ease. I shall return no more to the calamities of this life." When we are dead we are gone, to return no more, [1.] From our house under ground (*v.* 9): *He that goeth down to the grave shall come up no more* until the general resurrection, shall come up no more to his place in this world. Dying is work that is to be done but once, and therefore it had need be well done: an error there is past retrieve. This is illustrated by the blotting out and scattering of a cloud. It is consumed and vanisheth away, is resolved into air and never knits again. Other clouds arise, but the same cloud never returns: so a new generation of the children of men is raised up, but the former generation is quite consumed and vanishes away. When we see a cloud which looks great, as if it would eclipse the sun and drawn the earth, of a sudden dispersed and disappearing, let us say, "Just such a thing is the life of man; it is *a vapour that appears for a little while and then vanishes away."* [2.] To return no more to our house above ground (*v.* 10): *He shall return no more to his house,* to the possession and enjoyment of it, to the business and delights of it. Others will take possession, and keep it till they also resign to another generation. The rich man in hell desired that Lazarus might be sent to his house, knowing it was to no purpose to ask that he might have leave to go himself. Glorified saints shall return no more to the cares, and burdens, and sorrows of their house; nor damned sinners to the gaieties and pleasures of their house. Their place shall no more know them, no more own them, have no more acquaintance with them, nor be any more under their influence. It concerns us to secure a better place when we die, for this will no more own us.

2. The passionate inference he draws from it. From these premises he might have drawn a better conclusion that this (*v.* 11): *Therefore I will not refrain my mouth; I will speak; I will complain.* Holy David, when he had been meditating on the frailty of human life, made a contrary use of it (Ps. 39:9, *I was dumb, and opened not my mouth*); but Job, finding himself near expiring, hastens as much to make his complaint as if he had been to make his last will and testament or as if he could not die in peace until he had given vent to his passion. When we have but a few breaths to draw we should spend them in the holy gracious breathings of faith and prayer, not in the noisome noxious breathings of sin and corruption. Better die praying and praising than die complaining and quarrelling.

II. As a distempered man, sorely and grievously distempered both in body and mind. In this part of his representation is he is very peevish, as if God dealt hardly with him and laid upon him more than was meet: *"Am I a sea, or a whale* (*v.* 12), a raging sea, that must be kept within bounds, to check its proud waves, or an unruly whale, that must be restrained by force from devouring all the fishes of the sea? Am I so strong that there needs so much ado to hold me? so boisterous that no less than all these mighty bonds of affliction will serve to tame me and keep me within compass?" We are very apt, when we are in affliction, to complain of God and his providence, as if he laid more restraints upon us that there is occasion for; whereas we are never in heaviness but when there is need, nor more than the necessity demands. 1. He complains that he could not rest in his bed, *v.* 13, 14. There we promise ourselves some repose, when we are fatigued with labour, pain, or traveling: *"My bed shall comfort me, and my couch shall ease my complaint.* Sleep will for a time give me some relief;" it usually does so; it is appointed for that end; many a time it has eased us, and we have awaked refreshed, and with new vigour. When it is so we have great reason to be thankful; but it was not so with poor Job: his bed, instead of comforting him, terrified him; and his couch, instead of easing his complaint, added to it; for if he dropped asleep, he was disturbed with frightful dreams, and when those awaked him still he was haunted with dreadful apparitions. This was it that made the night so unwelcome and wearisome to him as it was (*v.* 4): When *shall I arise?* Note, God can, when he pleases, meet us with terror even where we promise ourselves ease and repose; nay, he can make us a terror to ourselves, and, as we have often contracted guilt by the rovings of an unsanctified fancy, he can likewise, by the power of our own imagination, create us much grief, and so make that our punishment which has often been our sin. In Job's dreams, though they might partly arise from his distemper (in fevers, or small pox, when the body is all over sore, it is common for the sleep to be unquiet), yet we have reason to think Satan had a hand, for he delights to terrify those whom it is out of his reach to destroy; but Job looked up to God, who permitted Satan to do this *(thou scarest me),* and mistook Satan's representations for the *terror of God setting themselves in array against him.* We have reason to pray to God that our dreams may neither defile nor disquiet us, neither tempt us to sin nor torment us with fear, that he who keeps Israel, and neither slumbers nor sleeps, may keep us when we slumber and sleep, that the devil may not then do us a mischief, either as an insinuating serpent or as a roaring lion, and to bless God if we lie down and our sleep is sweet and we are not thus scared. 2. He covets to rest in his grave, that bed where there are no tossings to and fro, nor any frightful dreams, *v.* 15, 16. (1.) He was sick of life, and hated the thoughts of it: *"I loathe it;* I have had enough of it. *I would not live always,* not only not live always in this condition, in pain and misery, but not live always in the most easy and prosperous condition, to be continually in danger of being thus reduced. *My days are vanity* at the best, empty of solid comfort, exposed to real griefs; and I would not be for ever tied to such uncertainty." Note, A good man would not (if he might) life always in this world, no, not though it smile upon him, because it is a world of sin and temptation and he has a better world in prospect. (2.) He was fond of death, and pleased himself with the thoughts of it: his *soul* (his judgment, he thought, but really it was his passion) *chose strangling and death rather than life;* any death rather than such a life as this. Doubtless this was Job's infirmity; for though a good man would not wish to live always in this world, and would choose strangling and death rather than sin, as the martyrs did, yet he will be content to live as long as pleases God, not choose death rather than life, because life is our opportunity of glorifying God and getting ready for heaven.

Verses 17–21

Job here reasons with God,

I. Concerning his dealings with man in general (*v.* 17, 18): *What is man, that thou shouldst magnify him?* This may be looked upon either, 1. As a passionate reflection upon the proceedings of divine justice; as if the great God did diminish and disparage himself in contending with man. "Great men think it below them to take cognizance of those who are much their inferiors so far as to reprove and correct their follies and indecencies; why then does God magnify man, by visiting him, and trying him, and making so much ado about him? Why will he thus pour all his forces upon one that is such an unequal match for him? Why will he visit him with afflictions, which, like a quotidian ague, return as duly and constantly as the morning light, and try, every moment, what he can bear?" We mistake God, and the nature of his providence, if we think it any lessening to him to take notice of the meanest of his creatures. Or, 2. As a pious admiration of the condescensions of divine grace, like that, Ps. 8:4; 144:3. He owns God's favour to man in general, even when he complains of his own particular troubles. *"What is man,* miserable man, a poor, mean, weak creature, *that thou,* the great and glorious God, shouldst deal with him as thou dost? What is man," (1.) "That thou shouldst put such honour upon him, *shouldst magnify him,* by taking him into covenant and communion with thyself?" (2.) "That thou shouldst concern thyself so much about him, *shouldst set thy heart upon him,* as dear to thee, and one that thou hast a kindness for?" (3.) *"That thou shouldst visit him* with thy compassions *every morning,* as we daily visit a particular friend, or as the physician visits his patients every morning to help them?" (4.) "That thou shouldst *try him,* shouldst feel his pulse and observe his looks, *every moment,* as in care about him and jealous over him?" That such a worm of the earth as man is should be the darling and favourite of heaven is what we have reason for ever to admire.

II. Concerning his dealings with him in particular. Observe,

1. The complaint he makes of his afflictions, which he here aggravates, and (as we are all too apt to do) makes the worst of, in three expressions: — (1.) That he was the butt to God's arrows: *"Thou hast set me as a mark against thee," v.* 20. "My case is singular, and none is shot at as I am." (2.) That he was a *burden to himself,* ready to sink under the load of his own life. How much delight soever we take in ourselves God can, when he pleases, make us burdens to ourselves. What comfort can we take in ourselves if God appear against us as an enemy and we have not comfort in him. (3.) That he had no intermission of his griefs (*v.* 19): *"How long* will it be ere thou cause thy rod to *depart from me,* or abate the rigour of the correction, at least for so long as that I may *swallow down my spittle?"* It should seem, Job's distemper lay much in his throat, and almost choked him, so that he could not swallow his spittle. He complains (*ch.* 30:18) that it *bound him about like the collar of his coat.* "Lord," says he, "wilt not thou give me some respite, some breathing time?" *ch.* 9:18.

2. The concern he is in about his sins. The best men have sin to complain of, and the better they are the more they will complain of it. (1.) He ingenuously owns himself guilty before God: *I have sinned.* God had said of him that he was a *perfect and an upright man;* yet he says of himself, *I have sinned.* Those may be upright who yet are not sinless; and those who are sincerely penitent are accepted, through a Mediator, as evangelically perfect. Job maintained, against his friends, that he was not a hypocrite, not a wicked man; and yet he owned to his God that he had sinned. If we have been kept from gross acts of sin, it does not therefore follow that we are innocent. The best must acknowledge, before God, that they have sinned. His calling God the *observer,* or *preserver,* of men, may be looked upon as designed for an aggravation of his sin: "Though God has had his eye upon me, his eye upon me for good, yet I have sinned against him." When we are in affliction it is seasonable to confess sin, as the procuring cause of our affliction. Penitent confessions would drown and silence passionate complaints. (2.) He seriously enquires how he may make his peace with God: *"What shall I do unto thee,* having done so much against thee?" Are we convinced that we have sinned, and are we brought to own it? We cannot but conclude that something must be done to prevent the fatal consequences of it. The matter must not rest as it is, but some course must be taken to undo what has been ill done. And, if we are truly sensible of the danger we have run ourselves into, we shall be willing to do any thing, to take a pardon upon any terms; and therefore shall be *inquisitive as to what we shall do* (Mic. 6:6, 7), what we shall do to God, not to satisfy the demands of his justice (that is done only by the Mediator), but to qualify ourselves for the tokens of his favour, according to the tenour of the gospel-covenant. In making this enquiry it is good to eye God as the preserver or Saviour of men, not their destroyer. In our repentance we must keep up good thoughts of God, as one that delights not in the ruin of his creatures, but would rather they should return and live. "Thou art the Saviour of men; be my Saviour, for I cast myself upon thy mercy." (3.) He earnestly begs for the forgiveness of his sins, *v.* 21. The heat of his spirit, as, on the one hand, it made his complaints the more bitter, so, on the other hand, it made his prayers the more lively and importunate; as here: *"Why dost thou not pardon my transgression?* Art thou not a God of infinite mercy, that art ready to forgive? Hast not thou wrought repentance in me? Why then dost thou not give me the pardon of my sin, and make me to hear the voice of that joy and gladness?" Surely he means more than barely the removing of his outward trouble, and is herein earnest for the return of God's favour, which he complained of the want of, *ch.* 6:4. "Lord, pardon my sins, and give me the comfort of that pardon, and then I can easily bear my afflictions," Mt. 9:2; Isa. 33:24. When the mercy of God pardons the transgression that is committed by us the grace of God takes away the iniquity that reigns in us. Wherever God removes the guilt of sin he breaks the power of sin. (4.) To enforce his prayer for pardon he pleads the prospect he had of dying quickly: *For now shall I sleep in the dust.* Death will lay us in the dust, will lay us to sleep there, and perhaps presently, now in a little time. Job had been complaining of restless nights, and that sleep departed from his eyes (*v.* 3, 4, 13, 14); but those who cannot sleep on a bed of down will shortly sleep in a bed of dust, and not be scared with dreams nor tossed to and fro: *"Thou shalt seek me in the morning,* to show me favour, but *I shall not be;* it will be too late then. If my sins be not pardoned while I live, I am lost and undone for ever." Note, The consideration of this, that we must shortly die, and perhaps may die suddenly, should make us all very solicitous to get our sins pardoned and our iniquity taken away.

CHAPTER 8

Job's friends are like Job's messengers: the latter followed one another close with evil tidings, the former followed him with harsh censures: both, unawares, served Satan's design; these to drive him from his integrity, those to drive him from the comfort of it. Eliphaz did not reply to what Job had said in answer to him, but left it to Bildad, whom he knew to be of the same mind with himself in this affair. Those are not the wisest of the company, but the weakest rather, who covet to have all the talk. Let others speak in their turn, and let the first keep silence, 1 Co. 14:30, 31. Eliphaz had undertaken to show that because Job was sorely afflicted he was certainly a wicked man. Bildad is much of the same mind, and will conclude Job a wicked man unless God do speedily appear for his relief. In this chapter he endeavours to convince Job, I. That he had spoken too passionately (*v.* 2). II. That he and his children had suffered justly (*v.* 3, 4). III. That, if he were a true penitent, God would soon turn his captivity (*v.* 5–7). IV. That it was a usual thing for Providence to extinguish the joys and hopes of wicked men as his were extinguished; and therefore that they had reason to suspect him for a hypocrite (*v.* 8–19). V. That they would be abundantly confirmed in their suspicion unless God did speedily appear for his relief (*v.* 20–22).

Verses 1–7

Here, I. Bildad reproves Job for what he had said (*v.* 2), checks his passion, but perhaps (as is too common) with greater passion. We thought Job spoke a great deal of good sense and much to the purpose, and that he had reason and right on his side; but Bildad, like an eager angry disputant, turns it all off with this, *How long wilt thou speak these things?* taking it for granted that Eliphaz had said enough to silence him, and that therefore all he said was impertinent. Thus (as Caryl observes) reproofs are often grounded upon mistakes. Men's meaning is not taken aright, and then they are gravely rebuked as if they were evil-doers. Bildad compares Job's discourse to a *strong wind.* Job had excused himself with this, that his speeches were but *as wind* (*ch.* 6:26), and therefore they should not make such ado about them: "Yea, but" (says Bildad) "they are as strong wind, blustering and threatening, boisterous and dangerous, and therefore we are concerned to fence against them."

II. He justifies God in what he had done. This he had no occasion to do at this time (for Job did not condemn God, as he would have it thought he did), or he might at least have done it without reflecting upon Job's children, as he does here. Could he not be an advocate for God but he must be an accuser of the brethren? 1. He is right in general, that *God doth not pervert judgment,* nor ever go contrary to any settled rule of justice, *v.* 3. Far be it from him that he should and from us that we should suspect him. He never oppresses the innocent, nor lays a greater load on the guilty than they deserve. He is God, the Judge; and shall not the Judge of all the earth do right? Gen. 18:25. If there should be unrighteousness with God, *how should he judge the world?* Rom. 3:5, 6. He is *Almighty, Shaddai — all sufficient.* Men pervert justice sometimes for fear of the power of others (but God is Almighty, and stands in awe of none), sometimes to obtain the favour of others; but God is all-sufficient, and cannot be benefited by the favour of any. It is man's weakness and impotency that he often is unjust; it is God's omnipotence that he cannot be so. 2. Yet he is not fair and candid in the application. He takes it for granted that Job's children (the death of whom was one of the greatest of his afflictions) had been guilty of some notorious wickedness, and that the unhappy circumstances of their death were sufficient evidence that they were sinners above all the children of the east, *v.* 4. Job readily owned that God did not pervert judgment; and yet it did not therefore follow either that his children were cast-aways or that they died for some great transgression. It is true that we and our children have sinned against God, and we ought to justify him in all he brings upon us and ours; but extraordinary afflictions are not always the punishment of extraordinary sins, but sometimes the trial of extraordinary graces; and, in our judgment of another's case (unless the contrary appears), we ought to take the more favourable side, as our Saviour directs, Lu. 13:2–4. Here Bildad missed it.

III. He put Job in hope that, if he were indeed upright, as he said he was, he should yet see a good issue of his present troubles: *"Although thy children have sinned against him, and are cast away in their transgression* (they have died in their own sin), yet if thou be pure and upright thyself, and as an evidence of that wilt now seek unto God and submit to him, all shall be well yet," *v.* 5–7. This may be taken two ways, either, 1. As designed to prove Job a hypocrite and a wicked man, though not by the greatness, yet the by the continuance, of his afflictions. "When thou wast impoverished, and thy children were killed, if thou hadst been pure and upright, and approved thyself so in the trial, God would before now have returned in mercy to thee and comforted thee according to the time of thy affliction; but, because he does not so, we have reason to conclude thou art not so *pure and upright* as thou pretendest to be. If thou hadst conducted thyself well under the former affliction, thou wouldst not have been struck with the latter." Herein Bildad was not in the right; for a good man may be afflicted for his trial, not only very sorely, but very long, and yet, if for life, it is in comparison with eternity but for a moment. But, since Bildad put it to this issue, God was pleased to join issue with him, and proved his servant Job an honest man by Bildad's own argument; for, soon after, he blessed his latter end more than his beginning. Or, 2. As designed to direct and encourage Job, that he might not thus run himself into despair, and give up all for gone; there might yet be hope if he would take the right course. I am apt to think Bildad here intended to condemn Job, yet would be thought to counsel and comfort him. (1.) He gives him good counsel, yet perhaps not expecting he would take it, the same that Eliphaz had given him (*ch.* 5:8), to *seek unto God,* and that *betimes* (that is, speedily and seriously), and not to be dilatory and trifling in his return and repentance. He advises him not to complain, but to petition, to *make* his *supplication to the Almighty* with humility and faith, and to see that there was (what he feared had hitherto been wanting) sincerity in his heart ("thou must be *pure and upright*") and honesty in his house — "that must be *the habitation of thy righteousness,* and not filled with ill-gotten goods, else God will not hear thy prayers," Ps. 66:18. It is only the prayer of the upright that is the acceptable and prevailing prayer, Prov. 15:8. (2.) He gives him good hopes that he shall yet again see good days, secretly suspecting, however, that he was not qualified to see them. He assures him that, if he would be early in seeking God, God would awake for his relief, would remember him and return to him, though now he seemed to forget him and forsake him — that if his habitation were righteous it should be prosperity. When we return to God in a way of duty we have reason to hope that he will return to us in a way of mercy. Let not Job object that he had so little left to being the world with again that it was impossible he should ever prosper as he had done; no, "Though thy beginning should be ever so small, a little meal in the barrel and a little oil in the cruse, God's blessing shall multiply that to a great increase." This is God's way of enriching the souls of his people with graces and comforts, not *per saltum — as by a bound,* but *per gradum — step by step.* The beginning is small, but the progress is to perfection. Dawning light grows to noonday, a grain of mustard seed to a great tree. Let us not therefore despise the day of small things, but hope for the day of great things.

Verses 8–19

Bildad here discourses very well on the sad catastrophe of hypocrites and evil-doers and the fatal period of all their hopes and joys. He will not be so bold as to say with Eliphaz that none that were righteous were ever cut off thus (*ch.* 4:7); yet he takes it for granted that God, in the course of his providence, does ordinarily bring wicked men, who seemed pious and were prosperous, to shame and ruin in this world, and that, by making their prosperity short, he discovers their piety to be counterfeit. Whether this will certainly prove that all who are thus ruined must be concluded to have been hypocrites he will not say, but rather suspect, and thinks the application is easy.

I. He proves this truth, of the certain destruction of all the hopes and joys of hypocrites, by an appeal to antiquity and the concurring sentiment and observation of all wise and good men; and an undoubted truth it is, if we take in the other world, that, if not in this life, yet in the life to come, hypocrites will be deprived of all their trusts and all their triumphs: whether Bildad so meant or no, we must so take it. Let us observe the method of his proof, *v.* 8–10.

1. He insists not on his own judgment and that of his companions: *We are but of yesterday, and know nothing, v.* 9. He perceived that Job had no opinion of their abilities, but thought they knew little. "We will own," says Bildad, "that we know nothing, are as ready to confess our ignorance as thou art to condemn it; for we are but of yesterday in comparison, *and our days upon earth are* short and transient, and hastening away as *a shadow.* And hence," (1.) "We are not so near the fountain-head of divine revelation" (which then for aught that appears, was conveyed by tradition) "as the former age was; and therefore we must enquire what they said and recount what we have been told of their sentiments." Blessed be God, now that we have the word of God in writing, and are directed to search that, we need not *enquire of the former age,* nor *prepare ourselves to the search of their fathers;* for, though we ourselves are but of yesterday, the word of God in the scripture is as nigh to us as it was to them (Rom. 10:8), and it is the *more sure word of prophecy, to which we must take heed.* If we study and keep God's precepts, we may by them *understand more than the ancients,* Ps. 119:99, 100. (2.) "We do not live so long as those of the former age did, to make observations upon the methods of divine providence, and therefore cannot be such competent judges as they in a cause of this nature." Note, The shortness of our lives is a great hindrance to the improvement of our knowledge, and so are the frailty and weakness of our bodies. *Vita brevis, ars longa — life is short, the progress of art boundless.*

2. He refers to the testimony of the ancients and to the knowledge which Job himself had of their sentiments. "Do thou *enquire of the former age,* and let them tell thee, not only their own judgment in this matter, but the judgment also of *their fathers, v.* 8. *They will teach thee,* and inform thee (*v.* 10), that all along, in their time, the judgments of God followed wicked men. This they will *utter out of their hearts,* that is, as that which they firmly believe themselves, which they are greatly affected with and desirous to acquaint and affect others with." Note, (1.) For the right understanding of divine Providence, and the unfolding of the difficulties of it, it will be of use to compare the observations and experiences of former ages with the events of our own day; and, in order thereto, to consult history, especially the sacred history, which is the most ancient, infallibly true, and written designedly for our learning. (2.) Those that would fetch knowledge from the former ages must search diligently, *prepare for the search,* and take pains for the search. (3.) Those words are most likely to reach to the hearts of the learners that come from the hearts of the teachers. *Those shall teach thee* best that *utter words out of their heart,* that speak by experience, and not by rote, of spiritual and divine things. The learned bishop Patrick suggests that Bildad being a Shuhite, descended from Shuah one of Abraham's sons by Keturah (Gen. 25:2), in this appeal which he makes to history he has a particular respect to the rewards which the blessing of God secured to the posterity of faithful Abraham (who hitherto, and long after, continued in his religion) and to the extirpation of those eastern people, neighbours to Job (in whose country they were settled), for their wickedness, whence he infers that it is God's usual way to prosper the just and root out the wicked, though for a while they may flourish.

II. He illustrates this truth by some similitudes.

1. The hopes and joys of the hypocrite are here compared to a rush or flag, *v.* 11–13. (1.) It grows up out of the mire and water. The hypocrite cannot gain his hope without some false rotten ground or other out of which to raise it, and with which to support it and keep it alive, any more than the rush can grow without mire. He grounds it on his worldly prosperity, the plausible profession he makes of religion, the good opinion of his neighbours, and his own good conceit of himself, which are no solid foundation on which to build his confidence. It is all but mire and water; and the hope that grows out of it is but rush and flag. (2.) It may look green and gay for a while (the rush outgrows the grass), but it is light and hollow, and empty, and good for nothing. It is green for show, but of no use. (3.) It withers presently, *before any other herb, v.* 12. Even *while it is in its greenness* it is dried away and gone in a little time. Note, The best state of hypocrites and evil-doers borders upon withering; even when it is green it is going. The grass is *cut down and withers* (Ps. 90:6); but the rush is *not cut down* and yet *withers, withers before it grows up* (Ps. 129:6): as it has no use, so it has no continuance. *So are the paths of all that forget God* (*v.* 13); they take the same way that the rush does, *for the hypocrite's hope shall perish.* Note, [1.] Forgetfulness of God is at the bottom of men's hypocrisy, and of the vain hopes with which they flatter and deceive themselves in their hypocrisy. Men would not be hypocrites if they did not forget that the God with whom they have to do searches the heart and requires truth there, that he is a Spirit and has his eye on our spirits; and hypocrites would have no hope if they did not forget that God is righteous, and will not be mocked with the torn and the lame. [2.] The hope of hypocrites is a great cheat upon themselves, and, though it may flourish for a while, it will certainly perish at last, and they with it.

2. They are here compared *to a spider's web,* or *a spider's house* (as it is in the margin), a cobweb, *v.* 14, 15. The hope of the hypocrite, (1.) Is woven out of his own bowels; it is the creature of his own fancy, and arises merely from a conceit of his own merit and sufficiency. There is a great deal of difference between the work of the bee and that of the spider. A diligent Christian, like the laborious bee, fetches in all his comfort from the heavenly dews of God's word; but the hypocrite, like the subtle spider, weaves his out of a false hypothesis of his own concerning God, as if he were altogether such a one as himself. (2.) He is very fond of it, as the spider of her web; pleases himself with it, wraps himself in it, calls it his house, *leans upon it,* and *holds it fast.* It is said of the spider that *she takes hold with her hands, and is in kings' palaces,* Prov. 30:28. So does a carnal worldling hug himself in the fulness and firmness of his outward prosperity; he prides himself in that house as his palace, fortifies himself in it as his castle, and makes use of it as the spider of her web, to ensnare those he has a mind to prey upon. So does a formal professor; he flatters himself in his own eyes, doubts not of his salvation, is secure of heaven, and cheats the world with his vain confidences. (3.) It will easily and certainly be swept away, as the cobweb with the besom, when God shall come to purge his house. The prosperity of worldly people will fail them when they expect to find safety and happiness in it. They seek to hold fast their estates, but God is plucking them out of their hands; and whose shall all those things be, which they have provided? or what the better they will be for them? The confidences of hypocrites will fail them. *I tell you, I know you not.* The house built on the sand will fall in the storm, when the builder most needs it and promised himself the benefit of

it. *When a wicked man dies his expectation perishes.* The ground of his hopes will prove false; he will be disappointed of the thing he hoped for, and his foolish hope with which he buoyed himself up will be turned into endless despair; and thus his hope will be cut off, his web, that refuge of lies, swept away, and he crushed in it.

3. The hypocrite is here compared to a flourishing and well-rooted tree, which, though it do not wither of itself, yet will easily be cut down and its place no it no more. The secure and prosperous sinner may think himself wronged when he is compared to a rush and a flag; he thinks he has a better root. "We will allow him his conceit," says Bildad, "and give him all the advantage he can desire, and bring him in suddenly cut off." He is here represented as Nebuchadnezzar was in his own dream (Dan. 4:10) by a great tree. (1.) See this tree fair and flourishing (*v.* 16) like a *green bay-tree* (Ps. 37:35), *green before the sun,* it keeps its greenness in defiance of the scorching sun-beams, and *his branch shoots forth* under the protection of his garden-wall and with the benefit of his garden-soil. See it fixed, and taking deep root, never likely to be overthrown by stormy winds, *for his roots are interwoven with the stones* (*v.* 17); it grows in firm ground, not, as the rush, of mire and water. Thus does a wicked man, when he prospers in the world, think himself secure; his wealth is a *high wall in his own conceit.* (2.) See this tree felled and forgotten notwithstanding, *destroyed from his place* (*v.* 18), and so entirely extirpated that there shall remain no sign or token where it grew. The very place say, *I have not seen thee;* and the standers by shall say the same. *I sought him, but he could not be found,* Ps. 36:36. He made a great show and a great noise for a time, but he is gone of a sudden, and *neither root nor branch is left him,* Mal. 4:1. *This is the joy* (that is, this is the end and conclusion) *of the wicked man's way* (*v.* 19); this is that which all his joy comes to. *The way of the ungodly shall perish,* Ps. 1:6. His hope, he thought, would in the issue be turned into joy; but this is the issue, this is the joy. *The harvest shall be a heap in the day of grief and of desperate sorrow,* Isa. 17:11. This is the best of it; and what then is the worst of it? But shall he not leave a family behind him to enjoy what he has? No, *out of the earth* (not out of his roots) *shall others grow,* that are nothing akin to him, and shall fill up his place, and rule over that for which he labored. Others (that is, others of the same spirit and disposition) shall grow up in his place, and be as secure as ever he was, not warned by his fall. The way of worldlings is their folly, and yet there is a race of those that *approve their sayings,* Ps. 49:13.

Verses 20–22

Bildad here, in the close of his discourse, sums up what he has to say in a few words, setting before Job life and death, the blessing and the curse, assuring him that as he was so he should fare, and therefore they might conclude that as he fared so he was. 1. On the one hand, if he were a perfect upright man, God would not *cast him away, v.* 20. Though now he seemed forsaken of God, he would yet return to him, and by degrees would *turn his mourning into dancing* (Ps. 30:11) and comforts should flow in upon him so plentifully that his *mouth* should be *filled with laughing, v.* 21. So affecting should the happy change be, Ps. 126:2. Those that loved him would rejoice with him; but those that hated him, and had triumphed in his fall, would be ashamed of their insolence, when they should see him restored to his former prosperity. Now it is true that *God will not cast away an upright man;* he may be cast down for a time, but he shall not be cast away for ever. It is true that, if not in this world, yet in another, the mouth of the righteous shall be *filled with rejoicing.* Though their sun should set under a cloud, yet it shall rise again clear, never more to be clouded; though they go mourning to the grave, that shall not hinder their entrance into the joy of their Lord. It is true that the enemies of the saints will be *clothed with shame* when they see them crowned with honour. But it does not therefore follow that, if Job were not perfectly restore to his former prosperity, he would forfeit the character of a perfect man. 2. On the other hand, if he were a wicked man and an evil-doer, God would not help him, but leave him to perish in his present distresses (*v.* 20), and his *dwelling-place* should *come to nought,* 22. And here also it is true that God *will not help the evil-doers;* they throw themselves out of his protection,

and forfeit his favour. He *will not take the ungodly by the hand* (so it is in the margin), will not have fellowship and communion with them; for *what communion* can there be *between light and darkness?* He will not lend them his hand to pull them out of the miseries, the eternal miseries, into which they have plunged themselves; they will then stretch out their hand to him for help, but it will be too late: he will not take them by the hand. *Between us and you there is a great gulf fixed.* It is true that *the dwelling-place of the wicked,* sooner or later, *will come to nought.* Those only *who make God their dwelling-place* are safe for ever, Ps. 90:1; 91:1. Those who make other things their refuge will be disappointed. Sin brings ruin on persons and families. Yet to argue (as Bildad, I doubt, slyly does) that because Job's family was sunk, and he himself at present seemed helpless, therefore he certainly was an ungodly wicked man, was neither just nor charitable, as long as there appeared no other evidence of his wickedness and ungodliness. Let us *judge nothing before the time,* but wait till the secrets of all hearts shall be made manifest, and the present difficulties of Providence be solved to universal and everlasting satisfaction, when the *mystery of God shall be finished.*

CHAPTER 9

In this and the following chapter we have Job's answer to Bildad's discourse, wherein he speaks honourably of God, humbly of himself, and feelingly of his troubles; but not one word by way of reflection upon his friends, or their unkindness to him, nor in direct reply to what Bildad had said. He wisely keeps to the merits of the cause, and makes no remarks upon the person that managed it, nor seeks occasion against him. In this chapter we have, I. The doctrine of God's justice laid down (*v.* 2). II. The proof of it, from his wisdom, and power, and sovereign dominion (*v.* 3–13). III. The application of it, in which, 1. He condemns himself, as not able to contend with God either in law or battle (*v.* 14–21). 2. He maintains his point, that we cannot judge of men's character by their outward condition (*v.* 22–24). 3. He complains of the greatness of his troubles, the confusion he was in, and the loss he was at what to say or do (*v.* 25–35).

Verses 1–13

Bildad began with a rebuke to Job for talking so much, *ch.* 8:2. Job makes no answer to that, though it would have been easy enough to retort it upon himself; but in what he next lays down as his principle, that God never perverts judgment, Job agrees with him: *I know it is so of a truth, v.* 2. Note, We should be ready to own how far we agree with those with whom we dispute, and should not slight, much less resist, a truth, though produced by an adversary and urged against us, but receive it in the light and love of it, though it may have been misapplied. *"It is so of a truth,* that wickedness brings men to ruin and the godly are taken under God's special protection. These are truths which I subscribe to; but how can any man make good his part with God?" *In his sight shall no flesh living be justified,* Ps. 143:2. *How should man be just with God?* Some understand this as a passionate complaint of God's strictness and severity, that he is a God whom there is no dealing with; and it cannot be denied that there are, in this chapter, some peevish expressions, which seem to speak such language as this. But I take this rather as a pious confession of man's sinfulness, and his own in particular, that, if God should deal with any of us according to the desert of our iniquities, we should certainly be undone.

I. He lays this down for a truth, that man is an unequal match for his Maker, either in dispute or combat.

1. In dispute (*v.* 3): *If he will contend with him,* either at law or at an argument, *he cannot answer him one of a thousand.* (1.) God can ask a thousand puzzling questions which those that quarrel with him, and arraign his proceedings, cannot give an answer to. When God spoke to Job out of the whirlwind he asked him a great many questions (*Dost thou know* this? *Canst thou do* that?) to none of which Job could give an answer, *ch.* 38, 39. God can easily manifest the folly of the greatest pretenders to wisdom. (2.) God can lay to our charge a thousand offences, can draw up against us a thousand articles of impeachment, and we cannot answer him so as to acquit ourselves from the imputation of any of them, but must, by silence, give consent that they are all true. We cannot set aside one as foreign, another as frivolous, and another as false. We cannot, as to one, deny the fact, and plead not guilty, and, as to another, deny the fault, confess and justify. No, we are not able to answer him, but must *lay our*

hand upon our mouth, as Job did (*ch.* 40:4, 5), and cry, Guilty, guilty.

2. In combat (*v.* 4): *"Who hath hardened himself against him and hath prospered?"* The answer is very easy. You cannot produce any instance, from the beginning of the world to this day, of any daring sinner who has *hardened himself against God,* has obstinately persisted in rebellion against him, who did not find God too hard for him and pay dearly for his folly. Such transgressors have not prospered or had peace; they have had no comfort in their way nor any success. What did ever man get by trials of skill, or trials of titles, with his Maker? All the opposition given to God is but setting briers and thorns before a consuming fire; so foolish, so fruitless, so destructive, is the attempt, Isa. 27:4; Eze. 28:24; 1 Co. 10:22. Apostate angels hardened themselves against God, but did not prosper, 2 Pt. 2:4. The dragon fights, but is cast out, Rev. 12:9. Wicked men harden themselves against God, dispute his wisdom, disobey his laws, are impenitent for their sins and incorrigible under their afflictions; they reject the offers of his grace, and resist the strivings of his Spirit; they make nothing of his threatenings, and make head against his interest in the world. But have they prospered? Can they prosper? No; they are but *treasuring up for themselves wrath against the day of wrath.* Those that roll this will find it return upon them.

II. He proves it by showing what a God he is with whom we have to do: *He is wise in heart,* and therefore we cannot answer him at law; he is *mighty in strength,* and therefore we cannot fight it out with him. It is the greatest madness that can be to think to contend with a God of infinite wisdom and power, who knows every thing and can do every thing, who can be neither outwitted nor overpowered. The devil promised himself that Job, in the day of his affliction, would curse God and speak ill of him, but, instead of that, he sets himself to honour God and to speak highly of him. As much pained as he is, and as much taken up with his own miseries, when he has occasion to mention the wisdom and power of God he forgets his complaints, dwells with delight, and expatiates with a flood of eloquence, upon that noble useful subject. Evidences of the wisdom and power of God he fetches,

1. From the kingdom of nature, in which the God of nature acts with an uncontrollable power and does what he pleases; for all the orders and all the powers of nature are derived from him and depend upon him.

(1.) When he pleases he alters the course of nature, and turns back its streams, *v.* 5–7. By the common law of nature the mountains are settled and are therefore called *everlasting mountains,* the earth is established and cannot be removed (Ps. 93:1) and the pillars there of are immovably fixed, the sun rises in its season, and the stars shed their influences on this lower world; but when God pleases he can not only drive out of the common track, but invert the order and change the law of nature. [1.] Nothing more firm than the mountains. When we speak of removing mountains we mean that which is impossible; yet the divine power can make them change their seat: *He removes them and they know not,* removes them whether they will or no; he can make them lower their heads; he can level them, and overturn them in his anger; he can spread the mountains as easily as the husbandman spreads the mole-hills, be they ever so high, and large, and rocky. Men have much ado to pass over them, but God, when he pleases, can make them pass away. He made Sinai shake, Ps. 68:8. *The hills skipped,* Ps. 114:4. *The everlasting mountains were scattered,* Hab. 3:6. [2.] Nothing more fixed than the earth on its axletree; yet God can, when he pleases, *shake the earth out of its place,* heave it off its centre, and make even *its pillars to tremble;* what seemed to support it will itself need support when God gives it a shock. See how much we are indebted to God's patience. God has power enough to shake the earth from under that guilty race of mankind which makes it groan under the burden of sin, and so to *shake the wicked out of it* (Job 38:13); yet he continues the earth, and man upon it, and does not make it, as once, to swallow up the rebels. [3.] Nothing more constant than the rising sun, it never misses its appointed time; yet God, when he pleases, can suspend it. He that at first commanded it to rise can countermand it. Once the sun was told to stand, and another time to retreat, to show that it is still under the check of its great Creator. Thus great is God's power; and how great then is his goodness, which causes his sun to shine even upon the evil and unthankful, though he could withhold it! He that made the stars also, can, if he pleases, seal them up, and hide them from our eyes. By earthquakes and subterraneous fires mountains have sometimes been removed and the earth shaken: in very dark and cloudy days and nights it seems to us as if the sun were forbidden to rise and the stars were sealed up, Acts 27:20. It is sufficient to say that Job here speaks of what God can do; but, if we must understand it of what he has done in fact, all these verses may perhaps be applied to Noah's flood, when the mountains of the earth were shaken, and the sun and stars were darkened; and the world that now is we believe to be reserved for that fire which will consume the mountains, and melt the earth, with its fervent heat, and which will turn the sun into darkness.

(2.) As long as he pleases he preserves the settled course and order of nature; and this is a continued creation. He himself alone, by his own power, and without the assistance of any other, [1.] *Spreads out the heaven* (*v.* 8), not only did spread them out at first, but still spreads them out (that is, keeps them spread out), for otherwise they would of themselves roll together like a scroll of parchment. [2.] *He treads upon the waves of the sea;* that is, he suppresses them and keeps them under, that they return not to deluge the earth (Ps. 104:9), which is given as a reason why we should all fear God and stand in awe of him, Jer. 5:22. He is mightier than the proud waves Ps. 93:4; 65:7. [3.] He makes the constellations; three are named for all the rest (*v.* 9), *Arcturus, Orion,* and *Pleiades,* and in general *the chambers of the south.* The stars of which these are composed he made at first, and put into that order, and he still makes them, preserves them in being, and guides their motions; he makes them to be what they are to man, and inclines the hearts of man to observe them, which the beasts are not capable of doing. Not only those stars which we see and give names to, but those also in the other hemisphere, about the antarctic pole, which never come in our sight, called here *the chambers of the south,* are under the divine direction and dominion. How wise is he then, and how mighty!

2. From the kingdom of Providence, that special Providence which is conversant about the affairs of the children of men. Consider what God does in the government of the world, and you will say, He is *wise in heart* and *mighty in strength.* (1.) He does many things and great, many and great to admiration, *v.* 10. Job here says the same that Eliphaz had said (*ch.* 5:9), and in the original in the very same words, not declining to speak after him, though now his antagonist. God is a great God, and *doeth great things,* a wonder-working God; his works of wonder are so many that we cannot number them and so mysterious that we cannot find them out. O the depth of his counsels! (2.) He acts invisibly and undiscerned, *v.* 11. *"He goes by me* in his operations, *and I see him not, I perceive him not.* His *way is in the sea,"* Ps. 77:19. The operations of second causes are commonly obvious to sense, but God does all about us and yet *we see him not,* Acts 17:23. Our finite understandings cannot fathom his counsels, apprehend his motions, or comprehend the measures he takes; we are therefore incompetent judges of God's proceedings, because we know not what he does or what he designs. The *arcana imperii — secrets of government,* are things above us, which therefore we must not pretend to expound or comment upon. (3.) He acts with an incontestable sovereignty, *v.* 12. He takes away our creature-comforts and confidences when and as he pleases, takes away health, estate, relations, friends, takes away life itself; whatever goes, it is he that takes it; by what hand so ever it is removed, his hand must be acknowledged in its removal. The Lord *takes away,* and *who can hinder him? Who can turn him away?* (Margin, *Who shall make him restore?*) Who can dissuade him or alter his counsels? Who can resist him or oppose his operations? Who can control him or call him to an account? What action can be brought against him? Or *who will say unto him, What dost thou?* Or, Why doest thou so? Dan. 4:35. God is not obliged to give us a reason of what he does. The meanings of his proceedings we know no now; it will be time enough to know hereafter, when it will appear that what seemed now to be done by prerogative was done in infinite wisdom and for the best. (4.) He acts with an irresistible power, which no creature can resist, *v.* 13. *If God will not withdraw his anger* (which he can do when he pleases, for he is *Lord of his anger,* lets it out or calls it in according to his will), *the proud helpers do stoop under him;* that is, He certainly breaks and crushes those that proudly help one another against him. Proud men set themselves against God and his proceedings. In this opposition they join hand in hand. *The kings of the earth set themselves, and the rulers take counsel together,* to throw off his yoke, to run down his truths, and to persecute his people. *Men of Israel, help,* Acts 21:28; Ps. 83:8. If one enemy of God's kingdom fall under his judgment, the rest come proudly to help that, and think to deliver that out of his hand: but in vain; unless he pleases to withdraw his anger (which he often does, for it is the day of his patience) the proud helpers stoop under him, and fall with those whom they designed to help. *Who knows the power of God's anger?* Those who think they have strength enough to help others will not be able to help themselves against it.

Verses 14–21

What Job had said of man's utter inability to contend with God he here applies to himself, and in effect despairs of gaining his favour, which (some think) arises from the hard thoughts he had of God, as one who, having set himself against him, right or wrong, would be too hard for him. I rather think it arises from the sense he had of the imperfection of his own righteousness, and the dark and cloudy apprehensions which at present he had of God's displeasure against him.

I. He durst not dispute with God (*v.* 14): *"If the proud helpers do stoop under him, how much less shall I* (a poor weak creature, so far from being a helper that I am very helpless) *answer him?* What can I say against that which God does? If I go about to reason with him, he will certainly be too hard for me." If the potter make the clay into a vessel of dishonour, or break in pieces the vessel he has made, shall the clay or the broken vessel reason with him? So absurd is the man who replies against God, or thinks to talk the matter out with him. No, let all flesh be silent before him.

II. He durst not insist upon his own justification before God. Though he vindicated his own integrity to his friends, and would not yield that he was a hypocrite and a wicked man, as they suggested, yet he would never plead it as his righteousness before God. "I will never venture upon the covenant of innocency, nor think to come off by virtue of that." Job knew so much of God, and knew so much of himself, that he durst not insist upon his own justification before God.

1. He knew so much of God that he durst not stand a trial with him, *v.* 15–19. He knew how to make his part good with his friends, and thought himself able to deal with them; but, though his cause had been better than it was, he knew it was to no purpose to debate it with God. (1.) God knew him better than he knew himself and therefore (*v.* 15), *"Though I were righteous* in my own apprehension, and my own heart did not condemn me, *yet God is greater than my heart,* and knows those secret faults and errors of mine which I do not and cannot understand, and is able to charge me with them, and therefore *I would not answer."* St. Paul speaks to the same purport: *I know nothing by myself,* am not conscious to myself of any reigning wickedness, and *yet I am not hereby justified,* 1 Co. 4:4. "I dare not put myself upon that issue, lest God should charge that upon me which I did not discover in myself." Job will therefore wave that plea, and *make supplication to his Judge,* that is, will cast himself upon God's mercy, and not think come off by his own merit. (2.) He had no reason to think that there was anything in his prayers to recommend them to the divine acceptance, or to fetch in an answer of peace, no worth or worthiness at all to which to ascribe their success, but it must be attributed purely to the grace and compassion of God, who answers before we call and not because we call, and gives gracious answers to our prayers, but not for our prayers (*v.* 16): *"If I had called, and he had answered,* had given the thing I called to him for, yet, so weak and defective are my best prayers, that *I would not believe he had* therein *hearkened to my voice;* I could not say that he had *saved with his right hand and answered me"* (Ps. 60:5), "but that he did it purely for his own name's sake." Bishop Patrick expounds it thus: "If I had made supplication, and he had granted my desire, I would not think my prayer had done the business." *Not for your sakes, be it known to you.* (3.) His present miseries, which God had brought him into notwithstanding his integrity, gave him too sensible a conviction that, in the ordering and disposing of men's outward condition in this world, God acts by sovereignty, and, though he never does wrong to any, yet he does not ever give full right to all (that is, the best do not always fare best, nor the worst fare worst) in this life, because he reserves the full and exact distribution of rewards and punishments for the future state. Job was not conscious to himself of any extraordinary guilt, and yet fell under extraordinary afflictions, *v.* 17, 18. Every man must expect the wind to blow upon him and ruffle him, but Job was *broken with a tempest.* Every man, in the midst of these thorns and briers, must expect to be scratched; but Job was wounded, and his wounds were multiplied. Every man must expect a cross daily, and to taste sometimes of the bitter cup; but poor Job's troubles came so thickly upon him that he had no breathing time, and he was filled with bitterness. And he presumes to say that all this was *without cause,* without any great provocation given. We have made the best of what Job said hitherto, though contrary to the judgment of many good interpreters; but here, no doubt, *he spoke unadvisedly with his lips;* he reflected on God's goodness in saying that he was not suffered *to take his breath* (while yet he had such good use of his reason and speech as to be able to talk thus) and on his justice in saying that it was without cause. Yet it is true that as, on the one hand, there are many who are chargeable with more sin than the common infirmities of human nature, and yet feel no more sorrow than that of the common calamities of human life, so, on the other hand, there are many who feel more than the common calamities of human life and yet are conscious to themselves of no more than the common infirmities of human nature. (4.) He was in no capacity at all to make his part good with God, *v.* 19. [1.] Not by force of arms. "I dare not enter the lists with the Almighty; for *if I speak of strength,* and think to come off by that, *lo, he is strong,* stronger than I, and will certainly overpower me." There is no disputing (said one once to Caesar) with him that commands legions. Much less is there any with him that has legions of angels at command. *Can thy heart endure* (thy courage and presence of mind) *or can thy hands be strong* to defend thyself, *in the days that I shall deal with thee?* Eze. 22:14. [2.] Not by force of arguments. "I dare not try the merits of the cause. *If I speak of judgment,* and insist upon my right, *who will set me a time to plead?* There is no higher power to which I may appeal, no superior court to appoint a hearing of the cause; for he is supreme and from him proceeds every man's judgment, which he must abide by."

2. He knew so much of himself the he durst not stand a trial, *v.* 20, 21. *"If I* go about to *justify myself,* and to plead a righteousness of my own, my defence will be my offence, and *my own mouth shall condemn me* even when it goes about to acquit me." A good man, who knows the deceitfulness of his own heart, and is jealous over it with a godly jealousy, and has often discovered that amiss there which had long lain undiscovered, is suspicious of more evil in himself than he is really conscious of, and therefore will by no means think of justifying himself before God. *If we say we have no sin, we* not only *deceive ourselves,* but we affront God; for we sin in saying so, and give the lie to the scripture, which has *concluded all under sin. "If I say, I am perfect,* I am sinless, God has nothing to lay to my charge, my very saying so shall *prove me perverse,* proud, ignorant, and presumptuous. Nay, *though I were perfect,* though God should pronounce me just, *yet would I not know my soul,* I would not be in care about the prolonging of my life while it is loaded with all these miseries." Or, "Though I were free from gross sin, though my conscience should not charge me with any enormous crime, yet would I not believe my own heart so far as to insist upon my innocency nor think my life worth striving for with God." In short, it is folly to contend with God, and our wisdom, as well as duty, to submit to him and throw ourselves at his feet.

Verses 22–24

Here Job touches briefly upon the main point now in dispute between him and his friends. They maintained that those who are righteous and good always prosper in this world, and none but the wicked are in misery and distress; he asserted, on the contrary, that it is a common thing for the wicked to prosper and the righteous to be greatly afflicted. This is the one thing, the chief thing, wherein he and his friends differed; and they had not proved their assertion, therefore he abides by his: "I said it, and day it again, that all things come alike to all." Now, 1. It must be owned that there is very much truth in what Job here means, that temporal judgments, when they are sent abroad, fall both upon good and bad, and the destroying angel seldom distinguishes (though once he did) between the houses of Israelites and the houses of Egyptians. In the judgment of Sodom indeed, which is called *the vengeance of eternal fire* (Jude 7), *far be it from* God to *slay the righteous with the wicked, and that the righteous should be as the wicked* (Gen. 18:25); but, in judgments merely temporal, the righteous have their share, and sometimes the greatest share. *The sword devours one as well as another,* Josiah as well as Ahab. Thus God *destroys the perfect and the wicked,* involves them both in the same common ruin; good and bad were sent together into Babylon, Jer. 24:5, 9. *If the scourge slay suddenly,* and sweep down all before it, God will be well pleased to see how the same scourge which is the perdition of the wicked is the trial of the innocent and of their faith, which *will be found unto praise, and honour, and glory,* 1 Pt. 1:7; Ps. 66:10.

Against the just th' Almighty's arrows fly,
For he delights the innocent to try,
To show their constant and their Godlike mind,
Not by afflictions broken, but refined.
— Sir R. Blackmore

Let this reconcile God's children to their troubles; they are but trials, designed for their honour and benefit, and, if God be pleased with them, let not them be displeased; if he *laugh at the trial of the innocent,* knowing how glorious the issue of it will be, at destruction and famine let them also laugh (*ch.* 5:22), and triumph over them, saying, *O death! where is thy sting?* On the other hand, the wicked are so far from being made the marks of God's judgments that *the earth is given into their hand, v.* 24 (they enjoy large possessions and great power, have what they will and do what they will), *into the hand of the wicked one* (in the original, the word is singular); the devil, that wicked one, is called *the god of this world,* and boasts that into his hands it is delivered, Lu. 4:6. Or *into the hand of a wicked man,* meaning (as bishop Patrick and the Assembly's Annotations conjecture) some noted tyrant then living in those parts, whose great wickedness and great prosperity were well known both to Job and his friends. The wicked have the earth given them, but the righteous have heaven given them, and which is better — heaven without earth or earth without heaven? God, in his providence, advances wicked men, while he *covers the faces of* those who are fit to be *judges,* who are wise and good, and qualified for government, and buries them alive in obscurity, perhaps suffers them to be run down and condemned, and to have their faces covered as criminals by those wicked ones into whose hand the earth is given. We daily see that this is done; *if* it be *not* God that does it, *where and who is he* that does it? To whom can it be ascribed but to him that rules in the kingdoms of men, and gives them to whom he will? Dan. 4:32. Yet, 2. It must be owned that there is too much passion in what Job here says. The manner of expression is peevish. When he meant that God afflicts he ought not to have said, *He destroys* both *the perfect and the wicked;* when he meant that God pleases himself with the trial of the innocent he ought not to have said, *He laughs at it,* for he doth not afflict willingly. When the spirit is heated, either with dispute or with discontent, we have need to set a watch before the door of our lips, that we may observe a due decorum in speaking of divine things.

Verses 25–35

Job here grows more and more querulous, and does not conclude this chapter with such reverent expressions of God's wisdom and justice as he began with. Those that indulge a complaining humour know not to what indecencies, nay, to what impieties, it will hurry them. *The beginning of* that *strife* with God *is as the letting forth of water; therefore leave it off before it be meddled with.* When we are in trouble we are allowed to complain to God, as the Psalmist often, but must by no means complain of God, as Job here.

I. His complaint here of the passing away of the days of his prosperity is proper enough (*v.* 25, 26): *"My days* (that is, all my good days) are gone, never to return, gone of a sudden, gone ere I was aware. Never did any courier that went express" (like Cushi and Ahimaaz) "with good tidings make such haste as all my comforts did from me. Never did ship sail to its port, never did eagle fly upon its prey, with such incredible swiftness; nor does there remain any trace of my prosperity, any more than there does of an eagle in the air or a ship in the sea," Prov. 30:19. See here, 1. How swift the motion of time is. It is always upon the wing, hastening to its period; it stays for no man. What little need have we of pastimes, and what great need to redeem time, when time runs out, runs on so fast towards eternity, which comes as time goes! 2. How vain the enjoyments of time are, which we may be quite deprived of while yet time continues. Our day may be longer than the sun-shine of our prosperity; and, when that is gone, it is as if it had not been. The remembrance of having done our duty will be pleasing afterwards; so will not the remembrance of our having got a great deal of worldly wealth when it is all lost and gone. *"They flee away,* past recall; *they see no good,* and leave none behind them."

II. His complaint of his present uneasiness is excusable, *v.* 27, 28. 1. It should seem, he did his endeavour to quiet and compose himself as his friends advised him. That was the good he would do: he would fain *forget his complaints* and praise God, would *leave off his heaviness and comfort himself,* that he might be fit for converse both with God and man; but, 2. He found he could not do it: *"I am afraid of all my sorrows.* When I strive most against my trouble it prevails most over me and proves too hard for me!" It is easier, in such a case, to know what we should do than to do it, to know what temper we should be in than to get into that temper and keep in it. It is easy to preach patience to those that are in trouble, and to tell them they must forget their complaints and comfort themselves; but it is not so soon done as said. Fear and sorrow are tyrannizing things, not easily brought into the subjection they ought to be kept in to religion and right reason. But,

III. His complaint of God as implacable and inexorable was by no means to be excused. It was the language of his corruption. He knew better, and, at another time, would have been far from harbouring any such hard thoughts of God as now broke in upon his spirit and broke out in these passionate complaints. Good men do not always speak like themselves; but God, who considers their frame and the strength of their temptations, gives them leave afterwards to unsay what was amiss by repentance and will not lay it to their charge.

1. Job seems to speak here, (1.) As if he despaired of obtaining from God any relief or redress of his grievances, though he should produce ever so good proofs of his integrity: *"I know that thou wilt not hold me innocent.* My afflictions have continued so long upon me, and increased so fast, that I do not expect thou wilt ever clear up my innocency by delivering me out of them and restoring me to a prosperous condition. Right or wrong, I must be treated as a wicked man; my friends will continue to think so of me, and God will continue upon me the afflictions which give them occasion to think so. *Why then do I labour in vain* to clear myself and maintain my own integrity?" *v.* 29. It is to no purpose to speak in a cause that is already prejudged. With men it is often labour in vain for the most innocent to go about to clear themselves; they must be adjudged guilty, though the evidence be ever so plain for them. But it is not so in our dealings with God, who is the patron of oppressed innocency and to whom it was never in vain to commit a righteous cause. Nay, he not only despairs of relief, but expects that his endeavour to clear himself will render him yet more obnoxious (*v.* 30, 31): *"If I wash myself with snow-water,* and make my integrity ever so evident, it will be all to no purpose; judgment must go against me. *Thou shalt plunge me in the ditch"* (the pit of destruction, so some, or rather the filthy kennel, or sewer), "which will make me so offensive in the nostrils of all about me that *my own clothes shall abhor me* and I shall even loathe to touch myself." He saw his afflictions coming from God. Those were the things that blackened him in the eye of his friends; and, upon that score, he complained of them, and of the continuance of them, as the ruin, not only of his comfort, but of his reputation. Yet these words are capable of a good construction. If we be ever so industrious to justify ourselves before men, and to preserve our credit with them, — if we keep our hands ever so clean from the pollutions of gross sin, which fall under the eye of the world, — yet God, who knows our hearts, can charge us with so much secret sin as will for ever take off all our pretensions to purity and innocency, and make us see ourselves odious in the sight of the holy God. Paul, while a Pharisee, made his hands very clean; but when the commandment came and discovered to him his heart-sins, made him know lust, that *plunged him in the ditch.* (2.) As if he despaired to have a fair hearing with God, and that were hard indeed. [1.] He complains that he was not upon even terms with God (*v.* 32): *"He is not a man, as I am.* I could venture to dispute with a man like myself (the potsherds may strive with the potsherds of the earth), but he is infinitely above me, and therefore I dare not enter the lists with him; I shall certainly be cast if I contend with him." Note, *First,* God is not a man as we are. Of the greatest princes we may say, "They are men as we are," but not of the great God. His thoughts and ways are infinitely above ours, and we must not measure him by ourselves. Man is foolish and weak, frail and fickle, but God is not. We are depending dying creatures; he is the independent an immortal Creator. *Secondly,* The consideration of this should keep us very humble and very silent before God. Let us not make ourselves equal with God, but always eye him as infinitely above us. [2.] That there was no arbitrator or umpire to adjust the differences between him and God and to determine the controversy (*v.* 33): *Neither is there any daysman between us.* This complaint that there was not is in effect a wish that there were, and so the Septuagint reads it: *O that there were a mediator between us!* Job would gladly refer the matter, but no creature was capable of being a referee, and therefore he must even refer it still to God himself and resolve to acquiesce in his judgment. Our Lord Jesus is the blessed days-man, who has mediated between heaven and earth, has laid his hand upon us both; to him the Father has committed all judgment, and we must. But this matter was not then brought to so clear a light as it is now by the gospel, which leaves no room for such a complaint as this. [3.] That the terrors of God, which set themselves in array against him, put him into such confusion that he knew not how to address God with the confidence with which he was formerly wont to approach him, *v.* 34, 35. "Besides the distance which I am kept at by his infinite transcendency, his present dealings with me are very discouraging: *Let him take his rod away from me."* He means not so much his outward afflictions as the load which lay upon his spirit from the apprehensions of God's wrath; that was *his fear* which *terrified him.* "Let that be removed; let me recover the sight of his mercy, and not be amazed with the sight of nothing but his terrors, and *then I would speak* and order my cause before him. *But it is not so with me;* the cloud is not at all dissipated; the wrath of God still fastens upon me, and preys on my spirits, as much as ever; and what to do I know not."

2. From all this let us take occasion, (1.) To stand in awe of God, and to fear the power of his wrath. If good men have been put into such consternation by it, *where shall the ungodly and the sinner appear?* (2.) To pity those that are wounded in spirit, and pray earnestly for them, because in that condition they know not how to pray for themselves. (3.) Carefully to keep up good thoughts of God in our minds, for hard thoughts of him are the inlets of much mischief. (4.) To bless God that we are not in such a disconsolate condition as poor Job was here in, but that we walk in the light of the Lord; let us rejoice therein, but *rejoice with trembling.*

CHAPTER 10

Job owns here that he was full of confusion (*v.* 15), and as he was so was his discourse: he knew not what to say, and perhaps sometimes scarcely knew what he said. In this chapter, I. He complains of the hardships he was under (*v.* 1–7), and then comforts himself with this, that he was in the hand of the God that made him, and pleads that (*v.* 8–13). II. He complains again of the severity of God's dealings with him (*v.* 14–17), and then comforts himself with this, that death would put an end to his troubles (*v.* 18–22).

Verses 1–7

Here is, I. A passionate resolution to persist in his complaint, *v.* 1. Being daunted with the dread of God's majesty, so that he could not plead his cause with him, he resolves to give himself some ease by giving vent to his resentments. He begins with vehement language: *"My soul is weary of my life,* weary of this body, and impatient to get clear of it, fallen out with life, and displeased at it, sick of it, and longing for death." Through the weakness of grace he went contrary to the dictates even of nature itself. We should act more like men did we act more like saints. Faith and patience would keep us from being weary of our lives (and *cruel to them,* as some read it), even when Providence has made them most wearisome to us; for that is to be weary of God's correction. Job, being weary of his life and having ease no other way, resolves to complain, resolves to speak. He will not give vent to his soul by violent hands, but he will give vent to the bitterness of his soul by violent words. Losers think they may have leave to speak; and unbridled passions, as well as unbridled appetites, are apt to think it an excuse for their excursions that they cannot help them: but what have we wisdom and grace for, but to keep the mouth as with a bridle? Job's corruption speaks here, yet grace puts in a word. 1. He will complain, but he will *leave his complaint upon himself.* He would not impeach God, nor charge him with unrighteousness or unkindness; but, though he knew not particularly the ground of God's controversy with him and the cause of action, yet, in the general, he would suppose it to be in himself and willingly bear all the blame. 2. He will speak, but it shall be the *bitterness of his soul* that he will express, not his settled judgment. If I speak amiss, it is *not I, but sin that dwells in me,* not my soul, but its bitterness.

II. A humble petition to God. He will speak, but the first word shall be a prayer, and, as I am willing to understand it, it is a good prayer, *v.* 2. 1. That he might be delivered from the sting of his afflictions, which is sin: *"Do not condemn me;* do not separate me for ever from thee. Though I lie under the cross, let me not lie under the curse; though I smart by the rod of a Father, let me not be cut off by the sword of a Judge. Thou dost correct me; I will bear that as well as I can; but O do not condemn me!" It is the comfort of those who are in Christ Jesus that, though they are in affliction, there is *no condemnation to them,* Rom. 8:1. Nay, they are *chastened of the Lord that they may not be condemned with the world,* 1 Co. 11:32. This therefore we should deprecate above any thing else, when we are in affliction. "However thou art pleased to deal with me, Lord, do not condemn me; my friends condemn me, but do not thou." 2. That he might be made acquainted with the true cause of his afflictions, and that is sin too: Lord, *show me wherefore thou contendest with me.* When God afflicts us he contends with us, and when he contends with us there is always a reason. He is never angry without a cause, though we are; and it is desirable to know what the reason is, that we may repent of, mortify, and forsake the sin for which God has a controversy with us. In enquiring it out, let conscience have leave to do its office and to deal faithfully with us, as Gen. 42:21.

III. A peevish expostulation with God concerning his dealings with him. Now he speaks in the bitterness of his soul indeed, not without some ill-natured reflections upon the righteousness of his God.

1. He thinks it unbecoming the goodness of God, and the mercifulness of his nature, to deal so hardly with his creature as to lay upon him more than he can bear (*v.* 3): *Is it good unto thee that thou shouldst oppress?* No, certainly it is not; what he approves no in men (Lam. 3:34–36) he will not do himself. "Lord, in dealing with me, thou seemest to oppress thy subject, to despise thy workmanship, and to countenance thy enemies. Now, Lord, what is the meaning of this? Such is thy nature that this cannot be a pleasure to thee; and such is thy name that it cannot be an honour to thee. Why then dealest thou thus with me? *What profit is there in my blood?"* Far be it from Job to think that God did him wrong, but he is quite at a loss how to reconcile his providences with his justice, as good men have often been, and must wait until the day shall declare it. Let us therefore now harbour no hard thoughts of God, because we shall then see there was no cause for them.

2. He thinks it unbecoming the infinite knowledge of God to put his prisoner thus upon the rack, as it were, by torture, to extort a confession from him, *v.* 4–6. (1.) He is sure that God does not discover things, nor judge of them, as men do: He has not *eyes of flesh* (*v.* 4), for he is a Spirit. Eyes of flesh cannot see in the dark, but darkness hides not from God. Eyes of flesh are but in one place at a time, and can see but a little way; but the *eyes of the Lord are in every place,* and *run to and fro through the whole earth.* Many things are hidden from eyes of flesh, the most curious and piercing; *there is a path which even the vulture's eye has not seen:* but nothing is, or can be, hidden from the eye of God, to which all things are naked and open. Eyes of flesh see the outward appearance only, and may be imposed upon by a *deceptio visus — an illusion of the senses;* but God sees every thing truly. His sight cannot be deceived, for he tries the heart, and is a witness to the thoughts and intents of that. Eyes of flesh discover things gradually, and, when we gain the sight of one thing, we lose the sight of another; but God sees every thing at one view. Eyes of flesh are soon tired, must be closed every night but the keeper of Israel neither slumbers nor sleeps, nor does his sight ever decay. *God sees not as man sees,* that is, he does not judge as man judges, at the best *secundum allegata et probata — according to what is alleged and proved,* as the thing appears rather than as it is, and too often according to the bias of the affections, passions, prejudices, and interest; *but we are sure that the judgment of God is according to truth,* and that he knows truth, not by information, but by his own inspection. Men discover secret things by search, and examination of witnesses, comparing evidence and giving conjectures upon it, wheedling or forcing the parties concerned to confess; but God needs not any of these ways of discovery: *he sees not as man sees.* (2.) He is sure that as God is not short-sighted, like man, so he is not short-lived (*v.* 5): *"Are thy days as the days of man,* few and evil? Do they roll on in succession, or are they subject to change, like the days of man? No, by no means." Men grow wiser by experience and more knowing by daily observation; with them truth is the daughter of time, and therefore they must take time for their searches, and, if one experiment fail, must try another. But it is not so with God; to him nothing is past, nothing future, but every thing present. The days of time, by which the life of man is measured, are nothing to the years of eternity, in which the life of God is wrapped up. (3.) He therefore thinks it strange that God should thus prolong his torture, and continue him under the confinement of this affliction, and neither bring him to a trial nor grant him a release, as if he must take time to *enquire after his iniquity* and use means to *search after his sin, v.* 6. Not as if Job thought that God did this torment him that he might find occasion against him; but his dealings with him had such an aspect, which was dishonourable to God, and would tempt men to think him a hard master. "Now, Lord, if thou wilt not consult my comfort, consult thy own honour; do something *for thy great name,* and *do not disgrace the throne of thy glory,"* Jer. 14:21.

3. He thinks it looked like an abuse of his omnipotence to keep a poor prisoner in custody, whom he knew to be innocent, only because there was none that could deliver him out of his hand (*v.* 7): *Thou knowest that I am not wicked.* He had already owned himself a sinner, and guilty before God; but he here stands to it that he was not wicked, not devoted to sin, not an enemy to God, not a dissembler in his religion, that *he had not wickedly departed from his God,* Ps. 18:21. *"But there is none that can deliver out of thy hand,* and therefore there is no remedy; I must be content to lie there, waiting thy time, and throwing myself on thy mercy, in submission to thy sovereign will." Here see, (1.) What ought to quiet us under our troubles — that it is to no purpose to contend with Omnipotence. (2.) What will abundantly comfort us — if we are able to appeal to God, as Job here, "Lord, *thou knowest that I am not wicked.* I cannot say that I am not wanting, or I am not weak; but, through grace, I can say, *I am not wicked:* thou knowest I am not, for *thou knowest I love thee."*

Verses 8–13

In these verses we may observe,

I. How Job eyes God as his Creator and preserver, and describes his dependence upon him as the author and upholder of his being. This is one of the first things we are all concerned to know and consider.

1. That God made us, he, and not our parents, who were only the instruments of his power and providence in our production. *He made us, and not we ourselves. His hands have made and fashioned* these bodies of ours and every part of them (*v.* 8), and they are *fearfully and wonderfully made.* The soul also, which animates the body, is his gift. Job takes notice of both here. (1.) The body is *made as the clay* (*v.* 9), cast into shape, into this shape, as the clay is formed into a vessel, according to the skill and will of the potter. We are earthen vessels, mean in our original, and soon broken in pieces, made *as the clay. Let not* therefore *the thing formed say unto him that formed it, Why hast thou made me thus?* We must not be proud of our bodies, because the matter is from the earth, yet not dishonour our bodies, because the mould and shape are from the divine wisdom. The formation of human bodies in the womb is described by an elegant similitude (*v.* 10, *Thou hast poured me out like milk, which is coagulated into cheese*), and by an induction of some particulars, *v.* 11. Though we come into the world naked, yet the body is itself both clothed and armed. The skin and flesh are its clothing; the bones and sinews are its armour, not offensive, but defensive. The vital parts, the heart and lungs, are thus clothed, not to he seen — thus fenced, not to be hurt. The admirable structure of human bodies is an illustrious instance of the wisdom, power, and goodness of the Creator. What a pity is it that these bodies should be instruments of unrighteousness which are capable of being temples of the Holy Ghost! (2.) The soul is the life, the soul is the man, and this is the gift of God: *Thou hast granted me life,* breathed into me the breath of life, without which the body would be but a worthless carcase. God is the Father of spirits: he made us living souls, and endued us with the power of reason; he gave us *life and favour,* and life is a favour — a great favour, more than meat, more than raiment — a distinguishing favour, a favour that puts us into a capacity of receiving other favours. Now Job was in a better mind than he was when he quarrelled with life as a burden, and asked, *Why died I not from the womb?* Or by life and favour may be meant life and all the comforts of life, referring to his former prosperity. Time was when he walked in the light of the divine favour, and thought, as David, that through that favour his mountain stood strong.

2. That God maintains us. Having lighted the lamp of life, he does not leave it to burn upon its own stock, but continually supplies it with fresh oil: *"Thy visitation has preserved my spirit,* kept me alive, protected me from the adversaries of life, the death we are in the midst of and the dangers we are continually exposed to, and blessed me with all the necessary supports of life and the daily supplies it needs and craves."

II. How he pleads this with God, and what use he makes of it. He reminds God of it (*v.* 9): *Remember, I beseech thee, that thou hast made me.* What then? Why, 1"Thou hast made me, and therefore thou hast a perfect knowledge of me (Ps. 139:1–13), and needest not to examine me by scourging, nor to put me upon the rack for the discovery of what is within me." 2. "Thou hast made me, as the clay, by an act of sovereignty; and wilt thou by a like act of sovereignty unmake me again? If so, I must submit." 3. "Wilt thou destroy the work of thy own hands?" It is a plea the saints have often used in prayer, *We are the clay and thou our potter,* Isa. 64:8. *Thy hands have made me and fashioned me,* Ps. 119:73. So here, *Thou madest me;* and wilt thou destroy me (*v.* 8), *wilt thou bring me into dust again? v.* 9. "Wilt thou not pity me? Wilt thou not spare and help me, and stand by *the work of thy own hands?* Ps. 138:8. Thou madest me, and knowest my strength; wilt thou then suffer me to be pressed above measure? Was I made to be made miserable? Was I preserved only to be reserved for these calamities?" If we plead this with ourselves as an inducement to duty, "God made me and maintains me, and therefore I will serve him and submit to him," we may plead it with God as an argument for mercy: *Thou hast made me,* new-make me; *I am thine, save me.* Job knew not how to reconcile God's former favours and his present frowns, but concludes (*v.* 13), *"These things hast thou hidden in thy heart.* Both are according to the counsel of thy own will, and therefore undoubtedly consistent, however they seem." When God thus strangely changes his way, though we cannot account for it, we are bound to believe there are good reasons for it hidden in his heart, which will be manifested shortly. It is not with us, or in our reach, to assign the cause, but I *know that this is with thee.* Known unto God are all his works.

Verses 14–22

Here we have,

I. Job's passionate complaints. On this harsh and unpleasant string he harps much, in which, though he cannot be justified, he may be excused. He complained not for nothing, as the murmuring Israelites, but had cause to complain. If we think it looks ill in him, let it be a warning to us to keep our temper better.

1. He complains of the strictness of God's judgment and the rigour of his proceedings against him, and is ready to call it *summum jus — justice bordering on severity.* (1.) That he took all advantages against him: *"If I sin, then thou markest me, v.* 14.(1.) If I do but take one false step, misplace a word, or cast a look awry, I shall be sure to hear of it. Conscience, thy deputy, will be sure to upbraid me with it, and to tell me that this gripe, this twitch of pain, is to punish me for that." If God should thus mark iniquities, we should be undone; but we must acknowledge the contrary, that, though we sin, God does not deal in extremity with us. (2.) That he prosecuted those advantages to the utmost: *Thou wilt not acquit me from my iniquity.* While his troubles he could not take the comfort of his pardon, nor hear that voice of joy and gladness; so hard is it to see love in God's heart when we see frowns in his face and a rod in his hand. (3.) That, whatever was his character, his case at present was very uncomfortable, *v.* 15. [1.] If he be wicked, he is certainly undone in the other world: *If I be wicked, woe to me.* Note, A sinful state is a woeful state. This we should each of us believe, as Job here, with application to ourselves: *"If I be wicked,* though prosperous and living in pleasure, yet woe to me." Some especially have reason to dread double woes if they be wicked. "I that have knowledge, that have made a great profession of religion, that have been so often under strong convictions, and have made so many fair promises — I that was born of such good parents, blessed with a good education, that have lived in good families, and long enjoyed the means of grace — *if I be wicked, woe,* and a thousand woes, *to me."* [2.] If he be *righteous,* yet he dares not *lift up his head,* dares not answer as before, *ch.* 9:15. He is so oppressed and overwhelmed with his troubles that he cannot look up with any comfort or confidence. Without were fightings, within were fears; so that, between both, he was full of confusion, not only confusion of face for the disgrace he was brought down to and the censures of his friends, but confusion of spirit; his mind was in a constant hurry, and he was almost distracted, Ps. 88:15.

2. He complains of the severity of the execution. God (he thought) did not only punish him for every failure, but punish him in a high degree, *v.* 16, 17. His affliction was, (1.) Grievous, very grievous, marvellous, exceedingly marvellous. God *hunted him* as a lion, *as a fierce lion* hunts and runs down his prey. God was not only strange to him, but *showed himself marvellous upon him,* by bringing him into uncommon troubles and so making him prodigy, a wonder unto many. All wondered that God would inflict and that Job could bear so much. That which made his afflictions most grievous was that he felt God's *indignation* in them; it was this that made them taste so bitter and lie so heavy. They were God's *witnesses* against him, tokens of his displeasure; this made the sores of his body wounds in his spirit. (2.) It was growing, still growing worse and worse. This he insists much upon; when he hoped the tide would turn, and begin to ebb, still it flowed higher and higher. His affliction increased, and God's indignation in the affliction. He found himself no better, no way better. These witnesses were renewed against him, that, if one did not reach to convict him, another might. *Changes and war* were against him. If there was any change with him, it was not for the better; still he was kept in a state of war. As long as we are here in this world we must expect that the clouds will return after the rain, and perhaps the sorest and sharpest trials may be reserved for the last. God was at war with him, and it was a great change. He did not use to be so, which aggravated the trouble and made it truly marvellous. God usually shows himself kind to his people; if at any time he shows himself otherwise, it is *his strange work, his strange act,* and he does in it show himself marvellous.

3. He complains of his life, and that ever he was born to all this trouble and misery (*v.* 18, 19): "If this was designed for my lot, *why was I brought out of the womb,* and not smothered there, or stifled in the birth?" This was the language of his passion, and it was a relapse into the same sin he fell into before. He had just now called life a *favour* (*v.* 12), yet now he calls it a *burden,* and quarrels with God for giving it, or rather laying it upon him. Mr. Caryl gives this a good turn in favour of Job. "We may charitably suppose," says he, "that what troubled Job was that he was in a condition of life which (as he conceived) hindered the main end of his life, which was the glorifying of God. His harp was hung on the willow-tress, and he was quite out of tun for praising God. Nay, he feared lest his troubles should reflect dishonour upon God and give occasion to his enemies to blaspheme; and therefore he wishes, *O that I had given up the ghost!* A godly man reckons that he lives to no purpose if he do not live to the praise and glory of God." If that was his meaning, it was grounded on a mistake; for we may *glorify the Lord in the fires.* But this use we may make of it, not to be over-fond of life, since the case has been such sometimes, even with wise and good men, that they have complained of it. Why should we dread giving up the ghost, or covet to be seen of men, since the time may come when we may be ready to wish we had given up the ghost and no eye had seen us? Why should we inordinately lament the death of our children in their infancy, that *are as if they had not been,* and are *carried from the womb to the grave,* when perhaps we ourselves may sometimes wish it had been our own lot?

II. Job's humble requests. He prays, 1. That God would *see his affliction* (*v.* 15), take cognizance of his case, and take it into his compassionate consideration. Thus David prays (Ps. 25:18), *Look upon my affliction and my pain.* Thus we should, in our troubles, refer ourselves to God, and may comfort ourselves with this, that he knows our souls in adversity. 2. That God would grant him some ease. If he could not prevail for the removal of his trouble, yet might he not have some intermission? "Lord, let me not be always upon the rack, always in extremity: *O let me alone, that I may take comfort a little! v.* 20. Grant me some respite, some breathing-time, some little enjoyment of myself." This he would reckon a great favour. Those that are not duly thankful for constant ease should think how welcome one hour's ease would be if they were in constant pain. Two things he pleads: — (1.) That life and its light were very short: *"Are not my days few? v.* 20. Yes, certainly they are, very few. Lord, let them not be all miserable, all in the extremity of misery. I have but a little time to live; let me have some comfort of life while it does last." This plea fastens on the goodness of God's nature, the consideration of which is very comfortable to an afflicted spirit. And, if we would use this as a plea with God for mercy (*"Are not my days few?* Lord, pity me"), we should use it as a plea with ourselves, to quicken us to duty: *"Are not my days few?* Then it concerns me to redeem time, to improve opportunities, what my hand finds to do to do it with all my might, that I may be ready for the days of eternity, which shall be many." (2.) That death and its darkness were very near and would be very long (*v.* 21, 22): "Lord, give me some ease before I die," that is, "lest I die of my pain." Thus David pleads (Ps. 13:3), *"Lest I sleep the sleep of death,* and then it will be too late to expect relief; for *wilt thou show wonders to the dead?"* Ps. 88:10. "Let me have a little comfort before I die, that I may take leave of this world calmly, and not in such confusion as I am now in." Thus earnest should we be for grace, and thus we should plead, "Lord, renew me in the inward man; Lord, sanctify me before I die, for otherwise it will never be done." See how he speaks here of the state of the dead. [1.] It is a fixed state, whence we shall not return ever again to live such a life as we now live, *ch.* 7:10. At death we must bid a final farewell to this world. The body must then be laid where it will lie long, and the soul adjudged to that state in which it must be for ever. That had need be well done which is to be done but once, and done for eternity. [2.] It is a very melancholy state; so it appears to us. Holy souls, at death, remove to a land of light, where there is no death; but their bodies they leave to a *land of darkness and the shadow of death.* He heaps up expressions here of the same import to show that he has as dreadful apprehensions of death and the grave as other men naturally have, so that it was only the extreme misery he was in that made him wish for it. Come and let us look a little into the grave, and we shall find, *First,* That there is no order there: it is *without any order,* perpetual night, and no succession of day. All there lie on the same level, and there is no distinction between prince and peasant, but *the servant is* there *free from his master, ch.* 3:19. No order is observed in bringing people to the grave, not the eldest first, not the richest, not the poorest, and yet every one in his own order, the order appointed by the God of life. *Secondly,* That there is no light there. In the grave there is thick darkness, darkness that cannot be felt indeed, yet cannot but be feared by those that enjoy the light of life. In the grave there is no knowledge, no comfort, no joy, no praising God, no working out our salvation, and therefore no light. Job was so much ashamed that others should see his sores, and so much afraid to see them himself, that the darkness of the grave, which would hide them and huddle them up, would upon that account be welcome to him. Darkness comes upon us; and therefore let us walk and work while we have the light with us. The grave being a land of darkness, it is well we are carried thither with our eyes closed, and then it is all one. The grave is a land of darkness to man; our friends that have gone thither we reckon removed into darkness, Ps. 88:18. But that it is not so to God will appear by this, that the dust of the bodies of the saints, though scattered, though mingled with other dust, will none of it be lost, for God's eye is upon every grain of it and it shall be forth-coming in the great day.

CHAPTER 11

Poor Job's wound's were yet bleeding, his sore still runs and ceases not, but none of his friends bring him any oil, any balm; Zophar, the third, pours into them as much vinegar as the two former had done. I. He exhibits a very high charge against Job, as proud and false in justifying himself (*v.* 1–4). II. He appeals to God for his conviction, and begs that God would take him to task (*v.* 5) and that Job might be made sensible, 1. Of God's unerring wisdom and his inviolable justice (*v.* 6). 2. Of his unsearchable perfections (*v.* 7–9). 3. Of his incontestable sovereignty and uncontrollable power (*v.* 10). 4. Of the cognizance he takes of the children of men (*v.* 11, 12). III. He assures him that, upon his repentance and reformation (*v.* 13, 14), God would restore him to his former prosperity and safety (*v.* 15–19); but that, if he were wicked it was in vain to expect it (*v.* 20).

Verses 1–6

It is sad to see what intemperate passions even wise and good men are sometimes betrayed into by the heat of disputation, of which Zophar here is an instance. Eliphaz began with a very modest preface, *ch.* 4:2. Bildad was a little more rough upon Job, *ch.* 8:2. But Zophar falls upon him without mercy, and gives him very bad language: *Should a man full of talk be justified? And should thy lies make men hold their peace?* Is this the way to comfort Job? No, nor to convince him neither. Does this become one that appears as an advocate for God and his justice? *Tantaene animis coelestibus irae? — In heavenly breasts can such resentment dwell?* Those that engage in controversy will find it very hard to keep their temper. All the wisdom, caution, and resolution they have will be little enough to prevent their breaking out into such indecencies as we here find Zophar guilty of.

I. He represents Job otherwise than what he was, *v.* 2, 3. He would have him thought idle and impertinent in his discourse, and one that loved to hear himself talk; he gives him the lie, and calls him *a mocker;* and all this that it might be looked upon as a piece of justice to chastise him. Those that have a mind to fall out with their brethren, and to fall foul upon them, find it necessary to put the worst colours they can upon them and their performances, and, right or wrong, to make them odious. We have read and considered Job's discourses in the foregoing chapters, and have found them full of good sense and much to the purpose, that his principles are right, his reasonings strong, many of his expressions weighty and very considerable, and that what there is in them of heat and passion a little candour and charity will excuse and overlook; and yet Zophar here invidiously represents him, 1. As a man that never considered what he said, but uttered what came uppermost, only to make a noise with the multitude of words, hoping by that means to carry his cause and run down his reprovers: *Should not the multitude of words be answered?* Truly, sometimes it is no great matter whether it be or no; silence perhaps is the best confutation of impertinence and puts the greatest contempt upon it. *Answer not a fool according to his folly.* But, if it be answered, let reason and grace have the answering of it, not pride and passion. *Should a man full of talk* (margin, *a man of lips,* that is all tongue, *vox et praeterea nihil — mere voice*) *be justified?* Should he be justified in his loquacity, as in effect he is if he be not reproved for it? No, for *in the multitude of words there wanteth not sin.* Should he be justified by it? Shall many words pass for valid pleas? Shall he carry the day with the flourishes of language? No, he shall not be accepted with God, or any wise men, *for his much speaking,* Mt. 6:7. 2. As a man that made no conscience of what he said — a liar, and one that hoped by the impudence of lies to silence his adversaries *(should thy lies make men hold their peace?)* — a mocker, one that bantered all mankind, and knew how to put false colours upon any thing, and was not ashamed to impose upon every one that talked with him: *When thou mockest shall no man make thee ashamed?* Is it not time to speak, to stem such a violent tide as this? Job was not mad, but spoke the words of truth and soberness, and yet was thus misrepresented. Eliphaz and Bildad had answered him, and said what they could to make him ashamed; it was therefore no instance of Zophar's generosity to set upon a man so violently who was already thus harassed. Here were three matched against one.

II. He charges Job with saying that which he had not said (*v.* 4): *Thou hast said, My doctrine is pure.* And what if he had said so? It was true that Job was sound in the faith, and orthodox in his judgment, and spoke better of God than his friends did. If he had expressed himself unwarily, yet it did not therefore follow but that his doctrine was true. But he charges him with saying, *I am clean in thy eyes.* Job had not said so: he had indeed said, *Thou knowest that I am not wicked* (*ch.* 10:7); but he had also said, *I have sinned,* and never pretended to a spotless perfection. He had indeed maintained that he was not a hypocrite as they charged him; but to infer thence that he would not own himself a sinner was an unfair insinuation. We ought to put the best construction on the words and actions of our brethren that they will bear; but contenders are tempted to put the worst.

III. He appeals to God, and wishes him to appear against Job. So very confident is he that Job is in the wrong that nothing will serve him but that God must immediately appear to silence and condemn him. We are commonly ready with too much assurance to interest God in our quarrels, and to conclude that, if he would but speak, he would take our part and speak for us, as Zophar here: *O that God would speak!* for he would certainly *open his lips against thee;* whereas, when God did speak, he opened his lips for Job against his three friends. We ought indeed to leave all controversies to be determined by the judgment of God, which we are sure *is according to truth;* but those are not always in the right who are most forward to appeal to that judgment and prejudge it against their antagonists. Zophar despairs to convince Job himself, and therefore desires God would convince him of two things which it is good for every one of us duly to consider, and under all our afflictions cheerfully to confess: —

1. The unsearchable depth of God's counsels. Zophar cannot pretend to do it, but he desires that God himself would show Job so much of the secrets of the divine wisdom as might convince him that *they are at least double to that which is, v.* 6. Note, (1.) There are secrets in the divine wisdom, *arcana imperii — state-secrets.* God's way is in the sea. Clouds and darkness are round about him. He has reasons of state which we cannot fathom and must not pry into. (2.) What we know of God is nothing to what we cannot know. What is hidden is more than double to what appears, Eph. 3:9. (3.) By employing ourselves in adoring the depth of those divine counsels of which we cannot find the bottom we shall very much tranquilize our minds under the afflicting hand of God. (4.) God knows a great deal more evil of us than we do of ourselves; so some understand it. When God gave David a sight and sense of sin he said that he had *in the hidden part made him to know wisdom,* Ps. 51:6.

2. The unexceptionable justice of his proceedings. "Know therefore that, how sore soever the correction is that thou art under, *God exacteth of thee less than thy iniquity deserves,*" or (as some read it), "he *remits thee part of thy iniquity,* and does not deal with thee according to the full demerit of it." Note, (1.) When the debt of duty is not paid it is justice to insist upon the debt of punishment. (2.) Whatever punishment is inflicted upon us in this world we must own that it is less than our iniquities deserve, and therefore, instead of complaining of our troubles, we must be thankful that we are out of hell, Lam. 3:39; Ps. 103:10.

Verses 7–12

Zophar here speaks very good things concerning God and his greatness and glory, concerning man and his vanity and folly: these two compared together, and duly considered, will have a powerful influence upon our submission to all the dispensations of the divine Providence.

I. See here what God is, and let him be adored.

1. He is an incomprehensible Being, infinite and immense, whose nature and perfections our finite understandings cannot possibly form any adequate conceptions of, and whose counsels and actings we cannot therefore, without the greatest presumption, pass a judgment upon. We that are so little acquainted with the divine nature are incompetent judges of the divine providence; and, when we censure the dispensations of it, we talk of things that we do not understand. We cannot find out God; how dare we then find fault with him? Zophar here shows, (1.) That God's nature infinitely exceeds the capacities of our understandings: *"Canst thou find out God, find him out to perfection?* No, *What canst thou do? What canst thou know?" v.* 7, 8. Thou, a poor, weak, short-sighted creature, a worm of the earth, that art but of yesterday? Thou, though ever so inquisitive after him, ever so desirous and industrious to find him out, yet darest thou attempt the search, or canst thou hope to speed in it? We may, by searching find God (Acts 17:27), but we cannot find him out in any thing he is pleased to conceal; we may apprehend him, but we cannot comprehend him; we may know that he is, but cannot know what he is. The eye can see the ocean but not see over it. We may, by a humble, diligent, and believing search, find out something of God, but cannot find him out to perfection; we may know, but cannot know fully, what God is, nor find out his work *from the beginning to the end,* Eccl. 3:11. Note, God is unsearchable. The ages of his eternity cannot be numbered, nor the spaces of his immensity measured; the depths of his wisdom cannot be fathomed, nor the reaches of his power bounded; the brightness of his glory can never be described, nor the treasures of his goodness reckoned up. This is a good reason why we should always speak of God with humility and caution and never prescribe to him nor quarrel with him, why we should be thankful for what he has revealed of himself and long to be where we shall see him as he is, 1 Co. 13:9, 10. (2.) That it infinitely exceeds the limits of the whole creation: *It is higher than heaven* (so some read it), *deeper than hell,* the great abyss, *longer than the earth, and broader than the sea,* many parts of which are to this day undiscovered, and more were then. It is quite out of our reach to comprehend God's nature. *Such knowledge is too wonderful for us,* Ps. 139:6. We cannot fathom God's designs, nor find out the reasons of his proceedings. His judgments are a great deep. Paul attributes such immeasurable dimensions to the divine love as Zophar here attributes to the divine wisdom, and yet recommends it to our acquaintance. Eph. 3:18, 19, *That you may know the breadth, and length, and depth, and height, of the love of Christ.*

2. God is a sovereign Lord (*v.* 10): *If he cut off* by death (margin, *If he make a change,* for death is a change; if he make a change in nations, in families, in the posture of our affairs), — if he *shut up* in prison, or in the net of affliction (Ps. 66:11), — if he seize any creature as a hunter his prey, he will gather it (so bishop Patrick) and who shall force him to restore? or if he *gather together,* as tares for the fire, or *if he gather to himself man's spirit and breath* (*ch.* 34:14), *then who can hinder him?* Who can either arrest the sentence or oppose the execution? Who can control his power or arraign his wisdom and justice? If he that made all out of nothing think fit to reduce all to nothing, or to their first chaos again, — if he that separated between light and darkness, dry land and sea, at first, please to gather them together again, — if he that made unmakes, *who can turn him away,* alter his mind or stay his hand, impede or impeach his proceedings?

3. God is a strict and just observer of the children of men (*v.* 11): *He knows vain men.* We know little of him, but he knows us perfectly: *He sees wickedness also,* not to approve it (Hab. 1:13), but to animadvert upon it. (1.) He observes vain men. Such all are *(every man, at his best estate, is altogether vanity),* and he considers it in his dealings with them. He knows what the projects and hopes of vain men are, and can blast and defeat them, the workings of their foolish fancies; he sits in heaven, and laughs at them. He takes knowledge of the vanity of men (that is, their little sins; so some) their vain thoughts and vain words, and unsteadiness in that which is good. (2.) He observes bad men: *He sees* gross *wickedness also,* though committed ever so secretly and ever so artfully palliated and disguised. All the wickedness of the wicked is naked and open before the all-seeing eye of God: *Will he not then consider it?* Yes, certainly he will, and will reckon for it, though for a time he seem to keep silence.

II. See here what man is, and let him be humbled, *v.* 12. God sees this concerning vain man that he *would be wise,* would be thought so, *though he is born like a wild ass's colt,* so sottish and foolish, unteachable and untameable. See what man is. 1. He is a vain creature — *empty;* so the word is. God made him full, but he emptied himself, impoverished himself, and now he is *raca,* a creature that has nothing in him. 2. He is a foolish creature, has become *like the beasts that perish* (Ps. 49:20, 73:22), an idiot, born like an ass, the most stupid animal, an ass's colt, not yet brought to any service. If ever he come to be good for any thing, it is owing to the grace of Christ, who once, in the day of his triumph, served himself by an ass's colt. 3. He is a wilful ungovernable creature. An ass's colt may be made good for something, but the wild ass's colt will never be reclaimed, nor regards the crying of the driver. See Job 39:5–7. Man thinks himself as much at liberty, and his own master, as the wild ass's colt does, that is *used to the wilderness* (Jer. 2:24), eager to gratify his own appetites and passions. 4. Yet he is a proud creature and self-conceited. He *would be wise,* would he thought so, values himself upon the honour of wisdom, though he will not submit to the laws of wisdom. He would be wise, that is, he reaches after forbidden wisdom, and, like his first parents, aiming to be wise above what is written, loses the tree of life for the tree of knowledge. Now is such a creature as this fit to contend with God or call him to an account? Did we but better know God and ourselves, we should better know how to conduct ourselves towards God.

Verses 13–20

Zophar, as the other two, here encourages Job to hope for better times if he would but come to a better temper.

I. He gives him good counsel (*v.* 13, 14), as Eliphaz did (*ch.* 5:8), and Bildad, *ch.* 8:5. He would have him repent and return to God. Observe the steps of that return. 1. He must look within, and get his mind changed and the tree made good. He must *prepare his heart;* there the work of conversion and reformation must begin. The heart that wandered from God must be reduced — that was defiled with sin and put into disorder must be cleansed and put in order again — that was wavering and unfixed must be settled and established; so the word here signifies. The heart is then prepared to seek God when it is determined and fully resolved to make a business of it and to go through with it. 2. He must look up, and *stretch out his hands towards God,* that is, must stir up himself to take hold on God, must pray to him with earnestness and importunity, striving in prayer, and with expectation to receive mercy and grace from him. To *give the hand to the Lord* signifies to yield ourselves to him and to covenant with him, 2 Chr. 30:8. This Job must do, and, for the doing of it, must prepare his heart. Job had prayed, but Zophar would have him to pray in a better manner, not as an appellant, but as a petitioner and humble suppliant. 3. He must amend what was amiss in his own conversation, else his prayers would be ineffectual (*v.* 14): *"If iniquity be in thy hand* (that is, if there be any sin which thou dost yet live in the practice of) *put it far away,* forsake it with detestation and a holy indignation, stedfastly resolving not to return to it, nor ever to have any thing more to do with it. Eze. 18:31; Hos. 14:9; Isa. 30:22. If any of the gains of iniquity, any goods gotten by fraud or oppression, be in thy hand, make restitution thereof" (as Zaccheus, Lu. 19:8), "and *shake thy hands from holding them,*" Isa. 33:15. The guilt of sin is not removed if the gain of sin be not restored. 4. He must do his utmost to reform his family too: *"Let not wickedness dwell in thy tabernacles;* let not thy house harbour or shelter any wicked persons, any wicked practices, or any wealth gotten by wickedness." He suspected that Job's great household had been ill-governed, and that, where there were many, there were many wicked, and the ruin of his family was the punishment of the wickedness of it; and therefore, if he expected God should return to him, he must reform what was amiss there, and, though wickedness might come into his tabernacles, he must not suffer it to dwell there, Ps. 101:3, etc.

II. He assures him of comfort if he took this counsel, *v.* 15, etc. If he would repent and reform, he should, without doubt, be easy and happy, and all would be well. Perhaps Zophar might insinuate that, unless God did speedily make such a change as this in his condition, he and his friends would be confirmed in their opinion of him as a hypocrite and a dissembler with God. A great truth, however, is conveyed, That, *the work of righteousness will be peace, and the effect of righteousness quietness and assurance for ever,* Isa. 32:17. Those that sincerely turn to God may expect,

1. A holy confidence towards God: *"Then shalt thou lift up thy face towards heaven* without spot; thou mayest come boldly to the throne of grace, and not with that terror and amazement expressed," *ch.* 9:34. If our hearts condemn us not for hypocrisy and impenitency, then have we confidence in our approaches to God and expectations from him, 1 Jn. 3:21. If we are looked upon in the face of the anointed, our faces, that were dejected, may be lifted up — that were polluted, being washed with the blood of Christ, may be lifted up without spot. We may *draw near in full assurance of faith* when we are *sprinkled from an evil conscience,* Heb. 10:22. Some understand this of the clearing up of his credit before men, Ps. 37:6. If we make our peace with God, we may with cheerfulness look our friends in the face.

2. A holy composedness in themselves: *Thou shalt be stedfast, and shalt not fear,* not *be afraid of evil tidings,* thy heart being fixed, Ps. 112:7. Job was now full of confusion (*ch.* 10:15), while he looked upon God as his enemy and quarrelled with him; but Zophar assures him that, if he would submit and humble himself, his mind would be composed, and he would be freed from those frightful apprehensions he had of God, which put him into such an agitation. The less we are frightened the more we are fixed, and consequently the more fit we are for our services and for our sufferings.

3. A comfortable reflection upon their past troubles (*v.* 16): *"Thou shalt forget thy misery,* as the mother forgets her travailing pains, for joy that the child is born; thou shalt be perfectly freed from the impressions it makes upon thee, and *thou shalt remember it as waters that pass away,* or are poured out of a vessel, which leave no taste or tincture behind them, as other liquors do. The wounds of thy present affliction shall be perfectly healed, not only without a remaining scar, but without a remaining pain." Job had endeavoured to forget his complaint (*ch.* 9:27), but found he could not; his soul *had still in remembrance the wormwood and the gall:* but here Zophar puts him in a way to forget it; let him by faith and prayer bring his griefs and cares to God, an leave them with him, and then he shall forget them. Where sin sits heavily affliction sits lightly. If we duly remember our sins, we shall, in comparison with them, forget our misery, much more if we obtain the comfort of a sealed pardon and a settled peace. He whose iniquity is forgiven shall *not say, I am sick,* but shall forget his sickness, Isa. 33:24.

4. A comfortable prospect of their future peace. This Zophar here thinks to please Job with, in answer to the many despairing expressions he had used, as if it were to no purpose for him to hope ever to see good days again in this world: "Yea, but thou mayest" (says Zophar) "and good nights too." A blessed change he here puts him in hopes of.

(1.) That though now his light was eclipsed it should shine out again, and more brightly than ever (*v.* 17), — that even his setting sun should out-shine his noon-day sun, and his evening be fair and clear as the morning, in respect both of honour and pleasure. — that his light should shine *out of obscurity* (Isa. 58:10), and the thick and dark cloud, from behind which his sun should break forth, would serve as a foil to its lustre, — that it should shine even in old age, and those evil days should be good days to him. Note, Those that truly turn to God then begin to shine forth; their path is as the shining light which increases, the period of their day will be the perfection of it, and their evening to this world will be their morning to a better.

(2.) That, though now he was in a continual fear and terror, he should live in a holy rest and security, and find himself continually safe and easy (*v.* 18): *Thou shalt be secure, because there is hope.* Note, Those who have a good hope, through grace, in God, and of heaven, are certainly safe, and have reason to be secure, how difficult soever the times are through which they pass in this world. He that walks uprightly may thus walk surely, because, though there are trouble and danger, yet there is hope that all will be well at last. Hope is *an anchor of the soul,* Heb. 6:19. *"Thou shalt dig about thee,"* that is, "Thou shalt be as safe as an army in its entrenchments." Those that submit to God's government shall be taken under his protection, and then they are safe both day and night. [1.] By day, when they employ themselves abroad: *"Thou shalt dig in safety,* thou and thy servants for thee, and not be again set upon by the plunderers, who fell upon thy servants at plough," *ch.* 1:14, 15. It is no part of the promised prosperity that he should live in idleness, but that he should have a calling and follow it, and, when he was about the business of it, should be under the divine protection. Thou shalt dig and be safe, not rob and be safe, revel and be safe. The way of duty is the way of safety. [2.] By night, when they repose themselves at home: *Thou shalt take thy rest* (and *the sleep of the labouring man is sweet*) *in safety,* notwithstanding the dangers of the darkness. The pillar of cloud by day shall be a pillar of fire by night: *"Thou shalt lie down* (*v.* 19), not forced to wander where there is no place to lay thy head on, nor forced to watch and sit up in expectation of assaults; but thou shalt go to bed at bedtime, and not only shall non hurt thee, but none shall make thee afraid nor so much as give thee an alarm." Note, It is a great mercy to have quiet nights and undisturbed sleeps; those say so that are within the hearing of the noise of war. And the way to be quiet is to seek unto God and keep ourselves in his love. Nothing needs make those afraid who *return to God as their rest* and take him for their habitation.

(3.) That, though now he was slighted, yet he should be courted: *"Many shall make suit to thee,* and think it their interest to secure thy friendship." Suit is made to those that are eminently wise or reputed to be so, that are very rich or in power. Zophar knew Job so well that he foresaw that, how low soever this present ebb was, if once the tide turned, it would flow as high as ever; and he would be again the darling of his country. Those that rightly make suit to God will probably see the day when others will make suit to them, as the foolish virgins to the wise, *Give us of your oil.*

III. Zophar concludes with a brief account of the doom of wicked people (*v.* 20): *But the eyes of the wicked shall fail.* It should seem, he suspected that Job would not take his counsel, and here tells him what would then come of it, setting death as well as life before him. See what will become of those who persist in their wickedness, and will not be reformed. 1. They shall not reach the good they flatter themselves with the hopes of in this world and in the other. Disappointments will be their doom, their shame, their endless torment. Their eyes shall fail with expecting that which will never come. *When a wicked man dies his expectation perishes,* Prov. 11:7. *Their hope shall be as a puff of breath* (margin), vanished and gone past recall. Or their hope will perish and expire as a man does when he gives up the ghost; it will fail them when they have most need of it and when they expected the accomplishment of it; it will die away, and leave them in utter confusion. 2. They shall not avoid the evil which sometimes they frighten themselves with the apprehensions of. They shall not escape the execution of the sentence passed upon them, can neither out-brave it nor outrun it. Those that will not fly to God will find it in vain to think of flying from him.

CHAPTER 12

In this and the two following chapters we have Job's answer to Zophar's discourse, in which, as before, he first reasons with his friends (see 13:19) and then turns to his God, and directs his expostulations to him, from thence to the end of his discourse. In this chapter he addresses himself to his friends, and, I. He condemns what they had said of him, and the judgment they had given of his character (*v.* 1–5). II. He contradicts and confronts what they had said of the destruction of wicked people in this world, showing that they often prosper (*v.* 6–11). III. He consents to what they had said of the wisdom, power, and sovereignty of God, and the dominion of his providence over the children of men and all their affairs; he confirms this, and enlarges upon it (*v.* 12–25).

Verses 1–5

The reproofs Job here gives to his friends, whether they were just or no, were very sharp, and may serve for a rebuke to all that are proud and scornful, and an exposure of their folly.

I. He upbraids them with their conceitedness of themselves, and the good opinion they seemed to have of their own wisdom in comparison with him, than which nothing is more weak and unbecoming, nor better deserves to be ridiculed, as it is here. 1. He represents them as claiming the monopoly of wisdom, *v.* 2. He speaks ironically: *"No doubt you are the people;* you think yourselves fit to dictate and give law to all mankind, and your own judgment to be the standard by which every man's opinion must be measured and tried, as if nobody could discern between truth and falsehood, good and evil, but you only; and therefore every top-sail must lower to you, and, right or wrong, we must all say as you say, and you three must be the people, the majority, to have the casting vote." Note, It is a very foolish and sinful thing for any to think themselves wiser than all mankind besides, or to speak and act confidently and imperiously, as if they thought so. Nay, he goes further: "You not only think there are none, but that there will be none, as wise as you, and therefore that *wisdom must die with you,* that all the world must be fools when you are gone, and in the dark when your sun has set." Note, It is folly for us to think that there will be any great irreparable loss of us when we are gone, or that we can be ill spared, since God has the residue of the Spirit, and can raise up others, more fit than we are, to do his work. When wise men and good men die it is a comfort to think that wisdom and goodness shall not die with them. Some think Job here reflects upon Zophar's comparing him (as he thought) and others to the wild ass's colt, *ch.* 11:12. "Yes," says he, "we must be asses; you are the only men." 2. He does himself the justice to put in his claim as a sharer in the gifts of wisdom (*v.* 3): *"But I have understanding (a heart) as well as you;* nay, *I fall not lower than you;"* as it is in the margin. "I am as well able to judge of the methods and meanings of the divine providence, and to construe the hard chapters of it, as you are." He says not this to magnify himself. It was no great applause of himself to say, *I have understanding as well as you;* no, nor to say, "I understand this matter as well as you;" for what reason had either he or they to be proud of understanding that which was obvious and level to the capacity of the meanest? *"Yea, who knows not such things as these?* What things you have said that are true are plain truths, and common themes, which there are many that can talk as excellently of as either you or I." But he says it to humble them, and check the value they had for themselves as doctors of the chair. Note, (1.) It may justly keep us from being proud of our knowledge to consider how many there are that know as much as we do, and perhaps much more and to better purpose. (2.) When we are tempted to be harsh in our censures of those we differ from and dispute with we ought to consider that they also have understanding as well as we, a capacity of judging, and a right of judging for themselves; nay, perhaps they are not inferior to us, but superior, and it is possible that they may be in the right and we in the wrong; and therefore we ought not to judge or despise them (Rom. 14:3), nor pretend to be masters (Jam. 3:1), while *all we are brethren,* Mt. 23:8. It is a very reasonable allowance to be made to all we converse with, all we contend with, that they are rational creatures as well as we.

II. He complains of the great contempt with which they had treated him. Those that are haughty and think too well of themselves are commonly scornful and ready to trample upon all about them. Job found it so, at least he thought he did (*v.* 4): *I am as one mocked.* I cannot say there was cause for this charge; we will not think Job's friends designed him any abuse, nor aimed at any thing but to convince him, and so, in the right method, to comfort him; yet he cries out, *I am as one mocked.* Note, We are apt to call reproofs reproaches, and to think ourselves mocked when we are but advised and admonished; this peevishness is our folly, and a great wrong to ourselves and to our friends. Yet we cannot but say there was colour for this charge; they came to comfort him, but they vexed him, gave him counsels and encouragements, but with no great opinion that either the one or the other would take effect; and therefore he thought they mocked him, and this added much to his grief. Nothing is more grievous to those that have fallen from the height of prosperity into the depth of adversity than to be trodden on, and insulted over, when they are down; and on this head they are too apt to be suspicious. Observe,

1. What aggravated this grievance to him. Two things: — (1.) That they were his *neighbours,* his friends, his companions (so the word signifies), and the scoffs of such are often most spitefully given, and always most indignantly received. Ps. 55:12, 13, *It was not an enemy that reproached me; then I would have* slighted it, and *so borne it; but it was thou, a man, my equal.* (2.) That they were professors of religion, such as *called upon God,* and said that he *answered them:* for some understand that of the persons mocking. "They are such as have a regard to heaven, and an interest in heaven, whose prayers I would therefore be glad of and thankful for, whose good opinion I cannot but covet, and therefore whose censures are the more grievous." Note, It is sad that any who call upon God should mock their brethren (Jam. 3:9, 10), and it cannot but lie heavily on a good man to be thought ill of by those whom he thinks well of, yet this is no new thing.

2. What supported him under it. (1.) That he had a God to go to, with whom he could lodge his appeal; for some understand those words of the person mocked, that he *calls upon God and he answers him;* and so it agrees with *ch.* 16:20. *My friends scorn me, but my eye poureth out tears to God.* If our friends be deaf to our complaints, God is not; if they condemn us, God knows our integrity; if they make the worst of us, he will make the best of us; if they give us cross answers, he will give us kind ones. (2.) That his case was not singular, but very common: *The just upright man is laughed to scorn.* By many he is laughed at even for his justice and his uprightness, his honesty towards men and his piety towards God; these are derided as foolish things, which silly people needlessly hamper themselves with, as if religion were a jest and therefore to be made a jest of. By most he is laughed at for any little infirmity or weakness, notwithstanding his justice and uprightness, without any consideration had of that which is so much his honour. Note, It was of old the lot of honest good people to be despised and derided; we are not therefore to think it strange (1 Pt. 4:12), no, nor to think it hard, if it be our lot; *so persecuted they* not only *the prophets,* but even the saints of the patriarchal age (Mt. 5:12), and can we expect to fare better than they?

3. What he suspected to be the true cause of it, and that was, in short, this: they were themselves rich and at ease, and therefore they despised him who had fallen into poverty. It is the way of the world; we see instances of it daily. Those that prosper are praised, but of those that are going down it is said, "Down with them." *He that is ready to slip with his feet* and fall into trouble, though he has formerly shone as a lamp, is then looked upon as a lamp going out like the snuff of a candle, which we throw to the ground and tread upon, and is accordingly *despised in the thought of him that is at ease, v.* 5. Even the just upright man, that is in his generation as a burning and shining light, if he enter into temptation (Ps. 73:2) or come under a cloud, is looked upon with contempt. See here, (1.) What is the common fault of those that live in prosperity. Being full, and easy, and merry themselves, they look scornfully upon those that are in want, pain, and sorrow; they overlook them, take no notice of them, and study to forget them. See Ps. 123:4. The chief butler drinks wine in bowls, but makes nothing of the afflictions of Joseph. Wealth without grace often makes men thus haughty, thus careless of their poor neighbours. (2.) What is the common fate of those that fall into adversity. Poverty serves to eclipse all their lustre; though they are lamps, yet, if taken out of golden candlesticks, and put, like Gideon's, into earthen pitchers, nobody values them as formerly, but those that live at ease despise them.

Verses 6–11

Job's friends all of them went upon this principle, that wicked people cannot prosper long in this world, but some remarkable judgment or other will suddenly light on them: Zophar had concluded with it, that *the eyes of the wicked shall fail, ch.* 11:20. This principle Job here opposes, and maintains that God, in disposing men's outward affairs, acts as a sovereign, reserving the exact distribution of rewards and punishments for the future state.

I. He asserts it as an undoubted truth that wicked people may, and often do, prosper long in this world, *v.* 6. Even great sinners may enjoy great prosperity. Observe, 1. How he describes the sinners. They are *robbers,* and such as provoke God, the worst kind of sinners, blasphemers and persecutors. Perhaps he refers to the Sabeans and Chaldeans, who had robbed him, and had always lived by spoil and rapine, and yet they prospered; all the world saw they did, and there is no disputing against sense; one observation built upon matter of fact is worth twenty notions framed by an hypothesis. Or more generally, All proud oppressors are robbers and pirates. It is supposed that what is injurious to men is provoking to God, the patron of right and the protector of mankind. It is not strange if those that violate the bonds of justice break through the obligations of all religion, bid defiance even to God himself, and make nothing of provoking him. 2. How he describes their prosperity. It is very great; for, (1.) Even *their tabernacles prosper,* those that live with them and those that come after them and descend from them. It seems as if a blessing were entailed upon their families; and that is sometimes preserved to succeeding generations which was got by fraud. (2.) They *are secure,* and not only feel no hurt, but fear none, are under no apprehensions of danger either from threatening providences or an awakened conscience. But those *that provoke God* are never the more safe for their being secure. (3.) *Into their hand God brings abundantly. They have more than heart could wish* (Ps. 73:7), not for necessity only, but for delight — not for themselves only, but for others — not for the present only, but for hereafter; and this from the hand of Providence too. God brings plentifully to them. We cannot therefore judge of men's piety by their plenty, nor of what they have in their heart by what they have in their hand.

II. He appeals even to the inferior creatures for the proof of this — the beasts, and fowls, and trees, and even the earth itself; consult these, and they shall tell thee, *v.* 7, 8. Many a good lesson we may learn from them, but what are they here to teach us?

1. We may from them learn that *the tabernacles of robbers prosper* (so some); for, (1.) Even among the brute creatures the greater devour the less and the stronger prey upon the weaker, and men are as the fishes of the sea, Hab. 1:14. If sin had not entered, we may suppose there would have been no such disorder among the creatures, but the wolf and the lamb would have lain down together. (2.) These creatures are serviceable to wicked men, and so they declare their prosperity. Ask the herds and the flocks to whom they belong, and they will tell you that such a robber, such an oppressor, is their owner: the fishes and fowls will tell you that they are served up to the tables, and feed the luxury, of proud sinners. The earth brings forth her fruits to them (*ch.* 9:24), and the whole creation groans under the burden of their tyranny, Rom. 8:20, 22. Note, All the creatures which wicked men abuse, by making them the food and fuel of their lusts, will witness against them another day, Jam. 5:3, 4.

2. We may from them learn the wisdom, power, and goodness of God, and that sovereign dominion of his into which plain and self-evident truth all these difficult dispensations must be resolved. Zophar had made a vast mystery of it, *ch.* 11:7. "So far from that," says Job, "that what we are concerned to know we may learn even from the inferior creatures; for *who knows not from all these? v.* 9. Any one may easily gather from the book of the creatures that *the hand of the Lord has wrought this,"* that is, "that there is a wise Providence which guides and governs all these things by rules which we are neither acquainted with nor are competent judges of." Note, From God's sovereign dominion over the inferior creatures we should learn to acquiesce in all his disposals of the affairs of the children of men, though contrary to our measures.

III. He resolves all into the absolute propriety which God has in all the creatures (*v.* 10): *In whose hand is the soul of every living thing.* All the creatures, and mankind particularly, derive their being from him, owe their being to him, depend upon him for the support of it, lie at his mercy, are under his direction and dominion and entirely at his disposal, and at his summons must resign their lives. All souls are his; and may he not do what he will with his own? The name *Jehovah* is used here (*v.* 9), and it is the only time that we meet with it in all the discourses between Job and his friends; for God was, in that age, more known by the name of *Shaddai — the Almighty.*

IV. Those words — (*v.* 11), *Doth not the ear try words, as the mouth tastes meat?* may be taken either as the conclusion to the foregoing discourse or the preface to what follows. The mind of man has as good a faculty of discerning between truth and error, when duly stated, as the palate has of discerning between what is sweet and what is bitter. Job therefore demands from his friends a liberty to judge for himself of what they had said, and desires them to use the same liberty in judging of what he had said; nay, he seems to appeal to any man's impartial judgment in this controversy; let the ear try the words on both sides, and it would be found that he was in the right. Note, The ear must try words before it receives them so as to subscribe to them. As by the taste we judge what food is wholesome to the body and what not, so by the spirit of discerning we must judge what doctrine is sound, and savoury, and wholesome, and what not, 1 Co. 10:15; 11:13.

Verses 12–25

This is a noble discourse of Job's concerning the wisdom, power, and sovereignty of God, in ordering and disposing of all the affairs of the children of men, according to the counsel of his own will, which none dares gainsay or can resist. Take both him and them out of the controversy in which they were so warmly engaged, and they all spoke admirably well; but, in *that,* we sometimes scarcely know what to make of them. It were well if wise and good men, that differ in their apprehensions about minor things, would see it to be for their honour and comfort, and the edification of others, to dwell most upon those great things in which they are agreed. On this subject Job speaks like himself. Here are no passionate complaints, no peevish reflections, but every thing masculine and great.

I. He asserts the unsearchable wisdom and irresistible power of God. It is allowed that among men there is *wisdom and understanding, v.* 12. But it is to be found only with some few, *with the ancient,* and those who are blessed with length of days, who get it by long experience and constant experience; and, when they have got the wisdom, they have lost their strength and are unable to execute the results of their wisdom. But now *with God there are* both *wisdom and strength,* wisdom to design the best and strength to accomplish what is designed. He does not get counsel or understanding, as we do, by observation, but he has it essentially and eternally in himself, *v.* 13. What is the wisdom of ancient men compared with the wisdom of the ancient of days! It is but little that we know, and less that we can do; but God can do every thing, and *no thought can be withheld from him.* Happy are those who have this God for their God, for they have infinite wisdom and strength engaged for them. Foolish and fruitless are all the attempts of men against him (*v.* 14): *He breaketh down, and it cannot be built again.* Note, There is no contending with the divine providence, nor breaking the measures of it. As he had said before (*ch.* 9:12), *He takes away, and who can hinder him?* so he says again. What God says cannot be gainsaid, nor what he does undone. There is no rebuilding what God will have to lie in ruins; witness the tower of Babel, which the undertakers could not go on with, and the desolations of Sodom and Gomorrah, which could never be repaired. See Isa. 25:2; Eze. 26:14; Rev. 18:21. There is no releasing those whom God has condemned to a perpetual imprisonment; if *he shut up* a man by sickness, reduce him to straits, and embarrass him in his affairs, *there can be no opening.* He shuts up in the grave, and none can break open those sealed doors — shuts up in hell, in chains of darkness, and none can pass that great gulf fixed.

II. He gives an instance, for the proof of this doctrine in nature, *v.* 15. God has the command of *the waters, binds them as in a garment* (Prov. 30:4), holds them *in the hollow of his hand* (Isa. 40:12); and he can punish the children of men either by the defect or by the excess of them. As men break the laws of virtue by extremes on each hand, both defects and excesses, while virtue is in the mean, so God corrects them by extremes, and denies them the mercy which is in the mean. 1. Great droughts are sometimes great judgments: *He withholds the waters, and they dry up;* if the heaven be as brass, the earth is as iron; if the rain be denied, fountains dry up and their streams are wanted, fields are parched and their fruits are wanted, Amos 4:7. 2. Great wet is sometimes a great judgment. He raises the waters, and *overturns the earth,* the productions of it, the buildings upon it. A sweeping rain is said to *leave no food,* Prov. 28:3. See how many ways God has of contending with a sinful people and taking from them abused, forfeited, mercies; and how utterly unable we are to contend with him. If we might invert the order, this verse would fitly refer to Noah's flood, that ever memorable instance of the divine power. God then, in wrath, sent the waters out, and they overturned the earth; but in mercy he withheld them, shut the windows of heaven and the fountains of the great deep, and then, in a little time, they dried up.

III. He gives many instances of it in God's powerful management of the children of men, crossing their purposes and serving his own by them and upon them, overruling all their counsels, overpowering all their attempts, and overcoming all their oppositions. What changes does God make with men! what turns does he give them! how easily, how surprisingly!

1. In general (*v.* 16): *With him are strength and reason* (so some translate it), strength and consistency with himself: it is an elegant word in the original. With him are the very quintessence and extract of wisdom. *With him are power and all that is;* so some read it. He is what he is of himself, and by him and in him all things subsist. Having this strength and wisdom, he knows how to make use, not only of those who are wise and good, who willingly and designedly serve him, but even of those who are foolish and bad, who, one would think, could be made no way serviceable to the designs of his providence: *The deceived and the deceiver are his;* the simplest men that are deceived are not below his notice; the subtlest men that deceive cannot with all their subtlety escape his cognizance. The world is full of deceit; the one half of mankind cheats the other, and God suffers it to be so, and from both will at last bring glory to himself. The deceivers make tools of the deceived, but the great God makes tools of them both, wherewith he works, and none can hinder him. He has wisdom and might enough to manage all the fools and knaves in the world, and knows how to serve his own purposes by them, notwithstanding the weakness of the one and the wickedness of the other. When Jacob by a fraud got the blessing the design of God's grace was served; when Ahab was drawn by a false prophecy into an expedition that was his ruin the design of God's justice was served; and in both *the deceived and the deceiver* were at his disposal. See Eze. 14:9. God would not suffer the sin of the deceiver, nor the misery of the deceived, if he knew not how to set bounds to both and bring glory to himself out of both. *Hallelujah, the Lord God omnipotent* thus reigns; and it is well he does, for otherwise there is so little wisdom and so little honesty in the world that it would all have been in confusion and ruin long ago.

2. He next descends to the particular instances of the wisdom and power of God in the revolutions of states and kingdoms; for thence he fetches his proofs, rather than from the like operations of Providence concerning private persons and families, because the more high and public the station is in which men are placed the more the changes that befal them are taken notice of, and consequently the more illustriously does Providence shine forth in them. And it is easy to argue, If God can thus turn and toss the great ones of the earth, like a ball in a large place (as the prophet speaks, Isa. 22:18), much more the little ones; and with him to whom states and kingdoms must submit it is surely the greatest madness for us to contend. Some think that Job here refers to the extirpation of those powerful nations, the Rephaim, the Zuzim, the Emim, and the Horites (mentioned Gen. 14:5, 6; Deu. 2:10, 20), in which perhaps it was particularly noticed how strangely they were infatuated and enfeebled: if so, it is designed to show that whenever the like is done in the affairs of nations it is God that does it, and we must therein observe his sovereign dominion, even over those that think themselves most powerful, politic, and absolute. Compare this with that of Eliphaz, *ch.* 5:12, etc. Let us gather up the particular changes here specified, which God makes upon persons, either for the destruction of nations and the planting of others in their room or for the turning out of a particular government and ministry and the elevation of another in its room, which may be a blessing to the kingdom; witness the glorious Revolution in our own land twenty years ago, in which we saw as happy an exposition as ever was given of this discourse of Job's. (1.) Those that were wise are sometimes strangely infatuated, and in this the hand of God must be acknowledged (*v.* 17): *He leadeth counsellors away spoiled,* as trophies of his victory over them, spoiled of all the honour and wealth they have got by their policy, nay, spoiled of the wisdom itself for which they have been celebrated and the success they promised themselves in their projects. His counsel stands, while all their devices are brought to nought and their designs baffled, and so they are spoiled both of the satisfaction and of the reputation of their wisdom. *He maketh the judges fools.* By a work on their minds he deprives them of their qualifications for business, and so they become really fools; and by his disposal of their affairs he makes the issue and event of their projects to be quite contrary to what they themselves intended, and so he makes them look like fools. The counsel of Ahithophel, one in whom this scripture was remarkably fulfilled, became foolishness, and he, according to his name, *the brother of a fool.* See Isa. 19:13, *The princes of Zoan have become fools; they have seduced Egypt, even those that are the stay of the tribes thereof.* Let not the wise man therefore glory in his wisdom, nor the ablest counsellors and judges be proud of their station, but humbly depend upon God for the continuance of their abilities. Even the aged, who seem to hold their wisdom by prescription, and think they have got it by their own industry and therefore have an indefeasible title to it, may yet be deprived of it, and often are, by the infirmities of age, which make them twice children: He *taketh away the understanding of the aged, v.* 20. The aged, who were most depended on for advice, fail those that depended on them. We read of an old and yet foolish king, Eccl. 4:13. (2.) Those that were high and in authority are strangely brought down, impoverished, and enslaved, and it is God that humbles them (*v.* 18): *He looseth the bond of kings,* and taketh from them the power wherewith they ruled their subjects, perhaps enslaved them and ruled them with rigour; he strips them of all the ensigns of their honour and authority, and all the supports of their tyranny, unbuckles their belts, so that the sword drops from their side, and then no marvel if the crown quickly drops from their head, on which immediately follows the *girding of their loins with a girdle,* a badge of servitude, for servants went with their loins girt. Thus *he leads* great *princes away spoiled* of all their power and wealth, and that in which they pleased and prided themselves, *v.* 19. Note, Kings are not exempt from God's jurisdiction. To us they are gods, but men to him, and subject to more than the common changes of human life. (3.) Those that were strong are strangely weakened, and it is God that weakens them (*v.* 21) and *overthrows the mighty. v.* 19. Strong bodies are weakened by age and sickness; powerful armies moulder and come to nothing, and their strength will not secure them from a fatal overthrow. No force can stand before Omnipotence, no, not that of Goliath. (4.) Those that were famed for eloquence, and entrusted with public business, are strangely silenced, and have nothing to say (*v.* 20): *He removeth away the speech of the trusty,* so that they cannot speak as they intended and as they used to do, with freedom and clearness, but blunder, and falter, and make nothing of it. Or they cannot speak what they intended, but the contrary, as Balaam, who blessed those whom he was called to curse. Let not the orator therefore be proud of his rhetoric, nor use it to any bad purposes, lest God take it away, who made man's mouth. (5.) Those that were honoured and admired strangely fall into disgrace (*v.* 21): He *poureth contempt upon princes.* He leaves them to themselves to do mean things, or alters the opinions of men concerning them. If princes themselves dishonour God and despise him, if they offer indignities to the people of God and trample upon them, they shall be lightly esteemed, and God will pour contempt upon them. See Ps. 107:40. Commonly none more abject in themselves, nor more abused by others when they are down, than those who were haughty and insolent when they were in power. (6.) That which was secret, and lay hidden, is strangely brought to light and laid open (*v.* 22): *He discovers deep things out of darkness.* Plots closely laid are discovered and defeated; wickedness closely committed and artfully concealed is discovered, and the guilty are brought to condign punishment — secret treasons (Eccl. 10:20), secret murders, secret whoredoms. The cabinet-councils of princes are before God's eye, 2 Ki. 6:11. (7.) Kingdoms have their ebbings and flowings, their waxings and wanings; and both are from God (*v.* 23): He sometimes *increases their numbers,* and enlarges their bounds, so that they make a figure among the nations and become formidable; but after a while, by some undiscerned cause perhaps, they are destroyed and straitened, made few and poor, cut short and many of them cut off, and so they are rendered despicable among their neighbours, and those that were the head become the tail of the nations. See Ps. 107:38, 39. (8.) Those that were bold and courageous, and made nothing of dangers, are strangely cowed and dispirited; and this also is the Lord's doing (*v.* 24): *He taketh away the heart cf the chief of the people,* that were their leaders and commanders, and were most famed for their martial fire and great achievements; when any thing is to be done they are heartless, and ready to flee at the shaking of a leaf. Ps. 76:5. (9.) Those that were driving on their projects with full speed are strangely bewildered and at a loss; they know not where they are nor what they do, are unsteady in their counsels and uncertain in their motions, off and on, this way and that way, wandering like men in a desert (*v.* 24), groping like men in the dark, and staggering like men in drink, *v.* 25. Isa. 59:10. Note, God can soon nonplus the deepest politicians and bring the greatest wits to their wits' end, to show that wherein they deal proudly he is above them.

Thus are the revolutions of kingdoms wonderfully brought about by an overruling Providence. Heaven and earth are shaken, but the Lord sits King for ever, and with him we look for *a kingdom that cannot be shaken.*

CHAPTER 13

Job here comes to make application of what he had said in the foregoing chapter; and now we have him not in so good a temper as he was in then: for, I. He is very bold with his friends, comparing himself with them, notwithstanding the mortifications he was under (*v.* 1, 2). Condemning them for their falsehood, their forwardness to judge, their partiality and deceitfulness under colour of pleading God's cause (*v.* 4–8), and threatening them with the judgments of God for their so doing (*v.* 9–12), desiring them to be silent (*v.* 5, 13, 17), and turning from them to God (*v.* 3). II. He is very bold with his God. 1. In some expressions his faith is very bold, yet that is not more bold than welcome (*v.* 15, 16, 18) But, 2. In other expressions his passion is rather too bold in expostulations with God concerning the deplorable condition he was in (*v.* 14, 19, etc.), complaining of the confusion he was in (*v.* 20–22), and the loss he was at to find out the sin that provoked God thus to afflict him, and in short of the rigour of God's proceedings against him (*v.* 23–28).

Verses 1–12

Job here warmly expresses his resentment of the unkindness of his friends.

I. He comes up with them as one that understood the matter in dispute as well as they, and did not need to be taught by them, *v.* 1, 2. They compelled him, as the Corinthians did Paul, to commend himself and his own knowledge, yet not in a way of self-applause, but of self-justification. All he had before said his eye had seen confirmed by many instances, and his ear had heard seconded by many authorities, and he well understood it and what use to make of it. Happy are those who not only see and hear, but understand, the greatness, glory, and sovereignty of God. This, he thought, would justify what he had said before (*ch.* 12:3), which he repeats here (*v.* 2): "*What you know, the same do I know also,* so that I need not come to you to be taught; *I am not inferior unto you* in wisdom." Note, Those who enter into disputation enter into temptation to magnify themselves and vilify their brethren more than is fit, and therefore ought to watch and pray against the workings of pride.

II. He turns from them to God (*v.* 3): *Surely I would speak to the Almighty;* as if he had said, "I can promise myself no satisfaction in talking to you. O that I might have liberty to *reason with God!* He would not be so hard upon me as you are." The prince himself will perhaps give audience to a poor petitioner with more mildness, patience, and condescension, than the servants will. Job would rather argue with God himself than with his friends. See here, 1. What confidence those have towards God whose hearts condemn them not of reigning hypocrisy: they can, with humble boldness, appear before him and appeal to him. 2. What comfort those have in God whose neighbours unjustly condemn them: if they may not speak to them with any hopes of a fair hearing, yet they may speak to the Almighty; they have easy access to him and shall find acceptance with him.

III. He condemns them for their unjust and uncharitable treatment of him, *v.* 4. 1. They falsely accused him, and that was unjust: *You are forgers of lies.* They framed a wrong hypothesis concerning the divine Providence, and misrepresented it, as if it did never remarkably afflict any but wicked men in this world, and thence they drew a false judgment concerning Job, that he was certainly a hypocrite. For this gross mistake, both in doctrine and application, he thinks an indictment of forgery lies against them. To speak lies is bad enough, though but at second hand, but to forge them with contrivance and deliberation is much worse; yet against this wrong neither innocency nor excellency will be a fence. 2. They basely deceived him, and that was unkind. They undertook his cure, and pretended to be his physicians; but they were all *physicians of no value,* "idol-physicians, who can do me no more good than an idol can." They were worthless physicians, who neither understood his case nor knew how to prescribe to him — mere empirics, who pretended to great things, but in conference added nothing to him: he was never the wiser for all they said. Thus to broken hearts and wounded consciences all creatures, without Christ, are physicians of no value, on which one may spend all and be never the better, but rather grow worse, Mk. 5:26.

IV. He begs they would be silent and give him a patient hearing, *v.* 5, 6. 1. He thinks it would be a credit to them if they would say no more, having said too much already: "*Hold your peace, and it shall be your wisdom,* for thereby you will conceal your ignorance and ill-nature, which now appear in all you say." They pleaded that they could not forbear speaking (*ch.* 4:2, 11:2, 3); but he tells them that they would better have consulted their own reputation if they had enjoined themselves silence. Better say nothing than nothing to the purpose or that which tends to the dishonour of God and the grief of our brethren. *Even a fool, when he holds his peace, is accounted wise,* because nothing appears to the contrary, Prov. 17:28. And, as silence is an evidence of wisdom, so it is a means of it, as it gives time to think and hear. 2. He thinks it would be a piece of justice to him to hear what he had to say: *Hear now my reasoning.* Perhaps, though they did not interrupt him in his discourse, yet they seemed careless, and did not much heed what he said. He therefore begged that they would not only hear, but hearken. Note, We should be very willing and glad to hear what those have to say for themselves whom, upon any account, we are tempted to have hard thoughts of. Many a man, if he could but be fairly heard, would be fairly acquitted, even in the consciences of those that run him down.

V. He endeavours to convince them of the wrong they did to God's honour, while they pretended to plead for him, *v.* 7, 8. They valued themselves upon it that they spoke for God, were advocates for him, and had undertaken to justify him and his proceedings against Job; and, being (as they thought) of counsel for the sovereign, they expected not only the ear of the court and the last word, but judgment on their side. But Job tells them plainly, 1. That God and his cause did not need such advocates: "*Will you* think to *contend for God,* as if his justice were clouded and want-

ed to be cleared up, or as if he were at a loss what to say and wanted you to speak for him? Will you, who are so weak and passionate, put in for the honour of pleading God's cause?" Good work ought not to be put into bad hands. *Will you accept his person?* If those who have not right on their side carry their cause, it is by the partiality of the judge in favour of their persons; but God's cause is so just that it needs no such methods for the support of it. He is a God, and can plead for himself (Jdg. 6:31); and, if you were for ever silent, the heavens would declare his righteousness. 2. That God's cause suffered by such management. Under pretence of justifying God in afflicting Job they magisterially condemned him as a hypocrite and a bad man. "This" (says he) "*is speaking wickedly*" (for uncharitableness and censoriousness are wickedness, great wickedness; it is an offence to God to wrong our brethren); "it is talking *deceitfully,* for you condemn one whom yet perhaps your own consciences, at the same time, cannot but acquit. Your principles are false and your arguings fallacious, and will it excuse you to say, *It is for God?*" No, for a good intention will not justify, much less will it sanctify, a bad word or action. God's truth needs not our lie, nor God's cause either our sinful policies or our sinful passions. The wrath of man works not the righteousness of God, nor may we *do evil that good may come,* Rom. 3:7, 8. Pious frauds (as they call them) are impious cheats; and devout persecutions are horrid profanations of the name of God, as theirs who *hated their brethren,* and *cast them out, saying, Let the Lord be glorified,* Isa. 66:5; Jn. 16:2.

VI. He endeavours to possess them with a fear of God's judgment, and so to bring them to a better temper. Let them not think to impose upon God as they might upon a man like themselves, nor expect to gain his countenance in their bad practices by pretending a zeal for him and his honour. "As one man mocks another by flattering him, do you think so to mock him and deceive him?" Assuredly those who think to put a cheat upon God will prove to have put a cheat upon themselves. *Be not deceived, God is not mocked.* That they might not think thus to jest with God, and affront him, Job would have them to consider both God and themselves, and then they would find themselves unable to enter into judgment with him.

1. Let them consider what a God he is into whose service they had thus thrust themselves, and to whom they really did so much disservice, and enquire whether they could give him a good account of what they did. Consider, (1.) The strictness of his scrutiny and enquiries concerning them (*v.* 9) "*Is it good that he should search you out?* Can you bear to have the principles looked into which you go upon in your censures, and to have the bottom of the matter found out?" Note, It concerns us all seriously to consider whether it will be to our advantage or no that God searches the heart. It is good to an upright man who means honestly that God should search him; therefore he prays for it: *Search me, O God! and know my heart.* God's omniscience is a witness of his sincerity. But it is bad to him who looks one way and rows another that God should search him out, and lay him open to his confusion. (2.) The severity of his rebukes and displeasure against them (*v.* 10): "*If you do accept persons,* though but secretly and in heart, *he will surely reprove you;* he will be so far from being pleased with your censures of me, though under colour of vindicating him, that he will resent them as a great provocation, as any prince or great man would if a base action were done under the sanction of his name and under the colour of advancing his interest." Note, What we do amiss we shall certainly be reproved for, one way or other, one time or other, though it be done ever so secretly. (3.) The terror of his majesty, which if they would duly stand in awe of they would not do that which would make them obnoxious to his wrath (*v.* 11): "*Shall not his excellency make you afraid?* You that have great knowledge of God, and profess religion and a fear of him, how dare you talk at this rate and give yourselves so great a liberty of speech? *Ought you not to walk* and talk *in the fear of God?* Neh. 5:9. *Should not his dread fall upon you,* and give a check to your passions?" Methinks Job speaks this as one that did himself know the terror of the Lord, and lived in a holy fear of him, whatever his friends suggested to the contrary. Note, [1.] There is in God a dreadful excellency. He is the most excellent Being, has all excellencies in himself and in each infinitely excels any creature. His excellencies in

themselves are amiable and lovely. He is the most beautiful Being; but considering man's distance from God by nature, and his defection and degeneracy by sin, his excellencies are dreadful. His power, holiness, justice, yea, and his goodness too, are dreadful excellencies. They shall fear the Lord and his goodness. [2.] A holy awe of this dreadful excellency should fall upon us and make us afraid. This would awaken impenitent sinners and bring them to repentance, and would influence all to be careful to please him and afraid of offending him.

2. Let them consider themselves, and what an unequal match they were for this great God (*v.* 12): "*Your remembrances* (all that in you for which you hope to be remembered when you are gone) *are like unto ashes,* worthless and weak, and easily trampled on and blown away. *Your bodies are like bodies of clay,* mouldering and coming to nothing. Your memories, you think, will survive your bodies, but, alas! they are like ashes which will be shovelled up with your dust." Note, the consideration of our own meanness and mortality should make us afraid of offending God, and furnishes a good reason why we should not despise and trample upon our brethren. Bishop Patrick gives another sense of this verse: "Your remonstrances on God's behalf are no better than dust, and the arguments you accumulate but like so many heaps of dirt."

Verses 13–22

Job here takes fresh hold, fast hold, of his integrity, as one that was resolved not to let it go, nor suffer it to be wrested from him. His firmness in this matter is commendable and his warmth excusable.

I. He entreats his friends and all the company to let him alone, and not interrupt him in what he was about to say (*v.* 13), but diligently to hearken to it, *v.* 17. He would have his own protestation to be decisive, for none but God and himself knew his heart. "Be silent therefore, and let me hear no more of you, but hearken diligently to what I say, and let my own oath for confirmation be an end of the strife."

II. He resolves to adhere to the testimony his own conscience gave of his integrity; and though his friends called it obstinacy that should not shake his constancy: "I will speak in my own defence, and *let come on me what will,* *v.* 13. Let my friends put what construction they please upon it, and think the worse of me for it; I hope God will not make my necessary defence to be my offence, as you do. He will justify me (*v.* 18) and then nothing can come amiss to me." Note, Those that are upright, and have the assurance of their uprightness, may cheerfully welcome every event. Come what will, *bene praeparatum pectus — they are ready for it.* He resolves (*v.* 15) that he will *maintain his own ways.* He would never part with the satisfaction he had in having walked uprightly with God; for, though he could not justify every word he had spoken, yet, in the general, his ways were good, and he would maintain his uprightness; and why should he not, since that was his great support under his present exercises, as it was Hezekiah's, *Now, Lord, remember how I have walked before thee?* Nay, he would not only not betray his own cause, or give it up, but he would openly avow his sincerity; for (*v.* 19) "*If hold my tongue,* and do not speak for myself, my silence now will for ever silence me, for *I shall certainly give up the ghost,*" *v.* 19. "If I cannot be cleared, yet let me be eased, by what I say," as Elihu, *ch.* 32:17, 20.

III. He complains of the extremity of pain and misery he was in (*v.* 14): *Wherefore do I take my flesh in my teeth?* That is, 1. "Why do I suffer such agonies? I cannot but wonder that God should lay so much upon me when he knows I am not a wicked man." He was ready, not only to rend his clothes, but even to tear his flesh, through the greatness of his affliction, and saw himself at the brink of death, and his life in his hand, yet his friends could not charge him with any enormous crime, nor could he himself discover any; no marvel then that he was in such confusion. 2. "Why do I stifle and smother the protestations of my innocency?" When a man with great difficulty keeps in what he would say, he bites his lips. "Now," says he, "why may not I take liberty to speak, since I do but vex myself, add to my torment, and endanger my life, by refraining?" Note, It would vex the most patient man, when he has lost every thing else, to be denied the comfort (if he deserves it) of a good conscience and a good name.

IV. He comforts himself in God, and still keeps hold of his confidence in him. Observe here,

1. What he depends upon God for — justification and salvation, the two great things we hope for through Christ. (1.) Justification (*v.* 18): *I have ordered my cause, and,* upon the whole matter, *I know that I shall be justified.* This he knew because he knew that his Redeemer lived, *ch.* 19:25. Those whose hearts are upright with God, in walking not after the flesh but after the Spirit, may be sure that through Christ there shall be no condemnation to them, but that, whoever lays any thing to their charge, they shall be justified: they may know that they shall. (2.) Salvation (*v.* 16): *He also shall be my salvation.* He means it not of temporal salvation (he had little expectation of that); but concerning his eternal salvation he was very confident that God would not only be his Saviour to make him happy, but his salvation, in the vision and fruition of whom he should be happy. And the reason why he depended on God for salvation was because *a hypocrite shall not come before him.* He knew himself not to be a hypocrite, and that none but hypocrites are rejected of God, and therefore concluded he should not be rejected. Sincerity is our evangelical perfection; nothing will ruin us but the want of that.

2. With what constancy he depends upon him: *Though he slay me, yet will I trust in him, v.* 15. This is a high expression of faith, and what we should all labour to come up to — to trust in God, though he slay us, that is, we must be well pleased with God as a friend even when he seems to come forth against us as an enemy, *ch.* 23:8–10. We must believe that all shall work for good to us even when all seems to make against us, Jer. 24:5. We must proceed and persevere in the way of our duty, though it cost us all that is dear to us in this world, even life itself, Heb. 11:35. We must depend upon the performance of the promise when all the ways leading to it are shut up, Rom. 4:18. We must rejoice in God when we have nothing else to rejoice in, and cleave to him, yea, though we cannot for the present find comfort in him. In a dying hour we must derive from him living comforts; and this is to trust in him though he slay us.

V. He wishes to argue the case even with God himself, if he might but have leave to settle the preliminaries of the treaty, *v.* 20–22. He had desired (*v.* 3) to *reason with God,* and is still of the same mind. He *will not hide himself,* that is, he will not decline the trial, nor dread the issue of it, but under two provisos: — 1. That his body might not be tortured with this exquisite pain: *"Withdraw thy hand far from me;* for, while I am in this extremity, I am fit for nothing. I can make a shift to talk with my friends, but I know not how to address myself to thee." When we are to converse with God we have need to be composed, and as free as possible from every thing that may make us uneasy. 2. That his mind might not be terrified with the tremendous majesty of God: *"Let not thy dread make me afraid;* either let the manifestations of thy presence be familiar or let me be enabled to bear them without disorder and disturbance." Moses himself trembled before God, so did Isaiah and Habakkuk. *O God! thou art terrible even in thy holy places.* "Lord," says Job, "let me not be put into such a consternation of spirit, together with this bodily affliction; for then I must certainly drop the cause, and shall make nothing of it." See what a folly it is for men to put off their repentance and conversion to a sick-bed and a death-bed. How can even a good man, much less a bad man, reason with God, so as to be justified before him, when he is upon the rack of pain and under the terror of the arrests of death? At such a time it is very bad to have the great work to do, but very comfortable to have it done, as it was to Job, who, if he might but have a little breathing-time, was ready either, (1.) To hear God speaking to him by his word, and return an answer: *Call thou, and I will answer;* or, (2.) To speak to him by prayer, and expect an answer: *Let me speak, and answer thou me, v.* 22. Compare this with *ch.* 9:34, 35, where he speaks to the same purport. In short, the badness of his case was at present such a damp upon him as he could not get over; otherwise he was well assured of the goodness of his cause, and doubted not but to have the comfort of it at last, when the present cloud was over. With such holy boldness may the upright come to the throne of grace, not doubting but to find mercy there.

Verses 23–28

Here, I. Job enquires after his sins, and begs to have them discovered to him. He looks up to God, and asks him what was the number of them *(How many are my iniquities?)* and what were the particulars of them: *Make me to know my transgressions, v.* 23. His friends were ready enough to tell him how numerous and how heinous they were, *ch.* 22:5. "But, Lord," says he, "let me know them from thee; *for thy judgment is according to truth,* theirs is not." This may be taken either, 1. As a passionate complaint of hard usage, that he was punished for his faults and yet was not told what his faults were. Or, 2. As a prudent appeal to God from the censures of his friends. He desired that all his sins might be brought to light, as knowing they would then appear not so many, nor so mighty, as his friends suspected him to be guilty of. Or, 3. As a pious request, to the same purport with that which Elihu directed him to, *ch.* 34:32. *That which I see not, teach thou me.* Note, A true penitent is willing to know the worst of himself; and we should all desire to know what our transgressions are, that we may be particular in the confession of them and on our guard against them for the future.

II. He bitterly complains of God's withdrawings from him (*v.* 24): *Wherefore hidest thou thy face?* This must be meant of something more than his outward afflictions; for the loss of estate, children, health, might well consist with God's love; when that was all, he blessed the name of the Lord; but *his soul was also sorely vexed,* and that is it which he here laments. 1. That the favours of the Almighty were suspended. God hid his face as one strange to him, displeased with him, shy and regardless of him. 2. That the terrors of the Almighty were inflicted and impressed upon him. God held him for his enemy, shot his arrows at him (*ch.* 6:4), and set him as a mark, *ch.* 7:20. Note, The Holy Ghost sometimes denies his favours and discovers his terrors to the best and dearest of his saints and servants in this world. This case occurs, not only in the production, but sometimes in the progress of the divine life. Evidences for heaven are eclipsed, sensible communications interrupted, dread of divine wrath impressed, and the returns of comfort, for the present, despaired of, Ps. 77:7–9; 88:7, 15, 16. These are grievous burdens to a gracious soul, that values God's loving-kindness as better than life, Prov. 18:14. *A wounded spirit who can bear?* Job, by asking here, *Why hidest thou thy face?* teaches us that, when at any time we are under the sense of God's withdrawings, we are concerned to enquire into the reason of them — what is the sin for which he corrects us and what the good he designs us. Job's sufferings were typical of the sufferings of Christ, from whom not only men hid their faces (Isa. 53:3), but God hid his, witness the darkness which surrounded him on the cross when he cried out, *My God, my God, why hast thou forsaken me?* If this were done to these green trees, what shall be done to the dry? They will for ever be forsaken.

III. He humbly pleads with God his own utter inability to stand before him (*v.* 25): *"Wilt thou break a leaf, pursue the dry stubble?* Lord, is it for thy honour to trample upon one that is down already, or to crush one that neither has nor pretends to any power to resist thee?" Note, We ought to have such an apprehension of the goodness and compassion of God as to believe that he will not *break the bruised reed,* Mt. 12:20.

IV. He sadly complains of God's severe dealings with him. He owns it was for his sins that God thus contended with him, but thinks it hard,

1. That his former sins, long since committed, should now be remembered against him, and he should he reckoned with for the old scores (*v.* 26): *Thou writest bitter things against me.* Afflictions are bitter things. Writing them denotes deliberation and determination, written as a warrant for execution; it denotes also the continuance of his affliction, for that which is written remains, and, "Herein *thou makest me to possess the iniquities of my youth,"* that is, "thou punishest me for them, and thereby puttest me in mind of them, and obligest me to renew my repentance for them." Note, (1.) God sometimes writes very bitter things against the best and dearest of his saints and servants, both in outward afflictions and inward disquiet; trouble in body and trouble in mind, that he may humble them, and prove them, and do them good in their latter end. (2.) That the sins of youth are often the smart of age both in respect of sorrow within (Jer. 31:18, 19) and suffering without, *ch.* 20:11. Time does not wear out the guilt of sin. (3.) That when God writes bitter things against us his design therein is to make us possess our iniquities, to bring forgotten sins to mind, and so to bring us to remorse for them as to break us off from them. *This is all the fruit, to take away our sin.*

2. That his present mistakes and miscarriages should be so strictly taken notice of, and so severely animadverted upon (*v.* 27): *"Thou puttest my feet also in the stocks,* not only to afflict me and expose me to shame, not only to keep me from escaping the strokes of thy wrath, but that thou mayest critically remark all my motions and look narrowly to all my paths, to correct me for every false step, nay, for but a look awry or a word misapplied; nay, thou *settest a print upon the heels of my feet,* scorest down every thing I do amiss, to reckon for it; or no sooner have I trodden wrong, though ever so little, than immediately I smart for it; the punishment treads upon the very heels of the sin. Guilt, both of the oldest and of the freshest date, is put together to make up the cause of my calamity." Now, (1.) It was not true that God did thus seek advantages against him. He is not thus extreme to mark what we do amiss; if he were, there were no abiding for us, Ps. 130:3. But he is so far from this that he deals not with us according to the desert, no, not of our manifest sins, which are not *found by secret search,* Jer. 2:34. This therefore was the language of Job's melancholy; his sober thoughts never represented God thus as a hard Master. (2.) But we should keep such a strict and jealous eye as this upon ourselves and our own steps, both for the discovery of sin past and the prevention of it for the future. It is good for us all to *ponder the path of our feet.*

V. He finds himself wasting away apace under the heavy hand of God, *v.* 28. *He* (that is, man) *as a rotten thing,* the principle of whose putrefaction is in itself, *consumes, even like a moth-eaten garment,* which becomes continually worse and worse. Or, *He* (that is, God) *like rottenness, and like a moth, consumes me.* Compare this with Hos. 5:12, *I will be unto Ephraim as a moth, and to the house of Judah as rottenness;* and see Ps. 39:11. Note, Man, at the best, wears fast; but, under God's rebukes especially, he is soon gone. While there is so little soundness in the soul, no marvel there is so little soundness in the flesh, Ps. 38:3.

CHAPTER 14

Job had turned from speaking to his friends, finding it to no purpose to reason with them, and here he goes on to speak to God and himself. He had reminded his friends of their frailty and mortality (*ch.* 13:12); here he reminds himself of his own, and pleads it with God for some mitigation of his miseries. We have here an account, I. Of man's life, that it is, 1. Short (*v.* 1). 2. Sorrowful (*v.* 1). 3. Sinful (*v.* 4). 4. Stinted (*v.* 5, 14). II. Of man's death, that it puts a final period to our present life, to which we shall not again return (*v.* 7–12), that it hides us from the calamities of life (*v.* 13), destroys the hopes of life (*v.* 18, 19), sends us away from the business of life (*v.* 20), and keeps us in the dark concerning our relations in this life, how much soever we have formerly been in care about them (*v.* 21, 22), III. The use Job makes of all this. 1. He pleads it with God, who, he thought, was too strict and severe with him (*v.* 16, 17), begging that, in consideration of his frailty, he would not contend with him (*v.* 3), but grant him some respite (*v.* 6). 2. He engages himself to prepare for death (*v.* 14), and encourages himself to hope that it would be comfortable to him (*v.* 15). This chapter is proper for funeral solemnities; and serious meditations on it will help us both to get good by the death of others and to get ready for our own.

Verses 1–6

We are here led to think,

I. Of the original of human life. God is indeed its great original, for he *breathed into man the breath of life* and in him we live; but we date it from our birth, and thence we must date both its frailty and its pollution. 1. Its frailty: *Man, that is born of a woman, is* therefore *of few days, v.* 1. This may refer to the first woman, who was called *Eve,* because she was the mother of all living. Of her, who being deceived by the tempter was first in the transgression, we are all born, and consequently derive from her that sin and corruption which both shorten our days and sadden them. Or it may refer to every man's immediate mother. The woman is the weaker vessel, and we know that *partus sequitur ventrem — the child takes after the mother.* Let not the strong man therefore glory in his strength, or in the strength of his father, but remember that he is born of a woman, and that, when God pleases, the *mighty men become as women,* Jer. 51:30. 2. Its pollution (*v.* 4): *Who can bring a clean thing out of an unclean?* If man be born of a woman that is a sinner, how can it be otherwise than that he should be a sinner? See *ch.* 25:4. *How can he be clean that is born of a woman?* Clean children cannot come from unclean parents any more than pure streams from an impure spring or grapes from thorns. Our habitual corruption is derived with our nature from our parents, and is therefore bred in the bone. Our blood is not only attainted by a legal conviction, but tainted with an hereditary disease. Our Lord Jesus, being made sin for us, is said to be *made of a woman,* Gal. 4:4.

II. Of the nature of human life: it is *a flower,* it is a *shadow, v.* 2. The flower is fading, and all its beauty soon withers and is gone. The shadow is fleeting, and its very being will soon be lost and drowned in the shadows of the night. Of neither do we make any account; in neither do we put any confidence.

III. Of the shortness and uncertainty of human life: Man is *of few days.* Life is here computed, not by months or years, but by days, for we cannot be sure of any day but that it may be our last. These days are few, fewer than we think of, few at the most, in comparison with the days of the first patriarchs, much more in comparison with the days of eternity, but much fewer to most, who come short of what we call *the age of man.* Man sometimes no sooner comes forth than he *is cut down* — comes forth out of the womb than he dies in the cradle — comes forth into the world and enters into the business of it than he is hurried away as soon as he has laid his hand to the plough. If not cut down immediately, yet *he flees as a shadow,* and never continues in one stay, in one shape, but the fashion of it passes away; so does this world, and our life in it, 1 Co. 7:31.

IV. Of the calamitous state of human life. Man, as he is short-lived, so he is sad-lived. Though he had but a few days to spend here, yet, if he might rejoice in those few, it were well (a short life and a merry one is the boast of some); but it is not so. During these few days he is *full of trouble,* not only troubled, but full of trouble, either toiling or fretting, grieving or fearing. No day passes without some vexation, some hurry, some disorder or other. Those that are fond of the world shall have enough of it. He is *satur tremore — full of commotion.* The fewness of his days creates him a continual trouble and uneasiness in expectation of the period of them, and he always hangs in doubt of his life. Yet, since man's days are so full of trouble, it is well that they are few, that the soul's imprisonment in the body, and banishment from the Lord, are not perpetual, are not long. When we come to heaven our days will be many, and perfectly free from trouble, and in the mean time faith, hope, and love, balance the present grievances.

V. Of the sinfulness of human life, arising from the sinfulness of the human nature. So some understand that question (*v.* 4), *Who can bring a clean thing out of an unclean?* — a clean performance from an unclean principle? Note, Actual transgressions are the natural product of habitual corruption, which is *therefore* called *original* sin, because it is the original of all our sins. This holy Job here laments, as all that are sanctified do, running up the streams to the fountain (Ps. 51:5); and some think he intends it as a plea with God for compassion: "Lord, be not extreme to mark my sins of human frailty and infirmity, for thou knowest my weakness. *O remember that I am flesh!*" The Chaldee paraphrase has an observable reading of this verse: *Who can make a man clean that is polluted with sin? Cannot one? that is, God. Or who but God, who is one, and will spare him?* God, by his almighty grace, can change the skin of the Ethiopian, the skin of Job, though clothed with worms.

VI. Of the settled period of human life, *v.* 5.

1. Three things we are here assured of: — (1.) That our life will come to an end; our days upon earth are not numberless, are not endless, no, they are numbered, and will soon be finished, Dan. 5:26. (2.) That it is determined, in the counsel and decree of God, how long we shall live and when we shall die. The number of our months is with God, at the disposal of his power, which cannot be controlled, and under the view of his omniscience, which cannot be deceived. It is certain that God's providence has the ordering of the period of our lives; our times are in his hand. The powers of nature depend upon him, and act under him. In him we live and move. Diseases are his servants; he kills and makes alive. Nothing comes to pass by chance, no, not the execution done by a bow drawn at a venture. It is therefore certain that God's prescience has determined it before; for *known unto God are all his works.* Whatever he does he determined, yet with a regard partly to the settled course of nature (the end and the means are determined together) and to the settled rules of moral government, punishing evil and rewarding good in this life. We are no more governed by the Stoic's blind fate than by the Epicurean's blind fortune. (3.) That the bounds God has fixed we cannot pass; for his counsels are unalterable, his foresight being infallible.

2. These considerations Job here urges as reasons, (1.) Why God should not be so strict in taking cognizance of him and of his slips and failings (*v.* 3): "Since I have such a corrupt nature within, and am liable to so much trouble, which is a constant temptation from without, *dost thou open thy eyes* and fasten them *upon such a one,* extremely to mark what I do amiss? *ch.* 13:27. And dost thou *bring me,* such a worthless worm as I am, *into judgment with thee* who art so quick sighted to discover the least failing, so holy to hate it, so just to condemn it, and so mighty to punish it?" The consideration of our own inability to contend with God, of our own sinfulness and weakness, should engage us to pray, *Lord, enter not into judgment with thy servant.* (2.) Why he should not be so severe in his dealings with him: "Lord, I have but a little time to live. I must certainly and shortly go hence, and the few days I have to spend here are, at the best, full of trouble. O let me have a little respite! *v.* 6. Turn from afflicting a poor creature thus, and let him rest awhile; allow him some breathing time, *until he shall accomplish as a hireling his day.* It is appointed to me once to die; let that one day suffice me, and let me not thus be continually dying, dying a thousand deaths. Let it suffice that my life, at best, is *as the day of a hireling,* a day of toil and labour. I am content to accomplish that, and will make the best of the common hardships of human life, the burden and heat of the day; but let me not feel those uncommon tortures, let not my life be as the day of a malefactor, all execution-day." Thus may we find some relief under great troubles by recommending ourselves to the compassion of that God who knows our frame and will consider it, and our being out of frame too.

Verses 7–15

We have seen what Job has to say concerning life; let us now see what he has to say concerning death, which his thoughts were very much conversant with, now that he was sick and sore. It is not unseasonable, when we are in health, to think of dying; but it is an inexcusable incogitancy if, when we are already taken into the custody of death's messengers, we look upon it as a thing at a distance. Job had already shown that death will come, and that its hour is already fixed. Now here he shows,

I. That death is a removal for ever out of this world. This he had spoken of before (*ch.* 7:9, 10), and now he mentions it again; for, though it be a truth that needs not be proved, yet it needs to be much considered, that it may be duly improved.

1. A man cut down by death will not revive again, as a tree cut down will. What hope there is of a tree he shows very elegantly, *v.* 7–9. If the body of the tree be cut down, and only the stem or stump left in the ground, though it seem dead and dry, yet it will shoot out young boughs again, as if it were but newly planted. The moisture of the earth and the rain of heaven are, as it were, scented and perceived by the stump of a tree, and they have an influence upon it to revive it; but the dead body of a man would not perceive them, nor be in the least affected by them. In Nebuchadnezzar's dream, when his being deprived of the use of his reason was signified by the cutting down of a tree, his return to it again was signified by the leaving of the stump in the earth with a band of iron and brass to be *wet with the dew of heaven,* Dan. 4:15. But man has no such prospect of a return to life. The vegetable life is a cheap and easy thing: the scent of water will recover it. The animal life, in some insects and fowls, is so: the heat of the sun retrieves it. But the rational soul, when once retired, is too great, too noble, a thing to be recalled by any of the powers of nature; it is out of the reach of sun or rain, and cannot be restored but by the immediate operations of Omnipotence itself; for (*v.* 10) *man dieth and wasteth, away, yea, man giveth up the ghost, and where is he?* Two words are here used for man: — *Geber, a mighty man,* though mighty, dies; *Adam, a man of the earth,* because earthy, gives up the ghost. Note, Man is a dying creature. He is here described by what occurs, (1.) Before death: he *wastes away;* he is continually wasting, dying daily, spending upon the quick stock of life. Sickness and old age are wasting things to the flesh, the strength, the beauty. (2.) In death: *he gives up the ghost;* the soul leaves the body, and returns to God who gave it, the Father of spirits. (3.) After death: *Where is he?* He is not where he was; his place knows him no more; but *is he nowhere?* So some read it. Yes, he is somewhere; and it is a very awful consideration to think where those are that have given up the ghost, and where we shall be when we give it up. It has gone to the world of spirits, gone into eternity, gone to return no more to this world.

2. A man laid down in the grave will not rise up again, *v.* 11, 12. Every night we lie down to sleep, and in the morning we awake and rise again; but at death we must lie down in the grave, not to awake or rise again to such a world, such a state, as we are now in, never to awake or arise *until the heavens,* the faithful measures of time, shall *be no more,* and consequently time itself shall come to an end and be swallowed up in eternity; so that the life of man may fitly be compared to the waters of a land-flood, which spread far and make a great show, but they are shallow, and when they are cut off from the sea or river, the swelling and overflowing of which was the cause of them, they soon decay and dry up, and their place knows them no more. The waters of life are soon exhaled and disappear. The body, like some of those waters, sinks and soaks into the earth, and is buried there; the soul, like others of them, is drawn upwards, to mingle with the waters above the firmament. The learned Sir Richard Blackmore makes this also to be a dissimilitude. If the waters decay and be dried up in the summer, yet they will return again in the winter; but it is not so with the life of man. Take part of his paraphrase in his own words: —

A flowing river, or a standing lake,
May their dry banks and naked shores forsake;
Their waters may exhale and upward move,
Their channel leave to roll in clouds above;
But the returning water will restore
What in the summer they had lost before:
But if, O man! thy vital streams desert
Their purple channels and defraud the heart,
With fresh recruits they ne'er will be supplied,
Nor feel their leaping life's returning tide.

II. That yet there will be a return of man to life again in another world, at the end of time, when *the heavens* are *no more.* Then *they shall awake and be raised out of their sleep.* The resurrection of the dead was doubtless an article of Job's creed, as appears, *ch.* 19:26, and to that, it should seem, he has an eye here, where, in the belief of that, we have three things: —

1. A humble petition for a hiding-place in the grave, *v.* 13. It was not only a passionate weariness of this life that he wished to die, but in a pious assurance of a better life, to which at length he should arise. *O that thou wouldst hide me in the grave!* The grave is not only a resting-place, but a hiding-place, to the people of God. God has the key of the grave, to let in now and to let out at the resurrection. He *hides men in the grave,* as we hide our treasure in a place of secresy and safety; and he who hides will find, and nothing shall be lost. "O that thou wouldst hide me, not only from the storms and troubles of this life, but for the bliss and glory of a better life! Let me lie in the grave, reserved for immortality, in secret from all the world, but not from thee, not from those eyes which saw my substance when first curiously wrought in *the lowest parts of the earth,*" Ps. 139:15, 16. There let me lie, (1.) *Until thy wrath be past.* As long as the bodies of the saints lie in the grave, so long there are some remains of that wrath which they were by nature children of, so long they are under some of the effects of sin; but, when the body is raised, it is wholly past — death, the last enemy, will then be totally destroyed. (2.) Until the *set time* comes for my being remembered, as Noah was remembered in the ark (Gen. 8:1), where God not only hid him from the destruction of the old world, but reserved him for the reparation of a new world. The bodies of the saints shall not be forgotten in the grave. There is a time appointed, a time set,

for their being enquired after. We cannot be sure that we shall look through the darkness of our present troubles and see good days after them in this world; but, if we can but get well to the grave, we may with an eye of faith look through the darkness of that, as Job here, and see better days on the other side of it, in a better world.

2. A holy resolution patiently to attend the will of God both in his death and his resurrection (*v.* 14): *If a man die, shall he live again? All the days of my appointed time will I wait until my change come.* Job's friends proving miserable comforters, he set himself to be the more his own comforter. His case was now bad, but he pleases himself with the expectation of a change. I think it cannot be meant of his return to a prosperous condition in this world. His friends indeed flattered him with the hopes of that, but he himself all along despaired of it. Comforts founded upon uncertainties at best must needs be uncertain comforts; and therefore, no doubt, it is something more sure than that which he here bears up himself with the expectation of. The change he waits for must therefore be understood either, (1.) Of the change of the resurrection, when the vile body shall be changed (Phil. 3:21), and a great and glorious change it will be; and then that question, *If a man die, shall he live again?* must be taken by way of admiration. "Strange! Shall these dry bones live! If so, all the time appointed for the continuance of the separation between soul and body my separate soul shall wait until that change comes, when it shall be united again to the body, *and my flesh also shall rest in hope.*" Ps. 16:9. Or, (2.) Of the change at death. *"If a man die, shall he live again?* No, not such a life as he now lives; and therefore I will patiently wait until that change comes which will put a period to my calamities, and not impatiently wish for the anticipation of it, as I have done." Observe here, [1.] That it is a serious thing to die; it is a work by itself. It is a change; there is a visible change in the body, its appearance altered, its actions brought to an end, but a greater change with the soul, which quits the body, and removes to the world of spirits, finishes its state of probation and enters upon that of retribution. This change will come, and it will be a final change, not like the transmutations of the elements, which return to their former state. No, we must die, not thus to live again. It is but once to die, and that had need be well done that is to be done but once. An error here is fatal, conclusive, and not again to be rectified. [2.] That therefore it is the duty of every one of us to wait for that change, and to continue waiting all the days of our appointed time. The time of life is an appointed time; that time is to be reckoned by days; and those days are to be spent in waiting for our change. That is, *First,* We must expect that it will come, and think much of it. *Secondly,* We must desire that it would come, as those that long to be with Christ. *Thirdly,* We must be willing to tarry until it does come, as those that believe God's time to be the best. *Fourthly,* We must give diligence to get ready against it comes, that it may be a blessed change to us.

3. A joyful expectation of bliss and satisfaction in this (*v.* 15): Then *thou shalt call, and I will answer thee.* Now, he was under such a cloud that he could not, he durst not, answer (*ch.* 9:15, 35; 13:22); but he comforted himself with this, that there would come a time when God would call and he should answer. Then, that is, (1.) At the resurrection, "Thou shalt call me out of the grave, by the voice of the archangel, and I will answer and come at the call." The body is the *work of God's hands,* and he will have a desire to that, having prepared a glory for it. Or, (2.) At death: "Thou shalt call my body to the grave, and my soul to thyself, and I will answer, Ready, Lord, ready — Coming, coming; here I am." Gracious souls can cheerfully answer death's summons, and appear to his writ. Their spirits are not forcibly required from them (as Lu. 12:20), but willingly resigned by them, and the earthly tabernacle not violently pulled down, but voluntarily laid down, with this assurance, "Thou *wilt have a desire to the work of thy hands.* Thou hast mercy in store for me, not only as made by thy providence, but new-made by thy grace;" otherwise *he that made them will not save them.* Note, Grace in the soul is the work of God's own hands, and therefore he will not forsake it in this world (Ps. 138:8), but will have a desire to it, to perfect it in the other, and to crown it with endless glory.

Verses 16–22

Job here returns to his complaints; and, though he is not without hope of future bliss, he finds it very hard to get over his present grievances.

I. He complains of the particular hardships he apprehended himself under from the strictness of God's justice, *v.* 16, 17. *Therefore* he longed to go hence to that world where God's wrath will be past, because now he was under the continual tokens of it, as a child, under the severe discipline of the rod, longs to be of age. "When shall my change come? *For now thou* seemest to me to *number my steps,* and *watch over my sin,* and *seal it up in a bag,* as bills of indictment are kept safely, to be produced against the prisoner." See Deu. 32:34. "Thou takest all advantages against me; old scores are called over, every infirmity is animadverted upon, and no sooner is a false step taken than I am beaten for it." Now, 1. Job does right to the divine justice in owning that he smarted for his sins and transgressions, that he had done enough to deserve all that was laid upon him; for there was sin in all his steps, and he was guilty of transgression enough to bring all this ruin upon him, if it were strictly enquired into: he is far from saying that he perishes being innocent. But, 2. He does wrong to the divine goodness in suggesting that God was extreme to mark what he did amiss, and made the worst of every thing. He spoke to this purport, *ch.* 13:27. It was unadvisedly said, and therefore we will not dwell too much upon it. God does indeed see all our sins; he sees sin in his own people; but he is not severe in reckoning with us, nor is the law ever stretched against us, but we are punished less than our iniquities deserve. God does indeed seal and sew up, against the day of wrath, the transgression of the impenitent, but the sins of his people he blots out as a cloud.

II. He complains of the wasting condition of mankind in general. We live in a dying world. *Who knows the power of God's anger, by which we are consumed and troubled, and in which all our days are passed away?* See Ps. 90:7–9, 11. And who can bear up against his rebukes? Ps. 39:11.

1. We see the decays of the earth itself. (1.) Of the strongest parts of it, *v.* 18. Nothing will last always, for we see even mountains moulder and come to nought; they wither and fall as a leaf; rocks wax old and pass away by the continual beating of the sea against them. *The waters wear the stones* with constant dropping, *non vi, sed saepe cadendo — not by the violence, but by the constancy with which they fall.* On this earth every thing is the worse for the wearing. *Tempus edax rerum — Time devours all things.* It is not so with the heavenly bodies. (2.) Of the natural products of it. The things which grow out of the earth, and seem to be firmly rooted in it, are sometimes by an excess of rain washed away, *v.* 19. Some think he pleads this for relief: "Lord, my patience will not hold out always; even rocks and mountains will fail at last; therefore cease the controversy."

2. No marvel then if we see the decays of man upon the earth, for he is of the earth, earthy. Job begins to think his case is not singular, and therefore he ought to reconcile himself to the common lot. We perceive by many instances, (1.) How vain it is to expect much from the enjoyments of life: *"Thou destroyest the hope of man,"* that is, "puttest an end to all the projects he had framed and all the prospects of satisfaction he had flattered himself with." Death will be the destruction of all those hopes which are built upon worldly confidences and confined to worldly comforts. Hope in Christ, and hope in heaven, death will consummate and not destroy. (2.) How vain it is to struggle against the assaults of death (*v.* 20): *Thou prevailest for ever against him.* Note, Man is an unequal match for God. Whom God contends with he will certainly prevail against, prevail for ever against so that they shall never be able to make head again. Note further, The stroke of death is irresistible; it is to no purpose to dispute its summons. God prevails against man and he passes away, and lo he is not. Look upon a dying man, and see, [1.] How his looks are altered: *Thou changest his countenance,* and this in two ways: — *First,* By the disease of his body. When a man has been a few days sick what a change is there in his countenance! How much more when he has been a few minutes dead! The countenance which was majestic and awful becomes mean and despicable — that was lovely and amiable becomes ghastly and frightful. *Bury my dead out of my sight.* Where then is the admired beauty? Death changes the countenance, and then sends us away out of this world, gives us one dismission hence, never to return. *Secondly,* By the discomposure of his mind. Note, The approach of death will make the strongest and stoutest to change countenance; it will make the most merry smiling countenance to look grave and serious, and the most bold daring countenance to look pale and timorous. [2.] How little he is concerned in the affairs of his family, which once lay so near his heart. When he is in the hands of the harbingers of death, suppose struck with a palsy or apoplexy, or delirious in a fever, or in conflict with death, tell him then the most agreeable news, or the most painful, concerning his children, it is all alike, he knows it not, he perceives it not, *v.* 21. He is going to that world where he will be a perfect stranger to all those things which here filled and affected him. The consideration of this should moderate our cares concerning our children and families. God will know what comes of them when we are gone. To him therefore let us commit them, with him let us leave them, and not burden ourselves with needless fruitless cares concerning them. [3.] How dreadful the agonies of death are (*v.* 22): *While his flesh is upon him* (so it may be read), that is, the body he soul is so loth to lay down,: *it shall have pain; and while his soul is within him,* that is, the spirit he is so loth to resign, it shall mourn. Note, Dying work is hard work; dying pangs are, commonly, sore pangs. It is folly therefore for men to defer their repentance to a death-bed, and to have that to do which is the one thing needful when they are really unfit to do any thing: but it is true wisdom by making our peace with God in Christ and keeping a good conscience, to treasure up comforts which will support and relieve us against the pains and sorrows of a dying hour.

CHAPTER 15

Perhaps Job was so clear, and so well satisfied, in the goodness of his own cause, that he thought, if he had not convinced, yet he had at least silenced all his three friends; but, it seems he had not: in this chapter they begin a second attack upon him, each of them charging him afresh with as much vehemence as before. It is natural to us to be fond of our own sentiments, and therefore to be firm to them, and with difficulty to be brought to recede from them. Eliphaz here keeps close to the principles upon which he had condemned Job, and, I. He reproves him for justifying himself, and fathers on him many evil things which are unfairly inferred thence (*v.* 2–13). II. He persuades him to humble himself before God and to take shame to himself (*v.* 14–16). III. He reads him a long lecture concerning the woeful estate of wicked people, who harden their hearts against God and the judgments which are prepared for them (*v.* 17–35). A good use may be made both of his reproofs (for they are plain) and of his doctrine (for it is sound), though both the one and the other are misapplied to Job.

Verses 1–16

Eliphaz here falls very foul upon Job, because he contradicted what he and his colleagues had said, and did not acquiesce in it and applaud it, as they expected. Proud people are apt thus to take it very much amiss if they may not have leave to dictate and give law to all about them, and to censure those as ignorant and obstinate, and all that is naught, who cannot in every thing say as they say. Several great crimes Eliphaz here charges Job with, only because he would not own himself a hypocrite.

I. He charges him with folly and absurdity (*v.* 2, 3), that, whereas he had been reputed a wise man, he had now quite forfeited his reputation; any one would say that his wisdom had departed from him, he talked so extravagantly and so little to the purpose. Bildad began thus (*ch.* 8:2), and Zophar, *ch.* 11:2, 3. It is common for angry disputants thus to represent one another's reasonings as impertinent and ridiculous more than there is cause, forgetting the doom of him that calls his brother *Raca,* and *Thou fool.* It is true, 1. That there is in the world a great deal of vain knowledge, science falsely so called, that is useless, and therefore worthless. 2. That this is the knowledge that puffs up, with which men swell in a fond conceit of their own accomplishments. 3. That, whatever vain knowledge a man may have in his head, if he would be thought a wise man he must not utter it, but let it die with himself as it deserves. 4. Unprofitable talk is evil talk. We must give an account in the great day not only for wicked words, but for idle words. Speeches therefore which do no good, which do no service either to God or our neighbour, or no justice to ourselves, which are no way to the use of edifying, were better unspoken. Those words which are as wind, light and empty, especially which are as the east wind, hurtful and pernicious, it will be pernicious to fill either ourselves or others with, for they will pass very ill in the account. 5. Vain knowledge or unprofitable talk ought to be reproved and checked, especially in a wise man, whom it worst becomes and who does most hurt by the bad example of it.

II. He charges him with impiety and irreligion (*v.* 4): *"Thou castest off fear,"* that is, "the fear of God, and that regard to him which thou shouldst have; and then *thou restrainest prayer."* See what religion is summed up in, fearing God and praying to him, the former the most needful principle, the latter the most needful practice. Where no fear of God is no good is to be expected; and those who live without prayer certainly live without God in the world. Those who restrain prayer do thereby give evidence that they cast off fear. Surely those have no reverence of God's majesty, no dread of his wrath, and are in no care about their souls and eternity, who make no applications to God for his grace. Those who are prayerless are fearless and graceless. When the fear of God is cast off all sin is let in and a door opened to all manner of profaneness. It is especially bad with those who have had some fear of God, but have now cast it off — have been frequent in prayer, but now restrain it. How have they fallen! How is their first love lost! It denotes a kind of force put upon themselves. The fear of God would cleave to them, but they throw it off; prayer would be uttered, but they restrain it; and, in both, they baffle their convictions. Those who either omit prayer or straiten and abridge themselves in it, quenching the spirit of adoption and denying themselves the liberty they might take in the duty, restrain prayer. This is bad enough, but it is worse to restrain others from prayer, to prohibit and discourage prayer, as Darius, Dan. 6:7. Now,

1. Eliphaz charges this upon Job, either, (1.) As that which was his own practice. He thought that Job talked of God with such liberty as if he had been his equal, and that he charged him so vehemently with hard usage of him, and challenged him so often to a fair trial, that he had quite thrown off all religious regard to him. This charge was utterly false, and yet wanted not some colour. We ought not only to take care that we keep up prayer and the fear of God, but that we never drop any unwary expressions which may give occasion to those who seek occasion to question our sincerity and constancy in religion. Or, (2.) As that which others would infer from the doctrine he maintained. "If this be true" (thinks Eliphaz) "which Job says, that a man may be thus sorely afflicted and yet be a good man, then farewell all religion, farewell prayer and the fear of God. If all things come alike to all, and the best men may have the worst treatment in this world, every one will be ready to say, *It is vain to serve God; and what profit is it to keep his ordinances?* Mal. 3:14. *Verily I have cleansed my hands in vain,* Ps. 73:13, 14. Who will be honest if the tabernacles of robbers prosper? *ch.* 12:6. If there be no forgiveness with God (*ch.* 7:21), who will fear him? Ps. 130:4. If he *laugh at the trial of the innocent* (*ch.* 9:23), if he be so difficult of access (*ch.* 9:32), who will pray to him?" Note, It is a piece of injustice which even wise and good men are too often guilty of, in the heat of disputation, to charge upon their adversaries those consequences of their opinions which are not fairly drawn from them and which really they abhor. This is not doing as we would be done by.

2. Upon this strained innuendo Eliphaz grounds that high charge of impiety (*v.* 5): *Thy mouth utters thy iniquity* — *teaches it,* so the word is. "Thou teachest others to have the same hard thoughts of God and religion that thou thyself hast." It is bad to *break even the least of the commandments,* but worse to *teach men so,* Mt. 5:19. If we ever thought evil, let us lay our hand upon our mouth to suppress the evil thought (Prov. 30:32), and let us by no means utter it; that is putting an *imprimatur* to it, publishing it with allowance, to the dishonour of God and the damage of others. Observe, When men have cast off fear and prayer their mouths utter iniquity. Those that cease to do good soon learn to do evil. What can we expect but all manner of iniquity from those that arm not themselves with the grace of God against it? But *thou choosest the tongue of the crafty,* that is, "Thou utterest thy iniquity with some show and pretence of piety, mixing some good words with the bad, as tradesmen do with their wares to help them

off." The mouth of iniquity could not do so much mischief as it does without the tongue of the crafty. The serpent beguiled Eve through his subtlety. See Rom. 16:18. The tongue of the crafty speaks with design and deliberation; and therefore those that use it may be said to *choose it,* as that which will serve their purpose better than the tongue of the upright: but it will be found, at last, that honesty is the best policy. Eliphaz, in his first discourse, had proceeded against Job upon mere surmise (*ch.* 4:6, 7), but now he has got proof against him from his own discourses (*v.* 6): *Thy own mouth condemns thee, and not I.* But he should have considered that he and his fellows had provoked him to say that which now they took advantage of; and that was not fair. Those are most effectually condemned that are condemned by themselves, Tit. 3:11; Lu. 19:22. Many a man needs no more to sink him than for his own tongue to fall upon him.

III. He charges him with intolerable arrogancy and self-conceitedness. It was a just, and reasonable, and modest demand that Job had made (*ch.* 12:3), Allow that *I have understanding as well as you;* but see how they seek occasion against him: that is misconstrued, as if he pretended to be wiser than any man. Because he will not grant to them the monopoly of wisdom, they will have it thought that he claims it to himself, *v.* 7–9. As if he thought he had the advantage of all mankind, 1. In length of acquaintance with the world, which furnishes men with so much the more experience: *"Art thou the first man that was born;* and, consequently, senior to us, and better able to give the sense of antiquity and the judgment of the first and earliest, the wisest and purest, ages? Art thou prior to Adam?" So it may be read. "Did not he suffer for sin; and yet wilt not thou, who art so great a sufferer, own thyself a sinner? *Wast thou made before the hills,* as Wisdom herself was? Prov. 8:23, etc. Must God's counsels, which are as the great mountains (Ps. 36:6), and immovable as the everlasting hills, be subject to thy notions and bow to them? Dost thou know more of the world than any of us do? No, thou art but of yesterday even as we are," *ch.* 8:9. Or, 2. In intimacy of acquaintance with God (*v.* 8): *"Hast thou heard the secret of God?* Dost thou pretend to be of the cabinet-council of heaven, that thou canst give better reasons than others can for God's proceedings?" There are secret things of God, which belong not to us, and which therefore we must not pretend to account for. Those are daringly presumptuous who do. He also represents him, (1.) As assuming to himself such knowledge as none else had: *"Dost thou restrain wisdom to thyself,* as if none were wise besides?" Job had said (*ch.* 13:2), *What you know, the same do I know also;* and now they return upon him, according to the usage of eager disputants, who think they have a privilege to commend themselves: *What knowest thou that we know not?* How natural are such replies as these in the heat of argument! But how simple do they look afterwards, upon the review! (2.) As opposing the stream of antiquity, a venerable name, under the shade of which all contending parties strive to shelter themselves: *"With us are the gray-headed and very aged men, v.* 10. We have the fathers on our side; all the ancient doctors of the church are of our opinion." A thing soon said, but not so soon proved; and, when proved, truth is not so soon discovered and proved by it as most people imagine. David preferred right scripture-knowledge before that of antiquity (Ps. 119:100): *I understand more than the ancients, because I keep thy precepts.* Or perhaps one or more, if not all three, of these friends of Job, were older than he (*ch.* 32:6), and therefore they thought he was bound to acknowledge them to be in the right. This also serves contenders to make a noise with to very little purpose. If they are older than their adversaries, and can say they knew such a thing before their opponents were born, this will not serve to justify them in being arrogant and overbearing; for the oldest are not always the wisest, *ch.* 32:9.

IV. He charges him with a contempt of the counsels and comforts that were given him by his friends (*v.* 11): *Are the consolations of God small with thee?* 1. Eliphaz takes it ill that Job did not value the comforts which he and his friends administered to him more than it seems he did, and did not welcome every word they said as true and important. It is true they had said some very good things, but, in their application to Job, they were miserable comforters. Note, We are apt to think that great and consid-

erable which we ourselves say, when others perhaps with good reason think it small and trifling. Paul found that those who *seemed to be somewhat, yet, in conference, added nothing to him,* Gal. 2:6. 2. He represents this as a slight put upon divine consolations in general, as if they were of small account with him, whereas really they were not. If he had not highly valued them, he could not have borne up as he did under his sufferings. Note, (1.) The consolations of God are not in themselves small. Divine comforts are great things, that is, the comfort which is from God, especially the comfort which is in God. (2.) The consolations of God not being small in themselves, it is very lamentable if they be small with us. It is a great affront to God, and an evidence of a degenerate depraved mind, to disesteem and undervalue spiritual delights and despise the pleasant land. "What!" (says Eliphaz) *"is there any secret thing with thee?* Hast thou some cordial to support thyself with, that is a *proprium,* an *arcanum,* that nobody else can pretend to, or knows any thing of?" Or, "Is there some secret sin harboured and indulged in thy bosom, which hinders the operation of divine comforts?" None disesteem divine comforts but those that secretly affect the world and the flesh.

V. He charges him with opposition to God himself and to religion (*v.* 12, 13): *"Why doth thy heart carry thee away into such indecent irreligious expressions?"* Note, *Every man is tempted when he is drawn away of his own lust,* Jam. 1:14. if we fly off from God and our duty, or fly out into any thing amiss, it is our own heart that carries us away. *If thou scornest, thou alone shalt bear it.* There is a violence, an ungovernable impetus, in the turnings of the soul; the corrupt heart carries men away, as it were, by force, against their convictions. "What is it that thy eyes wink at? Why so careless and mindless of what is said to thee, hearing it as if thou wert half asleep? Why so scornful, disdaining what we say, as if it were below thee to take notice of it? What have we said that deserves to be thus slighted — nay, *that thou turnest thy spirit against God?"* It was bad that his heart was carried away from God, but much worse that it was turned against God. But those that forsake God will soon break out in open enmity to him. But how did this appear? Why, "Thou lettest such words go out of thy mouth, reflecting on God, and his justice and goodness." It is the character of the wicked that they *set their mouth against the heavens* (Ps. 73:9), which is a certain indication that the spirit is turned against God. He thought Job's spirit was soured against God, and so turned from what it had been, and exasperated at his dealings with him. Eliphaz wanted candour and charity, else he would not have put such a harsh construction upon the speeches of one that had such a settled reputation for piety and was now in temptation. This was, in effect, to give the cause on Satan's side, and to own that Job had done as Satan said he would, had *cursed God to his face.*

VI. He charges him with justifying himself to such a degree as even to deny his share in the common corruption and pollution of the human nature (*v.* 14): *What is man, that he should be clean?* that is, that he should pretend to be so, or that any should expect to find him so. What is *he that is born of a woman,* a sinful woman, *that he should be righteous?* Note, 1. Righteousness is cleanness; it makes us acceptable to God and easy to ourselves, Ps. 18:24. 2. Man, in his fallen state, cannot pretend to be clean and righteous before God, either to acquit himself to God's justice or recommend himself to his favour. 3. He is to be adjudged unclean and unrighteous because born of a woman, from whom he derives a corrupt nature, which is both his guilt and his pollution. With these plain truths Eliphaz thinks to convince Job, whereas he had just now said the same (*ch.* 14:4): *Who can bring a clean thing out of an unclean?* But does it therefore follow that Job is a hypocrite, and a wicked man, which is all that he denied? By no means. Though man, as born of a woman, is not clean, yet, as born again of the Spirit, he is clean. 4. Further to evince this he here shows, (1.) That the brightest creatures are imperfect and impure before God, *v.* 15. God places no confidence in saints and angels; he employs both, but trusts neither with his service, without giving them fresh supplies of strength and wisdom for it, as knowing they are not sufficient of themselves, neither more nor better than his grace makes them. He takes no complacency in the heavens themselves. How pure soever they seem to us, in his eye they have many a speck and many a flaw: *The heavens are not clean in his sight.* If the stars (says Mr. Caryl) have no light in the sight of the sun, what light has the sun in the sight of God! See Isa. 24:23. (2.) That man is much more so (*v.* 16): *How much more abominable and filthy is man!* If saints are not to be trusted, much less sinners. If the heavens are not pure, which are as God made them, much less man, who is degenerated. Nay, he is abominable and filthy in the sight of God, and if ever he repent he is so in his own sight, and therefore he abhors himself. Sin is an odious thing, it makes men hateful. The body of sin is so, and is therefore called *a dead body,* a loathsome thing. Is it not a filthy thing, and enough to make any one sick, to see a man eating swine's food or drinking some nauseous and offensive stuff? Such is the filthiness of man that he *drinks iniquity* (that abominable thing which the Lord hates) as greedily, and with as much pleasure, as a man drinks water when he is thirsty. It is his constant drink; it is natural to sinners to commit iniquity. It gratifies, but does not satisfy, the appetites of the old man. It is like water to a man in a dropsy. The more men sin the more they would sin.

Verses 17–35

Eliphaz, having reproved Job for his answers, here comes to maintain his own thesis, upon which he built his censure of Job. His opinion is that those who are wicked are certainly miserable, whence he would infer that those who are miserable are certainly wicked, and that therefore Job was so. Observe,

I. His solemn preface to this discourse, in which he bespeaks Job's attention, which he had little reason to expect, he having given so little heed to and put so little value upon what Job had said (*v.* 17): "*I will show thee* that which is worth hearing, and not reason, as thou dost, with unprofitable talk." Thus apt are men, when they condemn the reasonings of others, to commend their own. He promises to teach him, 1. From his own experience and observation: "*That which I have* myself *seen,* in divers instances, *I will declare.*" It is of good use to take notice of the providences of God concerning the children of men, from which many a good lesson may be learned. What good observations we have made, and have found benefit by ourselves, we should be ready to communicate for the benefit of others; and we may speak boldly when we declare what we have seen. 2. From the wisdom of the ancients (*v.* 18): *Which wise men have told from their fathers.* Note, The wisdom and learning of the moderns are very much derived from those of the ancients. Good children will learn a good deal from their good parents; and what we have learned from our ancestors we must transmit to our posterity and not hide from the generations to come. See Ps. 78:3–6. If the thread of the knowledge of many ages be cut off by the carelessness of one, and nothing be done to preserve it pure and entire, all that succeed fare the worse. The authorities Eliphaz vouched were authorities indeed, men of rank and figure (*v.* 19), *unto whom alone the earth was given,* and therefore you may suppose them favourites of Heaven and best capable of making observations concerning the affairs of this earth. The dictates of wisdom come with advantage from those who are in places of dignity and power, as Solomon; yet there is a wisdom *which none of the princes of this world knew,* 1 Co. 2:7, 8.

II. The discourse itself. He here aims to show,

1. That those who are wise and good do ordinarily prosper in this world. This he only hints at (*v.* 19), that those of whose mind he was were such as had the earth given to them, and to them only; they enjoyed it entirely and peaceably, and no stranger passed among them, either to share with them or give disturbance to them. Job had said, *The earth is given into the hand of the wicked,* ch. 9:24. "No," says Eliphaz, "it is given into the hands of the saints, and runs along with the faith committed unto them; and they are not robbed and plundered by strangers and enemies making inroads upon them, as thou art by the Sabeans and Chaldeans." But because many of God's people have remarkably prospered in this world, as Abraham, Isaac, and Jacob, it does not therefore follow that those who are crossed and impoverished, as Job, are not God's people.

2. That wicked people, and particularly oppressors and

tyrannizing rulers, are subject to continual terrors, live very uncomfortably, and perish very miserably. On this head he enlarges, showing that even those who impiously dare God's judgments yet cannot but dread them and will feel them at last. He speaks in the singular number — *the wicked man,* meaning (as some think) Nimrod; or perhaps Chedorlaomer, or some such mighty hunter before the Lord. I fear he meant Job himself, whom he expressly charges both with the tyranny and with the timorousness here described, ch. 22:9, 10. Here he thinks the application easy, and that Job might, in this description, as in a glass, see his own face. Now,

(1.) Let us see how he describes the sinner who lives thus miserably. He does not begin with that, but brings it in as a reason of his doom, *v.* 25–28. It is no ordinary sinner, but one of the first rate, an *oppressor* (*v.* 20), a *blasphemer, and a persecutor,* one that *neither fears God nor regards man.* [1.] He bids defiance to God, and to his authority and power, *v.* 25. Tell him of the divine law, and its obligations; he breaks those bonds asunder, and will not have, no, not him that made him, to restrain him or rule over him. Tell him of the divine wrath, and its terrors; he bids the Almighty do his worst, he will have his will, he will have his way, in spite of him, and will not be controlled by law, or conscience, or the notices of a judgment to come. *He stretches out his hand against God,* in defiance of him and of the power of his wrath. God is indeed out of his reach, but he stretches out his hand against him, to show that, if it were in his power, he would ungod him. This applies to the audacious impiety of some sinners who are really *haters of God* (Rom. 1:30), and whose carnal mind is not only an enemy to him, but enmity itself, Rom. 8:7. But, alas! the sinner's malice is as impotent as it is impudent; what can he do? *He strengthens himself* (*he would be valiant,* so some read it) *against the Almighty.* He thinks with his exorbitant despotic power to *change times and laws* (Dan. 7:25), and, in spite of Providence, to carry the day for rapine and wrong, clear of the check of conscience. Note, It is the prodigious madness of presumptuous sinners that they enter the lists with Omnipotence. *Woe unto him that strives with his Maker.* That is generally taken for a further description of the sinner's daring presumption (*v.* 26): *He runs upon him,* upon God himself, in a direct opposition to him, to his precepts and providences, *even upon his neck,* as a desperate combatant, when he finds himself an unequal match for his adversary, flies in his face, though, at the same time, he falls on his sword's point, or the sharp spike of his buckler. Sinners, in general, run from God; but the presumptuous sinner, who sins with a high hand, runs upon him, fights against him, and bids defiance to him, and it is easy to foretel what will be the issue. [2.] He wraps himself up in security and sensuality (*v.* 27): *He covers his face with his fatness.* This signifies both the pampering of his flesh with daily delicious fare and the hardening of his heart thereby against the judgments of God. Note, The gratifying of the appetites of the body, feeding and feasting that to the full, often turns to the damage of the soul and its interests. Why is God forgotten and slighted, but because the belly is made a god of and happiness placed in the delights of sense? Those that fill themselves with wine and strong drink abandon all that is serious and flatter themselves with hopes that *tomorrow shall be as this day,* Isa. 56:12. Woe to those *that are thus at ease in Zion,* Amos 6:1, 3, 4; Lu. 12:19. The fat that covers his face makes him look bold and haughty, and that which covers his flanks makes him lie easy and soft, and feel little; but this will prove poor shelter against the darts of God's wrath. [3.] He enriches himself with the spoils of all about him, *v.* 28. He dwells in cities which he himself has made desolate by expelling the inhabitants out of them, that he might be placed alone in them, Isa. 5:8 Proud and cruel men take a strange pleasure in ruins, when they are of their own making, in *destroying cities* (Ps. 9:6) and triumphing in the destruction, since they cannot make them their own but by making them *ready to become heaps,* and frightening the inhabitants out of them. Note, Those that aim to engross the world to themselves, and grasp at all, lose the comfort of all, and make themselves miserable in the midst of all. How does this tyrant gain his point, and make himself master of cities that have all the marks of antiquity upon them? We are told (*v.* 35) that he does it by malice and falsehood,

the two chief ingredients of *his* wickedness who was a liar and a murderer from the beginning, *They conceive mischief,* and then they effect it by *preparing deceit,* pretending to protect those whom they design to subdue, and making leagues of peace the more effectually to carry on the operations of war. From such wicked men God deliver all good men.

(2.) Let us see now what is the miserable condition of this wicked man, both in spiritual and temporal judgments. [1.] His inward peace is continually disturbed. He seems to those about him to be easy, and they therefore envy him and wish themselves in his condition; but he who knows what is in men tells us that a wicked man has so little comfort and satisfaction in his own breast that he is rather to be pitied than envied. *First,* His own conscience accuses him, and with the pangs and throes of that *he travaileth in pain all his days, v.* 20. He is continually uneasy at the thought of the cruelties he as been guilty of and the blood in which he has imbrued his hands. His sins stare him in the face at every turn. *Diri conscia facti mens habet attonitos — Conscious guilt astonishes and confounds. Secondly,* He is vexed at the uncertainty of the continuance of his wealth and power: *The number of years is hidden to the oppressor.* He knows, whatever he pretends, that they will not last always, and has reason to fear that they will not last long and this he frets at. *Thirdly,* He is under a *certain fearful expectation of judgment and fiery indignation* (Heb. 10:27), which puts him into, and keeps him in, a continual terror and consternation, so that he dwells with Cain in the land of Nod, or *commotion* (Gen. 4:16), and is made like, *Pashur, Magor-missabib — a terror round about,* Jer. 20:3, 4. *A dreadful sound is in his ears, v.* 21. He knows that both heaven and earth are incensed against him, that God is angry with him and that all the world hates him; he has done nothing to make his peace with either, and therefore he thinks that every one who *meets him will slay him,* Gen. 4:14. Or he is like a man absconding for debt, who thinks every man a bailiff. Fear came in, at first, with sin (Gen. 3:10) and still attends it. Even in prosperity he is apprehensive that the destroyer will come upon him, either some destroying angel sent of God to avenge his quarrel or some of his injured subjects who will be their own avengers. Those who are the *terror of the mighty in the land of the living* usually *go down slain to the pit* (Eze. 32:25), the expectation of which makes them a terror to themselves. This is further set forth (*v.* 22): *He is,* in his own apprehension, *waited for of the sword;* for he knows that *he who killeth with the sword must be killed with the sword,* Rev. 13:10. A guilty conscience represents to the sinner a *flaming sword turning every way* (Gen. 3:24) and himself inevitably running on it. Again (*v.* 23): *He knows that the day of darkness* (or the *night* of darkness rather) *is ready at his hand,* that it is appointed to him and cannot be put by, that it is hastening on apace and cannot be put off. This day of darkness is something beyond death; it is that *day of the Lord* which to all wicked people will be darkness and not light and in which they will be doomed to utter, endless, darkness. Note, Some wicked people, though they seem secure, have already received the sentence of death, eternal death, within themselves, and plainly see hell gaping for them. No marvel that it follows (*v.* 24), *Trouble and anguish* (that inward tribulation and anguish of soul spoken of Rom. 2:8, 9, which are the effect of God's *indignation and wrath* fastening upon the conscience) *shall make him afraid* of worse to come. What is the hell before him if this be the hell within him? And though he would fain shake off his fears, drink them away, and jest them away, it will not do; *they shall prevail against him,* and overpower him, *as a king ready to the battle,* with forces too strong to be resisted. He that would keep his peace, let him keep a good conscience. *Fourthly,* If at any time he be in trouble, he despairs of getting out (*v.* 22): *He believeth not that he shall return out of darkness,* but he gives himself up for gone and lost in an endless night. Good men expect *light at evening time, light out of darkness;* but what reason have those to expect that they shall return out of the darkness of trouble who would not return from the darkness of sin, but *went on in it?* Ps. 82:5. It is the misery of damned sinners that they know they shall never return out of that utter darkness, nor pass the gulf there fixed. *Fifthly,* He perplexes himself with continual care, especially if Providence ever so little frown upon him, *v.* 23. Such a dread he has of poverty, and such a waste does he discern upon his estate, that he is already, in his own imagination, *wandering abroad for bread,* going a begging for a meal's meat, and *saying, Where is it?* The rich man, in his abundance, cried out, *What shall I do?* Lu. 12:17. Perhaps he pretends fear of wanting, as an excuse of his covetous practices; and justly may he be brought to this extremity at last. We read of those who *were full,* but have *hired out themselves for bread* (1 Sa. 2:5), which this sinner will not do. He cannot dig; he is too fat (*v.* 27): but to beg he may well be ashamed. See Ps. 109:10. David never saw the righteous so far forsaken as to beg their bread; for, verily, they shall be fed by the charitable unasked, Ps. 37:3, 25. But the wicked want it, and cannot expect it should be readily given them. How should those find mercy who never showed mercy?

[2.] His outward prosperity will soon come to an end, and all his confidence and all his comfort will come to an end with it. How can he prosper when God runs upon him? so some understand that, *v.* 26. Whom God runs *upon* he will certainly run *down;* for when he judges he will overcome. See how the judgments of God cross this worldly wicked man in all his cares, desires, and projects, and so complete his misery. *First,* He is in care to get, but *he shall not be rich, v.* 29. His own covetous mind keeps him from being truly rich. He is not rich that has not enough, and he has not enough that does not think he has. It is contentment only that is great gain. Providence remarkably keeps some from being rich, defeating their enterprises, breaking their measures, and keeping them always behindhand. Many that get much by fraud and injustice, yet do not grow rich: it goes as it comes; it is got by one sin and spent upon another. *Secondly,* He is in care to keep what he has got, but in vain: *His substance shall not continue;* it will dwindle and come to nothing. God blasts it, and what *came up in a night perishes in a night. Wealth gotten by vanity will certainly be diminished.* Some have themselves lived to see the ruin of those estates which have been raised by oppression; but, where this is not the case, that which is left goes with a curse to those who succeed. *De male quaesitis vix gaudet tertius haeres — Ill-gotten property will scarcely be enjoyed by the third generation.* He purchases estates *to him and his heirs for ever;* but to what purpose? *He shall not prolong the perfection thereof upon the earth;* neither the credit nor the comfort of his riches shall be prolonged; and, when those are gone, where is the perfection of them? How indeed can we expect the perfection of any thing to be prolonged upon the earth, where every thing is transitory, and we soon see the end of all perfection? *Thirdly,* He is in care to leave what he has got and kept to his children after him. But in this he is crossed; the branches of his family shall perish, in whom he hoped to live and flourish and to have the reputation of making them all great men. *They shall not be green, v.* 32. *The flame shall dry them up, v.* 30. he shall shake them off as blossoms that never knit, or as the *unripe grape, v.* 33. They shall die in the beginning of their days and never come to maturity. Many a man's family is ruined by his iniquity. *Fourthly,* He is in care to enjoy it a great while himself; but in that also he is crossed. 1. He may perhaps be taken from it (*v.* 30): *By the breath of God's mouth shall he go away,* and leave his wealth to others; that is, by God's wrath, which, *like a stream of brimstone, kindles* the fire that devours him (Isa. 30:33), or by his word; he speaks, and it is done immediately. *This night thy soul shall be required of thee;* and so *the wicked is driven away in his wickedness,* the worldling in his worldliness. 2. It may perhaps be taken from him, and fly away like an eagle towards heaven: *It shall be accomplished* (or cut off) *before his time* (*v.* 32); that is, he shall survive his prosperity, and see himself stripped of it. *Fifthly,* He is in care, when he is in trouble, how to get out of it (not how to get good by it); but in this also he is crossed (*v.* 30): *He shall not depart out of darkness.* When he begins to fall, like Haman, all men say, "Down with him." It was said of him (*v.* 22), *He believeth not that he shall return out of darkness.* He frightened himself with the perpetuity of his calamity, and God also shall *choose his delusions* and *bring his fears upon him* (Isa. 66:4), as he did upon Israel, Num. 14:28. God says *Amen* to his distrust and despair. *Sixthly,* He is in care to secure his partners, and hopes to secure himself by his partnership with them; but that is in vain too, *v.* 34, 35. *The congregation* of them, the whole confederacy, they and all their tabernacles, *shall be desolate* and consumed with fire. Hypocrisy and bribery are here charged upon them; that is, deceitful dealing both with God and man — God affronted under colour of religion, man wronged under colour of justice. It is impossible that these should end well. *Though hand join in hand* for the support of these perfidious practices, *yet shall not the wicked go unpunished.* (3.) The use and application of all this. Will the prosperity of presumptuous sinners end thus miserably? Then (*v.* 31) *let not him that is deceived trust in vanity.* Let the mischiefs which befal others be our warnings, and let not us rest on that broken reed which always failed those who leaned on it. [1.] Those who trust to their sinful ways of getting wealth *trust in vanity,* and *vanity will be their recompence,* for they shall not get what they expected. Their arts will deceive them and perhaps ruin them in this world. [2.] Those who trust to their wealth when they have gotten it, especially to the wealth they have gotten dishonestly, trust in vanity; for it will yield them no satisfaction. The guilt that cleaves to it will ruin the joy of it. They sow the wind, and will reap the whirlwind, and will own at length, with the utmost confusion, that *a deceived heart turned them aside,* and that they cheated themselves with *a lie in their right hand.*

CHAPTER 16

This chapter begins Job's reply to that discourse of Eliphaz which we had in the foregoing chapter; it is but the second part of the same song of lamentation with which he had before bemoaned himself, and is set to the same melancholy tune. I. He upbraids his friends with their unkind usage of him (*v.* 1–5). II. He represents his own case as very deplorable upon all accounts (*v.* 6–16). III. He still holds fast his integrity, concerning which he appeals to God's righteous judgment from the unrighteous censures of his friends (*v.* 14–22).

Verses 1–5

Both Job and his friends took the same way that disputants commonly take, which is to undervalue one another's sense, and wisdom, and management. The longer the saw of contention is drawn the hotter it grows; and the *beginning of* this sort of *strife is as the letting forth of water; therefore leave it off before it be meddled with.* Eliphaz had represented Job's discourses as idle, and unprofitable, and nothing to the purpose; and Job here gives his the same character. Those who are free in passing such censures must expect to have them retorted; it is easy, it is endless: but *cui bono? — what good does it do?* It will stir up men's passions, but will never convince their judgments, nor set truth in a clear light. Job here reproves Eliphaz, 1. For needless repetitions (*v.* 2): *"I have heard many such things.* You tell me nothing but what I knew before, nothing but what you yourselves have before said; you offer nothing new; it is the same thing over and over again." This Job thinks as great a trial of his patience as almost any of his troubles. The inculcating of the same things thus by an adversary is indeed provoking and nauseous, but by a teacher it is often necessary, and must not be grievous to the learner, to whom *precept must be upon precept, and line upon line.* Many things we have heard which it is good for us to hear again, that we may understand and remember them better, and be more affected with them and influenced by them. 2. For unskilful applications. They came with a design to comfort him, but they went about it very awkwardly, and, when they touched Job's case, quite mistook it: *"Miserable comforters are you all,* who, instead of offering any thing to alleviate the affliction, add affliction to it, and make it yet more grievous." The patient's case is sad indeed when his medicines are poisons and his physicians his worst disease. What Job says here of his friends is true of all creatures, in comparison with God, and, one time or other, we shall be made to see it and own it, that miserable comforters are they all. When we are under convictions of sin, terrors of conscience, and the arrests of death, it is only the blessed Spirit that can comfort effectually; all others, without him, do it miserably, and sing songs to a heavy heart, to no purpose. 3. For endless impertinence. Job wishes that *vain words might have an end, v.* 3. If vain, it were well that they were never begun, and the sooner they are ended the better. Those who are so wise as to speak to the purpose will be so wise as to know when they have said enough of a thing and when it is time to break off. 4. For causeless obstinacy. *What emboldeneth thee, that thou answerest?* It is a great piece of confidence, and unaccountable, to charge men with those crimes which we cannot prove upon them, to pass a judgment on men's spiritual state upon the view of their outward condition, and to re-advance those objections which have been again and again answered, as Eliphaz did. 5. For the violation of the sacred laws of friendship, doing by his brother as he would not have been done by and as his brother would not have done by him. This is a cutting reproof, and very affecting, *v.* 4, 5. (1.) He desires his friends, in imagination, for a little while, to change conditions with him, to put their souls in his soul's stead, to suppose themselves in misery like him and him at ease like them. This was no absurd or foreign supposition, but what might quickly become true in fact. So strange, so sudden, frequently, are the vicissitudes of human affairs, and such the turns of the wheel, that the spokes soon change places. Whatever our brethren's sorrows are, we ought by sympathy to make them our own, because we know not how soon they may be so. (2.) He represents the unkindness of their conduct towards him, by showing what he could do to them if they were in his condition: *I could speak as you do.* It is an easy thing to trample upon those that are down, and to find fault with what those say that are in extremity of pain and affliction: *"I could heap up words against you,* as you do against me; and how would you like it? how would you bear it?" (3.) He shows them what they should do, by telling them what in that case he would do (*v.* 5): *"I would strengthen you,* and say all I could to assuage your grief, but nothing to aggravate it." It is natural to sufferers to think what they would do if the tables were turned. But perhaps our hearts may deceive us; we know not what we should do. We find it easier to discern the reasonableness and importance of a command when we have occasion to claim the benefit of it than when we have occasion to do the duty of it. See what is the duty we owe to our brethren in their affliction. [1.] We should say and do all we can to strengthen them, suggesting to them such considerations as are proper to encourage their confidence in God and to support their sinking spirits. Faith and patience are the strength of the afflicted; whatever helps these graces confirms the feeble knees. [2.] To assuage their grief — the causes of their grief, if possible, or at least their resentment of those causes. Good words cost nothing; but they may be of good service to those that are in sorrow, not only as it is some comfort to them to see their friends concerned for them, but as they may be so reminded of that which, through the prevalency of grief, was forgotten. Though hard words (we say) break no bones, yet kind words may help to make broken bones rejoice; and those have the *tongue of the learned* that know how to *speak a word in season to the weary.*

Verses 6–16

Job's complaint is here as bitter as any where in all his discourses, and he is at a stand whether to smother it or to give it vent. Sometimes the one and sometimes the other is a relief to the afflicted, according as the temper or the circumstances are; but Job found help by neither, *v.* 6. 1. Sometimes giving vent to grief gives ease; but, *"Though I speak"* (says Job), *"my grief is not assuaged,* my spirit is never the lighter for the pouring out of my complaint; nay, what I speak is so misconstrued as to be turned to the aggravation of my grief." 2. At other times keeping silence makes the trouble the easier and the sooner forgotten; but (says Job) *though I forbear* I am never the nearer; *what am I eased?* If he complained he was censured as passionate; if not, as sullen. If he maintained his integrity, that was his crime; if he made no answer to their accusations, his silence was taken for a confession of his guilt.

Here is a doleful representation of Job's grievances. O what reason have we to bless God that we are not making such complaints! He complains,

I. That his family was scattered (*v.* 7): *"He hath made me weary,* weary of speaking, weary of forbearing, weary of my friends, weary of life itself; my journey through the world proves so very uncomfortable that I am quite tired with it." This made it as tiresome as any thing, that all his company was made desolate, his children and servants being killed and the poor remains of his great household dispersed. The company of good people that used to meet at his house for religious worship, was now scattered, and he spent his sabbaths in silence and solitude. He had company indeed, but such as he would rather have been without, for they seemed to triumph in his desolation. If lovers and friends are put far from us, we must see and own God's hand in it, making our company desolate.

II. That his body was worn away with diseases and pains, so that he had become a perfect skeleton, nothing but skin and bones, *v.* 8. His face was furrowed, not with age, but sickness: *Thou hast filled me with wrinkles.* His flesh was wasted with the running of his sore boils, so that *his leanness rose up in him,* that is, his bones, that before were not seen, stuck out, *ch.* 33:21. These are called *witnesses against him,* witnesses of God's displeasure against him, and such witnesses as his friends produced against him to prove him a wicked man. Or, "They are witnesses *for* me, that my complaint is not causeless," or "witnesses *to* me, that I am a dying man, and must be gone shortly."

III. That his enemy was a terror to him, threatened him, frightened him, looked sternly upon him, and gave all the indications of rage against him (*v.* 9): *He tears me in his wrath.* But who is this enemy? 1. Eliphaz, who showed himself very much exasperated against him, and perhaps had expressed himself with such marks of indignation as are here mentioned: at least, what he said tore Job's good name and thundered nothing but terror to him; his eyes were sharpened to spy out matter of reproach against Job, and very barbarously both he and the rest of them used him. Or, 2. Satan. He was his enemy that hated him, and perhaps, by the divine permission, terrified him with apparitions, as (some think) he terrified our Saviour, which put him into his agonies in the garden; and thus he aimed to make him curse God. It is not improbable that this is the enemy he means. Or, (3.) God himself. If we understand it of him, the expressions are indeed as rash as any he used. God hates none of his creatures; but Job's melancholy did thus represent to him the terrors of the Almighty: and nothing can be more grievous to a good man than to apprehend God to be his enemy. If the wrath of a king be as messengers of death, what is the wrath of the King of kings!

IV. That all about him were abusive to him, *v.* 10. They came upon him with open mouth to devour him, as if they would swallow him alive, so terrible were their threats and so scornful was their conduct to him. They offered him all the indignities they could invent, and even smote him *on the cheek;* and herein many were confederate. *They gathered themselves together against him,* even the abjects, Ps. 35:15. Herein Job was a type of Christ, as many of the ancients make him: these very expressions are used in the predictions of his sufferings, Ps. 22:13, *They gaped upon me with their mouths;* and (Mic. 5:1), *They shall smite the Judge of Israel with a rod upon the cheek,* which was literally fulfilled, Mt. 26:67. How were those increased that troubled him!

V. That God, instead of delivering him out of their hands, as he hoped, delivered him into their hands (*v.* 11): *He hath turned me over into the hands of the wicked.* They could have had no power against him if it had not been given them from above. He therefore looks beyond them to God who gave them their commission, as David did when Shimei cursed him; but he thinks it strange, and almost thinks it hard, that those should have power against him who were God's enemies as much as his. God sometimes makes use of wicked men as his sword to one another (Ps. 17:13) and his rod to his own children, Isa. 10:5. Herein also Job was a type of Christ, who was delivered into wicked hands, to be crucified and slain, by the *determinate counsel and fore-knowledge of God,* Acts 2:23.

VI. That God not only delivered him into the hands of the wicked, but took him into his own hands too, into which it is a fearful thing to fall (*v.* 12): *"I was at ease* in the comfortable enjoyment of the gifts of God's bounty, not fretting and uneasy, as some are in the midst of their prosperity, who thereby provoke God to strip them; yet *he has broken me asunder,* put me upon the rack of pain, and torn me limb from limb." God, in afflicting him, had seemed, 1. As if he were furious. Though fury is not in God, he thought it was, when he took him *by the neck* (as a strong man in a passion would take a child) and shook him to pieces, triumphing in the irresistible power he had to do what he would with him. 2. As if he were partial. "He has distinguished me from the rest of mankind by this hard usage of me: *He has set me up for his mark,* the butt at which he is pleased to let fly all his arrows: at me they are directed, and they come not by chance; against me they are levelled, as if I were the greatest sinner of all the men of the east or were singled out to be made an example." When God set him up for a mark *his archers* presently *compassed him round.* God has archers at command, who will be sure to hit the mark that he sets up. Whoever are our enemies, we must look upon them as God's archers, and see him directing the arrow. *It is the Lord; let him do what seemeth him good.* 3. As if he were cruel, and his wrath as relentless as his power was resistless. As if he contrived to touch him in the tenderest part, *cleaving his reins asunder* with acute pains; perhaps they were nephritic pains, those of the stone, which lie in the region of the kidneys. As if he had no mercy in reserve for him, he does not spare nor abate any thing of the extremity. And as if he aimed at nothing but his death, and his death in the midst of the most grievous tortures: *He pours out my gall upon the ground,* as when men have taken a wild beast, and killed it, they open it, and pour out the gall with a loathing of it. He thought his blood was poured out, as if it were not only not precious, but nauseous. 4. As if he were unreasonable and insatiable in his executions (*v.* 14): *"He breaketh me with breach upon breach,* follows me with one wound after another." So his troubles came at first; while one messenger of evil tidings was speaking another came: and so it was still; new boils were rising every day, so that he had no prospect of the end of his troubles. Thus he thought that God ran upon him *like a giant,* whom he could not possibly stand before or confront; as the giants of old ran down all their poor neighbours, and were too hard for them. Note, Even good men, when they are in great and extraordinary troubles, have much ado not to entertain hard thoughts of God.

VII. That he had divested himself of all his honour, and all his comfort, in compliance with the afflicting providences that surrounded him. Some can lessen their own troubles by concealing them, holding their heads as high and putting on as good a face as ever; but Job could not do so: he received the impressions of them, and, as one truly penitent and truly patient, he humbled himself under the mighty hand of God, *v.* 15, 16. 1. He now laid aside all his ornaments and soft clothing, consulted not either his ease or finery in his dress, but sewed sackcloth upon his skin; that clothing he thought good enough for such a defiled distempered body as he had. Silks upon sores, such sores, he thought, would be unsuitable; sackcloth would be more becoming. Those are fond indeed of gay clothing that will not be weaned from it by sickness and old age, and, as Job was (*v.* 8), by *wrinkles and leanness.* He not only put on sackcloth, but sewed it on, as one that resolved to continue his humiliation as long as the affliction continued. 2. He insisted not upon any points of honour, but humbled himself under humbling providences: *He defiled his horn in the dust,* and refused the respect that used to be paid to his dignity, power, and eminency. Note, When God brings down our condition, that should bring down our spirits. Better lay the horn in the dust than lift it up in contradiction to the designs of Providence and have it broken at last. Eliphaz had represented Job as high and haughty, and unhumbled under his affliction. "No," says Job, "I know better things; the dust is now the fittest place for me." 3. He banished mirth as utterly unseasonable, and set himself to sow in tears (*v.* 16): *"My face is foul with weeping* so constantly for my sins, for God's displeasure against me, and for my friends unkindness: this has brought a *shadow of death upon my eyelids."* He had not only wept away all his beauty, but almost wept his eyes out. In this also he was a type of Christ, who was a man of sorrows, and much in tears, and pronounced those blessed that mourn, *for they shall be comforted.*

Verses 17–22

Job's condition was very deplorable; but had he nothing to support him, nothing to comfort him? Yes, and he here tells us what it was.

I. He had the testimony of his conscience for him that he had walked uprightly, and had never allowed himself in any gross sin. None was ever more ready than he to acknowledge his sins of infirmity; but, upon search, he could not charge himself with any enormous crime, for which he should be made more miserable than other men, *v.* 17.

1. He had kept a conscience void of offence, (1.) Towards men: *"Not for any injustice in my hands,* any wealth that I have unjustly got or kept." Eliphaz had represented him as a tyrant and an oppressor. "No," says he, "I never did any wrong to any man, but always despised the gain of oppression." (2.) Towards God: *Also my prayer is pure;* but prayer cannot be pure as long as there is *injustice in our hands,* Isa. 1:15. Eliphaz had charged him with hypocrisy in religion, but he specifies prayer, the great act of religion, and professes that in that he was pure, though not from all infirmity, yet from reigning and allowed guile: it was not like the prayers of the Pharisees, who looked no further than to be seen of men, and to serve a turn.

2. This assertion of his own integrity he backs with a solemn imprecation of shame and confusion to himself if it were not true, *v.* 18. (1.) If there were any injustice in his hands, he wished it might not be concealed: *O earth! cover thou not my blood,* that is, "the innocent blood of others, which I am suspected to have shed." Murder will out; and "let it," says Job, "if I have ever been guilty if it," Gen. 4:10, 11. The day is coming when *the earth shall disclose her blood* (Isa. 26:21), and a good man as far from dreading that day. (2.) If there were any impurity in his prayers, he wished they might not be accepted: *Let my cry have no place.* He was willing to be judged by that rule, *If I regard iniquity in my heart, the Lord will not hear me,* Ps. 66:18. There is another probable sense of these words, that he does hereby, as it were, lay his death upon his friends, who broke his heart with their harsh censures, and charges the guilt of his blood upon them, begging of God to avenge it and that the cry of his blood might have no place in which to lie hid, but might come up to heaven and be heard by him that makes inquisition for blood.

II. He could appeal to God's omniscience concerning his integrity, *v.* 19. The witness in our own bosoms for us will stand us in little stead if we have not a witness in heaven for us too; for *God is greater than our hearts,* and we are not to be our own judges. This therefore is Job's triumph, *My witness is in heaven.* Note, It is an unspeakable comfort to a good man, when he lies under the censure of his brethren, that there is a God in heaven who knows his integrity and will clear it up sooner or later. See John *v.* 31, 37. This one witness is instead of a thousand.

III. He had a God to go to before whom he might unbosom himself, *v.* 20, 21. See here, 1. How the case stood between him and his friends. He knew not how to be free with them, nor could he expect either a fair hearing with them or fair dealing from them. "My friends (so they call themselves) scorn me; they set themselves not only to resist me, but to expose me; they are of counsel against me, and use all their art and eloquence" (so the word signifies) "to run me down." The scorns of friends are more cutting than those of enemies; but we must expect them, and provide accordingly. 2. How it stood between him and God. He doubted not but that, (1.) God did now take cognizance of his sorrows: *My eye pours out tears to God.* He had said (*v.* 16) that he wept much; here he tells us in what channel his tears ran, and which way they were directed. His sorrow was not that of the world, but he sorrowed after a godly sort, wept before the Lord, and offered to him the sacrifice of a broken heart. Note, Even tears, when sanctified to God, give ease to troubled spirits; and, if men slight our grief, this may comfort us, that God regards them. (2.) That he would in due time clear up his innocency (*v.* 21): *O that one might plead for a man with God!* If he could but now have the same freedom at God's bar that men commonly have at the bar of the civil magistrate, he doubted not but to carry his cause, for the Judge himself was a witness to his integrity. The language of this wish is like that in Isa. 50:7, 8, *I know that I shall not be ashamed, for he is near that justifies me.* Some give a gospel sense of this verse, and the original will very well bear it; *and he will plead* (that is, there is one that will plead) *for man with God, even the Son of man for his friend, or neighbour.* Those who pour out tears before God, though they cannot plead for themselves, by reason of their distance and defects, have a friend to plead for them, even the Son of man, and on this we must bottom all our hopes of acceptance with God.

IV. He had a prospect of death which would put a period to all his troubles. Such confidence had he towards God that he could take pleasure in thinking of the approach of death, when he should be determined to his everlasting state, as one that doubted not but it would be well with him then: *When a few years have come (the years of number* which are determined and appointed to me) *then I shall go the way whence I shall not return.* Note, 1. To die is to *go the way whence we shall not return.* It is to go a journey, a long journey, a journey for good and all, to remove from this to another country, from the world of sense to the world of spirits. It is a journey to our long home; there will be no coming back to out state in this world nor any change of our state in the other world. 2. We must all of us very certainly, and very shortly, go this journey; and it is comfortable to those who keep a good conscience to think of it, for it is the crown of their integrity.

CHAPTER 17

In this chapter, I. Job reflects upon the harsh censures which his friends had passed upon him, and looking upon himself as a dying man (v. 1), he appeals to God, and begs of him speedily to appear for him, and right him, because they had wronged him, and he knew not how to right himself (v. 2–7). But he hopes that, though it should be a surprise, it will be no stumbling-block, to good people, to see him thus abused (v. 8, 9). II. He reflects upon the vain hopes they had fed him with, that he should yet see good days, showing that his days were just at an end, and with his body all his hopes would be buried in the dust (v. 10–16). His friends becoming strange to him, which greatly grieved him, he makes death and the grave familiar to him, which yielded him some comfort.

Verses 1–9

Job's discourse is here somewhat broken and interrupted, and he passes suddenly from one thing to another, as is usual with men in trouble; but we may reduce what is here said to three heads: —

I. The deplorable condition which poor Job was now in, which he describes, to aggravate the great unkindness of his friends to him and to justify his own complaints. Let us see what his case was.

1. He was a dying man, v. 1. He had said (ch. 16:22), *"When a few years have come,* I shall go that long journey." But here he corrects himself. "Why do I talk of years to come? Alas! I am just setting out on that journey, am now ready to be offered, and the time of my departure is at hand. *My breath is already corrupt,* or broken off; my spirits are spent; I am a gone man." It is good for every one of us thus to look upon ourselves as dying, and especially to think of it when we are sick. We are dying, that is, (1.) Our life is going; for the breath of life is going. It is continually *going forth; it is in our nostrils* (Isa. 2:22), the door at which it entered (Gen. 2:7); there it is upon the threshold, ready to depart. Perhaps Job's distemper obstructed his breathing, and short breath will, after a while, be no breath. Let *the Anointed of the Lord be the breath of our nostrils,* and let us get spiritual life breathed into us, and that breath will never be corrupted. (2.) Our time is ending: *My days are extinct, are put out,* as a candle which, from the first lighting, is continually wasting and burning down, and will by degrees burn out of itself, but may by a thousand accidents be extinguished. Such is life. It concerns us therefore carefully to redeem the days of time, and to spend them in getting ready for the days of eternity, which will never be extinct. (3.) We are expected in our long home: *The graves are ready for me.* But would not one grave serve? Yes, but he speaks of the *sepulchres of his fathers,* to which he must be gathered: "The graves where they are laid are ready for me also," graves in consort, the congregation of the dead. Wherever we go there is but a step between us and the grave. Whatever is unready, that is ready; it is a bed soon made. If the graves be ready for us, it concerns us to be ready for the graves. *The graves for me* (so it runs), denoting not only his expectation of death, but his desire of it. "I have done with the world, and have nothing now to wish for but a grave."

2. He was a despised man (v. 6): "He" (that is, Eliphaz, so some, or rather God, whom he all along acknowledges to be the author of his calamities) *"has made me a byword of the people,* the talk of the country, a laughing-stock to many, a gazing-stock to all; *and aforetime* (or to men's faces, publicly) *I was as a tabret,* that whoever chose might play upon." They made ballads of him; his name became a proverb; it is so still, *As poor as Job.* "He has now *made me a byword,"* a reproach of men, whereas, aforetime, in my prosperity, I was as a tabret, *deliciae humani*

generis — the darling of the human race, whom they were all pleased with. It is common for those who were honoured in their wealth to be despised in their poverty.

3. He was a man of sorrows, v. 7. He wept so much that he had almost lost his sight: *My eye is dim by reason of sorrow, ch.* 16:16. The sorrow of the world thus works darkness and death. He grieved so much that he had fretted all the flesh away and become a perfect skeleton, nothing but skin and bones: *"All my members are as a shadow.* I have become so poor and thin that I am not to be called a man, but the *shadow of a man."*

II. The ill use which his friends made of his miseries. They trampled upon him, and insulted over him, and condemned him as a hypocrite, because he was thus grievously afflicted. Hard usage! Now observe,

1. How Job describes it, and what construction he puts upon their discourses with him. He looks upon himself as basely abused by them. (1.) They abused him with their foul censures, condemning him as a bad man, justly reduced thus and exposed to contempt, v. 2. "They are *mockers,* who deride my calamities, and insult over me, because I am thus brought low. They are *so with me,* abusing me to my face, pretending friendship in their visit, but intending mischief. I cannot get clear of them; they are continually tearing me, and they will not be wrought upon, either by reason or pity, to let fall the prosecution." (2.) They abused him too with their fair promises, for in them they did but banter him. He reckons them (v. 5) among those that speak flattery to their friends. They all came to mourn with him. Eliphaz began with a commendation of him, ch. 4:3. They had all promised him that he would be happy if he would take their advice. Now all this he looked upon as flattery, and as designed to vex him so much the more. All this he calls their *provocation, v.* 2. They did what they could to provoke him and then condemned him for his resentment of it; but he thinks himself excusable when his eye *continued* thus *in their provocation:* it never ceased, and he never could look off it. Note, The unkindness of those that trample upon their friends in affliction, that banter and abuse them then, is enough to try, if not to tire, the patience even of Job himself.

2. How he condemns it. (1.) It was a sign that *God had hidden their heart from understanding* (v. 4), and that in this matter they were infatuated, and their wonted wisdom had departed from them. Wisdom is a gift of God, which he grants to some and withholds from others, grants at some times and withholds at other times. Those that are void of compassion are so far void of understanding. Where there is not the tenderness of a man one may question whether there be the understanding of a man. (2.) It would be a lasting reproach and diminution to them: *Therefore shalt thou not exalt them.* Those are certainly kept back from honour whose hearts are hidden from understanding. When God infatuates men he will abase them. Surely those who discover so little acquaintance with the methods of Providence shall not have the honour of deciding this controversy! That is reserved for a man of better sense and better temper, such a one as Elihu afterwards appeared to be. (3.) It would entail a curse upon their families. He that thus violates the sacred laws of friendship forfeits the benefit of it, not only for himself, but for his posterity: *"Even the eyes of his children shall fail,* and, when they look for succour and comfort from their own and their father's friends, they shall look in vain as I have done, and be as much disappointed as I am in you." Note, Those that wrong their neighbours may thereby, in the end, wrong their own children more than they are aware of.

3. How he appeals from them to God (v. 3): *Lay down now, put me in a surety with thee,* that is, "Let me be assured that God will take the hearing and determining of the cause into his own hands, and I desire no more. Let some one engage for God to bring on this matter." Thus those whose hearts condemn them not have confidence towards God, and can with humble and believing boldness beg of him to search and try them. Some make Job here to glance at the mediation of Christ, for he speaks of a surety with God, without whom he durst not appear before God, nor try his cause at his bar; for, though his friends' accusations of him were utterly false, yet he could not justify himself before God but in a mediator. Our English annotations give this reading of the verse: *"Appoint, I pray thee, my surety with thee,* namely, Christ who is with

thee in heaven, and has undertaken to be my surety let him plead my cause, and stand up for me; and *who is he then that will strike upon my hand?"* that is, "Who dares then contend with me? Who shall lay any thing to my charge if Christ be an advocate for me?" Rom. 8:32, 33. Christ is the surety of the better testament (Heb. 7:22), a surety of God's appointing; and, if he undertake for us, we need not fear what can be done against us.

III. The good use which the righteous should make of Job's afflictions from God, from his enemies, and from his friends, v. 8, 9. Observe here,

1. How the saints are described. (1.) They are *upright men,* honest and sincere, and that act from a steady principle, with a single eye. This was Job's own character (ch. 1:1), and probably he speaks of such upright men especially as had been his intimates and associates. (2.) They are *the innocent,* not perfectly so, but innocence is what they aim at and press towards. Sincerity is evangelical innocency, and those that are upright are said to be *innocent from the great transgression,* Ps. 19:13. (3.) They are *the righteous,* who walk in the way of righteousness. (4.) They have *clean hands,* kept clean from the gross pollutions of sin, and, when spotted with infirmities, *washed with innocency,* Ps. 26:6.

2. How they should be affected with the account of Job's troubles. Great enquiry, no doubt, would be made concerning him, and every one would speak of him and his case; and what use will good people make of it? (1.) It will amaze them: *Upright men shall be astonished at this;* they will wonder to hear that so good a man as Job should be so grievously afflicted in body, name, and estate, that God should lay his hand so heavily upon him, and that his friends, who ought to have comforted him, should add to his grief, that such a remarkable saint should be such a remarkable sufferer, and so useful a man laid aside in the midst of his usefulness; what shall we say to these things? Upright men, though satisfied in general that God is wise and holy in all he does, yet cannot but be astonished at such dispensations of Providence, paradoxes which will not be unfolded till the mystery of God shall be finished. (2.) It will animate them. Instead of being deterred from and discouraged in the service of God, by the hard usage which this faithful servant of God met with, they shall be so much the more emboldened to proceed and persevere in it. That which was St. Paul's care (1 Th. 3:3) was Job's, that no good man should be moved, either from his holiness or his comfort, by these afflictions, that none should, for the sake hereof, think the worse of the ways or work of God. And that which was St. Paul's comfort was his too, that *the brethren in the Lord would wax confident by his bonds,* Phil. 1:14. They would hereby be animated, [1.] To oppose sin and to confront the corrupt and pernicious inferences which evil men would draw from Job's sufferings, as that God has forsaken the earth, that it is in vain to serve him, and the like: *The innocent shall stir up himself against the hypocrite,* will not bear to hear this (Rev. 2:2), but will withstand him to his face, will stir up himself to search into the meaning of such providences and study these hard chapters, that he may read them readily, will stir up himself to maintain religion's just but injured cause against all its opposers. Note, The boldness of the attacks which profane people make upon religion should sharpen the courage and resolution of its friends and advocates. It is time to stir when proclamation is made in the gate of the camp, *Who is on the Lord's side?* When vice is daring it is no time for virtue, through fear, to hide itself. [2.] To persevere in religion. *The righteous,* instead of drawing back, or so much as starting back, at this frightful spectacle, or standing still to deliberate whether he should proceed or no (allude to 2 Sa. 2:23), *shall* with so much the more constancy and resolution *hold on his way* and press forward. "Though in me he foresees that bonds and afflictions abide him, *yet none of these things shall move him,"* Acts 20:24. Those who keep their eye upon heaven as their end will keep their feet in the paths of religion as their way, whatever difficulties and discouragements they meet with in it [3.] In order thereunto to grow in grace. He will not only hold on his way notwithstanding, but will grow *stronger and stronger.* By the sight of other good men's trials, and the experience of his own, he will be made more vigorous and lively in his duty, more warm and affectionate, more resolute and undaunted; the worse others are the bet-

ter he will be; that which dismays others emboldens him. The blustering wind makes the traveller gather his cloak the closer about him and gird it the faster. Those that are truly wise and good will be continually growing wiser and better. Proficiency in religion is a good sign of sincerity in it.

Verses 10–16

Job's friends had pretended to comfort him with the hopes of his return to a prosperous estate again; now he here shows,

I. That it was their folly to talk so (*v.* 10): *"Return, and come now,* be convinced that you are in an error, and let me persuade you to be of my mind; *for I cannot find one wise man among you,* that knows how to explain the difficulties of God's providence or how to apply the consolations of his promises." Those do not go wisely about the work of comforting the afflicted who fetch their comforts from the possibility of their recovery and enlargement in this world; though that is not to be despaired of, it is at the best uncertain; and if it should fail, as perhaps it may, the comfort built upon it will fail too. It is therefore our wisdom to comfort ourselves, and others, in distress, with that which will not fail, the promise of God, his love and grace, and a well-grounded hope of eternal life.

II. That it would he much more his folly to heed them; for,

1. All his measures were already broken and he was full of confusion, *v.* 11, 12. He owns he had, in his prosperity, often pleased himself both with projects of what he should do and prospects of what he should enjoy; but now he looked upon his days as past, or drawing towards a period; all those purposes were broken off and those expectations dashed. He had had thoughts about enlarging his border, increasing his stock, and settling his children, and many pious thoughts, it is likely, of promoting religion in his country, redressing grievances, reforming the profane, relieving the poor, and raising funds perhaps for charitable uses; but he concluded that all these thoughts of his heart were now at an end, and that he should never have the satisfaction of seeing his designs effected. Note, The period of our days will be the period of all our contrivances and hopes for this world; but, if with full purpose of heart we cleave to the Lord, death will not break off that purpose. Job, being thus put upon new counsels, was under a constant uneasiness (*v.* 12): *The thoughts of his heart* being broken, they *changed the night into day and shortened the light.* Some, in their vanity and riot, turn night into day and day into night; but Job did so through trouble and anguish of spirit, which were a hindrance, (1.) To the repose of the night, keeping his eyes waking, so that the night was as wearisome to him as the day, and the tossings of the night tired him as much as the toils of the day. (2.) To the entertainments of the day. "The light of the morning is welcome, but, by reason of this inward darkness, the comfort of it is soon gone, and the day is to me as dismal as the black and dark night," Deu. 28:67. See what reason we have to be thankful for the health and ease which enable us to welcome both the shadows of the evening and the light of the morning.

2. All his expectations from this world would very shortly be buried in the grave with him; so that it was a jest for him to think of such mighty things as they had flattered him with the hopes of, *ch.* 5:19; 8:21; 11:17. "Alas! you do but make a fool of me."

(1.) He saw himself just dropping into the grave. A convenient house, an easy bed, and agreeable relations, are some of those things in which we take satisfaction in this world: Job expected not any of these above ground; all he felt, and all he had in view, was unpleasing and disagreeable, but under ground he expected them. [1.] He counted upon no house but the grave (*v.* 13): "If I wait, if there be any place where I shall ever be easy again, it must be in the grave. I should deceive myself if I should count upon any out-let from my trouble but what death will give me. Nothing is so sure as that." Note, In all our prosperity it is good to keep death in prospect. Whatever we expect, let us be sure to expect that; for that may prevent other things which we expect, but nothing will prevent that. But see how he endeavours not only to reconcile himself to the grave, but to recommend it to himself: "It is my house." The grave is a house; to the wicked it is a prison-house (*ch.* 24:19, 20); to the godly it is *Bethabara, a passage-house* in their way home. "It is my house, mine by descent, I am born to it; it is my father's house. It is mine by purchase. I have made myself obnoxious to it." We must every-one of us shortly remove to this house, and it is our wisdom to provide accordingly; let us think of removing, and send before to our long home. [2.] He counted upon no quiet bed but in the darkness: "There," says he, *"I have made my bed.* It is made, for it is ready, and I am just going to it." The grave is a bed, for we shall rest in it in the evening of our day on earth, and rise from it in the morning of our everlasting day, Isa. 57:2. Let this make good people willing to die; it is but going to bed; they are weary and sleepy, and it is time that they were in their beds. Why should they not go willingly, when their father calls? "Nay, *I have made my bed,* by preparation for it, have endeavoured to make it easy, by keeping conscience pure, by seeing Christ lying in this bed, and so turning it into a bed of spices, and by looking beyond it to the resurrection." [3.] He counted upon no agreeable relations but what he had in the grave (*v.* 14): *I have cried to corruption* (that is, to the grave, where the body will corrupt), *Thou art my father* (for our bodies were formed out of the earth), and *to the worms* there, *You are my mother and my sister,* to whom I am allied (for *man is a worm*) and with whom I must be conversant, for the *worms shall cover us, ch.* 21:26. Job complained that his kindred were estranged from him (*ch.* 19:13, 14); therefore here he claims acquaintance with other relations that would cleave to him when those disowned him. Note, *First,* We are all of us near akin to corruption and the worms. *Secondly,* It is therefore good to make ourselves familiar with them, by conversing much with them in our thoughts and meditations, which would very much help us above the inordinate love of life and fear of death.

(2.) He saw all his hopes from this world dropping into the grave with him (*v.* 15, 16): "Seeing I must shortly leave the world, *where is now my hope?* How can I expect to prosper who do not expect to live?" He is not hopeless, but his hope is not where they would have it be. *If in this life only* he had *hope,* he was *of all men most miserable.* "No, as for my hope, that hope which I comfort and support myself with, who shall see it? It is something out of sight that I hope for, not things that are seen, that are temporal, but things not seen, that are eternal." What is his hope he will tell us (*ch.* 19:25), *Non est mortale quod opto, immortale peto — I seek not for that which perishes, but for that which abides for ever.* "But, as for the hopes you would buoy me up with, they shall go down with me to the bars of the pit. You are dying men, and cannot make good your promises. I am a dying man, and cannot enjoy the good you promise. Since, therefore, our rest will be together in the dust, let us all lay aside the thoughts of this world and set our hearts upon another." We must shortly be in the dust, for dust we are, dust and ashes in the pit, under *the bars of the pit,* held fast there, never to loose the bands of death till the general resurrection. But we shall rest there; we shall rest together there. Job and his friends could not agree now, but they will both be quiet in the grave; the dust of that will shortly stop their mouths and put an end to the controversy. Let the foresight of this cool the heat of all contenders and moderate the disputers of this world.

CHAPTER 18

In this chapter Bildad makes a second assault upon Job. In his first discourse (*ch.* 8) he had given him encouragement to hope that all should yet be well with him. But here there is not a word of that; he has grown more peevish, and is so far from being convinced by Job's reasonings that he is but more exasperated. I. He sharply reproves Job as haughty and passionate, and obstinate in his opinion (*v.* 1–4). II. He enlarges upon the doctrine he had before maintained, concerning the miser of wicked people and the ruin that attends them (*v.* 5–21). In this he seems, all along, to have an eye to Job's complaints of the miserable condition he was in, that he was in the dark, bewildered, ensnared, terrified, and hastening out of the world. "This," says Bildad, "is the condition of a wicked man; and therefore thou art one."

Verses 1–4

Bildad here shoots his arrows, even bitter words, against poor Job, little thinking that, though he was a wise and good man, in this instance he was serving Satan's design in adding to Job's affliction.

I. He charges him with idle endless talk, as Eliphaz had done (*ch.* 15:2, 3): *How long will it be ere you make an end of words? v.* 2. Here he reflects, not only upon Job himself, but either upon all the managers of the conference (thinking perhaps that Eliphaz and Zophar did not speak so closely to the purpose as they might have done) or upon some that were present, who possibly took part with Job, and put in a word now and then in his favour, though it be not recorded. Bildad was weary of hearing others speak, and impatient till it came to his turn, which cannot be observed to any man's praise, for we ought to be swift to hear and slow to speak. It is common for contenders to monopolize the reputation of wisdom, and then to insist upon it as their privilege to be dictators. How unbecoming this conduct is in others every one can see; but few that are guilty of it can see it in themselves. Time was when Job had the last word in all debates (*ch.* 29:22): *After my words they spoke not again.* Then he was in power and prosperity; but now that he was impoverished and brought low he could scarcely be allowed to speak at all, and every thing he said was as much vilified as formerly it had been magnified. *Wisdom* therefore (as the world goes) *is good with an inheritance* (Eccl. 7:11); for *the poor man's wisdom is despised,* and, because he is poor, *his words are not heard,* Eccl. 9:16.

II. With a regardlessness of what was said to him, intimated in that, *Mark, and afterwards we will speak.* And it is to no purpose to speak, though what is said be ever so much to the purpose, if those to whom it is addressed will not mark and observe it. Let the *ear be opened to hear as the learned,* and then the tongues of the learned will do good service (Isa. 50:4) and not otherwise. It is an encouragement to those that speak of the things of God to see the hearers attentive.

III. With a haughty contempt and disdain of his friends and of that which they offered (*v.* 3): *Wherefore are we counted as beasts?* This was invidious. Job had indeed called them *mockers,* had represented them both as unwise and as unkind, wanting both in the reason and tenderness of men, but he did not count them beasts; yet Bildad so represents the matter, 1. Because his high spirit resented what Job had said as if it had been the greatest affront imaginable. Proud men are apt to think themselves slighted more than really they are. 2. Because his hot spirit was willing to find a pretence to be hard upon Job. Those that incline to be severe upon others will have it thought that others have first been so upon them.

IV. With outrageous passion: *He teareth himself in his anger, v.* 4. Herein he seems to reflect upon what Job had said (*ch.* 13:14): *Wherefore did I take my flesh in my teeth?* "It is thy own fault," says Bildad. Or he reflected upon what he said *ch.* 16:9, where he seemed to charge it upon God, or, as some think, upon Eliphaz: *He teareth me in his wrath.* "No," says Bildad; "thou alone shalt bear it." *He teareth himself in his anger.* Note, Anger is a sin that is its own punishment. Fretful passionate people tear and torment themselves. *He teareth his soul* (so the word is); every sin wounds the soul, tears that, wrongs that (Prov. 8:36), unbridled passion particularly.

V. With a proud and arrogant expectation to give law even to Providence itself: *"Shall the earth be forsaken for thee?* Surely not; there is no reason for that, that the course of nature should be changed and the settled rules of government violated to gratify the humour of one man. Job, dost thou think the world cannot stand without thee; but that, if thou art ruined, all the world is ruined and forsaken with thee?" Some make it a reproof of Job's justification of himself, falsely insinuating that either Job was a wicked man or we must deny a Providence and suppose that God has forsaken the earth and the rock of ages is removed. It is rather a just reproof of his passionate complaints. When we quarrel with the events of Providence we forget that, whatever befals us, it is, 1. According to the eternal purpose and counsel of God. 2. According to the written word. Thus it is written that in the world we must have tribulation, that, since we sin daily, we must expect to smart for it; and, 3. According to the usual way and custom, the track of Providence, nothing but what is common to men; and to expect that God's counsels should change, his method alter, and his word fail, to please us, is as absurd and unreasonable as to think *the earth should be forsaken for us and the rock removed out of its place.*

Verses 5–10

The rest of Bildad's discourse is entirely taken up in an elegant description of the miserable condition of a wicked man, in which there is a great deal of certain truth, and which will be of excellent use if duly considered — that a sinful condition is a sad condition, and that iniquity will be men's ruin if they do not repent of it. But it is not true that all wicked people are visibly and openly made thus miserable in this world; nor is it true that all who are brought into great distress and trouble in this world are *therefore* to be deemed and adjudged wicked men, when no other proof appears against them; and therefore, though Bildad thought the application of it to Job was easy, yet it was not safe nor just. In these verses we have,

I. The destruction of the wicked foreseen and foretold, under the similitude of darkness (*v.* 5, 6): *Yea, the light of the wicked shall be put out.* Even his *light,* the best and brightest part of him, shall be put out; even that which he rejoiced in shall fail him. Or the *yea* may refer to Job's complaints of the great distress he was in and the darkness he should shortly make his bed in. "Yea," says Bildad, "So it is; thou art clouded, and straitened, and made miserable, and no better could be expected; for *the light of the wicked shall be put out,* and therefore thine shall." Observe here, 1. The wicked may have some light for a while, some pleasure, some joy, some hope within, as well as wealth, and honour, and power without. But his light is but a spark (*v.* 5), a little thing and soon extinguished. It is but a candle (*v.* 6), wasting, and burning down, and easily blown out. It is not the light of the Lord (that is sunlight), but the *light of his own fire* and *sparks of his own kindling,* Isa. 50:11. 2. His light will certainly be put out at length, quite put out, so that not the least spark of it shall remain with which to kindle another fire. Even while he is in his tabernacle, while he is in the body, which is the tabernacle of the soul (2 Co. 5:1), the light shall be dark; he shall have no true solid comfort, no joy that is satisfying, no hope that is supporting. Even *the light that is in him is darkness;* and *how great is that darkness!* But, when he is put out of this tabernacle by death, *his candle shall be put out with him.* The period of his life will be the final period of all his days and will turn all his hopes into endless despair. *When a wicked man dies his expectation shall perish,* Prov. 11:7. *He shall lie down in sorrow.*

II. The preparatives for that destruction represented under the similitude of a beast or bird caught in a snare, or a malefactor arrested and taken into custody in order to his punishment, *v.* 7–10. 1. Satan is preparing for his destruction. He is *the robber that shall prevail against him* (*v.* 9); for, as he was a murderer, so he was a robber, from the beginning. He, as the tempter, lays snares for sinners in the way, wherever they go, and he shall prevail. If he make them sinful like himself, he will make them miserable like himself. He *hunts for the precious life.* 2. He is himself preparing for his own destruction by going on in sin, and so *treasuring up wrath against the day of wrath.* God gives him up, as he deserves and desires, to his own counsels, and then *his own counsels cast him down, v.* 7. His sinful projects and pursuits bring him into mischief. He is *cast into a net by his own feet* (*v.* 8), runs upon his own destruction, is *snared in the work of his own hands* (Ps. 9:16); his *own tongue falls upon him,* Ps. 64:8. *In the transgression of an evil man there is a snare.* 3. God is preparing for his destruction. The sinner by his sin is preparing the fuel and then God by his wrath is preparing the fire. See here, (1.) How the sinner is infatuated, to run himself into the snare; and whom God will destroy he infatuates. (2.) How he is embarrassed: *The steps of his strength,* his mighty designs and efforts, *shall be straitened,* so that he shall not compass what he intended; and the more he strives to extricate himself the more will he be entangled. Evil men wax worse and worse. (3.) How he is secured and kept from escaping the judgments of God that are in pursuit of him. *The gin shall take him by the heel.* He can no more escape the divine wrath that is in pursuit of him than a man, so held, can flee from the pursuer. God *knows how to reserve the wicked for the day of judgment,* 2 Pt. 2:9.

Verses 11–21

Bildad here describes the destruction itself which wicked people are reserved for in the other world, and which, in some degree, often seizes them in this world. Come, and see what a miserable condition the sinner is in when his day comes to fall.

I. See him disheartened and weakened by continual terrors arising from the sense of his own guilt and the dread of God's wrath (*v.* 11, 12): *Terror shall make him afraid on every side.* The terrors of his own conscience shall haunt him, so that he shall never be easy. Wherever he goes, these shall follow him; which way soever he looks, these shall stare him in the face. It will make him tremble to see himself fought against by the whole creation, to see Heaven frowning on him, hell gaping for him, and earth sick of him. He that carries his own accuser, and his own tormentor, always in his bosom, cannot but be afraid on every side. This will drive him to his feet, like the malefactor, who, being conscious of his own guilt, takes to his heels and *flees when none pursues,* Prov. 28:1. But his feet will do him no service; they are fast in the snare, *v.* 9. The sinner may as soon overpower the divine omnipotence as flee from the divine omniscience, Amos 9:2, 3. No marvel that the sinner is dispirited and distracted with fear, for, 1. He sees his ruin approaching: *Destruction shall be ready at his side,* to seize him whenever justice gives the word, so that he is *brought into desolation in a moment,* Ps. 73:19. 2. He feels himself utterly unable to grapple with it, either to escape it or to bear up under it. That which he relied upon as *his strength* (his wealth, power, pomp, friends, and the hardiness of his own spirit) *shall* fail him in the time of need, and *be hunger-bitten,* that is, it shall do him no more service than a famished man, pining away for hunger, would do in work or war. The case being thus with him, no marvel that he is a terror to himself. Note, The way of sin is a way of fear, and leads to everlasting confusion, of which the present terrors of an impure and unpacified conscience are earnests, as they were to Cain and Judas.

II. See him devoured and swallowed up by a miserable death; and miserable indeed a wicked man's death is, how secure and jovial soever his life was. 1. See him dying, arrested by *the first-born of death* (some disease, or some stroke that has in it a more than ordinary resemblance of death itself; *so great a death,* as it is called, 2 Co. 1:10, a messenger of death that has in it an uncommon strength and terror), weakened by the harbingers of death, which *devour the strength of his skin,* that is, it shall bring rottenness into his bones and consume them. *His confidence shall then be rooted out of his tabernacle* (*v.* 14), that is, all that he trusted to for his support shall be taken from him, and he shall have nothing to rely upon, no, not his own tabernacle. His own soul was his confidence, but that shall be rooted out of the tabernacle of the body, as a tree that cumbered the ground. "Thy soul shall be required of thee." 2. See him dead, and see his case then with an eye of faith. (1.) He is then brought to *the king of terrors.* He was surrounded with terrors while he lived (*v.* 11), and death was the king of all those terrors; they fought against the sinner in death's name, for it is by reason of death that sinners are *all their lifetime subject to bondage* (Heb. 2:15), and at length they will be brought to that which they so long feared, as a captive to the conqueror. Death is terrible to nature; our Saviour himself prayed, *Father, save me from this hour.* But to the wicked it is in a special manner *the king of terrors,* both as it is a period to that life in which they placed their happiness and a passage to that life where they will find their endless misery. How happy then are the saints, and how much indebted to the Lord Jesus, by whom death is so far abolished, and the property of it altered, that this king of terrors becomes a friend and servant! (2.) He is then *driven from the light into darkness* (*v.* 18), from the light of this world, and his prosperous condition in it, into darkness, the darkness of the grave, the darkness of hell, into utter darkness, never to see light (Ps. 49:19), not the least gleam, nor any hopes of it. (3.) He is then *chased out of the world,* hurried and dragged away by the messengers of death, sorely against his will, chased as Adam out of paradise, for the world is his paradise. It intimates that he would fain stay here; he is loth to depart, but go he must; all the world is weary of him, and therefore chases him out, as glad to get rid of him. This is death to a wicked man.

III. See his family sunk and cut off, *v.* 15. The wrath and curse of God light and lie, not only upon his head and heart, but upon his house too, to consume it with the *timber and stones thereof,* Zec. 5:4. Death itself shall dwell in his tabernacle, and, having expelled him, shall take possession of his house, to the terror and destruction of all that he leaves behind. Even the dwelling shall be ruined for the sake of its owner: *Brimstone shall be scattered upon his habitation,* rained upon it as upon Sodom, to the destruction of which this seems to have reference. Some think he here upbraids Job with the burning of his sheep and servants with fire from heaven. The reason is here given why his tabernacle is thus marked for ruin: *Because it is none of his;* that is, it was unjustly got, and kept, from the rightful owner, and therefore let him not expect either the comfort or the continuance of it. His children shall perish, either with him or after him, *v.* 16. So that, *his roots being* in his own person *dried up beneath, above his branch* (every child of his family) *shall be cut off.* Thus the houses of Jeroboam, Baasha, and Ahab, were cut off; none that descended from them were left alive. Those who take root in the earth may expect it will thus be dried up; but, if we be rooted in Christ, even our leaf shall not wither, much less shall our branch be cut off. Those who consult the true honour of their family, and the welfare of its branches, will be afraid of withering it by sin. The extirpation of the sinner's family is mentioned again (*v.* 19): *He shall neither have son nor nephew,* child nor grandchild, to enjoy his estate and bear up his name, *nor* shall there be *any remaining in his dwelling* akin to him. Sin entails a curse upon posterity, and the iniquity of the fathers is often visited upon the children. Herein, also, it is probable that Bildad reflects upon the death of Job's children and servants, as a further proof of his being a wicked man; whereas all that are written childless are not thereby written graceless; there is a name *better than that of sons and daughters.*

IV. See his memory buried with him, or made odious; he shall either be forgotten or spoken of with dishonour (*v.* 17): *His remembrance shall perish from the earth;* and, if it perish thence, it perishes wholly, for it was never written in heaven, as the names of the saints are, Lu. 10:20. All his honour shall be laid and lost in the dust, or stained with perpetual infamy, so that *he shall have no name in the street,* departing without being desired. Thus the judgments of God follow him, after death, in this world, as an indication of the misery his soul is in after death, and an earnest of that everlasting shame and contempt to which he shall rise in the great day. *The memory of the just is blessed, but the name of the wicked shall rot,* Prov. 10:7.

V. See a universal amazement at his fall, *v.* 20. Those that see it are affrighted, so sudden is the change, so dreadful the execution, so threatening to all about him: and those that come after, and hear the report of it, are astonished at it; their ears are made to tingle, and their hearts to tremble, and they cry out, *Lord, how terrible art thou in thy judgments!* A place or person utterly ruined is said to be *made an astonishment,* Deu. 28:37; 2 Chr. 7:21; Jer. 25:9, 18. Horrible sins bring strange punishments.

VI. See all this averred as the unanimous sense of the patriarchal age, grounded upon their knowledge of God and their many observations of his providence (*v.* 21): *Surely such are the dwellings of the wicked, and this is the place* (this the condition) *of him that knows not God!* See here what is the beginning, and what is the end, of the wickedness of this wicked world. 1. The beginning of it is ignorance of God, and it is a wilful ignorance, for there is that to be known of him which is sufficient to leave them for ever inexcusable. They know not God, and then they commit all iniquity. Pharaoh knows not the Lord, and therefore will not obey his voice. 2. The end of it, and that is utter destruction. *Such,* so miserable, *are the dwellings of the wicked.* Vengeance will be taken of those that *know not God,* 2 Th. 1:8. For those whom he has not honour from he will get himself honour upon. Let us therefore stand in awe and not sin, for it will certainly be bitterness in the latter end.

CHAPTER 19

This chapter is Job's answer to Bildad's discourse in the foregoing chapter. Though his spirit was grieved and much heated, and Bildad was very peevish, yet he gave him leave to say all he designed to say, and did not break in upon him in the midst of his argument; but, when he had done, he gave him a fair answer, in which, I. He complains of unkind usage. And very unkindly he takes it. 1. That his comforters added to his affliction (*v.* 2–7).

2. That his God was the author of his affliction (*v.* 8–12). 3. That his relations and friends were strange to him, and shy of him, in his affliction (*v.* 20–22). II. He comforts himself with the believing hopes of happiness in the other world, though he had so little comfort in this, making a very solemn confession of his faith, with a desire that it might be recorded as an evidence of his sincerity (*v.* 23–27). III. He concludes with a caution to his friends not to persist in their hard censures of him (*v.* 28, 29) If the remonstrance Job here makes of his grievances may serve sometimes to justify our complaints, yet his cheerful views of the future state, at the same time, may shame us Christians, and may serve to silence our complaints, or at least to balance them.

Verses 1–7

Job's friends had passed a very severe censure upon him as a wicked man because he was so grievously afflicted; now here he tells them how ill he took it to be so censured. Bildad had twice begun with a *How long* (*ch.* 8:2, 18:2), and therefore Job, being now to answer him particularly, begins with a *How long* too, *v.* 2. What is not liked is commonly thought long; but Job had more reason to think those long who assaulted him than they had to think him long who only vindicated himself. Better cause may be shown for defending ourselves, if we have right on our side, than for offending our brethren, though we have right on our side. Now observe here,

I. How he describes their unkindness to him and what account he gives of it. 1. They *vexed his soul,* and that is more grievous than the vexation of the bones, Ps. 6:2, 3. They were his friends; they came to comfort him, pretended to counsel him for the best; but with a great deal of gravity, and affectation of wisdom and piety, they set themselves to rob him of the only comfort he had now left him in a good God, a good conscience, and a good name; and this vexed him to his heart. 2. They *broke him in pieces with words,* and those were surely hard and very cruel words that would break a man to pieces: they grieved him, and so broke him; and therefore there will be a reckoning hereafter for all the hard speeches spoken against Christ and his people, Jude 15. 3. They *reproached him,* (*v.* 3), gave him a bad character and laid to his charge things that he knew not. To an ingenuous mind reproach is a cutting thing. 4. They *made themselves strange to him,* were shy of him now that he was in his troubles, and seemed as if they did not know him (*ch.* 2:12), were not free with him as they used to be when he was in his prosperity. Those are governed by the spirit of the world, and not by any principles of true honour or love, who make themselves strange to their friends, or God's friends, when they are in trouble. *A friend loves at all times.* 5. They not only estranged themselves from him, but *magnified themselves against him* (*v.* 5), not only looked shy of him, but looked big upon him, and insulted over him, magnifying themselves to depress him. It is a mean thing, it is a base thing, thus to trample upon those that are down. 6. *They pleaded against him his reproach,* that is, they made use of his affliction as an argument against him to prove him a wicked man. They should have pleaded for him his integrity, and helped him to take the comfort of that under his affliction, and so have pleaded that against his reproach (as St. Paul, 2 Co. 1:12); but, instead of that, they pleaded his reproach against his integrity, which was not only unkind, but very unjust; for where shall we find an honest man if reproach may be admitted for a plea against him?

II. How he aggravates their unkindness. 1. They had thus abused him often (*v.* 3): *These ten times you have reproached me,* that is, very often, as Gen. 31:7; Num. 14:22. Five times they had spoken, and every speech was a double reproach. He spoke as if he had kept a particular account of their reproaches, and could tell just how many they were. It is but a peevish and unfriendly thing to do so, and looks like a design of retaliation and revenge. We better befriend our own peace by forgetting injuries and unkindnesses than by remembering them and scoring them up. 2. They continued still to abuse him, and seemed resolved to persist in it: "How long will you do it?" *v.* 2, 5. "I see you will magnify yourselves against me, notwithstanding all I have said in my own justification." Those that speak too much seldom think they have said enough; and, when the mouth is opened in passion, the ear is shut to reason. 3. They were not ashamed of what they did, *v.* 3. They had reason to be ashamed of their hard-heartedness, so ill becoming men, of their uncharitableness, so ill becoming good men, and of their deceitfulness, so ill becoming friends: but were they ashamed? No, though they were told of it again and again, yet they could not blush.

III. How he answers their harsh censures, by showing them that what they condemned was capable of excuse, which they ought to have considered. 1. The errors of his judgment were excusable (*v.* 4): *"Be it indeed that I have erred,* that I am in the wrong through ignorance or mistake," which may well be supposed concerning men, concerning good men. *Humanum est errare — Error cleaves to humanity;* and we must be willing to suppose it concerning ourselves. It is folly to think ourselves infallible. "But be it so," said Job, *"my error remaineth with myself,"* that is, "I speak according to the best of my judgment, with all sincerity, and not from a spirit of contradiction." Or, "If I be in an error, I keep it to myself, and do not impose it upon others as you do. I only prove myself and my own work by it. I meddle not with other people, either to teach them or to judge them." Men's errors are the more excusable if they keep them to themselves, and do not disturb others with them. *Hast thou faith? Have it to thyself.* Some give this sense of these words: "If I be in an error, it is I that must smart for it; and therefore you need not concern yourselves: nay, it is I that do smart, and smart severely, for it; and therefore you need not add to my misery by your reproaches." 2. The breakings out of his passion, though not justifiable, yet were excusable, considering the vastness of his grief and the extremity of his misery. "If you will go on to cavil at every complaining word I speak, will make the worst of it and improve it against me, yet take the cause of the complaint along with you, and weigh that, before you pass a judgment upon the complaint, and turn it to my reproach: *Know then that God has overthrown me," v.* 6. Three things he would have them consider: — (1.) That his trouble was very great. He was overthrown, and could not help himself, enclosed as in a net, and could not get out. (2.) That God was the author of it, and that, in it, he fought against him: "It was his hand that overthrew me; it is in his net that I am enclosed; and therefore you need not appear against me thus. I have enough to do to grapple with God's displeasure; let me not have yours also. Let God's controversy with me be ended before you begin yours." It is barbarous to *persecute him whom God hath smitten and to talk to the grief of one whom he hath wounded,* Ps. 69:26. (3.) That he could not obtain any hope of the redress of his grievances, *v.* 7. He complained of his pain, but got no ease — begged to know the cause of his affliction, but could not discover it — appealed to God's tribunal for the clearing of his innocency, but could not obtain a hearing, much less a judgment, upon his appeal: *I cry out of wrong, but I am not heard.* God, for a time, may seem to turn away his ear from his people, to be angry at their prayers and overlook their appeals to him, and they must be excused if, in that case, they complain bitterly. Woe unto us if God be against us!

Verses 8–22

Bildad had very disingenuously perverted Job's complaints by making them the description of the miserable condition of a wicked man; and yet he repeats them here, to move their pity, and to work upon their good nature, if they had any left in them.

I. He complains of the tokens of God's displeasure which he was under, and which infused the wormwood and gall into the affliction and misery. How doleful are the accents of his complaints! *"He hath kindled his wrath against me,* which flames and terrifies me, which burns and pains me," *v.* 11. What is the fire of hell but the wrath of God? Seared consciences will feel it hereafter, but do not fear it now. Enlightened consciences fear it now, but shall not feel it hereafter. Job's present apprehension was that *God counted him as one of his enemies;* and yet, at the same time, God loved him, and gloried in him, as his faithful friend. It is a gross mistake, but a very common one, to think that whom God afflicts he treats as his enemies; whereas, on the contrary, *as many as he loves he rebukes and chastens;* it is the discipline of his sons. Which way soever Job looked he thought he saw the tokens of God's displeasure against him. 1. Did he look back upon his former prosperity? He saw God's hand putting an end to that (*v.* 9): *"He has stripped me of my glory,* my wealth, honour, power, and all the opportunity I had of doing good. My children were my glory, but I have lost them; and whatever was a crown to my head he has taken it from me, and has laid all my honour in the dust." See the vanity of worldly glory: it is what we may be soon stripped of; and, whatever strips us, we must see and own God's hand in it and comply with his design. 2. Did he look down upon his present troubles? He saw God giving them their commission, and their orders to attack him. They are *his troops,* that act by his direction, which *encamp against me, v.* 12. It did not so much trouble him that his miseries came upon him in troops as that they were *God's* troops, in whom it seemed as if God fought against him and intended his destruction. God's troops *encamped around his tabernacle,* as soldiers lay siege to a strong city, cutting off all provisions from being brought into it and battering it continually; thus was Job's tabernacle besieged. Time was when God's hosts encamped round him for safety: *Hast thou not made a hedge about him?* Now, on the contrary, they surrounded him, to his terror, and *destroyed him on every side, v.* 10. 3. Did he look forward for deliverance? He saw the hand of God cutting off all hopes of that (*v.* 8): *"He hath fenced up my way, that I cannot pass.* I have now no way left to help myself, either to extricate myself out of my troubles or to ease myself under them. Would I make any motion, take any steps towards deliverance? I find *my way hedged up;* I cannot do what I would; nay, if I would please myself with the prospect of a deliverance hereafter, I cannot do it; it is not only out of my reach, but out of my sight: God *hath set darkness in my paths,* and there is none to tell me how long," Ps. 74:9. He concludes (*v.* 10), "I am gone, quite lost and undone for this world; *my hope hath he removed like a tree* cut down, or plucked up by the roots, which will never grow again." Hope in this life is a perishing thing, but the hope of good men, when it is cut off from this world, is but removed like a tree, transplanted from this nursery to the garden of the Lord. We shall have no reason to complain if God thus remove our hopes from the sand to the rock, from things temporal to things eternal.

II. He complains of the unkindness of his relations and of all his old acquaintance. In this also he owns the hand of God (*v.* 13): *He has put my brethren far from me,* that is, "He has laid those afflictions upon me which frighten them from me, and make them stand aloof from my sores." As it was their sin God was not the author of it; it is Satan that alienates men's minds from their brethren in affliction. But, as it was Job's trouble, God ordered it for the completing of his trial. As we must eye the hand of God in all the injuries we receive from our enemies ("the Lord has bidden Shimei curse David"), so also in all the slights and unkindnesses we receive from our friends, which will help us to bear them the more patiently. Every creature is that to us (kind or unkind, comfortable or uncomfortable) which God makes it to be. Yet this does not excuse Job's relations and friends from the guilt of horrid ingratitude and injustice to him, which he had reason to complain of; few could have borne it so well as he did. He takes notice of the unkindness, 1. Of his kindred and acquaintance, his neighbours, and such as he had formerly been familiar with, who were bound by all the laws of friendship and civility to concern themselves for him, to visit him, to enquire after him, and to be ready to do him all the good offices that lay in their power; yet these were *estranged from him, v.* 13. They took no more care about him than if he had been a stranger whom they never knew. His kinsfolk, who claimed relation to him when he was in prosperity, now failed him; they came short of their former professions of friendship to him and his present expectations of kindness from them. Even his familiar friends, whom he was mindful of, had now forgotten him, had forgotten both his former friendliness to them and his present miseries: they had heard of his troubles, and designed him a visit; but truly they forgot it, so little affected were they with it. Nay, his inward friends, the men of his secret, whom he was most intimate with and laid in his bosom, not only forgot him, but abhorred him, kept as far off from him as they could, because he was poor and could not entertain them as he used to do, and because he was sore and a loathsome spectacle. Those whom he loved, and who therefore were worse than publicans if they did not love him now that he was in distress, not only turned from him, but were turned against him, and did all they could to make him odious, so to justify themselves in being so strange to him, *v.* 19. So uncertain is the friendship of men;

but, if God be our friend, he will not fail us in a time of need. But let none that pretend either to humanity or Christianity ever use their friends as Job's friends used him: adversity is the proof of friendship. 2. Of his domestics and family relations. Sometimes indeed we find that, beyond our expectation, there is a friend that sticks closer than a brother; but the master of a family ordinarily expects to be attended on and taken care of by those of his family, even when, through weakness of body or mind, he has become despicable to others. But poor Job was misused by his own family, and some of his worst foes were those of his own house. He mentions not his children; they were all dead, and we may suppose that the unkindness of his surviving relations made him lament the death of his children so much the more: "If they had been alive," would he think, "I should have had comfort in them." As for those that were now about him, (1.) His own servants slighted him. His maids did not attend him in his illness, but *counted him for a stranger and an alien, v.* 15. His other servants never heeded him; if he called to them they would not come at his call, but pretended that they did not hear him. If he asked them a question, they would not vouchsafe to *give him an answer, v.* 16. Job had been a good master to them, and did not *despise their cause when they pleaded with him* (*ch.* 31:13), and yet they were rude to him now, and despised his cause when he pleaded with them. We must not think it strange if we receive evil at the hand of those from whom we have deserved well. Though he was now sickly, yet he was not cross with his servants, and imperious, as is too common, but he entreated his servants with his mouth, when he had authority to command; and yet they would not be civil to him, neither kind nor just. Note, Those that are sick and in sorrow are apt to take things ill, and be jealous of a slight, and to lay to heart the least unkindness done to them: when Job was in affliction even his servants' neglect of him troubled him. (2.) But, one would think, when all forsook him, the wife of his bosom should have been tender of him: no, because he would not curse God and die, as she persuaded him, his breath was strange to her too; she did not care for coming near him, nor took any notice of what he said, *v.* 17. Though he spoke to her, not with the authority, but with the tenderness of a husband, did not command, but entreated her by that conjugal love which their children were the pledges of, yet she regarded him not. Some read it, "Though I lamented, or bemoaned myself, for the children," that is, "for the death of the children of my own body," an affliction in which she was equally concerned with him. Now, it appeared, the devil spared her to him, not only to be his tempter, but to be his tormentor. By what she said to him at first, *Curse God and die,* it appeared that she had little religion in her; and what can one expect that is kind and good from those that have not the fear of God before their eyes and are not governed by conscience? (3.) Even the little children who were born in his house, the children of his own servants, who were his servants by birth, despised him, and spoke against him (*v.* 18); though he arose in civility to speak friendly to them, or with authority to check them, they let him know that they neither feared him nor loved him.

III. He complains of the decay of his body; all the beauty and strength of that were gone. When those about him slighted him, if he had been in health, and at ease, he might have enjoyed himself. But he could take as little pleasure in himself as others took in him (*v.* 20): *My bone cleaves now to my skin,* as formerly it did to my flesh; it was this that filled *him with wrinkles* (*ch.* 16:8); he was a perfect skeleton, nothing but skin and bones. Nay, his skin too was almost gone, little remained unbroken but the *skin of his teeth,* his gums and perhaps his lips; all the rest was fetched off by his sore boils. See what little reason we have to indulge the body, which, after all our care, may be thus consumed by the diseases which it has in itself the seeds of.

IV. Upon all these accounts he recommends himself to the compassion of his friends, and justly blames their harshness with him. From this representation of his deplorable case, it was easy to infer, 1. That they ought to pity him, *v.* 21. This he begs in the most moving melting language that could be, enough (one would think) to break a heart of stone: *"Have pity upon me, have pity upon me, O you my friends!* if you will do nothing else for me, be sorry for me, and show some concern for me; *have pity upon me, for the hand of God hath touched me.* My case is sad indeed, for I have fallen into the hands of the living God, my spirit is touched with the sense of his wrath, a calamity of all other the most piteous." Note, It becomes friends to pity one another when they are in trouble, and not to shut up the bowels of compassion. 2. That, however, they ought not to persecute him; if they would not ease his affliction by their pity, yet they must not be so barbarous as to add to it by their censures and reproaches (*v.* 22): *"Why do you persecute me as God?* Surely his rebukes are enough for one man to bear; you need not add your wormwood and gall to the cup of affliction he puts into my hand, it is bitter enough without that: God has a sovereign power over me, and may do what he pleases with me; but do you think that you may do so too?" No, we must aim to be like the Most Holy and the Most Merciful, but not like the Most High and Most Mighty. God gives not account of any of his matters, but we must give account of ours. If they did delight in his calamity, let them be satisfied with his flesh, which was wasted and gone, but let them not, as if that were too little, wound his spirit, and ruin his good name. Great tenderness is due to those that are in affliction, especially to those that are troubled in mind.

Verses 23–29

In all the conferences between Job and his friends we do not find any more weighty and considerable lines than these; would one have expected it? Here is much both of Christ and heaven in these verses: and he that said such things as these *declared plainly that he sought the better country, that is, the heavenly;* as the patriarchs of that age did, Heb. 11:14. We have here Job's creed, or confession of faith. His belief in God the Father Almighty, the Maker of heaven and earth, and the principles of natural religion, he had often professed: but here we find him no stranger to revealed religion; though the revelation of the promised Seed, and the promised inheritance, was then discerned only like the dawning of the day, yet Job was taught of God to believe in a living Redeemer, and to *look for the resurrection of the dead and the life of the world to come,* for of these, doubtless, he must be understood to speak. These were the things he comforted himself with the expectation of, and not a deliverance from his trouble or a revival of his happiness in this world, as some would understand him; for besides that the expressions he here uses, of the Redeemer's *standing at the latter day upon the earth,* of his seeing God, and *seeing him for himself,* are wretchedly forced if they be understood of any temporal deliverance, it is very plain that he had no expectation at all of his return to a prosperous condition in this world. He had just now said that *his way was fenced up,* (*v.* 8) and his *hope removed like a tree, v.* 10. Nay, and after this he expressed his despair of any comfort in this life, *ch.* 23:8, 9; 30:23. So that we must necessarily understand him of the redemption of his soul from the power of the grave, and his reception to glory, which is spoken of, Ps. 49:15. We have reason to think that Job was just now under an extraordinary impulse of the blessed Spirit, which raised him above himself, gave him light, and gave him utterance, even to his own surprise. And some observe that, after this, we do not find Job's discourses such passionate, peevish, unbecoming, complaints of God and his providence as we have before met with: this hope quieted his spirit, stilled the storm and, having here cast anchor within the veil, his mind was kept steady from this time forward. Let us observe,

I. To what intent Job makes this confession of his faith here. Never did any thing come in more pertinently, or to better purpose. 1. Job was now accused, and this was his appeal. His friends reproached him as a hypocrite and contemned him as a wicked man; but he appeals to his creed, to his faith, to his hope, and to his own conscience, which not only acquitted him from reigning sin, but comforted him with the expectation of a blessed resurrection. *These are not the words of him that has a devil.* He appeals to the coming of the Redeemer, from this wrangle at the bar to the judgment of the bench, even to him to whom all judgment is committed, who he knew would right him. The consideration of God's day coming will make it a *very small thing with us to be judged of man's judgment,* 1 Co. 4:3, 4. How easily may we bear the unjust calumnies and reproaches of men while we expect the glorious appearance of our Redeemer, and his redeemed, at the last day, and that there will then be a resurrection of names, as well as bodies! 2. Job was now afflicted, and this was his cordial; when he was pressed above measure this kept him from fainting — he believed that he should *see the goodness of the Lord in the land of the living;* not in this world, for that is the land of the dying.

II. With what a solemn preface he introduces it, *v.* 23, 24. He breaks off his complaints abruptly, to triumph his comforts, which he does, not only for his own satisfaction, but for the edification of others. Those now about him, he feared, would little regard what he said, and so it proved, He therefore wished it might be recorded for the generations to come. *O that my words were now written,* the words I am now about to say! As if he had said, "I own I have spoken many unadvised words, which I could wish might be forgotten, for they will neither do me credit nor do others good. But I am now going to speak deliberately, and that which I desire may be published to all the world and preserved for the generations to come, *in perpetuam rei memoriam — for an abiding memorial,* and therefore that it may be written plainly and *printed,* or drawn out in large and legible characters, so that he that runs may read it; and that it may not be left in loose papers, but put into *a book;* or, if that should perish, that it may be *engraven* like an inscription upon a monument, *with an iron pen in lead, or in the stone;* let the engraver use all his art to make it a durable appeal to posterity." That which Job here somewhat passionately wished for God graciously granted him. His words are written; they are printed in God's book; so that, wherever that book is read, there shall this be told for a memorial concerning Job. He believed, therefore he spoke.

III. What his confession itself is; what are the words which he would have to be written; we here have them written, *v.* 25–27. Let us observe them.

1. He believes the glory of the Redeemer and his own interest in him (*v.* 25): *I know that my Redeemer liveth,* that he is in being and is my life, *and that he shall stand at last,* or stand the last, or at the latter day, *upon* (or above) *the earth.* He shall be raised up, or, He shall be, at the latter day, (that is, in the fulness of time: the gospel day is called *the last time* because that is the last dispensation) upon the earth: so it points at his incarnation; or, He shall be lifted up from the earth (so it points at his crucifixion), or raised up out of the earth (so it is applicable to his resurrection), or, as we commonly understand it, At the end of time he shall appear over the earth, for *he shall come in the clouds, and every eye shall see him,* so close shall he come to this earth. He shall stand *upon the dust* (so the word is), upon all his enemies, which shall be put a dust under his feet; and he shall tread upon them and triumph over them. Observe here, (1.) That there is a Redeemer provided for fallen man, and Jesus Christ is that Redeemer. The word is *Goël* which is used for the next of kin, to whom, by the law of Moses, the right of redeeming a mortgaged estate did belong, Lev. 25:25. Our heavenly inheritance was mortgaged by sin; we are ourselves utterly unable to redeem it; Christ is near of kin to us, the next kinsman that is able to redeem; he has paid our debt, satisfied God's justice for sin, and so has taken off the mortgage and made a new settlement of the inheritance. Our persons also want a Redeemer; we are sold for sin, and sold under sin; our Lord Jesus has wrought out a redemption for us, and proclaims redemption for us, and proclaims redemption to us, and so he is truly the Redeemer. (2.) He is a living Redeemer. As we are made by a living God, so we are saved by a living Redeemer, who is both almighty and eternal, and is therefore able to save to the uttermost. *Of him it is witnessed that he liveth,* Heb. 7:8; Rev. 1:18. We are dying, but he liveth, and hath assured us that *because he lives we shall live also,* Jn. 14:19. (3.) There are those that through grace have an interest in this Redeemer, and can, upon good grounds, call him theirs. When Job had lost all his wealth and all his friends, yet he was not separated from Christ, nor cut off from his relation to him: "Still he is my Redeemer." That next kinsman adhered to him when all his other kindred forsook him, and he had the comfort of it. (4.) Our interest in the Redeemer is a thing that may be known; and, where it is known, it may be triumphed in, as sufficient to balance all our griefs: *I know* (observe with what an air of assurance he speaks

it, as one confident of this very thing), *I know that my Redeemer lives.* His friends have often charged him with ignorance or vain knowledge; but he knows enough, and knows to good purpose, who knows Christ to be his Redeemer. (5.) There will be a latter day, a last day, a day when *time shall be no more,* Rev. 10:6. That is a day we are concerned to think of every day. (6.) Our Redeemer will at that day stand upon the earth, or over the earth, to summon the dead out of their graves, and determine them to an unchangeable state; for to him all judgment is committed. He shall stand, at the last, on the dust to which this earth will be reduced by the conflagration.

2. He believes the happiness of the redeemed, and his own title to that happiness, that, at Christ's second coming, believers shall be raised up in glory and so made perfectly blessed in the vision and fruition of God; and this he believes with application to himself. (1.) He counts upon the corrupting of his body in the grave, and speaks of it with a holy carelessness and unconcernedness: *Though, after my skin* (which is already wasted and gone, none of it remaining but *the skin of my teeth, v.* 20) *they destroy* (those that are appointed to destroy it, the grave and the worms in it of which he had spoken, *ch.* 17:14) *this body.* The word *body* is added: "Though they destroy this, this skeleton, this shadow (*ch.* 17:7), this that I lay my hand upon," or (pointing perhaps to his weak and withered limbs) "this that you see, call it what you will; I expect that shortly it will be a feast for the worms." Christ's body saw not corruption, but ours must. And Job mentions this, that the glory of the resurrection he believed and hoped for might shine the more brightly. Note, It is good for us often to think, not only of the approaching death of our bodies, but of their destruction and dissolution in the grave; yet let not that discourage our hope of their resurrection, for the same power that made man's body at first, out of common dust, can raise it out of its own dust. This body which we now take such care about, and make such provision for, will in a little time be destroyed. Even *my reins* (says Job) *shall be consumed within me* (*v.* 27); the innermost part of the body, which perhaps putrefies first. (2.) He comforts himself with the hopes of happiness on the other side death and the grave: *After I shall awake* (so the margin reads it), *though this body be destroyed, yet out of my flesh shall I see God.* [1.] Soul and body shall come together again. That body which must be destroyed in the grave shall be raised again, a glorious body: *Yet in my flesh I shall see God.* The separate soul has eyes wherewith to see God, eyes of the mind; but Job speaks of seeing him with eyes of flesh, *in my flesh, with my eyes;* the same body that died shall rise again, a true body, but a glorified body, fit for the employments and entertainments of that world, and therefore a *spiritual body,* 1 Co. 15:44. Let us *therefore* glorify God with our bodies because there is such a glory designed for them. [2.] Job and God shall come together again: *In my flesh shall I see God,* that is, the glorified Redeemer, who is God. *I shall see God in my flesh* (so some read it), the Son of God clothed with a body which will be visible even to eyes of flesh. Though the body, in the grave, seem despicable and miserable, yet it shall be dignified and made happy in the vision of God. Job now complained that he could not get a sight of God (*ch.* 23:8, 9), but hoped to see him shortly, never more to lose the sight of him, and that sight of him will be the more welcome after the present darkness and distance. Note, It is the blessedness of the blessed that they shall see God, shall see him as he is, see him face to face, and no longer through a glass darkly. See with what pleasure holy Job enlarges upon this (*v.* 27): *"Whom I shall see for myself,"* that is, "see and enjoy, see to my own unspeakable comfort and satisfaction. I shall see him as mine, as mine with an appropriating sight," Rev. 21:3. *God himself shall be with them and be their God;* they shall be *like him, for they shall see him as he is,* that is seeing for themselves, 1 Jn. 3:2. *My eyes shall behold him, and not another. First,* "He, and not another for him, shall be seen, not a type or figure of him, but he himself." Glorified saints are perfectly sure that they are not imposed upon; it is no *deceptio visus — illusion of the senses. Secondly,* "I, and not another for me, shall see him. Though my flesh and body be consumed, yet I shall not need a proxy; I shall see him with my own eyes." This was what Job hoped for, and what he earnestly desired, which, some think, is the meaning of the last clause: *My reins are spent in my bosom,* that is, "all my desires are summed up and concluded in this; this will crown and complete them all; let me have this, and I shall have nothing more to desire; it is enough; it is all." With this the prayers of David, the son of Jesse, are ended.

IV. The application of this to his friends. His creed spoke comfort to himself, but warning and terror to those that set themselves against him.

1. It was a word of caution to them not to proceed and persist in their unkind usage of him, *v.* 28. He had reproved them for what they had said, and now tells them what they should say for the reducing of themselves and one another to a better temper. *"Why persecute we him* thus? Why do we grieve him and vex him, by censuring and condemning him, *seeing the root of the matter,* or the root of the word, *is found in him?"* Let this direct us, (1.) In our care concerning ourselves. We are all concerned to see to it that the root of the matter be found in us. A living, quickening, commanding, principle of grace in the heart, is the root of the matter, as necessary to our religion as the root to the tree, to which it owes both its fixedness and its fruitfulness. Love to God and our brethren, faith in Christ, hatred of sin — these are the root of the matter; other things are but leaves in comparison with these. Serious godliness is the one thing needful. (2.) In our conduct towards our brethren. We are to believe that many have the root of the matter in them who are not in every thing of our mind — who have their follies, and weaknesses, and mistakes — and to conclude that it is at our peril if we persecute any such. Woe be to him that offends one of those little ones! God will resent and revenge it. Job and his friends differed in some notions concerning the methods of Providence, but they agreed in the root of the matter, the belief of another world, and therefore should not persecute one another for these differences.

2. It was a word of terror to them. Christ's second coming will be very dreadful to those that are found *smiting their fellow servants* (Mt. 24:49), and therefore (*v.* 29), *"Be you afraid of the sword,* the flaming sword of God's justice, which turns every way; fear, lest you make yourselves obnoxious to it." Good men need to be frightened from sin by the terrors of the Almighty, particularly from the sin of rashly judging their brethren, Mt. 7:1; Jam. 3:1. Those that are peevish and passionate with their brethren, censorious of them and malicious towards them, should know, not only that their wrath, whatever it pretends, works not the righteousness of God, but that, (1.) They may expect to smart for it in this world: *It brings the punishments of the sword.* Wrath leads to such crimes as expose men to the sword of the magistrate. God himself often takes vengeance for it, and those that showed no mercy shall find no mercy. (2.) If they repent not, that will be an earnest of worse. By these you may know there is a judgment, not only a present government, but a future judgment, in which hard speeches must be accounted for.

CHAPTER 20

One would have thought that such an excellent confession of faith as Job made, in the close of the foregoing chapter, would satisfy his friends, or at least mollify them; but they do not seem to have taken any notice of it, and therefore Zophar here takes his turn, enters the lists with Job, and attacks him with as much vehemence as before. I. His preface is short, but hot (*v.* 2, 3). II. His discourse is long, and all upon one subject, the very same that Bildad was large upon (*ch.* 18), the certain misery of wicked people and the ruin that awaits them. 1. He asserts, in general, that the prosperity of a wicked person is short, and his ruin sure (*v.* 4–9). 2. He proves the misery of his condition by many instances — that he should have a diseased body, a troubled conscience, a ruined estate, a beggared family, an infamous name and that he himself should perish under the weight of divine wrath: all this is most curiously described here in lofty expressions and lively similitudes; and it often proves true in this world, and always in another, without repentance (*v.* 10–29). But the great mistake was, and (as bishop Patrick expresses it) all the flaw in his discourse (which was common to him with the rest), that he imagined God never varied from this method, and therefore Job was, without doubt, a very bad man, though it did not appear that he was, any other way than by his infelicity.

Verses 1–9

Here, I. Zophar begins very passionately, and seems to be in a great heat at what Job had said. Being resolved to condemn Job for a bad man, he was much displeased that he talked so like a good man, and, as it should seem, broke in upon him, and began abruptly (*v.* 2): *Therefore do my thoughts cause me to answer.* He takes no notice of what Job had said to move their pity, or to evidence his own integrity, but fastens upon the reproof he gave them in the close of his discourse, counts that a reproach, and thinks himself *therefore* obliged to answer, because Job had bidden them be afraid of the sword, that he might not seem to be frightened by his menaces. The best counsel is too often ill taken from an antagonist, and therefore usually may be well spared. Zophar seemed more in haste to speak than became a wise man; but he excuses his haste with two things: — 1. That Job had given him strong provocation (*v.* 3): *"I have heard the check of my reproach,* and cannot bear to hear it any longer." Job's friends, I doubt, had spirits too high to deal with a man in his low condition; and high spirits are impatient of contradiction, and think themselves affronted if all about them do not say as they say; they cannot bear a check but they call it *the check of their reproach,* and then they are bound in honour to return it, if not to draw upon him that gave it. 2. That his own heart gave him a strong instigation. His thoughts caused him to answer (*v.* 2), for *out of the abundance of the heart the mouth speaks;* but he fathers the instigation (*v.* 3) upon *the spirit of his understanding:* that indeed should cause us to answer; we should rightly apprehend a thing and duly consider it before we speak of it; but whether it did so here or no is a question. Men often mistake the dictates of their passion for the dictates of their reason, and therefore think they do well to be angry.

II. Zophar proceeds very plainly to show the ruin and destruction of wicked people, insinuating that because Job was destroyed and ruined he was certainly a wicked man and a hypocrite. Observe,

1. How this doctrine is introduced, *v.* 4, where he appeals, (1.) To Job's own knowledge and conviction: *"Knowest thou not this?* Canst thou be ignorant of a truth so plain? Or canst thou doubt of a truth which has been confirmed by the suffrages of all mankind?" Those know little who do not know that the wages of sin is death. (2.) To the experience of all ages. It was known of old, since man was placed upon the earth; that is, ever since man was made he has had this truth written in his heart, that the sin of sinners will be their ruin; and ever since there were instances of wickedness (which there were soon after man was placed on the earth) there were instances of the punishments of it, witness the exclusions of Adam and Cain. When sin entered into the world death entered with it: all the world knows that evil pursues sinners, whom *vengeance suffers not to live* (Acts 28:4), and subscribes to that (Isa. 3:11), *Woe to the wicked; it shall be ill with him,* sooner or later.

2. How it is laid down (*v.* 5): *The triumphing of the wicked is short, and the joy of the hypocrite but for a moment.* Observe, (1.) He asserts the misery, not only of those who are openly wicked and profane, but of hypocrites, who secretly practice wickedness under a show and profession of religion, because such a wicked man he looked upon Job to be; and it is true that a form of godliness, if it be made use of for a cloak of maliciousness, does but make bad worse. Dissembled piety is double iniquity, and the ruin that attends it will be accordingly. The hottest place in hell will be the portion of hypocrites, as our Saviour intimates, Mt. 24:51. (2.) He grants that wicked men may for a time prosper, may be secure and easy, and very merry. You may see them in triumph and joy, triumphing and rejoicing in their wealth and power, their grandeur and success, triumphing and rejoicing over their poor honest neighbours whom they vex and oppress: they feel no evil, they fear none. Job's friends were loth to own, at first, that wicked people might prosper at all (*ch.* 4:9), until Job proved it plainly (*ch.* 9:24, 12:6), and now Zophar yields it; but, (3.) He lays it down for a certain truth that they will not prosper long. Their joy is but for a moment, and will quickly end in endless sorrow. Though he be ever so great, and rich, and jovial, the hypocrite will be humbled, and mortified, and made miserable.

3. How it is illustrated, *v.* 6–9. (1.) He supposes his prosperity to be very high, as high as you can imagine, *v.* 6. It is not his wisdom and virtue, but his worldly wealth or greatness, that he accounts *his excellency,* and values himself upon. We will suppose that *to mount up to the heavens,* and, since his spirit always rises with his condition, you may suppose that with it *his head reaches to the clouds.* He is every way advanced; the world has done the utmost it can for him. He looks down upon all about him

with disdain, while they look up to him with admiration, envy, or fear. We will suppose him to bid fair for a universal monarchy. And, though he cannot but have made himself many enemies before he arrived to this pitch of prosperity, yet he thinks himself as much out of the reach of their darts as if he were in the clouds. (2.) He is confident that his ruin will accordingly be very great, and his fall the more dreadful for his having risen so high: *He shall perish for ever, v.* 7. His pride and security were the certain presages of his misery. This will certainly be true of all impenitent sinners in the other world; they shall be undone, for ever undone. But Zophar means his ruin in this world; and indeed sometimes notorious sinners are remarkably cut off by present judgments; they have reason enough to fear what Zophar here threatens even the triumphant sinner with. [1.] A shameful destruction: *He shall perish like his own dung* or dunghill, so loathsome is he to God and all good men, and so willing will the world be to part with him, Ps. 119:119; Isa. 66:24. [2.] A surprising destruction. He will be brought into desolation in a moment (Ps. 73:19), so that those about him, that saw him but just now, will ask, *"Where is he?* Could he that made so great a figure vanish and expire so suddenly?" [3.] A swift destruction, *v.* 8. *He shall fly away* upon the wings of his own terrors, and be *chased away* by the just imprecations of all about him, who would gladly get rid of him. [4.] An utter destruction. It will be total; he shall go away *like a dream,* or *vision of the night,* which was a mere phantasm, and, whatever in it pleased the fancy, it is quite gone, and nothing of it remains but what serves us to laugh at the folly of. It will be final (*v.* 9): *The eye that saw him,* and was ready to adore him, *shall see him no more,* and the place he filled shall no more behold him, having given him an eternal farewell when he went to his own place, as Judas, Acts 1:25.

Verses 10–22

The instances here given of the miserable condition of the wicked man in this world are expressed with great fulness and fluency of language, and the same thing returned to again and repeated in other words. Let us therefore reduce the particulars to their proper heads, and observe,

I. What his wickedness is for which he is punished.

1. The lusts of the flesh, here called *the sins of his youth* (*v.* 11); for those are the sins which, at that age, people are most tempted to. The forbidden pleasures of sense are said to be *sweet in his mouth* (*v.* 12); he indulges himself in all the gratifications of the carnal appetite, and takes an inordinate complacency in them, as yielding the most agreeable delights. That is the satisfaction which *he hides under his tongue,* and rolls there, as the most dainty delicate thing that can be. *He keeps it still within his mouth* (*v.* 13); let him have that, and he desires no more; he will never part with that for the spiritual and divine pleasures of religion, which he has no relish or nor affection for. His keeping it still in his mouth denotes his obstinately persisting in his sin (*he spares it* when he should kill and mortify it, *and forsakes it not,* but holds it fast, and goes on frowardly in it), and also his re-acting of his sin by revolving it and remembering it with pleasure, as that adulterous woman (Eze. 23:19) who *multiplied her whoredoms by calling to remembrance the days of her youth;* so does this wicked man here. Or his hiding it and keeping it under his tongue denotes his industrious concealment of his beloved lust. Being a hypocrite, his haunts of sin are secret, that he may save the credit of his profession; but he who knows what is in the heart knows what is under the tongue too, and will discover it shortly.

2. The love of the world and the wealth of it. It is in worldly wealth that he places his happiness, and therefore he sets his heart upon it. See here, (1.) How greedy he is of it (*v.* 15): *He has swallowed down riches* as eagerly as ever a hungry man swallowed down meat; and is still crying, "Give, give." It is that which he desired (*v.* 20); it was, in his eye, the best gift, and that which he coveted earnestly. (2.) What pains he takes for it: It is *that which he laboured for* (*v.* 18), not by honest diligence in a lawful calling, but by an unwearied prosecution of all ways and methods, *per fas, per nefas — right or wrong,* to be rich. We must *labour,* not *to be rich* (Prov. 23:4), but to be charitable, *that we may have to give* (Eph. 4:28), not to spend. (3.) What great things he promises himself from it, intimated in *the rivers, the floods, the brooks of honey and butter* (*v.* 17); his being disappointed of them supposes that he had flattered himself with the hopes of them: he expected rivers of sensual delights.

3. Violence and oppression, and injustice in his poor neighbours, *v.* 19. This was the sin of the giants of the old world, and a sin that, as much as any, brings God's judgments upon nations and families. It is charged upon this wicked man, (1.) That *he has forsaken the poor,* taken no care of them, shown no kindness to them, nor made any provision for them. At first perhaps, for a pretence, he gave alms like the Pharisees, to gain a reputation; but, when he had served his turn by this practice, he left it off, and forsook the poor, whom before he seemed to be concerned for. Those who do good, but not from a good principle, though they may abound in it, will not abide in it. (2.) That he has *oppressed* them, crushed them, taken all advantages against them to do them a mischief. To enrich himself, he has robbed the spital, and made the poor poorer. (3.) That he has *violently taken away their houses,* which he had no right to, as Ahab took Naboth's vineyard, not by secret fraud, by forgery, perjury, or some trick in law, but avowedly, and by open violence.

II. What his punishment is for this wickedness.

1. He shall be disappointed in his expectations, and shall not find that satisfaction in his worldly wealth which he vainly promised himself (*v.* 17): *He shall never see the rivers, the floods, the brooks of honey and butter,* with which he hoped to glut himself. The world is not that to those who love it, and court it, and admire it, which they fancy it will be. The enjoyment sinks far below the raised expectation.

2. He shall be diseased and distempered in his body; and how little comfort a man has in riches if he has not health! Sickness and pain, especially it they be in extremity, embitter all his enjoyments. This wicked man has all the delights of sense wound up to the height of pleasurableness; but what real happiness can he enjoy when *his bones are full of the sins of his youth* (*v.* 11), that is, of the effects of those sins? By his drunkenness and gluttony, his uncleanness and wantonness, when he was young, he contracted those diseases which are painful to him long after, and perhaps make his life very miserable, and, as Solomon speaks, consume his flesh and his body, Prov. 5:11. Perhaps he was given to fight when he was young, and then made nothing of a cut or a bruise in a fray; but he feels it in his bones long after. But can he get no ease, no relief? No, he is likely to carry his pains and diseases with him to the grave, or rather they are likely to carry him thither, and so the sins of his youth shall *lie down with him in the dust;* the very putrefying of his body in the grave is to him the effect of sin (*ch.* 24:19), so that his iniquity is upon his bones there, Eze. 32:27. The sin of sinners follows them to the other side death.

3. He shall be disquieted and troubled in his mind: *Surely he shall not feel quietness in his belly, v.* 20. He has not that ease in his own mind that people think he has, but is in continual agitation. The ill-gotten wealth which he has swallowed down makes him sick, and, like undigested meat, is always upbraiding him. Let none expect to enjoy that comfortably which they have gotten unjustly. The unquietness of his mind arises, (1.) From his conscience looking back, and filling him with the fear of the wrath of God against him for his wickedness. Even that wickedness which was sweet in the commission, and was rolled under the tongue as a delicate morsel, becomes bitter in the reflection, and, when it is reviewed, fills him with horror and vexation. *In his bowels it is turned* (*v.* 14) like John's book, *in his mouth as sweet as honey,* but, *when he had eaten it, his belly was bitter,* Rev. 10:10. Such a thing is sin; it is turned into *the gall of asps,* than which nothing is more bitter, *the poison of asps* (*v.* 16), than which nothing more fatal, and so it will be to him; what he sucked so sweetly, and with so much pleasure, will prove to him the poison of asps; so will all unlawful gains be. The fawning tongue will prove the viper's tongue. All the charming graces that are thought to be in sin will, when conscience is awakened, turn into so many raging furies. (2.) From his cares, looking forward, *v.* 22. *In the fulness of his sufficiency,* when he thinks himself most happy, and most sure of the continuance of his happiness, *he shall be in straits,* that is, he shall think himself so, through the anxieties and perplexities of his own mind, as that rich man who, when his ground brought forth plentifully, cried out, *What shall I do?* Lu. 12:17.

4. He shall be dispossessed of his estate; that shall sink and dwindle away to nothing, so that *he shall not rejoice therein, v.* 18. He shall not only never rejoice truly, but not long rejoice at all. (1.) What he has unjustly swallowed he shall be compelled to disgorge (*v.* 15): *He swallowed down riches,* and then thought himself sure of them, and that they were as much his own as the meat he had eaten; but he was deceived: *he shall vomit them up again;* his own conscience perhaps may make him so uneasy in the keeping of what he has gotten that, for the quiet of his own mind, he shall make restitution, and that not with the pleasure of a virtue, but the pain of a vomit, and with the utmost reluctancy. Or, if he do not himself refund what he has violently taken away, God will, by his providence, force him to it, and bring it about, one way or other, that ill-gotten goods shall return to the right owners: *God shall cast them out of his belly,* while yet the love of the sin is not cast out of his heart. So loud shall the clamours of the poor, whom he has impoverished, be against him, that he shall be forced to send his children to them to soothe them and beg their pardon (*v.* 10): *His children shall seek to please the poor,* while his own hands shall restore them their goods with shame (*v.* 18): *That which he laboured for,* by all the arts of oppression, *shall he restore,* and shall not so swallow it down as to digest it; it shall not stay with him, but *according to his shame shall the restitution be;* having gotten a great deal unjustly, he shall restore a great deal, so that when every one has his own he will have but little left for himself. To be made to restore what was unjustly gotten, by the sanctifying grace of God, as Zaccheus was, is a great mercy; he voluntarily and cheerfully restored four-fold, and yet had a great deal left to *give to the poor,* Lu. 19:8. But to be forced to restore, as Judas was, merely by the horrors of a despairing conscience, has none of that benefit and comfort attending it, for he *threw down the pieces of silver and went and hanged himself.* (2.) He shall be stripped of all he has and become a beggar. He that spoiled others shall himself be spoiled (Isa. 33:1); for *every hand of the wicked shall be upon him.* The innocent, whom he has wronged, sit down by their loss, saying, as David, *Wickedness proceedeth from the wicked, but my hand shall not be upon him,* 1 Sa. 24:13. But though they have forgiven him, though they will make no reprisals, divine justice will, and often makes the wicked to avenge the quarrel of the righteous, and squeezes and crushes one bad man by the hand of another upon him. Thus, when he is plucked on all sides, *he shall not save of that which he desired* (*v.* 20), not only he shall not save it all, but he shall save nothing of it. *There shall none of his meat* (which he coveted so much, and fed upon with so much pleasure) *be left, v.* 21. All his neighbours and relations shall look upon him to be in such bad circumstances that, when he is dead, no man shall look for his goods, none of his kindred shall expect to be a penny the better for him, nor be willing to take out letters of administration for what he leaves behind him. In all this Zophar reflects upon Job, who had lost all and was reduced to the last extremity.

Verses 23–29

Zophar, having described the many embarrassments and vexations which commonly attend the wicked practices of oppressors and cruel men, here comes to show their utter ruin at last.

I. Their ruin will take its rise from God's wrath and vengeance, *v.* 23. The hand of the wicked was upon him (*v.* 22), *every hand of the wicked.* His hand was against every one, and therefore every man's hand will be against him. Yet, in grappling with these, he might go near to make his part good; but his heart cannot endure, nor his hands be strong, when *God shall deal with him* (Eze. 22:14), *when God shall cast the fury of his wrath upon him and rain it upon him.* Every word here speaks terror. It is not only the justice of God that is engaged against him, but his wrath, the deep resentment of provocations given to himself; it is *the fury of his wrath,* incensed to the highest degree; it is cast upon him with force and fierceness; it is rained upon him in abundance; it comes on his head like the fire and brimstone upon Sodom, to which the psalmist also refers, Ps. 11:6. *On the wicked God shall rain fire and brimstone.* There is no fence against this, but in Christ, who is the only covert from the storm and tempest, Isa. 32:2. This wrath shall be cast upon him *when he is about to fill his belly,* just going to glut himself with what he has gotten and promising himself abundant satisfaction in it. Then, when he is eating, shall this tempest surprise him, when he is secure and easy, and in apprehension of no danger; as the ruin of the old world and Sodom came when they were in the depth of their security, and the height of their sensuality, as Christ observes, Lu. 17:26, etc. Perhaps Zophar here reflects on the death of Job's children when they were eating and drinking.

II. Their ruin will be inevitable, and there will be no possibility of escaping it (*v.* 24): *He shall flee from the iron weapon.* Flight argues guilt. He will not humble himself under the judgments of God, nor seek means to make his peace with him. All his care is to escape the vengeance that pursues him, but in vain: if he escape the sword, yet *the bow of steel shall strike him through.* God has weapons of all sorts; he has both *whet his sword and bent his bow* (Ps. 7:12, 13); he can deal with his enemies *cominus vel eminus — at hand or afar off.* He has a sword for those that think to fight it out with him by their strength, and a bow for those that think to avoid him by their craft. See Isa. 24:17, 18; Jer. 48:43, 44. He that is marked for ruin, though he may escape one judgment, will find another ready for him.

III. It will be a total terrible ruin. When the dart that has struck him through (for when God shoots he is sure to hit his mark, when he strikes he strikes home) comes to be *drawn out of his body,* when *the glittering sword* (the *lightning,* so the word is), the flaming sword, the sword that is bathed in heaven (Isa. 34:5), *comes out of his gall,* O what *terrors are upon him!* How strong are the convulsions, how violent are the dying agonies! How terrible are the arrests of death to a wicked man!

IV. Sometimes it is a ruin that comes upon him insensibly, *v.* 26. 1. The darkness he is wrapped up in is a hidden darkness: it is *all darkness,* utter darkness, without the least mixture of light, and it is *hid in his secret place,* whither he has retreated and where he hopes to shelter himself; he never retires into his own conscience but he finds himself in the dark and utterly at a loss. 2. The fire he is consumed by is *a fire not blown,* kindled without noise, a consumption which every body sees the effect of, but nobody sees the cause of. It is plain that the gourd is withered, but the worm at the root, that causes it to wither, is out of sight. He is wasted by a soft gentle fire — surely, but very slowly. When the fuel is very combustible, the fire needs no blowing, and that is his case; he is ripe for ruin. *The proud, and those that do wickedly, shall be stubble,* Mal. 4:1. *An unquenchable fire shall consume him* (so some read it), and that is certainly true of hell-fire.

V. It is a ruin, not only to himself, but to his family: *It shall go ill with him that is left in his tabernacle,* for the curse shall reach him, and he shall be cut off perhaps by the same grievous disease. There is an entail of wrath upon the family, which will destroy both his heirs and his inheritance, *v.* 28. 1. His posterity will be rooted out: *The increase of his house shall depart,* shall either be cut off by untimely deaths or forced to run their country. Numerous and growing families, if wicked and vile, are soon reduced, dispersed, and extirpated, by the judgments of God. 2. His estate will be sunk. *His goods shall flow away* from his family as fast as ever they flowed into it, when *the day of God's wrath* comes, for which, all the while his estate was in the getting by fraud and oppression, he was treasuring up wrath.

VI. It is a ruin which will manifestly appear to be just and righteous, and what he has brought upon himself by his own wickedness; for (*v.* 27) *the heaven shall reveal his iniquity,* that is, the God of heaven, who sees all the secret wickedness of the wicked, will, by some means or other, let all the world know what a base man he has been, that they may own the justice of God in all that is brought upon him. *The earth* also *shall rise up against him,* both to discover his wickedness and to avenge it. *The earth shall disclose her blood,* Isa. 26:21. *The earth will rise up against him* (as the stomach rises against that which is loathsome), and will no longer keep him. *The heaven reveals his iniquity,* and therefore will not receive him. Whither then

must he go but to hell? If the God of heaven and earth be his enemy, neither heaven nor earth will show him any kindness, but all the hosts of both are and will be at war with him.

VII. Zophar concludes like an orator (*v.* 29): *This is the portion of a wicked man from God;* it is allotted him, it is designed him, as his portion. He will have it at last, as a child has his portion, and he will have it for a perpetuity; it is what he must abide by: *This is the heritage of his decree from God;* it is the settled rule of his judgment, and fair warning is given of it. *O wicked man! thou shalt surely die,* Eze. 33:8. Though impenitent sinners do not always fall under such temporal judgments as are here described (therein Zophar was mistaken), yet the wrath of God abides upon them, and they are made miserable by spiritual judgments, which are much worse, their consciences being either, on the one hand, a terror to them, and then they are in continual amazement, or, on the other hand, seared and silenced, and then they are given up to a reprobate sense and bound over to eternal ruin. Never was any doctrine better explained, or worse applied, than this by Zophar, who intended by all this to prove Job a hypocrite. Let us receive the good explication, and make a better application, for warning to ourselves to stand in awe and not to sin.

CHAPTER 21

This is Job's reply to Zophar's discourse, in which he complains less of his own miseries than he had done in his former discourses (finding that his friends were not moved by his complaints to pity him in the least), and comes closer to the general question that was in dispute between him and them, Whether outward prosperity, and the continuance of it, were a mark of the true church and the true members of it, so that the ruin of a man's prosperity is sufficient to prove him a hypocrite, though no other evidence appear against him: this they asserted, but Job denied. I. His preface here is designed for the moving of their affections, that he might gain their attention (*v.* 1–6). II. His discourse is designed for the convincing of their judgments and the rectifying of their mistakes. He owns that God does sometimes hang up a wicked man as it were in chains, *in terrorem* — as a terror to others, by some visible remarkable judgment in this life, but denies that he always does so; nay, he maintains that commonly he does otherwise, suffering even the worst of sinners to live all their days in prosperity and to go out of the world without any visible mark of his wrath upon them. 1. He describes the great prosperity of wicked people (*v.* 7–13). 2. He shows their great impiety, in which they are hardened by their prosperity (*v.* 14–16). 3. He foretels their ruin at length, but after a long reprieve (*v.* 17–21). 4. He observes a very great variety in the ways of God's providence towards men, even towards bad men (*v.* 22–26). 5. He overthrows the ground of their severe censures of him, by showing that the destruction of the wicked is reserved for the other world, and that they often escape to the last in this world (*v.* 27, to the end), and in this Job was clearly in the right.

Verses 1–6

Job here recommends himself, both his case and his discourse, both what he suffered and what he said, to the compassionate consideration of his friends. 1. That which he entreats of them is very fair, that they would suffer him to speak (*v.* 3) and not break in upon him, as Zophar had done, in the midst of his discourse. Losers, of all men, may have leave to speak; and, if those that are accused and censured are not allowed to speak for themselves, they are wronged without remedy, and have no way to come at their right. He entreats that they would hear diligently his speech (*v.* 2) as those that were willing to understand him, and, if they were under a mistake, to have it rectified; and that they would *mark him* (*v.* 5), for we may as well not hear as not heed and observe what we hear. 2. That which he urges for this is very reasonable. (1.) They came to comfort him. "No," says he, *"let this be your consolations* (*v.* 2); if you have no other comforts to administer to me, yet deny me not this; be so kind, so just, as to give me a patient hearing, and that shall pass for your consolations of me." Nay, they could not know how to comfort him if they would not give him leave to open his case and tell his own story. Or, "It will be a consolation to yourselves, in reflection, to have dealt tenderly with your afflicted friend, and not harshly." (2.) He would hear them speak when it came to their turn. "After I have spoken you may go on with what you have to say, and I will not hinder you, no, though you go on to mock me." Those that engage in controversy must reckon upon having hard words given them, and resolve to bear reproach patiently; for, generally, those that mock will mock on, whatever is said to them. (3.) He hoped to convince them. "If you will but give me a fair hearing, mock on if you can, but I believe I shall say that which will change your note and make you pity me rather than

mock me." (4.) They were not his judges (*v.* 4): *"Is my complaint to man?* No, if it were I see it would be to little purpose to complain. But my complaint is to God, and to him do I appeal. Let him be Judge between you and me. Before him we stand upon even terms, and therefore I have the privilege of being heard as well as you. If my complaint were to men, my spirit would be troubled, for they would not regard me, nor rightly understand me; but my complaint is to God, who will suffer me to speak, though you will not." It would be sad if God should deal as unkindly with us as our friends sometimes do. (5.) There was that in his case which was very surprising and astonishing, and therefore both needed and deserved their most serious consideration. It was not a common case, but a very extraordinary one. [1.] He himself was amazed at it, at the troubles God had laid upon him and the censures of his friends concerning him (*v.* 6): *"When I remember* that terrible day in which I was on a sudden stripped of all my comforts, that day in which I was stricken with sore boils, — when I remember all the hard speeches with which you have grieved me, — I confess *I am afraid, and trembling takes hold of my flesh,* especially when I compare this with the prosperous condition of many wicked people, and the applauses of their neighbours, with which they pass through the world." Note, The providences of God, in the government of the world, are sometimes very astonishing even to wise and good men, and bring them to their wits' end. [2.] He would have them wonder at it (*v.* 5): *"Mark me, and be astonished.* Instead of expounding my troubles, you should awfully adore the unsearchable mysteries of Providence in afflicting one thus of whom you know no evil; you should therefore *lay your hand upon your mouth,* silently wait the issue, and judge nothing before the time. *God's way is in the sea, and his path in the great waters.* When we cannot account for what he does, in suffering the wicked to prosper and the godly to be afflicted, nor fathom the depth of those proceedings, it becomes us to sit down and admire them. *Upright men shall be astonished at this,* ch. 17:8. Be you so."

Verses 7–16

All Job's three friends, in their last discourses, had been very copious in describing the miserable condition of a wicked man in this world. "It is true," says Job, "remarkable judgments are sometimes brought upon notorious sinners, but not always; for we have many instances of the great and long prosperity of those that are openly and avowedly wicked; though they are hardened in their wickedness by their prosperity, yet they are still suffered to prosper."

I. He here describes their prosperity in the height, and breadth, and length of it. "If this be true, as you say, pray tell me *wherefore do the wicked live?" v.* 7.

1. The matter of fact is taken for granted, for we see instances of it every day. (1.) They live, and are not suddenly cut off by the strokes of divine vengeance. Those yet speak who have set their mouths against the heavens. Those yet act who have stretched out their hands against God. Not only they live (that is, they are reprieved), but they *live in prosperity,* 1 Sa. 25:6. Nay, (2.) They *become old;* they have the honour, satisfaction, and advantage of living long, long enough to raise their families and estates. We read of a *sinner a hundred years old,* Isa. 65:20. But this is not all. (3.) They are *mighty in power,* are preferred to places of authority and trust, and not only make a great figure, but bear a great sway. *Vivit imo, et in senatum venit — He not only lives, but appears in the senate.* Now wherefore is it so? Note, It is worth while to enquire into the reasons of the outward prosperity of wicked people. It is not because God has forsaken the earth, because he does not see, or does not hate, or cannot punish their wickedness; but it is because the measure of their iniquities is not full. This is the day of God's patience, and, in some way or other, he makes use of them and their prosperity to serve his own counsels, while it ripens them for ruin; but the chief reason is because he will make it to appear there is another world which is the world of retribution, and not this.

2. The prosperity of the wicked is here described to be,

(1.) Complete and consummate. [1.] They are multiplied, and their family is built up, and they have the satisfaction of seeing it (*v.* 8): *Their seed is established in their sight,*

This is put first, as that which gives both a pleasant enjoyment and a pleasing prospect. [2.] They are easy and quiet, *v.* 9. Whereas Zophar had spoken of their continual frights and terrors, Job says, *Their houses are safe* both from danger and from the fear of it (*v.* 9), and so far are they from the killing wounds of God's sword or arrows that they do not feel the smart of so much as *the rod of God upon them.* [3.] They are rich and thrive in their estates. Of this he gives only one instance, *v.* 10. Their cattle increase, and they meet with no disappointment in them; not so much as a cow casts her calf, and then their much must needs grow more. This is promised, Ex. 23:26; Deu. 7:14. [4.] They are merry and live a jovial life (*v.* 11, 12): *They send forth their little ones* abroad among their neighbours, *like a flock,* in great numbers, to sport themselves. They have their balls and music-meetings, at which *their children dance;* and dancing is fittest for children, who know not better how to spend their time and whose innocency guards them against the mischiefs that commonly attend it. Though the parents are not so very youthful and frolicsome as to dance themselves, yet *they take the timbrel and harp;* they pipe, and their children dance after their pipe, and they know no grief to put their instruments out of tune or to withhold their hearts from any joy. Some observe that this is an instance of their vanity, as well as of their prosperity. Here is none of that care taken of their children which Abraham took of his, to *teach them the way of the Lord,* Gen. 18:19. Their children do not pray, or say their catechism, but dance, and sing, and *rejoice at the sound of the organ.* Sensual pleasures are all the delights of carnal people, and as men are themselves so they breed their children.

(2.) Continuing and constant (*v.* 13): *They spend their days,* all their days, *in wealth,* and never know what it is to want — in mirth, and never know what sadness means; and at last, without any previous alarms to frighten them, without any anguish or agony, *in a moment they go down to the grave,* and there are no bands in their death. If there were not another life after this, it were most desirable to die by the quickest shortest strokes of death. Since we must *go down to the grave,* if that were the furthest of our journey, we should wish to *go down in a moment,* to swallow the bitter pill, and not chew it.

II. He shows how they abuse their prosperity and are confirmed and hardened by it in their impiety, *v.* 14, 15.

1. Their gold and silver serve to steel them, to make them more insolent, and more impudent, in their wickedness. Now he mentions this either, (1.) To increase the difficulty. It is strange that any wicked people should prosper thus, but especially that those should prosper who have arrived at such a pitch of wickedness as openly to bid defiance to God himself, and tell him to his face that they care not for him; nay, and that their prosperity should be continued, though they bear up themselves upon that, in their opposition to God; with that weapon they fight against him, and yet are not disarmed. Or, (2.) To lessen the difficulty. God suffers them to prosper; but let us not wonder at it, for *the prosperity of fools destroys them,* by hardening them in sin, Prov. 1:32; Ps. 73:7–9.

2. See how light these prospering sinners make of God and religion, as if because they have so much of this world they had no need to look after another.

(1.) See how ill affected they are to God and religion; they abandon them, and cast off the thoughts of them. [1.] They dread the presence of God; they *say unto him, "Depart from us;* let us never be troubled with the apprehension of our being under God's eye nor be restrained by the fear of him." Or they bid him depart as one they do not need, nor have any occasion to make use of. The world is the portion they have chosen, and take up with, and think themselves happy in; while they have that they can live without God. Justly will God say *Depart* (Mt. 25:41) to those who have bidden him depart; and justly does he now take them at their word. [2.] They dread the knowledge of God, and of his will, and of their duty to him: *We desire not the knowledge of thy ways.* Those that are resolved not to walk in God's ways desire not to know them, because their knowledge will be a continual reproach to their disobedience, Jn. 3:19.

(2.) See how they argue against God and religion (*v.* 15): *What is the Almighty?* Strange that ever creatures should speak so insolently, that ever reasonable creatures should speak so absurdly and unreasonably. The two great bonds by which we are drawn and held to religion are those of duty and interest; now they here endeavour to break both these bonds asunder. [1.] They will not believe it is their duty to be religious: *What is the Almighty, that we should serve him?* Like Pharaoh (Ex. 5:2), *Who is the Lord, that I should obey his voice?* Observe, *First,* How slightly they speak of God: *What is the Almighty?* As if he were a mere name, a mere cipher, or one they have nothing to do with and that has nothing to do with them. *Secondly,* How hardly they speak of religion. They call it a *service,* and mean a hard service. Is it not enough, they think, to keep up a fair correspondence with the Almighty, but they must serve him, which they look upon as a task and drudgery. *Thirdly,* How highly they speak of themselves: *"That we should serve him;* we who are rich and mighty in power, shall we be subject and accountable to him? No, we are lords," Jer. 2:31. [2.] They will not believe it is their interest to be religious: *What profit shall we have if we pray unto him?* All the world are for what they can get, and *therefore* wisdom's merchandise is neglected, because they think there is nothing to be got by it. *It is vain to serve God,* Mal. 3:13, 14. Praying will not pay debts nor portion children; nay, perhaps serious godliness may hinder a man's preferment and expose him to losses; and what then? Is nothing to be called gain but the wealth and honour of this world? If we obtain the favour of God, and spiritual and eternal blessings, we have no reason to complain of losing by our religion. But, if we have not profit by prayer, it is our own fault (Isa. 58:3, 4), it is because we ask amiss, Jam. 4:3. Religion itself is not a vain thing; if it be so to us, we may thank ourselves for resting in the outside of it, Jam. 1:26.

III. He shows their folly herein, and utterly disclaims all concurrence with them (*v.* 19): *Lo, their good is not in their hand,* that is, they did not get it without God, and therefore they are very ungrateful to slight him thus. It was *not their might, nor the power of their hand,* that got them this wealth, and therefore they ought to remember God who gave it them. Nor can they keep it without God, and therefore they are very unwise to lose their interest in him and bid him to depart from them. Some give this sense of it: "Their good is in their barns and their bags, hoarded up there; it is not in their hand, to do good to others with it; and then what good does it do them?" "Therefore," says Job, *"the counsel of the wicked is far from me.* Far be it from me that I should be of their mind, say as they say, do as they do, and take my measures from them. Their *posterity approve their sayings,* though *their way* be *their folly* (Ps. 49:13); but I know better things than to walk in their counsel."

Verses 17–26

Job had largely described the prosperity of wicked people; now, in these verses,

I. He opposes this to what his friends had maintained concerning their certain ruin in this life. "Tell me *how often* do you see *the candle of the wicked put out?* Do you not as often see it burnt down to the socket, until it goes out of itself? *v.* 17. How often do you see *their destruction come upon them,* or *God distributing sorrows in his anger* among them? Do you not as often see their mirth and prosperity continuing to the last?" Perhaps there are as many instances of notorious sinners ending their days in pomp as ending them in misery, which observation is sufficient to invalidate their arguments against Job and to show that no certain judgment can be made of men's character by their outward condition.

II. He reconciles this to the holiness and justice of God. Though wicked people prosper thus all their days, yet we are not therefore to think that God will let their wickedness always go unpunished. No, 1. Even while they prosper thus they are *as stubble and chaff before the stormy wind, v.* 18. They are light and worthless, and of no account either with God or with wise and good men. They are fitted to destruction, and continually lie exposed to it, and in the height of their pomp and power there is but a step between them and ruin. 2. Though they spend all their days in wealth God is *laying up their iniquity for their children* (*v.* 19), and he will visit it upon their posterity when they are gone. The oppressor lays up his goods for his children, to make them gentlemen, but God lays up his iniquity for them, to make them beggars. He keeps an exact account of the fathers' sins, *seals them up among his treasures* (Deu. 32:34), and will justly punish the children, while the riches, to which the curse cleaves, are found as assets in their hands. 3. Though they prosper in this world, yet they shall be reckoned with in another world. God *rewards him* according to his deeds at last (*v.* 19), though the sentence passed against his evil works be not executed speedily. Perhaps he may not now be made to fear the wrath to come, but he may flatter himself with hopes that he shall have peace though he go on; but he shall be made to feel it in the day of the revelation of the righteous judgment of God. He shall know it (*v.* 20): *His eyes shall see his destruction* which he would not be persuaded to believe. They *will not see, but they shall see,* Isa. 26:11. The eyes that have been wilfully shut against the grace of God shall be opened to see his destruction. *He shall drink of the wrath of the Almighty;* that shall be the portion of his cup. Compare Ps. 11:6 with Rev. 14:10. The misery of damned sinners is here set forth in a few words, but very terrible ones. They lie under the wrath of an Almighty God, who, in their destruction, both shows his wrath and makes known his power; and, if this will be his condition in the other world, what good will his prosperity in this world do him? *What pleasure has he in his house after him? v.* 21. Our Saviour has let us know how little pleasure the rich man in hell had in his house after him, when the remembrance of the good things he had received in his life-time would not cool his tongue, but added much to his misery, as did also the sorrow he was in lest his five brethren, whom he left in his house after him, should follow him to that place of torment, Lu. 16:25–28. So little will the gain of the world profit him that has lost his soul.

III. He resolves this difference which Providence makes between one wicked man and another into the wisdom and sovereignty of God (*v.* 22): *Shall any pretend to teach God knowledge?* Dare we arraign God's proceedings or blame his conduct? Shall we take upon us to tell God how he should govern the world, what sinner he should spare and whom he should punish? He has both authority and ability to judge those that are high. Angels in heaven, princes and magistrates on earth, are accountable to God, and must receive their doom from him. He manages them, and makes what use he pleases of them. Shall he then be accountable to us, or receive advice from us? He is the Judge of all the earth, and therefore no doubt he will do right (Gen. 18:25, Rom. 3:6), and those proceedings of his providence which seem to contradict one another he can make, not only mutually to agree, but jointly to serve his own purposes. The little difference there is between one wicked man's dying so in pain and misery, when both will at last meet in hell, he illustrates by the little difference there is between one man's dying suddenly and another's dying slowly, when they will both meet shortly in the grave. So vast is the disproportion between time and eternity that, if hell be the lot of every sinner at last, it makes little difference if one goes singing thither and another sighing. See,

1. How various the circumstances of people's dying are. There is one way into the world, we say, but many out; yet, as some are born by quick and easy labour, others by that which is hard and lingering, so dying is to some much more terrible than to others; and, since the death of the body is the birth of the soul into another world, death-bed agonies may not unfitly be compared to child-bed throes. Observe the difference. (1.) One dies suddenly, *in his full strength,* not weakened by age or sickness (*v.* 23), *being wholly at ease and quiet,* under no apprehension at all of the approach of death, nor in any fear of it; but, on the contrary, because *his breasts are full of milk and his bones moistened with marrow* (*v.* 24), that is, he is healthful and vigorous, and of a good constitution (like a milch cow that is fat and in good liking), he counts upon nothing but to live many years in mirth and pleasure. Thus fair does he bid for life, and yet he is cut off in a moment by the stroke of death. Note, It is a common thing for persons to be taken away by death when they are in their full strength, in the highest degree of health, when they least expect death, and think themselves best armed against it, and are ready not only to set death at a distance, but to set it at defiance. Let us therefore never be secure; for we have known many well and dead in the same week, the same day, the same hour, nay, perhaps,

the same minute. Let us therefore be always ready. (2.) Another dies slowly, and with a great deal of previous pain and misery (*v.* 25), *in the betterness of his soul,* such as poor Job was himself now in, *and never eats with pleasure,* has no appetite to his food nor any relish of it, through sickness, or age, or sorrow of mind. What great reason have those to be thankful that are in health and always eat with pleasure! And what little reason have those to complain who sometimes do not eat thus, when they hear of many that never do!

2. How undiscernible this difference is in the grave. As rich and poor, so healthful and unhealthful, meet there (*v.* 26): *They shall lie down alike in the dust, and the worms shall cover them,* and feed sweetly on them. Thus, if one wicked man die in a palace and another in a dungeon, they will meet in the congregation of the dead and damned, and the worm that dies not, and the fire that is not quenched, will be the same to them, which makes those differences inconsiderable and not worth perplexing ourselves about.

Verses 27–34

In these verses,

I. Job opposes the opinion of his friends, which he saw they still adhered to, that the wicked are sure to fall into such visible and remarkable ruin as Job had now fallen into, and none but the wicked, upon which principle they condemned Job as a wicked man. *"I know your thoughts,"* says Job (*v.* 27); "I know you will not agree with me; for your judgments are tinctured and biassed by your piques and prejudices against me, *and the devices which you wrongfully imagine against* my comfort and honour: and how can such men be convinced?" Job's friends were ready to say, in answer to his discourse concerning the prosperity of the wicked, *"Where is the house of the prince? v.* 28. Where is Job's house, or the house of his eldest son, in which his children were feasting? Enquire into the circumstances of Job's house and family, and then ask, *Where are the dwelling-places of the wicked?* and compare them together, and you will soon see that Job's house is in the same predicament with the houses of tyrants and oppressors, and may therefore conclude that doubtless he was such a one."

II. He lays down his own judgment to the contrary, and, for proof of it, appeals to the sentiments and observations of all mankind. So confident is he that he is in the right that he is willing to refer the cause to the next man that comes by (*v.* 29): *"Have you not asked those that go by the way* — any indifferent person, any that will answer you? I say not, as Eliphaz (*ch.* 5:1), to which of the *saints,* but to which of *the children of men* will you turn? Turn to which you will, and you will find them all of my mind, that the punishment of sinners is designed more for the other world than for this, according to the prophecy of Enoch, the seventh from Adam, Jude 14. *Do you not know the tokens* of this truth, which all that have made any observations upon the providences of God concerning mankind in this world can furnish you with?" Now,

1. What is it that Job here asserts? Two things: — (1.) That impenitent sinners will certainly be punished in the other world, and, usually, their punishment is put off until then. (2.) That therefore we are not to think it strange if they prosper greatly in this world and fall under no visible token of God's wrath. *Therefore* they are spared now, because they are to be punished then; *therefore* the *workers of iniquity flourish, that they may be destroyed for ever,* Ps. 92:7. The sinner is here supposed, [1.] To live in a great deal of power, so as to be not only *the terror of the mighty in the land of the living* (Eze. 32:27), but the terror of the wise and good too, whom he keeps in such awe that none dares *declare his way to his face, v.* 31. None will take the liberty to reprove him, to tell him of the wickedness of his way, and what will be in the end thereof; so that he sins securely, and is not made to know either shame or fear. *The prosperity of fools destroys them,* by setting them (in their own conceit) above reproofs, by which they might be brought to that repentance which alone will prevent their ruin. Those are marked for destruction that are let alone in sin, Hos. 4:17. And, if none dares declare his way to his face, much less dare any repay him what he has done and make him refund what he has obtained by injustice. He is one of those great flies which break through the cobwebs of the law, that hold only the little ones. This emboldens sinners in their sinful ways that they can browbeat justice and make it afraid to meddle with them. But there is a day coming when those shall be told of their faults who now would not bear to hear of them, those shall have their sins set in order before them, and their way declared to their face, to their everlasting confusion, who would not have it done here, to their conviction, and those who would not repay the wrongs they had done shall have them repaid to them. [2.] To die, and be buried in a great deal of pomp and magnificence, *v.* 32, 33. There is no remedy; he must die; that is the lot of all men; but every thing you can think of shall be done to take off the reproach of death. *First,* He shall have a splendid funeral — a poor thing for any man to be proud of the prospect of; yet with some it passes for a mighty thing. Well, *he shall be brought to the grave* in state, surrounded with all the honours of the heralds' office and all the respect his friends can then pay to his remains. *The rich man died, and was buried,* but no mention is made of the poor man's burial, Lu. 16:22. *Secondly,* He shall have a stately monument erected over him. *He shall remain in the tomb* with a *Hic jacet — Here lies,* over him, and a large encomium. Perhaps it is meant of the embalming of his body to preserve it, which was a piece of honour anciently done by the Egyptians to their great men. He *shall watch in the tomb* (so the word is), shall abide solitary and quiet there, as a watchman in his tower. *Thirdly, The clods of the valley shall be sweet to him;* there shall be as much done as can be with rich odours to take off the noisomeness of the grave, as by lamps to set aside the darkness of it, which perhaps was referred to in the foregoing phrase of *watching in the tomb.* But it is all a jest; what is the light, or what the perfume, to a man that is dead? *Fourthly,* It shall be alleged, for the lessening of the disgrace of death, that it is the common lot: He has only yielded to fate, *and every man shall draw after him, as there are innumerable before him.* Note, Death is the way of all the earth: when we are to cross that darksome valley we must consider, 1. That there are innumerable before us; it is a tracked road, which may help to take off the terror of it. To die is *ire ad plures — to go to the great majority.* 2. That every man shall draw after us. As there is a plain track before, so there is a long train behind; we are neither the first nor the last that pass through that dark entry. Every one must go in his own order, the order appointed of God.

2. From all this Job infers the impertinency of their discourses, *v.* 34. (1.) Their foundation is rotten, and they went upon a wrong hypothesis: *"In your answers there remains falsehood;* what you have said stands not only unproved but disproved, and lies under such an imputation of falsehood as you cannot clear it from." (2.) Their building was therefore weak and tottering: *"You comfort me in vain.* All you have said gives me no relief; you tell me that I shall prosper again if I turn to God, but you go upon this presumption, that piety shall certainly be crowned with prosperity, which is false; and therefore how can your inference from it yield me any comfort?" Note, Where there is not truth there is little comfort to be expected.

CHAPTER 22

Eliphaz here leads on a third attack upon poor Job, in which Bildad followed him, but Zophar drew back, and quitted the field. It was one of the unhappinesses of Job, as it is of many an honest man, to be misunderstood by his friends. He had spoken of the prosperity of wicked men in this world as a mystery of Providence, but they took it for a reflection upon Providence, as countenancing their wickedness; and they reproached him accordingly. In this chapter, I. Eliphaz checks him for his complaints of God, and of his dealings with him, as if he thought God had done him wrong (*v.* 2–4). II. He charges him with many high crimes and misdemeanours, for which he supposes God was now punishing him. 1. Oppression and injustice (*v.* 5–11). 2. Atheism and infidelity (*v.* 12–14). III. He compares his case to that of the old world (*v.* 15–20). IV. He gives him very good counsel, assuring him that, if he would take it, God would return in mercy to him and he should return to his former prosperity (*v.* 21–30).

Verses 1–4

Eliphaz here insinuates that, because Job complained so much of his afflictions, he thought God was unjust in afflicting him; but it was a strained *innuendo.* Job was far from thinking so. What Eliphaz says here is therefore unjustly applied to Job, but in itself it is very true and good,

I. That when God does us good it is not because he is indebted to us; if he were, there might be some colour to say, when he afflicts us, "He does not deal fairly with us." But whoever pretends that he has by any meritorious action made God his debtor, let him prove this debt, and he shall be sure not to lose it, Rom. 11:35. *Who has given to him, and it shall be recompensed to him again?* But Eliphaz here shows that the righteousness and perfection of the best man in the world are no real benefit or advantage to God, and therefore cannot be thought to merit any thing from him. 1. Man's piety is no profit to God, no gain, *v.* 1, 2. If we could by any thing merit from God, it would be by our piety, our being righteous, and making our way perfect. If that will not merit, surely nothing else will. If a man cannot make God his debtor by his godliness, and honesty, and obedience to his laws, much less can he by his wit, and learning, and worldly policy. Now Eliphaz here asks whether any man can possibly be *profitable to God.* It is certain that he cannot. By no means. *He that is wise may be profitable to himself.* Note, Our wisdom and piety are that by which we ourselves are, and are likely to be, great gainers. *Wisdom is profitable to direct,* Eccl. 10:10. *Godliness is profitable to all things,* 1 Tim. 4:8. *If thou be wise, thou shalt be wise for thyself,* Prov. 9:12. The gains of religion are infinitely greater than the losses of it, and so it will appear when they are balanced. But can a man be thus profitable to God? No, for such is the perfection of God that he cannot receive any benefit or advantage by men; what can be added to that which is infinite? And such is the weakness and imperfection of man that he cannot offer any benefit or advantage to God. Can the light of a candle be profitable to the sun or the drop of the bucket to the ocean? He that is wise is profitable to himself, for his own direction and defence, his own credit and comfort; he can with his wisdom entertain himself and enrich himself; but can he so be profitable to God? No; God needs not us nor our services. We are undone, for ever undone, without him; but he is happy, for ever happy, without us. *Is it any gain to him,* any real addition to his glory or wealth, *if we make our way perfect?* Suppose it were absolutely perfect, yet what is God the better? Much less when it is so far short of being perfect. 2. It is no pleasure to him. God has indeed expressed himself in his word well pleased with the righteous; his countenance beholds them and his delight is in them and their prayers; but all that adds nothing to the infinite satisfaction and complacency which the Eternal Mind has in itself. God can enjoy himself without us, though we could have but little enjoyment of ourselves without our friends. This magnifies his condescension, in that, though our services be no real profit or pleasure to him, yet he invites, encourages, and accepts them.

II. That when God restrains or rebukes us it is not because he is in danger from us or jealous of us (*v.* 4): *"Will he reprove thee for fear of thee,* and take thee down from thy prosperity lest thou shouldst grow too great for him, as princes sometimes have thought it a piece of policy to curb the growing greatness of a subject, lest he should become formidable?" Satan indeed suggested to our first parents that God forbade them the tree of knowledge for fear of them, lest they should be as gods, and so become rivals with him; but it was a base insinuation. God rebukes the good because he loves them, but he never rebukes the great because he fears them. He does not *enter into judgment* with men, that is, pick a quarrel with them and seek occasion against them, through fear lest they should eclipse his honour or endanger his interest. Magistrates punish offenders for fear of them. Pharaoh oppressed Israel because he feared them. It was for fear that Herod slew the children of Bethlehem and that the Jews persecuted Christ and his apostles. But God does not, as they did, pervert justice for fear of any. See *ch.* 35:5–8.

Verses 5–14

Eliphaz and his companions had condemned Job, in general, as a wicked man and a hypocrite; but none of them had descended to particulars, nor drawn up any articles of impeachment against him, until Eliphaz did so here, where he positively and expressly charges him with many high crimes and misdemeanours, which, if he had really been guilty of them, might well have justified them in their harsh censures of him. "Come," says Eliphaz, "we have been too long beating about the bush, too tender of Job and afraid of grieving him, which has but confirmed him in his self-justification. It is high time to deal plainly with him. We have condemned him by parables, but that does not answer the end; he is not prevailed with to condemn himself. We must therefore plainly tell him, *Thou art the man,* the tyrant, the oppressor, the atheist, we have been speaking of all this while. *Is not thy wickedness great?* Certainly it is, or else thy troubles would not be so great. I appeal to thyself, and thy own conscience; are not *thy iniquities infinite,* both in number and heinousness?" Strictly taken, nothing is infinite but God; but he means this, that his sins were more than could be counted and more heinous than could be conceived. Sin, being committed against Infinite Majesty, has in it a kind of infinite malignity. But when Eliphaz charges Job thus highly, and ventures to descend to particulars too, laying to his charge that which he knew not, we may take occasion hence, 1. To be angry at those who unjustly censure and condemn their brethren. For aught I know, Eliphaz, in accusing Job falsely, as he does here, was guilty of as great a sin and as great a wrong to Job as the Sabeans and Chaldeans that robbed him; for a man's good name is more precious and valuable than his wealth. It is against all the laws of justice, charity, and friendship, either to raise or receive calumnies, jealousies, and evil surmises, concerning others; and it is the more base and disingenuous if we thus vex those that are in distress and add to their affliction. Eliphaz could produce no instances of Job's guilt in any of the particulars that follow here, but seems resolved to calumniate boldly, and throw all the reproach he could on Job, not doubting but that some would cleave to him. 2. To pity those who are thus censured and condemned. Innocency itself will be no security against a false and foul tongue. Job, whom God himself praised as the best man in the world, is here represented by one of his friends, and he a wise and good man too, as one of the greatest villains in nature. Let us not think it strange if at any time we be thus blackened, but learn how to pass by evil report as well as good, and commit our cause, as Job did his, to him that judgeth righteously.

Let us see the particular articles of this charge.

I. He charged him with oppression and injustice, that, when he was in prosperity, he not only did no good with his wealth and power, but did a great deal of hurt with them. This was utterly false, as appears by the account Job gives of himself (*ch.* 29:12, etc.) and the character God gave of him, *ch.* 1. And yet,

1. Eliphaz branches out this charge into divers particulars, with as much assurance as if he could call witnesses to prove upon oath every article of it. He tells him, (1.) That he had been cruel and unmerciful to the poor. As a magistrate he ought to have protected them and seen them provided for; but Eliphaz suspects that he never did them any kindness, but all the mischief his power enabled him to do, — that, for an inconsiderable debt, he demanded, and carried away by violence, a pawn of great value, even from his brother, whose honesty and sufficiency he could not but know (*v.* 6), *Thou hast taken a pledge from thy brother for nought,* or, as the Septuagint reads it, *Thou hast taken thy brethren for pledges,* and that for nought, imprisoned them, enslaved them, because they had nothing to pay, — that he had taken the very clothes of his insolvent tenants and debtors, so that he had *stripped them naked,* and left them so (the law of Moses forbade this, Ex. 22:26, Deu. 24:13), — he had not been charitable to the poor, no, not to poor travellers, and poor widows: *"Thou hast not given* so much as a cup of cold *water* (which would have cost thee nothing) *to the weary to drink,* when he begged for it (*v.* 7) and was ready to perish for want of it, nay, *thou hast withholden bread from the hungry* in their extremity, hast not only not given it, but hast forbidden the giving of it, which is *withholding good from those to whom it is really due,* Prov. 3:27. Poor widows, who while their husbands were living troubled nobody, but now were forced to seek relief, thou hast sent away empty from thy doors with a sad heart, *v.* 9. Those who came to thee for justice, thou didst send away unheard, unhelped; nay, though they came to thee full, thou didst squeeze them, and send them away empty; and, worst of all, *the arms of the fatherless have been broken;* those that could help themselves but little thou hast quite disabled to help themselves." This which is the blackest part of the charge, is but insinuated: *The arms of the fatherless have been broken.* He does not say, "Thou has broken them," but he would have it understood so, and if they be broken, and those who have power do not relieve them, they are chargeable with it. "They have been broken by those under thee, and thou hast connived at it, which brings thee under the guilt." (2.) That he had been partial to the rich and great (*v.* 8): *"As for the mighty man,* if he was guilty of any crime, he was never questioned for it: *he had the earth;* he *dwelt in it.* If he brought an action ever so unjustly, or if an action were ever so justly brought against him, yet he was sure to carry his cause in thy courts. The poor were not fed at thy door, while the rich were feasted at thy table." Contrary to this is Christ's rule for hospitality (Lu. 14:12–14); and Solomon says, *He that gives to the rich shall come to poverty.*

2. He attributes all his present troubles to these supposed sins (*v.* 10, 11): "Those that are guilty of such practices as these commonly bring themselves into just such a condition as thou art now in; and therefore we conclude thou hast been thus guilty." (1.) "The providence of God usually crosses and embarrasses such; and *snares are,* accordingly, *round about thee,* so that, which way soever thou steppest or lookest, thou findest thyself in distress; and others are as hard upon thee as thou hast been upon the poor." (2.) "Their consciences may be expected to terrify and accuse them. No sin makes a louder cry there than unmercifulness; and, accordingly, *sudden fear troubles thee;* and, though thou wilt not own it, it is guilt of this kind that creates thee all this terror." Zophar had insinuated this, *ch.* 20:19, 20. (3.) "They are brought to their wits' end, so amazed and bewildered that they know not what to do, and that also is thy case; for thou art *in darkness that thou canst not see* wherefore God contends with thee nor what is the best course for thee to take, *for abundance of waters cover thee,"* that is, "thou art in a mist, in the midst of dark waters, in the thick clouds of the sky." Note, Those that have not shown mercy may justly be denied the comfortable hope that they shall find mercy; and then what can they expect but snares, and darkness, and continual fear?

II. He charged him with atheism, infidelity, and gross impiety, and thought this was at the bottom of his injustice and oppressiveness: he that did not fear God did not regard man. He would have it thought that Job was an Epicurean, who did indeed own the being of God, but denied his providence, and fancied that he confined himself to the entertainments of the upper world and never concerned himself in the inhabitants and affairs of this.

1. Eliphaz referred to an important truth, which he thought, if Job had duly considered it, would have prevented him from being so passionate in his complaints and bold in justifying himself (*v.* 12): *Is not God in the height of heaven?* Yes, no doubt he is. No heaven so high but God is there; and in the highest heavens, the heavens of the blessed, the residence of his glory, he is present in a special manner. There he is pleased to manifest himself in a way peculiar to the upper world, and thence he is pleased to manifest himself in a way suited to this lower world. There is his throne; there is his court: he is called *the Heavens,* Dan. 4:26. Thus Eliphaz proves that a man cannot be profitable to God (*v.* 2), that he ought not to contend with God (it is his folly if he does), and that we ought always to address ourselves to God with very great reverence; for when we *behold the height of the stars, how high they are,* we should, at the same time, also consider the transcendent majesty of God, who is above the stars, and how high he is.

2. He charged it upon Job that he made a bad use of this doctrine, which he might have made so good a use of, *v.* 13. "This is *holding the truth in unrighteousness,* fighting against religion with its own weapons, and turning its own artillery upon itself: thou art willing to own that *God is in the height of heaven* but thence thou inferrest, *How doth God know?"* Bad men expel the fear of God out of their hearts by banishing the eye of God out of the world (Eze. 8:12), and care not what they do if they can but persuade themselves that God does not know. Eliphaz suspected that Job had such a notion of God as this, that, because he is in the height of heaven, (1.) It is therefore impossible for him to see and hear what is done at so great a distance as this earth, especially since there is a *dark cloud* (*v.* 13), many *thick clouds* (*v.* 14), that come between him and us, and *are a covering to him,* so that he cannot see, much less can he judge of, the affairs of this lower world; as if God had *eyes of flesh, ch.* 10:4. The interposing firmament is to him as transparent crystal, Eze. 1:22. Distance of place creates no difficulty to him who fills immensity, any more than distance of time to him who is eternal. Or, (2.) That it is therefore below him, and a diminution to his glory, to take cognizance of this inferior part of the creation: *He walks in the circuit of heaven,* and has enough to do to enjoy himself and his own perfections and glory in that bright and quiet world; why should he trouble himself about us? This is gross absurdity, as well as gross impiety, which Eliphaz here fathers upon Job; for it supposes that the administration of government is a burden and disparagement to the supreme governor and that the acts of justice and mercy are a toil to a mind infinitely wise, holy, and good. If the sun, a creature, and inanimate, can with his light and influence reach this earth, and every part of it (Ps. 19:6), even from that vast height of the visible heavens in which he is, and in the circuit of which he walks, and that through many a thick and dark cloud, shall we question it concerning the Creator?

Verses 15–20

Eliphaz, having endeavoured to convict Job, by setting his sins (as he thought) in order before him, here endeavours to awaken him to a sight and sense of his misery and danger by reason of sin; and this he does by comparing his case with that of the sinners of the old world; as if he had said, "Thy condition is bad now, but, unless thou repent, it will be worse, as theirs was — theirs *who were overflown with a flood,* as the old world (*v.* 16), and theirs the *remnant of whom the fire consumed"* (*v.* 20), namely, the Sodomites, who, in comparison of the old world, were but a remnant. And these two instances of the wrath of God against sin and sinners are more than once put together, for warning to a careless world, as by our Saviour (Lu. 17:26, etc.) and the apostle, 2 Pt. 2:5, 6. Eliphaz would have Job to *mark the old way which wicked men have trodden* (*v.* 15) and see what came of it, what the end of their way was. Note, There is an old way which wicked men have trodden. Religion had but newly entered when sin immediately followed it. But though it is an old way, a broad way, a tracked way, it is a dangerous way and it leads to destruction; and it is good for us to mark it, that we may not dare to walk in it. Eliphaz here puts Job in mind of it, perhaps in opposition to what he had said of the prosperity of the wicked; as if he had said, "Thou canst find out here and there a single instance, it may be, of a wicked man ending his days in peace; but what is that to those two great instances of the final perdition of ungodly men — the drowning of the whole world and the burning of Sodom?" destructions by wholesale, in which he thinks Job may, as in a glass, see his own face. Observe, 1. The ruin of those sinners (*v.* 16): *They were cut down out of time;* that is, they were cut off in the midst of their days, when, as man's time then went, many of them might, in the course of nature, have lived some hundreds of years longer, which made their immature extirpation the more grievous. They were *cut down out of time,* to be hurried into eternity. And their foundation, the earth on which they built themselves and all their hopes, was *overflown with a flood,* the flood which was *brought in upon the world of the ungodly,* 2 Pt. 2:5. Note, Those who build upon the sand choose a foundation which will be *overflown* when *the rains descend and the floods come* (Mt. 7:27), and then their building must needs fall and they perish in the ruins of it, and repent of their folly when it is too late. 2. The sin of those sinners, which brought that ruin (*v.* 17): *They said unto God, Depart from us.* Job had spoken of some who said so and yet prospered, *ch.* 21:14. "But these did not (says Eliphaz); they found to their cost what it was to set God at defiance. Those who were resolved to lay the reins on the neck of their appetites and passions began with this; they said unto God, *Depart;* they abandoned all religion, hated the thoughts of it, and desired to live *without God in the world;* they shunned his word, and silenced conscience, his deputy. *And what can the Almighty do for them?"* Some make this to denote the justness of their punishment. They said to God, *Depart from us;* and then *what could the Almighty do with them but cut them off?* Those who will not submit to God's golden sceptre must expect to be broken to pieces with his iron rod. Others make it to denote the injustice of their sin: But *what hath the Almighty done against them?* What iniquity have they found in him, or wherein has he wearied them? Mic. 6:3; Jer. 2:5. Others make it to denote the reason of their sin: They say unto God, *Depart,* asking *what the Almighty can do to them.* "What has he done to oblige us? What can he do in a way of wrath to make us miserable, or in a way of favour to make us happy?" As they argue, Zep. 1:12. *The Lord will not do good, neither will he do evil.* Eliphaz shows the absurdity of this in one word, and that is, calling God *the Almighty;* for, if he be so, what cannot he do? But it is not strange if those cast off all religion who neither dread God's wrath nor desire his favour. 3. The aggravation of this sin: *Yet he had filled their houses with good things, v.* 18. Both those of the old world and those of Sodom had great plenty of all the delights of sense; for *they ate, they drank, they bought, they sold,* etc. (Lu. 17:27), so that they had no reason to ask *what the Almighty could do for them,* for they lived upon his bounty, no reason to bid him depart from them who had been so kind to them. Many have their houses full of goods but their hearts empty of grace, and thereby are marked for ruin. 4. The protestation which Eliphaz makes against the principles and practices of those wicked people: *But the counsel of the wicked is far from me.* Job had said so (*ch.* 21:16) and Eliphaz will not be behind him. If they cannot agree in their own principles concerning God, yet they agree in renouncing the principles of those that live without God in the world. Note, Those that differ from each other in some matters of religion, and are engaged in disputes about them, yet ought unanimously and vigorously to appear against atheism and irreligion, and to take care that their disputes do not hinder either their vigour or unanimity in that common cause of God, that righteous cause. 5. The pleasure and satisfaction which the righteous shall have in this. (1.) In seeing the wicked destroyed, *v.* 19. They shall *see it,* that is, observe it, and take notice of it (Hos. 14:9); and they shall be *glad,* not to see their fellow-creatures miserable, or any secular turn of their own served, or point gained, but to see God glorified, the word of God fulfilled, the power of oppressors broken, and thereby the oppressed relieved — to see sin shamed, atheists and infidels confounded, and fair warning given to all others to shun such wicked courses. Nay, they shall *laugh them to scorn,* that is, they justly might do it, they shall do it, as God does it, in a holy manner, Ps. 2:4; Prov. 1:26. They shall take occasion thence to expose the folly of sinners and show how ridiculous their principles are, though they call themselves wits. *Lo, this is the man that made not God his strength;* and see what comes of it, Ps. 52:7. Some understand this of righteous Noah and his family, who beheld the destruction of the old world and rejoiced in it, as he had grieved for their impiety. Lot, who saw the ruin of Sodom, had the same reason to rejoice, 2 Pt. 2:7, 8. (2.) In seeing themselves distinguished (*v.* 20): *"Whereas our substance is not cut down,* as theirs was, and as thine is; we continue to prosper, which is a sign that we are the favourites of Heaven, and in the right." The same rule that served him to condemn Job by served him to magnify himself and his companions by. *His* substance is cut down; therefore he is a wicked man; *ours* is not; therefore we are righteous. But it is a deceitful rule to judge by; for none knows love or hatred by all that is before him. If others be consumed, and we be not, instead of censuring them and lifting up ourselves, as Eliphaz does here, we ought to be thankful to God and take it for a warning to ourselves to prepare for similar calamities.

Verses 21–30

Methinks I can almost forgive Eliphaz his hard censures of Job, which we had in the beginning of the chapter, though they were very unjust and unkind, for this good counsel and encouragement which he gives him in these verses with which he closes his discourse, and than which nothing could be better said, nor more to the purpose. Though he thought him a bad man, yet he saw reason to have hopes concerning him, that, for all this, he would be both pious and prosperous. But it is strange that out of the same mouth, and almost in the same breath, both sweet waters and bitter should proceed. Good men, though they may perhaps be put into a heat, yet sometimes will talk themselves into a better temper, and, it may be, sooner than another could talk them into it. Eliphaz had laid before Job the miserable condition of a wicked man, that he might frighten him into repentance. Here, on the other hand, he shows him the happiness which those may be sure of that do repent, that he might allure and encourage him to it. Ministers must try both ways in dealing with people, must speak to them from Mount Sinai by the terrors of the law, and from Mount Sion by the comforts of the gospel, must set before them both life and death, good and evil, the blessing and the curse. Now here observe,

I. The good counsel which Eliphaz gives to Job; and good counsel it is to us all, though, as to Job, it was built upon a false supposition that he was a wicked man and now a stranger and enemy to God. 1. *Acquaint now thyself with God. Acquiesce in God;* so some. It is our duty at all times, especially when we are in affliction, to accommodate ourselves to, and quiet ourselves in, all the disposals of the divine Providence. *Join thyself to him* (so some); fall in with his interests, and act no longer in opposition to him. Our translators render it well, *"Acquaint thyself with him;* be not such a stranger to him as thou hast made thyself by casting off the fear of him and restraining prayer before him." It is the duty and interest of every one of us to acquaint himself with God. We must get the knowledge of him, fix our affections on him, join ourselves to him in a covenant of friendship, and then set up, and keep up, a constant correspondence with him in the ways he has appointed. It is our honour that we are made capable of this acquaintance, our misery that by sin we have lost it, our privilege that through Christ we are invited to return to it; and it will be our unspeakable happiness to contract and cultivate this acquaintance. 2. *"Be at peace,* at peace with thyself, not fretful, uneasy, and in confusion; let not thy heart be troubled, but be quiet and calm, and well composed. Be at peace with thy God; be reconciled to him. Do not carry on this unholy war. Thou complainest that God is thy enemy; be thou his friend." It is the great concern of every one of us to make our peace with God, and it is necessary in order to our comfortable acquaintance with him; for *how can two walk together except they be agreed?* Amos 3:3. This we must do quickly, now, before it be too late. *Agree with thy adversary while thou art in the way.* This we are earnestly urged to do. Some read it, "Acquaint thyself, *I pray thee,* with him, and be at peace." God himself beseeches us; ministers, in Christ's stead, pray us to be reconciled. Can we gainsay such entreaties? 3. *Receive the law from his mouth, v.* 22. "Having made thy peace with God, submit to his government, and resolve to be ruled by him, that thou mayest keep thyself in his love." We receive our being and maintenance from God. From him we hope to receive our bliss, and from him we must receive law. *Lord, what wilt thou have me to do?* Acts 9:6. Which way soever we receive the intimations of his will we must have our eye to him; whether he speaks by scripture, ministers, conscience, or Providence, we must take the word as from his mouth and bow our souls to it. Though, in Job's time, we do not know that there was any written word, yet there was a revelation of God's will to be received. Eliphaz looked upon Job as a wicked man, and was pressing him to repent and reform. Herein consists the conversion of a sinner — his receiving the law from God's mouth and no longer from the world and the flesh. Eliphaz, being now in contest with Job, appeals to the word of God for the ending of the controversy. "Receive that, and be determined by it." *To the law and to the testimony.* 4. *Lay up his word in thy heart.* It is not enough to receive it, but we must retain it, Prov. 3:18. We must lay it up as a thing of great value, that it may be safe; and we must lay it up in our hearts, as a thing of great use, that it may be ready to us when there is occasion and we may neither lose it wholly nor be at a loss for it in a time of need. 5. *Return to the Almighty, v.* 23. "Do not only turn from sin, but turn to God and thy duty. Do not only turn towards the Almighty in some good inclinations and good beginnings, but *return to him;* return home to him, quite to him, so as to reach to the Almighty, by a universal reformation, an effectual thorough change of thy heart and life, and a firm resolution to cleave to him;" so Mr. Poole. 6. *Put away iniquity far from thy tabernacle.* This was the advice Zophar gave him, *ch.* 11:14. *"Let not wickedness dwell in thy tabernacle.* Put iniquity far off, the further the better, not only from thy heart and hand, but from thy house. Thou must not only not be wicked thyself, but must reprove and restrain sin in those that are under thy charge." Note, Family reformation is needful reformation; we and our house must serve the Lord.

II. The good encouragement which Eliphaz gives Job, that he shall be very happy, if he will but take this good counsel. In general, *"Thereby good shall come unto thee* (*v.* 21); the good that has now departed from thee, all the good thy heart can desire, temporal, spiritual, eternal good, shall come to thee. God shall come to thee, into covenant and communion with thee; and he brings all good with him, all good in him. Thou art now ruined and brought down, but, if thou return to God, *thou shalt be built up* again, and thy present ruins shall be repaired. Thy family shall be built up in children, thy estate in wealth, and thy soul in holiness and comfort." The promises which Eliphaz here encourages Job with are reducible to three heads: —

1. That his estate should prosper, and temporal blessings should be bestowed abundantly on him; for godliness has the promise of the life that now is. It is promised,

(1.) That he shall be very rich (*v.* 24): *"Thou shalt lay up gold as dust,* in such great abundance, and *shalt have plenty of silver* (*v.* 25), whereas now thou art poor and stripped of all." Job had been rich. Eliphaz suspected he got his riches by fraud and oppression, and therefore they were taken from him: but if he would return to God and his duty, [1.] He should have more wealth than ever he had, not only thousands of sheep and oxen, the wealth of farmers, but thousands of gold and silver, the wealth of princes, *ch.* 3:15. Abundantly more riches, true riches, are to be got by the service of God than by the service of the world. [2.] He should have it more sure to him: *"Thou shalt lay it up* in good hands, and hold that which is got by thy piety by a surer tenure than that which thou didst get by thy iniquity." *Thou shalt have silver of strength* (for so the word is), which, being honestly got, will wear well — silver like steel. [3.] He should, by the grace of God, be kept from setting his heart so much upon it as Eliphaz thought he had done; and then wealth is a blessing indeed when we are not ensnared with the love of it. Thou shalt *lay up gold;* but how? Not as thy treasure and portion, but *as dust,* and *as the stones of the brooks.* So little shalt thou value it or expect from it that thou shalt lay it at thy feet (Acts 4:35), not in thy bosom.

(2.) That yet he shall be very safe. Whereas men's riches usually expose them to danger, and he had owned that in his prosperity he *was not in safety* (*ch.* 3:26), now he might be secure; for *the Almighty shall be thy defender;* nay, he shall be *thy defence, v.* 25. He *shall be thy gold;* so it is in the margin, and it is the same word that is used (*v.* 24) for gold, but it signifies also a strong-hold, because *money is a defence,* Eccl. 7:12. Worldlings make gold their god, saints make God their gold; and those that are enriched with his favour and grace may truly be said *to have abundance of the best gold,* and best laid up. We read it, *"He shall be thy defence* against the incursions of neighbouring spoilers: thy wealth shall not then lie exposed as it did to Sabeans and Chaldeans," which, some think, is the meaning of that, *Thou shalt put away iniquity far from thy tabernacle,* taking it as a promise. "The iniquity or wrong designed against thee shall be put off and shall not reach thee." Note, Those must needs be safe that have Omnipotence itself for their defence, Ps. 91:1–3.

2. That his soul should prosper, and he should be enriched with spiritual blessings, which are the best blessings.

(1.) That he should live a life of complacency in God (*v.* 26): *"For then shalt thou have thy delight in the Almighty;* and *thus* the Almighty comes to be thy gold by thy delighting in him, as worldly people delight in their money. He shall be thy wealth, thy defence, thy dignity; for he shall be thy delight." The way to have our heart's desire is to make God our heart's delight, Ps. 37:4. If God give us himself to be our joy, he will deny us nothing that is good for us. "Now, God is a terror to thee; he is so by thy own confession (*ch.* 6:4; 16:9; 19:11); but, if thou wilt return to him, then, and not till then, *he will be thy delight;* and it shall be as much a pleasure to thee to think of him as ever it was a pain." No delight is comparable to the delight which gracious souls have in the Almighty; and those that acquaint themselves with him, and submit themselves entirely to him, shall find his favour to be, not only their strength, but their song.

(2.) That he should have a humble holy confidence towards God, such as those are said to have *whose hearts condemn them not,* 1 Jn. 3:21. "Then *shalt* thou *lift up thy face to God* with boldness, and not be afraid, as thou now art, to draw near to him. Thy countenance is now fallen, and thou lookest dejected; but, when thou hast made thy peace with God, thou shalt blush no more, tremble no more, and hang thy head no more, as thou dost now, but shalt cheerfully, and with a gracious assurance, show thyself to him, pray before him, and expect blessings from him."

(3.) That he should maintain a constant communion with God, "The correspondence, once settled, shall be kept up to thy unspeakable satisfaction. Letters shall be both statedly and occasionally interchanged between thee and heaven," *v.* 27. [1.] "Thou shalt by prayer send letters to God: *Thou shalt make thy prayer"* (the word is, *Thou shalt multiply* thy prayers) "unto him, and he will not think thy letters troublesome, though many and long. The oftener we come to the throne of grace the more welcome. Under all thy burdens, in all thy wants, cares, and fears, thou shalt send to heaven for guidance and strength, wisdom, and comfort, and good success." [2.] "He shall, by his providence and grace, answer those letters, and give thee what thou askest of him, either in kind or kindness: *He shall hear thee,* and make it to appear he does so by what he does for thee and in thee." [3.] "Then thou shalt by thy praises reply to the gracious answers which he sent thee: *Thou shalt pay thy vows,* and that shall be acceptable to him and fetch in further mercy." Note, When God performs that which in our distress we prayed for we must make conscience of performing that which we then promised, else we do not deal honestly. If we promised nothing else we promised to be thankful, and that is enough, for it includes all, Ps. 116:14.

(4.) That he should have inward satisfaction in the management of all his outward affairs (*v.* 28): *"Thou shalt decree a thing and it shall be established unto thee,"* that is, "Thou shalt frame all thy projects and purposes with so much wisdom, and grace, and resignation to the will of God, that the issue of them shall be to thy heart's content, just as thou wouldst have it to be. Thou shalt *commit thy works unto the Lord* by faith and prayer, and then *thy thoughts shall be established;* thou shalt be easy and pleased, whatever occurs, Prov. 16:3. This the grace of God shall work in thee; nay, sometimes the providence of God shall give thee the very thing thou didst desire and pray for, and give it thee in thy own way, and manner, and time. *Be it unto thee even as thou wilt."* When at any time an affair succeeds just according to the scheme we laid, and our measures are in nothing broken, nor are we put upon new counsels, then we must own the performance of this promise, *Thou shalt decree a thing and it shall be established unto thee.* "Whereas now thou complainest of darkness round about thee, then *the light shall shine on thy ways;"* that is, "God shall guide and direct thee, and then it will follow, of course, that he shall prosper and succeed thee in all thy undertakings. God's wisdom shall be thy guide, his favour thy comfort, and thy ways shall be so under both those lights that thou shalt have a comfortable enjoyment of what is present and a comfortable prospect of what is future," Ps. 90:17.

(5.) That even in times of common calamity and danger he should have abundance of joy and hope (*v.* 29): *"When men are cast down* round about thee, cast down in their affairs, cast down in their spirits, sinking, desponding, and ready to despair, *then shalt thou say, There is lifting up.* Thou shalt find that in thyself which will not only bear thee up under thy troubles, and keep thee from fainting, but lift thee up above thy troubles and enable thee to rejoice evermore." When men's *hearts fail them for fear,* then shall Christ's disciples *lift up their heads for joy,* Lu. 21:26–28. Thus are they made to *ride upon the high places of the earth* (Isa. 58:14), and that which will lift them up is the belief of this, that God will save the humble person. Those that humble themselves shall be exalted, not only in honour, but in comfort.

3. That he should be a blessing to his country and an instrument of good to many (*v.* 30): *God shall,* in answer to thy prayers, *deliver the island of the innocent,* and have a regard therein to *the pureness of thy hands,* which is necessary to the acceptableness of our prayers, 1 Tim. 2:8. But, because we may suppose the innocent not to need deliverance (it was guilty Sodom that wanted the benefit of Abraham's intercession), I incline to the marginal reading, *The innocent shall deliver the island,* by their advice (Eccl. 9:14, 15) and by their prayers and their interest in heaven, Acts 27:24. Or, *He shall deliver those that are not innocent, and they are delivered by the pureness of thy hands;* as it may be read, and most probably. Note, A good man is a public good. Sinners fare the better for saints, whether they are aware of it or no. If Eliphaz intended hereby (as some think he did) to insinuate that Job's prayers were not prevailing, nor his hands pure (for then he would have relieved others, much more himself), he was afterwards made to see his error, when it appeared that Job had a better interest in heaven than he had; for he and his three friends, who in this matter were not innocent, were delivered by *the pureness of Job's hands, ch.* 42:8.

CHAPTER 23

This chapter begins Job's reply to Eliphaz. In this reply he takes no notice of his friends, either because he saw it was to no purpose or because he liked the good counsel Eliphaz gave him in the close of his discourse so well that he would make no answer to the peevish reflections he began with; but he appeals to God, begs to have his cause heard, and doubts not but to make it good, having the testimony of his own conscience concerning his integrity. Here seems to be a struggle between flesh and spirit, fear and faith, throughout this chapter. I. He complains of his calamitous condition, and especially of God's withdrawings from him, so that he could not get his appeal heard (*v.* 2–5), nor discern the meaning of God's dealings with him (*v.* 8, 9), nor gain any hope of relief (*v.* 13, 14). This made deep impressions of trouble and terror upon him (*v.* 15–17). But, II. In the midst of these complaints he comforts himself with the assurance of God's clemency (*v.* 6, 7), and his own integrity, which God himself was a witness to (*v.* 10–12). Thus was the light of his day like that spoken of, Zec. 14:6, 7, neither perfectly clear nor perfectly dark, but "at evening time it was light."

Verses 1–7

Job is confident that he has wrong done him by his friends, and therefore, ill as he is, he will not give up the cause, nor let them have the last word. Here,

I. He justifies his own resentments of his trouble (*v.* 2): *Even to day,* I own, *my complaint is bitter;* for the affliction, the cause of the complaint, is so. There are *wormwood and gall in the affliction and misery; my soul has them still in remembrance* and is embittered by them, Lam. 3:19, 20. *Even to day is my complaint* counted *rebellion* (so some read it); his friends construed the innocent expressions of his grief into reflections upon God and his providence, and called them *rebellion.* "But," says he, "I do not complain more than there is cause; *for my stroke is heavier than my groaning.* Even today, after all you have said to convince and comfort me, still the pains of my body and the wounds of my spirit are such that I have reason enough for my complaints, if they were more bitter than they are." We wrong God if our groaning be heavier than our stroke, like froward children, who, when they cry for nothing, have justly something given them to cry for; but we do not wrong ourselves though our stroke be heavier than our groaning, for little said is soon amended.

II. He appeals from the censures of his friends to the just judgment of God; and this he thought was an evidence for him that he was not a hypocrite, for then he durst not have made such an appeal as this. St Paul comforted himself in this, that *he that judged him was the Lord,* and therefore he valued not man's judgment (1 Co. 4:3, 4), but he was willing to wait till the appointed day of decision came; whereas Job is impatient, and passionately wishes to have the judgment-day anticipated, and to have his cause tried quickly, as it were, by a special commission. The apostle found it necessary to press it much upon suffering Christians patiently to expect the Judge's coming, Jam. 5:7–9.

1. He is so sure of the equity of God's tribunal that he longs to appear before it (*v.* 3): *O that I knew where I might find him!* This may properly express the pious breathings of a soul convinced that it has by sin lost God and is undone for ever if it recover not its interest in his favour. "O that I knew how I might recover his favour! How I might come into his covenant and communion with him!" Mic. 6:6, 7. It is the cry of a poor deserted soul. *"Saw you him whom my soul loveth? O that I knew where I might find him!* O that he who has laid open the way to himself would direct me into it and lead me in it!" But Job here seems to complain too boldly that his friends wronged him and he knew not which way to apply himself to God to have justice done him, else he would go even to his seat, to demand it. A patient waiting for death and judgment is our wisdom and duty, and, if we duly consider things, that cannot be without a holy fear and trembling; but a passionate wishing for death or judgment, without any such fear and trembling, is our sin and folly, and ill becomes us. Do we know what death and judgment are, and are we so very ready for them, that we need not time to get readier? *Woe to those that* thus, in a heat, *desire the day of the Lord,* Amos 5:18.

2. He is so sure of the goodness of his own cause that he longs to be opening it at God's bar (*v.* 4): *"I would order my cause before him,* and set it in a true light. I would produce the evidences of my sincerity in a proper method, and would *fill my mouth with arguments* to prove it." We may apply this to the duty of prayer, in which we have *boldness to enter into the holiest* and to come even to the footstool of the throne of grace. We have not only liberty of access, but liberty of speech. We have leave, (1.) To be particular in our requests, *to order our cause before God,* to speak the whole matter, to lay before him all our grievances, in what method we think most proper; we durst not be so free with earthly princes as a humble holy soul may be with God. (2.) To be importunate in our requests. We are allowed, not only to pray, but to plead, not only to ask, but to argue; nay, to *fill our mouths with arguments,* not to move God (he is perfectly apprized of the merits of the cause without our showing), but to move ourselves, to excite our fervency and encourage our faith in prayer.

3. He is so sure of a sentence in favour of him that he even longed to hear it (*v.* 5): *"I would know the words which he would answer me,"* that is, "I would gladly hear what God will say to this matter in dispute between you and me, and will entirely acquiesce in his judgment." This becomes us, in all controversies; let the word of God determine them; let us know what he answers, and understand what he says. Job knew well enough what his friends would answer him; they would condemn him, and run him down. "But" (says he) *"I would* fain *know what God would answer me;* for I am sure his judgment is according to truth, which theirs is not. I cannot understand them; they talk so little to the purpose. But what he says I should understand and therefore be fully satisfied in."

III. He comforts himself with the hope that God would deal favourably with him in this matter, *v.* 6, 7. Note, It is of great use to us, in every thing wherein we have to do with God, to keep up good thoughts of him. He believes, 1. That God would not overpower him, that he would not deal with him either by absolute sovereignty or in strict justice, not with a high hand, nor with a strong hand: *Will he plead against me with his great power?* No. Job's friends pleaded against him with all the power they had; but will God do so? No; his power is all just and holy, whatever men's is. Against those that are obstinate in their unbelief and impenitency God will *plead with his great power;* their destruction will come *from the glory of his power.* But with his own people, that love him and trust in him, he will deal in tender compassion. 2. That, on the contrary, he would empower him to plead his own cause before God: *"He would put strength in me,* to support me and bear me up, in maintaining my integrity." Note, The same power that is engaged against proud sinners is engaged for humble saints, who prevail with God by strength derived from him, as Jacob did, Hos. 12:3. See Ps. 68:35. 3. That the issue would certainly be comfortable, *v.* 7. There, in the court of heaven, when the final sentence is to be given, *the righteous might dispute with him* and come off in his righteousness. Now, even the upright are often *chastened of the Lord,* and they cannot dispute against it; integrity itself is no fence either against calamity or calumny; but in that day *they shall not be condemned with the world,* though God may afflict by prerogative. *Then you shall discern between the righteous and the wicked* (Mal. 3:18), so vast will be the difference between them in their everlasting state; whereas now we can scarcely distinguish them, so little is the difference between them as to their outward condition, for all things come alike to all. Then, when the final doom is given, *"I shall be delivered for ever from my Judge,"* that is, "I shall be saved from the unjust censures of my friends and from that divine sentence which is now so much a terror to me." Those that are delivered up to God as their owner and ruler shall be for ever delivered from him as their judge and avenger; and there is no flying from his justice but by flying to his mercy.

Verses 8–12

Here, I. Job complains that he cannot understand the meaning of God's providences concerning him, but is quite at a loss about them (v. 8, 9): *I go forward, but he is not there*, etc. Eliphaz had bid him acquaint himself with God. "So I would, with all my heart," says Job, "If I knew how to get acquainted with him." He had himself a great desire to appear before God, and get a hearing of his case, but the Judge was not to be found. Look which way he would, he could see no sign of God's appearing for him to clear up his innocency. Job, no doubt, believed that God is every where present; but three things he seems to complain of here: — 1. That he could not fix his thoughts, nor form any clear judgment of things in his own mind. His mind was so hurried and discomposed with his troubles that he was like a man in a fright, or at his wits' end, who runs this way and that way, but, being in confusion, brings nothing to a head. By reason of the disorder and tumult his spirit was in he could not fasten upon that which he knew to be in God, and which, if he could but have mixed faith with it and dwelt upon it in his thoughts, would have been a support to him. It is the common complaint of those who are sick or melancholy that, when they would think of that which is good, they can make nothing of it. 2. That he could not find out the cause of his troubles, nor the sin which provoked God to contend with him. He took a view of his whole conversation, turned to every side of it, and could not perceive wherein he had sinned more than others, for which he should thus be punished more than others; nor could he discern what other end God should aim at in afflicting him thus. 3. That he could not foresee what would be in the end hereof, whether God would deliver him at all, nor, if he did, when or which way. He saw not his signs, nor was there any to tell him how long; as the church complains, Ps. 74:9. He was quite at a loss to know what God designed to do with him; and, whatever conjecture he advanced, still something or other appeared against it.

II. He satisfies himself with this, that God himself was a witness to his integrity, and therefore did not doubt but the issue would be good.

1. After Job had almost lost himself in the labyrinth of the divine counsels, how contentedly does he sit down, at length, with this thought: "Though *I* know not the way that he takes (for *his way is in the sea and his path in the great waters*, his thoughts and ways are infinitely above ours and it would be presumption in us to pretend to judge of them), yet *he knows the way that I take*," v. 10. That is, (1.) He is acquainted with it. His friends judged of that which they did not know, and therefore charged him with that which he was never guilty of; but God, who knew every step he had taken, would not do so, Ps. 139:3. Note, It is a great comfort to those who mean honestly that God understands their meaning, though men do not, cannot, or will not. (2.) He approves of it: "He knows that, however I may sometimes have *taken a false step*, yet I have still *taken a good way*, have *chosen the way of truth*, and therefore he knows it," that is, he accepts it, and is well pleased with it, as he is said to *know the way of the righteous*, Ps. 1:6. This comforted the prophet, Jer. 12:3. *Thou hast tried my heart towards thee*. From this Job infers, *When he hath tried me I shall come forth as gold*. Those that *keep the way of the Lord* may comfort themselves, when they are in affliction, with these three things: — [1.] That they are but tried. It is not intended for their hurt, but for their honour and benefit; *it is the trial of their faith*, 1 Pt. 1:7. [2.] That, when they are sufficiently tried, they shall come forth out of the furnace, and not be left to consume in it as dross or reprobate silver. The trial will have an end. *God will not contend for ever.* [3.] That they shall come forth as gold, pure in itself and precious to the refiner. They shall come forth as gold approved and improved, found to be good and made to be better. Afflictions are to us as we are; those that go gold into the furnace will come out no worse.

2. Now that which encouraged Job to hope that his present troubles would thus end well was the testimony of his conscience for him, that he had lived a good life in the fear of God.

(1.) That God's way was the way he walked in (v. 11): *"My foot hath held his steps,"* that is, "held to them, adhered closely to them; the steps he takes. I have endeavoured to conform myself to his example." Good people are followers of God. Or, "I have accommodated myself to his providence, and endeavoured to answer all the intentions of that, to follow Providence step by step." Or, "His steps are the steps he has appointed me to take; the way of religion and serious godliness — that way I have kept, and have not declined from it, not only not turned back from it by a total apostasy, but not turned aside out of it by any wilful transgression." His holding God's steps, and keeping his way, intimate that the tempter had used all his arts by fraud and force to draw him aside; but, with care and resolution, he had by the grace of God hitherto persevered, and those that will do so must hold and keep, hold with resolution and keep with watchfulness.

(2.) That God's word was the rule he walked by, v. 12. He governed himself by *the commandment of God's lips*, and would not go back from that, but go forward according to it. Whatever difficulties we may meet with in the way of God's commandments, though they lead us through a wilderness, yet we must never think of going back, but must press on towards the mark. Job kept closely to the law of God in his conversation, for both his judgment and his affection led him to it: *I have esteemed the words of his mouth more than my necessary food;* that is, he looked upon it as his necessary food; he could as well have lived without his daily bread as without the word of God. *I have laid it up* (so the word is), as those that lay up provision for a siege, or as Joseph laid up corn before the famine. Eliphaz had told him to *lay up God's words in his heart*, ch. 22:22. "I do," says he, "and always did, *that I might not sin against him,* and that, like the good householder, I might bring forth for the good of others." Note, The word of God is to our souls what our necessary food is to our bodies; it sustains the spiritual life and strengthens us for the actions of life; it is that which we cannot subsist without, and which nothing else can make up the want of: and we ought therefore so to esteem it, to take pains for it, hunger after it, feed upon it with delight, and nourish our souls with it; and this will be our rejoicing in the day of evil, as it was Job's here.

Verses 13–17

Some make Job to complain here that God dealt unjustly and unfairly with him in proceeding to punish him without the least relenting or relaxation, though he had such incontestable evidences to produce of his innocency. I am loth to think holy Job would charge the holy God with iniquity; but his complaint is indeed bitter and peevish, and he reasons himself into a sort of *patience per force*, which he cannot do without reflecting upon God as dealing hardly with him, but he must bear it because he cannot help it; the worst he says is that God deals unaccountably with him.

I. He lays down good truths, and truths which were capable of a good improvement, v. 13, 14. 1. That God's counsels are immutable: *He is in one mind, and who can turn him? He is one* (so some read it) or *in one;* he has no counsellors by whose interest he might be prevailed with to alter his purpose: he has no counsellors by whose interest he might be prevailed with to alter his purpose: he is one with himself, and never alters his mind, never alters his measures. Prayer has prevailed to change God's way and his providence, but never was his will or purpose changed; for *known unto God are all his works*. 2. That his power is irresistible: *What his soul desires* or designs *even that he does*, and nothing can stand in his way or put him upon new counsels. Men desire many things which they may not do, or cannot do, or dare not do. But God has an incontestable sovereignty; his will is so perfectly pure and right that it is highly fit he should pursue all its determinations. And he has an uncontrollable power. *None can stay his hand. Whatever the Lord pleased that did he* (Ps. 135:6), and always will, for it is always best. 3. That all he does is according to the counsel of his will (v. 14): *He performs the thing that is appointed for me.* Whatever happens to us, it is God that performs it (Ps. 57:2), and an admirable performance the whole will appear to be when the mystery of God shall be finished. He performs all that, and that only, which was appointed, and in the appointed time

and method. This may silence us, for what is appointed cannot be altered. But to consider that, when God was appointing us to eternal life and glory as our end, he was appointing to this condition, this affliction, whatever it is, in our way, this may do more than silence us, it may satisfy us that it is all for the best; though what he does we know not now, yet we shall know hereafter. 4. That all he does is according to the custom of his providence: *Many such things are with him*, that is, He does many things in the course of his providence which we can give no account of, but must resolve into his absolute sovereignty. Whatever trouble we are in others have been in the like. Our case is not singular; the same *afflictions are accomplished in our brethren*, 1 Pt. 5:9. Are we sick or sore, impoverished and stripped? Are our children removed by death or our friends unkind? This is what *God has appointed for us, and many such things are with him. Shall the earth be forsaken for us?*

II. He makes but a bad use of these good truths. Had he duly considered them, he might have said, "Therefore am I easy and pleased, and well reconciled to the way of my God concerning me; therefore will I rejoice in hope that my troubles will issue well at last." But he said, *Therefore am I troubled at his presence, v.* 15. Those are indeed of troubled spirits who are troubled at the presence of God, as the psalmist, who *remembered God and was troubled*, Ps. 77:3. See what confusion poor Job was now in, for he contradicted himself: just now he was troubled for God's absence (v. 8, 9); now he is troubled at his presence. *When I consider, I am afraid of him.* What he now felt made him fear worse. There is indeed that which, if we consider it, will show that we have cause to be afraid of God — his infinite justice and purity, compared with our own sinfulness and vileness; but if, withal, we consider his grace in a Redeemer, and our compliance with that grace, our fears will vanish and we shall see cause to hope in him. See what impressions were made upon him by the wounds of his spirit. 1. He was very fearful (v. 16): *The Almighty troubled him*, and so *made his heart soft*, that is, utterly unable to bear any thing, and afraid of every thing that stirred. There is a gracious softness, like that of Josiah, whose heart was tender, and trembled at the word of God; but this is meant of a grievous softness which apprehends every thing that is present to be pressing and every thing future to be threatening. 2. He was very fretful, peevish indeed, for he quarrels with God, (1.) Because he did not die before his troubles, that he might never have seen them (*Because I was not cut off before the darkness, v.* 17), and yet if, in the height of his prosperity, he had received a summons to the grave, he would have thought it hard. This may help to reconcile us to death, whenever it comes, that we do not know what evil we may be taken away from. But when trouble comes it is folly to wish we had not lived to see it and it is better to make the best of it. (2.) Because he was left to live so long in his troubles, and the darkness was not covered from his face by his being hidden in the grave. We should bear the darkness better than thus if we would but remember that to the upright there sometimes arises a marvellous light in the darkness; however, there is reserved for them a more marvellous light after it.

CHAPTER 24

Job having by his complaints in the foregoing chapter given vent to his passion, and thereby gained some ease, breaks them off abruptly, and now applies himself to a further discussion of the doctrinal controversy between him and his friends concerning the prosperity of wicked people. That many live at ease who yet are ungodly and profane, and despise all the exercises of devotion, he had shown, ch. 21. Now here he goes further, and shows that many who are mischievous to mankind, and live in open defiance to all the laws of justice and common honesty, yet thrive and succeed in their unrighteous practices; and we do not see them reckoned with in this world. What he had said before (ch. 12:6), "The tabernacles of robbers prosper," he here enlarges upon. He lays down his general proposition (v. 1), that the punishment of wicked people is not so visible and apparent as his friends supposed, and then proves it by an induction of particulars. I. Those that openly do wrong to their poor neighbours are not reckoned with, nor the injured righted (v. 2–12), though the former are very barbarous (v. 21, 22). II. Those that secretly practise mischief often go undiscovered and unpunished (v. 13–17). III. That God punished such by secret judgments and reserves them for future judgments (v. 18–20, and 23–25), so that, upon the whole matter, we cannot say that all who are in trouble are wicked; for it is certain that all who are in prosperity are not righteous.

Verses 1–12

Job's friends had been very positive in it that they

should soon see the fall of wicked people, how much soever they might prosper for a while. By no means, says Job; *though times are not hidden from the Almighty,* yet *those that know him do not presently see his day, v.* 1. 1. He takes it for granted that times are not hidden from the Almighty; past times are not hidden from his judgment (Eccl. 3:15), present times are not hidden from his providence (Mt. 10:29), future times are not hidden from his prescience, Acts 15:18. God governs the world, and therefore we may be sure he takes cognizance of it. Bad times are not hidden from him, though the bad men that make the times bad say one to another, He has *forsaken the earth,* Ps. 94:6, 7. Every man's times are in his hand, and under his eye, and therefore it is in his power to make the times of wicked men in this world miserable. He foresees the time of every man's death, and therefore, if wicked men die before they are punished for their wickedness, we cannot say, "They escaped him by surprise;" he foresaw it, nay, he ordered it. Before Job will enquire into the reasons of the prosperity of wicked men he asserts God's omniscience, as one prophet, in a similar case, asserts his righteousness (Jer. 12:1), another his holiness (Hab. 1:13), another his goodness to his own people, Ps. 73:1. General truths must be held fast, though we may find it difficult to reconcile them to particular events. 2. He yet asserts that those who know him (that is, wise and good people who are acquainted with him, and with whom his secret is) *do not see his day,* — the day of his judging for them; this was the thing he complained of in his own case (*ch.* 23:8), that he could not see God appearing on his behalf to plead his cause, — the day of his judging against open and notorious sinners, that is called *his day,* Ps. 37:13. We believe that day will come, but we do not see it, because it is future, and its presages are secret. 3. Though this is a mystery of Providence, yet there is a reason for it, and we shall shortly know why the judgment is deferred; even the wisest, and those who know God best, do not yet see it. God will exercise their faith and patience, and excite their prayers for the coming of his kingdom, for which they are to *cry day and night to him,* Lu. 18:7.

For the proof of this, that wicked people prosper, Job specifies two sorts of unrighteous ones, whom all the world saw thriving in their iniquity: —

I. Tyrants, and those that do wrong under pretence of law and authority. It is a melancholy sight which has often been *seen under the sun, wickedness in the place of judgment* (Eccl. 3:16), the unregarded *tears of the oppressed,* while *on the side of the oppressors there was power* (Eccl. 4:1), the *violent perverting of justice and judgment,* Eccl. 5:8. 1. They disseize their neighbours of their real estates, which came to them by descent from their ancestors. They *remove the land-marks,* under pretence that they were misplaced (*v.* 2), and so they encroach upon their neighbours' rights and think they effectually secure that to their posterity which they have got wrongfully, by making that to be an evidence for them which should have been an evidence for the rightful owner. This was forbidden by the law of Moses (Deu. 19:14), under a curse, Deu. 27:17. Forging or destroying deeds is now a crime equivalent to this. 2. They dispossess them of their personal estates, under colour of justice. *They violently take away flocks,* pretending they are forfeited, *and feed thereof;* as the rich man took the poor man's ewe lamb, 2 Sa. 12:4. If a poor fatherless child has but an ass of his own to get a little money with, they find some colour or other to take it away, because the owner is not able to contest with them. It is all one if a widow has but an ox for what little husbandry she has; under pretence of distraining for some small debt, or arrears of rent, this ox shall be taken for a pledge, though perhaps it is the widow's all. God has taken it among the titles of his honour to be a *Father of the fatherless and a judge of the widows;* and therefore those will not be reckoned his friends that do not to their utmost protect and help them; but those he will certainly reckon with as his enemies that vex and oppress them. 3. They take all occasions to offer personal abuses to them, *v.* 4. They will mislead them if they can when they meet them on the high-way, so that the poor and needy are forced to hide themselves from them, having no other way to secure themselves from them. They love in their hearts to banter people, and to make fools of them, and do them a mischief if they can, especially to triumph over poor people, whom they turn out of the way of getting relief, threaten to punish them as vagabonds, and so force them to abscond, and laugh at them when they have done. Some understand those barbarous actions (*v.* 9, 10) to be done by those oppressors that pretend law for what they do: *They pluck the fatherless from the breast;* that is, having made poor infants fatherless, they make them motherless too; having taken away the father's life, they break the mother's heart, and so starve the children and leave them to perish. Pharaoh and Herod plucked children from the breast to the sword; and we read of *children brought forth to the murderers,* Hos. 9:13. Those are inhuman murderers indeed that can with so much pleasure suck innocent blood. *They take a pledge of the poor,* and so they rob the spital; nay, they take the poor themselves for a pledge (as some read it), and probably it was under this pretence that they *plucked the fatherless from the breast,* distraining them for slaves, as Neh. 5:5. Cruelty to the poor is great wickedness and cries aloud for vengeance. Those who show no mercy to such as lie at their mercy shall themselves have judgment without mercy. Another instance of their barbarous treatment of those they have advantage against is that they take from them even their necessary food and raiment; they squeeze them so with their extortion that they *cause them to go naked without clothing* (*v.* 10) and so catch their death. And if a poor hungry family has gleaned a sheaf of corn, to make a little cake of, that they may eat it and die, even that they take away from them, being well pleased to see them perish for want, while they themselves are fed to the full. 4. They are very oppressive to the labourers they employ in their service. They not only give them no wages, though the labourer is worthy of his hire (and this is a crying sin, Jam. 5:4), but they will not so much as give them meat and drink: *Those that carry their sheaves are hungry;* so some read it (*v.* 10), and it agrees with *v.* 11, that those who *make oil within their walls,* and with a great deal of toil labour at the wine-presses, yet suffer thirst, which was worse than muzzling the mouth of the ox that treads out the corn. Those masters forget that they have a Master in heaven who will not allow the necessary supports of life to their servants and labourers, not caring whether they can live by their labour or no. 5. It is not only among the poor country people, but in the cities also, that we see the tears of the oppressed (*v.* 12): *Men groan from out of the city,* where the rich merchants and traders are as cruel with their poor debtors as the landlords in the country are with their poor tenants. In cities such cruel actions as these are more observed than in obscure corners of the country and the wronged have easier access to justice to right themselves; and yet the oppressors there fear neither the restraints of the law nor the just censures of their neighbours, but the oppressed groan and cry out like wounded men, and can no more ease and help themselves, for the oppressors are inexorable and deaf to their groans.

II. He speaks of robbers, and those that do wrong by downright force, as the bands of the Sabeans and Chaldeans, which had lately plundered him. He does not mention them particularly, lest he should seem partial to his own cause, and to judge of men (as we are apt to do) by what they are to us; but among the Arabians, the children of the east (Job's country), there were those that lived by spoil and rapine, making incursions upon their neighbours, and robbing travellers. See how they are described here, and what mischief they do, *v.* 5–8. 1. Their character is that they are *as wild asses in the desert,* untamed, untractable, unreasonable, Ishmael's character (Gen. 16:12), fierce and furious, and under no restraint of law or government, Jer. 2:23, 24. They choose the deserts for their dwelling, that they may be lawless and unsociable, and that they may have opportunity of doing the more mischief. The desert is indeed the fittest place for such wild people, *ch.* 39:6. But no desert can set men out of the reach of God's eye and hand. 2. Their trade is to steal, and to make a prey of all about them. They have chosen it as their trade; it is their work, because there is more to be got by it, and it is got more easily, than by an honest calling. They follow it as their trade; they follow it closely; *they go forth to* it as *their work,* as man goes forth to his labour, Ps. 104:23. They are diligent and take pains at it: They *rise betimes for a prey.* If a traveller be out early, they will be out as soon to rob him. They live by it as a man lives by his trade: *The wilderness* (not the grounds there but the roads there) *yieldeth food for them and for their children;* they maintain themselves and their families by robbing on the high-way, and bless themselves in it without any remorse of compassion or conscience, and with as much security as if it were honestly got; as Ephraim, Hos. 12:7, 8. 3. See the mischief they do to the country. They not only rob travellers, but they make incursions upon their neighbours, and *reap every one his corn in the field* (*v.* 6), that is, they enter upon other people's ground, cut their corn, and carry it away as freely as if it were their own. Even *the wicked gather the vintage,* and it is their wickedness; or, as we read it, They gather the vintage of the wicked, and so one wicked man is made a scourge to another. What the wicked got by extortion (which is their way of stealing) these robbers get from them in their way of stealing; thus oftentimes are the spoilers spoiled, Isa. 33:1. 4. The misery of those that fall into their hands (*v.* 7, 8): *They cause the naked,* whom they have stripped, not leaving them the clothes to their backs, *to lodge,* in the cold nights, *without clothing,* so that *they are wet with the showers of the mountains, and, for want of a* better *shelter, embrace the rock,* and are glad of a cave or den in it to preserve them from the injuries of the weather. Eliphaz had charged Job with such inhumanity as this, concluding that Providence would not thus have stripped him if he had not first *stripped the naked of their clothing, ch.* 22:6. Job here tells him there were those that were really guilty of those crimes with which he was unjustly charged and yet prospered and had success in their villanies, the curse they laid themselves under working invisibly; and Job thinks it more just to argue as he did, from an open notorious course of wickedness inferring a secret and future punishment, than to argue as Eliphaz did, who from nothing but present trouble inferred a course of past secret iniquity. The impunity of these oppressors and spoilers is expressed in one word (*v.* 12): *Yet God layeth not folly to them,* that is, he does not immediately prosecute them with his judgments for these crimes, nor make them examples, and so evince their folly to all the world. He that *gets riches, and not by right, at his end shall be a fool,* Jer. 17:11. But while he prospers he passes for a wise man, and God lays not folly to him until he saith, *Thou fool, this night thy soul shall be required of thee,* Lu. 12:20.

Verses 13–17

These verses describe another sort of sinners who *therefore* go unpunished, because they go undiscovered. *They rebel against the light, v.* 13. Some understand it figuratively: they sin against the light of nature, the light of God's law, and that of their own consciences; they profess to know God, but they rebel against the knowledge they have of him, and will not be guided and governed, commanded and controlled, by it. Others understand it literally: they have the day-light and choose the night as the most advantageous season for their wickedness. Sinful works are *therefore* called *works of darkness,* because he *that does evil hates the light* (Jn. 3:20), *knows not the ways thereof,* that is, keeps out of the way of it, or, if he happen to be seen, abides not where he thinks he is known. So that he here describes the worst of sinners, — those that sin wilfully, and against the convictions of their own consciences, whereby they add rebellion to their sin, — those that sin deliberately, and with a great deal of plot and contrivance, using a thousand arts to conceal their villanies, fondly imagining that, if they can but hide them from the eye of men, they are safe, but forgetting that *there is no darkness or shadow of death* in which *the workers of iniquity can hide themselves* from God's eye, *ch.* 34:22. In this paragraph Job specifies three sorts of sinners that shun the light: — 1. Murderers, *v.* 14. They *rise with the light,* as soon as ever the day breaks, to kill the poor travellers that are up early and abroad about their business, going to market with a little money or goods; and though it is so little that they are really to be called poor and needy, who with much ado get a sorry livelihood by their marketings, yet, to get it, the murderer will both take his neighbour's life and venture his own, will rather play at such small game than not play at all; nay, he kills for killing sake, thirsting more for blood than for booty. See what care and pains wicked men take to compass their wicked designs, and let the sight shame us out of our negligence and slothfulness in doing good.

> Ut jugulent homines, surgunt de nocte latrones,
> Tuque ut te serves non expergisceris? —
>
> Rogues nightly rise to murder men for pelf;
> Will you not rouse you to preserve yourself?

2. Adulterers. *The eyes* that are *full of adultery* (2 Pt. 2:14), the unclean and wanton eyes, *wait for the twilight, v.* 15. The eye of the adulteress did so, Prov. 7:9. Adultery hides its head for shame. The sinners themselves, even the most impudent, do what they can to hide their sin: *si non caste, tamen caute — if not chastely, yet cautiously;* and after all the wretched endeavours of the factors for hell to take away the reproach of it, it is and ever will be a *shame even to speak of those things which are done of them in secret,* Eph. 5:12. It hides its head also for fear, knowing that *jealousy is the rage of a husband,* who *will not spare in the day of vengeance,* Prov. 6:24, 25. See what pains those take that make provision for the flesh to fulfil the lusts of it, pains to compass, and then to conceal, that provision which, after all, will be death and hell at last. Less pains would serve to mortify and crucify the flesh, which would be life and heaven at last. Let the sinner change his heart, and then he needs not disguise his face, but may lift it up without spot. 3. House-breakers, *v.* 16. These *mark houses in the day-time,* mark the avenues of a house, and on which side they can most easily force their entrance, and then, in the night, dig through them, either to kill, or steal, or commit adultery. The night favours the assault, and makes the defence the more difficult; for the *good man of the house knows not what hour the thief will come* and therefore is asleep (Lu. 12:39) and he and his lie exposed. For this reason our law makes burglary, which is the breaking and entering of a dwelling-house in the night time with a felonious intent, to be felony without benefit of clergy.

And, *lastly,* Job observes (and perhaps observes it as part of the present, though secret, punishment of such sinners as these) that they are in a continual terror for fear of being discovered (*v.* 17): *The morning is to them even as the shadow of death.* The light of the day, which is welcome to honest people, is a terror to bad people. They curse the sun, not as the Moors, because it scorches them, but because it discovers them. *If one know them,* their consciences fly in their faces, and they are ready to become their own accusers; for *they are in the terrors of the shadow of death.* Shame came in with sin, and everlasting shame is at the end of it. See the misery of sinners — they are exposed to continual frights; and yet see their folly — they are afraid of coming under the eye of men, but have no dread of God's eye, which is always upon them: they are not afraid of doing that which yet they are so terribly afraid of being known to do.

Verses 18–25

Job here, in the conclusion of his discourse,

I. Gives some further instances of the wickedness of these cruel bloody men. 1. Some are pirates and robbers at sea. To this many learned interpreters apply those difficult expressions (*v.* 18), *He is swift upon the waters.* Privateers choose those ships that are the best sailors. In these swift ships they cruise from one channel to another, to pick up prizes; and this brings them in so much wealth that their *portion is cursed in the earth,* and they *behold not the way of the vineyards,* that is (as bishop Patrick explains it), they despise the employment of those who till the ground and plant vineyards as poor and unprofitable. But others make this a further description of the conduct of those sinners that are afraid of the light: if they be discovered, they get away as fast as they can, and choose to lurk, not in the vineyards, for fear of being discovered, but in some cursed portion, a lonely and desolate place, which nobody looks after. 2. Some are abusive to those that are in trouble, and add affliction to the afflicted. Barrenness was looked upon as a great reproach, and those that fall under that affliction they upbraid with it, as Peninnah did Hannah, on purpose to vex them and make them to fret, which is a barbarous thing. This is *evil entreating the barren that beareth not* (*v.* 21), or those that are childless, and so want the arrows others have in their quiver, which enable them to deal with their enemy in the gate, Ps. 127:5. They take that advantage against and are oppressive to them. As the fatherless, so the childless, are in some degree helpless. For the same reason it is a cruel thing to hurt the widow, to whom we ought to do good; and not doing good, when it is in our power, is doing hurt. 3. There are those who, by inuring themselves to cruelty, come at last to be so exceedingly boisterous that they are *the terror of the mighty in the land of the living* (*v.* 22): *"He draws the mighty* into a snare with his power; even the greatest are not able to stand before him when he is in his mad fits: *he rises up* in his passion, and lays about him with so much fury that *no man is sure of his life;* nor can he at the same time be sure of his own, for *his hand is against every man* and *every man's hand against him,"* Gen. 16:12. One would wonder how any man can take pleasure in making all about him afraid of him, yet there are those that do.

II. He shows that these daring sinners prosper, and are at ease for a while, nay, and often end their days in peace, as Ishmael, who, though he was a man of such a character as is here given, yet both *lived and died in the presence of all his brethren,* as we are told, Gen. 16:12; 25:18: Of these sinners here it is said, 1. That it is *given them to be in safety, v.* 23. They seem to be under the special protection of the divine Providence; and one would wonder how they escape with life through so many dangers as they run themselves into. 2. That they rest upon this, that is, they rely upon this as sufficient to warrant all their violences. *Because sentence against their evil works is not executed speedily* they think that there is no great evil in them, and that God is not displeased with them, nor will ever call them to an account. Their prosperity is their security. 3. That *they are exalted for a while.* They seem to be the favourites of heaven, and value themselves as making the best figure on earth. They are set up in honour, set up (as they think) out of the reach of danger, and lifted up in the pride of their own spirits. 4. That, at length, they are carried out of the world very silently and gently, and without any remarkable disgrace or terror. "They go down to the grave as easily as snow-water sinks into the dry ground when it is melted by the sun;" so bishop Patrick explains *v.* 19. To the same purport he paraphrases *v.* 20, *The womb shall forget him,* etc. "God sets no such mark of his displeasure upon him but that his mother may soon forget him. The hand of justice does not hang him on a gibbet for the birds to feed on; but he is carried to his grave like other men, to be the sweet food of worms. There he lies quietly, and neither he nor his wickedness is any more remembered than a tree which is broken to shivers." And *v.* 24, *They are taken out of the way as all others,* that is, "they are shut up in their graves like all other men; nay, they die as easily (without those tedious pains which some endure) as an ear of corn is cropped with your hand." Compare this with Solomon's observation (Eccl. 8:10), *I saw the wicked buried, who had come and gone from the place of the holy, and they were forgotten.*

III. He foresees their fall however, and that their death, though they die in ease and honour, will be their ruin. God's *eyes are upon their ways, v.* 23. Though he keep silence, and seem to connive at them, yet he takes notice, and keeps account of all their wickedness, and will make it to appear shortly that their most secret sins, which they thought *no eye should see* (*v.* 15), were under his eye and will be called over again. Here is no mention of the punishment of these sinners in the other world, but it is intimated in the particular notice taken of the consequences of their death. 1. The consumption of the body in the grave, though common to all, yet to them is in the nature of a punishment for their sin. The *grave shall consume those that have sinned;* that land of darkness will be the lot of those that *love darkness rather than light.* The bodies they pampered shall be a feast for worms, which shall feed as sweetly on them as ever they fed on the pleasures and gains of their sins. 2. Though they thought to make themselves a great name by their wealth, and power, and mighty achievements, yet *their memorial perished with them,* Ps. 9:6. He that made himself so much talked of *shall,* when he is dead, *be no more remembered* with honour; his *name shall rot,* Prov. 10:7. Those that durst not give him his due character while he lived shall not spare him when he is dead; so that the womb that bore him, his own mother, shall forget him, that is, shall avoid making mention of him, and shall think *that* the greatest kindness she can do him, since no good can be said of him. That honour which is got by sin will soon turn into shame. 3. The wickedness they thought to establish in their families shall be broken as a tree; all their wicked projects shall be blasted, and all their wicked hopes dashed and buried with them. 4. Their pride shall be brought down and laid in the dust (*v.* 24); and, in mercy to the world, they shall be taken out of the way, and all their power and prosperity shall be cut off. You may seek them, and they shall not be found. Job owns that wicked people will be miserable at last, miserable on the other side death, but utterly denies what his friends asserted, that ordinarily they are miserable in this life.

IV. He concludes with a bold challenge to all that were present to disprove what he had said if they could (*v.* 25): *"If it be not so now,* as I have declared, and if it do not thence follow that I am unjustly condemned and censured, let those that can undertake to prove that my discourse is either, 1. False in itself, and then they prove me a liar; or, 2. Foreign, and nothing to the purpose, and then they prove my speech frivolous and nothing worth." That indeed which is false is nothing worth; where there is not truth, how can there be goodness? But those that speak the words of truth and soberness need not fear having what they say brought to the test, but can cheerfully submit it to a fair examination, as Job does here.

CHAPTER 25

Bildad here makes a very short reply to Job's last discourse, as one that began to be tired of the cause. He drops the main question concerning the prosperity of wicked men, as being unable to answer the proofs Job had produced in the foregoing chapter: but, because he thought Job had made too bold with the divine majesty in his appeals to the divine tribunal (*ch.* 23), he in a few words shows the infinite distance there is between God and man, teaching us, I. To think highly and honourably of God (*v.* 2, 3, 5). II. To think meanly of ourselves (*v.* 4, 6). These, however misapplied to Job, are two good lessons for us all to learn.

Verses 1–6

Bildad is to be commended here for two things: — 1. For speaking no more on the subject about which Job and he differed. Perhaps he began to think Job was in the right, and then it was justice to say no more concerning it, as one that contended for truth, not for victory, and therefore, for the finding of truth, would be content to lose the victory; or, if he still thought himself in the right, yet he knew when he had said enough, and would not wrangle endlessly for the last word. Perhaps indeed one reason why he and the rest of them let fall this debate was because they perceived that Job and they did not differ so much in opinion as they thought: they owned that wicked people might prosper a while, and Job owned they would be destroyed at last; how little then was the difference! If disputants would understand one another better, perhaps they would find themselves nearer one another than they imagined. 2. For speaking so well on the matter about which Job and he were agreed. If we would all get our hearts filled with awful thoughts of God and humble thoughts of ourselves, we should not be so apt as we are to fall out about matters of doubtful disputation, which are trifling or intricate.

Two ways Bildad takes here to exalt God and abase man: —

I. He shows how glorious God is, and thence infers how guilty and impure man is before him, *v.* 2–4. Let us see then,

1. What great things are here said of God, designed to possess Job with a reverence of him, and to check his reflections upon him and upon his dealings with him: (1.) God is the sovereign Lord of all, and *with him is terrible majesty. Dominion and fear are with him, v.* 2. He that gave being has an incontestable authority to give laws, and can enforce the laws he gives. He that made all has a right to dispose of all according to his own will, with an absolute sovereignty. Whatever he will do he does, and may do; and none can say unto him, *What dost thou?* or *Why dost thou so?* Dan. 4:35. His having dominion (or being *Dominus — Lord*) bespeaks him both owner and ruler of all the creatures. They are all his, and they are all under his direction and at his disposal. Hence it follows that he is to be feared (that is, reverenced and obeyed), that he is feared by all that know him (the seraphim cover their faces before him), and that, first or last, all will be made to fear him. Men's dominion is often despicable, often de-

spised, but God is always terrible. (2.) The glorious inhabitants of the upper world are all perfectly observant of him and entirely acquiesce in his will: *He maketh peace in his high places.* He enjoys himself in a perfect tranquillity. The holy angels never quarrel with him, nor with one another, but entirely acquiesce in his will, and unanimously execute it without murmuring or disputing. Thus the will of God is done in heaven; and thus we pray that it may be done by us and others on earth. The sun, moon, and stars, keep their courses, and never clash with one another: nay, even in this lower region, which is often disturbed with storms and tempests, yet when God pleases he commands peace, by *making the storm a calm,* Ps. 107:29; 65:7. Observe, The high places are *his* high places; for *the heaven, even the heavens, are the Lord's* (Ps. 115:16) in a peculiar manner. Peace is God's work; where it is made it is he that makes it, Isa. 57:19. In heaven there is perfect peace; for there is perfect holiness, and there is God, who is love. (3.) He is a God of irresistible power: *Is there any number of his armies? v.* 3. The greatness and power of princes are judged of by their armies. God is not only himself almighty, but he has numberless numbers of armies at his beck and disposal, — standing armies that are never disbanded, — regular troops, and well disciplined, that are never to seek, never at a loss, that never mutiny, — veteran troops, that have been long in his service, — victorious troops, that never failed of success nor were ever foiled. All the creatures are his hosts, angels especially. He is Lord of all, Lord of hosts. He has numberless armies, and yet makes peace. He could make war upon us, but is willing to be at peace with us; and even the heavenly hosts were sent to proclaim *peace on earth* and *good will towards men,* Lu. 2:14. (4.) His providence extends itself to all: *Upon whom does not his light arise?* The light of the sun is communicated to all parts of the world, and, take the year round, to all equally. See Ps. 19:6. That is a faint resemblance of the universal cognizance and care God takes of the whole creation, Mt. 5:45. All are under the light of his knowledge and are naked and open before him. All partake of the light of his goodness: it seems especially to be meant of *that.* He is good to all; the earth is full of his goodness. He is *Deus optimus — God, the best of beings,* as well as *maximus — the greatest:* he has power to destroy; but his pleasure is to show mercy. All the creatures live upon his bounty.

2. What low things are here said of man, and very truly and justly (*v.* 4): *How then can man be justified with God? Or how can he be clean?* Man is not only mean, but vile, not only earthly, but filthy; he cannot be justified, he cannot be clean, (1.) In comparison with God. Man's righteousness and holiness, at the best, are nothing to God's, Ps. 89:6. (2.) In debate with God. He that will quarrel with the word and providence of God must unavoidably go by the worst. God will be justified, and then man will be condemned, Ps. 51:4; Rom. 3:4. There is no error in God's judgment, and therefore there lies no exception against it, nor appeal from it. (3.) In the sight of God. If God is so great and glorious, how can man, who is guilty and impure, appear before him? Note, [1.] Man, by reason of his actual transgressions, is obnoxious to God's justice and cannot in himself be justified before him: he can neither plead *Not guilty,* nor plead any merit of his own to balance or extenuate his guilt. The scripture has concluded all under sin. [2.] Man, by reason of his original corruption, as he is born of a woman, is odious to God's holiness, and cannot be clean in his sight. God sees his impurity, and it is certain that by it he is rendered utterly unfit for communion and fellowship with God in grace here and for the vision and fruition of him in glory hereafter. We have need therefore to be born again of water and of the Holy Ghost, and to be bathed again and again in the blood of Christ, that fountain opened.

II. He shows how dark and defective even the heavenly bodies are in the sight of God, and in comparison with him, and thence infers how little, and mean, and worthless, man is. 1. The lights of heaven, though beauteous creatures, are before God as clods of earth (*v.* 5): *Behold even to the moon,* walking in brightness, and the stars, those glorious lamps of heaven, which the heathen were so charmed with the lustre of that they worshipped them — yet, in God's sight, in comparison with him, they shine not, they are not pure; they have no glory, by reason of the glory which excelleth, as a candle, though it burn, yet does not shine when it is set in the clear light of the sun. The glory of God, shining in his providences, eclipses the glory of the brightest creatures, Isa. 24:23. *The moon shall be confounded, and the sun ashamed, when the Lord of hosts shall reign in Mount Sion.* The heavenly bodies are often clouded; we plainly see spots in the moon, and, with the help of glasses, may sometimes discern spots upon the sun too: but God sees spots in them that we do not see. How durst Job then so confidently appeal to God, who would discover that amiss in him which he was not aware of in himself? 2. The children of men, though noble creatures, are before God but as worms of the earth (*v.* 6): *How much less* does *man* shine in honour, how much less is he pure in righteousness *that is a worm, and the son of man,* whoever he be, *that is a worm! — a vermin* (so some), not only mean and despicable, but noxious and detestable; *a mite* (so others), the smallest animal, which cannot be discerned with the naked eye, but through a magnifying glass. Such a thing is man. (1.) So mean, and little, and inconsiderable, in comparison with God and with the holy angels: so worthless and despicable, having his original in corruption, and hastening to corruption. What little reason has man to be proud, and what great reason to be humble! (2.) So weak and impotent, and so easily crushed, and therefore a very unequal match for Almighty God. Shall man be such a fool as to contend with his Maker, who can tread him to pieces more easily than we can a worm? (3.) So sordid and filthy. Man is not pure for he is a worm, hatched in putrefaction, and therefore odious to God. Let us therefore wonder at God's condescension in taking such worms as we are into covenant and communion with himself, especially at the condescension of the Son of God, in emptying himself so far as to say, *I am a worm, and no man,* Ps. 22:6.

CHAPTER 26

This is Job's short reply to Bildad's short discourse, in which he is so far from contradicting him that he confirms what he had said, and out-does him in magnifying God and setting forth his power, to show what reason he had still to say, as he did (*ch.* 13:2), "What you know, the same do I know also." I. He shows that Bildad's discourse was foreign to the matter he was discoursing of — though very true and good, yet not to the purpose (*v.* 2–4). II. That it was needless to the person he was discoursing with; for he knew it, and believed it, and could speak of it as well as he and better, and could add to the proofs which he had produced of God's power and greatness, which he does in the rest of his discourse (*v.* 5–13), concluding that, when they had both said what they could, all came short of the merit of the subject and it was still far from being exhausted (*v.* 14).

Verses 1–4

One would not have thought that Job, when he was in so much pain and misery, could banter his friend as he does here and make himself merry with the impertinency of his discourse. Bildad thought that he had made a fine speech, that the matter was so weighty, and the language so fine, that he had gained the reputation both of an oracle and of an orator; but Job peevishly enough shows that his performance was not so valuable as he thought it and ridicules him for it. He shows,

I. That there was no great matter to be found in it (*v.* 3): *How hast thou plentifully declared the thing as it is?* This is spoken ironically, upbraiding Bildad with the good conceit he himself had of what he had said. 1. He thought he had spoken very clearly, had *declared the thing as it is.* He was very fond (as we are all apt to be) of his own notions, and thought they only were right, and true, and intelligible, and all other notions of the thing were false, mistaken, and confused; whereas, when we speak of the glory of God, we cannot declare the thing as it is, for we see it through a glass darkly, or but by reflection, and shall not see him as he is till we come to heaven. Here *we cannot order our speech concerning him, ch.* 37:19. 2. He thought he had spoken very fully, though in few words, that he had plentifully declared it, and, alas! it was but poorly and scantily that he declared it, in comparison with the vast compass and copiousness of the subject.

II. That there was no great use to be made of it. *Cui bono — What good hast thou done* by all that thou hast said? *How hast thou,* with all this mighty flourish, *helped him that is without power? v.* 2. *How hast thou,* with thy grave dictates, *counselled* him *that has no wisdom? v.* 3. Job would convince him, 1. That he had done God no service by it, nor made him in the least beholden to him. It is indeed our duty, and will be our honour, to speak on God's behalf; but we must not think that he needs our service, or is indebted to us for it, nor will he accept it if it come from a spirit of contention and contradiction, and not from a sincere regard to God's glory. 2. That he had done his cause no service by it. He thought his friends were mightily beholden to him for helping them, at a dead lift, to make their part good against Job, when they were quite at a loss, and had no strength, no wisdom. Even weak disputants, when warm, are apt to think truth more beholden to them than it really is. 3. That he had done him no service by it. He pretended to convince, instruct, and comfort, Job; but, alas! what he had said was so little to the purpose that it would not avail to rectify any mistakes, nor to assist him either in bearing his afflictions or in getting good by them: *"To whom hast thou uttered words? v.* 4. Was it to me that thou didst direct thy discourse? And dost thou take me for such a child as to need these instructions? Or dost thou think them proper for one in my condition?" Every thing that is true and good is not suitable and seasonable. To one that was humbled, and broken, and grieved in spirit, as Job was, he ought to have preached of the grace and mercy of God, rather than of his greatness and majesty, to have laid before him the consolations rather than the terrors of the Almighty. Christ knows how to speak what is proper for the weary (Isa. 50:4), and his ministers should learn rightly to divide the word of truth, and not make those sad whom God would not have made sad, as Bildad did; and therefore Job asks him, *Whose spirit came from thee?* that is, "What troubled soul would ever be revived, and relieved, and brought to itself, by such discourses as these?" Thus are we often disappointed in our expectations from our friends who should comfort us, but the Comforter, who is the Holy Ghost, never mistakes in his operations nor misses of his end.

Verses 5–14

The truth received a great deal of light from the dispute between Job and his friends concerning those points about which they differed; but now they are upon a subject in which they were all agreed, the infinite glory and power of God. How does truth triumph, and how brightly does it shine, when there appears no other strife between the contenders than which shall speak most highly and honourably of God and be most copious in showing forth his praise! It were well if all disputes about matters of religion might end thus, in *glorifying God* as Lord of all, and our Lord, *with one mind and one mouth* (Rom. 15:6); for to that we have all attained, in that we are all agreed.

I. Many illustrious instances are here given of the wisdom and power of God in the creation and preservation of the world.

1. If we look about us, to the earth and waters here below, we shall see striking instances of omnipotence, which we may gather out of these verses. (1.) *He hangs the earth upon nothing, v.* 7. The vast terraqueous globe neither rests upon any pillars nor hangs upon any axletree, and yet, by the almighty power of God, is firmly fixed in its place, poised with its own weight. The art of man could not hang a feather upon nothing, yet the divine wisdom hangs the whole earth so. It is *ponderibus librata suis — poised by its own weight,* so says the poet; it is *upheld by the word of God's power,* so says the apostle. What is hung upon nothing may serve us to set our feet on, and bear the weight of our bodies, but it will never serve us to set our hearts on, nor bear the weight of our souls. (2.) He *sets bounds to the waters of the sea,* and compasses them in (*v.* 10), that they may not *return to cover the earth;* and these bounds shall continue unmoved, unshaken, unworn, *till the day and night come to an end,* when time shall be no more. Herein appears the dominion which Providence has over the raging waters of the sea, and so it is an instance of his power, Jer. 5:22. We see too the care which Providence takes of the poor sinful inhabitants of the earth, who, though obnoxious to his justice and lying at his mercy, are thus preserved from being overwhelmed, as they were once by the waters of a flood, and will continue to be so, because they are reserved unto fire. (3.) He *forms dead things under the waters. Rephaim — giants, are formed under the waters,* that is, vast creatures, of prodigious bulk, as whales, giant-like creatures, among the innumerable inhabitants of the water. So bishop Patrick. (4.)

By mighty storms and tempests he shakes the mountains, which are here called *the pillars of heaven* (*v.* 11), and even *divides the sea, and smites through its proud waves, v.* 12. At the presence of the Lord the *sea flies* and the *mountains skip,* Ps. 114:3, 4. See Hab. 3:6, etc. A storm furrows the waters, and does, as it were, divide them; and then a calm smites through the waves, and lays them flat again. See Ps. 89:9, 10. Those who think Job lived at, or after, the time of Moses, apply this to the dividing of the Red Sea before the children of Israel, and the drowning of the Egyptians in it. *By his understanding he smiteth through Rahab;* so the word is, and Rahab is often put for Egypt; as Ps. 87:4; Isa. 51:9.

2. If we consider hell beneath, though it is out of our sight, yet we may conceive the instances of God's power there. By *hell and destruction* (*v.* 6) we may understand the grave, and those who are buried in it, that they are under the eye of God, though laid out of our sight, which may strengthen our belief of the resurrection of the dead. God knows where to find, and whence to fetch, all the scattered atoms of the consumed body. We may also consider them as referring to the place of the damned, where the separate souls of the wicked are in misery and torment. That is hell and destruction, which are said to be *before the Lord* (Prov. 15:11), and here to be *naked before him,* to which it is probable there is an allusion, Rev. 14:10, where sinners are to be tormented *in the presence of the holy angels* (who attended the Shechinah) and *in the presence of the Lamb.* And this may give light to *v.* 5, which some ancient versions read thus (and I think more agreeably to the signification of the word *Rephaim): Behold, the giants groan under the waters, and those that dwell with them;* and then follows, *Hell is naked before him,* typified by the drowning of the giants of the old world; so the learned Mr. Joseph Mede understands it, and with it illustrates Prov. 21:16, where hell is called *the congregation of the dead;* and it is the same word which is here used, and which he would there have rendered *the congregation of the giants,* in allusion to the drowning of the sinners of the old world. And is there any thing in which the majesty of God appears more dreadful than in the eternal ruin of the ungodly and the groans of the inhabitants of the land of darkness? Those that will not with angels fear and worship shall for ever with devils fear and tremble; and God therein will be glorified.

3. If we look up to heaven above, we shall see instances of God's sovereignty and power. (1.) *He stretches out the north over the empty place, v.* 7. So he did at first, when *he stretched out the heavens like a curtain* (Ps. 104:2); and he still continues to keep them stretched out, and will do so till the general conflagration, when they shall be *rolled together as a scroll,* Rev. 6:14. He mentions the north because his country (as ours) lay in the northern hemisphere; and the air is the empty place over which it is stretched out. See Ps. 89:12. What an empty place is this world in comparison with the other! (2.) He keeps the waters that are said to be *above the firmament* from pouring down upon the earth, as once they did (*v.* 8): *He binds up the waters in his thick clouds,* as if they were tied closely in a bag, till there is occasion to use them; and, notwithstanding the vast weight of water so raised and laid up, yet *the cloud is not rent under them,* for then they would burst and pour out as a spout; but they do, as it were, distil through the cloud, and so come drop by drop, in mercy to the earth, in small rain, or great rain, as he pleases. (3.) He conceals the glory of the upper world, the dazzling lustre of which we poor mortals could not bear (*v.* 9): *He holds back the face of his throne,* that light in which he dwells, *and spreads a cloud upon it,* through which *he judges, ch.* 22:13. God will have us to live by faith, not by sense; for this is agreeable to a state of probation. It were not a fair trial if the face of God's throne were visible now as it will be in the great day.

> Lest his high throne, above expression bright,
> With deadly glory should oppress our sight,
> To break the dazzling force he draws a screen
> Of sable shades, and spreads his clouds between.
> — Sir R. Blackmore

(4.) The bright ornaments of heaven are the work of his hands (*v.* 13): *By his Spirit,* the eternal Spirit that moved upon the face of the waters, *the breath of his mouth* (Ps. 33:6), *he has garnished the heavens,* not only made them, but beautified them, has curiously bespangled them with stars by night and painted them with the light of the sun by day. God, having made man to look upward *(Os homini sublime dedit — To man he gave an erect countenance),* has *therefore* garnished the heavens, to invite him to look upward, that, by pleasing his eye with the dazzling light of the sun and the sparkling light of the stars, their number, order, and various magnitudes, which, as so many golden studs, beautify the canopy drawn over our heads, he may be led to admire the great Creator, the Father and fountain of lights, and to say, "If the pavement be so richly inlaid, what must the palace be! If the visible heavens be so glorious, what are those that are out of sight!" From the beauteous garniture of the ante-chamber we may infer the precious furniture of the presence-chamber. If stars be so bright, what are angels! What is meant here by *the crooked serpent* which his hands have formed is not certain. Some make it part of the garnishing of the heavens, the milky-way, say some; some particular constellation, so called, say others. It is the same word that is used for leviathan (Isa. 27:1), and probably may be meant of the whale or crocodile, in which appears much of the power of the Creator; and why may not Job conclude with that inference, when God himself does so? *ch.* 41.

II. He concludes, at last, with an awful *et caetera* (*v.* 14): *Lo, these are parts of his ways,* the out-goings of his wisdom and power, the ways in which he walks and by which he makes himself known to the children of men. Here, 1. He acknowledges, with adoration, the discoveries that were made of God. These things which he himself had said, and which Bildad had said, are his ways, and this is heard of him; this is something of God. But, 2. He admires the depth of that which is undiscovered. This that we have said is but part of his ways, a small part. What we know of God is nothing in comparison with what is in God and what God is. After all the discoveries which God has made to us, and all the enquiries we have made after God, still we are much in the dark concerning him, and must conclude, *Lo, these are but parts of his ways.* Something we hear of him by his works and by his word; but, alas! *how little a portion is heard of him?* heard by us, heard from us! We know but in part; we prophesy but in part. When we have said all we can, concerning God, we must even do as St. Paul does (Rom. 11:33); despairing to find the bottom, we must sit down at the brink, and adore the depth: *O the depth of the wisdom and knowledge of God!* It is but a little portion that we hear and know of God in our present state. He is infinite and incomprehensible; our understandings and capacities are weak and shallow, and the full discoveries of the divine glory are reserved for the future state. Even *the thunder of his power* (that is, his powerful thunder), one of the lowest of his ways here in our own region, we cannot understand. See *ch.* 37:4, 5. Much less can we understand the utmost force and extent of his power, the terrible efforts and operations of it, and particularly *the power of his anger,* Ps. 90:11. God is great, and we know him not.

CHAPTER 27

Job had sometimes complained of his friends that they were so eager in disputing that they would scarcely let him put in a word: "Suffer me that I may speak;" and, "O that you would hold your peace!" But now, it seems, they were out of breath, and left him room to say what he would. Either they were themselves convinced that Job was in the right or they despaired of convincing him that he was in the wrong; and therefore they threw away their weapons and gave up the cause. Job was too hard for them, and forced them to quit the field; for great is the truth and will prevail. What Job had said (*ch.* 26) was a sufficient answer to Bildad's discourse; and now Job paused awhile, to see whether Zophar would take his turn again; but, he declining it, Job himself went on, and, without any interruption or vexation given him, said all he desired to say in this matter. I. He begins with a solemn protestation of his integrity and of his resolution to hold it fast (*v.* 2–6). II. He expresses the dread he had of that hypocrisy which they charged him with (*v.* 7–10). III. He shows the miserable end of wicked people, notwithstanding their long prosperity, and the curse that attends them and is entailed upon their families (*v.* 11–23).

Verses 1–6

Job's discourse here is called a *parable (mashal),* the title of Solomon's proverbs, because it was grave and weighty, and very instructive, and he spoke as one having authority. It comes from a word that signifies *to rule,* or *have dominion;* and some think it intimates that Job now triumphed over his opponents, and spoke as one that had baffled them. We say of an excellent preacher that he knows how *dominari in concionibus — to command his hearers.* Job did so here. A long strife there had been between Job and his friends; they seemed disposed to have the matter compromised; and therefore, since an *oath for confirmation is an end of strife* (Heb. 6:16), Job here backs all he had said in maintenance of his own integrity with a solemn oath, to silence contradiction, and take the blame entirely upon himself if he prevaricated. Observe,

I. The form of his oath (*v.* 2): *As God liveth, who hath taken away my judgment.* Here, 1. He speaks highly of God, in calling him *the living God* (which means *everliving,* the eternal God, that has life in himself) and in appealing to him as the sole and sovereign Judge. We can swear by no greater, and it is an affront to him to swear by any other. 2. Yet he speaks hardly of him, and unbecomingly, in saying that he had taken away his judgment (that is, refused to do him justice in this controversy and to appear in defence of him), and that by continuing his troubles, on which his friends grounded their censures of him, he had taken from him the opportunity he hoped ere now to have of clearing himself. Elihu reproved him for this word (*ch.* 34:5); for God is righteous in all his ways, and takes away no man's judgment. But see how apt we are to despair of favour if it be not shown us immediately, so poor-spirited are we and so soon weary of waiting God's time. He also charges it upon God that he had *vexed his soul,* had not only not appeared for him, but had appeared against him, and, by laying such grievous afflictions upon him had quite embittered his life to him and all the comforts of it. We, by our impatience, vex our own souls and then complain of God that he has vexed them. Yet see Job's confidence in the goodness both of his cause and of his God, that though God seemed to be angry with him, and to act against him for the present, yet he could cheerfully commit his cause to him.

II. The matter of his oath, *v.* 3, 4. 1. That he would not *speak wickedness, nor utter deceit* — that, in general, he would never allow himself in the way of lying, that, as in this debate he had all along spoken as he thought, so he would never wrong his conscience by speaking otherwise; he would never maintain any doctrine, nor assert any matter of fact, but what he believed to be true; nor would he deny the truth, how much soever it might make against him: and, whereas his friends charged him with being a hypocrite, he was ready to answer, upon oath, to all their interrogatories, if called to do so. On the one hand he would not, for all the world, deny the charge if he knew himself guilty, but would declare the truth, the whole truth, and nothing but the truth, and take to himself the shame of his hypocrisy. On the other hand, since he was conscious to himself of his integrity, and that he was not such a man as his friends represented him, he would never betray his integrity, nor charge himself with that which he was innocent of. He would not be brought, no, not by the rack of their unjust censures, falsely to accuse himself. If we must not bear false witness against our neighbour, then not against ourselves. 2. That he would adhere to this resolution as long as he lived (*v.* 3): *All the while my breath is in me.* Our resolutions against sin should be thus constant, resolutions for life. In things doubtful and indifferent, it is not safe to be thus peremptory. We know not what reason we may see to change our mind: God may reveal to us that which we now are not aware of. But in so plain a thing as this we cannot be too positive that we will never speak wickedness. Something of a reason for his resolution is here implied — that our breath will not be always in us. We must shortly breathe our last, and therefore, while our breath is in us, we must never breathe wickedness and deceit, nor allow ourselves to say or do any thing which will make against us when our breath shall depart. The breath in us is called *the spirit of God,* because he breathed it into us; and this is another reason why we must not speak wickedness. It is God that gives us life and breath, and therefore, while we have breath, we must praise him.

III. The explication of his oath (*v.* 5, 6): *"God forbid that I should justify you* in your uncharitable censures of me, by owning myself a hypocrite: no, *until I die I will not remove my integrity from me; my righteousness I hold fast, and will not let it go."* 1. He would always be an honest man, would hold fast his integrity, and not curse God, as Satan, by his wife, urged him to do, *ch.* 2:9. Job here thinks of dying, and of getting ready for death, and therefore resolves never to part with his religion, though he had lost all he had in the world. Note, The best preparative for death is perseverance to death in our integrity. *"Until I die,"* that is, "though I die by this affliction, I will not thereby be put out of conceit with my God and my religion. *Though he slay me, yet will I trust in him."* 2. He would always stand to it that he was an honest man; he would not remove, he would not part with, the conscience, and comfort, and credit of his integrity; he was resolved to defend it to the last. "God knows, and my own heart knows, that I always meant well, and did not allow myself in the omission of any known duty or the commission of any known sin. This is my rejoicing, and no man shall rob me of it; I will never lie against my right." It has often been the lot of upright men to be censured and condemned as hypocrites; but it well becomes them to bear up boldly against such censures, and not to be discouraged by them nor think the worse of themselves for them; as the apostle (Heb. 13:18): *We have a good conscience in all things, willing to live honestly.*

Hic murus aheneus esto, nil conscire sibi.
Be this thy brazen bulwark of defence,
Still to preserve thy conscious innocence.

Job complained much of the reproaches of his friends; but (says he) *my heart shall not reproach me,* that is, "I will never give my heart cause to reproach me, but will keep a conscience void of offence; and, while I do so, I will not give my heart leave to reproach me." *Who shall lay any thing to the charge of God's elect? It is God that justifies.* To resolve that our hearts shall not reproach us when we give them cause to do so is to affront God, whose deputy conscience is, and to wrong ourselves; for it is a good thing, when a man has sinned, to have a heart within him to smite him for it, 2 Sa. 24:10. But to resolve that our hearts shall not reproach us while we still hold fast our integrity is to baffle the designs of the evil spirit (who tempts good Christians to question their adoption, *If thou be the Son of God*) and to concur with the operations of the good Spirit, who witnesses to their adoption.

Verses 7–10

Job having solemnly protested the satisfaction he had in his integrity, for the further clearing of himself, here expresses the dread he had of being found a hypocrite.

I. He tells us how he startled at the thought of it, for he looked upon the condition of a hypocrite and a wicked man to be certainly the most miserable condition that any man could be in (*v.* 7): *Let my enemy be as the wicked,* a proverbial expression, like that (Dan. 4:19), *The dream be to those that hate thee.* Job was so far from indulging himself in any wicked way, and flattering himself in it, that, if he might have leave to wish the greatest evil he could think of to the worst enemy he had in the world, he would wish him the portion of a wicked man, knowing that worse he could not wish him. Not that we may lawfully wish any man to be wicked, or that any man who is not wicked should be treated as wicked; but we should all choose to be in the condition of a beggar, an out-law, a galley-slave, any thing, rather that in the condition of the wicked, though in ever so much pomp and outward prosperity.

II. He gives us the reasons of it.

1. Because the hypocrite's hopes will not be crowned (*v.* 8): *For what is the hope of the hypocrite?* Bildad had condemned it (*ch.* 8:13, 14), and Zophar (*ch.* 11:20), and Job here concurs with them, and reads the death of the hypocrite's hope with as much assurance as they had done; and this fitly comes in as a reason why he would not remove his integrity, but still hold it fast. Note, The consideration of the miserable condition of wicked people, and especially hypocrites, should engage us to be upright (for we are undone, for ever undone, if we be not) and also to get the comfortable evidence of our uprightness; for how can we be easy if the great concern lie at uncertainties? Job's friends would persuade him that all his hope was but the hope of the hypocrite, *ch.* 4:6. "Nay," says he, "I would not, for all the world, be so foolish as to build upon such a rotten foundation; for *what is the hope of the hypocrite?"* See here, (1.) The hypocrite deceived. *He has gained,* and he has hope; this is his bright side. It is allowed that he has gained by his hypocrisy, has gained the praise and applause of men and the wealth of this world. Jehu gained a kingdom by his hypocrisy and the Pharisees many a widow's house. Upon this gain he builds his hope, such as it is. He hopes he is in good circumstances for another world, because he finds he is so for this, and he blesses himself in his own way. (2.) The hypocrite undeceived. He will at last see himself wretchedly cheated; for, [1.] God shall *take away his soul,* sorely against his will. Lu. 12:20, *Thy soul shall be required of thee.* God, as the Judge, takes it away to be tried and determined to its everlasting state. He shall then fall into the hands of the living God, to be dealt with immediately. [2.] What will his hope be then? It will be vanity and a lie; it will stand him in no stead. The wealth of this world, which he hoped in, he must leave behind him, Ps. 49:17. The happiness of the other world, which he hoped for, he will certainly miss of. He hoped to go to heaven, but he will be shamefully disappointed; he will plead his external profession, privileges, and performances, but all his pleas will be overruled as frivolous: *Depart from me, I know you not.* So that, upon the whole, it is certain that a formal hypocrite, with all his gains and all his hopes, will be miserable in a dying hour.

2. Because the hypocrite's prayer will not be heard (*v.* 9): *Will God hear his cry when trouble comes upon him?* No, he will not; it cannot be expected he should. If true repentance come upon him, God will hear his cry and accept him (Isa. 1:18); but, if he continue impenitent and unchanged, let him not think to find favour with God. Observe, (1.) Trouble will come upon him, certainly it will. Troubles in the world often surprise those that are most secure of an uninterrupted prosperity. However, death will come, and trouble with it, when he must leave the world and all his delights in it. The judgment of the great day will come; fearfulness will surprise the hypocrites, Isa. 33:14. (2.) Then he will cry to God, will pray, and pray earnestly. Those who in prosperity slighted God, either prayed not at all or were cold and careless in prayer, when trouble comes will make their application to him and cry as men in earnest. But, (3.) Will God hear him then? In the troubles of this life, God has told us that he will not hear the prayers of those who regard iniquity in their hearts (Ps. 66:19) and set up their idols there (Eze. 14:4), nor of those who turn away their ear from hearing the law, Prov. 28:9. *Get you to the gods whom you have served,* Jdg. 10:14. In the judgment to come, it is certain, God will not hear the cry of those who lived and died in their hypocrisy. Their doleful lamentations will all be unpitied. *I will laugh at your calamity.* Their importunate petitions will all be thrown out and their pleas rejected. Inflexible justice cannot be biassed, nor the irreversible sentence revoked. See Mt. 7:22, 23; Lu. 13:26, and the case of the foolish virgins, Mt. 25:11.

3. Because the hypocrite's religion is neither comfortable nor constant (*v.* 10): *Will he delight himself in the Almighty?* No, not at any time (for his delight is in the profits of the world and the pleasures of the flesh, more than in God), especially not in the time of trouble. *Will he always call upon God?* No, in prosperity he will not call upon God, but slight him; in adversity he will not call upon God but curse him; he is weary of his religion when he gets nothing by it, or is in danger of losing. Note, (1.) Those are hypocrites who, though they profess religion, neither take pleasure in it nor persevere in it, who reckon their religion a task and a drudgery, a weariness, and snuff at it, who make use of it only to serve a turn, and lay it aside when the turn is served, who will call upon God while it is in fashion, or while the pang of devotion lasts, but leave it off when they fall into other company, or when the hot fit is over. (2.) The reason why hypocrites do not persevere in religion is because they have no pleasure in it. Those that do not delight in the Almighty will not always call upon him. The more comfort we find in our religion the more closely we shall cleave to it. Those who have no delight in God are easily inveigled by the pleasures of sense, and so drawn away from their religion; and they are easily run down by the crosses of this life, and so driven away from their religion, and will not always call upon God.

Verses 11–23

Job's friends had seen a great deal of the misery and destruction that attend wicked people, especially oppressors; and Job, while the heat of disputation lasted, had said as much, and with as much assurance, of their prosperity; but now that the heat of the battle was nearly over he was willing to own how far he agreed with them, and where the difference between his opinion and theirs lay. 1. He agreed with them that wicked people are miserable people, that God will surely reckon with cruel oppressors, and one time or other, one way or other, his justice will make reprisals upon them for all the affronts they have put upon God and all the wrongs they have done to their neighbours. This truth is abundantly confirmed by the entire concurrence even of these angry disputants in it. But, 2. In *this* they differed — they held that these deserved judgments are presently and visibly brought upon wicked oppressors, that *they travail with pain all their days,* that in prosperity *the destroyer comes upon them,* that they *shall not be rich,* nor their *branch green,* and that *their destruction shall be accomplished before their time* (so Eliphaz, *ch.* 15:20, 21, 29, 32), that the *steps of their strength shall be straitened,* that *terrors shall make them afraid on every side* (so Bildad, *ch.* 18:7, 11), that he himself *shall vomit up his riches,* and that *in the fulness of his sufficiency he shall be in straits,* so Zophar, *ch.* 20:15, 22. Now Job held that, in many cases, judgments do not fall upon them quickly, but are deferred for some time. That vengeance strikes slowly he had already shown (*ch.* 21 and 24); now he comes to show that it strikes surely and severely, and that reprieves are no pardons.

I. Job here undertakes to set this matter in a true light (*v.* 11, 12): *I will teach you.* We must not disdain to learn even from those who are sick and poor, yea, and peevish too, if they deliver what is true and good. Observe, 1. What he would teach them: *"That which is with the Almighty,"* that is, "the counsels and purposes of God concerning wicked people, which are hidden with him, and which you cannot hastily judge of; and the usual methods of his providence concerning them." This, says Job, *will I not conceal.* What God has not concealed from us we must not conceal from those we are concerned to teach. *Things revealed belong to us and our children.* 2. How he would teach them: *By the hand of God,* that is, by his strength and assistance. Those who undertake to teach others must look to the hand of God to direct them, to open their ear (Isa. 50:4), and to open their lips. Those whom God teaches with a strong hand are best able to teach others, Isa. 8:11. 3. What reason they had to learn those things which he was about to teach them (*v.* 12), that it was confirmed by their own observation — *You yourselves have seen it* (but what we have heard, and seen and known, we have need to be taught, that we may be perfect in our lesson), and that it would set them to rights in their judgment concerning him — *"Why then are you thus altogether vain,* to condemn me for a wicked man because I am afflicted?" Truth, rightly understood and applied, would cure us of that vanity of mind which arises from our mistakes. That particularly which he offers now to lay before them is *the portion of a wicked man with God,* particularly of *oppressors, v.* 13. Compare *ch.* 20:29. Their portion in the world may be wealth and preferment, but their portion with God is ruin and misery. They are above the control of any earthly power, it may be, but the Almighty can deal with them.

II. He does it, by showing that wicked people may, in some instances, prosper, but that ruin follows them in those very instances; and that is their portion, that is their heritage, that is it which they must abide by.

1. They may prosper in their children, but ruin attends them. *His children* perhaps *are multiplied* (*v.* 14) or *magnified* (so some); they are very numerous and are raised to honour and great estates. Worldly people are said to be *full of children* (Ps. 17:14), and, as it is in the margin there, *their children are full.* In them the parents hope to live and in their preferment to be honoured. But the more children they leave, and the greater prosperity they leave them in, the more and the fairer marks do they leave for the arrows of God's judgments to be levelled at, his three sore judgments, *sword, famine, and pestilence,* 2 Sa. 24:13. (1.) Some of them shall die by the sword, the sword of war perhaps (they brought them up to live by their sword, as Esau, Gen. 27:40, and those that do so commonly die by the sword, first or last), or by the sword of justice for their crimes, or the sword of the murderer for their estates. (2.) Others of them shall die by famine (*v.* 14): *His offspring shall not be satisfied with bread.* He thought he had secured to them large estates, but it may happen that they may be reduced to poverty, so as not to have the necessary sup-

ports of life, at least not to live comfortably. They shall be so needy that they shall not have a competency of necessary food, and so greedy, or so discontented, that what they have they shall not be satisfied with, because not so much, or not so dainty, as what they have been used to. *You eat, but you have not enough,* Hag. 1:6. (3.) Those that *remain shall be buried in death,* that is, shall die of the plague, which is called *death* (Rev. 6:8), and be buried privately and in haste, as soon as they are dead, without any solemnity, *buried with the burial of an ass;* and even their *widows shall not weep;* they shall not have wherewithal to put them in mourning. Or it denotes that these wicked men, as they live undesired, so they die unlamented, and even their widows will think themselves happy that they have got rid of them.

2. They may prosper in their estates, but ruin attends *them* too, *v.* 16–18. (1.) We will suppose them to be rich in money and plate, in clothing and furniture. *They heap up silver* in abundance *as the dust,* and *prepare raiment as the clay;* they have heaps of clothes about them, as plentiful as heaps of clay. Or it intimates that they have such abundance of clothes that they are even a burden to them. *They lade themselves with thick clay,* Hab. 2:6. See what is the care and business of worldly people — to heap up worldly wealth. Much would have more, until the silver is cankered and the garments are moth-eaten, Jam. 5:2, 3. But what comes of it? He shall never be the better for it himself; death will strip him, death will rob him, if he be not robbed and stripped sooner, Lu. 12:20. Nay, God will so order it that *the just shall wear his raiment and the innocent shall divide his silver.* [1.] They shall have it, and divide it among themselves. In some way or other Providence shall so order it that good men shall come honestly by that wealth which the wicked man came dishonestly by. *The wealth of the sinner is laid up for the just,* Prov. 13:22. God disposes of men's estates as he pleases, and often makes their wills against their wills. The just, whom he hated and persecuted, shall have rule over all his labour, and, in due time, recover with interest what was violently taken from him. The Egyptians' jewels were the Israelites' pay. Solomon observes (Eccl. 2:26) that God makes the sinners drudges to the righteous; for the *sinner he gives travail to gather and heap up, that he may give to him that is good before God.* [2.] They shall do good with it. The innocent shall not hoard the silver, as he did that gathered it, but shall divide it to the poor, shall *give a portion to seven and also to eight,* which is laying up the best securities. Money is like manure, good for nothing if it be not spread. When God enriches good men they must remember they are but stewards and must give an account. What bad men bring a curse upon their families with the ill-getting of good men bring a blessing upon their families with the well-using of. *He that by unjust gain increaseth his substance shall gather it for him that will pity the poor,* Prov. 28:8. (2.) We will suppose them to have built themselves strong and stately houses; but they are like the house which the moth makes for herself in an old garment, out of which she will soon be shaken, *v.* 18. He is very secure in it, as a moth, and has no apprehension of danger; but it will prove of as short continuance as *a booth which the keeper makes,* which will quickly be taken down and gone, and his place shall know him no more.

3. Destruction attends their persons, though they lived long in health and at ease (*v.* 19): *The rich man shall lie down* to sleep, to repose himself in the abundance of his wealth *(Soul, take thy ease),* shall lie down in it as his strong city, and seem to others to be very happy and very easy; *but he shall not be gathered,* that is, he shall not have his mind composed, and settled, and gathered in, to enjoy his wealth. He does not sleep so contentedly as people think he does. He *lies down,* but *his abundance will not suffer him to sleep,* at least not so sweetly as the *labouring man,* Eccl. 5:12. He lies down, but he is full of tossings to and fro till the dawning of the day, and then *he opens his eyes and he is not;* he sees himself, and all he has, hastening away, as it were, in the twinkling of an eye. His cares increase his fears, and both together make him uneasy, so that, when we attend him to his bed, we do not find him happy there. But, in the close, we are called to attend his exit, and see how miserable he is in death and after death.

(1.) He is miserable in death. It is to him the king of terrors, *v.* 20, 21. When some mortal disease seizes him what a fright is he in! *Terrors take hold of him as waters,* as if he were surrounded by the flowing tides. He trembles to think of leaving this world, and much more of removing to another. This mingles *sorrow and wrath with his sickness,* as Solomon observes, Eccl. 5:17. These terrors put him either [1.] Into a silent and sullen despair; and then the tempest of God's wrath, the tempest of death, may be said *to steal him away in the night,* when no one is aware or takes any notice of it. Or, [2.] Into an open and clamorous despair; and then he is said *to be carried away,* and hurled out of his place as with a storm, and with an east wind, violent, and noisy, and very dreadful. Death, to a godly man, is like a fair gale of wind to convey him to the heavenly country, but, to a wicked man, it is like an east wind, a storm, a tempest, that hurries him away in confusion and amazement, to destruction.

(2.) He is miserable after death. [1.] His soul falls under the just indignation of God, and it is the terror of that indignation which puts him into such amazement at the approach of death (*v.* 22): *For God shall cast upon him and not spare.* While he lived he had the benefit of sparing mercy; but now the day of God's patience is over, and he will not spare, but pour out upon him the full vials of his wrath. What God casts down upon a man there is no flying from nor bearing up under. We read of his *casting down great stones from heaven* upon the Canaanites (Jos. 10:11), which made terrible execution among them; but what was that to his casting down his anger in its full weight upon the sinner's conscience, like the *talent of lead?* Zec. 5:7, 8. The damned sinner, seeing the wrath of God break in upon him, would fain flee out of his hand; but he cannot: the gates of hell are locked and barred, and the great gulf fixed, and it will be in vain to call for the shelter of rocks and mountains. Those who will not be persuaded now to fly to the arms of divine grace, which are stretched out to receive them, will not be able to flee from the arms of divine wrath, which will shortly be stretched out to destroy them. [2.] His memory falls under the just indignation of all mankind (*v.* 23): *Men shall clap their hands at him,* that is, they shall rejoice in the judgments of God, by which he is cut off, and be well pleased in his fall. *When the wicked perish there is shouting,* Prov. 11:10. When God buries him men shall hiss him out of his place, and leave on his name perpetual marks of infamy. In the same place where he has been caressed and cried up he shall be laughed at (Ps. 52:7) and his ashes shall be trampled on.

CHAPTER 28

The strain of this chapter is very unlike the rest of this book. Job forgets his sores, and all his sorrows, and talks like a philosopher or a virtuoso. Here is a great deal both of natural and moral philosophy in this discourse; but the question is, How does it come in here? Doubtless it was not merely for an amusement, or diversion from the controversy; though, if it had been only so, perhaps it would not have been much amiss. When disputes grow hot, better lose the question than lose our temper. But this is pertinent and to the business in hand. Job and his friends had been discoursing about the dispensations of Providence towards the wicked and the righteous. Job had shown that some wicked men live and die in prosperity, while others are presently and openly arrested by the judgments of God. But, if any ask the reason why some are punished in this world and not others, they must be told it is a question that cannot be answered. The knowledge of the reasons of state in God's government of the world is kept from us, and we must neither pretend to it nor reach after it. Zophar had wished that God would show Job the "secrets of wisdom" (*ch.* 11:6). No, says Job, "secret things belong not to us, but things revealed," Deu. 29:29. And here he shows, I. Concerning worldly wealth, how industriously that is sought for and pursued by the children of men, what pains they take, what contrivances they have, and what hazards they run to get it (*v.* 1–11). II. Concerning wisdom (*v.* 12). In general, the price of it is very great; it is of inestimable value (*v.* 15–19). The place of it is very secret (*v.* 14, 20, 22). In particular, there is a wisdom which is hidden in God (*v.* 23–27) and there is a wisdom which is revealed to the children of men (*v.* 28). Our enquiries into the former must be checked, into the latter quickened, for that is it which is our concern.

Verses 1–11

Here Job shows, 1. What a great way the wit of man may go in diving into the depths of nature and seizing the riches of it, what a great deal of knowledge and wealth men may, by their ingenious and industrious searches, make themselves masters of. But does it therefore follow that men may, by their wit, comprehend the reasons why some wicked people prosper and others are punished, why some good people prosper and others are afflicted? No, by no means. The caverns of the earth may be discovered, but not the counsels of heaven. 2. What a great deal of care and pains worldly men take to get riches. He had observed concerning the wicked man (*ch.* 27:16) that he *heaped up silver as the dust;* now here he shows whence that silver came which he was so fond of and how it was obtained, to show what little reason wicked rich men have to be proud of their wealth and pomp. Observe here,

I. The wealth of this world is hidden in the earth. Thence the silver and the gold, which afterwards they refine, are fetched, *v.* 1. There they lay mixed with a great deal of dirt and dross, like a worthless thing, of no more account than common earth; and abundance of them will so lie neglected, till the earth and all the works therein shall be burnt up. Holy Mr. Herbert, in his poem called *Avarice,* takes notice of this, to shame men out of the love of money: —

> Money, thou bane of bliss, thou source of woe,
> Whence com'st thou, that thou art so fresh and fine?
> I know thy parentage is base and low;
> Man found thee poor and dirty in a mine.
>
> Surely thou didst so little contribute
> To this great kingdom which thou now hast got
> That he was fain, when thou wast destitute,
> To dig thee out of thy dark cave and grot.
>
> Man calleth thee his wealth, who made thee rich,
> And while he digs out thee falls in the ditch.

Iron and brass, less costly but more serviceable metals, are *taken out of the earth* (*v.* 2), and are there found in great abundance, which abates their price indeed, but is a great kindness to man, who could much better be without gold than without iron. Nay, *out of the earth comes bread,* that is, bread-corn, the necessary support of life, *v.* 5. Thence man's maintenance is fetched, to remind him of his own original; he is of the earth, and is hastening to the earth. *Under it is turned up as it were fire,* precious stones, that sparkle as fire — brimstone, that is apt to take fire — coal, that is proper to feed fire. As we have our food, so we have our fuel, out of the earth. There the sapphires and other gems are, and thence gold-dust is digged up;, *v.* 6. The wisdom of the Creator has placed these things, 1. Out of our sight, to teach us not to set our eyes upon them, Prov. 23:5. 2. Under our feet, to teach us not to lay them in our bosoms, nor to set our hearts upon them, but to trample upon them with a holy contempt. See how full the *earth is of God's riches* (Ps. 104:24) and infer thence, not only how great a God he is *whose the earth is* and *the fulness thereof* (Ps. 24:1), but how full heaven must needs be of God's riches, which is the city of the great King, in comparison with which this earth is a poor country.

II. The wealth that is hidden in the earth cannot be obtained but with a great deal of difficulty. 1. It is hard to be found out: there is but here and there *a vein for the silver, v.* 1. The precious stones, though bright themselves, yet, because buried in obscurity and out of sight, are called *stones of darkness and the shadow of death.* Men may search long before they light on them. 2. When found out it is hard to be fetched out. Men's wits must be set on work to contrive ways and means to get this hidden treasure into their hands. They must with their lamps *set an end to darkness;* and if one expedient miscarry, one method fail, they must try another, till they have *searched out all perfection,* and turned every stone to effect it, *v.* 3. They must grapple with subterraneous waters (*v.* 4, 10, 11), and force their way through rocks which are, as it were, the roots of the mountains, *v.* 9. Now God has made the getting of gold, and silver, and precious stones, so difficult, (1.) For the exciting and engaging of industry. *Dii laboribus omnia vendunt — Labour is the price which the gods affix to all things.* If valuable things were too easily obtained men would never learn to take pains. But the difficulty of gaining the riches of this earth may suggest to us what violence the kingdom of heaven suffers. (2.) For the checking and restraining of pomp and luxury. What is for necessity is had with a little labour from the surface of the earth; but what is for ornament must be dug with a great deal of pains out of the bowels of it. To be fed is cheap, but to be fine is chargeable.

III. Though the subterraneous wealth is thus hard to obtain, yet men will have it. He that loves silver is not satisfied with silver, and yet is not satisfied without it; but those that have much must needs have more. See here, 1. What inventions men have to get this wealth. They *search out all perfection, v.* 3. They have arts and engines to dry up the waters, and carry them off, when they break in upon them in their mines and threaten to drown the work, *v.* 4. They have pumps, and pipes, and canals, to clear their way, and, obstacles being removed, they tread *the path which no fowl knoweth* (*v.* 7, 8), unseen by the vulture's eye, which is piercing and quick-sighted, and untrodden by the lion's whelps, which traverse all the paths of the wilderness. 2. What pains men take, and what vast charge they are at, to get this wealth. They work their way through the rocks and undermine the mountains, *v.* 10. 3. What hazards they run. Those that dig in the mines have their lives in their hands; for they are obliged to *bind the floods from overflowing* (*v.* 11), and are continually in danger of being suffocated by damps or crushed or buried alive by the fall of the earth upon them. See how foolish man adds to his own burden. He is sentenced to eat bread in the sweat of his face; but, as if that were not enough, he will get gold and silver at the peril of his life, though the more is gotten the less valuable it is. In Solomon's time silver was as stones. But, 4. Observe what it is that carries men through all this toil and peril: *Their eye sees every precious thing, v.* 10. Silver and gold are precious things with them, and they have them in their eye in all these pursuits. They fancy they see them glittering before their faces, and, in the prospect of laying hold of them, they make nothing of all these difficulties; for they make something of their toil at last: *That which is hidden bringeth he forth to light, v.* 11. What was hidden under ground is laid upon the bank; the metal that was hidden in the ore is refined from its dross and brought forth pure out of the furnace; and then he thinks his pains well bestowed. Go to the miners then, thou sluggard in religion; consider their ways, and be wise. Let their courage, diligence, and constancy in seeking the wealth that perisheth shame us out of slothfulness and faint-heartedness in labouring for the true riches. *How much better is it to get wisdom than gold!* How much easier and safer! Yet gold is sought for, but grace neglected. Will the hopes of *precious things* out of the earth (so they call them, though really they are paltry and perishing) be such a spur to industry, and shall not the certain prospect of truly precious things in heaven be much more so?

Verses 12–19

Job, having spoken of the wealth of the world, which men put such a value upon and take so much pains for, here comes to speak of another more valuable jewel, and that is, *wisdom and understanding,* the knowing and enjoying of God and ourselves. Those that found out all those ways and means to enrich themselves thought themselves very wise; but Job will not own theirs to be wisdom. He supposes them to gain their point, and to bring to light what they sought for (*v.* 11), and yet asks, *"Where is wisdom?* for it is not here." This their way is their folly. We must therefore seek it somewhere else, and it will be found nowhere but in the principles and practices of religion. There is more true knowledge, satisfaction, and happiness, in sound divinity, which shows us the way to the joys of heaven, than in natural philosophy or mathematics, which help us to find a way into the bowels of the earth. Two things cannot be found out concerning this wisdom: —

I. The price of it, for that is inestimable; its worth is infinitely more than all the riches in this world: *Man knows not the price thereof* (*v.* 13), that is, 1. Few put a due value upon it. Men know not the worth of it, its innate excellency, their need of it, and of what unspeakable advantage it will be to them; and therefore, though they have many a price in their hand to get this wisdom, yet they *have no heart to it,* Prov. 17:16. The cock in the fable knew not the value of the precious stone he found in the dunghill, and therefore would rather have lighted on a barley-corn. Men know not the worth of grace, and therefore will take no pains to get it. 2. None can possibly give a valuable consideration for it, with all the wealth this world can furnish them with. This Job enlarges upon *v.* 15, etc., where he makes an inventory of the *bona notabilia — the most valuable treasures* of this world. Gold is five times mentioned; silver comes in also; and then several precious stones, the onyx and sapphire, pearls and rubies, and the topaz of Ethiopia. These are the things that are highest prized in the world's markets: but if a man would give, not only these, heaps of these, but all the substance of his house, all he is worth in the world, for wisdom, it would utterly be contemned. These may give a man some advantage in seeking wisdom, as they did to Solomon, but there is no purchasing wisdom with these. It is a gift of *the Holy Ghost,* which *cannot be bought with money,* Acts 8:20. As it does not run in the blood, and so come to us by descent, so it cannot be got for money, nor does it come to us by purchase. Spiritual gifts are conferred without money and without price, because no money can be a price for them. Wisdom is likewise a more valuable gift to him that has it, makes him richer and happier, than gold or precious stones. It is *better to get wisdom than gold.* Gold is another's, wisdom our own; gold is for the body and time, wisdom for the soul and eternity. Let that which is most precious in God's account be so in ours. See Prov. 3:14, etc.

II. The place of it, for that is undiscoverable. *Where shall wisdom be found? v.* 12. He asks this, 1. As one that truly desired to find it. This is a question we should all put. While the most of men are asking, "Where shall money be found?" we should ask, *Where may wisdom be found?* that we may seek it and find it, not vain philosophy, or carnal policy, but true religion; for that is the only true wisdom, that is it which best improves our faculties and best secures our spiritual and eternal welfare. This is that which we should cry after and dig for, Prov. 2:3, 4. 2. As one that utterly despaired of finding it any where but in God, and any way but by divine revelation: *It is not found in this land of the living, v.* 13. We cannot attain to a right understanding of God and his will, of ourselves and our duty and interest, by reading any books or men, but by reading God's book and the men of God. Such is the degeneracy of human nature that there is no true wisdom to be found with any but those who are born again, and who, through grace, partake of the divine nature. As for others, even the most ingenious and industrious, they can tell us no tidings of this lost wisdom. (1.) Ask the miners, and by them *the depth will say, It is not in me, v.* 14. Those who dig into the bowels of the earth, to rifle the treasures there, cannot in these dark recesses find this rare jewel, nor with all their art make themselves masters of it. (2.) Ask the mariners, and by them *the sea will say, It is not in me.* It can never be got either by trading on the waters or diving into them, can never be *sucked from the abundance of the seas or the treasures hidden in the sand.* Where there is a vein for the silver there is no vein for wisdom, none for grace. Men can more easily break through the difficulties they meet with in getting worldly wealth than through those they meet with in getting heavenly wisdom, and they will take more pains to learn how to live in this world than how to live for ever in a better world. So blind and foolish has man become that it is in vain to ask him, *Where is the place of wisdom,* and which is the road that leads to it?

Verses 20–28

The question which Job had asked (*v.* 12) he asks again here; for it is too worthy, too weighty, to be let fall, until we speed in the enquiry. Concerning this we must seek till we find, till we get some satisfactory account of it. By a diligent prosecution of this enquiry he brings it, at length, to this issue, that there is a twofold wisdom, one *hidden in God,* which is secret and *belongs not to us,* the other made known by him and revealed to man, which *belongs to us and to our children.*

I. The knowledge of God's secret will, the will of his providence, is out of our reach, and what God has reserved to himself. It *belongs to the Lord our God.* To know the particulars of what God will do hereafter, and the reasons of what he is doing now, is the knowledge Job first speaks of.

1. This knowledge is hidden from us. It is high, we cannot attain unto it (*v.* 21, 22): *It is hid from the eyes of all living,* even of philosophers, politicians, and saints; it is *kept close from the fowls of the air;* though they fly high and in the open firmament of heaven, though they seem somewhat nearer that upper world where the source of this wisdom is, though their eyes behold afar off (*ch.* 39:29), yet they cannot penetrate into the counsels of God. No, man is *wiser than the fowls of heaven,* and yet comes short of this wisdom. Even those who, in their speculations, soar highest, and think themselves, like the fowls of the air, above the heads of other people, yet cannot pretend to this knowledge. Job and his friends had been arguing about the methods and reasons of the dispensations of Providence in the government of the world. "What fools are we" (says Job) "to fight in the dark thus, to dispute about that which we do not understand!" The line and plummet of human reason can never fathom the abyss of the divine counsels. Who can undertake to give the rationale of Providence, or account for the maxims, measure, and methods of God's government, those *arcana imperii — cabinet counsels* of divine wisdom? Let us then be content not to know the future events of the Providence until time discover them (Acts 1:7) and not to know the secret reasons of Providence until eternity discover them. God is now a God that hideth himself (Isa. 45:15); *clouds and darkness are round about him.* Though this wisdom be hidden from all living, yet *destruction and death say, We have heard the fame of it.* Though they cannot give an account of themselves (for there is *no wisdom, nor device, nor knowledge at all in the grave,* much less this), yet there is a world on the other side death and the grave, on which those dark regions border, and to which we must pass through them, and there we shall see clearly what we are now in the dark about. "Have a little patience," says Death to the inquisitive soul: "I will fetch thee shortly to a place where even this wisdom will be found." When *the mystery of God shall be finished* it will be laid open, and we shall know as we are known; when the veil of flesh is rent, and the interposing clouds are scattered, we shall know what God does, though we know not now, Jn. 13:7.

2. This knowledge is hidden in God, as the apostle speaks, Eph. 3:9. *Known unto God are all his works,* though they are not known to us, Acts 15:18. There are good reasons for what he does, though we cannot assign them (*v.* 23): *God understands the way thereof.* Men sometimes do they know not what, but God never does. Men do what they did not design to do; new occurrences put them upon new counsels, and oblige them to take new measures. But God does all according to the purpose which he purposed in himself, and which he never alters. Men sometimes do that which they cannot give a good reason for, but in every will of God there is a counsel: he knows both what he does and why he does it, the whole series of events and the order and place of every occurrence. This knowledge he has in perfection, but keeps to himself. Two reasons are here given why God must needs understand his own way, and he only: —

(1.) Because all events are now directed by an all-seeing and almighty Providence, *v.* 24, 25. He that governs the world is, [1.] Omniscient; *for he looks to the ends of the earth,* both in place and time; distant ages, distant regions, are under his view. We do not understand our own way, much less can we understand God's way, because we are short-sighted. How little do we know of what is doing in the world, much less of what will be done? But *the eyes of the Lord are in every place;* nay, they *run to and fro through the earth.* Nothing is, or can be, hidden from him; and therefore the reasons why some wicked people prosper remarkably and others are remarkably punished in this world, which are secret to us, are known to him. One day's events, and one man's affairs, have such a reference to, and such a dependence upon, another's, that he only to whom all events and all affairs are naked and open, and who sees the whole at one entire and certain view, is a competent Judge of every part. [2.] He is omnipotent. He can do every thing, and is very exact in all he does. For proof of this Job mentions the winds and waters, *v.* 25. What is lighter than the wind? Yet God hath ways of poising it. He knows how *to make the weight for the winds,* which he *brings out of his treasuries* (Ps. 135:7), keeping a very particular account of what he draws out, as men do of what they pay out of their treasuries, not at random, as men bring out their trash. Nothing sensible is to us more unaccountable than the wind. We *hear the sound of it, yet cannot tell whence it comes, nor whither it goes;* but God gives it out by weight, wisely ordering both from what point it shall blow and with what strength. The waters of the sea, and the rain-waters, he both weighs and measures, allotting the proportion of every tide and every shower. A great and constant communication there is between clouds and seas, the waters above the firmament and those under it. Vapours go up, rains come down, air is condensed into water, water rarefied into air; but the great God keeps an exact account of all the stock with which this trade is carried on for the public benefit and sees that none of it be lost. Now if, in these things, Providence be so exact, much more in dispensing frowns and favours, rewards and punishments, to the children of men, according to the rules of equity.

(2.) Because all events were from eternity designed and determined by an infallible prescience and immutable decree, *v.* 26, 27. When he settled the course of nature he foreordained all the operations of his government. [1.] He settled the course of nature. Job mentions particularly *a decree for the rain* and *a way for the thunder and lightening.* The general manner and method, and the particular uses and tendencies, of these strange performances, both their causes and their effects, were appointed by the divine purpose; hence God is said to *prepare lightnings for the rain,* Ps. 135:7; Jer. 10:13. [2.] When he did that he laid all the measures of his providence, and drew an exact scheme of the whole work from first to last. Then, from eternity, did he see in himself, and declare to himself, the plan of his proceedings. Then he prepared it, fixed it, and established it, set every thing in readiness for all his works, so that, when any thing was to be done, nothing was to seek, nor could any thing unforeseen occur, to put it either out of its method or out of its time; for all was ordered as exactly as if he had studied it and searched it out, so that, whatever he does, *nothing can be put to it nor taken from it,* and therefore *it shall be for ever,* Eccl. 3:14. Some make Job to speak of wisdom here as a person, and translate it, *Then he saw her and showed her,* etc., and then it is parallel with that of Solomon concerning the essential wisdom of the Father, the eternal Word, Prov. 8:22, etc. *Before the earth was, then was I by him,* Jn. 1:1, 2.

II. The knowledge of God's revealed will, the will of his precept, and this is within our reach; it is level to our capacity, and will do us good (*v.* 28): *Unto man he said, Behold, the fear of the Lord that is wisdom.* Let it not be said that when God concealed his counsels from man, and forbade him that tree of knowledge, it was because he grudged him any thing that would contribute to his real bliss and satisfaction; no, he let him know as much as he was concerned to know in order to his duty and happiness; he shall be entrusted with as much of his sovereign mind as is needful and fit for a subject, but he must not think himself fit to be a privy-counsellor. He said to *Adam* (so some), to the first man, in the day in which he was created; he told him plainly it was not for him to amuse himself with over-curious searches into the mysteries of creation, nor to pretend to solve all the phenomena of nature; he would find it neither possible nor profitable to do so. No less wisdom (says archbishop Tillotson) than that which made the world can thoroughly understand the philosophy of it. But let him look upon this as his wisdom, to fear the Lord and to depart from evil; let him learn that, and he is learned enough; let this knowledge serve his turn. When God forbade man the tree of knowledge he allowed him the tree of life, and this is that tree, Prov. 3:18. We cannot attain true wisdom but by divine revelation. *The Lord giveth wisdom,* Prov. 2:6. Now the matter of that is not found in the secrets of nature or providence, but in the rules for our own practice. Unto man he said, not, "Go up to heaven, to fetch happiness thence;" or, "Go down to the deep, to draw it up thence." No, *the word is nigh thee,* Deu. 30:14. *He hath shown thee, O man!* not what is great, but *what is good,* not what the Lord thy God designs to do with thee, but what he *requires of thee,* Mic. 6:8. *Unto you, O men! I call,* Prov. 8:4. Lord, what is man that he should be thus minded, thus visited! Behold, mark, take notice of this; he that has ears let him hear what the God of heaven says to the children of men: *The fear of the Lord, that is the wisdom.* Here is, 1. The description of true religion, pure religion, and undefiled; it is to *fear the Lord and depart from evil,* which agrees with God's character of Job, *ch.* 1:1. The *fear of the Lord* is the spring and summary of all religion. There is a slavish fear of God, springing from hard thoughts of him, which is contrary to religion, Mt. 25:24. There is a selfish fear of God springing from dreadful thoughts of him, which may be a good step towards religion, Acts 9:5. But there is a filial fear of God, springing from great and high thoughts of him, which is the life and soul of all religion. And, wherever this reigns in the heart, it will appear by a constant care to *depart from evil,* Prov. 16:6. This is essential to religion. We must first cease to do evil, or we shall never learn to do well. *Virtus est vitium fugere — Even in our flight from vice some virtue lies.* 2. The commendation of religion: it is *wisdom* and *understanding.* To be truly religious is to be truly wise. As the wisdom of God appears in the institution of religion, so the wisdom of man appears in the institution of religion, so the wisdom of man appears in the practice and observance of it. It is understanding, for it is the best knowledge of truth; it is wisdom, for it is the best management of our affairs. Nothing more surely guides our way and gains our end than being religious.

CHAPTER 29

After that excellent discourse concerning wisdom in the foregoing chapter Job sat down and paused awhile, not because he had talked himself out of breath, but because he would not, without the leave of the company, engross the talk to himself, but would give room for his friends, if they pleased, to make their remarks on what he had said; but they had nothing to say, and therefore, after he had recollected himself a little, he went on with his discourse concerning his own affairs, as recorded in this and the two following chapters, in which, I. He describes the height of the prosperity from which he had fallen. And, II. The depth of the adversity into which he had fallen; and this he does to move the pity of his friends, and to justify, or at least excuse, his own complaints. But then, III. To obviate his friends' censures of him, he makes a very ample and particular protestation of his own integrity notwithstanding. In this chapter he looks back to the days of his prosperity, and shows, 1. What comfort and satisfaction he had in his house and family (*v.* 1–6). 2. What a great deal of honour and power he had in his country, and what respect was paid him by all sorts of people (*v.* 7–10). 3. What abundance of good he did in his place, as a magistrate (*v.* 11–17). 4. What a just prospect he had of the continuance of his comfort at home (*v.* 18–20) and of his interest abroad (*v.* 21–25). All this he enlarges upon, to aggravate his present calamities; like Naomi, "I went out full," but am brought "home again empty."

Verses 1–6

Losers may have leave to speak, and there is nothing they speak of more feelingly than of the comforts they are stripped of. Their former prosperity is one of the most pleasing subjects of their thoughts and talk. It was so to Job, who begins here with a wish (*v.* 2): *O that I were as in months past!* so he brings in this account of his prosperity. His wish is, 1. "O that I were in as good a state as I was in then, that I had as much wealth, honour, and pleasure, as I had then!" This he wishes, from a concern he had, not so much for his ease, as for his reputation and the glory of his God, which he thought were eclipsed by his present sufferings. "O that I might be restored to my prosperity, and then the censures and reproaches of my friends would be effectually silenced, even upon their own principles, and for ever rolled away!" If this be our end in desiring life, health, and prosperity, that God may be glorified, and the credit of our holy profession rescued, preserved, and advanced, the desire is not only natural, but spiritual. 2. "O that I were in as good a frame of spirit as I was in then!" That which Job complained most of now was a load upon his spirits, through God's withdrawing from him; and therefore he wishes he now had his spirit as much enlarged and encouraged in the service of God as he had then and that he had as much freedom and fellowship with him as then thought himself happy in. This was *in the days of his youth* (*v.* 4), when he was in the prime of his time for the enjoyment of those things and could relish them with the highest gust. Note, Those that prosper in the days of their youth know not what black and cloudy days they are yet reserved for. Two things made the months past pleasant to Job: —

I. That he had comfort in his God. This was the chief thing he rejoiced in, in his prosperity, as the spring of it and the sweetness of it, that he had the favour of God and the tokens of that favour. He did not attribute his prosperity to a happy turn of fortune, nor to his own might, nor to the power of his own hand, but makes the same acknowledgment that David does. Ps. 30:7, *Thou, by thy favour, hast made my mountain stand strong.* A gracious soul delights in God's smiles, not in the smiles of this world. Four things were then very pleasant to holy Job: — 1. The confidence he had in the divine protection. They were *the days when God preserved me, v.* 2. Even then he saw himself exposed, and did not make *his wealth his strong city* nor *trust in the abundance of his riches,* but *the name of the Lord was his strong tower;* in that only he thought himself safe, and to that he ascribed it that he was then safe and that his comforts were preserved to him. The devil saw a hedge about him of God's making (*ch.* 1:10), and Job saw it himself, and owned it was *God's visitation that preserved his spirit, ch.* 10:12. Those only whom God protects are safe and may be easy; and therefore those who have ever so much of this world must not think themselves safe unless God preserve them. 2. The complacency he had in the divine favour (*v.* 3): *God's candle shone upon his head,* that is, God lifted up the light of his countenance upon him, gave him the assurances and sweet relishes of his love. The best of the communications of the divine favour to the saints in this world is but the candle-light, compared with what is reserved for them in the future state. But such abundant satisfaction did Job take in the divine favour that, by the light of that, he walked through darkness; that guided him in his doubts, comforted him in his griefs, bore him up under his burdens, and helped him through all his difficulties. Those that have the brightest sun-shine of outward prosperity must yet expect some moments of darkness. They are sometimes crossed, sometimes at a loss, sometimes melancholy. But those that are interested in the favour of God, and know how to value it, can, by the light of that, walk cheerfully and comfortably through all the darkness of this vale of tears. That puts gladness into the heart enough to counterbalance all the grievances of this present time. 3. The communion he had with the divine word (*v.* 4): *The secret of God was upon my tabernacle,* that is, God conversed freely with him, as one bosom-friend with another. He knew God's mind, and was not in the dark about it, as, of late, he had been. *The secret of the Lord is* said to be *with those that fear him,* for *he shows them* that in *his covenant* which others see not, Ps. 25:14. God communicates his favour and grace to his people, and receives the return of their devotion in a way secret to the world. Some read it, *When the society of God was in my tabernacle,* which Rabbi Solomon understands of an assembly of God's people that used to meet at Job's house for religious worship, in which he presided; this he took a great deal of pleasure in, and the scattering of it was a trouble to him. Or it may be understood of the angels of God pitching their tents about his habitation. 4. The assurance he had of the divine presence (*v.* 5): *The Almighty was yet with me.* Now he thought God had departed from him, but in those days he was *with him,* and that was all in all to him. God's presence with a man in his house, though it be but a cottage, makes it both a castle and a palace.

II. That he had comfort in his family. Every thing was agreeable there: he had both mouths for his meat and meat for his mouths; the want of either is a great affliction. 1. He had a numerous offspring to enjoy his estate: *My children were about me.* He had many children, enough to compass him round, and they were observant of him and obsequious to him; they were about him, to know what he would have and wherein they might serve him. It is a comfort to tender parents to see their children about them. Job speaks very feelingly of this comfort now that he was deprived of it. He thought it an instance of God's being with him that his children were about him; and yet reckon amiss if, when we have lost our children, we cannot comfort ourselves with this, that we have not lost our God. 2. He had a plentiful estate for the support of this numerous family, *v.* 6. His dairy abounded to such a degree that he might, if he pleased, *wash his steps with butter;* and his olive-yards were so fruitful, beyond expectation, that it seemed as if the *rock poured him out rivers of oil.* He reckons his wealth, not by his silver and gold, which were for hoarding, but by his butter and oil, which were for use; for what is an estate good for unless we take the good of it ourselves and do good with it to others?

Verses 7–17

We have here Job in a post of honour and power. Though he had comfort enough in his own house, yet he did not confine himself to that. We are not born for ourselves, but for the public. When any business was to be done in the gate, the place of judgment, Job *went out to* it *through the city* (*v.* 7), not in an affectation of pomp, but in an affection to justice. Observe, Judgment was administered in the gate, in the street, in the places of concourse, to which every man might have a free access, that every one who would might be a witness to all that was said and done, and that when judgment was given against the guilty others might hear and fear. Job being a prince, a judge, a magistrate, a man in authority, among the children of the east, we are here told,

I. What a profound respect was paid to him by all sorts of people, not only for the dignity of his place, but for his personal merit, his eminent prudence, integrity, and good management. 1. The people honoured him and stood in awe of him, *v.* 8. The gravity and majesty of his looks and mien, and his known strictness in animadverting upon every thing that was evil and indecent, commanded all about him into due decorum. *The young men,* who could not keep their countenances, or, it may be, were conscious to themselves of something amiss, *hid themselves,* and got out of his way; *and the aged,* though they kept their ground, yet would not keep their seats: they *arose and stood up* to do homage to him; those who expected honour from others gave honour to him. Virtue and piety challenge respect from all, and usually have it; but those that not only *are* good, but *do* good, are worthy of double honour. Modesty becomes those that are young and in subjection as much as majesty becomes those that are aged and in power. Honour and fear are due to magistrates, and must be rendered to them, Rom. 13:7. But, if a great and good man was thus reverenced, how is the great and good God to be feared! 2. The princes and nobles paid great deference to him, *v.* 9, 10. Some think that these were inferior magistrates under him, and that the respect they paid him was due to his place, as their sovereign and supreme. It should rather seem that they were his equals in place, and joined in commission with him, and that the peculiar honour they gave him was gained by his extraordinary abilities and services. It was agreed that he excelled them all in quickness of apprehension, soundness of judgment, closeness of application, clearness and copiousness of expression; and therefore he was among his fellows an oracle of law, and counsel, and justice, and what he said all attended to and acquiesced in. When he came into court, especially when he stood up to speak to any business, *the princes refrained talking, the nobles held their peace,* that they might the more diligently hearken to what he said and might be sure to understand his meaning. Those that had been forward to speak their own thoughts, loved to hear themselves talk, and cared not much what any body else said, yet, when it came to Job's turn to speak, were as desirous to know his thoughts as ever they had been to vent their own. Those that suspected their own judgment were satisfied in his, and admired with what dexterity he split the hair and untied the knots which puzzled them and which they knew not what to make of. When the princes and nobles wrangled among themselves all agreed to refer the matters in dispute to Job and to abide by his judgment. Happy the men that are blessed with such eminent gifts as these; they have great opportunities of honouring God and doing good, but have great need to watch against pride. Happy the people that are blessed with such eminent men; it is a token for good to them.

II. What a great deal of good he did in his place. He was very serviceable to his country with the power he had; and here we shall see what it was which Job valued himself by in the day of his prosperity. It is natural to men to have some value for themselves, and we may judge something of our own character by observing what that is upon which we value ourselves. Job valued himself, not by the honour of his family, the great estate he had, his large income, his full table, the many servants he had at his command, the ensigns of his dignity, his equipage and retinue, the splendid entertainments he gave, and the court that was made to him, but by his usefulness. Goodness is God's glory, and it will be ours; if we are merciful as God is, we are perfect as he is.

1. He valued himself by the interest he had in the esteem, affections, and prayers, of sober people; not by the studied panegyrics of the wits and poets, but the unconstrained praises of all about him. All that heard what he said, and saw what he did, how he laid out himself for the public good with all the authority and tender affection of a father to his country, blessed him, and gave witness to him, *v.* 11. Many a good word they said of him, and many a good prayer they put up for him. He did not think it an honour to make every body fear him *(Oderint dum metuant — Let them hate, provided they also fear)* nor to be arbitrary, and to have his own will and way, not caring what people said of him; but, like Mordecai, to be *accepted of the multitude of his brethren,* Esth. 10:3. He did not so much value the applauses of those at a distance as the attestations of those that were the witnesses of his conduct, that constantly attended him, saw him, and heard him, and could speak of their own knowledge, especially theirs who had themselves been the better for him and could speak by their own experience: such was the blessing of him who was ready to perish (*v.* 13) and who by Job's means was rescued from perishing. Let great men, and men of estates, thus do good, and they shall have praise of the same; and let those who have good done to them look upon it as a just debt they owe to their protectors and benefactors to bless them and give witness to them, to use their interest on earth for their honour and in heaven for their comfort, to praise them and pray for them. Those are ungrateful indeed who grudge these small returns.

2. He valued himself by the care he took of those that were least able to help themselves, the poor and the needy, the widows and fatherless, the blind and the lame, who could not be supposed either to merit his favour or ever to be in a capacity to recompense it. (1.) If the poor were injured or oppressed, they might cry to Job, and, if he found the allegations of their petitions true, they had not only his ear and his bowels, but his hand too: He *delivered the poor that cried* (*v.* 12) and would not suffer them to be trampled upon and run down. Nay (*v.* 16), he was *a father to the poor,* not only a judge to protect them and to see that they were not wronged, but a father to provide for them and to see that they did not want, to counsel and direct them, and to appear and act for them upon all occasions. It is no disparagement to the son of a prince to be a father to the poor. (2.) The fatherless that had none to help them found Job ready to help them, and, if they were in straits, to deliver them. He helped them to make the best of what little they had, helped them to pay what they owed and to get in what was owing to them, helped them out into the world, helped them into business, helped them to it, and helped them in it; thus should the fatherless be helped. (3.) Those that were ready to perish he saved from perishing, relieving those that were hungry and ready to perish for want, taking care of those that were sick, that were outcasts, that were falsely accused, or in danger of being turned out of their estates unjustly, or, upon any other account, were ready to perish. The extremity of the peril, as it quickened Job to appear the more vigorously for them, so it made his seasonable kindness the more affecting and the more obliging, and brought their blessings the more abundantly upon him. (4.) The widows that were sighing for grief, and trembling for fear, he made to sing for joy, so carefully did he protect them and provide for them, and so heartily did he espouse their interest. It is a pleasure to a good man, and should be so to a great man, to give those occasion to rejoice that are most acquainted with grief. (5.) Those that were upon any account at a loss Job gave suitable and seasonable relief to (*v.* 15): *I was eyes to the blind,* counselling and advising those for the best that knew not what to do, and *feet to the lame,* assisting those with money and friends that knew what they should do, but knew not how to compass it. Those we best help whom we help out in that very thing wherein they are defective and most need help. We may come to be blind or lame ourselves, and therefore should pity and succour those that are so, Isa. 35:3, 4; Heb. 12:13.

3. He valued himself by the conscience he made of justice and equity in all his proceedings. His friends had unjustly censured him as an oppressor. "So far from that," says he, "I always made it my business to maintain and support right." (1.) He devoted himself to the administration of justice (*v.* 14): *I put on righteousness and it clothed me,* that is, he had an habitual disposition to execute justice and put on a fixed resolution to do it. It was *the girdle of his lions,* Isa. 11:5. It kept him tight and steady in all his motions. He always appeared in it, as in his clothing, and never without it. Righteousness will clothe those that put it on; it will keep them warm, and be comfortable to them; it will keep them safe, and fence them against the injuries of the season; it will adorn them, and recommend them to the favour both of God and man. (2.) He took pleasure in it, and, as I may say, a holy delight. He looked upon it as his greatest glory to do justice to all and injury to none: *My judgment was as a robe and a diadem.* Perhaps he did not himself wear a robe and a diadem; he was very indifferent to those ensigns of honour; those were most fond of them who had least intrinsic worth to recommend them. But the settled principles of justice, by which he was governed and did govern, were to him instead of all those ornaments. If a magistrate do the duty of his place, that is an honour to him far beyond his gold or purple, and should be, accordingly, his delight; and truly if he do not make conscience of his duty, and in some measure answer the end of his elevation, his robe and diadem, his gown and cap, his sword and mace, are but a reproach, like the purple robe and crown of thorns with which the Jews studied to ridicule our Saviour; for, as clothes on a dead man will never make him warm, so robes on a base man will never make him honourable. (3.) He took pains in the business of his place (*v.* 16): *The cause which I knew not I searched out.* He diligently enquired into the matters of fact, patiently and impartially heard both sides, set every thing in its true light, and cleared it from false colours; he laid all circumstances together, that he might find out the truth and the merits of every cause, and then, and not until then, gave judgment upon it. He never answered a matter before he heard it, nor did he judge a man to be righteous, however he seemed, for his being *first in his own cause,* Prov. 18:17.

4. He valued himself by the check he gave to the violence of proud and evil men (*v.* 17): *I broke the jaws of the wicked.* He does not say that he broke their necks. He did not take away their lives, but he broke their jaws, he took away their power of doing mischief; he humbled them, mortified them, and curbed their insolence, and so plucked the spoil out of their teeth, delivered the persons and estates of honest men from being made a prey of by them. When they had got the spoil between their teeth, and were greedily swallowing it down, he bravely rescued it, as David did the lamb out of the mouth of the lion, not fearing, though they roared and raged like a lion disappointed of his prey. Good magistrates must thus be a terror and restraint to evil-doers and a protection to the innocent, and, in order to this, they have need to arm themselves with zeal, and resolution, and an undaunted courage. A judge upon the bench has as much need to be bold and brave as a commander in the field.

Verses 18–25

That which crowned Job's prosperity was the pleasing prospect he had of the continuance of it. Though he knew, in general, that he was liable to trouble, and therefore was not secure (*ch.* 3:26, *I was not in safety, neither had I rest),* yet he had no particular occasion for fear, but as much reason as ever any man had to count upon the lengthening out of his tranquility.

I. See here what his thoughts were in his prosperity (*v.* 18): *Then I said, I shall die in my nest.* Having made himself a warm and easy nest, he hoped nothing would disturb him in it, nor remove him out of it, till death removed him. He knew he had never stolen any coal from the altar which might fire his nest; he saw no storm arising to shake down his nest; and therefore concluded, *To morrow shall be as this day;* as David (Ps. 30:6), *My mountain stands strong, and shall not be moved.* Observe, 1. In the midst of his prosperity he thought of dying, and the thought was not uneasy to him. He knew that, though his nest was high, it did not set him out of the reach of the darts of death. 2. Yet he flattered himself with vain hopes, (1.) That he should live long, should *multiply his days as the sand.* He means as the sand on the sea-shore; whereas we should rather reckon our days by the sand in the hourglass, which will have run out in a little time. See how apt even good people are to think of death as a thing at a distance, and to put far from them that evil day, which will really be to them a good day. (2.) That he should die in the same prosperous state in which he had lived. If such an expectation as this arise from a lively faith in the providence and promise of God, it is well, but if from a conceit of our own wisdom, and the stability of these earthly things, it is ill-grounded and turns into sin. We hope Job's confidence was like David's (Ps. 27:1, *Whom shall I fear?),* not like the rich fool's (Lu. 12:19), *Soul, take thy ease.*

II. See what was the ground of these thoughts.

1. If he looked at home, he found he had a good foundation. His stock was all his own, and none of all his neighbours had any demand upon him. He found no bodily dis-

temper growing upon him; his estate did not lie under any incumbrance; nor was he sensible of any worm at the root of it. He was getting forward in his affairs, and not going behind-hand; he lost no reputation, but gained rather; he knew no rival that threatened either to eclipse his honour or abridge his power. See how he describes this, *v.* 19, 20. He was like a tree whose root is not only spread out, which fixes it and keeps it firm, so that it is in no danger of being overturned, but *spread out by the waters,* which feed it, and make it fruitful and flourishing, so that it is in no danger of withering. And, as he thought himself blessed with the fatness of the earth, so also with the kind influences of heaven too; for the *dew lay all night upon his branch.* Providence favoured him, and made all his enjoyments comfortable and all his enterprises successful. Let none think to support their prosperity with what they draw from this earth without that blessing which is derived from above. God's favour being continued to Job, in the virtue of that his glory was still fresh in him. Those about him had still something new to say in his praise, and needed not to repeat the old stories: and it is only by constant goodness that men's glory is thus preserved fresh and kept from withering and growing stale. His *bow* also *was renewed in his hand,* that is, his power to protect himself and annoy those that assailed him still increased, so that he thought he had as little reason as any man to fear the insults of the Sabeans and Chaldeans.

2. If he looked abroad, he found he had a good interest and well confirmed. As he had no reason to dread the power of his enemies, so neither had he any reason to distrust the fidelity of his friends. To the last moment of his prosperity they continued their respect to him and their dependence on him. What had he to fear who so gave counsel as in effect to give law to all his neighbours? Nothing surely could be done against him when really nothing was done without him.

(1.) He was the oracle of his country. He was consulted as an oracle, and his dictates were acquiesced in as oracles, *v.* 21. When others could not be heard all men *gave ear* to him, *and kept silence at his counsel,* knowing that, as nothing could be said against it, so nothing needed to be added to it. And therefore, *after his words, they spoke not again, v.* 22. Why should men meddle with a subject that has already been exhausted?

(2.) He was the darling of his country. All about him were well pleased with every thing he said and did, as David's people were with him, 2 Sa. 3:36. He had the hearts and affections of all his neighbours, all his servants, tenants, subjects; never was man so much admired nor so well beloved. [1.] Those were thought happy to whom he spoke, and they thought themselves so. Never were the dews of heaven so acceptable to the parched ground as his wise discourses were to those that attended on them, especially to those to whom they were particularly accommodated and directed. His speech dropped upon them, and they waited for its as for the rain (*v.* 22, 23), wondering at the gracious words which proceeded out of his mouth, catching at them, laying hold on them, and treasuring them up as apophthegms. His servants that stood continually before him to hear his wisdom would not have envied Solomon's. Those are wise, or are likely to be so, that know how to value wise discourse, that wish for it, and wait for it, and drink it in as the earth does *the rain that comes often upon it,* Heb. 6:7. And those who have such an interest as Job had in the esteem of others whose *ipse dixit — bare assertion* goes so far, as they have a great opportunity of doing good, so they must take great care lest they do hurt, for a bad word out of their mouths is very infectious. [2.] Much more happy were those thought on whom he smiled, and they thought themselves so, *v.* 24. *"If I laughed on them,* designing thereby to show myself pleased in them, or pleasant with them, it was such a favour that *they believed it not* for joy," or because it was so rare a thing to see this grave man smile. *Many seek the ruler's favour.* Job was a ruler whose favour was courted and valued at a high rate. He to whom a great prince gave a kiss was envied by another to whom he only gave a golden cup. Familiarity often breeds contempt; but if Job at any time saw fit, for his own diversion, to make himself free with those about him, yet it did not in the least diminish the veneration they had for him: *The light of his countenance they cast not down.* So wisely did he dispense his favours as not to make them cheap, and so wisely did they receive them as not to make themselves unworthy of them another time.

(3.) He was the sovereign of his country, *v.* 25. He *chose out their way,* sat at the helm, and steered for them, all referring themselves to his conduct and submitting themselves to his command. To this perhaps, in many countries, monarchy owed its rise: such a man as Job, that so far excelled all his neighbours in wisdom and integrity, could not but sit chief, and the fool will, of course, be servant to the wise in heart: and, if the wisdom did but for a while run in the blood, the honour and power would certainly attend it and so by degrees become hereditary. Two things recommended Job to the sovereignty: — [1.] That he had the authority of a commander or general. He *dwelt as a king in the army,* giving orders which were not to be disputed. Every one that has the spirit of wisdom has not the spirit of government, but Job had both, and, when there was occasion, could assume state, as the king in the army does, and say, "Go," "Come," and "Do this," Mt. 8:9. [2.] That yet he had the tenderness of a comforter. He was as ready to succour those in distress as if it had been his office to comfort the mourners. Eliphaz himself owned he had been very good in that respect (*ch.* 4:3): *Thou hast strengthened the weak hands.* And this he now reflected upon with pleasure, when he was himself a mourner. But we find it easier to comfort others with the comforts wherewith we ourselves have been formerly comforted than to comfort ourselves with those comforts wherewith we have formerly comforted others.

I know not but we may look upon Job as a type and figure of Christ in his power and prosperity. Our Lord Jesus is such a King as Job was, the poor man's King, who loves righteousness and hates iniquity, and upon whom the blessing of a world ready to perish comes; see Ps. 72:2, etc. To him therefore let us give ear, and let him sit chief in our hearts.

CHAPTER 30

It is a melancholy "But now" which this chapter begins with. Adversity is here described as much to the life as prosperity was in the foregoing chapter, and the height of that did but increase the depth of this. God sets the one over-against the other, and so did Job, that his afflictions might appear the more grievous, and consequently his case the more pitiable. I. he had lived in great honour, but now he had fallen into disgrace, and was as much vilified, even by the meanest, as ever he had been magnified by the greatest; this he insists much on (*v.* 1–14). II. He had had much inward comfort and delight, but now he was a terror and burden to himself (*v.* 15, 16) and overwhelmed with sorrow (*v.* 28–31). III. He had long enjoyed a good state of health, but now he was sick and in pain (*v.* 17–18, 29, 30). IV. Time was when the secret of God was with him, but now his communication with heaven was cut off (*v.* 20–22). V. He had promised himself a long life, but now he saw death at the door (*v.* 23). One thing he mentions, which aggravated his affliction, that it surprised him when he looked for peace. But two things gave him some relief: — 1. That his troubles would not follow him to the grave (*v.* 24). 2. That his conscience witnessed for him that, in his prosperity, he had sympathized with those that were in misery (*v.* 25).

Verses 1–14

Here Job makes a very large and sad complaint of the great disgrace he had fallen into, from the height of honour and reputation, which was exceedingly grievous and cutting to such an ingenuous spirit as Job's was. Two things he insists upon as greatly aggravating his affliction: —

I. The meanness of the persons that affronted him. As it added much to his honour, in the day of his prosperity, that princes and nobles showed him respect and paid a deference to him, so it added no less to his disgrace in his adversity that he was spurned by the footmen, and trampled upon by those that were not only every way his inferiors, but were the meanest and most contemptible of all mankind. None can be represented as more base than those are here represented who insulted Job, upon all accounts. 1. They were young, younger than he (*v.* 1), *the youth* (*v.* 12), who ought to have behaved themselves respectfully towards him for his age and gravity. Even the children, in their play, played upon him, as the children of Bethel upon the prophet, *Go up, thou bald-head.* Children soon learn to be scornful when they see their parents so. 2. They were of a mean extraction. Their fathers were so very despicable that such a man as Job would have disdained to take them into the lowest service about his house, as that of tending the sheep and attending the shepherds with the dogs of his flock, *v.* 1. They were so shabby that they were not fit to be seen among his servants, so silly that they were not fit to be employed, and so false that they were not fit to be trusted in the meanest post. Job here speaks of what he might have done, not of what he did: he was not of such a spirit as to set any of the children of men with the dogs of his flock; he knew the dignity of human nature better than to do so. 3. They and their families were the unprofitable burdens of the earth, and good for nothing. Job himself, with all his prudence and patience, could make nothing of them, *v.* 2. The young were not fit for labour, they were so lazy, and went about their work so awkwardly: *Whereto might the strength of their hands profit me?* The old were not to be advised with in the smallest matters, for in them was old age indeed, but their *old age was perished,* they were twice children. 4. They were extremely poor, *v.* 3. They were ready to starve, for they would not dig, and to beg they were ashamed. Had they been brought to necessity by the providence of God, their neighbours would have sought them out as proper objects of charity and would have relieved them; but, being brought into straits by their own slothfulness and wastefulness, nobody was forward to relieve them. Hence they were forced to flee into the deserts both for shelter and sustenance, and were put to sorry shifts indeed, when they *cut up mallows by the bushes,* and were glad to eat them, for want of food that was fit for them, *v.* 4. See what hunger will bring men to: one half of the world does not know how the other half lives; yet those that have abundance ought to think sometimes of those whose fare is very coarse and who are brought to a short allowance of that too. But we must own the righteousness of God, and not think it strange, if slothfulness clothe men with rags and the idle soul be made to suffer hunger. This beggarly world is full of the devil's poor. 5. They were very scandalous wicked people, not only the burdens, but the plagues, of the places where they lived, arrant scoundrels, the scum of the country: *They were driven forth from among men, v.* 5. They were such lying, thieving, lurking, mischievous people, that the best service the magistrates could do was to rid the country of them, while the very mob cried after them as after a thief. *Away with such fellows from the earth; it is not fit they should live.* They were lazy and would not work, and therefore they were exclaimed against as thieves, and justly; for those that do not earn their own bread by honest labour do, in effect, steal the bread out of other people's mouths. An idle fellow is a public nuisance; but it is better to drive such into a workhouse than, as here, into a wilderness, which will punish them indeed, but never reform them. They were forced to dwell in *caves of the earth,* and *they brayed* like asses *among the bushes, v.* 6, 7. See what is the lot of those that have the cry of the country, the cry of their own conscience, against them; they cannot but be in a continual terror and confusion. *They groan among the trees* (so Broughton) *and smart among the nettles;* they are stung and scratched there, where they hoped to be sheltered and protected. See what miseries wicked people bring themselves to in this world; yet this is nothing to what is in reserve for them in the other world. 8. They had nothing at all in them to recommend them to any man's esteem. They were a vile kind; yea, a kind without fame, people that nobody could give a good word to nor had a good wish for; they were banished from the earth as being *viler than the earth.* One would not think it possible that ever the human nature should sink so low, and degenerate so far, as it did in these people. When we thank God that we are men we have reason to thank him that we are not such men. But such as these were abusive to Job, (1.) In revenge, because when he was in prosperity and power, like a good magistrate, he put in execution the laws which were in force against vagabonds, and rogues, and sturdy beggars, which these base people now remembered against him. (2.) In triumph over him, because they thought he had now become like one of them. Isa. 14:10, 11. The abjects, men of mean spirits, insult over the miserable, Ps. 35:15.

II. The greatness of the affronts that were given him. It cannot be imagined how abusive they were.

1. They made ballads on him, with which they made themselves and their companions merry (*v.* 9): *I am their song and their byword.* Those have a very base spirit that turn the calamities of their honest neighbours into a jest, and can sport themselves with their griefs.

2. They shunned him as a loathsome spectacle, abhorred him, fled far from him, (*v.* 10), as an ugly monster or as one infected. Those that were themselves driven out from among men would have had him driven out. For,

3. They expressed the greatest scorn and indignation against him. They spat in his face, or were ready to do so; they tripped up his heels, pushed away his feet (*v.* 12), kicked him, either in wrath, because they hated him, or in sport, to make themselves merry with him, as they did with their companions at foot-ball. The best of saints have sometimes received the worst of injuries and indignities from a spiteful, scornful, wicked world, and must not think it strange; our Master himself was thus abused.

4. They were very malicious against him, and not only made a jest of him, but made a prey of him — not only affronted him, but set themselves to do him all the real mischief they could devise: *They raise up against me the ways of their destruction;* or (as some read it), *They cast upon me the cause of their woe;* that is, "They lay the blame of their being driven out upon me;" and it is common for criminals to hate the judges and laws by which they are punished. But under this pretence, (1.) They accused him falsely, and misrepresented his former conversation, which is here called *marring his path.* They reflected upon him as a tyrant and an oppressor because he had done justice upon them; and perhaps Job's friends grounded their uncharitable censures of him (*ch.* 22:6, etc.) upon the unjust and unreasonable clamours of these sorry people; and it was an instance of their great weakness and inconsideration, for who can be innocent if the accusations of such persons may be heeded? (2.) They not only triumphed in his calamity, but set it forward, and did all they could to add to his miseries and make them more grievous to him. It is a great sin to forward the calamity of any, especially of good people. In this *they have no helper,* nobody to set them on or to countenance them in it, nobody to bear them out or to protect them, but they do it of their own accord; they are fools in other things, but wise enough to do mischief, and need no help in inventing that. Some read it thus, *They hold my heaviness a profit, though they be never the better.* Wicked people, though they get nothing by the calamities of others, yet rejoice in them.

5. Those that did him all this mischief were numerous, unanimous, and violent (*v.* 14): *They came upon me as a wide breaking in of waters,* when the dam is broken; or, "They came as soldiers into a broad breach which they have made in the wall of a besieged city, pouring in upon me with the utmost fury;" and in this they took a pride and a pleasure: *They rolled themselves in the desolation* as a man rolls himself in a soft and easy bed, and they rolled themselves upon him with all the weight of their malice.

III. All this contempt put upon him was caused by the troubles he was in (*v.* 11): *"Because he has loosed my cord,* has taken away the honour and power with which I was girded (*ch.* 12:18), has scattered what I had got together and untwisted all my affairs — because he has afflicted me, therefore *they have let loose the bridle before me,"* that is, "have given themselves a liberty to say and do what they please against me." Those that by Providence are stripped of their honour may expect to be loaded with contempt by inconsiderate ill-natured people. "Because he hath loosed *his* cord" (the original has that reading also), that is, "because he has taken off his bridle of restraint from off their malice, they cast away the bridle from me," that is, "they make no account of my authority, nor stand in any awe of me." It is owing to the hold God has of the consciences even of bad men, and the restraints he lays upon them, that we are not continually thus insulted and abused; and, if at any time we meet with such ill treatment, we must acknowledge the hand of God in taking off those restraints, as David did when Shimei cursed him: *So let him curse, for the Lord hath bidden him.* Now in all this, 1. We may see the uncertainty of worldly honour, and particularly of popular applause, how suddenly a man may fail from the height of dignity into the depth of disgrace. What little cause therefore have men to be ambitious or proud of that which may be so easily lost, and what little confidence is to be put in it! Those that to-day cry *Hosannah* may to-morrow cry *Crucify.* But there is an honour which comes from God, which if we secure, we shall find it not thus changeable and loseable. 2. We may see that it has often been the lot of very wise and good men to be trampled upon and abused. And, 3. That those who look only at the things that are seen despise those whom the world frowns upon, though they are ever so much the favourites of Heaven. Nothing is more grievous in poverty than that it renders men contemptible. *Turba Remi sequitur fortunam, ut semper odit damnatos — The Roman populace, faithful to the turns of fortune, still persecute the fallen.* 4. We may see in Job a type of Christ, who was thus made a *reproach of men* and *despised of the people* (Ps. 22:6; Isa. 53:3), and who hid not his face from shame and spitting, but bore the indignity better than Job did.

Verses 15–31

In this second part of Job's complaint, which is very bitter, and has a great many sorrowful accents in it, we may observe a great deal that he complains of and some little that he comforts himself with.

I. Here is much that he complains of.

1. In general, it was a day of great affliction and sorrow. (1.) Affliction seized him, and surprised him. It seized him (*v.* 16): *The days of affliction have taken hold upon me, have caught me* (so some); *they have arrested me,* as the bailiff arrests the debtor, claps him on the back, and secures him. When trouble comes with commission it will take fast hold, and not lose its hold. It surprised him (*v.* 27): *"The days of affliction prevented me,"* that is, "they came upon me without giving me any previous warning. I did not expect them, nor make any provision for such an evil day." Observe, He reckons his affliction by days, which will soon be numbered and finished, and are nothing to the ages of eternity, 2 Co. 4:17. (2.) He was in great sorrow by reason of it. His *bowels boiled* with grief, *and rested not, v.* 27. The sense of his calamities was continually preying upon his spirits without any intermission. He *went mourning* from day to day, always sighing, always weeping; and such cloud was constantly upon his mind that he went, in effect, *without the sun, v.* 28. He had nothing that he could take any comfort in. He abandoned himself to perpetual sorrow, as one that, like Jacob, resolved to go to the grave mourning. He walked out of the sun (so some) in dark shady places, as melancholy people use to do. If he went into the congregation, to join with them in solemn worship, instead of standing up calmly to desire their prayers, he *stood up and cried* aloud, through pain of body, or anguish of mind, like one half distracted. If he appeared in public, to receive visits, when the fit came upon him he could not contain himself, nor preserve due decorum, but stood up and shrieked aloud. Thus he was *a brother to dragons and owls* (*v.* 29), both in choosing solitude and retirement, as they do (Isa. 34:13), and in making a fearful hideous noise as they do; his inconsiderate complaints were fitly compared to their inarticulate ones.

2. The terror and trouble that seized his soul were the sorest part of his calamity, *v.* 15, 16. (1.) If he looked forward, he saw every thing frightful before him: if he endeavoured to shake off his terrors, they turned furiously upon him: if he endeavoured to escape from them, they pursued his soul as swiftly and violently as the wind. He complained, at first, of the *terrors of God setting themselves in array against him, ch.* 6:4. And still, which way soever he looked, they turned upon him; which way soever he fled, they pursued him. *My soul* (Heb., *my principal one, my princess*); the soul is the principal part of the man; it is our glory; it is every way more excellent than the body, and therefore that which pursues the soul, and threatens that, should be most dreaded. (2.) If he looked back, he saw all the good he had formerly enjoyed removed from him, and nothing left him but the bitter remembrance of it: *My welfare* and prosperity *pass away,* as suddenly, swiftly, and irrecoverably, *as a cloud.* (3.) If he looked within, he found his spirit quite sunk and unable to bear his infirmity, not only wounded, but *poured out upon him, v.* 16. He was not only weak as water, but, in his own apprehension, lost as water spilt upon the ground. Compare Ps. 22:14, *My heart is melted like wax.*

3. His bodily diseases were very grievous; for, (1.) He was full of pain, piercing pain, pain that went to the bone, to all his bones, *v.* 17. It was a *sword in his bones,* which *pierced him in the night season,* when he should have been refreshed with sleep. His nerves were affected with strong convulsions; his *sinews took no rest.* By reason of his pain, he could take no rest, but sleep departed from his eyes. *His bones were burnt with heat, v.* 30. He was in a constant fever, which dried up the radical moisture and even consumed the marrow in his bones. See how frail our bodies are, which carry in themselves the seeds of our own disease and death. (2.) He was full of sores. Some that are pained in their bones, yet sleep in a whole skin, but, Satan's commission against Job extending both to his bone and to his flesh, he spared neither. His *skin was black upon him, v.* 30. The blood settled, and the sores suppurated and by degrees scabbed over, which made his skin look black. Even his garment had its colour changed with the continual running of his boils, and the soft clothing he used to wear had now grown so stiff that all his garments were *like his collar, v.* 18. It would be noisome to describe what a condition poor Job was in for want of clean linen and good attendance, and what filthy rags all his clothes were. Some think that, among other diseases, Job was ill of a quinsy or swelling in his throat, and that it was this which bound him about like a stiff collar. Thus was he *cast into the mire* (*v.* 19), *compared to mire* (so some); his body looked more like a heap of dirt than any thing else. Let none be proud of their clothing nor proud of their cleanness; they know not but some disease or other may *change their garments,* and even *throw them into the mire,* and make them noisome both to themselves and others. *Instead of sweet smell, there shall be a stench,* Isa. 3:24. We are but dust and ashes at the best, and our bodies are vile bodies; but we are apt to forget it, till God, by some sore disease, makes us sensibly to feel and own what we are. *"I have become already like* that *dust and ashes* into which I must shortly be resolved: wherever I go I carry my grave about with me."

4. That which afflicted him most of all was that God seemed to be his enemy and to fight against him. It was *he* that *cast him into the mire* (*v.* 19), and seemed to trample on him when he had him there. This cut him to the heart more than any thing else, (1.) That God did not appear for him. He addressed himself to him, but gained no grant — appealed to him, but gained no sentence; he was very importunate in his applications, but in vain (*v.* 20): *"I cry unto thee,* as one in earnest, *I stand up,* and cry, as one waiting for an answer, but thou hearest not, *thou regardest not,* for any thing I can perceive." If our most fervent prayers bring not in speedy and sensible returns, we must not think it strange. Though the seed of Jacob did never seek in vain, yet they have often thought that they did and that God has not only been deaf, but angry, at the prayers of his people, Ps. 80:4. (2.) That God did appear against him. That which he here says of God is one of the worst words that ever Job spoke (*v.* 21): *Thou hast become cruel to me.* Far be it from the God of mercy and grace that he should be cruel to any (his compassions fail not), but especially that he should be so to his own children. Job was unjust and ungrateful when he said so of him: but harbouring hard thoughts of God was the sin which did, at this time, most easily beset him. Here, [1.] He thought God fought against him and stirred up his whole strength to ruin him: *With thy strong hand thou opposest thyself,* or art an adversary against me. He had better thoughts of God (*ch.* 23:6) when he concluded he would *not plead against him with his great power.* God has an absolute sovereignty and an irresistible strength, but he never uses either the one or the other for the crushing or oppressing of any. [2.] He thought he insulted over him (*v.* 22): *Thou liftest me up to the wind,* as a feather or the chaff which the wind plays with; so unequal a match did Job think himself for Omnipotence, and so unable was he to help himself when he was made to ride, not in triumph, but in terror, upon the wings of the wind, and the judgments of God did even *dissolve his substance,* as a cloud is dissolved and dispersed by the wind. Man's substance, take him in his best estate, is nothing before the power of God; it is soon dissolved.

5. He expected no other now than that God, by these troubles, would shortly make an end of him: "If I be made to ride upon the wind, I can count upon no other than to break my neck shortly;" and he speaks as if God had no other design upon him than that in all his dealings with him: *"I know that thou wilt bring me,* with so much the more terror, *to death,* though I might have been brought

thither without all this ado, for it is *the house appointed for all living,*" *v.* 23. The grave is a house, a narrow, dark, cold, ill-furnished house, but it will be our residence, where we shall rest and be safe. It is our long home, our own home; for it is our mother's lap, and in it we are gathered to our fathers. It is a house appointed for us by him that has appointed us the bounds of all our habitations. It is appointed for all the living. It is the common receptacle, where rich and poor meet; it is appointed for the general rendezvous. We must all be brought thither shortly. It is God that brings us to it, for the keys of death and the grave are in his hand, and we may all know that, sooner or later, he will bring us thither. It would be well for us if we would duly consider it. *The living know that they shall die;* let us, each of us, know it with application.

6. There were two things that aggravated his trouble, and made it the less tolerable: — (1.) That it was a very great disappointment to his expectation (*v.* 26): *"When I looked for good,* for more good, or at least for the continuance of what I had, *then evil came"* — such uncertain things are all our worldly enjoyments, and such a folly is it to feed ourselves with great expectations from them. Those that wait for light from the sparks of their creature comforts will be wretchedly disappointed and will *make their bed in the darkness.* (2.) That is was a very great change in his condition (*v.* 31): *"My harp is* not only laid by, and hung upon the willow-trees, but it is *turned to mourning, and my organ into the voice of those that weep."* Job, in his prosperity, had taken *the timbrel and harp,* and *rejoiced at the sound of the organ, ch.* 21:12. Notwithstanding his gravity and grace, he had found time to be cheerful; but now his tune was altered. Let those therefore that rejoice be *as though they rejoiced not,* for they know not how soon their *laughter* will be *turned into mourning and their joy into heaviness.* Thus we see how much Job complains of; but,

II. Here is something in the midst of all with which he comforts himself, and it is but a little. 1. He foresees, with comfort, that death will be the period of all his calamities (*v.* 24): Though God now, with a strong hand, opposed himself against him, "yet," says he, *"he will not stretch out his hand to the grave."* The hand of God's wrath would bring him to death, but would not follow him beyond death; his soul would be safe and happy in the world of spirits, his body safe and easy in the dust. Though men *cry in his destruction* (though, when they are dying, there is a great deal of agony and out-cry, many a sigh, and groan, and complaint), yet in the grave they feel nothing, they fear nothing, but all is quiet there. "Though in hell, which is called *destruction,* they cry, yet not in the grave; and, being delivered from the second death, the first to me will be an effectual relief." Therefore he wished he might be *hidden in the grave, ch.* 14:13. 2. He reflects with comfort upon the concern he always had for the calamities of others when he was himself at ease (*v.* 25): *Did not I weep for him that was in trouble?* Some think he herein complains of God, thinking it very hard that he who had shown mercy to others should not himself find mercy. I would rather take it as a quieting consideration to himself; his conscience witnessed for him that he had always sympathized with persons in misery and done what he could to help them, and therefore he had reason to expect that, at length, both God and his friends would pity him. Those who mourn with them that mourn will bear their own sorrows the better when it comes to their turn to drink of the bitter cup. *Did not my soul burn for the poor?* so some read it, comparing it with that of St. Paul, 2 Co. 11:29, *Who is offended, and I burn not?* As those who have been unmerciful and hard-hearted to others may expect to hear of it from their own consciences, when they are themselves in trouble, so those who have considered the poor and succoured them shall have the remembrance thereof to make their bed easy in their sickness, Ps. 41:1, 3.

CHAPTER 31

Job had often protested his integrity in general; here he does it in particular instances, not in a way of commendation (for he does not here proclaim his good deeds), but in his own just and necessary vindication, to clear himself from those crimes with which his friends had falsely charged him, which is a debt every man owes to his own reputation. Job's friends had been particular in their articles of impeachment against him, and therefore he is so in his protestation, which seems to refer especially to what Eliphaz had accused him of, *ch.* 22:6, etc. They had produced no witnesses against him, neither could they prove the things whereof they now accused him, and therefore he may well be admitted to purge himself upon oath, which he does very solemnly, and with many awful imprecations of God's wrath if he were guilty of those crimes. This protestation confirms God's character of him, that there was none like him in the earth. Perhaps some of his accusers durst not have joined with him; for he not only acquits himself from those gross sins which lie open to the eye of the world, but from many secret sins which, if he had been guilty of them, nobody could have charged him, with, because he will prove himself no hypocrite. Nor does he only maintain the cleanness of his practices, but shows also that in them he went upon good principles, that the reason of his eschewing evil was because he feared God, and his piety was at the bottom of his justice and charity; and this crowns the proof of his sincerity. I. The sins from which he here acquits himself are, 1. Wantonness and uncleanness of heart (*v.* 1–4). 2. Fraud and injustice in commerce (*v.* 4–8). 3. Adultery (*v.* 9–12). 4. Haughtiness and severity towards his servants (*v.* 13–15). 5. Unmercifulness to the poor, the widows, and the fatherless (*v.* 16–23). 6. Confidence in his worldly wealth (*v.* 24, 25). 7. Idolatry (*v.* 26–28). 8. Revenge (*v.* 29–31). 9. Neglect of poor strangers (*v.* 32). 10. Hypocrisy in concealing his own sins and cowardice in conniving at the sins of others (*v.* 33, 34). 11. Oppression, and the violent invasion of other people's rights (*v.* 38–40). And towards the close, he appeals to God's judgment concerning his integrity (*v.* 35–37). Now, II. In all this we may see, 1. The sense of the patriarchal age concerning good and evil and what was so long ago condemned as sinful, that is, both hateful and hurtful. 2. A noble pattern of piety and virtue proposed to us for our imitation, which, if our consciences can witness for us that we conform to it, will be our rejoicing, as it was Job's in the day of evil.

Verses 1–8

The lusts of the flesh, and the love of the world, are the two fatal rocks on which multitudes split; against these Job protests he was always careful to stand upon his guard.

I. Against the lusts of the flesh. He not only kept himself clear from adultery, from defiling his neighbour's wives (*v.* 9), but from all lewdness with any women whatsoever. He kept no concubine, no mistress, but was inviolably faithful to the marriage bed, though his wife was none of the wisest, best, or kindest. From the beginning it was so, that a man should have but one wife and cleave to her only; and Job kept closely to that institution and abhorred the thought of transgressing it; for, though his greatness might tempt him to it, his goodness kept him from it. Job was now in pain and sickness of body, and under that affliction it is in a particular manner comfortable if our consciences can witness for us that we have been careful to preserve our bodies in chastity and to possess those vessels in sanctification and honour, pure from the lusts of uncleanness. Now observe here,

1. What the resolutions were which, in this matter, he kept to (*v.* 1): *I made a covenant with my eyes,* that is, "I watched against the occasions of the sin; *why then should I think upon a maid?"* that is, "by that means, through the grace of God, I kept myself from the very first step towards it." So far was he from wanton dalliances, or any act of lasciviousness, that, (1.) He would not so much as admit a wanton look. *He made a covenant with his eyes,* made this bargain with them, that he would allow them the pleasure of beholding the light of the sun and the glory of God shining in the visible creation, provided they would never fasten upon any object that might occasion any impure imaginations, much less any impure desires, in his mind; and under this penalty, that, if they did, they must smart for it in penitential tears. Note, Those that would keep their hearts pure must guard their eyes, which are both the outlets and inlets of uncleanness. Hence we read of *wanton* eyes (Isa. 3:16) and *eyes full of adultery,* 2 Pt. 2:14. The first sin began in the eye, Gen. 3:6. What we must not meddle with we must not lust after; and what we must not lust after we must not look at; not the forbidden wealth (Prov. 23:5), not the forbidden wine (Prov. 23:31), not the forbidden woman, Mt. 5:28. (2.) He would not so much as allow a wanton thought: *"Why then should I think upon a maid* with any unchaste fancy or desire towards her?" Shame and sense of honour might restrain him from soliciting the chastity of a beautiful virgin, but only grace and the fear of God would restrain him from so much as thinking of it. Those are not chaste that are not so in spirit as well as body, 1 Co. 7:34. See how Christ's exposition of the seventh commandment agrees with the ancient sense of it, and how much better Job understood it than the Pharisees, though they sat in Moses's chair.

2. What the reasons were which, in this matter, he was governed by. It was not for fear of reproach among men, though that is to be considered (Prov. 6:33), but for fear of the wrath and curse of God. He knew very well, (1.) That uncleanness is a sin that forfeits all good, and shuts us out from the hope of it (*v.* 2): *What portion of God is there from above?* What blessing can such impure sinners expect from the pure and holy God, or what token of his favour? What inheritance of the Almighty can they look for from on high? There is no portion, no inheritance, no true happiness, for a soul, but what is in God, in the Almighty, and what comes from above, from on high. Those that wallow in uncleanness render themselves utterly unfit for communion with God, either in grace here or in glory hereafter, and become allied to unclean spirits, which are for ever separated from him; and then what portion, what inheritance, can they have with God? No unclean thing shall enter into the New Jerusalem, that holy city. (2.) It is a sin that incurs divine vengeance, *v.* 3. It will certainly be the sinner's ruin if it be not repented of in time. *Is not destruction,* a swift and sure destruction, *to* those *wicked* people, *and a strange punishment to the workers of* this *iniquity?* Fools make a mock at this sin, make a jest of it; it is with them a peccadillo, a trick of youth. But they deceive themselves with vain words, for because of these things, how light soever they make of them, the wrath of God, the unsupportable wrath of the eternal God, *comes upon the children of disobedience,* Eph. 5:6. There are some sinners whom God sometimes out of the common road of Providence to meet with; such are these. The destruction of Sodom is a strange punishment. *Is there not alienation* (so some read it) *to the workers of iniquity?* This is the sinfulness of the sin that it alienates the mind from God (Eph. 4:18, 19), and this is the punishment of the sinners that they shall be eternally set at a distance from him, Rev. 22:15. (3.) It cannot be hidden from the all-seeing God. A wanton thought cannot be so close, nor a wanton look so quick, as to escape his cognizance, much less any act of uncleanness so secretly done as to be out of his sight. If Job was at any time tempted to this sin, he restrained himself from it, and all approaches to it, with this pertinent thought (*v.* 4), *Doth not he see my ways;* as Joseph did (Gen. 39:9), *How can I do it, and sin against God?* Two things Job had an eye to: — [1.] God's omniscience. It is a great truth that God's eyes are *upon all the ways of men* (Prov. 5:20, 21); but Job here mentions it with application to himself and his own actions: *Doth not he see my ways? O God! thou hast searched me and known me.* God sees what rule we walk by, what company w walk with, what end we walk towards, and therefore what ways we walk in. [2.] His observance. "He not only sees, but takes notice; he *counts all my steps,* all my false steps in the way of duty, all my by-steps into the way of sin." He not only sees our ways in general, but takes cognizance of our particular steps in these ways, every action, every motion. He keeps account of all, because he will call us to account, will bring every work into judgment. God takes a more exact notice of us than we do of ourselves; for who ever counted his own steps? yet God counts them. Let us therefore walk circumspectly.

II. He stood upon his guard against the love of the world, and carefully avoided all sinful indirect means of getting wealth. He dreaded all forbidden profit as much as all forbidden pleasure. Let us see,

1. What his protestation is. In general, he had been honest and just in all his dealings, and never, to his knowledge, did any body any wrong. (1.) He never *walked with vanity* (*v.* 5), that is, he never durst tell a lie to get a good bargain. It was never his way to banter, or equivocate, or make many words in his dealings. Some men's constant walk is a constant cheat. They either make what they have more than it is, that they may be trusted, or less than it is, that nothing may be expected from them. But Job was a different man. His wealth was not acquired by vanity, though now diminished, Prov. 13:11. (2.) He never *hasted to deceit.* Those that deceive must be quick and sharp, but Job's quickness and sharpness were never turned that way. He never made haste to be rich by deceit, but always acted cautiously, lest, through inconsideration, he should do an unjust thing. Note, What we have in the world may be either used with comfort or lost with comfort if it was honestly obtained. (3.) His *steps never turned out of the way,* the way of justice and fair dealing; from that he never deviated, *v.* 7. He not only took care not to walk in a constant course and way of deceit, but he did not so much as take one step out of the way of honesty. In every particular action and affair we must closely tie ourselves up

to the rules of righteousness. (4.) His heart did not *walk after his eyes,* that is, he did not covet what he saw that was another's, nor wish it his own. Covetousness is called the *lust of the eye,* 1 Jn. 2:16. Achan saw, and then took, the accursed thing. That heart must needs wander that walks after the eyes; for then it looks no further than the things that are seen, whereas it ought to be in heaven whither the eyes cannot reach: it should follow the dictates of religion and right reason: if it follow the eye, it will be misled to that for which *God will bring men into judgment,* Eccl. 11:9. (5.) That *no blot had cleaved to his hands,* that is, he was not chargeable with getting any thing dishonestly, or keeping that which was another's, whenever it appeared to be so. Injustice is a blot, a blot to the estate, a blot to the owner; it spoils the beauty of both, and therefore is to be dreaded. Those that deal much in the world may perhaps have a blot come upon their hands, but they must wash it off again by repentance and restitution, and not let it *cleave to their hands.* See Isa. 33:15.

2. How he ratifies his protestation. So confident is he of his own honesty that, (1.) He is willing to have his goods searched (*v.* 6): *Let me be weighed in an even balance,* that is, "Let what I have got be enquired into and it will be found to weigh well" — a sign that it was not obtained by vanity, for then *Tekel* would have been written on it — *weighed in the balance and found too light.* An honest man is so far from dreading a trial that he desires it rather, being well assured that God knows his integrity and will approve it, and that the trial of it will be to his praise and honour. (2.) He is willing to forfeit the whole cargo if there be found any prohibited or contraband goods, any thing but what he came honestly by (*v.* 8): *"Let me sow, and let another eat,"* which was already agreed to be the doom of oppressors (*ch.* 5:5), "and *let my offspring,* all the trees that I have planted, *be rooted out."* This intimates that he believed the sin did deserve this punishment, that usually it is thus punished, but that though now his estate was ruined (and at such a time, if ever, his conscience would have brought his sin to his mind), yet he knew himself innocent and would venture all the poor remains of his estate upon the issue of the trial.

Verses 9–15

Two more instances we have here of Job's integrity: —

I. That he had a very great abhorrence of the sin of adultery. As he did not wrong his own marriage bed by keeping a concubine (he did not so much as think upon a maid, *v.* 1), so he was careful not to offer any injury to his neighbour's marriage bed. Let us see here, 1. How clear he was from this sin, *v.* 9. (1.) He did not so much as covet his neighbour's wife; for even *his heart was not deceived by a woman.* The beauty of another man's wife did not kindle in him any unchaste desires, nor was he ever moved by the allurements of an adulterous woman, such as is described, Prov. 7:6, etc. See the original of all the defilements of the life; they come from a deceived heart. Every sin is deceitful, and none more so than the sin of uncleanness. (2.) He never compassed or imagined any unchaste design. He never *laid wait at his neighbour's door,* to get an opportunity to debauch his wife in his absence, when the good man was not at home, Prov. 7:19. See *ch.* 24:15. 2. What a dread he had of this sin, and what frightful apprehensions he had concerning the malignity of it — that it was a *heinous crime* (*v.* 11), one of the greatest vilest sins a man can be guilty of, highly provoking to God, and destructive to the prosperity of the soul. With respect to the mischievousness of it, and the punishment it deserved, he owns that, if he were guilty of that heinous crime, (1.) His family might justly be made infamous in the highest degree (*v.* 10): *Let my wife grind to another.* Let her be a *slave* (so some), a *harlot,* so others. God often punishes the sins of one with the sin of another, the adultery of the husband with the adultery of the wife, as in David's case (2 Sa. 12:11), which does not in the least excuse the treachery of the adulterous wife; but, how unrighteous soever she is, God is righteous. See Hos. 4:13, *Your spouses shall commit adultery.* Note, Those who are not just and faithful to their relations must not think it strange if their relations be unjust and unfaithful to them. (2.) He himself might justly be made a public example: *For it is an iniquity to be punished by the judges;* yea, though those who are guilty of it are themselves judges, as Job was. Note, Adultery is a crime which the civil magistrate ought to take cognizance of and punish: so it was adjudged even in the patriarchal age, before the law of Moses made it capital. It is an evil work, to which the sword of justice ought to be a terror. (3.) It might justly become the ruin of his estate; nay, he knew it would be so (*v.* 12): *It is a fire.* Lust is a fire in the soul: those that indulge it are said to burn. It consumes all that is good there (the convictions, the comforts), and lays the conscience waste. It kindles the fire of God's wrath, which, if not extinguished by the blood of Christ, will burn to the lowest hell. It will *consume* even *to* that eternal *destruction.* It consumes the body, Prov. 5:11. It consumes the substance; it *roots out all the increase.* Burning lusts bring burning judgments. Perhaps it alludes to the burning of Sodom, which was intended for an example to those who should afterwards, in like manner, live ungodly.

II. That he had a very great tenderness for his servants and ruled them with a gentle hand. He had a great household and he managed it well. By this he evidenced his sincerity that he had grace to govern his passion as well as his appetite; and he that in these two things has the rule of his own spirit is *better than the mighty,* Prov. 16:32. Here observe, 1. What were Job's condescensions to his servants (*v.* 13): He did not *despise the cause of his man-servant,* no, nor of his *maid-servant, when they contended with him.* If they contradicted him in any thing, he was willing to hear their reasons. If they had offended him, or were accused to him, he would patiently hear what they had to say for themselves, in their own vindication or excuse. Nay, if they complained of any hardship he put upon them, he did not browbeat them, and bid them hold their tongues, but gave them leave to tell their story, and redressed their grievances as far as it appeared they had right on their side. He was tender of them, not only when they served and pleased him, but even when they contended with him. Herein he was a great example to masters, to *give to their servants that which is just and equal;* nay, to do the same things to them that they expect from them (Col. 4:1, Eph. 6:9), and not to rule them with rigour, and carry it with a high hand. Many of Job's servants were slain in his service (*ch.* 1:15–17); the rest were unkind and undutiful to him, and despised his cause, though he never despised theirs (*ch.* 19:15, 16); but he had this comfort that in his prosperity he had behaved well towards them. Note, When relations are either removed from us or embittered to us the testimony of our consciences that we have done our duty to them will be a great support and comfort to us. 2. What were the considerations that moved him to treat his servants thus kindly. He had, herein, an eye to God, both as his Judge and their Maker. (1.) As his Judge. He considered, "If I should be imperious and severe with my servants, *what then shall I do when God riseth up?"* He considered that he had a Master in heaven, to whom he was accountable, who will rise up and will visit; and *we* are concerned to consider *what we shall do in the day of his visitation* (Isa. 10:3), and, considering that we should be undone if God should then be strict and severe with us, we ought to be very mild and gentle towards all with whom we have to do. Consider what would become of us if God should be extreme to mark what we do amiss, should take all advantages against us and insist upon all his just demands from us — if he should visit every offence, and take every forfeiture — if he should always chide, and keep his anger for ever. And let not us be rigorous with our inferiors. Consider what will become of us if we be cruel and unmerciful to our brethren. The cries of the injured will be heard; the sins of the injurious will be punished. Those that showed no mercy shall find none; and what shall we do then? (2.) As his and his servants' Creator, *v.* 15. When he was tempted to be harsh with his servants, to deny them their right and turn a deaf ear to their reasonings, this thought came very seasonably into his mind, *"Did not he that made me in the womb make him?* I am a creature as well as he, and my being is derived and depending as well as his. He partakes of the same nature that I do and is the work of the same hand: *Have we not all one Father?"* Note, Whatever difference there is among men in their outward condition, in their capacity of mind, or strength of body, or place in the world, he that made the one made the other also, which is a good reason why we should not mock at men's natural infirmities, nor trample upon those that are in any way our inferiors, but, in every thing, do as we would be done by. It is a rule of justice, *Parium par sit ratio — Let equals be equally estimated and treated;* and therefore since there is so great a parity among men, they being all made of the same mould, by the same power, for the same end, notwithstanding the disparity of our outward condition, we are bound so far to set ourselves upon the level with those we deal with as to do to them, in all respects, as we would they should do to us.

Verses 16–23

Eliphaz had particularly charged Job with unmercifulness to the poor (*ch.* 22:6, etc.): Thou hast *withholden bread from the hungry, stripped the naked of their clothing,* and sent *widows away empty.* One would think he could not have been so very positive and express in his charge unless there had been some truth in it, some ground, for it; and yet it appears, by Job's protestation, that it was utterly false and groundless; he was never guilty of any such thing. See here,

I. The testimony which Job's conscience gave in concerning his constant behaviour towards the poor. He enlarges most upon this head because in this matter he was most particularly accused. He solemnly protests,

1. That he had never been wanting to do good to them, as there was occasion, to the utmost of his ability. He was always compassionate to the poor, and careful of them, especially the widows and fatherless, that were destitute of help. (1.) He was always ready to grant their desires and answer their expectations, *v.* 16. If a poor person begged a kindness of his, he was ready to gratify him; if he could but perceive by the widow's mournful craving look that she expected an alms from him, though she had not confidence enough to ask it, he had compassion enough to give it, and *never caused the eyes of the widow to fail.* (2.) He put a respect upon the poor, and did them honour; for he took the fatherless children to eat with him at his own table: they should fare as he fared, and be familiar with him, and he would show himself pleased with their company as if they had been his own, *v.* 17. As it is one of the greatest grievances of poverty that it exposes to contempt, so it is none of the least supports to the poor to be respected. (3.) He was very tender of them, and had a fatherly concern for them, *v.* 18. He was a father to the fatherless, took care of orphans, brought them up with him under his own eye, and gave them, not only maintenance, but education. He was a guide to the widow, who had lost the guide of her youth; he advised her in her affairs, took cognizance of them, and undertook the management of them. Those that need not our alms may yet have occasion for our counsel, and it may be a real kindness to them. This Job says he did *from his youth, from his mother's womb.* He had something of tenderness and compassion woven in his nature; he began betimes to do good, ever since he could remember; he had always some poor widow or fatherless child under his care. His parents taught him betimes to pity and relieve the poor, and brought up orphans with him. (4.) He provided food convenient for them; they ate of the same morsels that he did (*v.* 17), did not eat after him, of the crumbs that fell from his table, but with him, of the best dish upon his table. Those that have abundance must not eat their morsels alone, as if they had none but themselves to take care of, nor indulge their appetite with a dainty bit by themselves, but take others to share with them, as David took Mephibosheth. (5.) He took particular care to clothe those that were without covering, which would be more expensive to him than feeding them, *v.* 19. Poor people may perish for want of clothing as well as for want of food — for want of clothing to lie in by night or to go abroad in by day. If Job knew of any that were in this distress, he was forward to relieve them, and instead of giving rich and gaudy liveries to his servants, while the poor were turned off with rags that were ready to be thrown to the dunghill, he had good warm strong clothes made on purpose for them of *the fleece of his sheep* (*v.* 20), so that their *loins,* whenever they girt those garments about them, *blessed him;* they commended his charity, blessed God for him, and prayed God to bless him. Job's sheep were burned with fire from heaven, but this was his comfort that, when he had them, he came

honestly by them, and used them charitably, fed the poor with their flesh and clothed them with their wool.

2. That he had never been accessory to the wronging of any that were poor. It might be said, perhaps, that he was kind here and there to a poor orphan that was a favourite, but to others he was oppressive. No, he was tender to all and injurious to none. He never so much as *lifted up his hand against the fatherless* (*v.* 21), never threatened or frightened them, or offered to strike them; never used his power to crush those that stood in his way or squeeze what he could out of them, though he *saw his help in the gate,* that is, though he had interest enough, both in the people and in the judges, both to enable him to do it and to bear him out when he had done it. Those that have it in their power to do a wrong thing and go through with it, and a prospect of getting by it, and yet do justly, and love mercy, and are firm to both, may afterwards reflect upon their conduct with much comfort, as Job does here.

II. The imprecation with which he confirms this protestation (*v.* 22): "If I have been oppressive to the poor, *let my arm fall from my shoulder-blade and my arm be broken from the bone,*" that is, "let the flesh rot off from the bone and one bone be disjointed and broken off from another." Had he not been perfectly clear in this matter, he durst not thus have challenged the divine vengeance. And he intimates that it is a righteous thing with God to break the arm that is lifted up against the fatherless, as he withered Jeroboam's arm that was stretched out against a prophet.

III. The principles by which Job was restrained from all uncharitableness and unmercifulness. He durst not abuse the poor; for though, with his help in the gate, he could overpower them, yet he could not make his part good against that God who is the patron of oppressed poverty and will not let oppressors go unpunished (*v.* 23): *"Destruction from God was a terror to me,* whenever I was tempted to this sin, and *by reason of his highness I could not endure* the thought of making him my enemy." He stood in awe, 1. Of the majesty of God, as a God above him. He thought of his highness, the infinite distance between him and God, which possessed him with such a reverence of him as made him very circumspect in his whole conversation. Those who oppress the poor, and pervert judgment and justice, forget that *he who is higher than the highest regards,* and *there is a higher than they,* who is able to deal with them (Eccl. 5:8); but Job considered this. 2. Of the wrath of God, as a God that would certainly be against him if he should wrong the poor. *Destruction from God,* because it would be a certain and an utter ruin to him if he were guilty of this sin, was a constant terror to him, to restrain him from it. Note, Good men, even the best, have need to restrain themselves from sin with the fear of destruction from God, and all little enough. This should especially restrain us from all acts of injustice and oppression that God himself is the avenger thereof. Even when salvation from God is a comfort to us, yet destruction from God should be a terror to us. Adam, in innocency, was awed with a threatening.

Verses 24–32

Four articles more of Job's protestation we have in these verses, which, as all the rest, not only assure us what he was and did, but teach us what we should be and do: —

I. He protests that he never set his heart upon the wealth of this world, nor took the things of it for his portions and happiness. He had gold; he had fine gold. His *wealth was great,* and he *had gotten much.* Our wealth is either advantageous or pernicious to us according as we stand affected to it. If we make it our rest and our ruler, it will be our ruin; if we make it our servant, and an instrument of righteousness, it will be a blessing to us. Job here tells us how he stood affected to his worldly wealth. 1. He put no great confidence in it: he did not *make gold his hope, v.* 24. Those are very unwise that do, and enemies to themselves, who depend upon it as sufficient to make them happy, who think themselves safe and honourable, and sure of comfort, in having abundance of this world's goods. Some make it their hope and confidence for another world, as if it were a certain token of God's favour; and those who have so much sense as not to think so yet promise themselves that it will be a portion for them in this life, whereas the things themselves are uncertain and our satisfaction in them is much more so. It is hard to have riches and not to trust in riches; and it is this which makes it so difficult for *a rich man to enter into the kingdom of God,* Mt. 19:23; Mk. 10:24. 2. He took no great complacency in it (*v.* 25): *If I rejoiced because my wealth was great* and boasted that *my hand had gotten much.* He took no pride in his wealth, as if it added any thing to his real excellency, nor did he think that his might and the power of his hand obtained it for him, Deu. 8:17. He took no pleasure in it in comparison with the spiritual things which were the delight of his soul. His joy did not terminate in the gift, but passed through it to the giver. When he was in the midst of his abundance he never said, *Soul, take thy ease* in these things, *eat, drink, and be merry,* nor blessed himself in his riches. He did not inordinately rejoice in his wealth, which helped him to bear the loss of it so patiently as he did. The way to *weep as though we wept not* is to *rejoice as though we rejoiced not.* The less pleasure the enjoyment is the less pain the disappointment will be.

II. He protests that he never gave the worship and glory to the creature which are due to God only; he was never guilty of idolatry, *v.* 26–28. We do not find that Job's friends charged him with this. But there were those, it seems, at that time, who were so sottish as to worship the sun and moon, else Job would not have mentioned it. Idolatry is one of the old ways which wicked men have trodden, and the most ancient idolatry was the worshipping of the sun and moon, to which the temptation was most strong, as appears Deu. 4:19, where Moses speaks of the danger which the people were in of being driven to worship them. But as yet it was practised secretly, and durst not appear in open view, as afterwards the most abominable idolatries did. Observe,

1. How far Job kept from this sin. He not only never bowed the knee to Baal (which, some think, was designed to represent the sun), never fell down and worshipped the sun, but he kept his eye, his heart, and his lips, clean from this sin. (1.) He never so much as beheld the sun or the moon in their pomp and lustre with any other admiration of them than what led him to give all the glory of their brightness and usefulness to their Creator. Against spiritual as well as corporal adultery he made a covenant with his eyes; and this was his covenant, that, whenever he looked at the lights of heaven, he should by faith look through them, and beyond them, to the Father of lights. (2.) He kept his heart with all diligence, that that should not be secretly enticed to think that there is a divine glory in their brightness, or a divine power in their influence, and that therefore divine honours are to be paid to them. Here is the source of idolatry; it begins in the heart. Every man is tempted to that, as to other sins, when he is *drawn away by his own lust and enticed.* (3.) He did not so much as put a compliment upon these pretended deities, did not perform the least and lowest act of adoration: *His mouth did not kiss his hand,* which, it is likely, was a ceremony then commonly used even by some that yet would not be thought idolaters. It is an old-fashioned piece of civil respect among ourselves, in making a bow, to kiss the hand, a form which, it seems, was anciently used in giving divine honours to the sun and moon. They could not reach to kiss them, as *the men that sacrificed kissed the calves* (Hos. 13:2, 1 Ki. 19:18); but, to show their good will, they kissed their hand, reverencing those as their masters which God has made servants to this lower world, to hold the candle for us. Job never did it.

2. How ill Job thought of this sin, *v.* 28. (1.) He looked upon it as an affront to the civil magistrate: It *were an iniquity to be punished by the judge,* as a public nuisance, and hurtful to kings and provinces. Idolatry debauches men's minds, corrupts their manners, takes off the true sense of religion which is the great bond of societies, and provokes God to give men up to a reprobate sense, and to send judgments upon a nation; and therefore the conservators of the public peace are concerned to restrain it by punishing it. (2.) He looked upon it as a much greater affront to the God of heaven, and no less than high treason against his crown and dignity: For *I should have denied the God that is above,* denied his being as God and his sovereignty as God above. Idolatry is, in effect, atheism; hence the Gentiles are said to be *without God (atheists) in the world.* Note, We should be afraid of every thing that does but tacitly deny the God above, his providence, or any of his perfections.

III. He protests that he was so far from doing or designing mischief to any that he neither desired nor delighted in the hurt of the worst enemy he had. The forgiving of those that do us evil, it seems, was Old-Testament duty, though the Pharisees made the law concerning it of no effect, by teaching, *Thou shalt love thy neighbour and hate thy enemy,* Mt. 5:43. Observe here,

1. Job was far from revenge. He did not only not return the injuries that were done him, not only not destroy those who hated him; but, (1.) He did not so much as rejoice when any mischief befel them, *v.* 29. Many who would not wilfully hurt those who stand in their light, or have done them a diskindness, yet are secretly pleased and laugh in their sleeve (as we say) when hurt is done them. But Job was not of that spirit. Though Job was a very good man, yet, it seems, there were those that hated him; but evil found them. He saw their destruction, and was far from rejoicing in it; for that would justly have brought the destruction upon him, as it is intimated, Prov. 24:17, 18. (2.) He did not so much as wish in his own mind that evil might befel them, *v.* 30. He never *wished a curse to his soul* (curses to the soul are the worst of curses), never desired his death; he knew that, if he did, it would turn into sin to him. He was careful *not to offend with his tongue* (Ps. 39:1), would not *suffer his mouth to sin,* and therefore durst not imprecate any evil, no, not to his worst enemy. If others bear malice to us, that will not justify us in bearing malice to them.

2. He was violently urged to revenge, and yet he kept himself thus clear from it (*v.* 31): *The men of his tabernacle,* his domestics, his servants, and those about him, were so enraged at Job's enemy who hated him, that they could have eaten him, if Job would but have set them on or given them leave. *"O that we had of his flesh!* Our master is satisfied to forgive him, but *we cannot be so satisfied."* See how much beloved Job was by his family, how heartily they espoused his cause, and what enemies they were to his enemies; but see what a strict hand Job kept upon his passions, that he would not avenge himself, though he had those about him that blew the coals of his resentment. Note, (1.) A good man commonly does not himself lay to heart the affronts that are done him so much as his friends do for him. (2.) Great men have commonly those about them that stir them up to revenge. David had so, 1 Sa. 24:4; 26:8; 2 Sa. 16:9. But if they keep their temper, notwithstanding the spiteful insinuations of those about them, afterwards it shall be no grief of heart to them, but shall turn very much to their praise.

IV. He protests that he had never been unkind or inhospitable to strangers (*v.* 32): *The stranger lodged not in the street,* as angels might lately have done in the streets of Sodom if Lot alone had not entertained them. Perhaps by that instance Job was taught (as we are, Heb. 13:2) not to be forgetful to entertain strangers. He that is at home must consider those that are from home, and put his soul into their soul's stead, and then do as he would be done by. Hospitality is a Christian duty, 1 Pt. 4:9. Job, in his prosperity, was noted for good house-keeping: *He opened his door to the road* (so it may be read); he kept the street-door open, that he might see who passed by and invite them in, as Abraham, Gen. 18:1.

Verses 33–40

We have here Job's protestation against three more sins, together with his general appeal to God's bar and his petition for a hearing there, which, it is likely, was intended to conclude his discourse (and therefore we will consider it last), but that another particular sin occurred, from which he thought it requisite to acquit himself. He clears himself from the charge,

I. Of dissimulation and hypocrisy. The general crime of which his friends accused him was that, under the cloak of a profession of religion, he had kept up secret haunts of sin, and that really he was as bad as other people, but had the art of concealing it. Zophar insinuated (*ch.* 20:12) that he *hid his iniquity under his tongue.* "No," says Job, "I never did (*v.* 33), *I never covered my transgression as Adam,* never palliated a sin with frivolous excuses, nor made fig-leaves the shelter of my shame, nor ever *hid my iniquity in my bosom,* as a fondling, a darling, that I could by no means part with, or as stolen goods which I dreaded the discovery of." It is natural to us to cover our sins; we have it from our first parents. We are loth to confess our faults, willing to extenuate them and make the best of ourselves, to devolve the blame upon others, as Adam on his wife, not without a tacit reflection upon God himself. But *he that* thus *covers his sins shall not prosper,* Prov. 28:13. Job, in this protestation, intimates two things, which were certain evidences of his integrity: — 1. That he was not guilty of any great transgression or iniquity, inconsistent with sincerity, which he had now industriously concealed. In this protestation he had dealt fairly, and, while he denies some sins, was not conscious to himself that he allowed himself in any. 2. That what transgression and iniquity he had been guilty of *(Who is there that lives and sins not?)* he had always been ready to own it, and, as soon as ever he perceived he had said or done amiss, he was ready to unsay it and undo it, as far as he could, by repentance, confessing it both to God and man, and forsaking it: this is doing honestly.

II. From the charge of cowardice and base fear. His courage in that which is good he produces as an evidence of his sincerity in it (*v.* 34): *Did I fear a great multitude, that I kept silence?* No, all that knew Job knew him to be a man of undaunted resolution in a good cause, that boldly appeared, spoke, and acted, in defence of religion and justice, and did not fear the face of man nor was ever threatened or brow-beaten out of his duty, but set his face as a flint. Observe, 1. What great conscience Job had made of his duty as a magistrate, or a man of reputation, in the place where he lived. He did not, he durst not, keep silence when he had a call to speak in an honest cause, or keep within doors when he had a call to go abroad to do good. The case may be such that it may be our sin to be silent and retired, as when we are called to reprove sin and bear our testimony against it, to vindicate the truths and ways of God, to do justice to those who are injured or oppressed, or in any way to serve the public or to do honour to our religion. 2. What little account Job made of the discouragements he met with in the way of his duty. He valued not the clamours of the mob, feared not a great multitude, nor did he value the menaces of the mighty: *The contempt of families never terrified him.* He was not deterred by the number or quality, the scorns or insults, or the injurious from doing justice to the injured; no, he scorned to be swayed and biassed by any such considerations, nor ever suffered a righteous cause to be run down by a high hand. He feared the great God, not the multitude, and his curse, not the contempt of families.

III. From the charge of oppression and violence, and doing wrong to his poor neighbours. And here observe,

1. What his protestation is — that the estate he had he both got and used honestly, so that his *land* could not *cry out against him nor the furrows thereof complain* (*v.* 38), as they do against those who get the possession of them by fraud and extortion, Hab. 2:9–11. The whole creation is said to groan under the sin of man; but that which is unjustly gained and held cries out against a man, and accuses him, condemns him, and demands justice against him for the injury. Rather than his oppression shall go unpunished the very ground and the furrows of it shall witness against him, and be his prosecutors. Two things he could say safely concerning his estate: — (1.) That he *never ate the fruits of it without money, v.* 39. What he purchased he paid for, as Abraham for the land he bought (Gen. 23:16), and David, 2 Sa. 24:24. The labourers that he employed had their wages duly paid them, and, if he made use of the fruits of those lands that he let out, he paid his tenants for them, or allowed it in their rent. (2.) That he never caused the owners thereof to lose their life, never got an estate, as Ahab got Naboth's vineyard, by killing the heir and seizing the inheritance, never starved those that held lands of him nor killed them with hard bargains and hard usage. No tenant, no workman, no servant, he had, could complain of him.

2. How he confirms his protestation. He does it, as often before, with a suitable imprecation (*v.* 40): "If I have got my estate unjustly, *let thistles grow instead of wheat,* the worst of weeds instead of the best of grains." When men get estates unjustly they are justly deprived of the comfort of them, and disappointed in their expectations from them. They sow their land, but they sow not that body that shall be. God will give it a body. It was sown wheat, but shall come up thistles. What men do not come honestly by will never do them any good. Job, towards the close of his protestation, appeals to the judgment-seat of God concerning the truth of it (*v.* 35–37): *O that he would hear me,* even *that the Almighty would answer me!* This was what he desired and often complained that he could not obtain; and, now that he had drawn up his own defence so particularly, he leaves it upon record, in expectation of a hearing, files it, as it were, till his cause be called.

(1.) A trial is moved for, and the motion earnestly pressed: *"O that one,* any one, *would hear me;* my cause is so good, and my evidence so clear, that I am willing to refer it to any indifferent person whatsoever; but my desire is that the Almighty himself would determine it." An upright heart does not dread a scrutiny. He that means honestly wishes he had a window in his breast, that all men might see the intents of his heart. But an upright heart does particularly desire to be determined in every thing by the judgment of God, which we are sure is according to the truth. It was holy David's prayer, *Search me, O God! and know my heart;* and it was blessed Paul's comfort, *He that judgeth me is the Lord.*

(2.) The prosecutor is called, the plaintiff summoned, and ordered to bring in his information, to say what he has to say against the prisoner, for he stands upon his deliverance: *"O that my adversary had written a book* — that my friends, who charge me with hypocrisy, would draw up their charge in writing, that it might be reduced to a certainty, and that we might the better join issue upon it." Job would be very glad to see the libel, to have a copy of his indictment. He would not hide it under his arm, but *take it upon his shoulder,* to be seen and read of all men, nay, he would *bind it as a crown* to him, would be pleased with it, and look upon it as his ornament; for, [1.] If it discovered to him any sin he had been guilty of, which he did not yet see, he should be glad to know it, that he might repent of it and get it pardoned. A good man is willing to know the worst of himself and will be thankful to those that will faithfully tell him of his faults. [2.] If it charged him with what was false, he doubted not but to disprove the allegations, that his innocency would be cleared up as the light, and he should come off with so much the more honour. But, [3.] He believed that, when his adversaries came to consider the matter so closely as they must do if they put the charge in writing, the accusations would be trivial and minute, and every one that saw them would say, "If this was all they had to say against him, it was a shame they gave him so much trouble."

(3.) The defendant is ready to make his appearance and to give his accusers all the fair play they can desire. He will *declare unto them the number of his steps, v.* 37. He will let them into the history of his own life, will show them all the stages and scenes of it. He will give them a narrative of his conversation, what would make against him as well as what would make for him, and let them make what use they pleased of it; and so confident he is of his integrity that as a prince to be crowned, rather than a prisoner to be tried, he would *go near to him,* both to his accuser to hear his charge and to his judge to hear his doom. Thus the testimony of his conscience was his rejoicing.

> Hic murus aheneus esto, nil conscire sibi —
>
> Be this thy brazen bulwark of defence,
> Still to preserve thy conscience innocence.

Those that have kept their hands without spot from the world, as Job did, may lift up their faces without spot unto God, and may comfort themselves with the prospect of his judgment when they lie under the unjust censures of men. *If our hearts condemn us not, then have we confidence towards God.*

Thus *the words of Job are ended;* that is, he has now said all he would say in answer to his friends: he afterwards said something in a way of self-reproach and condemnation (*ch.* 40:4, 5, 42:2, etc.), but here ends what he had to say in a way of self-defence and vindication. If this suffice not he will say no more; he knows when he has said enough and will submit to the judgment of the bench. Some think the manner of expression intimates that he concluded with an air of assurance and triumph. He now keeps the field and doubts not but to win the field. *Who shall lay any thing to the charge of God's elect? It is God that justifies.*

CHAPTER 32

The stage is clear, for Job and his three friends have sat down, and neither he nor they have any thing more to say; it is therefore very seasonable for a moderator to interpose, and Elihu is the man. In this chapter we have, I. Some account of him, his parentage, his presence at this dispute, and his sentiments concerning it (*v.* 1–5). II. The apology he made for his bold undertaking to speak to a question which had been so largely and learnedly argued by his seniors. He pleads, 1. That, though he had not the experience of an old man, yet he had the understanding of a man (*v.* 6–10). 2. That he had patiently heard all they had to say (*v.* 11–13). 3. That he had something new to offer (*v.* 14–17). 4. That his mind was full of this matter, and it would be a refreshment to him to give it vent (*v.* 18–20). 5. That he was resolved to speak impartially (*v.* 21, 22). And he did speak so well to this matter that Job made no reply to him, and God gave him no rebuke when he checked both Job himself and his other three friends.

Verses 1–5

Usually young men are the disputants and old men the moderators; but here, when old men were the disputants, as a rebuke to them for their unbecoming heat, a young man is raised up to be the moderator. Divers of Job's friends were present, that came to visit him and to receive instruction. Now here we have,

I. The reason why his three friends were now silent. They *ceased to answer him,* and let him have his saying, *because he was righteous in his own eyes.* This was the reason they gave why they said no more, because it was to no purpose to argue with a man that was so opinionative, *v.* 1. Those that are self-conceited are indeed hard to be wrought upon; there is more hope of a fool (a fool of God's making) than of those who are fools of their own making, Prov. 26:12. But they did not judge fairly concerning Job: he was really righteous before God, and not righteous in his own eyes only; so that it was only to save their own credit that they made this the reason of their silence, as peevish disputants commonly do when they find themselves run a-ground and are not willing to own themselves unable to make their part good.

II. The reasons why Elihu, the fourth, now spoke. His name *Elihu* signifies *My God is he.* They had all tried in vain to convince Job, but *my God is he* that can and will do it, and did it at last: he only can open the understanding. He is said to be a *Buzite,* from Buz, Nahor's second son (Gen. 22:21), and *of the kindred of Ram,* that is, *Aram* (so some), whence the Syrians or Aramites descended and were denominated, Gen. 22:21. *Of the kindred of Abram;* so the Chaldee-paraphrase, supposing him to be first called *Ram — high,* then *Abram — a high father,* and lastly *Abraham — the high father of a multitude.* Elihu was not so well known as the rest, and therefore is more particularly described thus.

1. Elihu spoke because he was angry and thought he had good cause to be so. When he had made his observations upon the dispute he did not go away and calumniate the disputants, striking them secretly with a malicious censorious tongue, but what he had to say he would say before their faces, that they might vindicate themselves if they could. (1.) He was angry at Job, because he thought he did not speak so reverently of God as he ought to have done; and that was too true (*v.* 2): *He justified himself more than God,* that is, took more care and pains to clear himself from the imputation of unrighteousness in being thus afflicted than to clear God from the imputation of unrighteousness in afflicting him, as if he were more concerned for his own honour than for God's; whereas he should, in the first place, have justified God and cleared his glory, and then he might well enough have left his own reputation to shift for itself. Note, A gracious heart is jealous for the honour of God, and cannot but be angry when that is neglected or postponed, or when any injury is done it. Nor is it any breach of the law of meekness to be angry at our friends when they are offensive to God. *Get thee behind me, Satan,* says Christ to Simon. Elihu owned Job to be a good man, and yet would not say as he said when he thought he said amiss: it is too great a compliment to our friends not to tell them of their faults. (2.) He was angry at his friends because he thought they had not conducted themselves so charitably towards Job as they ought to have done (*v.* 3): *They had found no answer, and yet had condemned Job.* They had adjudged him to be a hypocrite, a wicked man, and would not recede from that sentence

concerning him; and yet they could not prove him so, nor disprove the evidences he produced of his integrity. They could not make good the premises, and yet held fast the conclusion. They had no reply to make to his arguments, and yet they would not yield, but, right or wrong, would run him down; and this was not fair. Seldom is a quarrel begun, and more seldom is a quarrel carried on to the length that this was, in which there is not a fault on both sides. Elihu, as became a moderator, took part with neither, but was equally displeased with the mistakes and mismanagement of both. Those that in good earnest seek for truth must thus be impartial in their judgments concerning the contenders, and not reject what is true and good on either side for the sake of what is amiss, nor approve or defend what is amiss for the sake of what is true and good, but must learn to separate between the precious and the vile.

2. Elihu spoke because he thought that it was time to speak, and that now, at length, it had come to his turn, *v.* 4, 5. (1.) He had waited on Job's speeches, had patiently heard him out, until the words of Job were ended. (2.) He had waited on his friends' silence, so that, as he would not interrupt him, so he would not prevent them, not because they were wiser than he, but because they were older than he, and therefore it was expected by the company that they should speak first; and Elihu was very modest, and would by no means offer to abridge them of their privilege. Some certain rules of precedency must be observed, for the keeping of order. Though inward real honour will attend true wisdom and worth, yet, since every man will think himself or his friend the wisest and worthiest, this can afford no certain rule for the outward ceremonial honour, which therefore must attend seniority either of age or office; and this respect the seniors may the better require because they paid it when they were juniors, and the juniors may the better pay because they shall have it when they come to be seniors.

Verses 6–14

Elihu here appears to have been,

I. A man of great modesty and humility. Though a young man, and a man of abilities, yet not pert, and confident, and assuming: his face shone, and, like Moses, he did not know it, which made it shine so much the brighter. Let it be observed by all, especially by young people, as worthy their imitation, 1. What a diffidence he had of himself and of his own judgment (*v.* 6): *"I am young, and therefore I was afraid, and durst not show you my opinion,* for fear I should either prove mistaken or do that which was unbecoming me." He was so observant of all that passed, and applied his mind so closely to what he heard, that he had formed in himself a judgment of it. He neither neglected it as foreign, nor declined it as intricate; but, how clear soever the matter was to himself, he was afraid to deliver his mind upon it, because he differed in his sentiments from those that were older than he. Note, It becomes us to be suspicious of our own judgment in matters of doubtful disputation, to be swift to hear the sentiments of others and slow to speak our own, especially when we go contrary to the judgment of those for whom, upon the score of their learning and piety, we justly have a veneration. 2. What a deference he paid to his seniors, and what great expectations he had from them, (*v.* 7): *I said, Days should speak.* Note, Age and experience give a man great advantage in judging of things, both as they furnish a man with so much the more matter for his thoughts to work upon and as they ripen and improve the facilities he is to work with, which is a good reason why old people should take pains both to learn themselves and to teach others (else the advantages of their age are a reproach to them), and why young people should attend on their instructions. It is a good *lodging with an old disciple,* Acts 21:16; Tit. 2:4. Elihu's modesty appeared in the patient attention he gave to what his seniors said, *v.* 11, 12. He waited for their words as one that expected much from them, agreeably to the opinion he had of these grave men. He gave ear to their reasons, that he might take their meaning, and fully understand what was the drift of their discourse and what the force of their arguments. He attended to them with diligence and care, and this, (1.) Though they were slow, and took up a great deal of time in searching out what to say. Though they had often to seek for matter and words, paused and hesitated, and were unready at their work, yet he overlooked that, and *gave ear to their reasons,* which, if really convincing, he would not think the less so for the disadvantages of the delivery of them. (2.) Though they trifled and made nothing of it, though none of them answered Job's words nor said what was proper to convince him, yet he attended to them, in hopes they would bring it to some head at last. We must often be willing to hear what we do not like, else we cannot prove all things. His patient attendance on their discourses he pleads, [1.] As that which entitled him to a liberty of speech in his turn and empowered him to require their attention. *Hanc veniam petimusque damusque vicissim — This liberty we mutually allow and ask.* Those that have heard may speak, and those that have learned may teach. [2.] As that which enabled him to pass a judgment upon what they had said. He had observed what they aimed at, and therefore knew what to say to it. Let us be thoroughly apprized of the sentiments of our brethren before we censure them; for *he that answers a matter before he hears it,* or when he has heard it only by halves, *it is folly and shame to him,* and bespeaks him both impertinent and imperious.

II. A man of great sense and courage, and one that knew as well when and how to speak as when and how to keep silence. Though he had so much respect to his friends as not to interrupt them with his speaking, yet he had so much regard to truth and justice (his better friends) as not to betray them by his silence. He boldly pleads,

1. That man is a rational creature, and therefore that every man has for himself a judgment of discretion and ought to be allowed a liberty of speech in his turn. He means the same that Job did (*ch.* 12:3, *But I have understanding as well as you)* when he says (*v.* 8), *But there is a spirit in man;* only he expresses it a little more modestly, that one man has understanding as well as another, and no man can pretend to have the monopoly of reason or to engross all the trade of it. Had he meant *I have revelation as well as you* (as some understand it), he must have proved it; but, if he meant only *I have reason as well as you,* they cannot deny it, for it is every man's honour, and it is no presumption to claim it, nor could they gainsay his inference from it (*v.* 10): *Therefore hearken to me.* Learn here, (1.) That the soul is a spirit, neither material itself nor dependent upon matter, but capable of conversing with things spiritual, which are not the objects of sense. (2.) It is an understanding spirit. It is able to discover and receive truth, to discourse and reason upon it, and to direct and rule accordingly. (3.) This understanding spirit is in every man; it is the light *that lighteth every man,* Jn. 1:9. (4.) It is the inspiration of the Almighty that gives us this understanding spirit; for he is the Father of spirits and fountain of understanding. See Gen. 2:7; Eccl. 12:7; Zec. 12:1.

2. That those who are advanced above others in grandeur and gravity do not always proportionably go beyond them in knowledge and wisdom (*v.* 9): *Great men are not always wise;* it is a pity but they were, for then they would never do hurt with their greatness and would do so much the more good with their wisdom. Men should be preferred for their wisdom, and those that are in honour and power have most need of wisdom and have the greatest opportunity of improving in it; and yet it does not follow that great men are always wise, and therefore it is folly to subscribe to the dictates of any with an implicit faith. The aged do not always understand judgment; even *they* may be mistaken, and therefore must not expect to bring every thought into obedience to them: nay, *therefore* they must not take it as an affront to be contradicted, but rather take it as a kindness to be instructed, by their juniors: *Therefore I said, hearken to me, v.* 10. We must be willing to hear reason from those that are every way inferior to us, and to yield to it. He that has a good eye can see further upon level ground than he that is purblind can from the top of the highest mountain. *Better is a poor and wise child then an old and foolish king,* Eccl. 4:13.

3. That it was requisite for something to be said, for the setting of this controversy in a true light, which, by all that had hitherto been said, was but rendered more intricate and perplexed (*v.* 13): "I must speak, *lest you should say, We have found out wisdom,* lest you should think your argument against Job conclusive and irrefragable, and that Job cannot be convinced and humbled by any other argument than this of yours, *That God casteth him down and not man,* that it appears by his extraordinary afflictions that God is his enemy, and therefore he is certainly a wicked man. I must show you that this is a false hypothesis and that Job may be convinced without maintaining it." Or, "Lest you should think you have found out the wisest way, to reason no more with him, but leave it to God to thrust him down." It is time to speak when we hear errors advanced and disputed for, especially under pretence of supporting the cause of God with them. It is time to speak when God's judgments are vouched for the patronizing of men's pride and passion and their unjust uncharitable censures of their brethren; then we must speak on God's behalf.

4. That he had something new to offer, and would endeavour to manage the dispute in a better manner than it had hitherto been managed, *v.* 14. He thinks he may expect a favourable hearing; for, (1.) He will not reply to Job's protestations of his integrity, but allows the truth of them, and therefore does not interpose as his enemy: *"He hath not directed his words against me.* I have nothing to say against the main scope of his discourse, nor do I differ from his principles. I have only a gentle reproof to give him for his passionate expressions." (2.) He will not repeat their arguments, nor go upon their principles: *"Neither will I answer him with your speeches* — not with the same matter, for should I only say what has been said I might justly be silenced as impertinent, — nor in the same manner; I will not be guilty of that peevishness towards him myself which I dislike in you." The controversy that has already been fully handled a wise man will let alone, unless he can amend and improve what has been done; why should he *actum agere — do that which has been done already?*

Verses 15–22

Three things here apologize for Elihu's interposing as he does in this controversy which had already been canvassed by such acute and learned disputants: —

1. That the stage was clear, and he did not break in upon any of the managers on either side: *They were amazed* (*v.* 15); *they stood still, and answered no more, v.* 16. They not only left off speaking themselves, but they stood still, to hear if any of the company would speak their minds, so that (as we say) he had room and fair play given him. They seemed not fully satisfied themselves with what they had said, else they would have adjourned the court, and not have stood still, expecting what might further be offered. And therefore *I said* (*v.* 17), *"I will answer also my part.* I cannot pretend to give a definitive sentence; no, the judgment is the Lord's, and by him it must be determined who is in the right and who is in the wrong; but, since you have each of you shown your opinion, I also will show mine, and let it take its fate with the rest." When what is offered, even by the meanest, is offered thus modestly, it is a pity but it should be fairly heard and considered. I see no inconvenience in supposing that Elihu here discovers himself to be the penman of this book, and that he here writes as an historian, relating the matter of fact, that, after he had bespoken their attention in the foregoing verses, they were amazed, they left off whispering among themselves, did not gainsay the liberty of speech he desired, but stood still to hear what he would say, being much surprised at the admirable mixture of boldness and modesty that appeared in his preface.

2. That he was uneasy, and even in pain, to be delivered of his thoughts upon this matter. They must give him leave to speak, for he cannot forbear; while he is *musing the fire burns* (Ps. 39:3), *shut up in his bones,* as the prophet speaks, Jer. 20:9. Never did nurse, when her breasts were gorged, so long to have them drawn as Elihu did to deliver his mind concerning Job's case, *v.* 18–20. If any of the disputants had hit that which he thought was the right joint, he would contentedly have been silent; but, when he thought they all missed it, he was eager to be trying his hand at it. He pleads, (1.) That he had a great deal to say: *"I am full of matter,* having carefully attended to all that has hitherto been said, and made my own reflections upon it." When aged men are drawn dry, and have spent their stock, in discoursing of the divine Providence, God can raise up others, even young men, and fill them with matter for the edifying of his church; for it is a subject that

can never be exhausted, though those that speak upon it may. (2.) That he was under a necessity of saying it: *"The spirit within me* not only instructs me what to say, but puts me on to say it; so that if I have not vent (such a ferment are my thoughts in) I shall *burst like bottles of new wine* when it is working," *v.* 19. See what a great grief it is to a good minister to be silenced and thrust into a corner; he is full of matter, full of Christ, full of heaven, and would speak of these things for the good of others, but he may not. (3.) That it would be an ease and satisfaction to himself to deliver his mind (*v.* 20): *I will speak, that I may be refreshed,* not only that I may be eased of the pain of stifling my thoughts, but that I may have the pleasure of endeavouring, according to my place and capacity, to do good. It is a great refreshment to a good man to have liberty to speak for the glory of God and the edification of others.

3. That he was resolved to speak, with all possible freedom and sincerity, what he thought was true, not what he thought would please (*v.* 21, 22): *"Let me not accept any man's person,* as partial judges do, that aim to enrich themselves, not to do justice. I am resolved to flatter no man." He would not speak otherwise than he thought, either, (1.) In compassion to Job, because he was poor and in affliction, would not make his case better than he really took it to be, for fear of increasing his grief; "but, let him bear it as he can, he shall be told the truth." Those that are in affliction must not be flattered, but dealt faithfully with. When trouble is upon any it is foolish pity to suffer sin upon them too (Lev. 19:17), for that is the worst addition that can be to their trouble. Thou shalt not countenance, any more than discountenance, *a poor man in his cause* (Ex. 23:3), nor regard a sad look any more than a big look, so as, for the sake of it, to pervert justice, for that is accepting persons. Or, (2.) In compliment to Job's friends, because they were in prosperity and reputation. Let them not expect that he should say as they said, any further than he was convinced that they say right, nor applaud their dictates for the sake of their dignities. No, though Elihu is a young man, and upon his preferment, he will not dissemble truth to court the favour of great men. It is a good resolution he has taken up — *"I know not to give flattering titles to men;* I never used myself to flattering language;" and it is a good reason he gives for that resolution — *in so doing my Maker would soon take my away.* It is good to keep ourselves in awe with a holy fear of God's judgments. He that made us will take us away in his wrath is we do not conduct ourselves as we should. He hates all dissimulation and flattery, and will soon *put lying lips to silence* and *cut off flattering lips,* Ps. 12:3. The more closely we eye the majesty of God as our Maker, and the more we dread his wrath and justice, the less danger shall we be in of a sinful fearing or flattering of men.

CHAPTER 33

Pompous prefaces, like the teeming mountain, often introduce poor performances; but Elihu's discourse here does not disappoint the expectations which his preface had raised. It is substantial, and lively, and very much to the purpose. He had, in the foregoing chapter, said what he had to say to Job's three friends; and now he comes up close to Job himself and directs his speech to him. I. He bespeaks Job's favourable acceptance of what he should say, and desires he would take him for that person whom he had so often wished for, that would plead with him, and receive his plea on God's behalf (*v.* 1–7). II. He does, in God's name, bring an action against him, for words which he had spoken, in the heat of disputation, reflecting upon God as dealing hardly with him (*v.* 8–11). III. He endeavours to convince him of his fault and folly herein, by showing him, 1. God's sovereign dominion over man (*v.* 12, 13). 2. The care God takes of man, and the various ways and means he uses to do his soul good, which we have reason to think he designs when he lays bodily afflictions upon him (*v.* 14). (1.) Job had sometimes complained of unquiet dreams, 7:14. "Why," says Elihu, "God sometimes speaks conviction and instruction to men by such dreams," (*v.* 15–18). (2.) Job had especially complained of his sicknesses and pains; and, as to these, he shows largely that they were so far from being tokens of God's wrath, as Job took them, or evidences of Job's hypocrisy, as his friends took them, that they were really wise and gracious methods, which divine grace took for the increase of his acquaintance with God, to work patience, experience, and hope (*v.* 19–30). And, lastly, he concludes with a request to Job, either to answer him or give him leave to go on (*v.* 31–33).

Verses 1–7

Several arguments Elihu here uses to persuade Job not only to give him a patient hearing, but to believe that he designed him a good office, and to take it kindly, and be willing to receive the instructions he was now about to give him. Let Job consider, 1. That Elihu does not join with his three friends against him. He has, in the foregoing chapter, declared his dislike of their proceedings, disclaimed their hypothesis, and quite set aside the method they took of healing Job. *"Wherefore, Job, I pray thee, hear my speech, v.* 1. They were all in the same song, all spoke in the same strain; but I am trying a new say, *therefore hearken to all my words,* and not to some of them only;" for we cannot judge of a discourse unless we take it entire and hearken to it all. 2. That he intended to make a solemn business of it, not to put in a word by the by, or give a short repartee, to show his wit: after long silence he *opened his mouth* (*v.* 2), with deliberation and design. Upon mature consideration he had already begun to speak, and was prepared to go on if Job would encourage him by his attention. 3. That he was resolved to speak as he thought and not otherwise (*v.* 3): *"My words shall be of the uprightness of my heart,* the genuine product of my convictions and sentiments." There was reason to suspect that Job's three friends did not think, in their consciences, that Job was so bad a man as they had in their discourses, merely for the support of their hypothesis, represented him to be; and that was not fair. It is a base thing to condemn those with our tongues, to serve a turn, whom at the same time we cannot but in our consciences think well of. Elihu is an honest man, and scorns to do so. 4. That what he said should be easy, and not dark and hard to be understood: *My lips shall utterly knowledge clearly.* Job shall readily comprehend his meaning, and perceive what he aims at. Those that speak of the things of God should carefully avoid all obscurity and perplexedness both of notion and expression, and speak as plainly and clearly as they can; for by that it will appear that they do themselves understand what they speak of, that they mean honestly, and design the edification of those they speak to. 5. That he would, in his discourse, make the best use he could of the reason and understanding God had given him, that life, that rational soul which he received from *the Spirit of God* and *the breath of the Almighty, v.* 4. He owns himself unfit to enter into the lists with his seniors, yet he desires they will not despise his youth, for that he is God's workmanship as well as they, made by the same hand, endued with the same noble powers and faculties, and designed for the same great end; and therefore why may not the God that made him make use of his as an instrument of good to Job? With this consideration also we should quicken ourselves (and perhaps Elihu made that use of it) to do good in our places according to our capacity. God has made us, and given us life, and therefore we should study to use our life to some good purpose, to spend it in glorifying God and serving our generation according to his will, that we may answer the end of our creation and it may not be said that we were made in vain. 6. That he would be very willing to hear what Job could object against what he had to say (*v.* 5): *"If thou canst, answer me.* If thou hast so much strength and spirit left thee, and art not quite spent with the distemper and the dispute, *set thy words in order,* and they shall have their due consideration." Those that can speak reason will hear reason. 7. That he had often wished for one that would appear for God, with whom he might freely expostulate, and to whom, as arbitrator, he might refer the matter, and such a one Elihu would be (*v.* 6): *I am, according to thy wish, in God's stead.* How pathetically had Job wished (*ch.* 16:21), *O that one might plead for a man with God!* and (*ch.* 22:3), *O that I knew where I might find him!* Only he would make it his bargain that *his dread should not make him afraid, ch.* 13:21. "Now," says Elihu, "look upon me, for this once, as in God's stead. I will undertake to plead his cause with thee and to show thee wherein thou hast affronted him and what he has against thee; and what appeals or complaints thou hast to make to God make them to me." 8. That he was not an unequal match for him: *"I also am formed out of the clay.* I also, as well as the first man (Gen. 2:7), I also as well as thou." Job had urged this with God as a reason why he should not bear hard upon him (*ch.* 10:9), *Remember that thou hast made me as the clay.* "I," says Elihu, "am *formed out of the clay* as well as thou," *formed of the same clay,* so some read it. It is good for us all to consider that we are formed out of the clay; and well for us it is that those who are to us in God's stead are so, that he speaks to us by men like ourselves, according to Israel's wish upon a full trial, Deu. 5:24. God has wisely deposited the treasure in earthen vessels like ourselves, 2 Co. 4:7. 9. That he would have no reason to be frightened at the assault he made upon him (*v.* 7): *"My terror shall not make thee afraid,"* (1.) "As thy friends have done with their arguings. I will not reproach thee as they have done, nor draw up such a heavy charge against thee, Nor," (2.) "As God would do if he should appear to reason with thee. I stand upon the same level with thee, and am made of the same mould, and therefore cannot impose that terror upon thee which thou mayest justly dread from the appearance of the divine Majesty." If we would rightly convince men, it must be by reason, not by terror, by fair arguing, not by a heavy hand.

Verses 8–13

In these verses,

I. Elihu particularly charges Job with some indecent expressions that had dropped from him, reflecting upon the justice and goodness of God in his dealings with him. He does not ground the charge upon report, but was himself an ear-witness of what he here reproves him for (*v.* 8): *"Thou hast spoken it in my hearing,* and in the hearing of all this company." He had it not at second hand; if so, he would have hoped it was not so bad as it was represented. He did not hear it from Job in private conversation, for then he would not have been so ill-bred as to repeat it thus publicly; but Job had said it openly, and therefore it was fit he should be openly reproved for it. *Those that sin before all rebuke before all.* When we hear any thing said that tends to God's dishonour we ought publicly to bear our testimony against it. What is said amiss in our hearing we are concerned to reprove; for *you are my witnesses, saith the Lord,* to confront the accuser. 1. Job had represented himself as innocent (*v.* 9): Thou hast said, *I am clean without transgression.* Job had not said this *totidem verbis — in so many words;* nay, he had owned himself to have sinned and to be impure before God; but he had indeed said, *Thou knowest that I am not wicked, my righteousness I hold fast,* and the like, on which Elihu might ground this charge. It was true that Job was a perfect and an upright man and not such a one as his friends had represented him; but he ought not to have insisted so much upon it, as if God had therefore done him wrong in afflicting him. Yet, it should seem, Elihu did not deal fairly in charging Job with saying that he was clean and innocent from all transgression, when he only pleaded that he was upright and innocent from the great transgression. But those that speak passionately and unwarily must thank themselves if they be misunderstood; they should have taken more care. 2. He had represented God as severe in marking what he did amiss and taking all advantages against him (*v.* 10, 11), as if he sought opportunity to pick quarrels with him. *He findeth occasions against me,* which supposes seeking them. To this purport Job had spoken, *ch.* 14:16, 17, *Dost thou not watch over my sin? He counteth me for his enemy;* so he had expressly said, *ch.* 13:24; 19:11. *"He putteth my feet in the stocks,* that, as I cannot contend with him, so I may not be able to flee from him;" this he had said, *ch.* 13:27. *He marketh all my paths;* so he had said, *ch.* 13:27.

II. He endeavours to convince him that he had spoken amiss in speaking thus, and that he ought to humble himself before God for it, and by repentance to unsay it (*v.* 12): *Behold, in this thou art not just. Here thou art not in the right,* so some read it. See; the difference between the charge which Elihu exhibited against Job and that which was preferred against him by his other friends; they would not own that he was just at all, but Elihu only says, "In this, in saying this, thou art not just." 1. "Thou dost not deal justly with God." To be just is to render to all their due; now we do not render to God his due, nor are we just to him, if we do not acknowledge his equity and kindness in all his dispensations of his providence towards us, that he is righteous in all his ways, and that, however it be, yet he is good. 2. "Thou dost not speak the language of a righteous man. I do not deny but thou art such a one, but in this thou dost not make it to appear." Many that are just yet, in some particular instances, do not speak and act like themselves; and as, on the one hand, we must not fail to tell even a good man wherein he mistakes and does amiss, nor flatter him in his errors and passions, for in that we ar not kind, so on the other hand we must not draw men's characters, nor pass a judgment on them, from one instance, or some few misplaced words, for in that we are not just. *In many things we all offend*, and therefore must be candid in our censures. Two things Elihu proposes to Job's consideration, to convince him that he had said amiss: — (1.) That God is infinitely above us, and therefore it is madness to contend with him; for if he plead against us with his great power we cannot stand before him. *I will answer thee*, says Elihu, in one word, which carries its own evidence along with it, *That God is greater than man;* no doubt he is, infinitely greater. Between God and man there is no proportion. Job had himself said a great deal, and admirably well, concerning the greatness of God, his irresistible power and incontestable sovereignty, his terrible majesty and unsearchable immensity. "Now," said Elihu, "do but consider what thou thyself hast said concerning the greatness of God, and apply it to thyself; if he is greater than man, he is greater than thou, and thou wilt see reason enough to repent of these ill-natures, ill-favoured, reflections upon him, and to blush at thy folly, and tremble to think of thy own presumption." Note, There is enough in this one plain unquestionable truth, *That God is greater than man*, if duly improved, for ever to put to silence and to shame all our complaints of his providence and our exceptions against his dealings with us. He is not only more wise and powerful than we are, and therefore it is to no purpose to contend with him who will be too hard for us, but more holy, just, and good, for these are the transcendent glories and excellencies of the divine nature; in these God is greater than man, and therefore it is absurd and unreasonable to find fault with him, for he is certainly in the right. (2.) That God is not accountable to us (v. 13): *Why dost thou strive against him?* Those that complain of God strive against him, implead him, impeach him, bring an action against him. And why do they do so? For what cause? To what purpose? Note, It is an unreasonable thing for us, weak, foolish, sinful, creatures, to strive with a God of infinite wisdom, power, and goodness. Woe to the clay that strives with the potter; *for he gives no account of any of his matters.* He is under no obligation to show us a reason for what he does, neither to tell us what he designs to do (in what method, at what time, by what instruments) nor to tell us why he deals thus with us. He is not bound either to justify his own proceedings or to satisfy our demands and enquiries; his judgments will certainly justify themselves. If we do not satisfy ourselves in them, it is our own fault. It is therefore daring impiety for us to arraign God at our bar, or challenge him to show cause for what he doeth, to say unto him, *What doest thou?* or, *Why doest thou so? He gives not account of all his matters* (so some read it); he reveals as much as it is fit for us to know, as follows here (v. 14), but still there are secret things, which belong not to us, which it is not for us to pry into.

Verses 14–18

Job had complained that God kept him wholly in the dark concerning the meaning of his dealings with him, and therefore concluded he dealt with him as his enemy. "No," says Elihu, "he speaks to you, but you do not perceive him; so that the fault is yours, not his; and he is designing your real good even in those dispensations which you put this harsh construction upon." Observe in general, 1. What a friend God is to our welfare: *He speaketh to us once, yea, twice, v.* 14. It is a token of his favour that, notwithstanding the distance and quarrel between us and him, yet he is pleased to speak to us. It is an evidence of his gracious design that he is pleased to speak to us of our own concerns, to show us what is our duty and what our interest, what he requires of us and what we may expect from him, to tell us of our faults and warn us of our danger, to show us the way and to lead us in it. This he does once, yea, twice, that is, again and again; when one warning is neglected he gives another, not willing that any should perish. *Precept must be upon precept, and line upon line;* it is so, that sinners may be left inexcusable. 2. What enemies we are to our own welfare: *Man perceives it not,* that is, he does not heed it or regard it, does not discern or understand it, is not aware that it is the voice of God, nor does he receive the things revealed, for they are foolishness to him; he stops his ear, stands in his own light, rejects the counsel of God against himself, and so is never

the wiser, no not for the dictates of wisdom itself. God speaks to us by conscience, by providences, and by ministers, of all which Elihu here discourses at large, to show Job that God was both telling him his mind and doing him a kindness, even now that he seemed to keep him in the dark and so treat him as a stranger, and to keep him in distress and so treat him as an enemy. There was not then, that we know of, any divine revelation in writing, and therefore that is not here mentioned among the ways by which God speaks to men, though now it is the principal way.

In these verses he shows how God teaches and admonishes the children of men by their own consciences. Observe,

I. The proper season and opportunity for these admonitions (v. 15): *In a dream, in slumberings upon the bed,* when men are retired from the world and the business and conversation of it. It is a good time for them to retire into their own hearts, and commune with them, when they are upon their beds, solitary and still, Ps. 4:4. It is the time God takes for dealing personally with men. 1. When he sent angels, extraordinary messengers, on his errands, he commonly chose that time for the delivery of their messages, when by deep sleep falling on men the bodily senses were all locked up and the mind more free to receive the immediate communications of divine light. Thus he made his mind known to the prophets by visions and dreams (Num. 12:6); thus he warned Abimelech (Gen. 20:3), Laban (Gen. 31:24), Joseph (Mt. 1:20); thus he made known to Pharaoh and Nebuchadnezzar things that should come to pass hereafter. 2. When he stirred up conscience, that ordinary deputy of his, in the soul, to do its office, he took that opportunity, either when deep sleep fell on men (for, though dreams mostly come from fancy, some may come from conscience) or in slumberings, when men are between sleeping and waking, reflecting at night upon the business of the foregoing day or projecting in the morning the business of the ensuing day; then is a proper time for their hearts to reproach them for what they have done ill and to admonish them what they should do. See Isa. 30:21.

II. The power and force with which those admonitions come, v. 16. When God designs men's good by the convictions and dictates of their own consciences, 1. He gives them admission, and makes them to be heeded: *Then he opens the ears of men*, which were before shut against the voice of this charmer, Ps. 58:5. He opens the heart, as he opened Lydia's, and so opens the ears. He takes away that which stopped the ear, so that the conviction finds or forces its way; nay, he works in the soul a submission to the regimen of conscience and a compliance with its rules, for that follows upon God's opening the ear, Isa. 50:5. *God has opened my ear, and I was not rebellious.* 2. He gives them a lodgment in the heart and makes them to abide: *He sealeth their instruction*, that is, the instruction that is designed for them and is suited to them; this he makes their souls to receive the deep and lasting impression of, as the wax of the seal. When the heart is delivered into divine instructions, as into a mould, then the work is done.

III. The end and design of these admonitions that are sent. 1. To keep men from sin, and particularly the sin of pride (v. 17). *That he may withdraw man from his purpose,* that is, from his evil purposes, may change the temper of his mind and the course of his life, his disposition and inclination, or prevent some particular sin he is in danger of falling into, that he may withdraw man from his work, may make him leave off man's work, which is working for the world and the flesh, and may set him to work the work of God. Many a man has been stopped in the full career of a sinful pursuit by the seasonable checks of his own conscience, saying, *Do not this abominable thing which the Lord hates.* Particularly, God does, by this means, *hide pride from man*, that is, hide those things from him which are the matter of his pride, and take his mind off from dwelling upon them, by setting before him what reason he has to be humble. That he may *take away pride from man* (so some read it), that he may pluck up that root of bitterness which is the cause of so much sin. All those whom God has mercy in store for he will humble and hide pride from. Pride makes people eager and resolute in the prosecution of their purposes; they will have their way, therefore God withdraws them from their purposes, by mortifying their pride. 2. To keep men from ruin,

v. 18. While sinners are pursuing their evil purposes, and indulging their pride, their souls are hastening apace to the pit, to the sword, to destruction, both in this world and that to come; but when God, by the admonitions of conscience, withdraws them from sin, he thereby *keeps back their souls from the pit*, from the bottomless pit, and saves them from perishing by *the sword* of divine vengeance, so iniquity shall not be their ruin. That which turns men from sin saves them from hell, *saves a soul from death,* James 5:20. See what a mercy it is to be under the restraints of an awakened conscience. Faithful are the wounds, and kind are the bonds, of that friend, for by them the soul is kept from perishing eternally.

Verses 19–28

God has spoken once to sinners by their own consciences, to keep them from the paths of the destroyer, but they perceive it not; they are not aware that the checks their own hearts give them in a sinful way are from God, but they are imputed to melancholy or the preciseness of their education; and therefore God speaks twice; he speaks a second time, and tries another way to convince and reclaim sinners, and that is by providences, afflictive and merciful (in which he speaks twice), and by the seasonable instructions of good ministers setting in with them. Job complained much of his diseases and judged by them that God was angry with him; his friends did so too: but Elihu shows that they were all mistaken, for God often afflicts the body in love, and with gracious designs of good to the soul, as appears in the issue. This part of Elihu's discourse will be of great use to us for the due improvement of sickness, in and by which God speaks to men. Here is,

I. The patient described in his extremity. See what work sickness makes (v. 19, etc.) when God sends it with commission. *Do this, and doeth it.* 1. The sick man is full of pain all over him (v. 19): *He is chastened with pain upon his bed,* such pain as confines him to his bed, or so extreme the pain is that he can get no ease, no, not on his bed, where he would repose himself. Pain and sickness will turn a bed of down into a bed of thorns, on which he that used to sleep now tosses to and fro till the dawning of the day. The case, as here put, is very bad. Pain is borne with more difficulty than sickness, and with that the patient here is chastened, not a dull heavy pain, but strong and acute; and frequently the stronger the patient the stronger the pain, for the more sanguine the complexion is the more violent, commonly, the disease is. It is not the smarting of the flesh that is complained of, but the aching of the bones. It is an inward rooted pain; and not only the bones of one limb, but *the multitude of the bones*, are thus chastened. See what frail, what vile bodies we have, which, though receiving no external hurt, may be thus pained from causes within themselves. See what work sin makes, what mischief it does. Pain is the fruit of sin; yet, by the grace of God, the pain of the body is often made a means of good to the soul. 2. He has quite lost his appetite, the common effect of sickness (v. 20): *His life abhorreth bread*, the most necessary food, *and dainty meat*, which he most delighted in, and formerly relished with a great deal of pleasure. This is a good reason why we should *not be desirous of dainties, because they are deceitful meat*, Prov. 23:3. We may be soon made as sick of them as we are now fond of them; and those who live in luxury when they are well, if ever they come, by reason of sickness, to loathe dainty meat, may, with grief and shame, read their sin in their punishment. Let us not inordinately love the taste of meat, for the time may come when we may even loathe the sight of meat, Ps. 107:18. 3. He has become a perfect skeleton, nothing but skin and bones, v. 21. By sickness, perhaps a few days' sickness, *his flesh*, which was fat, and fair, *is consumed away*, that it cannot be seen; it is strangely wasted and gone: *and his bones*, which were buried in flesh, now *stick out;* you may count his ribs, may tell all his bones. The soul that is well nourished with the bread of life sickness will not make lean, but it soon makes a change in the body.

> He who, before, had such a beauteous air,
> And, pampered with the ease, seemed plump and fair
> Doth all his friends (amazing change!) surprise
> With pale lean cheeks and ghastly hollow eyes;
> His bones (a horrid sight!) start through his skin,
> Which lay before, in flesh and fat, unseen.
> — Sir R. Blackmore

4. He is given up for gone, and his life despaired of (*v.* 22): *His soul draws near to the grave,* that is, he has all the symptoms of death upon him, and in the apprehension of all about him, as well as in his own, he is a dying man. The pangs of death, here called *the destroyers,* are just ready to seize him; they compass him about, Ps. 116:3. Perhaps it intimates the very dreadful apprehensions which those have of death as a destroying thing, when it stares them in the face, who, when it was at a distance, made light of it. All agree when it comes to the point, whatever they thought of it before, that it is a serious thing to die.

II. The provision made for his instruction, in order to a sanctified use of his affliction, that, when God in that way speaks to man, he may be heard and understood, and not speak in vain, *v.* 23. He is happy *if there be a messenger with him* to attend him in his sickness, to convince, counsel, and comfort him, *an interpreter* to expound the providence and give him to understand the meaning of it, *a man of wisdom* that knows the voice of the rod and its interpretation; for, when God speaks by afflictions, we are frequently so unversed in the language, that we have need of an interpreter, and it is well if we have such a one. The advice and help of a good minister are as needful and seasonable, and should be as acceptable, in sickness, as of a good physician, especially if he be well skilled in the art of explaining and improving providences; he is then *one of a thousand,* and to be valued accordingly. His business at such a time is *to show unto man his uprightness,* that is, God's uprightness, that in faithfulness he afflicts him and does him no wrong, which it is necessary to be convinced of in order to our making a due improvement of the affliction: or, rather, it may mean man's uprightness, or rectitude. 1. The uprightness that *is.* If it appear that the sick person is truly pious, the interpreter will not do as Job's friends had done, make it his business to prove him a hypocrite because he is afflicted, but on the contrary will show him his uprightness, notwithstanding his afflictions, that he may take the comfort of it, and be easy, whatever the event is. 2. The uprightness, the reformation, that *should be,* in order to life and peace. When men are made to see the way of uprightness to be the only way, and a sure way to salvation, and to choose it, and walk in it accordingly, the work is done.

III. God's gracious acceptance of him, upon his repentance, *v.* 24. When he sees that the sick person is indeed convinced that sincere repentance, and that uprightness which is gospel perfection, are his interest as well as his duty, then he that waits to be gracious, and shows mercy upon the first indication of true repentance, *is gracious unto him,* and takes him into his favour and thoughts for good. Wherever God finds a gracious heart he will be found a gracious God; and, 1. He will give a gracious order for his discharge. He says, *Deliver him* (that is, let him be delivered) *from going down to the pit,* from that death which is the wages of sin. When afflictions have done their work they shall be removed. When we return to God in a way of duty he will return to us in a way of mercy. Those shall be delivered from going down to the pit who receive God's messengers, and rightly understand his interpreters, so as to subscribe to his uprightness. 2. He will give a gracious reason for this order: *I have found a ransom,* or propitiation; Jesus Christ is that ransom, so Elihu calls him, as Job had called him his Redeemer, for he is both the purchaser and the price, the priest and the sacrifice; so high was the value put upon souls that nothing less would redeem them, and so great the injury done by sin that nothing less would atone for it than the blood of the Son of God, who *gave his life a ransom for many.* This is a ransom of God's finding, a contrivance of Infinite Wisdom; we could never have found it ourselves, and the angels themselves could never have found it. It is *the wisdom of God in a mystery, the hidden wisdom,* and such an invention as is and will be the everlasting wonder of those principalities and powers that desire to look into it. Observe how God glories in the invention here, ***heurēka, heurēka*** — *"I have found, I have found, the ransom;* I, even I, am he that has done it."

IV. The recovery of the sick man hereupon. Take away the cause and the effect will cease. When the patient becomes a penitent see what a blessed change follows. 1. His body recovers its health, *v.* 25. This is not always the consequence of a sick man's repentance and return to God, but sometimes it is; and recovery from sickness is a mercy indeed when it arises from the remission of sin; then it is in love to the soul that the body is *delivered from the pit of corruption* when God *casts our sins behind his back,* Isa. 38:17. That is the method of a blessed recovery. *Son, be of good cheer, thy sins be forgiven thee;* and then, *Rise, take up thy bed, and walk,* Mt. 9:2, 6. So here, interest him in the ransom, and then *his flesh shall be fresher than a child's* and there shall be no remains of his distemper, but *he shall return to the days of his youth,* to the beauty and strength which he had then. When the distemper that oppressed nature is removed how strangely does nature help itself, in which the power and goodness of the God of nature must be thankfully acknowledged! By such merciful providences as these, which afflictions give occasion for, God speaketh once, yea, twice, to the children of men, letting them know (if they would but perceive it) their dependence upon him and his tender compassion of them. 2. His soul recovers it peace, *v.* 26. (1.) The patient, being a penitent, is a supplicant, and has learned to pray. He knows God will be sought unto for his favours, and therefore *he shall pray unto God,* pray for pardon, pray for health. *Is any afflicted, and sick? Let him pray.* When he finds himself recovering he shall not then think that prayer is no longer necessary, for we need the grace of God as much for the sanctifying of a mercy as for the sanctifying of an affliction. (2.) His prayers are accepted. God *will be favourable to him,* and be well pleased with him; his anger shall be turned away from him, and the light of God's countenance shall shine upon his soul; and then it follows, (3.) That he has the comfort of communion with God. He shall now see the face of God, which before was hid from him, and he shall see it with joy, for what sight can be more reviving? See Gen. 33:10, *As though I had seen the face of God.* All true penitents rejoice more in the returns of God's favour than in any instance whatsoever of prosperity or pleasure, Ps. 4:6, 7. (4.) He has a blessed tranquility of mind, arising from the sense of his justification before God, who *will render unto this man his righteousness.* He shall receive the atonement, that is, the comfort of it, Rom. 5:11. Righteousness shall be imputed to him, and peace thereupon spoken, the joy and gladness of which he shall then be made to hear though he could not hear them in the day of his affliction. God will now deal with him as a righteous man, with whom it shall be well. He shall *receive the blessing from the Lord, even righteousness,* Ps. 24:5. God shall give him grace to go and sin no more. Perhaps this may denote the reformation of his life after his recovery. As he shall pray unto God, whom before he had slighted, so he shall render to man his righteousness, whom before he had wronged, shall make restitution, and for the future do justly.

V. The general rule which God will go by in dealing with the children of men inferred from this instance, *v.* 27, 28. As sick people, upon their submission, are restored, so all others that truly repent of their sins shall find mercy with God. See here, 1. What sin is, and what reason we have not to sin. Would we know the nature of sin and the malignity of it? It is the perverting of that which is right; it is a most unjust unreasonable thing; it is the rebellion of the creature against the Creator, the usurped dominion of the flesh over the spirit, and a contradiction to the eternal rules and reasons of good and evil. It is *perverting the right ways of the Lord* (Acts 13:10), and therefore the ways of sin are called *crooked ways,* Ps. 125:5. Would we know what is to be got by sin? *It profiteth us not.* The works of darkness are unfruitful works. When profit and loss come to be balanced all the gains of sin, put them all together, will come far short of countervailing the damage. All true penitents are ready to own this, and it is a mortifying consideration. Rom. 6:21, *What fruit had you then in those things whereof you are now ashamed?* 2. See what repentance is, and what reason we have to repent. Would we approve ourselves true penitents? We must then, with a broken and contrite heart, confess our sins to God, 1 Jn. 1:9. We must confess the fact of sin *(I have sinned)* and not deny the charge, or stand upon our own justification; we must confess the fault of sin, the iniquity, the dishonesty of it *(have perverted that which was right);* we must confess the folly of sin — "so foolish have I been and ignorant, for *it profited me not;* and therefore what have I to do any more with it?" Is there not good reason why we should make such a penitent confession as this? For, (1.) God expect it. *He looks upon men,* when they have sinned, to see what they will do next, whether they will go on in it or whether they will bethink themselves and return. He hearkens and hears whether any say, *What have I done?* Jer. 8:6. He looks upon sinners with an eye of compassion, desiring to hear this from them; for he has no pleasure in their ruin. He looks upon them, and, as soon as he perceives these workings of repentance in them, he encourages them and is ready to accept them (Ps. 32:5, 6), as the father went forth to meet the returning prodigal. (2.) It will turn to our unspeakable advantage. The promise is general. If any humble himself thus, whoever he be, [1.] He shall not come into condemnation, but be saved from the wrath to come: *He shall deliver his soul from going into the pit,* the pit of hell; iniquity shall not be his ruin. [2.] He shall be happy in everlasting life and joy: *His life shall see the light,* that is, all good, in the vision and fruition of God. To obtain this bliss, if the prophet had bidden us do some great thing, would we not have done it? How much more when he only says unto us, *Wash and be clean,* confess and be pardoned, repent and be saved?

Verses 29–33

We have here the conclusion of this first part of Elihu's discourse, in which, 1. He briefly sums up what he had said, showing that God's great and gracious design, in all the dispensations of his providence towards the children of men, is to save them from being for ever miserable and bring them to be for ever happy, *v.* 29, 30. *All these things God is working with the children of men.* He deals with them by conscience, by providences, by ministers, by mercies, by afflictions. He makes them sick, and makes them well again. All these are his operations; he has *set the one over the other* (Eccl. 7:14), but his hand is in all; it is he that performs all the things for us. All providences are to be looked upon as God's workings with man, his strivings with him. He uses a variety of methods to do men good; if one affliction do not do the work, he will try another; if neither do, he will try a mercy; and he will send a messenger to interpret both. He often works such things as these twice, thrice; so it is in the original, referring to *v.* 14. He *speaks once, yea, twice;* if that prevail not, he works twice, yea, thrice; he changes his method *(we have piped, we have mourned)* returns again to the same method, repeats the same applications. Why does he take all this pains with man? It is *to bring back his soul from the pit, v.* 30. If God did not take more care of us than we do of ourselves, we should be miserable; we would destroy ourselves, but he would have us saved, and devises means, by his grace, to undo that by which we were undoing ourselves. The former method, by dream and vision, was to *keep back the soul from the pit* (*v.* 18), that is, to prevent sin, that we might not fall into it. This, by sickness and the word, is to bring back the soul, to recover those that have fallen into sin, that they may not lie still and perish in it. With respect to all that by repentance are brought back from the pit, it is that they may be *enlightened with the light of the living,* that they may have present comfort and everlasting happiness. Whom God saves from sin and hell, which are darkness, he will bring to heaven, the inheritance of the saints in light; and this he aims at in all his institutions and all his dispensations. *Lord, what is man, that thou shouldst thus visit him!* This should engage us to comply with God's designs, to work with him for our own good, and not to counter-work him. This will render those that perish for ever inexcusable, that so much was done to save them and they would not be healed. 2. He bespeaks Job's acceptance of what he had offered and begs of him to *mark it well, v.* 31. What is intended for our good challenges our regard. If Job will observe what is said, (1.) He is welcome to make what objections he can against it (*v.* 32): *"If thou hast any thing to say* for thyself, in thy own vindication, *answer me;* though I am fresh, and thou art spent, I will not run thee down with words: *Speak, for I, desire to justify thee,* and am not as thy other friends that desired to condemn thee." Elihu contends for truth, not, as they did, for victory. Note, Those we reprove we should desire to justify, and be glad to see them clear themselves from the imputations they lie under, and therefore give them all possible advantage and encouragement to do so. (2.) If he has nothing to say against what is said, Elihu lets him know that he has something more to say, which he desires him patiently to attend to (v. 33): *Hold thy peace, and I will teach thee wisdom.* Those that would both show wisdom and learn wisdom must hearken and keep silence, be swift to hear and slow to speak. Job was wise and good; but those that are so may yet be wiser and better, and must therefore set themselves to improve by the means of wisdom and grace.

CHAPTER 34

Elihu, it is likely, paused awhile, to see if Job had any thing to say against his discourse in the foregoing chapter; but he sitting silent, and it is likely intimating his desire that he would go on, he here proceeds. And, I. He bespeaks not only the audience, but the assistance of the company (v. 2–4). II. He charges Job with some more indecent expressions that had dropped from him (v. 5–9). III. He undertakes to convince him that he had spoken amiss, by showing very fully, 1. God's incontestable justice (v. 10–12, 17, 19, 23). 2. His sovereign dominion (v. 13–15). 3. His almighty power (v. 20, 24). 4. His omniscience (v. 21, 22, 25). 5. His severity against sinners (v. 26–28). 6. His overruling providence (v. 29, 30). IV. He teaches him what he should say (v. 31, 32). And then, lastly, he leaves the matter to Job's own conscience, and concludes with a sharp reproof of him for his peevishness and discontent (v. 33–37). All this Job not only bore patiently, but took kindly, because he saw that Elihu meant well; and, whereas his other friends had accused him of that from which his own conscience acquitted him, Elihu charged him with that only for which, it is probable, his own heart, now upon the reflection, began to smite him.

Verses 1–9

Here, I. Elihu humbly addresses himself to the auditors, and endeavours, like an orator, to gain their good-will and their favourable attention. 1. He calls them *wise men,* and men that *had knowledge, v.* 2. It is comfortable dealing with such as understand sense. *I speak as to wise men,* who can *judge what I say,* 1 Co. 10:15. Elihu differed in opinion from them, and yet he calls them wise and knowing men. Peevish disputants think all fools that are not of their mind; but it is a piece of justice which we owe to those who are wise to acknowledge it, though our sentiments do not agree with theirs. 2. He appeals to their judgment, and therefore submits to their trial, v. 3. *The ear* of the judicious *tries words,* whether what is said be true or false, right or wrong, and he that speaks must stand the test of the intelligent. As we must prove all things we hear, so we must be willing that what we speak should be proved. 3. He takes them into partnership with him in the examination and discussion of this matter, v. 4. He does not pretend to be sole dictator, nor undertake to say what is just and good and what is not, but he is willing to join with them in searching it out, and desires a consultation: "Let us agree to lay aside all animosities and feuds, all prejudices and affectation of contradiction, and all stiffness in adhering to the opinion we have once espoused, and *let us choose to ourselves judgment;* let us fix right principles on which to proceed, and then take right methods for finding out truth; and *let us know among ourselves,* by comparing notes and communicating our reasons, *what is good* and what is otherwise." Note, We are then likely to discern what is right when we agree to assist one another in searching it out.

II. He warmly accuses Job for some passionate words which he had spoken, that reflected on the divine government, appealing to the house whether he ought not to be called to the bar and checked for them.

1. He recites the words which Job had spoken, as nearly as he can remember. (1.) He had insisted upon his own innocency. Job hath said, *I am righteous* (v. 5), and, when urged to confess his guilt, had stiffly maintained his plea of, *Not guilty: Should I lie against my right? v.* 6. Job had spoken to this purport, *My righteousness I hold fast, ch.* 27:6. (2.) He had charged God with injustice in his dealings with him, that he had wronged him in afflicting him and had not righted him: *God has taken away my judgment;* so Job had said, *ch.* 27:2. (3.) He had despaired of relief and concluded that God could not, or would not, help him: *My wound is incurable,* and likely to be mortal, and yet *without transgression; not for any injustice in my hand, ch.* 16:16, 17. (4.) He had, in effect, said that there is nothing to be got in the service of God and that no man will be the better at last for his (v. 9): *He hath said* that which gives occasion to suspect that he thinks *it profiteth a man nothing that he should delight himself with God.* It is granted that there is a present pleasure in religion; for what is it but to delight ourselves with God, in communion with

him, in concurrence with him, in walking with him as Enoch did? this is a true notion of religion, and bespeaks its ways to be pleasantness. Yet the advantage of it is denied, as if it were *vain to serve God,* Mal. 3:14. This Elihu gathers as Job's opinion, by an innuendo from what he said (*ch.* 9:22), *He destroys the perfect and the wicked,* which has a truth in it (for all things come alike to all), but it was ill expressed, and gave too much occasion for this imputation, and therefore Job sat down silently under it and attempted not his own vindication, whence Mr. Caryl well observes that good men sometimes speak worse than they mean, and that a good man will rather bear more blame than he deserves than to stand to excuse himself when he has deserved any blame.

2. He charges Job very high upon it. In general, *What man is like Job? v.* 7. "Did you ever know such a man as Job, or ever hear a man talk at such an extravagant rate?" He represents him, (1.) As sitting in the seat of the scornful: "He *drinketh up scorning like water,"* that is, "he takes a great deal of liberty to reproach both God and his friends, takes a pleasure in so doing, and is very liberal in his reflections." Or, "He is very greedy in receiving and hearkening to the scorns and contempts which others cast upon their brethren, is well pleased with them and extols them." Or, as some explain it, "By these foolish expressions of his he makes himself the object of scorn, lays himself very open to reproach, and gives occasion to others to laugh at him; while his religion suffers by them, and the reputation of that is wounded through his side." We have need to pray that God will never leave us to ourselves to say or do any thing which may *make us a reproach to the foolish,* Ps. 39:8. (2.) As walking in the course of the ungodly, and standing in the way of sinners: He *goes in company with the workers of iniquity* (v. 8), not that in his conversation he did associate with them, but in his opinion he did favour and countenance them, and strengthen their hands. If (as it follows, v. 9, for the proof of this) *it profits a man nothing to delight himself in God,* why should he not lay the reins on the neck of his lusts and herd with the workers of iniquity? He that says, I have *cleansed my hands in vain,* does not only *offend against the generation of God's children* (Ps. 72:13, 14), but gratifies his enemies, and says as they say.

Verses 10–15

The scope of Elihu's discourse to reconcile Job to his afflictions and to pacify his spirit under them. In order to this he had shown, in the foregoing chapter, that God meant him no hurt in afflicting him, but intended it for his spiritual benefit. In this chapter he shows that he did him no wrong in afflicting him, nor punished him more than he deserved. If the former could not prevail to satisfy him, yet this ought to silence him. In these verses he directs his discourse to all the company: *"Hearken to me, you men of understanding* (v. 10), and show yourselves to be intelligent by assenting to this which I say." And this is that which he says, That the righteous God never did, nor ever will do, any wrong to any of his creatures, but his ways are equal, ours are unequal. The truth here maintained respects the justice of equity of all God's proceedings. Now observe in these verses,

I. How plainly this truth is laid down, both negatively and positively. 1. He does wrong to none: *God cannot do wickedness,* nor *the Almighty commit iniquity, v.* 10. It is inconsistent with the perfection of his nature, and so it is also with the purity of his will (v. 12): *God will not do wickedly, neither will the Almighty pervert judgment.* He neither can nor will do a wrong thing, nor deal hardly with any man. He will never inflict the evil of punishment but where he finds the evil of sin, nor in any undue proportion, for that would be to commit iniquity and do wickedly. If appeals be made to him, or he be to give a definitive sentence, he will have an eye to the merits of the cause and not respect the person, for that were to pervert judgment. He will never either do any man wrong or deny any man right, but *the heavens will shortly declare his righteousness.* Because he is God, and therefore is infinitely perfect and holy, he can neither do wrong himself nor countenance it in others, nay more than he can die, or lie, or deny himself. Though he be Almighty, yet he never uses his power, as mighty men often do, for the support of injustice. He is *Shaddai* — God *all-sufficient,* and therefore

he cannot be *tempted with evil* (James 1:13), to do an unrighteous thing. 2. He ministers justice to all (v. 11): *The work of a man shall he render unto him.* Good works shall be rewarded and evil works either punished or satisfied for; so that sooner or later, in this world or in that to come, he will cause every man to find according to his ways. This is the standing rule of distributive justice, to give to every man according to his work. *Say to the righteous, it shall be well with them; woe to the wicked, it shall be ill with them.* If services persevered in now go unrewarded, and sins persisted in now go unpunished, yet there is a day coming when God will fully render to every man according to his works, with interest for the delay.

II. How warmly it is asserted, 1. With an assurance of the truth of it: *Yea, surely, v.* 12. It is a truth which none can deny or call in question; it is what we may take for granted and are all agreed in, That God will not do wickedly. 2. With an abhorrence of the very thought of the contrary (v. 10): *Far be it from God that he should do wickedness,* and from us that we should entertain the least suspicion of it or say any thing that looks like charging him with it.

III. How evidently it is proved by two arguments:

1. His independent absolute sovereignty and dominion (v. 13): *Who has given him a charge over the earth* and deputed him to manage the affairs of men upon the earth? Or, Who besides has disposed the whole world of mankind? He has the sole administration of the kingdoms of men, and has it of himself, nor is he entrusted with it by or for any other. (1.) It is certain that the government is his, and he does according to his will in all the hosts both of heaven and earth; and therefore he is not to be charged with injustice; for *shall not the Judge of all the earth do right?* Gen. 18:25. How shall God either rule or judge the world if there be, or could be, any *unrighteousness with him?* Rom. 3:5, 6. He that is entitled to such unlimited power most certainly have in himself unspotted purity. This is also a good reason why we should acquiesce in all God's dealings with us. Shall not he that disposes of the whole world dispose of us and our concerns? (2.) It is as certain that he does not derive his power from any, nor is it a dispensation that is committed to him, but his power is original, and, like his being, of himself; and therefore, if he were not perfectly just, all the world and the affairs of it would soon be in the utmost confusion. The highest powers on earth have a God above them, to whom they are accountable, because it is not far from them to do iniquity. But *therefore* God has none above him, because it is not possible that he should do any thing (such is the perfection of his nature) that should need to be controlled. And, if he be an absolute sovereign, we are bound to submit to him, for there is no higher power to which we may appeal, so that the virtue is a necessity.

2. His irresistible power (v. 14): *If he set his heart upon man,* to contend with him, much more *if* (as some read it) *he set his heart against man,* to ruin him, if he should deal with man either by *summa potestas* — mere *sovereignty,* or by *summum jus* — strict *justice,* there were no standing before him; man's spirit and breath would soon be gone and *all flesh would perish together, v.* 15. Many men's honesty is owing purely to their impotency; they do not do wrong because they cannot support it when it is done, or it is not in their power to do it. But God is able to crush any man easily and suddenly, and yet does not by arbitrary power crush any man, which therefore must be attributed to the infinite perfection of his nature, and that is immutable. See here, (1.) What God can do with us. He can soon bring us to dust; there needs not any positive act of his omnipotence to do it; if he do but withdraw that concurrence of his providence by which we live, *if he gather unto himself that spirit and breath* which was from his hand at first and is still in his hand, we expire immediately, like an animal in an air-pump when the air is exhausted. (2.) What he may do with us without doing us wrong. He may recall the being he gave, of which we are but tenants at will, and which also we have forfeited; and therefore, as long as that is continued of his mere favour, we have no reason to cry out of wrong, whatever other comforts are removed.

Verses 16–30

Elihu here addresses himself more directly to Job. He

had spoken to the rest (*v.* 10) as *men of understanding;* now, speaking to Job; he puts an *if* upon his understanding: *If thou hast understanding,* hear this and observe it, *v.* 16.

I. Hear this, That God is not to be quarrelled with for any thing that he does. It is daring presumption to arraign and condemn God's proceedings, as Job had done by his discontents. It was, 1. As absurd as it would be to advance one to power that is a professed enemy to justice: *Shall even he that hates right govern? v.* 17. The righteous Lord so loves righteousness that, in comparison with him, even Job himself, though a perfect and upright man, might be said to hate right; and shall he govern? Shall he pretend to direct God or correct what he does? Shall such unrighteous creatures as we are give law to the righteous God? or must he take his measures from us? When we consider the corruption of our nature, and the contrariety there is in us to the eternal rule of equity, we cannot but see it to be an impudent impious thing for us to prescribe to God. 2. It was as absurd as it would be to call a most righteous innocent person to the bar, and to give judgment against him, though it appeared ever so plainly, upon the trial, that he was most just: *Wilt thou condemn him that is righteous in all his ways,* and cannot but be so? 3. It is more absurd and unbecoming than it would be to say to a sovereign prince, *Thou art wicked,* and to judges upon the bench, *You are ungodly, v.* 18. This would be looked upon as an insufferable affront to majesty and to magistracy; no king, no prince, would bear it. In favour of government, we presume it is a right sentence that is passed, unless the contrary be very evident; but, whatever we think, it is not fit to tell a king to his face that he is wicked. Nathan reproved David by a parable. But, whatever a high priest or a prophet might do, it is not for an ordinary subject to make so bold with the powers that are. How absurd is then to say so to God — to impute iniquity to him, who, having no respect of persons, is in no temptation to do an unjust thing! *He regardeth not the rich more than the poor,* and therefore it is fit he should rule, and it is not fit we should find fault with him, *v.* 19. Note, Rich and poor stand upon the same level before God. A great man shall fare never the better, nor find any favour, for his wealth and greatness; nor shall a poor man fare ever the worse for his poverty, nor an honest cause be starved. Job, now that he was poor, should have as much favour with God, and be as much regarded by him, as when he was rich; *for they are all the work of his hands.* Their persons are so: the poor are made by the same hand, and of the same mould, as the rich. Their conditions are so: the poor were made poor by the divine providence, as well as the rich made rich; and therefore the poor shall fare never the worse for that which is their lot, not their fault.

II. Hear this, That God is to be acknowledged and submitted to in all that he does. Divers considerations Elihu here suggests to Job, to beget in him great and high thoughts of God, and so to persuade him to submit and proceed no further in his quarrel with him.

1. God is almighty, and able to deal with the strongest of men when he enters into judgment with them (*v.* 20); even *the people,* the body of a nation, though ever so numerous, *shall be troubled,* unhinged, and put into disorder, when God pleases; even *the mighty* man, the prince, though ever so honourable, ever so formidable among men, *shall,* if God speak the word, *be taken away* out of his throne, nay, out of the land of the living; they shall die; they shall pass away. What cannot he do that has all the powers of death at his command? Observe the suddenness of this destruction: *In a moment shall they die.* It is not a work of time, with God, to bring down his proud enemies, but, when he pleases, it is soon done; nor is he bound to give them warning, no, not an hour's warning. *This night thy soul shall be required.* Observe the season of it: *They shall be troubled at midnight,* when they are secure and careless, and unable to help themselves; as the Egyptians when their first-born were slain. This is the immediate work of God: they are taken away, *without hand,* insensibly, by secret judgments. God can himself humble the greatest tyrant, without the assistance or agency of any man. Whatever hand he sometimes uses in the accomplishing of his purposes, he needs none, but can do it without hand. Nor is it one single mighty man only that he can thus overpower, but even hosts of them (*v.* 24): *He shall*

break in pieces mighty men without number; for no combined power can stand it out against Omnipotence. Yet, when God destroys tyranny, he does not design anarchy; if those are brought down that ruled ill, it does not therefore follow that people must have no rulers; for, when he breaks mighty men, *he sets others in their stead,* that will rule better, or, if they do not, *he overturns them* also *in the night,* or in a night, *so that they are destroyed, v.* 25. Witness Belshazzar. Or, if he designs them space to repent, he does not presently destroy them, but *he strikes them as wicked men, v.* 26. Some humbling mortifying judgments are brought upon them; these wicked rulers are stricken as other wicked men, as surely, as sorely, stricken in their bodies, estates, or families, and this for warning to their neighbours; the stroke is given *in terrorem* — *as an alarm to others,* and therefore is given *in the open sight of others,* that they also may see and fear, and tremble before the justice of God. If kings stand not before him, how shall we stand!

2. God is omniscient, and can discover that which is most secret. As the strongest cannot oppose his arm, so the most subtle cannot escape his eye; and therefore, if some are punished either more or less than we think they should be, instead of quarrelling with God, it becomes us to ascribe it to some secret cause known to God only. For, (1.) Every thing is open before him (*v.* 21): *His eyes are upon the ways of man;* not only they are within reach of his eye, so that he can see them, but his eye is upon them, so that he actually observes and inspects them. He sees us all, and sees all our goings; go where we will, we are under his eye; all our actions, good and evil, are regarded and recorded and reserved to be brought into judgment when the books shall be opened. (2.) Nothing is or can be concealed from him (*v.* 22): *There is no darkness nor shadow of death* so close, so thick, so solitary, so remote from light or sight as that in it *the workers of iniquity may hide themselves* from the discovering eye and avenging hand of the righteous God. Observe here, [1.] The workers of iniquity would hide themselves if they could from the eye of the world for shame (and that perhaps they may do), and from the eye of God for fear, as Adam among the trees of the garden. The day is coming when mighty men, and chief captains, will call to the rocks and mountains to hide them. [2.] They would gladly be hid even by the shadow of death, be hid in the grave, and lie for ever there, rather than appear before the judgment-seat of Christ. (3.) It is in vain to think of flying from God's justice, or absconding when his wrath is in pursuit of us. The workers of iniquity may find ways and means to hide themselves from men, but not from God: *He knows their works* (*v.* 25), both what they do and what they design.

3. God is righteous, and, in all his proceedings, goes according to the rules of equity. Even when he is overturning mighty men, and breaking them in pieces, yet *he will not lay upon man more than right, v.* 23. As he will not punish the innocent, so he will not exact of those that are guilty more than their iniquities deserve; and of the proportion between the sin and the punishment Infinite Wisdom shall be the judge. He will not give any man cause to complain that he deals hardly with him, nor shall any man *enter into judgment with God,* or bring an action against him. If he do, God will be justified when he speaks and clear when he judges. Therefore Job was very much to be blamed for his complaints of God, and is here welladvised to let fall his action, for he would certainly be cast or non-suited. *It is not for man ever to purpose to enter into judgment with the Omnipotent;* so some read the whole verse. Job had often wished to plead his cause before God. Elihu asks, "To what purpose? The judgment already given concerning thee will certainly be affirmed; no errors can be found in it, nor any exceptions taken to it, but, after all, it must rest as it is." All is well that God does, and will be found so. To prove that when God destroys the mighty men, and *strikes them as wicked men,* he does not *lay upon them more than right,* he shows what their wickedness was (*v.* 27, 28); and let any compare that with their punishment, and then judge whether they did not deserve it. In short, these unjust judges, whom God will justly judge, neither *feared God nor regarded man,* Lu. 18:2. (1.) They were rebels to God: They *turned back from him,* cast off the fear of him, and abandoned the very thoughts of him; for *they would not consider any of his*

ways, took no heed either to his precepts or to his providences, but lived without God in the world. This is at the bottom of all the wickedness of the wicked, they turn back from God; and it is because they do not consider, not because they cannot, but because they will not. From inconsideration comes impiety, and thence all immorality. (2.) They were tyrants to all mankind, *v.* 28. They will not call upon God for themselves; but they *cause the cry of the poor to come to him,* and that cry is against them. They are injurious and oppressive to the poor, wrong them, crush them, impoverish them yet more, and add affliction to the afflicted, who cry unto God, make their complaint to him, and he hears them and pleads their cause. Their case is bad who have the prayers and tears of the poor against them; for the cry of the oppressed will, sooner or later, draw down vengeance on the heads of the oppressors, and no one can say that this is *more than right,* Ex. 22:23.

4. God has an uncontrollable dominion in all the affairs of the children of men, and so guides and governs whatever concerns both communities and particular persons, that, as what he designs cannot be defeated, so what he does cannot be changed, *v.* 29. Observe, (1.) The frowns of all the world cannot trouble those whom God quiets with his smiles. *When he gives quietness* who then *can make trouble? v.* 29. This is a challenge to all the powers of hell and earth to disquiet those to whom God speaks peace, and for whom he creates it. If God give outward peace to a nation, he can secure what he gives, and disable the enemies of it to give it any disturbance. If God give inward peace to a man only, the quietness and everlasting assurance which are the effect of righteousness, neither the accusations of Satan nor the afflictions of this present time, no, nor the arrests of death itself, can give trouble. What can make those uneasy whose *souls dwell at ease in God?* See Phil. 4:7. (2.) The smiles of all the world cannot quiet those whom God troubles with his frowns; for if he, in displeasure, *hide his face,* and withhold the comfort of his favour, *who then can behold him?* that is, Who can behold a displeased God, so as to bear up under his wrath or turn it away? Who can make him show his face when he resolves to hide it, or see through the clouds and darkness which are round about him? Or, Who can behold a disquieted sinner, so as to give him effectual relief? Who can stand a friend to him to whom God is an enemy? None can relieve the distresses of the outward condition without God. *If the Lord do not help thee, whence shall I?* 2 Ki. 6:27. Nor can any relieve the distresses of the mind against God and his terrors. If he impress the sense of his wrath upon a guilty conscience, all the comforts the creature can administer are ineffectual. *As vinegar upon nitre, so are songs to a heavy heart.* The irresistibleness of God's operations must be acknowledged in his dealings both with communities and with particular persons: what he does cannot be controlled, *whether it be done against a nation* in its public capacity *or against a man only* in his private affairs. The same Providence that governs mighty kingdoms presides in the concerns of the meanest individual; and neither the strength of a whole nation can resist his power nor the smallness of a single person evade his cognizance; but what he does shall be done effectually and victoriously.

5. God is wise, and careful of the public welfare, and therefore provides *that the hypocrite reign not, lest the people be ensnared, v.* 30. See here, (1.) The pride of hypocrites. They aim to reign; the praise of men, and power in the world, are their reward, what they aim at. (2.) The policy of tyrants. When they aim to set up themselves they sometimes make use of religion as a cloak and cover for their ambition and by their hypocrisy come to the throne. (3.) The danger the people are in when hypocrites reign. They are likely to be ensnared in sin, or trouble, or both. Power, in the hands of dissemblers, is often destructive to the rights and liberties of a people, which they are more easily wheedled out of than forced out of. Much mischief has been done likewise to the power of godliness under the pretence of a form of godliness. (4.) The care which divine Providence takes of the people, to prevent this danger, *that the hypocrite reign not,* either that he do not reign at all or that he do not reign long. If God has mercy in store for a people, he will either prevent the rise or hasten the ruin of hypocritical rulers.

Verses 31–37

In these verses,

I. Elihu instructs Job what he should say under his affliction, *v.* 31. 32. Having reproved him for his peevish passionate words, he here puts better words into his mouth. When we reprove for what is amiss we must direct to what is good, that our reproofs may be *the reproofs of instruction,* Prov. 6:23. He does not impose it upon Job to use these words, but recommends it to him, as that which was *meet to be said.* In general, he would have him repent of his misconduct, and indecent expressions, under his affliction. Job's other friends would have had him own himself a wicked man, and by overdoing they undid. Elihu will oblige him only to own that he had, in the management of this controversy, *spoken unadvisedly with his lips.* Let us remember this, in giving reproofs, and not make the matter worse than it is; for the stretching of the crime may defeat the prosecution. Elihu drives the right nail, and speeds accordingly. He directs Job, 1. To humble himself before God for his sins, and to accept the punishment of them: *"I have borne chastisement.* What I suffer comes justly upon me, and therefore I will bear it, and not only justify God in it, but acknowledge his goodness." Many are chastised that do not bear chastisement, do not bear it well, and so, in effect, do not bear it at all. Penitents, if sincere, will take all well that God does, and will bear chastisement as a medicinal operation intended for good. 2. To pray to God to discover his sins to him (*v.* 32): *"That which I see not teach thou me.* Lord, upon the review, I find much amiss in me and much done amiss by me, but I have reason to fear there is much more that I am not aware of, greater abominations, which through ignorance, mistake, and partiality to myself, I do not yet see; Lord, give me to see it, awaken by conscience to do its office faithfully." A good man is willing to know the worst of himself, and particularly, under affliction, desires to be told wherefore God contends with him and what God designs in correcting him. 3. To promise reformation (*v.* 31): *I will not offend any more. "If I have done iniquity (or seeing that I have), I will do so no more;* whatever thou shalt discover to me to have been amiss, by thy grace I will amend it for the future." This implies a confession that we have offended, true remorse and godly sorrow for the offence, and a humble compliance with God's design in afflicting us, which is to separate between us and our sins. The penitent here completes his repentance; for it is not enough to be sorry for our sins, but we must go and sin no more, and, as here, bind ourselves with the bond of a fixed resolution never more to return to folly. This is meet to be said in a stedfast purpose, and meet to be said to God in a solemn promise and vow.

II. He reasons with him concerning his discontent and uneasiness under his affliction, *v.* 23. We are ready to think every thing that concerns us should be just as we would have it; but Elihu here shows, 1. That it is absurd and unreasonable to expect this: *"Should it be according to thy mind?* No, what reason for that?" Elihu here speaks with a great deference to the divine will and wisdom, and a satisfaction therein: it is highly fit that every thing should be according to God's mind. He speaks also with a just disdain of the pretensions of those that are proud, and would be their own carvers: *Should it be according to thy mind?* Should we always have the good we have a mind to enjoy? We should then wrongfully encroach upon others and foolishly ensnare ourselves. Must we never be afflicted, because we have no mind to it? Is it fit that sinners should feel no smart, that scholars should be under no discipline? Or, if we must be afflicted, is it fit that we should choose what rod we will be beaten with? No; it is fit that every thing should be according to God's mind, and not ours; for he is the Creator, and we are creatures. He is infinitely wise and knowing; we are foolish and short-sighted. He is in one mind; we are in many. 2. That it is in vain, and to no purpose, to expect it: *"He will recompense it whether thou refuse or whether thou choose.* God will take his own way, fulfil his own counsel, and recompense according to the sentence of his own justice, whether thou art pleased or displeased; he will neither ask thy leave nor ask thy advice, but, what he pleases, that will he do. It is therefore thy wisdom to be easy, and make a virtue of necessity; *make the best of that which is,* because it is out of thy power to make it otherwise. If thou pretend to choose and refuse," that is, "to prescribe to God and except against what he does, so will not I — I will acquiesce in all he does; and *therefore speak what thou knowest;* say what thou wilt do, whether thou wilt oppose or submit. The matter lies plainly before thee; be at a point; thou art in God's hand, not in mine."

III. He appeals to all intelligent indifferent persons whether there was not a great deal of sin and folly in that which Job said. 1. He would have the matter thoroughly examined, and brought to an issue (*v.* 36): *"My desire is that Job may be tried unto the end.* If any will undertake to justify what he has said, let them do it; if not, let us all agree to bear our testimony against it." Many understand it of his trial by afflictions: "Let his troubles be continued till he be thoroughly humbled, and his proud spirit brought down, till he be made to see his error and to retract what he has so presumptuously said against God and his providence. Let the trial be continued till the end be obtained." 2. He appeals both to God and man, and desires the judgment of both upon it. (1.) Some read *v.* 36 as an appeal to God: *O, my Father! let Job be tried.* So the margin of our Bibles, for the same word signifies *my desire* and *my father;* and some suppose that he lifted up his eyes when he said this, meaning, *"O my Father who art in heaven!* let Job be tried till he be subdued." When we are praying for the benefit of afflictions either to ourselves or others we must eye God as a Father, because they are fatherly corrections and a part of our filial education, Heb. 12:7. (2.) He appeals to the by-standers (*v.* 34): *"Let men of understanding tell me* whether they can put any more favourable construction upon Job's words than I have put, and whether he has not spoken very ill and ought not to cry, *Peccavi — I have done wrong."* In what Job had said he thought it appeared, [1.] That he did not rightly understand himself, but had talked foolishly, *v.* 35. He cannot say that Job is without knowledge and wisdom; but, in this matter, *he has spoken without knowledge,* and, whatever his heart is, *his words were without prudence.* What he said to his wife may be retorted upon himself *(He speaks as one of the foolish men speak)* and for the same reason, *Shall we not receive evil as well as good* at God's hand? *ch.* 2:10. Sometimes we need and deserve those reproofs ourselves which we have given to others. Those that reproach God's wisdom really reproach their own. [2.] That he had not a due regard to God, but had talked wickedly. If what he had said *be tried to the end,* that is, if one put it to the utmost stretch and make the worst of it, it will be found, *First,* That he has taken part with God's enemies: *His answers* have been *for wicked men;* that is, what he had said tended to strengthen the hands and harden the hearts of wicked people in their wickedness, he having carried the matter of their prosperity much further than he needed. Let wicked men, like Baal, plead for themselves if they will, but far be it from us that we should answer for them, or say any thing in favour of them. *Secondly,* That he has insulted God's friends, and hectored over them: *"He clappeth his hands among us;* and, if he be not thoroughly tried and humbled, will grow yet more insolent and imperious, as if he had gotten the day and silenced us all." To speak ill is bad enough, but to clap our hands and triumph in it when we have done, as if error and passion had won the victory, is much worse. *Thirdly,* That he has spoken against God himself, and, by standing to what he had said, *added rebellion to his sin.* To speak, though but one word, against God, by whom we speak and for whom we ought to speak, is a great sin; what is it then to multiply words against him, as if we would out-talk him? What is it to repeat them, instead of unsaying them? Those that have sinned, and, when they are called to repent, thus go on frowardly, add rebellion to their sin and make it exceedingly sinful. *Errare possum, Haereticus esse nolo — I may fall into error, but I will not plunge into heresy.*

CHAPTER 35

Job being still silent, Elihu follows his blow, and here, a third time, undertakes to show him that he had spoken amiss, and ought to recant. Three improper sayings he here charges him with, and returns answer to them distinctly: — I. He had represented religion as an indifferent unprofitable thing, which God enjoins for his own sake, not for ours; Elihu evinces the contrary (*v.* 1–8). II. He had complained of God as deaf to the cries of the oppressed, against which imputation Elihu here justifies God (*v.* 9–13). III. He had despaired of the return of God's favour to him, because it was so long deferred, but Elihu shows him the true cause of the delay (*v.* 14–16).

Verses 1–8

We have here,

I. The bad words which Elihu charges upon Job, *v.* 2, 3. To evince the badness of them he appeals to Job himself, and his own sober thoughts, in the reflection: *Thinkest thou this to be right?* This intimates Elihu's confidence that the reproof he now gave was just, for he could refer the judgment of it even to Job himself. Those that have truth and equity on their side sooner or later will have every man's conscience on their side. It also intimates his good opinion of Job, that he thought better than he spoke, and that, though he had spoken amiss, yet, when he perceived his mistake, he would not stand to it. When we have said, in our haste, that which was not right, it becomes us to own that our second thoughts convince us that it was wrong. Two things Elihu here reproves Job for: — 1. For justifying himself more than God, which was the thing that first provoked him, *ch.* 32:2. "Thou hast, in effect, said, *My righteousness is more than God's,"* that is, "I have done more for God than ever he did for me; so that, when the accounts are balanced, he will be brought in debtor to me." As if Job thought his services had been paid less than they deserved and his sins punished more than they deserved, which is a most unjust and wicked thought for any man to harbour and especially to utter. When Job insisted so much upon his own integrity, and the severity of God's dealings with him, he did in effect say, *My righteousness is more than God's;* whereas, though we be ever so good and our afflictions ever so great, we are chargeable with unrighteousness and God is not. 2. For disowning the benefits and advantages of religion because he suffered these things: *What profit shall I have if I be cleansed from my sin? v.* 3. This is gathered from *ch.* 9:30, 31. *Though I make my hands ever so clean,* what the nearer am I? *Thou shalt plunge me in the ditch.* And *ch.* 10:15, *If I be wicked, woe to me;* but, if I be righteous, it is all the same. The psalmist, when he compared his own afflictions with the prosperity of the wicked, was tempted to say, *Verily I have cleansed my heart in vain,* Ps. 73:13. And, if Job said so, he did in effect say, *My righteousness is more than God's* (*v.* 9); for, if he got nothing by his religion, God was more beholden to him than he was to God. But, though there might be some colour for it, yet it was not fair to charge these words upon Job, when he himself had made them the wicked words of prospering sinners (*ch.* 21:15, *What profit shall we have if we pray to him?*) and had immediately disclaimed them. *The counsel of the wicked is far from me, ch.* 21:16. It is not a fair way of disputing to charge men with those consequences of their opinions which they expressly renounce.

II. The good answer which Elihu gives to this (*v.* 4): *"I will* undertake to *answer thee, and thy companions with thee,"* that is, "all those that approve thy sayings and are ready to justify thee in them, and all others that say as thou sayest: "I have that to offer which will silence them all." To do this he has recourse to his old maxim (*ch.* 33:12), *that God is greater than man.* This is a truth which, if duly improved, will serve many good purposes, and particularly this to prove that God is debtor to no man. The greatest of men may be a debtor to the meanest; but such is the infinite disproportion between God and man that the great God cannot possibly receive any benefit by man, and therefore cannot be supposed to lie under any obligation to man; for, if he be obliged by his purpose and promise, it is only to himself. That is a challenge which no man can take up (Rom. 11:35), *Who hath first given to God,* let him prove it, *and it shall be recompensed to him again.* Why should we demand it, as a just debt, to gain by our religion (as Job seemed to do), when the God we serve does not gain by it? 1. Elihu needs not prove that God is above man; it is agreed by all; but he endeavours to affect Job and us with it, by an ocular demonstration of the height of the heavens and the clouds, *v.* 5. They are far above us, and God is far above them; how much then is he set out of the reach either of our sins or of our services! *Look unto the heavens, and behold the clouds.* God made man erect, *coelumque tueri jussit — and bade him look up to heaven.* Idolaters looked up, and worshipped the hosts of heaven, the sun, moon, and stars; but we must look up to heaven, and worship the Lord of those hosts. They are higher than we, but God is infinitely above them. His *glory is above the heavens* (Ps. 8:1) and the knowledge of him higher than heaven, *ch.* 11:8. 2. But hence he infers that God is not affected, either one way or other, by any thing that we do. (1.) He owns that men may be either bettered or damaged by what we do (*v.* 8): *Thy wickedness,* perhaps, may *hurt a man as thou art,* may occasion him trouble in his outward concerns. A wicked man may wound, or rob, or slander his neighbour, or may draw him into sin and so prejudice his soul. Thy righteousness, thy justice, thy charity, thy wisdom, thy piety, may perhaps *profit the son of man.* Our goodness *extends to the saints that are in the earth,* Ps. 16:3. To men like ourselves we are in a capacity either of doing injury or of showing kindness; and in both these the sovereign Lord and Judge of all will interest himself, will reward those that do good and punish those that do hurt to their fellow-creatures and fellow-subjects. But, (2.) He utterly denies that God can really be either prejudiced or advantaged by what any, even the greatest men of the earth, do, or can do. [1.] The sins of the worst sinners are no damage to him (*v.* 6): *"If thou sinnest* wilfully, and of malice prepense, against him, with a high hand, nay, *if thy transgressions be multiplied,* and the acts of sin be ever so often repeated, yet *what dost thou against him?"* This is a challenge to the carnal mind, and defies the most daring sinner to do his worst. It speaks much for the greatness and glory of God that it is not in the power of his worst enemies to do him any real prejudice. Sin is said to *be against God* because so the sinner intends it and so God takes it, and it is an injury to his honour; yet it cannot *do any thing against him.* The malice of sinners is impotent malice: it cannot destroy his being or perfections, cannot dethrone him from his power and dominion, cannot disturb his peace and repose, cannot defeat his counsels and designs, nor can it derogate from his essential glory. Job therefore spoke amiss in saying *What profit is it that I am cleansed from my sin?* God was no gainer by his reformation; and who then would gain if he himself did not? [2.] The services of the best saints are no profit to him (*v.* 7): *If thou be righteous, what givest thou to him?* He needs not our service; or, if he did want to have the work done, he has better hands than ours at command. Our religion brings no accession at all to his felicity. He is so far from being beholden to us that we are beholden to him for making us righteous and accepting our righteousness; and therefore we can demand nothing from him, nor have any reason to complain if we have not what we expect, but to be thankful that we have better than we deserve.

Verses 9–13

Elihu here returns an answer to another word that Job had said, which, he thought, reflected much upon the justice and goodness of God, and therefore ought not to pass without a remark. Observe,

I. What it was that Job complained of; it was this, That God did not regard the cries of the oppressed against their oppressors (*v.* 9): *"By reason of the multitude of oppressions,* the many hardships which proud tyrants put upon poor people and the barbarous usage they give them, *they make the oppressed to cry;* but it is to no purpose: God does not appear to right them. They cry out, they cry on still, *by reason of the arm of the mighty,* which lies heavily upon them." This seems to refer to those words of Job (*ch.* 24:12), *Men groan from out of the city, and the soul of the wounded cries out* against the oppressors, *yet God lays not folly to them,* does not reckon with them for it. This is a thing that Job knows not what to make of, nor how to reconcile to the justice of God and his government. *Is there a righteous God, and can it be that he should so slowly hear, so slowly see?*

II. How Elihu solves the difficulty. If the cries of the oppressed be not heard, the fault is not in God; he is ready to hear and help them. But the fault is in themselves; they *ask and have not,* but it is *because they ask amiss,* James 4:3. *They cry out by reason of the arm of the mighty,* but it is a complaining cry, a wailing cry, not a penitent praying cry, the cry of nature and passion, not of grace. See Hos. 7:14, *They have not cried unto me with their heart when they howled upon their beds.* How then can we expect that they should be answered and relieved?

1. They do not enquire after God, nor seek to acquaint themselves with him, under their affliction (*v.* 10): *But none saith, Where is God my Maker?* Afflictions are sent to direct and quicken us to *enquire early after God,* Ps. 78:34. But many that groan under great oppressions never mind God, nor take notice of his hand in their troubles; if they did, they would bear their troubles more patiently and be more benefited by them. Of the many that are afflicted and oppressed, few get the good they might get by their affliction. It should drive them to God, but how seldom is this the case! It is lamentable to see so little religion among the poor and miserable part of mankind. Every one complains of his troubles; *but none saith, Where is God my Maker?* that is, none repent of their sins, none return to him that smites them, none seek the face and favour of God, and that comfort in him which would balance their outward afflictions. They are wholly taken up with the wretchedness of their condition, as if that would excuse them in living without God in the world which should engage them to cleave the more closely to him. Observe, (1.) God is our Maker, the author of our being, and, under that notion, it concerns us to regard and remember him, Eccl. 12:1. *God my makers,* in the plural number, which some think is, if not an indication, yet an intimation, of the Trinity of persons in the unity of the Godhead. *Let us make man.* (2.) It is our duty therefore to enquire after him. Where is he, that we may pay our homage to him, may own our dependence upon him and obligations to him? Where is he, that we may apply to him for maintenance and protection, may receive law from him, and may seek our happiness in his favour, from whose power we received our being? (3.) It is to be lamented that he is so little enquired after by the children of men. All are asking, Where is mirth? Where is wealth? Where is a good bargain? But none ask, *Where is God my Maker?*

2. They do not take notice of the mercies they enjoy in and under their afflictions, nor are thankful for them, and therefore cannot expect that God should deliver them out of their afflictions. (1.) He provides for our inward comfort and joy under our outward troubles, and we ought to make use of that, and wait his time for the removal of our troubles: He *gives songs in the night,* that is, when our condition is ever so dark, and sad, and melancholy, there is that in God, in his providence and promise, which is sufficient, not only to support us, but to fill us with joy and consolation, and enable us in every thing to give thanks, and even to rejoice in tribulation. When we only pore upon the afflictions we are under, and neglect the consolations of God which are treasured up for us, it is just with God to reject our prayers. (2.) He preserves to us the use of our reason and understanding (*v.* 11): *Who teaches us more than the beasts of the earth,* that is, who has endued us with more noble powers and faculties than they are endued with and has made us capable of more excellent pleasures and employments here and for ever. Now this comes in here, [1.] As that which furnishes us with matter for thanksgiving, even under the heaviest burden of affliction. Whatever we are deprived of, we have our immortal souls, those jewels of more worth than all the world, continued to us; even those that kill the body cannot hurt *them.* And if our affliction prevail not to disturb the exercise of their faculties, but we enjoy the use of our reason and the peace of our consciences, we have much reason to be thankful, how pressing soever our calamities otherwise are. [2.] As a reason why we should, under our afflictions, enquire after God our Maker, and seek unto him. This is the greatest excellency of reason, that it makes us capable of religion, and it is in that especially that we are *taught more than the beasts and the fowls.* They have wonderful instincts and sagacities in seeking out their food, their physic, their shelter; but none of them are capable of enquiring, *Where is God my Maker?* Something like logic, and philosophy, and politics, has been observed among the brute-creatures, but never any thing of divinity or religion; these are peculiar to man. If therefore the oppressed only *cry by reason of the arm of the mighty,* and do not look up to God, they do no more than the brutes (who complain when they are hurt), and they forget that instruction and wisdom by which they are advanced so far above them. God relieves the brute-creatures because they cry to him according to the best of their capacity, *ch.* 38:41; Ps. 104:21. But what reason have men to expect relief, who are capable of enquiring after God as their Maker and yet cry to him no otherwise than as brutes do?

3. They are proud and unhumbled under their afflictions, which were sent to mortify them and to hide pride from them (*v.* 12): *There they cry* — there they lie exclaiming against their oppressors, and filling the ears of all about them with their complaints, not sparing to reflect upon God himself and his providence — *but none gives answer.* God does not work deliverance for them, and perhaps men do not much regard them; and why so? It is *because of the pride of evil men;* they are evil men; they *regard iniquity in their hearts,* and therefore God will not hear their prayers, Ps. 66:18; Isa. 1:15. *God hears not* such *sinners.* They have, it may be, brought themselves into trouble by their own wickedness; they are the devil's poor; and then who can pity them? Yet this is not all: they are proud still, and *therefore* they do not seek unto God (Ps. 10:4), or, if they do cry unto him, *therefore* he does not give answer, for he hears only the *desire of the humble* (Ps. 10:17) and delivers those by his providence whom he has first by his grace prepared and made fit for deliverance, which we are not if, under humbling afflictions, our hearts remain unhumbled and our pride unmortified. The case is plain then, If we cry to God for the removal of the oppression and affliction we are under, and it is not removed, the reason is not because the Lord's hand is shortened or his ear heavy, but because the affliction has not done its work; we are not sufficiently humbled, and therefore must thank ourselves that it is continued.

4. They are not sincere, and upright, and inward with God, in their supplications to him, and therefore he does not hear and answer them (*v.* 13): *God will not hear vanity,* that is, the hypocritical prayer, which is a vain prayer, coming out of feigned lips. It is a vanity to think that God should hear it, who searches the heart and requires *truth in the inward part.*

Verses 14–16

Here is, I. Another improper word for which Elihu reproves Job (*v.* 14): *Thou sayest thou shalt not see him;* that is, 1. "Thou complainest that thou dost not understand the meaning of his severe dealings with thee, nor discern the drift and design of them," *ch.* 23:8, 9. And, 2. "Thou despairest of seeing his gracious returns to thee, of seeing better days again, and art ready to give up all for gone;" as Hezekiah (Isa. 38:11), *I shall not see the Lord.* As, when we are in prosperity, we are ready to think our mountain will never be brought low, so when we are in adversity we are ready to think our valley will never be filled, but, in both, to conclude that *to morrow must be as this day,* which is as absurd as to think, when the weather is either fair or foul, that is will be always so, that the flowing tide will always flow, or the ebbing tide will always ebb.

II. The answer which Elihu gives to this despairing word that Job had said, which is this, 1. That, when he looked up to God, he had no just reason to speak thus despairingly: *Judgment is before him,* that is, "He knows what he has to do, and will do all in infinite wisdom and justice; he has the entire plan and model of providence before him, and knows what he will do, which we do not, and therefore we understand not what he does. There is a day of judgment before him, when all the seeming disorders of providence will be set to rights and the dark chapters of it will be expounded. Then thou shalt see the full meaning of these dark events, and the final period of these dismal events; then thou shalt see his face with joy; *therefore trust in him,* depend upon him, wait for him, and believe that the issue will be good at last." When we consider that God is infinitely wise, and righteous, and faithful, and that he is a God of judgment (Isa. 30:18), we shall see no reason to despair of relief from him, but all the reason in the world to hope in him, that it will come in due time, in the best time. 2. That if he had not yet seen an end of his troubles, the reason was because he did not thus trust in God and wait for him (*v.* 15): *"Because it is not so,* because thou dost not thus trust in him, therefore the affliction which came at first from love has now displeasure mixed with it. Now God *has visited* thee *in his anger,* taking it very ill that thou canst not find in thy heart to trust him, but harbourest such hard misgiving thoughts of him." If there be any mixtures of divine wrath in our afflictions, we may thank ourselves; it is because we do not behave aright under them; we quarrel with God, and are fretful and impatient, and distrustful of the divine Providence. This was Job's case. *The foolishness of man perverts his way, and* then *his heart frets against the Lord,* Prov. 19:3. Yet Elihu thinks that Job, being in great extremity, did not know and consider this as he should, that it was his own fault that he was not yet delivered. He concludes therefore that *Job opens his mouth in vain* (*v.* 16) in complaining of his grievances and crying for redress, or in justifying himself and clearing up his own innocency; it is all in vain, because he does not trust in God and wait for him, and has not a due regard to him in his afflictions. He had said a great deal, had *multiplied words,* but all *without knowledge,* all to no purpose, because he did not encourage himself in God and humble himself before him. It is in vain for us either to appeal to God or to acquit ourselves if we do not study to answer the end for which affliction is sent, and in vain to pray for relief if we do not trust in God; for let not that man who distrusts God *think that he shall receive any thing from him,* James 1:7. Or this may refer to all that Job had said. Having shown the absurdity of some passages in his discourse, he concludes that there were many other passages which were in like manner the fruits of his ignorance and mistake. He did not, as his other friends, condemn him for a hypocrite, but charged him only with Moses's sin, *speaking unadvisedly with his lips* when his spirit was provoked. When at any time we do so (and who is there that offends not in word?) it is a mercy to be told of it, and we must take it patiently and kindly as Job did, not repeating, but recanting, what we have said amiss.

CHAPTER 36

Elihu, having largely reproved Job for some of his unadvised speeches, which Job had nothing to say in the vindication of, here comes more generally to set him to rights in his notions of God's dealings with him. His other friends had stood to it that, because he was a wicked man, therefore his afflictions were so great and so long. But Elihu only maintained that the affliction was sent for his trial, and that therefore it was lengthened out because Job was not, as yet, thoroughly humbled under it, nor had duly accommodated himself to it. He urges many reasons, taken from the wisdom and righteousness of God, his care of his people, and especially his greatness and almighty power, with which, in this and the following chapter, he persuades him to submit to the hand of God. Here we have, I. His preface, (*v.* 2–4). II. The account he gives of the methods of God's providence towards the children of men, according as they conduct themselves (*v.* 5–15). III. The fair warning and good counsel he gives to Job thereupon (*v.* 16–21). IV. His demonstration of God's sovereignty and omnipotence, which he gives instances of in the operations of common providence, and which is a reason why we should all submit to him in his dealings with us (*v.* 22–33). This he prosecutes and enlarges upon in the following chapter.

Verses 1–4

Once more Elihu begs the patience of the auditory, and Job's particularly, for he has not said all that he has to say, but he will not detain them long. *Stand about me a little* (so some read it), *v.* 2. "Let me have your attendance, your attention, awhile longer, and I will speak but this once, as plainly and as much to the purpose as I can." To gain this he pleads, 1. That he had a good cause, and a noble and very fruitful subject: *I have yet to speak on God's behalf.* He spoke as an advocate for God, and therefore might justly expect the ear of the court. Some indeed pretend to speak on God's behalf who really speak for themselves; but those who sincerely appear in the cause of God, and speak in behalf of his honour, his truths, his ways, his people, shall be sure neither to want instructions *(it shall be given them in that same hour what they shall speak)* nor to lose their cause or their fee. Nor need they fear lest they should exhaust their subject. Those that have spoken ever so much may yet find more to be spoken on God's behalf. 2. That he had something to offer that was uncommon, and out of the road of vulgar observation: *I will fetch my knowledge from afar* (*v.* 3), that is, "we will have recourse to our first principles and the highest notions we can make use of to serve any purpose." It is worth while to go far for this knowledge of God, to dig for it, to travel for it; it will recompense our pains, and, though far-fetched, is not dear-bought. 3. That his design was undeniably honest; for all he aimed at was to ascribe righteousness to his Maker, to maintain and clear this truth, that God is righteous in all his ways. In speaking of God, and speaking for him, it is good to remember that he is our Maker, to call him so, and therefore to be ready to do him and the interests of his kingdom the best service we can. If he be our Maker, we have our all from him, must use our all for him, and be very jealous for his honour. That his management should be very just and fair (*v.* 4): *"My words shall not be false,* neither disagreeable to the thing itself nor to my own thoughts and apprehensions. It is truth that I am contending for, and that for truth's sake, with all possible sincerity and plainness." He will make use of plain and solid arguments and not the subtleties and niceties of the schools. "He who is perfect or upright in knowledge is now reasoning with thee; and therefore let him not only have a fair hearing, but let what he says be taken in good part, as meant well." The perfection of our knowledge in this world is to be honest and sincere in searching out truth, in applying it to ourselves, and in making use of what we know for the good of others.

Verses 5–14

Elihu, being to speak on God's behalf, and particularly to ascribe righteousness to his Maker, here shows that the disposals of divine Providence are all, not only according to the eternal counsels of his will, but according to the eternal rules of equity. God acts as a righteous governor, for,

I. He does not think it below him to take notice of the meanest of his subjects, nor does poverty or obscurity set any at a distance from his favour. If men are mighty, they are apt to look with a haughty disdain upon those that are not of distinction and make no figure; but *God is mighty,* infinitely so, and yet he *despises not any, v.* 5. He humbles himself to take cognizance of the affairs of the meanest, to do them justice and to show them kindness. Job thought himself and his cause slighted because God did not immediately appear for him. "No," says Elihu, *God despises not any,* which is a good reason why we should honour all men. *He is mighty in strength and wisdom,* and yet does not look with contempt upon those that have but a little strength and wisdom, if they but mean honestly. Nay, for this reason he despises not any, because his wisdom and strength are incontestably infinite and therefore the condescensions of his grace can be no diminution to him. Those that are wise and good will not look upon any with scorn and disdain.

II. He gives no countenance to the greatest, if they be bad (*v.* 6): *He preserves not the life of the wicked.* Though their life may be prolonged, yet not under any special care of the divine Providence, but only its common protection. Job had said that *the wicked live, become old, and are mighty in power, ch.* 21:7. "No," says Elihu: "he seldom suffers wicked men to become old. He preserves not their life so long as they expected, nor with that comfort and satisfaction which are indeed our life; and their preservation is but a reservation for the day of wrath," Rom. 2:5.

III. He is always ready to right those that are any way injured, and to plead their cause (*v.* 6): He *gives right to the poor,* avenges their quarrel upon their persecutors and forces them to make restitution of what they have robbed them of. If men will not right the injured poor, God will.

IV. He takes a particular care for the protection of his good subjects, *v.* 7. He not only looks on them, but he never looks off them: *He withdraws not his eyes from the righteous.* Though they may seem sometimes neglected and forgotten, and that befals them which looks like an oversight of Providence, yet tender careful eye of their heavenly Father never withdraws from them. If our eye be ever towards God in duty, his eye will be ever upon us in mercy, and, when we are at the lowest, will not overlook us.

1. Sometimes he prefers good people to places of trust and honour (*v.* 7): *With kings are* they *on the throne,* and every sheaf is made to bow to theirs. When righteous persons are advanced to places of honour and power, it is in mercy to them; for God's grace in them will both arm them against the temptations that attend preferment and enable them to improve the opportunity it gives them of doing good. It is also in mercy to those over whom they are set: *When the righteous bear rule the city rejoices.* If the righteous be advanced, they are established. Those that in honour keep a good conscience stand upon sure ground, and high places are not such slippery ground to them as they are to others. But, because it is not often that we see good men made great men in this world, this may be supposed to refer to the honour to which the righteous shall rise when their Redeemer shall *stand at the latter day upon the earth;* for then only they shall be exalted for ever, and established for ever; then shall they all shine forth as the sun, and be made kings and priests to our God.

2. If at any time he bring them into affliction, it is for the good of their souls, *v.* 8–10. Some good people are preferred to honour and power, but others are in trouble. Now observe, (1.) The distress supposed (*v.* 8): *If they be bound in fetters,* laid in prison as Joseph was, or *holden in the cords of* any other *affliction,* confined by pain and sickness, hampered by poverty, bound in their counsels, and, notwithstanding all their struggles, held long in this distress. This was Job's case; he was caught, and kept fast, *in the cords of anguish* (as some read it); but observe, (2.) The design God has, in bringing his people into such distresses as these; it is for the benefit of their souls, the consideration of which should reconcile us to affliction and make us think well of it. Three things God intends when he afflicts us: — [1.] To discover past sins to us, and to bring them to our remembrance. Then he shows them that amiss in them which before they did not see. He discovers to them the fact of sin: *He shows them their work.* Sin is our own work. If there be any good in us, it is God's work; and we are concerned to see what work we have made by sin. He discovers the fault of sin, shows them *their transgressions* of the law of God, and withal the sinfulness of sin, *that they have exceeded,* and have been beyond measure sinful. True penitents lay a load upon themselves, do not extenuate, but aggravate, their sins, and own that they have exceeded in them. Affliction sometimes answers to the sin; it serves, however, to awaken the conscience and puts men upon considering. [2.] To dispose our hearts to receive present instructions: Then *he opens their ear to discipline, v.* 10. Whom God chastens *he teaches* (Ps. 94:12), and the affliction makes people willing to learn, softens the wax, that it may receive the impression of the seal; yet it does not do this of itself, but the grace of God working with and by it; it is he that opens the ear, that opens the heart, who has the key of David. [3.] To deter and draw us off from iniquity for the future. This is the errand on which the affliction is sent; it is a command to *return from iniquity,* to have no more to do with sin, to turn from it with an aversion to it and a resolution never to return to it any more, Hos. 14:8.

3. If the affliction do its work, and accomplish that for which it is sent, he will comfort them again, according to the time that he has afflicted them (*v.* 11): *If they obey and serve him,* — if they comply with his design and serve his purpose in these dispensations, — if, when the affliction is removed, they continue in the same good mind that they were in when they were under the smart of it and perform the vows they made then, — if they live in obedience to God's commands, particularly those which relate to his service and worship, and in all instances make conscience of their duty to him, — then *they shall spend their days in prosperity* again *and their years in* true *pleasures.* Piety is the only sure way to prosperity and pleasure; this is a certain truth, and yet few will believe it. If we faithfully serve God, (1.) We have the promise of outward prosperity, the promise of the life that now is, and the comforts of it, as far as is for God's glory and our good; and who would desire them any further? (2.) We have the possession of inward pleasures, the comfort of communion with God and a good conscience, and that great peace which those have that love God's law. If we rejoice not in the Lord always, and in hope of eternal life, it is our own fault; and what better pleasures can we spend our years in?

4. If the affliction do not do its work, let them expect the furnace to be heated seven times hotter till they are consumed (*v.* 12): *If they obey not,* if they are not bettered by their afflictions, are not reclaimed and reformed, they shall perish by the sword of God's wrath. Those whom his rod does not cure his sword will kill; and the consuming fire will prevail if the refining fire do not; for when God judges he will overcome. If *Ahaz, in his distress, trespass yet more against the Lord, this is that king Ahaz* that is marked for ruin, 2 Chr. 28:22; Jer. 6:29, 30. God would have instructed them by their afflictions, but they received not instruction, would not take the hints that were given them; and therefore *they shall die without knowledge,* ere they are aware, without any further previous notices given them; or *they shall die because they were without knowledge* notwithstanding the means of knowledge which they were

blessed with. Those that *die without knowledge* die without grace and are undone for ever.

V. He brings ruin upon hypocrites, the secret enemies of his kingdom (such as Elihu described, *v.* 12), who, though they were numbered among the righteous whom Elihu had spoken of before, yet did not obey God, but, being children of disobedience and darkness, become children of wrath and perdition; these are the *hypocrites in heart, who heap up wrath, v.* 13. See the nature of hypocrisy: it lies in the heart, which is for the world and the flesh when the outside seems to be for God and religion. Many that are saints in show and saints in word are hypocrites in heart. That spring is corrupt, and there is an evil treasure there. See the mischievousness of hypocrisy: hypocrites *heap up wrath.* They are doing that every day which is provoking to God, and will be reckoned with for it all together in the great day. *They treasure up wrath against the day of wrath,* Rom. 2:5. Their sins are *laid up in store with God among his treasures,* Deu. 32:34. Compare Jam. 5:3. As what goes up a vapour comes down a shower, so what goes up sin, if not repented of, will come down wrath. They think they are heaping up wealth, heaping up merits, but, when the treasures are opened, it will prove they were heaping up wrath. Observe, 1. What they do to heap up wrath. What is it that is so provoking? It is this, *They cry not when he binds them,* that is, when they are in affliction, bound with the cords of trouble, their hearts are hardened, they are stubborn and unhumbled, and will not cry to God nor make their application to him. They are stupid and senseless as stocks and stones, despising the chastening of the Lord. 2. What are the effects of that wrath? *They die in youth, and their life is among the unclean, v.* 14. This is the portion of hypocrites, whom Christ denounced many woes against. If they continue impenitent, (1.) They shall die a sudden death, *die in youth,* when death is most a surprise, and death (that is, the consequence of it) is always such to hypocrites; as those that die in youth die when they hoped to live, so hypocrites, at death, go to hell, when they hoped to go to heaven. *When a wicked man dies his expectations shall perish.* (2.) They shall die the second death. *Their life,* after death (for so it comes in here), *is among the unclean,* among the *fornicators* (so some), among the worst and vilest of sinners, notwithstanding their specious and plausible profession. It is among the *Sodomites* (so the margin), those filthy wretches, who *going after strange flesh, are set forth for an example, suffering the vengeance of eternal fire,* Jude 7. The souls of the wicked live after death, but they live among the unclean, the unclean spirits, the devil and his angels, forever separated from the new Jerusalem, into which *no unclean thing shall enter.*

Verses 15–23

Elihu here comes more closely to Job; and,

I. He tells him what God would have done for him before this if he had been duly humbled under his affliction. "We all know how ready God is to *deliver the poor in his affliction* (*v.* 15); he always was so. The poor in spirit, those that are of a broken and contrite heart, he looks upon with tenderness, and, when they are in affliction, is ready to help them. He *opens their ears,* and makes them to hear joy and gladness, even *in* their *oppressions;* while he does not yet deliver them he speaks to them good words and comfortable words, for the encouragement of their faith and patience, the silencing of their fears, and the balancing of their griefs; and *even so* (*v.* 16) would he have done to thee if thou hadst submitted to his providence and conducted thyself well; he would have delivered and comforted thee, and we should have had none of these complaints. If thou hadst accommodated thyself to the will of God, thy liberty and plenty would have been restored to thee with advantage." 1. "Thou wouldst have been enlarged, and not confined thus by thy sickness and disgrace: *He would have removed thee into a broad place where is no straitness,* and thou wouldst no longer have been cramped thus and have had all thy measures broken." 2. "Thou wouldst have been enriched, and wouldst not have been left in this poor condition; thou wouldst have had thy table richly spread, not only with food convenient, but with the finest of the wheat" (see Deu. 32:14) "and the fattest of the flesh." Note, It ought to silence us under our afflictions to consider that, if we were better, it would be every way better with us: if we had answered the ends of an affliction, the affliction would be removed; and deliverance would come if we were ready for it. God would have done well for us if we had conducted ourselves well; Ps. 81:13, 14; Isa. 48:18.

II. He charges him with standing in his own light, and makes him the cause of the continuance of his own trouble (*v.* 17): *"But thou hast fulfilled the judgment of the wicked,"* that is, "Whatever thou art really, in this thing thou hast conducted thyself like a wicked man, hast spoken and done like the wicked, hast gratified them and served their cause; and *therefore* judgment and justice take hold on thee as a wicked man, because thou goest in company with them, actest as if thou wert in their interest, aiding and abetting. *Thou hast maintained the cause of the wicked;* and such as a man's cause is such will the judgment of God be upon him;" so bishop Patrick. It is dangerous being on the wrong side: accessaries to treason will be dealt with as principals.

III. He cautions him not to persist in his frowardness. Several good cautions he gives him to this purport.

1. Let him not make light of divine vengeance, nor be secure, as if he were in no danger of it (*v.* 18): *"Because there is wrath"* (that is, "because God is a righteous governor, who resents all the affronts given to his government, because he has revealed his wrath from heaven against all ungodliness and unrighteousness of men, and because thou hast reason to fear that thou art under God's displeasure) therefore *beware lest he take thee away* suddenly *with his stroke,* and be so wise as to make thy peace with him quickly and get his anger turned away from thee." A warning to this purport Job had given his friends (*ch.* 19:29): *Be you afraid of the sword, for wrath brings the punishment of the sword.* Thus contenders are apt, with too much boldness, to bind one another over to the judgment of God and threaten one another with his wrath; but he that keeps a good conscience needs not fear the impotent menaces of proud men. But his was a friendly caution to Job, and necessary. Even good men have need to be kept to their duty by the fear of God's wrath. "Thou art a wise and good man, but beware lest he take thee away, for the wisest and best have enough in them to deserve his stroke."

2. Let him not promise himself that, if God's wrath should kindle against him, he could find out ways to escape the strokes of it. (1.) There is no escaping by money, no purchasing a pardon with silver, or gold, and such corruptible things: "Even *a great ransom cannot deliver thee* when God enters into judgment with thee. His justice cannot be bribed, nor any of the ministers of his justice. *Will he esteem thy riches,* and take from them a commutation of the punishment? *No, not gold, v.* 19. If thou hadst as much wealth as ever thou hadst, that would not ease thee, would not secure thee from the strokes of God's wrath, in the day of the revelation of which *riches profit not,"* Prov. 11:4. See Ps. 49:7, 8. (2.) There is no escaping by rescue: "If *all the forces of strength* were at thy command, if thou couldst muster ever so many servants and vassals to appear for thee to force thee out of the hands of divine vengeance, it were all in vain; God would not regard it. There is *none that can deliver out of his hand."* (3.) There is no escaping by absconding (*v.* 20): *"Desire not the night,* which often favours the retreat of a conquered army and covers it; think not that thou canst so escape the righteous judgment of God, for the *darkness hideth not from him,"* Ps. 139:11, 12. See *ch.* 34:22. "Think not, because in the night people retire to their place, go up to their beds, and it is then easy to escape being discovered by them, that God also ascends to his place, and cannot see thee. No; he *neither slumbers nor sleeps.* His eyes are open upon the children of men, not only in all places, but at all times. No rocks nor mountains can shelter us from his eye." Some understand it of the night of death; that is the night by which men are *cut off from their place,* and Job had earnestly breathed for that night, as the hireling desires the evening, *ch.* 7:2. "But do not do so," says Elihu; "for thou knowest not what the night of death is." Those that passionately wish for death, in hopes to make that their shelter from God's wrath, may perhaps be mistaken. There are those whom wrath pursues into that night.

3. Let him not continue his unjust quarrel with God and his providence, which hitherto he had persisted in when he should have submitted to the affliction (*v.* 21): *"Take heed,* look well to thy own spirit, and *regard not iniquity,* return not to it (so some), for it is at thy peril if thou do." Let us never dare to think a favourable thought of sin, never indulge it, nor allow ourselves in it. Elihu thinks Job had need of this caution, he having *chosen iniquity rather than affliction,* that is, having chosen rather to gratify his own pride and humour in contending with God than to mortify it by a submission to him and accepting the punishment. We may take it more generally, and observe that those who choose iniquity rather than affliction make a very foolish choice. Those that ease their cares by sinful pleasures, increase their wealth by sinful pursuits, escape their troubles by sinful projects, and evade sufferings for righteousness' sake by sinful compliances against their consciences, make a choice they will repent of; for there is more evil in the least sin than in the greatest affliction. It is an evil, and only evil.

4. Let him not dare to prescribe to God, nor give him his measures (*v.* 22, 23): *"Behold, God exalteth by his power,"* that is, "He does, may, and can set up and pull down whom he pleases, and therefore it is not for thee nor me to contend with him." The more we magnify God the more do we humble and abase ourselves. Now consider, (1.) That God is an absolute sovereign: *He exalts by his* own *power,* and not by strength derived from any other. He exalts whom he pleases, exalts those that were afflicted and cast down, by the strength and power which he gives his people; and therefore *who has enjoined him his way?* Who presides above him in his way? Is there any superior from whom he has his commission and to whom he is accountable? No; he himself is supreme and independent. *Who puts him in mind of his way?* so some. Does the eternal Mind need a remembrancer? No; his own way, as well as ours, is ever before him. He has not received orders or instructions from any (Isa. 60:13, 14), nor is he accountable to any. He enjoins to all the creatures their way; let not us then enjoin him his, but leave it to him to govern the world, who is fit to do it. (2.) That he is an incomparable teacher: *Who teaches like him?* It is absurd for us to teach him who is himself the fountain of light, truth, knowledge, and instruction. *He that teaches man knowledge,* and so as none else can, *shall not he know?* Ps. 94:9, 10. Shall we light a candle to the sun? Observe, When Elihu would give glory to God as a ruler he praises him as a teacher, for rulers must teach. God does so. He binds with the cords of a man. In this, as in other things, he is unequalled. None so fit to direct his own actions as he himself is. He knows what he has to do, and how to do it for the best, and needs no information nor advice. Solomon himself had a privy-council to advise him, but the King of kings has none. Nor is any so fit to direct our actions as he is. None teaches with such authority and convincing evidence, with such condescension and compassion, nor with such power and efficacy, as God does. He teaches by the Bible, and that is the best book, teaches by his Son, and he is the best Master. (3.) That he is unexceptionably just in all his proceedings: *Who can say, Thou hast wrought iniquity?* Not, Who *dares* say it? (many do iniquity, and those who tell them of it do so at their peril), but Who *can* say it? Who has any cause to say it? Who can say it and prove it? It is a maxim undoubtedly true, without limitation, that *the King of kings can do no wrong.*

Verses 24–33

Elihu is here endeavouring to possess Job with great and high thoughts of God, and so to persuade him into a cheerful submission to his providence.

I. He represents the work of God, in general, as illustrious and conspicuous, *v.* 24. His whole work is so. God does nothing mean. This is a good reason why we should acquiesce in all the operations of his providence concerning us in particular. His visible works, those of nature, and which concern the world in general, are such as we admire and commend, and in which we observe the Creator's wisdom, power, and goodness; shall we then find fault with his dispensations concerning us, and the counsels of his will concerning our affairs? We are here called to *consider the work of God,* Eccl. 7:13. 1. It is plain before our eyes, nothing more obvious: it is what *men behold.* Every man that has but half an eye may see it, may behold it afar off.

Look which way we will, we see the productions of God's wisdom and power; we see that done, and that doing, concerning which we cannot but say, This is *the work of God,* the finger of God; it is the Lord's doing. Every man may see, afar off, the heaven and all its lights, the earth and all its fruits, to be the work of Omnipotence; much more when we behold them nigh at hand. Look at the minutest works of nature through a microscope; do they not appear curious? The eternal power and godhead of the Creator are *clearly seen and understood* by the *things that are made,* Rom. 1:20. Every man, even those that have not the benefit of divine revelation, may see this; for *there is no speech or language where the voice* of these natural constant preachers *is not heard,* Ps. 19:3. 2. It ought to be marvellous in our eyes. The beauty and excellency of the work of God, and the agreement of all the parts of it, are what we must remember to magnify and highly to extol, not only justify it as right and good, and what cannot be blamed, but magnify it as wise and glorious, and such as no creature could contrive or produce. Man may see his works, and is capable of discerning his hand in them (which the beasts are not), and therefore ought to praise them and give him the glory of them.

II. He represents God, the author of them, as infinite and unsearchable, *v.* 26. The streams of being, power, and perfection should lead us to the fountain. *God is great,* infinitely so, — great in power, for he is omnipotent and independent, — great in wealth, for he is self-sufficient and all-sufficient, — great in himself, — great in all his works, — great, and therefore greatly to be praised, — great, and therefore *we know him not.* We know that he is, but not what he is. We know what he is not, but not what he is. We know in part, but not in perfection. This comes in here as a reason why we must not arraign his proceedings, nor find fault with what he does, because it is speaking evil of the things that we understand not and answering a matter before we hear if. We know not the duration of his existence, for it is infinite. *The number of his years cannot* possibly *be searched out,* for he is eternal; there is no number of them. He is a Being without beginning, succession, or period, who ever was, and ever will be, and ever the same, the great *I AM.* This is a good reason why we should not prescribe to him, nor quarrel with him, because, as he is, such are his operations, quite out of our reach.

III. He gives some instances of God's wisdom, power, and sovereign dominion, in the works of nature and the dispensations of common providence, beginning in this chapter with the clouds and the rain that descends from them. We need not be critical in examining either the phrase or the philosophy of this noble discourse. The general scope of it is to show that God is infinitely great, and the Lord of all, the first cause and supreme director of all the creatures, and *has all power in heaven and earth* (whom therefore we ought, with all humility and reverence, to adore, to speak well of, and to give honour to), and that it is presumption for us to prescribe to him the rules and methods of his special providence towards the children of men, or to expect from him an account of them, when the operations even of common providences about the meteors are so various and so mysterious and unaccountable. Elihu, to affect Job with God's sublimity and sovereignty, had directed him (*ch.* 35:5) to look unto the clouds. In these verses he shows us what we may observe in the clouds we see which will lead us to consider the glorious perfections of their Creator. Consider the clouds,

1. As springs to this lower world, the source and treasure of its moisture, and the great bank through which it circulates — a very necessary provision, for its stagnation would be as hurtful to this lower world as that of the blood to the body of man. It is worth while to observe in this common occurrence, (1.) That the clouds above distil upon the earth below. If the heavens become brass, the earth becomes iron; therefore thus the promise of plenty runs, *I will hear the heavens and they shall hear the earth.* This intimates to us that every good gift is from above, from him who is both Father of lights and Father of the rain, and it instructs us to direct our prayers to him and to look up. (2.) That they are here said to *distil upon man* (*v.* 28); for, though indeed God *causes it to rain in the wilderness where no man is* (*ch.* 38:26, Ps. 104:11), yet special respect is had to man herein, to whom the inferior creatures are all made serviceable and from whom the actual return of the tribute of praise is required. Among men, he *causes his rain to fall upon the just and upon the unjust,* Mt. 5:45. (3.) They are said to distil the water in *small drops,* not in spouts, as when the *windows of heaven were opened,* Gen. 7:11. God waters the earth with that with which he once drowned it, only dispensing it in another manner, to let us know how much we lie at his mercy, and how kind he is, in giving rain by drops, that the benefit of it may be the further and the more equally diffused, as by an artificial water-pot. (4.) Though sometimes the rain comes in very small drops, yet, at other times, it pours down in great rain, and this difference between one shower and another must be resolved into the divine Providence which orders it so. (5.) Though it comes down in drops, yet it distils upon man *abundantly* (*v.* 28), and therefore is called *the river of God which is full of water,* Ps. 65:9. (6.) The clouds *pour down according to the vapour* that they draw up, *v.* 27. So just the heavens are to the earth, but the earth is not so in the return it makes. (7.) The produce of the clouds is sometimes a great terror, and at other times a great favour, to the earth, *v.* 31. When he pleases *by them he judges the people* he is angry with. Storms, and tempests, and excessive rains, destroying the fruits of the earth and causing inundations, come from the clouds; but, on the other hand, from them, usually, he gives meat in abundance; they drop fatness upon the pastures that are clothed with flocks, and the valleys that are *covered with corn,* Ps. 65:11–13. (8.) Notice is sometimes given of the approach of rain, *v.* 33. *The noise thereof,* among other things, *shows concerning it.* Hence we read (1 Ki. 18:41) of *the sound of abundance of rain,* or (as it is in the margin) *a sound of a noise of rain,* before it came; and a welcome harbinger it was then. As the noise, so the face of the sky, shows concerning it, Lu. 12:56. The cattle also, by a strange instinct, are apprehensive of a change in the weather nigh at hand, and seek for shelter, shaming man, who will not foresee the evil and hide himself.

2. As shadows to the upper world (*v.* 29): *Can any understand the spreading of the clouds?* They are spread over the earth as a curtain or canopy; how they come to be so, how stretched out, and how poised, as they are, we cannot understand, though we daily see they are so. Shall we then pretend to understand the reasons and methods of God's judicial proceedings with the children of men, whose characters and cases are so various, when we cannot account for the spreadings of the clouds, which *cover the light? v.* 32. It is a cloud coming *betwixt, v.* 32; *ch.* 26:9. And this we are sensible of, that, by the interposition of the clouds between us and the sun, we are, (1.) Sometimes favoured; for they serve as an umbrella to shelter us from the violent heat of the sun, which otherwise would beat upon us. A *cloud of dew in the heat of harvest* is spoken of as a very great refreshment. Isa. 18:4. (2.) Sometimes we are by them frowned upon; for they darken the earth at noon-day and eclipse the light of the sun. Sin is compared to a cloud (Isa. 44:22), because it comes between us and the light of God's countenance and obstructs the shining of it. But though the clouds darken the sun for a time, and pour down rain, yet *(post nubila Phoebus — the sun shines forth after the rain),* after he has wearied the cloud, *he spreads his light upon it, v.* 30. There is a *clear shining after rain,* 2 Sa. 23:4. The sunbeams are darted forth, and reach to *cover* even *the bottom of the sea,* thence to exhale a fresh supply of vapours, and so raise recruits for the clouds, *v.* 30. In all this, we must remember to magnify the work of God.

CHAPTER 37

Elihu here goes on to extol the wonderful power of God in the meteors and all the changes of the weather: if, in those changes, we submit to the will of God, take the weather as it is and make the best of it, why should we not do so in other changes of our condition? Here he observes the hand of God, I. In the thunder and lightning (*v.* 1–5). II. In the frost and snow, the rains and wind (*v.* 6–13). III. He applies it to Job, and challenges him to solve the phenomena of these works of nature, that confessing his ignorance in them, he might own himself an incompetent judge in the proceedings of divine Providence, (*v.* 14–22). And then, IV. Concludes with his principle, which he undertook to make out, That God is great and greatly to be feared (*v.* 23, 24).

Verses 1–5

Thunder and lightning, which usually go together, are sensible indications of the glory and majesty, the power and terror, of Almighty God, one to the ear and the other to the eye; in these God leaves not himself without witness of his greatness, as, in the rain from heaven and fruitful seasons, he leaves not himself without witness of his goodness (Acts 14:17), even to the most stupid and unthinking. Though there are natural causes and useful effects of them, which the philosophers undertake to account for, yet they seem chiefly designed by the Creator to startle and awaken the slumbering world of mankind to the consideration of a God above them. The eye and the ear are the two learning senses; and therefore, though such a circumstance is possible, they say it was never known in fact that any one was born both blind and deaf. By the word of God divine instructions are conveyed to the mind through the ear, by his works through the eye; but, because those ordinary sights and sounds do not duly affect men, God is pleased sometimes to astonish men by the eye with his lightnings and by the ear with his thunder. It is very probable that at this time, when Elihu was speaking, it thundered and lightened, for he speaks of the phenomena as present; and, God being about to speak (*ch.* 38:1), these were, as afterwards on Mount Sinai, the proper prefaces to command attention and awe. Observe here, 1. How Elihu was himself affected, and desired to affect Job, with the appearance of God's glory in the thunder and lightning (*v.* 1, 2): "For my part," says Elihu, *"my heart trembles* at it; though I have often heard it, often seen it, yet it is still terrible to me, and makes every joint of me tremble, and my heart beat as if it would move *out of its place."* Thunder and lightning have been dreadful to the wicked: the emperor Caligula would run into a corner, or under a bed, for fear of them. Those who are very much astonished, we say, are *thunder-struck.* Even good people think thunder and lightning very awful; and that which makes them the more terrible is the hurt often done by lightning, many having been killed by it. Sodom and Gomorrah were laid in ruins by it. It is a sensible indication of what God could do to this sinful world, and what he *will do,* at last, by the fire to which it is reserved. Our hearts, like Elihu's should tremble at it for fear of God's judgments, Ps. 119:120. He also calls upon Job to attend to it (*v.* 2): *Hear attentively the noise of his voice.* Perhaps as yet it thundered at a distance, and could not be heard without listening: or rather, Though the thunder will be heard, and whatever we are doing we cannot help attending to it, yet, to apprehend and understand the instructions God thereby gives us, we have need to hear with great attention and application of mind. Thunder is called *the voice of the Lord* (Ps. 29:3, etc.), because by it God speaks to the children of men to fear before him, and it should put us in mind of that mighty word by which the world was at first made, which is called thunder. Ps. 104:7, *At the voice of thy thunder they hasted away,* namely, the waters, when God said, *Let them be gathered into one place.* Those that are themselves affected with God's greatness should labour to affect others. 2. How he describes them. (1.) Their original, not their second causes, but the first. God directs the thunder, and the lightning is his, *v.* 3. Their production and motion are not from chance, but from the counsel of God and under the direction and dominion of his providence, though to us they seem accidental and ungovernable. (2.) Their extent. The claps of thunder roll *under the whole heaven,* and are heard far and near; so are the lightnings darted to *the ends of the earth;* they come out of the one part under heaven and shine to the other, Lu. 17:24. Though the same lightning and thunder do not reach to all places, yet they reach to very distant places in a moment, and there is no place but, some time or other, has these alarms from heaven. (3.) Their order. The lightning is first directed, and *after it a voice roars, v.* 4. The flash of fire, and the noise it makes in a watery cloud, are really at the same time; but, because the motion of light is much quicker than that of sound, we see the lightning some time before we hear the thunder, as we see the firing of a great gun at a distance before we hear the report of it. The thunder is here called *the voice of God's excellency,* because by it he proclaims his transcendent power and greatness. *He sends forth his voice and that a mighty voice,* Ps. 68:33. (4.) Their violence. *He will not stay them,* that is, he does not need to check them, or hold them back, lest they should grow unruly and out of his power to restrain them, but lets them take their course, says to them, *Go, and they go — Come, and they come — Do this, and they do it.* He will not stay the rains and showers that usually follow upon the thunder (which he had spoken of, *ch.* 36:27, 29), so some, but will pour them out upon the earth *when his voice is heard.* Thunder-showers are sweeping rains, and for them he *makes the lightnings,* Ps. 135:7. (5.) The inference he draws from all this, *v.* 5. Does God thunder thus marvellously with his voice? We must then conclude that his other works are great, and such as we cannot comprehend. From this one instance we may argue to all, that, in the dispensations of his providence, there is that which is too great, too strong, for us to oppose or strive against, and too high, too deep, for us to arraign or quarrel with.

Verses 6–13

The changes and extremities of the weather, wet or dry, hot or cold, are the subject of a great deal of our common talk and observation; but how seldom do we think and speak of these things, as Elihu does here, with an awful regard to God the director of them, who shows his power and serves the purposes of his providence by them! We must take notice of the glory of God, not only in the thunder and lightning, but in the more common revolutions of the weather, which are not so terrible and which make less noise. As,

I. In the snow and rain, *v.* 6. Thunder and lightning happen usually in the summer, but here he takes notice of the winter-weather. Then *he saith to the snow, Be thou on the earth;* he commissions it, he commands it, he appoints it, where it shall light and how long it shall lie. He speaks, and it is done: as in the creation of the world, *Let there be light,* so in the works of common providence, *Snow, be thou on the earth.* Saying and doing are not two things with God, though they are with us. When he speaks the word *the small rain* distils and *the great rain* pours down as he pleases — *the winter-rain* (so the Septuagint), for in those countries, when the winter was past, the rain was over and gone, Cant. 2:11. The distinction in the Hebrew between the small rain and the great rain is this, that the former is called a shower of *rain,* the latter of *rains,* many showers in one; but all are the showers *of his strength:* the power of God is to be observed as much in the small rain that soaks into the earth as in the great rain that batters on the house-top and washes away all before it. Note, The providence of God is to be acknowledged, both by husbandmen in the fields and travellers upon the road, in every shower of rain, whether it does them a kindness of a diskindness. It is sin and folly to contend with God's providence in the weather; if he send the snow or rain, can we hinder them? Or shall we be angry at them? It is as absurd to quarrel with any other disposal of Providence concerning ourselves or ours. The effect of the extremity of the winter-weather is that it obliges both men and beasts to retire, making it uncomfortable and unsafe for them to go abroad. 1. Men retire to their houses from their labours in the field, and keep within doors (*v.* 7): *He seals up the hand of every man.* In frost and snow, husbandmen cannot follow their business, nor some tradesmen, nor travellers, when the weather is extreme. The plough is laid by, the shipping laid up, nothing is to be done, nothing to be got, that men, being taken off from their own work, *may know his work,* and contemplate that, and give him the glory of that, and, by the consideration of that work of his in the weather which seals up their hands, be led to celebrate his other great and marvellous works. Note, When we are, upon any account, disabled from following our worldly business, and taken off from it, we should spend our time rather in the exercises of piety and devotion (in acquainting ourselves with the works of God and praising him in them) than in foolish idle sports and recreations. When our hands are sealed up our hearts should be thus opened, and the less we have at any time to do in the world the more we should thereby be driven to our Bibles and our knees. 2. *The beasts* also *retire to* their *dens and remain in their* close *places, v.* 8. It is meant of the wild beasts, which, being wild, must seek a shelter for themselves, to which by instinct they are directed, while the tame beasts, which are serviceable to man, are housed and protected by his care, as Ex. 9:20. The ass has no den but his master's crib, and thither he goes, not only to be safe and warm, but to be fed. Nature directs all creatures to shelter themselves from a storm; and shall man alone be unprovided with an ark?

II. In the winds, which blow from different quarters and produce different effects (*v.* 9): *Out of the hidden place* (so it may be read) *comes the whirlwind;* it turns round, and so it is hard to say from which point it comes but it comes from *the secret chamber,* as the word signifies, which I am not so willing to understand of the *south,* because he says here (*v.* 17) that the wind out of the south is so far from being a whirlwind that it is a warming, quieting, wind. But at this time, perhaps, Elihu saw a whirlwind-cloud coming out of the south and making towards them, out of which the Lord spoke soon after, *ch.* 38:1. Or, if turbulent winds which bring showers come out of the south, cold and drying blasts come out of the north to scatter the vapours and clear the air of them.

III. In the frost, *v.* 10. See the cause of it: It *is given by the breath of God,* that is, by the word of his power and the command of his will; or, as some understand it, by the wind, which is the breath of God, as the thunder is his voice; it is caused by the cold freezing wind out of the north. See the effect of it: *The breadth of the waters is straitened,* that is, the waters that had spread themselves, and flowed with liberty, are congealed, benumbed, arrested, bound up in crystal fetters. This is such an instance of the power of God as, if it were not common, would be next to a miracle.

IV. In the clouds, the womb where all these watery meteors are conceived, of which he had spoken, *ch.* 36:28. Three sorts of clouds he here speaks of: — 1. Close, black, thick clouds, pregnant with showers; and these with watering *he wearies* (*v.* 11), that is, they spend themselves, and are exhausted by the rain into which they melt and are dissolved, pouring out water till they are weary and can pour out no more. See what pains, as I may say, the creatures, even those above us, take to serve man: the clouds water the earth till they are weary; they spend and are spent for our benefit, which shames and condemns us for the little good we do in our places, though it would be to our own advantage, for *he that watereth shall be watered also himself.* 2. Bright thin clouds, clouds without water; and these *he scattereth;* they are dispersed of themselves, and not dissolved into rain, but what becomes of them we know not. The bright cloud, in the evening, when the sky is red, is scattered, and proves an earnest of a fair day, Mt. 16:2. 3. Flying clouds, which do not dissolve, as the thick cloud, into a close rain, but are carried upon the wings of the wind from place to place, dropping showers as they go; and these are said to be *turned round about* by his counsels, *v.* 12. The common people say that the rain is determined by the planets, which is as bad divinity as it is philosophy, for it is guided and governed by the counsel of God, which extends even to those things that seem most casual and minute, *that they may do whatsoever he commands them;* for the stormy winds, and the clouds that are driven by them, fulfil his word; and by this means he *causes it to rain upon one city and not upon another,* Amos 4:7, 8. Thus his will is done *upon the face of the world in the earth,* that is, among the children of men, to whom God has an eye in all these things, of whom it is said that he *made them to dwell on the face of the earth,* Acts 17:26. The inferior creatures, being incapable of doing moral actions, are incapable of receiving rewards and punishments: but, among the children of men, God causes the rain to come, either for the correction of his land or for a mercy to it, *v.* 13. (1.) Rain sometimes turns into a judgment. It is a scourge to a sinful land; as once it was for the destruction of the whole world, so it is now often for the correction or discipline of some parts of it, by hindering seedness and harvest, raising the waters, and damaging the fruits. Some have said that our nation has received much more prejudice by the excess of rain than by the want of it. (2.) At other times it is a blessing. It is *for his land,* that this may be made fruitful; and, besides that which is just necessary, he gives *for mercy,* to fatten it and make it more fruitful. See what a necessary dependence we have upon God, when the very same thing, according to the proportion in which it is given, may be either a great judgment or a great mercy, and without God we cannot have either a shower or a fair gleam.

Verses 14–20

Elihu here addresses himself closely to Job, desiring him to apply what he had hitherto said to himself. He begs that he would hearken to this discourse (*v.* 14), that he would pause awhile: *Stand still, and consider the wondrous works of God.* What we hear is not likely to profit us unless we consider it, and we are not likely to consider things fully unless we stand still and compose ourselves to the consideration of them. The works of God, being wondrous, both deserve and need our consideration, and the due consideration of them will help to reconcile us to all his providences. Elihu, for the humbling of Job, shows him,

I. That he had no insight into natural causes, could neither see the springs of them nor foresee the effects of them (*v.* 15–17): *Dost thou know* this and know that which are *the wondrous works of him who is perfect in knowledge?* We are here taught, 1. The perfection of God's knowledge. It is one of the most glorious perfections of God that he is perfect in knowledge; he is omniscient. His knowledge is intuitive: he *sees,* and does not know by report. It is intimate and entire: he knows things truly, and not by their colours — thoroughly, and not by piecemeal. To his knowledge there is nothing distant, but all near — nothing future, but all present — nothing hid, but all open. We ought to acknowledge this in all his wondrous works, and it is sufficient to satisfy us in those wondrous works which we know not the meaning of that they are the works of one that knows what he does. 2. The imperfection of our knowledge. The greatest philosophers are much in the dark concerning the powers and works of nature. We are a paradox to ourselves, and every thing about us is a mystery. The gravitation of bodies, and the cohesion of the parts of matter, are most certain, and yet unaccountable. It is good for us to be made sensible of our own ignorance. Some have confessed their ignorance, and those that would not do this have betrayed it. But we must all infer from it what incompetent judges we are of the divine politics, when we understand so little even of the divine mechanics. (1.) We know not what orders God has given concerning the clouds, nor what orders he will give, *v.* 15. That all is done by determination and with design we are sure; but what is determined, and what designed, and when the plan was laid, we know not. God often *causes the light of his cloud to shine,* in the rainbow (so some), in the lightning (so others); but did we foresee, or could we foretel, when he would to it? If we foresee the change of weather a few hours before, by vulgar observation, or when second causes have begun to work by the weather-glass, yet how little do these show us of the purposes of God by these changes! (2.) We know not how the clouds are poised in the air, the *balancing* of them, which is one of the wondrous works of God. They are so balanced, so spread, that they never rob us of the benefit of the sun (even the cloudy day is day), so balanced that they do not fall at once, nor burst into cataracts or water-spouts. The rainbow is an intimation of God's favour in balancing the clouds so as to keep them from drowning the world. Nay, so are they balanced that they impartially distribute their showers on the earth, so that, one time or other, every place has its share. (3.) We know not how the comfortable change comes when the winter is past, *v.* 17. [1.] How the weather becomes warm after it has been cold. We know how our garment came to be warm upon us, that is, how we come to be warm in our clothes, by reason of the warmth of the air we breathe in. Without God's blessing we should clothe ourselves, yet not be warm, Hag. 1:6. But, when he so orders it, the clothes are warm upon us, which, in the extremity of cold weather, would not serve to keep us warm. [2.] How it becomes calm after it has been stormy: *He quiets the earth by the south wind,* when the spring comes. As he has a blustering freezing north wind, so he has a thawing, composing, south wind; the Spirit is compared to both, because he both convinces and comforts, Cant. 4:16.

II. That he had no share at all in the first making of the world (*v.* 18): *"Hast thou with him spread out the sky?* Thou canst not pretend to have stretched it out without him, no, nor to have stretched it out in conjunction with him; for he was far from needing any help either in contriving or in working." The creation of the vast expanse of the visible heavens (Gen. 1:6–8), which we see in being to this day, is a glorious instance of the divine power, considering, 1. That, though it is fluid, yet it is firm. It *is strong,* and has its name from its stability. It still is what it was, and suffers no decay, nor shall the ordinances of heaven be altered till the lease expires with time. 2. That, though it is large, it is bright and most curiously fine: It is a *molten looking-glass,* smooth and polished, and without the least flaw or crack. In this, as in a looking-glass, we may *behold the glory of God* and the wisdom of *his handy work,* Ps. 19:1. When we look up to heaven above we should remember it is a mirror or looking-glass, not to show us our own faces, but to be a faint representation of the purity, dignity, and brightness of the upper world and its glorious inhabitants.

III. That neither he nor they were able to speak of the glory of God in any proportion to the merit of the subject, *v.* 19, 20. 1. He challenges Job to be their director, if he durst undertake the task. He speaks it ironically: *"Teach us,* if thou canst, *what we shall say unto him, v.* 19. Thou hast a mind to reason with God, and wouldst have us to contend with him on thy behalf; teach us then what we shall say. Canst thou see further into this abyss than we can? If thou canst, favour us with thy discoveries, furnish us with instructions." 2. He owns his own insufficiency both in speaking to God and in speaking of him: *We cannot order our speech by reason of darkness.* Note, The best of men are much in the dark concerning the glorious perfections of the divine nature and the administrations of the divine government. Those that through grace know much of God, yet know little, yea, nothing, in comparison with what is to be known, and what will be known, when that which is perfect shall come and the veil shall be rent. When we would speak of God we speak confusedly and with great uncertainly, and are soon at a loss and run aground, not for want of matter, but for want of words. As we must always begin with fear and trembling, lest we speak amiss *(De Deo etiam vera dicere periculosum est — Even while affirming what is true concerning God we incur risk),* so we must conclude with shame and blushing, for having spoken no better. Elihu himself had, for his part, spoken well on God's behalf, and yet is so far from expecting a fee, or thinking that God was beholden to him for it, or that he was fit to be standing counsel for him, that (1.) He is even ashamed of what he has said, not of the cause, but of his own management of it: *"Shall it be told him that I speak? v.* 20. Shall it be reported to him as a meritorious piece of service, worthy his notice? By no means; let it never be spoken of," for he fears that the subject has suffered by his undertaking it, as a fine face is wronged by a bad painter, and his performance is so far from meriting thanks that it needs pardon. When we have done all we can for God we must acknowledge that we are unprofitable servants and have nothing at all to boast of. He is afraid of saying any more: *If a man speak,* if he undertake to plead for God, much more if he offer to plead against him, *surely he shall be swallowed up.* If he speak presumptuously, God's wrath shall soon consume him; but, if ever so well, he will soon lose himself in the mystery and be over powered by the divine lustre. Astonishment will strike him blind and dumb.

Verses 21–24

Elihu here concludes his discourse with some short but great sayings concerning the glory of God, as that which he was himself impressed, and desired to impress others, with a holy awe of. He speaks concisely, and in haste, because, it should seem, he perceived that God was about to take the work into his own hands. 1. He observes that God who has said that he will *dwell in the thick darkness* and *make that his pavilion* (2 Chr. 6:1, Ps. 18:11) is in that awful chariot advancing towards them, as if he were preparing his throne for judgment, surrounded with *clouds and darkness,* Ps. 97:2, 9. He saw the cloud, with a whirlwind in the bosom of it, coming out of the south; but now it hung so thick, so black, over their heads, that they could none of them *see the bright light which* just before *was in the clouds.* The light of the sun was now eclipsed. This reminded him of the darkness by reason of which he could not speak (*v.* 19), and made him afraid to go on, *v.* 20. Thus the disciples *feared when they entered into a cloud,* Lu. 9:34. Yet he looks to the north, and sees it clear that way, which gives him hope that the clouds are not gathering for a deluge; they are covered, but not surrounded, with them. He expects that *the wind will pass* (so it may be read) *and cleanse them,* such a wind as passed over the earth to clear it from the waters of Noah's flood (Gen. 8:1), in token of the return of God's favour; and then *fair weather will come out of the north* (*v.* 22) and all will be well. God will not always frown, nor contend for ever. 2. He hastens to conclude, now that God is about to speak; and therefore delivers much in a few words, as the sum of all that he had been discoursing of, which, if duly considered, would not only clench the nail he had been driving, but make way for what God would say. He observes, (1.) That *with God is terrible majesty.* He is a God of glory and such transcendent perfection as cannot but strike an awe upon all his attendants and a terror upon all his adversaries. *With God is terrible praise* (so some), for he is *fearful in praises,* Ex. 15. 11. (2.) That when we speak *touching the Almighty* we must own that *we cannot find him out;* our finite understandings cannot comprehend his infinite perfections, *v.* 23. Can we put the sea into an egg-shell? We cannot trace the steps he takes in his providence. *His way is in the sea.* (3.) That *he is excellent in power.* It is the excellency of his power that he can do whatever he pleases in heaven and earth. The universal extent and irresistible force of his power are the excellency of it; no creature has an arm like him, so long, so strong. (4.) That he is not less excellent in wisdom and righteousness, *in judgment and plenty of justice,* else there would be little excellency in his power. We may be sure that he who can do every thing will do every thing for the best, for he is infinitely wise, and will not in any thing do wrong, for he is infinitely just. When he executes judgment upon sinners, yet there is plenty of justice in the execution, and he inflicts not more than they deserve. (5.) That *he will not afflict,* that is, that he will not afflict willingly; it is no pleasure to him to grieve the children of men, much less his own children. He never afflicts but when there is cause and when there is need, and he does not overburden us with affliction, but considers our frame. Some read it thus: *"The Almighty, whom we cannot find out, is great in power, but he will not afflict in judgment, and with him is plenty of justice,* nor is he extreme to mark what we do amiss." (6.) He values not the censures of those who are wise in their own conceit: *He respecteth them not, v.* 24. He will not alter his counsels to oblige them, nor can those that prescribe to him prevail with him to do as they would have him do. He regards the prayer of the humble, but not the policies of the crafty. No, the foolishness of God is wiser than men, 1 Co. 1:15. (7.) From all this it is easy to infer that, since God is great, he is greatly to be feared; nay, because he is gracious and will not afflict, *men do therefore fear him,* for *there is forgiveness with him, that he may be feared,* Ps. 130. 4. It is the duty and interest of all men to fear God. *Men shall fear him* (so some); sooner or later they shall fear him. Those that will not fear the Lord and his goodness shall for ever tremble under the pourings out of the vials of his wrath.

CHAPTER 38

In most disputes the strife is who shall have the last word. Job's friends had, in this controversy, tamely yielded it to Job, and then he to Elihu. But, after all the wranglings of the counsel at bar, the judge upon the bench must have the last word; so God had here, and so he will have in every controversy, for every man's judgment proceeds from him and by his definitive sentence every man must stand or fall and every cause be won or lost. Job had often appealed to God, and had talked boldly how he would order his cause before him, and as a prince would he go near unto him; but, when God took the throne, Job had nothing to say in his own defence, but was silent before him. It is not so easy a matter as some think it to contest with the Almighty. Job's friends had sometimes appealed to God too: "O that God would speak!" 11:7. And now, at length, God does speak, when Job, by Elihu's clear and close arguings was mollified a little, and mortified, and so prepared to hear what God had to say. It is the office of ministers to prepare the way of the Lord. That which the great God designs in this discourse is to humble Job, and bring him to repent of, and to recant, his passionate indecent expressions concerning God's providential dealings with him; and this he does by calling upon Job to compare God's eternity with his own time, God's omniscience with his own ignorance, and God's omnipotence with his own impotency. I. He begins with an awakening challenge and demand in general (*v.* 2, 3). II. He proceeds in divers particular instances and proofs of Job's utter inability to contend with God, because of his ignorance and weakness: for, 1. He knew nothing of the founding of the earth (*v.* 4–7). 2. Nothing of the limiting of the sea (*v.* 8–11). 3. Nothing of the morning light (*v.* 12–15). 4. Nothing of the dark recesses of the sea and earth (*v.* 16–21). 5. Nothing of the springs in the clouds (*v.* 22–27), nor the secret counsels by which they are directed. 6. He could do nothing towards the production of the rain, or frost, or lightning (*v.* 28–30, 34, 35, 37, 38), nothing towards the directing of the stars and their influences (*v.* 31–33), nothing towards the making of his own soul (*v.* 36). And lastly, he could not provide for the lions and the ravens (*v.* 39–41). If, in these ordinary works of nature, Job was puzzled, how durst he pretend to dive into the counsels of God's government and to judge of them? In this (as bishop Patrick observes) God takes up the argument begun by Elihu (who came nearest to the truth) and prosecutes it in inimitable words, excelling his, and all other men's, in the loftiness of the style, as much as thunder does a whisper.

Verses 1–3

Let us observe here, 1. Who speaks — *The Lord,* Jehovah, not a created angel, but the eternal Word himself, the second person in the blessed Trinity, for it is he by whom the worlds were made, and that was no other than the Son of God. The same speaks here that afterwards spoke from Mount Sinai. Here he begins with the creation of the world, there with the redemption of Israel out of Egypt, and from both is inferred the necessity of our subjection to him. Elihu had said, *God speaks to men and they do not perceive it* (*ch.* 33:14); but this they could not but perceive, and yet we have *a more sure word of prophecy,* 2 Pt. 1:19. 2. When he spoke — *Then.* When they had all had their saying, and yet had not gained their point, then it was time for God to interpose, whose judgment is according to truth. When we know not who is in the right, and perhaps are doubtful whether we ourselves are, this may satisfy us, That God will determine shortly *in the valley of decision,* Joel 3:14. Job had silenced his three friends, and yet could not convince them of his integrity in the main. Elihu had silenced Job, and yet could not bring him to acknowledge his mismanagement of this dispute. But now God comes, and does both, convinces Job first of his unadvised speaking and makes him cry, *Peccavi — I have done wrong;* and, having humbled him, he puts honour upon him, by convincing his three friends that they had done him wrong. These two things God will, sooner or later, do for his people: he will show them their faults, that they may be themselves ashamed of them, and he will show others their righteousness, and bring it forth as the light, that they may be ashamed of their unjust censures of them. 3. How he spoke — *Out of the whirlwind,* the rolling and involving cloud, which Elihu took notice of, *ch.* 37:1, 2, 9. A whirlwind prefaced Ezekiel's vision (Eze. 1:4), and Elijah's, 1 Ki. 19:11. God is said to have *his way in the whirlwind* (Nah. 1:3), and, to show that even the stormy wind fulfils his word, here it was made the vehicle of it. This shows what a mighty voice God's is, that is was not lost, but perfectly audible, even in the noise of a whirlwind. Thus God designed to startled Job, and to command his attention. Sometimes God answers his own people in terrible corrections, as out of the whirlwind, but always in righteousness. 4. To whom he spoke: He *answered Job,* directed his speech to him, to convince him of what was amiss, before he cleared him from the unjust aspersions cast upon him. It is God only that can effectually convince of sin, and those shall so be humbled whom he designs to exalt. Those that desire to hear from God, as Job did, shall certainly hear from him at length. 5. What he said. We may conjecture that Elihu, or some other of the auditory, wrote down *verbatim* what was delivered out of the whirlwind, for we find (Rev. 10:4) that, when the thunders uttered their voices, John was prepared to write. Or, if it was not written then, yet, the penman of the book being inspired by the Holy Ghost, we are sure that we have here a very true and exact report of what was said. *The Spirit* (says Christ) *shall bring to your remembrance,* as he did here, *what I have said to you.* The preface is very searching. (1.) God charges him with ignorance and presumption in what he had said (*v.* 2): *"Who is this* that talks at this rate? Is it Job? What! a man? That weak, foolish, despicable, creature — shall he pretend to prescribe to me what I must do or to quarrel with me for what I have done? Is it Job? What! my servant Job, a perfect and an upright man? Can he so far forget himself, and act unlike himself? Who, where, is he *that darkens counsel thus by words without knowledge?* Let him show his face if he dare, and stand to what he has said." Note, Darkening the counsels of God's wisdom with our folly is a great affront and provocation to God. Concerning God's counsels we must own that we are without knowledge. They are a deep which we cannot fathom; we are quite out of our element, out of our aim, when we pretend to account for them. Yet we are too apt to talk of them as if we understood them, with a great deal of niceness and boldness; but, alas! we do but darken them, instead of explaining them. We confound and perplex ourselves and one another when we dispute of the order of God's decrees, and the designs, and reasons, and methods, of his operations of providence and grace. A humble faith and sincere obedience shall see further and better into the secret of the Lord than all the philosophy of the schools, and the searches of science, so called. This first word which God spoke is the more observable because Job, in his repentance, fastens upon it as that which silenced and humbled him, *ch.* 42:3. This he repeated and echoed as the arrow that stuck fast in him: "I am the fool that has darkened counsel." There was some colour to have turned it upon *Elihu,* as if God meant *him,* for he spoke last, and was speaking when the whirlwind began; but Job applied it to himself, as it becomes us to do when faithful reproofs are given, and not (as most do) to billet them upon other people. (2.) He challenges him to give such proofs of his knowledge as would serve to justify his enquiries into the divine counsels (*v.* 3): *"Gird up now thy loins like a stout man;* prepare thyself for the encounter; *I will demand of thee,* will put some questions to thee, *and answer me* if thou canst, before I answer thine." Those that go about to call God to an account must expect to be catechised and called to an account themselves, that they may be made sensible of their ignorance and arrogance. God here puts Job in mind of what he had said, *ch.* 13:22. *Call thou, and I will answer.* "Now make thy words good."

Verses 4–11

For the humbling of Job, God here shows him his ignorance even concerning the earth and the sea. Though so near, though so bulky, yet he could give no account of their origination, much less of heaven above or hell beneath, which are at such a distance, or of the several parts of matter which are so minute, and then, least of all, of the divine counsels.

I. Concerning the founding of the earth. "If he have such a mighty insight, as he pretends to have, into the counsels of God, let him give some account of the earth he goes upon, which is given to the children of men."

1. Let him tell where he was when this lower world was made, and whether he was advising of assisting in that wonderful work (*v.* 4): *"Where wast thou when I laid the foundations of the earth?* Thy pretensions are high; canst thou pretend to his? Wast thou present when the world was made?" See here, (1.) The greatness and glory of God: *I laid the foundations of the earth.* This proves him to be the only living and true God, and a God of power (Isa. 40:21, Jer. 10:11, 12), and encourages us to trust in him at all times, Isa. 51:13, 16. (2.) The meanness and contemptibleness of man: *"Where wast thou* then? Thou that hast made such a figure among the children of the east, and settest up for an oracle, and a judge of the divine counsels, where was thou when the foundations of the earth were laid?" So far were we from having any hand in the creation of the world, which might entitle us to a dominion in it, or so much as being witnesses of it, by which we might have gained an insight into it, that we were not then in being. The first man was not, much less were we. It is the honour of Christ that he was present when this was done (Prov. 8:22, etc., Jn. 1:1, 2); but *we are of yesterday and know nothing.* Let us not therefore find fault with the works of God, nor prescribe to him. He did not consult us in making the world, and yet it is well made; why should we expect then that he should take his measures from us in governing it?

2. Let him describe how this world was made, and give a particular account of the manner in which this strong and stately edifice was formed and erected: *"Declare, if thou hast* so much *understanding* as thou fanciest thyself to have, what were the advances of that work." Those that pretend to have understanding above others ought to give proof of it. Show my thy faith by thy works, thy knowledge by thy words. Let Job declare it if he can, (1.) How the world came to be so finely framed, with so much exactness, and such an admirable symmetry and proportion of all the parts of it (*v.* 5): "Stand forth, and *tell who laid the measures thereof* and *stretched out the line upon it.*" Wast thou the architect that formed the model and then drew the dimensions by rule according to it? The vast bulk

of the earth is moulded as regularly as if it had been done by line and measure; but who can describe how it was cast into this figure? Who can determine its circumference and diameter, and all the lines that are drawn on the terrestrial globe? It is to this day a dispute whether the earth stands still or turns round; how then can we determine by what measures it was first formed? (2.) How it came to be so firmly fixed. Though it is hung upon nothing, yet it is established, that it cannot be moved; but who can tell *upon what the foundations of it are fastened,* that it may not sink with its own weight, or *who laid the corner-stone thereof,* that the parts of it may not fall asunder? *v.* 6. *What God does, it shall be for ever* (Eccl. 3:14); and therefore, as we cannot find fault with God's work, so we need not be in fear concerning it; it will last, and answer the end, the works of his providence as well as the work of creation; the measures of neither can never be broken; and the work of redemption is no less firm, of which Christ himself is both the foundation and the corner-stone. The church stands as fast as the earth.

3. Let him repeat, if he can, the songs of praise which were sung at that solemnity (*v.* 7), *when the morning-stars sang together,* the blessed angels (the first-born of the Father of light), who, in the morning of time, shone as brightly as the morning star, going immediately before the light which God commanded to shine out of darkness upon the seeds of this lower world, the earth, which was without form and void. They were *the sons of God,* who *shouted for joy* when they saw the foundations of the earth laid, because, though it was not made for them, but for the children of men, and though it would increase their work and service, yet they knew that the eternal Wisdom and Word, whom they were to worship (Heb. 1:6), would *rejoice in the habitable parts of the earth,* and that much of his *delight would be in the sons of men,* Prov. 8:31. The angels are called *the sons of God* because they bear much of his image, are with him in his house above, and serve him as a son does his father. Now observe here, (1.) The glory of God, as the Creator of the world, is to be celebrated with joy and triumph by all his reasonable creatures; for they are qualified and appointed to be the collectors of his praises from the inferior creatures, who can praise him merely as objects that exemplify his workmanship. (2.) The work of angels is to praise God. The more we abound in holy, humble, thankful, joyful praise, the more we do the will of God as they do it; and, whereas we are so barren and defective in praising God, it is a comfort to think that they are doing it in a better manner. (3.) They were unanimous in singing God's praises; they sang together with one accord, and there was no jar in their harmony. The sweetest concerts are in praising God. (4.) They all did it, even those who afterwards fell and left their first estate. Even those who have praised God may, by the deceitful power of sin, be brought to blaspheme him, and yet God will be eternally praised.

II. Concerning the limiting of the sea to the place appointed for it, *v.* 8, etc. This refers to the third day's work, when God said (Gen. 1:9), *Let the waters under the heaven be gathered together unto one place, and it was so.* 1. Out of the great deep or chaos, in which earth and water were intermixed, in obedience to the divine command the waters *broke forth like a child out of the* teeming *womb, v.* 8. Then the waters that had covered the deep, and stood above the mountains, retired with precipitation. At *God's rebuke they fled,* Ps. 104:6, 7. 2. This newborn babe is clothed and swaddled, *v.* 9. *The cloud* is made the *garment thereof,* with which it is covered, and *thick darkness* (that is, shores vastly remote and distant from one another and quite in the dark one to another) *is a swaddling-band for it.* See with what ease the great God manages the raging sea; notwithstanding the violence of its tides, and the strength of its billows, he manages it as the nurse does the child in swaddling clothes. It is not said, He made *rocks and mountains* its swaddling bands, but *clouds and darkness,* something that we are not aware of and should think least likely for such a purpose. 3. There is a cradle too provided for this babe: *I broke up for it my decreed place, v.* 10. Valleys were sunk for it in the earth, capacious enough to receive it, and there it is laid to sleep; and, if it be sometimes tossed with winds, that (as bishop Patrick observes) is but the rocking of the cradle, which makes it sleep the faster. As for the sea, so for every one of us,

there is a decreed place; for he that determined the times before appointed determined also the bounds of our habitation. 4. This babe being made unruly and dangerous by the sin of man, which was the original of all unquietness and danger in this lower world, there is also a prison provided for it; *bars and doors are set, v.* 10. And it is said to it, by way of check to its insolence, *Hitherto shalt thou come, but no further.* The sea is God's for he made it, he restrains it; he says to it, *Here shall thy proud waves be stayed, v.* 11. This may be considered as an act of God's power over the sea. Though it is so vast a body, and though its motion is sometimes extremely violent, yet God has it under check. Its waves rise no higher, its tides roll no further, than God permits; and this is mentioned as a reason why we should stand in awe of God (Jer. 5:22), and yet why we should encourage ourselves in him, for he that stops the noise of the sea, even the noise of her waves, can, when he pleases, still the tumult of the people, Ps. 65:7. It is also to be looked upon as an act of God's mercy to the world of mankind and an instance of his patience towards that provoking grace. Though he could easily cover the earth again with the waters of the sea (and, methinks, every flowing tide twice a day threatens us, and shows what the sea could do, and would do, if God would give it leave), yet he restrains them, being not willing that any should perish, and having *reserved the world that now is unto fire,* 2 Pt. 3:7.

Verses 12–24

The Lord here proceeds to ask Job many puzzling questions, to convince him of his ignorance, and so to shame him for his folly in prescribing to God. If we will but try ourselves with such interrogatories as these, we shall soon be brought to own that what we know is nothing in comparison with what we know not. Job is here challenged to give an account of six things: —

I. Of the springs of the morning, the day-spring from on high, *v.* 12–15. As there is no visible being of which we may be more firmly assured that it is, so there is none which we are more puzzled in describing, nor more doubtful in determining what it is, than the light. We welcome the morning, and are glad of the day-spring; but, 1. It is not commanded since our days, but what it is it was long before we were born, so that it was neither made by us nor designed primarily for us, but we take it as we find it and as the many generations had it that went before us. The day-spring knew its place before we knew ours, for we are but of yesterday. 2. It was not we, it was not any man that commanded the morning-light at first, or appointed the place of its springing up and shining forth, or the time of it. The constant and regular succession of day and night was no contrivance of ours; it is the glory of God that it shows, and his handy work, not ours, Ps. 19:1, 2. 3. It is quite out of our power to alter this course: *"Hast thou countermanded the morning since thy days?* Hast thou at any time raised the morning light sooner than its appointed time, to serve thy purpose when thou hast waited for the morning, or ordered the day-spring for thy convenience to any other place than its own? No, never. Why then wilt thou pretend to direct the divine counsels, or expect to have the methods of Providence altered in favour of thee?" We may as soon break the covenant of the day and of the night as any part of God's covenant with his people, and particularly this, *I will chasten them with the rod of men.* 4. It is God that has appointed the day-spring to visit the earth, and diffuses the morning light through the air, which receives it as readily as the clay does the seal (*v.* 14), immediately admitting the impressions of it, so as of a sudden to be all over enlightened by it, as the seal stamps its image on the wax; *and they stand as a garment,* or as if they were clothed with a garment. The earth puts on a new face every morning, and dresses itself as we do, puts on light as a garment, and is then to be seen. 5. This is made a terror to evil-doers. Nothing is more comfortable to mankind than the light of the morning; it is pleasant to the eyes, it is serviceable to life and the business of it, and the favour of it is universally extended, for *it takes hold of the ends of the earth* (*v.* 13), and we should dwell, in our hymns to the light, on its advantages to the earth. But God here observes how unwelcome it is to those that do evil, and therefore hate the light. God makes the light a minister of his justice as well as of his mercy. It is designed *to shake the wicked out of the earth,* and for that purpose *it takes hold of the ends of it,* as we take hold of the ends of a garment to shake the dust and moths out of it. Job had observed what a terror the morning light is to criminals, because it discovers them (*ch.* 24:13, etc.), and God here seconds the observation, and asks him whether the world was indebted to him for that kindness? No, the great Judge of the world sends forth the beams of the morning light as his messengers to detect criminals, that they may not only be defeated in their purposes and put to shame, but that they may be brought to condign punishment (*v.* 15), that their light may be *withholden* from them (that is, that they may lose their comfort, their confidence, their liberties, their lives) and that their *high arm,* which they have lifted up against God and man, may be *broken,* and they deprived of their power to do mischief. Whether what is here said of the morning light was designed to represent, as in a figure, the light of the gospel of Christ, and to give a type of it, I will not say; but I am sure it may serve to put us in mind of the encomiums given to the gospel just at the rising of its morning-star by Zecharias in his *Benedictus* (Lu. 1:78, By the *tender mercy of our God the day-spring from on high has visited us, to give light to those that sit in darkness,* whose hearts are turned to it *as clay to the seal,* 2 Co. 4:6), and by the virgin Mary in her *Magnificat* (Lu. 1:51), showing that God, in his gospel, has *shown strength with his arm, scattered the proud, and put down the mighty,* by that light by which he designed to shake the wicked, to shake wickedness itself out of the earth, and break its high arm.

II. Of the springs of the sea (*v.* 16): *"Hast thou entered into* them, or *hast thou walked in the search of the depth?* Knowest thou what lies in the bottom of the sea, the treasures there hidden in the sands? Or canst thou give an account of the rise and original of the waters of the sea? Vapours are continually exhaled out of the sea. Dost thou know how the recruits are raised by which it is continually supplied? Rivers are constantly poured into the sea. Dost thou know how they are continually discharged, so as not to overflow the earth? Art thou acquainted with the secret subterraneous passages by which the waters circulate?" God's way in the government of the world is said to be *in the sea,* and *in the great waters* (Ps. 77:19), intimating that it is hidden from us and not to be pried into by us.

III. Of the gates of death: *Have* these *been open to thee? v.* 16. Death is a grand secret. 1. We know not beforehand when, and how, and by what means, we or others shall be brought to death, by what road we must go the way whence we shall not return, what disease or what disaster will be the door to let us into the house appointed for all living. *Man knows not his time.* 2. We cannot describe what death is, how the knot is untied between body and soul, nor how the *spirit of a man goes upward* (Eccl. 3:21), to be we know not what and live we know not how, as Mr. Norris expresses; with what dreadful curiosity (says he) does the soul launch out into the vast ocean of eternity and resign to an untried abyss! Let us make it sure that the gates of heaven shall be opened to us on the other side death, and then we need not fear the opening of the gates of death, though it is a way we are to go but once. 3. We have no correspondence at all with separate souls, nor any acquaintance with their state. It is an unknown undiscovered region to which they are removed; we can neither hear from them nor send to them. While we are here, in a world of sense, we speak of the world of spirits as blind men do of colours, and when we remove thither we shall be amazed to find how much we are mistaken.

IV. Of the breadth of the earth (*v.* 18): *Hast thou perceived* that? The knowledge of this might seem most level to him and within his reach; yet he is challenged to declare this if he can. We have our residence on the earth, God has given it to the children of men. But who ever surveyed it, or could give an account of the number of its acres? It is but a point to the universe? yet, small as it is, we cannot be exact in declaring the dimensions of it. Job had never sailed round the world, nor any before him; so little did men know the breadth of the earth that it was but a few ages ago that the vast continent of America was discovered, which had, time out of mind, lain hidden. The divine perfection is longer than the earth and broader than the sea; it is therefore presumption for us, who perceive not the breadth of the earth, to dive into the depth of God's counsels.

V. Of the place and way of light and darkness. Of the day-spring he had spoken before (*v.* 12) and he returns to speak of it again (*v.* 19): *Where is the way where light dwells?* And again (*v.* 24): *By what way is the light parted?* He challenges him to describe, 1. How the light and darkness were at first made. When God, in the beginning, first spread darkness upon the face of the deep, and afterwards commanded the light to shine out of darkness, by that mighty word, *Let there be light,* was Job a witness to the order, to the operation? can he tell where the fountains of light and darkness are, and where those mighty princes keep their courts distance, while in one world they rule alternately? Though we long ever so much either for the shining forth of the morning or the shadows of the evening, we know not whither to send, or go, to fetch them, nor can tell *the paths to the house thereof, v.* 20. We were not then born, nor is the number of our days so great that we can describe the birth of that first-born of the visible creation, *v.* 21. Shall we then undertake to discourse of God's counsels, which were from eternity, or to find out the paths to the house thereof, to solicit for the alteration of them? God glories in it that he forms the light and creates the darkness; and if we must take those as we find them, take those as they come, and quarrel with neither, but make the best of both, then we must, in like manner, accommodate ourselves to the peace and the evil which God likewise created. Isa. 45:7. 2. How they still keep their turns interchangeably. It is God that *makes the outgoings of the morning and of the evening to rejoice* (Ps. 65:8); for it is his order, and no order of ours, that is executed by the outgoings of the morning light and the darkness of the night. We cannot so much as tell whence they come nor whither they go (*v.* 24): *By what way is the light parted* in the morning, when, in an instant, it shoots itself into all the parts of the air above the horizon, as if the morning light flew upon the wings of an east wind, so swiftly, so strongly, is it carried, scattering the darkness of the night, as the east wind does the clouds? Hence we read of the *wings of the morning* (Ps. 139:9), on which the light is conveyed *to the uttermost parts of the sea,* and *scattered like an east wind upon the earth.* It is a marvellous change that passes over us every morning by the return of the light and every evening by the return of the darkness; but we expect them, and so they are no surprise nor uneasiness to us. If we would, in like manner, reckon upon changes in our outward condition, we should neither in the brightest noon expect perpetual day nor in the darkest midnight despair of the return of the morning. God has set the one over against the other, like the day and night; and so must we, Eccl. 7:14.

VI. Of the *treasures of the snow and hail* (*v.* 22, 23): *"Hast thou entered* into these and taken a view of them?" In the clouds the snow and hail are generated, and thence they come in such abundance that one would think there were treasures of them laid up in store there, whereas indeed they are produced *extempore — suddenly,* as I may say, and *pro re nata — for the occasion.* Sometimes they come so opportunely, to serve the purposes of Providence, in God's fighting for his people and against his and their enemies, that one would think they were laid up as magazines, or stores of arms, ammunition, and provisions, against the time of trouble, *the day of battle and war,* when God will either contend with the world in general (as in the deluge, when the windows of heaven were opened, and the waters fetched out of these treasures to drown a wicked world, that waged war with Heaven) or with some particular persons or parties, as when God out of these treasures fetched great hail-stones wherewith to fight against the Canaanites, Jos. 10:11. See what folly it is to strive against God, who is thus prepared for battle and war, and how much it is our interest to make our peace with him and to keep ourselves in his love. God can fight as effectually with snow and hail, if he please, as with thunder and lightning or the sword of an angel!

Verses 25–41

Hitherto God had put such questions to Job as were proper to convince him of his ignorance and shortsightedness. Now he comes, in the same manner, to show his impotency and weakness. As it is but little that he knows, and therefore he ought not to arraign the divine counsels, so it is but little that he can do, and therefore he ought not to oppose the proceedings of Providence. Let him consider what great things God does, and try whether he can do the like, or whether he thinks himself an equal match for him.

I. God has thunder, and lightning, and rain, and frost, at command, but Job has not, and therefore let him not dare to compare himself with God, or to contend with him. Nothing is more uncertain than what weather it shall be, nor more out of our reach to appoint; it shall be what weather pleases God, not what pleases us, unless, as becomes us, whatever pleases God pleases us. Concerning this observe here,

1. How great God is.

(1.) He has a sovereign dominion over the waters, has appointed them their course, even then when they seem to overflow and to be from under his check, *v.* 25. He has *divided a water-course,* directs the rain where to fall, even when the shower is most violent, with as much certainty as if it were conveyed by canals or conduit-pipes. Thus the hearts of kings are said to be *in God's hand;* and as the rains, those rivers of God, he turns them whithersoever he will. Every drop goes as it is directed. God has *sworn that the waters of Noah shall no more return to cover the earth;* and we see that he is able to make good what he has promised, for he has the rain in a water-course.

(2.) He has dominion over the lightning and the thunder, which go not at random, but in the way that he directs them. They are mentioned here because he *prepares the lightnings for the rain,* Ps. 135:7. Let not those that fear God be afraid of the lightning or the thunder, for they are not blind bullets, but go the way that God himself, who means no hurt to them, directs.

(3.) In directing the course of the rain he does not neglect the wilderness, the desert land (*v.* 26, 27), *where no man is.* [1.] Where there is no man to be employed in taking care of the productions. God's providence reaches further than man's industry. If he had not more kindness for many of the inferior creatures than man has, it would go ill with them. God can make the earth fruitful without any art or pains of ours, Gen. 2:5, 6. When *there was not a man to till the ground,* yet there went up a mist and watered it. But we cannot make it fruitful without God; it is he that gives the increase. [2.] Where there is no man to be provided for nor to take the benefit of the fruits that are produced. Though God does with very peculiar favour visit and regard man, yet he does not overlook the inferior creatures, but causes *the bud of the tender herb to spring forth for food for all flesh,* as well as *for the service of man.* Even the wild asses shall have their thirst quenched, Ps. 104:11. God has enough for all, and wonderfully provides even for those creatures that man neither has service from nor makes provision for.

(4.) He is, in a sense, *the Father of the rain, v.* 28. It has no other father. He produces it by his power; he governs and directs it, and makes what use he pleases of it. Even the small drops of the dew he distils upon the earth, as the God of nature; and, as the God of grace, he rains righteousness upon us and is himself as the dew unto Israel. See Hos. 14:5, 6; Mic. 5:7.

(5.) The ice and the frost, by which the waters are congealed and the earth incrustrated, are produced by his providence, *v.* 29, 30. These are very common things, which lessens the strangeness of them. But, considering what a vast change is made by them in a very little time, how the waters are hid as with a stone, as with a gravestone, laid upon them (so thick, so strong, is the ice that covers them), and the face even of the deep is sometimes frozen, we may well ask, *"Out of whose womb came the ice?* What created power could produce such a wonderful work?" No power but that of the Creator himself. Frost and snow come from him, and therefore should lead our thoughts and meditations to him who does such great things, past finding out. And we shall the more easily bear the inconveniences of winter-weather if we learn to make this good use of it.

2. How weak man is. Can he do such things as these? Could Job? No, *v.* 34, 35. (1.) He cannot command one shower of rain for the relief of himself or his friends: *"Canst thou lift up thy voice to the clouds,* those bottles of heaven, *that abundance of waters may cover thee,* to water thy

fields when they are dry and parched?" If we lift up our voice to God, to pray for rain, we may have it (Zec. 10:1); but if we lift up our voice to the clouds, to demand it, they will soon tell us they are not at our beck, and we shall go without it, Jer. 14:22. The heavens will not her the earth unless God hear them, Hos. 2:21. See what poor, indigent, depending creatures we are; we cannot do without rain, nor can we have it when we will. (2.) He cannot commission one flash of lightning, if he had a mind to make use of it for the terror of his enemies (*v.* 35): *"Canst thou send lightnings, that they may go* on thy errand, and do the execution thou desirest? Will they come at thy call, and say unto thee, *Here we are?"* No, the ministers of God's wrath will not be ministers of ours. Why should they, since the *wrath of man works not the righteousness of God?* See Lu. 9:55.

II. God has the stars of heaven under his command and cognizance, but we have them not under ours. Our meditations are now to rise higher, far above the clouds, to the glorious lights above. God mentions particularly, not the planets, which move in lower orbs, but the fixed stars, which are much higher. It is supposed that they have an influence upon this earth, notwithstanding their vast distance, not upon the minds of men or the events of providence (men's fate is not determined by their stars), but upon the ordinary course of nature; they are set for signs and seasons, for days and years, Gen. 1:14. And if the stars have such a dominion over this earth (*v.* 33), though they have their place in the heavens and are but mere matter, much more has he who is their Maker and ours, and who is an Eternal Mind. Now see how weak we are. 1. We cannot alter the influences of the stars (*v.* 31), not theirs that are instrumental to produce the pleasures of the spring: *Canst thou loose the bands of Orion?* — that magnificent constellation which makes so great a figure (none greater), and dispenses rough and unpleasing influences, which we cannot control nor repel. Both summer and winter will have their course. God can change them when he pleases, can make the spring cold, and so bind the sweet influences of Pleiades, and the winter warm, and so loose the bands of Orion; but we cannot. 2. It is not in our power to order the motions of the stars, nor are we entrusted with the guidance of them. God, who *calls the stars by their names* (Ps. 147:4), calls them forth in their respective seasons, appointing them the time of their rising and setting. But this is not our province; we cannot *bring forth Mazzaroth* — the stars in the southern signs, nor *guide Arcturus* — those in the northern, *v.* 32. God can bring forth the stars to battle (as he did when in their courses they fought against Sisera) and guide them in the attacks they are ordered to make; but man cannot do so. 3. We are not only unconcerned in the government of the stars (the government they are under, and the government they are entrusted with, for they both rule and are ruled), but utterly unacquainted with it; we *know not the ordinances of heaven, v.* 33. So far are we from being able to change them that we can give no account of them; they are a secret to us. Shall we then pretend to know God's counsels, and the reasons of them? If it were left to us to set the dominion of the stars upon the earth, we should soon be at a loss. Shall we then teach God how to govern the world?

III. God is the author and giver, the father and fountain, of all wisdom and understanding, *v.* 36. The souls of men are nobler and more excellent beings than the stars of heaven themselves, and shine more brightly. The powers and faculties of reason with which man is endued, and the wonderful performances of thought, bring him into some alliance to the blessed angels; and whence comes this light, but from the Father of lights? *Who* else *has put wisdom into the inner parts* of man, and *given understanding to the heart?* 1. The rational soul itself, and its capacities, come from him as the God of nature; for he forms the spirit of man within him. We did not make our own souls, nor can we describe how they act, nor how they are united to our bodies. He only that made them knows them, and knows how to manage them. He fashioneth men's hearts alike in some things, and yet unlike in others. 2. True wisdom, with its furniture and improvement, comes from him as the God of grace and the Father of every good and perfect gift. Shall we pretend to be wiser than God, when we have all our wisdom from him? Nay, shall we pretend to be wise above our sphere, and beyond the limits which he that gave us our understanding sets to it? He designed we should with it serve God and do our duty, but never intended we should with it set up for directors of the stars or the lightning.

IV. God has the clouds under his cognizance and government, but so have not we, *v.* 37. Can any man, with all his wisdom, undertake to *number the clouds,* or (as it may be read) to *declare and describe the nature of them?* Though they are near us, in our own atmosphere, yet we know little more of them than of the stars which are at so great a distance. And when the clouds have poured down rain in abundance, so that *the dust grows into* solid mire and *the clods cleave fast together* (*v.* 38), *who can stay the bottles of heaven?* Who can stop them, that it may not always rain? The power and goodness of God are herein to be acknowledged, that he gives the earth rain enough, but does not surfeit it, softens it, but does not drown it, makes it fit for the plough, but not unfit for the seed. As we cannot command a shower of rain, so we cannot command a fair day, without God; so necessary, so constant, is our dependence upon him.

V. God provides food for the inferior creatures, and it is by his providence, not by any care or pains of ours, that they are fed. The following chapter is wholly taken up with the instances of God's power and goodness about animals, and therefore some transfer to it the last three verses of this chapter, which speak of the provision made, 1. For the lions, *v.* 39, 40. "Thou dost not pretend that the clouds and stars have any dependence upon thee, for they are above thee; but on the earth thou thinkest thyself paramount; let us try that then: *Wilt thou hunt the prey for the lion?* Thou valuest thyself upon thy possessions of cattle which thou wast once owner of, the oxen, and asses, and camels, that were fed at thy crib; but wilt thou undertake the maintenance of the lions, and *the young lions, when they couch in their dens,* waiting for a prey? No, needest not do it, they can shift for themselves without thee: thou canst not do it, for thou hast not wherewithal to satisfy them: thou darest not do it; shouldst thou come to feed them, they would seize upon thee. But I do it." See the all-sufficiency of the divine providence: it has wherewithal to satisfy the desire of every living thing, even the most ravenous. See the bounty of the divine Providence, that, wherever it has given life, it will give livelihood, even to those creatures that are not only not serviceable, but dangerous, to man. And see its sovereignty, that it suffers some creatures to be killed for the support of other creatures. The harmless sheep are torn to pieces, to *fill the appetite of the young lions,* who yet sometimes are made to lack and suffer hunger, to punish them for their cruelty, while those that fear God want no good thing. 2. For the young ravens, *v.* 41. As ravenous beasts, so ravenous birds, are fed by the divine Providence. *Who* but God *provides for the raven his food?* Man does not; he takes care only of those creatures that are, or may be, useful to him. But God has a regard to all the works of his hands, even the meanest and least valuable. The ravens' *young ones* are in a special manner necessitous, and God supplies them, Ps. 147:9. God's feeding the fowls, especially these fowls (Mt. 6:26), is an encouragement to us to trust him for our daily bread. See here, (1.) What distress the young ravens are often in: *They wander for lack of meat.* The old ones, they say, neglect them, and do not provide for them as other birds do for their young: and indeed those that are ravenous to others are commonly barbarous to their own, and unnatural. (2.) What they are supposed to do in that distress: They *cry,* for they are noisy clamorous creatures, and this is interpreted as crying to God. It being the cry of nature, it is looked upon as directed to the God of nature. The putting of so favourable a construction as this upon the cries of the young ravens may encourage us in our prayers, though we can but cry, *Abba, Father.* (3.) What God does for them. Some way or other he provides for them, so that they grow up, and come to maturity. And he that takes this care of the young ravens certainly will not be wanting to his people or theirs. This, being but one instance of many of the divine compassion, may give us occasion to think how much good our God does, every day, beyond what we are aware of.

CHAPTER 39

God proceeds here to show Job what little reason he had to charge him with unkindness who was so compassionate to the inferior creatures and took such a tender care of them, or to boast of himself, and his own good deeds before God, which were nothing to the divine mercies. He shows him also what great reason he had to be humble who knew so little of the nature of the creatures about him and had so little influence upon them, and to submit to that God on whom they all depend. He discourses particularly, I. Concerning the wild goats and hinds (*v.* 1–4). II. Concerning the wild ass (*v.* 5–8). III. Concerning the unicorn (*v.* 9–12). IV. Concerning the horse (*v.* 19–25). VII. Concerning the hawk and the eagle (*v.* 26–30).

Verses 1–12

God here shows Job what little acquaintance he had with the untamed creatures that run wild in the deserts and live at large, but are the care of the divine Providence. As,

I. The *wild goats* and the *hinds.* That which is taken notice of concerning them is the bringing forth and bringing up of their young ones. For, as every individual is fed, so every species of animals is preserved, by the care of the divine Providence, and, for aught we know, none extinct to this day. Observe here, 1. Concerning the production of their young, (1.) Man is wholly ignorant of the time when they bring forth, *v.* 1, 2. Shall we pretend to tell what is in the womb of Providence, or what a day will bring forth, who know not the time of the pregnancy of a hind or a wild goat? (2.) Though they bring forth their young with a great deal of difficulty and sorrow, and have no assistance from man, yet, by the good providence of God, their young ones are safely produced, and their sorrows cast out and forgotten, *v.* 3. Some think it is intimated (Ps. 29:9) that God by thunder helps the hinds in calving. Let it be observed, for the comfort of women in labour, that God helps even the hinds to bring forth their young; and shall he not much more succour them, and save them in child-bearing, who are his children in covenant with him? 2. Concerning the growth of their young, (*v.* 4): *They are in good liking;* though they are brought forth in sorrow, after their dams have suckled them awhile they shift for themselves in the corn-fields, and are no more burdensome to them, which is an example to children, when they have grown up, not to be always hanging upon their parents and craving from them, but to put forth themselves to get their own livelihood and to requite their parents.

II. The *wild ass,* a creature we frequently read of in Scripture, some say untameable. Man is said to be born as the wild ass's colt, so hard to be governed. Two things Providence has allotted to the wild ass: — 1. An unbounded liberty (*v.* 5): *Who* but God *has sent out the wild ass free?* He has given a disposition to it, and therefore a dispensation for it. The tame ass is bound to labour; the wild ass has no bonds on him. Note, Freedom from service, and liberty to range at pleasure, are but the privileges of a wild ass. It is a pity that any of the children of men should covet such a liberty, or value themselves on it. It is better to labour and be good for something than ramble and be good for nothing. But if, among men, Providence sets some at liberty and suffers them to live at ease, while others are doomed to servitude, we must not marvel at the matter: it is so among the brute-creatures. 2. An unenclosed lodging (*v.* 6): *Whose house I have made the wilderness,* where he has room enough to traverse his ways, and snuff up the wind at his pleasure, as the wild ass is said to do (Jer. 2:24), as if he had to live upon the air, for it is *the barren land* that is *his dwelling.* Observe, The tame ass, that labours, and is serviceable to man, has his master's crib to go to both for shelter and food, and lives in a fruitful land: but the wild ass, that will have his liberty, must have it in a barren land. He that will not labour, let him not eat. He that will shall eat the labour of his hands, and have also to give to him that needs. Jacob, the shepherd, has good red pottage to spare, when Esau, a sportsman, is ready to perish for hunger. A further description of the liberty and livelihood of the wild ass we have, *v.* 7, 8. (1.) He has no owner, nor will he be in subjection: *He scorns the multitude of the city.* If they attempt to take him, and in order to that surround him with a multitude, he will soon get clear of them, and *the crying of the driver* is nothing to him. He laughs at those that live in the tumult and bustle of cities (so bishop Patrick), thinking himself happier in the wilderness; and opinion is the rate of things. (2.) Having no owner, he has no feeder, nor is any provision made for him, but he must shift for himself: *The range of the mountains is his pasture,* and a bare pasture it is; there he *searches after here and there a green thing,* as he can find it and pick it up; whereas the labouring asses have green things in plenty, without their searching for them. From the untameableness of this and other creatures we may infer how unfit we are to give law to Providence, who cannot give law even to a wild ass's colt.

III. The unicorn — *rhem,* a strong creature (Num. 23:22), a stately proud creature, Ps. 112:10. He is able to serve, but not willing; and God here challenges Job to force him to it. Job expected every thing should be just as he would have it. "Since thou dost pretend" (says God) "to bring every thing beneath thy sway, begin with the unicorn, and try thy skill upon him. Now that thy oxen and asses are all gone, try whether he will be willing to serve thee in their stead (*v.* 9) and whether he will be content with the provision thou usedst to make for them: *Will he abide by thy crib?* No;" 1. "Thou canst not tame him, nor *bind him with his band,* nor set him to *draw the harrow,*" *v.* 10. There are creatures that are willing to serve man, that seem to take a pleasure in serving him, and to have a love for their masters; but there are such as will never be brought to serve him, which is the effect of sin. Man has revolted from his subjection to his Maker, and is therefore justly punished with the revolt of the inferior creatures from their subjection to him; and yet, as an instance of God's good-will to man, there are some that are still serviceable to him. Though the wild bull (which some think is meant here by the unicorn) will not serve him, nor submit to his hand in the furrows, yet there are tame bullocks that will, and other animals that are not *ferae naturae — of a wild nature,* in whom man may have a property, for whom he provides, and to whose service he is entitled. *Lord, what is man, that thou art thus mindful of him?* 2. "Thou darest not trust him; though *his strength is great,* yet thou wilt not *leave thy labour to him,* as thou dost with thy asses or oxen, which a little child may lead or drive, leaving to them all the pains. Thou wilt never depend upon the wild bull, as likely to come to thy harvest-work, much less to go through it, to *bring home thy seed and gather it into thy barn,*" *v.* 11, 12. And, because he will not serve about the corn, he is not so well fed as the tame ox, whose mouth was not to be muzzled in treading out the corn; but *therefore* he will not draw the plough, because he that made him never designed him for it. A disposition to labour is as much the gift of God as an ability for it; and it is a great mercy if, where God gives strength for service, he gives a heart; it is what we should pray for, and reason ourselves into, which the brutes cannot do; for, as among beasts, so among men, those may justly be reckoned wild and abandoned to the deserts who have no mind either to take pains or to do good.

Verses 13–18

The ostrich is a wonderful animal, a very large bird, but it never flies. Some have called it *a winged camel.* God here gives an account of it, and observes,

I. Something that it has in common with the peacock, that is, beautiful feathers (*v.* 13): *Gavest thou proud wings unto the peacocks?* so some read it. Fine feathers make proud birds. The peacock is an emblem of pride; when he struts, and shows his fine feathers, Solomon in all his glory is not arrayed like him. The ostrich too has goodly feathers, and yet is a foolish bird; for wisdom does not always go along with beauty and gaiety. Other birds do not envy the peacock or the ostrich their gaudy colours, nor complain for want of them; why then should we repine if we see others wear better clothes than we can afford to wear? God gives his gifts variously, and those gifts are not always the most valuable that make the finest show. Who would not rather have the voice of the nightingale than the tail of the peacock, the eye of the eagle and her soaring wing, and the natural affection of the stork, than the beautiful wings and feathers of the ostrich, which can never rise above the earth, and is without natural affection?

II. Something that is peculiar to itself,

1. Carelessness of her young. It is well that this is peculiar to herself, for it is a very bad character. Observe, (1.) How she exposes her eggs; she does not retire to some private place, and make a nest there, as the sparrows and swallows do (Ps. 84:3), and there lay eggs and hatch her young. Most birds, as well as other animals, are strangely guided by natural instinct in providing for the preservation of their young. But the ostrich is a monster in nature, for she drops her eggs any where upon the ground and takes no care to hatch them. If the sand and the sun will hatch them, well and good; they may for her, for she will not warm them, *v.* 14. Nay, she takes no care to preserve them: *The foot* of the traveller *may crush them,* and *the wild beast break them, v.* 15. But how then are any young ones brought forth, and whence is it that the species has not perished? We must suppose either that God, by a special providence, with the heat of the sun and the sand (so some think), hatches the neglected eggs of the ostrich, as he feeds the neglected young ones of the raven, or that, though the ostrich *often* leaves her eggs thus, yet not *always.* (2.) The reason why she does thus expose her eggs. It is, [1.] For want of natural affection (*v.* 16): *She is hardened against her young ones.* To be hardened against any is unamiable, even in a brute-creature, much more in a rational creature that boasts of humanity, especially to be hardened against young ones, that cannot help themselves and therefore merit compassion, that give no provocation and therefore merit no hard usage: but it is worst of all for her to be hardened against her own young ones, as though they were not hers, whereas really they are parts of herself. Her labour in laying her eggs is in vain and all lost, because she has not that fear and tender concern for them that she should have. Those are most likely to lose their labour that are least in fear of losing it. [2.] For want of wisdom (*v.* 17): *God has deprived her of wisdom.* This intimates that the art which other animals have to nourish and preserve their young is God's gift, and that, where it exists not, God denies it, that by the folly of the ostrich, as well as by the wisdom of the ant, we may learn to be wise; for, *First,* As careless as the ostrich is of her eggs so careless many people are of their own souls; they make no provision for them, no proper nest in which they may be safe, leave them exposed to Satan and his temptations, which is a certain evidence that they are deprived of wisdom. *Secondly,* So careless are many parents of their children; some of their bodies, not providing for their own house, their own bowels, and therefore worse than infidels, and as bad as the ostrich; but many more are thus careless of their children's souls, take no care of their education, send them abroad into the world untaught, unarmed, forgetting what corruption there is in the world through lust, which will certainly crush them. Thus their labour in rearing them comes to be in vain; it were better for their country that they had never been born. *Thirdly,* So careless are too many ministers of their people, with whom they should reside; but they leave them in the earth, and forget how busy Satan is to sow tares while men sleep. They overlook those whom they should oversee, and are really hardened against them.

2. Care of herself. She leaves her eggs in danger, but, if she herself be in danger, no creature shall strive more to get out of the way of it than the ostrich, *v.* 18. Then she lifts up her wings on high (the strength of which then stands her in better stead than their beauty), and, with the help of them, runs so fast that a horseman at full speed cannot overtake her: *She scorneth the horse and his rider.* Those that are least under the law of natural affection often contend most for the law of self-preservation. Let not the rider be proud of the swiftness of his horse when such an animal as the ostrich shall out-run him.

Verses 19–25

God, having displayed his own power in those creatures that are strong and despise man, here shows it in one scarcely inferior to any of them in strength, and yet very tame and serviceable to man, and that is the horse, especially *the horse that is prepared against the day of battle* and is serviceable to man at a time when he has more than ordinary occasion for his service. It seems, there was, in Job's country, a noble generous breed of horses. Job, it is probable, kept many, though they are not mentioned among his possessions, cattle for use in husbandry being there valued more than those for state and war, which alone horses were then reserved for, and they were not then put to such mean services as with us they are commonly put to. Concerning the great horse, that stately beast, it is here observed, 1. That he has a great deal of strength and spirit (*v.* 19): *Hast thou given the horse strength?* He uses his strength for man, but has it not from him: God gave it to him, who is the fountain of all the powers of nature, and yet he himself *delights not in the strength of the horse* (Ps. 147:10), but has told us that *a horse is a vain thing for safety,* Ps. 33:17. For running, drawing, and carrying, no creature that is ordinarily in the service of man has so much strength as the horse has, nor is of so stout and bold a spirit, not to be made afraid as a grasshopper, but daring and forward to face danger. It is a mercy to man to have such a servant, which, though very strong, submits to the management of a child, and rebels not against his owner. But let not the strength of a horse be trusted to, Hos. 14:3; Ps. 20:7; Isa. 31:1, 3. 2. That his neck and nostrils look great. His neck is *clothed with thunder,* with a large and flowing mane, which makes him formidable and is an ornament to him. *The glory of his nostrils,* when he snorts, flings up his head, and throws foam about, *is terrible, v.* 20. Perhaps there might be at that time, and in that country, a more stately breed of horses than any we have now. 3. That he is very fierce and furious in battle, and charges with an undaunted courage, though he pushes on in imminent danger of his life. (1.) See how frolicsome he is (*v.* 21): *He paws in the valley,* scarcely knowing what ground he stands upon. He is proud of his strength, and he has much more reason to be so as using his strength in the service of man, and under his direction, than the wild ass that uses it in contempt of man, and in a revolt from him *v.* 8. (2.) See how forward he is to engage: *He goes on to meet the armed men,* animated, not by the goodness of the cause, or the prospect of honour, but only by *the sound of the trumpet, the thunder of the captains, and the shouting* of the soldiers, which are as bellows to the fire of his innate courage, and make him spring forward with the utmost eagerness, as if he cried, *Ha! ha! v.* 25. How wonderfully are the brute-creatures fitted for and inclined to the services for which they were designed. (3.) See how fearless he is, how he despises death and the most threatening dangers, (*v.* 22): *He mocks at fear,* and makes a jest of it; slash at him with a sword, rattle the quiver, brandish the spear, to drive him back, he will not retreat, but press forward, and even inspires courage into his rider. (4.) See how furious he is. He curvets and prances, and runs on with so much violence and heat against the enemy that one would think he even *swallowed the ground with fierceness and rage, v.* 24. High mettle is the praise of a horse rather than of a man, whom fierceness and rage ill become. This description of the war-horse will help to explain that character which is given of presumptuous sinners, Jer. 8:6. *Every one turneth to his course, as the horse rusheth into the battle.* When a man's heart is fully set in him to do evil, and he is carried on in a wicked way by the violence of inordinate appetites and passions, there is no making him afraid of the wrath of God and the fatal consequences of sin. Let his own conscience set before him the curse of the law, the death that is the wages of sin, and all the terrors of the Almighty in battle-array; he mocks at this fear, and is not affrighted, neither turns he back from the flaming sword of the cherubim. Let ministers lift up their voice like a trumpet, to proclaim the wrath of God against him, *he believes not that it is the sound of the trumpet,* nor that God and his heralds are in earnest with him; but what will be in the end hereof it is easy to foresee.

Verses 26–30

The birds of the air are proofs of the wonderful power and providences of God, as well as the beasts of the earth; God here refers particularly to two stately ones: — 1. The *hawk,* a noble bird of great strength and sagacity, and yet a bird of prey, *v.* 26. This bird is here taken notice of for her flight, which is swift and strong, and especially for the course she steers *towards the south,* whither she follows the sun in winter, out of the colder countries in the north, especially when she is to cast her plumes and renew them. This is her wisdom, and it was God that gave her this wisdom, not man. Perhaps the extraordinary wisdom of the hawk's flight after her prey was not used then for men's diversion and recreation, as it has been since. It is a pity that the reclaimed hawk, which is taught to fly at man's command and to make him sport, should at any time be abused to the dishonour of God, since it is from God that she receives that wisdom which makes her flight entertaining and serviceable. 2. The *eagle,* a royal bird, and yet a bird of prey too, the permission of which, nay, the giving of power to which, may help to reconcile us to the prosperity of oppressors among men. The eagle is here taken notice of, (1.) For the height of her flight. No bird soars so high, has so strong a wind, nor can so well bear the light of the sun. Now, *"Doth she mount at thy command?* *v.* 27. Is it by any strength she has from thee? or dost thou direct her flight? No; it is by the natural power and instinct God has given her that she will soar out of thy sight, much more out of thy call." (2.) For the strength of her nest. Her house is her castle and strong-hold; she makes it *on high* and *on the rock, the crag of the rock* (*v.* 28), which sets her and her young out of the reach of danger. Secure sinners think themselves as safe in their sins as the eagle in her nest on high, in the *clefts of the rock; but I will bring thee down thence, saith the Lord,* Jer. 49:16. The higher bad men sit above the resentments of the earth the nearer they ought to think themselves to the vengeance of Heaven. (3.) For her quicksightedness (*v.* 29): *Her eyes behold afar off,* not upwards, but downwards, in quest of her prey. In this she is an emblem of a hypocrite, who, while, in the profession of religion, he seems to rise towards heaven, keeps his eye and heart upon the prey on earth, some temporal advantage, some widow's house or other that he hopes to devour, under pretence of devotion. (4.) For the way she has of maintaining herself and her young. She preys upon living animals, which she seizes and tears to pieces, and thence carries to her young ones, which are taught to *suck up blood;* they do it by instinct, and know no better; but for men that have reason and conscience to thirst after blood is what could scarcely be believed if there had not been in every age wretched instances of it. She also preys upon the dead bodies of men: *Where the slain are, there is she,* These birds of prey (in another sense than the horse, *v.* 25) *smell the battle afar off.* Therefore, when a great slaughter is to be made among the enemies of the church, the fowls are invited to *the supper of the great God, to eat the flesh of kings and captains,* Rev. 19:17, 18. Our Saviour refers to this instinct of the eagle, Mt. 24:28. *Wheresoever the carcase is, there will the eagles be gathered together.* Every creature will make towards that which is its proper food; for he that provides the creatures their food has implanted in them that inclination. These and many such instances of natural power and sagacity in the inferior creatures, which we cannot account for, oblige us to confess our own weakness and ignorance and to give glory to God as the fountain of all being, power, wisdom, and perfection.

CHAPTER 40

Many humbling confounding questions God had put to Job, in the foregoing chapter; now, in this chapter, I. He demands an answer to them (*v.* 1, 2). II. Job submits in a humble silence (*v.* 3–5). III. God proceeds to reason with him, for his conviction, concerning the infinite distance and disproportion between him and God, showing that he was by no means an equal match for God. He challenges him (*v.* 6, 7) to vie with him, if he durst, for justice (*v.* 8), power (*v.* 9), majesty (*v.* 10), and dominion over the proud (*v.* 11–14), and he gives an instance of his power in one particular animal, here called "Behemoth," (*v.* 15–24).

Verses 1–5

Here is, I. A humbling challenge which God gave to Job. After he had heaped up many hard questions upon him, to show him, by his manifest ignorance in the works of nature, what an incompetent judge he was of the methods and designs of Providence, he clenches the nail with one demand more, which stands by itself here as the application of the whole. It should seem, God paused awhile, as Elihu had done, to give Job time to say what he had to say, or to think of what God had said; but Job was in such confusion that he remained silent, and therefore God here put him upon replying, *v.* 1, 2. This is not said to be spoken *out of the whirlwind,* as before; and therefore some think God said it in a still small voice, which wrought more upon Job than the whirlwind did, as upon Elijah, 1 Ki. 19:12, 13. *My doctrine shall drop as the rain,* and then it does wonders. Though Job had not spoken any thing, yet God is said to answer him; for he knows men's thoughts, and can return a suitable answer to their silence. Here, 1. God puts a convincing question to him: *"Shall he that contendeth with the Almighty instruct him?* Shall he pretend to dictate to God's wisdom or prescribe to his will? Shall God receive instruction from every peevish complainer, and change the measures he has taken to please him?" It is a question with disdain. *Shall any teach God knowledge? ch.* 21:22. It is intimated that those who quarrel with God do, in effect, go about to teach him how to mend his work. For if we contend with men like ourselves, as not having done well, we ought to instruct them how to do better; but is it a thing to be suffered that any man should teach his Maker? He that contends with God is justly looked upon as his enemy; and shall he pretend so far to have prevailed in the contest as to prescribe to him? We are ignorant and short-sighted, but before him all things are naked and open; we are depending creatures, but he is the sovereign Creator; and shall we pretend to instruct him? Some read it, *Is it any wisdom to contend with the Almighty?* The answer is easy. No; it is the greatest folly in the world. Is it wisdom to contend with him whom it will certainly be our ruin to oppose and unspeakably our interest to submit to? 2. He demands a speedy reply to it: *"He that reproaches God let him answer* this question to his own conscience, and answer it thus, *Far be it from me to contend with the Almighty* or to *instruct him.* Let him answer all those questions which I have put, if he can. Let him answer for his presumption and insolence, answer it at God's bar, to his confusion." Those have high thoughts of themselves, and mean thoughts of God, who reprove any thing he says or does.

II. Job's humble submission thereupon. Now Job came to himself, and began to melt into godly sorrow. When his friends reasoned with him he did not yield; but the voice of the Lord is powerful. *When the Spirit of truth shall come, he shall convince.* They had condemned him for a wicked man; Elihu himself had been very sharp upon him (*ch.* 34:7, 8, 37); but God had not given him such hard words. We may sometimes have reason to expect better treatment from God, and a more candid construction of what we do, than we meet with from our friends. This the good man is here overcome by, and yields himself a conquered captive to the grace of God. 1. He owns himself an offender, and has nothing to say in his own justification (*v.* 4): *"Behold, I am vile,* not only mean and contemptible, but vile and abominable, in my own eyes." He is now sensible that he has sinned, and therefore calls himself *vile.* Sin debases us, and penitents abase themselves, reproach themselves, are ashamed, yea, even confounded. "I have acted undutifully to my Father, ungratefully to my benefactor, unwisely for myself; and therefore I am vile." Job now vilifies himself as much as ever he had justified and magnified himself. Repentance changes men's opinion of themselves. Job had been too bold in demanding a conference with God, and thought he could make his part good with him: but now he is convinced of his error, and owns himself utterly unable to stand before God or to produce any thing worth his notice, the veriest dunghill-worm that ever crawled upon God's ground. While his friends talked with him, he answered them, for he thought himself as good as they; but, when God talked with him, he had nothing to say, for, in comparison with him, he sees himself nothing, less than nothing, worse than nothing, vanity and vileness itself; and therefore, *What shall I answer thee?* God demanded an answer, *v.* 2. Here he gives the reason of his silence; it was not because he was sullen, but because he was convinced he had been in the wrong. Those that are truly sensible of their own sinfulness and vileness dare not justify themselves before God, but are ashamed that ever they entertained such a thought, and, in token of their shame, lay their hand upon their mouth. 2. He promises not to offend any more as he had done; for Elihu had told him that this was meet to be said unto God. When we have spoken amiss we must repent of it and not repeat it nor stand to it. He enjoins himself silence (*v.* 4): *"I will lay my hand upon my mouth,* will keep that as with a bridle, to suppress all passionate thoughts which may arise in my mind, and keep them from breaking out in intemperate speeches." It is bad to think amiss, but it is much worse to speak amiss, for that is an allowance of the evil thought and gives it an *imprimatur — a sanction;* it is publishing the seditious libel; and therefore, *if thou hast thought evil, lay thy hand upon thy mouth* and let it go no further (Prov. 30:32) and that will be an evidence for thee that that which thou thoughtest thou allowest not. Job had suffered his evil thoughts to vent themselves: *"Once have I spoken* amiss, *yea, twice,"* that is, "divers times, in one discourse and in another; but I have done: *I will not answer;* I will not stand to what I have said, nor say it again; *I will proceed no further."* Observe here what true repentance is. (1.) It is to rectify our errors, and the false principles we went upon in doing as we did. What we have long, and often, and vigorously maintained, once, yea, twice, we must retract as soon as we are convinced that it is a mistake, not adhere to it any longer, but take shame to ourselves for holding it so long. (2.) It is to return from every by-path and to proceed not one step further in it: *"I will not add"* (so the word is); "I will never indulge my passion so much again, nor give myself such a liberty of speech, will never say as I have said nor do as I have done." Till it comes to this, we come short of repentance. Further observe, Those who dispute with God will be silenced at last. Job had been very bold and forward in demanding a conference with God, and talked very boldly, how plain he would make his case, and how sure he was that he should be justified. *As a prince he would go near unto him* (*ch.* 31:37); he would *come even to his seat* (*ch.* 23:3); but he has soon enough of it; he lets fall his plea and will not answer. "Lord, the wisdom and right are all on thy side, and I have done foolishly and wickedly in questioning them."

Verses 6–14

Job was greatly humbled for what God had already said, but not sufficiently; he was brought low, but not low enough; and therefore God here proceeds to reason with him in the same manner and to the same purport as before, *v.* 6. Observe, 1. Those who duly receive what they have heard from God, and profit by it, shall hear more from him. 2. Those who are truly convinced of sin, and penitent for it, yet have need to be more thoroughly convinced and to be made more deeply penitent. Those who are under convictions, who have their sins set in order before their eyes and their hearts broken for them, must learn from this instance not to catch at comfort too soon; it will be everlasting when it comes, and therefore it is necessary that we be prepared for it by deep humiliation, that the wound be searched to the bottom and not skinned over, and that we do not make more haste out of our convictions than good speed. When our hearts begin to melt and relent within us, let those considerations be dwelt upon and pursued which will help to make a thorough effectual thaw of it.

God begins with a challenge (*v.* 7), as before (*ch.* 38:3): *"Gird up thy loins now like a man;* if thou hast the courage and confidence thou hast pretended to, show them now; but thou wilt soon be made to see and own thyself no match for me." This is that which every proud heart must be brought to at last, either by its repentance or by its ruin; and thus low must every mountain and hill be, sooner or later, brought. We must acknowledge,

I. That we cannot vie with God for justice, that the Lord is righteous and holy in his dealings with us, but that we are unrighteous and unholy in our conduct towards him; we have a great deal to blame ourselves for, but nothing to blame him for (*v.* 8): *"Wilt thou disannul my judgment?* Wilt thou take exceptions to what I say and do, and bring a writ of error, to reverse the judgment I have given as erroneous and unjust?" Many of Job's complaints had too much of a tendency this way: *I cry out of wrong,* says he, *but I am not heard;* but such language as this is by no means to be suffered. God's judgment cannot, must not, be disannulled, for we are sure it is according to truth, and therefore it is a great piece of impudence and iniquity in us to call in question. *"Wilt thou,"* says God, *"condemn me, that thou mayest be righteous?* Must my honour suffer for the support of thy reputation? Must I be charged as dealing unjustly with thee because thou canst not otherwise clear thyself from the censures thou liest under?" Our duty is to condemn ourselves, that God may be righteous. David is *therefore* ready to own the evil he has done in God's sight, that *God may be justified when he speaks and clear when he judges,* Ps. 51:4. See Neh. 9:33; Dan. 9:7. But those are very proud, and very ignorant both of God and themselves, who, to clear themselves, will condemn God; and the day is coming when, if the mistake be not rectified in time by repentance, the eternal judgment will be both the confutation of the plea and the confusion of the prisoner, for the heavens shall declare God's righteousness and all the world shall become guilty before him.

II. That we cannot vie with God for power; and therefore, as it is great impiety, so it is great impudence to contest with him, and is as much against our interest as it is against reason and justice (*v.* 9): *"Hast thou an arm like God,* equal to his in length and strength? *Or canst thou thunder with a voice like him,* as he did (*ch.* 37:1, 2), or does now out of the whirlwind?" To convince Job that he was not so able as he thought himself to contest with God, he shows him, 1. That he could never fight it out with him, nor carry his cause by force of arms. Sometimes, among men, controversies have been decided by battle, and the victorious champion is adjudged to have justice on his side; but, if the controversy were put upon that issue between God and man, man would certainly go by the worse, for all the forces he could raise against the Almighty would be but like briers and thorns before a consuming fire, Isa. 27:4. "Hast thou, a poor weak worm of the earth, an arm comparable to his who upholds all things?" The power of creatures, even of angels themselves, is derived from God, limited by him, and dependent on him; but the power of God is original, independent, and unlimited. He can do every thing without us; we can do nothing without him; and therefore we have not an arm like God. 2. That he could never talk it out with him, nor carry his cause by noise and big words, which sometimes among men go a great way towards the gaining of a point: *"Canst thou thunder with a voice like him?* No; his voice will soon drown thine and one of his thunders will overpower and overrule all thy whispers." Man cannot speak so convincingly, so powerfully, nor with such a commanding conquering force as God can, who *speaks, and it is done.* his creating voice is called his *thunder* (Ps. 104:7), so is that voice of his with which he terrifies and discomfits his enemies, 1 Sa. 2:10. The wrath of a king may sometimes be like the roaring of a lion, but can never pretend to imitate God's thunder.

III. That we cannot vie with God for beauty and majesty, *v.* 10. "If thou wilt enter into a comparison with him, and appear more amiable, put on thy best attire: *Deck thyself now with majesty and excellency.* Appear in all the martial pomp, in all the royal pageantry that thou hast; make the best of every thing that will set thee off: *Array thyself with glory and beauty,* such as may awe thy enemies and charm thy friends; but what is it all to the divine majesty and beauty? No more than the light of a glow-worm to that of the sun when he goes forth in his strength." God decks himself with such majesty and glory as are the terror of devils and all the powers of darkness and make them tremble; he arrays himself with such glory and beauty as are the wonder of angels and all the saints in light and make them rejoice. David could dwell all his days in God's house, to behold the beauty of the Lord. But, in comparison with this, what is all the majesty and excellency by which princes think to make themselves feared, and all the glory and beauty by which lovers think to make themselves beloved? If Job think, in contending with God, to carry the day by looking great and making a figure, he is quite mistaken. *The sun shall be ashamed, and the moon confounded, when God shines forth.*

IV. That we cannot vie with God for dominion over the proud, *v.* 11–14. here the cause is put upon this short issue: if Job can humble and abase proud tyrants and oppressors as easily and effectually as God can, it shall be acknowledged that he has some colour to compete with God. Observe here,

1. The justice Job is here challenged to do, and that is to bring the proud low with a look. If Job will pretend to be a rival with God, especially if he pretend to be a judge of his actions, he must be able to do this.

(1.) It is here supposed that God can do it and will do it himself, else he would not have put it thus upon Job. By this God proves himself to be God, that he resists the proud, sits Judge upon them, and is able to bring them to ruin. Observe here, [1.] That proud people are wicked people, and pride is at the bottom of a great deal of the wickedness that is in this world both towards God and man. [2.] Proud people will certainly be abased and brought low; for *pride goes before destruction.* If they bend not, they will break; if they humble not themselves by true repentance, God will humble them, to their everlasting confusion. The wicked will be *trodden down in their place,* that is, Wherever they are found, though they pretend to have a place of their own, and to have taken root in it, yet even there they shall be trodden down, and all the wealth, and power, and interest, to which their place entitles them, will not be their security. [3.] The wrath of God, scattered among the proud, will humble them, and break them, and bring them down. If he casts abroad the rage of his wrath, as he will do at the great day and sometimes does in this life, the stoutest heart cannot hold out against him. *Who knows the power of his anger?* [4.] God can and does easily abase proud tyrants; he can *look upon them, and bring them low,* can overwhelm them with shame, and fear, and utter ruin, by one angry look, as he can, by a gracious look, revive the hearts of the contrite ones. [5.] He can and will at last do it effectually (*v.* 13), not only bring them to the dust, from which they might hope to arise, but *hide them in the dust,* like the proud Egyptian whom Moses slew and *hid in the sand* (Ex. 2:12), that is, they shall be brought not only to death, but to the grave, that pit out of which there is no return. They were proud of the figure they made, but they shall be buried in oblivion and be no more remembered than those that are hidden in the dust, out of sight and out of mind. They were linked in leagues and confederacies to do mischief, and are now bound in bundles. They are hidden *together;* not their rest, but their shame together *is in the dust, ch.* 17:16. Nay, they are treated as malefactors (who, when condemned, had their faces covered, as Haman's was: He *binds their faces in secret*) or as dead men: Lazarus, in the grave, had his face bound about. Thus complete will be the victory that God will gain, at last, over proud sinners that set themselves in opposition to him. Now by this he proves himself to be God. Does he thus hate proud men? Then he is holy. Will he thus punish them? Then he is the just Judge of the world. Can he thus humble them? Then he is the Lord Almighty. When he had abased proud Pharaoh, and hidden him in the sand of the Red Sea, Jethro thence inferred that doubtless *the Lord is greater than all gods, for wherein the proud* enemies of his *Israel dealt proudly he was above them,* he was too hard for them, Ex. 18:11. See Rev. 19:1, 2.

(2.) It is here proposed to Job to do it. He had been passionately quarrelling with God and his providence, casting abroad the rage of his wrath towards heaven, as if he thought thereby to bring God himself to his mind. "Come," says God, "try thy hand first upon proud men, and thou wilt soon see how little they value the rage of thy wrath; and shall I then regard it, or be moved by it?" Job had complained of the prosperity and power of tyrants and oppressors, and was ready to charge God with maladministration for suffering it; but he ought not to find fault, except he could mend. If God, and he only, has power enough to humble and bring down proud men, no doubt he has wisdom enough to know when and how to do it, and it is not for us to prescribe to him or to teach him how to prescribe to him or to teach him how to govern the world. Unless we had an arm like God we must not think to take his work out of his hands.

2. The justice which is here promised to be done him if he can perform such mighty works as these (*v.* 14): *"They will I also confess unto thee that thy right hand* is sufficient to save thee, though, after all, it would be too weak to contend with me." It is the innate pride and ambition of man that he would be his own saviour (would have his own hands sufficient for him and be independent), but it is presumption to pretend that he is. Our own hands cannot save us by recommending us to God's grace, much less by rescuing us from his justice. Unless we could by our own power humble our enemies, we cannot pretend by our own power to save ourselves; but, if we could, God himself would confess it. He never did nor ever will defraud any man of his just praise, nor deny him the honour he has merited. But, since we cannot do this, we must confess unto him that our own hands cannot save us, and therefore into his hand we must commit ourselves.

Verses 15–24

God, for the further proving of his own power and disproving of Job's pretensions, concludes his discourse with the description of two vast and mighty animals, far exceeding man in bulk and strength, one he calls *behemoth,* the other *leviathan.* In these verses we have the former described. *"Behold now behemoth,* and consider whether thou art able to contend with him who made that beast and gave him all the power he has, and whether it is not thy wisdom rather to submit to him and make thy peace with him." *Behemoth* signifies *beasts* in general, but must here be meant of some one particular species. Some understand it of the *bull;* others of an amphibious animal, well known (they say) in Egypt, called the *river-horse (hippopotamus),* living among the fish in the river Nile, but coming out to feed upon the earth. But I confess I see no reason to depart from the ancient and most generally received opinion, that it is the elephant that is here described, which is a very strong stately creature, of very large stature above any other, of wonderful sagacity, and of so great a reputation in the animal kingdom that among so many four-footed beasts as we have had the natural history of (*ch.* 38 and 39) we can scarcely suppose this should be omitted. Observe,

I. The description here given of the behemoth.

1. His body is very strong and well built. *His strength is in his loins, v.* 16. *His bones,* compared with those of other creatures, *are like bars of iron, v.* 18. His back-bone is so strong that, though his tail be not large, yet he moves it like a cedar, with a commanding force, *v.* 17. Some understand it of the trunk of the elephant, for the word signifies any extreme part, and in that there is indeed a wonderful strength. So strong is the elephant in his back and loins, and the sinews of his thighs, that he will carry a large wooden tower, and a great number of fighting men in it. No animal whatsoever comes near the elephant for strength of body, which is the main thing insisted on in this description.

2. He feeds on the productions of the earth and does not prey upon other animals: He *eats grass as an ox* (*v.* 15), the *mountains bring him forth food* (*v.* 20), and the beasts of the field do not tremble before him nor flee from him, as from a lion, but they play about him, knowing they are in no danger from him. This may give us occasion, (1.) To acknowledge the goodness of God in ordering it so that a creature of such bulk, which requires so much food, should not feed upon flesh (for then multitudes must die to keep him alive), but should be content with the grass of the field, to prevent such destruction of lives as otherwise must have ensued. (2.) To commend living upon herbs and fruits without flesh, according to the original appointment of man's food, Gen. 1:29. Even the strength of an elephant, as of a horse and an ox, may be supported without flesh; and why not that of a man? Though therefore we use the liberty God has allowed us, yet *be not among riotous eaters of flesh,* Prov. 23:20. (3.) To commend a quiet and peaceable life. Who would not rather, like the elephant, have his neighbours easy and pleasant about him, than, like the lion, have them all afraid of him?

3. He *lodges under the shady trees* (*v.* 21), which *cover him with their shadow* (*v.* 22), where he has a free and open air to breathe in, while lions, which live by prey, when they would repose themselves, are obliged to retire into a close and dark den, to live therein, and to abide in the covert of that, *ch.* 38:40. Those who are a terror to others cannot but be sometimes a terror to themselves too; but those will be easy who will let others be easy about them; and the reed and fens, and the willows of the brook, though a very weak and slender fortification, yet are sufficient for the defence and security of those who *therefore* dread no harm, because they design none.

4. That he is a very great and greedy drinker, not of wine or strong drink (to be greedy of that is peculiar to man, who by his drunkenness makes a beast of himself), but of fair water. (1.) His size is prodigious, and therefore he must have supply accordingly, *v.* 23. He drinks so much that one would think he could drink up a river, if you would give him time, and not hasten him. Or, when he drinks, *he hasteth not,* as those do that drink in fear; he is confident of his own strength and safety, and therefore makes no haste when he drinks, no more haste than good speed. (2.) His eye anticipates more than he can take; for, when he is very thirsty, having been long kept without water, *he trusts that he can drink up Jordan in his mouth,* and even *takes it with his eyes, v.* 24. As a covetous man causes his eyes to fly upon the wealth of this world, which he is greedy of, so this great beast is said to snatch, or draw up, even a river with his eyes. (3.) His nose has in it strength

enough for both; for, when he goes greedily to drink with it, he *pierces through snares* or nets, which perhaps are laid in the waters to catch fish. He makes nothing of the difficulties that lie in his way, so great is his strength and so eager his appetite.

II. The use that is to be made of this description. We have taken a view of this mountain of a beast, this overgrown animal, which is here set before us, not merely as a show (as sometimes it is in our country) to satisfy our curiosity and to amuse us, but as an argument with us to humble ourselves before the great God; for, 1. He made this vast animal, which is so fearfully and wonderfully made; it is the work of his hands, the contrivance of his wisdom, the production of his power; it is *behemoth which I made, v.* 15. Whatever strength this, or any other creature, has, it is derived from God, who therefore must be acknowledged to have all power originally and infinitely in himself, and such an arm as it is not for us to contest with. This beast is here called *the chief,* in its kind, *of the ways of God* (*v.* 19), an eminent instance of the Creator's power and wisdom. Those that will peruse the accounts given by historians of the elephant will find that his capacities approach nearer to those of reason than the capacities of any other brute-creature whatsoever, and therefore he is fitly called *the chief of the ways of God,* in the inferior part of the creation, no creature below man being preferable to him. 2. He made him with man, as he made other four-footed beasts, on the same day with man (Gen. 1:25, 26), whereas the fish and fowl were made the day before; he made him to live and move on the same earth, in the same element, and therefore man and beast are said to be jointly preserved by divine Providence as fellow-commoners, Ps. 36:6. "It is *behemoth, which I made with thee;* I made that beast as well as thee, and he does not quarrel with me; why then dost thou? Why shouldst thou demand peculiar favours because I made thee (*ch.* 10:9), when I made the *behemoth* likewise with thee? I made thee as well as that beast, and therefore can as easily manage thee at pleasure as that beast, and will do it whether thou refuse or whether thou choose. I made him with thee, that thou mayest look upon him and receive instruction." We need not go far for proofs and instances of God's almighty power and sovereign dominion; they are near us, they are with us, they are under our eye wherever we are. 3. *He that made him can make his sword to approach to him* (*v.* 19), that is, the same hand that made him, notwithstanding his great bulk and strength, can unmake him again at pleasure and kill an elephant as easily as a worm or a fly, without any difficulty, and without the imputation either of waste or wrong. God that gave to all the creatures their being may take away the being he gave; for may he not do what he will with his own? And he *can* do it; he that has power to create with a word no doubt has power to destroy with a word, and can as easily speak the creature into nothing as at first he spoke it out of nothing. The *behemoth* perhaps is here intended (as well as the *leviathan* afterwards) to represent those proud tyrants and oppressors whom God had just now challenged Job to abase and bring down. They think themselves as well fortified against the judgments of God as the elephant with his bones of brass and iron; but he that made the soul of man knows all the avenues to it, and can make the sword of justice, his wrath, to approach to it, and touch it in the most tender and sensible part. He that framed the engine, and put the parts of it together, knows how to take it in pieces. Woe to him therefore that strives with his Maker, for he that made him has therefore power to make him miserable, and will not make him happy unless he will be ruled by him.

CHAPTER 41

The description here given of the leviathan, a very large, strong, formidable fish, or water-animal, is designed yet further to convince Job of his own impotency, and of God's omnipotence, that he might be humbled for his folly in making so bold with him as he had done. I. To convince Job of his own weakness he is here challenged to subdue and tame this leviathan if he can, and make himself master of him (*v.* 1–9), and, since he cannot do this, he must own himself utterly unable to stand before the great God (*v.* 10). II. To convince Job of God's power and terrible majesty several particular instances are here given of the strength and terror of the leviathan, which is no more than what God has given him, nor more than he has under his check, (*v.* 11, 12). The face of the leviathan is here described to be terrible (*v.* 12, 14), his scales close (*v.* 15–17), his breath and neesings sparkling (*v.* 18–21), his flesh firm (*v.* 22–24), his strength and spirit, when he is attacked, insuperable (*v.* 25–30), his motions turbulent, and disturbing to the waters (*v.* 31, 32), so that, upon the whole, he is a very terrible creature, and man is no match for him (*v.* 33, 34).

Verses 1–10

Whether this leviathan be a whale or a crocodile is a great dispute among the learned, which I will not undertake to determine; some of the particulars agree more easily to the one, others to the other; both are very strong and fierce, and the power of the Creator appears in them. The ingenious Sir Richard Blackmore, though he admits the more received opinion concerning the *behemoth,* that it must be meant of the *elephant,* yet agrees with the learned Bochart's notion of the *leviathan,* that it is the *crocodile,* which was so well known in the river of Egypt. I confess that that which inclines me rather to understand it of the whale is not only because it is much larger and a nobler animal, but because, in the history of the Creation, there is such an express notice taken of it as is not of any other species of animals whatsoever (Gen. 1:21, *God created great whales*), by which it appears, not only that whales were well known in those parts in the time of Moses, who lived a little after Job, but that the creation of whales was generally looked upon as a most illustrious proof of the eternal power and godhead of the Creator; and we may conjecture that this was the reason (for otherwise it seems unaccountable) why Moses there so particularly mentions the creation of the whales, because God had so lately insisted upon the bulk and strength of that creature than of any other, as the proof of his power; and the *leviathan* is here spoken of as an inhabitant of the sea (*v.* 31), which the crocodile is not; and Ps. 104:25, 26, *there* in *the great and wide sea, is that leviathan.* Here in these verses,

I. He shows how unable Job was to master the leviathan. 1. That he could not catch him, as a little fish, with angling, *v.* 1, 2. He had no bait wherewith to deceive him, no hook wherewith to catch him, no fish-line wherewith to draw him out of the water, nor a thorn to run through his gills, on which to carry him home. 2. That he could not make him his prisoner, nor force him to cry for quarter, or surrender himself at discretion, *v.* 3, 4. "He knows his own strength too well to *make many supplications to thee,* and to *make a covenant with thee* to be thy servant on condition thou wilt save his life." 3. That he could not entice him into a cage, and keep him there as a bird for the children to play with, *v.* 5. There are creatures so little, so weak, as to be easily restrained thus, and triumphed over; but the leviathan is not one of these: he is made to be the terror, not the sport and diversion, of mankind. 4. That he could not have him served up to his table; he and his companions could not make a banquet of him; his flesh is too strong to be fit for food, and, if it were not, he is not easily caught. 5. That they could not enrich themselves with the spoil of him: *Shall they part him among the merchants,* the bones to one, the oil to another? If they can catch him, they will; but it is probable that the art of fishing for whales was not brought to perfection then, as it has been since. 6. That they could not destroy him, could not *fill his head with fish-spears, v.* 7. He kept out of the reach of their instruments of slaughter, or, if they touched him, they could not touch him to the quick. 7. That it was to no purpose to attempt it: *The hope of* taking *him is in vain, v.* 9. If men go about to seize him, so formidable is he that the very sight of him will appal them, and make a stout man ready to faint away: *Shall not one be cast down even at the sight of him?* and will not that deter the pursuers from their attempt? Job is told, at his peril, to *lay his hand upon him, v.* 8. "Touch him if thou dare; *remember the battle,* how unable thou art to encounter such a force, and what is therefore likely to be the issue of the battle, *and do no more,* but desist from the attempt." It is good to remember the battle before we engage in a war, and put off the harness in time if we foresee it will be to no purpose to gird it on. Job is hereby admonished not to proceed in his controversy with God, but to make his peace with him, remembering what the battle will certainly end in if he come to an engagement. See Isa. 27:4, 5.

II. Thence he infers how unable he was to contend with the Almighty. *None is so fierce,* none so fool-hardy, *that he dares* to *stir up* the leviathan (*v.* 10), it being known that he will certainly be too hard for them; and *who then is able to stand before God,* either to impeach and arraign his proceedings or to out-face the power of his wrath? If the inferior creatures that are put under the feet of man, and over whom he has dominion, keep us in awe thus, how terrible must the majesty of our great Lord be, who has a sovereign dominion over us and against whom man has been so long in rebellion! *Who can stand before him when once he is angry?*

Verses 11–34

God, having in the foregoing verses shown Job how unable he was to deal with the leviathan, here sets forth his own power in that massy mighty creature. Here is,

I. God's sovereign dominion and independency laid down, *v.* 11. 1. That he is indebted to none of his creatures. If any pretend he is indebted to them, let them make their demand and prove their debt, and they shall receive it in full and not by composition: *"Who has prevented me?"* that is, "who has laid any obligations upon me by any services he has done me? Who can pretend to be before-hand with me? If any were, I would not long be behind-hand with them; I would soon repay them." The apostle quotes this for the silencing of all flesh in God's presence, Rom. 11:35. *Who hath first given to him, and it shall be recompensed to him again?* As God does not inflict upon us the evils we have deserved, so he does bestow upon us the favours we have not deserved. 2. That he is the rightful Lord and owner of all the creatures: *"Whatsoever is under the whole heaven,* animate or inanimate, *is mine* (and particularly this leviathan), at my command and disposal, what I have an incontestable property in and dominion over." All is his; we are his, all we have and do; and therefore we cannot make God our debtor; but *of thy own, Lord, have we given thee.* All is his, and therefore, if he were indebted to any, he has wherewithal to repay them; the debt is in good hands. All is his, and therefore he needs not our services, nor can he be benefited by them. *If I were hungry I would not tell thee, for the world is mind and the fulness thereof,* Ps. 50:12.

II. The proof and illustration of it, from the wonderful structure of the leviathan, *v.* 12.

1. The parts of his body, the power he exerts, especially when he is set upon, and the comely proportion of the whole of him, are what God will not conceal, and therefore what we must observe and acknowledge the power of God in. Though he is a creature of monstrous bulk, yet there is in him a *comely proportion.* In our eye beauty lies in that which is small *(inest sua gratia parvis — little things have a gracefulness all their own)* because we ourselves are so; but in God's eye even the leviathan is comely; and, if he pronounce even the whale, event he crocodile, so, it is not for us to say of any of the works of his hands that they are ugly of ill-favoured; it is enough to say so, as we have cause, of our own works. God here goes about to give us an anatomical view (as it were) of the leviathan; for his works appear most beautiful and excellent, and his wisdom and power appear most in them, when they are taken in pieces and viewed in their several parts and proportions. (1.) The leviathan, even *prima facie — at first sight,* appears formidable and inaccessible, *v.* 13, 14. Who dares come so near him while he is alive as to discover or take a distinct view of *the face of the garment,* the skin with which he is clothed as with a garment, so near him as to bridle him like a horse and so lead him away, so near him as to be within reach of his jaws, which are like *a double bridle?* Who will venture to look into his mouth, as we do into a horse's mouth? He that *opens the doors of his face* will see *his teeth terrible round about,* strong and sharp, and fitted to devour; it would make a man tremble to think of having a leg or an arm between them. (2.) *His scales are* his beauty and strength, and therefore *his pride, v.* 15–17. The crocodile is indeed remarkable for his scales; if we understand it of the whale, we must understand by these *shields* (for so the word is) the several coats of his skin; or there might be whales in that country with scales. That which is remarkable concerning the scales is that *they stick* so close *together,* by which he is not only kept warm, for no air can pierce him, but kept safe, for no sword can pierce him through those scales. Fishes, that live in the water, are fortified accordingly by the wisdom of Providence, which gives clothes as it gives cold. (3.) He scatters

terror with his very breath and looks; if he sneeze or spout up water, it is like a light shining, either with the froth or the light of the sun shining through it, *v.* 18. The eyes of the whale are reported to shine in the night-time like a flame, or, as here, *like the eye-lids of the morning;* the same they say of the crocodile. The breath of this creature is so hot and fiery, from the great natural heat within, that *burning lamps and sparks of fire,* smoke and a flame, are said to *go out of his mouth,* even such as one would think sufficient to set coals on fire, *v.* 19–21. Probably these hyperbolical expressions are used concerning the leviathan to intimate the terror of the wrath of God, for that is it which all this is designed to convince us of. *Fire out of his mouth devours,* Ps. 18:7, 8. *The breath of the Almighty,* like a *stream of brimstone, kindles Tophet,* and will for ever keep it burning, Isa. 30:33. The wicked one shall be *consumed with the breath of his mouth,* 2 Th. 2:8. (4.) He is of invincible strength and most terrible fierceness, so that he frightens all that come in his way, but is not himself frightened by any. Take a view of his neck, and there remains strength, *v.* 22. his head and his body are well set together. *Sorrow rejoices* (or *rides in triumph) before him,* for he makes terrible work wherever he comes. Or, Those storms which are the sorrow of others are his joys; what is tossing to others is dancing to him. His flesh is well knit, *v.* 23. *The flakes* of it *are joined* so closely *together,* and *are so firm,* that it is hard to pierce it; he is as if he were all bone. *His flesh is of brass,* which Job had complained his was not, *ch.* 6:12. *His heart is as firm as a stone, v.* 24. He has spirit equal to his bodily strength, and, though he is bulky, he is sprightly, and not unwieldy. As his flesh and skin cannot be pierced, so his courage cannot be daunted; but, on the contrary, he daunts all he meets and puts them into a consternation (*v.* 25): *When he raises up himself* like a moving mountain in the great waters even *the mighty are afraid* lest he should overturn their ships or do them some other mischief. *By reason of the breakings* he makes in the water, which threaten death, *they purify themselves,* confess their sins, betake themselves to their prayers, and get ready for death. We read (*ch.* 3:8) of those who, when they raise up a leviathan, are in such a fright that they curse the day. It was a fear which, it seems, used to drive some to their curses and others to their prayers; for, as now, so then there were seafaring men of different characters and on whom the terrors of the sea have contrary effects; but all agree there is a great fright among them when the leviathan raises up himself. (5.) All the instruments of slaughter that are used against him do him no hurt and therefore are not error to him, *v.* 26–29. *The sword* and *the spear,* which wound nigh at hand, are nothing to him; the *darts, arrows,* and *sling-stones,* which wound at a distance, do him no damage; nature has so well armed him *cap-a-pie — at all points,* against them all. The defensive weapons which men use when they engage with the leviathan, as *the habergeon,* or breast-plate, often serve men no more than their offensive weapons; *iron and brass* are to him *as straw and rotten wood,* and he laughs at them. It is the picture of a hard-hearted sinner, that despises the terrors of the Almighty and laughs at all the threatenings of his word. The leviathan so little dreads the weapons that are used against him that, to show how hardy he is, he chooses to lie on the *sharp stones, the sharp-pointed things* (*v.* 30), and lies as easy there as if he lay on the soft mire. Those that would endure hardness must inure themselves to it. (6.) His very motion in the water troubles it and puts it into a ferment, *v.* 31, 32. When he rolls, and tosses, and makes a stir in the water, or is in pursuit of his prey, *he makes the deep to boil like a pot,* he raises a great froth and foam upon the water, such as is upon a boiling pot, especially *a pot of* boiling *ointment;* and *he makes a path to shine after him,* which even *a ship in the midst of the sea* does not, Prov. 30:19. One may trace the leviathan under water by the bubbles on the surface; and yet who can take that advantage against him in pursuing him? Men track hares in the snow and kill them, but he that tracks the leviathan dares not come near him.

2. Having given this particular account of *his parts, and his power, and his comely proportion,* he concludes with four things in general concerning this animal: — (1.) That he is a non-such among the inferior creatures: *Upon earth there is not his like, v.* 33. No creature in this world is comparable to him for strength and terror. Or the earth is here distinguished from the sea: *His dominion is not upon the earth* (so some), but *in the waters.* None of all the savage creatures upon earth come near him for bulk and strength, and it is well for man that he is confined to the waters and there has *a watch set upon him* (*ch.* 7:12) by the divine Providence, for, if such a terrible creature were allowed to roam and ravage upon this earth, it would be an unsafe and uncomfortable habitation for the children of men, for whom it is intended. (2.) That he is more bold and daring than any other creature whatsoever: He *is made without fear.* The creatures are as they are made; the leviathan has courage in his constitution, nothing can frighten him; other creatures, quite contrary, seem as much designed for flying as this for fighting. So, among men, some are in their natural temper bold, others are timorous. (3.) That he is himself very proud; though lodged in the deep, yet *he beholds all high things, v.* 34. The rolling waves, the impending rocks, the hovering clouds, and the ships under sail with top and top-gallant, this mighty animal beholds with contempt, for he does not think they either lessen him or threaten him. Those that are great are apt to be scornful. (4.) *That he is a king over all the children of pride,* that is, he is the proudest of all proud ones. He has more to be proud of (so Mr. Caryl expounds it) than the proudest people in the world have; and so it is a mortification to the haughtiness and lofty looks of men. Whatever bodily accomplishments men are proud of, and puffed up with, the leviathan excels them and is a *king over them.* Some read it so as to understand it of God: *He that beholds all high things, even he, is King over all the children of pride;* he can tame the behemoth (*ch.* 40:19) and the leviathan, big as they are, and stout-hearted as they are. This discourse concerning those two animals was brought in to prove that it is God only who can *look upon proud men and abase them, bring them low* and *tread them down,* and *hide them in the dust* (*ch.* 40:11–13), and so it concludes with a *quod erat demonstrandum — which was to be demonstrated;* there is one that *beholds all high things,* and, wherein men deal proudly, is above them; he is *King over all the children of pride,* whether brutal or rational, and can make them all either bend or break before him, Isa. 2:11. *The lofty looks of man shall be humbled, and the haughtiness of men shall be bowed down, and* thus *the Lord alone shall be exalted.*

CHAPTER 42

Solomon says, "Better is the end of a thing than the beginning thereof," Eccl. 7:8. It was so here in the story of Job; at the evening-time it was light. Three things we have met with in this book which, I confess , have troubled me very much; but we find all the three grievances redressed, thoroughly redressed, in this chapter, everything set to-rights. I. It has been a great trouble to us to see such a holy man as Job was so fretful, and peevish, and uneasy to himself, and especially to hear him quarrel with God and speak indecently to him; but, though he thus fall, he is not utterly cast down, for here he recovers his temper, comes to himself and to his right mind again by repentance, is sorry for what he has said amiss, unsays it, and humbles himself before God (*v.* 1–6). II. It has been likewise a great trouble to us to see Job and his friends so much at variance, not only differing in their opinions, but giving one another a great many hard words, and passing severe censures one upon another, though they were all very wise and good men; but here we have this grievance redressed likewise, the differences between them happily adjusted, the quarrel taken up, all the peevish reflections they had cast upon one another forgiven and forgotten, and all joining in sacrifices and prayers, mutually accepted of God (*v.* 7–9). III. It has troubled us to see a man of such eminent piety and usefulness as Job was so grievously afflicted, so pained, so sick, so poor, so reproached, so slighted, and made the very centre of all the calamities of human life; but here we have this grievance redressed too, Job healed of all his ailments, more honoured and beloved than ever, enriched with an estate double to what he had before, surrounded with all the comforts of life, and as great an instance of prosperity as ever he had been of affliction and patience (*v.* 10–17). All this is written for our learning, that we, under these and the like discouragements that we meet with, through patience and comfort of this scripture may have hope.

Verses 1–6

The words of Job justifying himself were ended, *ch.* 31:40. After that he said no more to that purport. The words of Job judging and condemning himself began, *ch.* 40:4, 5. Here he goes on with words to the same purport. Though his patience had not its perfect work, his repentance for his impatience had. He is here thoroughly humbled for his folly and unadvised speaking, and it was forgiven him. Good men will see and own their faults at last, though it may be some difficulty to bring them to do this. *Then,* when God had said all that to him concerning his own greatness and power appearing in the creatures, *then Job answered the Lord* (*v.* 1), not by way of contradiction (he had promised not so to answer again, *ch.* 40:5), but by way of submission; and thus we must all answer the calls of God.

I. He subscribes to the truth of God's unlimited power, knowledge, and dominion, to prove which was the scope of God's discourse out of the whirlwind, *v.* 2. Corrupt passions and practices arise either from some corrupt principles or from the neglect and disbelief of the principles of truth; and therefore true repentance begins in *the acknowledgement of the truth,* 2 Tim. 2:25. Job here owns his judgment convinced of the greatness, glory, and perfection of God, from which would follow the conviction of his conscience concerning his own folly in speaking irreverently to him. 1. He owns that God can do every thing. What can be too hard for him that made behemoth and leviathan, and manages both as he pleases? He knew this before, and had himself discoursed very well upon the subject, but now he knew it with application. *God had spoken* it once, and then he heard it twice, that *power belongs to God;* and therefore it is the greatest madness and presumption imaginable to contend with him. *"Thou canst do every thing,* and therefore canst raise me out of this low condition, which I have so often foolishly despaired of as impossible: I now believe thou art able to do this." 2. That *no thought can be withholden from him,* that is, (1.) There is no thought of ours that he can be hindered from the knowledge of. Not a fretful, discontented, unbelieving thought is in our minds at any time but God is a witness to it. It is in vain to contest with him; for we cannot hide our counsels and projects from him, and, if he discover them, he can defeat them. (2.) There is no thought of his that he can be hindered from the execution of. *Whatever the Lord pleased, that did he.* Job had said this passionately, complaining of it (*ch.* 23:13), *What his soul desireth even that he doeth;* now he says, with pleasure and satisfaction, that *God's counsels shall stand.* If God's thoughts concerning us be *thoughts of good, to give us an unexpected end,* he cannot be withheld from accomplishing his gracious purposes, whatever difficulties may seem to lie in the way.

II. He owns himself to be guilty of that which God had charged him with in the beginning of his discourse, *v.* 3. "Lord, the first word thou saidst was, *Who is this that darkens counsel by words without knowledge?* There needed no more; that word convinced me. I own *I am the man* that has been so foolish. That word reached my conscience, and set my sin in order before me. It is too plain to be denied, too bad to be excused. I have hidden *counsel without knowledge.* I have ignorantly overlooked the counsels and designs of God in afflicting me, and therefore have quarrelled with God, and insisted too much upon my own justification: *Therefore I uttered that which I understood not,"* that is, "I have passed a judgment upon the dispensations of Providence, though I was utterly a stranger to the reasons of them." Here, 1. He owns himself ignorant of the divine counsels; and so we are all. God's judgments are a great deep, which we cannot fathom, much less find out the springs of. We see what God does, but we neither know why he does it, what he is aiming at, nor what he will bring it to. These are things too wonderful for us, out of our sight to discover, out of our reach to alter, and out of our jurisdiction to judge of. They are things which we know not; it is quite above our capacity to pass a verdict upon them. The reason why we quarrel with Providence is because we do not understand it; and we must be content to be in the dark about it, until the mystery of God shall be finished. 2. He owns himself imprudent and presumptuous in undertaking to discourse of that which he did not understand and to arraign that which he could not judge of. *He that answereth a matter before he heareth it, it is folly and shame to him.* We wrong ourselves, as well as the cause which we undertake to determine, while we are no competent judges of it.

III. He will not answer, but he will *make supplication to his Judge,* as he had said, *ch.* 9:15. *"Hear, I beseech thee, and I will speak* (*v.* 4), not speak either as plaintiff or defendant (*ch.* 13:22), but as a humble petitioner, not as one that will undertake to teach and prescribe, but as one that desires to learn and is willing to be prescribed to. Lord, put no more hard questions to me, for I am not able to answer thee one of a thousand of those which thou hast put; but give me leave to ask instruction from thee, and do not deny it me, do not upbraid me with my folly and self-sufficiency," Jam. 1:5. Now he is brought to the prayer Elihu taught him, *That which I see not teach thou me.*

IV. He puts himself into the posture of a penitent, and therein goes upon a right principle. In true repentance there must be not only conviction of sin, but contrition and godly sorrow for it, sorrow *according to God,* 2 Co. 7:9. Such was Job's sorrow for his sins.

1. Job had an eye to God in his repentance, thought highly of him, and went upon that as the principle of it (*v.* 5): *"I have heard of thee by the hearing of the ear* many a time from my teachers when I was young, from my friends now of late. I have known something of thy greatness, and power, and sovereign dominion; and yet was not brought, by what I heard, to submit myself to thee as I ought. The notions I had of these things served me only to talk of, and had not a due influence upon my mind. *But now* thou hast by immediate revelation discovered thyself to me in thy glorious majesty; *now my eyes see thee;* now I feel the power of those truths which before I had only the notion of, and therefore now I repent, and unsay what I have foolishly said." Note, (1.) It is a great mercy to have a good education, and to know the things of God by the instructions of his word and ministers. *Faith comes by hearing,* and then it is most likely to come when we hear attentively and with the *hearing of the ear.* (2.) When the understanding is enlightened by the Spirit of grace our knowledge of divine things as far exceeds what we had before as that by ocular demonstration exceeds that by report and common fame. By the teachings of men God reveals his Son to us; but by the teachings of his Spirit he reveals his Son in us (Gal. 1:16), and so *changes us into the same image,* 2 Co. 3:18. (3.) God is pleased sometimes to manifest himself most fully to his people by the rebukes of his word and providence. "Now that I have been afflicted, now that I have been told of my faults, now my eye sees thee." *The rod and reproof give wisdom. Blessed is the man whom thou chastenest and teachest.*

2. Job had an eye to himself in his repentance, thought hardly of himself, and thereby expressed his sorrow for his sins (*v.* 6): *Wherefore I abhor myself, and repent in dust and ashes.* Observe, (1.) It concerns us to be deeply humbled for the sins we are convinced of, and not to rest in a slight superficial displeasure against ourselves for them. Even good people, that have no gross enormities to repent of, must be greatly afflicted in soul for the workings and breakings out of pride, passion, peevishness, and discontent, and all their hasty unadvised speeches; for these we must be pricked to the heart and be in bitterness. Till the enemy be effectually humbled, the peace will be insecure. (2.) Outward expressions of godly sorrow well become penitents; Job repented in dust and ashes. These, without an inward change, do but mock God; but, where they come from sincere contrition of soul, the sinner by them gives glory to God, takes shame to himself, and may be instrumental to bring others to repentance. Job's afflictions had brought him to the ashes (*ch.* 2:8, he *sat down among the ashes*), but now his sins brought him thither. True penitents mourn for their sins as heartily as ever they did for any outward afflictions, and are in bitterness as for an only son of a first-born, for they are brought to see more evils in their sins than in their troubles. (3.) Self-loathing is evermore the companion of true repentance. Eze. 6:9, *They shall loathe themselves for the evils which they have committed.* We must no only angry at ourselves for the wrong and damage we have by sin done to our own souls, but must abhor ourselves, as having by sin made ourselves odious to the pure and holy God, who cannot endure to look upon iniquity. If sin be truly an abomination to us, sin in ourselves will especially be so; the nearer it is to us the more loathsome it will be. (4.) The more we see of the glory and majesty of God, and the more we see of the vileness and odiousness of sin and of ourselves because of sin, the more we shall abase and abhor ourselves for it. "Now my eye sees what a God he is whom I have offended, the brightness of that majesty which by wilful sin I have spit in the face of, the tenderness of that mercy which I have spurned at the bowels of; now I see what a just and holy God he is whose wrath I have incurred; wherefore I abhor myself. *Woe is me, for I am undone,"* Isa. 6:5. God had challenged Job to *look upon proud men and abase them.* "I cannot," says Job, "pretend to do it; I have enough to do to get my own proud heart humbled, to abase that and bring that low." Let us leave it to God to govern the world, and make it our care, in the strength of his grace, to govern ourselves and our own hearts well.

Verses 7–9

Job, in his discourses, had complained very much of the censures of his friends and their hard usage of him, and had appealed to God as Judge between him and them, and thought it hard that judgment was not immediately given upon the appeal. While God was catechising Job out of the whirlwind one would have thought that he only was in the wrong, and that the cause would certainly go against him; but here, to our great surprise, we find it quite otherwise, and the definitive sentence given in Job's favour. Wherefore judge nothing before the time. Those who are truly righteous before God may have their righteousness clouded and eclipsed by great and uncommon afflictions, by the severe censures of men, by their own frailties and foolish passions, by the sharp reproofs of the word and conscience, and the deep humiliation of their own spirits under the sense of God's terrors; and yet, in due time, these clouds shall all blow over, and God will *bring forth their righteousness as the light and their judgment as the noon-day,* Ps. 37:6. He cleared Job's righteousness here, because he, like an honest man, held it fast and would not let it go. We have here,

I. Judgment given against Job's three friends, upon the controversy between them and Job. Elihu is not censured here, for he distinguished himself from the rest in the management of the dispute, and acted, not as a party, but as a moderator; and moderation will have its praise with God, whether it have with men or no. In the judgment here given Job is magnified and his three friends are mortified. While we were examining the discourses on both sides we could not discern, and therefore durst not determine, who was in the right; something of truth we thought they both had on their side, but we could not cleave the hair between them; nor would we, for all the world, have had to give the decisive sentence upon the case, lest we should have determined wrong. But it is well that the judgment is the Lord's, and we are sure that his judgment is according to truth; to it we will refer ourselves, and by it we will abide. Now, in the judgment here given,

1. Job is greatly magnified and comes off with honour. He was but one against three, a beggar now against three princes, and yet, having God on his side, he needed not fear the result, though thousands set themselves against him. Observe here, (1.) When God appeared for him: *After the Lord had spoken these words unto Job, v.* 7. After he had convinced and humbled him, and brought him to repentance for what he had said amiss, then he owned him in what he had said well, comforted him, and put honour upon him; not till then: for we are not ready for God's approbation till we judge and condemn ourselves; but then he thus pleaded his cause, for he that *has torn will heal* us, he that *has smitten will bind us.* The Comforter shall convince, Jn. 16:8. See in what method we are to expect divine acceptance; we must first be humbled under divine rebukes. After God, by speaking these words, had caused grief, he returned and had compassion, according to the multitude of his mercies; for he will not contend for ever, but will debate in measure, and stay his rough wind in the day of his east wind. Now that Job had humbled himself God exalted him. True penitents shall find favour with God, and what they have said and done amiss shall no more be mentioned against them. Then God is well pleased with us when we are brought to abhor ourselves. (2.) How he appeared for him. It is taken for granted that all his offences are forgiven; for if he be dignified, as we find he is here, no doubt he is justified. Job had sometimes intimated, with great assurance, that God would clear him at last, and he was not made ashamed of the hope. [1.] God calls him again and again *his servant Job,* four times in two verses, and he seems to take a pleasure in calling him so, as before his troubles (*ch.* 1:8), *"Hast thou considered my servant Job?* Though he is poor and despised, he is my servant notwithstanding, and as dear to me as when he was in prosperity. Though he has his faults, and has appeared to be a man subject to like passions as others, though he has contended with me, has gone about to disannul my judgment, and has darkened counsel by words without knowledge, yet he sees his error and retracts it, and therefore he is my servant Job still." If we still hold fast the integrity and fidelity of servants to God, as Job did, though we may for a time be deprived of the credit and comfort of the relation, we shall be restored to it at last, as he was. The devil had undertaken to prove Job a hypocrite, and his three friends had condemned him as a wicked man; but God will acknowledge those whom he accepts, and will not suffer them to be run down by the malice of hell or earth. If God says, *Well done, good and faithful servant,* it is of little consequence who says otherwise. [2.] He owns that he had *spoken of him the thing that was right,* beyond what his antagonists had done. He had given a much better and truer account of the divine Providence than they had done. They had wronged God by making prosperity a mark of the true church and affliction a certain indication of God's wrath; but Job had done him right by maintaining that God's love and hatred are to be judged of by what is in men, not by what is before them, Eccl. 9:1. Observe, *First,* Those do the most justice to God and his providence who have an eye to the rewards and punishments of another world more than to those of this, and with the prospect of those solve the difficulties of the present administration. Job had referred things to the future judgment, and the future state, more than his friends had done, and therefore he spoke of God that which was right, better than his friends had done. *Secondly,* Though Job had spoken some things amiss, even concerning God, whom he made too bold with, yet he is commended for what he spoke that was right. We must not only not reject that which is true and good, but must not deny it its due praise, though there appear in it a mixture of human frailty and infirmity. *Thirdly,* Job was in the right, and his friends were in the wrong, and yet he was in pain and they were at ease — a plain evidence that we cannot judge of men and their sentiments by looking in their faces or purses. He only can do it infallibly who sees men's hearts. [3.] He will pass his word for Job that, notwithstanding all the wrong his friends had done him, he is so good a man, and of such a humble, tender, forgiving spirit, that he will very readily pray for them, and use his interest in heaven on their behalf: *"My servant Job will pray for you.* I know he will. I have pardoned him, and he has the comfort of pardon, and therefore he will pardon you." [4.] He appoints him to be the priest of this congregation, and promises to accept him and his mediation for his friends. "Take your sacrifices to my servant Job, *for him will I accept."* Those whom God washes from their sins he makes to himself kings and priests. True penitents shall not only find favour as petitioners for themselves, but be accepted as intercessors for others also. It was a great honour that God hereby put upon Job, in appointing him to offer sacrifice for his friends, as formerly he used to do for his own children, *ch.* 1:5. And a happy presage it was of his restoration to his prosperity again, and indeed a good step towards it, that he was thus restored to the priesthood. Thus he became a type of Christ, through whom alone we and our spiritual sacrifices are *acceptable to God;* see 1 Pt. 2:5. *"Go to my servant Job,* to my servant Jesus" (from whom for a time he hid his face), "put your sacrifices into his hand, make use of him as your Advocate, for him will I accept, but, out of him, you must expect to be dealt with according to your folly." And, as Job prayed and offered sacrifice for those that had grieved and wounded his spirit, so Christ prayed and died for his persecutors, and ever lives *making intercession for the transgressors.*

2. Job's friends are greatly mortified, and come off with disgrace. They were good men and belonged to God, and therefore he would not let them lie still in their mistake any more than Job, but, having humbled him by a discourse out of the whirlwind, he takes another course to humble them. Job, who was dearest to him, was first chidden, but the rest in their turn. When they heard Job talked to, it is probable, they flattered themselves with a conceit that they were in the right and Job was in all the fault, but God soon took them to task, and made them know the contrary. In most disputes and controversies there is something amiss on both sides, either in the merits of the cause or in the management, if not in both; and it is fit that both sides should be told of it, and made to see their errors. God addresses this to Eliphaz, not only as the sen-

ior, but as the ringleader in the attack made upon Job. Now, (1.) God tells them plainly that they had *not spoken of him the thing that was right, like Job,* that is, they had censured and condemned Job upon a false hypothesis, had represented God fighting against Job as an enemy when really he was only trying him as a friend, and this was not right. Those do not say well of God who represent his fatherly chastisements of his own children as judicial punishments and who cut them off from his favour upon the account of them. Note, It is a dangerous thing to judge uncharitably of the spiritual and eternal state of others, for in so doing we may perhaps condemn those whom God has accepted, which is a great provocation to him; it is offending his little ones, and he takes himself to be wronged in all the wrongs that are done to them. (2.) He assures them he was angry with them: *My wrath is kindled against thee and thy two friends.* God is very angry with those who despise and reproach their brethren, who triumph over them, and judge hardly of them, either for their calamities or for their infirmities. Though they were wise and good men, yet, when they spoke amiss, God was angry with them and let them know that he was. (3.) He requires from them a sacrifice, to make atonement for what they had said amiss. They must bring each of them *seven bullocks,* and each of them *seven rams,* to be offered up to God for a *burnt-offering;* for it should seem that, before the law of Moses, all sacrifices, even those of atonement, were wholly burnt, and therefore were so called. They thought they had spoken wonderfully well, and that God was beholden to them for pleading his cause and owed them a good reward for it; but they are told that, on the contrary, he is displeased with them, requires from them a sacrifice, and threatens that, otherwise, he will deal with them after their folly. God is often angry at that in us which we are ourselves proud of and sees much amiss in that which we think was done well. (4.) He orders them to go to Job, and beg of him to offer their sacrifices, and pray for them, otherwise they should not be accepted. By this God designed, [1.] To humble them and lay them low. They thought that they only were the favourites of Heaven, and that Job had no interest there; but God gives them to understand that he had a better interest there than they had, and stood fairer for God's acceptance than they did. The day may come when those who despise and censure God's people will court their favour, and be *made to know that God has loved them,* Rev. 3:9. The foolish virgins will beg oil of the wise. [2.] To oblige them to make their peace with Job, as the condition of their making their peace with God. *If thy brother has aught against thee* (as Job had a great deal against them), *first be reconciled to thy brother and then come and offer thy gift.* Satisfaction must first be made for wrong done, according as the nature of the thing requires, before we can hope to obtain from God the forgiveness of sin. See how thoroughly God espoused the cause of his servant Job and engaged in it. God will not be reconciled to those that have offended Job till they have first begged his pardon and he be reconciled to them. Job and his friends had differed in their opinion about many things, and had been too keen in their reflections one upon another, but now they were to be made friends; in order to that, they are not to argue the matter over again and try to give it a new turn (that might be endless), but they must agree in a sacrifice and a prayer, and that must reconcile them: they must unite in affection and devotion when they could not concur in the same sentiments. Those who differ in judgments about minor things are yet one in Christ the great sacrifice, and meet at the same throne of grace, and therefore ought to love and bear with one another. Once more, observe, When God was angry with Job's friends, he did himself put them in a way to make their peace with him. Our quarrels with God always begin on our part, but the reconciliation begins on his.

II. The acquiescence of Job's friends in this judgment given, *v.* 9. They were good men, and, as soon as they understood what the mind of the Lord was, they did as he commanded them, and that speedily and without gainsaying, though it was against the grain to flesh and blood to court him thus whom they had condemned. Note, Those who would be reconciled to God must carefully use the prescribed means and methods of reconciliation. Peace with God is to be had only in his own way and upon his own terms, and they will never seem hard to those who know how to value the privilege, but they will be glad of it upon any terms, though ever so humbling. Job's friends had all joined in accusing Job, and now they join in begging his pardon. Those that have sinned together should repent together. Those that appeal to God, as both Job and his friends had often done, must resolve to stand by his award, whether pleasing or unpleasing to their own mind. And those that conscientiously observe God's commands need not doubt of his favour: *The Lord also accepted Job,* and his friends in answer to his prayer. It is not said, He accepted *them* (though that is implied), but, He accepted *Job* for them; so he has *made us accepted in the beloved,* Eph. 1:6; Mt. 3:17. Job did not insult over his friends upon the testimony God had given concerning him, and the submission they were obliged to make to him; but, God being graciously reconciled to him, he was easily reconciled to them, and then God accepted him. This is that which we should aim at in all our prayers and services, to be accepted of the Lord; this must be the summit of our ambition, not to have praise of men, but to please God.

Verses 10–17

You have heard of the patience of Job (says the apostle, Jam. 5:11) *and have seen the end of the Lord,* that is, what end the Lord, at length, put to his troubles. In the beginning of this book we had Job's patience under his troubles, for an example; here, in the close, for our encouragement to follow that example, we have the happy issue of his troubles and the prosperous condition to which he was restored after them, which confirms us in counting those happy which endure. Perhaps, too, the extraordinary prosperity which Job was crowned with after his afflictions was intended to be to us Christians a type and figure of the glory and happiness of heaven, which the afflictions of this present time are working for us, and in which they will issue at last; this will be more than double to all the delights and satisfactions we now enjoy, as Job's after-prosperity was to his former, though then he was the greatest of all the men of the east. He that rightly endures temptation, when he is tried, shall receive a *crown of life* (Jam. 1:12), as Job, when he was tried, received all the wealth, and honour, and comfort, which here we have an account of.

I. God returned in ways of mercy to him; and his thoughts concerning him *were thoughts of good and not of evil, to give the expected* (nay, the *unexpected*) *end,* Jer. 29:11. His troubles began in Satan's malice, which God restrained; his restoration began in God's mercy, which Satan could not oppose. Job's sorest complaint, and indeed the sorrowful accent of all his complaints, on which he laid the greatest emphasis, was that God appeared against him. But now God plainly appeared for him, and *watched over him to build and to plant, like as he had* (at least in his apprehension) *watched over him to pluck up and to throw down,* Jer. 31:28. This put a new face upon his affairs immediately, and every thing now looked as pleasing and promising as before it had looked gloomy and frightful. 1. God *turned his captivity,* that is, he redressed his grievances and took away all the causes of his complaints; he loosed him from the bond with which Satan had now, for a great while, bound him, and delivered him out of those cruel hands into which he had delivered him. We may suppose that now all his bodily pains and distempers were healed so suddenly and so thoroughly that the cure was next to miraculous: *His flesh became fresher than a child's, and he returned to the days of his youth;* and, what was more, he felt a very great alteration in his mind; it was calm and easy, and the tumult was all over, his disquieting thoughts had all vanished, his fears were silenced, and the consolations of God were now as much the delight of his soul as his terrors had been its burden. The tide thus turned, his troubles began to ebb as fast as they had flowed, just then *when he was praying for his friends,* praying over his sacrifice which he offered for them. Mercy did not return when he was disputing with his friends, no, not though he had right on his side, but when he was praying for them; for God is better served and pleased with our warm devotions than with our warm disputations. When Job completed his repentance by this instance of his *forgiving men their trespasses,* then God completed his remission by turning his captivity. Note, We are really doing our business when we are praying for our friends, if we pray in a right manner, for in those prayers there is not only faith, but love. Christ has taught us to pray with and for others in teaching us to say, *Our Father;* and, in seeking mercy for others, we may find mercy ourselves. Our Lord Jesus has his exaltation and dominion there, where he *ever lives making intercession.* Some, by the turning of Job's captivity, understand the restitution which the Sabeans and Chaldeans made of the cattle which they had taken from him, God wonderfully inclining them to do it; and with these he began the world again. Probably it was so; those spoilers had *swallowed down his riches,* but they were forced to *vomit them up again, ch.* 20:15. But I rather understand this more generally of the turn now given. 2. God doubled his possessions: *Also the Lord gave Job twice as much as he had before.* It is probable that he did at first, in some way or other, intimate to him that it was his gracious purpose, by degrees, in due time to bring him to such a height of prosperity that he should have twice as much as ever he had, for the encouraging of his hope and the quickening of his industry, and that it might appear that this wonderful increase was a special token of God's favour. And it may be considered as intended, (1.) To balance his losses. He suffered for the glory of God, and therefore God made it up to him with advantage, and allowed him more than interest upon interest. God will take care that none shall lose by him. (2.) To recompense his patience and his confidence in God, which (notwithstanding the workings of corruption) he did not cast away, but still held fast, and that is it which has *a great recompence of reward,* Heb. 10:35. Job's friends had often put their severe censure of Job upon this issue, *If thou wert pure and upright, surely now he would awake for thee, ch.* 8:6. But he does not awake for thee; therefore thou art not upright. "Well," says God, "though your argument be not conclusive, I will even by that demonstrate the integrity of my servant Job; his latter end shall greatly increase, and by that it shall appear, since you will have it so, that it was not for any injustice in his hands that he suffered the loss of all things." Now it appeared that Job had reason to bless God for taking away (as he did, *ch.* 1:21), since it made so good a return.

II. His old acquaintance, neighbours, and relations, were very kind to him, *v.* 11. They had been estranged from him, and this was not the least of the grievances of his afflicted state; he bitterly complained of their unkindness, *ch.* 19:13, etc. But now they visited him with all possible expressions of affection and respect. 1. They put honour upon him, in coming to dine with him as formerly, but (we may suppose) privately bringing their entertainment along with them, so that he had the reputation of feasting them without the expense. 2. They sympathized with him, and showed a tender concern for him, such as becomes brethren. They bemoaned him when they talked over all the calamities of his afflicted state, and comforted him when they took notice of God's gracious returns to him. They wept for his griefs, and rejoiced in his joys, and proved not such miserable comforters as his three friends, that, at first, were so forward and officious to attend him. These were not such great men nor such learned and eloquent men as those, but they proved much more skilful and kind in comforting Job. God sometimes chooses the foolish and weak things of the world, as for conviction, so for comfort. 3. They made a collection among them for the repair of his losses and the setting of him up again. They did not think it enough to say, *Be warmed, Be filled,* but gave him such things as would be of use to him, Jam. 2:16. *Every one gave him a piece of money* (some more, it is likely, and some less, according to their ability) *and every one an ear-ring of gold* (an ornament much used by the children of the east), which would be as good as money to him: this was a superfluity which they could well spare, and the rule is, That our abundance must be a supply to our brethren's necessity. But why did Job's relations now, at length, show this kindness to him? (1.) God put it in their hearts to do so; and every creature is that to us which he makes it to be. Job had acknowledged God in their estrangement from him, for which he now rewarded him in turning them to him again. (2.) Perhaps some of them withdrew from him because they thought him a hypocrite, but, now that his integrity was made manifest, they returned to him and to communion with him again. When God was friendly to him they were all willing to be friendly too, Ps. 119:74, 79. Others of them, it may be, withdrew because he was poor, and sore, and a rueful spectacle, but now that he began to recover they were willing to renew their acquaintance with him. Swallow-friends, that are gone in winter, will return in the spring, though their friendship is of little value. (3.) Perhaps the rebuke which God had given to Eliphaz and the other two for their unkindness to Job awakened the rest of his friends to return to their duty. Reproofs to others we should thus take as admonitions and instructions to us. 4. Job *prayed for his friends,* and then they flocked about him, overcome by his kindness, and every one desiring an interest in his prayers. The more we pray for our friends and relations the more comfort we may expect in them.

III. His estate strangely increased, by the blessing of God upon the little that his friends gave him. He thankfully received their courtesy, and did not think it below him to have his estate repaired by contributions. He did not, on the one hand, urge his friends to raise money for him; he acquits himself from that (*ch.* 6:22), *Did I say, Bring unto me or give me a reward of your substance?* Yet what they brought he thankfully accepted, and did not upbraid them with their former unkindnesses, nor ask them why they did not do this sooner. He was neither so covetous and griping as to ask their charity, nor so proud and ill-natured as to refuse it when they offered it; and, being in so good a temper, God gave him that which was far better than their money and ear-rings, and that was his blessing, *v.* 12. The Lord comforted him now according to the days wherein he had afflicted him, and *blessed his latter end more than his beginning.* Observe, 1. *The blessing of the Lord makes rich;* it is he that gives us power to get wealth and gives success in honest endeavours. Those therefore that would thrive must have an eye to God's blessing, and never to out of it, no, not into the warm sun; and those that have thriven must not sacrifice to their own net, but acknowledge their obligations to God for his blessing. 2. That blessing can make very rich and sometimes makes good people so. Those that become rich by getting think they can easily make themselves very rich by saving; but, as those that have little must depend upon God to make it much, so those that have much must depend upon God to make it more and to double it; else *you have sown much and bring in little,* Hag. 1:6. 3. The last days of a good man sometimes prove his best days, his last works his best works, his last comforts his best comforts; for his path, like that of the morning-light, shines more and more to the perfect day. Of a wicked man it is said, *His last state is worse than his first* (Lu. 11:26), but of the upright man, *His end is peace;* and sometimes the nearer it is the clearer are the views of it. In respect of outward prosperity God is pleased sometimes to make the latter end of a good man's life more comfortable than the former part of it has been, and strangely to outdo the expectations of his afflicted people, who thought they should never live to see better days, that we may not despair even in the depths of adversity. We know not what good times we may yet be reserved for in our latter end. *Non, si male nunc, et olim sic erit — It may yet be well with us, though now it is otherwise.* Job, in his affliction, had wished to be *as in months past,* as rich as he had been before, and quite despaired of that; but God is often better to us than our own fears, nay, than our own wishes, for Job's possessions were doubled to him; the number of his cattle, his sheep and camels, his oxen and she-asses, is just double here to what it was, *ch.* 1:3. This is a remarkable instance of the extent of the divine providence to things that seem minute, as this of the exact number of a man's cattle, as also of the harmony of providence, and the reference of one event to another; for *known unto God are all his works, from the beginning to the end.* Job's other possessions, no doubt, were increased in proportion to his cattle, lands, money, servants, etc. So that if, before, he was the greatest of all the men of the east, what was he now?

IV. His family was built up again, and he had great comfort in his children, *v.* 13–15. The last of his afflictions that are recorded (*ch.* 1), and the most grievous, was the death of all his children at once. His friends upbraided him with it (*ch.* 8:4), but God repaired even that breach in process of time, either by the same wife, or, she being dead, by another. 1. The number of his children was the same as before, *seven sons and three daughters.* Some give this reason why they were not doubled as his cattle were, because his children that were dead were not lost, but gone before to a better world; and therefore, if he have but the same number of them, they may be reckoned doubled, for he has two fleeces of children (as I may say) *mahanaim — two hosts,* one in heaven, the other on earth, and in both he is rich. 2. The names of his daughters are here registered (*v.* 14), because, in the significations of them, they seemed designed to perpetuate the remembrance of God's great goodness to him in the surprising change of his condition. He called the first *Jemima — The day* (whence perhaps *Diana* had her name), because of the shining forth of his prosperity after a dark night of affliction. The next *Kezia,* a spice of a very fragrant smell, because (says bishop Patrick) God had healed his ulcers, the smell of which was offensive. The third *Keren-happuch* (that is *Plenty restored,* or *A horn of paint*), because (says he) God had wiped away the tears which fouled his face, *ch.* 16:16. Concerning these daughters we are here told, (1.) That God adorned them with great beauty, *no women so fair as the daughters of Job, v.* 15. In the Old Testament we often find women praised for their beauty, as Sarah, Rebekah, and many others; but we never find any women in the New Testament whose beauty is in the least taken notice of, no, not the virgin Mary herself, because the beauty of holiness is that which is brought to a much clearer light by the gospel. (2.) That their father (God enabling him to do it) supplied them with great fortunes: *He gave them inheritance among their brethren,* and did not turn them off with small portions, as most did. It is probable that they had some extraordinary personal merit, which Job had an eye to in the extraordinary favour he showed them. Perhaps they excelled their brethren in wisdom and piety; and therefore, that they might continue in his family, to be a stay and blessing to it, he made them co-heirs with their brethren.

V. His life was long. What age he was when his troubles came we are nowhere told, but here we are told he lived 140 years, whence some conjecture that he was 70 when he was in his troubles, and that so his age was doubled, as his other possessions. 1. He lived to have much of the comfort of this life, for he saw his posterity to the fourth generation, *v.* 16. Though his children were not doubled to him, yet in his children's children (and those are the crown of old men) they were more than doubled. As God appointed to Adam another seed instead of that which was slain (Gen. 4:25), so he did to Job with advantage. God has ways to repair the losses and balance the griefs of those who are written childless, as Job was when he had buried all his children. 2. He lived till he was satisfied, for he died full of days, satisfied with living in this world, and willing to leave it; not peevishly so, as in the days of his affliction, but piously so, and thus, as Eliphaz had encouraged him to hope, he *came to his grave like a shock of corn in his season.*

AN EXPOSITION, WITH PRACTICAL OBSERVATIONS, OF

THE BOOK OF PSALMS

We have now before us one of the choicest and most excellent parts of all the Old Testament; nay, so much is there in it of Christ and his gospel, as well as of God and his law, that it had been called *the abstract,* or *summary, of both Testaments.* The History of Israel, which we were long upon, let us to camps and council-boards, and there entertained and instructed us in the knowledge of God. The book of Job brought us into the schools, and treated us with profitable disputations concerning God and his providence. But this book brings us into the sanctuary, draws us off from converse with men, with the politicians, philosophers, or disputers of this world, and directs us into communion with God, by solacing and reposing our souls in him, lifting up and letting out our hearts towards him. Thus may we be in the mount with God; and we understand not our interests if we say not, *It is good to be here.* Let us consider,

I. The title of this book. It is called, 1. The *Psalms;* under that title it is referred to, Lu. 24:44. The Hebrew calls it *Tehillim,* which properly signifies *Psalms of praise,* because many of them are such; but *Psalms* is a more general word, meaning all metrical compositions fitted to be sung, which may as well be historical, doctrinal, or supplicatory, as laudatory. Though singing be properly the voice of joy, yet the intention of songs is of a much greater latitude, to assist the memory, and both to express and to excite all the other affections as well as this of joy. The priests had a mournful muse as well as joyful ones; and the divine institution of singing psalms is thus largely intended; for we are directed not only to praise God, but to teach and admonish ourselves and one another *in psalms, and hymns, and spiritual songs,* Col. 3:16. 2. It is called the *Book of Psalms;* so it is quoted by St. Peter, Acts 1:20. It is a collection of psalms, of all the psalms that were divinely inspired, which, though composed at several times and upon several occasions, are here put together without any reference to or dependence upon one another; thus they were preserved from being scattered and lost, and were in so much greater readiness for the service of the church. See what a good master we serve, and what pleasantness there is in wisdom's ways, when we are not only commanded to sing at our work, and have cause enough given us to do so, but have words also put in our mouths and songs prepared to our hands.

II. The author of this book. It is, no doubt, derived originally from the blessed Spirit. They are spiritual songs, words which the Holy Ghost taught. The penman of most of them was David the son of Jesse, who is therefore called the *sweet psalmist of Israel,* 2 Sa. 23:1. Some that have not his name in their titles yet are expressly ascribed to him elsewhere, as Ps. 2 (Acts 4:25) and Ps. 96 and 105 (1 Chr. 16). One psalm is expressly said to be *the prayer of Moses* (Ps. 90); and that some of the psalms were penned by Asaph is intimated, 2 Chr. 29:30, where they are said to *praise the Lord in the words of David and Asaph,* who is there called a *seer* or *prophet.* Some of the psalms seem to have been penned long after, as Ps. 137, at the time of the captivity in Babylon; but the far greater part of them were certainly penned by David himself, whose genius lay towards poetry and music, and who was raised up, qualified, and animated, for the establishing of the ordinance of singing psalms in the church of God, as Moses and Aaron were, in their day, for the settling of the ordinances of sacrifice; theirs is superseded, but his remains, and will to the end of time, when it shall be swallowed up in the songs of eternity. Herein David was a type of Christ, who descended from him, not from Moses, because he came to take away sacrifice (the family of Moses was soon lost and extinct), but to establish and perpetuate joy and praise; for of the family of David in Christ there shall be no end.

III. The scope of it. It is manifestly intended, 1. To assist the exercises of natural religion, and to kindle in the souls of men those devout affections which we owe to God as our Creator, owner, ruler, and benefactor. The book of Job helps to prove our first principles of the divine perfections and providence; but this helps to improve them in prayers and praises, and professions of desire towards him, dependence on him, and an entire devotedness and resignation to him. Other parts of scripture show that God is infinitely above man, and his sovereign Lord; but this shows us that he may, notwithstanding, be conversed with by us sinful worms of the earth; and there are ways in which, if it be not our own fault, we may keep up communion with him in all the various conditions of human life. 2. To advance the excellencies of revealed religion, and in the most pleasing powerful manner to recommend it to the world. There is indeed little or nothing of the ceremonial law in all the book of *Psalms.* Though sacrifice and offering were yet to continue many ages, yet they are here represented as things which God did not desire (Ps. 40:6, 51:16), as things comparatively little, and which in time were to vanish away. But the word and law of God, those parts of it which are moral and of perpetual obligation are here all along magnified and made honourable, nowhere more. And Christ, the crown and centre of revealed religion, the foundation, corner, and top-stone, of that blessed building, is here clearly spoken of in type and prophecy, his sufferings and the glory that should follow, and the kingdom that he should set up in the world, in which God's covenant with David, concerning his kingdom, was to have its accomplishment. What a high value does this book put upon the word of God, his statutes and judgments, his covenant and the great and precious promises of it; and how does it recommend them to us as our guide and stay, and our heritage for ever!

IV. The use of it. All scripture, being given by inspiration of God, is profitable to convey divine light into our understandings; but this book is of singular use with that to convey divine life and power, and a holy warmth, into our affections. There is no one book of scripture that is more helpful to the devotions of the saints than this, and it has been so in all ages of the church, ever since it was written and the several parts of it were delivered to the chief musician for the service of the church. 1. It is of use to be sung. Further than David's psalms we *may* go, but we *need* not, for hymns and spiritual songs. What the rules of the Hebrew metre were even the learned are not certain. But these psalms ought to be rendered according to the metre of every language, at least so as that they may be sung for the edification of the church. And methinks it is a great comfort to us, when we are singing David's psalms, that we are offering the very same praises to God that were offered to him in the days of David and the other godly kings of Judah. So rich, so well made, are these divine poems, that they can never be exhausted, can never be worn thread-bare. 2. It is of use to be read and opened by the ministers of Christ, as containing great and excellent truths, and rules concerning good and evil. Our Lord Jesus expounded the psalms to his disciples, the gospel psalms, and opened their understandings (for he had the key of David) to understand them, Lu. 24:44. 3. It is of use to be read and meditated upon by all good people. It is a full fountain, out of which we may all be drawing water with joy. (1.) The Psalmist's experiences are of great use for our direction, caution, and encouragement. In telling us, as he often does, what passed between God and his soul, he lets us know what we may expect from God, and what he will expect, and require, and graciously accept, from us. David was a man after God's own heart, and therefore those who find themselves in some measure according to his heart have reason to hope that they are renewed by the grace of God, after the image of God, and many have much comfort in the testimony of their consciences for them that they can heartily say *Amen* to David's prayers and praises. (2.) Even the Psalmist's expressions too are of great use; and by them the Spirit helps our praying infirmities, because we know not what to pray for as we ought. In all our approaches to God, as well as in our first returns to God, we are directed to *take with us words* (Hos. 14:2), these word, words which the Holy Ghost teaches. If we make David's psalms familiar to us, as we ought to do, whatever errand we have at the throne of grace, by way of confession, petition, or thanksgiving, we may thence be assisted in the delivery of it; whatever devout affection is working in us, holy desire or hope, sorrow or joy, we may there find apt words wherewith to clothe it, sound speech which cannot be condemned. It will be good to collect the most proper and lively expressions of devotion which we find here, and to methodize them, and reduce them to the several heads of prayer, that they may be the more ready to us. Or we may take sometimes one choice psalm and sometimes another, and pray it over, that is, enlarge upon each verse in our own thoughts, and offer up our meditations to God as they arise from the expressions we find there. The learned Dr. Hammond, in his preface to his paraphrase on the Psalms (sect. 29), says, "That going over a few psalms with these interpunctions of mental devotion, suggested, animated, and maintained, by the native life and vigour which is in the psalms, is much to be preferred before the saying over the whole Psalter, since nothing is more fit to be averted in religious offices than their degenerating into heartless dispirited recitations." If, as St. Austin advises, we form our spirit by the affection of the psalm, we may then be sure of acceptance with God in using the language of it. Nor is it only our devotion, and the affections of our mind, that the book of Psalms assists, teaching us how to offer praise so as to glorify God, but, it is also a directory to the actions of our lives, and teaches us how to *order our conversation aright, so as that,* in the end, *we may see the salvation of God,* Ps. 1:23. The Psalms were thus serviceable to the Old-Testament church, but to us Christians they may be of more use than they could be to those who lived before the coming of Christ; for, as Moses's sacrifices, so David's songs, are expounded and made more intelligible by the gospel of Christ, which lets us within the veil; so that if to David's prayers and praises we all St. Paul's prayers in his epistles, and the new songs in the Revelation, we shall be thoroughly furnished for this good work; for the scripture, perfected, makes the man of God perfect.

As to the division of this book, we need not be solicitous; there is no connexion (or very seldom) between one psalm and another, nor any reason discernable for the placing of them in the order wherein we here find them; but it seems to be ancient, for that which is now the second psalm was so in the apostles' time, Acts 13:33. The vulgar Latin joins the 9th and 10th together; all popish authors quote by that, so that, thenceforward, throughout the book, their number is one short of ours; our 11 is their 10, our 119 is their 118. But they divide the 147th into two, and so make up the number of 150. Some have endeavoured to reduce the psalms to proper heads, according to the matter of them, but there is often such a variety of matter in one and the same psalm that this cannot be done with any certainty. But the seven penitential Psalms have been in a particular manner singled out by the devotions of many. They are reckoned to be Ps. 6, 32, 38, 51, 102, 130, and 143. The Psalms were divided into five books, each concluding with *Amen, Amen,* or *Hallelujah;* the first ending with Ps. 41, the second with Ps. 72, the third with Ps. 89, the fourth with Ps. 106, the fifth with Ps. 150. Others divide them into three fifties; others into sixty parts, two for every day of the month, one for the morning, the other for the evening. Let good Christians divide them for themselves, so as may best increase their acquaintance with them, that they may have them at hand upon all occasions and may sing them in the spirit and with the understanding.

PSALM 1

This is a psalm of instruction concerning good and evil, setting before us life and death, the blessing and the curse, that we may take the right way which leads to happiness and avoid that which will certainly end in our misery and ruin. The different character and condition of godly people and wicked people, those that serve God and those that serve him not, is here plainly stated in a few words; so that every man, if he will be faithful to himself, may here see his own face and then read his own doom. That division of the children of men into saints and sinners, righteous and unrighteous, the children of God and the children of the wicked one, as it is ancient, ever since the struggle began between sin and grace, the seed of the woman and the seed of the serpent, so it is lasting, and will survive all other divisions and subdivisions of men into high and low, rich and poor, bond and free; for by this men's everlasting state will be determined, and the distinction will last as long as heaven and hell. This psalm shows us, I. The holiness and happiness of a godly man (*v.* 1–3). II. The sinfulness and misery of a wicked man (*v.* 4, 5). III. The ground and reason of both (*v.* 6). Whoever collected the psalms of David (probably it was Ezra) with good reason put this psalm first, as a preface to the rest, because it is absolutely necessary to the acceptance of our devotions that we be righteous before God (for it is only the prayer of the upright that is his delight), and therefore that we be right in our notions of blessedness and in our choice of the way that leads to it. Those are not fit to put up good prayers who do not walk in good ways.

Verses 1–3

The psalmist begins with the character and condition of a godly man, that those may first take the comfort of that to whom it belongs. Here is,

I. A description of the godly man's spirit and way, by which we are to try ourselves. The Lord knows those that are his by name, but we must know them by their character; for that is agreeable to a state of probation, that we may study to answer to the character, which is indeed both the command of the law which we are bound in duty to obey and the condition of the promise which we are bound in interest to fulfil. The character of a good man is here given by the rules he chooses to walk by and to take his measures from. What we take at our setting out, and at every turn, for the guide of our conversation, whether the course of this world or the word of God, is of material consequence. An error in the choice of our standard and leader is original and fatal; but, if we be right here, we are in a far way to do well.

1. A godly man, that he may avoid the evil, utterly renounces the companionship of evil-doers, and will not be led by them (*v.* 1): *He walks not in the council of the ungodly, etc.* This part of his character is put first, because those that will keep the commandments of their God must say to evil-doers, *Depart from us* (Ps. 119:115), and departing from evil is that in which wisdom begins. (1.) He sees evil-doers round about him; the world is full of them; they walk on every side. They are here described by three characters, *ungodly, sinners,* and *scornful.* See by what steps men arrive at the height of impiety. *Nemo repente fit turpissimus — None reach the height of vice at once.* They are *ungodly* first, casting off their duty to him: but they rest not there. When the services of religion are laid aside, they come to be *sinners,* that is, they break out into open rebellion against God and engage in the service of sin and Satan. Omissions make way for commissions, and by these the heart is so hardened that at length they come to be *scorners,* that is, they openly defy all that is sacred, scoff at religion, and make a jest of sin. Thus is the way of iniquity down-hill; the bad grow worse, sinners themselves become tempters to others and advocates for Baal. The word which we translate *ungodly* signifies such as are unsettled, aim at no certain end and walk by no certain rule, but are at the command of every lust and at the beck of every temptation. The word for *sinners* signifies such as are determined for the practice of sin and set it up as their trade. The *scornful* are those that set *their mouths against the heavens.* These the good man sees with a sad heart; they are a constant vexation to his righteous soul. But, (2.) He shuns them wherever he sees them. He does not do as they do; and, that he may not, he does not converse familiarly with them. [1.] He does *not walk in the counsel of the ungodly.* He is not present at their councils, nor does he advise with them; though they are ever so witty, and subtle, and learned, if they are ungodly, they shall not be the men of his counsel. He does not consent to them, nor *say as they say,* Lu. 23:51. He does not take his measures from their principles, nor act according to the advice which they give and take. The ungodly are forward to give their advice against religion, and it is managed so artfully that we have reason to think ourselves happy if we escape being tainted and ensnared by it. [2.] He *stands not in the way of sinners;* he avoids doing as they do; their way shall not be his way; he will not come into it, much less will he continue in it, as the sinner does, who *sets himself in a way that is not good,* Ps. 36:4. He avoids (as much as may be) being where they are. That he may not imitate them, he will not associate with them, nor choose them for his companions. He does not stand in their way, to be picked up by them (Prov. 7:8), but keeps as far from them as from a place or person infected with the plague, for fear of the contagion, Prov. 4:14, 15. He that would be kept from harm must keep out of harm's way. [3.] He *sits not in the seat of the scornful;* he does not repose himself with those that sit down secure in their wickedness and please themselves with the searedness of their own consciences. He does not associate with those that sit in close cabal to find out ways and means for the support and advancement of the devil's kingdom, or that sit in open judgment, magisterially to condemn the generation of the righteous. The seat of the drunkards is the *seat of the scornful,* Ps. 69:12. Happy is the man that never sits in it, Hos. 7:5.

2. A godly man, that he may do that which is good and cleave to it, submits to the guidance of the word of God and makes that familiar to him, *v.* 2. This is that which keeps him out of the way of the ungodly and fortifies him against their temptations. *By the words of thy lips I have kept me from the path of the deceiver,* Ps. 17:4. We need not court the fellowship of sinners, either for pleasure or for improvement, while we have fellowship with the word of God and with God himself in and by his word. *When thou awakest it shall talk with thee,* Prov. 6:22. We may judge of our spiritual state by asking, "What is the law of God to us? What account do we make of it? What place has it in us?" See here, (1.) The entire affection which a good man has for the law of God: *His delight is in it.* He delights in it, though it be a law, a yoke, because it is the law of God, which is holy, just, and good, which he freely consents to, and so delights in, *after the inner man,* Rom.

7:16, 22. All who are well pleased that there is a God must be well pleased that there is a Bible, a revelation of God, of his will, and of the only way to happiness in him. (2.) The intimate acquaintance which a good man keeps up with the word of God: *In that law doth he meditate day and night;* and by this it appears that his delight is in it, for what we love we love to think of, Ps. 119:97. To meditate in God's word is to discourse with ourselves concerning the great things contained in it, with a close application of mind, a fixedness of thought, till we be suitably affected with those things and experience the savour and power of them in our hearts. This we must do *day and night;* we must have a constant habitual regard to the word of God as the rule of our actions and the spring of our comforts, and we must have it in our thoughts, accordingly, upon every occasion that occurs, whether night or day. No time is amiss for meditating on the word of God, nor is any time unseasonable for those visits. We must not only set ourselves to meditate on God's word morning and evening, at the entrance of the day and of the night, but these thought should be interwoven with the business and converse of every day and with the repose and slumbers of every night. *When I awake I am still with thee.*

II. An assurance given of the godly man's happiness, with which we should encourage ourselves to answer the character of such. 1. In general, he is *blessed,* Ps. 5:1. God blesses him, and that blessing will make him happy. Blessednesses are to him, blessings of all kinds, of the upper and nether springs, enough to make him completely happy; none of the ingredients of happiness shall be wanting to him. When the psalmist undertakes to describe a blessed man, he describes a good man; for, after all, those only are happy, truly happy, that are holy, truly holy; and we are more concerned to know the way to blessedness than to know wherein that blessedness will consist. Nay, goodness and holiness are not only the way to happiness (Rev. 22:14) but happiness itself; supposing there were not another life after this, yet that man is a happy man that keeps in the way of his duty. 2. His blessedness is here illustrated by a similitude (*v. 3*): *He shall be like a tree,* fruitful and flourishing. This is the effect, (1.) Of his pious practice; he meditates in the law of God, turns that *in succum et sanguinem — into juice and blood,* and that makes him like a tree. The more we converse with the word of God the better furnished we are for every good word and work. Or, (2.) Of the promised blessing; he is blessed of the Lord, and therefore *he shall be like a tree.* The divine blessing produces real effects. It is the happiness of a godly man, [1.] That he is planted by the grace of God. These trees were by nature wild olives, and will continue so till they are grafted anew, and so planted by a power from above. Never any good tree grew of itself; it is *the planting of the Lord,* and therefore he must in it be glorified. Isa. 61:3, *The trees of the Lord are full of sap.* [2.] That he is placed by the means of grace, here called *the rivers of water,* those rivers which *make glad the city of our God* (Ps. 46:4); from these a good man receives supplies of strength and vigour, but in secret undiscerned ways. [3.] That his practices shall be fruit, abounding to a good account, Phil. 4:17. To those whom God first blessed he said, *Be fruitful* (Gen. 1:22), and still the comfort and honour of fruitfulness are a recompense for the labour of it. It is expected from those who enjoy the mercies of grace that, both in the temper of their minds and in the tenour of their lives, they comply with the intentions of that grace, and then they bring forth fruit. And, be it observed to the praise of the great dresser of the vineyard, they bring forth their fruit (that which is required of them) *in due season,* when it is most beautiful and most useful, improving every opportunity of doing good and doing it in its proper time. [4.] That his profession shall be preserved from blemish and decay: *His leaf also shall not wither.* As to those who bring forth only the leaves of profession, without any good fruit, even their leaf will wither and they shall be as much ashamed of their profession as ever they were proud of it; but, if the word of God rule in the heart, that will keep the profession green, both to our comfort and to our credit; the laurels thus won shall never wither. [5.] That prosperity shall attend him wherever he goes, soul-prosperity. *Whatever he does,* in conformity to the law, it *shall prosper* and succeed to his mind, or above his hope.

In singing these verses, being duly affected with the malignant and dangerous nature of sin, the transcendent excellencies of the divine law, and the power and efficacy of God's grace, from which our fruit is found, we must teach and admonish ourselves, and one another, to watch against sin and all approaches towards it, to converse much with the word of God, and abound in the fruit of righteousness; and, in praying over them, we must seek to God for his grace both to fortify us against every evil word and work and to furnish us for every good word and work.

Verses 4–6

Here is, I. The description of the ungodly given, *v.* 4. 1. In general, they are the reverse of the righteous, both in character and condition: *They are not so.* The Septuagint emphatically repeats this: *Not so the ungodly; they are not so;* they are led by the counsel of the wicked, in the way of sinners, to the seat of the scornful; they have no delight in the law of God, nor ever think of it; they bring forth no fruit but grapes of Sodom; they cumber the ground. 2. In particular, whereas the righteous are like valuable, useful, fruitful trees, *they are like the chaff which the wind drives away,* the very lightest of the chaff, the dust which the owner of the floor desires to have driven away, as not capable of being put to any use. Would you value them? Would you weigh them? They are like chaff, of no worth at all in God's account, how highly soever they may value themselves. Would you know the temper of their minds? They are light and vain; they have no substance in them, no solidity; they are easily driven to and fro by every wind and temptation, and have no stedfastness. Would you know their end? The wrath of God will drive them away in their wickedness, as the wind does the chaff, which is never gathered nor looked after more. The chaff may be, for a while, among the wheat; but he is coming *whose fan is in his hand* and who will *thoroughly purge his floor.* Those that by their own sin and folly make themselves as chaff will be found so before the whirlwind and fire of divine wrath (Ps. 35:5), so unable to stand before it or to escape it, Isa. 17:13.

II. The doom of the ungodly read, *v.* 5. 1. They will be cast, upon their trial, as traitors convicted: *They shall not stand in the judgment,* that is, they shall be found guilty, shall hang down the head with shame and confusion, and all their peals and excuses will be overruled as frivolous. There is a judgment to come, in which every man's present character and work, though ever so artfully concealed and disguised, shall be truly and perfectly discovered, and appear in their own colours, and accordingly every man's future state will be, by an irreversible sentence, determined for eternity. The ungodly must appear in that judgment, to receive according to the things done in the body. They may hope to come off, nay, to come off with honour, but their hope will deceive them: *They shall not stand in the judgment,* so plain will the evidence be against them and so just and impartial will the judgment be upon it. 2. They will be for ever shut out from the society of the blessed. They shall not stand *in the congregation of the righteous,* that is, in the *judgment* (so some), that court wherein the saints, as assessors with Christ, shall judge the world, those holy myriads with which he shall come to execute *judgment upon all,* Jude 14; 1 Co. 6:2. Or in *heaven. There* will be seen, shortly, a *general assembly of the church of the first-born, a congregation of the righteous,* of all the saints, and none but saints, and saints made perfect, such a congregation of them as never was in this world, 2 Th. 2:1. The wicked shall not have a place in that congregation. Into the new Jerusalem none unclean nor unsanctified shall enter; they shall see the righteous enter into the kingdom, and themselves, to their everlasting vexation, thrust out, Lu. 13:27. The wicked and profane, in this world, ridiculed the righteous and their congregation, despised them, and cared not for their company; justly therefore will they be for ever separated from them. Hypocrites in this world, under the disguise of a plausible profession, may thrust themselves into the congregation of the righteous and remain undisturbed and undiscovered there; but Christ cannot be imposed upon, though his ministers may; the day is coming when he will separate *between the sheep and the goats, the tares and the wheat;* see Mt. 13:41, 49. That *great day* (so the Chaldee here calls it) will be a day of discovery, a day of distinction, and a day of final division.

Then you shall return and discern between the righteous and the wicked, which here it is sometimes hard to do, Mal. 3:18.

III. The reason rendered of this different state of the godly and wicked, *v.* 6. 1. God must have all the glory of the prosperity and happiness of the righteous. They are blessed because *the Lord knows their way;* he chose them into it, inclined them to choose it, leads and guides them in it, and orders all their steps. 2. Sinners must bear all the blame of their own destruction. *Therefore* the ungodly perish, because the very way in which they have chosen and resolved to walk leads directly to destruction; it naturally tends towards ruin and therefore must necessarily end in it. Or we may take it thus, The Lord approves and is well pleased with the way of the righteous, and therefore, under the influence of his gracious smiles, it shall prosper and end well; but he is angry at the way of the wicked, all they do is offensive to him, and therefore it shall perish, and they in it. It is certain that every man's judgment proceeds from the Lord, and it is well or ill with us, and is likely to be so to all eternity, accordingly as we are or are not accepted of God. Let this support the drooping spirits of the righteous, that the Lord knows their way, knows their hearts (Jer. 12:3), knows their secret devotions (Mt. 6:6), knows their character, how much soever it is blackened and blemished by the reproaches of men, and will shortly make them and their way manifest before the world, to their immortal joy and honour. Let this cast a damp upon the security and jollity of sinners, that their way, though pleasant now, will perish at last.

In singing these verses, and praying over them, let us possess ourselves with a holy dread of the wicked man's portion, and deprecate it with a firm and lively expectation of the judgment to come, and stir up ourselves to prepare for it, and with a holy care to approve ourselves to God in every thing, entreating his favour with our whole hearts.

PSALM 2

As the foregoing psalm was moral, and showed us our duty, so this is evangelical, and shows us our Saviour. Under the type of David's kingdom (which was of divine appointment, met with much opposition, but prevailed at last) the kingdom of the Messiah, the Son of David, is prophesied of, which is the primary intention and scope of the psalm; and I think there is less in it of the type, and more of the anti-type, than in any of the gospel psalms, for there is nothing in it but what is applicable to Christ, but some things that are not at all applicable to David (*v.* 6, 7): "Thou art my Son" (*v.* 8), "I will give thee the uttermost parts of the earth," and (*v.* 12), "Kiss the Son." It is interpreted of Christ Acts 4:24; 13:33; Heb. 1:5. The Holy Ghost here foretels, I. The opposition that should be given to the kingdom of the Messiah (*v.* 1–3). II. The baffling and chastising of that opposition (*v.* 4, 5). III. The setting up of the kingdom of Christ, notwithstanding that opposition (*v.* 6). IV. The confirmation and establishment of it (*v.* 7). V. A promise of the enlargement and success of it (*v.* 8, 9). VI. A call and exhortation to kings and princes to yield themselves the willing subjects of this kingdom, (*v.* 10–12). Or thus: We have here, I. Threatenings denounced against the adversaries of Christ's kingdom (*v.* 1–6). II. Promises made to Christ himself, the head of this kingdom (*v.* 7–9). III. Counsel given to all to espouse the interests of this kingdom (*v.* 10–12). This psalm, as the former, is very fitly prefixed to this book of devotions, because, as it is necessary to our acceptance with God that we should be subject to the precepts of his law, so it is likewise that we should be subject to the grace of his gospel, and come to him in the name of a Mediator.

Verses 1–6

We have here a very great struggle about the kingdom of Christ, hell and heaven contesting it; the seat of the war is this earth, where Satan has long had a usurped kingdom and exercised dominion to such a degree that he has been called *the prince of the power of the* very *air* we breathe in and *the god of the world* we live in. He knows very well that, as the Messiah's kingdom rises and gets ground, his falls and loses ground; and therefore, though it will be set up certainly, it shall not be set up tamely. Observe here,

I. The mighty opposition that would be given to the Messiah and his kingdom, to his holy religion and all the interests of it, *v.* 1–3. One would have expected that so great a blessing to this world would be universally welcomed and embraced, and that every sheaf would immediately bow to that of the Messiah and all the crowns and sceptres on earth would be laid at his feet; but it proves quite contrary. Never were the notions of any sect of philosophers, though ever so absurd, nor the powers of any prince or state, though ever so tyrannical, opposed with so much violence as the doctrine and government of Christ — a sign that it was from heaven, for the opposition was plainly from hell originally.

1. We are here told who would appear as adversaries to Christ and the devil's instruments in this opposition to his kingdom. Princes and people, court and country, have sometimes separate interests, but here they are united against Christ; not the mighty only, but the mob, the *heathen,* the *people,* numbers of them, communities of them; though usually fond of liberty, yet they were averse to the liberty Christ came to procure and proclaim. Not the mob only, but the mighty (among whom one might have expected more sense and consideration) appear violent against Christ. Though his kingdom is not of this world, nor in the least calculated to weaken their interests, but very likely, if they pleased, to strengthen them, yet the kings of the earth and rulers are up in arms immediately. See the effects of the old enmity in the seed of the serpent against the seed of the woman, and how general and malignant the corruption of mankind is. See how formidable the enemies of the church are; they are numerous; they are potent. The unbelieving Jews are here called *heathen,* so wretchedly had they degenerated from the faith and holiness of their ancestors; they stirred up the heathen, the Gentiles, to persecute the Christians. As the Philistines and their lords, Saul and his courtiers, the disaffected party and their ringleaders, opposed David's coming to the crown, so Herod and Pilate, the Gentiles and the Jews, did their utmost against Christ and his interest in men, Acts 4:27.

2. Who it is that they quarrel with, and muster up all their forces against; it is *against the Lord and against his anointed,* that is, against all religion in general and the Christian religion in particular. It is certain that all who are enemies to Christ, whatever they pretend, are enemies to God himself; they *have hated both me and my Father,* Jn. 15:24. The great author of our holy religion is here called *the Lord's anointed,* or *Messiah,* or *Christ,* in allusion to the anointing of David to be king. He is both authorized and qualified to be the church's head and king, is duly invested in the office and every way fitted for it; yet there are those that are against him; nay, *therefore* they are against him, because they are impatient of God's authority, envious at Christ's advancement, and have a rooted enmity to the Spirit of holiness.

3. The opposition they give is here described. (1.) It is a most spiteful and malicious opposition. They *rage* and fret; they gnash their teeth for vexation at the setting up of Christ's kingdom; it creates them the utmost uneasiness, and fills them with indignation, so that they have no enjoyment of themselves; see Lu. 13:14; Jn. 11:47; Acts 5:17, 33; 19:28. Idolaters raged at the discovery of their folly, the chief priests and Pharisees at the eclipsing of their glory and the shaking of their usurped dominion. Those that did evil raged at the light. (2.) It is a deliberate and politic opposition. They *imagine* or meditate, that is, they contrive means to suppress the rising interests of Christ's kingdom and are very confident of the success of their contrivances; they promise themselves that they shall run down religion and carry the day. (3.) It is a resolute and obstinate opposition. They *set themselves,* set their faces as a flint and their hearts as an adamant, in defiance of reason, and conscience, and all the terrors of the Lord; they are proud and daring, like the Babel-builders, and will persist in their resolution, come what will. (4.) It is a combined and confederate opposition. They *take counsel together,* to assist and animate one another in this opposition; they carry their resolutions *nemine contradicente — unanimously,* that they will push on the unholy war against the Messiah with the utmost vigour: and thereupon councils are called, cabals are formed, and all their wits are at work to find out ways and means for the preventing of the establishment of Christ's kingdom, Ps. 83:5.

4. We are here told what it is they are exasperated at and what they aim at in this opposition (*v.* 3): *Let us break their bands asunder.* They will not be under any government; they are children of Belial, that cannot endure the yoke, at least the yoke of the Lord and his anointed. They will be content to entertain such notions of the kingdom of God and the Messiah as will serve them to dispute of and to support their own dominion with: if the Lord and his anointed will make them rich and great in the world, they will bid them welcome; but if they will restrain their corrupt appetites and passions, regulate and reform their hearts and lives, and bring them under the government of a pure and heavenly religion, truly then *they will not have this man to reign over them,* Lu. 19:14. Christ has *bands and cords* for us; those that will be saved by him must be ruled by him; but they are *cords of a man,* agreeable to right reason, and *bands of love,* conducive to our true interest: and yet against those the quarrel is. Why do men oppose religion but because they are impatient of its restraints and obligations? They would break asunder the bands of conscience they are under and the cords of God's commandments by which they are called to tie themselves out from all sin and to themselves up to all duty; they will not receive them, but cast them away as far from them as they can.

5. They are here reasoned with concerning it, *v.* 1. Why do they do this? (1.) They can show no good cause for opposing so just, holy, and gracious a government, which will not interfere with the secular powers, nor introduce any dangerous principles hurtful to kings or provinces; but, on the contrary, if universally received, would bring a heaven upon earth. (2.) They can hope for no good success in opposing so powerful a kingdom, with which they are utterly unable to contend. It is *a vain thing;* when they have done their worst Christ will have a church in the world and that church shall be glorious and triumphant. It is *built upon a rock, and the gates of hell shall not prevail against it.* The moon walks in brightness, though the dogs bark at it.

II. The mighty conquest gained over all this threatening opposition. If heaven and earth be the combatants, it is easy to foretel which will be the conqueror. Those that make this mighty struggle are the people of the earth, and the kings of the earth, who, being of the earth, are earthy; but he whom they contest with is one that *sits in the heavens, v.* 4. He is in the heaven, a place of such a vast prospect that he can oversee them all and all their projects; and such is his power that he can overcome them all and all their attempts. He sits there, as one easy and at rest, out of the reach of all their impotent menaces and attempts. There he sits as Judge in all the affairs of the children of men, perfectly secure of the full accomplishment of all his own purposes and designs, in spite of all opposition, Ps. 29:10. The perfect repose of the Eternal Mind may be our comfort under all the disquietments of our mind. We are tossed on earth, and in the sea, but he sits in the heavens, where he has prepared his throne for judgment; and therefore,

1. The attempts of Christ's enemies are easily ridiculed. God *laughs* at them as a company of fools. He *has them,* and all their attempts, *in derision,* and therefore *the virgin, the daughter of Zion, has despised them,* Isa. 37:22. Sinners' follies are the just sport of God's infinite wisdom and power; and those attempts of the kingdom of Satan which in our eyes are formidable in his are despicable. Sometimes God is said to *awake,* and *arise,* and *stir up himself,* for the vanquishing of his enemies; here is said to *sit still* and vanquish them; for the utmost operations of God's omnipotence create no difficulty at all, nor the least disturbance to his eternal rest.

2. They are justly punished, *v.* 5. Though God despises them as impotent, yet he does not therefore wink at them, but is justly displeased with them as impudent and impious, and will make the most daring sinners to know that he is so and to tremble before him. (1.) Their sin is a provocation to him. He is wroth; he is sorely displeased. We cannot expect that God should be reconciled to us, or well pleased in us, but in and through the anointed; and therefore, if we affront and reject him, we sin against the remedy and forfeit the benefit of his interposition between us and God. (2.) His anger will be a vexation to them; if he but speak to them in his wrath, even the breath of his mouth will be their confusion, slaughter, and consumption, Isa. 11:4; 2 Th. 2:8. He speaks, and it is done; he speaks in wrath, and sinners are undone. As a word made us, so a word can unmake us again. *Who knows the power of his anger?* The enemies rage, but cannot vex God. God sits still, and yet vexes them, puts them into a consternation (as the word is), and brings them to their wits' end: his setting up this kingdom of his Son, in spite of them, is the greatest vexation to them that can be. They were vexatious to Christ's good subjects; but the day is coming when vexation shall be recompensed to them.

3. They are certainly defeated, and all their counsels turned headlong (*v.* 6): *Yet have I set my king upon my holy hill of Zion.* David was advanced to the throne, and became master of the strong-hold of Zion, notwithstanding the disturbance given him by the malcontents in his kingdom, and particularly the affronts he received from the garrison of Zion, who taunted him with their blind and their lame, their maimed soldiers, 2 Sa. 5:6. The Lord Jesus is exalted to the right hand of the Father, has all power both in heaven and in earth, and is head over all things to the church, notwithstanding the restless endeavours of his enemies to hinder his advancement. (1.) Jesus Christ is a King, and is invested by him who is the fountain of power with the dignity and authority of a sovereign prince in the kingdom both of providence and grace. (2.) God is pleased to call him *his* King, because he is appointed by him, and entrusted for him with the sole administration of government and judgment. He is his King, for he is dear to the Father, and one in whom he is well pleased. (3.) Christ took not this honour to himself, but was called to it, and he that called him owns him: *I have set him;* his commandment, his commission, he received from the Father. (4.) Being called to this honour, he was confirmed in it; high places (we say) are slippery places, but Christ, being raised, is fixed: *"I have set him,* I have settled him." (5.) He is set upon *Zion,* the hill of God's holiness, a type of the gospel church, for on that the temple was built, for the sake of which the whole mount was called *holy.* Christ's throne is set up in his church, that is, in the hearts of all believers and in the societies they form. The evangelical law of Christ is said to *go forth from Zion* (Isa. 2:3, Mic. 4:2), and therefore that is spoken of as the head-quarters of this general, the royal seat of this prince, in whom the children of men shall be joyful.

We are to sing these verses with a holy exultation, triumphing over all the enemies of Christ's kingdom (not doubting but they will all of them be quickly made his footstool), and triumphing in Jesus Christ as the great trustee of power; and we are to pray, in firm belief of the assurance here given, "Father in heaven, *Thy kingdom come;* let thy Son's kingdom come."

Verses 7–9

We have heard what the kings of the earth have to say against Christ's kingdom, and have heard it gainsaid by him that sits in heaven; let us now hear what the Messiah himself has to say for his kingdom, to make good his claims, and it is what all the powers on earth cannot gainsay.

I. The kingdom of the Messiah is founded upon a decree, an eternal decree, of God the Father. It was not a sudden resolve, it was not the trial of an experiment, but the result of the counsels of the divine wisdom and the determinations of the divine will, before all worlds, neither of which can be altered — the *precept* or *statute* (so some read it), the *covenant* or *compact* (so others), the federal transactions between the Father and the Son concerning man's redemption, represented by the covenant of royalty made with David and his seed, Ps. 89:3. This our Lord Jesus often referred to as that which, all along in his undertaking, he governed himself by; *This is the will of him that sent me,* Jn. 6:40. *This commandment have I received of my Father,* Jn. 10:18; 14:31.

II. There is a declaration of that decree as far as is necessary for the satisfaction of all those who are called and commanded to yield themselves subjects to this king, and to leave those inexcusable who will not have him to reign over them. The decree was secret; it was what the Father said to the Son, when he possessed him in the beginning of his way, before his works of old; but it is declared by a faithful witness, who had lain in the bosom of the Father from eternity, and came into the world as the prophet of the church, to declare him, Jn. 1:18. The fountain of all being is, without doubt, the fountain of all power; and it is by, from, and under him, that the Messiah claims. He has his right to rule from what Jehovah said to him, by whose word all things were made and are governed. Christ here makes a tow-fold title to his kingdom: — 1. A title by inheritance (*v.* 7): *Thou art my Son, this day have I begotten thee.* This scripture the apostle quotes (Heb. 1:5) to prove that Christ has a more excellent name than the angels, but that he *obtained it by inheritance, v.* 4. He is the Son of God, not by adoption, but his begotten Son, the only begotten of the Father, Jn. 1:14. And the Father owns him, and will have this declared to the world as the reason why he is constituted King upon the holy hill of Zion; he is therefore unquestionably entitled to, and perfectly qualified for, that great trust. He is the Son of God, and therefore of the same nature with the Father, has in him all the fulness of the godhead, infinite wisdom, power, and holiness. The supreme government of the church is too high an honour and too hard an undertaking for any mere creature; none can be fit for it but he who is *one with the Father* and was *from eternity by him as one brought up with him,* thoroughly apprized of all his counsels, Prov. 8:30. He is the Son of God, and therefore dear to him, his beloved Son, in whom he is well pleased; and upon this account we are to receive him as a King; for because *the Father loveth the Son he hath given all things into his hand,* Jn. 3:35; 5:20. Being a Son, he is heir of all things, and, the Father having made the worlds by him, it is easy to infer thence that by him also he governs them; for he is the eternal Wisdom and the eternal Word. If God hath said unto him, *"Thou art my Son,"* it becomes each of us to say to him, "Thou art my Lord, my sovereign." Further, to satisfy us that his kingdom is well-grounded upon his sonship, we are here told what his sonship is grounded on: *This day have I begotten thee,* which refers both to his eternal generation itself, for it is quoted (Heb. 1:5) to prove that he is the *brightness of his Father's glory and the express image of his person* (*v.* 3), and to the evidence and demonstration given of it by his resurrection from the dead, for to that also it is expressly applied by the apostle, Acts 13:33. *He hath raised up Jesus again, as it is written, Thou art my Son, this day have I begotten thee.* It was by the resurrection from the dead, that sign of the prophet Jonas, which was to be the most convincing of all, that he was *declared to be the Son of God with power,* Rom. 1:4. Christ is said to be the *first-begotten* and *first-born from the dead,* Rev. 1:5; Col. 1:18. Immediately after his resurrection he entered upon the administration of his mediatorial kingdom; it was then that he said, *All power is given unto me,* and to that especially he had an eye when he taught his disciples to pray, *Thy kingdom come.* 2. A title by agreement, *v.* 8, 9. The agreement is, in short, this: the Son must undertake the office of an intercessor, and, upon that condition, he shall have the honour and power of a universal monarch; see Isa. 53:12, *Therefore will I divide him a portion with the great, because he made intercession for the transgressors. He shall be a priest upon his throne, and the counsel of peace shall be between them both,* Zec. 6:13. (1.) The Son must ask. This supposes his putting himself voluntarily into a state of inferiority to the Father, by taking upon him the human nature; for, as God, he was equal in power and glory with the Father and had nothing to ask. It supposes the making of a satisfaction by the virtue of which the intercession must be made, and the paying of a price, on which this large demand was to be grounded; see Jn. 17:4, 5. The Son, in asking the heathen for his inheritance, aims, not only at his own honour, but at their happiness in him; so that he intercedes for them, ever lives to do so, and is therefore able to save to the uttermost. (2.) The Father will grant more than to the half of the kingdom, even to the kingdom itself. It is here promised him, [1.] That his government shall be universal: he shall have *the heathen* for his inheritance, not the Jews only, to whose nation the church had been long confined, but the Gentiles also. Those in *the uttermost parts of the earth* (as this nation of ours) shall be his *possession,* and he shall have multitudes of willing loyal subjects among them. Baptized Christians are the possession of the Lord Jesus; they are to him for a name and a praise. God the Father gives them to him when by his Spirit and grave he works upon them to submit their necks to the yoke of the Lord Jesus. This is in part fulfilled; a great part of the Gentile world received the gospel when it was first preached, and Christ's throne was set up there where Satan's seat had long been. But it is to be yet further accomplished when *the kingdoms of this world shall become the kingdoms of the Lord and of his Christ,* Rev. 11:15. *Who shall live when God doeth this?* [2.] That it shall be victorious: *Thou shalt break them* (those of them that oppose thy kingdom) *with a rod of iron, v.* 9. This was in part fulfilled when the nation of the Jews, those that persisted in unbelief and enmity to Christ's gospel, were destroyed by the Roman power, which was represented (Dan. 2:40) by feet of iron, as here by a rod of iron. It had a further accomplishment in the destruction of the Pagan powers, when the Christian religion came to be established; but it will not be completely fulfilled till all opposing rule, principality, and power, shall be finally put down, 1 Co. 15:24. See ex. 5, 6. Observe, How powerful Christ is and how weak the enemies of his kingdom are before him; he has a rod of iron wherewith to crush those that will not submit to his golden sceptre; they are but like a potter's vessel before him, suddenly, easily, and irreparably dashed in pieces by him; see Rev. 2:27. "Thou shalt do it, that is, thou shalt have *leave* to do it." Nations shall be ruined, rather than the gospel church shall not be built and established. *I have loved thee, therefore will I give men for thee,* Isa. 43:4. "Thou shalt have power to do it; none shall be able to stand before thee; and thou shalt do it effectually." Those that will not bow shall break.

In singing this, and praying it over, we must give glory to Christ as the eternal Son of God and our rightful Lord, and must take comfort from this promise, and plead it with God, that the kingdom of Christ shall be enlarged and established and shall triumph over all opposition.

Verses 10–12

We have here the practical application of this gospel doctrine concerning the kingdom of the Messiah, by way of exhortation to the kings and judges of the earth. They hear that it is in vain to oppose Christ's government; let them therefore be so wise for themselves as to submit to it. He that has power to destroy them shows that he has no pleasure in their destruction, for he puts them into a way to make themselves happy, *v.* 10. Those that would be wise must be instructed; and those are truly wise that receive instruction from the word of God. Kings and judges stand upon a level with common persons before God; and it is as necessary for them to be religious as for any others. Those that give law and judgment to others must receive law from Christ, and it will be their wisdom to do so. What is said to them is said to all, and is required of every one of us, only it is directed to kings and judges because of the influence which their example will have upon their inferiors, and because they were men of rank and power that opposed the setting up of Christ's kingdom, *v.* 2. We are exhorted,

I. To reverence God and to stand in awe of him, *v.* 11. This is the great duty of natural religion. God is great, and infinitely above us, just and holy, and provoked against us, and therefore we ought to fear him and tremble before him; yet he is our Lord and Master, and we are bound to serve him, our friend and benefactor, and we have reason to rejoice in him; and these are very well consistent with each other, for, 1. We must serve God in all ordinances of worship, and all instances of a godly conversation, but with a holy fear, a jealousy over ourselves, and a reverence of him. Even kings themselves, whom others serve and fear, must serve and fear God; there is the same indefinite distance between them and God that there is between the meanest of their subjects and him. 2. We must rejoice in God, and, in subordination to him, we may rejoice in other things, but still with a holy trembling, as those that know what a glorious and jealous God he is, whose eye is always upon us. Our salvation must be wrought out *with fear and trembling,* Phil. 2:12. We ought to rejoice in the setting up of the kingdom of Christ, but to *rejoice with trembling,* with a holy awe of him, a holy fear for ourselves, lest we come short, and a tender concern for the many precious souls to whom his gospel and kingdom are a savour of death unto death. Whatever we rejoice in, in this world, it must always be with trembling, lest we grow vain in our joy and be puffed up with the things we rejoice in, and because of the uncertainty of them and the damp which by a thousand accidents may soon be cast upon our joy. To *rejoice with trembling is to rejoice as though we rejoiced not,* 1 Co. 7:30.

II. To welcome Jesus Christ and to submit to him, *v.* 12. This is the great duty of the Christian religion; it is that which is required of all, even kings and judges, and it is our wisdom and interest to do it. Observe here,

1. The command given to this purport: *Kiss the Son.* Christ is called the *Son* because so he was declared (*v.* 7), *Thou art my Son.* He is the Son of God by eternal generation, and, upon that account, he is to be adored by us. He is the *Son of man* (that is, the Mediator, Jn. 5:27), and, upon that account, to be received and submitted to. He is called the *Son,* to include both, as God is often called emphatically the *Father,* because he is the Father of our Lord Jesus Christ, and in him our Father, and we must have an eye to him under both considerations. Our duty to Christ is here expressed figuratively: *Kiss the Son,* not with a betraying kiss, as Judas kissed him, and as all hypocrites, who pretend to honour him, but really affront him; but with a believing kiss. (1.) With a kiss of agreement and reconciliation. Kiss, and be friends, as Jacob and Esau; let the quarrel between us and God terminate; let the acts of hostility cease, and let us be at peace with God in Christ, who is our peace. (2.) With a kiss of adoration and religious worship. Those that worshipped idols kissed them, 1 Ki. 19:18; Hos. 13:2. Let us study how to do honour to the Lord Jesus, and to give unto him the glory due unto his name. *He is thy Lord, and worship thou him,* Ps. 45:11. We must *worship the Lamb,* as well as him that sits on the throne, Rev. 5:9–13. (3.) With a kiss of affection and sincere love: *"Kiss the Son;* enter into a covenant of friendship with him, and let him be very dear and precious to you; love him above all, love him in sincerity, love him much, as she did to whom much was forgiven, and, in token of it, kissed his feet," Lu. 7:38. (4.) With a kiss of allegiance and loyalty, as Samuel kissed Saul, 1 Sa. 10:1. Swear fealty and homage to him, submit to his government, take his yoke upon you, and give up yourselves to be governed by his laws, disposed of by his providence, and entirely devoted to his interest.

2. The reasons to enforce this command; and they are taken from our own interest, which God, in his gospel, shows a concern for. Consider,

(1.) The certain ruin we run upon if we refuse and reject Christ: *"Kiss the Son;* for it is at your peril if you do not." [1.] "It will be a great provocation to him. Do it, *lest he be angry."* The Father is angry already; the Son is the Mediator that undertakes to make peace; if we slight him, the *Father's wrath abides upon us* (Jn. 3:36), and not only so, but there is an addition of the Son's wrath too, to whom nothing is more displeasing than to have the offers of his grace slighted and the designs of it frustrated. The Son can be angry, though a Lamb; he is the lion of the tribe of Judah, and the wrath of this king, this King of kings, will be as the roaring of a lion, and will drive even mighty men and chief captains to seek in vain for shelter in rocks and mountains, Rev. 6:16. If the Son be angry, who shall intercede for us? There remains no more sacrifice, no other name by which we can be saved. Unbelief is a sin against the remedy. [2.] It will be utter destruction to yourselves: *Lest you perish from the way,* or *in* the way so some, *in* the way of your sins, and *from* the way of your vain hopes; *lest your way perish* (as Ps. 1:6), lest you prove to have missed the way to happiness. Christ is the way; take heed lest you be cut off from him as your way to God. It intimates that they were, or at least thought themselves, in the way; but, by neglecting Christ, they perished from it, which aggravates their ruin, that they go to hell from the way to heaven, are not far from the kingdom of God and yet never arrive there.

(2.) The happiness we are sure of if we yield ourselves to Christ. When his wrath is kindled, though *but a little,* the least spark of that fire is enough to make the proudest sinner miserable if it fasten upon his conscience; for it will burn to the lowest hell: one would think it should therefore follow, "When his wrath is kindled, woe be to those that despise him;" but the Psalmist startles at the thought, deprecates that dreadful doom and pronounces those blessed that escape it. Those that trust in him, and so kiss him, are truly happy; but they will especially appear to be so when the wrath of Christ is kindled against others. Blessed will those be in the day of wrath, who, by trusting in Christ, have made him their refuge and patron; when the hearts of others fail them for fear they shall lift up their heads with joy; and then those who now despise Christ and his followers will be forced to say, to their own greater confusion, "Now we see that *blessed are all those,* and those only, *that trust in him."*

In singing this, and praying it over, we should have our

hearts filled with a holy awe of God, but at the same time borne up with a cheerful confidence in Christ, in whose mediation we may comfort and encourage ourselves and one another. *We are the circumcision, that rejoice in Christ Jesus.*

PSALM 3

As the foregoing psalm, in the type of David in preferment, showed us the royal dignity of the Redeemer, so this, by the example of David in distress, shows us the peace and holy security of the redeemed, how safe they really are, and think themselves to be, under the divine protection. David, being now driven out from his palace, from the royal city, from the holy city, by his rebellious son Absalom, I. Complains to God of his enemies (*v.* 1, 2). II. Confides in God, and encourages himself in him as his God, notwithstanding (*v.* 3). III. Recollects the satisfaction he had in the gracious answers God gave to his prayers, and his experience of his goodness to him (*v.* 4, 5). IV. Triumphs over his fears (*v.* 6) and over his enemies, whom he prays against, (*v.* 7). V. Gives God the glory and takes to himself the comfort of the divine blessing and salvation which are sure to all the people of God (*v.* 8). Those speak best of the truths of God who speak experimentally; so David here speaks of the power and goodness of God, and of the safety and tranquility of the godly.

A psalm of David, when he fled from Absalom his son.

Verses 1–3

The title of this psalm and many others is as a key hung ready at the door, to open it, and let us into the entertainments of it; when we know upon what occasion a psalm was penned we know the better how to expound it. This was composed, or at least the substance of it was meditated and digested in David's thought, and offered up to God, when he fled from Absalom his son, who formed a conspiracy against him, to take away, not his crown only, but his life; we have the story, 2 Sa. 15, etc. 1. David was now in great grief; when, in his flight, he went up the Mount of Olives, he wept greatly, with his head covered, and marching bare-foot; yet *then* he composed this comfortable psalm. He wept and prayed, wept and sung, wept and believed; this was sowing in tears. Is any afflicted? Let him pray; nay, let him sing psalms, let him sing this psalm. Is any afflicted with undutiful disobedient children? David was; and yet that did not hinder his joy in God, nor put him out of tune for holy songs. 2. He was now in great danger; the plot against him was laid deep, the party that sought his ruin was very formidable, and his own son at the head of them, so that his affairs seemed to be at the last extremity; yet *then* he kept hold of his interest in God and improved that. Perils and frights should drive us to God, not drive us from him. 3. He had now a great deal of provocation given him by those from whom he had reason to expect better things, from his son, whom he had been indulgent of, from his subjects, whom he had been so great a blessing to; this he could not but resent, and it was enough to break in upon any man's temper; yet he was so far from any indecent expressions of passion and indignation that he had calmness enough for those acts of devotion which require the greatest fixedness and freedom of thought. The sedateness of his mind was evinced by the Spirit's coming upon him; for the Spirit chooses to move upon the still waters. Let no unkindness, no, not of a child or a friend, ever be laid so much to heart as to disfit us for communion with God. 4. He was now suffering for his sin in the matter of Uriah; this was the evil which, for that sin, God threatened to *raise up against him out of his own house* (2 Sa. 12:11), which, no doubt, he observed, and took occasion thence to renew his repentance for it. Yet he did not *therefore* cast away his confidence in the divine power and goodness, nor despair of succour. Even our sorrow for sin must not hinder either our joy in God or our hope in God. 5. He seemed cowardly in fleeing from Absalom, and quitting his royal city, before he had had one struggle for it; and yet, by this psalm, it appears he was full of true courage arising from his faith in God. True Christian fortitude consists more in a gracious security and serenity of mind, in patiently bearing and patiently waiting, than in daring enterprises with sword in hand.

In these three verses he applies to God. Whither else should we go but to him when any thing grieves us or frightens us? David was now at a distance from his own closet, and from the courts of God's house, where he used to pray; and yet he could find a way open heaven-ward. Wherever we are we may have access to God, and may draw nigh to him whithersoever we are driven. David, in his flight, attends his God,

I. With a representation of his distress, *v.* 1, 2. He looks round, and as it were takes a view of his enemies' camp, or receives information of their designs against him, which he brings to God, not to his own council-board. Two things he complains of, concerning his enemies: — 1. That they were very many: *Lord, how are they increased!* beyond what they were at first, and beyond whatever he thought they would have been. Absalom's faction, like a snow-ball, strangely gathered in its motion. He speaks of it as one amazed, and well he might, that a people he had so many ways obliged should almost generally revolt from him, rebel against him, and choose for their head such a foolish and giddy young man as Absalom was. How slippery and deceitful are the many! And how little fidelity and constancy are to be found among men! David had had the hearts of his subjects as much as ever any king had, and yet now, of a sudden, he had lost them. As people must not trust too much to princes (Ps. 146:3), so princes must not build too much upon their interest in the people. Christ, the Son of David, had many enemies. When a great multitude came to seize him, when the crowd cried, *Crucify him, Crucify him,* how were those then increased that troubled him! Even good people must not think it strange if the stream be against them and the powers that threaten them grow more and more formidable. 2. That they were very malicious. They rose up against him; they aimed to trouble him; but that was not all: they said of his soul, *There is no help for him in God.* That is, (1.) They put a spiteful and invidious construction upon his troubles, as Job's friends did upon him, concluding that, because his servants and subjects forsook him thus and did not help him, God had deserted him and abandoned his cause, and he was therefore to be looked *on,* or rather to be looked *off,* as a hypocrite and a wicked man. (2.) They blasphemously reflected upon God as unable to relieve him: "His danger is so great that God himself cannot help him." It is strange that so great unbelief should be found in any, especially in many, in Israel, as to think any party of men too strong for Omnipotence to deal with. (3.) They endeavoured to shake his confidence in God and drive him to despair of relief from him: "They have said it *to* my soul;" so it may be read; compare Ps. 11:1; 42:10. This grieved him worst of all, that they had so bad an opinion of him as to think it possible to take him off from that foundation. The mere temptation was a buffeting to him, *a thorn in his flesh,* nay, a *sword in his bones.* Note, A child of God startles at the very thought of despairing of help in God; you cannot vex him with any thing so much as if you offer to persuade him that *there is no help for him in God.* David comes to God, and tells him what his enemies said of him, as Hezekiah spread Rabshakeh's blasphemous letter before the Lord. "They say, *There is no help for me in thee;* but, Lord, if it be so, I am undone. They say to my soul, *There is no salvation*" (for so the word is) *"for him in God;* but, Lord, do thou say unto my soul, *I am thy salvation* (Ps. 35:3) and that shall satisfy me, and in due time silence them." To this complaint he adds *Selah,* which occurs about seventy times in the book of Psalms. Some refer it to the music with which, in David's time, the psalms were sung; others to the sense, and that it is a note commanding a solemn pause. *Selah — Mark that,* or, *"Stop there,* and consider a little." As here, they say, *There is no help for him in God, Selah.* "Take time for such a thought as this. *Get thee behind me, Satan. The Lord rebuke thee!* Away with such a vile suggestion!"

II. With a profession of his dependence upon God, *v.* 3. An active believer, the more he is beaten off from God, either by the rebukes of Providence or the reproaches of enemies, the faster hold he will take of him and the closer will he cleave to him; so David here, when his enemies said, *There is no help for him in God,* cries out with so much the more assurance, *"But thou, O Lord! art a shield for me;* let them say what they will, I am sure thou wilt never desert me, and I am resolved I will never distrust thee." See what God is to his people, what he will be, what they have found him, what David found in him. 1. Safety: *"Thou art a shield for me,* a shield *about* me" (so some), "to secure me on all sides, since my enemies surrounded me." Not only *my shield* (Gen. 15:1), which denotes an interest in the divine protection, but a shield *for* me, which denotes the present benefit and advantage of that protection. 2. Honour: *Thou art my glory.* Those whom God owns for his are not safe and easy, but really look great, and have true honour put upon them, far above that which the great ones of the earth are proud of. David was now in disgrace; the crown had fallen from his head; but he will not think the worse of himself while he has God for his glory, Isa. 60:19. *"Thou art my glory;* thy glory I reckon mine" (so some); "this is what I aim at, and am ambitious of, whatever my lot is, and whatever becomes of my honour — that I may be to my God for a name and a praise." 3. Joy and deliverance: *"Thou art the lifter up of my head;* thou wilt lift up my head *out of* my troubles, and restore me to my dignity again, in due time; or, at least, thou wilt lift up my head *under* my troubles, so that I shall not droop nor be discouraged, nor shall my spirits fail." If, in the worst of times, God's people can lift up their heads with joy, knowing that all shall work for good to them, they will own it is God that is the lifter up of their head, that gives them both cause to rejoice and hearts to rejoice.

In singing this, and praying it over, we should possess ourselves with an apprehension of the danger we are in from the multitude and malice of our spiritual enemies, who seek the ruin of our souls by driving us from our God, and we should concern ourselves in the distresses and dangers of the church of God, which is every where spoken again, every where fought against; but, in reference to both, we should encourage ourselves in our God, who owns and protects and will in due time crown his own interest both in the world and in the hearts of his people.

Verses 4–8

David, having stirred up himself by the irritations of his enemies to take hold on God as his God, and so gained comfort in looking upward when, if he looked round about him, nothing appeared but what was discouraging, here looks back with pleasing reflections upon the benefit he had derived from trusting in God and looks forward with pleasing expectations of a very bright and happy issue to which the dark dispensation he was now under would shortly be brought.

I. See with what comfort he looks back upon the communion he had had with God, and the communications of his favour to him, either in some former trouble he had been in, and through God's goodness got through, or in this hitherto. David had been exercised with many difficulties, often oppressed and brought very low; but still he had found God all-sufficient. He now remembered with pleasure,

1. That his troubles had always brought him to his knees, and that, in all his difficulties and dangers, he had been enabled to acknowledge God and to lift up his heart to him, and his voice too (this will be comfortable reflection when we are in trouble): *I cried unto God with my voice.* Care and grief do us good and no hurt when they set us a praying, and engage us, not only to speak to God, but to cry to him, as those that are in earnest. And though God understands the language of the heart, when the *voice is not heard* (1 Sa. 1:13), and values not the hypocritical prayers of those who *cause their voice to be heard on high* (Isa. 58:4), *vox et praeterea nihil — mere sound,* yet, when the earnestness of the voice comes from the fervency of the heart, it shall be taken notice of, in the account, that we cried unto God with our *voice.*

2. That he had always found God ready to answer his prayers: *He heard me out of his holy hill,* from heaven, the high and holy place, from the ark on Mount Sion, whence he used to give answers to those that sought to him. David had ordered Zadok to *carry back the ark into the city* when he was flying from Absalom (2 Sa. 15:25), knowing that God was not tied, no, not to the ark of his presence, and that, notwithstanding the distance of place, he could by faith receive answers of peace from the holy hill. No such things can fix a gulf between the communications of God's grace towards us and the operations of his grace in us, between his favour and our faith. The ark of the covenant was in Mount Zion, and all the answers to our prayers come from the promises of that covenant. Christ was *set King upon the holy hill of Zion* (Ps. 2:6), and it is through him, whom the Father hears always, that our prayers are heard.

3. That he had always been very safe and very easy under the divine protection (*v.* 5): *"I laid myself down and*

slept, composed and quiet; *and awaked* refreshed, *for the Lord sustained me."* (1.) This is applicable to the common mercies of every night, which we ought to give thanks for alone, and with our families, every morning. Many have not where to lay their head (but wander in deserts), or, if they have, dare not lie down for fear of the enemy; but we have laid ourselves down in peace. Many lie down and cannot sleep, but are full of tossings to and fro till the dawning of the day, through pain of body, or anguish of mind, or the continual alarms of fear in the night; but we lie down and sleep in safety, though incapable of doing any thing then for our own preservation. Many lie down and sleep, and never awake again, they sleep the sleep of death, as the first-born of the Egyptians; but we lie down and sleep, and awake again to the light and comfort of another day; and whence is it, but because the Lord has sustained us with sleep as with food? We have been safe under his protection and easy in the arms of his good providence. (2.) It seems here to be meant of the wonderful quietness and calmness of David's spirit, in the midst of his dangers. Having by prayer committed himself and his cause to God, and being sure of his protection, his heart was fixed, and he was easy. The undutifulness of his son, the disloyalty of his subjects, the treachery of many of his friends, the hazard of his person, the fatigues of his march, and the uncertainty of the event, never deprived him of an hour's sleep, nor gave any disturbance to his repose; for the Lord, by his grace and the consolations of his Spirit, powerfully sustained him and made him easy. It is a great mercy when we are in trouble to have our minds stayed upon God, so as never either to eat or sleep with trembling and astonishment. (3.) Some of the ancients apply it to the resurrection of Christ. In his sufferings he offered up strong cries, and was heard; and therefore, though he laid down and slept the sleep of death, yet he awaked the third day, for the Lord sustained him, that he should not see corruption.

4. That God had often broken the power and restrained the malice of his enemies, had *smitten them upon the cheek-bone* (v. 7), had silenced them and spoiled their speaking, blemished them and put them to shame, smitten them on the cheek reproachfully, had disabled them to do the mischief they intended; for he had broken their teeth. Saul and the Philistines, who were sometimes ready to swallow him up, could not effect what they designed. The teeth that are gnashed or sharpened against God's people shall be broken. When, at any time, the power of the church's enemies seems threatening, it is good to remember how often God has broken it; and we are sure that his arm is not shortened. He can stop their mouths and tie their hands.

II. See with what confidence he looks forward to the dangers he had yet in prospect. Having put himself under God's protection and often found the benefit of it, 1. His *fears were all stilled and silenced, v.* 6. With what a holy bravery does he bid defiance to the impotent menaces and attempts of his enemies! *"I will not be afraid of ten thousands of people,* that either in a foreign invasion or an intestine rebellion *set themselves,* or encamp, *against me round about."* No man seemed less safe (his enemies are numerous, *ten thousands;* they are spiteful and resolute, "They have set themselves against me; nay, they have prevailed far, and seem to have gained their point; for they are against me round about on every side, thousands against one"), and yet no man was more secure: "I will not be afraid, for all this; they cannot hurt me, and therefore they shall not frighten me; whatever prudent methods I take for my own preservation, I will not disquiet myself, distrust my God, nor doubt of a good issue at last." When David, in his flight from Absalom, bade Zadok carry back the ark, he spoke doubtfully of the issue of his present troubles, and concluded, like a humble penitent, *Here I am; let him do to me what seemeth to him good,* 2 Sa. 15:26. But now, like a strong believer, he speaks confidently, and has no fear concerning the event. Note, A cheerful resignation to God is the way to obtain a cheerful satisfaction and confidence in God. 2. His prayers were quickened and encouraged, *v.* 7. He believed God was his Saviour, and yet prays; nay, he *therefore* prays, *Arise, O Lord! save me, O my God!* Promises of salvation do not supersede, but engage, our petitions for it. He will for this be enquired of. 3. His faith became triumphant. He began the psalm with complaints of the strength and malice of his enemies, but

concludes it with exultation in the power and grace of his God, and now sees more with him than against him, *v.* 8. Two great truths he here builds his confidence upon and fetches comfort from. (1.) That *salvation belongeth unto the Lord;* he has power to save, be the danger ever so great; it is his prerogative to save, when all other helps and succours fail; it is his pleasure, it is his property, it is his promise to those that are his, whose salvation is not of themselves, but of the Lord. Therefore all that have the Lord for their God, according to the tenour of the new covenant, are sure of salvation; for he that is their God is the God of salvation. (2.) That his blessing is upon his people; he not only has power to save them, but he has assured them of his kind and gracious intentions towards them. He has, in his word, pronounced a blessing upon his people; and we are bound to believe that that blessing does accordingly rest upon them, though there be not the visible effects of it. Hence we may conclude that God's people, though they may lie under the reproaches and censures of men, are surely blessed of him, who blesses indeed, and therefore can command a blessing.

In singing this, and praying it over, we must own the satisfaction we have had in depending upon God and committing ourselves to him, and encourage ourselves, and one another to continue still hoping and quietly waiting for the salvation of the Lord.

PSALM 4

David was a preacher, a royal preacher, as well as Solomon; many of his psalms are doctrinal and practical as well as devotional; the greatest part of this psalm is so, in which Wisdom cries to men, to the sons of men (as Prov. 8:4, 5), to receive instruction. The title does not tell us, as that of the former did, that it was penned on any particular occasion, nor are we to think that all the psalms were occasional, though some were, but that many of them were designed in general for the instruction of the people of God, who attended in the courts of his house, the assisting of their devotions, and the directing of their conversations: such a one I take this psalm to be. Let us not make the prophecy of scripture to be of more private interpretation than needs must, 2 Pt. 1:20. Here I. David begins with a short prayer (v. 1) and that prayer preaches. II. He directs his speech to the children of men, and, 1. In God's name reproves them for the dishonour they do to God and the damage they do to their own souls (v. 2). 2. He sets before them the happiness of godly people for their encouragement to be religious (v. 3). 3. He calls upon them to consider their ways (v. 4). III. He exhorts them to serve God and trust in him (v. 5). IV. He gives an account of his own experiences of the grace of God working in him, 1. Enabling him to choose God's favour for his felicity (v. 6). 2. Filling his heart with joy therein (v. 7). 3. Quieting his spirit in the assurance of the divine protection he was under, night and day (v. 8).

To the chief musician on Neginoth. A psalm of David.

Verses 1-5

The title of the psalm acquaints us that David, having penned it by divine inspiration for the use of the church, delivered it to the chief musician, or master of the song, who (according to the divine appointment of psalmody made in his time, which he was chiefly instrumental in the establishment of) presided in that service. We have a particular account of the constitution, the modelling of the several classes of singers, each with a chief, and the share each bore in the work, 1 Chr. 25. Some *prophesied according to the order of the king, v.* 2. Others *prophesied with a harp, to give thanks, and to praise the Lord, v.* 3. Of others it is said that they were to *lift up the horn, v.* 5. But of them all, that they were *for song in the house of the Lord* (v. 6) and were *instructed in the songs of the Lord, v.* 7. This psalm was committed to one of the chiefs, to be sung on *neginoth — stringed instruments* (Hab. 3:19), which were played on with the hand; with music of that kind the choristers were to sing this psalm: and it should seem that then *they* only sung, not the people; but the New-Testament appoints all Christians to sing (Eph. 5:19; Col. 3:16), from whom it is expected that they do it decently, not artfully; and therefore there is not now so much occasion for musical instruments as there was then: the melody is to be made in the heart. In these verses,

I. David addresses himself to God, *v.* 1. Whether the *sons of men,* to whom he is about to speak, will hear, or whether they will forbear, he hopes and prays that God will give him a generous audience, and an answer of peace: *"Hear me when I call,* and accept my adorations, grant my petitions, and judge upon my appeals; *have mercy upon me, and hear me."* All the notice God is pleased to take of our prayers, and all the returns he is pleased to make to them, must be ascribed, not to our merit, but purely to his mercy.

"Hear me for thy mercy-sake" is our best plea. Two things David here pleads further: — 1. "Thou art *the God of my righteousness;* not only a righteous God thyself, but the author of my righteous dispositions, who hast by the grace wrought that good that is in me, hast made me a righteous man; therefore *hear men,* and so attest thy own work in me; thou art also the patron of my righteous cause, the protector of my wronged innocency, to whom I commit my way, and whom I trust to *bring forth my righteousness as the light."* When men condemn us unjustly, this is our comfort, *It is God that justifies;* he is the God of a believer's righteousness. 2. *"Thou has* formerly *enlarged me when I was in distress,* enlarged my heart in holy joy and comfort under my distresses, enlarged my condition by bringing me out of my distresses; therefore *now, Lord, have mercy upon me, and hear me."* The experience we have had of God's goodness to us in enlarging us when we have been in distress is not only a great encouragement to our faith and hope for the future, but a good plea with God in prayer. *"Thou hast; wilt thou not?* For thou art God, and changest not; thy work is perfect."

II. He addresses himself to the children of men, for the conviction and conversion of those that are yet strangers to God, and that will not have the Messiah, the Son of David, to reign over them.

1. He endeavours to convince them of the folly of their impiety (v. 2). *"O you sons of Men"* (of *great* men, so some, men of high degree, understanding it of the partisans of Saul or Absalom), *"how long will you* oppose me and my government, and continue disaffected to it, under the influence of the false and groundless suggestions of those that wish evil to me?"* Or it may be taken more generally. God, by the psalmist, here reasons with sinners to bring them to repentance. "You that go on in the neglect of God and his worship, and in contempt of the kingdom of Christ and his government, consider what you do." (1.) "You debase yourselves, for you are *sons of men"* (the word signifies man as a noble creature); "consider the dignity of your nature, and the excellency of those powers of reason with which you are endued, and do not act thus irrationally and unbecoming yourselves." Let the *sons of men* consider and show themselves men. (2.) "You dishonour your Maker, and *turn his glory into shame."* They may well be taken as God's own words, charging sinners with the wrong they do him in his honour: or, if David's words, the term glory may be understood of God, whom he called *his glory,* Ps. 3:3. Idolaters are charged with *changing the glory of God* into shame, Rom. 1:23. All wilful sinners do so by disobeying the commands of his law, despising the offers of his grace, and giving the affection and service to the creature which are due to God only. Those that profane God's holy name, that ridicule his word and ordinances, and, while they profess to know him, in works deny him, do what in them lies to *turn his glory into shame.* (3.) "You put a cheat upon yourselves: *You love vanity,* and *seek after leasing,* or *lying,* or that which is *a lie.* You are yourselves vain and lying, and you love to be so." Or, "You set your hearts upon that which will prove, at last, but vanity and a lie." Those that love the world, and seek the things that are beneath, love vanity, and seek lies; as those also do that please themselves with the delights of sense, and portion themselves with the wealth of this world; for these will deceive them, and so ruin them. "How long will you do this? Will you never be wise for yourselves, never consider your duty and interest? *When shall it once be?"* Jer. 13:27. The God of heaven thinks the time long that sinners persist in dishonouring him and in deceiving and ruining themselves.

2. He shows them the peculiar favour which God has for good people, the special protection they are under, and the singular privileges to which they are entitled, *v.* 3. This comes in here, (1.) As a reason why they should not oppose or persecute him that is godly, nor think to run him down. It is at their peril if they *offend one of these little ones,* whom God has *set apart for himself,* Mt. 18:6. God reckons that those who touch them touch the apple of his eye; and he will make their persecutors to know it, sooner or later. They have an interest in heaven, God will hear them, and therefore let none dare to do them any injury, for God will hear their cry and plead their cause, Ex. 22:23. It is generally supposed that David speaks of his own designation to the throne; he is the *godly* man whom *the Lord*

has set apart for that honour, and who does not usurp it or assume it to himself: "The opposition therefore which you give to him and to his advancement is very criminal, for therein you fight against God, and it will be vain and ineffectual." God has, in like manner, set apart the Lord Jesus for himself, that merciful One; and those that attempt to hinder his advancement will certainly be baffled, for the Father hears him always. Or, (2.) As a reason why they should themselves be good, and walk no longer in the counsel of the ungodly: "You have hitherto sought vanity; be truly religious, and you will be truly happy here and for ever; for," [1.] "God will secure to himself his interest in you." *The Lord has set apart him that is godly,* every particular godly man, *for himself,* in his eternal choice, in his effectual calling, in the special disposals of his providence and operations of his grace; his people are *purified unto him a peculiar people.* Godly men are God's separated, sealed, ones; he knows those that are his, and has set his image and superscription upon them; he distinguishes them with uncommon favours: *They shall be mine, saith the Lord, in that day when I make up my jewels. Know this;* let godly people know it, and let them never alienate themselves from him to whom they are thus appropriated; let wicked people know it, and take heed how they hurt those whom God protects. [2.] "God will secure to you an interest in himself." This David speaks with application: *The Lord will hear when I call unto him.* We should think ourselves happy if we had the ear of an earthly prince; and is it not worth while upon any terms, especially such easy ones, to gain the ear of the King of kings? Let us know this, and forsake lying vanities for our own mercies.

3. He warns them against sin, and exhorts them both to frighten and to reason themselves out of it (*v.* 4): *"Stand in awe and sin not"* (*be angry and sin not,* so the Septuagint, and some think the apostle takes that exhortation from him, Eph. 4:26); *"commune with your own hearts;* be converted, and, in order thereunto, consider and fear." Note, (1.) We must not sin, must not miss our way and so miss our aim. (2.) One good remedy against sin is to stand in awe. *Be moved* (so some), in opposition to carelessness and carnal security. "Always keep up a holy reverence of the glory and majesty of God, and a holy dread of his wrath and curse, and dare not to provoke him." (3.) One good means of preventing sin, and preserving a holy awe, is to be frequent and serious in *communing with our own hearts: "Talk with your hearts;* you have a great deal to say to them; they may be spoken with at any time; let it not be unsaid." A thinking man is in a fair way to be a wise and a good man. *"Commune with your hearts;* examine them by serious self-reflection, that you may acquaint yourselves with them and amend what is amiss in them; employ them in solemn pious meditations; let your thoughts fasten upon that which is good and keep closely to it. Consider your ways, and observe the directions here given in order to the doing of this work well and to good purpose." [1.] "Choose a solitary time; do it when you lie awake *upon your beds.* Before you turn yourself to go to sleep at night" (as some of the heathen moralists have directed) "examine your consciences with respect to what you have done that day, particularly what you have done amiss, that you may repent of it. When you awake in the night meditate upon God, and the things that belong to your peace." David himself practised what he here counsels others to do (Ps. 63:6), *I remember thee on my bed.* Upon a sick-bed, particularly, we should consider our ways and commune with our own hearts about them. [2.] "Compose yourselves into a serious frame: *Be still.* When you have asked conscience a question be silent, and wait for an answer; even in unquiet times keep you spirits calm and quiet."

4. He counsels them to make conscience of their duty (*v.* 5): *Offer to God the sacrifice of righteousness.* We must not only cease to do evil, but learn to do well. Those that were disaffected to David and his government would soon come to a better temper, and return to their allegiance, if they would but worship God aright; and those that know the concerns that lie between them and God will be glad of the Mediator, the Son of David. It is required here from every one of us, (1.) That we serve him: *"Offer sacrifices to him,* your own selves first, and your best sacrifices." But they must be *sacrifices of righteousness,* that is, good works, all the fruits of the reigning love of God and our neighbour, and all the instances of a religious conversation, which are better than all burnt-offerings and sacrifices. "Let all your devotions come from an upright heart; let all your alms be sacrifices of righteousness." The sacrifices of the unrighteous God will not accept; they are an abomination, Isa. 1:11, etc. (2.) That we confide in him. "First make conscience of offering the sacrifices of righteousness and then you are welcome to put your trust in the Lord. Serve God without any diffidence of him, or any fear of losing by him. Honour him, by trusting in him only, and not in your wealth nor in an arm of flesh; trust in his providence, and lean not to your own understanding; trust in his grace, and go not about to establish your own righteousness or sufficiency."

In singing these verses we must preach to ourselves the doctrine of the provoking nature of sin, the lying vanity of the world, and the unspeakable happiness of God's people; and we must press upon ourselves the duties of fearing God, conversing with our own hearts, and offering spiritual sacrifices; and in praying over these verses we must beg of God grace thus to think and thus to do.

Verses 6–8

We have here,

I. The foolish wish of worldly people: *There be many that say, Who will show us any good? Who will make us to see good?* What good they meant is intimated, *v.* 7. It was the increase of their corn and wine; all they desired was plenty of the wealth of this world, that they might enjoy abundance of the delights of sense. Thus far they are right, that they are desirous of good and solicitous about it; but there are these things amiss in this wish: — 1. They enquire, in general, "Who will make us happy?" but do not apply themselves to God who alone can; and so they expose themselves to be ill-advised, and show they would rather be beholden to any than to God, for they would willingly live without him. 2. They enquire for good that may be seen, seeming good, sensible good; and they show no concern for the good things that are out of sight and are the objects of faith only. The source of idolatry was a desire of gods that they might see, therefore they worshipped the sun; but, as we must be taught to worship an unseen God, so to seek an unseen good, 2 Co. 4:18. We look with an eye of faith further than we can see with an eye of sense. 3. They enquire for *any* good, not for the chief good; all they want is outward good, present good, partial good, good meat, good drink, a good trade, and a good estate; and what are all these worth without a good God and a good heart? Any good will serve the turn of most men, but a gracious soul will not be put off so. This way, this wish, of carnal worldlings is their folly, yet *many there be* that join in it; and their doom will be accordingly. *"Son, remember that thou in thy life-time receivedst thy good things,* the penny thou didst agree for."

II. The wise choice which godly people make. David, and the pious few that adhered to him, dissented from that wish, and joined in this prayer, *Lord, lift thou up the light of thy countenance upon us.* 1. He disagrees from the vote of the many. God had set him apart for himself by distinguishing favours, and therefore he sets himself apart by a distinguishing character. "They are for any good, for worldly good, but so am not I; I will not say as they say; any good will not serve my turn; the wealth of the world will never make a portion for my soul, and therefore I cannot take up with it." 2. He and his friends agree in their choice of God's favour as their felicity; it is this which in their account is better than life and all the comforts of life. (1.) This is what they most earnestly desire and seek after; this is the breathing of their souls, *"Lord, lift thou up the light of thy countenance upon us.* Most are for other things, but we are for this." Good people, as they are distinguished by their practices, so they are by their prayers, not the length and language of them, but the faith and fervency of them; those whom God has set apart have a prayer by themselves, which, though others may speak the words of it, they only offer up in sincerity; and this is a prayer which they all say *Amen* to; "Lord, let us have thy favour, and let us know that we have it, and we desire no more; that is enough to make us happy. Lord, be at peace with us, accept of us, manifest thyself to us, let us be satisfied *of* thy loving-kindness and we will be satisfied *with* it." Observe, Though David speaks of himself only in the 7th and 8th verses, he speaks, in this prayer, for others also, — *"upon us,"* as Christ taught us to pray, *"Our Father."* All the saints come to the throne of grace on the same errand, and in this they are one, they all desire God's favour as their chief good. We should beg it for others as well as for ourselves, for in God's favour there is enough for us all and we shall have never the less for others sharing in what we have. (2.) This is what, above any thing, they rejoice in (*v.* 7): *"Thou hast* hereby often *put gladness into my heart;* not only supported and refreshed me, but filled me with joy unspeakable; and therefore this is what I will still pursue, what I will seek after all the days of my life." When God puts grace in the heart he *puts gladness in the heart;* nor is any joy comparable to that which gracious souls have in the communications of the divine favour, no, not the joy of harvest, of a plentiful harvest, when the corn and wine increase. This is gladness in the heart, inward, solid, substantial joy. The mirth of worldly people is but a flash, a shadow; *even in laughter their heart is sorrowful,* Prov. 14:13. "Thou hast *given* gladness in my heart;" so the word is. True joy is God's gift, *not as the world giveth,* Jn. 14:27. The saints have no reason to envy carnal worldlings their mirth and joy, but should pity them rather, for they may know better and will not. (3.) This is what they entirely confide in, and in this confidence they are always easy, *v.* 8. He had laid himself down and slept (Ps. 3:5), and so he will still: *"I will lay myself down* (having the assurance of thy favour) *in peace,* and with as much pleasure as those whose corn and wine increase, and who lie down as Boaz did in his threshing-floor, at the end of the heap of corn, to sleep there when *his heart was merry* (Ruth 3:7), *for thou only makest me to dwell in safety.* Though I am alone, yet I am not alone, for God is with me; though I have no guards to attend me, the Lord alone is sufficient to protect me; he can do it himself when all other defences fail." If he have the light of God's countenance, [1.] He can enjoy himself. His soul returns to God, and reposes itself in him as its rest, and so he lays himself down and sleeps in peace. He has what he would have and is sure that nothing can come amiss to him. [2.] He fears no disturbance from his enemies, sleeps quietly, and is very secure, because God himself has undertaken to keep him safe. When he comes to sleep the sleep of death, and to lie down in the grave, and to make his bed in the darkness, he will then, with good old Simeon, *depart in peace* (Lu. 2:29), being assured that God will receive his soul, to be safe with himself, and that his body also shall be made to dwell in safety in the grave. [3.] He commits all his affairs to God, and contentedly leaves the issue of them with him. It is said of the husbandman that, having *cast his seed into the ground, he sleeps and rises night and day, and the seed springs and grows up, he knows not how,* Mk. 4:26, 27. So a good man, having by faith and prayer cast his care upon God, sleeps and rests night and day, and is very easy, leaving it to his God to perform all things for him and prepared to welcome his holy will.

In singing these verses, and praying over them, let us, with a holy contempt of the wealth and pleasure of this world, as insufficient to make us happy, earnestly seek the favour of God and pleasingly solace ourselves in that favour; and, with a holy indifferency about the issue of all our worldly concerns, let us commit ourselves and all our affairs to the guidance and custody of the divine Providence, and be satisfied that all shall be made to work for good to us if we keep ourselves in the love of God.

PSALM 5

The psalm is a prayer, a solemn address to God, at a time when the psalmist was brought into distress by the malice of his enemies. Many such times passed over David, nay, there was scarcely any time of his life to which this psalm may not be accommodated, for in this he was a type of Christ, that he was continually beset with enemies, and his powerful and prevalent appeals to God, when he was so beset, pointed at Christ's dependence on his Father and triumphs over the powers of darkness in the midst of his sufferings. In this psalm, I. David settles a correspondence between his soul and God, promising to pray, and promising himself that God would certainly hear him (*v.* 1–3). II. He gives to God the glory, and takes to himself the comfort, of God's holiness (*v.* 4–6). III. He declares his resolution to keep close to the public worship of God (*v.* 7). IV. He prayed, 1. For himself, that God would guide him, (*v.* 8). 2. Against his enemies, that God would destroy them (*v.* 9, 10). 3. For all the people of God, that God would give them joy, and keep them safe (*v.* 11, 12). And this is all of great use to direct us in prayer.

To the chief musician upon Nehiloth. A psalm of David.

Verses 1–6

The title of this psalm has nothing in it peculiar but that it is said to be upon *Nehiloth,* a word nowhere else used. It is conjectured (and it is but a conjecture) that is signifies *wind*-instruments, with which this psalm was sung, as *Neginoth* was supposed to signify the *stringed*-instruments. In these verses David had an eye to God,

I. As a prayer-hearing God; such he has always been ever since men began to call upon the name of the Lord, and yet is still as ready to hear prayer as ever. Observe how David here styles him: *O Lord* (*v.* 1, 3), *Jehovah,* a self-existent, self-sufficient, Being, whom we are bound to adore, and, *"my King and my God* (*v.* 2), whom I have avouched for my God, to whom I have sworn allegiance, and under whose protection I have put myself as my King." We believe that the God we pray to is a King, and a God. King of kings and God of gods; but that is not enough: the most commanding encouraging principle of prayer, and the most powerful or prevailing plea in prayer, is to look upon him as *our* King and *our* God, to whom we lie under peculiar obligations and from whom we have peculiar expectations. Now observe,

1. What David here prays for, which may encourage our faith and hopes in all our addresses to God. If we pray fervently, and in faith, we have reason to hope, (1.) That God will take cognizance of our case, the representation we make of it and the requests we make upon it; for so he prays here: *Give ear to my words, O Lord!* Though God is in heaven, he has an ear open to his people's prayers, and it is not heavy, that he cannot hear. Men perhaps will not or cannot hear us; our enemies are so haughty that they will not, our friends at such a distance that they cannot; but God, though high, though in heaven, can, and will. (2.) That he will take it into his wise and compassionate consideration, and will not slight it, or turn it off with a cursory answer; for so he prays: *Consider my meditation.* David's prayers were not his words only, but his meditations; as meditation is the best preparative for prayer, so prayer is the best issue of meditation. Meditation and prayer should go together, Ps. 19:14. It is when we thus consider our prayers, and then only, that we may expect that God will consider them, and take that to his heart which comes from ours. (3.) That he will, in due time, return a gracious answer of peace; for so he prays (*v.* 2): *Hearken to the voice of my cry.* His prayer was a *cry;* it was *the voice of his cry,* which denotes fervency of affection and importunity of expression; and such effectual fervent prayers of a righteous man avail much and do wonders.

2. What David here promises, as the condition on his part to be performed, fulfilled, and kept, that he might obtain this gracious acceptance; this may guide and govern us in our addresses to God, that we may present them aright, for we ask, and have not, if we ask amiss. Four things David here promises, and so must we: — (1.) That he will pray, that he will make conscience of praying, and make a business of it: *Unto thee will I pray.* "Others live without prayer, but I will pray." Kings on their own thrones (so David was) must be beggars at God's throne. "Others pray to strange gods, and expect relief from them, but to thee, to thee only, will I pray." The assurances God has given us of his readiness to hear prayer should confirm our resolution to live and die praying. (2.) That he will pray *in the morning.* His praying voice shall be heard then, and then shall his prayer be directed; that shall be the date of his letters to heaven, not that only ("Morning, and evening, and at noon, will I pray, nay, seven times a day, will I praise thee"), but that certainly. Morning prayer is our duty; we are the fittest for prayer when we are in the most fresh, and lively, and composed frame, got clear of the slumbers of the night, revived by them, and not yet filled with the business of the day. We have then most need of prayer, considering the dangers and temptations of the day to which we are exposed, and against which we are concerned; by faith and prayer, to fetch in fresh supplies of grace. (3.) That he will have his eye single and his heart intent in the duty: *I will direct my prayer,* as a marksman directs his arrow to the white; with such a fixedness and steadiness of mind should we address ourselves to God. Or as we direct a letter to a friend at such a place so must we direct our prayers to God as our Father in heaven; and let us always send them by the Lord Jesus, the great Mediator, and then they will be sure not to miscarry. All our prayers must be directed to God; his honour and glory must be aimed at as our highest end in all our prayers. Let our first petition be, *Hallowed,* glorified, *by thy name,* and then we may be sure of the same gracious answer to it that was given to Christ himself: *I have glorified it, and I will glorify it yet again.* (4.) That he will patiently wait for an answer of peace: "I *will look up,* will look after my prayers, and *hear what God the Lord will speak* (Ps. 85:8; Hab. 2:1), that, if he grant what I asked, I may be thankful — if he deny, I may be patient — if he defer, I may continue to pray and wait and may not faint." We must look *up,* or look *out,* as he that has shot an arrow looks to see how near it has come to the mark. We lose much of the comfort of our prayers for want of observing the returns of them. Thus praying, thus waiting, as the lame man looked stedfastly on Peter and John (Acts 3:4), we may expect that God will give ear to our words and consider them, and to him we may refer ourselves, as David here, who does not pray, "Lord, do this, or the other, for me;" but, "Hearken to me, consider my case, and do in it as seemeth good unto thee."

II. As a sin-hating God, *v.* 4–6. David takes notice of this, 1. As a warning to himself, and all other praying people, to remember that, as the God with whom we have to do is gracious and merciful, so he is pure and holy; though he is ready to hear prayer, yet, if we regard iniquity in our heart, he will not hear our prayers, Ps. 66:18. 2. As an encouragement to his prayers against his enemies; they were wicked men, and therefore enemies to God, and such as he had not pleasure in. See here. (1.) The holiness of God's nature. When he says, *Thou art not a God that has pleasure in wickedness,* he means, "Thou art a God that hates it, as directly contrary to thy infinite purity and rectitude, and holy will." Though the workers of iniquity prosper, let none thence infer that God has pleasure in wickedness, no, not in that by which men pretend to honour him, as those do that hate their brethren, and cast them out, and say, *Let the Lord be glorified.* God has no pleasure in wickedness, though covered with a cloak of religion. Let those therefore who delight in sin know that God has no delight in them; nor let any say, when he is tempted, *I am tempted of God,* for God is not the author of sin, neither *shall evil dwell with him,* that is, it shall not always be countenanced and suffered to prosper. Dr. Hammond thinks this refers to that law of Moses which would not permit strangers, who persisted in their idolatry, to dwell in the land of Israel. (2.) The justice of his government. The foolish *shall not stand in his sight,* that is, shall not be smiled upon by him, nor admitted to attend upon him, nor shall they be acquitted in the judgment of the great day. The workers of iniquity are very foolish. Sin is folly, and sinners are the greatest of all fools; not fools of God's making (those are to be pitied), for he hates nothing that he has made, but fools of their own making, and those he hates. Wicked people hate God; justly therefore are they hated of him, and it will be their endless misery and ruin. "Those whom thou hatest thou shalt destroy;" particularly two sorts of sinners, who are here marked for destruction: — [1.] Those that are fools, that speak leasing or lying, and that are deceitful. There is a particular emphasis laid on these sinners (Rev. 21:8), *All liars,* and (Ps. 22:15), *Whosoever loves and makes a lie;* nothing is more contrary than this, and therefore nothing more hateful to the God of truth. [2.] Those that are cruel: *Thou wilt abhor the bloody man;* for inhumanity is no less contrary, no less hateful, to the God of mercy, whom mercy pleases. Liars and murderers are in a particular manner said to resemble the devil and to be his children, and therefore it may well be expected that God should abhor them. These were the characters of David's enemies; and such as these are still the enemies of Christ and his church, men perfectly lost to all virtue and honour; and the worse they are the surer we may be of their ruin in due time.

In singing these verses, and praying them over, we must engage and stir up ourselves to the duty of prayer, and encourage ourselves in it, because we shall not seek the Lord in vain; and must express our detestation of sin, and our awful expectation of that day of Christ's appearing which will be the day of the perdition of ungodly men.

Verses 7–12

In these verses David gives three characters — of himself, of his enemies, and of all the people of God, and subjoins a prayer to each of them.

I. He gives an account of himself and prays for himself, *v.* 7, 8.

1. He is stedfastly resolved to keep closely to God and to his worship. Sinners go away from God, and so make themselves odious to his holiness and obnoxious to his justice: *"But, as for me,* that shall not keep me from thee." God's holiness and justice are so far from being a terror to the upright in heart, to drive them from God, that they are rather by them invited to cleave to him. David resolves, (1.) To worship God, to pay his homage to him, and give unto God the glory due unto his name. (2.) To worship him publicly: *"I will come into thy house,* the courts of thy house, to worship there with other faithful worshippers." David was much in secret worship, prayed often alone (*v.* 2, 3), and yet was very constant and devout in his attendance on the sanctuary. The duties of the closet are designed to prepare us for, not to excuse us from, public ordinances. (3.) To worship him reverently and with a due sense of the infinite distance there is between God and man: *"In thy fear will I worship,* with a holy awe of God upon my spirit," Heb. 12:28. God is greatly to be feared by all his worshippers. (4.) To take his encouragement, in worship, from God himself only. [1.] From his infinite mercy. It is in the multitude of God's mercy (the inexhaustible treasures of mercy that are in God and the innumerable proofs and instances of it which we receive from him) that David confides, and not in any merit or righteousness of his own, in his approaches to God. The mercy of God should ever be both the foundation of our hopes and the fountain of our joy in every thing wherein we have to do with him. [2.] From the instituted medium of worship, which was then the temple, here called *the temple of his holiness,* as a type of Christ, the great and only Mediator, who sanctifies the service as the temple sanctified the gold, and to whom we must have an eye in all our devotions as the worshippers then had to the temple.

2. He earnestly prays that God, by his grace, would guide and preserve him always in the way of his duty (*v.* 8): *Lead me in thy righteousness, because of my enemies —* Heb. *"Because of those who observe me,* who watch for my halting and seek occasion against me." See here, (1.) The good use which David made of the malice of his enemies against him. The more curious they were in spying faults in him, that they might have whereof to accuse him, the more cautious he was to avoid sin and all appearances of it, and the more solicitous to be always found in the good way of God and duty. Thus, by wisdom and grace, good may come out of evil. (2.) The right course which David took for the baffling of those who sought occasion against him. He committed himself to a divine guidance, begged of God both by his providence and by his grace to direct him in the right way, and keep him from turning aside out of it, at any time, in any instance whatsoever, that the most critical and captious of his enemies, like Daniel's, might find no occasion against him. The way of our duty is here called *God's way,* and *his righteousness,* because he prescribes to us by his just and holy laws, which if we sincerely set before us as our rule, we may in faith beg of God to direct us in all particular cases. How this prayer of David's was answered to him see 1 Sa. 18:14, 15.

II. He gives an account of his enemies, and prays against them, *v.* 9, 10. 1. If his account of them is true, as no doubt it is, they have a very bad character; and, if they had not been bad men indeed, they could not have been enemies to a man after God's own heart. He had spoken (*v.* 6) of God's hating the bloody and deceitful man. "Now, Lord," says he, "that is the character of my enemies: they are deceitful; there is no trusting them, for there is no faithfulness in their mouth." They thought it was no sin to tell a deliberate lie if it might but blemish David, and render him odious. *"Lord, lead me,"* says he (*v.* 8), "for such as these are the men I have to do with, against whose slanders innocency itself is no security. Do they speak fair? Do they talk of peace and friendship? *They flatter with their tongues;* it is designed to cover their malice, and to gain their point the more securely. Whatever they pretend of religion or friendship, two sacred things, they are true to neither: *Their inward part is wickedness* itself; it is *very wickedness.* They are likewise bloody; for *their throat is an open sepulchre, cruel as the grave, gaping to devour and to swallow up, insatiable as the grave, which never says, It is enough,"* Prov. 30:15, 16. This is quoted (Rom. 3:13) to show the general corruption of mankind; for they are all naturally prone to malice, Tit. 3:3. The grave is opened for them all, and yet they are as open graves to one another. 2. If his prayer against them is heard, as no doubt it is, they are in a bad condition. As men are, and do, so they must expect to fare. He prays to God to destroy them (according to what he had said *v.* 6, "Thou shalt destroy men of this character," so *let them fall;* and sinners would soon throw themselves into ruin if they were let alone), to *cast them out* of his protection and favour, out of the heritage of the Lord, out of the land of the living; and woe to those whom God casts out. "They have by their sins deserved destruction; there is enough to justify God in their utter rejection: *Cast them out in the multitude of their transgressions,* by which they have filled up the measure of their iniquity and have become ripe for ruin." Persecuting God's servants fills the measure as soon as any thing, 1 Th. 2:15, 16. Nay, they may be easily made to *fall by their own counsels;* that which they do to secure themselves, and do mischief to others, by the over-ruling providence of God may be made a means of their destruction, Ps. 7:15; 9:15. He pleads, *"They have rebelled against thee."* Had they been only my enemies, I could safely have forgiven them; but they are rebels against God, his crown and dignity; they oppose his government, and will not repent, to give him glory, and therefore I plainly foresee their ruin." His prayer for their destruction comes not from a spirit of revenge, but from a spirit of prophecy, by which he foretold that all who rebel against God will certainly be destroyed by their own counsels. If it is a righteous thing with God to recompense tribulation to those that trouble his people, as we are told it is (2 Th. 1:6), we pray that it may be done whenever we pray, *Father, thy will be done.*

III. He gives an account of the people of God, and prays for them, concluding with an assurance of their bliss, which he doubted not of his own interest in. Observe, 1. The description he gives of God's people. They are the righteous (*v.* 12); for they *put their trust in God,* are well assured of his power and all-sufficiency, venture their all upon his promise, and are confident of his protection in the way of their duty; and they *love his name,* are well pleased with all that by which God has made himself known, and take delight in their acquaintance with him. This is true and pure religion, to live a life of complacency in God and dependence on him. 2. His prayer for them: *"Let them rejoice;* let them have cause to rejoice and hearts to rejoice; fill them with joy, with great joy and unspeakable; let them shout for joy, with constant joy and perpetual; *let them ever shout for joy,* with holy joy, and that which terminates in God; *let them be joyful in thee,* in thy favour, in thy salvation, not in any creature. Let them rejoice *because thou defendest them,* coverest them, or overshadowest them, dwellest among them." Perhaps here is an allusion to the pillar of cloud and fire, which was to Israel a visible token of God's special presence with them and the special protection they were under. Let us learn of David to pray, not for ourselves only, but for others, for all good people, for all that trust in God and love his name, though not in every thing of our mind nor in our interest. Let all that are entitled to God's promises have a share in our prayers; grace be with all that love Christ in sincerity. This is to concur with God. 3. His comfort concerning them, *v.* 12. He takes them into his prayers because they are God's peculiar people; therefore he doubts not but his prayers shall be heard, and they shall always rejoice; for, (1.) They are happy in the assurance of God's blessing: *"Thou, Lord, wilt bless the righteous,* wilt command a blessing upon them. Thou hast in thy word pronounced them blessed, and therefore wilt make them truly so. *Those whom thou blessest are blessed indeed."* (2.) "They are safe under the protection of thy favour; with that thou wilt *crown* him" (so some read it); "it is his honour, will be to him a diadem of beauty, and make him truly great: with that thou *wilt compass him,* wilt surround him, on every side, *as with a shield."* A shield, in war, guards only one side, but the favour of God is to the saints a defence on every side; like the hedge about Job, round about, so that, while they keep themselves under

the divine protection, they are entirely safe and ought to be entirely satisfied.

In singing these verses, and praying them over, we must by faith put ourselves under God's guidance and care, and then please ourselves with his mercy and grace and with the prospect of God's triumphs at last over all his enemies and his people's triumphs in him and in his salvation.

PSALM 6

David was a weeping prophet as well as Jeremiah, and this psalm is one of his lamentations: either it was penned in a time, or at least calculated for a time, of great trouble, both outward and inward. Is any afflicted? Is any sick? Let him sing this psalm. The method of this psalm is very observable, and what we shall often meet with. He begins with doleful complaints, but ends with joyful praises; like Hannah, who went to prayer with a sorrowful spirit, but, when she had prayed, went her way, and her countenance was no more sad. Three things the psalmist is here complaining of: — 1. Sickness of body. 2. Trouble of mind, arising from the sense of sin, the meritorious cause of pain and sickness. 3. The insults of his enemies upon occasion of both. Now here, I. He pours out his complaints before God, deprecates his wrath, and begs earnestly for the return of his favour (*v.* 1–7). II. He assures himself of an answer of peace, shortly, to his full satisfaction (*v.* 8–10). This psalm is like the book of Job.

To the chief musician on Neginoth upon Sheminith. A psalm of David.

Verses 1–7

These verses speak the language of a heart truly humbled under humbling providences, of a broken and contrite spirit under great afflictions, sent on purpose to awaken conscience and mortify corruption. Those heap up wrath who cry not when God binds them; but those are getting ready for mercy who, under God's rebukes, sow in tears, as David does here. Let us observe here,

I. The representation he makes to God of his grievances. He pours out his complaint before him. Whither else should a child go with his complaints, but to his father? 1. He complains of bodily pain and sickness (*v.* 2): *My bones are vexed.* His bones and his flesh, like Job's, were touched. Though David was a king, yet he was sick and pained; his imperial crown could not keep his head from aching. Great men are men, and subject to the common calamities of human life. Though David was a stout man, a man of war from his youth, yet this could not secure him from distempers, which will soon make even the strong men to bow themselves. Though David was a good man, yet neither could his goodness keep him in health. *Lord, behold, he whom thou lovest is sick.* Let this help to reconcile us to pain and sickness, that it has been the lot of some of the best saints, and that we are directed and encouraged by their example to show before God our trouble in that case, who *is for the body,* and takes cognizance of its ailments. 2. He complains of inward trouble: *My soul is also sorely vexed;* and that is much more grievous than the vexation of the bones. *The spirit of a man will sustain his infirmity,* if that be in good plight; but, if that be wounded, the grievance is intolerable. David's sickness brought his sin to his remembrance, and he looked upon it as a token of God's displeasure against him; that was the vexation of his soul; that made him cry, *I am weak, heal me.* It is a sad thing for a man to have his bones and his soul vexed at the same time; but this has been sometimes the lot of God's own people: nay, and this completed his complicated trouble, that it was continued upon him a great while, which is here intimated in that expostulation (*v.* 3), *Thou, O Lord! how long?* To the living God we must, at such a time, address ourselves, who is the only physician both of body and mind, and not to the Assyrians, not to the god of Ekron.

II. The impression which his troubles made upon him. They lay very heavily; he *groaned till he was weary,* wept till he *made his bed to swim,* and *watered his couch* (*v.* 6), wept till he had almost wept his eyes out (*v.* 7): *My eye is consumed because of grief.* David had more courage and consideration than to mourn thus for any outward affliction; but, when sin sat heavily upon his conscience and he was made to possess his iniquities, when his soul was wounded with the sense of God's wrath and his withdrawings from him, then he thus grieves and mourns in secret, and even his soul refuses to be comforted. This not only kept his eyes waking, but kept his eyes weeping. Note, 1. It has often been the lot of the best of men to be men of sorrows; our Lord Jesus himself was so. Our way lies through a vale of tears, and we must accommodate our-

selves to the temper of the climate. 2. It well becomes the greatest spirits to be tender, and to relent, under the tokens of God's displeasure. David, who could face Goliath himself and many another threatening enemy with an undaunted bravery, yet melts into tears at the remembrance of sin and under the apprehensions of divine wrath; and it was no diminution at all to his character to do so. 3. True penitents weep in their retirements. The Pharisees disguised their faces, that they might *appear unto men to mourn;* but David mourned in the night upon the bed where he lay communing with his own heart, and no eye was a witness to his grief, but the eye of him who is all eye. Peter went out, covered his face, and wept. 4. Sorrow for sin ought to be great sorrow; so David's was; he wept so bitterly, so abundantly, that he watered his couch. 5. The triumphs of wicked men in the sorrows of the saints add very much to their grief. David's eye waxed old because of his enemies, who rejoiced in his afflictions and put bad constructions upon his tears. In this great sorrow David was a type of Christ, who often wept, and who cried out, *My soul is exceedingly sorrowful,* Heb. 5:7.

III. The petitions which he offers up to God in this sorrowful and distressed state. 1. That which he dreads as the greatest evil is the anger of God. This was the wormwood and the gall in the affliction and the misery; it was the infusion of this that made it indeed a bitter cup; and therefore he prays (*v.* 1), O Lord! rebuke me not in thy anger, though I have deserved it, *neither chasten me in thy hot displeasure.* He does not pray, "Lord, rebuke me not; Lord, chasten me not;" for, *as many as God loves he rebukes and chastens, as a father the son in whom he delights.* He can bear the rebuke and chastening well enough if God, at the same time, lift up the light of his countenance upon him and by his Spirit make him to hear the joy and gladness of his loving-kindness; the affliction of his body will be tolerable if he have but comfort in his soul. No matter though sickness make his bones ache, if God's wrath do not make his heart ache; therefore his prayer is, "Lord, rebuke me not in thy wrath; let me not lie under the impressions of that, for that will sink me." Herein David was a type of Christ, whose sorest complaint, in his sufferings, was of the trouble of his soul and of the suspension of his Father's smiles. He never so much as whispered a complaint of the rage of his enemies — "Why do they crucify me?" or the unkindness of his friends — "Why do they desert me?" But he *cried with a loud voice, My God, my God, why hast thou forsaken me?* Let us thus deprecate the wrath of God more than any outward trouble whatsoever and always beware of treasuring up wrath against a day of affliction. 2. That which he desires as the greatest good, and which would be to him the restoration of all good, is the favour and friendship of God. He prays, (1.) That God would pity him and look upon him with compassion. He thinks himself very miserable, and misery is the proper object of mercy. Hence he prays, "Have mercy upon me, O Lord! in wrath remember mercy, and deal not with me in strict justice." (2.) That God would pardon his sins; for that is the proper act of mercy, and is often chiefly intended in that petition, *Have mercy upon me.* (3.) That God would put forth his power for his relief: "*Lord, heal me* (*v.* 2), *save me* (*v.* 4), speak the word, and I shall be whole, and all will be well." (4.) That he would be at peace with him: "*Return, O Lord!* receive me into thy favour again, and be reconciled to me. Thou hast seemed to depart from me and neglect me, nay, to set thyself at a distance, as one angry; but now, Lord, return and show thyself nigh to me." (5.) That he would especially preserve the inward man and the interests of that, whatever might become of the body: "*O Lord! deliver my soul* from sinning, from sinking, from perishing for ever." It is an unspeakable privilege that we have a God to go to in our afflictions, and it is our duty to go to him, and thus to wrestle with him, and we shall not seek in vain.

IV. The pleas with which he enforces his petitions, not to move God (he knows our cause and the true merits of it better than we can state them), but to move himself. 1. He pleads God's mercy; and thence we take some of our best encouragements in prayer: *Save me, for thy mercies' sake.* 3. He pleads God's glory (*v.* 5): *"For in death there is no remembrance of thee.* Lord, if thou deliver me and comfort me, I will not only give thee thanks for my deliverance, and stir up others to join with me in these thanksgivings, but I will spend the new life thou shalt entrust me with in thy service and to thy glory, and all the remainder of my days I will preserve a grateful remembrance of thy favours to me, and be quickened thereby in all instances of service to thee; but, if I die, I shall be cut short of that opportunity of honouring thee and doing good to others, for *in the grave who will give the thanks?*" Not but that separate souls live and act, and the souls of the faithful joyfully remember God and give thanks to him. But, (1.) In the second death (which perhaps David, being now troubled in soul under the wrath of God, had some dreadful apprehensions of) there is no pleasing remembrance of God; devils and damned spirits blaspheme him and do not praise him. "Lord, let me not lie always under this wrath, for that is *sheol,* it is *hell* itself, and lays me under an everlasting disability to praise thee." Those that sincerely seek God's glory, and desire and delight to praise him, may pray in faith, "Lord, send me not to that dreadful place, where there is no devout remembrance of thee, nor are any thanks given to thee." (2.) Even the death of the body puts an end to our opportunity and capacity of glorifying God in this world, and serving the interests of his kingdom among men by opposing the powers of darkness and bringing many on this earth to know God and devote themselves to him. Some have maintained that the joys of the saints in heaven are more desirable, infinitely more so, than the comforts of saints on earth; yet the services of saints on earth, especially such eminent ones as David was, are more laudable, and redound more to the glory of the divine grace, than the services of the saints in heaven, who are not employed in maintaining the war against sin and Satan, nor in edifying the body of Christ. Courtiers in the royal presence are most happy, but soldiers in the field are more useful; and therefore we may, with good reason, pray that if it be the will of God, and he has any further work for us or our friends to do in this world, he will yet spare us, or them, to serve him. To depart and be with Christ is most happy for the saints themselves; but for them to abide in the flesh is more profitable for the church. This David had an eye to when he pleaded this, *In the grave who shall give thee thanks?* Ps. 30:9; 88:10; 115:17; Isa. 38:18. And this Christ had an eye to when he said, *I pray not that thou shouldst take them out of the world.*

We should sing these verses with a deep sense of the terrors of God's wrath, which we should therefore dread and deprecate above any thing; and with thankfulness if this be not our condition, and compassion to those who are thus afflicted: if we be thus troubled, let it comfort us that our case is not without precedent, nor, if we humble ourselves and pray, as David did, shall it be long without redress.

Verses 8–10

What a sudden change is here for the better! He that was groaning, and weeping, and giving up all for gone (*v.* 6, 7), here looks and speaks very pleasantly. Having made his requests known to God, and lodged his case with him, he is very confident the issue will be good and his sorrow is turned into joy.

I. He distinguishes himself from the wicked and ungodly, and fortifies himself against their insults (*v.* 8): *Depart from me, all you workers of iniquity.* When he was in the depth of his distress, 1. He was afraid that God's wrath against him would give him his portion with the workers of iniquity; but now that this cloud of melancholy had blown over he was assured that his soul would not be gathered with sinners, for they are not his people. He began to suspect himself to be one of them because of the heavy pressures of God's wrath upon him; but now that all his fears were silenced he bade them depart, knowing that his lot was among the chosen. 2. The workers of iniquity had teased him, and taunted him, and asked him, "Where is thy God?" triumphing in his despondency and despair; but now he had wherewith to answer those that reproached him, for God, who was about to return in mercy to him, had now comforted his spirit and would shortly complete his deliverance. 3. Perhaps they had tempted him to do as they did, to quit his religion and betake himself for ease to the pleasures of sin. But now, "*depart from me;* I will never lend an ear to your counsel; you would have had me to curse God and die, but I will bless him and live." This good use we should make of God's mercies to us, we should thereby have our resolution strengthened never to have any thing more to do with sin and sinners. David was a king, and he takes this occasion to renew his purpose of using his power for the suppression of sin and the reformation of manners, Ps. 75:4; 101:3. When God has done great things for us, this should put us upon studying what we shall do for him. Our Lord Jesus seems to borrow these words from the mouth of his father David, when, having all judgment committed to him, he shall say, *Depart from me, all you workers of iniquity* (Lu. 13:27), and so teaches us to say so now, Ps. 119:115.

II. He assures himself that God was, and would be, propitious to him, notwithstanding the present intimations of wrath which he was under. 1. He is confident of a gracious answer to this prayer which he is now making. While he is yet speaking, he is aware that God hears (as Isa. 65:24, Dan. 9:20), and therefore speaks of it as a thing done, and repeats it with an air of triumph, *"The Lord hath heard"* (*v.* 8), and again (*v.* 9), *"The Lord hath heard."* By the workings of God's grace upon his heart he knew his prayer was graciously accepted, and therefore did not doubt but it would in due time be effectually answered. His tears had a voice, a loud voice, in the ears of the God of mercy: *The Lord has heard the voice of my weeping.* Silent tears are not speechless ones. His prayers were cries to God: *"The Lord has heard the voice of my supplication,* has put his *Fiat — Let it be done,* to my petitions, and so it will appear shortly." 2. Thence he infers the like favourable audience of all his other prayers: "He *has heard the voice of my supplication,* and therefore he *will receive my prayer;* for he gives, and does not upbraid with former grants."

III. He either prays for the conversion or predicts the destruction of his enemies and persecutors, *v.* 10. 1. It may very well be taken as a prayer for their conversion: "Let them all be ashamed of the opposition they have given me and the censures they have passed upon me. Let them be (as all true penitents are) vexed at themselves for their own folly; let them return to a better temper and disposition of mind, and let them be ashamed of what they have done against me and take shame to themselves." 2. If they be not converted, it is a prediction of their confusion and ruin. *They shall be ashamed and sorely vexed* (so it maybe read), and that justly. They rejoiced that David was vexed (*v.* 2, 3), and therefore, as usually happens, the evil returns upon themselves; they also shall be sorely vexed. Those that will not give glory to God shall have their faces filled with everlasting shame.

In singing this, and praying over it, we must give glory to God, as a God ready to hear prayer, must own his goodness to us in hearing our prayers, and must encourage ourselves to wait upon him and to trust in him in the greatest straits and difficulties.

PSALM 7

It appears by the title that this psalm was penned with a particular reference to the malicious imputations that David was unjustly laid under by some of his enemies. Being thus wronged, I. He applies to God for favour (*v.* 1, 2). II. He appeals to God concerning his innocency as to those things whereof he was accused (*v.* 3–5). III. He prays to God to plead his cause and judge for him against his persecutors (*v.* 6–9). IV. He expresses his confidence in God that he would do so, and would return the mischief upon the head of those that designed it against him (*v.* 10–16). V. He promises to give God the glory of his deliverance (*v.* 17). In this David was a type of Christ, who was himself, and still is in his members, thus injured, but will certainly be righted at last.

Shiggaion of David, which he sang unto the Lord, concerning the words of Cush the Benjamite.

Verses 1–9

Shiggaion is a *song* or *psalm* (the word is used so only here and Hab. 3:1) — a *wandering* song (so some), the matter and composition of the several parts being different, but artificially put together — a *charming* song (so others), very delightful. David not only penned it, but sang it himself in a devout religious manner unto the Lord, *concerning the words* or affairs *of Cush the Benjamite,* that is, of Saul himself, whose barbarous usage of David bespoke him rather a Cushite, or Ethiopian, than a true-born Israelite. Or, more likely, it was some kinsman of Saul named *Cush,* who was an inveterate enemy to David, misrepresented him to Saul as a traitor, and (which was very needless) exasperated Saul against him, one of those children of men, children of Belial indeed, whom David complains of (1 Sa. 26:19), that made mischief between him and Saul. David, thus basely abused, has recourse to the Lord. The injuries men do us should drive us to God, for to him we may commit our cause. Nay, he sings to the Lord; his spirit was not ruffled by it, nor cast down, but so composed and cheerful that he was still in tune for sacred songs and it did not occasion one jarring string in his harp. Thus let the injuries we receive from men, instead of provoking our passions, kindle and excite our devotions. In these verses,

I. He puts himself under God's protection and flies to him for succour and shelter (*v.* 1): *"Lord, save me, and deliver me* from the power and malice of *all those that persecute me,* that they may not have their will against me." He pleads, 1. His relation to God. "Thou art *my God,* and therefore whither else should I go but to thee? Thou art my God, and therefore my shield (Gen. 15:1), my God, and therefore I am one of thy servants, who may expect to be protected." 2. His confidence in God: "Lord, save me, for I depend upon thee: *In thee do I put my trust,* and not in any arm of flesh." Men of honour will not fail those that repose a trust in them, especially if they themselves have encouraged them to do so, which is our case. 3. The rage and malice of his enemies, and the imminent danger he was in of being swallowed up by them: "Lord, save me, or I am gone; he will *tear my soul like a lion* tearing his prey," with so much pride, and pleasure, and power, so easily, so cruelly. St. Paul compares Nero to a lion (2 Tim. 4:17), as David here compares Saul. 4. The failure of all other helpers: "Lord, be thou pleased to deliver me, for otherwise *there is none to deliver,*" *v.* 2. It is the glory of God to help the helpless.

II. He makes a solemn protestation of his innocency as to those things whereof he was accused, and by a dreadful imprecation appeals to God, the searcher of hearts, concerning it, *v.* 3–5. Observe, in general, 1. When we are falsely accused by men it is a great comfort if our own consciences acquit us —

— Hic murus aheneus esto,
Nil conscire sibi. —
Be this thy brazen bulwark of defence,
Still to preserve thy conscious innocence. —

and not only they cannot prove their calumnies (Acts 24:13), but our hearts can disprove them, to our own satisfaction. 2. God is the patron of wronged innocency. David had no court on earth to appeal to. His prince, who should have righted him, was his sworn enemy. But he had the court of heaven to fly to, and a righteous Judge there, whom he could call *his God.* And here see, (1.) What the indictment is which he pleads not guilty to. He was charged with a traitorous design against Saul's crown and life, that he compassed and imagined to depose and murder him, and, in order to that, levied war against him. This he utterly denies. He never did this; there was no iniquity of this kind in his hand (*v.* 3); he abhorred the thought of it. He never *rewarded evil* to Saul when he was *at peace with him,* nor to any other, *v.* 4. Nay, as some think it should be rendered, he never rendered evil for evil, never did those mischief that had injured him. (2.) What evidence he produces of his innocency. It is hard to prove a negative, and yet this was a negative which David could produce very good proof of: *I have delivered him that without cause is my enemy, v.* 4. By *this* it appeared, beyond contradiction, that David had no design against Saul's life — that, once and again, Providence so ordered it that Saul lay at his mercy, and there were those about him that would soon have dispatched him, but David generously and conscientiously prevented it, when he cut off his skirt (1 Sa. 24:4) and afterwards when he took away his spear (1 Sa. 26:12), to attest for him what he could have done. Saul himself owned both these to be undeniable proofs of David's integrity and good affection to him. If we render good for evil, and deny ourselves the gratifications of our passion, our so doing may turn to us for a testimony, more than we think of, another day. (3.) What doom he would submit to if he were guilty (*v.* 5): *Let the enemy persecute my soul* to the death, and my good name when I am gone: let him *lay my honour in the dust.* This intimates, [1.] That, if he had been indeed injurious to others, he had reason to expect that they would repay him in the same coin. He that has his hand against every man must reckon upon it that every man's hand will be against him. [2.] That, in that case, he could not with any confidence go to God and beg of him to deliver him or plead his cause. It is a presumptuous dangerous thing for any that are guilty, and suffer justly, to appeal to God, as if they were innocent and suffered wrongfully; such must humble themselves and accept the punishment of their iniquity, and not expect that the righteous God will patronise their unrighteousness. [3.] That he was abundantly satisfied in himself concerning his innocency. It is natural to us to wish well to ourselves; and therefore a curse to ourselves, if we swear falsely, has been thought as awful a form of swearing as any. With such an oath, or imprecation, David here ratifies the protestation of his innocency, which yet will not justify us in doing the like for every light and trivial cause; for the occasion here was important.

III. Having this testimony of his conscience concerning his innocency, he humbly prays to God to appear for him against his persecutors, and backs every petition with a proper plea, as one that knew how to order his cause before God.

1. He prays that God would manifest his wrath against his enemies, and pleads their wrath against him: "Lord, they are unjustly angry at me, be thou justly angry with them and let them know that thou art so, v. 6. *In thy anger lift up thyself* to the seat of judgment, and make thy power and justice conspicuous, *because of the rage,* the furies, the outrages (the word is plural) *of my enemies.*" Those need not fear men's wrath against them who have God's wrath for them. *Who knows the power of his anger?*

2. He prays that God would plead his cause.

(1.) He prays, *Awake for me to judgment* (that is, let my cause have a hearing), to *the judgment which thou hast commanded;* this speaks, [1.] The divine power; as he blesses effectually, and is therefore said to *command the blessing,* so he judges effectually, and is therefore said to *command the judgment,* which is such as none can countermand; for it certainly carries execution along with it. [2.] The divine purpose and promise: "It is the judgment which thou hast determined to pass upon all the enemies of thy people. Thou hast commanded the princes and judges of the earth to give redress to the injured and vindicate the oppressed; Lord, awaken thyself to that judgment." He that loves righteousness, and requires it in others, will no doubt execute it himself. Though he seem to connive at wrong, as one asleep, he will awake in due time (Ps. 78:65) and will make it to appear that the delays were no neglects.

(2.) He prays (v. 7), "*Return thou on high,* maintain thy own authority, resume thy royal throne of which they have despised the sovereignty, and the judgment-seat of which they have despised the sentence. Return on high, that is, visibly and in the sight of all, that it may be universally acknowledged that heaven itself owns and pleads David's cause." Some make this to point at the resurrection and ascension of Jesus Christ, who, when he returned to heaven (returned on high in his exalted state), had all judgment committed to him. Or it may refer to his second coming, when he shall return on high to this world, to execute judgment upon all. This return his injured people wait for, and pray for, and to it they appeal from the unjust censures of men.

(3.) He prays again (v. 8), "*Judge me,* judge for me, give sentence on my side." To enforce this suit, [1.] He pleads that his cause was now brought into the proper court: *The Lord shall judge the people, v. 8.* He is the Judge of all the earth, and therefore no doubt he will do right and all will be obliged to acquiesce in his judgment. [2.] He insists upon his integrity as to all the matters in variance between him and Saul, and desires only to be judged, in this matter, according to his righteousness, and the sincerity of his heart in all the steps he had taken towards his preferment. [3.] He foretels that it would be much for the glory of God and the edification and comfort of his people if God would appear for him: "*So shall the congregation of the people compass thee about;* therefore do it for their sakes, that they may attend thee with their raises and services in the courts of thy house." *First,* They will do it of their own accord. God's appearing on David's behalf, and fulfilling his promise to him, would be such an instance of his righteousness, goodness, and faithfulness, as would greatly enlarge the hearts of all his faithful worshippers and fill their mouths with praise. David was the darling of his country, especially of all the good people in it; and therefore, when

they saw him in a fair way to the throne, they would greatly rejoice and give thanks to God; crowds of them would attend his footstool with their praises for such a blessing to their land. *Secondly,* If David come into power, as God has promised him, he will take care to bring people to church by his influence upon them, and the ark shall not be neglected, as it was *in the days of Saul,* 1 Chr. 13:3.

3. He prays, in general, for the conversion of sinners and the establishment of saints (v. 9): "*O let the wickedness,* not only of my wicked enemies, but *of all the wicked, come to an end! but establish the just.*" Here are two things which everyone of us must desire and may hope for: — (1.) The destruction of sin, that it may be brought to an end in ourselves and others. When corruption is mortified, when every wicked way and thought are forsaken, and the stream which ran violently towards the world and the flesh is driven back and runs towards God and heaven, then the wickedness of the wicked comes to an end. When there is a general reformation of manners, when atheists and profane are convinced and converted, when a stop is put to the spreading of the infection of sin, so that evil men proceed no further, their folly being made manifest, when the wicked designs of the church's enemies are baffled, and their power is broken, and the man of sin is destroyed, then the *wickedness of the wicked comes to an end.* And this is that which all that love God, and for his sake hate evil, desire and pray for. (2.) The perpetuity of righteousness: *But establish the just.* As we pray that the bad maybe made good, so we pray that the good may be made better, that they may not be seduced by the wiles of the wicked nor shocked by their malice, that they may be confirmed in their choice of the ways of God and in their resolution to persevere therein, may be firm to the interests of God and religion and zealous in their endeavours to bring the *wickedness of the wicked to an end.* His plea to enforce this petition is, *For the righteous God trieth the hearts and the reins;* and therefore he knows the secret wickedness of the wicked and knows how to bring it to an end, and the secret sincerity of the just he is witness to and has secret ways of establishing.

As far as we have the testimony of an unbiased conscience for us that in any instance we are wronged and injuriously reflected on, we may, in singing these verses, lodge our appeal with the righteous God, and be assured that he will own our righteous cause, and will one day, in the last day at furthest, bring forth our integrity as the light.

Verses 10–17

David having lodged his appeal with God by prayer and a solemn profession of his integrity, in the former part of the psalm, in this latter part does, as it were, take out judgment upon the appeal, by faith in the word of God, and the assurance it gives of the happiness and safety of the righteous and the certain destruction of wicked people that continue impenitent.

I. David is confident that he shall find God his powerful protector and Saviour, and the patron of his oppressed innocency (v. 10): "*My defence is of God.* Not only, God is my defender, and I shall find him so; but I look for defence and safety in no other; my hope for shelter in a time of danger is placed in God alone; if I have defence, it must be of God." *My shield is upon God* (so some read it); there is that in God which gives an assurance of protection to all that are his. His name is a strong tower, Prov. 18:10. Two things David builds this confidence upon: — 1. The particular favour God has for all that are sincere: *He saves the upright in heart,* saves them with an everlasting salvation, and therefore will *preserve them to his heavenly kingdom;* he saves them out of their present troubles, as far as is good for them; their integrity and uprightness will preserve them. The upright in heart are safe, and ought to think themselves so, under the divine protection. 2. The general respect he has for justice and equity: *God judgeth the righteous;* he owns every righteous cause, and will maintain it in every righteous man, and will protect him. *God is a righteous Judge* (so some read it), who not only doeth righteousness himself, but will take care that righteousness be done by the children of men and will avenge and punish all unrighteousness.

II. He is no less confident of the destruction of all his persecutors, even as many of them as would not *repent,*

to give glory to God. He reads their doom here, for their good, if possible, that they might cease from their enmity, or, however, for his own comfort, that he might not be afraid of them nor aggrieved at their prosperity and success for a time. He goes into the sanctuary of God, and there understands,

1. That they are children of wrath. They are not to be envied, for God is angry with them, is *angry with the wicked every day.* They are every day doing that which is provoking to him, and he resents it, and treasures it up *against the day of wrath.* As his mercies are new every morning towards his people, so his anger is new every morning against the wicked, upon the fresh occasions given for it by their renewed transgressions. God is angry with the wicked even in the merriest and most prosperous of their days, even in the days of their devotion; for, if they be suffered to prosper, it is in wrath; if they pray, their very prayers are an abomination. The wrath of God abides upon them (Jn. 3:36) and continual additions are made to it.

2. That they are children of death, as all the children of wrath are, sons of perdition, marked out for ruin. See their destruction.

(1.) God will destroy them. The destruction they are reserved for is *destruction from the Almighty,* which ought to be a terror to every one of us, for it comes from the *wrath of God, v.* 13, 14. It is here intimated, [1.] That the destruction of sinners may be prevented by their conversion, for it is threatened with that proviso: *If he turn not from his evil way,* if he do not let fall his enmity against the people of God, then let him expect it will be his ruin; but, if he turn, it is implied that his sin shall be pardoned and all shall be well. Thus even the threatenings of wrath are introduced with a gracious implication of mercy, enough to justify God for ever in the destruction of those that perish; they might have turned and lived, but they chose rather to go on and die and their blood is therefore upon their own heads. [2.] That, if it be not thus prevented by the conversion of the sinner, it will be prepared for him by the justice of God. In general (v. 13), *He has prepared for him the instruments of death,* of all that death which is the wages of sin. If God will slay, he will not want instruments of death for any creature; even the least and weakest may be made so when he pleases. *First,* Here is variety of instruments, all which breathe threatenings and slaughter. Here is a sword, which wounds and kills at hand, a bow and arrows, which wound and kill at a distance those who think to get out of the reach of God's vindictive justice. If the sinner *flees from the iron weapon,* yet the *bow of steel shall strike him through,* Job 20:24. *Secondly,* These instruments of death are all said to be made ready. God has them not to seek, but always at hand. *Judgments are prepared for scorners. Tophet is prepared of old. Thirdly,* While God is preparing his instruments of death, he gives the sinners timely warning of their danger, and space to repent and prevent it. He is slow to punish, and *long-suffering to us-ward, not willing that any should perish. Fourthly,* The longer the destruction is delayed, to give time for repentance, the sorer will it be and the heavier will it fall and lie for ever if that time be not so improved; while God is waiting the sword is in the whetting and the bow in the drawing. *Fifthly,* The destruction of impenitent sinners, though it come slowly, yet comes surely; for it is *ordained,* they are of old ordained to it. *Sixthly,* Of all sinners persecutors are set up as the fairest marks of divine wrath; against them, more than any other, God has ordained his arrows. They set God at defiance, but cannot set themselves out of the reach of his judgments.

(2.) They will destroy themselves, v. 14–16. The sinner is here described as taking a great deal of pains to ruin himself, more pains to damn his soul than, if directed aright, would save it. His conduct is described, [1.] By the pains of a labouring woman that brings forth a false conception, v. 14. The sinner's head with its politics *conceives mischief,* contrives it with a great deal of art, lays the plot deep, and keeps it close; the sinner's heart with its passions *travails with iniquity,* and is in pain to be delivered of the malicious projects it is hatching against the people of God. But what does it come to when it comes to the birth? It is falsehood; it is a cheat upon himself; it is a lie in his right hand. He cannot compass what he intended, nor, if he gain his point, will he gain the satisfaction he promised himself. He brings forth *wind* (Isa. 26:18), *stubble* (Isa. 33:11), *death* (James 1:15), that is, *falsehood.* [2.] By the pains of a labouring man that works hard to dig a pit, and then falls into it and perishes in it. *First,* This is true, in a sense of all sinners. They prepare destruction for themselves by preparing themselves for destruction, loading themselves with guilt and submitting themselves to their corruptions. *Secondly,* It is often remarkably true of those who contrive mischief against the people of God or against their neighbours; by the righteous hand of God it is made to *return upon their own heads.* What they designed for the shame and destruction of others proves to be their own confusion.

— Nec lex est jusitior ulla
Quam necis artifices arte perire sua —
There is not a juster law than that the author
of a murderous contrivance shall perish by it.

Some apply it to Saul, who fell upon his sword.

In singing this psalm we must do as David here does (*v.* 17), *praise the Lord according to his righteousness,* that is, give him the glory of that gracious protection under which he takes his afflicted people and of that just vengeance with which he will pursue those that afflict them. Thus we must sing to the praise of the Lord most high, who, when his enemies deal proudly, shows that he is above them.

PSALM 8

This psalm is a solemn meditation on, and admiration of, the glory and greatness of God, of which we are all concerned to think highly and honourably. It begins and ends with the same acknowledgment of the transcendent excellency of God's name. It is proposed for proof (*v.* 1) that God's name is excellent in all the earth, and then it is repeated as proved (with a "quod erat demonstrandum" — which was to be demonstrated) in the last verse. For the proof of God's glory the psalmist gives instances of his goodness to man; for God's goodness is his glory. God is to be glorified, I. For making known himself and his great name to us (*v.* 1). II. For making use of the weakest of the children of men, by them to serve his own purposes (*v.* 2). III. For making even the heavenly bodies useful to man (*v.* 3, 4). IV. For making him to have dominion over the creatures in this lower world, and thereby placing him but little lower then the angels (*v.* 5–8). This psalm is, in the New Testament, applied to Christ and the work of our redemption which he wrought out; the honour given by the children of men to him (*v.* 2, compared with Mt. 21:16) and the honour put upon the children of men by him, both in his humiliation, when he was made a little lower then the angels, and in his exaltation, when he was crowned with glory and honour. Compare *v.* 5, 6, with Heb. 2:6–8; 1 Co. 15:27. When we are observing the glory of God in the kingdom of nature and providence we should be led by that, and through that, to the contemplation of his glory in the kingdom of grace.

To the chief musician upon Gittith. A psalm of David.

Verses 1–2

The psalmist here sets himself to give to God the glory due to his name. Dr. Hammond grounds a conjecture upon the title of this psalm concerning the occasion of penning it. It is said to be upon *Gittith,* which is generally taken for the tune, or musical instrument, with which this psalm was to be sung; but he renders it upon the *Gittite,* that is, *Goliath the Gittite,* whom he vanquished and slew (1 Sa. 17); that enemy was stilled by him who was, in comparison, but a babe and a suckling. The conjecture would be probable enough but that we find two other psalms with the same title, Ps. 81 and 84. Two things David here admires: —

I. How plainly God displays his glory himself, *v.* 1. He addresses himself to God with all humility and reverence, as the Lord and his people's Lord: *O Lord our Lord!* If we believe that God is the Lord, we must avouch and acknowledge him to be ours. He is ours, for he made us, protects us, and takes special care of us. He must be ours, for we are bound to obey him and submit to him; we must own the relation, not only when we come to pray to God, as a plea with him to show us mercy, but when we come to praise him, as an argument with ourselves to give him glory: and we shall never think we can do that with affection enough if we consider, 1. How brightly God's glory shines even in this lower world: *How excellent is his name in all the earth!* The works of creation and Providence evince and proclaim to all the world that there is an infinite Being, the fountain of all being, power, and perfection, the sovereign ruler, powerful protector, and bountiful benefactor of all the creatures. How great, how illustrious, how magnificent, is his name in all the earth! The light of it shines in men's faces every where (Rom. 1:20); if they shut their eyes against it, that is their fault. There is no speech or language but the voice of God's name either is heard in it or may be. But this looks further, to the gospel of Christ, by which the name of God, as it is notified by divine revelation, which before was great in Israel only, came to be so in all the earth, the utmost ends of which have thus been made to *see God's great salvation,* Mk. 16:15, 16. 2. How much more brightly it shines in the upper world: *Thou hast set thy glory above the heavens.* (1.) God is infinitely more glorious and excellent than the noblest of creatures and those that shine most brightly. (2.) Whereas we, on this earth, only hear God's excellent name, and praise that, the angels and blessed spirits above see his glory, and praise that, and yet he is exalted far above even their blessing and praise. (3.) In the exaltation of the Lord Jesus to the right hand of God, who is the brightness of his Father's glory and the express image of his person, God set his glory above the heavens, far above all principalities and powers.

II. How powerfully he proclaims it by the weakest of his creatures (*v.* 2): *Out of the mouth of babes and sucklings hast thou ordained strength,* or perfected praise, the praise of thy strength, Mt. 21:16. This intimates the glory of God, 1. In the kingdom of nature. The care God takes of little children (when they first come into the world the most helpless of all animals), the special protection they are under, and the provision nature has made for them, ought to be acknowledged by every one of us, to the glory of God, as a great instance of his power and goodness, and the more sensibly because we have all had the benefit of it, for to this we owe it that we *died not from the womb,* that the knees then prevented us, *and the breasts, that we should suck.* "This is such an instance of thy goodness, as may for ever put to silence the enemies of thy glory, who say, There is no God." 2. In the kingdom of Providence. In the government of this lower world he makes use of the children of men, some that know him and others that do not (Isa. 45:4), and these such as have been babes and sucklings; nay, sometimes he is pleased to serve his own purposes by the ministry of such as are still, in wisdom and strength, little better than babes and sucklings. 3. In the kingdom of grace, the kingdom of the Messiah. It is here foretold that by the apostles, who were looked upon but as babes, *unlearned and ignorant men* (Acts 4:13), mean and despicable, and *by the foolishness of their preaching,* the devil's kingdom should be thrown down as Jericho's walls were by the sound of rams' horns. The gospel is called *the arm of the Lord* and *the rod of his strength;* this was ordained to work wonders, not out of the mouth of philosophers or orators, politicians or statesmen, but of a company of poor fishermen, who lay under the greatest external disadvantages; yea, we hear children crying, *Hosanna to the Son of David,* when the chief priests and Pharisees owned him not, but despised and rejected him; to that therefore our Saviour applied this (Mt. 21:16) and by it stilled the enemy. Sometimes the grace of God appears wonderfully in young children, and he *teaches* those *knowledge, and makes* those *to understand doctrine, who are* but *newly weaned from the milk and drawn from the breasts,* Isa. 28:9. Sometimes the power of God brings to pass great things in his church by very weak and unlikely instruments, and confounds the noble, wise, and mighty, by the base, and weak, and foolish things of the world, that no flesh may glory in his presence, but the excellency of the power may the more evidently appear to be of God, and not of man, 1 Co. 1:27, 28. This he does *because of his enemies,* because they are insolent and haughty, that he may still them, may put them to silence, and put them to shame, and so be justly avenged on the avengers; see Acts 4:14; 6:10. The devil is the great enemy and avenger, and by the preaching of the gospel he was in a great measure stilled, his oracles were silenced, the advocates of his cause were confounded, and unclean spirits themselves were not suffered to speak.

In singing this let us give God the glory of his great name, and of the great things he has done by the power of his gospel, in the chariot of which the exalted Redeemer rides forth conquering and to conquer, and ought to be attended, not only with our praises, but with our best wishes. Praise is perfected (that is, God is in the highest degree glorified) when strength is ordained out of the mouth of babes and sucklings.

Verses 3–9

David here goes on to magnify the honour of God by recounting the honours he has put upon man, especially the man Christ Jesus. The condescensions of the divine grace call for our praises as much as the elevations of the divine glory. How God has condescended in favour to man the psalmist here observes with wonder and thankfulness, and recommends it to our thoughts. See here,

I. What it is that leads him to admire the condescending favour of God to man; it is his consideration of the lustre and influence of the heavenly bodies, which are within the view of sense (*v.* 3): *I consider thy heavens,* and there, particularly, *the moon and the stars.* But why does he not take notice of the sun, which much excels them all? Probably because it was in a night-walk, but moon-light, that he entertained and instructed himself with this meditation, when the sun was not within view, but only the moon and the stars, which, though they are not altogether so serviceable to man as the sun is, yet are no less demonstrations of the wisdom, power, and goodness of the Creator. Observe, 1. It is our duty to consider the heavens. We see them, we cannot but see them. By this, among other things, man is distinguished from the beasts, that, while *they* are so framed as to look downwards to the earth, man is made erect to look upwards towards heaven. *Os homini sublime dedit, coelumque tueri jussit — To man he gave an erect countenance, and bade him gaze on the heavens,* that thus he may be directed to set his affections on things above; for what we see has not its due influence upon us unless we consider it. 2. We must always consider the heavens as God's heavens, not only as all the world is his, even the earth and the fulness thereof, but in a more peculiar manner. *The heavens, even the heavens, are the Lord's* (Ps. 115:16); they are the place of the residence of his glory and we are taught to call him *Our Father in heaven.* 3. They are *therefore* his, because they are the work of his fingers. He made them; he made them easily. The stretching out of the heavens needed not any outstretched arm; it was done with a word; it was but *the work of his fingers.* He made them with very great curiosity and fineness, like a nice piece of work which the artist makes with his fingers. 4. Even the inferior lights, the moon and stars, show the glory and power of the Father of lights, and furnish us with matter for praise. 5. The heavenly bodies are not only the creatures of the divine power, but subject to the divine government. God not only made them, but *ordained* them, and the ordinances of heaven can never be altered. But how does this come in here to magnify God's favour to man? (1.) When we consider how the glory of God shines in the upper world we may well wonder that he should take cognizance of such a mean creature as man, that he who resides in that bright and blessed part of the creation, and governs it, should humble himself to behold the things done upon this earth; see Ps. 113:5, 6. (2.) When we consider of what great use the heavens are to men on earth, and how the lights of heavens are *divided unto all nations* (Duet. 4:19, Gen. 1:15), we may well say, *"Lord, what is man* that thou shouldst settle the ordinances of heaven with an eye to him and to his benefit, and that his comfort and convenience should be so consulted in the making of the lights of heaven and directing their motions!"

II. How he expresses this admiration (*v.* 4): *"Lord, what is man* (*enosh,* sinful, weak, miserable man, a creature so forgetful of thee and his duty to thee) *that thou art* thus *mindful of him,* that thou takest cognizance of him and of his actions and affairs, that in the making of the world thou hadst a respect to him! What is the *son of man, that thou visitest him,* that thou not only feedest him and clothest him, protectest him and providest for him, in common with other creatures, but visited him as one friend visits another, art pleased to converse with him and concern thyself for him! What is man — (so mean a creature), that he should be thus honoured — (so sinful a creature), that he should be thus countenanced and favoured!" Now this refers,

1. To mankind in general. Though man is a worm, and the son of man is a worm (Job 25:6), yet God puts a respect upon him, and shows him abundance of kindness; man is, above all the creatures in this lower world, the favourite and darling of Providence. For, (1.) He is of a very honourable rank of beings. We may be sure he takes precedence of all the inhabitants of this lower world, for he

is made but a *little lower than the angels* (v. 5), lower indeed, because by his body he is allied to the earth and to the beasts that perish, and yet by his soul, which is spiritual and immortal, he is so near akin to the holy angels that he may be truly said to be but *a little lower than they,* and is, in order, next to them. He is but for a little while lower than the angels, while his great soul is cooped up in a house of clay, but the children of the resurrection shall be *isangeloi — angels' peers* (Lu. 20:36) and no longer lower than they. (2.) He is endued with noble faculties and capacities: *Thou hast crowned him with glory and honour.* He that gave him his being has distinguished him, and qualified him for a dominion over the inferior creatures; for, having *made him wiser than the beasts of the earth and the fowls of heaven* (Job 35:11), he has made him fit to rule them and it is fit that they should be ruled by him. Man's reason is his crown of glory; let him not profane that crown by disturbing the use of it nor forfeit that crown by acting contrary to its dictates. (3.) He is invested with a sovereign dominion over the inferior creatures, under God, and is constituted their lord. He that made them, and knows them, and whose own they are, has *made man to have dominion over them, v.* 6. His charter, by which he holds this royalty, bears equal date with his creation (Gen. 1:28) and was renewed after the flood, Gen. 9:2. God has put all things under man's feet, that he might serve himself, not only of the labour, but of the productions and lives of the inferior creatures; they are all delivered into his hand, nay, they are all *put under his feet.* He specifies some of the inferior animals (v. 7, 8), not only *sheep and oxen,* which man takes care of and provides for, but *the beasts of the field,* as well as those of the flood, yea, and those creatures which are most at a distance from man, as *the fowl of the air,* yea, *and the fish of the sea,* which live in another element and pass unseen through the paths of the seas. Man has arts to take these; though many of them are much stronger and many of them much swifter than he, yet, one way or other, he is too hard for them, Jam. 3:7. *Every kind of beasts, and birds, and things in the sea, is tamed, and has been tamed.* He has likewise liberty to use them as he has occasion. *Rise, Peter, kill and eat,* Acts 10:13. Every time we partake of fish or of fowl we realize this dominion which man has over the works of God's hands; and this is a reason for our subjection to God, our chief Lord, and to his dominion over us.

2. But this refers, in a particular manner, to Jesus Christ. Of him we are taught to expound it, Heb. 2:6–8, where the apostle, to prove the sovereign dominion of Christ both in heaven and in earth, shows that he is that man, that son of man, here spoken of, whom God *has crowned with glory and honour* and made to *have dominion over the works of his hands.* And it is certain that the greatest favour that ever was shown to the human race, and the greatest honour that ever was put upon the human nature, were exemplified in the incarnation and exaltation of the Lord Jesus; these far exceed the favours and honours done us by creation and providence, though they also are great and far more than we deserve. We have reason humbly to value ourselves by it and thankfully to admire the grace of God in it, (1.) That Jesus Christ assumed the nature of man, and, in that nature, humbled himself. He became the *Son of man,* a partaker of flesh and blood; being so, God visited him, which some apply to his sufferings for us, for it is said (Heb. 2:9), *For the suffering of death,* a visitation in wrath, *he was crowned with glory and honour.* God visited him; having laid upon him the iniquity of us all, he reckoned with him for it, visited him with a rod and with stripes, that we by them might be healed. He was, *for a little while* (so the apostle interprets it), made lower than the angels, when he took upon him the form of a servant and made himself of no reputation. (2.) That, in that nature, he is exalted to be Lord of all. God the Father exalted him, because he had humbled himself, *crowned him with glory and honour,* the glory which he had with him before the worlds were, set not only the *head of the church,* but *head over all things to the church,* and gave all things into his hand, entrusted him with the administration of the kingdom of providence in conjunction with and subserviency to the kingdom of grace. All the creatures are put under his feet; and, even in the days of his flesh, he gave some specimens of his power over them, as when he commanded the winds and the seas, and appointed a fish to pay

his tribute. With good reason therefore does the psalmist conclude as he began, *Lord, how excellent is thy name in all the earth,* which has been honoured with the presence of the Redeemer, and is still enlightened by his gospel and governed by his wisdom and power!

In singing this and praying it over, though we must not forget to acknowledge, with suitable affections, God's common favours to mankind, particularly in the serviceableness of the inferior creatures to us, yet we must especially set ourselves to give glory to our Lord Jesus, by confessing that he is Lord, submitting to him as our Lord, and waiting till we see all things put under him and all his enemies made his footstool.

PSALM 9

In this psalm, I. David praises God for pleading his cause, and giving him victory over his enemies and the enemies of his country (v. 1–6), and calls upon others to join with him in his songs of praise (v. 11, 12). II. He prays to God that he might have still further occasion to praise him, for his own deliverances and the confusion of his enemies (v. 13, 14, 19, 20). III. He triumphs in the assurance he had of God's judging the world (v. 7, 8), protecting his oppressed people (v. 9, 10, 18), and bringing his and their implacable enemies to ruin (v. 15–17). This is very applicable to the kingdom of the Messiah, the enemies of which have been in part destroyed already, and shall be yet more and more till they all be made his footstool, which we are to assure ourselves of, that God may have the glory and we may take the comfort.

To the chief musician upon Muth-labben. A psalm of David.

Verses 1–10

The title of this psalm gives a very uncertain sound concerning the occasion of penning it. It is upon *Muth-labben,* which some make to refer to the death of Goliath, others of Nabal, others of Absalom; but I incline to think it signifies only some tone, or some musical instrument, to which this psalm was intended to be sung; and that the enemies David is here triumphing in the defeat of are the Philistines, and the other neighbouring nations that opposed his settlement in the throne, whom he contested with and subdued in the beginning of his reign, 2 Sa. 5:8. In these verses,

I. David excites and engages himself to praise God for his mercies and the great things he had of late done for him and his government, v. 1, 2. Note, 1. God expects suitable returns of praise from those for whom he has done marvellous works. 2. If we would praise God acceptably, we must praise him in sincerity, with our hearts, and not only with our lips, and be lively and fervent in the duty, with our *whole heart.* 3. When we give thanks for some one particular mercy we should take occasion thence to remember former mercies and so to *show forth all his marvellous works.* 4. Holy joy is the life of thankful praise, as thankful praise is the language of holy joy: *I will be glad and rejoice in thee.* 5. Whatever occurs to make us glad, our joy must pass through it, and terminate in God only: *I will be glad and rejoice in thee,* not in the gift so much as in the giver. 6. Joy and praise are properly expressed by singing psalms. 7. When God has shown himself to be above the proud enemies of the church we must take occasion thence to give glory to him as the *Most High.* 8. The triumphs of the Redeemer ought to be the triumphs of the redeemed; see Rev. 12:10; 19:5; 15:3, 4.

II. He acknowledges the almighty power of God as that which the strongest and stoutest of his enemies were no way able to contest with or stand before, v. 3. But, 1. They are forced to turn back. Their policy and their courage fail them, so that they cannot, they dare not, push forward in their enterprises, but retire with precipitation. 2. When once they turn back, they fall and perish; even their retreat will be their ruin, and they will save themselves no more by flying than by fighting. If Haman begin to fall before Mordecai, he is a lost man, and shall prevail no more; see Esther 6:13. 3. The presence of the Lord, and the glory of his power, are sufficient for the destruction of his and his people's enemies. That is easily done which a man does with his very presence; with *that* God confounds his enemies, such a presence has he. This was fulfilled when our Lord Jesus, with one word, *I am he,* made his enemies to *fall back at his presence* (Jn. 18:6) and he could, at the same time, have made them perish. 4. When the enemies of God's church are put to confusion we must ascribe their discomfiture to the power, not of instruments, but of his presence, and give him all the glory.

III. He gives to God the glory of his righteousness, in his appearing on his behalf (v. 4): *"Thou hast maintained my right and my cause,* that is, my righteous cause; when that came on, *thou satest in the throne, judging right."* Observe, 1. God sits in the throne of judgment. To him it belongs to decide controversies, to determine appeals, to avenge the injured, and to punish the injurious; for he has said, *Vengeance is mine.* 2. We are sure that the judgment of God is according to truth and that with him there is no unrighteousness. Far be it from God that he should pervert justice. If there seem to us to be some irregularity in the present decisions of Providence, yet these, instead of shaking our belief of God's justice, may serve to strengthen our belief of the judgment to come, which will set all to-rights. 3. Whoever disown and desert a just and injured cause, we may be sure that the righteous God will maintain it and plead it with jealousy, and will never suffer it to be run down.

IV. He records, with joy, the triumphs of the God of heaven over all the powers of hell and attends those triumphs with his praises, v. 5. By three steps the power and justice of God had proceeded against the heathen, and wicked people, who were enemies to the king God had lately set up upon his holy hill of Zion. 1. He had checked them: *"Thou hast rebuked the heathen,* hast given them real proofs of thy displeasure against them." This he did before he destroyed them, that they might take warning by the rebukes of Providence and so prevent their own destruction. 2. He had cut them off: *Thou hast destroyed the wicked.* The wicked are marked for destruction, and some are made monuments of God's vindictive justice and destructive power in this world. 3. He had buried them in oblivion and perpetual infamy, had put out their name for ever, that they should never be remembered with any respect.

V. He exults over the enemy whom God thus appears against (v. 6): *Thou hast destroyed cities.* Either, "Thou, O enemy! hast destroyed our cities, at least in intention and imagination," or "Thou, O God! hast destroyed their cities by the desolation brought upon their country." It may be taken either way; for the psalmist will have the enemy to know, 1. That their destruction is just and that God was but reckoning with them for all the mischief which they had done and designed against his people. The malicious and vexatious neighbours of Israel, as the Philistines, Moabites, Ammonites, Edomites, and Syrians, had made incursions upon them (when there was no king in Israel to fight their battles), had destroyed their cities and done what they could to make their memorial perish with them. But now the wheel was turned upon them; their destructions of Israel had come to a perpetual end; they shall now cease to spoil and must themselves be spoiled, Isa. 33:1. 2. That it is total and final, such a destruction as should make a perpetual end of them, so that the very memorial of their cities should perish with them, So devouring a thing is time, and much more such desolations do the righteous judgments of God make upon sinners, that great and populous cities have been reduced to such ruins that their very memorial has perished, and those who have sought them could not find where they stood; but we look for a city that has stronger foundations.

VI. He comforts himself and others in God, and pleases himself with the thoughts of him. 1. With the thoughts of his eternity. On this earth we see nothing durable, even strong cities are buried in rubbish and forgotten; *but the Lord shall endure for ever, v.* 7. There is no change of his being; his felicity, power, and perfection, are out of the reach of all the combined forces of hell and earth; they may put an end to our liberties, our privileges, our lives, but our God is still the same, and sits even upon the floods, unshaken, undisturbed, Ps. 29:10; 93:2. 2. With the thoughts of his sovereignty both in government and judgment: *He has prepared his throne,* has fixed it by his infinite wisdom, has fixed it by his immutable counsel. It is the great support and comfort of good people, when the power of the church's enemies is threatening and the posture of its affairs melancholy and perplexed, that God now rules the world and will shortly judge the world. 3. With the thoughts of his justice and righteousness in all the administrations of his government. He does all every day, he will do all at the last day, according to the eternal unalterable rules of equity (v. 8): *He shall judge the world,* all

persons and all controversies, *shall minister judgment to the people* (shall determine their lot both in this and in the future state) in righteousness and *in uprightness,* so that there shall not be the least colour of exception against it.
4. With the thoughts of that peculiar favour which God bears to his own people and the special protection which he takes them under. The Lord, who endures for ever, is their everlasting strength and protection; he that judges the world will be sure to judge for them, when at any time they are injured or distressed (*v.* 9): *He will be a refuge for the oppressed,* a high place, a strong place, for the oppressed, *in times of trouble.* It is the lot of God's people to be oppressed in this world and to have troublous times appointed to them. Perhaps God may not immediately appear for them as their deliverer and avenger; but, in the midst of their distresses, they may by faith flee to him as their refuge and may depend upon his power and promise for their safety, so that no real hurt shall be done them.
5. With the thoughts of that sweet satisfaction and repose of mind which those have that make God their refuge (*v.* 10): *"Those that know thy name will put their trust in thee,* as I have done" (for the grace of God is the same in all the saints), "and then they will find, as I have found, that thou dost not forsake those that seek thee;" for the favour of God is the same towards all the saints. Note, (1.) The better God is known the more he is trusted. Those who know him to be a God of infinite wisdom will trust him *further than they can see him* (Job 35:14); those who know him to be a God of almighty power will trust him when creature-confidences fail and they have nothing else to trust to (2 Chr. 20:12); and those who know him to be a God of infinite grace and goodness will trust him *though he slay them,* Job 13:15. Those who know him to be a God of inviolable truth and faithfulness will rejoice in his word of promise, and rest upon that, though the performance be deferred and intermediate providences seem to contradict it. Those who know him to be the Father of spirits, and an everlasting Father, will trust him with their souls as their main care and trust in him at all times, even to the end. (2.) The more God is trusted the more he is sought unto. If we trust God we shall seek him by faithful and fervent prayer, and by a constant care to approve ourselves to him in the whole course of our conversations. (3.) God never did, nor ever will, disown or desert any that duly seek to him and trust in him. Though he afflict them, he will not leave them comfortless; though he seem to forsake them for a while, yet he will gather them with everlasting mercies.

Verses 11–20

In these verses,
I. David, having praised God himself, calls upon and invites others to praise him likewise, *v.* 11. Those who believe God is greatly to be praised not only desire to do that work better themselves, but desire that others also may join with them in it and would gladly be instrumental to bring them to it: *Sing praises to the Lord who dwelleth in Zion.* As the special residence of his glory is in heaven, so the special residence of his grace is in his church, of which Zion was a type. There he meets his people with his promises and graces, and there he expects they should meet him with their praises and services. In all our praises we should have an eye to God as dwelling in Zion, in a special manner present in the assemblies of his people, as their protector and patron. He resolved himself to show forth God's marvellous works (*v.* 1), and here he calls upon others to *declare among the people his doings.* He commands his own subjects to do it, for the honour of God, of their country, and of their holy religion: he courts his neighbours to do it, to sing praises not, as hitherto, to their false gods, but to Jehovah who dwelleth in Zion, to the God of Israel, and to own among the heathen that *the Lord has done great things for his people Israel,* Ps. 126:3, 4. Let them particularly take notice of the justice of God in avenging the blood of his people Israel on the Philistines and their other wicked neighbours, who had, in making war upon them, used them barbarously and given them no quarter, *v.* 12. When God comes to *make inquisition for blood* by his judgments on earth, before he comes to do it by the judgment of the great day, *he remembers them,* remembers every drop of the innocent blood which they have shed, and will return it sevenfold upon the head of

the blood-thirsty; he will give them blood to drink, for they are worthy. This assurance he might well build upon that word (Deu. 32:43), *He will avenge the blood of his servants.* Note, There is a day coming when God will make inquisition for blood, when he will discover what has been shed secretly, and avenge what has been shed unjustly; see Isa. 26:21; Jer. 51:35. In that day it will appear how precious the blood of God's people is to him (Ps. 72:14), when it must all be accounted for. It will then appear that he has not forgotten *the cry of the humble,* neither the cry of their blood nor the cry of their prayers, but that both are sealed up among his treasures.
II. David, having praised God for former mercies and deliverances, earnestly prays that God would still appear for him; for he sees not all things put under him.
1. He prays, (1.) That God would be compassionate to him (*v.* 13): *"Have mercy upon me,* who, having misery only, and no merit, to speak for me, must depend upon mercy for relief." (2.) That he would be concerned for him. He is not particular in his request, lest he should seem to prescribe to God; but submits himself to the wisdom and will of God in this modest request, *"Lord, consider my trouble,* and do for me as thou thinkest fit."
2. He pleads, (1.) The malice of his enemies, the trouble which he suffered from those that hated him, and hatred is a cruel passion. (2.) The experience he had had of divine succours and the expectation he now had of the continuance of them, as the necessity of his case required: *"O thou that liftest me up,* that canst do it, that hast done it, that wilt do it, whose prerogative it is to lift up thy people *from the gates of death!"* We are never brought so low, so near to death, but God can raise us up. If he has saved us from spiritual and eternal death, we may thence take encouragement to hope that in all our distresses he will be a very present help to us. (3.) His sincere purpose to praise God when his victories should be completed (*v.* 14): "Lord, save me, not that I may have the comfort and credit of the deliverance, but that thou mayest have the glory, *that I may show forth all thy praise,* and that publicly, *in the gates of the daughter of Zion;"* there God was said to dwell (*v.* 11) and there David would attend him, with joy in God's salvation, typical of the great salvation which was to be wrought out by the Son of David.
III. David by faith foresees and foretels the certain ruin of all wicked people, both in this world and in that to come.
1. In this world, *v.* 15, 16. God executes judgment upon them when the measure of their iniquities is full, and does it, (1.) So as to put shame upon them and make their fall inglorious; for they sink into the pit which they themselves digged (Ps. 7:15), they are taken in the net which they themselves laid for the ensnaring of God's people, and they are snared in the work of their own hands. In all the struggles David had with the Philistines they were the aggressors, 2 Sa. 5:17, 22. And other nations were subdued by those ward in which they embroiled themselves. The overruling providence of God frequently so orders it that persecutors and oppressors are brought to ruin by those very projects which they intended to be destructive to the people of God. Drunkards kill themselves; prodigals beggar themselves; the contentious bring mischief upon themselves. Thus men's sins may be read in their punishment, and it becomes visible to all that the destruction of sinners is not only meritoriously, but efficiently, of themselves, which will fill them with the utmost confusion. (2.) So as to get honour to himself: *The Lord is known,* that is, he makes himself known, by these judgments which he executes. It is known that there is a God who judges in the earth, that he is a righteous God, and one that hates sin and will punish it. In these judgments the wrath of God is revealed from heaven against all ungodliness and unrighteousness of men. The psalmist therefore adds here a note extraordinary, commanding special regard, *Higgaion;* it is a thing to be carefully observed and meditated upon. What we see of present judgments, and what we believe of the judgment to come, ought to be the subject of our frequent and serious meditations.
2. In the other world (*v.* 17): *The wicked shall be turned into hell,* as captives into the prison-house, even *all the nations that forget God.* Note, (1.) Forgetfulness of God is the cause of all the wickedness of the wicked. (2.) There are nations of those that forget God, multitudes that live without God in the world, many great and many mighty na-

tions, that never regard him nor desire the knowledge of his ways. (3.) Hell will, at last, be the portion of such, a state of everlasting misery and torment — *Sheol,* a pit of destruction, in which they and all their comforts will be for ever lost and buried. Though there be nations of them, yet they shall be turned into hell, like sheep into the slaughter-house (Ps. 49:14), and their being so numerous will not be any security or ease to them, nor any loss to God or the least impeachment of his goodness.
IV. David encourages the people of God to wait for his salvation, though it should be long deferred, *v.* 18. The needy may think themselves, and others may think them, forgotten for a while, and their expectation of help from God may seem to have perished and to have been for ever frustrated. But he that believes does not make haste; the vision is for an appointed time, and at the end it shall speak. We may build upon it as undoubtedly true that God's people, God's elect, shall not always be forgotten, nor shall they be disappointed of their hopes from the promise. God will not only remember them, at last, but will make it to appear that he never did forget them; it is impossible he should, though a woman may forget her sucking child.
V. He concludes with prayer that God would humble the pride, break the power, and blast the projects, of all the wicked enemies of his church: *"Arise, O Lord!* (*v.* 19), stir up thy self, exert thy power, take thy seat, and deal with all these proud and daring enemies of thy name, and cause, and people." 1. "Lord, restrain them, and set bounds to their malice: *Let not man prevail;* consult thy own honour, and let not weak and mortal men prevail against the kingdom and interest of the almighty and immortal God. *Shall mortal man be too hard for God, too strong for his Maker?"* 2. "Lord, reckon with them: *Let the heathen be judges in thy sight,* that is, let them be plainly called to an account for all the dishonour done to thee and the mischief done to thy people." Impenitent sinners will be punished in God's sight; and, when their day of grace is over, the bowels even of infinite mercy will not relent towards them, Rev. 14:10. 3. "Lord, frighten them: *Put them in fear, O Lord!* (*v.* 20), strike a terror upon them, make them afraid with thy judgments." God knows how to make the strongest and stoutest of men to tremble and to flee when none pursues, and thereby he makes them know and own that they are but men; they are but weak men, unable to stand before the holy God — sinful men, the guilt of whose consciences make them subject to alarms. Note, It is a very desirable thing, much for the glory of God and the peace and welfare of the universe, that men should know and consider themselves to be but men, depending creatures, mutable, mortal, and accountable.
In singing this psalm we must give to God the glory of his justice in pleading his people's cause against his and their enemies, and encourage ourselves to wait for the year of the redeemed and the year of recompences for the controversy of Zion, even the final destruction of all antichristian powers and factions, to which many of the ancients apply this psalm.

PSALM 10

The Septuagint translation joins this psalm with the ninth, and makes them but one; but the Hebrew makes it a distinct psalm, and the scope and style are certainly different. In this psalm, I. David complains of the wickedness of the wicked, describes the dreadful pitch of impiety at which they had arrived (to the great dishonour of God and the prejudice of his church and people), and notices the delay of God's appearing against them (*v.* 1–11). II. He prays to God to appear against them for the relief of his people and comforts himself with hopes that he would do so in due time (*v.* 12–18).

Verses 1–11

David, in these verses, discovers,
I. A very great affection to God and his favour; for, in the time of trouble, that which he complains of most feelingly is God's withdrawing his gracious presence (*v.* 1): *"Why standest thou afar off,* as one unconcerned in the indignities done to thy name and the injuries done to the people?" Note, God's withdrawings are very grievous to his people at any time, but especially in times of trouble. Outward deliverance is afar off and is hidden from us, and then we think God is afar off and we therefore want inward comfort; but that is our own fault; it is because we judge by outward appearance; we stand afar off from God

by our unbelief, and then we complain that God stands afar off from us.

II. A very great indignation against sin, the sins that made the times perilous, 2 Tim. 3:1. he beholds the transgressors and is grieved, is amazed, and brings to his heavenly Father their evil report, not in a way of vain-glory, boasting before God that he was not as *these publicans* (Lu. 18:11), much less venting any personal resentments, piques, or passions, of his own; but as one that laid to he art that which is offensive to God and all good men, and earnestly desired a reformation of manners. passionate and satirical invectives against bad men do more hurt than good; if we will speak of their badness, let it be to God in prayer, for he alone can make them better. This long representation of the wickedness of the wicked is here summed up in the first words of it (*v.* 2), *The wicked in his pride doth persecute the poor,* where two things are laid to their charge, pride and persecution, the former the cause of the latter. Proud men will have all about them to be of their mind, of their religion, to say as they say, to submit to their dominion, and acquiesce in their dictates; and those that either eclipse them or will not yield to them they malign and hate with an inveterate hatred. Tyranny, both in state and church, owes its origin to pride. The psalmist, having begun this description, presently inserts a short prayer, a prayer in a parenthesis, which is an advantage and no prejudice to the sense: *Let them be taken,* as proud people often are, *in the devices that they have imagined, v.* 2. Let their counsels be turned headlong, and let them fall headlong by them. These two heads of the charge are here enlarged upon.

1. They are proud, very proud, and extremely conceited of themselves; justly therefore did he wonder that God did not speedily appear against them, for he hates pride, and resists the proud. (1.) The sinner proudly glories in his power and success. He *boasts of his heart's desire,* boasts that he can do what he pleases (as if God himself could not control him) and that he has all he wished for and has carried his point. Ephraim said, *I have become rich, I have found me out substance,* Hos. 12:8. "Now, Lord, is it for thy glory to suffer a sinful man thus to pretend to the sovereignty and felicity of a God?" (2.) He proudly contradicts the judgment of God, which, we are sure, is according to truth; for he *blesses the covetous, whom the Lord abhors.* See how God and men differ in their sentiments of persons: God abhors covetous worldlings, who make money their God and idolize is; he looks upon them as his enemies, and will have no communion with them. *The friendship of the world is enmity to God.* But proud persecutors bless them, and approve their sayings, Ps. 49:13. They applaud those as wise whom God pronounces foolish (Lu. 12:20); they justify those as innocent whom God condemns as deeply guilty before him; and they admire those as happy, in having their portion in this life, whom God declares, upon that account, truly miserable. *Thou, in thy lifetime, receivedst thy good things.* (3.) He proudly casts off the thoughts of God, and all dependence upon him and devotion to him (*v.* 4): *The wicked, through the pride of his countenance,* that pride of his heart which appears in his very countenance (Prov. 6:17), *will not seek after God,* nor entertain the thoughts of him. *God is not in all his thoughts,* not in any of them. *All his thoughts are that there is not God.* See here, [1.] The nature of impiety and irreligion; it is *not seeking after God* and *not having him in our thoughts.* There is no enquiry made after him (Job 35:10, Jer. 2:6), no desire towards him, no communion with him, but a secret wish to have no dependence upon him and not to be beholden to him. Wicked people will not seek after God (that is, will not call upon him); they live without prayer, and that is living without God. They have many thoughts, many projects and devices, but no eye to God in any of them, no submission to his will nor aim at his glory. [2.] The cause of this impiety and irreligion; and that is pride. Men will not seek after God because they think they have no need of him, their own hands are sufficient for them; they think it a thing below them to be religious, because religious people are few, and mean, and despised, and the restraints of religion will be a disparagement to them. (4.) He proudly makes light of God's commandments and judgments (*v.* 5): *His wings are always grievous;* he is very daring and resolute in his sinful courses; he will have his way, though ever so tiresome to himself and vexatious to others; he travails with pain in his wicked courses, and yet his pride makes him wilful and obstinate in them. God's judgments (what he commands and what he threatens for the breach of his commands) are *far above out of his sight;* he is not sensible of his duty by the law of God nor of his danger by the wrath and curse of God. Tell him of God's authority over him, he turns it off with this, that he never saw God and therefore does not know that there is a God, he is *in the height of heaven,* and *quae supra nos nihil ad nos — we have nothing to do with things above us.* Tell him of God's judgments which will be executed upon those that go on still in their trespasses, and he will not be convinced that there is any reality in them; they are *far above out of his sight,* and therefore he thinks they are mere bugbears. (5.) He proudly despises all his enemies, and looks upon them with the utmost disdain; he puffs at those whom God is preparing to be a scourge and ruin to him, as if he could baffle them all, and was able to make his part good with them. But, as it is impolitic to despise an enemy, so it is impious to despise any instrument of God's wrath. (6.) He proudly sets trouble at defiance and is confident of the continuance of his own prosperity (*v.* 6): *He hath said in his heart,* and pleased himself with the thought, *I shall not be moved,* my goods are laid up for many years, and *I shall never be in adversity;* like Babylon, that said, *I shall be a lady for ever,* Isa. 47:7; Rev. 18:7. Those are nearest ruin who thus set it furthest from them.

2. They are persecutors, cruel persecutors. For the gratifying of their pride and covetousness, and in opposition to God and religion, they are very oppressive to all within their reach. Observe, concerning these persecutors, (1.) That they are very bitter and malicious (*v.* 7): *His mouth is full of cursing.* Those he cannot do a real mischief to, yet he will spit his venom at, and breathe out the slaughter which he cannot execute. Thus have God's faithful worshippers been anathematized and cursed, with bell, book, and candle. Where there is a heart full of malice there is commonly a mouth full of curses. (2.) They are very false and treacherous. There is mischief designed, but it is hidden under the tongue, not to be discerned, for *his mouth is full of deceit* and vanity. He has learned of the devil to deceive, and so to destroy; with this his hatred is covered, Prov. 26:26. He cares not what lies he tells, not what oaths he breaks, nor what arts of dissimulation he uses, to compass his ends. (3.) That they are very cunning and crafty in carrying on their designs. They have ways and means to concert what they intend, that they may the more effectually accomplish it. Like Esau, that cunning hunter, *he sits in the lurking places, in the secret places,* and *his eyes are privily set* to do mischief (*v.* 8), not because he is ashamed of what he does (if he blushed, there were some hopes he would repent), not because he is afraid of the wrath of God, for he imagines God will never call him to an account (*v.* 11), but because he is afraid lest the discovery of his designs should be the breaking of them. Perhaps it refers particularly to robbers and highwaymen, who lie in wait for honest travellers, to make a prey of them and what they have. (4.) That they are very cruel and barbarous. Their malice is against *the innocent,* who never provoked them — against *the poor,* who cannot resist them and over whom it will be no glory to triumph. Those are perfectly lost to all honesty and honour against whose mischievous designs neither innocence nor poverty will be any man's security. Those that have power ought to protect the innocent and provide for the poor; yet these will be the destroyers of those whose guardians they ought to be. And what do they aim at? It is to *catch the poor,* and *draw them into their net,* that is, get them into their power, not to strip them only, but to *murder them.* They hunt for the precious life. It is God's poor people that they are persecuting, against whom they bear a mortal hatred for his sake whose they are and whose image they bear, and therefore they lie in wait to murder them: *He lies in wait as a lion* that thirsts after blood, and feeds with pleasure upon the prey. The devil, whose agent he is, is compared to a roaring lion that seeks not what, but whom, he may devour. (5.) That they are base and hypocritical (*v.* 10): *He crouches and humbles himself,* as beasts of prey do, that they may get their prey within their reach. This intimates that the sordid spirits of persecutors and oppressors will stoop to any thing, though ever so mean, for the compassing of their wicked designs; witness the scandalous practices of Saul when he hunted David. It intimates, likewise, that they cover their malicious designs with the pretence of meekness and humility, and kindness to those they design the greatest mischief to; they seem to humble themselves to take cognizance of the poor, and concern themselves in their concernments, when it is in order to make them fall, to make a prey of them. (6.) That they are very impious and atheistical, *v.* 11. They could not thus break through all the laws of justice and goodness towards man if they had not first shaken off all sense of religion, and risen up in rebellion against the light of its most sacred and self-evident principles: *He hath said in his heart, God has forgotten.* When his own conscience rebuked him with the consequences of it, and asked how he would answer it to the righteous Judge of heaven and earth, he turned it off with this, *God has forsaken the earth,* Eze. 8:12; 9:9. This is a blasphemous reproach, [1.] Upon God's omniscience and providence, as if he could not, or did not, see what men do in this lower world. [2.] Upon his holiness and the rectitude of his nature, as if, though he did see, yet he did not dislike, but was willing to connive at, the most unnatural and inhuman villanies. [3.] Upon his justice and the equity of his government, as if, though he did see and dislike the wickedness of the wicked, yet he would never reckon with them, nor punish them for it, either because he could not or durst not, or because he was not inclined to do so. Let those that suffer by proud oppressors hope that God will, in due time, appear for them; for those that are abusive to them are abusive to God Almighty too.

In singing this psalm and praying it over, we should have our hearts much affected with a holy indignation at the wickedness of the oppressors, a tender compassion of the miseries of the oppressed, and a pious zeal for the glory and honour of God, with a firm belief that he will, in due time, give redress to the injured and reckon with the injurious.

Verses 12–18

David here, upon the foregoing representation of the inhumanity and impiety of the oppressors, grounds an address to God, wherein observe,

I. What he prays for. 1. That God would himself appear (*v.* 12): *"Arise, O Lord! O God! lift up thy hand,* manifest thy presence and providence in the affairs of this lower world. *Arise, O Lord!* to the confusion of those who say that thou hidest thy face. Manifest thy power, exert it for the maintaining of thy own cause, lift up thy hand to give a fatal blow to these oppressors; let thy everlasting arm be made bare." 2. That he would appear for his people: *"Forget not the humble, the afflicted,* that are poor, that are made poorer, and are poor in spirit. Their oppressors, in their presumption, say that thou hast forgotten them; and they, in their despair, are ready to say the same. Lord, make it to appear that they are both mistaken." 3. That he would appear against their persecutors, *v.* 15. (1.) That he would disable them from doing any mischief: *Break thou the arm of the wicked,* take away his power, *that the hypocrite reign not, lest the people be ensnared,* Job 34:30. We read of oppressors whose dominion was taken away, but their lives were prolonged (Dan. 7:12), that they might have time to repent. (2.) That he would deal with them for the mischief they had done: *"Seek out his wickedness;* let that be all brought to light which he thought should for ever lie undiscovered; let that be all brought to account which he thought should for ever go unpunished; bring it out *till thou find none,* that is, till none of his evil deeds remain unreckoned for, none of his evil designs undefeated, and none of his partisans undestroyed."

II. What he pleads for the encouraging of his own faith in these petitions.

1. He pleads the great affronts which these proud oppressors put upon God himself: "Lord, it is thy own cause that we beg thou wouldst appear in; the enemies have made it so, and therefore it is not for thy glory to let them go unpunished" (*v.* 13): *Wherefore do the wicked contemn God?* He does so; for he says, *"Thou wilt not require it;* thou wilt never call us to an account for what we do," than which they could not put a greater indignity upon the righteous God. The psalmist here speaks with astonishment, (1.) At the wickedness of the wicked: "Why do they speak

so impiously, why so absurdly?" It is a great trouble to good men to think what contempt is cast upon the holy God by the sin of sinners, upon his precepts, his promises, his threatenings, his favours, his judgments; all are despised and made light of. *Wherefore do the wicked thus contemn God?* It is because they do not know him. (2.) At the patience and forbearance of God towards them: "Why are they suffered thus to contemn God? Why does he not immediately vindicate himself and take vengeance on them?" It is because the day of reckoning is yet to come, when the measure of their iniquity is full.

2. He pleads the notice God took of the impiety and iniquity of these oppressors (v. 14): "Do the persecutors encourage themselves with a groundless fancy that thou wilt never see it? Let the persecuted encourage themselves with a well-grounded faith, not only that thou hast seen it, but that thou doest behold it, even all the mischief that is done by the hands, and all the spite and malice that lurk in the hearts, of these oppressors; it is all known to thee, and observed by thee; nay, not only thou hast seen it and dost behold it, but thou wilt requite it, wilt recompense it into their bosoms, by thy just and avenging hand."

3. He pleads the dependence which the oppressed had upon him: *"The poor commits himself unto thee,* each of them does so, I among the rest. They rely on thee as their patron and protector, they refer themselves to thee as their Judge, in whose determination they acquiesce and at whose disposal they are willing to be. *They leave themselves with thee"* (so some read it), "not prescribing, but subscribing, to thy wisdom and will. They thus give thee honour as much as their oppressors dishonour thee. They are thy willing subjects, and put themselves under thy protection; therefore protect them."

4. He pleads the relation in which God is pleased to stand to us, (1.) As a great God. He *is King for ever and ever, v.* 16. And it is the office of a king to administer justice for the restraint and terror of evil-doers and the protection and praise of those that do well. To whom should the injured subjects appeal but to the sovereign? *Help, my Lord, O King! Avenge me of my adversary.* "Lord, let all that pay homage and tribute to thee as their King have the benefit of thy government and find thee their refuge. Thou art an everlasting King, which no earthly prince is, and therefore canst and wilt, by an eternal judgment, dispense rewards and punishments in an everlasting state, when time shall be no more; and to that judgment the poor refer themselves." (2.) As a good God. He is the helper of the fatherless (v. 14), of those who have no one else to help them and have many to injure them. He has appointed kings to *defend the poor and fatherless* (Ps. 82:3), and therefore much more will he do so himself; for he has taken it among the titles of his honour to be a Father to the fatherless (Ps. 68:5), a helper of the helpless.

5. He pleads the experience which God's church and people had had of God's readiness to appear for them. (1.) He had dispersed and extirpated their enemies (v. 16): *"The heathen have perished out of his land;* the remainders of the Canaanites, the seven devoted nations, which have long been as thorns in the eyes and goads in the sides of Israel, are now, at length, utterly rooted out; and this is an encouragement to us to hope that God will, in like manner, break the arm of the oppressive Israelites, who were, in some respects, worse than heathens." (2.) He had heard and answered their prayers (v. 17): *"Lord, thou hast* many a time *heard the desire of the humble,* and never saidst to a distressed suppliant, *Seek in vain.* Why may not we hope for the continuance and repetition of the wonders, the favours, which our father told us of?"

6. He pleads their expectations from God pursuant to their experience of him: *"Thou hast heard,* therefore *thou will cause thy ear to hear,* as, Ps. 6:9. Thou art the same, and thy power, and promise, and relation to thy people are the same, and the work and workings of grace are the same in them; why therefore may we not hope that he who has been will still be, will ever be, a God hearing prayers?" But observe, (1.) In what method God hears prayer. He first prepares the heart of his people and then gives them an answer of peace; nor may we expect his gracious answer, but in this way; so that God's working upon us is the best earnest of his working for us. He prepares the heart for prayer by kindling holy desires, and strengthening our most holy faith, fixing the thoughts and

raising the affections, and then he graciously accepts the prayer; he prepares the heart for the mercy itself that is wanting and prayed for, makes us fit to receive it and use it well, and then gives it in to us. The preparation of the heart is from the Lord, and we must seek unto him for it (Prov. 16:1) and take that as a leading favour. (2.) What he will do in answer to prayer, v. 18. [1.] He will plead the cause of the persecuted, will judge the fatherless and oppressed, will judge for them, clear up their innocency, restore their comforts, and recompense them for all the loss and damage they have sustained. [2.] He will put an end to the fury of the persecutors. Hitherto they shall come, but no further; here shall the proud waves of their malice be stayed; an effectual course shall be taken *that the man of the earth may no more oppress.* See how light the psalmist now makes of the power of that proud persecutor whom he had been describing in this psalm, and how slightly he speaks of him now that he had been considering God's sovereignty. *First,* He is but *a man of the earth,* a man *out of* the earth (so the word is), sprung out of the earth, and therefore mean, and weak, and hastening to the earth again. Why then should we be afraid of the fury of the oppressor when he is but *man that shall die, a son of man that shall be as grass?* Isa. 51:12. He that protects us is the Lord of heaven; he that persecutes us is but a man of the earth. *Secondly,* God has him in a chain, and can easily restrain the remainder of his wrath, so that he cannot do what he would. When God speaks the word Satan shall by his instruments no more deceive (Rev. 20:3), no more oppress.

In singing these verses we must commit religion's just but injured cause to God, as those that are heartily concerned for its honour and interests, believing that he will, in due time, plead it with jealousy.

PSALM 11

In this psalm we have David's struggle with and triumph over a strong temptation to distrust God and betake himself to indirect means for his own safety in a time of danger. It is supposed to have been penned when he began to feel the resentments of Saul's envy, and had had the javelin thrown at him once and again. He was then advised to run his country. "No," says he, "I trust in God, and therefore will keep my ground." Observe, I. How he represents the temptation, and perhaps parleys with it, (v. 1–3). II. How he answers it, and puts it to silence with the consideration of God's dominion and providence (v. 4), his favour to the righteous, and the wrath which the wicked are reserved for (v. 5–7). In times of public fear, when the insults of the church's enemies are daring and threatening, it will be profitable to meditate on this psalm.

To the chief musician. A psalm of David.

Verses 1–3

Here is, I. David's fixed resolution to make God his confidence: *In the Lord put I my trust, v.* 1. Those that truly fear God and serve him are welcome to put their trust in him, and shall not be made ashamed of their doing so. And it is the character of the saints, who have taken God for their God, that they make him their hope. Even when they have other things to stay themselves upon, yet they do not, they dare not, stay upon them, but on God only. Gold is not their hope, nor are horses and chariots their confidence, but God only; and therefore, when second causes frown, yet their hopes do not fail them, because the first cause is still the same, is ever so. The psalmist, before he gives an account of the temptation he was in to distrust God, records his resolution to trust in him, as that which he was resolved to live and die by.

II. His resentment of a temptation to the contrary: *"How say you to my soul,* which has thus returned to God as its rest and reposes in him, *Flee as a bird to your mountain,* to be safe there out of the reach of the fowler?" This may be taken either,

1. As the serious advice of his timorous friends; so many understand it, and with great probability. Some that were hearty well-wishers to David, when they saw how much Saul was exasperated against him and how maliciously he sought his life, pressed him by all means to flee for the same to some place of shelter, and not to depend too much upon the anointing he had received, which, they thought, was more likely to occasion the loss of his head than to save it. That which grieved him in this motion was not that to flee now would savour of cowardice, and ill become a soldier, but that it would savour of unbelief and would ill become a saint who had so often said, *In the Lord put I*

my trust. Taking it thus, the two following verses contain the reason with which these faint-hearted friends of David backed this advice. They would have him flee, (1.) Because he could not be safe where he was, v. 2. "Observe," say they, "how *the wicked bend their bow;* Saul and his instruments aim at thy life, and the uprightness of thy heart will not be thy security." See what an enmity there is in the wicked against the upright, in the seed of the serpent against the seed of the woman; what pains they take, what preparations they make, to do them a mischief: *They privily shoot* at them, or, *in darkness,* that they may not see the evil designed, to avoid it, nor others, to prevent it, no, nor God himself, to punish it. (2.) Because he could be no longer useful where he was. "For," say they, *"if the foundations be destroyed"* (as they were by Saul's maladministration), "if the civil state and government be unhinged and all out of course" (Ps. 75:3, 82:5), "what canst thou do with thy righteousness to redress the grievances? Alas! it is to no purpose to attempt the saving of a kingdom so wretchedly shattered; whatever the righteous can do signifies nothing." *Abi in cellam, et dic, Miserere mei, Domine — Away to thy cell, and there cry, Pity me, O Lord!* Many are hindered from doing the service they might do to the public, in difficult times, by a despair of success.

2. It may be taken as a taunt wherewith his enemies bantered him, upbraiding him with the professions he used to make of confidence in God, and scornfully bidding him try what stead that would stand him in now. "You say, God is your mountain; flee to him now, and see what the better you will be." Thus they endeavoured to shame the counsel of the poor, saying, There is *no help for them in God,* Ps. 14:6; 3:2. The confidence and comfort which the saints have in God, when all the hopes and joys in the creature fail them, are a riddle to a carnal world and are ridiculed accordingly. Taking it thus, the two following verses are David's answer to this sarcasm, in which, (1.) He complains of the malice of those who did thus abuse him (v. 2): *They bend their bow and make ready their arrows;* and we are told (Ps. 64:3) what their arrows are, even bitter words, such words as these, by which they endeavour to discourage hope in God, which David felt as a sword in his bones. (2.) He resists the temptation with a gracious abhorrence, *v.* 3. He looks upon this suggestion as striking at the foundations which every Israelite builds upon: "If you destroy the foundations, if you take good people off from their hope in God, if you can persuade them that their religion is a cheat and a jest and can banter them out of that, you ruin them, and break their hearts indeed, and make them of all men the most miserable." The principles of religion are the foundations on which the faith and hope of the righteous are built. These we are concerned, in interest as well as duty, to hold fast against all temptations to infidelity; for, if these be destroyed, if we let these go, *What can the righteous do?* Good people would be undone if they had not a God to go to, a God to trust to, and a future bliss to hope for.

Verses 4–7

The shaking of a tree (they say) makes it take the deeper and faster root. The attempt of David's enemies to discourage his confidence in God engages him to cleave so much the more closely to his first principles, and to review them, which he here does, abundantly to his own satisfaction and the silencing of all temptations to infidelity. That which was shocking to his faith, and has been so to the faith of many, was the prosperity of wicked people in their wicked ways, and the straits and distresses which the best men are sometimes reduced to: hence such an evil thought as this was apt to arise, *Surely it is vain to serve God,* and we may call the proud happy. But, in order to stifle and shame all such thoughts, we are here called to consider,

I. That there is a God in heaven: *The Lord is in his holy temple* above, where, though he is out of our sight, we are not out of his. Let not the enemies of the saints insult over them, as if they were at a loss and at their wits' end: no, they have a God, and they know where to find him and how to direct their prayer unto him, as their Father in heaven. Or, He is in his holy temple, that is, in his church; he is a God in covenant and communion with his people, through a Mediator, of whom the temple was a type. We need not say, "Who shall go up to heaven, to fetch us thence a God to trust to?" No, the word is nigh us, and God in the word; his Spirit is in his saints, those living temples, and the Lord is that Spirit.

II. That this God governs the world. The Lord has not only his residence, but his throne, in heaven, and he has *set the dominion thereof in the earth* (Job 38:33); for, having *prepared his throne in the heavens, his kingdom ruleth over all,* Ps. 103:19. Hence the heavens are said *to rule,* Dan. 4:26. Let us by faith see God on this throne, on his throne of glory, infinitely transcending the splendour and majesty of earthly princes — on his throne of government, giving law, giving motion, and giving aim, to all the creatures — on his throne of judgment, rendering to every man according to his works — and on his throne of grace, to which his people may come boldly for mercy and grace; we shall then see no reason to be discouraged by the pride and power of oppressors, or any of the afflictions that attend the righteous.

III. That this God perfectly knows every man's true character: *His eyes behold, his eye-lids try, the children of men;* he not only sees them, but he sees through them, not only knows all they say and do, but knows what they think, what they design, and how they really stand affected, whatever they pretend. We may know what men seem to be, but he knows what they are, as the refiner knows what the value of the gold is when he has tried it. God is said to try *with his eyes,* and *his eye-lids,* because he knows men, not as earthly princes know men, by report and representation, but by his own strict inspection, which cannot err nor be imposed upon. This may comfort us when we are deceived in men, even in men that we think we have tried, that God's judgment of men, we are sure, is according to truth.

IV. That, if he afflict good people, it is for their trial and therefore for their good, *v.* 5. The Lord tries all the children of men that he may *do them good in their latter end,* Deu. 8:16. Let not that therefore shake our foundations nor discourage our hope and trust in God.

V. That, however persecutors and oppressors may prosper and prevail awhile, they now lie under, and will for ever perish under, the wrath of God. 1. He is a holy God, and therefore hates them, and cannot endure to look upon them: *The wicked, and him that loveth violence, his soul hateth;* for nothing is more contrary to the rectitude and goodness of his nature. Their prosperity is so far from being an evidence of God's love that their abuse of it does certainly make them the objects of his hatred. He that hates nothing that he has made, yet hates those who have thus ill-made themselves. Dr. Hammond offers another reading of this verse: *The Lord trieth the righteous and the wicked* (distinguishes infallibly between them, which is more than we can do), and *he that loveth violence hateth his own soul,* that is, persecutors bring certain ruin upon themselves (Prov. 8:36), as follows here. 2. He is a righteous Judge, and therefore he will punish them, *v.* 6. Their punishment will be, (1.) Inevitable: *Upon the wicked he shall rain snares.* Here is a double metaphor, to denote the unavoidableness of the punishment of wicked men. It shall be rained upon them from heaven (Job 20:23), against which there is no fence and from which there is no escape; see Jos. 10:11; 1 Sa. 2:10. It shall surprise them as a sudden shower sometimes surprises the traveller in a summer's day. It shall be as snares upon them, to hold them fast, and keep them prisoners, till the day of reckoning comes. (2.) Very terrible. It is *fire, and brimstone, and a horrible tempest,* which plainly alludes to the destruction of Sodom and Gomorrah, and very fitly, for that destruction was intended for a figure of *the vengeance of eternal fire,* Jude 7. The fire of God's wrath, fastening upon the brimstone of their own guilt, will burn certainly and furiously, will burn to the lowest hell and the utmost line of eternity. What a horrible tempest are the wicked hurried away in at death! What a lake of fire and brimstone must they make their bed in for ever, in the congregation of the dead and damned! It is this that is here meant; it is this that shall be the portion of their cup, the heritage appointed them by the Almighty and allotted to them, Job 20:29. This is the cup of trembling which shall be put into their hands, which they must *drink the dregs* of, Ps. 75:8. Every man has the portion of his cup assigned him. Those who choose the Lord for the portion of their cup shall have what they choose, and be for ever happy in their choice (Ps. 16:5); but those who reject his grace shall be made to drink the cup of his fury, Jer. 25:15; Isa. 51:17; Hab. 2:16.

VI. That, though honest good people may be run down and trampled upon, yet God does and will own them, and favour them, and smile upon them, and that is the reason why God will severely reckon with persecutors and oppressors, because those whom they oppress and persecute are dear to him; so that *whosoever toucheth them toucheth the apple of his eye, v.* 7. 1. He loves them and the work of his own grace in them. He is himself a righteous God, and therefore loves righteousness wherever he finds it and pleads the cause of the righteous that are injured and oppressed; he delights to execute judgment for them, Ps. 103:6. We must herein be followers of God, must love righteousness as he does, that we may keep ourselves always in his love. He looks graciously upon them: *His countenance doth behold the upright;* he is not only at peace with them, and puts gladness into their hearts, by letting them know that he is so. He, like a tender father, looks upon them with pleasure, and they, like dutiful children, are pleased and abundantly satisfied with his smiles. They walk in the light of the Lord.

In singing this psalm we must encourage and engage ourselves to trust in God at all times, must depend upon him to protect our innocence and make us happy, must dread his frowns as worse than death and desire his favour as better than life.

PSALM 12

It is supposed that David penned this psalm in Saul's reign, when there was a general decay of honesty and piety both in court and country, which he here complains of to God, and very feelingly, for he himself suffered by the treachery of his false friends and the insolence of his sworn enemies. I. He begs help of God, because there were none among men whom he durst trust (*v.* 1, 2). II. He foretels the destruction of his proud and threatening enemies (*v.* 3, 4). III. He assures himself and others that, how ill soever things went now (*v.* 8), God would preserve and secure to himself his own people (*v.* 5, 7), and would certainly make good his promises to them (*v.* 6). Whether this psalm was penned in Saul's reign or no, it is certainly calculated for a bad reign; and perhaps David, in spirit foresaw that some of his successors would bring things to as bad a pass as is here described, and treasured up this psalm for the use of the church then. "O tempora, O mores! — Oh the times! Oh the manners!"

To the chief musician upon Sheminith. A psalm of David.

Verses 1–8

This psalm furnishes us with good thoughts for bad times, in which, though the prudent will keep silent (Amos 5:13) because a man may then be made an offender for a word, yet we may comfort ourselves with such suitable meditations and prayers as are here got ready to our hand.

I. Let us see here what it is that makes the times bad, and when they may be said to be so. Ask the children of this world what it is in their account that makes the times bad, and they will tell you, Scarcity of money, decay of trade, and the desolations of war, make the times bad. But the scripture lays the badness of the times upon causes of another nature. 2 Tim. 3:1, *Perilous times shall come,* for iniquity shall abound; and that is the thing David here complains of.

1. When there is a general decay of piety and honesty among men the times are then truly bad (*v.* 1): *When the godly man ceases and the faithful fail.* Observe how these two characters are here put together, the godly and the faithful. As there is no true policy, so there is no true piety, without honesty. Godly men are faithful men, *fast* men, so they have sometimes been called; their word is as confirming as their oath, as binding as their bond; they make conscience of being true both to God and man. They are here said to cease and fail, either by death or by desertion, or by both. Those that were godly and faithful were taken away, and those that were left had sadly degenerated and were not what they had been; so that there were few or no good people that were Israelites indeed to be met with. Perhaps he meant that there were no godly faithful men among Saul's courtiers; if he meant there were few or none in Israel, we hope he was under the same mistake that Elijah was, who thought he only was left alone, when God had 7000 who kept their integrity (Rom. 11:3); or he meant that there were few in comparison; there was a general decay of religion and virtue (and the times are bad, very bad, when it is so), not a man to be found that executes judgment, Jer. 5:1.

2. When dissimulation and flattery have corrupted and debauched all conversation, then the times are very bad (*v.* 2), when men are generally so profligate that they make no conscience of a lie, are so spiteful as to design against their neighbours the worst of mischiefs, and yet so base as to cover the design with the most specious and plausible pretences and professions of friendship. Thus *they speak vanity* (that is, falsehood and a lie) *every one to his neighbour, with flattering lips and a double heart.* They will kiss and kill (as Joab did Abner and Amasa in David's own time), will smile in your face and cut your throat. This is the devil's image complete, a complication of malice and falsehood. The times are bad indeed when there is no such thing as sincerity to be met with, when an honest man knows not whom to believe nor whom to trust, nor dares put confidence in a friend, in a guide, Mic. 7:5, 6; Jer. 9:4, 5. Woe to those who help to make the times thus perilous.

3. When the enemies of God, and religion, and religious people, are impudent and daring, and threaten to run down all that is just and sacred, then the times are very bad, when proud sinners have arrived at such a pitch of impiety as to say, *"With our tongue will we prevail* against the cause of virtue; *our lips are our own* and we may say what we will; *who is lord over us,* either to restrain us or to call us to an account?" *v.* 4. This bespeaks, (1.) A proud conceit of themselves and confidence in themselves, as if the point were indeed gained by eating forbidden fruit, and they were as gods, independent and self-sufficient, infallible in their knowledge of good and evil and therefore fit to be oracles, irresistible in their power and therefore fit to be lawgivers, that could prevail with their tongues, and, like God himself, speak and it is done. (2.) An insolent contempt of God's dominion as if he had no propriety in them — *Our lips are our own* (an unjust pretension, for who made man's mouth, in whose hand is his breath, and whose is the air he breathes in?) and as if he had no authority either to command them or to judge them: *Who is Lord over us?* Like Pharaoh, Ex. 5:1. This is as absurd and unreasonable as the former; for he in whom we live, and move, and have our being, must needs be, by an indisputable title, Lord over us.

4. When the poor and needy are oppressed, and abused, and puffed at, then the times are very bad. This is implied (*v.* 5) where God himself takes notice of *the oppression of the poor* and *the sighing of the needy;* they are oppressed because they are poor, have all manner of wrong done them merely because they are not in a capacity to right themselves. Being thus oppressed, they dare not speak for themselves, lest their defence should be made their offence; but they sigh, secretly bemoaning their calamities, and pouring out their souls in sighs before God. If their oppressors be spoken to on their behalf, they puff at them, make light of their own sin and the misery of the poor, and lay neither to heart; see Ps. 10:5.

5. When wickedness abounds, and goes barefaced, under the protection and countenance of those in authority, then the times are very bad, *v.* 8. *When the vilest men are exalted* to places of trust and power (who, instead of putting the laws in execution against vice and injustice and punishing the wicked according to their merits, patronise and protect them, give them countenance, and support their reputation by their own example), then *the wicked walk on every side;* they swarm in all places, and go up and down seeking to deceive, debauch, and destroy others; they are neither afraid nor ashamed to discover themselves; they declare their sin as Sodom and there is none to check or control them. Bad men are base men, the vilest of men, and they are so though they are ever so highly exalted in this world. Antiochus the illustrious the scripture calls *a vile person,* Dan. 11:21. But it is bad with a kingdom when such are preferred; no marvel if wickedness then grows impudent and insolent. *When the wicked bear rule the people mourn.*

II. Let us now see what good thoughts we are here furnished with for such bad times; and what times we may yet be reserved for we cannot tell. When times are thus bad it is comfortable to think,

1. That we have a God to go to, from whom we may ask and expect the redress of all our grievances. This he begins with (*v.* 1): *"Help, Lord, for the godly man ceaseth.* All other helps and helpers fail; even the godly and faithful, who should lend a helping hand to support the dying

cause of religion, are gone, and therefore whither shall we seek but to thee?" Note, When godly faithful people cease and fail it is time to cry, *Help, Lord!* The abounding of iniquity threatens a deluge. "Help, Lord, help the virtuous; few seek to hold fast their integrity, and to stand in the gap; help to save thy own interest in the world from sinking. *It is time for thee, Lord, to work.*"

2. That God will certainly reckon with false and proud men, and will punish and restrain their insolence. They are above the control of men and set them at defiance. Men cannot discover the falsehood of flatterers, nor humble the haughtiness of those that speak proud things; but the righteous God will *cut off all flattering lips,* that give the traitor's kiss and speak words softer then oil when war is in the heart; he will pluck out *the tongue that speaks proud things* against God and religion, *v.* 3. Some translate it as a prayer, "May God cut off those false and spiteful lips." *Let lying lips be put to silence.*

3. That God will, in due time, work deliverance for his oppressed people, and shelter them from the malicious designs of their persecutors (*v.* 5): *Now, will I arise, saith the Lord.* This promise of God, which David here delivered by the spirit of prophecy, is an answer to that petition which he put up to God by the spirit of prayer. "Help, Lord," says he; "I will," says God; "here I am, with seasonable and effectual help." (1.) It is seasonable, in the fittest time. [1.] When the oppressors are in the height of their pride and insolence — when they say, *Who is lord over us?* — then is God's time to let them know, to their cost, that he is above them. [2.] When the oppressed are in the depth of their distress and despondency, when they are sighing like Israel in Egypt by reason of the cruel bondage, then is God's time to appear for them, as for Israel when they were most dejected and Pharaoh was most elevated. *Now will I arise.* Note, There is a time fixed for the rescue of oppressed innocency; that time will come, and we may be sure it is the fittest time, Ps. 102:13. (2.) It is effectual: *I will set him in safety,* or in salvation, not only protect him, but restore him to his former prosperity, will *bring him out into a wealthy place* (Ps. 66:12), so that, upon the whole, he shall lose nothing by his sufferings.

4. That, though men are false, God is faithful; though they are not to be trusted, God is. They speak vanity and flattery, but *the words of the Lord are pure words* (*v.* 6), not only all true, but all pure, like silver tried in a furnace of earth or a crucible. It denotes, (1.) The sincerity of God's word, every thing is really as it is there represented and not otherwise; it does not jest with us, not impose upon us, nor has it any other design towards us than our own good. (2.) The preciousness of God's word; it is of great and intrinsic value, like silver refined to the highest degree; it has nothing in it to depreciate it. (3.) The many proofs that have been given of its power and truth; it has been often tried, all the saints in all ages have trusted it and so tried it, and it never deceived them nor frustrated their expectation, but they have all set to their seal that God's word is true, with an *Experto crede — Trust one that has made trial;* they have found it so. Probably this refers especially to these promises of succouring and relieving the poor and oppressed. Their friends put them in hopes that they will do something for them, and yet prove a broken reed; but the words of God are what we may rely upon; and the less confidence is to be put in men's words let us with the more assurance trust in God's word.

5. That God will secure his chosen remnant to himself, how bad soever the times are (*v.* 7): *Thou shalt preserve them from this generation for ever.* This intimates that, as long as the world stands, there will be a generation of proud and wicked men in it, more or less, who will threaten by their wretched arts to ruin religion, by *wearing out the saints of the Most High,* Dan. 7:25. But let God alone to maintain his own interest and to preserve his own people. He will keep them from this generation, (1.) From being debauched by them and drawn away from God, from mingling with them and learning their works. In times of general apostasy the Lord knows those that are his, and they shall be enabled to keep their integrity. (2.) From being destroyed and rooted out by them. The church is built upon a rock, and so well fortified that the gates of hell shall not prevail against it. In the worst of times God has his remnant, and in every age will reserve to himself a holy seed and preserve that to his heavenly kingdom.

In singing this psalm, and praying it over, we must bewail the general corruption of manners, thank God that things are not worse than they are, but pray and hope that they will be better in God's due time.

PSALM 13

This psalm is the deserted soul's case and cure. Whether it was penned upon any particular occasion does not appear, but in general, I. David sadly complains that God had long withdrawn from him and delayed to relieve him (*v.* 1, 2). II. He earnestly prays to God to consider his case and comfort him (*v.* 3, 4). III. He assures himself of an answer of peace, and therefore concludes the psalm with joy and triumph, because he concludes his deliverance to be as good as wrought (*v.* 5, 6).

To the chief musician. A psalm of David.

Verses 1–6

David, in affliction, is here pouring out his soul before God; his address is short, but the method is very observable, and of use for direction and encouragement.

I. His troubles extort complaints (*v.* 1, 2); and the afflicted have liberty to *pour out their complaint before the Lord,* Ps. 102 *title.* It is some ease to a troubled spirit to give vent to its griefs, especially to give vent to them at the throne of grace, where we are sure to find one who is afflicted in the afflictions of his people and is troubled with the feeling of their infirmities; thither we have boldness of access by faith, and there we have *parrēsia — freedom of speech.* Observe here,

1. What David complains of. (1.) God's unkindness; so he construed it, and it was his infirmity. He thought God had forgotten him, had forgotten his promises to him, his covenant with him, his former lovingkindness which he had shown him and which he took to be an earnest of further mercy, had forgotten that there was such a man in the world, who needed and expected relief and succour from him. Thus Zion said, *My God has forgotten me* (Isa. 49:14), Israel said, *My way is hidden from the Lord,* Isa. 40:27. Not that any good man can doubt the omniscience, goodness, and faithfulness of God; but it is a peevish expression of prevailing fear, which yet, when it arises from a high esteem and earnest desire of God's favour, though it be indecent and culpable, shall be passed by and pardoned, for the second thought will retract it and repent of it. God hid his face from him, so that he wanted that inward comfort in God which he used to have, and herein was a type of Christ upon the cross, crying out, *My God, why hast thou forsaken me?* God sometimes hides his face from his own children, and leaves them in the dark concerning their interest in him; and this they lay to heart more than any outward trouble whatsoever. (2.) His own uneasiness. [1.] He was racked with care, which filled his head: *I take counsel in my soul;* "I am at a loss, and am *inops consilii — without a friend to advise with* that I can put any confidence in, and therefore am myself continually projecting what to do to help myself; but none of my projects are likely to take effect, so that I am at my wits' end, and in a continual agitation." Anxious cares are heavy burdens with which good people often load themselves more than they need. [2.] He was overwhelmed with sorrow, which filled his heart: *I have sorrow in my heart daily.* He had a constant disposition to sorrow and it preyed upon his spirits, not only in the night, when he was silent and solitary, but by day too, when lighter griefs are diverted and dissipated by conversation and business; nay, every day brought with it fresh occasions of grief; *the clouds returned after the rain.* The bread of sorrow is sometimes the saint's daily bread. Our Master himself was a man of sorrows. (3.) His enemies' insolence, which added to his grief. Saul his great enemy, and others under him, were exalted over him, triumphed in his distress, pleased themselves with his grief, and promised themselves a complete victory over him. This he complained of as reflecting dishonour upon God, and his power and promise.

2. How he expostulates with God hereupon: *"How long* shall it be thus?" And, "Shall it be thus *for ever?"* Long afflictions try our patience and often tire it. It is a common temptation, when trouble lasts long, to think it will last always; despondency then turns into despair, and those that have long been without joy begin, at last, to be without hope. "Lord, tell me how long thou wilt hide thy face, and assure me that it shall not be for ever, but that thou wilt return at length in mercy to me, and then I shall the more easily bear my present troubles."

II. His complaints stir up his prayers, *v.* 3, 4. We should never allow ourselves to make any complaints but what are fit to be offered up to God and what drive us to our knees. Observe here,

1. What his petitions are: *Consider* my case, *hear* my complaints, and *enlighten my eyes,* that is, (1.) "Strengthen my faith;" for faith is the eye of the soul, with which it sees above, and sees through, the things of sense. "Lord, enable me to look beyond my present troubles and to foresee a happy issue of them." (2.) "Guide my way; enable me to look about me, that I may avoid the snares which are laid for me." (3.) "Refresh my soul with the joy of thy salvation." That which revives the drooping spirits is said to *enlighten the eyes,* 1 Sa. 14:27; Ezra 9:8. "Lord, scatter the cloud of melancholy which darkens my eyes, and let my countenance be made pleasant."

2. What his pleas are. He mentions his relation to God and interest in him *(O Lord my God!)* and insists upon the greatness of the peril, which called for speedy relief and succour. If his eyes were not enlightened quickly, (1.) He concludes that he must perish: "I shall *sleep the sleep of death;* I cannot live under the weight of all this care and grief." Nothing is more killing to a soul then the want of God's favour, nothing more reviving than the return of it. (2.) That then his enemies would triumph: *"Lest my enemy say,* So would I have it; lest Saul, lest Satan, be gratified in my fall." It would gratify the pride of his enemy: He will say, *"I have prevailed,* I have gotten the day, and been too hard for him and his God." It would gratify the malice of his enemies: They will *rejoice when I am moved.* And will it be for God's honour to suffer them thus to trample upon all that is sacred both in heaven and earth?

III. His prayers are soon turned into praises (*v.* 5, 6): But *my heart shall rejoice and I will sing to the Lord.* What a surprising change is here in a few lines! In the beginning of the psalm we have him drooping, trembling, and ready to sink into melancholy and despair; but, in the close of it, rejoicing in God, and elevated and enlarged in his praises. See the power of faith, the power of prayer, and how good it is to draw near to God. If we bring our cares and griefs to the throne of grace, and leave them there, we may go away like Hannah, and our *countenance will be no more sad,* 1 Sa. 1:18. And here observe the method of his comfort. 1. God's mercy is the support of his faith. "My case is bad enough, and I am ready to think it deplorable, till I consider the infinite goodness of God; but, finding I have that to trust to, I am comforted, though I have no merit of my own. In former distresses *I have trusted in the mercy of God,* and I never found that it failed me; his mercy has in due time relieved me and my confidence in it has in the mean time supported me. Even in the depth of this distress, when God hid his face from me, when without were fightings and within were fears, yet *I trusted in the mercy of God* and that was as an anchor in a storm, by the help of which, though I was tossed, I was not overset." And still *I do trust in thy mercy;* so some read it. "I refer myself to that, with an assurance that it will do well for me at last." This he pleads with God, knowing what pleasure he takes *in those that hope in his mercy,* Ps. 147:11. 2. His faith in God's mercy filled his heart with *joy in his salvation;* for joy and peace come *by believing,* Rom. 15:13. *Believing, you rejoice,* 1 Pt. 1:8. Having put his trust in the mercy of God, he is fully assured of salvation, and that his heart, which was now daily grieving, should *rejoice in that salvation.* Though weeping endure long, joy will return. 3. His joy in God's salvation would fill his mouth with songs of praise (*v.* 6): *"I will sing unto the Lord,* sing in remembrance of what he has done formerly; though I should never recover the peace I have had, I will die blessing God that ever I had it. He has dealt bountifully with me formerly, and he shall have the glory of that, however he is pleased to deal with me now. I will sing in hope of what he will do for me at last, being confident that all will end well, will end everlastingly well." But he speaks of it as a thing past *(He has dealt bountifully with me),* because by faith he had received the earnest of the salvation and he was as confident of it as if it had been done already.

In singing this psalm and praying it over, if we have not the same complaints to make that David had, we must thank God that we have not, dread and deprecate his withdrawings, sympathize with those that are troubled in mind, and encourage ourselves in our most holy faith and joy.

PSALM 14

It does not appear upon what occasion this psalm was penned nor whether upon any particular occasion. Some say David penned it when Saul persecuted him; others, when Absalom rebelled against him. But they are mere conjectures, which have not certainty enough to warrant us to expound the psalm by them. The apostle, in quoting part of this psalm (Rom. 3:10, etc.) to prove that Jews and Gentiles are all under sin (*v.* 9) and that all the world is guilty before God (*v.* 19), leads us to understand it, in general, as a description of the depravity of human nature, the sinfulness of the sin we are conceived and born in, and the deplorable corruption of a great part of mankind, even of the world that lies in wickedness, 1 Jn. 5:19. But as in those psalms which are designed to discover our remedy in Christ there is commonly an allusion to David himself, yea, and some passages that are to be understood primarily of him (as in psalm 2, 16, 22, and others), so in this psalm, which is designed to discover our wound by sin, there is an allusion to David's enemies and persecutors, and other oppressors of good men at that time, to whom some passages have an immediate reference. In all the psalms from the 3rd to this (except the 8th) David had been complaining of those that hated and persecuted him, insulted him and abused him; now here he traces all those bitter streams to the fountain, the general corruption of nature, and sees that not his enemies only, but all the children of men, were thus corrupted. Here is, I. A charge exhibited against a wicked world (*v.* 1). II. The proof of the charge (*v.* 2, 3). III. A serious expostulation with sinners, especially with persecutors, upon it (*v.* 4–6). IV. A believing prayer for the salvation of Israel and a joyful expectation of it (*v.* 7).

To the chief musician. A psalm of David.

Verses 1–3

If we apply our hearts as Solomon did (Eccl. 7:25) *to search out the wickedness of folly, even of foolishness and madness,* these verses will assist us in the search and will show us that sin is exceedingly sinful. Sin is the disease of mankind, and it appears here to be malignant and epidemic.

1. See how malignant it is (*v.* 1) in two things: —

(1.) The contempt it puts upon the honour of God: for there is something of practical atheism at the bottom of all sin. *The fool hath said in his heart, There is no God.* We are sometimes tempted to think, "Surely there never was so much atheism and profaneness as there is in our days;" but we see the former days were no better; even in David's time there were those who had arrived at such a height of impiety as to deny the very being of a God and the first and self-evident principles of religion. Observe, [1.] The sinner here described. He is one that *saith in his heart, There is no God;* he is an atheist. "There is no *Elohim,* no Judge or governor of the world, no providence presiding over the affairs of men." They cannot doubt of the being of God, but will question his dominion. He says this *in his heart;* it is not his judgment, but his imagination. He cannot satisfy himself that there is none, but he wishes there were none, and pleases himself with the fancy that it is possible there may be none. He cannot be sure there is one, and therefore he is willing to think there is none. He dares not speak it out, lest he be confuted, and so undeceived, but he whispers it secretly *in his heart,* for the silencing of the clamours of his conscience and the emboldening of himself in his evil ways. [2.] The character of this sinner. He is a fool; he is simple and unwise, and this is an evidence of it; he is wicked and profane, and this is the cause of it. Note, Atheistical thoughts are very foolish wicked thoughts, and they are at the bottom of a great deal of the wickedness that is in this world. The word of God is a *discerner of these thoughts,* and puts a just brand on him that harbours them. *Nabal is his name, and folly is with him;* for he thinks against the clearest light, against his own knowledge and convictions, and the common sentiments of all the wise and sober part of mankind. No man will say, *There is no God* till he is so hardened in sin that it has become his interest that there should be none to call him to an account.

(2.) The disgrace and debasement it puts upon the nature of man. Sinners are corrupt, quite degenerated from what man was in his innocent estate: *They have become filthy* (*v.* 3), putrid. All their faculties are so disordered that they have become odious to their Maker and utterly incapable of answering the ends of their creation. *They are corrupt* indeed; for, [1.] They do no good, but are the unprofitable burdens of the earth; they do God no service, bring him no honour, nor do themselves any real kindness. [2.] They do a great deal of hurt. *They have done abominable works,* for such all sinful works are. Sin is an abomination to God; it is that *abominable thing which he hates* (Jer. 44:4), and, sooner or later, it will be so to the sinner; it will be *found to be hateful* (Ps. 36:2), an *abomination of desolation,* that is, making desolate, Mt. 24:15. This follows upon their saying, *There is no God;* for those that *profess they know God, but in works deny him, are abominable, and to every good work reprobate,* Tit. 1:16.

2. See how epidemic this disease is; it has infected the whole race of mankind. To prove this, God himself is here brought in for a witness, and he is an eye-witness, *v.* 2, 3. Observe, (1.) His enquiry: *The Lord looked down from heaven,* a place of prospect, which commands this lower world; thence, with an all-seeing eye, he took a view of all *the children of men,* and the question was, *Whether there were any* among them *that did understand* themselves aright, their duty and interests, and did seek God and set him before them. He that made this search was not only one that could find out a good man if he was to be found, though ever so obscure, but one that would be glad to find out one, and would be sure to take notice of him, as of Noah in the old world. (2.) The result of this enquiry, *v.* 3. Upon search, upon his search, it appeared, *They have all gone aside,* the apostasy is universal, *there is none that doeth good, no, not one,* till the free and mighty grace of God has wrought a change. Whatever good is in any of the children of men, or is done by them, it is not of themselves; it is God's work in them. When God had made the world he looked upon his own work, and *all was very good* (Gen. 1:31); but, some time after, he looked upon man's work, and, behold, all was very bad (Gen. 6:5), every operation of the thought of man's heart was evil, only evil, and that continually. They have gone aside from the right of their duty, the way that leads to happiness, and have turned into the paths of the destroyer.

In singing this let us lament the corruption of our own nature, and see what need we have of the grace of God; and, since that which is born of the flesh is flesh, let us not marvel that we are told we must be born again.

Verses 4–7

In these verses the psalmist endeavours,

I. To convince sinners of the evil and danger of the way they are in, how secure soever they are in that way. Three things he shows them, which, it may be, they are not very willing to see — their wickedness, their folly, and their danger, while they are apt to believe themselves very wise, and good, and safe. See here,

1. Their wickedness. This is described in four instances: — (1.) They are themselves *workers of iniquity;* they design it, they practise it, and take as much pleasure in it as ever any man did in his business. (2.) They *eat up God's people* with as much greediness *as they eat bread,* such an innate and inveterate enmity they have to them, and so heartily do they desire their ruin, because they really hate God, whose people they are. It is meat and drink to persecutors to be doing mischief; it is as agreeable to them as their necessary food. They eat up God's people easily, daily, securely, without either check of conscience when they do it or remorse of conscience when they have done it; as Joseph's brethren *cast him into a pit* and then *sat down to eat bread,* Gen. 37:24, 25. See Mic. 3:2, 3. (3.) They *call not upon the Lord.* Note, Those that care not for God's people, for God's poor, care not for God himself, but live in contempt of him. The reason why people run into all manner of wickedness, even the worst, is because they do not call upon God for his grace. What good can be expected from those that live without prayer? (4.) They *shame the counsel of the poor,* and upbraid them with making God their refuge, as David's enemies upbraided him, Ps. 11:1. Note, Those are very wicked indeed, and have a great deal to answer for, who not only shake off religion, and live without it themselves, but say and do what they can to put others out of conceit with it that are well-inclined — with the duties of it, as if they were mean, melancholy, and unprofitable, and with the privileges of it, as if they were insufficient to make a man safe and happy. Those that banter religion and religious people will find, to their cost, it is ill jesting with edged-tools and dangerous persecuting those that make God their refuge. *Be you not mockers, lest your bands be made strong.* He shows them,

2. Their folly: *They have no knowledge;* this is obvious, for if they had any knowledge of God, if they did rightly understand themselves, and would but consider things as men, they would not be so abusive and barbarous as they are to the people of God.

3. Their danger (*v.* 5): *There were they in great fear.* There, where they ate up God's people, their own consciences condemned what they did, and filled them with secret terrors; they sweetly sucked the blood of the saints, but in their bowels it is turned, and become the gall of asps. Many instances there have been of proud and cruel persecutors who have been made like Pashur, *Magormissabibs — terrors to themselves* and all about them. Those that will not fear God perhaps may be made to fear at the shaking of a leaf.

II. He endeavours to comfort the people of God, 1. With what they have. They have God's presence (*v.* 5): He *is in the generation of the righteous.* They have his protection (*v.* 6): *The Lord is their refuge.* This is as much their security as it is the terror of their enemies, who may jeer them for their confidence in God, but cannot jeer them out of it. In the judgment-day it will add to the terror and confusion of sinners to see God own the generation of the righteous, which they have hated and bantered. 2. With what they hope for; and that is the *salvation of Israel, v.* 7. When David was driven out by Absalom and his rebellious accomplices, he comforted himself with an assurance that god would in due time *turn again his captivity,* to the joy of all his good subjects. But surely this pleasing prospect looks further. He had, in the beginning of the psalm, lamented the general corruption of mankind; and, in the melancholy view of that, wishes for the salvation which should be wrought out by the Redeemer, who was expected *co come to Zion,* to *turn away ungodliness from Jacob,* Rom. 11:26. The world is bad; O that the Messiah would come and change its character! There is a universal corruption; O for the times of reformation! Those will be as joyful times as these are melancholy ones. Then shall God *turn again the captivity of his people;* for the Redeemer shall *ascend on high, and lead captivity captive,* and Jacob shall then rejoice. The triumphs of Zion's King will be the joys of Zion's children. The second coming of Christ, finally to extinguish the dominion of sin and Satan, will be the completing of this salvation, which is the hope, and will be the joy, of every Israelite indeed. With the assurance of that we should, in singing this, comfort ourselves and one another, with reference to the present sins of sinners and sufferings of saints.

PSALM 15

The scope of this short but excellent psalm is to show us the way to heaven, and to convince us that, if we would be happy, we must be holy and honest. Christ, who is himself the way, and in whom we must walk as our way, has also shown us the same way that is here prescribed, Mt. 19:17. "If thou wilt enter into life, keep the commandments." In this psalm, I. By the question (*v.* 1) we are directed and excited to enquire for the way. II. By the answer to that question, in the rest of the psalm, we are directed to walk in that way (*v.* 2–5). III. By the assurance given in the close of the psalm of the safety and happiness of those who answer these characters we are encouraged to walk in that way (*v.* 5).

A psalm of David.

Verses 1–5

Here is, I. A very serious and weighty question concerning the characters of a citizen of Zion (*v.* 1): *"Lord, who shall abide in thy tabernacle?* Let me know who shall go to heaven." Not, who by name (in this way the *Lord* only knows those that are his), but who by description: "What kind of people are those whom thou wilt own and crown with distinguishing and everlasting favours?" This supposes that it is a great privilege to be a citizen of Zion, an unspeakable honour and advantage, — that all are not thus privileged, but a remnant only, — and that men are not entitled to this privilege by their birth and blood: all shall not *abide in God's tabernacle* that have Abraham to their father, but, according as men's hearts and lives are, so will their lot be. It concerns us all to put this question to ourselves, *Lord, what shall I be, and do, that I may abide in thy tabernacle?* Lu. 18:18; Acts 16:30. 1. Observe to whom this enquiry is addressed — to God himself. Note, Those that would find the way to heaven must look up to God, must take direction from his word and beg direction from his Spirit. It is fit he himself should give laws to his servants, and appoint the conditions of his favours, and tell who are his and who not. 2. How it is expressed in Old-

Testament language. (1.) By the *tabernacle* we may understand the church militant, typified by Moses's tabernacle, fitted to a wilderness-state, mean and movable. There God manifests himself, and there he meets his people, as of old in the tabernacle of the testimony, the tabernacle of meeting. Who shall dwell in this tabernacle? Who shall be accounted a true living member of God's church, admitted among the spiritual priests to lodge in the courts of this tabernacle? We are concerned to enquire this, because many pretend to a place in this tabernacle who really have no part nor lot in the matter. (2.) By the *holy hill* we may understand the church triumphant, alluding to Mount Zion, on which the temple was to be built by Solomon. It is the happiness of glorified saints that they dwell in that holy hill; they are at home there: they shall be for ever there. It concerns us to know who shall dwell there, that we may make it sure to ourselves that we shall have a place among them, and may then take the comfort of it, and rejoice in prospect of that holy hill.

II. A very plain and particular answer to this question. Those that desire to know their duty, with a resolution to do it, will find the scripture a very faithful director and conscience a faithful monitor. Let us see then the particular characters of a citizen of Zion.

1. He is one that is sincere and entire in his religion: He *walketh uprightly,* according to the condition of the covenant (Gen. 17:1), *"Walk before me, and be thou perfect"* (it is the same word that is here used) "and then thou shalt find me a God all-sufficient." He is really what he professes to be, is sound at heart, and can approve himself to God, in his integrity, in all he does; his conversation is uniform, and he is of a piece with himself, and endeavours to stand complete in all the will of God. His eye perhaps is weak, but it is single; he has his spots indeed, but he does not paint; he is an *Israelite indeed in whom is no guile,* Jn. 1:47; 2 Co. 1:12. I know no religion but sincerity.

2. He is one that is conscientiously honest and just in all his dealings, faithful and fair to all with whom he has to do: He *worketh righteousness;* he walks in all the ordinances and commandments of the Lord, and takes care to give all their due, is just both to God and man; and, in speaking to both, he speaks that which is *the truth in his heart;* his prayers, professions, and promises, to God, come not out of feigned lips, nor dares he tell a lie, or so much as equivocate, in his converse or commerce with men. He walks by the rules of righteousness and truth, and scorns and abhors the gains of injustice and fraud. He reckons that that cannot be a good bargain, nor a saving one, which is made with a lie, and that he who wrongs his neighbour, though ever so plausibly, will prove, in the end, to have done the greatest injury to himself.

3. He is one that contrives to do all the good he can to his neighbours, but is very careful to do hurt to no man, and is, in a particular manner, tender of his neighbour's reputation, *v.* 3. He *does no evil* at all *to his neighbour* willingly or designedly, nothing to offend or grieve his spirit, nothing to prejudice the health or ease of his body, nothing to injure him in his estate or secular interests, in his family or relations; but walks by that golden rule of equity, To do as he would be done by. He is especially careful not to injure his neighbour in his good name, though many, who would not otherwise wrong their neighbours, make nothing of that. If any man, in this matter, bridles not his tongue, his religion is vain. He knows the worth of a good name, and therefore *he backbites not,* defames no man, speaks evil of no man, makes not others' faults the subject of his common talk, much less of his sport and ridicule, nor speaks of them with pleasure, nor at all but for edification. He makes the best of every body, and the worst of nobody. He does not *take up a reproach,* that is, he neither raises it nor receives it; he gives no credit nor countenance to a calumny, but frowns upon a backbiting tongue, and so silences it, Prov. 25:23. If an ill-natured character of his neighbour be given him, or an ill-natured story be told him, he will disprove it if he can; if not, it shall die with him and go no further. His *charity will cover a multitude of sins.*

4. He is one that values men by their virtue and piety, and not by the figure they make in the world, *v.* 5. (1.) He thinks the better of no man's wickedness for his pomp and grandeur: *In his eyes a vile person is contemned.* Wicked people are vile people, worthless and good for nothing (so the word signifies), as dross, as chaff, and as salt that has lost its savour. They are vile in their choices (Jer. 2:13), in their practices, Isa. 32:6. For this wise and good men contemn them, not denying them civil honour and respect as men, as men in authority and power perhaps (1 Pt. 2:17, Rom. 13:7), but, in their judgment of them, agreeing with the word of God. They are so far from envying them that they pity them, despising their gains (Isa. 33:15), as turning to no account, their dainties (Ps. 141:4), their pleasures (Heb. 11:24, 25) as sapless and insipid. They despise their society (Ps. 119:115; 2 Ki. 3:14); they despise their taunts and threats, and are not moved by them, nor disturbed at them; they despise the feeble efforts of their impotent malice (Ps. 2:1, 4), and will shortly triumph in their fall, Ps. 52:6, 7. God despises them, and they are of his mind. (2.) He thinks the worse of no man's piety for his poverty and meanness, *but he knows those that fear the Lord.* He reckons that serious piety, wherever it is found, puts an honour upon a man, and makes his face to shine, more than wealth, or wit, or a great name among men, does or can. He honours such, esteems them very highly in love, desires their friendship and conversation and an interest in their prayers, is glad of an opportunity to show them respect or do them a good office, pleads their cause and speaks of them with veneration, rejoices when they prosper, grieves when they are removed, and their memory, when they are gone, is precious with him. By this we may judge of ourselves in some measure. What rules do we go by in judging of others?

5. He is one that always prefers a good conscience before any secular interest or advantage whatsoever; for, if he has promised upon oath to do any thing, though afterwards it appear much to his damage and prejudice in his worldly estate, yet he adheres to it and *changes not, v.* 4. See how weak-sighted and short-sighted even wise and good men may be; they may *swear to their own hurt,* which they were not aware of when they took the oath. But see how strong the obligation of an oath is, that a man must rather suffer loss to himself and his family than wrong his neighbour by breaking his oath. An oath is a sacred thing, which we must not think to play fast and loose with.

6. He is one that will not increase his estate by any unjust practices, *v.* 5. (1.) Not by extortion: *He putteth not out his money to usury,* that he may live at ease upon the labours of others, while he is in a capacity for improving it by his own industry. Not that it is any breach of the law of justice or charity for the lender to share in the profit which the borrower makes of his money, any more than for the owner of the land to demand rent from the occupant, money being, by art and labour, as improvable as land. But a citizen of Zion will freely lend to the poor, according to his ability, and not be rigorous and severe in recovering his right from those that are reduced by Providence. (2.) Not by bribery: He will not *take a reward against the innocent;* if he be any way employed in the administration of public justice, he will not, for any gain, or hope of it, to himself, do any thing to the prejudice of a righteous cause.

III. The psalm concludes with a ratification of this character of the citizen of Zion. He is like Zion-hill itself, which cannot be moved, but abides for ever, Ps. 125:1. Every true living member of the church, like the church itself, is built upon a rock, which the gates of hell cannot prevail against: *He that doeth these things shall never be moved;* shall not be moved *for ever,* so the word is. The grace of God shall always be sufficient for him, to preserve him safe and blameless to the heavenly kingdom. Temptations shall not overcome him, troubles shall not overwhelm him, nothing shall rob him of his present peace nor his future bliss.

In singing this psalm we must teach and admonish ourselves, and one another, to answer the characters here given of the citizen of Zion, that we may never be moved from God's tabernacle on earth, and may arrive, at last, at that holy hill where we shall be for ever out of the reach of temptation and danger.

PSALM 16

This psalm has something of David in it, but much more of Christ. It begins with such expressions of devotion as may be applied to Christ; but concludes with such confidence of a resurrection (and so timely a one as to prevent corruption) as must be applied to Christ, to him only, and cannot be understood of David, as both St. Peter and St. Paul have observed, Acts 2:24; 13:36. For David died, and was buried, and saw corruption. I. David speaks of himself as a member of Christ, and so he speaks the language of all good Christians, professing his confidence in God (*v.* 1), his consent to him (*v.* 2), his affection to the people of God (*v.* 3), his adherence to the true worship of God (*v.* 4), and his entire complacency and satisfaction in God and the interest he had in him (*v.* 5–7). II. He speaks of himself as a type of Christ, and so he speaks the language of Christ himself, to whom all the rest of the psalm is expressly and at large applied (Acts 2:25, etc.). David speaks concerning him (not concerning himself), "I foresaw the Lord always before my face," etc. And this he spoke, being a prophet (*v.* 30, 31). He spoke, 1. Of the special presence of God with the Redeemer in his services and sufferings (*v.* 8). 2. Of the prospect which the Redeemer had of his own resurrection and the glory that should follow, which carried him cheerfully through his undertaking (*v.* 9–11).

Michtam of David.

Verses 1–7

This psalm is entitled *Michtam,* which some translate *a golden* psalm, a very precious one, more to be valued by us than gold, yea, than much fine gold, because it speaks so plainly of Christ and his resurrection, who is the true treasure hidden in the field of the Old Testament.

I. David here flies to God's protection with a cheerful believing confidence in it (*v.* 1): *"Preserve me, O God!* from the deaths, and especially from the sins, to which I am continually exposed; *for in thee,* and in thee only, *do I put my trust."* Those that by faith commit themselves to the divine care, and submit themselves to the divine guidance, have reason to hope for the benefit of both. This is applicable to Christ, who prayed, *Father, save me from this hour,* and trusted in God that he would deliver him.

II. He recognizes his solemn dedication of himself to God as his God (*v.* 2): *"O my soul! thou hast said unto the Lord, Thou art my Lord,* and therefore thou mayest venture to trust him." Note, 1. It is the duty and interest of every one of us to acknowledge the Lord for our Lord, to subject ourselves to him, and then to stay ourselves upon him. *Adonai* signifies *My stayer,* the strength of my heart. 2. This must be done with our souls: "O my soul! thou hast said it." Covenanting with God must be heart-work; all that is within us must be employed therein and engaged thereby. 3. Those who have avouched the Lord for their Lord should be often putting themselves in mind of what they have done. "Hast thou said unto the Lord, *Thou art my Lord?* Say it again then, stand to it, abide by it, and never unsay it. Hast thou said it? Take the comfort of it, and live up to it. He is thy Lord, and worship thou him, and let thy eye be ever towards him."

III. He devotes himself to the honour of God in the service of the saints (*v.* 2, 3): *My goodness extends not to thee, but to the saints.* Observe, 1. Those that have taken the lord for their Lord must, like him, be good and do good; we do not expect happiness without goodness. 2. Whatever good there is in us, or is done by us, we must humbly acknowledge that it extends not to God; so that we cannot pretend to merit any thing by it. God has no need of our services; he is not benefited by them, nor can they add any thing to his infinite perfection and blessedness. The wisest, and best, and most useful, men in the world cannot be profitable to God, Job 22:2; 35:7. God is infinitely above us, and happy without us, and whatever good we do it is all from him; so that we are indebted to him, not he to us: David owns it (1 Chr. 29:14), *Of thy own have we given thee.* 3. If God be ours, we must, for his sake, extend our goodness to those that are his, to the saints in the earth; for what is done to them he is pleased to take as done to himself, having constituted them his receivers. Note, (1.) There are saints in the earth; and saints on earth we must all be, or we shall never be saints in heaven. Those that are renewed by the grace of God, and devoted to the glory of God, are saints on earth. (2.) The saints in the earth are excellent ones, great, mighty, magnificent ones, and yet some of them so poor in the world that they need to have David's goodness extended to them. God makes them excellent by the grace he gives them. *The righteous is more excellent than his neighbour,* and then he accounts them excellent. They are precious in his sight and honourable; they are his jewels, his peculiar treasure. Their God is their glory, and a diadem of beauty to them. (3.) All that have taken the Lord for their God delight in his saints as excellent ones, because they bear his image, and because he loves them. David, though a king, was a *companion of all that feared God* (Ps. 119:63), even the meanest, which was a sign that his delight was in them. (4.) It is not enough for us to delight in the saints, but, as there is occasion, our goodness must extend to them; we must be ready to show them the kindness they need, distribute to their necessities, and abound in the labour of love to them. This is applicable to Christ. The salvation he wrought out for us was no gain to God, for our ruin would have been no loss to him; but the goodness and benefit of it extend to us men, in whom he delighteth, Prov. 8:31. *For their sakes,* says he, *I sanctify myself,* Jn. 17:19. Christ delights even in the saints on earth, notwithstanding their weaknesses and manifold informities, which is a good reason why we should.

IV. He disclaims the worship of all false gods and all communion with their worshippers, *v.* 4. Here, 1. He reads the doom of idolaters, who hasten after another God, being mad upon their idols, and pursuing them as eagerly as if they were afraid they would escape from them: *Their sorrows shall be multiplied,* both by the judgments they bring upon themselves from the true God whom they forsake and by the disappointment they will meet with in the false gods they embrace. Those that multiply gods multiply griefs to themselves; for, whoever thinks one God too little, will find two too many, and yet hundreds not enough. 2. He declares his resolution to have no fellowship with them nor with their unfruitful works of darkness: *"Their drink-offerings of blood will I not offer,* not only because the gods they are offered to are a lie, but because the offerings themselves are barbarous." At God's altar, because the blood made atonement, the drinking of it was most strictly prohibited, and the drink-offerings were of wine; but the devil prescribed to his worshippers to drink of the blood of the sacrifices, to teach them cruelty. "I will have nothing to do" (says David) "with those bloody deities, nor so much as take their names into my lips with any delight in them or respect to them." Thus must we hate idols and idolatry with a perfect hatred. Some make this also applicable to Christ and his undertaking, showing the nature of the sacrifice he offered (it was not the blood of bulls and goats, which was offered according to the law; that was never named, nor did he ever make any mention of it, but his own blood), showing also the multiplied sorrows of the unbelieving Jews, who hastened after another king, Caesar, and are still hastening after another Messiah, whom they in vain look for.

V. He repeats the solemn choice he had made of God for his portion and happiness (*v.* 5), takes to himself the comfort of the choice (*v.* 6), and gives God the glory of it, *v.* 7. This is very much the language of a devout and pious soul in its gracious exercises.

1. Choosing the Lord for its portion and happiness. "Most men take the world for their chief good, and place their felicity in the enjoyments of it; but this I say, *The Lord is the portion of my inheritance and of my cup,* the portion I make choice of, and will gladly take up with, how poor soever my condition is in this world. Let me have the love and favour of God, and be accepted of him; let me have the comfort of communion with God, and satisfaction in the communications of his graces and comforts; let me have an interest in his promises, and a title by promise to everlasting life and happiness in the future state; and I have enough, I need no more, I desire no more, to complete my felicity." Would we do well and wisely for ourselves, we must take God, in Christ, to be, (1.) The portion of our inheritance in the other world. Heaven is an inheritance. God himself is the inheritance of the saints there, whose everlasting bliss is to enjoy him. We must take that for our inheritance, our home, our rest, our lasting, everlasting, good, and look upon this world to be no more ours than the country through which our road lies when we are on a journey. (2.) The portion of our cup in this world, with which we are nourished, and refreshed, and kept from fainting. Those have not God for theirs who do not reckon his comforts the most reviving cordials, acquaint themselves with them, and make use of them as sufficient to counterbalance all the grievances of this present time and to sweeten the most bitter cup of affliction.

2. Confiding in him for the securing of this portion: *"Thou maintainest my lot.* Thou that hast by promise made over thy self to me, to be mine, wilt graciously make good what thou hast promised, and never leave me to myself to forfeit this happiness, nor leave it in the power of my enemies to rob me of it. Nothing shall pluck me out of thy hands, nor separate me from thy love, and the sure mercies of David." The saints and their bliss are kept by the power of God.

3. Rejoicing in this portion, and taking a complacency in it (*v.* 6): *The lines have fallen to me in pleasant places.* Those have reason to say so that have God for their portion; they have a worthy portion, a goodly heritage. What can they have better? What can they desire more? *Return unto thy rest, O my soul!* and look no further. Note, Gracious persons, though they still covet more of God, never covet more than God; but, being satisfied of his loving-kindness, they are abundantly satisfied with it, and envy not any their carnal mirth and sensual pleasures and delights, but account themselves truly happy in what they have, and doubt not but to be completely happy in what they hope for. Those whose lot is cast, as David's was, in a land of light, in a valley of vision, where God is known and worshipped, have, upon that account, reason to say, *The lines have fallen to me in pleasant places;* much more those who have not only the means, but the end, not only Immanuel's land, but Immanuel's love.

4. Giving thanks to God for it, and for grace to make this wise and happy choice (*v.* 7): *"I will bless the Lord who has given me counsel,* this counsel, to take him for my portion and happiness." So ignorant and foolish are we that, if we be left to ourselves, our hearts will follow our eyes, and we shall choose our own delusions, and forsake our own mercies for lying vanities; and therefore, if we have indeed taken God for our portion and preferred spiritual and eternal blessings before those that are sensible and temporal, we must thankfully acknowledge the power and goodness of divine grace directing and enabling us to make that choice. If we have the pleasure of it, let God have the praise of it.

5. Making a good use of it. God having given him counsel by his word and Spirit, his own *reins* also (his own thoughts) instructed him in the night-season; when he was silent and solitary, and retired from the world, then his own conscience (which is called the *reins,* Jer. 17:10) not only reflected with comfort upon the choice he had made, but instructed or admonished him concerning the duties arising out of this choice, catechized him, and engaged and quickened him to live as one that had God for his portion, by faith to live upon him and to live to him. Those who have God for their portion, and who will be faithful to him, must give their own consciences leave to deal thus faithfully and plainly with them.

All this may be applied to Christ, who made the Lord his portion and was pleased with that portion, made his Father's glory his highest end and made it his meat and drink to seek that and to do his will, and delighted to prosecute his undertaking, pursuant to his Father's counsel, depending upon him to maintain his lot and to carry him through his undertaking. We may also apply it to ourselves in singing it, renewing our choice of God as ours, with a holy complacency and satisfaction.

Verses 8–11

All these verses are quoted by St. Peter in his first sermon, after the pouring out of the Spirit on the day of pentecost (Acts 2:25–28); and he tells us expressly that David in them speaks concerning Christ and particularly of his resurrection. Something we may allow here of the workings of David's own pious and devout affections towards God, depending upon his grace to perfect every thing that concerned him, and looking for the blessed hope, and happy state on the other side death, in the enjoyment of God; but in these holy elevations towards God and heaven he was carried by the spirit of prophecy quite beyond the consideration of himself and his own case, to foretel the glory of the Messiah, in such expressions as were peculiar to that, and could not be understood of himself. The New Testament furnishes us with a key to let us into the mystery of these lines.

I. These verses must certainly be applied to Christ; of him speaks the prophet this, as did many of the Old-Testament prophets, who *testified beforehand the sufferings of Christ and the glory that should follow* (1 Pt. 1:11), and that is the subject of this prophecy here. It is foretold (as he himself showed concerning this, no doubt, among other prophecies in this psalm, Lu. 24:44, 46) that *Christ should suffer, and rise from the dead,* 1 Co. 15:3, 4.

1. That he should suffer and die. This is implied here when he says (*v.* 8), *I shall not be moved;* he supposed that he should be struck at, and have a dreadful shock given him, as he had in his agony, when his soul was exceedingly sorrowful, and he prayed that the cup might pass from him. When he says, *"My flesh shall rest,"* it is implied that he must put off the body, and therefore must go through the pains of death. It is likewise plainly intimated that his soul must go into a state of separation from the body, and that his body, so deserted, would be in imminent danger of seeing corruption — that he should not only die, but be buried, and abide for some time under the power of death.

2. That he should be wonderfully borne up by the divine power in suffering and dying. (1.) That he should not be moved, should not be driven off from his undertaking nor sink under the weight of it, that he should not fail nor be discouraged (Isa. 42:4), but should proceed and persevere in it, till he could say, *It is finished.* Though the service was hard and the encounter hot, and he trod the winepress alone, yet he was not moved, did not give up the cause, but set his face as a flint, Isa. 50:7–9. *Here am I, let these go their way.* Nay, (2.) That his heart should rejoice and his glory be glad, that he should go on with his undertaking, not only resolutely, but cheerfully, and with unspeakable pleasure and satisfaction, witness that saying (Jn. 17:11), *Now I am no more in the world, but I come to thee,* and that (Jn. 18:11), *The cup that my Father has given me, shall I not drink it?* and many the like. By his glory is meant his *tongue,* as appears, Acts 2:26. For our tongue is our glory, and never more so than when it is employed in glorifying God. Now there were three things which bore him up and carried him on thus cheerfully: — [1.] The respect he had to his Father's will and glory in what he did: *I have set the Lord always before me.* He still had an eye to his Father's commandment (Jn. 10:18, 14:31), the will of him that sent him. He aimed at his Father's honour and the restoring of the interests of his kingdom among men, and this kept him from being moved by the difficulties he met with; for he always did those things that pleased his Father. [2.] The assurance he had of his Father's presence with him in his sufferings: *He is at my right hand,* a present help to me, nigh at hand in the time of need. *He is near that justifieth me* (Isa. 50:8); he is at my right hand, to direct and strengthen it, and hold it up, Ps. 89:21. When he was in his agony an angel was sent from heaven to strengthen him, Lu. 22:43. To this the victories and triumphs of the cross were all owing; it was the Lord at his right hand that *struck through kings,* Ps. 110:5; Isa. 42:1, 2. [3.] The prospect he had of a glorious issue of his sufferings. It was *for the joy set before him* that *he endured the cross,* Heb. 12:2. He rested in hope, and that made his rest glorious, Isa. 11:10. He knew he should be justified in the Spirit by his resurrection, and straightway glorified. See Jn. 13:31, 32.

3. That he should be brought through his sufferings, and brought from under the power of death by a glorious resurrection. (1.) That his soul should not be left in hell, that is, his human spirit should not be long left, as other men's spirits are, in a state of separation from the body, but should, in a little time, return and be re-united to it, never to part again. (2.) That being God's holy One in a peculiar manner, sanctified to the work of redemption and perfectly free from sin, he should not see corruption nor feel it. This implies that he should not only be raised from the grave, but raised so soon that his dead body should not so much as being to corrupt, which, in the course of nature, it would have done if it had not been raised the third day. We, who have so much corruption in our souls, must expect that our bodies also will corrupt (Job 24:19); but that holy One of God who knew no sin saw no corruption. Under the law it was strictly ordered that those parts of the sacrifices which were not burnt upon the altar should by no means be kept till the third day, lest they should putrefy (Lev. 7:15, 18), which perhaps pointed at Christ's rising the third day, that he might not see corruption — neither was a bone of him broken.

4. That he should be abundantly recompensed for his sufferings, with the joy set before him, *v.* 11. he was well assured, (1.) That he should not miss of his glory: *"Thou wilt show me the path of life,* and lead me to that life through this darksome valley." In confidence of this, when

he gave up the ghost, he said, *Father, into thy hands I commit my spirit;* and, a little before, *Father, glorify me with thy own self.* (2.) That he should be received into the presence of God, to sit at his right hand. His being admitted into God's presence would be the acceptance of his service and his being set at his right hand the recompence of it. (3.) Thus, as a reward for the sorrows he underwent for our redemption, he should have a *fulness of joy, and pleasures for evermore;* not only the glory he had with God, as God, before all worlds, but the joy and pleasure of a Mediator, in seeing his seed, and the success and prosperity of his undertaking, Isa. 53:10, 11.

II. Christ being the Head of the body, the church, these verses may, for the most part, be applied to all good Christians, who are guided and animated by the Spirit of Christ; and, in singing them, when we have first given glory to Christ, in whom, to our everlasting comfort, they have had their accomplishment, we may then encourage and edify ourselves and one another with them, and may hence learn, 1. That it is our wisdom and duty to set the Lord always before us, and to see him continually at our right hand, wherever we are, to eye him as our chief good and highest end, our owner, ruler, and judge, our gracious benefactor, our sure guide and strict observer; and, while we do thus, we shall not be moved either from our duty or from our comfort. Blessed Paul set the Lord before him, when, though bonds and afflictions did await him, he could bravely say, *None of these things move me,* Acts 20:24. 2. That, if our eyes be ever towards God, our hearts and tongues may ever rejoice in him; it is our own fault if they do not. If the heart rejoice in God, out of the abundance of that let the mouth speak, to his glory, and the edification of others. 3. That dying Christians, as well as a dying Christ, may cheerfully put off the body, in a believing expectation of a joyful resurrection: *My flesh also shall rest in hope.* Our bodies have little rest in this world, but in the grave they shall rest as in their beds, Isa. 57:2. We have little to hope for from this life, but we shall rest in hope of a better life; we may put off the body in that hope. Death *destroys the hope of man* (Job 14:19), but not the hope of a good Christian, Prov. 14:32. He has hope in his death, living hopes in dying moments, hopes that the body shall not be left for ever in the grave, but, though it see corruption for a time, it shall, at the end of the time, be raised to immortality; Christ's resurrection is an earnest of ours if we be his. 4. That those who live piously with God in their eye may die comfortably with heaven in their eye. In this world sorrow is our lot, but in heaven there is joy. All our joys here are empty and defective, but in heaven there is a fulness of joy. Our pleasures here are transient and momentary, and such is the nature of them that it is not fit they should last long; but those at God's right hand are pleasures for evermore; for they are the pleasures of immortal souls in the immediate vision and fruition of an eternal God.

PSALM 17

David being in great distress and danger by the malice of his enemies, does, in this psalm, by prayer address himself to God, his tried refuge, and seeks shelter in him. I. He appeals to God concerning his integrity (*v.* 1–4). II. He prays to God still to be upheld in his integrity and preserved from the malice of his enemies (*v.* 5–8, 13). III. He gives a character of his enemies, using that as a plea with God for his preservation (*v.* 9–12, 14). IV. He comforts himself with the hopes of his future happiness (*v.* 15). Some make him, in this, a type of Christ, who was perfectly innocent, and yet was hated and persecuted, but, like David, committed himself and his cause to him that judgeth righteously.

A prayer of David.

Verses 1–7

This psalm is a prayer. As there is a time to weep and a time to rejoice, so there is a time for praise and a time for prayer. David was now persecuted, probably by Saul, who hunted him like a partridge on the mountains; without were fightings, within were fears, and both urged him as a suppliant to the throne of mercy. He addresses himself to God in these verses both by way of appeal (*Hear the right, O Lord!* let my righteous cause have a hearing before thy tribunal, and give judgment upon it) and by way of petition (*Give ear unto my prayer v.* 1, and again *v.* 6, *Incline thy ear unto me and hear my speech*); not that God needs to be thus pressed with our importunity, but he gives us leave thus to express our earnest desire of his gracious answers to our prayers. These things he pleads with God for audience, 1. That he was sincere, and did not dissemble with God in his prayer: *It goeth not out of feigned lips.* He meant as he spoke, and the feelings of his mind agreed with the expressions of his mouth. Feigned prayers are fruitless; but, if our hearts lead our prayers, God will meet them with his favour. 2. That he had been used to pray at other times, and it was not his distress and danger that now first brought him to his duty: *"I have called upon thee* formerly (*v.* 6); therefore, Lord, hear me now." It will be a great comfort to us if trouble, when it comes, find the wheels of prayer a-going, for then we may come with the more boldness to the throne of grace. Tradesmen are willing to oblige those that have been long their customers. 3. That he was encouraged by his faith to expect God would take notice of his prayers: "I know *thou wilt hear me,* and therefore, O God, *incline thy ear to me."* Our believing dependence upon God is a good plea to enforce our desires towards him. Let us now see,

I. What his appeal is; and here observe,

1. What the court is to the cognizance and determination of which he makes his appeal; it is the court of heaven. "Lord, do thou hear the right, for Saul is so passionate, so prejudiced, that he will not hear it. Lord, *let my sentence come forth from thy presence, v.* 2. Men sentence me to be pursued and cut off as an evil-doer. Lord, I appeal from them to thee." This he did in a public remonstrance before Saul's face (1 Sa. 24:12, *The Lord judge between me and thee*), and he repeats it here in his private devotions. Note, (1.) The equity and extent of God's government and judgment are a very great support to injured innocency. If we are blackened, and abused, and misrepresented, by unrighteous men, it is a comfort that we have a righteous God to go to, who will take our part, who is the patron of the oppressed, whose judgment is according to truth, by the discoveries of which every person and every cause will appear in a true light, stripped of all false colours, and by the decisions of which all unrighteous dooms will be reversed, and to every man will be rendered according to his work. (2.) Sincerity dreads no scrutiny, no, not that of God himself, according to the tenour of the covenant of grace: *Let thy eyes behold the things that are equal.* God's omniscience is as much the joy of the upright as it is the terror of hypocrites, and is particularly comfortable to those who are falsely accused and in any wise have wrong done them.

2. What the evidence is by which he hopes to make good his appeal; it is the trial God had made of him (*v.* 3): *Thou hast proved my heart.* God's sentence is *therefore* right, because he always proceeds upon his knowledge, which is more certain and infallible than that which men attain to by the closest views and the strictest investigations.

(1.) He knew God had tried him, [1.] By his own conscience, which is God's deputy in the soul. *The spirit of a man is the candle of the Lord,* with this God had searched him, and *visited him in the night,* when he *communed with his own heart upon his bed.* He had submitted to the search, and had seriously reviewed the actions of his life, to discover what was amiss, but could find nothing of that which his enemies charged him with. [2.] By providence. God had tried him by the fair opportunity he had, once and again, to kill Saul; he had tried him by the malice of Saul, the treachery of his friends, and the many provocations that were given him; so that, if he had been the man he was represented to be, it would have appeared; but, upon all these trials, there was nothing found against him, no proof at all of the things whereof they accused him.

(2.) God tried his heart, and could witness to the integrity of that; but, for the further proof of his integrity, he himself takes notice of two things concerning which his conscience bore him record: — [1.] That he had a fixed resolution against all sins of the tongue: *"I have purposed* and fully determined, in the strength of God's grace, *that my mouth shall not transgress."* He does not say, "I hope that it will not," or, "I wish that it may not," but, "I have fully purposed that it shall not:" with this bridle he kept his mouth, Ps. 39:1. Note, Constant resolution and watchfulness against sins of the tongue will be a good evidence of our integrity. *If any offend not in word, the same is a perfect man,* Jam. 3:2. He does not say, "My mouth never shall transgress" (for in many things we all offend), but, "I have purposed that it shall not;" and he that searches the heart knows whether the purpose be sincere. [2.] That he had been as careful to refrain from sinful actions as from sinful words (*v.* 4): *"Concerning the* common *works of men,* the actions and affairs of human life, *I have,* by the direction of thy word, *kept myself from the paths of the destroyer."* Some understand it particularly, that he had not been himself a destroyer of Saul, when it lay in his power, nor had he permitted others to be so, but said to Abishai, *Destroy him not,* 1 Sa. 26:9. But it may be taken more generally; he kept himself from all evil works, and endeavoured, according to the duty of his place, to keep others from them too. Note, *First,* The ways of sin are paths of the destroyer, of the devil, whose name is *Abaddon* and *Apollyon,* a destroyer, who ruins souls by decoying them into the paths of sin. *Secondly,* It concerns us all to keep out of the paths of the destroyer; for, if we walk in those ways that lead to destruction, we must thank ourselves if destruction and misery be our portion at last. *Thirdly,* It is by the word of God, as our guide and rule, that we must keep out of the paths of the destroyer, by observing its directions and admonitions, Ps. 119:9. *Fourthly,* If we carefully avoid all the paths of sin, it will be very comfortable in the reflection, when we are in trouble. If we *keep ourselves, that the wicked one touch us not* with his temptations (1 Jn. 5:18), we may hope he will not be able to touch us with his terrors.

II. What his petition is; it is, in short, this, That he might experience the good work of God in him, as an evidence of and qualification for the good will of God towards him: this is grace and peace from God the Father. 1. He prays for the work of God's grace in him (*v.* 5): *"Hold up my going in thy paths.* Lord, I have, by thy grace, kept myself from the paths of the destroyer; by the same grace let me be kept in thy paths; let me not only be restrained from doing that which is evil, but quickened to abound always in that which is good. Let my goings be held in thy paths, that I may not turn back from them nor turn aside out of them; let them be held up in thy paths, that I may not stumble and fall into sin, that I may not trifle and neglect my duty. Lord, as thou hast kept me hitherto, so keep me still." Those that are, through grace, going in God's paths, have need to pray, and do pray, that their goings may be held up in those paths; for we stand no longer than he is pleased to hold us, we go no further than he is pleased to lead us, bear us up, and carry us. David had been kept in the way of his duty hitherto, and yet he does not think that this would be his security for the future, and therefore prays, "Lord, still hold me up." Those that would proceed and persevere in the way of God must, by faith and prayer, fetch in daily fresh supplies of grace and strength from him. David was sensible that his way was slippery, that he himself was weak, and not so well fixed and furnished as he should be, that there were those who watched for his halting and would improve the least slip against him, and therefore he prays, "Lord, hold me up, that my foot slip not, that I may never say nor do any thing that looks either dishonest or distrustful of thee and thy providence and promise." 2. He prays for the tokens of God's favour to him, *v.* 7. Observe here, (1.) How he eyes God as the protector and Saviour of his people, so he calls him, and thence he takes his encouragement in prayer: *O thou that savest by thy right hand* (by thy own power, and needest not the agency of any other) *those who put their trust in thee from those that rise up against them.* It is the character of God's people that they trust in him; he is pleased to make them confidants, for his secret is with the righteous; and they make him their trust, for to him they commit themselves. Those that trust in God have many enemies, many that rise up against them and seek their ruin; but they have one friend that is able to deal with them all, and, if he be for them, no matter who is against them. He reckons it his honour to be their Saviour. His almighty power is engaged for them, and they have all found him ready to save them. The margin reads it, *O thou that savest those who trust in thee from those that rise up against thy right hand.* Those that are enemies to the saints are rebels against God and his right hand, and therefore, no doubt, he will, in due time, appear against them. (2.) What he expects and desires from God: *Show thy marvellous loving-kindness.* The word signifies, [1.] Distinguishing favours. "Set apart thy loving-kindnesses for me; put me not off with common mercies, but be gracious to me, *as thou usest* to do to those who love thy name." [2.] Wonderful favours. "O make thy loving-kindness admirable! Lord, testify thy favour to me in such a way that I and others may wonder at it." God's loving-kindness is marvellous for the freeness and the fulness of it; in some instances it appears, in a special manner, marvellous (Ps. 118:23), and it will certainly appear so in the salvation of the saints, when Christ shall come to be *glorified in the saints and to be admired in all those that believe.*

Verses 8–15

We may observe, in these verses,

I. What David prays for. Being compassed about with enemies that sought his life, he prays to God to preserve him safely through all their attempts against him, to the crown to which he was anointed. This prayer is both a prediction of the preservation of Christ through all the hardships and difficulties of his humiliation, to the glories and joys of his exalted state, and a pattern to Christians to commit the keeping of their souls to God, trusting him to *preserve them to his heavenly kingdom.* He prays,

1. That he himself might be protected (v. 8): "Keep me safe, hide me close, where I may not be found, where I may not be come at. Deliver my soul, not only my mortal life from death, but my immortal spirit from sin." Those who put themselves under God's protection may in faith implore the benefit of it.

(1.) He prays that God would keep him, [1.] With as much care as a man keeps the apple of his eye with, which nature has wonderfully fenced and teaches us to guard. If we keep God's law as the *apple of our eye* (Prov. 7:2), we may expect that God will so keep us; for it is said concerning his people that whoso *touches them touches the apple of his eye,* Zec. 2:8. [2.] With as much tenderness as the hen gathers her young ones under her wings with; Christ uses the similitude, Mt. 23:37. "*Hide me under the shadow of thy wings,* where I may be both safe and warm." Or, perhaps, it rather alludes to the wings of the cherubim shadowing the mercy-seat: "Let me be taken under the protection of that glorious grace which is peculiar to God's Israel." What David here prays for was performed to the Son of David, our Lord Jesus, of whom it is said (Isa. 49:2) that God hid *him in the shadow of his hand,* hid him as *a polished shaft in his quiver.*

(2.) David further prays, "Lord, keep me from the wicked, from men of the world," [1.] "From being, and doing, like them, from walking in their counsel, and standing in their way, and eating of their dainties." [2.] "From being destroyed and run down by them. Let them not have their will against me; let them not triumph over me."

2. That all the designs of his enemies to bring his either into sin or into trouble might be defeated (v. 13): "*Arise, O Lord!* appear for me, disappoint him, and cast him down in his own eyes by the disappointment." While Saul persecuted David, how often did he miss his prey, when he thought he had him sure! And how were Christ's enemies disappointed by his resurrection, who thought they had gained their point when they had put him to death!

II. What he pleads for the encouraging of his own faith in these petitions, and his hope of speeding. He pleads,

1. The malice and wickedness of his enemies: "They are such as are not fit to be countenanced, such as, if I be not delivered from them by the special care of God himself, will be my ruin. Lord, see what wicked men those are that oppress me, and waste me, and run me down." (1.) "They are very spiteful and malicious; they are *my deadly enemies,* that thirst after my blood, my heart's blood — *enemies against the soul,*" so the word is. David's enemies did what they could to drive him to sin and drive him away from God; they bade him *go serve other gods* (1 Sa. 26:19), and therefore he had reason to pray against them. Note, Those are our worst enemies, and we ought so to account them, that are enemies to our souls. (2.) "They are very secure and sensual, insolent and haughty (v. 10): *They are enclosed in their own fat,* wrap themselves, hug themselves, in their own honour, and power, and plenty, and then make light of God, and set his judgments at defiance, Ps. 73:7; Job 15:27. They wallow in pleasure, and promise themselves that to-morrow shall be as this day. And therefore with their mouth they speak proudly, glorying in themselves, blaspheming God, trampling upon his people, and insulting them." See Rev. 13:5, 6. "Lord,

are not such men as these fit to be mortified and humbled, and made to know themselves? Will it not be for thy glory *to look upon these proud men and abase them?*" (3.) "They are restless and unwearied in their attempts against me: They *compass me about, v.* 9. They have now in a manner gained their point; they have surrounded us, they have compassed us in our steps, they track us wherever we go, follow us as close as the hound does the hare, and take all advantages against us, being both too many and too quick for us. And yet they pretend to look another way, and set their eyes bowing down to the earth, as if they were meditating, retired into themselves, and thinking of something else;" or (as some think), "They are watchful and intent upon it, to do us a mischief; they are down-looked, and never let slip any opportunity of compassing their design." (4.) "The ringleader of them (that was Saul) is in a special manner bloody and barbarous, politic and projecting (v. 12), *like a lion* that lives by prey and is therefore greedy of it." It is as much the meat and drink of a wicked man to do mischief as it is of a good man to do good. He is like *a young lion lurking in secret places,* disguising his cruel designs. This is fitly applied to Saul, who sought David *on the rocks of the wild goats* (1 Sa. 24:2) and in *the wilderness of Ziph* (Ps. 26:2), where lions used to lurk for their prey.

2. The power God had over them, to control and restrain them. He pleads, (1.) "Lord, they are *thy sword; and* will any father suffer his sword to be drawn against his own children?" As this is a reason why we should patiently bear the injuries of men, that they are but the instruments of the trouble (it comes originally from God, to whose will we are bound to submit), so it is an encouragement to us to hope both that their wrath shall praise him and that the remainder thereof he will restrain, that they are God's sword, which he can manage as he pleases, which cannot move without him, and which he will sheathe when he has done his work with it. (2.) "They are *thy hand,* by which thou dost chastise thy people and make them feel thy displeasure." He therefore expects deliverance from God's hand because from God's hand the trouble came. *Una eademque manus vulnus opemque tulit — The same hand wounds and heals.* There is no flying from God's hand but by flying to it. It is very comfortable, when we are in fear of the power of man, to see it dependent upon and in subjection to the power of God; see Isa. 10:6, 7, 15.

3. Their outward prosperity (v. 14): "Lord, appear against them, for," (1.) "They are entirely devoted to the world, and care not for thee and thy favour. They are *men of the world,* actuated by the spirit of the world, walking according to the course of this world, in love with the wealth and pleasure of this world, eager in the pursuits of it (making them their business) and at ease in the enjoyments of it — making them their bliss. They *have their portion in this life;* they look upon the good things of this world as the best things, and sufficient to make them happy, and they choose them accordingly, place their felicity in them, and aim at them as their chief good; they rest satisfied with them, their souls take their ease in them, and they look no further, nor are in any care to provide for another life. These things are their consolation (Lu. 6:24), *their good things* (Lu. 16:25), *their reward* (Mt. 6:5), the penny they agreed for, Mt. 20:13. Now, Lord, shall men of this character be supported and countenanced against those who honour thee by preferring thy favour before all the wealth in this world, and taking thee for their portion?" Ps. 16:5. (2.) They have abundance of the world. [1.] They have enlarged appetites, and a great deal wherewith to satisfy them: *Their bellies thou fillest with thy hidden treasures.* The things of this world are called *treasures,* because they are so accounted; otherwise, to a soul, and in comparison with eternal blessings, they are but trash. They are hidden in the several parts of the creation, and hidden in the sovereign disposals of Providence. They are God's hidden treasures, for the earth is his and the fulness thereof, though the men of the world think it is their own and forget God's property in it. Those that fare deliciously every day have their *bellies filled with these hidden treasures;* and they will but *fill the belly* (1 Co. 6:13); they will not fill the soul; they are not bread for that, nor can they satisfy, Isa. 55:2. They are husks, and ashes, and wind; and yet most men, having no care for their souls, but all for their bellies, take up with

them. [2.] They have numerous families, and a great deal to leave to them: *They are full of children,* and yet their pasture is not overstocked; they have enough for them all, and *leave the rest of their substance to their babes,* to their grand-children; and this is their heaven, it is their bliss, it is their all. "Lord," said David, "*deliver me from them;* let me not have my portion with them. Deliver me from their designs against me; for, they having so much wealth and power, I am not able to deal with them unless the Lord be on my side."

4. He pleads his own dependence upon God as his portion and happiness. "They have their portion in this life, but as for me (v. 15) I am none of them, I have but little of the world. *Nec habeo, nec careo, nec curo — I neither have, nor need, nor care for it.* It is the vision and fruition of God that I place my happiness in; that is it I hope for, and comfort myself with the hopes of, and thereby distinguish myself from those who have their portion in this life." Beholding God's face with satisfaction may be considered, (1.) As our duty and comfort in this world. We must in righteousness (clothed with Christ's righteousness, having a good heart and a good life) by faith behold God's face and set him always before us, must entertain ourselves from day to day with the contemplation of the beauty of the Lord; and, when we awake every morning, we must be satisfied with his likeness set before us in his word, and with his likeness stamped upon us by his renewing grace. Our experience of God's favour to us, and our conformity to him, should yield us more satisfaction than those have whose belly is filled with the delights of sense. 2. As our recompence and happiness in the other world. With the prospect of that he concluded the foregoing psalm, and so this. That happiness is prepared and designed only for the righteous that are justified and sanctified. They shall be put in possession of it when they awake, when the soul awakes, at death, out of its slumber in the body, and when the body awakes, at the resurrection, out of its slumber in the grave. That blessedness will consist in three things: — [1.] The immediate vision of God and his glory: *I shall behold thy face,* not, as in this world, through a glass darkly. The knowledge of God will there be perfected and the enlarged intellect filled with it. [2.] The participation of his likeness. Our holiness will there be perfect. This results from the former (1 Jn. 3:2): *When he shall appear we shall be like him, for we shall see him as he is.* [3.] A complete and full satisfaction resulting from all this: *I shall be satisfied,* abundantly satisfied with it. There is no satisfaction for a soul but in God, and in his face and likeness, his good-will towards us and his good work in us; and even that satisfaction will not be perfect till we come to heaven.

PSALM 18

This psalm we met with before, in the history of David's life, 2 Sa. 22. That was the first edition of it; here we have it revived, altered a little, and fitted for the service of the church. It is David's thanksgiving for the many deliverances God had wrought for him; these he desired always to preserve fresh in his own memory and to diffuse and entail the knowledge of them. It is an admirable composition. The poetry is very fine, the images are bold, the expressions lofty, and every word is proper and significant; but the piety far exceeds the poetry. Holy faith, and love, and joy, and praise, and hope, are here lively, active, and upon the wing. I. He triumphs in God (v. 1–3). II. He magnifies the deliverances God had wrought for him (v. 4–19). III. He takes the comfort of his integrity, which God had thereby cleared up (v. 20–28). IV. He gives to God the glory of all his achievements (v. 29–42). V. He encourages himself with the expectation of what God would further do for him and his (v. 43–50).

To the chief musician, *A psalm* of David, the servant of the LORD, who spake unto the LORD the words of this song in the day *that* the LORD delivered him from the hand of all his enemies.

Verses 1–19

The title gives us the occasion of penning this psalm; we had it before (2 Sa. 22:1), only here we are told that the psalm was delivered *to the chief musician,* or precentor, in the temple-songs. Note, The private compositions of good men, designed by them for their own use, may be serviceable to the public, that others may not only borrow light from their candle, but heat from their fire. Examples sometimes teach better than rules. And David is here called *the servant of the Lord,* as Moses was, not only as every good man is God's servant, but because, with his sceptre, with his sword, and with his pen, he greatly promoted the interests of God's kingdom in Israel. It was more his honour that he was a servant of the Lord than that he was king of a great kingdom; and so he himself accounted it (Ps. 116:16): *O Lord! truly I am thy servant.* In these verses,

I. He triumphs in God and his relation to him. The first words of the psalm, *I will love thee, O Lord! my strength,* are here prefixed as the scope and contents of the whole. Love to God is the first and great commandment of the law, because it is the principle of all our acceptable praise and obedience; and this use we should make of all the mercies God bestows upon us, our hearts should thereby be enlarged in love to him. This he requires and will accept; and we are very ungrateful if we grudge him so poor a return. An interest in the person loved is the lover's delight; this string therefore he touches, and on this he harps with much pleasure (v. 2): *"The Lord Jehovah is my God;* and then he is my *rock, my fortress,* all that I need and can desire in my present distress." For there is that in God which is suited to all the exigencies and occasions of his people that trust in him. "He is my rock, and strength, and fortress;" that is, 1. "I have found him so in the greatest dangers and difficulties." 2. "I have chosen him to be so, disclaiming all others, and depending upon him alone to protect me." Those that truly love God may thus triumph in him as theirs, and may with confidence call upon him, v. 3. This further use we should make of our deliverances, we must not only love God the better, but love prayer the better — *call upon him as long as we live,* especially in time of trouble, with an assurance that so we shall be saved; for thus it is written, *Whosoever shall call upon the name of the Lord shall be saved,* Acts 2:21.

II. He sets himself to magnify the deliverances God had wrought for him, that he might be the more affected in his returns of praise. It is good for us to observe all the circumstances of a mercy, which magnify the power of God and his goodness to us in it.

1. The more imminent and threatening the danger was out of which we were delivered the greater is the mercy of the deliverance. David now remembered how the forces of his enemies poured in upon him, which he calls *the floods of Belial,* shoals of the children of Belial, likely to overpower him with numbers. They surrounded him, *compassed him about;* they surprised him, and by that means were very near seizing him; their snares prevented him, and, when without were fightings, within were fears and sorrows, v. 4, 5. His spirit was overwhelmed, and he looked upon himself as a lost man; see Ps. 116:3.

2. The more earnest we have been with God for deliverance, and the more direct answer it is to our prayers, the more we are obliged to be thankful. David's deliverances were so, v. 6. David was found a praying man, and God was found a prayer-hearing God. If we pray as he did, we shall speed as he did. Though distress drive us to prayer, God will not therefore be deaf to us; nay, being a God of pity, he will be the more ready to succour us.

3. The more wonderful God's appearances are in any deliverance the greater it is: such were the deliverances wrought for David, in which God's manifestation of his presence and glorious attributes is most magnificently described, v. 7, etc. Little appeared of man, but much of God, in these deliverances. (1.) He appeared a God of almighty power; for he made the earth shake and tremble, and moved even the *foundations of the hills* (v. 7), as of old at Mount Sinai. When the men of the earth were struck with fear, then the earth might be said to *tremble;* when the great men of the earth were put into confusion, then the hills moved. (2.) He showed his anger and displeasure against the enemies and persecutors of his people: *He was wroth,* v. 7. His wrath smoked, it burned, it was fire, it was devouring fire (v. 8), and *coals were kindled by it.* Those that by their own sins make themselves as coals (that is, fuel) to this fire will be consumed by it. He that ordains his arrows against the persecutors sends them forth when he pleases, and they are sure to hit the mark and do execution; for those arrows are lightnings, v. 14. (3.) He showed his readiness to plead his people's cause and work deliverance for them; for he rode upon a cherub and did fly, for the maintaining of right and the relieving of his distressed servants, v. 10. No opposition, no obstruction, can be given to him *who rides upon the wings of the wind, who rides on the heavens,* for the help of his people, and,

in his excellency, on the skies. (4.) He showed his condescension, in taking cognizance of David's case: *He bowed the heavens and came down* (v. 9), did not send an angel, but came himself, as one afflicted in the afflictions of his people. (5.) He wrapped himself in darkness, and yet commanded light to shine out of darkness for his people, Isa. 45:15. He is a God that hideth himself; for he *made darkness his pavilion,* v. 11. his glory is invisible, his counsels are unsearchable, and his proceedings unaccountable, and so, as to us, clouds and darkness are round about him; we know not the way that he takes, even when he is coming towards us in ways of mercy; but, when his designs are secret, they are kind; for, though he hide himself, he is the God of Israel, the Saviour. And, *at his brightness, the thick clouds pass* (v. 12), comfort returns, the face of affairs is changed, and that which was gloomy and threatening becomes serene and pleasant.

4. The greater the difficulties are that lie in the way of deliverance the more glorious the deliverance is. For the rescuing of David, the waters were to be divided till the very channels were seen; the earth was to be cloven till the very foundations of it were discovered, v. 15. There were waters deep and many, waters out of which he was to be drawn (v. 16), as Moses, who had his name from being drawn out of the water literally, as David was figuratively. His enemies were strong, and they hated him; had he been left to himself, they would have been too strong for him, v. 17. And they were too quick for him; for they *prevented him in the day of his calamity,* v. 18. But, in the midst of his troubles, the Lord was his stay, so that he did not sink. Note, God will not only deliver his people out of their troubles in due time, but he will sustain them and bear them up under their troubles in the mean time.

5. That which especially magnified the deliverance was that his comfort was the fruit of it and God's favour was the root and fountain of it. (1.) It was an introduction to his preferment, v. 19. "He brought me forth also out of my straits into a large place, where I had room, not only to turn, but to thrive in." (2.) It was a token of God's favour to him, and that made it doubly sweet: *"He delivered me because he delighted in me,* not for my merit, but for his own grace and good-will." Compare this with 2 Sa. 15:26, *If he thus say, I have no delight in thee, here I am.* We owe our salvation, that great deliverance, to the delight God had in the Son of David, in whom he has declared himself to be well pleased.

In singing this we must triumph in God, and trust in him: and we may apply it to Christ the Son of David. The sorrows of death surrounded him; in his distress he prayed (Heb. 5:7); God made the earth to shake and tremble, and the rocks to cleave, and brought him out, in his resurrection, into a large place, because he delighted in him and in his undertaking.

Verses 20–28

Here, I. David reflects with comfort upon his own integrity, and rejoices in the testimony of his conscience that he had had his conversation in godly sincerity and not with fleshly wisdom, 2 Co. 1:12. His deliverances were an evidence of this, and this was the great comfort of his deliverances. His enemies had misrepresented him, and perhaps, when his troubles continued long, he began to suspect himself; but, when God visibly took his part, he had both the credit and the comfort of his righteousness. 1. His deliverances cleared his innocency before men, and acquitted him from those crimes which he was falsely accused of. This he calls *rewarding him according to his righteousness* (v. 20, 24), that is, determining the controversy between him and his enemies, according to the justice of his cause and the cleanness of his hands, from that sedition, treason, and rebellion, with which he was charged. He had often appealed to God concerning his innocency; and now God had given judgment upon the appeal (as he always will) according to equity. 2. They confirmed the testimony of his own conscience for him, which he here reviews with a great deal of pleasure, v. 21–23. His own heart knows, and is ready to attest it, (1.) That he had kept firmly to his duty, and had not departed, not wickedly, not wilfully departed, from his God. Those that forsake the ways of the Lord do, in effect, depart from their God, and it is a wicked thing to do so. But though we are conscious to ourselves of many a stumble, and many a false step taken,

yet if we recover ourselves by repentance, and go on in the way of our duty, it shall not be construed into a departure, for it is not a wicked departure, from our God. (2.) That he had kept his eye upon the rule of God's commands (v. 22): *"All his judgments were before me;* and I had a respect to them all, despised none as little, disliked none as hard, but made it my care and business to conform to them all. His statutes I did not put away from me, out of my sight, out of my mind, but kept my eye always upon them, and did not as those who, because they would quit the ways of the Lord, desire not the knowledge of those ways." (3.) That he had kept himself from his iniquity, and thereby had approved himself upright before God. Constant care to abstain from that sin, whatever it be, which most easily besets us, and to mortify the habit of it, will be a good evidence for us that we are upright before God. As David's deliverances cleared his integrity, so did the exaltation of Christ clear his, and for ever roll away the reproach that was cast upon him; and therefore he is said to be *justified in the Spirit,* 1 Tim. 3:16.

II. He takes occasion thence to lay down the rules of God's government and judgment, that we may know not only what God expects from us, but what we may expect from him, v. 25, 26. 1. Those that show mercy to others (even they need mercy, and cannot depend upon the merit, no, not of their works of mercy) shall find mercy with God, Mt. 5:7. 2. Those that are faithful to their covenants with God, and the relations wherein they stand to him, shall find him all that to them which he has promised to be. Wherever God finds an upright man, he will be found an upright God. 3. Those that serve God with a pure conscience shall find that the words of the Lord are pure words, very sure to be depended on and very sweet to be delight in. 4. Those that resist God, and walk contrary to him, shall find that he will resist them, and walk contrary to them, Lev. 26:21, 24.

III. Hence he speaks comfort to the humble (*"Thou wilt save the afflicted people,* that are wronged and bear it patiently"), terror to the proud ("Thou *wilt bring down high looks,* that aim high, and look with scorn and disdain upon the poor and pious"), and encouragement to himself — *"Thou wilt light my candle,* that is, thou wilt revive and comfort my sorrowful spirit, and not leave me melancholy; thou wilt recover me out of my troubles and restore me to peace and prosperity; thou wilt make my honour bright, which is now eclipsed; thou wilt guide my way, and make it plain before me, that I may avoid the snares laid for me; thou wilt light my candle to work by, and give me an opportunity of serving thee and the interests of thy kingdom among men."

Let those that walk in darkness, and labour under many discouragements in singing these verses, encourage themselves that God himself will be a light to them.

Verses 29–50

In these verses,

I. David looks back, with thankfulness, upon the great things which God had done for him. He had not only wrought deliverance for him, but had given him victory and success, and made him triumph over those who thought to triumph over him. When we set ourselves to praise God for one mercy we must be led by that to observe the many more with which we have been compassed about, and followed, all our days. Many things had contributed to David's advancement, and he owns the hand of God in them all, to teach us to do likewise, in reviewing the several steps by which we have risen to our prosperity. 1. God had given him all his skill and understanding in military affairs, which he was not bred up to nor designed for, his genius leading him more to music, and poetry, and a contemplative life: *He teaches my hands to war,* v. 34. 2. God had given him bodily strength to go through the business and fatigue of war: God *girded him with strength* (v. 32, 39), to such a degree that he could break even a bow of steel, v. 34. What service God designs men for he will be sure to fit them for. 3. God had likewise given him great swiftness, not to flee from the enemies but to fly upon them (v. 33): *He makes my feet like hinds' feet,* v. 36. *"Thou hast enlarged my steps under me;* but" (whereas those that take large steps are apt to tread awry) "my feet did not slip." He was so swift that he pursued his enemies and overtook them, v. 37. 4. God had made him very bold and daring in his enterprises, and given him spirit proportionable to his strength. If a troop stood in his way, he made nothing of running through them; if a wall, he made nothing of leaping over it (*v.* 29); if ramparts and bulwarks, he soon mounted them, and by divine assistance set his feet upon the high places of the enemy, *v.* 33. 5. God had protected him, and kept him safe, in the midst of the greatest perils. Many a time he put his life in his hand, and yet it was wonderfully preserved: *"Thou hast given me the shield of thy salvation* (*v.* 35), and that has compassed me on every side. By that I have been delivered from the strivings of the people who aimed at my destruction (*v.* 43), particularly from the violent man" (*v.* 48), that is, Saul, who more than once threw a javelin at him. 6. God had prospered him in his designs; he it was that made his way perfect (*v.* 32) and it was his right hand that held him up, *v.* 35. 7. God had given him victory over his enemies, the Philistines, Moabites, Ammonites, and all that fought against Israel: those especially he means, yet not excluding the house of Saul, which opposed his coming to the crown, and the partisans of Absalom and Sheba, who would have deposed him. He enlarges much upon the goodness of God to him in defeating his enemies, attributing his victories, not to his own sword or bow, nor to the valour of his mighty men, but to the favour of God: *I pursued* them (*v.* 37), *I wounded them* (*v.* 38); *for thou hast girded me with strength* (*v.* 39), else I could not have done it. All the praise is ascribed to God: *Thou hast subdued them under me, v.* 39. Thou hast *given me their necks* (*v.* 40), not only to trample upon them (as Jos. 10:24), but to cut them off. Even those who hated David whom God loved, and were enemies to the Israel of God, in their distress cried unto the Lord: but in vain; he answered them not. How could they expect he should when it was he whom they fought against? And, when he disowned them (as he will all those that act against his people), no other succours could stand them in stead: *There was none to save them, v.* 41. Those whom God has abandoned are easily vanquished: *Then did I beat them small as the dust, v.* 42. But those whose cause is just he avenges (*v.* 47), and those whom he favours will certainly be *lifted up above those that rise up against them, v.* 48. 8. God had raised him to the throne, and not only delivered him and kept him alive, but dignified him and made him great (*v.* 35): *Thy gentleness has increased me* — thy *discipline* and *instruction;* so some. The good lessons David learned in his affliction prepared him for the dignity and power that were intended him; and the lessening of him helped very much to increase his greatness. God made him not only a great conqueror, but a great ruler: *Thou hast made me the head of the heathen* (*v.* 43); all the neighbouring nations were tributaries to him. See 2 Sa. 8:6, 11. In all this David was a type of Christ, whom the Father brought safely through his conflicts with the powers of darkness, and made victorious over them, and gave to be head over all things to his church, which is his body.

II. David looks up with humble and reverent adorations of the divine glory and perfection. When God had, by his providence, magnified him, he endeavours, with his praises, to magnify God, to bless him and exalt him, *v.* 46. He gives honour to him, 1. As a living God: *The Lord liveth, v.* 46. We had our lives at first from, and we owe the continuance of them to, that God who has life in himself and is therefore fitly called *the living God.* The gods of the heathen were dead gods. The best friends we have among men are dying friends. But God lives, lives for ever, and will not fail those that trust in him, but, because he lives, they shall live also; for he is their life. 2. As a finishing God: *As for God,* he is not only perfect himself, but *his way is perfect, v.* 30. He is known by his name *Jehovah* (Ex. 6:3), a God performing and perfecting what he begins in providence as well as creation, Gen. 2:1. If it was God that made David's way perfect (*v.* 32), much more is his own way so. There is no flaw in God's works, nor any fault to be found with what he does, Eccl. 3:14. And what he undertakes he will go through with, whatever difficulties lie in the way; what God begins to build he is able to finish. 3. As a faithful God: *The word of the Lord is tried.* "I have tried it" (says David), "and it has not failed me." All the saints, in all ages, have tried it, and it never failed any that trusted in it. It is tried as silver is tried, refined from all such mixture and alloy as lessen the value of men's words. David, in God's providences concerning him, takes notice of the performance of his promises to him, which, as it puts sweetness into the providence, so it puts honour upon the promise. 4. As the protector and defender of his people. David had found him so to him: *"He is the God of my salvation* (*v.* 46), by whose power and grace I am and hope to be saved; but not of mine only: he is *a buckler to all those that trust in him* (*v.* 30); he shelters and protects them all, is both able and ready to do so." 5. As a non-such in all this, *v.* 31. There is a God, and *who is God save Jehovah?* That God is a rock, for the support and shelter of his faithful worshippers; and *who is a rock save our God?* Thus he not only gives glory to God, but encourages his own faith in him. Note, (1.) Whoever pretends to be deities, it is certain that there is no God, save the Lord; all others are counterfeits, Isa. 44:8; Jer. 10:10. (2.) Whoever pretends to be our felicities, there is no rock, save our God; none that we can depend upon to make us happy.

III. David looks forward, with a believing hope that God would still do him good. He promises himself, 1. That his enemies should be completely subdued, and that those of them that yet remained should be made his footstool, — that his government should be extensive, so that even a people whom he had not known should serve him (*v.* 43), — that his conquests, and, consequently, his acquests, should be easy (*As soon as they hear of me they shall obey me, v.* 44), — and that his enemies should be convinced that it was to no purpose to oppose him; even those that had retired to their fastnesses should not trust to them, but be afraid out of their close places, having seen so much of David's wisdom, courage, and success. Thus the Son of David, though he sees not yet all things put under him, yet knows he shall reign till all opposing rule, principality, and power shall be quite put down. 2. That his seed should be forever continued in the Messiah, who, he foresaw, should come from his loins, *v.* 50. He *shows mercy to his anointed,* his Messiah, *to David* himself, the anointed of the God of Jacob in the type, *and to his seed for evermore. He saith not unto seeds, as of many, but to his seed, as of one, that is Christ,* Gal. 3:16. It is he only that shall reign for ever, and of the increase of whose government and peace there shall be no end. Christ is called *David,* Hos. 3:5. God has called him *his king,* Ps. 2:6. Great deliverance God does give, and will give to him, and to his church and people, here called *his seed, for evermore.*

In singing these verses we must give God the glory of the victories of Christ and his church hitherto and of all the deliverances and advancements of the gospel kingdom, and encourage ourselves and one another with an assurance that the church militant will be shortly triumphant, will be eternally so.

PSALM 19

There are two excellent books which the great God has published for the instruction and edification of the children of men; this psalm treats of them both, and recommends them both to our diligent study. I. The book of the creatures, in which we may easily read the power and godhead of the Creator (*v.* 1–6). II. The book of the scriptures, which makes known to us the will of God concerning our duty. He shows the excellency and usefulness of that book (*v.* 7–11) and then teaches us how to improve it (*v.* 12–14).

To the chief musician. A psalm of David.

Verses 1–6

From the things that are seen every day by all the world the psalmist, in these verses, leads us to the consideration of the invisible things of God, whose being appears incontestably evident and whose glory shines transcendently bright in the visible heavens, the structure and beauty of them, and the order and influence of the heavenly bodies. This instance of the divine power serves not only to show the folly of atheists, who see there is a heaven and yet say, "There is no God," who see the effect and yet say, "There is no cause," but to show the folly of idolaters also, and the vanity of their imagination, who, though the heavens declare the glory of God, yet gave that glory to the lights of heaven which those very lights directed them to give to God only, the Father of lights. Now observe here,

1. What that is which the creatures notify to us. They are in many ways useful and serviceable to us, but in nothing so much as in this, that they declare the glory of God, by showing his handy-works, *v.* 1. They plainly speak themselves to be God's handy-works; for they could not exist from eternity; all succession and motion must have had a beginning; they could not make themselves, that is a contradiction; they could not be produced by a casual hit of atoms, that is an absurdity, fit rather to be bantered than reasoned with: therefore they must have a Creator, who can be no other than an eternal mind, infinitely wise, powerful, and good. Thus it appears they are God's works, the *works of his fingers* (Ps. 8:3), and therefore they declare his glory. From the excellency of the work we may easily infer the infinite perfection of its great author. From the brightness of the heavens we may collect that the Creator is light; their vastness of extent bespeaks his immensity;, their height his transcendency and sovereignty, their influence upon this earth his dominion, and providence, and universal beneficence: and all declare his almighty power, by which they were at first made, and continue to this day according to the ordinances that were then settled.

II. What are some of those things which notify this? 1. The heavens and the firmament — the vast expanse of air and ether, and the spheres of the planets and fixed stars. Man has this advantage above the beasts, in the structure of his body, that whereas they are made to look downwards, as their spirits must go, he is made erect, to look upwards, because upwards his spirit must shortly go and his thoughts should now rise. 2. The constant and regular succession of day and night (*v.* 2): *Day unto day, and night unto night,* speak the glory of that God who first divided between the light and the darkness, and has, from the beginning to this day, preserved that established order without variation, according to God's covenant with Noah (Gen. 8:22), that, *while the earth remains, day and night shall not cease,* to which covenant of providence the covenant of grace is compared for its stability, Jer. 33:20; 31:35. The counterchanging of day and night, in so exact a method, is a great instance of the power of God, and calls us to observe that, as in the kingdom of nature, so in that of providence, *he forms the light and creates the darkness* (Isa. 45:7), and sets the one over-against the other. It is likewise an instance of his goodness to man; for he *makes the out-goings of the morning and evening to rejoice,* Ps. 65:8. He not only glorifies himself, but gratifies us, by this constant revolution; for as the light of the morning befriends the business of the day, so the shadows of the evening befriend the repose of the night; every day and every night speak the goodness of God, and, when they have finished their testimony, leave it to the next day, to the next night, to stay the same. 3. The light and influence of the sun do, in a special manner, declare the glory of God; for of all the heavenly bodies that is the most conspicuous in itself and most useful to this lower world, which would be all dungeon, and all desert, without it. It is not an improbable conjecture that David penned this psalm when he had the rising sun in view, and from the brightness of it took occasion to declare the glory of God. Concerning the sun observe here, (1.) The place appointed him. In the heavens God has *set a tabernacle for the sun.* The heavenly bodies are called *hosts of heaven,* and therefore are fitly said to *dwell in tents,* as soldiers in their encampments. The sun is said to have a tabernacle set him, no only because he is in continual motion and never has a fixed residence, but because the mansion he has will, at the end of time, be taken down like a tent, when the heavens shall be rolled together like a scroll and the sun shall be turned to darkness. (2.) The course assigned him. That glorious creature was not made to be idle, but *his going forth* (at least as it appears to our eye) *is from one point of the heavens, and his circuit* thence to the opposite point, and thence (to complete his diurnal revolution) to the same point again; and this with such steadiness and constancy that we can certainly foretel the hour and the minute at which the sun will rise at such a place, any day to come. (3.) The brightness wherein he appears. He is *as a bridegroom coming out of his chamber,* richly dressed and adorned, as fine as hands can make him, looking pleasantly himself and making all about him pleasant; for *the friend of the bridegroom rejoices greatly to hear the bridegroom's voice,* Jn. 3:29. (4.) The cheerfulness wherewith he makes this tour. Though it seems a vast round which he has to walk, and he has not a moment's rest, yet in obedience to the law of this creation, and for the service of man, he not only does it, but does it with a great deal of pleasure and *rejoices as a strong man to run a race.* With such satisfaction did Christ, the Sun of righteousness, finish the work that was given him to do. (5.) His universal influence on this earth: *There is nothing hidden from the heart thereof,* no, not metals in the bowels of the earth, which the sun has an influence upon.

III. To whom this declaration is made of the glory of God. It is made to all parts of the world (*v.* 3, 4): *There is no speech nor language* (no nation, for the nations were divided *after their tongues,* Gen. 10:31, 32) *where their voice is not heard. Their line has gone through all the earth* (the equinoctial line, suppose) *and* with it *their words to the end of the world,* proclaiming the eternal power of God of nature, *v.* 4. The apostle uses this as a reason why the Jews should not be angry with him and others for preaching the gospel to the Gentiles, because God had already made himself known to the Gentile world by the works of creation, and left not himself without witness among them (Rom. 10:18), so that they were without excuse if they were idolaters, Rom. 1:20, 21. And those were without blame, who, by preaching the gospel to them, endeavoured to turn them from their idolatry. If God used these means to prevent their apostasy, and they proved ineffectual, the apostles did well to use other means to recover them from it. *They have no speech or language* (so some read it) *and yet their voice is heard.* All people may hear these natural immortal preachers speak to them in their own tongue the wonderful works of God.

In singing these verses we must give God the glory of all the comfort and benefit we have by the lights of the heaven, still looking above and beyond them to the Sun of righteousness.

Verses 7–14

God's glory, (that is, his goodness to man) appears much in the works of creation, but much more in and by divine revelation. The holy scripture, as it is a rule both of our duty to God and of our expectation from him, is of much greater use and benefit to us than day or night, than the air we breathe in, or the light of the sun. The discoveries made of God by his works might have served if man had retained his integrity; but, to recover him out of his fallen state, another course must be taken; that must be done by the word of God. And here,

1. The psalmist gives an account of the excellent properties and uses of the word of God, in six sentences (*v.* 7–9), in each of which the name *Jehovah* is repeated, and no vain repetition, for the law has its authority and all its excellency from the law-maker. Here are six several titles of the word of God, to take in the whole of divine revelation, precepts and promises, and especially the gospel. Here are several good properties of it, which proves its divine original, which recommend it to our affection, and which extol it above all other laws whatsoever. Here are several good effects of the law upon the minds of men, which show what it is designed for, what use we are to make of it, and how wonderful the efficacy of divine grace is, going along with it, and working by it. 1. *The law of the Lord is perfect.* It is perfectly free from all corruption, perfectly filled with all good, and perfectly fitted for the end for which it is designed; and it will make the man of God perfect, 2 Tim. 3:17. Nothing is to be added to it nor taken from it. It is of use to *convert the soul,* to bring us back to ourselves, to our God, to our duty; for it shows us our sinfulness and misery in our departures from God and the indispensable necessity of our return to him. 2. *The testimony of the Lord* (which witnesses for him to us) *is sure,* incontestably and inviolably sure, what we may give credit to, may rely upon, and may be confident it will not deceive us. It is a sure discovery of the divine truth, a sure direction in the way of duty. It is a sure foundation of living comforts and a sure foundation of lasting hopes. It is of use to make us wise, wise to salvation, 2 Tim. 3:15. It will give us an insight into things divine and a foresight of things to come. It will employ us in the best work and secure to us our true interests. It will make even *the simple* (poor contrivers as they may be for the present world) wise for their souls and eternity. Those that are humbly simple, sensible of their own folly and willing to be taught, shall be made wise by the word of God, Ps. 25:9. 3. *The statutes of the Lord* (enacted by his authority, and binding on all wherever they come) *are right,* exactly agreeing with the eternal rules and principles of good and evil, that is, with the right reason of man and the right counsels of God. All God's precepts, concerning all things, are right (Ps. 119:128), just as they should be; and they will set us to rights if we receive them and submit to them; and, because they are right, they *rejoice the heart.* The law, as we see it in the hands of Christ, gives cause for joy; and, when it is written in our hearts, it lays a foundation for everlasting joy, by restoring us to our right mind. 4. *The commandment of the Lord is pure;* it is clear, without darkness; it is clean, without dross and defilement. It is itself purified from all alloy, and is purifying to those that receive and embrace it. It is the ordinary means which the Spirit uses in *enlightening the eyes;* it brings us to a sight and sense of our sin and misery, and directs us in the way of duty. 5. *The fear of the Lord* (true religion and godliness prescribed in the word, reigning in the heart, and practised in the life) *is clean,* clean itself, and will make us clean (Jn. 15:3); it will cleanse our way, Ps. 119:9. And it *endureth for ever;* it is of perpetual obligation and can never be repealed. The ceremonial law is long since done away, but the law concerning the fear of God is ever the same. Time will not alter the nature of moral good and evil. 6. *The judgments of the Lord* (all his precepts, which are framed in infinite wisdom) *are true;* they are grounded upon the most sacred and unquestionable truths; they are *righteous,* all consonant to natural equity; and they are so *altogether:* there is no unrighteousness in any of them, but they are all of a piece.

II. He expresses the great value he had for the word of God, and the great advantage he had, and hoped to have, from it, *v.* 10, 11.

1. See how highly he prized the commandments of God. It is the character of all good people that they prefer their religion and the word of God, (1.) Far before all the wealth of the world. It is *more desirable than gold,* than fine gold, *than much fine gold.* Gold is of the earth, earthly; but grace is the image of the heavenly. Gold is only for the body and the concerns of time; but grace is for the soul and the concerns of eternity. (2.) Far before all pleasures and delights of sense. The word of God, received by faith, is sweet to the soul, *sweeter than honey and the honey comb.* The pleasures of sense are the delight of brutes, and therefore debase the great soul of man; the pleasures of religion are the delight of angels, and exalt the soul. The pleasures of sense are deceitful, will soon surfeit, and yet never satisfy; but those of religion are substantial and satisfying, and there is no danger of exceeding in them.

2. See what use he made of the precepts of God's word: *By them is thy servant warned.* The word of God is a word of warning to the children of men; it warns us of the duty we are to do, the dangers we are to avoid, and the deluge we are to prepare for, Eze. 3:17; 33:7. It warns the wicked not to go on in his wicked way, and warns the righteous not to turn from his good way. All that are indeed God's servants take this warning.

3. See what advantage he promised himself by his obedience to God's precepts: *In keeping them there is great reward.* Those who make conscience of their duty will not only be no losers by it, but unspeakable gainers. There is a reward, not only after keeping, but in keeping, God's commandments, a present great reward of obedience. Religion is health and honour; it is peace and pleasure; it will make our comforts sweet and our crosses easy, life truly valuable and death itself truly desirable.

III. He draws some good inferences from this pious meditation upon the excellency of the word of God. Such thoughts as these should excite in us devout affections, and they are to good purpose.

1. He takes occasion hence to make a penitent reflection upon his sins; for *by the law is the knowledge of sin.* "Is the commandment thus holy, just, and good? Then *who can understand his errors?* I cannot, whoever can." From the rectitude of the divine law he learns to call his sins his *errors.* If the commandment be true and righteous, every transgressions of the commandment is an error, as grounded upon a mistake; every wicked practice takes rise from some corrupt principle; it is a deviation from the rule we are to work by, the way we are to walk in. From the extent, the strictness, and spiritual nature, of the divine law he learns that his sins are so many that he cannot understand the number of them, and so exceedingly sinful that he cannot understand the heinousness and malignity of them. We are guilty of many sins which, through our carelessness and partiality to ourselves, we are not aware of; many we have been guilty of which we have forgotten; so that, when we have been ever so particular in the confession of sin, we must conclude with an *et cetera — and such like;* for God knows a great deal more evil of us than we do of ourselves. In many things we all offend, and who can tell how often he offends? It is well that we are under grace, and not under the law, else we were undone.

2. He takes occasion hence to pray against sin. All the discoveries of sin made to us by the law should drive us to the throne of grace, there to pray, as David does here, (1.) For mercy to pardon. Finding himself unable to specify all the particulars of his transgressions, he cries out, *Lord, cleanse me from my secret faults;* not secret to God, so none are, nor only such as were secret to the world, but such as were hidden from his own observation of himself. The best of men have reason to suspect themselves guilty of many secret faults, and to pray to God to cleanse them from that guilt and not to lay it to their charge; for even our sins of infirmity and inadvertency, and our secret sins, would be our ruin if God should deal with us according to the desert of them. Even secret faults are defiling, and render us unfit for communion with God; but, when they are pardoned, we are cleansed from them, 1 Jn. 1:7. (2.) For grace to help in time of need. Having prayed that his sins of infirmity might be pardoned, he prays that presumptuous sins might be prevented, *v.* 13. All that truly repent of their sins, and have them pardoned, are in care not to relapse into sin, nor to return again to folly, as appears by their prayers, which concur with David's here, where observe, [1.] His petition: "Keep me from ever being guilty of a wilful presumptuous sin." We ought to pray that we may be kept from sins of infirmity, but especially from presumptuous sins, which most offend God and wound conscience, which wither our comforts and shock our hopes. "However, let none such *have dominion over me,* let me not be at the command of any such sin, nor be enslaved by it." [2.] His plea: *"So shall I be upright;* I shall appear upright; I shall preserve the evidence and comfort of my uprightness; and I *shall be innocent from the great transgression;"* so he calls a presumptuous sin, because no sacrifice was accepted for it, Num. 15:28–30. Note, *First,* Presumptuous sins are very heinous and dangerous. those that sin against the habitual convictions and actual admonitions of their consciences, in contempt and defiance of the law and its sanctions, that sin with a high hand, sin presumptuously, and it is a great transgression. *Secondly,* Even good men ought to be jealous of themselves, and afraid of sinning presumptuously, yea, though through the grace of God they have hitherto been kept from them. Let none be high-minded, but fear. *Thirdly,* Being so much exposed, we have great need to pray to God, when we are pushing forward towards a presumptuous sin, to keep us back from it, either by his providence preventing the temptation or by his grace giving us victory over it.

3. He takes occasion humbly to beg the divine acceptance of those his pious thoughts and affections, *v.* 14. Observe the connexion of this with what goes before. He prays to God to keep him from sin, and then begs he would accept his performances; for, if we favour our sins, we cannot expect God should favour us or our services, Ps. 66:18. Observe, (1.) What his services were — the *words of his mouth and the meditations of his heart,* his holy affections offered up to God. The pious meditations of the heart must not be smothered, but expressed in the words of our mouth, for God's glory and the edification of others; and the words of our mouth in prayer and praise must not be formal, but arising from the meditation of the heart, Ps. 45:1. (2.) What was his care concerning these services — that they might be acceptable with God; for, if our services be not acceptable to God, what do they avail us? Gracious souls must have all they aim at if they be accepted of God, for that is their bliss. (3.) What encouragement he had to hope for this, because God was his strength and his redeemer. If we seek assistance from God as our strength in our religious duties, we may hope to find acceptance with God in the discharge of our duties; for by his strength we have power with him.

In singing this we should get our hearts much affected with the excellency of the word of God and delivered into it, we should be much affected with the evil of sin, the danger we are in of it and the danger we are in by it, and we should fetch in help from heaven against it.

PSALM 20

It is the will of God that prayers, intercessions, and thanksgivings, should be made, in special manner, for kings and all in authority. This psalm is a prayer, and the next a thanksgiving, for the king. David was a martial prince, much in war. Either this psalm was penned upon occasion of some particular expedition of his, or, in general, as a form to be used in the daily service of the church for him. In this psalm we may observe, I. What it is they beg of God for the king (*v.* 1–4). II. With what assurance they beg it. The people triumph (*v.* 5), the prince (*v.* 6), both together (*v.* 7, 8), and so he concludes with a prayer to God for audience (*v.* 9). In this, David may well be looked upon as a type of Christ, to whose kingdom and its interests among men the church was, in every age, a hearty well-wisher.

To the chief musician. A psalm of David.

Verses 1–5

This prayer for David is entitled *a psalm of David;* nor was it any absurdity at all for him who was divinely inspired to draw up a directory, or form of prayer, to be used in the congregation for himself and those in authority under him; nay it is very proper for those who desire the prayers of their friends to tell them particularly what they would have to be asked of God for them. Note, Even great and good men, and those that know ever so well how to pray for themselves, must not despise, but earnestly desire, the prayers of others for them, even those that are their inferiors in all respects. Paul often begged of his friends to pray for him. Magistrates and those in power ought to esteem and encourage praying people, to reckon them their strength (Zec. 12:5, 10), and to do what they can for them, that they may have an interest in their prayers and may do nothing to forfeit it. Now observe here,

I. What it is that they are taught to ask of God for the king.

1. That God would answer his prayers: *The Lord hear thee in the day of trouble* (*v.* 1), and *the Lord fulfil all thy petitions, v.* 5. Note, (1.) Even the greatest of men may be much in trouble. It was often a day of trouble with David himself, of disappointment and distress, of treading down and of perplexity. Neither the crown on his head nor the grace in his heart would exempt him from the trouble. (2.) Even the greatest of men must be much in prayer. David, though a man of business, a man of war, was constant to his devotions; though he had prophets, and priests, and many good people among his subjects, to pray for him, he did not think that excused him from praying for himself. Let none expect benefit by the prayers of the church, or of their ministers or friends for them, who are capable of praying for themselves, and yet neglect it. The prayers of others for us must be desired, not to supersede, but to second, our own for ourselves. Happy the people that have praying princes, to whose prayers they may thus say, *Amen.*

2. That God would protect his person, and preserve his life, in the perils of war: *"The name of the God of Jacob defend thee,* and set thee out of the reach of thy enemies." (1.) "Let God by his providence keep thee safe, even the God who preserved Jacob in the days of his trouble." David had mighty men for his guards, but he commits himself, and his people commit him, to the care of the almighty God. (2.) "Let God by his grace keep thee easy from the fear of evil. — Prov. 18:10, *The name of the Lord is a strong tower, into which the righteous run* by faith, *and are safe;* let David be enabled to shelter himself in that strong tower, as he has done many a time."

3. That God would enable him to go on in his undertakings for the public good — that, in the day of battle, he would *send him help out of the sanctuary, and strength out of Zion,* not from common providence, but from the ark of the covenant and the peculiar favour God bears to his chosen people Israel. That he would help him, in performance of the promises and in answer to the prayers made in the sanctuary. Mercies out of the sanctuary are the sweetest mercies, such as are the tokens of God's peculiar love, the blessing of God, even our own God. Strength out of Zion is spiritual strength, strength in the soul, in the inward man, and that is what we should most desire both for ourselves and others in services and sufferings.

4. That God would testify his gracious acceptance of the sacrifices he offered with his prayers, according to the law of that time, before he went out on a dangerous expedition: *The Lord remember all thy offerings and accept thy burnt-sacrifices* (*v.* 3), or *turn them to ashes;* that is, "The Lord give thee the victory and success which thou didst by prayer with sacrifices ask of him, and thereby give as full proof of his acceptance of the sacrifice as ever he did by kindling it with fire from heaven." By this we may now know that God accepts our spiritual sacrifices, if by his Spirit he kindles in our souls a holy fire of pious and divine affection and with that makes our hearts burn within us.

5. That God would crown all his enterprises and noble designs for the public welfare with the desired success (*v.* 4): *The Lord grant thee according to thy own heart.* This they might in faith pray for, because they knew David was a man after God's own heart, and would design nothing but what was pleasing to him. Those who make it their business to glorify God may expect that God will, in one way or other, gratify them: and those who walk in his counsel may promise themselves that he will fulfil theirs. *Thou shalt devise a thing and it shall be established unto thee.*

II. What confidence they had of an answer of peace to these petitions for themselves and their good king (*v.* 5): *"We will rejoice in thy salvation.* We that are subjects will rejoice in the preservation and prosperity of our prince;" or, rather, "In thy salvation, O God! in thy power and promise to save, will we rejoice; that is it which we depend upon now, and which, in the issue, we shall have occasion greatly to rejoice in." Those that have their eye still upon the salvation of the Lord shall have their hearts filled with the joy of that salvation: *In the name of our God will we set up our banners.* 1. "We will wage war in his name; we will see that our cause be good and make his glory our end in every expedition; we will ask counsel at his mouth, and take him along with us; we will follow his direction, implore his aid and depend upon it, and refer the issue to him." David went against Goliath in the name of the Lord of hosts, 1 Sa. 17:45. (2.) "We will celebrate our victories in his name. When we lift up our banners in triumph, and set up our trophies, it shall be in the name of our God; he shall have all the glory of our success, and no instrument shall have any part of the honour that is due to him."

In singing this we ought to offer up to God our hearty good wishes to the good government we are under and to the prosperity of it. But we may look further; these prayers for David are prophecies concerning Christ the Son of David, and in him they were abundantly answered; he undertook the work of our redemption, and made war upon the powers of darkness. In the day of trouble, when his soul was exceedingly sorrowful, the Lord heard him, heard him in that he feared (Heb. 5:7), *sent him help out of the sanctuary,* sent an angel from heaven to strengthen him, took cognizance of his offering when he made his soul an offering for sin, and accepted his burnt-sacrifice, turned it to ashes, the fire that should have fastened upon the sinner fastening upon the sacrifice, with which God was well pleased. And he granted him according to his own heart, made him to see of the travail of his soul, to his satisfaction, prospered his good pleasure in his hand, fulfilled all his petitions for himself and us; for him the Father heareth always and his intercession is ever prevailing.

Verses 6–9

Here is, I. Holy David himself triumphing in the interest he had in the prayers of good people (*v.* 6): *"Now know I* (I that pen the psalm know it) *that the Lord saveth his anointed,* because he hath stirred up the hearts of the seed of Jacob to pray for him." Note, It bodes well to any prince and people, and may justly be taken as a happy presage, when God pours upon them a spirit of prayer. If he see us seeking him, he will be found of us; if he cause us to hope in his word, he will establish his word to us. Now that so many who have an interest in heaven are praying for him he doubts not but that God will hear him, and grant him an answer of peace, which will, 1. Take its rise from above: *He will hear him from his holy heaven,* of which the sanctuary was a type (Heb. 9:23), from the throne he hath prepared in heaven, of which the mercy-seat was a type. 2. It shall take its effect here below: He will hear him *with the saving strength of his right hand;* he will give a real answer to his prayers, and the prayers of his friends for him, not by letter, nor by word of mouth, but, which is much better, by his right hand, by the saving strength of his right hand. He will make it to appear that he hears him by what he does for him.

II. His people triumphing in God and their relation to him, and his revelation of himself to them, by which they distinguish themselves from those that live without God in the world. 1. See the difference between worldly people and godly people, in their confidences, *v.* 7. The children of this world trust in second causes, and think all is well if those do but smile upon them; they trust *in chariots and in horses,* and the more of them they can bring into the field the more sure they are of success in their wars; probably David has here an eye to the Syrians, whose forces consisted much of chariots and horsemen, as we find in the history of David's victories over them, 2 Sa. 8:4; 10:18. "But," say the Israelites, "we neither have chariots and horses to trust to nor do we want them, nor, if we had them, would we build our hopes of success upon that; *but we will remember,* and rely upon, *the name of the Lord our God,* upon the relation we stand in to him as the Lord our God and the knowledge we have of him by his name," that is, all that whereby he makes himself known; this we will remember and upon every remembrance of it will be encouraged. Note, those who make God and his name their praise may make God and his name their trust. 2. See the difference in the issue of their confidences and by that we are to judge of the wisdom of the choice; things are as they prove; see who will be ashamed of their confidence and who not, *v.* 8. "Those that trusted in their chariots and horses are brought down and fallen, and their chariots and horses were so far from saving them that they helped to sink them, and made them the easier and the richer prey to the conqueror, 2 Sa. 8:4. But we that trust in the name of the Lord our God not only stand upright, and keep our ground, but have risen, and have got ground against the enemy, and have triumphed over them." Note, A believing obedient trust in God and his name is the surest way both to preferment and to establishment, to rise and to stand upright, and this will stand us in stead when creature-confidences fail those that depend upon them.

III. They conclude their prayer for the king with a *Hosanna, "Save, now, we beseech thee,* O Lord!" *v.* 9. As we read this verse, it may be taken as a prayer that God would not only bless the king, "Save, Lord, give him success," but that he would make him a blessing to them, *"Let the king hear us* when we call to him for justice and mercy." Those that would have good of their magistrates must thus pray for them, for they, as all other creatures, are that to us (and no more) which God makes them to be. Or it may refer to the Messiah, that King, that King of kings; let him hear us when we call; let him come to us according to the promise, in the time appointed; let him, as the great Master of requests, receive all our petitions and present them to the Father. But many interpreters give another reading of this verse, by altering the pause, *Lord, save the king, and hear us when we call;* and so it is a summary of the whole psalm and is taken into our English Liturgy; *O Lord! save the king, and mercifully hear us when we call upon thee.*

In singing these verses we should encourage ourselves to trust in God, and stir up ourselves to pray earnestly, as we are in duty bound, for those in authority over us, that under them we may lead quiet and peaceable lives in all godliness and honesty.

PSALM 21

As the foregoing psalm was a prayer for the king that God would protect and prosper him, so this is a thanksgiving for the success God had blessed him with. Those whom we have prayed for we ought to give thanks for, and particularly for kings, in whose prosperity we share. They are here taught, I. To congratulate him on his victories, and the honour he had achieved (*v.* 1–6). II. To confide in the power of God for the completing of the ruin of the enemies of his kingdom (*v.* 7–13). In this there is an eye to Messiah the Prince, and the glory of his kingdom; for to him divers passages in this psalm are more applicable than to David himself.

To the chief musician. A psalm of David.

Verses 1–6

David here speaks for himself in the first place, professing that his joy was in God's strength and in his salvation, and not in the strength or success of his armies. He also directs his subjects herein to rejoice with him, and to give God all the glory of the victories he had obtained; and all with an eye to Christ, of whose triumphs over the powers of darkness David's victories were but shadows. 1. They here congratulate the king on his joys and concur with him in them (v. 1): *"The king rejoices,* he uses to rejoice *in thy strength,* and so do we; what pleases the king pleases us," 2 Sa. 3:36. Happy the people the character of whose king it is that he makes God's strength his confidence and God's salvation his joy, that is pleased with all the advancements of God's kingdom and trusts God to bear him out in all he does for the service of it. Our Lord Jesus, in his great undertaking, relied upon help from heaven, and pleased himself with the prospect of that great salvation which he was thereby to work out. 2. They gave God all the praise of those things which were the matter of their king's rejoicing. (1.) That God had heard his prayers (v. 2): *Thou hast given him his heart's desire* (and there is no prayer accepted but what is the heart's desire), the very thing they begged of God for him, Ps. 20:4. Note, God's gracious returns of prayer do, in a special manner, require our humble returns of praise. When God gives to Christ the heathen for his inheritance, gives him to see his seed, and accepts his intercession for all believers, he give him his heart's desire. (2.) That God had surprised him with favours, and much outdone his expectations (v. 3): *Thou preventest him with the blessings of goodness.* All our blessings are blessings of goodness, and are owing, not at all to any merit of ours, but purely and only to God's goodness. But the psalmist here reckons it in a special manner obliging that these blessings were given in a preventing way; this fixed his eye, enlarged his soul, and endeared his God, as one expresses it. When God's blessings come sooner and prove richer than we imagine, when they are given before we prayed for them, before we were ready for them, nay, when we feared the contrary, then it may be truly said that he prevented us with them. Nothing indeed prevented Christ, but to mankind never was any favour more preventing than our redemption by Christ and all the blessed fruits of his mediation. (3.) That God had advanced him to the highest honour and the most extensive power: *"Thou hast set a crown of pure gold upon his head* and kept it there, when his enemies attempted to throw it off." Note, Crowns are at God's disposal; no head wears them but God sets them there, whether in judgment to his land or for mercy the event will show. On the head of Christ God never set a crown of gold, but of thorns first, and then of glory. (4.) That God had assured him of the perpetuity of his kingdom, and therein had done more for him than he was able either to ask or think (v. 4): "When he went forth upon a perilous expedition *he asked* his *life of thee,* which he then put into his hand, *and thou* not only *gavest him that,* but withal gavest him *length of days for ever and ever,* didst not only prolong his life far beyond his expectation, but didst assure him of a blessed immortality in a future state and of the continuance of his kingdom in the Messiah that should come of his loins." See how God's grants often exceed our petitions and hopes, and infer thence how rich he is in mercy to those that call upon him. See also and rejoice in the length of the days of Christ's kingdom. He was dead, indeed, that we might live through him; but he is alive, and lives for evermore, and *of the increase of his government and peace there shall be no end;* and because he thus lives we shall thus live also. (5.) That God had advanced him to the highest honour and dignity (v. 5): *"His glory is great,* far transcending that of all the neighbouring princes, in the salvation thou hast wrought for him and by him." The glory which every good man is ambitious of is to see the salvation of the Lord. *Honour and majesty hast thou laid upon him,* as a burden which he must bear, as a charge which he must account for. Jesus Christ *received from God the Father honour and glory* (2 Pt. 1. 17), the glory which he had with him before the worlds were, Jn. 17:5. And on him is laid the charge of universal government and to him all power in heaven and earth is committed. (6.) That God had given him the satisfaction of being the channel of all bliss to mankind (v. 6): *"Thou hast set him to be blessings for ever"* (so the margin reads it), "thou hast made him to be a universal blessing to the world, in whom the families of the earth are, and shall be blessed; and so thou hast made him exceedingly glad with the countenance thou hast given to his undertaking and to him in the prosecution of it." See how the spirit of prophecy gradually rises here to that which is peculiar to Christ, for none besides is blessed for

ever, much less a blessing for ever to that eminency that the expression denotes: and of him it is said that God made him full of joy with his countenance.

In singing this we should rejoice in his joy and triumph in his exaltation.

Verses 7–13

The psalmist, having taught his people to look back with joy and praise on what God had done for him and them, here teaches them to look forward with faith, and hope, and prayer, upon what God would further do for them: *The king rejoices in God* (v. 1), and therefore we will be thankful; *the king trusteth in God* (v. 7), therefore will we be encouraged. The joy and confidence of Christ our King is the ground of all our joy and confidence.

I. They are confident of the stability of David's kingdom. *Through the mercy of the Most High,* and not through his own merit or strength, *he shall not be moved.* His prosperous state shall not be disturbed; his faith and hope in God, which are the stay of his spirit, shall not be shaken. The mercy of the Most High (the divine goodness, power, and dominion) is enough to secure our happiness, and therefore our trust in that mercy should be enough to silence all our fears. God being at Christ's right hand in his sufferings (Ps. 16:8) and he being at God's right hand in his glory, we may be sure he shall not, he cannot, be moved, but continues ever.

II. They are confident of the destruction of all the impenitent implacable enemies of David's kingdom. The success with which God had blessed David's arms hitherto was an earnest of the rest which God would give him from all his enemies round about, and a type of the total overthrow of all Christ's enemies who would not have him to reign over them. Observe, 1. The description of his enemies. They are such as hate him, v. 8. They hated David because God had set him apart for himself, hated Christ because they hated the light; but both were hated without any just cause, and in both God was hated, Jn. 15:23, 25. 2. The designs of his enemies (v. 11): *They intended evil against thee, and imagined a mischievous device;* they pretended to fight against David only, but their enmity was against God himself. Those that aimed to un-king David aimed, in effect, to un-God Jehovah. What is devised and designed against religion, and against the instruments God raises up to support and advance it, is very evil and mischievous, and God takes it as devised and designed against himself and will so reckon for it. (3.) The disappointment of them: "They devise what they are *not able to perform,"* v. 11. Their malice is impotent, and they *imagine a vain thing,* Ps. 2:1. (4.) The discovery of them (v. 8): *"Thy hand shall find them out.* Though ever so artfully disguised by the pretences and professions of friendship, though mingled with the faithful subjects of this kingdom and hardly to be distinguished from them, though flying from justice and absconding in their close places, yet thy hand shall find them out wherever they are." There is no escaping God's avenging eye, no going out of the reach of his hand; rocks and mountains will be no better shelter at last than fig-leaves were at first. (5.) The destruction of them; it will be an utter destruction (Lu. 19:27); they shall be swallowed up and devoured, v. 9. Hell, the portion of all Christ's enemies, is the complete misery both of body and soul. *Their fruit and their seed shall be destroyed,* v. 10. The enemies of God's kingdom, in every age, shall fall under the same doom, and the whole generation of them will at last be rooted out, and all opposing rule, principality, and power, shall be put down. The arrows of God's wrath shall confound them and put them to flight, being levelled at the face of them, v. 12. That will be the lot of daring enemies that face God. The fire of God's wrath will consume them (v. 9); they shall not only be cast into a furnace of fire (Mt. 13:42), but he shall make them themselves as a fiery oven or furnace; they shall be their own tormentors; the reflections and terrors of their own consciences will be their hell. Those that might have had Christ to rule and save them, but rejected him and fought against him, shall find that even the remembrance of that will be enough to make them, to eternity, a fiery oven to themselves: it is the worm that dies not.

III. In this confidence they beg of God that he would still appear for his anointed (v. 13), that he would act for him in his own strength, by the immediate operations of

his power as Lord of hosts and Father of spirits, making little use of means and instruments. And, 1. Hereby he would exalt himself and glorify his own name. "We have but little strength, and are not so active for thee as we should be, which is our shame; Lord, take the work into thy own hands, do it, without us, and it will be thy glory." 2. Hereupon they would exalt him: *"So will we sing, and praise thy power,* the more triumphantly." The less God has of our service when a deliverance is in the working the more he must have of our praises when it is wrought without us.

PSALM 22

The Spirit of Christ, which was in the prophets, testifies in this psalm, as clearly and fully as any where in all the Old Testament, "the sufferings of Christ and the glory that should follow" (1 Pt. 1:11); of him, no doubt, David here speaks, and not of himself, or any other man. Much of it is expressly applied to Christ in the New Testament, all of it may be applied to him, and some of it must be understood of him only. The providences of God concerning David were so very extraordinary that we may suppose there were some wise and good men who then could not but look upon him as a figure of him that was to come. But the composition of his psalms especially, in which he found himself wonderfully carried out by the spirit of prophecy far beyond his own thought and intention, was (we may suppose) an abundant satisfaction to himself that he was not only a father of the Messiah, but a figure of him. In this psalm he speaks, I. Of the humiliation of Christ (v. 1–21), where David, as a type of Christ, complains of the very calamitous condition he was in upon many accounts. 1. He complains, and mixes comforts with his complaints; he complains (v. 1, 2), but comforts himself (v. 3–5), complains again (v. 6–8), but comforts himself again, (v. 9, 10). 2. He complains, and mixes prayers with his complaints; he complains of the power and rage of his enemies (v. 12, 13, 16, 18), of his own bodily weakness and decay (v. 14, 15, 17); but prays that God would not be far from him (v. 11, 19), that he would save and deliver him (v. 19–21). II. Of the exaltation of Christ, that his undertaking should be for the glory of God (v. 22–25), for the salvation and joy of his people (v. 26–29), and for the perpetuating of his own kingdom (v. 30, 31). In singing this psalm we must keep our thoughts fixed upon Christ, and be so affected with his sufferings as to experience the fellowship of them, and so affected with his grace as to experience the power and influence of it.

To the chief musician upon Aijeleth Shahar.
A psalm of David.

Verses 1–10

Some think they find Christ in the title of this psalm, upon *Aijeleth Shahar — The hind of the morning.* Christ is as the swift hind upon the mountains of spices (Cant. 8:14), as the loving hind and the pleasant roe, to all believers (Prov. 5:19); he giveth goodly words like Naphtali, who is compared to a *hind let loose,* Gen. 49:21. He is the hind of the morning, marked out by the counsels of God from eternity, to be run down by those dogs that compassed him, v. 16. But others think it denotes only the tune to which the psalm was set. In these verses we have,

I. A sad complaint of God's withdrawings, v. 1, 2.

1. This may be applied to David, or any other child of God, in the want of the tokens of his favour, pressed with the burden of his displeasure, roaring under it, as one overwhelmed with grief and terror, crying earnestly for relief, and, in this case, apprehending himself forsaken of God, unhelped, unheard, yet calling him, again and again, *"My God,"* and continuing to cry day and night to him and earnestly desiring his gracious returns. Note, (1.) Spiritual desertions are the saints' sorest afflictions; when their evidences are clouded, divine consolations suspended, their communion with God interrupted, and the terrors of God set in array against them, how sad are their spirits, and how sapless all their comforts! (2.) Even their complaint of these burdens is a good sign of spiritual life and spiritual senses exercised. To cry out, "My God, why am I sick? Why am I poor?" would give cause to suspect discontent and worldliness. But, *Why has though forsaken me?* is the language of a heart binding up its happiness in God's favour. (3.) When we are lamenting God's withdrawings, yet still we must call him our God, and continue to call upon him as ours. When we want the faith of assurance we must live by a faith of adherence. "However it be, yet God is good, and he is mine; *though he slay me, yet I trust in him;* though he do not answer me immediately, I will continue praying and waiting; though he be silent, I will not be silent."

2. But is must be applied to Christ: for, in the first words of this complaint, he poured out his soul before God when he was upon the cross (Mt. 27:46); probably he proceeded to the following words, and, some think, repeated the

whole psalm, if not aloud (because they cavilled at the first words), yet to himself. Note, (1.) Christ, in his sufferings, cried earnestly to his Father for his favour and presence with him. He cried *in the day-time*, upon the cross, *and in the night-season*, when he was in agony in the garden. *He offered up strong crying and tears to him that was able to save him*, and with some fear too, Heb. 5:7. (2.) Yet God forsook him, was far from helping him, and did not hear him, and it was this that he complained of more than all his sufferings. God delivered him into the hands of his enemies; it was by his determinate counsel that he was crucified and slain, and he did not give in sensible comforts. But, Christ having made himself sin for us, in conformity thereunto the Father laid him under the present impressions of his wrath and displeasure against sin. *It pleased the Lord to bruise him and put him to grief*, Isa. 53:10. But even then he kept fast hold of his relation to his Father as his God, by whom he was now employed, whom he was now serving, and with whom he should shortly be glorified.

II. Encouragement taken, in reference hereunto, *v.* 3–5. Though God did not hear him, did not help him, yet, 1. He will think well of God: *"But thou art holy*, not unjust, untrue, nor unkind, in any of thy dispensations. Though thou dost not immediately come in to the relief of thy afflicted people, yet though lovest them, art true to thy covenant with them, and dost not countenance the iniquity of their persecutors, Hab. 1:13. And, as thou art infinitely pure and upright thyself, so thou delightest in the services of thy upright people: *Thou inhabitest the praises of Israel;* thou art pleased to manifest thy glory, and grace, and special presence with thy people, in the sanctuary, where they attend thee with their praises. There thou art always ready to receive their homage, and of the tabernacle of meeting thou hast said, *This is my rest for ever."* This bespeaks God's wonderful condescension to his faithful worshippers — (that, though he is attended with the praises of angels, yet he is pleased to inhabit the praises of Israel), and it may comfort us in all our complaints — that, though God seem, for a while, to turn a deaf ear to them, yet he is so well pleased with his people's praises that he will, in due time, give them cause to change their note: *Hope in God, for I shall yet praise him.* Our Lord Jesus, in his sufferings, had an eye to the holiness of God, to preserve and advance the honour of that, and of his grace in inhabiting the praises of Israel notwithstanding the iniquities of their holy things. 2. He will take comfort from the experiences which the saints in former ages had of the benefit of faith and prayer (*v.* 4, 5): *"Our fathers trusted in thee, cried unto thee, and thou didst deliver them;* therefore thou wilt, in due time, deliver me, for never any that hoped in thee were made ashamed of their hope, never any that sought thee sought thee in vain. And thou art still the same in thyself and the same to thy people that ever thou wast. They were our fathers, and thy people are *beloved for the fathers' sake,"* Rom. 11:28. The entail of the covenant is designed for the support of the seed of the faithful. He that was our fathers' God must be ours, and will therefore be ours. Our Lord Jesus, in his sufferings, supported himself with this — that all the fathers who were types of him in his sufferings, Noah, Joseph, David, Jonah, and others, were in due time delivered and were types of his exaltation too; therefore he knew that *he also should not be confounded*, Isa. 50:7.

III. The complaint renewed of another grievance, and that is the contempt and reproach of men. This complaint is by no means so bitter as that before of God's withdrawings; but, as that touches a gracious soul, so this a generous soul, in a very tender part, *v.* 6–8. Our fathers were honoured, the patriarchs in their day, first or last, appeared great in the eye of the world, Abraham, Moses, David; but Christ is *a worm, and no man.* It was great condescension that he became man, a step downwards, which is, and will be, the wonder of angels; yet, as if it were too much, too great, to be a man, he becomes a worm, and no man. He was *Adam — a mean man,* and *Enosh — a man of sorrows,* but *lo Ish — not a considerable man:* for he took upon him the form of a servant, and *his visage was marred more than any man's*, Isa. 52:14. Man, at the best, is a worm; but he became *a worm, and no man.* If he had not made himself a worm, he could not have been trampled

upon as he was. The word signifies such a worm as was used in dyeing scarlet or purple, whence some make it an allusion to his bloody sufferings. See what abuses were put upon him. 1. He was reproached as a bad man, as a blasphemer, a sabbath-breaker, a wine-bibber, a false prophet, an enemy to Caesar, a confederate with the prince of the devils. 2. He was despised of the people as a mean contemptible man, not worth taking notice of, his country in no repute, his relations poor mechanics, his followers none of the rulers, or the Pharisees, but the mob. 3. He was ridiculed as a foolish man, and one that not only deceived others, but himself too. Those that saw him hanging on the cross laughed him to scorn. So far were they from pitying him, or concerning themselves for him, that they added to his afflictions, with all the gestures and expressions of insolence upbraiding him with his fall. They make mouths at him, make merry over him, and make a jest of his sufferings: *They shoot out the lip, they shake their head,* saying, This was he that said *he trusted God would deliver him; now let him deliver him.* David was sometimes taunted for his confidence in God; but in the sufferings of Christ this was literally and exactly fulfilled. Those very gestures were used by those that reviled him (Mt. 27:39); they wagged their heads, nay, and so far did their malice make them forget themselves that they used the very words (*v.* 43), *He trusted in God; let him deliver him.* Our Lord Jesus, having undertaken to satisfy for the dishonour we had done to God by our sins, did it by submitting to the lowest possible instance of ignominy and disgrace.

IV. Encouragement taken as to this also (*v.* 9, 10): Men despise me, *but thou art he that took me out of the womb.* David and other good men have often, for direction to us, encouraged themselves with this, that God was not only the *God of their fathers,* as before (*v.* 4), but the God of their infancy, who began by times to take care of them, as soon as they had a being, and therefore, they hope, will never cast them off. He that did so well for us in that helpless useless state will not leave us when he has reared us and nursed us up into some capacity of serving him. See the early instances of God's providential care for us, 1. In the birth: *He took us also out of the womb,* else we had died there, or been stifled in the birth. Every man's particular time begins with this pregnant proof of God's providence, as time, in general, began with the creation, that pregnant proof of his being. 2. At the breast: *"Then didst thou make me hope;"* that is, "thou didst that for me, in providing sustenance for me and protecting me from the dangers to which I was exposed, which encourages me to hope in thee all my days." The blessings of the breasts, as they crown the blessings of the womb, so they are earnests of the blessings of our whole lives; surely he that fed us then will never starve us, Job 3:12. 3. In our early dedication to him: *I was cast upon thee from the womb,* which perhaps refers to his circumcision on the eighth day; he was then by his parents committed and given up to God as his God in covenant; for circumcision was a seal of the covenant; and this encouraged him to trust in God. Those have reason to think themselves safe who were so soon, so solemnly, *gathered under the wings of the divine majesty.* 4. In the experience we have had of God's goodness to us all along ever since, drawn out in a constant uninterrupted series of preservations and supplies: *Thou art my God,* providing me and watching over me for good, *from my mother's belly,* that is, from my coming into the world unto this day. And if, as soon as we became capable of exercising reason, we put our confidence in God and committed ourselves and our way to him, we need not doubt but he will always remember the *kindness of our youth and the love of our espousals,* Jer. 2:2. This is applicable to our Lord Jesus, over whose incarnation and birth the divine Providence watched with a peculiar care, when he was born in a stable, laid in a manger, and immediately exposed to the malice of Herod, and forced to flee into Egypt. *When he was a child God loved him and called him thence* (Hos. 11:1), and the remembrance of this comforted him in his sufferings. Men reproached him, and discouraged his confidence in God; but God had honoured him and encouraged his confidence in him.

Verses 11–21

In these verses we have Christ suffering and Christ pray-

ing, by which we are directed to look for crosses and to look up to God under them.

I. Here is Christ suffering. David indeed was often in trouble, and beset with enemies; but many of the particulars here specified are such as were never true of David, and therefore must be appropriated to Christ in the depth of his humiliation.

1. He is here deserted by his friends: *Trouble and distress are near,* and *there is none to help,* none to uphold, *v.* 11. He trod the wine-press alone; for all his disciples forsook him and fled. It is God's honour to help when all other helps and succours fail.

2. He is here insulted and surrounded by his enemies, such as were of a higher rank, who for their strength and fury, are compared to bulls, *strong bulls of Bashan* (*v.* 12), fat and fed to the full, haughty and sour; such were the chief priests and elders that persecuted Christ; and others of a lower rank, who are compared to dogs (*v.* 16), filthy and greedy, and unwearied in running him down. There was an assembly of the wicked plotting against him (*v.* 16); for the chief priests sat in council, to consult of ways and means to take Christ. These enemies were numerous and unanimous: "Many, and those of different and clashing interests among themselves, as Herod and Pilate, have agreed to compass me. They have carried their plot far, and seem to have gained their point, for they have *beset me round, v.* 12. They have enclosed me, *v.* 16. They are formidable and threatening (*v.* 13): *They gaped upon me with their mouths,* to show me that they would swallow me up; and this with as much strength and fierceness as a roaring ravening lion leaps upon his prey."

3. He is here crucified. The very manner of his death is described, though never in use among the Jews: *They pierced my hands and my feet* (*v.* 16), which were nailed to the accursed tree, and the whole body left so to hang, the effect of which must needs be the most exquisite pain and torture. There is no one passage in all the Old Testament which the Jews have so industriously corrupted as this, because it is such an eminent prediction of the death of Christ and was so exactly fulfilled.

4. He is here dying (*v.* 14, 15), dying in pain and anguish, because he was to satisfy for sin, which brought in pain, and for which we must otherwise have lain in everlasting anguish. Here is, (1.) The dissolution of the whole frame of his body: *I am poured out like water,* weak as water, and yielding to the power of death, emptying himself of all the supports of his human nature. (2.) The dislocation of his bones. Care was taken that not one of them should be broken (Jn. 19:36), but they were all out of joint by the violent stretching of his body upon the cross as upon a rack. Or it may denote the fear that seized him in his agony in the garden, when he began to be sore amazed, the effect of which perhaps was (as sometimes it has been of great fear, Dan. 5:6), that the *joints of his loins were loosed and his knees smote one against another.* His bones were put out of joint that he might put the whole creation into joint again, which sin had put out of joint, and might make our broken bones to rejoice. (3.) The colliquation of his spirits: *My heart is like wax,* melted to receive the impressions of God's wrath against the sins he undertook to satisfy for, melting away like the vitals of a dying man; and, as this satisfied for the hardness of our hearts, so the consideration of it should help to soften them. When Job speaks of his inward trouble he says, *The Almighty makes my heart soft,* Job 23:16, and see Ps. 58:2. (4.) The failing of his natural force: *My strength is dried up;* so that he became parched and brittle like a potsherd, the radical moisture being wasted by the fire of divine wrath preying upon his spirits. Who then can stand before God's anger? Or who knows the power of it? *If this was done in the green tree, what shall be done in the dry?* (5.) The clamminess of his mouth, a usual symptom of approaching death: *My tongue cleaveth to my jaws;* this was fulfilled both in his thirst upon the cross (Jn. 19:28) and in his silence under his sufferings; for, *as a sheep before the shearers is dumb, so he opened not his mouth,* nor objected against any thing done to him. (6.) His giving up the ghost: *"Thou hast brought me to the dust of death;* I am just ready to drop into the grave;" for nothing less would satisfy divine justice. The life of the sinner was forfeited, and therefore the life of the sacrifice must be the ransom for it. The sentence of death passed upon Adam was thus expressed: *Unto dust thou shalt return.* And

therefore Christ, having an eye to that sentence in his obedience to death, here uses a similar expression: *Thou hast brought me to the dust of death.*

5. He was stripped. The shame of nakedness was the immediate consequence of sin; and therefore our Lord Jesus was stripped of his clothes, when he was crucified, that he might clothe us with the robe of his righteousness, and that the shame of our nakedness might not appear. Now here we are told, (1.) How his body looked when it was thus stripped: *I may tell all my bones, v.* 17. His blessed body was lean and emaciated with labour, grief, and fasting, during the whole course of his ministry, which made him look as if he was nearly 50 years old when he was yet but 33, as we find, Jn. 8:57. His wrinkles now witnessed for him that he was far from being what was called, *a gluttonous man and a wine-bibber.* Or his bones might be numbered, because his body was distended upon the cross, which made it easy to count his ribs. *They look and stare upon me,* that is, my bones do, being distorted, and having no flesh to cover them, as Job says (*ch.* 16:8), *My leanness, rising up in me, beareth witness to my face.* Or "the standers by, the passers by, are amazed to see my bones start out thus; and, instead of pitying me, are pleased even with such a rueful spectacle." (2.) What they did with his clothes, which they took from him (*v.* 18): *They parted my garments among them,* to every soldier a part, and *upon my vesture,* the seamless coat, *do they cast lots.* This very circumstance was exactly fulfilled, Jn. 19:23, 24. And though it was no great instance of Christ's suffering, yet it is a great instance of the fulfilling of the scripture in him. *Thus it was written, and* therefore *thus it behoved Christ to suffer.* Let this therefore confirm our faith in him as the true Messiah, and inflame our love to him as the best of friends, who loved us and suffered all this for us.

II. Here is Christ praying, and with that supporting himself under the burden of his sufferings. Christ, in his agony, prayed earnestly, prayed that the cup might pass from him. When the prince of this world with his terrors set upon him, *gaped upon him as a roaring lion,* he fell upon the ground and prayed. And of that David's praying here was a type. He calls God his *strength, v.* 19. When we cannot rejoice in God as our song, yet let us stay ourselves upon him as out strength, and take the comfort of spiritual supports when we cannot come at spiritual delights. He prays, 1. That God would be with him, and not set himself at a distance from him: *Be not thou far from me* (*v.* 11), and again, *v.* 19. "Whoever stands aloof from my sore, Lord, do not thou." The nearness of trouble should quicken us to draw near to God and then we may hope that he will draw near to us. 2. That he would help him and make haste to help him, help him to bear up under his troubles, that he might not fail nor be discouraged, that he might neither shrink from his undertaking no sink under it. And the Father *heard him in that he feared* (Heb. 5:7) and enabled him to go through with his work. 3. That he would deliver him and save him, *v.* 20, 21. (1.) Observe what the jewel is which he is in care for, "The safety of my soul, my darling; let that be redeemed from the power of the grave, Ps. 49:15. Father, into thy hands I commit that, to be conveyed safely to paradise." The psalmist here calls his soul his *darling,* his *only one* (so the word is): *"My soul is my only one.* I have but one soul to take care of, and therefore the greater is my shame if I neglect it and the greater will the loss be if I let it perish. Being my only one, it ought to be my darling, for the eternal welfare of which I ought to be deeply concerned. I do not use my soul as my darling, unless I take care to preserve it from every thing that would hurt it and to provide all necessaries for it, and be entirely tender of its welfare." (2.) Observe what the danger is from which he prays to be delivered, *from the sword,* the flaming sword of divine wrath, which turns every way. This he dreaded more than any thing, Gen. 3:24. God's anger was the wormwood and the gall in the bitter cup that was put into his hands. "O deliver my soul from that. Lord, though I lose my life, let me not lose thy love. Save me from *the power of the dog,* and *from the lion's mouth."* This seems to be meant of Satan, that old enemy who bruised the heel of the seed of the woman, the prince of this world, with whom he was to engage in close combat and whom he saw coming, Jn. 14:30. "Lord, save me from being overpowered by his terrors." He pleads, "Thou hast formerly *heard me from the horns of the unicorn,"* that is, "saved me from him in answer to my prayer." This may refer to the victory Christ had obtained over Satan and his temptations (Mt. 4), when the devil left him for a season (Lu. 4:13), but now returned in another manner to attack him with his terrors. "Lord, thou gavest me the victory then, give it me now, that I may spoil principalities and powers, and *cast out the prince of this world."* Has God delivered us *from the horns of the unicorn,* that we be not tossed? Let that encourage us to hope that we shall be delivered from the lion's mouth, that we be not torn. He that has delivered doth and will deliver. This prayer of Christ, no doubt, was answered, for the Father heard him always. And, though he did not deliver him from death, yet he suffered him not to see corruption, but, the third day, raised him out of the dust of death, which was a greater instance of God's favour to him than if he had helped him down from the cross; for that would have hindered his undertaking, whereas his resurrection crowned it.

In singing this we should meditate on the sufferings and resurrection of Christ till we experience in our own souls the power of his resurrection and the fellowship of his sufferings.

Verses 22–31

The same that began the psalm complaining, who was no other than Christ in his humiliation, ends it here triumphing, and it can be no other than Christ in his exaltation. And, as the first words of the complaint were used by Christ himself upon the cross, so the first words of the triumph are expressly applied to him (Heb. 2:12) and are made his own words: *I will declare thy name unto my brethren, in the midst of the church will I sing praise unto thee.* The certain prospect which Christ had of the joy set before him not only gave him a satisfactory answer to his prayers, but turned his complaints into praises; he saw of the travail of his soul, and was well satisfied, witness that triumphant word wherewith he breathed his last: *It is finished.*

Five things are here spoken of, the view of which were the satisfaction and triumph of Christ in his sufferings: —

I. That he should have a church in the world, and that those that were given him from eternity should, in the fulness of time, be gathered in to him. This is implied here; that he should *see his seed,* Isa. 53:10. It pleased him to think, 1. That by the declaring of God's name, by the preaching of the everlasting gospel in its plainness and purity, many should be effectually called to him and to God by him. And for this end ministers should be employed to publish this doctrine to the world, and they should be much his messengers and his voice that their doing it should be accounted his doing it; their word is his, and by them he declares God's name. 2. That those who are thus called in should be brought into a very near and dear relation to him as his brethren; for he is not only not ashamed, but greatly well pleased, to call them so; not the believing Jews only, his countrymen, but those of the Gentiles also who became fellow-heirs and of the same body, Heb. 2:11. Christ is our elder brother, who takes care of us, and makes provision for us, and expects that our desire should be towards him and that we should be willing he should rule over us. 3. That these is brethren should be incorporated into a congregation, a great congregation; such is the universal church, the whole family that is named from him, unto which all the *children of God that were scattered abroad are collected,* and in which they are united (Jn. 11:52, Eph. 1:10), and that they should also be incorporated into smaller societies, members of that great body, many religious assemblies for divine worship, on which the face of Christianity should appear and in which the interests of it should be supported and advanced. 4. That these should be accounted the seed of Jacob and Israel (*v.* 23), that on them, though Gentiles, the blessing of Abraham might come (Gal. 3:14), and to them might pertain the adoption, the glory, the covenant, and the service of God, as much as ever they did to *Israel according to the flesh,* Rom. 9:4, Heb. 8:10. The gospel church is called *the Israel of God,* Gal. 6:16.

II. That God should be greatly honoured and glorified in him by that church. His Father's glory was that which he had in his eye throughout his whole undertaking (Jn. 17:4), particularly in his sufferings, which he entered upon with this solemn request, *Father, glorify thy name,* Jn. 12:27, 28. He foresees with pleasure, 1. That God would be glorified by the church that should be gathered to him, and that for this end they should be called and gathered in that they might be unto God *for a name and a praise.* Christ by his ministers will declare God's name to his brethren, as God's mouth to them, and then by them, as the mouth of the congregation to God, will God's name be praised. All that fear the Lord will praise him (*v.* 23), even every Israelite indeed. See Ps. 118:2–4; 135:19, 20. The business of Christians, particularly in their solemn religious assemblies, is to praise and glorify God with a holy awe and reverence of his majesty, and therefore those that are here called upon to praise God are called upon to fear him. 2. That God would be glorified in the Redeemer and in his undertaking. *Therefore* Christ is said to *praise God in the church,* not only because he is the Master of the assemblies in which God is praised, and the Mediator of all the praises that are offered up to God, but because he is the matter of the church's praise. See Eph. 3:21. All our praises must centre in the work of redemption and a great deal of reason we have to be thankful, (1.) That Jesus Christ was owned by his Father in his undertaking, notwithstanding the apprehension he was sometimes under that his Father had forsaken him. (*v.* 24): *For he hath not despised nor abhorred the affliction of the afflicted* one (that is, of the suffering Redeemer), but has graciously accepted it as a full satisfaction for sin, and a valuable consideration on which to ground the grant of eternal life to all believers. Though it was offered for us poor sinners, he did not despise nor abhor him that offered it for our sakes; no did he turn his face from him that offered it, as Saul was angry with his own son because he interceded for David, whom he looked upon as his enemy. But when he cried unto him, when his blood cried for peace and pardon for us, he heard him. This, as it is the matter of our rejoicing, ought to be the matter of our thanksgiving. Those who have thought their prayers slighted and unheard, if they continue to pray and wait, will find they have not sought in vain. (2.) That he himself will go on with his undertaking and complete it. Christ says, *I will pay my vows, v.* 25. Having engaged to bring many sons to glory, he will perform his engagement to the utmost, and will lose none.

III. That all humble gracious souls should have a full satisfaction and happiness in him, *v.* 26. It comforted the Lord Jesus in his sufferings that in and through him all true believers should have everlasting consolation. 1. The poor in spirit shall be rich in blessings, spiritual blessings; the hungry shall be filled with good things. Christ's sacrifice being accepted, the saints shall feast upon the sacrifice, as, under the law, upon the peace-offerings, and so partake of the altar: *The meek shall eat and be satisfied,* eat of the bread of life, feed with an appetite upon the doctrine of Christ's mediation, which is meat and drink to the soul that knows its own nature and case. Those that hunger and thirst after righteousness in Christ shall have all they can desire to satisfy them and make them easy, and shall not labour, as they have done, for that which satisfies not. 2. Those that are much in praying shall be much in thanksgiving: *Those shall praise the Lord that seek him,* because through Christ they are sure of finding him, in the hopes of which they have reason to praise him even while they are seeking him, and the more earnest they are in seeking him the more will their hearts be enlarged in his praises when they have found him. 3. The souls that are devoted to him shall be for ever happy with him: *"Your heart shall live for ever.* Yours that are meek, that are satisfied in Christ, that continue to seek God; what ever becomes of your bodies, *your hearts shall live for ever;* the graces and comforts you have shall be perfected in everlasting life. Christ has said, *Because I live, you shall live also,* (Jn. 14:19); and therefore that life shall be as sure and as long as his."

IV. That the church of Christ, and with it the kingdom of God among men, should extend itself to all the corners of the earth and should take in all sorts of people.

1. That it should reach far (*v.* 27, 28), that, whereas the Jews had long been the only professing people of God, now all the ends of the world should come into the church, and, the partition-wall being taken down, the Gentiles should be taken in. It is here prophesied, (1.) That they should be converted: They *shall remember, and turn to the Lord.* Note, Serious reflection is the first step, and a good step it is towards true conversion. We must consider and turn.

The prodigal came first to himself, and then to his father. (2.) That then they should be admitted into communion with God and with the assemblies that serve him; *They shall worship before thee,* for *in every place incense shall be offered to God,* Mal. 1:11; Isa. 66:23. Those that turn to God will make conscience of worshipping before him. And good reason there is why all the kindreds of nations should do homage to God, for (*v.* 28) *the kingdom is the Lord's;* his, and his only, is the universal monarchy. [1.] The kingdom of nature is the Lord Jehovah's, and his providence rules among the nations, and upon that account we are bound to worship him; so that the design of the Christian religion is to revive natural religion and its principles and laws. Christ died to bring us to God, the God that made us, from whom we had revolted, and to reduce us to our native allegiance. [2.] The kingdom of grace is the Lord Christ's, and he, as Mediator, is appointed governor among the nations, head over all things to his church. Let every tongue therefore confess that he is Lord.

2. That it should include many of different ranks, *v.* 29. High and low, rich and poor, bond and free, meet in Christ. (1.) Christ shall have the homage of many of the great ones. *Those that are fat upon the earth,* that live in pomp and power, *shall eat and worship;* even those that fare deliciously, when they have eaten and are full, shall bless the Lord their God for their plenty and prosperity. (2.) The poor also shall receive his gospel: *Those that go down to the dust,* that sit in the dust (Ps. 113:7), that can scarcely keep life and soul together, *shall bow before him,* before the Lord Jesus, who reckons it his honour to be the poor man's King (Ps. 72:12) and whose protection does, in a special manner, draw their allegiance. Or this may be understood in general of dying men, whether poor or rich. See then what is our condition — we are going down to the dust to which we are sentenced and where shortly we must make our bed. Nor can we keep alive our own souls; we cannot secure our own natural life long, nor can we be the authors of our own spiritual and eternal life. It is therefore our great interest, as well as duty, to bow before the Lord Jesus, to give up ourselves to him to be his subjects and worshippers; for this is the only way, and it is a sure way, to secure our happiness when we go down to the dust. Seeing we cannot keep alive our own souls, it is our wisdom, by an obedient faith, to commit our souls to Jesus Christ, who is able to save them and keep them alive for ever.

V. That the church of Christ, and with it the kingdom of God among men, should continue to the end, through all the ages of time. Mankind is kept up in a succession of generations; so that there is always a generation passing away and a generation coming up. Now, as Christ shall have honour from that which is passing away and leaving the world (*v.* 29, *those that go down to the dust shall bow before him,* and it is good to die bowing before Christ; *blessed are the dead who* thus *die in the Lord*), so he shall have honour from that which is rising up, and setting out, in the world, *v.* 30. Observe, 1. Their application to Christ: *A seed shall serve him,* shall keep up the solemn worship of him and profess and practice obedience to him as their Master and Lord. Note, God will have a church in the world to the end of time; and, in order to that, there shall be a succession of professing Christians and gospel ministers from generation to generation. *A seed shall serve him;* there shall be a remnant, more or less, to whom shall pertain the service of God and to whom God will give grace to serve him, — perhaps not the seed of the same persons, for grace does not run in a blood (he does not say *their* seed, but *a* seed), — perhaps but few, yet enough to preserve the entail. 2. Christ's acknowledgment of them: *They shall be accounted to him for a generation;* he will be the same to them that he was to those who went before them; his kindness to his friends shall not die with them, but shall be drawn out to their heirs and successors, and instead of the fathers shall be the children, whom all shall acknowledge to be a *seed that the Lord hath blessed,* Isa. 61:9; 65:23. The generation of the righteous God will graciously own as his treasure, his children. 3. Their agency for him (*v.* 31): *they shall come,* shall rise up in their day, not only to keep up the virtue of the generation that is past, and to do the work of their own generation, but to serve the honour of Christ and the welfare of souls in the generations to come; they shall transmit to them the gospel of Christ (that sacred deposit) pure and entire, even to a people that shall be born hereafter; to them they shall declare two things: — (1.) That there is an everlasting righteousness, which Jesus Christ has brought in. This righteousness of his, and not any of our own, they shall declare to be the foundation of all our hopes and the fountain of all our joys. See Rom. 1. 16, 17. (2.) That the work of our redemption by Christ is the Lord's own doing (Ps. 118:23) and no contrivance of ours. We must declare to our children that God has done this; it is his wisdom in a mystery; it is his arm revealed.

In singing this we must triumph in the name of Christ as above every name, must give him honour ourselves, rejoice in the honours others do him, and in the assurance we have that there shall be a people praising him on earth when we are praising him in heaven.

PSALM 23

Many of David's psalms are full of complaints, but this is full of comforts, and the expressions of delight in God's great goodness and dependence upon him. It is a psalm which has been sung by good Christians, and will be while the world stands, with a great deal of pleasure and satisfaction. I. The psalmist here claims relation to God, as his shepherd (*v.* 1). II. He recounts his experience of the kind things God had done for him as his shepherd (*v.* 2, 3, 5). III. Hence he infers that he should want no good (*v.* 1), that he needed to fear no evil (*v.* 4), that God would never leave nor forsake him in a way of mercy; and therefore he resolves never to leave nor forsake God in a way of duty (*v.* 6). In this he had certainly an eye, not only to the blessings of God's providence, which made his outward condition prosperous, but to the communications of God's grace, received by a lively faith, and returned in a warm devotion, which filled his soul with joy unspeakable. And, as in the foregoing psalm he represented Christ dying for his sheep, so here he represents Christians receiving the benefit of all the care and tenderness of that great and good shepherd.

A psalm of David.

Verses 1–6

From three very comfortable premises David, in this psalm, draws three very comfortable conclusions, and teaches us to do so too. We are saved by hope, and that hope will not make us ashamed, because it is well grounded. It is the duty of Christians to encourage themselves in the Lord their God; and we are here directed to take that encouragement both from the relation wherein he stands to us and from the experience we have had of his goodness according to that relation.

I. From God's being his shepherd he infers that he shall not want anything that is good for him, *v.* 1. See here, 1. The great care that God takes of believers. He is their shepherd, and they may call him so. Time was when David was himself a shepherd; he was taken from following the ewes great with young (Ps. 78:70, 71), and so he knew by experience the cares and tender affections of a good shepherd towards his flock. He remembered what need they had of a shepherd, and what a kindness it was to them to have one that was skilful and faithful; he once ventured his life to rescue a lamb. By this therefore he illustrates God's care of his people; and to this our Saviour seems to refer when he says, *I am the shepherd of the sheep; the good shepherd,* Jn. 10:11. He that is the shepherd of Israel, of the whole church in general (Ps. 80:1), is the shepherd of every particular believer; the meanest is not below his cognizance, Isa. 40:11. He takes them into his fold, and then takes care of them, protects them, and provides for them, with more care and constancy than a shepherd can, that makes it his business to keep the flock. If God be as a shepherd to us, we must be as sheep, inoffensive, meek, and quiet, silent before the shearers, nay, and before the butcher too, useful and sociable; we must know the shepherd's voice, and follow him. 2. The great confidence which believers have in God: "If the Lord is my shepherd, my feeder, I may conclude I shall not want any thing that is really necessary and good for me." If David penned this psalm before his coming to the crown, though destined to it, he had as much reason to fear wanting as any man. Once he sent his men a begging for him to Nabal, and another time went himself a begging to Ahimelech; and yet, when he considers that God is his shepherd, he can boldly say, *I shall not want.* Let not those fear starving that are at God's finding and have him for their feeder. More is implied than is expressed, not only, *I shall not want,* but, "I shall be supplied with whatever I need; and, if I have not every thing I desire, I may conclude it is either not fit for me or not good for me or I shall have it in due time."

II. From his performing the office of a good shepherd to him he infers that he needs not fear any evil in the greatest dangers and difficulties he could be in, *v.* 2–4. He experiences the benefit of God's presence with him and care of him now, and therefore expects the benefit of them when he most needs it. See here,

1. The comforts of a living saint. God is his shepherd and his God — a God all-sufficient to all intents and purposes. David found him so, and so have we. See the happiness of the saints as the sheep of God's pasture. (1.) They are well placed, well laid: *He maketh me to lie down in green pastures.* We have the supports and comforts of this life from God's good hand, our daily bread from him as our Father. The greatest abundance is but a dry pasture to a wicked man, who relishes that only in it which pleases the senses; but to a godly man, who tastes the goodness of God in all his enjoyments, and by faith relishes that, though he has but little of the world, it is a green pasture, Ps. 37:16; Prov. 15:16, 17. God's ordinances are the green pastures in which food is provided for all believers; the word of life is the nourishment of the new man. It is milk for babes, pasture for sheep, never barren, never eaten bare, never parched, but always a green pasture for faith to feed in. God makes his saints to lie down; he gives them quiet and contentment in their own minds, what ever their lot is; their souls dwell at ease in him, and that makes every pasture green. Are we blessed with the green pastures of the ordinances? Let us not think it enough to pass through them, but let us lie down in them, abide in them; this is my rest for ever. It is by a constancy of the means of grace that the soul is fed. (2.) They are well guided, well led. The shepherd of Israel guides Joseph like a flock; and every believer is under the same guidance: *He leadeth me beside the still waters.* Those that feed on God's goodness must follow his direction; he leads them by his providence, by his word, by his Spirit, disposes of their affairs for the best, according to his counsel, disposes their affections and actions according to his command, directs their eye, their way, and their heart, into his love. The still waters by which he leads them yield them, not only a pleasant prospect, but many a cooling draught, many a reviving cordial, when they are thirsty and weary. God provides for his people not only food and rest, but refreshment also and pleasure. The consolations of God, the joys of the Holy Ghost, are these still waters, by which the saints are led, streams which flow from the fountain of living waters and make glad the city of our God. God leads his people, not to the standing waters which corrupt and gather filth, not to the troubled sea, nor to the rapid rolling floods, but to the silent purling waters; for the still but running waters agree best with those spirits that flow out towards God and yet do it silently. The divine guidance they are under is stripped of its metaphor (*v.* 3): *He leadeth me in the paths of righteousness,* in the way of my duty; in that he instructs me by his word and directs me by conscience and providence. Theses are the paths in which all the saints desire to be led and kept, and never to turn aside out of them. And those only are led by the still waters of comfort that walk in the paths of righteousness. The way of duty is the truly pleasant way. It is the work of righteousness that is peace. In these paths we cannot walk unless God both lead us into them and lead us in them. (3.) They are well helped when any thing ails them: *He restoreth my soul.* [1.] "He restores me when I wander." No creature will lose itself sooner than a sheep, so apt is it to go astray, and then so unapt to find the way back. The best saints are sensible of their proneness to *go astray like lost sheep* (Ps. 119:176); they miss their way, and turn aside into by-paths; but when God shows them their error, gives them repentance, and brings them back to their duty again, he restores the soul; and, if he did not do so, they would wander endlessly and be undone. When, after one sin, David's heart smote him, and, after another, Nathan was sent to tell him, *Thou art the man,* God restored his soul. Though God may suffer his people to fall into sin, he will not suffer them to lie still in it. [2.] "He recovers me when I am sick, and revives me when I am faint, and so restores the soul which was ready to depart." He is the Lord our God that heals us, Ex. 15:26. Many a time we should have fainted unless we had believed; and it was the good shepherd that kept us from fainting.

2. See here the courage of a dying saint (*v.* 4): "Having had such experience of God's goodness to me all my days,

in six troubles and in seven, I will never distrust him, no, not in the last extremity; the rather because all he has done for me hitherto was not for any merit or desert of mine, but purely for his name's sake, in pursuance of his word, in performance of his promise, and for the glory of his own attributes and relations to his people. That name therefore shall still be my strong tower, and shall assure me that he who has led me, and fed me, all my life long, will not leave me at last." Here is,

(1.) Imminent danger supposed: *"Though I walk through the valley of the shadow of death,* that is, though I am in peril of death, though in the midst of dangers, deep as a valley, dark as a shadow, and dreadful as death itself," or rather, "though I am under the arrests of death, have received the sentence of death within myself, and have all the reason in the world to look upon myself as a dying man, yet I am easy." Those that are sick, those that are old, have reason to look upon themselves as in the valley of the shadow of death. Here is one word indeed which sounds terrible; it is *death,* which we must all count upon; *there is no discharge in that war.* But, even in the supposition of the distress, there are four words which lessen the terror: — It is death indeed that is before us; but, [1.] It is but the *shadow* of death; there is no substantial evil in it; the shadow of a serpent will not sting nor the shadow of a sword kill. [2.] It is the *valley* of the shadow, deep indeed, and dark, and dirty; but the valleys are fruitful, and so is death itself fruitful of comforts to God's people. [3.] It is but a *walk* in this valley, a gentle pleasant walk. The wicked are chased out of the world, and their souls are required; but the saints take a walk to another world as cheerfully as they take their leave of this. [4.] It is a walk *through* it; they shall not be lost in this valley, but get safely to the mountain of spices on the other side of it.

(2.) This danger made light of, and triumphed over, upon good grounds. Death is a king of terrors, but not to the sheep of Christ; they tremble at it no more than sheep do that are appointed for the slaughter. "Even in *the valley of the shadow of death I will fear no evil. None of these things move me."* Note, A child of God may meet the messengers of death, and receive its summons with a holy security and serenity of mind. The sucking child may play upon the hole of this asp; and the weaned child, that, through grace, is weaned from this world, may put his hand upon this cockatrice's den, bidding a holy defiance to death, as Paul, *O death! where is thy sting?* And there is ground enough for this confidence, [1.] Because there is no evil in it to a child of God; death cannot separate us from the love of God, and therefore it can do us no real harm; it kills the body, but cannot touch the soul. Why should it be dreadful when there is nothing in it hurtful? [2.] Because the saints have God's gracious presence with them in their dying moments; he is then at their right hand, and therefore why should they be moved? The good shepherd will not only conduct, but convoy, his sheep through the valley, where they are in danger of being set upon by the beasts of prey, the ravening wolves; he will not only convoy them, but comfort then when they most need comfort. His presence shall comfort them: *Thou art with me.* His word and Spirit shall comfort them — *his rod and staff,* alluding to the shepherd's crook, or the rod under which the sheep passed when they were counted (Lev. 27:32), or the staff with which the shepherds drove away the dogs that would scatter or worry the sheep. It is a comfort to the saints, when they come to die, that God takes cognizance of them *(he knows those that are his),* that he will rebuke the enemy, that he will guide them with his rod and sustain them with his staff. The gospel is called *the rod of Christ's strength* (Ps. 110:2), and there is enough in that to comfort the saints when they come to die, and *underneath* them are *the everlasting arms.*

III. From the good gifts of God's bounty to him now he infers the constancy and perpetuity of his mercy, *v.* 5, 6. Here we may observe,

1. How highly he magnifies God's gracious vouchsafements to him (*v.* 5): *"Thou preparest a table before me;* thou hast provided for me all things pertaining both to life and godliness, all things requisite both for body and soul, for time and eternity:" such a bountiful benefactor is God to all his people; and it becomes them abundantly to utter his great goodness, as David here, who acknowledges, (1.) That he had food convenient, a table spread, a cup filled, meat for his hunger, drink for his thirst. (2.) That he had it carefully and readily provided for him. His table was not spread with any thing that came next to hand, but prepared, and prepared *before him.* (3.) That he was not stinted, was not straitened, but had abundance: *"My cup runs over,* enough for myself and my friends too." (4.) That he had not only for necessity, but for ornament and delight: *Thou anointest my head with oil.* Samuel anointed him king, which was a certain pledge of further favor; but this is rather an instance of the plenty with which God had blessed him, or an allusion to the extraordinary entertainment of special friends, whose heads they anointed with oil, Lu. 7:46. Nay, some think he still looks upon himself as a sheep, but such a one as the *poor man's ewe-lamb* (2 Sa. 12:3), that did eat of his own meat, and drank of his own cup, and lay in his bosom; not only thus nobly, but thus tenderly, are the children of God looked after. Plentiful provision is made for their bodies, for their souls, for the life that now is and for that which is to come. If Providence do not bestow upon us thus plentifully for our natural life, it is our own fault if it be not made up to us in spiritual blessings.

2. How confidently he counts upon the continuance of God's favours, *v.* 6. He had said (*v.* 1), *I shall not want;* but now he speaks more positively, more comprehensively: *Surely goodness and mercy shall follow me all the days of my life.* His hope rises, and his faith is strengthened, by being exercised. Observe, (1.) What he promises himself — goodness and mercy, all the streams of mercy flowing from the fountain, pardoning mercy, protecting mercy, sustaining mercy, supplying mercy. (2.) The manner of the conveyance of it: It shall *follow* me, as the water out of the rock followed the camp of Israel through the wilderness; it shall follow into all places and all conditions, shall be always ready. (3.) The continuance of it: It shall follow me *all my life long,* even to the last; for whom God loves he loves to the end. (4.) The constancy of it: *All the days of my life,* as duly as the day comes; it shall be *new every morning* (Lam. 3:22, 23) like the manna that was given to the Israelites daily. (5.) The certainty of it: *Surely* it shall. It is as sure as the promise of the God of truth can make it; and we know whom we have believed. (6.) Here is a prospect of the perfection of bliss in the future state. So some take the latter clause: "Goodness and mercy having followed me all the days of my life on this earth, when that is ended I shall remove to a better world, to *dwell in the house of the Lord for ever,* in our Father's house above, where there are many mansions. *With what I have I am pleased much; with what I hope for I am pleased more."* All this, and heaven too! Then we serve a good Master.

3. How resolutely he determines to cleave to God and to his duty. We read the last clause as David's covenant with God: *"I will dwell in the house of the Lord for ever* (as long as I live), and I will praise him while I have any being." We must dwell in his house as servants, that desired to have their ears bored to the door-post, to serve him for ever. If God's goodness to us be like the morning light, which shines more and more to the perfect day, let not ours to him be like the morning cloud and the early dew that passeth away. Those that would be satisfied with the fatness of God's house must keep close to the duties of it.

PSALM 24

This psalm is concerning the kingdom of Jesus Christ, I. His providential kingdom, by which he rules the world (*v.* 1, 2). II. The kingdom of his grace, by which he rules in his church. 1. Concerning the subjects of that kingdom; their character (*v.* 4, 6), their charter (*v.* 5). 2. Concerning the King of that kingdom; and a summons to all to give him admission (*v.* 7–10). It is supposed that the psalm was penned upon occasion of David's bringing up the ark to the place prepared for it, and that the intention of it was to lead the people above the pomp of external ceremonies to a holy life and faith in Christ, of whom the ark was a type.

A psalm of David.

Verses 1–2

Here is, I. God's absolute propriety in this part of the creation where our lot is cast, *v.* 1. We are not to think that the heavens, even the heavens only, are the Lord's, and the numerous and bright inhabitants of the upper world, and that this earth, being so small and inconsiderable a part of the creation, and at such a distance from the royal palace above, is neglected, and that he claims no interest in it. No, even the earth is his, and this lower world; and, though he has prepared the throne of his glory in the heavens, yet his kingdom rules over all, and even the worms of this earth are not below his cognizance, nor from under his dominion. 1. When God gave the earth to the children of men he still reserved to himself the property, and only let it out to them as tenants, or usufructuaries: *The earth is the Lord's and the fulness thereof.* The mines that are lodged in the bowels of it, even the richest, the fruits it produces, all the beasts of the forest and the cattle upon a thousand hills, our lands and houses, and all the improvements that are made of this earth by the skill and industry of man, are all his. These indeed, in the kingdom of grace, are justly looked upon as emptiness; for they are vanity of vanities, nothing to a soul; but, in the kingdom of providence, they are fulness. *The earth is full of God's riches, so is the great and wide sea also.* All the parts and regions of the earth are the Lord's, all under his eye, all in his hand: so that, wherever a child of God goes, he may comfort himself with this, that he does not go off his Father's ground. That which falls to our share of the earth and its productions is but lent to us; it is the Lord's; what is our own against all the world is not so against his claims. That which is most remote from us, as that which passes through the paths of the sea, or is hidden in the bottom of it, is the Lord's and he knows where to find it. 2. The habitable part of this earth (Prov. 8:31) is his in a special manner — *the world and those that dwell therein.* We ourselves are not our own, our bodies, our souls, are not. *All souls are mine,* says God; for he is the former of our bodies and the Father of our spirits. Our tongues are not our own; they are to be at his service. Even those of the children of men that know him not, nor own their relation to him, are his. Now this comes in here to show that, though God is graciously pleased to accept the devotions and services of his peculiar chosen people (*v.* 3–5), it is not because he needs them, or can be benefited by them, for the earth is his and all in it, Ex. 19:5; Ps. 50:12. It is likewise to be applied to the dominion Christ has, as Mediator, over the utmost parts of the earth, which are given him for his possession: the Father loveth the Son and hath given all things into his hand, power over all flesh. The apostle quotes this scripture twice together in his discourse about things offered to idols, 1 Co. 10:26, 28. "If it be sold in the shambles, eat it, and ask no questions; *for the earth is the Lord's;* it is God's good creature, and you have a right to it. But, if one tell you it was offered to an idol, forbear, *for the earth is the Lord's,* and there is enough besides." This is a good reason why we should be content with our allotment in this world, and not envy others theirs; *the earth is the Lord's,* and may he not do what he will with his own, and give to some more of it, to others less, as it pleases him?

II. The ground of this propriety. The earth is his by an indisputable title, *for he hath founded it upon the seas* and *established it upon the floods, v.* 2. It is his; for, 1. He made it, formed it, founded it, and fitted it for the use of man. The matter is his, for he made it out of nothing; the form is his, for he made it according to the eternal counsels and ideas of his own mind. He made it himself, he made it for himself; so that he is sole, entire, and absolute owner, and none can let us a title to any part, but by, from, and under him; see Ps. 89:11, 12. 2. He made it so as no one else could. It is the creature of omnipotence, for it is founded upon the seas, upon the floods, a weak and unstable foundation (one would think) to build the earth upon, and yet, if almighty power please, it shall serve to bear the weight of this earth. The waters which at first covered the earth, and rendered it unfit to be a habitation for man, were ordered under it, that the dry land might appear, and so they are as a foundation to it; see Ps. 104:8, 9. 3. He continues it, he has *established* it, fixed it, so that, though one generation passes and another comes, the earth abides, Eccl. 1:4. And his providence is a continued creation, Ps. 119:90. The founding of the earth upon the floods should remind us how slippery and uncertain all earthly things are; their foundation is not only sand, but water; it is therefore our folly to build upon them.

Verses 3–6

From this world, and the fulness thereof, the psalmist's meditations rise, of a sudden to the great things of another world, the foundation of which is not on the seas, nor on the floods. The things of this world God has given to the children of men and we are much indebted to his providence for them; but they will not make a portion for us. And therefore,

I. Here is an enquiry after better things, *v.* 3. This earth is God's footstool; but, if we had ever so much of it, we must be here but a while, must shortly go hence, and *Who then shall ascend into the hill of the Lord?* Who shall go to heaven hereafter, and, as an earnest of that, shall have communion with God in holy ordinances now? A soul that knows and considers its own nature, origin, and immortality, when it has viewed the earth and the fulness thereof, will sit down unsatisfied; there is not found among all the creatures a help meet for man, and therefore it will think of ascending towards God, towards heaven, will ask, "What shall I do to rise to that high place, that hill, where the Lord dwells and manifests himself, that I may be acquainted with him, and to abide in that happy holy place where he meets his people and makes them holy and happy? What shall I do that I may be of those whom God owns for his peculiar people and who are his in another manner than the earth is his and its fulness?" This question is much the same with that, Ps. 15:1. The hill of Zion on which the temple was built typified the church, both visible and invisible. When the people attended the ark to its holy place David puts them in mind that these were but patterns of heavenly things, and therefore that by them they should be led to consider the heavenly things themselves.

II. An answer to this enquiry, in which we have,

1. The properties of God's peculiar people, who shall have communion with him in grace and glory. (1.) They are such as keep themselves from all the gross acts of sin. They have *clean hands;* not spotted with the pollutions of the world and the flesh. None that were ceremonially unclean might enter into the mountain of the temple, which signified that cleanness of conversation which is required in all those that have fellowship with God. The hands lifted up in prayer must be pure hands, no blot of unjust gain cleaving to them, nor any thing else that defiles the man and is offensive to the holy God. (2.) They are such as make conscience of being really (that is, of being inwardly) as good as they seem to be outwardly. They have *pure hearts.* We make nothing of our religion if we do not make heart-work of it. It is not enough that our hands be clean before men, but we must also wash our hearts from wickedness, and not allow ourselves in any secret heart-impurities, which are open before the eye of God. Yet in vain do those pretend to have pure and good hearts whose hands are defiled with the acts of sin. That is a pure heart which is sincere and without guile in covenanting with God, which is carefully guarded, that the wicked one, the unclean spirit, touch it not, which is purified by faith, and conformed to the image and will of God; see Mt. 5:8. (3.) They are such as do not set their affections upon the things of this world, do not *lift up their souls unto vanity,* whose hearts are not carried out inordinately towards the wealth of this world, the praise of men, or the delights of sense, who do not choose these things for their portion, nor reach forth after them, because they believe them to be vanity, uncertain and unsatisfying. (4.) They are such as deal honestly both with God and man. In their covenant with God, and their contracts with men, they have not sworn deceitfully, nor broken their promises, violated their engagements, nor taken any false oath. Those that have no regard to the obligations of truth or the honour of God's name are unfit for a place in God's holy hill. (5.) They are a praying people (*v.* 6): *This is the generation of those that seek him.* In every age there is a remnant of such as these, men of this character, who are *accounted to the Lord for a generation,* Ps. 22:30. And they are such as seek God, *that seek thy face, O Jacob!* [1.] They join themselves to God, to seek him, not only in earnest prayer, but in serious endeavours to obtain his favour and keep themselves in his love. Having made it the summit of their happiness, they make it the summit of their ambition to be accepted of him, and therefore take care and pains to approve themselves to him. It is to the hill of the Lord that we must ascend, and, the way being up-hill, we have need to put forth ourselves to the utmost, as those that seek diligently. [2.] They join themselves to the people of God, to seek God with them. Being brought into communion with God, they come into communion of saints; conforming to the patterns of the saints that have gone before (so some understand this), they seek God's face, as Jacob (so some), who was *therefore* surnamed *Israel,* because he wrestled with God and prevailed, sought him and found him; and, associating with the saints of their own day, they shall court the favour of God's church (Rev. 3:9), shall be glad of an acquaintance with God's people (Zec. 8:23), shall incorporate themselves with them, and, when they *subscribe with their hands to the Lord,* shall *call themselves by the name of Jacob,* Isa. 44:5. As soon as ever Paul was converted he *joined himself to the disciples,* Acts 9:26. They shall seek God's face *in Jacob* (so some), that is, in the assemblies of his people. *Thy face, O God of Jacob!* so our margin supplies it, and makes it easy. As all believers are the spiritual seed of Abraham, so all that strive in prayer are the spiritual seed of Jacob, to whom God never said, *Seek you me in vain.*

2. The privileges of God's peculiar people, *v.* 5. They shall be made truly and for ever happy. (1.) They shall be blessed: they shall receive the blessing from the Lord, all the fruits and gifts of God's favour, according to his promise; and those whom God blesses are blessed indeed, for it is his prerogative to command the blessing. (2.) They shall be justified and sanctified. These are the spiritual blessings in heavenly things which they shall receive, even righteousness, the very thing they hunger and thirst after, Mt. 5:6. Righteousness is blessedness, and it is from God only that we must expect it, for we have no righteousness of our own. They shall receive the reward of their righteousness (so some), the *crown of righteousness which the righteous Judge shall give,* 2 Tim. 4:8. (3.) They shall be saved; for God himself will be the God of their salvation. Note, Where God gives righteousness he certainly designs salvation. Those that are made meet for heaven shall be brought safely to heaven, and then they will find what they have been seeking, to their endless satisfaction.

Verses 7–10

What is spoken once is spoken a second time in these verses; such repetitions are usual in songs, and have much beauty in them. Here is, 1. Entrance once and again demanded for the King of glory; the doors and gates are to be thrown open, thrown wide open, to give him admission, for behold he stands at the door and knocks, ready to come in. 2. Enquiry once and again made concerning this mighty prince, in whose name entrance is demanded: *Who is this King of glory?* As, when any knock at our door, it is common to ask, *Who is there?* 3. Satisfaction once and again given concerning the royal person that makes the demand: *It is the Lord, strong and mighty, the Lord, mighty in battle, the Lord of hosts, v.* 8, 10. Now,

I. This splendid entry here described it is probable refers to the solemn bringing in of the ark into the tent David pitched for it or the temple Solomon built for it; for, when David prepared materials for the building of it, it was proper for him to prepare a psalm for the dedication of it. The porters are called upon to open the doors, and they are called *everlasting doors,* because much more durable than the door of the tabernacle, which was but a curtain. They are taught to ask, *Who is this King of glory?* And those that bore the ark are taught to answer in the language before us, and very fitly, because the ark was a symbol or token of God's presence, Jos. 3:11. Or it may be taken as a poetical figure designed to represent the subject more affectingly. God, in his word and ordinances, is thus to be welcomed by us, 1. With great readiness: the doors and gates must be thrown open to him. Let the word of the Lord come into the innermost and uppermost place in our souls; and, if we had 600 necks, we should bow them all to the authority of it. 2. With all reverence, remembering how great a God he is with whom we have to do, in all our approaches to him.

II. Doubtless it points at Christ, of whom the ark, with the mercy-seat, was a type. 1. We may apply it to the ascension of Christ into heaven and the welcome given to him there. When he had finished his work on earth he ascended *in the clouds of heaven,* Dan. 7:13, 14. The gates of heaven must then be opened to him, those doors that may be truly called *everlasting,* which had been shut against us, to keep the way of the tree of life, Gen. 3:24. Our Redeemer found them shut, but, having by his blood made atonement for sin and gained a title to *enter into the holy place* (Heb. 9:12), as one having authority, he demanded entrance, not for himself only, but for us; for, as the forerunner, he has for us entered and *opened the kingdom of heaven to all believers.* The keys not only of hell and death, but of heaven and life, must be put into his hand. His approach being very magnificent, the angels are brought in asking, *Who is this King of glory?* For angels keep the gates of the New Jerusalem, Rev. 21:12. When the first-begotten was brought into the upper world the angels were to worship him (Heb. 1:6); and accordingly, they here ask with wonder, "Who is he? — this that cometh *with dyed garments from Bozrah?* (Isa. 63:1–3), for he appears in that world *as a Lamb that had been slain."* It is answered that he is *strong and mighty, mighty in battle,* to save his people and subdue his and their enemies. 2. We may apply it to Christ's entrance into the souls of men by his word and Spirit, that they may be his temples. Christ's presence in them is like that of the ark in the temple; it sanctifies them. *Behold, he stands at the door and knocks,* Rev. 3:20. It is required that the gates and doors of the heart be opened to him, not only as admission is given to a guest, but as possession is delivered to the rightful owner, after the title has been contested. This is the gospel call and demand, that we let Jesus Christ, the King of glory, come into our souls, and welcome him with hosannas, *Blessed is he that cometh.* That we may do this aright we are concerned to ask, *Who is this King of glory?* — to acquaint ourselves with him, whom we are to believe in, and to love above all. And the answer is ready: He is *Jehovah,* and will be *Jehovah our righteousness,* an all-sufficient Saviour to us, if we give him entrance and entertainment. He is *strong and mighty,* and *the Lord of hosts;* and therefore it is at our peril if we deny him entrance; for he is able to avenge the affront; he can force his way, and can break those in pieces with his iron rod that will not submit to his golden sceptre.

In singing this let our hearts cheerfully answer to this call, as it is in the first words of the next psalm, *Unto thee, O Lord! do I lift up my soul.*

PSALM 25

This psalm is full of devout affection to God, the out-goings of holy desires towards his favour and grace and the lively actings of faith in his promises. We may learn out of it, I. What it is to pray (*v.* 1, 15). II. What we must pray for, the pardon of sin (*v.* 6, 7, 18), direction in the way of duty (*v.* 4, 5), the favour of God (*v.* 16), deliverance out of our troubles (*v.* 17, 18), preservation from our enemies (*v.* 20, 21), and the salvation of the church of God (*v.* 22). III. What we may plead in prayer, our confidence in God (*v.* 2, 3, 5, 20, 21), our distress and the malice of our enemies (*v.* 17, 19), our sincerity (*v.* 21). IV. What precious promises we have to encourage us in prayer, of guidance and instruction (*v.* 8, 9, 12), the benefit of the covenant (*v.* 10), and the pleasure of communion with God (*v.* 13, 14). It is easy to apply the several passages of this psalm to ourselves in the singing of it; for we have often troubles, and always sins, to complain of at the throne of grace.

A psalm of David.

Verses 1–7

Here we have David's professions of desire towards God and dependence on him. He often begins his psalms with such professions, not to move God, but to move himself, and to engage himself to answer those professions.

I. He professes his desire towards God: *Unto thee, O Lord! do I lift up my soul, v.* 1. In the foregoing psalm (*v.* 4) it was made the character of a good man that he *has not lifted up his soul to vanity;* and a call was given to the everlasting gates to lift up their heads for the *King of glory to come in, v.* 1. To this character, to this call, David here answers, "Lord, I lift up my soul, not to vanity, but to thee." Note, In worshipping God we must lift up our souls to him. Prayer is the ascent of the soul to God; God must be eyed and the soul employed. *Sursum corda — Up with you hearts,* was anciently used as a call to devotion. With a holy contempt of the world and the things of it, by a fixed thought and active faith, we must set God before us, and let out our desires towards him as the fountain of our happiness.

II. He professes his dependence upon God and begs for

the benefit and comfort of that dependence (*v.* 2): *O my God! I trust in thee.* His conscience witnessed for him that he had no confidence in himself nor in any creature, and that he had no diffidence of God or of his power or promise. He pleases himself with this profession of faith in God. Having put his trust in God, he is easy, is well satisfied, and quiet from the fear of evil; and he pleads it with God whose honour it is to help those that honour him by trusting in him. What men put a confidence in is either their joy or their shame, according as it proves. Now David here, under the direction of faith, prays earnestly, 1. That shame might not be his lot: *"Let me not be ashamed* of my confidence in thee; let me not be shaken from it by any prevailing fears, and let me not be, in the issue, disappointed of what I depend upon thee for; but, Lord, *keep what I have committed unto thee."* Note, If we make our confidence in God our stay, it shall not be our shame; and, if we triumph in him, our enemies shall not triumph over us, as they would if we should now sink under our fears, or should, in the issue, come short of our hopes. 2. That it might not be the lot of any that trusted in God. All the saints have obtained a like precious faith; and therefore, doubtless, it will be alike successful in the issue. Thus the communion of saints is kept up, even by their praying one for another. True saints will make supplication for all saints. It is certain that none who, by a believing attendance, wait on God, and, by a believing hope, wait for him, shall be made ashamed of it. 3. That it might be the lot of the transgressors; *Let those be ashamed that transgress without cause,* or *vainly,* as the word is. (1.) Upon no provocation. They revolt from God and their duty, from David and his government (so some), without any occasion given them, not being able to pretend any iniquity they have found in God, or that in any thing he has wearied them. The weaker the temptation is by which men are drawn to sin the stronger the corruption is by which they are driven by it. Those are the worst transgressors that sin for sinning-sake. (2.) To no purpose. They know their attempts against God are fruitless; they imagine a vain thing, and therefore they will soon be ashamed of it.

III. He begs direction from God in the way of his duty, *v.* 4, 5. Once and again he here prays to God to teach him. He was a knowing man himself, but the most intelligent, the most observant, both need and desire to be taught of God; from him we must be ever learning. Observe,

1. What he desired to learn: *"Teach me,* not fine words or fine notions, but *thy ways, thy paths, thy truth,* the ways in which thou walkest towards men, which are *all mercy and truth* (*v.* 10), and the ways in which thou wouldst have me to walk towards thee." Those are best taught who understand their duty, and know *the good things they should do,* Eccl. 2:3. God's *paths* and his *truth* are the same; divine laws are all founded upon divine truths. The way of God's precepts is the way of truth, Ps. 119:30. Christ is both the way and the truth, and therefore we must learn Christ.

2. What he desired of God, in order to this. (1.) That he would enlighten his understanding concerning his duty: *"Show me thy way,* and so *teach me."* In doubtful cases we should pray earnestly that God would make it plain to us what he would have us to do. (2.) That he would incline his will to do it, and strengthen him in it: *"Lead me,* and so teach me." Not only as we lead one that is dim-sighted, to keep him from missing his way, but as we lead one that is sick, and feeble, and faint, to help him forward in the way and to keep him from fainting and falling. We go no further in the way to heaven than God is pleased to lead us and to hold us up.

3. What he pleads, (1.) His great expectation from God: *Thou art the God of my salvation.* Note, Those that choose salvation of God as their end, and make him the God of their salvation, may come boldly to him for direction in the way that leads to that end. If God save us, he will teach us and lead us. He that gives salvation will give instruction. (2.) His constant attendance on God: *On thee do I wait all the day.* Whence should a servant expect direction what to do but from his own master, on whom he waits all the day? If we sincerely desire to know our duty, with a resolution to do it, we need not question but that God will direct us in it.

IV. He appeals to God's infinite mercy, and casts himself upon that, not pretending to any merit of his own (*v.* 6): *"Remember, O Lord! thy tender mercies,* and, for the sake of those mercies, lead me, and teach me; for they *have been ever of old."* 1. "Thou always wast a merciful God; it is thy name, it is thy nature and property, to show mercy." 2. "Thy counsels and designs of mercy were from everlasting; the vessels of mercy were, before all worlds, ordained to glory." 3. "The instances of thy mercy to the church in general, and to me in particular, were early and ancient, and constant hitherto; they began of old, and never ceased. Thou hast taught me from my youth up, teach me now."

V. He is in a special manner earnest for the pardon of his sins (*v.* 7): *"O remember not the sins of my youth.* Lord, remember thy mercies (*v.* 6), which speak for me, and not my sins, which speak against me." Here is, 1. An implicit confession of sin; he specifies particularly the sins of his youth. Note, Our youthful faults and follies should be matter of our repentance and humiliation long after, because time does not wear out the guilt of sin. Old people should mourn for the sinful mirth and be in pain for the sinful pleasures of their youth. He aggravates his sins, calling them his *transgressions;* and the more holy, just, and good the law is, which sin is the transgression of, the more exceedingly sinful it ought to appear to us. 2. An express petition for mercy, (1.) That he might be acquitted from guilt: *"Remember not the sins of my youth;* that is, remember them not against me, lay them not to my charge, enter not into judgment with me for them." When God pardons sin he is said to *remember it no more,* which denotes a plenary remission; he forgives and forgets. (2.) That he might be accepted in God's sight: "Remember thou me; think on me for good, and come in seasonably for my succour." We need desire no more to make us happy than for God to remember us with favour. His plea is, "according to thy mercy, and for thy goodness-sake." Note, It is God's goodness and not ours, his mercy and not our own merit, that must be our plea for the pardon of sin and all the good we stand in need of. This plea we must always rely upon, as those that are sensible of our poverty and unworthiness and as those that are satisfied of the riches of God's mercy and grace.

Verses 8–14

God's promises are here mixed with David's prayers. Many petitions there were in the former part of the psalm, and many we shall find in the latter; and here, in the middle of the psalm, he meditates upon the promises, and by a lively faith sucks and is satisfied from these breasts of consolation; for the promises of God are not only the best foundation of prayer, telling us what to pray for and encouraging our faith and hope in prayer, but they are a present answer to prayer. Let the prayer be made according to the promise, and then the promise may be read as a return to the prayer; and we are to believe the prayer is heard because the promise will be performed. But, in the midst of the promises, we fine one petition which seems to come in somewhat abruptly, and should have followed upon *v.* 7. It is that (*v.* 11), *Pardon my iniquity.* But prayers for the pardon of sin are never impertinent; we mingle sin with all our actions, and therefore should mingle such prayers with all our devotions. He enforces this petition with a double plea. The former is very natural: *"For thy name's sake pardon my iniquity,* because thou hast proclaimed thy name gracious and merciful, pardoning iniquity, for thy glory-sake, for thy promise-sake, for thy own sake," Isa. 43:25. But the latter is very surprising: *"Pardon my iniquity, for it is great,* and the greater it is the more will divine mercy be magnified in the forgiveness of it." It is the glory of a great God to forgive great sins, to forgive iniquity, transgression, and sin, Ex. 34:7. "It is great, and therefore I an undone, for ever undone, if infinite mercy do not interpose for the pardon of it. It is great; I see it to be so." The more we see of the heinousness of our sins the better qualified we are to find mercy with God. When we confess sin we must aggravate it.

Let us now take a view of the great and precious promises which we have in these verses, and observe,

I. To whom these promises belong and who may expect the benefit of them. We are all sinners; and can we hope for any advantage by them? Yes (*v.* 8), He will teach sinners, though they be sinners; for Christ came into the world to save sinners, and, in order to that, to teach sinners, to call sinners to repentance. These promises are sure to those who though they have been sinners, have gone astray, yet now keep God's word, 1. To such as keep his covenant and his testimonies (*v.* 10), such as take his precepts for their rule and his promises for their portion, such as, having taken God to be to them a God, live upon that, and, having given up themselves to be him a people, live up to that. Though, through the infirmity of the flesh, they sometimes break the command, yet by a sincere repentance when at any time they do amiss, and a constant adherence by faith to God as their God, they keep the covenant and do not break that. 2. To such as fear him (*v.* 12 and again *v.* 14), such as stand in awe of his majesty and worship him with reverence, submit to his authority and obey him with cheerfulness, dread his wrath and are afraid of offending him.

II. Upon what these promises are grounded, and what encouragement we have to build upon them. Here are two things which ratify and confirm all the promises: — 1. The perfections of God's nature. We value the promise by the character of him that makes its. We may therefore depend upon God's promises; for *good and upright is the Lord,* and therefore he will be as good as his word. He is so kind that he cannot deceive us, so true that he cannot break his promise. *Faithful is he who hath promised,* who also will do it. He was good in making the promise, and therefore will be upright in performing it. 2. The agreeableness of all he says and does with the perfections of his nature (*v.* 10): *All the paths of the Lord* (that is, all his promises and all his providences) *are mercy and truth;* they are, like himself, good and upright. All God's dealings with his people are according to the mercy of his purposes and the truth of his promises; all he does comes from love, covenant-love; and they may see in it his mercy displayed and his word fulfilled. What a rich satisfaction may this be to good people, that, whatever afflictions they are exercised with, *All the paths of the Lord are mercy and truth,* and so it will appear when they come to their journey's end.

III. What these promises are.

1. That God will instruct and direct them in the way of their duty. This is most insisted upon, because it is an answer to David's prayers (*v.* 4, 5), *Show me thy ways and lead me.* We should fix our thoughts, and act our faith, most on those promises which suit our present case. (1.) He will *teach sinners in the way,* because they are sinners, and therefore need teaching. When they see themselves sinners, and desire teaching, then he will teach them the way of reconciliation to God, the way to a well-grounded peace of conscience, and the way to eternal life. He does, by his gospel, make this way known to all, and, by his Spirit, open the understanding and guide penitent sinners that enquire after it. The devil leads men blindfold to hell, but God enlightens men's eyes, sets things before them in a true light, and so leads them to heaven. (2.) *The meek will he guide,* the meek will he teach, that is, those that are humble and low in their own eyes, that are distrustful of themselves, desirous to be taught, and honestly resolved to follow the divine guidance. *Speak, Lord, for thy servant hears.* These he will guide *in judgment,* that is, by the rule of the written word; he will guide them in that which is practical, which relates to sin and duty, so that they may keep conscience void of offence; and he will do it judiciously (so some), that is, he will suit his conduct to their case; he will teach sinners with wisdom, tenderness, and compassion, and as they are able to bear. He will teach them his way. All good people make God's way their way, and desire to be taught that; and those that do so shall be taught and led in that way. (3.) *Him that feareth the Lord he will teach in the way that he shall choose,* either in the way that God shall choose or that the good man shall choose. It comes all to one, for he that fears the Lord chooses the things that please him. If we choose the right way, he that directed our choice will direct our steps, and will lead us in it. If we choose wisely, God will give us grace to walk wisely.

2. That God will make them easy (*v.* 13): *His soul shall dwell at ease, shall lodge in goodness,* marg. Those that devote themselves to the fear of God, and give themselves to be taught of God, will be easy, if it be not their own fault. The soul that is sanctified by the grace of God, and, much more, that is comforted by the peace of God, dwells

at ease. Even when the body is sick and lies in pain, yet the soul may dwell at ease in God, may return to him, and repose in him as its rest. Many things occur to make us uneasy, but there is enough in the covenant of grace to counterbalance them all and to make us easy.

3. That he will give to them and theirs as much of this world as is good for them: *His seed shall inherit the earth.* Next to our care concerning our souls is our care concerning our seed, and God has a blessing in store for the generation of the upright. Those that fear God shall inherit the earth, shall have a competency in it and the comfort of it, and their children shall fare the better for their prayers when they are gone.

4. That God will admit them into the secret of communion with himself (*v.* 14): *The secret of the Lord is with those that fear him.* They understand his word; for, *if any man do his will, he shall know of the doctrine whether it be of God,* Jn. 7:17. Those that receive the truth in the love of it, and experience the power of it, best understand the mystery of it. They know the meaning of his providence, and what God is doing with them, better than others. *Shall I hide from Abraham the things that I do?* Gen. 18:17. He call them not *servants,* but *friends,* as he called Abraham. They know by experience the blessings of the covenant and the pleasure of that fellowship which gracious souls have with the Father and with his Son Jesus Christ. This honour have all his saints.

Verses 15–22

David, encouraged by the promises he had been meditating upon, here renews his addresses to God, and concludes the psalm, as he began, with professions of dependence upon God and desire towards him.

I. He lays open before God the calamitous condition he was in. His feet were in the net, held fast and entangled, so that he could not extricate himself out of his difficulties, *v.* 15. He was *desolate and afflicted, v.* 16. It is common for those that are afflicted to be desolate; their friends desert them then, and they are themselves disposed to sit alone and keep silence, Lam. 3:28. David calls himself *desolate and solitary* because he depended not upon his servants and soldiers, but relied as entirely upon God as if he had no prospect at all of help and succour from any creature. Being in distress, in many distresses, *the troubles of his heart were enlarged* (*v.* 17), he grew more and more melancholy and troubled in mind. Sense of sin afflicted him more than any thing else: this it was that broke and wounded his spirit, and made his outward troubles lie heavily upon him. He was in *affliction and pain, v.* 18. His enemies that persecuted him were many and malicious (they hated him), and very barbarous; it was *with a cruel hatred* that they hated him, *v.* 19. Such were Christ's enemies and the persecutors of his church.

II. He expresses the dependence he had upon God in these distresses (*v.* 15): *My eyes are ever towards the Lord.* Idolaters were for gods that they could see with their bodily eyes, and they had their eyes ever towards their idols, Isa. 17:7, 8. But it is an eye of faith that we must have towards God, who is a Spirit, Zec. 9:1. Our meditation of him must be sweet, and we must always set him before us: in all our ways we must acknowledge him and do all to his glory. Thus we must live a life of communion with God, not only in ordinances, but in providences, not only in acts of devotion, but in the whole course of our conversation. David had the comfort of this in his affliction; for, because his eyes were ever towards the Lord, he doubted not but he would pluck his feet out of the net, that he would deliver him from the corruptions of his own heart (so some), from the designs of his enemies against him, so others. Those that have their eye ever towards God shall not have their feet long in the net. He repeats his profession of dependence upon God (*v.* 20) — *Let me not be ashamed, for I put my trust in thee;* and of expectation from him — *I wait on thee, v.* 21. It is good thus to hope and quietly wait for the salvation of the Lord.

III. He prays earnestly to God for relief and succour, 1. For himself.

(1.) See how he begs, [1.] For the remission of sin (*v.* 18): *Forgive all my sins.* Those were his heaviest burdens, and which brought upon him all other burdens. He had begged (*v.* 7) for the pardon of the sins of his youth, and (*v.* 11) for the pardon of some one particular iniquity that was remarkably great, which some think, was his sin in the matter of Uriah. But her he prays, Lord, *forgive all, take away all iniquity.* It is observable that, as to his affliction, he asks for no more than God's regard to it: *"Look upon my affliction and my pain,* and do with it as thou pleasest." But, as to his sin, he asks for no less than a full pardon: *Forgive all my sins.* When at any time we are in trouble we should be more concerned about our sins, to get them pardoned, than about our afflictions, to get them removed. Yet he prays, [2.] For the redress of his grievances. His mind was troubled for God's withdrawings from him and under the sense he had of his displeasure against him for his sins; and therefore he prays (*v.* 16), *Turn thou unto me.* And, if God turn to us, no matter who turns from us. His condition was troubled, and, in reference to that, he prays, *"O bring thou me out of my distresses.* I see no way of deliverance open; but thou canst either find one or make one." His enemies were spiteful; and in reference to that, he prays, *"O keep my soul* from falling into their hands, or else *deliver me* out of their hands."

(2.) Four things he mentions by way of plea to enforce these petitions, and refers himself and them to God's consideration: — [1.] He pleads God's mercy: *Have mercy upon me.* Men of the greatest merits would be undone if they had not to do with a God of infinite mercies. [2.] He pleads his own misery, the distress he was in, his affliction and pain, especially the troubles of his heart, all which made him the proper object of divine mercy. [3.] He pleads the iniquity of his enemies: "Lord, consider them, how cruel they are, and deliver me out of their hands." [4.] He pleads his own integrity, *v.* 12. Though he had owned himself guilty before God, and had confessed his sins against him, yet, as to his enemies, he had the testimony of his conscience that he had done them no wrong, which was his comfort when they hated him with cruel hatred; and he prays that this might *preserve him,* This intimates that he did not expect to be safe any longer than he continued in his *integrity and uprightness,* and that, while he did continue in it, he did not doubt of being safe. Sincerity will be our best security in the worst of times. Integrity and uprightness will be a man's preservation more than the wealth and honour of the world can be. These will preserve us to the heavenly kingdom. We should therefore pray to God to preserve us in our integrity and then be assured that that will preserve us.

2. For the church of God (*v.* 22): *Redeem Israel, O God! out of all his troubles.* David was now in trouble himself, but he thinks it not strange, since trouble is the lot of all God's Israel. Why should any one member fare better than the whole body? David's troubles were enlarged, and very earnest he was with God to deliver him, yet he forgets not the distresses of God's church; for, when we have ever so much business of our own at the throne of grace, we must still remember to pray for the public. Good men have little comfort in their own safety while the church is in distress and danger. This prayer is a prophecy that God would, at length, give David rest, and therewith give Israel rest from all their enemies round about. It is a prophecy of the sending of the Messiah in due time to *redeem Israel from his iniquities* (Ps. 130:8) and so to redeem them from their troubles. It refers also to the happiness of the future state. In heaven, and in heaven only, will God's Israel be perfectly redeemed from all troubles.

PSALM 26

Holy David is in this psalm putting himself upon a solemn trial, not by God and his country, but by God and his own conscience, to both which he appeals touching his integrity (*v.* 1, 2), for the proof of which he alleges, I. His constant regard to God and his grace (*v.* 3). II. His rooted antipathy to sin and sinners (*v.* 4, 5). III. His sincere affection to the ordinances of God, and his care about them (*v.* 6–8). Having thus proved his integrity, 1. He deprecates the doom of the wicked (*v.* 9, 10). 2. He casts himself upon the mercy and grace of God, with a resolution to hold fast his integrity, and his hope in God (*v.* 11, 12). In singing this psalm we must teach and admonish ourselves, and one another, what we must be and do that we may have the favour of God, and comfort in our own consciences, and comfort ourselves with it, as David does, if we can say that in any measure we have, through grace, answered to these characters. The learned Amyraldus, in his argument of his psalm, suggests that David is here, by the spirit of prophecy, carried out to speak of himself as a type of Christ, of whom what he here says of his spotless innocence, was fully and eminently true, and of him only, and to him we may apply it in singing this psalm. "We are complete in him."

A psalm of David.

Verses 1–5

It is probable that David penned this psalm when he was persecuted by Saul and his party, who, to give some colour to their unjust rage, represented him as a very bad man, and falsely accused him of many high crimes and misdemeanors, dressed him up in the skins of wild beasts that they might bait him. Innocency itself is no fence to the name, though it is to the bosom, against the darts of calumny. Herein he was a type of Christ, who was made a reproach of men, and foretold to his followers that they also must have all manner of evil said against them falsely. Now see what David does in this case.

I. He appeals to God's righteous sentence (*v.* 1): *"Judge me, O God!* be thou Judge between me and my accusers, between the persecutor and the poor prisoner; bring me off with honour, and put those to shame that falsely accuse me." Saul, who was himself supreme judge in Israel, was his adversary, so that in a controversy with him he could appeal to no other then to God himself. As to his offences against God, he prays, *Lord, enter not into judgment with me* (Ps. 143:2), *remember not my transgressions* (Ps. 25:7), in which he appeals to God's mercy; but, as to his offences against Saul, he appeals to God's justice and begs of him to judge for him, as Ps. 43:1. Or thus: he cannot justify himself against the charge of sin; he owns his iniquity is great and he is undone if God, in his infinite mercy, do not forgive him; but he can justify himself against the charge of hypocrisy, and has reason to hope that, according to the tenour of the covenant of grace, he is one of those that may expect to find favour with God. Thus holy Job often owns he has sinned and yet he holds fast his integrity. Note, It is a comfort to those who are falsely accused that there is a righteous God, who, sooner or later, will clear up their innocency, and a comfort to all who are sincere in religion that God himself is a witness to their sincerity.

II. He submits to his unerring search (*v.* 2): *Examine me, O Lord! and prove me,* as gold is proved, whether it be standard. God knows every man's true character, for he knows the thoughts and intents of the heart, as sees through every disguise. David prays, *Lord, examine me,* which intimates that he was well pleased that God did know him and truly desirous that he would discover him to himself and discover him to all the world. So sincere was he in his devotion to his God and his loyalty to his prince (in both which he was suspected to be a pretender) that he wished he had a window in his bosom, that whoever would might look into his heart.

III. He solemnly protests his sincerity (*v.* 1): *"I have walked in my integrity;* my conversation had agreed with my profession, and one part of it has been of a piece with another." It is vain to boast of our integrity unless we can make it out that by the grace of God we have walked in our integrity, and that our conversation in the world has been in simplicity and godly sincerity. He produces here several proofs of his integrity, which encouraged him to trust in the Lord as his righteous Judge, who would patronise and plead his righteous cause, with an assurance that he should come off with reputation *(therefore I shall not slide),* and that those should not prevail who consulted to cast him down from his excellency, to shake his faith, blemish his name, and prevent his coming to the crown, Ps. 62:4. Those that are sincere in religion may trust in God that they shall not slide, that is, that they shall not apostasize from their religion.

1. He had a constant regard to God and to his grace, *v.* 3. (1.) He aimed at God's good favour as his end and chief good: *Thy loving-kindness is before my eyes.* This will be a good evidence of our sincerity, if what we do in religion we do from a principle of love to God, and good thoughts of him as the best of beings and the best of friends and benefactors, and from a grateful sense of God's goodness to us in particular, which we have had the experience of all our days. If we set God's loving-kindness before us as our pattern, to which we endeavour to conform ourselves, being *followers of him that is good,* in his goodness (1 Pt. 3:13), — if we set it before us as our great engagement and encouragement to our duty, and are afraid of doing any thing to forfeit God's favour and in care by all means to keep ourselves in his love, — this will not only

be a good evidence of our integrity, but will have a great influence upon our perseverance in it. (2.) He governed himself by the word of God as his rule: *"I have walked in thy truth,* that is, according to thy law, for thy law is truth." Note, Those only may expect the benefit of God's loving-kindness that live up to his truths, and his laws that are grounded upon them. Some understand it of his conforming himself to God's example in truth and faithfulness, as well as in goodness and loving-kindness. Those certainly walk well that are followers of God as dear children.

2. He had no fellowship with the unfruitful works of darkness, nor with the workers of those works, *v.* 4, 5. By this it appeared he was truly loyal to his prince that he never associated with those that were disaffected to his government, with any of those *sons of Belial that despised him,* 1 Sa. 10:27. He was in none of their cabals, nor joined with them in any of their intrigues; he cursed not the king, no, not in his heart. And this also was an evidence of his faithfulness to his God, that he never associated with those who he had any reason to think were disaffected to religion, or were open enemies, or false friends, to its interests. Note, Great care to avoid bad company is both a good evidence of our integrity and a good means to preserve us in it. Now observe here, (1.) That this part of his protestation looks both backward upon the care he had hitherto taken in this matter, and forward upon the care he would still take: *"I have not sat with them,* and I *will not go in with them."* Note, Our good practices hitherto are then evidence of our integrity when they are accompanied with resolutions, in God's strength, to persevere in them to the end, and not to draw back; and our good resolutions for the future we may then take the comfort of when they are the continuation of our good practices hitherto. (2.) That David shunned the company, not only of wicked persons, but of vain persons, that were wholly addicted to mirth and gaiety and had nothing solid or serious in them. The company of such may perhaps be the more pernicious of the two to a good man because he will not be so ready to stand upon his guard against the contagion of vanity as against that of downright wickedness. (3.) That the company of dissemblers is as dangerous company as any, and as much to be shunned, in prudence as well as piety. Evil-doers pretend friendship to those whom they would decoy into their snares, but they dissemble. *When they speak fair, believe them not.* (4.) Though sometimes he could not avoid being in the company of bad people, yet he would not *go in with them,* he would not choose such for his companions nor seek an opportunity of acquaintance and converse with them. He might fall in with them, but he would not, by appointment and assignation, go in with them. Or, if he happened to be with them, he would not sit with them, he would not continue with them; he would be in their company no longer than his business made it necessary: he would not concur with them, not say as they said, nor do as they did, as those that *sit in the seat of the scornful,* 1. 1. He would not sit in counsel with them upon ways and means to do mischief, nor sit in judgment with them to condemn the generation of the righteous. (5.) We must not only in our practice avoid bad company, but in our principles and affections we must have an aversion to it. David here says, not only "I have shunned it," but, *"I have hated it,"* Ps. 139:21. (6.) The congregation of evil-doers, the club, the confederacy of them, is in a special manner hateful to good people. I have hated *ecclesiam malignantium — the church of the malignant;* so the vulgar Latin reads its. As good men, in concert, make one another better, and are enabled to do so much the more good, so bad men, in combination, make one another worse, and do so much the more mischief. In all this David was a type of Christ, who, though he received sinners and ate with them, to instruct them and do them good, yet, otherwise, was holy, harmless, undefiled, and separate from sinners, particularly from the Pharisees, those dissemblers. He was also an example to Christians, when they join themselves to Christ, to *save themselves from this untoward generation,* Acts 2:40.

Verses 6–12

In these verses,

I. David mentions, as further evidence of his integrity, the sincere affection he had to the ordinances of God, the constant care he took about them, and the pleasure he took in them. Hypocrites and dissemblers may indeed be found attending on God's ordinances, as the proud Pharisee went up to the temple to pray with the penitent publican; but it is a good sign of sincerity if we attend upon them as David here tells us he did, *v.* 6–8.

1. He was very careful and conscientious in his preparation for holy ordinances: *I will wash my hands in innocency.* He not only refrained from the society of sinners, but kept himself clean from the pollutions of sin, and this with an eye to the place he had among those that compassed God's altar. "I will wash, and so will I compass the altar, knowing that otherwise I shall not be welcome." This is like that (1 Co. 11:28), *Let a man examine himself, and so let him eat,* so prepared. This denotes, (1.) Habitual preparation: *"I will wash my hands in innocency;* I will carefully watch against all sin, and keep my conscience pure from those dead works which defile it and forbid my drawing nigh to God." See Ps. 24:3, 4. (2.) Actual preparation. It alludes to the ceremony of the priests' washing when they went in to minister, Ex. 30:20, 21. Though David was no priest, yet, as every worshipper ought, he would look to the substance of that which the priests were enjoined the shadow of. In our preparation for solemn ordinances we must not only be able to clear ourselves from the charge of reigning infidelity or hypocrisy, and to protest our innocency of that (which was signified by *washing the hands,* Deu. 21:6), but we must take pains to cleanse ourselves from the spots of remaining iniquity by renewing our repentance, and making fresh application of the blood of Christ to our consciences for the purifying and pacifying of them. He that is washed (that is, in a justified state) has need thus to *wash his feet* (Jn. 13:10), to wash his hands, to wash them in innocency; he that is penitent is *pene innocens — almost innocent;* and he that is pardoned is so far innocent that his sins shall not be mentioned against him.

2. He was very diligent and serious in his attendance upon them: *I will compass thy altar,* alluding to the custom of the priests, who, while the sacrifice was in offering, walked round the altar, and probably the offerers likewise did so at some distance, denoting a diligent regard to what was done and a dutiful attendance in the service. *"I will compass it;* I will be among the crowds that do compass it, among the thickest of them." David, a man of honour, a man of business, a man of war, thought it not below him to attend with the multitude on God's altars and could find time for that attendance. Note, (1.) All God's people will be sure to wait on God's altar, in obedience to his commands and in pursuance of his favour. Christ is our altar, not as the altar in the Jewish church, which was fed by them, but an altar that we eat of and *live upon,* Heb. 13:10. (2.) It is a pleasant sight to see God's altar compassed and to see ourselves among those that compass it.

3. In all his attendance on God's ordinances he aimed at the glory of God and was much in the thankful praise and adoration of him. He had an eye to the place of worship as the place where God's honor dwelt (*v.* 8), and therefore made it his business there to honour God and to give him the glory due to his name, to publish with the voice of thanksgiving all God's wondrous works. God's gracious works, which call for thanksgiving, are all wondrous works, which call for our admiration. We ought to publish them, and tell of them, for his glory, and the excitement of others to praise him; and we ought to do it with the voice of thanksgiving, as those that are sensible of our obligations, by all ways possible, to acknowledge with gratitude the favours we have received from God.

4. He did this with delight and from a principle of true affection to God and his institutions. Touching this he appeals to God: *"Lord,* thou knowest how dearly *I have loved the habitation of thy house* (*v.* 8), the tabernacle where thou art pleased to manifest thy residence among thy people and receive their homage, *the place where thy honour dwells."* David was sometimes forced by persecution into the countries of idolaters and was hindered from attending God's altars, which perhaps his persecutors, that laid him under that restraint, did themselves upbraid him with as his crime. See 1 Sa. 20:27. "But, Lord," says he, "though I cannot come to the habitation of thy house, I love it; my heart is there, and it is my greatest trouble that I am not there." Note, All that truly love God truly love the ordinances of God, and *therefore* love them because in them he manifests his honour and they have an opportunity of honoring him. Our Lord Jesus loved his Father's honour, and made it his business to glorify him; he loved the habitation of his house, his church among men, loved it and gave himself for it, that he might build and consecrate it. Those who love communion with God, and delight in approaching him, find it to be a constant pleasure, a comfortable evidence of their integrity, and a comfortable earnest of their endless felicity.

II. David, having given proofs of his integrity, earnestly prays, with a humble confidence towards God (such as those have whose hearts condemn them not), that he might not fall under the doom of the wicked (*v.* 9, 10). *Gather not my soul with sinners,* Here, 1. David describes these sinners, whom he looked upon to be in a miserable condition, so miserable that he could not wish the worst enemy he had in the world to be in a worse. "They are *bloody men,* that thirst after blood and lie under a great deal of the guilt of blood. They do mischief, and mischief is always in their hands. Though they get by their wickedness (for *their right hand is full of bribes* which they have taken to pervert justice), yet that will make their case never the better; for *what is a man profited if he gain the world and lose his soul?"* 2. He dread having his lot with them. He never loved them, nor associated with them, in this world, and therefore could in faith pray that he might not have his lot with them in the other world. Our souls must shortly be gathered, to return to God that gave them and will call for them again. See Job 34:14. It concerns us to consider whether our souls will then be gathered with saints or with sinners, whether bound in the bundle of life with the Lord for ever, as the souls of the faithful are (1 Sa. 25:29), or bound in the bundle of tares for the fire, Mt. 13:30. Death gathers us to our people, to those that are our people while we live, whom we choose to associate with, and with whom we cast in our lot, to those death will gather us, and with them we must take our lot, to eternity. Balaam desired to die the death of the righteous; David dreaded dying the death of the wicked; so that both sides were of that mind, which if we be of, and will live up to it, we are happy for ever. Those that will not be companions with sinners in their mirth, nor eat of their dainties, may in faith pray not to be companions with them in their misery, nor to drink of their cup, their cup of trembling.

III. David, with a holy humble confidence, commits himself to the grace of God, *v.* 11, 12. 1. He promises that by the grace of God he would persevere in his duty: *"As for me,* whatever others do, *I will walk in my integrity."* Note, When the testimony of our consciences for us that we have walked in our integrity is comfortable to us this should confirm our resolutions to continue therein. 2. He prays for the divine grace both to enable him to do so and to give him the comfort of it: *"Redeem me* out of the hands of my enemies, *and be merciful to me,* living and dying." Be we ever so confident of our integrity, yet still we must rely upon God's mercy and the great redemption Christ has wrought out, and pray for the benefit of them. 3. He pleases himself with his steadiness: *"My foot stands in an even place,* where I shall not stumble and whence I shall not fall." This he speaks as one that found his resolutions fixed for God and godliness, not to be shaken by the temptations of the world, and his comforts firm in God and his grace, not to be disturbed by the crosses and troubles of the world. 4. He promises himself that he should yet have occasion to praise the Lord, that he should be furnished with matter for praise, that he should have a heart for praises, and that, though he was now perhaps banished from public ordinances, yet he should again have an opportunity of blessing God in the congregation of his people. Those that hate the congregation of evil-doers shall be joined to the congregation of the righteous and join with them in praising God; and it is pleasant doing that in good company; the more the better; it is the more like heaven.

PSALM 27

Some think David penned this psalm before his coming to the throne, when he was in the midst of his troubles, and perhaps upon occasion of the death of his parents; but the Jews think he penned it when he was old, upon occasion of the wonderful deliverance he had from the sword of the giant, when Abishai succoured him (2 Sa. 21:16, 17) and his people thereupon resolved he should never venture his life again in battle, lest he should quench the light of Israel. Perhaps it was not penned upon any particular occasion; but it is very expressive of the pious and devout affections with which gracious souls are carried out towards God at all times, especially in times of trouble. Here is, I. The courage and holy bravery of his faith (*v.* 1–3). II. The complacency he took in communion with God and the benefit he experienced by it (*v.* 4–6). III. His desire towards God, and his favour and grace (*v.* 7–9, 11, 12). IV. His expectations from God, and the encouragement he gives to others to hope in him (*v.* 10, 13, 14). And let our hearts be thus affected in singing this psalm.

A psalm of David.

Verses 1–6

We may observe here,

I. With what a lively faith David triumphs in God, glories in his holy name, and in the interest he had in him. 1. *The Lord is my light.* David's subjects called him *the light of Israel,* 2 Sa. 21:17. And he was indeed a burning and a shining light: but he owns that he shone, as the moon does, with a borrows light; what light God darted upon him reflected upon them: *The Lord is my light.* God is a light to his people, to show them the way when they are in doubt, to comfort and rejoice their hearts when they are in sorrow. It is in his light that they now walk on in their way, and in his light they hope to see light for ever. 2. "He is *my salvation,* in whom I am safe and by whom I shall be saved." 3. "He is *the strength of my life,* not only the protector of my exposed life, who keeps me from being slain, but the strength of my frail weak life, who keeps me from fainting, sinking, and dying away." God, who is a believer's light, is the strength of his life, not only by whom, but in whom, he lives and moves. In God therefore let us strengthen ourselves.

II. With what an undaunted courage he triumphs over his enemies; no fortitude like that of faith. If God be for him, who can be against him? *Whom shall I fear? Of whom shall I be afraid?* If Omnipotence be his guard, he has no cause to fear; if he knows it to be so, he has no disposition to fear. If God be his light, he fears no shades; if God be his salvation, he fears no colours. He triumphs over his enemies that were already routed, *v.* 2. His enemies came upon him, *to eat up his flesh,* aiming at no less and assured of that, but they fell; not, "He smote them and they fell," but, *"They stumbled and fell;"* they were so confounded and weakened that they could not go on with their enterprise. Thus those that came to take Christ with a word's speaking were made to stagger and fall to the ground, Jn. 18:6. The ruin of some of the enemies of God's people is an earnest of the complete conquest of them all. And therefore, these having fallen, he is fearless of the rest: "Though they be numerous, *a host* of them, — though they be daring and their attempts threatening, — though they *encamp against me,* an army against one man, — though they wage war upon me, yet *my heart shall not fear."* Hosts cannot hurt us if the Lord of hosts protect us. Nay, in this assurance that God is for me *"I will be confident."* Two things he will be confident of: — 1. That he shall be safe. "If God is my salvation, *in the time of trouble he shall hide me;* he shall set me out of danger and above the fear of it." God will not only find out a shelter for his people in distress (as he did Jer. 36:26), but he will himself be their hiding-place, Ps. 32:7. His providence will, it may be, keep them safe; at least his grace will make them easy. His name is the strong tower into which by faith they run, Prov. 18:10. *"He shall hide me,* not in the strongholds of En-gedi (1 Sa. 23:29), but *in the secret of his tabernacle."* The gracious presence of God, his power, his promise, his readiness to hear prayer, the witness of his Spirit in the hearts of his people — these are the secret of his tabernacle, and in these the saints find cause for that holy security and serenity of mind in which they dwell at ease. This sets them upon a rock which will not sink under them, but on which they find firm footing for their hopes; nay, it sets them *up upon a rock* on high, where the raging threatening billows of a stormy sea cannot touch them; it is a rock that is *higher than we,* Ps. 61:2. 2. That he shall be victorious (*v.* 6): *"Now shall my head be lifted up above my enemies,* not only so as that they cannot reach it with their darts, but so as that I shall be exalted to bear rule over them." David here, by faith in the promise of God, triumphs before the victory, and is as sure, not only of the laurel, but of the crown, as if it were already upon his head.

III. With what a gracious earnestness he prays for a constant communion with God in holy ordinances, *v.* 4. It greatly encouraged his confidence in God that he was conscious to himself of an entire affection to God and to his ordinances, and that he was in his element when in the way of his duty and in the way of increasing his acquaintance with him. If our hearts can witness for us that we delight in God above any creature, that may encourage us to depend upon him; for it is a sign we are of those whom he protects as his own. Or it may be taken thus: He desired to dwell in the house of the Lord that there he might be safe from the enemies that surrounded him. Finding himself surrounded by threatening hosts, he does not say, *"One thing have I desired,* in order to my safety," that I may have my army augmented to such a number," or that I may be master of such a city or such a castle, but *"that I may dwell in the house of the Lord,* and then I am well." Observe,

1. What it is he desires — *to dwell in the house of the Lord.* In the courts of God's house the priests had their lodgings, and David wished he had been one of them. Disdainfully as some look upon God's ministers, one of the greatest and best of kings that ever was would gladly have taken his lot, have taken his lodging, among them. Or, rather, he desires that he might duly and constantly attend on the public service of God, with other faithful Israelites, according as the duty of every day required. He longed to see an end of the wars in which he was now engaged, not that he might live at ease in his own palace, but that he might have leisure and liberty for a constant attendance in God's courts. Thus Hezekiah, a genuine son of David, wished for the recovery of his health, not that he might go up to the thrones of judgment, but that he might *go up to the house of the Lord,* Isa. 38:22. Note, All God's children desire to dwell in God's house; where should they dwell else? Not to sojourn there as a wayfaring man, that turns aside to tarry but for a night, nor to dwell there for a time only, as the servant that abides not in the house for ever, but to dwell there all the days of their life; for there the Son abides ever. Do we hope that praising God will be the blessedness of our eternity? Surely them we ought to make it the business of our time.

2. How earnestly he covets this: "This is the *one thing I have desired of the Lord* and which I will seek after." If he were to ask but one thing of God, this should be it; for this he had at heart more than any thing. He desired it as a good thing; he desired it of the Lord as his gift and a token of his favour. And, having fixed his desire upon this as the one thing needful, he sought after it; he continued to pray for it, and contrived his affairs so as that he might have this liberty and opportunity. Note, Those that truly desire communion with God will set themselves with all diligence to seek after it, Prov. 18:1.

3. What he had in his eye in it. He would dwell in God's house, not for the plenty of good entertainment that was there, in the feasts upon the sacrifices, nor for the music and good singing that were there, but *to behold the beauty of the Lord and to enquire in his temple.* He desired to attend in God's courts, (1.) That he might have the pleasure of meditating upon God. He knew something of the beauty of the Lord, the infinite and transcendent amiableness of the divine being and perfections; his holiness is his beauty (Ps. 110:3), his goodness is his beauty, Zec. 9:17. The harmony of all his attributes is the beauty of his nature. With an eye of faith and holy love we with pleasure behold this beauty, and observe more and more in it that is amiable, that is admirable. When with fixedness of thought, and a holy flame of devout affections, we contemplate God's glorious excellencies, and entertain ourselves with the tokens of his peculiar favour to us, this is that view of the beauty of the Lord which David here covets, and it is to be had in his ordinances, for there he manifests himself. (2.) That he might have the satisfaction of being instructed in his duty; for concerning this he would *enquire in God's temple.* Lord, *what wilt thou have me to do?* For the sake of these two things he desired that one thing, to *dwell in the house of the Lord all the days of his life;* for blessed are those that do so; they will be still praising him (Ps. 84:4), both in speaking to him and in hearing from him. Mary's sitting at Christ's feet to hear his word Christ calls the *one thing needful,* and *the good part.*

4. What advantage he promised himself by it. Could he but have a place in God's house, (1.) There he should be quiet and easy: there troubles would not find him, for he should be hid in secret; there troubles would not reach him, for he should be set on high, *v.* 5. Joash, one of David's seed, was hidden in the house of the Lord six years, and there not only preserved from the sword, but reserved to the crown, 2 Ki. 11:3. The temple was thought a safe place for Nehemiah to abscond in, Neh. 6:10. The safety of believers however is not in the walls of the temple, but in the God of the temple and their comfort in communion with him. (2.) There he should be pleasant and cheerful: there he would offer sacrifices of joy, *v.* 6. For God's work is its own wages. There *he would sing, yea, he would sing praises to the Lord.* Note, Whatever is the matter of our joy ought to be the matter of our praise; and, when we attend upon God in holy ordinances, we ought to be much in joy and praise. It is for the glory of our God that we should sing in his ways; and, whenever God lifts us up above our enemies, we ought to exalt him in our praises. *Thanks be to God, who always causeth us to triumph,* 2 Co. 2:14.

Verses 7–14

David in these verses expresses,

I. His desire towards God, in many petitions. If he cannot now go up to the house of the Lord, yet, wherever he is, he can find a way to the throne of grace by prayer.

1. He humbly bespeaks, because he firmly believes he shall have, a gracious audience: *"Hear, O Lord, when I cry,* not only with my heart, but, as one in earnest, *with my voice too."* He bespeaks also an answer of peace, which he expects, not from his own merit, but God's goodness: *Have mercy upon me, and answer me, v.* 7. If we pray and believe, God will graciously hear and answer.

2. He takes hold of the kind invitation God had given him to this duty, *v.* 8. It is presumption for us to come into the presence of the King of kings uncalled, nor can we draw near with any assurance unless he *hold forth to us the golden sceptre.* David therefore going to pray fastens, in his thoughts, upon the call God had given him to the throne of his grace, and reverently touches, as it were, the top of the golden sceptre which was thereby held out to him. *My heart said unto thee* (so it begins in the original) or *of* thee, *Seek you my face;* he first revolved that, and preached that over again to himself (and that is the best preaching: it is hearing twice what God speaks once) — *Thou saidst* (so it may be supplied), *Seek you my face;* and then he returns what he had so meditated upon, in this pious resolution, *Thy face, Lord, will I seek.* Observe here, (1.) The true nature of religious worship; it is seeking the face of God. This it is in God's precept: *Seek you my face;* he would have us seek him for himself, and make his favour our chief good; and this it is in the saint's purpose and desire: *"Thy face, Lord, will I seek,* and nothing less will I take up with." The opening of his hand will satisfy the desire of other living things (Ps. 145:16), but it is only the shining of his face that will satisfy the desire of a living soul, Ps. 4:6, 7. (2.) The kind of invitation of a gracious God to this duty: *Thou saidst, Seek you my face;* it is not only permission, but a precept; and his commanding us to seek implies a promise of finding; for he is too kind to say, *Seek you me in vain.* God calls us to seek his face in our conversion to him and in our converse with him. He calls us, by the whispers of his Spirit to and with our spirits, to seek his face; he calls us by his word, by the stated returns of opportunities for his worship, and by special providences, merciful and afflictive. When we are foolishly making our court to lying vanities God is, in love to us, calling us in him to seek our own mercies. (3.) The ready compliance of a gracious soul with this invitation. The call is immediately returned: *My heart answered, Thy face, Lord, will I seek.* The call was general; *"Seek you my face;"* but, like David, we must apply it to ourselves, *"I will seek it."* The word does us no good when we transfer it to others, and do not ourselves accept the exhortation. The call was, *Seek you my face;* the answer is express, *Thy face, Lord, will I seek;* like that (Jer. 3:22), *Behold, we come unto thee.* A gracious heart readily echoes to the call of a gracious God, being made willing in the day of his power.

3. He is very particular in his requests. (1.) For the favour of God, that he might not be shut out from that (*v.* 9): *"Thy face, Lord, will I seek,* in obedience to thy command; therefore *hide not thy face from me;* let me never want

the reviving sense of the favour; love me, and let me know that thou lovest me; *put not thy servant away in anger.*" He owns he had deserved God's displeasure, but begs that, however God might correct him, he would not cast him away from his presence; for what is hell but that? (2.) For the continuance of his presence with him: "*Thou hast been my help* formerly, and *thou are the God of my salvation;* and therefore whither shall I go but to thee? *O leave me not, neither forsake me;* withdraw not the operations of they power from me, for then I am helpless; withdraw not the tokens of thy good-will to me, for then I am comfortless." (3.) For the benefit of divine guidance (*v.* 11): "*Teach me thy way, O Lord!* give me to understand the meaning of thy providences towards me and make them plain to me; and give me to know my duty in every doubtful case, that I may not mistake it, but may walk rightly, and that I may not do it with hesitation, but may walk surely." It is not policy, but plainness (that is, downright honesty) that will direct us into and keep us in the way of our duty. He begs to be guided *in a plain path, because of his enemies,* or (as the margin reads it) his *observers.* His enemies watched for his halting, that they may find occasion against him. Saul eyed David, 1 Sa. 18:9. This quickened him to pray, "Lord, *lead me in a plain path,* that they may have nothing ill, or nothing that looks ill, to lay to my charge." (4.) For the benefit of a divine protection (*v.* 12): "*Deliver me not over to the will of my enemies.* Lord, let them not gain their point, for it aims at my life, and no less, and in such a way as that I have no fence against them, but thy power over their consciences; for *false witnesses have risen up against me,* that aim further than to take away my reputation or estate, for they *breathe out cruelty;* it is the blood, the precious blood, they thirst after." Herein David was a type of Christ; for false witnesses rose up against him, and such as breathed out cruelty; but though he was delivered into their wicked hands, he was not delivered over to their will, for they could not prevent his exaltation.

II. He expresses his dependence upon God,

1. That he would help and succour him when all other helps and succours failed him (*v.* 10): "*When my father and my mother forsake me,* the nearest and dearest friends I have in the world, from whom I may expect most relief and with most reason, when they die, or are at a distance from me, or are disabled to help me in time of need, or are unkind to me or unmindful of me, and will not help me, when I am as helpless as ever poor orphan was that was left fatherless and motherless, then I know *the Lord will take me up,* as a poor wandering sheep is taken up, and saved from perishing." His time to help those that trust in him is when all other helpers fail, when it is most for his honour and their comfort. With him *the fatherless find mercy.* This promise has often been fulfilled in the letter of it. Forsaken orphans have been taken under the special care of the divine Providence, which has raised up relief and friends for them in a way that one would not have expected. God is a surer and better friend than our earthly parents are or can be.

2. That in due time he should see the displays of his goodness, *v.* 13. He believed he should *see the goodness of the Lord in the land of the living;* and, if he had not done so, he would *have fainted* under his afflictions. Even the best saints are subject to faint when their troubles become grievous and tedious, their spirits are overwhelmed, and their flesh and heart fail. But then faith is a sovereign cordial; it keeps them from desponding under their burden and from despairing of relief, keeps them hoping, and praying, and waiting, and keeps up in them good thoughts of God, and the comfortable enjoyment of themselves. But what was it the belief of which kept David from fainting? — *that he should see the goodness of the Lord,* which now seemed at a distance. Those that walk by faith in the goodness of the Lord shall in due time walk in the sight of that goodness. This he hopes to see in the land of the living, that is, (1.) In this world, that he should outlive his troubles and not perish under them. It is his comfort, not so much that he shall see the land of the living as that he shall see the goodness of God in it; for that is the comfort of all creature-comforts to a gracious soul. (2.) In the land of Canaan, and in Jerusalem where the lively oracles were. In comparison with the heathen, that were dead in sin, the land of Israel might fitly be called *the land of the living;* there God was known, and there David hoped to see his goodness; see 2 Sa. 15:25, 26. Or, (3.), In heaven. It is that alone that may truly be called *the land of the living,* where there is no more death. This earth is the land of the dying. There is nothing like the believing hope of eternal life, the foresights of that glory, and foretastes of those pleasures, to keep us from fainting under all the calamities of this present time.

3. That in the mean time he should be strengthened to bear up under his burdens (*v.* 14); whether he says it to himself, or to his friends, it comes all to one; this is that which encourages him: *He shall strengthen thy heart,* shall sustain thy spirit, and then the spirit shall sustain the infirmity. In that strength, (1.) Keep close to God and to your duty. *Wait on the Lord* by faith, and prayer, and a humble resignation to his will; *wait, I say, on the Lord;* whatever you do, grow not remiss in your attendance upon God. (2.) Keep up your spirits in the midst of the greatest dangers and difficulties: *Be of good courage;* let your hearts be fixed, trusting in God, and your minds stayed upon him, and then let none of these things move you. Those that wait upon the Lord have reason to be of good courage.

PSALM 28

The former part of this psalm is the prayer of a saint militan and now in distress (*v.* 1–3), to which is added the doom of God's implacable enemies (*v.* 4, 5). The latter part of the psalm is the thanksgiving of a saint triumphant, and delivered out of his distresses (*v.* 6–8), to which is added a prophetical prayer for all God's faithful loyal subjects (*v.* 9). So that it is hard to say which of these two conditions David was in when he penned it. Some think he was now in trouble seeking God, but at the same time preparing to praise him for his deliverance, and by faith giving him thanks for it, before it was wrought. Others think he was now in triumph, but remembered, and recorded for his own and others' benefit, the prayers he made when he was in affliction, that the mercy might relish the better, when it appeared to be an answer to them.

A psalm of David.

Verses 1–5

In these verses David is very earnest in prayer.

I. He prays that God would graciously hear and answer him, now that, in his distress, he called upon him, *v.* 1, 2. Observe his faith in prayer: *O Lord, my rock,* denoting his belief of God's power (he is a rock) and his dependence upon that power — "He is *my rock,* on whom I build my hope." Observe his fervency in prayer: "*To thee will I cry,* as one in earnest, being ready to sink, unless thou come in with seasonable succour." And observe how solicitous he is to obtain an answer: "*Be not silent to me,* as one angry at my prayers, Ps. 80:4. Lord, speak to me, answer me *with good words and comfortable words* (Zec. 1:13); though the thing I pray for has not been given me, yet let God speak to me joy and gladness, and make me to hear them. Lord, speak for me, in answer to my prayers, plead my cause, command deliverances for me, and thus hear and answer the voice of my supplications." Two things he pleads: — 1. The sad despair he should be in if God slighted him: "*If thou be silent to me,* and I have not the tokens of thy favour, I am *like those that go down into the pit* (that is, I am a dead man, lost and undone); if God be not my friend, appear not to me and appear not for me, my hope and my help will have perished." Nothing can be so cutting, so killing, to a gracious soul, as the want of God's favour and the sense of his displeasure. *I shall be like those that go down to hell* (so some understand it); for what is the misery of the damned but this, that God is ever silent to them and deaf to their cry? Those are in some measure qualified for God's favour, and may expect it, who are thus possessed with a dread of his wrath, and to whom his frowns are worse than death. 2. The good hopes he had that God would favour him: *I lift up my hands towards thy holy oracle,* which denotes, not only an earnest desire, but an earnest expectation, thence to receive an answer of peace. The most holy place within the veil is here, as elsewhere, called the *oracle;* there the ark and the mercy-seat were, there God was said to *dwell between the cherubim,* and thence he spoke to his people, Num. 7:89. That was a type of Christ, and it is to him that we must lift up our eyes and hands, for through him all good comes from God to us. It was also a figure of heaven (Heb. 9:24); and from God as our Father in heaven we are taught to expect an answer to our prayers. The scriptures are called *the oracles of God,* and to them we must have an eye in our prayers and expectations. There is the word on which God hath caused and encouraged us to hope.

II. He deprecates the doom of wicked people, as before (Ps. 26:9, "*Gather not my soul with sinners*"): Lord, I attend thy holy oracle, *draw me not away* from that *with the wicked, and with the workers of iniquity,*" *v.* 3. 1. "Save me from being entangled in the snares they have laid for me. They flatter and cajole me, and speak peace to me; but they have a design upon me, for *mischief is in their heart;* they aim to disturb me, nay, to destroy me. Lord, suffer me not to be drawn away and ruined by their cursed plots; for they have, can have, no power, no success, against me, except it be given them from above." 2. "Save me from being infected with their sins and from doing as they do. Let me not be drawn away by their fallacious arguments, or their allurements, from the holy oracle (where I desire to dwell all the days of my life), to practise any wicked works;" see Ps. 141:4. "Lord, never leave me to myself, to use such arts of deceit and treachery for my safety as they use to my ruin. Let no event of Providence be an invincible temptation to me, to draw me either into the imitation or into the interest of wicked people." Good men dread the way of sinners; the best are sensible of the danger they are in of being drawn aside into it; and therefore we should all pray earnestly to God for his grace to keep us in our integrity. 3. "Save me from being involved in their doom; let me not be led forth with the workers of iniquity, for I am not one of those that speak peace while war is in their hearts." Note, Those that are careful not to partake with sinners in their sins have reason to hope that they shall not partake with them in their plagues, Rev. 18:4.

III. He imprecates the just judgments of God upon the workers of iniquity (*v.* 4): *Give them according to their deeds.* This is not the language of passion or revenge, nor is it inconsistent with the duty of praying for our enemies. But, 1. Thus he would show how far he was from complying with the workers of iniquity, and with what good reason he had begged not to be drawn away with them, because he was convinced that they could not be made more miserable then to be dealt with according to their deeds. 2. Thus he would express his zeal for the honour of God's justice in the governing world. "Lord, they think all well that they do, and justify themselves in their wicked practices. Lord, *give them after the work of their hands,* and so undeceive those about them, who think there is no harm in what they do because it goes unpunished," Ps. 94:1,2. 3. This prayer is a prophecy that God will, sooner or later, render to all impenitent sinners according to their deserts. If what has been done amiss be not undone by repentance, there will certainly come a reckoning day, when God will render to every man who persists in his evil deeds according to them. It is a prophecy particularly of the destruction of destroyers: "*They speak peace to their neighbours, but mischief is in their hearts;* Lord, *give them according to their deeds,* let the spoilers be spoiled, and let those be treacherously dealt with who have thus dealt treacherously;" see Isa. 33:1; Rev. 18:6; 13:10. Observe, He foretels that God will reward them, not only according to their deed, but *according to the wickedness of their endeavours;* for sinners shall be reckoned with, not only for the mischief they have done, but for the mischief they would have done, which they designed, and did what they could to effect. And, if God go by this rule in dealing with the wicked, surely he will do so in dealing with the righteous, and will reward them, not only for the good they have done, but for the good they have endeavoured to do, though they could not accomplish it.

IV. He foretels their destruction for their contempt of God and his hand (*v.* 5): "*Because they regard not the works of the Lord and the operations of his hands,* by which he manifests himself and speaks to the children of men, *he will destroy them* in this world and in the other, *and not build them up.*" Note, A stupid regardlessness of the works of God is the cause of their ruin. Why do men question the being or attributes of God, but because they do not duly regard his handiworks, which declare his glory, and in which the invisible things of him are clearly seen? Why do men forget God, and live without him, nay, affront God, and live in rebellion against him, but because they consider not the instances of that wrath of his which is revealed *from heaven against all ungodliness and unrighteousness of men?* Why do the enemies of God's people hate and persecute them, and devise mischief against them, but because they regard not the works God has wrought for his church, by which he has made it appear how dear it is to him? See Isa. 5:12.

In singing this we must arm ourselves against all temptations to join with the workers of iniquity, and animate ourselves against all the troubles we may be threatened with by the workers of iniquity.

Verses 6–9

In these verses,

I. David gives God thanks for the audience of his prayers as affectionately as a few verses before he had begged it: *Blessed be the Lord, v.* 6. How soon are the saints' sorrows turned into songs and their prayers into praises! It was in faith that David prayed (*v.* 2), *Hear the voice of my supplications;* and by the same faith he gives thanks (*v.* 6) that *God has heard the voice of his supplications.* Note, 1. Those that pray in faith may rejoice in hope. "He hath heard me (graciously accepted me) and I am as sure of a real answer as if I had it already." 2. What we win by prayer we must wear by praise. Has God heard our supplications? Let us then bless his name.

II. He encourages himself to hope in God for the perfecting of every thing that concerned him. Having given to God the glory of his grace (*v.* 6), he is humbly bold to take the comfort of it, *v.* 7. This is the method of attaining peace: let us begin with praise that is attainable. Let us first bless God and then bless ourselves. Observe, 1. His dependence upon God: *"The Lord is my strength,* to support me, and carry me on, through all my services and sufferings. He is *my shield,* to protect me from all the malicious designs of my enemies against me. I have chosen him to be so, I have always found him so, and I expect he will still be so." 2. His experience of the benefits of that dependence: *"My heart trusted in him,* and in his power and promise; and it has not been in vain to do so, for *I am helped,* I have been often helped; not only God has given to me, in his due time, the help I trusted to him for, but my very trusting in him has helped me, in the mean time, and kept me from fainting." Ps. 27:13. The very actings of faith are present aids to a dropping spirit, and often help it at a dead lift. 3. His improvement of this experience. (1.) He had the pleasure of it: *Therefore my heart greatly rejoices.* The joy of a believer is seated in the heart, while, in the laughter of the fool, the heart is sorrowful. It is great joy, *joy unspeakable and full of glory.* The heart that truly believes shall in due time greatly rejoice; it is *joy and peace in believing* that we are to expect. (2.) God shall have the praise of it: when *my heart greatly rejoices, with my song will I praise him.* This must we express our gratitude; it is the least we can do; and others will hereby be invited and encouraged to trust in him too.

III. He pleases himself with the interest which all good people, through Christ, have in God (*v.* 8): *"The Lord is their strength;* not mine only, but the strength of every believer." Note, The saints rejoice in their friends' comforts as well as their own; for, as we have not the less benefit from the light of the sun, so neither from the light of Gods' countenance, for others' sharing therein; for we are sure there is enough for all and enough for each. This is our communion with all saints, that God is their strength and ours, Christ their Lord and ours, 1 Co. 1:2. He is their strength, the strength of all Israel, because he is *the saving strength of his anointed,* that is, 1. Of David in the type. God, in strengthening him that was their king and fought their battles, strengthened the whole kingdom. He calls himself God's *anointed* because it was the unction he had received that exposed him to the envy of his enemies, and therefore entitled him to the divine protection. 2. Of Christ, his anointed, his Messiah, in the anti-type. God was his saving strength, qualified him for his undertaking and carried him through it; see Ps. 89:21; Isa. 49:5; 50:7, 9. And so he becomes their strength, the strength of all the saints; he strengthened him that is the church's head, and from him diffuses strength to all the members, has commanded his strength, and so *strengthens what he has wrought for us;* Ps. 68:28; 80:17, 18.

IV. He concludes with a short but comprehensive prayer for the church of God, *v.* 9. He prays for Israel, not as his people ("save my people, and bless my inheritance"), though they were so, but, *"thine."* God's interest in them lay nearer his heart than his own. *We are thy people* is a good plea, Isa. 64:9; 63:19. *I am thine, save me.* God's people are his inheritance, dear to him, and precious in his eyes; what little glory he has from this world he has from them. *The Lord's portion is his people.* That which he begs of God for them is, 1. That he would save them from their enemies and the dangers they were exposed to. 2. That he would bless them with all good, flowing from his favour, in performance of his promise, and amounting to a happiness for them. 3. That he would *feed them,* bless them with plenty, and especially the plenty of his ordinances, which are food to the soul. *Rule them;* so the margin. "Direct their counsels and actions aright, and overrule their affairs for good. Feed them, and rule them; sets pastors, set rulers, over them, that shall do their office with wisdom and understanding." 4. That he would *lift them up for ever,* lift them up out of their troubles and distresses, and do this, not only for those of that age, but for his people in every age to come, even to the end. "Lift them up into thy glorious kingdom, lift them up as high as heaven." There, and there only, will the saints be lifted up for ever, never more to sink or be depressed. Observe, Those, and those only, whom God feeds and rules, who are willing to be taught, and guided, and governed, by him, shall be saved, and blessed, and lifted up for ever.

PSALM 29

It is the probable conjecture of some very good interpreters that David penned this psalm upon occasion, and just at the time, of a great storm of thunder, lightning, and rain, as the eighth psalm was his meditation in a moon-light night and the nineteenth in a sunny morning. It is good to take occasion from the sensible operations of God's power in the kingdom of nature to give glory to him. So composed was David, and so cheerful, even in a dreadful tempest, when others trembled, that then he penned this psalm; for, "though the earth be removed, yet will we not fear." I. He calls upon the great ones of the world to give glory to God (*v.* 1, 2). II. To convince them of the goodness of that God whom they were to adore, he takes notice of his power and terror in the thunder, and lightning, and thunder-showers (*v.* 3–9), his sovereign dominion over the world (*v.* 10), and his special favour to his church (*v.* 11). Great and high thoughts of God should fill us in singing this psalm.

A psalm of David.

Verses 1–11

In this psalm we have,

I. A demand of the homage of the great men of the earth to be paid to the great God. Every clap of thunder David interpreted as a call to himself and other princes to give glory to the great God. Observe, 1. Who they are that are called to this duty: *"O you mighty* (*v.* 1), you sons of the mighty, who have power, and on whom that power is devolved by succession and inheritance, who have royal blood running in your veins!" It is much for the honour of the great God that the men of this world should pay their homage to him; and they are bound to do it, not only because, high as they are, he is infinitely above them, and therefore they must bow to him, but because they have their power from him, and are to use it for him, and this tribute of acknowledgment they owe to him for it. 2. How often this call is repeated; *Give unto the Lord,* and again, and a third time, *Give unto the Lord.* This intimates that the mighty men are backward to this duty and are with difficulty persuaded to it, but that it is of great consequence to the interests of God's kingdom among men that princes should heartily espouse them. Jerusalem flourishes when the *kings of the earth bring their glory and honour into it,* Rev. 21:24. 3. What they are called to do — to *give unto the Lord,* not as if he needed any thing, or could be benefited by any gifts of ours, nor as if we had any thing to give him that is not his own already *(Who hath first given to him?),* but the recognition of his glory, and of his dominion over us, he is pleased to interpret as a gift to him: *"Give unto the Lord* your own selves, in the first place, and then your services. *Give unto the Lord glory and strength;* acknowledge his glory and strength, and give praise to him as a God of infinite majesty and irresistible power; and whatever glory or strength he has by his providence entrusted you with offer it to him, to be used for his honour, in his service. Give him your crowns; let them be laid at his feet; give him your sceptres, your swords, your keys, put all into his hand, that you, in the use of them, may be to him for a name and a praise." Princes value themselves by their glory and strength; these they must ascribe to God, owning him to be infinitely more glorious and powerful than they. This demand of homage from the mighty must be looked upon as directed either to the grandees of David's own kingdom, the peers of the realm, the princes of the tribes (and it is to excite them to a more diligent and constant attendance at God's altars, in which he had observed them very remiss), or to the neighbouring kings whom he by his sword had made tributaries to Israel and now would persuade to become tributaries to the God of Israel. Crowned heads must bow before the King of kings. What is here said to the mighty is said to all: *Worship God;* it is the sum and substance of the everlasting gospel, Rev. 14:6, 7. Now we have here, (1.) The nature of religious worship; it is *giving to the Lord the glory due to his name, v.* 2. God's name is that whereby he has made himself known. There is a glory due to his name. It is impossible that we should give him all the glory due to his name; when we have said and done out best for the honour of God's name, still we come infinitely short of the merit of the subject; but when we answer that revelation which he has made of himself, with suitable affections and adorations, then we give him some of that glory which is due to his name. If we would, in hearing and praying, and other acts of devotion, receive grace from God, we must make it our business to give glory to God. (2.) The rule of the performance of religious exercises; *Worship the Lord in the beauty of holiness,* which denotes, [1.] The object of our worship; the glorious majesty of God is called *the beauty of holiness,* 2 Chr. 20:21. In the worship of God we must have an eye to his beauty, and adore him, not only as infinitely awful and therefore to be feared above all, but as infinitely amiable and therefore to be loved and delighted in above all; especially we must have an eye to the beauty of his holiness; this the angels fasten upon in their praises, Rev. 4:8. Or, [2.] The place of worship. The sanctuary then was the *beauty of holiness,* Ps. 48:1, 2; Jer. 17:12. The beauty of the sanctuary was the exact agreement of the worship there performed with the divine appointment — the pattern in the mount. Now, under the gospel, solemn assemblies of Christians (which purity is the beauty of) are the places where God is to be worshipped. Or, [3.] The manner of worship. We must be holy in all our religious performances, devoted to God, and to his will and glory. There is a beauty in holiness, and it is that which puts an acceptable beauty upon all the acts of worship.

II. Good reason given for this demand. We shall see ourselves bound to give glory to God if we consider,

1. His sufficiency in himself, intimated in his name *Jehovah — I am that I am,* which is repeated here no fewer than eighteen times in this short psalm, twice in every verse but three, and once in two of those three; I do not recollect that there is the like in all the book of psalms. Let the mighty ones of the earth know him by this name and give him the glory due to it.

2. His sovereignty over all things. Let those that rule over men know there is a God that rules over them, that rules over all. The psalmist here sets forth God's dominion,

(1.) In the kingdom of nature. In the wonderful effects of natural causes, and the operations of the powers of nature, we ought to take notice of God's glory and strength, which we are called upon to ascribe to him; in the thunder, and lightning, and rain, we may see, [1.] His glory. It is the God of glory that thunders (thunders is the *noise of his voice,* Job 37:2), and it declares him a God of glory, so awful is the sound of the thunder, and so bright the flash of its companion, the lightning; to the hearing and to the sight nothing is more affecting than these, as if by those two learning senses God would have such proofs of his glory to the minds of men as should leave the most stupid inexcusable. Some observe that there were then some particular reasons why thunder should be called *the voice of the Lord,* not only because it comes from above, is not under the direction or foresight of any man, speaks aloud, and reaches far, but because God often spoke in thunder, particularly at Mount Sinai, and by thunder discomfited the enemies of Israel. To speak it the voice of the God of glory, it is here said to be *upon the water,* upon *many waters* (*v.* 3); it reaches over the vast ocean, the waters under the firmament; it rattles among the thick clouds, the waters above the firmament. Every one that hears the thunder (his ear being made to tingle with it) will own that *the voice of the Lord is full of majesty* (Ps. 29:4), enough to make the highest humble (for none can *thunder with a voice like him*) and the proudest tremble — for, if his voice be so terrible, what is his arm? Every time we hear it thunder, let our hearts be thereby filled with great, and high, and honourable thoughts of God, in the holy adorings and admirings of whom the power of godliness does so much consist. *O Lord our God! thou art very great.* [2.] His power (*v.* 4.): *The voice of the Lord is powerful,* as appears by the effects of it; for it works wonders. Those that write natural histories relate the prodigious effects of thunder and lightning, even out of the ordinary course of natural causes, which must be resolved into the omnipotence of the God of nature. *First,* Trees have been rent and split by thunderbolts, *v.* 5, 6. *The voice of the Lord,* in the thunder, often *broke the cedars,* even those of Lebanon, the strongest, the stateliest. Some understand it of the violent winds which shook the cedars, and sometimes tore off their aspiring tops. Earthquakes also shook the ground itself on which the trees grew, and made *Lebanon and Sirion* to dance; *the wilderness of Kadesh* also was in like manner shaken (*v.* 8), the trees by winds, the ground by earthquakes, and both by thunders, of which I incline rather to understand it. The learned Dr. Hammond understands it of the consternations and conquest of neighbouring kingdoms that warred with Israel and opposed David, as the Syrians, whose country lay near the forest of Lebanon, the Amorites that bordered on Mount Hermon, and the Moabites and Ammonites that lay about the wilderness of Kadesh. *Secondly,* Fires have been kindled by lightnings and houses and churches thereby consumed; hence we read of hot thunderbolts (Ps. 78:48); accordingly the voice of the Lord, in the thunder, is here said to *divide the flames of fire* (*v.* 7), that is, to scatter them upon the earth, as God sees fit to direct them and do execution by them. *Thirdly,* The terror of thunder makes the hinds to calve sooner, and some think more easily, than otherwise they would. The hind is a timourous creature, and much affected with the noise of thunder; and no marvel, when sometimes proud and stout men have been made to tremble at it. The emperor Caligula would hide himself under his bed when it thundered. Horace, the poet, owns that he was reclaimed from atheism by the terror of thunder and lightning, which he describes somewhat like this of David, *lib.* 1, *ode* 34. The thunder is said here to *discover the forest,* that is, it so terrifies the wild beasts of the forest that they quit the dens and thickets in which they hid themselves are so are discovered. Or it throws down the trees, and so discovers the ground that was shaded by them. Whenever it thunders let us think of this psalm; and, whenever we sing this psalm, let us think of the dreadful thunder-claps we have sometimes heard, and thus bring God's words and his works together, that by both we may be directed and quickened to give unto him the glory due unto his name; and let us bless him that there is another voice of his besides this dreadful one, by which God now speaks to us, even the still small voice of his gospel, the terror of which shall not make us afraid.

(2.) In the kingdom of providence, *v.* 10. God is to be praised as the governor of the world of mankind. He *sits upon the flood; he sits King for ever.* He not only sits at rest in the enjoyment of himself, but he sits as King in the throne which he has *prepared in the heavens* (Ps. 103:19), where he takes cognizance of, and gives orders about, all the affairs of the children of men, and does all according to his will, according to the counsel of his will. Observe, [1.] The power of his kingdom: He *sits upon the flood.* As he has founded the earth, so he has founded his own throne, upon the floods, Ps. 24:2. The ebbings and flowings of this lower world, and the agitations and revolutions of the affairs in it, give not the least shake to the repose nor to the counsels of the Eternal Mind. The opposition of his enemies is compared to the flood (Ps. 93:3, 4); but the Lord sits upon it; he crushes it, conquers it, and completes his own purposes in despite of all the devices that are in men's hearts. The word here translated *the flood* is never used but concerning Noah's flood; and therefore some think it is that which is here spoken of. God did sit upon that flood as a Judge executing the sentence of his justice upon the world of the ungodly that was swept away by it. And he still sits upon the flood, restraining the waters of Noah, that they turn not again to cover the earth, according to his promise never to *destroy the earth any*

more by a flood, Gen. 9:11; Isa. 54:9. [2.] The perpetuity of his kingdom; *He sits King for ever;* no period can, or shall, be put to his government. The administration of his kingdom is consonant to his counsels from eternity and pursuant to his designs for eternity.

(3.) In the kingdom of grace. Here his glory shines most brightly, [1.] In the adorations he receives from the subjects of that kingdom (*v.* 9). *In his temple,* where people attend his discoveries of himself and his mind and attend him with their praises, *every one speaks of his glory.* In the world every man sees it, or at least *may behold it afar off* (Job 36:25); but it is only in the temple, in the church, that it is spoken of to his honour. *All his works do praise him* (that is, they minister matter for praise), but his saints only do bless him, and speak of his glory of his works, Ps. 145:10. [2.] In the favours he bestows upon the subjects of that kingdom, *v.* 11. *First,* He will qualify them for his service: *He will give strength to his people,* to fortify them against every evil work and to furnish them for every good work; out of weakness they shall be made strong; nay, he will perfect strength in weakness. *Secondly,* He will encourage them in his service: *He will bless his people with peace.* Peace is a blessing of inestimable value, which God designs for all his people. The *work of righteousness is peace (great peace have those that love thy law);* but much more the crown of righteousness: the end of righteousness is peace; it is endless peace. When the thunder of God's wrath shall make sinners tremble the saints shall lift up their heads with joy.

PSALM 30

This is a psalm of thanksgiving for the great deliverances which God had wrought for David, penned upon occasion of the dedicating of his house of cedar, and sung in that pious solemnity, though there is not any thing in it that has particular reference to that occasion. Some collect from divers passages in the psalm itself that it was penned upon his recovery from a dangerous fit of sickness, which might happen to be about the time of the dedication of his house. I. He here praises God for the deliverances he had wrought for him (*v.* 1–3). II. He calls upon others to praise him too, and encourages them to trust in him (*v.* 4, 5). III. He blames himself for his former security (*v.* 6, 7). IV. He recollects the prayers and complaints he had made in his distress (*v.* 8–10). With them he stirs up himself to be very thankful to God for the present comfortable change (*v.* 11, 12). In singing this psalm we ought to remember with thankfulness any like deliverances wrought for us, for which we must stir up our selves to praise him and by which we must be engaged to depend upon him.

A psalm *and song at* the dedication of the house of David.

Verses 1–5

It was the laudable practice of the pious Jews, and, though not expressly appointed, yet allowed and accepted, when they had built a new house, to *dedicate it to God,* Deu. 20:5. David did so when his house was built, and he took possession of it (2 Sa. 5:11); for royal palaces do as much need God's protection, and are as much bound to be at his service, as ordinary houses. Note, The houses we dwell in should, at our first entrance upon them, be dedicated to God, as little sanctuaries. We must solemnly commit ourselves, our families, and all our family affairs, to God's guidance and care, must pray for his presence and blessing, must devote ourselves and all ours to his glory, and must resolve both that we put away iniquity far from our tabernacles and that we and our houses will serve the Lord both in the duties of family worship and in all instances of gospel obedience. Some conjecture that this psalm was sung at the re-dedication of David's house, after he had been driven out of it by Absalom, who had defiled it with his incest, and that it is a thanksgiving for the crushing of that dangerous rebellion. In these verses,

I. David does himself give God thanks for the great deliverances he had wrought for him (*v.* 1): "*I will extol thee, O Lord!* I will exalt thy name, will praise thee as one high and lifted up, I will do what I can to advance the interest of thy kingdom among men. I will extol thee, for thou hast lifted me up, not only up out of the pit in which I was sinking, but up to the throne of Israel." He *raiseth up the poor out of the dust.* In consideration of the great things God has done to exalt us, both by his providence and by his grace, we are bound, in gratitude, to do all we can to extol his name, though the most we can do is but little. Three thing magnify David's deliverance: — 1. That it was the defeat of his enemies. They were not suffered to triumph over him, as they would have done (though it is a bar-

barous thing) if he had died of this sickness or perished in this distress: see Ps. 41:11. 2. That it was an answer to his prayers (*v.* 2): *I cried unto thee.* All the expressions of the sense we have of our troubles should be directed to God, and every cry be a cry to him; and giving way, in this manner, to our grief, will ease a burdened spirit. "*I cried to thee, and thou hast* not only heard me, but *healed me,* healed the distempered body, healed the disturbed and disquieted mind, healed the disordered distracted affairs of the kingdom." This is what God glories in, *I am the Lord that healeth thee* (Ex. 15:26), and we must give him the glory of it. 3. That it was the saving of his life; for he was brought to the last extremity, dropping into the grave, and ready *to go down into the pit,* and yet rescued and kept alive, *v.* 3. The more imminent our dangers have been, the more eminent our deliverances have been, the more comfortable are they to ourselves and the more illustrious proofs of the power and goodness of God. A life from the dead ought to be spent in extolling the God of our life.

II. He calls upon others to join with him in praise, not only for the particular favours God has bestowed upon him, but for the general tokens of his good-will to all his saints (*v.* 4): *Sing unto the Lord, O you saints of his!* All that are truly saints he owns for his. There is a remnant of such in this world, and from them it is expected that they sing unto him; for they are created and sanctified, made and made saints, that they may be to him for a name and a praise. His saints in heaven sing to him; why should not those on earth be doing the same work, as well as they can, in concert with them? 1. They believe him to be a God of unspotted purity; and therefore let them sing to him; "Let them *give thanks at the remembrance of his holiness;* let them praise his holy name, for holiness is his memorial throughout all generations." God is a holy God; his holiness is his glory; that is the attribute which the holy angels, in their praises, fasten most upon, Isa. 6:3; Rev. 4:8. We ought to be much in the mention and remembrance of God's holiness. It is a matter of joy to the saints that God is a holy God; for then they hope he will make them holy, more holy. None of all God's perfections carries in it more terror to the wicked, nor more comfort to the godly, than his holiness. It is a good sign that we are in some measure partakers of his holiness if we can heartily rejoice and give thanks at the remembrance of it. 2. They have experienced him to be a God gracious and merciful; and therefore let them sing to him. (1.) We have found his frowns very short. Though we have deserved that they should be everlasting, and that he should be angry with us till he had consumed us, and should never be reconciled, yet *his anger endureth but for a moment, v.* 5. When we offend him he is angry; but, as he is slow to anger and not soon provoked, so when he is angry, upon our repentance and humiliation his anger is soon turned away and he is willing to be at peace with us. If he hide his face from his own children, and suspend the wonted tokens of his favour, it is but *in a little wrath,* and *for a small moment;* but he will *gather them with everlasting kindness,* Isa. 54:7, 8. If *weeping endureth for a night,* and it be a wearisome night, yet as sure as the light of the morning returns after the darkness of the night, so sure will joy and comfort return in a short time, in due time, to the people of God; for the covenant of grace is as firm as the covenant of the day. This word has often been fulfilled to us in the letter. Weeping has endured for a night, but the grief has been soon over and the grievance gone. Observe, As long as God's anger continues so long the saints' weeping continues; but, if that be but for a moment, the affliction is but for a moment, and when the light of God's countenance is restored the affliction is easily pronounced light and momentary. (2.) We have found his smiles very sweet; *In his favour is life,* that is, all good. The return of his favour to an afflicted soul is as life from the dead; nothing can be more reviving. Our happiness is bound up in God's favour; if we have that, we have enough, whatever else we want. It is the life of the soul, it is spiritual life, the earnest of life eternal.

Verses 6–12

We have, in these verses, an account of three several states that David was in successively, and of the workings of his heart towards God in each of those states — what he said and did, and how his heart stood affected; in the first of these we may see what we are too apt to be, and in the other two what we should be.

I. He had long enjoyed prosperity, and then he grew secure and over-confident of the continuance of it (*v.* 6, 7): *"In my prosperity,* when I was in health of body and God had *given me rest from all my enemies, I said I shall never be moved;* I never thought either of having my body distempered or my government disturbed, not had any apprehensions of danger upon any account." Such complete victories had he obtained over those that opposed him, and such a confirmed interest had he in the hearts of his people, such a firmness of mind and such a strong constitution of body, that he thought his prosperity fixed like a mountain; yet this he ascribes, not to his own wisdom or fortitude, but to the divine goodness. *Thou, through thy favour, hast made my mountain to stand strong, v.* 7. He does not look upon it as his *heaven* (as worldly people do, who make their prosperity their felicity), only his *mountain;* it is earth still, only raised a little higher than the common level. This he thought, by the favour of God, would be perpetuated to him, imagining perhaps that, having had so many troubles in the beginning of his days, he had had his whole share and should have none in his latter end, or that God, who had given him such tokens of his favour, would never frown upon him. Note, 1. We are very apt to dream, when things are well with us, that they will always be so, and never otherwise. *To-morrow shall be as this day.* As if we should think, when the weather is once fair, that it will be even fair; whereas nothing is more certain than that it will change. 2. When we see ourselves deceived in our expectations, it becomes us to reflect, with shame, upon our security, as our folly, as David does here, that we may be wiser another time and may rejoice in our prosperity as though we rejoiced not, because the fashion of it passes away.

II. On a sudden he fell into trouble, and then he prayed to God, and pleaded earnestly for relief and succour.

1. His mountain was shaken and he with it; it proved, when he grew secure, that he was least safe: *"Thou didst hide thy face and I was troubled,* in mind, body, or estate." In every change of his condition he still kept his eye upon God, and, as he ascribed his prosperity to God's favour, so in his adversity he observed the hiding of God's face, to be the cause of it. If God hide his face, a good man is certainly troubled, though no other calamity befal him; when the sun sets night certainly follows, and the moon and all the stars cannot make day.

2. When his mountain was shaken he lifted up his eyes above the hills. Prayer is a salve for every sore; he made use of it accordingly. *Is any afflicted?* Is any troubled? *Let him pray.* Though God hid his face from him, yet he prayed. If God, in wisdom and justice, turn from us, yet it will be in us the greatest folly and injustice imaginable if we turn from him. No; let us learn to pray in the dark (*v.* 8): *I cried to thee, O Lord!* It seems God's withdrawings made his prayers the more vehement. We are here told, for it seems he kept account of it,

(1.) What he pleaded, *v.* 9. [1.] That God would be no gainer by his death: *What profit is there in my blood?* implying that he would willingly die if he could thereby do any real service to God or his country (Phil. 2:17), but he saw not what good could be done by his dying in the bed of sickness, as might be if he had died in the bed of honour. "Lord," says he, "wilt thou sell one of thy own *people for nought and not increase thy wealth by the price?"* Ps. 44:12. Nay [2.] That, in his honour, God would seem to be a loser by his death: *Shall the dust praise thee?* The sanctified spirit, which returns to God, shall praise him, shall be still praising him; but the dust, which returns to the earth, shall not praise him, nor declare his truth. The services of God's house cannot be performed by the dust; it cannot praise him; there is none of that device or working in the grave, for it is the land of silence. The promises of God's covenant cannot be performed to the dust. "Lord," says David, "if I die now, what will become of the promise made to me? Who shall declare the truth of that?" The best pleas in prayer are those that are taken from God's honour; and then we ask aright for life when we have that in view, that we may live and praise him.

(2.) What he prayed for, *v.* 10. He prayed for mercy to pardon *(Have mercy upon me),* and for grace to help in time of need — *Lord, be thou my helper.* On these two errands we also may come boldly to the throne of grace, Heb. 4:16.

III. In due time God delivered him out of his troubles and restored him to his former prosperity. His prayers were answered and his *mourning was turned into dancing, v.* 11. God's anger now endured but for a moment, and David's weeping but for a night. The sackcloth with which, in a humble compliance with the divine Providence, he had clad himself, was loosed; his griefs were balanced; his fears were silenced; his comforts returned; and he was girded with gladness: joy was made his ornament, was made his strength, and seemed to cleave to him, as the girdle cleaves to the loins of a man. As David's plunge into trouble from the height of prosperity, and then when he least expected it, teaches us to rejoice as though we rejoiced not, because we know not how near trouble may be, so his sudden return to a prosperous condition teaches us to weep as though we wept not, because we know not how soon the storm may become a calm and the formidable blast may become a favourable gale. But what temper of mind was he in upon this happy change of the face of his affairs? What does he say now? He tells us, *v.* 12. 1. His complaints were turned into praises. He looked upon it that God girded him with gladness to the end that he might be the *sweet psalmist of Israel* (2 Sa. 23:1), that his *glory might sing praise to God,* that is, his tongue (for our tongue is our glory, and never more so than when it is employed in praising God) or his soul, for that is our glory above the beasts, that must be employed in blessing the Lord, and with that we must make melody to him in singing psalms. Those that are kept from being silent in the pit must not be silent in the land of the living, but fervent, and constant, and public, in praising God. 2. These praises were likely to be everlasting: *I will give thanks unto thee for ever.* This bespeaks a gracious resolution that he would persevere to the end in praising God and a gracious hope that he should never want fresh matter for praise and that he should shortly be where this would be the everlasting work. *Blessed are those that dwell in God's house; they will be still praising him.* Thus must we learn to accommodate ourselves to the various providences of God that concern us, to want and to abound, to sing of mercy and judgment, and to sing unto God for both.

PSALM 31

It is probable that David penned this psalm when he was persecuted by Saul; some passages in it agree particularly to the narrow escapes he had, at Keilah (1 Sa. 23:13), then in the wilderness of Maon, when Saul marched on one side of the hill and he on the other, and, soon after, in the cave in the wilderness of En-gedi; but that it was penned upon any of those occasions we are not told. It is a mixture of prayers, and praises, and professions of confidence in God, all which do well together and are helpful to one another. I. David professes his cheerful confidence in God, and, in that confidence, prays for deliverance out of his present troubles (*v.* 1–8). II. He complains of the very deplorable condition he was in, and, in the sense of his calamities, still prays that God would graciously appear for him against his persecutors (*v.* 9–18). III. He concludes the psalm with praise and triumph, giving glory to God, and encouraging himself and others to trust in him (*v.* 19–24).

To the chief musician. A psalm of David.

Verses 1–8

Faith and prayer must go together. He that believes, let his pray — *I believe, therefore I have spoken:* and he that prays, let him believe, for the prayer of faith is the prevailing prayer. We have both here.

I. David, in distress, is very earnest with God in prayer for succour and relief. This eases a burdened spirit, fetches in promised mercies, and wonderfully supports and comforts the soul in the expectation of them. He prays, 1. That God would deliver him (*v.* 1), that his life might be preserved from the malice of his enemies, and that an end might be put to their persecutions of him, that God, not only in his mercy, but in righteousness, would deliver him, as a righteous Judge betwixt him and his unrighteous persecutors, that he would bow down his ear to his petitions, to his appeals, and deliver him, *v.* 2. It is condescension in God to take cognizance of the case of the greatest and best of men; he humbles himself to do it. The psalmist prays also that he would deliver him speedily, lest, if the deliverance were long deferred, his faith should fail. 2. That if he did not immediately deliver him out of his troubles, yet he would protect and shelter him in his troubles; *"Be thou my strong rock,* immovable, impregnable, as a fastness framed by nature, and my *house of defence,* a fortress framed by art, and all *to save me."* Thus we may pray that God's providence would secure to us our lives and comforts, and that by his grace we may be enabled to think ourselves safe in him, Prov. 18:10. 3. That his case having much in it of difficulty, both in respect of duty and in respect of prudence, he might be under the divine guidance: *"Lord, lead me and guide me* (*v.* 3), so order my steps, so order my spirit, that I may never do any thing unlawful and unjustifiable — against my conscience, nor unwise and indiscreet — against my interest." Those that resolve to follow God's direction may in faith pray for it. 4. That his enemies being very crafty, as well as very spiteful, God would frustrate and baffle their designs against him (*v.* 4): *"Pull me out of the net that they have laid privily for me,* and keep me from the sin, the trouble, the death, they aim to entrap me in."

II. In this prayer he gives glory to God by a repeated profession of his confidence in him and dependence on him. This encouraged his prayers and qualified him for the mercies he prayed for (*v.* 1): *"In thee, O Lord! do I put my trust,* and not in myself, or any sufficiency of my own, or in any creature; *let me never be ashamed,* let me not be disappointed of any of that good which thou hast promised me and which therefore I have promised myself in thee." 1. He had chosen God for his protector, and God had, by his promise, undertaken to be so (*v.* 3): *"Thou art my rock and my fortress,* by thy covenant with me and my believing consent to that covenant; therefore *be my strong rock," v.* 2. Those that have in sincerity avouched the Lord for theirs may expect the benefit of his being so; for God's relations to us carry with them both name and thing. *Thou art my strength, v.* 4. If God be our strength, we may hope that he will both put his strength in us and put forth his strength for us. 2. He gave up his soul in a special manner to him (*v.* 5): *Into thy hands I commit my spirit.* (1.) If David here looks upon himself as a dying man, by these words he resigns his departing soul to God who gave it, and to whom, at death, the spirit returns. "Men can but kill the body, but I trust in God to *redeem my soul from the power of the grave,"* Ps. 49:15. He is willing to die if God will have it so; but let my soul *fall into the hands of the Lord, for his mercies are great.* With these words our Lord Jesus yielded up the ghost upon the cross, and made his soul an offering, a free-will offering for sin, voluntarily laying down his life a ransom. By Stephen's example we are taught in, our dying moment, to eye Christ at God's right hand, and to commit our spirits to him: *Lord Jesus, receive my spirit.* But, 2. David is here to be looked upon as a man in distress and trouble. And, [1.] His great care is about his soul, his spirit, his better part. Note, Our outward afflictions should increase our concern for our souls. Many think that while they are perplexed about their worldly affairs, and Providence multiplies their cares about them, they may be excused if they neglect their souls; whereas the greater hazard our lives and secular interests lie at the more we are concerned to look to our souls, that, though the outward man perish, the inward man may suffer no damage (2 Co. 4:16), and that we may keep possession of our souls when we can keep possession of nothing else, Lu. 21:19. [2.] He thinks the best he can do for the soul is to commit it into the hand of God, and lodge that great trust with him. He had prayed (*v.* 4) to be plucked out of the net of outward trouble, but, as not insisting upon that (God's will be done), he immediately lets fall that petition, and commits the spirit, the inward man, into God's hand. "Lord, however it goes with me, as to my body, let it go well with my soul." Note, It is the wisdom and duty of every one of us solemnly to commit our spirits into the hands of God, to be sanctified by his grace, devoted to his honour, employed in his service, and fitted for his kingdom. That which encourages us to commit our spirits into the hand of God is that he has not only created, but redeemed, them; the particular redemptions of the Old-Testament church and the Old-Testament saints were typical of our redemption by Jesus Christ, Gen. 48:16. The redemption of the soul is so precious that it must have ceased for ever if Christ had not undertaken it; but, by redeeming our souls, he has not only acquired an additional right and title to them, which obliges us to commit them to him as his own, but has shown the extraordinary kindness and concern he has for them, which encourages us to commit them to him, to be preserved to his heavenly kingdom (2 Tim. 1:12): *"Thou hast redeemed me, O Lord God of truth!* redeem me according to a promise which thou wilt be true to."

III. He disclaimed all confederacy with those that made an arm of flesh their confidence (*v.* 6): *I have hated those that regard lying vanities* — idolaters (to some), who expect aid from false gods, which are vanity and a lie — astrologers, and those that give heed to them, so others. David abhorred the use of enchantments and divinations; he consulted not, nor even took notice of, the flight of birds or entrails of beasts, good omens or bad omens; they are lying vanities, and he not only did not regard them himself, but hated the wickedness of those that did. He trusted in God only, and not in any creature. His interest in the court or country, his retreats or strongholds, even Goliath's sword itself — these were lying vanities, which he could not depend upon, but trusted in the Lord only. See Ps. 40:4; Jer. 17:5.

IV. He comforted himself with his hope in God, and made himself, not only easy, but cheerful, with it, *v.* 7. Having relied on God's mercy, he will be glad and rejoice in it; and those know not how to value their hope in God who cannot find joy enough in that hope to counterbalance their grievances and silence their griefs.

V. He encouraged himself in this hope with the experiences he had had of late, and formerly, of God's goodness to him, which he mentions to the glory of God; he that has delivered doth and will. 1. God had taken notice of his afflictions and all the circumstances of them: *"Thou hast considered my trouble,* with wisdom to suit relief to it, with condescension and compassion regarding the low estate of they servant." 2. He had observed the temper of his spirit and the workings of his heart under his afflictions: *"Thou hast known my soul in adversities,* with a tender concern and care for it." God's eye is upon our souls when we are in trouble, to see whether they be humbled for sin, submissive to the will of God, and bettered by the affliction. If the soul, when cast down under affliction, has been lifted up to him in true devotion, he knows it. 3. He had rescued him out of the hands of Saul when he had him safe enough in Keilah (1 Sa. 23:7): *"Thou hast not shut me up into the hand of the enemy,* but set me at liberty, in a *large room,* where I may shift for my own safety," *v.* 8. Christ's using those words (*v.* 5) upon the cross may warrant us to apply all this to Christ, who trusted in his Father and was supported and delivered by him, and (because he humbled himself) highly exalted, which it is proper to think of when we sing these verses, as also therein to acknowledge the experience we have had of God's gracious presence with us in our troubles and to encourage ourselves to trust in him for the future.

Verses 9–18

In the foregoing verses David had appealed to God's righteousness, and pleaded his relation to him and dependence on him; here he appeals to his mercy, and pleads the greatness of his own misery, which made his case the proper object of that mercy. Observe,

I. The complaint he makes of his trouble and distress (*v.* 9): *"Have mercy upon me, O Lord! for I am in trouble,* and need thy mercy." The remembrance he makes of his condition is not much unlike some even of Job's complaints. 1. His troubles had fixed a very deep impression upon his mind and made him a man of sorrows. So great was his grief that his very soul was consumed with it, and his life spent with it, and he was continually sighing, *v.* 9, 10. Herein he was a type of Christ, — who was intimately acquainted with grief and often in tears. We may guess by David's complexion, which was ruddy and sanguine, by his genius for music, and by his daring enterprises in his early days, that his natural disposition was both cheerful and firm, that he was apt to be cheerful, and not to lay trouble to his heart; yet here we see what he is brought to: he has almost wept out his eyes, and sighed away his breath. Let those that are airy and gay take heed of running into extremes, and never set sorrow at defiance; God can find out ways to make them melancholy if they will not otherwise learn to be serious. 2. His body was afflicted with the sorrows of his mind (*v.* 10): *My strength fails, my bones are consumed,* and all *because of my iniquity.* As to Saul, and the quarrel he had with him, he could confidently insist upon his righteousness; but, as it was an affliction God laid upon him, he owns he had deserved it, and freely confesses his iniquity to have been the procuring cause of all his trouble; and the sense of sin touched him to the quick and wasted him more than all his calamities. 3. His friends were unkind and became shy of him. He was *a fear to his acquaintance,* when they saw him they *fled from him, v.* 11. They durst not harbour him nor give him any assistance, durst not show him any countenance, nor so much as be seen in his company, for fear of being brought into trouble by it, now that Saul had proclaimed him a traitor and outlawed him. They saw how dearly Ahimelech the priest had paid for aiding and abetting him, though ignorantly; and therefore, though they could not but own he had a great deal of wrong done him, yet they had not the courage to appear for him. He was forgotten by them, *as a dead man out of mind* (*v.* 12), and looked upon with contempt *as a broken vessel.* Those that showed him all possible respect when he was in honour at court, now that he had fallen into disgrace, though unjustly, were strange to him. Such swallow-friends the world is full of, that are gone in winter. Let those that fall on the losing side not think it strange if they be thus deserted, but make sure a friend in heaven, that will not fail them, and make use of him. 4. His enemies were unjust in their censures of him. They would not have persecuted him as they did if they had not first represented him as a bad man; he was a *reproach among all his enemies, but especially among his neighbours, v.* 11. Those that had been the witnesses of his integrity, and could not but be convinced in their consciences that he was an honest man, were the most forward to represent him quite otherwise, that they might curry favour with Saul. Thus he *heard the slander of many;* every one had a stone to throw at him, because *fear was in every side;* that is, they durst not do otherwise, for he that would not join with his neighbours to accuse David was looked upon as disaffected to Saul. Thus the best of men have been represented under the worst characters by those that resolved to give them the worst treatment. 5. His life was aimed at and he went in continual peril of it. Fear was on every side, and he knew that, whatever counsel his enemies took against him, the design was not to take away his liberty, but to take away his life (*v.* 13), a life so valuable, so useful, to the good services of which all Israel owed so much, and which was never forfeited. Thus, in all the plots of the Pharisees and Herodians against Christ, still the design was to take away his life, such are the enmity and cruelty of the serpent's seed.

II. His confidence in God in the midst of these troubles. Every thing looked black and dismal round about him, and threatened to drive him to despair: *"But I trusted in thee, O Lord!* (*v.* 14) and was thereby kept from sinking." His enemies robbed him of his reputation among men, but they could not rob him of his comfort in God, because they could not drive him from his confidence in God. Two things he comforted himself with in his straits, and he went to God and pleaded them with him: — 1. *"Thou art my God;* I have chosen thee for mine, and thou hast promised to be mine;" and, if he be ours and we can by faith call him so, it is enough, when we can call nothing else ours. "Thou art my God; and therefore to whom shall I go for relief but to thee?" Those need not be straitened in their prayers who can plead this; for, if God undertake to be our God, he will do that for us which will answer the compass and vast extent of the engagement. 2. *My times are in thy hand.* Join this with the former and it makes the comfort complete. If God have our times in his hand, he can help us; and, if he be our God, he will help us; and then what can discourage us? It is a great support to those who have God for their God that their times are in his hand and he will be sure to order and dispose of them for the best, to all those who commit their spirits also into his hand, to suit them to their times, as David here, *v.* 5. The time of life is in God's hands, to lengthen or shorten, embitter or sweeten, as he pleases, according to the counsel of his will. Our times (all events that concern us, and the timing of them) are at God's disposal; they are not in our own hands, for the way of man is not in himself, not in our friends' hands, nor in our enemies' hands, but in God's; *every man's judgment proceedeth from him.* David does not, in his prayers, prescribe to God, but subscribe to him. "Lord, my times are in thy hand, and I am well pleased that they are so; they could not be in a better hand. Thy will be done."

III. His petitions to God, in this faith and confidence, 1. He prays that God would deliver him out of the hand of his enemies (*v.* 15), and save him (*v.* 16), and this for his mercies' sake, and not for any merit of his own. Our opportunities are in God's hand (so some read it), and therefore he knows how to choose the best and fittest time for our deliverance, and we must be willing to wait that time. When David had Saul at his mercy in the cave those about him said, *"This is the time* in which God will deliver thee," 1 Sa. 24:4. "No," says David, "the time has not come for my deliverance till it can be wrought without sin; and I will wait for that time; for it is God's time, and that is the best time." 2. That God would give him the comfort of his favour in the mean time (*v.* 16): *"Make they face to shine upon thy servant;* let me have the comfortable tokens and evidences of thy favour to me, and that shall put gladness in my heart in the midst of all my griefs." 3. That his prayers to God might be answered and his hopes in God accomplished (*v.* 17): *"Let me not be ashamed* of my hopes and prayers, *for I have called upon thee,* who never saidst to thy people, Seek in vain, and hope in vain." 4. That shame and silence might be the portion of wicked people, and particularly of his enemies. They were confident of their success against David, and that they should run him down and ruin him. "Lord," says he, "let them be made ashamed of that confidence by the disappointment of their expectations," as those that opposed the building of the wall about Jerusalem, when it was finished, were *much cast down in their own eye,* Neh. 6:16. *Let them be silent in the grave.* Note, Death will silence the rage and clamour of cruel persecutors, whom reason would not silence. In the grave the wicked cease from troubling. Particularly, he prays for (that is, he prophesies) the silencing of those that reproach and calumniate the people of God (*v.* 18): *Let lying lips be put to silence, that speak grievous things proudly and contemptuously against the righteous.* This is a very good prayer which, (1.) We have often occasion to put up to God; for those that set their mouth against the heavens commonly revile the heirs of heaven. Religion, in the strict and serious professors of it, are every where spoken against, [1.] With a great deal of malice: They speak *grievous things,* on purpose to vex them, and hoping, with what they say, to do them a real mischief. They speak *hard things* (so the word is), which bear hard upon them, and by which they hope to fasten indelible characters of infamy upon them. [2.] With a great deal of falsehood: They are *lying lips,* taught by the father of lies and serving his interest. [3.] With a great deal of scorn and disdain: They speak *proudly and contemptuously,* as if the righteous, whom God has honoured, were the most despicable people in the world, and not worthy to be set with the dogs of their flock. One would think they thought it no sin to tell a deliberate lie if it might but serve to expose a good man either to hatred or contempt. *Hear, O our God! for we are despised.* (2.) We may pray in faith; for these lying lips shall be put to silence. God has many ways of doing it. Sometimes he convinces the consciences of those that reproach his people, and turns their hearts. Sometimes by his providence he visibly confutes their calumnies, and brings forth the righteousness of his people as the light. However, there is a day coming when God will convince ungodly sinners of the falsehood of all the hard speeches that have spoken against his people and will execute judgment upon them, Jude 14, 15. Then shall this prayer be fully answered, and to that day we should have an eye in the singing of it, engaging ourselves likewise by welldoing, if possible, to *silence the ignorance of foolish men,* 1 Pt. 2:15.

Verses 19–24

We have three things in these verses: —

I. The believing acknowledgment which David makes of God's goodness to his people in general, *v.* 19, 20.

1. God is good to all, but he is, in a special manner, good to Israel. His goodness to them is wonderful, and will be, to eternity, matter of admiration: *O how great is thy goodness!* How profound are the counsels of it! how rich are the treasures of it! how free and extensive are the communications of it! Those very persons whom men load with slanders God loads with benefits and honours. Those who

are interested in this goodness are described to be such as fear God and trust in him, as stand in awe of his greatness and rely on his grace. This goodness is said to be *laid up for them* and *wrought for them.* (1.) There is a goodness laid up for them in the other world, an inheritance *reserved in heaven* (1 Pt. 1:4), and there is a goodness wrought for them in this world, goodness wrought in them. There is enough in God's goodness both for the portion and inheritance of all his children when they come to their full age, and for their maintenance and education during their minority. There is enough in bank and enough in hand. (2.) This goodness is laid up in his promise for all that fear God, to whom assurance is given that they shall want no good thing. But it is wrought, in the actual performance of the promise, for those that trust in him — that by faith take hold of the promise, put it in suit, and draw out to themselves the benefit and comfort of it. If what is laid up for us in the treasures of the everlasting covenant be not wrought for us, it is our own fault, because we do not believe. But those that trust in God, as they have the comfort of his goodness in their own bosoms, so they have the credit of it (and the credit of an estate goes far with some); it is wrought for them *before the sons of men.* God's goodness to them puts an honour upon them and rolls away their reproach; *for all that see them shall acknowledge them, that they are the seed which the Lord hath blessed,* Isa. 61:9.

2. God preserves man and beast; but he is, in a special manner, the protector of his own people (*v.* 20): *Thou shalt hide them.* As his goodness is hid and reserved for them, so they are hid and preserved for it. The saints are God's hidden ones. See here, (1.) The danger they are in, which arises from the pride of man and from the strife of tongues; proud men insult over them and would trample on them and tread them down; contentious men pick quarrels with them; and, when tongues are at strife, good people often go by the worst. The pride of men endangers their liberty; the strife of tongues in perverse disputings endangers truth. But, (2.) See the defence they are under: *Thou shalt hide them in the secret of thy presence, in a pavilion.* God's providence shall keep them safe form the malice of their enemies. He has many ways of sheltering them. When Baruch and Jeremiah were sought for *the Lord hid them,* Jer. 36:26. God's grace shall keep them safe from the evil of the judgments that are abroad; to them they have no sting; and they shall hidden in the day of the Lord's anger, for there is no anger at them. His comforts shall keep them easy and cheerful; his sanctuary, where they have communion with him, shelters then from the fiery darts of terror and temptation; and the mansions in his house above shall be shortly, shall be eternally, their hiding-place from all danger and fear.

II. The thankful returns which David makes for God's goodness to him in particular, *v.* 21, 22. Having admired God's goodness to all the saints, he here owns how good he had found him. 1. Without were fightings; but God had wonderfully preserved his life: *"He has shown me his marvellous loving-kindness,* he has given me an instance of his care for me and favour to me, beyond what I could have expected." God's loving-kindness to his people, all things considered, is wonderful; but some instances of it, even in this world, are in a special manner marvelous in their eyes; as this here, when God preserved David from the sword of Saul, in caves and woods, as safe as if he had been in a strong city. In Keilah, that strong city, God showed him great mercy, both in making him an instrument to rescue the inhabitants out of the hands of the Philistines and then in rescuing him from the same men who would have ungratefully delivered him up into the hand of Saul, 1 Sa. 23:5, 12. This was marvellous loving-kindness indeed, upon which he writes, with wonder and thankfulness, *Blessed be the Lord.* Special preservations call for particular thanksgivings. 2. Within were fears; but God was better to him than his fears, *v.* 22. He here keeps an account, (1.) Of his own folly, in distrusting God, which he acknowledges, to his shame. Though he had express promises to build upon, and great experience of God's care concerning him in many straits, yet he had entertained this hard and jealous thought of God, and could not forbear telling it him to his face. *"I am cut off before thy eyes;* thou hast quite forsaken me, and I must not expect to be looked upon or regarded by thee any more. *I shall one day perish by the hand of Saul,* and so be cut off before thy eyes, be ruined while thou lookest on," 1 Sa. 27:1. This he said in his *flight* (so some read it), which denotes the distress of his affairs. Saul was just at his back, and ready to seize him, which made the temptation strong. *In my haste* (so we read it), which denotes the disturbance and discomposure of his mind, which made the temptation surprising, so that it found him off his guard. Note, It is a common thing to speak amiss when we speak in haste and without consideration; but what we speak amiss in haste we must repent of at leisure, particularly that which we have spoken distrustfully of God. (2.) Of God's wonderful goodness to him notwithstanding. Though his faith failed, God's promise did not: *Thou hearest the voice of my supplication,* for all this. He mentions his own unbelief as a foil to God's fidelity, serving to make his loving-kindness the more marvellous, the more illustrious. When we have thus distrusted God he might justly take us at our word, and bring our fears upon us, as he did on Israel, Num. 14:28; Isa. 66:4. But he has pitied and pardoned us, and our unbelief has not made his promise and grace of no effect; for he knows our frame.

III. The exhortation and encouragement which he hereupon gives to all the saints, *v.* 23, 24. 1. He would have them set their love on God (*v.* 23): *O love the Lord! all you his saints.* Those that have their own hearts full of love to God cannot but desire that others also may be in love with him; for in his favour there is no need to fear a rival. It is the character of the saints that they do love God; and yet they must still be called upon to love him, to love him more and love him better, and give proofs of their love. We must love him, not only for his goodness, because *he preserves the faithful,* but for his justice, because he *plentifully rewards the proud doer* (who would ruin those whom he preserves), according to their pride. Some take it in a good sense; he plentifully rewards the magnificent (or excellent) doer, that is daringly good, whose heart, like Jehoshaphat's, is lifted up in the ways of the Lord. He rewards him that does well, but plentifully rewards him that does excellently well. 2. He would have them set their hope in God (*v.* 24): *"Be of good courage;* have a good heart on it; whatever difficulties or dangers you may meet with, the God you trust in shall by that trust strengthen your heart." Those that hope in God have reason to be of good courage, and let their hearts be strong, for, as nothing truly evil can befal them, so nothing truly good for them shall be wanting to them.

In singing this we should animate ourselves and one another to proceed and persevere in our Christian course, whatever threatens us, and whoever frowns upon us.

PSALM 32

This psalm, though it speaks not of Christ, as many of the psalms we have hitherto met with have done, has yet a great deal of gospel in it. The apostle tells us that David, in this psalm, describes "the blessedness of the man unto whom God imputes righteousness without words," Rom. 4:6. We have here a summary, I. Of gospel grace in the pardon of sin (*v.* 1, 2), in divine protection (*v.* 7), and divine guidance (*v.* 8). II. Of gospel duty. To confess sin (*v.* 3–5), to pray (*v.* 6), to govern ourselves well (*v.* 9, 10), and to rejoice in God (*v.* 11). The way to obtain these privileges is to make conscience of these duties, which we ought to think of — of the former for our comfort, of the latter for our quickening, when we sing this psalm. Grotius thinks it was designed to be sung on the day of atonement.

A psalm of David, Maschil.

Verses 1–6

This psalm is entitled *Maschil,* which some take to be only the name of the tune to which it was set and was to be sung. But others think it is significant; our margin reads it, *A psalm of David giving instruction,* and there is nothing in which we have more need of instruction than in the nature of true blessedness, wherein it consists and the way that leads to it — what we must do that we may be happy. There are several things in which these verses instruct us. In general, we are here taught that our happiness consists in the favour of God, and not in the wealth of this world — in spiritual blessings, and not the good things of this world. When David says (Ps. 1:1), *Blessed is the man that walks not in the counsel of the ungodly,* and (Ps. 119:1), *Blessed are the undefiled in the way,* the meaning is, "This is the character of the blessed man; and he that has not this character cannot expect to be happy:" but when it is here said, *Blessed is the man whose iniquity is forgiven,* the meaning is, "This is the ground of his blessedness: this is that fundamental privilege from which all the other ingredients of his blessedness flow." In particular, we are here instructed,

I. Concerning the nature of the pardon of sin. This is that which we all need and are undone without; we are therefore concerned to be very solicitous and inquisitive about it. 1. It is the forgiving of transgression. *Sin is the transgression of the law.* Upon our repentance, the transgression is forgiven; that is, the obligation to punishment which we lay under, by virtue of the sentence of the law, is vacated and cancelled; it is *lifted off* (so some read it), that by the pardon of it we may be eased of a burden, a heavy burden, like a load on the back, that makes us stoop, or a load on the stomach, that makes us sick, or a load on the spirits, that makes us sink. The remission of sins gives rest and relief to those that were *weary and heavily laden,* Mt. 11:28. 2. It is the covering of sin, as nakedness is covered, that it may not appear to our shame, Rev. 3:18. One of the first symptoms of guilt in our first parents was blushing at their own nakedness. Sin makes us loathsome in the sight of God and utterly unfit for communion with him, and, when conscience is awakened, it makes us loathsome to ourselves too; but, when sin is pardoned, it is covered with the robe of Christ's righteousness, like the coats of skins wherewith God clothed Adam and Eve (an emblem of the remission of sins), so that God is no longer displeased with us, but perfectly reconciled. They are not covered from us (no; *My sin is ever before me*) nor covered from God's omniscience, but from his vindictive justice. When he pardons sin he *remembers it no more,* he *casts it behind his back,* it *shall be sought for and not found,* and the sinner, being thus reconciled to God, begins to be reconciled to himself. 3. It is the not imputing of iniquity, not laying it to the sinner's charge, not proceeding against him for it according to the strictness of the law, not dealing with him as he deserves. The righteousness of Christ being imputed to us, and we being made *the righteousness of God in him,* our iniquity is not imputed, God having *laid upon him the iniquity of us all* and made him *sin for us.* Observe, Not to impute iniquity is God's act, for he is the Judge. *It is God that justifies.*

II. Concerning the character of those whose sins are pardoned: *in whose spirit there is no guile.* He does not say, "There is no *guilt"* (for who is there that lives and sins not?), but no *guile;* the pardoned sinner is one that does not dissemble with God in his professions of repentance and faith, nor in his prayers for peace or pardon, but in all these is sincere and means as he says — that does not repent with a purpose to sin again, and then sin with a purpose to repent again, as a learned interpreter glosses upon it. Those that design honestly, that are really what they profess to be, are Israelites indeed, in whom is no guile.

III. Concerning the happiness of a justified state: *Blessednesses are to the man whose iniquity is forgiven,* all manner of blessings, sufficient to make him completely blessed. That is taken away which incurred the curse and obstructed the blessing; and then God will pour out blessings till there be no room to receive them. The forgiveness of sin is that article of the covenant which is the reason and ground of all the rest. *For I will be merciful to their unrighteousness,* Heb. 8:12.

IV. Concerning the uncomfortable condition of an unhumbled sinner, that sees his guilt, but is not yet brought to make a penitent confession of it. This David describes very pathetically, from his own sad experience (*v.* 3, 4): *While I kept silence my bones waxed old.* Those may be said to keep silence who stifle their convictions, who, when they cannot but see the evil of sin and their danger by reason of it, ease themselves by not thinking of it and diverting their minds to something else, as Cain to the building of a city, — who *cry not when God binds them,* — who will not unburden their consciences by a penitent confession, nor seek for peace, as they ought, by faithful and fervent prayer, — and who choose rather to pine away in their iniquities than to take the method which God has appointed of finding rest for their souls. Let such expect that their smothered convictions will be a fire in their bones, and the wounds of sin, not opened, will fester, and grow intolerably painful. If conscience be seared, the case is so much the more dangerous; but if it be startled and awake, it will be heard. The hand of divine wrath will be felt lying heavily upon the soul, and the anguish of the spirit will affect the body; to the degree David experienced it, so that when he was young his bones waxed old; and even his silence made him *roar all the day long,* as if he had been under some grievous pain and distemper of body, when really the cause of all his uneasiness was the struggle he felt in his own bosom between his convictions and his corruptions. Note, *He that covers his sin shall not prosper;* some inward trouble is required in repentance, but there is much worse in impenitency.

V. Concerning the true and only way to peace of conscience. We are here taught to confess our sins, that they may be forgiven, to declare them, that we may be justified. This course David took: *I acknowledged my sin unto thee,* and no longer *hid my iniquity, v.* 5. Note, Those that would have the comfort of the pardon of their sins must take shame to themselves by a penitent confession of them. We must confess the fact of sin, and be particular in it *(Thus and thus have I done),* confess the fault of sin, aggravate it, and lay a load upon ourselves for it *(I have done very wickedly),* confess the justice of the punishment we have been under for it *(The Lord is just in all that is brought upon us),* and that we deserve much worse — *I am no more worthy to be called thy son.* We must confess sin with shame and holy blushing, with fear and holy trembling.

VI. Concerning God's readiness to pardon sin to those who truly repent of it: *"I said, I will confess* (I sincerely resolved upon it, hesitated no longer, but came to a point, that I would make a free and ingenuous confession of my sins) *and* immediately *thou forgavest the iniquity of my sin,* and gavest me the comfort of the pardon in my own conscience; immediately I found rest to my soul." Note, God is more ready to pardon sin, upon our repentance, than we are to repent in order to the obtaining of pardon. It was with much ado that David was here brought to confess his sins; he was put to the rack before he was brought to do it (*v.* 3, 4), he held out long, and would not surrender till it came to the last extremity; but, when he did offer to surrender, see how quickly, how easily, he obtained good terms: "I did but say, *I will confess, and thou forgavest."* Thus the father of the prodigal saw his returning son *when he was yet afar off,* and ran to meet him with the kiss that sealed his pardon. What an encouragement is this to poor penitents, and what an assurance does it give us that, *if we confess our sins,* we shall find God, not only *faithful and just,* but gracious and kind, *to forgive us our sins!*

VII. Concerning the good use that we are to make of the experience David had had of God's readiness to forgive his sins (*v.* 6): *For this shall every one that is godly pray unto thee.* Note, 1. All godly people are praying people. As soon as ever Paul was converted, *Behold, he prays,* Acts 9:11. You may as soon find a living man without breath as a living Christian without prayer. 2. The instructions given us concerning the happiness of those whose sins are pardoned, and the easiness of obtaining the pardon, should engage and encourage us to pray, and particularly to pray, *God be merciful to us sinners.* For this shall every one that is well inclined be earnest with God in prayer, and *come boldly to the throne of grace,* with hopes to *obtain mercy,* Heb. 4:16. 3. Those that would speed in prayer must seek the Lord in *a time when he will be found.* When, by his providence, he calls them to seek him, and by his Spirit stirs them up to seek him, they must *go speedily to seek the Lord* (Zec. 8:21) and lose no time, lest death cut them off, and then it will be too late to seek him, Isa. 55:6. *Behold, now is the accepted time,* 2 Co. 6:2, 4. Those that are sincere and abundant in prayer will find the benefit of it when they are in trouble: *Surely in the floods of great waters,* which are very threatening, *they shall not come nigh them,* to terrify them, or create them any uneasiness, much less shall they overwhelm them. Those that have God *nigh unto them in all that which they call upon him for,* as all upright, penitent, praying people have, are so guarded, so advanced, that no waters — no, not great waters — no, not floods of them, can come nigh them, to hurt them. As the temptations of the *wicked one touch them not* (1 Jn. 5:18), so neither do the troubles of this evil world; these fiery darts of both kinds, drop short of them.

Verses 7–11

David is here improving the experience he had had of the comfort of pardoning mercy.

I. He speaks to God, and professes his confidence in him and expectation from him, *v.* 7. Having tasted the sweetness of divine grace to a penitent sinner, he cannot doubt of the continuance of that grace to a praying saint, and that in that grace he should find both safety and joy. 1. Safety: *"Thou art my hiding-place;* when by faith I have recourse to thee I see all the reason in the world to be easy, and to think myself out of the reach of any real evil. *Thou shalt preserve me from trouble,* from the sting of it, and from the strokes of it as far as is good for me. *Thou shalt preserve me from* such trouble as I was in *while I kept silence," v.* 3. When God has pardoned our sins, if he leaves us to ourselves, we shall soon run as far in debt again as ever and plunge ourselves again into the same gulf; and therefore, when we have received the comfort of our remission, we must fly to the grace of God to be preserved from returning to folly again, and having our hearts again hardened through the deceitfulness of sin. God keeps his people from trouble by keeping them from sin. 2. Joy: "Thou shalt not only deliver me, but *compass me about with songs of deliverance;* which way soever I look I shall see occasion to rejoice and to praise God; and my friends also shall compass me about in the great congregation, to join with me in songs of praise: they shall join their songs of deliverance with mine. As *every one that is godly shall pray with me,* so they shall give thanks with me."

II. He turns his speech to the children of men. Being himself converted, he does what he can to *strengthen his brethren* (Lu. 22:32): *I will instruct thee,* whoever thou art that desirest instruction, *and teach thee in the way which thou shalt go, v.* 8. This, in another of his penitential psalms, he resolves that when God should have restored to him the joy of his salvation he would teach transgressors his ways, and do what he could to convert sinners to God, as well as to comfort those that were converted, Ps. 51:12, 13. When Solomon became a penitent he immediately became a preacher, Eccl. 1:1. Those are best able to teach others the grace of God who have themselves had the experience of it: and those who are themselves taught of God ought to *tell others what he has done for their souls* (Ps. 66:16) and so teach them. *I will guide thee with my eye.* Some apply this to God's conduct and direction. He teaches us by his word and guides us with his eye, by the secret intimations of his will in the hints and turns of Providence, which he enables his people to understand and take direction from, as a master makes a servant know his mind by a wink of his eye. When Christ turned and looked upon Peter he guided him with his eye. But it is rather to be taken as David's promise to those who sat under his instruction, his own children and family especially: *"I will counsel thee; my eye shall be upon thee"* (so the margin reads it); "I will give thee the best counsel I can and then observe whether thou takest it or no." Those that are taught in the word should be under the constant inspection of those that teach them; spiritual guides must be overseers. In this application of the foregoing doctrine concerning the blessedness of those whose sins are pardoned we have a word to sinners and a word to saints; and this is rightly dividing the word of truth and giving to each their portion.

1. Here is a word of caution to sinners, and a good reason is given for it. (1.) The caution is, not to be unruly and ungovernable: *Be you not as the horse and the mule, which have no understanding, v.* 9. When the psalmist would reproach himself for the sins he repented of he compared himself to a *beast before God* (*so foolish have I been and ignorant,* Ps. 73:22) and therefore warns others not to be so. It is our honour and happiness that we have understanding, that we are capable of being governed by reason and of reasoning with ourselves. Let us therefore use the faculties we have, and act rationally. The horse and mule must be managed *with bit and bridle, lest they come near* us, to do us a mischief, or (as some read it) that they may come near to us, to do us service, that they *may obey us,* Jam. 3:3. Let us not be like them; let us not be hurried by appetite and passion, at any time, to go contrary to the dictate of right reason and to our true interest. If sinners would be governed and determined by these, they would soon become saints and would not go a step further in their sinful courses; where there is renewing grace there is no need of the bit and bridle of restraining grace. (2.) The reason for this caution is because the way of sin which we would persuade you to forsake will certainly end in sorrow (*v.* 10): *Many sorrows shall be to the wicked,* which will not only spoil their vain and carnal mirth, and put an end to it, but will make them pay dearly for it. Sin will have sorrow, if not repented of, everlasting sorrow. It was part of the sentence, *I will greatly multiply thy sorrows.* "Be wise for yourselves therefore, and turn from your wickedness, that you may prevent those sorrows, those many sorrows."

2. Here is a word of comfort to saints, and a good reason is given for that too. (1.) They are assured that if they will but trust in the Lord, and keep closely to him, *mercy shall compass them about* on every side (*v.* 10), so that they shall not depart from God, for that mercy shall keep them in, nor shall any real evil break in upon them, for that mercy shall keep it out. (2.) They are therefore commanded to *be glad in the Lord, and* to *rejoice* in him, to such a degree as even to *shout for joy, v.* 11. Let them be so transported with this holy joy as not to be able to contain themselves; and let them affect others with it, that they also may see that a life of communion with God is the most pleasant and comfortable life we can live in this world. This is that present bliss which the upright in heart, and they are only, are entitled to and qualified for.

PSALM 33

This is a psalm of praise; it is probable that David was the penman of it, but we are not told so, because God would have us look above the penmen of sacred writ, to that blessed Spirit that moved and guided them. The psalmist, in this psalm, I. Calls upon the righteous to praise God (*v.* 1–3). II. Furnishes us with matter for praise. We must praise God, 1. For his justice, goodness, and truth, appearing in his word, and in all his works (*v.* 4, 5). 2. For his power appearing in the work of creation (*v.* 6–9). 3. For the sovereignty of his providence in the government of the world (*v.* 10, 11) and again (*v.* 13–17). 4. For the peculiar favour which he bears to his own chosen people, which encourages them to trust in him (*v.* 12) and again (*v.* 18–22). We need not be at a loss for proper thoughts in singing this psalm, which so naturally expresses the pious affections of a devout soul towards God.

Verses 1–11

Four things the psalmist expresses in these verses:

I. The great desire he had that God might be praised. He did not think he did it so well himself, but that he wished others also might be employed in this work; the more the better, in this concert: it is the more like heaven. 1. Holy joy is the heart and soul of praise, and that is here pressed upon all good people (*v.* 1): *Rejoice in the Lord, you righteous;* so the foregoing psalm concluded and so this begins; for all our religious exercises should both begin and end with a holy complacency and triumph in God as the best of being and best of friends. 2. Thankful praise is the breath and language of holy joy; and that also is here required of us (*v.* 2): *"Praise the Lord;* speak well of him, and give him the glory due to his name." 3. Religious songs are the proper expressions of thankful praise; those are here required (*v.* 3): *"Sing unto him a new song,* the best you have, not that which by frequent use is worn, thread-bare, but that which, being new, is most likely to move the affections, a new song for new mercies and upon every new occasion, for those compassions which are new every morning." Music was then used, by the appointment of David, with the temple-songs, that they might be the better sung; and this also is here called for (*v.* 2): *Sing unto him with the psaltery.* Here is, (1.) A good rule for this duty: "Do it *skilfully,* and *with a loud noise;* let it have the best both of head and heart; let it be done intelligently and with a clear head, affectionately and with a warm heart." (2.) A good reason for this duty: *For praise is comely for the upright.* It is well pleasing to God (the garments of praise add much to the comeliness which God puts upon his people) and it is an excellent ornament to our profession. *It becomes the upright,* whom God has put so much honour upon, to give honour to him. The upright praise God in a comely manner, for they praise him with their hearts, that is praising him with their glory; whereas the praises of hypocrites are awkward and uncomely, like *a parable in the mouth of fools,* Prov. 26:7.

II. The high thoughts he had of God, and of his infinite perfections, *v.* 4, 5. God makes himself known to us, 1. In his *word,* here put for all divine revelation, all that which God at sundry times and in divers manners spoke to the children of men, and that is all *right,* there is nothing amiss in it; his commands exactly agree with the rules of equity and the eternal reasons of good and evil. His promises are all wise and good and inviolably sure, and there is no iniquity in his threatenings, but even those are designed for our good, by deterring us from evil. God's word is right, and therefore all our deviations from it are wrong, and we are then in the right when we agree with it. 2. In his *works,* and those are all *done in truth,* all according to his counsels, which are called the *scriptures of truth,* Dan. 10:21. The copy in all God's works agrees exactly with the great original, the plan laid in the Eternal Mind, and varies not in the least jot. God has made it to appear in his works, (1.) That he is a God of inflexible justice: *He loveth righteousness and judgment.* There is nothing but righteousness in the sentence he passes and judgment in the execution of it. He never did nor can do wrong to any of his creatures, but is always ready to give redress to those that are wronged, and does it with delight. He takes pleasure in those that are righteous. He is himself the righteous Lord, and therefore loveth righteousness. (2.) That he is a God of inexhaustible bounty: *The earth is full of his goodness,* that is, of the proofs and instances of it. The benign influences which the earth receives from above, and the fruits it is thereby enabled to produce, the provision that is made both for man and beast, and the common blessings with which all the nations of the earth are blessed, plainly declare that *the earth is full of his goodness* — the darkest, the coldest, the hottest, and the most dry and desert part of it not excepted. What a pity is it that this earth, which is so full of God's goodness, should be so empty of his praises, and that of the multitudes that live upon his bounty there are so few that live to his glory!

III. The conviction he was under of the almighty power of God, evidenced in the creation of the world. We "believe in God," and therefore we praise him as "the Father Almighty, maker of heaven and earth," so we are here taught to praise him. Observe,

1. How God made the world, and brought all things into being. (1.) How easily: All things were made *by the word of the Lord and by the breath of his mouth.* Christ is the Word, the Spirit is the breath, so that God the Father made the world, as he rules it and redeems it, by his Son and Spirit. *He spoke, and he commanded* (*v.* 9), and that was enough; there needed no more. With men saying and doing are two things, but it is not so with God. By the Word and Spirit of God as the world was made, so was man, that little world. God said, *Let us make man,* and he *breathed into him the breath of life.* By the Word and Spirit the church is built, that new world, and grace wrought in the soul, that new man, that new creation. What cannot that power do which with a word made a world! (2.) How effectually it was done: *And it stood fast.* What God does he does to purpose; he does it and it stands fast. *Whatsoever God doeth, it shall be for ever,* Eccl. 3:14. It is by virtue of that command to stand fast that things *continue to this day according to God's ordinance,* Ps. 119:91.

2. What he made. He made all things, but notice is here taken, (1.) of *the heavens, and the host of them, v.* 6. The visible heavens, and the sun, moon, and stars, their hosts — (2.) Of the waters, and the treasures of them, *v.* 7. The earth was at first covered with the water, and, being heavier, must of course subside and sink under it; but, to show from the very first that the God of nature is not tied to the ordinary method of nature, and the usual operations of his powers, with a word's speaking *he gathered the waters together on a heap,* that the dry land might appear, yet left them not to continue on a heap, but *laid up the depth in store-houses,* not only in the flats where the seas make their beds, and in which they are locked up by the sand on the shore as in storehouses, but in secret subterraneous caverns, where they are hidden from the eyes of all living, but were reserved as in a store-house for that day when those fountains of the great deep were to be broken up; and they are still laid up there in store, for which use the great Master of the house knows best.

3. What use is to be made of this (*v.* 8): *Let all the earth fear the Lord,* and *stand in awe of him;* that is, let all the children of men worship him and give glory to him, Ps. 95:5, 6. The everlasting gospel gives this as the reason why we must worship God, because he made the heaven, and the earth, and the sea, Rev. 14:6, 7. Let us all fear him, that is, dread his wrath and displeasure, and be afraid of having him our enemy and of standing it out against him. Let us not dare to offend him who having this power no doubt has all power in his hand. It is dangerous being at war with him who has the host of heaven for his armies and the depths of the sea for his magazines, and therefore it is wisdom to desire conditions of peace, see Jer. 5:22.

IV. The satisfaction he had of God's sovereignty and dominion, *v.* 10, 11. He over-rules all the counsels of men, and makes them, contrary to their intention, serviceable to his counsels. Come and see with an eye of faith God in the throne, 1. Frustrating the devices of his enemies: *He bringeth the counsel of the heathen to nought,* so that what they imagine against him and his kingdom proves *a vain thing* (Ps. 2:1); the counsel of Ahithophel is turned into foolishness; Haman's plot is baffled. Though the design be laid ever so deep, and the hopes raised upon it ever so high, yet, if God says it *shall not stand, neither shall it come to pass;* it is all to no purpose. 2. Fulfilling his own decrees: *The counsel of the Lord standeth for ever.* It is immutable in itself, *for he is in one mind, and who can turn him?* The execution of it may be opposed, but cannot in the least be obstructed by any created power. Through all the revolutions of time God never changed his measures, but in every event, even that which to us is most surprising, the eternal counsel of God is fulfilled, nor can any thing prevent its being accomplished in its time. With what pleasure to ourselves may we in singing this give praise to God! How easy may this thought make us at all times, that God governs the world, that he did it in infinite wisdom before we were born, and will do it when we are silent in the dust!

Verses 12–22

We are here taught to give to God the glory,

I. Of his common providence towards all the children of men. Though he has endued man with understanding and freedom of will, yet he reserves to himself the government of him, and even of those very faculties by which he is qualified to govern himself. 1. The children of men are all under his eye, even their hearts are so; and all the motions and operations of their souls, which none know but they themselves, he knows better than they themselves, *v.* 13, 14. Though the residence of God's glory is in the highest heavens, yet thence he not only has a prospect of all the earth, but a particular inspection of all the inhabitants of the earth. He not only beholds them, but he *looks upon them;* he looks narrowly upon them (so the word here used is sometimes rendered), so narrowly that not the least thought can escape his observation. Atheists think that, because he dwells above in heaven, he cannot, or will not, take notice of what is done here in this lower world; but thence, high as it is, he sees us all, and all persons and thing are naked and open before him. 2. Their hearts, as well as their times, are all in his hand: *He fashions their hearts.* He made them at first, formed the spirit of each man within him, then when he brought him into being. Hence he is called *the Father of spirits:* and this is a good argument to prove that he perfectly knows them. The artist that made the clock, can account for the motions of every wheel. David uses this argument with application to himself, Ps. 139:1, 14. He still moulds the hearts of men, turns them as the rivers of water, which way soever he pleases, to serve his own purposes, darkens or enlightens men's understandings, stiffens or bows their wills, according as he is pleased to make use of them. He that fashions men's hearts fashions them alike. It is in hearts as in faces, though there is a great difference, and such a variety as that no two faces are exactly of the same features, nor any two hearts exactly of the same temper, yet there is such a similitude that, in some things, all faces and all hearts agree, *as in water face answers to face,* Prov. 27:19. He *fashions them together* (so some read it); as the wheels of a watch, though of different shapes, sizes, and motions, are yet all put together, to serve one and the same purpose, so the hearts of men and their dispositions, however varying from each other and seeming to contradict one another, are yet all overruled to serve the divine purpose, which is one. 3. They, and all they do, are obnoxious to his judgment; *for he considers all their works,* not only knows them, but weighs them, that he may render to every man according to his works, in the day, in the world, of retribution, in the judgment, and to eternity. 4. All the powers of the creature have a dependence upon him, and are of no account, of no avail at all, without him, *v.* 16, 17. It is much for the honour of God that not only no force can prevail in opposition to him, but that no force can act but in dependence on him and by a power derived from him. (1.) The strength of a king is nothing without God. No king is sacred by his royal prerogatives, or the authority with which he is invested; for the powers that are, of that kind, are ordained of God, and are what he makes them, and no more. David was a king, and a man of war from his youth, and yet acknowledged God to be his only protector and Saviour. (2.) The strength of an army is nothing without God. *The multitude of a host* cannot secure those under whose command they act, unless God make them a security to them. A great army cannot be sure of victory; for, when God pleases, one shall chase a thousand. (3.) The strength of a giant is nothing without God. *A mighty man,* such as Goliath was, *is not delivered by* his *much strength,* when his day comes to fall. Neither the firmness and activity of his body nor the stoutness and resolution of his mind will stand him in any stead, any further than God is pleased to give him success. *Let not the strong man* then *glory in his strength,* but let us all strengthen ourselves in the Lord our God, go forth, and go on, in his strength. (4.) The strength of a horse is nothing without God (*v.* 17): *A horse is a vain thing for safety.* In war horses were then so highly accounted of, and so much depended on, that God forbade the kings of Israel to *multiply horses* (Deu. 17:16), lest they should be tempted to trust to them and their confidence should thereby be taken off from God. David houghed the horses of the Syrians (2 Sa. 8:4); here he houghs all the horses in the world, by pronouncing a horse a vain thing for safety in the day of battle. If the war-horse be unruly and ill-managed, he may hurry his rider into danger instead of carrying him out of danger. If he be killed under him, he may be his death, instead of saving his life. It is therefore our interest to make sure God's favour towards us, and then we may be sure of his power engaged for us, and need not fear whatever is against us.

II. We are to give God the glory of his special grace. In the midst of his acknowledgements of God's providence he pronounces those blessed that have Jehovah for their God, who governs the world, and has wherewithal to help them in every time of need, while those were miserable who had this and the other Baal for their god, which was so far from being able to hear and help them that is was itself senseless and helpless (*v.* 12): *Blessed is the nation whose God is the Lord,* even Israel, who had the knowledge of the true God and were taken into covenant with him, and all others who own God for theirs and are owned by him; for they also, whatever nation they are of, are of the spiritual seed of Abraham. 1. It is their wisdom that they take the Lord for their God, that they direct their homage and adoration there where it is due and where the payment of it will not be in vain. 2. It is their happiness that they are the people whom God has chosen for his own inheritance, whom he is pleased with, and honoured in, and whom he protects and takes care of, whom he cultivates and improves as a man does his inheritance, Deu. 32:9. Now let us observe here, to the honour of divine grace, (1.) The regard which God has to his people, *v.* 18, 19. God beholds all the sons of men with an eye of observation, but his eye of favour and complacency is upon those that fear him. He looks upon them with delight, as the father on his children, as the bridegroom on his spouse, Isa. 62:5. While those that depend on arms and armies, on chariots and horses, perish in the disappointment of their expectations, God's people, under his protection, are safe, for he shall deliver their soul from death when there seems to be but a step between them and it. If he do not deliver the body from temporal death, yet he will deliver the soul from spiritual and eternal death. Their souls, whatever happens, shall live and praise him, either in this world or in a better. From his bounty they shall be supplied with all necessaries. he shall *keep them alive in famine;* when others die for want, they shall live, which shall make it a distinguishing mercy. When visible means fail, God will find out some way or other to supply them. He does not say that he will give them abundance (they have no reason either to desire it or to expect it), but he will keep them alive; they shall not starve; and, when destroying judgments are abroad, it ought to be reckoned a great favour, for it is a very striking one, and lays us under peculiar obligations, to have our lives given us for a prey. Those that have the Lord for their God shall find him their help and their shield, v. 20. In their difficulties he will assist them; they shall be helped over them, helped through them. In their dangers he will secure them; they shall be helped over them, helped through them. In their dangers he will secure them, so that they shall not receive any real damage. (2.) The regard which God's people have to him and which we ought to have in consideration of this. [1.] We must wait for God. We must attend the motions of his providence, and accommodate ourselves to them, and patiently accommodate ourselves to them, and patiently expect the issue of them. Our souls must wait for him, v. 20. We must not only in word and tongue profess a believing regard to God, but it must be inward and sincere, a secret and silent attendance on him. [2.] We must rely on God, hope in his mercy, in the goodness of his nature, though we have not an express promise to depend upon. Those that fear God and his wrath must hope in God and his mercy; for there is no flying from God, but by flying to him. These pious dispositions will not only consist together, but befriend each other, a holy fear of God and yet at the same time a hope in his mercy. This is trusting in his holy name (v. 21), in all that whereby he has made known himself to us, for our encouragement to serve him. [3.] We must rejoice in God, v. 21. Those do not truly rest in God, or do not know the unspeakable advantage they have by so doing, who do not rejoice in him at all times; because those that hope in God hope for an eternal fulness of joy in his presence. [4.] We must seek to him for that mercy which we hope in, v. 22. Our expectations from God are not to supersede, but to quicken and encourage, our applications to him; he will be sought unto for that which he has promised, and therefore the psalm concludes with a short but comprehensive prayer, "Let thy mercy, O Lord! be upon us; let us always have the comfort and benefit of it, not according as we merit from thee, but according as we hope in thee, that is, according to the promise which thou hast in thy word given to us and according to the faith which thou hast by thy Spirit and grace wrought in us." If, in singing these verses, we put forth a dependence upon God, and let out our desires towards him, we make melody with our hearts to the Lord.

PSALM 34

This psalm was penned upon a particular occasion, as appears by the title, and yet there is little in it peculiar to that occasion, but that which is general, both by way of thanksgiving to God an instruction to us. I. He praises God for the experience which he and others had had of his goodness (v. 1–6). II. He encourages all good people to trust in God and to seek to him (v. 7–10). III. He gives good counsel to us all, as unto children, to take heed of sin, and to make conscience of our duty both to God and man (v. 11–14). IV. To enforce this good counsel he shows God's favour to the righteous and his displeasure against the wicked, in which he sets before us good and evil, the blessing and the curse (v. 15–22). So that, in singing this psalm, we are both to give glory to God and to teach and admonish ourselves and one another.

A psalm of David when he changed his behaviour before Abimelech, who drove him away, and he departed.

Verses 1–10

The title of this psalm tells us both who penned it and upon what occasion it was penned. David, being forced to flee from his country, which was made too hot for him by the rage of Saul, sought shelter as near it as he could, in the land of the Philistines. There it was soon discovered who he was, and he was brought before the king, who, in the narrative, is called Achish (his proper name), here Abimelech (his title); and lest he should be treated as a spy, or one that came thither upon design, he feigned himself to be a madman (such there have been in every age, that even by idiots men might be taught to give God thanks for the use of their reason), that Achish might dismiss him as a contemptible man, rather than take cognizance of him as a dangerous man. And it had the effect he desired; by this stratagem he escaped the hand that otherwise would have handled him roughly. Now, 1. We cannot justify David in this dissimulation. It ill became an honest man to feign himself to be what he was not, and a man of honour to feign himself to be a fool and a mad-man. If, in sport, we mimic those who have not so good an understanding as we think we have, we forget that God might have made their case ours. 2. Yet we cannot but wonder at the composure of his spirit, and how far he was from any change of that, when he changed his behaviour. Even when he

was in that fright, or rather in that danger only, his heart was so fixed, trusting in God, that even then he penned this excellent psalm, which has as much in it of the marks of a calm sedate spirit as any psalm in all the book; and there is something curious too in the composition, for it is what is called an alphabetical psalm, that is, a psalm in which every verse begins with each letter in its order as it stands in the Hebrew alphabet. Happy are those who can thus keep their temper, and keep their graces in exercise, even when they are tempted to change their behaviour. In this former part of the psalm,

I. David engages and excites himself to praise God. Though it was his fault that he changed his behaviour, yet it was God's mercy that he escaped, and the mercy was so much the greater in that God did not deal with him according to the desert of his dissimulation, and we must in every thing give thanks. He resolves, 1. That he will praise God constantly: I will bless the Lord at all times, upon all occasions. He resolves to keep up stated times for this duty, to lay hold of all opportunities for it, and to renew his praises upon every fresh occurrence that furnished him with matter. If we hope to spend our eternity in praising God, it is fit that we should spend as much as may be of our time in this work. 2. That he will praise him openly: His praise shall continually be in my mouth. Thus he would show how forward he was to own his obligations to the mercy of God and how desirous to make others also sensible of theirs. 3. That he will praise him heartily: "My soul shall make her boast in the Lord, in my relation to him, my interest in him, and expectations from him." It is not vainglory to glory in the Lord.

II. He calls upon others to join with him herein. He expects they will (v. 2): "The humble shall hear thereof, both of my deliverance and of my thankfulness, and be glad that a good man has so much favour shown him and a good God so much honour done him." Those have most comfort in God's mercies, both to others and to themselves, that are humble, and have the least confidence in their own merit and sufficiency. It pleased David to think that God's favours to him would rejoice the heart of every Israelite. Three things he would have us all to concur with him in: —

1. In great and high thoughts of God, which we should express in magnifying him and exalting his name, v. 3. We cannot make God greater or higher than he is; but if we adore him as infinitely great, and higher than the highest, he is pleased to reckon this magnifying and exalting him. This we must do together. God's praises sound best in concert, for so we praise him as the angels do in heaven. Those that share in God's favour, as all the saints do, should concur in his praises; and we should be as desirous of the assistance of our friends in returning thanks for mercies as in praying for them. We have reason to join in thanksgiving to God,

(1.) For his readiness to hear prayer, which all the saints have had the comfort of; for he never said to any of them, Seek you me in vain. [1.] David, for his part, will give it under his hand that he has found him a prayer-hearing God (v. 4): "I sought the Lord, in my distress, entreated his favour, begged his help, and he heard me, answered my request immediately, and delivered me from all my fears, both from the death I feared and from the disquietude and disturbance produced by fear of it." The former he does by his providence working for us, the latter by his grace working in us, to silence our fears and still the tumult of the spirits; this latter is the greater mercy of the two, because the thing we fear is our trouble only, but our unbelieving distrustful fear of it is our sin; nay, it is often more our torment too than the thing itself would be, which perhaps would only touch the bone and the flesh, while the fear would prey upon the spirits and put us out of the possession of our own soul. David's prayers helped to silence his fears; having sought the Lord, and left his case with him, he could wait the event with great composure. "But David was a great and eminent man, we may not expect to be favoured as he was; have any others ever experienced the like benefit by prayer?" Yes, [2.] Many besides him have looked unto God by faith and prayer, and have been lightened by it, v. 5. It has wonderfully revived and comforted them; witness Hannah, who, when she had prayed, went her way, and did eat, and her countenance was no more sad. When we look to the world we are dark-

ened, we are perplexed, and at a loss; but, when we look to God, from him we have the light both of direction and joy, and our way is made both plain and pleasant. These here spoken of, that looked unto God, had their expectations raised, and the event did not frustrate them: Their faces were not ashamed of their confidence. "But perhaps these also were persons of great eminence, like David himself, and upon that account were highly favoured, or their numbers made them considerable;" nay, [3.] This poor man cried, a single person, mean and inconsiderable, whom no man looked upon with any respect or looked after with any concern; yet he was as welcome to the throne of grace as David or any of his worthies: The Lord heard him, took cognizance of his case and of his prayers, and saved him out of all his troubles, v. 6. God will regard the prayer of the destitute, Ps. 102:17. See Isa. 57:15.

(2.) For the ministration of the good angels about us (v. 7): The angel of the Lord, a guard of angels (so some), but as unanimous in their service as if they were but one, or a guardian angel, encamps round about those that fear God, as the life-guard about the prince, and delivers them. God makes use of the attendance of the good spirits for the protection of his people from the malice and power of evil spirits; and the holy angels do us more good offices every day than we are aware of. Though in dignity and in capacity of nature they are very much superior to us, — though they retain their primitive rectitude, which we have lost; — though they have constant employment in the upper world, the employment of praising God, and are entitled to a constant rest and bliss there, — yet in obedience to their Maker, and in love to those that bear his image, they condescend to minister to the saints, and stand up for them against the powers of darkness; they not only visit them, but encamp round about them, acting for their good as really, though not as sensibly, as for Jacob's (Gen. 32:1), and Elisha's, 2 Ki. 6:17. All the glory be to the God of the angels.

2. He would have us to join with him in kind and good thoughts of God (v. 8): O taste and see that the Lord is good! The goodness of God includes both the beauty and amiableness of his being and the bounty and beneficence of his providence and grace; and accordingly, (1.) We must taste that he is a bountiful benefactor, relish the goodness of God in all his gifts to us, and reckon that the savour and sweetness of them. Let God's goodness be rolled under the tongue as a sweet morsel. (2.) We must see that he is a beautiful being, and delight in the contemplation of his infinite perfections. By taste and sight we both make discoveries and take complacency. Taste and see God's goodness, that is, take notice of it and take the comfort of it, 1 Pt. 2:3. he is good, for he makes all those that trust in him truly blessed; let us therefore be so convinced of his goodness as thereby to be encouraged in the worst of times to trust in him.

3. He would have us join with him in a resolution to seek God and serve him, and continue in his fear (v. 9): O fear the Lord! you his saints. When we taste and see that he is good we must not forget that he is great and greatly to be feared; nay, even his goodness is the proper object of a filial reverence and awe. They shall fear the Lord and his goodness, Hos. 3:5. Fear the Lord; that is, worship him, and make conscience of your duty to him in every thing, not fear him and shun him, but fear him and seek him (v. 10) as a people seek unto their God; address yourselves to him and portion yourselves in him. To encourage us to fear God and seek him, it is here promised that those that do so, even in this wanting world, shall want no good thing (Heb. They shall not want all good things); they shall so have all good things that they shall have no reason to complain of the want of any. As to the things of the other world, they shall have grace sufficient for the support of the spiritual life (2 Co. 12:9; Ps. 84:11); and, as to this life, they shall have what is necessary to the support of it from the hand of God: as a Father, he will feed them with food convenient. What further comforts they desire they shall have, as far as Infinite Wisdom sees good, and what they want in one thing shall be made up in another. What God denies them he will give them grace to be content without and then they do not want it, Deu. 3:26. Paul had all and abounded, because he was content, Phil. 4:11, 18. Those that live by faith in God's all-sufficiency want nothing; for in him they have enough. The young lions often lack and

suffer hunger — those that live upon common providence, as the lions do, shall want that satisfaction which those have that live by faith in the promise; those that trust to themselves, and think their own hands sufficient for them, shall want (for *bread is not always to the wise*) — but verily those shall be fed that trust in God and desire to be at his finding. Those that are ravenous, and prey upon all about them, shall want; but *the meek shall inherit the earth.* Those shall not want who with quietness work and mind their own business; plain-hearted Jacob has pottage enough, when Esau, the cunning hunter, is ready to perish for hunger.

Verses 11–22

David, in this latter part of the psalm, undertakes to teach children. Though a man of war, and anointed to be king, he did not think it below him; though now he had his head so full of cares and his hands of business, yet he could find heart and time to give good counsel to young people, from his own experience. It does not appear that he had now any children of his own, at least any that were grown up to a capacity of being taught; but, by divine inspiration, he instructs the children of his people. Those that were in years would not be taught by him, though he had offered them his service (Ps. 32:8); but he had hopes that the tender branches will be more easily bent and that children and young people will be more tractable, and therefore he calls together a congregation of them (*v.* 11): *"Come, you children,* that are now in your learning age, and are now to lay up a stock of knowledge which you must live upon all your days, you children that are foolish and ignorant, and need to be taught." Perhaps he intends especially those children whose parents neglected to instruct and catechise them; and it is as great a piece of charity to put those children to school whose parents are not in a capacity to teach them as to feed those children whose parents have not bread for them. Observe, 1. What he expects from them: *"Hearken unto me,* leave your play, lay by your toys, and hear what I have to say to you; not only give me the hearing, but observe and obey me." 2. What he undertakes to teach them — *the fear of the Lord,* inclusive of all the duties of religion. David was a famous musician, a statesman, a soldier; but he does not say to the children, "I will teach you to play on the harp, or to handle the sword or spear, or to draw the bow, or I will teach you the maxims of state policy;" but I will teach you *the fear of the Lord,* which is better than all arts and sciences, better than all burnt-offerings and sacrifices. That is it which we should be solicitous both to learn ourselves and to teach our children.

I. He supposes that we all aim to be happy (*v.* 12): *What man is he that desireth life?* that is, as it follows, not only to see many days, but to see good comfortable days. *Non est vivere, sed valere, vita — It is not being, but well being, that constitutes life.* It is asked, "Who wishes to live a long and pleasant life?" and it is easily answered, *Who does not?* Surely this must look further than time and this present world; for man's life on earth at best consists but of few days and those full of trouble. What man is he that would be eternally happy, that would see many days, as many as the days of heaven, that would see good in that world where all bliss is in perfection, without the least alloy? Who would see the good before him now, by faith and hope, and enjoy it shortly? Who would? Alas! very few have that in their thoughts. Most ask, *Who will show us any good?* But few ask, *What shall we do to inherit eternal life?* This question implies that there are some such.

II. He prescribes the true and only way to happiness both in this world and that to come, *v.* 13, 14. Would we pass comfortably through this world, and out of the world, our constant care must be to keep a good conscience; and, in order to that, 1. We must learn to bridle our tongues, and be careful what we say, that we never speak amiss, to God's dishonour or our neighbours prejudice: *Keep thy tongue from evil speaking, lying, and slandering.* So great a way does this go in religion that, *if any offend not in word, the same is a perfect man;* and so little a way does religion go without this that of him who *bridles not his tongue* it is declared, *His religion is vain.* 2. We must be upright and sincere in every thing we say, and not double-tongued. Our words must be the indications of our minds; our lips must be kept from speaking guild either to God or man. 3. We must leave all our sins, and resolve we will have no more to do with them. We must *depart from evil,* from evil works and evil workers; from the sins others commit and which we have formerly allowed ourselves in. 4. It is not enough not to do hurt in the world, but we must study to be useful, and live to some purpose. We must not only depart from evil, but we must *do good,* good for ourselves, especially for our own souls, employing them well, furnishing them with a good treasure, and fitting them for another world; and, as we have ability and opportunity, we must do good to others also. 5. Since nothing is more contrary to that love which never fails (which is the summary both of law and gospel, both of grace and glory) than strife and contention, which bring confusion and every evil work, we must *seek peace and pursue it;* we must show a peaceable disposition, study the things that make for peace, do nothing to break the peace and to make mischief. If peace seem to flee from us, we must pursue it; *follow peace with all men,* spare no pains, no expense, to preserve and recover peace; be willing to deny ourselves a great deal, both in honour and interest, for peace' sake. These excellent directions in a way to life and good are transcribed into the New Testament and made part of our gospel duty, 1 Pt. 3:10, 11. And, perhaps David, in warning us that we speak no guile, reflects upon his own sin in changing his behaviour. Those that truly repent of what they have done amiss will warn others to take heed of doing likewise.

III. He enforces these directions by setting before us the happiness of the godly in the love and favour of God and the miserable state of the wicked under his displeasure. Here are life and death, good and evil, the blessing and the curse, plainly stated before us, that we may choose life and live. See Isa. 3:10, 11.

1. *Woe to the wicked, it shall be ill with them,* however they may bless themselves in their own way. (1.) God is against them, and then they cannot but be miserable. Sad is the case of that man who by his sin has made his Maker his enemy, his destroyer. *The face of the Lord is against those that do evil, v.* 16. Sometimes God is said to *turn his face from them* (Jer. 18:17), because they have forsaken him; here he is said to *set his face against them,* because they have fought against him; and most certainly God is able to out-face the most proud and daring sinners and can frown them into hell. (2.) Ruin is before them; this will follow of course if God be against them, for he is able both to kill and to cast into hell. [1.] The land of the living shall be no place for them nor theirs. When God sets his face against them he will not only cut them off, but *cut off the remembrance of them;* when they are alive he will bury them in obscurity, when they are dead he will bury them in oblivion. He will root out their posterity, by whom they would be remembered. He will pour disgrace upon their achievements, which they gloried in and for which they thought they should be remembered. It is certain that there is no lasting honour but that which comes from God. [2.] There shall be a sting in their death: *Evil shall slay the wicked, v.* 21. Their death shall be miserable; and so it will certainly be, though they die on a bed of down or on the bed of honour. Death, to them, has a curse in it, and is the king of terrors; to them it is evil, only evil. It is very well observed by Dr. Hammond that the *evil* here, which slays the wicked, is the same word, in the singular number, that is used (*v.* 19) for the afflictions of the righteous, to intimate that godly people have many troubles, and yet they do them no hurt, but are made to work for good to them, for God will deliver them out of them all; whereas wicked people have fewer troubles, fewer evils befal them, perhaps but one, and yet that one may prove their utter ruin. One trouble with a curse in it kills and slays, and does execution; but many, with a blessing in them, are harmless, nay, gainful. [3.] Desolation will be their everlasting portion. Those that are wicked themselves often hate the righteous, name and thing, have an implacable enmity to them and their righteousness; but they *shall be desolate,* shall be condemned as guilty, and laid waste for ever, shall be for ever forsaken and abandoned of God and all good angels and men; and those that are so are desolate indeed.

2. Yet *say to the righteous, It shall be well with them.* All good people are under God's special favour and protection. We are here assured of this under a great variety of instances and expressions.

(1.) God takes special notice of good people, and takes notice who have their eyes ever to him and who make conscience of their duty to him: *The eyes of the Lord are upon the righteous* (*v.* 15), to direct and guide them, to protect and keep them. Parents that are very fond of a child will not let it be out of their sight; none of God's children are ever from under his eye, but on them he looks with a singular complacency, as well as with a watchful and tender concern.

(2.) They are sure of an answer of peace to their prayers. All God's people are a praying people, and they cry in prayer, which denotes great importunity; but is it to any purpose? Yes, [1.] God takes notice of what we say (*v.* 17): They *cry, and the Lord hears them,* and hears them so as to make it appear he has a regard to them. *His ears are open to their prayers,* to receive them all, and to receive them readily and with delight. Though he has been a God hearing prayer ever since men began to call upon the name of the Lord, yet his ear is not heavy. There is no rhetoric, nothing charming, in a cry, yet God's ears are open to it, as the tender mother's to the cry of her sucking child, which another would take no notice of: *The righteous cry, and the Lord heareth, v.* 17. This intimates that it is the constant practice of good people, when they are in distress, to cry unto God, and it is their constant comfort that God hears them. [2.] He not only takes notice of what we say, but is ready for us to our relief (*v.* 18): *He is nigh to those that are of a broken heart, and saves them.* Note, *First,* It is the character of the righteous, whose prayers God will hear, that they are of a broken heart and a contrite spirit (that is, humbled for sin and emptied of self); they are low in their own eyes, and have no confidence in their own merit and sufficiency, but in God only. *Secondly,* Those who are so have God nigh unto them, to comfort and support them, that the spirit may not be broken more than is meet, lest it should fail before him. See Isa. 57:15. Though God is high, and dwells on high, yet he is near to those who, being of a contrite spirit, know how to value his favour, and will save them from sinking under their burdens; he is near them to good purpose.

(3.) They are taken under the special protection of the divine government (*v.* 20): *He keepeth all his bones;* not only his soul, but his body; not only his body in general, but every bone in it: *Not one of them is broken.* He that has a broken heart shall not have a broken bone; for David himself had found that, when he had a contrite heart, the *broken bones* were *made to rejoice,* Ps. 51:8, 17. One would not expect to meet with any thing of Christ here, and yet this scripture is said to be fulfilled in him (Jn. 19:36) when the soldiers broke the legs of the two thieves that were crucified with him, but did not break his, they being under the protection of this promise as well as of the type, even the paschal-lamb *(a bone of him shall not be broken);* the promises, being made good to Christ, through him are sure to all the seed. It does not follow but that a good man may have a broken bone; but, by the watchful providence of God concerning him, such a calamity is often wonderfully prevented, and the preservation of his bones is the effect of this promise; and, if he have a broken bone, sooner or later it shall be made whole, at furthest at the resurrection, when that which is sown in weakness shall be raised in power.

(4.) They are, and shall be, delivered out of their troubles. [1.] It is supposed that they have their share of crosses in this world, perhaps a greater share than others. In the world they must have tribulation, that they may be conformed both to the will of God and to the example of Christ (*v.* 19); *Many are the afflictions of the righteous,* witness David and his afflictions, Ps. 132:1. There are those that hate them (*v.* 21) and they are continually aiming to do them a mischief; their God loves them, and therefore corrects them; so that, between the mercy of heaven and the malice of hell, the afflictions of the righteous must needs be many. [2.] God has engaged for their deliverance and salvation: *He delivers them out of all their troubles* (*v.* 17, 19); he saves them (*v.* 18), so that, though they may fall into trouble, it shall not be their ruin. This promise of their deliverance is explained, *v.* 22. Whatever troubles befal them, *First,* They shall not hurt their better part. *The Lord redeemeth the soul of his servants* from the power of the grave (Ps. 49:15) and from the sting of every affliction. He keeps them from sinning in their troubles, which is the only thing that would do them a mischief, and keeps them from despair, and from being put out of the possession of their own souls. *Secondly,* They shall not hinder their everlasting bliss. *None of those that trust in him shall be desolate;* that is, they shall not be comfortless, for they shall not be cut off from their communion with God. No man is desolate but he whom God has forsaken, nor is any man undone till he is in hell. Those that are God's faithful servants, that make it their care to please him and their business to honour him, and in doing so trust him to protect and reward them, and, with good thoughts of him, refer themselves to him, have reason to be easy whatever befals them, for they are safe and shall be happy.

In singing these verses let us be confirmed in the choice we have made of the ways of God; let us be quickened in his service, and greatly encouraged by the assurances he has given of the particular care he takes of all those that faithfully adhere to him.

PSALM 35

David, in this psalm, appeals to the righteous Judge of heaven and earth against his enemies that hated and persecuted him. It is supposed that Saul and his party are the persons he means, for with them he had the greatest struggles. I. He complains to God of the injuries they did him; they strove with him, fought against him (*v.* 1), persecuted him (*v.* 3), sought his ruin (*v.* 4, 7), accused him falsely (*v.* 11), abused him basely (*v.* 15, 16), and all his friends (*v.* 20), and triumphed over him, (*v.* 21, 25, 26). II. He pleads his own innocency, that he never gave them any provocation (*v.* 7, 19), but, on the contrary, had studied to oblige them (*v.* 12-14). III. He prays to God to protect and deliver him, and appear for him (*v.* 1, 2), to comfort him (*v.* 3), to be nigh to him and rescue him (*v.* 17, 22), to plead his cause (*v.* 23, 24), to defeat all the designs of his enemies against him (*v.* 3, 4), to disappoint their expectations of his fall (*v.* 19, 25, 26), and, lastly, to countenance all his friends, and encourage them (*v.* 27). IV. He prophesies the destruction of his persecutors (*v.* 4-6, 8). V. He promises himself that he shall yet see better days (*v.* 9, 10), and promises God that he will then attend him with his praises (*v.* 18, 28). In singing this psalm, and praying over it, we must take heed of applying it to any little peevish quarrels and enmities of our own, and of expressing by it any uncharitable revengeful resentments of injuries done to us; for Christ has taught us to forgive our enemies and not to pray against them, but to pray for them, as he did; but, 1. We may comfort ourselves with the testimony of our consciences concerning our innocency, with reference to those that are any way injurious to us, and with hopes that God will, in his own way and time, right us, and, in the mean time, support us. 2. We ought to apply it to the public enemies of Christ and his kingdom, typified by David and his kingdom, to resent the indignities done to Christ's honour, to pray to God to plead the just and injured cause of Christianity and serious godliness, and to believe that God will, in due time, glorify his own name in the ruin of all the irreconcilable enemies of his church, that will not repent to give him glory.

A psalm of David.

Verses 1-10

In these verses we have,

I. David's representation of his case to God, setting forth the restless rage and malice of his persecutors. He was God's servant, expressly appointed by him to be what he was, followed his guidance, and aimed at his glory in the way of duty, had lived (as St. Paul speaks) *in all good conscience before God unto this day;* and yet there were those that strove with him, that did their utmost to oppose his advancement, and made all the interest they could against him; they fought against him (*v.* 1), not only undermined him closely and secretly, but openly avowed their opposition to him and set themselves to do him all the mischief they could. They persecuted him with an unwearied enmity, *sought after his soul* (*v.* 4), that is, his life, no less would satisfy their bloody minds; they aimed to disquiet his spirit and put that into disorder. Nor was it a sudden passion against him that they harboured, but inveterate malice: They *devised his hurt,* laid their heads together, and set their wits on work, not only to do him a mischief, but to find out ways and means to ruin him. They treated him, who was the greatest blessing of his country, as if he had been the curse and plague of it; they hunted him as a dangerous beast of prey; they digged a pit for him and laid a net in it, that they might have him at their mercy, *v.* 7. They took a great deal of pains in persecuting him, for they digged a pit (Ps. 7:15); and very close and crafty they were in carrying on their designs; the old serpent taught them subtlety: they hid their net from David and his friends; but in vain, for they could not hide it from God. And, *lastly,* he found himself an unequal match for them. His enemy, especially Saul, was *too strong for him* (*v.* 10), for he had the army at his command, and assumed to himself the sole power of making laws and giving judgment,

attainted and condemned whom he pleased, carried not a sceptre, but a javelin, in his hand, to cast at any man that stood in his way; such was the manner of the king, and all about him were compelled to do as he bade them, right or wrong. The king's word is a law, and every thing must be carried with a high hand; he has fields, and vineyards, and preferments, at his disposal, 1 Sa. 22:7. but David is poor and needy, has nothing to make friends with, and therefore has none to take his part but men (as we say) of broken fortunes (1 Sa. 22:2); and therefore no marvel that Saul spoiled him of what little he had got and the interest he had made. If the kings of the earth set themselves against the Lord and his anointed, who can contend with them? Note, It is no new thing for the most righteous men, and the most righteous cause, to meet with many mighty and malicious enemies: Christ himself is striven with and fought against, and war is made upon the holy seed; and we are not to marvel at the matter: it is a fruit of the old enmity in the seed of the serpent against the seed of the woman.

II. His appeal to God concerning his integrity and the justice of his cause. If a fellow-subject had wronged him, he might have appealed to his prince, as St. Paul did to Caesar; but, when his prince wronged him, he appealed to his God, who is prince and Judge of the kings of the earth: *Plead my cause, O Lord! v.* 1. Note, A righteous cause may, with the greatest satisfaction imaginable, be laid before a righteous God, and referred to him to give judgment upon it; for he perfectly knows the merits of it, holds the balance exactly even, and with him there is no respect of persons. God knew that they were, without cause, his enemies, and that they had, without cause, digged pits for him, *v.* 7. Note, It will be a comfort to us, when men do us wrong, if our consciences can witness for us that we have never done them any. It was so to St. Paul. Acts 25:10, *To the Jews have I done no wrong.* We are apt to justify our uneasiness at the injuries men do us by this, That we never gave them any cause to use us so; whereas this should, more than any thing, make us easy; for then we may the more confidently expect that God will plead our cause.

III. His prayer to God to manifest himself both for him and to him, in this trial. 1. For him. He prays that God would *fight against* his enemies, so as to disable them to hurt him, and defeat their designs against him (*v.* 1), that he would *take hold of shield and buckler,* for the Lord is a man of war (Ex. 15:3), *and* that he would *stand up for his help* (*v.* 2), for he had few that would stand up for him, and, if he had ever so many, they would stand him in no stead without God. he prays that God would *stop their way* (*v.* 3), that they might not overtake him when he fled from them. This prayer we may put up against our persecutors, that God would restrain them and stop their way. 2. To him: *"Say unto my soul, I am thy salvation;* let me have inward comfort under all these outward troubles, to support my soul which they strike at. Let God be my salvation, not only my Saviour out of my present troubles, but my everlasting bliss. Let me have that salvation not only which he is the author of, but which consists in his favour; and let me know my interest in it; let me have the comfortable assurance of it in my own breast." If God, by his Spirit, witness to our spirits that he is our salvation, we have enough, we need desire no more to make us happy; and this is a powerful support when men persecute us. If God be our friend, no matter who is our enemy.

IV. His prospect of the destruction of his enemies, which he prays for, not in malice or revenge. We find how patiently he bore Shimei's curses (*so let him curse, for the Lord has bidden him*); and we cannot suppose that he who was so meek in his conversation would give vent to any intemperate heat or passion in his devotion; but, by the spirit of prophecy, he foretells the just judgments of God that would come upon them for their great wickedness, their malice, cruelty, and perfidiousness, and especially the enmity to the counsels of God, the interests of religion, and that reformation which they knew David, if ever he had power in his hand, would be an instrument of. They seemed to be hardened in their sins, and to be of the number of those who have sinned unto death and are not to be prayed for, Jer. 7:16; 11:14; 14:11; 1 Jn. 5:16. As for Saul himself, David, it is probable, knew that God had rejected him and had forbidden Samuel to mourn for him, 1 Sa.

16:1. And these predictions look further, and read the doom of the enemies of Christ and his kingdom, as appears by comparing Rom. 11:9, 10. David here prays, 1. Against his many enemies (*v.* 4-6): *Let them be confounded,* etc. Or, as Dr. Hammond reads it, *They shall be confounded, they shall be turned back.* This may be taken as a prayer for their repentance, for all penitents are put to shame for their sins and turned back from them. Or, if they were not brought to repentance, David prays that they might be defeated and disappointed in their designs against him and so put to shame. Though they should in some degree prevail, yet he foresees that it would be to their own ruin at last: *They shall be as chaff before the wind,* so unable will wicked men be to stand before the judgments of God and so certainly will they be driven away by them, Ps. 1:4. Their way shall be *dark and slippery, darkness and slipperiness* (so the margin reads it); the way of sinners is so, for they walk in darkness and in continual danger of falling into sin, into hell; and it will prove so at last, for *their foot shall slide in due time,* Deu. 32:35. But this is not the worst of it. Even chaff before the wind may perhaps be stopped, and find a place of rest, and, though the way be dark and slippery, it is possible that a man may keep his footing; but it is here foretold that the *angel of the Lord shall chase them* (*v.* 5) so that they shall find no rest, *shall persecute them* (*v.* 6) so that they cannot possibly escape the pit of destruction. As God's angels encamp against those that fight against him. They are the ministers of his justice, as well as of his mercy. Those that make God their enemy make all the holy angels their enemies. 2. Against his one mighty enemy (*v.* 8): *Let destruction come upon him.* It is probable that he means Saul, who laid snares for him and aimed at his destruction. David vowed that his hand should not be upon him; he would not be judge in his own cause. But, at the same time, he foretold that *the Lord would smite him* (1 Sa. 26:10), and here that the net he had hidden should catch himself, and into *that very destruction he should fall.* This was remarkably fulfilled in the ruin of Saul; for he had laid a plot to make David *fall by the hand of the Philistines* (1 Sa. 18:25), that was the net which he hid for him under pretence of doing him honour, and in that very net was he himself taken, for he fell by the hand of the Philistines when his day came to fall.

V. His prospect of his own deliverance, which, having committed his cause to God, he did not doubt of, *v.* 9, 10. 1. He hoped that he should have the comfort of it: *"My soul shall be joyful,* not in my own ease and safety, but *in the Lord* and in his favour, in his promise and *in his salvation according to the promise."* Joy in God and in his salvation is the only true, solid, satisfying joy. Those whose souls are sorrowful in the Lord, who sow in tears and sorrow after a godly sort, need not question but that in due time their souls shall be joyful in the Lord; for gladness is sown for them, and they shall at last *enter into the joy of their Lord.* 2. He promised that then God should have the glory of it (*v.* 10): *All my bones shall say, Lord, who is like unto thee?* (1.) He will praise God with the whole man, with all that is within him, and with all the strength and vigour of his soul, intimated by his bones, which are within the body and are the strength of it. (2.) He will praise him as one of peerless and unparalleled perfection. We cannot express how great and good God is, and therefore must praise him by acknowledging him to be a non-such. *Lord, who is like unto thee?* No such patron of oppressed innocency, no such punisher of triumphant tyranny. The formation of our bones so wonderfully, so curiously (Eccl. 11:5; Ps. 139:16), the serviceableness of our bones, and the preservation of them, and especially the life which, at the resurrection, shall be breathed upon the dry bones and make them flourish as a herb, oblige every bone in our bodies, if it could speak, to say, *Lord, who is like unto thee?* and willingly to undergo any services or sufferings for him.

Verses 11-16

Two very wicked things David here lays to the charge of his enemies, to make good his appeal to God against them — perjury and ingratitude.

I. Perjury, *v.* 11. When Saul would have David attainted of treason, in order to his being outlawed, perhaps he did it with the formalities of a legal prosecution, produced witnesses who swore some treasonable words or overt acts against him, and he being not present to clear himself (or, if he was, it was all the same), Saul adjudged him a traitor. This he complains of here as the highest piece of injustice imaginable: *False witnesses did rise up,* who would swear anything; *they laid to my charge things that I knew not,* nor ever thought of. See how much the honours, estates, liberties, and lives, even of the best men, lie at the mercy of the worst, against whose false oaths innocency itself is no fence; and what reason we have to acknowledge with thankfulness the hold God has of the consciences even of bad men, to which it is owing that there is not more mischief done in that way than is. This instance of the wrong done to David was typical, and had its accomplishment in the Son of David, against whom false witnesses did arise, Mt. 26:60. If we be at any time charged with what we are innocent of let us not think it strange, as though some new thing happened to us; so persecuted they the prophets, even the great prophet.

II. Ingratitude. Call a man ungrateful and you can call him no worse. This was the character of David's enemies (*v.* 12): *They rewarded me evil for good.* A great deal of good service he had done to his king, witness his harp, witness Goliath's sword, witness the foreskins of the Philistines; and yet his king vowed his death, and his country was made too hot for him. This is *to the spoiling of his soul;* this base unkind usage robs him of his comfort, and cuts him to the heart, more than any thing else. Nay, he had deserved well not only of the public in general, but of those particular persons that were now most bitter against him. Probably it was then well known whom he meant; it may be Saul himself for one, whom he was sent for to attend upon when he was melancholy and ill, and to whom he was serviceable to drive away the evil spirit, not with his harp, but with his prayers; to others of the courtiers, it is likely, he had shown this respect, while he lived at court, who now were, of all others, most abusive to him. Herein he was a type of Christ, to whom this wicked world was very ungrateful. Jn. 10:32. *Many good works have I shown you from my Father; for which of those do you stone me?* David here shows,

1. How tenderly, and with what a cordial affection, he had behaved towards them in their afflictions (*v.* 13, 14): *They were sick.* Note, Even the palaces and courts of princes are not exempt from the jurisdiction of death and the visitation of sickness. Now when these people were sick, (1.) David mourned for them and sympathized with them in their grief. They were not related to him; he was under no obligations to them; he would lose nothing by their death, but perhaps be a gainer by it; and yet he behaved himself as though they had been his nearest relations, purely from a principle of compassion and humanity. David was a man of war, and of a bold stout spirit, and yet was thus susceptible of the impressions of sympathy, forgot the bravery of the hero, and seemed wholly made up of love and pity; it was a rare composition of hardiness and tenderness, courage and compassion, in the same breast. Observe, He mourned as for a brother or mother, which intimates that it is our duty, and well becomes us, to lay to heart the sickness, and sorrow, and death of our near relations. Those that do not are justly stigmatized as without natural affection. (2.) He prayed for them. He discovered not only the tender affection of a man, but the pious affection of a saint. He was concerned for their precious souls, and, since he helped them with his prayers to God for mercy and grace; and the prayers of one who had so great an interest in heaven were of more value than perhaps they knew or considered. With his prayers he joined humiliation and self-affliction, both in his diet (he fasted, at least from pleasant bread) and in his dress; he clothed himself with sackcloth, thus expressing his grief, not only for their affliction, but for their sin; for this was the guise and practice of a penitent. We ought to mourn for the sins of those that do not mourn for them themselves. His fasting also put an edge upon his praying, and was an expression of the fervour of it; he was so intent in his devotions that he had no appetite to meat, nor would allow himself time for eating: *"My prayer returned into my own bosom;* I had the comfort of having done my duty, and of having approved myself a loving neighbour, though I could not thereby win upon them nor make them my friends." We shall not lose by the good offices we have done to any, how ungrateful soever they are; for our rejoicing will be this, *the testimony of our conscience.*

2. How basely and insolently and with what a brutish enmity, and worse than brutish, they had behaved towards him (*v.* 15, 16); *In my adversity they rejoiced.* When he fell under the frowns of Saul, was banished the court, and persecuted as a criminal, they were pleased, were glad at his calamities, and got together in their drunken clubs to make themselves and one another merry with the disgrace of this great favourite. Well, might he call them *abjects,* for nothing could be more vile and sordid than to triumph in the fall of a man of such unstained honour and consummate virtue. But this was not all. (1.) They tore him, rent his good name without mercy, said all the ill they could of him and fastened upon him all the reproach their cursed wit and malice could reach to. (2.) *They gnashed upon him with their teeth;* they never spoke of him but with the greatest indignation imaginable, as those that would have eaten him up if they could. David was the fool in the play, and his disappointment all the table-talk of the hypocritical mockers at feasts; it was the song of the drunkards. The comedians, who may fitly be called *hypocritical mockers* (for which does a hypocrite signify but a stage-player?) and whose comedies, it is likely, were acted at feasts and balls, chose David for their subject, bantered and abused him, while the auditory, in token of their agreement with the plot, hummed, and *gnashed upon him with their teeth.* Such has often been the hard fate of the best of men. The apostles were made a spectacle to the world. David was looked upon with ill-will for no other reason than because he was caressed by the people. It is a vexation of spirit which attends even a right work that *for this a man is envied of his neighbour,* Eccl. 4:4. And *who can stand before envy?* Prov. 27:4.

Verses 17–28

In these verses, as before,

I. David describes the great injustice, malice, and insolence, of his persecutors, pleading this with God as a reason why he should protect him from them and appear against them. 1. They were very unrighteous; they were his enemies wrongfully, for he never gave them any provocation: *They hated him without a cause;* nay, for that for which they ought rather to have loved and honoured him. This is quoted, with application to Christ, and is said to be fulfilled in him. Jn. 15:25, *They hated me without cause.* 2. They were very rude; they could not find in their hearts to show him common civility: *They speak not peace;* if they met him, they had not the good manners to give him the time of day; like Joseph's brethren, that could not *speak peaceably to him,* Gen. 37:4. 3. They were very proud and scornful (*v.* 21): *They opened their mouth wide against me;* they shouted and huzzaed when they saw his fall; they bawled after him when he was forced to quit the court, "Aha! aha! this is the day we longed to see." 4. They were very barbarous and base, for they trampled upon him when he was down, rejoiced at his hurt, and *magnified themselves against him, v.* 26. *Turba Remi sequitur fortunam, ut semper, et odit damnatos — The Roman crowd, varying their opinions with every turn of fortune, are sure to execrate the fallen.* Thus, when the Son of David was run upon by the rulers, the people cried, *Crucify him, crucify him.* 5. They set themselves against all the sober good people that adhered to David (*v.* 20): *They devised deceitful matters,* to trepan and ruin *those that were quiet in the land.* Note, (1.) It is the character of the godly in the land that they are the quiet in the land, that they live in all dutiful subjection to government and governors, in the Lord, and endeavour, as much as in them lies, to live peaceably with all men, however they may have been misrepresented as enemies to Caesar and hurtful to kings and provinces. *I am for peace,* Ps. 120:7. (2.) Though the people of God are, and study to be, a quiet people, yet it has been the common practice of their enemies to devise deceitful matters against them. All the hellish arts of malice and falsehood are made use of to render them odious or despicable; their words and actions are misconstrued, even that which they abhor is fathered upon them, laws are made to ensnare them (Dan. 6:4, etc.), and all to ruin them and root them out. Those that hated David thought scorn, like Haman, to lay hands on him alone, but contrived to involve all the religious people of the land in the same ruin with him.

II. He appeals to God against them, the *God to whom vengeance belongs,* appeals to his knowledge (*v.* 22): *This thou hast seen.* They had falsely accused him, but God, who knows all things, knew that he did not falsely accuse them, nor make them worse than really they were. They had carried on their plots against him with a great degree of secresy (*v.* 15): "I knew it not, till long after, when they themselves gloried in it; but thy eye was upon them in their close cabals and thou art a witness of all they have said and done against me and thy people." He appeals to God's justice: *Awake to my judgment, even to my cause,* and let it have a hearing at thy bar, *v.* 23. *"Judge me, O Lord my God!* pass sentence upon this appeal, *according to the righteousness* of thy nature and government," *v.* 24. See this explained by Solomon, 1 Ki. 7:31, 32. When thou art appealed to, *hear in heaven, and judge, by condemning the wicked and justifying the righteous.*

III. He prays earnestly to God to appear graciously for him and his friends, against his and their enemies, that by his providence the struggle might issue to the honour and comfort of David and to the conviction and confusion of his persecutors. 1. He prays that God would act for him, and not stand by as a spectator (*v.* 17): *"Lord, how long wilt thou look on?* How long wilt thou connive at the wickedness of the wicked? *Rescue my soul from the destructions* they are plotting against it; rescue *my darling,* my only one, *from the lions.* My soul is my only one, and therefore the greater is the shame if I neglect it and the greater the loss if I lose it: it is my only one, and therefore ought to be my darling, ought to be carefully protected and provided for. It is my soul that is in danger; Lord, rescue it. It does, in a peculiar manner, belong to the Father of spirits, therefore claim thy own; it is thine, save it. *Lord, keep not silence,* as if thou didst consent to what is done against me! *Lord, be not far from me* (*v.* 22), as if I were a stranger that thou wert not concerned for; let not me beheld afar off, as the proud are." 2. He prays that his enemies might not have cause to rejoice (*v.* 19): *Let them not rejoice over me* (and again, *v.* 24); not so much because it would be a mortification to him to be trampled upon the abjects, as because it would turn to the dishonour of God and the reproach of his confidence in God. It would harden the hearts of his enemies in their wickedness and confirm them in their enmity to him, and would be a great discouragement to all the pious Jews that were friends to his righteous cause. He prays that he might never be in such imminent danger as that they should *say in their hearts, Ah! so would we have it* (*v.* 25), much more that he might not be reduced to such extremity that they should say, *We have swallowed him up;* for then they will reflect upon God himself. But, on the contrary, that they might be *ashamed and brought to confusion together* (*v.* 26, as before, *v.* 4); he desires that his innocency might be so cleared that they might be ashamed of the calumnies with which they had loaded him, that his interest might be so confirmed that they might be ashamed of their designs against him and their expectations of his ruin, that they might either be brought to that shame which would be a step towards their reformation or that that might be their portion which would be their everlasting misery. 3. He prays that his friends might have cause to rejoice and give glory to God, *v.* 27. Notwithstanding the arts that were used to blacken David, and make him odious, and to frighten people from owning him, there were some that favoured his righteous cause, that knew he was wronged and bore a good affection to him; and he prays for them, (1.) That they might rejoice with him in his joys. It is a great pleasure to all that are good to see an honest man, and an honest cause, prevail and prosper; and those that heartily espouse the interests of God's people, and are willing to take their lot with them even when they are run down and trampled upon, shall in due time shout for joy and be glad, for the righteous cause will at length be a victorious cause. (2.) That they might join with him in his praises: *Let them say continually, The Lord be magnified,* by us and others, *who hath pleasure in the prosperity of his servant.* Note, [1.] The great God has pleasure in this prosperity of good people, not only of his family, the church in general, but of every particular servant in his family. He has pleasure in the prosperity both of their temporal and of their spiritual affairs, and delights not in their griefs; for he does not afflict willingly; and we ought therefore to have pleasure in their prosperity, and not to envy it. [2.] When God in his providence shows his good-will to the prosperity of his servants, and the pleasure he takes in it, we ought to acknowledge it with thankfulness, to his praise, and to say, *The Lord be magnified.*

IV. The mercy he hoped to win by prayer he promises to wear with praise: "*I will give thee thanks,* as the author of my deliverance (*v.* 18), *and my tongue shall speak of thy righteousness,* the justice of thy judgments and the equity of all thy dispensations;" and this, 1. Publicly, as one that took a pleasure in owning his obligations to his God, so far was he from being ashamed of them. he will do it in the great congregation, and among much people, that God might be honoured and many edified. 2. Constantly. he will speak God's praise *every day* (so it may be read) and *all the day long;* for it is a subject that will never be exhausted, no, not by the endless praises of saints and angels.

PSALM 36

It is uncertain when, and upon what occasion, David penned this psalm, probably when he was struck at either by Saul or by Absalom; for in it he complains of the malice of his enemies against him, but triumphs in the goodness of God to him. We are here led to consider, and it will do us good to consider seriously, I. The sinfulness of sin, and how mischievous it is (*v.* 1–4). II. The goodness of God, and how gracious he is, 1. To all his creatures in general (*v.* 5, 6). 2. To his own people in a special manner (*v.* 7–9). By this the psalmist is encouraged to pray for all the saints (*v.* 10), for himself in particular and his own preservation (*v.* 11), and to triumph in the certain fall of his enemies (*v.* 12). If, in singing this psalm, our hearts be duly affected with the hatred of sin and satisfaction in God's lovingkindness, we sing it with grace and understanding.

To the chief Musician. A psalm of David the servant of the Lord.

Verses 1–4

David, in the title of this psalm, is styled *the servant of the Lord;* why in this, and not in any other, except in Ps. 18 *(title),* no reason can be given; but so he was, not only as every good man is God's servant, but as a king, as a prophet, as one employed in serving the interests of God's kingdom among men more immediately and more eminently than any other in his day. He glories in it, Ps. 116:16. It is no disparagement, but an honour, to the greatest of men, to be the servants of the great God; it is the highest preferment a man is capable of in this world.

David, in these verses, describes the wickedness of the wicked; whether he means his persecutors in particular, or all notorious gross sinners in general, is not certain. But we have here sin in its causes and sin in its colours, in its root and in its branches.

I. Here is the root of bitterness, from which all the wickedness of the wicked comes. It takes rise, 1. From their contempt of God and the want of a due regard to him (*v.* 1): "*The transgression of the wicked* (as it is described afterwards, *v.* 3, 4) *saith within my heart* (makes me to conclude within myself) *that there is no fear of God before his eyes;* for, if there were, he would not talk and act so extravagantly as he does; he would not, he durst not, break the laws of God, and violate his covenants with him, if he had any awe of his majesty or dread of his wrath." Fitly therefore is it brought into the form of indictments by our law that the criminal, *not having the fear of God before his eyes,* did so and so. The wicked did not openly renounce the fear of God, but their transgression whispered it secretly into the minds of all those that knew any thing of the nature of piety and impiety. David concluded concerning those who lived at large that they lived without God in the world. 2. From their conceit of themselves and a cheat they wilfully put upon their own souls (*v.* 2): *He flattereth himself in his own eyes;* that is, while he goes on in sin, he thinks he does wisely and well for himself, and either does not see or will not own the evil and danger of his wicked practices; he calls evil good and good evil; his licentiousness he pretends to be but his just liberty, his fraud passes for his prudence and policy, and his persecuting the people of God, he suggests to himself, is a piece of necessary justice. If his own conscience threaten him for what he does, he says, *God will not require it; I shall have peace though I go on.* Note, Sinners are self-destroyers by being self-flatterers. Satan could not deceive them if they did not deceive themselves. Buy will the cheat last always? No; the day is coming when the sinner will be undeceived, when *his iniquity shall be found to be hate-*ful. Iniquity is a hateful thing; it is that *abominable thing which the Lord hates,* and which his pure and jealous eye cannot endure to look upon. It is hurtful to the sinner himself, and therefore ought to be hateful to him; but it is not so; he rolls it under his tongue as a sweet morsel, because of the secular profit and sensual pleasure which may attend it; yet *the meat in his bowels will be turned, it will be the gall of asps,* Job 20:13, 14. When their consciences are convinced, and sin appears in its true colours and makes them a terror to themselves — when the cup of trembling is put into their hands and they are made to drink the dregs of it — then their iniquity will be found hateful, and their self-flattery their unspeakable folly, and an aggravation of their condemnation.

II. Here are the cursed branches which spring from this root of bitterness. The sinner defies God, and even deifies himself, and then what can be expected but that he should go all to naught? These two were the first inlets of sin. Men do not fear God, and therefore they flatter themselves, and then, 1. They make no conscience of what they say, true of false, right or wrong (*v.* 3): *The words of his mouth are iniquity and deceit,* contrived to do wrong, and yet to cover it with specious and plausible pretences. It is no marvel if those that deceive themselves contrive how to deceive all mankind; for to whom will those be true who are false to their own souls? 2. What little good there has been in them is gone; the sparks of virtue are extinguished, their convictions baffled, their good beginnings come to nothing: They have *left off to be wise and to do good.* They seemed to be under the direction of wisdom and the government of religion, but they have broken these bonds asunder; they have shaken off their religion, and therewith their wisdom. Note, Those that leave off to do good leave off to be wise. 3. Having left off to do good, they contrive to do hurt and to be vexatious to those about them that are good and do good (*v.* 4): *He devises mischief upon his bed.* Note, (1.) Omissions make way for commissions. When men leave off doing good, leave off praying, leave off their attendance on God's ordinances and their duty to him, the devil easily makes them his agents, his instruments to draw those that will be drawn into sin, and, with respect to those that will not, to draw them into trouble. Those that leave off to do good begin to do evil; the devil, being an apostate from his innocency, soon became a tempter to Eve and a persecutor of righteous Abel. (2.) It is bad to do mischief, but it is worse to devise it, to do it deliberately and with resolution, to set the wits on work to contrive to do it most effectually, to do it with plot and management, with the subtlety, as well as the malice, of the old serpent, to devise it upon the bed, where we should be meditating upon God and his word, Mic. 2:1. This argues the sinner's heart fully set in him to do evil. 4. Having entered into the way of sin, that way that is not good, that has good neither in it nor at the end of it, they persist and resolve to persevere in that way. *He sets himself* to execute the mischief he has devised, and nothing shall be withholden from him which he has purposed to do, though it be ever to contrary both to his duty and to his true interest. If sinners did not steel their hearts and brazen their faces with obstinacy and impudence, they could not go on in their evil ways, in such a direct opposition to all that is just and good. 5. Doing evil themselves, they have no dislike at all of it in others: *He abhors not evil,* but on the contrary, takes pleasure in it, and is glad to see others as bad as himself. Or this may denote his impenitency in sin. Those that have done evil, if God give them repentance, abhor the evil they have done and themselves because of it; it is bitter in the reflection, however sweet it was in the commission. But these hardened sinners have such seared stupefied consciences that they never reflect upon their sings afterwards with any regret or remorse, but stand to what they have done, as if they could justify it before God himself.

Some think that David, in all this, particularly means Saul, who had cast off the fear of God and left off all goodness, who pretended kindness to him when he gave him his daughter to wife, but at the same time was devising mischief against him. But we are under no necessity of limiting ourselves so in the exposition of it; there are too many among us to whom the description agrees, which is to be greatly lamented.

Verses 5–12

David, having looked round with grief upon the wickedness of the wicked, here looks up with comfort upon the goodness of God, a subject as delightful as the former was distasteful and very proper to be set in the balance against it. Observe,

I. His meditations upon the grace of God. He sees the world polluted, himself endangered, and God dishonoured, by the transgressions of the wicked; but, of a sudden, he turns his eye, and heart, and speech, to God "However it be, yet thou art good." He here acknowledges,

1. The transcendent perfections of the divine nature. Among men we have often reason to complain, There is *no truth nor mercy,* (Hos. 4:1), *no judgment nor justice,* Isa. *v.* 7. But all these may be found in God without the least alloy. Whatever is missing, or amiss, in the world, we are sure there is nothing missing, nothing amiss, in him that governs it. (1.) He is a God of inexhaustible goodness: *Thy mercy, O Lord! is in the heavens.* If men shut up the bowels of their compassion, yet with God, at the throne of his grace, we shall find mercy. When men are devising mischief against us God's thoughts concerning us, if we cleave closely to him, are thoughts of good. On earth we meet with little content and a great deal of disquiet and disappointment; but in the heavens, where the mercy of God reigns in perfection and to eternity, there is all satisfaction; there therefore, if we would be easy, let us have our conversation, and there let us long to be. How bad soever the world is, let us never think the worse of God nor of his government; but, from the abundance of wickedness that is among men, let us take occasion, instead of reflecting upon God's purity, as if he countenanced sin, to admire his patience, that he bears so much with those that so impudently provoke him, nay, and causes his sun to shine and his rain to fall upon them. If God's mercy were not in the heavens (that is, infinitely above the mercies of any creature), he would, long ere this, have drowned the world again. See Isa. 55:8, 9; Hos. 11:9. (2.) He is a God of inviolable truth: *Thy faithfulness reaches unto the clouds.* Though God suffers wicked people to do a great deal of mischief, yet he is and will be faithful to his threatenings against sin, and there will come a day when he will reckon with them; he is faithful also to his covenant with his people, which cannot be broken, nor one jot or tittle of the promises of it defeated by all the malice of earth and hell. This is matter of great comfort to all good people, that, though men are false, God is faithful; men speak vanity, but the words of the Lord are pure words. God's faithfulness reaches so high that it does not change with the weather, as men's does, for it reaches to the *skies* (so it should be read, as some think), above the clouds, and all the changes of the lower region. (3.) He is a God of incontestable justice and equity: *Thy righteousness is like the great mountains,* so immovable and inflexible itself and so conspicuous and evident to all the world; for no truth is more certain nor more plain than this, That the Lord is righteous in all his ways, and that he never did, nor ever will do, any wrong to any of his creatures. Even *when clouds and darkness are round about him, yet judgment and justice are the habitation of his throne,* Ps. 97:2. (4.) He is a God of unsearchable wisdom and design: "*Thy judgments are a great deep,* not to be fathomed with the line and plummet of any finite understanding." As his power is sovereign, which he owes not any account of to us, so his method is singular and mysterious, which cannot be accounted for by us: *His way is in the sea and his path in the great waters.* We know that he does all wisely and well; but what he does we know not now; it will be time enough to know hereafter.

2. The extensive care and beneficence of the divine Providence: "*Thou preservest man and beast,* not only protectest them from mischief, but suppliest them with that which is needful for the support of life." The beasts, though not capable of knowing and praising God, are yet graciously provided for; their eyes wait on him, and he gives them their meat in due season. Let us not wonder that God gives food to bad men, for he feeds the brute-creatures; and let us not fear but that he will provide well for good men; he that feeds the young lions will not starve his own children.

3. The peculiar favour of God to the saints. Observe, (1.) Their character, *v.* 7. They are such as are allured

by the *excellency of God's loving-kindness to put their trust under the shadow of his wings.* [1.] God's loving-kindness is precious to them. They relish it; they taste a transcendent sweetness in it; they admire God's beauty and benignity above any thing in this world, nothing so amiable, so desirable. Those know not God that do not admire his loving-kindness; and those know not themselves that do not earnestly covet it. [2.] They therefore repose an entire confidence in him. They have recourse to him, put themselves under his protection, and then think themselves safe and find themselves easy, as the chickens under the wings of the hen, Mt. 23:37. It was the character of proselytes that they came to *trust under the wings of the God of Israel* (Ruth 2:12); and what more proper to gather proselytes than the excellency of his loving-kindness? What more powerful to engage our complacency to him and on him? Those that are thus drawn by love will cleave to him.

(2.) Their privilege. Happy, thrice happy, the people whose God is the Lord, for in him they have, or may have, or shall have, a complete happiness. [1.] Their desires shall be answered, (*v.* 8): *They shall be abundantly satisfied with the fatness of thy house,* their wants supplied; their cravings gratified, and their capacities filled. In God all-sufficient they shall have enough, all that which an enlightened enlarged soul can desire or receive. The gains of the world and the delights of sense will surfeit, but never satisfy, Isa. 55:2. But the communications of divine favour and grace will satisfy, but never surfeit. A gracious soul, though still desiring more of God, never desires more than God. The gifts of Providence so far satisfy them that they are content with such things as they have. *I have all, and abound,* Phil. 4:18. The benefit of holy ordinances is the fatness of God's house, sweet to a sanctified soul and strengthening to the spiritual and divine life. With this they are abundantly satisfied; they desire nothing more in this world than to live a life of communion with God and to have the comfort of the promises. But the full, the abundant satisfaction is reserved for the future state, the house not made with hands, eternal in the heavens. Every vessel will be full there. [2.] Their joys shall be constant: *Thou shalt make them drink of the river of thy pleasures. First,* There are pleasures that are truly divine. "They are *thy pleasures,* not only which come from thee as the giver of them, but which terminate in thee as the matter and centre of them." Being purely spiritual, they are of the same nature with those of the glorious inhabitants of the upper world, and bear some analogy even to the delights of the Eternal Mind. *Secondly,* There is a river of these pleasures, always full, always fresh, always flowing. There is enough for all, enough for each; see Ps. 46:4. The pleasures of sense are putrid puddle-water; those of faith are pure and pleasant, *clear as crystal,* Rev. 22:1. *Thirdly,* God has not only provided this river of pleasures for his people, but he makes them to drink of it, works in them a gracious appetite to these pleasures, and by his Spirit fills their souls with joy and peace in believing. In heaven they shall be for ever drinking of those *pleasures that are at God's right hand,* satiated with a *fulness of joy,* Ps. 16:11. [3.] Life and light shall be their everlasting bliss and portion, *v.* 9. Having God himself for their felicity, *First,* In him they have a fountain of life, from which those rivers of pleasure flow, *v.* 8. The God of nature is the fountain of natural life. In him we live, and move, and have our being. The God of grace is the fountain of spiritual life. All the strength and comfort of a sanctified soul, all its gracious principles, powers, and performances, are from God. He is the spring and author of all its sensations of divine things, and all its motions towards them: he quickens whom he will; and whosoever will may come, and take from him of the waters of life freely. He is the fountain of eternal life. The happiness of glorified saints consists in the vision and fruition of him, and in the immediate communications of his love, without interruption or fear of cessation. *Secondly,* In him they have light in perfection, wisdom, knowledge, and joy, all included in this light: *In thy light we shall see light,* that is, 1. "In the knowledge of thee in grace, and the vision of thee in glory, we shall have that which will abundantly suit and satisfy our understandings." That divine light which shines in the scripture, and especially in the face of Christ, the light of the world, has all truth in it. When we come to see God face to face, within the veil, we shall see light in perfection, we shall know enough then, 1 Co. 13:12; 1 Jn. 3:2. 2. "In communion with thee now; by the communications of thy grace to us and the return of our devout affections to thee, and in the fruition of thee shortly in heaven, we shall have a complete felicity and satisfaction. In thy favour we have all the good we can desire." This is a dark world; we see little comfort in it; but in the heavenly light there is true light, and no false light, light that is lasting and never wastes. In this world we see God, and enjoy him by creatures and means; but in heaven *God himself shall be with us* (Rev. 21:3) and we shall see and enjoy him immediately.

II. We have here David's prayers, intercessions, and holy triumphs, grounded upon these meditations.

1. He intercedes for all saints, begging that they may always experience the benefit and comfort of God's favour and grace, *v.* 10. (1.) The persons he prays for are those that know God, that are acquainted with him, acknowledge him, and avouch him for theirs — the upright in heart, that are sincere in their profession of religion, and faithful both to God and man. Those that are not upright with God do not know him as they should. (2.) The blessing he begs for them is God's loving-kindness (that is, the tokens of his favour towards them) and his righteousness (that is, the workings of his grace in them); or his loving-kindness and righteousness are his goodness according to promise; they are mercy and truth. (3.) The manner in which he desires this blessing may be conveyed: *O continue it, draw it out,* as the mother draws out her breasts to the child, and then the child draws out the milk from the breasts. Let it be drawn out to a length equal to the line of eternity itself. The happiness of the saints in heaven will be in perfection, and yet in continual progression (as some thing); for the fountain there will be always full and the streams always flowing. *In these is continuance,* Isa. 64:5.

2. He prays for himself, that he might be preserved in his integrity and comfort (*v.* 11): *"Let not the foot of pride come against me,* to trip up my heels, or trample upon me; *and let not the hand of the wicked,* which is stretched out against me, prevail to *remove me,* either from my purity and integrity, by any temptation, or from my peace and comfort, by any trouble." Let not those who fight against God triumph over those who desire to cleave to him. Those that have experienced the pleasure of communion with God cannot but desire that nothing may ever remove them from him.

3. He rejoices in hope of the downfall of all his enemies in due time (*v.* 12): "*There,* where they thought to gain the point against me, *they have* themselves *fallen,* been taken in that snare which they laid for me." *There,* in the other world (so some), where the saints stand in the judgment, and have a place in God's house, the workers of iniquity are cast in the judgment, *are cast down* into hell, into the bottomless pit, out of which they shall assuredly never be able to rise from under the insupportable weight of God's wrath and curse. It is true we are not to rejoice when any particular enemy of ours falls; but the final overthrow of all the workers of iniquity will be the everlasting triumph of glorified saints.

PSALM 37

This psalm is a sermon, and an excellent useful sermon it is, calculated not (as most of the psalms) for our devotion, but for our conversation; there is nothing in it of prayer or praise, but it is all instruction; it is "Maschil — a teaching psalm;" it is an exposition of some of the hardest chapters in the book of Providence, the advancement of the wicked and the disgrace of the righteous, a solution of the difficulties that arise thereupon, and an exhortation to conduct ourselves as becomes us under such dark dispensations. The work of the prophets (and David was one) was to explain the law. Now the law of Moses had promised temporal blessings to the obedient, and denounced temporal miseries against the disobedient, which principally referred to the body of the people, the nation as a nation; for, when they came to be applied to particular persons, many instances occurred of sinners in prosperity and saints in adversity; to reconcile those instances with the word that God had spoken is the scope of the prophet in this psalm, in which, I. He forbids us to fret at the prosperity of the wicked in their wicked ways (*v.* 1, 7, 8). II. He gives very good reasons why we should not fret at it. 1. Because of the scandalous character of the wicked (*v.* 12, 14, 21, 32) notwithstanding their prosperity, and the honourable character of the righteous (*v.* 21, 26, 30, 31). 2. Because of the destruction and ruin which the wicked are nigh to (*v.* 2, 9, 10, 20, 35, 36, 38) and the salvation and protection which the righteous are sure of from all the malicious designs of the wicked (*v.* 13, 15, 17, 28, 33, 39, 40). 3. Because of the particular mercy God has in store for all good people and the favour he shows them (*v.* 11, 16, 18, 19, 22–25, 28, 29, 37). III. He prescribes very good remedies against this sin of envying the prosperity of the wicked, and great encouragement to use those remedies (*v.* 3–6, 27, 34). In singing this psalm we must teach and admonish one another rightly to understand the providence of God and to accommodate ourselves to it, at all times carefully to do our duty and then patiently to leave the event with God and to believe that, how black soever things may look for the present, it shall be "well with those that fear God, that fear before him."

A psalm of David.

Verses 1–6

The instructions here given are very plain; much need not be said for the exposition of them, but there is a great deal to be done for the reducing of them to practice, and there they will look best.

I. We are here cautioned against discontent at the prosperity and success of evil-doers (*v.* 1, 2): *Fret not thyself, neither be thou envious.* We may suppose that David speaks this to himself first, and preaches it to his own heart (in his communing with that upon his bed), for the suppressing of those corrupt passions which he found working there, and then leaves it in writing for instruction to others that might be in similar temptation. That is preached best, and with most probability of success, to others, which is first preached to ourselves. Now, 1. When we look abroad we see the world full of evil-doers and workers of iniquity, that flourish and prosper, that have what they will and do what they will, that live in ease and pomp themselves and have power in their hands to do mischief to those about them. So it was in David's time; and therefore, if it is so still, let us not marvel at the matter, as though it were some new or strange thing. 2. When we look within we find ourselves tempted to fret at this, and to be envious against these scandals and burdens, these blemishes and common nuisances, of this earth. We are apt to fret at God, as if he were unkind to the world and unkind to his church in permitting such men to live, and prosper, and prevail, as they do. We are apt to fret ourselves with vexation at their success in their evil projects. We are apt to envy them the liberty they take in getting wealth, and perhaps by unlawful means, and in the indulgence of their lusts, and to wish that we could shake off the restraints of conscience and do so too. We are tempted to think them the only happy people, and to incline to imitate them, and to join ourselves with them, that we may share in their gains and eat of their dainties; and this is that which we are warned against: *Fret not thyself, neither be thou envious.* Fretfulness and envy are sins that are their own punishments; they are the uneasiness of the spirit and the rottenness of the bones; it is therefore in kindness to ourselves that we are warned against them. Yet that is not all; for, 3. When we look forward with an eye of faith we shall see no reason to envy wicked people their prosperity, for their ruin is at the door and they are ripening apace for it, *v.* 2. They flourish, but as the grass, and as the green herb, which nobody envies nor frets at. The flourishing of a godly man is like that of a fruitful tree (Ps. 1:3), but that of the wicked man is like grass and herbs, which are very short-lived. (1.) They will soon wither of themselves. Outward prosperity is a fading thing, and so is the life itself to which it is confined. (2.) They will sooner be cut down by the judgments of God. Their triumphing is short, but their weeping and wailing will be everlasting.

II. We are here counselled to live a life on confidence and complacency in God, and that will keep us from fretting at the prosperity of evil-doers; if we do well for our own souls, we shall see little reason to envy those that do so ill for theirs. Here are three excellent precepts, which we are to be ruled by, and, to enforce them, three precious promises, which we may rely upon.

1. We must make God our hope in the way of duty and then we shall have a comfortable subsistence in this world, *v.* 3. (1.) It is required that we *trust in the Lord and do good,* that we confide in God and conform to him. The life of religion lies much in a believing reliance on God, his favour, his providence, his promise, his grace, and a diligent care to serve him and our generation, according to his will. We must not think to trust in God and then live as we list. No; it is not trusting God, but tempting him, if we do not make conscience of our duty to him. Nor must we think to do good, and then to trust to ourselves, and our own righteousness and strength. No; we must both trust in the Lord and do good. And then, (2.) It is promised that we

shall be well provided for in this world: *So shalt thou dwell in the land, and verily thou shalt be fed.* He does not say, "So shalt thou get preferment, dwell in a palace, and be feasted." This is not necessary; a man's life consists not in the abundance of these things; but, "Thou shalt have a place to live in, and that in the land, in Canaan, the valley of vision, and thou shalt have food convenient for thee." This is more than we deserve; it is as much as a good man will stipulate for (Gen. 28:20) and it is enough for one that is going to heaven. "Thou shalt have a settlement, a quiet settlement, and a maintenance, a comfortable maintenance: *Verily thou shalt be fed.*" Some read it, *Thou shalt be fed by faith,* as the just are said to live by faith, and it is good living, good feeding, upon the promises. *"Verily thou shalt be fed,* as Elijah in the famine, with what is needful for thee." God himself is a shepherd, a feeder, to all those that trust in him, Ps. 23:1.

2. We must make God our heart's delight and then we shall have our heart's desire, *v.* 4. We must not only depend upon God, but solace ourselves in him. We must be well pleased that there is a God, that he is such a one as he has revealed himself to be, and that he is our God in covenant. We must delight ourselves in his beauty, bounty, and benignity; our souls must return to him, and repose in him, as their rest, and their portion for ever. Being satisfied of his loving-kindness, we must be satisfied with it, and make that our exceeding joy, Ps. 43:4. We were commanded (*v.* 3) to do good, and then follows this command to delight in God, which is as much a privilege as a duty. If we make conscience of obedience to God, we may then take the comfort of a complacency in him. And even this pleasant duty of delighting in God has a promise annexed to it, which is very full and precious, enough to recompense the hardest services: *He shall give thee the desires of thy heart.* He has not promised to gratify all the appetites of the body and the humours of the fancy, but to grant all the desires of the heart, all the cravings of the renewed sanctified soul. What is the desire of the heart of a good man? It is this, to know, and love, and live to God, to please him and to be pleased in him.

3. We must make God our guide, and submit in every thing to his guidance and disposal; and then all our affairs, even those that seem most intricate and perplexed, shall be made to issue well and to our satisfaction, *v.* 5, 6. (1.) The duty is very easy; and, if we do it aright, it will make us easy: *Commit thy way unto the Lord; roll thy way upon the Lord* (so the margin reads it), Prov. 16:3; Ps. 55:22. *Cast thy burden upon the Lord,* the burden of thy care, 1 Pt. 5:7. We must roll it off ourselves, so as not to afflict and perplex ourselves with thoughts about future events (Mt. 6:25), not to cumber and trouble ourselves either with the contrivance of the means or with expectation of the end, but refer it to God, leave it to him by his wise and good providence to order and dispose of all our concerns as he pleases. *Retreat thy way unto the Lord* (so the Septuagint), that is, "By prayer spread thy case, and all thy cares about it, before the Lord" (as Jephthah *uttered all his words before the Lord in Mizpeh,* Jdg. 11:11), "and then trust in him to bring it to a good issue, with a full satisfaction that all is well that God does." We must do our duty (that must be our care) and then leave the event with God. *Sit still, and see how the matter will fall,* Ruth 3:18. We must follow Providence, and not force it, subscribe to Infinite Wisdom and not prescribe. (2.) The promise is very sweet. [1.] In general, *"He shall bring that to pass,* whatever it is, which thou hast committed to him, if not to thy contrivance, yet to thy content. He will find means to extricate thee out of thy straits, to prevent thy fears, and bring about thy purposes, to thy satisfaction." [2.] In particular, "He will take care of thy reputation, and bring thee out of thy difficulties, not only with comfort, but with credit and honour: *He shall bring forth thy righteousness as the light and thy judgment as the noon-day."* (*v.* 6), that is, "he shall make it to appear that thou art an honest man, and that is honour enough." *First,* It is implied that the righteousness and judgment of good people may, for a time, be clouded and eclipsed, either by remarkable rebukes of Providence (Job's great afflictions darkened his righteousness) or by the malicious censures and reproaches of men, who give them bad names which they no way deserve, and lay to their charge things which they know not. *Secondly,* It is promised that God will, in due time, roll away the reproach they are under, clear up their innocency, and bring forth their righteousness, to their honour, perhaps in this world, at furthest in the great day, Mt. 13:43. Note, If we take care to keep a good conscience, we may leave it to God to take care of our good name.

Verses 7–20

In these verses we have,

I. The foregoing precepts inculcated; for we are so apt to disquiet ourselves with needless fruitless discontents and distrusts that it is necessary there should be precept upon precept, and line upon line, to suppress them and arm us against them. 1. Let us compose ourselves by believing in God: *"Rest in the Lord, and wait patiently for him* (*v.* 7), that is, be well reconciled to all he does and acquiesce in it, for that is best that is, because it is what God has appointed; and be well satisfied that he will still make all to work for good to us, though we know not how or which way." *Be silent to the Lord* (so the word is), not with a sullen, but a submissive silence. A patient bearing of what is laid upon us, with a patient expectation of what is further appointed for us, is as much our interest as it is our duty, for it will make us always easy; and there is a great deal of reason for it, for it is making a virtue of necessity. 2. Let us not discompose ourselves at what we see in this world: *"Fret not thyself because of him who prospers in his wicked way,* who, though he is a bad man, yet thrives and grows rich and great in the world; no, nor because of him who does mischief with his power and wealth, and brings wicked devices to pass against those that are virtuous and good, who seems to have gained his point and to have run them down. If thy heart begins to rise at it, stroke down thy folly, and *cease from anger* (*v.* 8), check the first stirrings of discontent and envy, and do not harbour any hard thoughts of God and his providence upon this account. Be not angry at any thing that God does, but forsake that wrath; it is the worst kind of wrath that can be. *Fret not thyself in any wise to do evil;* do not envy them their prosperity, lest thou be tempted to fall in with them and to take the same evil course that they take to enrich and advance themselves or some desperate course to avoid them and their power." Note, A fretful discontented spirit lies open to many temptations; and those that indulge it are in danger of doing evil.

II. The foregoing reasons, taken from the approaching ruin of the wicked notwithstanding their prosperity, and the real happiness of the righteous notwithstanding their troubles, are here much enlarged upon and the same things repeated in a pleasing variety of expression. We were cautioned (*v.* 7) not to envy the wicked either worldly prosperity or the success of their plots against the righteous, and the reasons here given respect these two temptations severally: —

1. Good people have no reason to envy the worldly prosperity of wicked people, nor to grieve or be uneasy at it, (1.) Because the prosperity of the wicked will soon be at an end (*v.* 9): *Evil-doers shall be cut off* by some sudden stroke of divine justice in the midst of their prosperity; what they have got by sin will not only flow away from them (Job 20:28), but they shall be carried away with it. See the end of these men (Ps. 73:17), how dear their ill-got gain will cost them, and you will be far from envying them or from being willing to espouse their lot, for better, for worse. Their ruin is sure, and it is very near (*v.* 10): *Yet a little while, and the wicked shall not be* what they now are; *they are brought into desolation in a moment,* Ps. 73:19. Have a little patience, for *the Judge stands before the door,* Jam. 5:8, 9. Moderate your passion, *for the Lord is at hand,* Phil. 4:5. And when their ruin comes it will be an utter ruin; he and his shall be extirpated; the day that comes shall *leave him neither root nor branch* (Mal. 4:1): *Thou shalt diligently consider his place,* where but the other day he made a mighty figure, but *it shall not be,* you will not find it; he shall leave nothing valuable, nothing honourable, behind. him. To the same purport (*v.* 20), *The wicked shall perish;* their death is their perdition, because it is the termination of all their joy and a passage to endless misery. *Blessed are the dead that die in the Lord;* but undone, for ever undone, are the dead that die in their sins. The wicked are the enemies of the Lord; such those make themselves who will not have him to reign over them, and as such he will reckon with them: *They shall consume as the fat of lambs, they shall consume into smoke.* Their prosperity, which gratifies their sensuality, is like the fat of lambs, not solid or substantial, but loose and washy; and, when their ruin comes, they shall fall as sacrifices to the justice of God and be consumed as the fat of the sacrifices was upon the altar, whence it ascended in smoke. The day of God's vengeance on the wicked is represented as a *sacrifice of the fat of the kidneys of rams* (Isa. 34:6); for he will be honoured by the ruin of his enemies, as he was by the sacrifices. Damned sinners are sacrifices, Mk. 9:49. This is a good reason why we should not envy them their prosperity; while they are fed to the full, they are but in the fattening for the day of sacrifice, *like a lamb in a large place* (Hos. 4:16), and the more they prosper the more will God be glorified in their ruin. (2.) Because the condition of the righteous, even in this life, is every way better and more desirable than that of the wicked, *v.* 16. In general, *a little that a righteous man has* of the honour, wealth, and pleasure of this world, *is better than the riches of many wicked.* Observe, [1.] The wealth of the world is so dispensed by the divine Providence that it is often the lot of good people to have but a little of it, and of wicked people to have abundance of it; for thus God would show us that the things of this world are not the best things, for, if they were, those would have most that are best and dearest to God. [2.] That a godly man's little is really better than a wicked man's estate, though ever so much; for it comes from a better hand, from a hand of special love and not merely from a hand of common providence, — it is enjoyed by a better title (God gives it to them by promise, Gal. 3:18), — it is theirs by virtue of their relation to Christ, who is the heir of all things, — and it is put to better use; it is sanctified to them by the blessing of God. *Unto the pure all things are pure,* Tit. 1:15. A little wherewith God is served and honoured is better than a great deal prepared for Baal or for a base lust. The promises here made to the righteous secure them such a happiness that they need not envy the prosperity of evil-doers. Let them know to their comfort, *First,* That *they shall inherit the earth,* as much of it as Infinite Wisdom sees good for them; they have the promise of the *life that now is,* 1 Tim. 4:8. If all the earth were necessary to make them happy, they should have it. All is theirs, even *the world,* and *things present,* as well as *things to come,* 1 Co. 3:21, 22. They have it by inheritance, a safe and honourable title, not by permission only and connivance. When evil-doers are cut off the righteous sometimes inherit what they gathered. *The wealth of the sinner is laid up for the just,* Job 27:17; Prov. 13:22. This promise is here made, 1. To those that live a life of faith (*v.* 9); *Those that wait upon the Lord,* as dependents on him, expectants from him, and suppliants to him, *shall inherit the earth,* as a token of his present favour to them and an earnest of better things intended for them in the other world. God is a good Master, that provides plentifully and well, not only for his working servants, but for his waiting servants. 2. To those that live a quiet and peaceable life (*v.* 11): *The meek shall inherit the earth.* They are in least danger of being injured and disturbed in the possession of what they have and they have most satisfaction in themselves and consequently the sweetest relish of their creature-comforts. Our Saviour has made this a gospel promise, and a confirmation of the blessings he pronounced on the meek, Mt. *v.* 5. *Secondly,* That they *shall delight themselves in the abundance of peace, v.* 11. Perhaps they have not abundance of wealth to delight in; but they have that which is better, abundance of peace, inward peace and tranquility of mind, peace with God, and then peace in God, that great peace which those have that love God's law, whom *nothing shall offend* (Ps. 119:165), that abundance of peace which is in the kingdom of Christ (Ps. 72:7), that peace which the world cannot give (Jn. 14:27), and which the wicked cannot have, Isa. 57:21. This they shall delight themselves in, and in it they shall have a continual feast; while those that have abundance of wealth do but cumber and perplex themselves with it and have little delight in it. *Thirdly,* That God *knows their days, v.* 18. He takes particular notice of them, of all they do and of all that happens to them. He keeps account of the days of their service, and not one day's work shall go unrewarded, and of the days of their suffering, that for those also they may receive a recompence. He knows their bright days, and has pleasure in their prosperity; he

knows their cloudy and dark days, the days of their affliction, and as the day is so shall the strength be. *Fourthly,* That *their inheritance shall be for ever;* not their inheritance in the earth, but that incorruptible indefeasible one which is laid up for them in heaven. Those that are sure of an everlasting inheritance in the other world have no reason to envy the wicked their transitory possessions and pleasures in this world. *Fifthly,* That in the worst of times it shall go well with them (*v.* 19): *They shall not be ashamed* of their hope and confidence in God, nor of the profession they have made of religion; for the comfort of that will stand them in stead, and be a real support to them, in evil times. When others droop they shall lift up their heads with joy and confidence: Even *in the days of famine,* when others are dying for hunger round about them, *they shall be satisfied,* as Elijah was; in some way or other God will provide food convenient for them, or give them hearts to be satisfied and content without it, so that, if they should be hardly bestead and hungry, they shall not (as the wicked do) *fret themselves and curse their king and their God* (Isa. 7:21), but rejoice in God as the God of their salvation even when *the fig-tree does not blossom,* Hab. 3:17, 18.

2. Good people have no reason to fret at the occasional success of the designs of the wicked against the just. Though they do bring some of their wicked devices to pass, which makes us fear they will gain their point and bring them all to pass, yet let us cease from anger, and not fret ourselves so as to think of giving up the cause. For,

(1.) Their plots will be their shame, *v.* 12, 13. It is true *the wicked plotteth against the just;* there is a rooted enmity in the seed of the wicked one against the righteous seed; their aim is, if they can, to destroy their righteousness, or, if that fail, then to destroy them. With this end in view they have acted with a great deal both of cursed policy and contrivance (they plot, they practice, against the just), and of cursed zeal and fury — *they gnash upon them with their teeth,* so desirous are they, if they could get it into their power, to eat them up, and so full of rage and indignation are they because it is not in their power; but by all this they do but make themselves ridiculous. *The Lord shall laugh at them,* Ps. 2:4, 5. They are proud and insolent, but God shall pour contempt upon them. he is not only displeased with them, but he despises them and all their attempts as vain and ineffectual, and their malice as impotent and in a chain; *for he sees that his day is coming,* that is, [1.] The day of God's reckoning, the day of the revelation of his righteousness, which now seems clouded and eclipsed. Men have their day now. *This is your hour,* Lu. 22:53. But God will have his day shortly, a day of recompences, a day which will set all to rights, and render that ridiculous which now passes for glorious. *It is a small thing to be judged of man's judgment,* 1 Co. 4:3. God's day will give a decisive judgment. [2.] The day of their ruin. The wicked man's day, the day set for his fall, that day *is coming,* which denotes delay; it has not yet come, but certainly it will come. The believing prospect of that day will enable the virgin, the daughter of Zion, to despise the rage of her enemies and *laugh them to scorn,* Isa. 37:22.

(2.) Their attempts will be their destruction, *v.* 14, 15. See here, [1.] How cruel they are in their designs against good people. They prepare instruments of death, *the sword* and *the bow,* no less will serve; they hunt for the precious life. That which they design is *to cast down and slay;* it is the blood of the saints they thirst after. They carry on the design very far, and it is near to be put in execution: They *have drawn the sword, and bent the bow;* and all these military preparations are made against the helpless, *the poor and needy* (which proves them to be very cowardly), and against the guiltless, *such as are of upright conversation,* that never gave them any provocation, nor offered injury to them or any other person, which proves them to be very wicked. Uprightness itself will be no fence against their malice. But, [2.] How justly their malice recoils upon themselves: *Their sword shall turn into their own heart,* which implies the preservation of the righteous from their malice and the filling up of the measure of their own iniquity by it. Sometimes that very thing proves to be their own destruction which they projected against their harmless neighbours; however, God's sword, which their provocations have drawn against them, will give them their death's wound.

(3.) Those that are not suddenly cut off shall yet be so disabled for doing any further mischief that the interests of the church shall be effectually secured: *Their bows shall be broken* (v. 15); the instruments of their cruelty shall fail them and they shall lose those whom they had made tools of to serve their bloody purposes with; nay, *their arms shall be broken,* so that they shall not be able to go on with their enterprises, v. 17. *But the Lord upholds the righteous,* so that they neither sink under the weight of their afflictions nor are crushed by the violence of their enemies. He upholds them both in their integrity and in their prosperity; and those that are so upheld by the rock of ages have no reason to envy the wicked the support of their broken reeds.

Verses 21–33

These verses are much to the same purport with the foregoing verses of this psalm, for it is a subject worthy to be dwelt upon. Observe here,

I. What is required of us as the way to our happiness, which we may learn both from the characters here laid down and from the directions here given. If we would be blessed of God, 1. We must make conscience of giving every body his own; for *the wicked borrows and pays not again,* v. 21. It is the first thing which the Lord our God requires of us, that we do justly, and render to all their due. It is not only a shameful paltry thing, but a sinful wicked thing, not to repay what we have borrowed. Some make this an instance, not so much of the wickedness of the wicked as of the misery and poverty to which they are reduced by the just judgment of God, that they shall be necessitated to borrow for their supply and then be in no capacity to repay it again, and so lie at the mercy of their creditors. Whatever some men seem to think of it, as it is a great sin for those that are able to deny the payment of their just debts, so it is a great misery not to be able to pay them. 2. We must be ready to all acts of charity and beneficence; for, as it is an instance of God's goodness to the righteous that he puts it into the power of his hand to be kind and to do good (and so some understand it, God's blessing increases his little to such a degree that he has abundance to spare for the relief of others), so it is an instance of the goodness of the righteous man that he has a heart proportionable to his estate: *He shows mercy, and gives,* v. 21. *He is ever merciful,* or every day, or all the day, merciful, *and lends,* and sometimes there is as true charity in lending as in giving; and giving and lending are acceptable to God when they proceed from a merciful disposition in the heart, which, if it be sincere, will be constant, and will keep us from being weary of well-doing. he that is truly merciful will be ever merciful. 3. We must leave our sins, and engage in the practice of serious godliness (v. 27): *Depart from evil and do good.* Cease to do evil and abhor it; learn to do well and cleave to it; this is true religion. 4. We must abound in good discourse, and with our tongues must glorify God and edify others. It is part of the character of a righteous man (v. 30) that his *mouth speaketh wisdom;* not only he speaks wisely, but he speaks wisdom, like Solomon himself, for the instruction of those about him. *His tongue talks* not of things idle and impertinent, but *of judgment,* that is, of the word and providence of God and the rules of wisdom for the right ordering of the conversation. Out of the abundance of a good heart will the mouth speak that which is good and to the use of edifying. 5. We must have our wills brought into an entire subjection to the will and word of God (v. 31): *The law of God,* of his God, *is in his heart;* and in vain do we pretend that God is our God if we do not receive his law into our hearts and resign ourselves to the government of it. It is but a jest and a mockery to speak wisdom, and to talk of judgment (v. 30), unless we have the law in our hearts, and we think as we speak. The law of God must be a commanding ruling principle in the heart; it must be a light there, a spring there, and then the conversation will be regular and uniform: *None of his steps will slide;* it will effectually prevent backsliding into sin, and the uneasiness that follows from it.

II. What is assured to us, as instances of our happiness and comfort, upon these conditions.

1. That we shall have the blessing of God, and that blessing shall be the spring, and sweetness, and security of all our temporal comforts and enjoyments (v. 22): *Such as are*

blessed of God, as all the righteous are, with a Father's blessing, by virtue of that *shall inherit the earth,* or *the land* (for so the same word is translated, v. 29), the land of Canaan, that glory of all lands. Our creature-comforts are comforts indeed to us when we see them flowing from the blessing of God, we are sure not to want any thing that is good for us in this world. *The earth shall yield us her increase* if God, as *our own God, give us his blessing,* Ps. 67:6. And as *those whom God blesses are thus blessed indeed (for they shall inherit the land),* so *those whom he curses are cursed indeed;* they *shall be cut off* and rooted out, and their extirpation by the divine curse will set off the establishment of the righteous by the divine blessing and be a foil to it.

2. That God will direct and dispose of our actions and affairs so as may be most for his glory (v. 23): *The steps of a good man are ordered by the Lord.* By his grace and Holy Spirit he directs the thoughts, affections, and designs of good men. He has all hearts in his hand, but theirs by their own consent. By his providence he overrules the events that concern them, so as to make their way plain before them, both what they should do and what they may expect. Observe, God orders the steps of a good man; not only his way in general, by his written word, but his particular steps, by the whispers of conscience, saying, *This is the way, walk in it.* He does not always show him his way at a distance, but leads him step by step, as children are led, and so keeps him in a continual dependence upon his guidance; and this, (1.) Because *he delights in his way,* and is well pleased with the paths of righteousness wherein he walks. *The Lord knows the way of the righteous* (Ps. 1:6), knows it with favour, and therefore directs it. (2.) That he may delight in his way. Because God orders his way according to his own will, therefore he delights in it; for, as he loves his own image upon us, so he is well pleased with what we do under his guidance.

3. That God will keep us from being ruined by our falls either into sin or into trouble (v. 24): *Though he fall, he shall not be utterly cast down.* (1.) A good man may be overtaken in a fault, but the grace of God shall recover him to repentance, so that he shall not be utterly cast down. Though he may, for a time, lose the joys of God's salvation, yet they shall be restored to him; for God shall uphold him with his hand, uphold him with his free Spirit. The root shall be kept alive, though the leaf wither; and there will come a spring after the winter. (2.) A good man may be in distress, his affairs embarrassed, his spirits sunk, but he shall not be utterly cast down; God will be the strength of his heart when his flesh and heart fail, and will uphold him with his comforts, so that the spirit he has made shall not fail before him.

4. That we shall not want the necessary supports of this life (v. 25): *"I have been young and now am old,* and, among all the changes I have seen in men's outward condition and the observations I have made upon them, *I never saw the righteous forsaken* of God and man, as I have sometimes seen wicked people abandoned both by heaven and earth; nor do I ever remember to have seen the seed of the righteous reduced to such an extremity as to beg their bread." David had himself begged his bread of Abimelech the priest, but it was when Saul hunted him; and our Saviour has taught us to except the case of persecution for righteousness' sake out of all the temporal promises (Mk. 10:30), because that has such peculiar honours and comforts attending it as make it rather a gift (as the apostle reckons it, Phil. 1:29) than a loss or grievance. But there are very few instances of good men, or their families, that are reduced to such extreme poverty as many wicked people bring themselves to by their wickedness. He had not *seen the righteous forsaken, nor his seed begging their bread.* Forsaken (so some expound it); if they do want God will raise them up friends to supply them, without a scandalous exposing of themselves to the reproach of common beggars; or, if they go from door to door for meat, it shall not be with despair, as the wicked man *that wanders abroad for bread, saying, Where is it?* Job 15:23. Nor shall he be denied, as the prodigal, that *would fain have filled his belly, but no man gave unto him,* Lu. 15:16. Nor shall he grudge if he be not satisfied, as David's enemies, when they *wandered up and down for meat,* Ps. 59:15. Some make this promise relate especially to those that are charitable and liberal to the poor, and

to intimate that David never observed any that brought themselves to poverty by their charity. It is *withholding more than is meet that tends to poverty,* Prov. 11:24.

5. That God will not desert us, but graciously protect us in our difficulties and straits (*v.* 28): *The Lord loves judgment;* he delights in doing justice himself and he delights in those that do justice; and therefore he forsakes not his saints in affliction when others make themselves strange to them and become shy of them, but he takes care that they be *preserved for ever,* that is, that the saint in every age be taken under his protection, that the succession be preserved to the end of time, and that particular saints be preserved from all the temptations and through all the trials of this present time, to that happiness which shall be for ever. He will *preserve them to his heavenly kingdom;* that is a preservation for ever, 2 Tim. 4:18; Ps. 12:7.

6. That we shall have a comfortable settlement in this world, and in a better when we leave this. That we shall *dwell for evermore* (*v.* 27), and not be *cut off* as the *seed of the wicked, v.* 28. Those shall not be tossed that make God their rest and are at home in him. But on this earth there is no dwelling for ever, no continuing city; it is in heaven only, that city which has foundations, that the righteous shall dwell for ever; that will be their everlasting habitation.

7. That we shall not become a prey to our adversaries, who seek our ruin, *v.* 32, 33. There is an adversary that takes all opportunities to do us a mischief, a wicked one that watches the righteous (as a roaring lion watches his prey) and seeks to slay him. There are wicked men that do so, that are very subtle (they watch the righteous, that they may have an opportunity to do them a mischief effectually and may have a pretence wherewith to justify themselves in the doing of it), and very spiteful, for they seek to slay him. But it may very well be applied to the wicked one, the devil, that old serpent, who has his wiles to entrap the righteous, his devices which we should not be ignorant of, — that great red dragon, who seeks to slay them, — that roaring lion, who goes about continually, restless and raging, and seeking whom he may devour. But it is here promised that he shall not prevail, neither Satan nor his instruments. (1.) He shall not prevail as a field-adversary: *The Lord will not leave him in his hand;* he will not permit Satan to do what he would, nor will he withdraw his strength and grace from his people, but will enable them to resist and overcome him, and *their faith shall not fail,* Lu. 22:31, 32. A good man may fall into the hands of a messenger of Satan, and be sorely buffeted, but God will not leave him in his hands, 1 Co. 10:13. (2.) He shall not prevail as a law-adversary: *God will not condemn him when he is judged,* though urged to do it by the accuser of the brethren, who *accuses them before our God day and night.* His false accusations will be thrown out, as those exhibited against Joshua (Zec. 3:1, 2), *The Lord rebuke thee, O Satan! It is God that justifies,* and then *who shall lay any thing to the charge of God's elect?*

Verses 34–40

The psalmist's conclusion of this sermon (for that is the nature of this poem) is of the same purport with the whole, and inculcates the same things.

I. The duty here pressed upon us is still the same (*v.* 34): *Wait on the Lord and keep his way.* Duty is ours, and we must mind it and make conscience of it, keep God's way and never turn out of it nor loiter in it, keep close, keep going; but events are God's and we must refer ourselves to him for the disposal of them; we must wait on the Lord, attend the motions of his providence, carefully observe them, and conscientiously accommodate ourselves to them. If we make conscience of *keeping God's way,* we may with cheerfulness wait on him and commit to him our way; and we shall find him a good Master both to his working servants and to his waiting servants.

II. The reasons to enforce this duty are much the same too, taken from the certain destruction of the wicked and the certain salvation of the righteous. This good man, being tempted to envy the prosperity of the wicked, that he might fortify himself against the temptation, *goes into the sanctuary of God* and leads us thither (Ps. 73:17); there he understands their end, and thence gives us to understand it, and, by comparing that with the end of the righteous, baffles the temptation and puts it to silence. Observe,

1. The misery of the wicked at last, however they may prosper awhile: *The end of the wicked shall be cut off* (*v.* 38); and that cannot be well that will undoubtedly end so ill. The wicked, in their end, will be cut off from all good and all hopes of it; a final period will be put to all their joys, and they will be for ever separated from the fountain of life to all evil. (1.) Some instances of the remarkable ruin of wicked people David had himself observed in this world — that the pomp and prosperity of sinners would not secure them from the judgments of God when their day should come to fall (*v.* 36, 35): *I have seen a wicked man* (the word is singular), suppose Saul or Ahithophel (for David was an old man when he penned this psalm), *in great power, formidable* (so some render it), *the terror of the mighty in the land of the living,* carrying all before him with a high hand, and seeming to be firmly fixed and finely flourishing, *spreading himself like a green bay-tree,* which produces all leaves and no fruit; like a native home-born Israelite (so Dr. Hammond), likely to take root. But what became of him? Eliphaz, long before, had learned, when he saw the foolish taking root, to curse his habitation, Job 5:3. And David saw cause for it; for this bay-tree withered away as soon as the fig-tree. Christ cursed: *He passed away as a dream,* as a shadow, such was he and all the pomp and power he was so proud of. He was gone in an instant: *He was not; I sought him* with wonder, *but he could not be found.* He had acted his part and then quitted the stage, and there was no miss of him. (2.) The total and final ruin of sinners, of all sinners, will shortly be made as much a spectacle to the saints as they are now sometimes made a spectacle to the world (*v.* 34): *When the wicked are cut off* (and cut off they certainly will be) *thou shalt see it,* with awful adorations of the divine justice. *The transgressors shall be destroyed together, v.* 38. In this world God singles out here one sinner and there another, out of many, to be made an example *in terrorem — as a warning;* but in the day of judgment there will be a general destruction of all the transgressors, and not one shall escape. Those that have sinned together shall be damned together. *Bind them in bundles, to burn them.*

2. The blessedness of the righteous, at last. Let us see what will be the end of God's poor despised people. (1.) Preferment. There have been times the iniquity of which has been such that men's piety has hindered their preferment in this world, and put them quite out of the way of raising estates; but those that keep God's way may be assured that in due time he will *exalt them, to inherit the land* (*v.* 34); he will advance them to a place in the heavenly mansions, to dignity, and honour, and true wealth, in the New Jerusalem, to inherit that good land, that land of promise, of which Canaan was a type; he will exalt them above all contempt and danger. (2.) Peace, *v.* 37. Let all people *mark the perfect man, and behold the upright;* take notice of him to admire him and imitate him, keep your eye upon him to observe what comes of him, and you will find that *the end of that man is peace.* Sometimes the latter end of his days proves more comfortable to him than the beginning was; the storms blow over, and he is comforted again, after the time that he was afflicted. However, if all his days continue dark and cloudy, perhaps his dying day may prove comfortable to him and his sun may set in brightness; or, if it should set under a cloud, yet his future state will be peace, everlasting peace. Those that walk in their uprightness while they live shall enter into peace when they die, Isa. 57:2. A peaceful death has concluded the troublesome life of many a good man; and all is well that thus ends everlastingly well. Balaam himself wished that his death and his last end might be like that of the righteous Num. 23:10. (3.) Salvation, *v.* 39, 40. *The salvation of the righteous* (which may be applied to the great salvation of which *the prophets enquired and searched diligently,* 1 Pt. 1:10) *is of the Lord;* it will be the Lord's doing. The eternal salvation, that salvation of God which those shall see that *order their conversation aright* (Ps. 50:23), is likewise of the Lord. And he that intends Christ and heaven for them will be a God all-sufficient to them: *He is their strength in time of trouble,* to support them under it and carry them through it. *He shall help them and deliver them,* help them to do their duties, to bear their burdens, and to maintain their spiritual conflicts, help them to bear their troubles well and get good by them, and, in due time, shall deliver them out of their troubles. He shall deliver them from the wicked that would overwhelm them and swallow them up, shall secure them there, where the wicked cease from troubling. He shall *save them,* not only keep them safe, but make them happy, *because they trust in him,* not because they have merited it from him, but because they have committed themselves to him and reposed a confidence in him, and have thereby honoured him.

PSALM 38

This is one of the penitential psalms; it is full of grief and complaint from the beginning to the end. David's sins and his afflictions are the cause of his grief and the matter of his complaints. It should seem he was now sick and in pain, which reminded him of his sins and helped to humble him for them; he was, at the same time, deserted by his friends and persecuted by his enemies; so that the psalm is calculated for the depth of distress and a complication of calamities. He complains, I. Of God's displeasure, and of his own sin which provoked God against him (*v.* 1–5). II. Of his bodily sickness (*v.* 6–10). III. Of the unkindness of his friends (*v.* 11). IV. Of the injuries which his enemies did him, pleading his good conduct towards them, yet confessing his sins against God (*v.* 12–20). Lastly, he concludes the psalm with earnest prayers to God for his gracious presence and help (*v.* 21, 22). In singing this psalm we ought to be much affected with the malignity of sin; and, if we have not such troubles as are here described, we know not how soon we may have, and therefore must sing of them by way of preparation and we know that others have them, and therefore we must sing of the by way of sympathy.

A psalm of David to bring to remembrance.

Verses 1–11

The title of this psalm is very observable; it is a psalm *to bring to remembrance;* the 70th psalm, which was likewise penned in a day of affliction, is so entitled. It is designed, 1. To bring to his own remembrance. We will suppose it penned when he was sick and in pain, and then it teaches us that times of sickness are times to bring to remembrance, to bring the sin to remembrance, for which God contended with us, to awaken our consciences to deal faithfully and plainly with us, and set our sins in order before us, for our humiliation. *In a day of adversity consider.* Or we may suppose it penned after his recovery, but designed as a record of the convictions he was under and the workings of his heart when he was in affliction, that upon every review of this psalm he might call to mind the good impressions then made upon him and make a fresh improvement of them. To the same purport was the writing of Hezekiah when he had been sick. 2. To put others in mind of the same things which he was himself mindful of, and to teach them what to think and what to say when they are sick and in affliction; let them think as he did, and speak as he did.

I. He deprecates the wrath of God and his displeasure in his affliction (*v.* 1): *O Lord! rebuke me not in thy wrath.* With this same petition he began another prayer for the visitation of the sick, Ps. 6:1. This was most upon his heart, and should be most upon ours when we are in affliction, that, however God rebukes and chastens us, it may not be in wrath and displeasure, for that will be wormwood and gall in the affliction and misery. Those that would escape the wrath of God must pray against that more than any outward affliction, and be content to bear any outward affliction while it comes from, and consists with, the love of God.

II. He bitterly laments the impressions of God's displeasure upon his soul (*v.* 2): *Thy arrows stick fast in me.* Let Job's complaint (*ch.* 7:4) expound this of David. By the arrows of the Almighty he means the terrors of God, which did set themselves in array against him. He was under a very melancholy frightful apprehension of the wrath of God against him for his sins, and thought he could look for nothing but judgment and fiery indignation to devour him. God's arrows, as they are sure to hit the mark, so they are sure to stick where they hit, to stick fast, till he is pleased to draw them out and to bind up with his comforts the wound he has made with his terrors. This will be the everlasting misery of the damned — the arrows of God's wrath will stick fast in them and the wound will be incurable. *"Thy hand,* thy heavy hand, *presses me sore,* and I am ready to sink under it; it not only lies hard upon me, but it lies long; and who knows the power of God's anger, the weight of his hand?" Sometimes God shot his arrows, and stretched forth his hand, for David (Ps. 18:14), but now against him; so uncertain is the continuance of divine comforts, where yet the continuance of divine grace is assured. He complains of God's wrath as that which inflicted the bodily distemper he was under (*v.* 3): *There is no soundness in my flesh because of thy anger.* The bitterness of it, infused in his mind, affected his body; but that was not the worst: it caused the disquietude of his heart, by reason of which he forgot the courage of a soldier, the dignity of a prince, and all the cheerfulness of the sweet psalmist of Israel, and roared terribly, *v.* 8. Nothing will disquiet the heart of a good man so much as the sense of God's anger, which shows what a fearful thing it is to fall into his hands. The way to keep the heart quiet is to keep ourselves in the love of God and to do nothing to offend him.

III. He acknowledges his sin to be the procuring provoking cause of all his troubles, and groans more under the load of guilt than any other load, *v.* 3. He complains that his flesh had no soundness, his bones had no rest, so great an agitation he was in. "It is *because of thy anger;* that kindles the fire which burns so fiercely;" but, in the next words, he justifies God herein, and takes all the blame upon himself: "It is *because of my sin.* I have deserved it, and so have brought it upon myself. My own iniquities do correct me." If our trouble be the fruit of God's anger, we may thank ourselves; it is our sin that is the cause of it. Are we restless? It is sin that makes us so. If there were not sin in our souls, there would be no pain in our bones, no illness in our bodies. It is sin therefore that this good man complains most of, 1. As a burden, a heavy burden (*v.* 4): *"My iniquities have gone over my head,* as proud waters over a man that is sinking and drowning, or as a heavy burden upon my head, pressing me down more than I am able to bear or to bear up under." Note, Sin is a burden. The power of sin dwelling in us is a weight, Heb. 12:1. All are clogged with it; it keeps men from soaring upward and pressing forward. All the saints are complaining of it as a body of death they are loaded with, Rom. 7:24. The guilt of sin committed by us is a burden, a heavy burden; it is a burden to God (he is pressed under it, Amos 2:13), a burden to the whole creation, which groans under it, Rom. 8:21, 22. It will, first or last, be a burden to the sinner himself, either a burden of repentance when he is pricked to the heart for it, labours, and is heavy-laden, under it, or a burden of ruin when it sinks him to the lowest hell and will for ever detain him there; it will be a talent of lead upon him, Zec. 5:8. Sinners are said to bear their iniquity. Threatenings are burdens. 2. As wounds, dangerous wounds (*v.* 5): *"My wounds stink and are corrupt* (as wounds in the body rankle, and fester, and grow foul, for want of being dressed and looked after), and it is through my own *foolishness."* Sins are wounds (Gen. 4:23), painful mortal wounds. Our wounds by sin are often in a bad condition, no care taken of them, no application made to them, and it is owing to the sinner's foolishness in not confessing sin, Ps. 32:3, 4. A slight sore, neglected, may prove of fatal consequence, and so may a slight sin slighted and left unrepented of.

IV. He bemoans himself because of his afflictions, and gives ease to his grief by giving vent to it and pouring out his complaint before the Lord.

1. He was troubled in mind, his conscience was pained, and he had no rest in his own spirit; and a wounded spirit who can bear? He was *troubled,* or distorted, *bowed down greatly,* and went *mourning all the day long, v.* 6. He was always pensive and melancholy, which made him a burden and terror to himself. His spirit was feeble and sorely broken, and his heart disquieted, *v.* 8. Herein David, in his sufferings, was a type of Christ, who, being in his agony, cried out, *My soul is exceedingly sorrowful.* This is a sorer affliction than any other in this world; whatever God is pleased to lay upon us, we have no reason to complain as long as he preserves to us the use of our reason and the peace of our consciences.

2. He was sick and weak in body; his loins were filled with a loathsome disease, some swelling, or ulcer, or inflammation (some think a plague-sore, such as Hezekiah's boil), and there was *no soundness in his flesh,* but, like Job, he was all over distempered. See (1.) What vile bodies these are which we carry about with us, what grievous diseases they are liable to, and what an offence and grievance they may soon be made by some diseases to the souls that animate them, as they always are a cloud and cog. (2.) That the bodies both of the greatest and of the best of men have in them the same seeds of diseases that the bodies of others have, and are liable to the same disasters. David himself, though so great a prince and so great a saint, was not exempt from the most grievous diseases: there was no soundness even in his flesh. Probably this was after his sin in the matter of Uriah, and thus did he smart in his flesh for his fleshly lusts. When, at any time, we are distempered in our bodies, we ought to remember how God has been dishonoured in and by our bodies. He was *feeble and sorely broken, v.* 8. His *heart panted,* and was in a continual palpitation, *v.* 10. His *strength* and limbs *failed* him. As for *the light of his eyes,* that *had gone from him,* either with much weeping or by a defluxion of rheum upon them, or perhaps through the lowness of his spirits and the frequent returns of fainting. Note, Sickness will tame the strongest body and the stoutest spirit. David was famed for his courage and great exploits; and yet, when God contended with him by bodily sickness and the impressions of his wrath upon his mind, his hair is cut, his heart fails him, and he becomes weak as water. Therefore let not the strong man glory in his strength, nor any man set grief at defiance, however it may be thought at a distance.

3. His friends were unkind to him (*v.* 11): *My lovers* (such as had been merry with him in the day of his mirth) now *stand aloof from my sore;* they would not sympathize with him in his griefs, nor so much as come within hearing of his complaints, but, like the priest and Levite (Lu. 10:31), *passed on the other side.* Even *his kinsmen,* that were bound to him by blood and alliance, *stood afar off.* See what little reason we have to trust in man or to wonder if we disappointed in our expectations of kindness from men. Adversity tries friendship, and separates between the precious and the vile. It is our wisdom to make sure a friend in heaven, who will not stand aloof from our sore and from whose love no tribulation nor distress shall be able to separate us. David, in his troubles, was a type of Christ in his agony, Christ, on his cross, feeble and sorely broken, and then deserted by his friends and kinsmen, who beheld afar off.

V. In the midst of his complaints, he comforts himself with the cognizance God graciously took both of his griefs and of his prayers (*v.* 9): *"Lord, all my desire is before thee.* Thou knowest what I want and what I would have: *My groaning is not hidden from thee.* Thou knowest the burdens I groan under and the blessings I groan after." The *groanings which cannot be uttered* are not hidden from him that *searches the heart and knows what is the mind of the Spirit,* Rom. 8:26, 27.

In singing this, and praying it over, whatever burden lies upon our spirits, we would by faith cast it upon God, and all our care concerning it, and then be easy.

Verses 12–22

In these verses,

I. David complains of the power and malice of his enemies, who, it should seem, not only took occasion from the weakness of his body and the trouble of his mind to insult over him, but took advantage thence to do him a mischief. He has a great deal to say against them, which he humbly offers as a reason why God should appear for him, as Ps. 25:19, *Consider my enemies.* 1. "They are very spiteful and cruel: *They seek my hurt;* nay, they *seek after my life," v.* 12. That life which was so precious in the sight of the Lord and all good men was aimed at, as if it had been forfeited, or a public nuisance. Such is the enmity of the serpent's seed against the seed of the woman; it would wound the head, though it can but reach the heel. It is the blood of the saints that is thirsted after. 2. "They are very subtle and politic. They *lay snares,* they *imagine deceits,* and herein they are restless and unwearied: they do it *all the day long.* They speak mischievous things one to another; every one has something or other to propose that may be a mischief to me." Mischief, covered and carried on by deceit, may well be called a *snare.* 3. "They are very insolent and abusive: *When my foot slips,* when I fall into any trouble, or when I make any mistake, misplace a word, or take a false step, they magnify themselves against me; they are pleased with it, and promise themselves that it will ruin my interest, and that if I slip I shall certainly fall and be undone." 4. "They are not only unjust, but very ungrateful: They *hate me wrongfully, v.* 19. I never did them any ill turn, nor so much as bore them any ill-will, nor ever gave them any provocation; nay, *they render evil for good, v.* 20. Many a kindness I have done them, for which I might have expected a return of kindness; but *for my love they are my adversaries,"* Ps. 109:4. Such a rooted enmity there is in the hearts of wicked men to goodness for its own sake that they hate it, even when they themselves have the benefit of it; they hate prayer even in those that pray for them, and hate peace even in those that would be at peace with them. Very ill-natured indeed those are whom no courtesy will oblige, but who are rather exasperated by it. 5. "They are very impious and devilish: *They are my adversaries* merely *because I follow the thing that good is."* They hated him, not only for his kindness to them, but for his devotion and obedience to God; they hated him because they hated God and all that bear his image. If we suffer ill for doing well, we must not think it strange; from the beginning it was so (Cain slew Abel, because his works were righteous); nor must we think it hard, because it will not be always so; for so much the greater will our reward be. 6. "They are many and mighty: They *are lively; they are strong; they are multiplied, v.* 19. Lord, how are those increased that trouble me?" Ps. 3:1. Holy David was weak and faint; his heart panted, and his strength failed; he was melancholy and of a sorrowful spirit, and persecuted by his friends; but at the same time his wicked enemies were strong and lively, and their number increased. Let us not therefore pretend to judge of men's characters by their outward condition; none knows love or hatred by all that is before him. It should seem that David in this, as in other complaints he makes of his enemies, has an eye to Christ, whose persecutors were such as are here described, perfectly lost to all honour and virtue. None hate Christianity but such as have first divested themselves of the first principles of humanity and broken through its most sacred bonds.

II. He reflects, with comfort, upon his own peaceable and pious behaviour under all the injuries and indignities that were done him. It is then only that our enemies do us a real mischief when they provoke us to sin (Neh. 6:13), when they prevail to put us out of the possession of our own souls, and drive us from God and our duty. If by divine grace we are enabled to prevent this mischief, we quench their fiery darts, and are saved from harm. If still we hold fast our integrity and our peace, who can hurt us? This David did here. 1. He kept his temper, and was not ruffled nor discomposed by any of the slights that were put upon him or the mischievous things that were said or done against him (*v.* 13, 14): *"I, as a deaf man, heard not;* I took no notice of the affronts put upon me, did not resent them, nor was put into disorder by them, much less did I meditate revenge, or study to return the injury." Note, The less notice we take of the unkindness and injuries that are done us the more we consult the quiet of our own minds. Being deaf, he was dumb, as a man *in whose mouth there are no reproofs;* he was as silent as if he had nothing to say for himself, for fear of putting himself into a heat and incensing his enemies yet more against him; he would not only not recriminate upon them, but not so much as vindicate himself, lest his necessary defence should be construed his offence. Though they sought after his life, and his silence might be taken for a confession of his guilt, yet he was as a dumb man that opens not his mouth. Note, When our enemies are most clamorous it is generally our prudence to be silent, or to say little, lest we make bad worse. David could not hope by his mildness to win upon his enemies, nor by his soft answers to turn away their wrath; for they were men of such base spirits that they rendered him evil for good; and yet he conducted himself thus meekly towards them, that he might prevent his own sin and might have the comfort of it in the reflection. Herein David was a type of Christ, who was as a sheep dumb before the shearer, and, when he was reviled, reviled not again; and both are examples to us not to render railing for railing. 2. He kept close to his God by faith and prayer, and so both supported himself under these injuries and silenced his own resentments of them. (1.) He trusted in God (*v.* 15): *"I was as a man that opens not his mouth, for in thee, O Lord! do I hope.* I depend upon thee to plead my cause and clear my innocency, and, some way or other, to put my enemies to silence and shame." His lovers and friends, that should have owned him, and stood by him, and appeared as witnesses for him, withdrew from him, *v.* 10. but God is a friend that will never fail us if we hope in him. *"I was as a man that heareth not, for thou wilt hear.* Why need I hear, and God hear too?" *He careth for you* (1 Pt. 5:7), and why need you care and God care too? *"Thou wilt answer"* (so some) "and therefore I will say nothing." Note, It is a good reason why we should bear reproach and calumny with silence and patience, because God is a witness to all the wrong that is done us, and, in due time, will be a witness for us and against those that do us wrong; therefore let us be silent, because, if we be, then we may expect that God will appear for us, for this is an evidence that we trust in him; but, if we undertake to manage for ourselves, we take God's work out of his hands and forfeit the benefit of his appearing for us. Our Lord Jesus, when he suffered, threatened not, because he *committed himself to him that judges righteously* (1 Pt. 2:23); and we shall lose nothing, at last, by doing so. *Thou shalt answer, Lord, for me.* (2.) He called upon God (*v.* 16): *For I said,* Hear me (that is supplied); *"I said so"* (as *v.* 15); "in thee do I hope, for thou wilt hear, lest they should rejoice over me. I comforted myself with that when I was apprehensive that they would overwhelm me." It is a great support to us, when men are false and unkind, that we have a God to go to whom we may be free with and who will be faithful to us.

III. He here bewails his own follies and infirmities. 1. He was very sensible of the present workings of corruption in him, and that he was now ready to repine at the providence of God and to be put into a passion by the injuries men did him: *I am ready to halt, v.* 17. This will best be explained by a reflection like this which the psalmist made upon himself in a similar case (Ps. 73:2): *My feet were almost gone, when I saw the prosperity of the wicked.* So here: *I was ready to halt,* ready to say, *I have cleansed my hands in vain.* His sorrow was continual: *All the day long have I been plagued.* (Ps. 73:13, 14), and it was continually before him; he could not forbear poring upon it, and that made him almost ready to halt between religion and irreligion. The fear of this drove him to his God: "In thee do I hope, not only that thou wilt plead my cause, but that thou wilt prevent my falling into sin." Good men, by setting their sorrow continually before them, have been ready to halt, who, by setting God always before them, have kept their standing. 2. He remembered against himself his former transgressions, acknowledging that by them he had brought these troubles upon himself and forfeited the divine protection. Though before men he could justify himself, before God he will judge and condemn himself (*v.* 18): *"I will declare my iniquity,* and not cover it; *I will be sorry for my sin,* and not make a light matter of it;" and this helped to make him silent under the rebukes of Providence and the reproaches of men. Note, If we be truly penitent for sin, that will make us patient under affliction, and particularly under unjust censures. Two things are required in repentance: — (1.) Confession of sin: *"I will declare my iniquity;* I will not only in general own myself a sinner, but I will make a particular acknowledgment of what I have done amiss." We must declare our sins before God freely and fully, and with their aggravating circumstances, that we may give glory to God and take shame to ourselves. (2.) Contrition for sin: *I will be sorry for it.* Sin will have sorrow; every true penitent grieves for the dishonour he has done to God and the wrong he has done to himself. "I will be in care or fear about my sin" (so some), "in fear lest it ruin me and in care to get it pardoned."

IV. He concludes with very earnest prayers to God for his gracious presence with him and seasonable powerful succour in his distress (*v.* 21, 11): *"Forsake me not, O Lord!* though my friends forsake me, and though I deserve to be forsaken by thee. Be not far from me, as my unbelieving heart is ready to fear thou art." Nothing goes nearer to the heart of a good man in affliction than to be under the apprehension of God's deserting him in wrath; nor does any thing therefore come more feelingly from his heart than this prayer: *"Lord, be not thou far from me; make haste for my help;* for I am ready to perish, and in danger of being lost if relief do not come quickly." God gives us leave, not only to call upon him when we are in trouble, but to hasten him. He pleads, "Thou art *my God,* whom I serve, and on whom I depend to bear me out; and *my salvation,* who alone art able to save me, who hast engaged thyself by promise to save me, and from whom alone I expect salvation." Is any afflicted? let him thus pray, let him thus plead, let him thus hope, in singing this psalm.

PSALM 39

David seems to have been in a great strait when he penned this psalm, and, upon some account or other, very uneasy; for it is with some difficulty that he conquers his passion, and composes his spirit himself to take that good counsel which he had given to others (37) to rest in the Lord, and wait patiently for him, without fretting; for it is easier to give the good advice than to give the good example of quietness under affliction. What was the particular trouble which gave occasion for the conflict David was now in does not appear. Perhaps it was the death of some dear friend or relation that was the trial of his patience, and that suggested to him these meditations of morality; and at the same time, it should seem too, he himself was weak and ill, and under some prevailing distemper. His enemies likewise were seeking advantages against him, and watched for his halting, that they might have something to reproach him for. Thus aggrieved, I. He relates the struggle that was in his breast between grace and corruption, between passion and patience (*v.* 1–3). II. He meditates upon the doctrine of man's frailty and mortality, and prays to God to instruct him in it (*v.* 4–6). III. He applies to God for the pardon of his sons, the removal of his afflictions, and the lengthening out of his life till he was ready for death (*v.* 7–13). This is a funeral psalm, and very proper for the occasion; in singing it we should get our hearts duly affected with the brevity, uncertainty, and calamitous state of human life; and those on whose comforts God has, by death, made breaches, will find this psalm of great use to them, in order to their obtaining what we ought much to aim at under such an affliction, which is to get it sanctified to us for our spiritual benefit and to get our hearts reconciled to the holy will of God in it.

To the chief musician, *even* to Jeduthun. A psalm of David.

Verses 1–6

David here recollects, and leaves upon record, the workings of his heart under his afflictions; and it is good for us to do so, that what was thought amiss may be amended, and what was well thought of may be improved the next time.

I. He remembered the covenants he had made with God to walk circumspectly, and to be very cautious both of what he did and what he said. When at any time we are tempted to sin, and are in danger of falling into it, we must call to mind the solemn vows we have made against sin, against the particular sin we are upon the brink of. God can, and will, remind us of them (Jer. 2:20, *Thou saidst, I will not transgress*), and therefore we ought to remind ourselves of them. So David did here.

1. He remembers that he had resolved, in general, to be very cautious and circumspect in his walking (*v.* 1): *I said, I will take heed to my ways;* and it was well said, and what he would never unsay and therefore must never gainsay. Note, (1.) It is the great concern of every one of us to take heed to our ways, that is, to walk circumspectly, while others walk at all adventures. (2.) We ought stedfastly to resolve that we will take heed to our ways, and frequently to renew that resolution. Fast bind, fast find. (3.) Having resolved to take heed to our ways, we must, upon all occasions, remind ourselves of that resolution, for it is a covenant never to be forgotten, but which we must be always mindful of.

2. He remembers that he had in particular covenanted against tongue-sins — that he would not sin with his tongue, that he would not speak amiss, either to offend God or *offend the generation of the righteous,* Ps. 73:15. it is not so easy as we could wish not to sin in thought; but, if an evil thought should arise in his mind, he would lay his hand upon his mouth, and suppress it, that it should go no further: and this is so great an attainment that, *if any offend not in word, the same is a perfect man;* and so needful a one that of him who *seems to be religious, but bridles not his tongue,* it is declared *His religion is vain.* David had resolved, (1.) That he would at all times watch against tongue-sins: *"I will keep a bridle,* or muzzle, *upon my mouth."* He would keep a bridle upon it, as upon the head; watchfulness in the act and exercise is the hand upon the bridle. he would keep a muzzle upon it, as upon an unruly dog that is fierce and does mischief; by particular stedfast resolution corruption is restrained from breaking out at the lips, and so is muzzled. (2.) That he would double his guard against them when there was most danger of scandal — *when the wicked is before me.* When he was in company with the wicked he would take heed of saying any thing that might harden them or give occasion to them to blaspheme. If good men fall into bad company, they must take heed what they say. Or, *when the wicked is before me,* in my thoughts. When he was contemplating the pride and power, the prosperity and flourishing estate, of evil-doers, he was tempted to speak amiss; and therefore then he would take special care what he said. Note, The stronger the temptation to a sin is the stronger the resolution must be against it.

II. Pursuant to these covenants he made a shift with much ado to bridle his tongue (*v.* 2): *I was dumb with silence; I held my peace even from good.* His silence was commendable; and the greater the provocation was the more praiseworthy was his silence. Watchfulness and resolution, in the strength of God's grace, will do more towards the bridling of the tongue than we can imagine, though it be an unruly evil. But what shall we say of his keeping silence *even from good?* Was it his wisdom that he refrained from good discourse when the wicked were before him, because he would not cast pearls before swine? I rather think it was his weakness; because he might not say any thing, he would say nothing, but ran into an extreme, which was a reproach to the law, for that prescribes a mean between extremes. The same law which forbids all corrupt communication requires *that which is good and to the use of edifying,* Eph. 4:29.

III. The less he spoke the more he thought and the more warmly. Binding the distempered part did but draw the humour to it: *My sorrow was stirred, my heart was hot within me, v.* 3. He could bridle his tongue, but he could not keep his passion under; though he suppressed the smoke, that was as a fire in his bones, and, while he was musing upon his afflictions and upon the prosperity of the wicked, the fire burned. Note, Those that are of a fretful discontented spirit ought not to pore much, for, while they suffer their thoughts to dwell upon the causes of the calamity, the fire of their discontent is fed with fuel and burns the more furiously. Impatience is a sin that has its ill cause within ourselves, and that is musing, and its ill effects upon ourselves, and that is no less than burning. If therefore we would prevent the mischief of ungoverned passions, we must redress the grievance of ungoverned thoughts.

IV. When he did speak, at last, it was to the purpose: *At the last I spoke with my tongue.* Some make what he said to be the breach of his good purpose, and conclude that, in what he said, he sinned with his tongue; and so they make what follows to be a passionate wish *that he might die,* like Elijah (1 Ki. 19:4) and Job, *ch.* 6:8, 9. But I rather take it to be, not the breach of his good purpose, but the reformation of his mistake in carrying it too far; he had kept silence from good, but now he would so keep silence no longer. He had nothing to say to the wicked that were before him, for to them he knew not how to place his words, but, after long musing, the first word he said was a prayer, and a devout meditation upon a subject which it will be good for us all to think much of.

1. He prays to God to make him sensible of the shortness and uncertainty of life and the near approach of death (*v.* 4): *Lord, make me to know my end and the measure of my days.* He does not mean, "Lord, let me know how long I shall live and when I shall die." We could not, in faith, pray such a prayer; for God has nowhere promised to let us know, but has, in wisdom, locked up that knowledge among the secret things which belong not to us, nor would it be good for us to know it. But, *Lord, make me to know my end,* means, "Lord, give me wisdom and grace to consider it (Deu. 32:29) and to improve what I know concerning it." *The living know that they shall die* (Eccl. 9:5), but few care for thinking of death; we have therefore need to pray that God by his grace would conquer that aversion which is in our corrupt hearts to the thoughts of death. "Lord, make me to consider," (1.) "What death is. It is my end, the end of my life, and all the employments and enjoyments of life. It is the end of all men," Eccl. 7:2. It is a final period to our state of probation and preparation, and an awful entrance upon a state of recompence and retribution. To the wicked man it is the end of all joys; to a godly man it is the end of all griefs. "Lord, give me to know my end, to be better acquainted with death, to make it more familiar to me (Job 17:14), and to be more affected with the greatness of the change. Lord, give me to consider what a serious thing it is to die." (2.) "How near it is. Lord, give me to consider the measure of my days, that they are measured in the counsel of God" (the end is a fixed end, so the word signifies; *my days are determined,* Job 14:5) "and that the measure is but short: My days will soon be numbered and finished." When we look upon death as a thing at a distance we are tempted to adjourn the necessary preparations for it; but, when we con-

sider how short life is, we shall see ourselves concerned to do what our hand finds to do, not only with all our might, but with all possible expedition. (3.) That it is continually working in us: "Lord, give me to consider how frail I am, how scanty the stock of life is, and how faint the spirits which are as the oil to keep that lamp burning." We find by daily experience that the earthly house of this tabernacle is mouldering and going to decay: "Lord, make us to consider this, that we may secure mansions in the house not made with hands."

2. He meditates upon the brevity and vanity of life, pleading them with God for relief under the burdens of life, as Job often, and pleading them with himself for his quickening to the business of life.

(1.) Man's life on earth is short and of no continuance, and that is a reason why we should sit loose to it and prepare for the end of it (*v.* 5): *Behold, thou hast made my days as a hand-breadth,* the breadth of four fingers, a certain dimension, a small one, and the measure whereof we have always about us, always before our eyes. We need no rod, no pole, no measuring line, wherewith to take the dimension of our days, nor any skill in arithmetic wherewith to compute the number of them. No; we have the standard of them at our fingers' end, and there is no multiplication of it; it is but one hand-breadth in all. Our time is short, and God has made it so; for *the number of our months is with him.* It is short, and he knows it to be so: It *is as nothing before thee.* he remembers *how short our time is,* Ps. 79:47. *It is nothing in comparison with thee;* so some. All time is nothing to God's eternity, much less our share of time.

(2.) Man's life on earth is vain and of no value, and therefore it is folly to be fond of it and wisdom to make sure of a better life. Adam is Abel — *man is vanity,* in his present state. He is not what he seems to be, has not what he promised himself. He and all his comforts lie at a continual uncertainty; and if there were not another life after this, all things considered, he were made in vain. He is vanity; he is mortal, he is mutable. Observe, [1.] How emphatically this truth is expressed here. *First, Every man is vanity,* without exception; high and low, rich and poor, all meet in this. *Secondly,* He is *so at his best estate,* when he is young, and strong, and healthful, in wealth and honour, and the height of prosperity; when he is most easy, and merry, and secure, and thinks his mountain stands strong. *Thirdly,* He is *altogether vanity,* as vain as you can imagine. *All man is all vanity* (so it may be read); every thing about him is uncertain; nothing is substantial and durable but what relates to the new man. *Fourthly, Verily* he is so. This is a truth of undoubted certainty, but which we are very unwilling to believe and need to have solemnly attested to us, as indeed it is by frequent instances. *Fifthly, Selah* is annexed, as a note commanding observation. "Stop here, and pause awhile, that you may take time to consider and apply this truth, that every man is vanity." We ourselves are so. [2.] For the proof of the vanity of man, as mortal, he here mentions three things, and shows the vanity of each of them, *v.* 6. *First,* The vanity of our joys and honours: *Surely every man walks* (even when he walks in state, when he walks in pleasure) in a shadow, in an image, *in a vain show.* When he makes a figure his fashion passes away, and his great pomp is but great fancy, Acts 25:23. It is but a show, and therefore a vain show, like the rainbow, the gaudy colours of which must needs vanish and disappear quickly when the substratum is but a cloud, a vapour; such is life (Jam. 4:14), and therefore such are all the gaieties of it. *Secondly,* The vanity of our griefs and fears. *Surely they are disquieted in vain.* Our disquietudes are often groundless (we vex ourselves without any just cause, and the occasions of our trouble are often the creatures of our own fancy and imagination), and they are always fruitless; we disquiet ourselves in vain, for we cannot, with all our disquietment, alter the nature of things nor the counsel of God; things will be as they are when we have disquieted ourselves ever so much about them. *Thirdly,* The vanity of our cares and toils. Man takes a great deal of pains to *heap up riches,* and they are but like heaps of manure in the furrows of the field, good for nothing unless they be spread. but, when he has filled his treasures with his trash, he *knows not who shall gather them,* nor to whom they shall descend when he is gone; for he shall not take them away with him. He asks not, *For whom do I labour?* and that is his folly, Eccl. 4:8. but, if he did ask, he could not tell whether he should be a wise man or a fool, a friend or a foe, Eccl. 2:19. *This is vanity.*

Verses 7–13

The psalmist, having meditated on the shortness and uncertainty of life, and the vanity and vexation of spirit that attend all the comforts of life, here, in these verses, turns his eyes and heart heaven-ward. When there is no solid satisfaction to be had in the creature it is to be found in God, and in communion with him; and to him we should be driven by our disappointments in the world. David here expresses,

I. His dependence on God, *v.* 7. Seeing all is vanity, and man himself is so, 1. He despairs of a happiness in the things of the world, and disclaims all expectations from it: *"Now, Lord, what wait I for?* Even nothing from the things of sense and time; I have nothing to wish for, nothing to hope for, from this earth." Note, The consideration of the vanity and frailty of human life should deaden our desires to the things of this world and lower our expectations from it. "If the world be such a thing as this, God deliver me from having, or seeking, my portion in it." We cannot reckon upon constant health and prosperity, nor upon comfort in any relation; for it is all as uncertain as our continuance here. "Though I have sometimes foolishly promised myself this and the other from the world, I am now of another mind." 2. He takes hold of happiness and satisfaction in God: *My hope is in thee.* Note, When creature-confidences fail, it is our comfort that we have a God to go to, a God to trust to, and we should thereby be quickened to take so much the faster hold of him by faith.

II. His submission to God, and his cheerful acquiescence in his holy will, *v.* 9. If our hope be in God for a happiness in the other world, we may well afford to reconcile ourselves to all the dispensations of his providence concerning us in this world: *"I was dumb; I opened not my mouth* in a way of complaint and murmuring." He now again recovered that serenity and sedateness of mind which were disturbed, *v.* 2. Whatever comforts he is deprived of, whatever crosses he is burdened with, he will be easy. *"Because thou didst it;* it did not come to pass by chance, but according to thy appointment." We may here see, 1. A good God doing all, and ordering all events concerning us. Of every event we may say, "This is the finger of God; it is the Lord's doing," whoever were the instruments. 2. A good man, for that reason, saying nothing against it. He is dumb, he has nothing to object, no question to ask, no dispute to raise upon it. All that God does is well done.

III. His desire towards God, and the prayers he puts up to him. *Is any afflicted? let him pray,* as David here,

1. For the pardoning of his sin and the preventing of his shame, *v.* 8. Before he prays (*v.* 10), *Remove thy stroke from me,* he prays (*v.* 8), *"Deliver me from all my offences,* from the guilt I have contracted, the punishment I have deserved, and the power of corruption by which I have been enslaved." When God forgives our sins he delivers us from them, he delivers us from them all. He pleads, *Make me not a reproach to the foolish.* Wicked people are foolish people; and they then show their folly most when they think to show their wit, by scoffing at God's people. When David prays that God would pardon his sins, and not make him a reproach, it is to be taken as a prayer for peace of conscience ("Lord, leave me not to the power of melancholy, which the foolish will laugh at me for"), and as a prayer for grace, that God would never leave him to himself, so far as to do any thing that might make him a reproach to bad men. Note, This is a good reason why we should both watch and pray against sin, because the credit of our profession is nearly concerned in the preservation of our integrity.

2. For the removal of his affliction, that he might speedily be eased of his present burdens (*v.* 10): *Remove thy stroke away from me.* Note, When we are under the correcting hand of God our eye must be to God himself, and not to any other, for relief. He only that inflicts the stroke can remove it; and we may then in faith, and with satisfaction, pray that our afflictions may be removed, when our sins are pardoned (Isa. 38:17), and when, as here, the affliction is sanctified and has done its work, and we are humbled under the hand of God.

(1.) He pleads the great extremity he was reduced to by his affliction, which made him the proper object of God's compassion: *I am consumed by the blow of thy hand.* His sickness prevailed to such a degree that his spirits failed, his strength was wasted, and his body emaciated. "The blow, or conflict, of thy hand has brought me even to the gates of death." Note, The strongest, and boldest, and best of men cannot bear up under, much less make head against, the power of God's wrath. It was not his case only, but any man will find himself an unequal match for the Almighty, *v.* 11. When God, at any time, contends with us, when with rebukes he corrects us, [1.] We cannot impeach the equity of his controversy, but must acknowledge that he is righteous in it; for, whenever he corrects man, it is for iniquity. Our ways and our doings procure the trouble to ourselves, and we are beaten with a rod of our own making. It is the yoke of our transgressions, though it be *bound with his hand,* Lam. 1:14. [2.] We cannot oppose the effects of his controversy, but he will be too hard for us. As we have nothing to move in arrest of his judgment, so we have no way of escaping the execution. God's rebukes make man's *beauty to consume away like a moth;* we often see, we sometimes feel, how much the body is weakened and decayed by sickness in a little time; the countenance is changed; where are the ruddy cheek and lip, the sprightly eye, the lively look, the smiling face? It is the reverse of all this that presents itself to view. What a poor thing is beauty; and what fools are those that are proud of it, or in love with it, when it will certainly, and may quickly, be consumed thus! Some make the moth to represent man, who is as easily crushed as a moth with the touch of a finger, Job 4:19. Others make it to represent the divine rebukes, which silently and insensibly waste and consume us, as the moth does the garment. All this abundantly proves what he had said before, that surely every man is vanity, weak and helpless; so he will be found when God comes to contend with him.

(2.) He pleads the good impressions made upon him by his affliction. He hoped that the end was accomplished for which it was sent, and that therefore it would be removed in mercy; and unless an affliction has done its work, though it may be removed, it is not removed in mercy. [1.] It had set him a weeping, and he hoped God would take notice of that. When the Lord God called to mourning, he answered the call and accommodated himself to the dispensation, and therefore could, in faith, pray, *Lord, hold not thy peace at my tears, v.* 12. He that does not willingly afflict and grieve the children of men, much less his own children, will not hold his peace at their tears, but will either speak deliverance for them (and, if he speak, it is done) or in the mean time speak comfort to them and make them to hear joy and gladness. [2.] It had set him a praying; and afflictions are sent to stir up prayer. If they have that effect, and when we are afflicted we pray more, and pray better, than before, we may hope that God will hear our prayer and give ear to our cry; for the prayer which by his providence he gives occasion for, and which by his Spirit of grace he indites, shall not return void. [3.] It had helped to wean him from the world and to take his affections off from it. Now he began, more than ever, to look upon himself as *a stranger and sojourner* here, like all his fathers, not at home in this world, but travelling through it to another, to a better, and would never reckon himself at home till he came to heaven. He pleads it with God: "Lord, take cognizance of me, and of my wants and burdens, for I am a stranger here, and therefore meet with strange usage; I am slighted and oppressed as a stranger; and whence should I expect relief but from thee, from that other country to which I belong?"

3. He prays for a reprieve yet a little longer (*v.* 13): *"O spare me,* ease me, raise me up from this illness that I may recover strength both in body and mind, that I may get into a more calm and composed frame of spirit, and may be better prepared for another world, *before I go hence* by death, *and* shall *be no more* in this world." Some make this to be a passionate wish that God would send him help quickly or it would be too late, like that, Job 10:20, 21. But I rather take it as a pious prayer that God would continue him here till by his grace he had made him fit to go hence, and that he might finish the work of life before his life was finished. *Let my soul live, and it shall praise thee.*

PSALM 40

It should seem David penned this psalm upon occasion of his deliverance, by the power and goodness of God, from some great and pressing trouble, by which he was in danger of being overwhelmed; probably it was some trouble of mind arising from a sense of sin and of God's displeasure against him for it; whatever it was, the same Spirit that indited his praises for that deliverance was in him, at the same time, a Spirit of prophecy, testifying of the sufferings of Christ and the glory that should follow; or, ere he was aware, he was led to speak of his undertaking, and the discharge of his undertaking, in words that must be applied to Christ only; and therefore how far the praises that here go before that illustrious prophecy, and the prayers that follow, may safely and profitably be applied to him it will be worth while to consider. In this psalm, I. David records God's favour to him in delivering him out of his deep distress, with thankfulness to his praise (v. 1–5). II. Thence he takes occasion to speak of the work of our redemption by Christ (v. 6–10). III. That gives him encouragement to pray to God for mercy and grace both for himself and for his friends (v. 11–17). If, in singing this psalm, we mix faith with the prophecy of Christ, and join in sincerity with the praises and prayers here offered up, we make melody wit our hearts to the Lord.

To the chief musician. A psalm of David.

Verses 1–5

In these verses we have,

I. The great distress and trouble that the psalmist had been in. He had been plunged into a horrible pit and into miry clay (v. 2), out of which he could not work himself, and in which he found himself sinking yet further. He says nothing here either of the sickness of his body or the insults of his enemies, and therefore we have reason to think it was some inward disquiet and perplexity of spirit that was now his greatest grievance. Despondency of spirit under the sense of God's withdrawings, and prevailing doubts and fears about the eternal state, are indeed a horrible pit and miry clay, and have been so to many a dear child of God.

II. His humble attendance upon God and his believing expectations from him in those depths: *I waited patiently for the Lord, v.* 1. Waiting, I waited. He expected relief from no other than from God; the same hand that tears must heal, that smites must bind up (Hos. 6:1), or it will never be done. From God he expected relief, and he was big with expectation, not doubting but it would come in due time. There is power enough in God to help the weakest, and grace enough in God to help the unworthiest, of all his people that trust in him. But he waited patiently, which intimates that the relief did not come quickly; yet he doubted not but it would come, and resolved to continue believing, and hoping, and praying, till it did come. Those whose expectation is from God may wait with assurance, but must wait with patience. Now this is very applicable to Christ. His agony, both in the garden and on the cross, was the same continued, and it was a horrible pit and miry clay. Then was his soul troubled and exceedingly sorrowful; but then he prayed, *Father, glorify thy name; Father, save me;* then he kept hold of his relation to his Father, "My God, my God," and thus waited patiently for him.

III. His comfortable experience of God's goodness to him in his distress, which he records for the honour of God and his own and others' encouragement.

1. God answered his prayers: *He inclined unto me and heard my cry.* Those that wait patiently for God, though they may wait long, do not wait in vain. Our Lord Jesus was *heard in that he feared,* Heb. v. 7. Nay, he was sure that the Father heard him always.

2. He silenced his fears, and stilled the tumult of his spirits, and gave him a settled peace of conscience (v. 2): "He *brought me up out of that horrible pit* of despondency and despair, scattered the clouds, and shone brightly upon my soul, with the assurances of his favour; and not only so, but *set my feet upon a rock and established my goings.*" Those that have been under the prevalency of a religious melancholy, and by the grace of God have been relieved, may apply this very feelingly to themselves; they are brought up out of a horrible pit. (1.) The mercy is completed by the setting of their feet upon a rock, where they find firm footing, are as much elevated with the hopes of heaven as they were before cast down with the fears of hell. Christ is the rock on which a poor soul may stand fast, and on whose meditation alone between us and God we can build any solid hopes or satisfaction. (2.) It is continued in the establishment of their goings. Where God has given a stedfast hope he expects there should be a steady

regular conversation; and, if that be the blessed fruit of it, we have reason to acknowledge, with abundance of thankfulness, the riches and power of his grace.

3. He filled him with joy, as well as peace, in believing: *"He has put a new song in my mouth;* he has given me cause to rejoice and a heart to rejoice." He was brought, as it were, into a new world, and that filled his mouth with a new song, *even praise to our God;* for to his praise and glory must all our songs be sung. Fresh mercies, especially such as we never before received, call for new songs. This is applicable to our Lord Jesus in his reception to paradise, his resurrection from the grave, and his exaltation to the joy and glory set before him; he was brought out of the horrible pit, set upon a rock, and had a new song put into his mouth.

IV. The good improvement that should be made of this instance of God's goodness to David.

1. David's experience would be an encouragement to many to hope in God, and, for that end, he leaves it here upon record: *Many shall see, and fear, and trust in the Lord.* They shall fear the Lord and his justice, which brought David, and the Son of David, into that horrible pit, and shall say, *If this be done to the green tree, what shall be done to the dry?* They shall fear the Lord and his goodness, in filling the mouth of David, and the Son of David, with new songs of joy and praise. There is a holy reverent fear of God, which is not only consistent with, but the foundation of, our hope in him. They shall not fear him and shun him, but fear him and trust in him in their greatest straits, not doubting but to find him as able and ready to help as David did in his distress. God's dealings with our Lord Jesus are our great encouragement to trust in God; when it pleased the Lord to bruise him, and put him to grief for our sins, he demanded our debt from him; and when he raised him from the dead, and set him at his own right hand, he made it to appear that he had accepted the payment he made and was satisfied with it; and what greater encouragement can we have to fear and worship God and to *trust in him?.* See Rom. 4:25; v. 1, 2. The psalmist invites others to make God their hope, as he did, by pronouncing those happy that do so (v. 4): *"Blessed is the man that makes the Lord his trust,* and him only (that has great and good thoughts of him, and is entirely devoted to him), *and respects not the proud,* does not do as those do that trust in themselves, nor depends upon those who proudly encourage others to trust in them; for both the one and the other turn aside to lies, as indeed all those do that turn aside from God." This is applicable, particularly, to our faith in Christ. Blessed are those that trust in him, and in his righteousness alone, and respect not the proud Pharisees, that set up their own righteousness in competition with that, that will not be governed by their dictates, nor turn aside to lies, with the unbelieving Jews, who *submit not to the righteousness of God,* Rom. 10:3. Blessed are those that escape this temptation.

2. The joyful sense he had of this mercy led him to observe, with thankfulness, the many other favours he had received from God, v. 5. When God puts new songs into our mouth we must not forget our former songs, but repeat them: *"Many, O Lord my God! are thy wonderful works which thou hast done,* both for me and others; this is but one of many." Many are the benefits with which we are daily loaded both by the providence and by the grace of God. (1.) They are his works, not only the gifts of his bounty, but the operations of his power. He works for us, he works in us, and thus he favours us with matter, not only for thanks, but for praise. (2.) They are his wonderful works, the contrivance of them admirable, his condescension to us in bestowing them upon us admirable; eternity itself will be short enough to be spent in the admiration of them. (3.) All his wonderful works are the product of his thoughts to us-ward. He does all *according to the counsel of his own will* (Eph. 1:11), the purposes of his grace *which he purposed in himself,* Eph. 3:11. They are the projects of infinite wisdom, the designs of everlasting love (1 Co. 2:7, Jer. 31:3), *thoughts of good and not of evil,* Jer. 29:11. His gifts and callings will *therefore* be without repentance, because they are not sudden resolves, but the result of his thoughts, his many thoughts, to us-ward. (4.) They are innumerable; they cannot be methodized or *reckoned up in order.* There is an order in all God's works, but there are so many that present themselves to our view at once that

we know not where to begin nor which to name next; the order of them, and their natural references and dependencies, and how the links of the golden chain are joined, are a mystery to us, and what we shall not be able to account for till the veil be rent and the mystery of God finished. Nor can they be counted, not the very heads of them. When we have said the most we can of the wonders of divine love to us we must conclude with an *et caetera — and such like,* and adore the depth, despairing to find the bottom.

Verses 6–10

The psalmist, being struck with amazement at the wonderful works that God had done for his people, is strangely carried out here to foretel that work of wonder which excels all the rest and is the foundation and fountain of all, that of our redemption by our Lord Jesus Christ. God's thoughts, which were to us-ward concerning that work, were the most curious, the most copious, the most gracious, and therefore to be most admired. This paragraph is quoted by the apostle (Heb. 10:5, etc.) and applied to Christ and his undertaking for us. As in the institutions, so in the devotions, of the Old Testament saints were aware of; and, when the apostle would show us the Redeemer's voluntary undertaking of his work, he does not fetch his account out of the book of God's secret counsels, which belong not to us, but from the things revealed. Observe,

I. The utter insufficiency of the legal sacrifices to atone for sin in order to our peace with God and our happiness in him: *Sacrifice and offering thou didst not desire;* thou wouldst not have the Redeemer to offer them. Something he must have to offer, but not these (Heb. 8:3); therefore he must not be of the house of Aaron, Heb. 7:14. Or, In the days of the Messiah burnt-offering and sin-offering will be no longer required, but all those ceremonial institutions will be abolished. But that is not all: even while the law concerning them was in full force it might be said, God did not desire them, nor accept them, for their own sake. They could not take away the guilt of sin by satisfying God's justice. The life of a sheep, which is so much inferior in value to that of a man (Mt. 12:12), could not pretend to be an equivalent, much less an expedient to preserve the honour of God's government and laws and repair the injury done to that honour by the sin of man. They could not take away the terror of sin by pacifying the conscience, nor the power of sin by sanctifying the nature; it was impossible, Heb. 9:9; 10:1–4. What there was in them that was valuable resulted from their reference to Jesus Christ, of whom they were types — shadows indeed, but shadows of good things to come, and trials of the faith and obedience of God's people, of their obedience of God's people, of their obedience to the law and their faith in the gospel. But the substance must come, which is Christ, who must bring that glory to God and that grace to man which it was impossible those sacrifices should ever do.

II. The designation of our Lord Jesus to the work and office of Mediator: *My ears hast thou opened.* God the Father disposed him to the undertaking (Isa. 50:5, 6) and then obliged him to go through with it. *My ear hast thou digged.* It is supposed to allude to the law and custom of binding servants to serve for ever by boring their ear to the doorpost; see Ex. 21:6. Our Lord Jesus was so in love with his undertaking that he would not go out free from it, and therefore engaged to persevere for ever in it; and for this reason *he is able to save us to the uttermost,* because he has engaged to serve his Father to the uttermost, who upholds him in it, Isa. 42:1.

III. His own voluntary consent to this undertaking: *"Then said I, Lo, I come;* then, when sacrifice and offering would not do, rather than the work should be undone; I said, Lo, I come, to enter the lists with the powers of darkness, and to advance the interests of God's glory and kingdom." This intimates three things: — 1. That he freely offered himself to this service, to which he was under no obligation at all prior to his own voluntary engagement. It was no sooner proposed to him than, with the greatest cheerfulness, he consented to it, and was wonderfully well pleased with the undertaking. Had he not been perfectly voluntary in it, he could not have been a surety, he could not have been a sacrifice; for it is by this will (this *animus offerentis — mind of the offerer*) that we are sanctified, Heb. 10:10. 2. That he firmly obliged himself to it: "I come; I promise to come in the fulness of time." And therefore the apostle says, "It was when he came into the world that he had an actual regard to this promise, by which he had *engaged his heart to approach unto God.*" He thus entered into bonds, not only to show the greatness of his love, but because he was to have the honour of his undertaking before he had fully performed it. Though the price was not paid, it was secured to be paid, so that he was the Lamb slain from the foundation of the world. 3. That he frankly owned himself engaged: He said, *Lo, I come,* said it all along to the Old Testament saints, who therefore knew him by the title of *ho erchomenos — He that should come.* This word was the foundation on which they built their faith and hope, and which they looked and longed for the accomplishment of.

IV. The reason why he came, in pursuance of his undertaking — because *in the volume of the book it was written of him,* 1. In the close rolls of the divine decree and counsel; there it was written that his ear was opened, and he said, *Lo, I come;* there the covenant of redemption was recorded, the counsel of redemption was recorded, the counsel of peace between the Father and the Son; and to that he had an eye in all he did, the commandment he received of his Father. 2. In the letters patent of the Old Testament. Moses and all the prophets testified of him; in all the volumes of that book something or other was written of him, which he had an eye to, that all might be accomplished, Jn. 19:28.

V. The pleasure he took in his undertaking. Having freely offered himself to it, he did not fail, nor was discouraged, but proceeded with all possible satisfaction to himself (*v.* 8. 9): *I delight to do thy will, O my God!* It was to Christ his meat and drink to go on with the work appointed to him (Jn. 4:34); and the reason here given is, *Thy law is within my heart;* it is written there, it rules there. It is meant of the law concerning the work and office of the Mediator, what he was to do and suffer; this law was dear to him and had an influence upon him in his whole undertaking. Note, When the law of God is written in our hearts our duty will be our delight.

VI. The publication of the gospel to the children of men, even *in the great congregation, v.* 9, 10. The same that as a priest wrought out redemption for us, as a prophet, by his own preaching first, then by his apostles, and still by his word and Spirit, makes it know to us. The *great salvation began to be spoken by the Lord,* Heb. 2:3. It is the gospel of Christ that is preached to all nations. Observe, 1. What it is that is preached: It is *righteousness* (*v.* 9), God's righteousness (*v.* 10), the everlasting righteousness which Christ has brought in (Dan. 9:24); compare Rom. 1:16, 17. It is God's *faithfulness* to his promise, and the salvation which had long been looked for. It is God's *lovingkindness* and his *truth,* his mercy according to his word. Note, In the work of our redemption we ought to take notice how brightly all the divine attributions shine, and give to God the praise of each of them. 2. To whom it is preached — *to the great congregation, v.* 9 and again *v.* 10. When Christ was here on earth he preached to multitudes, thousands at a time. The gospel was preached both to Jews and Gentiles, to great congregations of both. Solemn religious assemblies are a divine institution, and in them the glory of God, in the face of Christ, ought to be both praised to the glory of God and preached for the edification of men. 3. How it is preached — freely and openly: *I have not refrained my lips; I have not hid it; I have not concealed it.* This intimates that whoever undertook to preach the gospel of Christ would be in great temptation to hide it and conceal it, because it must be preached with great contention and in the face of great opposition; but Christ himself, and those whom he called to that work, set their faces *as a flint* (Isa. 50:7) and were wonderfully carried on in it. It is well for us that they were so, for by this means our eyes come to see this joyful light and our ears to hear this joyful sound, which otherwise we might for ever have perished in ignorance of.

Verses 11–17

The psalmist, having meditated upon the work of redemption, and spoken of it in the person of the Messiah, now comes to make improvement of the doctrine of his mediation between us and God, and therefore speaks in his own person. Christ having done his Father's will, and finished his work, and given orders for the preaching of the gospel to every creature, we are encouraged to come boldly to the throne of grace, for mercy and grace.

I. This may encourage us to pray for the mercy of God, and to put ourselves under the protection of that mercy, *v.* 11. "Lord, thou hast not spared thy Son, nor withheld him; *withhold not thou thy tender mercies* then, which thou hast laid up for us in him; for wilt thou not *with him also freely give us all things?* Rom. 8:32. *Let thy lovingkindness and thy truth continually preserve me.*" The best saints are in continual danger, and see themselves undone if they be not continually preserved by the grace of God; and the everlasting lovingkindness and truth of God are what we have to depend upon for our preservation to the heavenly kingdom, Ps. 61:7.

II. This may encourage us in reference to the guilt of sin, that Jesus Christ has done that towards our discharge from it which sacrifice and offering could not do. See here, 1. The frightful sight he had of sin, *v.* 12. This was it that made the discovery he was now favoured with of a Redeemer very welcome to him. He saw his iniquities to be evils, the worst of evils; he saw that they *compassed him about;* in all the reviews of his life, and his reflections upon each step of it, still he discovered something amiss. The threatening consequences of his sin surrounded him. Look which way he would, he saw some mischief or other waiting for him, which he was conscious to himself his sins had deserved. He saw them taking hold of him, arresting him, as the bailiff does the poor debtor; he saw them to be innumerable and *more than the hairs of his head.* Convinced awakened consciences are apprehensive of danger from the numberless number of the sins of infirmity which seem small as hairs, but, being numerous, are very dangerous. *Who can understand his errors?* God numbers our hairs (Mt. 10:30), which yet we cannot number; so he keeps an account of our sins, which we keep no account of. The sight of sin so oppressed him that he could not hold up his head — *I am not able to look up;* much less could he keep up his heart — *therefore my heart fails me.* Note, The sight of our sins in their own colours would drive us to distraction, if we had not at the same time some sight of a Saviour. 2. The careful recourse he had to God under the sense of sin (*v.* 13); seeing himself brought by his sins to the very brink of ruin, eternal ruin, with what a holy passion does he cry out, *"Be pleased, O Lord! to deliver me* (*v.* 13); O save me from the wrath to come, and the present terrors I am in through the apprehensions of that wrath! I am undone, I die, I perish, without speedy relief. In a case of this nature, where the bliss of an immortal soul is concerned, delays are dangerous; therefore, *O Lord! make haste to help me."*

III. This may encourage us to hope for victory over our spiritual enemies that seek after our souls to destroy them (*v.* 14), the roaring lion that goes about continually seeking to devour. If Christ has triumphed over them, we through him, shall be more than conquerors. In the belief of this we may pray, with humble boldness, *Let them be ashamed and confounded together,* and *driven backward, v.* 14. *Let them be desolate, v.* 15. Both the conversion of a sinner and the glorification of a saint are great disappointments to Satan, who does his utmost, with all his power and subtlety, to hinder both. Now, our Lord Jesus having undertaken to bring about the salvation of all his chosen, we may in faith pray that, in both these ways, that great adversary may be confounded. When a child of God is brought into that horrible pit, and the miry clay, Satan cries *Aha! aha!* thinking he has gained his point; but he shall rage when he sees the brand plucked out of the fire, and shall be *desolate, for a reward of his shame. The Lord rebuke thee, O Satan! The accuser of the brethren is cast out.*

IV. This may encourage all that seek God, and love his salvation, to rejoice in him and to praise him, *v.* 16. See here, 1. The character of good people. Conformably to the laws of natural religion, they seek God, desire his favour, and in all their exigencies apply to him, as a people should seek unto their God; and conformably to the laws of revealed religion they *love his salvation,* that great salvation of which the prophets enquired and searched diligently, which the Redeemer undertook to work out when he said, *Lo, I come.* All that shall be saved love the salvation not only as a salvation from hell, but a salvation from sin. 2. The happiness secured to good people by this prophetic prayer. Those that seek God shall *rejoice and be glad in him,* and with good reason, for he will not only be found of them but will be their bountiful rewarder. Those that love his salvation shall be filled with the joy of his salvation, and shall *say continually, The Lord be magnified;* and thus they shall have a heaven upon earth. Blessed are those that are thus still praising God.

V. This may encourage the saints, in distress and affliction, to trust in God and comfort themselves in him, *v.* 17. David himself was one of these: *I am poor and needy* (a king, perhaps now on the throne, and yet, being troubled in spirit, he calls himself *poor and needy,* in want and distress, lost and undone without a Saviour), *yet the Lord thinketh upon me* in and through the Mediator, by whom we are made accepted. Men forget the poor and needy, and seldom think of them; but God's thoughts, towards them (which he had spoken of *v.* 5) are their support and comfort. They may assure themselves that God is their help under their troubles, and will be, in due time, their deliverer out of their troubles, and will make no long tarrying; for *the vision is for an appointed time,* and therefore, *though it tarry,* we may *wait for it,* for it shall come; *it will come, it will not tarry.*

PSALM 41

God's kindness and truth have often been the support and comfort of the saints when they have had most experience of man's unkindness and treachery. David here found them so, upon a sick-bed; he found his enemies very barbarous, but his God very gracious. I. He here comforts himself in his communion with God under his sickness, by faith receiving and laying hold of God's promises to him (v 1–3) and lifting up his heart in prayer to God (*v.* 4). II. He here represents the malice of his enemies against him, their malicious censures of him, their spiteful reflections upon him, and their insolent conduct towards him (*v.* 5–9). III. He leaves his case with God, not doubting but that he would own and favour him (*v.* 10–12), and so the psalm concludes with a doxology (*v.* 13). Is any afflicted with sickness? let him sing the beginning of this psalm. Is any persecuted by enemies? let him sing the latter end of it; and we may any of us, in singing it, meditate upon both the calamities and comforts of good people in this world.

To the chief musician. A psalm of David.

Verses 1–4

In these verses we have,

I. God's promises of succour and comfort to those that consider the poor; and,

1. We may suppose that David makes mention of these with application either, (1.) To his friends, who were kind to him, and very considerate of his case, now that he was in affliction: *Blessed is he that considers* poor David. Here and there he met with one that sympathized with him, and was concerned for him, and kept up his good opinion of him and respect for him, notwithstanding his afflictions, while his enemies were so insolent and abusive to him; on these he pronounced this blessing, not doubting but that God would recompense to them all the kindness they had done him, particularly when they also came to be in affliction. The provocations which his enemies gave him did but endear his friends so much the more to him. Or, (2.) To himself. He had the testimony of his conscience for him that he had considered the poor, that when he was in honour and power at court he had taken cognizance of the wants and miseries of the poor and had provided for their relief, and therefore was sure God would, according to his promise, strengthen and comfort him in his sickness.

2. We must regard them more generally with application to ourselves. Here is a comment upon that promise, *Blessed are the merciful, for they shall obtain mercy.* Observe, (1.) What the mercy is which is required of us. It is to consider the poor or afflicted, whether in mind, body, or estate. These we are to consider with prudence and tenderness; we must take notice of their affliction and enquire into their state, must sympathize with them and judge charitably concerning them. We must wisely consider the poor; that is, we must ourselves be instructed by the poverty and affliction of others; it must be *Maschil* to us, that is the word here used. (2.) What the mercy is that is promised to us if we thus show mercy. He that considers the poor (if he cannot relieve them, yet he considers them, and has a compassionate concern for them, and in relieving them acts considerately and with discretion) shall be considered by his God: he shall not only be recompensed

in the resurrection of the just, but he *shall be blessed upon the earth* This branch of godliness, as much as any, has the promise of the life that now is and is usually recompensed with temporal blessings. Liberality to the poor is the surest and safest way of thriving; such as practise it may be sure of seasonable and effectual relief from God, [1.] In all troubles: He *will deliver them in the day of evil,* so that when the times are at the worst it shall go well with them, and they shall not fall into the calamities in which others are involved; if any be hidden in the day of the Lord's anger, *they,* shall. Those who thus distinguish themselves from those that have hard hearts God will distinguish from those that have hard usage. Are they in danger? he will preserve and keep them alive; and those who have a thousand times forfeited their lives, as the best have, must acknowledge it as a great favour if they have their *lives given them for a prey.* He does not say, "They shall be preferred," but, *"They shall be preserved and kept alive,* when the arrows of death fly thickly round about them." Do their enemies threaten them? God will not *deliver them into the will of their enemies;* and the most potent enemy we have can have no power against us but what is given him from above. The good-will of a God that loves us is sufficient to secure us from the ill-will of all that hate us, men and devils; and that good-will we may promise ourselves an interest in if we have considered the poor and helped to relieve and rescue them. [2.] Particularly in sickness (*v.* 3): *The Lord will strengthen him,* both in body and mind, *upon the bed of languishing,* on which he had long lain sick, and *he will make all his bed* — a very condescending expression, alluding to the care of those that nurse and tend sick people, especially of mothers for their children when they are sick, which is to make their beds easy for them; and that bed must needs be well made which God himself has the making of. He will make all his bed from head to foot, so that no part shall be uneasy; he will *turn* his bed (so the word is), to shake it up and make it very easy; or he will turn it into a bed of health. Note, God has promised his people that he will strengthen them, and make them easy, under their bodily pains and sicknesses. He has not promised that they shall never be sick, nor that they shall not lie long languishing, nor that their sickness shall not be unto death; but he has promised to enable them to bear their affliction with patience, and cheerfully to wait the issue. The soul shall by his grace be made to dwell at ease when the body lies in pain.

II. David's prayer, directed and encouraged by these promises (*v.* 4): *I said, Heal my soul.* It is good for us to keep some account of our prayers, that we may not unsay, in our practices, any thing that we said in our prayers. Here is, 1. His humble petition: *Lord be merciful to me.* He appeals to mercy, as one that knew he could not stand the test of strict justice. The best saints, even those that have been merciful to the poor, have not made God their debtor, but must throw themselves on his mercy. When we are under the rod we must thus recommend ourselves to the tender mercy of our God: *Lord, heal my soul.* Sin is the sickness of the soul; pardoning mercy heals it; renewing grace heals it; and this spiritual healing we should be more earnest for than for bodily health. 2. His penitent confession: *"I have sinned against thee,* and therefore my soul needs healing. I am a sinner, a miserable sinner; therefore, *God be merciful to me,"* Lu. 18:13. It does not appear that this has reference to any particular gross act of sin, but, in general, to his many sins of infirmity, which his sickness set in order before him, and the dread of the consequences of which made him pray, *Heal my soul.*

Verses 5–13

David often complains of the insolent conduct of his enemies towards him when he was sick, which, as it was very barbarous in them, so it could not but be very grievous to him. They had not indeed arrived at that modern pitch of wickedness of poisoning his meat and drink, or giving him something to make him sick; but, when he was sick, they insulted over him (*v.* 5): *My enemies speak evil of me,* designing thereby to grieve his spirit, to ruin his reputation, and so to sink his interest. Let us enquire,

I. What was the conduct of his enemies towards him. 1. They longed for his death: *When shall he die, and his name perish* with him? He had but an uncomfortable life, and yet they grudged him that. But it was a useful life;

he was, upon all accounts, the greatest ornament and blessing of his country; and yet, it seems, there were some who were sick of him, as the Jews were of Paul, crying out, *Away with such a fellow from the earth.* We ought not to desire the death of any; but to desire the death of useful men, for their usefulness, has much in it of the venom of the old serpent. They envied him his name, and the honour he had won, and doubted not but, if he were dead, that would be laid in the dust with him; yet see how they were mistaken: when he had served his generation he did die (Acts 13:36), but did his name perish? No; it lives and flourishes to this day in the sacred writings, and will to the end of time; for *the memory of the just is,* and shall be, *blessed.* 2. They picked up every thing they could to reproach him with (*v.* 6): *"If he come to see me"* (as it has always been reckoned a piece of neighbourly kindness to visit the sick) *"he speaks vanity;* that is, he pretends friendship, and that his errand is to mourn with me and to comfort me; he tells me he is very sorry to see me so much indisposed, and wishes me my health; but it is all flattery and falsehood." We complain, and justly, of the want of sincerity in our days, and that there is scarcely any true friendship to be found among men; but it seems, by this, that the former days were no better than these. David's friends were all compliment, and had nothing of that affection for him in their hearts which they made profession of. Nor was that the worst of it; it was upon a mischievous design that they came to see him, that they might make invidious remarks upon every thing he said or did, and might represent it as they pleased to others, with their own comments upon it, so as to render him odious or ridiculous: *His heart gathereth iniquity to itself,* puts ill constructions upon every thing; and the, when he goes among his companions, he tells it to them, that they may tell it to others. *Report, say they, and we will report it,* Jer. 20:10. If he complained much of his illness, they would reproach him for his pusillanimity; if he scarcely complained at all, they would reproach him for his stupidity. If he prayed, or gave them good counsel, they would banter it, and call it *canting;* if he kept silence from good, when the wicked were before him, they would say that he had forgotten his religion now that he was sick. There is no fence against those whose malice thus gathers iniquity. 3. They promised themselves that he would never recover from this sickness, nor ever wipe off the odium with which they had loaded him. They *whispered together against him* (*v.* 7), speaking that secretly in one another's ears which they could not for shame speak out, and which, if they did, they knew would be confuted. Whisperers and backbiters are put together among the worst of sinners, Rom. 1:29, 30. They whispered, that their plot against him might not be discovered and so defeated; there is seldom whispering (we say) but there is lying, or some mischief on foot. Those whisperers devised evil to David. Concluding he would die quickly, they contrived how to break all the measures he had concerted for the public good, to prevent the prosecution of them, and to undo all that he had hitherto been doing. This he calls *devising hurt against him;* and they doubted not but to gain their point: *An evil disease (a thing of Belial),* say they, *cleaves fast to him.* The reproach with which they had loaded his name, they hoped, would cleave so fast to it that it would perish with him, and then they should gain their point. They went by a modern maxim, *Fortiter calumniari, aliquid adhaerebit* — *Fling an abundance of calumny, and some will be sure to stick.* "The disease he is now under will certainly make an end of him; for it is the punishment of some great enormous crime, which he will not be brought to repent of, and proves him, however he has appeared, a son of Belial." Or, "It is inflicted by Satan, who is called *Belial," the wicked one,* 2 Co. 6:15. *"It is"* (according to a loose way of speaking some have) "a devilish disease, and therefore it will *cleave fast to him;* and *now that he lieth,* now that his distemper prevails so far as to oblige him to keep his bed, *he shall rise up no more;* we shall get rid of him, and divide the spoil of his preferments." We are not to think it strange if, when good men are sick, there be those that fear it, which makes the world not worthy of them, Rev. 11:10. 4. There was one particularly, in whom he had reposed a great deal of confidence, that took part with his enemies and was as abusive to him as any of them (*v.* 9): *My own familiar friend;* probably he means Ahithophel, who had been his

bosom-friend and prime-minister of state, in whom he trusted as one inviolably firm to him, whose advice he relied much upon in dealing with his enemies, and who *did eat of his bread,* that is, with whom he had been very intimate and whom he had taken to sit at the table with hi, nay, whom he had maintained and given a livelihood to, and so obliged, both in gratitude and interest, to adhere to him. Those that had their *maintenance from the king's palace* did not think it *meet for them to see the king's dishonour* (Ezra 4:14), much less to do him dishonour. Yet this base and treacherous confidant of David's forgot all the eaten bread, and *lifted up his heel against him* that had lifted up his head; not only deserted him, but insulted him, kicked at him, endeavoured to supplant him. Those are wicked indeed whom no courtesy done them, nor confidence reposed in them, will oblige; and let us not think it strange if we receive abuses from such: David did, and the Son of David; for of Judas the traitor David here, in the Spirit, spoke; our Saviour himself so expounds this, and *therefore* gave Judas the sop, that the scripture might be fulfilled, *He that eats bread with me has lifted up his heel against me,* Jn. 13:18, 16. Nay, have not we ourselves behaved thus perfidiously and disingenuously towards God? We *eat of his bread* daily, and yet *lift up the heel against him,* as Jeshurun, that *waxed fat and kicked,* Deu. 32:15.

II. How did David bear this insolent ill-natured conduct of his enemies towards him?

1. He prayed to God that they might be disappointed. He said nothing to them, but turned himself to God: *O Lord! be thou merciful to me,* for they are unmerciful, *v.* 10. He had prayed in reference to the insults of his enemies, *Lord, be merciful to me,* for this is a prayer which will suit every case. God's mercy has in it a redress for every grievance, "They endeavour to run me down, but, Lord, do thou raise me up from this bed of languishing, from which they think I shall never arise. Raise me up *that I may requite them,* that I may render them good for evil" (so some), for that was David's practice, Ps. 7:4; 35:13. A good man will even wish for an opportunity of making it to appear that he bears no malice to those that have been injurious to him, but, on the contrary, that he is ready to do them any good office. Or, "That, as a king, I may put them under the marks of my just displeasure, banish them the court, and forbid them my table for the future," which would be a necessary piece of justice, for warning to others. Perhaps in this prayer is couched a prophecy of the exaltation of Christ, whom God raised up, that he might be a just avenger of all the wrongs done to him and to his people, particularly by the Jews, whose utter destruction followed not long after.

2. He assured himself that they would be disappointed (*v.* 11): *"By this I know that thou favourest me and my interest, because my enemy doth not triumph over me."* They hoped for his death, but he found himself, through mercy, recovering, and this would add to the comfort of his recovery, (1.) That it would be a disappointment to his adversaries; they would be crest-fallen and wretchedly ashamed, and there would be no occasion to upbraid them with their disappointment; they would fret at it themselves. Note. Though we may not take a pleasure in the fall of our enemies, we may take a pleasure in the frustrating of their designs against us. (2.) That is would be a token of God's favour to him, and a certain evidence that he did favour him, and would continue to do so. Note, When we can discern the favour of God to us in any mercy, personal or public, that doubles it and sweetens it.

3. He depended upon God, who had thus delivered him from many an evil work, to *preserve him to his heavenly kingdom,* as blessed Paul, 2 Tim. 4:18. "As for me, forasmuch as thou favourest me, as a fruit of that favour, and to qualify me for the continuance of it, *thou upholdest me in my integrity, and,* in order to that, *settest me before thy face,* hast thy eye always upon me for good;" or, "Because thou dost, by thy grace, uphold me in my integrity, I know that thou wilt, in thy glory, set me for ever before thy face." Note, (1.) When at any time we suffer in our reputation our chief concern should be about our integrity, and then we may cheerfully leave it to God to secure our reputation. David knows that, if he can but persevere in his integrity, he needs not fear his enemies' triumphs over him. (2.) The best man in the world holds his integrity no longer then God upholds him in it; for by his grace we are what

we are; if we be left to ourselves, we shall not only fall, but fall away. (3.) It is a great comfort to us that, however weak we are, God is able to uphold us in our integrity, and will do it if we commit the keeping of it to him. (4.) If the grace of God did not take a constant care of us, we should not be upheld in our integrity; his eye is always upon us, else we should soon start aside from him. (5.) Those whom God now upholds in their integrity he will set before his face for ever, and make happy in the vision and fruition of himself. *He that endures to the end shall be saved.*

4. The psalm concludes with a solemn doxology, or adoration of God as *the Lord God of Israel, v.* 13. It is not certain whether this verse pertains to this particular psalm (if so, it teaches us this, That a believing hope of our preservation through grace to glory is enough to fill our hearts with joy and our mouths with everlasting praise, even in our greatest straits) or whether it was added as the conclusion of the first book of *Psalms,* which is reckoned to end here (the like being subjoined to Ps. 72, 89, 106), and then it teaches us to make God the Omega who is the Alpha, to make him the end who is the beginning of every good work. We are taught, (1.) To give glory to God as the *Lord God of Israel,* a God in covenant with his people, who has done great and kind things for them and has more and better in reserve. (2.) To give him glory as an eternal God, that has both his being and his blessedness *from everlasting and to everlasting.* (3.) To do this with great affection and fervour of spirit, intimated in the double seal set to it — *Amen, and Amen.* Be it so now, be it so to all eternity. We say *Amen* to it, and let all others say *Amen* too.

PSALM 42

If the book of Psalms be, as some have styled it, a mirror or looking-glass of pious and devout affections, this psalm in particular deserves, as much as any one psalm, to be so entitled, and is as proper as any to kindle and excite such in us: gracious desires are here strong and fervent; gracious hopes and fears, joys and sorrows, are here struggling, but the pleasing passion comes off a conqueror. Or we may take it for a conflict between sense and faith, sense objecting and faith answering. I. Faith begins with holy desires towards God and communion with him (*v.* 1, 2). II. Sense complains of the darkness and cloudiness of the present condition, aggravated by the remembrance of the former enjoyments (*v.* 3, 4). III. Faith silences the complaint with the assurance of a good issue at last (*v.* 5). IV. Sense renews its complaints of the present dark and melancholy state (*v.* 6, 7). V. Faith holds up the heart, notwithstanding, with hope that the day will dawn (*v.* 8). VI. Sense repeats its lamentations (*v.* 9, 10) and sighs out the same remonstrance it had before made of its grievances. VII. Faith gets the last word (*v.* 11), for the silencing of the complaints of sense, and, though it be almost the same with that (*v.* 5) yet now it prevails and carries the day. The title does not tell us who was the penman of this psalm, but most probably it was David, and we may conjecture that it was penned by him at a time when, either by Saul's persecution or Absalom's rebellion, he was driven from the sanctuary and cut off from the privilege of waiting upon God in public ordinances. The strain of it is much the same with 63, and therefore we may presume it was penned by the same hand and upon the same or a similar occasion. In singing it, if we be either in outward affliction or in inward distress, we may accommodate to ourselves the melancholy expressions we find here; if not, we must, in singing them, sympathize with those whose case they speak too plainly, and thank God it is not our own case; but those passages in it which express and excite holy desires towards God, and dependence on him, we must earnestly endeavour to bring our minds up to.

To the chief musician, Maschil, for the sons of Korah.

Verses 1–5

Holy love to God as the chief good and our felicity is the power of godliness, the very life and soul of religion, without which all external professions and performances are but a shell and carcase: now here we have some of the expressions of that love. Here is,

I. Holy love thirsting, love upon the wing, soaring upwards in holy desires towards the Lord and towards the remembrance of his name (*v.* 1, 2): "*My soul panteth, thirsteth, for God,* for nothing more than God, but still for more and more of him." Now observe,

1. When it was that David thus expressed his vehement desire towards God. It was, (1.) When he was debarred from his outward opportunities of waiting on God, when he was banished to the land of Jordan, a great way off from the courts of God's house. Note, Sometimes God teaches us effectually to know the worth of mercies by the want of them, and whets our appetite for the means of grace by cutting us short in those means. We are apt to loathe that manna, when we have plenty of it, which will be very precious to us if ever we come to know the scarcity of it. (2.) When he was deprived, in a great measure, of the inward comfort he used to have in God. He now

went mourning, but he went on panting. Note, If God, by his grace, has wrought in us sincere and earnest desires towards him, we may take comfort from these when we want those ravishing delights we have sometimes had in God, because lamenting after God is as sure an evidence that we love him as rejoicing in God. Before the psalmist records his doubts, and fears, and griefs, which had sorely shaken him, he premises this, That he looked upon the living God as his chief good, and had set his heart upon him accordingly, and was resolved to live and die by him; and, casting anchor thus at first, he rides out the storm.

2. What is the object of his desire and what it is he thus thirsts after. (1.) He pants after God, he thirsts for God, not the ordinances themselves, but the God of the ordinances. A gracious soul can take little satisfaction in God's courts if it do not meet with God himself there: "*O that I knew where I might find him!* that I might have more of the tokens of his favour, the graces and comforts of his Spirit, and the earnests of his glory." (2.) He has, herein, an eye to God as the living God, that has life in himself, and is the fountain of life and all happiness to those that are his, the living God, not only in opposition to dead idols, the works of men's hands, but to all the dying comforts of this world, which perish in the using. Living souls can never take up their rest any where short of a living God. (3.) He longs to *come and appear before God,* — to make himself known to him, as being conscious to himself of his own sincerity, — to attend on him, as a servant appears before his master, to pay his respects to him and receive his commands, — to give an account to him, as one from whom our judgment proceeds. To appear before God is as much the desire of the upright as it is the dread of the hypocrite. The psalmist knew he could not come into God's courts without incurring expense, for so was the law, that *none should appear before God empty;* yet he longs to come, and will not grudge the charges.

3. What is the degree of this desire. It is very importunate; it is his soul that pants, his soul that thirsts, which denotes not only the sincerity, but the strength, of his desire. His longing for the water of the well of Bethlehem was nothing to this. He compares it to the *panting of a hart,* or deer, which is naturally hot and dry, especially of a hunted buck, *after the water-brooks.* Thus earnestly does a gracious soul desire communion with God, thus impatient is it in the want of that communion, so impossible does it find it to be satisfied with any thing short of that communion, and so insatiable is it in taking the pleasures of that communion when the opportunity of it returns, still thirsting after the full enjoyment of him in the heavenly kingdom.

II. Holy love mourning for God's present withdrawings and the want of the benefit of solemn ordinances (*v.* 3): "*My tears have been my meat day and night* during this forced absence from God's house." His circumstances were sorrowful, and he accommodated himself to them, received the impressions and returned the signs of sorrow. Even the royal prophet was a weeping prophet when he wanted the comforts of God's house. His tears were mingled with his meat; nay, they were *his meat day and night;* he fed, he feasted, upon his own tears, when there was such just cause for them; and it was a satisfaction to him that he found his heart so much affected with a grievance of this nature. Observe, He did not think it enough to shed a tear or two at parting from the sanctuary, to weep a farewell-prayer when he took his leave, but, as long as he continued under a forced absence from that place of his delight, he never looked up, but wept day and night. Note, Those that are deprived of the benefit of public ordinances constantly miss them, and therefore should constantly mourn for the want of them, till they are restored to them again. Two things aggravated his grief: —

1. The reproaches with which his enemies teased him: *They continually say unto me, Where is thy God?* (1.) Because he was absent from the ark, the token of God's presence. Judging of the God of Israel by the gods of the heathen, they concluded he had lost his God. Note, Those are mistaken who think that when they have robbed us of our Bibles, and our ministers, and our solemn assemblies, they have robbed us of our God; for, though God has tied us to them when they are to be had, he has not tied himself to them. We know where our God is, and where to find him, when we know not where his ark is, nor where

to find that. Wherever we are there is a way open heavenward. (2.) Because God did not immediately appear for his deliverance they concluded that he had abandoned him; but herein also they were deceived: it does not follow that the saints have lost their God because they have lost all their other friends. However, by this base reflection on God and his people, they added affliction to the afflicted, and that was what they aimed at. Nothing is more grievous to a gracious soul than that which is intended to shake its hope and confidence in God.

2. The remembrance of his former liberties and enjoyments, *v.* 4. *Son, remember thy good things,* is a great aggravation of evil things, so much do our powers of reflection and anticipation add to the grievance of this present time. David remembered the *days of old,* and then *his soul was poured out in him;* he melted away, and the thought almost broke his heart. he poured out his soul within him in sorrow, and then poured out his soul before God in prayer. But what was it that occasioned this painful melting of spirit? It was not the remembrance of the pleasures at court, or the entertainments of his own house, from which he was now banished, that afflicted him, but the remembrance of the free access he had formerly had to God's house and the pleasure he had in attending the sacred solemnities there. (1.) He *went to the house of God,* though in his time it was but a tent; nay, if this psalm was penned, as many think it was, at the time of his being persecuted by Saul, the ark was then in a private house, 2 Sa. 6:3. But the meanness, obscurity, and inconveniency of the place did not lessen his esteem of that sacred symbol of the divine presence. David was a courtier, a prince, a man of honour, a man of business, and yet very diligent in attending God's house and joining in public ordinances, even in the days of Saul, when he and his great men *enquired not at it,* 1 Chr. 13:3. Whatever others did, David and his house would serve the Lord. (2.) He *went with the multitude,* and thought it no disparagement to his dignity to be at the head of a crowd in attending upon God. Nay, this added to the pleasure of it, that he was accompanied with a multitude, and therefore it is twice mentioned, as that which he greatly lamented the want of now. The more the better in the service of God; it is the more like heaven, and a sensible help to our comfort in the communion of saints. (3.) He went *with the voice of joy and praise,* not only with joy and praise in his heart, but with the outward expressions of it, proclaiming his joy and speaking forth the high praises of his God. Note, When we wait upon God in public ordinances we have reason to do it both with cheerfulness and thankfulness, to take to ourselves the comfort and give to God the glory of our liberty of access to him. (4.) He went to keep holy-days, not to keep them in vain mirth and recreation, but in religious exercises. Solemn days are spent most comfortably in solemn assemblies.

III. Holy love hoping (*v.* 5): *Why art thou cast down, O my soul?* His sorrow was upon a very good account, and yet it must not exceed its due limits, nor prevail to depress his spirits; he therefore communes with his own heart, for his relief. "Come, my soul, I have something to say to thee in thy heaviness." Let us consider, 1. The cause of it. "Thou art cast down, as one stooping and sinking under a burden, Prov. 12:25. Thou art disquieted, in confusion and disorder; now why are thou so?" This may be taken as an enquiring question: "Let the cause of this uneasiness be duly weighed, and see whether it be a just cause." Our disquietudes would in many cases vanish before a strict scrutiny into the grounds and reasons of them. *"Why am I cast down?* Is there a cause, a real cause? Have not others more cause, that do not make so much ado? Have not we, at the same time, cause to be encouraged?" Or it may be taken as an expostulating question; those that commune much with their own hearts will often have occasion to chide them, as David here. "Why do I thus dishonour God by my melancholy dejections? Why do I discourage others and do so much injury to myself? Can I give a good account of this tumult?" 2. The cure of it: *Hope thou in God, for I shall yet praise him.* A believing confidence in God is a sovereign antidote against prevailing despondency and disquietude of spirit. And therefore, when we chide ourselves to hope in God; when the soul embraces itself it sinks; if it catch hold on the power and promise of God, it keeps the head above water. *Hope in*

God, (1.) That he shall have glory from us: *"I shall yet praise him,"* I shall experience such a change in my state that I shall not want matter for praise, and such a change in my spirit that I shall not want a heart for praise." It is the greatest honour and happiness of a man, and the greatest desire and hope of every good man, to be unto God for a name and a praise. What is the crown of heaven's bliss but this, that there we shall be for ever praising God? And what is our support under our present woes but this, that we shall yet praise God, that they shall not prevent nor abate our endless hallelujahs? (2.) That we shall have comfort in him. We shall praise him *for the help of his countenance,* for his favour, the support we have by it and the satisfaction we have in it. Those that know how to value and improve the light of God's countenance will find in that a suitable, seasonable, and sufficient help, in the worst of times, and that which will furnish them with constant matter for praise. David's believing expectation of this kept him from sinking, nay, it kept him from drooping; his harp was a palliative cure of Saul's melancholy, but his hope was an effectual cure of his own.

Verses 6–11

Complaints and comforts here, as before, take their turn, like day and night in the course of nature.

I. He complains of the dejections of his spirit, but comforts himself with the thoughts of God, *v.* 6. 1. In his troubles. His soul was dejected, and he goes to God and tells him so: *O my God! my soul is cast down within me.* It is a great support to us, when upon any account we are distressed, that we have liberty of access to God, and liberty of speech before him, and may open to him the causes of our dejection. David had communed with his own heart about its own bitterness, and had not as yet found relief; and therefore he turns to God, and opens before him the trouble. Note, When we cannot get relief for our burdened spirits by pleading with ourselves, we should try what we can do by praying to God and leaving our case with him. We cannot still these winds and waves; but we know who can. 2. In his devotions. His soul was elevated, and, finding the disease very painful, he had recourse to that as a sovereign remedy. "My soul is plunged; therefore, to prevent its sinking, I will remember thee, meditate upon thee, and call upon thee, and try what that will do to keep up my spirit." Note, The way to forget the sense of our miseries is to remember the God of our mercies. It was an uncommon case when the psalmist *remembered God and was troubled,* Ps. 77:3. He had often remembered God and was comforted, and therefore had recourse to that expedient now. He was now driven to the utmost borders of the land of Canaan, to shelter himself there from the rage of his persecutors — sometimes *to the country about Jordan,* and, when discovered there, to *the land of the Hermonites,* or to a hill called *Mizar,* or *the little hill;* but, (1.) Wherever he went he took his religion along with him. In all these places, he remembered God, and lifted up his heart to him, and kept his secret communion with him. This is the comfort of the banished, the wanderers, the travellers, of those that are strangers in a strange land, that *undique ad caelos tantundem est viae — wherever they are there is a way open heavenward.* (2.) Wherever he was he retained his affection for the courts of God's house; from the land of Jordan, or from the top of the hills, he used to look a long look, a longing look, towards the place of the sanctuary, and wish himself there. Distance and time could not make him forget that which his heart was so much upon and which lay so near it.

II. He complains of the tokens of God's displeasure against him, but comforts himself with the hopes of the return of his favour in due time.

1. He saw his troubles coming from God's wrath, and that discouraged him (*v.* 7): "Deep calls unto deep, one affliction comes upon the neck of another, as if it were called to hasten after it; and thy water-spouts give the signal and sound the alarm of war." It may be meant of the terror and disquietude of his mind under the apprehensions of God's anger. One frightful thought summoned another, and made way for it, as is usual in melancholy people. He was overpowered and overwhelmed with a deluge of grief, like that of the old world, when the windows of heaven were opened and the fountains of the great deep were broken up. Or it is an allusion to a ship at sea in a great storm,

tossed by the roaring waves, which go over it, Ps. 107:25. Whatever waves and billows of affliction go over us at any time we must call them God's waves and his billows, that we may humble ourselves under his mighty hand, and may encourage ourselves to hope that though we be threatened we shall not be ruined; for the waves and billows are under a divine check. *The Lord on high is mightier than the noise of these many waters.* Let not good men think it strange if they be exercised with many and various trials, and if they come thickly upon them; God knows what he does, and so shall they shortly. Jonah, in the whale's belly, made use of these words of David, Jonah 2:3 (they are exactly the same in the original), and of him they were literally true, *All thy waves and thy billows have gone over me;* for the book of psalms is contrived so as to reach every one's case.

2. He expected his deliverance to come from God's favour (*v.* 8): *Yet the Lord will command his lovingkindness.* Things are bad, but they shall not always be so. *Non si male nunc et olim sic erit — Though affairs are now in an evil plight, they may not always be so.* After the storm there will come a calm, and the prospect of this supported him when deep called unto deep. Observe (1.) What he promised himself from God: *The Lord will command his lovingkindness.* He eyes the favour of God as the fountain of all the good he looked for. That is life; that is better than life; and with that God will gather those from whom he has, *in a little wrath, hid his face,* Isa. 54:7, 8. God's conferring his favour is called his *commanding* it. This intimates the freeness of it; we cannot pretend to merit it, but it is bestowed in a way of sovereignty, he gives like a king. It intimates also the efficacy of it; he speaks his lovingkindness, and makes us to hear it; speaks, and it is done. He *commands deliverance* (Ps. 44:4), *commands the blessing* (Ps. 133:3), as one having authority. By commanding his lovingkindness, he commands down the waves and the billows, and they shall obey him. This he will do *in the daytime,* for God's lovingkindness will make day in the soul at any time. Though *weeping* has *endured for a night,* a long night, yet *joy will come in the morning.* (2.) What he promised for himself to God. If God command his lovingkindness for him, he will meet it, and bid it welcome, with his best affections and devotions. [1.] He will rejoice in God: *In the night his song shall be with me.* The mercies we receive in the day we ought to return thanks for at night; when others are sleeping we should be praising God. See Ps. 119:62, *At midnight will I rise to give thanks.* In silence and solitude, when we are retired from the hurries of the world, we must be pleasing ourselves with the thoughts of God's goodness. Or in the night of affliction: "Before the day dawns, in which God commands his lovingkindness, I will sing songs of praise in the prospect of it." Even in tribulation the saints can *rejoice in hope of the glory of God,* sing in hope, and praise in hope, Rom. *v.* 2, 3. It is God's prerogative to *give songs in the night,* Job 35:10. [2.] He will seek to God in a constant dependence upon him: *My prayer shall be to the God of my life.* Our believing expectation of mercy must not supersede, but quicken, our prayers for it. God is the God of our life, in whom we live and move, the author and giver of all our comforts; and therefore to whom should we apply by prayer, but to him? And from him what good may not we expect? It would put life into our prayers in them to eye God as the God of our life; for then it is for our lives, and the lives of our souls, that we stand up to make request.

III. He complains of the insolence of his enemies, and yet comforts himself in God as his friend, *v.* 9–11.

1. His complaint is that his enemies oppressed and reproached him, and this made a great impression upon him. (1.) They oppressed him to such a degree that he went mourning from day to day, from place to place, *v.* 9. He did not break out into indecent passions, though abused as never man was, but he silently wept out his grief, and went mourning; and for this we cannot blame him: it must needs grieve a man that truly loves his country, and seeks the good of it, to see himself persecuted and hardly used, as if he were an enemy to it. Yet David ought not hence to have concluded that God had forgotten him and cast him off, nor thus to have expostulated with him, as if he did him as much wrong in suffering him to be trampled upon as those did that trampled upon him: *Why go I mourning?* and *why hast thou forgotten me?* We may com-

plain to God, but we are not allowed thus to complain of him. (2.) They reproached him so cuttingly that it was a *sword in his bones, v.* 10. He had mentioned before what the reproach was that touched him thus to the quick, and here he repeats it: *They say daily unto me, Where is thy God?* — a reproach which was very grievous to him, both because it reflected dishonour upon God and was intended to discourage his hope in God, which he had enough to do to keep up in any measure, and which was but too apt to fail of itself.

2. His comfort is that God is his *rock* (*v.* 9) — a rock to build upon, a rock to take shelter in. The rock of ages, in whom is everlasting strength, would be his rock, his strength in the inner man, both for doing and suffering. To him he had access with confidence. To God his rock he might say what he had to say, and be sure of a gracious audience. he therefore repeats what he had before said (*v.* 5), and concludes with it (*v.* 11): *Why art thou cast down, O my soul?* His griefs and fears were clamorous and troublesome; they were not silenced though they were again and again answered. But here, at length, his faith came off a conqueror and forced the enemies to quit the field. And he gains this victory, (1.) By repeating what he had before said, chiding himself, as before, for his dejections and disquietudes, and encouraging himself to trust in the name of the Lord and to stay himself upon his God. Note, It may be of great use to us to think our good thoughts over again, and, if we do not gain our point with them at first, perhaps we may the second time; however, where the heart goes along with the words, it is no vain repetition. We have need to press the same thing over and over again upon our hearts, and all little enough. (2.) By adding one word to it; *there* he hoped to praise God for the salvation that was in his countenance; *here,* "I will praise him," says he, "as the salvation of my countenance from the present cloud that is upon it; if God smile upon me, that will make me look pleasant, look up, look forward, look round, with pleasure." He adds, *and my God,* "related to me, in covenant with me; all that he is, all that he has, is mine, according to the true intent and meaning of the promise." This thought enabled him to triumph over all his griefs and fears. God's being with the saints in heaven, and being their God, is that which will *wipe away all tears from their eyes,* Rev. 21:3, 4.

PSALM 43

This psalm, it is likely, was penned upon the same occasion with the former, and having no title, may be looked upon as an appendix to it; the malady presently returning, he had immediate recourse to the same remedy, because he had entered it in his book, with a "probatum est — it has been proved," upon it. The second verse of this psalm is almost the very same with the ninth verse of the foregoing psalm, as the fifth of this is exactly the same with the eleventh of that. Christ himself, who had the Spirit without measure, when there was occasion prayed a second and third time "saying the same words," Mt. 26:44. In this psalm. I. David appeals to God concerning the injuries that were done him by his enemies (*v.* 1, 2). II. He prays to God to restore to him the free enjoyment of public ordinances again, and promises to make a good improvement of them (*v.* 3, 4). III. He endeavours to still the tumult of his own spirit with a lively hope and confidence in God (*v.* 5), and if, in singing this psalm, we labour after these, we sing with grace in our hearts.

Verses 1–5

David here makes application to God, by faith and prayer, as his judge, his strength, his guide, his joy, his hope, with suitable affections and expressions.

I. As his Judge, his righteous Judge, who he knew would judge him, and who (being conscious of his own integrity) he knew would judge for him (*v.* 1): *Judge me, O God! and plead my cause.* There were those that impeached him; against them he is defendant, and from their courts, where he stood unjustly convicted and condemned, he appeals to the court of heaven, the supreme judicature, praying to have their judgment given against him reversed and his innocency cleared. There were those that had injured him; against them he is plaintiff, and exhibits his complaint to him who is the avenger of wrong, praying for justice for himself and upon them. Observe, 1. Who his enemies were with whom he had this struggle. Here was a sinful body of men, whom he calls an *ungodly* or *unmerciful nation.* Those that are unmerciful make it appear that they are ungodly; for, those that have any fear or love of their master will have compassion on their fellow-servants. And here was one bad man the head of them, a deceitful and unjust man, most probably Saul, who not only showed no kindness to David, but dealt most perfidiously and dishonestly with him. If Absalom was the man he meant, his character was no better. As long as there are such bad men out of hell, and nations of them, it is not strange that good men, who are yet out of heaven, meet with hard and base treatment. Some think that David, by the spirit of prophecy, calculated this psalm for the use of the Jews in their captivity in Babylon, and that the Chaldeans are the ungodly nation here meant; to them it was very applicable, but only as other similar scriptures, none of which are of private interpretation. God might design it for their use, whether David did or no. 2. What is his prayer with reference to them: *Judge me.* As to the quarrel God had with him for sin, he prays, *"Enter not into judgment with me,"* for then I shall be condemned;" but, as to the quarrel his enemies had with him he prays, *"Lord, judge me,* for I know that I shall be justified; *plead my cause against them,* take my part, and in thy providence appear on my behalf." He that has an honest cause may expect that God will plead it. "Plead my cause so as to deliver me from them, that they may not have their will against me." We must reckon our cause sufficiently pleaded if we be delivered, though our enemies be not destroyed.

II. As his strength, his all-sufficient strength; so he eyes God (*v.* 2): *"Thou art the God of my strength, my God, my strength,* from whom all my strength is derived, in whom I strengthen myself, who hast often strengthened me, and without whom I am weak as water and utterly unable either to do or suffer any thing for thee." David now went mourning, destitute of spiritual joys, yet he found God to be the God of his strength. If we cannot comfort ourselves in God, we may stay ourselves upon him, and may have spiritual supports when we want spiritual delights. David here pleads this with God: "Thou art the God on whom I depend as my strength; why then dost thou cast me off?" This was a mistake; for God never cast off any that trusted in him, whatever melancholy apprehensions they may have had of their own state. "Thou art the God of my strength; why then is my enemy too strong for me, and why go I mourning because of his oppressive power?" It is hard to reconcile the mighty force of the church's enemies with the almighty power of the church's God; but the day will reconcile them when all his enemies shall become his footstool.

III. As his guide, his faithful guide (*v.* 3): *Lead me, bring me to thy holy hill.* He prays, 1. That God by his providence would bring him back from his banishment, and open a way for him again to the free enjoyment of the privileges of God's sanctuary. His heart is upon *the holy hill and the tabernacles,* not upon his family-comforts, his court-preferments, or his diversions; he could bear the want of these, but he is impatient to see God's tabernacles again; nothing so amiable in his eyes as those; thither he would gladly be brought back. In order to this he prays, *"Send out thy light and thy truth;* let me have this as a fruit of thy favour, which is light, and the performance of thy promise, which is truth." We need desire no more to make us happy than the good that flows from God's favour and is included in his promise. That mercy, that truth, is enough, is all; and, when we see these in God's providences, we see ourselves under a very safe conduct. Note, Those whom God leads he leads to his holy hill, and to his tabernacles; those therefore who pretend to be led by the Spirit, and yet turn their backs upon instituted ordinances, certainly deceive themselves. 2. That God by his grace would bring him into communion with himself, and prepare him for the vision and fruition of himself in the other world. Some of the Jewish writers by the *light* and *truth* here understand Messiah the Prince and Elias his forerunner: these have come, in answer to the prayers of the Old Testament; but we are still to pray for God's light and truth, the Spirit of light and truth, who supplies the want of Christ's bodily presence, to lead us into the mystery of godliness and to guide us in the way to heaven. When God sends his light and truth into our hearts, these will guide us to the upper world in all our devotions as well as in all our aims and expectations; and, if we conscientiously follow that light and that truth, they will certainly bring us to the holy hill above.

IV. As his joy, his exceeding joy. If God guide him to his tabernacles, if he restore him to his former liberties, he knows very well what he has to do: *Then will I go unto*

the altar of God, *v.* 4. He will get as near as he can unto God, his exceeding joy. Note, 1. Those that come to the tabernacles should come to the altar; those that come to ordinances should qualify themselves to come, and then come to special ordinances, to those that are most affecting and most binding. The nearer we come, the closer we cleave, to God, the better. 2. Those that come to the altar of God must see to it that therein they come unto God, and draw near to him with the heart, with a true heart: we come in vain to holy ordinances if we do not in them come to the holy God. 3. Those that come unto God must come to him as their exceeding joy, not only as their future bliss, but as their present joy, and that not a common, but an exceeding joy, far exceeding all the joys of sense and time. The phrase, in the original, is very emphatic — *unto God the gladness of my joy,* or of my triumph. Whatever we rejoice or triumph in God must be the joy of it; all our joy in it must terminate in him, and must pass through the gift to the giver. 4. When we come to God as our exceeding joy our comforts in him must be the matter of our praises to him as God, and our God: *Upon the harp will I praise thee, O God! my God.* David excelled at the harp (1 Sa. 16:16, 18), and with that in which he excelled he would praise God; for God is to be praised with the best we have; it is fit he should be, for he is the best.

V. As his hope, his never-failing hope, *v.* 5. Here, as before, David quarrels with himself for his dejections and despondencies, and owns he did ill to yield to them, and that he had no reason to do so: *Why art thou cast down, O my soul?* He then quiets himself in the believing expectation he had of giving glory to God *(Hope in God, for I shall yet praise him)* and of enjoying glory with God: *He is the health of my countenance and my God.* That is what we cannot too much insist upon, for it is what we must live and die by.

PSALM 44

We are not told either who was the penmen of this psalm or when and upon what occasion it was penned, upon a melancholy occasion, we are sure, not so much to the penman himself (then we could have found occasions enough for it in the history of David and his afflictions), but to the church of God in general; and therefore, if we suppose it penned by David, yet we must attribute it purely to the Spirit of prophecy, and must conclude that the Spirit (whatever he himself had) had in view the captivity of Babylon, or the sufferings of the Jewish church under Antiochus, or rather the afflicted state of the Christian church in its early days (to which *v.* 22 is applied by the apostle, Rom. 8:36), and indeed in all its days on earth, for it is its determined lot that it must enter into the kingdom of heaven through many tribulations. And, if we have any gospel-psalms pointing at the privileges and comforts of Christians, why should we not have one pointing at their trials and exercises? It is a psalm calculated for a day of fasting and humiliation upon occasion of some public calamity, either pressing or threatening. In it the church is taught, I. To own with thankfulness, to the glory of God, the great things God has done for their fathers (*v.* 1–8). II. To exhibit a memorial of their present calamitous estate (*v.* 9–16). III. To file a protestation of their integrity and adherence to God notwithstanding (*v.* 17–22). IV. To lodge a petition at the throne of grace for succour and relief (*v.* 22–26). In singing this psalm we ought to give God the praise of what he has formerly done for his people, to represent our own grievances, or sympathize with those parts of the church that are in distress, to engage ourselves, whatever happens, to cleave to God and duty, and then cheerfully to wait the event.

To the chief musician for the sons of Korah, Maschil.

Verses 1–8

Some observe that most of the psalms that are entitled *Maschil — psalms of instruction,* are sorrowful psalms; for afflictions give instructions, and sorrow of spirit opens the ear to them. *Blessed is the man whom thou chastenest and teachest.*

In these verses the church, though now trampled upon, calls to remembrance the days of her triumph, of her triumph in God and over her enemies. This is very largely mentioned here, 1. As an aggravation of the present distress. The yoke of servitude cannot but lie very heavily on the necks of those that used to wear the crown of victory; and the tokens of God's displeasure must needs be most grievous to those that have been long accustomed to the tokens of his favour. 2. As an encouragement to hope that God would yet turn again their captivity and return in mercy to them; accordingly he mixes prayers and comfortable expectations with his record of former mercies. Observe,

I. Their commemoration of the great things God had formerly done for them.

1. In general (*v.* 1): *Our fathers have told us what work*

thou didst in their days. Observe, (1.) The many operations of providence are here spoken of as one work — "They have told us the *work* which thou didst;" for there is a wonderful harmony and uniformity in all that God does, and the many wheels make but one wheel (Eze. 10:13), many works make but one work. (2.) It is a debt which every age owes to posterity to keep an account of God's works of wonder, and to transmit the knowledge of them to the next generation. Those that went before us told us what God did in their days, we are bound to tell those that come after us what he has done in our days, and let them do the like justice to those that shall succeed them; thus shall *one generation praise his works to another* (Ps. 145:4), the *fathers to the children shall make known his truth,* Isa. 38:19. (3.) We must not only make mention of the work God has done in our own days, but must also acquaint ourselves and our children with what he did in the times of old, long before our own days; and of this we have in the scripture a sure word of history, as sure as the word of prophecy. (4.) Children must diligently attend to what their parents tell them of the wonderful works of God, and keep it in remembrance, as that which will be of great use to them. (5.) Former experiences of God's power and goodness are strong supports to faith and powerful pleas in prayer under present calamities. See how Gideon insists upon it (Jdg. 6:13): *Where are all his miracles which our fathers told us of?*

2. In particular, their fathers had told them,

(1.) How wonderfully God planted Israel in Canaan at first, *v.* 2, 3. He drove out the natives, to make room for Israel, afflicted them, and cast them out, gave them as dust to Israel's sword and as driven stubble to their bow. The many complete victories which Israel obtained over the Canaanites, under the command of Joshua, were not to be attributed to themselves, nor could they challenge the glory of them. [1.] They were not owing to their own merit, but to God's favour and free grace: It was *through the light of thy countenance, because thou hadst a favour to them. Not for thy righteousness, or the uprightness of thy heart, doth God drive them out from before thee* (Deu. 9:5, 6), but because God would *perform the oath which he swore unto their fathers,* Deu. 7:8. The less praise this allows us the more comfort it administers to us, that we may see all our successes and enlargements coming to us from the favour of God and the light of his countenance. [2.] They were not owing to their own might, but to God's power engaged for them, without which all their own efforts and endeavours would have been fruitless. It was not by their own sword that they got the land in possession, though they had great numbers of mighty men; nor did their own arm save them from being driven back by the Canaanites and put to shame; but it was God's *right hand* and his *arm.* He fought for Israel, else they would have fought in vain; it was through him that they did valiantly and victoriously. It was God that planted Israel in that good land, as the careful husbandman plants a tree, from which he promises himself fruit. See Ps. 80:8. This is applicable to the planting of the Christian church in the world, by the preaching of the gospel. Paganism was wonderfully driven out, as the Canaanites, not all at once, but by little and little, not by any human policy or power (for God chose to do it by the weak and foolish things of the world), but by the wisdom and power of God — Christ by his Spirit went forth conquering and to conquer; and the remembrance of that is a great support and comfort to those that groan under the yoke of antichristian tyranny, for to the state of the church under the power of the New-Testament Babylon, some think (and particularly the learned Amyraldus), the complaints in the latter part of this psalm may very fitly be accommodated. He that by his power and goodness planted a church for himself in the world will certainly support it by the same power and goodness; and the *gates of hell shall not prevail against it.*

(2.) How frequently he had given them success against their enemies that attempted to disturb them in the possession of that good land (*v.* 7): *Thou hast,* many a time, *saved us from our enemies,* and hast put to flight, and so put to shame, *those that hated us,* witness the successes of the judges against the nations that oppressed Israel. Many a time have the persecutors of the Christian church, and those that hate it, been put to shame by the power of truth, Acts 6:10.

II. The good use they make of this record, and had formerly made of it, in consideration of the great things God had done for their fathers of old.

1. They had taken God for their sovereign Lord, had sworn allegiance to him, and put themselves under his protection (*v.* 4): *Thou art my King, O God!* He speaks in the name of the church, as (Ps. 74:12), *Thou art my King of old.* God, as a king, has made laws for his church, provided for the peace and good order of it, judged for it, pleaded its cause, fought its battles, and protected it; it is his kingdom in the world, and ought to be subject to him, and to pay him tribute. Or the psalmist speaks for himself here: "Lord, *Thou art my King;* whither shall I go with my petitions, but to thee? The favour I ask is not for myself, but for thy church." Note, It is every one's duty to improve his personal interest at the throne of grace for the public welfare and prosperity of the people of God; as Moses, *"If I have found grace in thy sight,* guide thy people," Ex. 33:13.

2. They had always applied to him by prayer for deliverance when at any time they were in distress: *Command deliverances for Jacob.* Observe, (1.) The enlargedness of their desire. They pray for deliverances, not one, but many, as many as they had need of, how many soever they were, a series of deliverances, a deliverance from every danger. (2.) The strength of their faith in the power of God. They do not say, *Work deliverances,* but *Command them,* which denotes his doing it easily and instantly — *Speak and it is done* (such was the faith of the centurion, Mt. 8:8, *Speak the word only, and my servant shall be healed);* it denotes also his doing it effectually: "Command it, as one having authority, whose command will be obeyed." *Where the word of a king is there is power,* much more the word of the King of kings.

3. They had trusted and triumphed in him. As they owned it was not their own sword and bow that had saved them (*v.* 3), so neither did they trust to their own sword or bow to save them for the future (*v.* 6): *"I will not trust in my bow,* nor in any of my military preparations, as if those would stand me in stead without God. No; *through thee will we push down our enemies* (*v.* 5); we will attempt it in thy strength, relying only upon that, and not upon the number or valour of our forces; and, having thee on our side, we will not doubt of success in the attempt. *Through thy name* (by virtue of thy wisdom directing us, thy power strengthening us and working for us, and thy promise securing success to us) we shall, we *will, tread those under that rise up against us."*

4. They had made him their joy and praise (*v.* 8): *"In God we have boasted;* in him we do and will boast, every day, and all the day long." When their enemies boasted of their strength and successes, as Sennacherib and Rabshakeh hectored Hezekiah, they owned they had nothing to boast of, in answer thereunto, but their relation to God and their interest in him; and, if he were for them, they could set all the world at defiance. *Let him that glories glory in the Lord,* and let that for ever exclude all other boasting. Let those that trust in God make their boast in him, for they know whom they have trusted; let them *boast in him all the day long,* for it is a subject that can never be exhausted. But let them withal *praise his name for ever;* if they have the comfort of his name, let them give unto him the glory due to it.

Verses 9–16

The people of God here complain to him of the low and afflicted condition that they were now in, under the prevailing power of their enemies and oppressors, which was the more grievous to them because *they* were now trampled upon, who had always been used, in their struggles with their neighbours, to win the day and get the upper hand, and because those were now their oppressors whom they had many a time triumphed over and made tributaries, and especially because they had boasted in their God with great assurance that he would still protect and prosper them, which made the distress they were in, and the disgrace they were under, the more shameful. Let us see what the complaint is.

I. That they wanted the usual tokens of God's favour to them and presence with them (*v.* 9): *"Thou hast cast off;* thou seemest to have cast us off and our cause, and to have cast off thy wonted care of us and concern for us, and so hast put us to shame, for we boasted of the constancy and perpetuity of thy favour. Our armies go forth as usual, but they are put to flight; we gain no ground, but lose what we have gained, for thou goest not forth with them, for, if thou didst, which way soever they turned they would prosper; but it is quite contrary." Note, God's people, when they are cast down, are tempted to think themselves cast off and forsaken of God; but it is a mistake. *Hath God cast away his people? God forbid,* Rom. 11:1.

II. That they were put to the worst before their enemies in the field of battle (*v.* 10): *Thou makest us to turn back from the enemy,* as Joshua complained when they met with a repulse at Ai (Jos. 7:8): "We are dispirited, and have lost the ancient valour of Israelites; we flee, we fall, before those that used to flee and fall before us; and then those that hate us have the plunder of our camp and of our country; they spoil for themselves, and reckon all their own that they can lay their hands on. Attempts to shake off the Babylonish yoke have been ineffectual, and we have rather lost ground by them."

III. That they were doomed to the sword and to captivity (*v.* 11): *"Thou hast given us like sheep appointed for meat.* They make no more scruple of killing an Israelite than of killing a sheep; nay, like the butcher, they make a trade of it, they take a pleasure in it as a hungry man in his meat; and we are led with as much ease, and as little resistance, as a lamb to the slaughter; many are slain, and the rest scattered among the heathen, continually insulted by their malice or in danger of being infected by their iniquities." They looked upon themselves as bought and sold, and charged it upon God, *Thou sellest thy people,* when they should have charged it upon their own sin. *For your iniquities have you sold yourselves,* Isa. 50:1. However, thus far was right that they looked above the instruments of their trouble and kept their eye upon God, as well knowing that their worst enemies had no power against them *but what was given them from above;* they own it was God that *delivered them into the hand of the ungodly,* as that which is sold is delivered to the buyer. *Thou sellest them for nought, and dost not increase in their price* (so it may be read); "thou dost not sell them by auction, to those that will bid most for them, but in haste, to those that will bid first for them; any one shall have them that will." Or, as we read it, *Thou dost not increase thy wealth by their price,* intimating that they could have suffered this contentedly if they had been sure that it would redound to the glory of God and that his interest might be some way served by their sufferings; but it was quite contrary: Israel's disgrace turned to God's dishonour, so that he was so far from being a gainer in his glory by the sale of them that it should seem he was greatly a loser by it; see Isa. 52:5; Eze. 36:20.

IV. That they were loaded with contempt, and all possible ignominy was put upon them. In this also they acknowledge God: *"Thou makest us a reproach;* thou bringest those calamities upon us which occasion the reproach, and thou permittest their virulent tongues to smite us." They complain, 1. That they were ridiculed and bantered, and were looked upon as the most contemptible people under the sun; their troubles were turned to their reproach, and upon the account of them they were derided. 2. That their neighbours, those about them, from whom they could not withdraw, were most abusive to them, *v.* 13. 3. That the heathen, the people that were strangers to the commonwealth of Israel and aliens to the covenants of promise, made them a by-word, and shook the head at them, as triumphing in their fall, *v.* 14. 4. That the reproach was constant and incessant (*v.* 15): *My confusion is continually before me.* The church in general, the psalmist in particular, were continually teased and vexed with the insults of the enemy. Concerning those that are going down every one cries, "Down with them." 5. That it was very grievous, and in a manner overwhelmed him: *The shame of my face has covered me.* He blushed for sin, or rather for the dishonour done to God, and then it was a holy blushing. 6. That it reflected upon God himself; the reproach which the enemy and the avenger cast upon them was downright blasphemy against God, *v.* 16, and 2 Ki. 19:3. There was therefore strong reason to believe that God would appear for them. As there is no trouble more grievous to a generous and ingenuous mind than reproach and calumny, so there is none more grievous to a holy gracious soul than blasphemy and dishonour done to God.

Verses 17–26

The people of God, being greatly afflicted and oppressed, here apply to him; whither else should they go?

I. By way of appeal, concerning their integrity, which he only is an infallible judge of, and which he will certainly be the rewarder of. Two things they call God to witness to: —

1. That, though they suffered these hard things, yet they kept close to God and to their duty (*v.* 17): *"All this has come upon us,* and it is as bad perhaps as bad can be, *yet have we not forgotten thee,* neither cast off the thoughts of thee nor deserted the worship of thee; for, though we cannot deny but that we have dealt foolishly, yet we have not *dealt falsely in thy covenant,* so as to cast thee off and take to other gods. Though idolaters were our conquerors, we did not therefore entertain any more favourable thoughts of their idols and idolatries; though thou hast seemed to forsake us and withdraw from us, yet we have not therefore forsaken thee." The trouble they had been long in was very great: "We have been *sorely broken in the place of dragons,* among men as fierce, and furious, and cruel, as dragons. We have been *covered with the shadow of death,* that is, we have been under deep melancholy and apprehensive of nothing short of death. We have been wrapped up in obscurity, and buried alive; and thou hast thus broken us, thou hast thus covered us (*v.* 19), yet we have not harboured any hard thoughts of thee, nor meditated a retreat from thy service. Though thou hast slain us, we have continued to trust in thee: *Our heart has not turned back;* we have not secretly withdrawn our affections from thee, neither have our steps, either in our religious worship or in our conversation, *declined from thy way* (*v.* 18), the way which thou hast appointed us to walk in." When the heart turns back the steps will soon decline; for it is the evil heart of unbelief that inclines to depart from God. Note, We may the better bear our troubles, how pressing soever, if in them we still hold fast our integrity. While our troubles do not drive us from our duty to God we should not suffer them to drive us from our comfort in God; for he will not leave us if we do not leave him. For the proof of their integrity they take God's omniscience to witness, which is as much the comfort of the upright in heart as it is the terror of hypocrites (*v.* 20, 21): *"If we have forgotten the name of our God,* under pretence that he had forgotten us, or in our distress have *stretched out our hands to a strange god,* as more likely to help us, *shall not God search this out?* Shall he not know it more fully and distinctly than we know that which we have with the greatest care and diligence searched out? Shall he not judge it, and call us to an account for it?" Forgetting God was a heart-sin, and stretching our the hand to a strange god was often a secret sin, Eze. 8:12. But heart-sins and secret sins are known to God, and must be reckoned for; for *he knows the secrets of the heart,* and therefore is a infallible judge of the words and actions.

2. That they suffered these hard things because they kept close to God and to their duty (*v.* 22): "It is *for thy sake that we are killed all the day long,* because we stand related to thee, are called by thy name, call upon thy name, and will not worship other gods." In this the Spirit of prophecy had reference to those who suffered even unto death for the testimony of Christ, to whom it is applied, Rom. 8:36. So many were killed, and put to such lingering deaths, that they were in the killing all the day long; so universally was this practised that when a man became a Christian he reckoned himself as a *sheep appointed for the slaughter.*

II. By way of petition, with reference to their present distress, that God would, in his own due time, work deliverance for them. 1. Their request is very importunate: *Awake, arise, v.* 23. *Arise for our help; redeem us* (*v.* 26); come speedily and powerfully to our relief, Ps. 80:2. *Stir up thy strength, and come and save us.* They had complained (*v.* 12) that God had sold them; here they pray (*v.* 26) that God would redeem them; for there is no appealing from God, but by appealing to him. If he sell us, it is not any one else that can redeem us; the same hand that tears must heal, that smites must bind up, Hos. 6:1. They had complained (*v.* 9), *Thou hast cast us off;* but here they pray (*v.* 23), *"Cast us not off forever;* let us not be finally forsaken of God." 2. The expostulations are very moving: *Why sleepest thou? v.* 23. He that keeps Israel neither slumbers nor sleeps; but, when he does not immediately appear for the deliverance of his people, they are tempted to think he sleeps. The expression is figurative (as Ps. 78:65, *Then the Lord awaked as one out of sleep);* but it was applicable to Christ in the letter (Mt. 8:24); he was asleep when his disciples were in a storm, and they awoke him, saying, *Lord, save us, we perish. "Wherefore hidest thou thy face,* that we may not see thee and the light of thy countenance?" Or, "that thou mayest not see us and our distresses? Thou forgettest our affliction and our oppression, for it still continues, and we see no way open for our deliverance." And, 3. The pleas are very proper, not their own merit and righteousness, though they had the testimony of their consciences concerning their integrity, but they plead the poor sinner's pleas. (1.) Their own misery, which made them the proper objects of the divine compassion (*v.* 25): *"Our soul is bowed down to the dust* under prevailing grief and fear. We have become as creeping things, the most despicable animals: *Our belly cleaves unto the earth;* we cannot lift up ourselves, neither revive our own drooping spirits nor recover ourselves out of our low and sad condition, and we lie exposed to be trodden on by every insulting foe." 2. God's mercy: *"O redeem us for thy mercies' sake;* we depend upon the goodness of thy nature, which is the glory of thy name (Ex. 34:6), and upon those sure mercies of David which are conveyed by the covenant to all his spiritual seed."

PSALM 45

This psalm is an illustrious prophecy of Messiah the Prince: it is all over gospel, and points at him only, as a bridegroom espousing the church to himself and as a king ruling in it and ruling for it. It is probable that our Saviour has reference to this psalm when he compares the kingdom of heaven, more than once, to a nuptial solemnity, the solemnity of a royal nuptial, Mt. 22:2; 25:1. We have no reason to think it has any reference to Solomon's marriage with Pharaoh's daughter; if I thought that it had reference to any other than the mystical marriage between Christ and his church, I would rather apply it to some of David's marriages, because he was a man of war, such a one as the bridegroom here is described to be, which Solomon was not. But I take it to be purely and only meant of Jesus Christ; of him speaks the prophet this, of him and of no other man; and to him (*v.* 6, 7) it is applied in the New Testament (Heb. 1:8), nor can it be understood of any other. The preface speaks the excellency of the song (*v.* 1). The psalm speaks, I. Of the royal bridegroom, who is Christ. 1. The transcendent excellency of his person (*v.* 2). 2. The glory of his victories (*v.* 3–5). 3. The righteousness of his government (*v.* 6, 7). 4. The splendour of his court (*v.* 8, 9). II. Of the royal bride, which is the church. 1. Her consent gained (*v.* 10, 11). 2. The nuptials solemnized (*v.* 12–15). 3. The issue of this marriage (*v.* 16, 17). In singing this psalm our hearts must be filled with high thoughts of Christ, with an entire submission to and satisfaction in his government, and with an earnest desire of the enlarging and perpetuating of his church in the world.

To the chief musician upon Shoshannim, for the sons of Korah, Maschil. A song of loves.

Verses 1–5

Some make *Shoshannim,* in the title, to signify an instrument of six strings; others take it in its primitive signification for lilies or roses, which probably were strewed, with other flowers, at nuptial solemnities; and then it is easily applicable to Christ who calls himself the *rose of Sharon and the lily of the valleys,* Cant. 2:1. It is *a song of loves,* concerning the holy love that is between Christ and his church. It is a *song of the well-beloved,* the virgins, the companions of the bride (*v.* 14), prepared to be sung by them. The virgin-company that attend the Lamb on Mount Zion are said to *sing a new song,* Rev. 14:3, 4.

I. The preface (*v.* 1) speaks, 1. The dignity of the subject. It is *a good matter,* and it is a pity that such a moving art as poetry should every be employed about a bad matter. It is *touching the King,* King Jesus, and his kingdom and government. Note, Those that speak of Christ speak of a good matter, no subject so noble, so copious, so fruitful, so profitable, and so well-becoming us; it is a shame that this good matter is not more the matter of our discourse. 2. The excellency of the management. This song was a confession with the mouth of faith in the heart concerning Christ and his church. (1.) The matter was well digested, as it well deserved: *My heart is inditing it,* which perhaps is meant of that Spirit of prophecy that dictated the psalm to David, that Spirit of Christ which was in the prophets, 1 Pt. 1:11. But it is applicable to his devout meditations and affections in his heart, out of the abundance of which his mouth spoke. Things concerning Christ ought to be thought of by us with all possible seriousness, with fixedness of thought and a fire of holy love, especially when we are to speak of those things. We then speak best of Christ and divine things when we speak from the heart that which has warmed and affected us; and we should never be rash in speaking of the things of Christ, but weigh well beforehand what we have to say, lest we speak amiss. See Eccl. 5:2. (2.) It was well expressed: *I will speak of the things which I have made.* He would express himself, [1.] With all possible clearness, as one that did himself understand and was affected with the things he spoke of. Not, "I will speak the things I have heard from others," that is speaking by rote; but, "the things which I have myself studied." Note, What God has wrought in our souls, as well as what he has wrought for them, we must declare to others, Ps. 66:16. [2.] With all possible cheerfulness, freedom, and fluency: *"My tongue is as the pen of a ready writer,* guided by my heart in every word as the pen is by the hand." We call the prophets the *penmen* of scripture, whereas really they were but the pen. The tongue of the most subtle disputant, and the most eloquent orator, is but the pen with which God writes what he pleases. Why should we quarrel with the pen if bitter things be written against us, or idolize the pen if it write in our favour? David not only spoke what he thought of Christ, but wrote it, that it might spread the further and last the longer. His tongue was as the pen of a ready writer, that lets nothing slip. When the heart is inditing a good matter it is a pity but the tongue should be as *the pen of a ready writer,* to leave it upon record.

II. In these verses the Lord Jesus is represented,

1. As most beautiful and amiable in himself. It is a marriage-song; and therefore the transcendent excellencies of Christ are represented by the beauty of the royal bridegroom (*v.* 2): *Thou art fairer than the children of men,* than any of them. He proposed (*v.* 1) to speak of the King, but immediately directs his speech to him. Those that have an admiration and affection for Christ love to go to him and tell him so. Thus we must profess our faith, that we see his beauty, and our love, that we are pleased with it: *Thou are fair,* thou art *fairer than the children of men.* Note, Jesus Christ is in himself, and in the eyes of all believers, more amiable and lovely than the children of men. The beauties of the Lord Jesus, as God, as Mediator, far surpass those of human nature in general and those which the most amiable and excellent of the children of men are endowed with; there is more in Christ to engage our love than there is or can be in any creature. Our beloved is more than another beloved. The beauties of this lower world, and its charms, are in danger of drawing away our hearts from Christ, and therefore we are concerned to understand how much he excels them all, and how much more worthy he is of our love.

2. As the great favourite of heaven. He is *fairer than the children of men,* for God has done more for him than for any of the children of men, and all his kindness to the children of men is for his sake, and passes through his hands, through his mouth. (1.) He has grace, and he has it for us; *Grace is poured into thy lips.* By his word, his promise, his gospel, the good-will of God is made known to us and the good work of God is begun and carried on in us. He received all grace from God, all the endowments that were requisite to qualify him for his work and office as Mediator, that from his fulness we might receive, Jn. 1:16. It was not only poured into his heart, for his own strength and encouragement, but poured into his lips, that by the words of his mouth in general, and the kisses of his mouth to particular believers, he might communicate both holiness and comfort. From this grace poured into his lips proceeded those gracious words which all admired, Lu. 4:22. The gospel of grace is poured into his lips; for it *began to be spoken by the Lord,* and from him we receive it. He has the words of eternal life. *The spirit of prophecy is put into thy lips;* so the Chaldee. (2.) He has the blessing, and he has it for us. "Therefore, because thou art the great trustee of divine grace for the use and benefit of the children of men, *therefore God has blessed thee for ever,* has made thee an everlasting blessing, so as that in thee all the nations of the earth shall be blessed." Where God gives his grace he will give his blessing. We are blessed with spiritual blessings in Christ Jesus, Eph. 1:3.

3. As victorious over all his enemies. The royal bridegroom is a man of war, and his nuptials do not excuse him from the field of battle (as was allowed by the law, Deu. 24:5); nay, they bring him to the field of battle, for he is to rescue his spouse by dint of sword out of her captivity, to conquer her, and to conquer for her, and then to marry her. Now we have here,

(1.) His preparations for war (*v.* 3): *Gird thy sword upon thy thigh, O Most Mighty!* The word of God is the sword of the Spirit. By the promises of that word, and the grace contained in those promises, souls are made willing to submit to Jesus Christ and become his loyal subjects; by the threatenings of that word, and the judgments executed according to them, those that stand it out against Christ will, in due time, be brought down and ruined. By the gospel of Christ many Jews and Gentiles were converted, and, at length, the Jewish nation was destroyed, according to the predictions of it, for their implacable enmity to it; and paganism was quite abolished. The sword here girt on Christ's thigh is the same which is said to *proceed out of his mouth,* Rev. 19:15. When the gospel was sent fort to be preached to all nations, then our Redeemer girded his sword upon his thigh.

(2.) His expedition to this holy war: He goes forth *with his glory and his majesty,* as a great king takes the field with abundance of pomp and magnificence — his sword, his glory, and majesty. In his gospel he appears transcendently great and excellent, bright and blessed, in the honour and majesty which the Father had laid upon him. Christ, both in his person and in his gospel, had nothing of external glory or majesty, nothing to charm men (for he had no form nor comeliness), nothing to awe men, for he *took upon him the form of a servant;* it was all spiritual glory, spiritual majesty. There is so much grace, and therefore glory, in that word, *He that believes shall be saved,* so much terror, and therefore majesty, in that word, *He that believes shall not be damned,* that we may well say, in the chariot of that gospel, which these words are the sum of, the Redeemer rides forth in glory and majesty. *In thy majesty ride prosperously, v.* 4. *Prosper thou; ride thou.* This speaks the promise of his Father, that he should prosper according to *the good pleasure of the Lord,* that he should *divide the spoil with the strong,* in recompence of his sufferings. Those cannot but prosper to whom God says, Prosper, Isa. 52:10–12. And it denotes the good wishes of his friends, praying that he may prosper in the conversion of souls to him, and the destruction of all the powers of darkness that rebel against him. *"Thy kingdom come;* Go on and prosper."

(3.) The glorious cause in which he is engaged — *because of truth, and meekness, and righteousness,* which were, in a manner, sunk and lost among men, and which Christ came to retrieve and rescue. [1.] The gospel itself is *truth, meekness, and righteousness;* it commands by the power of truth and righteousness; for Christianity has these, incontestably, on its side, and yet it is to be promoted by meekness and gentleness, 1 Co. 4:12, 13; 2 Tim. 2:25. [2.] Christ appears in it in his *truth, meekness,* and *righteousness,* and these are his glory and majesty, and because of these he shall prosper. Men are brought to believe on him because he is true, to learn of him because he is meek, Mt. 11:29 (the gentleness of Christ is of mighty force, 2 Co. 10:1), and to submit to him because he is righteous and rules with equity. [3.] The gospel, as far as it prevails with men, sets up in their hearts *truth, meekness, and righteousness,* rectifies their mistakes by the light of truth, controls their passions by the power of meekness, and governs their hearts and lives by the laws of righteousness. Christ came, by setting up his kingdom among men, to restore those glories to a degenerate world, and to maintain the cause of those just and rightful rulers under him that by error, malice, and iniquity, had been deposed.

(4.) The success of his expedition: *"Thy right hand shall teach thee terrible things;* thou shalt experience a wonderful divine power going along with thy gospel, to make it victorious, and the effects of it will be terrible things." [1.] In order to the conversion and reduction of souls to him, there are terrible things to be done; the heart must be pricked, conscience must be startled, and the terrors of the Lord must make way for his consolations. This is done by the right hand of Christ. The Comforter shall continue, Jn. 16:8. [2.] In the conquest of the gates of hell and its supporters, in the destruction of Judaism and Paganism, terrible things will be done, which will make *men's hearts fail them for fear* (Lu. 21:26) and great men and chief captains call to the *rocks and mountains to fall on them,* Rev. 6:15. The next verse describes these terrible things (*v.* 5): *Thy arrows are sharp in the heart of the king's enemies. First,* Those that were by nature enemies are thus wounded, in order to their being subdued and reconciled. Convictions are like the arrows of the bow, which are sharp in the heart on which they fasten, and bring people to fall under Christ, in subjection to his laws and government. Those that thus fall on this stone shall by broken, Mt. 21:44. *Secondly,* Those that persist in their enmity are thus wounded, in order to their being ruined. The arrows of God's terrors are sharp in their hearts, whereby they shall fall under him, so as to be made his footstool, Ps. 110:1. Those that would not have him to reign over them shall be brought forth and slain before him (Lu. 19:27); those that would not submit to his golden sceptre shall be broken to pieces by his iron rod.

Verses 6–9

We have here the royal bridegroom filling his throne with judgment and keeping his court with splendour.

I. He here fills his throne with judgment. It is God the Father that says to the Son here, *Thy throne, O God! is for ever and ever,* as appears Heb. 1:8, 9, where this is quoted to prove that he is God and has a *more excellent name than the angels.* The Mediator is God, else he neither would have been able to do the Mediator's work nor fit to wear the Mediator's crown. Concerning his government observe, 1. The eternity of it; it is *for ever and ever.* It shall continue on earth throughout all the ages of time, in despite of all the opposition of the gates of hell; and in the blessed fruits and consequences of it it shall last as long as the days of heaven, and run parallel with the line of eternity itself. Perhaps even then the glory of the Redeemer, and the blessedness of the redeemed, shall be in a continual infinite progression; for it is promised that not only of his government, but of *the increase of his government and peace, there shall be no end* (Isa. 9:7); even when the kingdom shall be *delivered up to God even the Father* (1 Co. 15:24) the throne of the Redeemer will continue. 2. The equity of it: *The sceptre of thy kingdom,* the administration of thy government, *is right,* exactly according to the eternal counsel and will of God, which is the eternal rule and reason of good and evil. Whatever Christ does he does none of his subjects any wrong, but gives redress to those that do suffer wrong: *He loves righteousness, and hates wickedness, v.* 7. He himself loves to do righteousness, and hates to do wickedness; and he loves those that do righteousness, and hates those that do wickedness. By the holiness of his life, the merit of his death, and the great design of his gospel, he has made it to appear that he loves righteousness (for by his example, his satisfaction, and his precepts, he has brought in an everlasting righteousness), and that he hates wickedness, for never did God's hatred of sin appear so conspicuously as it did in the sufferings of Christ. 3. The establishment and elevation of it: *Therefore God, even thy God* (Christ, as Mediator, called God *his God,* Jn. 20:17, as commissioned by him, and the head of those that are taken into covenant with him), *has anointed thee with the oil of gladness. Therefore,* that is, (1.) "In order to this righteous government of thine, God has given thee his Spirit, that divine unction, to qualify thee for thy undertaking," Isa. 61:1. 1. *The Spirit of the Lord God is upon me, because he has anointed me.* What God called him to he fitted him for, Isa. 11:2. The Spirit is called *the oil of gladness* because of the delight wherewith Christ was filled in carrying on his undertaking. He was anointed with the Spirit *above all his fellows,* above all those that were anointed, whether priests or kings. (2.) "In recompence of what thou has done and suffered for the advancement of righteousness and the destruction of sin God has anointed thee with the oil of gladness, has brought thee to all the honours and all the joys of thy exalted state." *Because he humbled himself, God has highly exalted him,* Phil. 2:8, 9. His anointing him denotes the power and glory to which he is exalted; he is invested in all the dignities and authorities of the Messiah. And his anointing him with the oil of gladness denotes *the joy that was set before him* (so his exaltation is expressed, Heb. 12:2) both in the light of his *Father's countenance* (Acts 2:28) and in the success of his undertaking, which he shall *see, and be satisfied,* Isa. 53:11. This he is anointed with *above all his fellows,* above all believers, who are his brethren, and who partake of the anointing — they by measure, he without measure. But the apostle brings it to prove his pre-eminence above the angels, Heb. 1:4, 9. The salvation of sinners is the joy of angels (Lu. 15:10), but much more of the Son.

II. He keeps his court with splendour and magnificence. 1. His robes of state, wherein he appears, are taken notice of, not for their pomp, which might strike an awe upon the spectator, but their pleasantness and the gratefulness of the odours with which they were perfumed (*v.* 8): *They smell of myrrh, aloes, and cassia* (the *oil of gladness* with which he and his garments were anointed): these were some of the ingredients of the holy anointing oil which God appointed, the like to which was not to be made up for any common use (Ex. 30:23, 24), which was typical of the unction of the Spirit which Christ, the great high priest of our profession, received, and to which therefore there seems here to be a reference. It is the savour of these good ointments, his graces and comforts, that draws souls to him (Cant. 1:3, 4) and makes him *precious to believers,* 1 Pt. 2:7. 2. His royal palaces are said to be *ivory* ones, such as were then reckoned most magnificent. We read of an ivory house that Ahab made, 1 Ki. 22:39. The mansions of light above are the *ivory palaces,* whence all the joys both of Christ and believers come, and where they will be for ever in perfection; for by them he is made glad, and all that are his with him; for they shall enter into the joy of their Lord. 3. The beauties of his court shine very brightly. In public appearances at court, when the pomp of it is shown, nothing is supposed to contribute so much to it as the splendour of the ladies, which is alluded to here, *v.* 9. (1.) Particular believers are here compared to the ladies at court, richly dressed in honour of the sovereign: *Kings' daughters are among thy honourable women,* whose looks, and mien, and ornaments, we may suppose, from the height of their extraction, to excel all others. All true believers are born from above; they are the children of the King of kings. These attend the throne of the Lord Jesus daily with their prayers and praises, which is really their honour, and he is pleased to reckon it his. The numbering of kings' daughters among his honourable women, or maids of honour, intimates that the kings whose daughters they were should be tributaries to him and dependents on him, and would therefore think it a preferment to their daughters to attend him. (2.) The church in general, constituted of these particular believers, is here compared to the queen herself — the queen-consort, whom, by an everlasting covenant, he hath betrothed to himself. She stands *at his right hand,* near to him, and receives honour from him, in the richest array, *in gold of Ophir,* in robes woven with golden thread or with a gold chain and other ornaments of gold. This is *the bride, the Lamb's wife,* whose graces, which are her ornaments, are compared to *fine linen, clean and white* (Rev. 19:8), for their purity, here to *gold of Ophir,* for their costliness; for, as we owe our redemption, so we owe our adorning, not to corruptible things, but to *the precious blood of the Son of God.*

Verses 10–17

This latter part of the psalm is addressed to the royal bride, standing on the right hand of the royal bridegroom. God, who said to the Son, *Thy throne is for ever and ever,* says this to the church, which, upon the account of her espousals to the Son, he here calls his *daughter.*

I. He tells her of the duties expected from her, which ought to be considered by all those that come into relation to the Lord Jesus: *"Hearken,* therefore, *and consider* this, *and incline thy ear,* that is, submit to those conditions of thy espousals, and bring thy will to comply with them." This is the method of profiting by the word of God. *He that has ears, let him hear,* let him hearken diligently; he that hearkens, let him consider and weigh it duly; he that considers, let him incline and yield to the force of what is laid before him. And what is it that is here required?

1. She must renounce all others.

(1.) Here is the law of her espousals: *"Forget thy own people and thy father's house,* according to the law of marriage. Retain not the affection thou hast had for them, nor covet to return to them again; banish all such remembrance (not only of thy people that were dear to thee, but of thy father's house that were dearer) as may incline thee to look back, as Lot's wife to Sodom." When Abraham, in obedience to God's call, had quitted his native soil, he was not so much as *mindful of the country whence he came out.* This shows, [1.] How necessary it was for those who were converted from Judaism or paganism to the faith of Christ wholly to cast out the old leaven, and not to bring into their Christian profession either the Jewish ceremonies or the heathen idolatries, for these would make such a mongrel religion in Christianity as the Samaritans had. [2.] How necessary it is for us all, when we give up our names to Jesus Christ, to hate father and mother, and all that is dear to us in this world, in comparison, that is, to love them less than Christ and his honour, and our interest in him, Lu. 14:26.

(2.) Here is good encouragement given to the royal bride thus entirely to break off from her former alliances: *So shall the king greatly desire thy beauty,* which intimates that the mixing of her old rites and customs, whether Jewish or Gentile, with her religion, would blemish her beauty and would hazard her interest in the affections of the royal bridegroom, but that, if she entirely conformed to his will, he would delight in her. The beauty of holiness, both on the church and on particular believers, is in the sight of Christ of great price and very amiable. Where that is he says, *This is my rest for ever; here will I dwell, for I have desired it.* Among the golden candlesticks he walks with pleasure, Rev. 2:1.

2. She must reverence him, must love, honour, and obey him: *He is thy Lord, and worship thou him.* The church is to be subject to Christ as the wife to the husband (Eph. 5:24), to call him *Lord,* as Sarah called Abraham, and to obey him (1 Pt. 3:6), and so not only to submit to his government, but to give him divine honours. We must worship him as God, and our Lord; for this is the will of God, that *all men should honour the Son even as they honour the Father;* nay, in so doing it is reckoned that they honour the Father. If we confess that Christ is Lord, and pay our homage to him accordingly, it is *to the glory of God the Father,* Phil. 2:11.

II. He tells her of the honours designed for her.

1. Great court should be made to her, and rich presents brought her (*v.* 12): *"The daughter of Tyre,"* a rich and splendid city, "the *daughter of the King of Tyre* shall be *there with a gift;* every royal family round about shall send a branch, as a representative of the whole, to seek thy favour and to make an interest in thee; *even the rich among the people,* whose wealth might be thought to exempt them from dependence at court, even they shall entreat thy favour, for his sake to whom thou art espoused, that by thee they may make him their friend." The Jews, the pretending Jews, who are rich to a proverb (as rich as a Jew), shall come and worship before the church's feet in the Philadelphian period, and shall *know that Christ has loved her,* Rev. 3:9. When the Gentiles, being converted to the faith of Christ, join themselves to the church, they then *come with a gift,* 2 Co. 8:5; Rom. 15:16. When with themselves they devote all they have to the honour of Christ, and the service of his kingdom, they then *come with a gift.*

2. She shall be very splendid, and highly esteemed in the eyes of all, (1.) For her personal qualifications, the endowments of her mind, which every one shall admire (*v.* 13): *The king's daughter is all glorious within.* Note, The glory of the church is spiritual glory, and that is indeed all glory; it is the glory of the soul, and that is the man; it is glory in God's sight, and it is an earnest of eternal glory. The glory of the saints falls not within the view of a carnal eye. As their life, so their glory, is hidden with Christ in God, neither can the natural man know it, for it is spiritually discerned; but those who do so discern it highly value it. Let us see here what is that true glory which we should be ambitious of, not that which *makes a fair show in the flesh,* but which is in *the hidden man of the heart, in that which is not corruptible* (1 Pt. 3:4), *whose praise is not of men, but of God,* Rom. 2:29. (2.) For her rich apparel. Though all her glory is within, that for which she is truly valuable, yet *her clothing* also *is of wrought gold;* the conversation of Christians, in which they appear in the world, must be enriched with good works, not gay and gaudy ones, like paint and flourish, but substantially good, like gold; and it must be accurate and

exact, like wrought gold, which is worked with a great deal of care and caution.

3. Her nuptials shall be celebrated with a great deal of honour and joy (*v.* 14, 15): *She shall be brought to the king,* as the Lord God brought the woman to the man (Gen. 2:22), which was a type of this mystical marriage between Christ and his church. None are brought to Christ but whom the Father brings, and he has undertaken to do it; none besides are so brought *to the king* (*v.* 14) as to *enter into the king's palace, v.* 15.

(1.) This intimates a two-fold bringing of the spouse to Christ. [1.] In the conversion of souls to Christ; then they are espoused to him, privately contracted, as chaste virgins, 2 Co. 11:2; Rom. 7:4. [2.] In the completing of the mystical body, and the glorification of all the saints, at the end of time; then the *bride, the Lamb's wife,* shall be made completely ready, when all that belong to the election of grace shall be called in and called home, and all gathered together to Christ, 2 Th. 2:1. Then is the marriage of the Lamb come (Rev. 19:7; 21:2), and the virgins *go forth to meet the bridegroom,* Mt. 25:1. Then they shall *enter into the king's palaces,* into the heavenly mansions, to be ever with the Lord.

(2.) In both these espousals, observe, to the honour of the royal bride, [1.] Her wedding clothes — *raiment of needle-work,* the righteousness of Christ, the graces of the Spirit; both curiously wrought by divine wisdom. [2.] Her bride-maids — *the virgins her companions,* the wise virgins who have oil in their vessels as well as in their lamps, those who, being joined to the church, cleave to it and follow it, these shall go in to the marriage. [3.] The mirth with which the nuptials will be celebrated: *With gladness and rejoicing shall she be brought.* When the prodigal is brought home to his father *it is meet that we should make merry and be glad* (Lu. 15:32); and when the marriage of the Lamb has come *let us be glad and rejoice* (Rev. 19:7); for the *day of his espousals is the day of the gladness of his heart,* Cant. 3:11.

4. The progeny of this marriage shall be illustrious (*v.* 16): *Instead of thy fathers shall be thy children.* Instead of the Old-Testament church, the economy of which had waxed old, and ready to *vanish away* (Heb. 8:13), as the fathers that are going off, there shall be a New-Testament church, a Gentile-church, that shall be grafted into the same olive and partake of its *root and fatness* (Rom. 11:17); more and more eminent shall be *the children of the desolate* than *the children of the married wife,* Isa. 54:1. This promise to Christ is of the same import with that Isa. 53:10, *He shall see his seed;* and these shall be made *princes in all the earth;* there shall be some of all nations brought into subjection to Christ, and so made princes, *made to our God kings and priests,* Rev. 1:6. Or it may intimate that there should be a much greater number of Christian kings than ever there was of Jewish kings (those in Canaan only, these in all the earth), nursing fathers and nursing mothers to the church, which shall *suck the breasts of kings.* They are princes of Christ's making; for *by him kings reign and princes decree justice.*

5. The praise of this marriage shall be perpetual in the praises of the royal bridegroom (*v.* 18): *I will make thy name to be remembered.* His Father has given him *a name above every name,* and here promises to make it perpetual, by keeping up a succession of ministers and Christians in every age, that shall bear up his name, which shall thus *endure for ever* (Ps. 72:17), by being remembered in all the generations of time; for the entail of Christianity shall not be cut off. "Therefore, because they shall remember thee in all generations, they shall praise thee for ever and ever." Those that help to support the honour of Christ on earth shall in heaven see his glory, and share in it, and be for ever praising him. In the believing hope of our everlasting happiness in the other world let us always keep up the remembrance of Christ, as our only way thither, in our generation; and, in assurance of the perpetuating of the kingdom of the Redeemer in the world, let us transmit the remembrance of him to succeeding generations, that his name *may endure for ever and be as the days of heaven.*

PSALM 46

This psalm encourages us to hope and trust in God, and his power, and providence, and gracious presence with his church in the worst of times, and directs us to give him the glory of what he has done for us and what he will do: probably it was penned upon occasion of David's victories over the neighbouring nations (2 Sa. 8), and the rest which God gave him from all his enemies round about. We are here taught, I. To take comfort in God when things look very black and threatening (*v.* 1–5). II. To mention, to his praise, the great things he had wrought for his church against its enemies (*v.* 6–9). III. To assure ourselves that God who has glorified his own name will glorify it yet again, and to comfort ourselves with that (*v.* 10, 11). We may, in singing it, apply it either to our spiritual enemies, and be more than conquerors over them, or to the public enemies of Christ's kingdom in the world and their threatening insults, endeavouring to preserve a holy security and serenity of mind when they seem most formidable. It is said of Luther that, when he heard any discouraging news, he would say, Come let us sing the forty-sixth psalm.

To the chief musician for the sons of Korah.
A song upon Alamoth.

Verses 1–5

The psalmist here teaches us by his own example.

I. To triumph in God, and his relation to us and presence with us, especially when we have had some fresh experiences of his appearing in our behalf (*v.* 1): *God is our refuge and strength;* we have found him so, he has engaged to be so, and he ever will be so. Are we pursued? God is our refuge to whom we may flee, and in whom we may be safe and think ourselves so; secure upon good grounds, Prov. 18:10. Are we oppressed by troubles? Have we work to do and enemies to grapple with? God is our strength, to bear us up under our burdens, to fit us for all our services and sufferings; he will by his grace put strength into us, and on him we may stay ourselves. Are we in distress? He is a help, to do all that for us which we need, *a present help, a help found* (so the word is), one whom we have found to be so, a help on which we may write *Probatum est — It is tried,* as Christ is called a *tried stone,* Isa. 28:16. Or, *a help at hand,* one that never is to seek for, but that is always near. Or, a *help sufficient,* a help accommodated to every case and exigence; whatever it is, he is a very present help; we cannot desire a better help, nor shall ever find the like in any creature.

II. To triumph over the greatest dangers: *God is our strength and our help,* a God all-sufficient to us; *therefore will not we fear.* Those that with a holy reverence fear God need not with any amazement to be afraid of the power of hell or earth. *If God be for us, who can be against us;* to do us any harm? It is our duty, it is our privilege, to be thus fearless; it is an evidence of a clear conscience, of an honest heart, and of a lively faith in God and his providence and promise: *"We will not fear, though the earth be removed,* though all our creature-confidences fail us and sink us; nay, though that which should support us threaten to swallow us up, as the earth did Korah," for whose sons this psalm was penned, and, some think, by them; yet while we keep close to God, and have him for us, we will not fear, for we have no cause to fear;

— Si fractus illabatur orbis,
Impavidum ferient ruinae — Hor.
— Let Jove's dread arm
With thunder rend the spheres,
Beneath the crush of worlds undaunted he appears.

Observe here, 1. How threatening the danger is. We will suppose the earth to be removed, and thrown into the sea, even the mountains, the strongest and firmest parts of the earth, to lie buried in the unfathomed ocean; we will suppose the sea to roar and rage, and make a dreadful noise, and its foaming billows to insult the shore with so much violence as even to *shake the mountains, v.* 3. Though kingdoms and states be in confusion, embroiled in wars, tossed with tumults, and their governments in continual revolution — though their powers combine against the church and people of God, aim at no less than their ruin, and go very near to gain their point — yet will not we fear, knowing that all these troubles will end well for the church. See Ps. 93:4. If the earth be removed, those have reason to fear who have laid up their treasures on earth, and set their hearts upon it; but not those who have laid up for themselves treasures in heaven, and who expect to be most happy when *the earth and all the works that are therein shall be burnt up.* Let those be troubled at the troubling of the waters who build their confidence on such a floating foundation, but not those who are led to *the rock that is higher than they,* and find firm footing upon that rock. 2. How well-grounded the defiance of this danger is, considering how well guarded the church is, and that interest which we are concerned for. It is not any private particular concern of our own that we are in pain about; no, it is the city of God, *the holy place of the tabernacles of the Most High;* it is the ark of God for which our hearts tremble. But, when we consider what God has provided for the comfort and safety of his church, we shall see reason to have our hearts fixed, and set above the fear of evil tidings. Here is, (1.) Joy to the church, even in the most melancholy and sorrowful times (*v.* 4): *There is a river the streams whereof shall make* it *glad,* even then when the waters of the sea roar and threaten it. It alludes to the waters of Siloam, which *went softly by Jerusalem* (Isa. 8:6, 7): though of no great depth or breadth, yet the waters of it were made serviceable to the defence of Jerusalem in Hezekiah's time, Isa. 22:10, 11. But this must be understood spiritually; the covenant of grace is the river, the promises of which are the streams; or the Spirit of grace is the river (Jn. 7:38, 39), the comforts of which are *the streams, that make glad the city of our God.* God's word and ordinances are rivers and streams with which God makes his saints glad in cloudy and dark days. God himself is to his church a place of *broad rivers and streams,* Isa. 33:21. The streams that make glad the city of God are not rapid, but gentle, like those of Siloam. Note, The spiritual comforts which are conveyed to the saints by soft and silent whispers, and which come not with observation, are sufficient to counterbalance the most loud and noisy threatenings of an angry and malicious world. (2.) Establishment to the church. Though heaven and earth are shaken, yet *God is in the midst of her, she shall not be moved, v.* 5. God has assured his church of his special presence with her and concern for her; his honour is embarked in her, he has set up his tabernacle in her and has undertaken the protection of it, and therefore she shall not be moved, that is, [1.] Not destroyed, not removed, as the earth may be *v.* 2. The church shall survive the world, and be in bliss when that is in ruins. It is *built upon a rock,* and the *gates of hell shall not prevail against it.* [2.] Not disturbed, not much moved, with fears of the issue. If God be for us, if God be with us, we need not be moved at the most violent attempts made against us. (3.) Deliverance to the church, though her dangers be very great: *God shall help her;* and who then can hurt her? He shall help her under her troubles, that she shall not sink; nay, that the more she is afflicted the more she shall multiply. God shall help her out of her troubles, *and that right early* — when the morning appears; that is, very speedily, for he is *a present help* (*v.* 1), and very seasonably, when things are brought to the last extremity and when the relief will be most welcome. This may be applied by particular believers to themselves; if God be in our hearts, in the midst of us, by his word dwelling richly in us, we shall be established, we shall be helped; let us therefore trust and not be afraid; all is well, and will end well.

Verses 6–11

These verses give glory to God both as King of nations and as King of saints.

I. As King of nations, ruling the world by his power and providence, and overruling all the affairs of the children of men to his own glory; he does according to his will among the inhabitants of the earth, and none may say, *What doest thou?* 1. He checks the rage and breaks the power of the nations that oppose him and his interests in the world (*v.* 6): *The heathen raged* at David's coming to the throne, and at the setting up of the kingdom of the Son of David; compare Ps. 2:1, 2. *The kingdoms were moved* with indignation, and rose in a tumultuous furious manner to oppose it; but God *uttered his voice, spoke to them in his wrath,* and they were moved in another sense, they were struck into confusion and consternation, put into disorder, and all their measures broken; the earth itself melted under them, so that they found no firm footing; their earthly hearts failed them for fear, and dissolved like snow before the sun. Such a melting of the spirits of the enemies is described, Jdg. 5:4, 5; and see Lu. 21:25, 26. 2. When he pleases to draw his sword, and give it commission, he can make great havoc among the nations and lay all waste (*v.* 8): *Come, behold the works of the Lord;* they are to be observed (Ps. 66:5), and to be sought out, Ps. 111:2. All the operations of Providence must be considered as the works of the Lord, and his attributes and purposes must be taken notice of in them. Particularly take notice of the *desolations he has made in the earth,* among the enemies of his church, who thought to lay the land of Israel desolate. The destruction they designed to bring upon the church has been turned upon themselves. War is a tragedy which commonly destroys the stage it is acted on; David carried the war into the enemies' country; and O what desolations did it make there! Cities were burnt, countries laid waste, and armies of men cut off and laid in heaps upon heaps. Come and see the effects of desolating judgments, and stand in awe of God; say, *How terrible art thou in thy works!* Ps. 66:3. Let all that oppose him see this with terror, and expect the same cup of trembling to be put into their hands; let all that fear him and trust in him see it with pleasure, and not be afraid of the most formidable powers armed against the church. Let them gird themselves, but *they shall be broken to pieces.* 3. When he pleases to sheathe his sword, he puts an end to the wars of the nations and crowns them with peace, *v.* 9. War and peace depend on his word and will, as much as storms and calms at sea do, Ps. 107:25, 29. *He makes wars to cease unto the end of the earth,* sometimes in pity to the nations, that they may have a breathing-time, when, by long wars with each other, they have run themselves out of breadth. Both sides perhaps are weary of the war, and willing to let it fall; expedients are found out for accommodation; martial princes are removed, and peacemakers set in their room; and then the bow is broken by consent, the spear cut asunder and turned into a pruning-hook, the sword beaten into a ploughshare, and the chariots of war are burned, there being no more occasion for them; or, rather, it may be meant of what he does, at other times, in favour of his own people. He makes those wars to cease that were waged against them and designed for their ruin. He breaks the enemies' bow that was drawn against them. *No weapon formed against Zion shall prosper,* Isa. 54:17. The total destruction of Gog and Magog is prophetically described by the burning of their weapons of war (Eze. 39:9, 10), which intimates likewise the church's perfect security and assurance of lasting peace, which made it needless to lay up those weapons of war for their own service. The bringing of a long war to a good issue is a work of the Lord, which we ought to behold with wonder and thankfulness.

II. As King of saints, and as such we must own that *great and marvellous are his works,* Rev. 15:3. He does and will do great things,

1. For his own glory (*v.* 10): *Be still, and know that I am God.* (1.) Let his enemies be still, and threaten no more, but know it, to their terror, that he is God, one infinitely above them, and that will certainly be too hard for them; let them rage no more, for it is all in vain: *he that sits in heaven, laughs at them;* and, in spite of all their impotent malice against his name and honour, he will be exalted among the heathen and not merely among his own people, he will be exalted in the earth and not merely in the church. Men will set up themselves, will have their own way and do their own will; but let them know that God will be exalted, he will have his way will do his own will, will glorify his own name, and *wherein they deal proudly he will be above them,* and make them know that he is so. (2.) Let his own people be still; let them be calm and sedate, and tremble no more, but know, to their comfort, that the Lord is God, he is God alone, and will be exalted above the heathen; let him alone to maintain his honour, to fulfil his own counsels and to support his own interest in the world. Though we be depressed, yet let us not be dejected, for we are sure that God will be exalted, and that may satisfy us; he will work for his great name, and then no matter what becomes of our little names. When we pray, *Father, glorify thy name,* we ought to exercise faith upon the answer given to that prayer when Christ himself prayed it, *I have both glorified it and I will glorify it yet again.* Amen, Lord, so be it.

2. For his people's safety and protection. He triumphs in the former: *I will be exalted;* they triumph in this, *v.* 7 and again *v.* 11. It is the burden of the song, *"The Lord of hosts is with us;* he is on our side, he takes our part, is present with us and president over us; *the God of Jacob is our refuge,* to whom we may flee, and in whom we may confide and be sure of safety." Let all believers triumph in this. (1.) They have the presence of a God of power, of all power: *The Lord of hosts is with us.* God is the Lord of hosts, for he has all the creatures which are called *the hosts of heaven and earth* at his beck and command, and he makes what use he pleases of them, as the instruments either of his justice or of his mercy. This sovereign Lord is with us, sides with us, acts with us, and has promised he will never leave us. Hosts may be against us, but we need not fear them if the Lord of hosts be with us. (2.) They are under the protection of a God in covenant, who not only is able to help them, but is engaged in honour and faithfulness to help them. He is the God of Jacob, not only Jacob the person, but Jacob the people; nay, and of all praying people, the spiritual seed of wrestling Jacob; and he is our refuge, by whom we are sheltered and in whom we are satisfied, who by his providence secures our welfare when without are fightings, and who by his grace quiets our minds, and establishes them, when within are fears. The Lord of hosts, the God of Jacob, has been, is, and will be with us — has been, is and will be our refuge: the original includes all; and well may *Selah* be added to it. Mark this, and take the comfort of it, and say, *If God be for us, who can be against us?*

PSALM 47

The scope of this psalm is to stir us up to praise God, to stir up all people to do so; and, I. We are directed in what manner to do it, publicly, cheerfully, and intelligently (*v.* 1, 6, 7). II. We are furnished with matter for praise. 1. God's majesty (*v.* 2). 2. His sovereign and universal dominion (*v.* 2, 7–9). 3. The great things he had done, and will do, for his people (*v.* 3–5). Many suppose that this psalm was penned upon occasion of the bringing up of the ark to Mount Zion which *v.* 5 seems to refer to ("God has gone up with a shout"); — but it looks further, to the ascension of Christ into the heavenly Zion, after he had finished his undertaking on earth, and to the setting up of his kingdom in the world, to which the heathen should become willing subjects. In singing this psalm we are to give honour to the exalted Redeemer, to rejoice in his exaltation, and to celebrate his praises, confessing that he is Lord, to the glory of God the Father.

To the chief musician. A psalm for the sons of Korah.

Verses 1–4

The psalmist, having his own heart filled with great and good thoughts of God, endeavours to engage all about him in the blessed work of praise, as one convinced that God is worthy of all blessing and praise, and as one grieved at his own and others' backwardness to and barrenness in this work. Observe, in these verses,

I. Who are called upon to praise God: *"All you people,* all you people of Israel;" those were his own subjects, and under his charge, and therefore he will engage them to praise God, for on them he has an influence. Whatever others do, he and his house, he and his people, shall praise the Lord. Or, "All you people and nations of the earth;" and so it may be taken as a prophecy of the conversion of the Gentiles and the bringing of them into the church; see Rom. 15:11.

II. What they are called upon to do: *"O clap your hands,* in token of your own joy and satisfaction in what God has done for you, of your approbation, nay, your admiration, of what God has done in general, and of your indignation against all the enemies of God's glory, Job 27:23. *Clap your hands,* as men transported with pleasure, that cannot contain themselves; *shout unto God,* not to make him hear (his ear is not heavy), but to make all about you hear, and take notice how much you are affected and filled with the works of God. Shout *with the voice of triumph* in him, and in his power and goodness, that others may join with you in the triumph." Note, Such expressions of pious and devout affections as to some may seem indecent and imprudent ought not to be hastily censured and condemned, much less ridiculed, because, if they come from an upright heart, God will accept the strength of the affection and excuse the weakness of the expressions of it.

III. What is suggested to us as matter for our praise. 1. That the God with whom we have to do is a God of awful majesty (*v.* 2): *The Lord most high is terrible.* He is infinitely above the noblest creatures, higher than the highest; there are those perfections in him that are to be reverenced by all, and particularly that power, holiness, and justice, that are to be dreaded by all those that contend with him. 2. That he is a God of sovereign and universal dominion. He is a King that reigns alone, and with an absolute power, *a King over all the earth;* all the creatures, being made by him, are subject to him, and therefore he is *a great King,* the King of kings. 3. That he takes a particular care of his people and their concerns, has done so and ever will; (1.) In giving them victory and success (*v.* 3), subduing the people and nations under them, both those that stood in their way (Ps. 44:2) and those that made attempts upon them. This God had done for them, witness the planting of them in Canaan, and their continuance there unto this day. This they doubted not but he would still do for them by his servant David, who prospered which way soever he turned his victorious arms. But this looks forward to the kingdom of the Messiah, which was to be set over all the earth, and not confined to the Jewish nation. Jesus Christ shall subdue the Gentiles; he shall bring *them in as sheep into the fold* (so the word signifies), not for slaughter, but for preservation. He shall subdue their affections, and make them a *willing people in the day of his power,* shall bring their thoughts into obedience to him, and reduce those who had gone astray, under the guidance of the *great shepherd and bishop of souls,* 1 Pt. 2:25. (2.) In giving them rest and settlement (*v.* 4): *He shall choose our inheritance for us.* He had chosen the land of Canaan to be an inheritance for Israel; it was the land which the Lord their God spied out for them; see Deu. 32:8. This justified their possession of that land, an d gave them a good title; and this sweetened their enjoyment of it, and made it comfortable; they had reason to think it a happy lot, and to be satisfied in it, when it was that which Infinite Wisdom chose for them. And the setting up of God's sanctuary in it made it *the excellency,* the honour, *of Jacob* (Amos 6:8); and he chose so good an inheritance for Jacob because he loved him, Deu. 7:8. Apply this spiritually, and it bespeaks, [1.] The happiness of the saints, that God himself has chosen their inheritance for them, and it is a goodly heritage: *he* has chosen it who knows the soul, and what will serve to make it happy; and he has chosen so well that he himself has undertaken to be the *inheritance of his people* (Ps. 16:5), and he has laid up for them in the other world an inheritance incorruptible, 1 Pt. 1:4. This will be indeed the excellency of Jacob, for whom, because he loved them, he prepared such a happiness as eye has not seen. [2.] The faith and submission of the saints to God. This is the language of every gracious soul, "God shall choose my inheritance for me; let him appoint me my lot, and I will acquiesce in the appointment. He knows what is good for me better than I do for myself, and therefore I will have no will of my own but what is resolved into his."

Verses 5–9

We are here most earnestly pressed to praise God, and to sing his praises; so backward are we to this duty that we have need to be urged to it by precept upon precept, and line upon line; so we are here (*v.* 6): *Sing praises to God,* and again, *Sing praises, Sing praises to our King,* and again, *Sing praises.* This intimates that it is a very necessary and excellent duty, that it is a duty we ought to be frequent and abundant in; we may sing praises again and again in the same words, and it is no vain repetition if it be done with new affections. Should not a people praise their God? Dan. 5:4. Should not subjects praise their king? God is our God, our King, and therefore we must praise him; we must sing his praises, as those that are pleased with them and that are not ashamed of them. But here is a needful rule subjoined (*v.* 7): *Sing you praises with understanding,* with *Maschil.* 1. "Intelligently; as those that do yourselves understand why and for what reasons you praise God and what is the meaning of the service." This is the gospel-rule (1 Co. 14:15), *to sing with the spirit and with the understanding also;* it is only with the heart that we make melody to the Lord, Eph. 5:19. It is not an acceptable service if it be not a reasonable service. 2. "Instructively, as those that desire to make others understand God's glorious perfections, and to teach them to praise him." Three things are mentioned in these verses as just matter for our praises, and each of them will admit of a double sense: —

I. We must praise God going up (*v.* 5): *God has gone up with a shout,* which may refer, 1. To the carrying up of the ark to the hill of Zion, which was done with great solemnity, David himself dancing before it, the priests, it is likely, blowing the trumpets, and the people following with their loud huzzas. The ark being the instituted token of God's special presence with them, when that was brought up by warrant from him he might be said to *go up.* The emerging of God's ordinances out of obscurity, in order to the more public and solemn administration of them, is a great favour to any people, which they have reason to rejoice in and give thanks for. 2. To the ascension of our Lord Jesus into heaven, when he had finished his work on earth, Acts 1:9. Then *God went up with a shout,* the shout of a King, of a conqueror, as one who, having *spoiled principalities and powers,* then *led captivity captive,* Ps. 68:18. He went up as a Mediator, typified by the ark and the mercy-seat over it, and was brought as the ark was into the most holy place, *into heaven itself;* see Heb. 9:24. We read not of a shout, or of the sound of a trumpet, at the ascension of Christ, but they were the inhabitants of the upper world, those sons of God, that then shouted for joy, Job 38:7. He shall come again in the same manner as he went (Acts 1:11) and we are sure that he shall come again with a shout and the sound of a trumpet.

II. We must praise God reigning, *v.* 7. 8. God is not only our King, and therefore we owe our homage to him, but he is *King of all the earth* (*v.* 7), over all the kings of the earth, and therefore in every place the incense of praise is to be offered up to him. Now this may be understood, 1. Of the kingdom of providence. God, as Creator, and the God of nature, *reigns over the heathen,* disposes of them and all their affairs, as he pleases, though they know him not, nor have any regard to him: *He sits upon the throne of his holiness,* which he has prepared in the heavens, and there he rules over all, even over the heathen, serving his own purposes by them and upon them. See here the extent of God's government; all are born within his allegiance; even the heathen that serve other gods are ruled by the true God, our God, whether they will or no. See the equity of his government; it is a throne of holiness, on which he sits, whence he gives warrants, orders, and judgment, in which we are sure there is no iniquity. 2. Of the kingdom of the Messiah. Jesus Christ, who is God, and whose *throne is for ever and ever reigns over the heathen;* not only he is entrusted with the administration of the providential kingdom, but he shall set up the kingdom of his grace in the Gentile world, and rule in the hearts of multitudes that were bred up in heathenism, Eph. 2:12, 13. This the apostle speaks of as a great mystery that the *Gentiles should be fellow-heirs,* Eph. 3:6. Christ *sits upon the throne of his holiness,* his throne in the heavens, where all the administrations of his government are intended to show forth God's holiness and to advance holiness among the children of men.

III. We must praise God as attended and honoured by *the princes of the people, v.* 9. This may be understood, 1. Of the congress or convention of the states of Israel, the heads and rulers of the several tribes, at the solemn feasts, or to despatch the public business of the nation. It was the honour of Israel that they were *the people of the God of Abraham,* as they were Abraham's seed and taken into his covenant; and, thanks be to God, this blessing of Abraham has come upon the isles of the Gentiles, Gal. 3:14. It was their happiness that they had a settled government, *princes of their people,* who were the *shields of their land.* Magistracy is the shield of a nation, and it is a great mercy to any people to have this shield, especially when their princes, *their shields, belong unto the Lord,* are devoted to his honour, and their power is employed in his service, for then he is greatly exalted. It is likewise the honour of God that, in another sense, the *shields of the earth do belong to him;* magistracy is his institution, and he serves his own purposes by it in the government of the world, turning the hearts of kings as the rivers of water, which way soever he pleases. It was well with Israel when the princes of their people were gathered together to consult for the public welfare. The unanimous agreement of the great ones of a nation in the things that belong to its peace is a very happy omen, which promises abundance of blessings. 2. It may be applied to the calling of the Gentiles into the church of Christ, and taken as a prophecy that in the days of the Messiah the kings of the earth and their people should join themselves to the church, and bring their glory and power into the New Jerusalem, that they should all become *the people of the God of Abraham,* to whom it was promised that he should be *the father of many nations.* The *volunteers* of the people (so it may be read); it is the same word that is used in Ps. 110:3, *Thy people shall be willing;* for those that are gathered to Christ are not forced, but made freely willing, to be his. When the *shields of the earth,* the ensigns of royal dignity (1 Ki. 14:27, 28,), are surrendered to the Lord Jesus, as the keys of a city are presented to the conqueror or sovereign, when princes use their power for the advancement of the interests of religion, then Christ is greatly exalted.

PSALM 48

This psalm, as the two former, is a triumphant song; some think it was penned on occasion of Jehoshaphat's victory (2 Chr. 20), others of Sennacherib's defeat, when his army laid siege to Jerusalem in Hezekiah's time; but, for aught I know, it might be penned by David upon occasion of some eminent victory obtained in his time; yet not so calculated for that but that it might serve any other similar occasion in aftertimes, and be applicable also to the glories of the gospel church, of which Jerusalem was a type, especially when it shall come to be a church triumphant, the "heavenly Jerusalem" (Heb. 12:22), "the Jerusalem which is above," Gal. 4:26. Jerusalem is here praised, I. For its relation to God (*v.* 1, 2). II. For God's care of it (*v.* 3). III. For the terror it strikes upon its enemies (*v.* 4–7). IV. For the pleasure it gives to its friends, who delight to think, 1. Of what God has done, does, and will do for it (*v.* 3). 2. Of the gracious discoveries he makes of himself in and for that holy city (*v.* 9, 10). 3. Of the effectual provision which is made for its safety (*v.* 11–13). 4. Of the assurance we have of the perpetuity of God's covenant with the children of Zion (*v.* 14). In singing this psalm we must be affected with the privilege we have as members of the gospel church, and must express and excite our sincere good-will to all its interests.

A song *and* psalm for the sons of Korah.

Verses 1–7

The psalmist is designing to praise Jerusalem and to set forth the grandeur of that city; but he begins with the praises of God and his greatness (*v.* 1), and ends with the praises of God and his goodness, *v.* 14. For, whatever is the subject of our praises, God must be both the Alpha and Omega of them. And, particularly, whatever is said to the honour of the church must redound to the honour of the church's God.

What is here said to the honour of Jerusalem is,

I. That the King of heaven owns it: it is *the city of our God* (*v.* 1), which he chose out of all the cities of Israel to put his name there. Of Zion he said kinder things than ever he said of place upon earth. *This is my rest for ever; here will I dwell, for I have desired it,* Ps. 132:13, 14. It is *the city of the great King* (*v.* 2), the King of all the earth, who is pleased to declare himself in a special manner present there. This our Saviour quotes to prove that to swear by Jerusalem is profanely to swear by God himself (Mt. 5:35), *for it is the city of the great King,* who has chosen it for the special residence of his grace, as heaven is of his glory. 1. It is enlightened with the knowledge of God. *In Judah God is known, and his name is great,* but especially in Jerusalem, the head-quarters of the priests, whose lips were to keep this knowledge. In Jerusalem *God is great* (*v.* 1) who in other places was made little of, was made nothing of. Happy the kingdom, the city, the family, the heart, in which God is great, in which he is uppermost, in which he is all. There *God is known* (*v.* 3) and where he is known he will be great; none contemn God but those that are ignorant of him. 2. It is devoted to the honour of God. It is therefore called *the mountain of his holiness,* for *holiness to the Lord* is written upon it and all the furniture of it, Zec. 14:20, 21. This is the privilege of the church of Christ, that it is *a holy nation, a peculiar people;* Jerusalem, the type of it, is called *the holy city,* bad as it was (Mt. 27:53), till that was set up, but never after. 3. It is the place appointed for the solemn service and worship of God; there he is greatly praised, and *greatly to be praised, v.* 1. Note, The clearer discoveries are made to us of God and his greatness the more it is expected that we should abound in his praises. Those that from all parts of the country brought their offerings to Jerusalem had reason to be thankful that God would not only permit them thus to attend him, but promise to accept them, and meet them with a blessing, and reckon himself praised and honoured by their services. Herein Jerusalem typified the gospel church; for what little tribute of praise God has from this earth arises from that church upon earth, which is therefore his tabernacle among men. 4. It is taken under his special protection (*v.* 3): He is *known for a refuge;* that is, he has approved himself such a one, and as such a one he is there applied to by his worshippers. Those that know him will *trust in him, and seek to him,* Ps. 9:10. God was known, not only in the streets, but even in the palaces of Jerusalem, for a refuge; the great men had recourse to God and acquaintance with him. And then religion was likely to flourish in the city when it reigned in the palaces. 5. Upon all these accounts, Jerusalem, and especially Mount Zion, on which the temple was built, were universally beloved and admired — *beautiful for situation,* and *the joy of the whole earth, v.* 2. The situation must needs be every way agreeable, when Infinite Wisdom chose it for the place of the sanctuary; and that which made it beautiful was that it was the mountain of holiness, for there is a beauty in holiness. This earth is, by sin, covered with deformity, and therefore justly might that spot of ground which was thus beautified with holiness he called *the joy of the whole earth,* that is, what the whole earth had reason to rejoice in, that God would thus in very deed dwell with man upon the earth. Mount Zion was on the north side of Jerusalem, and so was a shelter to the city from the cold and bleak winds that blew from that quarter; or, if fair weather was expected out of the north, they were thus directed to look Zion-ward for it.

II. That the kings of the earth were afraid of it. That God was known in their palaces for a refuge they had had a late instance, and a very remarkable one. Whatever it was, 1. They had had but too much occasion to fear their enemies; for *the kings were assembled, v.* 4. The neighbouring princes were confederate against Jerusalem; their heads and horns, their policies and powers, were combined for its ruin; they were assembled with all their forces; they passed, advanced, and marched on together, not doubting but they should soon make themselves masters of that city which should have been the joy, but was the envy of the whole earth. 2. God made their enemies to fear them. The very sight of Jerusalem struck them into a consternation and gave check to their fury, as the sight of the tents of Jacob frightened Balaam from his purpose to curse Israel (Num. 24:2): *They saw it and marvelled, and hasted away, v.* 5. Not *Veni, vidi, vici — I came, I saw, I conquered;* but, on the contrary, *Veni vidi victus sum — I came, I saw, I was defeated.* Not that there was any thing to be seen in Jerusalem that was so very formidable; but the sight of it brought to mind what they had heard concerning the special presence of God in that city and the divine protection it was under, and God impressed such terrors on their minds thereby as made them retire with precipitation. Though they were kings, though they were many in confederacy, yet they knew themselves an unequal match for Omnipotence, and therefore *fear came upon them, and pain, v.* 6. Note, God can dispirit the stoutest of his church's enemies, and soon put those in pain that live at ease. The fright they were in upon the sight of Jerusalem is here compared to the throes of a woman in travail, which are sharp and grievous, which sometimes come suddenly (1 Th. 5:3), which cannot be avoided, and which are effects of sin and the curse. The defeat hereby given to their designs upon Jerusalem is compared to the dreadful work made with a fleet of ships by a violent storm, when some are split, others shattered, all dispersed (*v.* 7): *Thou breakest the ships of Tarshish with an east wind;* effects at sea lie thus exposed. The terrors of God are compared to an east wind (Job 27:20, 21); these shall put them into confusion, and break all their measures. *Who knows the power of God's anger?*

Verses 8–14

We have here the good use and improvement which the people of God are taught to make of his late glorious and gracious appearances for them against their enemies, that they might work for their good.

I. Let our faith in the word of God be hereby confirmed. If we compare what God has done with what he has spoken, we shall find that, as *we have heard,* so *have we seen* (*v.* 8), and what we have seen obliges us to believe what we have heard. 1. "As we have heard done in former providences, in the days of old, so have we seen done in our own days." Note, God's latter appearances for his people against his and their enemies are consonant to his former appearances, and should put us in mind of them. 2. "As we have heard in the promise and prediction, so have we seen in the performance and accomplishment. We have heard that God is the Lord of hosts, and that Jerusalem is the city of our God, is dear to him, is his particular care; and now we have seen it; we have seen the power of our God; we have seen his goodness; we have seen his care and concern for us, that he is a *wall of fire round about Jerusalem and the glory in the midst of her.*" Note, In the great things that God has done, and is doing, for his church, it is good to take notice of the fulfilling of the scriptures; and this would help us the better to understand both the providence itself and the scripture that is fulfilled in it.

II. Let our hope of the stability and perpetuity of the church be hereby encouraged. "From what we have seen, compared with what we have heard, in the city of our God, we may conclude that God will establish it for ever." This was not fulfilled in Jerusalem (that city was long since destroyed, and all its glory laid in the dust), but has its accomplishment in the gospel church. We are sure that that shall be established for ever; it is built upon a rock, and the gates of hell cannot prevail against it, Mt. 16:18. God himself has undertaken the establishment of it; it is the Lord that has founded Zion, Isa. 14:32. And what we have seen, compared with what we have heard, may encourage us to hope in that promise of God upon which the church is built.

III. Let our minds be hereby filled with good thoughts of God. "From what we have heard, and seen, and hope for, we may take occasion to think much of God's lovingkindness, whenever we meet *in the midst of his temple,*" *v.* 9. All the streams of mercy that flow down to us must be traced up to the fountain of God's lovingkindness. It is not owing to any merit of ours, but purely to his mercy, and the peculiar favour he bears to his people. This therefore we must think of with delight, think of frequently and fixedly. What subject can we dwell upon more noble, more pleasant, more profitable? We must have God's lovingkindness always before our eyes (Ps. 26:3), especially when we attend upon him in his temple. When we enjoy the benefit of public ordinances undisturbed, when we meet in his temple and there is none to make us afraid, we should take occasion thence to think of his lovingkindness.

IV. Let us give to God the glory of the great things which he has done for us, and mention them to his honour (*v.* 10): *"According to thy name, O God! so is thy praise,* not only in Jerusalem, but to the ends of the earth." By the late signal deliverance of Jerusalem God had made himself a name; that is, he had gloriously discovered his wisdom, power, and goodness, and made all the nations about sensible of it; and *so was his praise;* that is, some in all parts would be found giving glory to him accordingly. As far as his name goes his praise will go, at least it should go, and, at length, it shall go, when all the ends of the world shall praise him, Ps. 22:27; Rev. 11:15. Some, by his *name,* understand especially that glorious name of his, *the Lord of hosts;* according to that name, so is his praise; for all the creatures, even to the ends of the earth, are under his command. But his people must, in a special manner, acknowledge his justice in all he does for them. *"Righteousness fills thy right hand;"* that is, all the operations of thy power are consonant to the eternal rules of equity.

V. Let all the members of the church in particular take to themselves the comfort of what God does for his church in general (*v.* 11): *"Let Mount Zion rejoice,* the priests and Levites that attend the sanctuary, and then *let* all *the daughters of Judah,* the country towns, and the inhabitants of them, be glad: let the women in their songs and dances, as usual on occasion of public joys, celebrate with thankfulness the great salvation which God has wrought for us." Note, When we have given God the praise we may then take the pleasure of the extraordinary deliverances of the church, and *be glad because of God's judgments* (that is, the operations of his providence), all which we may see wrought in wisdom (therefore called *judgments*) and working for the good of his church.

VI. Let us diligently observe the instances and evidences of the church's beauty, strength, and safety, and faithfully transmit our observations to those that shall come after us (*v.* 12, 13): *Walk about Zion.* Some think this refers to the ceremony of the triumph; let those who are employed in that solemnity walk round the walls (as they did, Neh. 12:31), singing and praising God. In doing this let *them tell the towers and mark well the bulwarks,* 1. That they might magnify the late wonderful deliverance God had wrought for them. Let them observe, with wonder, that the towers and bulwarks are all in their full strength and none of them damaged, the palaces in their beauty and none of them blemished; there is not the least damage done to the city by the kings that were assembled against it (*v.* 4): *Tell this to the generation following,* as a wonderful instance of God's care of his holy city, that the enemies should not only not ruin or destroy it, but not so much as hurt or deface it. 2. That they might fortify themselves against the fear of the like threatening danger another time. And so, (1.) We may understand it literally of Jerusalem, and the strong-hold of Zion. Let the daughters of Judah see the towers and bulwarks of Zion, with a pleasure equal to the terror with which the kings their enemies saw them, *v.* 5. Jerusalem was generally looked upon as an impregnable place, as appears, Lam. 4:12. *All the inhabitants of the world would not have believed that an enemy should enter the gates of Jerusalem;* nor could they have entered if the inhabitants had not sinned away their defence. *Set your heart to her bulwarks.* This intimates that the principal bulwarks of Zion were not the objects of sense, which they might set their eye upon, but the objects of faith, which they must set their hearts upon. It was well enough fortified indeed both by nature and art; but its bulwarks that were mostly to be relied upon were the special presence of God in it, the beauty of holiness he had put upon it, and the promises he had made concerning it. "Consider Jerusalem's strength, and tell it to the generations to come, that they may do nothing to weaken it, and that, if at any time it be in distress, they may not basely surrender it to the enemy as not tenable." Calvin observes here that when they are directed to transmit to posterity a particular account of the towers, and bulwarks, and palaces of Jerusalem, it is intimated that in process of time they would all be destroyed and remain no longer to be seen; for, otherwise, what need was thee to preserve the description and history of them? When the disciples were admiring the buildings of the temple their Master told them that in a little time one stone of it should not be *left upon another,* Mt. 24:1, 2. Therefore, (2.) This must certainly be applied to the gospel church, that Mount Zion, Heb. 12:22. "Consider the towers, and bulwarks, and palaces of that, that you may be invited and encouraged to join yourselves to it and embark in it. See it founded on Christ, the rock fortified by the divine power, guarded by him that neither slumbers nor sleeps. See what precious ordinances are its palaces, what precious promises are its bulwarks; tell this to the generation following, that they may with purpose of heart espouse its interests and cleave to it."

VII. Let us triumph in God, and in the assurances we have of his everlasting lovingkindness, *v.* 14. Tell this to the generation following; transmit this truth as a sacred deposit to your posterity, That *this God,* who has now done such great things for us, *is our God for ever and ever;* he is constant and unchangeable in his love to us and care for us. 1. If God be our God, he is ours for ever, not only through all the ages of time, but to eternity; for it is the everlasting blessedness of glorified saints that *God himself will be with them and will be their God,* Rev. 21:3. 2. If he be our God, *he will be our guide,* our faithful constant guide, to show us our way and to lead us in it; he will be so, *even unto death,* which will be the period of our way, and will bring us to our rest. He will lead and keep us even to the last. He will be our guide *above* death (so some); he will so guide us as to set us above the reach of death, so that it shall not be able to do us any real hurt. He will be our guide *beyond* death (so others); he will conduct us safely to a happiness on the other side death, to a life in which there shall be no more death. If we take the Lord for our God, he will conduct and convey us safely to death, through death, and beyond death — down to death and up again to glory.

PSALM 49

This psalm is a sermon, and so is the next. In most of the psalms we have the penman praying or praising; in these we have him preaching; and it is our duty, in singing psalms, to teach and admonish ourselves and one another. The scope and design of this discourse is to convince the men of this world of their sin and folly in setting their hearts upon the things of this world, and so to persuade them to seek the things of a better world; as also to comfort the people of God, in reference to their own troubles and the grief that arises from the prosperity of the wicked. I. In the preface he proposes to awaken worldly people out of their security (*v.* 1–3) and to comfort himself and other godly people in a day of distress (*v.* 4, 5). II. In the rest of the psalm, 1. He endeavours to convince sinners of their folly in doting upon the wealth of this world, by showing them (1.) That they cannot, with all their wealth, save their friends from death (*v.* 6–9). (2.) They cannot save themselves from death (*v.* 10). (3.) They cannot secure to themselves a happiness in this world (*v.* 11, 12). Much less, (4.) Can they secure to themselves a happiness in the other world (*v.* 14). 2. He endeavours to comfort himself and other good people, (1.) Against the fear of death (*v.* 15). (2.) Against the fear of the prospering power of wicked people (*v.* 16–20). In singing this psalm let us receive these instructions, and be wise.

To the chief musician. A psalm for the sons of Korah.

Verses 1–5

This is the psalmist's preface to his discourse concerning the vanity of the world and its insufficiency to make us happy; and we seldom meet with an introduction more solemn than this is; for there is no truth of more undoubted certainty, nor of greater weight and importance, and the consideration of which will be of more advantage to us.

I. He demands the attention of others to that which he was about to say (*v.* 1, 2): *Hear this, all you people;* hear it and heed it, hear it and consider it; what is spoken once, hear twice. *Hear and give ear,* Ps. 62:9, 11. Not only, "Hear, all you Israelites, and give ear all the inhabitants of Canaan," but, *Hear, all you people, and give ear, all you inhabitants of the world;* for this doctrine is not peculiar to those that are blessed with divine revelation, but even the light of nature witnesses to it. All men may know, and therefore let all men consider, that their riches will not profit them in the day of death. *Both low and high,* both *rich and poor,* must come together, to hear the word of God; let both therefore hear this with application. Let those that are high and rich in the world hear of the vanity of their worldly possessions and not be proud of them, nor secure in the enjoyment of them, but lay them out in doing good, that with them they may make to themselves friends; let those that are poor and low hear this and be content with their little, and not envy those that have abundance. Poor people are as much in danger from an inordinate desire towards the wealth of the world as rich people from an inordinate delight in it. He gives a good reason why his discourse should be regarded (*v.* 3): *My mouth shall speak of wisdom;* what he had to say, 1. Was true and good. It is wisdom and understanding; it will make those wise and intelligent that receive it and submit to it. It is not doubtful but certain, not trivial but weighty, not a matter of nice speculation but of admirable use to guide us in the right way to our great end. 2. It was what he had himself well digested. What his mouth spoke was the *meditation of his heart* (as Ps. 19:14; 45:1); it was what God put into his mind, what he had himself seriously considered, and was fully apprized of the meaning of and convinced of the truth of. That which ministers speak from their own hearts is most likely to reach the hearts of their hearers.

II. He engages his own attention (*v.* 4): *I will incline my ear to a parable.* It is called a *parable,* not because it is figurative and obscure, but because it is a wise discourse and very instructive. It is the same word that is used concerning Solomon's proverbs. The psalmist will himself incline his ear to it. This intimates, 1. That he was taught it by the Spirit of God and did not speak of himself. Those that undertake to teach others must first learn themselves. 2. That he thought himself nearly concerned in it, and was resolved not to venture his own soul upon that bottom which he dissuaded others from venturing theirs upon. 3. That he would not expect others should attend to that which he himself did not attend to as a matter of the greatest importance. Where God *gives the tongue of the learned* he first *wakens the ear to hear as the learned,* Isa. 50:4.

III. He promises to make the matter as plain and as affecting as he could: *I will open my dark saying upon the harp.* What he learned for himself he would not conceal or confine to himself, but would communicate, for the benefit of others. 1. Some understood it not, it was a riddle to them; tell them of the vanity of the things that are seen, and of the reality and weight of invisible things, and they say, *Ah Lord God! doth he not speak parables?* For the sake of such, he would open this dark saying, and make it so plain that he that runs might read it. 2. Others understood it well enough, but they were not moved by it, it never affected them, and for their sake he would open it upon the harp, and try that expedient to work upon them, to win upon them. *A verse may find him who a sermon flies.* Herbert.

IV. He begins with the application of it to himself, and that is the right method in which to treat of divine things. We must first preach to ourselves before we undertake to admonish or instruct others. Before he comes to set down the folly of carnal security (*v.* 6), he here lays down, from his own experience, the benefit and comfort of a holy gracious security, which those enjoy who trust in God, and not in their worldly wealth: *Wherefore should I fear?* he means, *Wherefore should I fear their fear* (Isa. 8:12), the fears of worldly people. 1. "Wherefore should I be afraid of them? Wherefore should I fear in the days of trouble and persecution, *when the iniquity of my heels,* or of my supplanters that endeavour to trip up my heels, *shall compass me about,* and they shall surround me with their mischievous attempts? Why should I be afraid of those all whose power lies in their wealth, which will not enable them to redeem their friends? I will not fear their power, for it cannot enable them to ruin me." The great men of the world will not appear at all formidable when we consider what little stead their wealth will stand them in. We need not fear their casting us down from our excellency who cannot support themselves in their own excellency. 2. "Wherefore should I be afraid like them?" The days of old age and death are the *days of evil,* Eccl. 12:1. In the day of judgment *the iniquity of our heels* (or of our steps, our past sins) will compass us about, will be set in order before us. *Every work will be brought into judgment, with every secret thing;* and *every one of us must give account of himself.* In these days worldly wicked people will be afraid; nothing more dreadful to those that have set their hearts upon the world than to think of leaving it; death to them is the king of terrors, because, after death, comes the judgment, when their sins will surround them as so many furies; but wherefore should a good man fear death, who has God with him? Ps. 23:4. When his iniquities compass him about, he sees them all pardoned, his conscience is purified and pacified, and then even in the judgment-day, when the hearts of others fail them for fear, he can lift up his head with joy, Lu. 21:26, 28. Note, The children of God, though ever so poor, are in this truly happy, above the most prosperous of the children of this world, that they are well guarded against the terrors of death and the judgment to come.

Verses 6–14

In these verses we have,

I. A description of the spirit and way of worldly people, whose portion is in this life, Ps. 17:14. It is taken for granted that they have wealth, and a multitude of riches (*v.* 6), houses and lands of inheritance, which they call their own, *v.* 11. God often gives abundance of the good things of this world to bad men who live in contempt of him and rebellion against him, by which it appears that they are not the best things in themselves (for then God would give most of them to his best friends), and that they are not the best things for us, for then those would not have so much of them who, being marked for ruin, are to be ripened for it by their prosperity, Prov. 1:32. A man may have abundance of the wealth of this world and be made better by it, may thereby have his heart enlarged in love, and thankfulness, and obedience, and may do that good with it which will be fruit abounding to his account; and therefore it is not men's having riches that denominates them worldly, but their setting their hearts upon them as the best things; and so these worldly people are here described. 1. They repose a confidence in their riches: *They trust in their wealth* (*v.* 6); they depend upon it as their portion and happiness, and expect that it will secure them from all evil and supply them with all good, and that they need nothing else, no, not God himself. Their gold is their hope (Job 31:24), and so it becomes their God. Thus our Saviour explains the difficulty of the salvation of rich people (Mk. 10:24): *How hard is it for those that trust in riches to enter into the kingdom of God!* See 1 Tim. 6:17. 2. They take a pride in their riches: *They boast themselves in the multitude of them,* as if they were sure tokens of God's favour and certain proofs of their own ingenuity and industry *(my might, and the power of my hand, have gotten me this wealth),* as if they made them truly great and happy, and more really excellent than their neighbours. They boast that they have all they would have (Ps. 10:3) and can set all the world at defiance *(I sit as a queen, and shall be a lady for ever);* therefore *they call their lands after their own names,* hoping thereby to perpetuate their memory; and, if their lands do retain the names by which they called them, it is but a poor honour; but they often change their names when they change their owners. 3. They flatter themselves with an expectation of the perpetuity of their worldly possessions (*v.* 11): *Their inward thought is that their houses shall continue for ever,* and with this thought they please themselves. Are not all thoughts inward? Yes; but it intimates, (1.) That this thought is deeply rooted in their minds, is rolled and revolved there, and carefully lodged in the innermost recesses of their hearts. A godly man has thoughts of the world, but they are his outward thoughts; his inward thought is reserved for God and heavenly things: but a worldly man has only some floating foreign thoughts of the things of God, while his fixed thought, his inward thought, is about the world; that lies nearest his heart, and is upon the throne there. (2.) There it is industriously concealed. They cannot, for shame, say that they expect their houses to continue for ever, but inwardly they think so. If they cannot persuade themselves that they shall continue for ever, yet they are so foolish as to think *their houses* shall, and their dwelling-places; and suppose they should, what good will that do them when they shall be no longer theirs? But they will not; for the world passes away, and the fashion of it. All things are devoured by the teeth of time.

II. A demonstration of their folly herein. In general (*v.* 13), *This their way is their folly.* Note, The way of worldliness is a very foolish way: those that lay up their treasure on earth, and set their affections on things below, act contrary both to right reason and to their true interest. God himself pronounced him *a fool* who thought his goods were laid up for many years, and that they would be a portion for his soul, Lu. 12:19, 20. And yet their posterity approve their sayings, agree with them in the same sentiments, say as t hey say and do as they do, and tread in the steps of their worldliness. Note, The love of the world is a disease that runs in the blood; men have it by kind, till the grace of God cures it. To prove the folly of carnal worldlings he shows,

1. That with all their wealth they cannot save the life of the dearest friend they have in the world, nor purchase a reprieve for him when he is under the arrest of death (*v.* 7–9): *None of them can by any means redeem his brother,* his brother worldling, who would give counter-security out of his own estate, if he would but be bail for him: and gladly he would, in hopes that he might do the same kindness for him another time. But their words will not be taken one for another, nor will one man's estate be the ransom of another man's life. God does not value it; it is of no account with him; and the true value of things is as they stand in his books. His justice will not accept it by way of commutation or equivalent. The Lord of our brother's life is the Lord of our estate, and may take both if he please, without either difficulty to himself or wrong to us; and therefore one cannot be ransom for another. We cannot bribe death, that our brother should still live, much less that he should live for ever, in this world, nor bribe the grave, that he should not see corruption; for we must needs die, and return to the dust, and there is no discharge from that war. What folly is it to trust to that, and boast of that, which will not enable us so much as for one hour to respite the execution of the sentence of death upon a parent, a child, or friend that is to us as our own soul! It is certainly true that *the redemption of the soul is precious and ceaseth for ever;* that is, life, when it is going, cannot be arrested, and when it is gone it cannot be recalled, by any human art, or worldly price. But this looks further, to the eternal redemption which was to be wrought out by the Messiah, whom the Old-testament saints had an eye to as the Redeemer. Everlasting life is a jewel of too great a value to be purchased by the wealth of this world. We are *not redeemed with corruptible things, such as silver and gold,* 1 Pt. 1:18, 19. The learned Dr. Hammond applies the 8th and 9th verses expressly to Christ: *"The redemption of the soul shall be precious,* shall be high-prized, it shall cost very dear; but, being once wrought, it shall cease for ever, it shall never need to be repeated, Heb. 9:25, 26; 10:12. And he (that is, the Redeemer) *shall yet live for ever, and shall not see corruption;* he shall rise again before he sees corruption, and then shall live for evermore," Rev. 1:18. Christ did that for us which all the riches of the world could not do; well therefore may he be dearer to us than any worldly things. Christ did that for us which a brother, a friend, could not do for us, no, not one of the best estate or interest; and therefore those that *love father or brother more than him are not worthy of him.* This likewise shows the folly of worldly people, who sell their souls for that which would never buy them.

2. That with all their wealth they cannot secure themselves from the stroke of death. The worldling sees, and it vexes him to see it, that *wise men die, likewise the fool and the brutish person perish, v.* 10. Therefore he cannot but expect that it will, at length, come to his own turn; he cannot find any encouragement to hope that he himself shall continue for ever, and therefore foolishly comforts himself with this, that, though he shall not, his house shall. Some rich people are wise, they are politicians, but they cannot out-wit death, nor evade his stroke, with all their art and management; others are fools and brutish *(Fortuna favet fatuis — Fools are Fortune's favourites);* these, though they do no good, yet perhaps do no great hurt in the world: but that shall not excuse them; they shall perish, and be taken away by death, as well as the wise that did mischief with their craft. Or by the wise and the foolish we may understand the godly and the wicked; the godly die, and their death is their deliverance; the wicked perish, and their death is their destruction; but, however, they leave their wealth to others. (1.) They cannot continue with it, nor will it serve to procure them a reprieve. That is a frivolous plea, though once it served a turn (Jer. 41:8), *Slay us not, for we have treasures in the field.* (2.) They cannot carry it away with them, but must leave it behind them. (3.) They cannot foresee who will enjoy it when they have left it; they must leave it to others, but to whom they know not, perhaps to a fool (Eccl. 2:19), perhaps to an enemy.

3. That, as their wealth will stand them in no stead in a dying hour, so neither will their honour (*v.* 12): *Man, being in honour, abides not.* We will suppose a man advanced to the highest pinnacle of preferment, as great and happy as the world can make him, man in splendour, man at his best estate, surrounded and supported with all the advantages he can desire; yet then he abides not. His honour does not continue; that is a fleeting shadow. He himself does not, he tarries not all night; this world is an inn, in which his stay is so short that he can scarcely be said to get a night's lodging in it; so little rest is there in these things; he has but a baiting time. *He is like the beasts that perish;* that is, he must as certainly die as the beasts, and his death will be as final a period to his state in this world as theirs is; his dead body likewise will putrefy as theirs does; and (as Dr. Hammond observes) frequently the greatest honours and wealth, unjustly gotten by the parent, descend not to any one of his posterity (as the beasts, when they die, leave nothing behind them to their young ones, but the wide world to feed in), but fall into other hands immediately, for which he never designed to gather them.

4. That their condition on the other side of death will be very miserable. The world they dote upon will not only not save them from death, but will sink them so much the lower into hell (*v.* 14): *Like sheep they are laid in the grave.* Their prosperity did but feed them like sheep for the slaughter (Hos. 4:16), and then death comes, and shuts them up in the grave like fat sheep in a fold, *to be brought forth to the day of wrath,* Job 21:30. Multitudes of them, like flocks of sheep dead of some disease, are thrown into the grave, and there death shall feed on them, the second death, *the worm that dies not,* Job 24:20. Their own guilty consciences, like so many vultures, shall be continually preying upon them, with, *Son, remember,* Lu. 16:25. Death insults and triumphs over them, as it is represented in the fall of the king of Babylon, at which *hell from beneath is moved,* Isa. 14:9, etc. While a saint can ask proud Death, *Where is thy sting?* Death will ask the proud sinner, *Where is thy wealth, thy pomp?* and the more he was fattened with prosperity the more sweetly will death feed on him. And in the morning of the resurrection, when all that sleep in the dust shall awake (Dan. 12:2), *the upright shall have dominion over them,* shall not only be advanced to the highest dignity and honour when they are filled with ever-

lasting shame and contempt, elevated to the highest heavens when they are sunk to the lowest hell, but they shall be assessors with Christ in passing judgment upon them, and shall applaud the justice of God in their ruin. When the rich man in hell begged that Lazarus might bring him a drop of water to cool his tongue he owned that that upright man had dominion over him, as the foolish virgins also owned the dominion of the wise, and that they lay much at their mercy, when the begged, *Give us of your oil.* Let this comfort us in reference to the oppressions which the upright are now often groaning under, and the dominion which the wicked have over them. The day is coming when the tables will be turned (Esther 9:1) and the upright will have the dominion. Let us now judge of things as they will appear at that day. But what will become of all the beauty of the wicked? Alas! that shall all be *consumed in the grave from their dwelling;* all that upon which they valued themselves, and for which others caressed and admired them, was adventitious and borrowed; it was paint and varnish, and they will rise in their own native deformity. The beauty of holiness is that which the grave, that consumes all other beauty, cannot touch, or do any damage to. Their beauty shall consume, the grave (or hell) being a habitation to every one of them; and what beauty can be there where there is nothing but the blackness of darkness for ever?

Verses 15–20

Good reason is here given to good people,

I. Why they should not be afraid of death. There is no cause for that fear if they have such a comfortable prospect as David here has of a happy state on the other side death, *v.* 15. He had shown (*v.* 14) how miserable the dead are that die in their sins, where he shows how blessed the dead are that die in the Lord. The distinction of men's outward condition, how great a difference soever it makes in life, makes none at death; rich and poor meet in the grave. But the distinction of men's spiritual state, though, in this life, it makes a small difference, where all things come alike to all, yet, at and after death, it makes a very great one. *Now he is comforted, and thou art tormented.* The righteous has hope in his death, so has David here hope in God concerning his soul. Note, The believing hopes of the soul's redemption from the grave, and reception to glory, are the great support and joy of the children of God in a dying hour. They hope,

I. That God will redeem their souls from the power of the grave, which includes, (1.) The preserving of the soul from going to the grave with the body. The grave has a power over the body, by virtue of the sentence (Gen. 3:19), and it is cruel enough in executing that power (Cant. 8:6); but is has no such power over the soul. It has power to silence, and imprison, and consume the body; but the soul then moves, and acts, and converses, more freely than ever (Rev. 6:9, 10); it is immaterial and immortal. When death breaks the dark lantern, yet it does not extinguish the candle that was pent up in it. (2.) The reuniting of the soul and body at the resurrection. The soul is often put for the life; that indeed falls under the power of the grave for a time, but is hall, at length, be redeemed from it, when *mortality shall be swallowed up of life.* The God of life, that was its Creator at first, can and will be its Redeemer at last. (3.) The salvation of the soul from eternal ruin: *"God shall redeem my soul from the sheol of hell* (*v.* 15), the wrath to come, that pit of destruction into which the wicked shall be cast," *v.* 14. It is a great comfort to dying saints that they shall not be hurt of the second death (Rev. 2:11), and therefore the first death has no sting and the grave no victory.

2. That he will receive them to himself. He redeems their souls, that he may receive them. Ps. 31:5, *Into thy hands I commit my spirit, for thou has redeemed it.* He will receive them into his favour, will admit them into his kingdom, into the mansions that he prepared for them (Jn. 14:2, 3), those everlasting habitations, Lu. 16:9.

II. Why they should not be afraid of the prosperity and power of wicked people in this world, which, as it is their pride and joy, has often been the envy, and grief, and terror of the righteous, which yet, all things considered, there is no reason for.

1. He supposes the temptation very strong to envy the prosperity of sinners, and to be afraid that they will carry all before them with a high hand, that with their wealth and interest they will run down religion and religious people, and that they will be found the truly happy people; for he supposes, (1.) That they are made rich, and so are enabled to give law to all about them and have every thing at command. *Pecuniae obediunt omnes et omnia — Every person and every thing obey the commanding influence of money.* (2.) That the glory of their house, from very small beginnings, is increased greatly, which naturally makes men haughty, insolent, and imperious, Ps. 5:16. Thus they seem to be the favourites of heaven, and therefore formidable. (3.) That they are very easy and secure in themselves and in their own minds (*v.* 18): *In his life-time he blessed his soul;* that is, he thought himself a very happy man, such a one as he would be, and a very good man, such a one as he should be, because he prospered in the world. He blessed his soul, as that rich fool who said to his soul, *"Soul, take thy ease,* and be not disturbed either with cares and fears about the world or with the rebukes and admonitions of conscience. All is well, and will be well for ever." Note, [1.] It is of great consequence to consider what that is in which we bless our souls, upon the score of which we think well of ourselves. Believers *bless themselves in the God of truth* (Isa. 65:16) and think themselves happy if he be theirs; carnal people bless themselves in the wealth of the world, and think themselves happy if they have abundance of that. [2.] There are many whose precious souls lie under God's curse, and yet they do themselves bless them; they applaud that in themselves which God condemns, and speak peace to themselves when God denounces war against them. Yet this is not all. (4.) They are in good reputation among their neighbours: *"Men will praise thee,* and cry thee up, as having done well for thyself in raising such an estate and family." This is the sentiment of all the children of this world, that those do best for themselves that do most for their bodies, by heaping up riches, though, at the same time, nothing is done for the soul, nothing for eternity; and accordingly they *bless the covetous, whom the Lord abhors,* Ps. 10:3. If men were to be our judges, it were our wisdom thus to recommend ourselves to their good opinion: but what will it avail us to be approved of men if God condemn us? Dr. Hammond understands this of the good man here spoken to, for it is the second person, not of the wicked man spoken of: *"He, in his life-time, blessed his soul, but thou shalt be praised for doing well unto thyself.* The worldling magnified himself; but thou that dost not, like him, speak well of thyself, but do well for thyself, in securing thy eternal welfare, thou shalt be praised, if not of men, yet of God, which will be thy everlasting honour."

2. He suggests that which is sufficient to take off the strength of the temptation, by directing us to look forward to the end of prosperous sinners (Ps. 73:17): "Think what they will be in the other world, and you will see no cause to envy them what they are and have in this world."

(1.) In the other world they will be never the better for all the wealth and prosperity they are now so fond of. It is a miserable portion, which will not last so long as they must (*v.* 17): *When he dies* it is taken for granted that he goes into another world himself, but *he shall carry nothing away with him* of all that which he has been so long heaping up. The greatest and wealthiest cannot therefore be the happiest, because they are never the better for their living in this world; as they came naked into it, they shall go naked out of it. But those have something to show in the other world for their living in this world who can say, through grace, that though they came corrupt, and sinful, and spiritually naked, into it, they go renewed, and sanctified, and well clothed with the righteousness of Christ, out of it. Those that are rich in the graces and comforts of the Spirit have something which, when they die, they shall carry away with them, something which death cannot strip them of, nay, which death will be the improvement of; but, as for worldly possessions, as we *brought nothing into the world* (what we have we had from others), so it is certain that we shall carry nothing out, but leave it to others, 1 Tim. 6:7. They shall descend, but *their glory,* that which they called and counted their glory, and gloried in, *shall not descend after them* to lessen the disgrace of death and the grave, to bring them off in the judgment, or abate the torments of hell. Grace is glory that will ascend with us, but no earthly glory will descend after us.

(2.) In the other world they will be infinitely the worse for all their abuses of the wealth and prosperity they enjoyed in this world (*v.* 19): *The soul shall go to the generation of his fathers,* his worldly wicked fathers, whose sayings he approved and whose steps he trod in, his fathers who would not hearken to the word of God, Zec. 1:4. He shall go to be there where they are that shall never see light, shall never have the least glimpse of comfort and joy, being condemned to utter darkness. Be not afraid then of the pomp and power of wicked people; for the end of the man that is in honour, if he be not wise and good, will be miserable; if he understand not, he is to be pitied rather than envied. A fool, a wicked man, in honour, is really as despicable an animal as any under the sun; he is *like the beasts that perish* (*v.* 20); nay, it is better to be a beast than to be a man that makes himself like a beast. Men in honour that understand, that know and do their duty and make conscience of it, are as gods, and children of the Most High. But men in honour that understand not, that are proud, and sensual, and oppressive, are as beasts, and they shall perish, like the beasts, ingloriously as to this world, though not, like the beasts, indemnified as to another world. Let prosperous sinners therefore be afraid for themselves, but let not even suffering saints be afraid of them.

PSALM 50

This psalm, as the former, is a psalm of instruction, not of prayer or praise; it is a psalm of reproof and admonition, in singing which we are to teach and admonish one another. In the foregoing psalm, after a general demand of attention, God by his prophet deals (*v.* 3) with the children of this world, to convince them of their sin and folly in setting their hearts upon the wealth of this world; in this psalm, after a like preface, he deals with those that were, in profession, the church's children, to convince them of their sin and folly in placing their religion in ritual services, while they neglected practical godliness; and this is as sure a way to ruin as the other. This psalm is intended, 1. As a proof to the carnal Jews, both those that rested in the external performances of their religion, and were remiss in the more excellent duties of prayer and praise, and those that expounded the law to others, but lived wicked lives themselves. 2. As a prediction of the abolishing of the ceremonial law, and of the introducing of a spiritual way of worship in and by the kingdom of the Messiah, Jn. 4:23, 24. 3. As a representation of the day of judgment, in which God will call men to an account concerning their observance of those things which they have thus been taught; men shall be judged "according to what is written in the books;" and therefore Christ is fitly represented speaking as a Judge, then when he speaks as a Lawgiver. Here is, I. The glorious appearance of the Prince that gives law and judgment (*v.* 1–6). II. Instruction given to his worshippers, to turn their sacrifices into prayers (*v.* 7–15). III. A rebuke to those that pretend to worship God, but live in disobedience to his commands (*v.* 16–20), their doom read (*v.* 21, 22), and warning given to all to look to their conversation as well as to their devotions (*v.* 23). These instructions and admonitions we must take to ourselves, and give to one another, in singing this psalm.

A psalm of Asaph.

Verses 1–6

It is probable that Asaph was not only the chief musician, who was to put a tune to this psalm, but that he was himself the penman of it; for we read that in Hezekiah's time they praised God *in the words of David and of Asaph the seer,* 2 Chr. 29:30. Here is,

I. The court called, in the name of the King of kings (*v.* 2): *The mighty God, even the Lord, hath spoken* — El, Elohim, Jehovah, the God of infinite power justice and mercy, Father, Son, and Holy Ghost. God is the Judge, the Son of God came for judgement into the world, and the Holy Ghost is the Spirit of judgment. All the earth is called to attend, not only because the controversy God had with his people Israel for their hypocrisy and ingratitude might safely be referred to any man of reason (nay, let the house of Israel itself *judge between God and his vineyard,* Isa. 5:3), but because all the children of men are concerned to know the right way of worshipping God, in spirit and in truth, because when the kingdom of the Messiah should be set up all should be instructed in the evangelical worship, and invited to join in it (see Mal. 1:11, Acts 10:34), and because in the day of final judgment all nations shall be gathered together to receive their doom, and every man shall give an account of himself unto God.

II. The judgment set, and the Judge taking his seat. As, when God gave the law to Israel in the wilderness, it is said, *He came from Sinai, and rose up from Seir, and shone forth from Mount Paran, and came with ten thousands of his saints, and then from his right hand went a fiery law* (Deu. 33:2), so, with allusion to that, when God comes to reprove them for their hypocrisy, and to send forth his gospel to supersede the legal institutions, it is said here, 1. That *he shall shine out of Zion,* as then from the top of Sinai, *v.* 2. Because in Zion his oracle was now fixed, thence his judgments upon that provoking people denounced, and thence the orders issued for the execution of them (Joel 2:1): *Blow you the trumpet in Zion.* Sometimes there are more than ordinary appearances of God's presence and power working with and by his word and ordinances, for the convincing of men's consciences and the reforming and refining of his church; and then God, who always dwells in Zion, may be said to *shine out of Zion.* Moreover, he may be said to *shine out of Zion* because the gospel, which set up spiritual worship, was to *go forth from Mount Zion* (Isa. 2:3, Mic. 4:2), and the preachers of it were to *begin at Jerusalem* (Lu. 24:47), and Christians are said to come unto Mount Zion, to receive their instructions, Heb. 12:22, 28. Zion is here called *the perfection of beauty,* because it was the holy hill; and holiness is indeed the perfection of beauty. 2. That he *shall come, and not keep silence,* shall no longer seem to wink at the sins of men, as he had done (*v.* 21), but shall show his displeasure at them, and shall also cause that mystery to be published to the world by his holy apostles which had long *lain hid, that the Gentiles should be fellow-heirs* (Eph. 3:5, 6) and that the partition-wall of the ceremonial law should be taken down; this shall now no longer be concealed. In the great day *our God shall come and shall not keep silence,* but shall make those to hear his judgment that would not hearken to his law. 3. That his appearance should be very majestic and terrible: *A fire shall devour before him.* The fire of his judgments shall make way for the rebukes of his word, in order to the awakening of the hypocritical nation of the Jews, that the sinners in Zion, being afraid of that devouring fire (Isa. 33:14), might be startled out of their sins. When his gospel kingdom was to be set up Christ *came to send fire on the earth,* Lu. 12:49. The Spirit was given in cloven tongues as of fire, introduced by a rushing mighty wind, which was very tempestuous, Acts 2:2, 3. And in the last judgment Christ shall come in flaming fire, 2 Th. 1:8. See Dan. 7:9; Heb. 10:27. 4. That as on Mount Sinai he came with *ten thousands of his saints,* so he shall now *call to the heavens from above,* to take notice of this solemn process (*v.* 4), as Moses often *called heaven and earth to witness* against Israel (Deu. 4:26, 31:28, 32:1), and God by his prophets, Isa. 1:2; Mic. 6:2. The equity of the judgment of the great day will be attested and applauded by heaven and earth, by saints and angels, even all the holy myriads.

III. The parties summoned (*v.* 5): *Gather my saints together unto me.* This may be understood either, 1. Of saints indeed: "Let them be gathered to God through Christ; let the few pious Israelites be set by themselves;" for to them the following denunciations of wrath do not belong; rebukes to hypocrites ought not to be terrors to the upright. When God will reject the services of those that only offered sacrifice, resting in the outside of the performance, he will graciously accept those who, in sacrificing, *make a covenant with him,* and so attend to and answer the end of the institution of sacrifices. The design of the preaching of the gospel, and the setting up of Christ's kingdom, was to gather together in one the children of God, Jn. 11:52. And at the second coming of Jesus Christ all his saints shall be *gathered together unto him* (2 Th. 2:1) to be assessors with him in the judgment; for *the saints shall judge the world,* 1 Co. 6:2. Now it is here given as a character of the saints that they have made a covenant with God by sacrifice. Note, (1.) Those only shall be gathered to God as his saints who have, in sincerity, covenanted with him, who have taken him to be their God and given up themselves to him to be his people, and thus have joined themselves unto the Lord. (2.) It is only by sacrifice, by Christ the great sacrifice (from whom all the legal sacrifices derived what value they had), that we poor sinners can covenant with God so as to be accepted of him. There must be an atonement made for the breach of the first covenant before we can be admitted again into covenant. Or, 2. It may be understood of saints in profession, such as the people of Israel were, who are called *a kingdom of priests* and *a holy nation,* Ex. 19:6. They were, as a body politic, taken into covenant with God, the covenant of peculiarity; and it was done with great solemnity, *by sacrifice,* Ex. 24:8. "Let them come and hear what God has to say to them; let them receive the reproofs God sends them now by his prophets, and the gospel he will, in due time, send them by his Son, which shall supersede the ceremonial law. If these be slighted, let them expect to hear from God another way, and to be judged by that word which they will not be ruled by."

IV. The issue of this solemn trial foretold (*v.* 6): *The heavens shall declare his righteousness,* those heavens that were called to be witnesses to the trial (*v.* 4); the *people in heaven shall say, Hallelujah. True and righteous are his judgments,* Rev. 19:1, 2. The righteousness of God in all the rebukes of his word and providence, in the establishment of his gospel (which *brings in an everlasting righteousness,* and in which *the righteousness of God is revealed*), and especially in the judgment of the great day, is what the heavens will declare; that is, 1. It will be universally known, and proclaimed to all the world. *As the heavens declare the glory,* the wisdom and power, of God the Creator (Ps. 19:1), so they shall no less openly declare the glory, the justice and righteousness, of God the *Judge;* and so loudly do they proclaim both that *there is no speech nor language where their voice is not heard,* as it follows there, *v.* 3. 2. It will be incontestably owned and proved; who can deny what the heavens declare? Even sinners' own consciences will subscribe to it, and hell as well as heaven will be forced to acknowledge the righteousness of God. The reason given is, *for God is Judge himself,* and therefore, (1.) He will be just; for it is impossible he should do any wrong to any of his creatures, he never did, nor ever will. When men are employed to judge for him they may do unjustly; but, when he is Judge himself, there can be no injustice done. *Is God unrighteous, who takes vengeance?* The apostle, for this reason, startles at the thought of it; *God forbid! for then how shall God judge the world?* Rom. 3:5, 6. These decisions will be perfectly just, for against them there will lie no exception, and from them there will lie no appeal. (2.) He will be justified; *God is Judge,* and therefore he will not only execute justice, but he will oblige all to own it; for he *will be clear when he judges,* Ps. 51:4.

Verses 7–15

God is here dealing with those that placed all their religion in the observances of the ceremonial law, and thought those sufficient.

I. He lays down the original contract between him and Israel, in which they had avouched him to be their God, and he them to be his people, and so both parties were agreed (*v.* 7): *Hear, O my people! and I will speak.* Note, It is justly expected that whatever others doe, when he speaks, his people should give ear; who will, if they do not? And then we may comfortably expect that God will speak to us when we are ready to hear what he says; even when he testifies against us in the rebukes and threatenings of his word and providences we must be forward to hear what he says, to hear even *the rod and him that has appointed it.*

II. He puts a slight upon the legal sacrifices, *v.* 8, etc. Now,

1. This may be considered as looking back to the use of these under the law. God had a controversy with the Jews; but what was the ground of the controversy? Not their neglect of the ceremonial institutions; no, they had not been wanting in the observance of them, their burnt-offerings had been continually before God, they took a pride in them, and hoped by their offerings to procure a dispensation for their lusts, as the adulterous woman, Prov. 7:14. Their constant sacrifices, they thought, would both expiate and excuse their neglect of the weightier matters of the law. Nay, if they had, in some degree, neglected these institutions, yet that should not have been the cause of God's quarrel with them, for it was but a small offence in comparison with the immoralities of their conversation. They thought God was mightily beholden to them for the many sacrifices they had brought to his altar, and that they had made him very much their debtor by them, as if he could not h have maintained his numerous family of priests without their contributions; but God here shows them the contrary, (1.) That he did not need their sacrifices. What occasion had he for their bullocks and goats who has the command of all *the beasts of the forest,* and the *cattle upon a thousand hills* (*v.* 9, 10), has an incontestable propriety in them and dominion over them, has them all always under his eye and within his reach, and can make what use he pleases of them; they all wait on him, and are all at his disposal? Ps. 104:27–29. Can we add any thing to his store whose all the wild fowl and wild beasts are, the world itself and the fulness thereof? *v.* 11, 12. God's infinite self-sufficiency proves our utter insufficiency to add any thing to him. (2.) That he could not be benefited by their sacrifices. Their goodness, of this kind, could not possibly extend to him, nor, if they were in this matter righteous, was he the better (*v.* 13): *Will I eat the flesh of bulls?* It is as absurd to think that their sacrifices could, of themselves, and by virtue of any innate excellency in them, add any pleasure of praise to God, as it would be to imagine that an infinite Spirit could be supported by meat and drink, as our bodies are. It is said indeed of the demons whom the Gentiles worshipped that they did *eat the fat of their sacrifices, and drink the wine of their drink-offerings* (Deu. 32:38): they regaled themselves in the homage they robbed the true God of; but will the great Jehovah be thus entertained? No; *to obey is better than sacrifice,* and to love God and our neighbour *better than all burnt-offerings,* so much better that God by his prophets often told them that their sacrifices were not only not acceptable, but abominable, to him, while they lived in sin; instead of pleasing him, he looked upon them as a mockery, and therefore an affront and provocation to him; see Prov. 15:8; Isa. 1:11, etc.; 66:3; Jer. 6:20; Amos 5:21. They are therefore here warned not to rest in these performances; but to conduct themselves, in all other instances, towards God as their God.

2. This may be considered as looking forward to the abolishing of these by the gospel of Christ. Thus Dr. Hammond understands it. When God shall set up the kingdom of the Messiah he shall abolish the old way of worship by sacrifice and offerings; he will no more have those to be *continually before him* (*v.* 8); he will no more require of his worshippers to bring him their bullocks and their goats, to be burnt upon his altar, *v.* 9. For indeed he never appointed this as that which he had any need of, or took any pleasure in, for, besides that all we have is his already, he has far more beasts in the forest and upon the mountains, which we know nothing of nor have any property in, than we have in our folds; but he instituted it to prefigure the great sacrifice which his own Son should in the fulness of time offer upon the cross, to make atonement for sin, and all the other spiritual sacrifices of acknowledgment with which God, through Christ, will be well pleased.

III. He directs to the best sacrifices of prayer and praise as those which, under the law, were preferred before all burn-offerings and sacrifices, and on which then the greatest stress was laid, and which now, under the gospel, come in the room of those carnal ordinances which were imposed until the times of reformation. He shows us here (*v.* 14, 15) what is good, and what the Lord our God requires of us, and will accept, when sacrifices are slighted and superseded. 1. We must make a penitent acknowledgment of our sins: *Offer to God confession,* so some read it, and understand it of the confession of sin, in order to our giving glory to God and taking shame to ourselves, that we may never return to it. *A broken and contrite heart* is the sacrifice which *God will not despise,* Ps. 51:17. If the sin was not abandoned the sin-offering was not accepted. 2. We must give God thanks for his mercies to us: *Offer to God thanksgiving,* every day, often every day *(seven times a day will I praise thee),* and upon special occasions; and *this shall please the Lord,* if it come from a humble thankful heart, full of love to him and joy in him, *better than an ox or bullock that has horns and hoofs,* Ps. 69:30, 31. 3. We must make conscience of performing our covenants with him: *Pay thy vows to the Most High,* forsake thy sins, and do thy duty better, pursuant to the solemn promises thou has made him to that purport. When we give God thanks for any mercy we have received we must be sure to pay the vows we made to him when we were in the pursuit of the mercy, else our thanksgivings will not be accepted. Dr. Hammond applies this to the great gospel ordinance of the eucharist, in which we are to give thanks to God for his great love in sending his Son to save us, and to pay our vows of love and duty to him, and to give alms. Instead of all the Old Testament types of a Christ to come, we have that blessed memorial of a Christ already come. 4. In the day of distress we must address ourselves to God by faithful and fervent prayer (*v.* 15): *Call upon me in the day of trouble,* and not upon any other god. Our troubles, though we see them coming from God's hand, must drive us to him, and not drive us from him. We must thus acknowledge him in all our ways, depend upon his wisdom, power, and goodness, and refer ourselves entirely to him, and so give him glory. This is a cheaper, easier, readier way of seeking his favour than by a peace-offering, and yet more acceptable. 5. When he, in answer to our prayers, delivers us, as he has promised to do in such way and time as he shall think fit, we must glorify him, not only by a grateful mention of his favour, but by living to his praise. Thus must we keep up our communion with God, meeting him with our prayers when he afflicts us and with our praises when he delivers us.

Verses 16–23

God, by the psalmist, having instructed his people in the right way of worshipping him and keeping up their communion with him, here directs his speech to the wicked, to hypocrites, whether they were such as professed the Jewish or the Christian religion: hypocrisy is wickedness for which God will judge. Observe here,

I. The charge drawn up against them. 1. They are charged with invading and usurping the honours and privileges of religion (*v.* 16): *What has thou to do,* O wicked man! *to declare my statutes?* This is a challenge to those that rare really profane, but seemingly godly, to show what title they have to the cloak of religion, and by what authority they wear it, when they use it only to cover and conceal the abominable impieties of their hearts and lives. Let them make out their claim to it if they can. Some think it points prophetically at the scribes and Pharisees that were the teachers and leaders of the Jewish church at the time when the kingdom of the Messiah, and that evangelical way of worship spoken of in the foregoing verses, were to be set up. They violently opposed that great revolution, and used all the power and interest which they had by siting in Moses's seat to hinder it; but the account which our blessed Saviour gives of them (Mt. 23), and St. Paul (Rom. 2:21, 22), makes this expostulation here agree very well to them. They took on them to declare God's statues, but they hated Christ's instruction; and therefore what had they to do to expound the law, when they rejected the gospel? But it is applicable to all those that are practicers of iniquity, and yet professors of piety, especially if withal they be preachers of it. Note, It is very absurd in itself, and a great affront to the God of heaven, for those that are wicked and ungodly to declare his statutes and to take his covenant in their mouths. It is very possible, and too common, for those that declare God's statutes to others to live in disobedience to them themselves, and for those that take God's covenant in their mouths yet in their hearts to continue their covenant with sin and death; but they are guilty of a usurpation, they take to themselves an honour which they have no title to, and there is a day coming when they will be thrust out as intruders. *Friend, how camest thou in hither?* 2. They are charged with transgressing and violating the laws and precepts of religion. (1.) They are charged with a daring contempt of the word of God (*v.* 17): *Thou hatest instruction.* They loved to give instruction, and to tell others what they should do, for this fed their pride and made them look great, and by this craft they got their living; but they hated to receive instruction from God himself, for that would be a check upon them and a mortification to them. "Thou hatest discipline, the reproofs of the word and the rebukes of Providence." No wonder that those who hate to be reformed hate the means of reformation. *Thou castest my words behind thee.* They seemed to set God's words before them, when they sat in Moses's seat, and undertook to teach others out of the law (Rom. 2:19); but in their conversations they cast God's word behind them, and did not care for seeing that rule which they were resolved not to be ruled by. This is despising the commandment of the Lord. (2.) A close confederacy with the worst of sinners (*v.* 18): *"When thou sawest a thief,* instead of reproving him and witnessing against him, as those should do that declare God's statutes, *thou consentedst with him,* didst approve of his practices, and desire to be a partner with him and to share in the profits of his cursed trade; *and thou hast been partaker with adulterers,* hast done as they did, and encouraged them to go on in their wicked courses, hast done these things and hast *had pleasure in those that do them,"* Rom. 1:32. (3.) A constant persisting in the worst of tongue-sins (*v.* 19): *"Thou givest thy mouth to evil,* not only allowest thyself in, but addictest thyself wholly to, all manner of evil-speaking." [1.] Lying: *Thy tongue frames deceit,* which denotes contrivance and deliberation in lying. It *knits* or *links* deceit, so some. One lie begets another, and one fraud requires another to cover it. [2.] Slandering (*v.* 20): *"Thou sittest, and speakest against thy brother,* dost basely abuse and misrepresent him, magisterially judge and censure him, and pass sentence upon him, as if you wert his master to whom he must stand or fall, whereas he is thy brother, as good as thou art, and upon the level with thee, for he is *thy own mother's son.* He is thy near relation, whom thou oughtest to love, to vindicate, and stand up for, if others abused him; yet thou dost thyself abuse him, whose faults thou oughtest to cover and make the best of; if really he had done amiss, yet thou dost most falsely and unjustly charge him with that which he is innocent of; *thou sittest* and doest this, as a judge upon the bench, with authority; thou sittest in the seat of the scornful, to deride and backbite those whom thou oughtest to respect and be kind to." Those that do ill themselves commonly delight in speaking ill of others.

II. The proof of this charge (*v.* 21): *"These things thou hast done;* the fact is too plain to be denied, the fault too bad to be excused; these things God knows, and thy own heart knows, thou hast done." The sins of sinners will be proved upon them, beyond contradiction, in the judgment of the great day: *"I will reprove thee,* or convince thee, so that thou shalt have not one word to say for thyself." The day is coming when impenitent sinners will have their mouths for ever stopped and be struck speechless. What confusion will they be filled with when God shall set their sins in order before their eyes! They would not see their sins to their humiliation, but cast them behind their backs, covered them, and endeavoured to forget them, nor would they suffer their own consciences to put them in mind of them; but the day is coming when God will make them see their sins to their everlasting shame and terror; he will set them in order, original sin, actual sins, sins against the law, sins against the gospel, against the first table, against the second table, sins of childhood and youth, of riper age, and old age. He will set them in order, as the witnesses are set in order, and called in order, against the criminal, and asked what they have to say against him.

III. The Judge's patience, and the sinner's abuse of that patience: *"I kept silence,* did not give thee any disturbance in thy sinful way, but let thee alone to take thy course; sentence against thy evil works was respited, and not executed speedily." Note, The patience of God is very great towards provoking sinners. He sees their sins and hates them; it would be neither difficulty nor damage to him to punish them, and yet he waits to be gracious and gives them space to repent, that he may render them inexcusable if they repent not. His patience is the more wonderful because the sinner makes such an ill use of it: *"Thou thoughtest that I was altogether such a one as thyself,* as weak and forgetful as thyself, as false to my word as thyself, nay, as much a friend to sin as thyself." Sinners take God's silence for consent and his patience for connivance; and therefore the longer they are reprieved the more are their hearts hardened; but, if they turn not, they shall be made to see their error when it is too late, and that the God they provoke is just, and holy, and terrible, and not such a one as themselves.

IV. The fair warning given of the dreadful doom of hypocrites (*v.* 22): *"Now consider this, you that forget God,* consider that God knows and keeps account of all your sins, that he will call you to an account for them, that patience abused will turn into the greater wrath, that though you forget God and your duty to him he will not forget you and your rebellions against him: consider this in time, before it be too late; for if these things be not considered, and the consideration of them improved, he will *tear you in pieces, and there will be none to deliver."* It is the doom of hypocrites to be *cut asunder,* Mt. 24:51. Note, 1. Forgetfulness of God is at the bottom of all the wickedness of the wicked. Those that know God, and yet do not obey him, do certainly forget him. 2. Those that forget God forget themselves; and it will never be right with them till they consider, and so recover themselves. Consideration is the first step towards conversion. 3. Those that will not consider the warnings of God's word will certainly be torn in pieces by the executions of his wrath. 4. When God comes to tear sinners in pieces, there is no delivering them out of his hand. They cannot deliver themselves, nor can any friend they have in the world deliver them.

V. Full instructions given to us all how to prevent this fearful doom. Let us hear the conclusion of the whole matter; we have it, *v.* 23, which directs us what to do that we may attain our chief end. 1. Man's chief end is to glorify God, and we are here told that *whoso offers praise glorifies him;* whether he be Jew or Gentile, those spiritual sacrifices shall be accepted from him. We must praise God, and we must sacrifice praise, direct it to God, as every sacrifice was directed; put it into the hands of the priest, our Lord Jesus, who is also the altar; see that it be made by fire, sacred fire, that it be kindled with the flame of holy and devout affection; we must be fervent in spirit, praising the Lord. This he is pleased, in infinite condescension, to interpret as glorifying him. Hereby we give him the glory due to his name and do what we can to advance the interests of his kingdom among men. 2. Man's chief end, in conjunction with this, is to enjoy God; and we are here told that those who *order their conversation aright shall see his salvation.* (1.) It is not enough for us to offer praise, but we must withal order our conversation aright. Thanksgiving is good, but thanks-living is better. (2.) Those that would have their conversation right must take care and pains to order it, to dispose it according to rule, to understand their way and to direct it. (3.) Those that take care of their conversation make sure their salvation; them God will make to see his salvation, for it is a salvation ready to be revealed; he will make them to see it and enjoy it, to see it, and to see themselves happy for ever in it. Note, The right ordering of the conversation is the only way, and it is a sure way, to obtain the great salvation.

PSALM 51

Though David penned this psalm upon a very particular occasion, yet, it is of as general use as any of David's psalms; it is the most eminent of the penitential psalms, and most expressive of the cares and desires of a repenting sinner. It is a pity indeed that in our devout addresses to God we should have any thing else to do than to praise God, for that is the work of heaven; but we make other work for ourselves by our own sins and follies: we must come to the throne of grace in the posture of penitents, to confess our sins and sue for the grace of God; and, if therein we would take with us words, we can nowhere find any more apposite than in this psalm, which is the record of David's repentance for his sin in the matter of Uriah, which was the greatest blemish upon his character: all the rest of his faults were nothing to this; it is said of him (1 Ki. 15:5), That "he turned not aside from the commandment of the Lord all the days of his life, save only in the matter of Uriah the Hittite." In this psalm, I. He confesses his sin (*v.* 3–6). II. He prays earnestly for the pardon of his sin (*v.* 1, 2, 7, 9). III. For peace of conscience (*v.* 8, 12). IV. For grace to go and sin no more (*v.* 10, 11, 14). V. For liberty of access to God (*v.* 15). IV. He promises to do what he could for the good of the souls of others (*v.* 13) and for the glory of God (*v.* 16, 17, 19). And, lastly, concludes with a prayer for Zion and Jerusalem (*v.* 18). Those whose consciences charge them with any gross sin should, with a believing regard to Jesus Christ, the Mediator, again and again pray over this psalm; nay, though we have not been guilty of adultery and murder, or any the like enormous crime, yet in singing it, and praying over it, we may very sensibly apply it all to ourselves, which if we do with suitable affections we shall, through Christ, find mercy to pardon and grace for seasonable help.

To the chief musician. A psalm of David, when Nathan the prophet came unto him, after he had gone in to Bath-sheba.

Verses 1–6

The title has reference to a very sad story, that of David's fall. But, though he fell, he was not utterly cast down, for God graciously upheld him and raised him up. 1. The sin which, in this psalm, he laments, was the folly and wickedness he committed with his neighbour's wife, a sin not to be spoken of, nor thought of, without detestation. His debauching of Bathsheba was the inlet to all the other sins that followed; it was as the letting forth of water. This sin of David's is recorded for warning to all, that he who thinks he stands may take heed lest he fall. 2. The repentance which, in this psalm, he expresses, he was brought to by the ministry of Nathan, who was sent of God to convince him of his sin, after he had continued above nine months (for aught that appears) without any particular expressions of remorse and sorrow for it. But though God may suffer his people to fall into sin, and to lie a great while in it, yet he will, by some means or other, recover them to repentance, bring them to himself and to their right mind again. Herein, generally, he uses the ministry of the word, which yet he is not tied to. But those that have been overtaken in any fault ought to reckon a faithful reproof the greatest kindness that can be don them and a wise reprover their best friend. *Let the righteous smite me, and it shall be excellent oil.* 3. David, being convinced of his sin, poured out his soul to God in prayer for mercy and grace. Whither should backsliding children return, but to the Lord their God, from whom they have backslidden, and who alone can heal their backslidings? 4. He drew up, by divine inspiration, the workings of his heart towards God, upon this occasion, into a psalm, that it might be often repeated, and long after reviewed; and this he committed to the chief musician, to be sung in the public service of the church. (1.) As a profession of his own repentance, which he would have to be generally taken notice of, his sin having been notorious, that the plaster might be as wide as the wound. Those that truly repent of their sins will not be ashamed to own their repentance; but, having lost the honour of innocents, they will rather covet the honour of penitents. (2.) As a pattern to others, both to bring them to repentance by his example and to instruct them in their repentance what to do an what to say. Being converted himself, he thus *strengthens his brethren* (Lu. 22:32), and *for this cause he obtained mercy,* 1 Tim. 1:16.

In these words we have,

I. David's humble petition, *v.* 1, 2. His prayer is much the same with that which our Saviour puts into the mouth of his penitent publican in the parable: *God be merciful to me a sinner!* Lu. 18:13. David was, upon many accounts, a man of great merit; he had not only done much, but suffered much, in the cause of God; and yet, when he is convinced of sin, he does not offer to balance his evil deeds with his good deeds, nor can he think that his services will atone for his offences; but he flies to God's infinite mercy, and depends upon that only for pardon and peace: *Have mercy upon me, O God!* He owns himself obnoxious to God's justice, and therefore casts himself upon his mercy; and it is certain that the best man in the world will be undone if God be not merciful to him. Observe,

1. What his plea is for this mercy: *"have mercy upon me, O God!* not according to the dignity of my birth, as descended from the prince of the tribe of Judah, not according to my public services as Israel's champion, or my public honours as Israel's king;" his plea is not, *Lord, remember David and all his afflictions, how he vowed to build a place for the ark* (Ps. 132:1, 2); a true penitent will make no mention of any such thing; but "Have mercy upon me for mercy's sake. I have nothing to plead with thee but," (1.) "The freeness of thy mercy, according to thy lovingkindness, thy clemency, the goodness of thy nature, which inclines thee to pity the miserable." (2.) "The fulness of thy mercy. There are in thee not only lovingkindness and tender mercies, but abundance of them, a multitude of tender mercies for the forgiveness of many sinners, of many sins, to multiply pardons as we multiply transgressions."

2. What is the particular mercy that he begs — the pardon of sin. *Blot out my transgressions,* as a debt is blotted or crossed out of the book, when either the debtor has paid it or the creditor has remitted it. "Wipe out my transgressions, that they may not appear to demand judgment against me, nor stare me in the face to my confusion and terror." The blood of Christ, sprinkled upon the conscience, to purify and pacify that, blots out the transgression, and, having reconciled us to God, reconciles up to ourselves, *v.* 2. *"Wash me thoroughly from my iniquity;* wash my soul from the guilt and stain of my sin by thy mercy and grace, for it is only from a ceremonial pollution that the water of separation will avail to cleanse me. Multiple to wash me; the stain is deep, for I have lain long soaking in the guilt, so that it will not easily be got out. O wash me much, wash me thoroughly. *Cleanse me from my sin."* Sin defiles us, renders us odious in the sight of the holy God, and uneasy to ourselves; it unfits us for communion with God in grace or glory. When God pardons sin he cleanses us from it, so that we become acceptable to him, easy to ourselves, and have liberty of access to him. Nathan had assured David, upon his first profession of repentance, that his win was pardoned. *The Lord has taken away thy sin; thou shalt not die,* 2 Sa. 12:13. Yet he prays, *Wash me, cleanse, blot out my transgressions;* for God will be sought unto even for that which he has promised; and those whose sins are pardoned must pray that the pardon may be more and more cleared up to them. God had forgiven him, but he could not forgive himself; and therefore he is thus importunate for pardon, as one that thought himself unworthy of it and knew how to value it.

II. David's penitential confessions, *v.* 3–5.

1. He was very free to own his guilt before God: *I acknowledge my transgressions;* this he had formerly found the only way of easing his conscience, Ps. 32:4, 5. Nathan said, *Thou art the man. I am,* says David; *I have sinned.*

2. He had such a deep sense of it that the was continually thinking of it with sorrow and shame. His contrition for his sin was not a slight sudden passion, but an abiding grief: *"My sin is ever before me,* to humble me and mortify me, and make me continually blush and tremble. It is *ever against me"* (so some); "I see it before me as an enemy, accusing and threatening me." David was, upon all occasions, put in mid of his sin, and was willing to be so, for his further abasement. He never walked on the roof of his house without a penitent reflection on his unhappy walk there when thence he saw Bathsheba; he never lay down to sleep without a sorrowful thought of the bed of his uncleanness, never sat down to meat, never sent his servant on an errand, or took his pen in hand, but it put him in mind of his making Uriah drunk, the treacherous message he sent by him, and the fatal warrant he wrote and signed for his execution. Note, The acts of repentance, even for the same sin, must be often repeated. It will be of good use for us to have our sins ever before us, that by the remembrance of our past sins we may be kept humble, may be armed against temptation, quickened to duty, and made patient under the cross.

(1.) He confesses his actual transgressions (*v.* 4): *Against thee, thee only, have I sinned.* David was a very great man, and yet, having done amiss, submits to the discipline of a penitent, and thinks not his royal dignity will excuse him from it. Rich and poor must here meet together; there is one law of repentance for both; the greatest must be judged shortly, and therefore must judge themselves now. David was a very good man, and yet, having sinned, he willingly accommodates himself to the place and posture of a penitent. The best men, if they sin, should give the best example of repentance. [1.] His confession is particular; *"I have done this evil,* this that I am now reproved for, this that my own conscience now upbraids me with." Note, It is good to be particular in the confession of sin, that we may be the more express in praying for pardon, and so may have the more comfort in it. We ought to reflect upon the particular heads of our sins of infirmity and the particular circumstances of our gross sins. [2.] He aggravates the sin which he confesses and lays a load upon himself for it: *Against thee, and in thy sight.* Hence our Saviour seems to borrow the confession which he puts into the mouth of the returning prodigal: *I have sinned against heaven, and before thee,* Lu. 15:18. Two things David laments in his sin: — *First,* That it was committed against God. To him the affront is given, and he is the party wronged. It is his truth that by wilful sin we deny, his conduct that we despise, his command that we disobey, his promise that we distrust, his name that we dishonour, and it is with him that we deal deceitfully and disingenuously. From this topic Joseph fetched the great argument against sin (Gen. 39:9), and David here the great aggravation of it: *Against thee only.* Some make this to intimate the prerogative of his crown, that, as a king, he was not accountable to any but God; but it is more agreeable to his present temper to suppose that it expresses the deep contrition of his soul for his sin, and that it was upon right grounds. He here sinned against Bathsheba and Uriah, against his own soul, and body, and family, against his kingdom, and against the church of God, and all this helped to humble him; but none of these were sinned against so as God was, and therefore this he lays the most sorrowful accent upon: *Against thee only have I sinned. Secondly,* That it was committed in God's sight. "This not only proves it upon me, but renders it exceedingly sinful." This should greatly humble us for all our sins, that they have been committed under the eye of God, which argues either a disbelief of his omniscience or a contempt of his justice. [3.] He justifies God in the sentence passed upon him — that *the sword should never depart from his house,* 2 Sa. 12:10, 11. He is very forward to own his sin, and aggravate it, not only that he might obtain the pardon of it himself, but that by his confession he might give honour to God. *First,* That God might be justified in the threatenings he had spoken by Nathan. "Lord, I have nothing to say against the justice of them; I deserve what is threatened, and a thousand times worse." Thus Eli acquiesced in the like threatenings (1 Sa. 3:18), *It is the Lord.* And Hezekiah (2 Ki. 20:19), *Good is the word of the Lord, which thou hast spoken. Secondly,* That God might be clear when he judged, that is, when he executed those threatenings. David published his confession of sin that when hereafter he should come into trouble none might say God had done him any wrong; for he owns the Lord is righteous: thus will all true penitents justify God by condemning themselves. *Thou art just in all that is brought upon us.*

(2.) He confesses his original corruption (*v.* 5): *Behold, I was shapen in iniquity.* He does not call upon God to behold it, but upon himself. "Come, my soul, look unto the rock out of which I was hewn, and thou wilt find I was shapen in iniquity. Had I duly considered this before, I find I should not have made so bold with the temptation, nor have ventured among the sparks with such tinder in my heart; and so the sin might have been prevented. Let me consider it now, not to excuse or extenuate the sin — *Lord, I did so; but indeed I could not help it, my inclination led me to it"* (for as that plea is false, with due care and watchfulness, and improvement of the grace of God, he might have helped it, so it is what a true penitent never offers to put in), "but let me consider it rather as an aggravation of the sin: Lord, I have not only been guilty of adultery and murder, but I have an adulterous murderous nature; therefore I abhor myself." David elsewhere speaks of the admirable structure of his body (Ps. 139:14, 15); it was *curiously wrought;* and yet here he says it was shapen in iniquity, sin was twisted in with it; not as it came out of God's hands, but as it comes through our parents' loins. He elsewhere speaks of the piety of his mother, that she was God's handmaid, and he pleads his relation to her (Ps. 116:16, 86:16), and yet here he says *she conceived him in sin;* for though she was, by grace, a child of God, she was, by nature, a daughter of Eve, and not excepted from the common character. Note, It is to be sadly lamented by every one of us that we brought into the world with us a corrupt nature, wretchedly degenerated from its primitive purity and rectitude; we have from our birth the snares of sin in our bodies, the seeds of sin in our souls, and a stain of sin upon both. This is what we call *original sin,* because it is as ancient as our original, and because it is the original of all our actual transgressions. This is that foolishness which is bound in the heart of a child, that proneness of evil and backwardness to good which is the burden of the regenerate and the ruin of the unregenerate; it is a bent to backslide from God.

III. David's acknowledgment of the grace of God (*v.* 6), both his good-will towards us (*"thou desirest truth in the inward parts,* thou wouldst have us all honest and sincere, and true to our profession") and his good work in us — *"In the hidden part thou hast made,"* or shalt make, *"me to know wisdom."* Note, 1. Truth and wisdom will go very far towards making a man a good man. A clear head and a sound heart (prudence and sincerity) bespeak the man of God perfect. 2. What God requires of us he himself works in us, and he works it in the regular way, enlightening the mind, and so gaining the will. But how does this come in here? (1.) God is hereby justified and cleared: "Lord, thou was not the author of my sin; there is no blame to be laid upon thee; but I alone must bear it; for thou has many a time admonished me to be sincere, and hast made me to know that which, if I had duly considered it, would have prevented my falling into this sin; had I improved the grace thou hast given me, I should have kept my integrity." (2.) The sin is hereby aggravated: "Lord, thou desirest truth; but where was it when I dissembled with Uriah? *Thou hast made me to know wisdom;* but I have not lived up to what I have known." (3.) He is hereby encouraged, in his repentance, to hope that God would graciously accept him; for, [1.] God had made him sincere in his resolutions never to return to folly again: *Thou desirest truth in the inward part;* this is that which God has an eye to in a returning sinner, that *in his spirit there be no guile,* Ps. 32:2. David was conscious to himself of the uprightness of his heart towards God in his repentance, and therefore doubted not but God would accept him. [2.] He hoped that God would enable him to make good his resolutions, that in the hidden part, in the new man, which is called the *hidden man of the heart* (1 Pt. 3:4), he would make him to know wisdom, so as to discern and avoid the designs of the tempter another time. Some read it as a prayer: "Lord, in this instance, I have done foolishly; for the future make me to know wisdom." Where there is truth God will give wisdom; those that sincerely endeavour to do their duty shall be taught their duty.

Verses 7–13

I. See here what David prays for. Many excellent petitions he here puts up, to which if we do but add, "for Christ's sake," they are as evangelical as any other.

1. He prays that God would cleanse him from his sins and the defilement he had contracted by them (*v.* 7): *"Purge me with hyssop;* that is, pardon my sins, and let me know that they are pardoned, that I may be restored to those privileges which by sin I have forfeited and lost." The expression here alludes to a ceremonial distinction, that of cleansing the leper, or those that were unclean by the touch of a body by sprinkling water, or blood, or both upon them with a bunch of hyssop, by which they were, at length, discharged from the restraints they were laid under by their pollution. "Lord, let me be as well assured of my restoration to thy favour, and to the privilege of communion with thee, as they were thereby assured of their readmission to their former privileges." But it is founded upon gospel-grace: *Purge me with hyssop,* that is, with the blood of Christ applied to my soul by a lively faith, as water of purification was sprinkled with a bunch of hyssop. It is the blood of Christ (which is therefore called *the blood of sprinkling,* Heb. 12:24), that purges the conscience from dead works, from that guilt of sin and dread of God which shut us out of communion with him, as the touch of a dead body, under the law, shut a man out from the courts of God's house. If this blood of Christ, which cleanses from all sin, cleanse us from our sin, then we shall be clean indeed, Heb. 10:2. If we be washed in this fountain opened, we shall be whiter than snow, not only acquitted but accepted; so those are that are justified. Isa. 1:18, *Though your sins have been as scarlet, they shall be white as snow.*

2. He prays that, his sins being pardoned, he might have the comfort of that pardon. He asks not to be comforted till first he is cleansed; but if sin, the bitter root of sorrow, be taken away, he can pray in faith, *"Make me to hear joy and gladness* (*v.* 8), that is, let me have a well-grounded peace, of thy creating, thy speaking, so that the bones which thou hast broken by convictions and threatenings may rejoice, may not only be set again, and eased from the pain, but may be sensibly comforted, and, as the prophet speaks, may flourish as a herb." Note, (1.) The pain of a heart truly broken for sin may well be compared to that of a broken bone; and it is the same Spirit who as a Spirit of bondage smites and wounds and as a Spirit of adoption heals and binds up. (2.) The comfort and joy that arise from a sealed pardon to a penitent sinner are as refreshing as perfect ease from the most exquisite pain. (3.) It is God's work, not only to speak this joy and gladness, but to make us hear it and take the comfort of it. He earnestly desires that God would lift up the light of his countenance upon him, and so put gladness into his heart, that he would not only be reconciled to him, but, which is a further act of grace, let him know that he was so.

3. He prays for a complete and effectual pardon. This is that which he is most earnest for as the foundation of his comfort (*v.* 9): *"Hide thy face from my sins,* that is, be not provoked by them to deal with me as I deserve; they are ever before me, let them be cast behind thy back. *Blot out all my iniquities* out of the book of thy account; blot them out, as a cloud is blotted out and dispelled by the beams of the sun," Isa. 44:22.

4. He prays for sanctifying grace; and this every true penitent is as earnest for as for pardon and peace, *v.* 10. He does not pray, "Lord, preserve me my reputation," as Saul, *I have sinned, yet honour me before this people.* No; his great concern is to get his corrupt nature changed: the sin he had been guilty of was, (1.) An evidence of its impurity, and therefore he prays, *Create in me a clean heart, O God!* He now saw, more than ever, what an unclean heart he had, and sadly laments it, but sees it is not in his own power to amend it, and therefore begs of God (whose prerogative it is to create) that he would create in him a clean heart. He only that made the heart can new-make it; and to his power nothing is impossible. He created the world by the word of his power as the God of nature, and it is by the word of his power as the God of grace that *we are clean* (Jn. 15:3), that we *are sanctified,* Jn. 17:17. (2.) It was the cause of its disorder, and undid much of the good work that had been wrought in him; and therefore he prays, *"Lord, renew a right spirit within me;* repair the decays of spiritual strength which this sin has been the cause of, and set me to rights again." Renew a *constant* spirit within me, so some. He had, in this matter, discovered much inconstancy and inconsistency with himself, and therefore he prays, "Lord, fix me for the time to come, that I may never in like manner depart from thee."

5. He prays for the continuance of God's good-will towards him and the progress of his good work in him, *v.* 11. (1.) That he might never be shut out from God's favour: *"Cast me not away from thy presence,* as one whom thou abhorrest and canst not endure to look upon." He prays that he might not be thrown out of God's protection, but that wherever he went, he might have the divine presence with him, might be under the guidance of his wisdom and in the custody of his power, and that he might not be forbidden communion with God: "Let me not be banished thy courts, but always have liberty of access to thee by prayer." He does not deprecate the temporal judgments which God by Nathan had threatened to bring upon him. "God's will be done; but, Lord, rebuke me no in thy wrath. If the sword come into my house never to depart from it, yet let me have a God to go to in my distresses, and all shall be well." (2.) That he might never be deprived of God's grace: *Take not thy Holy Spirit from me.* He knew he had by his sin grieved the Spirit and provoked him to with draw, and that because he also was flesh God might justly have said that his Spirit should no more strive with him nor work upon him, Gen. 6:3. This he dreads more than any thing. We are undone if God take his Holy Spirit from us. Saul was a sad instance of this. How exceedingly sinful, how exceedingly miserable, was he, when the Spirit of the Lord had departed from him! David knew it, and therefore begs thus earnestly: "Lord, whatever thou take from me, my children, my crown, my life, yet *take not thy Holy Spirit from me"* (see 2 Sa. 7:15), "but continue thy Holy Spirit with me, to perfect the work of my repentance, to prevent my relapse into sin, and to enable me to discharge my duty both as a prince and as a psalmist."

6. He prays for the restoration of divine comforts and the perpetual communications of divine grace, *v.* 12. David finds two ill effects of his sin: — (1.) It had made him sad, and therefore he prays, *Restore unto me the joy of thy salvation.* A child of God knows no true nor solid joy but the joy of God's salvation, joy in God his Saviour and in the hope of eternal life. By wilful sin we forfeit this joy and deprive ourselves of it; our evidences cannot but be clouded and our hopes shaken. When we give ourselves so much cause to doubt of our interest in the salvation, how can we expect the joy of it? But, when we truly repent, we may pray and hope that God will restore to us those joys. Those that sow in penitential tears shall reap in the joys of God's salvation when the times of refreshing shall come. (2.) It had made him weak, and therefore he prays, *"Uphold me with the free Spirit:* I am ready to fall, either into sin or into despair; Lord, sustain me; my own spirit" (though the spirit of a man will go far towards the sustaining of his infirmity) "is not sufficient; if I be left to myself, I shall certainly sink; therefore uphold me with thy Spirit, let him counterwork the evil spirit that would cast me down from my excellency. Thy Spirit is a free spirit, a free gent himself, working freely" (and that makes those free whom he works upon, for where the Spirit of the Lord is there is liberty) — "thy ingenuous princely Spirit." He was conscious to himself of having acted, in the matter of Uriah, very disingenuously and unlike a prince; his behaviour was base and paltry: "Lord," says he, "let thy Spirit inspire my soul with noble and generous principles, that I may always act as becomes me." A free spirit will be a firm and fixed spirit, and will uphold us. The more cheerful we are in our duty the more constant we shall be to it.

II. See what David here promises, *v.* 13. Observe,

1. What good work he promises to do: *I will teach transgressors thy ways.* David had been himself a transgressor, and therefore could speak experimentally to transgressors, and resolves, having himself found mercy with God in the way of repentance, to teach others God's ways, that is, (1.) Our way to God by repentance; he would teach others that had sinned to take the same course that he had taken, to humble themselves, to confess their sins, and seek God's face; and, (2.) God's way towards us in pardoning mercy; how ready he is to receive those that return to him. He taught the former by his own example, for the direction of sinners in repenting; he taught the latter by his own experience, for their encouragement. By this psalm he is, and will be to the world's end, teaching transgressors, telling them what God had done for his soul. Note, Penitents should be preachers. Solomon was so, and blessed Paul.

2. What good effect he promises himself from his doing this: *"Sinners shall be converted unto thee,* and shall neither persist in their wanderings from thee, nor despair of finding mercy in their returns to thee." The great thing to be aimed at in teaching transgressors is their conversion to God; that is a happy point gained, and happy are those that are instrumental to contribute towards it, Jam. 5:20.

Verses 14–19

I. David prays against the guilt of sin, and prays for the grace of God, enforcing both petitions from a plea taken from the glory of God, which he promises with thankfulness to show forth. 1. He prays against the guilt of sin, that he might be delivered from that, and promises that then he would praise God, *v.* 14. The particular sin he prays against is blood-guiltiness, the sin he had now been guilty of, having slain Uriah with the sword of the children of Ammon. Hitherto perhaps he had stopped the mouth of conscience with that frivolous excuse, that he did not kill him himself; but now he was convinced that he was the murderer, and, hearing the blood cry to God for vengeance, he cries to God for mercy: *"Deliver me from blood-guiltiness;* let me not lie under the guilt of this kind which I have contracted, but let it be pardoned to me, and let me never be left to myself to contract the like guilt again." Note, It concerns us all to pray earnestly against the guilt of blood. In this prayer he eyes God as the God of salvation. Note, Those to whom God is the God of salvation he will deliver from guilt; for the salvation he is the God of is salvation from sin. We may therefore plead this with him, "Lord, thou art the God of my salvation, therefore deliver me from the dominion of sin." He promises that, if God would deliver him, *his tongue should sing aloud of his righteousness;* God should have the glory both of pardoning mercy and of preventing grace. God's righteousness is often put for his grace, especially in the great business of justification and sanctification. This he would comfort himself in and therefore sing of; and this he would endeavour both to acquaint and to affect others with; he would *sing aloud* of it. This all those should do that have had the benefit of it, and owe their all to it. 2. He prays for the grace of God and promises to improve that grace to his glory (*v.* 15): *"O Lord! open thou my lips,* not only that I may teach and instruct sinners" (which the best preacher cannot do to any purpose unless God give him the opening of the mouth, and the tongue of the learned), "but *that my mouth may show forth thy praise,* not only that I may have abundant matter for praise, but a heart enlarged in praise." Guilt had closed his lips, had gone near to stop the mouth of prayer; he could not for shame, he could not for fear, come into the presence of that God whom he knew he had offended, much less speak to him; his heart condemned him, and therefore he had little confidence towards God. It cast a damp particularly upon his praises; when he had lost the joys of his salvation his harp was hung upon the willow-trees; therefore he prays, *"Lord, open my life,* put my heart in tune for praise again." To those that are tongue-tied by reason of guilt the assurance of the forgiveness of their sins says effectually, *Ephphatha — Be opened;* and, when the lips are opened, what should they speak but the praises of God, as Zacharias did? Lu. 1:64.

II. David offers the sacrifice of a penitent contrite heart, as that which he knew God would be pleased with. 1. He knew well that the sacrificing of beasts was in itself of no account with God (*v.* 16): *Thou desirest not sacrifice (else would I give it* with all my heart to obtain pardon and peace); *thou delightest not in burnt-offering.* Here see how glad David would have been to give thousands of rams to make atonement for sin. Those that are thoroughly convinced of their misery and danger by reason of sin would spare no cost to obtain the remission of it, Mic. 6:6, 7. But see how little God valued this. As trials of obedience, and types of Christ, he did indeed require sacrifices to be offered; but he had no delight in them for any intrinsic worth or value they had. *Sacrifice and offering thou wouldst not.* As they cannot make satisfaction for sin, so God cannot take any satisfaction in them, any otherwise than as the offering of them is expressive of love and duty to him. 2. He knew also how acceptable true repentance is to God (*v.* 17): *The sacrifices of God are a broken spirit.* See here, (1.) What the good work is that is wrought in every true penitent — a broken spirit, a broken and a contrite heart. It is a work wrought upon the heart; that is it that God looks at, and requires, in all religious exercises, particularly in the exercises of repentance. It is a sharp work wrought there, no less than the breaking of the heart; not in despair (as we say, when a man is undone, His heart is broken), but in necessary humiliation and sorrow for sin. It is a heart breaking with itself, and breaking from its sin; it is a heart pliable to the word of God, and patient under the rod of God, a heart subdued and brought into obedience; it is a heart that is tender, like Josiah's, and trembles at God's word. Oh that there were such a heart in us! (2.) How graciously God is pleased to accept of this. It is *the sacrifices of God,* not one, but many; it is instead of all burnt-offering and sacrifice. The breaking of Christ's body for sin is the only sacrifice of atonement, for no sacrifice but that could take away sin; but the breaking of our hearts for sin is a sacrifice of acknowledgment, a sacrifice of God, for to him it is offered up; he requires it, he prepares it (he provides this lamb for a burnt-offering), and he will accept of it. That which pleased God was not the feeding of a beast, and making much of it, but killing it; so it is not the pampering of our flesh, but the mortifying of it, that God will accept. The sacrifice was bound, was bled, was burnt; so the penitent heart is bound by convictions, bleeds in contrition, and then burns in holy zeal against sin and for God. The sacrifice was offered upon the altar that sanctified the gift; so the broken heart is acceptable to God only through Jesus Christ; there is no true repentance without faith in him; and this is the sacrifice which he will not despise. Men despise that which is broken, but God will not. He despised the sacrifice of torn and broken beasts, but he will not despise that of a torn and broken heart. He will not overlook it; he will not refuse or reject it; though it make God no satisfaction for the wrong done him by sin, yet he does not despise it. The proud Pharisee despised the broken-hearted publican, and he thought very meanly of himself; but God did not despise him. More is implied than is expressed; the great God overlooks heaven and earth, to look with favour upon a *broken and contrite heart,* Isa. 66:1, 2; 57:15.

III. David intercedes for Zion and Jerusalem, with an eye to the honour of God. See what a concern he had,

1. For the good of the church of God (*v.* 18): *Do good in thy good pleasure unto Zion,* that is, (1.) "To all the particular worshippers in Zion, to all that love and fear thy name; keep them from falling into such wounding wasting sins as these of mine; defend and succour all that fear thy name." Those that have been in spiritual troubles themselves know how to pity and pray for those that are in like manner afflicted. Or, (2.) To the public interests of Israel. David was sensible of the wrong he had done to Judah and Jerusalem by his sin, how it had weakened the hands and saddened the hearts of good people, and opened the mouths of their adversaries; he was likewise afraid lest, he being a public person, his sin should bring judgments upon the city and kingdom, and therefore he prays to God to secure and advance those public interests which he had damaged and endangered. He prays that God would prevent those national judgments which his sin had deserved, that he would continue those blessings, and carry on that good work, which it had threatened to retard and put a stop to. He prays, not only that God would do good to Zion, as he did to other places, by his providence, but that he would do it in his *good pleasure,* with the peculiar favour he bore to that place which he had chosen to put his name there, that the walls of Jerusalem, which perhaps were now in the building, might be built up, and that good work finished. Note, [1.] When we have most business of our own, and of greatest importance at the throne of grace, yet then we must not forget to pray for the church of God; nay, or Master has taught us in our daily prayers to begin with that, *Hallowed be thy name, Thy kingdom come.* [2.] The consideration of the prejudice we have done to the public interests by our sins should engage us to do them all the service we can, particularly by our prayers.

2. For the honour of the churches of God, *v.* 19. If God would show himself reconciled to him and his people, as he had prayed, then they should go on with the public services of his house, (1.) Cheerfully to themselves. The sense of God's goodness to them would enlarge their hearts in all the instances and expressions of thankfulness and obedience. They will then come to his tabernacle with burnt-offerings, with whole burnt-offerings, which were intended purely for the glory of God, and they shall offer, not lambs and rams only, but bullocks, the costliest sacrifices, upon his altar. (2.) Acceptably to God: *"Thou shalt be pleased with them,* that is, we shall have reason to hope so when we perceive the sin taken away which threatened to hinder thy acceptance." Note, It is a great comfort to a good man to think of the communion that is between God and his people in their public assemblies, how he is honoured by their humble attendance on him and they are happy in his gracious acceptance of it.

PSALM 52

David, no doubt, was in very great grief when he said to Abiathar (1 Sa. 22:22), "I have occasioned the death of all the persons of thy father's house," who were put to death upon Doeg's malicious information; to give some vent to that grief, and to gain some relief to his mind under it, he penned this psalm, wherein, as a prophet, and therefore with as good an authority as if he had been now a prince upon the throne, I. He arraigns Doeg for what he had done (*v.* 1). II. He accuses him, convicts him, and aggravates his crimes (*v.* 2–4). III. He passes sentence upon him (*v.* 5). IV. He foretels the triumphs of the righteous in the execution of the sentence (*v.* 6, 7). V. He comforts himself in the mercy of God and the assurance he had that he should yet praise him (*v.* 8, 9). In singing this psalm we should conceive a detestation of the sin of lying, foresee the ruin of those that persist in it, and please ourselves with the assurance of the preservation of God's church and people, in spite of all the malicious designs of the children of Satan, that father of lies.

To the chief musician, Maschil. *A psalm* of David, when Doeg the Edomite came and told Saul, and said unto him, David is come to the house of Ahimelech.

Verses 1–5

The title is a brief account of the story which the psalm refers to. David now, at length, saw it necessary to quit the court, and shift for his own safety, for fear of Saul, who had once and again attempted to murder him. Being unprovided wit harms and victuals, he, by a wile, got Ahimelech the priest to furnish him with both. Doeg an Edomite happened to be there, and he went and informed Saul against Ahimelech, representing him as confederate with a traitor, upon which accusation Saul grounded a very bloody warrant, to kill all the priests; and Doeg, the prosecutor, was the executioner, 1 Sa. 22:9, etc. In these verses,

I. David argues the case fairly with this proud and mighty man, *v.* 1. Doeg, it is probably, was mighty in respect of bodily strength; but, if he was, he gained no reputation to it by his easy victory over the unarmed priests of the Lord; it is no honour for those that wear a sword to hector those that wear an ephod. However, he was, by his office, a *mighty man,* for he was set over the servants of Saul, chamberlain of the household. This was he that boasted himself, not only in the power he had to do mischief, but in the mischief he did. Note, It is bad to do ill, but it is worse to boast of it and glory in it when we have done, not only not to be ashamed of a wicked action, but to justify it, not only to justify it, but to magnify it and value ourselves upon it. Those that glory in their sin glory in their shame, and then it becomes yet more shameful; might men are often mischievous men, and *boast of their heart's desire,* Ps. 10:3. It is uncertain how the following words come in: *The goodness of God endures continually.* Some make it the wicked man's answer to this question. The patience and forbearance of God (those great proofs of his goodness) are abused by sinners to the hardening of their hearts in their wicked ways; because sentence against their evil works is not executed speedily, nay, because God is continually doing them good, therefore they boast in mischief; as if their prosperity in their wickedness were an evidence that there is no harm in it. But it is rather to be taken as an argument against him, to show, 1. The sinfulness of his sin: "God is continually doing good, and those that therein are like him have reason to glory in their being so; but thou art continually doing mischief, and therein art utterly unlike him, and contrary to him, and yet gloriest in being so." 2. The folly of it: "Thou thinkest, with the mischief which thou boastest of (so artfully contrived and so successfully carried on), to run down and ruin the people of God; but thou wilt find thyself mistaken: *the goodness of God endures continually* for their preservation, and then they need *not fear what man can do unto them."* The enemies in vain boast in their mischief while we have God's mercy to boast in.

II. He draws up a high charge against him in the court of heaven, as he had drawn up a high charge against Ahimelech in Saul's court, *v.* 2–4. He accuses him of the wickedness of his tongue (that unruly evil, full of deadly poison) and the wickedness of his heart, which that was an evidence of. Four things he charges him with: — 1. Malice. His tongue does *mischief,* not only pricking like a needle, but cutting *like a sharp razor.* Scornful bantering words would not content him; he loved devouring words, words that would ruin the priests of the Lord, whom he hated. 2. Falsehood. It was a *deceitful tongue* that he did this mischief with (*v.* 4); he loved lying (*v.* 3), and this sharp razor did *work deceitfully* (*v.* 2), that is, before he had this occasion given him to discover his malice against the priests, he had acted very plausibly towards them; though he was an Edomite, he attended the altars, and brought his offerings, and paid his respects to the priests, as decently as any Israelite; therein he put a force upon himself (for he was *detained before the Lord*), but thus he gained an opportunity of doing them so much the greater mischief. Or it may refer to the information itself which he gave in against Ahimelech; for the matter of fact was, in substance, true, yet it was misrepresented, and false colours were put upon it, and therefore he might well be said to love lying, and to have a deceitful tongue. He told the truth, but not all the truth, as a witness ought to do; had he told that David made Ahimelech believe he was then going upon Saul's errand, the kindness he showed him would have appeared to be not only not traitorous against Saul, but respectful to him. It will not save us from the guilt of lying to be able to say, "There was some truth in what we said," if we pervert it, and make it to appear otherwise than it was. 3. Subtlety in sin: *"Thy tongue devises mischiefs;* that is, it speaks the mischief which thy heart devises." The more there is of craft and contrivance in any wickedness the more there is of the devil in it. 4. Affection to sin: *"Thou lovest evil more than good;* that is, thou lovest evil, and hast no love at all to that which is good; thou takest delight in lying, and makest no conscience of doing right. Thou wouldst rather please Saul by telling a lie than please God by speaking truth." Those are of Doeg's spirit who, instead of being pleased (as we ought all to be) with an opportunity of doing a man a kindness in his body, estate, or good name, are glad when they have a fair occasion to do a man a mischief, and readily close with an opportunity of that kind; that is loving evil more than good. It is bad to speak devouring words, but it is worse to love them either in others or in ourselves.

III. He reads his doom and denounces the judgments of God against him for his wickedness (*v.* 5): "Thou hast destroyed the priests of the Lord and cut them off, and therefore *God shall likewise destroy thee for ever."* Sons of perdition actively shall be sons of perdition passively, as Judas and the man of sin. Destroyers shall be destroyed; those especially that hate, and persecute, and destroy the priests of the Lord, his ministers and people, who are made to our God priests, a royal priesthood, shall be taken away with a swift and everlasting destruction. Doeg is here condemned, 1. To be driven out of the church: *He shall pluck thee out of the tabernacle,* not thy dwelling-place, but God's (so it is most probably understood); "thou shalt be cut off from the favour of God, and his presence, and all communion with him, and shalt have no benefit either by oracle or offering." Justly was he deprived of all the privileges of God's house who had been so mischievous to his servants; he had come sometimes to God's tabernacle, and attended in his courts, but he was detained there; he was weary of his service, and sought an opportunity to defame his family; it was very fit therefore that he should be taken away, and plucked out thence; we should forbid any one our house that should serve us so. Note, We forfeit the benefit of ordinances if we make an ill use of them. 2. To be driven out of the world; *"He shall root thee out of the land of the living,* in which thou thoughtest thyself so deeply rooted." When good men die they are transplanted from the land of the living on earth, the nursery of the plants of righteousness, to that in heaven, the garden of the Lord, where they shall take root for ever; but, when wicked men die, they are rooted out of the land of the living, to perish for ever, as fuel to the fire of divine wrath. This will be the portion of those that contend with God.

Verses 6–9

David was at this time in great distress; the mischief Doeg had done him was but the beginning of his sorrows; and yet here we have him triumphing, and that is more than rejoicing, in tribulation. Blessed Paul, in the midst of his troubles, is in the midst of his triumphs, 2 Co. 2:14. David here triumphs,

I. In the fall of Doeg. Yet, lest this should look like personal revenge, he does not speak of it as how own act, but the language of other righteous persons. They shall observe God's judgments on Doeg, and speak of them, 1. To the glory of God: *They shall see and fear* (*v.* 6); that is, they shall reverence the justice of God, and stand in awe of him, as a God of almighty power, before whom the proudest sinner cannot stand and before whom therefore we ought every one of us to humble ourselves. Note, God's judgments on the wicked should strike an awe upon the righteous and make them afraid of offending God and incurring his displeasure, Ps. 119:120; Rev. 15:3, 4. 2. To the shame of Doeg. They shall laugh at him, not with a ludicrous, but a rational serious laughter, as *he that sits in heaven shall laugh at him,* Ps. 2:4. He shall appear ridiculous, and worthy to be laughed at. We are told how they shall triumph in God's just judgments on him (*v.* 7): *Lo, this is the man that made not God his strength.* The fall and ruin of a wealthy mighty man cannot but be generally taken notice of, and every one is apt to make his remarks upon it; now this is the remark which the righteous should make upon Doeg's fall, that no better could come of it, since he took the wrong method of establishing himself in his wealth and power. If a newly-erected fabric tumbles down, every one immediately enquires where was the fault in the building of it. Now that which ruined Doeg's prosperity was, (1.) That he did not build it upon a rock: *He made not God his strength,* that is, he did not think that the continuance of his prosperity depended upon the favour of God, and therefore took no care to make sure that favour nor to keep himself in God's love, made no conscience of his duty to him nor sought him in the least. Those wretchedly deceive themselves that think to support themselves in their power and wealth without God and religion. (2.) That he did build it upon the sand. He thought his wealth would support itself: *He trusted in the abundance of his riches,* which, he imagined, were *laid up for many years;* nay, he thought his wickedness would help to support it. He was resolved to stick at nothing for the securing and advancing of his honour and power. Right or wrong, he would get what he could and keep what he had, and be the ruin of any one that stood in his way; and this, he thought, would strengthen him. Those may have any thing that will make conscience of nothing. But now see what it comes to; see what untempered mortar he built his house with, now that it has fallen and he is himself buried in the ruins of it.

II. In his own stability, *v.* 8, 9. "This mighty man is plucked up by the roots; *but I am like a green olive-tree,* planted and rooted, fixed and flourishing; he is turned out of God's dwelling-place, but I am established in it, not detained, as Doeg, by any thing but the abundant satisfaction I meet with there." Note, Those that by faith and love dwell in the house of God shall be like green olive-trees there; the wicked are said to flourish like a green bay-tree (Ps. 37:35), which bears no useful fruit, though it has abundance of large leaves; but the righteous flourish like a green olive-tree, which is fat as well as flourishing (Ps. 92:14) and with *its fatness honours God and man* (Jdg. 9:9), deriving its root and fatness from the good olive, Rom. 11:17. Now what must we do that we may be as green olive-trees? 1. We must live a life of faith and holy confidence in God and his grace? "I see what comes of men's trusting in the abundance of their riches, and therefore *I trust in the mercy of God for ever and ever* — not in the world, but in God, not in my own merit, but in God's mercy, which dispenses its gifts freely, even to the unworthy, and has in it an all-sufficiency to be our portion and happiness." This mercy is for ever; it is constant and unchangeable, and its gifts will continue to all eternity. We must therefore for ever trust in it, and never come off from that foundation. 2. We must live a life of thankfulness and holy joy in God (*v.* 9): *"I will praise thee for ever, because thou hast done it,* has avenged the blood of thy priests upon their bloody enemy, and given him blood to drink, and hast performed thy promise to me," which he was as sure would be done in due time as if it were done already. It contributes very much to the beauty of our profession, and to our fruitfulness in every grace, to be much in praising God; and it is certain that we never want matter for praise. 3. We must live a life of expectation and humble dependence upon God: *"I will wait on thy name;* I will attend upon thee in all those ways wherein thou hast made thyself known, hoping for the discoveries of thy favour to me and willing to tarry till the time appointed for them; *for it is good before thy saints,"* or *in the opinion and judgment of thy saints,* with whom David heartily concurs. *Communis sensus fidelium — All the saints are of this mind,* (1.) That God's name is good in itself, that God's manifestations of himself to his people are gracious and very kind; there is no other name given than his that can be our refuge and strong tower. (2.) That it is very good for us to wait on that name, that there is nothing better to calm and quiet our spirits when they are ruffled and disturbed, and to keep us in the way of duty when we are tempted to use any indirect courses for our own relief, than to *hope and quietly wait for the salvation of the Lord,* Lam. 3:26. All the saints have experienced the benefit of it, who never attended him in vain, never followed his guidance but it ended well, nor were ever made ashamed of their believing expectations from him. What is good before all the saints let us therefore abide and abound in, and in this particularly: *Turn thou to thy God; keep mercy and judgment, and wait on thy God continually,* Hos. 12:6.

PSALM 53

God speaks once, yea, twice, and it were well if man would even then perceive it; God, in this psalm, speaks twice, for this is the same almost verbatim with the fourteenth psalm. The scope of it is to convince us of our sins, to set us a blushing and trembling because of them; and this is what we are with so much difficulty brought to that there is need of line upon line to this purport. The word, as a convincing word, is compared to a hammer, the strokes whereof must be frequently repeated. God, by the psalmist here, I. Shows us how bad we are (*v.* 1). II. Proves it upon us by his own certain knowledge (*v.* 2, 3). III. He speaks terror to persecutors, the worst of sinners (*v.* 4, 5). IV. He speaks encouragement to God's persecuted people (*v.* 6). Some little variation there is between Ps. 14 and this, but none considerable, only between *v.* 5, 6, there, and *v.* 5 here; some expressions there used are here left out, concerning the shame which the wicked put upon God's people, and instead of that, is here foretold the shame which God would put upon the wicked, which alteration, with some others, he made by divine direction when he delivered it the second time to the chief musician. In singing it we ought to lament the corruption of the human nature, and the wretched degeneracy of the world we live in, yet rejoicing in hope of the great salvation.

To the chief musician upon Mahalath, Maschil.
A psalm of David.

Verses 1–6

This psalm was opened before, and therefore we shall here only observe, in short, some things concerning sin, in order to the increasing of our sorrow for it and hatred of it. 1. The fact of sin. Is that proved? Can the charge be made out? Yes, God is a witness to it, an unexceptionable witness: from the place of his holiness he looks on the children of men, and sees how little good there is among them, *v.* 2. All the sinfulness of their hearts and lives in naked and open before him. 2. The fault of sin. Is there any harm in it? Yes, it is iniquity (*v.* 1, 4); it is an unrighteous thing; it is that which there is no good in (*v.* 1, 3); it is an evil thing; it is the worst of evils; it is that which makes this world such an evil world as it is; it is going back from God, *v.* 3. 3. The fountain of sin. How comes it that men are so bad? Surely it is because *there is no fear of God before their eyes:* they *say in their hearts, "There is no God* at all to call us to an account, none that we need to stand in awe of." Men's bad practices flow from their bad principles; if they profess to know God, yet in works, because in thoughts, they deny him. 4. The folly of sin. He is a fool (in the account of God, whose judgment we are sure is right) that harbours such corrupt thoughts. Atheists, whether in opinion or practice, are the greatest fools in the world. Those that do not seek God do not understand; they are like brute-beasts that have no understanding; for man is distinguished from the brutes, not so much by the powers of reason as by a capacity for religion. *The workers of iniquity,* whatever they pretend to, *have no knowledge;* those may truly be said to know nothing that do not know God, *v.* 4. 5. The filthiness of sin. Sinners are corrupt (*v.* 1); their nature is vitiated and spoiled, and the more noble the nature is the more vile it is when it is depraved, as that of the angels. *Corruptio optimi est pessima — The best things, when corrupted, become the worst.* Their iniquity is abominable; it is odious to the holy God, and it renders them so; whereas otherwise he *hates nothing that he has made.* It makes men filthy, altogether filthy. Wilful sinners are offensive in the nostrils of the God of heaven and of the holy angels. What decency soever proud sinners pretend to, it is certain that wickedness is the greatest defilement in the world. 6. The fruit of sin. See to what a degree of barbarity it brings men at last; when men's hearts are hardened through the deceitfulness of sin see their cruelty to their brethren, that are bone of their bone — because they will not *run with them to the same excess of riot,* they *eat them up as they eat bread;* as if they had not only become beasts, but beasts of prey. And see their contempt of God at the same time. *They have not called upon* him, but scorn to be beholden to him. 7. The fear and shame that attend sin (*v.* 5): *There were those in great fear* who had made God their enemy; their own guilty consciences frightened them, and filled them with horror, though otherwise there was no apparent cause of fear. *The wicked flees when none pursues.* See the ground of this fear; it is because God has formerly *scattered the bones of those that encamped against* his people, not only broken their power and dispersed their forces, but slain them, and reduced their bodies to dry bones, like those *scattered at the grave's mouth,* Ps. 141:7. Such will be the fate of those that lay siege to the *camp of the saints and the beloved city,* Rev. 20:9. The apprehensions of this cannot but put those into frights that eat up God's people. This enables the virgin, the daughter of Zion, to put them to shame, and expose them, *because God has despised them,* to laugh at them, because he that sits in heaven laughs at them. We need not look upon those enemies with fear whom God looks upon with contempt. If he despises them, we may. 8. The faith of the saints, and their hope and power touching the cure of this great evil, *v.* 6. There will come a Saviour, a great salvation, a salvation from sin. Oh that it might be hastened! for it will bring in glorious and joyful times. There were those in the Old-Testament times that looked and hoped, that prayed and waited, for this redemption. (1.) God will, in due time, save his church from the sinful malice of its enemies, which will bring joy to Jacob and Israel, that have long been in a mournful melancholy state. Such salvations were often wrought, and all typical of the everlasting triumphs of the glorious church. (2.) He will save all believers from their own iniquities, that they may not be led captive by them, which will be everlasting matter of joy to them. From this work the Redeemer had his name — *Jesus,* for *he shall save his people from their sins,* Mt. 1:21.

PSALM 54

The key of this psalm hangs at the door, for the title tells us upon what occasion it was penned — when the inhabitants of Ziph, men of Judah (types of Judas the traitor), betrayed David to Saul, by informing him where he was and putting him in a way how to seize him. This they did twice (1 Sa. 23:19; 26:1), and it is upon record to their everlasting infamy. The psalm is sweet; the former part of it, perhaps, was meditated when he was in his distress and put into writing when the danger was over, with the addition of the last two verses, which express his thankfulness for the deliverance, which yet might be written in faith, even when he was in the midst of his fright. Here, I. He complains to God of the malice of his enemies, and prays for help against them (*v.* 1–3). II. He comforts himself with an assurance of the divine favour and protection, and that, in due time, his enemies should be confounded and be delivered (*v.* 4–7). What time we are in distress we may comfortable sing this psalm.

To the chief musician on Neginoth, Maschil. *A psalm* of David, when the Ziphim came and said to Saul, Doth not David hide himself with us?

Verses 1–3

We may observe here, 1. The great distress that David was now in, which the title gives an account of. The Ziphim came of their own accord, and informed Saul where David was, with a promise to deliver him into his hand. One would have thought that when David had retired into the country he would not be pursued, into a desert country he would not be discovered, and into his own country he would not be betrayed; and yet it seems he was. Never let a good man expect to be safe an easy till he comes to heaven. How treacherous, how officious, were these Ziphim! It is well that God is faithful, for men are not to be trusted, Mic. 7:5. 2. His prayer to God for succour and deliverance, *v.* 1, 2. He appeals to God's strength, by which he was able to help him, and to his name, by which he was engaged to help him, and begs he would save him from his enemies and judge him, that is, plead his cause and judge for him. David has no other plea to depend upon than God's name, no other power to depend upon than God's strength, and those he makes his refuge and confidence. This would be the effectual answer of his prayers (*v.* 2), which even in his flight, when he had not opportunity for solemn address to God, he was ever and anon lifting up to heaven: *Hear my prayer,* which comes from my heart, and *give ear to the words of my mouth.* 3. His plea, which is taken from the character of his enemies, *v.* 3. (1.) They are *strangers;* such were the Ziphites, unworthy the name of Israelites. "They have used me more basely and barbarously than the Philistines themselves would have done." The worst treatment may be expected from those who, having broken through the bonds of relation and alliance, make themselves strangers. (2.) They are *oppressors;* such was Saul, who, as a king, should have used his power for the protection of all his good subjects, but abused it for their destruction. Nothing is so grievous as oppression in *the seat of judgment,* Eccl. 3:16. Paul's greatest perils were by his *own countrymen* and by *false brethren* (2 Co. 11:26), and so were David's. (3.) They were very formidable and threatening; they not only hated him and wished him ill, but they rose up against him in a body, joining their power to do him a mischief. (4.) They were very spiteful and malicious: *They seek after my soul;* they hunt for the precious life; no less will satisfy them. We may, in faith, pray that God would not by his providence give success, lest it should look like giving countenance, to such cruel bloody men. (5.) They were very profane and atheistical, and, for this reason, he thought God was concerned in honour to appear against them: *They have not set God before them,* that is, they have quite cast off the thoughts of God; they do not consider that his eye is upon them, that, in fighting against his people, they fight against him, nor have they any dread of the certain fatal consequences of such an unequal engagement. Note, From those who do not set God before them no good is to be expected; nay, what wickedness will not such men be guilty of? What bonds of nature, or friendship, or gratitude, or covenant, will hold those that have broken through the fear of God? *Selah — Mark this.* Let us all be sure to set God before us at all times; for, if we do not we are in danger of becoming desperate.

Verses 4–7

We have here the lively actings of David's faith in his prayer, by which he was assured that the issue would be comfortable, though the attempt upon him was formidable.

I. He was sure that he had God on his side, that God took his part (*v.* 4); he speaks it with an air of triumph and exultation, *Behold, God is my helper.* If we be for him, he is for us; and, if he be for us, we shall have such help in him that we need not fear any power engaged against us. Though men and devils aim to be our destroyers, they shall not prevail while God is our helper: *The Lord is with those that uphold my soul.* Compare Ps. 118:7, *"The Lord taketh my part with those that help me.* There are some that uphold me, and God is one of them; he is the principal one; none of them could help me if he did not help them." Every creature is that to us (and no more) that God makes it to be. He means, "The Lord is he that upholds my soul, and keeps me from tiring in my work and sinking under my burdens." He that by his providence upholds all things by his grace upholds the souls of his people. God, who will in due time save his people, does, in the mean time, sustain them and bear them up, so that the spirit he has made shall not fail before him.

II. God taking part with him, he doubted not but his enemies should both flee and fall before him (*v.* 5): *"He shall reward evil unto my enemies that observe me,* seeking an opportunity to do me a mischief. The evil they designed against me the righteous God will return upon their own heads." David would not render evil to them, but he knew God would: *I as a deaf man heard not, for thou wilt hear.* The enemies we forgive, if they repent not, God will judge; and for this reason we must not avenge ourselves, because God has said, *Vengeance is mine.* But he prays, *Cut them off in thy truth.* This is not a prayer of malice, but a prayer of faith; for it has an eye to the word of God, and only desires the performance of that. There is truth in God's threatenings as well as in his promises, and sinners that repent not will find it so to their cost.

III. He promises to give thanks to God for all the experiences he had had of his goodness to him (*v.* 6): *I will sacrifice unto thee.* Though sacrifices were expensive, yet, when God required that his worshippers should in that way praise him, David would not only offer them, but offer them freely and without grudging. All our spiritual sacrifices must, in this sense, be free-will-offerings; for God loves a cheerful giver. Yet he will not only bring his sacrifice, which was but the shadow, the ceremony; he will mind the substance: *I will praise thy name.* A thankful heart, and the calves of our lips giving thanks to his name, are the sacrifices God will accept: *"I will praise thy name, for it is good.* Thy name is not only great but good, and therefore to be praised. To praise thy name is not only what we are bound to, but it is good, it is pleasant, it is profitable; it is good for us (Ps. 92:1); therefore *I will praise thy name."*

IV. He speaks of his deliverance as a thing done (*v.* 7): I will praise thy name, and say, *"He has delivered me;* this shall be my song then." That which he rejoices in is a complete deliverance — *He has delivered me from all trouble;* and a deliverance to his heart's content — *My eye has seen its desire upon my enemies,* not seen them cut off and ruined, but forced to retreat, tidings being brought to Saul that the Philistines were upon him, 1 Sa. 23:27, 28. All David desired was to be himself safe; when he saw Saul draw off his forces he saw his desire. *He has delivered me from all trouble.* Either, 1. With this thought David comforted himself when he was in distress: *"He has delivered me from all trouble* hitherto, and many a time I have gained my point, and seen my desire on my enemies; therefore he will deliver me out of this trouble." We should thus, in our greatest straits, encourage ourselves with our past experiences. Or, 2. With this thought he magnified his present deliverance when the fright was over, that it was an earnest of further deliverance. He speaks of the completing of his deliverance as a thing done, though he had as yet many troubles before him, because, having God's promise for it, he was as sure of it as if it had been done already. "He that has begun to deliver me from all troubles, and will at length give me to see my desire upon my enemies." This may perhaps point at Christ, of whom David was a type; God would deliver him out of all the troubles of his state of humiliation, and he was perfectly sure of it; and all things are said to be put under his feet; for, though we see not yet all things put under him, yet we are sure he shall reign till all his enemies be made his footstool, and he shall see his desire upon them. However, it is an encouragement to all believers to make that use of their particular deliverances which St. Paul does (like David here), 2 Tim. 4:17, 18, *He that delivered me from the mouth of the lion shall deliver me from every evil work, and will preserve me to his heavenly kingdom.*

PSALM 55

It is the conjecture of many expositors that David penned this psalm upon occasion of Absalom's rebellion, and that the particular enemy he here speaks of, that dealt treacherously with him, was Ahithophel; and some will therefore make David's troubles here typical of Christ's sufferings, and Ahithophel's treachery a figure of Judas's, because they both hanged themselves. But there is nothing in it particularly applied to Christ in the New Testament. David was in great distress when he penned this psalm. I. He prays that God would manifest his favour to him, and pleads his own sorrow and fear (*v.* 1–8). II. He prays that God would manifest his displeasure against his enemies, and pleads their great wickedness and treachery (*v.* 9–15 and again *v.* 20, 21). III. He assures himself that God would, in due time, appear for him against his enemies, comforts himself with the hopes of it, and encourages others to trust in God (*v.* 16–19 and again *v.* 22, 23). In singing this psalm we may, if there be occasion, apply it to our own troubles; if not, we may sympathize with those to whose case it comes nearer, foreseeing that there will be, at last, indignation and wrath to the persecutors, salvation and joy to the persecuted.

To the chief musician on Neginoth, Maschil. *A psalm* of David.

Verses 1–8

In these verses we have,

I. David praying. Prayer is a salve for every sore and a relief to the spirit under every burden: *Give ear to my prayer, O God! v.* 1, 2. He does not set down the petitions he offered up to God in his distress, but begs that God would hear the prayers which, at every period, his heart lifted up to God, and grant an answer of peace to them: *Attend to me, hear me.* Saul would not hear his petitions; his other enemies regarded not his pleas; but, "Lord, be thou pleased to hearken to me. *Hide not thyself from my supplication,* either as one unconcerned and not regarding it, nor seeming to take any notice of it, or as one displeased, angry at me, and therefore at my prayer." If we, in our prayers, sincerely lay open ourselves, our case, our hearts, to God, we have reason to hope that he will not hide himself, his favours, his comforts, from us.

II. David weeping; for in this he was a type of Christ that he was a man of sorrows and often in tears (*v.* 2): *"I mourn in my complaint"* (or in my *meditation,* my *melancholy musings*), "and I make a noise; I cannot forbear such sighs and groans, and other expressions of grief, as discover it to those about me." Great griefs are sometimes noisy and clamorous, and thus are, in some measure, lessened, while those increase that are stifled, and have no vent given them. But what was the matter? *v.* 3. It is *because of the voice of the enemy,* the menaces and insults of Absalom's party, that swelled, and hectored, and stirred up the people to cry out against David, and shout him out of his palace and capital city, as afterwards the chief priests stirred up the mob to cry out against the Son of David, *Away with him — Crucify him.* Yet it was not the voice of the enemy only that fetched tears from David's eyes, but their oppression, and the hardship he was thereby reduced to: *They cast iniquity upon me.* They could not justly charge David with any mal-administration in his government, could not prove any act of oppression or injustice upon him, but they loaded him with calumnies. Though they found no iniquity in him relating to his trust as a king, yet they cast all manner of iniquity upon him, and represented him to the people as a tyrant fit to be expelled. Innocency itself is no security against violent and lying tongues. They hated him themselves, nay, in wrath they hated him; there was in their enmity both the heat and violence of anger, or sudden passion, and the implacableness of hatred and rooted malice; and therefore they studied to make him odious, that others also might hate him. This made him mourn, and the more because he could remember the time when he was the darling of the people, and answered to his name, *David — a beloved one.*

III. David trembling, and in great consternation. We may well suppose him to be so upon the breaking out of Absalom's conspiracy and the general defection of the people, even those that he had little reason to suspect. 1. See what fear seized him. David was a man of great boldness, and in some very eminent instances had signalized his courage, and yet, when the danger was surprising and imminent, his heart failed him. Let not the stout man therefore glory in his courage any more than the strong man in his strength. Now David's *heart is sorely pained within him; the terrors of death have fallen upon him, v.* 4. Fearfulness of mind and trembling of body came upon him, and horror covered and overwhelmed him, *v.* 5. When without are fightings no marvel that within are fears; and, if it was upon the occasion of Absalom's rebellion, we may suppose that the remembrance of his sin in the matter of

Uriah, which God was now reckoning with him for, added as much more to the fright. Sometimes David's faith made him, in a manner, fearless, and he could boldly say, when surrounded with enemies, *I will not be afraid what man can do unto me.* But at other times his fears prevail and tyrannise; for the best men are not always alike strong in faith. 2. See how desirous he was, in this fright, to retire into a desert, any where to be far enough from hearing the voice of the enemy and seeing their oppressions. He said (*v.* 6), said it to God in prayer, said it to himself in meditation, said it to his friends in complaint, *O that I had wings like a dove!* Much as he had been sometimes in love with Jerusalem, now that it had become a rebellious city he longed to get clear of it, and, like the prophet, wished he had *in the wilderness a lodging place of way-faring men, that he might leave his people and go from them; for they were an assembly of treacherous men,* Jer. 9:2. This agrees very well with David's resolution upon the breaking out of that plot, *Arise, let us flee, and make speed to depart,* 2 Sa. 15:14. Observe, (1.) How he would make his escape. He was so surrounded with enemies that he saw not how he could escape but upon the wing, and therefore he wishes, *O that I had wings!* not like a hawk that flies swiftly; he wishes for wings, not to fly upon the prey, but to fly from the birds of prey, for such his enemies were. The wings of a dove were most agreeable to him who was of a dove-like spirit, and therefore the wings of an eagle would not become him. The dove flies low, and takes shelter as soon as she can, and thus would David fly. (2.) What he would make his escape from — *from the wind, storm, and tempest,* the tumult and ferment that the city was now in, and the danger to which he was exposed. Herein he was like a dove, that cannot endure noise. (3.) What he aimed at in making this escape, not victory but rest: *"I would fly away and be at rest, v.* 6. I would fly any where, if it were to a barren frightful wilderness, ever so far off, so I might be quiet," *v.* 7. Note, Peace and quietness in silence and solitude are what the wisest and best of men have most earnestly coveted, and the more when they have been vexed and wearied with the noise and clamour of those about them. Gracious souls wish to retire from the hurry and bustle of this world, that they may sweetly enjoy God and themselves; and, if there be any true peace on this side heaven, it is they that enjoy it in those retirements. This makes death desirable to a child of God, that it is a final escape from all the storms and tempests of this world to perfect and everlasting rest.

Verses 9–15

David here complains of his enemies, whose wicked plots had brought him, though not to his faith's end, yet to his wits' end, and prays against them by the spirit of prophecy. Observe here,

I. The character he gives of the enemies he feared. They were of the worst sort of men, and his description of them agrees very well with Absalom and his accomplices. 1. He complains of the city of Jerusalem, which strangely fell in with Absalom and fell off from David, so that he had none there but how own guards and servants that he could repose any confidence in: *How has that faithful city become a harlot!* David did not take the representation of it from others; but with his own eyes, and with a sad heart, did himself see nothing but *violence and strife in the city* (*v.* 9); for, when they grew disaffected and disloyal to David, they grew mischievous one to another. If he walked the rounds upon the walls of the city, he saw that violence and strife went about it day and night, and mounted its guards, *v.* 10. All the arts and methods which the rebels used for the fortifying of the city were made up on violence and strife, and there were no remains of honesty or love among them. If he looked into the heart of the city, mischief and injury, mutual wrong and vexation, were in the midst of it: *Wickedness,* all manner of wickedness, *is in the midst thereof. Jusque datum sceleri — Wickedness was legalized.* Deceit and guile, and all manner of treacherous dealing, *departed not from her streets, v.* 11. It may be meant of their base and barbarous usage of David's friends and such as they knew were firm and faithful to him; they did them all the mischief they could, by fraud or force. Is this the character of Jerusalem, the royal city, and, which is more, the holy city, and in David's time too, so soon after the thrones of judgment and the testimony of Israel were both placed there? *Is this the city that men call the perfection of beauty?* Lam. 2:15. Is Jerusalem, the head-quarters of God's priests, so ill taught? Can Jerusalem be ungrateful to David himself, its own illustrious founder, and be made too hot for him, so that he cannot reside in it? Let us not be surprised at the corruptions and disorders of this church on earth, but long to see the New Jerusalem, where there is no violence nor strife, no mischief nor guilt, and into which no unclean thing shall enter, nor any thing that disquiets. 2. He complains of one of the ringleaders of the conspiracy, that had been very industrious to foment jealousies, to misrepresent him and his government, and to incense the city against him. It was one that reproached him, as if he either abused his power or neglected the use of it, for that was Absalom's malicious suggestion: *There is no man deputed of the king to hear thee,* 2 Sa. 15:3. That and similar accusations were industriously spread among the people; and who was most active in it? "Not a sworn enemy, not Shimei, nor any of the nonjurors; then I could have borne it, for I should not have expected better from them" (and we find how patiently he did bear Shimei's curses); "not one that professed to hate me, then I would have stood upon my guard against him, would have hidden myself and counsels from him, so that it would not have been in his power to betray me. *But it was thou, a man, my equal," v.* 13. The Chaldee-paraphrase names Ahithophel as the person here meant, and nothing in that plot seems to have discouraged David so much as to hear that Ahithophel was *among the conspirators with Absalom* (2 Sa. 15:31), for he was *the king's counsellor,* 1 Chr. 27:33. *"It was thou, a man, my equal,* one whom I esteemed as myself, a friend as my own soul, whom I had laid in my bosom and made equal with myself, to whom I had communicated all my secrets and who knew my mind as well as I myself did, — my guide, with whom I advised and by whom I was directed in all my affairs, whom I made president of the council and prime-minister of state, — my intimate acquaintance and familiar friend; this is the man that now abuses me. I have been kind to him, but I find him thus basely ungrateful. I have put a trust in him, but I find him thus basely treacherous; nay, and he could not have done me the one-half of the mischief he does if I had not shown him so much respect." All this must needs be very grievous to an ingenuous mind, and yet this was not all; this traitor had seemed a saint, else he had never been David's bosom-friend (*v.* 14): *"We took counsel together,* spent many an hour together, with a great deal of pleasure, in religious discourse," or, as Dr. Hammond reads it, *"We joined ourselves together to the assembly;* I gave him the right hand of fellowship in holy ordinances, and then *we walked to the house of God in company,* to attend the public service." Note, (1.) There always has been, and always will be, a mixture of good and bad, sound and unsound, in the visible church, between whom, perhaps for a long time, we can discern no difference; but the searcher of hearts does. David, who went to the house of God in his sincerity, had Ahithophel in company with him, who went in his hypocrisy. The Pharisee and the publican went together to the temple to pray; but, sooner or later, those that are perfect and those that are not will be made manifest. (2.) Carnal policy may carry men on very far and very long in a profession of religion while it is in fashion, and will serve a turn. In the court of pious David none was more devout than Ahithophel, and yet his heart was not right in the sight of God. (3.) We must not wonder if we be sadly deceived in some that have made great pretensions to those two sacred things, religion and friendship; David himself, though a very wise man, was thus imposed upon, which may make similar disappointments the more tolerable to us.

II. His prayers against them, which we are both to stand in awe of and to comfort ourselves in, as prophecies, but not to copy into our prayers against any particular enemies of our own. He prays, 1. That God would disperse them, as he did the Babel-builders (*v.* 9): *"Destroy, O Lord! and divide their tongues;* that is, blast their counsels, by making them to disagree among themselves, and clash with one another. Send an evil spirit among them, that they may not understand one another, but be envious and jealous one of another." This prayer was answered in the turning of Ahithophel's counsel into foolishness, by setting up the counsel of Hushai against it. God often destroys the church's enemies by dividing them; nor is there a surer way to the destruction of any people than their division. A kingdom, an interest, divided against itself, cannot long stand. 2. That God would destroy them, as he did Dathan and Abiram, and their associates, who were confederate against Moses, whose throat being an open sepulchre, the earth therefore opened and swallowed them up. This was then a new thing which God executed, Num. 16:30. But David prays that it might now be repeated, or something equivalent (*v.* 15): *"Let death seize upon them* by divine warrant, and *let them go down quickly into hell;* let them be dead, and buried, and so utterly destroyed, in a moment; for wickedness is wherever they are; it is in the midst of them." The souls of impenitent sinners go down quick, or alive, into hell, for they have a perfect sense of their miseries, and shall *therefore* live still, that they may be still miserable. This prayer is a prophecy of the utter, the final, the everlasting ruin of all those who, whether secretly or openly, oppose and rebel against the Lord's Messiah.

Verses 16–23

In these verses,

I. David perseveres in his resolution to call upon God, being well assured that he should not seek him in vain (*v.* 16): *"As for me,* let them take what course they please to secure themselves, let violence and strife be their guards, prayer shall be mind; this I have found comfort in, and therefore this will I abide by: *I will call upon God,* and commit myself to him, and *the Lord shall save me;"* for whosoever shall call on the name of the Lord, in a right manner, shall be saved, Rom. 10:13. He resolves to be both fervent and frequent in this duty. 1. He will pray fervently: *"I will pray and cry aloud. I will meditate"* (so the former word signifies); "I will speak with my own heart, and the prayer shall come thence." Then we pray aright when we pray with all that is within us, think first and then pray over our thoughts; for the true nature of prayer is lifting up the heart to God. Having meditated, he will cry, he will cry aloud; the fervour of his spirit in prayer shall be expressed and yet more excited by the intenseness and earnestness of his voice. 2. He will pray frequently, every day, and three times a day — *evening, and morning, and at noon.* It is probable that this had been his constant practice, and he resolves to continue it now that he is in his distress. Then we may come the more boldly to the throne of grace in trouble when we do not then first begin to seek acquaintance with God, but it is what we have constantly practised, and the trouble finds the wheels of prayer going. Those that think three meals a day little enough for the body ought much more to think three solemn prayers a day little enough for the soul, and to count it a pleasure, not a task. As it is fit that in the morning we should begin the day with God, and in the evening close it with him, so it is fit that in the midst of the day we should retire awhile to converse with him. It was Daniel's practice to pray three times a day (Dan. 6:10), and noon was one of Peter's hours of prayer, Acts 10:9. Let not us be weary of praying often, for God is not weary of hearing. "He shall hear my voice, and not blame me for coming too often, but the oftener the better, the more welcome."

II. He assures himself that God would in due time give an answer of peace to his prayers.

1. That he himself should be delivered and his fears prevented; those fears with which he was much disordered (*v.* 4, 5) by the exercise of faith were now silenced, and he begins to rejoice in hope (*v.* 18): *God has delivered my soul in peace,* that is, he will deliver it; David is as sure of the deliverance as if it were already wrought. His enemies were at war with him, and the battle was against him, but God delivered him in peace, that is, brought him off with as much comfort as if he had never been in danger. If he did not deliver him in victory, yet he delivered him in peace, inward peace. He delivered his soul in peace; by patience and holy joy in God he kept possession of that. Those are safe and easy whose hearts and minds are kept by that peace of God which *passes all understanding,* Phil. 4:7. David, in his fright, thought all were against him; but now he sees there were many with him, more than he imagined; his interest proved better than he expected, and this he gives to God the glory of: for it is he that raises us up friends when we need them, and makes them faithful to us. There were many with him; for though his sub-

jects deserted him, and went over to Absalom, yet God was with him and the good angels. With an eye of faith he now sees himself surrounded, as Elisha was, with chariots of fire and horses of fire, and therefore triumphs thus, *There are many with me,* more *with me than against me,* 2 Ki. 6:16, 17.

2. That his enemies should be reckoned with, and brought down. They had frightened him with their menaces (*v.* 3), but here he says enough to frighten them and make them tremble with more reason, and no remedy; for they could not ease themselves of their fears as David could, by faith in God.

(1.) David here gives their character as the reason why he expected God would bring them down. [1.] They are impious and profane, and stand in no awe of God, of his authority or wrath (*v.* 19): *"Because they have no changes* (no afflictions, no interruption to the constant course of their prosperity, no crosses to empty them from vessel to vessel) *therefore they fear not God;* they live in a constant neglect and contempt of God and religion, which is the cause of all their other wickedness, and by which they are certainly marked for destruction." [2.] They are treacherous and false, and will not be held by the most sacred and solemn engagements (*v.* 20): *"He has put forth his hand against such as are at peace with him,* that never provoked him, nor gave him any cause to quarrel with them; nay, to whom he had given all possible encouragement to expect kindness from him. He has put forth his hand against those whom he had given his hand to, and has broken his covenant both with God and man, has perfidiously violated his engagement to both," than which nothing makes men riper for ruin. [3.] They are base and hypocritical, pretending friendship while they design mischief (*v.* 21): *"The words of his mouth"* (probably, he means Ahithophel particularly) *"were smoother than butter and softer than oil,* so courteous was he and obliging, so free in his professions of respect and kindness and the proffers of his service; yet, at the same time, *war was in his heart,* and all this courtesy was but a stratagem of war, and those very words had such a mischievous design in them that they were as *drawn swords* designed to stab." They smile in a man's face, and cut his throat at the same time, as Joab, that kissed and killed. Satan is such an enemy; he flatters men into their ruin. *When he speaks fair, believe him not.*

(2.) David here foretels their ruin. [1.] God shall afflict them, and bring them into straits and frights, and recompense tribulation to those that have troubled his people, and this in answer to the prayers of his people: *God shall hear and afflict them,* hear the cries of the oppressed and speak terror to their oppressors, *even he that abides of old,* who is God from everlasting, and world without end, and who sits Judge from the beginning of time, and has always presided in the affairs of the children of men. Mortal men, though ever so high and strong, will easily be crushed by an eternal God and are a very unequal match for him. This the saints have comforted themselves with in reference to the threatening power of the church's enemies (Hab. 1:12): *Art thou not from everlasting, O Lord?* [2.] God shall *bring them down,* not only to the dust, but *to the pit of destruction* (*v.* 23), to the bottomless pit, which is called *destruction,* Job 26:6. He afflicted them (*v.* 19) to see if that would humble and reform them; but, they not being wrought upon by that, he shall at last bring them to ruin. Those that are not reclaimed by the rod of affliction will certainly be brought down into the pit of destruction. They are *bloody and deceitful men* (that is, the worst of men) and therefore *shall not live out half their days,* not half so long as men ordinarily live, and as they might have lived in a course of nature, and as they themselves expected to live. They shall live as long as the Lord of life, the righteous Judge, has appointed, with whom the number of our months is; but he has determined to cut them off by an untimely death in the midst of their days. They were bloody men, and cut others off, and therefore God will justly cut them off: they were deceitful men, and defrauded others of the one-half perhaps of what was their due, and now God will cut them short, though not of that which was their due, yet of that which they counted upon.

III. He encourages himself and all good people to commit themselves to God, with confidence in him. He himself resolves to do so (*v.* 23): *"I will trust in thee,* in thy providence, and power, and mercy, and not in my own prudence, strength, or merit; when bloody and deceitful men are cut off in the midst of their days I shall still live by faith in thee." And this he will have others to do (*v.* 22): *"Cast thy burden upon the Lord,"* whoever thou art that art burdened, and whatever the burden is. *"Cast thy gift upon the Lord"* (so some read it); "whatever blessings God has bestowed upon thee to enjoy commit them all to his custody, and particularly commit the keeping of thy soul to him." Or, "Whatever it is that thou desirest God should give thee, leave it to him to give it to thee in his own way and time. *Cast thy care upon the Lord,"* so the Septuagint, to which the apostle refers, 1 Pt. 5:7. Care is a burden; it makes the heart stoop (Prov. 12:25); we must cast it upon God by faith and prayer, commit our way and works to him; let him do as seemeth him good, and we will be satisfied. To cast our burden upon God is to stay ourselves on his providence and promise, and to be very easy in the assurance that all shall work for good. If we do so, it is promised, 1. That he will sustain us, both support and supply us, will himself carry us in the arms of his power, as the nurse carries the sucking-child, will strengthen our spirits so by his Spirit as that they shall sustain the infirmity. He has not promised to free us immediately from that trouble which gives rise to our cares and fears; but he will provide that we be not tempted above what we are able, and that we shall be able according as we are tempted. 2. That he will never suffer the righteous to be moved, to be so shaken by any troubles as to quit either their duty to God or their comfort in him. However, he will not suffer them to be moved for ever (as some read it); though they fall, they shall not be utterly cast down.

PSALM 56

It seems by this, and many other psalms, that even in times of the greatest trouble and distress David never hung his harp upon the willow-trees, never unstrung it or laid it by; but that when his dangers and fears were greatest he was still in tune for singing God's praises. He was in imminent peril when he penned this psalm, at least when he meditated it; yet even then his meditation of God was sweet. I. He complains of the malice of his enemies, and begs mercy for himself and justice against them (*v.* 1, 2, 5–7). II. He confides in God, being assured that he took his part, comforting himself with this, that therefore he was safe and should be victorious, and that while he lived he should praise God (*v.* 3, 4, 8–13). How pleasantly may a good Christian, in singing this psalm, rejoice in God, and praise him for what he will do, as well as for what he has done.

To the chief musician upon Jonath-elem-rechokim, Michtam of David, when the Philistines took him in Gath.

Verses 1–7

David, in this psalm, by his faith throws himself into the hands of God, even when he had by his fear and folly thrown himself into the hands of the Philistines; it was when they took him in Gath, whither he fled for fear of Saul, forgetting the quarrel they had with him for killing Goliath; but they soon put him in mid of it, 1 Sa. 21:10, 11. Upon that occasion he changed his behaviour, but with so little ruffle to his temper that then he penned both this psalm and the 34th. This is called *Michtam — a golden psalm.* So some other psalms are entitled, but this has something peculiar in the title; it is upon *Jonath-elem-rechokim,* which signifies *the silent dove afar off.* Some apply this to David himself, who wished for the wings of a dove on which to fly away. He was innocent and inoffensive, mild and patient, as a dove, was at this time driven from his nest, from the sanctuary (Ps. 84:3), was forced to wander afar off, to seek for shelter in distant countries; there he was like the doves of the valleys, mourning and melancholy; but silent, neither murmuring against God nor railing at the instruments of his trouble; herein a type of Christ, who was as a sheep, dumb before the shearers, and a pattern to Christians, who, wherever they are and whatever injuries are done them, ought to be as silent doves. In this former part of the psalm,

I. He complains to God of the malice and wickedness of his enemies, to show what reason he had to fear them, and what cause, what need, there was that God should appear against them (*v.* 1): *Be merciful unto me, O God!* That petition includes all the good we come to the throne of grace for; if we obtain mercy there, we obtain all we can desire, and need no more to make us happy. It implies likewise our best plea, not our merit, but God's mercy, his free rich mercy. He prays that he might find mercy with God, for with men he could find no mercy. When he fled [illegible] no[illegible] flee to [illegible] rounded [illegible] plains, 1. T[illegible] *are many th*[illegible] me with numbe[illegible] and make it to app[illegible] art above them." It is [illegible] help of one against man[illegible] many soever they are that [illegible] good grounds, boast that the[illegible] that great general said) "How ma[illegible] 2. That they were very barbarous: [illegible] *up, v.* 1 and again *v.* 2. They sought to [illegible] would serve; they came upon him with [illegible] like beasts of prey, to eat up his flesh, Ps. 2[illegible] swallow him up, those of his own kind, fro[illegible] might have expected humanity. The ravenous [illegible] not upon those of their own species; yet a bad ma[illegible] devour a good man if he could. "They are men, wea[illegible] frail; make them to know that they are so," Ps. 9:20. 3. T[illegible] they were very unanimous (*v.* 6): *They gather themselves together;* though they were many, and of different interests among themselves, yet they united and combined against David, as Herod and Pilate against the Son of David. 4. That they were very powerful, quite too hard for him if God did not help him: *"They fight against me* (*v.* 2); *they oppress me, v.* 1. I am almost overcome and borne down by them, and reduced to the last extremity." 5. That they were very subtle and crafty (*v.* 6): *"They hide themselves;* they industriously cover their designs, that they may the more effectually prosecute and pursue them. They hide themselves as a lion in his den, that they may mark my steps;" that is, "they observe every thing I say and do with a critical eye, that they may have something to accuse me of" (thus Christ's enemies watched him, Lu. 20:20), or "they have an eye upon all my motions, that they may gain an opportunity to do me a mischief, and may lay their snares for me." 6. That they were very spiteful and malicious. They put invidious constructions upon every thing he said, though ever so honestly meant and prudently expressed (*v.* 5): *"They wrest my words,* put them upon the rack, to extort that out of them which was never in them;" and so they made him an offender for a word (Isa. 29:21), misrepresenting it to Saul, and aggravating it, to incense him yet more against him. They made it their whole business to ruin David; all their thoughts were against him for evil, which put evil interpretations upon all his words. 7. That they were very restless and unwearied. They continually waited for his soul; it was the life, the precious life, they hunted for; it was his death they longed for, *v.* 6. They fought daily against him (*v.* 1), and would daily swallow him up (*v.* 2), and every day they wrested his words, *v.* 5. Their malice would not admit the least cessation of arms, or the acts of hostility, but they were continually pushing at him. Such as this is the enmity of Satan and his agents against the kingdom of Christ and the interests of his holy religion, which if we cordially espouse, we must not think it strange to meet with such treatment as this, as though some strange thing happened to us. Our betters have been thus used. So persecuted they the prophets.

II. He encourages himself in God, and in his promises, power, and providence, *v.* 3, 4. In the midst of his complaints, and before he has said what he has to say of his enemies, he triumphs in the divine protection. 1. He resolves to make God his confidence, then when dangers were most threatening and all other confidences failed: *"What time I am afraid,* in the day of my fear, when I am most terrified from without and most timorous within, then *I will trust in thee,* and thereby my fears shall be silenced." Note, There are some times which are, in a special manner, times of fear with God's people; in these times it is their duty and interest to trust in God as their God, and to know whom they have trusted. This will fix the heart, and keep it in peace. 2. He resolves to make God's promises the matter of his praises, and so we have reason to make them (*v.* 4): *"In God I will praise,* not only his work which he has done, but *his word* which he has spoken; I will give him thanks for a promise, though not yet performed. *In God* (in his strength and by his assistance) I will from the cruel hands of Saul he fell into the cruel hands of the Philistines. "Lord" (says he), "be thou merciful to me ... or I am undone." The mercy of God is what we may ... and trust to, and in faith pray for, when we are surrounded on all sides with difficulties and dangers. He complains ... that his enemies were very numerous (v. 2); "They ... fight against me, and think to overpower ...; take notice of this, O thou Most High! ... that wherein they deal proudly thou ... a point of honour to come in to the ... And, if God be on our side, how ... fight against us, we may upon ... re are more with us; for (as ... hey would swallow him ... 2. Men would ... devour him; no less ... whom he ... easts prey ...

Psalm 56:1-7

Verses 8-13

Several things David here comforts himself with in the day of his distress and fear.

I. That God took particular notice of all his grievances and all his griefs, *v.* 8. 1. Of all the inconveniences of his state: *Thou tellest my wanderings,* my *flittings,* so the old translation. David was now but a young (under thirty) and yet he had had many removes, from his father's house to the court, thence to the camp, and now driven out to sojourn where he could find a place, but not allowed to rest any where; he was hunted like a partridge upon the mountains; continual terrors and toils attended him; but this comforted him, that God kept a particular account of all his motions, and numbered all the weary steps he took, by night or by day. Note, God takes cognizance of all the afflictions of his people; and he does not cast out from his care and love those whom men have cast out from their acquaintance and converse. 2. Of all the impressions thus made upon his spirit. When he was wandering he was often weeping, and therefore prays, "Put thou my tears into thy bottle, to be preserved and looked upon; nay, I know they are in thy book, the book of thy remembrance." God has a bottle and a book for his people's tears, both those for their sins and those for their afflictions. This intimates, (1.) That he observes them with compassion and tender concern; he is afflicted in their afflictions, and knows their souls in adversity. As the blood of his saints, and their deaths, are precious in the sight of the Lord, so are their tears, not one of them shall fall to the ground. *I have seen thy tears,* 2 Ki. 20:5. *I have heard Ephraim bemoaning himself,* Jer. 31:18. (2.) That he will remember them and review them, as we do the accounts we have booked. Paul was mindful of Timothy's tears (2 Tim. 1:4), and God will not forget the sorrows of his people. The tears of God's persecuted people are bottled up and sealed among God's treasures; and, when these books come to be opened, they will be found vials of wrath, which will be poured out upon their persecutors, whom God will surely reckon with for all the tears they have forced from his people's eyes; and they will be breasts of consolation to God's mourners, whose sackcloth will be turned into garments of praise. God will comfort his people according to the time wherein he has afflicted them, and give to those to reap in joy who sowed in tears. What was sown a tear will come up a pearl.

II. That his prayers would be powerful for the defeat and discomfiture of his enemies, as well as for his own support and encouragement (*v.* 9): "*When I cry unto thee, then shall my enemies turn back;* I need no other weapons than prayers and tears; *this I know, for God is for me,* to plead my cause, to protect and deliver me; and, if God be for me, who can be against me so as to prevail?" The saints have God for them; they may know it; and to him they must cry when they are surrounded with enemies; and, if they do this in faith, they shall find a divine power exerted and engaged for them; their enemies shall be made

their spiritual enemies, against whom we fight [on our] knees, Eph. 6:18.

[...] is faith in God would set him above the fear [...], 11. Here he repeats, with a strong pathos, [...] said (*v.* 4), "*In God will I praise his word;* that [...]ly depend upon the promise for the sake of [...]de it, who is true and faithful, and has wisdom and goodness enough to make it good." When [...] it to a man's bill we honour him that drew [...]ve do, and suffer, for God, in a dependence [...]mise, not staggering at it, we give glory to [...]se his word, and so give praise to him. Having this trust in God, he looks with a holy contempt on the threatening power of man: "*In God have* [...]*t,* and in him only, and therefore *I will not* [...]*t man can do unto me* (*v.* 111), though I know [...]at he would do if he could," *v.* 1, 2. This triumph, so expressive of a holy magnanimity, is put into the mouth of every true believer, whom [...] Christian hero, Heb. 13:6. We may each of us [...] *e Lord is my helper,* and then *I will not fear* [...] *all do unto me;* for he has no power but what [...] him from above.

[...]e is in bonds to God (*v.* 12): "*Thy vows are* [...] *God!* — not upon me as a burden which I [...] loaded with, but as a badge which I glory in, as that by which I am known to be thy menial servant — not upon me as fetters that hamper me (such are superstitious vows), but upon me as a bridle that restrains me from what would be hurtful to me, and directs me in the way of my duty. Thy vows are upon me, the vows I have made to thee, to which thou art not only a witness, but a party, and which thou hast commanded and encouraged me to make." It is probably that he means especially those vows which he had made to God in the day of his trouble and distress, which he would retain the remembrance of, and acknowledge the obligations of, when his fright was over. Note, It ought to be the matter of our consideration and joy that *the vows of God are upon us* — our baptismal vows renewed at the Lord's table, our occasional vows under convictions, under corrections, by these we are bound to live to God.

V. That he should still have more and more occasion to praise him: *I will render praises unto thee.* This is part of the performance of his vows; for vows of thankfulness properly accompany prayers for mercy, and when the mercy is received must be made good. When we study what we shall render this is the least we can resolve upon, to render praises to God — poor returns for rich receivings! Two things he will praise God for: — 1. For what he had done for him (*v.* 13): "*Thou has delivered my soul,* my life, *from death,* which was just ready to seize me." If God have delivered us from sin, either from the commission of it by preventing grace or from the punishment of it by pardoning mercy, we have reason to own that he has thereby delivered our souls from death, which is the wages of sin. If we, who were by nature dead in sin, are quickened together with Christ, and are made spiritually alive, we have reason to own that God has delivered our souls from death. 2. For what he would do for him: "*Thou hast delivered my soul from death,* and so hast given me a new life, and thereby hast given me an earnest of further mercy, that thou wilt *deliver my feet from falling;* thou hast done the greater, and therefore thou wilt do the less; thou hast begun a good work, and therefore thou wilt carry it on and perfect it." This may be taken either as the matter of his prayer, pleading his experience, or as the matter of his praise, raising his expectations; and those that know how to praise in faith will give God thanks for mercies in promise and prospect, as well as in possession. See here, (1.) What David hopes for, that God would deliver his feet from falling either into sin, which would wound his conscience, or into the appearance of sin, from which his enemies would take occasion to wound his good name. Those that think the stand must take heed lest they fall, because the best stand no longer than God is pleased to uphold them. We are weak, our way is slippery, many stumbling-blocks are in it, our spiritual enemies are industrious to thrust us down, and therefore we are concerned by faith and prayer to commit ourselves to his care who *keeps the feet of his saints.* (2.) What he builds this hope upon: "*Thou hast delivered my soul from death,* and therein hast mag-

nified thy power and goodness, and put me into a capacity of receiving further mercy from thee; and now wilt thou not secure and crown thy own work?" God never brought his people out of Egypt to slay them in the wilderness. He that in conversion delivers the soul from so great a death as sin is will not fail *to preserve it to his heavenly kingdom.* (3.) What he designs in these hopes: *That I may walk before God in the light of the living,* that is, [1.] "That I may get to heaven, the only land of light and life; for in this world darkness and death reign." [2.] "That I may do my duty while this life lasts." Note, This we should aim at, in all our desires and expectations of deliverance both from sin and trouble, that we may do God so much the better service — *that, being delivered out of the hands of our enemies, we may serve him without fear.*

PSALM 57

This psalm is very much like that which goes next before it; it was penned upon a like occasion, when David was both in danger of trouble and in temptation to sin; it begins as that did, "Be merciful to me;" the method also is the same. I. He begins with prayer and complaint, yet not without some assurance of speeding in his request (*v.* 1-6). II. He concludes with joy and praise (*v.* 7-11). So that hence we may take direction and encouragement, both in our supplications and in our thanksgivings, and may offer both to God, in singing this psalm.

To the chief musician, Al-taschith, Michtam of David, when he fled from Saul in the cave.

Verses 1-6

The title of this psalm has one word new in it, *Al-taschith — Destroy not.* Some make it to be only some known tune to which this psalm was set; others apply it to the occasion and matter of the psalm. *Destroy not;* that is, David would not let Saul be destroyed, when now in the cave there was a fair opportunity of killing him, and his servants would fain have done so. No, says David, *destroy him not,* 1 Sa. 24:4, 6. Or, rather, God would not let David be destroyed by Saul; he suffered him to persecute David, but still under this limitation, *Destroy him hot;* as he permitted Satan to afflict Job, *Only save his life.* David must not be destroyed, for *a blessing is in him* (Isa. 65:8), even Christ, the best of blessings. When David was in the cave, in imminent peril, he here tells us what were the workings of his heart towards God; and happy are those that have such good thoughts as these in their minds when they are in danger!

I. He supports himself with faith and hope in God, and prayer to him, *v.* 1, 2. Seeing himself surrounded with enemies, he looks up to God with that suitable prayer: *Be merciful to me, O Lord!* which he again repeats, and it is no vain repetition: *Be merciful unto me.* It was the publican's prayer, Lu. 18:13. It is a pity that any should use it slightly and profanely, should cry, *God be merciful to us,* or, *Lord, have mercy upon us,* when they mean only to express their wonder, or surprise, or vexation, but God and his mercy are not in all their thoughts. It is with much devout affection that David here prays, "*Be merciful unto me, O Lord!* look with compassion upon me, and in thy love and pity redeem me." To recommend himself to God's mercy, he here professes,

1. That all his dependence is upon God: *My soul trusteth in thee, v.* 1. He did not only profess to trust in God, but his soul did indeed rely on God only, with a sincere devotion and self-dedication, and an entire complacency and satisfaction. He goes to God, and, at the footstool of the throne of his grace, humbly professes his confidence in him: *In the shadow of thy wings will I make my refuge,* as the chickens take shelter under the wings of the hen when the birds of prey are ready to strike at them, *until these calamities be over-past.* (1.) He was confident his troubles would end well, in due time; *these calamities will be over-past;* the storm will blow over. *Non si male nunc et olim sic erit — Though now distressed, I shall not always be so.* Our Lord Jesus comforted himself with this in his sufferings, Lu. 22:37. *The things concerning me have an end.* (2.) He was very easy under the divine protection in the mean time. [1.] He comforted himself in the goodness of God's nature, by which he is inclined to succour and protect his people, as the hen is by instinct to shelter her young ones. God comes upon the wing to the help of his people, which denotes a speedy deliverance (Ps. 18:10); and he takes them under his wing, which denotes warmth and

refreshment, even when the calamities are upon them; see Mt. 23:37. [2.] In the promise of his word and the covenant of his grace; for it may refer to the out-stretched *wings of the cherubim,* between which God is said to dwell (Ps. 80:1) and whence he gave his oracles. "To God, as the God of grace, will I fly, and his promise shall be my refuge, and a sure passport it will be through all these danger." God, by his promise, offers himself to us, to be trusted; we by our faith must accept of him, and put our trust in him.

2. That all his desire is towards God (*v.* 2): "*I will cry unto God most high,* for succour and relief; to him that is most high will I lift up my soul, and pray earnestly, even *unto God that performs all things for me.*" Note, (1.) In every thing that befalls us we ought to see and own the hand of God; whatever is done is of his performing; in it his counsel is accomplished and the scripture is fulfilled. (2.) Whatever God performs concerning his people, it will appear, in the issue, to have been performed for them and for their benefit. Though God be high, *most high,* yet he condescends so low as to take care that all things be made to work for good to them. (3.) This is a good reason why we should, in all our straits and difficulties, cry unto him, not only pray, but pray earnestly.

3. That all his expectation is from God (*v.* 3): *He shall send from heaven, and save me.* Those that make God their only refuge, and fly to him by faith and prayer, may be sure of salvation, in his way and time. Observe here, (1.) Whence he expects the salvation — from heaven. Look which way he will, in this earth, refuge fails, no help appears; but he looks for it from heaven. Those that lift up their hearts to things above may thence expect all good. (2.) What the salvation is that he expects. He trusts that God will save him *from the reproach of those that would swallow him up,* that aimed to ruin him, and, in the mean time, did all they could to vex him. Some read it, *He shall send from heaven and save me, for he has put to shame him that would swallow me up;* he has disappointed their designs against me hitherto, and therefore he will perfect my deliverance. (3.) What he will ascribe his salvation to: *God shall send forth his mercy and truth.* God is good in himself and faithful to every word that he has spoken, and so he makes it appear when he works deliverance for his people. We need no more to make us happy than to have the benefit of the mercy and truth of God, Ps. 25:10.

II. He represents the power and malice of his enemies (*v.* 4): *My soul is among lions.* So fierce and furious was Saul, and those about him, against David, that he might have been as safe in a den of lions as among such men, who were continually roaring against him and ready to make a prey of him. They are set on fire, and breathe nothing but flame; they set on fire the course of nature, inflaming one another against David, and *they were themselves set on fire of hell,* Jam. 3:6. They were sons of men, from whom one might have expected something of the reason and compassion of a man; but they were beasts of prey in the shape of men; their *teeth,* which they gnashed upon him, and with which they hoped to tear him to pieces and to eat him up, *were spears and arrows* fitted for mischiefs and murders; and their *tongue,* with which they cursed him and wounded his reputation, was *as a sharp sword* to cut and kill; see Ps. 42:10. A spiteful tongue is a dangerous weapon, wherewith Satan's instruments fight against God's people. He describes their malicious projects against him (*v.* 6) and shows the issue of them: "*They have prepared a net for my steps,* in which to take me, that I might not again escape out of their hands; *they have digged a pit before me,* that I might, ere I was aware, run headlong into it." See the policies of the church's enemies; see the pains they take to do mischief. But let us see what comes of it. 1. It is indeed some disturbance to David: *My soul is bowed down.* It made him droop, and hang the head, to think that there should be those that bore him so much ill-will. But, 2. It was destruction to themselves; they dug a pit for David, *into the midst whereof they have fallen.* The mischief they designed against David returned upon themselves, and they were embarrassed in their counsels; then when Saul was pursuing David the Philistines were invading *him;* nay, in the cave, when Saul thought David should fall into his hands, he fell into the hands of David, and lay at his mercy.

III. He prays to God to glorify himself and his own great

name (*v.* 5): "Whatever becomes of me and my interest, *be thou exalted, O God! above the heavens,* be thou praised by the holy angels, those glorious inhabitants of the upper world; *and let thy glory be above* or over *all the earth;* let all the inhabitants of this earth be brought to know and praise thee." Thus God's glory should lie hearer our hearts, and we should be more concerned for it, than for any particular interests of our own. When David was in the greatest distress and disgrace he did not pray, *Lord, exalt me,* but, *Lord, exalt thy own name.* Thus the Son of David, when his soul was troubled, and he prayed, *Father, save me from this hour,* immediately withdrew that petition, and presented this in the room of it, *For this cause came I to this hour; Father, glorify thy name,* Jn. 12:27, 28. Or it may be taken as a plea to enforce his petition for deliverance: "Lord, *send from heaven to save me,* and thereby thou wilt glorify thyself as the God both of heaven and earth." Our best encouragement in prayer is taken from the glory of God, and to that therefore, more than our own comfort, we should have an eye in all our petitions for particular mercies; for this is made the first petition in the Lord's prayer, as that which regulates and directs all the rest, *Father in heaven, hallowed by thy name.*

Verses 7–11

How strangely is the tune altered here! David's prayers and complaints, by the lively actings of faith, are here, all of a sudden, turned into praises and thanksgivings; his sack-cloth is loosed, he is girded with gladness, and his hallelujahs are as fervent as his hosannas. This should make us in love with prayer, that, sooner or later, it will be swallowed up in praise. Observe,

I. How he prepares himself for the duty of praise (*v.* 7): *My heart is fixed, O God! my heart is fixed.* My heart is *erect,* or *lifted up* (so some), which was bowed down, *v.* 6. *My heart is fixed,* 1. With reference to God's providences; it is prepared for every event, being *stayed upon God,* Ps. 112:7; Isa. 26:3. *My heart is fixed,* and then *none of these things move me,* Acts 20:24. If by the grace of God we be brought into this even composed frame of spirit, we have great reason to be thankful. 2. With reference to the worship of God: *My heart is fixed* to *sing and give praise.* It is implied that the heart is the main thing required in all acts of devotion; nothing is done to purpose, in religion, further than it is done with the heart. The heart must be fixed, fixed for the duty, fitted and put in frame for it, fixed in the duty by a close application, *attending on the Lord without distraction.*

II. How he excites himself to the duty of praise (*v.* 8): *Awake up my glory,* that is, my tongue (our tongue is our glory, and never more so than when it is employed in praising God), or my soul, that must be first awakened; dull and sleepy devotions will never be acceptable to God. We must stir up ourselves, and all that is within us, to praise God; with a holy fire must that sacrifice be kindled, and ascend in a holy flame. David's tongue will lead, and his psaltery and harp will follow, in these hymns of praise. *I myself will awake,* not only, "I will not be dead, and drowsy, and careless, in this work," but, "I will be in the most lively frame, as one newly awakened out of a refreshing sleep." He will awake *early* to this work, early in the morning, to begin the day with God, early in the beginnings of a mercy. When God is coming towards us with his favours we must go forth to meet him with our praises.

III. How he pleases himself, and (as I may say) even prides himself, in the work of praise; so far is he from being ashamed to own his obligations to God, and dependence upon him, that he resolves to *praise him among the people* and to *sing unto him among the nations,* *v.* 9. This intimates, 1. That his own heart was much affected and enlarged in praising God; he would even make the earth ring with his sacred songs, that all might take notice how much he thought himself indebted to the goodness of God. 2. That he desired to bring others in to join with him in praising God. He will publish God's praises *among the people,* that the knowledge, and fear, and love of God might be propagated, and the ends of the earth might see his salvation. When David was driven out into heathen lands he would not only not worship their gods, but he would openly avow his veneration for the God of Israel, would take his religion along with him wherever he went, would endeavour to bring others in love with it, and leave the sweet

savour of it behind him. David, in his psalms, which fill the universal church, and will to the end of time, may be said to be still *praising God among the people* and *singing to him among the nations;* for all good people make use of his words in praising God. Thus St. John, in his writings, is said to *prophesy again before many peoples and nations,* Rev. 10:11.

IV. How he furnishes himself with matter for praise, *v.* 10. That which was the matter of his hope and comfort (*God shall send forth his mercy and his truth, v.* 3) is here the matter of his thanksgiving: *Thy mercy is great unto the heavens,* great beyond conception and expression; and *thy truth unto the clouds,* great beyond discovery, for what eye can reach that which is wrapped up in the clouds? God's mercy and truth reach to the heavens, for they will bring all such to heaven as lay up their treasure in them and build their hopes upon them. God's mercy and truth are praised even to the heavens, that is, by all the bright and blessed inhabitants of the upper world, who are continually exalting God's praises to the highest, while David, on earth, is endeavouring to spread his praises to the furthest, *v.* 9.

V. How he leaves it at last to God to glorify his own name (*v.* 11): *Be thou exalted, O God!* The same words which he had used (*v.* 5) to sum up his prayers in he here uses again (and no vain repetition) to sum up his praises in: "Lord, I desire to exalt thy name, and that all the creatures may exalt it; but what can the best of us do towards it? Lord, take the work into thy own hands; do it thyself: *Be thou exalted, O God!* In the praises of the church triumphant thou art exalted to the heavens, and in the praises of the church militant thy glory is throughout all the earth; but thou art above all the blessing and praise of both (Neh. 9:5), and therefore, Lord, exalt thyself *above the heavens* and *above all the earth. Father, glorify thy own name.* Thou hast glorified it, glorify it yet again."

PSALM 58

It is the probable conjecture of some (Amyraldus particularly) that before Saul began to persecute David by force of arms, and raised the militia to seize him, he formed a process against him by course of law, upon which he was condemned unheard, and attainted as a traitor, by the great council, or supreme court of judicature, and then proclaimed "qui caput gerit lupinum — an outlawed wolf," whom any man might kill and no man might protect. The elders, in order to curry favour with Saul, having passed this bill of attainder, it is supposed that David penned this psalm on the occasion. I. He describes their sin, and aggravates that (*v.* 1–5). II. He imprecates and foretels their ruin, and the judgments which the righteous God would bring upon them for their injustice (*v.* 6–9) which would redound, 1. To the comfort of the saints (*v.* 10). 2. To the glory of God (*v.* 11). Sin appears here both exceedingly sinful and exceedingly dangerous, and God a just avenger of wrong, with which we should be affected in singing this psalm.

To the chief musician, Al-taschith, Michtam of David.

Verses 1–5

We have reason to think that this psalm refers to the malice of Saul and his janizaries against David, because it bears the same inscription (*Al-taschith,* and *Michtam of David*) with that which goes before and that which follows, both which appear, by the title, to have been penned with reference to that persecution through which God preserved him (*Al-taschith — Destroy not),* and therefore the psalms he then penned were precious to him, *Michtams — David's jewels,* as Dr. Hammond translates it.

In these verses David, not as a king, for he had not yet come to the throne, but as a prophet, in God's name arraigns and convicts his judges, with more authority and justice than they showed in prosecuting him. Two things he charges them with:

I. The corruption of their government. They were a congregation, a bench of justices, nay, perhaps, a congress or convention of the states, from whom one might have expected fair dealing, for they were men learned in the laws, had been brought up in the study of these statutes and judgments, which were so righteous that those of other nations were not to be compared with them. One would not have thought a congregation of such could be bribed and biassed with pensions, and yet, it seems, they were, because the son of Kish could do that for them which the son of Jesse could not, 1 Sa. 22:7. He had vineyards, and fields, and preferments, to give them, and, therefore, to please him, they would do any thing, right or wrong. Of all the melancholy views which Solomon took of this earth and its grievances, nothing vexed him so much as to see that in the *place of judgment wickedness was there,* Eccl. 3:16. So it was in Saul's time. 1. The judges would not do right, would not protect or vindicate oppressed innocency (*v.* 1): "*Do you indeed speak righteousness, or judge uprightly?* No; you are far from it; your own consciences cannot but tell you that you do not discharge the trust reposed in you as magistrates, by which you are bound to be *a terror to evil-doers and a praise to those that do well.* Is this the justice you pretend to administer? Is this the patronage, this the countenance, which an honest man and an honest cause may expect from you? Remember you are sons of men; mortal and dying, and that you stand upon the same level before God with the meanest of those you trample upon, and must yourselves be called to an account and judged. You are *sons of men,* and therefore we may appeal to yourselves, and to that law of nature which is written in every man's heart: *Do you indeed speak righteousness?* And will not your second thoughts correct what you have done?" Note, It is good for us often to reflect upon what we say with this serious question, *Do we indeed speak righteousness?* that we may unsay what we have spoken amiss and may proceed no further in it. 2. They did a great deal of wrong; they used their power for the support of injury and oppression (*v.* 2): *In heart you work wickedness* (all the wickedness of the life is wrought in the heart). It intimates that they wrought with a great deal of plot and management, not by surprise, but with premeditation and design, and with a strong inclination to it and resolution in it. The moire there is of the heart in any act of wickedness the worse it is, Eccl. 8:11. And what was their wickedness? It follows, "*You weigh the violence of your hands in the earth*" (or *in the land*), "the peace of which you are appointed to be the conservators of." They did all the violence and injury they could, either to enrich or avenge themselves, and they weighed it; that is, 1. They did it with a great deal of craft and caution: "*You frame it by rule and lines*" (so the word signifies), "that it may effectually answer your mischievous intentions; such masters are you of the art of oppression." 2. They did it under colour of justice. They held the balances (the emblem of justice) in their hands, as if they designed to do right, and right is expected from them, but the result is violence and oppression, which are practised the more effectually for being practised under the pretext of law and right.

II. The corruption of their nature. This was the root of bitterness from which that gall and wormwood sprang (*v.* 3): *The wicked,* who in heart work wickedness, *are estranged from the womb,* estranged from God and all good, *alienated from the divine life,* and its principles, powers, and pleasures, Eph. 4:18. A sinful state is a state of estrangement from that acquaintance with God and service of him which we were made for. Let none wonder that these wicked men dare do such things, for wickedness is bred in the bone with them; they brought it into the world with them; they have in their natures a strong inclination to it; they learned it from their wicked parents, and have been trained up in it by a bad education. They are called, and not miscalled, *transgressors from the womb;* one can therefore expect no other than that they will *deal very treacherously;* see Isa. 48:8. They go astray from God and their duty as soon as they are born, (that is, as soon as possibly they can); the foolishness that is bound up in their hearts appears with the first operations of reason; as the wheat springs up, the tares spring up with it. Three instances are here given of the corruption of nature: — 1. Falsehood. They soon learn to speak lies, and *bend their tongues, like their* bows, for that purpose, Jer. 9:3. How soon will little children tell a lie to excuse a fault, or in their own commendation! No sooner can they speak than they speak to God's dishonour; tongue-sins are some of the first of our actual transgressions. 2. Malice. *Their poison* (that is, their ill-will, and the spite they bore to goodness and all good men, particularly to David) was *like the poison of a serpent,* innate, venomous, and very mischievous, and that which they can never be cured of. We pity a dog that is poisoned by accident, but hate a serpent that is poisonous by nature. Such as the cursed enmity in this serpent's brood against the Lord and his anointed. 3. Untractableness. They are malicious, and nothing will work upon them, no reason, no kindness, to mollify them, and bring them to a better temper. *They are like the deaf adder*

that stops her ear, v. 4, 5. The psalmist, having compared these wicked men, whom he here complains of, to serpents, for their poisonous malice, takes occasion thence, upon another account, to compare them to the deaf adder or viper, concerning which there was then this vulgar tradition, that whereas, by music or some other art, they had a way of charming serpents, so as either to destroy them or at least disable them to do mischief, this deaf adder would lay one ear to the ground and stop the other with her tail, so that she could not hear the voice of the enchantment, and so defeated the intention of it and secured herself. The using of this comparison neither verifies the story, nor, if it were true, justifies the use of this enchantment; for it is only an allusion to the report of such a thing, to illustrate the obstinacy of sinners in a sinful way. God's design, in his word and providence, is to cure serpents of their malignity; to this end how wise, how powerful, how well-chosen are the charms! How forcible the right words! But all in vain with most men; and what is the reason? It is because they will not hearken. None so deaf as those that will not hear. We *have piped unto men, and they have not danced;* how should they, when they have stopped their ears?

Verses 6–11

In these verses we have,

I. David's prayers against his enemies, and all the enemies of God's church and people; for it is as such that he looks upon them, so that he was actuated by a public spirit in praying against them, and not by any private revenge. 1. He prays that they might be disabled to do any further mischief (*v.* 6): *Break their teeth, O God!* Not so much that they might not feed themselves as that they might not be able to make prey of others, Ps. 3:7. He does not say, "Break their necks" (no; let them live to repent, *slay them not, lest my people forget*), but, "Break their teeth, for they are lions, they are young lions, that live by rapine." 2. That they might be disappointed in the plots they had already laid, and might not gain their point: "*When he bends his bow,* and takes aim *to shoot his arrows* at the upright in heart, *let them be as cut in pieces, v.* 7. Let them fall at his feet, and never come near the mark." 3. That they and their interest might waste and come to nothing, that they might *melt away as waters that run continually;* that is, as the waters of a land-flood, which, though they seem formidable for a while, soon soak into the ground or return to their channels, or, in general, as water spilt upon the ground, which cannot be gathered up again, but gradually dries away and disappears. Such shall the *floods of ungodly men* be, which sometimes *make us afraid* (Ps. 18:4); so shall the proud waters be reduced, which threaten to go over our soul, Ps. 124:4, 5. Let us by faith then see what they shall be and then we shall not fear what they are. He prays (*v.* 8) that they might *melt as a snail,* which wastes by its own motion, in every stretch it makes leaving some of its moisture behind, which, by degrees, must needs consume it, though it makes a path to shine after it. He that like a snail in her house is *plenus sui* — *full of himself,* that pleases himself and trusts to himself, does but consume himself, and will quickly bring himself to nothing. And he prays that they might be *like the untimely birth of a woman,* which dies as soon as it begins to live and never *sees the sun.* Job, in his passion, wished he himself had been such a one (Job 3:16), but he knew not what he said. We may, in faith, pray against the designs of the church's enemies, as the prophet does (Hos. 9:14, *Give them, O Lord! what wilt thou give them? Give them a miscarrying womb and dry breasts*), which explains this prayer of the psalmist.

II. His prediction of their ruin (*v.* 9): "*Before your pots can feel the* heat of a fire of *thorns* made under them (which they will presently do, for it is a quick fire and violent while it lasts), so speedily, with such a hasty and violent flame, God shall hurry them away, as terribly and as irresistibly as with a whirlwind, as it were alive, as it were in fury."

1. The proverbial expressions are somewhat difficult, but the sense is plain, (1.) That the judgments of God often surprise wicked people in the midst of their jollity, and hurry them away of a sudden. When they are beginning to walk in the light of their own fire, and the sparks of their own kindling, they are made to *lie down in sorrow*

(Isa. 50:11), and their laughter proves like the crackling of thorns under a pot, the comfort of which is soon gone, ere they can say, *Alas! I am warm,* Eccl. 7:6. (2.) That there is no standing before the destruction that comes from the Almighty; for *who knows the power of God's anger?* When God will take sinners away, dead or alive, they cannot contest with him. *The wicked are driven away in their wickedness.* Now,

2. There are two things which the psalmist promises himself as the good effects of sinners' destruction: — (1.) That saints would be encouraged and comforted by it (*v.* 10): *The righteous shall rejoice when he sees the vengeance.* The pomp and power, the prosperity and success, of the wicked, are a discouragement to the righteous; they sadden their hearts, and weaken their hands, and are sometimes a strong temptation to them to question their foundations, Ps. 73:2, 13. But when they see the judgments of God hurrying them away, and just vengeance taken on them for all the mischief they have done to the people of God, they rejoice in the satisfaction thereby given to their doubts and the confirmation thereby given to their faith in the providence of God and his justice and righteousness in governing the world; they shall rejoice in the victory thus gained over that temptation by seeing *their end,* Ps. 73:17. *He shall wash his feet in the blood of the wicked;* that is, there shall be abundance of bloodshed (Ps. 68:23), and it shall be as great a refreshment to the saints to see God glorified in the ruin of sinners as it is to a weary traveller to have his feet washed. It shall likewise contribute to their sanctification; the sight of the vengeance shall make them tremble before God (Ps. 119:120) and shall convince them of the evil of sin, and the obligations they lie under to that God who pleads their cause and will suffer no man to do them wrong and go unpunished for it. The joy of the saints in the destruction of the wicked is then a holy joy, and justifiable, when it helps to make them holy and to purify them from sin. (2.) That sinners would be convinced and converted by it, *v.* 11. The vengeance God sometimes takes on the wicked in this world will bring men to say, *Verily, there is a reward for the righteous.* Any man may draw this inference from such providences, and many a man shall, who before denied even these plain truths or doubted of them. Some shall have this confession extorted from them, others shall have their minds so changed that they shall willingly own it, and thank God who has given them to see it and see it with satisfaction, That God is, and, [1.] That he is the bountiful rewarder of his saints and servants: *Verily (however it be,* so it may be read) *there is a fruit to the righteous;* whatever damage he may run, and whatever hardship he may undergo for his religion, he shall not only be no loser by it, but an unspeakable gainer in the issue. Even in this world there is a reward for the righteous; they shall be recompensed in the earth. Those shall be taken notice of, honoured, and protected, that seemed slighted, despised, and abandoned. [2.] That he is the righteous governor of the world, and will surely reckon with the enemies of his kingdom: *Verily,* however it be, though wicked people prosper, and bid defiance to divine justice, yet it shall be made to appear, to their confusion, that the world is not governed by chance, but by a Being of infinite wisdom and justice; *there is a God that judges in the earth,* though he has prepared his throne in the heavens. He presides in all the affairs of the children of men, and directs and disposes them according to the counsel of his will, to his own glory; and he will punish the wicked, not only in the world to come, but *in the earth,* where they have laid up their treasure and promised themselves a happiness — *in the earth,* that the Lord may be known by the judgments which he executes, and that they may be taken as earnests of a judgment to come. *He is a God* (so we read it), not a weak man, not an angel, not a mere name, not (as the atheists suggest) a creature of men's fear and fancy, not a deified hero, not the sun and moon, as idolaters imagined, but a God, a self-existent perfect Being; he it is that judges the earth; his favour therefore let us seek, from whom every man's judgment proceeds, and to him let all judgment be referred.

PSALM 59

This psalm is of the same nature and scope with six or seven foregoing psalms; they are all filled with David's complaints of the malice of his enemies and of their cursed and cruel designs against him, his prayers and prophecies against them, and his comfort and confidence in God as his God. The first is the language of nature, and may be allowed; the second of a prophetical spirit, looking forward to Christ and the enemies of his kingdom, and therefore not to be drawn into a precedent; the third of grace and a most holy faith, which ought to be imitated by every one of us. In this psalm, I. He prays to God to defend and deliver him from his enemies, representing them as very bad men, barbarous, malicious, and atheistical (*v.* 1–7). II. He foresees and foretels the destruction of his enemies, which he would give to God the glory of (*v.* 8–17). As far as it appears that any of the particular enemies of God's people fall under these characters, we may, in singing this psalm, read their doom and foresee their ruin.

To the chief musician, Al-taschith, Michtam of David, when Saul sent and they watched the house to kill him.

Verses 1–7

The title of this psalm acquaints us particularly with the occasion on which it was penned; it was when Saul sent a party of his guards to beset David's house in the night, that they might seize him and kill him; we have the story 1 Sa. 19:11. It was when his hostilities against David were newly begun, and he had but just before narrowly escaped Saul's javelin. These first eruptions of Saul's malice could not but put David into disorder and be both grievous and terrifying, and yet he kept up his communion with God, and such a composure of mind as that he was never out of frame for prayer and praises; happy are those whose intercourse with heaven is not intercepted nor broken in upon by their cares, or griefs, or fears, or any of the hurries (whether outward or inward) of an afflicted state. In these verses,

I. David prays to be delivered out of the hands of his enemies, and that their cruel designs against him might be defeated (*v.* 1, 2): *"Deliver me from my enemies, O my God!* thou art *God,* and cast deliver me, *my* God, under whose protection I have put myself; and thou hast promised me to be a God all-sufficient, and therefore, in honour and faithfulness, thou wilt deliver me. Set me on high out of the reach of the power and malice of those that rise up against me, and above the fear of it. Let me be safe, and see myself so, safe and easy, safe and satisfied. O deliver me! and save me." He cries out as one ready to perish, and that had his eye to God only for salvation and deliverance. He prays (*v.* 4), *"Awake to help me,* take cognizance of my case, behold that with an eye of pity, and exert thy power for my relief." Thus the disciples, in the storm, awoke Christ, saying, *Master, save us, we perish.* And thus earnestly should we pray daily to be defended and delivered form our spiritual enemies, the temptations of Satan, and the corruptions of our own hearts, which war against our spiritual life.

II. He pleads for deliverance. Our God gives us leave not only to pray, but to plead with him, to order our cause before him and to fill our mouth with arguments, not to move him, but to move ourselves. David does so here.

1. He pleads the bad character of his enemies. They are *workers of iniquity,* and therefore not only his enemies, but God's enemies; they are *bloody men,* and therefore not only his enemies, but enemies to all mankind. "Lord, let not the workers of iniquity prevail against one that is a worker of righteousness, nor bloody men against a merciful man."

2. He pleads their malice against him, and the imminent danger he was in from them, *v.* 3. "Their spite is great; they aim at my soul, my life, my better part. They are subtle and very politic: *They lie in wait,* taking an opportunity to do me a mischief. They are all mighty, men of honour and estates, and interest in court and country. They are in a confederacy; they are united by league, and actually *gathered* together *against me,* combined both in consultation and action. They are very ingenious in their contrivances, and very industrious in the prosecution of them (*v.* 4): *They run and prepare themselves,* with the utmost speed and fury, to do me a mischief." He takes particular notice of the brutish conduct of the messengers that Saul sent to take him (*v.* 6): *"They return at evening* from the posts assigned them in the day, to apply themselves to their works of darkness (their night-work, which may well be their day-shame), and then *they make a noise like a hound* in pursuit of the hare." Thus did David's enemies, when they came to take him, raise an out cry against him as a rebel, and traitor, a man not fit to live; with this clamour they went *round about the city,* to bring a bad reputation upon David, if possible to set the mob against him, at least to prevent their being incensed against them, which otherwise they had reason to fear they would be, so much was David their darling. Thus the persecutors of our Lord Jesus, who are compared to dogs (Ps. 22:16), ran him down with noise; for else they could not have taken him, at least *no on the feast-day, for there would have been an uproar among the people. They belch out with their mouth* the malice that boils in their hearts, *v.* 7. *Swords are in their lips;* that is, reproaches that would my heart with grief (Ps. 42:10), and slanders that stab and wound my reputation. They were continually suggesting that which drew and whetted Saul's sword against him, and the fault is laid upon the false accusers. The sword perhaps would not have been in Saul's hand if it had not been first in their lips.

3. He pleads his own innocency, not as to God (he was never backward to own himself guilty before him), but as to his persecutors;. what they charged him with was utterly false, nor had he ever said or done any thing to deserve such treatment from them (*v.* 3): *"Not for my transgression, nor for my sin, O Lord!* thou knowest, who knowest all things." And again (*v.* 4), *without my fault.* Note, (1.) The innocency of the godly will not secure them from the malignity of the wicked. Those that are harmless like doves, yet, for Christ's sake, are hated of all men, as if they were noxious like serpents, and obnoxious accordingly. (2.) Though our innocency will not secure us from troubles, yet it will greatly support and comfort us under our troubles. The testimony of our conscience for us that we have behaved ourselves well towards those that behave themselves ill towards us will be very much our rejoicing in the day of evil. (3.) If we are conscious to ourselves of our innocency, we may with humble confidence appeal to God and beg of him to plead our injured cause, which he will do in due time.

4. He pleads that his enemies were profane and atheistical, and bolstered themselves up in their enmity to David, with the contempt of God: *For who,* say they, *doth hear? v.* 7. Not God himself, Ps. 10:11; 94:7. Note, It is not strange if those regard not what they say who have made themselves believe the God regards not what they say.

III. He refers himself and his cause to the just judgment of God, *v.* 5. "The Lord, the Judge, be Judge between me and my persecutors." In this appeal to God he has an eye to him as *the Lord of hosts,* that has power to execute judgment, having all creatures, even hosts of angels, at his command; he views him also as *the God of Israel,* to whom he was, in a peculiar manner, King and Judge, not doubting that he would appear on the behalf of those that were upright, that were Israelites indeed. When Saul's hosts persecuted him, he had recourse to God as *the Lord of all hosts;* when those maligned him who in spirit were strangers to the commonwealth of Israel he had recourse to God as *the God of Israel.* He desires (that is, he is very sure) that God will *awake to visit all the nations,* will make an early and exact enquiry into the controversies and quarrels that are among the children of men; there will be a day of visitation (Isa. 10:3), and to that day David refers himself, with this solemn appeal, *Be not merciful to any wicked transgressors. Selah — Mark that.* 1. If David had been conscious to himself that he was a wicked transgressor, he would not have expected to find mercy; but, as to his enemies, he would say he was no transgressor at all (*v.* 3, 4): *"Not for my transgression,* and therefore thou wilt appear for me." As to God, he could say he was no *wicked* transgressor; for, though he had transgressed, he was a penitent transgressor, and did not obstinately persist in what he had done amiss. 2. He knew his enemies were wicked transgressors, wilful, malicious, and hardened in their transgressions both against God and man, and therefore he sues for justice against them, judgment without mercy. Let not those expect to find mercy who never showed mercy, for such are wicked transgressors.

Verses 8–17

David here encourages himself, in reference to the threatening power of his enemies, with a pious resolution to wait upon God and a believing expectation that he should yet praise him.

I. He resolves to wait upon God (*v.* 9): *"Because of his strength"* (either the strength of his enemies, the fear of which drove him to God, or because of God's strength, the hope of which drew him to God) *"Will I wait upon thee,* with a believing dependence upon thee and confidence in thee." It is our wisdom and duty, in times of danger and difficulty, to wait upon God; for he is our defence, our high place, in whom we shall be safe. He hopes, 1. That God will be to him a God of mercy (*v.* 10): *"The God of my mercy shall prevent me* with the blessings of his goodness and the gifts of his mercy, prevent my fears, prevent my prayers, and be better to me than my own expectations." It is very comfortable to us, in prayer, to eye God, not only as the God of mercy, but as the God of our mercy, the author of all good in us and the giver of all good to us. Whatever mercy there is in God, it is laid up for us, and is ready to be laid out upon us. Justly does the psalmist call God's mercy *his mercy,* for all the blessings of the new covenant are called *the sure mercies of David* (Isa. 55:3); and they are *sure to all the seed.* 2. That he will be to his persecutors a God of vengeance. His expectation of this he expresses partly by way of prediction and partly by way of petition, which come all to one; for his prayer that it might be so amounts to a prophecy that it shall be so. Here are several things which he foretels concerning his enemies, or observers, that sought occasions against him and opportunity to do him a mischief, in all which he should see his desire, not a passionate or revengeful desire, but a believing desire upon them, *v.* 10. (1.) He foresees that God would expose them to scorn, as they had indeed made themselves ridiculous, *v.* 8. "They think *God does not hear them,* does not heed them; *but thou, O Lord! shalt laugh at them* for their folly, to think that he who planted the ear shall not hear, and *thou shalt have* not them only, but all such other heathenish people that live without God in the world, *in derision."* Note, Atheists and persecutors are worthy to be laughed at and had in derision. See Ps. 2:4; Prov. 1:26; Isa. 37:22. (2.) That God would make them standing monuments of his justice (*v.* 11): *Slay them not;* let them not be killed outright, *lest my people forget.* If the execution be soon done, the impressions of it will not be keep, and therefore will not be durable, but will quickly wear off. Swift destructions startle men for the present, but they are soon forgotten, for which reason he prays that this might be gradual: *"Scatter them by thy power,* and let them carry about with them, in their wanderings, such tokens of God's displeasure as may spread the notice of their punishment to all parts of the country." Thus Cain himself, though a murderer, was not slain, lest the vengeance should be forgotten, but was sentenced to be *a fugitive and a vagabond.* Note, When we think God's judgments come slowly upon sinners we must conclude that God has wise and holy ends in the gradual proceedings of his wrath. "So scatter them as that they may never again unite to do mischief, *bring them down, O Lord, our shield!"* If God has undertaken the protection of his people as their shield, he will doubtless humble and abase all those that fight against them. (3.) That they might be dealt with according to their deserts (*v.* 12): *For the sin of their mouth, even for the words of their lips* (for every word they speak has sin in it), *let them* for this *be taken in their pride,* even for their cursing others and themselves (a sin Saul was subject to, 1 Sa. 14:28, 44), and lying. Note, There is a great deal of malignity in tongue-sins, more than is commonly thought of. Note, further, Cursing, and lying, and speaking proudly, are some of the worst of the sins of the tongue; and that man is truly miserable whom God deals with according to the deserts of these, *making his own tongue to fall on him.* (4.) That God would glorify himself, as Israel's God and King, in their destruction (*v.* 13): *"Consume them in wrath, consume them;* that is, follow them with one judgment after another, till they be utterly ruined; let them be sensibly, but gradually wasted, that they themselves, while they are in the consuming, may know, and that the standers-by may likewise draw this inference form it, *That God ruleth in Jacob unto the ends of the earth."* Saul and his party think to rule and carry all before them, but they shall be made to know that there is a higher than they, that there is one who does and will overrule them. The design of God's judgments is to convince men that the Lord reigns, that he fulfils his own counsels, gives law to all the creatures, and disposes all things to his own glory, so that the greatest of men are under his check, and he makes what use he pleases of them. He *rules in Jacob;* for there he keeps his court; there it is known, and his name is great. But he *rules to the end of the earth;* for all nations are within the territories of his kingdom. He *rules to the ends of the earth,* even over those that know him not, but he *rules for Jacob* (so it may be read); he has an eye to the good of his church in the government of the world; the administrations of that government, even to the ends of the earth, are *for Jacob his servant's sake and for Israel's his elect,* Isa. 45:4. (5.) That he would make their sin their punishment, *v.* 14, compare *v.* 6. Their sin was their hunting for David to make a prey of him; their punishment should be that they should be reduced to such extreme poverty that they should hunt about for meat to satisfy their hunger, and should miss of it as they missed of David. Thus they should be, not cut off at once, but scattered (*v.* 11), and gradually consumed (*v.* 13); those that die by famine die by inches, and feel themselves die, Lam. 4:9. He foretels that they should be forced to beg their bread from door to door. [1.] That they should do it with the greatest regret and reluctancy imaginable. *To beg they are ashamed* (which makes it the greater punishment to them), and therefore they do it at evening, when it begins to be dark, that they may not be seen, at the time when other beasts of prey creep forth, Ps. 104:20. [2.] That yet they should be very clamorous and loud in their complaints, which would proceed from a great indignation at their condition, which they cannot in the least degree reconcile themselves to: *They shall make a noise like a dog.* When they were in quest of David they made a noise like an angry dog snarling and barking; now, when they are in quest of meat, they shall make a noise like a hungry dog howling and wailing. Those that repent of their sins *mourn,* when in trouble, *like doves;* those whose hearts are hardened make a noise, when in trouble, like dogs, *like a wild bull in a net, full of the fury of the Lord.* See Hos. 7:14, *They have not cried unto me with their heart when they howled on their beds for corn and wine.* [3.] That they should meet with little relief, but the hearts of people should be very much hardened towards them, so that they should *go round about the city,* and *wander up and down for meat* (*v.* 15), and should get nothing but by dint of importunity (according to our marginal reading, *If they be not satisfied, they will tarry all night*), so that what people do give them is not with good-will, but only to get rid of them, lest by their continual coming they weary them. [4.] That they should be insatiable, which is the greatest misery of all in a poor condition. *They are greedy dogs which can never have enough* (Isa. 56:11), and *they grudge if they be not satisfied.* A contented man, if he has not what he would have, yet does not grudge, does not quarrel with Providence, nor fret within himself; but those whose God is their belly, if that be not filled and its appetites gratified, fall out both with God and themselves. It is not poverty, but discontent, that makes a man unhappy.

II. He expects to praise God, that God's providence would find him matter for praise and that God's grace would work in him a heart for praise, *v.* 16, 17. Observe,

1. What he would praise God for. (1.) He would praise his power and his mercy; both should be the subject-matter of his song. Power, without mercy, is to be dreaded; mercy, without power, is not what a man can expect much benefit from; but God's power by which he is able to help us, and his mercy by which he is inclined to help us, will justly be the everlasting praise of all the saints. (2.) He would praise him because he had, many a time, and all along, found him his defence and his refuge in the day of trouble. God brings his people into trouble, that they may experience his power and mercy in protecting and sheltering them, and may have occasion to praise him. (3.) He would praise him because he had still a dependence upon him and a confidence in him, as his strength to support him and carry him on in his duty, his defence to keep him safe from evil, and the God of his mercy to make him happy and easy. He that is all this to us is certainly worthy of our best affections, praises, and services.

2. How he would praise God. (1.) He would *sing.* As that is a natural expression of joy, so it is an instituted ordinance for the exerting and exciting of holy joy and thankfulness. (2.) He would *sing aloud,* as one much affected with the glory of God, that was not ashamed to own it, and that desired to affect others with it. He will sing of God's power, but he will sing aloud of his mercy; the consideration of that raises his affections more than any thing else. (3.) He would sing aloud *in the morning,* when his spirits were most fresh and lively. God's compassions are new every morning, and therefore it is fit to begin the day with his praises. (4.) He would *sing unto God* (*v.* 17), to his honour and glory, and with him in his eye. As we must direct our prayers to God, so to him we must direct our praises, and must look up, making melody to the Lord.

PSALM 60

After many psalms which David penned in a day of distress this comes which was calculated for a day of triumph; it was penned after he was settled in the throne, upon occasion of an illustrious victory which God blessed his forces with over the Syrians and Edomites; it was when David was in the zenith of his prosperity, and the affairs of his kingdom seem to have been in a better posture then ever they were either before or after. See 2 Sa. 8:3, 13; 1 Chr. 18:3, 12. David, in prosperity, was as devout as David in adversity. In this psalm, I. He reflects upon the bad state of the public interests, for many years, in which God had been contending with them (*v.* 1–3). II. He takes notice of the happy turn lately given to their affairs (*v.* 4). III. He prays for the deliverance of God's Israel from their enemies (*v.* 5). IV. He triumphs in hope of their victories over their enemies, and begs of God to carry them on and complete them (*v.* 6–12). In singing this psalm we may have an eye both to the acts of the church and to the state of our own souls, both which have their struggles.

To the chief musician upon Shushan-eduth, Michtam of David, to teach, when he strove with Aram-naharaim, and with Aramzobah, when Joab returned, and smote of Edom in the valley of salt 12,000.

Verses 1–5

The title gives us an account, 1. Of the general design of the psalm. It is *Michtam — David's jewel,* and it is *to teach.* The Levites must teach it to the people, and by it teach them both to trust in God and to triumph in him; we must, in it, teach ourselves and one another. In a day of public rejoicing we have need to be taught to direct our joy to God and to terminate it in him, to give none of that praise to the instruments of our deliverance which is due to him only, and to encourage our hopes with our joys. 2. Of the particular occasion of it. It was at a time, (1.) When he was at war with the Syrians, and still had a conflict with them, both those of Mesopotamia and those of Zobah. (2.) When he had gained a great victory over the Edomites, by his forces, under the command of Joab, who had left 12,000 of the enemy dead upon the spot. David has an eye to both these concerns in this psalm: he is in care about his strife with the Assyrians, and in reference to that he prays; he is rejoicing in his success against the Edomites, and in reference to that he triumphs with a holy confidence in God that he would complete the victory. We have our cares at the same time that we have our joys, and they may serve for a balance to each other, that neither may exceed. They may likewise furnish us with matter both for prayer and praise, for both must be laid before God with suitable affections and emotions. If one point be gained, yet in another we are still striving: the Edomites are vanquished, but the Syrians are not; therefore *let not him that girds on the harness boast as if he had put it off.*

In these verses, which begin the psalm, we have,

I. A melancholy memorial of the many disgraces and disappointments which God had, for some years past, put the people under. During the reign of Saul, especially in the latter end of it, and during David's struggle with the house of Saul, while he reigned over Judah only, the affairs of the kingdom were much perplexed, and the neighbouring nations were vexatious to them. 1. He complains of *hard things* which they had seen (that is, which they had suffered), while the Philistines and other ill-disposed neighbours took all advantages against them, *v.* 3. God sometimes shows even his own people hard things in this world, that they may not take up their rest in it, but may dwell at ease in him only. 2. He owns God's displeasure to be the cause of all the hardships they had undergone: *"Thou hast been displeased* by us, displeased against us (*v.* 1), and in thy displeasure hast cast us off and scattered us, hast put us out of thy protection, else our enemies could not have prevailed thus against us. They would never have picked us up and made a prey of us if thou hadst not broken *the staff of bands* (Zec. 11:14) by which we were united, and so scattered us." Whatever our trouble is, and whoever are the instruments of it, we must own the hand of God, his righteous hand, in it. 3. He laments the ill effects and consequences of the miscarriages of the late years. The whole nation was in a convulsion: *Thou hast made the earth* (or *the land) to tremble, v.* 2. The generality of the people had dreadful apprehensions of the issue of these things. The good people themselves were in a consternation: *"Thou hast made us to drink the wine of astonishment* (*v.* 3); we were like men intoxicated, and at our wits' end, not knowing how to reconcile these dispensations with God's promises and his relation to his people; we are amazed, can do nothing, nor know we what to do." Now this is mentioned here *to teach,* that is, for the instruction of the people. When God is turning his hand in our favour, it is good to remember our former calamities, (1.) That we may retain the good impressions they made upon us, and may have them revived. Our souls must still have the affliction and the misery in remembrance, that they may be *humbled within us,* Lam. 3:19, 20. (2.) That God's goodness to us, in relieving us and raising us up, may be more magnified; for it is as life from the dead, so strange, so refreshing. Our calamities serve as foils to our joys. (3.) That we may not be secure, but may always rejoice with trembling, as those that know not how soon we may be returned into the furnace again, which we were lately taken out of as the silver is when it is not thoroughly refined.

II. A thankful notice of the encouragement God had given them to hope that, though things had been long bad, they would now begin to mend (*v.* 4): *"Thou hast given a banner to those that fear thee* (for, as bad as the times are, there is a remnant among us that desire to fear thy name, for whom thou hast a tender concern), *that it may be displayed* by thee, *because of the truth* of thy promise which thou wilt perform, and to be displayed by them, in defense of truth and equity," Ps. 45:4. This banner was David's government, the establishment and enlargement of it over all Israel. The pious Israelites, who feared God and had a regard to the divine designation of David to the throne, took his elevation as a token for good, and like the lifting up of a banner to them, 1. It united them, as soldiers are gathered together to their colours. Those that were *scattered* (*v.* 1), divided among themselves, and so weakened and exposed, coalesced in him when he was fixed upon the throne. 2. It animated them, and put life and courage into them, as the soldiers are animated by the sight of their banner. 3. It struck a terror upon their enemies, to whom they could now hang out a flag of defiance. Christ, the Son of David, is given *for an ensign of the people* (Isa. 11:10), for a banner to those that fear God; in him, as the centre of their unity, they are gathered together in one; to him they seek, in him they glory and take courage. His love is the banner over them; in his name and strength they wage war with the powers of darkness, and under him the church becomes terrible as an army with banners.

III. A humble petition for seasonable mercy. 1. That God would be reconciled to them, though he had been displeased with them. In his displeasure their calamities began, and therefore in his favour their prosperity must begin: *O turn thyself to us again!* (*v.* 1) smile upon us, and take part with us; be at peace with us, and in that peace we shall have peace. *Tranquillus Deus tranquillat omnia — A God at peace with us spreads peace over all the scene.* 2. That they might be reconciled to one another, though they had been broken and wretchedly divided among themselves: *"Heal the breaches of our land* (*v.* 2), not only the breaches made upon us by our enemies, but the breaches made among ourselves by our unhappy divisions." Those are breaches which the folly and corruption of man makes, and which nothing but the wisdom and grace of God can make up and repair, by pouring out a spirit of love and peace, by which only a shaken shattered kingdom is set to rights and saved from ruin. 3. That thus they might be preserved out of the hands of their enemies (*v.* 5): *"That thy beloved may be delivered,* and not made a prey of, *save with thy right hand,* with thy own power and by such instruments as thou art pleased to make the men of thy right hand, *and hear me."* Those that fear God are his beloved; they are dear to him as the apple of his eye. They are often in distress, but they shall be delivered. God's own right hand shall save them; for those that have his heart have his hand. *Save them, and hear me.* Note, God's praying people may take the general deliverances of the church as answers to their payers in particular. If we improve what interest we have at the throne of grace for blessings for the public, and those blessings be bestowed, besides the share we have with others in the benefit of them we may each of us say, with peculiar satisfaction, "God has therein heard me, and answered me."

Verses 6–12

David is here rejoicing in hope and praying in hope; such are the triumphs of the saints, not so much upon the account of what they have in possession as of what they have in prospect (*v.* 6): *"God has spoken in his holiness* (that is, he has given me his word of promise, has *sworn by his holiness, and he will not lie unto David,* Ps. 89:35), therefore *I will rejoice,* and please myself with the hopes of the performance of the promise, which was intended for more than a pleasing promise," Note, God's word of promise, being a firm foundation of hope, is a full fountain of joy to all believers.

I. David here rejoices; and it is in prospect of two things: —

1. The perfecting of this revolution in his own kingdom. God having *spoken in his holiness* that David shall be king, he doubts not but the kingdom is all his own, as sure as if it were already in his hand: *I will divide Shechem* (a pleasant city in Mount Ephraim) *and mete out the valley of Succoth,* as my own. *Gilead is mine, and Manasseh is mine,* and both are entirely reduced, *v.* 7. Ephraim would furnish him with soldiers for his life-guards and his standing forces; Judah would furnish him with able judges for his courts of justice; and thus Ephraim would be *the strength of his head* and Judah *his lawgiver.* Thus may an active believer triumph in the promises, and take the comfort of all the good contained in them; for they are all yea and amen in Christ. *"God has spoken in his holiness,* and then pardon is mine, peace mine, grace mine, Christ mine, heaven mine, God himself mine." *All is yours, for you are Christ's,* 1 Co. 3:22, 23.

2. The conquering of the neighbouring nations, which had been vexatious to Israel, were still dangerous, and opposed the throne of David, *v.* 8. Moab shall be enslaved, and put to the meanest drudgery. *The Moabites became David's servants,* 2 Sa. 8:2. Edom shall be made a dunghill to throw old shoes upon; at least David shall take possession of it as his own, which was signified by *drawing off his shoe* over it, Ruth 4:7. As for the Philistines, let them, if they dare, triumph over him as they had done; he will soon force them to change their note. Rather let those that know their own interest triumph because of him; for it would be the greatest kindness imaginable to them to be brought into subjection to David and communion with Israel. But the war is not yet brought to an end; there is a *strong city,* Rabbah (perhaps) of the children of Ammon, which yet holds out; Edom is not yet subdued. Now, (1.) David is here enquiring for help to carry on the ark: *"Who will bring me into the strong city?* What allies, what auxiliaries, can I depend upon, to make me master of the enemies' country and their strongholds?" Those that have begun a good work cannot but desire to make a thorough work of it, and to bring it to perfection. (2.) He is expecting it from God only: *"Wilt not thou, O God?* For thou hast *spoken in thy holiness;* and wilt not thou be as good as thy word?" He takes notice of the frowns of Providence they had been under: *Thou hadst,* in appearance, *cast us off; thou didst not go forth with our armies.* When they were defeated and met with disappointments, they owned it was because they wanted (that is, because they had forfeited) the gracious presence of God with them; yet they do not therefore fly off from him, but rather take so much the faster hold of him; and the less he has done for them of late the more they hoped he would do. At the same time that they own God's justice in what was past they hope in his mercy for what was to come: "Though *thou hadst cast us off,* yet thou wilt not contend for ever, thou wilt not always chide; though *thou hadst cast us off,* yet thou hast begun to show mercy; and wilt thou not perfect what thou hast begun?" The Son of David, in his sufferings, seemed to be cast off by his Father when he cried out, *Why hast thou forsaken me?* and yet even then he obtained a glorious victory over the powers of darkness and their strong city, a victory which will undoubtedly be completed at last; for he has gone forth conquering and to conquer. The Israel of God, his spiritual Israel, are likewise, through him, more than conquerors. Though sometimes they may be tempted to think that God has cast them off, and may be foiled in particular conflicts, yet God will bring them into the strong city at last. *Vincimur in praelio, sed non in bello — We are foiled in a battle, but not in the whole war.* A lively faith in the promise will assure us, not only that *the God of peace shall tread Satan under our feet shortly,* but that *it is our Father's good pleasure to give us the kingdom.*

II. He prays in hope. His prayer is, *Give us help from trouble, v.* 11. Even in the day of their triumph they see themselves in trouble, because still in war, which is troublesome even to the prevailing side. None therefore can delight in war but those that love to fish in troubled waters. The *help from trouble* they pray for is preservation from those they were at war with. Though now they were conquerors, yet (so uncertain are the issues of war), unless God gave them help in the next engagement, they might be defeated; therefore, *Lord, send us help from the sanctuary. Help from trouble* is rest from war, which they prayed for, as those that contended for equity, not for victory. *Sic quaerimus pacem — Thus we seek for peace.* The hope with which they support themselves in this prayer has two things in it: — 1. A diffidence of themselves and all their creature-confidences: *Vain is the help of man.* Then only we are qualified to receive help from God when we are brought to own the insufficiency of all creatures to do that for us which we expect him to do. 2. A confidence in God, and in his power and promise (*v.* 12): *"Through God we shall do valiantly,* and so we shall do victoriously; for *he it is,* and he only, *that shall tread down our enemies,* and shall have the praise of doing it." Note, (1.) Our confidence in God must be so far from superseding that it must encourage and quicken our endeavours in the way of our duty. Though *it is God that performs all things for us,* yet there is something to be done by us. (2.) Hope in God is the best principle of true courage. Those that do their duty under his conduct may afford to do it valiantly; for what need those fear who have God on their side? (3.) It is only through God, and by the influence of his grace, that we do valiantly; it is he that puts strength into us, and inspires us, who of ourselves are weak and timorous, with courage and resolution. (4.) Though we do ever so valiantly, the success must be attributed entirely to him; for *he it is that shall tread down our enemies,* and not we ourselves. All our victories, as well as our valour, are from him, and therefore at his feet all our crown must be cast.

PSALM 61

David, in this psalm, as in many others, begins with a sad heart, but concludes with an air of pleasantness — begins with prayers and tears, but ends with songs of praise. Thus the soul, by being lifted up to God, returns to the enjoyment of itself. It should seem David was driven out and banished when he penned this psalm, wether by Saul or Absalom is uncertain: some think by Absalom, because he calls himself "the king" (*v.* 6), but that refers to the King Messiah. David, in this psalm, resolves to persevere in his duty, encouraged thereto both by his experience an by his expectations. I. He will call upon God because God had protected him (*v.* 1–3). II. He will call upon God because God had provided well for him (*v.* 4, 5). III. He will praise God because he had an assurance of the continuance of God's favour to him (*v.* 6–8). So that, in singing this psalm, we may find that which is very expressive both of our faith and of our hope, of our prayers and of our praises; and some passages in this psalm are very peculiar.

To the chief musician upon Neginah. *A psalm* of David.

Verses 1–4

In these verses we may observe,

I. David's close adherence and application to God by prayer in the day of his distress and trouble: "Whatever comes, *I will cry unto thee* (*v.* 2), — not cry unto other gods, but to thee only, — not fall out with thee because thou afflictest me, but still look unto thee, and wait upon thee, — not speak to thee in a cold and careless manner, but cry to thee with the greatest importunity and fervency of spirit, as one that will not let thee go except thou bless me." This he will do, 1. Notwithstanding his distance from the sanctuary, the house of prayer, where he used to attend as in the court of requests: *"From the end of the earth,* or of *the land,* from the most remote and obscure corner of the country, *will I cry unto thee."* Note, Wherever we are we may have liberty of access to God, and may find a way open to the throne of grace. *Undique ad coelos tantundem est viae — Heaven is equally accessible from all places.* "Nay, because I am here in the end of the earth, in sorrow and solitude, therefore *I will cry unto thee."* Note, That which separates us from our other comforts should drive us so much the nearer to God, the fountain of all comfort. 2. Notwithstanding the dejection and despondency of his spirit: "Though *my heart is overwhelmed,* it is not so sunk, so burdened, but that it may be lifted up to God in prayer; if it is not capable of being thus raised, it is certainly too much cast down. Nay, because my heart is ready to be overwhelmed, therefore *I will cry unto thee,* for by that means it will be supported and relived." Note, Weeping must quicken praying, and not deaden it. *Is any afflicted? Let him pray,* Jam. 5:13; Ps. 102, title.

II. The particular petition he put up to God when his heart was overwhelmed and he was ready to sink: *Lead me to the rock that is higher than I;* that is, 1. "To the rock which is too high for me to get up to unless thou help me to it. Lord, give me such an assurance and satisfaction of my own safety as I can never attain to but by thy special grace working such a faith in me." 2. "To the rock on the top of which I shall be set further out of the reach of my troubles, and nearer the serene and quiet region, than I can be by any power or wisdom of my own." God's power and promise are a rock that is higher than we. This rock is Christ; those are safe that are in him. We cannot get upon this rock unless God by his power lead us. *I will put thee in the cleft of the rock,* Ex. 33:22. We should therefore by faith and prayer put ourselves under the divine management, that we may be taken under the divine protection.

III. His desire and expectation of an answer of peace. He begs in faith (*v.* 1): *"Hear my cry, O God! attend unto my prayer;* that is, let me have the present comfort of knowing that I am heard (Ps. 20:6), and in due time let me have that which I pray for."

IV. The ground of this expectation, and the plea he uses to enforce his petition (*v.* 3): *"Thou hast been a shelter for me;* I have found in thee a rock higher than I: therefore I trust thou wilt still lead me to that rock." Note, Past experiences of the benefit of trusting in God, as they should engage us still to keep close to him, so they should encourage us to hope that it will not be in vain. "Thou hast been my *strong tower from the enemy,* and thou art as strong a ever, and thy name is as much a refuge to the righteous as ever it was." Prov. 18:10.

V. His resolution to continue in the way of duty to God and dependence on him, *v.* 4. 1. The service of God shall be his constant work and business. All those must make it so who expect to find God their shelter and strong tower: none but his menial servants have the benefit of his protection. *I will abide in thy tabernacle for ever.* David was now banished from the tabernacle, which was his greatest grievance, but he is assured that God by his providence would bring him back to his tabernacle, because he had by his grace wrought in him such a kindness for the tabernacle as that he was resolved to make it his perpetual residence, Ps. 27:4. He speaks of abiding in it *for ever* because that tabernacle was a type and figure of heaven, Heb. 9:8, 9, 24. Those that dwell in God's tabernacle, as it is a house of duty, during their short *ever* on earth, shall dwell in that tabernacle which is the house of glory during an endless *ever.* 2. The grace of God and the covenant of grace shall be his constant comfort: *I will make my refuge in the covert of his wings,* as the chickens seek both warmth and safety under the wings of the hen. Those that have found God a shelter to them ought still to have recourse to him in all their straits. This advantage those have that abide in God's tabernacle, that in the time of trouble he shall there hide them.

Verses 5–8

In these verses we may observe,

I. With what pleasure David looks back upon what God had done for him formerly (*v.* 5): *Thou, O God! hast heard my vows,* that is, 1. "The vows themselves which I made, and with which I bound my soul: thou hast taken notice of them; thou hast accepted them, because made in sincerity, and been well pleased with them; thou hast been mindful of them, and put me in mind of them." God put Jacob in mind of his vows, Gen. 31:13; 35:1. note, God is a witness to all our vows, all our good purposes, and all our solemn promises of new obedience. He keeps an account of them, which should be a good reason with us, as it was with David here, why we should perform our vows, *v.* 8. For he that hears the vows we made will make us hear respecting them if they be not made good. 2. "The prayers that went along with those vows; those thou hast graciously heard and answered," which encouraged him now to pray, *O God! hear my cry.* He that never did say to the seed of Jacob, Seek you me in vain, will not now begin to say so. "Thou hast heard my vows, and given a real answer to them; for *thou hast given me a heritage of those that fear thy name.*" Note, (1.) There is a peculiar people in the world that fear God name, that with a holy awe and reverence accept of and accommodate themselves to all the discoveries he is pleased to make of himself to the children of men. (2.) There is a heritage peculiar to that peculiar people, present comforts, earnests of their future bliss. God himself is their inheritance, their portion for ever. The Levites that had God for their inheritance must take up with him, and not expect a lot like their brethren; so those that fear God have enough in him, and therefore must not complain if they have but little of the world. (3.) We need desire no better heritage than that of those who fear God. If God deal with us as he uses to deal with those that love his name we need not desire to be any better dealt with.

II. With what assurance he looks forward to the continuance of his life (*v.* 6): *Thou shalt prolong the king's life.* This may be understood either, 1. Of himself. If it was penned before he came to the crown, yet, being anointed by Samuel, and knowing what God had spoken in his holiness, he could in faith call himself *the king,* though now persecuted as an out-law; or perhaps it was penned when Absalom sought to dethrone him, and force him into exile. There were those that aimed to shorten his life, but he trusted to God to prolong his life, which he did to the age of man set by Moses (namely, seventy years), which, being spent in serving his generation according to the will of God (Acts 13:36), might be reckoned *as many generations,* because many generations would be the better for him. His resolution was to abide in God's tabernacle for ever (*v.* 4), in a way of duty; and now his hope is that he shall abide before God for ever, in a way of comfort. Those abide to good purpose in this world that abide before God, that serve him and walk in his fear; and those that do so shall abide before him for ever. He speaks of himself in the third person, because the psalm was delivered to the chief musician for the use of the church, and he would have the people, in singing it, to be encouraged with an assurance that, notwithstanding the malice of his enemies, their king, as they wished, should live for ever. Or, 2. Of the Messiah, the King of whom he was a type. It was a comfort to David to think, whatever became of him, that the years of the Lord's Anointed would be as many generations, and that *of the increase of his government and peace there should be no end.* The Mediator shall abide before God for ever, for he always appears in the presence of God for us, and ever lives, making intercession; and, because he lives, we shall live also.

III. With what importunity he begs of God to take him and keep him always under his protection: *O prepare mercy and truth which may preserve him!* God's promises and our faith in them are not to supersede, but to quicken and encourage prayer. David is sure that God will prolong his life, and therefore prays that he would preserve it, not that he would prepare him a strong lifeguard, or a well-fortified castle, but that he would prepare mercy and truth for his preservation; that is, that God's goodness would provide for his safety according to the promise. We need not desire to be better secured than under the protection of God's mercy and truth. This may be applied to the Messiah: "Let him be sent in the fulness of time, in *performance of the truth to Jacob and the mercy to Abraham.*" Micah 7:20; Lu. 1:72, 73.

IV. With what cheerfulness he vows the grateful returns of duty to God (*v.* 8): *So will I sing praise unto thy name for ever.* Note, God's preservation of us calls upon us to praise him; and *therefore* we should desire to live, that we may praise him: *Let my soul live, and it shall praise thee.* We must make praising God the work of our time, even to the last (as long as our lives are prolonged we must continue praising God), and then it shall be made the work of our eternity, and we shall be praising him for ever. *That I may daily perform my vows.* His praising God was itself the performance of his vows, and it disposed his heart to the performance of his vows in other instances. Note, 1. The vows we have made we must conscientiously perform. 2. Praising God and paying our vows to him must be our constant daily work; every day we must be doing something towards it, because it is all but little in comparison with what is due, because we daily receive fresh mercies, and because, if we think much to do it daily, we cannot expect to be doing it eternally.

PSALM 62

This psalm has nothing in it directly either of prayer or praise, nor does it appear upon what occasion it was penned, nor whether upon any particular occasion, whether mournful or joyful. But in it, I. David with a great deal of pleasure professes his own confidence in God and dependence upon him, and encourages himself to continue waiting on him (*v.* 1–7). II. With a great deal of earnestness he excites and encourages others to trust in God likewise, and not in any creature (*v.* 8–12). In singing it we should stir up ourselves to wait on God.

To the chief musician, to Jeduthun. A psalm of David.

Verses 1–7

In these verses we have,

I. David's profession of dependence upon God, and upon him only, for all good (*v.* 1): *Truly my soul waiteth upon God. Nevertheless* (so some) or *"However it be,* whatever difficulties or dangers I may meet with, though God frown upon me and I meet with discouragements in my attendance on him, yet still my soul waits upon God" (or *is silent to God,* as the word is), "Says nothing against what he does, but quietly expects what he will do." We are in the way both of duty and comfort when our souls wait upon God, when we cheerfully refer ourselves, and the disposal of all our affairs, to his will and wisdom, when we acquiesce in and accommodate ourselves to all the dispensations of his providence, and patiently expect a doubtful event, with an entire satisfaction in his righteousness and goodness, *however it be. Is not my soul subject go God?* So the Septuagint. So it, certainly so it ought to be; our wills must be melted into his will. *My soul has respect to God, for from him cometh my salvation.* He doubts not but his salvation will come, though now he was threatened and in danger, and he expects it to come from God, and from him only; for *in vain is it hoped for from hills and mountains,* Jer. 3:23; Ps. 121:1, 2. "From him I know it will come, and therefore on him will I patiently wait till it does come, for his time is the best time." We may apply it to our eternal salvation, which is called *the salvation of God* (Ps. 50:23); from him it comes; he prepared it for us, he prepares us for it, and preserves us to it, and therefore let our souls wait on him, to be conducted through this world to that eternal salvation, in such way as he thinks fit.

II. The ground and reason of this dependence (*v.* 2): *He only is my rock and my salvation; he is my defence.* 1. "He has been so many a time; in him I have found shelter, and strength, and succour. He has by his grace supported me and borne me up under my troubles, and by his providence defended me from the insults of my enemies and delivered me out of the troubles into which I was plunged; and therefore *I trust he will deliver me,*" 2 Co. 1:10. 2. "He only can be my rock and my salvation. Creatures are insufficient; they are nothing without him, and therefore I will look above them to him." 3. "He has by covenant undertaken to be so. Even he that is the rock of ages is my rock; he that is the God of salvation is my salvation; he that is the Most High is my high place; and therefore I have all the reason in the world to confide in him."

III. The improvement he makes of his confidence in God.

1. Trusting in God, his heart is fixed. "If God is my strength and mighty delivered, *I shall not be greatly moved* (that is, I shall not be undone and ruined); I may be shocked, but I shall not be sunk." Or, "I shall not be much disturbed and disquieted in my own breast. I may be put into some fright, but I shall not be afraid with any amazement, nor so as to be put out of the possession of my own soul. I may be perplexed, but not in despair," 2 Co. 4:8. This hope in God will be an anchor of the soul, sure and stedfast.

2. His enemies are slighted, and all their attempts against him looked upon by him with contempt, *v.* 3, 4. If God be for us, we need not fear what man can do against us, though ever so mighty and malicious. He here, (1.) Gives a character of his enemies: *They imagine mischief,* design it with a great deal of the serpent's venom and contrive it with a great deal of the serpent's subtlety, and this *against a man,* one of their own kind, against one single man, that is not an equal match for them, for they are many; they continued their malicious persecution though Providence had often defeated their mischievous designs. *"How long will you* do it? Will you never be convinced of your error? Will your malice never have spent itself?" They are unanimous in their consultations to cast an excellent man *down from his excellency,* to draw an honest man from his integrity, to entangle him in sin, which is the only thing that can effectually cast us down from our excellency, to thrust a man, whom God has exalted, down from his dignity, and so to fight against God. Envy was at the bottom of their malice; they were grieved at David's advancement, and therefore plotted, by diminishing his character and blackening that (which was casting him down from his excellency) to hinder his preferment. In order to this they calumniate him, and love to hear such bad characters given of him and such bad reports raised and spread concerning him as they themselves know to be false: *They delight in lies.* And as they make no conscience of lying concerning him, to do him a mischief, so they make no conscience of lying to him, to conceal the mischief they design, and accomplish it the more effectually: *They bless with their mouth* (they compliment David to his face), *but they curse inwardly;* in their hearts they wish him all mischief, and privately they are plotting against him and in their cabals carrying on some evil design or other, by which they hope to ruin him. It is dangerous putting our trust in men who are thus false; but God is faithful. (2.) He reads their doom, pronounces a sentence of death upon them, not as a king, but as a prophet: *You shall be slain all of you,* by the righteous judgments of God. Saul and his servants were slain by the Philistines on Mount Gilboa, according to this prediction. Those who seek the ruin of God's chosen are but preparing ruin for themselves. God's church is built upon a rock which will stand, but those that fight against it, and its patrons and protectors, shall be *as a bowing wall and a tottering fence,* which, having a rotten foundation, sinks with its own weight, falls of a sudden, and buries those in the ruins of it that put themselves under the shadow and shelter of it. David, having put his confidence in God, thus foresees the overthrow of his enemies, and, in effect, sets them at defiance and bids them do their worst.

3. He is himself encouraged to continue waiting upon God (*v.* 5–7): *My soul, wait thou only upon God.* Note, The good we do we should stir up ourselves to continue doing, and to do yet more and more, as those that have, through grace, experienced the comfort and benefit of it. We have found it good to wait upon God, and therefore should charge our souls, and even charm them, into such a constant dependence upon him as may make us always easy. He had said (*v.* 1), *From him cometh my salvation;* he says (*v.* 5), *My expectation is from him.* His salvation was the principal matter of his expectation; let him have that from God, and he expects no more. His salvation being from God, all his other expectations are from him. "If God will save my soul, as to every thing else let him do what he pleases with me, and I will acquiesce in his disposals, knowing they shall *all turn to my salvation,*" Phil. 1:19. He repeats (*v.* 6) what he had said concerning God (*v.* 2), as one that was not only assured of it, but greatly pleased with it, and that dwelt much upon it in his thoughts: *He only is my rock and my salvation; he is my defence,* I know he is; but there he adds, *I shall not be greatly moved,* here, *I shall not be moved at all.* Note, The more faith is acted the more active it is. *Crescit eundo — It grows by being exercised.* The more we meditate upon God's attributes and promises, and our own experience, the more ground we get of our fears, which, like Haman, when they begin to fall, shall fall before us, and we shall be *kept in perfect peace,* Isa. 26:3. And, as David's faith in God advances to an unshaken stayedness, so his joy in God improves itself into a holy triumph (*v.* 7): *In God is my salvation and my glory.* Where our salvation is there our glory is; for what is our salvation but the glory to be revealed, the eternal weight of glory? And there our glorying must be. In God let us boast all the day long. "The *rock of my strength* (that is, my strong rock, on which I build my hopes and stay myself) *and my refuge,* to which I flee for shelter when I am pursued, *is in God,* and in him only. I have no other

to flee to, no other to trust to; the more I think of it the better satisfied I am in the choice I have made." Thus does he *delight himself in the Lord, and then ride upon the high places of the earth,* Isa. 58:14.

Verses 8–12

Here we have David's exhortation to others to trust in God and wait upon him, as he had done. Those that have found the comfort of the ways of God themselves will invite others into those ways; there is enough in God for all the saints to draw from, and we shall have never the less for others sharing with us.

I. He counsels all to wait upon God, as he did, *v.* 8. Observe,

1. To whom he gives this good counsel: *You people* (that is, all people); all shall be welcome to trust in God, for he is *the confidence of all the ends of the earth,* Ps. 65:5. *You people of the house of Israel* (so the Chaldee); they are especially engaged and invited to trust in God, for he is the God of Israel; and should not a people seek unto their God?

2. What the good counsel is which he gives. (1.) To confide in God: *"Trust in him;* deal with him, and be willing to deal upon trust; depend upon him to perform all things for you, upon his wisdom and goodness, his power and promise, his providence and grace. Do this *at all times."* We must have an habitual confidence in God always, must live a life of dependence upon him, must so trust in him at all times as not at any time to put that confidence in ourselves, or in any creature, which is to be put in him only; and we must have an actual confidence in God upon all occasions, trust in him upon every emergency, to guide us when we are in doubt, to protect us when we are in danger, to supply us when we are in want, to strengthen us for every good word and work. (2.) To converse with God: *Pour out your heart before him.* The expression seems to allude to the pouring out of the drink-offerings before the Lord. When we make a penitent confession of sin our hearts are therein *poured out before God,* 1 Sa. 7:6. But here it is meant of prayer, which, if it be as it should be, is the pouring out of the heart before God. We must lay our grievances before him, offer up our desires to him with all humble freedom, and then entirely refer ourselves to his disposal, patiently submitting our wills to his: this is pouring out our hearts.

3. What encouragement he gives us to take this good counsel: *God is a refuge for us,* not only my refuge (*v.* 7), but a refuge for us all, even as many as will flee to him and take shelter in him.

II. He cautions us to take heed of misplacing our confidence, in which, as much as in any thing, *the heart is deceitful,* Jer. 17:5–9. Those that trust in God truly (*v.* 1) will trust in him only, *v.* 5. 1. Let us not trust in the men of this world, for they are broken reeds (*v.* 9): *Surely men of low degree are vanity,* utterly unable to help us, and *men of high degree are a lie,* that will deceive us if we trust to them. Men of low degree, one would think, might be relied on for their multitude and number, their bodily strength and service, and men of high degree for their wisdom, power, and influence; but neither the one nor the other are to be depended on. Of the two, men of high degree are mentioned as the more deceiving; for they are *a lie,* which denotes not only vanity, but iniquity. We are not so apt to depend upon men of low degree as upon the king and the captain of the host, who, by the figure they make, tempt us to trust in them, and so, when they fail us, prove a lie. But lay them *in the balance,* the balance of the scripture, or rather make trial of them, see how they will prove, whether they will answer your expectations from them or no, and you will write *Tekel* upon them; they are alike *lighter than vanity;* there is no depending upon their wisdom to advise us, their power to act for us, their good-will to us, no, nor upon their promises, in comparison with God, nor otherwise than in subordination to him. 2. Let us not trust in the wealth of this world, let not that be made our strong city (*v.* 10): *Trust not in oppression;* that is, in riches got by fraud and violence, because where there is a great deal it is commonly got by indirect scraping or saving (our Saviour calls it the *mammon of unrighteousness,* Lu. 16:9), or in the arts of getting riches. "Think not, either because you have got abundance or are in the way of getting, that therefore you are safe enough; for this is becoming *vain in rob-*

bery, that is, cheating yourselves while you think to cheat others." He that *trusted in the abundance of his riches strengthened himself in his wickedness* (Ps. 52:7); but at his end he will be a fool, Jer. 17:11. Let none be so stupid as to think of supporting themselves in their sin, much less of supporting themselves in this sin. Nay, because it is hard to have riches and not to trust in them, if they increase, though by lawful and honest means, we must take heed lest we let out our affections inordinately towards them: *"Set not your heart upon them;* be not eager for them, do not take a complacency in them as the rest of your souls, nor put a confidence in them as your portion; be not over-solicitous about them; do not value yourselves and others by them; make not the wealth of the world your chief good and highest end: in short, do not make an idol of it." This we are most in danger of doing when riches increase. When the grounds of the rich man brought forth plentifully, then he said to his soul, *Take thy ease* in these things, Lu. 12:19. It is a smiling world that is most likely to draw the heart away from God, on whom only it should be set.

III. He gives a very good reason why we should make God our confidence, because he is a God of infinite power, mercy, and righteousness, *v.* 11, 12. This he himself was well assured of and would have us be assured of it: *God has spoken once; twice have I heard this;* that is, 1. "God has spoken it, and I have heard it, once, yea, twice. He has spoken it, and I have heard it by the light of reason, which easily infers it from the nature of the infinitely perfect Being and from his works both of creation and providence. He has spoken it, and I have heard once, yea, twice (that is, many a time), by the events that have concerned me in particular. He has spoken it and I have heard it by the light of revelation, by dreams and visions (Job 4:15), by the glorious manifestation of himself upon Mount Sinai" (to which, some think, it does especially refer), "and by the written word." God has often told us what a great and good God he is, and we ought as often to take notice of what he has told us. Or, 2. "Though God spoke it but once, I heard it twice, heard it diligently, not only with my outward ears, but with my soul and mind." To some God speaks twice and they will not hear once; but to others he speaks but once, and they hear twice. Compare Job 33:14. Now what is it which is thus spoken and thus heard? (1.) That the God with whom we have to do is infinite in power. *Power belongs to God;* he is almighty, and can do every thing; with him nothing is impossible. All the powers of all the creatures are derived form him, depend upon him, and are used by him as he pleases. His is the power, and to him we must ascribe it. This is a good reason why we should trust in him at all times and live in a constant dependence upon him; for he is able to do all that for us which we trust in him for. (2.) That he is a God of infinite goodness. Here the psalmist turns his speech to God himself, as being desirous to give him the glory of his goodness, which is his glory: *Also unto thee, O Lord! belongeth mercy.* God is not only the greatest, but the best, of beings. Mercy is with him, Ps. 130:4, 7. He is merciful in a way peculiar to himself; he is the *Father of mercies,* 2 Co. 1:3. This is a further reason why we should trust in him, and answers the objections of our sinfulness and unworthiness; though we deserve nothing but his wrath, yet we may hope for all good from his mercy, which is over all his works. (3.) That he never did, nor ever will do, any wrong to any of his creatures: *For thou renderest to every man according to his work.* Though he does not always do this visibly in this world, yet he will do it in the day of recompence. No service done him shall go unrewarded, nor any affront given him unpunished, unless it be repented of. By this it appears that power and mercy belong to him. If he were not a God of power, there are sinners that would be too great to be punished. And if he were not a God of mercy there are services that would be too worthless to be rewarded. This seems especially to bespeak the justice of God in judging upon appeals made to him by wronged innocency; he will be sure to judge according to truth, in giving redress to the injured and avenging them on those that have been injurious to them, 1 Ki. 8:32. Let those therefore that are wronged commit their cause to him and trust to him to plead it.

PSALM 63

This psalm has in it as much of warmth and lively devotion as any of David's psalms in so little a compass. As the sweetest of Paul's epistles were those that bore date out of a prison, so some of the sweetest of David's psalms were those that were penned, as this was, in a wilderness. That which grieved him most in his banishment was the want of public ordinances; these he here longs to be restored to the enjoyment of; and the present want did but whet his appetite. Yet it is not the ordinances, but the God of the ordinances, that his heart is upon. And here we have, I. His desire towards God (*v.* 1, 2). II. His esteem of God (*v.* 3, 4). III. His satisfaction in God (*v.* 5). IV. His secret communion with God (*v.* 6). V. His joyful dependence upon God (*v.* 7, 8). IV. His holy triumph in God over his enemies and in the assurance of his own safety (*v.* 9–11). A devout and pious soul has little need of direction how to sing this psalm, so naturally does it speak its own genuine language; and an unsanctified soul, that is unacquainted and unaffected with divine things, is scarcely capable of singing it with understanding.

A psalm of David, when he was in the wilderness of Judah.

Verses 1–2

The title tells us when the psalm was penned, when David was *in the wilderness of Judah;* that is, *in the forest of Hareth* (1 Sa. 22:5) or in *the wilderness of Ziph,* 1 Sa. 23:15. 1. Even in Canaan, though a fruitful land and the people numerous, yet there were wildernesses, places less fruitful and less inhabited than other places. It will be so in the world, in the church, but not in heaven; there it is all city, all paradise, and no desert ground; *the wilderness* there *shall blossom as the rose.* 2. The best and dearest of God's saints and servants may sometimes have their lot cast in a wilderness, which speaks them lonely and solitary, desolate and afflicted, wanting, wandering, and unsettled, and quite at a loss what to do with themselves. 3. All the straits and difficulties of a wilderness must not put us out of tune for sacred songs; but even then it is our duty and interest to keep up a cheerful communion with God. There are psalms proper for a wilderness, and we have reason to thank God that it is the wilderness of Judah we are in, not the wilderness of Sin.

David, in these verses, *stirs up himself to take hold on God,*

I. By a lively active faith: *O God! thou art my God.* Note, In all our addresses to God we must eye him as God, and our God, and this will be our comfort in a wilderness-state. We must acknowledge that God is, that we speak to one that really exists and is present with us, when we say, *O God!* which is a serious word; pity it should ever be used as a by-word. And we must own his authority over us and propriety in us, and our relation to him: *"Thou art my God,* mine by creation and therefore my rightful owner and ruler, mine by covenant and my own consent." We must speak it with the greatest pleasure to ourselves, and thankfulness to God, as those that are resolved to abide by it: *O God! thou art my God.*

II. By pious and devout affections, pursuant to the choice he had made of God and the covenant he had made with him.

1. He resolves to seek God, and his favour and grace: *Thou art my God,* and therefore *I will seek thee;* for *should not a people seek unto their God?* Isa. 8:19. We must seek him; we must covet his favour as our chief good and consult his glory as our highest end; we must seek acquaintance with him by his word and seek mercy from him by prayer. We must seek him, (1.) Early, with the utmost care, as those that are afraid of missing him; we must begin our days with him, begin every day with him: *Early will I seek thee.* (2.) Earnestly: *"My soul thirsteth for thee* and *my flesh longeth for thee* (that is, my whole man is affected with this pursuit) here *in a dry and thirsty land."* Observe, [1.] His complaint in the want of God's favourable presence. He was in a dry and thirsty land; so he reckoned it, not so much because it was a wilderness as because it was at a distance from the ark, from the word and sacraments. This world is a *weary land* (so the word is); it is so to the worldly that have their portion in it — it will yield them no true satisfaction; it is so to the godly that have their passage through it — it is a valley of Baca; they can promise themselves little from it. [2.] His importunity for that presence of God: *My soul thirsteth, longeth, for thee.* His want quickened his desires, which were very intense; he thirsted as the hunted hart for the water-brooks; he would take up with nothing short of it. His desires were almost impatient; he longed, he languished, till he should be re-

stored to the liberty of God's ordinances. Note, Gracious souls look down upon the world with a holy disdain and look up to God with a holy desire.

2. He longs to enjoy God. What is it that he does so passionately wish for? What is his petition and what is his request? It is this (*v.* 2), *To see thy power and thy glory, so as I have seen thee in the sanctuary.* That is, (1.) "To see it here in this wilderness as I have seen it in the tabernacle; to see it in secret as I have seen it in the solemn assembly." Note, When we are deprived of the benefit of public ordinances we should desire and endeavour to keep up the same communion with God in our retirements that we have had in the great congregation. A closet may be turned into a little sanctuary. Ezekiel had the visions of the Almighty in Babylon, and John in the isle of Patmos. When we are alone we may have the Father with us, and that is enough. (2.) "To see it again in the sanctuary as I have formerly seen it there." He longs to be brought out of the wilderness, not that he might see his friends again and be restored to the pleasures and gaieties of the court, but that he might have access to the sanctuary, not to see the priests there, and the ceremony of the worship, but *to see thy power and glory* (that is, thy glorious power, or thy powerful glory, which is put for all God's attributes and perfections), "that I may increase in my acquaintance with them and have the agreeable impressions of them made upon my heart" — so to *behold the glory of the Lord* as to *be changed into the same image,* 2 Co. 3:18. "That I may see thy power and glory," he does not say, as I have seen them, but "as I have seen *thee.*" We cannot see the essence of God, but we see him in seeing by faith his attributes and perfections. These sights David here pleases himself with the remembrance of. Those were precious minutes which he spent in communion with God; he loved to think them over again; these he lamented the loss of, and longed to be restored to. Note, That which has been the delight and is the desire of gracious souls, in their attendance on solemn ordinances, is to see God and his power and glory in them.

Verses 3–6

How soon are David's complaints and prayers turned into praises and thanksgivings! After two verses that express his desire in seeking God, here are some that express his joy and satisfaction in having found him. Faithful prayers may quickly be turned into joyful praises, if it be not our own fault. *Let the hearts of those rejoice that seek the Lord* (Ps. 105:3), and let them praise him for working those desires in them, and giving them assurance that he will satisfy them. David was now in a wilderness, and yet had his heart much enlarged in blessing God. Even in affliction we need not want matter for praise, if we have but a heart to it. Observe,

I. What David will praise God for (*v.* 3): *Because thy lovingkindness is better than life,* than *lives,* life and all the comforts of life, life in its best estate, long life and prosperity. God's lovingkindness is in itself, and in the account of all the saints, better than life. It is our spiritual life, and that is better than temporal life, Ps. 30:5. It is better, a thousand times, to die in God's favour than to live under his wrath. David in the wilderness finds, by comfortable experience, that God's lovingkindness is better than life; and *therefore* (says he) *my lips shall praise thee.* Note, Those that have their hearts refreshed with the tokens of God's favour ought to have them enlarged in his praises. A great deal of reason we have to bless God that we have better provisions and better possessions than the wealth of this world can afford us, and that in the service of God, and in communion with him, we have better employments and better enjoyments than we can have in the business and converse of this world.

II. How he will praise God, and how long, *v.* 4. He resolves to live a life of thankfulness to God and dependence on him. Observe, 1. His manner of blessing God: *"Thus will I bless thee,* thus as I have now begun; the present devout affections shall not pass away, like the morning cloud, but shine more and more, like the morning sun." Or, "I will bless thee with the same earnestness and fervency with which I have prayed to thee." 2. His continuance and perseverance therein: *I will bless thee while I live.* Note, Praising God must be the work of our whole lives; we must always retain a grateful sense of his former

favours and repeat our thanksgivings for them. We must every day give thanks to him for the benefits with which we are daily loaded. We must in every thing give thanks, and not be put out of frame for this duty by any of the afflictions of this present time. Whatever days we live to see, how dark and cloudy soever, though the days come of which we say, *We have no pleasure in them,* yet still every day must be a thanksgiving-day, even to our dying-day. In this work we must spend our time because in this work we hope to spend a blessed eternity. 3. His constant regard to God upon all occasions, which should accompany his praises of him: *I will lift up my hands in thy name.* We must have an eye to God's name (to all that by which he has made himself known) in all our prayers and praises, which we are taught to begin with, — *Hallowed be thy name,* and to conclude with, — *Thine is the glory.* This we must have an eye to in our work and warfare; we must lift up our hands to our duty and against our special enemies in God's name, that is, in the strength of his Spirit and grace, Ps. 71:16; Zec. 10:12. We must make all our vows in God's name; to him we must engage ourselves and in a dependence upon his grace. And when we lift up the hands that hang down, in comfort and joy, it must be in God's name; from him our comforts must be fetched, and to him they must be devoted. *In thee do we boast all the day long.*

III. With what pleasure and delight he would praise God, *v.* 5. 1. With inward complacency: *My soul shall be satisfied as with marrow and fatness,* not only as with bread, which is nourishing, but as with marrow, which is pleasant and delicious, Isa. 25:6. David hopes he shall return again to the enjoyment of God's ordinances, and then he shall thus be satisfied, and the more for his having been for a time under restraint. Or, if not, yet in God's loving kindness, and in conversing with him in solitude, he shall be thus satisfied. Note, There is that in a gracious God, and in communion with him, which gives abundant satisfaction to a gracious soul, Ps. 36:8; 65:4. And there is that in a gracious soul which takes abundant satisfaction in God and communion with him. The saints have a contentment with God; they desire no more than his favour to make them happy; and they have a transcendent complacency in God, in comparison with which all the delights of sense are sapless and without relish, as puddle-water in comparison with the wine of this consolation. 2. With outward expressions of this satisfaction; he will praise God *with joyful lips.* He will praise him, (1.) Openly. His mouth and lips shall praise God. When with the heart man believes and is thankful, with the mouth confession must be made of both, to the glory of God; not that the performances of the mouth are accepted without the heart (Mt. 15:8), but out of the abundance of the heart the mouth must speak (Ps. 45:1), both for the exciting of our own devout affections and for the edification of others. (2.) Cheerfully. We must praise God with joyful lips; we must address ourselves to that and other duties of religion with great cheerfulness, and speak forth the praises of God from a principle of holy joy. Praising lips must be joyful lips.

IV. How he would entertain himself with thoughts of God when he was most retired (*v.* 6): I will praise thee *when I remember thee upon my bed.* We must praise God upon every remembrance of him. Now that David was shut out from public ordinances he abounded the more in secret communion with God, and so did something towards making up his loss. Observe here, 1. How David employed himself in thinking of God. God was in all his thoughts, which is the reverse of the wicked man's character, Ps. 10:4. The thoughts of God were ready to him: "*I remember thee;* that is, when I go to think, I find thee at my right hand, present to my mind." This subject should first offer itself, as that which we cannot forget or overlook. And they were fixed in him: "*I meditate on thee.*" Thoughts of God must not be transient thoughts, passing through the mind, but abiding thoughts, dwelling in the mind. 2. When David employed himself thus — *upon his bed* and in the night-watches. David was now wandering and unsettled, but, wherever he came, he brought his religion along with him. Upon my *beds* (so some); being hunted by Saul, he seldom lay two nights together in the same bed; but wherever he lay, if, as Jacob, upon the cold ground and with a stone for his pillow, good thoughts of God lay down with him. David was so full of business all day, shifting for his

own safety, that he had scarcely leisure to apply himself solemnly to religious exercises, and therefore, rather than want time for them, he denied himself his necessary sleep. He was now in continual peril of his life, so that we may suppose care and fear many a time held his eyes waking and gave him wearisome nights; but then he entertained and comforted himself with thoughts of God. Sometimes we find David in tears upon his bed (Ps. 6:6), but thus he wiped away his tears. When sleep departs from our eyes (through pain, or sickness of body, or any disturbance in the mind) our souls, by remembering God, may be at ease, and repose themselves. Perhaps an hour's pious meditation will do us more good than an hour's sleep would have done. See Ps. 16:7; 17:3; 4:4; 119:62. There were night-watches kept in the tabernacle for praising God (Ps. 134:1), in which, probably, David, when he had liberty, joined with the Levites; and now that he could not keep place with them he kept time with them, and wished himself among them.

Verses 7–11

David, having expressed his desires towards God and his praises of him, here expresses his confidence in him and his joyful expectations from him (*v.* 7): *In the shadow of thy wings I will rejoice,* alluding either to the wings of the cherubim stretched out over the ark of the covenant, between which God is said to dwell ("I will rejoice in thy oracles, and in covenant and communion with thee"), or to the wings of a fowl, under which the helpless young ones have shelter, as the eagle's young ones (Ex. 19:4, Deu. 32:11), which speaks the divine power, and the young ones of the common hen (Mt. 23:37), which speaks more of divine tenderness. It is a phrase often used in the psalms (Ps. 17:8; 36:7; 57:1; 61:4; 91:4), and no where else in this sense, except Ruth 2:12, where Ruth, when she became a proselyte, is said to *trust under the wings of the God of Israel.* It is our duty to *rejoice in the shadow of God's wings,* which denotes our recourse to him by faith and prayer, as naturally as the chickens, when they are cold or frightened, run by instinct under the wings of the hen. It intimates also our reliance upon him as able and ready to help us and our refreshment and satisfaction in his care and protection. Having committed ourselves to God, we must be easy and pleased, and quiet from the fear of evil. Now let us see further,

I. What were the supports and encouragements of David's confidence in God. Two things were as props to that hope which the word of God was the only foundation of: —

1. His former experiences of God's power in relieving him: "*Because thou hast been my help* when other helps and helpers failed me, therefore I will still rejoice in thy salvation, will trust in thee for the future, and will do it with delight and holy joy. Thou hast been not only my helper, but my help;" for we could never have helped ourselves, nor could any creature have been helpful to us, but by him. Here we may set up our Ebenezer, saying, *Hitherto the Lord has helped us,* and must therefore resolve that we will never desert him, never distrust him, nor ever droop in our walking with him.

2. The present sense he had of God's grace carrying him on in these pursuits (*v.* 8): *My soul follows hard after thee,* which speaks a very earnest desire and a serious vigorous endeavour to keep up communion with God; if we cannot always have God in our embraces, yet we must always have him in our eye, reaching forth towards him as our prize, Phil. 3:14. To press hard after God is to follow him closely, as those that are afraid of losing the sight of him, and to follow him swiftly, as those that long to be with him. This David did, and he owns, to the glory of God, *Thy right hand upholds me.* God upheld him, (1.) Under his afflictions, that he might not sink under them. *Underneath are the everlasting arms.* (2.) In his devotions. God upheld him in his holy desires and pursuits, that he might not grow weary in well-doing. Those that follow hard after God would soon fail and faint if God's right hand did not uphold them. It is he that strengthens us in the pursuit of him, quickens our good affections, and comforts us while we have not yet attained what we are in the pursuit of. It is by the power of God (that is his right hand) that we are kept from falling. Now this was a great encouragement to the psalmist to hope that he would, in due time,

give him that which he so earnestly desired, because he had by his grace wrought in him those desires and kept them up.

II. What it was that David triumphed in the hopes of.

1. That his enemies should be ruined, *v.* 9, 10. There were those that *sought his soul to destroy it,* not only his life (which they struck at, both to prevent his coming to the crown and because they envied and hated him for his wisdom, piety, and usefulness), but his soul, which they sought to destroy by banishing him from God's ordinances, which are the nourishment and support of the soul (so doing what they could to starve it), and by sending him to serve other gods, so doing what they could to poison it, 1 Sa. 26:19. But he foresees and foretels, (1.) That they shall *go into the lower parts of the earth,* to the grave, to hell; their enmity to David would be their death and their damnation, their ruin, their eternal ruin. (2.) That they shall fall by the sword, by the sword of God's wrath and his justice, by the sword of man, Job 19:28, 29. They shall die a violent death, Rev. 13:10. This was fulfilled in Saul, who fell by the sword, his own sword; David foretold this, yet he would not execute it when it was in the power of his hand, once and again; for precepts, not prophecies, are our rule. (3.) That *they shall be a portion for foxes;* either their dead bodies shall be a prey to ravenous beasts (Saul lay a good while unburied) or their houses and estates shall be a habitation for wild beasts, Isa. 34:14. Such as this will be the doom of Christ's enemies, that oppose his kingdom and interest in the world; *Bring them forth and slay them before me,* Lu. 19:27.

2. That he himself should gain his point at last (*v.* 11), that he should be advanced to the throne to which he had been anointed: *The king shall rejoice in God.* (1.) He calls himself *the king,* because he knew himself to be so in the divine purpose and designation; thus Paul, while yet in the conflict, writes himself *more than a conqueror,* Rom. 8:37. Believers are made kings, though they are not to have the dominion till the morning of the resurrection. (2.) He doubts not but that though he was now sowing in tears he should reap in joy. *The king shall rejoice.* (3.) He resolves to make God the Alpha and Omega of all his joys. He shall *rejoice in God.* Now this is applicable to the glories and joys of the exalted Redeemer. Messiah the Prince shall rejoice in God; he has already entered into the joy set before him, and his glory will be completed at his second coming. Two things would be the good effect of David's advancement: — [1.] It would be the consolation of his friends. *Every one that swears to him* (that is, to David), that comes into his interest and takes an oath of allegiance to him, *shall glory* in his success; or *every one that swears by him* (that is, by the blessed name of God, and not by any idol, Deu. 6:13), and then it means all good people, that make a sincere and open profession of God's name; they shall glory in God; they shall glory in David's advancement. *Those that fear thee will be glad when they see me.* Those that heartily espouse the cause of Christ shall glory in its victory at last. *If we suffer with him, we shall reign with him.* [2.] It would be the confutation of his enemies: *The mouth of those that speak lies,* of Saul, and Doeg, and others that misrepresented David and insulted over him, as if his cause was desperate, *shall be* quite *stopped;* they shall not have one word more to say against him, but will be for ever silenced and shamed. Apply this to Christ's enemies, to those that speak lies to him, as all hypocrites do, that tell him they love him while their hearts are not with him; their mouth shall be stopped with that word, *I know you not whence you are;* they shall be for ever speechless, Mt. 22:12. The mouths of those also that speak lies against him, that *pervert the right ways of the Lord* and speak ill of his holy religion, will be stopped in that day when the Lord shall come to reckon for all the hard speeches which ungodly sinners have spoken against him. Christ's second coming will be the everlasting triumph of all his faithful friends and followers, who may therefore now triumph in the believing hopes of it.

PSALM 64

This whole psalm has reference to David's enemies, persecutors, and slanderers; many such there were, and a great deal of trouble they gave him, almost all his days, so that we need not guess at any particular occasion of penning this psalm. I. He prays to God to preserve him from their malicious designs against him (*v.* 1, 2). II. He gives a very bad character of them, as men marked for ruin by their own wickedness (*v.* 3–6). III. By the spirit of prophecy he foretels their destruction, which would redound to the glory of God and the encouragement of his people (*v.* 7–10). In singing this psalm we must observe the effect of the old enmity that is in the seed of the woman against the seed of the serpent, and assure ourselves that the serpent's head will be broken, at last, to the honour and joy of the holy seed.

To the chief musician. A psalm of David.

Verses 1–6

David, in these verses, puts in before God a representation of his own danger and of his enemies' character, to enforce his petition that God would protect him and punish them.

I. He earnestly begs of God to preserve him (*v.* 1, 2): *Hear my voice, O God! in my prayer;* that is, grant me the thing I pray for, and this is it, *Lord, preserve my life from fear of the enemy,* that is, fro the enemy that I am in fear of. He makes request for his life, which is, in a particular manner, dear to him, because he knows it is designed to be very serviceable to God and his generation. When his life is struck at it cannot be thought he should altogether hold his peace, Est. 7:2, 4. And, if he plead his fear of the enemy, it is no disparagement to his courage; his father Jacob, that prince with God, did so before him. Gen. 32:11, *Deliver me from the hand of Esau, for I fear him. Preserve my life from fear,* not only from the thing itself which I fear, but from the disquieting fear of it; this is, in effect, the preservation of the life, for fear has torment, particularly the fear of death, by reason of which some are all their life-time subject to bondage. He prays, *"Hide me from the secret counsel of the wicked,* from the mischief which they secretly consult among themselves to do against me, and *from the insurrection of the workers of iniquity,* who join forces, as they join counsels, to do me a mischief." Observe, The secret counsel ends in an insurrection; treasonable practices begin in treasonable confederacies and conspiracies. "Hide me from them, that they may not find me, that they may not reach me. Let me be safe under thy protection."

II. He complains of the great malice and wickedness of his enemies: "Lord, hide me from them, for they are the worst of men, not fit to be connived at; they are dangerous men, that will stick at nothing; so that I am undone if thou do not take my part."

1. They are very spiteful in their calumnies and reproaches, *v.* 3, 4. They are described as military men, with their sword and bow, archers that take aim exactly, secretly, and suddenly, and shoot at the harmless bird that apprehends not herself in any danger. But, (1.) Their tongues are their swords, flaming swords, two-edged swords, drawn swords, drawn in anger, with which they cut, and wound, and kill, the good name of their neighbours. The tongue is a little member, but, like the sword, it *boasts great things,* Jam. 3:5. It is a dangerous weapon. (2.) *Bitter words* are *their arrows* — scurrilous reflections, opprobrious nicknames, false representations, slanders, and calumnies, the fiery darts of the wicked one, set on fire to hell. For these their malice *bends their bows,* to send out these arrows with so much the more force. (3.) The upright man is their mark; against him their spleen is, and they cannot speak peaceably either of him or to him. The better any man is the more he is envied by those that are themselves bad, and the more ill is said of him. (4.) They manage it with a great deal of art and subtlety. They *shoot in secret,* that those they shoot at may not discover them and avoid the danger, for *in vain is the net spread in the sight of any bird.* And *suddenly do they shoot,* without giving a man lawful warning or any opportunity to defend himself. *Cursed be he that thus smites his neighbour secretly* in his reputation, Deu. 27:24. There is no guard against a pass made by a false tongue. (5.) Herein *they fear not,* that is, they are confident of their success, and doubt not but by these methods they shall gain the point which their malice aims at. Or, rather, they fear not the wrath of God, which they will be the portion of a false tongue. They are impudent and daring in the mischief they do to good people, as if they must never be called to an account for it.

2. They are very close and very resolute in their malicious projects, *v.* 5. (1.) They strengthen and corroborate themselves and one another in this evil matter, and by joining together in it they make one another the more bitter and the more bold. *Fortiter calumniari, aliquid adhaerebit — Lay on an abundance of reproach; part will be sure to stick.* It is bad to do a wrong thing, but worse to encourage ourselves and one another in doing it; this is doing the devil's work for him. It is a sign that the heart is hardened to the highest degree when it is thus fully set to do evil and fears no colours. It is the office of conscience to discourage men in an evil matter, but, when that is baffled, the case is desperate. (2.) They consult with themselves and one another how to do the most mischief and most effectually: *They commune of laying snares privily.* All their communion is in sin and all their communication is how to sin securely. They hold councils of war for finding out the most effectual expedients to do mischief; every snare they lay was talked of before, and was laid with all the contrivance of their wicked wits combined. (3.) They please themselves with an atheistical conceit that God himself takes no notice of their wicked practices: *They say, Who shall see them?* A practical disbelief of God's omniscience is at the bottom of all the wickedness of the wicked.

3. They are very industrious in putting their projects in execution (*v.* 6): *"They search out iniquity;* they take a great deal of pains to find out some iniquity or other to lay to my charge; they dig deep, and look far back, and put things to the utmost stretch, that they may have something to accuse me of;" or, "They are industrious to find out new arts of doing mischief to me; in this they accomplish a diligent search; they go through with it, and spare neither cost nor labour." *Evil men dig up mischief.* Half the pains that many take to damn their souls would serve to save them. They are masters of all the arts of mischief and destruction, for *the inward thought of every one of them, and the heart, are keep,* deep as hell, desperately wicked, who can know it? By the unaccountable wickedness of their wit and of their will, they show themselves to be, both in subtlety and malignity, the genuine offspring of the old serpent.

Verses 7–10

We may observe here,

I. The judgments of God which should certainly come upon these malicious persecutors of David. Though they encouraged themselves in their wickedness, here is that which, if they would believe and consider it, was enough to discourage them. And it is observable how the punishment answers the sin. 1. They shot at David secretly and suddenly, to wound him; but God shall shoot at them, for the *ordains his arrows against the persecutors* (Ps. 7:13), *against the face of them,* Ps. 21:12. And God's arrows will hit surer, and fly swifter, and pierce deeper, than theirs do or can. They have many arrows, but they are only bitter words, and words are but wind: the curse causeless shall not come. But God has one arrow that will be their death, his curse which is never causeless, and therefore shall come; with it they shall be suddenly wounded, that is, their wound by it will be a surprise upon them, because they were secure and not apprehensive of any danger. 2. Their tongues fell upon him, but God shall *make their tongues to fall upon themselves.* They do it by the desert of their sin; God does it by the justice of his wrath, *v.* 8. When God deals with men according to the desert of their tongue-sins, and brings those mischiefs upon them which they have passionately and maliciously imprecated upon others, then he makes their own tongues to fall upon them; and it is weight enough to sink a man to the lowest hell, like a talent of lead. Many have cut their own throats, and many more have damned their own souls, with their tongues, and it will be an aggravation of their condemnation. *O Israel! thou hast destroyed thyself,* art *snared in the words of thy mouth. If thou scornest, thou alone shalt bear it.* Those that love cursing, it shall come unto them. Sometimes men's secret wickedness is brought to light by their own confession, and then their own tongue falls upon them.

II. The influence which these judgments should have upon others; for it is done *in the open sight of all,* Job 34:26.

1. Their neighbours shall shun them and shift for their own safety. They *shall flee away,* as the men of Israel did from the tents of Korah, Dathan, and Abiram, Num. 16:27. Some think this was fulfilled in the death of Saul, when

not only his army was dispersed, but the inhabitants of the neighbouring country were so terrified with the fall, not only of their king but of his three sons, that they quitted their cities and fled, 1 Sa. 31:7.

2. Spectators shall reverence the providence of God therein, *v.* 9. (1.) They shall understand and observe God's hand in all (and, unless we do so, we are not likely to profit by the dispensations of Providence, Hos. 14:9): *They shall wisely consider his doing.* There is need of consideration and serious thought rightly to apprehend the matter of fact, and need of wisdom to put a true interpretation upon it. God's doing is well worth our considering (Eccl. 7:13), but it must be considered wisely, that we put not a corrupt gloss upon a pure text. (2.) They shall be affected with a holy awe of God upon the consideration of it. All men (all that have any thing of the reason of a man in them) shall fear and tremble because of God's judgments, Ps. 119:120. They shall fear to do the like, fear being found persecutors of God's people. *Smite the scorner and the simple shall beware.* (3.) They shall declare the work of God. They shall speak to one another and to all about them of the justice of God in punishing persecutors. What we wisely consider ourselves we should wisely declare to others, for their edification and the glory of God. *This is the finger of God.*

3. Good people shall in a special manner take notice of it, and it shall affect them with a holy pleasure, *v.* 10. (1.) It shall increase their joy: *The righteous shall be glad in the Lord,* not glad of the misery and ruin of their fellow-creatures, but glad that God is glorified, and his word fulfilled, and the cause of injured innocency pleaded effectually. (2.) It shall encourage their faith. They shall commit themselves to him in the way of duty and be willing to venture for him with an entire confidence in him. (3.) Their joy and faith shall both express themselves in a holy boasting: *All the upright in heart,* that keep a good conscience and approve themselves to God, *shall glory,* not in themselves, but in the favour of God, in his righteousness and goodness, their relation to him and interest in him. *Let him that glories glory in the Lord.*

PSALM 65

In this psalm we are directed to give to God the glory of his power and goodness, which appear, I. In the kingdom of grace (*v.* 1), hearing prayer (*v.* 2), pardoning sin (*v.* 3), satisfying the souls of the people (*v.* 4), protecting and supporting them (*v.* 5). II. In the kingdom of Providence, fixing the mountains (*v.* 6), calming the sea (*v.* 7), preserving the regular succession of day and night (*v.* 8), and making the earth fruitful (*v.* 9–13). These are blessings we are all indebted to God for, and therefore we may easily accommodate this psalm to ourselves in singing it.

To the chief musician. A psalm *and* song of David.

Verses 1–5

The psalmist here has no particular concern of his own at the throne of grace, but begins with an address to God, as the master of an assembly and the mouth of a congregation; and observe,

I. How he gives glory to God, *v.* 1. 1. By humble thankfulness: *Praise waiteth for thee, O God! in Zion,* waits till it arrives, that it may be received with thankfulness at its first approach. When God is coming towards us with his favours we must go forth to meet him with our praises, and wait till the day dawn. "Praise waits, with an entire satisfaction in thy holy will and dependence on thy mercy." When we stand ready in every thing to give thanks, then praise waits for God. "Praise waits thy acceptance" the *Levites* by night *stood in the house of the Lord,* ready to sing their songs of praise at the hour appointed (Ps. 134:1, 2), and thus their praise waited for him. *Praise is silent unto thee* (so the word is), as wanting words to express the great goodness of God, and being struck with a silent admiration at it. As there are holy *groanings which cannot be uttered,* so there are holy adorings which cannot be uttered, and yet shall be accepted by him that *searches the heart and knows what is the mind of the spirit.* Our praise is silent, that the praises of the blessed angels, who excel in strength, may be heard. Let it not be told him that I speak, for if a man offer to *speak forth all God's praise surely he shall be swallowed up,* Job 37:20. *Before thee praise is reputed as silence* (so the Chaldee), so far exalted is God above all our blessing and praise. Praise is due to God from all the world, but it waits for him in Zion only, in his church, among his people. All his works praise him (they minister matter for praise), but only his saints bless him by actual adorations. The redeemed church sing their new song upon Mount Zion, Rev. 14:1, 3. In Zion was God's dwelling-place, Ps. 76:2. Happy are those who dwell with him there, for they will be still praising him. 2. By sincere faithfulness: *Unto thee shall the vow be performed,* that is, the sacrifice shall be offered up which was vowed. We shall not be accepted in our thanksgivings to God for the mercies we have received unless we make conscience of paying the vows which we made when we were in pursuit of the mercy; for better it is not to vow than to vow and not to pay.

II. What he gives him glory for.

1. For hearing prayer (*v.* 2): *Praise waits for thee;* and why is it so ready? (1.) "Because thou art ready to grant our petitions. *O thou that hearest prayer!* thou canst answer every prayer, for thou art able to do for us more than we are able to ask or think (Eph. 3:20), and thou wilt answer every prayer of faith, either in kind or kindness." It is much for the glory of God's goodness, and the encouragement of ours, that he is a God hearing prayer, and has taken it among the titles of his honour to be so; and we are much wanting to ourselves if we do not take all occasions to give him his title. (2.) Because, for that reason, we are ready to run to him when we are in our straits. "*Therefore,* because thou art a God hearing prayer, *unto thee shall all flesh come;* justly does every man's praise wait for thee, because every man's prayer waits on thee when he is in want or distress, whatever he does at other times. Now only the seed of Israel come to thee, and the proselytes to their religion; but, when thy *house shall be called a house of prayer to all people,* then unto thee shall all flesh come, and be welcome," Rom. 10:12, 13. To him let us come, and come boldly, because he is a God that hears prayer.

2. For pardoning sin. In this *who is a God like unto him?* Micah 7:18. By this he proclaims his name (Ex. 34:7), and therefore, upon this account, praise waits for him, *v.* 3. "Our sins reach to the heavens, *iniquities prevail against* us, and appear so numerous, so heinous, that when they are set in order before us we are full of confusion and ready to fall into despair. They prevail so against us that we cannot pretend to balance them with any righteousness of our own, so that when we appear before God our own consciences accuse us and we have no reply to make; and yet, *as for our transgressions, thou shalt,* of thy own free mercy and for the sake of a righteousness of thy own providing, *purge them away,* so that we shall not come into condemnation for them." Note, The greater our danger is by reason of sin the more cause we have to admire the power and riches of God's pardoning mercy, which can invalidate the threatening force of our manifold transgressions and our mighty sins.

3. For the kind entertainment he gives to those that attend upon him and the comfort they have in communion with him. Iniquity must first be purged away (*v.* 3) and then we are welcome to compass God's altars, *v.* 4. Those that come into communion with God shall certainly find true happiness and full satisfaction in that communion.

(1.) They are blessed. Not only blessed is the nation (Ps. 33:12), but *blessed is the man,* the particular person, how mean soever, *whom thou choosest, and causest to approach unto thee, that he may dwell in thy courts;* he is a happy man, for he has the surest token of the divine favour and the surest pledge and earnest of everlasting bliss. Observe here, [1.] What it is to come into communion with God, in order to this blessedness. *First,* It is to approach to him by laying hold on his covenant, setting our best affections upon him, and letting out our desires towards him; it is to converse with him as one we love and value. *Secondly,* It is to dwell in his courts, as the priests and Levites did, that were at home in God's house; it is to be constant in the exercises of religion, and apply ourselves closely to them as we do to that which is the business of our dwelling-place. [2.] How we come into communion with God, not recommended by any merit of our own, nor brought in by any management of our own, but by God's free choice: "*Blessed is the man whom thou choosest,* and so distinguishest from others who are left to themselves;" and it is by his effectual special grace pursuant to that choice; whom he chooses he causes to approach, not only invites them, but inclines and enables them, to draw nigh to him. He draws them, Jn. 6:44.

(2.) They shall be satisfied. Here the psalmist changes the person, not, *He* shall be satisfied (the man whom thou choosest), but, *We* shall, which teaches us to apply the promises to ourselves and by an active faith to put our own names into them: *We shall be satisfied with the goodness of thy house, even of thy holy temple.* Note, [1.] God's holy temple is his house; there he dwells, where his ordinances are administered. [2.] God keeps a good house. There is abundance of goodness in his house, righteousness, grace, and all the comforts of the everlasting covenant; there is enough for all, enough for each; it is ready, always ready; and all on free cost, without money and without price. [3.] In those things there is that which is satisfying to a soul, and with which all gracious souls will be satisfied. Let them have the pleasure of communion with God, and that suffices them; they have enough, they desire no more.

4. For the glorious operations of his power on their behalf (*v.* 5): *By terrible things in righteousness wilt thou answer us, O God of our salvation!* This may be understood of the rebukes which God in his providence sometimes gives to his own people; he often answers them by terrible things, for the awakening and quickening of them, but always in righteousness; he neither does them any wrong nor means them any hurt, for even then he is the God of their salvation. See Isa. 45:15. But it is rather to be understood of his judgments upon their enemies; God answers his people's prayers by the destructions made, for their sakes, among the heathen, and the recompence he renders to their proud oppressors, as a righteous God, the God to whom vengeance belongs, and as the God that protects and saves his people. By *wonderful* things (so some read it), things which are very surprising, and which we looked not for, Isa. 64:3. Or, "By things which strike an awe upon us thou wilt answer us." The holy freedom that we are admitted to in God's courts, and the nearness of our approach to him, must not at all abate our reverence and godly fear of him; for he is *terrible in his holy places.*

5. For the care he takes of all his people, however distressed, and whithersoever dispersed. He is *the confidence of all the ends of the earth* that is, of all the saints all the world over and not theirs only that were of the seed of Israel; for he is the God of the Gentiles as well as of the Jews, the confidence *of those that are afar off* from his holy temple and its courts, that dwell in the islands of the Gentiles, or that are in distress *upon the sea.* They trust in thee, and cry to thee, when they are at their wits' end, Ps. 107:27, 28. By faith and prayer we may keep up our communion with God, and fetch in comfort from him, wherever we are, not only in the solemn assemblies of his people, but also afar off upon the sea.

Verses 6–13

That we may be the more affected with the wonderful condescensions of the God of grace, it is of use to observe his power and sovereignty as the God of nature, the riches and bounty of his providential kingdom.

I. He establishes the earth and it abides, Ps. 119:90. *By his own strength* he *setteth fast the mountains* (*v.* 6), did set them fast at first and still keeps them firm, though they are sometimes shaken by earthquakes.

— Feriuntque summos. Fulmina montes.
The lightning blasts and loftiest hills.

Hence they are called *everlasting mountains,* Hab. 3:6. yet God's covenant with his people is said to stand more firmly than they, Isa. 54:10.

II. He stills the sea, and it is quiet, *v.* 7. The sea in a storm makes a great noise, which adds to its threatening terror; but, when God pleases, he commands silence among the waves and billows, and lays them to sleep, turns the storm into a calm quickly, Ps. 107:29. And by this change in the sea, as well as by the former instance of the unchangeableness of the earth, it appears that he whose the sea and the dry land are is girded with power. And by this our Lord Jesus gave a proof of his divine power, that he *commanded the winds and waves, and they obeyed him.* To this instance of the quieting of the sea he adds, as a thing much of the same nature, that he stills *the tumult of the people,* the common people. Nothing is more unruly and disagreeable than the insurrections of the mob, the insults of the rabble; yet even these God can pacify, in secret ways, which they themselves are not aware of. Or it may be meant of the outrage of the people that were enemies to Israel, Ps. 2:1. God has many ways to still them and will for ever silence their tumults.

III. He renews the morning and evening, and their revolution is constant, *v.* 8. This regular succession of day and night may be considered, 1. As an instance of God's great power, and so it strikes an awe upon all: *Those that dwell in the uttermost parts of the earth are afraid at thy* signs or *tokens;* they are by them convinced that there is a supreme deity, a sovereign monarch, before whom they ought to fear and tremble; for in these things the invisible things of God are clearly seen; and therefore they are said to be *set for signs,* Gen. 1:14. Many of those that dwell in the remote and dark corners of the earth were so afraid at these tokens that they were driven to worship them (Deu. 4:19), not considering that they were God's tokens, undeniable proofs of his power and godhead, and therefore they should have been led by them to worship him. 2. As an instance of God's great goodness, and so it brings comfort to all: *Thou makest the outgoings of the morning,* before the sun rises, *and of the evening,* before the sun sets, *to rejoice.* As it is God that scatters the light of the morning and draws the curtains of the evening, so he does both in favour to man, and makes both to rejoice, gives occasion to us to rejoice in both; so that how contrary soever light and darkness are to each other, and how inviolable soever the partition between them (Gen. 1:4), both are equally welcome to the world in their season. It is hard to say which is more welcome to us, the light of the morning, which befriends the business of the day, or the shadows of the evening, which befriend the repose of the night. Does the watchman wait for the morning? So does the hireling earnestly desire the shadow. Some understand it of the morning and evening sacrifice, which good people greatly rejoiced in and in which God was constantly honoured. Thou makest them to *sing* (so the word is); for every morning and every evening songs of praise were sung by the Levites; it was that which the duty of every day required. We are to look upon our daily worship, alone and with our families, to be both the most needful of our daily occupations and the most delightful of our daily comforts; and, if therein we keep up our communion with God, the outgoings both of the morning and of the evening are thereby made truly to rejoice.

IV. He waters the earth and makes it fruitful. On this instance of God's power and goodness he enlarges very much, the psalm being probably penned upon occasion either of a more than ordinarily plentiful harvest or of a seasonable rain after long drought. How much the fruitfulness of this lower part of the creation depends upon the influence of the upper is easy to observe; if the heavens be as brass, the earth is as iron, which is a sensible intimation to a stupid world that every good and perfect gift is from above, *omnia desuper — all from above;* we must lift up our eyes above the hills, lift them up to the heavens, where the original springs of all blessings are, out of sight, and thither must our praises return, as the first-fruits of the earth were in the heave-offerings lifted up towards heaven by way of acknowledgment that thence they were derived. All God's blessings, even spiritual ones, are expressed by his raining righteousness upon us. Now observe how the common blessing of rain from heaven and fruitful seasons is here described.

1. How much there is in it of the power and goodness of God, which is here set forth by a great variety of lively expressions. (1.) God that made the earth hereby visits it, sends to it, gives proof of his care of it, *v.* 9. It is a visit in mercy, which the inhabitants of the earth ought to return in praises. (2.) God, that made it dry land, hereby waters it, in order to its fruitfulness. Though the productions of the earth flourished before God had caused it to rain, yet even then there was a mist which answered the intention, and *watered the whole face of the ground,* Gen. 2:5, 6. Our hearts are dry and barren unless God himself be as the dew to us and water us; and the plants of his own planting he will water and make them to increase. (3.) Rain is *the river of God, which is full of water;* the clouds are the springs of this river, which do not flow at random, but in the channel which God cuts out for it. The showers of rain, as the rivers of water, he turns which way soever he pleases. (4.) This river of God enriches the earth,

which without it would quickly be a poor thing. The riches of the earth, which are produced out of its surface, are abundantly more useful and serviceable to man than those which are hidden in its bowels; we might live well enough without silver and gold, but not without corn and grass.

2. How much benefit is derived from it to the earth and to man upon it. (1.) To the earth itself. The rain in season gives it a new face; nothing is more reviving, more refreshing, than the *rain upon the new-mown grass,* Ps. 72:6. Even *the ridges* of the earth, off which the rain seems to slide, are watered *abundantly,* for they drink in the rain which comes often upon them; *the furrows* of it, which are turned up by the plough, in order to the seedness, are settled by the rain and made fit to receive the seed (*v.* 10); they are settled by being made soft. That which makes the soil of the heart tender settles it; for the heart is established with that grace. Thus the springing of the year is blessed; and if the spring, that first quarter of the year, be blessed, that is an earnest of a blessing upon the whole year, which God is therefore said to *crown with his goodness* (*v.* 11), to compass it on every side as the head is compassed with a crown, and to complete the comforts of it as the end of a thing is said to crown it. And his paths are said to *drop fatness;* for whatever fatness there is in the earth, which impregnates its productions, it comes from the out-goings of the divine goodness. Wherever God goes he leaves the tokens of his mercy behind him (Joel 2:13, 14) and makes his path thus to shine after him. These communications of God's goodness to this lower world are very extensive and diffusive (*v.* 12): *They drop upon the pastures of the wilderness,* and not merely upon the pastures of the inhabited land. The deserts, which man takes no care of and receives no profit from, are under the care of the divine Providence, and the profits of them redound to the glory of God, as the great benefactor of the whole creation, though not immediately to the benefit of man; and we ought to be thankful not only for that which serves us, but for that which serves any part of the creation, because thereby it turns to the honour of the Creator. The wilderness, which makes not such returns as the cultivated grounds do, receives as much of the rain of heaven as the most fruitful soil; for God does good to the evil and unthankful. So extensive are the gifts of God's bounty that in them the hills, *the little hills, rejoice on every side,* even the north side, that lies most from the sun. Hills are not above the need of God's providence; little hills are not below the cognizance of it. But as, when he pleases, he can make them tremble (Ps. 114:6), so when he pleases he can make them rejoice. (2.) To man upon the earth. God, by providing rain for the earth, prepares corn for man, *v.* 9. *As for the earth, out of it comes bread* (Job 28:5), for out of it comes corn; but every grain of corn that comes out of it God himself prepared; and therefore he provides rain for the earth, that thereby he may prepare corn for man, under whose feet he has put the rest of the creatures and for whose use he has fitted them. When we consider that the yearly produce of the corn is not only an operation of the same power that raises the dead, but an instance of that power not much unlike it (as appears by that of our Saviour, Jn. 12:24), and that the constant benefit we have from it is an instance of that goodness which endures for ever, we shall have reason to think that it is no less than a God that prepares corn for us. Corn and cattle are the two staple commodities with which the husbandman, who deals immediately in the fruits of the earth, is enriched; and both are owing to the divine goodness in watering the earth, *v.* 13. To this it is owing that the pastures are clothed with flocks, *v.* 13. So well stocked are the pastures that they seem to be covered over with the cattle that are laid in them, and yet the pasture not overcharged; so well fed are the cattle that they are the ornament and the glory of the pastures in which they are fed. The valleys are so fruitful that they seem to be *covered over with corn,* in the time of harvest. The lowest parts of the earth are commonly the most fruitful, and one acre of the humble valleys is worth five of the lofty mountains. But both corn-ground and pasture-ground, answering the end of their creation, are said to *shout for joy and sin,* because they are serviceable to the honour of God and the comfort of man, and because they furnish us with matter for joy and praise: as there is no earthly joy above the joy of harvest, so there was none of the feasts of the Lord, among

the Jews, solemnized with greater expressions of thankfulness than the *feast of in-gathering at the end of the year,* Ex. 23:16. Let all these common gifts of the divine bounty, which we yearly and daily partake of, increase our love to God as the best of beings, and engage us to glorify him with our bodies, which he thus provides so well for.

PSALM 66

This is a thanksgiving-psalm, and it is of such a general use and application that we need not suppose it penned upon any particular occasion. All people are here called upon to praise God, I. For the general instances of his sovereign dominion and power in the whole creation (*v.* 1-7). II. For the special tokens of his favour to the church, his peculiar people (*v.* 8-12). And then, III. The psalmist praises God for his own experiences of his goodness to him in particular, especially in answering his prayers (*v.* 13-20). If we have learned in every thing to give thanks for ancient and modern mercies, public and personal mercies, we shall know how to sing this psalm with grace and understanding.

To the chief musician. A song or psalm.

Verses 1–7

I. In these verses the psalmist calls upon all people to praise God, *all lands, all the earth,* all the inhabitants of the world that are capable of praising God, *v.* 1. 1. This speaks the glory of God, that he is worthy to be praised by all, for he is good to all and furnishes every nation with matter for praise. 2. The duty of man, that all are obliged to praise God; it is part of the law of creation, and therefore is required of every creature. 3. A prediction of the conversion of the Gentiles to the faith of Christ; the time should come when all lands should praise God, and this incense should in every place be offered to him. 4. A hearty good-will which the psalmist had to this good work of praising God. He will abound in it himself, and wishes that God might have his tribute paid him by all the nations of the earth and not by the land of Israel only. He excites all lands, (1.) To *make a joyful noise to God.* Holy joy is that devout affection which should animate all our praises; and, though it is not making a noise in religion that God will accept of (hypocrites are said to *cause their voice to be heard on high,* Isa. 58:4), yet, in praising God, [1.] We must be hearty and zealous, and must do what we do with all our might, with all that is within us. [2.] We must be open and public, as those that are not ashamed of our Master. And both these are implied in making a noise, a joyful noise. (2.) To sing with pleasure, and to *sing forth,* for the edification of others, *the honour of his name,* that is, of all that whereby he has made himself known, *v.* 2. That which is the honour of God's name ought to be the matter of our praise. (3.) To *make his praise glorious* as far as we can. In praising God we must do it so as to glorify him, and that must be the scope and drift of all our praises. *Reckon it your greatest glory to praise God,* so some. It is the highest honour the creature is capable of to be to the Creator for a name and a praise.

II. He had called upon all lands to praise God (*v.* 1), and he foretels (*v.* 4) that they shall do so: *All the earth shall worship thee;* some in all parts of the earth, even the remotest regions, for *the everlasting gospel shall be preached to every nation and kindred;* and this is the purport of it, *Worship him that made heaven and earth,* Rev. 14:6, 7. Being thus sent forth, it shall not return void, but shall bring all the earth, more or less, to worship God, and sing unto him. In gospel times God shall be worshipped by the singing of Psalms. They shall *sing to God,* that is, *sing to his name,* for it is only to his declarative glory, that by which he has made himself known, not to his essential glory, that we can contribute any thing by our praises.

III. That we may be furnished with matter for praise, we are here called upon *to come and see the works of God;* for *his own works praise him,* whether we do or no; and the reason why we do not praise him more and better is because we do not duly and attentively observe them. Let us therefore see God's works and observe the instances of his wisdom, power, and faithfulness in them (*v.* 5), and then speak of them, and speak of them to him (*v.* 3): *Say unto God, How terrible art thou in thy works, terrible in thy doings!* 1. God's works are wonderful in themselves, and such as, when duly considered, may justly fill us with amazement. God *is terrible* (that is, admirable) in his works, through the greatness of his power, which is such, and shines so brightly, so strongly, in all he does, that it may be truly said there are *not any works like unto his works.*

Hence he is said to be *fearful in praises,* Ex. 15:11. In all his doings towards the children of men he is terrible, and to be eyed with a holy awe. Much of religion lies in a reverence for the divine Providence. 2. They are formidable to his enemies, and have many a time forced and frightened them into a feigned submission (*v.* 3): *Through the greatness of thy power,* before which none can stand, *shall thy enemies submit themselves unto thee; they shall lie unto thee* (so the word is), that is, they shall be compelled, sorely against their wills, to make their peace with thee upon any terms. Subjection extorted by fear is seldom sincere, and therefore force is no proper means of propagating religion, nor can there be much joy of such proselytes to the church as will in the end be found liars unto it, Deu. 33:29. 3. They are comfortable and beneficial to his people, *v.* 6. When Israel came out of Egypt, *he turned the sea into dry land* before them, which encouraged them to follow God's guidance through the wilderness; and, when they were to enter Canaan, for their encouragement in their wars Jordan was divided before them, and *they went through that flood on foot;* and such foot, so signally owned by heaven, might well pass for cavalry, rather than infantry, in the wars of the Lord. There did the enemies tremble before them (Ex. 15:14, 15; Jos. 5:1), but *there did we rejoice in him,* both trust his power (for relying on God is often expressed by rejoicing in him) and sing his praise, Ps. 106:12. There did we rejoice; that is, our ancestors did, and we in their loins. The joys of our fathers were our joys, and we ought to look upon ourselves as sharers in them. 4. They are commanding to all. God by his works keeps up his dominion in the world (*v.* 7): *He rules by his power for ever; his eyes behold the nations.* (1.) God has a commanding eye; from the height of heaven his eye commands all the inhabitants of the world, and he has a clear and full view of them all. *His eyes run to and fro through the earth;* the most remote and obscure nations are under his inspection. (2.) He has a commanding arm; his power rules, rules for ever, and is never weakened, never obstructed. *Strong is his hand, and high is his right hand.* Hence he infers, *Let not the rebellious exalt themselves;* let not those that have revolting and rebellious hearts dare to rise up in any overt acts of rebellion against God, as Adonijah exalted himself, saying, *I will be king.* Let not those that are in rebellion against God exalt themselves as if there were any probability that they should gain their point. No; let them be still, for God hath said, *I will be exalted,* and man cannot gainsay it.

Verses 8–12

In these verses the psalmist calls upon God's people in a special manner to praise him. Let all lands do it, but Israel's land particularly. Bless our God; bless him as ours, a God in covenant with us, and that takes care of us as his own. Let them *make the voice of his praise to be heard* (*v.* 8); for from whom should it be heard but from those who are his peculiar favourites and select attendants? Two things we have reason to bless God for: —

I. Common protection (*v.* 9): *He holdeth our soul in life,* that it may not drop away of itself; for, being continually in our hands, it is apt to slip through our fingers. We must own that it is the good providence of God that keeps life and soul together and his visitation that preserves our spirit. *He puts our soul in life,* so the word is. He that gave us our being, by a constant renewed act upholds us in our being, and his providence is a continued creation. When we are ready to faint and perish he restores our soul, and so puts it, as it were, into a new life, giving new comforts. *Non est vivere, sed valere, vita — It is not existence, but happiness, that deserves the name of life.* But we are apt to stumble and fall, and are exposed to many destructive accidents, killing disasters as well as killing diseases, and therefore as to these also we are guarded by the divine power. He *suffers not our feet to be moved,* preventing many unforeseen evils, which we ourselves were not aware of our danger from. To him we owe it that we have not, long ere this, fallen into endless ruin. *He will keep the feet of his saints.*

II. Special deliverance from great distress. Observe,

1. How grievous the distress and danger were, *v.* 11, 12. What particular trouble of the church this refers to does not appear; it might be the trouble of some private persons or families only. But, whatever it was, they were surprised with it as a bird with a snare, enclosed and entangled in it as a fish in a net; they were pressed down with it, and kept under as with a load *upon their loins, v.* 11. But they owned the hand of God in it. We are never in the net but God brings us into it, never under affliction but God lays it upon us. Is any thing more dangerous than fire and water? *We went through both,* that is, afflictions of different kinds; the end of one trouble was the beginning of another; when we had got clear of one sort of dangers we found ourselves involved in dangers of another sort. Such may be the troubles of the best of God's saints, but he has promised, *When thou passest through the waters, through the fire, I will be with thee,* Isa. 43:1. Yet proud and cruel men may be as dangerous as fire and water, and more so. *Beware of men,* Mt. 10:17. When men rose up against us, that was fire and water, and all that is threatening (Ps. 124:2, 3, 4), and that was the case here: *"Thou hast caused men to ride over our heads,* to trample upon us and insult over us, to hector and abuse us, nay, and to make perfect slaves of us; they have said to our souls, *Bow down, that we may go over,"* Isa. 51:23. While it is the pleasure of good princes to rule in the hearts of their subjects it is the pride of tyrants to ride over their heads; yet the afflicted church in this also owns the hand of God: "Thou hast caused them thus to abuse us;" for the most furious oppressor has no power but what is given him from above.

2. How gracious God's design was in bringing them into this distress and danger. See what the meaning of it is (*v.* 10): *Thou, O God! hast proved us, and tried us.* Then we are likely to get good by our afflictions, when we look upon them under this notion, for then we may see God's grace and love at the bottom of them and our own honour and benefit in the end of them. By afflictions we are proved as silver in the fire. (1.) That our graces, by being tried, may be made more evident and so we may be approved, as silver, when it is touched and marked sterling, and this will be *to our praise at the appearing of Jesus Christ* (1 Pt. 1:7) and perhaps in this world. Job's integrity and constancy were manifested by his afflictions. (2.) That our graces, by being exercised, may be made more strong and active, and so we may be improved, as silver when it is refined by the fire and made more clear from its dross; and this will be to our unspeakable advantage, for thus we are made partakers of God's holiness, Heb. 12:10. Public troubles are for the purifying of the church, Dan. 11:35; Rev. 2:10; Deu. 8:2.

3. How glorious the issue was at last. The troubles of the church will certainly end well; these do so, for (1.) The outlet of the trouble is happy. They are in fire and water, but they get through them: *"We went through fire and water,* and did not perish in the flames or floods." Whatever the troubles of the saints are, blessed be God, there is a way through them. (2.) The inlet to a better state is much more happy: *Thou broughtest us out into a wealthy place,* into a *well-watered* place (so the word is), *like the gardens of the Lord,* and therefore fruitful. God brings his people into trouble that their comforts afterwards may be the sweeter and that their affliction may thus yield the peaceable fruit of righteousness, which will make the poorest place in the world a wealthy place.

Verses 13–20

The psalmist, having before stirred up all people, and all God's people in particular, to bless the Lord, here stirs up himself and engages himself to do it.

I. In his devotions to his God, *v.* 13–15. He had called upon others to sing God's praises and to make a joyful noise with them; but, for himself, his resolutions go further, and he will praise God, 1. By costly sacrifices, which, under the law, were offered to the honour of God. All people had not wherewithal to offer these sacrifices, or wanted zeal to be at such an expense in praising God; but David, for his part, being able, is as willing, in this chargeable way to pay his homage to God (*v.* 13): *I will go into thy house with burnt-offerings.* His sacrifices should be public, in the place which God had chosen: "I will go into thy house with them." Christ is our temple, to whom we must bring our spiritual gifts, and by whom they are sanctified. They should be the best of the king — *burnt-sacrifices,* which were wholly consumed upon the altar, to the honour of God, and of which the offerer had no share; and burnt-sacrifices *of fatlings,* not the lame or the lean, but the best fed, and such as would be most acceptable at his own table. God, who is the best, must be served with the best we have. The feast God makes for us is a *feast of fat things, full of marrow* (Isa. 25:6), and such sacrifices should we bring to him. He will *offer bullocks with goats,* so liberal will he be in his return of praise, and not strait-handed: he would not offer that which cost him nothing, but that which cost him a great deal. And this *with the incense of rams,* that is, with the fat of rams, which being burnt upon the altar, the smoke of it would ascend like the smoke of incense. Or *rams with incense.* The incense typifies Christ's intercession, without which the fattest of our sacrifices will not be accepted. 2. By a conscientious performance of his vows. We do not acceptably praise God for our deliverance out of trouble unless we make conscience of paying the vows we made when we were in trouble. This was the psalmist's resolution (*v.* 13, 14), *I will pay thee my vows, which my lips have uttered when I was in trouble.* Note, (1.) It is very common, and very commendable, when we are under the pressure of any affliction, or in the pursuit of any mercy, to make vows, and solemnly to speak them before the Lord, to bind ourselves out from sin and bind ourselves more closely to our duty; not as if this were an equivalent, or valuable consideration, for the favour of God, but a qualification for receiving the tokens of that favour. (2.) The vows which we made when we were in trouble must not be forgotten when the trouble is over, but be carefully performed, for better it is not to vow than to vow and not pay.

II. In his declarations to his friends, *v.* 16. He calls together a congregation of good people to hear his thankful narrative of God's favours to him: *"Come and hear, all you that fear God,* for, 1. You will join with me in my praises and help me in giving thanks." And we should be as desirous of the assistance of those that fear God in returning thanks for the mercies we have received as in praying for those we want. 2. "You will be edified and encouraged by that which I have to say. *The humble shall hear of it and be glad,* Ps. 34:2. *Those that fear thee will be glad when they see me* (Ps. 119:74), and therefore let me have their company, and I will declare to them, not to vain carnal people that will banter it and make a jest of it" (pearls are not to be cast before swine); "but to those that fear God, and will make a good use of it, I will declare what God has done for my soul," not in pride and vain-glory, that he might be thought more a favourite of heaven than other people, but for the honour of God, to which we owe this as a just debt, and for the edification of others. Note, God's people should communicate their experiences to each other. We should take all occasions to tell one another of the great and kind things which God has done for us, especially which he has done for our souls, the spiritual blessings with which he has blessed us in heavenly things; these we should be most affected with ourselves, and therefore with these we should be desirous to affect others. Now what was it that God had done for his soul? (1.) He had wrought in him a love to the duty of prayer, and had by his grace enlarged his heart in that duty (*v.* 17): *I cried unto him with my mouth.* But if God, among other things done for our souls, had not given us the Spirit of adoption, teaching and enabling us to cry, *Abba, Father,* we should never have done it. That God has given us leave to pray, a command to pray, encouragements to pray, and (to crown all) a heart to pray, is what we have reason to mention with thankfulness to his praise; and the more if, when we cried to him with our mouth, *he was extolled with our tongue,* that is, if we were enabled by faith and hope to give glory to him when we were seeking for mercy and grace from him, and to praise him for mercy in prospect though not yet in possession. By crying to him we do indeed extol him. He is pleased to reckon himself honoured by the humble believing prayers of the upright, and this is a great thing which he has done for our souls, that he has been pleased so far to unite interests with us that, in seeking our own welfare, we seek his glory. *His exaltation was under my tongue* (so it may be read); that is, I was considering in my mind how I might exalt and magnify his name. When prayers are in our mouths praises must be in our hearts. (2.) He had wrought in him a dread of sin as an enemy to prayer (*v.* 18): *If I regard iniquity in my heart,* I know very well *the Lord will not hear me.* The Jewish writers, some of them that have the leaven of the Pharisees, which is hypocrisy, put a very corrupt gloss upon these words: *If I regard iniquity in my heart,* that is (say they), If I allow myself only in heart-sins, and iniquity does not break out in my words and actions, *God will not hear me,* that is, he will not be offended with me, will take no notice of it, so as to lay it to my charge; as if heart-sins were no sins in God's account. The falsehood of this our Saviour has shown in his spiritual exposition of the law, Mt. 5. But the sense of this place is plain: *If I regard iniquity in my heart,* that is, "If I have favourable thoughts of it, if I love it, indulge it, and allow myself in it, if I treat it as a friend and bid it welcome, make provision for it and am loth to part with it, if I roll it under my tongue as a sweet morsel, though it be but a heart sin that is thus countenanced and made much of, if I delight in it after the inward man, God will not hear my prayer, will not accept it, nor be pleased with it, nor can I expect an answer of peace to it." Note, Iniquity, regarded in the heart, will certainly spoil the comfort and success of prayer; for *the sacrifice of the wicked is an abomination to the Lord.* Those that continue in love and league with sin have no interest either in the promise or in the Mediator, and therefore cannot expect to speed in prayer. (3.) He had graciously granted him an answer of peace to his prayers (v. 19): *"But verily God has heard me;* though, being conscious to myself of much amiss in me, I began to fear that my prayers would be rejected, yet, to my comfort, I found that God was pleased to regard them." This God did for his soul, by answering his prayer, he gave him a token of his favour and an evidence that he had wrought a good work in him. And therefore he concludes (v. 20), *Blessed be God.* The two foregoing verses are the major and minor propositions of a syllogism: *If I regard iniquity in my heart, God will not hear my prayer;* that is the proposition: *but verily God has heard me;* that is the assumption, from which he might have rationally inferred, "Therefore I do not regard iniquity in my heart;" but, instead of taking the comfort to himself, he gives the praise to God: *Blessed be God.* Whatever are the premises, God's glory must always be the conclusion. *God has heard me,* and therefore *blessed be God.* Note, What we win by prayer we must wear with praise. Mercies in answer to prayer do, in a special manner, oblige us to be thankful. He has *not turned away my prayer, nor his mercy.* Lest it should be thought that the deliverance was granted for the sake of some worthiness in his prayer, he ascribes it to God's mercy. This he adds by way of correction: "It was not my prayer that fetched the deliverance, but his mercy that sent it." *Therefore* God does not turn away our prayer, because he does not turn away his own mercy, for that is the foundation of our hopes and the fountain of our comforts, and therefore ought to be the matter of our praises.

PSALM 67

This psalm relates to the church and is calculated for the public. Here is, I. A prayer for the prosperity of the church of Israel (v. 1). II. A prayer for the conversion of the Gentiles and the bringing of them into the church (v. 2-5). III. A prospect of happy and glorious times when God shall do this (v. 6, 7). Thus was the psalmist carried out by the spirit of prophecy to foretel the glorious estate of the Christian church, in which Jews and Gentiles should unite in one flock, the beginning of which blessed work ought to be the matter of our joy and praise, and the completing of it of our prayer and hope, in singing this psalm.

To the chief musician on Neginoth. A psalm *or song.*

Verses 1-7

The composition of this psalm is such as denotes the penman's affections to have been very warm and lively, by which spirit of devotion he was elevated to receive the spirit of prophecy concerning the enlargement of God's kingdom.

I. He begins with a prayer for the welfare and prosperity of the church then in being, in the happiness of which he should share, and think himself happy, v. 1. Our Saviour, in teaching us to say, *Our Father,* has intimated that we ought to pray with and for others; so the psalmist here prays not, *God be merciful to me, and bless me,* but to *us,* and bless *us;* for we must make supplication for all saints, and be willing and glad to take our lot with them. We are here taught, 1. That all our happiness comes from God's mercy and takes rise in that; and therefore the first thing prayed for is, *God be merciful to us,* to us sinners,

and pardon our sins (Lu. 18:13), to us miserable sinners, and help us out of our miseries. 2. That it is conveyed by God's blessing, and secured in that: *God bless us;* that is, give us an interest in his promises, and confer upon us all the good contained in them. God's speaking well to us amounts to his doing well for us. *God bless us* is a comprehensive prayer; it is a pity such excellent words should ever be used slightly and carelessly, and as a byword. 3. That it is completed in the light of his countenance: *God cause his face to shine upon us;* that is, God by his grace qualify us for his favour and then give us the tokens of his favour. We need desire no more to make us happy than to have God's face shine upon us, to have God love us, and let us know that he loves us: *To shine with us* (so the margin reads it); *with us* doing our endeavour, and let it crown that endeavour with success. If we by faith walk with God, we may hope that his face will shine with us.

II. He passes from this to a prayer for the conversion of the Gentiles (v. 2): *That thy way may be known upon earth.* "Lord, I pray not only that thou wilt be merciful to us and bless us, but that thou wilt be merciful to all mankind, *that thy way may be known upon earth."* Thus publicspirited must we be in our prayers. *Father in heaven, hallowed be thy name, thy kingdom come.* We shall have never the less of God's mercy, and blessing, and favour, for others coming in to share with us. Or it may be taken thus: *"God be merciful to us Jews, and bless us, that* thereby thy way may be known upon earth, that by the peculiar distinguishing tokens of thy favour to us others may be allured to come and join themselves to us, saying, *We will go with you, for we have heard that God is with you,"* Zec. 8:23.

1. These verses, which point at the conversion of the Gentiles, may be taken, (1.) As a prayer; and so it speaks the desire of the Old-Testament saints; so far were they from wishing to monopolize the privileges of the church that they desired nothing more than the throwing down of the enclosure and the laying open of the advantages. See then how the spirit of the Jews, in the days of Christ and his apostles, differed from the spirit of their fathers. The Israelites indeed that were of old desired that God's name might be known among the Gentiles; those counterfeit Jews were enraged at the preaching of the gospel to the Gentiles; nothing in Christianity exasperated them so much as that did. (2.) As a prophecy that it shall be as he here prays. Many scripture-prophecies and promises are wrapped up in prayers, to intimate that the answer of the church's prayer is as sure as the performance of God's promises.

2. Three things are here prayed for, with reference to the Gentiles:—

(1.) That divine revelation might be sent among them, v. 2. Two things he desires might be know upon earth, even among all nations, and not to the nation of the Jews only:—[1.] God's way, the rule of duty: "Let them all know, as well as we do, *what is good and what the Lord our God requires of them;* let them be blessed and honoured with the same righteous statutes and judgments which are so much the praise of our nation and the envy of all its neighbours," Deu. 4:8. [2.] His saving health, or his salvation. The former is wrapped up in his law, this in his gospel. If God make known his way to us, and we walk in it, he will show us his saving health, Ps. 50:23. Those that have themselves experimentally known the pleasantness of God's ways, and the comforts of his salvation, cannot but desire and pray that they may be known to others, even among all nations. All upon earth are bound to walk in God's way, all need his salvation, and there is in it enough for all; and therefore we should pray that both the one and the other may be made known to all.

(2.) That divine worship may be set up among them, as it will be where divine revelation is received and embraced (v. 3): *"Let the people praise thee, O God!* let them have matter for praise, let them have hearts for praise; yea, let not only some, but *all the people, praise thee,"* all nations in their national capacity, some of all nations. It is again repeated (v. 5) as that which the psalmist's heart was very much upon. Those that delight in praising God themselves cannot but desire that others also may be brought to praise him, that he may have the honour of it and they may have the benefit of it. It is a prayer, [1.] That the gospel might be preached to them, and then they would have

cause enough to praise God, as for the day-spring after a long and dark night. *Ortus est sol — The sun has risen.* Acts 8:8. [2.] That they might be converted and brought into the church, and then they would have a disposition to praise God, the living and true God, and not the dumb and dunghill deities they had worshipped, Dan. 5:4. Then their hard thoughts of God would be silenced, and they would see him, in the gospel glass, to be love itself, and the proper object of praise. [3.] That they might be incorporated into solemn assemblies, and might praise God in a body, that they might all together praise him with one mind and one mouth. Thus a face of religion appears upon a land when God is publicly owned and the ordinances of religious worship are duly celebrated in religious assemblies.

(3.) That the divine government may be acknowledged and cheerfully submitted to (v. 4): *O let the nations be glad, and sing for joy!* Holy joy, joy in God and in his name, is the heart and soul of thankful praise. That *all the people* may *praise thee, let the nations be glad.* Those that *rejoice in the Lord always will in every thing give thanks.* The joy he wishes to the nations is holy joy; for it is joy in God's dominion, joy that *God has taken to himself his great power and has reigned,* which the unconverted *nations are angry at,* Rev. 11:17, 18. Let them be glad, [1.] That *the kingdom is the Lord's* (Ps. 22:28), that he, as an absolute sovereign, shall govern the nations upon earth, that by the kingdom of his providence he shall overrule the affairs of kingdoms according to the counsel of his will, though they neither know him nor own him, and that in due time he shall disciple all nations by the preaching of his gospel (Mt. 28:19) and set up the kingdom of his grace among them upon the ruin of the devil's kingdom — that he shall make them a willing people in the day of his power, and even *the kingdoms of this world shall become the kingdoms of the Lord and of his Christ.* [2.] That *every man's judgment proceeds from the Lord.* "Let them be glad that *thou shalt judge the people righteously,* that thou shalt give a law and gospel which shall be a righteous rule of judgment, and shalt pass an unerring sentence, according to that rule, upon all the children of men, against which there will lie no exception." Let us all be glad that we are not to be one another's judges, but that he that judges us is the Lord, whose judgment we are sure is according to truth.

III. He concludes with a joyful prospect of all good when God shall do this, when the nations shall be converted and brought to praise God.

1. The lower world shall smile upon them, and they shall have the fruits of that (v. 6): *Then shall the earth yield her increase.* Not but that God gave rain from heaven and fruitful seasons to the nations when they *sat in darkness* (Acts 14:17); but when they were converted the earth yielded its increase to God; the meat and the drink then became a *meat-offering and a drink-offering to the Lord our God* (Joel 2:14); and then it was fruitful to some good purpose. Then it yielded its increase more than before to the comfort of men, who through Christ acquired a covenant-title to the fruits of it and had a sanctified use of it. Note, The success of the gospel sometimes brings outward mercies along with it; righteousness exalts a nation. See Isa. 4:2; 62:9.

2. The upper world shall smile upon them, and they shall have the favours of that, which is much better: *God, even our own God, shall bless us,* v. 6. And again (v. 7), *God shall bless us.* Note, (1.) There are a people in the world that can, upon good grounds, call God their God. (2.) Believers have reason to glory in their relation to God and the interest they have in him. It is here spoken with an air of triumph. *God, even our own God.* (2.) Those who through grace call God their own may with a humble confidence expect a blessing from him. If he be our God, he will bless us with special blessings. (4.) The blessing of God, as ours in covenant, is that which sweetens all our creature-comforts to us, and makes them comforts indeed; then we receive the increase of the earth as a mercy indeed when with it God, even our own God, gives us his blessing.

3. All the world shall hereby be brought to do like them: *The ends of the earth shall fear him,* that is, worship him, which is to be done with a godly fear. The blessings God bestows upon us call upon us not only to love him, but to fear him, to keep up high thoughts of him and to be afraid of offending him. When the gospel begins to spread

it shall get ground more and more, till it reach to the ends of the earth. The leaven hidden in the meal shall diffuse itself, till the whole be leavened. And the many blessings which those will own themselves to have received that are brought into the church invite others to join themselves to them. It is good to cast in our lot with those that are the blessed of the Lord.

PSALM 68

This is a most excellent psalm, but in many places the genuine sense is not easy to come at; for in this, as in some other scriptures, there are things dark and hard to be understood. It does not appear when, or upon what occasion, David penned this psalm; but probably it was when, God having given him rest from all his enemies round about, he brought the ark (which was both the token of God's presence and a type of Christ's mediation) from the house of Obed-edom to the tent he had pitched for it in Zion; for the first words are the prayer which Moses used at the removing of the ark, Num. 10:35. From this he is led, by the Spirit of prophecy, to speak glorious things concerning the Messiah, his ascension into heaven, and the setting up of his kingdom in the world. I. He begins with prayer, both against God's enemies (*v.* 1, 2) and for his people (*v.* 3). II. He proceeds to praise, which takes up the rest of the psalm, calling upon all to praise God (*v.* 4, 26, 32) and suggesting many things as matter for praise. 1. The greatness and goodness of God (*v.* 4–6). 2. The wonderful works God had wrought for his people formerly, bringing them through the wilderness (*v.* 7, 8), settling them in Canaan (*v.* 9, 10), giving them victory over their enemies (*v.* 11, 12), and delivering them out of the hands of their oppressors (*v.* 13, 14). 3. The special presence of God in his church (*v.* 15–17). 4. The ascension of Christ (*v.* 18) and the salvation of his people by him (*v.* 19, 20). 5. The victories which Christ would obtain over his enemies, and the favours he would bestow upon his church (*v.* 21–28). 6. The enlargement of the church by the accession of the Gentiles to it (*v.* 29–31). And so he concludes the psalm with an awful acknowledgment of the glory and grace of God (*v.* 32–35). With all these great things we should endeavour to be duly affected in singing this psalm.

To the chief musician. A psalm *or* song of David.

Verses 1–6

In these verses,

I. David prays that God would appear in his glory,

1. For the confusion of his enemies (*v.* 1, 2): *"Let God arise,* as a judge to pass sentence upon them, as a general to take the field and do execution upon them; *and let them be scattered,* and flee before him, as unable to keep their ground, much less to make head against him. Let God arise, as the sun when he goes forth in his strength; and the children of darkness shall be scattered, as the shadows of the evening flee before the rising sun. Let them be driven away as smoke by the wind, which ascends as if it would eclipse the sun, but is presently dispelled, and there appears to remainder of it. Let them melt *as wax before the fire,* which is quickly dissolved." Thus does David comment upon Moses's prayer, and not only repeat it with application to himself and his own times, but enlarge upon it, to direct us how to make use of scripture-prayers. Nay, it looks further, to the Redeemer's victory over the enemies of this kingdom, for he was the angel of the covenant, that guided Israel through the wilderness. Note, (1.) There are, and have been, and ever will be, such as are enemies to God and hate him, that join in with the old serpent against the kingdom of God among men and against the seed of the woman. (2.) They are the wicked, and none but the wicked, that are enemies to God, the children of the wicked one. (3.) Though we are to pray for our enemies as such, yet we are to pray against God's enemies as such, against their enmity to him and all their attempts upon his kingdom. (4.) If God but arise, all his impenitent and implacable enemies, that will not repent to give him glory, will certainly and speedily be scattered, and driven away, and made to perish at his presence; for none ever hardened his heart against God and prospered. The day of judgment will be the day of the complete and final *perdition of ungodly men* (2 Pt. 3:7), who shall melt like wax before that flaming fire in which the Lord shall then appear, 2 Th. 1:8.

2. For the comfort and joy of his own people (*v.* 3): *"Let the righteous be glad,* that are now in sorrow; *let them rejoice before God* in his favourable presence. God is the joy of his people; let them rejoice whenever they come before God, yea, let them exceedingly rejoice, let them rejoice with gladness." Note, Those who rejoice in God have reason to rejoice with exceeding joy; and this joy we ought to wish to all the saints, for it belongs to them. *Light is sown for the righteous.*

II. He praises God for his glorious appearances, and calls upon us to praise him, to sing to his name, and extol him,

1. As a great God, infinitely great (*v.* 4): He *rides upon the heavens, by his name JAH.* He is the spring of all the motions of the heavenly bodies, directs and manages them, as he that rides in the chariot sets it a-going, has a supreme command of the influences of heaven; he rides upon the heavens for the help of his people (Deu. 33:26), so swiftly, so strongly, and so much above the reach of opposition. He rules these by his name *Jah,* or *Jehovah,* a self-existent self-sufficient being; the fountain of all being, power, motion, and perfection; this is his name for ever. When we thus extol God we must *rejoice before him.* Holy joy in God will very well consist with that reverence and godly fear wherewith we ought to worship him.

2. As a gracious God, a God of mercy and tender compassion. He is great, but he despises not any, no, not the meanest; nay, being a God of great power, he uses his power for the relief of those that are distressed, *v.* 5, 6. The fatherless, the widows, the solitary, find him a God all-sufficient to them. Observe how much God's goodness is his glory. He that *rides on the heavens by his name Jah,* one would think should immediately have been adored as King of kings and Lord of lords, and the sovereign director of all the affairs of states and nations; he is so, but this he rather glories in, that he is *a Father of the fatherless. Though God be high, yet has he respect unto the lowly.* Happy are those that have an interest in such a God as this. He that *rides upon the heavens* is a Father worth having; thrice *happy are the people whose God is the Lord.* (1.) When families are bereaved of their head God takes care of them, and is himself their head; and the widows and the fatherless children shall find that in him which they have lost in the relation that is removed, and infinitely more and better. He is *a Father of the fatherless,* to pity them, to bless them, to teach them, to provide for them, to portion them. He will *preserve them alive* (Jer. 49:11), and with him they shall *find mercy,* Hos. 14:3. They have liberty to call him Father, and to plead their relation to him as their guardian, Ps. 146:9; 10:14, 18. He is a judge or patron of the widows, to give them counsel and to redress their grievances, to own them and plead their cause, Prov. 22:23. He has an ear open to all their complaints and a hand open to all their wants. He is so *in his holy habitation,* which may be understood either of the habitation of his glory in heaven (there he has prepared his throne of judgment, which the fatherless and widow have free recourse to, and are taken under the protection of, Ps. 9:4, 7), or of the habitation of his grace on earth; and so it is a direction to the widows and fatherless how to apply to God; let them go to his holy habitation, to his word and ordinances; there they may find him and find comfort in him. (2.) When families are to be built up he is the founder of them: *God sets the solitary in families,* brings those into comfortable relations that were lonely, gives those a convenient settlement that were unsettled (Ps. 113:9); he *makes those dwell at home that were* forced to *seek* for relief *abroad* (so Dr. Hammond), putting those that were destitute into a way of getting their livelihood, which is a very good way for man's charity, as it is of God's bounty.

3. As a righteous God, (1.) In relieving the oppressed. He *brings out those that are bound with chains,* and sets those at liberty who were unjustly imprisoned and brought into servitude. No chains can detain those whom God will make free. (2.) In reckoning with the oppressors: *The rebellious dwell in a dry land* and have no comfort in that which they have got by fraud and injury. The best land will be a dry land to those that by their rebellion have forfeited the blessing of God, which is the juice and fatness of all our enjoyments. The Israelites were brought out of Egypt into the wilderness, but were there better provided for than the Egyptians themselves, whose land, if Nilus failed them, as it sometimes did, was a dry land.

Verses 7–14

The psalmist here, having occasion to give God thanks for the great things he had done for him and his people of late, takes occasion thence to praise him for what he had done for their fathers in the days of old. Fresh mercies should put us in mind of former mercies and revive our grateful sense of them. Let it never be forgotten,

I. That God himself was the guide of Israel through the wilderness; when he had brought them out of their chains he did not leave them in the dry land, but he himself went before them in a *march through the wilderness, v.* 7. It was not a journey, but a march, for they went as soldiers, as an army with banners. The Egyptians promised themselves that the wilderness had shut them in, but they were deceived; God's Israel, having him for their leader, marched through the wilderness and were not lost in it. Note, If God bring his people into a wilderness, he will be sure to go before them in it and bring them out of it. Cant. 8:5.

II. That he manifested his glorious presence with them at Mount Sinai, *v.* 8. Never did any people see the glory of God, nor hear his voice, as Israel did, Deu. 4:32, 33. Never had any people such an excellent law given them, so expounded, so enforced. Then the *earth shook,* and the neighbouring countries, it is likely, felt the shock; terrible thunders there were, accompanied no doubt with thunder-showers, in which the heavens seemed to drop; while the divine doctrine *dropped as the rain,* Deu. 32:2. *Sinai itself,* that vast mountain, that long ridge of mountains, *was moved at the presence of God;* see Jdg. 5:4, 5; Deu. 33:2; Hab. 3:3. This terrible appearance of the Divine Majesty, as it would possess them with a fear and dread of him, so it would encourage their faith in him and dependence upon him. Whatever mountains of difficulty lay in the way of their happy settlement, he that could move Sinai itself could remove them, could get over them.

III. That he provided very comfortably for them both in the wilderness and in Canaan (*v.* 9, 10): *Thou didst send a plentiful rain and hast prepared of thy goodness for the poor.* This may refer, 1. To the victualling of their camp with manna in the wilderness, which was rained upon them, as were also the quails (Ps. 78:24, 27), and it might be fitly called a rain of liberality or munificence, for it was a memorable instance of the divine bounty. This confirmed the camp of Israel (here called *God's inheritance,* because he had chosen them to be a peculiar treasure to himself) *when it was weary* and ready to perish: this confirmed their faith, and was a standing proof of God's power and goodness. Even in the wilderness God found a comfortable dwelling for Israel, which was his congregation. Or, 2. To the seasonable supplies granted them in Canaan, that land *flowing with mild and honey,* which is said to *drink water of the rain of heaven,* Deu. 11:11. When sometimes that fruitful land was ready to be turned into barrenness, for the iniquity of those that dwelt therein, God, in judgment, remembered mercy, and sent them a plentiful rain, which refreshed it again, so that the congregation of Israel dwelt therein, and there was provision enough, even to satisfy their poor with bread. This looks further to the spiritual provision made for God's Israel; the Spirit of grace and the gospel of grace are the plentiful rain with which God confirms his inheritance, and from which their fruit is found, Isa. 45:8. Christ himself is this rain, Ps. 72:6. *He shall come as showers that water the earth.*

IV. That he often gave them victory over their enemies; armies, and kings of armies, appeared against them, from their first coming into Canaan, and all along in the times of the judges, till David's days, but, first or last, they gained their point against them, *v.* 11, 12, 14. Observe here, 1. That God was their commander-in-chief: *The Lord gave the word,* as general of their armies. He raised up judges for them, gave them their commissions and instructions, and assured them of success. *God spoke in his holiness,* and then *Gilead is mine.* 2. That they had prophets, as God's messengers, to make known his mind to them. God gave them his word (*the word of the Lord* came unto them) and then *great was the company of the preachers* — prophets and *prophetesses,* for the word is feminine. When God has messages to send he will not want messengers. Or perhaps it may allude to the women's joining in the triumph when the victory was obtained, as was usual (Ex. 15:20, 1 Sa. 18:7), in which they took notice of the word of God, triumphing in that as much as in his works. 3. That their enemies were defeated, and put to confusion: *Kings of armies did flee,* did flee with the greatest terror and precipitation imaginable, did not fight and flee, but flee and flee, retired without striking a stroke; they fled apace, fled and never rallied again. 4. That they were enriched with the plunder of the field: *She that tarried at home divided the spoil.* Not only the men, the soldiers that abode by the stuff, who were, by a statute of distributions, to share the prey (1 Sa. 30:24), but even the women that tarried at home had a share, which intimates the abundance of spoil that should be taken. 5. That these great things which God did for them were sanctified to them and contributed to their reformation (*v.* 14): *When the Almighty scattered kings for her* (for the church) *she was white as snow in Salmon,* purified and refined by the mercies of God; *when the host went forth against the enemy they kept themselves from every wicked thing,* and so the host returned victorious, and Israel by the victory were confirmed in their purity and piety. This account of Israel's victories is applicable to the victories obtained by the exalted Redeemer for those that are his, over death and hell. By the resurrection of Christ our spiritual enemies were made to flee, their power was broken, and they were for ever disabled to hurt any of God's people. This victory was first notified by the women (the she-publishers) to the disciples (Mt. 28:7) and by them it was preached to all the world, while believers that tarry at home, that did not themselves contribute any thing towards it, enjoy the benefit of it, and divide the spoil.

V. That from a low and despised condition they had been advanced to splendour and prosperity. When they were bond-slaves in Egypt, and afterwards when they were oppressed sometimes by one potent neighbour and sometimes by another, they did, as it were, *lie among the pots* or rubbish, as despised broken vessels, or as vessels in which there was no pleasure — they were black, and dirty, and discoloured. But God, at length, *delivered them from the pots* (Ps. 81:6), and in David's time they were in a fair way to be one of the most prosperous kingdoms in the world, amiable in the eyes of all about them, *like the wings of a dove covered with silver, v.* 13. "And so," says Dr. Hammond, "under Christ's kingdom, the heathen idolaters that were brought to the basest and most despicable condition of any creatures, worshipping wood and stone, and given up to the vilest lusts, should from that detestable condition be advanced to the service of Christ, and the practice of all Christian virtues, the greatest inward beauties in the world." It may be applied also to the deliverance of the church out of a suffering state and the comforts of particular believers after their despondencies.

Verses 15–21

David, having given God praise for what he had done for Israel in general, as the God of Israel (*v.* 8), here comes to give him praise as Zion's God in a special manner; compare Ps. 9:11. *Sing praises to the Lord who dwelleth in Zion,* for which reason Zion is called *the hill of God.*

I. He compares it with the hill of Bashan and other high and fruitful hills, and prefers it before them, *v.* 15, 16. It is true, Zion was but little and low in comparison with them, and was not covered over with flocks and herds as they were, yet, upon this account, it has the pre-eminence above them all, that it is *the hill of God,* the hill *which he desires to dwell in,* and where he chooses to manifest the tokens of his peculiar presence, Ps. 132:13, 14. Note, It is much more honourable to be holy to God than to be high and great in the world. *"Why leap you, you high hills?* Why do you insult over poor Zion, and boast of your own height? This is the hill which God has chosen, and therefore though you exceed it in bulk, and be first-rates, yet, because on this the royal flag is hoisted, you must all strike sail to it." Zion was especially honourable because it was a type of the gospel church, which is therefore called Mount Zion (Heb. 12:22), and this is intimated here, when he said, *The Lord will dwell in it for ever,* which must have its accomplishment in the gospel Zion. There is no kingdom in the world comparable to the kingdom of the Redeemer, no city comparable to that which is incorporated by the gospel charter, for there God dwells and will dwell for ever.

II. He compares it with Mount Sinai, of which he had spoken (*v.* 8), and shows that it has the Shechinah or divine presence in it as really, though not as sensibly, as Sinai itself had, *v.* 17. Angels are *the chariots of God,* his chariots of war, which he make use of against his enemies, his chariots of conveyance, which he sends for his friends, as he did for Elijah (and Lazarus is said to be carried by the angels), his chariots of state, in the midst of which he shows his glory and power. They are vastly numerous: *Twenty thousands,* even thousands multiplied. There is an *innumerable company of angels* in the heavenly Jerusalem, Heb. 12:22. The enemies David fought with had chariots (2 Sa. 8:4), but what were they, for number or strength, to the chariots of God? While David had these on his side he needed not to fear those that trusted in *chariots and horses,* Ps. 20:7. God appeared on Mount Sinai, attended with myriads of angels, by whose dispensation the law was given, Acts 7:53. *He comes with ten thousands of saints,* Deu. 33:2. And still in Zion God manifests his glory, and is really present, with a numerous retinue of his heavenly hosts, signified by the cherubim between which God is said *to dwell.* So that, as some read the last words of the verse, *Sinai is in the sanctuary;* that is, the sanctuary was to Israel instead of Mount Sinai, whence they received divine oracles. Our Lord Jesus has these chariots at command. When the first-begotten was brought into the world it was with this charge, *Let all the angels of God worship him* (Heb. 1:6); they attended him upon all occasions, and he is now among them, *angels, principalities, and powers, being made subject to him,* 1 Pt. 3:22. And it is intimated in the New Testament that the angels are present in the solemn religious assemblies of Christians, 1 Co. 11:10. Let the woman have a veil on her head *because of the angels;* and see Eph. 3:10.

III. The glory of Mount Zion was the King whom God *set on that holy hill* (Ps. 2:6), who *came to the daughter of Zion,* Mt. 21:5. Of his ascension the psalmist here speaks, and to it his language is expressly applied (Eph. 4:8): *Thou hast ascended on high* (*v.* 18); compare Ps. 47:5, 6. Christ's ascending on high is here spoken of as a thing past, so sure was it; and spoken of to his honour, so great was it. It may include his whole exalted state, but points especially at his ascension into heaven to the right hand of the Father, which was as much our advantage as his advancement. For, 1. He then triumphed over the gates of hell. He led *captivity captive;* that is, he led his captives in triumph, as great conquerors used to do, *making a show of them openly,* Col. 2:15. He led those captive who had led us captive, and who, if he had not interposed, would have held us captive for ever. Nay, he *led captivity itself captive,* having quite broken the power of sin and Satan. As he was the death of death, so he was the captivity of captivity, Hos. 13:14. This intimates the complete victory which Jesus Christ obtained over our spiritual enemies; it was such that through him *we also are more than conquerors,* that is, triumphers, Rom. 8:37. 2. He then opened the gates of heaven to all believers: *Thou hast received gifts for men.* He *gave gifts to men,* so the apostle reads it, Eph. 4:8. For he received that he might give; on his head the anointing of the Spirit was poured, that from him it might descend to the skirts of his garments. And he gave what he had received; having received power to give eternal life, he bestows it upon *as many as were given him,* Jn. 17:2. *Thou hast received gifts for men,* not for angels; fallen angels were not to be made saints, nor standing angels made gospel ministers, Heb. 2:5. Not for Jews only, but for all men; whoever will may reap the benefit of these gifts. The apostle tells us what these gifts were (Eph. 4:11), *prophets, apostles, evangelists, pastors and teachers,* the institution of a gospel ministry and the qualification of men for it, both which are to be valued as the gifts of heaven and the fruits of Christ's ascension. *Thou hast received gifts in man* (so the margin), that is, in the human nature which Christ was pleased to clothe himself with, that he might be a *merciful and faithful high priest in things pertaining to God.* In him, as Mediator, *all fulness dwells,* that *from his fulness we might receive.* To magnify the kindness and love of Christ to us in receiving these gifts for us, the psalmist observes, (1.) The forfeiture we had made of them. He received them for the *rebellious also,* for those that had been rebellious; so all the children of men had been in their fallen state. Perhaps it is especially meant of the Gentiles, that had been *enemies in their minds by wicked works,* Col. 1:21. For them these gifts are received, to them they are given, that they might lay down their arms, that their enmity might be slain, and that they might return to their allegiance. This magnifies the grace of Christ exceedingly that through him rebels are, upon their submission, not only pardoned, but preferred. They have commissions given them under Christ, which some say, in our law, amounts to the reversing of an attainder. Christ came to a rebellious world, not to condemn it, but that through him it might be saved. (2.) The favour designed us in them: He *received gifts for the rebellious,* that *the Lord God might dwell among them,* that he might set up a church in a rebellious world, in which he would dwell by his word and ordinances, as of old in the sanctuary, that he might set up his throne, and Christ might dwell in the hearts of particular persons that had been rebellious. The gracious intention of Christ's undertaking was to rear up the *tabernacle of God among men,* that he might dwell with them and they might themselves be living temples to his praise, Eze. 37:27.

IV. The glory of Zion's King is that he is a Saviour and benefactor to all his willing people and a consuming fire to all those that persist in rebellion against him, *v.* 19–21. We have here good and evil, life and death, the blessing and the curse, set before us, like that (Mk. 16:16), *He that believes shall be saved; he that believes not shall be damned.*

1. Those that take God for their God, and so give up themselves to him to be his people, shall be loaded with his benefits, and to them he will be a God of salvation. If in sincerity we avouch God to be our God, and seek to him as such, (1.) He will continually do us good and furnish us with occasion for praise. Having mentioned the gifts Christ received for us (*v.* 18), fitly does he subjoin, in the next words, *Blessed be the Lord;* for it is owing to the mediation of Christ that we live, and live comfortably, and are daily loaded with benefits. So many, so weighty, are the gifts of God's bounty to us that he may be truly said to *load us* with them; he *pours out blessings till there is no room to receive them,* Mal. 3:10. So constant are they, and so unwearied is he in doing us good, that he *daily* loads us with them, according as the necessity of every day requires. (2.) He will at length be unto us the God of salvation, of everlasting salvation, the *salvation of God,* which he will *show to those that order their conversation aright* (Ps. 50:23), the salvation of the soul. He that *daily loads us with benefits* will not put us off with present things for a portion, but will be the God of our salvation; and what he gives us now he gives as the God of salvation, pursuant to the great design of our salvation. *He is our God,* and therefore he will be the God of eternal salvation to us; for that only will answer the vast extent of his covenant-relation to us as our God. But has he power to complete this salvation? Yes, certainly; *for unto God the Lord belong the issues from death.* The keys of hell and death are put into the hand of the Lord Jesus, Rev. 1:18. He, having made an escape from death himself in his resurrection, has both authority and power to rescue those that are his from the dominion of death, by altering the property of it to them when they die and giving them a complete victory over it when they shall rise again; for *the last enemy that shall be destroyed is death.* And to those that shall thus for ever escape death, and shall find such an outlet from it as not to be hurt of the second death, to them surely deliverances from temporal death are mercies indeed and come from God as the God of their salvation. 2 Co. 1:10.

2. Those that persist in their enmity to him will certainly be ruined (*v.* 21): *God shall wound the head of his enemies,* — of Satan the old serpent (of whom it was by the first promise foretold that *the seed of the woman* should *break his head,* Gen. 3:15), — of all the powers of the nations, whether Jews or Gentiles, that oppose him and his kingdom among men (Ps. 110:6, *He shall wound the heads over many countries*), — of all those, whoever they are, that will *not have him to reign over them,* for those he accounts his enemies, and they shall be *brought forth* and *slain before him,* Lu. 19:27. He will *wound the hairy scalp of such a one as goeth on still in his trespasses.* Note, Those who go on still in their trespasses, and hate to be reformed, God looks upon as his enemies and will treat them accordingly. In calling the head *the hairy scalp* perhaps there is an allusion to Absalom, whose bushy hair was his halter. Or it denotes either the most fierce and barbarous of his enemies, who let their hair grow, to make themselves look the more frightful, or the most fine and delicate of his enemies, who are nice about their hair: neither the one nor the other can secure themselves from the fatal wounds which divine justice will give to the heads of those that go on in their sins.

Verses 22–31

In these verses we have three things: —

I. The gracious promise which God makes of the redemption of his people, and their victory over his and their enemies (*v.* 22, 23): *The Lord said,* in his own gracious purpose and promise, "I will do great things for my people, as the God of their salvation," *v.* 20. God will not fail the expectations of those who by faith take him for their God. It is promised, 1. That he will set them in safety from their danger, as he had done formerly: "I will *again bring them from the depths of the sea,"* as he did Israel when he brought them out of the slavery of Egypt into the ease and liberty of the wilderness; "and *I will again bring them from Bashan,"* as he did Israel when he brought them from their wants and wanderings in the wilderness into the fulness and settlement of the land of Canaan; for the land of Bashan was on the other side Jordan, where they had wars with Sihon and Og, and whence their next removal was into Canaan. Note, The former appearances of God's power and goodness for his people should encourage their faith and hope in him for the future, that what he has done he will do again. He will *set his hand again the second time to recover the remnant of his people* (Isa. 11:11); and we may perhaps see repeated *all the wonders which our fathers told us of.* But this is not all: 2. That he will make them victorious over their enemies (*v.* 23): *That thy feet may be dipped,* as thou passest along, *in the blood of thy enemies,* shed like water in great abundance, and the *tongue of thy dogs* may lap *in the same.* Dogs licked the blood of Ahab; and, in the destruction of the anti-christian generation, we read of blood up *to the horses' bridles,* Rev. 14:20. The victories with which God blessed David's forces over the enemies of Israel are here prophesied of, but as types of Christ's victory over death and the grave for himself and for all believers, in his resurrection (and theirs by virtue of his) out of the earth, and of the destruction of the enemies of Christ and his church, who shall have blood given them to drink, for they are worthy.

II. The welcome entertainment which God's own people shall give to these glorious discoveries of his grace, both in his word and in his works. Has he spoken in his holiness? Has he said he will *bring again from Bashan?* What then is required of us in return to this?

1. That we observe his motions (*v.* 24): *"They have seen,* thy people have seen, *thy goings, O God!* While others regard not the work of the Lord, nor the operation of his hands, they have seen *the goings of my God, my King, in the sanctuary."* See here, (1.) How an active faith appropriates God; he is God and King; but that is not all, he is *my* God and *my* King. Those who thus take him for theirs may see him, in all his outgoings, acting as their God, as their King, for their good, and in answer to their prayers. (2.) Where God's most remarkable outgoings are, even in the sanctuary, in and by his word and ordinances, and among his people in the gospel church especially, in and by which is made known the manifold wisdom of God. These outgoings of his *in the sanctuary* far outshine the outgoings of the morning and the evening, and more loudly proclaim his eternal power and godhead. (3.) What is our duty in reference to these outgoings, which is to observe them. *This is the finger of God. Surely God is with us of a truth.*

2. That we give him glory in the most devout and solemn manner. When we see *his goings in his sanctuary,* (1.) Let those that are immediately employed in the service of the temple praise him, *v.* 25. It was expected that the Levites, some of whom were singers and others players on instruments, who had the nearest views of his *outgoings in his sanctuary,* should lead in his praises. And, it being a day of extraordinary triumph, *among them were damsels playing with timbrels,* to complete the concert. "Thus (says Dr. Hammond) when Christ has gone up to heaven the apostles shall celebrate and publish it to all the world, and even the women that were witnesses of it shall affectionately join with them in divulging it." (2.) Let all the people of Israel in their solemn religious assembly give glory to God: *Bless God,* not only in temples, but in the synagogues, or schools of the prophets, or wherever there is a congregation of those that *come forth from the fountain of Israel,* that are of the seed of Jacob, let them concur in blessing God. Public mercies, which we jointly share in, call for public thanksgivings, which all should join in. "Thus (says Dr. Hammond) all Christians shall be obliged solemnly to magnify the name of the Messiah, and, to that end, frequently to assemble together in congregations." And, (3.) Let those among them who, upon any account, are the most eminent, and make a figure, go before the rest in praising God, *v.* 27. There was *little Benjamin* (that was the royal tribe in Saul's time) *with their rulers, the princes of Judah* (that was the royal tribe in David's time), and *their council,* their captains or leaders. In the beginning of David's reign there had been long war between Judah and Benjamin, but now they both join in praises for success against the common enemy. But why are the tribes of Zebulun and Naphtali particularly mentioned? Perhaps because those tribes, lying towards the north, lay most exposed to the incursions of the Syrians, and other neighbours that molested them, and therefore should be in a particular manner thankful for these victories over them. Dr. Hammond gives another reason, That these were the two learned tribes. *Naphtali giveth goodly words* (Gen. 49:21) and Zebulun had those that *handle the pen of the writer,* Jdg. 5:14. These shall join in praising God, their princes especially. It is much for the honour of God when those that are above others in dignity, power, and reputation, go before them in the worship of God and are forward in using their influence and interest for the advancing of any service that is to be done to him. Dr. Hammond notes hence that the kingdom of the Messiah should, at length, be submitted to by all the potentates and learned men in the world.

3. That we seek unto him, and depend upon him, for the perfecting of what he has begun, *v.* 28. In the former part of the verse the psalmist speaks to Israel: *"Thy God has commanded thy strength;* that is, whatever is done for thee, or whatever strength thou hast to help thyself, it comes from God, his power and grace, and the word which he has commanded; thou hast no reason to fear while thou hast strength of God's commanding, and no reason to boast while thou hast no strength but what is of his commanding." In the latter part he speaks to God, encouraged by his experiences: *"Strengthen, O God! that which thou hast wrought for us.* Lord, confirm what thou hast commanded, perform what thou hast promised, and bring to a happy end that good work which thou hast so gloriously begun." What God has wrought he will strengthen; where he has given true grace he will give more grace. Some make this whole verse to be a believer's address to the Messiah, whom David calls *God,* as he had done, Ps. 45:6, 8. *"Thy God"* (God the Father) *"has commanded thy strength,* has made thee strong for himself, as the *man of his right hand* (Ps. 80:17), has treasured up strength in thee for us; therefore we pray that thou, *O God* the Son! wilt *strengthen what thou hast wrought for us,* wilt accomplish thy undertaking for us by finishing thy good work in us."

III. The powerful invitation and inducement which would hereby be given to those that are without to come in and join themselves to the church, *v.* 29–31. This was in part fulfilled by the accession of many proselytes to the Jewish religion in the days of David and Solomon; but it was to have its full accomplishment in the conversion of the Gentile nations to the faith of Christ, and the making of them fellow-heirs, and of the same body, with the seed of Israel, Eph. 3:6. 1. Some shall submit for fear (*v.* 30): *"The company of spearmen,* that stand it out against Christ and his gospel, that are not willing to be ruled by him, that persecute the preachers and professors of his name, that are furious and outrageous as a multitude of bulls, fat and wanton as the calves of the people" (which is a description of those Jews and Gentiles that opposed the gospel of Christ and did what they could to prevent the setting up of his kingdom in the world), "Lord, rebuke them, abate their pride, assuage their malice, and confound their devices, till, conquered by the convictions of their consciences and the many checks of providence, they be every one of them brought, at length, to *submit themselves with pieces of silver,* as being glad to make their peace with the church upon any terms." Even Judas submitted himself with pieces of silver when he returned them with this confession, *I have betrayed innocent blood.* And see Rev. 3:9. Many, by being rebuked, have been happily saved from being ruined. But as for those that will not submit, notwithstanding these rebukes, he prays for their dispersion, which amounts to a prophecy of it: *Scatter thou the people that delight in war,* who take such a pleasure in opposing Christ that they will never be reconciled to him. This may refer to the unbelieving Jews, who delighted in making war upon the holy seed, and would not submit themselves, and were therefore scattered over the face of the earth. David had himself been a man of war, but could appeal to God that he never delighted in war and bloodshed for its own sake; as for those that did, and therefore would not submit to the fairest terms of peace, he does not doubt but God would scatter them. Those are lost to all the sacred principles of humanity, as well as Christianity, that can delight in war and take a pleasure in contention let them expect that, sooner or later, they shall have enough of it, Isa. 33:1; Rev. 13:10. 2. Others shall submit willingly (*v.* 29, 31): *Because of thy temple at Jerusalem* (this David speaks of in faith, for the temple of Jerusalem was not built in his time, only the materials and model were prepared) *kings shall bring presents unto thee;* rich presents shall be brought, such as are fit for kings to bring; even kings themselves, that stand much upon the punctilios of honour and prerogative, shall court the favour of Christ at a great expense. There is that in God's temple, that beauty and benefit in the service of God and in communion with him, and in the gospel of Christ which went forth from Jerusalem, that is enough to invite kings themselves to bring presents to God, to present themselves to him as living sacrifices, and with themselves the best performances. He mentions *Egypt* and *Ethiopia,* two countries out of which subjects and suppliants were least to be expected (*v.* 31): *Princes shall come out of Egypt* as ambassadors to seek God's favour and submit to him; and they shall be accepted, for *the Lord of hosts shall* thereupon *bless them, saying, Blessed by Egypt my people,* Isa. 19:25. Even Ethiopia, that had stretched out her hands against God's Israel (2 Chr. 14:9), should now *stretch out her hands unto God,* in prayer, in presents, and to take hold on him, and that soon. *Agree with thy adversary quickly.* Out of all nations some shall be gathered in to Christ and be owned by him.

Verses 32–35

The psalmist, having prayed for and prophesied of the conversion of the Gentiles, here invites them to come in and join with the devout Israelites in praising God, intimating that their accession to the church would be the matter of their joy and praise (*v.* 32): Let the *kingdoms of the earth sing praises to the Lord;* they all ought to do it, and, when they become the kingdoms of the Lord and of his Christ, they will do it. God is here proposed to them as the proper object of praise upon several accounts:

I. Because of his supreme and sovereign dominion: *He rides upon the heavens of heavens which were of old* (*v.* 33); compare *v.* 4. He has from the beginning, nay from before all time, prepared his throne; he sits on the circuit of heaven, guides all the motions of the heavenly bodies; and from the highest heavens, which are the residence of his glory, he dispenses the influences of his power and goodness to this lower world.

II. Because of his awful and terrible majesty: *He sends out his voice, and that a mighty voice.* This may refer either generally to the thunder, which is called *the voice of the Lord* and is said to be *powerful and full of majesty* (Ps. 29:3, 4), or in particular to that thunder in which God spoke to Israel at Mount Sinai.

III. Because of his mighty power: *Ascribe you strength unto God* (*v.* 34); acknowledge him to be a God of such irresistible power that it is folly to contend with him and wisdom to submit to him; acknowledge that he has power sufficient both to protect his faithful subjects and to destroy his stubborn adversaries; and give him the glory of all the instances of his omnipotence. *Thine is the kingdom and power,* and therefore *thine is the glory.* We must acknowledge his power, 1. In the kingdom of grace: *His excellency is over Israel;* he shows his sovereign care in protecting and governing his church; that is the excellency of his power, which is employed for the good of his people. 2. In the kingdom of providence: *His strength is in the clouds,* whence comes the thunder of his power, the *small rain, and the great rain of his strength.* Though God has his strength in the clouds, yet he condescends to gather his Israel under the shadow of his wings, Deu. 33:26.

IV. Because of the glory of his sanctuary and the wonders wrought there (*v.* 35): *O God! thou art terrible out of thy holy places.* God is to be admired and adored with reverence and godly fear by all those that attend him in his holy places, that receive his oracles, that observe his operations according to them, and that pay their homage to him. He displays that out of his holy places which declares aloud that he will be sanctified in those that come nigh unto him. Out of heaven, his holy place above, he does, and will, show himself a terrible God. Nor is any attribute of God more dreadful to sinners than his holiness.

V. Because of the grace bestowed upon his people: *The God of Israel is he that gives strength and power unto his people,* which the gods of the nations, that were vanity and a lie, could not give to their worshippers; how should they help them, when they could not help themselves? All Israel's strength against their enemies came from God; they owned they had *no might of their own,* 2 Chr. 20:12. And all our sufficiency for our spiritual work and warfare is from the grace of God. It is through Christ strengthening us that we can do all things, and not otherwise; and therefore he must have the glory of all we do (Ps. 115:1) and our humble thanks for enabling us to do it and accepting the work of his own hands in us. If it be the God of Israel that vies strength and power unto his people, they ought to say, *Blessed be God.* If all be from him, let all be to him.

PSALM 69

David penned this psalm when he was in affliction; and in it, I. He complains of the great distress and trouble he was in and earnestly begs of God to relieve and succour him (*v.* 1–21). II. He imprecates the judgments of God upon his persecutors (*v.* 22–29). III. He concludes with the voice of joy and praise, in an assurance that God would help and succour him, and would do well for the church (*v.* 30–36). Now, in this, David was a type of Christ, and divers passages in this psalm are applied to Christ in the new Testament and are said to have their accomplishment in him (*v.* 4, 9, 21), and *v.* 22 refers to the enemies of Christ. So that (like the twenty-second psalm) it begins with the humiliation and ends with the exaltation of Christ, one branch of which was the destruction of the Jewish nation for persecuting him, which the imprecations here are predictions of. In singing this psalm we must have an eye to the sufferings of Christ, and the glory that followed, not forgetting the sufferings of Christians too, and the glory that shall follow them; for it may lead us to think of the ruin reserved for the persecutors and the rest reserved for the persecuted.

To the chief musician upon Shoshannim. *A psalm* of David.

Verses 1–12

In these verses David complains of his troubles, intermixing with those complaints some requests for relief.

I. His complaints are very sad, and he pours them out before the Lord, as one that hoped thus to ease himself of a burden that lay very heaven upon him.

1. He complains of the deep impressions that his troubles made upon his spirit (*v.* 1, 2): "The *waters of affliction,* those bitter waters, *have come unto my soul,* not only threaten my life, but disquiet my mind; they fill my head with perplexing cares and my heart with oppressive grief, so that I cannot enjoy God and myself as I used to do." We shall bear up under our troubles if we can but keep them from our hearts; but, when they put us out of the possession of our own souls, our case is bad. *The spirit of a man will sustain his infirmity;* but what shall we do when the spirit is wounded? That was David's case here. His thoughts sought for something to confide in, and with which to support his hope, but he found nothing: He sunk *in keep mire, where there was no standing,* no firm footing; the considerations that used to support and encourage him now failed him, or were out of the way, and he was ready to give himself up for gone. He sought for something to comfort himself with, but found himself *in deep waters* that *overflowed* him, overwhelmed him; he was like a sinking drowning man, in such confusion and consternation. This points at Christ's sufferings in his soul, and the inward agony he was in when he said, *Now is my soul troubled;* and, *My soul is exceedingly sorrowful;* for it was his soul that he made an offering for sin. And it instructs us, when we are in affliction, to commit the keeping of our souls to God, that we may be neither soured with discontent nor sink into despair.

2. He complains of the long continuance of his troubles (*v.* 3): *I am weary of my crying.* Though he could not keep his head above water, yet he cried to his God, and the more death was in his view the more life was in his prayers; yet he had not immediately an answer of peace given in, no, nor so much of that support and comfort in praying which God's people used to have; so that he was almost weary of crying, grew hoarse, and his *throat so dried* that he could cry no more. Nor had he his wonted satisfaction in believing, hoping, and expecting relief: *My eyes fail while I wait for my God;* he had almost looked

his eyes out, in expectation of deliverance. Yet his pleading this with God is an indication that he is resolved not to give up believing and praying. His throat is dried, but his heart is not; his eyes fail, but his faith does not. Thus our Lord Jesus, on the cross, cried out, *Why hast thou forsaken me?* yet, at the same time, he kept hold of his relation to him: *My God, my God.*

3. He complains of the malice and multitude of his enemies, their injustice and cruelty, and the hardships they put upon him, *v.* 4. They hated him, they would destroy him, for hatred aims at the destruction of the person hated; but what was his iniquity, what was his sin, what provocation had he given them, that they were so spiteful towards him? None at all: *"They hate me without a cause;* I never did them the least injury, that they should bear me such ill-will." Our Saviour applies this to himself (Jn. 15:25): *They hated me without a cause.* We are apt to use this in justification of our passion against those that hate us, that we never gave them cause to hate us. But it is rather an argument why we should bear it patiently, because then we suffer as Christ did, and may then expect that God will give us redress. "They are *my enemies wrongfully,* for I have been no enemy to them." In a world where unrighteousness reigns so much we must not wonder if we meet with those that are our enemies wrongfully. Let us take care that we never do wrong and then we may the better bear it if we receive wrong. These enemies were not to be despised, but were very formidable both for their number — *They are more than the hairs of my head* (Christ's enemies were numerous; those that came to seize him were a great multitude; how were those increased that troubled him!) and for their strength — They *are mighty* in authority and power. We are weak, but our enemies are strong; for *we wrestle against principalities and powers.* Then *I restored that which I took not away.* Applying this to David, it was what his enemies compelled him to (they made him suffer for that offence which he had never been guilty of); and it was what he consented to, that, if possible, he might pacify them and make them to be at peace with him. He might have insisted upon the laws of justice and honour, the former not requiring and the latter commonly thought to forbid the restoring of that which we took not away, for that is to wrong ourselves both in our wealth and in our reputation. Yet the case may be such sometimes that it may become our duty. Blessed Paul, though free from all men, yet, for the honour of Christ and the edification of the church, made himself a servant to all. But, applying it to Christ, it is an observable description of the satisfaction which he made to God for our sin by his blood: *Then he restored that which he took not away;* he underwent the punishment that was due to us, paid our debt, suffered for our offence. God's glory, in some instances of it, was taken away by the sin of man; man's honour, and peace, and happiness, were taken away; it was not he that took them away, and yet by the merit of his death he restored them.

4. He complains of the unkindness of his friends and relations, and this is a grievance which with an ingenuous mind cuts as deeply as any (*v.* 8): *"I have become a stranger to my brethren;* they make themselves strange to me and use me as a stranger, are shy of conversing with me and ashamed to own me." This was fulfilled in Christ, whose *brethren did not believe on him* (Jn. 7:5), who *came to his own and his own received him not* (Jn. 1:11), and who was forsaken by his disciples, whom he had been free with as his brethren.

5. He complains of the contempt that was put upon him and the reproach with which he was continually loaded. And in this especially his complaint points at Christ, who for our sakes submitted to the greatest disgrace and made himself of no reputation. We having by sin injured God in his honour, Christ made him satisfaction, not only by divesting himself of the honours due to an incarnate deity, but by submitting to the greatest dishonours that could be done to any man. Two things David here takes notice of as aggravations of the indignities done him: — (1.) The ground and matter of the reproach, *v.* 10, 11. They ridiculed him for that by which he both humbled himself and honoured God. When men lift up themselves in pride and vain glory they are justly laughed at for their folly; but David chastened his soul, and clothed himself with sackcloth, and from his abasing himself they took occasion to

trample upon him. When men dishonour God it is just that their so doing should turn to their dishonour; but when David, purely in devotion to God and to testify his respect to him, *wept, and chastened his soul with fasting,* and *made sackcloth his garment,* as humble penitents used to do, instead of commending his devotion and recommending it as a great example of piety, they did all they could both to discourage him in it and to prevent others from following his good example; for *that was to his reproach.* They laughed at him as a fool for mortifying himself thus; and even for this he *became a proverb to them;* they made him the common subject of their banter. We must not think it strange if we be ill spoken of for that which is well done, and in which we have reason to hope that we are accepted of God. Our Lord Jesus was stoned for his good works (Jn. 10:32), and when he cried, *Eli, Eli — My God, my God,* was bantered, as if he called for Elias. (2.) The persons that reproached him, *v.* 12. [1.] Even the gravest and the most honourable, from whom better was expected: *Those that sit in the gate speak against me,* and their reproaches pass for the dictates of senators and the decrees of judges, and are credited accordingly. [2.] The meanest, and the most despicable, the abjects (Ps. 35:15), and scum of the country, the *children of fools,* yea, the *children of base men,* Job 30:8. Such drunkards as these make themselves vile, and he was the song of the drunkards; they made themselves and their companions merry with him. See the bad consequences of the sin of drunkenness; it makes men *despisers of those that are good,* 2 Tim. 3:3. When *the king was made sick with bottles of wine he stretched out his hand with scorners,* Hos. 7:5. The bench of the drunkards is the seat of the scornful. See what is commonly the lot of the best of men: those that are the praise of the wise are the song of fools. But it is easy to those that rightly judge of things to despise being thus despised.

II. His confessions of sin are very serious (*v.* 5): *"O God! thou knowest my foolishness,* what is and what is not; my sins that I am guilty of are not hidden from thee, and therefore thou knowest how innocent I am of those crimes which they charge upon me." Note, Even when, as to men's unjust accusations, we plead *Not guilty,* yet, before God, we must acknowledge ourselves to have deserved all that is brought upon us, and much worse. This is the genuine confession of a penitent, who knows that he cannot prosper in covering his sin, and that *therefore* it is his wisdom to acknowledge it, because it is naked and open before God. 1. He knows the corruption of our nature: *Thou knowest the foolishness* that is bound up in my heart. All our sins take rise from our foolishness. 2. He knows the transgressions of our lives; they are not hidden from him, no, not our heart-sins, no, not those that are committed most secretly. They are all done in his sight, and are never cast behind his back till they are repented of and pardoned. This may aptly be applied to Christ, for he knew no sin, yet he was made sin for us; and God knew it, nor was it hidden from him, when it pleased the Lord to bruise him and put him to grief.

III. His supplications are very earnest. 1. For himself (*v.* 1): *"Save me, O God!* save me from sinking, from despairing." Thus Christ was heard in that he feared, for he was saved from letting fall his undertaking, Heb. 5:7. 2. For his friends (*v.* 6): *Let not those that wait on thee, O Lord God of hosts! and that seek thee, O God of Israel!* (under these two characters we ought to seek God, and in seeking him to wait on him, as the *God of hosts,* who has all power to help, and as the *God of Israel* in covenant with his people, whom therefore he is engaged in honour and truth to help) *be ashamed and confounded for my sake.* This intimates his fear that if God did not appear for him it would be a discouragement to all other good people and would give their enemies occasion to triumph over them, and his earnest desire that whatever became of him all that seek God, and wait upon him, might be kept in heart and kept in countenance, and might neither be discouraged in themselves nor exposed to contempt from others. If Jesus Christ had not been owned and accepted of his Father in his sufferings, all that seek God, and wait for him, would have been ashamed and confounded; but they have confidence towards God, and in his name come boldly to the throne of grace.

IV. His plea is very powerful, *v.* 7, 9. Reproach was one of the greatest of his burdens: "Lord, roll away the reproach, and plead my cause, for, 1. It is for thee that I am reproached, for serving thee and trusting in thee: *For thy sake I have borne reproach.*" Those that are evil spoken of for well-doing may with a humble confidence leave it to God to *bring forth their righteousness as the light.* 2. "It is with thee that I am reproached: *The zeal of thy house has eaten me up,* that is, has made me forget myself, and do that which they wickedly turn to my reproach. Those that hate thee and thy house for that reason hate me, because they know how zealously affected I am to it. It is this that has made them ready to eat me up and has eaten up all the love and respect I had among them." Those that blasphemed God, and spoke ill of his word and ways, did therefore reproach David for believing in his word and walking in his ways. Or it may be construed as an instance of David's zeal for God's house, that he resented all the indignities done to God's name as if they had been done to his own name. He laid to heart all the dishonour done to God and the contempt cast upon religion; these he laid nearer to his heart than any outward troubles of his own. And *therefore* he had reason to hope God would interest himself in the reproaches cast upon him, because he had always interested himself in the reproaches cast upon God. Both the parts of his verse are applied to Christ. (1.) It was an instance of his love to his Father that *the zeal of his house did even eat him up* when he whipped the buyers and sellers out of the temple, which reminded his disciples of this text, Jn. 2:17. (2.) It was an instance of his self-denial, and that he pleased not himself, that the *reproaches of those that reproached God fell upon him* (Rom. 15:3), and therein he set us an example.

Verses 13–21

David had been speaking before of the spiteful reproaches which his enemies cast upon him; here he adds, *But, as for me, my prayer is unto thee.* They spoke ill of him for his fasting and praying, and for that he was made the song of the drunkards; but, notwithstanding that, he resolves to continue praying. Note, Though we may be jeered for well-doing, we must never be jeered out of it. Those can bear but little for God, and their confessing his name before men, that cannot bear a scoff and a hard word rather than quit their duty. David's enemies were very abusive to him, but this was his comfort, that he had a God to go to, with whom he would lodge his cause. "They think to carry their cause by insolence and calumny; but I use other methods. Whatever they do, *As for me, my prayer is unto thee, O Lord!*" And it was in an acceptable time, not the less acceptable for being a time of affliction. God will not drive us from him, though it is need that drives us to him; nay, it is the more acceptable, because the misery and distress of God's people make them so much the more the objects of his pity: it is seasonable for him to help them when all other helps fail, and they are undone, and feel that they are undone, if he do not help them. We find this expression used concerning Christ. Isa. 49:8, *In an acceptable time have I heard thee.* Now observe,

I. What his requests are. 1. That he might have a gracious audience given to his complaints, the cry of his affliction, and the desire of his heart. *Hear me* (*v.* 13), and again, *Hear me, O Lord!* (*v.* 16), *Hear me speedily* (*v.* 17), not only hear what I say, but grant what I ask. Christ knew that *the Father heard him always,* Jn. 11:42. 2. That he might be rescued out of his troubles, might be saved from sinking under the load of grief (*Deliver me out of the mire;* let me not stick in it, so some, but help me out, and *set my feet on a rock,* Ps. 40:2), might be saved from his enemies, that they might not swallow him up, nor have their will against him: *"Let me be delivered from those that hate me,* as a lamb from the paw of a lion, *v.* 14. Though I have come into keep waters (*v.* 2), where I am ready to conclude that the floods will overflow me, yet let my fears be prevented and silenced; let not the waterflood, though it flow upon me, overflow me, *v.* 15. Let me not fall into the gulf of despair; let not that deep swallow me up; let not that pit shut her mouth upon me, for then I am undone." He gave himself up for lost in the beginning of the psalm; yet now he has his head above water, and is not so weary of crying as he thought himself. 3. That God would turn to him (*v.* 16), that he would smile upon him, and not hide his face from him, *v.* 17. The tokens of God's favour to us, and the light of his countenance shining upon us, are enough to keep our spirits from sinking in the deepest mire of outward troubles, nor need we desire any more to make us safe and easy, *v.* 18. "Draw nigh to my soul, to manifest thyself to it, and that shall redeem it."

II. What his pleas are to enforce these petitions. 1. He pleads God's mercy and truth (*v.* 13): *In the multitude of thy mercy hear me.* There is mercy in God, a multitude of mercies, all kinds of mercy, inexhaustible mercy, mercy enough for all, enough for each; and hence we must take our encouragement in praying. The truth also of his salvation (the truth of all those promises of salvation which he has made to those that trust in him) is a further encouragement. He repeats his argument taken from the mercy of God: *"Hear me,* for *thy lovingkindness of good.* It is so in itself; it is rich and plentiful and abundant. It is so in the account of all the saints; it is very precious to them, it is their life, their joy, their all. O let me have the benefit of it! Turn to me, *according to the multitude of thy tender mercies," v.* 16. See how highly he speaks of the goodness of God: in him there are mercies, tender mercies, and a multitude of them. If we think well of God, and continue to do so under the greatest hardships, we need not fear but God will do well for us; for *he takes pleasure in those that hope in his mercy,* Ps. 147:11. 2. He pleads his own distress and affliction: *"Hide not thy face* from me, *for I am in trouble* (*v.* 17), and therefore need thy favour; therefore it will come seasonably, and therefore I shall know how to value it." He pleads particularly the reproach he was under and the indignities that were done him (*v.* 19): *Thou hast known my reproach, my shame, and my dishonour.* See what a stress is laid upon this; for, in the sufferings of Christ for us, perhaps nothing contributed more to the satisfaction he made for sin, which had been so injurious to God in his honour, than the reproach, and shame, and dishonour he underwent, which God took notice of, and accepted as more than an equivalent for the everlasting shame and contempt which our sins had deserved, and therefore we must by repentance take shame to ourselves and bear the reproach of our youth. And if at any time we be called out to suffer reproach, and shame, and dishonour, for his sake, this may be our comfort, that he knows it, and, as he is before-hand with us, so he will not be behind-hand with us. The Psalmist speaks the language of an ingenuous nature when he says (*v.* 20): *Reproach has broken my heart; I am full of heaviness;* for it bears hard upon one that knows the worth of a good name to be put under a bad character; but when we consider what an honour it is to be dishonoured for God, and what a favour to be counted worthy to suffer shame for his name (as they deemed it, Acts 5:41), we shall see there is no reason at all why it should sit so heavily or be any heart-breaking to us. 3. He pleads the insolence and cruelty of his enemies (*v.* 18): *Deliver me because of my enemies,* because they were such as he had before described them, *v.* 4. *"My adversaries are all before thee* (*v.* 19); thou knowest what sort of men they are, what danger I am in from them, what enemies they are to thee, and how much thou art reflected upon in what they do and design against me." One instance of their barbarity is given (*v.* 21): *They gave me gall for my meat* (the word signifies a bitter herb, and is often joined with wormwood) *and in my thirst they gave me vinegar to drink.* This was literally fulfilled in Christ, and did so directly point to him that he would not say *It is finished* till this was fulfilled; and, in order that his enemies might have occasion to fulfil it, he said, *I thirst,* Jn. 19:28, 29. Some think that the hyssop which they put to his mouth with the vinegar was the bitter herb which they gave him with the vinegar for his meat. See how particularly the sufferings of Christ were foretold, which proves the scripture to be the word of God, and how exactly the predictions were fulfilled in Jesus Christ, which proves him to be the true Messiah. This is he that should come, and we are to look for no other. 4. He pleads the unkindness of his friends and his disappointment in them (*v.* 20): *I looked for some to take pity, but there was none;* they all failed him like the brooks in summer. This was fulfilled in Christ, for in his sufferings all his disciples forsook him and fled. We cannot expect too little from men (miserable comforters are they all); nor can we expect too much from God, for he is the Father of mercy and the God of all comfort and consolation.

Verses 22–29

These imprecations are not David's prayers against his enemies, but prophecies of the destruction of Christ's persecutors, especially the Jewish nation, which our Lord himself foretold with tears, and which was accomplished about forty years after the death of Christ. The first two verses of this paragraph are expressly applied to the judgments of God upon the unbelieving Jews by the apostle (Rom. 11:9, 10), and therefore the whole must look that way. The rejection of the Jews for rejecting Christ, as it was a signal instance of God's justice and an earnest of the vengeance which God will at last take on all that are obstinate in their infidelity, so it was, and continues to be, a convincing proof of the truth of the Christian religion. One great objection against it, at first, was, that it set aside the ceremonial law; but its doing so was effectually justified, and that objection removed, when God so remarkably set it aside by the utter destruction of the temple, and the sinking of those, with the Mosaic economy, that obstinately adhered to it in opposition to the gospel of Christ. Let us observe here,

I. What the judgments are which should come upon the crucifiers of Christ; not upon all of them, for there were those who had a hand in his death and yet repented and found mercy (Acts 2:23; 3:14, 15), but upon those of them and their successors who justified it by an obstinate infidelity and rejection of his gospel, and by an inveterate enmity to his disciples and followers. See 1 Th. 2:15, 16. It is here foretold,

1. That their sacrifices and offerings should be a mischief and prejudice to them (*v.* 22): *Let their table become a snare.* This may be understood of the altar of the Lord, which is called *his table and theirs* because in feasting upon the sacrifices they were partakers of the altar. This should have been for their welfare or peace (for they were peace-offerings), but it became a snare and a trap to them; for by their affection and adherence to the altar they were held fast in their infidelity and hardened in their prejudices against Christ, that altar which those had no right to eat of who continued to serve the tabernacle, Heb. 13:10. Or it may be understood of their common creature-comforts, even their necessary food; they had given Christ gall and vinegar, and therefore justly shall their meat and drink be made gall and vinegar to them. When the supports of life and delights of sense, through the corruption of our nature, become an occasion of sin to us, and are made the food and fuel of our sensuality, then our table is a snare, which is a good reason why we should never feed ourselves without fear, Jude 12.

2. That they should never have the comfort either of that knowledge or of that peace which believers are blessed with in the gospel of Christ (*v.* 23), that they should be given up, (1.) To a judicial blindness: *Let their eyes be darkened,* that they see not the glory of God in the face of Christ. Their sin was that they would not see, but shut their eyes against the light, loving darkness rather; their punishment was that they should not see, but be given up to their own hearts' lusts, which were hardening, and the god of this world should be permitted to blind their minds, 2 Co. 4:4. This was foretold concerning them (Isa. 6:10), and Christ ratified it, Mt. 13:14, 15; Jn. 12:40. (2.) To a judicial terror. There is a gracious terror, which opens the way to comfort, such as that of Paul (Acts 9:6); he trembled and was astonished. But this is a terror that shall never end in peace, but shall make their loins continually to shake, through horror of conscience, as Belshazzar, when the joints of his loins were loosed. "Let them be driven to despair, and filled with constant confusion." This was fulfilled in the desperate counsels of the Jews when the Romans came upon them.

3. That they should fall and lie under God's anger and fiery indignation (*v.* 24): *Pour out thy indignation upon them.* Note, Those who reject God's great salvation proffered to them may justly fear that his indignation will be poured out upon them; for those that submit not to the Son of his love will certainly be made the generation of his wrath. It is the doom passed on those who believe not in Christ that the *wrath of God abideth on them* (Jn. 3:36); it takes hold of them, and will never let them go. Salvation itself will not save those that are not willing to be ruled by it. Behold the goodness and severity of God!

4. That their place and nation should be utterly taken away, the very thing they were afraid of, and to prevent

which, as they pretended, they persecuted Christ (Jn. 11:48): *Let their habitation be desolate* (*v.* 25), which was fulfilled when their country was laid waste by the Romans, and *Zion, for their sakes, was ploughed as a field,* Mic. 3:12. The temple was the house which they were in a particular manner proud of, but this was *left unto them desolate,* Mt. 23:38. Yet that is not all; it ought to be some satisfaction to us, if we be cut off from the enjoyment of our possessions, that others will have the benefit of them when we are dislodged: but it is here added, *Let none dwell in their tents,* which was remarkably fulfilled in Judah and Jerusalem, for after the destruction of the Jews it was long ere the country was inhabited to any purpose. But this is applied particularly to Judas, by St. Peter, Acts 1:20. For, he being *felo de se — a suicide,* we may suppose his estate was confiscated, so that *his habitation was desolate and no man* of his own kindred *dwelt therein.*

5. That their way to ruin should be downhill, and nothing should stop them, nor interpose to prevent it (*v.* 27): "Lord, leave them to themselves, to *add iniquity to iniquity.*" Those that are bad, if they be given up to their own hearts' lusts, will certainly be worse; they will add sin to sin, nay, they will *add rebellion to their sin,* Job 34:37. It is said of the Jews that they *filled up their sin always,* 1 Th. 2:16. *Add the punishment of iniquity to their iniquity* (so some read it), for the same word signifies both sin and punishment, so close is their connexion. If men will sin, God will reckon for it. But those that have multiplied to sin may yet find mercy, for God multiplies to pardon, through the righteousness of the Mediator; and therefore, that they might be precluded from all hopes of mercy, he adds, *Let them not come into thy righteousness,* to receive the benefit of the righteousness of God, which is by faith in a Mediator, Phil. 3:9. Not that God shuts out any from that righteousness, for the gospel excludes none that do not by their unbelief exclude themselves; but let them be left to take their own course and they will never come into this government; for being ignorant of the demands of God's righteousness, and going about to establish the merit of their own, they *have not submitted themselves to the righteousness of God,* Rom. 10:3. And those that are so proud and self-willed that they will not come into God's righteousness shall have their doom accordingly; they themselves have decided it: they *shall not come into his righteousness.* Let not those expect any benefit by it that are not willing and glad to be beholden to it.

6. That they should be cut off from all hopes of happiness (*v.* 28): *Let them be blotted out of the book of the living;* let them not be suffered to live any longer, since, the longer they live, the more mischief they do. Multitudes of the unbelieving Jews fell by sword and famine, and none of those who had embraced the Christian faith perished among them; the nation, as a nation, was blotted out, and became not a people. Many understand it of their rejection from God's covenant and all the privileges of it; that is *the book of the living:* "Let the commonwealth of Israel itself, Israel according to the flesh, now become alienated from that covenant of promise which hitherto it has had the monopoly of. Let it appear that they were never written in the Lamb's book of life, but reprobate silver let *men call them, because the Lord has rejected them.* Let them *not be written with the righteous;* that is, let them not have a place in the congregation of the saints when they shall all be gathered in the general assembly of those whose names are written in heaven," Ps. 1:5.

II. What the sin is for which these dreadful judgments should be brought upon them (*v.* 26): *They persecute him whom thou hast smitten, and talk to the grief of thy wounded.* 1. Christ was he whom God had smitten, for *it pleased the Lord to bruise him,* and he was esteemed *stricken, smitten of God, and afflicted,* and therefore men *hid their faces from him,* Isa. 53:3, 4, 10. They persecuted him with a rage reaching up to heaven; they cried, *Crucify him, crucify him.* Compare that of St. Peter with this, Acts 2:23. Though he was *delivered by the counsel and foreknowledge of God,* it was *with wicked hands that they crucified and slew him.* They talked to the grief of the Lord Jesus when he was upon the cross, saying, *He trusted in God, let him deliver him,* than which nothing could be said more grieving. 2. The suffering saints were God's wounded, wounded in his cause and for his sake, and them they persecuted, and *talked to their grief.* For these things *wrath came upon them to the uttermost,* 1 Th. 2:16; and see Mt. 23:34, etc. This may be understood more generally, and it teaches us that nothing is more provoking to God than to insult over those whom he has smitten, and to add affliction to the afflicted, upon which it justly follows here, *Add iniquity to iniquity;* see Zec. 1:15. Those that are of a wounded spirit, under trouble and fear about their spiritual state, ought to be very tenderly dealt with, and care must be taken not to *talk to their grief and not to make the heart of the righteous sad.*

III. What the psalmist thinks of himself in the midst of all (*v.* 29): *"But I am poor and sorrowful;* that is the worst of my case, under outward afflictions, yet *written among the righteous,* and not under God's indignation as they are." It is better to be poor and sorrowful, with the blessing of God, than rich and jovial and under his curse. For those who come into God's righteousness shall soon see an end of their poverty and sorrow, and his salvation shall set them up on high, which is the thing that David here prays for, Isa. 61:10. This may be applied to Christ. He was, in his humiliation, poor and sorrowful, a man of sorrows, and that had not where to lay his head. But God highly exalted him; the salvation wrought for him, the salvation wrought by him, *set him up on high, far above all principalities and powers.*

Verses 30–36

The psalmist here, both as a type of Christ and as an example to Christians, concludes a psalm with holy joy and praise which he began with complaints and remonstrances of his griefs.

I. He resolves to praise God himself, not doubting but that therein he should be accepted of him (*v.* 30, 31): *"I will praise the name of God,* not only with my heart, but with my song, and *magnify him with thanksgiving;"* for he is pleased to reckon himself magnified by the thankful praises of his people. It is intimated that all Christians ought to glorify God with their praises, *in psalms, and hymns, and spiritual songs.* And *this shall please the Lord,* through Christ the Mediator of our praises as well as of our prayers, better than the most valuable of the legal sacrifices (*v.* 31), *an ox or bullock.* This is a plain intimation that in the days of the Messiah an end should be put, not only to the sacrifices of atonement, but to those of praise and acknowledgment which were instituted by the ceremonial law; and, instead of them, spiritual sacrifices of praise and thanksgiving are accepted — the calves of our lips, not the calves of the stall, Heb. 13:15. It is a great comfort to us that humble and thankful praises are more pleasing to God than the most costly pompous sacrifices are or ever were.

II. He encourages other good people to rejoice in God and continue seeking him (*v.* 32, 33): *The humble shall see this and be glad.* They shall observe, to their comfort, 1. The experiences of the saints. They shall see how ready God is to hear the poor when they cry to him, and to give them that which they call upon him for, how far he is from despising his prisoners; though men despise them, he favours them with his gracious visits and will find a time to enlarge them. *The humble shall see this and be glad,* not only because when one member is honoured all the members rejoice with it, but because it is an encouragement to them in their straits and difficulties to trust in God. It shall revive the hearts of those who seek God to see more seals and subscriptions to this truth, that Jacob's God never said to Jacob's seed, *Seek you me in vain.* 2. The exaltation of the Saviour, for of him the psalmist had been speaking, and of himself as a type of him. When his sorrows are over, and he enters into the joy that was set before him, when he is heard and discharged from his imprisonment in the grave, the humble shall look upon it and be glad, and those that seek God through Christ shall live and be comforted, concluding that, if they suffer with him, they shall also reign with him.

III. He calls upon all the creatures to praise God, the heaven, and earth, and sea, and the inhabitants of each, *v.* 34. Heaven and earth, and the hosts of both, were made by him, and therefore *let heaven and earth praise him.* Angels in heaven, and saints on earth, may each of them in their respective habitations furnish themselves with matter enough for constant praise. Let the fishes of the sea, though mute to a proverb, praise the Lord, for the sea is his, and he made it. The praises of the world must be offered for God's favours to his church, *v.* 35, 36. For God will save Zion, the holy mountain, where his service was kept up. He will save all that are sanctified and set apart to him, all that employ themselves in his worship, and all those over whom Christ reigns; for he was King upon the holy hill of Zion. He has mercy in store for the cities of Judah, of which tribe Christ was. God will do great things for the gospel church, in which let all that wish well to it rejoice. For, 1. It shall be peopled and inhabited. There shall be added to it such as shall be saved. *The cities of Judah shall be built,* particular churches shall be formed and incorporated according to the gospel model, that there may be a remnant to *dwell there* and to *have it in possession,* to enjoy the privileges conferred upon it and to pay the tributes and services required from it. Those that love his name, that have a kindness for religion in general, shall embrace the Christian religion, and take their place in the Christian church; they shall dwell therein, as citizens, and of the household of God 2. It shall be perpetuated and inherited. Christianity was not to be *res unius aetatis — a transitory thin.* No: *The seed of his servants shall inherit it.* God will secure and raise up for himself a seed to serve him, and they shall inherit the privileges of their fathers; for the promise is to you and your children, as it was of old. *I will be a God to thee, and thy seed after thee.* The land of promise shall never be lost for want of heirs, for God *can out of stones raise up children unto Abraham* and will do so rather than the entail shall be cut off. David shall never want a man to stand before him. The Redeemer shall see his seed, and prolong his days in them, till the mystery of God shall be finished and the mystical body completed. And since the holy seed is the substance of the world, and if that were all gathered in the world would be at an end quickly, it is just that for this assurance of the preservation of it heaven and earth should praise him.

PSALM 70

This psalm is adapted to a state of affliction; it is copied almost word for word from the fortieth, and, some think for that reason, is entitled, "a psalm to bring to remembrance;" for it may be of use sometimes to pray over the prayers we have formerly made to God upon similar occasions, which may be done with new affections. David here prays that God would send, I. Help to himself (*v.* 1, 5). II. Shame to his enemies (*v.* 2, 3). III. Joy to his friends (*v.* 4). These five verses were the last five verses of Ps. 40. He seems to have intended this short prayer to be both for himself and us a salve for every sore, and therefore to be always in mind; and in singing we may apply it to our particular troubles, whatever they are.

To the chief musician. *A psalm* of David, to bring to remembrance.

Verses 1–5

The title tells us that this psalm was designed to bring to remembrance; that is, to put God in remembrance of his mercy and promises (for so we are said to do when we pray to him and plead with him. Isa. 43:26, *Put me in remembrance*) — not that the Eternal Mind needs a remembrancer, but this honour he is pleased to put upon the prayer of faith. Or, rather, to put himself and others in remembrance of former afflictions, that we may never be secure, but always in expectation of troubles, and of former devotions, that when the clouds return after the rain we may have recourse to the same means which we have formerly found effectual for fetching in comfort and relief. We may in prayer use the words we have often used before: our Saviour in his agony prayed thrice, saying the same words; so David here uses the words he had used before, yet not without some alterations, to show that he did not design to tie himself or others to them as a form. God looks at the heart, not at the words.

I. David here prays that God would make haste to relieve and succour him (*v.* 1, 5): *I am poor and needy,* in want and distress, and much at a loss within myself. Poverty and necessity are very good pleas in prayer to a God of infinite mercy, who despises not the sighing of a contrite heart, who has pronounced a blessing upon the poor in spirit, and who fills the hungry with good things. He prays, 1. That God would appear for him to deliver him from his troubles in due time. 2. That in the mean time he would come in to his aid, to help him under his troubles, that he might not sink and faint. 3. That he would do this quickly: *Make haste* (*v.* 1), and again (*v.* 5), *Make haste, make no tarrying.* Sometimes God seems to delay helping his own people, that he may excite such earnest desires as these. *He that believes does not make haste,* so as to anticipate or outrun the divine counsels, so as to force a way of escape or to take any unlawful methods of relief; but he may make haste by going forth to meet God in humble prayer that he would hasten the desired succour. *"Make haste unto me,* for the longing desire of my soul is towards thee; I shall perish if I be not speedily helped. I have no other to expect relief from: *Thou art my help and my delivered.* Thou hast engaged to be so to all that seek thee; I depend upon thee to be so to me; I have often found thee so; and thou art sufficient, all-sufficient, to be so; therefore make haste to me."

II. He prays that God would fill the faces of his enemies with shame, *v.* 2, 3. Observe, 1. How he describes them; they sought after his soul — his life, to destroy that — his mind, to disturb that, to draw him from God to sin and to despair. They desired his hurt, his ruin; when any calamity befel him or threatened him they said, *"Aha, aha! so would we have it;* we shall gain our point now, and see him ruined." Thus spiteful, thus insolent, were they. 2. What his prayer is against them: *"Let them be ashamed;* let them be brought to repentance, so filled with shame as that they may seek thy name (Ps. 83:16); let them see their fault and folly in fighting against those whom thou dost protect, and be *ashamed of their envy,* Isa. 26:11. However, let their designs against me be frustrated and their measures broken; let them be turned back from their malicious pursuits, and then they will be ashamed and confounded, and, like the enemies of the Jews, *much cast down in their own eyes,"* Gen. 6:16.

III. He prays that God would fill the hearts of his friends with joy (*v.* 4), that all those who seek God and love his salvation, who desire it, delight in it, and depend upon it, may have continual matter for joy and praise and hearts for both; and then he doubts not but that he should put in for a share of the blessing he prays for; and so may we if we answer the character. 1. Let us make the service of God our great business and the favour of God our great delight and pleasure, for that is seeking him and loving his salvation. Let the pursuit of a happiness in God be our great care and the enjoyment of it our great satisfaction. A heart to love the salvation of the Lord, and to prefer it before any secular advantages whatsoever, so as cheerfully to quit all rather than hazard our salvation, is a good evidence of our interest in it and title to it. 2. Let us then be assured that, if it be not our own fault, the joy of the Lord shall fill our minds and the high praises of the Lord shall fill our mouths. Those that seek God, if they seek him early and seek him diligently, shall rejoice and be glad in him, for their seeking him is an evidence of his good-will to them and an earnest of their finding him, 105:3. There is pleasure and joy even in seeking God, for it is one of the fundamental principles of religion that God is the *rewarder of all those that diligently seek him.* Those that love God's salvation shall say with pleasure, with constant pleasure (for praising God, if we make it our continual work, will be our continual feast), *Let God be magnified,* as he will be, to eternity, in the salvation of his people. All who wish well to the comfort of the saints, and to the glory of God, cannot but say a hearty *amen* to this prayer, that those who love God's salvation may say continually, *Let God be magnified.*

PSALM 71

David penned this psalm in his old age, as appears by several passages in it, which makes many think that it was penned at the time of Absalom's rebellion; for that was the great trouble of his later days. It might be occasioned by Sheba's insurrection, or some trouble that happened to him in that part of his life of which it was foretold that the sword should not depart from his house. But he is not over-particular in representing his case, because he intended it for the general use of God's people in their afflictions, especially those they meet with in their declining years; for this psalm, above any other, is fitted for the use of the old disciples of Jesus Christ. I. He begins the psalm with believing prayers, with prayers that God would deliver him and save him (*v.* 2, 4), and not cast him off (*v.* 9) or be far from him (*v.* 12), and that his enemies might be put to shame (*v.* 13). He pleads his confidence in God (*v.* 1, 3, 5, 7), the experience he had had of help from God (*v.* 6), and the malice of his enemies against him (*v.* 10, 11). II. He concludes the psalm with believing praises (*v.* 14, etc.). Never was his hope more established (*v.* 16, 18, 20, 21). Never were his joys and thanksgivings more enlarged (*v.* 15, 19, 22–24). He is in an ecstasy of joyful praise; and, in the singing of it, we too should have our faith in God encouraged and our hearts raised in blessing his holy name.

Verses 1–13

Two things in general David here prays for — that he might not be confounded and that his enemies and persecutors might be confounded.

I. He prays that he might never be made ashamed of his dependence upon God nor disappointed in his believing expectations from him. With this petition every true believer may come boldly to the throne of grace; for God will never disappoint the hope that is of his own raising. Now observe here,

1. How David professes his confidence in God, and with what pleasure and grateful variety of expression he repeats his profession of that confidence, still presenting the profession of it to God and pleading it with him. We praise God, and so please him, by telling him (if it be indeed true) what an entire confidence we have in him (*v.* 1): *"In thee, O Lord!* and in thee only, *do I put my trust.* Whatever others do, I choose the God of Jacob for my help." Those that are entirely satisfied with God's all-sufficiency and the truth of his promise, and in dependence upon that, as sufficient to make them amends, are freely willing to do and suffer, to lose and venture, for him, may truly say, *In thee, O Lord! do I put my trust.* Those that will deal with God must deal upon trust; if we are shy of dealing with him, it is a sign we do not trust him. *Thou art my rock and my fortress* (*v.* 3); and again, *"Thou art my refuge, my strong refuge"* (*v.* 7); that is, "I fly to thee, and am sure to be safe in thee, and under thy protection. If thou secure me, none can hurt me. *Thou art my hope and my trust"* (*v.* 5); that is, "thou hast proposed thyself to me in thy word as the proper object of my hope and trust; I have hoped in thee, and never found it in vain to do so."

2. How his confidence in God is supported and encouraged by his experiences (*v.* 5, 6): *"Thou hast been my trust from my youth;* ever since I was capable of discerning between my right hand and my left, I stayed myself upon thee, and saw a great deal of reason to do so; for *by thee have I been holden up from the womb."* Ever since he had the use of his reason he had been a dependent upon God's goodness, because ever since he had had a being he had been a monument of it. Note, The consideration of the gracious care which the divine Providence took of us in our birth and infancy should engage us to an early piety and constant devotedness to his honour. He that was our help from our birth ought to be our hope from our youth. If we received so much mercy from God before we were capable of doing him any service, we should lose no time when we are capable. This comes in here as a support to the psalmist in his present distress; not only that God had given him his life and being, bringing him out of his mother's bowels into the world, and providing that he should not die from the womb, nor give up the ghost when he came out of the belly, but that he had betimes made him one of his family: "Thou art he that took me out of my mother's bowels into the arms of thy grace, under the shadow of thy wings, into the bond of thy covenant; thou tookest me into thy church, as a son of thy handmaid, and born in thy house, Ps. 116:16. And therefore," (1.) "I have reason to hope that thou wilt protect me; thou that hast held me up hitherto wilt not let me fall now; thou that madest me wilt not forsake the work of thy own hands; thou that helpedst me when I could not help myself wilt not abandon me now that I am as helpless as I was then." (2.) "Therefore I have reason to resolve that I will devote myself unto thee: *My praise shall therefore be continually of thee;"* that is, "I will make it my business every day to praise thee and will take all occasions to do it."

3. What his requests to God are, in this confidence.

(1.) That he might *never be put to confusion* (*v.* 1), that he might not be disappointed of the mercy he expected and so made ashamed of his expectation. Thus we may all pray in faith that our confidence in God may not be our confusion. Hope of the glory of God is hope that makes not ashamed.

(2.) That he might be delivered out of the hand of his enemies (*v.* 2): *"Deliver me in thy righteousness.* As thou art the righteous Judge of the world, pleading the cause of the injured and punishing the injurious, cause me in some way or other to escape" (God will, with the temptation, make a way to escape, 1 Co. 10:13): *"Incline thy ear unto my prayers,* and, in answer to them, save me out of my troubles, *v.* 4. Deliver me, O my God! out of the hands of those that are ready to pull me in pieces." Three things he pleads for deliverance: — [1.] The encouragement God had given him to expect it: *Thou hast given commandment to save me* (*v.* 3); that is, thou hast promised to do it, and such efficacy is there in God's promises that they are often spoken of as commands, like that, *Let there be light, and there was light.* He speaks, and it is done. [2.] The character of his enemies; they are *wicked, unrighteous, cruel men,* and it will be for the honour of God to appear against them (*v.* 4), for he is a holy, just, and good God. [3.] The many eyes that were upon him (*v.* 7): *"I am as a wonder unto many;* every one waits to see what will be the issue of such extraordinary troubles as I have fallen into and such extraordinary confidence as I profess to have in God." Or, "I am looked upon as a monster, am one whom every body shuns, and therefore am undone if the Lord be not my refuge. Men abandon me, but God will not."

(3.) That he might always find rest and safety in God (*v.* 3): *Be thou my strong habitation;* by thou to me *a rock of repose, whereto I may continually resort.* Those that are at home in God, that live a life of communion with him and confidence in him, that continually resort unto him by faith and prayer, having their eyes ever towards him, may promise themselves a strong habitation in him, such as will never fall of itself nor can ever be broken through by any invading power; and they shall be welcome to resort to him continually upon all occasions, and not be upbraided as coming too often.

(4.) That he might have continual matter for thanksgiving to God, and might be continually employed in that pleasant work (*v.* 8): *"Let my mouth be filled with thy praise,* as now it is with my complaints, and then I shall not be ashamed of my hope, but my enemies will be ashamed of their insolence." Those that love God love to be praising him, and desire to be doing it all the day, not only in their morning and evening devotions, not only *seven times a day* (Ps. 119:164), but *all the day,* to intermix with all they say something or other that may redound to the honour and praise of God. They resolve to do it while they live; they hope to be doing it eternally in a better world.

(5.) That he might not be neglected now in his declining years (*v.* 9): *Cast me not off* now *in the time of* my *old gage; forsake me not when my strength fails.* Observe here, [1.] The natural sense he had of the infirmities of age: *My strength fails.* Where there was strength of body and vigour of mind, strong sight, a strong voice, strong limbs, alas! in old age they fail; the life is continued, but the strength is gone, or that which is his *labour and sorrow,* Ps. 90:10. [2.] The gracious desire he had of the continuance of God's presence with him under these infirmities: *Lord, cast me not off;* do *not then forsake me.* This intimates that he should look upon himself as undone if God should abandon him. To be cast off and forsaken of God is a thing to be dreaded at any time, especially in the time of old age and when our strength fails us; for it is God that is the strength of our heart. But it intimates that he had reason to hope God would not desert him; the faithful servants of God may be comfortably assured that he will not cast them off in old age, nor forsake them when their strength fails them. He is a Master that is not wont to cast off old servants. In this confidence David here prays again (*v.* 12): *"O God! be not far from me;* let me not be under the apprehension of thy withdrawings, for then I am miserable. *I my God!* a God in covenant with me, *make haste for my help,* lest I perish before help come."

II. He prays that his enemies might be made ashamed of their designs against him. Observe, 1. What it was which they unjustly said against him, *v.* 10, 11. Their plot was deep and desperate; it was against his life: *They lay wait for my soul* (*v.* 10), and are adversaries to that, *v.* 13. Their powers and policies were combined: *They take counsel together.* And very insolent they were in their deportment: They say, *God has forsaken him; persecute and take him.* Here their premises are utterly false, that because a good man was in great trouble and had continued long in it, and was not so soon delivered as perhaps he expected, therefore God had forsaken him and would have no more to do with him. All are not forsaken of God who think themselves so or whom others think to be so. And, as their premises were false, so their inference was barbarous. If God has forsaken him, then persecute and take him, and doubt not but to make a prey of him. This is *talking to the grief of* one whom God has smitten, Ps. 69:26. But thus they endeavour to discourage David, as Sennacherib endeavoured to intimidate Hezekiah by suggesting that God was his enemy and fought against him. *Have I now come up without the Lord against this city, to destroy it?* Isa. 36:10. It is true, if God has forsaken a man, there is none to deliver him; but *therefore* to insult over him ill becomes those who are conscious to themselves that they deserve to be for ever forsaken of God. But *rejoice not against me, O my enemy! though I fall, I shall rise.* He that seems to forsake for a small moment will gather with everlasting kindness. 2. What it was which he justly prayed for, from a spirit of prophecy, not a spirit of passion (v. 13): *"Let them be confounded and consumed that are adversaries to my soul.* If they will not be confounded by repentance, and so saved, let them be confounded with everlasting dishonour, and so ruined." God will turn into shame the glory of those who turn into shame the glory of God and his people.

Verses 14–24

David is here in a holy transport of joy and praise, arising from his faith and hope in God; we have both together v. 14, where there is a sudden and remarkable change of his voice; his fears are all silenced, his hopes raised, and his prayers turned into thanksgivings. "Let my enemies say what they will, to drive me to despair, *I will hope continually,* hope in all conditions, in the most cloudy and dark day; I will live upon hope and will hope to the end." Since we hope in one that will never fail us, let not our hope in him fail us, and then we shall praise him yet more and more. "The more they reproach me the more closely will I cleave to thee; I *will praise thee more* and better than ever I have done yet." The longer we live the more expert we should grow in praising God and the more we should abound in it. *I will add over and above all thy praise,* all the praise I have hitherto offered, for it is all too little. When we have said all we can, to the glory of God's grace, there is still more to be said; it is a subject that can never be exhausted, and therefore we should never grow weary of it. Now observe, in these verses,

I. How his heart is established in faith and hope; and it is a good thing that the heart be so established. Observe,

1. What he hopes in, v. 16. (1.) In the power of God: *"I will go in the strength of the Lord God,* not sit down in despair, but stir up myself to and exert myself in my work and warfare, will go forth and go on, not in any strength of my own, but in God's strength — disclaiming my own sufficiency and depending on him only as all-sufficient — in the strength of his providence and in the strength of his grace." We must always go about God's work in his strength, having our eyes up unto him to work in us both to will and to do. (2.) In the promise of God: *"I will make mention of thy righteousness,* that is, thy faithfulness to every word which thou hast spoken, the equity of thy disposals, and thy kindness to thy people that trust in thee. This I will make mention of as my plea in prayer for thy mercy." We may very fitly apply it to the righteousness of Christ, which is called the *righteousness of God by faith,* and which is *witnessed by the law and the prophets;* we must depend upon God's strength for assistance and upon Christ's righteousness for acceptance. *In the Lord have I righteousness and strength,* Isa. 45:24.

2. What he hopes for.

(1.) He hopes that God will not leave him in his old age, but will be the same to him to the end that he had been all along, v. 17, 18. Observe here, [1.] What God had done for him when he was young: *Thou hast taught me from my youth.* The good education and good instructions which his parents gave him when he was young he owns himself obliged to give God thanks for as a great favour. It is a blessed thing to be taught of God from our youth, from our childhood to know the holy scriptures, and it is what we have reason to bless God for. [2.] What he had done for God when he was middle-aged: He had *declared all God's wondrous works.* Those that have not good when they are young must be doing good when they are grown up, and must continue to communicate what they have received. We must own that all the works of God's goodness to us are wondrous works, admiring he should do so much for us who are so undeserving, and we must make it our business to declare them, to the glory of God and the good of others. [3.] What he desired of God now that

he was old: *Now that I am old and gray-headed,* dying to this world and hastening to another, *O God! forsake me not.* This is what he earnestly desires and confidently hopes for. Those that have been taught of God from their youth, and have made it the business of their lives to honour him, may be sure that he will not leave them when they are old and gray-headed, will not leave them helpless and comfortless, but will make the evil days of old age their best days, and such as they shall have occasion to say they have pleasure in. [4.] What he designed to do for God in his old age: "I will not only *show thy strength,* by my own experience of it, *to this generation,* but I will leave my observations upon record for the benefit of posterity, and so who it *to every one that is to come."* As long as we live we should be endeavouring to glorify God and edify one another; and those that have had the largest and longest experience of the goodness of God to them should improve their experiences for the good of their friends. It is a debt which the old disciples of Christ owe to the succeeding generations to leave behind them a solemn testimony to the power, pleasure, and advantage of religion, and the truth of God's promises.

(2.) He hopes that God would revive him and raise him up out of his present low and disconsolate condition (v. 20): *Thou who hast made me to see and feel great and sore troubles,* above most men, *shalt quicken me again.* Note, [1.] The best of God's saints and servants are sometimes exercised with great and sore troubles in this world. [2.] God's hand is to be eyed in all the troubles of the saints, and that will help to extenuate them and make them seem light. He does not say, "Thou hast burdened me with those troubles," but "shown them to me," as the tender father shows the child the rod to keep him in awe. [3.] Though God's people be brought ever so low he can revive them and raise them up. Are they dead? he can quicken them again. See 2 Co. 1:9. Are they buried, as dead men out of mind? he can bring *them up again from the depths of the earth,* can cheer the most drooping spirit and raise the most sinking interest. [4.] If we have a due regard to the hand of God in our troubles, we may promise ourselves, in due time, a deliverance out of them. Our present troubles, though great and sore, shall be no hindrance to our joyful resurrection from the depths of the earth, witness our great Master, to whom this may have some reference; his Father showed him great and sore troubles, but quickened him and brought him up from the grave.

(3.) He hopes that God would not only deliver him out of his troubles, but would advance his honour and joy more than ever (v. 21): "Thou shalt not only restore me to *my greatness* again, but shalt *increase* it, and give me a better interest, after this shock, than before; thou shalt not only comfort me, but *comfort me on every side,* so that I shall see nothing black or threatening on any side." Note, Sometimes God makes his people's troubles contribute to the increase of their greatness, and their sun shines the brighter for having been under a cloud. If he make them contribute to the increase of their goodness, that will prove in the end the increase of their greatness, their glory; and if he comfort them on every side, according to the time and degree wherein he has afflicted them on every side, they will have no reason to complain. When our Lord Jesus was quickened again, and brought back from the depths of the earth, his greatness was increased, and he entered on the joy set before him.

(4.) He hopes that all his enemies would be put to confusion, v. 24. He speaks of it with the greatest assurance as a thing done, and triumphs in it accordingly: *They are confounded, they are brought to shame, that seek my hurt.* His honour would be their disgrace and his comfort their vexation.

II. Let us now see how his heart is enlarged in joy and praises, how he rejoices in hope, and sings in hope for we are saved by hope.

1. He will speak of God's righteousness and his salvation, as great things, things which he was well acquainted with, and much affected with, which he desired God might have the glory of and others might have the comfortable knowledge of (v. 15): *My mouth shall show forth thy righteousness and thy salvation;* and again (v. 24), *My tongue shall talk of thy righteousness,* and this *all the day.* God's righteousness, which David seems here to be in a particular manner affected with, includes a great deal: the rec-

titude of his nature, the equity of his providential disposals, the righteous laws he has given us to be ruled by, the righteous promises he has given us to depend upon, and the everlasting righteousness which his Son has brought in for our justification. God's righteousness and his salvation are here joined together; let no man think to put them asunder, nor expect salvation without righteousness, Ps. 50:23. If these two are made the objects of our desire, let them be made the subjects of our discourse all the day, for they are subjects that can never be exhausted.

2. He will speak of them with wonder and admiration, as one astonished at the dimensions of divine love and grace, the height and depth, the length and breadth, of it: *"I know not the numbers thereof, v.* 15. Though I cannot give a particular account of thy favours to me, they are so many, so great (if *I would count them, they are more in number than the sand,* Ps. 40:5), yet, knowing them to be numberless, I will be still speaking of them, for in them I shall find new matter," *v.* 19. The righteousness that is in God is very high; that which is done by him for his people is very great: put both together, and we shall say, *O God! who is like unto thee?* This is praising God, acknowledging his perfections and performances to be, (1.) Above our conception; they are very high and great, so high that we cannot apprehend them, so great that we cannot comprehend them. (2.) Without any parallel; no being like him, no works like his: *O God! who is like unto thee?* None in heaven, none on earth, no angel, no king. God is a nonsuch; we do not rightly praise him if we do not own him to be so.

3. He will speak of them with all the expressions of joy and exultation, v. 22, 23. Observe,

(1.) How he would eye God in praising him. [1.] As a faithful God: *I will praise thee, even thy truth.* God is made known by his word; if we praise that, and the truth of that, we praise him. By faith we set to our seal that God is true; and so we praise his truth. [2.] As a God in covenant with him: *"O my God!* whom I have consented to and avouched for mine." As in our prayers, so in our praises, we must look up to God as our God, and give him the glory of our interest in him and relation to him. [3.] As the *Holy One of Israel,* Israel's God in a peculiar manner, glorious in his holiness among that people and faithful to his covenant with them. It is God's honour that he is a Holy One; it is his people's honour that he is the Holy One of Israel.

(2.) How he will express his joy and exultation. [1.] With his hand, in sacred music — *with the psaltery, with the harp;* at these David excelled, and the best of his skill shall be employed in setting forth God's praises to such advantage as might affect others. [2.] With his lips, in sacred songs: *"Unto thee will I sing,* to thy honour, and with a desire to be accepted of thee. *My lips shall greatly rejoice when I sing unto thee,* knowing they cannot be better employed." [3.] In both with his heart: *"My soul shall rejoice which thou hast redeemed."* Note, *First,* Holy joy is the very heart and life of thankful praise. *Secondly,* We do not make melody to the Lord, in singing his praises, if we do not do it with our hearts. My lips shall rejoice, but that is nothing; lip-labour, though ever so well laboured, if that be all, is but lost labour in serving God; the soul must be at work, and with all that is within us we must bless his holy name, else all about us is worth little. *Thirdly,* Redeemed souls ought to be joyful thankful souls. The work of redemption ought, above all God's works, to be celebrated by us in our praises. The Lamb that was slain, and has redeemed us to God, must therefore be counted worthy of all blessing and praise.

PSALM 72

The foregoing psalm was penned by David when he was old, and, it should seem, so was this too; for Solomon was now standing fair for the crown; that was his prayer for himself, this for his son and successor, and with these two the prayers of David the son of Jesse are ended, as we find in the close of this psalm. If we have but God's presence with us while we live, and good hopes concerning those that shall come after us that they shall be praising God on earth when we are praising him in heaven, it is enough. This is entitled "a psalm for Solomon;" it is probable that David dictated it, or, rather, that it was by the blessed Spirit dictated to him, when, a little before he died, by divine direction he settled the succession, and gave orders to proclaim Solomon king, 1 Ki. 1:30, etc. But, though Solomon's name is here made use of, Christ's kingdom is here prophesied of under the type and figure of Solomon's. David knew what the divine oracle was, That "of the fruit of his loins, according to the flesh, he would raise up Christ to sit on his throne," Acts 2:30. To him he here bears witness, and with the prospect of the glories of his kingdom he comforted himself in his dying moments when he foresaw that his house would not be so with God, not so great not so good, as he wished. David, in spirit, I. Begins with a short prayer for his successor (v. 1). II. He passes immediately into a long prediction of the glories of his reign (v. 2–17). And, III. He concludes with praise to the God of Israel (v. 18–20). In singing this psalm we must have an eye to Christ, praising him as a King, and pleasing ourselves with our happiness as his subjects.

A psalm for Solomon.

Verse 1

This verse is a prayer for the king, even the king's son. I. We may apply it to Solomon: *Give him thy judgments, O God! and thy righteousness;* make him a man, a king; make him a good man, a good king. 1. It is the prayer of a father for his child, a dying blessing, such as the patriarchs bequeathed to their children. The best thing we can ask of God for our children is that God will give them wisdom and grace to know and do their duty; that is better than gold. Solomon learned to pray for himself as his father had prayed for him, not that God would give him riches and honour, but a wise and understanding heart. It was a comfort to David that his own son was to be his successor, but more so that he was likely to be both judicious and righteous. David had given him a good education (Prov. 4:3), had taught him *good judgment and righteous,* yet that would not do unless God gave him his judgments. Parents cannot give grace to their children, but may by prayer bring them to the God of grace, and shall not seek him in vain, for their prayer shall either be answered or it shall return with comfort into their own bosom. 2. It is the prayer of a king for his successor. David had executed judgment and justice during his reign, and now he prays that his son might do so too. Such a concern as this we should have for posterity, desiring and endeavouring that those who come after us may do God more and better service in their day than we have done in ours. Those have little love either to God or man, and are of a very narrow selfish spirit, who care not what becomes of the world and the church when they are gone. 3. It is the prayer of subjects for their king. It should seem, David penned this psalm for the use of the people, that they, in singing, might pray for Solomon. Those who would live quiet and peaceable lives must pray for kings and all in authority, that God would give them his judgments and righteousness.

II. We may apply it to Christ; not that he who intercedes for us needs us to intercede for him; but, 1. It is a prayer of the Old-Testament church for sending the Messiah, as the church's King, King *on the holy hill of Zion,* of whom the King of kings had said, *Thou art my Son,* Ps. 2:6, 7. "Hasten his coming to whom all judgment is committed;" and we must thus hasten the second coming of Christ, when he shall *judge the world in righteousness.* 2. It is an expression of the satisfaction which all true believers take in the authority which the Lord Jesus has received from the Father: "Let him have all power both in heaven and earth, and be the Lord our righteousness; let him be the great trustee of divine grace for all that are his; give it to him, that he may give it to us."

Verses 2–17

This is a prophecy of the prosperity and perpetuity of the kingdom of Christ under the shadow of the reign of Solomon. It comes in, 1. As a plea to enforce the prayer: "Lord, *give him thy judgments and thy righteousness,* and then *he shall judge thy people with righteousness,* and so shall answer the end of his elevation, v. 2. Give him thy grace, and then thy people, committed to his charge, will have the benefit of it." *Because God loved Israel, he made him king over them to do judgment and justice,* 2 Chr. 9:8. We may in faith wrestle with God for that grace which we have reason to think will be of common advantage to his church. 2. As an answer of peace to the prayer. As by the prayer of faith we return answers to God's promises of mercy, so by the promises of mercy God returns answers to our prayers of faith. That this prophecy must refer to the kingdom of the Messiah is plain, because there are many passages in it which cannot be applied to the reign of Solomon. There was indeed a great deal of righteousness and peace, at first, in the administration of his government; but, before the end of his reign, there were both

trouble and unrighteousness. The kingdom here spoken of is to last as long as the sun, but Solomon's was soon extinct. Therefore even the Jewish expositors understand it of the kingdom of the Messiah.

Let us observe the many great and precious promises here made, which were to have their full accomplishment only in the kingdom of Christ; and yet some of them were in part fulfilled in Solomon's reign.

I. That it should be a *righteous government* (v. 2): *He shall judge thy people with righteousness.* Compare Isa. 11:4. All the laws of Christ's kingdom are consonant to the eternal rules of equity; the chancery it erects to relieve against the rigours of the broken law is indeed a court of equity; and against the sentence of his last judgment there will lie no exception. The peace of his kingdom shall be supported by righteousness (v. 3); for then only is the peace like a river, when the *righteousness is as the waves of the sea.* The world will be judged in righteousness, Acts 17:31.

II. That it should be a peaceable government: *The mountains shall bring peace, and the little hills* (v. 3); that is (says Dr. Hammond), both the superior and the inferior courts of judicature in Solomon's kingdom. There shall be *abundance of peace, v.* 7. Solomon's name signifies *peaceable,* and such was his reign; for in it Israel enjoyed the victories of the foregoing reign and preserved the tranquillity and repose of that reign. But peace is, in a special manner, the glory of Christ's kingdom; for, as far as it prevails, it reconciles men to God, to themselves, and to one another, and slays all enmities; for he is our peace.

III. That the poor and needy should be, in a particular manner, taken under the protection of this government: *He shall judge thy poor, v.* 2. Those are God's poor that are impoverished by keeping a good conscience, and those shall be provided for with a distinguishing care, shall be judged for with judgment, with a particular cognizance taken of their case and a particular vengeance taken for their wrongs. *The poor of the people,* and *the children of the needy,* he will be sure so to judge as to save, v. 4. This is insisted upon again (v. 12, 13), intimating that Christ will be sure to carry his cause on behalf of his injured poor. *He will deliver the needy* that lie at the mercy of their oppressors, *the poor also,* both because they have *no helper* and it is for his honour to help them and because they cry unto him and he has promised, in answer to their prayers, to help them; they by prayer *commit themselves unto him,* Ps. 10:14. *He will spare the needy* that throw themselves on his mercy, and will not be rigorous and severe with them; he *will save their souls,* and that is all they desire. *Blessed are the poor in spirit, for theirs is the kingdom of heaven.* Christ is the poor man's King.

IV. That proud oppressors shall be reckoned with: *He shall break them in pieces* (v. 4), shall take away their power to hurt, and punish them for all the mischief they have done. This is the office of a good king, *Parcere subjectis, et debellare superbos — To spare the vanquished and debase the proud.* The devil is the great oppressor, whom Christ will break in pieces and of whose kingdom he will be the destruction. *With the breath of his mouth shall he slay that wicked one* (Isa. 11:4), and shall deliver the souls of his people *from deceit and violence, v.* 14. He shall save from the power of Satan, both as an old serpent working by deceit to ensnare them and as a roaring lion working by violence to terrify and devour them. So *precious shall their blood be unto him* that not a drop of it shall be shed, by the deceit or violence of Satan or his instruments, without being reckoned for. Christ is a King, who, though he calls his subjects sometimes to resist unto blood for him, yet is not prodigal of their blood, nor will ever have it parted with but upon a valuable consideration to his glory and theirs, and the filling up of the measure of their enemies' iniquity.

V. That religion shall flourish under Christ's government (v. 5): *They shall fear thee as long as the sun and moon endure.* Solomon indeed built the temple, and the fear and worship of God were well kept up, for some time, under his government, but it did not last long; this therefore must point at Christ's kingdom, all the subjects of which are brought to and kept in the fear of God; for the Christian religion has a direct tendency to, and a powerful influence upon, the support and advancement of natural religion. Faith in Christ will set up, and keep up, the fear of God; and therefore this is the everlasting gospel that

is preached, *Fear God, and give honour to him,* Rev. 14:7. And, as Christ's government promotes devotion towards God, so it promotes both justice and charity among men (v. 7): *In his days shall the righteous flourish;* righteousness shall be practised, and those that practise righteousness shall be preferred. Righteousness shall abound and be in reputation, shall command and be in power. The law of Christ, written in the heart, disposes men to be honest and just, and to render to all their due; it likewise disposes men to live in love, and so it produces abundance of peace and beats swords into ploughshares. Both holiness and love shall be perpetual in Christ's kingdom, and shall never go to decay, for the subjects of it shall *fear God as long as the sun and moon endure;* Christianity, in the profession of it, having got footing in the world, shall keep its ground till the end of time, and having, in the power of it, got footing in the heart, it will continue there till, by death, the sun, and the moon, and the stars (that is, the bodily senses) are darkened. Through all the changes of the world, and all the changes of life, Christ's kingdom will support itself; and, if the fear of God continue as long as the sun and moon, abundance of peace will. The peace of the church, the peace of the soul, shall run parallel with its purity and piety, and last as long as these last.

VI. That Christ's government shall be very comfortable to all his faithful loving subjects (v. 6): *He shall,* by the graces and comforts of his Spirit, *come down like rain upon the mown grass;* not on that which is cut down, but that which is left growing, that it may spring again, though it was beheaded. The gospel of Christ distils as the rain, which softens the ground that was hard, moistens that which was dry, and so makes it green and fruitful, Isa. 55:10. Let our hearts *drink in the rain,* Heb. 6:7.

VII. That Christ's kingdom shall be extended very far, and greatly enlarged; considering,

1. The extent of his territories (v. 8): *He shall have dominion from sea to sea* (from the South Sea to the North, or from the Red Sea to the Mediterranean) *and from the river* Euphrates, or Nile, *to the ends of the earth.* Solomon's dominion was very large (1 Ki. 4:21), according to the promise, Gen. 15:18. But no sea, no river, is named, that it might, by these proverbial expressions, intimate the universal monarchy of the Lord Jesus. His gospel has been, or shall be, preached *to all nations* (Mt. 24:14), and the *kingdoms of the world* shall *become his kingdoms* (Rev. 11:15) when the fulness of the Gentiles shall be brought in. His territories shall be extended to those countries, (1.) That were strangers to him: *Those that dwell in the wilderness,* out of all high roads, that seldom hear news, shall hear the glad tidings of the Redeemer and redemption by him, *shall bow before him,* shall believe in him, accept of him, worship him, and take his yoke upon them. Before the Lord Jesus we must all either bow or break; if we break, we are ruined — if we bow, we are certainly made for ever. (2.) That were enemies to him, and had fought against him: *They shall lick the dust;* they shall be brought down and laid in the dust, shall bite the ground for vexation, and be so hunger-bitten that they shall be glad of dust, the serpent's meat (Gen. 3:15), for of his seed they are; and over whom shall not he rule, when his enemies themselves are thus humbled and brought low?

2. The dignity of his tributaries. He shall not only reign over those that dwell in the wilderness, the peasants and cottagers, but over those that dwell in the palaces (v. 10): *The kings of Tarshish, and of the isles,* that lie most remote from Israel and are *the isles of the Gentiles* (Gen. 10:5), *shall bring presents* to him as their sovereign Lord, by and under whom they hold their crowns and all their crown lands. They shall court his favour, and make an interest in him, that they may hear his wisdom. This was literally fulfilled in Solomon (for *all the kings of the earth sought the wisdom of Solomon, and brought every man his present,* 2 Chr. 9:23, 24), and in Christ too, when the wise men of the east, who probably were men of the first rank in their own country, came to worship him and *brought him presents,* Mt. 2:11. They shall present themselves to him; that is the best present we can bring to Christ, and without that no other present is acceptable, Rom. 12:1. They *shall offer gifts,* spiritual sacrifices of prayer and praise, offer them to Christ as their God, on Christ as their altar, which sanctifies every gift. Their conversion to God is called the *offering up,* or *sacrificing, of the Gentiles,* Rom.

15:16. Yea, all kings shall, sooner or later, *fall down before him,* either to do their duty to him or to receive their doom from him, *v.* 11. They shall fall before him, either as his willing subjects or as his conquered captives, as suppliants for his mercy or expectants of his judgment. And, when the kings submit, the people come in of course: *All nations shall serve him;* all shall be invited into his service; some of all nations shall come into it, and in every nation *incense shall be offered to him and a pure offering,* Mal. 1:11; Rev. 7:9.

VIII. That he shall be honoured and beloved by all his subjects (*v.* 15): *He shall live;* his subjects shall desire his life *(O king! live for ever)* and with good reason; for he has said, *Because I live, you shall live also; and of him it is witnessed that he liveth, ever liveth, making intercession,* Heb. 7:8, 25. He shall live, and live prosperously; and, 1. Presents shall be made to him. Though he shall be able to live without them, for he needs neither the gifts nor the services of any, yet to him *shall be given of the gold of Sheba* — gold, the best of metals, gold of Sheba, which probably was the finest gold; for he that is best must be served with the best. Those that have abundance of the wealth of this world, that have gold at command, must give it to Christ, must serve him with it, do good with it. *Honour the Lord with thy substance.* 2. Prayers shall be made for him, and that continually. The people prayed for Solomon, and that helped to make him and his reign so great a blessing to them. It is the duty of subjects to make prayers, intercessions, and giving of thanks, for kings and all in authority, not in compliment to them, as is too often done, but in concern for the public welfare. But how is this applied to Christ? He needs not our prayers, nor can have any benefit by them. But the Old-Testament saints prayed for his coming, prayed continually for it; for they called him, *He that should come.* And now that he has come we must pray for the success of his gospel and the advancement of his kingdom, which he calls praying for him (Hosanna to the Son of David, prosperity to his reign), and we must pray for his second coming. It may be read, *Prayer shall be made through him,* or for his sake; whatsoever we ask of the Father shall be in his name and in dependence upon his intercession. 3. Praises shall be made of him, and high encomiums given of his wisdom, justice, and goodness: *Daily shall he be praised.* By praying daily in his name we give him honour. Subjects ought to speak well of the government that is a blessing to them; and much more ought all Christians to praise Jesus Christ, daily to praise him; for they owe their all to him, and to him they lie under the highest obligations.

IX. That under his government there shall be a wonderful increase both of meat and mouths, both of the fruits of the earth in the country and of the people inhabiting the cities, *v.* 16. 1. The country shall grow rich. Sow but a *handful of corn on the top of the mountains,* whence one would expect but little, and yet *the fruit of it shall shake like Lebanon;* it shall come up like a wood, so thick, and tall, and strong, like the cedars of Lebanon. Even upon the tops of the mountains the earth shall bring forth by handfuls; that is an expression of great plenty (Gen. 41:47), as the grass upon the house top is said to be that wherewith the mower fills not his hand. This is applicable to the wonderful productions of the seed of the gospel in the days of the Messiah. A handful of that seed, sown in the mountainous and barren soil of the Gentile world, produced a wonderful harvest gathered in to Christ, fruit that shook like Lebanon. The fields were *white to the harvest,* Jn. 4:35; Mt. 9:37. The grain of mustard-seed grew up to a great tree. 2. The towns shall grow populous: *Those of the city shall flourish like grass,* for number, for verdure. The gospel church, the city of God among men, shall have all the marks of prosperity, many shall be added to it, and those that are shall be happy in it.

X. That his government shall be perpetual, both to his honour and to the happiness of his subjects. The Lord Jesus shall reign for ever, and of him only this must be understood, and not at all of Solomon. It is Christ only that shall *be feared throughout all generations* (*v.* 5) and *as long as the sun and moon endure, v.* 7. 1. The honour of the princes is immortal and shall never be sullied (*v.* 17): *His name shall endure for ever,* in spite of all the malicious attempts and endeavours of the powers of darkness to eclipse the lustre of it and to cut off the line of it; it shall be preserved; it shall be perpetuated; it shall be propagated. As the names of earthly princes are continued in their posterity, so Christ's in himself. *Filiabitur nomen ejus — His name shall descend to posterity.* All nations, while the world stands, shall call him blessed, shall bless God for him, continually speak well of him, and think themselves happy in him. To the end of time, and to eternity, his name shall be celebrated, shall be made use of; every tongue shall confess it and every knee shall bow before it. 2. The happiness of the people if universal too; it is complete and everlasting: *Men shall be blessed,* truly and for ever blessed, *in him.* This plainly refers to the promise made unto the fathers that in the Messiah all the nations of the earth should be blessed. Gen. 12:3.

Verses 18–20

Such an illustrious prophecy as is in the foregoing verses of the Messiah and his kingdom may fitly be concluded, as it is here, with hearty prayers and praises.

I. The psalmist is here enlarged in thanksgivings for the prophecy and promise, *v.* 18, 19. So sure is every word of God, and with so much satisfaction may we rely upon it, that we have reason enough to give thanks for what he has said, though it be not yet done. We must own that for all the great things he has done for the world, for the church, for the children of men, for his own children, in the kingdom of providence, in the kingdom of grace, for all the power and trust lodged in the hands of the Redeemer, God is worthy to be praised; we must stir up ourselves and all that is within us to praise him after the best manner, and desire that all others may do it. *Blessed be the Lord,* that is, *blessed be his glorious name;* for it is only in his name that we can contribute any thing to his glory and blessedness, and yet that is also *exalted above all blessing and praise.* Let it be blessed for ever, it shall be blessed for ever, it deserves to be blessed for ever, and we hope to be for ever blessing it. We are here taught to bless the name of Christ, and to bless God in Christ, for all that which he has done for us by him. We must bless him, 1. As the Lord God, as a self-existent self-sufficient Being, and our sovereign Lord. 2. As the God of Israel, in covenant with that people and worshipped by them, and who does this in performance of the truth unto Jacob and the mercy to Abraham, 3. As the God *who only does wondrous things,* in creation and providence, and especially this work of redemption, which excels them all. Men's works are little, common, trifling things, and even these they could not do without him. But God does all by his own power, and they are wondrous things which he does, and such as will be the eternal admiration of saints and angels.

II. He is earnest in prayer for the accomplishment of this prophecy and promise: *Let the whole earth be filled with his glory,* as it will be when the *kings of Tarshish, and the isles, shall bring presents to him.* It is sad to think how empty the earth is of the glory of God, how little service and honour he has from a world to which he is such a bountiful benefactor. All those, therefore, that wish well to the honour of God and the welfare of mankind, cannot but desire that the earth may be filled with the discoveries of his glory, suitably returned in thankful acknowledgments of his glory. Let every heart, and every mouth, and every assembly, be filled with the high praises of God. We shall see how earnest David is in this prayer, and how much his heart is in it, if we observe, 1. How he shuts up the prayer with a double seal: *"Amen and amen;* again and again I say, I say it and let all others say the same, so be it. Amen to my prayer; Amen to the prayers of all the saints to this purport — *Hallowed be thy name; thy kingdom come."* 2. How he ever shuts up his life with this prayer, *v.* 20. This was the last psalm that ever he penned, though not placed last in this collection; he penned it when he lay on his death-bed, and with this he breathes his last: "Let God be glorified, let the kingdom of the Messiah be set up, and kept up, in the world, and I have enough, I desire no more. With this let *the prayers of David the son of Jesse* be *ended.* Even so, come, Lord Jesus, come quickly."

PSALM 73

This psalm, and the ten that next follow it, carry the name of Asaph in the titles of them. If he was the penman of them (as many think), we rightly call them psalms of Asaph. If he was only the chief musician, to whom they were delivered, our marginal reading is right, which calls them psalms for Asaph. It is probable that he penned them; for we read of the words of David and of Asaph the seer, which were used in praising God in Hezekiah's time, 2 Chr. 29:30. Though the Spirit of prophecy by sacred songs descended chiefly on David, who is therefore styled "the sweet psalmist of Israel," yet God put some of that Spirit upon those about him. This is a psalm of great use; it gives us an account of the conflict which the psalmist had with a strong temptation to envy the prosperity of wicked people. He begins his account with a sacred principle, which he held fast, and by the help of which he kept his ground and carried his point (*v.* 1). He then tells us, I. How he got into the temptation (*v.* 2–14). II. How he got out of the temptation and gained a victory over it (*v.* 15–20). III. How he got by the temptation and was the better for it (*v.* 21–23). If, in singing this psalm, we fortify ourselves against the life temptation, we do not use it in vain. The experiences of others should be our instructions.

A psalm of Asaph.

Verses 1–14

This psalm begins somewhat abruptly: *Yet God is good to Israel* (so the margin reads it); he had been thinking of the prosperity of the wicked; while he was thus musing the fire burned, and at last he spoke by way of check to himself for what he had been thinking of. "However it be, yet God is good." Though wicked people receive many of the gifts of his providential bounty, yet we must own that he is, in a peculiar manner, good to Israel; they have favours from him which others have not.

The psalmist designs an account of a temptation he was strongly assaulted with — to envy the prosperity of the wicked, a common temptation, which has tried the graces of many of the saints. Now in this account,

I. He lays down, in the first place, that great principle which he is resolved to abide by and not to quit while he was parleying with this temptation, *v.* 1. Job, when he was entering into such a temptation, fixed for his principle the omniscience of God: *Times are not hidden from the Almighty,* Job 24:1. Jeremiah's principle is the justice of God: *Righteous art thou, O God! when I plead with thee,* Jer. 12:1. Habakkuk's principle is the holiness of God: *Thou art of purer eyes than to behold iniquity,* Hab. 1:13. The psalmist's, here, is the goodness of God. These are truths which cannot be shaken and which we must resolve to live and die by. Though we may not be able to reconcile all the disposals of Providence with them, we must believe they are reconcilable. Note, Good thoughts of God will fortify us against many of Satan's temptations. *Truly God is good;* he had had many thoughts in his mind concerning the providences of God, but this word, at last, settled him: "For all this, God is good, *good to Israel, even to those that are of a clean heart."* Note, 1. Those are the Israel of God that are of a clean heart, purified by the blood of Christ, cleansed from the pollutions of sin, and entirely devoted to the glory of God. An upright heart is a clean heart; cleanness is truth in the inward part. 2. God, who is good to all, is in a special manner good to his church and people, as he was to Israel of old. God was good to Israel in redeeming them out of Egypt, taking them into covenant with himself, giving them his laws and ordinances, and in the various providences that related to them; he is, in like manner, good to all those that are of a clean heart, and, whatever happens, we must not think otherwise.

II. He comes now to relate the shock that was given to his faith in God's distinguishing goodness to Israel by a strong temptation to envy the prosperity of the wicked, and therefore to think that the Israel of God are no happier than other people and that God is no kinder to them than to others.

1. He speaks of it as a very narrow escape that he had not been quite foiled and overthrown by this temptation (*v.* 2): *"But as for me,* though I was so well satisfied in the goodness of God to Israel, yet *my feet were almost gone* (the tempter had almost tripped up my heels), *my steps had well-nigh slipped* (I had like to have quitted my religion, and given up all my expectations of benefit by it); *for I was envious at the foolish."* Note, 1. The faith even of strong believers may sometimes be sorely shaken and ready to fail them. There are storms that will try the firmest anchors. 2. Those that shall never be quite undone are sometimes very near it, and, in their own apprehension, as good as gone. Many a precious soul, that shall live for ever, had once a very narrow turn for its life; almost and well-nigh ruined, but a step between it and fatal apostasy, and yet snatched as a brand out of the burning, which will

for ever magnify the riches of divine grace in the nations of those that are saved. Now,

2. Let us take notice of the process of the psalmist's temptation, what he was tempted with and tempted to.

(1.) He observed that foolish wicked people have sometimes a very great share of outward prosperity. He *saw*, with grief, *the prosperity of the wicked, v.* 3. Wicked people are really foolish people, and act against reason and their true interest, and yet every stander-by sees their prosperity. [1.] They seem to have the least share of the troubles and calamities of this life (*v.* 5): *They are not in the troubles of other men*, even of wise and good men, *neither are they plagued like other men*, but seem as if by some special privilege they were exempted from the common lot of sorrows. If they meet with some little trouble, it is nothing to what others endure that are less sinners and yet greater sufferers. [2.] They seem to have the greatest share of the comforts of this life. They live at ease, and bathe themselves in pleasures, so that *their eyes stand out with fatness, v.* 7. See what the excess of pleasure is; the moderate use of it enlightens the eyes, but those that indulge themselves inordinately in the delights of sense have their eyes ready to start out of their heads. Epicures are really their own tormentors, by putting a force upon nature, while they pretend to gratify it. And well may those feed themselves to the full who have *more than heart could wish*, more than they themselves ever thought of or expected to be masters of. They have, at least, more than a humble, quiet, contented heart could wish, yet not so much as they themselves wish for. There are many who have a great deal of this life in their hands, but nothing of the other life in their hearts. They are ungodly, live without the fear and worship of God, and yet they prosper and get on in the world, and not only are rich, but *increase in riches, v.* 12. They are looked upon as thriving men; while others have much ado to keep what they have, they are still adding more, more honour, power, pleasure, by increasing in riches. *They are the prosperous of the age*, so some read it. [3.] Their end seems to be peace. This is mentioned first, as the most strange of all, for peace in death was every thought to be the peculiar privilege of the godly (Ps. 37:37), yet, to outward appearance, it is often the lot of the ungodly (*v.* 4): *There are no bands in their death*. They are not taken off by a violent death; they are foolish, and yet die not as fools die; for *their hands are not bound nor their feet put into fetters*, 2 Sa. 3:33, 34. They are not taken off by an untimely death, like the fruit forced from the tree before it is ripe, but are left to hang on, till, through old age, they gently drop of themselves. They do not die of sore and painful diseases: *There are no pangs, no agonies, in their death, but their strength is firm* to the last, so that they scarcely feel themselves die. They are of those who *die in their full strength, being wholly at ease and quiet*, not of those that *die in the bitterness of their souls and never eat with pleasure*, Job 21:23, 25. Nay, they are not bound by the terrors of conscience in their dying moments; they are not frightened either with the remembrance of their sins or the prospect of their misery, but die securely. We cannot judge of men's state on the other side death either by the manner of their death or the frame of their spirits in dying. Men may die like lambs, and yet have their place with the goats.

(2.) He observed that they made a very bad use of their outward prosperity and were hardened by it in their wickedness, which very much strengthened the temptation he was in to fret at it. If it had done them any good, if it had made them less provoking to God or less oppressive to man, it would never have vexed him; but it had quite a contrary effect upon them. [1.] It made them very proud and haughty. Because they live at ease, *pride compasses them as a chain, v.* 6. They show themselves (to all that see them) to be puffed up with their prosperity, as men show their ornaments. *The pride of Israel testifies to his face*, Hos. 5:5; Isa. 3:9. *Pride ties on their chain*, or necklace; so Dr. Hammond reads it. It is no harm to wear a chain or necklace; but when pride ties it on, when it is worn to gratify a vain mind, it ceases to be an ornament. It is not so much what the dress or apparel is (though we have rules for that, 1 Tim. 2:9) as what principle ties it on and with what spirit it is worn. And, as the pride of sinners appears in their dress, so it does in their talk: *They speak loftily* (*v.* 8); they affect *great swelling words of van-*

ity (2 Pt. 2:18), bragging of themselves and disdaining all about them. Out of the abundance of the pride that is in their heart they speak big. [1.] It made them oppressive to their poor neighbours (*v.* 6): *Violence covers them as a garment*. What they have got by fraud and oppression they keep and increase by the same wicked methods, and care not what injury they do to others, nor what violence they use, so they may but enrich and aggrandize themselves. *They are corrupt*, like the giants, the sinners of the old world, when *the earth was filled with violence*, Gen. 6:11, 13. They care not what mischief they do, either for mischief-sake or for their own advantage-sake. *They speak wickedly concerning oppression*; they oppress, and justify themselves in it. Those that speak well of sin speak wickedly of it. *They are corrupt*, that is, dissolved in pleasures and every thing that is luxurious (so some), and then they deride and speak maliciously; they care not whom they wound with the poisoned darts of calumny; from on high they speak oppression. [3.] It made them very insolent in their demeanour towards both God and man (*v.* 9): *They set their mouth against the heavens*, putting contempt upon God himself and his honour, bidding defiance to him and his power and justice. They cannot reach the heavens with their hands, to shake God's throne, else they would; but they show their ill-will by setting their mouth against the heavens. *Their tongue* also *walks through the earth*, and they take liberty to abuse all that come in their way. No man's greatness or goodness can secure him from the scourge of the virulent tongue. They take a pride and pleasure in bantering all mankind; they are pests of the country, for they neither fear God nor regard man. [4.] In all this they were very atheistical and profane. They could not have been thus wicked if they had not learned to say (*v.* 11), *How doth God know? And is there knowledge in the Most High?* So far were they from desiring the knowledge of God, who gave them all the good things they had and would have taught them to use them well, that they were not willing to believe God had any knowledge of them, that he took any notice of their wickedness or would ever call them to an account. As if, because he is *Most High*, he could not or would not see them, Job 22:12, 13. Whereas because he is *Most High* therefore he can, and will, take cognizance of all the children of men and of all they do, or say, or think. What an affront is it to the God of infinite knowledge, from whom all knowledge is, to ask, *Is there knowledge in him?* Well may he say (*v.* 12), *Behold, these are the ungodly*.

(3.) He observed that while wicked men thus prospered in their impiety, and were made more impious by their prosperity, good people were in great affliction, and he himself in particular, which very much strengthened the temptation he was in to quarrel with Providence. [1.] He looked abroad and saw many of God's people greatly at a loss (*v.* 10): "Because the wicked are so very daring *therefore his people return hither*; they are at the same pause, the same plunge, that I am at; they know not what to say to it any more than I do, and the rather because *waters of a full cup are wrung out to them*; they are not only made to drink, and to drink deeply, of the bitter cup of affliction, but to drink all. Care is taken that they lose not a drop of that unpleasant potion; the waters are wrung out unto them, that they may have the dregs of the cup. They pour out abundance of tears when they hear wicked people blaspheme God and speak profanely," as David did, Ps. 119:136. These are the waters wrung out to them. [2.] He looked at home, and felt himself under the continual frowns of Providence, while the wicked were sunning themselves in its smiles (*v.* 14): "For my part," says he, "*all the day long have I been plagued* with one affliction or another, *and chastened every morning*, as duly as the morning comes." His afflictions were great — he was chastened and plagued; the returns of them were constant, *every morning* with the morning, and they continued, without intermission, *all the day long*. This he thought was very hard, that, when those who blasphemed God were in prosperity, he that worshipped God was under such great affliction. He spoke feelingly when he spoke of his own troubles; there is no disputing against sense, except by faith.

(4.) From all this arose a very strong temptation to cast off his religion. [1.] Some that observed the prosperity of the wicked, especially comparing it with the afflictions of the righteous, were tempted to deny a providence and to

think that God had forsaken the earth. In this sense some take *v.* 11. There are those, even among God's professing people, that say, "*How does God know? Surely all things are left to blind fortune, and not disposed of by an all-seeing God.*" Some of the heathen, upon such a remark as this, have asked, *Quis putet esse deos? — Who will believe that there are gods?* [2.] Though the psalmist's feet were not so far gone as to question God's omniscience, yet he was tempted to question the benefit of religion, and to say (*v.* 13), *Verily, I have cleansed my heart in vain*, and have, to no purpose, *washed my hands in innocency*. See here what it is to be religious; it is to cleanse our hearts, in the first place, by repentance and regeneration, and then to wash our hands in innocency by a universal reformation of our lives. It is not in vain to do this, not in vain to serve God and keep his ordinances; but good men have been sometimes tempted to say, "It is in vain," and "Religion is a thing that there is nothing to be got by," because they see wicked people in prosperity. But, however the thing may appear now, when the pure in heart, those blessed ones, shall see God (Mt. 5:8), they will not say that they cleansed their hearts in vain.

Verses 15–20

We have seen what a strong temptation the psalmist was in to envy prospering profaneness; now here we are told how he kept his footing and got the victory.

I. He kept up a respect for God's people, and with that he restrained himself from speaking what he had thought amiss, *v.* 15. He got the victory by degrees, and this was the first point he gained; he was ready to say, *Verily, I have cleansed my heart in vain*, and thought he had reason to say it, but he kept his mouth with this consideration, "*If I say, I will speak thus, behold, I should myself revolt and apostatize from, and so give the greatest offence imaginable to, the generation of thy children.*" Observe here, 1. Though he thought amiss, he took care not to utter that evil thought which he had conceived. Note, It is bad to think ill, but it is worse to speak it, for that is giving the evil thought an *imprimatur* — *a sanction*; it is allowing it, giving consent to it, and publishing it for the infection of others. But it is a good sign that we repent of the evil imagination of the heart if we suppress it, and the error remains with ourselves. If therefore thou hast been so foolish as to think evil, be so wise as to *lay thy hand upon thy mouth*, and let it go no further, Prov. 30:32. *If I say, I will speak thus*. Observe, Though his corrupt heart made this inference from the prosperity of the wicked, yet he did not mention it to those whether it were fit to be mentioned or no. Note, We must think twice before we speak once, both because some things may be thought which yet may not be spoken and because the second thoughts may correct the mistakes of the first. 2. The reason why he would not speak it was for fear of giving offence to those whom God owned for his children. Note, (1.) There are a people in the world that are the generation of God's children, a set of men that hear and love God as their Father. (2.) We must be very careful not to say or do any thing which may justly offend *any of these little ones* (Mt. 18:6), especially which may offend *the generation of them*, may sadden their hearts, or weaken their hands, or shake their interest. (3.) There is nothing that can give more general offence to the generation of God's children than to say that *we have cleansed our heart in vain* or that it is vain to serve God; for there is nothing more contrary to their universal sentiment and experience nor any thing that grieves them more than to hear God thus reflected on. (4.) Those that wish themselves in the condition of the wicked do in effect quit the tents of God's children.

II. He foresaw the ruin of wicked people. By this he baffled the temptation, as by the former he gave some check to it. Because he durst not speak what he had thought, for fear of giving offence, he began to consider whether he had any good reason for that thought (*v.* 16): "I endeavoured to understand the meaning of this unaccountable dispensation of Providence; but *it was too painful for me*. I could not conquer it by the strength of my own reasoning." It is a problem, not to be solved by the mere light of nature, for, if there were not another life after this, we could not fully reconcile the prosperity of the wicked with the justice of God. But (*v.* 17) *he went into the sanctuary of God*; he applied to his devotions, meditated upon the attributes of God, and the *things revealed, which belong to us and to our children;* he consulted the scriptures, and the lips of the priests who attended the sanctuary; he prayed to God to make this matter plain to him and to help him over this difficulty; and, at length, he understood the wretched end of wicked people, which he plainly foresaw to be such that even in the height of their prosperity they were rather to be pitied than envied, for they were but ripening for ruin. Note, There are many great things, and things needful to be known, which will not be known otherwise than by going into the sanctuary of God, by the word and prayer. The sanctuary must therefore be the resort of a tempted soul. Note, further, We must judge of persons and things as they appear by the light of divine revelation, and then we shall judge righteous judgment; particularly we must judge by the end. All is well that ends well, everlastingly well; but nothing well that ends ill, everlastingly ill. The righteous man's afflictions end in peace, and therefore he is happy; the wicked man's enjoyments end in destruction, and therefore he is miserable.

1. The prosperity of the wicked is short and uncertain. The high places in which Providence sets them are *slippery places* (*v.* 18), where they cannot long keep footing; but, when they offer to climb higher, that very attempt will be the occasion of their sliding and falling. Their prosperity has no firm ground; it is not built upon God's favour or his promise; and they have not the satisfaction of feeling that it rests on firm ground.

2. Their destruction is sure, and sudden, and very great. This cannot be meant of any temporal destruction; for they were supposed to *spend all their days in wealth* and their death itself had no bands in it: *In a moment they go down to the grave,* so that even that could scarcely be called *their destruction;* it must therefore be meant of eternal destruction on the other side death — hell and destruction. They flourish for a time, but are undone for ever. (1.) Their ruin is sure and inevitable. He speaks of it as a thing done — *They are cast down;* for their destruction is as certain as if it were already accomplished. He speaks of it as God's doing, and therefore it cannot be resisted: *Thou castest them down.* It is *destruction from the Almighty* (Joel 1:15), from *the glory of his power,* 2 Th. 1:9. Who can support those whom God will cast down, on whom God will lay burdens? (2.) It is swift and sudden; their damnation slumbers not; for *how are they brought into desolation as in a moment! v.* 19. It is easily effected, and will be a great surprise to themselves and all about them. (3.) It is severe and very dreadful. It is a total and final ruin: *They are utterly consumed with terrors,* It is the misery of the damned that the terrors of the Almighty, whom they have made their enemy, fasten upon their guilty consciences, which can neither shelter themselves from them nor strengthen themselves under them; and therefore not their being, but their bliss, must needs be utterly consumed by them; not the least degree of comfort or hope remains to them; the higher they were lifted up in their prosperity the sorer will their fall be when they are cast down into *destructions* (for the word is plural) and suddenly *brought into desolation.*

3. Their prosperity is therefore not to be envied at all, but despised rather, *quod erat demonstrandum — which was the point to be established, v.* 20. *As a dream when one awaketh, so, O Lord! when thou awakest,* or when they awake (as some read it), *thou shalt despise their image,* their shadow, *and make it to vanish. In the day of the great judgment* (so the Chaldee paraphrase reads it), when they are awaked out of their graves, thou shalt, in wrath, despise their image; for *they shall rise to shame and everlasting contempt.* See here, (1.) What their prosperity now is; it is but an image, a vain show, a fashion of the world that passes away; it is not real, but imaginary, and it is only a corrupt imagination that makes it a happiness; it is not substance, but a mere shadow; it is not what it seems to be, nor will it prove what we promise ourselves from it; it is as a dream, which may please us a little, while we are asleep, yet even then it disturbs our repose; but, how pleasing soever it is, it is all but a cheat, all false; when we awake we find it so. A hungry man *dreams that he eats, but he awakes and his soul is empty,* Isa. 29:8. A man is never the more rich or honourable for dreaming he is so. Who therefore will envy a man the pleasure of a dream? (2.) What will be the issue of it; God will awake to judgment, to plead his own and his people's injured cause; they shall be made to awake out of the sleep of their carnal security, and then God shall despise their image; he shall make it appear to all the world how despicable it is; so that the righteous shall laugh at them, Ps. 52:6, 7. How did God despise that rich man's image when he said, *Thou fool, this night thy soul shall be required of thee!* Lu. 12:19, 20. We ought to be of God's mind, for his judgment is according to truth, and not to admire and envy that which he despises and will despise; for, sooner or later, he will bring all the world to be of his mind.

Verses 21–28

Behold Samson's riddle again unriddled, *Out of the eater came forth meat, and out of the strong sweetness;* for we have here an account of the good improvement which the psalmist made of that sore temptation with which he had been assaulted and by which he was almost overcome. He that stumbles and does not fall, by recovering himself takes so much the longer steps forward. It was so with the psalmist here; many good lessons he learned from his temptation, his struggles with it, and his victories over it. Nor would God suffer his people to be tempted if his grace were not sufficient for them, not only to save them from harm, but to make them gainers by it; even this shall work for good.

I. He learned to think very humbly of himself and to abase and accuse himself before God (*v.* 21, 22); he reflects with shame upon the disorder and danger he was in, and the vexation he gave himself by entertaining the temptation and parleying with it: *My heart was grieved, and I was pricked in my reins,* as one afflicted with the acute pain of the stone in the region of the kidneys. If evil thoughts at any time enter into the mind of a good man, he does not roll them under his tongue as a sweet morsel, but they are grievous and painful to him; temptation was to Paul as a thorn in the flesh, 2 Co. 12:7. This particular temptation, the working of envy and discontent, is as painful as any; where it constantly rests it is the *rottenness of the bones* (Prov. 14:30); where it does but occasionally come it is the pricking of the reins. Fretfulness is a corruption that is its own correction. Now in the reflection upon it, 1. He owns it was his folly thus to vex himself: *"So foolish was I* to be my own tormentor." Let peevish people thus reproach themselves for, and shame themselves out of, their discontents. "What a fool am I thus to make myself uneasy without a cause?" 2. He owns it was his ignorance to vex himself at this: "So ignorant was I of that which I might have known, and which, if I had known it aright, would have been sufficient to silence my murmurs. *I was as a beast (Behemoth — a great beast) before thee.* Beasts mind present things only, and never look before at what is to come; and so did I. If I had not been a great fool, I should never have suffered such a senseless temptation to prevail over me so far. What! to envy wicked men upon account of their prosperity! To be ready to wish myself one of them, and to think of changing conditions with them! *So foolish was I."* Note, If good men do at any time, through the surprise and strength of temptation, think, or speak, or act amiss, when they see their error they will reflect upon it with sorrow, and shame, and self-abhorrence, will call themselves *fools* for it. *Surely I am more brutish than any man,* Prov. 30:2; Job 42:5, 6. Thus David, 2 Sa. 24:10.

II. He took occasion hence to own his dependence on and obligations to the grace of God (*v.* 23): *"Nevertheless,* foolish as I am, *I am continually with thee* and in thy favour; *thou hast holden me by my right hand."* This may refer either, 1. To the care God had taken of him, and the kindness he had shown him, all along from his beginning hitherto. He had said, in the hour of temptation (*v.* 14), *All the day long have I been plagued;* but here he corrects himself for that passionate complaint: "Though God has chastened me, he has not cast me off; notwithstanding all the crosses of my life, *I have been continually with thee;* I have had thy presence with me, and thou hast been nigh unto me in all that which I have called upon thee for; and therefore, though perplexed, yet not in despair. Though God has sometimes written bitter things against me, yet he has still *holden me by my right hand,* both to keep me, that I should not desert him or fly off from him, and to prevent my sinking and fainting under my burdens, or losing my way in the wildernesses through which I have walked." If we have been kept in the way with God, kept closely in our duty and upheld in our integrity, we must own ourselves indebted to the free grace of God for our preservation: *Having obtained help of God, I continue hitherto.* And, if he has thus maintained the spiritual life, the earnest of eternal life, we ought not to complain, whatever calamities of this present time we have met with. Or, 2. To the late experience he had had of the power of divine grace in carrying him through this strong temptation and bringing him off a conqueror: "I was foolish and ignorant, and yet thou hast had compassion on me and taught me (Heb. 5:2), and kept me under thy protection;" for the unworthiness of man is no bar to the free grace of God. We must ascribe our safety in temptation, and our victory over it, not to our own wisdom, for we are foolish and ignorant, but to the gracious presence of God with us and the prevalency of Christ's intercession for us, that our faith may not fail: *"My feet were almost gone,* and they would have quite gone, past recovery, but that thou hast holden me by my right hand and so kept me from falling."

III. He encouraged himself to hope that the same God who had delivered him from this evil work would *preserve him to his heavenly kingdom,* as St. Paul does (2 Tim. 4:18): "I am now upheld by thee, therefore *thou shalt guide me with thy counsel,* leading me, as thou hast done hitherto, many a difficult step; and, since I am now continually with thee, thou *shalt afterwards receive me to glory" v.* 24. This completes the happiness of the saints, so that they have no reason to envy the worldly prosperity of sinners. Note, 1. All those who commit themselves to God shall be guided with his counsel, with the counsel both of his word and of his Spirit, the best counsellors. The psalmist had like to have paid dearly for following his own counsels in this temptation and therefore resolves for the future to take God's advice, which shall never be wanting to those that duly seek it with a resolution to follow it. 2. All those who are guided and led by the counsel of God in this world shall be received to his glory in another world. If we make God's glory in us the end we aim at, he will make our glory with him the end we shall for ever be happy in. Upon this consideration, let us never envy sinners, but rather bless ourselves in our own blessedness. If God direct us in the way of our duty, and prevent our turning aside out of it, he will afterwards, when our state of trial and preparation is over, receive us to his kingdom and glory, the believing hopes and prospects of which will reconcile us to all the dark providences that now puzzle and perplex us, and ease us of the pain we have been put into by some threatening temptations.

IV. He was hereby quickened to cleave the more closely to God, and very much confirmed and comforted in the choice he had made of him, *v.* 25, 26. His thoughts here dwell with delight upon his own happiness in God, as much greater then the happiness of the ungodly that prospered in the world. He saw little reason to envy them what they had in the creature when he found how much more and better, surer and sweeter, comforts he had in the Creator, and what cause he had to congratulate himself on this account. He had complained of his afflictions (*v.* 14); but this makes them very light and easy, *All is well if God be mine.* We have here the breathings of a sanctified soul towards God, and its repose in him, as that to a godly man really which the prosperity of a worldly man is to him in conceit and imagination: *Whom have I in heaven but thee?* There is scarcely a verse in all the psalms more expressive than this of the pious and devout affections of a soul to God; here it soars up towards him, follows hard after him, and yet, at the same time, has an entire satisfaction and complacency in him.

1. It is here supposed that God alone is the felicity and chief good of man. He, and he only, that made the soul, can make it happy; there is none in heaven, none in earth, that can pretend to do it besides.

2. Here are expressed the workings and breathings of a soul towards God accordingly. If God be our felicity,

(1.) Then we must have him *(Whom have I but thee?),* we must choose him, and make sure to ourselves an interest in him. What will it avail us that he is the felicity of souls if he be not the felicity of our souls, and if we do not by a lively faith make him ours, by joining ourselves to him in an everlasting covenant?

(2.) Then our desire must be towards him and our delight in him (the word signifies both); we must delight in what we have of God and desire what we yet further hope for. Our desires must not only be offered up to God, but they must all terminate in him, desiring nothing more than God, but still more and more of him. This includes all our prayers, *Lord, give us thyself;* as that includes all the promises, *I will be to them a God. The desire of our souls is to thy name.*

(3.) We must prefer him in our choice and desire before any other. [1.] *"There is none in heaven but thee,* none to seek to or trust in, none to court or covet acquaintance with, but thee." God is in himself more glorious than any celestial being (Ps. 89:6), and must be, in our eyes, infinitely more desirable. Excellent beings there are in heaven, but God alone can make us happy. His favour is infinitely more to us than the refreshment of the dews of heaven or the benign influence of the stars of heaven, more than the friendship of the saints in heaven or the good offices of the angels there. [2.] *I desire none on earth besides thee;* not only none in heaven, a place at a distance, which we have but little acquaintance with, but none on earth neither, where we have many friends and where much of our present interest and concern lie. "Earth carries away the desires of most men, and yet I have none on earth, no persons, no things, no possessions, no delights, that I desire besides thee or with thee, in comparison or competition with thee." We must desire nothing besides God but what we desire for him *(nil praeter te nisi propter te — nothing besides thee except for thy sake),* nothing but what we desire from him, and can be content without so that it be made up in him. We must desire nothing besides God as needful to be a partner with him in making us happy.

(4.) Then we must repose ourselves in God with an entire satisfaction, *v.* 26. Observe here, [1.] Great distress and trouble supposed: *My flesh and my heart fail.* Note, Others have experienced and we must expect, the failing both of flesh and heart. The body will fail by sickness, age, and death; and that which touches the bone and the flesh touches us in a tender part, that part of ourselves which we have been but too fond of; when the flesh fails the heart is ready to fail too; the conduct, courage, and comfort fail. [2.] Sovereign relief provided in this distress: *But God is the strength of my heart and my portion for ever.* Note, Gracious souls, in their greatest distresses, rest upon God as their spiritual strength and their eternal portion. *First, "He is the strength of my heart,* the rock of my heart, a firm foundation, which will bear my weight and not sink under it. *God is the strength of my heart;* I have found him so; I do so still, and hope ever to find him so." In the distress supposed, he had put the case of a double failure, both *flesh and heart fail;* but, in the relief, he fastens on a single support: he leaves out the flesh and the consideration of that, it is enough that God is *the strength of his heart.* He speaks as one careless of the body (let that fail, there is no remedy), but as one concerned about the soul, to be *strengthened in the inner man. Secondly, "He is my portion for ever;* he will not only support me while I am here, but make me happy when I go hence." The saints choose God for their portion, they have him for their portion, and it is their happiness that he will be their portion, a portion that will last as long as the immortal soul lasts.

V. He was fully convinced of the miserable condition of all wicked people. This he learned in the sanctuary upon this occasion, and he would never forget it (*v.* 27): *"Lo, those that are far from thee,* in a state of distance and estrangement, that desire the Almighty to depart from them, *shall* certainly *perish;* so shall their doom be; they choose to be far from God, and they shall be far from him for ever. *Thou wilt* justly *destroy all those that go a whoring from thee,* that is, all apostates, that in profession have been betrothed to God, but forsake him, their duty to him and their communion with him, to embrace the bosom of a stranger." The doom is sever, no less than perishing and being destroyed. It is universal: "They shall all be destroyed without exception." It is certain: *"Thou hast destroyed;* it is as sure to be done as if done already; and the destruction of some ungodly men is an earnest of the perdition of all." God himself undertakes to do it, into whose hands it is a fearful thing to fall: "Thou, though infinite in goodness, wilt reckon for thy injured honour and abused patience, and wilt destroy those that go a whoring from thee."

VI. He was greatly encouraged to cleave to God and to confide in him, *v.* 28. *If those that are far from God shall perish,* then, 1. Let this constrain us to live in communion with God; "if it fare so ill with those that live at a distance from him, then it is good, very good, the chief good, that good for a man, in this life, which he should most carefully pursue and secure, it is best for me to draw near to God, and to have God draw near to me;" the original may take in both. *But for my part* (so I would read it) *the approach of God is good for me.* Our drawing near to God takes rise from his drawing near to us, and it is the happy meeting that makes the bliss. Here is a great truth laid down, That it is good to draw near to God; but the life of it lies in the application, "It is good for *me."* Those are the wise who know what is good for themselves: *"It is good,* says he (and every good man agrees with him in it), *it is good for me to draw near to God;* it is my duty; it is my interest." 2. Let us therefore live in a continual dependence upon him: *"I have put my trust in the Lord God,* and will never go a whoring from him after any creature confidences." If wicked men, notwithstanding all their prosperity, shall perish and be destroyed, then let us trust in the Lord God, in him, not in them (see Ps. 146:3–5), in him, and not in our worldly prosperity; let us trust in God, and neither fret at them nor be afraid of them; let us trust in him for a better portion than theirs is. 3. While we do so, let us not doubt but that we shall have occasion to praise his name. Let us trust in the Lord, that we may declare all his works. Note, Those that with an upright heart put their trust in God shall never want matter for thanksgiving to him.

PSALM 74

This psalm does so particularly describe the destruction of Jerusalem and the temple, by Nebuchadnezzar and the army of the Chaldeans, and can so ill be applied to any other event we meet with in the Jewish history, that interpreters incline to think that either it was penned by David, or Asaph in David's time, with a prophetical reference to that sad event (which yet is not so probable), or that it was penned by another Asaph, who lived at the time of the captivity, or by Jeremiah (for it is of a piece with his Lamentations,) or some other prophet, and, after the return out of captivity, was delivered to the sons of Asaph, who were called by his name, for the public service of the church. That was the most eminent family of the singers in Ezra's time. See Ezra 2:41; 3:10; Neh. 11:17, 22; 12:35, 46. The deplorable case of the people of God at that time is here spread before the Lord, and left with him. The prophet, in the name of the church I. Puts in complaining pleas of the miseries they suffered, for the quickening of their desires in prayer (*v.* 1–11). II. He puts in comfortable pleas for the encouraging of their faith in prayer (*v.* 12–17). III. He concludes with divers petitions to God for deliverances (*v.* 18–23). In singing it we must be affected with the former desolations of the church, for we are members of the same body, and may apply it to any present distresses or desolations of any part of the Christian church.

Maschil of Asaph.

Verses 1–11

This psalm is entitled *Maschil — a psalm to give instruction,* for it was penned in a day of affliction, which is intended for instruction; and this instruction in general it gives us, That when we are, upon any account, in distress, it is our wisdom and duty to apply to God by faithful and fervent prayer, and we shall not find it in vain to do so. Three things the people of God here complain of: —

I. The displeasure of God against them, as that which was the cause and bitterness of all their calamities. They look above the instruments of their trouble, who, they knew, could have no power against them unless it were given them from above, and keep their eye upon God, by whose determined counsel they were delivered up into the hands of wicked and unreasonable men. Observe the liberty they take to expostulate with God (*v.* 1), we hope not too great a liberty, for Christ himself, upon the cross, cried out, *My God my God, why hast thou forsaken me?* So the church here, *O God! why hast thou forsaken us for ever?* Here they speak according to their present dark and melancholy apprehensions; for otherwise, *Has God cast away his people? God forbid,* Rom. 11:1. The people of God must not think that because they are cast down they are therefore cast off, that because men cast them off therefore God does, and that because he seems to cast them off for a time therefore they are really cast off for ever: yet this expostulation intimates that they dreaded God's casting them off more than any thing, that they desired to be owned of him, whatever they suffered from men, and were desirous to know wherefore he thus contended with them: *Why does thy anger smoke?* that is, why does it rise up to such a degree that all about us take notice of it, and ask, *What means the heat of this great anger?* Deu. 29:24. Compare *v.* 20, where the anger of the Lord and his jealousy are said to smoke against sinners. Observe what they plead with God, now that they lay under the tokens and apprehensions of his wrath. 1. They plead their relation to him: "We are *the sheep of thy pasture,* the sheep wherewith thou hast been pleased to stock the pasture, thy peculiar people whom thou art pleased to set apart for thyself and design for thy own glory. That the wolves worry the sheep is not strange; but was ever any shepherd thus displeased at his own sheep? *Remember,* we are *thy congregation* (*v.* 2), incorporated by thee and for thee, and devoted to thy praise; we are *the rod,* or tribe, *of thy inheritance,* whom thou hast been pleased to claim a special property in above other people (Deu. 32:9), and from whom thou hast received the rents and issues of praise and worship more than from the neighbouring nations. Nay, a man's inheritance may lie at a great distance, but we are pleading for *Mount Zion, wherein thou hast dwelt,* which has been the place of thy peculiar delight and residence, thy demesne and mansion." 2. They plead the great things God had done for them and the vast expense he had been at upon them: "It is *thy congregation,* which thou hast not only made with a word's speaking, but *purchased of old* by many miracles of mercy when they were first formed into a people; it is *thy inheritance, which thou hast redeemed* when they were sold into servitude." God *gave Egypt* to ruin *for their ransom, gave men for them,* and *people for their life,* Isa. 43:3, 4. "Now, Lord, wilt thou now abandon a people that cost thee so dear, and has been so dear to thee?" And, if the redemption of Israel out of Egypt was an encouragement to hope that he would not cast them off, much more reason have we to hope that God will not cast off any whom Christ has redeemed with his own blood; but the people of his purchase shall be for ever the people of his praise. 3. They plead the calamitous state that they were in (*v.* 3): *"Lift up thy feet;* that is, come with speed to repair the desolations that are made in thy sanctuary, which otherwise will be perpetual an irreparable." It has been sometimes said that the divine vengeance strikes with iron hands, yet it comes with leaden feet; and then those who wait for the day of the Lord, cry, *Lord, lift up thy feet; exalt thy steps;* magnify thyself in the outgoing of thy providence. When the desolations of the sanctuary have continued long we are tempted to think they will be perpetual; but it is a temptation; for God will avenge his own elect, will avenge them speedily, though he bear long with their oppressors and persecutors.

II. They complain of the outrage and cruelty of their enemies, not so much, no, not at all, of what they had done to the prejudice of their secular interests; here are no complaints of the burning of their cities and ravaging of their country, but only what they had done against the sanctuary and the synagogue. The concerns of religion should lie nearer our hearts and affect us more than any worldly concern whatsoever. The desolation of God's house should grieve us more than the desolation of our own houses; for the matter is not great what becomes of us and our families in this world provided God's name may be sanctified, his kingdom may come, and his will be done.

1. The psalmist complains of the desolations of the sanctuary, as Daniel, *ch.* 9:17. The temple at Jerusalem was the *dwelling-place of God's name,* and therefore the *sanctuary,* or *holy place, v.* 7. In this the enemies did wickedly (*v.* 3), for they destroyed it in downright contempt of God and affront to him. (1.) They *roared in the midst of God's congregations, v.* 4. There where God's faithful people attended on him with a humble reverent silence, or softly speaking, they roared in a riotous revelling manner, being elated with having made themselves masters of that sanctuary of which they had sometimes heard formidable things. (2.) *They set up their ensigns for signs.* The banners of their army they set up in the temple (Israel's strongest castle, as long as they kept closely to God) as trophies of their victory. There, where the signs of God's presence used to be, now the enemy had set up their ensigns. This daring defiance of God and his power touched his people in a tender part. (3.) They took a pride in destroying *the carved work* of the temple. As much as formerly men thought it an honour to lend a hand to the building of the temple, and he was thought famous that helped to fell tim-

ber for that work, so much now they valued themselves upon their agency in destroying it, *v.* 5, 6. Thus, as formerly those were celebrated for wise men that did service to religion, so now those are applauded as wits that help to run it down. Some read it thus: *They show themselves, as one that lifts up axes on high in a thicket of trees,* for so do they break down the carved work of the temple they make no more scruple of breaking down the rich wainscot of the temple than woodcutters do of hewing trees in the forest; such indignation have they at the sanctuary that the most curious carving that ever was seen is beaten down by the common soldiers without any regard had to it, either as a dedicated thing or as a piece of exquisite art. (4.) They set fire to it, and so violated or *destroyed it to the ground, v.* 7. The Chaldeans burnt the house of God, that stately costly fabric, 2 Chr. 36:19. And the Romans *left not there one stone upon another* (Mt. 24:2), rasing it, rasing it, even to the foundations, till Zion, the holy mountain, was, by Titus Vespasian, ploughed as a field.

2. He complains of the desolations of the synagogues, or schools of the prophets, which, before the captivity, were in use, though much more afterwards. There God's word was read and expounded, and his name praised and called upon, without altars or sacrifices. These also they had a spite to (*v.* 8): *Let us destroy them together;* not only the temple, but all the places of religious worship and the worshippers with them. *Let us destroy them together;* let them be consumed in the same flame. Pursuant to this impious resolve they *burnt up all the synagogues of God in the land* and laid them all waste. So great was their rage against religion that the religious houses, because religious, were all levelled with the ground, that God's worshippers might not glorify God, and edify one another, by meeting in solemn assemblies.

III. The great aggravation of all these calamities was that they had no prospect at all of relief, nor could they foresee an end of them (*v.* 9): "We see our enemy's sign set up in the sanctuary, but *we see not our signs,* none of the tokens of God's presence, no hopeful indications of approaching deliverance. *There is no more any prophet* to tell us how long the trouble will last and when things concerning us shall have an end, that the hope of an issue at last may support us under our troubles." In the captivity in Babylon they had prophets, and had been told how long the captivity should continue, but the day was cloudy and dark (Eze. 34:12), and they had not as yet the comfort of these gracious discoveries. God spoke once, yea, twice, good words and comfortable words, but they perceived them not. Observe, They do not complain, "We see not our armies; there are no men of war to command our forces, nor any to go forth with our hosts;" but, "no prophets, none to tell us how long." This puts them upon expostulating with God, as delaying, 1. To assert his honour (*v.* 10): *How long shall the adversary reproach and blaspheme thy name?* In the desolations of the sanctuary our chief concern should be for the glory of God, that it may not be injured by the blasphemies of those who persecute his people for his sake, because they are his; and therefore our enquiry should be, not "How long shall we be troubled?" but "How long shall God be blasphemed?" 2. To exert his power (*v.* 11): *"Why withdrawest thou thy hand,* and dost not stretch it out, to deliver thy people and destroy thy enemies? *Pluck it out of thy bosom,* and be not *as a man astonished, as a mighty man that cannot save,* or will not," Jer. 14:9. When the power of enemies is most threatening it is comfortable to fly to the power of God.

Verses 12–17

The lamenting church fastens upon something here which she calls to mind, and *therefore hath she hope* (as Lam. 3:21), with which she encourages herself and silences her own complaints. Two things quiet the minds of those that are here sorrowing for the solemn assembly: —

I. That God is the God of Israel, a God in covenant with his people (*v.* 12): *God is my King of old.* This comes in both as a plea in prayer to God (Ps. 44:4, *thou art my King, O God!*) and as a prop to their own faith and hope, to encourage themselves to expect deliverance, considering the *days of old,* Ps. 77:5. The church speaks as a complex body, the same in every age, and therefore calls God, "My King, my King of old," or, "from antiquity;" he of old put himself into that relation to them and appeared and acted for them in that relation. As Israel's King, he wrought salvation in the midst of the nations of the earth; for what he did, in the government of the world, tended towards the salvation of his church. Several things are here mentioned which God had done for his people as their King of old, which encouraged them to commit themselves to him and depend upon him.

1. He had divided the sea before them when they came out of Egypt, not by the strength of Moses or his rod, but by his own strength; and he that could do that could do any thing.

2. He had destroyed Pharaoh and the Egyptians. Pharaoh was the *leviathan;* the Egyptians were *the dragons,* fierce and cruel. Observe, (1.) The victory obtained over these enemies. God broke their heads, baffled their politics, as when Israel, the more they were afflicted by them, multiplied the more. God crushed their powers, though complicated, ruined their country by ten plagues, and at last drowned them all in the Red Sea. *This is Pharaoh and all his multitude,* Eze. 31:18. It was the Lord's doing; none besides could do it, and he did it with a strong hand and an outstretched arm. This was typical of Christ's victory over Satan and his kingdom, pursuant to the first promise, that the seed of the woman should break the serpent's head. (2.) The improvement of this victory for the encouragement of the church: *Thou gavest him to be meat to the people* of Israel, now going to *inhabit the wilderness.* The spoil of the Egyptians enriched them; they stripped their slain, and so got the Egyptians' arms and weapons, as before they had got their jewels. Or, rather, this providence was meat to their faith and hope, to support and encourage them in reference to the other difficulties they were likely to meet with in the wilderness. It was part of the spiritual meat which they were all made to eat of. Note, The breaking of the heads of the church's enemies is the joy and strength of the hearts of the church's friends. Thus the companions make a banquet even of leviathan, Job 41:6.

3. God had both ways altered the course of nature, both in fetching streams out of the rock and turning streams into rock, *v.* 15. (1.) He had dissolved the rock into waters: *Thou didst bring out the fountain and the flood* (so some read it); and every one knows whence it was brought, out of the rock, out of the flinty rock. Let this never be forgotten, but let it especially be remembered that the rock was Christ, and the waters out of it were spiritual drink. (2.) He had congealed the waters into rock: *Thou driedst up mighty* rapid *rivers,* Jordan particularly at the time when it overflowed all its banks. He that did these things could now deliver his oppressed people, and break the yoke of the oppressors, as he had done formerly; nay, he would do it, for his justice and goodness, his wisdom and truth, are still the same, as well as his power.

II. That the God of Israel is the God of nature, *v.* 16, 17. It is he that orders the regular successions and revolutions, 1. Of day and night. He is the Lord of all time. The evening and the morning are of his ordaining. It is he that opens the eyelids of the morning light, and draws the curtains of the evening shadow. *He has prepared the moon and the sun* (so some read it), the two great lights, to rule by day and by night alternately. The preparing of them denotes their constant readiness and exact observance of their time, which they never miss a moment. 2. Of summer and winter: "Thou hast *appointed all the bounds of the earth,* and the different climates of its several regions, for *thou hast made summer and winter,* the frigid and the torrid zones; or, rather, the constant revolutions of the year and its several seasons." Herein we are to acknowledge God, from whom all the laws and powers of nature are derived; but how does this come in here? (1.) He that had power at first to settle, and still to preserve, this course of nature by the diurnal and annual motions of the heavenly bodies, has certainly all power both to save and to destroy, and with him nothing is impossible, nor are any difficulties or oppositions insuperable. (2.) He that is faithful to his covenant with the day and with the night, and preserves the ordinances of heaven inviolable will certainly make good his promise to his people and never cast off those whom he has chosen, Jer. 31:35, 36; 33:20, 21. His covenant with Abraham and his seed is as firm as that with Noah and his sons, Gen. 8:21. (3.) Day and night, summer and winter, being counterchanged in the course of nature, throughout all the borders of the earth, we can expect no other than that trouble and peace, prosperity and adversity, should be, in like manner, counterchanged in all the borders of the church. We have as much reason to expect affliction as to expect night and winter. But we have then no more reason to despair of the return of comfort than we have to despair of day and summer.

Verses 18–23

The psalmist here, in the name of the church, most earnestly begs that God would appear fro them against their enemies, and put an end to their present troubles. To encourage his own faith, he interests God in this matter (*v.* 22): *Arise, O God! plead thy own cause.* This we may be sure he will do, for he is jealous for his own honour; whatever is his own cause he will plead it with a strong hand, will appear against those that oppose it and with and for those that cordially espouse it. He will arise and plead it, though for a time he seems to neglect it; he will stir up himself, will manifest himself, will do his own work in his own time. Note, The cause of religion is God's own cause and he will certainly plead it. Now, to make it out that the cause is God's, he pleads,

I. That the persecutors are God's sworn enemies: "Lord, they have not only abused us, but they have been, and are, abusive to thee; what is done against us, for thy sake, does, by consequence, reflect upon thee. But that is not all; they have directly and immediately reproached thee, and *blasphemed thy name," v.* 18. This was that which they roared in the sanctuary; they triumphed as if they had now got the mastery of the God is Israel, of whom they had heard such great things. As nothing grieves the saints more than to hear God's name blasphemed, so nothing encourages them more to hope that God will appear against their enemies than when they have arrived at such a pitch of wickedness as to reproach God himself; this fills the measure of their sins apace and hastens their ruin. The psalmist insists much upon this: "We dare not answer their reproaches; Lord, do thou answer them. Remember that the *foolish people have blasphemed thy name* (*v.* 18) and that still *the foolish man reproaches thee daily."* Observe the character of those that reproach God; they are foolish. As atheism is folly (Ps. 14:1), profaneness and blasphemy are no less so. Perhaps those are cried up as the wits of the age that ridicule religion and sacred things; but really they are the greatest fools, and will shortly be made to appear so before all the world. And yet see their malice — They reproach God daily, as constantly as his faithful worshippers pray to him and praise him; see their impudence — They do not hide their blasphemous thoughts in their own bosoms, but proclaim them with a loud voice (*forget not the voice of thy enemies, v.* 23), and this with a daring defiance of divine justice; they *rise up against thee,* and by their blasphemies even wage war with heaven and take up arms against the Almighty. Their noise and *tumult ascend continually* (so some), as the cry of Sodom came up before God, calling for vengeance, Gen. 18:21. *It increases continually* (so we read it); they grow worse and worse, and are hardened in their impieties by their successes. Now, Lord, *remember this; do not forget it.* God needs not to be put in remembrance by us of what he has to do, but thus we must show our concern for his honour and believe that he will vindicate us.

II. That the persecuted are his covenant-people. 1. See what distress they are in. They have fallen into the hands of *the multitude of the wicked, v.* 19. *How are those increased that trouble them!* There is no standing before an enraged multitude, especially like these, armed with power; and, as they are numerous, so they are barbarous: *The dark places of the earth are full of the habitations of cruelty.* The land of the Chaldeans, where there was none of the light of the knowledge of the true God (though otherwise it was famed for learning and arts), was indeed a dark place; the inhabitants of it were *alienated from the life of God through the ignorance that was in them,* and therefore they were cruel: where there was no true divinity there was scarcely to be found common humanity. They were especially cruel to the people of God; certainly those have no knowledge who *eat them up,* Ps. 14:4. They are oppressed (*v.* 21) because they are poor and unable to help themselves; they are oppressed, and so impoverished and made poor. 2. See what reason they had to hope that God would appear for their relief and not suffer them to be always thus trampled upon. Observe how the psalmist pleads with God for them. (1.) "It is *thy turtle-dove* that is ready to be swallowed up by the multitude of the wicked," *v.* 19. The church is a dove for harmlessness and mildness, innocency and inoffensiveness, purity and fruitfulness, a dove for mournfulness in a day of distress, a turtle-dove for fidelity and the constancy of love: turtle-doves and pigeons were the only fowls that were offered in sacrifice to God. "Shall thy turtle-dove, that is true to thee and devoted to thy honour, be delivered, its life and soul and all, into the *hand of the multitude of the wicked,* to whom it will soon become an easy and acceptable prey? Lord, it will be thy honour to help the weak, especially to help thy own." (2.) "It is *the congregation of thy poor,* and they are not the less thine for their being poor (for God has *chosen the poor of this world,* Jam. 2:5), but they have the more reason to expect thou wilt appear for them because they are many: it is *the congregation of thy poor;* let them not be abandoned and forgotten for ever." (3.) "They are in covenant with thee; and wilt thou not *have respect unto the covenant? v.* 20. Wilt thou not perform the promises thou hast, in thy covenant, made to them? Wilt thou not own those whom thou hast brought into the bond of the covenant?" When God delivers his people it is *in remembrance of his covenant,* Lev. 26:42. "Lord, though we are unworthy to be respected, yet have respect to the covenant." (4.) "They trust in thee, and boast of their relation to thee and expectations from thee. O let not them return ashamed of their hope (*v.* 21), as they will be if they be disappointed." (5.) "If thou deliver them, they will praise thy name and give thee the glory of their deliverance. Appear, Lord, for those that will praise thy name, against those that blaspheme it."

PSALM 75

Though this psalm is attributed to Asaph in the title, yet it does so exactly agree with David's circumstances, at his coming to the crown after the death of Saul, that most interpreters apply it to that juncture, and suppose that either Asaph penned it, in the person of David, as his poet-laureat (probably the substance of the psalm was some speech which David made to a convention of the states, at his accession to the government, and Asaph turned it into verse, and published it in a poem, for the better spreading of it among the people), or that David penned it, and delivered it to Asaph as precentor of the temple. In this psalm, I. David returns God thanks for bringing him to the throne (*v.* 1, 9). II. He promises to lay out himself for the public good, in the use of the power God had given him (*v.* 2, 3, 10). III. He checks the insolence of those that opposed his coming to the throne (*v.* 4, 5). IV. He fetches a reason for all this from God's sovereign dominion in the affairs of the children of men (*v.* 6–8). In singing this psalm we must give to God the glory of all the revolutions of states and kingdoms, believing that they are all according to his counsel and that he will make them all to work for the good of his church.

To the chief musician, Al-taschith. A psalm *or* song of Asaph.

Verses 1–5

In these verses,

I. The psalmist gives to God the praise of his advancement to honour and power, and the other great things he had done for him and for his people Israel (*v.* 1): *Unto thee, O God! do we give thanks* for all the favours thou hast bestowed upon us; and again, *unto thee do we give thanks;* for our thanksgivings must be often repeated. Did not we often pray for mercy when we were in pursuit of it; and shall we think it will suffice once or twice to give thanks when we have obtained it? Not only *I* do give thanks, but *we* do, and I and all my friends. If we share with others in their mercies, we must join with them in their praises. *"Unto thee, O God!* the author of our mercies (and we will not give that glory to the instruments which is due to thee only), *we give thanks; for that thy name is near* (that the complete accomplishment of thy promise made to David is not far off) *thy wondrous works,* which thou hast already done for him, *declare."* Note, 1. There are many works which God does for his people that may truly be called *wondrous works,* out of the common course of providence and quite beyond our expectation. 2. These wondrous works declare the nearness of his name; they show that he himself is at hand, nigh to us in what we call upon him for, and that he is about to do some great things for his people, in pursuance of his purpose and promise. 3. When God's wondrous works declare the nearness of his name it is our duty to give him thanks, again and again to give him thanks.

II. He lays himself under an obligation to use his power well, pursuant to the great trust reposed in him (*v.* 2): *When I shall receive the congregation I will judge uprightly.* Here he takes it for granted that God would, in due time, perfect that which concerned him, that though the congregation was very slow in gathering to him, and great opposition was made to it, yet, at length, he should receive it; for what God has spoken in his holiness he will perform by his wisdom and power. Being thus in expectation of the mercy, he promises to make conscience of his duty: "When I am a judge I will judge, and *judge uprightly;* not as those that went before me, who either neglected judgment or, which was worse, perverted it, either did no good with their power or did hurt." Note, 1. Those that are advanced to posts of honour must remember they are posts of service, and must set themselves with diligence and application of mind to do the work to which they are called. He does not say, *"When I shall receive the congregation* I will take my ease, and take state upon me, and leave the public business to others;" but, "I will mind it myself." 2. Public trusts are to be managed with great integrity; those that judge must judge uprightly, according to the rules of justice, without respect of persons.

III. He promises himself that his government would be a public blessing to Israel, *v.* 3. The present state of the kingdom was very bad: *The earth and all the inhabitants thereof are dissolved;* and no marvel, when the former reign was so dissolute that all went to wrack and ruin. There was a general corruption of manners, for want of putting the laws in execution against vice and profaneness. They were divided one from another for want of centering, as they ought to have done, in the government God had appointed. They were all to pieces, two against three and three against two, crumbled into factions and parties, which was likely to issue in their ruin; but *I bear up the pillars of it.* Even in Saul's time David did what he could for the public welfare; but he hoped that when he had himself received the congregation he should do much more, and should not only prevent the public ruin, but recover the public strength and beauty. Now, 1. See the mischief of parties; they melt and dissolve a land and the inhabitants of it. 2. See how much one head frequently holds up. The fabric would have sunk if David had not held up the pillars of it. This may well be applied to Christ and his government. The *world and all the inhabitants of it* were dissolved by sin; man's apostasy threatened the destruction of the whole creation. But Christ bore up the pillars of it; he saved the whole world from utter ruin by saving his people from their sins, and into his hand the administration of the kingdom of Providence is committed, for *he upholds all things by the word of his power,* Heb. 1:3.

IV. He checks those that opposed his government, that were against his accession to it and obstructed the administration of it, striving to keep up that vice and profaneness which he had made it his business to suppress (*v.* 4, 5): *I said unto the fools, Deal not foolishly.* He had said so to them in Saul's time. When he had not power to restrain them, yet he had wisdom and grace to reprove them, and to give them good counsel; though they bore themselves high, upon the favour of that unhappy prince, he cautioned them not to be too presumptuous. Or, rather, he does now say so to them. As soon as he came to the crown he issued out a proclamation against vice and profaneness, and here we have the contents of it. 1. To the simple sneaking sinners, the fools in Israel, that corrupted themselves, to them he said, *"Deal not foolishly;* do not act so directly contrary both to your reason and to your interest as you do while you walk contrary to the laws God has given to Israel and the promises he has made to David." Christ, the son of David, gives us this counsel, issues out this edict, *Deal not foolishly.* He who is made of God to us wisdom bids us be wise for ourselves, and not make fools of ourselves. 2. To the proud daring sinners, the wicked, that set God himself at defiance, he says, *"Lift not up the horn;* boast not of your power and prerogatives; persist not in your contumacy and contempt of the government set over you; *lift not up your horn on high,* as though you could have what you will and do what you will; *speak not with a stiff neck,* in which is an iron sinew, that will never bend to the will of God in the government; for those that will not bend shall break; those whose necks are stiffened are so to their own destruction." This is Christ's word of command in his gospel, that *every mountain will be brought low before him,* Isa. 40:4. Let not the antichristian power, with its heads and horns, lift up itself against him, for it shall certainly be broken to pieces; what is said with a stiff neck must be unsaid again with a broken heart, or we are undone. Pharaoh said with a stiff neck, *Who is the Lord?* But God made him know to his cost.

Verses 6–10

In these verses we have two great doctrines laid down and two good inferences drawn from them, for the confirmation of what he had before said.

I. Here are two great truths laid down concerning God's government of the world, which we ought to mix faith with, both pertinent to the occasion: —

1. That from God alone kings receive their power (*v.* 6, 7), and therefore to God alone David would give the praise of his advancement; having his power from God he would use it for him, and therefore those were fools that lifted up the horn against him. We see strange revolutions in states and kingdoms, and are surprised at the sudden disgrace of some and elevation of others; we are all full of such changes, when they happen; but here we are directed to look at the author of them, and are taught where the original of power is, and whence promotion comes. Whence comes preferment to kingdoms, to the sovereignty of them? And whence come preferments in kingdoms, to places of power and trust in them? The former depends not upon the will of the people, nor the latter on the will of the prince, but both on the will of God, who has all hearts in his hands; to him therefore those must look who are in pursuit of preferment, and then they begin aright. We are here told, (1.) Negatively, which way we are not to look for the fountain of power: *Promotion comes not from the east, nor from the west, nor from the desert,* that is, neither from the desert on the north of Jerusalem nor from that on the south; so that the fair gale of preferment is not to be expected to blow from any point of the compass, but only from above, directly thence. Men cannot gain promotion either by the wisdom or wealth of the children of the east, nor by the numerous forces of the isles of the Gentiles, that lay westward, nor those of Egypt or Arabia, that lay south; no concurring smiles of second causes will raise men to preferment without the first cause. The learned bishop Lloyd *(Serm. in loc.)* gives this gloss upon it: "All men took the original of power to be from heaven, but from whom there many knew not; the eastern nations, who were generally given to astrology, took it to come from their stars, especially the sun, their god. No, says David, it comes neither from the east nor from the west, neither from the rising nor from the setting of such a planet, or such a constellation, nor from the south, nor from the exaltation of the sun or any star in the midheaven." He mentions not the north, because none supposed it to come thence; or because the same word that signifies the north signifies the secret place, and from the secret of God's counsel it does come, or from the oracle in Zion, which lay on the north side of Jerusalem. Note, No wind is so good as to blow promotion, but as he directs who has the winds in his fists. (2.) Positively: *God is the judge,* the governor or umpire. When parties contend for the prize, he *puts down one and sets up another* as he sees fit, so as to serve his own purposes and bring to pass his own counsels. Herein he acts by prerogative, and is not accountable to us for any of these matters; nor is it any damage, danger, or disgrace that he, who is infinitely wise, holy, and good, has an arbitrary and despotic power to set up and put down whom, and when, and how he pleases. This is a good reason why magistrates should rule for God as those that must give account to him, because it is by him that kings reign.

2. That from God alone all must receive their doom (*v.* 8): *In the hand of the Lord there is a cup,* which he puts into the hands of the children of men, a cup of providence, mixed up (as he thinks fit) of many ingredients, a cup of affliction. The sufferings of Christ are called a *cup,* Mt. 20:22; Jn. 18:11. The judgments of God upon sinners are *the cup of the Lord's right hand,* Hab. 2:16. *The wine is red,* denoting the wrath of God, which is infused into the judg-

ments executed on sinners, and is the wormwood and the gall in the affliction and the misery. It is read as fire, red as blood, for it burns, it kills. It is *full of mixture,* prepared in wisdom, so as to answer the end. There are mixtures of mercy and grace in the cup of affliction when it is put into the hands of God's own people, mixtures of the curse when it is put into the hands of the wicked; it is wine mingled with gall. These vials, (1.) Are poured out upon all; see Rev. 15:7; 16:1; where we read of the angels pouring out the vials of God's wrath upon the earth. Some drops of this wrath may light on good people; when God's judgments are abroad, they have their share in common calamities; but, (2.) The dregs of the cup are reserved for the wicked. The calamity itself is but the vehicle into which the wrath and curse is infused, the top of which has little of the infusion; but the sediment is pure wrath, and that shall fall to the share of sinners; they have the dregs of the cup now in the terrors of conscience, and hereafter in the torments of hell. They shall *wring them out,* that not a drop of the wrath may be left behind, *and they shall drink them,* for the curse shall *enter into their bowels like water and like oil into their bones.* The cup of the Lord's indignation will be to them a cup of trembling, everlasting trembling, Rev. 14:10. The wicked man's cup, while he prospers in the world, is full of mixture, but the worst is at the bottom. The wicked are reserved unto the day of judgment.

II. Here are two good practical inferences drawn from these great truths, and they are the same purposes of duty that he began the psalm with. This being so, 1. He will praise God, and give him glory, for the power to which he has advanced him (*v.* 9): *I will declare for ever* that which *thy wondrous works declare, v.* 1. He will praise God for his elevation, not only at first, while the mercy was fresh, but for ever, so long as he lives. The exaltation of the Son of David will be the subject of the saints' everlasting praises. He will give glory to God, not only as his God, but as the God of Jacob, knowing it was for Jacob his servant's sake, and because he loved his people Israel, that he made him king over them. 2. He will use the power with which he is entrusted for the great ends for which it was put into his hands, *v.* 10, as before, *v.* 2, 4. According to the duty of the higher powers, (1.) He resolves to be a terror to evildoers, to humble their pride and break their power: "Though not all the heads, yet *all the horns, of the wicked will I cut off,* with which they push their poor neighbours; I will disable them to do mischief." Thus God promises to raise up carpenters who should *fray the horns of the Gentiles that had scattered Judah and Israel,* Zec. 1:18–21. (2.) He resolves to be a protection and praise to those that do well: *The horns of the righteous shall be exalted;* they shall be preferred and be put into places of power; and those that are good, and have hearts to do good, shall not want ability and opportunity for it. This agrees with David's resolutions, Ps. 101:3, etc. Herein David was a type of Christ, who with the breath of his mouth shall slay the wicked, but shall *exalt with honour the horn of the righteous,* Ps. 112:9.

PSALM 76

This psalm seems to have been penned upon occasion of some great victory obtained by the church over some threatening enemy or other, and designed to grace the triumph. The Septuagint calls it, "A song upon the Assyrians," whence many good interpreters conjecture that it was penned when Sennacherib's army, then besieging Jerusalem, was entirely cut off by a destroying angel in Hezekiah's time; and several passages in the psalm are very applicable to that work of wonder: but there was a religious triumph upon occasion of another victory, in Jehoshaphat's time, which might as well be the subject of this psalm (2 Chr. 20:28), and it might be called "a song of Asaph" because always sung by the sons of Asaph. Or it might be penned by Asaph who lived in David's time, upon occasion of the many triumphs with which God delighted to honour that reign. Upon occasion of this glorious victory, whatever it was, I. The psalmist congratulates the happiness of the church in having God so nigh (*v.* 1–3). II. He celebrates the glory of God's power, which this was an illustrious instance of (*v.* 4–6). III. He infers hence what reason all have to fear before him (*v.* 7–9). And, IV. What reason his people have to trust in him and to pay their vows to him (*v.* 10–12). It is a psalm proper for a thanksgiving day, upon the account of public successes, and not improper at other times, because it is never out of season to glorify God for the great things he has done for his church formerly, especially for the victories of the Redeemer over the powers of darkness, which all those Old-Testament victories were types of, at least those that are celebrated in the psalms.

To the chief musician on Neginoth. A psalm *or* song of Asaph.

Verses 1–6

The church is here triumphant even in the midst of its militant state. The psalmist, in the church's name, triumphs here in God, the centre of all our triumphs.

I. In the revelation God had made of himself to them, *v.* 1. It is the honour and privilege of Judah and Israel that among them *God is known,* and where he is known *his name* will be *great.* God is known as he is pleased to make himself known; and those are happy to whom he discovers himself — happy people that have their land filled with the knowledge of God, happy persons that have their hearts filled with that knowledge. In Judah God was known as he was not known in other nations, which made the favour the greater, inasmuch as it was distinguishing, Ps. 147:19, 20.

II. In the tokens of God's special presence with them in his ordinances, *v.* 2. In the whole land of Judah and Israel God was known and his name was great; but *in Salem, in Zion,* were *his tabernacle* and *his dwelling-place.* There he kept court; there he received the homage of his people by their sacrifices and entertained them by the feasts upon the sacrifices; thither they came to address themselves to him, and thence by his oracles he issued out his orders; there he recorded his name, and of that place he said, *Her will I dwell, for I have desired it.* It is the glory and happiness of a people to have God among them by his ordinances; but his dwelling-place is a tabernacle, a movable dwelling. *Yet a little while is that light with us.*

III. In the victories they had obtained over their enemies (*v.* 3): *There broke he the arrows of the bow.* Observe how threatening the danger was. Though Judah and Israel, Salem and Zion, were thus privileged, yet war is raised against them, and the weapons of war are furbished.

1. Here are bow and arrows, shield and sword, and all for battle; but all are broken and rendered useless. And it was done there, (1.) In Judah and in Israel, in favour of that people near to God. While the weapons of war were used against other nations they answered their end, but, when turned against that holy nation, they were immediately broken. The Chaldee paraphrases it thus: When the house of Israel did his will he placed his majesty among them, and there he broke the arrows of the bow; while they kept closely to his service they were great and safe, and every thing went well with them. Or, (2.) In the tabernacle and dwelling-place in Zion, there he broke the arrows of the bow; it was done in the field of battle, and yet it is said to be done in the sanctuary, because done in answer to the prayers which God's people there made to him and in the performance of the promises which he there made to them, of both which see that instance, 2 Chr. 20:5, 14. Public successes are owing as much to what is done in the church as to what is done in the camp. Now,

2. This victory redounded very much, (1.) To the immortal honour of Israel's God (*v.* 4): *Thou art,* and hast manifested thyself to be, *more glorious and excellent than the mountains of prey.* [1.] "Than the great and mighty ones of the earth in general, who are high, and think themselves firmly fixed like mountains, but are really mountains of prey, oppressive to all about them. It is their glory to destroy; it is thine to deliver." [2.] "Than our invaders in particular. When they besieged the cities of Judah, they cast up mounts against them, and raised batteries; but thou art more able to protect us than they are to annoy us." Wherein the enemies of the church deal proudly it will appear that God is above them. (2.) To the perpetual disgrace of the enemies of Israel, *v.* 5, 6. They were *stouthearted,* men of great courage and resolution, flushed with their former victories, enraged against Israel, confident of success; they were *men of might,* robust and fit for service; they had *chariots and horses,* which were then greatly valued and trusted to in war, Ps. 20:7. But all this force was of no avail when it was levelled against Jerusalem. [1.] *The stouthearted have despoiled and disarmed themselves* (so some read it); when God pleases he can make his enemies to weaken and destroy themselves. *They have slept,* not the sleep of the righteous, who sleep in Jesus, but *their sleep,* the sleep of sinners, that shall awake to everlasting shame and contempt. [2.] The men of might can no more *find their hands* than the stout-hearted can their spirit. As the bold men are cowed, so the strong men are lamed, and cannot so much as find their hands, to save their own heads, much less to hurt their enemies. [3.] The chariots and horses may be truly said to be *cast into a dead sleep* when their drivers and their riders were so. God did but speak the word, as the God of Jacob that commands deliverances for Jacob, and, at his rebuke, the chariot and horse were both cast into a dead sleep. When the men were laid dead upon the spot by the destroying angel the chariot and horse were not at all formidable. See the power and efficacy of God's rebukes. With what pleasure may we Christians apply all this to the advantages we enjoy by the Redeemer! It is through him that God is known; it is in him that God's name is great; to him it is owing that God has a tabernacle and a dwelling-place in his church. He it was that vanquished the strong man armed, spoiled principalities and powers, and made a show of them openly.

Verses 7–12

This glorious victory with which God had graced and blessed his church is here made to speak three things: —

I. Terror to God's enemies (*v.* 7–9): *"Thou, even thou, art to be feared;* thy majesty is to be reverenced, thy sovereignty to be submitted to, and thy justice to be dreaded by those that have offended thee." Let all the world learn by this event to stand in awe of the great God. 1. Let all be afraid of his wrath against the daring impiety of sinners: *Who may stand in thy sight from the minute that thou art angry?* If God be a consuming fire, how can chaff and stubble stand before him, though his *anger be kindled but a little?* Ps. 2:12. 2. Let all be afraid of his jealousy for oppressed innocency and the injured cause of his own people: *"Thou didst cause judgment to be heard from heaven,* then *when thou didst arise to save all the meek of the earth* (*v.* 8, 9); and then *the earth feared and was still,* waiting what would be the issue of those glorious appearances of thine." Note, (1.) God's people are the *meek of the earth* (Zec. 2:3), the *quiet in the land* (Ps. 35:20), that can bear any wrong, but do none. (2.) Though the meek of the earth are by their meekness exposed to injury, yet God will, sooner or later, appear for their salvation, and plead their cause. (3.) When God comes to save *all the meek of the earth,* he will *cause judgment to be heard from heaven;* he will make the world know that he is angry at the oppressors of his people, and takes what is done against them as done against himself. The righteous God long seems to keep silence, yet, sooner or later, he will make judgment to be heard. (4.) When God is speaking judgment from heaven it is time for the earth to compose itself into an awful and reverent silence: *The earth feared and was still,* as silence is made by proclamation when the court sits. *Be still and know that I am God,* Ps. 46:10. *Be silent, O all flesh! before the Lord, for he is raised* up to judgment, Zec. 2:13. Those that suppose this psalm to have been penned upon the occasion of the routing of Sennacherib's army take it for granted that the descent of the destroying angel, who did the execution, was accompanied with thunder, by which *God caused judgment to be heard from heaven,* and that the earth feared (that is, there was an earthquake), but it was soon over. But this is altogether uncertain.

II. Comfort to God's people, *v.* 10. We live in a very angry provoking world; we often feel much, and are apt to fear more, from the wrath of man, which seems boundless. But this is a great comfort to us, 1. That as far as God permits the wrath of man to break forth at any time he will make it turn to his praise, will bring honour to himself and serve his own purposes by it: *Surely the wrath of man shall praise thee,* not only by the checks given to it, when it shall be forced to confess its own impotency, but even by the liberty given to it for a time. The hardships which God's people suffer by the wrath of their enemies are made to redound to the glory of God and his grace; and the more *the heathen rage* and plot *against the Lord and his anointed* the more will God be praised for setting *his King upon his holy hill of Zion* in spite of them, Ps. 2:1, 6. When the heavenly hosts make this the matter of their thanksgiving-song that God has *taken to himself his great power and has reigned, though the nations were angry* (Rev. 11:17, 18), then the wrath of man adds lustre to the praises of God. 2. That what will not turn to his praise shall not be suffered to break out: *The remainder of wrath shalt thou restrain.* Men must never permit sin, because they cannot check it when they will; but God can. He can set bounds to the wrath of man, as he does to the raging sea. *Hitherto it shall come and no further; here shall its proud waves be stayed.* God restrained the remainder of Sennacherib's rage, for he put *a hook in his nose and a bridle in his jaws* (Isa. 37:29); and, though he permitted him to talk big, he restrained him from doing what he designed.

III. Duty to all, *v.* 11, 12. Let all submit themselves to this great God and become his loyal subjects. Observe, 1. The duty required of us all, all that are about him, that have any dependence upon him or any occasion to approach to him; and who is there that has not? We are therefore every one of us commanded to do our homage to the King of kings: *Vow and pay;* that is, take an oath of allegiance to him and make conscience of keeping it. Vow to be his, and pay what you vow. Bind your souls with a bond to him (for that is the nature of a vow), and then live up to the obligations you have laid upon yourselves; for *better it is not to vow than to vow and not to pay.* And, having taken him for our King, let us bring presents to him, as subjects to their sovereign, 1 Sa. 10:27. *Send you the lamb to the ruler of the land,* Isa. 16:1. Not that God needs any present we can bring, or can be benefited by it; but thus we must give him honour and own that we have our all from him. Our prayers and praises, and especially our hearts, are the presents we should bring to the Lord our God. 2. The reasons to enforce this duty: *Render to all their due, fear to whom fear is due;* and is it not due to God? Yes; (1.) He ought to be feared: *He is the fear* (so the word is); his name is glorious and fearful,; and he is the proper object of our fear; with him is terrible majesty. The God of Abraham is called *the fear of Isaac* (Gen. 31:42), and we are commanded to *make him our fear,* Isa. 8:13. When we bring presents to him we must have an eye to him as greatly to be feared; for he is terrible in his holy places. (2.) He will be feared, even by those who think it their own sole prerogative to be feared (*v.* 12): He shall *cut off the spirit of princes;* he shall slip it off as easily as we slip off a flower from the stalk or a bunch of grapes from the vine; so the word signifies. He can dispirit those that are most daring and make them heartless; for he is, or will be, *terrible to the kings of the earth;* and sooner or later, if they be not so wise as to submit themselves to him, he will force them to call in vain to *rocks and mountains to fall on them and hide them from his wrath,* Rev. 6:16. Since there is no contending with God, it is as much our wisdom as it is our duty to submit to him.

PSALM 77

This psalm, according to the method of many other psalms, begins with sorrowful complaints but ends with comfortable encouragements. The complaints seem to be of personal grievances, but the encouragements relate to the public concerns of the church, so that it is not certain whether it was penned upon a personal or a public account. If they were private troubles that he was groaning under, it teaches us that what God has wrought for his church in general may be improved for the comfort of particular believers; if it was some public calamity that he is here lamenting, his speaking of it so feelingly, as if it had been some particular trouble of his own, shows how much we should lay to heart the interests of the church of God and make them ours. One of the rabbin says, This psalm is spoken in the dialect of the captives; and therefore some think it was penned in the captivity in Babylon. I. The psalmist complains here of the deep impressions which his troubles made upon his spirits, and the temptation he was in to despair of relief (*v.* 1–10). II. He encourages himself to hope that it would be well at last, by the remembrance of God's former appearances for the help of his people, of which he gives several instances (*v.* 11–20). In singing this psalm we must take shame to ourselves for all our sinful distrusts of God, and of his providence and promise, and give to him the glory of his power and goodness by a thankful commemoration of what he has done for us formerly and a cheerful dependence on him for the future.

To the chief musician, to Jeduthun. A psalm of Asaph.

Verses 1–10

We have here the lively portraiture of a good man under prevailing melancholy, fallen into and sinking in that horrible pit and that miry clay, but struggling to get out. Drooping saints, that are of a sorrowful spirit, may here as in a glass see their own faces. The conflict which the psalmist had with his griefs and fears seems to have been over when he penned this record of it; for he says (*v.* 1), *I cried unto God, and he gave ear unto me,* which, while the struggle lasted, he had not the comfortable sense of, as he had afterwards; but he inserts it in the beginning of his narrative as an intimation that his trouble did not end in despair; for God heard him, and, at length, he knew that he heard him. Observe,

I. His melancholy prayers. Being afflicted, he prayed (Jam. 5:13), and, being in an agony, he prayed more earnestly (*v.* 1): *My voice was unto God, and I cried, even with my voice unto God.* He was full of complaints, loud complaints, but he directed them to God, and turned them all into prayers, vocal prayers, very earnest and importunate. Thus he gave vent to his grief and gained some ease; and thus he took the right way in order to relief (*v.* 2): *In the day of my trouble I sought the Lord.* Note, Days of trouble must be days of prayer, days of inward trouble especially, when God seems to have withdrawn from us; we must seek him and seek till we find him. In the day of his trouble he did not seek for the diversion of business or recreation, to shake off his trouble that way, but he sought God, and his favour and grace. Those that are under trouble of mind must not think to drink it away, or laugh it away, but must pray it away. *My hand was stretched out in the night and ceased not;* so Dr. Hammond reads the following words, as speaking the incessant importunity of his prayers. Compare Ps. 143:5, 6.

II. His melancholy grief. Grief may then be called melancholy indeed, 1. When it admits of no intermission; such was his: *My sore,* or wound, *ran in the night,* and bled inwardly, and it ceased not, no, not in the time appointed for rest and sleep. 2. When it admits of no consolation; and that also as his case: *My soul refused to be comforted;* he had no mind to hearken to those that would be his comforters. *As vinegar upon nitre, so is he that sings songs to a heavy heart,* Prov. 25:20. Nor had he any mind to think of those things that would be his comforts; he put them far from him, as one that indulged himself in sorrow. Those that are in sorrow, upon any account, do not only prejudice themselves, but affront God, if they refuse to be comforted.

III. His melancholy musings. He pored so much upon the trouble, whatever it was, personal or public, that, 1. The methods that should have relieved him did but increase his grief, *v.* 3. (1.) One would have thought that the remembrance of God would comfort him, but it did not: *I remembered God and was troubled,* as poor Job (ch. 23:15), *I am troubled at his presence; when I consider I am afraid of him.* When he remembered God his thoughts fastened only upon his justice, and wrath, and dreadful majesty, and thus God himself became a terror to him. (2.) One would have thought that pouring out his soul before God would give him ease, but it did not; he *complained, and yet his spirit was overwhelmed,* and sank under the load. 2. The means of his present relief were denied him, *v.* 4. He could not enjoy sleep, which, if it be quiet and refreshing, is a parenthesis to our griefs and cares: *"Thou holdest my eyes waking* with thy terrors, which make me full of *tossings to and fro until the dawning of the day."* He could not speak, by reason of the disorder of his thoughts, the tumult of his spirits, and the confusion his mind was in: He *kept silence even from good* while his *heart was hot within him;* he was *ready to burst like a new bottle* (Job 32:19), and yet so troubled that he could not speak and refresh himself. Grief never preys so much upon the spirits as when it is thus smothered and pent up.

IV. His melancholy reflections (*v.* 5, 6): *"I have considered the days of old,* and compared them with the present days; and our former prosperity does but aggravate our present calamities: for we see not the wonders that our fathers told us off."* Melancholy people are apt to pore altogether upon the days of old and the years of ancient times, and to magnify them, for the justifying of their own uneasiness and discontent at the present posture of affairs. But *say not thou* that *the former days were better than these,* because it is more than thou knowest whether they were or no, Eccl. 7:10. Neither let the remembrance of the comforts we have lost make us unthankful for those that are left, or impatient under our crosses. Particularly, he *called to remembrance his song in the night,* the comforts with which he had supported himself in his former sorrows and entertained himself in his former solitude. These songs he remembered, and tried if he could not sing them over again; but he was out of tune for them, and the remembrance of them did but *pour out his soul in him,* Ps. 43:4. See Job 35:10.

V. His melancholy fears and apprehensions: *"I communed with my own heart, v.* 6. Come, my soul, what will be the issue of these things? What can I think of them and what can I expect they will come to at last? I made dil-

igent search into the causes of my trouble, enquiring wherefore God contended with me and what would be the consequences of it. And thus I began to reason, *Will the Lord cast off for ever,* as he does for the present? He is not now favourable; and *will he be favourable no more? His mercy* is now gone; *and is it clean gone for ever? His promise* now fails; and *does it fail for evermore?* God is not now gracious; but *has he forgotten to be gracious?* His *tender mercies* have been withheld, perhaps in wisdom; but *are they shut up,* shut up *in anger?" v.* 7–9. This is the language of a disconsolate deserted soul, walking in darkness and having no light, a case not uncommon even with those that *fear the Lord and obey the voice of his servant,* Isa. 50:10. He may here be looked upon, 1. As groaning under a sore trouble. God hid his face from him, and withdrew the usual tokens of his favour. Note, Spiritual trouble is of all trouble most grievous to a gracious soul; nothing wounds and pierces it like the apprehensions of God's being angry, the suspending of his favour and the superseding of his promise; this wounds the spirit; and who can bear that? 2. As grappling with a strong temptation. Note, God's own people, in a cloudy and dark day, may be tempted to make desperate conclusions about their own spiritual state and the condition of God's church and kingdom in the world, and, as to both, to give up all for gone. We may be tempted to think that God has abandoned us and cast us off, that the covenant of grace fails us, and that the tender mercy of our God shall be for ever withheld from us. But we must not give way to such suggestions as these. If fear and melancholy ask such peevish questions, let faith answer them from the Scripture: *Will the Lord cast off for ever?* God forbid, Rom. 11:1. No; *the Lord will not cast off his people,* Ps. 94:14. *Will he be favourable no more?* Yes, he will; *for, though he cause grief, yet will he have compassion,* Lam. 3:32. *Is his mercy clean gone for ever?* No; his *mercy endures for ever;* as it is *from everlasting,* it is *to everlasting,* Ps. 103:17. *Doth his promise fail for evermore?* No; *it is impossible for God to lie,* Heb. 6:18. *Hath God forgotten to be gracious?* No; he cannot deny himself, and his own name which he hath proclaimed *gracious and merciful,* Ex. 34:6. *Has he in anger shut up his tender mercies?* No; they are *new every morning* (Lam. 3:23); and therefore, *How shall I give thee up, Ephraim?* Hos. 11:8, 9. Thus was he going on with his dark and dismal apprehensions when, on a sudden, he first checked himself with that word, *Selah,* "Stop there; go no further; let us hear no more of these unbelieving surmises;" and he then chid himself (*v.* 10): *I said, This is my infirmity.* He is soon aware that it is not well said, and therefore, *"Why art thou cast down, O my soul?* I said, *This is my affliction"* (so some understand it); "This is the calamity that falls to my lot and I must make the best of it; every one has his affliction, his trouble in the flesh; and this is mine, the cross I must take up." Or, rather, "This is my sin; it is my iniquity, the plague of my own heart." These doubts and fears proceed from the want and weakness of faith and the corruption of a distempered mind. note, (1.) We all know that concerning ourselves of which we must say, "This is our infirmity," a sin that most easily besets us." (2.) Despondency of spirit, and distrust of God, under affliction, are too often the infirmities of good people, and, as such, are to be reflected upon by us with sorrow and shame, as by the psalmist here: *This is my infirmity.* When at any time it is working in us we must thus suppress the rising of it, and not suffer the evil spirit to speak. We must argue down the insurrections of unbelief, as the psalmist here: *But I will remember the years of the right hand of the Most High.* He had been considering the *years of ancient times* (*v.* 5), the blessings formerly enjoyed, the remembrance of which did only add to his grief; but now he considered them as *the years of the right hand of the Most High,* that those blessings of ancient times came from the Ancient of days, from the power and sovereign disposal of his right hand who is *over all, God, blessed for ever,* and this satisfied him; for may not the Most High with his right hand make what changes he pleases?

Verses 11–20

The psalmist here recovers himself out of the great distress and plague he was in, and silences his own fears of God's casting off his people by the remembrance of the great things he had done for them formerly, which though he had in vain tried to quiet himself with (v. 5, 6) yet he tried again, and, upon this second trial, found it not in vain. It is good to persevere in the proper means for the strengthening of faith, though they do not prove effectual at first: "*I will remember, surely I will,* what God has done for his people of old, till I can thence infer a happy issue of the present dark dispensation," v. 11, 12. Note, 1. The works of the Lord, for his people, have been wondrous works. 2. They are recorded for us, that they may be remembered by us. 3. That we may have benefit by the remembrance of them we must meditate upon them, and dwell upon them in our thoughts, and must talk of them, that we may inform ourselves and others further concerning them. 4. The due remembrance of the works of God will be a powerful antidote against distrust of his promise and goodness; for he is God and changes not. If he begin, he will finish his work and bring forth the top-stone.

Two things, in general, satisfied him very much:

I. That *God's way is in the sanctuary, v.* 13. It is *in holiness,* so some. When we cannot solve the particular difficulties that may arise in our constructions of the divine providence, this we are sure of, in general, that God is holy in all his works, that they are all worthy of himself and consonant to the eternal purity and rectitude of his nature. He has holy ends in all he does, and will be sanctified in every dispensation of his providence. His way is according to his promise, which he has spoken in his holiness and made known in the sanctuary. What he has done is according to what he has said and may be interpreted by it; and from what he has said we may easily gather that he will not cast off his people for ever. God's way is for the sanctuary, and for the benefit of it. All he does is intended for the good of his church.

II. That God's *way is in the sea.* Though God is holy, just, and good, in all he does, yet we cannot give an account of the reasons of his proceedings, nor make any certain judgment of his designs: *His path is in the great waters and his footsteps are not known, v.* 19. God's ways are like the deep waters which cannot be fathomed (Ps. 36:6), like the way of a ship in the sea, which cannot be tracked, Prov. 30:18, 19. God's proceedings are always to be acquiesced in, but cannot always be accounted for. He specifies some particulars, for which he goes as far back as the infancy of the Jewish church, and from which he gathers, 1. That there is no God to be compared with the God of Israel (v. 13): *Who is so great a God as our God?* Let us first give to God the glory of the great things he has done for his people, and acknowledge him, therein, great above all comparison; and then we may take to ourselves the comfort of what he has done and encourage ourselves with it. 2. That he is a God of almighty power (v. 14): *"Thou art the God that* alone *doest wonders,* above the power of any creature; *thou hast* visibly, and beyond any contradiction, *declared thy strength among the people."* What God has done for his church has been a standing declaration of his almighty power, for therein he has made bare his everlasting arm. (1.) God brought Israel out of Egypt, v. 15. This was the beginning of mercy to them, and was yearly to be commemorated among them in the passover: *"Thou hast with thy arm,* stretched out in so many miracles, *redeemed thy people* out of the hand of the Egyptians." Though they were delivered by power, yet they are said to be redeemed, as if it had been done by price, because it was typical of the great redemption, which was to be wrought out, in the fulness of time, both by price and power. Those that were redeemed are here called not only *the sons of Jacob,* to whom the promise was made, but *of Joseph* also, who had a most firm and lively belief of the performance of it; for, when he was dying, he made mention of the departing of the children of Israel out of Egypt, and gave commandment concerning his bones. (2.) He divided the Red Sea before them (v. 16): *The waters gave way, and a lane was made through that crowd instantly, as if they had seen God himself at the head of the armies of Israel, and had retired for fear of him. Not only the surface of the waters, but the depths, were troubled,* and opened to the right and to the left, in obedience to his word of command. (3.) He destroyed the Egyptians (v. 17): *The clouds poured out water* upon them, while the pillar of fire, like an umbrella over the camp of Israel, sheltered it from the shower, in which, as in the deluge, the waters that were above the firmament concurred with those that

were beneath the firmament to destroy the rebels. Then *the skies sent out a sound; thy arrows also went abroad,* which is explained (v. 18): *The voice of thy thunder was heard in the heaven* (that was the sound which the skies sent forth); *the lightnings lightened the world* — those were the arrows which went abroad, by which the host of the Egyptians was discomfited, with so much terror that *the earth* of the adjacent coast *trembled and shook.* Thus God's way was in the sea, for the destruction of his enemies, as well as for the salvation of his people; and yet when the waters returned to their place *his footsteps were not known* (v. 19); there was no mark set upon the place, as there was, afterwards, in Jordan, Jos. 4:9. We do not read in the story of Israel's passing through the Red Sea that there were thunders and lightning, and an earthquake; yet there might be, and Josephus says there were, such displays of the divine terror upon that occasion. But it may refer to the thunders, lightnings, and earth quakes, that were at Mount Sinai when the law was given. (4.) He took his people Israel under his own guidance and protection (v. 20): *Thou leddest thy people like a clock.* They being weak and helpless, and apt to wander like a flock of sheep, and lying exposed to the beasts of prey, God went before them with all the care and tenderness of a shepherd, that they might not fail. The pillar of cloud and fire led them; yet that is not here taken notice of, but the agency of Moses and Aaron, by whose hand God led them; they could not do it without God, but God did it with and by them. Moses was their governor, Aaron their high priest; they were guides, overseers, and rulers to Israel, and by them God led them. The right and happy administration of the two great ordinances of magistracy and ministry is, though not so great a miracle, yet as great a mercy to any people as the pillar of cloud and fire was to Israel in the wilderness.

The psalm concludes abruptly, and does not apply those ancient instances of God's power to the present distresses of the church, as one might have expected. But as soon as the good man began to meditate on these things he found he had gained his point; his very entrance upon this matter *gave him light* and joy (Ps. 119:130); his fears suddenly and strangely vanished, so that he needed to go no further; he *went his way, and did eat,* and *his countenance was no more sad,* like Hannah, 1 Sa. 1:18.

PSALM 78

This psalm is historical; it is a narrative of the great mercies God had bestowed upon Israel, the great sins wherewith they had provoked him, and the many tokens of his displeasure they had been under for their sins. The psalmist began, in the foregoing psalm, to relate God's wonders of old, for his own encouragement in a difficult time; there he broke off abruptly, but here resumes the subject, for the edification of the church, and enlarges much upon it, showing not only how good God had been to them, which was an earnest of further finishing mercy, but how basely they had conducted themselves towards God, which justified him in correcting them as he did at this time, and forbade all complaints. Here is, I. The preface to this church history, commanding the attention of the present age to it and recommending it to the study of the generations to come (v. 1–8). II. The history itself from Moses to David; it is put into a psalm or song that it might be the better remembered and transmitted to posterity, and that the singing of it might affect them with the things here related, more than they would be with a bare narrative of them. The general scope of this psalm we have (v. 9–11) where notice is taken of the present rebukes they were under (v. 9), the sin which brought them under those rebukes (v. 10), and the mercies of God to them formerly, which aggravated that sin (v. 11). As to the particulars, we are here told, 1. What wonderful works God had wrought for them in bringing them out of Egypt (v. 12–16), providing for them in the wilderness (v. 23–29), plaguing and ruining their enemies (v. 43–53), and at length putting them in possession of the land of promise (v. 54, 55). 2. How ungrateful they were to God for his favours to them and how many and great provocations they were guilty of. How they murmured against God and distrusted him (v. 17–20), and did but counterfeit repentance and submission when he punished them (v. 34–37), thus grieving and tempting him (v. 40–42). How they affronted God with their idolatries after they came to Canaan (v. 56–58). 3. How God had justly punished them for their sins (v. 21, 22) in the wilderness, making their sin their punishment (v. 29–33), and now, of late, when the ark was taken by the Philistines (v. 59–64). 4. How graciously God had spared them and returned in mercy to them, notwithstanding their provocations. He had forgiven them formerly (v. 38, 39), and now, of late, had removed the judgments they had brought upon themselves, and brought them under a happy establishment both in church and state (v. 65–72). As the general scope of this psalm may be of use to us in the singing of it, to put us upon recollecting what God has done for us and for his church formerly, and what we have done against him, so the particulars also may be of use to us, for warning against those sins of unbelief and ingratitude which Israel of old was notoriously guilty of, and the record of which was preserved for our learning. "These things happened unto them for ensamples," 1 Co. 10:11; Heb. 4:11.

Maschil of Asaph.

Verses 1–8

These verses, which contain the preface to this history, show that the psalm answers the title; it is indeed *Maschil* — *a psalm to give instruction;* if we receive not the instruction it gives, it is our own fault. Here,

I. The psalmist demands attention to what he wrote (v. 1): *Give ear, O my people! to my law.* Some make these the psalmist's words. David, as a king, or Asaph, in his name, as his secretary of state, or scribe to the sweet singer of Israel, here calls upon the people, as his people committed to his charge, to give ear to his law. He calls his instructions his *law* or *edict;* such was their commanding force in themselves. Every good truth, received in the light and love of it, will have the power of a law upon the conscience; yet that was not all: David was a king, and he would interpose his royal power for the edification of his people. If God, by his grace, make great men good men, they will be capable of doing more good than others, because their word will be a law to all about them, who must therefore give ear and hearken; for to what purpose is divine revelation brought our ears if we will not incline our ears to it, both humble ourselves and engage ourselves to hear it and heed it? Or the psalmist, being a prophet, speaks as God's mouth, and so calls them *his people,* and demands subjection to what was said as to a law. Let him that has an ear thus *hear what the Spirit saith unto the churches,* Rev. 2:7.

II. Several reasons are given why we should diligently attend to that which is here related. 1. The things here discoursed of are weighty, and deserve consideration, strange, and need it (v. 2): *I will open my mouth in a parable,* in that which is sublime and uncommon, but very excellent and well worthy your attention; *I will utter dark sayings,* which challenge your most serious regards as much as the enigmas with which the eastern princes and learned men used to try one another. These are called *dark sayings,* not because they are hard to be understood, but because they are greatly to be admired and carefully to be looked into. This is said to be fulfilled in the parables which our Saviour put forth (Mt. 13:35), which were (as this) representations of the state of the kingdom of God among men. 2. They are the monuments of antiquity — *dark sayings of old which our fathers have told us, v.* 3. They are things of undoubted certainty; we have heard them and known them, and there is no room left to question the truth of them. The gospel of Luke is called a *declaration of those things which are most surely believed among us* (Lu. 1:1), so were the things here related. The honour we owe to our parents and ancestors obliges us to attend to that which our fathers have told us, and, as far as it appears to be true and good, to receive it with so much the more reverence and regard. 3. They are to be transmitted to posterity, and it lies as a charge upon us carefully to hand them down (v. 4); because our fathers told them to us *we will not hide them from their children.* Our children are called *theirs,* for they were in care for their seed's seed, and looked upon them as theirs; and, in teaching our children the knowledge of God, we repay to our parents some of that debt we owe to them for teaching us. Nay, if we have no children of our own, we must declare the things of God to *their* children, the children of others. Our care must be for posterity in general, and not only for our own posterity; and for the generation to come hereafter, the children that shall be born, as well as for the generation that is next rising up and the children that are born. That which we are to transmit to our children is not only the knowledge of languages, arts and sciences, liberty and property, but especially the praises of the Lord, and his strength appearing in the wonderful works he has done. Our great care must be to lodge our religion, that great deposit, pure and entire in the hands of those that succeed us. There are two things the full and clear knowledge of which we must preserve the entail of to our heirs: — (1.) The law of God; for this was given with a particular charge to teach it diligently to their children (v. 5): *He established a testimony* or covenant, and enacted a law, in Jacob and Israel, gave them precepts and promises, which he *commanded them to make known to their children,* Deu. 6:7, 20. The church of God, as the historian says of the Roman commonwealth, was not to be *res unius aetatis* — *a thing of one age* but was to be kept up from one generation to another; and therefore, as God provided for a succession of ministers in the tribe of Levi and the house of Aaron, so he appointed that parents should train up their children in the knowledge of his law: and, when they had grown up, they must arise *and declare them to their children* (*v.* 6), that, as one generation of God's servants and worshippers passes away, another generation may come, and the church, as the earth, may abide for ever; and thus God's name among men may be as the days of heaven. (2.) The providences of God concerning them, both in mercy and in judgment. The former seem to be mentioned for the sake of this; since God gave order that his laws should be made known to posterity, it is requisite that with them his works also should be made known, the fulfilling of the promises made to the obedient and the threatenings denounced against the disobedient. Let these be told to our children and our children's children, [1.] That they may take encouragement to conform to the will of God (*v.* 7): *that, not forgetting the works of God* wrought in former days, *they* might *set their hope in God and keep his commandments,* might make his command their rule and his covenant their stay. Those only may with confidence hope for God's salvation that make conscience of doing his commandments. The works of God, duly considered, will very much strengthen our resolution both to set our hope in him and to keep his commandments, for he is able to bear us out in both. [2.] That they may take warning not to conform to the example of their fathers (*v.* 8): *That they might not be as their fathers, a stubborn and rebellious generation.* See here, *First,* What was the character of their fathers. Though they were the seed of Abraham, taken into covenant with God, and, for aught we know, the only professing people he had then in the world, yet they were stubborn and rebellious, and walked contrary to God, in direct opposition to his will. They did indeed profess relation to him, but they did not set their hearts aright; they were not cordial in their engagements to God, nor inward with him in their worship of him, and therefore their *spirit was not stedfast with him,* but upon every occasion they flew off from him. Note, Hypocrisy is the high road to apostasy. Those that do not set their hearts aright will not be stedfast with God, but play fat and loose. *Secondly,* What was a charge to the children: *That they be not as their fathers.* Note, Those that have descended from wicked and ungodly ancestors, if they will but consider the word and works of God, will see reason enough not to tread in their steps. It will be no excuse for a vain conversation that it was received by tradition from our fathers (1 Pt. 1:18); for what we know of them that was evil must be an admonition to us, that we dread that which was so pernicious to them as we would shun those courses which they took that were ruinous to their health or estates.

Verses 9–39

In these verses,

I. The psalmist observes the late rebukes of Providence that the people of Israel had been under, which they had brought upon themselves by their dealing treacherously with God, *v.* 9–11. *The children of Ephraim,* in which tribe Shiloh was, though they were well armed and shot with bows, yet *turned back in the day of battle.* This seems to refer to that shameful defeat which the Philistines gave them in Eli's time, when they took the ark prisoner, 1 Sa. 4:10, 11. Of this the psalmist here begins to speak, and, after a long digression, returns to it again, *v.* 61. Well might that event be thus fresh in mind in David's time, above forty years after, for the ark, which in that memorable battle was seized by the Philistines, though it was quickly brought out of captivity, was never brought out of obscurity till David fetched it from Kirjath-jearim to his own city. Observe, 1. The shameful cowardice of the children of Ephraim, that warlike tribe, so famed for valiant men, Joshua's tribe; the children of that tribe, though as well armed as ever, turned back when they came to face the enemy. Note, Weapons of war stand men in little stead without a martial spirit, and that is gone if God be gone. Sin dispirits men and takes away the heart. 2. The causes of their cowardice, which were no less shameful; and these were, (1.) A shameful violation of God's law and their covenant with him (*v.* 10); they were basely treacherous and perfidious, for *they kept not the covenant of God,* and basely stubborn and rebellious (as they were described, *v.* 8), for they peremptorily refused to walk in his law, and, in effect, told him to his face they would not be ruled by him. (2.) A shameful ingratitude to God for the favours he had bestowed upon them: They *forgot his works and his wonders,* his works of wonder which they ought to have admired, *v.* 11. Note, Our forgetfulness of God's works is at the bottom of our disobedience to his laws.

II. He takes occasion hence to consult precedents and to compare this with the case of their fathers, who were in like manner unmindful of God's mercies to them and ungrateful to their founder and great benefactor, and were therefore often brought under his displeasure. The narrative in these verses is very remarkable, for it relates a kind of struggle between God's goodness and man's badness, and mercy, at length, rejoices against judgment.

1. God did great things for his people Israel when he first incorporated them and formed them into a people: *Marvellous things did he in the sight of their fathers,* and not only in their sight, but in their cause, and for their benefit, so strange, so kind, that one would think they should never be forgotten. What he did for them in the land of Egypt is only just mentioned here (*v.* 12), but afterwards resumed, *v.* 43. He proceeds here to show, (1.) How he made a lane for them through the Red Sea, and caused them, gave them courage, to pass through, though the waters stood over their heads as a heap, *v.* 13. See Isa. 63:12, 13, where God is said to *lead them by the hand,* as it were, *through the deep that they should not stumble.* (2.) How he provided a guide for them through the untrodden paths of the wilderness (*v.* 14); he led them step by step, *in the day time by a cloud,* which also sheltered them from the heat, and *all the night with a light of fire,* which perhaps warmed the air; at least it made the darkness of night less frightful, and perhaps kept off wild beasts, Zec. 2:5. (3.) How he furnished their camp with fresh water in a dry and thirsty land where no water was, not by opening the bottles of heaven (that would have been a common way), but by broaching a rock (*v.* 15, 16): *He clave the rocks in the wilderness,* which yielded water, though they were not capable of receiving it either from the clouds above or the springs beneath. Out of the dry and hard rock he gave them drink, not distilled as out of an alembic, drop by drop, but in streams *running down like rivers,* and as out of the great depths. God gives abundantly, and is rich in mercy; he gives seasonably, and sometimes makes us to feel the want of mercies that we may the better know the worth of them. This water which God gave Israel out of the rock was the more valuable because it was spiritual drink. *And that rock was Christ.*

2. When God began thus to bless them they began to affront him (*v.* 17): *They sinned yet more against him,* more than they had done in Egypt, though there they were bad enough, Eze. 20:8. They bore the miseries of their servitude better than the difficulties of their deliverance, and never murmured at their taskmasters so much as they did at Moses and Aaron; as if they were *delivered to do all these abominations,* Jer. 7:10. As sin sometimes takes occasion by the commandment, so at other times it takes occasion by the deliverance, to become more exceedingly sinful. *They provoked the Most High.* Though he is most high, and they knew themselves an unequal match for him, yet they provoked him and even bade defiance to his justice; and this in the wilderness, where he had them at his mercy and therefore they were bound in interest to please him, and where he showed them so much mercy and therefore they were bound in gratitude to please him; yet there they said and did that which they knew would provoke him: *They tempted God in their heart, v.* 18. Their sin began in their heart, and thence it took its malignity. *They do always err in their heart,* Heb. 3:10. Thus they tempted God, tried his patience to the utmost, whether he would bear with them or no, and, in effect, bade him do his worst. Two ways they provoked him: — (1.) By desiring, or rather demanding, that which he had not thought fit to give them: *They asked meat for their lust.* God had given them meat for their hunger, in the manna, wholesome pleasant food and in abundance; he had given them meat for their faith out of the heads of leviathan which *he broke in pieces,* Ps. 74:14. But all this would not serve; they must have meat for their lust, dainties and varieties to gratify a luxurious appetite. Nothing is more provoking to God than our quarrelling with our allotment and indulging the desires of the flesh. (2.) By distrusting his power to give them what they desired. This was tempting God indeed. They challenged him to give them flesh; and, if he did not, they would say it was because he could not, not because he did not see it fit for them (*v.* 19): *They spoke against God.* Those that set bounds to God's power speak against him. It was as injurious a reflection as could be cat upon God to say, *Can God furnish a table in the wilderness?* They had manna, but the did not think they had a table furnished unless they had boiled and roast, a first, a second, and a third course, as they had in Egypt, where they had both flesh and fish, and sauce too (Ex. 16:3, Num. 11:5), dishes of meat and salvers of fruit. What an unreasonable insatiable thin is luxury! Such a mighty thing did these epicures think a table well furnished to be that they thought it was more than God himself could give them in that wilderness; whereas the *beasts of the forest,* and all the *fowls of the mountains,* are his, Ps. 50:10, 11. Their disbelief of God's power was so much the worse in that they did at the same time own that he had done as much as that came to (*v.* 20): *Behold, he smote the rock, that the waters gushed out,* which they and their cattle drank of. And which is easier, to furnish a table in the wilderness, which a rich man can do, or to fetch water out of a rock, which the greatest potentate on the earth cannot do? Never did unbelief, though always unreasonable, ask so absurd a question: "Can he that melted down a rock into streams of water give bread also? Or can he that has given bread provide flesh also?" Is any thing too hard for Omnipotence? When once the ordinary powers of nature are exceeded God has made bare his arm, and we must conclude that nothing is impossible with him. Be it ever so great a thing that we ask, it becomes us to own, *Lord, if thou wilt, thou canst.*

3. God justly resented the provocation and was much displeased with them (*v.* 21): *The Lord heard this, and was wroth.* Note, God is a witness to all our murmurings and distrusts; he hears them and is much displeased with them. *A fire was kindled* for this *against Jacob;* the *fire of the Lord burnt among them,* Num. 11:1. Or it may be understood of the fire of God's anger which came up against Israel. To unbelievers our God is himself a consuming fire. Those that will not believe the power of God's mercy shall feel the power of his indignation, and be made to confess that *it is a fearful thing to fall into his hands.* Now here we are told, (1.) Why God thus resented the provocation (*v.* 22): *Because* by this it appeared that *they believed not in God;* they did not give credit to the revelation he had made of himself to them, for they durst not commit themselves to him, nor venture themselves with him: *They trusted not in the salvation* he had begun to work for them; for then they would not thus have questioned its progress. Those cannot be said to trust in God's salvation as their felicity at last who cannot find in their hearts to trust in his providence for food convenient in the way to it. That which aggravated their unbelief was the experience they had had of the power and goodness of God, *v.* 23–25. He had given them undeniable proofs of his power, not only on earth beneath, but in heaven above; for *he commanded the clouds from above,* as one that had created them and commanded them into being; he made what use he pleased of them. Usually by their showers they contribute to the earth's producing corn; but now, when God so commanded them, they showered down corn themselves, which is therefore called here *the corn of heaven;* for heaven can do the work without the earth, but not the earth without heaven. God, who has the key of the clouds, *opened the doors of heaven,* and that is more than *opening the windows,* which yet is spoken of as a great blessing, Mal. 3:10. To all that by faith and prayer ask, seek, and knock, these doors shall at any time be opened; for the God of heaven is rich in mercy to all that call upon him. He not only keeps a good house, but keeps open house. Justly might God take it ill that they should distrust him when he had been so very kind to them that he *had rained down manna upon them to eat,* substantial food, daily, duly, enough for all, enough for each. *Man did eat angels' food,* such as angels, if they had occasion for food, would eat and be thankful for; or rather such as was given by the ministry of angels, and (as the *Chaldee* reads it) such as descended from the dwelling of angels. Every one, even the least child in Israel, did *eat the bread of the mighty* (so the margin reads it); the weakest stomach could digest it, and yet it was so nourishing that it was strong meat for

strong men. And, though the provision was so good, yet they were not stinted, nor ever reduced to short allowance; for *he sent them meat to the full.* If they gathered little, it was their own fault; and yet even then they had no lack, Ex. 16:18. The daily provision God makes for us, and has made ever since we came into the world, though it has not so much of miracle as this, has no less of mercy, and is therefore a great aggravation of our distrust of God. (2.) How he expressed his resentment of the provocation, not in denying them what they so inordinately lusted after, but in granting it to them. [1.] Did they question his power? He soon gave them a sensible conviction that he could *furnish a table in the wilderness.* Though the winds seem to blow where they list, yet, when he pleased, he could make them his caterers to fetch in provisions, *v.* 26. *He caused an east wind to blow and a south wind,* either a south-east wind, or an east wind first to bring in the quails from that quarter and then a south wind to bring in more from that quarter; so that *he rained flesh upon them,* and that of the most delicate sort, not butchers' meat, but wild-fowl, and abundance of it, *as dust, as the sand of the sea* (*v.* 27), so that the meanest Israelite might have sufficient; and it cost them nothing, no, not the pains of fetching it from the mountains, for *he let it fall in the midst of their camp, round about their habitation, v.* 28. We have the account Num. 11:31, 32. See how good God is even to the evil and unthankful, and wonder that his goodness does not overcome their badness. See what little reason we have to judge of God's love by such gifts of his bounty as these; dainty bits are no tokens of his peculiar favour. Christ gave dry bread to the disciples that he loved, but a sop dipped in the sauce to Judas that betrayed him. [2.] Did they defy his justice and boast that they had gained their point? He made them pay dearly for their quails; for, though he *gave them their own desire, they were not estranged from their lust* (*v.* 29, 30); their appetite was insatiable; they were well filled and yet they were not satisfied; for they knew not what they would have. Such is the nature of lust; it is content with nothing, and the more it is humoured the more humoursome it grows. Those that indulge their lust will never be estranged from it. Or it intimates that God's liberality did not make them ashamed of their ungrateful lustings, as it would have done if they had had any sense of honour. But what came of it? *While the meat was yet in their mouth,* rolled under the tongue as a sweet morsel, *the wrath of God came upon them and slew the fattest of them* (*v.* 31), those that were most luxurious and most daring. See Num. 11:33, 34. They were fed *as sheep for the slaughter:* the butcher takes the fattest first. We may suppose there were some pious and contented Israelites, that did eat moderately of the quails and were never the worse; for it was not the meat that poisoned them, but their own lust. Let epicures and sensualists here read their doom. The end of those who make a *god of their belly is destruction,* Phil. 3:19. *The prosperity of fools shall destroy them,* and their ruin will be the greater.

4. The judgments of God upon them did not reform them, nor attain the end, any more than his mercies (*v.* 32): *For all this, they sinned still;* they murmured and quarrelled with God and Moses as much as ever. Though God *was wroth and smote them, yet they went on frowardly in the way of their heart* (Isa. 57:17); *they believed not for his wondrous works.* Though his works of justice were as wondrous and as great proofs of his power as his works of mercy, yet they were not wrought upon by them to fear God, nor convinced how much it was their interest to make him their friend. Those hearts are hard indeed that will neither be melted by the mercies of God nor broken by his judgments.

5. They persisting in their sins, God proceeded in his judgments, but they were judgments of another nature, which wrought not suddenly, but slowly. He punished them not now with such acute diseases as that was which *slew the fattest of them,* but a lingering chronical distemper (*v.* 33): *Therefore their days did he consume in vanity* in the wilderness *and their years in trouble.* By an irreversible doom they were condemned to wear out thirty-eight tedious years in the wilderness, which indeed were consumed in vanity; for in all those years there was not a step taken nearer Canaan, but they were turned back again, and wandered to and fro as in a labyrinth, not one stroke struck towards the conquest of it: and not only in vanity, but in trouble, for their carcases were condemned to fall in the wilderness and there they all perished but Caleb and Joshua. Note, Those that sin still must expect to be in trouble still. And the reason why we spend our days in so much vanity and trouble, why we live with so little comfort and to so little purpose, is because we do not live by faith.

6. Under these rebukes they professed repentance, but they were not cordial and sincere in this profession. (1.) Their profession was plausible enough (*v.* 34, 35): *When he slew them,* or condemned them to be slain, *then they sought him;* they confessed their fault, and begged his pardon. When some were slain others in a fright cried to God for mercy, and promised they would reform and be very good; then *they returned to God, and enquired early after him.* So one would have taken them to be such as desired to find him. And they pretended to do this because, however they had forgotten it formerly, now *they remembered that God was their rock* and therefore now that they needed him they would fly to him and take shelter in him, *and* that *the high God* was *their Redeemer,* who brought them out of Egypt and to whom therefore they might come with boldness. Afflictions are sent to put us in mind of God as our rock and our redeemer; for, in prosperity, we are apt to forget him. (2.) They were not sincere in this profession (*v.* 36, 37): *They did but flatter him with their mouth,* as if they thought by fair speeches to prevail with him to revoke the sentence and remove the judgment, with a secret intention to break their word when the danger was over; they did not *return to God with their whole heart, but feignedly,* Jer. 3:10. All their professions, prayers, and promises, were extorted by the rack. It was plain that they did not mean as they said, for they did not adhere to it. They thawed in the sun, but froze in the shade. They did but *lie to God with their tongues, for their heart was not with him,* was not right with him, as appeared by the issue, for *they were not stedfast in his covenant.* They were not sincere in their reformation, for they were not constant; and, by thinking thus to impose upon a heart-searching God, they really put as great an affront upon him as by any of their reflections.

7. God hereupon, in pity to them, put a stop to the judgments which were threatened and in part executed (*v.* 38, 39): *But he, being full of compassion, forgave their iniquity.* One would think this counterfeit repentance should have filled up the measure of their iniquity. What could be more provoking than to *lie thus to the holy God,* than thus to *keep back part of the price,* the chief part? Acts 5:3. And *yet he, being full of compassion, forgave their iniquity* thus far, that he did not destroy them and cut them off from being a people, as he justly might have done, but spared their lives till they had reared another generation which should enter into the promised land. *Destroy it not, for a blessing is in it,* Isa. 65:8. *Many a time he turned his anger away* (for he is Lord of his anger) *and did not stir up all his wrath,* to deal with them as they deserved: and why did he not? Not because their ruin would have been any loss to him, but, (1.) Because he was *full of compassion* and, when he was going to destroy them, *his repentings were kindled together,* and he said, *How shall I give thee up, Ephraim? How shall I deliver thee, Israel?* Hos. 11:8. (2.) Because, though they did not rightly remember that he was their rock, he *remembered that they were but flesh.* He considered the corruption of their nature, which inclined them to evil, and was pleased to make that an excuse for his sparing them, though it was really no excuse for their sin. See Gen. 6:3. He considered the weakness and frailty of their nature, and what an easy thing it would be to crush them: *They are as a wind that passeth away and cometh not again.* They may soon be taken off, but, when they are gone, they are gone irrecoverably, and then what will become of the covenant with Abraham? They are flesh, they are wind; whence it were easy to argue they may justly, they may immediately, be cut off, and there would be no loss of them: but God argues, on the contrary, therefore he will not destroy them; for the true reason is, *He is full of compassion.*

Verses 40–72

The matter and scope of this paragraph are the same with the former, showing what great mercies God had bestowed upon Israel, how provoking they had been, what judgments he had brought upon them for their sins, and yet how, in judgment, he remembered mercy at last. Let not those that receive mercy from God be thereby emboldened to sin, for the mercies they receive will aggravate their sin and hasten the punishment of it; yet let not those that are under divine rebukes for sin be discouraged from repentance, for their punishments are means of repentance, and shall not prevent the mercy God has yet in store for them. Observe,

I. The sins of Israel in the wilderness again reflected on, because written for our admonition (*v.* 40, 41): *How often did they provoke him in the wilderness!* Note once, nor twice, but many a time; and the repetition of the provocation was a great aggravation of it, as well as the place, *v.* 17. God kept an account how often they provoked him, though they did not. Num. 14:22, *They have tempted me these ten times.* By provoking him they did not so much anger him as grieve him, for he looked upon them as his children *(Israel is my son, my first-born),* and the undutiful disrespectful behaviour of children does more grieve than anger the tender parents; they lay it to heart, and take it unkindly, Isa. 1:2. They grieved him because they put him under a necessity of afflicting them, which he did not willingly. After they had humbled themselves before him they *turned back and tempted God,* as before, and *limited the Holy One of Israel,* prescribing to him what proofs he should give of his power and presence with them and what methods he should take in leading them and providing for them. They limited him to their way and their time, as if he did not observe that they quarrelled with him. It is presumption for us to limit *the Holy One of Israel;* for, being *the Holy One,* he will do what is most for his own glory; and, being *the Holy One of Israel,* he will do what is most for their good; and we both impeach his wisdom and betray our own pride and folly if we go about to prescribe to him. That which occasioned their limiting God for the future was their forgetting his former favours (*v.* 42): *They remembered not his hand,* how strong it is and how it had been stretched out for them, nor *the day when he delivered them from the enemy,* Pharaoh, that great enemy who sought their ruin. There are some days made remarkable by signal deliverances, which ought never to be forgotten; for the remembrance of them would encourage us in our greatest straits.

II. The mercies of God to Israel, which they were unmindful of when they tempted God and limited him; and this catalogue of the works of wonder which God wrought for them begins higher, and is carried down further, than that before, *v.* 12, etc.

1. This begins with their deliverance out of Egypt, and the plagues with which God compelled the Egyptians to let them go: these were the *signs* God *wrought in Egypt* (*v.* 43), the *wonders* he wrought *in the field of Zoan,* that is, in the country of Zoan, as we say, *in Agro N.,* meaning in such a country.

(1.) Several of the plagues of Egypt are here specified, which speak aloud the power of God and his favour to Israel, as well as terror to his and their enemies. As, [1.] The turning of the waters into blood; they had made themselves drunk with the bloods of God's people, even the infants, and now God gave them blood to drink, *for they were worthy, v.* 44. [2.] The flies and frogs which infested them, mixtures of insects in swarms, in shoals, *which devoured them, which destroyed them, v.* 45. For God can make the weakest and most despicable animals instruments of his wrath when he pleases; what they want in strength may be made up in number. [3.] The plague of locusts, which devoured their increase, and that which they had laboured for, *v.* 46. They are called *God's great army,* Joel 2:25. [4.] The *hail,* which *destroyed* their trees, especially *their vines,* the weakest of trees (*v.* 47), and *their cattle,* especially *their flocks* of sheep, the weakest of their cattle, which were killed with *hot thunder-bolts* (*v.* 48), and the *frost,* or congealed rain (as the word signifies), was so violent that it destroyed even the *sycamore-trees.* [5.] The death of the first-born was the last and sorest of the plagues of Egypt, and that which perfected the deliverance of Israel; it was first in intention (Ex. 4:23), but last in execution; for, if gentler methods would have done the work, this would have been prevented: but it is here largely described, *v.* 49–51. *First,* The anger of God was the cause of it. Wrath had now come upon the Egyptians to the uttermost; Pharaoh's heart having been often hardened after less judgments had softened it, God now *stirred up all his wrath;* for he *cast upon them the fierceness of his anger,* anger in the highest degree, *wrath and indignation* the cause, *and trouble (tribulation and anguish,* Rom. 2:8, 9) the effect. This from on high he cast upon them and did not spare, and they could not *flee out of his hands,* Job 27:22. *He made a way,* or (as the word is) *he weighed a path, to his anger.* He did not cast it upon them uncertainly, but by weight. His anger was weighed with the greatest exactness in the balances of justice; for, in his greatest displeasure, he never did, nor ever will do, any wrong to any of his creatures: the path of his anger is always weighed. *Secondly,* The angels of God were the instruments employed in this execution: *He sent evil angels among them,* not evil in their own nature, but in respect to the errand upon which they were sent; they were destroying angels, or angels of punishment, which passed through all the land of Egypt, with orders, according to the weighed paths of God's anger, not to kill all, but the first-born only. Good angels become evil angels to sinners. Those that make the holy God their enemy must never expect the holy angels to be their friends. *Thirdly,* The execution itself was very severe: *He spared not their soul from death,* but suffered death to ride in triumph among them and *gave their life over to the pestilence,* which cut the thread of life off immediately; for *he smote all the first-born in Egypt* (*v.* 51), *the chief of their strength,* the hopes of their respective families; children are the parents' strength, and the first-born the *chief of their strength.* Thus, because Israel was precious in God's sight, he *gave men for them and people for their life,* Isa. 43:4.

(2.) By these plagues on the Egyptians God made a way for *his own people to go forth like sheep,* distinguishing between them and the Egyptians, *as the shepherd divides between the sheep and the goats,* having set his own mark on these sheep by the blood of the lamb sprinkled on their door-posts. *He made them go forth like sheep,* not knowing whither they went, and *guided them in the wilderness,* as a shepherd guides his flock, with all possible care and tenderness, *v.* 52. *He led them on safely,* though in dangerous paths, so that *they feared not,* that is, they needed not to fear; they were indeed frightened at the Red Sea (Ex. 14:10), but that was said to them, and done for them, which effectually silenced their fears. *But the sea overwhelmed their enemies* that ventured to pursue them into it, *v.* 63. It was a lane to them, but a grave to their persecutors.

2. It is carried down as far as their settlement in Canaan (*v.* 54): *He brought them to the border of his sanctuary,* to that land in the midst of which he set up his sanctuary, which was, as it were, the centre and metropolis, the crown and glory, of it. That is a happy land which is the border of God's sanctuary. It was the happiness of that land that there God was known, and there were his sanctuary and dwelling-place, Ps. 76:1, 2. The whole land in general, and Zion in particular, was *the mountain which his right hand had purchased,* which by his own power he had set apart for himself. See Ps. 44:3. He *made them to ride on the high places of the earth,* Isa. 58:14; Deu. 32:13. They found the Canaanites in the full and quiet possession of that land, but God *cast out the heathen before them,* not only took away their title to it, as the Lord of the whole earth, but himself executed the judgment given against them, and, as Lord of hosts, turned them out of it, and made his people *Israel tread upon their high places, dividing* each tribe *an inheritance by line,* and making them *to dwell* in the houses of those whom they had destroyed. God could have turned the uninhabited uncultivated wilderness (which perhaps was nearly of the same extent as Canaan) into fruitful soil, and have planted them there; but the land he designed for them was to be a type of heaven, and therefore must be *the glory of all lands;* it must likewise be fought for, for *the kingdom of heaven suffers violence.*

III. The sins of Israel after they were settled in Canaan, *v.* 56–58. The children were *like their fathers,* and brought their old corruptions into their new habitations. Though God had done so much for them, yet *they tempted and provoked the most high God* still. He gave them his testimonies, but they did not keep them; they began very promisingly, but they turned back, gave God good words, but dealt unfaithfully, and were *like a deceitful bow,* which seemed likely to send the arrow to the mark, but, when it is drawn, breaks, and drops the arrow at the archer's foot, or perhaps makes it recoil in his face. There was no hold of them, nor any confidence to be put in their promises or professions. They seemed sometimes devoted to God, but they presently *turned aside,* and *provoked him to anger with their high places and their graven images.* Idolatry was the sin that did most easily beset them, and which, though they often professed their repentance for, they as often relapsed into. It was spiritual adultery either to worship idols or to worship God by images, as if he had been an idol, and therefore by it they are said to *move him to jealousy,* Deu. 32:16, 21.

IV. The judgments God brought upon them for these sins. Their place in Canaan would no more secure them in a sinful way than their descent from Israel. *You only have I known of all the families of the earth, therefore I will punish you,* Amos 3:2. Idolatry is winked at among the Gentiles, but not in Israel, 1. God was displeased with them (*v.* 59): *When God heard this,* when he heard the cry of their iniquity, which came up before him, *he was wroth,* he took it very heinously, as well he might, and he greatly abhorred Israel, whom he had greatly loved and delighted in. Those that had been the people of his choice became the generation of his wrath. Presumptuous sins, idolatries especially, render even Israelites odious to God's holiness and obnoxious to his justice. 2. He deserted his tabernacle among them, and removed the defence which was upon that glory, *v.* 60. God never leaves us till we leave him, never withdraws till we have driven him from us. His name is *Jealous,* and he is a jealous God; and therefore no marvel if a people whom he had betrothed to himself be loathed and rejected, and he refuse to cohabit with them any longer, when they have embraced the bosom of a stranger. The *tabernacle at Shiloh* was *the tent God had placed among men,* in which God would *in very deed dwell with men upon the earth;* but, when his people treacherously forsook it, he justly forsook it, and then all its glory departed. Israel has small joy of the tabernacle without the presence of God in it. 3. He gave up all into the hands of the enemy. Those whom God forsakes become an easy prey to the destroyer. The Philistines are sworn enemies to the Israel of God, and no less so to the God of Israel, and yet God will make use of them to be a scourge to his people. (1.) God permits them to take the ark prisoner, and carry it off as a trophy of their victory, to show that he had not only forsaken the tabernacle, but even the ark itself, which shall now be no longer a token of his presence (*v.* 61): *He delivered his strength into captivity,* as if it had been weakened and overcome, *and his glory* fell under the disgrace of being abandoned *into the enemy's hand.* We have the story 1 Sa. 4:11. When the ark has become as a stranger among Israelites, no marvel if it soon be made a prisoner among Philistines. (2.) He suffers the armies of Israel to be routed by the Philistines (*v.* 62, 63): *He gave his people over unto the sword,* to the sword of his own justice and of the enemy's rage, for he *was wroth with his inheritance;* and that wrath of his was the *fire which consumed their young men,* in the prime of their time, by the sword or sickness, and made such a devastation of them that *their maidens were not praised,* that is, *were not given in marriage* (which is honourable in all), because there were no young men for them to be given to, and because the distresses and calamities of Israel were so many and great that the joys of marriage-solemnities were judged unseasonable, and it was said, *Blessed is the womb that beareth not.* General destructions produce a scarcity of men. Isa. 13:12, *I will make a man more precious than fine gold,* so that *seven women shall take hold of one man,* Isa. 4:1; 3:25. Yet this was not the worst: (3.) Even *their priests,* who attended the ark, *fell by the sword,* Hophni and Phinehas. Justly they fell, for they made themselves vile, and were sinners before the Lord exceedingly; and their priesthood was so far from being their protection that it aggravated their sin and hastened their fall. Justly did they fall by the sword, because they exposed themselves in the field of battle, without call or warrant. We throw ourselves out of God's protection when we go out of our place and out of the way of our duty. When the priests fell *their widows made no lamentation, v.* 64. All the ceremonies of mourning were lost and buried in substantial grief; the widow of Phinehas, instead of lamenting her husband's death, died herself, when she had called her son *Ichabod,* 1 Sa. 4:19, etc.

V. God's return, in mercy, to them, and his gracious appearances for them after this. We read not of their repentance and return to God, but God was *grieved for the miseries of Israel* (Jdg. 10:16) and concerned for his own honour, *fearing the wrath of the enemy, lest they should behave themselves strangely,* Deu. 32:27. And therefore *then the Lord awaked as one out of sleep* (*v.* 65), *and like a mighty man that shouteth by reason of wine,* not only like one that is raised out of sleep and recovers himself from the slumber which by drinking he was overcome with, who then regards that which before he seemed wholly to neglect, but like one that is refreshed with sleep, and whose heart is made glad by the sober and moderate use of wine, and is therefore the more lively and vigorous, and fit for business. When God had delivered the ark of his strength into captivity, as one jealous of his honour, he soon put forth the arm of his strength to rescue it, stirred up his strength to do great things for his people.

1. He plagued the Philistines who held the ark in captivity, *v.* 66. He smote them with emerods *in the hinder parts,* wounded them behind, as if they were fleeing from him, even when they thought themselves more than conquerors. He put them to reproach, and they themselves helped to make it a perpetual reproach by the golden images of their emerods, which they returned with the ark for a trespass-offering (1 Sa. 6:5), to remain *in perpetuam rei memoriam — as a perpetual memorial.* Note, Sooner or later God will glorify himself by putting disgrace upon his enemies, even when they are most elevated with their successes.

2. He provided a new settlement for his ark after it had been some months in captivity and some years in obscurity. He did indeed *refuse the tabernacle of Joseph;* he never sent it back to Shiloh, in the tribe of Ephraim, *v.* 67. The ruins of that place were standing monuments of divine justice. *God, see what I did to Shiloh,* Jer. 7:12. But he did not wholly take away the glory from Israel; the moving of the ark is not the removing of it. Shiloh has lost it, but Israel has not. God will have a church in the world, and a kingdom among men, though this or that place may have its candlestick removed; nay, the rejection of Shiloh is the election of Zion, as, long after, the fall of the Jews was the riches of the Gentiles, Rom. 11:12. When God *chose not the tribe of Ephraim,* of which tribe Joshua was, he *chose the tribe of Judah* (*v.* 68), because of that tribe Jesus was to be, who is greater than Joshua. Kirjath-jearim, the place to which the ark was brought after its rescue out of the hands of the Philistines, was in the tribe of Judah. There it took possession of that tribe; but thence it was removed to Zion, *the Mount Zion which he loved* (*v.* 68), which was *beautiful for situation, the joy of the whole earth;* there it was that he *built his sanctuary like high palaces* and *like the earth, v.* 69. David indeed erected only a tent for the ark, but a temple was then designed and prepared for, and finished by his son; and that was, (1.) A very stately place. It was built like the palaces of princes, and the great men of the earth, nay, it excelled them all in splendour and magnificence. Solomon built it, and yet here it is said *God built its,* for his father had taught him, perhaps with reference to this undertaking, that *except the Lord build the house those labour in vain* that build it, Ps. 127:1, which is a psalm for Solomon. (2.) A very stable place, like the earth, though not to continue as long as the earth, yet while it was to continue it was as firm as the earth, which God *upholds by the word of his power,* and it was not finally destroyed till the gospel temple was erected, which is to continue *as long as the sun and moon endure* (Ps. 89:36, 37) and against which the *gates of hell shall not prevail.*

3. He set a good government over them, a monarchy, and a monarch after his own heart: *He chose David his servant* out of all the thousands of Israel, and put the sceptre into his hand, out of whose loins Christ was to come, and who was to be a type of him, *v.* 70. Concerning David observe here, (1.) The meanness of his beginning. His extraction indeed was great, for he descended from the prince of the tribe of Judah, but his education was poor. He was bred not a scholar, not a soldier, but a shepherd. He was *taken from the sheep-folds,* as Moses was; for God delights to put honour upon the humble and diligent, to raise the poor out of the dust and to set them among

princes; and sometimes he finds those most fit for public action that have spent the beginning of their time in solitude and contemplation. The Son of David was upbraided with the obscurity of his original: *Is not this the carpenter?* David was taken, he does not say from leading the rams, but *from following the ewes*, especially those *great with young*, which intimated that of all the good properties of a shepherd he was most remarkable for his tenderness and compassion to those of his flock that most needed his care. This temper of mind fitted him for government, and made him a type of Christ, who, when he feeds his flock like a shepherd, does with a particular care *gently lead those that are with young*, Isa. 40:11. (2.) The greatness of his advancement. God preferred him to *feed Jacob his people*, v. 71. It was a great honour that God put upon him, in advancing him to be a king, especially to be king over Jacob and Israel, God's peculiar people, near and dear to him; but withal it was a great trust reposed in him when he was charged with the government of those that were God's own inheritance. God advanced him to the throne that he might feed them, not that he might feed himself, that he might do good, not that he might make his family great. It is the charge given to all the undershepherds, both magistrates and ministers, that they *feed the flock of God*. (3.) The happiness of his management. David, having so great a trust put into his hands, obtained mercy of the Lord to be found both skilful and faithful in the discharge of it (v. 72): *So he fed them;* he ruled them and taught them, guided and protected them, [1.] Very honestly; he did it *according to the integrity of his heart*, aiming at nothing but the glory of God and the good of the people committed to his charge; the principles of his religion were the maxims of his government, which he administered, not with carnal policy, but with *godly sincerity, by the grace of God*. In every thing he did he meant well and had no by-end in view. [2.] Very discreetly; he did it *by the skilfulness of his hands*. He was not only very sincere in what he designed, but very prudent in what he did, and chose out the most proper means in pursuit of his end, for his God did instruct him to discretion. Happy the people that are under such a government! With good reason does the psalmist make this the finishing crowning instance of God's favour to Israel, for David was a type of Christ the great and good Shepherd, who was humbled first and then exalted, and of whom it was foretold that he should be filled with the *spirit of wisdom and understanding* and should *judge and reprove with equity*, Isa. 11:3, 4. On the integrity of his heart and the skilfulness of his hands all his subjects may entirely rely, and *of the increase of his government* and people *there shall be no end*.

PSALM 79

This psalm, if penned with any particular event in view, is with most probability made to refer to the destruction of Jerusalem and the temple, and the woeful havoc made of the Jewish nation by the Chaldeans under Nebuchadnezzar. It is set to the same tune, as I may say, with the Lamentations of Jeremiah, and that weeping prophet borrows two verses out of it (v. 6, 7) and makes use of them in his prayer, Jer. 10:25. Some think it was penned long before by the spirit of prophecy, prepared for the use of the church in that cloudy and dark day. Others think that it was penned then by the spirit of prayer, either by a prophet named Asaph or by some other prophet for the sons of Asaph. Whatever the particular occasion was, we have here, I. A representation of the very deplorable condition that the people of God were in at this time (v. 1–5). II. A petition to God for succour and relief, that their enemies might be reckoned with (v. 6, 7, 10, 12), that their sins might be pardoned (v. 8, 9), and that they might be delivered (v. 11). III. A plea taken from the readiness of his people to praise him (v. 13). In times of the church's peace and prosperity this psalm may, in the singing of it, give us occasion to bless God that we are not thus trampled on and insulted. But it is especially seasonable in a day of treading down and perplexity, for the exciting of our desires towards God and the encouragement of our faith in him as the church's patron.

A psalm of Asaph.

Verses 1–5

We have here a sad complaint exhibited in the court of heaven. The world is full of complaints, and so is the church too, for it suffers, not only with it, but from it, as *a lily among thorns*. God is complained to; whither should children go with their grievances, but to their father, to such a father as is able and willing to help? The heathen are complained of, who, being themselves aliens from the commonwealth of Israel, were sworn enemies to it. Though they knew not God, nor owned him, yet, God having them

in chain, the church very fitly appeals to him against them; for he is King of nations, to overrule them, to judge among the heathen, and King of saints, to favour and protect them.

I. They complain here of the anger of their enemies and the outrageous fury of the oppressor, exerted,

1. Against places, v. 1. They did all the mischief they could, (1.) To the holy land; they invaded that, and made inroads into it: *"The heathen have come into thy inheritance,* to plunder that, and lay it waste." Canaan was dearer to the pious Israelites as it was God's inheritance than as it was their own, as it was the land in which God was known and his name was great rather than as it was the land in which they were bred and born and which they and their ancestors had been long in possession of. note, Injuries done to religion should grieve us more than even those done to common right, nay, to our own right. We should better bear to see our own inheritance wasted than God's inheritance. This psalmist had mentioned it in the foregoing psalm as an instance of God's great favour to Israel that he had *cast out the heathen before them*, Ps. 78:55. But see what a change sin made; now the heathen are suffered to pour in upon them. (2.) To the holy city: *They have laid Jerusalem on heaps*, heaps of rubbish, such heaps as are raised over graves, so some. The inhabitants were buried in the ruins of their own houses, and their dwelling places became their sepulchres, their long homes. (3.) To the holy house. That sanctuary which God had built like high palaces, and which was thought to be established as the earth, was now laid level with the ground: *They holy temple have they defiled*, by entering into it and laying it waste. God's own people had defiled it by their sins, and therefore God suffered their enemies to defile it by their insolence.

2. Against persons, against the bodies of God's people; and further their malice could not reach. (1.) They were prodigal of their blood, and killed them without mercy; their eye did not spare, nor did they give any quarter (v. 3): *Their blood have they shed like water*, wherever they met with them, *round about Jerusalem*, in all the avenues to the city; whoever *went out or came in* was *waited for of the sword*. Abundance of human blood was shed, so that the channels of water ran with blood. And they shed it with no more reluctancy or regret than if they had spilt so much water, little thinking that every drop of it will be reckoned for in the day when *God shall make inquisition for blood*. (2.) They were abusive to their dead bodies. When they had killed them they would let none bury them. Nay, those that were buried, even the *dead bodies of God's servants, the flesh of his saints*, whose names and memories they had a particular spite at, they dug up again, and *gave them to be meat to the fowls of the heaven and to the beasts of the earth;* or, at least, they left those so exposed whom they slew; they hung them in chains, which was in a particular manner grievous to the Jews to see, because God had given them an express law against this, as a barbarous thing, Deu. 21:23. This inhuman usage of Christ's witnesses is foretold (Rev. 11:9), and thus even the dead bodies were witnesses against their persecutors. This is mentioned (says Austin, *De Civitate Dei, lib.* 1 *cap.* 12) not as an instance of the misery of the persecuted (for the bodies of the saints shall rise in glory, however they became meat to the birds and the fowls), but of the malice of the persecutors.

3. Against their names (v. 4): *"We that survive have become a reproach to our neighbours;* they all study to abuse us and load us with contempt, and represent us as ridiculous, or odious, or both, upbraiding us with our sins and with our sufferings, or giving the lie to our relation to God and expectations from him; so that we have become a *scorn and derision to those that are round about us."* If God's professing people degenerate from what themselves and their fathers were, they must expect to be told of it; and it is well if a just reproach will help to bring us to a true repentance. But it has been the lot of the gospel-Israel to be made unjustly a reproach and derision; the apostles themselves were *counted as the offscouring of all things*.

II. They wonder more at God's anger, v. 5. This they discern in the anger of their neighbours, and this they complain most of: *How long, Lord, wilt thou be angry?* Shall it be *for ever?* This intimates that they desired no more than that God would be reconciled to them, that his anger might be turned away, and then the remainder of men's

wrath would be restrained. Note, Those who desire God's favour as better than life cannot but dread and deprecate his wrath as worse than death.

Verses 6–13

The petitions here put up to God are very suitable to the present distresses of the church, and they have pleas to enforce them, interwoven with them, taken mostly from God's honour.

I. They pray that God would so turn away his anger from them as to turn it upon those that persecuted and abused them (v. 6): *"Pour out thy wrath*, the full vials of it, *upon the heathen;* let them wring out the dregs of it, and drink them." This prayer is in effect a prophecy, in which the *wrath of God is revealed from heaven against all ungodliness and unrighteousness of men*. Observe here, 1. The character of those he prays against; they are such as have not known God, nor called upon his name. The reason why men do not call upon God is because they do not know him, how able and willing he is to help them. Those that persist in ignorance of God, and neglect of prayer, are the ungodly, who live *without God in the world*. There are kingdoms that know not God and obey not the gospel, but neither their multitude nor their force united will secure them from his just judgments. 2. Their crime: *They have devoured Jacob, v.* 7. That is crime enough in the account of him who reckons that those who touch his people touch the apple of his eye. They have not only disturbed, but devoured, Jacob, not only encroached upon his dwelling place, the land of Canaan, but laid it waste by plundering and depopulating it. (3.) Their condemnation: *"Pour out thy wrath* upon them; do not only restrain them from doing further mischief, but reckon with them for the mischief they have done."

II. They pray for the pardon of sin, which they own to be the procuring cause of all their calamities. How unrighteous soever men were, God was righteous in permitting them to do what they did. They pray, 1. That God would not *remember against them their former iniquities* (v. 8), either their own former iniquities, that now, when they were old, they might not be made to possess the iniquities of their youth, or the former iniquities of their people, the sins of their ancestors. In the captivity of Babylon former iniquities were brought to account; but God promises not again to do so (Jer. 31:29, 30), and so they pray, "Remember not against us our first sins," which some make to look as far back as the golden calf, because God said, *In the day when I visit I will visit for this sin* of theirs *upon them*, Ex. 32:34. If the children by repentance and reformation cut off the entail of the parents' sin, they may in faith pray that God will not *remember them against them*. When God pardons sin he blots it out and remembers it no more. 2. That he would purge away the sins they had been lately guilty of, by the guilt of which their minds and consciences had been defiled: *Deliver us, and purge away our sins, v.* 9. Then deliverances from trouble are granted in love, and are mercies indeed, when they are grounded upon the pardon of sin and flow from that; we should therefore be more earnest with God in prayer for the removal of our sins than for the removal of our afflictions, and the pardon of them is the foundation and sweetness of our deliverances.

III. They pray that God would work deliverance for them, and bring their troubles to a good end and that speedily: *Let thy tender mercies speedily prevent us, v.* 8. They had no hopes but from God's mercies, his tender mercies; their case was so deplorable that they looked upon themselves as the proper objects of divine compassion, and so near to desperate that, unless divine mercy did speedily interpose to prevent their ruin, they were undone. This whets their importunity: *"Lord, help us; Lord, deliver us;* help us under our troubles, that we may bear them well; help us out of our troubles, that the spirit may not fail. Deliver us from sin, from sinking." Three things they plead: — 1. The great distress they were reduced to: *"We are brought very low*, and, being low, shall be lost if thou help us not." The lower we are brought the more need we have of help from heaven and the more will divine power be magnified in raising us up. 2. Their dependence upon him: "Thou art the *God of our salvation*, who alone canst help. *Salvation belongs to the Lord*, from whom we expect help; for *in the Lord alone is the salvation of his people."* Those who make God the God of their salvation shall find him so. 3. The interest of his own honour in their case. They plead no merit of theirs; they pretend to none; but, *"Help us for the glory of thy name;* pardon us for thy name's sake." The best encouragements in prayer are those that are taken from God only, and those things whereby he has made himself known. Two things are insinuated in this plea: — (1.) That God's name and honour would be greatly injured if he did not deliver them; for those that derided them blasphemed God, as if he were weak and could not help them, or had withdrawn and would not; therefore they plead (*v.* 10), *"Wherefore should the heathen say, Where is their God?* He has forsaken them, and forgotten them; and this they get by worshipping a God whom they cannot see." (*Nil praeter nubes et coeli numen adorant.* Juv. — *They adore no other divinity than the clouds and the sky.*) That which was their praise (that they served a God that is every where) was now turned to their reproach and his too, as if they served a God that is nowhere. "Lord," say they, "Make it to appear that thou art by making it to appear that thou art with us and for us, that when we are asked, *Where is your God?* we may be able to say, He is nigh unto us in all that which we call upon him for, and you see he is so by what he does for us." (2.) That God's name and honour would be greatly advanced if he did deliver them; his mercy would be glorified in delivering those that were so miserable and helpless. By making bare his everlasting arm on their behalf he would make unto himself an everlasting name; and their deliverance would be a type and figure of the great salvation, which in the fulness of time Messiah the Prince would work out, to the glory of God's name.

IV. They pray that God would avenge them on their adversaries, 1. For their cruelty and barbarity (*v.* 10): "Let the avenging of our blood" (according to the ancient law, Gen. 9:6) "be known among the heathen; let them be made sensible that what judgments are brought upon them are punishments of the wrong they have done to us; let this be in our sight, and by this means *let God be known among the heathen* as *the God to whom vengeance belongs* (Ps. 94:1) and the God that espouses his people's cause." Those that have intoxicated themselves with the blood of the saints shall have *blood given them to drink,* for they are worthy. 2. For their insolence and scorn (*v.* 12): *"Render to them their reproach.* The indignities which by word and deed they have done to the people of God himself and his name let them be repaid to them with interest." The reproach wherewith men have reproached us only we must leave it to God whether he will render to them or no, and must pray that he would forgive them; but the reproach wherewith they have blasphemed God himself we may in faith pray that God would render seven-fold into their bosoms, so as to strike at their hearts, to humble them, and bring them to repentance. This prayer is a prophecy, of the same import with that of Enoch, that God will convince sinners of all their hard speeches which they have spoken against him (Jude 15) and will return them into their own bosoms by everlasting terrors at the remembrance of them.

V. They pray that God would find out a way for the rescue of his poor prisoners, especially the condemned prisoners, *v.* 11. The case of their brethren who had fallen into the hands of the enemy was very sad; they were kept close prisoners, and, because they durst not be heard to bemoan themselves, they vented their griefs in deep and silent sighs. All their breathing was sighing, and so was their praying. They were appointed to die, as sheep for the slaughter, and had received the sentence of death within themselves. This deplorable case the psalmist recommends, 1. To the divine pity: *"Let their sighs come up before thee,* and be thou pleased to take cognizance of their moans." 2. To the divine power: *"According to the greatness of thy arm,* which no creature can contest with, *preserve thou those that are appointed to die* from the death to which they are appointed." Man's extremity is God's opportunity to appear for his people. See 2 Co. 1:8–10.

Lastly, They promise the returns of praise for the answers of prayer (*v.* 13): *So we will give thee thanks for ever.* Observe, 1. How they please themselves with their relation to God. "Though we are oppressed and brought low, yet we are the sheep of thy pasture, not disowned and cast off by thee for all this: *We are thine; save us."* 2. How they promise themselves an opportunity of praising God for their deliverance, which they *therefore* desired, and would bid welcome, because it would furnish them with matter for thanksgiving and put their hearts in tune for that excellent work, the work of heaven. 3. How they oblige themselves not only to give God thanks at present, but to *show forth his praise unto all generations,* that is, to do all they could both to perpetuate the remembrance of God's favours to them and to engage their posterity to keep up the work of praise. 4. How they plead this with God: "Lord, appear for us against our enemies; for, if they get the better, they will *blaspheme thee* (*v.* 12); but, if we be delivered, we will praise thee. Lord, we are that people of thine which thou hast *formed for thyself, to show forth thy praise;* if we be cut off, whence shall that rent, that tribute, be raised?" Note, Those lives that are entirely devoted to God's praise are assuredly taken under his protection.

PSALM 80

This psalm is much to the same purport with the foregoing. Some think it was penned upon occasion of the desolation and captivity of the ten tribes, as the foregoing psalm of the two. But many were the distresses of the Israel of God, many perhaps which are not recorded in the sacred history some whereof might give occasion for the drawing up of this psalm, which is proper to be sung in the day of Jacob's trouble, and if, in singing it, we express a true love to the church and a hearty concern for its interest, with a firm confidence in God's power to help it out of its greatest distresses, we make melody with our hearts to the Lord. The psalmist here, I. Begs for the tokens of God's presence with them and favour to them (*v.* 1–3). II. He complains of the present rebukes they were under (*v.* 4–7). III. He illustrates the present desolations of the church, by the comparison of a vine and a vineyard, which had flourished, but was now destroyed (*v.* 8–16). IV. He concludes with prayer to God for the preparing of mercy for them and the preparing of them for mercy (*v.* 17–19). This, as many psalms before and after, relates to the public interests of God's Israel, which ought to lie nearer to our hearts than any secular interest of our own.

To the chief musician upon Shoshannim, Eduth.
A psalm of Asaph.

Verses 1–7

The psalmist here, in the name of the church, applies to God by prayer, with reference to the present afflicted state of Israel.

I. He entreats God's favour for them (*v.* 1, 2); that is all in all to the sanctuary when it is desolate, and is to be sought in the first place. Observe, 1. How he eyes God in his address as the Shepherd of Israel, whom he had called the *sheep of his pasture* (Ps. 79:13), under whose guidance and care Israel was, as the sheep are under the care and conduct of the shepherd. Christ is the great and good Shepherd, to whom we may in faith commit the custody of his sheep that were given to him. He *leads Joseph like a flock,* to the best pastures, and out of the way of danger; if Joseph follow him not as obsequiously as the sheep do the shepherd, it is his own fault. He *dwells between the cherubim,* where he is ready to receive petitions and to give directions. The mercy-seat was between the cherubim; and it is very comfortable in prayer to look up to God as sitting on a throne of grace, and that it is so to us is owning to the great propitiation, for the mercy-seat was the propitiatory. 2. What he expects and desires from God, that he would give ear to the cry of their miseries and of their prayers, that he would shine forth both in his own glory and in favour and kindness to his people, that he would show himself and smile on them, that he would *sir up his strength,* that he would excite it and exert it. It had seemed to slumber: "Lord, awaken it." His cause met with great opposition and the enemies threatened to overpower it: "Lord, put forth thy strength so much the more, and come for salvation to us; be to thy people a powerful help and a present help; Lord, do this *before Ephraim, Benjamin, and Manasseh,"* that is, "In the sight of all the tribes of Israel; let them see it to their satisfaction." Perhaps these three tribes are named because they were the tribes which formed that squadron of the camp of Israel that in their march through the wilderness followed next after the tabernacle; so that before them the ark of God's strength rose to scatter their enemies.

II. He complains of God's displeasure against them. God was angry, and he dreads that more than any thing, *v.* 4. 1. It was great anger. He apprehended that God was *angry against the prayer of his people,* not only that he was angry notwithstanding their prayers, by which they hoped to turn away his wrath from them, but that he was angry with their prayers, though they were his own people that prayed. That God should be angry at the sins of his people and at the prayers of his enemies is not strange; but that he should be angry at the prayers of his people is strange indeed. He not only delayed to answer them (that he often does in love), but he was displeased at them. If he be really angry at the prayers of his people, we may be sure it is because they ask amiss, Jam. 4:3. They pray, but they do not wrestle in prayer; their ends are not right, or there is some secret sin harboured and indulged in them; they do not lift up pure hands, or they lift them up with wrath and doubting. But perhaps it is only in their own apprehension; he seems angry with their prayers when really he is not; for thus he will try their patience and perseverance in prayer, as Christ tried the woman of Canaan when he said, *It is not meet to take the children's bread and cast it to dogs.* 2. It was anger that had continued a great while: *"How long wilt thou be angry?* We have still continued praying and yet are still under thy frowns." Now the tokens of God's displeasure which they had been long under were both their sorrow and shame. (1.) Their sorrow (*v.* 5): *Thou feedest them with the bread of tears;* they eat their meat from day to day in tears; this is the vinegar in which they *dipped their morsel,* Ps. 42:3. They had tears given them to drink, not now and then a taste of that bitter cup, but in great measure. Note, There are many that spend their time in sorrow who yet shall spend their eternity in joy. (2.) It was their shame, *v.* 6. God, by frowning upon them, made them a strife unto their neighbours; each strove which should expose them most, and such a cheap and easy prey were they made to them that all the strife was who should have the stripping and plundering of them. Their enemies laughed among themselves to see the frights they were in, the straits they were reduced to, and the disappointments they met with. When God is displeased with his people we must expect to see them in tears and their enemies in triumph.

III. He prays earnestly for converting grace in order to their acceptance with God, and their salvation: *Turn us again, O God! v.* 3. *Turn us again, O God of hosts!* (*v.* 7) and then *cause thy face to shine and we shall be saved.* It is the burden of the song, for we have it again, *v.* 19. They are conscious to themselves that they have gone astray from God and their duty, and have turned aside into sinful ways, and that it was this that provoked God to hide his face from them and to give them up into the hand of their enemies; and therefore they desire to begin their work at the right end: "Lord, turn us to thee in a way of repentance and reformation, and then, no doubt, thou wilt return to us in a way of mercy and deliverance." Observe, 1. No salvation but from God's favour: *"Cause thy face to shine,* let us have thy love and the light of thy countenance, and then we shall be saved." 2. No obtaining favour with God unless we be converted to him. We must turn again to God from the world and the flesh, and then he will cause his face to shine upon us. 3. No conversion to God but by his own grace; we must frame our doings to turn to him (Hos. 5:4) and then pray earnestly for his grace, *Turn thou me, and I shall be turned,* pleading that gracious promise (Prov. 1:23), *Burn you at my reproof; behold, I will pour out my Spirit unto you.* The prayer here is for a national conversion; in this method we must pray for national mercies, that what is amiss may be amended, and then our grievances would be soon redressed. National holiness would secure national happiness.

Verses 8–19

The psalmist is here presenting his suit for the Israel of God, and pressing it home at the throne of grace, pleading with God for mercy and grace for them. The church is here represented as a vine (*v.* 8, 14) and a vineyard, *v.* 15. The root of this vine is Christ, Rom. 11:18. The branches are believers, Jn. 15:5. The church is like a vine, weak and needing support, unsightly and having an unpromising outside, but spreading and fruitful, and its fruit most excellent. The church is a choice and noble vine; we have reason to acknowledge the goodness of God that he has planted such a vine in the wilderness of this world, and preserved it to this day. Now observe here,

I. How the vine of the Old-Testament church was planted at first. It was *brought out of Egypt* with a high hand; *the heathen were cast out* of Canaan to make room for it, seven nations to make room for that one. *Thou didst sweep before it* (so some read *v.* 9), to make clear work; the nations were swept away as dirt with the besom of destruction. God, having made room for it, and planted it, cause it to take deep root by a happy establishment of their government both in church and state, which was so firm that, though their neighbours about them often attempted it, they could not prevail to pluck it up.

II. How it spread and flourished. 1. The land of Canaan itself was fully peopled. At first they were not so numerous as to replenish it, Ex. 23:29. But in Solomon's time *Judah and Israel were many as the sand of the sea;* the land was filled with them, and yet such a fruitful land that it was not over-stocked, *v.* 10. The hills of Canaan were covered with their shadow, and the branches, though they extended themselves far, like those of the vine, yet were not weak like them, but as strong as those of the goodly cedars. Israel not only had abundance of men, but those mighty men of valour. 2. They extended their conquests and dominion to the neighbouring countries (*v.* 11): *She sent out her boughs to the sea,* the great sea westward, and *her branches to the river,* to the river of Egypt southward, the river of Damascus northward, or rather the river Euphrates eastward, Gen. 15:18. Nebuchadnezzar's greatness is represented by a flourishing tree, Dan. 4:20, 21. But it is observable here concerning this vine that it is praised for its *shadow,* its *boughs,* and its *branches,* but not a word of its fruit, for *Israel was an empty vine,* Hos. 10:1. God came looking for grapes, but, behold, wild grapes, Isa. 5:2. And, if a vine do not bring forth fruit, no tree so useless, so worthless, Eze. 15:2, 6.

III. How it was wasted and ruined: "Lord, thou hast done great things for this vine, and why shall it be all undone again? If it were a plant not of God's planting, it were not strange to see it rooted up; but will God desert and abandon that which he himself gave being to?" *v.* 12. *Why hast thou then broken down her hedges?* There was a good reason for this change in God's way towards them. This noble vine had become *the degenerate plant of a strange vine* (Jer. 2:21), to the reproach of its great owner, and then no marvel if he *took away its hedge* (Isa. 5:5); yet God's former favours to this vine are urged as pleas in prayer to God, and improved as encouragements to faith, that, notwithstanding all this, God would not wholly cast them off. Observe, 1. The malice and enmity of the Gentile nations against Israel. As soon as ever God *broke down their hedges* and left them exposed troops of enemies presently broke in upon them, that waited for an opportunity to destroy them. Those that passed by the way plucked at them; the *board out of the wood* and the *wild beast of the field* were ready to ravage it, *v.* 13. But, 2. See also the restraint which these cruel enemies were under; for till God had *broken down their hedges* they could not pluck a leaf of this vine. The devil could not hurt Job so long as God continued the *hedge round about him,* Job 1:10. See how much it is the interest of any people to keep themselves in the favour of God and then they need not fear any wild beast of the field, Job 5:23. If we provoke God to withdraw, *our defence has departed from us,* and we are undone. The deplorable state of Israel is described (*v.* 16): *It is burnt with fire; it is cut down;* the people are treated like thorns and briers, that are nigh unto cursing and whose end is to be burned, and no longer like vines that are protected and cherished. They perish not through the rage of the wild beast and the boar, but *at the rebuke of thy countenance;* that was it which they dreaded and to which they attributed all their calamities. It is well or ill with us according as we are under God's smiles or frowns.

IV. What their requests were to God hereupon. 1. That God would help the vine (*v.* 14, 15), that he would graciously take cognizance of its case and do for it as he thought fit: *"Return, we beseech thee, O Lord of hosts!* for thou hast seemed to go away from us. *Look down from heaven,* to which thou hast retired, — from heaven, that place of prospect, whence thou seest all the wrongs that are done us, that place of power, whence thou canst send effectual relief, — from heaven, where thou hast prepared thy throne of judgment, to which we appeal, and where thou hast prepared a better country for those that are Israelites indeed, — thence give a gracious look, thence make a gracious visit, to this vine. Take our woeful condition into thy compassionate consideration, and for the particular fruits of thy pity we refer ourselves to thee. Only behold the vineyard, or rather the root, which *thy right hand hath planted,* and which therefore we hope thy right hand will protect, that *branch which thou madest strong for thyself,* to show forth thy praise (Isa. 43:21), that with the fruit of it thou mightest be honoured. Lord, it is formed by thyself and for thyself, and therefore it may with a humble confidence be committed to thyself and to thy own care." *As for God, his work is perfect.* What we read the *branch* in the Hebrew is the *son (Ben),* whom in thy counsel thou hast made strong for thyself. That branch was to come out of the stock of Israel (*my servant the branch,* Zec. 3:8), and therefore, till he should come, Israel in general, and the house of David in particular, must be preserved, and upheld, and kept in being. *He is the true vine,* Jn. 15:1; Isa. 11:1. *Destroy it not for that blessing is in it,* Isa. 65:8. 2. That he would help the vine-dresser (*v.* 17, 18): *"Let thy hand be upon the man of thy right hand,"* that king (whoever it was) of the house of David that was now to go in and out before them; "let they hand be upon him, not only to protect and cover him, but to own him, and strengthen him, and give him success." We have this phrase, Ezra 7:28, *And I was strengthened as the hand of the Lord my God was upon me.* Their king is called the *man of God's right hand* as he was the representative of their state, which was dear to God, as his Benjamin, the *son of his right hand,* as he was president in their affairs and an instrument in God's right hand of much good to them, defending them from themselves and from their enemies and directing them in the right way, and as he was under-shepherd under him who was the great shepherd of Israel. Princes, who have power, must remember that they are *sons of men,* of *Adam* (so the word is), that, if they are strong, it is God that has made them strong, and he has made them so for himself, for they are his ministers to serve the interests of his kingdom among men, and, if they do this in sincerity, *his hand shall be upon them;* and we should pray in faith that it may be so, adding this promise, that, if God will adhere to our governors, we will adhere to him: *So will not we go back from thee;* we will never desert a cause which we see that God espouses and is the patron of. Let God be our leader and we will follow him. Adding also this prayer, *"Quicken us,* put life into us, revive our dying interests, revive our drooping spirits, and then *we will call upon thy name.* We will continue to do so upon all occasions, having found it not in vain to do so." We cannot call upon God's name in a right manner unless he quicken us; but it is he that puts life into our souls, that puts liveliness into our prayers. But many interpreters, both Jewish and Christian, apply this to the Messiah, the Son of David, the protector and Saviour of the church and the keeper of the vineyard. (1.) He is the man of God's right hand, to whom he has *sworn by his right hand* (so the Chaldee), whom he has exalted to his right hand, and who is indeed his right hand, the arm of the Lord, for all power is given to him. (2.) He is that son of man whom he *made strong for himself,* for the glorifying of his name and the advancing of the interests of his kingdom among men. (3.) God's hand is upon him throughout his whole undertaking, to bear him out and carry him on, to protect and animate him, that the *good pleasure of the Lord might prosper in his hand.* (4.) The stability and constancy of believers are entirely owing to the grace and strength which are laid up for us in Jesus Christ, Ps. 68:28. In him is our strength found, by which we are enabled to persevere to the end. Let thy hand be upon him; on him let our help be laid who is mighty; let him be made able to save to the uttermost and that will be our security; *so will not we go back from thee.*

Lastly, The psalm concludes with the same petition that had been put up twice before, and yet it is no vain repetition (*v.* 19): *Turn us again.* The title given to God rises, *v.* 3, *O God! v.* 7, *O God of hosts! v.* 19, *O Lord (Jehovah) God of hosts!* When we come to God for his grace, his good-will towards us and his good work in us, we should pray earnestly, continue instant in prayer, and pray more earnestly.

PSALM 81

This psalm was penned, as is supposed, not upon occasion of any particular providence, but for the solemnity of a particular ordinance, either that of the new-moon in general or that of the feast of trumpets on the new moon of the seventh month, Lev. 23:24; Num. 29:1. When David, by the Spirit, introduced the singing of psalms into the temple-service this psalm was intended for that day, to excite and assist the proper devotions of it. All the psalms are profitable; but, if one psalm be more suitable than another to the day and observances of it, we should choose that. The two great intentions of our religious assemblies, and which we ought to have in our eye in our attendance on them, are answered in this psalm, which are, to give glory to God and to receive instruction from God, to "behold the beauty of the Lord and to enquire in his temple;" accordingly by this psalm we are assisted on our solemn feast days, I. In praising God for what he is to his people (*v.* 1–3), and has done for them (*v.* 4–7). II. In teaching and admonishing one another concerning the obligations we lie under to God (*v.* 8–10), the danger of revolting from him (*v.* 11, 12), and the happiness we should have if we would but keep close to him (*v.* 13–16). This, though spoken primarily of Israel of old, is written for our learning, and is therefore to be sung with application.

To the chief musician upon Gittith. *A psalm* of Asaph.

Verses 1–7

When the people of God were gathered together in *the solemn day, the day of the feast of the Lord,* they must be told that they had business to do, for we do not go to church to sleep nor to be idle; no, there is that which the duty of every day requires, work of the day, which is to be done in its day. And here,

I. The worshippers of God are excited to their work, and are taught, by singing this psalm, to stir up both themselves and one another to it, *v.* 1–3. Our errand is, to give unto God the glory due unto his name, and in all our religious assemblies we must mind this as our business. 1. In doing this we must eye God as *our strength,* and as *the God of Jacob, v.* 1. He is the strength of Israel, as a people; for he is a God in covenant with them, who will powerfully protect, support, and deliver them, who fights their battles and makes them do valiantly and victoriously. He is the strength of every Israelite; by his grace we are enabled to go through all our services, sufferings, and conflicts; and to him, as our strength, we must pray, and we must sing praise to him as the God of all the wrestling seed of Jacob, with whom we have a spiritual communion. 2. We must do this by all the expressions of holy joy and triumph. It was then to be done by musical instruments, the *timbrel, harp, and psaltery;* and by blowing *the trumpet,* some think in remembrance of the sound of the trumpet on Mount Sinai, which waxed louder and louder. It was then and is now to be done by singing psalms, singing *aloud,* and making *a joyful noise.* The pleasantness of the harp and the awfulness of the trumpet intimate to us that God is to be worshipped with cheerfulness and joy with reverence and godly fear. Singing aloud and making a noise intimate that we must be warm and affectionate in praising God, that we must with a hearty good-will show forth his praise, as those that are not ashamed to own our dependence on him and obligations to him, and that we should join many together in this work; the more the better; it is the more like heaven. 3. This must be done in the time appointed. No time is amiss for praising God (*Seven times a day will I praise thee;* nay, *at midnight will I rise and give thanks unto thee*); but some are times appointed, not for God to meet us (he is always ready), but for us to meet one another, that we may join together in praising Do. The solemn feast-day must be a day of praise; when we are receiving the gifts of God's bounty, and rejoicing in them, then it is proper to sing his praises.

II. They are here directed in their work. 1. They must look up to the divine institution which it is the observation of. In all religious worship we must have an eye to the command (*v.* 4): *This was a statute for Israel,* for the keeping up of a face of religion among them; it was *a law of the God of Jacob,* which all the seed of Jacob are bound by, and must be subject to. Note, Praising God is not only a good thing, which we do well to do, but it is our indispensable duty, which we are obliged to do; it is at our peril if we neglect it; and in all religious exercises we must have an eye to the institution as our warrant and rule: "This I do because God has commanded me; and therefore I hope he will accept me;" then it is done in faith. 2. They must look back upon those operations of divine Providence which it is the memorial of. This solemn service was *ordained for a testimony* (*v.* 5), a standing traditional evidence, for the attesting of the matters of fact. It was a testimony to Israel, that they might know and remember what God had done for their fathers, and would be a testimony against them if they should be ignorant of them and forget them. (1.) The psalmist, in the people's name, puts himself in mind of the general work of God on Israel's behalf, which was kept in remembrance by this and other solemnities, v. 5. When God went out against the land of Egypt, to lay it waste, that he might force Pharaoh to let Israel go, then he ordained solemn feast-days to be observed by a statute for ever in their generations, as a memorial of it, particularly the passover, which perhaps is meant by the *solemn feast-day* (v. 3); that was appointed just then when God went out through the land of Egypt to destroy the first-born, and passed over the houses of the Israelites, Ex. 12:23, 24. By it that work of wonder was to be kept in perpetual remembrance, that all ages might in it behold the goodness and severity of God. The psalmist, speaking for his people, takes notice of this aggravating circumstance of their slavery in Egypt that there they heard a language that they understood not; there they were strangers in a strange land. The Egyptians and the Hebrews understood not one another's language; for Joseph spoke to his brethren by an interpreter (Gen. 42:23), and the Egyptians are said to be to the house of Jacob *a people of a strange language*, Ps. 114:1. To make a deliverance appear the more gracious, the more glorious, it is good to observe every thing that makes the trouble we are delivered from appear the more grievous. (2.) The psalmist, in God's name, puts the people in mind of some of the particulars of their deliverance. Here he changes the person, v. 6. God speaks by him, saying, *I removed the shoulder from the burden*. Let him remember this on the feast-day, [1.] That God had brought them out of the house of bondage, had removed their shoulder from the burden of oppression under which they were ready to sink, *had delivered their hands from the pots*, or panniers, or baskets, in which they carried clay or bricks. Deliverance out of slavery is a very sensible mercy and one which ought to be had in everlasting remembrance. But this was not all. [2.] God had delivered them at the Red Sea; then they called in trouble, and he rescued them and disappointed the designs of their enemies against them, Ex. 14:10. Then he answered them with a real answer, out of *the secret place of thunder;* that is, out of the pillar of fire, through which God looked upon the host of the Egyptians and troubled it, Ex. 14:24, 25. Or it may be meant of the giving of the law at Mount Sinai, which was the secret place, for it was death to gaze (Ex. 19:21), and it was in thunder that God then spoke. Even the terrors of Sinai were favours to Israel, Deu. 4:33. [3.] God had borne their manners in the wilderness: *"I proved thee at the waters of Meribah; thou didst there show thy temper, what an unbelieving murmuring people thou wast, and yet I continued my favour to thee." Selah — Mark that;* compare God's goodness and man's badness, and they will serve as foils to each other. Now if they, on their solemn feast-days, were thus to call to mind their redemption out of Egypt, much more ought we, on the Christian sabbath, to call to mind a more glorious redemption wrought out for us by Jesus Christ from worse than Egyptian bondage, and the many gracious answers he has given to us, notwithstanding our manifold provocations.

Verses 8–16

God, by the psalmist, here speaks to Israel, and in them to us, on whom the ends of the world are come.

I. He demands their diligent and serious attention to what he was about to say (v. 8): *"Hear, O my people!* and who should hear me if my people will not? I have heard and answered thee; now wilt thou hear me? Hear what is said with the greatest solemnity and the most unquestionable certainty, for it is what *I will testify unto thee*. Do not only give me the hearing, but *hearken unto me*, that is, be advised by me, be ruled by me." Nothing could be more reasonably nor more justly expected, and yet God puts an *if* upon it: *"If thou wilt hearken unto me*. It is thy interest to do so, and yet it is questionable whether thou wilt or no; for thy neck is an iron sinew."

II. He puts them in mind of their obligation to him as the Lord their God and Redeemer (v. 10): *I am the Lord thy God, who brought thee out of the land of Egypt;* this is the preface to the ten commandments, and a powerful reason for the keeping of them, showing that we are bound to it in duty, interest, and gratitude, all which bonds we break asunder if we be disobedient.

III. He gives them an abstract both of the precepts and of the promises which he gave them, as the Lord and their God, upon their coming out of Egypt. 1. The great command was that they should have no other gods before him (v. 9): *There shall no strange god be in thee,* none besides thy own God. Other gods might well be called strange gods, for it was very strange that ever any people who had the true and living God for their God should hanker after any other. God is jealous in this matter, for he will not suffer his glory to be given to another; and therefore in this matter they must be circumspect, Ex. 23:13. 2. The great promise was that God himself, as a God all-sufficient, would be nigh unto them in all that which they called upon him for (Deu. 4:7), that, if they would adhere to him as their powerful protector and ruler, they should always find him their bountiful benefactor: *"Open thy mouth wide and I will fill it,* as the young ravens that cry open their mouths wide and the old ones fill them." See here, (1.) What is our duty — to raise our expectations from God and enlarge our desires towards him. We cannot look for too little from the creature nor too much from the Creator. We are not straitened in him; why therefore should we be straitened in our own bosoms? (2.) What is God's promise. I will fill thy mouth with good things, Ps. 103:5. There is *enough in God to fill our treasures* (Prov. 8:21), to *replenish every hungry soul* (Jer. 31:25), to supply all our wants, to answer all our desires, and to make us completely happy. The pleasures of sense will surfeit and never satisfy (Isa. 55:2); divine pleasures will satisfy and never surfeit. And we may have enough from God if we pray for it in faith. *Ask, and it shall be given you.* He *gives liberally, and upbraids not.* God assured his people Israel that it would be their own fault if he did not do as great and kind things for them as he had done for their fathers. Nothing should be thought too good, too much, to give them, if they would but keep close to God. He *would moreover have given them such and such things,* 2 Sa. 12:8.

IV. He charges them with a high contempt of his authority as their lawgiver and his grace and favour as their benefactor, v. 11. He had done much for them, and designed to do more; but all in vain: *"My people would not hearken to my voice,* but turned a deaf ear to all I said." Two things he complains of: — 1. Their disobedience to his commands. They did hear his voice, so as never any people did; but they would not hearken to it, they would not be ruled by it, neither by the law nor by the reason of it. 2. Their dislike of his covenant-relation to them: *They would none of me. They acquiesced not in my word* (so the Chaldee); God was willing to be to them a God, but they were not willing to be to him a people; they did not like his terms. "I would have gathered them, but they would not." They had none of him; and why had they not? It was not because they might not; they were fairly invited into covenant with God. It was not because they could not; for the word was nigh them, even in their mouth and in their heart. But it was purely because they would not. God calls them hi people, for they were bought by him, bound to him, his by a thousand ties, and yet even they had not hearkened, had not obeyed. "Israel, the seed of Jacob my friend, set me at nought, and *would* have *none of me."* Note, All the wickedness of the wicked world is owing to the wilfulness of the wicked will. The reason why people are not religious is because they will not be so.

V. He justifies himself with this in the spiritual judgments he had brought upon them (v. 12): *So I gave them up unto their own hearts' lusts,* which would be more dangerous enemies and more mischievous oppressors to them than any of the neighbouring nations ever were. God withdrew his Spirit from them, took off the bridle of restraining grace, left them to themselves, and justly; they will do as they will, and therefore let them do as they will. *Ephraim is joined to idols; let him alone.* It is a righteous thing with God to give those up to their own hearts' lusts that indulge them, and give up themselves to be led by them; for why should his Spirit always strive? His grace is his own, and he is debtor to no man, and yet, as he never gave his grace to any that could say they deserved it, so he never took it away from any but such as had first forfeited it: They would none of me, so I gave them up; let them take their course. And see what follows: *They walked in their own counsels,* in the way of their heart and in the sight of their eye, both in their worships and in their conversations. "I left them to do as they would, and then they did all that

was ill;" they walked in their own counsels, and not according to the counsels of God and his advice. God therefore was not the author of their sin; he left them to the lusts of their own hearts and the counsels of their own heads; if they do not well, the blame must lie upon their own hearts and the blood upon their own heads.

VI. He testifies his good-will to them in wishing they had done well for themselves. He saw how sad their case was, and how sure their ruin, when they were delivered up to their own lusts; that is worse than being given up to Satan, which may be in order to reformation (1 Tim. 1:20) and to salvation (1 Co. 5:5); but to be delivered up to their own hearts' lusts is to be sealed under condemnation. *He that is filthy, let him be filthy still.* What fatal precipices will not these hurry a man to! Now here God looks upon them with pity, and shows that it was with reluctance that he thus abandoned them to their folly and fate. *How shall I give thee up, Ephraim?* Hos. 11:8, 9. So here, *O that my people had hearkened!* See Isa. 48:18. Thus Christ lamented the obstinacy of Jerusalem. *If thou hadst known,* Lu. 19:42. The expressions here are very affecting (v. 13–16), designed to show how unwilling God is that any should perish and desirous that all should come to repentance (he delights not in the ruin of sinful persons or nations), and also what enemies sinners are to themselves and what an aggravation it will be of their misery that they might have been happy upon such easy terms. Observe here,

1. The great mercy God had in store for his people, and which he would have wrought for them if they had been obedient. (1.) He would have given them victory over their enemies and would soon have completed the reduction of them. They should not only have kept their ground, but have gained their point, against the remaining Canaanites, and their encroaching vexatious neighbours (v. 14): *I should have subdued their enemies;* and it is God only that is to be depended on for the subduing of our enemies. Not would had have put them to the expense and fatigue of a tedious war: he would *soon* have done it; for he would have *turned his hand against their adversaries,* and then they would not have been able to stand before them. It intimates how easily he would have done it and without any difficulty. With the turn of a hand, nay, *with the breath of his mouth, shall he slay the wicked,* Isa. 11:4. If he but turn his hand, the *haters of the Lord will submit themselves to him* (v. 15); and, though they are not brought to love him, yet they shall be made to fear him and to confess that he is too hard for them and that it is in vain to contend with him. God is honoured, and so is his Israel, by the submission of those that have been in rebellion against them, though it be but a forced and feigned submission. (2.) He would have confirmed and perpetuated their posterity, and established it upon sure and lasting foundations. In spite of all the attempts of their enemies against them, *their time should have endured for ever,* and they should never have been disturbed in the possession of the good land God had given them, much less evicted and turned out of possession. (3.) He would have given them great plenty of all good things (v. 16): *He should have fed them with the finest of the wheat,* with the best grain and the best of the kind. Wheat was the staple commodity of Canaan, and they exported a great deal of it, Eze. 27:17. He would not only have provided for them the best sort of bread, but *with honey out of the rock would he have satisfied them.* Besides the precious products of the fruitful soil, that there might not be a barren spot in all their land, even the clefts of the rock should serve for bee-hives and in them they should find honey in abundance. See Deu. 32:13, 14. In short, God designed to make them every way easy and happy.

2. The duty God required from them as the condition of all this mercy. He expected no more than that they should *hearken to him,* as a scholar to his teacher, to receive his instructions — as a servant to his master, to receive his commands; and that they should *walk in his ways,* those ways of the Lord which are right and pleasant, that they should observe the institutions of his ordinances and attend the intimations of his providence. There was nothing unreasonable in this.

3. Observe how the reason of the withholding of the mercy is laid in their neglect of the duty: If they had *hearkened to me, I would soon have subdued their enemies.* Na-

tional sin or disobedience is the great and only thing that retards and obstructs national deliverance. *When I would have healed Israel,* and set every thing to-rights among them, then *the iniquity of Ephraim was discovered,* and so a stop was put to the cure, Hos. 7:1. We are apt to say, "If such a method had been taken, such an instrument employed, we should soon have subdued our enemies:" but we mistake; if we had hearkened to God, and kept to our duty, the thing would have been done, but it is sin that makes our troubles long and salvation slow. And this is that which God himself complains of, and wishes it had been otherwise. Note, *Therefore* God would have us do our duty to him, that we may be qualified to receive favour from him. He delights in our serving him, not because he is the better for it, but because we shall be.

PSALM 82

This psalm is calculated for the meridian of princes' courts and courts of justice, not in Israel only, but in other nations; yet it was probably penned primarily for the use of the magistrates of Israel, the great Sanhedrim, and their other elders who were in places of power, and perhaps by David's direction. This psalm is designed to make kings wise, and "to instruct the judges of the earth" (as 2 and 10), to tell them their duty as (2 Sa. 23:3), and to tell them of their faults as 58:1. We have here, I. The dignity of magistracy and its dependence upon God (*v.* 1). II. The duty of magistrates (*v.* 3, 4). III. The degeneracy of bad magistrates and the mischief they do (*v.* 2, 5). IV. Their doom read (*v.* 6, 7). V. The desire and prayer of all good people that the kingdom of God may be set up more and more (*v.* 8). Though magistrates may most closely apply this psalm to themselves, yet we may any of us sing it with understanding when we give glory to God, in singing it, as presiding in all public affairs, providing for the protection of injured innocency, and ready to punish the most powerful injustice, and when we comfort ourselves with a belief of his present government and with the hopes of his future judgment.

A psalm of Asaph.

Verses 1–5

We have here,

I. God's supreme presidency and power in all councils and courts asserted and laid down, as a great truth necessary to be believed both by princes and subjects (*v.* 1): *God stands,* as chief director, *in the congregation of the mighty,* the mighty One, *in coetu fortis — in the councils of the prince,* the supreme magistrate, and he judges among the gods, the inferior magistrates; both the legislative and the executive power of princes is under his eye and his hand. Observe here, 1. The power and honour of magistrates; they are the *mighty.* They are so in authority, for the public good (it is a great power that they are entrusted with), and they ought to be so in wisdom and courage. They are, in the Hebrew dialect, called *gods;* the same word is used for these subordinate governors that is used for the sovereign ruler of the world. They are *elohim.* Angels are so called both because they are great in power and might and because God is pleased to make use of their service in the government of this lower world; and magistrates in an inferior capacity are likewise the ministers of his providence in general, for the keeping up of order and peace in human societies, and particularly of his justice and goodness in punishing evil-doers and protecting those that do well. Good magistrates, who answer the ends of magistracy, are as God; some of his honour is put upon them; they are his vicegerents, and great blessings to any people. *A divine sentence is in the lips of the king,* Prov. 16:10. But, as *roaring lions and ranging bears,* so are *wicked rulers over the poor people,* Prov. 28:15. 2. A good form and constitution of government intimated, and that is a mixed monarchy like ours; here is the might one, the sovereign, and here is his congregation, his privy-council, his parliament, his bench of judges, who are called the *gods.* 3. God's incontestable sovereignty maintained in and over all the congregations of the mighty. *God stands,* he *judges among them;* they have their power from him and are accountable to him. *By him kings reign.* He is present at all their debates, and inspects all they say and do, and what is said and done amiss will be called over again, and they reckoned with for their mal-administrations. God has their hearts in his hands, and their tongues too, and he directs them *which way soever he will,* Prov. 21:1. So that he has a negative voice in all their resolves, and his counsels shall stand, whatever devices are in men's hearts. He makes what use

he pleases of them, and serves his own purposes and designs by them; though their hearts little think so, Isa. 10:7. Let magistrates consider this and be awed by it; God is with them in the judgment, 2 Chr. 19:6; Deu. 1:17. Let subjects consider this and be comforted with it; for good princes and good judges, who mean well, are under a divine direction, and bad ones, who mean ever so ill, are under a divine restraint.

II. A charge given to all magistrates to do good with their power, as they will answer it to him by whom they are entrusted with it, *v.* 3, 4. 1. They are to be the protectors of those who lie exposed to injury and the patrons of those who want advice and assistance: *Defend the poor,* who have no money wherewith to make friends or fee counsel, *and the fatherless,* who, while they are young and unable to help themselves, have lost those who would have been the guides of their youth. Magistrates, as they must be fathers to their country in general, so particularly to those in it who are fatherless. Are they called *gods?* Herein they must be followers of him, they must be *fathers of the fatherless.* Job was so, Job 29:12. 2. They are to administer justice impartially, and do *right to the afflicted and needy,* who, being weak and helpless, have often wrongs done them; and will be in danger of losing all if magistrates do not, *ex officio* — officially, interpose for their relief. If a poor man has an honest cause, his poverty must be no prejudice to his cause, how great and powerful soever those are that contend with him. 3. They are to rescue those who have already fallen into the hands of oppressors and deliver them. (*v.* 4): *Rid them out of the hand of the wicked. Avenge them of their adversary,* Lu. 18:3. These are clients whom there is nothing to be got by, no pay for serving them, no interest by obliging them; yet these are those whom judges and magistrates must concern themselves for, whose comfort they must consult and whose cause they must espouse.

III. A charge drawn up against bad magistrates, who neglect their duty and abuse their power, forgetting that God standeth among them, *v.* 2, 5. Observe, 1. What the sin is they are here charged with; they *judge unjustly,* contrary to the rules of equity and the dictates of their consciences, giving judgment against those who have right on their side, out of malice and ill-will, or for those who have an unrighteous cause, out of favour and partial affection. To do unjustly is bad, but to judge unjustly is much worse, because it is doing wrong under colour of right; against such acts of injustice there is least fence for the injured and by them encouragement is given to the injurious. It was as great an evil as any Solomon saw under the sun when he observed *the place of judgment, that iniquity was there,* Eccl. 3:16; Isa. 5:7. They not only accepted the persons of the rich because they were rich, though that is bad enough, but (which is much worse) they *accepted the persons of the wicked* because they were wicked; they not only countenanced them in their wickedness, but loved them the better for it, and fell in with their interests. Woe unto thee, O land! when thy judges are such as these. 2. What was the cause of this sin. They were told plainly enough that it was their office and duty to protect and deliver the poor; it was many a time given them in charge; yet they judge unjustly, for *they know not, neither will they understand.* They do not care to hear their duty; they will not take pains to study it; they have no desire to take things right, but are governed by interest, not by reason or justice. *A gift in secret blinds their eyes.* They know not because they will not understand. None so blind as those that will not see. They have baffled their own consciences, and so they walk on in darkness, not knowing nor caring what they do nor whither they go. Those that walk on in darkness are walking on to everlasting darkness. 3. What were the consequences of this sin: *All the foundations of the earth* (or *of the land*) *are out of course.* When justice is perverted what good can be expected? *The earth and all the inhabitants thereof are dissolved,* as the psalmist speaks in a like case, Ps. 75:3. The miscarriages of public persons are public mischiefs.

Verses 6–8

We have here,

I. Earthly gods abased and brought down, *v.* 6, 7. The dignity of their character is acknowledged (*v.* 6): *I have said, You are gods.* They have been honoured with the

name and title of gods. God himself called them so in the statute against treasonable words Ex. 22:28, *Thou shalt not revile the gods.* And, if they have this style from the fountain of honour, who can dispute it? But what is man, that he should be thus magnified? He called them *gods* because *unto them the word of God came,* so our Saviour expounds it (Jn. 10:35); they had a commission from God, and were delegated and appointed by him to be the shields of the earth, the conservators of the public peace, and revengers to execute wrath upon those that disturb it, Rom. 13:4. All of them are in this sense *children of the Most High.* God has put some of his honour upon them, and employs them in his providential government of the world, as David made his sons chief rulers. Or, "Because *I said, You are gods,* you have carried the honour further than was intended and have imagined yourselves to be *the children of the Most High,*" as the king of Babylon (Isa. 14:14), *I will be like the Most High,* and the king of Tyre (Eze. 28:2), *Thou hast set thy heart as the heart of God.* It is a hard thing for men to have so much honour put upon them by the hand of God, and so much honour paid them, as ought to be by the children of men, and not to be proud of it and puffed up with it, and so to think of themselves above what is meet. But here follows a mortifying consideration: *You shall die like men.* This may be taken either, 1. As the punishment of bad magistrates, such as judged unjustly, and by their misrule put the *foundations of the earth out of course.* God will reckon with them, and will cut them off in the midst of their pomp and prosperity; they shall die like other wicked men, *and fall like one of the* heathen *princes* (and their being Israelites shall not secure them anymore than their being judges) or like one of the angels that sinned, or like one of the giants of the old world. Compare this with that which Elihu observed concerning the mighty oppressors in his time. Job 34:26, *He striketh them as wicked men in the open sight of others.* Let those that abuse their power know that God will take both it and their lives from them; for wherein they deal proudly he will *show himself above them.* Or, 2. As the period of the glory of all magistrates in this world. Let them not be puffed up with their honour nor neglect their work, but let the consideration of their mortality be both mortifying to their pride and quickening to their duty. "You are called gods, but you have no patent for immortality; *you shall die like men,* like common men; and *like one of them, you, O princes! shall fall."* Note, Kings and princes, all the judges of the earth, though they are gods to us, are men to God, and shall die like men, and all their honour shall be laid in the dust. *Mors sceptra ligonibus aequat — Death mingles sceptres with spades.*

II. The God of heaven exalted and raised high, *v.* 8. The psalmist finds it to little purpose to reason with these proud oppressors; they turned a deaf ear to all he said and walked on in darkness; and therefore he looks up to God, appeals to him, and begs of him to *take unto himself his great power: Arise, O God! judge the earth;* and, when he prays that he would do it, he believes that he will do it: *Thou shalt inherit all nations.* This has respect, 1. To the kingdom of providence. God governs the world, sets up and puts down whom he pleases; he inherits all nations, has an absolute dominion over them, to dispose of them as a man does of his inheritance. This we are to believe and to comfort ourselves with, that the earth is not given so much *into the hands of the wicked,* the wicked rulers, as we are tempted to think it is, Job 9:24. But God has reserved the power to himself and overrules them. In this faith we must pray, "*Arise, O God! judge the earth,* appear against those that judge unjustly, and set shepherds over thy people after thy own heart." There is a righteous God to whom we may have recourse, and on whom we may depend for the effectual relief of all that find themselves aggrieved by unjust judges. 2. To the kingdom of the Messiah. It is a prayer for the hastening of that, that Christ would come, who is to judge the earth, and that promise is pleaded, that God shall *give him the heathen for his inheritance.* Thou, O Christ! shalt *inherit all nations,* and be the governor over them, Ps. 2:8; 22:28. Let the second coming of Christ set to-rights all these disorders. There are two words with which we may comfort ourselves and one another in reference to the mismanagements of power among men: one is Rev. 19:6, *Hallelujah, the Lord God omnipotent reigneth;* the other is Rev. 22:20, *Surely, I come quickly.*

PSALM 83

This psalm is the last of those that go under the name of Asaph. It is penned, as most of those, upon a public account, with reference to the insults of the church's enemies, who sought its ruin. Some think it was penned upon occasion of the threatening descent which was made upon the land of Judah in Jehoshaphat's time by the Moabites and Ammonites, those children of Lot here spoken of (*v.* 8), who were at the head of the alliance and to whom all the other states here mentioned were auxiliaries. We have the story 2 Chr. 20:1, where it is said, The children of Moab and Ammon, and others besides them, invaded the land. Others think it was penned with reference to all the confederacies of the neighbouring nations against Israel, from first to last. The psalmist here makes an appeal and application, I. To God's knowledge, by a representation of their designs and endeavours to destroy Israel (*v.* 1–8). II. To God's justice and jealousy, both for his church and for his own honour, by an earnest prayer for the defeat of their attempt, that the church might be preserved, the enemies humbled, and God glorified (*v.* 9–18). This, in the singing of it, we may apply to the enemies of the gospel-church, all anti-christian powers and factions, representing to God their confederacies against Christ and his kingdom, and rejoicing in the hope that all their projects will be baffled and the gates of hell shall not prevail against the church.

A song *or* psalm of Asaph.

Verses 1–8

The Israel of God were now in danger, and fear, and great distress, and yet their prayer is called, *A song or psalm;* for singing psalms is not unseasonable, no, not when the harps are hung upon the willow-trees.

I. The psalmist here begs of God to appear on the behalf of his injured threatened people (*v.* 1): *"Keep not thou silence, O God!* but give judgment for us against those that do us an apparent wrong." Thus Jehoshaphat prayed upon occasion of that invasion (2 Chr. 20:11), *Behold, how they reward us, to come to cast us out of thy possession.* Sometimes God seems to connive at the unjust treatment which is given to his people; he keeps silence, as one that either did not observe it or did not concern himself in it; he holds his peace, as if he would observe an exact neutrality, and let them fight it out; he is still, and gives not the enemies of his people any disturbance or opposition, but seems to sit by *as a man astonished, or as a mighty man that cannot save.* Then he gives us leave to call upon him, as here, *"Keep not thou silence, O God!* Lord, speak to us by the prophets for our encouragement against our fears" (as he did in reference to that invasion, 2 Chr. 20:14, etc.); "Lord, speak for us by the providence and speak against our enemies; speak deliverance to us and disappointment to them." God's speaking is his acting; for with him saying and doing are the same thing.

II. He here gives an account of the grand alliance of the neighbouring nations against Israel, which he begs of God to break, and blast the projects of. Now observe here,

1. Against whom this confederacy is formed; it is against the Israel of God, and so, in effect, against the God of Israel. Thus the psalmist takes care to interest God in their cause, not doubting but that, if it appeared that they were for God, God would make it to appear that he was for them, and then they might set all their enemies at defiance; for whom then could be against them? "Lord," says he, "they are thy enemies, and they hate thee." All wicked people are God's enemies (the *carnal mind is enmity against God*), but especially wicked persecutors; they hated the religious worshippers of God, because they hated God's holy religion and the worship of him. This was that which made God's people so zealous against them — that they fought against God: *They are confederate against thee, v.* 5. Were our interest only concerned, we could the better bear it; but, when God himself is struck at, it is time to cry, Help, Lord. *Keep not thou silence, O God!* He proves that they are confederate against God, for they are so against the people of God, who are near and dear to him, his son, his first-born, his portion, and the lot of his inheritance; he may truly be said to fight against me that endeavours to destroy my children, to root out my family, and to ruin my estate. "Lord," says the psalmist, "they are thy enemies, for they consult against thy hidden ones." Note, God's people are his hidden ones, hidden, (1.) In respect of secresy. Their life is *hid with Christ in God;* the *world knows them not;* if they knew them, they would not hate them as they do. (2.) In respect of safety. God takes them under his special protection, hides them in the hollow of his hand; and yet, in defiance of God and his power and promise to secure his people, they will consult to ruin them and *cast them down from their excellency* (Ps. 62:4), and to make a prey of those whom the *Lord has set apart for himself,* Ps. 4:3. They resolve to destroy those whom God resolves to preserve.

2. How this confederacy is managed. The devil is at the bottom of it, and therefore it is carried on, (1.) With a great deal of heat and violence: *Thy enemies make a tumult, v.* 2. *The heathen rage,* Ps. 2:1. *The nations are angry,* Rev. 11:18. They are noisy in their clamours against the people whom they hope to run down with their loud calumnies. This comes in as a reason why God should not keep silence: "The enemies talk big and talk much; Lord, let them not talk all, but do thou *speak to them in thy wrath,"* Ps. 2:5. (2.) With a great deal of pride and insolence: *They have lifted up the head.* In confidence of their success, they are so elevated as if they could over-top the Most High and overpower the Almighty. (3.) With a great deal of art and policy: They have *taken crafty counsel, v.* 3. The subtlety of the old serpent appears in their management, and they contrive by all possible means, though ever so base, ever so bad, to gain their point. They are*profound to make slaughter* (Hos. 5:2), as if they could outwit Infinite Wisdom. (4.) With a great deal of unanimity. Whatever separate clashing interest they have among themselves, against the people of God they *consult with one consent* (*v.* 5), nor is *Satan's kingdom divided against itself.* To push on this unholy war, they lay their heads together, and their horns, and their hearts too. *Fas est et ab hoste doceri — Even an enemy may instruct.* Do the enemies of the church act with one consent to destroy it? Are the kings of the earth of one mind to give their power and honour to the beast? And shall not the church's friends be unanimous in serving her interests? If Herod and Pilate are made friends, that they may join in crucifying Christ, surely Paul and Barnabas, Paul and Peter, will soon be made friends, that they may join in preaching Christ.

3. What it is that is aimed at in this confederacy. They consult not like the Gibeonites to make a league with Israel, that they might strengthen themselves by such a desirable alliance, which would have been their wisdom. They consult, not only to clip the wings of Israel, to recover their new conquests, and check the progress of their victorious arms, not only to keep the balance even between them and Israel, and to prevent their power from growing exorbitant; this will not serve. It is no less than the utter ruin and extirpation of Israel that they design (*v.* 4): *"Come, let us cut them off from being a nation,* as they cut off the seven nations of Canaan; let us leave them neither root nor branch, but lay their country so perfectly waste *that the name of Israel may be no more in remembrance,* no, not in history;" for with them they would destroy their Bibles and burn all their records. Such is the enmity of the serpent's seed against the seed of the woman. It is the secret wish of many wicked men that the church of God might not have a being in the world, that there might be no such thing as religion among mankind. Having banished the sense of it out of their own hearts, they would gladly see the whole earth as well rid of it, all its laws and ordinances abolished, all its restraints and obligations shaken off, and all that preach, profess, or practise it cut off. This they would bring it to if it were in their power; but *he that sits in heaven shall laugh at them.*

4. Who they are that are drawn into this confederacy. The nations that entered into this alliance are here mentioned (*v.* 6–8); the Edomites and Ishmaelites, both descendants from Abraham, lead the van; for apostates from the church have been its most bitter and spiteful enemies, witness Julian. These were allied to Israel in blood and yet in alliance against Israel. There are no bonds of nature so strong but the spirit of persecution has broken through them. *The brother shall betray the brother to death.* Moab and Ammon were the children of righteous Lot; but, as an incestuous, so a degenerate race. The Philistines were long a thorn in Israel's side, and very vexatious. How the inhabitants of Tyre, who in David's time were Israel's firm allies, come in among their enemies, I know not; but that *Assur* (that is, the Assyrian) *also is joined with them* is not strange, or that (as the word is) they were *an arm to the children of Lot.* See how numerous the enemies of God's church have always been. *Lord, how are those increased that trouble it!* God's heritage was as a speckled bird; all *the birds round about were against her* (Jer. 12:9), which highly magnifies the power of God in preserving to himself a church in the world, in spite of the combined force of earth and hell.

Verses 9–18

The psalmist here, in the name of the church, prays for the destruction of those confederate forces, and, in God's name, foretels it; for this prayer that it might be so amounts to a prophecy that it shall be so, and this prophecy reaches to all the enemies of the gospel-church; whoever they be that oppose the kingdom of Christ, here they may read their doom. The prayer is, in short, that these enemies, who were confederate against Israel, might be defeated in all their attempts, and that they might prove their own ruin, and so God's Israel might be preserved and perpetuated. Now this is here illustrated,

I. By some precedents. Let that be their punishment which has been the fate of others who have formerly set themselves against God's Israel. The defeat and discomfiture of former combinations may be pleaded in prayer to God and improved for the encouragement of our own faith and hope, because God is the same still that ever he was, the same to his people and the same against his and their enemies; with him is no variableness. 1. He prays that their armies might be destroyed as the armies of former enemies had been (*v.* 9, 10): *Do to them as to the Midianites;* let them be routed by their own fears, for so the Midianites were, more than by Gideon's 300 men. Do to them as to the army under the command of Sisera (who was general under Jabin king of Canaan) which God discomfited (Jdg. 4:15) at the brook Kishon, near to which was Endor. *They became as dung on the earth;* their dead bodies were thrown like dung laid in heaps, or spread, to fatten the ground; they were trodden to dirt by Barak's small but victorious army; and this was fitly made a precedent here, because Deborah made it so to aftertimes when it was fresh. Jdg. 5:31, *So let all thy enemies perish, O Lord!* that is, So they shall perish. 2. He prays that their leaders might be destroyed as they had been formerly. The common people would not have been so mischievous if their princes had not set them on, and therefore they are particularly prayed against, *v.* 11, 12. Observe, (1.) What their malice was against the Israel of God. They said, *Let us take to ourselves the houses of God in possession* (*v.* 12), the *pleasant places* of God (so the word is), by which we may understand the land of Canaan, which was a pleasant land and was Immanuel's land, or the temple, which was indeed God's pleasant place (Isa. 64:11), or (as Dr. Hammond suggests) the pleasant pastures, which these Arabians, who traded in cattle, did in a particular manner seek after. The princes and nobles aimed to enrich themselves by this war; and their armies must be made as dung for the earth, to serve their covetousness and their ambition. (2.) What their lot should be. They shall be made *like Oreb and Zeeb* (two princes of the Midianites, who, when their forces were routed, were taken in their flight by the Ephraimites and slain, Jdg. 7:25), and *like Zeba and Zalmunna,* whom Gideon himself slew, Jdg. 8:21. "Let these enemies of ours be made as easy a prey to us as they were to the conquerors then." We may not prescribe to God, but we may pray to God that he will deal with the enemies of his church in our days as he did with those in the days of our fathers.

II. He illustrates it by some similitudes, and prays, 1. That God would *make them like a wheel* (*v.* 13), that they might be in continual motion, unquiet, unsettled, and giddy in all their counsels and resolves, that they might roll down easily and speedily to their own ruin. Or, as some think, that they might be broken by the judgments of God, as the corn is broken, or beaten out, by the wheel which was then used in threshing. Thus, when a *wise king scatters the wicked,* he is said to *bring the wheel over them,* Prov. 20:26. Those that trust in God have their hearts fixed; those that fight against him are unfixed, like a wheel. 2. That they might be chased as *stubble,* or chaff, *before the* fierce *wind.* "The wheel, though it continually turn round, is fixed on its own axis; but let them have no more fixation than the light stubble has, which the wind hurries away, and nobody desires to save it, but is willing it should go," Ps. 1:4. Thus shall *the wicked be driven away in his wickedness, and chased out of the world.* 3. That they might be consumed, as wood by the fire, or as briers and thorns, as fern or furze, upon the mountains, by the flames, *v.* 14. When the stubble is driven by the wind it will rest, at last, under some hedge, in some ditch or other; but he prays that they might not only be driven away as stubble, but burnt up as stubble. And this will be the end of wicked men (Heb. 6:8) and particularly of all the enemies of God's church. The application of these comparisons we have (*v.* 15): *So persecute them with thy tempest,* persecute them to their utter ruin, and make *them afraid with thy storm.* See how sinners are made miserable; the storm of God's wrath raises terrors in their own hearts, and so they are made completely miserable. God can deal with the proudest and most daring sinner that has bidden defiance to his justice, and can make him afraid as a grasshopper. It is the torment of devils that they tremble.

III. He illustrates it by the good consequences of their confusion, *v.* 16–18. He prays here that God, having filled their hearts with terror, would thereby fill their faces with shame, that they might be ashamed of their enmity to the people of God (Isa. 26:11), ashamed of their folly in acting both against Omnipotence itself and their own true interest. They did what they could to put God's people to shame, but the shame will at length return upon themselves. Now, 1. The beginning of this shame might be a means of their conversion: "Let them be broken and baffled in their attempts, *that they may seek thy name, O Lord!* Let them be put to a stand, that they may have both leisure and reason to pause a little, and consider who it is that they are fighting against and what an unequal match they are for him, and may therefore humble and submit themselves and desire conditions of peace. Let them be made to fear thy name, and perhaps that will bring them to seek thy name." Note, That which we should earnestly desire and beg of God for our enemies and persecutors is that God would bring them to repentance, and we should desire their abasement in order to this, no other confusion to them than what may be a step towards their conversion. 2. If it did not prove a means of their conversion, the perfecting of it would redound greatly to the honour of God. If they will not be ashamed and repent, let them be put to shame and perish; if they will not be troubled and turned, which would soon put an end to all their trouble, a happy end, *let them be troubled for ever,* and never have peace: this will be for God's glory (*v.* 18), that other men may know and own, if they themselves will not, *that thou, whose name alone is JEHOVAH* (that incommunicable, though not ineffable name) *art the Most High over all the earth.* God's triumphs over his and his church's enemies will be incontestable proofs, (1.) That he is, according to his name JEHOVAH, a self-existent self-sufficient Being, that has all power and perfection in himself. (2.) That he is the most high God, sovereign Lord of all, above all gods, above all kings, above all that exalt themselves and pretend to be high. (3.) That he is so, not only over the land of Israel, but *over all the earth,* even those nations of the earth that do not know him or own him; for his kingdom rules over all. These are great and unquestionable truths, but men will hardly be persuaded to know and believe them; therefore the psalmist prays that the destruction of some might be the conviction of others. The final ruin of all God's enemies, in the great day, will be the effectual proof of this, before angels and men, when the everlasting shame and contempt to which sinners shall rise (Dan. 12:2) shall redound to the everlasting honour and praise of that God to whom vengeance belongs.

PSALM 84

Though David's name be not in the title of this psalm, yet we have reason to think he was the penman of it, because it breathes so much of his excellent spirit and is so much like the sixty-third psalm which was penned by him; it is supposed that David penned this psalm when he was forced by Absalom's rebellion to quit his city, which he lamented his absence from, not so much because it was the royal city as because it was the holy city, witness this psalm, which contains the pious breathings of a gracious soul after God and communion with him. Though it be not entitled, yet it may fitly be looked upon as a psalm or song for the sabbath day, the day of our solemn assemblies. The psalmist here with great devotion expresses his affection, I. To the ordinances of God; his value for them (*v.* 1), his desire towards them (*v.* 2, 3), his conviction of the happiness of those that did enjoy them (*v.* 4–7), and his placing his own happiness so very much in the enjoyment of them (*v.* 10). II. To the God of the ordinances; his desire towards him (*v.* 8, 9), his faith in him (*v.* 11), and his conviction of the happiness of those that put their confidence in him (*v.* 12). In singing this psalm we should have the same devout affections working towards God that David had, and then the singing of it will be very pleasant.

To the chief musician upon Gittith. A psalm for the sons of Korah.

Verses 1–7

The psalmist here, being by force restrained from waiting upon God in public ordinances, by the want of them is brought under a more sensible conviction than ever of the worth of them. Observe,

I. The wonderful beauty he saw in holy institutions (*v.* 1): *How amiable are thy tabernacles, O Lord of hosts!* Some think that he here calls God the *Lord of hosts* (that is, in a special manner of the angels, the heavenly hosts) because of the presence of the angels in God's sanctuary; they attended the Shechinah, and were (as some think) signified by the cherubim. God is the Lord of these hosts, and his the tabernacle is: it is spoken of as more than one *(thy tabernacles)* because there were several courts in which the people attended, and because the tabernacle itself consisted of a holy place and a most holy. How amiable are these! How lovely is the sanctuary in the eyes of all that are truly sanctified! Gracious souls see a wonderful, an inexpressible, beauty in holiness, and in holy work. A tabernacle was a mean habitation, but the disadvantage of external circumstances makes holy ordinances not at all the less amiable; for the beauty of holiness is spiritual, and their glory is within.

II. The longing desire he had to return to the enjoyment of public ordinances, or rather of God in them, *v.* 2. It was an entire desire; body, soul, and spirit concurred in it. He was not conscious to himself of any rising thought to the contrary. It was an intense desire; it was like the desire of the ambitious, or covetous, or voluptuous. He longed, he fainted, he cried out, importunate to be restored to his place in God's courts, and almost impatient of delay. Yet it was not so much the courts of the Lord that he coveted, but he cried out, in prayer, *for the living God* himself. O that I might know him, and be again taken into communion with him! 1 Jn. 1:3. Ordinances are empty things if we meet not with God in the ordinances.

III. His grudging the happiness of the little birds that made their nests in the buildings that were adjoining to God's altars, *v.* 3. This is an elegant and surprising expression of his affection to God's altars: *The sparrow has found a house and the swallow a nest for herself.* These little birds, by the instinct and direction of nature, provide habitations for themselves in houses, as other birds do in the woods, both for their own repose and in which to lay their young; some such David supposes there were in the buildings about the courts of God's house, and wishes himself with them. He would rather live in a bird's nest nigh God's altars than in a palace at a distance from them. He sometimes wished for *the wings of a dove,* on which to *fly into the wilderness* (Ps. 55:6); here for the wings of a sparrow, that he might fly undiscovered into God's courts; and, though to *watch as a sparrow alone upon the house-top* is the description of a very melancholy state and spirit (Ps. 102:7), yet David would be glad to take it for his lot, provided he might be near God's altars. It is better to be serving God in solitude than serving sin with a multitude. The word for a sparrow signifies any little bird, and (if I may offer a conjecture) perhaps when, in David's time, music was introduced so much into the sacred service, both vocal and instrumental, to complete the harmony they had singing-birds in cages hung about the courts of the tabernacle (for we find the singing of birds taken notice of to the glory of God, Ps. 104:12), and David envies the happiness of these, and would gladly change places with them. Observe, David envies the happiness not of those birds that flew over the altars, and had only a transient view of God's courts, but of those that had nests for themselves there. David will not think it enough to sojourn in God's house *as a way-faring man that turns aside to tarry for a night;* but let this be his rest, his home; here he will dwell. And he takes notice that these birds not only have nests for themselves there, but that there they lay their young; for those who have a place in God's courts themselves cannot but desire that their children also may have in God's house, and within his walls, a place and a name, that they may *feed their kids beside the shepherds' tents.* Some give another sense of this verse: "Lord, by thy providence thou hast furnished the birds with nests and resting-places, agreeable to their nature, and to them they have free recourse; but thy altar, which is my nest, my resting-place, which I am as desirous of as ever the wandering bird was of her nest, I cannot have access to. Lord, wilt thou provide better for thy birds than for thy babes? *As a bird that wanders from her nest* so am I, now that I wander from the place of God's altars, for that is my place (Prov. 27:8); I shall never be easy till I return to my place again." Note, Those whose souls are at home, at rest, in God, cannot but desire a settlement near his ordinances. There were two altars, one for sacrifice, the other for incense, and David, in his desire of a place in God's courts, has an eye to both, as we also must, in all our attendance on God, have an eye both to the satisfaction and to the intercession of Christ. And, *lastly,* Observe how he eyes God in this address: Thou art the *Lord of hosts, my King and my God.* Where should a poor distressed subject seek for protection but with his king? *And should not a people seek unto their God?* My King, my God, is Lord of hosts; by him and his altars let me live and die.

IV. His acknowledgment of the happiness both of the ministers and of the people that had liberty of attendance on God's altars: *"Blessed are they.* O when shall I return to the enjoyment of that blessedness?" 1. Blessed are the ministers, the priests and Levites, who have their residence about the tabernacle and are in their courses employed in the service of it (*v.* 4): *Blessed are those that dwell in thy house,* that are at home there, and whose business lies there. He is so far from pitying them, as confined to a constant attendance and obliged to perpetual seriousness, that he would sooner envy them than the greatest princes in the world. There are those that bless the covetous, but he blesses the religious. *Blessed are those that dwell in thy house* (not because they have good wages, a part of every sacrifice for themselves, which would enable them to keep a good table, but because they have good work): *They will be still praising thee;* and, if there be a heaven upon earth, it is in praising God, in continually praising him. Apply this to his house above; blessed are those that dwell there, angels and glorified saints, for they *rest not day nor night from praising God.* Let us therefore spend as much of our time as may be in that blessed work in which we hope to spend a joyful eternity. 2. Blessed are the people, the inhabitants of the country, who, though they do not constantly dwell in God's house as the priests do, yet have liberty of access to it at the times appointed for their solemn feasts, the three great feasts, at which all the males were obliged to give their attendance, Deu. 16:16. David was so far from reckoning this an imposition, and a hardship put upon them, that he envies the happiness of those who might thus attend, *v.* 5–7. Those whom he pronounces blessed are here described. (1.) They are such as act in religion from a rooted principle of dependence upon God and devotedness to him: *Blessed is the man whose strength is in thee,* who makes thee his strength and strongly stays himself upon thee, who makes thy name his strong tower into which he runs for safety, Prov. 18:10. *Happy is the man whose hope is in the Lord his God,* Ps. 40:4; 146:5. Those are truly happy who go forth, and go on, in the exercises of religion, not in their own strength (for then the work is sure to miscarry), but in the strength of the grace of Jesus Christ, from whom all our sufficiency is. David wished to return to God's tabernacles again, that there he might strengthen himself in the Lord his God for service and suffering. (2.) They are such as have a love for holy ordinances: *In whose heart are the ways of them,* that is, who, having placed their happiness in God as their end, rejoice in all the ways that lead to him, all those means by which their graces are strengthened and their communion with him kept up. They not only walk in these ways, but they have them in their hearts, they lay them near their hearts; no care or concern, no pleasure or delight, lies nearer than this. Note, Those who have the new Jerusalem in their eye must have the ways that lead to it in their heart, must mind them, their eyes must look straight forward in them, must ponder the paths of them, must keep close to them, and be afraid of turning aside to the right hand or to the left. If we make God's promise our strength, we must make God's word our rule, and walk by it. (3.) They are such as will break through difficulties and discouragements in waiting upon God in holy ordinances, *v.* 6. When they come up out of the country to worship at the feasts their way lies through many a dry and sandy valley (so some), in which they are ready to perish for thirst; but, to guard against that inconvenience, they dig little pits to receive and keep the rain-water, which is ready to them and others for their refreshment. When they make the pools the ram of heaven fills them. If we be ready to receive the grace of God, that grace shall not be wanting to us, but shall be sufficient for us at all times. Their way lay through many a weeping valley, so Baca signifies, that is (as others understand it), many watery valleys, which in wet weather, when *the rain filled the pools,* either through the rising of the waters or through the dirtiness of the way were impassable; but, by draining and trenching them, they made a road through them for the benefit of those who went up to Jerusalem. Care should be taken to keep those roads in repair that lead to church, as well as those that lead to market. But all this is intended to show, [1.] That they had a good will to the journey. When they were to attend the solemn feasts at Jerusalem, they would not be kept back by bad weather, or bad ways, nor make those an excuse for staying at home. Difficulties in the way of duty are designed to try our resolution; and *he that observes the wind shall not sow.* [2.] That they made the best of the way to Zion, contrived and took pains to mend it where it was bad, and bore, as well as they could, the inconveniences that could not be removed. Our way to heaven lies through a valley of Baca, but even that may be made a well if we make a due improvement of the comforts God has provided for the pilgrims to the heavenly city. (4.) They are such as are still pressing forward till they come to their journey's end at length, and do not take up short of it (*v.* 7): *They go from strength to strength;* their company increases by the accession of more out of every town they pass through, till they become very numerous. Those that were near staid till those that were further off called on them, saying, *Come, and let us go to the house of the Lord* (Ps. 122:1, 2), that they might go together in a body, in token of their mutual love. Or the particular persons, instead of being fatigued with the tediousness of their journey and the difficulties they met with, the nearer they came to Jerusalem the more lively and cheerful they were, and so went on *stronger and stronger,* Job 17:9. Thus it is promised that those that *wait on the Lord shall renew their strength,* Isa. 40:31. Even where they are weak, there they are strong. They go *from virtue to virtue* (so some); it is the same word that is used for the virtuous woman. Those that press forward in their Christian course shall find God adding grace to their graces, Jn. 1:16. They shall be changed from glory to glory (2 Co. 3:18), from one degree of glorious grace to another, till, at length, *every one of them appears before God in Zion,* to give glory to him and receive blessings from him. Note, Those who grow in grace shall, at last, be perfect in glory. The Chaldee reads it, *They go from the house of the sanctuary to the house of doctrine; and the pains which they have taken about the law shall appear before God, whose majesty dwells in Zion.* We must go from one duty to another, from prayer to the word, from practising what we have learned to learn more; and, if we do this, the benefit of it will appear, to God's glory and our own everlasting comfort.

Verses 8–12

Here, I. The psalmist prays for audience and acceptance with God, not mentioning particularly what he desired God would do for him. He needed to say no more when he had professed such an affectionate esteem for the ordinances of God, which now he was restrained and banished from. All his desire was, in that profession, plainly before God, and his longing, his groaning, was not hidden from him; therefore he prays (*v.* 8, 9) only that God would hear his prayer and give ear, that he would behold his condition, behold his good affection, and look upon his face, which way it was set, and how his countenance discovered the longing desire he had towards God's courts. He calls himself (as many think) *God's anointed,* for David was anointed by him and anointed for him. In this petition, 1. He has an eye to God under several of his glorious titles — as *the Lord God of hosts,* who has all the creatures at his command, and therefore has all power both in heaven and in earth, — as the *God of Jacob,* a God in covenant with his own people, a God who never said to the praying seed of Jacob, *Seek you me in vain,* — and as *God our shield,* who takes his people under his special protection, pursuant to his covenant with Abraham their father. Gen. 15:1, *Fear not, Abraham, I am thy shield.* When David could not be hidden in the secret of God's tabernacle (Ps. 27:5), being at a distance from it, yet he hoped to find God his shield ready to him wherever he was. 2. He has an eye to the Mediator; for of him I rather understand those words, *Look upon the face of thy Messiah,* thy anointed one, for of his anointing David spoke, Ps. 45:7. In all our addresses to God we must desire that he would look upon the face of Christ, accept us for his sake, and be well-pleased with us in him. We must look with an eye of faith, and then God will with an eye of favour look *upon the face of the anointed,* who does show his face when we without him dare not show ours.

II. He pleads his love to God's ordinances and his dependence upon God himself.

1. God's courts were his choice, *v.* 10. A very great regard he had for holy ordinances: he valued them above any thing else, and he expresses his value for them, (1.) By preferring the time of God's worship before all other time: *A day spent in thy courts,* in attending on the services of religion, wholly abstracted from all secular affairs, *is better than a thousand,* not than a thousand in thy courts, but any where else in this world, though in the midst of all the delights of the children of men. Better than a thousand, he does not say *days,* you may supply it with years, with ages, if you will, and yet David will set his hand to it. "A day in thy courts, a sabbath day, a holy day, a feast-day, though but one day, would be very welcome to me; nay" (as some of the rabbin paraphrase it), "though I were to die for it the next day, yet that would be more sweet than years spent in the business and pleasure of this world. One of these days shall with its pleasure *chase a thousand, and two put ten thousand to flight,* to shame, as not worthy to be compared." (2.) By preferring the place of worship before any other place: *I would rather be a door-keeper,* rather be in the meanest place and office, *in the house of my God, than dwell* in state, as master, *in the tents of wickedness.* Observe, He calls even the tabernacle a house, for the presence of God in it made even those curtains more stately than a palace and more strong than a castle. It is the house of my God; the covenant-interest he had in God as his God was the sweet string on which he loved dearly to be harping; those, and those only, who can, upon good ground, call God theirs, delight in the courts of his house. I would rather be a porter in God's house than a prince in those tents where wickedness reigns, rather lie at the threshold (so the word is); that was the beggar's place (Acts 3:2): "no matter" (says David), "let that be my place rather than none." The Pharisees loved synagogues well enough, provided they might have the uppermost seats there (Mt. 23:6), that they might make a figure. Holy David is not solicitous about that; if he may but be admitted to the threshold, he will say, *Master, it is good to be here.* Some read it, *I would rather be fixed to a post in the house of my God than live at liberty in the tents of wickedness,* alluding to the law concerning servants, who, if they would not go out free, were to have their ear bored to the door-post, Ex. 21:5, 6. David loved his master and loved his work so well that he desired to be tied to this service for ever, to be more free to it, but never to go out free from it, preferring bonds to duty far before the greatest liberty to sin. Such a superlative delight have holy hearts in holy duties; no satisfaction in their account comparable to that in communion with God.

2. God himself was his hope, and joy, and all. *Therefore* he loved the house of his God, because his expectation was from his God, and there he used to communicate himself, *v.* 11. See, (1.) What God is, and will be, to his people: *The Lord God is a sun and shield.* We are here in darkness, but, if God be our God, he will be to us a sun, to enlighten and enliven us, to guide and direct us. We are here in danger, but he will be to us a shield to secure us from the fiery darts that fly thickly about us. *With his favour he will compass us as with a shield.* Let us therefore always *walk in the light of the Lord,* and never throw ourselves out of his protection, and we shall find him a sun to supply us with all good and a shield to shelter us from all evil. (2.) What he does, and will, bestow upon them: *The Lord will give grace and glory.* Grace signifies both the good-will of God towards us and the good work of God in us; glory signifies both the honour which he now puts upon us, in giving us the adoption of sons, and that which he has prepared for us in the inheritance of sons. God will give them grace in this world as a preparation for glory, and glory in the other world as the perfection of grace; both are God's gift, his free gift. And as, on the one hand, wherever God gives grace he will give glory (for grace is glory begun, and is an earnest of it), so, on the other hand, he will give glory hereafter to none to whom he does not give grace now, or who receive his grace in vain. And if God will give grace and glory, which are the two great things that concur to make us happy in both worlds, we may be sure that *no good thing will be withheld from those that walk uprightly.* It is the character of all good people that they walk uprightly, that they worship God in spirit and in truth, and have their conversation in the world in simplicity and godly sincerity; and such may be sure that God will withhold *no good thing from them,* that is requisite to their comfortable passage through this world. Make sure grace and glory, and *other things shall be added.* This is a comprehensive promise, and is such an assurance of the present comfort of the saints that, whatever they desire, and think they need, they may be sure that either Infinite Wisdom sees it is not good for them or Infinite Goodness will give it to them in due time. Let it be our care to walk uprightly, and then let us trust God to give us every thing that is good for us.

Lastly, He pronounces those blessed who put their confidence in God, as he did, *v.* 12. Those are blessed who have the liberty of ordinances and the privileges of God's house. But, though we should be debarred from them, yet we are not therefore debarred from blessedness if we trust in God. If we cannot go to the house of the Lord, we may go by faith to the Lord of the house, and in him we shall be happy and may be easy.

PSALM 85

Interpreters are generally of the opinion that this psalm was penned after the return of the Jews out of their captivity in Babylon, when they still remained under some tokens of God's displeasure, which they here pray for the removal of. And nothing appears to the contrary, but that it might be penned then, as well as Ps. 137. They are the public interests that lie near the psalmist's heart here, and the psalm is penned for the great congregation. The church was here in a deluge; above were clouds, below were waves; every thing was dark and dismal. The church is like Noah in the ark, between life and death, between hope and fear; being so, I. Here is the dove sent forth in prayer. The petitions are against sin and wrath (*v.* 4) and for mercy and grace (*v.* 7). The pleas are taken from former favours (*v.* 1–3) and present distresses (*v.* 5, 6). II. Here is the dove returning with an olive branch of peace and good tidings; the psalmist expects her return (*v.* 8) and then recounts the favours to God's Israel which by the spirit of prophecy he gave assurance of to others, and by the spirit of faith he took the assurance of to himself (*v.* 9–13). In singing this psalm we may be assisted in our prayers to God both for his church in general and for the land of our nativity in particular. The former part will be of use to direct our desires, the latter to encourage our faith and hope in those prayers.

To the chief musician. A psalm for the sons of Korah.

Verses 1–7

The church, in affliction and distress, is here, by direction from God, making her application to God. So ready is God to hear and answer the prayers of his people that by his Spirit in the word, and in the heart, he indites their petitions and puts words into their mouths. The people of God, in a very low and weak condition, are here taught how to address themselves to God.

I. They are to acknowledge with thankfulness the great things God had done for them (*v.* 1–3): "Thou has done so and so for us and our fathers." Note, The sense of present afflictions should not drown the remembrance of former mercies; but, even when we are brought very low, we must call to remembrance past experiences of God's goodness, which we must take notice of with thankfulness, to his praise. They speak of it here with pleasure, 1. That God had shown himself propitious to their land, and had smiled upon it as his own: *"Thou hast been favourable to thy land,* as thine, with distinguishing favours." Note, The favour of God is the spring-head of all good, and the fountain of happiness, to nations, as well as to particular persons. It was by the favour of God that Israel got and kept possession of Canaan (Ps. 44:3); and, if he had not continued very favourable to them, they would have been ruined many a time. 2. That he had rescued them out of the hands of their enemies and restored them to their liberty: *"Thou hast brought back the captivity of Jacob,* and settled those in their own land again that had been driven out and were strangers in a strange land, prisoners in the land of their oppressors." The captivity of Jacob, though it may continue long, will be brought back in due time. 3. That he had not dealt with them according to the desert of their provocations (*v.* 2): *"Thou hast forgiven the iniquity of thy people,* and not punished them as in justice thou mightest. *Thou hast covered all their sin."* When God forgives sin he covers it; and, when he covers the sin of his people, he covers it all. The bringing back of their captivity was *then* an instance of God's favour to them, when it was accompanied with the pardon of their iniquity. 4. That he had not continued his anger against them so far, and so long, as they had reason to fear (*v.* 3): "Having *covered all their sin,* thou hast *taken away all thy wrath;"* for when sin is set aside God's anger ceases; God is pacified if we are purified. See what the pardon of sin is: *Thou hast forgiven the iniquity of thy people,* that is, *"Thou hast turned thy anger from waxing hot,* so as to consume us in the flame of it. In compassion to us thou hast not stirred up all thy wrath, but, when an intercessor has stood before thee in the gap, thou hast turned away thy anger."

II. They are taught to pray to God for grace and mercy, in reference to their present distress; this is inferred from the former: "Thou hast done well for our fathers; do well for us, for we are the children of the same covenant." 1. They pray for converting grace: *"Turn us, O God of our salvation!* in order to the turning of our captivity; turn us from iniquity; turn us to thyself and to our duty; turn us, and we shall be turned." All those whom God will save sooner or later he will turn. If no conversion, no salvation. 2. They pray for the removal of the tokens of God's displeasure which they were under: *"Cause thine anger towards us to cease,* as thou didst many a time cause it to cease in the days of our fathers, when thou didst take away thy wrath from them." Observe the method, "First turn us to thee, and then cause thy anger to turn from us." When we are reconciled to God, then, and not till then, we may expect the comfort of his being reconciled to us. 3. They pray for the manifestation of God's goodwill to them (*v.* 7): *"Show us thy mercy, O Lord!* show thyself merciful to us; not only have mercy on us, but let us have the comfortable evidences of that mercy; let us know that thou hast mercy on us and mercy in store for us." 4. They pray that God would, graciously to them and gloriously to himself, appear on their behalf: *"Grant us thy salvation;* grant it by thy promise, and then, no doubt, thou wilt work it by thy providence." Note, The vessels of God's mercy are the heirs of his salvation; he shows mercy to those to whom he grants salvation; for salvation is of mere mercy.

III. They are taught humbly to expostulate with God concerning their present troubles, *v.* 5, 6. Here observe, 1. What they dread and deprecate: *"Wilt thou be angry with us for ever?* We are undone if thou art, but we hope thou wilt not. *Wilt thou draw out thy anger unto all generations?* No; thou art gracious, slow to anger, and swift to show mercy, and wilt not contend for ever. Thou wast not angry with our fathers for ever, but didst soon turn thyself from the fierceness of thy wrath; why then wilt thou be angry with us for ever? Are not thy mercies and compassions as plentiful and powerful as ever they were? Impenitent sinners God will be angry with for ever; for what is hell but the wrath of God drawn out unto endless generations? But shall a hell upon earth be the lot of thy people?" 2. What they desire and hope for: *"Wilt thou not revive us again* (*v.* 6), revive us with comforts spoken to us, revive us with deliverances wrought for us? Thou hast been favourable to thy land formerly, and that revived it; wilt thou not again be favourable, and so revive it again?" God had granted to the children of the captivity *some reviving in their bondage,* Ezra 9:8. Their return out of Babylon was as *life from the dead,* Eze. 37:11, 12. Now, Lord (say they), *wilt thou not revive us again,* and *put thy hand again the second time* to gather us in? Isa. 11:11; Ps. 126:1, 4. *Revive thy work in the midst of the years,* Hab. 3:2. "Revive us again," (1.) "That thy people may rejoice; and so we shall have the comfort of it," Ps. 14:7. Give them life, that they may have joy. (2.) "That they may rejoice in thee; and so thou wilt have the glory of it." If God be the fountain of all our mercies, he must be the centre of all our joys.

Verses 8–13

We have here an answer to the prayers and expostulations in the foregoing verses.

I. In general, it is an answer of peace. This the psalmist is soon aware of (*v.* 8), for he *stands upon his watch-tower* to *hear what God will say unto him,* as the prophet, Hab. 2:1, 2. *I will hear what God the Lord will speak.* This intimates, 1. The stilling of his passions — his grief, his fear — and the tumult of his spirit which they occasioned: "Compose thyself, O my soul! in a humble silence to attend upon God and wait his motions. I have spoken enough, or too much; now I will hear what God will speak, and welcome his holy will. *What saith my Lord unto his servant?"* If we would have God to hear what we say to him by prayer, we must be ready to hear what he says to us by his word. 2. The raising of his expectation; now that he has been at prayer he looks for something very great, and very kind, from the God that hears prayer. When we have prayed we should look after our prayers, and stay for an answer. Now observe here, (1.) What it is that he promises himself from God, in answer to his prayers: *He will speak peace to his people, and to his saints.* There are a people in the world who are God's people, set apart for him, subject to him, and who shall be saved by him. All his people are his saints, sanctified by his grace and devoted to his glory; these may sometimes want peace, when without are fightings and within are fears; but, sooner or later, God will speak peace to them; if he do not command outward peace, yet he will suggest inward peace, speaking that to their hearts by his Spirit which he has spoken to their ears by his word and ministers and making them to hear joy and gladness. (2.) What use he makes of this expectation. [1.] He takes the comfort of it; and so must we: *"I will hear what God the Lord will speak,* hear the assurances he gives of peace, in answer to prayer." When God speaks peace we must not be deaf to it, but with all humility and thankfulness receive it. [2.] He cautions the saints to do the duty which this calls for: *But let them not turn again to folly;* for it is on these terms, and no other, that peace is to be expected. To those, and those only, peace is spoken, who turn from sin; but, if they return to it again, it is at their peril. All sin is folly, but especially backsliding; it is egregious folly to turn to sin after we have seemed to turn from it, to turn to it after God has spoken peace. God is for peace, but, when he speaks, such are for war.

II. Here are the particulars of this answer of peace. He doubts not but all will be well in a little time, and therefore gives us the pleasing prospect of the flourishing estate of the church in the last five verses of the psalm, which describe the peace and prosperity that God, at length, blessed the children of the captivity with, when, after a great deal of toil and agitation, at length they gained a settlement in their own land. But it may be taken both as a promise also to all who fear God and work righteousness, that they shall be easy and happy, and as a prophecy of the kingdom of the Messiah and the blessings with which that kingdom should be enriched. Here is,

1. Help at hand (*v.* 9): *"Surely his salvation is nigh,* nigh to us, nigher than we think it is: it will soon be effected, how great soever our difficulties and distresses are, when God's time shall come, and that time is not far off." When the tale of bricks is doubled, then Moses comes. It is nigh to all who fear him; when trouble is nigh salvation is nigh, for God is a very present help in time of trouble to all who are his; whereas *salvation is far from the wicked,* Ps. 119:155. This may fitly be applied to Christ the author of eternal salvation: it was the comfort of the Old-Testament saints that, though they lived not to see that redemption in Jerusalem which they waited for, yet they were sure it was nigh, and would be welcome, to all that fear God.

2. Honour secured: *"That glory may dwell in our land,* that we may have the worship of God settled and established among us; for that is the glory of a land. When that goes, *Ichabod — the glory has departed;* when that stays glory dwells." This may refer to the Messiah, who was to be *the glory of his people Israel,* and who came and dwelt among them (Jn. 1:4), for which reason their land is called *Immanuel's land,* Isa. 8:8.

3. Graces meeting, and happily embracing (*v.* 10, 11): *Mercy and truth, righteousness and peace, kiss each other.* This may be understood, (1.) Of the reformation of the people and of the government, in the administration of which all those graces should be conspicuous and commanding. The rulers and ruled shall all be merciful and true, righteous and peaceable. When there is no truth nor mercy all goes to ruin (Hos. 4:1; Isa. 59:14, 15); but when these meet in the management of all affairs, when these give aim, when these give law, when there is such plenty of truth that it sprouts up like the grass of the earth, and of righteousness that it is showered down like rain from heaven, then things go well. When in every congress mercy and truth meet, in every embrace righteousness and peace kiss, and common honesty is indeed common, then glory dwells in a land, as the sin of reigning dishonesty is a reproach to any people. (2.) Of the return of God's favour, and the continuance of it, thereupon. When a people return to God and adhere to him in a way of duty he will return to them and abide with them in a way of mercy. So some understand this, man's truth and God's mercy, man's righteousness and God's peace, meet together. If God find us true to him, to one another, to ourselves, we shall find him merciful. If we make conscience of righteousness, we shall have the comfort of peace. If *truth spring out of the earth,* that is (as Dr. Hammond expounds it), out of the hearts of men, the proper soil for it to grow in, righteousness (that is, God's mercy) shall look down from heaven, as the sun does upon the world when it sheds its influences on the productions of the earth and cherishes them. (3.) Of the harmony of the divine attributes in the Messiah's undertaking. In him who is both our salvation and our glory *mercy and truth have met together;* God's mercy and truth, and his *righteousness and peace, have kissed each other;* that is, the great affair of our salvation is so well contrived, so well concerted, that God may have mercy upon poor sinners, and be at peace with them, without any wrong to his truth and righteousness. He is true to the threatening, and just in his government, and yet pardons sinners and takes them into covenant with himself. Christ, as Mediator, brings heaven and earth together again, which sin had set at variance; through him *truth springs out of the earth,* that truth which God *desires in the inward part,* and then *righteousness looks down from heaven;* for God is *just, and the justifier of those who believe in Jesus.* Or it may denote that in the kingdom of the Messiah these graces shall flourish and prevail and have a universal command.

4. Great plenty of every thing desirable (*v.* 12): *The Lord shall give that which is good,* every thing that he sees to be good for us. All good comes from God's goodness; and when mercy, truth, and righteousness, have a sovereign influence on men's hearts and lives, all good may be expected. If we thus *seek the righteousness of God's kingdom, other things shall be added;* Mt. 6:33. When the glory of the gospel dwells in our land, then it shall yield its increase, for soul-prosperity will either bring outward prosperity along with it or sweeten the want of it. See Ps. 67:6.

5. A sure guidance in the good way (*v.* 13): *The righteousness* of his promise which he has made to us, assuring us of happiness, and the righteousness of sanctification, that good work which he has wrought in us, these shall go before him to prepare his way, both to raise our expectations of his favour and to qualify us for it; and these shall go before us also, and be our guide to *set us in the way of his steps,* that is, to encourage our hopes and guide our practice, that we may go forth to meet him when he is coming towards us in ways of mercy. Christ, the sun of righteousness, shall bring us to God, and put us into the way that leads to him. John Baptist, a preacher of righteousness, shall go before Christ to prepare his way. Righteousness is a sure guide both in meeting God and in following him.

PSALM 86

This psalm is entitled "a prayer of David;" probably it was not penned upon any particular occasion, but was a prayer he often used himself, and recommended to others for their use, especially in a day of affliction. Many think that David penned this prayer as a type of Christ, "who in the days of his flesh offered up strong cries," Heb. 5:7. David, in this prayer (according to the nature of that duty), I. Gives glory to God (*v.* 8–10, 12, 13). II. Seeks for grace and favour from God, that God would hear his prayers (*v.* 1, 6, 7), preserve and save him, and be merciful to him (*v.* 2, 3, 16), that he would give him joy, and grace, and strength, and put honour upon him (*v.* 4, 11, 17). He pleads God's goodness (*v.* 5, 15) and the malice of his enemies (*v.* 14). In singing this we must, as David did, lift up our souls to God with application.

A Prayer of David.

Verses 1-7

This psalm was published under the title of *a prayer of David;* not as if David sung all his prayers, but into some of his songs he inserted prayers; for a psalm will admit the expressions of any pious and devout affections. But it is observable how very plain the language of this psalm is, and how little there is in it of poetic flights or figures, in comparison with some other psalms; for the flourishes of wit are not the proper ornaments of prayer. Now here we may observe,

I. The petitions he puts up to God. It is true, prayer accidentally may preach, but it is most fit that (as it is in this prayer) every passage should be directed to God, for such is the nature of prayer as it is here described (v. 4): *Unto thee, O Lord! do I lift up my soul,* as he had said Ps. 25:1. In all the parts of prayer the soul must ascend upon the wings of faith and holy desire, and be lifted up to God, to meet the communications of his grace, and in an expectation raised very high of great things from him. 1. He begs that God would give a gracious audience to his prayers (v. 1): *Bow down thy ear, O Lord! hear me.* When God hears our prayers it is fitly said that he *bows down his ear* to them, for it is admirable condescension in God that he is pleased to take notice of such mean creatures as we are and such defective prayers as ours are. He repeats this again (v. 6): "*Give ear, O Lord! unto my prayer,* a favourable ear, though it be whispered, though it be stammered; *attend to the voice of my supplications.*" Not that God needs to have his affection stirred up by any thing that we can say; but thus we must express our desire of his favour. The Son of David spoke it with assurance and pleasure (Jn. 11:41, 42), *Father, I thank thee that thou hast heard me; and I know that thou hearest me always.* 2. He begs that God would take him under his special protection, and so be the author of his salvation (v. 2): *Preserve my soul; save thy servant.* It was David's soul that was God's servant; for those only serve God acceptably that *serve him with their spirits.* David's concern is about his soul; if we understand it of his natural life, it teaches us that the best self-preservation is to commit ourselves to God's keeping and by faith and prayer to make our Creator our preserver. But it may be understood of his spiritual life, the life of the soul as distinct from the body: "Preserve my soul from that one evil and dangerous thing to souls, even from sin; preserve my soul, and so save me." All those whom God will save he preserves, and will preserve them to his heavenly kingdom. 3. He begs that God would look upon him with an eye of pity and compassion (v. 3): *Be merciful to me, O Lord!* It is mercy in God to pardon our sins and to help us out of our distresses; both these are included in this prayer, *God be merciful to me.* "Men show no mercy; we ourselves deserve no mercy, but, Lord, for mercy-sake, be *merciful unto me.*" 4. He begs that God would fill him with inward comfort (v. 4): *Rejoice the soul of thy servant.* It is God only that can *put gladness into the heart and make the soul to rejoice,* and then, and not till then, the joy is full; and, as it is the duty of those who are God's servants to *serve him with gladness,* so it is their privilege to be *filled with joy and peace in believing,* and they may in faith pray, not only that God will preserve their souls, but that he will rejoice their souls, and the *joy of the Lord* will be *their strength.* Observe, When he prays, *Rejoice my soul,* he adds, *For unto thee do I lift up my soul.* Then we may expect comfort from God when we take care to keep up our communion with God: prayer is the nurse of spiritual joy.

II. The pleas with which he enforces these petitions. 1. He pleads his relation to God and interest in him: "Thou art my God, to whom I have devoted myself, and on whom I depend, and I am thy servant (v. 2), in subjection to thee, and therefore looking for protection from thee." 2. He pleads his distress: "*Hear me, for I am poor and needy,* therefore I want thy help, therefore none else will hear me." God is the poor man's King, whose glory it is to *save the souls of the needy;* those who are poor in spirit, who see themselves empty and necessitous, are most welcome to the God of all grace. 3. He pleads God's good will towards all that seek him (v. 5): "To thee do I *lift up my soul* in desire and expectation; *for thou, Lord, art good;*" and whither should beggars go but to the door of the good house-keeper? The goodness of God's nature is a great encouragement to us in all our addresses to him. His goodness appears in two things, giving and forgiving. (1.) He is a sin-pardoning God; not only he can forgive, but he is ready to forgive, more ready to forgive than we are to repent. *I said, I will confess, and thou forgavest,* Ps. 32:5. (2.) He is a prayer-hearing God; he is plenteous in mercy, very full, and very free, both rich and liberal unto *all those that call upon him;* he has wherewithal to supply all their needs and is openhanded in granting that supply. 4. He pleads God's good work in himself, by which he had qualified him for the tokens of his favour. Three things were wrought in him by divine grace, which he looked upon as earnests of all good: — (1.) A conformity to God (v. 2): *I am holy,* therefore preserve my soul; for those whom the Spirit sanctifies he will preserve. He does not say this in pride and vain glory, but with humble thankfulness to God. *I am one whom thou favourest* (so the margin reads it), whom thou hast *set apart for thyself.* If God has begun a good work of grace in us, we must own that *the time was a time of love. Then was I in his eyes as one that found favour,* and whom God hath taken into his favour he will take under his protection. *All his saints are in thy hand,* Deu. 33:3. Observe, *I am needy* (v. 1), yet *I am holy* (v. 2), holy and yet needy, *poor in the world, but rich in faith.* Those who preserve their purity in their greatest poverty may assure themselves that God will preserve their comforts, will preserve their souls. (2.) A confidence in God: *Save thy servant that trusteth in thee.* Those that are holy must nevertheless not trust in themselves, nor in their own righteousness, but only in God and his grace. Those that trust in God may expect salvation from him. (3.) A disposition to communion with God. He hopes God will answer his prayers, because he had inclined him to pray. [1.] To be constant in prayer: *I cry unto thee daily, and all the day,* v. 3. It is thus our duty to pray always, without ceasing, and to continue instant in prayer; and then we may hope to have our prayers heard which we make in the time of trouble, if we have made conscience of the duty at other times, at all times. It is comfortable if an affliction finds the wheels of prayer a-going, and that hey are not then to be set a-going. [2.] To be inward with God in prayer, to *lift up his soul* to him, v. 4. Then we may hope that God will meet us with his mercies, when we in our prayers send forth our souls as it were to meet him. [3.] To be in a special manner earnest with God in prayer when he was in affliction (v. 7): "*In the day of my trouble,* whatever others do, *I will call upon thee,* and commit my case to thee, for thou wilt hear and answer me, and I shall not seek in vain, as those did who cried, *O Baal! hear us; but there was no voice, nor any that regarded,*" 1 Ki. 18:29.

Verses 8-17

David is here going on in his prayer.

I. He gives glory to God; for we ought in our prayers to praise him, ascribing kingdom, power, and glory, to him, with the most humble and reverent adorations. 1. As a being of unparalleled perfection, such a one that there is none like him nor any to be compared with him, v. 8. *Among the gods,* the false gods, whom the heathens worshipped, the angels, the kings of the earth, among them all, *there is none like unto thee, O Lord!* none so wise, so mighty, so good; *neither are there any works like unto thy works,* which is an undeniable proof that there is none like him; his own works praise him, and the best way we have of praising him is by acknowledging that there is none like him. 2. As the fountain of all being and the centre of all praise (v. 9): "*Thou hast made all nations,* made them all of one blood; they all derive their being from thee, and have a constant dependence on thee, and therefore *they shall come and worship before thee and glorify thy name.*" This was in part fulfilled in the multitude of proselytes to the Jewish religion in the days of David and Solomon, but was to have its full accomplishment in the days of the Messiah, when some out of every kingdom and nation should be effectually brought in to praise God, Rev. 7:9. It was by Christ that God made all nations, for without him was not any thing made that was made, and therefore through Christ, and by the power of his gospel and grace, all nations shall be brought to *worship before God,* Isa. 66:23. 3. As a being infinitely great (v. 10): "Therefore all nations shall worship before thee, because as King of nations thou

art great, thy sovereignty absolute and incontestable, thy majesty terrible and insupportable, thy power universal and irresistible, thy riches vast and inexhaustible, thy dominion boundless and unquestionable; and, for the proof of this, *thou doest wondrous things,* which all nations admire, and whence they might easily infer that thou art God alone, not only none like thee, but none besides thee." Let us always entertain great thoughts of this great God, and be filled with holy admiration of this God who doeth wonders; and let him alone have our hearts who is God alone. 4. As a being infinitely good. Man is bad, very wicked and vile (v. 14); no mercy is to be expected from him; *but thou, O Lord! art a God full of compassion, and gracious, v.* 15. This is that attribute by which he proclaims his name, and by which we are therefore to proclaim it, Ex. 34:6, 7. It is his goodness that is over all his works, and therefore should fill all our praises; and this is our comfort, in reference to the wickedness of the world we live in, that, however it be, God is good. Men are barbarous, but God is gracious; men are false, but God is faithful. God is not only compassionate, but full of compassion, and in him *mercy rejoiceth against judgment.* He is long-suffering towards us, though we forfeit his favour and provoke him to anger, and he is *plenteous in mercy and truth,* as faithful in performing as he was free in promising. 5. As a kind friend and bountiful benefactor to him. We ought to praise God as good in himself, but we do it most feelingly when we observe how good he has been to us. This therefore the psalmist dwells upon with most pleasure, v. 12, 13. He had said (v. 9), *All nations shall praise thee, O Lord! and glorify thy name.* It is some satisfaction to a good man to think that others shall praise and glorify God, but it is his greatest care and pleasure to do it himself. "Whatever others do" (says David), "*I will praise thee, O Lord my God!* not only as the Lord, but as my God; and I will do it with all my heart; I will be ready to do it and cordial in it; I will do it with cheerfulness and liveliness, with a sincere regard to thy honour; for *I will glorify thy name,* not for a time, but for evermore. I will do it as long as I live, and hope to be doing it to eternity." With good reason does he resolve to be thus particular in praising God, because God had shown him particular favours: *For great is thy mercy towards me.* The fountain of mercy is inexhaustibly full; the streams of mercy are inestimably rich. When we speak of God's mercy to us, it becomes us thus to magnify it: *Great is thy mercy towards me.* Of the greatness of God's mercy he gives this instance, *Thou hast delivered my soul from the lowest hell,* from death, from so great a death, as St. Paul (2 Co. 1:10), from eternal death, so even some of the Jewish writers understand it. David knew he deserved to be cast off for ever into the lowest hell for his sin in the matter of Uriah; but Nathan assured him that the Lord had *taken away his sin,* and by that word he was delivered from the lowest hell, and herein God's mercy was great towards him. Even the best saints owe it, not to their own merit, but to the mercy of God, that they are saved from the lowest hell; and the consideration of that should greatly enlarge their hearts in praising the mercy of God, which they are obliged to glorify for evermore. So glorious; so gracious, a rescue from everlasting misery, justly requires the return of everlasting praise.

II. He prays earnestly for mercy and grace from God. He complains of the restless and implacable malice of his enemies against him (v. 14): "Lord, be thou for me; for there are many against me." He then takes notice of their character; they were *proud men* that looked with disdain upon poor David. (Many are made persecutors by their pride.) They were *violent men,* that would carry all before them by force, right or wrong. They were *terrible formidable men* (so some), that did what they could to frighten all about them. He notices their number: There were *assemblies* of them; they were men in authority and met in councils and courts, or men for conversation, and met in clubs; but, being assembled, they were the more capable of doing mischief. He notices their enmity to him: They *rise up against me* in open rebellion; they not only plot, but they put their plots in execution as far as they can; and the design is not only to depose me, but to destroy me: they seek after my life, to slay me; after my soul, to damn me, if it lay in their power." And, *lastly,* He notices their distance and estrangement from God, which were at the bottom of their enmity to David: "*They have not set thee before *them;* and what good can be expected from those that have no fear of God before their eyes? Lord, appear against them, for they are thy enemies as well as mine." His petitions are,

1. For the operations of God's grace in him, *v.* 11. He prays that God would give him, (1.) An understanding heart, that he would inform and instruct him concerning his duty: *"Teach me thy way, O Lord!* the way that thou hast appointed me to walk in; when I am in doubt concerning it, make it plain to me what I should do; let me hear the voice saying, *This is the way,"* Isa. 30:21. David was well taught in the things of God, and yet was sensible he needed further instruction, and many a time could not trust his own judgment: *Teach me thy way; I will walk in thy truth.* One would think it should be, *Teach me thy truth, and I will walk in thy way;* but it comes all to one; it is the way of truth that God teaches and that we must choose to walk in, Ps. 119:30. Christ is the way and the truth, and we must both learn Christ and walk in him. We cannot walk in God's way and truth unless he teach us; and, if we expect he should teach us, we must resolve to be governed by his teachings, Isa. 2:3. (2.) An upright heart: *"Unite my heart to fear thy name.* Make me sincere in religion. A hypocrite has a double heart; let mine be single and entire for God, not divided between him and the world, not straggling from him." Our hearts are apt to wander and hang loose; their powers and faculties wander after a thousand foreign things; we have therefore need of God's grace to unite them, that we may serve God with all that is within us, and all little enough to be employed in his service. "Let my heart be fixed for God, and firm and faithful to him, and fervent in serving him; that is a united heart."

2. For the tokens of God's favour to him, *v.* 16, 17. Three things he here prays for: — (1.) That God would speak peace and comfort to him: *"O turn unto me,* as to one thou lovest and hast a kind and tender concern for. My enemies turn against me, my friends turn from me; Lord, do thou turn to me and have mercy upon me; it will be a comfort to me to know that thou pitiest me." (2.) That God would work deliverance for him, and set him in safety: "Give me *thy strength;* put strength into me, that I may help myself, and put forth thy strength for me, that I may be saved out of the hands of those that seek my ruin." He pleads relation: "I am *thy servant;* I am so by birth, as *the son of thy handmaid,* born in thy house, and therefore thou art my rightful owner and proprietor, from whom I may expect protection. *I am thine; save me."* The children of godly parents, who were betimes dedicated to the Lord, may plead it with him; if they come under the discipline of his family, they are entitled to the privileges of it. (3.) That God would put a reputation on him: *"Show me a token for good;* make it to appear to others as well as to myself that thou art doing me good, and designing further good for me. Let me have some unquestionable illustrious instances of thy favour to me, *that those who hate me may see it, and be ashamed* of their enmity to me, as they will have reason to be when they perceive that *thou, Lord, hast helped me and comforted me,* and that therefore they have been striving against God, opposing one whom he owns, and that they have been striving in vain to ruin and vex one whom God himself has undertaken to help and comfort." The joy of the saints shall be the shame of their persecutors.

PSALM 87

The foregoing psalm was very plain and easy, but in this are things dark and hard to be understood. It is an encomium of Zion, as a type and figure of the gospel-church, to which what is here spoken is very applicable. Zion, for the temple's sake, is here preferred, I. Before the rest of the land of Canaan, as being crowned with special tokens of God's favour (*v.* 1–3). II. Before any other place or country whatsoever, as being replenished with more eminent men and with a greater plenty of divine blessings (*v.* 4–7). Some think it was penned to express the joy of God's people when Zion was in a flourishing state; others think it was penned to encourage their faith and hope when Zion was in ruins and was to be rebuilt after the captivity. Though no man cared for her (Jer. 30:17, "This is Zion whom no man seeketh after"), yet God had done great things for her, and spoken glorious things of her, which should all have their perfection and accomplishment in the gospel-church; to that therefore we must have an eye in singing this psalm.

A psalm *or* song for the sons of Korah.

Verses 1–3

Some make the first words of the psalm to be part of the title; it is a psalm or song whose subject is the holy mountains — the temple built in Zion upon Mount Moriah. This is the foundation of the argument, or beginning of the psalm. Or we may suppose the psalmist had now the tabernacle or temple in view and was contemplating the glories of it, and at length he breaks out into this expression, which has reference, though not to what he had written before, yet to what he had thought of; every one knew what he meant when he said thus abruptly, *Its foundation is in the holy mountains.* Three things are here observed, in praise of the temple: — 1. That it was founded on the holy mountains, *v.* 1. The church has a foundation, so that it cannot sink or totter; Christ himself is the foundation of it, which God has laid. The Jerusalem above is a city that has foundations. The foundation is upon the mountains. It is built high; the *mountain of the Lord's house is established upon the top of the mountains,* Isa. 2:2. It is built firmly; the mountains are rocky, and on a rock the church is built. The world is founded upon the seas (Ps. 24:2), which are continually ebbing and flowing, and are a very weak foundation; Babel was built in a plain, where the ground was rotten. But the church is built upon the everlasting mountains and the perpetual hills; for sooner shall the mountains depart, and the hills be removed, than the covenant of God's peace shall be disannulled, and on that the church is built, Isa. 54:10. The foundation is upon the holy mountains. Holiness is the strength and stability of the church: it is this that will support it and keep it from sinking; not so much that it is built upon mountains as that it is built upon holy mountains — upon the promise of God, for the confirming of which he has sworn by his holiness, upon the sanctification of the Spirit, which will secure the happiness of all the saints. 2. That God had expressed a particular affection for it (*v.* 2): *The Lord loveth the gates of Zion,* of the temple, of *the houses of doctrine* (so the Chaldee), *more than all the dwellings of Jacob,* whether in Jerusalem or any where else in the country. God had said concerning Zion, *This is my rest for ever; here will I dwell.* There he met his people, and conversed with them, received their homage, and showed them the tokens of his favour, and therefore we may conclude how well he loves those gates. Note, (1.) God has a love for the dwellings of Jacob, has a gracious regard to religious families and accepts their family-worship. (2.) Yet he loves the gates of Zion better, not only better than any, but better than all, of the dwellings of Jacob. God was worshipped in the dwellings of Jacob, and family-worship is family-duty, which must by no means be neglected; yet, when they come in competition, public worship *(caeteris paribus — other things being equal)* is to be preferred before private. 3. That there was much said concerning it in the word of God (*v.* 3): *Glorious things are spoken of thee, O city of God!* We are to judge of things and persons by the figure they make and the estimate put upon them in and by the scripture. Many base things were spoken of the city of God by the enemies of it, to render it mean and odious; but by him whose judgment we are sure is according to truth glorious things are spoken of it. God said of the temple, *My eyes and my heart shall be there perpetually; I have sanctified this house, that my name may be there for ever,* 2 Chr. 7:16. *Beautiful for situation is Mount Zion,* Ps. 48:2. These are glorious things. Yet more glorious things are spoken of the gospel-church. It is the spouse of Christ, the purchase of his blood; it is a *peculiar people, a holy nation, a royal priesthood,* and the *gates of hell shall not prevail against it.* Let us not be ashamed of the church of Christ in its meanest condition, nor of any that belong to it, nor disown our relation to it, though it be turned ever so much to our reproach, since such glorious things are spoken of it, and not on iota or tittle of what is said shall fall to the ground.

Verses 4–7

Zion is here compared with other places, and preferred before them; the church of Christ is more glorious and excellent than the nations of the earth. 1. It is owned that other places have their glories (*v.* 4): *"I will make mention of Rahab"* (that is, *Egypt*) *"and Babylon, to those that know me* and are about me, and with whom I discourse about public affairs; *behold Philistia and Tyre, with Ethiopia"* (or rather Arabia), "we will observe that *this man was born there;* here and there one famous man, eminent for knowledge and virtue, may be produced, that was a native of these countries; here and there one that becomes a proselyte and worshipper of the true God." But some give another sense of it, supposing that it is a prophecy or promise of bringing the Gentiles into the church and of uniting them in one body with the Jews. God says, *"I will reckon Egypt and Babylon with those that know me.* I will reckon them my people as much as Israel when they shall receive the gospel of Christ, and own them as born in Zion, born again there, and admitted to the privileges of Zion as freely as a true-born Israelite." Those that were strangers and foreigners became *fellow-citizens with the saints,* Eph. 2:19. A Gentile convert shall stand upon a level with a native Jew; compare Isa. 19:23–25. *The Lord shall say, Blessed be Egypt my people, and Assyria the work of my hands, and Israel my inheritance.* 2. It is proved that the glory of Zion outshines them all, upon many accounts; for, (1.) Zion shall produce many great and good men that shall be famous in their generation, *v.* 5. Of Zion it shall be said by all her neighbours that *this and that man were born in her,* many men of renown for wisdom and piety, and especially for acquaintance with the words of God and the visions of the Almighty — many prophets and kings, who should be greater favourites of heaven, and greater blessings to the earth, than ever were bred in Egypt or Babylon. The worthies of the church far exceed those of heathen nations, and their names will shine brighter than in perpetual records. *A man, a man was born in her,* by which some understand Christ, that man, that son of man, who is fairer than the children of men; he was born at Bethlehem near Zion, and was the glory of his people Israel. The greatest honour that ever was put upon the Jewish nation was, that of them, *as concerning the flesh, Christ came,* Rom. 9:5. Or this also may be applied to the conversion of the Gentiles. Of Zion it shall be said that the law which went forth out of Zion, the gospel of Christ, shall be an instrument to beget many souls to God, and the Jerusalem that is from above shall be acknowledged the mother of them all. (2.) Zion's interest shall be strengthened and settled by an almighty power. *The Highest himself shall* undertake to *establish her,* who can do it effectually; the accession of proselytes out of various nations shall be so far from occasioning discord and division that it shall contribute greatly to Zion's strength; for, God himself having founded her upon an everlasting foundation, whatever convulsions and revolutions there are of states and kingdoms, and however heaven and earth may be shaken, these are things which cannot be shaken, but must remain. (3.) Zion's sons shall be registered with honour (*v.* 6): *"The Lord shall count, when he writes up the people,* and takes a catalogue of his subjects, *that this man was born there,* and so is a subject by birth, by the first birth, being born in his house — by the second birth, being born again of his Spirit." When God comes to reckon with the children of men, that he may render to every man according to his works, he will observe who was born in Zion, and consequently enjoyed the privileges of God's sanctuary, to whom pertained the adoption, and the glory, and the covenants, and the service of God, Rom. 9:4; 3:1, 2. For to them much was given, and therefore of them much will be required, and the account will be accordingly; five talents must be improved by those that were entrusted with five. *I know thy works, and where thou dwellest,* and where thou was born. *Selah.* Let those that dwell in Zion *mark this,* and live up to their profession. (4.) Zion's songs shall be sung with joy and triumph: *As well the singers as the players on instruments shall be there* to praise God, *v.* 7. It was much to the honour of Zion, and is to the honour of the gospel-church, that there God is served and worshipped with rejoicing: his work is done, and done cheerfully; see Ps. 68:25. *All my springs are in thee,* O Zion! So God says; he has deposited treasures of grace in his holy ordinances; there are the springs from which those streams take rise *which make glad the city of our God,* Ps. 46:4. So the psalmist says, reckoning the springs from which his dry soul must be watered to lie in the sanctuary, in the word and ordinances, and in the communion of saints. The springs of the joy of a carnal worldling lie in wealth and pleasure; but the springs of the joy of a gracious soul lie in the word of God and prayer. Christ is the true temple; all our springs are in him, and from him all our streams flow. *It pleased the*

Father, and all believers are well pleased with it too, *that in him should all fulness dwell.*

PSALM 88

This psalm is a lamentation, one of the most melancholy of all the psalms; and it does not conclude, as usually the melancholy psalms do, with the least intimation of comfort or joy, but, from first to last, it is mourning and woe. It is not upon a public account that the psalmist here complains (here is no mention of the afflictions of the church), but only upon a personal account, especially trouble of mind, and the grief impressed upon his spirits both by his outward afflictions and by the remembrance of his sins and the fear of God's wrath. It is reckoned among the penitential psalms, and it is well when our fears are thus turned into the right channel, and we take occasion from our worldly grievances to sorrow after a godly sort. In this psalm we have, I. The great pressure of spirit that the psalmist was under (*v.* 3–6). II. The wrath of God, which was the cause of that pressure (*v.* 7, 15–17). III. The wickedness of his friends (*v.* 8, 18). IV. The application he made to God by prayer (*v.* 1, 2, 9, 13). V. His humble expostulations and pleadings with God (*v.* 10, 12, 14). Those who are in trouble of mind may sing this psalm feelingly; those that are not ought to sing it thankfully, blessing God that it is not their case.

A song *or* psalm for the sons of Korah, to the chief musician upon Mahalath Leannoth, Maschil of Heman the Ezrahite.

Verses 1–9

It should seem, by the titles of this and the following psalm, that Heman was the penman of the one and Ethan of the other. There were two, of these names, who were sons of Zerah the son of Judah, 1 Chr. 2:4, 6. There were two others famed for wisdom, 1 Ki. 4:31, where, to magnify Solomon's wisdom, he is said to be *wiser than Heman and Ethan.* Whether the Heman and Ethan who were Levites and precentors in the songs of Zion were the same we are not sure, nor which of these, nor whether any of these, were the penmen of these psalms. There was a Heman that was one of the chief singers, who is called *the king's seer, or prophet,* in the words of God (1 Chr. 25:5); it is probable that this also was a seer, and yet could see no comfort for himself, an instructor and comforter of others, and yet himself putting comfort away from him. The very first words of the psalm are the only words of comfort and support in all the psalm. There is nothing about him but clouds and darkness; but, before he begins his complaint, he calls God *the God of his salvation,* which intimates both that he looked for salvation, bad as things were, and that he looked up to God for the salvation and depended upon him to be the author of it. Now here we have the psalmist,

I. A man of prayer, one that gave himself to prayer at all times, but especially now that he was in affliction; for *is any afflicted? let him pray.* It is his comfort that he had prayed; it is his complaint that, notwithstanding his prayer, he was still in affliction. He was, 1. Very earnest in prayer: *"I have cried unto thee* (*v.* 1), and have *stretched out my hands unto thee* (*v.* 9), as one that would take hold on thee, and even catch at the mercy, with a holy fear of coming short and missing of it." 2. He was very frequent and constant in prayer: *I have called upon thee daily* (*v.* 9), nay, *day and night, v.* 1. For thus men ought always to pray, and not to faint; God's own elect cry day and night to him, not only morning and evening, beginning every day and every night with prayer, but spending the day and night in prayer. This is indeed praying always; and then we shall speed in prayer, when we continue instant in prayer. 3. He directed his prayer to God, and from him expected and desired an answer (*v.* 2): *"Let my prayer come before thee,* to be accepted of thee, not before men, to be seen of them, as the Pharisees' prayers." He does not desire that men should hear them, but, "Lord, *incline thy ear unto my cry,* for to that I refer myself; give what answer to it thou pleasest."

II. He was a man of sorrows, and therefore some make him, in this psalm, a type of Christ, whose complaints on the cross, and sometimes before, were much to the same purport with this psalm. He cries out (*v.* 3): *My soul is full of troubles;* so Christ said, *Now is my soul troubled;* and, in his agony, *My soul is exceedingly sorrowful even unto death,* like the psalmist's here, for he says, *My life draws nigh unto the grave.* Heman was a very wise man, and a very good man, a man of God, and a singer too, and one may therefore suppose him to have been a man of a cheerful spirit, and yet now a man of sorrowful spirit, troubled in mind, and upon the brink of despair. Inward trouble is the sorest trouble, and that which, sometimes, the best of God's saints and servants have been severely exercised with. *The spirit of man,* of the greatest of men, will not always sustain his infirmity, but will droop and sink under it; *who then can bear a wounded spirit?*

III. He looked upon himself as a dying man, whose heart was ready to break with sorrow (*v.* 5): *"Free among the dead* (one of that ghastly corporation), *like the slain that lie in the grave,* whose rotting and perishing nobody takes notice of or is concerned for, nay, whom thou rememberest no more, to protect or provide for the dead bodies, but they become an easy prey to corruption and the worms; they are *cut off from thy hand,* which used to be employed in supporting them and reaching out to them; but, now there is no more occasion for this, they are cut off from it and cut off by it" (*for God will not stretch out his hand to the grave,* Job 30:24); *"thou hast laid me in the lowest pit,* as low as possible, my condition low, my spirits low, *in darkness, in the deep* (*v.* 6), sinking, and seeing no way open of escape, brought to the last extremity, and ready to give up all for gone." Thus greatly may good men be afflicted, such dismal apprehensions may they have concerning their afflictions, and such dark conclusions may they sometimes be ready to make concerning the issue of them, through the power of melancholy and the weakness of faith.

IV. He complained most of God's displeasure against him, which infused the wormwood and the gall into the affliction and the misery (*v.* 7): *Thy wrath lies hard upon me.* Could he have discerned the favour and love of God in his affliction, it would have lain light upon him; but it lay hard, very hard, upon him, so that he was ready to sink and faint under it. The impressions of this wrath upon his spirits were God's *waves* with which he afflicted him, which rolled upon him, one on the neck of another, so that he scarcely recovered from one dark thought before he was oppressed with another; these waves beat against him with noise and fury; not some, but all, of God's waves were made use of in afflicting him and bearing him down. Even the children of God's love may sometimes apprehend themselves children of wrath, and no outward trouble can lie so hard upon them as that apprehension.

V. It added to his affliction that his friends deserted him and made themselves strange to him. When we are in trouble it is some comfort to have those about us that love us, and sympathize with us; but this good man had none such, which gives him occasion, not to accuse them, or charge them with treachery, ingratitude, and inhumanity, but to complain to God, with an eye to his hand in this part of the affliction (*v.* 8): *Thou hast put away my acquaintance far from me.* Providence had removed them, or rendered them incapable of being serviceable to him, or alienated their affections from him; for every creature is that to us (and no more) that God makes it to be. If our old acquaintance be shy of us, and those we expect kindness from prove unkind, we must bear that with the same patient submission to the divine will that we do other afflictions, Job 19:13. Nay, his friends were not only strange to him, but even hated him, because he was poor and in distress: *"Thou hast made me an abomination to them;* they are not only shy of me, but sick of me, and I am looked upon by them, not only with contempt, but with abhorrence." Let none think it strange concerning such a trial as this, when Heman, who was so famed for wisdom, was yet, when the world frowned upon him, neglected, as a vessel in which is no pleasure.

VI. He looked upon his case as helpless and deplorable: *"I am shut up, and I cannot come forth,* a close prisoner, under the arrests of divine wrath, and no way open of escape." He therefore lies down and sinks under his troubles, because he sees not any probability of getting out of them. For thus he bemoans himself (*v.* 9): *My eye mourneth by reason of affliction.* Sometimes giving vent to grief by weeping gives some ease to a troubled spirit. Yet weeping must not hinder praying; we must sow in tears: *My eye mourns,* but *I cry unto thee daily.* Let prayers and tears go together, and they shall be accepted together. *I have heard thy prayers, I have seen thy tears.*

Verses 10–18

In these verses,

I. The psalmist expostulates with God concerning the present deplorable condition he was in (*v.* 10–12): *"Wilt thou do a miraculous work to the dead,* and raise them to life again? Shall those that are dead and buried *rise up to praise thee?* No; they leave it to their children to rise up in their room to praise God; none expects that they should do it; and wherefore should they rise, wherefore should they live, but to praise God? The life we are born to at first, and the life we hope to rise to at last, must thus be spent. But *shall thy lovingkindness to thy people be declared in the grave,* either by those or to those that lie buried there? And thy faithfulness to thy promise, shall that be told in destruction? *shall thy wonders be wrought in the dark,* or known there, *and thy righteousness in* the grave, which is *the land of forgetfulness,* where men remember nothing, nor are themselves remembered? Departed souls may indeed know God's wonders and declare his faithfulness, justice, and lovingkindness; but deceased bodies cannot; they can neither receive God's favours in comfort nor return them in praise." Now we will not suppose these expostulations to be the language of despair, as if he thought God could not help him or would not, much less do they imply any disbelief of the resurrection of the dead at the last day; but he thus pleads with God for speedy relief: "Lord, thou art good, thou art faithful, thou art righteous; these attributes of thine will be made known in my deliverance, but, if it be not hastened, it will come too late; for I shall be dead and past relief, dead and not capable of receiving any comfort, very shortly." Job often pleaded thus, Job 7:8; 10:21.

II. He resolves to continue instant in prayer, and the more so because the deliverance was deferred (*v.* 13): *"Unto thee have I cried* many a time, and found comfort in so doing, and therefore I will continue to do so; *in the morning shall my prayer prevent thee."* Note, Though our prayers be not answered immediately, yet we must not therefore give over praying, because *the vision is for an appointed time, and at the end it shall speak and not lie.* God delays the answer in order that he may try our patience and perseverance in prayer. He resolves to seek God early, in the morning, when his spirits were lively, and before the business of the day began to crowd in — in the morning, after he had been tossed with cares, and sorrowful thoughts in the silence and solitude of the night; but how could he say, *My prayer shall prevent thee?* Not as if he could wake sooner to pray than God to hear and answer; for he neither slumbers nor sleeps; but it intimates that he would be up earlier than ordinary to pray, would *prevent* (that is, go before) his usual hour of prayer. The greater our afflictions are the more solicitous and serious we should be in prayer. "My prayer shall present itself before thee, and be betimes with thee, and shall not stay for the encouragement of the beginning of mercy, but reach towards it with faith and expectation even before the day dawns." God often prevents our prayers and expectations with his mercies; let us prevent his mercies with our prayers and expectations.

III. He sets down what he will say to God in prayer. 1. He will humbly reason with God concerning the abject afflicted condition he was now in (*v.* 14): *"Lord, why castest thou off my soul?* What is it that provokes thee to treat me as one abandoned? *Show me wherefore thou contendest with me."* He speaks it with wonder that God should cast off an old servant, should cast off one that was resolved not to cast him off: "No wonder men cast me off; but, Lord, why dost thou, whose gifts and callings are without repentance? *Why hidest thou thy face,* as one angry at me, that either hast no favour for me or wilt not let me know that thou hast?" Nothing grieves a child of God so much as God's hiding his face from him, nor is there any thing he so much dreads as God's casting off his soul. If the sun be clouded, that darkens the earth; but if the sun should abandon the earth, and quite cast it off, what a dungeon would it be! 2. He will humbly repeat the same complaints he had before made, until God have mercy on him. Two things he represents to God as his grievances: — (1.) That God was a terror to him: *I suffer thy terrors, v.* 15. He had continual frightful apprehensions of the wrath of God against him for his sins and the consequences of that wrath. It terrified him to think of God, of falling into his hands and appearing before him to receive his doom from him. He perspired and trembled at the apprehension of God's displeasure against him, and the terror of his majesty. Note, Even those that are designed for God's favours may yet, for a time, suffer his terrors. The spirit of adoption is first a spirit of bondage to fear. Poor Job complained of the terrors of *God setting themselves in array against him,* Job 6:4. The psalmist here explains himself, and tells us what he means by God's terrors, even his *fierce wrath.* Let us see what dreadful impressions those terrors made upon him, and how deeply they wounded him. [1.] They had almost taken away his life: *"I am so afflicted* with them that I am *ready to die,* and" (as the word is) *"to give up the ghost. Thy terrors have cut me off," v.* 16. What is hell, that eternal excision, by which damned sinners are for ever cut off from God and all happiness, but God's terrors fastening and preying upon their guilty consciences? [2.] They had almost taken away the use of his reason: *When I suffer thy terrors I am distracted.* This sad effect the terrors of the Lord have had upon many, and upon some good men, who have thereby been put quite out of the possession of their own souls, a most piteous case, and which ought to be looked upon with great compassion. [3.] This had continued long: *From my youth up I suffer thy terrors.* He had been from his childhood afflicted with melancholy, and trained up in sorrow under the discipline of that school. If we begin our days with trouble, and the days of our mourning have been prolonged a great while, let us not think it strange, but let tribulation work patience. It is observable the Heman, who became eminently wise and good, was *afflicted and ready to die,* and suffered God's terrors, *from his youth up.* Thus many have found it was good for them to bear the yoke in their youth, that sorrow has been much better for them than laughter would have been, and that being much afflicted, and often ready to die, when they were young, they have, by the grace of God, got such an habitual seriousness and weanedness from the world as have been of great use to them all their days. Sometimes those whom God designs for eminent services are prepared for them by exercises of this kind. [4.] His affliction was now extreme, and worse than ever. God's terrors now came round about him, so that from all sides he was assaulted with variety of troubles, and he had no comfortable gale from any point of the compass. They broke in upon him together like an inundation of water; and this daily, and all the day; so that he had no rest, no respite, not the lest breathing-time, no lucid intervals, nor any gleam of hope. Such was the calamitous state of a very wise and good man; he was so surrounded with terrors that he could find no place of shelter, nor lie any where under the wind. (2.) That no friend he had in the world was a comfort to him (*v.* 18): *Lover and friend hast thou put far from me;* some are dead, others at a distance, and perhaps many unkind. Next to the comforts of religion are those of friendship and society; therefore to be friendless is (as to this life) almost to be comfortless; and to those who have had friends, but have lost them, the calamity is the more grievous. With this the psalmist here closes his complaint, as if this were that which completed his woe and gave the finishing stroke to the melancholy piece. If our friends are put far from us by scattering providences, nay, if by death our acquaintance are removed into darkness, we have reason to look upon it as a sore affliction, but must acknowledge and submit to the hand of God in it.

PSALM 89

Many psalms that begin with complaint and prayer end with joy and praise, but this begins with joy and praise and ends with sad complaints and petitions; for the psalmist first recounts God's former favours, and then with the consideration of them aggravates the present grievances. It is uncertain when it was penned; only, in general, that it was at a time when the house of David was woefully eclipsed; some think it was at the time of the captivity of Babylon, when king Zedekiah was insulted over, and abused, by Nebuchadnezzar, and then they make the title to signify no more than that the psalm was set to the tune of a song of Ethan the son of Zerah, called Maschil; others suppose it to be penned by Ethan, who is mentioned in the story of Solomon, who, outliving that glorious prince, thus lamented the great disgrace done to the house of David in the next reign by the revolt of the ten tribes. I. The psalmist, in the joyful pleasant part of the psalm, gives glory to God, and takes comfort to himself and his friends. This he does more briefly, mentioning God's mercy and truth (*v.* 1) and his covenant (*v.* 2–4), but more largely in the following verses, wherein, 1. He adores the glory and perfection of God (*v.* 5–14). 2. He pleases himself in the happiness of those that are admitted into communion with him (*v.* 15–18). 3. He builds all his hope upon God's covenant with David, as a type of Christ (*v.* 19–37). II. In the melancholy part of the psalm he laments the present calamitous state of the prince and royal family (*v.* 38–45), expostulates with God upon it (*v.* 46–49), and then concludes with prayer for redress (*v.* 50, 51). In singing this psalm we must have high thoughts of God, a lively faith in his covenant with the Redeemer, and a sympathy with the afflicted parts of the church.

Maschil of Ethan the Ezrahite.

Verses 1–4

The psalmist has a very sad complaint to make of the deplorable condition of the family of David at this time, and yet he begins the psalm with songs of praise; for we must, in every thing, in every state, give thanks; thus we must glorify the Lord in the fire. We think, when we are in trouble, that we get ease by complaining; but we do more — we get joy, by praising. Let our complaints therefore be turned into thanksgivings; and in these verses we find that which will be matter of praise and thanksgiving for us in the worst of times, whether upon a personal or a public account, 1. However it be, the everlasting God is good and true, *v.* 1. Though we may find it hard to reconcile present dark providences with the goodness and truth of God, yet we must abide by this principle, That God's mercies are inexhaustible and his truth is inviolable; and these must be the matter of our joy and praise: *"I will sing of the mercies of the Lord for ever,* sing a praising song to God's honour, a pleasant song for my own solace, and *Maschil,* an instructive song, for the edification of others." We may be for ever singing God's mercies, and yet the subject will not be drawn dry. We must sing of God's mercies as long as we live, train up others to sing of them when we are gone, and hope to be singing them in heaven world without end; and this is *singing of the mercies of the Lord for ever. With my mouth,* and with my pen (for by that also do we speak), *will I make known thy faithfulness to all generations,* assuring posterity, from my own observation and experience, that God is true to every word that he has spoken, that they may learn to *put their trust in God,* Ps. 78:6. 2. However it be, the everlasting covenant is firm and sure, *v.* 2–4. Here we have, (1.) The psalmist's faith and hope: "Things now look black, and threaten the utter extirpation of the house of David; but *I have said,* and I have warrant from the word of God to say it, that *mercy shall be built up for ever."* As the goodness of God's nature is to be the matter of our song (*v.* 1), so much more the mercy that is built for us in the covenant; it is still increasing, like a house in the building up, and shall still continue our rest for ever, like a house built up. It shall be built up for ever; for the everlasting habitations we hope for in the new Jerusalem are of this building. If mercy shall be built for ever, then the *tabernacle of David, which has fallen down,* shall *be raised out of its ruins,* and *built up as in the days of old,* Amos 9:11. *Therefore* mercy shall be built up for ever, because *thy faithfulness shalt thou establish in the very heavens.* Though our expectations are in some particular instances disappointed, yet God's promises are not disannulled; they are *established in the very heavens* (that is, in his eternal counsels); they are above the changes of this lower region and out of the reach of the opposition of hell and earth. The stability of the material heavens is an emblem of the truth of God's word; the heavens may be clouded by vapours arising out of the earth, but they cannot be touched, they cannot be changed. (2.) An abstract of the covenant upon which this faith and hope are built: *I have said it,* says the psalmist, for *God hath sworn it,* that the heirs of promise might be entirely satisfied of the immutability of his counsel. He brings in God speaking (*v.* 3), owning, to the comfort of his people, *"I have made a covenant,* and therefore will make it good." The covenant is made with David; the covenant of royalty is made with him, as the father of his family, and with his seed through him and for his sake, representing the covenant of grace made with Christ as head of the church and with all believers as his spiritual seed. David is here called *God's chosen* and *his servant;* and, as God is not changeable to recede from his own choice, so he is not unrighteous to cast off one that served him. Two things encourage the psalmist to build his faith on this covenant: — [1.] The ratification of it; it was confirmed with an oath: *The Lord has sworn, and he will not repent.* [2.] The perpetuity of it; the blessings of the covenant were not only secured to David himself, but were entailed on his family; it was promised that his family should continue — *Thy seed will I establish for ever,* so that *David shall not want a son to reign* (Jer. 33:20, 21); and that it should continue a royal family — *I will build up thy throne to all generations,* to all the generations of time. This has its accomplishment only in Christ, of the seed of David, who lives for ever, to whom God has given the throne of his father David, and of the increase of whose government and peace there shall be no end. Of this covenant the psalmist will return to speak more largely, *v.* 19, etc.

Verses 5–14

These verses are full of the praises of God. Observe,

I. Where, and by whom, God is to be praised. 1. God is praised by the angels above: *The heavens shall praise thy wonders, O Lord! v.* 5; that is, "the glorious inhabitants of the upper world continually celebrate thy praises." *Bless the Lord, you his angels,* Ps. 103:20. The works of God are wonders even to those that are best acquainted and most intimately conversant with them; the more God's works are known the more they are admired and praised. This should make us love heaven, and long to be there, that there we shall have nothing else to do but to praise God and his wonders. 2. God is praised by the assemblies of his saints on earth *(praise waits for him in Zion);* and, though their praises fall so far short of the praises of angels, yet God is pleased to take notice of them, and accept of them, and reckon himself honoured by them. "Thy faithfulness and the truth of thy promise, that rock on which the church is built, shall be praised in the congregation of the saints, who owe their all to that faithfulness, and whose constant comfort it is that there is a promise, and that he is faithful who has promised." It is expected from God's saints on earth that they praise him; who should, if they do not? Let every saint praise him, but especially the congregation of saints; when they come together, let them join in praising God. The more the better; it is the more like heaven. Of the honour done to God by the assembly of the saints he speaks again (*v.* 7): *God is greatly to be feared in the assembly of the saints.* Saints should assemble for religious worship, that they may publicly own their relation to God and may stir up one another to give honour to him, and, in keeping up communion with God, may likewise maintain the communion of saints. In religious assemblies God has promised the presence of his grace, but we must also, in them, have an eye to his glorious presence, that the familiarity we are admitted to may not breed the least contempt; for he is terrible in his holy places, and therefore greatly to be feared. A holy awe of God must fall upon us, and fill us, in all our approaches to God, even in secret, to which something may very well be added by the solemnity of public assemblies. God must be had *in reverence of all that are about him,* that attend him continually as his servants or approach him upon any particular errand. See Lev. 10:3. Those only serve God acceptably who serve him with *reverence and godly fear,* Heb. 12:28.

II. What it is to praise God; it is to acknowledge him to be a being of unparalleled perfection, such a one that there is none like him, nor any to be compared with him, *v.* 6. If there be any beings that can pretend to vie with God, surely they must be found among the angels; but they are all infinitely short of him: *Who in the heaven can be compared with the Lord,* so as to challenge any share of the reverence and adoration which are due to him only, or to set up in rivalship with him for the homage of the children of men? They are sons of the mighty, but which of them can be likened unto the Lord? Nobles are princes' peers; some parity there is between them. But there is none between God and the angels; they are not his peers. *To whom will you liken me, or shall I be equal? saith the Holy One,* Isa. 40:25. This is insisted on again (*v.* 8): *Who is a strong Lord like unto thee?* No angel, no earthly potentate, whatsoever, is comparable to God, or *has an arm like him,* or can *thunder with a voice like him.* Thy *faithfulness is round about thee;* that is, "thy angels who are round about thee, attending thee with their praises and ready to go on thy errands, are all faithful." Or, rather, "In every thing thou doest, on all sides, thou approvest thyself faithful to thy word, above whatever prince or potentate was." Among men it is too often found that those who are most able to break their word are least careful to keep it; but God is both strong and faithful; he can do every thing, and yet will never do an unjust thing.

III. What we ought, in our praises, to give God the glory of. Several things are here mentioned. 1. The command God has of the most ungovernable creatures (*v.* 9): *Thou* rulest the raging of the sea, than which nothing is more frightful or threatening, nor more out of the power of man to give check to; it can swell no higher, roll no further, beat no harder, continue no longer, nor do any more hurt, than God suffers it. *"When the waves thereof arise* thou canst immediately hush them asleep, still them, and make them quiet, and turn the storm into a calm." This coming in here as an act of omnipotence, what manner of man then was the Lord Jesus, whom the *winds and seas obeyed?* 2. The victories God has obtained over the enemies of his church. His ruling the raging of the sea and quelling its billows was an emblem of this (v. 10): *Thou hast broken Rahab,* many a *proud enemy* (so it signifies), Egypt in particular, which is sometimes called *Rahab,* broken it in pieces, as one that is slain and utterly unable to make head again. "The head being broken, thou hast scattered the remainder with the arm of thy strength." God has more ways than one to deal with his and his church's enemies. We think he should slay them immediately, but sometimes he scatters them, that he may send them abroad to be monuments of his justice, Ps. 59:11. The remembrance of the breaking of Egypt in pieces is a comfort to the church, in reference to the present power of Babylon; for God is still the same. 3. The incontestable property he has in all the creatures of the upper and lower world (v. 11, 12): "Men are honoured for their large possessions; but *the heavens are thine, O Lord! the earth also is thine;* therefore we praise thee, therefore we trust in thee, therefore we will not fear what man can do against us. *The world and the fulness thereof,* all the riches contained in it, all the inhabitants of it, both the tenements and the tenants, are all thine; for *thou hast founded them,"* and the founder may justly claim to be the owner. He specifies, (1.) The remotest parts of the world, the north and south, the countries that lie under the two poles, which are uninhabited and little known: *"Thou hast created them,* and therefore knowest them, takest care of them, and hast tributes of praise from them." The north is said to be *hung over the empty place;* yet what fulness there is there God is the owner of it. (2.) The highest parts of the world. He mentions the two highest hills in Canaan — *"Tabor and Hermon"* (one lying to the west, the other to the east); "these shall rejoice in thy name, for they are under the care of thy providence, and they produce offerings for thy altar." The little hills are said to rejoice in their own fruitfulness, Ps. 65:12. Tabor is commonly supposed to be that high mountain in Galilee on the top of which Christ was transfigured; and then indeed it might be said to rejoice in that voice which was there heard, *This is my beloved Son.* 4. The power and justice, the mercy and truth, with which he governs the world and rules in the affairs of the children of men, v. 13, 14. (1.) God is able to do every thing; for his is the Lord God Almighty. His arm, his hand, is mighty and strong, both to save his people and to destroy his and their enemies; none can either resist the force or bear the weight of his mighty hand. *High is his right hand,* to reach the highest, even those that *set their nests among the stars* (Amos 9:2, 3; Obad. 4); his *right hand is exalted* in what he has done, for in thousands of instances he has signalized his power, Ps. 118:16. (2.) He never did, nor ever will do, any thing that is either unjust or unwise; for *righteousness and judgment are the habitation of his throne.* None of all his dictates or decrees ever varied from the rules of equity and wisdom, nor could ever any charge God with unrighteousness or folly. Justice and judgment are the *preparing* of his throne (so some), the *establishment* of it, so others. The preparations for his government in his counsels from eternity, and the establishment of it in its consequences to eternity, are all justice and judgment. (3.) He always does that which is kind to his people and consonant to the word which he has spoken: *"Mercy and truth shall go before thy face,* to prepare thy way, as harbingers to make room for thee — mercy in promising, truth in performing — truth in being as good as thy word, mercy in being better." How praiseworthy are these in great men, much more in the great God, in whom they are in perfection!

Verses 15–18

The psalmist, having largely shown the blessedness of the God of Israel, here shows the blessedness of the Israel of God. As *there is none like unto the God of Jeshurun, so, happy art thou, O Israel! there is none like unto thee,*

O people! especially as a type of the gospel-Israel, consisting of all true believers, whose happiness is here described.

I. Glorious discoveries are made to them, and glad tidings of good brought to them; they hear, *they know, the joyful sound, v.* 15. This may allude, 1. To the shout of a victorious army, the shout of a king, Num. 23:21. Israel have the tokens of God's presence with them in their wars; the sound of the *going in the top of the mulberry-trees* was indeed a *joyful sound* (2 Sa. 5:24); and they often returned making the earth ring with their songs of triumph; these were joyful sounds. Or, 2. To the sound that was made over the sacrifices and on the solemn feast-day, Ps. 81:1–3. This was the happiness of Israel, that they had among them the free and open profession of God's holy religion, and abundance of joy in their sacrifices. Or, 3. To the sound of the jubilee-trumpet; a joyful sound it was to servants and debtors, to whom it proclaimed release. The gospel is indeed a joyful sound, a sound of victory, of liberty, of communion with God, and the *sound of abundance of rain;* blessed are the people that hear it, and know it, and bid it welcome.

II. Special tokens of God's favour are granted them: *"They shall walk, O Lord! in the light of thy countenance;* they shall govern themselves by thy directions, shall be guided by the eye; and they shall delight themselves in thy consolations. They shall have the favour of God; they shall know that they have it, and it shall be continual matter of joy and rejoicing to them. They shall go through all the exercises of a holy life under the powerful influences of God's lovingkindness, which shall make their duty pleasant to them and make them sincere in it, aiming at this, as their end, to be accepted of the Lord." We then walk in the light of the Lord when we fetch all our comforts from God's favour and are very careful to keep ourselves in his love.

III. They never want matter for joy: Blessed are God's people, for in his name, in all that whereby he has made himself known, if it be not their own fault, *they shall rejoice all the day.* Those that rejoice in Christ Jesus, and make God their exceeding joy, have enough to counterbalance their grievances and silence their griefs; and therefore their joy is full (1 Jn. 1:4) and constant; it is their duty to rejoice evermore.

IV. Their relation to God is their honour and dignity. They are happy, for they are high. *Surely in the Lord,* in the Lord Christ, *they have righteousness and strength,* and so are recommended by him to the divine acceptance; and therefore *in him shall all the seed of Israel glory,* Isa. 45:24, 25. So it is here, v. 16, 17. 1. "In *thy righteousness shall they be exalted,* and not in any righteousness of their own." We are exalted out of danger, and into honour, purely by the righteousness of Christ, which is a clothing both for dignity and for defence. 2. "Thou art the *glory of their strength,"* that is, "thou art their strength, and it is their glory that thou art so, and what they glory in." *Thanks be to God who always causes us to triumph.* 3. "In thy favour, which through Christ we hope for, our *horn shall be exalted."* The horn denotes beauty, plenty, and power; these those have who are made accepted in the beloved. What greater preferment are men capable of in this world than to be God's favourites?

V. Their relation to God is their protection and safety (v. 18): *"For our shield is of the Lord"* (so the margin) "and our *king is from the Holy One of Israel.* If God be our ruler, he will be our defender; and who is he than that can harm us?" It was the happiness of Israel that God himself had the erecting of their bulwarks and the nominating of their king (so some take it); or, rather, that he was himself a *wall of fire round about them,* and, as a Holy One, the author and centre of their holy religion; he was their King, and so their glory in the midst of them. Christ is the Holy One of Israel, that holy thing; and in nothing was that peculiar people more blessed than in this, that *he* was born King of the Jews. Now this account of the blessedness of God's Israel comes in here as that to which it was hard to reconcile their present calamitous state.

Verses 19–37

The covenant God made with David and his seed was mentioned before (v. 3, 4); but in these verses it is enlarged upon, and pleaded with God, for favour to the royal family, now almost sunk and ruined; yet certainly it looks at

Christ, and has its accomplishment in him much more than in David; nay, some passages here are scarcely applicable at all to David, but must be understood of Christ only (who is therefore called *David our king,* Hos. 3:5), and very great and precious promises they are which are here made to the Redeemer, which are strong foundations for the faith and hope of the redeemed to build upon. The comforts of our redemption flow from the covenant of redemption; all our springs are in that, Isa. 55:3. *I will make an everlasting covenant with you, even the sure mercies of David,* Acts 13:34. Now here we have an account of those sure mercies. Observe,

I. What assurance we have of the truth of the promise, which may encourage us to build upon it. We are here told, 1. How it was spoken (v. 19): *Thou didst speak in vision to thy Holy One.* God's promise to David, which is especially referred to here, was spoken in vision to Nathan the prophet, 2 Sa. 7:12–17. *Then,* when the *Holy One of Israel was their king* (v. 18), he appointed David to be his viceroy. But to all the prophets, those holy ones, he *spoke in vision* concerning Christ, and to him himself especially, who had lain in his bosom from eternity, and was made perfectly acquainted with the whole design of redemption, Mt. 11:27. 2. How it was sworn to and ratified (v. 35): *Once have I sworn by my holiness,* that darling attribute. In swearing by his holiness, he swore by himself; for he will as soon cease to be as be otherwise than holy. His swearing once is enough; he needs not swear again, as David did (1 Sa. 20:17); for his word and oath are two immutable things. As Christ was made a priest, so he was made a king, *by an oath* (Heb. 7:21); for his kingdom and priesthood are both unchangeable.

II. The choice made of the person to whom the promise is given, v. 19, 20. David was a king of God's own choosing, so is Christ, and therefore both are called *God's kings,* Ps. 2:6. David was mighty, a man of courage and fit for business; he was chosen out of the people, not out of the princes, but the shepherds. God found him out, exalted him, laid help upon him, and ordered Samuel to anoint him. But this is especially to be applied to Christ. 1. He is one that is mighty, every way qualified for the great work he was to undertake, *able to save to the uttermost —* mighty in strength, for he is the Son of God — mighty in love, for he is able experimentally to compassionate those that are tempted. He is *the mighty God,* Isa. 9:6. 2. He is *chosen out of the people,* one of us, bone of our bone, that takes part with us of flesh and blood. Being ordained for men, he is taken from among men, that his terror might not make us afraid. 3. God has found him. He is a Saviour of God's own providing; for the salvation, from first to last, is purely the Lord's doing. *He has found the ransom,* Job 33:24. We could never have found a person fit to undertake this great work, Rev. 5:3, 4. 4. God has *laid help upon him,* not only helped him, but treasured up help in him for us, laid it as a charge upon him to help fallen man up again, to help the chosen remnant to heaven. *In me is thy help,* Hos. 13:9. 5. He has exalted him, by constituting him the prophet, priest, and king of his church, clothing him with power, raising him from the dead, and setting him at his own right hand. Whom God chooses and uses he will exalt. 6. He has anointed him, has qualified him for his office, and so confirmed him in it, by giving him the Spirit, not by measure, but without measure, infinitely above his fellows. He is called *Messiah,* or *Christ,* the *Anointed.* 7. In all this he designed him to be his own servant, for the accomplishing of his eternal purpose and the advancement of the interests of his kingdom among men.

III. The promises made to this chosen one, to David in the type and the Son of David in the antitype, in which not only gracious, but glorious things are spoken of him.

1. With reference to himself, as king and God's servant: and what makes for him makes for all his loving subjects. It is here promised, (1.) That God would stand by him and strengthen him in his undertaking (v. 21): *With him my hand* not only shall be, but *shall be established,* by promise, shall be so established that he shall by it be established and confirmed in all his offices, so that none of them shall be undermined and overthrown, though by the man of sin they shall all be usurped and fought against. Christ had a great deal of hard work to do and hard usage to go through; but he that gave him commission gave him forces sufficient for the execution of his commission: *"My arm*

also shall strengthen him to break through and bear up under all his difficulties." No good work can miscarry in the hand of those whom God himself undertakes to strengthen. (2.) That he should be victorious over his enemies, that they should not encroach upon him (*v.* 22): *The son of wickedness shall not exact upon him,* nor afflict him. He that at first broke the peace would set himself against him that undertook to make peace, and do what he could to blast his design: but he could only reach to bruise his heel; further he could not exact upon him nor afflict him. Christ became a surety for our debt, and thereby Satan and death thought to gain advantage against him; but he satisfied the demands of God's justice, and then they could not exact upon him. *The prince of this world cometh, but he has nothing in me,* Jn. 14:30. Nay, they not only shall not prevail against him, but they shall fall before him (*v.* 23): *I will bend down his foes before his face;* the prince of this world shall be cast out, principalities and powers spoiled, and he shall be the death of death itself, and the destruction of the grave, Hos. 13:14. Some apply this to the ruin which God brought upon the Jewish nation, that persecuted Christ and put him to death. But all Christ's enemies, who hate him and will not have him to reign over them, shall be brought forth and slain before him, Lu. 19:27. (3.) That he should be the great trustee of the covenant between God and men, that God would be gracious and true to us (*v.* 24): *My faithfulness and my mercy shall be with him.* They were with David; God continued merciful to him, and so approved himself faithful. They were with Christ; God made good all his promises to him. But that is not all; God's mercy to us, and his faithfulness to us, are with Christ; he is not only pleased with him, but with us in him; and it is in him that all the promises of God are yea and amen. So that if any poor sinners hope for benefit by the faithfulness and mercy of God, let them know it is with Christ; it is lodged in his hand, and to him they must apply for it (*v.* 28): *My mercy will I keep for him,* to be disposed of by him, *for evermore;* in the channel of Christ's mediation all the streams of divine goodness will for ever run. Therefore it is *the mercy of our Lord Jesus Christ* which we *look for unto eternal life,* Jude 21; Jn. 17:2. And, as the mercy of God flows to us through him, so the promise of God is, through him, firm to us: *My covenant shall stand fast with him,* both the covenant of redemption made with him and the covenant of grace made with us in him. The new covenant is *therefore* always new, and firmly established, because it is lodged in the hands of a Mediator, Heb. 8:6. The covenant stands fast, because it stands upon this basis. And this redounds to the everlasting honour of the Lord Jesus, that to him the great cause between God and man is entirely referred and the Father has committed all judgment to him, that *all men might honour him* (Jn. 5:22, 23); therefore it is here said, *In my name shall his horn be exalted;* this shall be his glory, that God's *name is in him* (Ex. 23:21), and that he acts in God's name. *As the Father gave me commandment, so I do.* (4.) That his kingdom should be greatly enlarged (*v.* 25): *I will set his hand in the sea* (he shall have the dominion of the seas, and the isles of the sea), and *his right hand in the rivers,* the inland countries that are watered with rivers. David's kingdom extended itself to the Great Sea, and the Red Sea, to the river of Egypt and the river Euphrates. But it is in the kingdom of the Messiah that this has its full accomplishment, and shall have more and more, when *the kingdoms of this world shall become the kingdoms of the Lord and of his Christ* (Rev. 11:15), and *the isles shall wait for his law.* (5.) That he should own God as his Father, and God would own him as his Son, his firstborn, *v.* 26, 27. This is a comment upon these words in Nathan's message concerning Solomon (for he also was a type of Christ as well as David), *I will be his Father and he shall be my Son* (2 Sa. 7:14), and the relation shall be owned on both sides. [1.] *He shall cry unto me, Thou art my Father.* It is probable that Solomon did so; but we are sure Christ did so, in the days of his flesh, when he offered up strong cries to God, and called him *holy Father, righteous Father,* and taught us to address ourselves to him as *our Father in heaven.* Christ, in his agony, cried unto God, *Thou art my Father* (Mt. 26:39, 42, *O my Father*), and, upon the cross, *Father, forgive them; Father, into thy hands I commend my spirit.* He looked upon him likewise as his God, and therefore he perfectly obeyed him, and submitted to his will in his whole undertaking (he is*my God and your God,* Jn. 20:17), and as the rock of his salvation, who would bear him up and bear him out in his undertaking, and make him more than a conqueror, even a complete Saviour; and therefore with an undaunted resolution he *endured the cross, despising the shame,* for he knew he should be both justified and glorified. [2.] *I will make him my firstborn.* I see not how this can be applied to David; it is Christ's prerogative to be *the firstborn of every creature,* and, as such, the *heir of all things,* Col. 1:15; Heb. 1:2, 6. When *all power was given to Christ both in heaven and in earth, and all things were delivered unto him by the Father,* then god made him his firstborn, and far higher, more great and honourable, than the kings of the earth; for he is the King of kings, *angels, authorities, and powers, being made subject to him,* 1 Pt. 3:22.

2. With reference to his seed. God's covenants always took in the seed of the covenanters; this does so (*v.* 29, 36): *His seed shall endure for ever,* and with it his throne. Now this will be differently understood according as we apply it to Christ or David.

(1.) If we apply it to David, by his seed we are to understand his successors, Solomon and the following kings of Judah, who descended from the loins of David. It is supposed that they might degenerate, and not walk in the spirit and steps of their father David; in such a case they must expect to come under divine rebukes, such as the house of David was at this time under, *v.* 38. But let this encourage them, that, though they were corrected, they should not be abandoned or disinherited. This refers to that part of Nathan's message (2 Sa. 7:14, 15), *If he commit iniquity, I will chasten him,* but *my mercy shall not depart from him.* Thus far David's seed and throne did endure for ever, that, notwithstanding the wickedness of many of his posterity, who were the scandals of his house, yet his family continued, and continued in the imperial dignity, a very long time, — that, as long as Judah continued a kingdom, David's posterity were kings of it, and the royalty of that kingdom was never in any other family, as that of the ten tribes was, in Jeroboam's first, then in Baasha's, etc., — and that the family of David continued a family of distinction till that Son of David came whose throne should endure for ever; see Lu. 1:27, 32; 2:4, 11. If David's posterity, in after-times, should forsake God and their duty and revolt to the ways of sin, God would bring desolating judgments upon them and ruin the family; and yet he would not take away his lovingkindness from David, nor break his covenant with him; for, in the Messiah, who should come out of his loins, all these promises shall have their accomplishment to the full. Thus, when the Jews were rejected, the apostle shows that God's covenant with Abraham was not broken, because it was fulfilled in his spiritual seed, the heirs of the righteousness of faith, Rom. 11:7.

(2.) If we apply it to Christ, by his seed we are to understand his subjects, all believers, his spiritual seed, the children which God has given him, Heb. 2:13. This is that seed which shall be made to endure for ever, and his throne in the midst of them, in the church in the heart, *as the days of heaven.* To the end Christ shall have a people in the world to serve and honour him. *He shall see his seed; he shall prolong his days.* This holy seed shall endure for ever in a glorified state, when time and days shall be no more; and thus Christ's throne and kingdom shall be perpetuated: the kingdom of his grace shall continue through all the ages of time and the kingdom of his glory to the endless ages of eternity.

[1.] The continuance of Christ's kingdom is here made doubtful by the sins and afflictions of his subjects; their iniquities and calamities threaten the ruin of it. This case is here put, that we may not be offended when it comes to be a case in fact, but that we may reconcile it with the stability of the covenant and be assured of that notwithstanding. *First,* It is here supposed that there will be much amiss in the subjects of Christ's kingdom. His children may *forsake God's law* (*v.* 30) by omissions, and *break his statutes* (*v.* 31) by commissions. There are spots which are the spots of God's children, Deu. 32:5. Many corruptions there are in the bowels of the church, as well as in the hearts of those who are the members of it, and these corruptions break out. *Secondly,* They are here told that they must smart for it (*v.* 32): *I will visit their transgression with a rod,* their transgression sooner than that of others. *You only have I known, and therefore I will punish you,* Amos 3:2. Their being related to Christ shall not excuse them from being called to an account. But observe what affliction is to God's people. 1. It is but a rod, not an axe, not a sword; it is for correction, not for destruction. This denotes gentleness in the affliction; it is the rod of men, such a rod as men use in correcting their children; and it denotes a design of good in and by the affliction, such a rod as yields the peaceable fruit of righteousness. 2. It is a rod on the hand of God *(I will visit them),* he who is wise, and knows what he does, gracious, and will do what is best. 3. It is a rod which they shall never feel the smart of but when there is great need: *If they break my law, then I will visit their transgression with the rod,* but not else. Then it is requisite that God's honour be vindicated, and that they be humbled and reduced.

[2.] The continuance of Christ's kingdom is made certain by the inviolable promise and oath of God, notwithstanding all this (*v.* 33): *Nevertheless, my kindness will I not* totally and finally *take from him. First,* "Notwithstanding their provocations, yet my covenant shall not be broken." Note, Afflictions are not only consistent with covenant-love, but to the people of God they flow from it. Though David's seed be chastened, it does not follow that they are disinherited; they may be cast down, but they are not cast off. God's favour is continued to his people, 1. For Christ's sake; in him the mercy is laid up for us, and God says, *I will not take it from him* (*v.* 33), *I will not lie unto David, v.* 35. We are unworthy, but he is worthy. 2. For the covenant's sake: *My faithfulness shall not fail, my covenant will I not break.* It was supposed that they had broken God's statutes, *profaned and polluted* them (so the word signifies); "But," says God, "I will not break, I will not profane and pollute, my covenant;" it is the same word. That which is said and sworn is that God will have a church in the world as long as sun and moon endure, *v.* 36, 37. The sun and moon are faithful witnesses in heaven of the wisdom, power, and goodness of the Creator, and shall continue while time lasts, which they are the measurers of; but the *seed of Christ shall be established for ever,* as *lights of the world* while the world stands, to shine in it, and, when it is at an end, they shall be established lights shining in the firmament of the Father.

Verses 38–52

In these verses we have,

I. A very melancholy complaint of the present deplorable state of David's family, which the psalmist thinks hard to be reconciled to the covenant God made with David. "Thou saidst thou wouldst not *take away thy lovingkindness, but thou hast cast off.*" Sometimes, it is no easy thing to reconcile God's providences with his promises, and yet we are sure they are reconcilable; for God's works fulfil his word and never contradict it. 1. David's house seemed to have lost its interest in God, which was the greatest strength and beauty of it. God had been pleased with his anointed, but now he was *wroth with him* (*v.* 38), had entered into covenant with the family, but now, for aught he could perceive, he had made void the covenant, not broken some of the articles of it, but cancelled it, *v.* 39. We misconstrue the rebukes of Providence if we think they make void the covenant. When the great anointed one, Christ himself, was upon the cross, God seemed to have cast him off, and was wroth with him, and yet did not make void his covenant with him, for that was established for ever. 2. The honour of the house of David was lost and laid in the dust: *Thou hast profaned his crown* (which was always looked upon as sacred) by *casting it to the ground,* to be trampled on, *v.* 39. *Thou hast made his glory to cease* (so uncertain is all earthly glory, and so soon does it wither) and *thou hast cast his throne down to the ground,* not only dethroned the king, but put a period to the kingdom, *v.* 44. If it was penned in Rehoboam's time, it was true as to the greatest part of the kingdom, five parts of six; if in Zedekiah's time, it was more remarkably true of the poor remainder. Note, Thrones and crowns are tottering things, and are often laid in the dust; but there is a crown of glory reserved for Christ's spiritual seed which fadeth not away. 3. It was exposed and made a prey to all the neighbours, who insulted over that ancient and honourable family (*v.* 40): *Thou hast broken down all his hedges* (all those things that were a defence to them, and particularly that hedge of protection which they thought God's covenant and promise had made about them) and thou *hast made even his strong-holds a ruin,* so that they were rather a reproach to them than any shelter; and then, *All that pass by the way spoil him* (*v.* 41) and make an easy prey of him; see Ps. 80:12, 13. The enemies talk insolently: *He is a reproach to his neighbours,* who triumph in his fall from so great a degree of honour. Nay, every one helps forward the calamity (*v.* 42): *"Thou hast set up the right hand of his adversaries,* not only given them power, but inclined them to turn their power this way." If the enemies of the church lift up their hand against it, we must see God setting up their hand; for they could have *no power unless it were given them from above.* But, when God does permit them to do mischief to his church, it pleases them: *"Thou hast made all his enemies to rejoice;* and this is for thy glory, that those who hate thee should have the pleasure to see the tears and troubles of those that love thee." 4. It was disabled to help itself (*v.* 43): *"Thou hast turned the edge of his sword,* and made it blunt, that it cannot do execution as it has done; and (which is worse) thou hast turned the edge of his spirit, and taken off his courage, *and hast not made him to stand* as he used to do *in the battle."* The spirit of men is what the Father and former of spirits makes them; nor can we stand with any strength or resolution further than God is pleased to uphold us. If men's hearts fail them, it is God that dispirits them; but it is sad with the church when those cannot stand who should stand up for it. 5. It was upon the brink of an inglorious exit (*v.* 45): *The days of his youth hast thou shortened;* it is ready to be cut off, like a young man in the flower of his age. This seems to intimate that the psalm was penned in Rehoboam's time, when the house of David was but in the days of its youth, and yet waxed old and began to decay already. Thus it was covered with shame, and it was turned very much to its reproach that a family which, in the first and second reign, looked so great, and made such a figure, should, in the third, dwindle and look so little as the house of David did in Rehoboam's time. But it may be applied to the captivity in Babylon, which, in comparison with what was expected, was but the day of the youth of that kingdom. However, the kings then had remarkably the *days of their youth shortened,* for it was in the days of their youth, when they were about thirty years old, that Jehoiachin and Zedekiah were carried captives to Babylon.

From all this complaint let us learn, 1. What work sin makes with families, noble royal families, with families in which religion has been uppermost; when posterity degenerates, it falls into disgrace, and iniquity stains their glory. 2. How apt we are to place the promised honour and happiness of the church in something external, and to think the promise fails, and the covenant is made void, if we be disappointed of that, a mistake which we now are inexcusable if we fall into, since our Master has so expressly told us that his kingdom is not of this world.

II. A very pathetic expostulation with God upon this. Four things they plead with God for mercy: —

1. The long continuance of the trouble (*v.* 46): *How long, O Lord! wilt thou hide thyself? For ever?* That which grieved them most was that God himself, as one displeased, did not appear to them by his prophets to comfort them, did not appear for them by his providences to deliver them, and that he had kept them long in the dark; it seemed an eternal night, when God had withdrawn: *Thou hidest thyself for ever.* Nay, God not only hid himself from them, but seemed to set himself against them: *"Shall thy wrath burn like fire?* How long shall it burn? Shall it never be put out? What is hell, but the wrath of God, burning for ever? And is that the lot of thy anointed?"

2. The shortness of life, and the certainty of death: "Lord, let thy anger cease, and return thou, in mercy to us, remembering how short my time is and how sure the period of my time. Lord, since my life is so transitory, and will, ere long, be at an end, let it not be always so miserable that I should rather choose no being at all than such a being." Job pleads thus, *ch.* 10:20, 21. And probably the psalmist here urges it in the name of the house of David, and the present prince of that house, the *days of whose youth* were *shortened, v.* 45.

(1.) He pleads the shortness and vanity of life (*v.* 47): *Remember how short my time is, how transitory I am* (say some), therefore unable to bear the power of thy wrath, and therefore a proper object of thy pity. *Wherefore hast thou made all men in vain?* or, *Unto what vanity hast thou created all the sons of Adam!* Now, this may be understood either, [1.] As declaring a great truth. If the ancient lovingkindnesses spoken of (*v.* 49) be forgotten (those relating to another life), man is indeed made in vain. Considering man as mortal, if there were not a future state on the other side of death, we might be ready to think that man was made in vain, and was in vain endued with the noble powers and faculties of reason and filled with such vast designs and desires; but God would not make man in vain; therefore, Lord, *remember those lovingkindnesses.* Or, [2.] As implying a strong temptation that the psalmist was in. It is certain *God has not made all men,* nor any man, *in vain,* Isa. 45:18. For, *First,* If we think that God has made men in vain because so many have short lives, and long afflictions, in this world, it is true that God has made them so, but it is not true that *therefore* they are made in vain. For those whose days are few and full of trouble may yet glorify God and do some good, may keep their communion with God and get to heaven, and then they are not made in vain. *Secondly,* If we think that God has made men in vain because the most of men neither serve him nor enjoy him, it is true that, as to themselves, they were made in vain, better for them had they not been born than not to be born again; but it was not owing to God that they were made in vain; it was owing to themselves; nor are they made in vain as to him, for he has *made all things for himself, even the wicked for the day of evil,* and those whom he is not glorified by he will be glorified upon.

(2.) He pleads the universality and unavoidableness of death (*v.* 48): *"What man"* (what *strong man,* so the word is) *"is he that liveth and shall not see death?* The king himself, of the house of David, is not exempted from the sentence, from the stroke. Lord, since he is under a fatal necessity of dying, let not his whole life be made thus miserable. *Shall he deliver his soul from the hand of the grave?* No, he shall not when his time has come. Let him not therefore be delivered into the hand of the grave by the miseries of a dying life, till his time shall come." We must learn here that death is the end of all men; our eyes must shortly be closed to see death; there is no discharge from that war, nor will any bail be taken to save us from the prison of the grave. It concerns us therefore to make sure a happiness on the other side of death and the grave, that, *when we fail, we may be received into everlasting habitations.*

3. The next plea is taken from the kindness God had for and the covenant he made with his servant David (*v.* 49): *"Lord, where are thy former lovingkindnesses,* which thou showedst, nay, *which thou swaredst, to David in thy truth?* Wilt thou fail of doing what thou hast promised? Wilt thou undo what thou hast done? Art not thou still the same? Why then may not we have the benefit of the former sure mercies of David?" God's unchangeableness and faithfulness assure us that God will not cast off those whom he has chosen and covenanted with.

4. The last plea is taken from the insolence of the enemies and the indignity done to God's anointed (*v.* 50, 51): *"Remember, Lord, the reproach,* and let it be rolled away from us and returned upon our enemies." (1.) They were God's servants that were reproached, and the abuses done to them reflected upon their master, especially since it was for serving him that they were reproached. (2.) The reproach cast upon God's servants was a very grievous burden to all that were concerned for the honour of God: *"I bear in my bosom the reproach of all the mighty people,* and am even overwhelmed with it; it is what I lay much to heart and can scarcely keep up my spirits under the weight of." (3.) "They are thy enemies who do thus reproach us; and wilt thou not appear against them as such?" (4.) *They have reproached the footsteps of thy anointed.* They reflected upon all the steps which the king had taken in the course of his administration, tracked him in all his motions, that they might make invidious remarks upon every thing he had said and done. Or, if we may apply it to Christ, the Lord's Messiah, they reproached the Jews with his footsteps, the slowness of his coming. They have reproached the delays of the Messiah; so Dr. Hammond. They called him, *He that should come;* but, because he had not yet come, because he did not now come to deliver them out of the hands of their enemies, when they had none to deliver them, they told them he would never come, they must give over looking for him. The scoffers of the latter days do, in like manner, reproach the footsteps of the Messiah when they ask, *Where is the promise of his coming?* 2 Pt. 3:3, 4. The reproaching of the footsteps of the anointed some refer to the serpent's *bruising the heel of the seed of the woman,* or to the sufferings of Christ's followers, who tread in his footsteps, and are reproached for his name's sake.

III. The psalm concludes with praise, even after this sad complaint (*v.* 52): *Blessed be the Lord for evermore, Amen, and amen.* Thus he confronts the reproaches of his enemies. The more others blaspheme God the more we should bless him. Thus he corrects his own complaints, chiding himself for quarrelling with God's providences and questioning his promises; let both these sinful passions be silenced with the praises of God. However it be, yet God is good, and we will never think hardly of him; God is true, and we will never distrust him. Though the glory of David's house be stained and sullied, this shall be our comfort, that God is blessed for ever, and his glory cannot be eclipsed. If we would have the comfort of the stability of God's promise, we must give him the praise of it; in blessing God, we encourage ourselves. Here is a double *Amen,* according to the double signification. *Amen — so it is,* God is blessed for ever. *Amen — be it so,* let God be blessed for ever. He began the psalm with thanksgiving, before he made his complaint (*v.* 1); and now he concludes it with a doxology. Those who give God thanks for what he has done may give him thanks also for what he will do; God will follow those with his mercies who, in a right manner, follow him with their praises.

PSALM 90

The foregoing psalm is supposed to have been penned as late as the captivity in Babylon; this, it is plain, was penned as early as the deliverance out of Egypt, and yet they are put close together in this collection of divine songs. This psalm was penned by Moses (as appears by the title), the most ancient penman of sacred writ. We have upon record a praising song of his (Ex. 15, which is alluded to Rev. 15:3), and an instructing song of his, Deu. 32. But this is of a different nature from both, for it is called a prayer. It is supposed that this psalm was penned upon occasion of the sentence passed upon Israel in the wilderness for their unbelief, murmuring, and rebellion, that their carcases should fall in the wilderness, that they should be wasted away by a series of miseries for thirty-eight years together, and that none of them that were then of age should enter Canaan. This was calculated for their wanderings in the wilderness, as that other song of Moses (Deu. 31:19, 21) was for their settlement in Canaan. We have the story to which this psalm seems to refer, Num. 14. Probably Moses penned this prayer to be daily used, either by the people in their tents, or, at lest, by the priests in the tabernacle-service, during their tedious fatigue in the wilderness. In it, I. Moses comforts himself and his people with the eternity of God and their interest in him (*v.* 1, 2). II. He humbles himself and his people with the consideration of the frailty of man (*v.* 3–6). III. He submits himself and his people to the righteous sentence of God passed upon them (*v.* 7–11). IV. He commits himself and his people to God by prayer for divine mercy and grace, and the return of God's favour (*v.* 12–17). Though it seems to have been penned upon this particular occasion, yet it is very applicable to the frailty of human life in general, and, in singing it, we may easily apply it to the years of our passage through the wilderness of this world, and it furnishes us with meditations and prayers very suitable to the solemnity of a funeral.

A Prayer of Moses the man of God.

Verses 1–6

This psalm is entitled *a prayer of Moses.* Where, and in what volume, it was preserved from Moses's time till the collection of psalms was begun to be made, is uncertain; but, being divinely inspired, it was under a special protection: perhaps it was written in the book of Jasher, or the book of the wars of the Lord. Moses taught the people of Israel to pray, and put words into their mouths which they might make use of in turning to the Lord. Moses is here called *the man of God,* because he was a prophet, the father of prophets, and an eminent type of the great prophet. In these verses we are taught,

I. To give God the praise of his care concerning his people at all times, and concerning us in our days (*v.* 1): *Lord, thou hast been to us a habitation,* or *dwelling-place, a refuge* or *help, in all generations.* Now that they had fallen under God's displeasure, and he threatened to abandon them, they plead his former kindnesses to their ancestors. Canaan was a land of pilgrimage to their fathers the patriarchs, who dwelt there in tabernacles; but then God was their habitation, and, wherever they went, they were at home, at rest, in him. Egypt had been a land of bondage to them for many years, but even then God was their refuge; and in him that poor oppressed people lived and were kept in being. Note, True believers are at home in God, and that is their comfort in reference to all the toils and tribulations they meet with in this world. In him we may repose and shelter ourselves as in our dwelling-place.

II. To give God the glory of his eternity (v. 2): *Before the mountains were brought forth, before he made the highest part of the dust of the world* (as it is expressed, Prov. 8:26), *before the earth fell in travail,* or, as we may read it, *before thou hadst formed the earth and the world* (that is, before the beginning of time) thou hadst a being; *even from everlasting to everlasting thou art God,* an eternal God, whose existence has neither its commencement nor its period with time, nor is measured by the successions and revolutions of it, but who art *the same yesterday, to-day, and for ever,* without beginning of days, or end of life, or change of time. Note, Against all the grievances that arise from our own mortality, and the mortality of our friends, we may take comfort from God's immortality. We are dying creatures, and all our comforts in the world are dying comforts, but God is an everliving God, and those shall find him so who have him for theirs.

III. To own God's absolute sovereign dominion over man, and his irresistible incontestable power to dispose of him as he pleases (v. 3): *Thou turnest man to destruction,* with a word's speaking, when thou pleasest, to the destruction of the body, of the earthly house; *and* thou *sayest, Return, you children of men.* 1. When God is, by sickness or other afflictions, turning men to destruction, he does thereby call men to return unto him, that is, to repent of their sins and live a new life. This God *speaketh once, yea, twice.* "Return unto me, from whom you have revolted," Jer. 4:1. 2. When God is threatening to *turn men to destruction,* to bring them to death, and they have received a sentence of death within themselves, sometimes he wonderfully restores them, and says, as the old translation reads it, *Again thou sayest, Return* to life and health again. For God kills and makes alive again, brings down to the grave and brings up. 3. When God turns men to destruction, it is according to the general sentence passed upon all, which is this, "*Return, you children of men,* one, as well as another, return to your first principles; let the body return to the earth as it was (*dust to dust,* Gen. 3:19) and let the soul *return to God who gave it,*" Eccl. 12:7. 4. Though God turns all men to destruction, yet he will again say, *Return, you children of men,* at the general resurrection, when, though a man dies, yet he shall live again; and "*then shalt thou call and I will answer* (Job 14:14, 15); thou shalt bid me return, and I shall return." The body, the soul, shall both return and unite again.

IV. To acknowledge the infinite disproportion there is between God and men, v. 4. Some of the patriarchs lived nearly a thousand years; Moses knew this very well, and had recorded it: but what is their long life to God's eternal life? "A thousand years, to us, are a long period, which we cannot expect to survive; or, if we could, it is what we could not retain the remembrance of; but it is, *in thy sight, as yesterday,* as one day, as that which is freshest in mind; nay, it is but as a *watch of the night,*" which was but three hours. 1. A thousand years are nothing to God's eternity; they are less than a day, than an hour, to a thousand years. Betwixt a minute and a million of years there is some proportion, but betwixt time and eternity there is none. The long lives of the patriarchs were nothing to God, not so much as the life of a child (that is born and dies the same day) is to theirs. 2. All the events of a thousand years, whether past or to come, are as present to the Eternal Mind as what was done yesterday, or the last hour, is to us, and more so. God will say, at the great day, to those whom he has *turned to destruction, Return — Arise you dead.* But it might be objected against the doctrine of the resurrection that it is a long time since it was expected and it has not yet come. Let that be no difficulty, for a thousand years, in God's sight, are but as one day. *Nullum tempus occurrit regi — To the king all periods are alike.* To this purport these words are quoted, 2 Pt. 3:8.

V. To see the frailty of man, and his vanity even at his best estate (v. 5, 6): look upon all the children of men, and we shall see, 1. That their life is a dying life: *Thou carriest them away as with a flood,* that is, they are continually gliding down the stream of time into the ocean of eter-

nity. The flood is continually flowing, and they are carried away with it; as soon as we are born we begin to die, and every day of our life carries us so much nearer death; or we are carried away violently and irresistibly, as with a flood of waters, as with an inundation, which sweeps away all before it; or as the old world was carried away with Noah's flood. Though God promised not so to drown the world again, yet death is a constant deluge. 2. That it is a dreaming life. Men are carried away as with a flood and yet *they are as a sleep;* they consider not their own frailty, nor are aware how near they approach to an awful eternity. Like men asleep, they imagine great things to themselves, till death wakes them, and puts an end to the pleasing dream. Time passes unobserved by us, as it does with men asleep; and, when it is over, it is as nothing. 3. That it is a short and transient life, like that of the grass which grows up and flourishes, in the morning looks green and pleasant, but in the evening the mower cuts it down, and it immediately withers, changes its colour, and loses all its beauty. Death will change us shortly, perhaps suddenly; and it is a great change that death will make with us in a little time. Man, in his prime, does but flourish as the grass, which is weak, and low, and tender, and exposed, and which, when the winter of old age comes, will wither of itself: but he may be mown down by disease or disaster, as the grass is, in the midst of summer. *All flesh is as grass.*

Verses 7–11

Moses had, in the foregoing verses, lamented the frailty of human life in general; the children of men *are as a sleep and as the grass.* But here he teaches the people of Israel to confess before God that righteous sentence of death which they were under in a special manner, and which by their sins they had brought upon themselves. Their share in the common lot of mortality was not enough, but they are, and must live and die, under peculiar tokens of God's displeasure. Here they speak of themselves: *We Israelites are consumed and troubled,* and *our days have passed away.*

I. They are here taught to acknowledge the wrath of God to be the cause of all their miseries. *We are consumed, we are troubled,* and it is *by thy anger,* by *thy wrath* (v. 7); *our days have passed away in thy wrath,* v. 9. The afflictions of the saints often come purely from God's love, as Job's; but the rebukes of sinners, and of good men for their sins, must be seen coming from the anger of God, who takes notice of, and is much displeased with, the sins of Israel. We are too apt to look upon death as no more than a debt owing to nature; whereas it is not so; if the nature of man had continued in its primitive purity and rectitude, there would have been no such debt owing to it. It is a debt to the justice of God, a debt to the law. *Sin entered into the world, and death by sin.* Are we consumed by decays of nature, the infirmities of age, or any chronic disease? We must ascribe it to God's anger. Are we troubled by any sudden or surprising stroke? That also is the fruit of God's wrath, which is thus revealed from heaven against the *ungodliness* and *unrighteousness of men.*

II. They are taught to confess their sins, which had provoked the wrath of God against them (v. 8): *Thou hast set our iniquities before thee, even our secret sins.* It was not without cause that God was angry with them. He had said, *Provoke me not, and I will do you no hurt;* but they had provoked him, and will own that, in passing this severe sentence upon them, he justly punished them, 1. For their open contempts of him and the daring affronts they had given him: *Thou hast set our iniquities before thee.* God had herein an eye to their unbelief and murmuring, their distrusting his power and their despising the pleasant land: these he set before them when he passed that sentence on them; these kindled the fire of God's wrath against them and kept good things from them. 2. For their more secret departures from him: "*Thou hast set our secret sins* (those which go no further than the heart, and which are at the bottom of all the overt acts) *in the light of thy countenance;* that is, thou hast discovered these, and brought these also to the account, and made us to see them, who before overlooked them." Secret sins are known to God and shall be reckoned for. Those who in heart return into Egypt, who set up idols in their heart, shall be dealt with as revolters

or idolaters. See the folly of those who go about to cover their sins, for they cannot cover them.

III. They are taught to look upon themselves as dying and passing away, and not to think either of a long life or of a pleasant one; for the decree gone forth against them was irreversible (v. 9): *All our days are* likely to be *passed away in thy wrath,* under the tokens of thy displeasure; and, though we are not quite deprived of the residue of our years, yet we are likely to *spend* them *as a tale that is told.* The thirty-eight years which, after this, they wore away in the wilderness, were not the subject of the sacred history; for little or nothing is recorded of that which happened to them from the second year to the fortieth. After they came out of Egypt their time was perfectly trifled away, and was not worthy to be the subject of a history, but only of *a tale that is told;* for it was only to pass away time, like telling stories, that they spent those years in the wilderness; all that while they were in the consuming, and another generation was in the raising. When they came out of Egypt *there was not one feeble person among their tribes* (Ps. 105:37); but now they were feeble. Their joyful prospect of a prosperous glorious life in Canaan was turned into the melancholy prospect of a tedious inglorious death in the wilderness; so that their whole life was now as impertinent a thing as ever any winter-tale was. That is applicable to the state of every one of us in the wilderness of this world: *We spend our years, we bring them to an end,* each year, and all at last, *as a tale that is told — as the breath of our mouth in winter* (so some), which soon disappears — *as a thought* (so some), than which nothing more quick — *as a word,* which is soon spoken, and then vanishes into air — or *as a tale that is told.* The spending of our years is like the telling of a tale. A year, when it past, is like a tale when it is told. Some of our years are a pleasant story, others as a tragical one, most mixed, but all short and transient: that which was long in the doing may be told in a short time. Our years, when they are gone, can no more be recalled than the word that we have spoken can. The loss and waste of our time, which are our fault and folly, may be thus complained of: we should spend our years like the despatch of business, with care and industry; but, alas! we do spend them like the telling of a tale, idle, and to little purpose, carelessly, and without regard. Every year passed *as a tale that is told;* but what was the number of them? As they were vain, so they were few (v. 10), seventy or eighty at most, which may be understood either, 1. Of the lives of the Israelites in the wilderness; all those that were numbered when they came out of Egypt, above twenty years old, were to die within thirty-eight years; they numbered those only that *were able to go forth to war,* most of whom, we may suppose, were between twenty and forty, who therefore must have all died before eighty years old, and many before sixty, and perhaps much sooner, which was far short of the years of the lives of their fathers. And those that lived to seventy or eighty, yet, being under a sentence of consumption and a melancholy despair of ever seeing through this wilderness-state, their strength, their life, was nothing but *labour and sorrow,* which otherwise would have been made a new life by the joys of Canaan. See what work sin made. Or, 2. Of the lives of men in general, ever since the days of Moses. Before the time of Moses it was usual for men to live about 100 years, or nearly 150; but, since, seventy or eighty is the common stint, which few exceed and multitudes never come near. We reckon those to have lived to the age of man, and to have had as large a share of life as they had reason to expect, who live to be seventy years old; and how short a time is that compared with eternity! Moses was the first that committed divine revelation to writing, which, before, had been transmitted by tradition; now also both the world and the church were pretty well peopled, and therefore there were not now the same reasons for men's living long that there had been. If, by reason of a strong constitution, some reach to eighty years, yet their strength then is what they have little joy of; it does but serve to prolong their misery, and make their death the more tedious; for even *their strength then is labour and sorrow,* much more their weakness; for the years have come which they have no pleasure in. Or it may be taken thus: *Our years are seventy, and the years of some, by reason of strength, are eighty; but the breadth of our years* (for so the latter word signifies, rather than strength), *the whole extent of them, from infancy to old age, is but labour and sorrow.* In the sweat of our face we must eat bread; our whole life is toilsome and troublesome; and perhaps, in the midst of the years we count upon, *it is soon cut off, and we fly away,* and do not live out half our days.

IV. They are taught by all this to stand in awe of the wrath of God (*v.* 11): *Who knows the power of thy anger?* 1. None can perfectly comprehend it. The psalmist speaks as one afraid of God's anger, and amazed at the greatness of the power of it; who knows how far the power of God's anger can reach and how deeply it can wound? The angels that sinned knew experimentally the power of God's anger; damned sinners in hell know it; but which of us can fully comprehend or describe it? 2. Few do seriously consider it as they ought. *Who knows it,* so as to improve the knowledge of it? Those who make a mock at sin, and make light of Christ, surely do not know the power of God's anger. For, *according to thy fear, so is thy wrath;* God's wrath is equal to the apprehensions which the most thoughtful serious people have of it; let men have ever so great a dread upon them of the wrath of God, it is not greater than there is cause for and than the nature of the thing deserves. God has not in his word represented his wrath as more terrible than really it is; nay, what is felt in the other world is infinitely worse than what is feared in this world. *Who among us can dwell with that devouring fire?*

Verses 12–17

These are the petitions of this prayer, grounded upon the foregoing meditations and acknowledgments. *Is any afflicted? Let him* learn thus to *pray.* Four things they are here directed to pray for: —

I. For a sanctified use of the sad dispensation they were now under. Being condemned to have our days shortened, *"Lord, teach us to number our days* (*v.* 12); Lord, give us grace duly to consider how few they are, and how little a while we have to live in this world." Note, 1. It is an excellent art rightly *to number our days,* so as not to be out in our calculation, as he was who counted upon many years to come when, that night, his soul was required of him. We must live under a constant apprehension of the shortness and uncertainty of life and the near approach of death and eternity. We must so number our days as to compare our work with them, and mind it accordingly with a double diligence, as those that have no time to trifle. 2. Those that would learn this arithmetic must pray for divine instruction, must go to God, and beg of him to teach them by his Spirit, to put them upon considering and to give them a good understanding. 3. We then number our days to good purpose when thereby our hearts are inclined and engaged to true wisdom, that is, to the practice of serious godliness. To be religious is to be wise; this is a thing to which it is necessary that we apply our hearts, and the matter requires and deserves a close application, to which frequent thoughts of the uncertainty of our continuance here, and the certainty of our removal hence, will very much contribute.

II. For the turning away of God's anger from them, that though the decree had gone forth, and was past revocation, there was no remedy, but they must die in the wilderness: *"Yet return, O Lord!* be thou reconciled to us, and *let it repent thee concerning thy servants* (*v.* 13); send us tidings of peace to comfort us again after these heavy tidings. How long must we look upon ourselves as under thy wrath, and when shall we have some token given us of our restoration to thy favour? *We are thy servants, thy people* (Isa. 64:9); when wilt thou change thy way toward us?" In answer to this prayer, and upon their profession of repentance (Num. 14:39, 40), God, in the next chapter, proceeding with the laws concerning sacrifices (Num. 15:1, etc.), which was a token that it repented him concerning his servants; for, *if the Lord had been pleased to kill them, he would not have shown them such things as these.*

III. For comfort and joy in the returns of God's favour to them, *v.* 14, 15. They pray for the mercy of God; for they pretend not to plead any merit of their own. *Have mercy upon us, O God!* is a prayer we are all concerned to say *Amen* to. Let us pray for early mercy, the seasonable communications of divine mercy, that God's *tender mercies may speedily prevent us, early in the morning* of our days, when we are young and flourishing, *v.* 6. Let us pray for the true satisfaction and happiness which are to be had only in the favour and mercy of God, Ps. 4:6, 7. A gracious soul, if it may but be satisfied of God's lovingkindness, will be satisfied with it, abundantly satisfied, will take up with that, and will take up with nothing short of it. Two things are pleaded to enforce this petition for God's mercy: — 1. That it would be a full fountain of future joys: *"O satisfy us with thy mercy,* not only that we may be easy and at rest within ourselves, which we can never be while we lie under thy wrath, but that we *may rejoice and be glad,* not only for a time, upon the first indications of thy favour, but *all our days,* though we are to spend them in the wilderness." With respect to those that make God their chief joy, as their joy may be full (1 Jn. 1:4), so it may be constant, even in this vale of tears; it is their own fault if they are not glad all their days, for his mercy will furnish them with joy in tribulation and nothing can separate them from it. 2. That it would be a sufficient balance to their former griefs: *"Make us glad according to the days wherein thou has afflicted us;* let the days of our joy in thy favour be as many as the days of our pain for thy displeasure have been and as pleasant as those have been gloomy. *Lord, thou usest to set the one over-against the other* (Eccl. 7:14); do so in our case. Let it suffice that we have drunk so long of the cup of trembling; now put into our hands the cup of salvation." God's people reckon the returns of God's lovingkindness a sufficient recompence for all their troubles.

IV. For the progress of the work of God among them notwithstanding, *v.* 16, 17. 1. That he would manifest himself in carrying it on: *"Let thy work appear upon thy servants;* let it appear that thou hast wrought upon us, to bring us home to thyself and to fit us for thyself." God's servants cannot work for him unless he work upon them, and work in them both to will and to do; and then we may hope the operations of God's providence will be apparent for us when the operations of his grace are apparent upon us. "Let thy work appear, and in it thy glory will appear to us and those that shall come after us." In praying for God's grace God's glory must be our end; and we must therein have an eye to our children as well as to ourselves, that they also may experience God's glory appearing upon them, so as to change them into the same image, from glory to glory. Perhaps, in this prayer, they distinguish between themselves and their children, for so God distinguished in his late message to them (Num. 14:31, *Your carcases shall fall in this wilderness, but your little ones I will bring into Canaan):* "Lord," say they, "let *thy work appear upon us,* to reform us, and bring us to a better temper, and then *let thy glory appear to our children,* in performing the promise to them which we have forfeited the benefit of." 2. That he would countenance and strengthen them in carrying it on, in doing their part towards it. (1.) That he would smile upon them in it: *Let the beauty of the Lord our God be upon us;* let it appear that God favours us. Let us have God's ordinances kept up among us and the tokens of God's presence with his ordinances; so some. We may apply this petition both to our sanctification and to our consolation. Holiness is *the beauty of the Lord our God;* let that be upon us in all we say and do; let the grace of God in us, and the light of our good works, make our faces to shine (that is the comeliness God puts upon us, and those are comely indeed who are so beautified), and then let divine consolations put gladness into our hearts, and a lustre upon our countenances, and that also will be the beauty of the Lord upon us, as our God. (2.) That he would prosper them in it: *Establish thou the work of our hands upon us.* God's working upon us (*v.* 16) does not discharge us from using our utmost endeavours in serving him and working out our salvation. But, when we have done all, we must wait upon God for the success, and beg of him to *prosper our handy works,* to give us to compass what we aim at for his glory. We are so unworthy of divine assistance, and yet so utterly insufficient to bring any thing to pass without it, that we have need to be earnest for it and to repeat the request: *Yea, the work of our hands, establish thou it,* and, in order to that, establish us in it.

PSALM 91

Some of the ancients were of opinion that Moses was the penman, not only of the foregoing psalm, which is expressly said to be his, but also of the eight that next follow it; but that cannot be, for Ps. 95 is expressly said to be penned by David, and long after Moses, Heb. 4:7. It is probable that this psalm also was penned by David; it is a writ of protection for all true believers, not in the name of king David, or under his broad seal; he needed it himself, especially if the psalm was penned, as some conjecture it was, at the time of the pestilence which was sent for his numbering the people; but in the name of the King of kings, and under the broad seal of Heaven. Observe, I. The psalmist's own resolution to take God for his keeper (*v.* 2), from which he gives both direction and encouragement to others (*v.* 9). II. The promises which are here made, in God's name, to all those that do so in sincerity. 1. They shall be taken under the peculiar care of Heaven (*v.* 1, 4). 2. They shall be delivered from the malice of the powers of darkness (*v.* 3, 5, 6), and that by a distinguishing preservation (*v.* 7, 8). 3. They shall be the charge of the holy angels (*v.* 10–12). 4. They shall triumph over their enemies (*v.* 13). 5. They shall be the special favourites of God himself (*v.* 14–16). In singing this we must shelter ourselves under, and then solace ourselves in, the divine protection. Many think that to Christ, as Mediator, these promises do primarily belong (Isa. 49:2), not because to him the devil applied one of these promises (Mt. 4:6), but because to him they are very applicable, and, coming through him, they are more sweet and sure to all believers.

Verses 1–8

In these verses we have,

I. A great truth laid down in general, That all those who live a life of communion with God are constantly safe under his protection, and may therefore preserve a holy serenity and security of mind at all times (*v.* 1): *He that dwells,* that sits down, *in the secret place of the Most High, shall abide under the shadow of the Almighty;* he that by faith chooses God for his guardian shall find all that in him which he needs or can desire. Note, 1. It is the character of a true believer that he *dwells in the secret place of the Most High;* he is at home in God, returns to God, and reposes in him as his rest; he acquaints himself with inward religion, and makes heart-work of the service of God, worships within the veil, and loves to be alone with God, to converse with him in solitude. 2. It is the privilege and comfort of those that do so that they *abide under the shadow of the Almighty;* he shelters them, and comes between them and every thing that would annoy them, whether storm or sunshine. They shall not only have an admittance, but a residence, under God's protection; he will be their rest and refuge for ever.

II. The psalmist's comfortable application of this to himself (*v.* 2): *I will say of the Lord,* whatever others say of him, *"He is my refuge;* I choose him as such, and confide in him. Others make idols their refuge, but I will say of Jehovah, the true and living God, He is *my refuge:* any other is a *refuge of lies.* He is a refuge that will not fail me; for he is *my fortress and strong-hold."* Idolaters called their idols *Mahuzzim,* their *most strong-hold* (Dan. 11:39), but therein they deceived themselves; those only secure themselves that make the Lord their God, their fortress. There being no reason to question his sufficiency, fitly does it follow, *In him will I trust.* If Jehovah be our God, our refuge, and our fortress, what can we desire which we may not be sure to find in him? He is neither fickle nor false, neither weak nor mortal; he is God and not man, and therefore there is no danger of being disappointed in him. *We know whom we have trusted.*

III. The great encouragement he gives to others to do likewise, not only from his own experience of the comfort of it (for in that there might possibly be a fallacy), but from the truth of God's promise, in which there neither is nor can be any deceit (*v.* 3, 4, etc.): *Surely he shall deliver thee.* Those who have themselves found the comfort of making God their refuge cannot but desire that others may do so. Now here it is promised,

1. That believers shall be kept from those mischiefs which they are in imminent danger of, and which would be fatal to them (*v.* 3), *from the snare of the fowler,* which is laid unseen and catches the unwary prey on a sudden, and *from the noisome pestilence,* which seizes men unawares and against which there is no guard. This promise protects, (1.) The natural life, and is often fulfilled in our preservation from those dangers which are very threatening and very near, while yet we ourselves are not apprehensive of them, any more than the bird is of *the snare of the fowler.* We owe it, more than we are sensible, to the care of the divine Providence that we have been kept from infectious diseases and out of the hands of the wicked and unreasonable. (2.) The spiritual life, which is protected by divine grace from the temptations of Satan, which are as the *snares of the fowler,* and from the contagion of sin, which is the *noisome pestilence.* He that has given grace to be the glory of the soul will create a defence upon all that glory.

2. That God himself will be their protector; those must needs be safe who have him for their keeper, and successful for whom he undertakes (*v.* 4): *He shall cover thee,* shall keep thee *secret* (Ps. 31:20), and so keep thee safe, Ps. 27:5. God protects believers, (1.) With the greatest tenderness and affection, which is intimated in that, *He shall cover thee with his feathers, under his wings,* which alludes to the hen *gathering her chickens under wings,* Mt. 23:37. By natural instinct she not only protects them, but calls them under that protection when she sees them in danger, not only keeps them safe, but cherishes them and keeps them warm. To this the great God is pleased to compare his care of his people, who are helpless as the chickens, and easily made a prey of, but are invited to trust under the shadow of the wings of the divine promise and providence, which is the periphrasis of a proselyte to the true religion, that he has come to *trust under the wings of the God of Israel,* Ruth 2:12. (2.) With the greatest power and efficacy. Wings and feathers, though spread with the greatest tenderness, are yet weak, and easily broken through, and therefore it is added, *His truth shall be thy shield and buckler,* a strong defence. God is willing to guard his people as the hen is to guard the chickens, and as able as a man of war in armour.

3. That he will not only keep them from evil, but from the fear of evil, *v.* 5, 6. Here is, (1.) Great danger supposed; the mention of it is enough to frighten us; night and day we lie exposed, and those that are apt to be timorous will in neither period think themselves safe. When we are retired into our chambers, our beds, and have made all as safe as we can about us, yet there is terror by night, from thieves and robbers, winds and storms, besides those things that are the creatures of fancy and imagination, which are often most frightful of all. We read of *fear in the night,* Cant. 3:8. There is also a *pestilence that walketh in darkness,* as that was which slew the first-born of the Egyptians, and the army of the Assyrians. No locks nor bars can shut out diseases, while we carry about with us in our bodies the seeds of them. But surely in the day-time, when we can look about us, we are not so much in danger; yes, there is an *arrow that flieth by day* too, and yet flies unseen; there is a destruction that wasteth at high-noon, when we are awake and have all our friends about us; even then we cannot secure ourselves, nor can they secure us. It was in the day-time that that pestilence wasted which was sent to chastise David for numbering the people, on occasion of which some think this psalm was penned. But, (2.) Here is great security promised to believers in the midst of this danger: *"Thou shalt not be afraid.* God by his grace will keep thee from disquieting distrustful fear (that fear which hath torment) in the midst of the greatest dangers. Wisdom shall keep thee from being causelessly afraid, and faith shall keep thee from being inordinately afraid. Thou shalt not be afraid of the arrow, as knowing that though it may hit thee it cannot hurt thee; if it take away the natural life, yet it shall be so far from doing any prejudice to the spiritual life that it shall be its perfection." A believer *needs not* fear, and therefore *should not* fear, any arrow, because the point is off, the poison is out. *O death! where is thy sting?* It is also under divine direction, and will hit where God appoints and not otherwise. Every bullet has its commission. Whatever is done our heavenly Father's will is done; and we have no reason to be afraid of that.

4. That they shall be preserved in common calamities, in a distinguishing way (*v.* 7): "When death rides in triumph, and diseases rage, so that *thousands and ten thousands* fall, fall by sickness, or fall by the sword in battle, *fall at thy side, at thy right hand,* and the sight of their fall is enough to frighten thee, and if they fall by the pestilence their falling so near thee may be likely to infect thee, *yet it shall not come nigh thee,* the death shall not, the fear of death shall not." Those that preserve their purity in times of general corruption may trust God with their safety in times of general desolation. When multitudes die round about us, though thereby we must be awakened to prepare for our own death, yet we must not be *afraid with any amazement,* nor make ourselves subject to bondage, as many do all their life-time, *through fear of death,* Heb. 2:15. The sprinkling of blood secured the first-born of Israel when thousands fell. Nay, it is promised to God's people that they shall have the satisfaction of seeing, not only God's promises fulfilled to them, but his threatenings fulfilled upon those that hate them (*v.* 8): *Only with thy eyes shalt thou behold and see the just reward of the wicked,* which perhaps refers to the destruction of the first-born of Egypt by the pestilence, which was both the punishment of the oppressors and the enlargement of the oppressed; this Israel saw when they saw themselves unhurt, untouched. As it will aggravate the damnation of sinners that with their eyes they shall behold and see the reward of the righteous (Lu. 13:28), so it will magnify the salvation of the saints that with their eyes they shall behold and see the destruction of the wicked, Isa. 66:24; Ps. 58:10.

Verses 9–16

Here are more promises to the same purport with those in the foregoing verses, and they are exceedingly great and precious, and sure to all the seed.

I. The psalmist assures believers of divine protection, from his own experience; and that which he says is the word of God, and what we may rely upon. Observe, 1. The character of those who shall have the benefit and comfort of these promises; it is much the same with that, *v.* 1. They are such as make *the Most High their habitation* (*v.* 9), as are continually with God and rest in him, as make his name both their temple and their strong tower, as dwell in love and so dwell in God. It is our duty to be at home in God, to make our choice of him, and then to live our life in him as our habitation, to converse with him, and delight in him, and depend upon him; and then it shall be our privilege to be at home in God; we shall be welcome to him as a man to his own habitation, without any let, hindrance, or molestation, from the arrests of the law or the clamours of conscience; then too we shall be safe in him, shall be kept in *perfect peace,* Isa. 26:3. To encourage us to make the Lord our habitation, and to hope for safety and satisfaction in him, the psalmist intimates the comfort he had had in doing so: "He whom thou makest thy *habitation is my refuge;* and I have found him firm and faithful, and in him there is room enough, and shelter enough, both for thee and me." *In my father's house* there *are many mansions,* one needs not crowd another, much less crowd out another. 2. The promises that are sure to all those who have thus made *the Most High* their *habitation.* (1.) That, whatever happens to them, nothing shall hurt them (*v.* 10): *"There shall no evil befal thee;* though trouble or affliction befal thee, yet there shall be no real evil in it, for it shall come from the love of God and shall be sanctified; it shall come, not for thy hurt, but for thy good; and though, for *the present, it be not joyous but grievous,* yet, in the end, it shall yield so well that thou thyself shalt own *no evil befel thee.* It is not an evil, an only evil, but there is a mixture of good in it and a product of good by it. Nay, not thy person only, but thy dwelling, shall be taken under the divine protection: *There shall no plague come nigh* that, nothing to do thee or thine any damage." *Nihil accidere bono viro mali potest — No evil can befal a good man.* Seneca *De Providentia.* (2.) That the angels of light shall be serviceable to them, *v.* 11, 12. This is a precious promise, and speaks a great deal both of honour and comfort to the saints, nor is it ever the worse for being quoted and abused by the devil in tempting Christ, Mt. 4:6. Observe, [1.] The charge given to the angels concerning the saints. He who is the Lord of the angels, who gave them their being and gives laws to them, whose they are and whom they were made to serve, *he shall give his angels a charge over thee,* not only over the church in general, but over every particular believer. The angels *keep the charge of the Lord their God;* and this is the charge they receive from him. It denotes the great care God takes of the saints, in that the angels themselves shall be charged with them, and employed for them. The charge is *to keep thee in all thy ways;* here is a limitation of the promise: They *shall keep thee in thy ways,* that is, "as long as thou keepest in the way of thy duty;" those that go out of that way put themselves out of God's protection. This word the devil left out when he quoted the promise to enforce a temptation, knowing how much it made against him. But observe the extent of the promise; it is *to keep thee in all thy ways:* even where there is no apparent danger yet we need it, and where there is the most imminent danger we shall have it. Wherever the saints go the angels are charged with them, as the servants are with the children. [2.] The care which the angels take of the saints, pursuant to this charge: *They shall bear thee up in their hands,* which denotes both their great ability and their great affection. They are able to bear up the saints out of the reach of danger, and they do it with all the tenderness and affection wherewith the nurse carries the little child about in her arms; it speaks us helpless and them helpful. They are condescending in their ministrations; they keep the feet of the saints, lest they *dash them against a stone,* lest they stumble and fall into sin and into trouble. [3.] That the powers of darkness shall be triumphed over by them (*v.* 13): *Thou shalt tread upon the lion and adder.* The devil is called *a roaring lion, the old serpent, the red dragon;* so that to this promise the apostle seems to refer in that (Rom. 16:20), *The God of peace shall tread Satan under your feet.* Christ has broken the serpent's head, spoiled our spiritual enemies (Col. 2:15), and through him *we are more than conquerors;* for Christ calls us, as Joshua called the captains of Israel, to come and set our feet on the necks of vanquished enemies. Some think that this promise had its full accomplishment in Christ, and the miraculous power which he had over the whole creation, healing the sick, casting out devils, and particularly putting it into his disciples' commission that they should *take up serpents,* Mk. 16:18. It may be applied to that care of the divine Providence by which we are preserved from ravenous noxious creatures (*the wild beasts of the field shall be at peace with thee,* Job 5:23); nay, and have ways and means of taming them, Jam. 3:7.

II. He brings in God himself speaking words of comfort to the saints, and declaring the mercy he had in store for them, *v.* 14–16. Some make this to be spoken to the angels as the reason of the charge given them concerning the saints, as if he had said, "Take care of them, for they are dear to me, and I have a tender concern for them." And now, as before, we must observe,

1. To whom these promises do belong; they are described by three characters: — (1.) They are such as know God's name. His nature we cannot fully know; but by his name he has made himself known, and with that we must acquaint ourselves. (2.) They are such as have set their love upon him; and those who rightly know him will love him, will place their love upon him as the only adequate object of it, will let out their love towards him with pleasure and enlargement, and will fix their love upon him with a resolution never to remove it to any rival. (3.) They are such as call upon him, as by prayer keep up a constant correspondence with him, and in every difficult case refer themselves to him.

2. What the promises are which God makes to the saints. (1.) That he will, in due time, deliver them out of trouble: *I will deliver him* (*v.* 14 and again *v.* 15), denoting a double deliverance, living and dying, a deliverance in trouble and a deliverance out of trouble. If God proportions the degree and continuance of our troubles to our strength, if he keeps us from offending him in our troubles, and makes our death our discharge, at length, from all our troubles, then this promise is fulfilled. See Ps. 34:19; 2 Tim. 3:11; 4:18. (2.) That he will, in the mean time, *be with them in trouble, v.* 15. If he does not immediately put a period to their afflictions, yet they shall have his gracious presence with them in their troubles; he will take notice of their sorrows, and *know their souls in adversity,* will visit them graciously by his word and Spirit, and converse with them, will take their part, will support and comfort them, and sanctify their afflictions to them, which will be the surest token of his presence with them in their troubles. (3.) That herein he will answer their prayers: *He shall call upon me;* I will pour upon him the spirit of prayer, *and* then *I will answer,* answer by promises (Ps. 85:8), answer by providences, bringing in seasonable relief, and answer by graces, *strengthening them with strength in their souls* (Ps. 138:3); thus he answered Paul with *grace sufficient,* 2 Co. 12:9. (4.) That he will exalt and dignify them: *I will set him on high,* out of the reach of trouble, above the stormy region, on a rock *above the waves,* Isa. 33:16. They shall be enabled, by the grace of God, to look down upon the things of this world with a holy contempt and indifference, to look up to the things of the other world with a holy ambition and concern; and then they are set on high. *I will honour him;* those are truly honourable whom God puts honour upon by taking them into covenant and communion with himself and designing them for his kingdom and glory, Jn. 12:26. (5.) That they shall

have a sufficiency of life in this world (*v.* 16): *With length of days will I satisfy him;* that is, [1.] They shall live long enough: they shall be continued in this world till they have done the work they were sent into this world for and are ready for heaven, and that is long enough. Who would wish to live a day longer than God has some work to do, either by him or upon him? [2.] They shall think it long enough; for God by his grace shall wean them from the world and make them willing to leave it. A man may die young, and yet die full of days, *satur dierum — satisfied with living.* A wicked worldly man is not satisfied, no, not with long life; he still cries, *Give, give.* But he that has his treasure and heart in another world has soon enough of this; he would not live always. (6.) That they shall have an eternal life in the other world. This crowns the blessedness: *I will show him my salvation,* show him *the Messiah* (so some); good old Simeon was then satisfied with long life when he could say, *My eyes have seen thy salvation,* nor was there any greater joy to the Old-Testament saints than to see Christ's day, though at a distance. It is more probably that the word refers to the better country, that is, the heavenly, which the patriarchs desired and sought: he *will show him* that, bring him to that blessed state, the felicity of which consists so much in seeing that face to face which we here see through a glass darkly; and, in the mean time, he will give him a prospect of it. All these promises, some think, point primarily at Christ, and had their accomplishment in his resurrection and exaltation.

PSALM 92

It is a groundless opinion of some of the Jewish writers (who are usually free of their conjectures) that this psalm was penned and sung by Adam in innocency, on the first sabbath. It is inconsistent with the psalm itself, which speaks of the workers of iniquity, when as yet sin had not entered. It is probable that it was penned by David, and, being calculated for the sabbath day, I. Praise, the business of the sabbath, is here recommended (*v.* 1–3). II. God's works, which gave occasion for the sabbath, are here celebrated as great and unsearchable in general (*v.* 4–6). In particular, with reference to the works both of providence and redemption, the psalmist sings unto God both of mercy and judgment, the ruin of sinners and the joy of saints, three times counterchanged. 1. The wicked shall perish (*v.* 7), but God is eternal (*v.* 8). 2. God's enemies shall be cut off, but David shall be exalted (*v.* 9, 10). 3. David's enemies shall be confounded (*v.* 11), but all the righteous shall be fruitful and flourishing (*v.* 12–15). In singing this psalm we must take pleasure in giving to God the glory due to his name, and triumph in his works.

A psalm *or* song for the sabbath day.

Verses 1–6

This psalm was appointed to be sung, at least it usually was sung, in the house of the sanctuary on the sabbath day, that day of rest, which was an instituted memorial of the work of creation, of God's rest from that work, and the continuance of it in his providence; for *the Father worketh hitherto.* Note, 1. The sabbath day must be a day, not only of holy rest, but of holy work, and the rest is in order to the work. 2. The proper work of the sabbath is praising God; every sabbath day must be a thanksgiving-day; and the other services of the day must be in order to this, and therefore must by no means thrust this into a corner. One of the Jewish writers refers it to the kingdom of the Messiah, and calls it, *A psalm or song for the age to come,* which shall be all sabbath. Believers, through Christ, enjoy that *sabbatism which remains for the people of God* (Heb. 4:9), the beginning of the everlasting sabbath. In these verses,

I. We are called upon and encouraged to praise God (*v.* 1–3): *It is a good thing to give thanks unto the Lord.* Praising God is good work: it is good in itself and good for us. It is our duty, the rent, the tribute, we are to pay to our great Lord; we are unjust if we withhold it. It is our privilege that we are admitted to praise God, and have hope to be accepted in it. It is good, for it is pleasant and profitable, work that is its own wages; it is the work of angels, the work of heaven. It is good to give thanks for the mercies we have received, for that is the way of fetching in further mercy: it is fit to sing to his name who is Most High, exalted above all blessing and praise. Now observe here, 1. How we must praise God. We must do it by *showing forth his lovingkindness and his faithfulness.* Being convinced of his glorious attributes and perfections, we must show them forth, as those that are greatly affected with them ourselves and desire to affect others with them likewise. We must show forth, not only his greatness and majesty, his holiness and justice, which magnify him and strike an awe upon us, but his lovingkindness and his faithfulness; for his goodness is his glory (Ex. 33:18, 19), and by these he proclaims his name. His mercy and truth are the great supports of our faith and hope, and the great encouragements of our love and obedience; these therefore we must show forth as our pleas in prayer and the matter of our joy. This was then done, not only by singing, but by music joined with it, *upon an instrument of ten strings* (*v.* 3); but then it was to be *with a solemn sound,* not that which was gay, and apt to dissipate the spirits, but that which was grave, and apt to fix them. 2. When we must praise God — *in the morning and every night,* not only on sabbath days, but every day; it is that which the duty of every day requires. We must praise God, not only in public assemblies, but in secret, and in our families, showing forth, to ourselves and those about us, his lovingkindness and faithfulness. We must begin and end every day with praising God, must give him thanks every morning, when we are fresh and before the business of the day comes in upon us, and every night, when we are again composed and retired, and are recollecting ourselves; we must give him thanks every morning for the mercies of the night and every night for the mercies of the day; going out and coming in we must bless God.

II. We have an example set before us in the psalmist himself, both to move us to and to direct us in this work (*v.* 4): *Thou, Lord, hast made me glad through thy work.* Note, 1. Those can best recommend to others the duty of praise who have themselves experienced the pleasantness of it. "God's works are to be praised, for they have many a time rejoiced my heart; and therefore, whatever others may think of them, I must think well and speak well of them." 2. If God has given us the joy of his works, there is all the reason in the world why we should give him the honour of them. Has he made our hearts glad? Let us then make his praises glorious. Has God made us glad through the works of his providence for us, and of his grace in us, and both through the great work of redemption? (1.) Let us thence fetch encouragement for our faith and hope; so the psalmist does: *I will triumph in the works of thy hands.* From a joyful remembrance of what God has done for us we may raise a joyful prospect of what he will do, and triumph in the assurance of it, triumph over all opposition, 2 Th. 2:13, 14. (2.) Let us thence fetch matter for holy adorings and admirings of God (*v.* 5): *O Lord! how great are thy works* — great beyond conception, beyond expression, the products of great power and wisdom, of great consequence and importance! men's works are nothing to them. We cannot comprehend the greatness of God's works, and therefore must reverently and awfully wonder at them, and even stand amazed at the magnificence of them. "Men's works are little and trifling, for their thoughts are shallow; but, Lord, *thy works are great* and such as cannot be measured; for *thy thoughts are very deep* and such as cannot be fathomed." God's counsels as much exceed the contrivances of our wisdom as his works do the efforts of our power. *His thoughts are above our thoughts,* as his *ways* are *above our ways,* Isa. 55:9. *O the depth* of God's designs! Rom. 11:33. The greatness of God's works should lead us to consider the depth of his thoughts, that counsel of his own will according to which he does all things — what a compass his thoughts fetch and to what a length they reach!

III. We are admonished not to neglect the works of God, by the character of those who do so, *v.* 6. Those are fools, they are brutish, who do not know, who do not understand, how great God's works are, who will not acquaint themselves with them, nor give him the glory of them; they *regard not the work of the Lord* nor *consider the operation of his hands* (Ps. 28:5); particularly, they understand not the meaning of their own prosperity (which is spoken of *v.* 7); they take it as a pledge of their happiness, whereas it is a preparative for their ruin. If there are so many who know not the designs of Providence, nor care to know them, those who through grace are acquainted with them, and love to be so, have the more reason to be thankful.

Verses 7–15

The psalmist had said (*v.* 4) that from the works of God he would take occasion to triumph; and here he does so.

I. He triumphs over God's enemies (*v.* 7, 9, 11), triumphs in the foresight of their destruction, not as it would be the misery of his fellow-creatures, but as it would redound to the honour of God's justice and holiness. He is confident of the ruin of sinners, 1. Though they are flourishing (*v.* 7): *When the wicked spring as the grass* in spring (so numerous, so thickly sown, so green, and growing so fast), *and all the workers of iniquity do flourish* in pomp, and power, and all the instances of outward prosperity, are easy and many, and succeed in their enterprises, one would think that all this was in order to their being happy, that it was a certain evidence of God's favour and an earnest of something as good or better in reserve: but it is quite otherwise; it is *that they shall be destroyed for ever.* The very *prosperity of fools shall slay them,* Prov. 1:32. The sheep that are designed for the slaughter are put into the fattest pasture. 2. Though they are daring, *v.* 9. They are thy enemies, and impudently avow themselves to be so. They are contrary to God, and they fight against God. They are in rebellion against his crown and dignity, and therefore it is easy to foresee that they shall perish; for *who ever hardened his heart against God and prospered?* Note, All the impenitent workers of iniquity shall be deemed and taken as God's enemies, and as such they shall perish and be scattered. Christ reckons those his enemies that will not have him to reign over them; and they shall be brought forth and slain before him. The workers of iniquity are now associated, and closely linked together, in a combination against God and religion; but they shall be scattered, and disabled to help one another against the just judgment of God. *In the world to come they shall be separated from the congregation of the righteous;* so the Chaldee, Ps. 1:5. 3. Though they had a particular malice against the psalmist, and, upon that account, he might be tempted to fear them, yet he triumphs over them (*v.* 11): *"My eye shall see my desire on my enemies that rise up against me;* I shall see them not only disabled from doing me any further mischief, but reckoned with for the mischief they have done me, and brought either to repentance or ruin:" and this was his desire concerning them. In the Hebrew it is no more than thus, *My eye shall look on my enemies, and my ear shall hear of the wicked.* He does not say what he shall see or what he shall hear, but he shall see and hear that in which God will be glorified and in which he will therefore be satisfied. This perhaps has reference to Christ, to his victory over Satan, death, and hell, the destruction of those that persecuted and crucified him, and opposed his gospel, and to the final ruin of the impenitent at the last day. Those that rise up against Christ will fall before him and be made his footstool.

II. He triumphs in God, and his glory and grace. 1. In the glory of God (*v.* 8): *"But thou, O Lord! art most high for evermore.* The workers of iniquity who fight against us may be high for a time, and think to carry all before them with a high hand, but *thou art high, most high, for evermore.* Their height will be humbled and brought down, but thine is everlasting." Let us not therefore fear the pride and power of evil men, nor be discouraged by their impotent menaces, for the moth shall eat them up as a garment, but *God's righteousness shall be for ever,* Isa. 51:7, 8. 2. In the grace of God, his favour and the fruits of it, (1.) To himself (*v.* 10): "Thou, O Lord! that art thyself most high, *shalt exalt my horn."* The great God is the fountain of honour, and he, being *high for evermore,* himself will exalt his people for ever, for *he is the praise of all his saints,* Ps. 148:14. The wicked are forbidden to *lift up the horn* (Ps. 75:4, 5), but those that serve God and the interest of his kingdom with their honour or power, and commit it to him to keep it, to raise it, to use it, and to dispose of it, as he pleases, may hope that he will *exalt their horn as the horn of a unicorn,* to the greatest height, either in this world or the other: *My horn shalt thou exalt,* when *thy enemies perish; for then shall the righteous shine forth as the sun,* when the wicked shall be doomed to *shame and everlasting contempt.* He adds, *I shall be anointed with fresh oil,* which denotes a fresh confirmation in his office to which he had been anointed, or abundance of plenty, so that he should have fresh oil as often as he pleased, or renewed comforts to revive him when his spirits drooped. Grace is the anointing of the Spirit; when this is given to help in the time of need, and is received, as there is occasion, from the fulness that is in Christ Jesus, we are then anointed with fresh oil. Some read it, *When*

I grow old thou shalt anoint me with fresh oil. My old age shalt thou exalt with rich mercy; so the Septuagint. Compare *v.* 14, *They shall bring forth fruit in old age.* The comforts of God's Spirit, and the joys of his salvation, shall be a refreshing oil to the *hoary heads that are found in the way of righteousness.* (2.) To all the saints. They are here represented as *trees of righteousness,* Isa. 61:3; Ps. 1:3. Observe, [1.] The good place they are fixed in; they are *planted in the house of the Lord, v.* 13. The trees of righteousness do not grow of themselves; they are *planted,* not in common soil, but in paradise, *in the house of the Lord.* Trees are not usually planted in a house; but God's trees are said to be planted in his house because it is from his grace, by his word and Spirit, that they receive all the sap and virtue that keep them alive and make them fruitful. They fix themselves to holy ordinances, take root in them, abide by them, put themselves under the divine protection, and bring forth all their fruits to God's honour and glory. [2.] The good plight they shall be kept in. It is here promised, *First,* That they shall grow, *v.* 12. Where God gives true grace he will give more grace. God's trees shall grow higher, like the cedars, the tall cedars in Lebanon; they shall grow nearer heaven, and with a holy ambition shall aspire towards the upper world; they shall grow stronger, like the cedars, and fitter for use. *He that has clean hands shall be stronger and stronger. Secondly,* That they shall flourish, both in the credit of their profession and in the comfort and joy of their own souls. They shall be cheerful themselves and respected by all about them. *They shall flourish like the palm-tree,* which has a stately body (Cant. 7:7), and large boughs, Lev. 23:40; Jdg. 4:5. Dates, the fruit of it, are very pleasant, but it is especially alluded to here as being ever green. The wicked flourish as the grass (*v.* 7), which is soon withered, but the righteous as the palm-tree, which is long-lived and which the winter does not change. It has been said of the palm-tree, *Sub pondere crescit — The more it is pressed down the more it grows;* so the righteous flourish under their burdens; the more they are afflicted the more they multiply. Being planted in *the house of the Lord* (there their root is), *they flourish in the courts of our God* — there their branches spread. *Their life is hid with Christ in God.* But their light also shines before men. It is desirable that those who have a place should have a name in God's house, and within his walls, Isa. 56:5. Let good Christians aim to excel, that they may be eminent and may flourish, and so may adorn the doctrine of God our Saviour, as flourishing trees adorn the courts of a house. And let those who flourish in God's courts give him the glory of it; it is by virtue of this promise, *They shall be fat and flourishing.* Their flourishing without is from a fatness within, from the *root and fatness of the good olive,* Rom. 11:17. Without a living principle of grace in the heart the profession will not be long flourishing; but where that is *the leaf also shall not wither,* Ps. 1:3. *The trees of the Lord are full of sap,* Ps. 104:16. See Hos. 14:5, 6. *Thirdly,* That they shall be fruitful. Were there nothing but leaves upon them, they would not be trees of any value; but *they shall still bring forth fruit.* The products of sanctification, all the instances of a lively devotion and a useful conversation, good works, by which God is glorified and others are edified, these are the fruits of righteousness, in which it is the privilege, as well as the duty, of the righteous to abound; and their abounding in them is the matter of a promise as well as of a command. It is promised that they shall bring forth fruit in old age. Other trees, when they are old, leave off bearing, but in God's trees the strength of grace does not fail with the strength of nature. The last days of the saints are sometimes their best days, and their last work is their best work. This indeed shows that they are upright; perseverance is the surest evidence of sincerity. But it is here said *to show that the Lord is upright* (*v.* 15), that he is true to his promises and faithful to every word that he has spoken, and that he is constant to the work which he has begun. As it is by the promises that believers first partake of a divine nature, so it is by the promises that that divine nature is preserved and kept up; and therefore the power it exerts is an evidence that the *Lord is upright,* and so he will show himself *with an upright man,* Ps. 18:25. This the psalmist triumphs in: *"He is my rock and there is no unrighteousness in him.* I have chosen him for my rock on which to build, in the clefts of which to take shelter, on the top of which to set my feet. I have found him a rock, strong and stedfast, and his word as firm as a rock. I have found" (and let every one speak as he finds) "that there is no unrighteousness in him." He is as able, and will be as kind, as his word makes him to be. All that ever trusted in God found him faithful and all-sufficient, and none were ever made ashamed of their hope in him.

PSALM 93

This short psalm sets forth the honour of the kingdom of God among men, to his glory, the terror of his enemies, and the comfort of all his loving subjects. It relates both to the kingdom of his providence, by which he upholds and governs the world, and especially to the kingdom of his grace, by which he secures the church, sanctifies and preserves it. The administration of both these kingdoms is put into the hands of the Messiah, and to him, doubtless, the prophet here hears witness, and to his kingdom, speaking of it as present, because sure; and because, as the eternal Word, even before his incarnation he was Lord of all. Concerning God's kingdom glorious things are here spoken. I. Have other kings their royal robes? So has he (*v.* 1). II. Have they their thrones? So has he (*v.* 2). III. Have they their enemies whom they subdue and triumph over? So has he (*v.* 3, 4). IV. Is it their honour to be faithful and holy? So it is his (*v.* 5). In singing this psalm we forget ourselves if we forget Christ, to whom the Father has given all power both in heaven and in earth.

Verses 1–5

Next to the being of God there is nothing that we are more concerned to believe and consider than God's dominion, that Jehovah is God, and that this God reigns (*v.* 1), not only that he is King of right, and is the owner and proprietor of all persons and things, but that he is King in fact, and does direct and dispose of all the creatures and all their actions according to the counsel of his own will. This is celebrated here, and in many other psalms: *The Lord reigns.* It is the song of the gospel church, of the glorified church (Rev. 19:6), *Hallelujah; the Lord God omnipotent reigns.* Here we are told how he reigns.

I. The Lord reigns gloriously: *He is clothed with majesty.* The majesty of earthly princes, compared with God's terrible majesty, is but like the glimmerings of a glow-worm compared with the brightness of the sun when he goes forth in his strength. Are the enemies of God's kingdom great and formidable? Yet let us not fear them, for God's majesty will eclipse theirs.

II. He reigns powerfully. He is not only clothed with majesty, as a prince in his court, but he is *clothed with strength,* as a general in the camp. He has wherewithal to support his greatness and to make it truly formidable. See him not only clad in robes, but clad in armour. Both *strength and honour are his clothing.* He can do every thing, and with him nothing is impossible. 1. With this power *he has girded himself;* it is not derived from any other, nor does the executing of it depend upon any other, but he has it of himself and with it does whatsoever he pleases. Let us not fear the power of man, which is borrowed and bounded, but fear him who has power to kill and cast into hell. 2. To this power it is owing that the world stands to this day. The world also is established; it was so at first, by the creating power of God, when he founded it upon the seas; it is so still, by that providence which upholds all things and is a continued creation; it is so established that though he has *hanged the earth upon nothing* (Job 26:7) yet *it cannot be moved;* all things *continue to this day, according to his ordinance.* Note, The preserving of the powers of nature and the course of nature is what the God of nature must have the glory of; and we who have the benefit thereof daily are very careless and ungrateful if we give him not the glory of it. Though God clothes himself with majesty, yet he condescends to take care of this lower world and to settle its affairs; and, if he established the world, much more will he establish his church, that it cannot be moved.

III. He reigns eternally (*v.* 2): *Thy throne is established of old.* 1. God's right to rule the world is founded in his making it; he that gave being to it, no doubt, may give law to it, and so his title to the government is incontestable: *Thy throne is established;* it is a title without a flaw in it. And it is ancient: it is *established of old,* from the beginning of time, before any other rule, principality, or power was erected, as it will continue when all other rule, principality, and power shall be put down, 1 Co. 15:24. 2. The whole administration of his government was settled in his eternal counsels before all worlds; for he does all according to the purpose which he purposed in himself; The chariots of Providence came down from between the mountains of brass, from those decrees which are fixed as the everlasting mountains (Zec. 6:1): *Thou art from everlasting,* and therefore *thy throne is established of old;* because God himself was from everlasting, his throne and all the determinations of it were so too; for in an eternal mind there could not but be eternal thoughts.

IV. He reigns triumphantly, *v.* 3, 4. We have here, 1. A threatening storm supposed: *The floods have lifted up, O Lord!* (to God himself the remonstrance is made) *the floods have lifted up their voice,* which speaks terror; nay, they have *lifted up their waves,* which speaks real danger. It alludes to a tempestuous sea, such as the wicked are compared to, Isa. 57:20. The *heathen rage* (Ps. 2:1) and think to ruin the church, to overwhelm it like a deluge, to sink it like a ship at sea. The church is said to *be tossed with tempests* (Isa. 54:11), and the *floods of ungodly men* make the saints *afraid,* Ps. 18:4. We may apply it to the tumults that are sometimes in our own bosoms, through prevailing passions and frights, which put the soul into disorder, and are ready to overthrow its graces and comforts; but, if the Lord reign there, even the winds and seas shall obey him. 2. An immovable anchor cast in this storm (*v.* 4): *The Lord himself is mightier.* Let this keep our minds fixed, (1.) That God is on high, above them, which denotes his safety (they cannot reach him, Ps. 29:10) and his sovereignty; they are ruled by him, they are overruled, and, wherein they rebel, overcome, Ex. 18:11. (2.) That he *is mightier,* does more *wondrous things* than *the noise of many waters;* they cannot disturb his rest or rule; they cannot defeat his designs and purposes. Observe, The power of the church's enemies is but *as the noise of many waters;* there is more of sound than substance in it. *Pharaoh king of Egypt is but a noise,* Jer. 46:17. The church's friends are commonly more frightened than hurt. God is mightier than this noise; he is mighty to preserve his people's interests from being ruined by these many waters and his people's spirits from being terrified by the noise of them. He can, when he pleases, command peace to the church (Ps. 65:7), peace in the soul, Isa. 26:3. Note, The unlimited sovereignty and irresistible power of the great Jehovah are very encouraging to the people of God, in reference to all the noises and hurries they meet with in this world, Ps. 46:1, 2.

V. He reigns in truth and holiness, *v.* 5. 1. All his promises are inviolably faithful: *Thy testimonies are very sure.* As God is able to protect his church, so he is true to the promises he has made of its safety and victory. His word is passed, and all the saints may rely upon it. Whatever was foretold concerning the kingdom of the Messiah would certainly have its accomplishment in due time. Those testimonies upon which the faith and hope of the Old-Testament saints were built were very sure, and would not fail them. 2. All his people ought to be conscientiously pure: *Holiness becomes thy house, O Lord! for ever.* God's church is his house; it is a holy house, cleansed from sin, consecrated by God, and employed in his service. The holiness of it is its beauty (nothing better becomes the saints than conformity to God's image and an entire devotedness to his honour), and it is its strength and safety; it is the holiness of God's house that secures it against the many waters and their noise. Where there is purity there shall be peace. Fashions change, and that which is becoming at one time is not so at another; but holiness always becomes God's house and family, and those who belong to it; it is perpetually decent; and nothing so ill becomes the worshippers of the holy God as unholiness.

PSALM 94

This psalm was penned when the church of God was under hatches, oppressed and persecuted; and it is an appeal to God, as the judge of heaven and earth, and an address to him, to appear for his people against his and their enemies. Two things this psalm speaks: — I. Conviction and terror to the persecutors (*v.* 1–11), showing them their danger and folly, and arguing with them. II. Comfort and peace to the persecuted (*v.* 12–23), assuring them, both from God's promise and from the psalmist's own experience, that their troubles would end well, and God would, in due time, appear to their joy and the confusion of those who set themselves against them. In singing this psalm we must look abroad upon the pride of oppressors with a holy indignation, and the tears of the oppressed with a holy compassion; but, at the same time, look upwards to the righteous Judge with an entire satisfaction, and look forward, to the end of all these things, with a pleasing hope.

Verses 1–11

In these verses we have,

I. A solemn appeal to God against the cruel oppressors

of his people, *v.* 1, 2. This speaks terror enough to them, that they have the prayers of God's people against them, who cry day and night to him to avenge them of their adversaries; and shall he not avenge them speedily? Lu. 18:3, 7. Observe here,

1. The titles they give to God for the encouraging of their faith in this appeal: *O God! to whom vengeance belongeth;* and *thou Judge of the earth.* We may with boldness appeal to him; for, (1.) He is judge, supreme judge, judge alone, from whom every man's judgment proceeds. He that gives law gives sentence upon every man according to his works, by the rule of that law. He has prepared his throne for judgment. He has indeed appointed magistrates to be avengers under him (Rom. 13:4), but he is the avenger in chief, to whom even magistrates themselves are accountable; his throne is the last refuge (the *dernier ressort,* as the law speaks) of oppressed innocency. He is universal judge, not of this city or country only, but *judge of the earth,* of the whole earth: none are exempt from his jurisdiction; nor can it be alleged against an appeal to him in any court that it is *coram non judice — before a person not judicially qualified.* (2.) He is just. As he has authority to avenge wrong, so it is his nature, and property, and honour. This also is implied in the title here given to him and repeated with such an emphasis, *O God! to whom vengeance belongs,* who wilt not suffer might always to prevail against right. This is a good reason why we must not avenge ourselves, because God has said, *Vengeance is mine;* and it is daring presumption to usurp his prerogative and step into his throne, Rom. 12:19. Let this alarm those who do wrong, whether with a close hand, so as not to be discovered, or with a high hand, so as not to be controlled, There is a God to whom vengeance belongs, who will certainly call them to an account; and let it encourage those who suffer wrong to bear it with silence, committing themselves to him who judges righteously.

2. What it is they ask of God. (1.) That he would *glorify himself,* and get honour to his own name. Wicked persecutors thought God had withdrawn and had forsaken the earth. "Lord," say they, "show thyself; make them know that thou art and that thou art ready to *show thyself strong on the behalf of those whose hearts are upright with thee.*" The enemies thought God was conquered because his people were. "Lord," say they, *"lift up thyself, be thou exalted in thy own strength.* Lift up thyself, to be seen, to be feared; and suffer not thy name to be trampled upon and run down." (2.) That he would mortify the oppressors: *Render a reward to the proud;* that is, "Reckon with them for all their insolence, and the injuries they have done to thy people." These prayers are prophecies, which speak terror to all the sons of violence. The righteous God will deal with them according to their merits.

II. A humble complaint to God of the pride and cruelty of the oppressors, and an expostulation with him concerning it, *v.* 3–6. Here observe,

1. The character of the enemies they complain against. They are wicked; they are *workers of iniquity;* they are bad, very bad, themselves, and therefore they hate and persecute those whose goodness shames and condemns them. Those are wicked indeed, and *workers of the worst iniquity,* lost to all honour and virtue, who are cruel to the innocent and hate the righteous.

2. Their haughty barbarous carriage which they complain of. (1.) They are insolent, and take a pleasure in magnifying themselves. They talk high and talk big; they triumph; they speak loud things; they boast themselves, as if their tongues were their own and their hands too, and they were accountable to none for what they say or do, and as if the day were their own, and they doubted not but to carry the cause against God and religion. Those that speak highly of themselves, that triumph and boast, are apt to speak hardly of others; but there will come a day of reckoning for all their hard speeches which ungodly sinners have spoken against God, his truths, and ways, and people, Jude 15. (2.) They are impious, and take a pleasure in running down God's people because they are his (*v.* 5): *"They break in pieces thy people, O Lord!* break their assemblies, their estates, their families, their persons, in pieces, and do all they can to afflict thy heritage, to grieve them, to crush them, to run them down, to root them out." God's people are his heritage; there are those that, for his sake, hate them, and seek their ruin. This is a very good plea with God, in our intercessions for the church: "Lord, it is thine; thou hast a property in it. It is thy heritage; thou hast a pleasure in it, and out of it the rent of thy glory in this world issues. And wilt thou suffer these wicked men to trample upon it thus?" (3.) They are inhuman, and take a pleasure in wronging those that are least able to help themselves (*v.* 6); they not only oppress and impoverish, but *they slay the widow and the stranger;* not only neglect the fatherless, and make a prey of them, but murder them, because they are weak and exposed, and sometimes lie at their mercy. Those whom they should protect from injury they are most injurious to, perhaps because God has taken them into his particular care. Who would think it possible that any of the children of men should be thus barbarous?

3. A modest pleading with God concerning the continuance of the persecution: "Lord, *how long* shall they do thus?" And again, *How long?* When shall this wickedness of the wicked come to an end?

III. A charge of atheism exhibited against the persecutors, and an expostulation with them upon that charge.

1. Their atheistical thoughts are here discovered (*v.* 7): *Yet they say, The Lord shall not see.* Though the cry of their wickedness is very great and loud, though they rebel against the light of nature and the dictates of their own consciences, yet they have the confidence to say, *"The Lord shall not see;* he will not only wink at small faults, but shut his eyes at great ones too." Or they think they have managed it so artfully, under colour of justice and religion perhaps, that it will not be adjudged murder. "The God of Jacob, though his people pretend to have such an interest in him, does not regard it either as against justice or as against his own people; he will never call us to an account for it." Thus they deny God's government of the world, banter his covenant with his people, and set the judgment to come at defiance.

2. They are here convicted of folly and absurdity. He that says either that Jehovah the living God shall not see or that the God of Jacob shall not regard the injuries done to his people, *Nabal* is his name and folly is with him; and yet here he is fairly reasoned with, for his conviction and conversion, to prevent his confusion (*v.* 8): *"Understand, you brutish among the people,* and let reason guide you." Note, The atheistical, though they set up for wits, and philosophers, and politicians, yet are really the *brutish among the people;* if they would but understand, they would believe. God, by the prophet, speaks as if he thought the time long till men would be men, and show themselves so by understanding and considering: *"You fools, when will you be wise,* so wise as to know that God sees and regards all you say and do, and to speak and act accordingly, as those that must give account?" Note, None are so bad but means are to be used for the reclaiming and reforming of them, none so brutish, so foolish, but it should be tried whether they may not yet be made wise; while there is life there is hope. To prove the folly of those that question God's omniscience and justice the psalmist argues,

(1.) From the works of creation (*v.* 9), the formation of human bodies, which as it proves that there is a God, proves also that God has infinitely and transcendently in himself all those perfections that are in any creature. *He that planted the ear* (and it is planted in the head, as a tree in the ground) *shall he not hear?* No doubt he shall, more and better than we can. *He that formed the eye* (and how curiously it is formed above any part of the body anatomists know and let us know by their dissections) *shall he not see?* Could he give, would he give, that perfection to a creature which he has not in himself? Note, [1.] The powers of nature are all derived from the God of nature. See Ex. 4:11. [2.] By the knowledge of ourselves we may be led a great way towards the knowledge of God — if by the knowledge of our own bodies, and the organs of sense, so as to conclude that if we can see and hear much more can God, then certainly by the knowledge of our own souls and their noble faculties. The gods of the heathen had eyes and saw not, ears and heard not; our God has no eyes nor ears, as we have, and yet we must conclude he both sees and hears, because we have our sight and hearing from him, and are accountable to him for our use of them.

(2.) From the works of providence (*v.* 10): *He that chastises the heathen* for their polytheism and idolatry, *shall not he* much more *correct* his own people for their atheism and profaneness? He that chastises the children of men for oppressing and wronging one another, shall not he correct those that profess to be his own children, and call themselves so, and yet persecute those that are really so? Shall not we be under his correction, under whose government the whole world is? Does he regard as King of nations, and shall he not much more regard as the God of Jacob? Dr. Hammond gives another very probably sense of this: *"He that instructs the nations* (that is, gives them his law), *shall not he correct,* that is, shall not he judge them according to that law, and call them to an account for their violations of it? In vain was the law given if there will not be a judgment upon it." And it is true that the same word signifies to chastise and to instruct, because chastisement is intended for instruction and instruction should go along with chastisement.

(3.) From the works of grace: *He that teaches man knowledge, shall he not know?* He not only, as the God of nature, has given the light of reason, but, as the God of grace, has given the light of revelation, has shown man what is true wisdom and understanding; and he that does this, shall he not know? Job 28:23, 28. The flowing of the streams is a certain sign of the fulness of the fountain. If all knowledge is from God, no doubt all knowledge is in God. From this general doctrine of God's omniscience, the psalmist not only confutes the atheists, who said, *"The Lord shall not see* (*v.* 7), he will not take cognizance of what we do;" but awakens us all to consider that God will take cognizance even of what we think (*v.* 11): *The Lord knows the thoughts of man, that they are vanity.* [1.] He knows those thoughts in particular, concerning God's conniving at the wickedness of the wicked, and knows them to be vain, and laughs at the folly of those who by such fond conceits buoy themselves up in sin. [2.] He knows all the thoughts of the children of men, and knows them to be, for the most part, vain, that the imaginations of the thoughts of men's hearts are evil, only evil, and that continually. Even in good thoughts there is a fickleness and inconstancy which may well be called *vanity.* It concerns us to keep a strict guard upon our thoughts, because God takes particular notice of them. Thoughts are words to God, and vain thoughts are provocations.

Verses 12–23

The psalmist, having denounced tribulation to those that trouble God's people, here assures those that are troubled of rest. See 2 Th. 1:6, 7. He speaks comfort to suffering saints from God's promises and his own experience.

I. From God's promises, which are such as not only save them from being miserable, but secure a happiness to them (*v.* 12): *Blessed is the man whom thou chastenest.* Here he looks above the instruments of trouble, and eyes the hand of God, which gives it another name and puts quite another color upon it. The enemies break in pieces God's people (*v.* 5); they aim at no less; but the truth of the matter is that God by them chastens his people, as the father the son in whom he delights, and the persecutors are only the rod he makes use of. *Howbeit they mean not so, neither doth their heart think so,* Isa. 10:5–7. Now it is here promised,

1. That God's people shall get good by their sufferings. When he chastens them he will teach them, and blessed is the man who is thus taken under a divine discipline, for *none teaches like God.* Note, (1.) The afflictions of the saints are fatherly chastenings, designed for their instruction, reformation, and improvement. (2.) When the teachings of the word and Spirit go along with the rebukes of Providence they then both manifest men to be blessed and help to make them so; for then they are marks of adoption and means of sanctification. When we are chastened we must pray to be taught, and look into the law as the best expositor of Providence. It is not the chastening itself that does good, but the teaching that goes along with it and is the exposition of it.

2. That they shall see through their sufferings (*v.* 13): *That thou mayest give him rest from the days of adversity.* Note, (1.) There is a rest remaining for the people of God after the days of their adversity, which, though they may be many and long, shall be numbered and finished in due time, and shall not last always. He that sends the trouble

will send the rest, that he may comfort them according to the time that he has afflicted them. (2.) God *therefore* teaches his people by their troubles, that he may prepare them for deliverance, and so give them rest from their troubles, that, being reformed, they may be relieved, and that the affliction, having done its work, may be removed.

3. That they shall see the ruin of those that are the instruments of their sufferings, which is the matter of a promise, not as gratifying any passion of theirs, but as redounding to the glory of God: *Until the pit is digged* (or rather while the pit is digging) *for the wicked,* God is ordering peace for them at the same time that he is ordaining his arrows against the persecutors.

4. That, though they may be cast down, yet certainly they shall not be cast off, *v.* 14. Let God's suffering people assure themselves of this, that, whatever their friends do, God will not cast them off, nor throw them out of his covenant or out of his care; he will not forsake them, because they are his inheritance, which he will not quit his title to nor suffer himself to be disseised of. St. Paul comforted himself with this, Rom. 11:1.

5. That, bad as things are, they shall mend, and, though they are now out of course, yet they shall return to their due and ancient channel (*v.* 15): *Judgment shall return unto righteousness;* the seeming disorders of Providence (for real ones there never were) shall be rectified. God's judgment, that is, his government, looks sometimes as if it were at a distance from righteousness, while the wicked prosper, and the best men meet with the worst usage; but it shall return to righteousness again, either in this world or at the furthest in the judgment of the great day, which will set all to-rights. Then *all the upright in heart shall be after it;* they shall follow it with their praises, and with entire satisfaction; they shall return to a prosperous and flourishing condition, and shine forth out of obscurity; they shall accommodate themselves to the dispensations of divine Providence, and with suitable affections attend all its motions. *They shall walk after the Lord,* Hos. 11:10. Dr. Hammond thinks this was most eminently fulfilled in the destruction of Jerusalem first, and afterwards of heathen Rome, the crucifiers of Christ and persecutors of Christians, and the rest which the churches had thereby. *Then judgment returned even to righteousness,* to mercy and goodness, and favour to God's people, who then were as much countenanced as before they had been trampled on.

II. From his own experiences and observations.

1. He and his friends had been oppressed by cruel and imperious men, that had power in their hands and abused it by abusing all good people with it. They were themselves *evil-doers* and *workers of iniquity* (*v.* 16); they abandoned themselves to all manner of impiety and immorality, and then their throne was a *throne of iniquity, v.* 20. Their dignity served to put a reputation upon sin, and their authority was employed to support it, and to bring about their wicked designs. It is a pity that ever a throne, which should be a terror to evil-doers and a protection and praise to those that do well, should be the seat and shelter of iniquity. That is a throne of iniquity which by the policy of its council *frames mischief,* and by its sovereignty enacts it and turns it into a law. Iniquity is daring enough even when human laws are against it, which often prove too weak to give an effectual check to it; but how insolent, how mischievous, is it when it is backed by a law! Iniquity is not the better, but much the worse, for being enacted by law; nor will it excuse those that practise it to say that they did but do as they were bidden. These workers of iniquity, having *framed mischief by a law, take care to see the law executed;* for *they gather themselves together against the soul of the righteous,* who dare not *keep the statutes of Omri* nor *the law of the house of Ahab;* and they *condemn the innocent blood* for violating their decrees. See an instance in Daniel's enemies; they *framed mischief by a law* when the obtained an impious edict against prayer (Dan. 6:7), and, when Daniel would not obey it, they *assembled together against* him (*v.* 11) and *condemned his innocent blood* to the lions. The best benefactors of mankind have often been thus treated, under colour of law and justice, as the worst of malefactors.

2. The oppression they were under bore very hard upon them, and oppressed their spirits too. Let not suffering saints despair, though, when they are persecuted, they find themselves perplexed and cast down; it was so with the psalmist here: His *soul had almost dwelt in silence* (*v.* 17); he was at his wits' end, and knew not what to say or do; he was, in his own apprehensions, at his life's end, ready to drop into the grave, that land of silence. St. Paul, in a like case, *received a sentence of death within himself,* 2 Co. 1:8, 9. He said, *"My foot slippeth* (*v.* 18); I am going irretrievably; there is no remedy; I must *fall.* I *shall one day perish by the hand of Saul.* My hope fails me; I do not find such firm footing for my faith as I have sometimes found." Ps. 73:2. He had a multitude of perplexed entangled thoughts within him concerning the case he was in and the construction to be made of it, and concerning the course he should take and what was likely to be the issue of it.

3. In this distress they sought for help, and succour, and some relief. (1.) They looked about for it and were disappointed (*v.* 16): *"Who will rise up for me against the evil-doers?* Have I any friend who, in love to me, will appear for me? Has justice any friend who, in a pious indignation at unrighteousness, will plead my injured cause?" He looked, but there was none to save, there was none to uphold. Note, When on the side of the oppressors there is power it is no marvel if the oppressed have no comforter, none that dare own them, or speak a good word for them, Eccl. 4:1. When St. Paul was brought before Nero's throne of iniquity *no man stood by him,* 2 Tim. 4:16. (2.) They looked up for it, *v.* 20. They humbly expostulate with God: "Lord, *shall the throne of iniquity have fellowship with thee?* Wilt thou countenance and support these tyrants in their wickedness? We know thou wilt not." A throne has fellowship with God when it is a throne of justice and answers the end of the erecting of it; for by him kings reign, and when they reign for him their judgments are his, and he owns them as his ministers, and whoever resist them, or rise up against them, shall receive to themselves damnation; but, when it becomes a *throne of iniquity,* it has no longer fellowship with God. Far be it from the just and holy God that he should be the patron of unrighteousness, even in princes and those that sit in thrones, yea, though they be the *thrones of the house of David.*

4. They found succour and relief in God, and in him only. When other friends failed, in him they had a faithful and powerful friend; and it is recommended to all God's suffering saints to trust in him. (1.) God helps at a dead lift (*v.* 17): "When I had almost *dwelt in silence,* then the Lord was *my help,* kept me alive, kept me in heart; and *unless I had* made him *my help,* by putting my trust in him and expecting relief from him, I could never have kept possession of my own soul; but living by faith in him has kept my head above water, has given me breath, and something to say." (2.) God's goodness is the great support of sinking spirits (*v.* 18): *"When I said, My foot slips* into sin, into ruin, into despair, then *thy mercy, O Lord! held me up,* kept me from falling, and defeated the design of those who consulted to *cast me down from my excellency,"* Ps. 62:4. We are beholden not only to God's power, but to his pity, for spiritual supports: *Thy mercy,* the gifts of thy mercy and my hope in thy mercy, *held me up.* God's right hand sustains his people when they look on their right hand and on their left and there is none to uphold; and we are then prepared for his gracious supports when we are sensible of our own weakness and inability to stand by our own strength, and come to God, to acknowledge it, and to tell him how *our foot slips.* (3.) Divine consolations are the effectual relief of troubled spirits (*v.* 19): *"In the multitude of my thoughts within me,* which are noisy like a multitude, crowding and jostling one another like a multitude, and very unruly and ungovernable, in the multitude of my sorrowful, solicitous, timorous thoughts, *thy comforts delight my soul;* and they are never more delightful than when they come in so seasonably to silence my unquiet thoughts and keep my mind easy." The world's comforts give but little delight to the soul when it is hurried with melancholy thoughts; they are songs to a heavy heart. But God's comforts will reach the soul, and not the fancy only, and will bring with them that peace and that pleasure which the smiles of the world cannot give and which the frowns of the world cannot take away.

5. God is, and will be, as a righteous Judge, the patron and protector of right and the punisher and avenger of wrong; this the psalmist had both the assurance of and the experience of. (1.) He will give redress to the injured (*v.* 22): "When none else will, nor can, nor dare, shelter me, *the Lord is my defence,* to preserve me from the evil of my troubles, from sinking under them and being ruined by them; and he is *the rock of my refuge,* in the clefts of which I may take shelter, and on the top of which I may set my feet, to be out of the reach of danger." God is his people's refuge, to whom they may flee, in whom they are safe and may be secure; he is the rock of their refuge, so strong, so firm, impregnable, immovable, as a rock: natural fastnesses sometimes exceed artificial fortifications. (2.) He will reckon with the injurious (*v.* 23): *He shall render to them their own iniquity;* he shall deal with them according to their deserts, and that very mischief which they did and designed against God's people shall be brought upon themselves: it follows, *He shall cut them off in their wickedness.* A man cannot be more miserable than his own wickedness will make him if God visit it upon him: it will cut him in the remembrance of it; it will cut him off in the recompence of it. This the psalm concludes with the triumphant assurance of: *Yea, the Lord our God,* who takes our part and owns us for his, *shall cut them off* from any fellowship with him, and so shall make them completely miserable and their pomp and power shall stand them in no stead.

PSALM 95

For the expounding of this psalm we may borrow a great deal of light from the apostle's discourse, Heb. 3 and 4, where it appears both to have been penned by David and to have been calculated for the days of the Messiah; for it is there said expressly (Heb. 4:7) that the day here spoken of (*v.* 7) is to be understood of the gospel day, in which God speaks to us by his Son in a voice which we are concerned to hear, and proposes to us a rest besides that of Canaan. In singing psalms it is intended, I. That we should "make melody unto the Lord;" this we are here excited to do, and assisted in doing, being called upon to praise God (*v.* 1, 2) as a great God (*v.* 3–5) and as our gracious benefactor (*v.* 6, 7). II. That we should teach and admonish ourselves and one another; and we are here taught and warned to hear God's voice (*v.* 7), and not to harden our hearts, as the Israelites in the wilderness did (*v.* 8, 9), lest we fall under God's wrath and fall short of his rest, as they did (*v.* 10, 11). This psalm must be sung with a holy reverence of God's majesty and a dread of his justice, with a desire to please him and a fear to offend him.

Verses 1–7a

The psalmist here, as often elsewhere, stirs up himself and others to praise God; for it is a duty which ought to be performed with the most lively affections, and which we have great need to be excited to, being very often backward to it and cold in it. Observe,

I. How God is to be praised. 1. With holy joy and delight in him. The praising song must be *a joyful noise, v.* 1 and again *v.* 2. Spiritual joy is the heart and soul of thankful praise. It is the will of God (such is the condescension of his grace) that when we give glory to him as a being infinitely perfect and blessed we should, at the same time, *rejoice in him* as our Father and King, and a God in covenant with us. 2. With humble reverence, and a holy awe of him (*v.* 6): *"Let us worship, and bow down, and kneel before him,* as becomes those who know what an infinite distance there is between us and God, how much we are in danger of his wrath and in need of his mercy." Though *bodily exercise,* alone, *profits little,* yet certainly it is our duty to glorify God with our bodies by the outward expressions of reverence, seriousness, and humility, in the duties of religious worship. 3. We must praise God with our voice; we must speak forth, sing forth, his praises out of the abundance of a heart filled with love, and joy, and thankfulness — *Sing to the Lord; make a noise, a joyful noise to him, with psalms* — as those who are ourselves much affected with his greatness and goodness, are forward to own ourselves so, are desirous to be more and more affected therewith, and would willingly be instrumental to kindle and inflame the same pious and devout affection in others also. 4. We must praise God in concert, in the solemn assemblies: *"Come, let us sing;* let us join in singing to the Lord; not others without me, nor I alone, but others with me. *Let us come* together *before his presence,* in the courts of his house, where his people are wont to attend him and to expect his manifestations of himself." Whenever we come into God's presence we must come with thanksgiving that we are admitted to such a favour; and, whenever we have thanks to give, we must *come before God's presence,* set ourselves before him, and present ourselves to him in the ordinances which he has appointed.

II. Why God is to be praised and what must be the matter of our praise. We do not want matter; it were well if we did not want a heart. We must praise God,

1. Because he is *a great God,* and sovereign Lord of all, *v.* 3. He is great, and therefore *greatly to be praised.* He is infinite and immense, and has all perfection in himself. (1.) He has great power: *He is a great King above all gods,* above all deputed deities, all magistrates, to whom he said, *You are gods* (he manages them all, and serves his own purposes by them, and to him they are all accountable), above all counterfeit deities, all pretenders, all usurpers; he can do that which none of them can do; he can, and will, famish and vanquish them all. (2.) He has great possessions. This lower world is here particularly specified. We reckon those great men who have large territories, which they call their own against all the world, which yet are a very inconsiderable part of the universe: how great then is that God whose *the whole earth is, and the fulness thereof,* not only under whose feet it is, as he has an incontestable dominion over all the creatures and a propriety in them, but in whose hand it is, as he has the actual directing and disposing of all (*v.* 4); even *the deep places of the earth,* which are out of our sight, subterraneous springs and mines, *are in his hand;* and *the height of the hills* which are out of our reach, whatever grows or feeds upon them, *is his also.* This may be taken figuratively: the meanest of the children of men, who are as the low places of the earth, are not beneath his cognizance; and the greatest, who are as the strength of the hills, are not above his control. Whatever strength is in any creature it is derived from God and employed for him (*v.* 5): *The sea is his,* and all that is in it (the waves fulfil his word); it is his, for *he made it,* gathered its waters and fixed its shores; *the dry land,* though given to the children of men, is his too, for he still reserved the property to himself; it is his, for *his hands formed* it, when his word made *the dry land* appear. His being the Creator of all makes him, without dispute, the owner of all. This being a gospel psalm, we may very well suppose that it is the Lord Jesus whom we are here taught to praise. He *is a great God;* the mighty God is one of his titles, and *God over all, blessed for evermore.* As Mediator, he is *a great King above all gods;* by him kings reign; and angels, principalities, and powers, are subject to him; *by him,* as the eternal Word, *all things were made* (Jn. 1:3), and it was fit he should be the restorer and reconciler of all who was the Creator of all, Col. 1:16, 20. To him all power is given both in heaven and in earth, and into his hand all things are delivered. It is he that sets one foot on the sea and the other on the earth, as sovereign Lord of both (Rev. 10:2), and therefore to him we must sing our songs of praise, and before him we must *worship and bow down.*

2. Because he is our God, not only has a dominion over us, as he has over all the creatures, but stands in special relation to us (*v.* 7): *He is our God,* and therefore it is expected we should praise him; who will, if we do not? What else did he make us for but that we should *be to him for a name and a praise?* (1.) He is our Creator, and the author of our being; we must *kneel before the Lord our Maker, v.* 6. Idolaters kneel before gods which they themselves made; we kneel before a God who made us and all the world and who is therefore our rightful proprietor; for his we are, and not our own. (2.) He is our Saviour, and the author of our blessedness. He is here called *the rock of our salvation* (*v.* 1), not only the founder, but the very foundation, of that work of wonder, on whom it is built. *That rock is Christ;* to him therefore we must sing our songs of praises, *to him that sits upon the throne and to the Lamb.* (3.) We are therefore his, under all possible obligations: *We are the people of his pasture and the sheep of his hand.* All the children of men are so; they are fed and led by his Providence, which cares for them, and conducts them, as the shepherd the sheep. We must praise him, not only because he made us, but because he preserves and maintains us, and our breath and ways are in his hand. All the church's children are in a special manner so; Israel *are the people of his pasture and the sheep of his hand;* and therefore he demands their homage in a special manner. The gospel church is his flock. Christ is the great and good Shepherd of it. We, as Christians, are led by his hand into the green pastures, by him we are protected and well provided for, to his honour and service we are entirely devoted as a peculiar people, and therefore to him must be *glory in the churches* (whether it be in the world or no) *throughout all ages,* Eph. 3:21.

Verses 7b–11

The latter part of this psalm, which begins in the middle of a verse, is an exhortation to those who sing gospel psalms to live gospel lives, and to hear the voice of God's word; otherwise, how can they expect that he should hear the voice of their prayers and praises? Observe,

I. The duty required of all those that *are the people of* Christ's *pasture and the sheep of his hand.* He expects that they *hear his voice,* for he has said, *My sheep hear my voice,* Jn. 10:27. *We are his people,* say they. Are you so? Then *hear his voice.* If you call him *Master,* or *Lord,* then *do the things which he says,* and be his willing obedient people. Hear the voice of his doctrine, of his law, and, in both, of his Spirit; hear and heed; hear and yield. *Hear his voice,* and not the *voice of a stranger. If you will hear his voice;* some take it as a wish, *O that you would hear his voice!* that you would be so wise, and do so well for yourselves; like that, *If thou hadst known* (Lu. 19:42), that is, O that thou hadst known! Christ's voice must be heard *to-day;* this the apostle lays much stress upon, applying it to the gospel day. While he is speaking to you see that you attend to him, for this day of your opportunities will not last always; improve it, therefore, *while it is called today,* Heb. 3:13, 15. Hearing the voice of Christ is the same with believing. *To-day,* if by faith you accept the gospel offer, well and good, but to-morrow it may be too late. In a matter of such vast importance nothing is more dangerous than delay.

II. The sin they are warned against, as inconsistent with the believing obedient ear required, and that is hardness of heart. *If you will hear his voice,* and profit by what you hear, then do *not harden your hearts;* for the seed sown on the rock never brought any fruit to perfection. The Jews *therefore* believed not the gospel of Christ because *their hearts were hardened;* they were not convinced of the evil of sin, and of their danger by reason of sin, and therefore they regarded not the offer of salvation; they would not bend to the yoke of Christ, nor yield to his demands; and, if the sinner's heart be hardened, it is his own act and deed (he hardening it himself) and he alone shall bear the blame for ever.

III. The example they are warned by, which is that of the Israelites in the wilderness.

1. "Take heed of sinning as they did, lest you be shut out of the everlasting rest as they were out of Canaan." *Be not, as your fathers, a stubborn and rebellious generation,* Ps. 78:8. Thus here, *Harden not your heart as* you did (that is, your ancestors) *in the provocation,* or in *Meribah,* the place where they quarrelled with God and Moses (Ex. 17:2–7), *and in the day of temptation in the wilderness, v.* 8. So often did they provoke God by their distrusts and murmurings that the whole time of their continuance in the wilderness might be called a *day of temptation,* or *Massah,* the other name given to that place (Ex. 17:7), because they tempted the Lord, saying, *Is the Lord among us or is he not?* This was in the wilderness, where they could not help themselves, but lay at God's mercy, and where God wonderfully helped them and gave them such sensible proofs of his power and tokens of his favour as never any people had before or since. Note, (1.) Days of temptation are days of provocation. Nothing is more offensive to God than disbelief of his promise and despair of the performance of it because of some difficulties that seem to lie in the way. (2.) The more experience we have had of the power and goodness of God the greater is our sin if we distrust him. What, to tempt him in the wilderness, where we live upon him! This is as ungrateful as it is absurd and unreasonable. (3.) Hardness of heart is at the bottom of all our distrusts of God and quarrels with him. That is a hard heart which receives not the impressions of divine discoveries and conforms not to the intentions of the divine will, which will not melt, which will not bend. (4.) The sins of others ought to be warnings to us not to tread in their steps. The murmurings of Israel *were written for our admonition,* 1 Co. 10:11.

2. Now here observe,

(1.) The charge drawn up, in God's name, against the unbelieving Israelites, *v.* 9, 10. God here, many ages after, complains of their ill conduct towards him, with the expressions of high resentment. [1.] Their sin was unbelief: they *tempted* God and *proved* him; they questioned whether they might take his word, and insisted upon further security before they would go forward to Canaan, by sending spies; and, when those discouraged them, they protested against the sufficiency of the divine power and promise, and would make a captain and return into Egypt, Num. 14:3, 4. This is called *rebellion,* Deu. 1:26, 32. [2.] The aggravation of this sin was that they *saw God's work;* they saw what he had done for them in bringing them out of Egypt, nay, what he was now doing for them every day, this day, in the bread he rained from heaven for them and the water out of the rock that followed them, than which they could not have more unquestionable evidences of God's presence with them. With them even seeing was not believing, because they *hardened their hearts,* though they had seen what Pharaoh got by hardening his heart. [3.] The causes of their sin. See what God imputed it to: *It is a people that do err in their hearts, and they have not known my ways.* Men's unbelief and distrust of God, their murmurings and quarrels with him, are the effect of their ignorance and mistake. *First,* Of their ignorance: *They have not known my ways.* They saw his work (*v.* 9) and he *made known his acts to them* (Ps. 103:7); and yet they *did not know his ways,* the ways of his providence, in which he walked towards them, or the ways of his commandments, in which he would have them to walk towards him: they did not know, they did not rightly understand and therefore did not approve of these. Note, The reason why people slight and forsake the ways of God is because they do not know them. *Secondly,* Of their mistake: *They do err in their heart;* they wander out of the way; in heart they turn back. Note, Sins are errors, practical errors, errors in heart; such there are, and as fatal as errors in the head. When the corrupt affections pervert the judgment, and so lead the soul out of the ways of duty and obedience, there is an error of the heart. [4.] God's resentment of their sin: *Forty years long was I grieved with this generation.* Not, The sins of God's professing people do not only anger him, but grieve him, especially their distrust of him; and God keeps an account how often (Num. 14:22) and how long they grieve him. See the patience of God towards provoking sinners; he was grieved with them forty years, and yet those years ended in a triumphant entrance into Canaan made by the next generation. If our sins have grieved God, surely they should grieve us, and nothing in sin should grieve us so much as that.

(2.) The sentence passed upon them for their sin (*v.* 11): *"Unto whom I swore in my wrath, If they shall enter into my rest,* then say I am changeable and untrue:" see the sentence at large, Num. 14:21, etc. Observe, [1.] Whence this sentence came — from the wrath of God. He *swore solemnly in his wrath,* his just and holy wrath; but let not men therefore swear profanely in their wrath, their sinful brutish wrath. God is not subject to such passions as we are; but he is said to be angry, very angry, at sin and sinners, to show the malignity of sin and the justice of God's government. That is certainly an evil thing which deserves such a recompence of revenge as may be expected from a provoked Deity. [2.] What it was: *That they should not enter into his rest,* the rest which he had prepared and designed for them, a settlement for them and theirs, that none of those who were enrolled when they came out of Egypt should be found written in the roll of the living at their entering into Canaan, but Caleb and Joshua. [3.] How it was ratified: *I swore it.* It was not only a purpose, but a decree; the oath showed the *immutability of his counsel; the Lord swore, and will not repent.* It cut off the thought of any reserve of mercy. God's threatenings are as sure as his promises.

Now this case of Israel may be applied to those of their posterity that lived in David's time, when this psalm was penned; let them hear God's voice, and not harden their hearts as their fathers did, lest, if they were stiffnecked like them, God should be provoked to forbid them the privileges of his temple at Jerusalem, of which he had said, *This is my rest.* But it must be applied to us Christians, because so the apostle applies it. There is a spiritual and eternal rest set before us, and promised to us, of which Canaan was a type; we are all (in profession, at least) bound for this rest; yet many that seem to be so come short and shall never enter into it. And what is it that puts a bar in their door? It is sin; it is unbelief, that sin against the remedy, against our appeal. Those that, like Israel, distrust God, and his power and goodness, and prefer the garlick and onions of Egypt before the milk and honey of Canaan, will justly be shut out from his rest: so shall their doom be; they themselves have decided it. *Let us therefore fear,* Heb. 4:1.

PSALM 96

This psalm is part of that which was delivered into the hand of Asaph and his brethren (1 Chr. 16:7), by which it appears both that David was the penman of it and that it has reference to the bringing up of the ark to the city of David; whether that long psalm was made first, and this afterwards taken out of it, or this made first and afterwards borrowed to make up that, is not certain. But this is certain, that, though it was sung at the translation of the ark, it looks further, to the kingdom of Christ, and is designed to celebrate the glories of that kingdom, especially the accession of the Gentiles to it. Here is, I. A call given to all people to praise God, to worship him, and give glory to him, as a great and glorious God (*v.* 1–9). II. Notice given to all people of God's universal government and judgment, which ought to be the matter of universal joy (*v.* 10–13). In singing this psalm we ought to have our hearts filed with great and high thoughts of the glory of God and the grace of the gospel, and with an entire satisfaction in Christ's sovereign dominion and in the expectation of the judgment to come.

Verses 1–9

These verses will be best expounded by pious and devout affections working in our souls towards God, with a high veneration for his majesty and transcendent excellency. The call here given us to praise God is very lively, the expressions are raised and repeated, to all which the echo of a thankful heart should make agreeable returns.

I. We are here required to honour God,

1. With songs, *v.* 1, 2. Three times we are here called to *sing unto the Lord;* sing to the Father, to the Son, to the Holy Ghost, as it was *in the beginning,* when *the morning stars sang together, is now,* in the church militant, and *ever shall be,* in the church triumphant. We have reason to do it often, and we have need to be often reminded of it, and stirred up to it. *Sing unto the Lord,* that is, *"Bless his name,* speak well of him, that you may bring others to think well of him." (1.) *Sing a new song,* an excellent song, the product of new affections, clothed with new expressions. We speak of nothing more despicable than "an old song," but the newness of a song recommends it; for there we expect something surprising. A new song is a song for new favours, for those compassions which are new every morning. A new song is New-Testament song, a song of praise for the new covenant and the precious privileges of that covenant. A new song is a song that shall be ever new, and shall never wax old nor vanish away; it is an everlasting song, that shall never be antiquated or out of date. (2.) Let all the earth sing this song, not the Jews only, to whom hitherto the service of God had been appropriated, who could not *sing the Lord's song in* (would not sing it to) *a strange land;* but let *all the earth,* all that are *redeemed from the earth, learn* and sing *this new song,* Rev. 14:3. This is a prophecy of the calling of the Gentiles; all the earth shall have this *new song put into their mouths,* shall have both cause and call to sing it. (3.) Let the subject-matter of this song be *his salvation,* the great salvation which was to be wrought out by the Lord Jesus; that must be shown forth as the cause of this joy and praise. (4.) Let this song be sung constantly, not only in the times appointed for the solemn feasts, but from day to day; it is a subject that can never be exhausted. Let day unto day utter this speech, that, under the influence of gospel devotions, we may daily exemplify a gospel conversation.

2. With sermons (*v.* 3): *Declare his glory among the heathen,* even *his wonders among all people.* (1.) Salvation by Christ is here spoken of as a work of wonder, and that in which the glory of God shines very brightly; in showing forth that salvation we declare God's glory as it shines in the face of Christ. (2.) This salvation was, in the Old-Testament times, as heaven's happiness is now, *a glory to be revealed;* but in the fulness of time it was declared, and a full discovery made of that, even to babes, which prophets and kings desired and wished to see and might not. (3.) What was then discovered was declared only among the Jews, but it is now declared *among the heathen, among all people;* the nations which long sat in darkness now see this great light. The apostles' commission to preach the gospel to every creature is copied from this: *Declare his glory among the heathen.*

3. With religious services, *v.* 7–9. Hitherto, though in every nation those that feared God and wrought righteousness were accepted of him, yet instituted ordinances were the peculiarities of the Jewish religion; but, in gospel-times, the kindreds of the people shall be invited and admitted into the service of God and be as welcome as ever the Jews were. The court of the Gentiles shall no longer be an outward court, but shall be laid in common with the court of Israel. All the earth is here summoned to fear before the Lord, to worship him according to his appointment. *In every place incense shall be offered to his name,* Mal. 1:11; Zec. 14:17; Isa. 66:23. This indeed spoke mortification to the Jews, but, withal, it gave a prospect of that which would redound very much to the glory of God and to the happiness of mankind. Now observe how the acts of devotion to God are here described. (1.) We must *give unto the Lord;* not as if God needed any thing, or could receive any thing, from us or any creature, which was not his own before, much less be benefited by it; but we must in our best affections, adorations, and services, return to him what we have received from him, and do it freely, as what we give; for *God loves a cheerful giver.* It is debt, it is rent, it is tribute, it is what must be paid, and, if not, will be recovered, and yet, if it come from holy love, God is pleased to accept it as a gift. (2.) We must acknowledge God to be the sovereign Lord and pay homage to him accordingly (*v.* 7): *Give unto the Lord glory and strength, glory and empire,* or *dominion,* so some. As a king, he is clothed with robes of glory and girt with the girdle of power, and we must subscribe to both. *Thine is the kingdom,* and therefore *thine is the power and the glory.* "Give the glory to God; do not take it to yourselves, nor give it to any creature." (3.) We must *give unto the Lord the glory due unto his name,* that is, to the discovery he has been pleased to make of himself to the children of men. In all the acts of religious worship this is that which we must aim at, to honour God, to pay him some of that reverence which we owe him as the best of beings and the fountain of our being. (4.) We must *bring an offering into his courts.* We must bring ourselves, in the first place, the *offering up of the Gentiles,* Rom. 15:16. We must offer up the *sacrifices of praise continually* (Heb. 13:15), must often appear before God in public worship and never appear before him empty. (5.) We must *worship him in the beauty of holiness,* in the solemn assembly where divine institutions are religiously observed, the beauty of which is their holiness, that is, their conformity to the rule. We must worship him with holy hearts, sanctified by the grace of God, devoted to the glory of God, and purified from the pollutions of sin. (6.) We must *fear before him;* all the acts of worship must be performed from a principle of the fear of God and with a holy awe and reverence.

II. In the midst of these calls to praise God and give glory to him glorious things are here said of him, both as motives to praise and matter of praise: *The Lord is great, and* therefore *greatly to be praised* (*v.* 4) and *to be feared,* great and honourable to his attendants, great and terrible to his adversaries. Even the new song proclaims God great as well as good; for his goodness is his glory; and, when the everlasting gospel is preached, it is this, *Fear God, and give glory to him,* Rev. 14:6, 7. 1. He is great in his sovereignty over all that pretend to be deities; none dare vie with him: *He is to be feared above all gods* — all princes, who were often deified after their deaths, and even while they lived were adored as petty gods — or rather all idols, *the gods of the nations v.* 5. All the earth being called to sing the new song, they must be convinced that the Lord Jehovah, to whose honour they must sing it, is the one only living and true God, infinitely above all rivals and pretenders; he is great, and they are little; he is all, and they are *nothing;* so the word used for idols signifies, for we know that *an idol is nothing in the world,* 1 Co. 8:4. 2. He is great in his right, even to the noblest part of the creation; for it is his own work and derives its being from him: *The Lord made the heavens* and all their hosts; they *are the work of his fingers* (Ps. 8:3), so nicely, so curiously, are they made. The gods of the nations were all made-gods, the creatures of men's fancies; but our God is the Creator of the sun, moon, and stars, those lights of heaven, which they imagined to be gods and worshipped as such. 3. He is great in the manifestation of his glory both in the upper and lower world, among his angels in heaven and his saints on earth (*v.* 6): *Splendour and majesty are before him,* in his immediate presence above, where the angels cover their faces, as unable to bear the dazzling lustre of his glory. *Strength and beauty are in his sanctuary,* both that above and this below. In God there is every thing that is awful and yet every thing that is amiable. If we attend him in his sanctuary, we shall behold his beauty, for *God is love,* and experience his strength, for *he is our rock.* Let us therefore go forth in his strength, enamoured with his beauty.

Verses 10–13

We have here instructions given to those who were to preach the gospel to the nations what to preach, or to those who had themselves received the gospel what account to give of it to their neighbours, what to *say among the heathen;* and it is an illustrious prophecy of the setting up of the kingdom of Christ upon the ruins of the devil's kingdom, which began immediately after his ascension and will continue in the doing till the mystery of God be finished.

I. Let it be told *that the Lord reigns,* the Lord Christ reigns, that King whom God determined to set upon his holy hill of Zion. See how this was first said *among the heathen* by Peter, Acts 10:42. Some of the ancients added a gloss to this, which by degrees crept into the text, *The Lord reigneth from the tree* (so Justin Martyr, Austin, and others, quote it), meaning the cross, when he had this title written over him, *The King of the Jews.* It was because he became obedient to death, even the death of the cross, that God exalted him, and gave him a name above every name, a throne above every throne. Some of the heathen came betimes to enquire after him that was *born King of the Jews,* Mt. 2:2. Now let them know that he has come and his kingdom is set up.

II. Let it be told that Christ's government will be the world's happy settlement. *The world also shall be established, that it shall not be moved.* The natural world shall be established. The standing of the world, and its stability, are owing to the mediation of Christ. Sin had given it a shock, and still threatens it; but Christ, as Redeemer, upholds all things, and preserves the course of nature. The world of mankind shall be established, shall be preserved, till all that belong to the election of grace are called in, though a guilty provoking world. The Christian religion, as far as it is embraced, shall establish states and kingdoms, and preserve good order among men. The church in the world shall be established (so some), that it *cannot be moved; for it is built upon a rock, and the gates of hell shall never prevail against it;* it is a *kingdom that cannot be shaken.*

III. Let them be told that Christ's government will be incontestably just and righteous: *He shall judge the people righteously* (*v.* 10), *judge the world with righteousness, and with his truth, v.* 13. Judging is here put for ruling; and though this may be extended to the general judgment of the world at the last day, which will be *in righteousness* (Acts 17:31), yet it refers more immediately to Christ's first coming, and the setting up of his kingdom in the world by the gospel. He says himself, *For judgment have I come into this world* (Jn. 9:39; 12:31), and declares that *all judgment was committed to him,* Jn. 5:22, 27. His ruling and judging with righteousness and truth signify, 1. That all the laws and ordinances of his kingdom shall be consonant to the rules and principles of eternal truth and equity, that is, to the rectitude and purity of the divine nature and will. 2. That all his administrations of government shall be just and faithful, and according to what he has said. 3. That he shall rule in the hearts and consciences of men by the commanding power of truth and the Spirit of righteousness and sanctification. When Pilate asked our Saviour, *Art thou a king?* he answered, *For this cause came I into the world, that I should bear witness unto the truth* (Jn. 18:37); for he rules by truth, commands men's wills by informing their judgments aright.

IV. Let them be told that his coming draws nigh, that this King, this Judge, *standeth before the door; for he cometh, for he cometh.* Enoch, the seventh from Adam, said so. *Behold, the Lord cometh,* Jude 14. Between this and his first coming the revolutions of many ages intervened, and yet he came at the set time, and so sure will his second coming be; though it is now long since it was said, *Behold, he comes in the clouds* (Rev. 1:7) and he has not yet come. See 2 Pt. 3:4, etc.

V. Let them be called upon to rejoice in this honour that is put upon the Messiah, and this great trust that is to be lodged in his hand (*v.* 11, 12): *Let heaven and earth rejoice, the sea, the field,* and *all the trees of the wood.* The dialect here is poetical; the meaning is, 1. That the days of the Messiah will be joyful days, and, as far as his grace and government are submitted to, will bring joy along with them. We have reason to give that place, that soul, joy into which Christ is admitted. See an instance of both, Acts 8. When Samaria received the gospel *there was great joy in that city* (*v.* 8), and, when the eunuch was baptized, *he went on his way rejoicing, v.* 39. 2. That it is the duty of every one of us to bid Christ and his kingdom welcome; for, though he comes conquering and to conquer, yet he comes peaceably. *Hosanna, Blessed is he that cometh;* and again, *Hosanna, Blessed be the kingdom of our father David* (Mk. 11:9, 10); not only *let the daughter of Zion rejoice that her King comes* (Zec. 9:9), but let all rejoice. 3. That the whole creation will have reason to rejoice in the setting up of Christ's kingdom, even *the sea* and *the field;* for, as by the sin of the first Adam the whole creation was made *subject to vanity,* so by the grace of the second Adam it shall, some way or other, first or last, be *delivered from the bondage of corruption into the glorious liberty of the children of God,* Rom. 8:20, 21. 4. That there will, in the first place, be *joy in heaven, joy in the presence of the angels of God;* for, when the First-begotten was brought into the world, they sang their anthems to his praise, Lu. 2:14. 5. That God will graciously accept the holy joy and praises of all the hearty well-wishers to the kingdom of Christ, be their capacity ever so mean. *The sea* can but *roar,* and how *the trees of the wood* can show that they *rejoice* I know not; but *he that searches the heart knows what is the mind of the Spirit,* and understands the language, the broken language, of the weakest.

PSALM 97

This psalm dwells upon the same subject, and is set to the same tune, with the foregoing psalm. Christ is the Alpha and the Omega of both; they are both penned, and are both to be sung to his honour; and we make nothing of them if we do not, in them, make melody with our hearts to the Lord Jesus. He it is that reigns, to the joy of all mankind (*v.* 1); and his government speaks, I. Terror to his enemies; for he is a prince of inflexible justice and irresistible power (*v.* 2–7). II. Comfort to his friends and loyal subjects, arising from his sovereign dominion, the care he takes of his people, and the provision he makes for them (*v.* 8–12). In singing this psalm we must be affected with the glory of the exalted Redeemer, must dread the lot of his enemies, and think ourselves happy if we are of those that "kiss the son."

Verses 1–7

What was to be said among the heathen in the foregoing psalm (*v.* 10) is here said again (*v.* 1) and is made the subject of this psalm, and of psalm 99. *The Lord reigns;* that is the great truth here laid down. The Lord Jehovah reigns, he that made the world governs it; he that gave being gives motion and power, gives law and commission, gives success and event. Every man's judgment proceeds from the Lord, from his counsel and providence, and in all affairs, both public and private, he performs the thing which he himself has appointed. The Lord Jesus reigns; the providential kingdom is twisted in with the mediatorial and the administration of both is in the hand of Christ, who therefore is both the *head of the church* and *head over all things to the church.* The kingdom of Christ is so constituted that,

I. It may be matter of joy to all; and it will be so if it be not their own fault. *Let the earth rejoice,* for hereby it is *established* (Ps. 96:10); it is honoured and enriched, and, in part, rescued from the vanity which by sin it is made subject to. Not only let the people of Israel rejoice in him as King of the Jews, and the daughter of Zion as her King, but let all the earth rejoice in his elevation; for the kingdoms of the world shall, more or less, sooner or later, become his kingdoms: *Let the multitude of isles,* the many or great isles, *be glad thereof.* This is applicable to our country, which is a great isle, and has many belonging to it; at least, it speaks comfort in general to the Gentiles, whose countries are called *the isles of the Gentiles,* Gen. 10:5. There is enough in Christ for the multitude of the isles to rejoice in; for, though many have been made happy in him, yet still there is room. All have reason to rejoice in Christ's government. 1. In the equity of it. There is an incontestable justice in all the acts of his government, both legislative and judicial. Sometimes indeed *clouds and darkness are round about him;* his dispensations are altogether unaccountable; *his way is in the sea and his path in the great waters.* We are not aware of what he designs, what he drives at; nor is it fit that we should be let into the secrets of his government. There is a depth in his counsels, which we must not pretend to fathom. But still *righteousness and judgment are the habitation of his throne;* a golden thread of justice runs through the whole web of his administration. In this he resides, for it is his habitation. In this he rules, for it is *the habitation of his throne. His commandments are,* and will be, *all righteous. Righteousness and judgment are the basis of his throne* (so Dr. Hammond); for *therefore* his *throne is for ever and ever,* because his *sceptre is a right sceptre,* Ps. 45:6. *The throne is established in righteousness.* Even *the heavens declare his righteousness* (*v.* 6); it is as conspicuous and as illustrious as the heavens themselves. The angels of heaven will declare it, who are employed as messengers in the administration of his government and therefore know more of it than any of his creatures. His righteousness is incontestable; for who can contradict or dispute what the *heavens declare?* Ps. 50:6. 2. In the extent of it in the upper and lower world. (1.) All the men on earth are under his government; either he is served by them or he serves himself by them. *All the people see his glory,* or may see it. The glory of God, in the face of Christ, was made to shine in distant countries, among many people, more or less among all people; the gospel was preached, for aught we know, in all languages, Acts 2:5, 11. Miracles were wrought in all nations, and so *all the people saw his glory. Have they not heard?* Rom. 10:18. (2.) All the angels in heaven are so. Perhaps we should not have found this truth in those words (*v.* 7), *Worship him, all you gods,* if we had not been directed to it by the inspired apostle, who, from the Septuagint version of those words, makes the Messiah to be introduced into the upper world at the ascension with this charge (Heb. 1:6), *Let all the angels of God worship him,* which helps us to a key to this whole psalm, and shows us that it must be applied to the exalted Redeemer, who has gone into heaven, *and is on the right hand of God,* which intimates that all power is given him both in heaven and earth, *angels, authorities, and powers, being made subject unto him,* 1 Pt. 3:22. This speaks the honour of Christ, that he has such worshippers, and the honour of all good Christians, that they have such fellow-worshippers.

II. Christ's government, though it may be matter of joy to all, will yet be matter of terror to some, and it is their own fault that it is so, *v.* 3–5, 7. Observe,

1. When the kingdom of Christ was to be set up in the world, after his ascension, it would meet with many enemies, and much opposition would be given to it. He that reigns, to the *joy of the whole earth,* yet, as he has his subjects, so he has *his enemies* (*v.* 3), that not only will not have him to reign over them, but would not have him to reign at all, that not only will not *enter into the kingdom of heaven themselves,* but do all they can to *hinder those that are entering,* Mt. 23:13. This was fulfilled in the enmity of the unbelieving Jews to the gospel of Christ, and the violent persecution which in all places they stirred up against the preachers and professors of it. These enemies are here called *hills* (*v.* 5), for their height, and strength, and immovable obstinacy. It was the *princes of this world* that *crucified the Lord of glory,* 1 Co. 2:8; Ps. 2:2.

2. The opposition which the Jews gave to the setting up of Christ's kingdom turned to their own ruin. Their persecuting the apostles, and *forbidding them to speak to the Gentiles,* filled up their sin, and brought *wrath upon them to the uttermost,* 1 Th. 2:15, 16. That wrath is here compared, (1.) To consuming fire, which *goes before him, and burns up his enemies,* that have made themselves like chaff and stubble, and have *set the briers and thorns before him in battle,* Isa. 27:4. This fire of divine wrath will not only burn the rubbish upon the hills, but will even *melt the hills* themselves *like wax, v.* 5. When our God appears as a consuming fire even rocks will be wax before him. The most resolute and daring opposition will be baffled *at the presence of the Lord.* His very presence is enough to shame and sink it, for he is *the Lord of the whole earth,* by whom all the children of men are manageable and to whom they are accountable. Men hate and persecute God's people, because they think him absent, that the Lord has *forsaken the earth;* but, when he manifests his presence, they melt. (2.) To amazing *lightnings* (*v.* 4), which strike a terror upon many. The judgments God brought upon the enemies of Christ's kingdom were such as all the world took notice of with terror: *The earth saw and trembled,* and the ears of all that heard were made to tingle. This was fulfilled in the destruction of Jerusalem and the Jewish nation by the Romans, about forty years after Christ's resurrection, which, like fire, wholly destroyed that people, and, like lightning, astonished all their neighbours (Deu. 29:24); but the heavens declare God's righteousness in it, and all the people, to this day, see his glory, in those lasting monuments of his justice, the scattered Jews.

3. Idolaters also would be put to confusion by the setting up of Christ's kingdom (*v.* 7): *Confounded be all those who serve graven images,* the Gentile world, who *did service to those that by nature are no gods* (Gal. 4:8), who boasted themselves of idols as their protectors and benefactors. Did those that served idols boast of them, and shall the servants of the living God distrust him, or be ashamed of him? *Let those be ashamed that serve graven images.* (1.) This is a prayer for the conversion of the Gentiles, that those who have been so long serving dumb idols may be convinced of their error, ashamed of their folly, and may, by the power of Christ's gospel, be brought to serve the only living and true God, and may be as much ashamed of their idols as ever they were proud of them. See Isa. 2:20, 21. (2.) This is a prophecy of the ruin of those that would not be reformed and reclaimed from their idolatry; they shall be confounded by the destruction of Paganism in the Roman empire, which was fulfilled about 300 years after Christ, so much to the terror of idolaters that some think it was the revolution under Constantine that made even the mighty men say to the rocks, *Fall on us and hide us,* Rev. 6:15, 16. This prayer and prophecy are still in force against antichristian idolaters, who may here read their doom: *Confounded be all those that worship graven images, v.* 7. See Jer. 48:13.

Verses 8–12

The kingdom of the Messiah, like the pillar of cloud and fire, as it has a dark side towards the Egyptians, so it has a bright side towards the Israel of God. It is set up in spite of opposition; and then *the earth saw and trembled* (*v.* 4), but *Zion heard and was glad,* very glad, to hear of the conversion of some and of the confusion of others, that is, the conquest of all that stood it out against Christ. *Rejoice greatly, O daughter of Zion! for behold thy king comes unto thee,* Zec. 9:9. And not Zion only, where the temple was, but even *the daughters of Judah, rejoiced;* the common people, the inhabitants of the villages, they shall triumph in Christ's victories. The command (*v.* 1) is, *Let the earth rejoice;* but it is only the sons of Zion and the daughters of Judah that do rejoice. All should bid the kingdom of the Messiah welcome, but few do. Now here observe,

I. The reasons that are given for Zion's joy in the government of the Redeemer. The faithful servants of God may well *rejoice* and be *glad,* 1. Because God is glorified, and whatever redounds to his honour is very much his people's pleasure. They rejoice *because of thy judgments, O Lord!* which may take in both the judgments of his mouth and the judgments of his hand, the word of his gospel and his works wrought for the propagating of it, miracles and marvellous providences; for in these we must own, *"Thou, Lord, art high above all the earth* (*v.* 9); thou hast manifested thy sovereignty in the kingdom of nature, and thy command of all its powers, and thy dominion over all nations, over all hearts; thou art *exalted far above all gods"* — all deputed gods, that is, princes — all counterfeit gods, that is, idols. The exaltation of Christ, and the advancement of God's glory among men thereby, are the rejoicing of all the saints. 2. Because care is taken for their safety. Those that pay allegiance to Christ as a King shall be sure of his protection. Princes are the shields of the earth; Christ is so to his subjects; they may put their trust under his shadow and rejoice in it, for (*v.* 10) *He preserves the souls of the saints;* he preserves their lives as long as he has any work for them to do, and wonderfully *delivers them* many a time *out of the hand of the wicked,* their persecutors that thirst after their blood; for *precious in the sight of the Lord is the death of his saints.* But something more is meant than their lives; for those that will be his disciples must be willing to lay down their lives, and not indent for the securing of them. It is the *immortal soul* that Christ preserves, the *inward man,* which may be renewed more and more when the *outward man decays.* He will *preserve the souls of his saints* from sin, from apostasy, and despair, under their greatest trials; he will *deliver them out of the hands of the wicked one* that *seeks to devour them; he will preserve them* safely *to his heavenly kingdom,* 2 Tim. 4:18. They have therefore reason to be glad, being thus safe. 3. Because provision is made for their comfort. Those that rejoice in Christ Jesus, and in his exaltation, have fountains of joy treasured up for them, which will be opened sooner or later (*v.* 11): *Light is sown for the righteous,* that is, *gladness for the upright in heart.* The subjects of Christ's kingdom are told to expect tribulation in the world. They must suffer by its malice, and must not share in its mirth; yet let them know, to their comfort, that *light is sown* for them; it is designed and prepared for them. What is sown will come up again in due time; though, like a winter seedness, it may lie long under the clods, and seem to be lost and buried, yet it will return in a rich and plentiful increase. God's goodness shall be sure of a *harvest* in the *appointed weeks. Those that sow in tears shall,* without fail, *reap in joy,* Ps. 126:5, 6. Christ told his disciples, at parting (Jn. 16:20), *You shall be sorrowful, but your sorrow shall be turned into joy.* Gladness is sure to the *upright in heart,* to those only that are sincere in religion. *The joy of the hypocrite is but for a moment.* There is no serenity without a lasting sincerity,

II. The rules that are given for Zion's joy. 1. Let it be a pure and holy joy. "You that love the Lord Jesus, that *love his appearing* and kingdom, that love his word and his exaltation, see that you hate evil, the evil of sin, every thing that is offensive to him and will throw you out of his favour." Note, A true love to God will show itself in a real hatred of all sin, as that abominable thing which he hates. The joy of the saints should likewise confirm their antipathy to sin and divine comforts should put their mouths out of taste for sensual pleasures. 2. Let the joy terminate in God (*v.* 12): *Rejoice in the Lord, you righteous.* Let all the streams of comfort, which flow to us in the channel of Christ's kingdom, lead us to the fountain, and oblige us to *rejoice in the Lord.* All the lines of joy must meet in him as in the centre. See Phil. 3:3; 4:4. 3. Let it express itself in praise and thanksgiving: *Give thanks at the remembrance of his holiness.* Whatever is the matter of our rejoicing ought to be the matter of our thanksgiving, and particularly the holiness of God. Those that hate sin themselves are glad that God does so, in hopes that therefore he will not suffer it to have dominion over them. Note, (1.) We ought to be much in the remembrance of God's holiness, the infinite purity, rectitude, and perfection of the divine nature. We must be ever mindful of his holy covenant, which he has confirmed with an oath *by his holiness.* (2.) We ought to give thanks at the remembrance of his holiness, not only give him the glory of it as it is an honour to him, but give him thanks for it as it is a favour to us; and an unspeakable favour it will be if, through grace, we are *partakers of his holiness.* It is God's holiness which, above all his attributes, the angels celebrate. Isa. 6:3, *Holy, holy, holy.* Sinners tremble, but saints rejoice, *at the remembrance of God's holiness,* Ps. 30:4.

PSALM 98

This psalm is to the same purport with the two foregoing psalms; it is a prophecy of the kingdom of the Messiah, the settling of it up in the world, and the bringing of the Gentiles into it. The Chaldee entitles it a prophetic psalm. It sets forth, I. The glory of the Redeemer (*v.* 1–3). II. The joy of the redeemed (*v.* 4–9). If we in a right manner give to Christ this glory, and upon right grounds take to ourselves this joy, in singing this psalm, we sing it with understanding. If those who saw Christ's triumph thus, much more reason have we to do so who see these things accomplished and share in the better things provided for us, Heb. 11:40.

A psalm.

Verses 1–3

We are here called upon again to *sing unto the Lord a new song,* as before, Ps. 96:1. "Sing a most excellent song, the best song you have." Let the song of Christ's love be like Solomon's on that subject, a *song of songs.* A song of praise for redeeming love is a *new song,* such a song as had not been sung before; for this is a mystery which was hidden from ages and generations. Converts sing a *new song,* very different from what they had sung; they change their wonder and change their joy, and therefore change their note. If the grace of God put a new heart into our breasts, it will therewith put a new song into our mouths. In the new Jerusalem there will be new songs sung, that will be new to eternity, and never wax old. Let this new song be sung to the praise of God, in consideration of these four things: —

I. The wonders he has wrought: *He has done marvellous things, v.* 1. Note, The work of our salvation by Christ is a work of wonder. If we take a view of all the steps of it from the contrivance of it, and the counsels of God concerning it before all time, to the consummation of it, and its everlasting consequences when time shall be no more, we shall say, God has in it *done marvellous things;* it is all his doing and it is *marvellous in our eyes.* The more it is known the more it will be admired.

II. The conquests he has won: *His right hand and his holy arm have gotten him the victory.* Our Redeemer has surmounted all the difficulties that lay in the way of our redemption, has broken through them all, and was not discouraged by the services or sufferings appointed him. He has subdued all the enemies that opposed it, has gotten the victory over Satan, disarmed him, and cast him out of his strong-holds, has *spoiled principalities and powers* (Col. 2:15), has *taken the prey from the mighty* (Isa. 49:24), and given death his death's wound. He has gotten a clear and complete victory, not only for himself, but for us also, for we through him are more than conquerors. He got this victory by his own power; there was *none to help, none to uphold,* none that durst venture into the service; but his *right hand and his holy arm,* which are always stretched out with good success, because they are never stretched out but in a good cause, these have *gotten him the victory,* have *brought him relief or deliverance.* God's power and faithfulness, called here *his right hand and his holy arm,* brought relief to the Lord Jesus, in raising him from the dead, and exalting him personally to the right hand of God; so Dr. Hammond.

III. The discoveries he has made to the world of the work of redemption. What he has wrought for us he has revealed to us, and both by his Son; the gospel-revelation is that on which the gospel-kingdom is founded — *the word which God sent,* Acts 10:36. The *opening of the sealed book* is that which is to be celebrated with songs of praise (Rev. 5:8), because by it was brought to light the mystery which had long been hid in God. Observe, 1. The subject of this discovery — his salvation and his righteousness, *v.* 3. Righteousness and salvation are often put together; as Isa. 61:10; 46:13; 51:5, 6, 8. Salvation denotes the redemption itself, and righteousness the way in which it was wrought, by the righteousness of Christ. Or the salvation includes all our gospel-privileges and the righteousness all our gospel-duties; both are made known, for God has joined them together, and we must not separate them. Or righteousness is here put for the way of our justification by Christ, which is revealed in the gospel to be by faith, Rom. 1:17. 2. The plainness of this discovery. He has openly shown it, not in types and figures as under the law, but it is written as with a sunbeam, that he that runs may read it. Ministers are appointed to preach it with all plainness of speech. 3. The extent of this discovery. It is made in the sight of the heathen, and not of the Jews only: *All the ends of the earth have seen the salvation of our God;* for to the Gentiles was the word of salvation sent.

IV. The accomplishment of the prophecies and promises of the Old Testament, in this (*v.* 3): *He has remembered his mercy and his truth towards the house of Israel.* God had mercy in store for the seed of Abraham, and had given them many and great assurances of the kindness he designed them in the latter days; and it was in pursuance of all those that he raised up his Son Jesus to be not only a *light to lighten the Gentiles,* but *the glory of his people Israel;* for he sent him, in the first place, to bless *them.* God is said, in sending Christ, to *perform the mercy promised to our fathers, and to remember the holy covenant,* Lu. 1:72. It was in consideration of that, and not of their merit.

Verses 4–9

The setting up of the kingdom of Christ is here represented as a matter of joy and praise.

I. Let all the children of men rejoice in it, for they all have, or may have, benefit by it. Again and again we are here called upon by all ways and means possible to express our joy in it and give God praise for it: *Make a joyful noise,* as before, Ps. 95:1, 2. *Make a loud noise,* as those that are affected with those glad tidings and are desirous to affect others with them. *Rejoice and sing praise,* sing *Hosannas* (Mt. 21:9), sing *Hallelujahs,* Rev. 19:6. Let him be welcomed to the throne, as new kings are, with acclamations of joy and loud shouts, till the earth ring again, as when Solomon was proclaimed, 1 Ki. 1:40. And let the shouts of the crowd be accompanied with the *singers and players on instruments* (Ps. 87:7; 68:25), as is usual in such solemnities. 1. Let sacred songs attend the new King: *"Sing praise, sing with the voice of a psalm.* Express your joy; thus proclaim it, thus excite it yet more, and thus propagate it among others." 2. Let these be assisted with sacred music, not only with the soft and gentle melody of *the harp,* but since it is a victorious King whose glory is to be celebrated, who goes forth conquering and to conquer, let him be proclaimed with the martial sound of the *trumpet* and *cornet, v.* 6. Let all this joy be directed to God, and expressed in a solemn religious manner: *Make a joyful noise to the Lord, v.* 4. *Sing to the Lord,* (*v.* 5); do it *before the Lord, the King, v.* 6. Carnal mirth is an enemy to this holy joy. When David danced before the ark he pleaded that *it was before the Lord;* and the piety and devotion of the intention not only vindicated what he did, but commended it. We must rejoice *before the Lord* whenever we draw near to him (Deu. 12:12), before *the Lord Jesus,* and before him, not only as the Saviour, but as the King, the King of kings, the church's King, and our King.

II. Let the inferior creatures rejoice in it, *v.* 7–9. This is to the same purport with what we had before (Ps. 96:11–13): *Let the sea roar,* and let that be called, not as it used to be, a *dreadful noise,* but a *joyful noise;* for the coming of Christ, and the salvation wrought out by him, have quite altered the property of the troubles and terrors of this world, so that when the floods *lift up their voice, lift up their waves,* we must not construe that to be the sea roaring against us, but rather rejoicing with us. Let the *floods* express their joy, as men do when they *clap their hands;* and let the hills, that trembled for fear before God when he came down to give the law at Mount Sinai, dance for joy before him when his gospel is preached and that word of the Lord goes forth from Zion in a still small voice: *Let the hills be joyful together before the Lord.* This intimates that the kingdom of Christ would be a blessing to the whole creation; but that, as the inferior creatures declare the glory of the Creator (Ps. 19:1), so they declare the glory of the Redeemer, for by him all things not only subsist in their being, but consist in their order. It intimates likewise that the children of men would be wanting in paying their due respects to the Redeemer, and therefore that he must look for his honour from the sea and the floods, which would shame the stupidity and ingratitude of mankind. And perhaps respect is here had to the *new heavens* and the *new earth,* which we yet, according to his promise, look for (2 Pt. 3:13), and this second mention of his coming (after the like, Ps. 96) may principally refer to his second coming, when all these things shall be so dissolved as to be refined; then shall he come to *judge the world with righteousness.* In the prospect of that day all that are sanctified do rejoice, and even the sea, and the floods, and the hills, would rejoice if they could. One would think that Virgil had these psalms in his eye, as well as the oracles of the Cumean Sibyl, in his fourth eclogue, where he either ignorantly or basely applies to Asinius Pollio the ancient prophecies, which at that time were expected to be fulfilled; for he lived in the reign of Augustus Caesar, a little before our Saviour's birth. He owns they looked for the birth of a child from heaven that should be a great blessing to the world, and restore the golden age: —

> Jam nova progenies coelo demittitur alto —
> A new race descends from the lofty sky;

and that should take away sin: —

Te duce, si qua manent sceleris vestigia nostri,
Irrita perpetua solvent formidine terras —
Thy influence shall efface every stain of corruption,
And free the world from alarm.

Many other things he says of this long-looked-for child, which Ludovicus Vives, in his notes on that eclogue, thinks applicable to Christ; and he concludes, as the psalmist here, with a prospect of the rejoicing of the whole creation herein: —

Aspice, venturo laetentur ut omnia saeclo —
See how this promis'd age makes all rejoice.

And, if all rejoice, why should not we?

PSALM 99

Still we are celebrating the glories of the kingdom of God among men, and are called upon to praise him, as in the foregoing psalms; but those psalms looked forward to the times of the gospel, and prophesied of the graces and comforts of those times; this psalm seems to dwell more upon the Old-Testament dispensation and the manifestation of God's glory and grace in that. The Jews were not, in expectation of the Messiah's kingdom and the evangelical worship, to neglect the divine regimen they were then under, and the ordinances that were then given them, but in them to see God reigning, and to worship before him according to the law of Moses. Prophecies of good things to come must not lessen our esteem of good things present. To Israel indeed pertained the promises, which they were bound to believe; but to them pertained also the giving of the law, and the service of God, which they were also bound dutifully and conscientiously to attend to, Rom. 9:4. And this they are called to do in this psalm, where yet there is much of Christ, for the government of the church was in the hands of the eternal Word before he was incarnate; and, besides, the ceremonial services were types and figures of evangelical worship. The people of Israel are here required to praise and exalt God, and to worship before him, in consideration of these two things: — I. The happy constitution of the government they were under, both in sacred and civil things (*v.* 1–5). II. Some instances of the happy administration of it (*v.* 6–9). In singing this psalm we must set ourselves to exalt the name of God, as it is made known to us in the gospel, which we have much more reason to do than those had who lived under the law.

Verses 1–5

The foundation of all religion is laid in this truth, That *the Lord reigns.* God governs the world by his providence, governs the church by his grace, and both by his Son. We are to believe not only that *the Lord lives,* but that *the Lord reigns.* This is the triumph of the Christian church, and here it was the triumph of the Jewish church, that Jehovah was their King; and hence it is inferred, *Let the people tremble,* that is, 1. Let even the subjects of this kingdom tremble; for the Old-Testament dispensation had much of terror in it. At Mount Sinai Israel, and even Moses himself, did *exceedingly fear and quake;* and then God was *terrible in his holy places.* Even when he appeared in his people's behalf, he did terrible things. But we are not now come to *that mount that burned with fire,* Heb. 12:18. Now that *the Lord reigns let the earth rejoice.* Then he ruled more by the power of holy fear; now he rules by the power of holy love. 2. Much more let the enemies of this kingdom tremble; for he will either bring them into obedience to his golden sceptre or crush them with his iron rod. *The Lord reigns, though the people be stirred with indignation* at it; though they fret away all their spirits, their rage is all in vain. He will set his King upon his holy hill of Zion in spite of them (Ps. 2:1–6); first, or last, he will make them *tremble,* Rev. 6:15, etc. *The Lord reigns, let the earth be moved.* Those that submit to him shall be established, and not *moved* (Ps. 96:10); but those that oppose him will be moved. Heaven and earth shall be shaken, and all nations; but the kingdom of Christ is what cannot be moved; the *things which cannot be shaken shall remain,* Heb. 12:27. *In these is continuance,* Isa. 64:5.

God's kingdom, set up in Israel, is here made the subject of the psalmist's praise.

I. Two things the psalmist affirms: — 1. God presided in the affairs of religion: *He sitteth between the cherubim* (*v.* 1), as on his throne, to give law by the oracles thence delivered — as on the mercy-seat, to receive petitions. This was the honour of Israel, that they had among them the Shechinah, or special presence of God, attended by the holy angels; the temple was the royal palace, and the Holy of holies was the presence-chamber. *The Lord is great in Zion* (*v.* 2); there he is known and praised (Ps. 76:1, 2); there he is served as great, more than any where else. *He is high* there *above all people;* as that which is high is exposed to view, and looked up to, so in Zion the perfections of the divine nature appear more conspicuous and more illustrious than any where else. Therefore *let those* that dwell in Zion, and worship there, *praise thy great and terrible name,* and give thee the glory due unto it, *for it is holy.* The holiness of God's name makes it truly great to his friends and terrible to his enemies, *v.* 3. This is that which those above adore — *Holy, holy, holy.* 2. He was all in all in their civil government, *v.* 4. As in Jerusalem was the testimony of Israel, whither the tribes went up, so *there were set thrones of judgment,* Ps. 122:4, 5. Their government was a theocracy. God raised up David to rule over them (and some think this psalm was penned upon occasion of his quiet and happy settlement in the throne) and he is *the king* whose *strength loves judgment.* He is strong; all his strength he has from God; and *his strength* is not abused for the support of any wrong, as the power of great princes often is, but it *loves judgment.* He does justice with his power, and does it with delight; and herein he was a type of Christ, to whom God would give *the throne of his father David, to do judgment and justice.* He has power to crush, but his *strength loves judgment;* he does not rule with rigour, but with moderation, with wisdom, and with tenderness. The people of Israel had a good king; but they are here taught to look up to God as he by whom their king reigns: *Thou dost establish equity* (that is, God gave them those excellent laws by which they were governed), and *thou executest judgment and righteousness in Jacob;* he not only by his immediate providences often executed and enforced his own laws, but took care for the administration of justice among them by civil magistrates, who reigned by him and by him did decree justice. Their judges judged for God, and their judgment was his, 2 Chr. 19:6.

II. Putting these two things together, we see what was the happiness of Israel above any other people, as Moses had described it (Deu. 4:7, 8), that they had *God so night unto them,* sitting between the cherubim, and that they had *statutes and judgments so righteous,* by which equity was established, and God himself ruled in Jacob, from which he infers this command to that happy people (*v.* 5): *"Exalt you the Lord our God, and worship at his footstool;* give him the glory of the good government you are under, as it is now established, both in church and state." Note, 1. The greater the public mercies are which we have a share in the more we are obliged to bear a part in the public homage paid to God: the setting up of the kingdom of Christ, especially, ought to be the matter of our praise. 2. When we draw night to God, to worship him, our hearts must be filled with high thoughts of him, and he must be exalted in our souls. 3. The more we abase ourselves, and the more prostrate we are before God, the more we exalt him. We must *worship at his footstool,* at his ark, which was as the footstool to the mercy-seat between the cherubim; or we must cast ourselves down upon the pavement of his courts; and good reason we have to be thus reverent, *for he is holy,* and his holiness should strike an awe upon us, as it does on the angels themselves, Isa. 6:2, 3.

Verses 6–9

The happiness of Israel in God's government is here further made out by some particular instances of his administration, especially with reference to those that were, in their day, the prime leaders and most active useful governors of that people — Moses, Aaron, and Samuel, in the two former of whom the theocracy or divine government began (for they were employed to form Israel into a people) and in the last of whom that form of government, in a great measure, ended; for when the people rejected Samuel, and urged him to resign, they are said to reject God himself, that he should not be so immediately their king as he had been (1 Sa. 8:7), for now they would have a king, like all the nations. Moses, as well as Aaron, is said to be *among his priests,* for he executed the priest's office till Aaron was settled in it and he consecrated Aaron and his sons; therefore the Jews call him the *priest of the priests.* Now concerning these three chief rulers observe,

I. The intimate communion they had with God, and the wonderful favour to which he admitted them. None of all the nations of the earth could produce three such men as these, that had such an intercourse with Heaven, and whom God *knew by name,* Ex. 33:17. Here is, 1. Their gracious observance of God. No kingdom had men that honoured God as these three men of the kingdom of Israel did. They honoured him, (1.) By their prayers. Samuel, though not among his priests, yet was *among those that called on his name;* and for *this* they were all famous, *They called upon the Lord;* they relied not on their own wisdom or virtue, but in every emergency had recourse to God, towards him was their desire, and on him their dependence. (2.) By their obedience: *They kept his testimonies, and the ordinances that he gave them;* they made conscience of their duty, and in every thing made God's word and law their rule, as knowing that unless they did so they could not expect their prayers should be answered, Prov. 28:9. Moses did all according to the pattern shown him; it is often repeated, *According to all that God commanded Moses, so did he.* Aaron and Samuel did likewise. Those were the greatest men and most honourable that were most eminent for keeping God's testimonies and conforming to the rule of his word. 2. God's gracious acceptance of them: *He answered them,* and granted them the things which they called upon him for. They all wonderfully prevailed with God in prayer; miracles were wrought at their special instance and request; nay, he not only condescended to do that for them which they desired, as a prince for a petitioner, but he communed with them as one friend familiarly converses with another (*v.* 7): *He spoke unto them in the cloudy pillar.* He often spoke to Samuel; from his childhood the word of the Lord came to him, and, probably, sometimes he spoke to him by a bright cloud overshadowing him: however, to Moses and Aaron he often spoke out of the famous *cloudy pillar,* Ex. 16:10; Num. 12:5. Israel are now reminded of this, for the confirming of their faith, that though they had not every day such sensible tokens of God's presence as the cloudy pillar was, yet to those that were their first founders, and to him that was their great reformer, God was pleased thus to manifest himself.

II. The good offices they did to Israel. They interceded for the people, and for them also they obtained many an answer of peace. *Moses stood in the gap,* and *Aaron between the living and the dead;* and, when Israel was in distress, Samuel cried unto the Lord for them, 1 Sa. 7:9. This is here referred to (*v.* 8): *"Thou answeredst them, O Lord our God!* and, at their prayer, *thou wast a God that forgavest* the people they prayed for; and, *though thou tookest vengeance of their inventions,* yet thou didst not cut them off from being a people, as their sin deserved." *"Thou wast a God that wast propitious for them* (so Dr. Hammond), for their sakes, and sparedst the people at their request, even when thou wast about to *take vengeance of their inventions,* that is, when thy wrath was so highly provoked against them that it was just ready to break in upon them, to their utter overthrow." These were some of the many remarkable instances of God's dominion in Israel, more than in any other nation, for which the people are again called upon to praise God (*v.* 9): *"Exalt the Lord our God,* on account of what he has done for us formerly, as well as of late, *and worship at his holy hill* of Zion, on which he has now set his temple and will shortly *set his King* (Ps. 2:6), the former a type of the latter; there, as the centre of unity, let all God's Israel meet, with their adorations, *for the Lord our God is holy,* and appears so, not only in his holy law, but in his holy gospel."

PSALM 100

It is with good reason that many sing this psalm very frequently in their religious assemblies, for it is very proper both to express and to excite pious and devout affections towards God in our approach to him in holy ordinances; and, if our hearts go along with the words, we shall make melody in it to the Lord. The Jews say it was penned to be sung with their thank-offerings; perhaps it was; but we say that as there is nothing in it peculiar to their economy so its beginning with a call to all lands to praise God plainly extends it to the gospel-church. Here, I. We are called upon to praise God and rejoice in him (*v.* 1, 2, 4). II. We are furnished with matter for praise; we must praise him, considering his being and relation to us (*v.* 3) and his mercy and truth (*v.* 5). These are plain and common things, and therefore the more fit to be the matter of devotion.

A psalm of praise.

Verses 1–5

Here, I. The exhortations to praise are very importunate. The psalm does indeed answer to the title, *A psalm of praise;* it begins with that call which of late we have several times met with (*v.* 1), *Make a joyful noise unto the Lord, all you lands,* or *all the earth,* all the inhabitants of the earth. When all nations shall be discipled, and the gospel preached to every creature, then this summons will be fully answered to. But, if we take the foregoing psalm to be (as we have opened it) a call to the Jewish church to rejoice in the administration of God's kingdom, which they were under (as the four psalms before it were calculated for the days of the Messiah), this psalm, perhaps, was intended for proselytes, that came over out of all lands to the Jews' religion. However, we have here, 1. A strong invitation to worship God; not that God needs us, or any thing we have or can do, but it is his will that we should *serve the Lord*, should devote ourselves to his service and employ ourselves in it; and that we should not only serve him in all instances of obedience to his law, but that we should *come before his presence* in the ordinances which he has appointed and in which he has promised to manifest himself (v. 2), that we should *enter into his gates and into his courts* (v. 4), that we should attend upon him among his servants, and keep there where he keeps court. In all acts of religious worship, whether in secret or in our families, we come into God's presence, and serve him; but it is in public worship especially that we *enter into his gates and into his courts*. The people were not permitted to enter into the holy place; there the priests only went in to minister. But let the people be thankful for their place in the courts of God's house, to which they were admitted and where they gave their attendance. 2. Great encouragement given us, in worshipping God, to do it cheerfully (v. 2): *Serve the Lord with gladness*. This intimates a prediction that in gospel-times there should be special occasion for joy; and it prescribes this as a rule of worship: Let God be *served with gladness*. By holy joy we do really serve God; it is an honour to him to rejoice in him; and we ought to serve him with holy joy. Gospel-worshippers should be joyful worshippers; if we serve God in uprightness, let us serve him with gladness. We must be willing and forward to it, glad when we are called to *go up to the house of the Lord* (Ps. 122:1), looking upon it as the comfort of our lives to have communion with God; and we must be pleasant and cheerful in it, must say, *It is good to be here*, approaching to God, in every duty, as *to God our exceeding Joy*, Ps. 43:4. We must *come before his presence with singing*, not only songs of joy, but songs of praise. *Enter into his gates with thanksgiving*, v. 4. We must not only comfort ourselves, but glorify God, with our joy, and let him have the praise of that which we have the pleasure of. Be *thankful to him and bless his name*; that is, (1.) We must take it as a favour to be admitted into his service, and give him thanks that we have liberty of access to him, that we have ordinances instituted and opportunity continued of waiting upon God in those ordinances. (2.) We must intermix praise and thanksgiving with all our services. This golden thread must run through every duty (Heb. 13:15), for it is the work of angels. *In every thing give thanks*, in every ordinance, as well as in every providence.

II. The matter of praise, and motives to it, are very important, v. 3, 5. Know you what God is in himself and what he is to you. Note, Knowledge is the mother of devotion and of all obedience: blind sacrifices will never please a seeing God. "Know it; consider and apply it, and then you will be more close and constant, more inward and serious, in the worship of him." Let us know then these seven things concerning the Lord Jehovah, with whom we have to do in all the acts of religious worship: — 1. *That the Lord he is God*, the only living and true God — that he is a Being infinitely perfect, self-existent, and self-sufficient, and the fountain of all being; he is God, and not a man as we are. He is an eternal Spirit, incomprehensible and independent, the first cause and last end. The heathen worshipped the creature of their own fancy; the workmen made it, therefore it is not God. We worship him that made us and all the world; he is God, and all other pretended deities are vanity and a lie, and such as he has triumphed over. 2. That he is our Creator: *It is he that has made us, and not we ourselves*. I find that I am, but cannot say, *I am that I am*, and therefore must ask, Whence am I? Who made me? *Where is God my Maker?* And it is the Lord Jehovah. He gave us being, he gave us this being; he is both the former of our bodies and the Father of our spirits. We did not, we could not, make ourselves. It is God's prerogative to be his own cause; our being is derived and depending. 3. That therefore he is our rightful owner. The Masorites, by altering one letter in the Hebrew, read it, *He made us, and his we are*, or to him we belong. Put both

the readings together, and we learn that because God *made us, and not we ourselves*, therefore we are not our own, but his. He has an incontestable right to, and property in, us and all things. His we are, to be actuated by his power, disposed of by his will, and devoted to his honour and glory. 4. That he is our sovereign ruler: *We are his people* or subjects, and he is our prince, our rector or governor, that gives law to us as moral agents, and will call us to an account for what we do. *The Lord is our judge; the Lord is our lawgiver*. We are not at liberty to do what we will, but must always make conscience of doing as we are bidden. 5. That he is our bountiful benefactor. We are not only his sheep, whom he is entitled to, but *the sheep of his pasture*, whom he takes care of; the *flock of his feeding* (so it may be read); therefore the *sheep of his hand*; at his disposal because the *sheep of his pasture*, Ps. 95:7. He that made us maintains us, and gives us all good things richly to enjoy. 6. That he is a God of infinite mercy and goodness (v. 5): *The Lord is good*, and therefore does good; *his mercy is everlasting*; it is a fountain that can never be drawn dry. The saints, who are now the sanctified vessels of mercy, will be, to eternity, the glorified monuments of mercy. 7. That he is a God of inviolable truth and faithfulness: *His truth endures to all generations*, and no word of his shall fall to the ground as antiquated or revoked. The promise is sure to all the seed, from age to age.

PSALM 101

David was certainly the penman of this psalm, and it has in it the genuine spirit of the man after God's own heart; it is a solemn vow which he made to God when he took upon him the charge of a family and of the kingdom. Whether it was penned when he entered upon the government, immediately after the death of Saul (as some think), or when he began to reign over all Israel, and brought up the ark to the city of David (as others think), is not material; it is an excellent plan or model for the good government of a court, or the keeping up of virtue and piety, and, by that means, good order, in it: but it is applicable to private families; it is the householder's psalm. It instructs all that are in any sphere of power, whether larger or narrower, to use their power so as to make it a terror to evil-doers, but a praise to those that do well. Here is, I. The general scope of David's vow (v. 1, 2). II. The particulars of it, that he would detest and discountenance all manner of wickedness (v. 3-5, 7, 8) and that he would favour and encourage such as were virtuous (v. 6). Some think this may fitly be accommodated to Christ, the Son of David, who governs his church, the city of the Lord, by these rules, and who loves righteousness and hates wickedness. In singing this psalm families, both governors and governed, should teach, and admonish, and engage themselves and one another to walk by the rule of it, that peace may be upon them and God's presence with them.

A psalm of David.

Verses 1-8

David here cuts out to himself and others a pattern both of a good magistrate and a good master of a family; and, if these were careful to discharge the duty of their place, it would contribute very much to a universal reformation. Observe,

I. The chosen subject of the psalm (v. 1): *I will sing of mercy and judgment*, that is,

1. Of God's mercy and judgment, and then it looks back upon the dispensations of Providence concerning David since he was first anointed to be king, during which time he had met with many a rebuke and much hardship on the one hand, and yet, on the other hand, had had many wonderful deliverances wrought for him and favours bestowed upon him; of these he will sing unto God. Note, (1.) God's providences concerning his people are commonly mixed — *mercy and judgment*; God has set the one over-against the other, and appointed them April-days, showers and sunshine. It was so with David and his family; when there was mercy in the return of the ark there was judgment in the death of Uzza. (2.) When God in his providence exercises us with a mixture of mercy and judgment it is our duty to sing, and sing unto him, both of the one and of the other; we must be suitably affected with both, and make suitable acknowledgments to God for both. The Chaldee-paraphrase of this is observable: *If thou bestowest mercy upon me, or If thou bring any judgment upon me, before thee, O Lord! will I sing my hymns for all*. Whatever our outward condition is, whether joyful or sorrowful, still we must give glory to God, and sing praises to him; neither the laughter of a prosperous condition nor the tears of an afflicted condition must put us out of tune for sacred songs. Or,

2. It may be understood of David's mercy and judg-

ment; he would, in this psalm, promise to be merciful and just, or wise, for judgment is often put for discretion. To do justly and love mercy is the sum of our duty; these he would covenant to make conscience of in that place and relation to which God had called him and this in consideration of the various providences of God that had occurred to him. Family-mercies and family-afflictions are both of them calls to family-religion. David put his vow into a song or psalm, that he might the better keep it in his own mind and frequently repeat it, and that it might the better be communicated to others and preserved in his family, for a pattern to his sons and successors.

II. The general resolution David took up to conduct himself carefully and conscientiously in his court, v. 2. We have here,

1. A good purpose concerning his conversation — concerning his conversation in general (how he would behave himself in every thing; he would live by rule, and not at large, not walk at all adventures; he would, though a king, by a solemn covenant bind himself to his good behaviour), and concerning his conversation in his family particularly, not only how he would walk when he appeared in public, when he sat in the throne, but how he would *walk within his house*, where he was more out of the eye of the world, but where he still saw himself under the eye of God. It is not enough to put on our religion when we go abroad and appear before men; but we must govern ourselves by it in our families. Those that are in public stations are not thereby excused from care in governing their families; nay, rather, they are more concerned to set a good example of *ruling their own houses well*, 1 Tim. 3:4. When David had his hands full of public affairs, yet he returned to bless his house, 2 Sa. 6:20. He resolves, (1.) To act conscientiously and with integrity, to *walk in a perfect way*, in the way of God's commandments; that is *a perfect way*, for *the law of the Lord is perfect*. This he will walk in *with a perfect heart*, with all sincerity, not dissembling either with God or men. When we make the word of God our rule, and are ruled by it, the glory of God our end, and aim at it, then we walk in *a perfect way with a perfect heart*. (2.) To act considerately and with discretion: *I will behave myself wisely; I will understand* or *instruct myself* in a perfect way, so some. I will walk circumspectly. Note, We must all resolve to walk by the rules of Christian prudence in the ways of Christian piety. We must never turn aside out of the perfect way, under pretence of *behaving ourselves wisely*; but, while we keep to the good way, we must be *wise as serpents*.

2. A good prayer: *O when wilt thou come unto me?* Note, It is a desirable thing, when a man has a house of his own, to have God come to him and dwell with him in it; and those may expect God's presence that walk with *a perfect heart* in *a perfect way*. If we compare the account which the historian gives of David (1 Sa. 18:14), we shall find how exactly it answers his purpose and prayer, and that neither was in vain. David, as he purposed, *behaved himself wisely in all his ways; and*, as he prayed, *the Lord was with him*.

III. His particular resolution to practise no evil himself (v. 3): "*I will set no wicked thing before my eyes; I will not design nor aim at any thing but what is for the glory of God and the public welfare.*" He will never have it in his eye to enrich himself by impoverishing his subjects, or enlarge his own prerogative by encroaching on their property. In all our worldly business we must see that what we set our eyes upon be right and good and not any forbidden fruit, and that we never seek that which we cannot have without sin. It is the character of a good man that he shuts his eyes from seeing evil, Isa. 33:15. "Nay, I *hate the work of those that turn aside* from the paths of equity (Job 31:7), not only I avoid it, but I abhor it; *it shall not cleave to me*. If any blot of injustice should come on my hands, it shall be washed off quickly."

IV. His further resolution not to keep bad servants, nor to employ those about him that were vicious. He will not countenance them, nor show them any favour, lest thereby he should harden them in their wickedness, and encourage others to do like them. He will not converse with them himself, nor admit them into the company of his other servants, lest they should spread the infection of sin in his family. He will not confide in them, nor put them in power under him; for those who hated to be reformed would certainly hinder every thing that is good. When he comes to mention particulars he does not mention drunkards, adulterers, murderers or blasphemers; such gross sinners as these he was in no danger of admitting into his house, nor did he need to covenant particularly against having fellowship with them; but he mentions those whose sins were less scandalous, but no less dangerous, and in reference to whom he needed to stand upon his guard with caution and to behave himself wisely. He will have nothing to do, 1. With spiteful malicious people, who are ill-natured, and will bear a grudge a great while, and care not what mischief they do to those they have a pique against (*v.* 4): *"A froward heart* (one that delights to be cross and perverse) *shall depart from me,* as not fit for society, the bond of which is love. *I will not know,"* that is, "I will have no acquaintance or conversation, if I can help it, with such *a wicked person;* for a little of the leaven of malice and wickedness will leaven the whole lump." 2. With slanderers, and those who take a pleasure in wounding their neighbour's reputation secretly (*v.* 5): *"Whoso privily slanders his neighbour,* either raises or spreads false stories, to the prejudice of his good name, *him will I cut off* from my family and court." Many endeavour to raise themselves into the favour of princes by unjust representations of persons and things, which they think will please their prince. *If a ruler hearken to lies, all his servants are wicked,* Prov. 29:12. But David will not only not hearken to them, but will prevent the preferment of those that hope thus to curry favour with him: he will punish not only him that falsely accuses another in open court, but him that privily slanders another. I wish David had remembered this vow in the case of Mephibosheth and Ziba. 3. With haughty, conceited, ambitious people; none do more mischief in a family, in a court, in a church, for *only by pride comes contention:* "Therefore him *that has a high look and a proud heart will I not suffer;* I will have no patience with those that are still grasping at all preferments, for it is certain that they do not aim at doing good, but only at aggrandizing themselves and their families." God resists the proud, and so will David. 4. With false deceitful people, that scruple not to tell lies, or commit frauds (*v.* 7): *"He that worketh deceit,* though he may insinuate himself into my family, yet, as soon as he is discovered, *shall not dwell within my house."* Some great men know how to serve their own purposes by such as are skilful to deceive, and they are fit tools for them to work by; but David will make use of no such persons as agents for him: *He that tells lies shall not tarry in my sight,* but shall be expelled the house with indignation. Herein David was *a man after God's own heart,* for a proud look and a lying tongue are things which God hates; and he was also a type of Christ, who will, in the great day, banish from his presence *all that love and make a lie,* Rev. 22:15.

V. His resolution to put those in trust under him that were honest and good (*v.* 6): *My eyes shall be upon the faithful in the land.* In choosing his servants and ministers of state he kept to the land of Israel and would not employ foreigners; none shall be preferred but true-born Israelites, and those such as were Israelites indeed, the *faithful in the land;* for even in that land there were those that were unfaithful. These faithful ones his eyes shall be upon, to discover them and find them out; for they were modest, did not crowd into the city to court preferment, but lived retired in the land, in the country, out of the way of it. Those are commonly most fit for places of honour and trust that are least fond of them; and therefore wise princes will spy out such in their recesses and privacies, and take them to dwell with them and act under them. *He that walks in a perfect way,* that makes conscience of what he says and does, *shall serve me.* The kingdom must be searched for honest men to make courtiers of; and, if any man is better than another, he must be preferred. This was a good resolution of David's; but either he did not keep to it or else his judgment was imposed upon when he made Ahithophel his right hand. It should be the care and endeavour of all masters of families, for their own sakes and their children's, to take such servants into their families as they have reason to hope fear God. The Son of David has his eyes upon *the faithful in the land;* his secret is with them, and they *shall dwell with him.* Saul chose servants for their goodliness (1 Sa. 8:16), but David for their goodness.

VI. His resolution to extend his zeal to the reformation of the city and country, as well as of the court (*v.* 8): *"I will early destroy all the wicked of the land,* all that are discovered and convicted; the law shall have its course against them." He would do his utmost to *destroy all the wicked,* so that there might be none left that were notoriously wicked. He would do it early; he would lose no time and spare no pains; he would be forward and zealous in promoting the reformation of manners and suppression of vice; and those must rise betimes that will do anything to purpose in the work. That which he aimed at was not only the securing of his own government and the peace of the country, but the honour of God in the purity of his church, *That I may cut off all wicked doers from the city of the Lord.* Not Jerusalem only, but the whole land, was the *city of the Lord;* so is the gospel-church. It is the interest of the *city of the Lord* to be purged from *wicked doers,* who both blemish it and weaken it; and it is therefore the duty of all to do what they can, in their places, towards so good a work, and to be zealously affected in it. The day is coming when the Son of David shall cut off all wicked doers from the new Jerusalem, for there shall not enter into it any that do iniquity.

PSALM 102

Some think that David penned this psalm at the time of Absalom's rebellion; others that Daniel, Nehemiah, or some other prophet, penned it for the use of the church, when it was in captivity in Babylon, because it seems to speak of the ruin of Zion and of a time set for the rebuilding of it, which Daniel understood by books, Dan. 9:2. Or perhaps the psalmist was himself in great affliction, which he complains of in the beginning of the psalm, but (as in Ps. 77 and elsewhere) he comforts himself under it with the consideration of God's eternity, and the church's prosperity and perpetuity, how much soever it was now distressed and threatened. But it is clear, from the application of *v.* 25, 26, to Christ (Heb. 1:10–12), that the psalm has reference to the days of the Messiah, and speaks either of his affliction or of the afflictions of his church for his sake. In the psalm we have, I. A sorrowful complaint which the psalmist makes, either for himself or in the name of the church, of great afflictions, which were very pressing (*v.* 1–11). II. Seasonable comfort fetched in against these grievances, 1. From the eternity of God (*v.* 12, 24, 27). 2. From a believing prospect of the deliverance which God would, in due time, work for his afflicted church (*v.* 13–22) and the continuance of it in the world (*v.* 28). In singing this psalm, if we have not occasion to make the same complaints, yet we may take occasion to sympathize with those that have, and then the comfortable part of this psalm will be the more comfortable to us in the singing of it.

A prayer of the afflicted, when he is overwhelmed, and poureth out his complaint before the Lord.

Verses 1–11

The title of this psalm is very observable; it is *a prayer of the afflicted.* It was composed by one that was himself afflicted, afflicted with the church and for it; and on those that are of a public spirit afflictions of that kind lie heavier than any other. It is calculated for an afflicted state, and is intended for the use of others that may be in the like distress; for *whatsoever things were written aforetime were written* designedly *for our use.* The whole word of God is of use to direct us in prayer; but here, as often elsewhere, the Holy Ghost has drawn up our petition for us, has put words into our mouths. Hos. 14:2, *Take with you words.* Here is a prayer put into the hands of the afflicted: let them set, not their hands, but their hearts to it, and present it to God. Note, 1. It is often the lot of the best saints in this world to be sorely affected. 2. Even good men may be almost overwhelmed with their afflictions, and may be ready to faint under them. 3. When our state is afflicted, and our spirits are overwhelmed, it is our duty and interest to pray, and by prayer to *pour out our complaints before the Lord,* which intimates the leave God gives us to be free with him and the liberty of speech we have before him, as well as liberty of access to him; it intimates also what an ease it is to an afflicted spirit to unburden itself by a humble representation of its grievances and griefs. Such a representation we have here, in which,

I. The psalmist humbly begs of God to take notice of his affliction, and of his prayer in his affliction, *v.* 1, 2. When we pray in our affliction, 1. It should be our care that God would graciously hear us; for, if our prayers be not pleasing to God, they will be to no purpose to ourselves. Let this therefore be in our eye that our prayer may *come unto God,* even *to his ears* (Ps. 18:6); and, in order to that, let us *lift up the prayer,* and our souls with it. 2. It may be our hope that God will graciously hear us, because he has appointed us to seek him and has promised we shall not seek him in vain. If we put up a *prayer in faith,* we may in faith say, *Hear my prayer, O Lord!* "Hear me," that is, (1.) "Manifest thyself to me, *hide not thy face from me* in displeasure, *when I am in trouble.* If thou dost not quickly free me, yet let me know that thou favourest me; if I see not the operations of thy hand for me, yet let me see the smiles of thy face upon me." God's hiding his face is trouble enough to a good man even in his prosperity (Ps. 30:7, *Thou didst hide thy face, and I was troubled);* but if, when we are in trouble, God hides his face, the case is sad indeed. (2.) "Manifest thyself for me; not only hear me, but answer me; grant me the deliverance I am in want of and in pursuit of; answer me speedily, even *in the day when I call."* When troubles press hard upon us, God gives us leave to be thus pressing in prayer, yet with humility and patience.

II. He makes a lamentable complaint of the low condition to which he was reduced by his afflictions. 1. His body was macerated and emaciated, and he had become a perfect skeleton, nothing but skin and bones. As prosperity and joy are represented by *making fat the bones,* and the *bones flourishing like a herb,* so great trouble and grief are here represented by the contrary: *My bones are burnt as a hearth* (*v.* 3); they *cleave to my skin* (*v.* 5); nay, *my heart is smitten, and withered like grass* (*v.* 4); it touches the vitals, and there is a sensible decay there. *I am withered like grass* (*v.* 11), scorched with the burning heat of my troubles. If we be thus brought low by bodily distempers, let us not think it strange; the body is like grass, weak and of the earth, no wonder then that it withers. 2. He was very melancholy and of a sorrowful spirit. He was so taken up with the thoughts of his troubles that he *forgot to eat his bread* (*v.* 4); he had no appetite to his necessary food nor could he relish it. When God hides his face from a soul the delights of sense will be sapless things. He was always *sighing* and *groaning,* as one pressed above measure (*v.* 5), and this wasted him and exhausted his spirits. He affected solitude, as melancholy people do. His friends deserted him and were shy of him, and he cared as little for their company (*v.* 6, 7): *"I am like a pelican of the wilderness,* or a *bittern* (so some) that make a doleful noise; *I am like an owl,* that affects to lodge in deserted ruined buildings; *I watch, and am as a sparrow upon the house-top.* I live in a garret, and there spend my hours in poring on my troubles and bemoaning myself." Those who do thus, when they are in sorrow, humour themselves indeed; but they prejudice themselves, and know not what they do, nor what advantage they hereby give to the tempter. In affliction we should sit alone to consider our ways (Lam. 3:28), but not sit alone to indulge an inordinate grief. 3. He was evil-spoken of by his enemies, and all manner of evil was said against him. When his friends went off from him his foes set themselves against him (*v.* 8): *My enemies reproach me all the day,* designing thereby both to create vexation to him (for an ingenuous mind regrets reproach) and to bring an odium upon him before men. When they could not otherwise reach him they shot these arrows at him, even *bitter words.* In this they were unwearied; they did it *all the day;* it was a continual dropping. His enemies were very outrageous: *They* are *mad against me,* and very obstinate and implacable. *They* are *sworn against me;* as the Jews that bound themselves with an oath that they would kill Paul; or, *They have sworn against me* as accusers, to take away my life. 4. He fasted and wept under the tokens of God's displeasure (*v.* 9, 10): *"I have eaten ashes like bread;* instead of eating my bread, I have lain down in dust and ashes, and *I have mingled my drink with weeping;* when I should have refreshed myself with drinking I have only eased myself with weeping." And what is the matter? He tells us (*v.* 10): *Because of thy wrath.* It was not so much the trouble itself that troubled him as the wrath of God which he was under the apprehensions of as the cause of the trouble. This, this was the *wormwood and the gall* in the affliction and the misery: *Thou hast lifted me up and cast me down,* as that which we cast to the ground with a design to dash it to pieces; we lift up first, that we may throw it down with the more violence; or, "Thou hast formerly lifted me up in honour, and joy, and uncommon prosperity; but the remembrance of that aggravates the present grief and makes it the more grievous." We must eye the hand of God both in lifting us up and casting us down, and say, "Blessed be the name of the Lord, who both gives and takes away." 5. He looked upon himself as a dying man: *My days are consumed like smoke* (*v.* 3), which vanishes away quickly. Or, They are consumed *in smoke,* of which nothing remains; they are *like a shadow that declines* (*v.* 11), like the evening-shadow, or a forerunner of approaching night. Now all this, though it seems to speak the psalmist's personal calamities, and therefore is properly a prayer for a particular person afflicted, yet is supposed to be a description of the afflictions of the church of God, with which the psalmist sympathizes, making public grievances his own. The mystical body of Christ is sometimes, like the psalmist's body here, *withered* and *parched,* nay, like *dead and dry bones.* The church sometimes is forced *into the wilderness,* seems lost, and gives up herself for gone, under the tokens of God's displeasure.

Verses 12–22

Many exceedingly great and precious comforts are here thought of, and mustered up, to balance the foregoing complaints; for *unto the upright there arises light in the darkness,* so that, though they are cast down, they are not in despair. It is bad with the psalmist himself, bad with the people of God; but he has many considerations to revive himself with.

I. We are dying creatures, and our interests and comforts are dying, but God is an everliving everlasting God (*v.* 12): *"My days are like a shadow;* there is no remedy; night is coming upon me; but, *thou, O Lord! shalt endure for ever.* Our life is transient, but thine is permanent; our friends die, but thou our God diest not; what threatened us cannot touch thee; our names will be written in the dust and buried in oblivion, but *thy remembrance shall be unto all generations;* to the end of time, nay, to eternity, thou shalt be known and honoured." A good man loves God better than himself, and therefore can balance his own sorrow and death with the pleasing thought of the unchangeable blessedness of the Eternal Mind. God *endures for ever,* his church's faithful patron and protector; and, his honour and perpetual remembrance being very much bound up in her interests, we may be confident that they shall not be neglected.

II. Poor Zion is now in distress, but there will come a time for her relief and succour (*v.* 13): *Thou shalt arise and have mercy upon Zion.* The hope of deliverance is built upon the goodness of God — "Thou wilt *have mercy upon Zion,* for she has become an object of thy pity;" and upon the power of God — "Thou shalt arise and have mercy, shalt stir up thyself to do it, shalt do it in contempt of all the opposition made by the church's enemies." *The zeal of the Lord of hosts shall do this.* That which is very encouraging is that there is a time set for the deliverance of the church, which not only will come some time, but will come at the time appointed, the time which Infinite Wisdom has appointed (and therefore it is the best time) and which Eternal Truth has fixed it to, and therefore it is a certain time, and shall not be forgotten nor further adjourned. At the end of seventy years, the time to favour Zion, by delivering her from the daughter of Babylon, was to come, and at length it did come. Zion was now in ruins, that is, the temple that was built in the city of David: the favouring of Zion is the building of the temple up again, as it is explained, *v.* 16. This is expected from the favour of God; that will set all to rights, and nothing but that, and therefore Daniel prays (Dan. 9:17), *Cause thy face to shine upon thy sanctuary, which is desolate.* The building up of Zion is as great a favour to any people as they can desire. No blessing more desirable to a ruined state than the restoring and re-establishing of their church-privileges. Now this is here wished for and longed for, 1. Because it would be a great rejoicing to Zion's friends (*v.* 14): *Thy servants take pleasure* even in *the stones* of the temple, though they were thrown down and scattered, and *favour the dust,* the very rubbish and ruins of it. Observe here, When the temple was ruined, yet the stones of it were to be had for a new building, and there were those who encouraged themselves with that, for they had a favour even for the dust of it. Those who truly love the church of God love it when it is in affliction as well as when it is in prosperity; and it is a good ground to hope that God will favour the ruins of Zion when he puts it into the heart of his people to favour them, and to show that they do so by their prayers and by their endeavours; as it is also a good plea with God for mercy for Zion that there are those who are so affectionately concerned for her, and are *waiting for the salvation of the Lord.* 2. Because it would have a good influence upon Zion's neighbours, *v.* 15. It will be a happy means perhaps of their conversion, at least of their conviction; for *so the heathen shall fear the name of the Lord,* shall have high thoughts of him and his people, and even the kings of the earth shall be affected with his glory. They shall have better thoughts of the church of God than they have had, when God by his providence thus puts an honour upon it; they shall be afraid of doing any thing against it when they see God taking its part; nay, they shall say, We will go with you, for we have *seen that God is with you,* Zec. 8:23. Thus it is said (Est. 8:17) that *many of the people of the land became Jews, for the fear of the Jews fell upon them.* 3. Because it would redound to the honour of Zion's God (*v.* 16): *When the Lord shall build up Zion.* They take it for granted it will be done, for God himself has undertaken it, and *he shall then appear in his glory;* and for that reason all that have made his glory their highest end desire it and pray for it. Note, The edifying of the church will be the glorifying of God, and therefore we may be assured it will be done in the set time. Those that pray in faith, *Father, glorify thy name,* may receive the same answer to that prayer which was given to Christ himself by a voice from heaven, *I have both glorified it and I will glorify it yet again,* though now for a time it may be eclipsed.

III. The prayers of God's people now seem to be slighted and no notice taken of them, but they will be reviewed and greatly encouraged (*v.* 17): *He will regard the prayer of the destitute.* It was said (*v.* 16) that God will *appear in his glory,* such a glory as kings themselves shall *stand in awe of, v.* 15. When great men *appear in their glory* they are apt to look with disdain upon the poor that apply to them; but the great God will not do so. Observe, 1. The meanness of the petitioners; they are the *destitute.* It is an elegant word that is here used, which signifies the heath in the wilderness, a low shrub, or bush, like the hyssop of the wall. They are supposed to be in a low and broken state, enriched with spiritual blessings, but destitute of temporal good things — the poor, the weak, the desolate, the stripped; thus variously is the word rendered; or it may signify that low and broken spirit which God looks for in all that draw nigh to him and which he will graciously look upon. This will bring them to their knees. Destitute people should be praying people, 1 Tim. 5:5. 2. The favour of God to them, notwithstanding their meanness: *He will regard their prayer,* and will look at it, will peruse their petition (2 Chr. 6:40), and he *will not despise their prayer.* More is implied than is expressed: he will value it and be well pleased with it, and will return an answer of peace to it, which is the greatest honour that can be put upon it. But it is thus expressed because others despise their praying, they themselves fear God will despise it, and he was thought to despise it while their affliction was prolonged and their prayers lay unanswered. When we consider our own meanness and vileness, our darkness and deadness, and the manifold defects in our prayers, we have cause to suspect that our prayers will be received with disdain in heaven; but we are here assured of the contrary, for we have an advocate with the Father, and are under grace, not under the law. This instance of God's favour to his praying people, though they are destitute, will be a lasting encouragement to prayer (*v.* 18): *This shall be written for the generation to come, that none may despair,* though they be destitute, nor think their prayers forgotten because they have not an answer to them immediately. The experiences of others should be our encouragements to seek unto God and trust in him. And, if we have the comfort of the experiences of others, it is fit that we should give God the glory of them: *The people who shall be created shall praise the Lord* for what he has done both for them and for their predecessors. Many that are now unborn shall, by reading the history of the church, be wrought upon to turn proselytes. The people that shall be created anew by divine grace, that are a kind of *first-fruits of his creatures,* shall praise the Lord for his answers to their prayers when they were more destitute.

IV. The prisoners under condemnation unjustly seem as sheep appointed for the slaughter, but care shall be taken for their discharge (*v.* 19, 20): God has *looked down from the height of his sanctuary, from heaven,* where he has prepared his throne, that high place, that holy place; thence did *the Lord behold the earth,* for it is a place of prospect, and nothing on this earth is or can be hidden from his all-seeing eye; he looks down, not to take a view of the kingdoms of the world and the glory of them, but to do acts of grace, *to hear the groaning of the prisoners* (which we desire to be out of the hearing of), and not only to hear them, but to help them, *to loose those that are appointed to death,* then when there is but a step between them and it. Some understand it of the release of the Jews out of their captivity in Babylon. God heard their groaning there as he did when they were in Egypt (Ex. 3:7, 9) and came down to deliver them. God takes notice not only of the prayers of his afflicted people, which are the language of grace, but even of their groans, which are the language of nature. See the divine pity in hearing the prisoner's groans, and the divine power in loosing the prisoner's bonds, even when they are appointed to death and are pinioned and double-shackled. We have an instance in Peter, Acts 12:6. Such instances as these of the divine condescension and compassion will help, 1. *To declare the name of the Lord in Zion,* and to make it appear that he answers to his name, which he himself proclaimed, *The Lord God, gracious and merciful;* and this declaration of his name in Zion shall be the matter of his praise in Jerusalem, *v.* 21. If God by his providences declare his name, we must by our acknowledgments of them declare his praise, which ought to be the echo of his name. God will discharge his people that were prisoners and captives in Babylon, *that they may declare his name in Zion,* the place he has chosen to put his name there, *and his praise in Jerusalem,* at their return thither; in the land of their captivity they could not sing the songs of Zion (Ps. 137:3, 4), and God brought them again to Jerusalem in order that they might sing them there. For this end God gives liberty from bondage (*Bring my soul out of prison, that I may praise thy name,* Ps. 142:7), and life from the dead. *Let my soul live, and it shall praise thee,* Ps. 119:175. 2. They will help to draw in others to the worship of God (*v.* 22): *When the people of God are gathered together* at Jerusalem (as they were after their return out of Babylon) many out of the kingdoms joined with them *to serve the Lord.* This was fulfilled Ezra 6:21, where we find that not only the children of Israel that had come out of captivity, but many that had *separated themselves from them among the heathen,* did *keep the feast of unleavened bread with joy.* But it may look further, at the conversion of the Gentiles to the faith of Christ in the latter days. Christ has proclaimed *liberty to the captives,* and *the opening of the prison to those that were bound,* that they may declare the name of the Lord in the gospel-church, in which Jews and Gentiles shall unite.

Verses 23–28

We may here observe,

I. The imminent danger that the Jewish church was in of being quite extirpated and cut off by the captivity in Babylon (*v.* 23): *He weakened my strength in the way.* They were for many ages in the way to the performance of the great promise made to their fathers concerning the Messiah, longing as much for it as ever a traveller did to be at his journey's end. The legal institutions led them in the way; but when the ten tribes were lost in Assyria, and the two almost lost in Babylon, the strength of that nation was weakened, and, in all appearance, its day shortened; for they said, *Our hope is lost; we are cut off for our parts,* Eze. 37:11. And then what becomes of the promise that Shiloh should arise out of Judah, the star out of Jacob, and the Messiah out of the family of David? If these fail, the promise fails. This the psalmist speaks of as in his own person, and it is very applicable to two of the common afflictions of this time: — 1. To be sickly. Bodily distempers soon *weaken our strength in the way,* make the keepers of the house to tremble and the strong men to bow themselves. 2. To be short-lived. Where the former is felt, this is feared; when in the midst of our days, according to a course of nature, our strength is weakened, what can we expect but that the *number of our months should be cut off in the midst?* and what should we do but provide accordingly? We must own God's hand in it (for in his hand our strength and time are), and must reconcile it to his love, for it has often been the lot of those that have used their strength well to have it weakened, and of those that could very ill be spared to have their days shortened.

II. A prayer for the continuance of it (*v.* 24): "*O my God! take me not away in the midst of my days;* let not this poor church be cut off in the midst of the days assigned it by the promise; let it not be cut off till the Messiah shall come. *Destroy it not, for that blessing is in it,*" Isa. 65:8. She is a criminal, but, for the sake of that blessing which is in her, she pleads for a reprieve. This is a prayer for the afflicted, and which, with submission to the will of God, we may in faith put up, that God would not *take us away in the midst of our days,* but that, if it be his will, he would spare us to do him further service and to be made riper for heaven.

III. A plea to enforce this prayer taken from the eternity of the Messiah promised, *v.* 25–27. The apostle quotes these verses (Heb. 1:10–12) and tells us, *He saith this to the Son,* and in that exposition we must acquiesce. It is very comfortable, in reference to all the changes that pass over the church, and all the dangers it is in, that *Jesus Christ is the same yesterday, to-day, and for ever. Thy years are throughout all generations,* and cannot be shortened. It is likewise comfortable in reference to the decay and death of our own bodies, and the removal of our friends from us, that God is an everliving God, and that therefore, if he be ours, in him we may have everlasting consolation. In this plea observe how, to illustrate the eternity of the Creator, he compares it with the mutability of the creature; for it is God's sole prerogative to be unchangeable. 1. God made the world, and therefore had a being before it from eternity. The Son of God, the eternal Word, made the world. It is expressly said, *All things were made by him, and without him was not any thing made that was made;* and *therefore the same was in the beginning* from eternity *with God, and was God,* Jn. 1:1–3; Col. 1:16; Eph. 3:9; Heb. 1:2. Earth and heaven, and the hosts of both, include the universe and its fulness, and these derive their being from God by his Son (*v.* 25): "*Of old hast thou laid the foundation of the earth,* which is founded *on the seas* and *on the floods* and yet *it abides;* much more shall the church, which is *built upon a rock.* The *heavens are the work of thy hands,* and by thee are all their motions and influences directed;" God is therefore the fountain, not only of all being, but of all power and dominion. See how fit the great Redeemer is to be entrusted with all power, both in heaven and in earth, since he himself, as Creator of both, perfectly knows both and is entitled to both. 2. God will unmake the world again, and therefore shall have a being to eternity (*v.* 26, 27): *They shall perish,* for *thou shalt change them* by the same almighty power that made them, and therefore, no doubt, *thou shalt endure; thou art the same.* God and the world, Christ and the creature, are rivals for the innermost and uppermost place in the soul of man, the immortal soul; now what is here said, one would think, were enough to decide the controversy immediately and to determine us for God and Christ. For, (1.) A portion in the creature is fading and dying: *They shall perish;* they will not last so long as we shall last. The day is coming when *the earth and all the works that are therein shall be burnt up;* and then what will become of those that have laid up their treasure in it? Heaven and earth shall *wax old as a garment,* not by a gradual decay, but, when the set time comes, they shall be laid aside like an old garment that we have no more occasion for: *As a vesture shalt thou change them, and they shall be changed,* not annihilated, but altered, it may be so that they shall not be at all the same, but *new heavens and a new earth.* See God's sovereign dominion over heaven and earth. He can change them as he pleases and when he pleases; and the constant changes they are subject to, in the revolutions of day and night, summer and winter, are earnests of their last and final change, when *the heavens* and *time* (which is measured by them) *shall be no more.* (2.) A portion in God is perpetual and everlasting: *Thou art the same,* subject to no change; and *thy years have no end, v.* 27. Christ will be the same in the performance that he was in the promise, the same to his church in captivity that he was to his church at liberty. Let not the church fear the weakening of her strength, or the shortening of her days, while Christ himself is both her strength and her life; he is the same, and has said, *Because I live you shall live also.* Christ came in the fulness of time, and set up his kingdom in spite of the power of the Old-Testament Babylon, and he will keep it up in spite of the power of the New-Testament Babylon.

IV. A comfortable assurance of an answer to this prayer (*v.* 28): *The children of thy servants shall continue;* since Christ is the same, the church shall continue from one generation to another; from the eternity of the head we may infer the perpetuity of the body, though often weak and distempered, and even at death's door. Those that hope to *wear out the saints of the Most High* will be mistaken. Christ's servants shall have children; those children shall have a seed, a succession, of professing people; the church, as well as the world, is under the influence of that blessing, *Be fruitful and multiply.* These *children shall continue,* not in their own persons, by reason of death, but in their seed, which shall be established before God (that is, in his service, and by his grace); the entail of religion shall not be cut off while the world stands, but, as one generation of good people passes away, another shall come, and thus the throne of Christ shall endure.

PSALM 103

This psalm calls more for devotion than exposition; it is a most excellent psalm of praise, and of general use. The psalmist, I. Stirs up himself and his own soul to praise God (*v.* 1, 2) for his favour to him in particular (*v.* 3–5), to the church in general, and to all good men, to whom he is, and will be, just, and kind, and constant (*v.* 6–18), and for his government of the world (*v.* 19). II. He desires the assistance of the holy angels, and all the works of God, in praising him (*v.* 20–22). In singing this psalm we must in a special manner get our hearts affected with the goodness of God and enlarged in love and thankfulness.

A psalm of David.

Verses 1–5

David is here communing with his own heart, and he is no fool that thus talks to himself and excites his own soul to that which is good. Observe,

I. How he stirs up himself to the duty of praise, *v.* 1, 2. 1. It is the Lord that is to be blessed and spoken well of; for he is the fountain of all good, whatever are the channels or cisterns; it is to his name, his holy name, that we are to consecrate our praise, *giving thanks at the remembrance of his holiness.* 2. It is the soul that is to be employed in blessing God, *and all that is within* us. We make nothing of our religious performances if we do not make heart-work of them, if that which is within us, nay, if *all that is within* us, be not engaged in them. The work requires the inward man, the whole man, and all little enough. 3. In order to our return of praises to God, there must be a grateful remembrance of the mercies we have received from him: *Forget not all his benefits.* If we do not give thanks for them, we do forget them; and that is unjust as well as unkind, since in all God's favours there is so much that is memorable. "O my soul! to thy shame be it spoken, thou hast forgotten many of his benefits; but surely thou wilt not forget them all, for thou shouldst not have forgotten any."

II. How he furnishes himself with abundant matter for praise, and that which is very affecting: "Come, my soul, consider what God has done for thee." 1. "He has pardoned thy sins (*v.* 3); he has forgiven, and *does forgive, all thy iniquities.*" This is mentioned first because by the pardon of sin that is taken away which kept good things from us, and we are restored to the favour of God, which bestows good things on us. Think what the provocation was; it was iniquity, and yet pardoned; how many the provocations were, and yet all pardoned. *He has forgiven all our trespasses.* It is a continued act; he is still forgiving, as we are still sinning and repenting. 2. "He has cured thy sickness." The corruption of nature is the sickness of the soul; it is its disorder, and threatens its death. This is cured in sanctification; when sin is mortified, the disease is healed; though complicated, it is all healed. Our crimes were capital, but God saves our lives by pardoning them; our diseases were mortal, but God saves our lives by healing them. These two go together; for, as for God, his work is perfect and not done by halves; if God take away the guilt of sin by pardoning mercy, he will break the power of it by renewing grace. Where Christ is made righteousness to any soul he is made sanctification, 1 Co. 1:30. 3. "He has rescued thee from danger." A man may be in peril of life, not only by his crimes, or his diseases, but by the power of his enemies; and therefore here also we experience the divine goodness: *Who redeemed thy life from destruction* (*v.* 4), from the destroyer, *from hell* (so the Chaldee), from the second death. *The redemption of the soul is precious;* we cannot compass it, and therefore are the more indebted to divine grace that has wrought it out, to him who has *obtained eternal redemption for us.* See Job 33:24, 28. 4. "He has not only saved thee from death and ruin, but has made thee truly and completely happy, with honour, pleasure, and long life." (1.) "He has given thee true honour and great honour, no less than a crown: *He crowns thee with his lovingkindness and tender mercies;*" and what greater dignity is a poor soul capable of than to be advanced into the love and favour of God? *This honour have all his saints.* What is the crown of glory but God's favour? (2.) "He has given thee true pleasure: *He satisfies thy mouth with good things*" (*v.* 5); it is only the favour and grace of God that can give satisfaction to a soul, can suit its capacities, supply its needs, and answer to its desires. Nothing but divine wisdom can undertake to *fill its treasures* (Prov. 8:21); other things will surfeit, but not *satiate,* Eccl. 6:7; Isa. 55:2. (3.) "He has given thee a prospect and pledge of long life: *Thy youth is renewed like the eagle's.*" The eagle is long-lived, and, as naturalists say, when she is nearly 100 years old, casts all her feathers (as indeed she changes them in a great measure every year at moulting time), and fresh ones come, so that she becomes young again. When God, by the graces and comforts of his Spirit, recovers his people from their decays, and fills them with new life and joy, which is to them an earnest of eternal life and joy, then they may be said to *return to the days of their youth,* Job 33:25.

Verses 6–18

Hitherto the psalmist had only looked back upon his own experiences and thence fetched matter for praise; here he looks abroad and takes notice of his favour to others also; for in them we should rejoice and give thanks for them, all the saints being fed at a common table and sharing in the same blessings.

I. Truly God is good to all (*v.* 6): He *executes righteousness and judgment,* not only for his own people, but *for all that are oppressed;* for even in common providence he is the patron of wronged innocency, and, one way or other, will plead the cause of those that are injured against their oppressors. It is his honour to humble the proud and help the helpless.

II. He is in a special manner good to Israel, to every Israelite indeed, that is of a clean and upright heart.

1. He has revealed himself and his grace to us (*v.* 7): *He made known his ways unto Moses,* and by him *his acts to the children of Israel,* not only by his rod to those who then lived, but by his pen to succeeding ages. Note, Divine revelation is one of the first and greatest of divine favours with which the church is blessed; for God restores us to himself by revealing himself to us, and gives us all good by giving us knowledge. He has *made known his acts and his ways* (that is, his nature, and the methods of his dealing with the children of men), that they may know both what to conceive of him and what to expect from him; so Dr. Hammond. Or by his *ways* we may understand his precepts, the way which he requires us to walk in; and by his *acts,* or *designs* (as the word signifies), his promises and purposes as to what he will do with us. Thus fairly does God deal with us.

2. He has never been rigorous and severe with us, but always tender, full of compassion, and ready to forgive.

(1.) It is in his nature to be so (*v.* 8): *The Lord is merciful and gracious;* this was his way which he made known unto Moses at Mount Horeb, when he thus proclaimed his name (Ex. 34:6, 7), in answer to Moses's request (*ch.* 33:13), *I beseech thee, show me thy way, that I may know thee.* It is my way, says God, to pardon sin. [1.] He is not soon angry, *v.* 8. He is *slow to anger,* not extreme to mark what we do amiss nor ready to take advantage against us. He bears long with those that are very provoking, defers punishing, that he may give space to repent, and does not speedily execute the sentence of his law; and he could not be thus *slow to anger* if he were not *plenteous in mercy,* the very *Father of mercies.* [2.] He is not long angry; for (*v.* 9) *he* will not always chide, though we always offend and deserve chiding. Though he signify his displeasure against us for our sins by the rebukes of Providence, and the reproaches of our own consciences, and thus cause grief, yet he will have compassion, and will not always keep us in pain and terror, no, not for our sins, but, after the spirit of bondage, will give the spirit of adoption. How unlike are those to God who always chide, who take every occasion to chide, and never know when to cease! What would become of us if God should deal so with us? *He will not keep his anger for ever* against his own people, but will gather them with *everlasting mercies,* Isa. 54:8; 57:16.

(2.) We have found him so; we, for our parts, must own that *he has not dealt with us after our sins, v.* 10. The scripture says a great deal of the mercy of God, and we may all set to our seal that it is true, that we have experienced it. If he had not been a God of patience, we should have been in hell long ago; but *he has not rewarded us after our iniquities;* so those will say who know what sin deserves. He has not inflicted the judgments which we have merited, nor deprived us of the comforts which we have forfeited, which should make us think the worse, and not the better, of sin; for *God's patience should lead us to repentance,* Rom. 2:4.

3. He has pardoned our sins, not only my *iniquity (v.* 3), but *our transgressions, v.* 12. Though it is of our own benefit, by the pardoning mercy of God, that we are to take the comfort, yet of the benefit others have by it we must give him the glory. Observe, (1.) The transcendent riches of God's mercy (v. 11): *As the heaven is high above the earth* (so high that the earth is but a point to the vast expanse), so God's mercy is above the merits of those that fear him most, so much above and beyond them that there is no proportion at all between them; the greatest performances of man's duty cannot demand the least tokens of God's favour as a debt, and therefore all the seed of Jacob will join with him in owning themselves *less than the least of all God's mercies,* Gen. 32:10. Observe, God's mercy is thus great *towards those that fear him,* not towards those that trifle with him. We must fear the Lord and his goodness. (2.) The fulness of his pardons, an evidence of the riches of his mercy (v. 12): *As far as the east is from the west* (which two quarters of the world are of greatest extent, because all known and inhabited, and therefore geographers that way reckon their longitudes) *so far has he removed our transgressions from us,* so that they shall never be laid to our charge, nor rise up in judgment against us. The sins of believers shall be remembered no more, shall not be mentioned unto them; they shall be sought for, and not found. If we thoroughly forsake them, God will thoroughly forgive them.

4. He has pitied our sorrows, *v.* 13, 14. Observe, (1.) Whom he pities — *those that fear him,* that is, all good people, who in this world may become objects of pity on account of the grievances to which they are not only born, but born again. Or it may be understood of those who have not yet received the spirit of adoption, but are yet *trembling at his word;* those he *pities,* Jer. 31:18, 20. (2.) How he pities — *as a father pities his children,* and does them good as there is occasion. God is a Father to those that fear him and owns them for his children, and he is tender of them as a father. The father pities his children that are weak in knowledge and instructs them, pities them when they are froward and bears with them, pities them when they are sick and comforts them (Isa. 66:13), pities them when they have fallen and helps them up again, pities them when they have offended, and, upon their submission, forgives them, pities them when they are wronged and gives them redress; thus *the Lord pities those that fear him.* (3.) Why he pities — *for he knows our frame.* He has reason to know our frame, for he framed us; and, having himself made man of the dust, *he remembers that he is dust,* not only by constitution, but by sentence. *Dust thou art.* He considers the frailty of our bodies and the folly of our souls, how little we can do, and expects accordingly from us, how little we can bear, and lays accordingly upon us, in all which appears the tenderness of his compassion.

5. He has perpetuated his covenant-mercy and thereby provided relief for our frailty, *v.* 15–18. See here, (1.) How short man's life is and of what uncertain continuance. The lives even of great men and good men are so, and neither their greatness nor their goodness can alter the property

of them: *As for man, his days are as grass,* which grows out of the earth, rises but a little way above it, and soon withers and returns to it again. See Isa. 40:6, 7. Man, in his best estate, seems somewhat more than grass; he flourishes and looks gay; yet then he is but *like a flower of the field,* which, though distinguished a little from the grass, will wither with it. The flower of the garden is commonly more choice and valuable, and, though in its own nature withering, will last the longer for its being sheltered by the garden wall and the gardener's care; but the flower of the field (to which life is here compared) is not only withering in itself, but exposed to the cold blasts, and liable to be cropped and trodden on by the beasts of the field. Man's life is not only wasting of itself, but its period may be anticipated by a thousand accidents. When the flower is in its perfection a blasting wind, unseen, unlooked for, *passes over it, and it is gone;* it hangs the head, drops the leaves, dwindles into the ground again, *and the place thereof,* which was proud of it, now *knows it no more.* Such a thing is man: God considers this, and pities him; let him consider it himself, and be humble, dead to this world and thoughtful of another. (2.) How long and lasting God's mercy is to his people (v. 17, 18): it will continue longer than their lives, and will survive their present state. Observe, [1.] The description of those to whom this mercy belongs. They are such as fear God, such as are truly religious, from principle. *First,* They live a life of faith; for they *keep God's covenant;* having taken hold of it, they keep hold of it, fast hold, and will not let it go. They keep it as a treasure, keep it as their portion, and would not for all the world part with it, for it is their life. *Secondly,* They live a life of obedience; they *remember his commandments to do them,* else they do not *keep his covenant.* Those only shall have the benefit of God's promises that make conscience of his precepts. See who those are that have a good memory, as well as a *good understanding* (Ps. 111:10), those that *remember God's commandments,* not to talk of them, but *to do them,* and to be ruled by them. [2.] The continuance of the mercy which belongs to such as these; it will last them longer than their lives on earth, and therefore they need not be troubled though their lives be short, since death itself will be no abridgment, no infringement, of their bliss. God's mercy is better than life, for it will out-live it. *First,* To their souls, which are immortal; to them the mercy of the Lord is *from everlasting to everlasting;* from everlasting in the councils of it to everlasting in the consequences of it, in their election before the world was and their glorification when this world shall be no more; for they are predestinated to the *inheritance* (Eph. 1:11) and *look for the mercy of the Lord,* the Lord Jesus, unto eternal life. *Secondly,* To their seed, which shall be kept up to the end of time (Ps. 102:28): *His righteousness,* the truth of his promise, shall be *unto children's children;* provided they tread in the steps of their predecessors' piety, and *keep his covenant,* as they did, then shall mercy be preserved to them, even to *a thousand generations.*

Verses 19–22

Here is, I. The doctrine of universal providence laid down, *v.* 19. He has secured the happiness of his peculiar people by promise and covenant, but the order of mankind, and the world in general, he secures by common providence. *The Lord has a throne of his own,* a throne of glory, a throne of government. He that made all rules all, and both by a word of power: *He has prepared his throne,* has fixed and established it that it cannot be shaken; he has afore-ordained all the measures of his government and does all according to the counsel of his own will. He *has prepared* it *in the heavens,* above us, and out of sight; for he *holds back the face of his throne,* and *spreads a cloud upon it* (Job 26:9); yet he can himself *judge through the dark cloud,* Job 22:13. Hence *the heavens are said to rule* (Dan. 4:26), and we are led to consider this by the influence which even the visible heavens have upon this earth, their *dominion,* Job 38:33; Gen. 1:16. But though God's throne is in heaven, and there he keeps his court, and thither we are to direct to him *(Our Father who art in heaven),* yet *his kingdom rules over all.* He takes cognizance of all the inhabitants, and all the affairs, of this lower world, and disposes all persons and things according to the counsel of his will, to his own glory (Dan. 4:35):

His kingdom rules over all kings and all kingdoms, and from it there is no exempt jurisdiction.

II. The duty of universal praise inferred from it: if all are under God's dominion, all must do him homage.

1. Let the holy angels praise him *(v.* 20, 21): *Bless the Lord, you his angels;* and again, *Bless the Lord, all you his hosts, you ministers of his.* David had been stirring up himself and others to praise God, and here, in the close, he calls upon the angels to do it; not as if they needed any excitement of ours to praise God, they do it continually; but thus he expresses his high thoughts of God as worthy of the adorations of the holy angels, thus he quickens himself and others to the duty with this consideration, That it is the work of angels, and comforts himself in reference to his own weakness and defect in the performance of this duty with this consideration, That there is a world of holy angels who dwell in God's house and are still praising him. In short, the blessed angels are glorious attendants upon the blessed God. Observe, (1.) How well qualified they are for the post they are in. They are able; for they *excel in strength;* they are *mighty in strength* (so the word is); they are able to bring great things to pass, and to abide in their work without weariness. And they are as willing as they are able; they are willing to know their work; for they *hearken to the voice of his word;* they stand expecting commission and instructions from their great Lord, and *always behold his face* (Mt. 18:10), that they may take the first intimation of his mind. They are willing to do their work: They *do his commandments (v.* 20); they *do his pleasure (v.* 21); they dispute not any divine commands, but readily address themselves to the execution of them. Nor do they delay, but fly swiftly: They *do his commandments at hearing,* or *as soon as they hear the voice of his word;* so Dr. Hammond. *To obey is better than sacrifice;* for angels obey, but do not sacrifice. (2.) What their service is. They are *his angels,* and *ministers of his* — his, for he made them, and made them for himself — his, for he employs them, though he does not need them — his, for he is their owner and Lord; they belong to him and he has them at his beck. All the creatures are his servants, but not as the angels that attend the presence of his glory. Soldiers, and seamen, and all good subjects, serve the king, but not as the courtiers do, the ministers of state and those of the household. [1.] The angels occasionally serve God in this lower world; they *do his commandments,* go on his errands (Dan. 9:21), fight his battles (2 Ki. 6:17), and minister for the good of his people, Heb. 1:14. [2.] They *continually praise him* in the upper world; they began betimes to do it (Job 38:7), and it is still their business, from which they rest not *day nor night,* Rev. 4:8. It is God's glory that he has such attendants, but more his glory that he neither needs them nor is benefited by them.

2. Let *all his works* praise him *(v.* 22), all *in all places of his dominion;* for, because they are his works, they are under his dominion, and they were made and are ruled that they may be unto him *for a name and a praise. All his works,* that is, all the children of men, in all parts of the world, let them all praise God; yea, and the inferior creatures too, which are God's works also; let them praise him objectively, though they cannot praise him actually, Ps. 145:10. Yet all this shall not excuse David from praising God, but rather excite him to do it the more cheerfully, that he may bear a part in this concert; for he concludes, *Bless the Lord, O my soul!* as he began, *v.* 1. Blessing God and giving him glory must be the alpha and the omega of all our services. He began with *Bless the Lord, O my soul!* and, when he had penned and sung this excellent hymn to his honour, he does not say, Now, O my soul! thou hast blessed the Lord, sit down, and rest thee, but, *Bless the Lord, O my soul!* yet more and more. When we have done ever so much in the service of God, yet still we must stir up ourselves to do more. God's praise is a subject that will never be exhausted, and therefore we must never think this work done till we come to heaven, where it will be for ever in the doing.

PSALM 104

It is very probable that this psalm was penned by the same hand, and at the same time, as the former; for as that ended this begins, with "Bless the Lord, O my soul!" and concludes with it too. The style indeed is somewhat different, because the matter is so: the scope of the foregoing psalm was to celebrate the goodness of God and his tender mercy and compassion, to which a soft and sweet style was most agreeable; the scope of this is to celebrate his greatness, and majesty, and sovereign dominion, which ought to be done in the most stately lofty strains of poetry. David, in the former psalm, gave God the glory of his covenant-mercy and love to his own people; in this he gives him the glory of his works of creation and providence, his dominion over, and his bounty to, all the creatures. God is there praised as the God of grace, here as the God of nature. And this psalm is wholly bestowed on that subject; not as Ps. 19, which begins with it, but passes from it to the consideration of the divine law; nor as Ps. 8, which speaks of this but prophetically, and with an eye to Christ. This noble poem is thought by very competent judges greatly to excel, not only for piety and devotion (that is past dispute), but for flight of fancy, brightness of ideas, surprising turns, and all the beauties and ornaments of expression, the Greek and Latin poets upon any subject of this nature. Many great things the psalmist here gives God the glory of I. The splendour of his majesty in the upper world (*v.* 1–4). II. The creation of the sea and the dry land (*v.* 5–9). III. The provision he makes for the maintenance of all the creatures according to their nature (*v.* 10–18, 27, 28). IV. The regular course of the sun and moon (*v.* 19–24). V. The furniture of the sea (*v.* 25, 26). IV. God's sovereign power over all the creatures (*v.* 29–32). And, lastly, he concludes with a pleasant and firm resolution to continue praising God (*v.* 33–35), with which we should heartily join in singing this psalm.

Verses 1–9

When we are addressing ourselves to any religious service we must *stir up ourselves to take hold on God* in it (Isa. 64:7); so David does here. "Come, my soul, where art thou? What art thou thinking of? Here is work to be done, good work, angels' work; set about it in good earnest; let all the powers and faculties be engaged and employed in it: *Bless the Lord, O my soul!*" In these verses,

I. The psalmist looks up to the divine glory shining in the upper world, of which, though it is one of the things not seen, faith is the evidence. With what reverence and holy awe does he begin his meditation with that acknowledgment: *O Lord my God! thou art very great!* It is the joy of the saints that he who is their God is a great God. The grandeur of the prince is the pride and pleasure of all his good subjects. The majesty of God is here set forth by various instances, alluding to the figure which great princes in their public appearances covet to make. Their equipage, compared with his (even of the eastern kings, who most affected pomp), is but as the light of a glow-worm compared with that of the sun, when he goes forth in his strength. Princes appear great, 1. In their robes; and what are God's robes? *Thou art clothed with honour and majesty, v.* 1. God is seen in his works, and these proclaim him infinitely wise and good, and all that is great. Thou *coverest thyself with light as with a garment, v.* 2. God *is light* (1 Jn. 1:5), the *Father of lights* (Jam. 1:17); he *dwells in light* (1 Tim. 6:16); he clothes himself with it. The residence of his glory is in the highest heaven, that light which was created the first day, Gen. 1:3. Of all visible beings light comes nearest to the nature of a spirit, and therefore with that God is pleased to cover himself, that is, to reveal himself under that similitude, as men are seen in the clothes with which they cover themselves; and so only, for his face cannot be seen. 2. In their palaces or pavilions, when they take the field; and what is God's palace and his pavilion? He *stretches out the heavens like a curtain, v.* 2. So he did at first, when he made the firmament, which in the Hebrew has its name from its being expanded, or *stretched out,* Gen. 1:7. He made it to divide the waters as a curtain divides between two apartments. So he does still: he now *stretches out the heavens like a curtain,* keeps them upon the stretch, and they *continue to this day according to his ordinance.* The regions of the air are stretched out about the earth, like a curtain about a bed, to keep it warm, and drawn between us and the upper world, to break its dazzling light; for, though God *covers himself with light,* yet, in compassion to us, *he makes darkness his pavilion. Thick clouds are a covering to him.* The vastness of this pavilion may lead us to consider how great, how very great, he is that *fills heaven and earth.* He has his *chambers,* his *upper rooms* (so the word signifies), *the beams* whereof *he lays in the waters,* the waters that are above the firmament (*v.* 3), as he has *founded the earth upon the seas and floods,* the waters beneath the firmament. Though air and water are fluid bodies, yet, by the divine power, they are kept as tight and as firm in the place assigned them as a chamber is with beams and rafters. How great a God is he whose presence-chamber is thus reared, thus fixed! 3. In their coaches of state, with their stately horses, which add much to the magnificence of their entries; but God *makes the clouds his chariots,* in which he rides strongly, swiftly, and far above out of the reach of opposition, when at any time he will act by uncommon providences in the government of this world. He descended in a cloud, as in a chariot, to Mount Sinai, to give the law, and to Mount Tabor, to proclaim the gospel (Mt. 17:5), and he *walks* (a gentle pace indeed, yet stately) *upon the wings of the wind.* See Ps. 18:10, 11. He commands the winds, directs them as he pleases, and serves his own purposes by them. 4. In their retinue or train of attendants; and here also God is very great, for (*v.* 4) he *makes his angels spirits.* This is quoted by the apostle (Heb. 1:7) to prove the pre-eminence of Christ above the angels. The angels are here said to be *his angels* and *his ministers,* for they are under his dominion and at his disposal; they are *winds,* and *a flame of fire,* that is, they appeared in wind and fire (so some), or they are as swift as winds, and pure as flames; or he *makes them spirits,* so the apostle quotes it. They are spiritual beings; and, whatever vehicles they may have proper to their nature, it is certain they have not bodies as we have. Being spirits, they are so much the further removed from the encumbrances of the human nature and so much the nearer allied to the glories of the divine nature. And they are bright, and quick, and ascending, as fire, as *a flame of fire.* In Ezekiel's vision they ran and returned *like a flash of lightning,* Eze. 1:14. Thence they are called *seraphim — burners.* Whatever they are, they are what God made them, what he still makes them; they derive their being from him, having the being he gave them, are held in being by him, and he makes what use he pleases of them.

II. He looks down, and looks about, to the power of God shining in this lower world. He is not so taken up with the glories of his court as to neglect even the remotest of his territories; no, not the sea and dry land.

1. He has founded the earth, *v.* 5. Though he has *hung it upon nothing* (Job 26:2), *ponderibus librata suis — balanced by its own weight,* yet it is as immovable as if it had been laid upon the surest foundations. He has built the earth upon her basis, so that though it has received a dangerous shock by the sin of man, and the malice of hell strikes at it, yet *it shall not be removed for ever,* that is, not till the end of time, when it must give way to the new earth. Dr. Hammond's paraphrase of this is worth noting: "God has fixed so strange a place for the earth, that, being a heavy body, one would think it should fall every minute; and yet, which way soever we would imagine it to stir, it must, contrary to the nature of such a body, fall upwards, and so can have no possible ruin but by tumbling into heaven."

2. He has set bounds to the sea; for that also is his. (1.) He brought it within bounds in the creation. At first the earth, which, being the more ponderous body, would subside of course, was *covered with the deep* (*v.* 6): *The waters were above the mountains;* and so it was unfit to be, as it was designed, a habitation for man; and therefore, on the third day, God said, *Let the waters under the heaven be gathered to one place, and let the dry land appear,* Gen. 1:9. This command of God is here called his *rebuke,* as if he gave it because he was displeased that the earth was thus covered with water and not fit for man to dwell on. Power went along with this word, and therefore it is also called here *the voice of* his *thunder,* which is a mighty voice and produces strange effects, *v.* 7. *At thy rebuke,* as if they were made sensible that they were out of their place, *they fled; they hasted away* (they called, and not in vain, to the rocks and mountains to cover them), as it is said on another occasion (Ps. 77:16), *The waters saw thee, O God! the waters saw thee; they were afraid.* Even those fluid bodies received the impression of God's terror. But *was the Lord displeased against the rivers?* No; it was *for the salvation of his people,* Hab. 3:8, 13. So here; God rebuked the waters for man's sake, to prepare room for him; for *men must not be made as the fishes of the sea* (Hab. 1:14); they must have air to breathe in. Immediately therefore, with all speed, the waters retired, *v.* 8. *They* go over hill and dale (as we say), *go up by the mountains* and *down by the valleys;* they will neither stop at the former nor lodge in the latter, but make the best of their way *to the place which thou hast founded for them,* and there they make their bed. Let the obsequiousness even of the unstable waters teach us obedience to the word and will of God; for shall man alone of all the creatures be obstinate? Let their retiring to and resting in the place assigned them teach us to acquiesce in the disposals of that wise providence which appoints us the bounds of our habitation. (2.) He keeps it within bounds, *v.* 9. The waters are forbidden to pass over the limits set them; they may not, and therefore they do not, *turn again to cover the earth.* Once they did, in Noah's flood, because God bade them, but never since, because he forbids them, having promised not to drown the world again. God himself glorifies in this instance of his power (Job 38:8, etc.) and uses it as an argument with us to fear him, Jer. 5:22. This, if duly considered, would keep the world in awe of the Lord and his goodness, That the waters of the sea would soon cover the earth if God did not restrain them.

Verses 10–18

Having given glory to God as the powerful protector of this earth, in saving it from being deluged, here he comes to acknowledge him as its bountiful benefactor, who provides conveniences for all the creatures.

I. He provides fresh water for their drink: *He sends the springs into the valleys, v.* 10. There is water enough indeed in the sea, that is, enough to drown us, but not one drop to refresh us, be we ever so thirsty — it is all so salt; and therefore God has graciously provided water fit to drink. Naturalists dispute about the origin of fountains; but, whatever are their second causes, here is their first cause; it is God that *sends the springs into the* brooks, *which* walk by easy steps between *the hills,* and receive increase from the rain-water that descends from them. These *give drink,* not only to man, and those creatures that are immediately useful to him, but *to every beast of the field* (*v.* 11); for where God has given life he provides a livelihood and takes care of all the creatures. Even *the wild asses,* though untameable and therefore of no use to man, are welcome to *quench their thirst;* and we have no reason to grudge it them, for we are better provided for, though *born like the wild ass's colt.* We have reason to thank God for the plenty of fair water with which he has provided the habitable part of his earth, which otherwise would not be habitable. That ought to be reckoned a great mercy the want of which would be a great affliction; and the more common it is the greater mercy it is. *Usus communis aquarum — water is common for all.*

II. He provides food convenient for them, both for man and beast: *The heavens drop fatness;* they *hear the earth,* but God *hears them,* Hos. 2:21. *He waters the hills from his chambers* (*v.* 13), from those chambers spoken of (*v.* 3), *the beams of* which *he lays in the waters,* those storechambers, the clouds that distil fruitful showers. The hills that are not watered by the rivers, as Egypt was by the Nile, are watered by the rain from heaven, which is called *the river of God* (Ps. 65:9), as Canaan was, Deu. 11:11, 12. Thus *the earth is satisfied with the fruit of his works,* either with the rain it drinks in (the earth knows when it has enough; it is a pity that any man should not) or with the products it brings forth. It is a satisfaction to the earth to bear the fruit of God's works for the benefit of man, for thus it answers the end of its creation. The *food* which God *brings forth out of the earth* (*v.* 14) is *the fruit of his works,* which *the earth is satisfied with.* Observe how various and how valuable its products are.

1. For the cattle there is grass, and the beasts of prey, that live not on grass, feed on those that do; for man there is herb, a better sort of grass (and a dinner of herbs and roots is not to be despised); nay, he is furnished with *wine, and oil, and bread, v.* 15. We may observe here, concerning our food, that which will help to make us both humble and thankful. (1.) To make us humble let us consider that we have a necessary dependence upon God for all the supports of this life (we live upon alms; we are at his finding, for our own hands are not sufficient for us), — that our food comes all out of the earth, to remind us whence we ourselves were taken and whither we must return, — and that therefore we must not think to *live by bread alone,* for that will feed the body only, but must look into the word of God for the meat that endures to eternal life. Let us also consider that we are in this respect fellow-commoners with the beasts; the same earth, the same spot of ground, that brings grass for the cattle, brings corn for man. (2.) To make us thankful let us consider, [1.] That God not only provides for us, but for our servants. The cattle that are of use to man are particularly taken care of; grass

is made to grow in great abundance for them, when *the young lions,* that are not for the service of man, often *lack and suffer hunger.* [2.] That our food is nigh us, and ready to us. Having our habitation on the earth, there we have our storehouse, and depend not on the *merchant-ships that bring food from afar,* Prov. 31:14. [3.] That we have even from the products of the earth, not only for necessity, but for ornament and delight, so good a Master do we serve. *First,* Does nature call for something to support it, and repair its daily decays? Here is *bread, which strengthens man's heart,* and is therefore called *the staff of life;* let none who have that complain of want. *Secondly,* Does nature go further, and covet something pleasant? Here is *wine, that makes glad the heart,* refreshes the spirits, and exhilarates them, when it is soberly and moderately used, that we may not only go through our business, but go through it cheerfully. It is a pity that that should be abused to overcharge the heart, and unfit men for their duty, which was given to revive their heart and quicken them in their duty. *Thirdly,* Is nature yet more humoursome, and does it crave something for ornament too? Here is that also out of the earth — *oil to make the face to shine,* that the countenance may not only be cheerful but beautiful, and we may be the more acceptable to one another.

2. Nay, the divine providence not only furnishes animals with their proper food, but vegetables also with theirs (*v.* 16): *The trees of the Lord are full of sap,* not only men's trees, which they take care of and have an eye to, in their orchards, and parks, and other enclosures, but God's trees, which grow in the wildernesses, and are taken care of only by his providence; they *are full of sap* and want no nourishment. Even *the cedars of Lebanon,* an open forest, though they are high and bulky, and require a great deal of sap to feed them, have enough from the earth; they are trees *which he has planted,* and which therefore he will protect and provide for. We may apply this to the trees of righteousness, which are the planting of the Lord, planted in his vineyard; these *are full of sap,* for what God plants he will water, and those that *are planted in the house of the Lord shall flourish in the courts of our God,* Ps. 92:13.

III. He takes care that they shall have suitable habitations to dwell in. To men God has given discretion to build for themselves and for the cattle that are serviceable to them; but there are some creatures which God more immediately provides a settlement for. 1. The birds. Some birds, by instinct, make their nests in the bushes near rivers (*v.* 12): *By the springs* that *run among the hills* some of the *fowls of heaven have their habitation, which sing among the branches.* They sing, according to their capacity, to the honour of their Creator and benefactor, and their singing may shame our silence. Our *heavenly Father feeds them* (Mt. 6:26), and therefore they are easy and cheerful, and take no thought for the morrow. The birds being made to *fly above the earth* (as we find, Gen. 1:20), they *make their nests* on high, in the tops of trees (*v.* 17); it should seem as if nature had an eye to this in *planting the cedars of Lebanon,* that they might be receptacles for the birds. Those that fly heavenward shall not want resting-places. *The stork* is particularly mentioned; *the fir-trees,* which are very high, *are her house,* her castle. 2. The smaller sort of beasts (*v.* 18): *The wild goats,* having neither strength nor swiftness to secure themselves, are guided by instinct to *the high hills,* which are a refuge to them; and *the rabbits,* which are also helpless animals, find shelter in *the rocks,* where they can set the beasts of prey at defiance. Does God provide thus for the inferior creatures; and will he not himself be a refuge and dwelling-place to his own people?

Verses 19–30

We are here taught to praise and magnify God,

I. For the constant revolutions and succession of day and night, and the dominion of sun and moon over them. The heathen were so affected with the light and influence of the sun and moon, and their serviceableness to the earth, that they worshipped them as deities; and therefore the scripture takes all occasions to show that the gods they worshipped are the creatures and servants of the true God (*v.* 19): *He appointed the moon for seasons,* for the measuring of the months, the directing of the seasons for the business of the husbandman, and the governing of the tides. The full and change, the increase and decrease, of the moon, exactly observe the appointment of the Creator; so does the sun, for he keeps as punctually to the time and place of his going down as if he were an intellectual being and knew what he did. God herein consults the comfort of man. 1. The shadows of the evening befriend the repose of the night (*v.* 20): *Thou makes darkness and it is night,* which, though black, contributes to the beauty of nature, and is as a foil to the light of the day; and under the protection of the night *all the beasts of the forest creep forth* to feed, which they are afraid to do in the day, God having put the *fear* and *dread of man upon every beast of the earth* (Gen. 9:2), which contributes as much to man's safety as to his honour. See how nearly allied those are to the disposition of the wild beasts who *wait for the twilight* (Job 24:15) and have fellowship with the unfruitful works of darkness; and compare to this the danger of ignorance and melancholy, which are both as darkness to the soul; when, in either of those ways, *it is night,* then *all the beasts of the forest creep forth.* Satan's temptations then assault us and have advantage against us. Then the *young lions roar after their prey;* and, as naturalists tell us, their roaring terrifies the timorous beasts so that they have not strength nor spirit to escape from them, which otherwise they might do, and so they become an easy prey to them. They are said to *seek their meat from God,* because it is not prepared for them by the care and forecast of man, but more immediately by the providence of God. The roaring of the young lions, like the crying of the young ravens, is interpreted *asking their meat of God.* Does God put this construction upon the language of mere nature, even in venomous creatures? and shall he not much more interpret favourably the language of grace in his own people, though it be weak and broken, *groanings which cannot be uttered?* 2. The light of the morning befriends the business of the day (*v.* 22, 23): *The sun arises* (for, as he *knows his going down,* so, thanks be to God, he knows his rising again), and then the wild beasts betake themselves to their rest; even they have some society among them, for they *gather themselves together* and *lay down in their dens,* which is a great mercy to the children of men, that while they are abroad, as becomes honest travellers, between sun and sun, care is taken that they shall not be set upon by wild beasts, for they are then drawn out of the field, and the sluggard shall have no ground to excuse himself from the business of the day with this, That there is *a lion in the way.* Therefore then *man goes forth to his work and to his labour.* The beasts of prey creep forth with fear; man goes forth with boldness, as one that has dominion. The beasts creep forth to spoil and do mischief; man goes forth to work and do good. There is the work of every day, which is to be done in its day, which man must apply to every morning (for the lights are set up for us to work by, not to play by) and which he must stick to till evening; it will be time enough to rest when the night comes, in which *no man can work.*

II. For the replenishing of the ocean (*v.* 25, 26): As *the earth is full of God's riches,* well stocked with animals, and those well provided for, so that it is seldom that any creature dies merely for want of food, *so is this great and wide sea* which seems a useless part of the globe, at least not to answer the room it takes up; yet God has appointed it its place and made it serviceable to man both for navigation (*there go the ships,* in which goods are conveyed, to countries vastly distant, speedily and much more cheaply than by land-carriage) and also to be his storehouse for fish. God made not the sea in vain, any more than the earth; he *made it to be inherited,* for *there are things swimming innumerable, both small and great animals,* which serve for man's dainty food. The whale is particularly mentioned in the history of the creation (Gen. 1:21) and is here called the *leviathan,* as Job 41:1. He is made to *play in the sea;* he has nothing to do, as man has, who *goes forth to his work;* he has nothing to fear, as the beasts have, that lie down in their dens; and therefore he plays with the waters. It is a pity that any of the children of men, who have nobler powers and were made for nobler purposes, should live as if they were sent into the world, like leviathan into the waters, to play therein, spending all their time in pastime. The leviathan is said to *play in the waters,* because he is so well armed against all assaults that he sets them at defiance and *laughs at the shaking of a spear,* Job 41:29.

III. For the seasonable and plentiful provision which is made for all the creatures, *v.* 27, 28. 1. God is a bountiful benefactor to them: He *gives them their meat;* he *opens his hand and they are filled with good.* He supports the armies both of heaven and earth. Even the meanest creatures are not below his cognizance. He is open-handed in the gifts of his bounty, and is a great and good housekeeper that provides for so large a family. 2. They are patient expectants from him: They *all wait upon him.* They seek their food, according to the natural instinct God has put into them and in the proper season for it, and affect not any other food, or at any other time, than nature has ordained. They do their part for the obtaining of it: what God gives them *they gather,* and expect not that Providence should put it into their mouths; and what they gather they are satisfied with — *they are filled with good.* They desire no more than what God sees fit for them, which may shame our murmurings, and discontent, and dissatisfaction with our lot.

IV. For the absolute power and sovereign dominion which he has over all the creatures, by which every species is still continued, though the individuals of each are daily dying and dropping off. See here, 1. All the creatures perishing (*v.* 29): *Thou hidest thy face,* withdrawest thy supporting power, thy supplying bounty, and *they are troubled* immediately. Every creature has as necessary a dependence upon God's favours as every saint is sensible he has and therefore says with David (Ps. 30:7), *Thou didst hide thy face and I was troubled.* God's displeasure against this lower world for the sin of man is the cause of all the vanity and burden which the whole creation groans under. *Thou takest away their breath,* which is in thy hand, and then, and not till then, *they die and return to their dust,* to their first principles. The *spirit of the beast, which goes downward,* is at God's command, as well as *the spirit of a man, which goes upward.* The death of cattle was one of the plagues of Egypt, and is particularly taken notice of in the drowning of the world. 2. All preserved notwithstanding, in a succession (*v.* 30): *Thou sendest forth thy spirit, they are created.* The same spirit (that is, the same divine will and power) by which they were all created at first still preserves the several sorts of creatures in their being, and place, and usefulness; so that, though one generation of them passes away, another comes, and from time to time they are created; new ones rise up instead of the old ones, and this is a continual creation. Thus the *face of the earth is renewed* from day to day by the light of the sun (which beautifies it anew every morning), from year to year by the products of it, which enrich it anew every spring and put quite another face upon it from what it had all winter. The world is as full of creatures as if none died, for the place of those that die is filled up. This (the Jews say) is to be applied to the resurrection, which every spring is an emblem of, when a new world rises out of the ashes of the old one.

In the midst of this discourse the psalmist breaks out into wonder at the works of God (*v.* 24): *O Lord! how manifold are thy works!* They are numerous, they are various, of many kinds, and many of every kind; and yet *in wisdom hast thou made them all.* When men undertake many works, and of different kinds, commonly some of them are neglected and not done with due care; but God's works, though many and of very different kinds, are all made in wisdom and with the greatest exactness; there is not the least flaw nor defect in them. The works of art, the more closely they are looked upon with the help of microscopes, the more rough they appear; the works of nature through these glasses appear more fine and exact. They are all made in wisdom, for they are all made to answer the end they were designed to serve, the good of the universe, in order to the glory of the universal Monarch.

Verses 31–35

The psalmist concludes this meditation with speaking,

I. Praise to God, which is chiefly intended in the psalm.

1. He is to be praised, (1.) As a great God, and a God of matchless perfection: *The glory of the Lord shall endure for ever, v.* 31. It shall endure to the end of time in his works of creation and providence; it shall endure to eternity in the felicity and adorations of saints and angels. Man's glory is fading; God's glory is everlasting. Creatures change, but with the Creator there is no variableness. (2.) As a gracious God: *The Lord shall rejoice in his works.* He

continues that complacency in the products of his own wisdom and goodness which he had when he *saw every thing that he had made, and behold it was very good,* and *rested the seventh day.* We often do that which, upon the review, we cannot rejoice in, but are displeased at, and wish undone again, blaming our own management. But God always *rejoices in his works,* because they are all done in wisdom. We regret our bounty and beneficence, but God never does; he rejoices in the works of his grace: his *gifts and callings* are *without repentance.* (3.) As a God of almighty power (*v.* 32): *He looks on the earth, and it trembles,* as unable to bear his frowns —trembles, as Sinai did, *at the presence of the Lord. He touches the hills, and they smoke.* The volcanoes, or burning mountains, such as Aetna, are emblems of the power of God's wrath fastening upon proud unhumbled sinners. If an angry look and a touch have such effects, what will the weight of his heavy hand do and the operations of his outstretched arm? *Who knows the power of his anger?* Who then dares set it at defiance? God rejoices in his works because they are all so observant of him; and he will in like manner *take pleasure in those that fear him and that tremble at his word.*

2. The psalmist will himself be much in praising him (*v.* 33): *"I will sing unto the Lord, unto my God,* will praise him as Jehovah, the Creator, and as *my God,* a God in covenant with me, and this not now only, but *as long as I live,* and *while I have my being."* Because we have our being from God, and depend upon him for the support and continuance of it, as long as we live and have our being we must continue to praise God; and when we have no life, no being, on earth, we hope to have a better life and better being in a better world and there to be doing this work in a better manner and in better company.

II. Joy to himself (*v.* 34): *My meditation of him shall be sweet;* it shall be fixed and close; it shall be affecting and influencing; and therefore it shall be sweet. Thoughts of God will *then* be most pleasing, when they are most powerful. Note, Divine meditation is a very sweet duty to all that are sanctified: *"I will be glad in the Lord;* it shall be a pleasure to me to praise him; I will be glad of all opportunities to set forth his glory; and I will *rejoice in the Lord always* and in him only." All my joys shall centre in him, and in him they shall be full.

III. Terror to the wicked (*v.* 35): *Let the sinners be consumed out of the earth; and let the wicked be no more.* 1. Those that oppose the God of power, and fight against him, will certainly be consumed; none can prosper that harden themselves against the Almighty. 2. Those that rebel against the light of such convincing evidence of God's being, and refuse to serve him whom all the creatures serve, will justly be consumed. Those that make that earth to groan under the burden of their impieties which God thus fills with his riches deserve to be consumed out of it, and that it should spue them out. 3. Those that heartily desire to praise God themselves cannot but have a holy indignation at those that blaspheme and dishonour him, and a holy satisfaction in the prospect of their destruction and the honour that God will get to himself upon them. Even this ought to be the matter of their praise: "While *sinners* are *consumed out of the earth,* let *my soul bless the Lord* that I am not cast away with the workers of iniquity, but distinguished from them by the special grace of God. When *the wicked* are *no more* I hope to be praising God world without end; and therefore, *Praise you the Lord;* let all about me join with me in praising God. *Hallelujah;* sing praise to Jehovah." This is the first time that we meet with *Hallelujah;* and it comes in here upon occasion of the destruction of the wicked; and the last time we meet with it is upon a similar occasion. When the New-Testament Babylon is consumed, this is the burden of the song, *Hallelujah,* Rev. 19:1, 3, 4, 6.

PSALM 105

Some of the psalms of praise are very short, others very long, to teach us that, in our devotions, we should be more observant how our hearts work than how the time passes and neither overstretch ourselves by coveting to be long nor over-stint ourselves by coveting to be short, but either the one or the other as we find in our hearts to pray. This is a long psalm; the general scope is the same with most of the psalms, to set forth the glory of God, but the subject-matter is particular. Every time we come to the throne of grace we may, if we please, furnish ourselves out of the word of God (out of the history of the New Testament, as this out of the history of the Old) with new songs, with fresh thoughts — so copious, so various, so inexhaustible is the subject. In the foregoing psalm we are taught to praise God for his wondrous works of common providence with reference to the world in general. In this we are directed to praise him for his special favours to his church. We find the first eleven verses of this psalm in the beginning of that psalm which David delivered to Asaph to be used (as it should seem) in the daily service of the sanctuary when the ark was fixed in the place he had prepared for it, by which it appears both who penned it and when and upon what occasion it was penned, 1 Chr. 16:7, etc. David by it designed to instruct his people in the obligations they lay under to adhere faithfully to their holy religion. Here is the preface (*v.* 1–7) and the history itself in several articles. I. God's covenant with the patriarchs (*v.* 8–11). II. His care of them while they were strangers (*v.* 12–15). III. His raising up Joseph to be the shepherd and stone of Israel (*v.* 16–22). IV. The increase of Israel in Egypt and their deliverance out of Egypt (*v.* 23–38). V. The care he took of them in the wilderness and their settlement in Canaan (*v.* 39–45). In singing this we must give to God the glory of his wisdom and power, his goodness and faithfulness, must look upon ourselves as concerned in the affairs of the Old-Testament church, both because to it were committed the oracles of God, which are our treasure, and because out of it Christ arose, and these things happened to it for ensamples.

Verses 1–7

Our devotion is here warmly excited; and we are stirred up, that we may stir up ourselves to praise God. Observe,

I. The duties to which we are here called, and they are many, but the tendency of them all is to give unto God the glory due unto his name. 1. We must *give thanks to him,* as one who has always been our bountiful benefactor and requires only that we give him thanks for his favours — poor returns for rich receivings. 2. *Call upon his name,* as one whom you depend upon for further favours. Praying for further mercies is accepted as an acknowledgment of former mercies. *Because he has inclined his ear unto me, therefore will I call upon him.* 3. *Make known his deeds* (*v.* 1), that others may join with you in praising him. *Talk of all his wondrous works* (*v.* 2), as we talk of things that we are full of, and much affected with, and desire to fill others with. God's wondrous works ought to be the subject of our familiar discourses with our families and friends, and we should talk of them *as we sit in the house and as we go by the way* (Deu. 6:7), not merely for entertainment, but for the exciting of devotion and the encouraging of our own and others' faith and hope in God. Even sacred things may be the matter of common talk, provided it be with due reverence. 4. *Sing psalms* to God's honour, as those that rejoice in him, and desire to testify that joy for the encouragement of others and to transmit it to posterity, as memorable things anciently were handed down by songs, when writing was scarce. 5. *Glory in his holy name;* let those that are disposed to glory not boast of their own accomplishments and achievements, but of their acquaintance with God and their relation to him, Jer. 9:23, 24. *Praise you his holy name,* so some; but it comes all to one, for in glorying in him we give glory to him. 6. *Seek him;* place your happiness in him, and then pursue that happiness in all the ways that he has appointed. *Seek the Lord and his strength,* that is, the *ark of his strength;* seek him in the sanctuary, in the way wherein he has appointed us to seek him. *Seek his strength,* that is, his grace, the strength of his Spirit to work in you that which is good, which we cannot do but by strength derived from him, for which he will be enquired of. *Seek the Lord and be strengthened;* so divers ancient versions read it. Those that would be *strengthened in the inward man* must fetch in strength from God by faith and prayer. Seek *his strength,* and then *seek his face;* for by his strength, we hope to prevail with him for his favour, as Jacob did, Hos. 12:3. *"Seek his face evermore;* seek to have his favour to eternity, and therefore continue seeking it to the end of the time of your probation. Seek it while you live in this world, and you shall have it while you live in the other world, and even there shall be for ever seeking it in an infinite progression, and yet be for ever satisfied in it." 7. *Let the hearts of those rejoice that do seek him* (*v.* 3); for they have chosen well, are well fixed, and well employed, and they may be sure that their labour will not be in vain, for he will not only be found, but he will be found the *rewarder of those that diligently seek him.* If those have reason to rejoice that *seek the Lord,* much more those that have *found him.*

II. Some arguments to quicken us to these duties. 1. "Consider both what he has said and what he has done to engage us for ever to him. You will see yourselves under all possible obligations to give thanks to him, and call upon his name, if you remember the wonders which should make deep and durable impressions upon you, — the wonders of his providence which he has *wrought for you* and those who are gone before you, the *marvellous works that he has done,* which will be had in everlasting remembrance with the thoughtful and with the grateful, — the wonders of his law, which he has written to you, and entrusted you with, *the judgments of his mouth,* as well as the judgments of his hand," *v.* 5. 2. "Consider the relation you stand in to him (*v.* 6): *You are the seed of Abraham his servant;* you are born in his house, and being thereby entitled to the privilege of his servants, protection and provision, you are also bound to do the duty of servants, to attend your Master, consult his honour, obey his commands, and do what you can to advance his interests. You are *the children of Jacob his chosen,* and are *chosen* and *beloved* for the fathers' sake, and therefore ought to tread in the steps of those whose honours you inherit. You are the children of godly parents; do no degenerate. You are God's church upon earth, and, if you do not praise him, who should?" 3. Consider your interest in him: *He is the Lord our God, v.* 7. We depend upon him, are devoted to him, and from him our expectation is. *Should not a people seek unto their God* (Isa. 8:19) and praise their God? Dan. 5:4. He is *Jehovah our God.* He that is our God is self-existent and self-sufficient, has an irresistible power and incontestable sovereignty: *His judgments are in all the earth;* he governs the whole world in wisdom, and gives law to all nations, even to those that know him not. The earth is full of the proofs of his power.

Verses 8–24

We are here taught, in praising God, to look a great way back, and to give him the glory of what he did for his church in former ages, especially when it was in the founding and forming, which those in its latter ages enjoy the benefit of and therefore should give thanks for. Doubtless we may fetch as proper matter for praise from the histories of the gospels, and the acts of the apostles, which relate the birth of the Christian church, as the psalmist here does from the histories of Genesis and Exodus, which relate the birth of the Jewish church; and our histories greatly outshine theirs. Two things are here made the subject of praise: —

I. God's promise to the patriarchs, that great promise that he would give to their seed the land of Canaan for an inheritance, which was a type of the promise of eternal life made in Christ to all believers. In all the marvellous works which God did for Israel *he remembered his covenant* (*v.* 8) and he will remember it *for ever;* it is *the word which he commanded to a thousand generations.* See here the power of the promise; it is the word which he commanded and which will take effect. See the perpetuity of the promise; it is commanded *to a thousand generations,* and the entail of it shall not be cut off. In the parallel place it is expressed as our duty (1 Chr. 16:15), *Be you mindful always of his covenant.* God will not forget it and therefore we must not. The promise is here called a *covenant,* because there was something required on man's part as the condition of the promise. Observe, 1. The persons with whom this covenant was made — with Abraham, Isaac, and Jacob, grandfather, father, and son, all eminent believers, Heb. 11:8, 9. 2. The ratifications of the covenant; it was made sure by all that is sacred. Is that sure which is sworn to? It is his oath to Isaac and to Abraham. See to whom God *swore by himself,* Heb. 6:13, 14. Is that sure which has passed *into a law?* He *confirmed the same for a law,* a law never to be repealed. Is that sure which is reduced to a mutual contract and stipulation? This is confirmed *for an everlasting covenant,* inviolable. 3. The covenant itself: *Unto thee will I give the land of Canaan, v.* 11. The patriarchs had a right to it, not by providence, but by promise; and their seed should be put in possession of it, not by the common ways of settling nations, but by miracles; God will give it to them himself, as it were with his own hand; it shall be given to them as their lot which God assigns them and measures out to them, as *the lot of their inheritance,* a sure title, by virtue of their birth; it shall come to them by descent, not by purchase, by the favour of God, and not any merit of their own. Heaven is the inheritance we have obtained, Eph. 1:11. And *this is the prom-*

ise which God has promised us (as Canaan was the promise he promised them), *even eternal life*, 1 Jn. 2:25; Tit. 1:2.

II. His providences concerning the patriarchs while they were waiting for the accomplishment of this promise, which represent to us the care God takes of his people in this world, while they are yet on this side the heavenly Canaan; for these things *happened unto them for examples* and encouragements to all the heirs of promise, that life by faith as they did.

1. They were wonderfully protected and sheltered, and (as the Jewish masters express it) *gathered under the wings of the divine Majesty*. This is accounted for, *v.* 12–15. Here we may observe,

(1.) How they were exposed to injuries from men. To the three renowned patriarchs, Abraham, and Isaac, and Jacob, God's promises were very rich; again and again he told them he would be their God; but his performances in this world were so little proportionable that, if he had not *prepared for them a city* in the other world, he would have been *ashamed to be called their God* (see Heb. 11:16), because he was always generous; and yet even in this world he was not wanting to them, but that he might appear, to do uncommon things for them, he exercised them with uncommon trials. [1.] They were few, very few. Abraham was called alone (Isa. 51:2); he had but two sons, and one of them he cast out; Isaac had but two, and one of them was forced for many years to flee from his country; Jacob had more, but some of them, instead of being a defence to him, exposed him, when (as he himself pleads, Gen. 34:30) he was but few in number, and therefore might easily be destroyed by the natives, he and his house. God's chosen are but a little flock, few, very few, and yet upheld. [2.] They were strangers, and therefore were the most likely to be abused and to meet with strange usage, and the less able to help themselves. Their religion made them to be looked upon as strangers (1 Pt. 4:4) and to be hooted at as *speckled birds*, Jer. 12:9. Though the whole land was theirs by promise, yet they were so far from producing and pleading their grant that they *confessed themselves strangers in it*, Heb. 11:13. [3.] They were unsettled (*v.* 13): *They went from one nation to another*, from one part of that land to another (for it was then in the holding and occupation of divers nations, Gen. 12:8; 13:3, 18); nay, *from one kingdom to another people*, from Canaan to Egypt, from Egypt to the land of the Philistines, which could not but weaken and expose them; yet they were forced to it by famine. Note, Though frequent removals are neither desirable nor commendable, yet sometimes there is a just and necessary occasion for them, and they may be the lot of some of the best men.

(2.) How they were guarded by the special providence of God, the wisdom and power of which were the more magnified by their being so many ways exposed, *v.* 14, 15. They were not able to help themselves and yet, [1.] No men were suffered to wrong them, but even those that hated them, and would gladly have done them a mischief, had their hands tied, and could not do what they would. This may refer to Gen. 35:5, where we find that *the terror of God* (an unaccountable restraint) *was upon the cities that were round about them*, so that, though provoked, *they did not pursue after the sons of Jacob*. [2.] Even crowned heads, that did offer to wrong them, were not only checked and chidden for it, but controlled and baffled: *He reproved kings for their sakes* in dreams and visions, *saying, "Touch not my anointed;* it is at your peril if you do, nay, it shall not be in your power to do it; *do my prophets no harm."* Pharaoh king of Egypt was plagued (Gen. 12:17) and Abimelech king of Gerar was sharply rebuked (Gen. 20:6) for doing wrong to Abraham. Note, *First*, Even kings themselves are liable to God's rebukes if they do wrong. *Secondly*, God's prophets are his anointed, for they have the unction *of the Spirit*, that *oil of gladness*, 1 Jn. 2:27. *Thirdly*, Those that offer to touch God's prophets, with design to harm them, may expect to hear of it one way or other. God is jealous for his prophets; whoso *touches them touches the apple of his eye*. *Fourthly*, Even those that *touch the prophets*, nay that *kill the prophets* (as many did), cannot *do them any harm*, any real harm. *Lastly*, God's anointed prophets are dearer to him than anointed kings themselves. Jeroboam's hand was withered when it was stretched out against a prophet.

2. They were wonderfully provided for and supplied.

And here also, (1.) They were reduced to great extremity. Even in Canaan, the land of promise, *he called for a famine*, *v.* 16. Note, All judgments are at God's call, and no place is exempt from their visitation and jurisdiction when God sends them forth with commission. To try the faith of the patriarchs, God *broke the whole staff of bread*, even in that good land, that they might plainly see God designed them a better country than that was. (2.) God graciously took care for their relief. It was in obedience to his precept, and in dependence upon his promise, that they were now sojourners in Canaan, and therefore he could not in honour suffer any evil to befal them or any good thing to be wanting to them. As he restrained one Pharaoh from doing them wrong, so he raised up another to do them a kindness, by preferring and entrusting Joseph, of whose story we have here an abstract. He was to be the shepherd and stone of Israel and to save that holy *seed alive*, Gen. 49:24; 50:20. In order to this, [1.] He was humbled, greatly humbled (*v.* 17, 18): *God sent a man before them, even Joseph*. Many years before the famine began, he was sent before them, to nourish them in the famine; so vast are the foresights and forecasts of Providence, and so long its reaches. But in what character did *he* go to Egypt who was to provide for the reception of the church there? He went not in quality of an ambassador, no, nor so much as a factor or commissary; but *he was sold* thither *for a servant*, a slave for term of life, without any prospect of being ever set at liberty. This was low enough, and, one would think, set him far enough from any probability of being great. And yet he was brought lower; he was made a prisoner (*v.* 18): *His feet they hurt with fetters.* Being unjustly charged with a crime no less heinous than a rape upon his mistress, *the iron entered into his soul*, that is, was very painful to him; and the false accusation which was the cause of his imprisonment did in a special manner grieve him, and went to his heart; yet all this was the way to his preferment. [2.] He was exalted, highly exalted. He continued a prisoner, neither tried nor bailed, *until the time* appointed of God for his release (*v.* 19), when *his word came*, that is, his interpretations of the dreams came to pass, and the report thereof came to Pharaoh's ears by the chief butler. And then *the word of the Lord cleared him;* that is, the power God gave him to foretel things to come rolled away the reproach his mistress had loaded him with; for it could not be thought that God would give such a power to so bad a man as he was represented to be. *God's word tried him*, tried his faith and patience, and then it came in power to give command for his release. There is a time set when God's word will come for the comfort of all that trust in it, Hab. 2:3. *At the end it shall speak, and not lie.* God gave the word, and then *the king sent and loosed him;* for the king's heart is in the hand of the Lord. Pharaoh, finding him to be a favourite of Heaven, *First*, Discharged him from his imprisonment (*v.* 20): He *let him go free*. God has often, by wonderful turns of providence, pleaded the cause of oppressed innocency. *Secondly*, He advanced him to the highest posts of honour, *v.* 21, 22. He made him lord high chamberlain of his household (he *made him lord of his house);* nay, he put him into the office of lord-treasurer, *the ruler of all his substance*. He made him prime-minister of state, lord-president of his council, to *command his princes at his pleasure* and *teach them wisdom*, and general of his forces. *According to thy word shall all my people be ruled*, Gen. 41:40, 43, 44. He made him lord chief justice, to judge even his senators and punish those that were disobedient. In all this Joseph was designed to be, 1. A father to the church that then was, to save the house of Israel from perishing by the famine. He was made great, that he might *do good, especially* in *the household of faith*. 2. A figure of Christ that was to come, who, because he humbled himself and took upon him the form of a servant, was highly exalted, and has all judgment committed to him. Joseph being thus sent before, and put into a capacity of maintaining all his father's house, *Israel also came into Egypt* (*v.* 23), where he and all his were very honourably and comfortably provided for many years. Thus the New-Testament church has a place provided for her even in the wilderness, where *she is nourished for a time, times, and half a time*, Rev. 12:14. Verily she shall be fed.

3. They were wonderfully multiplied, according to the promise made to Abraham that his seed should be as the

sand of the sea for multitude, *v.* 24. In Egypt *he increased his people greatly;* they multiplied like fishes, so that in a little time they became *stronger than their enemies* and formidable to them. Pharaoh took notice of it. Ex. 1:9, *The children of Israel are more and mightier than we.* When God pleases *a little one shall become a thousand;* and God's promises, though they work slowly, work surely.

Verses 25–45

After the history of the patriarchs follows here the history of the people of Israel, when they grew into a nation.

I. Their affliction in Egypt (*v.* 25): *He turned the heart* of the Egyptians, who had protected them, *to hate* them and *deal subtilely* with them. God's goodness to his people exasperated the Egyptians against them; and, though their old antipathy to the Hebrews (which we read of Gen. 43:32; 46:34) was laid asleep for a while, yet now it revived with more violence than ever: formerly they hated them because they despised them, now because they feared them. They *dealt subtilely* with them, set all their politics on work to find out ways and means to weaken them, and waste them, and prevent their growth; they made their burdens heavy and their lives bitter, and slew their male children as soon as they were born. Malice is crafty to destroy: Satan has the serpent's subtlety, with his venom. It was God that turned the hearts of the Egyptians against them; for every creature is that to us that he makes it to be, a friend or an enemy. Though God is not the author of the sins of men, yet he serves his own purposes by them.

II. Their deliverance out of Egypt, that work of wonder, which, that it might never be forgotten, is put into the preface to the ten commandments. Observe,

1. The instruments employed in that deliverance (*v.* 26): *He sent Moses his servant* on this errand and joined Aaron in commission with him. Moses was designed to be their lawgiver and chief magistrate, Aaron to be their chief priest; and therefore, that they might respect them the more and submit to them the more cheerfully, God made use of them as their deliverers.

2. The means of accomplishing that deliverance; these were the plagues of Egypt. Moses and Aaron observed their orders, in summoning them just as God appointed them, and *they rebelled not against his word* (*v.* 28) as Jonah did, who, when he was sent to denounce God's judgments against Nineveh, went to Tarshish. Moses and Aaron were not moved, either with a foolish fear of Pharaoh's wrath or a foolish pity of Egypt's misery, to relax or retard any of the plagues which God ordered them to inflict on the Egyptians, but stretched forth their hand to inflict them as God appointed. Those that are instructed to execute judgment will find their remissness construed as a rebellion against God's word. The plagues of Egypt are here called God's *signs, and his wonders* (*v.* 27); they were not only proofs of his power, but tokens of his wrath, and to be looked upon with admiration and holy awe. *They showed the words of his signs* (so it is in the original), for every plague had an exposition going along with it; they were not, as the common works of creation and providence, silent signs, but speaking ones, and they spoke aloud. They are all or most of them here specified, though not in the order in which they were inflicted. (1.) The plague of darkness, *v.* 28. This was one of the last, though here mentioned first. God *sent darkness*, and, coming with commission, it came with efficacy; his command *made it dark. And then they* (that is, the people of Israel) *rebelled not against God's word*, namely, a command which some think was given them to circumcise all among them that had not been circumcised, in doing which the three days' darkness would be a protection to them. The old translation follows the Septuagint, and reads it, *They were not obedient to his word*, which may be applied to Pharaoh and the Egyptians, who, notwithstanding the terror of this plague, *would not let the people go;* but there is no ground for it in the Hebrew. (2.) The turning of the river Nilus (which they idolized) *into blood*, and all their other waters, which *slew their fish* (*v.* 29), and so they were deprived, not only of their drink, but of the daintiest of their meat, Num. 11:5. (3.) The frogs, shoals of which their land brought forth, which poured in upon them, not only in such numbers, but with such fury, that they could not keep them out of the *chambers of their kings* and great men, whose

hearts had been full of vermin, more nauseous and more noxious — contempt of, and enmity to, both God and his Israel. (4.) Flies of divers sorts swarmed in their air, and lice in their clothes, *v.* 31; Ex. 8:17, 24. Note, God can make use of the meanest, and weakest, and most despicable animals, for the punishing and humbling of proud oppressors, to whom the impotency of the instrument cannot but be a great mortification, as well as an undeniable conviction of the divine omnipotence. (5.) Hail-stones shattered their trees, even the strongest timber-trees in *their coasts,* and killed their vines, and their other fruit-trees, *v.* 32, 33. Instead of rain to cherish their trees, he gave them hail to crush them, and with it thunder and lightning, to such a degree that the *fire ran along upon the ground,* as if it had been a stream of kindled brimstone, Ex. 9:23. (6.) *Locusts and caterpillars* destroyed *all the* herbs which were made for the service of man and ate the bread out of their mouths, *v.* 34, 35. See what variety of judgments God has, wherewith to plague proud oppressors, that will not let his people go. God did not bring the same plague twice, but, when there was occasion for another, it was still a new one; for he has many arrows in his quiver. Locusts and caterpillars are God's armies; and, how weak soever they are singly, he can raise such numbers of them as to make them formidable, Joel 1:4, 6. (7.) Having mentioned all the plagues but those of the murrain and boils, he concludes with that which gave the conquering stroke, and that was the death of *the first-born, v.* 36. In the dead of the night the joys and hopes of their families, *the chief of their strength* and flower of their land, were all struck dead by the destroying angel. They would not release God's first-born, and therefore God seized theirs by way of reprisal, and thereby forced them to dismiss his too, when it was too late to retrieve their own; for *when God judges he will overcome,* and those will certainly sit down losers at last that contend with him.

3. The mercies that accompanied this deliverance. In their bondage, (1.) They had been impoverished, and yet they came out rich and wealthy. God not only brought them forth, but he *brought them forth with silver and gold, v.* 37. God empowered them to ask and collect the contributions of their neighbours (which were indeed but part of payment for the service they had done them) and inclined the Egyptians to furnish them with what they asked. Their wealth was his, and therefore he might, their hearts were in his hand, and therefore he could, give it to the Israelites. (2.) Their lives had been made bitter to them, and their bodies and spirits broken by their bondage; and yet, when God brought them forth, *there was not one feeble person,* none sick, none so much as sickly, *among their tribes.* They went out that very night that the plague swept away all the first-born of Egypt, and yet they went out all in good health, and brought not with them any of the diseases of Egypt. Surely never was the like, that among so many thousands there was not one sick! So false was the representation which the enemies of the Jews, in after-ages, gave of this matter, that they were all sick of a leprosy, or some loathsome disease, and that therefore the Egyptians thrust them out of their land. (3.) They had been trampled upon and insulted over; and yet they were brought out with honour (*v.* 38): *Egypt was glad when they departed;* for God had so wonderfully owned them, and pleaded their cause, that *the fear of Israel fell upon them,* and they owned themselves baffled and overcome. God can and will make his church *a burdensome stone* to all that *heave at it* and seek to displace it, so that those shall think themselves happy that get out of its way, Zec. 12:3. *When God judges, he will overcome.* (4.) They had spent their days in sorrow and in sighing, by reason of their bondage; but now he brought them forth *with joy and gladness, v.* 43. When Egypt's cry for grief was loud, their first-born being all slain, Israel's shouts for joy were as loud, both when they looked back upon the land of slavery out of which they were rescued and when they looked forward to the pleasant land to which they were hastening. God now put a new song into their mouth.

4. The special care God took of them in the wilderness. (1.) For their shelter. Besides the canopy of heaven, he provided them another heavenly canopy: He *spread a cloud for a covering* (*v.* 39), which was to them not only a screen and umbrella, but a cloth of state. A cloud was often God's pavilion (Ps. 18:11) and now it was Israel's; for they also were his hidden ones. (2.) For their guidance and refreshment in the dark. He appointed a pillar of *fire to give light in the night,* that they might never be at a loss. Note, God graciously provides against all the grievances of his people, and furnishes them with convenient succours for every condition, for day and night, till they come to heaven, where it will be all day to eternity. (3.) He fed them both with necessaries and dainties. Sometimes he furnished their tables with wild fowl (*v.* 40): *The people asked, and he brought quails;* and, when they were not thus feasted, yet they were abundantly satisfied *with the bread of heaven.* Those are curious and covetous indeed who will not be so satisfied. Man did eat angels' food, and that constantly and on free-cost. And, as every bit they ate had miracle in it, so had every drop they drank: *He opened the rock, and the waters gushed out, v.* 41. Common providence fetches waters from heaven, and bread out of the earth; but for Israel the divine power brings bread from the clouds and water from the rocks: so far is the God of nature from being tied to the laws and courses of nature. The water did not only gush out once, but it ran *like a river,* plentifully and constantly, and attended their camp in all their removes; hence they are said to have the *rock follow them* (1 Co. 10:4), and, which increased the miracle, this *river of God* (so it might be truly called) *ran in dry places,* and yet was not drunk in and lost, as one would have expected it to be, by the sands of the desert of Arabia. To this that promise alludes, *I will give rivers in the desert, to give drink to my chosen,* Isa. 43:19, 20.

5. Their entrance, at length, into Canaan (*v.* 44): *He gave them the lands of the heathen,* put them in possession of that which they had long been put in hopes of; and what the Canaanites had taken pains for God's Israel had the enjoyment of: *They inherited the labour of the people;* and the wealth of the sinner is laid up for the just. The Egyptians had long inherited their labours, and now they inherited the labours of the Canaanites. Thus sometimes one enemy of the church is made to pay another's scores.

6. The reasons why God did all this for them. (1.) Because he would himself perform the promises of the word, *v.* 42. They were unworthy and unthankful, yet he did those great things in their favour *because he remembered the word of his holiness* (that is, his covenant) *with Abraham his servant,* and he would not suffer one iota or tittle of that to fall to the ground. See Deu. 7:8. (2.) Because he would have them to perform the precepts of the word, to bind them to which was the greatest kindness he could put upon them. He put them in possession of Canaan, not that they might live in plenty and pleasure, in ease and honour, and might make a figure among the nations, but *that they might observe his statutes and keep his laws,* — that, being formed into a people, they might be under God's immediate government, and revealed religion might be the basis of their national constitution, — that, having a good land given them, they might out of the profits of it bring sacrifices to God's altar, — and that, God having thus done them good, they might the more cheerfully receive his law, concluding that also designed for their good, and might be sensible of their obligations in gratitude to live in obedience to him. We are *therefore* made, maintained, and redeemed, that we may live in obedience to the will of God; and the hallelujah with which the psalm concludes may be taken both as a thankful acknowledgment of God's favours and as a cheerful concurrence with this great intention of them. Has God done so much for us, and yet does he expect so little from us? *Praise you the Lord.*

PSALM 106

We must give glory to God by making confession, not only of his goodness but our own badness, which serve as foils to each other. Our badness makes his goodness appear the more illustrious, as his goodness makes our badness the more heinous and scandalous. The foregoing psalm was a history of God's goodness to Israel; this is a history of their rebellions and provocations, and yet it begins and ends with Hallelujah; for even sorrow for sin must not put us out of tune for praising God. Some think it was penned at the time of the captivity in Babylon and the dispersion of the Jewish nation thereupon, because of that prayer in the close (*v.* 47). I rather think it was penned by David at the same time with the foregoing psalm, because we find the first verse and the last two verses in that psalm which David delivered to Asaph, at the bringing up of the ark to the place he had prepared for it (1 Chr. 16:34-36), "Gather us from among the heathen;" for we may suppose that in Saul's time there was a great dispersion of pious Israelites, when David was forced to wander. In this psalm we have, I. The preface to the narrative, speaking honour to God (*v.* 1, 2), comfort to the saints (*v.* 3), and the desire of the faithful towards God's favour (*v.* 4, 5). II. The narrative itself of the sins of Israel, aggravated by the great things God did for them, an account of which is intermixed. Their provocations at the Red Sea (*v.* 6–12), lusting (*v.* 13–15), mutinying (*v.* 16–18), worshipping the golden calf (*v.* 19–23), murmuring (*v.* 24–27), joining themselves to Baal-peor (*v.* 28–31), quarrelling with Moses (*v.* 32, 33), incorporating themselves with the nations of Canaan (*v.* 34–39). To this is added an account how God had rebuked them for their sins, and yet saved them from ruin (*v.* 40–46). III. The conclusion of the psalm with prayer and praise (*v.* 47, 48). It may be of use to us to sing this psalm, that, being put in mind by it of our sins, the sins of our land, and the sins of our fathers, we may be humbled before God and yet not despair of mercy, which even rebellious Israel often found with God.

Verses 1–5

We are here taught,

I. To bless God (*v.* 1, 2): *Praise you the Lord,* that is, 1. Give him thanks for his goodness, the manifestation of it to us, and the many instances of it. *He is good* and *his mercy endures for ever;* let us therefore own our obligations to him and make him a return of our best affections and services. 2. Give him the glory of his greatness, his *mighty acts,* proofs of his almighty power, wherein he has done great things, and such as would be opposed. *Who can utter these?* Who is worthy to do it? Who is able to do it? They are so many that they cannot be numbered, so mysterious that they cannot be described; when we have said the most we can of the mighty acts of the Lord, the one half is not told; still there is more to be said; it is a subject that cannot be exhausted. We must *show forth his praise;* we may show forth some of it, but *who can show forth all?* Not the angels themselves. This will not excuse us in not doing what we can, but should quicken us to do all we can.

II. To bless the people of God, to call and account them happy (*v.* 3): *Those that keep judgment are blessed,* for they are fit to be employed in praising God. God's people are those whose principles are sound — *They keep judgment* (they adhere to the rules of wisdom and religion, and their practices are agreeable); they *do righteousness,* are just to God and to all men, and herein they are steady and constant; they do it *at all times,* in all manner of conversation, at every turn, in every instance, and herein persevering to the end.

III. To bless ourselves in the favour of God, to place our happiness in it, and to seek it, accordingly, with all seriousness, as the psalmist here, *v.* 4, 5. 1. He has an eye to the lovingkindness of God, as the fountain of all happiness: *"Remember me, O Lord!* to give me that mercy and grace which I stand in need of, *with the favour which thou bearest to thy people."* As there are a people in the world who are in a peculiar manner God's people, so there is a peculiar favour which God bears to that people, which all gracious souls desire an interest in; and we need desire no more to make us happy. 2. He has an eye to the salvation of God, the great salvation, that of the soul, as the foundation of happiness: *O visit me with thy salvation.* "Afford me (says Dr. Hammond) that pardon and that grace which I stand in need of, and can hope for from none but thee." Let that salvation be my portion for ever, and the pledges of it my present comfort. 3. He has an eye to the blessedness of the righteous, as that which includes all good (*v.* 5): *"That I may see the good of thy chosen* and be as happy as the saints are; and happier I do not desire to be." God's people are here called his *chosen,* his *nation,* his *inheritance;* for he has set them apart for himself, incorporated them under his own government, is served by them and glorified in them. The chosen people of God have a good which is peculiar to them, which is the matter both of their gladness and of their glorying, which is their pleasure, and their praise. God's people have reason to be a cheerful people, and to boast in their God all the day long; and those who have that gladness, that glory, need not envy any of the children of men their pleasure or pride. The gladness of God's nation, and the glory of his inheritance, are enough to satisfy any man; for they have everlasting joy and glory at the end of them.

Verses 6–12

Here begins a penitential confession of sin, which was in a special manner seasonable now that the church was in distress; for thus we must justify God in all that he brings upon us, acknowledging that *therefore* he has done right, because *we have done wickedly;* and the remembrance of former sins, notwithstanding which God did not cast off his people, is an encouragement to us to hope that, though we are justly corrected for our sins, yet we shall not be utterly abandoned.

I. God's afflicted people here own themselves guilty before God (*v.* 6): "*We have sinned with our fathers,* that is, like our fathers, after the similitude of their transgression. We have added to the stock of hereditary guilt, and filled up the measure of our fathers' iniquity, *to augment yet the fierce anger of the Lord,*" Num. 32:14; Mt. 23:32. And see how they lay a load upon themselves, as becomes penitents: "*We have committed iniquity,* that which is in its own nature sinful, and *we have done wickedly;* we have sinned with a high hand presumptuously." Or this is a confession, not only of their imitation of, but their interest in, their fathers' sins: *We have sinned with our fathers,* for we were in their loins and we *bear their iniquity,* Lam. 5:7.

II. They bewail the sins of their fathers when they were first formed into a people, which, since children often smart for, they are concerned to sorrow for, even further than to the third and fourth generation. Even we now ought to take occasion from the history of Israel's rebellions to lament the depravity and perverseness of man's nature and its unaptness to be amended by the most probable means. Observe here,

1. The strange stupidity of Israel in the midst of the favours God bestowed upon them (*v.* 7): *They understood not thy wonders in Egypt.* They saw them, but they did not rightly apprehend the meaning and design of them. *Blessed are those that have not seen, and yet have* understood. They thought the plagues of Egypt were intended for their deliverance, whereas they were intended also for their instruction and conviction, not only to force them out of their Egyptian slavery, but to cure them of their inclination to Egyptian idolatry, by evidencing the sovereign power and dominion of the God of Israel, above all gods, and his particular concern for them. We lose the benefit of providences for want of understanding them. And, as their understandings were dull, so their memories were treacherous; though one would think such astonishing events should never have been forgotten, yet they remembered them not, at least *they remembered not the multitude of* God's *mercies* in them. *Therefore* God is distrusted because his favours are not remembered.

2. Their perverseness arising from this stupidity: *They provoked him at the sea, even at the Red Sea.* The provocation was, despair of deliverance (because the danger was great) and wishing they had been left in Egypt still, Ex. 14:11, 12. Quarrelling with God's providence, and questioning his power, goodness, and faithfulness, are as great provocations to him as any whatsoever. The place aggravated the crime; it was *at the sea, at the Red Sea,* when they had newly come out of Egypt and the wonders God had wrought for them were fresh in their minds; yet they reproach him, as if all that power had no mercy in it, but he had brought them out of Egypt on purpose to *kill them in the wilderness.* They never lay at God's mercy so immediately as in their passage through the Red Sea, yet there they affront it, and provoke his wrath.

3. The great salvation God wrought for them notwithstanding their provocations, *v.* 8–11. (1.) He forced a passage for them through the sea: *He rebuked the Red Sea* for standing in their way and retarding their march, *and it was dried up* immediately; as, in the creation, *at God's rebuke the waters fled,* Ps. 104:7. Nay, he not only prepared them a way, but, by the pillar of cloud and fire, he *led them* into the sea, and, by the conduct of Moses, led them through it as readily as *through the wilderness.* He encouraged them to take those steps, and subdued their fears, when those were their most dangerous and threatening enemies. See Isa. 63:12–14. (2.) He interposed between them and their pursuers, and prevented them from cutting them off, as they designed. The Israelites were all on foot, and the Egyptians had all of them chariots and horses, with which they were likely to overtake them quickly, but God *saved them from the hand of him that hated them,* namely, Pharaoh, who never loved them, but now hated them the more for the plagues he had suffered on their account. *From the hand of* his *enemy,* who was just ready to seize them, *God redeemed them* (*v.* 10), interposing himself, as it were, in the pillar of fire, between the persecuted and the persecutors. (3.) To complete the mercy, and turn the deliverance into a victory, the Red Sea, which was a lane to them, was a grave to the Egyptians (*v.* 11): *The waters covered their enemies,* so as to slay them, but not so as to conceal their shame; for, the next tide, they were thrown up dead upon the shore, Ex. 14:30. *There was not one of them left* alive, to bring tidings of what had become of the rest. And why did God do this for them? Nay, why did he not cover them, as he did their enemies, for their unbelief and murmuring? He tells us (*v.* 8): it was *for his name's sake.* Though they did not deserve this favour, he designed it; and their undeservings should not alter his designs, nor break his measures, nor make him withdraw his promise, or fail in the performance of it. He did this for his own glory, *that he might make his mighty power to be known,* not only in dividing the sea, but in doing it notwithstanding their provocations. Moses prays (Num. 14:17, 19), *Let the power of my Lord be great and pardon the iniquity of this people.* The power of the God of grace in pardoning sin and sparing sinners is as much to be admired as the power of the God of nature in dividing the waters.

4. The good impression this made upon them for the present (*v.* 12): *Then believed they his words,* and acknowledged that God was with them of a truth, and had, in mercy to them, brought them out of Egypt, and not with any design to slay them in the wilderness; then *they feared the Lord and his servant Moses,* Ex. 14:31. Then *they sang his praise,* in that song of Moses penned on this great occasion, Ex. 15:1. See in what a gracious and merciful way God sometimes silences the unbelief of his people, and turns their fears into praises; and so it is written, *Those that erred in spirit shall come to understanding,* and *those that murmured shall learn doctrine,* Isa. 29:24.

Verses 13–33

This is an abridgment of the history of Israel's provocations in the wilderness, and of the wrath of God against them for those provocations: and this abridgment is abridged by the apostle, with application to us Christians (1 Co. 10:5, etc.); for these things were *written for our admonition,* that we sin not like them, lest we suffer like them.

I. The cause of their sin was disregard to the works and word of God, *v.* 13. 1. They minded not what he had done for them: *They soon forgot his works,* and lost the impressions they had made upon them. Those that do not improve God's mercies to them, nor endeavour in some measure to render according to the benefit done unto them, do indeed forget them. This people soon forgot them (God took notice of this, Ex. 32:8, *They have turned aside quickly): They made haste, they forgot his works* (so it is in the margin), which some make to be two separate instances of their sin. *They made haste;* their expectations anticipated God's promises; they expected to be in Canaan shortly, and because they were not they questioned whether they should ever be there and quarrelled with all the difficulties they met with in their way; whereas *he that believeth does not make haste,* Isa. 28:16. And, withal, *they forgot his works,* which were the undeniable evidences of his wisdom, power, and goodness, and denied the conclusion as confidently as if they had never seen the premises proved. This is mentioned again (*v.* 21, 22): *They forgot God their Saviour;* that is, they forgot that he had been their Saviour. Those that forget the works of God forget God himself, who makes himself known by his works. They forgot what was done but a few days before, which we may suppose they could not but talk of, even then, when, because they did not make a good use of it, they are said to forget it: it was what God did for them *in Egypt, in the land of Ham,* and *by the Red Sea,* things which we at this distance cannot, or should not, be unmindful of. They are called *great things* (for, though the great God does nothing mean, yet he does some things that are in a special manner great), *wondrous works,* out of the common road of Providence, therefore observable, therefore memorable, and *terrible things,* awful to them, and dreadful to their enemies, and yet soon forgotten. Even miracles that were seen passed away with them as tales that are told. 2. They minded not what God had said to them nor would they depend upon it: *They waited not for his counsel,* did not attend his word, though they had Moses to be his mouth to them; they took up resolves about which they did not consult him and made demands without calling upon him. They would be in Canaan directly, and had not patience to tarry God's time. The delay was intolerable, and therefore the difficulties were looked upon as insuperable. This is explained (*v.* 24): *They believed not his word,* his promise that he would make them masters of Canaan; and (*v.* 25), *They hearkened not to the voice of the Lord,* who gave them counsel which they would not wait for, not only by Moses and Aaron, but by Caleb and Joshua, Num. 14:6, 7, etc. Those that will not wait for God's counsel shall justly be given up to their own hearts' lusts, to walk in their own counsels.

II. Many of their sins are here mentioned, together with the tokens of God's displeasure which they fell under for those sins.

1. They would have flesh, and yet would not believe that God could give it to them (*v.* 14): *They lusted a lust* (so the word is) *in the wilderness;* there, where they had bread enough and to spare, yet nothing would serve them but they must have flesh to eat. They were now purely at God's finding, being supported entirely by miracles, so that this was a reflection upon the wisdom and goodness of their Creator. They were also, in all probability, within a step of Canaan, yet had not patience to stay for dainties till they came thither. They had flocks and herds of their own, but they will not kill them; God must give them flesh as he gave them bread, or they will never give him credit, or their good word. They did not only wish for flesh, *but* they *lusted exceedingly* after it. A desire, even of lawful things, when it is inordinate and violent, becomes sinful; and therefore this is called *lusting after evil things* (1 Co. 10:6), though the quails, as God's gift, were good things, and were so spoken of, Ps. 105:40. Yet this was not all: *They tempted God in the desert,* where they had had such experience of his goodness and power, and questioned whether he could and would gratify them herein. See Ps. 78:19, 20. Now how did God show his displeasure against them for this. We are told how (*v.* 15): *He gave them their request,* but gave it them in anger, and with a curse, for he *sent leanness into their soul;* he filled them with uneasiness of mind, and terror of conscience, and a self-reproach, occasioned by their bodies being sick with the surfeit, such as sometimes drunkards experience after a great debauch. Or this is put for that great plague with which the Lord smote them, *while the flesh was yet between their teeth,* as we read, Num. 11:33. It was the consumption of the life. Note, (1.) What is asked in passion is often given in wrath. (2.) Many that fare deliciously every day, and whose bodies are healthful and fat, have, at the same time, leanness in their souls, no love to God, no thankfulness, no appetite to the bread of life, and then the soul must needs be lean. Those wretchedly forget themselves that feast their bodies and starve their souls. *Then* God gives the good things of this life in love, when with them he gives grace to glorify him in the use of them; for then *the soul delights itself in fatness,* Isa. 55:2.

2. They quarrelled with the government which God had set over them both in church and state (*v.* 16): *They envied Moses* his authority *in the camp,* as generalissimo of the armies of Israel and chief justice in all their courts; they envied *Aaron* his power, as *saint of the Lord,* consecrated to the office of high priest, and Korah would needs put in for the pontificate, while Dathan and Abiram, as princes of the tribe of Reuben, Jacob's eldest son, would claim to be chief magistrates, by the so-much-admired right of primogeniture. Note, Those are preparing ruin for themselves who envy those whom God has put honour upon and usurp the dignities they were never designed for. And justly will contempt be poured upon those who put contempt upon any of the saints of the Lord. How did God show his displeasure for this? We are told how, and it is enough to make us tremble (*v.* 17, 18); we have the story, Num. 16:32, 35. (1.) Those that flew in the face of the civil authority were punished by *the earth,* which *opened and swallowed them up,* as not fit to go upon God's ground, because they would not submit to God's government. (2.) Those that would usurp the ecclesiastical authority in things pertaining to God suffered the vengeance of heaven, for *fire came out from the Lord and consumed them,* and the pretending sacrificers were themselves sacrificed to divine justice. *The flame burnt up the wicked;* for though they vied with

Aaron, the saint of the Lord, for holiness (Num. 16:3, 5), yet God adjudged them wicked, and as such cut them off, as in due time he will destroy the man of sin, that wicked one, notwithstanding his proud pretensions to holiness.

3. They made and worshipped the golden calf, and this in Horeb, where the law was given, and where God had expressly said, *Thou shalt* neither *make any graven image* nor *bow down* to it; they did both: *They made a calf and worshipped* it, *v.* 19.

(1.) Herein they bade defiance to, and put an affront upon, the two great lights which God has made to rule the moral world: — [1.] That of human reason; for *they changed their glory,* their God, at least the manifestation of him, which always had been in a cloud (either a dark cloud or a bright one), without any manner of visible similitude, *into the similitude of* Apis, one of the Egyptian idols, *an ox that eateth grass,* than which nothing could be more grossly and scandalously absurd, *v.* 20. Idolaters are perfectly besotted, and put the greatest disparagement possible both upon God, in representing him by the image of a beast, and upon themselves, in worshipping it when they have so done. That which is here said to be the changing of their glory is explained by St. Paul (Rom. 1:23) to be the *changing of the glory of the incorruptible God.* [2.] That of divine revelation, which was afforded to them, not only in the words God spoke to them, but in the works he wrought for them, *wondrous works,* which declared aloud that the Lord Jehovah is the only true and living God and is alone to be worshipped, *v.* 21, 22.

(2.) For this God showed his displeasure by declaring the decree that he would cut them off from being a people, as they had, as far as lay in their power, in effect cut him off from being a God; he *spoke of destroying them* (*v.* 23), and certainly he would have done it if *Moses, his chosen, had not stood before him in the breach* (*v.* 23), if he had not seasonably interposed to deal with God as an advocate about the breach or ruin God was about to devote them to and wonderfully prevailed to turn away his wrath. See here the mercy of God, and how easily his anger is turned away, even from a provoking people. See the power of prayer, and the interest which God's chosen have in heaven. See a type of Christ, God's *chosen,* his *elect, in whom his soul delights,* who *stood before him in the breach* to *turn away* his wrath from a provoking world, and ever lives, for this end, making intercession.

4. They gave credit to the report of the evil spies concerning the land of Canaan, in contradiction to the promise of God (*v.* 24): *They despised the pleasant land.* Canaan was a pleasant land, Deu. 8:7. They undervalued it when they thought it not worth venturing for, no, not under the guidance of God himself, and therefore were for making a captain and returning to Egypt again. They *believed not God's word* concerning it, but *murmured in their tents,* basely charging God with a design upon them in bringing them thither that they might become a prey to the Canaanites, Num. 14:2, 3. And, when they were reminded of God's power and promise, they were so far from hearkening to that voice of the Lord that they attempted to stone those who spoke to them, Num. 14:10. The heavenly Canaan is a pleasant land. A promise is left us of entering into it; but there are many that despise it, that neglect and refuse the offer of it, that prefer the wealth and pleasure of this world before it, and grudge the pains and hazards of this life to obtain that. This also was so displeasing to God that *he lifted up his hand against them,* in a way of threatening, *to destroy them in the wilderness;* nay, in a way of swearing, for he swore in his wrath that they should not enter into his rest (Ps. 95:11; Num. 14:28); nay, and he threatened that their children also should be *overthrown and scattered* (*v.* 26, 27), and the whole nation dispersed and disinherited; but Moses prevailed for mercy for their seed, that they might enter Canaan. Note, Those who despise God's favours, and particularly the pleasant land, forfeit his favours, and will be shut out for ever from the pleasant land.

5. They were guilty of a great sin in the matter of Peor; and this was the sin of the new generation, when they were within a step of Canaan (*v.* 28): *They joined themselves to Baal-peor,* and so were entangled both in idolatry and in adultery, in corporeal and in spiritual whoredom, Num. 25:1–3. Those that did often partake of the altar of the living God now *ate the sacrifices of the dead,* of the idols of Moab (that were dead images, or dead men canonized or deified), or sacrifices to the infernal deities on the behalf of their dead friends. *Thus they provoked God to anger with their inventions* (*v.* 29), in contempt of him and his institutions, his commands, and his threatenings. The iniquity of Peor was so great that, long after, it is said, *They were not cleansed from it,* Jos. 22:17. God testified his displeasure at this, (1.) By sending a plague among them, which in a little time swept away 24,000 of those impudent sinners. (2.) By stirring up Phinehas to use his power as a magistrate for the suppressing of the sin and checking the contagion of it. He stood up in his zeal for the Lord of hosts, and executed judgment upon Zimri and Cozbi, sinners of the first rank, genteel sinners; he put the law in execution upon them, and this was a service so pleasing to God that upon it *the plague was stayed, v.* 30. By this, and some other similar acts of public justice on that occasion (Num. 25:4, 5), the guilt ceased to be national, and the general controversy was let fall. When the proper officers did their duty God left it to them, and did not any longer keep the work in his own hands by the plague. Note, National justice prevents national judgments. But, Phinehas herein signalizing himself, a special mark of honour was put upon him, for what he did was *counted to him for righteousness to all generations* (*v.* 31), and, in recompence of it, the priesthood was entailed on his family. *He* shall make an atonement by offering up the sacrifices, who had so bravely made an atonement (so some read it, *v.* 30) by offering up the sinners. Note, It is the honour of saints to be zealous against sin.

6. They continued their murmurings to the very last of their wanderings; for in the fortieth year they *angered God at the waters of strife* (*v.* 32), which refers to that story, Num. 20:3–5. And that which aggravated it now was that *it went ill with Moses for their sakes;* for, though he was the meekest of all the men in the earth, yet their clamours at that time were so peevish and provoking that they put him into a passion, and, having now grown very old and off his guard, *he spoke unadvisedly with his lips* (*v.* 33), and not as became him on that occasion; for he said in a heat, *Hear now, you rebels, must we fetch water out of this rock for you?* This was Moses's infirmity, and is written for our admonition, that we may learn, when we are in the midst of provocation, to keep our mouth as with a bridle (Ps. 39:1–3), and to *take heed to our spirits,* that they admit not resentments too much; for, when the spirit is provoked, it is much ado, even for those that have a great deal of wisdom and grace, not to *speak unadvisedly.* But it is charged upon the people as their sin: *They provoked his spirit* with that with which they angered God himself. Note, We must answer not only for our own passions, but for the provocation which by them we give to the passions of others, especially of those who, if not greatly provoked, would be meek and quiet. God shows his displeasure against this sin of theirs by shutting Moses and Aaron out of Canaan for their misconduct upon this occasion, by which, (1.) God discovered his resentment of all such intemperate heats, even in the dearest of his servants. If he deals thus severely with Moses for one unadvised word, what does their sin deserve who have spoken so many presumptuous wicked words? *If this was done in the green tree, what shall be done in the dry?* (2.) God deprived them of the blessing of Moses's guidance and government at a time when they most needed it, so that his death was more a punishment to them than to himself. It is just with God to remove those relations from us that are blessings to us, when we are peevish and provoking to them and grieve their spirits.

Verses 34–48

Here, I. The narrative concludes with an account of Israel's conduct in Canaan, which was of a piece with that in the wilderness, and God's dealings with them, wherein, as all along, both justice and mercy appeared.

1. They were very provoking to God. The miracles and mercies which settled them in Canaan made no more deep and durable impressions upon them than those which fetched them out of Egypt; for by the time they were just settled in Canaan they corrupted themselves, and forsook God. Observe,

(1.) The steps of their apostasy. [1.] They spared the nations which God had doomed to destruction (*v.* 34); when they had got the good land God had promised them they had no zeal against the wicked inhabitants whom the Lord commanded them to extirpate, pretending pity; but so merciful is God that no man needs to be in any case more compassionate than he. [2.] When they spared them they promised themselves that, notwithstanding this, they would not join in any dangerous affinity with them. But the way of sin is down-hill; omissions make way for commissions; when they neglect to *destroy the heathen* the next news we hear is, They were *mingled among the heathen,* made leagues with them and contracted an intimacy with them, so that they *learned their works, v.* 35. That which is rotten will sooner corrupt that which is sound than be cured or made sound by it. [3.] When they mingled with them, and learned some of their works that seemed innocent diversions and entertainments, yet they thought they would never join with them in their worship; but by degrees they learned that too (*v.* 36): *They served their idols* in the same manner, and with the same rites, that they served them; and they became *a snare to them.* That sin drew on many more, and brought the judgments of God upon them, which they themselves could not but be sensible of and yet knew not how to recover themselves. [4.] When they joined with them in some of their idolatrous services, which they thought had least harm in them, they little thought that ever they should be guilty of that barbarous and inhuman piece of idolatry the sacrificing of their living children to their dead gods; but they came to that at last (*v.* 37, 38), in which Satan triumphed over his worshippers, and regaled himself in blood and slaughter: *They sacrificed their sons and daughters,* pieces of themselves, to devils, and added murder, the most unnatural murder, to their idolatry; one cannot think of it without horror. They *shed innocent blood,* the most innocent, for it was infant-blood, nay, it was the *blood of their sons and their daughters.* See the power of the spirit that works in the children of disobedience, and see his malice. The beginning of idolatry and superstition, like that of strife, is as the letting forth of water, and there is no villany which those that venture upon it can be sure they shall stop short of, for God justly *gives them up to a reprobate mind,* Rom. 1:28.

(2.) Their sin was, in part, their own punishment; for by it, [1.] They wronged their country: *The land was polluted with blood, v.* 38. That pleasant land, that holy land, was rendered uncomfortable to themselves, and unfit to receive those kind tokens of God's favour and presence in it which were designed to be its honour. [2.] They wronged their consciences (*v.* 39): *They went a whoring with their own inventions,* and so debauched their own minds, and were *defiled with their own works,* and rendered odious in the eyes of the holy God, and perhaps of their own consciences.

2. God brought his judgments upon them; and what else could be expected? For his name is Jealous, and he is a jealous God. (1.) He fell out with them for it, *v.* 40. He was angry with them: *The wrath of God,* that consuming fire, *was kindled against his people;* for from them he took it as more insulting and ungrateful than from the heathen that never knew him. Nay, he was sick of them: *He abhorred his own inheritance,* which once he had taken pleasure in; yet the change was not in him, but in them. This is the worst thing in sin, that it makes us loathsome to God; and the nearer any are to God in profession the more loathsome are they if they rebel against him, like a dunghill at our door. (2.) Their enemies then fell upon them, and, their defence having departed, made an easy prey of them (*v.* 41, 42): *He gave them into the hands of the heathen.* Observe here how the punishment answered to the sin: They *mingled with the heathen and learned their works;* from them they willingly took the infection of sin, and therefore God justly made use of them as the instruments of their correction. Sinners often see themselves ruined by those by whom they have suffered themselves to be debauched. Satan, who is a tempter, will be a tormentor. The heathen hated them. Apostates lose all the love on God's side, and get none on Satan's; and when those that *hated them ruled over them,* and they were brought into subjection under them, no marvel that they oppressed them and ruled them with rigour; and thus God made them know the difference between *his service and the service of the kings of the countries,* 2 Chr. 12:8. (3.) When God granted them some relief, yet they went on in their sins, and their trou-

bles also were continued, *v.* 43. This refers to the days of the Judges, when God often raised up deliverers and wrought deliverances for them, and yet they relapsed to idolatry and *provoked God with their counsel,* their idolatrous inventions, to deliver them up to some other oppressor, so that at last they *were brought* very *low for their iniquity.* Those that by sin disparage themselves, and will not by repentance humble themselves, are justly debased, and humbled, and brought low, by the judgments of God. (4.) At length they cried unto God, and God returned in favour to them, *v.* 44–46. They were chastened for their sins, but not destroyed, cast down, but not cast off. God appeared for them, [1.] As a God of mercy, who looked upon their grievances, *regarded their affliction, beheld when distress was upon them* (so some), who looked over their complaints, for he *heard their cry* with tender compassion (Ex. 3:7) and overlooked their provocations; for though he had said, and had reason to say it, that he would destroy them, yet he *repented, according to the multitude of his mercies,* and reversed the sentence. Though he is not a *man that he should repent,* so as to change his mind, yet he is a gracious God, who pities us, and changes his way. [2.] As a God of truth, who *remembered for them his covenant,* and made good every word that he had spoken; and therefore, bad as they were, he would not break with them, because he would not break his own promise. [3.] As a God of power, who has all hearts in his hand, and turns them which way soever he pleases. *He made them to be pitied even of those that carried them captives,* and hated them, and ruled them with rigour. He not only restrained the remainder of their enemies' wrath, that it should not utterly consume them, but he infused compassion even into their stony hearts, and made them relent, which was more than any art of man could have done with the utmost force of rhetoric. Note, God can change lions into lambs, and, *when a man's ways please the Lord,* will make even *his enemies to pity him* and *be at peace with him.* When God pities men shall. *Tranquillus Deus tranquillat omnia — A God at peace with us makes every thing at peace.*

II. The psalm concludes with prayer and praise. 1. Prayer for the completing of his people's deliverance. Even when the Lord brought back the captivity of his people still there was occasion to pray, *Lord, turn again our captivity* (Ps. 126:1, 4); so here (*v.* 47), *Save us, O Lord our God! and gather us from among the heathen.* We may suppose that many who were forced into foreign countries, in the times of the Judges (as Naomi was, Ruth 1:1), had not returned in the beginning of David's reign, Saul's time being discouraging, and therefore it was seasonable to pray, Lord, gather the dispersed Israelites *from among the heathen, to give thanks to thy holy name,* not only that they may have cause to give thanks and hearts to give thanks, that they may have opportunity to do it in the courts of the Lord's house, from which they were now banished, and so may *triumph in thy praise,* over those that had in scorn challenged them to *sing the Lord's song in a strange land.* 2. Praise for the beginning and progress of it (*v.* 48): *Blessed be the Lord God of Israel from everlasting to everlasting.* He is a blessed God from eternity, and will be so to eternity, and so let him be praised by all his worshippers. Let the priests say this, and then *let all the people say, Amen, Hallelujah,* in token of their cheerful concurrence in all these prayers, praises, and confessions. According to this rubric, or directory, we find that when this psalm (or at least the closing verses of it) was sung all the people said *Amen,* and praised the Lord by saying, *Hallelujah.* By these two comprehensive words it is very proper, in religious assemblies, to testify their joining with their ministers in the prayers and praises which, as their mouth, they offer up to God, according to his will, saying *Amen* to the prayers and *Hallelujah* to the praises.

PSALM 107

The psalmist, having in the two foregoing psalms celebrated the wisdom, power, and goodness of God, in his dealings with his church in particular, here observes some of the instances of his providential care of the children of men in general, especially in their distresses; for he is not only King of saints, but King of nations, not only the God of Israel, but the God of the whole earth, and a common Father to all mankind. Though this may especially refer to Israelites in their personal capacity, yet there were those who pertained not to the commonwealth of Israel and yet were worshippers of the true God; and even those who worshipped images had some knowledge of a supreme "Numen," to whom, when they were in earnest, they looked above all their false gods. And of these, when they prayed in their distresses, God took a particular care, I. The psalmist specifies some of the most common calamities of human life, and shows how God succours those that labour under them, in answer to their prayers. I. Banishment and dispersion (*v.* 2–9). 2. Captivity and imprisonment (*v.* 10–16). 3. Sickness and distemper of body (*v.* 17–22). 4. Danger and distress at sea (*v.* 23–32). These are put for all similar perils, in which those that cry unto God have ever found him a very present help. II. He specifies the varieties and vicissitudes of events concerning nations and families, in all which God's hand is to be eyed by his own people, with joyful acknowledgments of his goodness (*v.* 33–43). When we are in any of these or the like distresses it will be comfortable to sing this psalm, with application; but, if we be not, others are, and have been, of whose deliverances it becomes us to give God the glory, for we are members one of another.

Verses 1–9

Here is, I. A general call to all to give thanks to God, *v.* 1. Let all that sing this psalm, or pray over it, set themselves herein to *give thanks to the Lord;* and those that have not any special matter for praise may furnish themselves with matter enough from God's universal goodness. In the fountain *he is good;* in the streams *his mercy endures for ever* and never fails.

II. A particular demand hereof from *the redeemed of the Lord,* which may well be applied spiritually to those that have an interest in the great Redeemer and are saved by him from sin and hell. They have, of all people, most reason to say that God is good, and his mercy everlasting; these are the *children of God that were scattered abroad,* whom Christ died to *gather together in one,* out of all lands, Jn. 11:52; Mt. 24:31. But it seems here to be meant of a temporal deliverance, wrought for them when in their distress *they cried unto the Lord, v.* 6. *Is any afflicted? Let him pray.* Does any pray? God will certainly hear and help. When troubles become extreme that is man's time to cry; those who but whispered prayer before then cry aloud, and then it is God's time to succour. In the mount he will be seen. 1. They were in an enemy's country, but God wrought out their rescue: *He redeemed them from the hand of the enemy* (*v.* 2), not by *might or power,* it may be (Zec. 4:6), nor by *price or reward* (Isa. 45:13), *but by the Spirit of God* working on the spirits of men. 2. They were dispersed as out-casts, but God gathered them out of all the countries whither they were scattered in the cloudy and dark day, that they might again be incorporated, *v.* 3. See Deu. 30:4; Eze. 34:12. God knows those that are his, and where to find them. 3. They were bewildered, had no road to travel in, no dwelling place to rest in, *v.* 4. *When they were redeemed* out of the *hand of the enemy, and gathered out of the lands,* they were in danger of perishing in their return home through the dry and barren deserts. *They wandered in the wilderness,* where there was no trodden path, no company, but *a solitary way,* no lodging, no conveniences, no accommodations, no inhabited city where they might have quarters or refreshment. But *God led them forth by the right way* (*v.* 7), directed them to an inn, nay, directed them to a home, *that they might go to a city of habitation,* which was inhabited, nay which them themselves should inhabit. This may refer to poor travellers in general, those particularly whose way lay through the wilds of Arabia, where we may suppose they were often at a loss; and yet many in that distress were wonderfully relieved, so that few perished. Note, We ought to take notice of the good hand of God's providence over us in our journeys, going out and coming in, directing us in our way, and providing for us places both to bait in and rest in. Or (as some think) it has an eye to the wanderings of the children of Israel in the wilderness for forty years; it is said (Deu. 32:10), *God led them about,* and yet here *he led them by the right way.* God's way, though to us it seems about, will appear at last to have been the right way. It is applicable to our condition in this world; we are here as in a wilderness, have here *no continuing city,* but dwell in tents as strangers and pilgrims. But we are under the guidance of his wise and good providence, and, if we commit ourselves to it, we shall be *led in the right way to the city that has foundations.* 4. They were ready to perish for hunger (*v.* 5): *Their soul even fainted in them.* They were spent with the fatigues of their journey and ready to drop down for want of refreshment. Those that have constant plenty, and are every day fed to the full, know not what a miserable case it is to be *hungry and thirsty,* and to have no supply. This was sometimes the case of Israel in the wilderness, and perhaps of other poor travellers; but God's providence finds out ways to *satisfy the longing soul and fill the hungry soul with goodness, v.* 9. Israel's wants were seasonably supplied, and many have been wonderfully relieved when they were ready to perish. The same God that has led us has fed us all our life long unto this day, has fed us with food convenient, has provided food for the soul, *and filled the hungry soul with goodness. Those that hunger and thirst after righteousness,* after God, the living God, and communion with him, shall be abundantly *replenished with the goodness of his house,* both in grace and glory. Now for all this those who receive mercy are called upon to return thanks (*v.* 8): *Oh that men* (it is meant especially of those men whom God has graciously relieved) *would praise the Lord for his goodness* to them in particular, *and for his wonderful works to* others of *the children of men!* Note, (1.) God's works of mercy are wonderful works, works of wonderful power considering the weakness, and of wonderful grace considering the unworthiness, of those he shows mercy to. (2.) It is expected of those who receive mercy from God that they return praise to him. (3.) We must acknowledge God's goodness to the children of men as well as to the children of God, to others as well as to ourselves.

Verses 10–16

We are to take notice of the goodness of God towards prisoners and captives. Observe, 1. A description of this affliction. Prisoners are said to *sit in darkness* (*v.* 10), in dark dungeons, close prisons, which intimates that they are desolate and disconsolate; they sit *in the shadow of death,* which intimates not only great distress and trouble, but great danger. Prisoners are many times appointed to die; they sit despairing to get out, but resolving to make the best of it. They are *bound in affliction, and* many times *in iron,* as Joseph. Thus sore a calamity is imprisonment, which should make us prize liberty, and be thankful for it. 2. The cause of this affliction, *v.* 11. It is *because they rebelled against the words of God.* Wilful sin is rebellion against the words of God; it is a contradiction to his truths and a violation of his laws. *They contemned the counsel of the Most High,* and thought they neither needed it nor could be the better for it; and those that will not be counselled cannot be helped. Those that despise prophesying, that regard not the admonitions of their own consciences nor the just reproofs of their friends, contemn the counsel of the Most High, and for this they are bound in affliction, both to punish them for and to reclaim them from their rebellions. 3. The design of this affliction, and that is to bring *down their heart* (*v.* 12), to humble them for sin, to make them low in their own eyes, to cast down every high, proud, aspiring thought. Afflicting providences must be improved as humbling providences; and we not only lose the benefit of them, but thwart God's designs and walk contrary to him in them if our hearts be unhumbled and unbroken, as high and hard as ever under them. Is the estate brought down with labour, the honour sunk? Have those that exalted themselves fallen down, and is there none to help them? Let this bring down the spirit to confess sin, to accept the punishment of it, and humbly to sue for mercy and grace. 4. The duty of this afflicted state, and that is to pray (*v.* 13): *Then they cried unto the Lord in their trouble,* though before perhaps they had neglected him. Prisoners have time to pray, who, when they were at liberty, could not find time; they see they have need of God's help, though formerly they thought they could do well enough without him. Sense will make men cry when they are in trouble, but grace will direct them to cry unto the Lord, from whom the affliction comes and who alone can remove it. 5. Their deliverance out of the affliction: *They cried unto the Lord, and he saved them, v.* 13. *He brought them out of darkness into light,* welcome light, and then doubly sweet and pleasant, *brought them out of the shadow of death* to the comforts of life, and their liberty was to them life from the dead, *v.* 14. Were they *fettered? He broke their bands asunder.* Were they imprisoned in strong castles? *He broke the gates of brass* and the *bars of iron* wherewith those gates were made fast; he did not put back, but *cut in sunder.* Note, When God will work deliverance the greatest difficulties that lie in the way shall be made nothing of. Gates of brass and bars of iron, as they cannot keep him out from him people (he was with Joseph in the prison), so they cannot keep them in when the time, the set-time, for their enlargement, comes. 6. The return that is required from those whose bands God has loosed (*v.* 15): *Let them praise the Lord for his goodness,* and take occasion from their own experience of it, and share in it, to bless him for that goodness which the earth is full of, *the world and those that dwell therein.*

Verses 17–22

Bodily sickness is another of the calamities of this life which gives us an opportunity of experiencing the goodness of God in recovering us, and of that the psalmist speaks in these verses, where we may observe,

I. That we, by our sins, bring sickness upon ourselves and then it is our duty to pray, *v.* 17–19. 1. It is the sin of the soul that is the cause of sickness; we bring it upon ourselves both meritoriously and efficiently; *Fools, because of their transgression, are thus afflicted;* they are thus corrected for the sins they have committed and thus cured of their evil inclinations to sin. If we knew no sin, we should know no sickness; but the transgression of our life, and the iniquity of our heart, make it necessary. Sinners are fools; they wrong themselves, and all against their own interest, not only their spiritual, but their secular interest. They prejudice their bodily health by intemperance and endanger their lives by indulging their appetites. This their way is their folly, and they need the rod of correction to drive out the foolishness that is bound up in their hearts. 2. The weakness of the body is the effect of sickness, *v.* 18. When people are sick *their soul abhors all manner of meat;* they not only have no desire to eat nor power to digest it, but they nauseate it, and their stomach is turned against it. And here they may read their sin in their punishment: those that doted most on the meat that perishes, when they come to be sick are sick of it, and the dainties they loved are loathed; what they took too much of now they can take nothing of, which commonly follows upon the overcharging of the heart with surfeiting and drunkenness. And when the appetite is gone the life is as good as gone: *They draw near unto the gates of death;* they are, in their own apprehension and in the apprehension of all about them, at the brink of the grave, as ready to be turned to destruction. 3. Then is a proper time for prayer: *Then they cry unto the Lord,* v. 19. Is any sick? Let him pray; let him be prayed for. Prayer is a salve for every sore.

II. That it is by the power and mercy of God that we are recovered from sickness, and then it is our duty to be thankful. Compare with this Job 33:18, 28. 1. When those that are sick call upon God he returns them an answer of peace. They cry unto him and he *saves them out of their distresses* (*v.* 19); he removes their griefs and prevents their fears. (1.) He does it easily: *He sent his word and healed them, v.* 20. This may be applied to the miraculous cures which Christ wrought when he was upon earth, by a word's speaking; he said, *Be clean, Be whole,* and the work was done. It may also be applied to the spiritual cures which the Spirit of grace works in regeneration; he sends his word, and heals souls, convinces, converts, sanctifies them, and all by the word. In the common instances of recovery from sickness God in his providence does but speak, and it is done. (2.) He does it effectually: *He delivereth them out of their destructions,* that they shall neither be destroyed nor distressed with the fear of being so. Nothing is too hard for that God to do who kills and makes alive again, brings down to the grave and raises up, who *turneth man* almost *to destruction,* and yet saith, *Return.* 2. When those that have been sick are restored they must return to God an answer of praise (*v.* 21, 22): *Let all men praise the Lord for his goodness,* and let those, particularly, to whom God has thus granted a new life, spend it in his service; *let them sacrifice with thanksgiving,* not only bring a thank-offering to the altar, but a thankful heart to God. Thanksgivings are the best thank-offerings, and shall please the Lord better than an ox or bullock. *And let them declare his works with rejoicing,* to his honour and for the encouragement of others. *The living, the living, they shall praise him.*

Verses 23–32

The psalmist here calls upon those to give glory to God who are delivered from dangers at sea. Though the Israelites dealt not much in merchandise, yet their neighbours

the Tyrians and Zidonians did, and for them perhaps this part of the psalm was especially calculated.

I. Much of the power of God appears at all times in the sea, 23, 24. It appears to those *that go down to the sea in ships,* as mariners, merchants, fishermen, or passengers, *that do business in great waters.* And surely none will expose themselves there but those that have business (among all Solomon's pleasant things we do not read of any pleasure-boat he had), but those that go on business, lawful business, may, in faith, put themselves under the divine protection. *These see the works of the Lord, and his wonders,* which are the more surprising, because most are born and bred upon land, and what passes at sea is new to them. The deep itself is a wonder, its vastness, its saltness, its ebbing and flowing. The great variety of living creatures in the sea is wonderful. Let those that go to sea be led, by all the wonders they observe there, to consider and adore the infinite perfections of that God whose the sea is, for he made it and manages it.

II. It especially appears in storms at sea, which are much more terrible than at land. Observe here, 1. How dangerous and dreadful a tempest at sea is. *Then* wonders begin to appear in the deep, when God *commands and raises the strong wind,* which *fulfils his word,* Ps. 148:8. He raises the winds, as a prince by his commission raises forces. Satan pretends to be the *prince of the power of the air;* but he is a pretender; the powers of the air are at God's command, not at his. When the wind becomes stormy it *lifts up the waves* of the sea, *v.* 25. Then the ships are kicked like tennis-balls on the tops of the waves; they seem to *mount up to the heavens,* and then they couch again, as if they would *go down to the depths, v.* 26. A stranger, who had never seen it, would not think it possible for a ship to live at sea, as it will in a storm, and ride it out, but would expect that the next wave would bury it and it would never come up again; and yet God, who taught man discretion to make ships that should so strangely keep above water, does by his special providence preserve them, that they answer the end to admiration. When the ships are thus tossed the *soul* of the seaman *melts because of trouble;* and, when the storm is very high, even those that are used to the sea can neither shake off nor dissemble their fears, but *they reel to and fro,* and tossing makes them giddy, *and* they *stagger* and are sick, it may be, *like a drunken man;* the whole ship's crew are in confusion *and* quite *at their wits' end* (*v.* 27), not knowing what to do more for their preservation; all their wisdom is swallowed up, and they are ready to give up themselves for gone, Jonah 1:5, etc. 2. How seasonable it is at such a time to pray. Those that go to sea must expect such perils as are here described, and the best preparation they can make for them is to make sure a liberty of access to God by prayer, for *then they* will *cry unto the Lord, v.* 28. We have a saying, "Let those that would learn to pray go to sea;" I say, Let those that will go to sea learn to pray, and accustom themselves to pray, that they may come with the more boldness to the throne of grace when they are in trouble. Even heathen mariners, in a storm, *cried every man to his god;* but those that have the Lord for their God have a present and powerful help in that and every other time of need, so that when they are at their wits' end they are not at their faith's end. 3. How wonderfully God sometimes appears for those that are in distress at sea, in answer to their prayers: *He brings them out* of the danger; and, (1.) The sea is still: *He makes the storm a calm,* v. 29. The winds fall, and only by their soft and gentle murmurs serve to lull the waves asleep again, so that the surface of the sea becomes smooth and smiling. By this Christ proved himself to be more than a man *that even the winds and the seas obeyed him.* (2.) The seamen are made easy: *They are glad because they are quiet,* quiet from the noise, quiet from the fear of evil. Quietness after a storm is a very desirable thing, and sensibly pleasant. (3.) The voyage becomes prosperous and successful: *So he brings them to their desired haven, v.* 30. Thus he carries his people safely through all the storms and tempests that they meet with in their voyage heaven-ward, and lands them, at length, in the desired harbour. 4. How justly it is expected that all those who have had a safe passage over the sea, and especially who have been delivered from remarkable perils at sea, should acknowledge it with thankfulness, to the glory of God. Let them do it privately in their closets and

families. Let them *praise the Lord for his goodness* to themselves and others, *v.* 31. Let them do it publicly (*v.* 32), *in the congregation of the people and in the assembly of the elders;* there let them erect the memorials of their deliverance, to the honour of God, and for the encouragement of others to trust him.

Verses 33–43

The psalmist, having given God the glory of the providential reliefs granted to persons in distress, here gives him the glory of the revolutions of providence, and the surprising changes it sometimes makes in the affairs of the children of men.

I. He gives some instances of these revolutions.

1. Fruitful countries are made barren and barren countries are made fruitful. Much of the comfort of this life depends upon the soil in which our lot is cast. Now, (1.) The sin of man has often marred the fruitfulness of the soil and made it unserviceable, *v.* 33, 34. Land watered with *rivers* is sometimes *turned into a wilderness,* and that which had been full of water-springs now has not so much as water-streams; it is turned *into dry* and *sandy ground,* that has not consistency and moisture enough to produce any thing valuable. Many *a fruitful land* is turned into saltness, not so much from natural causes as from the just judgment of God, who thus punished *the wickedness of those that dwell therein;* as the vale of Sodom became a salt sea. Note, If the land be bad, it is because the inhabitants are so. Justly is the ground made unfruitful to those that bring not forth fruit unto God, but serve Baal with their corn and wine. (2.) The goodness of God has often mended the barrenness of the soil, and turned a *wilderness,* a land o drought, *into water-springs, v.* 35. The land of Canaan, which was once the glory of all lands for fruitfulness, is said to be, at this day, a fruitless, useless, worthless spot of ground, as was foretold, Deu. 29:23. This land of ours, which formerly was much of it an uncultivated desert, is now full of all good things, and *more abundant honour is given to that part which lacked.* Let the plantations in America, and the colonies settled there, compared with the desolations of many countries in Asia and Europe, that formerly were famous, expound this.

2. Necessitous families are raised and enriched, while prosperous families are impoverished and go to decay. If we look broad in the world, (1.) We see many greatly increasing whose beginning was small, and whose ancestors were mean and made no figure, *v.* 36–38. Those that were *hungry* are made to *dwell* in fruitful lands; there they take root, and gain a settlement, and *prepare a city for habitation* for themselves and theirs after them. Providence puts good land under their hands, and they build upon it. Cities took rise from rising families. But as lands, will not serve for men without lodgings, and therefore they must *prepare a city of habitation,* so lodgings, though ever so convenient, will not serve without lands, and therefore they must *sow the fields, and plant vineyards* (*v.* 37), for the king himself is served of the field. And yet the fields, though favoured with water-springs, will not *yield fruits of increase,* unless they be sown, nor will vineyards be had, unless they be planted; man's industry must attend God's blessing, and then God's blessing will crown man's industry. The fruitfulness of the soil should engage, for it does encourage, diligence; and, ordinarily, *the hand of the diligent,* by the blessing of God, *makes rich, v.* 38. He blesses them also, *so that they are,* in a little time, *multiplied greatly, and he diminishes not their cattle.* As in the beginning, so still it is, by the blessing of God, that the earth and all the creatures *increase and multiply* (Gen. 1:22), and we depend upon God for the increase of the cattle as well as for the increase of the ground. Cattle would decrease many ways if God should permit it, and men would soon suffer by it. (2.) We see many that have thus suddenly risen as suddenly sunk and brought to nothing (*v.* 39): *Again they are diminished and brought low* by adverse providences, and end their days as low as they began them; or their families, after them lose as fast a they got, and scatter what they heaped together. Note, Worldly wealth is an uncertain thing, and often those that are filled with it, ere they are aware, grow so secure and sensual with it that, ere they are aware, they lose it again. Hence it is called *deceitful riches* and the *mammon of unrighteousness.* God has many ways of making men poor; he can do it by *oppression,*

affliction, and sorrow, as he tempted Job and brought him low.

3. Those that were high and great in the world are abased, and those that were mean and despicable are advanced to honour, *v.* 40, 41. We have seen, (1.) Princes dethroned and reduced to straits. *He pours contempt upon* them, even among those that have idolized them. Those that exalt themselves God will abase, and, in order thereunto, will infatuate: He makes *them to wander in the wilderness, where there is no way.* He baffles those counsels by which they thought to support themselves, and their own power and pomp, and drives them headlong, so that they know not what course to steer, nor what measures to take. We met with this before, Job 12:24, 25. (2.) Those of low degree advanced to the posts of honour (*v.* 41): *Yet setteth he the poor on high,* raiseth *from the dust* to the *throne of glory,* 1 Sa. 2:8; Ps. 113:7, 8. Those that were afflicted and trampled on are not only delivered, but set on high out of the reach of their troubles, above their enemies, and have dominion over those to whom they had been in subjection. That which adds to their honour, and strengthens them in their elevation, is the multitude of their children: *He maketh him families like a flock* of sheep, so numerous, so useful, so sociable with one another, and so meek and peaceable. He that sent them meat sent them mouths. *Happy is the man that has his quiver filled* with arrows, for he shall boldly *speak with the enemy in the gate,* Ps. 127:5. God is to be acknowledged both in setting up families and in building them up. Let not princes be envied, nor the poor despised, for God has many ways of changing the condition of both.

II. He makes some improvement of these remarks; such surprising turns as these are of use, 1. For the solacing of saints. They observe these dispensations with pleasure (*v.* 42): *The righteous shall see it and rejoice* in the glorifying of God's attributes and the manifesting of his dominion over the children of men. It is a great comfort to a good man to see how God manages the children of men, as the potter does the clay, so as to serve his own purposes by them, to see despised virtue advanced and impious pride brought low to the dust, to see it evinced beyond dispute that *verily there is a God that judges in the earth.* 2. For the silencing of sinners: *All iniquity shall stop her mouth;* it shall be a full conviction of the folly of atheists, and of those that deny the divine providence; and, forasmuch as practical atheism is at the bottom of all sin, it shall in effect *stop the mouth of all iniquity.* When sinners see how their punishment answers to their sin, and how justly God deals with them in taking away from them those gifts of his which they had abused, they shall not have one word to say for themselves; for God will be justified, he will be clear. 3. For the satisfying of all concerning the divine goodness (*v.* 43): *Whoso is wise, and will observe these things,* these various dispensations of divine providence, *even they shall understand the lovingkindness of the Lord.* Here is, (1.) A desirable end proposed, and that is, rightly to *understand the lovingkindness of the Lord.* It is of great use to us, in religion, to be fully assured of God's goodness, to be experimentally acquainted and duly affected with it, that his *lovingkindness* may be *before our eyes,* Ps. 26:3. (2.) A proper means prescribed for attaining this end, and that is a due observance of God's providence. We must lay up these things, mind them, and keep them in mind, Lu. 2:19. (3.) A commendation of the use of this means as an instance of true wisdom: *Whoso is wise,* let him by this both prove his wisdom and improve it. A prudent observance of the providences of God will contribute very much to the accomplishing of a good Christian.

PSALM 108

This psalm begins with praise and concludes with prayer, and faith is at work in both. I. David here gives thanks to God for mercies to himself (*v.* 1–5). II. He prays to God for mercies for the land, pleading the promises of God and putting them in suit (*v.* 6–13). The former part it taken out of Ps. 57:7, etc., the latter out of Ps. 60:5, etc., and both with very little variation, to teach us that we may in prayer use the same words that we have formerly used, provided it be with new affections. It intimates likewise that it is not only allowable, but sometimes convenient, to gather some verses out of one psalm and some out of another, and to put them together, to be sung to the glory of God. In singing this psalm we must give glory to God and take comfort to ourselves.

A song or psalm of David.

Verses 1–5

We may here learn how to praise God from the example of one who was master of the art. 1. We must praise God with fixedness of heart. Our heart must be employed in the duty (else we make nothing of it) and engaged to the duty (*v.* 1): *O God! my heart is fixed,* and then *I will sing and give praise.* Wandering straggling thoughts must be gathered in, and kept close to the business; for they must be told that here is work enough for them all. 2. We must praise God with freeness of expression: I will praise him *with my glory,* that is, with my tongue. Our tongue is our glory, and never more so than when it is employed in praising God. When the *heart is inditing* this *good matter* our *tongue* must be as *the pen of a ready writer,* Ps. 45:1. David's skill in music was his glory, it made him famous, and this should be consecrated to the praise of God; and therefore it follows, *Awake* my *psaltery and harp.* Whatever gift we excel in we must praise God with. 3. We must praise God with fervency of affection, and must stir up ourselves to do it, that it may be done in a lively manner and not carelessly (*v.* 2): *Awake, psaltery and harp;* let it not be done with a dull and sleepy tune, but let the airs be all lively. *I myself will awake early* to do it, with all that is within me, and all little enough. Warm devotions honour God. 4. We must praise God publicly, as those that are not ashamed to own our obligations to him and our thankful sense of his favours, but desire that others also may be in like manner affected with the divine goodness (*v.* 3): *I will praise thee among the people* of the Jews; nay, *I will sing to thee among the nations* of the earth. Whatever company we are in we must take all occasions to speak well of God; and we must not be shy of singing psalms, though our neighbours hear us, for it looks like being ashamed of our Master. 5. We must, in our praises, magnify the mercy and truth of God in a special manner (*v.* 4), mercy in promising, truth in performing. The heavens are vast, but the mercy of God is more capacious; the skies are high and bright, but the truth of God is more eminent, more illustrious. We cannot see further than the heavens and clouds; whatever we see of God's mercy and truth there is still more to be seen, more reserved to be seen, in the other world. 6. Since we find ourselves so, defective in glorifying God, we must beg of him to glorify himself, to do all, to dispose all, to his own glory, to get himself honour and make himself a name (*v.* 5): *Be thou exalted, O God! above the heavens,* higher than the angels themselves can exalt thee with their praises, *and* let *thy glory* be spread over *all the earth. Father, glorify thy own name. Thou hast glorified it; glorify it again.* It is to be our first petition, *Hallowed be thy name.*

Verses 6–13

We may here learn how to pray as well as praise. 1. We must be public-spirited in prayer, and bear upon our hearts, at the throne of grace, the concerns of the church of God, *v.* 6. It is God's *beloved,* and therefore must be ours; and therefore we must pray for its deliverance, and reckon that we are answered if God grant what we ask for his church, though he delay to give us what we ask for ourselves. *"Save* thy church, *and* thou *answerest me;* I have what I would have." *Let the earth be filled with God's glory, and the prayers of David are ended* (Ps. 72:19, 20); he desires no more. 2. We must, in prayer, act faith upon the power and promise of God — upon his power (*Save with thy right hand,* which is mighty to save), and upon his promise: *God has spoken in his holiness,* in his holy word, to which he has sworn by his holiness, and therefore *I will rejoice, v.* 7. What he has promised he will perform, for it is the word both of his truth and of his power. An active faith can rejoice in what God has said, though it be not yet done; for with him saying and doing are not two things, whatever they are with us. 3. We must, in prayer, take the comfort of what God has secured to us and settled upon us, though we are not yet put in possession of it. God had promised David to give him, (1.) The hearts of his subjects; and therefore he surveys the several parts of the country as his own already: *"Shechem* and *Succoth, Gilead* and *Manasseh, Ephraim* and *Judah,* are all my own," *v.* 8. With such assurance as this we may speak of the performance of what God has promised to the Son of David; he will, without fail, give him the heathen for his *inheritance* and *the utmost parts of the earth for his possession,* for so has he *spoken in his holiness;* nay, of all the particular persons that were given him he will *lose none;* he also, as David, shall have the hearts of his subjects, Jn. 6:37. And, (2.) The *necks of his enemies.* These are promised, and therefore David looks upon *Moab,* and *Edom,* and *Philistia,* as his own already (*v.* 9): *Over Philistia will I triumph,* which explains Ps. 60:8, *Philistia, triumph thou because of me,* which some think should be read, *O my soul! triumph thou over Philistia.* Thus the exalted Redeemer is set down at God's right hand, in a full assurance that all his enemies shall in due time *be made his footstool, though all things are not yet put under him,* Heb. 2:8. 4. We must take encouragement from the beginnings of mercy to pray and hope for the perfecting of it (*v.* 10, 11): *"Who will bring me into the strong cities* that are yet unconquered? Who will make me master of the country of *Edom,* which is yet unsubdued?" The question was probably to be debated in his privy council, or a council of war, what methods they should take to subdue the Edomites and to reduce that country; but he brings it into his prayers, and leaves it in God's hands: *Wilt not thou, O God?* Certainly thou wilt. It is probable that he spoke with the more assurance concerning the conquest of Edom because of the ancient oracle concerning Jacob and Esau, that *the elder should serve the younger,* and the blessing of Jacob, by which he was made Esau's lord, Gen. 27:37. 5. We must not be discouraged in prayer, nor beaten off from our hold of God, though Providence has in some instances frowned upon us: "Though thou hast *cast us off,* yet thou wilt now *go forth with our hosts, v.* 11. Thou wilt *comfort us again* after the time that thou *hast afflicted us."* Adverse events are sometimes intended for the trial of the constancy of our faith and prayer, which we ought to persevere in whatever difficulties we meet with, and not to *faint.* 6. We must seek help from God, renouncing all confidence in the creature (*v.* 12): *"Lord, give us help from trouble,* prosper our designs, and defeat the designs of our enemies against us." It is not unseasonable to talk of trouble at the same time that we talk of triumphs, especially when it is to quicken prayer for help from heaven; and it is a good plea, *Vain is the help of man.* "It is really so, and therefore we are undone if thou do not help us; we apprehend it to be so, and therefore depend upon thee for help and have the more reason to expect it." 7. We must depend entirely upon the favour and grace of God, both for strength and success in our work and warfare, *v.* 13. (1.) We must do our part, but we can do nothing of ourselves; it is only *through God that we shall do valiantly.* Blessed Paul will own that even he can *do nothing,* nothing to purpose, *but through Christ strengthening him,* Phil. 4:13. (2.) When we have acquitted ourselves ever so well, yet we cannot speed by any merit or might of our own; it is God himself that *treads down our enemies,* else we with all our valour cannot do it. Whatever we do, whatever we gain, God must have all the glory.

PSALM 109

Whether David penned this psalm when he was persecuted by Saul, or when his son Absalom rebelled against him, or upon occasion of some other trouble that was given him, is uncertain; and whether the particular enemy he prays against was Saul, or Doeg, or Ahithophel, or some other not mentioned in the story, we cannot determine; but it is certain that in penning it he had an eye to Christ, his sufferings and his persecutors, for that imprecation (*v.* 8) is applied to Judas, Acts 1:20. The rest of the prayers here against his enemies were the expressions, not of passion, but of the Spirit of prophecy. I. He lodges a complaint in the court of heaven of the malice and base ingratitude of his enemies and with it an appeal to the righteous God (*v.* 1–5). II. He prays against his enemies, and devotes them to destruction (*v.* 6–20). III. He prays for himself, that God would help and succour him in his low condition (*v.* 21–29). IV. He concludes with a joyful expectation that God would appear for him (*v.* 30, 31). In singing this psalm we must comfort ourselves with the believing foresight of the certain destruction of all the enemies of Christ and his church, and the certain salvation of all those that trust in God and keep close to him.

To the chief Musician. A psalm of David.

Verses 1–5

It is the unspeakable comfort of all good people that, whoever is against them, God is for them, and to him they may apply as to one that is pleased to concern himself for them. Thus David here.

I. He refers himself to God's judgment (*v.* 1): *"Hold not thy peace,* but *let my sentence come forth from thy presence,* Ps. 17:2. Delay not to give judgment upon the appeal made to thee." God saw what his enemies did against him, but seemed to connive at it, and to keep silence: "Lord," says he, "do not always do so." The title he gives to God is observable: *"O God of my praise! the God in whom I glory,* and not in any wisdom or strength of my own, from whom I have every thing that is my praise, or the God whom I have praised, and will praise, and hope to be for ever praising." He had before called God the *God of his mercy* (Ps. 59:10), here he calls him *the God of his praise.* Forasmuch as God is the *God of our mercies* we must make him the *God of our praises;* if all is of him and from him, all must be to him and for him.

II. He complains of his enemies, showing that they were such as it was fit for the righteous God to appear against. 1. They were very spiteful and malicious: They are *wicked;* they delight in doing mischief (*v.* 2); their words are *words of hatred, v.* 3. They had an implacable enmity to a good man because of his goodness. "They open their mouths against me to swallow me up, and *fight against me* to cut me off if they could." 2. They were notorious liars; and lying comprehends two of the seven things which the Lord hates. "They are *deceitful* in their protestations and professions of kindness, while at the same time they speak against me behind my back, *with a lying tongue."* They were equally false in their flatteries and in their calumnies. 3. They were both public and restless in their designs; "They *compassed me about* on all sides, so that, which way soever I looked, I could see nothing but what made against me." 4. They were unjust; their accusations of him, and sentence against him, were all groundless: *"They have fought against me without a cause;* I never gave them any provocation." Nay, which was worst of all, 5. They were very ungrateful, and *rewarded him evil for good, v.* 5. Many a kindness he had done them, and was upon all occasions ready to do them, and yet he could not work upon them to abate their malice against him, but, on the contrary, they were the more exasperated because they could not provoke him to give them some occasion against him (*v.* 4): *For my love they are my adversaries.* The more he endeavoured to gratify them the more they hated him. We may wonder that it is possible that any should be so wicked; and yet, since there have been so many instances of it, we should not wonder if any be so wicked against us.

III. He resolves to keep close to his duty and take the comfort of that: *But I give myself unto prayer* (*v.* 4), *I prayer* (so it is in the original); "I am for prayer, I am a man of prayer, I love prayer, and prize prayer, and practise prayer, and make a business of prayer, and am in my element when I am at prayer." A good man is made up of prayer, *gives himself to prayer,* as the apostles, Acts 6:4. When David's enemies falsely accused him, and misrepresented him, he applied to God and by prayer committed his cause to him. Though they were his adversaries for his love, yet he continued to pray for them; if others are abusive and injurious to us, yet let not us fail to do our duty to them, nor *sin against the Lord in ceasing to pray for them,* 1 Sa. 12:23. Though they hated and persecuted him for his religion, yet he kept close to it; they laughed at him for his devotion, but they could not laugh him out of it. "Let them say what they will, *I give myself unto prayer."* Now herein David was a type of Christ, who was compassed about with *words of hatred* and lying words, whose enemies not only persecuted him without cause, but for his love and his *good works* (Jn. 10:32); and yet he *gave himself to prayer,* to pray for them. *Father, forgive them.*

Verses 6–20

David here fastens upon some one particular person that was worse than the rest of his enemies, and the ringleader of them, and in a devout and pious manner, not from a principle of malice and revenge, but in a holy zeal for God and against sin and with an eye to the enemies of Christ, particularly Judas who betrayed him, whose sin was greater than Pilate's that condemned him (Jn. 19:11), he imprecates and predicts his destruction, foresees and pronounces him completely miserable, and such a one as our Saviour calls him, *A son of perdition.* Calvin speaks of it as a detestable piece of sacrilege, common in his time among Franciscan friars and other monks, that if any one had malice against a neighbour he might hire some of them to curse him every day, which he would do in the words of these verses; and particularly he tells of a lady

in France who, being at variance with her own and only son, hired a parcel of friars to curse him in these words. Greater impiety can scarcely be imagined than to vent a devilish passion in the language of sacred writ, to kindle strife with coals snatched from God's altar, and to call for fire from heaven with a tongue set on fire of hell.

I. The imprecations here are very terrible — woe, and a thousand woes, to that man against whom God says *Amen* to them; and they are all in full force against the implacable enemies and persecutors of God's church and people, that *will not repent, to give him glory.* It is here foretold concerning this bad man,

1. That he should be cast and sentenced as a criminal, with all the dreadful pomp of a trial, conviction, and condemnation (*v.* 6, 7): *Set thou a wicked man over him,* to be as cruel and oppressive to him as he has been to others; for God often makes one wicked man a scourge to another, to spoil the spoilers and to deal treacherously with those that have dealt treacherously. *Set the wicked one over him* (so some), that is, Satan, as it follows; and then it was fulfilled in Judas, into whom Satan entered, to hurry him into sin first and then into despair. Set his own wicked heart over him, set his own conscience against him; let that fly in his face. *Let Satan stand on his right hand,* and be let loose against him to deceive him, as he did Ahab to his destruction, and then to accuse him and resist him, and then he is certainly cast, having no interest in that advocate who alone can say, *The Lord rebuke thee, Satan* (Zec. 3:1, 2); when he shall be judged at men's bar let not his usual arts to evade justice do him any service, but let his sin find him out and *let him be condemned;* nor shall he escape before God's tribunal, but be condemned there when the day of inquisition and recompence shall come. *Let his prayer become sin,* as the clamours of a condemned malefactor not only find no acceptance, but are looked upon as an affront to the court. The prayers of the wicked now become sin, because soured with the leaven of hypocrisy and malice; and so they will in the great day, because then it will be too late to cry, *Lord, Lord, open to us.* Let every thing be turned against him and improved to his disadvantage, even his prayers.

2. That, being condemned, he should be executed as a most notorious malefactor. (1.) That he should lose his life, and the number of his months be cut off in the midst, by the sword of justice: *Let his days be few,* or shortened, as a condemned criminal has but a few days to live (*v.* 8); such bloody and *deceitful men shall not live out half their days.* (2.) That consequently all his places should be disposed of to others, and they should enjoy his preferments and employments: *Let another take his office.* This Peter applies to the filling up of Judas's place in the truly sacred college of the apostles, by the choice of Matthias, Acts 1:20. Those that mismanage their trusts will justly have their office taken from them and given to those that will approve themselves faithful. (3.) That his family should be beheaded and beggared, that *his wife* should be made *a widow* and *his children fatherless,* by his untimely death, *v.* 9. Wicked men, by their wicked courses, bring ruin upon their wives and children, whom they ought to take care of and provide for. Yet his children, if, when they lost their father, they had a competency to live upon, might still subsist in comfort; but they shall be *vagabonds and shall beg;* they shall not have a house of their own to live in, nor any certain dwelling-place, nor know where to have a meal's-meat, but shall creep *out of their desolate places* with fear and trembling, like beasts out of their dens, to *seek their bread* (*v.* 10), because they are conscious to themselves that all mankind have reason to hate them for their father's sake. (4.) That his estate should be ruined, as the estates of malefactors are confiscated (*v.* 11): *Let the extortioner,* the officer, seize *all that he has and let the stranger,* who was nothing akin to his estate, *spoil his labour,* either for his crimes or for his debts, Job 5:4, 5. (5.) That his posterity should be miserable. Fatherless children, though they have nothing of their own, yet sometimes are well provided for by the kindness of those whom God inclines to pity them; but this wicked man having never shown mercy there shall *be none to extend mercy to him,* by *favouring his fatherless children* when he is gone, *v.* 12. The children of wicked parents often fare the worse for their parents' wickedness in this way that the bowels of men's compassion are shut up from them, which yet ought

not to be, for why should children suffer for that which was not their fault, but their infelicity? (6.) That his memory should be infamous, and buried in oblivion and disgrace (*v.* 13): *Let his posterity be cut off; let his end be to destruction* (so Dr. Hammond); *and in the* next *generation let their name be blotted out,* or remembered with contempt and indignation, and (*v.* 15) let an indelible mark of disgrace be left upon it. See here what hurries some to shameful deaths, and brings the families and estates of others to ruin, makes them and their despicable and odious, and entails poverty, and shame, and misery, upon their posterity; it is sin, that mischievous destructive thing. The learned Dr. Hammond applies this to the final dispersion and desolation of the Jewish nation for their crucifying Christ; their princes and people were cut off, their country was laid waste, and their posterity were made fugitives and vagabonds.

II. The ground of these imprecations bespeaks them very just, though they sound very severe. 1. To justify the imprecations of vengeance upon the sinner's posterity, the sin of his ancestors is here brought into the account (*v.* 14, 15), *the iniquity of his fathers* and *the sin of his mother.* These God often visits even upon the children's children, and is not unrighteous therein: when wickedness has long run in the blood justly does the curse run along with it. Thus all the innocent blood that had been shed upon the earth, from that of righteous Abel, was required from that persecuting generation, who, by putting Christ to death, *filled up the measure of their fathers,* and left as long a train of vengeance to follow them as the train of guilt was that went before them, which they themselves agreed to by saying, *His blood be upon us and on our children.* 2. To justify the imprecations of vengeance upon the sinner himself, his own sin is here charged upon him, which called aloud for it. (1.) He had loved cruelty, and therefore give him blood to drink (*v.* 16): *He remembered not to show mercy,* remembered not those considerations which should have induced him to show mercy, remembered not the objects of compassion that had been presented to him, but persecuted the poor, whom he should have protected and relieved, and *slew the broken in heart,* whom he should have comforted and healed. Here is a barbarous man indeed, not it to live. (2.) He had loved cursing, and therefore let the curse come upon his head, *v.* 17–19. Those that were out of the reach of his cruelty he let fly at with his curses, which were impotent and ridiculous; but they shall return upon him. *He delighted not in blessing;* he took no pleasure in wishing well to others, nor in seeing others do well; he would give nobody a good word or a good wish, much less would he do any body a good turn; and *so let all good be far from him. He clothed himself with cursing;* he was proud of it as an ornament that he could frighten all about him with the curses he was liberal of; he confided in it as armour, which would secure him from the insults of those he feared. And let him have enough of it. Was he fond of cursing? *Let* God's curse *come into his bowels like water* and swell him as with a dropsy, *and* let it soak *like oil into his bones.* The word of the curse *is quick and powerful, and divides between the joints and the marrow;* it works powerfully and effectually; it fastens on the soul; it is a piercing thing, and there is no antidote against it. Let is compass him on every side *as a garment, v.* 19. Let God's cursing him be his shame, as his cursing his neighbour was his pride; let it cleave to him as *a girdle,* and let him never be able to get clear of it. Let it be to him like the waters of jealousy, which caused the *belly to swell* and the *thigh to rot.* This points at the utter ruin of Judas, and the spiritual judgments which fell on the Jews for crucifying Christ. The psalmist concludes his imprecations with a terrible *Amen,* which signifies not only, "I wish it may be so," but "I know it shall be so." *Let this be the reward of my adversaries from the Lord, v.* 20. And this will be the reward of all the adversaries of the Lord Jesus; his enemies that will not have him to reign over them shall be *brought forth and slain before him.* And he will one day recompense tribulation to those that trouble his people.

Verses 21–31

David, having denounced God's wrath against his enemies, here takes God's comforts to himself, but in a very humble manner, and without boasting.

I. He pours out his complaint before God concerning

the low condition he was in, which, probably, gave advantage to his enemies to insult over him: "*I am poor and needy,* and therefore a proper object of pity, and one that needs and craves thy help." 1. He was troubled in mind (*v.* 22): *My heart is wounded within me,* not only broken with outward troubles, which sometimes prostrate and sink the spirits, but wounded with a sense of guilt; and *a wounded spirit who can bear?* who can heal? 2. He apprehended himself drawing near to his end: *I am gone like the shadow when it declines,* as good as gone already. Man's life, at best, is like a shadow; sometimes it is like the evening shadow, the presage of night approaching, *like the shadow when it declines.* 3. He was unsettled, *tossed up and down like the locust,* his mind fluctuating and unsteady, still putting him upon new counsels, his outward condition far from any fixation, but still upon the remove, hunted like a partridge on the mountains. 4. His body was wasted, and almost worn away (*v.* 24): *My knees are weak through fasting,* either forced fasting (for want of food when he was persecuted, or for want of appetite when he was sick) or voluntary fasting, when he chastened his soul either for sin or affliction, his own or other's, Ps. 35:13; 69:10. "*My flesh fails of fatness;* that is, it has lost the fatness it had, so that I have become a skeleton, nothing but skin and bones." But it is better to have this leanness in the body, while the soul prospers and is in health, than, like Israel, to have leanness sent into the soul, while the body is feasted. 5. He was ridiculed and reproached by his enemies (*v.* 25); his devotions and his afflictions they made the matter of their laughter, and, upon both those accounts, God's people have been exceedingly filled with the scorning of those that were at ease. In all this David was a type of Christ, who in his humiliation was thus wounded, thus weakened, thus reproached; he was also a type of the church, which is often *afflicted, tossed with tempests, and not comforted.*

II. He prays for mercy for himself. In general (*v.* 21): "*Do thou for me, O God the Lord!* appear for me, act for me." If God be for us, he will do for us, will do *more abundantly for us than we are able either to ask or think.* He does not prescribe to God what he should do for him, but refers himself to his wisdom: "Lord, do for me what seems good in thy eyes. Do that which thou knowest will be for me, really for me, in the issue for me, though for the present it may seem to make against me." More particularly, he prays (*v.* 26): "*Help me, O Lord my God! O save me!* Help me under my trouble, save me out of my trouble; save me from sin, help me to do my duty." He prays (*v.* 28), Though they *curse, bless thou.* Here (1.) He despises the causeless curses of his enemies: *Let them curse.* He said of Shimei, *So let him curse.* They can but show their malice; they can do him no more mischief than *the bird by wandering* or *the swallow by flying,* Prov. 26:2. He values the blessing of God as sufficient to counterbalance their curses: *Bless thou,* and then it is no matter though they *curse.* If God bless us, we need not care who curses us; for *how can they curse those whom God has not cursed,* nay, whom he has blessed? Num. 23:8. Men's curses are impotent; God's blessings are omnipotent; and those whom we unjustly curse may in faith expect and pray for God's blessing, his special blessing. When the Pharisees cast out the poor man for his confessing Christ, *Christ found him,* Jn. 9:35. When men without cause say all the ill they can of us, and wish all the ills they can to us, we may with comfort lift up our heart to God in this petition: *Let them curse, but bless thou.* He prays (*v.* 28), *Let thy servant rejoice.* Those that know how to value God's blessing, let them but be sure of it, and they will be glad of it.

III. He prays that his enemies might *be ashamed* (*v.* 28), *clothed with shame* (*v.* 29), that they might *cover themselves with their own confusion,* that they might be left to themselves, to do that which would expose them and *manifest their folly before all men,* or rather that they might be disappointed in their designs and enterprises against David, and thereby might be *filled with shame,* as the adversaries of the Jews were, Neh. 6:16. Nay, in this he prays that they might be brought to repentance, which is the chief thing we should beg of God for our enemies. Sinners indeed bring shame upon themselves, but they are true penitents that take shame to themselves and *cover themselves with their own confusion.*

IV. He pleads God's glory, the honour of his name: —

Do for me, for thy name's sake (*v.* 21), especially the honour of his goodness, by which he has proclaimed his name: "*Deliver me, because thy mercy is good;* it is what thou thyself dost delight in, and it is what I do depend upon. Save me, not according to my merit, for I have none to pretend to, but *according to thy mercy;* let that be the fountain, the reason, the measure, of my salvation."

Lastly, He concludes the psalm with joy, the joy of faith, joy in assurance that his present conflicts would end in triumphs. 1. He promises God that he will praise him (*v.* 30): "*I will greatly praise the Lord,* not only with my heart, but with my mouth; I will praise him, not in secret only, but *among the multitude.*" 2. He promises himself that he shall have cause to praise God (*v.* 31): *He shall stand at the right hand of the poor,* night to him, a present help; he shall stand at his right hand as his patron and advocate to plead his cause against his accusers and to bring him off, *to save him from those that condemn his soul* and would execute their sentence if they could. God was David's protector in his sufferings, and was present also with the Lord Jesus in his, *stood at his right hand,* so that he was *not moved* (Ps. 16:8), saved his soul from those that pretended to be the judges of it, and received it into his own hands. Let all those that *suffer according to the will of God commit the keeping of their souls to him.*

PSALM 110

This psalm is pure gospel; it is only, and wholly, concerning Christ, the Messiah promised to the fathers and expected by them. It is plain that the Jews of old, even the worst of them, so understood it, however the modern Jews have endeavoured to pervert it and to rob us of it; for when the Lord Jesus proposed a question to the Pharisees upon the first words of this psalm, where he takes it for granted that David, in spirit, calls Christ his Lord though he was his Son, they chose rather to say nothing, and to own themselves gravelled, than to make it a question whether David does indeed speak of the Messiah or no; for they freely yield so plain a truth, though they foresee it will turn to their own disgrace, Mt. 22:41, etc. Of him therefore, no doubt, the prophet here speaks of him and of no other man. Christ, as our Redeemer, executes the office of a prophet, of a priest, and of a king, with reference both to his humiliation and his exaltation; and of each of these we have here an account. I. His prophetical office (*v.* 2). II. His priestly office (*v.* 4). III. His kingly office (*v.* 1, 3, 5, 6). IV. His estates of humiliation and exaltation (*v.* 7). In singing this psalm we must act faith upon Christ, submit ourselves entirely to him, to his grace and government, and triumph in him as our prophet, priest, and king, by whom we hope to be ruled, and taught, and saved, for ever, and as the prophet, priest, and king, of the whole church, who shall reign till he has put down all opposing rule, principality, and power, and delivered up the kingdom to God the Father.

A psalm of David.

Verses 1–4

Some have called this psalm *David's creed,* almost all the articles of the Christian faith being found in it; the title calls it *David's psalm,* for in the believing foresight of the Messiah he both praised God and solaced himself, much more may we, in singing it, to whom that is fulfilled, and therefore more clearly revealed, which is here foretold. Glorious things are here spoken of Christ, and such as oblige us to consider how great he is.

I. That he is David's Lord. We must take special notice of this because he himself does. Mt. 22:43, *David, in spirit, calls him Lord.* And as the apostle proves the dignity of Melchizedek, and in him of Christ, by this, that so great a man as Abraham was paid him *tithes* (Heb. 7:4), so we may be this prove the dignity of the Lord Jesus that David, that great man, *called him* his *Lord;* by him that king acknowledges himself to reign, and to him to be acceptable as a servant to his lord. Some think he calls him his *Lord* because he was the Lord that was to descend from him, his son and yet his Lord. Thus him immediate mother calls him her *Saviour* (Lu. 1:47); even his parents were his subjects, his saved ones.

II. That he is constituted a sovereign Lord by the counsel and decree of God himself: *The Lord,* Jehovah, *said unto him, Sit* as a king. He *receives of the Father* this honour and glory (2 Pt. 1:17), from him who is the fountain of honour and power, and *takes it not to himself.* He is therefore rightful Lord, and his title is incontestable; for what God has said cannot be gainsaid. He is therefore everlasting Lord; for what God has said shall not be unsaid. He will certainly take and keep possession of that kingdom which the Father has committed to him, and none can hinder.

III. That he was to be advanced to the highest honour, and entrusted with an absolute sovereign power both in

heaven and in earth: *Sit thou at my right hand.* Sitting is a resting posture; after his services and sufferings, he entered into rest from all his labours. It is a ruling posture; he sits to give law, to give judgment. It is a remaining posture; he sits like a king for ever. Sitting at the right hand of God denotes both his dignity and his dominion, the honour put upon him and the trusts reposed in him by the Father. All the favours that come from God to man, and all the service that comes from man to God, pass through his hand.

IV. That all his enemies were in due time to be made his footstool, and not till then; but then also he must reign in the glory of the Mediator, though the work of the Mediator will be, in a manner, at an end. Note, 1. Even Christ himself has enemies that fight against his kingdom and subjects, his honour and interest, in the world. There are those that will not have him to reign over them, and thereby they join themselves to Satan, who will not have him to reign at all. 2. These enemies will *be made his footstool;* he will subdue them and triumph over them; he will do it easily, as easily as we put a footstool in its proper place, and such a propriety there will be in it. He will make himself easy by the doing of it, as a man that sits with a footstool under his feet; he will subdue them in such a way as shall be most for his honour and their perpetual disgrace; he will *tread down the wicked,* Mal. 4:3. 3. God the Father has undertaken to do it: *I will make them thy footstool,* who can do it. 4. It will not be done immediately. All his enemies are now in a chain, but not yet made his footstool. This the apostle observes. Heb. 2:8, *We see not yet all things put under him.* Christ himself must wait for the completing of his victories and triumphs. 5. He shall wait till it is done; and all their might and malice shall not give the least disturbance to his government. His sitting at God's right hand is a pledge to him of his setting his feet, at last, on the necks of all his enemies.

V. That he should have a kingdom set up in the world, beginning at Jerusalem (*v.* 2): "*The Lord shall send the rod* or *sceptre of thy strength out of Zion,* by which thy kingdom shall be erected, maintained, and administered." The Messiah, when he sits on the right hand of the Majesty in the heavens, will have a church on earth, and will have an eye to it; for he is *King upon the holy hill of Zion* (Ps. 2:6), in opposition to Mount Sinai, that frightful mountain, on which the law was given, Heb. 12:18, 24; Gal. 4:24, 25. The kingdom of Christ took rise from Zion, the city of David, for he was the Son of David, and was to have the *throne of his father David.* By the rod of his strength, or his strong rod, is meant his everlasting gospel, and the power of the Holy Ghost going along with it — the report of the word, and the arm of the Lord accompanying it (Isa. 53:1; Rom. 1:16), — the gospel coming in word, and in power, and *in the holy Ghost,* 1 Th. 1:5. By the word and Spirit of God souls were to be reduced first, and brought into obedience to God, and then ruled and governed according to the will of God. This strong rod God sent forth; he poured out the Spirit, and gave both commissions and qualifications to those that preached the word, and *ministered the Spirit,* Gal. 3:5. It was sent out of Zion, for there the Spirit was given, and there the preaching of the gospel among all nations must begin, at Jerusalem. See Lu. 24:47, 49. *Out of Zion* must go forth the law of faith, Isa. 2:3. Note, The gospel of Christ, being sent of God, is *mighty through God* to do wonders, 2 Co. 10:4. It is *the rod of Christ's strength.* Some make it to allude not only to the sceptre of a prince, denoting the glory of Christ shining in the gospel, but to a shepherd's crook, his rod and staff, denoting the tender care of Christ takes of his church; for he is both *the great and the good Shepherd.*

VI. That his kingdom, being set up, should be maintained and kept up in the world, in spite of all the oppositions of the power of darkness. 1. Christ shall rule, shall give laws, and govern his subjects by them, shall perfect them, and make them easy and happy, shall do his own will, fulfil his own counsels, and maintain his own interests among men. His kingdom is of God, and it shall stand; his crown sits firmly on his head, and there it shall flourish. 2. He shall rule *in the midst of his enemies.* He sits in heaven in the midst of his friends; his throne of glory there is surrounded with none but faithful worshippers of him, Rev. 5:11. But he rules on earth in the midst of his enemies, and his throne of government here is surrounded with those that hate him and fight against him. Christ's church is a lily among thorns, and his disciples are sent forth *as sheep in the midst of wolves;* he knows *where they dwell, even where Satan's seat is* (Rev. 2:13), and this redounds to his honour that he not only keeps his ground, but gains his point, notwithstanding all the malignant policies and powers of hell and earth, which cannot shake the rock on which the church is built. *Great is the truth, and will prevail.*

VII. That he should have a great number of subjects, who should be to him for a name and a praise, *v.* 3.

1. That they should be his own people, and such as he should have an incontestable title to. They are given to him by the Father, who gave them their lives and beings, and to whom their lives and beings were forfeited. *Thine they were and thou gavest them me,* Jn. 17:6. They are redeemed by him; he has purchased them to be to himself *a peculiar people,* Tit. 2:14. They are his by right, antecedent to their consent. He *had much people in Corinth* before they were converted, Acts 18:10.

2. That they should be *a willing people,* a people of willingness, alluding to servants that choose their service and are not coerced to it (they love their masters and would not go out free), to soldiers that are volunteers and not pressed men ("Here am I, send me"), to sacrifices that are free-will offerings and not offered of necessity; we *present ourselves living sacrifices.* Note, Christ's people are a willing people. The conversion of a soul consists in its being willing to be Christ's, coming under his yoke and into his interests, with an entire compliancy and satisfaction.

3. That they should be so *in the day of his power, in the day of thy muster* (so some); when thou art enlisting soldiers thou shalt find a multitude of volunteers forward to be enlisted; let but the standard be set up and the *Gentiles will seek to it,* Isa. 11:10; 60:3. Or when thou art drawing them out to battle they shall be willing to *follow the Lamb whithersoever he goes,* Rev. 14:4. *In the day of thy armies* (so some); "when the first preachers of the gospel shall be sent forth, as Christ's armies, to reduce apostate men, and to ruin the kingdom of apostate angels, then all that are *thy people shall be willing;* that will be thy time of setting up thy kingdom." *In the day of thy strength,* so we take it. There is a general power which goes along with the gospel to all, proper to make them willing to be Christ's people, arising from the supreme authority of its great author and the intrinsic excellency of the things themselves contained in it, besides the undeniable miracles that were wrought for the confirmation of it. And there is also a particular power, the power of the Spirit, going along with the power of the word, to the people of Christ, which is effectual to make them willing. The former leaves sinners without matter of excuse; this leaves saints without matter of boasting. Whoever are willing to be Christ's people, it is the free and mighty grace of God that makes them so.

4. That they should be so *in the beauty of holiness,* that is, (1.) They shall be allured to him by the beauty of holiness; they shall be charmed into a subjection to Christ by the sight given them of his beauty, who is the holy Jesus, and the beauty of the church, which is the holy nation. (2.) They shall be admitted by him into the beauty of holiness, as spiritual priests, to minister in his sanctuary; for *by the blood of Jesus we have boldness to enter into the holiest.* (3.) They shall attend upon him in the beautiful attire or ornaments of grace and sanctification. Note, Holiness is the livery of Christ's family and that which *becomes his house for ever.* Christ's soldiers are all thus clothed; these are the colours they wear. The armies of heaven *follow him in fine linen, clean and white,* Rev. 19:14.

5. That he should have great numbers of people devoted to him. The multitude of the people is the honour of the prince, and that shall be the honour of this prince. *From the womb of the morning thou hast the dew of thy youth,* that is, abundance of young converts, like the drops of dew in a summer's morning. In the early days of the gospel, in the morning of the New Testament, the youth of the church, great numbers flocked to Christ, and there were *multitudes that believed,* a *remnant of Jacob,* that was as *dew from the Lord,* Mic. 5:7; Isa. 64:4, 8. Or thus? *"From the womb of the morning* (from their very childhood) *thou hast the dew of thy* people's *youth,* that is, their hearts and affections when they are young; it is thy youth, because it is dedicated to thee." *The dew of the youth* is a numer-

ous, illustrious, hopeful show of young people flocking to Christ, which would be to the world as dew to the ground, to make it fruitful. Note, The dew of our youth, even in the morning of our days, ought to be consecrated to our Lord Jesus.

6. That he should be not only a king, but a priest, *v.* 4. The same Lord that said, *Sit thou at my right hand, swore, and will not repent, Thou art a priest,* that is, *Be thou a priest;* for by the word of his oath he was consecrated. Note, (1.) Our Lord Jesus Christ is a priest. He was appointed to that office and faithfully executes it; he is *ordained for men in things pertaining to God, to offer gifts and sacrifices for sin* (Heb. 5:1), to make atonement for our sins and to recommend our services to God's acceptance. He is God's minister to us, and our advocate with God, and so is a Mediator between us and God. (2.) He is *a priest for ever.* He was designed for a priest, in God's eternal counsels; he was a priest to the Old-Testament saints, and will be a priest for all believers to the end of time, Heb. 13:8. He is said to be *a priest for ever,* not only because we are never to expect any other dispensation of grace than this by the priesthood of Christ, but because the blessed fruits and consequences of it will remain to eternity. (3.) He is made a priest with an oath, which the apostle urges to prove the pre-eminence of his priesthood above that of Aaron, Heb. 7:20, 21. *The Lord has sworn,* to show that in the commission there was no implied reserve of a power of revocation; for *he will not repent,* as he did concerning Eli's priesthood, 1 Sa. 2:30. This was intended for the honour of Christ and the comfort of Christians. The priesthood of Christ is confirmed by the highest ratifications possible, that it might be an unshaken foundation for our faith and hope to build upon. (4.) He is a priest, not of the order of Aaron, but of that of Melchizedek, which, as it was prior, so it was upon many accounts superior, to that of Aaron, and a more lively representation of Christ's priesthood. Melchizedek was *a priest upon his throne,* so is Christ (Zec. 6:13), king of righteousness and king of peace. Melchizedek had no successor, nor has Christ; his is an unchangeable priesthood. The apostle comments largely upon these words (Heb. 7) and builds on them his discourse of Christ's priestly office, which he shows was no new notion, but built upon this most sure word of prophecy. For, as the New Testament explains the Old, so the Old Testament confirms the New, and Jesus Christ is the Alpha and Omega of both.

Verses 5–7

Here we have our great Redeemer,

I. Conquering his enemies (*v.* 5, 6) in order to the making of them *his footstool, v.* 1. Our Lord Jesus will certainly bring to nought all the opposition made to his kingdom, and bring to ruin all those who make that opposition and persist in it. He will be too hard for those, whoever they may be, that fight against him, against his subjects and the interest of his kingdom among men, either by persecutions or by perverse disputings. Observe here,

1. The conqueror: *The Lord — Adonai,* the Lord Jesus, he to whom all judgment is committed, he shall make his own part good against his enemies. *The Lord at thy right hand, O church!* so some; that is, the Lord that is nigh unto his people, and a very present help to them, that is at their right hand, to strengthen and succour them, shall appear for them against his and their enemies. See Ps. 109:31. *He shall stand at the right hand of the poor,* Ps. 16:8. Some observe that when Christ is said to do his work at the right hand of his church it intimates that, if we would have Christ to appear for us, we must *bestir ourselves,* 2 Sa. 5:24. Or, rather, *At thy right hand, O God!* referring to *v.* 1, in the dignity and dominion to which he is advanced. Note, Christ's sitting at the right hand of God speaks as much terror to his enemies as happiness to his people.

2. The time fixed for this victory: *In the day of his wrath,* that is, the time appointed for it, when the measure of their iniquities is full and they are ripe for ruin. When the day of his patience has expired, when the day of his wrath comes. Note, (1.) Christ has wrath of his own, as well as grace. It concerns us to *kiss the Son,* for he can be *angry* (Ps. 2:12) and we read of the *wrath of the Lamb,* Rev. 6:16. (2.) There is a day of wrath set, a year of *recompences for the controversy of Zion, the year of the redeemed.* The time is set for the destruction of particular enemies, and when

that time shall come it shall be done, how unlikely soever it may seem; but the great day of his wrath will be at the end of time, Rev. 6:17.

3. The extent of this victory. (1.) It shall reach very high: He *shall strike through kings.* The greatest of men, that set themselves against Christ, shall be made to fall before him. Though they be *kings of the earth,* and rulers, accustomed to carry their point, they cannot carry it against Christ, they do but make themselves ridiculous by the attempt, Ps. 2:2–5. Be their power among men ever so despotic, Christ will call them to an account; be their strength ever so great, their policies ever so deep, Christ will be too hard for them, and wherein they deal proudly he will be above them. Satan is the prince of this world, Death the king of terrors, and we read of kings that make war with the Lamb; but they shall all be brought down and broken. (2.) It shall reach very far. The trophies of Christ's victories will be set up *among the heathen,* and in many countries, wherever any of his enemies are, not his eye only, but his *hand, shall find them out* (Ps. 21:8) and his wrath shall follow them. He will *plead with all nations,* Joel 3:2.

4. The equity of this victory: *He shall judge among them.* It is not a military execution, which is done in fury, but a judicial one. Before he condemns and slays, he will judge; he will make it appear that they have brought this ruin upon themselves, and have themselves rolled the stone which returns upon them, that he may be *justified when he speaks* and the *heavens may declare his righteousness.* See Rev. 19:1, 2.

5. The effect of this victory; it shall be the complete and utter ruin of all his enemies. He shall strike them through, for he strikes home and gives an incurable wound: He shall *wound the heads,* which seems to refer to the first promise of the Messiah (Gen. 3:15), that he should *bruise the serpent's head.* He shall *wound the head of his enemies,* Ps. 68:21. Some read it, *He shall wound* him that is *the head over many countries,* either Satan or Antichrist, whom *the Lord shall consume with the breath of his mouth.* He shall make such destruction of his enemies that he shall *fill the places with the dead bodies.* The slain of the Lord shall be many. See Isa. 34:3, etc.; Eze. 39:12, 14; Rev. 14:20; 19:17, 18. The filling of *the valleys* (for so some read it) *with dead bodies,* perhaps denotes the *filling of hell* (which is sometimes compared to the valley of *Hinnom,* Isa. 30:33; Jer. 7:32) with *damned souls,* for that will be the portion of those that persist in their enmity to Christ.

II. We have here the Redeemer saving his friends and comforting them (*v.* 7); for their benefit, 1. He shall be humbled: *He shall drink of the brook in the way,* that bitter cup which the Father put into his hand. He shall be so abased and impoverished, and withal so intent upon his work, that he shall drink puddle-water out of the lakes in the highway; so some. The wrath of God, running in the channel of the curse of the law, was *the brook in the way,* in the way of his undertaking, which must go through, or which ran in the way of our salvation and obstructed it, which lay between us and heaven. Christ drank of this brook when he was made a curse for us, and therefore, when he entered upon his suffering, he *went over the brook Kidron,* Jn. 18:1. He drank deeply of this *black brook* (so Kidron signifies), this bloody brook, so drank of the *brook in the way* as to take it out of the way of our redemption and salvation. 2. He shall be exalted: *Therefore shall he lift up the head.* When he died he *bowed the head* (Jn. 19:30), but he soon lifted up the head by his own power in his resurrection. He lifted up the head as a conqueror, yea, more than a conqueror. This denotes not only his exaltation, but his exultation; not only his elevation, but his triumph in it. Col. 2:15, *Having spoiled principalities and powers, he made a show of them.* David spoke as a type of him in this (Ps. 27:6), *Now shall my head be lifted up above my enemies.* His exaltation was the reward of his humiliation; because he *humbled himself, therefore God also highly exalted him,* Phil. 2:9. Because he drank of the brook in the way therefore he lifted up his own head, and so lifted up the heads of all his faithful followers, who, *if they suffer with him, shall also reign with him.*

PSALM 111

This and divers of the psalms that follow it seem to have been penned by David for the service of the church in their solemn feasts, and not upon any particular occasion. This is a psalm of praise. The title of it is "Hallelujah — Praise you the Lord," intimating that we must address ourselves to the use of this psalm with hearts disposed to praise God. It is composed alphabetically, each sentence beginning with a several letter of the Hebrew alphabet, in order exactly, two sentences to each verse, and three a piece to the last two. The psalmist, exhorting to praise God, I. Sets himself for an example (*v.* 1). II. Furnishes us with matter for praise from the works of God. 1. The greatness of his works and the glory of them. 2. The righteousness of them. 3. The goodness of them. 4. The power of them. 5. The conformity of them to his word of promise. 6. The perpetuity of them. These observations are intermixed (*v.* 2–9). III. He recommends the holy fear of God, and conscientious obedience to his commands, as the most acceptable way of praising God (*v.* 10).

Verses 1–5

The title of the psalm being *Hallelujah,* the psalmist (as every author ought to have) has an eye to his title, and keeps to his text.

I. He resolves to praise God himself, *v.* 1. What duty we call others to we must oblige and excite ourselves to; nay, whatever others do, whether they will praise God or no, we and our houses must determine to do it, we and our hearts; for such is the psalmist's resolution here: *I will praise the Lord with my whole heart.* My heart, my whole heart, being devoted to his honour, shall be employed in this work; and this *in the assembly,* or secret, *of the upright,* in the cabinet-council, *and in the congregation* of Israelites. Note, We must praise God both in private and in public, in less and greater assemblies, in our own families and in the courts of the Lord's house; but in both it is most comfortable to do it in concert with the upright, who will heartily join in it. Private meetings for devotion should be kept up as well as more public and promiscuous assemblies.

II. He recommends to us the *works of the Lord* as the proper subject of our meditations when we are praising him — the dispensations of his providence towards the world, towards the church, and towards particular persons. 1. God's works are very magnificent, great like himself; there is nothing in them that is mean or trifling: they are the products of infinite wisdom and power, and we must say this upon the first view of them, before we come to enquire more particularly into them, that the *works of the Lord are great, v.* 2. There is something in them surprising, and that strikes an awe upon us. All the *works of the Lord* are spoken of as one (*v.* 3); it is *his work,* such is the beauty and harmony of Providence and so admirably do all its dispensations centre in one design; it was cried to *the wheels, O wheel!* Eze. 10:13. Take all together, and it is *honourable and glorious,* and such as becomes him. 2. They are entertaining and exercising to the inquisitive — *sought out of all those that have pleasure therein.* Note, (1.) All that truly love God have pleasure in his works, and reckon all well that he does; nor do their thoughts dwell upon any subject with more delight than on the works of God, which the more they are looked into the more they give us of a pleasing surprise. (2.) Those that have pleasure in the works of God will not take up with a superficial transient view of them, but will diligently search into them and observe them. In studying both natural and political history we should have this in our eye, to discover the greatness and glory of God's works. (3.) These works of God, that are humbly and diligently sought into, shall be *sought out;* those that *seek shall find* (so some read); *they are found of all those that have pleasure in them,* or found in all their parts, designs, purposes, and several concernments (so Dr. Hammond), for the *secret of the Lord is with those that fear him,* Ps. 25:14. 3. They are all justly and holy; *His righteousness endures for ever.* Whatever he does, he never did, nor ever will do, any wrong to any of his creatures; and *therefore* his works *endure for ever* (Eccl. 3:14) because the righteousness of them endures. 4. They are admirable and memorable, fit to be registered and kept on record. Much that we do is so trifling that it is not fit to be spoken of or told again; the greatest kindness is to forget it. But notice is to be taken of God's works, and an account to be kept of them (*v.* 4). *He has made his wonderful works to be remembered;* he has done that which is worthy to be remembered, which cannot but be remembered, and he has instituted ways and means for the keeping of some of them in remembrance, as the deliverance of Israel out of Egypt by the passover. *He has made himself a memorial by his wonderful works* (so some read it); see Isa. 63:10. By that which God did with his *glorious arm he made himself an everlasting name.* 5. They are very kind. In them the Lord shows that he is *gracious and full of compassion.* As of the works of creation, so of the works of providence, we must say, They are not only all very great, but all very good. Dr. Hammond takes this to be the name which God has made to himself by his wonderful works, the same with that which he proclaimed to Moses, *The Lord God is gracious and merciful,* Ex. 24:6. God's pardoning sin is the most wonderful of all his works and which ought to be remembered to his glory. It is a further instance of his grace and compassion that *he has given meat to those that fear him, v.* 5. He gives them their daily bread, food convenient for them; so he does to others by common providence, but to those that fear him he gives it by covenant and in pursuance of the promise, for it follows, *He will be ever mindful of his covenant;* so that they can taste covenant-love even in common mercies. Some refer this to the manna with which God fed his people Israel in the wilderness, others to the spoil they got from the Egyptians when they came out with great substance, according to the promise, Gen. 15:14. When God *broke the heads of leviathan* he gave him to be *meat to his people,* Ps. 74:14. *He has given* prey *to those that fear him* (so the margin has it), not only fed them, but enriched them, and given their enemies to be a prey to them. 6. They are earnests of what he will do, according to his promise: *He will ever be mindful of his covenant,* for he has ever been so; and, as he never did, so he never will, let one jot or tittle of it fall to the ground. Though God's people have their infirmities, and are often unmindful of his commands, yet he *will ever be mindful of his covenant.*

Verses 6–10

We are here taught to give glory to God,

I. For the great things he has done for his people, for his people Israel, of old and of late: *He has shown his people the power of his works* (*v.* 6), in what he has wrought for them; many a time he has given proofs of his omnipotence, and shown them what he can do, and that there is nothing too hard for him to do. Two things are specified to show *the power of his works:* — 1. The possession God gave to Israel in the land of Canaan, *that he might give them,* or in giving them, *the heritage of the heathen.* This he did in Joshua's time, when the seven nations were subdued, and in David's time, when the neighbouring nations were many of them brought into subjection to Israel and became tributaries to David. Herein God showed his sovereignty, in disposing of kingdoms as he pleases, and his might, in making good his disposals. If God will make the heritage of the heathen to be the heritage of Israel, who can either arraign his counsel or stay his hand? 2. The many deliverances which he wrought for his people when by their iniquities they had sold themselves into the hand of their enemies (*v.* 9): *He sent redemption unto his people,* not only out of Egypt at first, but often afterwards; and these redemptions were typical of the great redemption which in the fulness of time was to be wrought out by the Lord Jesus, that redemption in Jerusalem which so many waited for.

II. For the stability both of his word and of his works, which assure us of the great things he will do for them. 1. What God has done shall never be undone. He will not undo it himself, and men and devils cannot (*v.* 7): *The works of his hand are verity and judgment* (*v.* 8), that is, they *are done in truth and uprightness;* all he does is consonant to the eternal rules and reasons of equity, all according to the counsel of his wisdom and the purpose of his will, all well done and therefore there is nothing to be altered or amended, but his works are firm and unchangeable. Upon the beginning of his works we may depend for the perfecting of them; work that is done properly will last, will neither go to decay nor sink under the stress that is laid upon it. 2. What God has said shall never be unsaid: *All his commandments are sure,* all straight and therefore all steady. His purposes, the rule of his actions, shall all have their accomplishment: *Has he spoken, and will he not make it good?* No doubt he will; whether he commands light or darkness, it is done as he commands. His precepts, the rule of our actions, are unquestionably just and good, and therefore unchangeable and not to be repealed; his promises and threatenings are all sure, and will be made good; nor shall the unbelief of man make either the one or the other of no effect. They are established, and therefore *they stand fast for ever and ever,* and the scripture cannot be broken. The wise God is never put upon new counsels, nor obliged to take new measures, either in his laws or in his providences. All is said, as all is done, in truth and uprightness, and therefore it is immutable. Men's folly and falsehood make them *unstable in all their ways,* but infinite wisdom and truth for ever exclude retraction and revocation: *He has commanded his covenant for ever.* God's covenant is commanded, for he has made it as one that has an incontestable authority to prescribe both what we must do and what we must expect, and an unquestionable ability to perform both what he has promised in the blessings of the covenant and what he has threatened in the curses of it, Ps. 105:8.

III. For the setting up and establishing of religion among men. Because *holy and reverend is his name, and the fear of* him *is the beginning of wisdom,* therefore *his praise endureth for ever,* that is, he is to be everlastingly praised. 1. Because the discoveries of religion tend so much to his honour. Review what he has made known of himself in his word and in his works, and you will see, and say, that God is great and greatly to be feared; for his name is holy, his infinite purity and rectitude appear in all that whereby he has made himself known, and because it is holy therefore it is reverend, and to be thought of and mentioned with a holy awe. Note, What is holy is reverend; the angels have an eye to God's holiness when they cover their faces before him, and nothing is more man's honour than his sanctification. It is in his holy places that God appears most terrible, Ps. 68:35; Lev. 10:3. 2. Because the dictates of religion tend so much to man's happiness. We have reason to praise God that the matter is so well contrived that our reverence of him and obedience to him are as much our interest as they are our duty. (1.) Our reverence of him is so: *The fear of the Lord is the beginning of wisdom.* It is not only reasonable that we should fear God, because his name is reverend and his nature is holy, but it is advantageous to us. It is wisdom; it will direct us to speak and act as becomes us, in a consistency with ourselves, and for our own benefit. It is the head of wisdom, that is (as we read it), it *is the beginning of wisdom.* Men can never begin to be wise till they begin to fear God; all true wisdom takes its rise from true religion, and has its foundation in it. Or, as some understand it, it is the chief wisdom, and the most excellent, the first in dignity. It is the principal wisdom, and the principal of wisdom, to worship God and give honour to him as our Father and Master. Those manage well who always act under the government of his holy fear. (2.) Our obedience to him is so: *A good understanding have all those that do his commandments.* Where the fear of the Lord rules in the heart there will be a constant conscientious care to keep his commandments, not to talk of them, but to do them; and such have a good understanding, that is, [1.] They are well understood; their obedience is graciously accepted as a plain indication of their mind that they do indeed fear God. Compare Prov. 3:4, *So shalt thou find favour and good understanding.* God and man will look upon those as meaning well, and approve of them, who make conscience of their duty, though they have their mistakes. What is honestly intended shall be well taken. [2.] They understand well. *First,* It is a sign that they do understand well. The most obedient are accepted as the most intelligent; those understand themselves and their interest best that make God's law their rule and are in every thing ruled by it. A great understanding those have that know God's commandments and can discourse learnedly of them, but a good understanding have those that do them and walk according to them. *Secondly,* It is the way to understand better: *A good understanding are they to all that do them;* the fear of the Lord and the laws of that give men a good understanding, and are able to make them *wise unto salvation. If any man will do his will, he shall know* more and more clearly of the doctrine of Christ, Jn. 7:17. *Good success have all those that do them* (so the margin), according to what was promised to Joshua if he would observe to do according to the law. Jos. 1:8, *Then thou shalt make thy way prosperous and shalt have good success.* We have reason to praise God, to praise him for ever, for putting man into such a fair way to happiness. Some apply the last words rather to the good man who fears the Lord than to the good God: *His praise endures for ever.* It is *not of men* perhaps, *but* it is *of God*

(Rom. 2:29), and that praise which is of God endures for ever when the praise of men is withered and gone.

PSALM 112

This psalm is composed alphabetically, as the former is, and is (like the former) entitled "Hallelujah," though it treats of the happiness of the saints, because it redounds to the glory of God, and whatever we have the pleasure of he must have the praise of. It is a comment upon the last verse of the foregoing psalm, and fully shows how much it is our wisdom to fear God and do his commandments. We have here, I. The character of the righteous (v. 1). II. The blessedness of the righteous. 1. There is a blessing entailed upon their posterity (v. 2). 2. There is a blessing conferred upon themselves. (1.) Prosperity outward and inward (v. 3). (2.) Comfort (v. 4). (3.) Wisdom (v. 5). (4.) Stability (v. 6–8). (5.) Honour (v. 6, 9). III. The misery of the wicked (v. 10). So that good and evil are set before us, the blessing and the curse. In singing this psalm we must not only teach and admonish ourselves and one another to answer to the characters here given of the happy, but comfort and encourage ourselves and one another with the privileges and comforts here secured to the holy.

Verses 1–5

The psalmist begins with a call to us to praise God, but immediately applies himself to praise the people of God; for whatever glory is acknowledged to be on them it comes from God, and must return to him; as he is their praise, so they are his. We have reason to praise the Lord that there are a people in the world who fear him and serve him, and that they are a happy people, both which are owing entirely to the grace of God. Now here we have,

I. A description of those who are here pronounced blessed, and to whom these promises are made.

1. They are well-principled with pious and devout affections. Those have the privileges of God's subjects, not who cry, *Lord, Lord,* but who are indeed well affected to his government. (1.) They are such as stand in awe of God and have a constant reverence for his majesty and deference to his will. The happy man is he *that fears the Lord,* v. 1. (2.) They are such as take a pleasure in their duty. He *that fears the Lord,* as a Father, with the disposition of a child, not of a slave, *delights greatly in his commandments,* is well pleased with them and with the equity and goodness of them; they are written in his heart; it is his choice to be under them, and he calls them an easy, a pleasant, yoke; it is his delight to be searching into and conversing with God's commandments, by reading, hearing, and meditation, Ps. 1:2. He delights not only in God's promises, but in his precepts, and thinks himself happy under God's government as well as in his favour. It is a pleasure to him to be found in the way of his duty, and he is in his element when he is in the service of God. Herein he delights greatly, more than in any of the employments and enjoyments of this world. And what he does in religion is done from principle, because he sees amiableness in religion and advantage by it.

2. They are honest and sincere in their professions and intentions. They are called *the upright* (v. 2, 4), who are really as good as they seem to be, and deal faithfully both with God and man. There is no true religion without sincerity; that is gospel-perfection.

3. They are both just and kind in all their dealings: *He is gracious, full of compassion, and righteous* (v. 4), dares not do any wrong to any man, but does to every man all the good he can, and that from a principle of compassion and kindness. It was said of God, in the foregoing psalm (v. 4), He *is gracious, and full of compassion;* and here it is said of the good man that he is so; for herein we must be *followers of God as dear children;* be merciful as he is. He is *full of compassion, and yet righteous;* what he does good with is what he came honestly by. God hates robbery for burnt-offerings, and so does he. One instance is given of his beneficence (v. 5): He *shows favour and lends.* Sometimes there is as much charity in lending as in giving, as it obliges the borrower both to industry and honesty. He is *gracious and lends* (Ps. 37:26); he does it from a right principle, not as the usurer lends for his own advantage, nor merely out of generosity, but out of pure charity; he does it in a right manner, not grudgingly, but pleasantly, and with a cheerful countenance.

II. The blessedness that is here entailed upon those that answer to these characters. Happiness, all happiness, to *the man that feareth the Lord.* Whatever men think or say of them, God says that they are blessed; and his saying so makes them so.

1. The posterity of good men shall fare the better for his goodness (v. 2): *His seed shall be mighty on earth.* Per-

haps he himself shall not be so great in the world, nor make such a figure, as his seed after him shall for his sake. Religion has been the raising of many a family, if not so as to advance it high, yet so as to fix it firmly. When good men themselves are happy in heaven their seed perhaps are considerable on earth, and will themselves own that it is by virtue of a blessing descending from them. *The generation of the upright shall be blessed;* if they tread in their steps, they shall be the more blessed for their relation to them, *beloved for the Father's sake* (Rom. 11:28), for so runs the covenant — *I will be a God to thee, and to thy seed;* while *the seed of evil-doers shall never be renowned.* Let the children of godly parents value themselves upon it, and take heed of doing any thing to forfeit the blessing entailed upon the generation of the upright.

2. They shall prosper in the world, and especially their souls shall prosper, v. 3. (1.) They shall be blessed with outward prosperity as far as is good for them: *Wealth and riches shall be in* the upright man's *house,* not in his heart (for he is none of those in whom the love of money reigns), perhaps not so much in his hand (for he only begins to raise the estate), but in his house; his family shall grow rich when he is gone. But, (2.) That which is much better is that they shall be blessed with spiritual blessings, which are the true riches. His *wealth shall be in his house,* for he must leave that to others; but *his righteousness* he himself shall have the comfort of to himself, it *endures for ever.* Grace is better than gold, for it will outlast it. He shall have wealth and riches, and yet shall keep up his religion, and in a prosperous condition shall *still hold fast his integrity,* which many, who kept it in the storm, throw off and let go in the sunshine. *Then* worldly prosperity is a blessing when it does not make men cool in their piety, but they still persevere in that; and when this endures in the family, and goes along with the wealth and riches, and the heirs of the father's estate inherit his virtues too, that is a happy family indeed. However, the good man's *righteousness endures for ever* in the *crown of righteousness which fades not away.*

3. They shall have comfort in affliction (v. 4): *Unto the upright there arises light in the darkness.* It is here implied that good men may be in affliction; the promise does not exempt them from that. They shall have their share in the common calamities of human life; but, *when they sit in darkness, the Lord shall be a light to them,* Mic. 7:8. They shall be supported and comforted under their troubles; their spirits shall be lightsome when their outward condition is clouded. *Sat lucis intus — There is light enough within.* During the Egyptian darkness the Israelites had *light in their dwellings.* They shall be in due time, and perhaps when they least expect it, delivered out of their troubles; when the night is darkest the day dawns; nay, at *evening-time,* when night was looked for, *it shall be light.*

4. They shall have wisdom for the management of all their concerns, v. 5. He that does good with his estate shall, through the providence of God, increase it, not by miracle, but by his prudence: *He shall guide his affairs with discretion,* and his God *instructs him to discretion and teaches him,* Isa. 28:26. It is part of the character of a good man that he will use his discretion in managing his affairs, in getting and saving, that he may have to give. It may be understood of the affairs of his charity: He *shows favour and lends;* but then it is with discretion, that his charity may not be misplaced, that he may give to proper objects what is proper to be given and in due time and proportion. And it is part of the promise to him who thus uses discretion that God will give him more. Those who most use their wisdom see most of their need of it, and *ask it of God,* who has promised to *give it liberally,* Jam. 1:5. *He will guide his words with judgment* (so it is in the original); and there is nothing in which we have more occasion for wisdom than in the government of the tongue; blessed is he to whom God gives that wisdom.

Verses 6–10

In these verses we have,

I. The satisfaction of saints, and their stability. It is the happiness of a good man that *he shall not be moved for ever,* v. 6. Satan and his instruments endeavour to move him, but his foundation is firm and he shall never be moved, at least *not moved for ever;* if he be shaken for a time, yet he settles again quickly.

1. A good man will have a settled reputation, and that is a great satisfaction. A good man shall have a good name, a name for good things, with God and good people: *The righteous shall be in everlasting remembrance* (v. 6); in this sense *his righteousness* (the memorial of it) *endures for ever,* v. 9. There are those that do all they can to sully his reputation and to load him with reproach; but his integrity shall be cleared up, and the honour of it shall survive him. Some that have been eminently righteous are *had in a lasting remembrance* on earth; wherever the scripture is read their good deeds are *told for a memorial* of them. And the memory of many a good man that is dead and gone is still blessed; but in heaven their remembrance shall be truly everlasting, and the honour of their righteousness shall there endure for ever, with the reward of it, in the *crown of glory that fades not away.* Those that are forgotten on earth, and despised, are remembered there, and honoured, and *their righteousness found unto praise, and honour, and glory* (1 Pt. 1:7); then, at furthest, shall the horn of a good man *be exalted with honour,* as that of the unicorn when he is a conqueror. Wicked men, now in their pride, *lift up their horns on high,* but they shall all be *cut off,* Ps. 75:5, 10. The godly, in their humility and humiliation, have *defiled their horn in the dust* (Job 16:15); but the day is coming when it *shall be exalted with honour.* That which shall especially turn to the honour of good men is their liberality and bounty to the poor: *He has dispersed, he has given to the poor;* he has not suffered his charity to run all in one channel, or directed it to some few objects that he had a particular kindness for, but he has dispersed it, *given a portion to seven and also to eight,* has *sown beside all waters,* and by thus scattering he has increased: and this is *his righteousness,* which *endures for ever.* Alms are called *righteousness,* not because they will justify us by making atonement for our evil deeds, but because they are good deeds, which we are bound to perform; so that if we are not charitable we are not just; we *withhold good from those to whom it is due.* The honour of this endures for ever, for it shall be taken notice of in the great day. *I was hungry, and you gave me meat.* This is quoted as an inducement and encouragement to charity, 2 Co. 9:9.

2. A good man shall have a settled spirit, and that is a much greater satisfaction than the former; for *so shall a man have rejoicing in himself alone, and not in another. Surely he shall not be moved,* whatever happens, not moved either from his duty or from his comfort; for *he shall not be afraid; his heart is established,* v. 7, 8. This is a part both of the character and of the comfort of good people. It is their endeavour to keep their minds stayed upon God, and so to keep them calm, and easy, and undisturbed; and God has promised them both cause to do so and grace to do so. Observe, (1.) It is the duty and interest of the people of God not to *be afraid of evil tidings,* not to be afraid of hearing bad news; and, when they do, not to be put into confusion by it and into an amazing expectation of worse and worse, but whatever happens, whatever threatens, to be able to say, with blessed Paul, *None of these things move me,* neither will I *fear, though the earth be removed,* Ps. 46:2. (2.) The fixedness of the heart is a sovereign remedy against the disquieting fear of evil tidings. If we keep our thoughts composed, and ourselves masters of them, our wills resigned to the holy will of God, our temper sedate, and our spirits even, under all the unevenness of Providence, we are well fortified against the agitations of the timorous. (3.) Trusting in the Lord is the best an surest way of fixing and establishing the heart. By faith we must cast anchor in the promise, in the word of God, and so return to him and repose in him as our rest. The heart of man cannot fix any where, to its satisfaction, but in the truth of God, and there it finds firm footing. (4.) Those whose hearts are established by faith will patiently wait till they have gained their point: *He shall not be afraid, till he see his desire upon his enemies,* that is, till he come to heaven, where he shall see Satan, and all his spiritual enemies, trodden under his feet, and, as Israel saw the Egyptians, dead on the sea-shore. *Till he look upon his oppressors* (so Dr. Hammond), till he behold them securely, and look boldly in their faces, as being now no longer under their power. It will complete the satisfaction of the saints, when they shall look back upon their troubles and pressures, and be able to say with St. Paul, when he had

recounted the persecutions he endured (2 Tim. 3:11), *But out of them all the Lord delivered me.*

II. The vexation of sinners, *v.* 10. Two things shall fret them: — 1. The felicity of the righteous: *The wicked shall see* the righteous in prosperity and honour and shall *be grieved.* It will vex them to see their innocency cleared and their low estate regarded, and those whom they hated and despised, and whose ruin they sought and hoped to see, the favourites of Heaven, and advanced to have *dominion over them* (Ps. 49:14); this will make them *gnash with their teeth and pine away.* This is often fulfilled in this world. The happiness of the saints is the envy of the wicked, and that envy is the *rottenness of their bones.* But it will most fully be accomplished in the other world, when it shall make damned sinners *gnash with their teeth,* to see *Abraham afar off, and Lazarus in him bosom,* to see *all the prophets in the kingdom of God and themselves thrust out.* 2. Their own disappointment: *The desire of the wicked shall perish.* Their desire was wholly to the world and the flesh, and they ruled over them; and therefore, when these perish, their joy is gone, and their expectations from them are cut off, to their everlasting confusion; their hope is as a spider's web.

PSALM 113

This psalm begins and ends with "Hallelujah;" for, as many others, it is designed to promote the great and good work of praising God. I. We are here called upon and urged to praise God (*v.* 1–3). II. We are here furnished with matter for praise, and words are put into our mouths, in singing which we must with holy fear and love give to God the glory of, 1. The elevations of his glory and greatness (*v.* 4, 5). 2. The condescensions of his grace and goodness (*v.* 6–9), which very much illustrate one another, that we may be duly affected with both.

Verses 1–9

In this psalm,

I. We are extorted to give glory to God, to give him the glory due to his name.

1. The invitation is very pressing: *praise you the Lord,* and again and again, *Praise him, praise him; blessed be his name,* for it is to be praised, *v.* 1–3. This intimates, (1.) That it is a necessary and most excellent duty, greatly pleasing to God, and has a large room in religion. (2.) That it is a duty we should much abound in, in which we should be frequently employed and greatly enlarged. (3.) That it is work which we are very backward to, and which we need to be engaged and excited to by precept upon precept and line upon line. (4.) That those who are much in praising God themselves will court others to it, both because they find the weight of the work, and that there is need of all the help they can fetch in (there is employment for all hearts, all hands, and all little enough), and because they find the pleasure of it, which they wish all their friends may share in.

2. The invitation is very extensive. Observe, (1.) From whom God has praise — from his own people; they are here called upon to praise God, as those that will answer the call: *Praise, O you servants of the Lord!* They have most reason to praise him; for those that attend him as his servants know him best and receive most of his favours. And it is their business to praise him; that is the work required of them as his servants: it is easy pleasant work to speak well of their Master, and do him what honour they can; if they do not, who should? Some understand it of the Levites; but, if so, all Christians are a royal priesthood, *to show forth the praises of him that has called them,* 1 Pt. 2:9. The angels are the servants of the Lord; they need not be called upon by us to praise God, yet it is a comfort to us that they do praise him, and that they praise him better than we can. (2.) From whom he ought to have praise. [1.] From all ages (*v.* 2) — *from this time forth for evermore.* Let not this work die with us, but let us be doing it in a better world, and let those that come after us be doing it in this. Let not our seed degenerate, but let God be praised through all the generations of time, and not in this only. We must bless the Lord in our day, by saying, with the psalmist, *Blessed be his name now and always.* [2.] From all places — *from the rising of the sun to the going down of the same,* that is, throughout the habitable world. Let all that enjoy the benefit of the sun rising (and those that do so must count upon it that the sun will set) give thanks for that light to the Father of lights. God's *name is to be praised;* it ought to be praised by all nations; for in every place, from east to west, there appear the manifest proofs and products of his wisdom, power, and goodness; and it is to be lamented that so great a part of mankind are ignorant of him, and give that praise to others which is due to him alone. But perhaps there is more in it; as the former verse gave us a glimpse of the kingdom of glory, intimating that God's name shall be *blessed for ever* (when time shall be no more that praise shall be the work of heaven), so this verse gives us a glimpse of the kingdom of grace in the gospel-dispensation of it. When the church shall no longer be confined to the Jewish nation, but shall spread itself all the world over, when in *every place* spiritual *incense shall be offered to our God* (Mal. 1:11), then from *the rising to the setting of the sun the Lord's name shall be praised* by some in all countries.

II. We are here directed what to give him the glory of.

1. Let us look up with an eye of faith, and see how high his glory is in the upper world, and mention that to his praise, *v.* 4, 5. We are, in our praises, to exalt his name, for he is high, his glory is high. (1.) *High above all nations,* their kings though ever so pompous, their people though ever so numerous. Whether it be true of an earthly king or no that though he is *major singulis — greater than individuals,* he is *minor universis — less than the whole,* we will not dispute; but we are sure it is not true of the King of kings. Put all the nations together, and he is above them all; they are before him as the *drop of the bucket and the small dust of the balance,* Isa. 60:15, 17. Let all nations think and speak highly of God, for he is high above them all. (2.) High *above the heavens;* the throne of his glory is in the highest heavens, which should raise our hearts in praising him, Lam. 3:41. *His glory is above the heavens,* that is, above the angels; he is above what they are, for their brightness is nothing to his, — above what they do, for they are under his command and do his pleasure, — and above what even they can speak him to be. He is exalted above *all blessing and praise,* not only all ours, but all theirs. We must therefore say, with holy admiration, *Who is like unto the Lord our God?* who of all the princes and potentates of the earth? who of all the bright and blessed spirits above? None can equal him, none dare compare with him. God is to be praised as transcendently, incomparably, and infinitely great; for he *dwells on high,* and from on high sees all, and rules all, and justly attracts all praise to himself.

2. Let us look around with an eye of observation, and see how extensive his goodness is in the lower world, and mention that to his praise. He is a God *who exalts himself to dwell, who humbles himself in heaven, and in earth.* Some think there is a transposition, *He exalts himself to dwell in heaven,* he *humbles himself to behold on earth;* but the sense is plain enough as we take it, only observe, God is said to *exalt himself* and to *humble himself,* both are his own act and deed; as he is self-existent, so he is both the fountain of his own honour and the spring of his own grace; God's condescending goodness appears,

(1.) In the cognizance he takes of the world below him. His glory is *above the nations* and *above the heavens,* and yet neither is neglected by him. *God is great,* yet *he despises not any,* Job 36:5. *He humbles himself to behold* all his creatures, all his subjects, though he is infinitely above them. Considering the infinite perfection, sufficiency, and felicity of the divine nature, it must be acknowledged as an act of wonderful condescension that God is pleased to take into the thoughts of his eternal counsel, and into the hand of his universal Providence, both the armies of heaven and the inhabitants of the earth (Dan. 4:35); even in this dominion he humbles himself. [1.] It is condescension in him to behold the things in heaven, to support the beings, direct the motions, and accept the praises and services, of the angels themselves; for he needs them not, nor is benefited by them. [2.] Much more is it condescension in him to *behold the things that are in the earth,* to visit the sons of men, and regard them, to order and overrule their affairs, and to take notice of what they say and do, that he may fill the earth with his goodness, and so set us an example of stooping to do good, of taking notice of, and concerning ourselves about, our inferiors. If it be such condescension for God to behold things in heaven and earth, what an amazing condescension was it for the Son of God to come from heaven to earth and take our nature upon him, that he might *seek and save those that were lost!* Herein indeed he humbled himself.

(2.) In the particular favour he sometimes shows to the least and lowest of the inhabitants of this meaner lower world. He not only beholds the great things in the earth, but the meanest, and those things which great men commonly overlook. Not does he merely behold them, but does wonders for them, and things that are very surprising, out of the common road of providence and chain of causes, which shows that the world is governed, not by a course of nature, for that would always run in the same channel, but by a God of nature, who delights in doing things we looked not for. [1.] Those that have been long despicable are sometimes, on a sudden, made honourable (*v.* 7, 8): *He raises up the poor out of the dust, that he may set him with princes. First,* Thus God does sometimes magnify himself, and his own wisdom, power, and sovereignty. When he has some great work to do he chooses to employ those in it that were least likely, and least thought of for it by themselves or others, to the highest post of honour: Gideon is fetched from threshing, Saul from seeking the asses, and David from keeping the sheep; the apostles are sent from fishing to be *fishers of men.* The treasure of the gospel is put into earthen vessels, and the weak and foolish ones of the world are pitched upon to be preachers of it, to confound the *wise and mighty* (1 Co. 1:27, 28), that the excellency of the power may be of God, and all may see that promotion comes from him. *Secondly,* Thus God does sometimes reward the eminent piety and patience of his people who have long groaned under the burden of poverty and disgrace. When Joseph's virtue was tried and manifested he was raised from the prison-dust and *set with princes.* Those that are wise will observe such returns of Providence, and will understand by them *the loving-kindness of the Lord.* Some have applied this to the work of redemption by Jesus Christ, and not unfitly; for through him poor fallen men are raised out of the dust (one of the Jewish rabbies applies it to the resurrection of the dead), nay, out of the dunghill of sin, and *set among princes,* among angels, those princes of his people. Hannah had sung to this purport, 1 Sa. 2:6–8. [2.] Those that have been long barren are sometimes, on a sudden, made fruitful, *v.* 9. This may look back to Sarah and Rebecca, Rachel, Hannah, and Samson's mother, or forward to Elizabeth; and many such instances there have been, in which God has looked on the affliction of his handmaids and taken away their reproach. *He makes the barren woman to keep house,* not only builds up the family, but thereby finds the heads of the family something to do. Note, Those that have the comfort of a family must take the care of it; *bearing children* and *guiding the house* are put together, 1 Tim. 5:14. When God *sets the barren in a family* he expects that she should *look well to the ways of her household,* Prov. 31:27. She is said to *be a joyful mother of children,* not only because, even in common cases, the pain is forgotten, *for joy that a man-child is born into the world,* but there is particular joy when a child is born to those that have been long childless (as Lu. 1:14) and therefore there ought to be particular thanksgiving. *Praise you the Lord.* Yet, in this case, *rejoice with trembling;* for, though the sorrowful mother be made joyful, the joyful mother may be made sorrowful again, if the children be either removed from her or embittered to her. This, therefore, may be applied to the gospel-church among the Gentiles (the building of which is illustrated by this similitude, Isa. 54:1, *Sing, O barren! thou that didst not bear,* and Gal. 4:27), for which we, who, being sinners of the Gentiles, are children of the desolate, have reason to say, *Praise you the Lord.*

PSALM 114

The deliverance of Israel out of Egypt gave birth to their church and nation, which were then founded, then formed; that work of wonder ought therefore to be had in everlasting remembrance. God gloried in it, in the preface to the ten commandments, and Hos. 11:1, "Out of Egypt have I called my son." In this psalm it is celebrated in lively strains of praise; it was fitly therefore made a part of the great Hallelujah, or song of praise, which the Jews were wont to sing at the close of the passover-super. It must never be forgotten, I. That they were brought out of slavery (*v.* 1). II. That God set up his tabernacle among them (*v.* 2). III. That the sea and Jordan were divided before them (*v.* 3, 5). IV. That the earth shook at the giving of the law, when God came down on Mount Sinai (*v.* 4, 6, 7). V. That

God gave them water out of the rock (*v.* 8). In singing this psalm we must acknowledge God's power and goodness in what he did for Israel, applying it to the much greater work of wonder, our redemption by Christ, and encouraging ourselves and others to trust in God in the greatest straits.

Verses 1–8

The psalmist is here remembering *the days of old, the years of the right hand of the Most High,* and the wonders which their fathers told them of (Jdg. 6:13), for time, as it does not wear out the guilt of sin, so it should not wear out the sense of mercy. Let it never be forgotten,

I. That God brought Israel out of the house of bondage with a high hand and a stretched-out arm: *Israel went out of Egypt, v.* 1. They did not steal out clandestinely, nor were they driven out, but fairly went out, marched out with all the marks of honour; they went out from a barbarous people, that had used them barbarously, from *a people of a strange language,* Ps. 81:5. The Israelites, it seems, preserved their own language pure among them, and cared not for learning the language of their oppressors. By this distinction from them they kept up an earnest of their deliverance.

II. That he himself framed their civil and sacred constitution (*v.* 2): *Judah and Israel were his sanctuary, his dominion.* When he delivered them out of the hand of their oppressors it was *that they might serve him* both *in holiness and in righteousness,* in the duties of religious worship and in obedience to the moral law, in their whole conversation. *Let my people go, that they may serve me.* In order to this, 1. He set up his sanctuary among them, in which he gave them the special tokens of his presence with them and promised to receive their homage and tribute. Happy are the people that have God's sanctuary among them (see Ex. 25:8, Eze. 37:26), much more those that, like Judah here, are his *sanctuaries,* his living temples, on whom *Holiness to the Lord* is written. 2. He set up his dominion among them, was himself their lawgiver and their judge, and their government was a theocracy: *The Lord was their King.* All the world is God's dominion, but Israel was so in a peculiar manner. What is God's sanctuary must be his dominion. Those only have the privileges of his house that submit to the laws of it; and for this end Christ has redeemed us that he might bring us into God's service and engage us for ever in it.

III. That the Red Sea was divided before them at their coming out of Egypt, both for their rescue and the ruin of their enemies; and the river Jordan, when they entered into Canaan, for their honour, and the confusion and terror of their enemies (*v.* 3): *The sea saw it,* saw there that *Judah was God's sanctuary, and Israel his dominion, and* therefore *fled;* for nothing could be more awful. It was this that *drove Jordan back,* and was an invincible dam to his streams; God was at the head of that people, and therefore they must give way to them, must make room for them, they must retire, contrary to their nature, when God speaks the word. To illustrate this the psalmist asks, in a poetical strain (*v.* 5), *What ailed thee, O thou sea! that thou fleddest?* And furnishes the sea with an answer (*v.* 7); it was *at the presence of the Lord.* This is designed to express, 1. The reality of the miracle, that it was not by any power of nature, or from any natural cause, but it was *at the presence of the Lord,* who gave the word. 2. The mercy of the miracle: *What ailed thee?* Was it in a frolic? Was it only to amuse men? No; it was *at the presence of the God of Jacob;* it was in kindness to the Israel of God, *for the salvation* of that chosen people, that God was thus *displeased against the rivers,* and his *wrath was against the sea,* as the prophet speaks, Hab. 3:8–13; Isa. 51:10; 63:11, etc. 3. The wonder and surprise of the miracle. Who would have thought of such a thing? Shall the course of nature be changed, and its fundamental laws dispensed with, to serve a turn for God's Israel? Well may the *dukes of Edom be amazed* and the *mighty men of Moab tremble,* Ex. 15:15. 4. The honour hereby put upon Israel, who are taught to triumph over the sea, and Jordan, as unable to stand before them. Note, There is no sea, no Jordan, so deep, so broad, but, when God's time shall come for the redemption of his people, it shall be divided and driven back if it stand in their way. Apply this, (1.) To the planting of the Christian church in the world. What ailed Satan and the powers of darkness, that they trembled and truckled as they did? Mk. 1:34. What ailed the heathen oracles, that they were silenced, struck dumb, struck dead? What ailed their idolatries and witchcrafts, that they died away before the gospel, and melted like snow before the sun? What ailed the persecutors and opposers of the gospel, that they gave up their cause, hid their guilty heads, and called to rocks and mountains for shelter? Rev. 6:15. It was *at the presence of the Lord,* and that power which went along with the gospel. (2.) To the work of grace in the heart. What turns the stream in a regenerate soul? What ails the lusts and corruptions, that they fly back, that the prejudices are removed and the whole man has become new? It is at the presence of God's Spirit that imaginations are *cast down,* 2 Co. 10:5.

IV. That the earth shook and trembled when God came down on Mount Sinai to give the law (*v.* 4): *The mountains skipped like rams, and* then *the little hills* might well be excused if they skipped *like lambs,* either when they are frightened or when they sport themselves. The same power that fixed the fluid waters and made them stand still shook the stable mountains and made them tremble for all the powers of nature are under the check of the God of nature. Mountains and hills are, before God, but like rams and lambs; even the bulkiest and the most rocky are as manageable by him as *they* are by the shepherd. The trembling of the mountains before the Lord may shame the stupidity and obduracy of the children of men, who are not moved at the discoveries of his glory. The psalmist asks the mountains and hills what ailed them to skip thus; and he answers for them, as for the seas, it was *at the presence of the Lord,* before whom, not only those mountains, but the earth itself, may well tremble (*v.* 7), since it has lain under a curse for man's sin. See Ps. 104:32; Isa. 64:3, 4. He that made the hills and mountains to skip thus can, when he pleases, dissipate the strength and spirit of the proudest of his enemies and make them tremble.

V. That God supplied them with water out of the rock, which followed them through the dry and sandy deserts. Well may the earth and all its inhabitants tremble before that God who *turned the rock into a standing water* (*v.* 8), and what cannot he do who did that? The same almighty power that turned waters into a rock to be a wall to Israel (Ex. 14:22) turned the rock into waters to be a well to Israel: as they were protected, so they were provided for, by miracles, standing miracles; for such was the standing water, that fountain of waters into which the rock, the flinty rock, was turned, *and that rock was Christ,* 1 Co. 10:4. For he is a fountain of living waters to his Israel, from whom they receive grace for grace.

PSALM 115

Many ancient translations join this psalm to that which goes next before it, the Septuagint particularly, and the vulgar Latin; but it is, in the Hebrew, a distinct psalm. In it we are taught to give glory, I. To God, and not to ourselves (*v.* 1). II. To God, and not to idols (*v.* 2–8). We must give glory to God, 1. By trusting in him, and in his promise and blessing (*v.* 9–15). 2. By blessing him (*v.* 16–18). Some think this psalm was penned upon occasion of some great distress and trouble that the church of God was in, when the enemies were in insolent and threatening, in which case the church does not so much pour out her complaint to God as place her confidence in God, and triumph in doing so; and with such a holy triumph we ought to sing this psalm.

Verses 1–8

Sufficient care is here taken to answer both the pretensions of self and the reproaches of idolaters.

I. Boasting is here for ever excluded, *v.* 1. Let no opinion of our own merits have any room either in our prayers or in our praises, but let both centre in God's glory. 1. Have we received any mercy, gone through any service, or gained any success? We must not assume the glory of it to ourselves, but ascribe it wholly to God. We must not imagine that we do any thing for God by our own strength, or deserve any thing from God by our own righteousness; but all the good we do is done by the power of his grace, and all the good we have is the gift of his mere mercy, and therefore he must have all the praise. Say not, *The power of my hand has gotten me this wealth,* Deu. 8:17. Say not, *For my righteousness the Lord has* done these great and kind things for me, Deu. 9:4. No; all our songs must be sung to this humble tune, *Not unto us, O Lord!* and again, *Not unto us, but to thy name,* let all the glory be given; for whatever good is wrought in us, or wrought for us, it is for his mercy and his truth's sake, because he will glorify his mercy and fulfil his promise. All our crowns must be cast at the feet of *him that sits upon the throne,* for that is the proper place for them. 2. Are we in pursuit of any mercy and wrestling with God for it? We must take our encouragement, in prayer, from God only, and have an eye to his glory more than to our own benefit in it. "Lord, do so and so for us, not that we may have the credit and comfort of it, but that thy mercy and truth may have the glory of it." This must be our highest and ultimate end in our prayers, and therefore it is made the first petition in the Lord's prayer, as that which guides all the rest, *Hallowed be thy name;* and, in order to that, *Give us our daily bread,* etc. This also must satisfy us, if our prayers be not answered in the letter of them. Whatever becomes of us, *unto thy name give glory.* See Jn. 12:27, 28.

II. The reproach of the heathen is here for ever silenced and justly retorted.

1. The psalmist complains of the reproach of the heathen (*v.* 2): *Wherefore should they say, Where is now their God?* (1.) "Why do they say so? Do they not know that our God is every where by his providence, and always nigh to us by his promise and grace?" (2.) "Why does God permit them to say so? Nay, why is Israel brought so low that they have some colour for saying so? Lord, appear for our relief, that thou mayest vindicate thyself, and glorify thy own name."

2. He gives a direct answer to their question, *v.* 3. "Do they ask where is our God? We can tell where he is." (1.) "In the upper world is the presence of his glory: *Our God is in the heavens,* where the gods of the heathen never were, *in the heavens,* and therefore out of sight; but, though his majesty be unapproachable, it does not therefore follow that his being is questionable." (2.) "In the lower world are the products of his power: *He has done whatsoever he pleased,* according to the counsel of his will; he has a sovereign dominion and a universal uncontrollable influence. Do you ask where he is? He is at the beginning and end of every thing, *and not far from any of us."*

3. He returns their question upon themselves. They asked, Where is the God of Israel? because he is not seen. He does in effect ask, What are the gods of the heathen? because they are seen. (1.) He shows that their gods, though they are not shapeless things, are senseless things. Idolaters, at first, worshipped the sun and moon (Job 31:26), which was bad enough, but not so bad as that which they were now come to (for evil men grow worse and worse), which was the worshipping of images, *v.* 4. The matter of them was *silver and gold,* dug out of the earth (*man found them poor and dirty in a mine,* Herbert), proper things to make money of, but not to make gods of. The make of them was from the artificer; they are creatures of men's vain imaginations and *the works of men's hands,* and therefore can have no divinity in them. If man is the work of God's hands (as certainly he is, and it was his honour that he was made *in the image of God*) it is absurd to think that that can be God which is the work of men's hands, or that it can be any other than a dishonour to God to make him in the image of man. The argument is irrefragable: *The workmen made it, therefore it is not God,* Hos. 8:6. These idols are represented here as the most ridiculous things, a mere jest, that would seem to be something, but were really nothing, fitter for a toy shop than a temple, for children to play with than for men to pray to. The painter, the carver, the statuary, did their part well enough; they made them with *mouths* and *eyes, ears* and *noses, hands* and *feet,* but they could put no life into them and therefore no sense. They had better have worshipped a dead carcase (for that had life in it once) than a dead image, which neither has life nor can have. *They speak not,* in answer to those that consult them; the crafty priest must speak for them. In Baal's image there was *no voice, neither any that answered. They see not* the prostrations of their worshippers before them, much less their burdens and wants. *They hear not* their prayers, though ever so loud; *they smell not* their incense, though ever so strong, ever so sweet; *they handle not* the gifts presented to them, much less have they any gifts to bestow on their worshippers; they cannot *stretch forth their hands to the needy. They walk not,* they cannot stir a step for the relief of those that apply to them. Nay, they do not so much as *breathe through their throat;* they have not the least sign of symptom of life, but are as dead, after the priest has pretended to consecrate them and call a deity into them, as they were

before. (2.) He thence infers the sottishness of their worshippers (*v.* 8): *Those that make them* images show their ingenuity, and doubtless are sensible men; but *those that make them* gods show their stupidity and folly, and *are like unto them,* as senseless blockish things; *they see not* the invisible things of the true and living God in the works of creation; *they hear not* the voice of the day and the night, which in every speech and language declare his glory, Ps. 19:2, 3. By worshipping these foolish puppets, they make themselves more and more foolish like them, and set themselves at a greater distance from every thing that is spiritual, sinking themselves deeper into the mire of sense; and withal they provoke God to *give them up to a reprobate mind, a mind void of judgment,* Rom. 1:28. Those *that trust in them* act very absurdly and very unreasonably, are senseless, helpless, useless, like them; and they will find it so themselves, to their own confusion. We shall know where our God is, and so shall they, to their cost, when their gods are gone, Jer. 10:3–11; Isa. 44:9, etc.

Verses 9–18

In these verses,

I. We are earnestly exhorted, all of us, to repose our confidence in God, and not suffer our confidence in him to be shaken by the heathens' insulting over us upon the account of our present distresses. It is folly to trust in dead images, but it is wisdom to trust in the living God, for he is a *help and a shield* to those that do *trust in them,* a help to furnish them with and forward them in that which is good, and a shield to fortify them against and protect them from every thing that is evil. Therefore, 1. Let Israel trust in the Lord; the body of the people, as to their public interests, and every particular Israelite, as to his own private concerns, let them leave it to God to dispose of all for them, and believe it will dispose of all for the best and will be *their help and shield.* 2. Let the priests, the Lord's ministers, and all the families of the *house of Aaron, trust in the Lord,* (*v.* 10); they are most maligned and struck at by the enemies and therefore of them God takes particular care. They ought to be examples to others of a cheerful confidence in God, and a faithful adherence to him in the worst of times. 3. Let the proselytes, who are not of the seed of Israel, but *fear the Lord,* who worship him and make conscience of their duty to him, let them *trust in him,* for he will not fail nor forsake them, *v.* 11. Note, Wherever there is an awful fear of God, there may be a cheerful faith in him: those that reverence his word may rely upon it.

II. We are greatly encouraged to trust in God, and good reason is given us why we should stay ourselves upon him with an entire satisfaction. Consider, 1. What we have experienced (*v.* 12): *The Lord has been mindful of us,* and never unmindful, has been so constantly, has been so remarkably upon special occasions. He has been mindful of our case, our wants and burdens, mindful of our prayers to him, his promises to us, and the covenant-relation between him and us. All our comforts are derived from God's *thoughts to us-ward;* he *has been mindful of us,* though we have forgotten him. Let *this* engage us to trust in him, that we have found him faithful. 2. What we may expect. From what he has done for us we may infer, *He will bless us;* he that has been our *help and our shield* will be so; he that has *remembered us in our low estate* will not forget us; for he is still the same, his power and goodness the same, and his promise inviolable; so that we have reason to hope that he who has delivered, and does, will yet deliver. Yet this is not all: *He will bless us;* he has promised that he will; he has pronounced a blessing upon all his people. God's blessing us is not only speaking good to us, but doing well for us; those whom he blesses are blessed indeed. It is particularly promised that *he will bless the house of Israel,* that is, he will bless the commonwealth, will bless his people in their civil interests. *He will bless the house of Aaron,* that is, the church, the ministry, will bless his people in their religious concerns. The priests were to bless the people; it was their office (Num. 6:23); but God blessed them, and so blessed their blessings. Nay (*v.* 13), *he will bless those that fear the Lord,* though they be not of the house of Israel or the house of Aaron; for it was a truth, before Peter perceived it, *That in every nation he that fears God is accepted or him,* and blessed, Acts 10:34, 35. *He will bless them both small and great,* both young and old. God has blessings in store for those that are good betimes and for those that are old disciples, both those that are poor in the world and those that make a figure. The greatest need his blessing, and it shall not be denied to the meanest that fear him. Both the weak in grace and the strong shall be blessed of God, the lambs and the sheep of his flock. It is promised (*v.* 14), *The Lord shall increase you.* Whom God blesses he increases; that was one of the earliest and most ancient blessings, *Be fruitful and multiply.* God's blessing gives an increase — increase in number, building up the family — increase in wealth, adding to the estate and honour — especially an increase in spiritual blessings, with the increasings of God. He will bless you with the increase of knowledge and wisdom, of grace, holiness, and joy; those are blessed indeed whom God thus increases, who are made wiser and better, and fitter for God and heaven. It is promised that this shall be, (1.) A constant continual increase: *"He shall increase you more and more;* so that, as long as you live, you shall be still increasing, till you come to perfection, as the shining light," Prov. 4:18. (2.) An hereditary increase: *"You and your children;* you in your children." It is a comfort to parents to see their children increasing in wisdom and strength. There is a blessing entailed upon the seed of those that fear God even in their infancy. For (*v.* 15), *You are blessed of the Lord,* you and your children are so; *all that see them shall acknowledge them, that they are the seed which the Lord has blessed,* Isa. 59:9. Those that are the blessed of the Lord have encouragement enough to *trust in the Lord,* as *their help and shield,* for it is he that *made heaven and earth;* therefore his blessings are free, for he needs not any thing himself; and therefore they are rich, for he has all things at command for us if we fear him and trust in him. He that *made heaven and earth* can doubtless make those happy that trust in him, and will do it.

III. We are stirred up to praise God by the psalmist's example, who concludes the psalm with a resolution to persevere in his praises. 1. God is to be praised, *v.* 16. He is greatly to be praised; for, (1.) His glory is high. See how stately his palace is, and the throne he has prepared in the heavens: *The heaven, even the heavens are the Lord's;* he is the rightful owner of all the treasures of light and bliss in the upper and better world, and is in the full possession of them, for he is himself infinitely bright and happy. (2.) His goodness is large, for *the earth he has given to the children of men,* having designed it, when he made it, for their use, to find them with meat, drink, and lodging. Not but that still he is proprietor in chief; *the earth is the Lord's, and the fulness thereof;* but he has let out that vineyard to these unthankful husbandmen, and from them he expects the rents and services; for, though he has given them the earth, his eye is upon them, and he will call them to render an account how they use it. Calvin complains that profane wicked people, in his days, perverted this scripture, and made a jest of it, which some in our days do, arguing, in banter, that God, having given the earth to the children of men, will no more look after it, nor after them upon it, but they may do what they will with it, and make the best of it as their portion; it is as it were thrown like a prey among them, Let him seize it that can. It is a pity that such an instance as this gives of God's bounty to man, and such a proof as arises from it of man's obligation to God, should be thus abused. From the highest heavens, it is certain, God beholds all the children of men; to them he has given the earth; but to the children of God heaven is given. 2. The dead are not capable of praising him (*v.* 17), nor *any that go into silence.* The soul indeed lives in a state of separation from the body and is capable of praising God; and *the souls of the faithful, after they are delivered from the burdens of the flesh,* do praise God, are still praising him; for they go up to the land of perfect light and constant business. But the dead body cannot praise God; death puts an end to our glorifying God in this world of trial and conflict, to all our services in the field; the grave is a land of darkness and silence, where there is no work or device. This they plead with God for deliverance out of the hand of their enemies, "Lord, if they prevail to cut us off, the idols will carry the day, and there will be none to praise thee, to bear thy name, and to bear a testimony against the worshippers of idols." *The dead praise not the Lord,* so as we do in the business and for the comforts of this life. See Ps. 30:9; 88:10. 3. Therefore it concerns us to praise him (*v.* 18): *"But we,* we that are alive, *will bless the Lord;* we and those that shall come after us, will do it, *from this time forth and for evermore,* to the end of time; we and those we shall remove to, *from this time forth* and to eternity. *The dead praise not the Lord,* therefore we will do it the more diligently." (1.) Others are dead, and an end is thereby put to their service, and therefore we will lay out ourselves to do so much the more for God, that we may fill up the gap. *Moses my servant is dead, now therefore, Joshua, arise.* (2.) We ourselves must shortly go to the land of silence; *but, while we do live, we will bless the Lord,* will improve our time and work that work of him that sent us into the world to praise him before the night comes, and because *the night comes, wherein no man can work. The Lord will bless us* (*v.* 12); he will do well for us, and therefore *we will bless* him, we will speak well of him. Poor returns for such receivings! Nay, we will not only do it ourselves, but will engage others to do it. *Praise the Lord;* praise him with us; praise him in your places, as we in ours; praise him when we are gone, that he may be praised *for evermore. Hallelujah.*

PSALM 116

This is a thanksgiving psalm; it is not certain whether David penned it upon any particular occasion or upon a general review of the many gracious deliverances God had wrought for him, out of six troubles and seven, which deliverances draw from him many very lively expressions of devotion, love, and gratitude; and with similar pious affections our souls should be lifted up to God in singing it. Observe, I. The great distress and danger that the psalmist was in, which almost drove him to despair (*v.* 3, 10, 11). II. The application he made to God in that distress (*v.* 4). III. The experience he had of God's goodness to him, in answer to prayer; God heard him (*v.* 1, 2), pitied him (*v.* 5, 6), delivered him (*v.* 8). IV His care respecting the acknowledgments he should make of the goodness of God to him (*v.* 12). 1. He will love God (*v.* 1). 2. He will continue to call upon him (*v.* 2, 13, 17). 3. He will rest in him (*v.* 7). 4. He will walk before him (*v.* 9). 5. He will pay his vows of thanksgiving, in which he will own the tender regard God had to him, and this publicly (*v.* 13–15, 17–19). Lastly, He will continue God's faithful servant to his life's end (*v.* 16). These are such breathings of a holy soul as bespeak it very happy.

Verses 1–9

In this part of the psalm we have,

I. A general account of David's experience, and his pious resolutions (*v.* 1, 2), which are as the contents of the whole psalm, and give an idea of it. 1. He had experienced God's goodness to him in answer to prayer: *He has heard my voice and my supplications.* David, in straits, had humbly and earnestly begged mercy of God, and God had heard him, that is, had graciously accepted his prayer, taken cognizance of his case, and granted him an answer of peace. *He has inclined his ear to me.* This intimates his readiness and willingness to hear prayer; he lays his ear, as it were, to the mouth of prayer, to hear it, though it be but whispered *in groanings that cannot be uttered.* He *hearkens and hears,* Jer. 8:6. Yet it implies, also, that it is wonderful condescension in God to hear prayer; it is bowing his ear. Lord, what is man, that God should thus stoop to him! — 2. He resolved, in consideration thereof, to devote himself entirely to God and to his honour. (1.) He will love God the better. He begins the psalm somewhat abruptly with a profession of that which his heart was full of: *I love the Lord* (as Ps. 18:1); and fitly does he begin with this, in compliance with the first and great commandment and with God's end in all the gifts of his bounty to us. "I love him only, and nothing besides him, but what I love for him." God's love of compassion towards us justly requires our love of complacency in him. (2.) He will love prayer the better: *Therefore I will call upon him.* The experiences we have had of God's goodness to us, in answer to prayer, are great encouragements to us to continue praying; we have sped well, notwithstanding our unworthiness and our infirmities in prayer, and therefore why may we not? God answers prayer, to make us love it, and expects this from us, in return for his favour. Why should we glean in any other field when we have been so well treated in this? Nay, *I will call upon him as long as I live* (Heb., *In my days*), every day, to the last day. Note, As long as we continue living we must continue praying. This breath we must breathe till we breathe our last, because then we shall take our leave of it, and till then we have continual occasion for it.

II. A more particular narrative of God's gracious dealings with him and the good impressions thereby made upon him.

1. God, in his dealings with him, showed himself a good

God, and therefore he bears this testimony to him, and leaves it upon record (*v.* 5): *"Gracious is the Lord, and righteous.* He is righteous, and did me no wrong in afflicting me; he is gracious, and was very kind in supporting and delivering me." Let us all speak of God as we have found; and have we ever found him otherwise than just and good? No; *our God is merciful,* merciful to us, and *it is of his mercies that we are not consumed.*

(1.) Let us review David's experiences. [1.] He was in great distress and trouble (*v.* 3): *The sorrows of death compassed me,* that is, such sorrows as were likely to be his death, such as were thought to be the very pangs of death. Perhaps the extremity of bodily pain, or trouble of mind, is called here *the pains of hell,* terror of conscience arising from sense of guilt. Note, The sorrows of death are great sorrows, and the pains of hell great pains. Let us *therefore* give diligence to prepare for the former, that we may escape the latter. These *compassed* him on every side; they arrested him, *got hold upon him,* so that he could not escape. *Without were fightings, within were fears. "I found trouble and sorrow;* not only they found me, but I found them." Those that are melancholy have a great deal of sorrow of their own finding, a great deal of trouble which they create to themselves, by indulging fancy and passion; this has sometimes been the infirmity of good men. When God's providence makes our condition bad let us not by our own imprudence make it worse. [2.] In his trouble he had recourse to God by faithful and fervent prayer, *v.* 4. He tells us that he prayed: *Then called I upon the name of the Lord;* then, when he was brought to the last extremity, then he made use of this, not as the last remedy, but as the old and only remedy, which he had found a salve for every sore. He tells us what his prayer was; it was short, but to the purpose: *"O Lord! I beseech thee, deliver my soul;* save me from death, and save me from sin, for that is it that is killing to the soul." Both the humility and the fervency of his prayer are intimated in these words, *O Lord! I beseech thee.* When we come to the throne of grace we must come as beggars for an alms, for necessary food. The following words (*v.* 5), *Gracious is the Lord,* may be taken as part of his prayer, as a plea to enforce his request and encourage his faith and hope: "Lord *deliver my soul,* for thou art *gracious* and *merciful,* and that only I depend upon for relief." [3.] God, in answer to his prayer, came in with seasonable and effectual relief. He found by experience that God is gracious and merciful, and in his compassion *preserves the simple, v.* 6. Because they are simple (that is, sincere, and upright, and without guile) therefore God preserves them, as he preserved Paul, who had his conversation in the world *not with fleshly wisdom, but in simplicity and godly sincerity.* Though they are simple (that is, weak, and helpless, and unable to shift for themselves, men of no depth, no design) yet God preserves them, because they commit themselves to him and have no confidence in their own sufficiency. Those who by faith put themselves under God's protection shall be safe.

(2.) Let David speak his own experience. [1.] God supported him under his troubles: *"I was brought low,* was plunged into the depth of misery, and then *he helped me,* helped me both to bear the worst and to hope the best, helped me to pray, else desire had failed, helped me to wait, else faith had failed. I was one of the simple ones whom God preserved, the poor man who *cried and the Lord heard him,"* Ps. 34:6. Note, God's people are never brought so low but that everlasting arms are under them, and those cannot sink who are thus sustained. Nay, it is in the time of need, at the dead lift, that God chooses to help, Deu. 32:36. [2.] God saved him out of his troubles (*v.* 8): *Thou hast delivered,* which means either the preventing of the distress he was ready to fall into or the recovering of him from the distress he was already in. God graciously delivered, *First,* His *soul from death.* Note, It is God's great mercy to us that we are alive; and the mercy is the more sensible if we have been at death's door and yet have been spared and raised up, just turned to destruction and yet ordered to return. That a life so often forfeited, and so often exposed, should yet be lengthened out, is a miracle of mercy. The deliverance of the soul from spiritual and eternal death is especially to be acknowledged by all those who are now sanctified and shall be shortly glorified. *Secondly,* His *eyes from tears,* that is, his heart from inordinate grief. It is a great mercy to be kept either from the occasions of sorrow, the evil that causes grief, or, at least, from being swallowed up with overmuch sorrow. When God comforts those that are cast down, looses the mourners' sackcloth and girds them with gladness, then he delivers *their eyes from tears,* which yet will not be perfectly done till we come to that world where God shall *wipe away all tears from our eyes. Thirdly,* His *feet from falling,* from falling into sin and so into misery. It is a great mercy, when our feet are almost gone, to have God *hold us by the right hand* (Ps. 72:2, 23), so that though we enter into temptation we are not overcome and overthrown by the temptation. Or, "Thou *hast delivered my feet from falling* into the grave, when I had one foot there already."

2. David, in his returns of gratitude to God, showed himself a good man. God had done all this for him, and therefore,

(1.) He will live a life of delight in God (*v.* 7): *Return unto thy rest, O my soul!* [1.] "Repose thyself and be easy, and do not agitate thyself with distrustful disquieting fears as thou hast sometimes done. Quiet thyself, and then enjoy thyself. God has dealt kindly with thee, and therefore thou needest not fear that ever he will deal hardly with thee." [2.] "Repose thyself in God. Return to him as thy rest, and seek not for that rest in the creature which is to be had in him only." God is the soul's rest; in him only it can *dwell at ease;* to him therefore it must retire, and rejoice in him. He has *dealt bountifully with us;* he has provided sufficiently for our comfort and refreshment, and encouraged us to come to him for the benefit of it, at all times, upon all occasions; let us therefore be satisfied with that. Return to that rest which Christ gives to *the weary and heavy-laden,* Mt. 11:28. Return to thy Noah; his name signifies *rest,* as the dove, when she found no rest, returned to the ark. I know no word more proper to close our eyes with at night, when we go to sleep, nor to close them with at death, that long sleep, than this, *Return to thy rest, O my soul!*

(2.) He will live a life of devotedness to God (*v.* 9): *I will walk before the Lord in the land of the living,* that is, in this world, as long as I continue to live in it. Note, [1.] It is our great duty to *walk before the Lord,* to do all we do as becomes us in his presence and under his eye, to approve ourselves to him as a holy God by conformity to him as our sovereign Lord, by subjection to his will, and, as a God all-sufficient, by a cheerful confidence in him. *I am the almighty God; walk before me,* Gen. 17:1. *We must walk worthy of the Lord unto all well-pleasing.* [2.] The consideration of this, that we are in the land of the living, should engage and quicken us to do so. We are spared and continued in the land of the living by the power, and patience, and tender mercy of our God, and therefore must make conscience of our duty to him. The *land of the living* is a land of mercy, which we ought to be thankful for; it is a land of opportunity, which we should improve. Canaan is called the *land of the living* (Eze. 26:20), and those whose lot is cast in such a valley of vision are in a special manner concerned to *set the Lord always before them.* If God has delivered our soul from death, we must walk before him. A new life must be a new life indeed.

Verses 10–19

The Septuagint and some other ancient versions make these verses a distinct psalm separate from the former; and some have called it the *Martyr's psalm,* I suppose for the sake of *v.* 15. Three things David here makes confession of: —

I. His faith (*v.* 10): *I believed, therefore have I spoken.* This is quoted by the apostle (2 Co. 4:13) with application to himself and his fellow-ministers, who, though they suffered for Christ, were not ashamed to own him. David believed the being, providence, and promise of God, particularly the assurance God had given him by Samuel that he should exchange his crook for a sceptre: a great deal of hardship he went through in the belief of this, and therefore he spoke, spoke to God by prayer (*v.* 4), by praise, *v.* 12. Those that believe in God will address themselves to him. He spoke to himself; because he believed, he said to his soul, *Return to thy rest.* He spoke to others, told his friends what his hope was, and what the ground of it, though it exasperated Saul against him and he was greatly afflicted for it. Note, Those that believe with the heart must confess with the mouth, for the glory of God, the encouragement of others, and to evidence their own sincerity, Rom. 10:10; Acts 9:19, 20. Those that live in hope of the kingdom of glory must neither be afraid nor ashamed to own their obligation to him that purchased it for them, Mt. 10:22.

II. His fear (*v.* 11): *I was greatly afflicted,* and then *I said in my haste* (somewhat rashly and inconsiderately — in my *amazement* (so some), when I was in a consternation — *in my flight* (so others), when Saul was in pursuit of me), *All men are liars,* all with whom he had to do, Saul and all his courtiers; his friends, who he thought would stand by him, deserted him and disowned him when he fell into disgrace at court. And some think it is especially a reflection on Samuel, who had promised him the kingdom, but deceived him; for, says he, *I shall one day perish by the hand of Saul,* 1 Sa. 27:1. Observe, 1. The faith of the best of saints is not perfect, nor always alike strong and active. David *believed* and *spoke well* (*v.* 10), but now, through unbelief, he spoke amiss. 2. When we are under great and sore afflictions, especially if they continue long, we are apt to grow weary, to despond, and almost to despair of a good issue. Let us not therefore be harsh in censuring others, but carefully watch over ourselves when we are in trouble, Ps. 39:1–3. 3. If good men speak amiss, it is in their haste, through the surprise of a temptation, not deliberately and with premeditation, as the wicked man, who *sits in the seat of the scornful* (Ps. 1:1), sits and *speaks against his brother,* Ps. 50:19, 20. 4. What we speak amiss, in haste, we must by repentance unsay again (as David, Ps. 31:22), and then it shall not be laid to our charge. Some make this to be no rash word of David's. He was greatly afflicted and forced to fly, but he did not trust in man, nor make flesh his arm. No: he said, *"All men are liars;* as *men of low degree are vanity,* so *men of high degree are a lie,* and therefore my confidence was in God only, and in him I cannot be disappointed." In this sense the apostle seems to take it. Rom. 3:4, *Let God be true and every man a liar* in comparison with God. All men are fickle and inconstant, and subject to change; and therefore let us cease from man and cleave to God.

III. His gratitude, *v.* 12, etc. God had been better to him than his fears, and had graciously delivered him out of his distresses; and, in consideration hereof,

1. He enquires what returns he shall make (*v.* 12): *What shall I render unto the Lord for all his benefits towards me?* Here he speaks, (1.) As one sensible of many mercies received from God — *all his benefits.* This psalm seems to have been penned upon occasion of some one particular benefit (*v.* 6, 7), but in that one he saw many and that one brought many to mind, and therefore now he thinks of all God's benefits towards him. Note, When we speak of God's mercies we should magnify them and speak highly of them. (2.) As one solicitous and studious how to express his gratitude: *What shall I render unto the Lord?* Not as if he thought he could render any thing proportionable, or as a valuable consideration for what he had received; we can no more pretend to give a recompense to God than we can to merit any favour from him; but he desired to render something acceptable, something that God would be pleased with as the acknowledgment of a grateful mind. He asks God, *What shall I render?* Asks the priest, asks his friends, or rather asks himself, and communes with his own heart about it. Note, Having received many benefits from God, we are concerned to enquire, *What shall we render?*

2. He resolves what returns he will make.

(1.) He will in the most devout and solemn manner offer up his praises and prayers to God, *v.* 13, 17. [1.] *"I will take the cup of salvation,* that is, I will offer the drink-offerings appointed by the law, in token of my thankfulness to God, and rejoice with my friends in God's goodness to me;" this is called *the cup of deliverance* because drunk in memory of his deliverance. The pious Jews had sometimes a *cup of blessing,* at their private meals, which the master of the family drank first of, with thanksgiving to God, and all at his table drank with him. But some understand it not of the cup that he would present to God, but of the cup that God would put into his hand. *I will receive, First,* The *cup of affliction.* Many good interpreters understand it of that cup, that bitter cup, which is yet sanctified to the saints, so that to them it is a cup of salvation. Phil. 1:19, *This shall turn to my salvation;* it is a means of spiritual health. David's sufferings were typical of Christ's, and we, in ours, have communion with his, and his cup was indeed a cup of salvation. "God, having bestowed so many benefits upon me, whatever cup he shall put into my hands I will readily take it, and not dispute it; welcome his holy will." Herein David spoke the language of the Son of David. Jn. 18:11, *The cup that my Father has given me, shall I not* take it and *drink it? Secondly,* The cup of consolation: "I will receive the benefits God bestows upon me as from his hand, and taste his love in them, as that which is *the portion* not only *of my inheritance* in the other world, but *of my cup* in this." [2.] *I will offer to thee the sacrifice of thanksgiving,* the thank-offerings which God required, Lev. 7:11, 12, etc. Note, Those whose hearts are truly thankful will express their gratitude in thank-offerings. We must first *give our ownselves* to God as *living sacrifices* (Rom. 12:1, 2 Co. 8:5), and then lay out of what we have for his honour in works of piety and charity. *Doing good* and *communicating* are *sacrifices* with which *God is well pleased* (Heb. 13:15, 16) and this must accompany our *giving thanks to his name.* If God has been bountiful to us, the least we can do in return is to be bountiful to the poor, Ps. 16:2, 3. Why should we offer that to God which costs us nothing? [3.] *I will call upon the name of the Lord.* This he had promised (*v.* 2) and here he repeats it, *v.* 13 and again *v.* 17. If we have received kindness from a man like ourselves, we tell him that we hope we shall never trouble him again; but God is pleased to reckon the prayers of his people an honour to him, and a delight, and no trouble; and therefore, in gratitude for former mercies, we must seek to him for further mercies, and continue to *call upon him.*

(2.) He will always entertain good thoughts of God, as very tender of the lives and comforts of his people (*v.* 15): *Precious in the sight of the Lord is the death of his saints,* so precious that he will not gratify Saul, nor Absalom, nor any of David's enemies, with his death, how earnestly soever they desire it. This truth David had comforted himself with in the depth of his distress and danger; and, the event having confirmed it, he comforts others with it who might be in like manner exposed. God has a people, even in this world, that are his saints, his merciful ones, or men of mercy, that have received mercy from him and show mercy for his sake. The saints of God are mortal and dying; nay, there are those that desire their death, and labour all they can to hasten it, and sometimes prevail to be the death of them; but it is *precious in the sight of the Lord; their life* is so (2 Ki. 1:13); their *blood* is so, Ps. 72:14. God often wonderfully prevents the death of his saints when there is but a step between them and it; he takes special care about their death, to order it for the best in all the circumstances of it; and whoever kills them, how light soever they may make of it, they shall be made to pay dearly for it when inquisition is made for the blood of the saints, Mt. 23:35. Though *no man lays it to heart* when *the righteous perish,* God will make it to appear that he lays it to heart. This should make us willing to die, to die for Christ, if we are called to it, that our death shall be registered in heaven; and let that be precious to us which is so to God.

(3.) He will oblige himself to be God's servant all his days. Having asked, *What shall I render?* here he surrenders himself, which was *more than all burnt-offerings and sacrifice* (*v.* 16): *O Lord! truly I am thy servant.* Here is, [1.] The relation in which David professes to stand to God: *"I am thy servant;* I choose to be so; I resolve to be so; I will live and die in thy service." He had called God's people, who are dear to him, *his saints;* but, when he comes to apply it to himself, he does not say, *Truly I am thy saint* (that looked too high a title for himself), but, *I am thy servant.* David was a king, and yet he glories in this, that he was God's servant. It is no disparagement, but an honour, to the greatest kings on earth, to be the servants of the God of heaven. David does not here compliment God, as it is common among men to say, *I am your servant, Sir.* No; "Lord, I am *truly thy servant; thou knowest all things, thou knowest that I am so."* And he repeats it, as that which he took pleasure in the thoughts of and which he was resolved to abide by: *"I am thy servant, I am thy servant.* Let others serve what master they will, *truly I am* they *servant."* [2.] The ground of that relation. Two ways men came to be servants: — *First,* by birth. "Lord, I was born in thy house; I am *the son of thy handmaid,* and therefore thine." It, is a great mercy to be the children of godly parents, as it obliges us to duty and is pleadable with God for mercy. *Secondly,* By redemption. He that procured the release of a captive took him for his servant. *"Lord, thou hast loosed my bonds;* those sorrows of death that compassed me, thou hast discharged me from them, and therefore *I am thy servant,* and entitled to thy protection as well as obliged to thy work." *The very bonds which thou hast loosed shall tie me faster unto thee.* Patrick.

(4.) He will make conscience of paying his vows and making good what he had promised, not only that he would offer the sacrifices of praise, which he had vowed to bring, but perform all his other engagements to God, which he had laid himself under in the day of his affliction (*v.* 14): *I will pay my vows;* and again, (*v.* 18), *now in the presence of all his people.* Note, Vows are debts that must be paid, for it is better not to vow than to vow and not pay. He will pay his vows, [1.] Presently; he will not, like sorry debtors, delay the payment of them, or beg a day; but, *"I will pay them now,"* Eccl. 5:4. [2.] Publicly; he will not huddle up his praises in a corner, but what service he has to do for God he will do it *in the presence of all his people;* nor for ostentation, but to show that he was not ashamed of the service of God, and that others might be invited to join with him. He will pay his vows in the courts of the tabernacle, where there was a crowd of Israelites attending, *in the midst of Jerusalem,* that he might bring devotion into more reputation.

PSALM 117

This psalm is short and sweet; I doubt the reason why we sing it so often as we do is for the shortness of it; but, if we rightly understood and considered it, we should sing it oftener for the sweetness of it, especially to us sinners of the Gentiles, on whom it casts a very favourable eye. Here is, I. A solemn call to all nations to praise God (*v.* 1). II. Proper matter for that praise suggested (*v.* 2). We are soon weary indeed of well-doing if, in singing this psalm, we keep not up those pious and devout affections with which the spiritual sacrifice of praise ought to be kindled and kept burning.

Verses 1–2

There is a great deal of gospel in this psalm. The apostle has furnished us with a key to it (Rom. 15:11), where he quotes it as a proof that the gospel was to be preached to, and would be entertained by, the Gentile nations, which yet was so great a stumbling-block to the Jews. Why should that offend them when it is said, and they themselves had often sung it, *Praise the Lord, all you Gentiles, and laud him, all you people.* Some of the Jewish writers confess that this psalm refers to the kingdom of the Messiah; nay, one of them has a fancy that it consists of two verses to signify that in the days of the Messiah God should be glorified by two sorts of people, by the Jews, according to the law of Moses, and by the Gentiles, according to the seven precepts of the sons of Noah, which yet should make one church, as these two verses make one psalm. We have here,

I. The vast extent of the gospel church, *v.* 1. For many ages in Judah only was God known and his name praised. The sons of Levi and the seed of Israel praised him, but the rest of the nations *praised gods of wood and stone* (Dan. 5:4), while there was no devotion at all paid, at least none openly, that we know of, to the living and true God. But here *all nations* are called to praise the Lord, which could not be applied to the Old-Testament times, both because this call was not then given to any of the Gentile nations, much less to all, in a language they understood, and because, unless the people of the land became Jews and were circumcised, they were not admitted to praise God with them. But the gospel of Christ is ordered to be preached to all nations, and by him the partition-wall is taken down, and those that were *afar off* are *made nigh.* This was the mystery which was hidden in prophecy for many ages, but was at length revealed in the accomplishment, *That the Gentiles should be fellow-heirs,* Eph. 3:3, 6. Observe here, 1. Who should be admitted into the church — *all nations* and *all people.* The original words are the same that are used for the *heathen that rage* and *the people that imagine* against Christ (Ps. 2:1); those that had been enemies to his kingdom should become his willing subjects. The gospel of the kingdom was to be preached *to all the world, for a witness to all nations,* Mt. 24:14; Mk. 16:15. All nations shall be called, and to some of all nations the call shall be effectual, and they shall be discipled. 2. How their admission into the church is foretold — by a repeated call to *praise him.* The tidings of the gospel, being sent to all nations, should give them cause to praise God; the institution of gospel-ordinances would give them leave and opportunity to praise God; and the power of gospel-grace would give them hearts to praise him. Those are highly favoured whom God invites by his word and inclines by his Spirit to praise him, and so makes to be to him for a name and a praise, Jer. 13:11. See Rev. 7:9, 10.

II. The unsearchable riches of gospel-grace, which are to be the matter or our praise, *v.* 2. In the gospel, those celebrated attributes of God, his mercy and his truth, shine most brightly in themselves and most comfortably to us; and the apostle, where he quotes this psalm, takes notice of these as the two great things for which the Gentiles should glorify God (Rom. 15:8, 9), for *the truth of God* and for *his mercy.* We that enjoy the gospel have reason to praise the Lord, 1. For the power of his mercy: *His merciful kindness is great towards us;* it is *strong* (so the word signifies); it is *mighty* for the pardon of *mighty sins* (Amos 5:12) and for the working out of a mighty salvation. 2. For the perpetuity of his truth: *The truth of the Lord endures for ever.* It was mercy, mere mercy, to the Gentiles, that the gospel was sent among them. It was merciful kindness prevailing towards them above their deserts; and in it the *truth of the Lord,* of his promise made unto the fathers, *endures for ever;* for, though the Jews were hardened and expelled, yet the promise took its effect in the believing Gentiles, the spiritual seed of Abraham. God's mercy is the fountain of all our comforts and his truth the foundation of all our hopes, and therefore for both we must praise the Lord.

PSALM 118

It is probable that David penned this psalm when he had, after many a story, weathered his point at last, and gained a full possession of the kingdom to which he had been anointed. He then invites and stirs up his friends to join with him, not only in a cheerful acknowledgment of God's goodness and a cheerful dependence upon that goodness for the future, but in a believing expectation of the promised Messiah, of whose kingdom and his exaltation to it his were typical. To him, it is certain, the prophet here bears witness, in the latter part of the psalm. Christ himself applies it to himself (Mt. 21:42), and the former part of the psalm may fairly, and without forcing, be accommodated to him and his undertaking. Some think it was first calculated for the solemnity of the bringing of the ark to the city of David, and was afterwards sung at the feast of tabernacles. In it, I. David calls upon all about him to give to God the glory of his goodness (*v.* 1–4). II. He encourages himself and others to trust in God, from the experience he had had of God's power and pity in the great and kind things he had done for him (*v.* 5–18). III. He gives thanks for his advancement to the throne, as it was a figure of the exaltation of Christ (*v.* 19–23). IV. The people, the priests, and the psalmist himself, triumph in the prospect of the Redeemer's kingdom (*v.* 24–29). In singing this psalm we must glorify God for his goodness, his goodness to us, and especially his goodness to us in Jesus Christ.

Verses 1–18

It appears here, as often as elsewhere, that David had his heart full of the goodness of God. He loved to think of it, loved to speak of it, and was very solicitous that God might have the praise of it and others the comfort of it. The more our hearts are impressed with a sense of God's goodness the more they will be enlarged in all manner of obedience. In these verses,

I. He celebrates God's mercy in general, and calls upon others to acknowledge it, from their own experience of it (*v.* 1): *O give thanks unto the Lord, for he is* not only good in himself, but good to you, and *his mercy endures for ever,* not only in the everlasting fountain, God himself, but in the never-failing streams of that mercy, which shall run parallel with the longest line of eternity, and in the chosen *vessels of mercy,* who will be everlasting monuments of it. Israel, and the house of Aaron, and all that *fear* God, were called upon to *trust in God* (Ps. 115:9–11); here they are called upon to confess that *his mercy endures for ever,* and so to encourage themselves to trust in him, *v.* 2–4. Priests and people, Jews and proselytes, must all own God's goodness, and all join in the same thankful song; if they can say no more, let them say this for him, that *his mercy endures for ever,* that they have had experience of it all their days, and confide in it for good things that shall last for ever. The praises and thanksgivings of all that truly *fear the Lord* shall be as pleasing to him as those of the house of Israel or the house of Aaron.

II. He preserves an account of God's gracious dealings with him in particular, which he communicates to others, that they might thence fetch both songs of praise and supports of faith, and both ways God would have the glory. David had, in his time, waded through a great deal of difficulty, which gave him great experience of God's goodness. Let us therefore observe here,

1. The great distress and danger that he had been in, which he reflects upon for the magnifying of God's goodness to him in his present advancement. There are many who, when they are lifted up, care not for hearing or speaking of their former depressions; but David takes all occasions to remember his own low estate. He was *in distress* (v. 5), greatly straitened and at a loss; there were many that *hated him* (v. 7), and this could not but be a great grief to one of an ingenuous spirit, that strove to gain the good affections of all. *All nations compassed me about, v.* 10. All the nations adjacent to Israel set themselves to give disturbance to David, when he had newly come to the throne, Philistines, Moabites, Syrians, Ammonites, etc. We read of *his enemies round about;* they were confederate against him, and thought to cut off all succours from him. This endeavour of his enemies to surround him is repeated (v. 11): *They compassed me about, yea, they compassed me about,* which intimates that they were virulent and violent, and, for a time, prevalent, in their attempts against him, and when put into disorder they rallied again and pushed on their design. *They compassed me about like bees,* so numerous were they, so noisy, so vexatious; they came flying upon him, came upon him in swarms, set upon him with their malignant stings; but it was to their own destruction, as the bee, they say, loses her life with her sting, *Animamque in vulnere ponit — She lays down her life in the wound. Lord, how are those increased that trouble me!* Two ways David was brought into trouble: — (1.) By the injuries that men did him (v. 13): *Thou* (O enemy!) *hast thrust sore at me,* with many a desperate push, *that I might fall* into sin and into ruin. *Thrusting thou hast thrust at me* (so the word is), so that I was *ready to fall.* Satan is the great enemy that thrusts sorely at us by his temptations, to cast us down from our excellency, that we may fall from our God and from our comfort in him; and, if Go had not upheld us by his grace, his thrusts would have been fatal to us. (2.) By the afflictions which God laid upon him (v. 18): *The Lord has chastened me sore.* Men thrust at him for his destruction; God chastened him for his instruction. They thrust at him with the malice of enemies; God chastened him with the love and tenderness of a Father. Perhaps he refers to the same trouble which God, the author of it, designed for his profit, that by it he *might partake of his holiness* (Heb. 12:10, 11); howbeit, men, who were the instruments of it, meant not so, *neither did their heart think so, but it was in their heart to cut off and destroy,* Isa. 10:7. What men intend for the greatest mischief God intends for the greatest good, and it is easy to say whose counsel shall stand. God will sanctify the trouble to his people, as it is his chastening, and secure the good he designs; and he will guard them against the trouble, as it is the enemies' thrusting, and secure them from the evil they design, and then we need not fear.

This account which David gives of his troubles is very applicable to our Lord Jesus. Many there were that *hated him,* hated him without a cause. They *compassed him about;* Jews and Romans surrounded him. *They thrust sorely at him;* the devil did so when he tempted him; his persecutors did so when they reviled him; nay, the Lord himself *chastened him sorely,* bruised him, and put him to grief, that *by his stripes we might be healed.*

2. The favour God vouchsafed to him in his distress. (1.) God heart his prayer (v. 5): *"He answered me* with enlargements; he did more for me than I was able to ask; he enlarged my heart in prayer and yet gave more largely than I desired." *He answered me, and set me in a large place* (so we read it), where I had room to bestir myself, room to enjoy myself, and room to thrive; and the large place was the more comfortable because he was brought to it out of distress, Ps. 4:1. (2.) God baffled the designs of his enemies against him: They are *quenched as the fire of thorns* (v. 12), which burns furiously for a while, makes a great noise and a great blaze, but is presently out, and cannot do the mischief that it threatened. Such was the fury of David's enemies; such is *the laughter of the fool,* like the *crackling of thorns under a pot* (Eccl. 7:6), and such is the anger of the fool, which therefore is not to be feared, any more than his laughter is to be envied, but both to

be pitied. They thrust sorely at him, but *the Lord helped him* (v. 13), helped him to keep his feet and maintain his ground. Our spiritual enemies would, long before this, have been our ruin if God had not been our helper. (3.) God preserved his life when there was but a step between him and death (v. 18): "He has *chastened me,* but he has not *given me over unto death,* for he has not given me over to the will of my enemies." To this St. Paul seems to refer in 2 Co. 6:9. *As dying, and behold we live; as chastened, and not killed.* We ought not therefore, when we are chastened sorely, immediately to despair of life, for God sometimes, in appearance, *turns men to destruction,* and yet says, *Return; says unto them, Live.*

This also is applicable to Jesus Christ. God *answered him, and set him in a large place.* He quenched the fire of his enemies; rage, which did but consume themselves; for *through death he destroyed him that had the power of death.* He helped him through his undertaking; and thus far he did not *give him over unto death* that he did *not leave him in the grave,* nor *suffer him to see corruption. Death had no dominion over him.*

3. The improvement he made of this favour. (1.) It encouraged him to trust in God; from his own experience he can say, *It is better,* more wise, more comfortable, and more safe, there is more reason for it, and it will speed better, *to trust in the Lord, than to put confidence in man,* yea, though it be *in princes, v.* 8, 9. He that devotes himself to God's guidance and government, with an entire dependence upon God's wisdom, power, and goodness, has a better security to make him easy than if all the kings and potentates of the earth should undertake to protect him. (2.) It enabled him to triumph in that trust. [1.] He triumphs in God, and in his relation to him and interest in him (v. 6): *"The Lord is on my side.* He is a righteous God, and therefore espouses my righteous cause and will plead it." If we are on God's side, he is on ours; if we be for him and with him, he will be for us and with us (v. 7): *"The Lord takes my part,* and stands up for me, *with those that help me.* He is to me among my helpers, and so one of them that he is all in all both to them and me, and without him I could not help myself nor could any friend I have in the world help me." Thus (v. 14), *"The Lord is my strength and my song;* that is, I make him so (without him I am weak and sad, but on him I stay myself as my strength, both for doing and suffering, and in him I solace myself as my song, by which I both express my joy and ease my grief), and, making him so, I find him so: he strengthens my heart with his graces and gladdens my heart with his comforts." If God be our strength, he must be our song; if he work all our works in us, he must have all praise and glory from us. God is sometimes the strength of his people when he is not their song; they have spiritual supports when they want spiritual delights. But, if he be both to us, we have abundant reason to triumph in him; for, he be our strength and our song, he has become not only our Saviour, but our salvation; for his being our strength is our protection to the salvation, and his being our song is an earnest and foretaste of the salvation. [2.] He triumphs over his enemies. Now shall his head be lifted up above them; for, *First,* He is sure they cannot hurt him: "God is for me, and then *I will not fear what man can do against me,"* v. 6. He can set them all at defiance, and is not disturbed at any of their attempts. "They can do nothing to me but what God permits them to do; they can do no real damage, for they cannot separate between me and God; they cannot do any thing but what God can make to work for my good. The enemy is a man, a depending creature, whose power is limited, and subordinate to a higher power, and therefore I will not fear him." *Who art thou, that thou shouldst be afraid of a man that shall die?* Isa. 51:12. The apostle quotes this, with application to all Christians, Heb. 13:6. They may boldly say, as boldly as David himself, *The Lord is my helper,* and *I will not fear what man shall do unto me;* let him do his worst. *Secondly,* He is sure that he shall be too hard for them at last: "I shall see my desire upon those that hate me (v. 7); I shall see them defeated in their designs against me; nay, *In the name of the Lord I will destroy them* (v. 10–12); I trust in the name of the Lord that I shall destroy them, and in his name I will go forth against them, depending on his strength, by warrant from him, and with an eye to his glory, not confiding in myself nor taking vengeance for myself." Thus he went forth

against Goliath, *in the name of the God of Israel,* 1 Sa. 17:45. David says this as a type of Christ, who triumphed over the powers of darkness, destroyed them, and *made a show of them openly.* [3.] He triumphs in an assurance of the continuance of his comfort, his victory, and his life. *First,* Of his comfort (v. 15): *The voice of rejoicing and salvation is in the tabernacles of the righteous,* and in mine particularly, in my family. The dwellings of the righteous in this world are but tabernacles, mean and movable; here we have no city, *no continuing city.* But these tabernacles are more comfortable to them than the palaces of the wicked are to them; for in the house where religion rules, 1. There is salvation; safety from evil, earnests of eternal salvation, which *has come to this house,* Lu. 19:9. 2. Where there is salvation there is cause for rejoicing, for continual joy in God. Holy joy is called *the joy of salvation,* for in that there is abundant matter for joy. 3. Where there is rejoicing there ought to be *the voice* of rejoicing, that is, praise and thanksgiving. Let God be served with joyfulness and gladness of heart, and let the voice of that rejoicing be heard daily in our families, to the glory of God and encouragement of others. *Secondly,* Of his victory: *The right hand of the Lord does valiantly* (v. 15) and *is exalted;* for (as some read it) *it has exalted me.* The right hand of God's power is engaged for his people, and it acts vigorously for them and therefore victoriously. For what difficulty can stand before the divine valour? We are weak, and act but cowardly for ourselves; but God is mighty, and acts valiantly for us, with jealousy and resolution, Isa. 63:5, 6. There is spirit, as well as strength, in all God's operations for his people. And, when God's right hand does valiantly for our salvation, it ought to be exalted in our praises. *Thirdly,* Of his life (v. 17): *"I shall not die* by the hands of my enemies that seek my life, *but live and declare the works of the Lord;* I shall live a monument of God's mercy and power; his works shall be declared in me, and I will make it the business of my life to praise and magnify God, looking upon that as the end of my preservation." Note, It is not worth while to live for any other purpose than to *declare the works of God,* for his honour and the encouragement of others to serve him and trust in him. Such as these were the triumphs of the Son of David in the assurance he had of the success of his undertaking and that the *good pleasure of the Lord* should *prosper in his hand.*

Verses 19–29

We have here an illustrious prophecy of the humiliation and exaltation of our Lord Jesus, his sufferings, and the glory that should follow. Peter thus applies it directly to the chief priests and scribes, and none of them could charge him with misapplying it, Acts 4:11. Now observe here,

I. The preface with which this precious prophecy is introduced, v. 19–21. 1. The psalmist desires admission into the sanctuary of God, there to celebrate the glory of him *that cometh in the name of the Lord: Open to me the gates of righteousness.* So the temple-gates are called, because they were shut against the uncircumcised, and forbade the stranger to come nigh, as the sacrifices there offered are called *sacrifices of righteousness.* Those that would enter into communion with God in holy ordinances must become humble suitors to God for admission. And when the gates of righteousness are opened to us we must *go into them,* must enter into the holiest, as far as we have leave, *and praise the Lord.* Our business within God's gates is to praise God; *therefore* we should long till the gates of heaven be opened to us, that we may go into them to dwell in God's house above, where we shall be still praising him. 2. He sees admission granted him (v. 20): *This is the gate of the Lord,* the gate of his appointing, *into which the righteous shall enter;* as if he had said, "The gate you knocked at is opened, and you are welcome. *Knock, and it shall be opened unto you."* Some by this gate understand Christ, by whom we are taken into fellowship with God and our praises are accepted; he is *the way;* there is no coming to the Father but by him (Jn. 14:6), he is the *door of the sheep* (Jn. 10:9); he is the gate of the temple, by whom, and by whom only, the righteous, and they only, shall enter, and *come into God's righteousness,* as the expression is, Ps. 69:27. The psalmist triumphs in the discovery that the gate of righteousness, which had been so long shut, and so long knocked at, was now at length opened. 3. He promises to give thanks to God for this favour (*v.* 21): *I will praise thee.* Those that saw Christ's day at so great a distance saw cause to praise God for the prospect; for in him they saw that God had heard them, had heard the prayers of the Old-Testament saints for the coming of the Messiah, and would be their salvation.

II. The prophecy itself, *v.* 22, 23. This may have some reference to David's preferment; he was the stone which Saul and his courtiers rejected, but was by the wonderful providence of God advanced to be the headstone of the building. But its principal reference is to Christ; and here we have, 1. His humiliation. He is *the stone which the builders refused;* he is the *stone cut out of the mountain without hands,* Dan. 2:34. He is a stone, not only for strength, and firmness, and duration, but for life, in the building of the spiritual temple; and yet a *precious stone* (1 Pt. 2:6), for the foundation of the gospel-church must be *sapphires,* Isa. 54:11. This stone was *rejected by the builders,* by the rulers and people of the Jews (Acts 4:8, 10, 11); they refused to own him as the stone, the Messiah promised; they would not build their faith upon him nor join themselves to him; they would make no use of him, but go on in their building without him; they *denied him in the presence of Pilate* (Acts 3:13) when they said, *We have no king but Caesar.* They trampled upon this stone, threw it among the rubbish out of the city; nay, they stumbled at it. This was a disgrace to Christ, but it proved the ruin of those that thus made light of him. Rejecters of Christ are rejected of God. 2. His exaltation. He *has become the headstone of the corner;* he is advanced to the highest degree both of honour and usefulness, to be above all, and all in all. He is the chief corner-stone in the foundation, in whom Jew and Gentile are united, that they may be built up one holy house. He is the chief top-stone in the corner, in whom the building is completed, and who must in all things have the pre-eminence, as the *author and finisher of our faith.* Thus highly *has God exalted him, because he humbled himself;* and we, in compliance with God's design, must make him the foundation of our hope, the centre of our unity, and the end of our living. *To me to live is Christ.* 3. The hand of God in all this: *This is the Lord's doing;* it is from the Lord; it is with the Lord; it is the product of his counsel; it is his contrivance. Both the humiliation and the exaltation of the Lord Jesus were his work, Acts 2:23; 4:27, 28. He sent him, sealed him; his hand went with him throughout his whole undertaking, and from first to last he did his Father's will; and this ought to be *marvellous in our eyes.* Christ's name is *Wonderful;* and the redemption he wrought out is the most amazing of all God's works of wonder; it is what the angels *desire to look into,* and will be admiring to eternity; much more ought we to admire it, who owe our all to it. *Without controversy, great is the mystery of godliness.*

III. The joy wherewith it is entertained and the acclamations which attend this prediction.

1. Let the day be solemnized to the honour of God with great joy (*v.* 24): *This is the day the Lord has made.* The whole time of the gospel-dispensation, that *accepted time,* that *day of salvation,* is what the Lord has made so; it is a continual feast, which ought to be kept with joy. Or it may very fitly be understood of the Christian sabbath, which we sanctify in remembrance of Christ's resurrection, when the rejected stone began to be exalted; and so, (1.) Here is the doctrine of the Christian sabbath: *It is the day which the Lord has made,* has made remarkable, made holy, has distinguished from other days; he has made it for man: it is therefore called *the Lord's day,* for it bears his image and superscription. (2.) The duty of the sabbath, the work of the day that is to be done in his day: *We will rejoice and be glad in it,* not only in the institution of the day, that there is such a day appointed, but in the occasion of it, Christ's becoming the *head of the corner.* This we ought to rejoice in both as his honour and our advantage. Sabbath days must be rejoicing days, and then they are to us as the days of heaven. See what a good Master we serve, who, having instituted a day for his service, appoints it to be spent in holy joy.

2. Let the exalted Redeemer be met, and attended, with joyful hosannas, *v.* 25, 26.

(1.) Let him have the acclamations of the people, as is usual at the inauguration of a prince. Let every one of his loyal subjects shout for joy, *Save now, I beseech thee, O Lord!* This is like *Vivat rex — Long live the king,* and expresses a hearty joy for his accession to the crown, an entire satisfaction in his government, and a zealous affection to the interests and honour of it. *Hosanna* signifies, *Save now, I beseech thee.* [1.] "Lord, save me, I beseech thee; let this Saviour be my Saviour, and, in order to that, my ruler; let me be taken under his protection and owned as one of his willing subjects. His enemies are my enemies; Lord, I beseech thee, save me from them. Send me an interest in that prosperity which his kingdom brings with it to all those that entertain it. Let my soul prosper and be in health, in that peace and righteousness which his government brings, Ps. 72:3. Let me have victory over those lusts *that war against my soul,* and let divine grace go on in my heart *conquering and to conquer.*" [2.] "Lord, preserve him, I beseech thee, even the Saviour himself, and *send him prosperity* in all his undertakings; give success to his gospel, and let it be *mighty, through God, to the pulling down of strong-holds* and reducing souls to their allegiance to him. Let his name be sanctified, his *kingdom come,* his *will be done.*" Thus *let prayer be made for him continually,* Ps. 72:15. On the Lord's day, when we rejoice and are glad in his kingdom, we must pray for the advancement of it more and more, and its establishment upon the ruins of the devil's kingdom. When Christ made his public entry into Jerusalem he was thus met by his well-wishers (Mt. 21:9): *Hosanna to the Son of David;* long live King Jesus; let him reign for ever.

(2.) Let the priests, the Lord's ministers, do their part in this great solemnity, *v.* 26. [1.] Let them bless the prince with their praises: *Blessed is he that cometh in the name of the Lord.* Jesus Christ is *he that cometh — ho erchomenos,* he that was to come and is yet to come again, Rev. 1:8. He *comes in the name of the Lord,* with a commission from him, to act for him, to do his will and to seek his glory; and therefore we must say, *Blessed be he that cometh;* we must rejoice that he has come; we must speak well of him, admire him, and esteem him highly, as one we are eternally obliged to, call him blessed Jesus, blessed for ever, Ps. 45:2. We must bid him welcome into our hearts, saying, "Come in, thou blessed of the Lord; come in by thy grace and Spirit, and take possession of me for thy own." We must bless his faithful ministers that come in his name, and receive them for his sake, Isa. 52:7; Jn. 13:20. We must pray for the enlargement and edification of his church, for the ripening of things for his second coming, and then that he who has said, *Surely I come quickly,* would *even so come.* [2.] Let them bless the people with their prayers: *We have blessed you out of the house of the Lord.* Christ's ministers are not only warranted, but appointed to pronounce a blessing, in his name, upon all his loyal subjects that love him and his government in sincerity, Eph. 6:24. We assure you that in and through Jesus Christ you are blessed; for he came to bless you. "You are *blessed out of the house of the Lord,* that is, *with spiritual blessings in heavenly places* (Eph. 1:3), and therefore have reason to bless him who has thus blessed you."

3. Let sacrifices of thanksgiving be offered to his honour who offered for us the great atoning sacrifice, *v.* 27. Here is, (1.) The privilege we enjoy by Jesus Christ: *God is the Lord who has shown us light.* God is Jehovah, is known by that name, a God performing what he has promised and perfecting what he has begun, Ex. 6:3. *He has shown us light,* that is, he has given us the knowledge of himself and his will. He *has shined upon us* (so some); he has favoured us, and lifted up upon us the light of his countenance; he has given us occasion for joy and rejoicing, which is light to the soul, by giving us a prospect of everlasting light in heaven. *The day which the Lord has made* brings light with it, true light. (2.) The duty which this privilege calls for: *Bind the sacrifice with cords,* that, being killed, the blood of it may be sprinkled *upon the horns of the altar,* according to the law; or perhaps it was the custom (though we read not of it elsewhere) to *bind the sacrifice to the horns of the altar* while things were getting ready for the slaying of it. Or this may have a peculiar significancy here; the sacrifice we are to offer to God, in gratitude for redeeming love, is ourselves, not to be slain upon the altar, but *living sacrifices* (Rom. 12:1), to be bound to the altar, spiritual sacrifices of prayer and praise, in which our hearts must be fixed and engaged, as the sacrifice was bound *with cords to the horns of the altar,* not to start back.

4. The psalmist concludes with his own thankful acknowledgments of divine grace, in which he calls upon others to join with him, *v.* 28, 29. (1.) He will praise God himself, and endeavour to exalt him in his own heart and in the hearts of others, and this because of his covenant-relation to him and interest in him: *"Thou art my God,* on whom I depend, and to whom I am devoted, who ownest me and art owned by me; *and* therefore *I will praise thee."* (2.) He will have all about him to give thanks to God for these glad tidings of great joy to all people, that there is a Redeemer, even Christ the Lord. In him it is that God *is good* to man and that *his mercy endures for ever;* in him the covenant of grace is made, and in him it is made sure, made good, and made an everlasting covenant. He concludes this psalm as he began it (*v.* 1), for God's glory must be the Alpha and Omega, the beginning and the end, of all our addresses to him. *Hallowed by thy name,* and *thine is the glory.* And this fitly closes a prophecy of Christ. The angels give thanks for man's redemption. *Glory to God in the highest* (Lu. 2:14), for there is *on earth peace,* to which we must echo with our hosannas, as they did, Lu. 19:38. *Peace in heaven* to us through Christ, and therefore *glory in the highest.*

PSALM 119

This is a psalm by itself, like none of the rest; it excels them all, and shines brightest in this constellation. It is much longer than any of them more than twice as long as any of them. It is not making long prayers that Christ censurers, but making them for a pretence, which intimates that they are in themselves good and commendable. It seems to me to be a collection of David's pious and devout ejaculations, the short and sudden breathings and elevations of his soul to God, which he wrote down as they occurred, and, towards the latter end of his time, gathered out of his day-book where they lay scattered, added to them many like words, and digested them into this psalm, in which there is seldom any coherence between the verses, but, like Solomon's proverbs, it is a chest of gold rings, not a chain of gold links. And we may not only learn, by the psalmist's example, to accustom ourselves to such pious ejaculations, which are an excellent means of maintaining constant communion with God, and keeping the heart in frame for the more solemn exercises of religion, but we must make use of the psalmist's words, both for the exciting and for the expressing of our devout affections; what some have said of this psalm is true, "He that shall read it considerately, it will either warm him or shame him." The composition of it is singular and very exact. It is divided into twenty-two parts, according to the number of the letters of the Hebrew alphabet, and each part consists of eight verses, all the verses of the first part beginning with Aleph, all the verses of the second with Beth, and so on, without any flaw throughout the whole psalm. Archbishop Tillotson says, It seems to have more of poetical skill and number in it than we at this distance can easily understand. Some have called it the saints' alphabet; and it were to be wished we had it as ready in our memories as the very letters of our alphabet, as ready as our A B C. Perhaps the penman found it of use to himself to observe this method, as it obliged him to seek for thoughts, and search for them, that he might fill up the quota of every part; and the letter he was to begin with might lead him to a word which might suggest a good sentence; and all little enough to raise any thing that is good in the barren soil of our hearts. However, it would be of use to the learners, a help to them both in committing it to memory and in calling it to mind upon occasion; by the letter the first word would be got, and that would bring in the whole verse; thus young people would the more easily learn it by heart and retain it the better even in old age. If any censure it as childish and trifling, because acrostics are now quite out of fashion, let them know that the royal psalmist despises their censure; he is a teacher of babes, and, if this method may be beneficial to them, he can easily stoop to it; if this to be vile, he will be yet more vile.

II. The general scope and design of it is to magnify the law, and make it honourable; to set forth the excellency and usefulness of divine revelation, and to recommend it to us, not only for the entertainment, but for the government, of ourselves, by the psalmist's own example, who speaks by experience of the benefit of it, and of the good impressions made upon him by it, for which he praises God, and earnestly prays, from first to last, for the continuance of God's grace with him, to direct and quicken him in the way of his duty. There are ten different words by which divine revelation is called in this psalm, and they are synonymous, each of them expressive of the whole compass of it (both that which tells us what God expects from us and that which tells us that we may expect from him) and of the system of religion which is founded upon it and guided by it. The things contained in the scripture, and drawn from it, are here called, 1. God's law, because they are enacted by him as our Sovereign. 2. His way, because they are the rule both of his providence and of our obedience. 3. His testimonies, because they are solemnly declared to the world and attested beyond contradiction. 4. His commandments, because given with authority, and (as the word signifies) lodged with us as a trust. 5. His precepts, because prescribed to us and not left indifferent. 6. His word, or saying, because it is the declaration of his mind, and Christ, the essential eternal Word, is all in all in it. 7. His judgments, because framed in infinite wisdom, and because by them we must both judge and be judged. 8. His righteousness, because it is all holy, just, and good, and the rule and standard of righteousness. 9. His statutes, because they are fixed and determined, and of perpetual obligation. His truth, or faithfulness, because the principles upon which the divine law is built are eternal truths. And I think there is but one verse (it is *v.* 122) in all this long psalm in which there is not one or other of these ten words; only in three or four they are used concerning God's providence or David's practice (as *v.* 75, 84, 121), and *v.* 132 they are called God's name. The great esteem and affection David had for the word of God is the more admirable considering how little he had of it, in comparison with what we have, no more perhaps in writing than the first books of Moses, which were but the dawning of this day, which may shame us who enjoy the full discoveries of divine revelation and yet are so cold towards it. In singing this psalm there is work for all the devout affections of a sanctified soul, so copious, so various, is the matter of it. We here find that in which we must give glory to God both as our ruler and great benefactor, that in which we are to teach and admonish ourselves and one another (so many are the instructions which we here find about a religious life), and that in which we are to comfort and encourage ourselves and one another, so many are the sweet experiences of one that lived such a life. Here is something or other to suit the case of every Christian. Is any afflicted? Is any merry? Each will find that here which is proper for him. And it is so far from being a tedious repetition of the same thing, as may seem to those who look over it cursorily, that, if we duly meditate upon it, we shall find almost every verse has a new thought and something in it very lively. And this, as many other of David's psalms, teaches us to be sententious in our devotions, both alone and when others join with us; for, ordinarily, the affections, especially of weaker Christians, are more likely to be raised and kept by short expressions, the sense of which lies in a little compass, than by long and laboured periods.

1. ALEPH.

Verses 1–3

The psalmist here shows that godly people are happy people; they are, and shall be, blessed indeed. Felicity is the thing we all pretend to aim at and pursue. He does not say here wherein it consists; it is enough for us to know what we must do and be that we may attain to it, and that we are here told. All men would be happy, but few take the right way; God has here laid before us the right way, which we may be sure will end in happiness, though it be strait and narrow. Blessednesses are to the righteous; all manner of blessedness. Now observe the characters of the happy people. Those are happy, 1. Who make the will of God the rule of all their actions, and govern themselves, in their whole conversation, by that rule: They *walk in the law of the Lord, v.* 1. God's word is a law to them, not only in this or that instance, but in the whole course of their conversation; they walk within the hedges of that law, which they dare not break through by doing any thing it forbids; and they walk in the paths of that law, which they will not trifle in, but *press forward* in them *towards the mark,* taking every step by rule and never walking at all adventures. This is *walking in God's ways (v.* 3), the ways which he has marked out to us and has appointed us to walk in. It will not serve us to make religion the subject of our discourse, but we must make it the rule of our walk; we must walk *in his ways,* not in the way of the world, or of our own hearts, Job 23:10, 11; 31:7. 2. Who are upright and honest in their religion — *undefiled in the way,* not only who keep themselves pure from the pollutions of actual sin, *unspotted from the world,* but who are habitually sincere in their intentions, *in whose spirit there is no guile,* who are really as good as they seem to be and row the same way as they look. 3. Who are true to the trust reposed in them as God's professing people. It was the honour of the Jews that *to them were committed the oracles of God;* and blessed are those who preserve pure and entire that sacred deposit, *who keep his testimonies* as a treasure of inestimable value, keep them as the apple of their eye, so keep them as to carry the comfort of them themselves to another world and leave the knowledge and profession of them to those who shall come after them in this world. Those who would *walk in the law of the Lord* must *keep his testimonies,* that is, his truths. Those will not long make conscience of good practices who do not adhere to good principles. Or *his testimonies* may denote his covenant; the ark of the covenant is called *the ark of the testimony.* Those do not keep covenant with God who do not keep the commandments of God. 4. Who have a single eye to God as their chief good and highest end in all they do in religion (*v.* 2): They *seek him with their whole heart.* They do not seek themselves and their own things, but God only; this is that which they aim at, that God may be glorified in their obedience and that they may be happy in God's acceptance. he is, and will be, the rewarder, the reward, of all those who thus *seek him diligently, seek him*

with the heart, for that is it that God looks at and requires; and *with the whole heart,* for if the heart be divided between him and the world it is faulty. 5. Who carefully avoid all sin (*v.* 3): *They do no iniquity;* they do not allow themselves in any sin; they do not commit it as those do who are the servants of sin; they do not make a practice of it, do not make a trade of it. They are conscious to themselves of much iniquity that clogs them in the ways of God, but not of that iniquity which draws them out of those ways. Blessed and holy are those who thus exercise themselves *to have always consciences void of offence.*

Verses 4–6

We are here taught, 1. To own ourselves under the highest obligations to walk in God's law. The tempter would possess men with an opinion that they are at their liberty whether they will make the word of God their rule or no, that, though it may be good, yet it is not so necessary as they are made to believe it is. He taught our first parents to question the command: *Hath God said, You shall not eat?* And therefore we are concerned to be well established in this (*v.* 4): *Thou hast commanded us to keep thy precepts,* to make religion our rule; and *to keep them diligently,* to make religion our business and to mind it carefully and constantly. We are bound, and must obey at our peril. 2. To look up to God for wisdom and grace to do so (*v.* 5): *O that my ways were directed* accordingly! not only that all events concerning us may be so ordered and disposed by the providence of God as not to be in any thing a hindrance to us, but a furtherance rather, in the service of God, but that our hearts may be so guided and influenced by the Spirit of God that we may not in any thing transgress God's commandments — not only that our eyes may be directed to behold God's statutes, but our hearts directed to keep them. See how the desire and prayer of a good man exactly agree with the will and command of a good God: "Thou wouldest have me keep thy precepts, and, Lord, I fain would keep them." *This is the will of God, even our sanctification;* and it should be our will. 3. To encourage ourselves in the way of our duty with a prospect of the comfort we shall find in it, *v.* 6. Note, (1.) It is the undoubted character of every good man that he has a *respect to all* God's *commandments.* He has a respect to the command, eyes it as his copy, aims to conform to it, is sorry wherein he comes short; and what he does in religion he does with a conscientious regard to the command, because it is his duty. He has *respect to all* the *commandments,* one as well as another, because they are all backed with the same authority (Jam. 2:10, 11) and all levelled at the same end, the glorifying of God in our happiness. Those who have a sincere respect to any command will have a general respect to every command, to the commands of both testaments and both tables, to the prohibitions and the precepts, to those that concern both the inward and the outward man, both the head and the heart, to those that forbid the most pleasant and gainful sins and to those that require the most difficult and hazardous duties. (2.) Those who have a sincere *respect to all* God's *commandments shall not be ashamed,* not only they will thereby be kept from doing that which will turn to their shame, but they shall have *confidence towards God* and boldness of access to the throne of his grace, 1 Jn. 3:21. They shall have credit before men; their honesty will be their honour. And they shall have clearness and courage in their own souls; they shall not be ashamed to retire into themselves, nor to reflect upon themselves, for their hearts shall not condemn them. David speaks this with application to himself. Those that are upright may take the comfort of their uprightness. "As, if I be wicked, woe to me; so, if I be sincere, it is well with me."

Verses 7–8

Here is, I. David's endeavour to perfect himself in his religion, and to make himself (as we say) master of his business. He hopes to *learn* God's *righteous judgments.* He knew much, but he was still pressing forward and desired to know more, as knowing this, that *he had not yet attained;* but as far as perfection is attainable in this life he reached towards it, and would not take up short of it. As long as we live we must be scholars in Christ's school, and sit at his feet; but we should aim to be head-scholars, and to get into the highest form. God's judgments are all right-

eous, and therefore it is desirable not only to learn them, but to be learned in them, *mighty in the scriptures.*

II. The use he would make of his divine learning. He coveted to be learned in the laws of God, not that he might make himself a name and interest among men, or fill his own head with entertaining speculations, but, 1. That he might give God the glory of his learning: *I will praise thee when I have learned thy judgments,* intimating that he could not learn unless God taught him, and that divine instructions are special blessings, which we have reason to be thankful for. Though Christ keeps a free-school, and teaches without money and without price, yet he expects his scholars should give him thanks both for his word and for his Spirit; surely it is a mercy worth thanks to be taught so gainful a calling as religion is. Those have learned a good lesson who have learned to praise God, for that is the work of angels, the work of heaven. It is an easy thing to praise God in word and tongue; but those only are well learned in this mystery who have learned to *praise* him *with uprightness of heart,* that is, are inward with him in praising him, and sincerely aim at his glory in the course of their conversation as well as in the exercises of devotion. God accepts only the praises of the upright. 2. That he might himself come under the government of that learning: *When I shall have learned thy righteous judgments I will keep thy statutes.* We cannot keep them unless we learn them; but we learn them in vain if we do not keep them. Those have well learned God's statutes who have come up to a full resolution, in the strength of his grace, to keep them.

III. His prayer to God not to leave him: "*O forsake me not!* that is, leave me not to myself, withdraw not thy Spirit and grace from me, for then *I shall* not *keep thy statutes.*" Good men see themselves undone if God forsakes them; for then the tempter will be too hard for them. "Though thou seem to forsake me, and threaten to forsake me, and dost, for a time, withdraw from me, yet let not the desertion be total and final; for that is hell. *O forsake me not utterly!* for woe unto me if God departs from me."

2. BETH.

Verse 9

Here is, 1. A weighty question asked. By what means may the next generation be made better than this? *Wherewithal shall a young man cleanse his way?* Cleansing implies that it is polluted. Besides the original corruption we all brought into the world with us (from which we are not cleansed unto this day), there are many particular sins which young people are subject to, by which they defile their way, *youthful lusts* (2 Tim. 2:22); these render their way offensive to God and disgraceful to themselves. Young men are concerned to cleanse their way — to get their hearts renewed and their lives reformed, to make clean, and keep clean, from the *corruption that is in the world through lust,* that they may have both a good conscience and a good name. Few young people do themselves enquire by what means they may recover and preserve their purity; and therefore David asks the question for them. 2. A satisfactory answer given to this question. Young men may effectually *cleanse their way by taking heed thereto according to* the word of God; and it is the honour of the word of God that it has such power and is of such use both to particular persons and to communities, whose happiness lies much in the virtue of their youth. (1.) Young men must make the word of God their rule, must acquaint themselves with it and resolve to conform themselves to it; that will do more towards the cleansing of young men that the laws of princes or the morals of philosophers. (2.) They must carefully apply that rule and make use of it; they must take heed to their way, must examine it by the word of God, as a touchstone and standard, must rectify what is amiss in it by that regulator and steer by that chart and compass. God's word will not do without our watchfulness, and a constant regard both to it and to our way, that we may compare them together. The ruin of young men is either living at large (or by no rule at all) or choosing to themselves false rules: let them ponder the path of their feet, and walk by scripture-rules; so their way shall be clean, and they shall have the comfort and credit of it here and for ever.

Verse 10

Here is, 1. David's experience of a good work God had wrought in him, which he takes the comfort of and pleads with God: *"I have sought thee,* sought to thee as my oracle, sought after thee as my happiness, sought thee as my God; for *should not a people seek unto their God?* If I have not yet found thee, *I have sought thee,* and thou never saidst, Seek in vain, nor wilt say so to me, for *I have sought thee with my heart, with my whole heart,* sought thee only, sought thee diligently." 2. His prayer for the preservation of that work: "Thou that hast inclined me to seek thy precepts, never suffer me to wander from them." The best are sensible of their aptness to wander; and the more we have found of the pleasure there is in keeping God's commandments the more afraid we shall be of wandering from them and the more earnest we shall be in prayer to God for his grace to prevent our wanderings.

Verse 11

Here is, 1. The close application which David made of the word of God to himself: *He hid it in his heart,* laid it up there, that it might be ready to him whenever he had occasion to use it; he laid it up as that which he valued highly, and had a warm regard for, and which he was afraid of losing and being robbed of. God's word is a treasure worth laying up, and there is no laying it up safely but in our hearts; if we have it only in our houses and hands, enemies may take it from us; if only in our heads, our memories may fail us: but if our hearts be delivered into the mould of it, and the impressions of it remain on our souls, it is safe. 2. The good uses he designed to make of it: *That I might not sin against thee.* Good men are afraid of sin, and are in care to prevent it; and the most effectual way to prevent is to hide God's word in our hearts, that we may answer every temptation, as our Master did, with, *It is written,* may oppose God's precepts to the dominion of sin, his promises to its allurements, and his threatenings to its menaces.

Verse 12

Here, 1. David gives glory to God: *"Blessed art thou, O Lord!* Thou art infinitely happy in the enjoyment of thyself and hast no need of me or my services; yet thou art pleased to reckon thyself honoured by them; assist me therefore, and then accept me." In all our prayers we should intermix praises. 2. He asks grace from God: *"Teach me thy statutes;* give me to know and do my duty in every thing. Thou art the fountain of all blessedness; O let me have this drop from that fountain, this blessing from that blessedness: *Teach me thy statutes,* that I may know how to bless thee, who art a blessed God, and that I may be blessed in thee."

Verses 13–16

Here, I. David looks back with comfort upon the respect he had paid to the word of God. He had the testimony of his conscience for him, 1. That he had edified others with what he had been taught out of the word of God (*v.* 13): *With my lips have I declared all the judgments of thy mouth.* This he did, not only as a king in making orders, and giving judgment, according to the word of God, nor only as a prophet by his psalms, but in his common discourse. Thus he showed how full he was of the word of God, and what a holy delight he took in his acquaintance with it; for it is *out of the abundance of the heart* that *the mouth speaks.* Thus he did good with his knowledge; he did not hide God's word from others, but hid it for them; and, out of that *good treasure in his heart,* brought *forth good things,* as the householder out of his store *things new and old.* Those whose hearts are fed with the bread of life should with their lips feed many. He had prayed (*v.* 12) that God would teach him; and here he pleads, "Lord, I have endeavoured to make a good use of the knowledge thou hast given me, therefore increase it;" for *to him that has shall be given.* 2. That he had entertained himself with it: *"Lord, teach me thy statutes;* for I desire no greater pleasure than to know and do them (*v.* 14): *I have rejoiced in the way of thy commandments,* in a constant even course of obedience to thee; not only in the speculations and histories of thy word, but in the precepts of it, and in that path of serious godliness which they chalk out to me. *I have rejoiced in* this *as much as in all riches,* as much as ever any worldling rejoiced in the increase of his wealth. In the way of God's commandments I can truly say, *Soul, take thy ease;"* in true religion there is all riches, the unsearchable riches of Christ.

II. He looks forward with a holy resolution never to cool in his affection to the word of God; what he *does that he will do,* 2 Co. 11:12. Those that have found pleasure in the ways of God are likely to proceed and persevere in them. 1. He will dwell much upon them in his thoughts (*v.* 15): *I will meditate in thy precepts.* He not only discoursed of them to others (many do that only to show their knowledge and authority), but he communed with his own heart about them, and took pains to digest in his own thoughts what he had declared, or had to declare, to others. Note, God's words ought to be very much the subject of our thoughts. 2. He will have them always in his eye: *I will have respect unto thy ways,* as the traveller has to his road, which he is in care not to miss and always aims and endeavours to hit. We do not meditate on God's precepts to good purpose unless we have respect to them as our rule and our good thoughts produce good works and good intentions in them. 3. He will take a constant pleasure in communion with God and obedience to him. It is not for a season that he rejoices in this light, but *"I will* still, I will for ever, *delight myself in thy statutes,* not only think of them, but do them with delight," *v.* 16. David took more delight in God's statutes than in the pleasures of his court or the honours of his camp, more than in his sword or in his harp. When the law is written in the heart duty becomes a delight. 4. He will never forget what he has learned of the things of God: *"I will not forget thy word,* not only I will not quite forget it, but I will be mindful of it when I have occasion to use it." Those that meditate in God's word, and delight in it, are in no great danger of forgetting it.

3. GIMEL.

Verse 17

We are here taught, 1. That we owe our lives to God's mercy. David prays, *Deal bountifully with* me, *that I may live.* It was God's bounty that gave us life, that gave us this life; and the same bounty that gave it continues it, and gives all the supports and comforts of it; if these be withheld, we die, or, which is equivalent, our lives are embittered and we become weary of them. If God deals in strict justice with us, we die, we perish, we all perish; if these forfeited lives be preserved and prolonged, it is because God deals bountifully with us, according to his mercy, not according to our deserts. The continuance of the most useful life is owing to God's bounty, and on that we must have a continual dependence. 2. That therefore we ought to spend our lives in God's service. Life is *therefore* a choice mercy, because it is an opportunity of obeying God in this world, where there are so few that do glorify him; and this David had in his eye: "Not *that I may live* and grow rich, live and be merry, but *that I may live and keep thy word,* may observe it myself and transmit it to those that shall come after, which the longer I live the better I shall do."

Verse 18

Observe here, 1. That there are *wondrous things* in God's *law,* which we are all concerned, and should covet, to *behold,* not only strange things, which are very surprising and unexpected, but excellent things, which are to be highly esteemed and valued, and things which were long *hidden from the wise and prudent,* but are now *revealed unto babes.* If there were wonders in the law, much more in the gospel, where Christ is all in all, whose name is *Wonderful.* Well may we, who are so nearly interested, desire to behold these wondrous things, when the angels themselves reach *to look into them,* 1 Pt. 1:12. Those that would see the wondrous things of God's law and gospel must beg of him to *open their eyes* and to give them an understanding. We are by nature blind to the things of God, till his grace cause the scales to fall from our eyes; and even those in whose hearts God has said, *Let there be light,* have yet need to be further enlightened, and must still pray to God to open their eyes yet more and more, that those who at first *saw men as trees walking* may come to see all things clearly; and the more God opens our eyes the more wonders we see in the word of God, which we saw not before.

Verse 19

Here we have, 1. The acknowledgment which David makes of his own condition: *I am a stranger in the earth.* We all are so, and all good people confess themselves to be so; for heaven is their home, and the world is but their inn, the land of their pilgrimage. David was a man that knew as much of the world, and was as well known in it, as most men. God built him a house, established his throne; strangers submitted to him, and people that he had not known served him; he had a name like the names of the great men, and yet he calls himself a stranger. We are all strangers on earth and must so account ourselves. 2. The request he makes to God thereupon: *Hide not thy commandments from me.* He means more: "Lord, show thy commandments to me; let me never know the want of the word of God, but, as long as I live, give me to be growing in my acquaintance with it. *I am a stranger,* and therefore stand in need of a guide, a guard, a companion, a comforter; let me have thy commandments always in view, for they will be all this to me, all that a poor stranger can desire. *I am a stranger* here, and must be gone shortly; by thy commandments let me be prepared for my removal hence."

Verse 20

David had prayed that God would open his eyes (*v.* 18) and open the law (*v.* 19); now here he pleads the earnestness of his desire for knowledge and grace, for it is the fervent prayer that avails much. 1. His desire was importunate: *My soul breaketh for the longing it hath to thy judgments,* or (as some read it) *"It is taken up, and wholly employed, in longing for thy judgments;* the whole stream of its desires runs in this channel. I shall think myself quite broken and undone if I want the word of God, the direction, converse, and comfort of it." 2. It was constant — *at all times.* It was not now and then, in a good humour, that he was so fond of the word of God; but it is the habitual temper of every sanctified soul to hunger after the word of God as its necessary food, which there is no living without.

Verse 21

Here is, 1. The wretched character of wicked people. The temper of their minds is bad. They are *proud;* they magnify themselves above others. And yet that is not all: they magnify themselves against God, and set up their wills in competition with and opposition to the will of God, as if their hearts, and tongues, and all, were their own. There is something of pride at the bottom of every wilful sin, and the tenour of their lives is no better: They *do err from thy commandments,* as Israel, that did *always err in their hearts;* they err in judgment, and embrace principles contrary to thy commandments, and then no wonder that they err in practice, and wilfully turn aside out of the good way. This is the effect of their pride; for they say, *What is the Almighty, that we should serve him?* As Pharaoh, *Who is the Lord?* 2. The wretched case of such. They are certainly cursed, for *God resists the proud;* and those that throw off the commands of the law lay themselves under its curse (Gal. 3:10), and he that now *beholds them afar off* will shortly say to them, *Go, you cursed.* The proud sinners bless themselves; God curses them; and, though the most direful effects of this curse are reserved for the other world, yet they are often severely rebuked in this world: Providence crosses them, vexes them, and, wherein they dealt proudly, God shows himself above them; and these rebukes are earnests of worse. David took notice of the rebukes proud men were under, and it made him cleave the more closely to the word of God and pray the more earnestly that he might not *err from God's commandments.* Thus saints get good by God's judgments on sinners.

Verse 22

Here, 1. David prays against the reproach and contempt of men, that they might be *removed,* or (as the word is) *rolled, from off him.* This intimates that they lay upon him, and that neither his greatness nor his goodness could secure him from being libelled and lampooned. Some despised him and endeavoured to make him mean; others reproached him and endeavoured to make him odious. It has often been the lot of those that do well to be ill-spoken of. It intimates that they lay heavily upon him. Hard and foul words indeed break no bones, and yet they are very grievous to a tender and ingenuous spirit; therefore David prays, "Lord, *remove* them from me, that I may not be thereby either driven from my duty or discouraged in it." God has all men's hearts and tongues in his hand, and can silence lying lips, and raise up a good name that is trodden in the dust. To him we may appeal as the assertor of right and avenger of wrong, and may depend on his promise that he will clear up our *righteousness as the light,* Ps. 37:6. Reproach and contempt may humble us and do us good and then it shall be removed. 2. He pleads his constant adherence to the word and way of God: *For I have kept thy testimonies.* He not only pleads his innocency, that he was unjustly censured, but, (1.) That he was jeered for well-doing. He was despised and abused for his strictness and zeal in religion; so that it was for God's name's sake that he suffered reproach, and therefore he could with the more assurance beg of God to appear for him. The reproach of God's people, if it be not removed now, will be turned into the greater honour shortly. (2.) That he was not jeered out of well-doing: "Lord, remove it from me, *for I have kept thy testimonies* notwithstanding." If in a day of trial we still retain our integrity, we may be sure it will end well.

Verse 23

See here, 1. How David was abused even by great men, who should have known better his character and his case, and have been more generous: *Princes did sit,* sit in council, sit in judgment, and *speak against me.* What even princes say is not always right; but it is sad when judgment is thus turned to wormwood, when those that should be the protectors of the innocent are their betrayers. Herein David was a type of Christ, for they were the princes of this world that vilified and *crucified the Lord of glory,* 1 Co. 2:8. 2. What method he took to make himself easy under these abuses: he *meditated in God's statutes,* went on in his duty, and did not regard them; as a deaf man, he heard not. When they spoke against him, he found that in the word of God which spoke for him, and spoke comfort to him, and then none of these things moved him. Those that have pleasure in communion with God may easily despise the censures of men, even of princes.

Verse 24

Here David explains his meditating in God's statutes (*v.* 23), which was of such use to him when princes sat and spoke against him. 1. Did the affliction make his sad? The word of God comforted him, and was *his delight,* more his delight than any of the pleasures either of court or camp, of city or country. Sometimes it proves that the comforts of the word of God are most pleasant to a gracious soul when other comforts are embittered. 2. Did it perplex him? Was he at a loss what to do when the princes spoke against him? God's statutes were *his counsellors,* and they counselled him to bear it patiently and commit his cause to God. God's *testimonies* will be the best counsellors both to princes and private persons. *They are the men of my counsel;* so the word is. There will be found more safety and satisfaction in consulting them than in the multitude of other counsellors. Observe here, Those that would have God's testimonies to be their delight must take them for their counsellors and be advised by them; and let those that take them for their counsellors in close walking take them for their delight in comfortable walking.

4. DALETH.

Verse 25

Here is, I. David's complaint. We should have thought his soul soaring to heaven; but he says himself, *My soul* not only rolls in the dust, but *cleaves to the dust,* which is a complaint either, 1. Of his corruptions, his inclination to the world and the body (both which are dust), and that which follows upon it, a deadness to holy duties. When he would *do good evil was present with him.* God intimated that Adam was not only mortal, but sinful, when he said, *Dust thou art,* Gen. 3:19. David's complaint here is like St. Paul's of a body of death that he carried about

with him. The remainders of in-dwelling corruption are a very grievous burden to a gracious soul. Or, 2. Of his afflictions, either trouble of mind or outward trouble. *Without were fightings, within were fears,* and both together brought him even to the *dust of death* (Ps. 22:15), and his soul clave inseparably to it.

II. His petition for relief, and his plea to enforce that petition: "*Quicken thou me according to thy word.* By thy providence put life into my affairs, by thy grace put life into my affections; cure me of my spiritual deadness and make me lively in my devotion." Note, When we find ourselves dull we must go to God and beg of him to quicken us; he has an eye to God's word as a means of quickening (for the words which God speaks, *they are spirit and they are life* to those that receive them), and as an encouragement to hope that God would quicken him, having promised grace and comfort to all the saints, and to David in particular. God's word must be our guide and plea in every prayer.

Verses 26–27

We have here, 1. The great intimacy and freedom that had been between David and his God. David had opened his case, opened his very heart to God: "*I have declared my ways,* and acknowledged thee in them all, have taken thee along with me in all my designs and enterprises." Thus *Jephthah uttered all his words,* and Hezekiah spread his letters, *before the Lord.* "*I have declared my ways,* my wants, and burdens, and troubles, that I meet with in my way, or my sins, my by-ways (I have made an ingenuous confession of them), and *thou heardest me,* heardest patiently all I had to say, and tookedst cognizance of my case." It is an unspeakable comfort to a gracious soul to think with what tenderness all its complaints are received by a gracious God, 1 Jn. 5:14, 15. 2. David's earnest desire of the continuance of that intimacy, not by visions and voices from heaven, but by the word and Spirit in an ordinary way: *Teach me thy statutes,* that is, *Make me to understand the way of thy precepts.* When he knew God had heard his declaration of his ways he did not say, "Now, Lord, tell me my lot, and let me know what the event will be;" but, "Now, Lord, tell me my duty; let me know what thou wouldst have me to do as the case stands." Note, Those who in all their ways acknowledge God may pray in faith that he will *direct their steps* in the right way. And the surest way of keeping up our communion with God is by learning his statutes and walking intelligently in the *way of his precepts.* See 1 Jn. 1:6, 7. 3. The good use he would make of this for the honour of God and the edification of others: "Let me have a good understanding of *the way of thy precepts;* give me a clear, distinct, and methodical knowledge of divine things; *so shall I talk* with the more assurance, and the more to the purpose, *of thy wondrous works.*" We can talk with a better grace of God's wondrous works, the wonders of providence, and especially the wonders of redeeming love, when we understand the way of God's precepts and walk in that way.

Verses 28–29

Here is, 1. David's representation of his own griefs: *My soul melteth for heaviness,* which is to the same purport with *v.* 25, *My soul cleaveth to the dust.* Heaviness in the heart of man makes it to melt, to drop away like a candle that wastes. The penitent soul melts in sorrow for sin, and even the patient soul may melt in the sense of affliction, and it is then its interest to pour out its supplication before God. 2. His request for God's grace. (1.) That God would enable him to bear his affliction well and graciously support him under it: "*Strengthen thou me* with strength in my soul, *according to thy word,* which, as the bread of life, strengthens man's heart to undergo whatever God is pleased to inflict. Strengthen me to do the duties, resist the temptations, and bear up under the burdens, of an afflicted state, that the spirit may not fail. *Strengthen me according to* that *word* (Deu. 33:25), *As thy days so shall thy strength be.*" (2.) That God would keep him from using any unlawful indirect means for the extricating of himself out of his troubles (*v.* 29): *Remove from me the way of lying.* David was conscious to himself of a proneness to this sin; he had, in a strait, cheated Ahimelech (1 Sa. 21:2), and Achish, *v.* 13 and *ch.* 27:10. Great difficulties are great temptations to palliate a lie with the colour of a pious fraud

and a necessary self-defence; therefore David prays that God would prevent him from falling into this sin any more, lest he should settle in the way of it. A course of lying, of deceit and dissimulation, is that which every good man dreads and which we are all concerned to beg of God by his grace to keep us from. (3.) That he might always be under the guidance and protection of God's government: *Grant me thy law graciously;* grant me that to keep me from the *way of lying.* David had the law written with his own hand, for the king was obliged to transcribe a copy of it for his own use (Deu. 17:18); but he prays that he might have it written in his heart; for then, and then only, we have it indeed, and to good purpose. "Grant it me more and more." Those that know and love the law of God cannot but desire to know it more and love it better. "Grant it me *graciously;*" he begs it as a special token of God's favour. Note, We ought to reckon God's law a grant, a gift, an unspeakable gift, to value it, and pray for it, and to give thanks for it accordingly. The divine code of institutes and precepts is indeed a charter of privileges; and God is truly gracious to those whom he makes gracious by giving them his law.

Verses 30–32

Observe, I. That those who will make anything to purpose of their religion must first make it their serious and deliberate choice; so David did: *I have chosen the way of truth.* Note, 1. The way of serious godliness is the way of truth; the principles it is founded on are principles of eternal truth, and it is the only true way to happiness. 2. We must choose to walk in this way, not because we know no other way, but because we know no better; nay we know no other safe and good way. Let us choose that way for our way, which we will walk in, though it be narrow.

II. That those who have chosen the way of truth must have a constant regard to the word of God as the rule of their walking: *Thy judgments have I laid before me,* as he who learns to write lays his copy before him, that he may write according to it, as the workman lays his model and platform before him, that he may do his work exactly. As we must have the word in our heart by an habitual conformity to it, so we must have it in our eye by an actual regard to it upon all occasions, that we may walk accurately and by rule.

III. That those who make religion their choice and rule are likely to adhere to it faithfully: "*I have stuck to thy testimonies* with unchanged affection and an unshaken resolution, stuck to them at all times, through all trials. *I have chosen them,* and therefore *I have stuck to* them." Note, The choosing Christian is likely to be the steady Christian; while those that are Christians by chance tack about if the wind turn.

IV. That those who stick to the word of God may in faith expect and pray for acceptance with God; for David means this when he begs, "*Lord, put me not to shame;* that is, never leave me to do that by which I shall shame myself, and do thou not reject my services, which will put me to the greatest confusion."

V. That the more comfort God gives us the more duty he expects from us, *v.* 32. Here we have, 1. His resolution to go on vigorously in religion: *I will run the way of thy commandments.* Those that are going to heaven should make haste thither and be still pressing forward. It concerns us to redeem time and take pains, and to go on in our business with cheerfulness. We *then* run the way of our duty, when we are ready to it, and pleasant in it, and *lay aside every weight,* Heb. 12:1. 2. His dependence upon God for grace to do so: "I shall *then* abound in thy work, *when thou shalt enlarge my heart.*" God, by his Spirit, enlarges the hearts of his people when he gives them wisdom (for that is called *largeness of heart,* 1 Ki. 4:29), when he *sheds abroad the love of God* in the heart, and puts gladness there. The joy of our Lord should be wheels to our obedience.

5. HE.

Verses 33–34

Here, I. David prays earnestly that God himself would be his teacher; he had prophets, and wise men, and priests, about him, and was himself well instructed in the law of God, yet he begs to be taught of God, as knowing that *none* teaches like him, Job 36:22. Observe here, 1. What he desires to be taught, not the notions or language of God's statutes, but *the way* of them — "the way of applying them to myself and governing myself by them; teach me the way of my duty which thy statutes prescribe, and in every doubtful case let me know what thou wouldst have me to do, let me hear the word behind me, saying, *This is the way, walk in it*" Isa. 30:21. 2. How he desires to be taught, in such a way as no man could teach him: *Lord, give me understanding.* As the God of nature, he has given us intellectual powers and faculties; but here we are taught to pray that, as the God of grace, he would give us understanding to use those powers and faculties about the great things which belong to our peace, which, through the corruption of nature, we are averse to: *Give me understanding,* an enlightened understanding; for it is as good to have no understanding at all as not to have it sanctified. Nor will the spirit of revelation in the word answer the end unless we have the spirit of wisdom in the heart. This is that which we are indebted to Christ for; for the *Son of God has come and has given us understanding,* 1 Jn. 5:20.

II. He promises faithfully that he would be a good scholar. If God would teach him, he was sure he should learn to good purpose: "*I shall keep thy law,* which I shall never do unless I be taught of God, and therefore I earnestly desire that I may be taught." If God, by his Spirit, give us a right and good understanding, we shall be, 1. Constant in our obedience: "*I shall keep it to the end,* to the end of my life, which will be the surest proof of sincerity." It will not avail the traveller to keep the way for a while, if he do not keep it to the end of his journey. 2. Cordial in our obedience: *I shall observe it with my whole heart,* with pleasure and delight, and with vigour and resolution. That way which the whole heart goes the whole man goes; and that should be the way of God's commandments, for the keeping of them is the whole of man.

Verses 35–36

He had before prayed to God to enlighten his understanding, that he might know his duty, and not mistake concerning it; here he prays to God to bow his will, and quicken the active powers of his soul, that he might do his duty; for *it is God that works in us both to will and to do,* as well as to understand, what is good, Phil. 2:13. Both the good head and the good heart are from the good grace of God, and both are necessary to every good work. Observe here,

I. The grace he prays for. 1. That God would make him able to do his duty: "*Make me to go;* strengthen me for every good work." Since we are not sufficient of ourselves, our dependence must be upon the grace of God, for from him all our sufficiency is. God puts his Spirit within us, and so causes us to *walk in his statutes* (Eze. 36:27), and this is that which David here begs. 2. That God would make him willing to do it, and would, by his grace, subdue the aversion he naturally had to it: "*Incline my heart to thy testimonies,* to those things which thy testimonies prescribe; not only make me willing to do my duty, as that which I must do and therefore am concerned to make the best of, but make me desirous to do my duty as that which is agreeable to the new nature and really advantageous to me." Duty is then done with delight when the heart is inclined to it: it is God's grace that inclines us, and the more backward we find ourselves to it the more earnest we must be for that grace.

II. The sin he prays against, and that is covetousness: "*Incline my heart to keep thy testimonies,* and restrain and mortify the inclination there is in me to *covetousness.*" That is a sin which stands opposed to all God's testimonies; for the love of money is such a sin as is the root of much sin, of all sin. Those therefore that would have the love of God rooted in them must get the love of the world rooted out of them; for *the friendship of the world is enmity with God.* See in what way God deals with men, not by compulsion, but he draws with the cords of a man, working in them an inclination to that which is good and an aversion to that which is evil.

III. His plea to enforce this prayer: "Lord, bring me to, and keep me in, *the way of thy commandments, for therein do I delight;* and therefore I pray thus earnestly for grace to walk in that way. Thou hast wrought in me this delight in the way of thy commandments; wilt thou not work

in me an ability to walk in them, and so crown thy own work?"

Verse 37

Here, 1. David prays for restraining grace, that he might be prevented and kept back from that which would hinder him in the way of his duty: *Turn away my eyes from beholding vanity.* The honours, pleasures, and profits of the world are the vanities, the aspect and prospect of which draw multitudes away from the paths of religion and godliness. The eye, when fastened on these, infects the heart with the love of them, and so it is alienated from God and divine things; and therefore, as we ought to *make a covenant with our eyes,* and lay a charge upon them, that they shall not wander after, much less fix upon, that which is dangerous (Job 31:1), so we ought to pray that God by his providence would keep vanity out of our sight and that by his grace he would keep us from being enamoured with the sight of it. 2. He prays for constraining grace, that he might not only be kept from every thing that would obstruct his progress heaven-ward, but might have that grace which was necessary to forward him in that progress: "*Quicken thou me in thy way;* quicken me to redeem time, to improve opportunity, to press forward, and to do every duty with liveliness and fervency of spirit." Beholding vanity deadens us and slackens our pace; a traveller that stands gazing upon every object that presents itself to his view will not rid ground; but, if our eyes be kept from that which would divert us, our hearts will be kept to that which will excite us.

Verse 38

Here is 1. The character of a good man, which is the work of God's grace in him; he is *God's servant,* subject to his law and employed in his work, that is, *devoted to his fear,* given up to his direction and disposal, and taken up with high thoughts of him and all those acts of devotion which have a tendency to his glory. Those are truly God's servants who, though they have their infirmities and defects, are sincerely *devoted to the fear of God* and have all their affections and motions governed by that fear; they are engaged and addicted to religion. 2. The confidence that a good man has towards God, in dependence upon the word of his grace to him. Those that are God's servants may, in faith and with humble boldness, pray that God would *establish his word to them,* that is, that he would fulfil his promises to them in due time, and in the mean time give them an assurance that they shall be fulfilled. What God has promised we must pray for; we need not be so aspiring as to ask more; we need not be so modest as to ask less.

Verse 39

Here, 1. David prays against *reproach,* as before, *v.* 22. David was conscious to himself that he had done that which might give *occasion to the enemies of the Lord to blaspheme,* which would blemish his own reputation and turn to the dishonour of his family; now he prays that God, who has all men's hearts and tongues in his hands, would be pleased to prevent this, to *deliver him from all his transgressions,* that he *might not be the reproach of the foolish,* which he feared (Ps. 39:8); or he means that reproach which his enemies unjustly loaded him with. Let their *lying lips be put to silence.* 2. He pleads the goodness of God's judgments: "Lord, thou sittest in the throne, and *thy judgments are right* and *good,* just and kind, to those that are wronged, and therefore to thee I appeal from the unjust and unkind censures of men." It is a small thing to be judged of man's judgment, while *he that judges us is the Lord.* Or thus: "Thy word, and ways, and thy holy religion, are very good, but the reproaches cast on me will fall on them; therefore, *Lord, turn them away;* let not religion be wounded through my side."

Verse 40

Here, 1. David professes the ardent affection he had to the word of God: "*I have longed after thy precepts,* not only loved them, and delighted in what I have already attained, but I have earnestly desired to know them more and do them better, and am still pressing forward towards perfection." Tastes of the sweetness of God's precepts will but set us a longing after a more intimate acquaintance with them.

He appeals to God concerning this passionate desire after his precepts: "*Behold, I have* thus loved, thus *longed;* thou knowest all things, thou knowest that I am thus affected." 2. He prays for grace to enable him to answer this profession. "Thou hast wrought in me this languishing desire, put life into me, that I may prosecute it; *quicken me in thy righteousness,* in thy righteous ways, according to thy righteous promise." Where God has wrought to will he will work to do, and where he has wrought to desire he will satisfy the desire.

6. VAU.

Verses 41–42

Here is, 1. David's prayer for the salvation of the Lord. "Lord, thou art my Saviour; I am miserable in myself, and thou only canst make me happy; *let thy salvation come to me.* Hasten temporal salvation to me from my present distresses, and hasten me to the eternal salvation, by giving me the necessary qualifications for it and the comfortable pledges and foretastes of it." 2. David's dependence upon the grace and promise of God for that salvation. These are the two pillars on which our hope is built, and they will not fail us:: — (1.) The grace of God: *Let thy mercies come, even thy salvation.* Our salvation must be attributed purely to God's mercy, and not to any merit of our own. Eternal life must be expected as the *mercy of our Lord Jesus Christ,* Jude 21. "Lord, I have by faith thy mercies in view; let me by prayer prevail to have them come to me." (2.) The promise of God: "*Let it come according to thy word,* thy word of promise. *I trust in thy word,* and therefore may expect the performance of the promise." We are not only allowed to trust in God's word, but our trusting in it is the condition of our benefit by it. 3. David's expectation of the good assurance which that grace and promise of God would give him: "*So shall I have wherewith to answer him that reproaches me* for my confidence in God, as if it would deceive me." When God saves those out of their troubles who trusted in him he effectually silences those who would have *shamed that counsel of the poor* (Ps. 14:6), and their reproaches will be for ever silenced when the salvation of the saints is completed; then it will appear, beyond dispute, that it was not in vain to trust in God.

Verses 43–44

Here is, 1. David's humble petition for the tongue of the learned, that he might know how to *speak a word in season* for the glory of God: *Take not the word of truth utterly out of my mouth.* He means, "Lord, let the word of truth be always in my mouth; let me have the wisdom and courage which are necessary to enable me both to use my knowledge for the instruction of others, and, like the good householder, to bring out of my treasury *things new and old,* and to make profession of my faith whenever I am called to it." We have need to pray to God that we may never be afraid or ashamed to own his truths and ways, nor deny him before men. David found that he was sometimes at a loss, that the *word of truth* was not so ready to him as it should have been, but he prays, "Lord, let it not be taken utterly from me; let my always have so much of it at hand as will be necessary to the due discharge of my duty." 2. His humble profession of the heart of the upright, without which the tongue of the learned, however it may be serviceable to others, will stand us in no stead. (1.) David professes his confidence in God: "Lord, make me ready and mighty in the scriptures, *for I have hoped in those judgments* of thy mouth, and, if they be not at hand, my support and defence have departed from me." (2.) He professes his resolution to adhere to his duty in the strength of God's grace: "*So shall I keep thy law continually.* If I have thy word not only in my heart, but in my mouth, I shall do all I should do, stand complete in thy whole will." Thus shall the *man of God be perfect, thoroughly furnished for every good word and work,* 2 Tim. 3:17; Col. 3:16. Observe how he resolves to keep God's law, [1.] Continually, without trifling. God must be served in a constant course of obedience every day, and all the day long. [2.] *For ever and ever,* without backsliding. We must never be *weary of well-doing.* If we serve him to the end of our time on earth, we shall be serving him in heaven to the endless ages of eternity; so shall we *keep his law* for ever and ever. Or thus: "Lord, let me have the word of truth in *my mouth*, that I may commit that sacred deposit to the rising generation (2 Tim. 2:2) and by them it may be transmitted to succeeding ages; so shall thy law be kept *for ever and ever*," that is, from one generation to another, according to that promise (Isa. 59:21), *My word in thy mouth shall not depart out of the mouth of thy seed, nor thy seed's seed.*

Verses 45–48

We may observe in these verses, 1. What David experienced of an affection to the law of God: "*I seek thy precepts, v.* 45. I desire to know and do my duty, and consult thy word accordingly; I do all I can to *understand what the will of the Lord is* and to discover the intimations of his mind. *I seek thy precepts,* for *I have loved them, v.* 47, 48. I not only give consent to them as good, but take complacency in them as good for me." All that love God love his government and therefore love all his commandments. 2. What he expected from this. Five things he promises himself here in the strength of God's grace: — (1.) That he should be free and easy in his duty: "*I will walk at liberty,* freed from that which is evil, not hampered with the fetters of my own corruptions, and free to that which is good, doing it not by constraint, but willingly." The service of sin is perfect slavery; the service of God is perfect liberty. Licentiousness is bondage to the greatest of tyrants; conscientiousness is freedom to the meanest of prisoners, Jn. 8:32, 36; Lu. 1:74, 75. (2.) That he should be bold and courageous in his duty: *I will speak of thy testimonies also before kings.* Before David came to the crown kings were sometimes his judges, as Saul, and Achish; but, if he were called before them to give a reason of the hope that was in him, he would *speak of God's testimonies,* and profess to build his hope upon them and make them his council, his guards, his crown, his all. We must never be afraid to own our religion, though it should expose us to the wrath of kings, but speak of it as that which we will live and die by, like the three children before Nebuchadnezzar, Dan. 3:16; Acts 4:20. After David came to the crown kings were sometimes his companions; they visited him and he returned their visits; but he did not, in complaisance to them, talk of every thing but religion, for fear of affronting them and making his conversation uneasy to them. No; God's testimonies shall be the principal subject of his discourse with the kings, not only to show that he was not ashamed of his religion, but to instruct them in it and bring them over to it. It is good for kings to hear of God's testimonies, and it will adorn the conversation of princes themselves to speak of them. (3.) That he should be cheerful and pleasant in his duty (*v.* 47): "*I will delight myself in thy commandments,* in conversing with them, in conforming to them. I will never be so well pleased with myself as when I do that which is pleasing to God. The more delight we take in the service of God the nearer we come to the perfection we aim at. (4.) That he should be diligent and vigorous in his duty: *I will lift up my hands to thy commandments,* which denotes not only a vehement desire towards them (Ps. 143:6) — "I will lay hold of them as one afraid of missing them, or letting them go;" but a close application of mind to the observance of them — "I will lay my hands to the command, not only to praise it, but practise it; nay, I will lift up my hands to it, that is, I will put forth all the strength I have to do it." The hands that hang down, through sloth and discouragement, shall be lifted up, Heb. 12:12. (5.) That he should be thoughtful and considerate in his duty (*v.* 48): "*I will meditate in thy statutes,* not only entertain myself with thinking of them as matters of speculation, but contrive how I may observe them in the best manner." By *this* it will appear that we truly love God's commandments, if we apply both our minds and our hands to them.

7. ZAIN.

Verse 49

Two things David here pleads with God in prayer for that mercy and grace which he hoped for, according to the word, by which his requests were guided: — 1. That God had given him the promise on which he hoped: "Lord, I desire no more than that thou wouldst *remember thy word unto thy servant,* and *do as thou hast said;"* see 1 Chr. 17:23. "Thou art wise, and therefore wilt perfect what thou hast purposed, and not change thy counsel. Thou art faithful, and therefore wilt perform what thou hast promised, and not break thy word." Those that make God's promises their portion may with humble boldness make them their plea. "Lord, is not that the word which thou hast spoken; and wilt thou not make it good?" Gen. 32:9; Ex. 33:12. 2. That God, who had given him the promise in the word, had by his grace wrought in him a hope in that promise and enabled him to depend upon it, and had raised his expectations of great things from it. Has God kindled in us desires towards spiritual blessings more than towards any temporal good things, and will he not be so kind as to satisfy those desires? Has he filled us with hopes of those blessings, and will he not be so just as to accomplish these hopes? He that did by his Spirit work faith in us will, according to our faith, work for us, and will not disappoint us.

Verse 50

Here is David's experience of benefit by the word. 1. As a means of his sanctification: "*Thy word has quickened me.* It made me alive when I was dead in sin; it has many a time made me lively when I was dead in duty; it has quickened me to that which is good when I was backward and averse to it, and it has quickened me in that which is good when I was cold and indifferent." 2. Therefore as a means of his consolation when he was in affliction and needed something to support him: "Because thy word has quickened my at other times, it has comforted me then." The word of God has much in it that speaks *comfort in affliction;* but those only may apply it to themselves who have experienced in some measure the quickening power of the word. If through grace it make us holy, there is enough in it to make us easy, in all conditions, under all events.

Verse 51

David here tells us, and it will be of use to us to know it, 1. That he had been jeered for his religion. Though he was a man of honour, a man of great prudence, and had done eminent services to his country, yet, because he was a devout conscientious man, *the proud had him greatly in derision;* they ridiculed him, bantered him, and did all they could to expose him to contempt; they laughed at him for his praying, and called it *cant,* for his seriousness, and called it *mopishness,* for his strictness, and called it *needless preciseness.* They were the proud that sat in the scorner's seat and valued themselves on so doing. 2. That yet he had not been jeered out of his religion: "They have done all they could to make me quit it for shame, but none of these things move me: *I have not declined from thy law* for all this; but, *if this be to be vile"* (as he said when Michal had him greatly in derision), *"I will be yet more vile."* He not only had not quite forsaken the law, but had not so much as declined from it. We must never shrink from any duty, nor let slip an opportunity of doing good, for fear of the reproach of men, or their revilings. The traveller goes on his way though the dogs bark at him. Those can bear but little for Christ that cannot bear a hard word for him.

Verse 52

When David was derided for his godliness he not only held fast his integrity, but, 1. He comforted himself. He not only bore reproach, but bore it cheerfully. It did not disturb his peace, nor break in upon the repose of his spirit in God. It was a comfort to him to think that it was for God's sake that he bore reproach, and that his worst enemies could find *no occasion against him, save only in the matter of his God,* Dan. 6:5. Those that are derided for their adherence to God's law may comfort themselves with this, that *the reproach of Christ* will prove, in the end, *greater riches* to them *than the treasures of Egypt.* 2. That which he comforted himself with was the remembrance of God's *judgments of old,* the providences of God concerning his people formerly, both in mercy to them and in justice against their persecutors. God's judgments of old, in our own early days and in the days of our fathers, are to be remembered by us for our comfort and encouragement in the way of God, for he is still the same.

Verse 53

Here is, 1. The character of wicked people; he means those that are openly and grossly wicked: *They forsake thy law.* Every sin is a transgression of the law, but a course and way of wilful and avowed sin is downright forsaking it and throwing it off. 2. The impression which the wickedness of the wicked made upon David; it frightened him, it put him into an amazement. He trembled to think of the dishonour thereby done to God, the gratification thereby given to Satan, and the mischiefs thereby done to the souls of men. He dreaded the consequences of it both to the sinners themselves (and cried out, *O gather not my soul with sinners! let my enemy be as the wicked*) and to the interests of God's kingdom among men, which he was afraid would be thereby sunk and ruined. He does not say, *"Horror has taken hold on me* because of their cruel designs against me," but "because of the contempt they put on God and his law." Sin is a monstrous horrible thing in the eyes of all that are sanctified, Jer. 5:30; 23:14; Hos. 6:10; Jer. 2:12.

Verse 54

Here is, 1. David's state and condition; he was *in the house of his pilgrimage,* which may be understood either as his peculiar trouble (he was often tossed and hurried, and forced to fly) or as his lot in common with all. This world is the house of our pilgrimage, the house in which we are pilgrims; it is our tabernacle; it is our inn. We must confess ourselves *strangers and pilgrims upon earth,* who are not at home here, nor must be here long. Even David's palace is but the house of his pilgrimage. 2. His comfort in this state: "*Thy statutes have been my songs,* with which I here entertain myself," as travellers are wont to divert the thoughts of their weariness, and take off something of the tediousness of their journey, by singing a pleasant song now and then. David was the sweet singer of Israel, and here we are told whence he fetched his songs; they were all borrowed from the word of God. God's statutes were as familiar to him as the songs which a man is accustomed to sing; and he conversed with them in his pilgrimage-solitudes. They were as pleasant to him as songs, and *put gladness into his heart* more than those have that *chant to the sound of the viol,* Amos 6:5. *Is any afflicted* then? Let him sing over God's statutes, and try if he cannot so *sing away sorrow,* Ps. 138:5.

Verses 55–56

Here is, 1. The converse David had with the word of God; he kept it in mind, and upon every occasion he called it to mind. God's name is the discovery he has made of himself to us in and by his word. *This is his memorial unto all generations,* and therefore we should always keep it in memory — remember it *in the night,* upon a waking bed, when we are communing with our own hearts. When others were sleeping David was remembering God's name, and, by repeating that lesson, increasing his acquaintance with it; in the night of affliction this he called to mind. 2. The conscience he made of conforming to it. The due remembrance of God's name, which is prefixed to his law, will have a great influence upon our observance of the law: *I remembered thy name in the night,* and therefore was careful to *keep thy law* all day. How comfortable will it be in the reflection if our own hearts can witness for us that we have thus remembered God's name, and kept his law! 3. The advantage he got by it (*v.* 56): *This I had because I kept thy precepts.* Some understand this indefinitely: *This I had* (that is I had that which satisfied me; I had every thing that is comfortable) *because I kept thy precepts.* Note, All that have made a business of religion will own that it has turned to a good account, and that they have been unspeakable gainers by it. Others refer it to what goes immediately before: "I had the comfort of keeping thy law because I kept it." Note, God's work is its own wages. A heart to obey the will of God is a most valuable reward of obedience; and the more we do the more we may do, and shall do, in the service of God; the branch that bears fruit is made *more fruitful,* Jn. 15:2.

8. CHETH.

Verse 57

We may hence gather the character of a godly man.

1. He makes the favour of God his felicity: *Thou art my portion, O Lord!* Others place their happiness in the wealth and honours of this world. Their portion is in this life; they look no further; they desire no more; these are *their good things,* Lu. 16:25. But all that are sanctified take the Lord for the portion of their inheritance and their cup, and nothing less will satisfy them. David can appeal to God in this matter: "Lord, thou knowest that I have chosen thee for my portion, and depend upon thee to make me happy." 2. He makes the law of God his rule: *"I have said that I would keep thy words;* and what I have said by thy grace I will do, and will abide by it to the end." Note, Those that take God for their portion must take him for their prince, and swear allegiance to him; and, having promised to *keep his word,* we must often put ourselves in mind of our promise, Ps. 39:1.

Verse 58

David, having in the foregoing verse reflected upon his covenants with God, here reflects upon his prayers to God, and renews his petition. Observe, 1. What he prayed for. Having taken God for his portion, he *entreated his favour,* as one that knew he had forfeited it, was unworthy of it, and yet undone without it, but for ever happy if he could obtain it. We cannot demand God's favour as a debt, but must be humble suppliants for it, that God will not only be reconciled to us, but accept us and smile upon us. He prays, *"Be merciful to me,* in the forgiveness of what I have done amiss, and in giving me grace to do better for the future." 2. How he prayed — *with his whole heart,* as one that knew how to value the blessing he prayed for. The gracious soul is entirely set upon the favour of God, and is therefore importunate for it. *I will not let thee go except thou bless me.* 3. What he pleaded — the promise of God: *"Be merciful to me, according to thy word.* I desire the mercy promised, and depend upon the promise for it." Those that are governed by the precepts of the word and are resolved to keep them (*v.* 57) may plead the promises of the word and take the comfort of them.

Verses 59–60

David had said he *would keep God's word* (*v.* 57), and it was well said; now here he tells us how and in what method he pursued that resolution. 1. He *thought on his ways.* He thought beforehand what he should do, pondering the path of his feet (Prov. 4:26), that he might walk surely, and not at all adventures. He thought after what he had done, reflected upon his life past, and recollected the paths he had walked in and the steps he had taken. The word signifies a fixed abiding thought. Some make it an allusion to those who work embroidery, who are very exact and careful to cover the least flaw, or to those who cast up their accounts, who reckon with themselves, What do I owe? What am I worth? *"I thought* not on my wealth (as the covetous man, Ps. 49:11) but *on my ways,* not on what I have, but what I do:" for what we do will follow us into another world when what we have must be left behind. Many are critical enough in their remarks upon other people's ways who never think of their own: but *let every man prove his own work.* 2. He *turned his feet to God's testimonies.* He determined to make the word of God his rule, and to walk by that rule. He turned from the by-paths to which he had turned aside, and returned to God's testimonies. He turned not only his eye to them, but his feet, his affections to the love of God's word and his conversation to the practice of it. The bent and inclinations of his soul were towards God's testimonies and his conversation was governed by them Penitent reflections must produce pious resolutions. 3. He did this immediately and without demur (*v.* 60): *I made haste and delayed not.* When we are under convictions of sin we must strike while the iron is hot, and not think to defer the prosecution of them, as Felix did, to *a more convenient season.* When we are called to duty we must lose no time, but set about it *to-day, while it is called to-day.* Now this account which David here gives of himself may refer either to his constant practice every day (he reflected on his ways at night, directed his feet to God's testimonies in the morning, and what his hand found to do that was good he did it without delay), or it may refer to his first acquaintance with God and religion, when he began to throw off the vanity of childhood and youth, and to remember his Creator; that blessed change was, by the grace of God, thus wrought. Note, (1.) Conversion begins in serious consideration, Eze. 18:28; Lu. 15:17. (2.) Consideration must end in a sound conversion. To what purpose have we thought on our ways if we do not turn our feet with all speed to God's testimonies?

Verse 61

Here is, 1. The malice of David's enemies against him. They were wicked men, who hated him for his godliness. There were bands or troops of them confederate against him. They did him all the mischief they could; they robbed him; having endeavoured to take away his good name (*v.* 51), they set upon his goods, and spoiled him of them, either by plunder in time of war or by fines and confiscations under colour of law. Saul (it is likely) seized his effects, Absalom his palace, and the Amalekites rifled Ziklag. Worldly wealth is what we may be robbed of. David, though a man of war, could not keep his own. *Thieves break through and steal.* 2. The testimony of David's conscience for him that he had held fast his religion when he was stripped of every thing else, as Job did when the bands of the Chaldeans and Sabeans had robbed him: *But I have not forgotten thy law.* No care nor grief should drive God's word out of our minds, or hinder our comfortable relish of it and converse with it. Nor must we ever think the worse of the ways of God for any trouble we meet with in those ways, nor fear being losers by our religion at last, however we may be losers for it now.

Verse 62

Though David is, in this psalm, much in prayer, yet he did not neglect the duty of thanksgiving; for those that pray much will have much to give thanks for. See, 1. How much God's hand was eyed in his thanksgivings. He does not say, *"I will give thanks* because of thy favours to me, which I have the comfort of," but, *"Because of thy righteous judgments,* all the disposals of thy providence in wisdom and equity, which thou hast the glory of." We must give thanks for the asserting of God's honour and the accomplishing of his word in all he does in the government of the world. 2. How much David's heart was set upon his thanksgivings. He would *rise at midnight to give thanks* to God. Great and good thoughts kept him awake, and refreshed him, instead of sleep; and so zealous was he for the honour of God that when others were in their beds he was upon his knees at his devotions. He did not affect to be seen of men in it, but gave thanks in secret, where our heavenly Father sees. He had praised God *in the courts of the Lord's house,* and yet he will do it in his bed-chamber. Public worship will not excuse us from secret worship. When David found his heart affected with God's judgments, he immediately offered up those affections to God, in actual adorations, not deferring, lest they should cool. Yet observe his reverence; he did not lie still and give thanks, but rose out of his bed, perhaps in the cold and in the dark, to do it the more solemnly. And see what a good husband he was of time; when he could not lie and sleep, he would rise and pray.

Verse 63

David had often expressed the great love he had to God; here he expresses the great love he had to the people of God; and observe, 1. Why he loved them; not so much because they were his best friends, most firm to his interest and most forward to serve him, but because they were such as *feared God* and *kept his precepts,* and so did him honour and helped to support his kingdom among men. Our love to the saints is *then* sincere when we love them for the sake of what we see of God in them and the service they do to him. 2. How he showed his love to them: He was *a companion of them.* He had not only a spiritual communion with them in the same faith and hope, but he joined with them in holy ordinances in the courts of the Lord, where rich and poor, prince and peasant, meet together. He sympathized with them in their joys and sorrows (Heb. 10:33); he conversed familiarly with them, communicated his experiences to them, and consulted theirs. He not only took such to be his companions as did fear God, but he vouchsafed himself to be a companion with all, with any, that did so, wherever he met with them. Though he was a king, he would associate with the poorest of his subjects that feared God, Ps. 15:4: Jam. 2:1.

Verse 64

Here, 1. David pleads that God is good to all the creatures according to their necessities and capacities; as the heaven is full of God's glory, so *the earth is full of his mercy,* full of the instances of his pity and bounty. Not only the land of Canaan, where God is known and worshipped, but the whole earth, in many parts of which he has no homage paid him, is full of his mercy. Not only the children of men upon the earth, but even the inferior creatures, taste of God's goodness. *His tender mercies are over all his works.* 2. He therefore prays that God would be good to him according to his necessity and capacity: *"Teach me thy statutes.* Thou feedest the young ravens that cry, with food proper for them; and wilt thou not feed me with spiritual food, the bread of life, which my soul needs and craves, and cannot subsist without? *The earth is full of thy mercy;* and is not heaven too? Wilt thou not then give me spiritual blessings in heavenly places?" A gracious heart will fetch an argument from any thing to enforce a petition for divine teaching. Surely he that will not let his birds be unfed will not let his children be untaught.

9. TETH.

Verses 65–66

Here, 1. David makes a thankful acknowledgment of God's gracious dealings with him all along: *Thou hast dealt well with thy servant.* However God has dealt with us, we must own he has dealt *well* with us, better than we deserve, and all in love and with design to work for our good. In many instances God has done well for us beyond our expectations. He has done well for all his servants; never any of them complained that he had used them hardly. *Thou hast dealt well with* me, not only according to thy mercy, but *according to thy word.* God's favours look best when they are compared with the promise and are seen flowing from that fountain. 2. Upon these experiences he grounds a petition for divine instruction: *"Teach me good judgment and knowledge,* that, by thy grace, I may render again, in some measure, according to the benefit done unto me." Teach me *a good taste* (so the word signifies), a good relish, to discern things that differ, to distinguish between truth and falsehood, good and evil; for *the ear tries words, as the mouth tastes meat.* We should pray to God for a sound mind, that we may have *spiritual senses exercised,* Heb. 5:14. Many have knowledge who have little judgment; those who have both are well fortified against the snares of Satan and well furnished for the service of God and their generation. 3. This petition is backed with a plea: *"For I have believed thy commandments,* received them, and consented to them that they are good, and submitted to their government; therefore, Lord, *teach me."* Where God has given a good heart a good head too many in faith be prayed for.

Verse 67

David here tells us what he had experienced, 1. Of the temptations of a prosperous condition: *"Before I was afflicted,* while I lived in peace and plenty, and knew no sorrow, *I went astray* from God and my duty." Sin is going astray; and we are most apt to wander from God when we are easy and think ourselves at home in the world. Prosperity is the unhappy occasion of much iniquity; it makes people conceited of themselves, indulgent of the flesh, forgetful of God, in love with the world, and deaf to the reproofs of the word. See Ps. 30:6. It is good for us, when we are afflicted, to remember how and wherein we went astray *before we were afflicted,* that we may answer the end of the affliction. 2. Of the benefit of an afflicted state: *"Now have I kept thy word,* and so have been recovered from my wanderings." God often makes use of afflictions as a means to reduce those to himself who have wandered from him. Sanctified afflictions humble us for sin and show us the vanity of the world; they soften the heart, and open the ear to discipline. The prodigal's distress brought him to himself first and then to his father.

Verse 68

Here, 1. David praises God's goodness and gives him the glory of it: *Thou art good and doest good.* All who have any knowledge of God and dealings with him wilt own that he does good, and therefore will conclude that he is good. The streams of God's goodness are so numerous, and run so full, so strong, to all the creatures, that we must conclude the fountain that is in himself to be inexhaustible. We cannot conceive how much good our God does every day, much less can we conceive how good he is. Let us acknowledge it with admiration and with holy love and thankfulness. 2. He prays for God's grace, and begs to be under the guidance and influence of it: *Teach me thy statutes.* "Lord, thou doest good to all, art the bountiful benefactor of all the creatures; this is the good I beg thou wilt do to me, — Instruct me in my duty, incline me to it, and enable me to do it. *Thou art good, and doest good;* Lord, *teach me thy statutes,* that I may be good and do good, may have a good heart and live a good life." It is an encouragement to poor sinners to hope that God will *teach them his way* because he is *good and upright,* Ps. 25:8.

Verses 69–70

David here tells us how he was affected as to the proud and wicked people that were about him. 1. He did not fear their malice, nor was he by it deterred from his duty: *They have forged a lie against me.* Thus they aimed to take away his good name. Nay, all we have in the world, even life itself, may be brought into danger by those who make no conscience of forging a lie. Those that were proud envied David's reputation, because it eclipsed them, and therefore did all they could to blemish him. They took a pride in trampling upon him. They therefore persuaded themselves it was no sin to tell a deliberate lie if it might but expose him to contempt. Their wicked wit forged lies, invented storied which there was not the least colour for, to serve their wicked designs. And what did David do when he was thus belied? He will bear it patiently; he will keep that precept which forbids him to render railing for railing, and will with all his heart sit down silently. He will go on in his duty with constancy and resolution: "Let them say what they will, *I will keep thy precepts,* and not dread their reproach." 2. He did not envy their prosperity, nor was he by it allured from his duty. *Their heart is as fat as grease.* The proud are *at ease* (Ps. 123:4); they are full of the world, and the wealth and pleasures of it; and this makes them, (1.) Senseless, secure, and stupid; they are past feeling: thus the phrase is used, Isa. 6:10. *Make the heart of this people fat.* They are not sensible of the touch of the word of God or his rod. (2.) Sensual and voluptuous: *"Their eyes stand out with fatness* (Ps. 73:7); they roll themselves in the pleasures of sense, and take up with them as their chief good; and much good may it do them. I would not change conditions with them. *I delight in thy law;* I build my security upon the promises of God's word and have pleasure enough in communion with God, infinitely preferable to all their delights." The children of God, who are acquainted with spiritual pleasures, need not envy the children of this world their carnal pleasures.

Verse 71

See here, 1. That it has been the lot of the best saints to be afflicted. The proud and the wicked lived in pomp and pleasure, while David, though he kept close to God and his duty, was still in affliction. *Waters of a full cup are wrung out to* God's people, Ps. 73:10. 2. That it has been the advantage of God's people to be afflicted. David could speak experimentally: *It was good for me;* many a good lesson he had learnt by his afflictions, and many a good duty he had been brought to which otherwise would have been unlearnt and undone. *Therefore* God visited him with affliction, that he might learn God's statutes; and the intention was answered: the afflictions had contributed to the improvement of his knowledge and grace. He that chastened him taught him. *The rod and reproof give wisdom.*

Verse 72

This is a reason why David reckoned that when by his afflictions he learned God's statutes, an the profit did so much counterbalance the loss, he was really a gainer by them; for God's *law,* which he got acquaintance with by his affliction, was *better* to him than all the *gold and silver* which he lost by his affliction. 1. David had but a little of the word of God in comparison with what we have, yet see how highly he valued it; how inexcusable then are we, who have both the Old and New Testament complete, and yet account them as a strange thing! Observe, *Therefore* he valued the law, because it is *the law of God's mouth,* the revelation of his will, and ratified by his authority. 2. He had a great deal of gold and silver in comparison with what we have, yet see how little he valued it. His riches increased, and yet he did not set his heart upon them, but upon the word of God. That was better to him, yielded him better pleasures, and better maintenance, and a better inheritance, than all the treasures he was master of. Those that have read, and believe, David's *Psalms* and Solomon's *Ecclesiastes,* cannot but prefer the word of God far before the wealth of this world.

10. JOD.

Verse 73

Here, 1. David adores God as the God of nature and the author of his being: *Thy hands have made me and fashioned me,* Job 10:8. Every man is as truly the work of God's hands as the first man was, Ps. 139:15, 16. *"Thy hands have* not only *made me,* and given me a being, otherwise I should never have been, but *fashioned me,* and given me this being, this noble and excellent being, endued with these powers and faculties;" and we must own that we are *fearfully and wonderfully made.* 2. He addresses himself to God as the God of grace, and begs he will be the author of his new and better being. God made us to serve him and enjoy him; but by sin we have made ourselves unable for his service and indisposed for the enjoyment of him; and we must have a new and divine nature, otherwise we had the human nature in vain; therefore David prays, "Lord, since thou hast made me by thy power for thy glory, make me anew by thy grace, that I may answer the ends of my creation and live to some purpose: *Give me understanding, that I may learn thy commandments."* The way in which God recovers and secures his interest in men is by giving them an understanding; for by that door he enters into the soul and gains possession of it.

Verse 74

Here is, 1. The confidence of this good man in the hope of God's salvation: *"I have hoped in thy word;* and I have not found it in vain to do so; it has not failed me, nor have I been disappointed in my expectations from it. It is a hope that *maketh not ashamed;* but is present satisfaction, and fruition at last." 2. The concurrence of other good men with him in the joy of that salvation: *"Those that fear thee will be glad when they see me* relieved by my hope in thy word and delivered according to my hope." The comforts which some of God's children have in God, and the favours they have received from him, should be matter of joy to others of them. Paul often expressed the hope that for God's grace to him thanks would be rendered by many, 2 Co. 1:11; 4:15. Or it may be taken more generally; good people are glad to see one another; they are especially pleased with those who are eminent for their hope in God's word.

Verse 75

Still David is in affliction, and being so he owns, 1. That his sin was justly corrected: *I know, O Lord! that thy judgments are right,* are righteousness itself. However God is pleased to afflict us, he does us no wrong, nor can we charge him with any iniquity, but most acknowledge that it is less than we have deserved. We know that God is holy in his nature and wise and just in all the acts of his government, and therefore we cannot but know, in the general, that his *judgments are right,* though, in some particular instances, there may be difficulties which we cannot easily resolve. 2. That God's promise was graciously performed. The former may silence us under our afflictions, and forbid us to repine, but this may satisfy us, and enable us to rejoice; for afflictions are in the covenant, and therefore they are not only not meant for our hurt, but they are really intended for our good: *"In faithfulness thou hast afflicted me,* pursuant to the great design of my salvation." It is easier to own, in general, that God's *judgments are right,* than to own it when it comes to be our own case; but David subscribes to it with application, "Even my afflictions are just and kind."

Verses 76–77

Here is, 1. An earnest petition to God for his favour. Those that own the justice of God in their afflictions (as David had done, *v.* 75) may, in faith, and with humble boldness, be earnest for the mercy of God, and the tokens and fruits of that mercy, in their affliction. He prays for God's *merciful kindness* (*v.* 76), his *tender mercies, v.* 77. He can claim nothing as his due, but all his supports under his affliction must come from mere mercy and compassion to one in misery, one in want. "Let these *come to me,"* that is, "the evidence of them (clear it up to me that thou hast a kindness for me, and mercy in store), and the effects of them; let them work my relief and deliverance." 2. The benefit he promised himself from God's lovingkindness: "Let it *come to me for my comfort* (*v.* 76); that will comfort me when nothing else will; that will comfort me whatever grieves me." Gracious souls fetch all their comfort from a gracious God, as the fountain of all happiness and joy: "Let it *come to me, that I may live,* that is, that I may be revived, and my life may be made sweet to me, for I have no joy of it while I am under God's displeasure. *In his favour is life;* in his frowns are death." A good man cannot live with any satisfaction any longer than he has some tokens of God's favour to him. 3. his pleas for the benefits of God's favour. He pleads, (1.) God's promise: "Let me have thy kindness, *according to thy word unto thy servant,* the kindness which thou hast promised and because thou hast promised it." Our Master has passed his word to all his servants that he will be kind to them, and they may plead it with him. (2.) His own confidence and complacency in that promise: *"Thy law is my delight;* I hope in thy word and rejoice in that hope." Note, Those that delight in the law of God may depend upon the favour of God, for it shall certainly make them happy.

Verses 78–79

Here David shows,

I. How little he valued the will-will of sinners. There were those that dealt perversely with him, that were peevish and ill-conditioned towards him, that sought advantages against him, and misconstrued all he said and did. Even those that deal most fairly may meet with those that deal perversely. But David regarded it not, for, 1. He knew it was *without cause,* and that for his love they were his adversaries. The causeless reproach, like the curse causeless, may be easily slighted; it does not hurt us, and therefore should not move us. 2. He could pray, in faith, that they might *be ashamed* of it; God's dealing favourably with him might make them ashamed to think that they had dealt perversely with him. *"Let* them *be ashamed,* that is, let them be brought either to repentance or to ruin." 3. He could go on in the way of his duty, and find comfort in that. "However they deal with me, *I will meditate in thy precepts,* and entertain myself with them."

II. How much he valued the good-will of saints, and how desirous he was to stand right in their opinion, and keep up his interest in them and communion with them: *Let those that fear thee turn to me.* He does not mean so much that they might side with him, and take up arms in his cause, as that they might love him, and pray for him, and associate with him. Good men desire the friendship and society of those that are good. Some think it intimates that when David had been guilty of that foul sin in the murder of Uriah, though he was a king, those that feared God grew strange to him and turned from him, for they were ashamed of him; this troubled him, and therefore he prays, Lord, let them *turn to me again.* He desires especially the company of those that were not only honest, but intelligent, *that have known thy testimonies,* have good heads as well as good hearts, and whose conversation will be edifying. It is desirable to have an intimacy with such.

Verse 80

Here is, 1. David's prayer for sincerity, that his heart might be brought to God's *statutes,* and that it might be *sound* in them, not rotten and deceitful, that he might not rest in the form of godliness, but be acquainted with the subject to the power of it, — that he might be hearty and constant in religion, and that his soul might be in health. 2. His dread of the consequences of hypocrisy: *That I be not ashamed.* Shame is the portion of hypocrites, either here, if it be repented of, or hereafter, if it be not: *"Let my heart be sound,* that I fall not into scandalous sin, that I fall not quite off from the ways of God, and so shame myself. *Let my heart be sound,* that I may come *boldly to the throne of grace,* and may lift up my face without spot at the great day."

11. CAPH.

Verses 81–82

Here we have the psalmist,

I. Longing for help from heaven: *My soul faints; my eyes fail.* He longs *for the salvation of the Lord* and *for his word,* that is, salvation according to the word. He is not thus eager for the creatures of fancy, but for the objects of faith, salvation from the present calamities under which he was groaning and the doubts and fears which he was oppressed with. It may be understood of the coming of the Messiah, and so he speaks in the name of the Old-Testament church; the souls of the faithful even *fainted to see* that salvation of which the prophets testified. (1 Pt. 1:10); their eyes failed for it. Abraham saw it at a distance, and so did others, but at such a distance that it put their eyes to the stretch and they could not stedfastly see it. David was now under prevailing dejections, and, having been long so, his eyes cried our, *"When wilt thou comfort me?* Comfort me with *thy salvation,* comfort me with *thy word."* Observe, 1. The salvation and consolation of God's people are secured to them by the word, which will certainly be fulfilled in its season. 2. The promised salvation and comfort may be, and often are, long deferred, so that they are ready to faint and fall in the expectation of them. 3. Though we think the time long ere the promised salvation and comfort come, yet we must still keep our eye upon that salvation, and resolve to take up with nothing short of it. "Thy salvation, thy word, thy comfort, are what my heart is still upon."

II. Waiting for that help, assured that it will come, and tarrying till it come: *But I hope in thy word;* and but for hope the heart would break. When the *eyes fail* yet the faith must not; for *the vision is for an appointed time, and at the end it shall speak and shall not lie.*

Verse 83

David begs God would make haste to comfort him, 1. Because his affliction was great, and therefore he was an object of God's pity: Lord, make haste to help me, *for I have become like a bottle in the smoke,* a leathern bottle, which, if it hung any while in the smoke, was not only blackened with soot, but dried, and parched, and shrivelled up. David was thus wasted by age, and sickness, and sorrow. See how affliction will mortify the strongest and stoutest of men! David had been of a ruddy countenance, as fresh as a rose; but now he is withered, his colour is gone, his cheeks are furrowed. Thus does man's beauty consume under God's rebukes, as a moth fretting a garment. A bottle, when it is thus wrinkled with smoke, is thrown by, and there is no more use of it. Who will put wine into such old bottles? Thus was David, in his low estate, looked upon *as a despised broken vessel,* and as *a vessel in which there was no pleasure.* Good men, when they are drooping and melancholy, sometimes think themselves more slighted than really they are. 2. Because, though his affliction was great, yet it had not driven him from his duty, and therefore he was within the reach of God's promise: *Yet do I not forget thy statutes.* Whatever our outward condition is we must not cool in our affection to the word of God, nor let that slip out of our minds; no care, no grief, must crowd that out. As some *drink and forget the law* (Prov. 31:5), so others weep and forget the law; but we must in every condition, both prosperous and adverse, have the things of God in remembrance; and, if we be mindful of God's statutes, we may pray and hope that he will be mindful of our sorrows, though for a time he seems to forget us.

Verse 84

Here, I. David prays against the instruments of his troubles, that God would make haste to execute judgment on those that persecuted him. He prays not for power to avenge himself (he bore no malice to any), but that God would take to himself the vengeance that belonged to him, and *would repay* (Rom. 12:19), as the God that *sits in the throne judging right.* There is a day coming, and a great and terrible day it will be, when God will execute judgment on all the proud persecutors of his people, *tribulation to those that troubled them;* Enoch foretold it (Jude 14), whose prophecy perhaps David here had an eye to; and that day we are to look for and pray for the hastening of. *Come, Lord Jesus, come quickly.* 2. He pleads the long continuance of his trouble: *"How many are the days of thy servant? The days of my life are but few"* (so some); "therefore let them not all be miserable, and therefore make haste to appear for me against my enemies, *before I go hence and shall be seen no more."* Or rather, *"The days of my affliction are many;* thou seest, Lord, how many they be; when wilt thou return in mercy to me? Sometimes, for the elect's sake, *the days of trouble are shortened.* O let the days of my trouble be shortened; I am *thy servant;* and therefore, as the eyes of a servant are to the hand of his master, so are mine to thee, until thou have mercy on me."

Verses 85–87

David's state was *herein* a type and figure of the state both of Christ and Christians that he was grievously persecuted; as there are many of his psalms, so there are many of the verses of this psalm, which complain of this, as those here. Here observe,

I. The account he gives of his persecutors and their malice against him. 1. They were *proud,* and in their pride *they persecuted him,* glorying in this, that they could trample upon one who was so much cried up, and hoping to raise themselves on his ruins. 2. They were unjust: *They persecuted him wrongfully;* so far was he from giving them any provocation that he had studied to oblige them; but *for his love they were his adversaries.* 3. They were spiteful: *They dug pits for him,* which intimates that they were deliberate in their designs against him and that what they did was of malice prepense; it intimates likewise that they were subtle and crafty, and had the serpent's head as well as the serpent's venom, that they were industrious and would refuse no pains to do him a mischief, and treacherous, laying snares in secret for him, as hunters do take wild beasts, Ps. 35:7. Such has been the enmity of the serpent's seed to the seed of the woman. 4. They herein showed their enmity to God himself. The pits they *dug for him* were *not after God's law;* he means they were very much against his law, which forbids to *devise evil to our neighbour,* and has particularly said, *Touch not my anointed.* The law appointed that, if a man dug a pit which occasioned any mischief, he should answer for the mischief (Ex. 21:33, 34), much more when it was dug with a mischievous design. 5. They carried on their designs against him so far that *they had almost consumed him upon earth;* they went near to ruin him and all his interests. It is possible that those who shall shortly be consummate in heaven may be, for the present, *almost consumed on earth;* and *it is of the Lord's mercies* (and, considering the malice of their enemies, it is a miracle of mercy) *that they are not quite consumed.* But the bush in which God is, though it burns, shall not be burnt up.

II. His application to God in his persecuted state. 1. He acknowledges the truth and goodness of his religion, though he suffered: "However it be, *all thy commandments are faithful,* and therefore, whatever I lose for my observance of them, I know I shall not lose by it." True religion, if it be worth any thing, is worth every thing, and therefore worth suffering for. "Men are false; I find them do; men of low degree, men of high degree, are so, there is no trusting them. But *all thy commandments are faithful;* on them I may rely." 2. He begs that God would stand by him, and succour him: *"They persecute me; help thou me;* help me under my troubles, that I may bear them patiently, and as becomes me, and may still hold fast my integrity, and in due time help me out of my troubles." *God help me* is an excellent comprehensive prayer; it is a pity that it should ever be used lightly and as a by-word.

III. His adherence to his duty notwithstanding all the malice of his persecutors (*v.* 87): *But I forsook not thy precepts.* That which they aimed at was to frighten him from the ways of God, but they could not prevail; he would sooner forsake all that was dear to him in this world than forsake the word of God, would sooner lose his life than lose the comfort of doing his duty.

Verse 88

Here is, 1. David in care to be found in the way of his duty. His constant desire and design are to *keep the testimony of God's mouth,* to keep to it as his rule and to keep hold of it as his confidence and portion for ever. This we must keep, whatever we lose. 2. David at prayer for divine grace to assist him therein: *"Quicken me after thy lovingkindness* (make me alive and make me lively), *so shall I keep thy testimonies,"* implying that otherwise he should not keep them. We cannot proceed, nor persevere, in the good way, unless God quicken us and put life into us; we are therefore here taught to depend upon the grace of God for strength to do every good work, and to depend upon it as grace, as purely the fruit of God's favour. He had prayed before, *Quicken me in thy righteousness* (*v.* 40); but here, *Quicken me after thy lovingkindness.* The surest token of God's good-will toward us is his good work in us.

12. LAMED.

Verses 89–91

Here, 1. The psalmist acknowledges the unchangeableness of the word of God and of all his counsels: *"For ever, O Lord! thy word is settled. Thou art for ever thyself* (so some read it); thou art the same, and with thee there is no variableness, and this is a proof of it. *Thy word,* by which the heavens were made, *is settled* there in the abiding products of it;" or the settling of God's word in heaven is opposed to the changes and revolutions that are here upon earth. *All flesh is grass;* but *the word of the Lord endures for ever.* It *is settled in heaven,* that is, in the secret counsel of God, which is hidden in himself and is far above out of our sight, and is immovable, *as mountains of brass.* And his revealed will is as firm as his secret will; as he will fulfil the thoughts of his heart, so no word of his shall *fall to the ground;* for it follows here, *Thy faithfulness is unto all generations,* that is, the promise is sure to every age of the church and it cannot be antiquated by lapse of time. The promises that look ever so far forward shall be performed in their season. 2. He produces, for proof of it, the constancy of the course of nature: *Thou hast established the earth for ever and it abides;* it is what it was at first made, and where it was at first placed, poised with its own weight, and notwithstanding the convulsions in its own bowels, the agitations of the sea that is interwoven with it, and the violent concussions of the atmosphere that surrounds it, it remains unmoved. *"They"* (the heavens and the earth and all the hosts of both) *"continue to this day according to thy ordinances;* they remain in the posts wherein thou hast set them; they fill up the place assigned them, and answer the purposes for which they were intended." The stability of the ordinances of the day and night, of heaven and earth, is produced to prove the perpetuity of God's covenant, Jer. 31:35, 36; 33:20, 21. It is by virtue of God's promise to Noah (Gen. 8:22) that *day and night, summer and winter,* observe a steady course. "They have continued to this day, and shall still continue to the end of time, acting according to the ordinances which were at first given them; for all are thy servants; they do thy will, and set forth thy glory, and in both *are thy servants."* All the creatures are, in their places, and according to their capacities, serviceable to their Creator, and answer the ends of their creation; and shall man be the only rebel, the only revolter from his allegiance, and the only unprofitable burden of the earth.?

Verse 92

Here is, 1. The great distress that David was in. He was in affliction, and ready to *perish in his affliction,* not likely to die, so much as likely to despair; he was ready to give up all for gone, and to look upon himself as cut off from God's sight; he therefore admires the goodness of God to him, that he had not perished, that he kept the possession of his own soul, and was not driven out of his wits by his troubles, but especially that he was enabled to keep close to his God and was not driven off from his religion by them. Though we are not kept from affliction, yet, if we are kept from perishing in our affliction, we have no reason to say, *We have cleansed our hands in vain;* or, *What profit is it that we have served God?* 2. His support in this distress. God's law was his delight, (1.) It had been so formerly, and the remembrance of that was a comfort to him, as it afforded him a good evidence of his integrity. (2.) It was so now in his affliction; it afforded him abundant matter of comfort, and from these fountains of life he drew living waters, when the cisterns of the creature were broken or dried up. His converse with God's law, and his meditations on it, were his delightful entertainment in solitude and sorrow. A Bible is a pleasant companion at any time if we please.

Verse 93

Here is, 1. A very good resolution: *"I will never forget thy precepts,* but will always retain a remembrance of and regard to thy word as my rule." It is a resolution for perpetuity, never to be altered. Note, The best evidence of our love to the word of God is never to forget it. We must resolve that we will never, at any time, cast off our religion, and never, upon any occasion, lay aside our religion, but that we will be constant to it and persevere in it. 2. A very good reason for it: *"For by them thou hast quickened me;* not only they are quickening, but," (1.) "They have been so to me; I have found them so." Those speak best of the things of God who speak by experience, who can say that by the word the spiritual life has been begun in them, maintained and strengthened in them, excited and comforted in them. (2.) "Thou hast made them so;" the word of itself, without the grace of God, would not quicken us. Ministers can but prophesy upon the dry bones, they cannot put life into them; but, ordinarily, the grace of God works by the word and makes use of it as a means of quickening, and this is a good reason why we should never forget it, but should highly value what God has put such honour upon, and dearly love what we have found and hope still to find such benefit by. See here what is the best help for bad memories, namely, good affections. If we are quickened by the word, we shall never forget it; nay, that word that does really quicken us to and in our duty is not forgotten; though the expressions be lost, if the impressions remain, it is well.

Verse 94

Here, 1. David claims relation to God: *"I am thine,* devoted to thee and owned by thee, thine in covenant." He does not say, *Thou art mine* (as Dr. Manton observes), though that follows of course, because that were a higher challenge; but, *I am thine,* expressing himself in a more humble and dutiful way of resignation; nor does he say, *I am thus,* but, *I am thine,* not pleading his own good property or qualification, but God's propriety in him: *"I am thine,* not my own, not the world's." 2. He proves his claim: *"I have sought thy precepts;* I have carefully enquired concerning my duty and diligently endeavoured to do it." This will be the best evidence that we belong to God; all that are his, though they have not found perfection, are seeking it. 3. He improves his claim: *"I am thine; save me;* save me from sin, save me from ruin." Those that have in sincerity given up themselves to God to be his may be sure that he will protect them and preserve them to his heavenly kingdom, Mal. 3:18.

Verse 95

Here, 1. David complains of the malice of his enemies: *The wicked* (and none but such would be enemies to so good a man) *have waited for me to destroy me.* They were very cruel, and aimed at no less than his destruction; they were very crafty, and sought all opportunities to do him a mischief; and they were *confident* (they *expected,* so some read it), that they should destroy him; they thought themselves sure of their prey. 2. He comforts himself in the word of God as his protection: "While they are contriving my destruction, *I consider thy testimonies,* which secure to me my salvation." God's testimonies are *then* likely to be our support, when we consider them, and dwell in our thoughts upon them.

Verse 96

Here we have David's testimony from his own experience, 1. Of the vanity of the world and its insufficiency to make us happy: *I have seen an end of all perfection.* Poor perfection which one sees an end of! Yet such are all those things in this world which pass for perfections. David, in his time, had seen Goliath, the strongest, overcome, Asahel, the swiftest, overtaken, Ahithophel, the wisest, befooled, Absalom, the fairest, deformed; and, in short, he had *seen an end of perfection,* of *all perfection.* He saw it by faith; he saw it by observation; he saw an end of the perfection of the creature both in respect of sufficiency (it

was scanty and defective; there is that to be done for us which the creature cannot do) and in respect of continuance; it will not last our time, for it will not last to eternity as we must. The glory of man is but as the flower of the grass. 2. Of the fulness of the word of God, and its sufficiency for our satisfaction: *But thy commandment is broad, exceedingly broad.* The word of God reaches to all cases, to all times. The divine law lays a restraint upon the whole man, is designed to sanctify us wholly. There is a great deal required and forbidden in every commandment. The divine promise (for that also is commanded) extends itself to all our burdens, wants, and grievances, and has that in it which will make a portion and happiness for us when we *have seen an end of all perfection.*

13. MEM.

Verse 97

Here is, 1. David's inexpressible love to the word of God: *O how love I thy law!* He protests his affection to the word of God with a holy vehemency; he found that love to it in his heart which, considering the corruption of his nature and the temptations of the world, he could not but wonder at, and at that grace which had wrought it in him. He not only loved the promises, but loved the law, and delighted in it after the inner man. 2. An unexceptionable evidence of this. What we love we love to think of; by *this* it appeared that David loved the word of God that it was his *meditation.* He not only read the book of the law, but digested what he read in his thoughts, and was delivered into it as into a mould: it was his meditation not only in the night, when he was silent and solitary, and had nothing else to do, but in the day, when he was full of business and company; nay, and *all the day;* some good thoughts were interwoven with his common thoughts, so full was he of the word of God.

Verses 98–100

We have here an account of David's learning, not that of the Egyptians, but of the *Israelites indeed.*

I. The good method by which he got it. In his youth he minded business in the country as a shepherd; from his youth he minded business in the court and camp. Which way then could he get any great stock of learning? He tells us here how he came by it; he had it from God as the author: *Thou hast made me wise.* All true wisdom is from God. He had it by the word of God as the means, by *his commandments* and *his testimonies.* These are able to *make us wise to salvation* and to furnish *the man of God for every good work.* 1. These David took for his constant companions: *"They are ever with me,* ever in my mind, ever in my eye." A good man, wherever he goes, carries his Bible along with him, if not in his hands, yet in his head and in his heart. 2. These he took for the delightful subject of his thoughts; they were his *meditation,* not only as matters of speculation for his entertainment, as scholars meditate on their notions, but as matters of concern, for his right management, as men of business think of their business, that they may do it in the best manner. 3. These he took for the commanding rules of all his actions: *I keep thy precepts,* that is, I make conscience of doing my duty in every thing. The best way to improve in knowledge is to abide and abound in all the instances of serious godliness; for, *if any man do his will, he shall know of the doctrine* of Christ, shall know more and more of it, Jn. 7:17. The love of the truth prepares for the light of it; the *pure in heart shall see God* here.

II. The great eminency he attained to in it. By studying and practising God's commandments, and making them his rule, he learnt to *behave himself wisely in all his ways,* 1 Sa. 18:14. 2. He outwitted his enemies; God, by these means, made him wiser to baffle and defeat their designs against him than they were to lay them. Heavenly wisdom will carry the point, at last, against carnal policy. By keeping the commandments we secure God on our side and make him our friend, and therein are certainly wiser than those that make him their enemy. By keeping the commandments we preserve in ourselves that peace and quiet of mind which our enemies would rob us of, and so are wise for ourselves, wiser than they are for themselves, for this world as well as for the other. 2. He outstripped his *teachers,* and had more understanding than all of them.

He means either those who would have been his teachers, who blamed his conduct and undertook to prescribe to him (by keeping God's commandments he managed his matters so that it appeared, in the event, he had taken the right measures and they had taken the wrong), or those who should have been his teachers, the priests and Levites, who sat in Moses's chair, and whose lips ought to have kept knowledge, but who neglected the study of the law, and minded their honours and revenues, and the formalities only of their religion; and so David, who conversed much with the scriptures, by that means became more intelligent than they. Or he may mean those who had been his teachers when he was young; he built so well upon the foundation which they had laid that, with the help of his Bible, he became able to teach them, to teach them all. He was not now a babe that needed milk, but had *spiritual senses exercised,* Heb. 5:14. It is no reflection upon our teachers, but rather an honour to them, to improve so as really to excel them, and not to need them. By meditation we preach to ourselves, and so we come to *understand more than our teachers,* for we come to understand our own hearts, which they cannot. 3. He outdid *the ancients,* either those of his day (he was young, like Elihu, and they were very old, but his keeping God's precepts taught more wisdom than the multitude of their years, Job 32:7, 8) or those of former days; he himself quotes the proverb of the ancients (1 Sa. 24:13), but the word of God gave him to understand things better than he could do by tradition and all the learning that was handed down from preceding ages. In short, the written word is a surer guide to heaven than all the doctors and fathers, the teachers and ancients, of the church; and the sacred writings kept, and kept to, will teach us more wisdom than all their writings.

Verse 101

Here is, 1. David's care to avoid the ways of sin: *"I have refrained my feet from the evil ways* they were ready to step aside into. I checked myself and drew back as soon as I was aware that I was entering into temptation." Though it was a broad way, a green way, a pleasant way, and a way that many walked in, yet, being a sinful way, it was an evil way, and he refrained his feet from it, foreseeing the end of that way. And his care was universal; he shunned every evil way. *By the words of thy lips I have kept myself from the paths of the destroyer,* Ps. 17:4. 2. His care to be found in the way of duty; *That I might keep thy word,* and never transgress it. His abstaining from sin was, (1.) An evidence that he did conscientiously aim to keep God's word and had made that his rule. (2.) It was a means of his keeping God's word in the exercises of religion; for we cannot with any comfort or boldness attend on God in holy duties, so as in them to keep his word, while we are under guilt or in any by-way.

Verse 102

Here is, 1. David's constancy in his religion. He had *not departed from God's judgments;* he had not chosen any other rule than the word of God, nor had he wilfully deviated from that rule. A constant adherence to the ways of God in trying times will be a good evidence of our integrity. 2. The cause of his constancy: *"For thou hast taught me;* that is, they were divine instructions that I learned; I was satisfied that the doctrine was of God, and therefore I stuck to it." Or rather, "It was divine grace in my heart that enabled me to receive those instructions." All the saints are taught of God, for he it is that gives the understanding; and those, and those only, that are taught of God, will continue to the end in the things that they have learned.

Verses 103–104

Here is, 1. The wonderful pleasure and delight which David took in the word of God; it was *sweet to his taste, sweeter than honey.* There is such a thing as a spiritual taste, an inward savour and relish of divine things, such an evidence of them to ourselves, by experience, as we cannot give to others. We have *heard him ourselves,* Jn. 4:42. To this scripture-taste the word of God is sweet, very sweet, sweeter than any of the gratifications of sense, even those that are most delicious. David speaks as if he wanted words to express the satisfaction he took in the discoveries of the divine will and grace; no pleasure was comparable to it. 2. The unspeakable profit and advantage he gained by the word of God. (1.) It helped him to a good head: *"Through thy precepts I get understanding* to discern between truth and falsehood, good and evil, so as not to mistake either in the conduct of my own life or in advising others." (2.) It helped him to a good heart: *"Therefore,* because I have got understanding of the truth, *I hate every false way,* and am stedfastly resolved not to turn aside into it." Observe here, [1.] The way of sin is a false way; it deceives, and will ruin, all that walk in it; it is the wrong way, and yet it seems to a man right, Prov. 14:12. [2.] It is the character of every good man that he hates the way of sin, and hates it because it is a false way; he not only refrains his feet from it (*v.* 101), but he *hates it,* has an antipathy to it and a dread of it. [3.] Those who hate sin as sin will hate all sin, hate every false way, because every false way leads to destruction. And, [4.] The more understanding we get by the word of God the more rooted will our hatred of sin be (for *to depart from evil, that is understanding,* Job 28:28), and the more ready we are in the scriptures the better furnished we are with answers to temptation.

14. NUN.

Verse 105

Observe here, 1. The nature of the word of God, and the great intention of giving it to the world; it is a *lamp and a light.* It discovers to us, concerning God and ourselves, that which otherwise we could not have known; it shows us what is amiss, and will be dangerous; it directs us in our work and way, and a dark place indeed the world would be without it. It is a lamp which we may set up by us, and take into our hands for our own particular use, Prov. 6:23. The commandment is a lamp kept burning with the oil of the Spirit; it is like the lamps in the sanctuary, and the pillar of fire to Israel. 2. The use we should make of it. It must be not only a *light to out eyes,* to gratify them, and fill our heads with speculations, but a *light to our feet* and *to our path,* to direct us in the right ordering of our conversation, both in the choice of our way in general and in the particular steps we take in that way, that we may not take a false way nor a false step in the right way. We are then truly sensible of God's goodness to us in giving us such a lamp and light when we make it a guide to our feet, our path.

Verse 106

Here is, 1. The notion David had of religion; it is *keeping God's righteous judgments.* God's commands are his judgments, the dictates of infinite wisdom. They are righteous judgments, consonant to the eternal rules of equity, and it is our duty to keep them carefully. 2. The obligation he here laid upon himself to be religious, binding himself, by his own promise, to that which he was already bound to by the divine precept, and all little enough. *"I have sworn (I have lifted up my head to the Lord, and I cannot go back)* and therefore must go forward: *I will perform it."* Note, (1.) It is good for us to bind ourselves with a solemn oath to be religious. We must swear to the Lord as subjects swear allegiance to their sovereign, promising fealty, appealing to God concerning our sincerity in this promise, and owning ourselves liable to the curse of we do not perform it. (2.) We must often call to mind the vows of God that are upon us, and remember that we have sworn. (3.) We must make conscience of performing unto the Lord our oaths (an honest man will be as good as his word; nor have we sworn to our own hurt, but it will be unspeakably to our hurt if we do not perform.

Verse 107

Here is, 1. The representation David makes of the sorrowful condition he was in: *I am afflicted very much,* afflicted in spirit; he seems to mean that especially. He laboured under many discouragements; without were fightings, within were fears. This is often the lot of the best saints; therefore think it not strange if sometimes it be ours. 2. The recourse he has to God in this condition; he prays for his grace: *"Quicken me, O Lord!* make me lively, make me cheerful; quicken me by afflictions to greater diligence in my work. *Quicken me,* that is, deliver me out of my afflictions, which will be as life from the dead." He pleads

the promise of God, guides his desires by it, and grounds his hopes upon it: *Quicken me according to thy word.* David resolved to perform his promises to God (*v.* 106) and therefore could, with humble boldness, beg of God to make good his word to him.

Verse 108

Two things we are here taught to pray for, in reference to our religious performances: — 1. Acceptance of them. This we must aim at in all we do in religion, that, whether present or absent, we may be accepted of the Lord. What David here earnestly prays for the acceptance of are the *free-will-offerings,* not of his purse, but of his *mouth,* his prayers and praises. *The calves of our lips* (Hos. 14:2), *the fruit of our lips* (Heb. 1:15), these are the spiritual offerings which all Christians, as spiritual priests, must offer to God; and they must be *free-will-offerings,* for we must offer them abundantly and cheerfully, and it is this willing mind that is accepted. The more there is of freeness and willingness in the service of God the more pleasing it is to him. 2. Assistance in them: *Teach me thy judgments.* We cannot offer any thing to God which we have reason to think he will accept of, but what he is pleased to instruct us in the doing of; and we must be as earnest for the grace of God in us as for the favour of God towards us.

Verses 109–110

Here is, 1. David in danger of losing his life. There is but a step between him and death, for the *wicked have laid a snare* for him; Saul did so many a time, because he hated him for his piety. Wherever he was he found some design or other laid against him to take away his life, for it was that they aimed at. What they could not effect by open force they hoped to compass by treachery, which made him say, *My soul is continually in my hand.* It was so with him, not only as a *man* (so it is true of us all; wherever we are we lie exposed to the strokes of death; what we carry in our hands is easily snatched away from us by violence, or if sandy, as our life is, it easily of itself slips through our fingers), but as a *man of war,* a soldier, who often jeoparded his life in the high places of the field, and especially as *a man after God's own heart,* and, as such, hated and persecuted, and *always delivered to death* (2 Co. 4:11), *killed all the day long.* 2. David in no danger of losing his religion, notwithstanding this, thus in jeopardy every hour and yet constant to God and his duty. None of these things move him; for, (1.) He *does not forget the law,* and therefore he is likely to persevere. In the multitude of his cares for his own safety he finds room in his head and heart for the word of God, and has that in his mind as fresh as ever; and where that dwells richly it will be a *well of living water.* (2.) He has not yet erred from God's precepts, and therefore it is to be hoped he will not. He had stood many a shock and kept his ground, and surely that grace which had helped him hitherto would not fail him, but would still prevent his wanderings.

Verses 111–112

The psalmist here in a most affectionate manner, like an Israelite indeed, resolves to stick to the word of God and to live and die by it.

I. He resolves to portion himself in it, and there to seek his happiness, nay, there to enjoy it; *"Thy testimonies* (the truths, the promises, of thy word) *have I taken as a heritage for ever, for they are the rejoicing of my heart."* The present delight he took in them was an evidence that the good things contained in them were in his account the best things, and the treasure which he set his heart upon. 1. He expected an eternal happiness in God's testimonies. The covenant God had made with him was an everlasting covenant, and therefore he took it as a *heritage for ever.* If he could not yet say, "They are my heritage," yet he could say, "I have made choice of them for my heritage; and will never take up with a portion in this life," Ps. 17:14, 15. God's testimonies are a heritage to all that have received the Spirit of adoption; for, *if children, then heirs.* They are a *heritage for ever,* and that no earthly heritage is (1 Pt. 1:4); all the saints accept them as such, take up with them, live upon them, and can therefore be content with but little of this world. 2. He enjoyed a present satisfaction in them: *They are the rejoicing of my heart,* because they will be *my heritage for ever.* It requires the heart of a good man

to see his portion in the promise of God and not in the possessions of this world.

II. He resolves to govern himself by it and thence to take his measures: *I have inclined my heart to do thy statutes.* Those that would have the blessings of God's testimonies must come under the bonds of his statutes. We must look for comfort only in the way of duty, and that duty must be done, 1. With full consent and complacency: *"I have,* by the grace of God, *inclined my heart to it,* and conquered the aversion I had to it." A good man brings his heart to his work and then it is done well. A gracious disposition to do the will of God is the acceptable principle of all obedience. 2. With constancy and perseverance. He would perform God's statutes always, in all instances, in the duty of every day, in a constant course of holy walking, and this *to the end,* without weariness. This is following the Lord fully.

15. SAMECH.

Verse 113

Here we have, 1. David's dread of the risings of sin, and the first beginnings of it: *I hate vain thoughts.* He does not mean that he hated them in others, for there he could not discern them, but he hated them in his own heart. Every good man makes conscience of his thoughts, for they are words to God. Vain thoughts, how light soever most make of them, are sinful and hurtful, and therefore we should account them hateful and dreadful, for they do not only divert the mind from that which is good, but open the door to all evil, Jer. 4:14. Though David could not say that he was free from vain thoughts, yet he could say that he hated them; he did not countenance them, nor give them any entertainment, but did what he could to keep them out, at least to keep them under. *The evil I do I allow not.* 2. David's delight in the rule of duty: *But thy law do I love,* which forbids those vain thoughts, and threatens them. The more we love the law of God the more we shall get the mastery of our vain thoughts, the more hateful they will be to us, as being contrary to the whole law, and the more watchful we shall be against them, lest they draw us from that which we love.

Verse 114

Here is, 1. God's care of David to protect and defend him, which he comforted himself with when his enemies were very malicious against him: *Thou art my hiding-place and my shield.* David, when Saul pursued him, often betook himself to close places for shelter; in war he guarded himself with his shield. Now God was both these to him, a hiding-place to preserve him from danger and a shield to preserve him in danger, his life from death and his soul from sin. Good people are safe under God's protection. He is their *strength and their shield,* their *help and their shield,* their *sun and their shield,* their *shield and their great reward,* and here their *hiding-place and their shield.* They may by faith retire to him, and repose in him as their hiding-place, where they are kept in secret. They may by faith oppose his power to all the might and malice of their enemies, as their shield to quench every fiery dart. 2. David's confidence in God. He is safe, and therefore he is easy, under the divine protection: *"I hope in thy word,* which has acquainted me with thee and assured me of thy kindness to me." Those who depend on God's promise shall have the benefit of his power and be taken under his special protection.

Verse 115

Here is, 1. David's firm and fixed resolution to live a holy life: *I will keep the commandments of my God.* Bravely resolved! like a saint, like a soldier; for true courage consists in a steady resolution against all sin and for all duty. Those that would keep God's commandments must be often renewing their resolutions to do so: *"I will keep them.* Whatever others do, this I will do; though I be singular, though all about me be evil-doers, and desert me; whatever I have done hitherto, I will for the future walk closely with God. They are the commandments of God, of my God, and therefore I will keep them. He is God and may command me, my God and will command me nothing but what is for my good." 2. His farewell to bad company, pursuant to this resolution: *Depart from me, you evil-doers.* Though

David, as a good magistrate, was a terror to evil-doers, yet there were many such, even about court, intruding near his person; these he here abdicates, and resolves to have no conversation with them. Note, Those that resolve to keep the commandments of God must have no society with evil-doers; for bad company is a great hindrance to a holy life. We must not choose wicked people for our companions, nor be intimate with them; we must not do as they do nor do as they would have us do, Ps. 1:1; Eph. 5:11.

Verses 116–117

Here, 1. David prays for sustaining grace; for this grace sufficient he besought the Lord twice: *Uphold me;* and again, *Hold thou me up.* He sees himself not only unable to go on in his duty by any strength of his own, but in danger of falling into sin unless he was prevented by divine grace; and therefore he is thus earnest for that grace to uphold him in his integrity (Ps. 41:12), to keep him from falling and to keep him from tiring, that he might neither turn aside to evil-doing nor be weary of well-doing. We stand no longer than God holds us and go no further than he carries us. 2. He pleads earnestly for this grace. (1.) He pleads the promise of God, his dependence upon the promise, and his expectation from it: *"Uphold me, according to thy word,* which word I hope in; and, if it be not performed, I shall be made *ashamed of my hope,* and be called a fool for my credulity." But those that hope in God's word may be sure that the word will not fail them, and therefore their hope will not make them ashamed. (2.) He pleads the great need he had of God's grace and the great advantage it would be of to him: *Uphold me, that I may live,* intimating that he could not live without the grace of God; he should fall into sin, into death, into hell, if God did not hold him up; but, supported by his hand, he shall live; his spiritual life shall be maintained and be an earnest of eternal life. *Hold me up, and I shall be safe,* out of danger and out of the fear of danger. Our holy security is grounded on divine supports. (3.) He pleads his resolution, in the strength of this grace, to proceed in his duty: *"Hold me up,* and then *I will have respect unto thy statutes continually* and never turn my eyes or feet aside from them." *I will employ myself* (so some), I *will delight myself* (so others) *in thy statutes.* If God's right hand uphold us, we must, in his strength, go on in our duty both with diligence and pleasure.

Verses 118–120

Here is, I. God's judgment on wicked people, on those that *wander from his statutes,* that take their measures from other rules and will not have God to reign over them. All departure from God's statutes is certainly an error, and will prove a fatal one. These are *the wicked of the earth;* they mind earthly things, lay up their treasures in the earth, live in pleasure on the earth, and are strangers and enemies to heaven and heavenly things. Now see how God deals with them, that you may neither fear them nor envy them. 1. He *treads them all down.* He brings them to ruin, to utter ruin, to shameful ruin; he makes them his footstool. Though they are ever so high, he can bring them low (Amos 2:9); he has done it many a time, and he will do it, for he resists the proud and will triumph over those that oppose his kingdom. Proud persecutors trample upon his people, but, sooner or later, he will trample upon them. 2. He *puts them all away like dross.* Wicked people are as dross, which, though it be mingled with the good metal in the ore, and seems to be of the same substance with it, must be separated from it. And in God's account they are worthless things, the scum and refuse of the earth, and no more to be compared with the righteous than dross with fine gold. There is a day coming which will put them away from among the righteous (Mt. 13:49), so that they shall have no place *in their congregation* (Ps. 1:5), which will put them away into everlasting fire, the fittest place for the dross. Sometimes, in this world, the wicked are, by the censures of the church, or the sword of the magistrate, or the judgments of God, *put away as dross,* Prov. 25:4, 5.

II. The reasons of these judgments. God casts them off because they *err from his statutes* (those that will not submit to the commands of the word shall feel the curses of it) and because *their deceit is falsehood,* that is, because they deceive themselves by setting up false rules, in opposition to God's statutes, which they err from, and because they go about to deceive others with their hypocritical pretences of good and their crafty projects of mischief. *Their cunning is falsehood,* so Dr. Hammond. The utmost of their policy is treachery and perfidiousness; this the God of truth hates and will punish.

III. The improvement David made of these judgments. He took notice of them and received instruction from them. The ruin of the wicked helped to increase, 1. His love to the word of God. "I see what comes of sin; *therefore I love thy testimonies,* which warn me to take heed of those dangerous courses and *keep me from the paths of the destroyer."* We see the word of Go fulfilled in his judgments on sin and sinners, and therefore we should love it. 2. His fear of the wrath of God: *My flesh trembles for fear of thee.* Instead of insulting over those who fell under God's displeasure, he humbled himself. What we read and hear of the judgments of God upon wicked people would make us, (1.) To reverence his terrible majesty, and to stand in awe of him: *Who is able to stand before this holy Lord God?* 1 Sa. 6:20. (2.) To fear lest we offend him and become obnoxious to his wrath. Good men have need to be restrained from sin by *the terrors of the Lord,* especially when judgment *begins at the house of God* and hypocrites are discovered and *put away as dross.*

16. AIN.

Verses 121–122

David here appeals to God, 1. As his witness that he had not done wrong; he could truly say, *"I have done judgment and justice,* that is, I have made conscience of rendering to all their due, and have not by force or fraud hindered any of their right." Take him as a king, he *executed judgment and justice to all his people,* 2 Sa. 8:15. Take him in a private capacity, he could appeal to Saul himself that *there was no evil or transgression in his hand,* 1 Sa. 24:11. Note, Honesty is the best policy and will be our rejoicing in the day of evil. 2. As his Judge, that he might not be wronged. Having done justice for others that were oppressed, he begs that God would do him justice and avenge him of his adversaries: *"Be surety for thy servant, for good;* undertake for me against those that would run me down and ruin me." He is sensible that he cannot make his part good himself, and therefore begs that God would appear for him. Christ is our surety with God; and, if he be so, Providence shall be our surety against all the world. Who or what shall harm us if God's power and goodness be engaged for our protection and rescue? He does not prescribe to God what he should do for him; only let it be *for good,* in such way and manner as Infinite Wisdom sees best; "only *let me not be left to my oppressors."* Though David had *done judgment and justice,* yet he had many enemies; but, having God for his friend, he hoped they should not have their will against him; and in that hope he prayed again, *Let not the proud oppress me.* David, one of the best of men, was oppressed by the proud, whom God beholds afar off; the condition therefore of the persecuted is better than that of the persecutors, and will appear so at last.

Verse 123

David, being oppressed, is here waiting and wishing for the salvation of the Lord, which would make him easy. 1. He cannot but think that it comes slowly: *My eyes fail for thy salvation.* His eyes were towards it and had been long so. He looked for help from heaven (and we deceive ourselves if we look for it any other way), but it did not come so soon as he expected, so that his eyes began to fail, and he was sometimes ready to despair, and to think that, because the salvation did not come when he looked for it, it would never come. It is often the infirmity even of good men to be weary of waiting God's time when *their* time has elapsed. 2. Yet he cannot hope that it comes surely; for he expects *the word of God's righteousness,* and no other salvation than what is secured by that word, which cannot fall to the ground because it is a word of righteousness. Though our eyes fail, yet God's word does not, and therefore those that build upon it, though now discouraged, shall in due time see his salvation.

Verses 124–125

Here is, 1. David's petition for divine instruction: *"Teach me thy statutes;* give me to know all my duty; when I am in doubt, and know not for certain what is my duty, direct me, and make it plain to me; now that I am afflicted, oppressed, and *my eyes* are ready to *fail for thy salvation,* let me know what my duty is in this condition." In difficult times we should desire more to be told what we must do than what we may expect, and should pray more to be led into the knowledge of scripture-precepts than of scripture-prophecies. If God, who gave us his statutes, do not teach us, we shall never learn them. How God teaches is implied in the next petition: *Give me understanding* (a renewed understanding, apt to receive divine light), *that I may know thy testimonies.* It is God's prerogative to give an understanding, that understanding without which we cannot know God's testimonies. Those who know most of God's testimonies desire to know more, and are still earnest with God to teach them, never thinking they know enough. 2. His pleas to enforce this petition. (1.) He pleads God's goodness to him: *Deal with me according to thy mercy.* The best saints count this their best plea for any blessing, "Let me have it according to thy mercy;" for we deserve no favour from God, nor can we claim any as a debt, but we are most likely to be easy when we cast ourselves upon God's mercy and refer ourselves to it. Particularly, when we come to him for instruction, we must beg it as a mercy, and reckon that in being taught we are well dealt with. (2.) He pleads his relation to God: *"I am thy servant,* and have work to do for thee; therefore *teach me* tod o it and to do it well." The servant has reason to expect that, if he be at a loss about his work, his master should teach him, and, if it were in his power, give him an understanding. "Lord," says David, "I desire to serve thee; show me how." If any man resolve to do God's will as his servant, he shall be made to know his testimonies, Jn. 7:17; Ps. 25:14.

Verse 126

Here is, 1. A complaint of the daring impiety of the wicked. David, having in himself a holy indignation at it, humbly represents it to God: "Lord, there are those that *have made void thy law,* have set thee and thy government at defiance, and have done what in them lay to cancel and vacate the obligation of thy commands." Those that sin through infirmity transgress the law, but presumptuous sinners do in effect make void the law, saying, *Who is the Lord? What is the Almighty, that we should fear him?* It is possible a godly man may sin against the commandment, but a wicked man would sin away the commandment, would repeal God's laws and enact his own lusts. This is the sinfulness of sin and the malignity of the carnal mind. 2. A desire that God would appear, for the vindication of his own honour: *"It is time for thee, Lord, to work,* to do something for the effectual confutation of atheists and infidels, and the silencing of those that set their mouth against the heavens." God's time to work is when vice has become most daring and the measure of iniquity is full. *Now will I arise, saith the Lord.* Some read it, and the original will bear it, *It is time to work for thee, O Lord!* it is time for every one in his place to appear on the Lord's side — against the threatening growth of profaneness and immorality. We must do what we can for the support of the sinking interests of religion, and, after all, we must beg of God to take the work into his own hands.

Verses 127–128

David here, as often in this psalm, professes the great love he had to the word and law of God; and, to evidence the sincerity of it, observe, 1. The degree of his love. He loved his Bible better than he loved his money — *above gold, yea, above fine gold.* Gold, fine gold, is what most men set their hearts upon; nothing charms them and dazzles their eyes so much as gold does. It is fine gold, a fine thing in their eyes; they will venture their souls, their God, their all, to get and keep it. But David saw that the word of God answers all purposes better than money does, for it enriches the soul towards God; and therefore he loved it better than gold, for it had done that for him which gold could not do, and would stand him in stead when the wealth of the world would fail him. 2. The ground of his love. He loved all God's commandments because he esteemed them to be right, all reasonable and just, and suited to the end for which they were made. They are all as they should be, and no fault can be found with them; and we must love them because they bear God's image and are the revelations of his will. If we thus *consent to the law that it is good,* we shall delight in it after the inner man. 3. The fruit and evidence of this love: He *hated every false way.* The way of sin being directly contrary to God's precepts, which are right, is a false way, and therefore those that have a love and esteem for God's law hate it and will not be reconciled to it.

17. PE.

Verse 129

See here how David was affected towards the word of God. 1. He admired it, as most excellent in itself: *Thy testimonies are wonderful.* The word of God gives us admirable discoveries of God, and Christ, and another world; admirable proofs of divine love and grace. The majesty of the style, the purity of the matter, the harmony of the parts, are all wonderful. Its effects upon the consciences of men, both for conviction and comfort, are wonderful; and it is a sign that we are not acquainted with God's testimonies, or do not understand them, if we do not admire them. 2. He adhered to it as of constant use to him: *"Therefore doth my soul keep them,* as a treasure of inestimable value, which I cannot be without." We do not keep them to any purpose unless our souls keep them. There they must be deposited, as the tables of testimony in the ark, there they must have the innermost and uppermost place. Those that see God's word to be admirable will prize it highly and preserve it carefully, as that which they promise themselves great things from.

Verse 130

Here is, 1. The great use for which the word of God was intended, to give light, that is, to give understanding, to give us to understand that which will be of use to us in our travels through this world; and it is the outward and ordinary means by which the Spirit of God enlightens the understanding of all that are sanctified. God's testimonies are not only wonderful for the greatness of them, but useful, as a light in a dark place. 2. Its efficacy for this purpose. It admirably answers the end; for, (1.) Even *the entrance of God's word gives light.* If we begin at the beginning, and take it before us, we shall find that the very first verses of the Bible give us surprising and yet satisfying discoveries of the origin of the universe, about which, without that, the world is utterly in the dark. As soon as the word of God enters into us, and has a place in us, it enlightens us; we find we begin to see when we begin to study the word of God. The very first principles of the oracles of God, the plainest truths, the milk appointed for the babes, bring a great light into the soul, much more will the soul be illuminated by the sublime mysteries that are found there. "The exposition or explication of thy word gives light;" then it is most profitable when ministers do their part *in giving the sense,* Neh. 8:8. Some understand it of the New Testament, which is the opening or unfolding of the Old, which would give light concerning life and immortality. (2.) It would *give understanding* even *to the simple,* to the weakest capacities; for it shows us a way to heaven so plain that the *wayfaring men, though fools, shall not err therein.*

Verse 131

Here is, 1. The desire David had towards the word of God: *I longed for thy commandments.* When he was under a forced absence from God's ordinances he longed to be restored to them again; when he enjoyed ordinances he greedily sucked in the word of God, *as new-born babes desire the milk.* When Christ is formed in the soul there are gracious longings, unaccountable to one that is a stranger to the work. 2. The degree of that desire appearing in the expressions of it: *I opened my mouth and panted,* as one overcome with hear, or almost stifled, pants for a mouthful of fresh air. Thus strong, thus earnest, should our desires be towards God and the remembrance of his name, Ps. 42:1, 2. Lu. 12:50.

Verse 132

Here is, 1. David's request for God's favour to himself: *"Look* graciously *upon me;* let me have thy smiles, and the light of thy countenance. Take cognizance of me and my affairs, *and be merciful to me;* let me taste the sweetness of thy mercy and receive the gifts of thy mercy." See how humble his petition is. He asks not for the operations of God's hand, only for the smiles of his face; a good look is enough; and for that he does not plead merit, but implores mercy. 2. His acknowledgment of his favour to all his people: *As thou usest to do unto those that love thy name.* This is either, (1.) A plea for mercy: "Lord, I am one of *those that love thy name,* love thee and thy word, and thou usest to be kind to those that do so; and wilt thou be worse to me than to others of thy people?" Or, (2.) A description of the favour and mercy he desired — "that which thou usest to bestow on those that love thy name, which *thou bearest to thy chosen,"* Ps. 106:4, 5. He desires no more, no better, than neighbour's fare, and he will take up with no less; common looks and common mercies will not serve, but such as are reserved for those that love him, which are such as *eye has not seen,* 1 Co. 2:9. Note, The dealings of God with those that love him are such that a man needs not desire to be any better dealt with, for he will make them truly and eternally happy. And as long as God deals with us no otherwise than as he uses to deal with those that love him we have no reason to complain, 1 Co. 10:13.

Verse 133

Here David prays for two great spiritual blessings, and is, in this verse, as earnest for the good work of God in him as, in the verse before, for the good-will of God towards him. He prays, 1. For direction in the paths of duty: *"Order my steps in thy word;* having led me into the right way, let every step I take in that way be under the guidance of thy grace." We ought to walk by rule; all the motions of the soul must not only be kept within the bounds prescribed by the word, so as not to transgress them, but carried out in the paths prescribed by the word, so as not to trifle in them. And therefore we must beg of God that by his good Spirit he would order our steps accordingly. 2. For deliverance from the power of sin: *"Let no iniquity have dominion over me,* so as to gain my consent to it, and that I should be led captive by it." The dominion of sin is to be dreaded and deprecated by every one of us; and, if in sincerity we pray against it, we may receive that promise as an answer to the prayer (Rom. 6:14), *Sin shall not have dominion over you.*

Verse 134

Here, 1. David prays that he might live a quiet and peaceable life, and might not be harassed and discomposed by those that studied to be vexatious: *"Deliver me from the oppression of man* — man, whom God can control, and whose power is limited. Let them know themselves to be *but men* (Ps. 9:20), and let me be delivered out of the hands of my enemies, that I may serve God without fear; *so will I keep thy precepts."* Not but that he would keep God's precepts, though he should be continued under oppression; "but so shall I keep thy precepts more cheerfully and with more enlargement of heart, my bonds being loosed." *Then* we may expect temporal blessings when we desire them with this in our eye, that we may serve God the better.

Verse 135

David here, as often as elsewhere, writes himself God's servant, a title he gloried in, though he was a king; now here, as became a good servant, 1. He is very ambitious of his Master's favour, accounting that his happiness and chief good. He asks not for corn and wine, for silver and gold, but, *"Make thy face to shine upon thy servant;* let me be accepted of thee, and let me know that I am so. Comfort me with the light of thy countenance in every cloudy and dark day. If the world frown upon me, yet do thou smile." 2. He is very solicitous about his Master's work, accounting that his business and chief concern. This he would be instructed in, that he might do it, and do it well, so as to be accepted in the doing of it: *Teach me thy statutes.* Note, We must pray as earnestly for grace as for comfort. If God hides his face from us, it is because we have been careless in keeping his statutes; and therefore, that we may be qualified for the returns of his favour, we must pray for wisdom to do our duty.

Verse 136

Here we have David in sorrow. 1. It is a great sorrow, to such a degree that he weeps *rivers of tears.* Commonly, where there is a gracious heart, there is a weeping eye, in conformity to Christ, who was a man of sorrows and acquainted with grief. David had prayed for comfort in God's favour (*v.* 135), now he pleads that he was qualified for that comfort, and had need of it, for he was one of those that mourned in Zion, and those that do so shall be comforted, Isa. 61:3. 2. It is godly sorrow. He wept not for his troubles, though they were many, but for the dishonour done to God: *Because they keep not thy law,* either *because my eyes keep not thy law,* so some (the eye is the inlet and outlet of a great deal of sin, and therefore it ought to be a weeping eye), or, rather, *they,* that is, those about me, *v.* 139. Note, The sins of sinners are the sorrows of saints. We must mourn for that which we cannot mend.

18. TZADDI.

Verses 137–138

Here is, 1. The righteousness of God, the infinite rectitude and perfection of his nature. As he is what he is, so he is what he should be, and in every thing acts as becomes him; there is nothing wanting, nothing amiss, in God; his will is the eternal rule of equity, and he is righteous, for he does all according to it. 2. The righteousness of his government. He rules the world by his providence, according to the principles of justice, and never did, nor ever can do, any wrong to any of his creatures: *Upright are thy judgments,* the promises and threatenings and the executions of both. Every word of God is pure, and he will be true to it; he perfectly knows the merits of every cause and will judge accordingly. 3. The righteousness of his commands, which he has given to be the rule of our obedience: *"Thy testimonies that thou hast commanded,* which are backed with thy sovereign authority, and to which thou dost require our obedience, *are* exceedingly *righteous and faithful,* righteousness and faithfulness itself." As he acts like himself, so his law requires that we act like ourselves and like him, that we be just to ourselves and to all we deal with, true to all the engagements we lay ourselves under both to God and man. That which we are commanded to practise is righteous; that which we are commanded to believe is faithful. It is necessary to our faith and obedience that we be convinced of this.

Verse 139

Here is, 1. The great contempt which wicked men put upon religion: *My enemies have forgotten thy words.* They have often heard them, but so little did they heed them that they soon forgot them, they willingly forgot them, not only through carelessness let them slip out of their minds, but contrived how to cast them behind their backs. This is at the bottom of all the wickedness of the wicked, and particularly of their malignity and enmity to the people of God; they have forgotten the words of God, else those would give check to their sinful courses. 2. The great concern which godly men show for religion. David reckoned those his enemies who forgot the words of God because they were enemies to religion, which he had entered into a league with, offensive and defensive. And therefore his *zeal* even *consumed him,* when he observed their impieties. He conceived such an indignation at their wickedness as preyed upon his spirits, even *ate them up* (as Christ's zeal, Jn. 2:17), swallowed up all inferior considerations, and made him forget himself. *My zeal has pressed or constrained me* (so Dr. Hammond reads it), Acts 18:5. Zeal against sin should constrain us to do what we can against it in our places, at least to do so much the more in religion ourselves. The worse others are the better we should be.

Verse 140

Here is, 1. David's great affection for the word of God: *Thy servant loves it.* Every good man, being a servant of God, loves the word of God, because it lets him know his Master's will and directs him in his Master's work. Wherever there is grace there is a warm attachment to the word of God. 2. The ground and reason of that affection; he saw it to be *very pure,* and therefore he loved it. Our love to the word of God is *then* an evidence of our love to God when we love it for the sake of its purity, because it bears the image of God's holiness and is designed to make us partakers of his holiness. It commands purity, and, as it is itself refined from all corrupt mixture, so if we receive it in the light and love of it it will refine us from the dross of worldliness and fleshly-mindedness.

Verse 141

Here is, 1. David pious and yet poor. He was a man after God's own heart, one whom the King of kings did delight to honour, and yet *small and despised* in his own account and in the account of many others. Men's excellency cannot always secure them from contempt; nay, it often exposes them to the scorn of others and always makes them low in their own eyes. *God has chosen the foolish things of the world,* and it has been the common lot of his people to be a despised people. 2. David poor and yet pious, *small and despised* for his strict and serious godliness, yet his conscience can witness for him that he did *not forget God's precepts.* He would not throw off his religion, though it exposed him to contempt, for he knew that was designed to try his constancy. When we are small and despised we have the more need to remember God's precepts, that we may have them to support us under the pressures of a low condition.

Verse 142

Observe, 1. That God's word *is righteousness,* and it *is an everlasting righteousness.* It is the rule of God's judgment, and it is consonant to his counsels from eternity and will direct his sentence for eternity. The word of God will judge us, it will judge us in righteousness, and by it our everlasting state will be determined. This should possess us with a very great reverence for the word of God that it is righteousness itself, the standard of righteousness, and it is everlasting in its rewards and punishments. 2. That God's word is a law, and that law is truth. See the double obligation we are under to be governed by the word of God. We are reasonable creatures, and as such we must be ruled by truth, acknowledging the force and power of it. If the principles be true, the practices must be agreeable to them, else we do not act rationally. We are creatures, and therefore subjects, and must be ruled by our Creator; and whatever he commands we are bound to obey as a law. See how these obligations are here twisted, these cords of a man. Here is truth brought to the understanding, there to sit chief, and direct the motions of the whole man; but, lest the authority of that should become weak through the flesh, here is a law to bind the will and bring that into subjection. God's truth is a law (Jn. 18:37) *and* God's *law is the truth;* surely we cannot break such words as these asunder.

Verses 143–144

These two verses are almost a repetition of the two foregoing verses, but with improvement. 1. David again professes his constant adherence to God and his duty, notwithstanding the many difficulties and discouragements he met with. He had said (*v.* 14), *I am small and despised,* and yet adhere to my duty. Here he finds himself not only mean, but miserable, as far as this world could make him so: *Trouble and anguish have taken hold on me* — trouble without, anguish within; they surprised him, they seized him, they held him. Sorrows are often the lot of saints in this vale of tears; they are *in heaviness through manifold temptations.* There he had said, *Yet do I not forget thy precepts;* here he carries his constancy much higher: *Yet thy commandments are my delights.* All this trouble and anguish did not put his mouth out of taste for the comforts of the word of God, but he could still relish them and find that peace and pleasure in them which all the calamities of this present time could not deprive him of. There are delights, variety of delights, in the word of God, which the saints have often the sweetest enjoyment of when they are in trouble and anguish, 2 Co. 1:5. 2. He again acknowledges the everlasting righteousness of God's word as before (*v.* 142): *The righteousness of thy testimonies is everlasting* and cannot be altered; and, when it is admitted in its power into a soul, it is there an abiding principle, *a well of living water,* Jn. 4:14. We ought to meditate much and often upon the equity and the eternity of the word of God. Here he adds, by way of inference, (1.) His prayer for grace: *Give me understanding.* Those that know much of the word of God should still covet to know more; for there is more to be known. He does not say, "Give me a further revelation," but, *Give me a further understanding;* what is revealed we should desire to understand, and what we know to know better; and we must go to God for a heart to know. (2.) His hope of glory: "Give me this renewed understanding, and then *I shall live,* shall live for ever, shall be eternally happy, and shall be comforted, for the present, in the prospect of it." *This is life eternal, to know God,* Jn. 17:3.

19. KOPH.

Verses 145–146

Here we have, I. David's good prayers, by which he sought to God for mercy; these he mentions here, not as boasting of them, or trusting to any merit in them, but reflecting upon them with comfort, that he had taken the appointed way to comfort. Observe here, 1. That he was inward with God in prayer; he prayed *with his heart,* and prayer is acceptable no further than the heart goes along with it. Lip-labour, if that be all, is lost labour. 2. He was importunate with God in prayer; he *cried,* as one in earnest, with fervour of affection and a holy vehemence and vigour of desire. *He cried with his whole heart;* all the powers of his soul were not only engaged and employed, but exerted to the utmost, in his prayers. *Then* we are likely to speed when we thus strive and wrestle in prayer. 3. That he directed his prayer to God: *I cried unto thee.* Whither should the child go but to his father when any thing ails him? 4. That the great thing he prayed for was salvation: *Save me.* A short prayer (for we mistake if we think we shall be heard for our much speaking), but a comprehensive prayer: "Not only rescue me from ruin, but make me happy." We need desire no more than God's salvation (Ps. 50:23) and the *things that accompany* it, Heb. 6:9. 5. That he was earnest for an answer; and not only looked up in his prayers, but looked up after them, to see what became of them (Ps. 5:3): "Lord, *hear me,* and let me know that thou hearest me."

II. David's good purposes, by which he bound himself to duty when he was in the pursuit of mercy. *"I will keep thy statutes;* I am resolved that by thy grace I will;" for, *if we turn away our ear from hearing the law,* we cannot expect an answer of peace to our prayers, Prov. 28:9. This purpose is used as a humble plea (*v.* 146): *"Save me* from my sins, my corruptions, my temptations, all the hindrances that lie in my way, that I may *keep thy testimonies."* We must cry for salvation, not that we may have the ease and comfort of it, but that we may have an opportunity of serving God the more cheerfully.

Verses 147–148

David goes on here to relate how he had abounded in the duty of prayer, much to his comfort and advantage: he cried unto God, that is, offered up to him his pious and devout affections with all seriousness. Observe,

I. The handmaids of his devotion. The two great exercises that attended his prayers, and were helpful to them, were, 1. Hope in God's word, which encouraged him to continue instant in prayer, though the answer did not come immediately: "I cried, and hoped that at last I should speed, because *the vision is for an appointed time, and at the end it will speak and not lie. I hoped in thy word,* which I knew would not fail me." 2. Meditation in God's word. The more intimately we converse with the word of God, and the more we dwell upon it in our thoughts, the better able we shall be to speak to God in his own language and the better we shall know what to pray for as we ought. Reading the word will not serve, but we must meditate in it.

II. The hours of his devotion. *He anticipated the dawning of the morning,* nay, and *the night-watches.* See here, 1. That David was an early riser, which perhaps contributed to his eminency. He was none of those that say, *Yet a little sleep.* 2. That he began the day with God. The first thing he did in the morning, before he admitted any business, was to pray, when his mind was most fresh and in the best frame. If our first thoughts in the morning be of God they will help to keep us in his fear all the day long. 3. That his mind was so full of God, and the cares and delights of his religion, that a little sleep served his turn. Even in *the night-watches,* when he awaked from his first sleep, he would rather meditate and pray than turn himself and go to sleep again. He *esteemed the words of God's mouth more than his necessary* repose, which we can as ill spare as our *food,* Job 23:12. 4. That he would redeem time for religious exercises. He was full of business all day, but that will excuse no man from secret devotion; it is better to take time from sleep, as David did, than not to find time for prayer. And this is our comfort, when we pray in the night, that we can never come unseasonably to the throne of grace; for we may have access to it at all hours. Baal may be asleep, but Israel's God never slumbers, nor are there any hours in which he may not be spoken with.

Verse 149

Here, 1. David applies to God for grace and comfort with much solemnity. He begs of God to hear his voice: "Lord, I have something to say to thee; shall I obtain a gracious audience?" Well, what has he to say? What is his petition and what is his request? It is not long, but it has much in a little: *"Lord, quicken me;* stir me up to that which is good, and make me vigorous, and lively, and cheerful in it. Let habits of grace be drawn out into act." 2. He encourages himself to hope that he shall obtain his request; for he depends, (1.) Upon God's lovingkindness: "He is good, therefore he will be good to me, who hope in his mercy. His lovingkindness manifested to me will help to quicken me, and put life into me." (2.) Upon God's *judgment,* that is, his wisdom ("He knows what I need, and what is good for me, and therefore will quicken me"), or his promise, the word which he has spoken, mercy secured by the new covenant: *Quicken me according to* the tenour of that covenant.

Verses 150–151

Here is, I. The apprehension David was in of danger from his enemies. 1. They were very malicious, and industrious in prosecuting their malicious designs: They *follow after mischief,* any mischief they could do to David or his friends; they would let slip no opportunity nor let fall any pursuit that might be to his hurt. 2. They were very impious, and had no fear of God before their eyes: *They are far from thy law,* setting themselves as far as they can out of the reach of its convictions and commands. The persecutors of God's people are such as make light of God himself; we may therefore be sure that God will take his people's part against them. 3. They followed him closely and he was just ready to fall into their hands: *They draw nigh,* nigher than they were; so that they got ground of him. They were at his heels, just upon his back. God sometimes suffers persecutors to prevail very far against his people, so that, as David said (1 Sa. 20:3), *There is but a step between them and death.* Perhaps this comes in here as a reason why David was so earnest in prayer, *v.* 149. God brings us into imminent perils, as he did Jacob, that, like him, we may wrestle for a blessing.

II. The assurance David had of protection with God: *"They draw nigh* to destroy me, but *thou art near, O Lord!* to save me, not only mightier than they and therefore able to help me against them, but nearer than they and therefore ready to help." It is the happiness of the saints that, when trouble is near, God is near, and no trouble can separate between them and him. He is never far to seek, but he is within our call, and means are within his call, Deu. 4:7. *All thy commandments are truth.* The enemies thought to defeat the promises God had made to David, but he was sure it was out of their power; they were inviolably true, and would be infallibly performed.

Verse 152

This confirms what he had said in the close of the foregoing verses, *All thy commandments are truth;* he means the covenant, the word which God has commanded to a thousand generations. This is firm, as true as truth itself. For, 1. God has founded it so; he has framed it for a perpetuity. Such is the constitution of it, and so well ordered is it in all things, that it cannot but be sure. The promises are *founded for ever,* so that when heaven and earth shall have passed away every iota and tittle of the promise shall stand firm, 2 Co. 1:20. 2. David had found it so, both by a work of God's grace upon his heart (begetting in him a full persuasion of the truth of God's word and enabling him to rely upon it with a full satisfaction) and by the works of his providence on his behalf, fulfilling the promise beyond what he expected. Thus he *knew of old,* from the days of his youth, ever since he began to look towards God, that the word of God is what one may venture one's all upon. This assurance was confirmed by the observations and experiences of his own life all along, and of others that had gone before him in the ways of God. All that ever dealt with God, and trusted in him will own that they have found him faithful.

20. RESH.

Verses 153–154

Here, I. David prays for succour in distress. *Is any afflicted? let him pray;* let him pray as David does here. 1. He has an eye to God's pity, and prays, *"Consider my affliction;* take it into thy thoughts, and all the circumstances of it, and sit not by as one unconcerned." God is never unmindful of his people's afflictions, but he will have us to *put him in remembrance* (Isa. 43:26), to spread our case before him, and then leave it to his compassionate consideration to do in it as in his wisdom he shall think fit, in his own time and way. 2. He has an eye to God's power and prays, *Deliver me;* and again, *"Deliver me;* consider my troubles and bring me out of them." God has promised deliverance (Ps. 50:15) and we may pray for it, with submission to his will and with regard to his glory, that we may serve him the better. 3. He has an eye to God's righteousness, and prays, *"Plead my cause;* be thou my patron and advocate, and take me for thy client." David had a just cause, but his adversaries were many and mighty, and he was in danger of being run down by them; he therefore begs of God to clear his integrity and silence their false accusations. If God do not plead his people's cause, who will? He is righteous, and they commit themselves to him, and therefore he will do it, and do it effectually, Isa. 51:22; Jer. 50:34. (4.) He has an eye to God's grace, and prays, *"Quicken me.* Lord, I am weak, and unable to bear my troubles; my spirit is apt to droop and sink. O that thou wouldst revive and comfort me, till the deliverance is wrought!"

II. He pleads his dependence upon the word oaf God and his obedient regard to its directions: *Quicken* and *deliver me according to thy word* of promise, *for I do not forget thy precepts.* The more closely we cleave to the word of God, both as our rule and as our stay, the more assurance we may have of deliverance in due time.

Verse 155

Here is, 1. The description of wicked men. They do not only do God's statutes, but they do not so much as seek them; they do not acquaint themselves with them, nor so much as desire to know their duty, nor in the least endeavour to do it. Those are wicked indeed who do not think the law of God worth enquiring after, but are altogether regardless of it, being resolved to live at large and to walk in the way of their heart. 2. Their doom: *Salvation is far from* them. They cannot upon any good grounds promise themselves temporal deliverance. *Let not that man think that he shall receive any thing of the Lord.* How can those expect to seek God's favour with success, when they are in adversity, who never sought his statutes when they were in prosperity? But eternal salvation is certainly far from them. They flatter themselves with a conceit that it is near, and that they are going to heaven; but they are mistaken: it is far from them. They thrust it from them by thrusting the Saviour from them; it is so far from them that they cannot reach it, and the longer they persist in sin the further it is; nay, while salvation is far from them, damnation is near; it slumbers not. *Behold, the Judge stands before the door.*

Verse 156

Here, 1. David admires God's grace: *Great are thy tender mercies, O Lord!* The goodness of God's nature, as it is his glory, so it is the joy of all the saints. His mercies are tender, for he is full of compassion; they are many, they are great, a fountain that can never be exhausted. He is rich in mercy to all that call upon him. David had spoken of the misery of the wicked (*v.* 155); but God is good notwithstanding; there were tender mercies sufficient in God to have saved them, if they had not *"despised the riches of those mercies."* Those that are delivered from the sinner's doom are bound for ever to own the greatness of God's mercies which delivered them. 2. He begs for God's grace, reviving quickening grace, *according to his judgments,* that is, according to the tenour of the new covenant (that established rule by which he goes in dispensing that grace) or according to his manner, his custom or usage, with those that love his name, *v.* 132.

Verse 157

Here is, 1. David surrounded with difficulties and dangers: *Many are my persecutors and my enemies.* When Saul the king was his persecutor and enemy no marvel that many more were so: multitudes will follow the pernicious ways of abused authority. David, being a public person, had many enemies, but withal he had many friends, who loved him and wished him well; let him set the one over-against the other. In this David was a type both of Christ and his church. The enemies, the persecutors, of both, are many, very many. 2. David established in the way of his duty, notwithstanding: *"Yet do I not decline from thy testimonies,* as knowing that while I adhere to them God is for me; and then no matter who is against me." A man who is steady in the way of his duty, though he may have many enemies, needs fear none.

Verse 158

Here is, 1. David's sorrow for the wickedness of the wicked. Though he conversed much at home, yet sometimes he looked abroad, and could not but see the wicked walking on every side. He *beheld the transgressors,* those whose sins were open before all men, and it *grieved* him to see them dishonour God, serve Satan, debauch the world, and ruin their own souls, to see the transgressors so numerous, so daring, so very impudent, and so industrious to draw unstable souls into their snares. All this cannot but be a grief to those who have any regard to the glory of God and the welfare of mankind. 2. The reason of that sorrow. He was grieved, not because they were vexatious to him, but because they were provoking to God: *They kept not thy word.* Those that hate sin truly hate it as sin, as a transgression of the law of God and a violation of his word.

Verse 159

Here is, 1. David's appeal to God concerning his love to his precepts: "Lord, thou knowest all things, thou knowest that I love them; consider it then, and deal with me as thou usest to deal with those that love thy word, which thou hast magnified above all thy name." He does not say, "Consider how I fulfil thy precepts;" he was conscious to himself that in many things he came short; but, "Consider how I love them." Our obedience is pleasing to God, and pleasant to ourselves, only when it comes from a principle of love. 2. His petition thereupon: *"Quicken me,* to do my duty with vigour; revive me, keep me alive, not according to any merit of mine, though I love thy word, *but according to thy lovingkindness;"* to that we owe our lives, nay, that is better than live itself. We need not desire to be quickened any further than God's lovingkindness will quicken us.

Verse 160

David here comforts himself with the faithfulness of God's word, for the encouragement of himself and others to rely upon it. 1. It has always been found faithful hitherto, and never failed any that ventured upon it; *It is true from the beginning.* Ever since God began to reveal himself to the children of men all he said was true and to be trusted. The church, from its beginning, was built upon this rock. It has not gained its validity by lapse of time, as many governments, whose best plea is prescription and long usage, *Quod initio non valet, tractu temporis convalescit — That which, at first, wanted validity, in the progress of time acquired it.* But the *beginning of God's word was true* (so some read it); his government was laid on a sure foundation. And all, in every age, that have received God's word in faith and love, have found every saying in it *faithful and well worthy of all acceptation.* 2. It will be found faithful to the end, because righteous: *"Every one of thy judgments remains for ever* unalterable and of perpetual obligation, adjusting men's everlasting doom."

21. SCHIN.

Verse 161

David here lets us know, 1. How he was discouraged in his duty by the fear of man: *Princes persecuted him.* They looked upon him as a traitor and an enemy to the government, and under that notion sought his life, and bade him *go serve other gods,* 1 Sa. 26:19. It has been the common lot of the best men to be persecuted; and the case is the worse if princes be the persecutors, for they have not only the sword in their hand, and therefore can do the more hurt, but they have the law on their side, and can do it with reputation and a colour of justice. It is sad that the power which magistrates have from God, and should use for him, should ever be employed against him. But *marvel not at the matter,* Eccl. 5:8. It was a comfort to David that when princes persecuted him he could truly say it was without cause, he never gave them any provocation. 2. How he was kept to his duty, notwithstanding, by the fear of God: "They would make me stand in awe of them and their word, and do as they bid me; but *my heart stands in awe of thy word,* and I am resolved to please God, and keep in with him, whoever is displeased and falls out with me." Every gracious soul stands in awe of the word of God, of the authority of its precepts and the terror of its threatenings; and to those that do so nothing appears, in the power and wrath of man, at all formidable. We ought to obey God rather than men, and to make sure of God's favour, though we throw ourselves under the frowns of all the world, Lu. 12:4, 5. The heart that stands in awe of God's word is armed against the temptations that arise from persecution.

Verse 162

Here is, 1. The pleasure David took in the word of God. He rejoiced at it, rejoiced that God had made such a discovery of his mind, that Israel was blessed with that light when other nations sat in darkness, that he was himself let into the understanding of it and had had experience of the power of it. He took a pleasure in reading it, hearing it, and meditating on it, and every thing he met with in it was agreeable to him. He had just now said that his heart stood in awe of his word, and yet here he declares that he rejoiced in it. The more reverence we have for the word of God the more joy we shall find in it. 2. The degree of that pleasure — *as one that finds great spoil.* This supposes a victory over the enemy. It is through much opposition that a soul comes to this, to *rejoice in God's word.* But, besides the pleasure and honour of a conquest, there is great advantage gained by the plunder of the field, which adds much to the joy. By the word of God we become more than conquerors, that is, unspeakable gainers.

Verse 163

Love and hatred are the leading affections of the soul; if those be fixed aright, the rest move accordingly. Here we have them fixed aright in David. 1. He had a rooted antipathy to sin; he could not endure to think of it: *I hate and abhor lying,* which may be taken for all sin, inasmuch as by it we deal treacherously and perfidiously with God and put a cheat upon ourselves. Hypocrisy is lying; false doctrine is lying; breach of faith is lying. Lying, in commerce or conversation, is a sin which every good man hates and abhors, hates and doubly hates, because of the seven things which the Lord hates *one* is a *lying tongue* and *another* is a *false witness that speaks lies,* Prov. 6:16. Every man hates to have a lie told him; but we should more hate telling a lie because by the former we only receive an affront from men, by the latter we give an affront to God. 2. He had a rooted affection to the word of God: *Thy law do I love.* And therefore he abhorred lying, for lying is contrary to the whole law of God; and the reason why he loved the law of God was because of the truth of it. The more we see of the amiable beauty of truth the more we shall see of the detestable deformity of a lie.

Verse 164

David, in this psalm, is full of complaints, yet those did neither jostle out his praises nor put him out of tune for them; whatever condition a child of God is in he does not want matter for praise and therefore should not want a heart. See here, 1. How often David praised God — *Seven times a day,* that is, very frequently, not only every day, but often every day. Many think that once a week will serve, or once or twice a day, but David would praise God seven times a day at least. Praising God is a duty which we should very much abound in. We must praise God at every meal, praise him upon all occasions, in every thing give thanks. We should praise God seven times a day, for the subject can never be exhausted and our affections should never be tired. See *v.* 62. 2. What he praised God for — *because of thy righteous judgments.* We must praise God for his precepts, which are all just and good, for his promises and threatenings and the performance of both in his providence. We are to praise God even for our afflictions, if through grace we get good by them.

Verse 165

Here is an account of the happiness of good men, who are governed by a principle of love to the word of God, who make it their rule and are ruled by it. 2. They are easy, and have a holy serenity; none enjoy themselves more than they do: *Great peace have those that love thy law,* abundant satisfaction in doing their duty and pleasure in reflecting upon it. *The work of righteousness is peace* (Isa. 32:17), such peace as the world can neither give nor take away. They may be in great troubles without and yet enjoy great peace within, *sat lucis intus — abundance of internal light.* Those that love the world have great vexation, for it does not answer their expectation; those that love God's word have great peace, for it outdoes their expectation, and in it they have sure footing. 2. They are safe, and have a holy security: *Nothing shall offend them;* nothing shall be a scandal, snare, or stumbling-block, to them, to entangle them either in guilt or grief. No event of providence shall be either an invincible temptation or an intolerable affliction to them, but their love to the word of God shall enable them both to hold fast their integrity and to preserve their tranquility. They will make the best of that which is, and not quarrel with any thing that God does. Nothing shall offend or hurt them, for every thing shall work for good to them, and therefore shall please them, and they shall reconcile themselves to it. Those in whom this holy love reigns will not be apt to perplex themselves with needless scruples, nor to take offence at their brethren, 1 Co. 13:6, 7.

Verse 166

Here is the whole duty of man; for we are taught, 1. To keep our eye upon God's favour as our end: *"Lord, I have hoped for thy salvation,* not only temporal but eternal salvation. I have hoped for that as my happiness and laid up my treasure in it; I have hoped for it as thine, as a happiness of thy preparing, thy promising, and which consists in being with thee. Hope of this has raised me above the world, and borne me up under all my burdens in it." 2. To keep our eye upon God's word as our rule: *I have done thy commandments,* that is, I have made conscience of conforming myself to thy will in every thing. Observe here how God has joined these two together, and let no man put them asunder. We cannot, upon good grounds, hope for God's salvation, unless we set ourselves to do his commandments, Rev. 22:14. But those that sincerely endeavour to do his commandments ought to keep up a good hope of the salvation; and that hope will both engage and enlarge the heart in doing the commandments. The more lively the hope is the more lively the obedience will be.

Verses 167–168

David's conscience here witnesses for him,

I. That his practices were good. 1. He loved God's testimonies, he loved them exceedingly. Our love to the word of God must be a superlative love (we must love it better than the wealth and pleasure of this world), and it must be a victorious love, such as will subdue and mortify our lusts and extirpate carnal affections. 2. He kept them, his soul kept them. Bodily exercise profits little in religion; we must make heart-work of it or we make nothing of it. The soul must be sanctified and renewed, and delivered into the mould of the word; the soul must be employed in glorifying God, for he will be worshipped in the spirit. We must keep both the precepts and the testimonies, the com-

mands of God by our obedience to them and his promises by our reliance on them.

II. That he was governed herein by a good principle: *"Therefore* I have kept thy precepts, because by faith I have seen thy eye always upon me; *all my ways are before thee;* thou knowest every step I take and strictly observest all I say and do. Thou dost see and accept all that I say and do well; thou dost see and art displeased with all I say and do amiss." Note, The consideration of this, that God's eye is upon us at all times, should make us very careful in every thing to keep his commandments, Gen. 17:1.

22. TAU.

Verses 169–170

Here we have, I. A general petition for audience repeated: *Let my cry come near before thee;* and again, *Let my supplication come before thee.* He calls his prayer his *cry,* which denotes the fervency and vehemence of it, and his *supplication,* which denotes the humility of it. We must come to God as beggars come to our doors for an alms. He is concerned that his prayer might come before God, might come near before him, that is, that he might have grace and strength by faith and fervency to lift up his prayers, that no guilt might interpose to shut out his prayers and to separate between him and God, and that God would graciously receive his prayers and take notice of them. His prayer that his supplication might come before God implied a deep sense of his unworthiness, and a holy fear that his prayer should come short or miscarry, as not fit to come before God; nor would any of out prayers have had access to God if Jesus Christ had not approached to him as an advocate for us.

II. Two particular requests, which he is thus earnest to present: — 1. That God, by his grace, would give him wisdom to conduct himself well under his troubles: *Give me understanding;* he means that wisdom of the prudent which is to understand his way; "Give me to know thee and myself, and my duty to thee." 2. That God, by his providence, would rescue him out of his troubles: *Deliver me,* that is, with the temptation make a way to escape, 1 Co. 10:13.

III. The same general plea to enforce these requests —*according to thy word.* This directs and limits his desires: "Lord, give me such an understanding as thou hast promised and such a deliverance as thou hast promised; I ask for no other." It also encourages his faith and expectation: "Lord, that which I pray for is what thou hast promised, and wilt not thou be as good as thy word?"

Verse 171

Here is, 1. A great favour which David expects from God, that he will teach him his *statutes.* This he had often prayed for in this psalm, and urged his petition for it with various arguments; and now that he is drawing towards the close of the psalm he speaks of it as taken for granted. Those that are humbly earnest with God for his grace, and resolve with Jacob that they will not let him go unless he bless them with spiritual blessings, may be humbly confident that they shall at length obtain what they are so importunate for. The God of Israel will grant them those things which they request of him. 2. The grateful sense he promises to have of that favour: *My lips shall utter praise when thou hast taught me.* (1.) Then he shall have cause to praise God. Those that are taught of God have a great deal of reason to be thankful, for this is the foundation of all these spiritual blessings, which are the best blessings, and the earnest of eternal blessings. (2.) Then he shall know how to praise God, and have a heart to do it. All that are taught of God are taught this lesson; when God opens the understanding, opens the heart, and so opens the lips, it is that the mouth may show forth his praise. We have learned nothing to purpose if we have not learned to praise God. (3.) *Therefore* he is thus importunate for divine instructions, that he might praise God. Those that pray for God's grace must aim at God's glory, Eph. 1:12.

Verse 172

Observe here, 1. The good knowledge David had of the word of God; he knew it so well that he was ready to own, with the utmost satisfaction, that all God's commandments are not only righteous, but righteousness itself, the rule

and standard of righteousness. 2. The good use he resolved to make of that knowledge: *My tongue shall speak of thy word,* not only utter praise for it to the glory of God, but discourse of it for the instruction and edification of others, as that which he himself was full of (for out of the abundance of the heart the mouth will speak) and as that which he desired others also might be filled with. The more we see of the righteousness of God's commandments the more industrious we should be to bring others acquainted with them, that they may be ruled by them. We should always make the word of God the governor of our discourse, so as never to transgress it by sinful speaking or sinful silence; and we should often make it the subject-matter of our discourse, that it may feed many and *minister grace to the hearers.*

Verses 173–174

Here, 1. David prays that divine grace would work for him: *Let thy hand help me.* He finds his own hands are not sufficient for him, nor can any creature lend him a helping hand to any purpose; therefore he looks up to God in hopes that the hand that had made him would help him; for, if the Lord do not help us, whence can any creature help us? All our help must be expected from God's hand, from his power and his bounty. 2. He pleads what divine grace had already wrought in him as a pledge of further mercy, being a qualification for it. Three things he pleads: — (1.) That he had made religion his serious and deliberate choice: *"I have chosen thy precepts.* I took them for my rule, not because I knew no other, but because, upon trial, I knew no better." Those are good, and do good indeed, who are good and do good, not by chance, but from choice; and those who have thus chosen God's precepts may depend upon God's helping hand in all their services and under all their sufferings. (2.) That his heart was upon heaven: *I have longed for thy salvation.* David, when he had got to the throne, met with enough in the world to court his stay, and to make him say, "It is good to be here;" but still he was looking further, and longing for something better in another world. There is an eternal salvation which all the saints are longing for, and therefore pray that God's hand would help them forward in their way to it. (3.) That he took pleasure in doing his duty: *"Thy law is my delight.* Not only I delight in it, but it is my delight, the greatest delight I have in this world." Those that are cheerful in their obedience may in faith beg help of God to carry them on in their obedience; and those that expect God's salvation must take delight in his law and their hopes must increase their delight.

Verse 175

David's heart is still upon praising God; and therefore, 1. He prays that God would give him time to praise him: *"Let my soul live, and it shall praise thee,* that is, let my life be prolonged, that I may live to thy glory." The reason why a good man desires to live is that he may praise God in the land of the living, and do something to his honour. Not, "Let me live and serve my country, live and provide for my family;" but, "Let me live that, in doing this, I may praise God here in this world of conflict and opposition." When we die we hope to go to a better world to praise him, and that is more agreeable for us, though here there is more need of us. And therefore one would not desire to live any longer than we may do God some service here. *Let my soul live,* that is, let me be sanctified and comforted, for sanctification and comfort are the life of the soul, *and then it shall praise thee.* Our souls must be employed in praising God, and we must pray for grace and peace that we may be fitted to praise God. 2. He prays that God would give him strength to praise him: *"Let thy judgments help me;* let all ordinances and all providences" (both are God's judgments) "further me in glorifying God; let them be the matter of my praise and let them help to fit me for that work."

Verse 176

Here is, 1. A penitent confession: *I have gone astray,* or wander up and down, *like a lost sheep.* As unconverted sinners are like lost sheep (Lu. 15:4), so weak unsteady saints are like lost sheep, Mt. 18:12, 13. We are apt to wander like sheep, and very unapt, when we have gone astray, to find the way again. By going astray we lose the comfort of the green pastures and expose ourselves to a thousand mischiefs. 2. A believing petition: *Seek thy servant,* as the good shepherd seeks a wandering sheep to bring it back again, Eze. 34:12. "Lord, seek me, as I used to seek my sheep when they went astray;" for David had been himself a tender shepherd. "Lord, own me for one of thine; for, though I am a stray sheep, I have thy mark; concern thyself for me, send after me by the word, and conscience, and providences; bring me back by thy grace." *Seek me,* that is, *find me;* for God never seeks in vain. *Turn me, and I shall be turned.* 3. An obedient plea: "Though I have gone astray, yet I have not wickedly departed, *I do not forget thy commandments."* Thus he concludes the psalm with a penitent sense of his own sin and believing dependence on God's grace. With these a devout Christian will conclude his duties, will conclude his life; he will live and die repenting and praying. Observe here, (1.) It is the character of good people that they do not *forget God's commandments,* being well pleased with their convictions and well settled in their resolutions. (2.) Even those who, through grace, are mindful of their duty, cannot but own that they have in many instances wandered from it. (3.) Those that have wandered from their duty, if they continue mindful of it, may with a humble confidence commit themselves to the care of God's grace.

PSALM 120

This psalm is the first of those fifteen which are here put together under the title of "songs of degrees." It is well that it is not material what the meaning of that title should be, for nothing is offered towards the explication of it, no, not by the Jewish writers themselves, but what is conjectural. These psalms do not seem to be composed all by the same hand, much less all at the same time. Four of them are expressly ascribed to David, and one is said to be designed for Solomon, and perhaps penned by him; yet 126 and 129 seem to be of a much later date. Some of them are calculated for the closet (as 120 and 130), some for the family (as 127 and 128), some for the public assembly (as 122 and 134), and some occasional, as 124, and 132. So that it should seem, they had not this title from the author, but from the publisher. Some conjecture that they are so called from their singular excellency (as the song of songs, so the song of degrees, is a most excellent song, in the highest degree), others from the tune they were set to, or the musical instruments they were sung to, or the raising of the voice in singing them. Some think they were sung on the fifteen steps or stairs, by which they went up from the outward court of the temple to the inner, others at so many stages of the people's journey, when they returned out of captivity. I shall only observe, 1. That they are all short psalms, all but one very short (three of them have but three verses apiece), and that they are placed next to Ps. 119, which is by much the longest of all. Now as that was one psalm divided into many parts, so these were many psalms, which, being short, were sometimes sung all together, and made, as it were, one psalm, observing only a pause between each; as many steps make one pair of stairs. 2. That, in the composition of them, we frequently meet with the figure they call climax, or an ascent, the preceding word repeated, and then rising to something further, as 120, "With him that hated peace. I peace." 121, "Whence cometh my help; my help cometh." "He that keepeth thee shall not slumber; he that keepeth Israel." 122, "Within thy gates, O Jerusalem. Jerusalem is builded." 123, "Until that he have mercy upon us. Have mercy upon us." And the like in most of them, if not all. Perhaps for one of these reasons they are called songs of degrees.

This psalm is supposed to have been penned by David upon occasion of Doeg's accusing him and the priests to Saul, because it is like 52, which was penned upon that occasion, and because the psalmist complains of his being driven out of the congregation of the Lord and his being forced among barbarous people. I. He prays to God to deliver him from the mischief designed him by false and malicious tongues (*v.* 1, 2). II. He threatens the judgments of God against such (*v.* 3, 4). III. He complains of his wicked neighbours that were quarrelsome and vexatious (*v.* 5–7). In singing this psalm we may comfort ourselves in reference to the scourge of the tongue, when at any time we fall unjustly under the lash of it, that better than we have smarted from it.

A song of degrees.

Verses 1–4

Here is, I. Deliverance from a false tongue obtained by prayer. David records his own experience of this.

1. He was brought into distress, into great distress, by *lying lips and a deceitful tongue.* There were those that sought his ruin, and had almost effected it, by lying. (1.) By telling lies to him. They flattered him with professions and protestations of friendships, and promises of kindness and service to him, that they might the more securely and without suspicion carry on their designs against him, and might have an opportunity, by betraying his counsels, to do him a mischief. They smiled in his face and kissed him, even when they were aiming to smite him under the fifth rib. The most dangerous enemies, and those which it is most hard to guard against, are such as carry on their malicious designs under the colour of friendship. The Lord deliver every good man from such lying lips. (2.) By telling lies of him. They forged false accusations against him and *laid to his charge things that he knew not.* This has often been the lot not only of the innocent, but of the excellent ones, of the earth, who have been greatly distressed by lying lips, and have not only had their names blackened and made odious by calumnies in conversation, but their lives, and all that is dear to them in this world, endangered by false-witness-bearing in judgment. David was herein a type of Christ, who was distressed by lying lips and deceitful tongues.

2. In this distress he had recourse to God by faithful and fervent prayer: *I cried unto the Lord.* Having no fence against false tongues, he appealed to him who has all men's hearts in his hand, who has power over the consciences of bad men, and can, when he pleases, bridle their tongues. His prayer was, *"Deliver my soul, O Lord! from lying lips,* that my enemies may not by these cursed methods work my ruin." He that had prayed so earnestly to be kept from lying (Ps. 119:29) and hated it so heartily in himself (*v.* 163) might with the more confidence pray to be kept from being belied by others, and from the ill consequences of it.

3. He obtained a gracious answer to this prayer. God heard him; so that his enemies, though they carried their designs very far, were baffled at last, and could not prevail to do him the mischief they intended. The God of truth is, and will be, the protector of his people from lying lips, Ps. 37:6.

II. The doom of a false tongue foretold by faith, *v.* 3, 4. As God will preserve his people from this mischievous generation, so he will reckon with their enemies, Ps. 12:3, 7. The threatening is addressed to the sinner himself, for the awakening of his conscience, if he have any left: "Consider *what shall be given unto thee, and what shall be done unto thee,* by the righteous Judge of heaven and earth, *thou false tongue."* Surely sinners durst not do as they do if they knew, and would be persuaded to think, what will be in the end thereof. Let liars consider what shall be given to them: *Sharp arrows of the Almighty, with coals of juniper,* that is, they will fall and lie for ever under the wrath of God, and will be made miserable by the tokens of his displeasure, which will fly swiftly like arrows, and will strike the sinner ere he is aware and when he sees not who hurts him. This is threatened against liars, Ps. 64:7. *God shall shoot at them with an arrow; suddenly shall they be wounded.* They set God at a distance from them, but from afar his arrows can reach them. They are sharp arrows, and arrows of the mighty, the Almighty; for they will pierce through the strongest armour and strike deep into the hardest heart. The terrors of the Lord are his arrows (Job 6:4), and his wrath is compared to burning coals of juniper, which do not flame or crackle, like thorns under a pot, but have a vehement heat, and keep fire very long (some say, a year round) even when they seem to be gone out. This is the portion of the false tongue; for all that love and make a lie shall have their portion in the lake that burns eternally, Rev. 22:15.

Verses 5–7

The psalmist here complains of the bad neighbourhood into which he was driven; and some apply the two foregoing verses to this: "What shall the deceitful tongue give, what shall it do to those that lie open to it? What shall a man get by living among such malicious deceitful men? Nothing but *sharp arrows* and *coals of juniper,"* all the mischiefs of a false and spiteful tongue, Ps. 57:4. *Woe is me,* says David, that I am forced to dwell among such, *that I sojourn in Mesech and Kedar.* Not that David dwelt in the country of Mesech or Kedar; we never find him so far off from his own native country; but he dwelt among rude and barbarous people, like the inhabitants of Mesech and Kedar: as, when we would describe an ill neighbourhood, we say, We dwell among Turks and heathens. This made him cry out, *Woe is me!* 1. He was forced to live at a distance from the ordinances of God. While he was in banishment, he looked upon himself as a sojourner, never at home but when he was near God's altars; and he cries out, *"Woe is me* that my sojourning is prolonged, that I cannot get home to my resting-place, but am still kept at a distance!" So some read it. Note, A good man cannot think himself at home while he is banished from God's ordinances and has not them within reach. And it is a great grief to all that love God to be without the means of grace and of communion with God: when they are under a force of that kind they cannot but cry out, as David here, *Woe to me!* 2. He was forced to live among wicked people, who were, upon many accounts, troublesome to him. He *dwell in the tents of Kedar,* where the shepherds were probably in an ill name for being litigious, like the herdsmen of Abraham and Lot. It is a very grievous burden to a good man to be cast into, and kept in, the company of those whom he hopes to be for ever separated from (like Lot in Sodom; 2 Pt. 2:8); to dwell long with such is grievous indeed, for they are thorns, vexing, and scratching, and tearing, and they will show the old enmity that is in the *seed of the serpent* against the *seed of the woman.* Those that David dwelt with were such as not only hated him, but hated peace, and proclaimed war with it, who might write on their weapons of war not *Sic sequimur pacem — Thus we aim at peace,* but *Sic persequimur — Thus we persecute.* Perhaps Saul's court was the Mesech and Kedar in which David dwelt, and Saul was the man he meant that hated peace, whom David studied to oblige and could not, but the more service he did him the more exasperated he was against him. See here, (1.) The character of a very good man in David, who could truly say, though he was a man of war, *I am for peace;* for living peaceably with all men and unpeaceably with none. *I peace* (so it is in the original); "I love peace and pursue peace; my disposition is to peace and my delight is in it. I pray for peace and strive for peace, will do any thing, submit to any thing, part with any thing, in reason, for peace. *I am for peace,* and have made it to appear that I am so." *The wisdom that is from above is first pure, then peaceable.* (2.) The character of the worst of bad men in David's enemies, who would pick quarrels with those that were most peaceably disposed: *"When I speak they are for war;* and the more forward for war the more they find me inclined to peace." He spoke with all the respect and kindness that could be, proposed methods of accommodation, spoke reason, spoke love; but they would not so much as hear him patiently, but cried out, "To arms! to arms!" so fierce and implacable were they, and so bent to mischief. Such were Christ's enemies: for his love they were his adversaries, and for his good words, and good works, they stoned him. If we meet with such enemies, we must not think it strange, nor love peace the less for our seeking it in vain. *Be not overcome of evil,* no, not of such evil as this, *but,* even when thus tried, still try to *overcome evil with good.*

PSALM 121

Some call this the soldier's psalm, and think it was penned in the camp, when David was hazarding his life in the high places of the field, and thus trusted God to cover his head in the day of battle. Others call it the traveller's psalm (for there is nothing in it of military dangers) and think David penned it when he was going abroad, and designed it *pro vehiculo — for the carriage,* for a good man's convoy and companion in a journey or voyage. But we need not thus appropriate it; wherever we are, at home or abroad, we are exposed to danger more than we are aware of; and this psalm directs and encourages us to repose ourselves and our confidence in God, and by faith to put ourselves under his protection and commit ourselves to his care, which we must do, with an entire resignation and satisfaction, in singing this psalm. I. David here assures himself of help from God (*v.* 1, 2). II. He assures others of it (*v.* 3–8).

A song of degrees.

Verses 1–8

This psalm teaches us,

I. To stay ourselves upon God as a God of power and a God all-sufficient for us. David did so and found the benefit of it. 1. We must not rely upon creatures, upon men and means, instruments and second causes, nor make flesh our arm: *"Shall I lift up my eyes to the hills?"* — so some read it. "Does my help come thence? Shall I depend upon the powers of the earth, upon the strength of the hills, upon princes and great men, who, like hills, fill the earth, and hold up their heads towards heaven? No; *in vain is salvation hoped for from hills and mountains,* Jer. 3:23. I never expect help to come from them; my confidence is in God only." *We must lift up our eyes above the hills* (so some read it); we must look beyond instruments to God, who makes them that to us which they are. 2. We must see all our help laid up in God, in his power and goodness, his providence and grace; and from him we must expect it to come: *"My help comes from the Lord;* the help

I desire is what he sends, and from him I expect it in his own way and time. If he do not help, no creature can help; if he do, no creature can hinder, can hurt." 3. We must fetch in help from God, by faith in his promises, and a due regard to all his institutions: *"I will lift up my eyes to the hills"* (probably he meant the hills on which the temple was built, Mount Moriah, and the holy hill of Zion, where the ark of the covenant, the oracle, and the altars were); "I will have an eye to the special presence of God in his church, and with his people (his presence by promise) and not only to his common presence." When he was at a distance he would look towards the sanctuary (Ps. 28:2; 42:6); thence *comes* our *help*, from the word and prayer, from the secret of his tabernacle. *My help cometh from the Lord* (so the word is, *v.* 2), *from before the Lord,* or *from the sight and presence of the Lord.* "This (says Dr. Hammond) may refer to Christ incarnate, with whose humanity the Deity being inseparably united, God is always present with him, and, through him, with us, for whom, sitting at God's right hand, he constantly maketh intercession." Christ is called the *angel of his presence,* that saved his people, Isa. 63:9. 4. We must encourage our confidence in God with this that he *made heaven and earth,* and he who did that can do any thing. He made the world out of nothing, himself alone, by a word's speaking, in a little time, and *all very good,* very excellent and beautiful; and therefore, how great soever our straits and difficulties are, he has power sufficient for our succour and relief. He that made heaven and earth is sovereign Lord of all the hosts of both, and can make use of them as he pleases for the help of his people, and restrain them when he pleases from hurting his people.

II. To comfort ourselves in God when our difficulties and dangers are greatest. It is here promised that if we put our trust in God, and keep in the way of our duty, we shall be safe under his protection, so that no real evil, no mere evil, shall happen to us, nor any affliction but what God sees good for us and will do us good by. 1. God himself has undertaken to be our protector: *The Lord is thy keeper, v.* 5. Whatever charge he gives his angels to keep his people, he has not thereby discharged himself, so that, whether every particular saint has an angel for his guardian or no, we are sure he has God himself for his guardian. It is infinite wisdom that contrives, and infinite power that works, the safety of those that have put themselves under God's protection. Those must needs be well kept that have *the Lord* for their *keeper.* If, by affliction, they be made his prisoners, yet still he is their keeper. 2. The same that is the protector of the church in general is engaged for the preservation of every particular believer, the same wisdom, the same power, the same promises. *He that keepeth Israel (v.* 4) *is thy keeper, v.* 5. The shepherd of the flock is the shepherd of every sheep, and will take care that not one, even of the little ones, shall perish. 3. He is a wakeful watchful keeper: *"He that keepeth Israel,* that keepeth thee, O Israelite! *shall neither slumber nor sleep;* he never did, nor ever will, for he is never weary; he not only does not sleep, but he does not so much as slumber; he has not the least inclination to sleep." 4. He not only protects those whom he is the keeper of, but he refreshes them: He *is their shade.* The comparison has a great deal of gracious condescension in it; the eternal Being who is infinite substance is what he is in order that he may speak sensible comfort to his people, promises to be their *umbra* — their *shadow,* to keep as close to them as the shadow does to the body, and to shelter them from the scorching heat, as *the shadow of a great rock in a weary land,* Isa. 32:2. Under this shadow they may sit with delight and assurance, Cant. 2:3. 5. He is always near to his people for their protection and refreshment, and never at a distance; he *is* their *keeper and shade on their right hand;* so that he is never far to seek. The right hand is the working hand; let them but turn themselves dexterously to their duty, and they shall find God ready to them, to assist them and give them success, Ps. 16:8. 6. He is not only at their right hand, but he will also *keep the feet of his saints,* 1 Sa. 2:9. He will have an eye upon them in their motions: *He will not suffer thy foot to be moved.* God will provide that his people shall not be tempted above what they are able, shall not fall into sin, though they may be very near it (Ps. 73:2, 23), shall not fall into trouble, though there be many endeavouring to undermine them by fraud or over throw them

by force. He will keep them from being frightened, as we are when we slip or stumble and are ready to fall. 7. He will protect them from all the malignant influences of the heavenly bodies (*v.* 6): *The sun shall not smite thee* with his heat *by day nor the moon* with her cold and moisture *by night.* The sun and moon are great blessings to mankind, and yet (such a sad change has sin made in the creation) even the sun and moon, though worshipped by a great part of mankind, are often instruments of hurt and distemper to human bodies; God by them often smites us; but his favour shall interpose so that they shall not damage his people. He will keep them *night and day* (Isa. 27:3), as he kept Israel in the wilderness by *a pillar of cloud by day,* which screened them from the heat of the sun, *and of fire by night,* which probably diffused a genial warmth over the whole camp, that they might not be prejudiced by the cold and damp of the night, their father Jacob having complained (Gen. 31:40) that *by day the drought consumed him and the frost by night.* It may be understood figuratively: "Thou shalt not be hurt either by the open assaults of thy enemies, which are as visible as the scorching beams of the sun, or by their secret treacherous attempts, which are like the insensible insinuations of the cold by night." 8. His protection will make them safe in every respect: *"The Lord shall preserve thee from all evil,* the evil of sin and the evil of trouble. He shall prevent the evil thou fearest, and shall sanctify, remove, or lighten, the evil thou feelest. He will keep thee from doing evil (2 Co. 13:7), and so far from suffering evil that whatever affliction happens to thee there shall be no evil in it. Even that which kills shall not hurt." 9. It is the spiritual life, especially, that God will take under his protection: *He shall preserve thy soul.* All souls are his; and the soul is the man, and therefore he will with a peculiar care preserve them, that they be not defiled by sin and disturbed by affliction. He will keep them by keeping us in the possession of them; and he will preserve them from perishing eternally. 10. He will keep us in all our ways: *"He shall preserve thy going out and thy coming in.* Thou shalt be under his protection in all thy journeys and voyages, outward-bound or homeward-bound, as he kept Israel in the wilderness, in their removes and rests. He will prosper thee in all thy affairs at home and abroad, in the beginning and in the conclusion of them. He will keep thee in life and death, thy going out and going on while thou livest and thy coming in when thou diest, going out to thy labour in the morning of thy days and coming home to thy rest when the evening of old age calls thee in," Ps. 104:23. 11. He will continue his care over us *from this time forth and even for evermore.* It is a protection for life, never out of date. "He will be thy guide *even unto death,* and will then hide thee in the grave, hide thee in heaven. He will *preserve thee in his heavenly kingdom.*" God will protect his church and his saints always, *even to the end of the world.* The Spirit, who is their preserver and comforter, shall abide with them for ever.

PSALM 122

This psalm seems to have been penned by David for the use of the people of Israel, when they came up to Jerusalem to worship at the three solemn feasts. It was in David's time that Jerusalem was first chosen to be the city where God would record his name. It being a new thing, this, among other means, was used to bring the people to be in love with Jerusalem, as the holy city, though it was but the other day in the hands of the Jebusites. Observe, I. The joy with which they were to go up to Jerusalem (*v.* 1, 2). II. The great esteem they were to have of Jerusalem (*v.* 3-5). III. The great concern they were to have for Jerusalem, and the prayers they were to put up for its welfare (*v.* 6-9). In singing this psalm we must have an eye to the gospel church, which is called the "Jerusalem that is from above."

A song of degrees of David.

Verses 1-5

Here we have,

I. The pleasure which David and other pious Israelites took in approaching to and attending upon God in public ordinances, *v.* 1, 2.

1. The invitation to them was very welcome. David was himself glad, and would have every Israelite to say that he *was glad, when* he was called upon to *go up to the house of the Lord.* Note, (1.) It is the will of God that we should worship him in concert, that many should join together to wait upon him in public ordinances. We ought to worship God in our own houses, but that is not enough;

we must *go into the house of the Lord,* to pay our homage to him there, and *not forsake the assembling of ourselves together.* (2.) We should not only agree with one another, but excite and stir up one another, to go to worship God in public. *Let us go;* not, "Do you go and pray for us, and we will stay at home;" but, *We will go also,* Zec. 8:21. Not, "Do you go before, and we will follow at our leisure;" or, "We will go first, and you shall come after us;" but, *"Let us go* together, for the honour of God and for our mutual edification and encouragement." We ourselves are slow and backward, and others are so too, and therefore we should thus quicken and sharpen one another to that which is good, as iron sharpens iron. (3.) Those that rejoice in God will rejoice in calls and opportunities to wait upon him. David himself, though he had as little need of a spur to his zeal in religious exercises as any, yet was so far from taking it as an affront that he was glad of it as a kindness when he was called upon to *go up to the house of the Lord* with the meanest of his subjects. We should desire our Christian friends, when they have any good work in hand, to call for us and take us along with them.

2. The prospect of them was very pleasing. They speak it with a holy triumph (*v.* 2): *Our feet shall stand within thy gates, O Jerusalem!* Those that came out of the country, when they found the journey tedious, comforted themselves with this, that they should be in Jerusalem shortly, and that would make amends for all the fatigues of their journey. We shall stand there as servants; it is desirable to have a place in Jerusalem, though it be *among those that stand by* (Zec. 3:7), though it be the door keeper's place, Ps. 84:10. We have now got a resting-place for the ark, and where it is there will we be.

II. The praises of Jerusalem, as Ps. 48:12.

1. It is the beautiful city, not only for situation, but for building. It is built into *a city,* the houses not scattered, but contiguous, and the streets fair and spacious. It is built uniform, *compact together,* the houses strengthening and supporting one another. Though the city was divided into the higher and lower town, yet the Jebusites being driven out, and it being entirely in the possession of God's people, it is said to be compact together. It was a type of the gospel-church, which is compact together in holy love and Christian communion, so that it is all as one city.

2. It is the holy city, *v.* 4. It is the place where all Israel meet one another: *Thither the tribes go up,* from all parts of the country, as one man, under the character of *the tribes of the Lord,* in obedience to his command. It is the place appointed for their general rendezvous; and they come together, (1.) To receive instruction from God; they come *to the testimony of Israel,* to hear what God has to say to them and to consult his oracle. (2.) To ascribe the glory to God, *to give thanks to the name of the Lord,* which we have all reason to do, especially those that have the testimony of Israel among them. If God speak to us by his word, we have reason to answer him by our thanksgivings. See on what errand we go to public worship, *to give thanks.*

3. It is the royal city (*v.* 5): *There are set thrones of judgment.* Therefore the people had reason to be in love with Jerusalem, because justice was administered there by a man after God's own heart. The civil interests of the people were as well secured as their ecclesiastical concerns; and very happy they were in their courts of judicature, which were erected in Jerusalem, as with us in Westminster Hall. Observe, What a goodly sight it was to see *the testimony of Israel* and the *thrones of judgment* such near neighbours, and they are good neighbours, which may greatly befriend one another. Let the testimony of Israel direct the thrones of judgment, and the thrones of judgment protect the testimony of Israel.

Verses 6-9

Here, I. David calls upon others to which well to Jerusalem, *v.* 6, 7. *Pray for the peace of Jerusalem,* for the welfare of it, for all good to it, particularly for the uniting of the inhabitants among themselves and their preservation from the incursions of enemies. This we may truly desire, that in the peace thereof we may have peace; and this we must earnestly pray for, for it is the gift of God, and for it he will be enquired of. Those that can do nothing else for the peace of Jerusalem can pray for it, which is something more than showing their good-will; it is the appointed way of fetching in mercy. The peace and welfare of the gospel church, particularly in our land, is to be earnestly desired and prayed for by every one of us. Now, 1. We are here encouraged in our prayers for Jerusalem's peace: *Those shall prosper that love thee.* We must pray for Jerusalem, not out of custom, nor for fashion's sake, but out of a principle of love to God's government of man and man's worship of God; and, in seeking the public welfare, we seek our own, for so well does God *love the gates of Zion* that he will love all those that do love them, and therefore they cannot but prosper; at least their souls shall prosper by the ordinances they so dearly love. 2. We are here directed in our prayers for it and words are put into our mouths (*v.* 7): *Peace be within thy walls.* He teaches us to pray, (1.) For all the inhabitants in general, all within the walls, from the least to the greatest. Peace be in thy fortifications; let them never be attacked, or, if they be, let them never be taken, but be an effectual security to the city. (2.) For the princes and rulers especially: Let *prosperity* be *in the palaces* of the great men that sit at the helm and have the direction of public affairs; for, if they prosper, it will be well for the public. The poorer sort are apt to envy the prosperity of the palaces, but they are here taught to pray for it.

II. He resolves that whatever others do he will approve himself a faithful friend to Jerusalem, 1. In his prayers: "*I will now say,* now I see the tribes so cheerfully resorting hither to *the testimony of Israel,* and the matter settled, that Jerusalem must be the place where God will record his name, now I will say, *Peace be within thee.*" He did not say, "Let others pray for the public peace, the priests and the prophets, whose business it is, and the people, that have nothing else to do, and I will fight for it and rule for it." No; "I will pray for it too." 2. In his endeavours, with which he will second his prayers: "*I will,* to the utmost of my power, *seek thy good.*" Whatever lies within the sphere of our activity to do for the public good we must do it, else we are not sincere in praying for it. Now it might be said, No thanks to David to be so solicitous for the welfare of Jerusalem; it was his own city, and the interests of his family were lodged in it. This is true; yet he professes that this was not the reason why he was in such care for the welfare of Jerusalem, but it proceeded from the warm regard he had, (1.) To the communion of saints: It is *for my brethren and companions' sakes,* that is, for the sake of all true-hearted Israelites, whom I look upon as my brethren (so he called them, 1 Chr. 28:2) and who have often been my companions in the worship of God, which has knit my heart to them. (2.) To the ordinances of God: He had *set his affections to the house of his God* (1 Chr. 29:3); he took a great pleasure in public worship, and for that reason would pray for the good of Jerusalem. *Then* our concern for the public welfare is right when it is the effect of a sincere love to God's institutions and his faithful worshippers.

PSALM 123

This psalm was penned at a time then the church of God was brought low and trampled upon; some think it was when the Jews were captives in Babylon, though that was not the only time that they were insulted over by the proud. The psalmist begins as if he spoke for himself only (*v.* 1), but presently speaks in the name of the church. Here is, I. Their expectation of mercy from God (*v.* 1, 2). II. Their plea for mercy with God, (*v.* 3, 4). In singing it we must have our eye up to God's favour with a holy concern, and then an eye down to men's reproach with a holy contempt.

A song of degrees.

Verses 1–4

We have here,

I. The solemn profession which God's people make of faith and hope in God, *v.* 1, 2. Observe, 1. The title here given to God: *O thou that dwellest in the heavens.* Our Lord Jesus has taught us, in prayer, to have an eye to God as *our Father in heaven;* not that he is confined there, but there especially he manifests his glory, as the King in his court. Heaven is a place of prospect and a place of power; he that dwells there beholds thence all the calamities of his people and thence can send to save them. Sometimes God seems to have forsaken the earth, and the enemies of God's people ask, *Where is now your God?* But then they can say with comfort, *Our God is in the heavens. O thou that sittest in the heavens* (so some), sittest as Judge there; for *the Lord has prepared his throne in the heavens,* and to that throne injured innocency may appeal. 2. The regard here had to God. The psalmist himself *lifted up his eyes* to him. The eyes of a good man are *ever towards the Lord,* Ps. 25:15. In every prayer we lift up our soul, the eye of our soul, to God, especially in trouble, which was the case here. The *eyes* of the people *waited on the Lord, v.* 2. We find mercy coming towards a people *when the eyes of man, as of all the tribes of Israel, are towards the Lord,* Zec. 9:1. The eyes of the body are heaven-ward. *Os homini sublime dedit — To man he gave an erect mien,* to teach us which way to direct the eyes of the mind. *Our eyes wait on the Lord,* the eye of desire and prayer, the begging eye, and the eye of dependence, hope, and expectation, the longing eye. Our eyes must wait upon God as *the Lord,* and *our God, until that he have mercy upon us.* We desire mercy from him, we hope he will show us mercy, and we will continue our attendance on him till the mercy come. This is illustrated (*v.* 2) by a similitude: Our eyes are to God *as the eyes of a servant,* and *handmaid, to the hand of their master and mistress.* The eyes of a servant are, (1.) To his master's directing hand, expecting that he will appoint him his work, and cut it out for him, and show him how he must do it. *Lord, what wilt thou have me to do?* (2.) To his supplying hand. Servants look to their master, or their mistress, for their portion of meat in due season, Prov. 31:15. And to God must we look for daily bread, for grace sufficient; from him we must receive it thankfully. (3.) To his assisting hand. If the servant cannot do his work himself, where must he look for help but to his master? And in the strength of the Lord God we must go forth and go on. (4.) To his protecting hand. If the servant meet with opposition in his work, if he be questioned for what he does, if he be wronged and injured, who should bear him out and right him, but his master that set him on work? The people of God, when they are persecuted, may appeal to their Master, *We are thine; save us.* (5.) To his correcting hand. If the servant has provoked his master to beat him, he does not call for help against his master, but looks at the hand that strikes him, till it shall say, "It is enough; I will not contend for ever." The people of God were now under his rebukes; and whither should they turn but to him that *smote them?* Isa. 9:13. To whom should they make supplication but to their Judge? They will not do as Hagar did, who ran away from her mistress when she put some hardships upon her (Gen. 16:6), but they submit themselves to and humble themselves under God's mighty hand. (6.) To his rewarding hand. The servant expects his wages, his *well-done,* from his master. Hypocrites have their eye to the world's hand; thence *they have their reward* (Mt. 6:2); but true Christians have their eye to God as their rewarder.

II. The humble address which God's people present to him in their calamitous condition (*v.* 3, 4), wherein, 1. They sue for mercy, not prescribing to God what he shall do for them, nor pleading any merit of their own why he should do it for them, but, *Have mercy upon us, O Lord! have mercy upon us.* We find little mercy with men; their *tender mercies are cruel;* there are *cruel mockings.* But this is our comfort, that *with the Lord there is mercy* and we need desire no more to relieve us, and make us easy, than the mercy of God. Whatever the troubles of the church are, God's mercy is a sovereign remedy. 2. They set forth their grievances: *We are exceedingly filled with contempt.* Reproach is the wound, the burden, they complain of. Observe, (1.) Who were reproached: "We, who have our eyes up to thee." Those who are owned of God are often despised and trampled on by the world. Some translate the words which we render, *those that are at ease,* and *the proud,* so as to signify the persons that are scorned and contemned. "Our soul is troubled to see how those that are at peace, and the excellent ones, are scorned and despised." The saints are a peaceable people and yet are abused (Ps. 35:20), the excellent ones of the earth and yet undervalued, Lam. 4:1, 2. (2.) Who did reproach them. Taking the words as we read them, they were the epicures who lived at ease, carnal sensual people, Job 12:5. The scoffers are such as walk after their own lusts and serve their own bellies, and the proud such as set God himself at defiance and had a high opinion of themselves; they trampled on God's people, thinking they magnified themselves by vilifying them. (3.) To what degree they were reproached: "*We are filled,* we are surfeited with it. *Our soul is exceedingly filled with it.*" The enemies thought they could never jeer them enough, nor say enough to make them despicable; and they could not but lay it to heart; it was a sword in their bones, Ps. 42:10. Note, [1.] Scorning and contempt have been, and are, and are likely to be, the lot of God's people in this world. Ishmael mocked Isaac, which is called *persecuting* him; and so it is now, Gal. 4:29. [2.] In reference to the scorn and contempt of men it is matter of comfort that there is mercy with God, mercy to our good names when they are barbarously used. *Hear, O our God! for we are despised.*

PSALM 124

David penned this psalm (we suppose) upon occasion of some great deliverance which God wrought for him and his people from some very threatening danger, which was likely to have involved them all in ruin, whether by foreign invasion, or intestine insurrection, is not certain; whatever it was he seems to have been himself much affected, and very desirous to affect others, with the goodness of God, in making a way for them to escape. To him he is careful to give all the glory, and takes none to himself as conquerors usually do. I. He here magnifies the greatness of the danger they were in, and of the ruin they were at the brink of (*v.* 1–5). II. He gives God the glory of their escape (*v.* 6, 7 compared with *v.* 1, 2). III. He takes encouragement thence to trust in God (*v.* 8). In singing this psalm, besides the application of it to any particular deliverance wrought for us and our people, in our days and the days of our fathers, we may have in our thoughts the great work of our redemption by Jesus Christ, by which we were rescued from the powers of darkness.

A song of degrees of David.

Verses 1–5

The people of God, being here called upon to praise God for their deliverance, are to take notice,

I. Of the malice of men, by which they were reduced to the very brink of ruin. Let Israel say that there was but a step between them and death: the more desperate the disease appears to have been the more does the skill of the Physician appear in the cure. Observe, 1. Whence the threatening danger came: *Men rose up against us,* creatures of our own kind, and yet bent upon our ruin. *Homo homini lupus — Man is a wolf to man.* No marvel that the red dragon, the roaring lion, should seek to swallow us up; but that men should thirst after the blood of men, Absalom after the blood of his own father, that a woman should be drunk with the blood of saints, is what, with St. John, we may wonder at with great admiration. From men we may expect humanity, yet there are those whose *tender mercies are cruel.* But what was the matter with these men? Why *their wrath was kindled against us* (*v.* 3); something or other they were angry at, and then no less would serve than the destruction of those they had conceived a displeasure against. *Wrath is cruel and anger is outrageous.* Their wrath was kindled as fire ready to consume us. They were proud; and *the wicked in his pride doth persecute the poor.* They were daring in their attempt; they *rose up against us,* rose in rebellion, with a resolution to *swallow us up* alive. 2. How far it went, and how fatal it would have been if it had gone a little further: "We should have been devoured as a lamb by a lion, not only slain, but *swallowed up,* so that there would have been no relics of us remaining, swallowed up with so much haste, ere we were aware, that we should have gone down alive to the pit. We should have been deluged as the low grounds by a land-flood or the sands by a high spring-tide." This similitude he dwells upon, with the ascents which bespeak this a song of degrees, or risings, like the rest. *The waters had overwhelmed us.* What of us? Why *the stream had gone over our souls,* our lives, our comforts, all that is dear to us. What waters? Why *the proud waters.* God suffers the enemies of his people sometimes to prevail very far against them, that his own power may appear the more illustrious in their deliverance.

II. Of the goodness of God, by which they were rescued from the very brink of ruin: "*The Lord was on our side;* and, *if he had not been so,* we should have been undone." 1. "God was on our side; he took our part, espoused our cause, and appeared for us. He was our helper, and a very present help, a help on our side, nigh at hand. He was with us, not only for us, but among us, and commander-in-chief of our forces." 2. That God was Jehovah; there the emphasis lies. "If it had not been Jehovah himself, a God of infinite power and perfection, that had undertaken our deliverance, our enemies would have overpowered us." Happy the people, therefore, whose God is Jehovah, a God all-sufficient. Let Israel say this, to his honour, and resolve never to forsake him.

Verses 6–8

Here the psalmist further magnifies the great deliverance God had lately wrought for them.

I. That their hearts might be the more enlarged in thankfulness to him (*v.* 6): *Blessed be the Lord.* God is the author of all our deliverances, and therefore he must have the glory of them. We rob him of his due if we do not return thanks to him. And we are the more obliged to praise him because we had such a narrow escape. We were delivered, 1. Like a lamb out of the very jaws of a beast of prey: God *has not given us as a prey to their teeth,* intimating that they had no power over God's people but what was given them from above. They could not be a prey to their teeth unless God gave them up, and *therefore* they were rescued, because God would not suffer them to be ruined. 2. Like *a bird,* a little bird (the word signifies a sparrow), *out of the snare of the fowler.* The enemies are very subtle and spiteful; they lay snares for God's people, to bring them into sin and trouble, and to hold them there. Sometimes they seem to have prevailed so far as to gain their point. God's people are taken in the snare, and are as unable to help themselves out as any weak and silly bird is; and *then* is God's time to appear for their relief, when all other friends fail; then God breaks the snare, and turns the counsel of the enemies into foolishness: *The snare is broken and so we are delivered.* Isaac was saved when he lay ready to be sacrificed. *Jehovah-jireh — in the mount of the Lord it shall be seen.*

II. That their hearts, and the hearts of others, might be the more encouraged to trust in God in the like dangers (*v.* 8): *Our help is in the name of the Lord.* David had directed us (Ps. 121:2) to depend upon God for help as to our personal concerns — *My help is in the name of the Lord;* here as to the concerns of the public — Our *help is so.* It is a comfort to all that lay the interests of God's Israel near their hearts that Israel's God is the same that made the world, and therefore will have a church in the world, and can secure that church in times of the greatest danger and distress. In him therefore let the church's friends put their confidence, and they shall not be put to confusion.

PSALM 125

This short psalm may be summed up in those words of the prophet (Isa. 3:10, 11), "Say you to the righteous, It shall be well with him. Woe to the wicked, it shall be will with him." Thus are life and death, the blessing and the curse, set before us often in the psalms, as well as in the law and the prophets. I. It is certainly well with the people of God; for, 1. They have the promises of a good God that they shall be fixed (*v.* 1), and safe (*v.* 2), and not always under the hatches (*v.* 3). 2. They have the prayers of a good man, which shall be heard for them (*v.* 4). II. It is certainly ill with the wicked, and particularly with the apostates (*v.* 5). Some of the Jewish rabbies are of opinion that it has reference to the days of the Messiah; however, we that are members of the gospel-church may certainly, in singing this psalm, take comfort of these promises, and the more so if we stand in awe of the threatening.

A song of degrees.

Verses 1–3

Here are three very precious promises made to the people of God, which, though they are designed to secure the welfare of the church in general, may be applied by particular believers to themselves, as other promises of this nature may. Here is,

I. The character of God's people, to whom these promises belong. Many call themselves God's people who have no part nor lot in this matter. But those shall have the benefit of them and may take the comfort of them, (1.) Who are *righteous* (*v.* 3), righteous before God, righteous to God, and righteous to all men, for his sake justified and sanctified. (2.) Who *trust in the Lord,* who depend upon his care and devote themselves to his honour. All that deal with God must deal upon trust, and he will give comfort to those only that give credit to him, and make it to appear they do so by quitting other confidences, and venturing to the utmost for God. The closer our expectations are confined to God the higher our expectations may be raised from him.

II. The promises themselves.

1. That their hearts shall be established by faith: those minds shall be truly stayed that are stayed on God: *They shall be as Mount Zion.* The church in general is called *Mount Zion* (Heb. 12:22), and it shall in *this* respect be like *Mount Zion,* it shall be built upon a rock, and its interests shall be so well secured that *the gates of hell shall not prevail against it.* The stability of the church is the satisfaction of all its well-wishers. Particular persons, who trust in God, shall be established (Ps. 112:7); their faith shall be their fixation, Isa. 7:9. *They shall be as Mount Zion,* which is firm as it is a mountain supported by providence, much more as a holy mountain supported by promise. (1.) They *cannot be removed* by the prince of the power of the air, nor by all his subtlety and strength. They cannot be removed from their integrity nor from their confidence in God. (2.) They *abide for ever* in that grace which is the earnest of their everlasting continuance in glory.

2. That, committing themselves to God, they shall be safe, under his protection, from all the insults of their enemies, as Jerusalem had a natural fastness and fortification in the *mountains* that *were round about it, v.* 2. Those mountains not only sheltered it from winds and tempests, and broke the force of them, but made it also very difficult of access for an enemy; such a defence is God's providence to his people. Observe, (1.) The compass of it: *The Lord is round about his people* on every side. There is no gap in the hedge of protection which he makes round about his people, at which the enemy, who goes about them, seeking to do them a mischief, can find entrance, Job 1:10. (2.) The continuance of it — *henceforth even for ever.* Mountains may moulder and *come to nought, and rocks* be *removed out of their place* (Job 14:18), but God's covenant with his people cannot be *broken* (Isa. 54:10) nor his care of them cease. Their being said to stand fast *for ever* (*v.* 1), and here to have God *round about them for ever,* intimates that the promises of the stability and security of God's people will have their full accomplishment in their everlasting state. In heaven they shall *stand fast for ever,* shall be as *pillars in the temple of our God and go no more out* (Rev. 3:12), and there God himself, with his glory and favour, will be *round about them for ever.*

3. That their troubles shall last no longer than their strength will serve to bear them up under them, *v.* 3. (1.) It is supposed that the *rod of the wicked* may come, may fall, *upon the lot of the righteous.* The rod of their power may oppress them; the rod of their anger may vex and torment them. It may fall upon their persons, their estates, their liberties, their families, their names, any thing that falls to their lot, only it cannot reach their souls. (2.) It is promised that, though it may come upon their lot, it shall not rest there; it shall not continue so long as the enemies design, and as the people of God fear, but God will cut the work short in righteousness, so short that even *with the temptation he will make a way for them to escape.* (3.) It is considered as a reason of this promise that if the trouble should continue over-long the righteous themselves would be in temptation to *put forth their hands to iniquity,* to join with wicked people in their wicked practices, to say as they say and do as they do. There is danger lest, being long persecuted for their religion, at length they grow weary of it and willing to give it up, lest, being kept long in expectation of promised mercies, they begin to distrust the promise, and to think of casting God off, upon suspicion of his having cast them off. See Ps. 73:13, 14. Note, God considers the frame of his people, and will proportion their trials to their strength by the care of his providence, as well as their strength to their trials by the power of his grace. *Oppression makes a wise man mad,* especially if it continue long; therefore *for the elect's sake* the days shall be shortened, that, whatever becomes of their lot in this world, they may not lose their lot among the chosen.

Verses 4–5

Here is, 1. The prayer the psalmist puts up for the happiness of those that are sincere and constant (*v.* 4): *Do good, O Lord! unto those that are good.* This teaches us to pray for all good people, to *make supplication for all saints;* and we may pray in faith for them, being assured that those who do well shall certainly be well dealt with. Those that are as they should be shall be as they would be, provided they be *upright in heart,* that they be really as good as they seem to be. *With the upright God will show himself upright.* He does not say, Do good, O Lord! to those that are perfect, that are sinless and spotless, but to those that are sincere and honest. God's promises should quicken our prayers. It is comfortable wishing well to those for whom God has engaged to do well. 2. The prospect he has of the ruin of hypocrites and deserters; he does not pray for it *(I have not desired the woeful day, thou knowest),* but he predicts it: *As for those,* who having known the way of righteousness, for fear of the rod of the wicked, basely turn aside out of it *to their wicked ways,* use indirect ways to prevent trouble or extricate themselves out of it, or those who, instead of reforming, grow worse and worse and are more obstinate and daring in their impieties, God shall *send them away, cast them out,* and *lead them forth with the workers of iniquity,* that is, he will appoint them their portion with the worst of sinners. Note, (1.) Sinful ways are *crooked ways;* sin is the perverting of that which is right. (2.) The doom of those who turn aside to those crooked ways out of the right way will be the same with theirs who have all along walked in them, nay, and more grievous, for if any place in hell be hotter than another that shall be the portion of hypocrites and apostates. God shall *lead them forth,* as prisoners are led forth to execution. *Go, you cursed, into everlasting fire;* and *these shall go away;* all their former righteousness shall not be mentioned unto them. The last words, *Place upon Israel,* may be taken as a prayer: "God preserve his Israel in peace, when his judgments are abroad reckoning with evil-doers." We read them as a promise: *Peace shall be upon Israel;* that is, [1.] When those who have treacherously deserted the ways of God meet with their own destruction those who faithfully adhere to them, though they may have trouble in their way, shall have peace in the end. [2.] The destruction of those who walk in crooked ways will contribute to the peace and safety of the church. When Herod was cut off *the word of God grew,* Acts 12:23, 24. [3.] The peace and happiness of God's Israel will be the vexation, and will add much to the torment, of those who perish in their wickedness, Lu. 13:28; Isa. 65:13. *My servants shall rejoice, but you shall be ashamed.*

PSALM 126

It was with reference to some great and surprising deliverance of the people of God out of bondage and distress that this psalm was penned, most likely their return out of Babylon in Ezra's time. Though Babylon be not mentioned here (as it is, Ps. 137) yet their captivity there was the most remarkable captivity both in itself and as their return out of it was typical of our redemption by Christ. Probably this psalm was penned by Ezra, or some of the prophets that came up with the first. We read of singers of the children of Asaph, that famous psalmist, who returned then, Ezra 2:41. It being a song of ascents, in which the same things are twice repeated with advancement (*v.* 2, 3, and *v.* 4, 5), it is put here among the rest of the psalms that bear that title. I. Those that had returned out of captivity are here called upon to be thankful (*v.* 1–3). II. Those that were yet remaining in captivity are here prayed for (*v.* 4) and encouraged (*v.* 5, 6). It will be easy, in singing this psalm, to apply it either to any particular deliverance wrought for the church or our own land or to the great work of our salvation by Christ.

A song of degrees.

Verses 1–3

While the people of Israel were captives in Babylon their harps were hung upon the willow-trees, for then God called to weeping and mourning, then he mourned unto them and they lamented; but now that their captivity is turned they resume their harps; Providence pipes to them, and they dance. Thus must we accommodate ourselves to all the dispensations of Providence and be suitably affected with them. And the harps are never more melodiously tunable than after such a melancholy disuse. The long want of mercies greatly sweetens their return. Here is, 1. The deliverance God has wrought for them: He *turned again the captivity of Zion.* It is possible that Zion may be in captivity for the punishment of her degeneracy, but her captivity shall be turned again when the end is answered and the work designed by it is effected. Cyrus, for reasons of state, proclaimed liberty to God's captives, and yet it was *the Lord's doing,* according to his word many years before. God sent them into captivity, not as dross is put into the fire to be consumed, but as gold to be refined. Observe, The release of Israel is called *the turning again of the captivity of Zion,* the holy hill, where God's tabernacle and dwelling-place were; for the restoring of their sacred interests, and the reviving of the public exercise of their religion, were the most valuable advantages of their return out of captivity. 2. The pleasing surprise that this was to them. They were amazed at it; it came so suddenly that at first they were in confusion, not knowing what to make of it, nor what it was tending to: "We thought ourselves *like men that dream;* we thought it too good news to be true, and began to question whether we were well awake or no, and whether it was not still" (as sometimes it had been to the prophets) "only a representation of it in vision," as St. Peter for a while thought his deliverance was, Acts 12:9. Sometimes the people of God are thus prevented with the blessings of his goodness before they are aware. *We were like those that are recovered to health* (so Dr. Hammond reads it); "such a comfortable happy change it was to us, as life from the dead or sudden ease from exquisite pain; we thought ourselves in a new world." And the surprise of it put them into such an ecstasy and transport of joy that they could scarcely contain themselves within the bounds of decency in the expressions of it: *Our mouth was filled with laughter and our tongue with singing.* Thus they gave vent to their joy, gave glory to their God, and gave notice to all about them what wonders God had wrought for them. Those that were laughed at now laugh and a *new song is put into their mouths.* It was a laughter of joy in God, not scorn of their enemies. 3. The notice which their neighbours took of it: *They said among the heathen,* Jehovah, the God of Israel, *has done great things* for that people, such as our gods cannot do for us. The heathen had observed their calamity and had triumphed in it, Jer. 22:8, 9; Ps. 137:7. Now they could not but observe their deliverance and admire that. It put a reputation upon those that had been scorned and despised, and made them look considerable; besides, it turned greatly to the honour of God, and extorted from those that set up other gods in competition with him an acknowledgment of his wisdom, power, and providence. 4. The acknowledgments which they themselves made of it, *v.* 3. The heathen were but spectators, and spoke of it only as matter of news; they had no part nor lot in the matter; but the people of God spoke of it as sharers in it, (1.) With application: "He has *done great things for us,* things that we are interested in and have advantage by." Thus it is comfortable speaking of the redemption Christ has wrought out as wrought out for us. *Who loved me, and gave himself for me.* (2.) With affection: "*Whereof we are glad.* The heathen are amazed at it, and some of them angry, but we are glad." While Israel went a whoring from their God joy was forbidden them (Hos. 9:1); but now that the iniquity of Jacob was purged by the captivity, and their sin taken away, now God makes them to rejoice. It is the repenting reforming people that are, and shall be, the rejoicing people. Observe here, [1.] God's appearances for his people are to be looked upon as great things. [2.] God is to be eyed as the author of all the great things done for the church. [3.] It is good to observe how the church's deliverances are for us, that we may rejoice in them.

Verses 4–6

These verses look forward to the mercies that were yet wanted. Those that had come out of captivity were still in distress, even in their own land (Neh. 1:3), and many yet remained in Babylon; and therefore they rejoiced with trembling, and bore upon their hearts the grievances that were yet to be redressed. We have here, 1. A prayer for the perfecting of their deliverance (*v.* 4): "*Turn again our captivity.* Let those that have returned to their own land be eased of the burdens which they are yet groaning under. Let those that remain in Babylon have their hearts stirred up, as ours were, to take the benefit of the liberty granted." The beginnings of mercy are encouragements to us to pray for the completing of it. And while we are here in this world there will still be matter for prayer, even when we are most furnished with matter for praise. And, when we are free and in prosperity ourselves, we must not be unmindful of our brethren that are in trouble and under restraint. The bringing of those that were yet in captivity to join with their brethren that had returned would be as welcome to both sides as streams of water in those countries, which, lying far south, were parched and dry. As cold water to a thirsty soul, so would this good news be from that far country, Prov. 25:25. 2. A promise for their encouragement to wait for it, assuring them that, though they had now a sorrowful time, yet it would end well. But the promise is expressed generally, that all the saints may comfort themselves with this confidence, that their seedness of tears will certainly end in a harvest of joy at last, *v.* 5, 6. (1.) Suffering saints have a seedness of tears. They are in tears often; they share in the calamities of human life, and commonly have a greater share in them than others. But they *sow in tears;* they do the duty of an afflicted state and so answer the intentions of the providences they are under. Weeping must not hinder sowing; when we suffer ill we must be doing well. Nay, as the ground is by the rain prepared for the seed, and the husbandman sometimes chooses to sow in the wet, so we must improve times of affliction, as disposing us to repentance, and prayer, and humiliation. Nay, there are tears which are themselves the seed that we must sow, tears of sorrow for sin, our own and others, tears of sympathy with the afflicted church, and the tears of tenderness in prayer and under the word. These are precious seed, such as the husbandman sows when corn is dear and he has but little for his family, and therefore weeps to part with it, yet buries it under ground, in expectation of receiving it again with advantage. Thus does a good man sow in tears. (2.) They shall have a harvest of joy. The troubles of the saints will not last always, but, when they have done their work, shall have a happy period. The captives in Babylon were long sowing in tears, but at length they were brought forth with joy, and then they reaped the benefit of their patient suffering, and brought their sheaves with them to their own land, in their experiences of the goodness of God to them. Job, and Joseph, and David, and many others, had harvests of joy after a sorrowful seedness. Those that sow in the tears of godly sorrow shall reap in the joy of a sealed pardon and a settled peace. Those that *sow to the spirit,* in this vale of tears, *shall of the spirit reap life everlasting,* and that will be a joyful harvest indeed. *Blessed are those that mourn, for they shall be* for ever *comforted.*

PSALM 127

This is a family-psalm, as divers before were state-poems and church-poems. It is entitled (as we read it) "for Solomon," dedicated to him by his father. He having a house to build, a city to keep, and seed to raise up to his father, David directs him to look up to God, and to depend upon his providence, without which all his wisdom, care, and industry, would not serve. Some take it to have been penned by Solomon himself, and it may as well be read, "a song of Solomon," who wrote a great many; and they compare it with the Ecclesiastes, the scope of both being the same, to show the vanity of worldly care and how necessary it is that we keep in favour with God. On him we must depend, I. For wealth (*v.* 1, 2). II. For heirs to leave it to (*v.* 3–5). In singing this psalm we must have our eye up unto God for success in all our undertakings and a blessing upon all our comforts and enjoyments, because every creature is that to us which he makes it to be and no more.

A song of degrees for Solomon.

Verses 1–5

We are here taught to have a continual regard to the divine Providence in all the concerns of this life. Solomon was cried up for a wise man, and would be apt to lean to his own understanding and forecast, and therefore his father teaches him to look higher, and to take God along with him in his undertakings. He was to be a man of business, and therefore David instructed him how to manage his business under the direction of his religion. Parents, in teaching their children, should suit their exhortations to their condition and occasions. We must have an eye to God,

I. In all the affairs and business of the family, even of the royal family, for kings' houses are no longer safe than while God protects them. We must depend upon God's blessing and not our own contrivance, 1. For the raising of a family: *Except the Lord build the house,* by his providence and blessing, *those labour in vain,* though ever so ingenious, *that build it.* We may understand it of the material house: except the Lord bless the building it is to no purpose for men to build, any more than for the builders of Babel, who attempted in defiance of heaven, or Hiel, who built Jericho under a curse. If the model and design be laid in pride and vanity, or if the foundations be laid in oppression and injustice (Hab. 2:11, 12), God certainly does not build there; nay, if God be not acknowledged, we have no reason to expect his blessing, and without his blessing all is nothing. Or, rather, it is to be understood of the making of a family considerable that was mean; men labour to do this by advantageous matches, offices, employments, purchases; but all in vain, unless God build up the family, and *raise the poor out of the dust.* The best-laid project fails unless God crown it with success. See Mal. 1:4. 2. For the securing of a family or a city (for this is what the psalmist particularly mentions): if the guards of the city cannot secure it without God, much less can the good man of the house save his house from being broken up. *Except the Lord keep the city* from fire, from enemies, *the watchmen,* who *go about the city,* or patrol upon the walls of it, though they neither slumber nor sleep, *wake but in vain,* for a raging fire may break out, the mischief of which the timeliest discoveries may not be able to prevent. The guards may be slain, or the city betrayed and lost, by a thousand accidents, which the most watchful sentinel or most cautious governor could not obviate. 3. For the enriching of a family; this is a work of time and thought, but cannot be effected without the favour of Providence any more than that which is the product of one happy turn: "*It is vain for you to rise up early and sit up late,* and so to deny yourselves your bodily refreshments, in the eager pursuit of the wealth of the world." Usually, those that rise early do not care for sitting up late, nor can those that sit up late easily persuade themselves to rise early; but there are some so hot upon the world that they will do both, will rob their sleep to pay their cares. And they have as little comfort in their meals as in their rest; they *eat the bread of sorrows.* It is part of our sentence that we eat our bread in the sweat of our face; but those go further: *all their days they eat in darkness,* Eccl. 5:17. They are continually fell of care, which embitters their comforts, and makes their lives a burden to them. All this is to get money, and all in vain except God prosper them, for *riches are* not always *to men of understanding,* Eccl. 9:11. Those that love God, and are beloved of him, have their minds easy and live very comfortably without this ado. Solomon was called *Jedidiah — Beloved of the Lord* (2 Sa. 12:25); to him the kingdom was promised, and then it was in vain for Absalom to rise up early, to wheedle the people, and for Adonijah to make such a stir, and to say, *I will be king.* Solomon sits still, and, being *beloved of the Lord,* to him he gives sleep and the kingdom too. Note, (1.) Inordinate excessive care about the things of this world is a vain a d fruitless thing. We weary ourselves for vanity if we have it, and often weary ourselves in vain for it, Hag. 1:6, 9. (2.) Bodily sleep is God's gift to his beloved. We owe it to his goodness that our sleep is safe (Ps. 4:8), that it is sweet, Jer. 31:25, 26. God gives us sleep as he gives it to his beloved when with it he gives us grace to lie down in his fear (our souls returning to him and reposing in him as our rest), and when we awake to be still with him and to use the refreshment we have by sleep in his service. *He gives his beloved sleep,* that is, quietness and contentment of mind, and comfortable enjoyment of what is present and a comfortable expectation of what is to come. Our care must be to *keep ourselves in the love of God,* and then we may be easy whether we have little or much of this world.

II. In the increase of the family. He shows, 1. That children are *God's gift, v.* 3. If children are withheld it is God that withholds them (Gen. 30:2); if they are given, it is God that gives them (Gen. 33:5); and they are to us what he makes them, comforts or crosses. Solomon multiplied wives, contrary to the law, but we never read of more than one son that he had; for those that desire children as a heritage from the Lord must receive them in the way that he is pleased to give them, by lawful marriage to one wife. Mal. 2:15, *therefore one, that he might seek a seed of God.* But *they shall commit whoredom and shall not increase. Children are a heritage,* and a *reward,* and are so to be accounted, blessings and not burdens; for he that sends mouths will send meat if we trust in him. Obed-edom had eight sons, for the Lord blessed him because he had entertained the ark, 1 Chr. 26:5. Children are a heritage for the Lord, as well as from him; they are *my children* (says God) *which thou hast borne unto me* (Eze. 16:20); and they are most our honour and comfort when they are accounted to him for a generation. 2. That they are a good gift, and a great support and defence to a family: *As arrows are in the hand of a mighty man,* who knows how to use them for his own safety and advantage, so are children of the youth, that is, children born to their parents when they are young, which are the strongest and most healthful children, and are grown up to serve them by the time they need their service; or, rather, children who are themselves young; they are instruments of much good to their parents and families, which may fortify themselves with them against their enemies. The family that has a large stock of children is like a quiver full of arrows, of different sizes we may suppose, but all of use one time or other; children of different capacities and inclinations may be several ways serviceable to the family. He that has a numerous issue may boldly *speak with his enemy in the gate* in judgment; in battle he needs not fear, having so many good seconds, so zealous, so faithful, and in the vigour of youth, 1 Sa. 2:4, 5. Observe here, *Children of the youth are arrows in the hand,* which, with prudence, may be directed aright to the mark, God's glory and the service of their generation; but afterwards, when they have gone abroad into the world, they are arrows out of the hand; it is too late to bend them then. But these arrows in the hand too often prove arrows in the heart, a constant grief to their godly parents, whose gray hairs they bring with sorrow to the grave.

PSALM 128

This, as the former, is a psalm for families. In that we were taught that the prosperity of our families depends upon the blessing of God; in this we are taught that the only way to obtain that blessing which will make our families comfortable is to live in the fear of God and in obedience to him. Those that do so, in general, shall be blessed (*v.* 1, 2, 4), In particular, I. They shall be prosperous and successful in their employments (*v.* 2). II. Their relations shall be agreeable (*v.* 3). III. They shall live to see their families brought up (*v.* 6). IV. They shall have the satisfaction of seeing the church of God in a flourishing condition (*v.* 5, 6). We must sing this psalm in the firm belief of this truth, That religion and piety are the best friends to outward prosperity, giving God the praise that it is so and that we have found it so, and encouraging ourselves and others with it.

A song of degrees.

Verses 1–6

It is here shown that godliness has the promise of the life that now is and of that which is to come.

I. It is here again and again laid down as an undoubted truth that *those who are truly holy are truly happy.* Those whose blessed state we are here assured of are such as *fear the Lord* and *walk in his ways,* such as have a deep reverence of God upon their spirits and evidence it by a regular and constant conformity to his will. Where the fear of God is a commanding principle in the heart the tenour of the conversation will be accordingly; and in vain do we pretend to be of those that fear God if we do not make conscience both of keeping to his ways and not trifling in them or drawing back. Such are blessed (*v.* 1), and shall be blessed, *v.* 4. God blesses them, and his pronouncing them blessed makes them so. They are blessed now, they shall be blessed still, and for ever. This blessedness, arising from this blessing, is here secured, 1. To all the saints universally: *Blessed is everyone that fears the Lord,* whoever he be; in every nation he that fears God and works righteousness is accepted of him, and therefore is blessed whether he be high or low, rich or poor, in the world; if religion rule him, it will protect and enrich him. 2. To such a saint in particular: *Thus shall the man be blessed,* not only the nation, the church in its public capacity, but the particular person in his private interests. 3. We are encouraged to apply it to ourselves (*v.* 2): *"Happy shalt thou be;* thou mayest take the comfort of the promise, and expect the benefit of it, as if it were directed to thee by name, if thou *fear God and walk in his ways. Happy shalt thou be,* that is, *It shall be well with thee;* whatever befals thee, good shall be brought out of it; it shall be well with thee while thou livest, better when thou diest, and best of all to eternity."* It is asserted (*v.* 4) with a note commanding attention: *Behold, thus shall the man be blessed;* behold it by faith in the promise; behold it by observation in the performance of the promise; behold it with assurance that it shall be so, for God is faithful, and with admiration that it should be so, for we merit no favour, no blessing, from him.

II. Particular promises are here made to godly people, which they may depend upon, as far as is for God's glory and their good; and that is enough.

1. That, by the blessing of God, they shall get an honest livelihood and live comfortably upon it. It is not promised that they shall live at ease, without care or pains, but, *Thou shalt eat the labour of thy hands.* Here is a double

promise, (1.) That they shall have something to do (for an idle life is a miserable uncomfortable life) and shall have health, and strength, and capacity of mind to do it, and shall not be forced to be beholden to others for necessary food, and to live, as the disabled poor do, upon the labours of other people. It is as much a mercy as it is a duty *with quietness* to *work and eat our own bread,* 2 Th. 3:12. (2.) That they shall succeed in their employments, and they and theirs shall enjoy what they get; others shall not come and eat the bread out of their mouths, nor shall it be taken from them either by oppressive rulers or invading enemies. God will not blast it and blow upon it (as he did, Hag. 1:9), and his blessing will make a little go a great way. It is very pleasant to enjoy the fruits of our own industry; as the sleep, so the food, of a labouring man is sweet.

2. That they shall have abundance of comfort in their family-relations. As a wife and children are very much a man's care, so, if by the grace of God they are such as they should be, they are very much a man's delight, as much as any creature-comfort. (1.) The *wife* shall be *as a vine by the sides of the house,* not only as a spreading vine which serves for an ornament, but as a fruitful vine which is for profit, and with the fruit whereof both God and man are honoured, Jdg. 9:13. The vine is a weak and tender plant, and needs to be supported and cherished, but it is a very valuable plant, and some think (because all the products of it were prohibited to the Nazarites) it was the *tree of knowledge* itself. The wife's place is the husband's house; there her business lies, and that is her castle. *Where is Sarah thy wife? Behold, in the tent;* where should she be else? Her place is *by the sides of the house,* not under-foot to be trampled on, nor yet upon the house-top to domineer (if she be so, she is but *as the grass upon the house-top,* in the next psalm), but on the side of the house, being a rib out of the side of the man. She shall be a loving wife, as the vine, which cleaves to the house-side, an obedient wife, as the vine, which is pliable, and grows as it is directed. She shall be fruitful as the vine, not only in children, but in the fruits of wisdom, and righteousness, and good management, the *branches* of which *run over the wall* (Gen. 49:22; Ps. 80:11), *like a fruitful vine,* not cumbering the ground, nor bringing forth sour grapes, or grapes of Sodom, but good fruit. (2.) The *children* shall be *as olive plants,* likely in time to be olive-trees, and, though *wild by nature,* yet grafted into the good olive, and partaking of its *root and fatness,* Rom. 11:17. It is pleasant to parents who have a table spread, though but with ordinary fare, to see their children round about it, to have many children, enough to surround it, and those with them, and not scattered, or the parents forced from them. Job makes it one of the first instances of his former prosperity that *his children were about him,* Job 29:5. Parents love to have their children at table, to keep up the pleasantness of the table-talk, to have them in health, craving food and not physic, to have them like *olive-plants,* straight and green, sucking in the sap of their good education, and likely in due time to be serviceable.

3. That they shall have those things which God has promised and which they pray for: *The Lord shall bless thee out of Zion,* where the ark of the covenant was, and where the pious Israelites attended with their devotions. *Blessings out of Zion* are the best-blessings, which flow, not from common providence, but from special grace, Ps. 20:2.

4. That they shall live long, to enjoy the comforts of the rising generations: "Thou shalt *see thy children's children,* as Joseph, Gen. 50:23. Thy family shall be built up and continued, and thou shalt have the pleasure of seeing it." *Children's children,* if they be good children, *are the crown of old men* (Prov. 17:6), who are apt to be fond of their grandchildren.

5. That they shall see the welfare of God's church, and the land of their nativity, which every man who fears God is no less concerned for than for the prosperity of his own family. "Thou shalt be blessed in Zion's blessing, and wilt think thyself so. Thou shalt *see the good of Jerusalem* as long as thou shalt live, though thou shouldest live long, and shalt not have thy private comforts allayed and embittered by public troubles." A good man can have little comfort in seeing his children's children, unless withal he see peace upon Israel, and have hopes of transmitting the entail of religion pure and entire to those that shall come after him, for that is the best inheritance.

PSALM 129

This psalm relates to the public concerns of God's Israel. It is not certain when it was penned, probably when they were in captivity in Babylon, or about the time of their return. I. They look back with thankfulness for the former deliverances God had wrought for them and their fathers out of the many distresses they had been in from time to time (*v.* 1–4). II. They look forward with a believing prayer for and a prospect of the destruction of all the enemies of Zion (*v.* 5–8). In singing this psalm we may apply it both ways to the Gospel-Israel, which, like the Old-Testament Israel, has weathered many a storm and is still threatened by many enemies.

A song of degrees.

Verses 1–4

The church of God, in its several ages, is here spoken of, or, rather, here speaks, as one single person, now old and gray-headed, but calling to remembrance the former days, and reflecting upon the times of old. And, upon the review, it is found, 1. That the church has been often greatly distressed by its enemies on earth: *Israel may now say,* "I am the people that has been oppressed more than any people, that has been *as a speckled bird,* pecked at by *all the birds round about,"* Jer. 12:9. It is true, they brought their troubles upon themselves by their sins; it was for them that God punished them; but it was for the peculiarity of their covenant, and the singularities of their religion, that their neighbours hated and persecuted them. "For these *many a time have they afflicted me from my youth."* Note, God's people have always had many enemies, and the state of the church, from its infancy, has frequently been an afflicted state. Israel's youth was in Egypt, or in the times of the Judges; then they were afflicted, and thenceforward more or less. The gospel-church, ever since it had a being, has been at times afflicted; and it bore this yoke most of all in its youth, witness the ten persecutions which the primitive church groaned under. *The ploughers ploughed upon my back, v.* 3. We read (Ps. 125:3) of *the rod of the wicked upon the lot of the righteous,* where we rather expected the plough, to mark it out for themselves; here we read of the *plough* of the wicked *upon the back of the righteous,* where we rather expected to find the rod. But the metaphors in these places may be said to be *crossed;* the sense however of both is the same, and is too plain, that the enemies of God's people have all along used them very barbarously. They tore them, as the husbandman tears the ground with his plough-share, to pull them to pieces and get all they could out of them, and so to *wear out the saints of the Most High,* as the ground is worn out that has been long tilled, tilled (as we say) quite out of heart. When God permitted them to plough thus he intended it for his people's good, that, their fallow ground being thus broken up, he might sow the seeds of his grace upon them, and reap a harvest of good fruit from them: howbeit, the enemies meant not so, neither did their hearts think so (Isa. 10:7); *they made long their furrows,* never knew when to have done, aiming at nothing less than the destruction of the church. Many by the *furrows* they made on the backs of God's people understand the stripes they gave them. *The cutters cut upon my back,* so they read it. The saints have often *had trials of cruel scourgings* (probably the captives had) *and cruel mockings* (for we read of the scourge or lash of the tongue, Heb. 11:36), and so it was fulfilled in Christ, who *gave his back to the smiters,* Isa. 50:6. Or it may refer to the desolations they made of the cities of Israel. *Zion shall, for your sake, be ploughed as a field,* Mic. 3:12. 2. That the church has been always graciously delivered by her friend in heaven. (1.) The enemies' projects have been defeated. They have afflicted the church, in hopes to ruin it, but they have not gained their point. Many a storm it has weathered; many a shock, and many a brunt, it has borne; and yet it is in being: *They have not prevailed against me.* One would wonder how this ship has lived at sea, when it has been tossed with tempests, and all the waves and billows have gone over it. Christ has built his church upon a rock, and the gates of hell have not prevailed against it, nor ever shall. (2.) The enemies' power has been broken: God *has cut asunder the cords of the wicked,* has cut their gears, their traces, and so spoiled their ploughing, has cut their scourges, and so spoiled their lashing, has cut the bands of union by which they were combined together, has cut the bands of captivity in which they held God's people. God has many ways of disabling wicked men to do the mischief they design against his church and shaming their counsels. These words, *The Lord is righteous,* may refer either to the distresses or to the deliverances of the church. [1.] *The Lord is righteous* in suffering Israel to be afflicted. This the people of God were always ready to own, that, how unjust soever their enemies were, God was *just in all that was brought upon them,* Neh. 9:33. [2.] *The Lord is righteous* in not suffering Israel to be ruined; for he has promised to preserve it a people to himself, and he will be as good as his word. He is righteous in reckoning with their persecutors, and rendering to them *a recompence,* 2 Th. 1:6.

Verses 5–8

The psalmist, having triumphed in the defeat of the many designs that had been laid as deep as hell to ruin the church, here concludes his psalm as Deborah did her song, *So let all thy enemies perish, O Lord!* Jdg. 5:31.

I. There are many that hate Zion, that hate Zion's God, his worship, and his worshippers, that have an antipathy to religion and religious people, that seek the ruin of both, and do what they can that God may not have a church in the world.

II. We ought to pray that all their attempts against the church may be frustrated, that in them they may be *confounded* and *turned back* with shame, as those that have not been able to bring to pass their enterprise and expectation: *Let them all be confounded* is as much as, *They shall be* all confounded. The confusion imprecated and predicted is illustrated by a similitude; while God's people shall flourish as the loaded palm-tree, or the green and fruitful olive, their enemies shall *wither as the grass upon the house-top.* As men they are not to be feared, for they shall be made as grass, Isa. 51:12. But as they are enemies to Zion they are so certainly marked for ruin that they may be looked upon with as much contempt as the grass on the house-tops, which is little, and short, and sour, and good for nothing. 1. It perishes quickly: It *withers before it grows up* to any maturity, having no root; and the higher its place is, which perhaps is its pride, the more it is exposed to the scorching heat of the sun, and consequently the sooner does it wither. *It withers before it is plucked up,* so some read it. The enemies of God's church wither of themselves, and stay not till they are rooted out by the judgments of God. 2. It is of no use to any body; nor are *they* any thing but the unprofitable burdens of the earth, nor will their attempts against Zion ever ripen or come to any head, nor, whatever they promise themselves, will they get any more by them than the husbandman does by the grass on his house-top. Their *harvest will be a heap in the day of grief,* Isa. 17:11.

III. No wise man will pray God to bless the mowers or reapers, *v.* 8. Observe, 1. It has been an ancient and laudable custom not only to salute and wish a good day to strangers and travellers, but particularly to pray for the prosperity of harvest-labourers. Thus Boas prayed for his reapers. Ruth 2:4, *The Lord be with you.* We must thus acknowledge God's providence, testify our good-will to our neighbours, and commend their industry, and it will be accepted of God as a pious ejaculation if it come from a devout and upright heart. 2. Religious expressions, being sacred things, must never be made use of in light and ludicrous actions. Mowing the grass on the house-top would be a jest, and therefore those that have a reverence for the name of God will not prostitute to it the usual forms of salutation, which savoured of devotion; for holy things must not be jested with. 3. It is a dangerous thing to let the church's enemies have our good wishes in their designs against the church. If we *wish them God speed, we are partakers of their evil deeds,* 2 Jn. 11. When it is said, None will bless them, and show them respect, more is implied, namely, that all wise and good people will cry out shame on them, and beg of God to defeat them; and woe to those that have the prayers of the saints against them. *I cursed his habitation,* Job 5:3.

PSALM 130

This psalm relates not to any temporal concern, either personal or public, but it is wholly taken up with the affairs of the soul. It is reckoned one of the seven penitential psalms, which have sometimes been made use of by penitents, upon their admission into the church; and, in singing it, we are all concerned to apply it to ourselves. The psalmist here expresses, I. His desire towards God (*v.* 1, 2). II. His repentance before God (*v.* 3, 4). III. His attendance upon God (*v.* 5, 6). IV. His expectations from God (*v.* 7, 8). And, as in water face answers to face, so does the heart of one humble penitent to another.

A song of degrees.

Verses 1–4

In these verses we are taught,

I. Whatever condition we are in, though ever so deplorable, to continue calling upon God, *v.* 1. The best men may sometimes be in *the depths,* in great trouble and affliction, and utterly at a loss what to do, in the depths of distress and almost in the depths of despair, the spirit low and dark, sinking and drooping, cast down and disquieted. But, in the greatest depths, it is our privilege that we may cry unto God and be heard. A prayer may reach the heights of heaven, though not out of the depths of hell, yet out of the depths of the greatest trouble we can be in in this world, Jeremiah's out of the dungeon, Daniel's out of the den, and Jonah's out of the fish's belly. It is our duty and interest to cry unto God, for that is the likeliest way both to prevent our sinking lower and to recover us out of the *horrible pit and miry clay,* Ps. 40:1, 2.

II. While we continue calling upon God to assure ourselves of an answer of peace from him; for this is that which David in faith prays for (*v.* 2): *Lord, hear my voice,* my complaint and prayer, and *let thy ears be attentive* to the voice both of my afflictions and *of my supplications.*

III. We are taught to humble ourselves before the justice of God as guilty in his sight, and unable to answer him for one of a thousand of our offences (*v.* 3): *If thou, Lord, shouldst mark iniquities, O Lord! who shall stand?* His calling God *Lord* twice, in so few words, *Jah* and *Adonai,* is very emphatic, and intimates a very awful sense of God's glorious majesty and a dread of his wrath. Let us learn here, 1. To acknowledge our iniquities, that we cannot justify ourselves before God, or plead Not guilty. There is that which is remarkable in our iniquities and is liable to be animadverted upon. 2. To own the power and justice of God, which are such that, if he were extreme to mark what we do amiss, there would be no hopes of coming off. His eye can discover enough in the best man to ground a condemnation upon; and, if he proceed against us, we have no way to help ourselves, we cannot stand, but shall certainly be cast. If God deal with us in strict justice, we are undone; if he make remarks upon our iniquities, he will find them to be many and great, greatly aggravated and very provoking; and then, if he should proceed accordingly, he would shut us out from all hope of his favour and shut us up under his wrath; and what could we do to help ourselves? We could not make our escape, nor resist not bear up under his avenging hand. 3. Let us admire God's patience and forbearance; we should be undone if he were to mark iniquities, and he knows it, and therefore bears with us. *It is of his mercy that we are not consumed* by his wrath.

IV. We are taught to cast ourselves upon the pardoning mercy of God, and to comfort ourselves with that when we see ourselves obnoxious to his justice, *v.* 4. Here is, 1. God's grace discovered, and pleaded with him, by a penitent sinner: *But there is forgiveness with thee.* It is our unspeakable comfort, in all our approaches to God, that there is forgiveness with him, for that is what we need. He has put himself into a capacity to pardon sin; he has declared himself gracious and merciful, and ready to forgive, Ex. 34:6, 7. He has promised to forgive the sins of those that do repent. Never any that dealt with him found him implacable, but easy to be entreated, and swift to show mercy. With us there is iniquity, and therefore it is well for us that with him there is forgiveness. *There is a propitiation with thee,* so some read it. Jesus Christ is the great propitiation, the ransom which God has found; he is ever with him, as advocate for us, and through him we hope to obtain forgiveness. 2. Our duty designed in that discovery, and inferred from it: *"There is forgiveness with thee,* not that thou mayest be made bold with and presumed upon, but *that thou mayest be feared* — in general, that thou mayest be worshipped and served by the children of men, who, being sinners, could have no dealings with God, if he were not a Master that could pass by a great many faults." But this encourages us to come into his service that we shall not be turned off for every misdemeanour; no, nor for any, if we truly repent. This does in a special manner invite those who have sinned to repent, and return to the fear of God, that he is gracious and merciful, and will receive them upon their repentance, Joel 2:13; Mt. 3:2. And, particularly, we are to have a holy awe and reverence of God's pardoning mercy (Hos. 3:5, *They shall fear the Lord, and his goodness*); and *then* we may expect the benefit of the forgiveness that is with God when we make it the object of our holy fear.

Verses 5–8

Here, I. The psalmist engages himself to trust in God and to wait for him, *v.* 5, 6. Observe, 1. His dependence upon God, expressed in a climax, it being a a song of degrees, or ascents: *"I wait for the Lord;* from him I expect relief and comfort, believing it will come, longing till it does come, but patiently bearing the delay of it, and resolving to look for it from no other hand. *My soul doth wait;* I wait for him in sincerity, and not in profession only. I am an expectant, and it is *for the Lord* that *my soul waits,* for the gifts of his grace and the operations of his power." 2. The ground of that dependence: *In his word do I hope.* We must hope for that only which he has promised in his word, and not for the creatures of our own fancy and imagination; we must hope for it because he has promised it, and not from any opinion of our own merit. 3. The degree of that dependence — *"more than those that watch for the morning,* who are, (1.) Well-assured that the morning will come; and so am I that God will return in mercy to me, according to his promise; for God's covenant is more firm than the ordinances of day and night, for they shall come to an end, but that is everlasting." (2.) Very desirous that it would come. Sentinels that keep guard upon the walls, those that watch with sick people, and travellers that are abroad upon their journey, long before day wish to see the dawning of the day; but more earnestly does this good man long for the tokens of God's favour and the visits of his grace, and more readily will he be aware of his first appearances than they are of day. Dr. Hammond reads it thus, *My soul hastens to the Lord, from the guards in the morning, the guards in the morning,* and gives this sense of it, "To thee I daily betake myself, early in the morning, addressing my prayers, and my very soul, before thee, at the time that the priests offer their morning sacrifice."

II. He encourages all the people of God in like manner to depend upon him and trust in him: *Let Israel hope in the Lord* and *wait for* him; not only the body of the people, but every good man, who *surnames himself by the name of Israel,* Isa. 44:5. Let all that devote themselves to God cheerfully stay themselves upon him (*v.* 7, 8), for two reasons: — 1. Because the light of nature discovers to us that *there is mercy with him,* that the God of Israel is a merciful God and *the Father of mercies. Mercy is with* him; not only inherent in his nature, but it is his delight, it is his darling attribute; it is with him in all his works, in all his counsels. 2. Because the light of the gospel discovers to us that *there is redemption with him,* contrived by him, and to be wrought out *in the fulness of time;* it was in the beginning hidden in God. See here, (1.) The nature of this redemption; it is redemption from sin, from all sin, and therefore can be no other than that eternal redemption which Jesus Christ became the author of; for it is he *that saves his people from their sins* (Mt. 1:21), that *redeems them from all iniquity* (Tit. 2:14), and *turns away ungodliness from Jacob,* Rom. 11:26. It is he that redeems us both from the condemning and from the commanding power of sin. (2.) The riches of this redemption; it *is plenteous redemption;* there is an all-sufficient fulness of merit and grace in the Redeemer, enough for all, enough for each; enough for me, says the believer. Redemption from sin includes redemption from all other evils, and therefore is a plenteous redemption. (3.) The persons to whom the benefits of this redemption belong: *He shall redeem Israel,* Israel according to the spirit, all those who are in covenant with God, as Israel was, and who are *Israelites indeed, in whom is no guile.*

PSALM 131

This psalm is David's profession of humility, humbly made, with thankfulness to God for his grace, and not in vain-glory. It is probable enough that (as most interpreters suggest) David made this protestation in answer to the calumnies of Saul and his courtiers, who represented David as an ambitious aspiring man, who, under pretence of a divine appointment, sought the kingdom, in the pride of his heart. But he appeals to God, that, on the contrary, I. He aimed at nothing high nor great (*v.* 1). II. He was very easy in every condition which God allotted him (*v.* 2); and therefore, III. He encourages all good people to trust in God as he did (*v.* 3). Some have made it an objection against singing David's psalms that there are many who cannot say, "My heart is not haughty," etc. It is true there are; but we may sing it for the same purpose that we read it, to teach and admonish ourselves, and one another, what we ought to be, with repentance that we have come short of being so, and humble prayer to God for his grace to make us so.

A song of degrees of David.

Verses 1–3

Here are two things which will be comforts to us: —

I. Consciousness of our integrity. This was David's rejoicing, that his heart could witness for him that he had walked humbly with his God, notwithstanding the censures he was under and the temptations he was in.

1. He aimed not at a high condition, nor was he desirous of making a figure in the world, but, if God had so ordered, could have been well content to spend all his days, as he did in the beginning of them, in the sheep-folds. His own brother, in a passion, charged him with pride (1 Sa. 17:28), but the charge was groundless and unjust. God, who searches the heart, knew, (1.) That he had no conceited opinion of himself, or his own merits: *Lord, my heart is not haughty.* Humble saints cannot think so well of themselves as others think of them, are not in love with their own shadow, nor do they magnify their own attainments or achievements. The love of God reigning in the heart will subdue all inordinate self-love. (2.) That he had neither a scornful nor an aspiring look: *"My eyes are not lofty,* either to look with envy upon those that are above me or to look with disdain upon those that are below me." Where there is a proud heart there is commonly a proud look (Prov. 6:17), but the humble publican will not so much as lift up his eyes. (3.) That he did not employ himself in things above his station, *in things too great or too high for* him. He did not employ himself in studies too high; he made God's word his meditation, and did not amuse himself with matters of nice speculation or doubtful disputation, or covet to be wise above what is written. To know God and our duty is learning sufficiently high for us. He did not employ himself in affairs too great; he followed his ewes, and never set up for a politician; no, nor for a soldier; for, when his brethren went to the wars, he staid at home to keep the sheep. It is our wisdom, and will be our praise, to keep within our sphere, and not to intrude into things which we have not seen, or meddle with that which does not belong to us. Princes and scholars must not exercise themselves in matters too great, too high, for men: and those in a low station, and of ordinary capacities, must not pretend to that which is out of their reach, and which they were not cut out for. Those will fall under due shame that affect undue honours.

2. He was well reconciled to every condition that God placed him in (*v.* 2): *I have behaved and quieted myself as a child that is weaned of his mother.* As he had not proudly aimed at the kingdom, so, since God had appointed him to it, he had not behaved insolently towards any, nor been restless in his attempts to get the crown before the time set; but, (1.) He had been as humble as a little child about the age of a weanling, as manageable and governable, and as far from aiming at high things; as entirely at God's disposal as the child at the disposal of the mother or nurse; as far from taking state upon him, though anointed to be king, or valuing himself upon the prospect of his future advancement, as a child in the arms. Our Saviour has taught us humility by this comparison (Mt. 18:3); we must *become as little children.* (2.) He had been as indifferent to the wealth and honour of this world as a child is to the breast when it is thoroughly weaned from it. *I have levelled and quieted myself* (so Dr. Hammond reads it) *as a child that is weaned.* This intimates that our hearts are naturally as desirous of worldly things as the babe is of the breast, and in like manner relish them, cry for them, are fond of them, play with them, and cannot live without them. But, by the grace of God, a soul that is sanctified, is weaned from those things. Providence puts wormwood upon the breast, and that helps to wean us. The child is perhaps cross and fretful while it is in the weaning and

thinks itself undone when it has lost the breast. But in a day or two it is forgotten; the fret is over, and it accommodates itself well enough to a new way of feeding, cares no longer for milk, but can bear strong meat. Thus does a gracious soul quiet itself under the loss of that which it loved and disappointment in that which it hoped for, and is easy whatever happens, lives, and lives comfortably, upon God and the covenant-grace, when creatures prove dry breasts. When our condition is not to our mind we must bring our mind to our condition; and then we are easy to ourselves and all about us; then our souls are *as a weaned child.*

II. Confidence in God; and this David recommends to all Israel of God, no doubt from his own experience of the benefit of it (*v.* 3): *Let Israel hope in the Lord,* and let them continue to do so *henceforth and for ever.* Though David could himself wait patiently and quietly for the crown designed him, yet perhaps Israel, the people whose darling he was, would be ready to attempt something in favour of him before the time; and therefore endeavours to quiet them too, and bids them *hope in the Lord* that they should see a happy change of the face of affairs in due time. *Thus it is good to hope and quietly to wait for the salvation of the Lord.*

PSALM 132

It is probable that this psalm was penned by Solomon, to be sung at the dedication of the temple which he built according to the charge his father gave him, 1 Chr. 28:2, etc. Having fulfilled his trust, he begs of God to own what he had done. I. He had built this house for the honour and service of God; and when he brings the ark into it, the token of God's presence, he desires that God himself would come and take possession of it (*v.* 8–10). With these words Solomon concluded his prayer, 2 Chr. 6:41, 42. II. He had built it in pursuance of the orders he had received from his father, and therefore his pleas to enforce these petitions refer to David. 1. He pleads David's piety towards God (*v.* 1–7). 2. He pleads God's promise to David (*v.* 11–18). The former introduces his petition: the latter follows it as an answer to it. In singing this psalm we must have a concern for the gospel church as the temple of God, and a dependence upon Christ as David our King, in whom the mercies of God are sure mercies.

A song of degrees.

Verses 1–10

In these verses we have Solomon's address to God for his favour to him and to his government, and his acceptance of his building a house to God's name. Observe,

I. What he pleads — two things: —

1. That what he had done was in pursuance of the pious vow which his father David had made to build a house for God. Solomon was a wise man, yet pleads not any merit of his own: "I am not worthy, for whom thou shouldst do this; but, *Lord, remember David,* with whom thou madest the covenant" (as Moses prayed, Ex. 32:13, *Remember Abraham,* the first trustee of the covenant); "remember *all his afflictions,* all the troubles of his life, which his being anointed was the occasion of," or his care and concern about the ark, and what an uneasiness it was to him that the ark was in curtains, 2 Sa. 7:2. *Remember all his humility and meekness* (so some read it), all that pious and devout affection with which he had made the following vow. Note, It is not amiss for us to put God in mind of our predecessors in profession, of their afflictions, their services, and their sufferings, of God's covenant with them, the experiences they have had of his goodness, the care they took of, and the many prayers they put up for, those that should come after them. We may apply it to Christ, the Son of David, and to all his afflictions: "Lord, remember the covenant made with him and the satisfaction made by him. *Remember all his offerings* (Ps. 20:3), that is, all his sufferings." He especially pleads the solemn vow that David had made as soon as ever he was settled in his government, and before he was well settled in a house of his own, that he would build a house for God. Observe, (1.) Whom he bound himself to, *to the Lord, to the mighty God of Jacob.* Vows are to be made to God, who is a party as well as a witness. The Lord is the Mighty One of Jacob, Jacob's God, and a mighty one, whose power is engaged for Jacob's defence and deliverance. Jacob is weak, but the God of Jacob is a mighty one. (2.) What he bound himself to do, to *find out a place for the Lord,* that is, for the ark, the token of his presence. He had observed in the law frequent mention of the *place that God would choose to put his name there,* to which all the tribes should resort. When

he came to the crown there was no such place; Shiloh was deserted, and no other place was pitched upon, for want of which the feasts of the Lord were not kept with due solemnity. "Well," says David, "I will find out such a place for the general rendezvous of all the tribes, a place of *habitation for the Mighty* One *of Jacob,* a place for the ark, where there shall be room both for the priests and people to attend upon it." (3.) How intent he was upon it; he would not settle in his bed, till he had brought this matter to some head, *v.* 3, 4. The thing had been long talked of, and nothing done, till at last David, when he went out one morning about public business, made a vow that before night he would come to a resolution in this matter, and would determine the place either where the tent should be pitched for the reception of the ark, at the beginning of his reign, or rather where Solomon should build the temple, which was not fixed till the latter end of his reign, just after the pestilence with which he was punished for numbering the people (1 Chr. 22:1, *Then David said, This is the house of the Lord*); and perhaps it was upon occasion of that judgment that he made this vow, being apprehensive that one of God's controversies with him was for his dilatoriness in this matter. Note, When needful work is to be done for God it is good for us to task ourselves, and tie ourselves to a time, because we are apt to put off. It is good in the morning to cut out work for the day, binding ourselves that we will do it before we sleep, only with submission to Providence; for we *know not what a day may bring forth.* Especially in the great work of conversion to God we must be thus solicitous, thus zealous; we have good reason to resolve that we will not enjoy the comforts of this life till we have laid a foundation for hopes of a better.

2. That it was in pursuance of the expectations of the people of Israel, *v.* 6, 7. (1.) They were inquisitive after the ark; for they lamented its obscurity, 1 Sa. 7:2. They *heard of it at Ephratah* (that is, at Shiloh, in the tribe of Ephraim); there they were told it had been, but it was gone. They *found it,* at last, *in the fields of the wood,* that is, in Kirjathjearim, which signifies *the city of woods.* Thence all Israel fetched it, with great solemnity, in the beginning of David's reign (1 Chr. 13:6), so that in building his house for the ark Solomon had gratified all Israel. They needed not to go about to seek the ark anymore; they now knew where to find it. (2.) They were resolved to attend it: "Let us but have a convenient place, and *we will go into his tabernacle,* to pay our homage there; *we will worship at his footstool* as subjects and suppliants, which we neglected to do, for want of such a place, *in the days of Saul,*" 1 Chr. 13:3.

II. What he prays for, *v.* 8–10. 1. That God would vouchsafe, not only to take possession of, but to take up his residence in, this temple which he had built: *Arise, O Lord! into thy rest,* and let this be it, *thou,* even *the ark of thy strength,* the pledge of thy presence, thy mighty presence. 2. That God would give grace to the ministers of the sanctuary to do their duty: *Let thy priests be clothed with righteousness;* let them appear righteous both in their administrations and in their conversations, and let both be according to the rule. Note, Righteousness is the best ornament of a minister. Holiness towards God, and goodness towards all men, are habits for ministers of the necessity of which there is no dispute. "They are *thy priests,* and will therefore discredit their relation to thee if they *be not clothed with righteousness.*" 3. That the people of God might have the comfort of the due administration of holy ordinances among them: *Let thy saints shout for joy.* They did so when the ark was brought into the city of David (2 Sa. 6:15); they will do so when the priests are clothed with righteousness. A faithful ministry is the joy of the saints; it is the matter of it; it is a friend and a furtherance to it; we are *helpers of your joy,* 2 Co. 1:24. 4. That Solomon's own prayer, upon occasion of the dedicating of the temple, might be accepted of God: *"Turn not away the face of thy anointed,* that is, deny me not the things I have asked of thee, send me not away ashamed." He pleads, (1.) That he was the anointed of the Lord, and this he pleads as a type of Christ, the great anointed, who, in his intercession, urges his designation to his office. He is God's anointed, and therefore the Father hears him always. (2.) That he was the son of David: "For his sake do not deny me;" and this is the Christian's plea: "For the sake of Christ (our David), *in whom thou art well pleased,* accept me." He is David, whose name signifies *beloved;* and we are made accepted in the beloved. He is God's servant, whom he *upholds,* Isa. 42:1. "We have no merit of our own to plead, but for his sake, in whom there is a fulness of merit, let us find favour." When we pray for the prosperity of the church we may pray with great boldness, for Christ's sake, who purchased the church with his own blood. "Let both ministers and people do their duty."

Verses 11–18

These are precious promises, *confirmed by an oath,* that the heirs of them might have *strong consolation,* Heb. 6:17, 18. It is all one whether we take them as pleas urged in the prayer or as answers returned to the prayer; believers know how to make use of the promises both ways, with them to speak to God and in them to hear what God the Lord will speak to us. These promises relate to the establishment both in church and state, both to the throne of the house of David and to the testimony of Israel fixed on Mount Zion. The promises concerning Zion's hill are as applicable to the gospel-church as these concerning David's seed are to Christ, and therefore both pleadable by us and very comfortable to us. Here is,

I. The choice God made of David's house and Zion hill. Both were of divine appointment.

1. God chose David's family for the royal family and confirmed his choice by an oath, *v.* 11, 12. David, being a type of Christ, was made king with an oath: *The Lord hath sworn and will not repent,* will not turn from it. Did David swear to the Lord (*v.* 2) that he would find him a house? The Lord swore to David that he would build him a house; for God will be behind with none of his people in affections or assurances. The promise made to David refers, (1.) To a long succession of kings that should descend from his loins: *Of the fruit of thy body will I set upon thy throne,* which was fulfilled in Solomon; David himself lived to see it with great satisfaction, 1 Ki. 1:48. The crown was also entailed conditionally upon his heirs for ever: *If thy children,* in following ages, *will keep my covenant and my testimony that I shall teach them.* God himself engaged to teach them, and he did his part; they had Moses and the prophets, and all he expects is that they should keep what he taught them, and keep to it, and then *their children shall sit upon thy throne for evermore.* Kings are before God upon their good behaviour, and their commission from him runs *quamdiu se bene gesserint — during good behaviour.* The issue of this was that they did not keep God's covenant, and so the entail was at length cut off, and *the sceptre departed from Judah* by degrees. (2.) To an everlasting successor, a king that should descend from his loins of *the increase of whose government and peace there shall be no end.* St. Peter applies this to Christ, nay, he tells us that David himself so understood it. Acts 2:30, *He knew that God had sworn with an oath to him that of the fruit of his loins, according to the flesh, he would raise up Christ to sit on his throne;* and in the fulness of time he did so, and *gave him the throne of his father David,* Lu. 1:32. He did fulfill the condition of the promise; he kept God's covenant and his testimony, did his Father's will, and in all things pleased him; and therefore to him, and his spiritual seed, the promise shall be made good. He, and the children God has given him, all believers, shall *sit upon the throne for evermore,* Rev. 3:21.

2. God chose Zion hill for the holy hill, and confirmed his choice by the delight he took in it, *v.* 13, 14. He *chose the Mount Zion which he loved* (Ps. 78:68); he chose it for the habitation of his ark, and said of it, *This is my rest for ever,* and not merely my residence for a time, as Shiloh was. Zion was the city of David; he chose it for the royal city because God chose it for the holy city. God said, *Here will I dwell,* and therefore David said, *Here will I dwell,* for here he adhered to his principle, *It is good for me to be near to God.* Zion must be here looked upon as a type of the gospel-church, which is called *Mount Zion* (Heb. 12:22), and in it what is here said of Zion has its full accomplishment. Zion was long since ploughed as a field, but the church of Christ *is the house of the living God* (1 Tim. 3:15), and it is his *rest for ever,* and shall be blessed with his presence always, even to the end of the world. The delight God takes in his church, and the continuance of his presence with his church, are the comfort and joy of all its members.

II. The choice blessings God has in store for David's house and Zion hill. Whom God chooses he will bless.

1. God, having chosen Zion hill, promises to bless that,

(1.) With the blessings of the life that now is; for godliness has the promise of them, *v.* 15. The earth shall yield her increase; where religion is set up there shall be provision, and in blessing God will bless it (Ps. 67:6); he will surely and abundantly bless it. And a little provision, with an abundant blessing upon it, will be more serviceable, as well as more comfortable, than a great deal without that blessing. God's people have a special blessing upon common enjoyments, and that blessing puts a peculiar sweetness into them. Nay, the promise goes further: *I will satisfy her poor with bread.* Zion has her own poor to keep; and it is promised that God will take care even of them. [1.] By his providence they shall be kept from wanting; they shall have provision enough. If there be scarcity, the poor are the first that feel it, so that it is a sure sign of plenty if they have sufficient. Zion's poor shall not want, for God has obliged all the sons of Zion to be charitable to the poor, according to their ability, and the church must take care that they be not *neglected,* Acts 6:1. [2.] By his grace they shall be kept from complaining; though they have but dry bread, yet they shall be satisfied. Zion's poor have, of all others, reason to be content with a little of this world, because they have better things prepared for them. And this may be understood spiritually of the provision that is made for the soul in the word and ordinances; God will abundantly bless that for the nourishment of the new man, and satisfy the poor in spirit with the bread of life. What God sanctifies to us we shall and may be satisfied with.

(2.) With the blessings of the life that is to come, things pertaining to godliness (*v.* 16), which is an answer to the prayer, *v.* 9. [1.] It was desired that the priests might be *clothed with righteousness;* it is here promised that God will *clothe them with salvation,* not only save them, but make them and their administrations instrumental for the salvation of his people; they shall both *save themselves and those that hear them,* and *add those to the church that shall be saved.* Note, Whom God clothes with righteousness he will clothe with salvation; we must pray for righteousness and then with it God will give salvation. [2.] It was desired that the saints might *shout for joy;* it is promised that they *shall shout aloud for joy.* God gives more than we ask, and when he gives salvation he will give an abundant joy.

2. God, having chosen David's family, here promises to bless that also with suitable blessings. (1.) Growing power: *There,* in Zion, *will I make the horn of David to bud, v.* 17. The royal dignity shall increase more and more, and constant additions he made to the lustre of it. Christ is the *horn of salvation* (denoting a plentiful and powerful salvation) which God has raised up, and made to bud, *in the house of his servant David.* David had promised to use his power for God's glory, to cut off the horns of the wicked, and to exalt the horns of the righteous (Ps. 75:10); in recompence for it God here promises to make his horn to bud, for to those that have power, and use it well, more shall be given. (2.) Lasting honour: *I have ordained a lamp for my anointed.* Thou wilt *light my candle,* Ps. 18:28. That lamp is likely to burn brightly which God ordains. A lamp is a successor, for, when a lamp is almost out, another may be lighted by it; it is a succession, for by this means David shall not want a man to stand before God. Christ is the lamp and the light of the world. (3.) Complete victory: *"His enemies,* who have formed designs against him, *will I clothe with shame,* when they shall see their designs baffled." Let the enemies of all good governors expect to be clothed with shame, and especially the enemies of the Lord Jesus and his government, who shall rise, in the great day, *to everlasting shame and contempt.* (4.) Universal prosperity: *Upon himself shall his crown flourish,* that is, his government shall be more and more his honour. This was to have its full accomplishment in Jesus Christ, whose crown of honour and power shall never fade, nor the flowers of it wither. The crowns of earthly princes *endure not to all generations* (Prov. 27:24), but Christ's crown shall endure to all eternity and the crowns reserved for his faithful subjects are such as *fade not away.*

PSALM 133

This psalm is a brief encomium on unity and brotherly love, which, if we did not see the miseries of discord among men, we should think needless; but we cannot say too much, it were well if we could say enough, to persuade people to live together in peace. Some conjecture that David penned this psalm upon occasion of the union between the tribes when they all met unanimously to make him king. It is a psalm of general use to all societies, smaller and larger, civil and sacred. Here is, I. The doctrine laid down of the happiness of brotherly love (*v.* 1). II. The illustration of that doctrine, in two similitudes (*v.* 2, 3). III. The proof of it, in a good reason given for it (*v.* 3); and then we are left to make the application, which we ought to do in singing it, provoking ourselves and one another to holy love. The contents of this psalm in our Bibles, are short, but very proper; it is "the benefit of the communion of saints."

A song of degrees of David.

Verses 1–3

Here see, I. What it is that is commended — *brethren's dwelling together in unity,* not only not quarrelling, and devouring one another, but delighting in each other with mutual endearments, and promoting each other's welfare with mutual services. Sometimes it is chosen, as the best expedient for preserving peace, that brethren should live asunder and at a distance from each other; that indeed may prevent enmity and strife (Gen. 13:9), but the goodness and pleasantness are *for brethren to dwell together* and so *to dwell in unity, to dwell even as one* (so some read it), as having one heart, one soul, one interest. David had many sons by many wives; probably he penned this psalm for their instruction, to engage them to love another, and, if they had done this, much of the mischief that arose in his family would have been happily prevented. The tribes of Israel had long had separate interests during the government of the Judges, and it was often of bad consequence; but now that they were united under one common head he would have them sensible how much it was likely to be for their advantage, especially since now the ark was fixed, and with it the place of their rendezvous for public worship and the centre of their unity. Now let them live in love.

II. How commendable it is: *Behold, how good and how pleasant it is!* It is good in itself, agreeable to the will of God, the conformity of earth to heaven. It is good for us, for our honour and comfort. It is pleasant and pleasing to God and all good men; it brings constant delight to those who do thus live in unity. *Behold, how good!* We cannot conceive or express the goodness and pleasantness of it. Behold it is a rare thing, and therefore admirable. Behold and wonder that there should be so much goodness and pleasantness among men, so much of heaven on this earth! Behold it is an amiable thing, which will attract our hearts. Behold it is an exemplary thing, which, where it is, is to be imitated by us with a holy emulation.

III. How the pleasantness of it is illustrated.

1. It is fragrant as the holy anointing oil, which was strongly perfumed, and diffused its odours, to the great delight of all the bystanders, when it was poured upon the head of Aaron, or his successor the high priest, so plentifully that it ran down the face, even to the collar or binding of the garment, *v.* 2. (1.) This ointment was holy. So must our brotherly love be, with a pure heart, devoted to God. We must love those that are begotten *for his sake that begat,* 1 Jn. 5:1. (2.) This ointment was a composition made up by a divine dispensatory; God appointed the ingredients and the quantities. Thus believers are *taught of God to love one another;* it is a grace of his working in us. (3.) It was very precious, and the like to it was not to be made for any common use. Thus holy love is, in the sight of God, of great price; and that is precious indeed which is so in God's sight. (4.) It was grateful both to Aaron himself and to all about him. So is holy love; it is like *ointment and perfume which rejoice the heart.* Christ's love to mankind was part of that *oil of gladness* with which he was *anointed above his fellows.* (5.) Aaron and his sons were not admitted to minister unto the Lord till they were anointed with this ointment, nor are our services acceptable to God without this holy love; if we have it not we are nothing, 1 Co. 13:1, 2.

2. It is fructifying. It is profitable as well as pleasing; it is *as the dew;* it brings abundance of blessings along with it, as numerous as the drops of dew. It cools the scorching heat of men's passions, as the evening dews cool the air and refresh the earth. It contributes very much to our fruitfulness in every thing that is good; it moistens the heart, and makes it tender and fit to receive the good seed of the word; as, on the contrary, *malice and bitterness* unfit

us to receive it, 1 Pt. 2:1. It is *as the dew of Hermon,* a common hill (for brotherly love is the beauty and benefit of civil societies), *and as the dew that descended upon the mountains of Zion,* a holy hill, for it contributes greatly to the fruitfulness of sacred societies. Both Hermon and Zion will wither without this dew. It is said of the dew that it *tarrieth not for man, nor waiteth for the sons of men,* Mic. 5:7. Nor should our love to our brethren stay for theirs to us (that is publican's love), but should go before it —that is divine love.

IV. The proof of the excellency of brotherly love. Loving people are blessed people. For, 1. They are blessed of God, and therefore blessed indeed: *There,* where brethren dwell together in unity, *the Lord commands the blessing,* a complicated blessing, including all blessings. It is God's prerogative to command the blessing, man can but beg a blessing. Blessings according to the promise are commanded blessings, for he has commanded *his covenant for ever.* Blessings that take effect are commanded blessings, for *he speaks and it is done.* 2. They are everlastingly blessed. The blessing which God commands on those that dwell in love is *life for evermore;* that is the blessing of blessings. Those that dwell in love not only dwell in God, but do already dwell in heaven. As the perfection of love is the blessedness of heaven, so the sincerity of love is the earnest of that blessedness. Those that live in love and peace shall have the God of love and peace with them now, and they shall be with him shortly, with him for ever, in the world of endless love and peace. How good then is it, and how pleasant!

PSALM 134

This is the last of the fifteen songs of degrees; and, if they were at any time sung all together in the temple-service, it is fitly made the conclusion of them, for the design of it is to stir up the ministers to go on with their work in the night, when the solemnities of the day were over. Some make this psalm to be a dialogue. I. In the first two verses, the priests or Levites who sat up all night to keep the watch of the house of the Lord are called upon to spend their time while they were upon the guard, not in idle talk, but in the acts of devotion. II. In the last verse those who were thus called upon to praise God pray for him that gave them the exhortation, either the high priest or the captain of the guard. Or thus: those who did that service did mutually exhort one another and pray for one another. In singing this psalm we must both stir up ourselves to give glory to God and encourage ourselves to hope for mercy and grace from him.

A song of degrees.

Verses 1–3

This psalm instructs us concerning a two-fold blessing:—

I. Our blessing God, that is, speaking well of him, which here we are taught to do, *v.* 1, 2. 1. It is a call to the *Levites* to do it. They were *the servants of the Lord* by office, appointed to minister in holy things; they attended the sanctuary, and kept the charge of the house of the Lord, Num. 3:6, etc. Some of them did *by night stand in the house of the Lord,* to guard the holy things of the temple, that they might not be profaned, and the rich things of the temple, that they might not be plundered. While the ark was in curtains there was the more need of guards upon it. They attended likewise to see that neither the fire on the altar nor the lamps in the candlestick went out. Probably it was usual for some devout and pious Israelites to sit up with them; we read of one that *departed not from the temple night or day,* Lu. 2:37. Now these are here called upon to *blesss the Lord.* Thus they must keep themselves awake by keeping themselves employed. Thus they must redeem time for holy exercises; and how can we spend our time better than in praising God? It would be an excellent piece of husbandry to fill up the vacancies of time with pious meditations and ejaculations; and surely it is a very modest and reasonable to converse with God when we have nothing else to do. Those who stood *in the house of the Lord* must remember where they were, and that holiness and holy work became that house. Let them therefore *bless the Lord;* let them all do it in concert, or each by himself; let them *lift up* their *hands* in the doing of it, in token of the lifting up of their hearts. *Let them lift up their hands in holiness* (so Dr. Hammond reads it) or in sanctification, as it is fit when they lift them up *in the sanctuary;* and let them remember that when they were appointed to wash before they went in to minister they were thereby taught to *lift up holy hands* in prayer and praise. 2. It is a call to us to do it, who, as Christians, are made priests to our God, and Levites, Isa. 66:21. We are the *servants of the Lord;* we have a place and a name in his house, in his sanctuary; we stand before him to minister to him. Even by night we are under his eye and have access to him. Let us therefore *bless the Lord,* and again bless him; think and speak of his glory and goodness. Let us *lift up* our *hands* in prayer, in praise, in vows; let us do our work with diligence and cheerfulness, and an elevation of mind. This exhortation is ushered in with *Behold!* a note commanding attention. Look about you, Sirs, when you are in God's presence, and conduct yourselves accordingly.

II. God's blessing us, and that is doing well for us, which we are here taught to desire, *v.* 3. Whether it is the watchmen's blessing their captain, or the Levites' blessing the high priest, or whoever was their chief (as many take it, because it is in the singular number, *The Lord bless thee*), or whether the blessing is pronounced by one upon many ("*The Lord bless thee,* each of you in particular, thee and thee; you that are blessing God, the Lord bless you"), is not material. We may learn, 1. That we need desire no more to make us happy than to be blessed of the Lord, for those whom he blesses are blessed indeed. 2. That blessings out of Zion, spiritual blessings, the blessings of the covenant, and of communion with God, are the best blessings, which we should be most earnest for. 3. It is a great encouragement to us, when we come to God for a blessing, that it is he who *made heaven and earth,* and therefore has all the blessings of both at his disposal, the upper and nether springs. 4. We ought to beg these blessings, not only for ourselves, but for others also; not only, The Lord bless *me,* but, The Lord bless *thee,* thus testifying our belief of the fulness of divine blessings, that there is enough for others as well as for us, and our good-will also to others. We must pray for those that exhort us. Though *the less is blessed of the greater* (Heb. 7:7), yet the greater must be prayed for by the less.

PSALM 135

This is one of the Hallelujah-psalms; that is the title of it, and that is the Amen of it, both its Alpha and its Omega. I. It begins with a call to praise God, particularly a call to the "servants of the Lord" to praise him, as in the foregoing psalm (*v.* 1–3). II. It goes on to furnish us with matter for praise. God is to be praised, 1. As the God of Jacob (*v.* 4). 2. As the God of gods (*v.* 5). 3. As the God of the whole world (*v.* 6, 7). 4. As a terrible God to the enemies of Israel (*v.* 8–11). 5. As a gracious God to Israel, both in what he had done for them and what he would do (*v.* 12–14). 6. As the only living God, all other gods being vanity and a lie (*v.* 15–18). III. It concludes with another exhortation to all persons concerned to praise God (*v.* 19–21). In singing this psalm our hearts must be filled, as well as our mouths, with the high praises of God.

Verses 1–4

Here is, 1. The duty we are called to — to *praise the Lord,* to *praise his name; praise him,* and again *praise him.* We must not only thank him for what he has done for us, but praise him for what he is in himself and has done for others; take all occasions to speak well of God and to give his truths and ways a good word. 2. The persons that are called upon to do this — the *servants of the Lord,* the priests and Levites *that stand in his house,* and all the devout and pious Israelites that stand *in the courts of his house* to worship there, *v.* 2. Those that have most reason to praise God who are admitted to the privileges of his house, and those see most reason who there behold his beauty and taste his bounty; from them it is expected, for to that end they enjoy their places. Who should praise him if they do not? 3. The reasons why we should praise God. (1.) Because he whom we are to praise *is good,* and goodness is that which every body will speak well of. He is good to all, and we must give him the praise of that. His goodness is his glory, and we must make mention of it to his glory. (2.) Because the work is its own wages: *Sing praises to his name, for it is pleasant.* It is best done with a cheerful spirit, and we shall have the pleasure of having done our duty. It is a heaven upon earth to be praising God; and the pleasure of that should quite put our mouths out of taste for the pleasures of sin. (3.) Because of the peculiar privileges of God's people (*v.* 4): *The Lord hath chosen Jacob to himself,* and therefore Jacob is bound to praise him; for *therefore* God chose a people to himself that they might be unto him *for a name and a praise* (Jer. 13:11), and *therefore* Jacob has abundant matter for praise, being thus dignified and distinguished. *Israel* is God's *peculiar treasure* above all people (Ex. 19:5); they are his *Segullah,* a people appropriated to him, and that he has a delight in, *precious in his sight and honourable.* For this distinguishing surprising favour, if the seed of Jacob do not praise him, they are the most unworthy ungrateful people under the sun.

Verses 5–14

The psalmist had suggested to us the goodness of God, as the proper matter of our cheerful praises; here he suggests to us the greatness of God as the proper matter of our awful praises; and on this he is most copious, because this we are less forward to consider.

I. He asserts the doctrine of God's greatness (*v.* 5): *The Lord is great,* great indeed, who knows no limits of time or place. He asserts it with assurance, "I know that he is so; know it not only by observation of the proofs of it, but by belief of the revelation of it. I know it; I am sure of it; I know it by my own experience of the divine greatness working on my soul." He asserts it with a holy defiance of all pretenders, though they should join in confederacy against him. He is not only above any god, but above all gods, infinitely above them, between him and them there is no comparison.

II. He proves him to be a great God by the greatness of his power, *v.* 6. 1. He has an absolute power, and may do what he will: *Whatsoever the Lord pleased, that did he,* and none could control him, or say unto him, *What dost thou?* He does what he pleases, because he pleases, and gives not an account of any of his matters. 2. He has an almighty power and can do what he will; if he will work, none shall hinder. 3. This absolute almighty power is of universal extent; he does what he will *in heaven, in earth, in the seas,* and in *all the deep places* that are in the bottom of the sea or the bowels of the earth. The gods of the heathen can do nothing; but our God can do any thing and does do every thing.

III. He gives instances of his great power,

1. In the kingdom of nature, *v.* 7. All the powers of nature prove the greatness of the God of nature, from whom they are derived and on whom they depend. The chain of natural causes was not only framed by him at first, but is still preserved by him. (1.) It is by his power that exhalations are drawn up from the terraqueous globe. The heat of the sun raises them, but it has that power from God, and therefore it is given as an instance of the glory of God that *nothing is hidden from the heat* of the sun, Ps. 19:6. *He causes the vapours to ascend* (not only unhelped, but unseen, by us) from the earth, *from the ends of the earth,* that is, from the seas, by which the earth is surrounded. (2.) It is he who, out of those vapours so raised, forms the rain, so that the earth is no loser by the vapours it sends up, for they are returned with advantage in fruitful showers. (3.) Out of the same vapours (such is his wonderful power) he *makes lightnings or the rain;* by them he opens the bottles of heaven, and shakes the clouds, that they may water the earth. Here are fire and water thoroughly reconciled by divine omnipotence. They come together, and yet the water does not quench the fire, nor the fire lick up the water, as fire from heaven did when God pleased, 1 Ki. 18:38. (4.) The same exhalations, to serve another purpose, are converted into winds, which blow where they list, from what point of the compass they will, and we are so far from directing them that we cannot tell whence they come nor whither they go, but God *brings them out of his treasuries* with as much exactness and design as a prudent prince orders money to issue out of his exchequer.

2. In the kingdoms of men; and here he mentions the great things God had formerly done for his people Israel, which were proofs of God's greatness as well as of his goodness, and confirmations of the truth of the scriptures of the Old Testament, which began to be written by Moses, the person employed in working those miracles. Observe God's sovereign dominion and irresistible power, (1.) In bringing Israel out of Egypt, humbling Pharaoh by many plagues, and so forcing him to let them go. These plagues are called *tokens* and *wonders,* because they came not in the common course of providence, but there was something miraculous in each of them. They were *sent upon Pharaoh and all his servants,* his subjects; but the Israelites, whom God claimed for his servants, his son, his first-born, his free-born, were exempted from them, and no plague came nigh their dwelling. The death of the first-

born both of men and cattle was the heaviest of all the plagues, and that which gained the point. (2.) In destroying the kingdoms of Canaan before them, *v.* 10. Those that were in possession of the land designed for Israel had all possible advantages for keeping possession. The people were numerous, and warlike, and confederate against Israel. They were great nations. Yet, if a great nation has a meek and mean-spirited prince, it lies exposed; but these great nations had *mighty kings,* and yet they were all smitten and slain — *Sihon* and *Og,* and *all the kingdoms of Canaan, v.* 10, 11. No power of hell or earth can prevent the accomplishment of the promise of God when the time, the set time, for it has come. (3.) In settling them in the land of promise. He that gives kingdoms to whomsoever he pleases gave Canaan to be a heritage to Israel his people. It came to them by inheritance, for their ancestors had the promise of it, though not the possession; and it descended as an inheritance to their seed. This was done long before, yet God is now praised for it; and with good reason, for the children were now enjoying the benefit of it.

IV. He triumphs in the perpetuity of God's glory and grace. 1. Of his glory (*v.* 13): *Thy name, O God! endures for ever.* God's manifestations of himself to his people have everlasting fruits and consequences. *What God doeth it shall be for ever,* Eccl. 3:14. His name endures for ever in the constant and everlasting praises of his people; his memorial endures, has endured hitherto, and shall still endure throughout all generations of the church. This seems to refer to Ex. 3:15, where, when God had called himself *the God of Abraham, Isaac, and Jacob,* he adds, *This is my name for ever and this is my memorial unto all generations.* God is, and will be, always the same to his church, a gracious, faithful, wonder-working God; and his church is, and will be, the same to him, a thankful praising people; and thus his name *endures for ever.* 2. Of his grace. He will be kind to his people. (1.) He will plead their cause against others that contend with them. *He will judge his people,* that is, he will judge for them, and will not suffer them to be run down. (2.) He will not himself contend for ever with them, but will *repent himself concerning his servants,* and not proceed in his controversy with them; he will be entreated for them, or he will be comforted concerning them; he will return in ways of mercy to them and will delight to do them good. This verse is taken from the song of Moses, Deu. 32:36.

Verses 15–21

The design of these verses is,

I. To arm the people of God against idolatry and all false worship, by showing what sort of gods they were that the heathen worshipped, as we had it before, Ps. 115:4, etc. 1. They were gods of their own making; being so, they could have no power but what their makers gave them, and then what power could their makers receive from them? The images were the *work of men's hands,* and the deities that were supposed to inform them were as much the creatures of men's fancy and imagination. 2. They had the shape of animals, but could not perform the least act, no, not of the *animal* life. They could neither *see,* nor *hear,* nor *speak,* nor so much as *breathe;* and therefore to make them with *eyes,* and *ears,* and *mouths,* and *nostrils,* was such a jest that one would wonder how reasonable creatures could suffer themselves to be so imposed upon as to expect any good from such mock-deities. 3. Their worshippers were therefore as stupid and senseless as they were, both those that made them to be worshipped and those that trusted in them when they were made, *v.* 18. The worshipping of such gods as were the objects of sense, and senseless, made the worshippers sensual and senseless. Let our worshipping a God that is a Spirit make us spiritual and wise.

II. To stir up the people of God to true devotion in the worship of the true God, *v.* 19–21. The more deplorable the condition of the Gentile nations that worship idols is the more are we bound to thank God that we know better. Therefore, 1. Let us set ourselves about the acts of devotion, and employ ourselves in them: *Bless the Lord,* and again and again, *bless the Lord.* In the parallel place (Ps. 115:9–11), by way of inference from the impotency of idols, the duty thus pressed upon us is to *trust in the Lord;* here to *bless him;* by putting our trust in God we give glory to him, and those that depend upon God shall not want matter of thanksgiving to him. All persons that knew God are here called to praise him — the *house of Israel* (the nation in general), the *house of Aaron* and the *house of Levi* (the Lord's ministers that attended in his sanctuary), and all others *that feared the Lord,* though they were not of the house of Israel. 2. Let God have the glory of all: *Blessed be the Lord.* The tribute of praise arises *out of Zion.* All God's works do praise him, but his saints bless him; and they need not go far to pay their tribute, for he *dwells in Jerusalem,* in his church, which they are members of, so that he is always nigh unto them to receive their homage. The condescensions of his grace, in dwelling with men upon the earth, call for our grateful and thankful returns, and our repeated Hallelujahs.

PSALM 136

The scope of this psalm is the same with that of the foregoing psalm, but there is something very singular in the composition of it; for the latter half of each verse is the same, repeated throughout the psalm, "for his mercy endureth for ever," and yet no vain repetition. It is allowed that such burdens, or "keepings," as we call them, add very much to the beauty of a song, and help to make it moving and affecting; nor can any verse contain more weighty matter, or more worthy to be thus repeated, than this, that God's mercy endureth for ever; and the repetition of it here twenty-six times intimates, 1. That God's mercies to his people are thus repeated and drawn, as it were, with a continuando from the beginning to the end, with a progress and advance in infinitum. 2. That in every particular favour we ought to take notice of the mercy of God, and to take favour we ought to take notice of the mercy of God, and to take notice of it as enduring still, the same now that it has been, and enduring for ever, the same always that it is. 3. That the everlasting continuance of the mercy of God is very much his honour and that which he glories in, and very much the saints' comfort and that which they glory in. It is that which therefore our hearts should be full of and greatly affected with, so that the most frequent mention of it, instead of cloying us, should raise us the more, because it will be the subject of our praise to all eternity. This most excellent sentence, that God's mercy endureth for ever, is magnified above all the truths concerning God, not only by the repetition of it here, but by the signal tokens of divine acceptance with which God owned the singing of it, both in Solomon's time (2 Chr. 5:13, when they sang these words, "for his mercy endureth for ever," the house was filled with a cloud) and in Jehoshaphat's time (when they sang these words, God gave them victory, 2 Chr. 20:21, 22), which should make us love to sing, "His mercies sure do still endure, eternally." We must praise God, I. As great and good in himself (*v.* 1–3). II. As the Creator of the world (*v.* 5–9). III. As Israel's God and Saviour (*v.* 10–22). IV. As our Redeemer (*v.* 23, 24). V. As the great benefactor of the whole creation, and God over all, blessed for evermore (*v.* 25, 26).

Verses 1–9

The duty we are here again and again called to is to *give thanks,* to *offer the sacrifice of praise continually,* not the fruits of our ground or cattle, but *the fruit of our lips, giving thanks to his name,* Heb. 13:15. We are never so earnestly called upon to pray and repent as to *give thanks;* for it is the will of God that we should abound most in the most pleasant exercises of religion, in that which is the work of heaven. Now here observe, 1. Whom we must give thanks to — to him that we receive all good from, *to the Lord,* Jehovah, Israel's God (*v.* 1), *the God of gods,* the God whom angels adore, from whom magistrates derive their power, and by whom all pretended deities are and shall be conquered (*v.* 2), *to the Lord of lords,* the Sovereign of all sovereigns, the stay and supporter of all supports; *v.* 3. In all our adorations we must have an eye to God's excellency as transcendent, and to his power and dominion as incontestably and uncontrollably supreme. 2. What we must give thanks for, not as the Pharisee that made all his thanksgivings terminate in his own praise (*God, I thank thee,* that I am so and so), but directing them all to God's glory. (1.) We must give thanks to God for his goodness and mercy (*v.* 1): *Give thanks to the Lord,* not only because he does good, but because he is good (all the streams must be traced up to the fountain), not only because he is merciful to us, but because his mercy endures for ever, and will be drawn out to those that shall come after us. We must give thanks to God, not only for that mercy which is now handed out to us here on earth, but for that which shall endure for ever in the glories and joys of heaven. (2.) We must give God thanks for the instances of his power and wisdom. In general (*v.* 4), he *along does great wonders.* The contrivance is wonderful, the design being laid by infinite wisdom; the performance is wonderful, being put in execution by infinite power. He alone does marvellous things; none besides can do such things, and he does them without the assistance or advice of any other. More particularly, [1.] He made the heavens, and stretched them out, and in them we not only see his wisdom and power, but we taste his mercy in their benign influences; as long as the heavens endure the mercy of God endures in them, *v.* 5. [2.] He raised the earth out of the waters when he caused the dry land to appear, that it might be fit to be a habitation for man, and therein also his mercy to man still endures (*v.* 6); for *the earth hath he given to the children of men,* and all its products. [3.] Having made both heaven and earth, he settled a correspondence between them, notwithstanding their distance, by making the sun, moon, and stars, which he placed in the firmament of heaven, to shed their light and influences upon this earth, *v.* 7–9. These are called the *great lights* because they appear so to us, for otherwise astronomers could tell us that the moon is less than many of the stars, but, being nearer to the earth, it seems much greater. They are said to *rule,* not only because they govern the seasons of the year, but because they are useful to the world, and benefactors are the best rulers, Lu. 22:25. But the empire is divided, one *rules by day,* the *other by night* (at least, *the stars*), and yet all are subject to God's direction and disposal. Those rulers, therefore, which the Gentiles idolized, are the world's servants and God's subjects. *Sun, stand thou still, and thou moon.*

Verses 10–22

The great things God for Israel, when he first formed them into a people, and set up his kingdom among them, are here mentioned, as often elsewhere in the psalms, as instances both of the power of God and of the particular kindness he had for Israel. See Ps. 135:8, etc. 1. He brought them out of Egypt, *v.* 10–12. That was a mercy which endured long to them, and our redemption by Christ, which was typified by that, does indeed endure for ever, for it is an eternal redemption. Of all the plagues of Egypt, none is mentioned but the death of the first-born, because that was the conquering plague; by that God, who in all the plagues distinguished the Israelites from the Egyptians, brought them at last from among them, not by a wile, but with a strong hand and an arm stretched out to reach far and do great things. These miracles of mercy, as they proved Moses's commission to give law to Israel, so they laid Israel under lasting obligations to obey that law, Ex. 20:2. 2. He forced them a way through the Red Sea, which obstructed them at their first setting out. By the power he has to control the common course of nature he *divided the sea into two parts,* between which he opened a path, and made Israel to pass between the parts, now that they were to enter into covenant with him; see Jer. 34:18. He not only divided the sea, but gave his people courage to go through it when it was divided, which was an instance of God's power over men's hearts, as the former of his power over the waters. And, to make it a miracle of justice as well as mercy, the same Red Sea that was a lane to the Israelites was a grave to their pursuers. There he shook off Pharaoh and his host. 3. He conducted them through a vast howling wilderness (*v.* 16); there he led them and fed them. Their camp was victualled and fortified by a constant series of miracles for forty years; though they loitered and wandered there, they were not lost. And in this the mercy of God, and the constancy of that mercy, were the more observable because they often provoked him in the wilderness and grieved him in the desert. 4. He destroyed kings before them, to make room for them (*v.* 17, 18), not deposed and banished them, but smote and slew them, in which appeared his wrath against them, but his mercy, his never-failing mercy, to Israel. And that which magnified it was that they were *great kings* and *famous kings,* yet God subdued them as easily as if they had been the least, and weakest, and meanest, of the children of men. They were wicked kings, and then their grandeur and lustre would not secure them from the justice of God. The more great and famous they were the more did God's mercy to Israel appear in giving such kings for them. Sihon and Og are particularly mentioned, because they were the first two that were conquered on the other side Jordan, *v.* 19, 20. It is good to enter into the detail of God's favours and not to view them in the gross, and in each instance to observe, and own, that God's *mercy endureth for ever.* 5. He put them in possession of a good land, *v.* 21, 22. He whose the earth is, and the fulness thereof, the world and those that dwell therein, took land from one people and gave it to another, as pleased him. The *iniquity of the Amorites was now full,* and therefore it was taken from them.

Israel was his *servant,* and, though they had been provoking in the wilderness, yet he intended to have some service out of them, for *to them pertained the service of God.* As he said to the Egyptians, *Let my people go,* so to the Canaanites, *Let my people in,* that they may serve me. In this *God's mercy* to them *endureth for ever,* because it was a figure of the heavenly Canaan, the *mercy of our Lord Jesus Christ unto eternal life.*

Verses 23–26

God's everlasting mercy is here celebrated, 1. In the redemption of his church, *v.* 23, 24. In the many redemptions wrought for the Jewish church out of the hands of their oppressors (when, in the years of their servitude, their estate was very low, God remembered them, and raised them up saviours, the judges, and David, at length, by whom God gave them rest from all their enemies), but especially in the great redemption of the universal church, of which these were types, we have a great deal of reason to say, *"He remembered us,* the children of men, *in our low estate,* in our lost estate, *for his mercy endureth for ever;* he sent his Son to redeem us from sin, and death, and hell, and all our spiritual enemies, *for his mercy endureth for ever;* he was sent to redeem us, and not the angels that sinned, for his mercy endureth for ever." 2. In the provision he makes for all the creatures (*v.* 25): *He gives food to all flesh.* It is an instance of the mercy of God's providence that wherever he has given life he gives food agreeable and sufficient; and he is a good housekeeper that provides for so large a family. 3. In all his glories, and all his gifts (*v.* 26): *Give thanks to the God of heaven.* This denotes him to be a glorious God, and the glory of his mercy is to be taken notice of in our praises. The *riches of his glory* are displayed in the *vessels of his mercy,* Rom. 9:23. It also denotes him to be the great benefactor, *for every good and perfect gift is from above,* from the Father of lights, the *God of heaven;* and we should trace every stream to the fountain. This and that particular mercy may perhaps endure but a while, but the mercy that is in God *endures for ever;* it is an inexhaustible fountain.

PSALM 137

There are divers psalms which are thought to have been penned in the latter days of the Jewish church, when prophecy was near expiring and the canon of the Old Testament ready to be closed up, but none of them appears so plainly to be of a late date as this, which was penned when the people of God were captives in Babylon, and there insulted over by these proud oppressors; probably it was towards the latter end of their captivity; for now they saw the destruction of Babylon hastening on apace (*v.* 8), which would be their discharge. It is a mournful psalm, a lamentation; and the Septuagint makes it one of the lamentations of Jeremiah, naming him for the author of it. Here I. The melancholy captives cannot enjoy themselves (*v.* 1, 2). II. They cannot humour their proud oppressors (*v.* 3, 4). III. They cannot forget Jerusalem (*v.* 5, 6). IV. They cannot forgive Edom and Babylon (*v.* 7–9). In singing this psalm we must be much affected with the concernments of the church, especially that part of it that is in affliction, laying the sorrows of God's people near our hearts, comforting ourselves in the prospect of the deliverance of the church and the ruin of its enemies, in due time, but carefully avoiding all personal animosities, and not mixing the leaven of malice with our sacrifices.

Verses 1–6

We have here the daughter of Zion covered with a cloud, and dwelling with the daughter of Babylon; the people of God in tears, but sowing in tears. Observe,

I. The mournful posture they were in as to their affairs and as to their spirits. 1. They were posted *by the rivers of Babylon,* in a strange land, a great way from their own country, whence they were brought as prisoners of war. The land of Babylon was now a house of bondage to that people, as Egypt had been in their beginning. Their conquerors quartered them *by the rivers,* with design to employ them there, and keep them to work in their galleys; or perhaps they chose it as the most melancholy place, and therefore most suitable to their sorrowful spirits. If they must build houses there (Jer. 29:5), it shall not be in the cities, the places of concourse, but by the rivers, the places of solitude, where they might mingle their tears with the streams. We find some of them by the *river Chebar* (Eze. 1:3), others by the *river Ulai,* Dan. 8:2. 2. There they *sat down* to indulge their grief by poring on their miseries. Jeremiah had taught them under this yoke to *sit alone,* and *keep silence,* and *put their mouths in the dust,* Lam. 3:28, 29. "We sat down, as those that expected to stay, and were content, since it was the will of God that it must be so." 3. Thoughts of Zion drew tears from their eyes; and it was not a sudden passion of weeping, such as we are sometimes put into by a trouble that surprises us, but they were deliberate tears (we *sat down and wept*), tears with consideration — we *wept when we remembered Zion,* the holy hill on which the temple was built. Their affection to God's house swallowed up their concern for their own houses. They remembered Zion's former glory and the satisfaction they had had in Zion's courts, Lam. 1:7. *Jerusalem remembered, in the days of her misery, all her pleasant things which she had in the days of old,* Ps. 42:4. They remembered Zion's present desolations, and *favoured the dust thereof,* which was a good sign that the time for God to favour it was not far off, Ps. 102:13, 14. 4. They laid by their instruments of music (*v.* 2): *We hung our harps upon the willows.* (1.) The harps they used for their own diversion and entertainment. These they laid aside, both because it was their judgment that they ought not to use them now that God called to weeping and mourning (Isa. 22:12), and their spirits were so sad that they had no hearts to use them; they brought their harps with them, designing perhaps to use them for the alleviating of their grief, but it proved so great that it would not admit the experiment. Music makes some people melancholy. *As vinegar upon nitre, so is he that sings songs to a heavy heart.* (2.) The harps they used in God's worship, the Levites' harps. These they did not throw away, hoping they might yet again have occasion to use them, but they laid them aside because they had no present use for them; God had cut them out other work by *turning their feasting into mourning and their songs into lamentations,* Amos 8:10. Every thing is beautiful in its season. They did not hide their harps in the bushes, or the hollows of the rocks; but hung them up in view, that the sight of them might affect them with this deplorable change. Yet perhaps they were faulty in doing this; for praising God is never out of season; it is his will that we should *in every thing give thanks,* Isa. 24:15, 16.

II. The abuses which their enemies put upon them when they were in this melancholy condition, *v.* 3. They had *carried them away captive* from their own land and then *wasted them* in the land of their captivity, took what little they had from them. But this was not enough; to complete their woes they insulted over them: They *required of us mirth and a song.* Now, 1. This was very barbarous and inhuman; even an enemy, in misery, is to be pitied and not trampled upon. It argues a base and sordid spirit to upbraid those that are in distress either with their former joys or with their present griefs, or to challenge those to be merry who, we know, are out of tune for it. This is adding affliction to the afflicted. 2. It was very profane and impious. No songs would serve them but the *songs of Zion,* with which God had been honoured; so that in this demand they reflected upon God himself as Belshazzar, when he drank wine in temple-bowls. Their enemies *mocked at their sabbaths,* Lam. 1:7.

III. The patience wherewith they bore these abuses, *v.* 4. They had laid by their harps, and would not resume them, no, not to ingratiate themselves with those at whose mercy they lay; they would not answer those fools according to their folly. Profane scoffers are not to be humoured, nor pearls cast before swine. David prudently *kept silence even from good* when the *wicked were before him,* who, he knew, would ridicule what he said and make a jest of it, Ps. 39:1, 2. The reason they gave is very mild and pious: *How shall we sing the Lord's song in a strange land?* They do not say, "How shall we sing when we are so much in sorrow?" If that had been all, they might perhaps have put a force upon themselves so far as to oblige their masters with a song; but "It is the *Lord's song;* it is a sacred thing; it is peculiar to the temple-service, and therefore we dare not sing it in the land of a stranger, among idolaters." We must not serve common mirth, much less profane mirth, with any thing that is appropriated to God, who is sometimes to be honoured by a religious silence as well as by religious speaking.

IV. The constant affection they retained for Jerusalem, the city of their solemnities, even now that they were in Babylon. Though their enemies banter them for talking so much of Jerusalem, and even doting upon it, their love to it is not in the least abated; it is what they may be jeered for, but will never be jeered out of, *v.* 5, 6. Observe,

1. How these pious captives stood affected to Jerusalem. (1.) Their heads were full of it. It was always in their minds; they remembered it; they did not forget it, though they had been long absent from it; many of them had never seen it, nor knew any thing of it but by report, and by what they had read in the scripture, yet it was graven upon the palms of their hands, and even its ruins were continually before them, which was ann evidence of their faith in the promise of its restoration in due time. In their daily prayers they opened their windows towards Jerusalem; and how then could they forget it? (2.) Their hearts were full of it. They *preferred* it *above* their *chief joy,* and therefore they remembered it and could not forget it. What we love we love to think of. Those that rejoice in God do, for his sake, make Jerusalem their joy, and prefer it before that, whatever it is, which is the head of their joy, which is dearest to them in this world. A godly man will prefer a public good before any private satisfaction or gratification whatsoever.

2. How stedfastly they resolved to keep up this affection, which they express by a solemn imprecation of mischief to themselves if they should let it fall: "Let me be for ever disabled either to sing or play on the harp if I so far forget the religion of my country as to make use of my songs and harps for the pleasing of Babylon's sons or the praising of Babylon's gods. *Let my right hand forget her art"* (which the hand of an expert musician never can, unless it be withered), "nay, *let my tongue cleave to the roof of my mouth,* if I have not a good word to say for Jerusalem wherever I am." Though they dare not sing Zion's songs among the Babylonians, yet they cannot forget them, but, as soon as ever the present restraint is taken off, they will sing them as readily as ever, notwithstanding the long disuse.

Verses 7–9

The pious Jews in Babylon, having afflicted themselves with the thoughts of the ruins of Jerusalem, here please themselves with the prospect of the ruin of her impenitent implacable enemies; but this not from a spirit of revenge, but from a holy zeal for the glory of God and the honour of his kingdom.

I. The Edomites will certainly be reckoned with, and all others that were accessaries to the destruction of Jerusalem, that were aiding and abetting, that *helped forward the affliction* (Zec. 1:15) and triumphed in it, that *said, in the day of Jerusalem,* the day of her judgment, *"Rase it, rase it to the foundations;* down with it, down with it; do not leave one stone upon another." Thus they made the Chaldean army more furious, who were already so enraged that they needed no spur. Thus they put shame upon Israel, who would be looked upon as a people worthy to be cut off when their next neighbours had such an ill-will to them. And all this was a fruit of the old enmity of Esau against Jacob, because he got the birthright and the blessing, and a branch of that more ancient enmity between the seed of the woman and the seed of the serpent: *Lord, remember* them, says the psalmist, which is an appeal to his justice against them. Far be it from us to avenge ourselves, if ever it should be in our power, but we will leave it to him who has said, *Vengeance is mine.* Note, Those that are glad at calamities, especially the calamities of Jerusalem, shall not go unpunished. Those that are confederate with the persecutors of good people, and stir them up, and set them on, and are pleased with what they do, shall certainly be called to an account for it against another day, and God will remember it against them.

II. Babylon is the principal, and it will come to her turn too to drink of the cup of tremblings, the very dregs of it (*v.* 8, 9): *O daughter of Babylon!* proud and secure as thou art, we know well, by the scriptures of truth, thou *art to be destroyed,* or (as Dr. Hammond reads it) *who art the destroyer.* The destroyers shall be destroyed, Rev. 13:10. And perhaps it is with reference to this that the man of sin, the head of the New-Testament Babylon, is called a *son of perdition,* 2 Th. 2:3. The destruction of Babylon being foreseen as a sure destruction (thou *art to be destroyed*), it is spoken of, 1. As a just destruction. She shall be paid in her own coin: "Thou shalt be served *as thou hast served us,* as barbarously used by the destroyers as we have been by thee," See Rev. 18:6. Let not those expect to find mercy who, when they had power, did not show mercy. 2. As an utter destruction. The very little ones of Babylon, when it is taken by storm, and all in it are put to the sword, shall be dashed to pieces by the enraged and merciless conqueror. None escape if these little ones perish. Those are the seed of another generation; so that, if they be cut off, the ruin will be not only total, as Jerusalem's was, but final. It is sunk like a millstone into the sea, never to rise. 3. As a destruction which should reflect honour upon the instruments of it. Happy shall those be that do it; for they are fulfilling God's counsels; and therefore he calls Cyrus, who did it, his *servant*, his *shepherd*, his *anointed* (Isa. 44:28; 45:1), and the soldiers that were employed in it his *sanctified ones*, Isa. 13:3. They are making way for the enlargement of God's Israel, and happy are those who are in any way serviceable to that. The fall of the New-Testament Babylon will be the triumph of all the saints, Rev. 19:1.

PSALM 138

It does not appear, nor is it material to enquire, upon what occasion David penned this psalm; but in it, I. He looks back with thankfulness upon the experiences he had had of God's goodness to him (*v.* 1–3). II. He looks forward with comfort, in hopes, 1. That others would go on to praise God like him (*v.* 4, 5). 2. That God would go on to do good to him (*v.* 6–8). In singing this psalm we must in like manner devote ourselves to God's praise and glory and repose ourselves in his power and goodness.

A psalm of David.

Verses 1–5

I. How he would praise God, compare Ps. 111:1. 1. He will praise him with sincerity and zeal — "*With my heart, with my whole heart,* with that which is within me and with all that is within me, with uprightness of intention and fervency of affection, inward impressions agreeing with outward expressions." 2. With freedom and boldness: *Before the gods will I sing praise unto thee,* before the princes, and judges, and great men, either those of other nations that visited him or those of his own nation that attended on him, even in their presence. He will not only praise God with his heart, which we may do by pious ejaculations in any company, but will sing praise if there be occasion. Note, Praising God is work which the greatest of men need not be ashamed of; it is the work of angels, the work of heaven. *Before the angels* (so some understand it), that is, in religious assemblies, where there is a special presence of angels, 1 Co. 11:10. 3. In the way that God had appointed: *I will worship towards thy holy temple.* The priests alone went into the temple; the people, at the nearest, did but worship towards it, and that they might do at a distance. Christ is our temple, and towards him we must look with an eye of faith, as Mediator between us and God, in all our praises of him. Heaven is God's holy temple, and thitherward we must lift up our eyes in all our addresses to God. *Our Father in heaven.*

II. What he would praise God for. 1. For the fountain of his comforts — *for thy lovingkindness and for thy truth,* for thy goodness and for thy promise, mercy hidden in thee and mercy revealed by thee, that God is a gracious God in himself and has engaged to be so to all those that trust in him. *For thou hast magnified thy word* (thy promise, which is truth) *above all thy name.* God has made himself known to us in many ways in creation and providence, but most clearly by his word. The judgments of his mouth are magnified even above those of his hand, and greater things are done by them. The wonders of grace exceed the wonders of nature; and what is discovered of God by revelation is much greater than what is discovered by reason. In what God had done for David his faithfulness to his work appeared more illustriously, and redounded more to his glory, than any other of his attributes. Some good interpreters understand it of Christ, the essential Word, and of his gospel, which are magnified above all the discoveries God had before made of himself to the fathers. He that magnified the law, and made that honourable, magnifies the gospel much more. 2. For the streams flowing from that fountain, in which he himself had tasted that the Lord is gracious, *v.* 3. He had been in affliction, and he remembers, with thankfulness, (1.) The sweet communion he then had with God. He cried, he prayed, and prayed earnestly, and God answered him, gave him to understand that his prayer was accepted and should have a gracious return in due time. The intercourse between God and his saints is carried on by his promises and their prayers. (2.) The sweet communications he then had from God: *Thou strength-*

enedst me with strength in my soul. This was the answer to his prayer, for God gives more than good words, Ps. 20:6. Observe, [1.] It was a speedy answer: *In the day when I cried.* Note, Those that trade with heaven by prayer grow rich by quick returns. *While we are yet speaking God hears,* Isa. 65:24. [2.] It was a spiritual answer. God gave him strength in his soul, and that is a real and valuable answer to the prayer of faith in the day of affliction. If God give us strength in our souls to bear the burdens, resist the temptations, and do the duties of an afflicted state, if he strengthen us to keep hold of himself by faith, to maintain the peace of our own minds and to wait with patience for the issue, we must own that he has answered us, and we are bound to be thankful.

III. What influence he hoped that his praising God would have upon others, *v.* 4, 5. David was himself a king, and therefore he hoped that kings would be wrought upon by his experiences, and his example, to embrace religion; and, if kings became religious, their kingdoms would be every way better. Now, 1. This may have reference to the kings that were neighbours to David, as Hiram and others. "They shall all praise thee." When they visited David, and, after his death, when they sought the presence of Solomon (as *all the kings of the earth* are expressly said to have done, 2 Chr. 9:23), they readily joined in the worship of the God of Israel. 2. It may look further, to the calling of the Gentiles and the discipling of all nations by the gospel of Christ, of whom it is said that *all kings shall fall down before him,* Ps. 72:11. Now it is here foretold, (1.) That *the kings of the earth shall hear the words of God.* All that came near David should hear them from him, Ps. 119:46. In the latter days the preachers of the gospel should be sent into all the world. (2.) That then they shall praise God, as all those have reason to do that hear his word, and receive it in the light and love of it, Acts 13:48. (3.) That they shall *sing in the ways of the Lord,* in the ways of his providence and grace towards them; they shall rejoice in God, and give glory to him, however he is pleased to deal with them in the ways of their duty and obedience to him. Note, Those that walk in the ways of the Lord have reason to sing in those ways, to go on in them with a great deal of cheerfulness, for they are ways of pleasantness, and it becomes us to be pleasant in them; and, if we are so, *great is the glory of the Lord.* It is very much for the honour of God that kings should walk in his ways, and that all those who walk in them should sing in them, and so proclaim to all the world that he is a good Master and his work its own wages.

Verses 6–8

David here comforts himself with three things: —

I. The favour God bears to his humble people (*v.* 6): *Though the Lord be high,* and neither needs any of his creatures nor can be benefited by them, *yet has he respect unto the lowly,* smiles upon them as well pleased with them, overlooks heaven and earth to cast a gracious look upon them (Isa. 57:15; 66:1), and, sooner or later, he will put honour upon them, while *he knows the proud afar off,* knows them, but disowns them and rejects them, how proudly soever they pretend to his favour. Dr. Hammond makes this to be the sum of that gospel which the kings of the earth shall hear and welcome — that penitent sinners shall be accepted of God, but the impenitent cast out; witness the instance of the Pharisee and the publican, Lu. 18.

II. The care God takes of his afflicted oppressed people, *v.* 7. David, though a great and good man, expects to *walk in the midst of trouble,* but encourages himself with hope, 1. That God would comfort him: "When my spirit is ready to sink and fail, *thou* shalt *revive me,* and make me easy and cheerful under my troubles." Divine consolations have enough in them to revive us even when we walk in the midst of troubles and are ready to die away for fear. 2. That he would protect him, and plead his cause: "*Thou* shalt *stretch forth thy hand,* though not against my enemies to destroy them, yet *against the wrath of my enemies,* to restrain that and set bounds to it." 3. That he would in due time work deliverance for him: *Thy right hand shall save me.* As he has one hand to stretch out against his enemies, so he has another to save his own people. Christ is the right hand of the Lord, that shall save all those who serve him.

III. The assurance we have that whatever good work

God has begun in and for his people he will perform it (*v.* 8): *The Lord will perfect that which concerns me,* 1. That which is most needful for me; and he knows best what is so. We *are careful and cumbered about many things* that do not concern us, but he knows what are the things that really are of consequence to us (Mt. 6:32) and he will order them for the best. 2. That which we are most concerned about. Every good man is most concerned about his duty to God and his happiness in God, that the former may be faithfully done and the latter effectually secured; and if indeed these are the things that our hearts are most upon, and concerning which we are most solicitous, there is a good work begun in us, and he that has begun it will perfect it, we may be confident he will, Phil. 1:6. Observe, (1.) What ground the psalmist builds this confidence upon: *Thy mercy, O Lord! endures for ever.* This he had made very much the matter of his praise (Ps. 136), and therefore he could here with the more assurance make it the matter of his hope. For, if we give God the glory of his mercy, we may take to ourselves the comfort of it. Our hopes that we shall persevere must be founded, not upon our own strength, for that will fail us, but upon the mercy of God, for that will not fail. It is well pleaded, "*Lord, thy mercy endures for ever;* let me be for ever a monument of it." (2.) What use he makes of this confidence; it does not supersede, but quicken prayer; he turns his expectation into a petition: "*Forsake not,* do not let go, *the work of thy own hands.* Lord, I am the work of thy own hands, my soul is so, do not forsake me; my concerns are so, do not lay by thy care of them." Whatever good there is in us it is the work of God's own hands; *he works in us both to will and to do;* it will fail if he forsake it; but his glory, as Jehovah, a perfecting God, is so much concerned in the progress of it to the end that we may in faith pray, "Lord, do not forsake it." Whom he loves he loves to the end; and, as for God, his work is perfect.

PSALM 139

Some of the Jewish doctors are of opinion that this is the most excellent of all the psalms of David; and a very pious devout meditation it is upon the doctrine of God's omniscience, which we should therefore have our hearts fixed upon and filled with in singing this psalm. I. This doctrine is here asserted, and fully laid down (*v.* 1–6). II. It is confirmed by two arguments: — 1. God is every where present; therefore he knows all (*v.* 7–12). 2. He made us, therefore he knows us (*v.* 13–16). III. Some inferences are drawn from this doctrine. 1. It may fill us with pleasing admiration of God (*v.* 17, 18). 2. With a holy dread and detestation of sin and sinners (*v.* 19–22). 3. With a holy satisfaction in our own integrity, concerning which we may appeal to God (*v.* 23, 24). This great and self-evident truth, That God knows our hearts, and the hearts of all the children of men, if we did but mix faith with it and seriously consider it and apply it, would have a great influence upon our holiness and upon our comfort.

To the chief musician. A psalm of David.

Verses 1–6

David here lays down this great doctrine, That the God with whom we have to do has a perfect knowledge of us, and that all the motions and actions both of our inward and of our outward man are naked and open before him.

I. He lays down this doctrine in the way of an address to God; he says it to him, acknowledging it to him, and giving him the glory of it. Divine truths look fully as well when they are prayed over as when they are preached over, and much better than when they are disputed over. When we speak of God to him himself we shall find ourselves concerned to speak with the utmost degree both of sincerity and reverence, which will be likely to make the impressions the deeper.

II. He lays it down in a way of application to himself, not, "Thou hast known *all;*" but, "Thou hast known *me;* that is it which I am most concerned to believe and which it will be most profitable for me to consider." Then we know these things for our good when we know them *for ourselves,* Job 5:27. When we acknowledge, "Lord, all souls are thine," we must add, "My soul is thine; thou that hatest all sin hatest my sin; thou that art good to all, good to Israel, art good to me." So here, "*Thou hast searched me, and known me;* known me as thoroughly as we know that which we have most diligently and exactly searched into." David was a king, and *the hearts of kings are unsearchable* to their subjects (Prov. 25:3), but they are not so to their Sovereign.

III. He descends to particulars: "Thou knowest me wherever I am and whatever I am doing, me and all that belongs to me." 1. *"Thou knowest* me and all my motions, *my down-sitting* to rest, *my up-rising* to work, with what temper of mind I compose myself when I sit down and stir up myself when I rise up, what my soul reposes itself in as its stay and support, what it aims at and reaches towards as its felicity and end. Thou knowest me when I come home, how I walk before my house, and when I go abroad, on what errands I go." 2. "Thou knowest all my imaginations. Nothing is more close and quick than thought; it is always unknown to others; it is often unobserved by ourselves, and yet *thou understandest my thought afar off.* Though my thoughts be ever so foreign and distant from one another, thou understandest the chain of them, and canst make out their connexion, when so many of them slip my notice that I myself cannot." Or, *"Thou understandest them afar off,* even before I think them, and long after I have thought them and have myself forgotten them." Or, *"Thou understandest them from afar;* from the height of heaven thou seest into the depths of the heart," Ps. 33:14. 3. "Thou knowest me and all my designs and undertakings; *thou compassest* every particular *path; thou siftest* (or *winnowest*) *my path"* (so some), "so as thoroughly to distinguish between the good and evil of what I do," as by sifting we separate between the corn and the chaff. All our actions are ventilated by the judgment of God, Ps. 17:3. God takes notice of every step we take, every right step and every by-step. He is *acquainted with all* our *ways,* intimately acquainted with them; he knows what rule we walk by, what end we walk towards, what company we walk with. 4. *"Thou knowest* me in all my retirements; thou knowest *my lying down;* when I am withdrawn from all company, and am reflecting upon what has passed all day and composing myself to rest, thou knowest what I have in my heart and with what thought I go to bed." 5. "Thou knowest me, and all I say (*v.* 4): *There is not a word in my tongue,* not a vain word, nor a good word, *but thou knowest it altogether,* knowest what it meant, from what thought it came, and with what design it was uttered. There is not a word at my tongue's end, ready to be spoken, yet checked and kept in, but thou knowest it." *When there is not a word in my tongue, O Lord! thou knowest all* (so some read it); for thoughts are words to God. 6. "Thou knowest me in every part of me: *Thou hast beset me behind and before,* so that, go which way I will, I am under thy eye and cannot possibly escape it. Thou hast *laid thy hand upon me,* and I cannot run away from thee." Wherever we are we are under the eye and hand of God. perhaps it is an allusion to the physician's laying his hand upon his patient to feel how his pulse beats or what temper he is in. God knows us as we know not only what we see, but what we feel and have our hands upon. *All his saints are in his hand.*

IV. He speaks of it with admiration (*v.* 6): *It is too wonderful for me; it is high.* 1. "Thou hast such a knowledge of me as I have not of myself, nor can have. I cannot take notice of all my own thoughts, nor make such a judgment of myself as thou makest of me."? 2. "It is such a knowledge as I cannot comprehend, much less describe. That thou knowest all things I am sure, but how I cannot tell." We cannot by searching find out how God searches and finds out us; nor do we know how we are known.

Verses 7–16

It is of great use to us to know the certainty of the things wherein we have been instructed, that we may not only believe them, but be able to tell why we believe them, and to give a reason of the hope that is in us. David is sure that God perfectly knows him and all his ways,

I. Because he is always under his eye. If God is omnipresent, he must needs be omniscient; but he is omnipresent; this supposes the infinite and immensity of his being, from which follows the ubiquity of his presence; heaven and earth include the whole creation, and the Creator fills both (Jer. 23:24); he not only knows both, and governs both, but he fills both. Every part of the creation is under God's intuition and influence. David here acknowledges this also with application and sees himself thus open before God.

1. No flight can remove us out of God's presence: *"Whither shall I go from thy Spirit, from thy presence,* that is, from thy spiritual presence, from thyself, who art a Spirit?" *God is a Spirit,* and therefore it is folly to think that because we cannot see him he cannot see us: *Whither shall I flee from thy presence?* Not that he desired to go away from God; no, he desired nothing more than to be near him; but he only puts the case, "Suppose I should be so foolish as to think of getting out of thy sight, that I might shake off the awe of thee, suppose I should think of revolting from my obedience to thee, or of disowning a dependence on thee and of shifting for myself, alas! whither can I go?" A heathen could say, *Quocunque te flexeris, ibi Deum videbis occurrentem tibi — Whithersoever thou turnest thyself, thou wilt see God meeting thee.* Seneca. He specifies the most remote and distant places, and counts upon meeting God in them. (1.) In heaven: *"If I ascend* thither, as I hope to do shortly, *thou art there,* and it will be my eternal bliss to be with thee there." Heaven is a vast large place, replenished with an innumerable company, and yet there is no escaping God's eye there, in any corner, or in any crowd. The inhabitants of that world have as necessary a dependence upon God, and lie as open to his strict scrutiny, as the inhabitants of this. (2.) *In hell* — in *Sheol,* which may be understood of the depth of the earth, the very centre of it. Should we dig as deep as we can under ground, and think to hide ourselves there, we should be mistaken; God knows that path which the vulture's eye never saw, and to him the earth is all surface. Or it may be understood of the state of the dead. When we are removed out of the sight of all living, yet not out of the sight of the living God; from his eye we cannot hide ourselves in the grave. Or it maybe understood of the place of the damned: *If I make my bed in hell* (an uncomfortable place to make a bed in, where there is no rest day or night, yet thousands will make their bed for ever in those flames), *behold, thou art there,* in thy power and justice. God's wrath is the fire which will there burn everlastingly, Rev. 14:10. (3.) In the remotest corners of this world: *"If I take the wings of the morning,* the rays of the morning-light (called the wings of the sun, Mal. 4:2), than which nothing more swift, and flee upon them to *the uttermost parts of the sea,* or of the earth (Job 38:12, 13), should I flee to the most distant and obscure islands (the *ultima Thule,* the *Terra incognita*), I should find thee there; *there shall thy hand lead me,* as far as I go, *and thy right hand hold me,* that I can go no further, that I cannot go out of thy reach." God soon arrested Jonah when *he fled to Tarshish from the presence of the Lord.*

2. No veil can hide us from God's eye, no, not that of the thickest darkness, *v.* 11, 12. *"If I say,* Yet *the darkness shall cover me,* when nothing else will, alas! I find myself deceived; the curtains of the evening will stand me in no more stead than the wings of the morning; *even the night shall be light about me.* That which often favours the escape of a pursued criminal, and the retreat of a beaten army, will do me no kindness in fleeing from them." When God divided between the light and darkness it was with a reservation of this prerogative, that to himself *the darkness and the light* should still be *both alike. "The darkness* darkeneth *not from thee,* for there is no darkness nor shadow of death where the workers of iniquity may hide themselves." No hypocritical mask or disguise, how specious soever, can save any person or action from appearing in a true light before God. Secret haunts of sin are as open before God as the most open and barefaced villanies.

II. Because he is the work of his hands. He that framed the engine knows all the motions of it. God made us, and therefore no doubt he knows us; he saw us when we were in the forming, and can we be hidden from him now that we are formed? This argument he insists upon (*v.* 13–16): *"Thou hast possessed my reins;* thou art Master of my most secret thoughts and intentions, and the innermost recesses of my soul; thou not only knowest, but governest, them, as we do that which we have possession of; and the possession thou hast of my reins is a rightful possession, *for thou coveredst me in my mother's womb,* that is, thou madest me (Job 10:11), thou madest me in secret. The soul is concealed form all about us. *Who knows the things of a man, save the spirit of a man?"* 1 Co. 2:11. Hence we read of *the hidden man of the heart.* But it was God himself that thus covered us, and therefore he can, when he pleases, discover us; when he hid us from all the world he did not intend to hide us from himself. Concerning the formation of man, of each of us,

1. The glory of it is here given to God, entirely to him; *for it is he that has made us and not we ourselves. "I will praise thee,* the author of my being; my parents were only the instruments of it." It was done, (1.) Under the divine inspection: *My substance,* when hid in the womb, nay, when it was yet but *in fieri — in the forming,* an unshapen embryo, *was not hidden from thee; thy eyes did see my substance.* (2.) By the divine operation. As the eye of God saw us then, so his hand wrought us; we were his work. (3.) According to the divine model: *In thy book all my members were written.* Eternal wisdom formed the plan, and by that almighty power raised the noble structure.

2. Glorious things are here said concerning it. The generation of man is to be considered with the same pious veneration as his creation at first. Consider it, (1.) As a great marvel, a great miracle we might call it, but that it is done in the ordinary course of nature. We are *fearfully and wonderfully made;* we may justly be astonished at the admirable contrivance of these living temples, the composition of every part, and the harmony of all together. (2.) As a great mystery, a mystery of nature: *My soul knows right well* that it is marvellous, but how to describe it for any one else I know not; for *I was made in secret, and curiously wrought* in the womb as *in the lowest parts of the earth,* so privately, and so far out of sight. (3.) As a great mercy, that all our members *in continuance were fashioned,* according as they were written in the book of God's wise counsel, *when as yet there was none of them;* or, as some read it, *and none of them was left out.* If any of our members had been wanting in God's book, they would have been wanting in our bodies, but, through his goodness, we have all our limbs and sense, the want of any of which might have made us burdens to ourselves. See what reason we have then to praise God for our creation, and to conclude that he who saw our substance when it was unfashioned sees it now that it is fashioned.

Verses 17–24

Here the psalmist makes application of the doctrine of God's omniscience, divers ways.

I. He acknowledges, with wonder and thankfulness, the care God had taken of him all his days, *v.* 17, 18. God, who knew him, thought of him, and his thoughts towards him were thoughts of love, *thought of good, and not of evil,* Jer. 29:11. God's omniscience, which might justly have watched over us to do us hurt, has been employed for us, and has watched over us to do us good, Jer. 31:28. God's counsels concerning us and our welfare have been, 1. Precious to admiration: *How precious* are they! They are deep in themselves, such as cannot possibly be fathomed and comprehended. Providence has had a vast reach in its dispensations concerning us, and has brought things about for our good quite beyond our contrivance and foresight. They are dear to us; we must think of them with a great deal of reverence, and yet with pleasure and thankfulness. Our thoughts concerning God must be delightful to us, above any other thoughts. 2. Numerous to admiration: *How great is the sum of them!* We cannot conceive how many God's kind counsels have been concerning us, how many good turns he has done us, and what variety of mercies we have received from him. *If* we would *count them,* the heads of them, much more the particulars of them, *they are more in number than the sand,* and yet every one great and very considerable, Ps. 40:5. We cannot conceive the multitude of God's compassions, which are all new every morning. 3. Constant at all times: *"When I awake,* every morning, *I am still with thee,* under thy eye and care, safe and easy under thy protection." This bespeaks also the continual devout sense David had of the eye of God upon him: *When I awake I am with thee,* in my thoughts; and it would help to keep us in the fear of the Lord all the day long if, when we awake in the morning, our first thoughts were of him and we did then set him before us.

II. He concludes from this doctrine that ruin will certainly be the end of sinners. God knows all the wickedness of the wicked, and therefore he will reckon for it: *"Surely thou wilt slay the wicked, O God!* for all their wickedness is open before thee, however it may be artfully disguised and coloured over, to hide it from the eye of the world. However thou suffer them to prosper for a while, *surely thou wilt slay* them at last." Now observe, 1. The reason why God will punish them, because they daringly affront him and set him at defiance (*v.* 20): *They speak against thee wickedly;* they *set their mouth against the heavens* (Ps. 73:9), and shall be called to account for the hard speeches they have *spoken against him,* Jude 15. They are his *enemies,* and declare their enmity by *taking his name in vain,* as we show our contempt of a man if we make a by-word of his name, and never mention him but in a way of jest and banter. Those that profane the sacred forms of swearing or praying by using them in an impertinent irreverent manner take God's name in vain, and thereby show themselves enemies to him. Some make it to be a description of hypocrites: "They speak of thee for mischief; they talk of God, pretending to piety, but it is with some ill design, for a cloak of maliciousness; and, being enemies to God, while they pretend friendship, they *take* his *name in vain;* they swear falsely." 2. The use David makes of this prospect which he has of the ruin of the wicked. (1.) He defies them: *"Depart from me, you bloody men;* you shall not debauch me, for I will not admit your friendship nor have fellowship with you; and you cannot destroy me, for, being under God's protection, he shall force you to depart from me." (2.) He detests them (*v.* 21, 22): "Lord, thou knowest the heart, and canst witness for me; *do not I hate those that hate thee,* and for that reason, because they hate thee? I hate them because I love thee, and hate to see such affronts and indignities put upon thy blessed name. *Am not I grieved with those that rise up against thee,* grieved to see their rebellion and to foresee their ruin, which it will certainly end in?" Note, Sin is hated, and sinners are lamented, by all that fear God. *"I hate them"* (that is, *"I hate the work of them that turn aside,"* as he explains himself, Ps. 101:3) *"with a* sincere and *perfect hatred; I count those* that are enemies to God as enemies to me, and will not have any intimacy with them," Ps. 69:8.

III. He appeals to God concerning his sincerity, *v.* 23, 24. 1. He desires that as far as he was in the wrong God would discover it to him. Those that are upright can take comfort in God's omniscience as a witness of their uprightness, and can with a humble confidence beg of him to search and try them, to discover them to themselves (for a good man desires to know the worst of himself) and to discover them to others. He that means honestly could wish he had a window in his breast that any man may look into his heart: "Lord, I hope I am not in a wicked way, but *see if there be any wicked way in me,* any corrupt inclination remaining; let me see it; and root it out of me, for I do not allow it." 2. He desires that, as far as he was in the right, he might be forwarded in it, which he that knows the heart knows how to do effectually: *Lead me in the way everlasting.* Note, (1.) The way of godliness is an everlasting way; it is everlastingly true and good, pleasing to God and profitable to us, and will end in everlasting life. *It is the way of antiquity* (so some), *the good old way.* (2.) All the saints desire to be kept and led in this way, that they may not miss it, turn out of it, nor tire in it.

PSALM 140

This and the four following psalms are much of a piece, and the scope of them the same with many that we met with in the beginning and middle of the book of Psalms, though with but few of late. They were penned by David (as it should seem) when he was persecuted by Saul; one of them is said to be his "prayer when he was in the cave," and it is probable that all the rest were penned about the same time. In this psalm, I. David complains of the malice of his enemies, and prays to God to preserve him from them (*v.* 1–5). II. He encourages himself in God as his God (*v.* 6, 7). III. He prays for, and prophesies, the destruction of his persecutors (*v.* 8–11). IV. He assures all God's afflicted people that their troubles would in due time end well (*v.* 12, 13), with which assurance we must comfort ourselves, and one another, in singing this psalm.

To the chief musician. A psalm of David.

Verses 1–7

In *this,* as in other things, David was a type of Christ, that he suffered before he reigned, was humbled before he was exalted, and that as there were many who loved and valued him, and sought to do him honour, so there were many who hated and envied him, and sought to do him mischief, as appears by these verses, where,

I. He gives a character of his enemies, and paints them out in their own colours, as dangerous men, whom he had reason to be afraid of, but wicked men, whom he had no reason to think the righteous God would countenance. There was one that seems to have been the ring-leader of them, whom he calls *the evil man* and *the man of violences* (*v.* 1, 4), probably he means Saul. The Chaldee paraphrast (*v.* 9) names both Doeg and Ahithophel; but between them there was a great distance of time. Violent men are evil men. But there were many besides this one who were confederate against David, who are here represented as the genuine offspring and seed of the serpent. For, 1. They are very subtle, crafty to do mischief; they have imagined it (*v.* 2), have laid the scheme with all the art and cunning imaginable. They *have purposed* and plotted *to overthrow the goings* of a good man (*v.* 4), to draw him into sin and trouble, to ruin him by blasting his reputation, crushing his interest, and taking away his life. For this purpose *they have,* like mighty hunters, *hidden a snare,* and *spread a net,* and *set gins* (*v.* 5), that their designs against him, being kept undiscovered, might be the more likely to take effect, and he might fall into their hands ere he was aware. Great persecutors have often been great politicians, which has indeed made them the more formidable; but *the Lord preserves the simple* without all those arts. 2. They are very spiteful, as full of malice as Satan himself: *They have sharpened their tongues like a serpent,* that infuses his venom with his tongue; and there is so much malignity in all they say that one would think there was nothing *under their lips* but *adders' poison, v.* 3. With their calumnies, and with their counsels, they aimed to destroy David, but secretly, as a man is stung with a serpent, or a snake in the grass. And they endeavoured likewise to infuse their malice into others, and to make them seven times more the children of hell than themselves. A malignant tongue makes men like the old serpent; and poison in the lips is a certain sign of poison in the heart. 3. They are confederate; they are many of them; but they are all *gathered together* against me *for war, v.* 2. Those who can agree in nothing else can agree to persecute a good man. Herod and Pilate will unite in this, and in this they resemble Satan, who is not divided against himself, all the devils agreeing in Beelzebub. 4. They are *proud* (*v.* 5), conceited of themselves and confident of their success; and herein also they resemble Satan, whose reigning ruining sin was pride. The pride of persecutors, though at present it be the terror, yet may be the encouragement, of the persecuted, for the more haughty they are the faster are they ripening for ruin. *Pride goes before destruction.*

II. He prays to God to keep him from them and from being swallowed up by them: "Lord, *deliver me, preserve me, keep me* (*v.* 1, 4); let them not prevail to take away my life, my reputation, my interest, my comfort, and to prevent my coming to the throne. *Keep me* from doing as they do, or as they would have me do, or as they promise themselves I shall do." Note, The more malice appears in our enemies against us the more earnest we should be in prayer to God to take us under his protection. In him believers may count upon a security, and may enjoy it and themselves with a holy serenity. Those are safe whom God preserves. If he be for us, who can be against us?

III. He triumphs in God, and thereby, in effect, he triumphs over his persecutors, *v.* 6, 7. When his enemies sharpened their tongues against him, did he sharpen his against them? No; *adders' poison* was *under their lips,* but grace was poured into his lips, witness what he here said unto the Lord, for to him he looked, to him he directed himself, when he saw himself in so much danger, through the malice of his enemies: and it is well for us that we have a God to go to. He comforted himself, 1. In his interest in God: *"I said, Thou art my God;* and, if my God, then my shield and mighty protector." In troublous dangerous times it is good to claim relation to God, and by faith to keep hold of him. 2. In his access to God. This comforted him, that he was not only taken into covenant with God, but into communion with him, that he had leave to speak to him, and might expect an answer of peace from him, and could say, with a humble confidence, *Hear the voice of my supplications, O Lord!* 3. In the assurance he had of help from God and happiness in him: *"O God the Lord — Jehovah Adonai!* as *Jehovah* thou art self-existent and self-sufficient, an infinitely perfect being; as *Adonai* thou art my stay and support, my ruler and governor, and therefore *the strength of my salvation,* my strong Saviour; nay, not only my Saviour, but my salvation itself, from whom, in whom, my salvation is; not only a strong Saviour, but the very strength of my salvation, on whom the stress of my hope is laid; all in all, to make me happy, and to preserve me to my happiness." 4. In the experience he had had formerly of God's care of him: *Thou hast covered my head in the day of battle.* As he pleaded with Saul, that, for the service of his country, he many a time jeoparded his life in the high places of the field, so he pleads with God that, in those services, he had wonderfully protected him, and provided him a better helmet for the securing of his head than Goliath's was: "Lord, thou hast kept me *in the day of battle* with the Philistines, suffer me not to fall by the treacherous intrigues of false-hearted Israelites." God is as able to preserve his people from secret fraud as from open force; and the experience we have had of his power and care, in dangers of one kind, may encourage us to trust in him and depend upon him in dangers of another nature; for nothing can shorten the Lord's right hand.

Verses 8–13

Here is the believing foresight David had,

I. Of the shame and confusion of persecutors.

1. Their disappointment. This he prays for (*v.* 8), that their lusts might not be gratified, their lust of ambition, envy, and revenge: *"Grant not, O Lord! the desires of the wicked,* but frustrate them; let them not see the ruin of my interest, which they so earnestly wish to see; but *hear the voice of my supplications."* He prays that their projects might not take effect, but be blasted: *"O further not his wicked device;* let not Providence favour any of his designs, but cross them; suffer *not his wicked device* to proceed, but chain his wheels, and stop him in the career of his pursuits." Thus we are to pray against the enemies of God's people, that they may not succeed in any of their enterprises. Such was David's prayer against Ahithophel, that God would turn his counsels into foolishness. The plea is, *lest they exalt themselves,* value themselves upon their success as if it were an evidence that God favoured them. Proud men, when they prosper, are made prouder, grow more impudent against God and insolent against his people, and *therefore,* "Lord, do not prosper them."

2. Their destruction. This he prays for (as we read it); but some choose to read it rather as a prophecy, and the original will bear it. If we take it as a prayer, that proceeds from a spirit of prophecy, which comes all to one. He foretels the ruin,

(1.) Of his own enemies: *"As for those that compass me about,* and seek my ruin," [1.] *"The mischief of their own lips* shall *cover* their heads (*v.* 9); the evil they have wished to me shall come upon themselves, their curses shall be blown back into their own faces, and the very designs which they have laid against me shall turn to their own ruin," Ps. 7:15, 16. Let those that make mischief, by slandering, tale-bearing, misrepresenting their neighbours, and spreading ill-natured characters and stories, dread the consequence of it, and think how sad their condition will be when all the mischief they have been accessory to shall be made to return upon themselves. [2.] The judgments of God shall *fall upon them,* compared here to *burning coals,* in allusion to the destruction of Sodom; nay, as in the deluge the waters from above, and those from beneath, met for the drowning of the world, both the windows of heaven were opened and the fountains of the great deep were broken up, so here, to complete the ruin of the enemies of Christ and his kingdom, they shall not only have *burning coals* cast upon them from above (Job 20:23; 27:22), but they themselves shall *be cast into the fire* beneath; both heaven and hell, the wrath of God the Judge and the rage of Satan the tormentor, shall concur to make them miserable. And the fire they shall be cast into is not a furnace of fire, out of which perhaps they might escape, but a *deep pit,* out of which they cannot rise. Tophet is said to be *deep and large,* Isa. 30:33.

(2.) Of all others that are like them, *v.* 11. [1.] Evil speakers must expect to be shaken, for they shall never *be established in the earth.* What is got by fraud and falsehood, by calumny and unjust accusation, will not prosper, will not last. Wealth gotten by vanity will be diminished. Let not such men as Doeg think to reign long, for his doom will be theirs, Ps. 2:5. A lying tongue is but for a moment, but the *lip of truth shall be established for ever.* [2.] Evil doers must expect to be destroyed: *Evil shall hunt the violent man,* as the blood-hound hunts the murderer to discover him, as the lion hunts his prey to tear it to pieces.

Mischievous men will be brought to light, and brought to ruin; the destruction appointed shall run them down and overthrow them. *Evil pursues sinners.*

II. Here is his foresight of the deliverance and comfort of the persecuted, *v.* 12, 13. 1. God will do those justice, in delivering them, who, being wronged, commit themselves to him: *"I know that the Lord will maintain the* just and injured *cause of* his *afflicted* people, and will not suffer might always to prevail against right, though it be but *the right of the poor,* who have but little that they can pretend a right to." God is, and will be, the patron of oppressed innocence, much more of persecuted piety; those that know him cannot but know this. 2. They will do him justice (if I may so speak), in ascribing the glory of their deliverance to him: *"Surely the righteous* (who make conscience of rendering to God his due, as well as to men theirs) *shall give thanks unto thy name* when they find their cause pleaded with jealousy and prosecuted with effect." The closing words, *The upright shall dwell in thy presence,* denote both God's favour to them ("Thou shalt admit them to dwell in thy presence in grace here, in glory hereafter, and it shall be their safety and happiness") and their duty to God: "They shall attend upon thee as servants that keep in the presence of their masters, both to do them honour and to receive their commands." This is true thanksgiving, even thanksliving; and this use we should make of all our deliverance, we should serve God the more closely and cheerfully.

PSALM 141

David was in distress when he penned this psalm, pursued, it is most likely, by Saul, that violent man. Is any distressed? Let him pray; David did so, and had the comfort of it. I. He prays for God's favourable acceptance (*v.* 1, 2). II. For his powerful assistance (*v.* 3, 4). III. That others might be instrumental of good to his soul, as he hoped to be to the souls of others (*v.* 5, 6). IV. That he and his friends being now brought to the last extremity God would graciously appear for their relief and rescue (*v.* 7-10). The mercy and grace of God are as necessary to us as they were to him, and therefore we should be humbly earnest for them in singing this psalm.

A psalm of David.

Verses 1-4

Mercy to accept what we do well, and grace to keep us from doing ill, are the two things which we are here taught by David's example to pray to God for.

I. David loved prayer, and he begs of God that his prayers might be heard and answered, *v.* 1, 2. *David cried unto God.* His crying denotes fervency in prayer; he prayed as one in earnest. His crying to God denotes faith and fixedness in prayer. And what did he desire as the success of his prayer? 1. That God would take cognizance of it: *"Give ear to my voice;* let me have a gracious audience." Those that cry in prayer may hope to be heard in prayer, not for their loudness, but their liveliness. 2. That he would visit him upon it: *Make haste unto me.* Those that know how to value God's gracious presence will be importunate for it and humbly impatient of delays. He that believes does not make haste, but he that prays may be earnest with God to make haste. 3. That he would be well pleased with him in it, well pleased with his *praying* and the *lifting up of his hands in prayer,* which denotes both the elevation and enlargement of his desire and the out-goings of his hope and expectation, the lifting up of the hand signifying the lifting up of the heart, and being used instead of lifting up the sacrifices which were heaved and waved before the Lord. Prayer is a spiritual sacrifice; it is the offering up of the soul, and its best affections, to God. Now he prays that this may be set forth and directed before God *as the incense* which was daily burnt upon the golden altar, and *as the evening sacrifice,* which he mentions rather than the morning sacrifice, perhaps because this was an evening prayer, or with an eye to Christ, who, in the evening of the world and in the evening of the day, was to offer up himself a sacrifice of atonement, and establish the spiritual sacrifices of acknowledgement, having abolished all the carnal ordinances of the law. Those that pray in faith may expect it will please God better than an ox or bullock. David was now banished from God's court, and could not attend the sacrifice and incense, and therefore begs that his prayer might be instead of them. Note, Prayer is of a sweet-smelling savour to God, as incense, which yet has no

savour without fire; nor has prayer without the fire of holy love and fervour.

II. David was in fear of sin, and he begs of God that he might be kept from sin, knowing that his prayers would not be accepted unless he took care to watch against sin. We must be as earnest for God's grace in us as for his favour towards us. 1. He prays that he might not be surprised into any sinful words (*v.* 3): *"Set a watch, O Lord! before my mouth,* and, nature having made my lips to be a door to my words, let grace keep that door, that no word may be suffered to go out which may in any way tend to the dishonour of God or the hurt of others." Good men know the evil of tongue-sins, and how prone they are to them (when enemies are provoking we are in danger of carrying our resentment too far, and of speaking unadvisedly, as Moses did, though the meekest of men), and therefore they are earnest with God to prevent their speaking amiss, as knowing that no watchfulness or resolution of their own is sufficient for the governing of their tongues, much less of their hearts, without the special grace of God. We must *keep our mouths as with a bridle;* but that will not serve: we must pray to God to keep them. Nehemiah prayed to the Lord when he set a watch, and so must we, for without him the watchman walketh but in vain. 2. That he might not be inclined to any sinful practices (*v.* 4): *"Incline not my heart to any evil thing;* whatever inclination there is in me to sin, let it be not only restrained, but mortified, by divine grace." The example of those about us, and the provocations of those against us, are apt to stir up and draw out corrupt inclinations. We are ready to do as others do, and to think that if we have received injuries we may return them; and therefore we have need to pray that we may never be left to ourselves to practise any wicked work, either in confederacy with or in opposition to the *men that work iniquity.* While we live in such an evil world, and carry about with us such evil hearts, we have need to pray that we may neither be drawn in by any allurement nor driven on by any provocation to do any sinful thing. 3. That he might not be ensnared by any sinful pleasures: *"Let me not eat of their dainties.* Let me not join with them in their feasts and sports, lest thereby I be inveigled into their sins." *Better is a dinner of herbs,* out of the way of temptation, than a *stalled ox* in it. Sinners pretend to find dainties in sin. *Stolen waters are sweet;* forbidden fruit is pleasant to the eye. But those that consider how soon the dainties of sin will turn into wormwood and gall, how certainly it will, at last, *bite like a serpent* and *sting like an adder,* will dread those dainties, and pray to God by his providence to take them out of their sight, and by his grace to turn them against them. Good men will pray even against the sweets of sin.

Verses 5-10

Here, I. David desires to be told of his faults. His enemies reproached him with that which was false, which he could not but complain of; yet, at the same time, he desired his friends would reprove him for that which was really amiss in him, particularly if there was any thing that gave the least colour to those reproaches (*v.* 5): *let the righteous smite me; it shall be a kindness.* The righteous God (so some); "I will welcome the rebukes of his providence, and be so far from quarrelling with them that I will receive them as tokens of love and improve them as means of grace, and will pray for those that are the instruments of my trouble." But it is commonly taken for the reproofs given by righteous men; and it best becomes those that are themselves righteous to reprove the unrighteousness of others, and from them reproof will be best taken. But if the reproof be just, though the reprover be not so, we must make a good use of it and learn obedience by it. We are here taught how to receive the reproofs of the righteous and wise. 1. We must desire to be reproved for whatever is amiss in us, or is done amiss by us: "Lord, put it into the heart of the righteous to smite me and reprove me. If my own heart does not *smite me,* as it ought, let my friend do it; let me never fall under that dreadful judgment of being let alone in sin." 2. We must account it a piece of friendship. We must not only bear it patiently, but take it as a kindness; for *reproofs of instruction are the way of life* (Prov. 6:23), are means

of good to us, to bring us to repentance for the sins we have committed, and to prevent relapses into sin. Though reproofs cut, it is in order to a cure, and therefore they are much more desirable than the kisses of an enemy (Prov. 27:6) or the song of fools, Eccl. 7:5. David blessed God for Abigail's seasonable admonition, 1 Sa. 25:32. 3. We must reckon ourselves helped and healed by it: It *shall be as an excellent oil* to a wound, to mollify it and close it up; *it shall not break my head,* as some reckon it to do, who could as well bear to have their heads broken as to be told of their faults; but, says David, "I am not of that mind; it is my sin that has broken my head, that has broken my bones, Ps. 51:8. The reproof is an excellent oil, to cure the bruises sin has given me. It shall not *break my head,* if it may but help to break my heart." 4. We must requite the kindness of those that deal thus faithfully, thus friendly with us, at least by our *prayers for them in their calamities,* and hereby we must show that we take it kindly. Dr. Hammond gives quite another reading of this verse: *"Reproach will bruise me that am righteous,* and rebuke me; *but that poisonous oil shall not break my head* (shall not destroy me, shall not do me the mischief intended), *for yet my prayer shall be in their mischiefs,* that God would preserve me from them, and my prayer shall not be in vain."

II. David hopes his persecutors will, some time or other, bear to be told of their faults, as he was willing to be told of his (*v.* 6): *"When their judges"* (Saul and his officers who judged and condemned David, and would themselves be sole judges) *"are overthrown in stony places,* among the rocks in the wilderness, then *they shall hear my words, for they are sweet."* Some think this refers to the relentings that were in Saul's breast when he said, with tears, *Is this thy voice, my son David?* 1 Sa. 24:16; 26:21. Or we may take it more generally: even judges, great as they are, may come to be overthrown. Those that make the greatest figure in this world do not always meet with level smooth ways through it. And those that slighted the word of God before will relish it, and be glad of it, when they are in affliction, for that opens the ear to instruction. When the world is bitter the word is sweet. Oppressed innocency cannot gain a hearing with those that live in pomp and pleasure, but when they come to be overthrown themselves they will have more compassionate thoughts of the afflicted.

III. David complains of the great extremity to which he and his friends were reduced (*v.* 7): *Our bones are scattered at the grave's mouth,* out of which they are thrown up, so long have we been dead, or into which they are ready to be thrown, so near are we to the pit; and they are as little regarded as chips among the hewers of wood, which are thrown in neglected heaps: *As one that cuts and cleaves the earth* (so some read it), alluding to the ploughman who tears the earth in pieces with his plough-share, Ps. 129:3. *Can these dry bones live?*

IV. David casts himself upon God, and depends upon him for deliverance: *"But my eyes are unto thee (v.* 8); for, when the case is ever so deplorable, thou canst redress all the grievances. From thee I expect relief, bad as things are, and in *thee is my trust."* Those that have their eye towards God may have their hopes in him.

V. He prays that God would succour and relieve him as his necessity required. 1. That he would comfort him: *"Leave not my soul desolate and destitute;* still let me see where my help is." 2. That he would prevent the designs of his enemies against him (*v.* 9): *"Keep me from being taken in the snare they have laid for me;* give me to discover it and to evade it." Be the gin placed with ever so much subtlety, God can and will secure his people from being taken in it. 3. That God would, in justice, turn the designs of his enemies upon themselves, and, in mercy, deliver him from being ruined by them (*v.* 10): *let the wicked fall into their own net,* the net which, intentionally, they procured for me, but which, meritoriously, they prepared for themselves. *Nec lex est justioir ulla quam necis artifices arte perire sua — No law can be more just than that the architects of destruction should perish by their own contrivances.* All that are bound over to God's justice are held in the cords of their own iniquity. But let me at the same time obtain a discharge. The entangling and ensnaring of the wicked sometimes prove the escape and enlargement of the righteous.

PSALM 142

This psalm is a prayer, the substance of which David offered up to God when he was forced by Saul to take shelter in a cave, and which he afterwards penned in this form. Here is, I. The complaint he makes to God (*v.* 1, 2) of the subtlety, strength, and malice, of his enemies (*v.* 3, 6), and the coldness and indifference of his friends (*v.* 4). II. The comfort he takes in God that he knew his case (*v.* 3) and was his refuge (*v.* 5). III. His expectation from God that he would hear and deliver him (*v.* 6, 7). IV His expectation from the righteous that they would join with him in praises (*v.* 7). Those that are troubled in mind, body, or estate, may, in singing this psalm (if they sing it in some measure with David's spirit), both warrant his complaints and fetch in his comforts.

Maschil of David. A prayer when he was in the cave.

Verses 1–3

Whether it was in the cave of *Adullam,* or that of *Engedi,* that David prayed this prayer, is not material; it is plain that he was in distress. It was a great disgrace to so great a soldier, so great a courtier, to be put to such shifts for his own safety, and a great terror to be so hotly pursued and every moment in expectation of death; yet then he had such a presence of mind as to pray this prayer, and, wherever he was, still had his religion about him. Prayers and tears were his weapons, and, when he durst not stretch forth his hands against his prince, he lifted them up to his God. There is no cave so deep, so dark, but we may out of it send up our prayers, and our souls in prayer, to God. He calls this prayer *Maschil — a psalm of instruction,* because of the good lessons he had himself learnt in the cave, learnt on his knees, which he desired to teach others. In these verses observe,

I. How David complained to God, *v.* 1, 2. When the danger was over he was not ashamed to own (as great spirits sometimes are) the fright he had been in and the application he had made to God. Let no men of the first rank think it any diminution or disparagement to them, when they are in affliction, to cry to God, and to cry like children to their parents when any thing frightens them. *David poured out his complaint,* which denotes a free and full complaint; he was copious and particular in it. His heart was as full of his grievances as it could hold, but he made himself easy by pouring them out before the Lord; and this he did with great fervency: *He cried unto the Lord with his voice,* with the voice of his mind (so some think), for, being hidden in the cave, he durst not speak with an audible voice, lest that should betray him; but mental prayer is vocal to God, and he hears the groanings which cannot, or dare not, be uttered, Rom. 8:26. Two things David laid open to God, in this complaint: — 1. His distress. He exhibited a remonstrance or memorial of his case: *I showed before him my trouble,* and all the circumstances of it. He did not prescribe to God, nor show him his trouble, as if God did not know it without his showing; but as one that put a confidence in God, desired to keep up communion with him, and was willing to refer himself entirely to him, he unbosomed himself to him, humbly laid the matter before him, and then cheerfully left it with him. We are apt to show our trouble too much to ourselves, aggravating it, and poring upon it, which does us no service, whereas by showing it to God we might cast the care upon him who careth for us, and thereby ease ourselves. Nor should we allow of any complaint to ourselves or others which we cannot with due decency and sincerity of devotion make to God, and stand to before him. 2. His desire. When he made his complaint he *made his supplication* (*v.* 1), not claiming relief as a debt, but humbly begging it as a favour. Complainants must be suppliants, for God will be sought unto.

II. What he complained of: *"In the way wherein I walked,* suspecting no danger, *have they privily laid a snare for me,* to entrap me." Saul gave Michal his daughter to David on purpose that she might be *a snare to him,* 1 Sa. 18:21. This he complains of to God, that every thing was done with a design against him. If he had gone out of his way, and met with snares, he might have thanked himself; but when he met with them in the way of his duty he might with humble boldness tell God of them.

III. What comforted him in the midst of these complaints (*v.* 3): *"When my spirit was overwhelmed within me,* and ready to sink under the burden of grief and fear, when I was quite at a loss and ready to despair, *then thou knewest my path,* that is, then it was a pleasure to me to think that thou knewest it. Thou knewest my sincerity, the right path which I have walked in, and that I am not such a one as my persecutors represent me. Thou knewest my condition in all the particulars of it; when my spirit was so overwhelmed that I could not distinctly show it, this comforted me, that thou knewest it, Job 23:10. Thou knewest it, that is, thou didst protect, preserve, and secure it," Ps. 31:7; Deu. 2:7.

Verses 4–7

The psalmist here tells us, for our instruction, 1. How he was disowned and deserted by his friends, *v.* 4. When he was in favour at court he seemed to have a great interest, but when he was made an out-law, and it was dangerous for any one to harbour him (witness Ahimelech's fate), then *no man would know him,* but every body was shy of him. He looked *on his right hand* for an advocate (Ps. 109:31), some friend or other to speak a good word for him; but, since Jonathan's appearing for him had like to have cost him his life, nobody was willing to venture in defence of his innocency, but all were ready to say they knew nothing of the matter. He looked round to see if any would open their doors to him; but *refuge failed him.* None of all his old friends would give him a night's lodging, or direct him to any place of secresy and safety. How many good men have been deceived by such swallow-friends, who are gone when winter comes! David's life was exceedingly precious, and yet, when he was unjustly proscribed, *no man cared for it,* nor would move a hand for the protection of it. Herein he was a type of Christ, who, in his sufferings for us, was forsaken of all men, even of his own disciples, and trod the wine-press alone, for there was *none to help, none to uphold,* Isa. 63:5. 2. How he then found satisfaction in God, *v.* 5. Lovers and friends stood aloof from him, and it was in vain to call to them. "But," said he, *"I cried unto thee, O Lord!* who knowest me, and carest for me, when none else will, and wilt not fail me nor forsake me when men do;" for God is constant in his love. David tells us what he said to God in the cave: *"Thou art my refuge and my portion in the land of the living;* I depend upon thee to be so, *my refuge* to save me from being miserable, *my portion* to make me happy. The cave I am in is but a poor refuge. Lord, *thy name* is the *strong tower* that *I run into.* Thou art *my refuge,* in whom alone I shall think myself safe. The crown I am in hopes of is but a poor portion; I can never think myself well provided for till I know that *the Lord is the portion of my inheritance and of my cup."* Those who in sincerity take the Lord for their God shall find him all-sufficient both as a refuge and as a portion, so that, as no evil shall hurt them, so no good shall be wanting to them; and they may humbly claim their interest: *"Lord, thou art my refuge and my portion;* every thing else is a refuge of lies and a portion of no value. Thou art so *in the land of the living,* that is, while I live and have my being, whether in this world or in a better." There is enough in God to answer all the necessities of this present time. We live in a world of dangers and wants; but what danger need we fear if God is our refuge, or what wants if he be our portion? Heaven, which alone deserves to be called *the land of the living,* will be to all believers both a refuge and a portion. 3. How, in this satisfaction, he addressed himself to God (*v.* 5, 6): "Lord, give a gracious *ear to my cry,* the cry of my affliction, the cry of my supplication, for *I am brought very low,* and, if thou help me not, I shall be quite sunk. Lord, *deliver me from my persecutors,* either tie their hands or turn their hearts, break their power or blast their projects, restrain them or rescue me, *for they are stronger than I,* and it will be thy honour to take part with the weakest. Deliver me from them, or I shall be ruined by them, for I am not yet myself a match for them. Lord, *bring my soul out of prison,* not only bring me safe out of this cave, but bring me out of all my perplexities." We may apply it spiritually: the souls of good men are often straitened by doubts and fears, cramped and fettered through the weakness of faith and the prevalency of corruption; and it is then their duty and interest to apply themselves to God, and beg of him to set them at liberty and to enlarge their hearts, that they may *run the way of his commandments.* 4. How much he expected his deliverance would redound to the glory of God. (1.) By his own thanksgivings, into which his present complaints would then be turned: *"Bring my soul out of prison,* not that I may enjoy myself and my friends and live at ease, no, nor that I may secure my country, but *that I may praise thy name."* This we should have an eye to, in all our prayers to God for deliverance out of trouble, that we may have occasion to praise God and may live to his praise. This is the greatest comfort of temporal mercies that they furnish us with matter, and give us opportunity, for the excellent duty of praise. (2.) By the thanksgivings of many on his behalf (2 Co. 1:11): "When I am enlarged *the righteous shall encompass me about;* for *my cause they shall make thee a crown of praise,* so the Chaldee. They shall flock about me to congratulate me on my deliverance, to hear my experiences, and to receive (Maschil) instructions from me; they shall encompass me, to join with me in my thanksgivings, *because thou shalt* have dealt *bountifully with me."* Note, The mercies of others ought to be the matter of our praises to God; and the praises of others, on our behalf, ought to be both desired and rejoiced in by us.

PSALM 143

This psalm, as those before, is a prayer of David, and full of complaints of the great distress and danger he was in, probably when Saul persecuted him. He did not only pray in that affliction, but he prayed very much and very often, not the same over again, but new thoughts. In this psalm, I. He complains of his troubles, through the oppression of his enemies (*v.* 3) and the weakness of his spirit under it, which was ready to sink notwithstanding the likely course he took to support himself (*v.* 4, 5). II. He prays, and prays earnestly (*v.* 6), 1. That God would hear him (*v.* 1–7). 2. That he would not deal with him according to his sins (*v.* 2). 3. That he would not hide his face from him (*v.* 7), but manifest his favour to him (*v.* 8). 4. That he would guide and direct him in the way of his duty (*v.* 8, 10) and quicken him in it (*v.* 11). 5. That he would deliver him out of his troubles (*v.* 9, 11). 6. That he would in due time reckon with his persecutors (*v.* 12). We may more easily accommodate this psalm to ourselves, in the singing of it, because most of the petitions in it are for spiritual blessings (which we all need at all times), mercy and grace.

A psalm of David.

Verses 1–6

Here, I. David humbly begs to be heard (*v.* 1), not as if he questioned it, but he earnestly desired it, and was in care about it, for, having desired it, and was in care about it, for having directed his prayer, he looked up to see how it sped, Hab. 2:1. He is a suppliant to his God, and he begs that his requests may be granted: *Hear my prayer; give ear to my supplications.* He is an appellant against his persecutors, and he begs that his case may be brought to hearing and that God will give judgment upon it, in his faithfulness and righteousness, as the Judge of right and wrong. Or, "Answer my petitions in thy faithfulness, according to the promises thou hast made, which thou wilt be just to." We have no righteousness of our own to plead, and therefore must plead God's righteousness, the word of promise which he has freely given us and caused us to hope in.

II. He humbly begs not to be proceeded against in strict justice, *v.* 2. He seems here, if not to correct, yet to explain, his plea (*v.* 1), Deliver me *in thy righteousness;* "I mean," says he, "the righteous promises of the gospel, not the righteous threatenings of the law; if I be answered according to the righteousness of this broken covenant of innocency, I am quite undone;" and therefore, 1. His petition is, *"Enter not into judgment with thy servant;* do not deal with me in strict justice, as I deserve to be dealt with." In this prayer we must own ourselves to be God's servants, bound to obey him, accountable to him, and solicitous to obtain his favour, and we must approve ourselves to him. We must acknowledge that in many instances we have offended him, and have come short of our duty to him, that he might justly enquire into our offences, and proceed against us for them according to law, and that, if he should do so, judgment would certainly go against us; we have nothing to move in arrest or mitigation of it, but execution would be taken out and awarded and then we should be ruined for ever. But we must encourage ourselves with a hope that there is mercy and forgiveness with God, and be earnest with him for the benefit of that mercy. *"Enter not into judgment with thy servant,* for thou hast already entered into judgment with thy Son, and laid upon him the iniquity of us all. *Enter not into judgment with thy servant,* for thy servant enters into judgment with himself;" and, if *we will judge ourselves, we shall not be judged.* 2. His plea is, *"In thy sight shall no man living be justified* upon those terms, for no man can plead innocency nor any righteousness of his own, either that he has not sinned or that he does not deserve to die for his sins; nor that he has any satisfaction of his own to offer;" nay, if God contend with us, *we are not able to answer him for one of a thousand,* Job 9:3; 15:20. David, before he prays for the removal of his trouble, prays for the pardon of his sin, and depends upon mere mercy for it.

III. He complains of the prevalency of his enemies against him (*v.* 3): "Saul, that great enemy, *has persecuted my soul,* sought my life, with a restless malice, and has carried the persecution so far that he has already *smitten it down to the ground.* Though I am not yet under ground, I am struck to the ground, and that is next door to it; he has forced me to *dwell in darkness,* not only in dark caves, but in dark thoughts and apprehensions, in the clouds of melancholy, *as* helpless and hopeless as *those that have been long dead.* Lord, let me find mercy with thee, for I find no mercy with men. They condemn me; but, Lord, do not thou condemn me. Am not I an object of thy compassion, fit to be appeared for; and is not my enemy an object of thy displeasure, fit to be appeared against?"

IV. He bemoans the oppression of his mind, occasioned by his outward troubles (*v.* 4): *Therefore is my spirit* overpowered and *overwhelmed within me,* and I am almost plunged in despair; when without are fightings within are fears, and those fears greater tyrants and oppressors than Saul himself and not so easily out-run. It is sometimes the lot of the best men to have their spirits for a time almost overwhelmed and their hearts desolate, and doubtless it is their infirmity. David was not only a great saint, but a great soldier, and yet even he was sometimes ready to faint in a day of adversity. *Howl, fir-trees, if the cedars be shaken.*

V. He applies himself to the use of proper means for the relief of his troubled spirit. He had no force to muster up against the oppression of the enemy, but, if he can keep possession of nothing else, he will do what he can to keep possession of his own soul and to preserve his inward peace. In order to this, 1. He looks back, and *remembers the days of old* (*v.* 5), God's former appearances for his afflicted people and for him in particular. It has been often a relief to the people of God in their straits to think of the wonders which their fathers told them of, Ps. 77:5, 11. 2. He looks round, and takes notice of the works of God in the visible creation, and the providential government of the world: *I meditate on all thy works.* Many see them, but do not see the footsteps of God's wisdom, power, and goodness in them, and do not receive the benefit they might by them because they do not meditate upon them; they do not dwell on that copious curious subject, but soon quit it, as if they had exhausted it, when they have scarcely touched upon it. *I muse on,* or (as some read it) *I discourse of, the* operation *of thy hands,* how great, how good, it is! The more we consider the power of God the less we shall fear the face or force of man, Isa. 51:12, 13. 3. He looks up with earnest desires towards God and his favour (*v.* 6): *"I stretch forth my hands unto thee,* as one begging an alms, and big with expectation to receive something great, standing ready to lay hold on it and bid it welcome. *My soul thirsteth after thee; it is to thee* (so the word is), entire for thee, intent on thee; it is *as a thirsty land,* which, being parched with excessive heat, gapes for rain; so do I need, so do I crave, the support and refreshment of divine consolations under my afflictions, and nothing else will relieve me." This is the best course we can take when our spirits are overwhelmed; and justly do those sink under their load who will not take such a ready way as this to ease themselves.

Verses 7–12

David here tells us what he said when he stretched forth his hands unto God; he begins not only as one in earnest, but as one in haste: *"Hear me speedily,* and defer no longer, for *my spirit faileth.* I am just ready to faint; reach the cordial — quickly, quickly, or I am gone." It was not a haste of unbelief, but of vehement desire and holy love. *Make haste, O God! to help me.* Three things David here prays for: —

I. The manifestations of God's favour towards him, that God would be well pleased with him and let him know that he was so; this he prefers before any good, Ps. 4:6. 1. He dreads God's frowns: "Lord, *hide not thy face from me;* Lord, be not angry with me, do not turn from me, as we do from one we are displeased with; Lord, let me not be left under the apprehensions of thy anger or in doubt concerning thy favour; if I have thy favour, let it not be hidden from me." Those that have the truth of grace cannot but desire the evidence of it. He pleads the wretchedness of his case if God withdrew from him: "Lord, let me not lie under thy wrath, for then I am *like those that go down to the pit,* that is, down to the grave (I am a dead man, weak, and pale, and ghastly; thy frowns are worse than death), or down to hell, the bottomless pit." Even those who through grace are delivered from going down to the pit may sometimes, when the terrors of the Almighty set themselves in array against them, look like those who are going to the pit. Disconsolate saints have sometimes cried out of the wrath of God, as if they had been damned sinners, Job 6:4; Ps. 88:6. 2. He entreats God's favour (*v.* 8): *Cause me to hear thy lovingkindness in the morning.* He cannot but think that God has a kindness for him, that he has some kind things to say to him, some good words and comfortable words; but the present hurry of his affairs, and tumult of his spirits, drowned those pleasing whispers; and therefore he begs, "Lord, do not only speak kindly to me, but cause me to hear it, to *hear joy and gladness,"* Ps. 51:8. God speaks to us by his word and by his providence, and in both we should desire and endeavour to *hear his lovingkindness* (Ps. 107:43), that we may set that always before us: *"Cause me to hear* it *in the morning,* every morning; let my waking thoughts be of God's lovingkindness, that the sweet relish of that may abide upon my spirits all the day long." His plea is, *"For in thee do I trust,* and in thee only; I look not for comfort in any other." God's goodness is commonly wrought *for those who trust in him* (Ps. 31:8), who by faith draw it out.

II. The operations of God's grace in him. Those he is as earnest for as for the tokens of God's favour to him, and so should we be. He prays,

1. That he might be enlightened with the knowledge of God's will; and this is the first work of the Spirit, in order to his other works, for God deals with men as men, as reasonable creatures. Here are three petitions to this effect: — (1.) *Cause me to know the way wherein I should walk.* Sometimes those that are much in care to walk right are in doubt, and in the dark, which is the right way. Let them come boldly to the throne of grace, and beg of God, by his word, and Spirit, and providence, to show them the way, and prevent their missing it. A good man does not ask what is the way in which he must walk, or in which is the most pleasant walking, but what is the right way, the way in which he should walk. He pleads, *"I lift up my soul unto thee,* to be moulded and fashioned according to thy will." He did not only importunately, but impartially, desire to know his duty; and those that do so shall be taught. (2.) *"Teach me to do thy will,* not only show me what thy will is, but teach me how to do it, how to turn my hand dexterously to my duty." It is the desire and endeavour of all God's faithful servants to know and to do his will, and to stand complete in it. He pleads, *"Thou art my God,* and therefore my oracle, by whom I may expect to be advised — my God, and therefore my ruler, whose will I desire to do." If we do in sincerity take God for our God, we may depend upon him to teach us to do his will, as a master does his servant. (3.) *Lead me into the land of uprightness,* into the communion of saints, that pleasant land of the upright, or into a settled course of holy living, which will lead to heaven, that land of uprightness where holiness will be in perfection, and he that is holy shall be holy still. We should desire to be led, and kept safe, to heaven, not only because it is a land of blessedness, but because it is a land of uprightness; it is the perfection of grace. We cannot find the way that will bring us to that land unless God show us, nor go in that way unless he take us by the hand and lead us, as we lead those that are weak, or lame, or timorous, or dim-sighted; so necessary is the grace of God, not only to put us into the good way, but to keep us and carry us on in it. The plea is, *"Thy Spirit is good,* and able to make me good," good and willing to help those that are at a loss. Those that have the Lord for their God have his Spirit for their guide; and it is both their character and their privilege that they are *led by the Spirit.*

2. He prays that he might be enlivened to do his will (*v.* 11): *"Quicken me, O Lord!* — quicken my devotions, that they may be lively; quicken me to my duty, and quicken me in it; and this *for thy name's sake."* The best saints often find themselves dull, and dead, and slow, and therefore pray to God to quicken them.

III. The appearance of God's providence for him, 1. That God would, in his own way and time, give him rest from his troubles (*v.* 9): *"Deliver me, O Lord! from my enemies,* that they may not have their will against me; *for I flee unto thee to hide me;* I trust to thee to defend me in my trouble, and therefore to rescue me out of it." Preservations are pledges of salvation, and those shall find God their hiding-place who by faith make him such. He explains himself (*v.* 11): *"For thy righteousness-sake, bring my soul out of trouble,* for thy promise-sake, nay, for thy mercy-sake" (for some by *righteousness* understand *kindness* and *goodness*); "do not only deliver me from my outward trouble, but from the trouble of my soul, the trouble that threatens to overwhelm my spirit. Whatever trouble I am in, Lord, let not my heart be troubled," Jn. 14:1. 2. That he would reckon with those that were the instruments of his trouble (*v.* 12): *"Of thy mercy* to me *cut off my enemies,* that I may be no longer in fear of them; *and destroy all those,* whoever they be, how numerous, how powerful, soever, *who afflict my soul,* and create vexation to that; *for I am thy servant,* and am resolved to continue such, and therefore may expect to be owned and protected in thy service." This prayer is a prophecy of the utter destruction of all the impenitent enemies of Jesus Christ and his kingdom, who will not have him to reign over them, who grieve his Spirit, and afflict his soul, by afflicting his people, in whose afflictions he is afflicted.

PSALM 144

The four preceding psalms seem to have been penned by David before his accession to the crown, when he was persecuted by Saul; this seems to have been penned afterwards, when he was still in trouble (for there is no condition in this world privileged with an exemption from trouble), the neighbouring nations molesting him and giving him disturbance, especially the Philistines, 2 Sa. 5:17. In this psalm, I. He acknowledges, with triumph and thankfulness, the great goodness of God to him in advancing him to the government (*v.* 1–4). II. He prays to God to help him against the enemies who threatened him (*v.* 5–8 and again *v.* 11). III. He rejoices in the assurance of victory over them (*v.* 9, 10). IV. He prays for the prosperity of his own kingdom, and pleases himself with the hopes of it (*v.* 12–15). In singing this psalm we may give God the glory of our spiritual privileges and advancements, and fetch in help from him against our spiritual enemies; we may pray for the prosperity of our souls, of our families, and of our land; and, in the opinion of some of the Jewish writers, we may refer the psalm to the Messiah and his kingdom.

A psalm of David.

Verses 1–8

Here, I. David acknowledges his dependence upon God and his obligations to him, *v.* 1, 2. A prayer for further mercy is fitly begun with a thanksgiving for former mercy; and when we are waiting upon God to bless us we should stir up ourselves to bless him. He gives to God the glory of two things: —

1. What he was to him: *Blessed be the Lord my* rock (*v.* 1), *my goodness, my fortress, v.* 2. He has in the covenant engaged himself to be so, and encouraged us, accordingly, to depend upon him; all the saints, who by faith have made him theirs, have found him not only to answer but to out do their expectations. David speaks of it here as the matter of his trust, and that which made him easy, as the matter of his triumph, and that which made him glad, and in which he gloried. See how he multiplies words to express the satisfaction he had in God and his interest in him. (1.) "He is *my strength,* on whom I stay, and from whom I have power both for my work and for my warfare, my rock to build on, to take shelter in." Even when we are weak we may *be strong in the Lord and in the power of his might.* (2.) *"My goodness,* not only good to me, but my chief good, in whose favour I place my felicity, and who is the author of all the goodness that is in me, and *from whom comes every good and perfect gift."* (3.) *"My fortress,* and *my high tower,* in whom I think myself as safe as ever any prince thought himself in a castle or stronghold." David had formerly sheltered himself in strong-holds at En-gedi (1 Sa. 23:29), which perhaps were natural fastnesses. He had lately made himself master of the stronghold of Zion, which was fortified by art, and he *dwelt in the fort* (2 Sa. 5:7, 9), but he depends not on these. "Lord," says he, "thou art *my fortress* and *my high tower."* The di-

vine attributes and promises are fortifications to a believer, far exceeding those either of nature or art. (4.) *My deliverer,* and, as it is in the original, very emphatically, *my deliverer to me,* "not only a deliverer I have interest in, but who is always nigh unto me and makes all my deliverances turn to my real benefit." (5.) *"My shield,* to guard me against all the malignant darts that my enemies let fly at me, not only *my fortress* at home, but *my shield* abroad in the field of battle." Wherever a believer goes he carries his protection along with him. *Fear not, Abram, I am thy shield.*

2. What he had done for him. He was bred a shepherd, and seems not to have been designed by his parents, or himself for any thing more. But, (1.) God had made him a soldier. His hands had been used to the crook and his fingers to the harp, but God *taught his hands to war and his fingers to fight,* because he designed him for Israel's champion; and what God calls men to he either finds them or makes them fit for. Let the men of war give God the glory of all their military skill; the same that teaches the meanest husbandman his art teaches the greatest general his. It is a pity that any whose fingers God has taught to fight should fight against him or his kingdom among men. Those have special reason to acknowledge God with thankfulness who prove to be qualified for services which they themselves never thought of. (2.) God had made him a sovereign prince, had taught him to wield the sceptre as well as the sword, to rule as well as fight, the harder and nobler art of the two: He *subdueth my people under me.* The providence of God is to be acknowledged in making people subject to their prince, and so preserving the order and benefit of societies. There was a special hand of God inclining the people of Israel to be subject to David, pursuant to the promise God had made him; and it was typical of that great act of divine grace, the bringing of souls into subjection to the Lord Jesus and making them willing in the day of his power.

II. He admires God's condescension to man and to himself in particular (*v.* 3, 4): *"Lord, what is man,* what a poor little thing is he, *that thou takest knowledge of him, that thou makest account of him,* that he falls so much under thy cognizance and care, and that thou hast such a tender regard to any of that mean and worthless race as thou hast had to me!" Considering the many disgraces which the human nature lies under, we have reason to admire the honours God has put upon mankind in general (the saints especially, some in a particular manner, as David) and upon the Messiah (to whom those words are applied, Heb. 2:6), who was *highly exalted because he humbled himself to be found in fashion as a man,* and *has authority to execute judgment because he is the Son of man.* A question to this purport David asked (Ps. 8:4), and he illustrated the wonder by the consideration of the great dignity God has placed man in (Ps. 8:5), *Thou hast crowned him with glory and honour.* Here he illustrates it by the consideration of the meanness and mortality of man, notwithstanding the dignity put upon him (*v.* 4): *Man is like to vanity;* so frail is he, so weak, so helpless, compassed about with so many infirmities, and his continuance here so very short and uncertain, that he is as like as may be to vanity itself. Nay, he is vanity, he is so at his best estate. *His days* have little substance in them, considering how many of the thoughts and cares of an immortal soul are employed about a poor dying body; they *are as a shadow,* dark and flitting, transitory and finishing with the sun, and, when that sets, resolving itself into all shadow. They *are as a shadow that passeth away,* and there is no loss of it. David puts himself into the number of those that are thus mean and despicable.

III. He begs of God to strengthen him and give him success against the enemies that invaded him, *v.* 5–8. He does not specify who they were that he was in fear of, but says, *Scatter them, destroy them.* God knew whom he meant, though he did not name them. But afterwards he describes them (*v.* 7, 8): "They are *strange children,* Philistines, aliens, bad neighbours to Israel, heathens, whom we are bound to be strange to and not to make any leagues with, and who therefore carry it strangely towards us." Notwithstanding the advantages with which God had blessed David's arms against them, they were still vexatious and treacherous, and men that one could put no confidence in: "One cannot take their word, for their *mouth speaketh vanity;* nay, if they give their hand upon it, or offer their hand to help you, there is no trusting them; for *their right hand is a right hand of falsehood."* Against such as these we cannot defend ourselves, but we may depend on the God of truth and justice, who hates falsehood, to defend us from them. 1. David prays that God would appear, that he would do something extraordinary, for the conviction of those who preferred their dunghill-deities before the God of Israel (*v.* 5): *"Bow thy heavens, O Lord!* and make it evident that they are indeed thine, and that thou art the Lord of them, Isa. 66:1. Let thy providence threaten my enemies, and look black upon them, as the clouds do on the earth when they are thick, and hang very low, big with a storm. Fight against those that fight against us, so that it may visibly appear that thou art for us. *Touch the mountains,* our strong and stately enemies, *and* let them *smoke.* Show thyself by the ministry of thy angels, as thou didst upon Mount Sinai." 2. That he would appear against his enemies, that he would fight from heaven against them, as sometimes he had done, by lightnings, which are his arrows (his fiery darts, against which the hardest steel is no armour of proof, so penetrating is the force of lightning), that he himself would shoot these arrows, who, we are sure, never misses his mark, but hits where he aims. 3. That he would appear for him, *v.* 7. He begs for their destruction, in order to his own deliverance and the repose of his people: *"Send thy hand,* thy power, *from above,* for that way we look for help; *rid me and deliver me out of* these *great waters* that are ready to overflow me." God's time to help his people is when they are sinking and all other helps fail.

Verses 9–15

The method is the same in this latter part of the psalm as in the former; David first gives glory to God and then begs mercy from him.

I. He praises God for the experiences he had had of his goodness to him and the encouragements he had to expect further mercy from him, *v.* 9, 10. In the midst of his complaints concerning the power and treachery of his enemies, here is a holy exultation in his God: *I will sing a new song to thee, O God!* a song of praise for new mercies, for those compassions that are new every morning. Fresh favours call for fresh returns of thanks; nay, we must praise God for the mercies we hope for by his promise as well as those we have received by his providence, 2 Chr. 20:20, 21. He will join music with his songs of praise, to express and excite his holy joy in God; he will praise God *upon a psaltery of ten strings,* in the best manner, thinking all little enough to set forth the praises of God. He tells us what this new song shall be (*v.* 10): *It is he that giveth salvation unto kings.* This intimates, 1. That great kings cannot save themselves without him. Kings have their life-guards, and have armies at command, and all the means of safety that can be devised; but, after all, it is God that gives them their salvation, and secures them by those means, which he could do, if there were occasion, without them, Ps. 33:16. Kings are the protectors of their people, but it is God that is their protector. How much service do they owe him then with their power who gives them all their salvations! 2. That good kings, who are his ministers for the good of their subjects, shall be protected and saved by him. He has engaged to give salvation to those kings that are his subjects and rule for him; witness the great things he had done for *David his servant,* whom he had many a time *delivered from the hurtful sword,* to which Saul's malice, and his own zeal for the service of his country, had often exposed him. This may refer to Christ the Son of David, and then it is a new song indeed, a New-Testament song. God delivered him from the hurtful sword, upheld him as his servant, and brought him off a conqueror over all the powers of darkness, Isa. 42:1; 49:8. To him he gave salvation, not for himself only, but for us, raising him up to be *a horn of salvation.*

II. He prays for the continuance of God's favour.

1. That he might be delivered from the public enemies, *v.* 11. Here he repeats his prayer and plea, *v.* 7, 8. His persecutors were still of the same character, false and perfidious, and who would certainly over-reach an honest man and be too hard for him: "Therefore, Lord, do thou *deliver me from* them, for they are a strange sort of people."

2. That he might see the public peace and prosperity: "Lord, let us have victory, that we may have quietness, which we shall never have while our enemies have it in their power to do us mischief." David, as a king, here expresses the earnest desire he had of the welfare of his people, wherein he was a type of Christ, who provides effectually for the good of his chosen. We have here,

(1.) The particular instances of that public prosperity which David desired for his people. [1.] A hopeful progeny (*v.* 12): *"That our sons* and *our daughters may be* in all respects such as we could wish." He means not those only of his own family, but those of his subjects, that are the seed of the next generation. It adds much to the comfort and happiness of parents in this world to see their children promising and likely to do well. *First,* It is pleasant to see *our sons as plants grown up in their youth,* as olive-plants (Ps. 128:), the *planting of the Lord* (Isa. 61:3), — to see them as plants, not as weeds, not as thorns, — to see them as plants growing great, not withered and blasted, — to see them of a healthful constitution, a quick capacity, a towardly disposition, and especially of a pious inclination, likely to bring forth fruit unto God in their day, — to see them *in their youth,* their growing time, increasing in every thing that is good, growing wiser and better, till they grow strong in spirit. *Secondly,* It is no less desirable to see *our daughters as corner-stones,* or corner-pillars, *polished after the similitude of a palace,* or temple. By daughters families are united and connected, to their mutual strength, as the parts of a building are by the corner-stones; and when they are graceful and beautiful both in body and mind they are then polished after the similitude of a nice and curious structure. When we see our daughters well-established and stayed with wisdom and discretion, as corner-stones are fastened in the building, — when we see them by faith united to Christ, as the chief corner-stone, adorned with the graces of God's Spirit, which are the polishing of that which is naturally rough, and *become women professing godliness,* — when we see them purified and consecrated to God as living temples, we think ourselves happy in them. [2.] Great plenty. Numerous families increase the care, perhaps more than the comfort, where there is not sufficient for their maintenance; and therefore he prays for a growing estate with a growing family. *First,* That their store-houses might be well-replenished with the fruits and products of the earth: *That our garners may be full,* like those of the good householder, who brings out of them things new and old (those things that are best new he has in that state, those that are best when they are kept he has in that state), — that we may have in them *all manner of stores,* for ourselves and our friends, — that, living plentifully, we may live not luxuriously, for then we abuse our plenty, but cheerfully and usefully, — that, having abundance, we may be thankful to God, generous to our friends, and charitable to the poor; otherwise, what profit is it to have our garners full? Jam. 5:3. *Secondly,* That their flocks might greatly increase: *That our sheep may bring forth thousands, and ten thousands, in our* folds. Much of the wealth of their country consisted in their flocks (Prov. 27:26), and this is the case with ours too, else wool would not be, as it is, a staple commodity. The increase of our cattle is a blessing in which God is to be acknowledged. *Thirdly,* That their beasts designed for service might be fit for it: *That our oxen may be strong to labour* in the plough, *that they may be fat and fleshy* (so some), in good working case. We were none of us made to be idle, and therefore we should pray for bodily health, not that we may be easy and take our pleasures, but that we *may be strong to labour,* that we may do the work of our place and day, else we are worse than the beasts; for when they are strong it is for labour. [3.] An uninterrupted peace. *First,* That there be no war, *no breaking in* of invaders, *no going out* of deserters. "Let not our enemies break in upon us; let us not have occasion to march out against them." War brings with it abundance of mischiefs, whether it be offensive or defensive. *Secondly,* That there be no oppression nor faction — *no complaining in our streets,* that the people may have no cause to complain either of their government or of one another, nor may be so peevish as to complain without cause. It is desirable thus to dwell in quiet habitations.

(2.) His reflection upon this description of the prosperity of the nation, which he so much desired (*v.* 15): *Happy are the people that are in such a case* (but it is seldom so, and never long so), *yea, happy are the people whose God is the Lord.* The relation of a people to God as theirs is here spoken of either, [1.] As that which is the fountain whence all those blessings flow. Happy are the Israelites if they faithfully adhere to the Lord as their God, for they may expect to be *in such a case.* National piety commonly brings national prosperity; for nations as such, in their national capacity, are capable of rewards and punishments only in this life. Or, [2.] As that which is abundantly preferable to all these enjoyments. The psalmist began to say, as most do, *Happy are the people that are in such a case;* those are blessed that prosper in the world. But he immediately corrects himself: *Yea, rather, happy are the people whose God is the Lord,* who have his favour, and love, and grace, according to the tenour of the covenant, though they have not abundance of this world's goods. As all this, and much more, cannot make us happy, unless the Lord be our God, so, if he be, the want of this, the loss of this, nay, the reverse of this, cannot make us miserable.

PSALM 145

The five foregoing psalms were all of a piece, all full of prayers; this, and the five that follow it to the end of the book, are all of a piece too, all full of praises; and though only this is entitled David's psalm yet we have no reason to think but that they were all his as well as all the foregoing prayers. And it is observable, 1. That after five psalms of prayer follow six psalms of praise; for those that are much in prayer shall not want matter for praise, and those that have sped in prayer must abound in praise. Our thanksgivings for mercy, when we have received it, should even exceed our supplications for it when we were in pursuit of it. David, in the last of his begging psalms, had promised to praise God (144:9), and here he performs his promise. 2. That the book of Psalms concludes with psalms of praise, all praise, for praise, is the conclusion of the whole matter; it is that in which all the psalms centre. And it intimates that God's people, towards the end of their life, should abound much in praise, and the rather because, at the end of their life, they hope to remove to the world of everlasting praise, and the nearer they come to heaven the more they should accustom themselves to the work of heaven. This is one of those psalms which are composed alphabetically (as Ps. 25 and 34, etc.), that it might be the more easily committed to memory, and kept in mind. The Jewish writers justly extol this psalm as a star of the first magnitude in this bright constellation; and some of them have an extravagant saying concerning it, not much unlike some of the popish superstitions, That whosoever will sing this psalm constantly three times a day shall certainly be happy in the world to come. In this psalm, I. David engages himself and others to praise God (v. 1, 2, 4–7, 10–12). II. He fastens upon those things that are proper matter for praise, God's greatness (v. 3), his goodness (v. 8, 9), the proofs of both in the administration of his kingdom (v. 13), the kingdom of providence (v. 14–16), the kingdom of grace (v. 17–20), and then he concludes with a resolution to continue praising God (v. 21) with which resolution our hearts must be filled, and in which they must be fixed, in singing this psalm.

David's *psalm* of praise.

Verses 1–9

The entitling of this *David's psalm of praise* may intimate not only that he was the penman of it, but that he took a particular pleasure in it and sung it often; it was his companion wherever he went. In this former part of the psalm God's glorious attributes are praised, as, in the latter part of the psalm, his kingdom and the administration of it. Observe,

I. Who shall be employed in giving glory to God.

1. Whatever others do, the psalmist will himself be much in praising God. To this good work he here excites himself, engages himself, and has his heart much enlarged in it. What he does, that he will do, having more and more satisfaction in it. It was his duty; it was his delight. Observe, (1.) How he expresses the work itself: "*I will extol thee, and bless thy name* (v. 1); I will speak well of thee, as thou hast made thyself known, and will therein express my own high thoughts of thee and endeavour to raise the like in others." When we speak honourably of God, this is graciously interpreted and accepted as an extolling of him. Again (v. 2): *I will bless thee, I will praise thy name;* the repetition intimates the fervency of his affection to this work, the fixedness of his purpose to abound in it, and the frequency of his performances therein. Again (v. 5): *I will speak of thy honour,* and (v. 6) *I will declare thy greatness.* He would give glory to God, not only in his solemn devotions, but in his common conversation. If the heart be full of God, out of the abundance of that the mouth will speak with reverence, to his praise, upon all occasions. What subject of discourse can we find more noble, more copious, more pleasant, useful, and unexceptionable, than the glory of God? (2.) How he expresses his resolution to persevere in it. [1.] He will be constant to this work: *Every*

day will I bless thee. Praising God must be our daily work. No day must pass, though ever so busy a day, though ever so sorrowful a day, without praising God. We ought to reckon it the most needful of our daily employments, and the most delightful of our daily comforts. God is every day blessing us, doing well for us; there is therefore reason that we should be every day blessing him, speaking well of him. [2.] He will continue in it: *I will bless* thee *for ever and ever, v.* 1 and again *v.* 2. This intimates, *First,* That he resolved to continue in this work to the end of his life, throughout *his ever* in this world. *Secondly,* That the psalms he penned should be made use of in praising God by the church to the end of time, 2 Chr. 29:30. *Thirdly,* That he hoped to be praising God to all eternity in the other world. Those that make praise their constant work on earth shall have it their everlasting bliss in heaven.

2. He doubts not but others also would be forward to this work. (1.) "They shall concur in it now; they shall join with me in it: When *I declare thy greatness men shall speak of* it (v. 6); *they shall abundantly utter it"* (v. 7), or *pour it out* (as the word is); they shall praise God with a gracious fluency, better than the most curious oratory. David's zeal would provoke many, and it has done so. (2.) "They shall keep it up when I am gone, in an uninterrupted succession (v. 4): *One generation shall praise thy works to another."* The generation that is going off shall tell them to that which is rising up, shall tell what they have seen in their days and what they have heard from their fathers; they *shall* fully and particularly *declare thy mighty acts* (Ps. 78:3); and the generation that is rising up shall follow the example of that which is going off: so that the death of God's worshippers shall be no diminution of his worship, for a new generation shall rise up in their room to carry on that good work, more or less, to the end of time, when it shall be left to that world to do it in which there is no succession of generations.

II. What we must give to God the glory of.

1. Of his greatness and his great works. We must declare, *Great is the Lord,* his presence infinite, his power irresistible, his brightness insupportable, his majesty awful, his dominion boundless, and his sovereignty incontestable; and therefore there is no dispute, but *great is the Lord, and,* if great, then *greatly to be praised,* with all that is within us, to the utmost of our power, and with all the circumstances of solemnity imaginable. His greatness indeed cannot be comprehended, for it is unsearchable; who can conceive or express how great God is? But then it is so much the more to be praised. When we cannot, by searching, find the bottom, we must sit down at the brink, and adore the depth, Rom. 11:33. God is great, for, (1.) His majesty is glorious in the upper world, above the heavens, where he has set his glory; and when we are declaring his greatness we must not fail to *speak of the glorious honour of his majesty,* the splendour of the glory of his majesty (v. 5), how brightly he shines in the upper world, so as to dazzle the eyes of the angels themselves, and oblige them to cover their faces, as unable to bear the lustre of it. (2.) His works are wondrous in this lower world. The preservation, maintenance, and government of all the creatures, proclaim the Creator very great. When therefore we declare his greatness we must observe the unquestionable proofs of it, and must *declare his mighty acts* (v. 4), *speak of his wondrous works* (v. 5), *the might of his terrible acts, v.* 6. We must see God acting and working in all the affairs of this lower world. Various instruments are used, but in all events God is the supreme director; it is he that performs all things. Much of his power is seen in the operations of his providence (they are *mighty acts,* such as cannot be paralleled by the strength of any creature), and much of his justice — they are *terrible acts,* awful to saints, dreadful to sinners. These we should take all occasions to speak of, observing the finger of God, his hand, his arm, in all, that we may marvel.

2. Of his goodness; this is his glory, Ex. 33:19. It is what he glories in (Ex. 34:6, 7), and it is what we must give him the glory of: *They shall abundantly utter the memory of thy great goodness, v.* 7. God's goodness is great goodness, the treasures of it can never be exhausted, nay, they can never be lessened, for he ever will be as rich in mercy as he ever was. It is memorable goodness; it is what we ought always to lay before us, always to have in mind and preserve the memorials of, for it is *worthy to be had in ever-*

lasting remembrance; and the remembrance we retain of God's goodness we should utter, we should *abundantly utter,* as those who are full of it, very full of it, and desire that others may be acquainted and affected with it. But, whenever we utter God's great goodness, we must not forget, at the same time, to *sing of his righteousness;* for, as he is gracious in rewarding those that serve him faithfully, so he is righteous in punishing those that rebel against him. Impartial and inflexible justice is as surely in God as inexhaustible goodness; and we must sing of both together, Rom. 11:22. (1.) There is a fountain of goodness in God's nature (v. 8): *The Lord is gracious* to those that serve him; he is *full of compassion* to those that need him, *slow to anger* to those that have offended him, *and of great mercy* to all that seek him and sue to him. he is ready to give, and ready to forgive, more ready than we are to ask, than we are to repent. (2.) There are streams of goodness in all the dispensations of his providence, v. 9. As he is good, so he does good; he *is good to all,* to all his creatures, from the highest angel to the meanest worm, to all but devils and damned sinners, that have shut themselves out from his goodness. *His tender mercies are over all his works.* [1.] All his works, all his creatures, receive the fruits of his merciful care and bounty. It is extended to them all; he hates nothing that he has made. [2.] The works of his mercy out-shine all his other works, and declare him more than any of them. In nothing will the glory of God be for ever so illustrious as in the vessels of mercy ordained to glory. To the divine goodness will the everlasting hallelujahs of all the saints be sung.

Verses 10–21

The greatness and goodness of him who is *optimus et maximus — the best and greatest* of beings, were celebrated in the former part of the psalm; here, in these verses, we are taught to give him *the glory of his kingdom,* in the administration of which his greatness and goodness shine so clearly, so very brightly. Observe, as before,

I. From whom the tribute of praise is expected (v. 10): *All* God's *works shall praise* him. They all minister to us matter for praise, and so praise him according to their capacity; even those that refuse to give him honour he will get himself honour upon. But his *saints* do bless him, not only as they have peculiar blessings from him, which other creatures have not, but as they praise him actively, while his other works praise him only objectively. They bless him, for they collect the rent or tribute of praise from the inferior creatures, and pay it into the treasury above. All God's works do praise him, as the beautiful building praises the builder or the well-drawn picture praises the painter; but the saints bless him as the children of prudent tender parents rise up and call them blessed. Of all God's works, his saints, the workmanship of his grace, the first-fruits of his creatures, have most reason to bless him.

II. For what this praise is to be given: *They shall speak of thy kingdom.* The kingdom of God among men is a thing to be often thought of and often spoken of. As, before, he had magnified God's greatness and goodness in general, so here he magnifies them with application to his kingdom. Consider then,

1. The greatness of his kingdom. It is great indeed, for all the kings and kingdoms of the earth are under his control. To show the greatness of God's kingdom, he observes, (1.) The pomp of it. Would we by faith look within the veil, we should see, and, believing, we should *speak of the glory of his kingdom* (v. 11), *the glorious majesty of* it (v. 12), for he has prepared his throne in the heavens, and it is high and lifted up, and surrounded with an innumerable company of angels. The courts of Solomon and Ahasuerus were magnificent; but, compared with the glorious majesty of God's kingdom, they were but as glow-worms to the sun. The consideration of this should strike an awe upon us in all our approaches to God. (2.) The power of it: When *they speak of the glory of* God's *kingdom* they must *talk of his power,* the extent of it, the efficacy of it — his power, by which he can do any thing and does every thing he pleases (v. 11); and, as a proof of it, let them *make known his mighty acts* (v. 12), that *the sons of men* may be invited to yield themselves his willing subjects and so put themselves under the protection of such a mighty potentate. (3.) The perpetuity of it, v. 13. The thrones of earthly princes totter, and the flowers of their crowns wither, mon-

archies come to an end; but, Lord, *thy kingdom is an everlasting kingdom.* God will govern the world to the end of time, when the Mediator, who is now entrusted with the administration of his kingdom, shall deliver it up to God, even the Father, that he may be all in all to eternity. His *dominion endures throughout all generations,* for he himself is eternal, and his counsels are unchangeable and uniform; and Satan, who has set up a kingdom in opposition to him, is conquered and in a chain.

2. The goodness of his kingdom. His royal style and title are, *The Lord God, gracious and merciful;* and his government answers to his title. The goodness of God appears in what he does,

(1.) For all the creatures in general (*v.* 15, 16): He *provides food for all flesh,* and therein appears his everlasting mercy, Ps. 136:25. All the creatures live upon God, and, as they had their being from him at first, so from him they have all the supports of their being and on him they depend for the continuance of it. [1.] The eye of their expectation attends upon him: *The eyes of all wait on thee.* The inferior creatures indeed have not the knowledge of God, nor are capable of it, and yet they are said to *wait upon God,* because they seek their food according to the instinct which the God of nature has put into them (and *they sow not, neither do they reap,* Mt. 6:26), and because they take what the God of nature has provided for them, in the time and way that he has appointed, and are content with it. [2.] The hand of his bounty is stretched out to them: *Thou givest them their meat in due season,* the meat proper for them, and in the proper time, when they need it; so that none of the creatures ordinarily perish for want of food, no, not in the winter. *Thou openest thy hand* freely and liberally, *and satisfiest the desire of every living thing,* except some of the unreasonable children of men, that will be satisfied with nothing, but are still complaining, still crying, *Give, give.*

(2.) For the children of men in particular, whom he governs as reasonable creatures.

[1.] He does none of them any wrong, for (*v.* 17) *the Lord is righteous in all his ways,* and not unrighteous in any of them; he is *holy,* and acts like himself, with a perfect rectitude *in all his works.* In all the acts of government he is just, injurious to none, but administering justice to all. *The ways of the lord are equal,* though ours are unequal. In giving laws, in deciding controversies, in recompensing services, and punishing offences, he is incontestably just, and we are bound to own that he is so.

[2.] He does all of them good, his own people in a special manner.

First, He supports those that are sinking, and it is his honour to help the weak, *v.* 14. He *upholds all that fall,* in that, though they fall, they are not utterly cast down. Many of the children of men are brought very low by sickness and other distresses, and seem ready to drop into the grave, and yet Providence wonderfully upholds them, raises them up, and says, *Return,* Ps. 110:3. If all had died who once seemed dying, the world would have been very thin. Many of the children of God, who have been ready to fall into sin, to fall into despair, have experienced his goodness in preventing their falls, or recovering them speedily by his graces and comforts, so that, though they fell, they were *not utterly cast down,* Ps. 37:24. If those who were *bowed down* by oppression and affliction are *raised up,* it was God that raised them. And, with respect to all those *that are heavy-laden* under the burden of sin, if they come to Christ by faith, he will ease them, he will raise them.

Secondly, He is very ready to hear and answer the prayers of his people, *v.* 18, 19. In this appears the grace of his kingdom, that his subjects have not only liberty of petitioning, but all the encouragement that can be to petition. 1. The grant is very rich, that God will be *nigh to all that call upon him;* he will be always within call of their prayers, and they shall always find themselves within reach of his help. If *a neighbour that is near is better than a brother afar off* (Prov. 27:10), much more a God that is near. Nay, he will not only be *nigh to them,* that they may have the satisfaction of being heard, but *he will fulfil* their *desires;* they shall have what they ask and find that they seek. It was said (*v.* 16) that he *satisfies the desire of every living thing,* much more *will he fulfil the desire of those that fear him;* for he that feeds his birds will not starve his babes. *He will hear their call and will save them;* that is hearing them to purpose, as he heard David (that is, saved him) *from the horn of the unicorn,* Ps. 22:21. 2. The proviso is very reasonable. He will hear and help us, (1.) If we *fear him,* if we worship and serve him with a holy awe of him; for otherwise how can we expect that he should accept us? (2.) If we *call upon him in truth;* for he desires truth in the inward part. We must be faithful to God, and sincere in our professions of dependence on him, and devotedness to him. In all devotions inward impressions must be answerable to the outward expressions, else they are not performed in truth.

Thirdly, He takes those under his special protection who have a confidence and complacency in him (*v.* 20): *The Lord preserves all those that love him;* they lie exposed in this world, but he, by preserving them in their integrity, will effectually secure them, that no real evil shall befal them.

[3.] If any are destroyed they may thank themselves: *All the wicked he will destroy,* but they have by their wickedness fitted themselves for destruction. This magnifies his goodness in the protection of the righteous, that *with their eyes they shall see the reward of the wicked* (Ps. 91:8); and God will by this means preserve his people, even by destroying the wicked that would do them a mischief.

Lastly, The psalmist concludes, 1. With a resolution to give glory to God himself (*v.* 21): *My mouth shall speak the praise of the Lord.* When we have said what we can, in praising God, still there is more to be said, and therefore we must not only begin our thanksgivings with this purpose, as he did (*v.* 1), but conclude them with it, as he does here, because we shall presently have occasion to begin again. As the end of one mercy is the beginning of another, so should the end of one thanksgiving be. While I have breath to draw, my mouth shall still speak God's praises. 2. With a call to others to do so too: *Let all flesh,* all mankind, *bless his holy name for ever and ever.* Some of mankind shall be blessing God for ever; it is a pity but that they should be all so engaged.

PSALM 146

This and all the rest of the psalms that follow begin and end with Hallelujah, a word which puts much of God's praise into a little compass; for in it we praise him by his name Jah, the contraction of Jehovah. In this excellent psalm of praise, I. The psalmist engages himself to praise God (*v.* 1, 2). II. He engages others to trust in him, which is one necessary and acceptable way of praising him. 1. He shows why we should not trust in men (*v.* 3, 4). 2. Why we should trust in God (*v.* 5), because of his power in the kingdom of nature (*v.* 6), his dominion in the kingdom of providence (*v.* 7), and his grace in the kingdom of the Messiah (*v.* 8, 9), that everlasting kingdom (*v.* 10), to which many of the Jewish writers refer this psalm, and to which therefore we should have an eye, in the singing of it.

Verses 1–4

David is supposed to have penned this psalm; and he was himself a prince, a mighty prince; as such, it might be thought, 1. That he should be exempted from the service of praising God, that it was enough for him to see that his priests and people did it, but that he needed not to do it himself in his own person. Michal thought it a disparagement to him to *dance before the ark;* but he was so far from being of this mind that he would himself be first and foremost in the work, *v.* 1, 2. He considered his dignity as so far from excusing him from it that it rather obliged him to lead in it, and he thought it so far from lessening him that it really magnified him; therefore he stirred up himself to it and to make a business of it: *Praise the Lord, O my soul!* and he resolved to abide by it: "I will praise him with my heart, *I will sing praises* to him with my mouth. Herein I will have an eye to him as *the Lord,* infinitely blessed and glorious in himself, and as *my God,* in covenant with me." Praise is most pleasant when, in praising God, we have an eye to him as ours, whom we have an interest in and stand in relation to. "This I will do constantly while I live, every day of my life, and to my life's end; nay, I will do it *while I have any being,* for when I have no being on earth I hope to have a being in heaven, a better being, to be doing it better." That which is the great end of our being ought to be our great employment and delight while we have any being. "In thee must our time and powers be spent." 2. It might be thought that he himself, having been so great a blessing to his country, should be adored, according to the usage of the heathen nations, who deified their heroes, that they should all come and *trust in his shadow* and make him their *stay* and *strong-hold.* "No," says David, *"Put not your trust in princes* (*v.* 3), not in me, not in any other; do not repose your confidence in them; do not raise your expectations from them. Be not too sure of their sincerity; some have thought they knew better how to reign by knowing how to dissemble. Be not too sure of their constancy and fidelity; it is possible they may both change their minds and break their words." But, though we suppose them very wise and as good as David himself, yet we must not be too sure of their ability and continuance, for they are sons of Adam, weak and mortal. There is indeed a Son of man in whom there is help, in whom there is salvation, and who will not fail those that trust in him. But all other sons of men are like the man they are sprung of, who, being in honour, did not abide. (1.) We cannot be sure of their ability. Even the power of kings may be so straitened, cramped, and weakened, that they may not be in a capacity to do that for us which we expect. David himself owned (2 Sa. 3:39), *I am this day weak, though anointed king.* So that *in the son of man there is* often *no help,* no salvation; he is at a loss, at his wits' end, as *a man astonished,* and then, though *a mighty man,* he *cannot save,* Jer. 14:9. (2.) We cannot be sure of their continuance. Suppose he has it in his power to help us while he lives, yet he may be suddenly taken off when we expect most from him (*v.* 4): *His breath goes forth,* so it does every moment, and comes back again, but that is an intimation that it will shortly go for good and all, and then *he returns to his earth.* The earth is his, in respect of his original as a man, the earth out of which he was taken, and to which therefore he must return, according to the sentence, Gen. 3:19. It is his, if he be a worldly man, in respect of choice, his earth which he has chosen for his portion, and on the things of which he has set his affections. He shall go to his own place. Or, rather, it is his earth because of the property he has in it; and though he has had large possessions on earth a grave is all that will remain to him. *The earth God has given to the children of men,* and great striving there is about it, and, as a mark of their authority, men *call their lands by their own names.* But, after a while, no part of the earth will be their own but that in which the dead body shall make its bed, and that shall be theirs *while the earth remains.* But, when he returns to his earth, *in that very day his thoughts perish;* all the projects and designs he had of kindness to us vanish and are gone, and he cannot take one step further in them; all his purposes are cut off and buried with him, Job 17:11. And then what becomes of our expectations from him? Princes are mortal, as well as other men, and therefore we cannot have that assurance of help from them which we may have from that Potentate who hath immortality. *Cease from man, whose breath is in his nostrils* and will not be there long.

Verses 5–10

The psalmist, having cautioned us not to trust in princes (because, if we do, we shall be miserably disappointed), here encourages us to put our confidence in God, because, if we do so, we shall be happily secured: *Happy is he that has the God of Jacob for his help,* that has an interest in his attributes and promises, and has them engaged for him, and *whose hope is in the Lord his God.*

I. Let us take a view of the character here given of those whom God will uphold. Those shall have God for their help, 1. Who take him for their God, and serve and worship him accordingly. 2. Who have their hope in him, and live a life of dependence upon him, who have good thoughts of him, and encourage themselves in him, when all other supports fail. Every believer may look upon him as the God of Jacob, of the church in general, and therefore may expect relief from him, in reference to public distresses, and as his God in particular, and therefore may depend upon him in all personal wants and straits. We must hope, (1.) In the providence of God for all the good things we need, which relate to the life that now is. (2.) In the grace of Christ for all the good things which relate to the life that is to come. To this especially the learned Dr. Hammond refers this and the following verses, looking upon the latter part of this psalm to have a most visible remarkable aspect towards the eternal Son of God in his incarnation. He quotes one of the rabbies, who says of *v.* 10 that it belongs to the days of the Messiah. And that it does so he thinks will appear by comparing *v.* 7, 8, with the characters Christ gives of the Messiah (Mt. 11:5, 6), *The blind receive their sight, the lame walk;* and the closing words there, *Blessed is he whosoever shall not be offended in me,* he thinks may very well be supposed to refer to *v.* 5. *Happy is the man that hopes in the Lord his God,* and who is not offended in him.

II. Let us take a view of the great encouragements here given us to hope in *the Lord our God.* 1. He is the *Maker of the world,* and therefore has all power in himself, and the command of the powers of all the creatures, which, being derived from him, depend upon him (*v.* 6): *He made heaven and earth, the sea, and all that in them is,* and therefore his arm is not shortened, that it cannot save. It is very applicable to Christ, by whom God made the world, and *without whom was not any thing made that was made.* It is a great support to faith that the Redeemer of the world is the same that was the Creator of it, and therefore has a good-will to it, a perfect knowledge of its case, and power to help it. 2. He is a God of inviolable fidelity. We may venture to take God's word, for he *keepeth truth for ever,* and therefore no word of his shall fall to the ground; it is true *from the beginning,* and therefore true *to the end.* Our Lord Jesus is the Amen, *the faithful witness,* as well as *the beginning,* the author and principle, *of the creation of God,* Rev. 3:14. The keeping of God's truth for ever is committed to him, for *all the promises* are in him *yea and amen.* 3. He is the patron of injured innocency: *He pleads the cause of the oppressed,* and (as we read it) he *executes judgment* for them. He often does it in his providence, giving redress to those that suffer wrong and clearing up their integrity. He will do it in the judgment of the great day. The Messiah came to rescue the children of men out of the hands of Satan the great oppressor, and, all judgment being committed to him, the executing of judgment upon persecutors is so among the rest, Jude 15. 4. He is a bountiful benefactor to the necessitous: *He gives food to the hungry;* so God does in an ordinary way for the answering of the cravings of nature; so he has done sometimes in an extraordinary way, as when ravens fed Elijah; so Christ did more than once when he fed thousands miraculously with that which was intended but for one meal or two for his own family. This encourages us to hope in him as the nourisher of our souls with the bread of life. 5. He is the author of liberty to those that were bound: *The Lord looseth the prisoners.* He brought Israel out of the house of bondage in Egypt and afterwards in Babylon. The miracles Christ wrought, in making the dumb to speak and the deaf to hear with that one word, *Ephphatha — Be opened,* his cleansing lepers, and so discharging them from their confinements, and his raising the dead out of their graves, may all be included in this one of *loosing the prisoners;* and we may take encouragement from those to hope in him for that spiritual liberty which he came to proclaim, Isa. 61:1, 2. 6. He gives sight to those that have been long deprived of it; *The Lord can open the eyes of the blind,* and has often given to his afflicted people to see that comfort which before they were not aware of; witness Gen. 21:19, and the prophet's servant, 2 Ki. 6:17. But this has special reference to Christ; for *since the world began was it not heard that any man opened the eyes of one that was born blind* till Christ did it (Jn. 9:32) and thereby encouraged us to hope in him for spiritual illumination. 7. He sets that straight which was crooked, and makes those easy that were pained and ready to sink: He *raises those that are bowed down,* by comforting and supporting them under their burdens, and, in due time, removing their burdens. This was literally performed by Christ when he made a poor woman straight that had been *bowed together, and could in no wise lift up herself* (Lu. 13:12); and he still does it by his grace, giving rest to those that were weary and heavily laden, and raising up with his comforts those that were humbled and cast down by convictions. 8. He has a constant kindness for all good people: *The Lord loveth the righteous,* and they may with the more confidence depend upon his power when they are sure of his good-will. Our Lord Jesus showed his love to the righteous *by fulfilling all righteousness.* 9. He has a tender concern for those that stand in special need of his care: *The Lord preserves the strangers.* It ought not to pass without remark that the name of *Jehovah* is repeated here five times in five lines, to intimate that it is an almighty power (that of Jehovah) that is engaged and exerted for the relief of the oppressed, and that it is as much the glory of God to succour those that are in misery as it is to *ride on the heavens by his name Jah,* Ps. 68:4. (1.) Strangers are exposed, and are commonly destitute of friends, but *the Lord preserves them,* that they be not run down and ruined. Many a poor stranger has found the benefit of the divine protection and been kept alive by it. (2.) *Widows and fatherless children,* that have lost the head of the family, who took care of the affairs of it, often fall into the hands of those that make a prey of them, that will not do them justice, nay, that will do them injustice; but *the Lord relieveth them,* and raiseth up friends for them. See Ex. 22:22, 23. Our Lord Jesus came into the world to help the helpless, to receive Gentiles, strangers, into his kingdom, and that with him poor sinners, that are as fatherless, *may find mercy,* Hos. 14:3. 10. He will appear for the destruction of all those that oppose his kingdom and oppress the faithful subjects of it: *The way of the wicked he turns upside down,* and therefore let us *hope in him,* and not be *afraid of the fury of the oppressor,* as though he were *ready to destroy.* It is the glory of the Messiah that he will subvert all the counsels of hell and earth that militate against his church, so that, having him for us, we need not fear any thing that can be done against us. 11. His kingdom shall continue through all the revolutions of time, to the utmost ages of eternity, *v.* 10. Let *this* encourage us to trust in God at all times that *the Lord shall reign for ever,* in spite of all the malignity of the powers of darkness, *even thy God, O Zion! unto all generations.* Christ is set King on the holy hill of Zion, and his kingdom shall continue in an endless glory. It cannot be destroyed by an invader; it shall not be left to a successor, either to a succeeding monarch or a succeeding monarchy, but it shall stand for ever. It is matter of unspeakable comfort that *the Lord reigns* as Zion's God, as Zion's king, that the Messiah is head over all things to the church, and will be so while the world stands.

PSALM 147

This is another psalm of praise. Some think it was penned after the return of the Jews from their captivity; but it is so much of a piece with Ps. 145 that I rather think it was penned by David, and what is said (*v.* 2, 13) may well enough be applied to the first building and fortifying of Jerusalem in his time, and the gathering in of those that had been out-casts in Saul's time. The Septuagint divides it into two; and we may divide it into the first and second part, but both of the same import. I. We are called upon to praise God (*v.* 1, 7, 12). II. We are furnished with matter for praise, for God is to be glorified, 1. As the God of nature, and so he is very great (*v.* 4, 5, 8, 9, 15–18). 2. As the God of grace, comforting his people (*v.* 3, 6, 10, 11). 3. As the God of Israel, Jerusalem, and Zion, settling their civil state (*v.* 2, 13, 14), and especially settling religion among them (*v.* 19, 20). It is easy, in singing this psalm, to apply it to ourselves, both as to personal and national mercies, were it but as easy to do so with suitable affections.

Verses 1–11

Here, I. The duty of praise is recommended to us. It is not without reason that we are thus called to it again and again: *Praise you the Lord* (*v.* 1), and again (*v.* 7), *Sing unto the Lord with thanksgiving, sing praise upon the harp to our God* (let all our praises be directed to him and centre in him), *for it is good* to do so; it is our duty, and therefore good in itself; it is our interest, and therefore good for us. It is acceptable to our Creator and it answers the end of our creation. The law for it is holy, just, and good; the practice of it will turn to a good account. It is good, for 1. It is pleasant. Holy joy or delight are required as the principle of it, and that is pleasant to us as men; giving glory to God is the design and business of it, and that is pleasant to us as saints that are devoted to his honour. Praising God is work that is its own wages; it is heaven upon earth; it is what we should be in as in our element. 2. It is comely; it is that which becomes us as reasonable creatures, much more as people in covenant with God. In giving honour to God we really do ourselves a great deal of honour.

II. God is recommended to us as the proper object of our most exalted and enlarged praises, upon several accounts.

1. The care he takes of his chosen people, *v.* 2. Is Jerusalem to be raised out of small beginnings? Is it to be recovered out of its ruins? In both cases, *The Lord builds up Jerusalem.* The gospel-church, the Jerusalem that is from above, is of this building. He framed the model of it in his own counsels; he founded it by the preaching of his gospel; he adds to it daily such as shall be saved, and so increases it. He will build it up unto perfection, build it up as high as heaven. Are any of his people outcasts? Have they made themselves so by their own folly? He gathers them by giving them repentance and bringing them again into the communion of saints. Have they been forced out by war, famine, or persecution? He opens a door for their return; many that were missing, and thought to be lost, are brought back, and those that were scattered in the cloudy and dark day are gathered together again.

2. The comforts he has laid up for true penitents, *v.* 3. They are *broken in heart,* and wounded, humbled, and troubled, for sin, inwardly pained at the remembrance of it, as a man is that is sorely wounded. Their very hearts are not only pricked, but rent, under the sense of the dishonour they have done to God and the injury they have done to themselves by sin. To those whom God heals with the consolations of his Spirit he speaks peace, assures them that their sins are pardoned and that he is reconciled to them, and so makes them easy, pours the balm of Gilead into the bleeding wounds, and then binds them up, and makes them to rejoice. Those who have had experience of this need not be called upon to praise the Lord; for when he brought them *out of the horrible pit,* and *set their feet upon a rock,* he *put a new song into their mouths,* Ps. 40:2, 3. And for this let others praise him also.

3. The sovereign dominion he has over the lights of heaven, *v.* 4, 5. The stars are innumerable, many of them being scarcely discernible with the naked eye, and yet he counts them, and knows the exact number of them, for they are all the work of his hands and the instruments of his providence. Their bulk and power are very great; but *he calleth them all by their names,* which shows his dominion over them and the command he has them at, to make what use of them he pleases. They are his servants, his soldiers; he musters them, he marshals them; they come and go at his bidding, and all their motions are under his direction. He mentions this as one instance of many, to show that *great is our Lord and of great power* (he can do what he pleases), and of *his understanding there is no computation,* so that he can contrive every thing for the best. Man's knowledge is soon drained, and you have his utmost length; hitherto his wisdom can reach and no further. But God's knowledge is a depth that can never be fathomed.

4. The pleasure he takes in humbling the proud and exalting those of low degree (*v.* 6): *The Lord lifts up the meek,* who abase themselves before him, and whom men trample on; but *the wicked,* who conduct themselves insolently towards God and scornfully towards all mankind, who lift up themselves in pride and folly, he *casteth down to the ground,* sometimes by very humbling providences in this world, at furthest in the day when their faces shall be *filled with everlasting shame.* God proves himself to be God by *looking on the proud and abasing them,* Job 40:12.

5. The provision he makes for the inferior creatures. Though he is so great as to command the stars, he is so good as not to forget even the fowls, *v.* 8, 9. Observe in what method he feeds man and beast. (1.) *He covereth the heaven with clouds,* which darken the air and intercept the beams of the sun, and yet in them he *prepareth* that *rain for the earth* which is necessary to its fruitfulness. Clouds look melancholy, and yet without them we could have no rain and consequently no fruit. Thus afflictions, for the present, look black, and dark, and unpleasant, and we are in heaviness because of them, as sometimes when the sky is overcast it makes us dull; but they are necessary, for from these clouds of affliction come those showers that make the harvest to *yield the peaceable fruits of righteousness* (Heb. 12:11), which should help to reconcile us to them. Observe the necessary dependence which the earth has upon the heavens, which directs us on earth to depend on God in heaven. All the rain with which the earth is watered is of God's preparing. (2.) By the rain which distils on the earth he *makes grass to grow upon the mountains,* even the high mountains, which man neither takes care of nor reaps the benefit of. The mountains, which are not watered with the springs and rivers, as the valleys are, are yet watered so that they are not barren. (3.) This grass he *gives* to *the beast* for *his food,* the beast of the mountains which runs wild, which man makes no provision for. And even the *young ravens,* which, being forsaken by their old ones, *cry,* are heard by him, and ways are found to feed them, so that they are kept from perishing in the nest.

6. The complacency he takes in his people, *v.* 10, 11. In times when great things are doing, and there are great expectations of the success of them, it concerns us to know (since the issue proceeds from the Lord) whom, and what, God will delight to honour and crown with victory. It is not the strength of armies, but the strength of grace, that God is pleased to own. (1.) Not the strength of armies — not in the cavalry, *for he delighteth not in the strength of the horse,* the war-horse, noted for his courage (Job 39:19,. etc.) — nor in the infantry, for he *taketh no pleasure in the legs of a man;* he does not mean the swiftness of them for flight, to quit the field, but the steadiness of them for charging, to stand the ground. If one king, making war with another king, goes to God to pray for success, it will not avail him to plead, "Lord, I have a gallant army, the horse and foot in good order; it is a pity that they should suffer any disgrace;" for that is no argument with God, Ps. 20:7. Jehoshaphat's was much better: *Lord, we have no might,* 2 Chr. 20:12. But, (2.) God is pleased to own the strength of grace. A serious and suitable regard to God is that which is, in the sight of God, of great price in such a case. The Lord accepts and *takes pleasure* in those that *fear him and that hope in his mercy.* Observe, [1.] A holy fear of God and hope in God not only may consist, but must concur. In the same heart, at the same time, there must be both a reverence of his majesty and a complacency in his goodness, both a believing dread of his wrath and a believing expectation of his favour; not that we must hang in suspense between hope and fear, but we must act under the gracious influences of hope and fear. Our fear must save our hope from swelling into presumption, and our hope must save our fear from sinking into despair; thus must we take our work before us. [2.] We must *hope in God's mercy,* his general mercy, even when we cannot find a particular promise to stay ourselves upon. A humble confidence in the goodness of God's nature is very pleasing to him, as that which turns to the glory of that attribute in which he most glories. Every man of honour loves to be trusted.

Verses 12–20

Jerusalem, and Zion, the holy city, the holy hill, are here called upon to *praise God, v.* 12. For where should praise be offered up to God but where his altar is? Where may we expect that glory should be given to him but in the beauty of holiness? Let the inhabitants of Jerusalem praise the Lord in their own houses; let the priests and Levites, who attend in Zion, the city of their solemnities, in a special manner praise the Lord. They have more cause to do it than others, and they lie under greater obligations to do it than others; for it is their business, it is their profession. *"Praise thy God, O Zion!* he is thine, and therefore thou art bound to praise him; his being thine includes all happiness, so that thou canst never want matter for praise." Jerusalem and Zion must praise God,

I. For the prosperity and flourishing state of their civil interests, *v.* 13, 14. 1. For their common safety. They had gates, and kept their gates barred in times of danger; but that would not have been an effectual security to them if God had not *strengthened the bars of their gates* and fortified their fortifications. The most probable means we can devise for our own preservation will not answer the end, unless God give his blessing with them; we must therefore in the careful and diligent use of those means, depend upon him for that blessing, and attribute the undisturbed repose of our land more to the wall of fire than to the wall of water round about us, Zec. 2:5. 2. For the increase of their people. This strengthens the bars of the gates as much as any thing: *He hath blessed thy children within thee,* with that first and great blessing, *Be fruitful, and multiply, and replenish the land.* It is a comfort to parents to see their children blessed of the Lord (Isa. 61:9), and a comfort to the generation that is going off to see the rising generation numerous and hopeful, for which blessing God must be blessed. 3. For the public tranquillity, that they were delivered from the terrors and desolations of war: *He makes peace in thy borders,* by putting an end to the wars that were, and preventing the wars that were threatened and feared. *He makes peace within thy borders,* that is, in all parts of the country, by composing differences among neighbours, that there may be no intestine broils and animosities, and *upon thy borders,* that they may not be attacked by invasions from abroad. If there be trouble any where, it is in the borders, the marches of a country; the frontier-towns lie most exposed, so that, if there be peace in the borders, there is a universal peace, a mercy we can never be sufficiently thankful for. 4. For great plenty, the common effect of peace: He *filleth thee with the finest of the wheat* — wheat, the most valuable grain, the fat, the finest of that, and a fulness thereof. What would they more? Canaan abounded with the best wheat (Deu. 32:14) and exported it to the countries abroad, as appears, Eze. 27:17. The land of Israel was not enriched with precious stones nor spices, but with *the finest of the wheat,* with bread, which strengthens man's heart. This made it the glory of all lands, and for this God was praised in Zion.

II. For the wonderful instances of his power in the weather, particularly the winter-weather. He that protects Zion and Jerusalem is that God of power from whom all the powers of nature are derived and on whom they depend, and who produces all the changes of the seasons, which, if they were not common, would astonish us.

1. In general, whatever alterations there are in this lower world (and it is that world that is subject to continual changes) they are produced by the will, and power, and providence of God (*v.* 15): *He sendeth forth his commandment upon earth,* as one that has an incontestable authority to give orders, and innumerable attendants ready to carry his orders and put them in execution. As the world was at first made, so it is still upheld and governed, by a word of almighty power. *God speaks and it is done,* for all are his servants. That word takes effect, not only surely, but speedily. *His word runneth very swiftly,* for nothing can oppose or retard it. As the lightning, which passes through the air in an instant, such is the word of God's providence, and such the word of his grace, when it is sent forth with commission, Lu. 17:24. Angels, who carry his word and fulfil it, *fly swiftly,* Dan. 9:21.

2. In particular, frosts and thaws are both of them wonderful changes, and in both we must acknowledge the word of his power.

(1.) Frosts are from God. With him are the *treasures of the snow and the hail* (Job 38:22, 23), and out of these treasures he draws as he pleases. [1.] *He giveth snow like wool.* It is compared to wool for its whiteness (Isa. 1:18), and its softness; it falls silently, and makes no more noise than the fall of a lock of wool; it covers the earth, and keeps it warm like a fleece of wool, and so promotes its fruitfulness. See how God can work by contraries, and bring meat out of the eater, can warm the earth with cold snow. [2.] *He scatters the hoar-frost,* which is dew congealed, as the snow and hail are rain congealed. This looks like ashes scattered upon the grass, and is sometimes prejudicial to the products of the earth and blasts them as if it were hot ashes, Ps. 78:47. [3.] *He casts forth his ice like morsels,* which may be understood either of large hail-stones, which are as ice in the air, or of the ice which covers the face of the waters, and when it is broken, though naturally it was as drops of drink, it is as morsels of meat, or crusts of bread. [4.] When we see the frost, and snow, and ice, we feel it in the air: *Who can stand before his cold?* The beasts cannot; they retire into dens (Job 37:8); they are easily conquered then, 2 Sa. 23:20. Men cannot, but are forced to protect themselves by fires, or furs, or both, and all little enough where and when the cold is in extremity. We see not the causes when we feel the effects; and therefore we must call it *his cold;* it is of his sending, and therefore we must bear it patiently, and be thankful for warm houses, and clothes, and beds, to relieve us against the rigour of the season, and must give him the glory of his wisdom and sovereignty, his power and faithfulness, which shall not cease any more than summer, Gen. 8:22. And let us also infer from it, If we cannot stand before the cold of his frosts, how can we stand before the heat of his wrath?

(2.) Thaws are from God. When he pleases (*v.* 18) *he sends out his word and melts them;* the frost, the snow, the ice, are all dissolved quickly, in order to which he *causes the wind,* the *south wind, to blow,* and *the waters,* which were frozen, *flow* again as they did before. We are soon sensible of the change, but we see not the causes of it, but must resolve it into the will of the First Cause. And in it we must take notice not only of the power of God, that he can so suddenly, so insensibly, make such a great and universal alteration in the temper of the air and the face of the earth (what cannot he do that does this every winter, perhaps often every winter?) but also of the goodness of God. Hard weather does not always continue; it would be sad if it should. He does not *contend for ever,* but *renews the face of the earth.* As he remembered Noah, and released him (Gen. 8:1), so he remembers the earth, and his covenant with the earth, Cant. 2:11, 12. This thawing word may represent the gospel of Christ, and this thawing wind the Spirit of Christ (for the Spirit is compared to the wind, Jn. 3:8); both are sent for the melting of frozen souls. Converting grace, like the thaw, softens the heart that was hard, moistens it, and melts it into tears of repentance; it warms good affections, and makes them to flow, which, before, were chilled and stopped up. The change which the thaw makes is universal and yet gradual; it is very evident, and yet how it is done is unaccountable: such is the change wrought in the conversion of a soul, when God's word and Spirit are sent to melt it and restore it to itself.

III. For his distinguishing favour to Israel, in giving them his word and ordinances, a much more valuable blessing than their peace and plenty (*v.* 14), as much as the soul is more excellent than the body. Jacob and Israel had God's statutes and judgments among them. They were under his peculiar government; the municipal laws of their nation were of his framing and enacting, and their constitution was a theocracy. They had the benefit of divine revelation; the great things of God's law were written to them. They had a priesthood of divine institution for all things pertaining to God, and prophets for all extraordinary occasions. No people besides went upon sure grounds in their religion. Now this was, 1. A preventing mercy. They did not find out God's statutes and judgments of themselves, but *God showed his word unto Jacob,* and by that word he made known to them his *statutes and judgments.* It is a great mercy to any people to have the word of God among them; for *faith comes by hearing* and reading that word, that faith without which it is impossible to please God. 2. A distinguishing mercy, and upon that account the more obliging: *"He hath not dealt so with every nation,* not with *any* nation; and, *as for his judgments, they have not known them,* nor are likely to know them till the Messiah shall come and take down the partition-wall between Jew and Gentile, that the gospel may be preached to every creature." Other nations had plenty of outward good things; some nations were very rich, others had pompous powerful princes and polite literature, but none were blessed with God's statutes and judgments as Israel were. Let *Israel* therefore *praise the Lord* in the observance of these statutes. *Lord, how is it that thou wilt manifest thyself to us, and not to the world! Even so, Father, because it seemed good in thy eyes.*

PSALM 148

This psalm is a most solemn and earnest call to all the creatures, according to their capacity, to praise their Creator, and to show forth his eternal power and Godhead, the invisible things of which are manifested in the things that are seen. Thereby the psalmist designs to express his great affection to the duty of praise; he is highly satisfied that God is praised, is very desirous that he may be more praised, and therefore does all he can to engage all about him in this pleasant work, yea, and all who shall come after him, whose hearts must be very dead and cold if they be not raised and enlarged, in praising God, by the lofty flights of divine poetry which we find in this psalm. I. He calls upon the higher house, the creatures that are placed in the upper world, to praise the Lord, both those that are intellectual beings, and are capable of doing it actively (*v.* 1, 2), and those that are not, and are therefore capable of doing it only objectively (*v.* 3–6). II. He calls upon the lower house, the creatures of this lower world, both those that can only minister matter of praise (*v.* 7–10) and those that, being endued with reason, are capable of offering up this sacrifice (*v.* 11–13), especially his own people, who have more cause to do it, and are more concerned to do it, than any other (*v.* 14).

Verses 1–6

We, in this dark and depressed world, know but little of the world of light and exaltation, and, conversing within narrow confines, can scarcely admit any tolerable conceptions of the vast regions above. But this we know,

I. That there is above us a world of blessed angels by whom God is praised, an innumerable company of them. *Thousand thousands minister unto him, and ten thousand times ten thousand stand before him;* and it is his glory that he has such attendants, but much more his glory that he neither needs them, nor is, nor can be, any way benefited by them. To that bright and happy world the psalmist has an eye here, v. 1, 2. In general, to *the heavens*, to *the heights*. The heavens are the heights, and therefore we must lift up our souls above the world unto God in *the heavens*, and *on things above* we must *set our affections*. It is his desire that God may be praised *from the heavens*, that thence a praising frame may be transmitted to this world in which we live, that while we are so cold, and low, and flat, in praising God, there are those above who are doing it in a better manner, and that while we are so often interrupted in this work they rest not day nor night from it. In particular, he had an eye to God's *angels*, to *his hosts*, and calls upon them to praise God. That God's angels are his hosts is plain enough; as soon as they were made they were enlisted, armed, and disciplined; he employs them in fighting his battles, and they keep ranks, and know their place, and observe the word of command as his hosts. But what is meant by the psalmist's calling upon them, and exciting them to praise God, is not so easy to account for. I will not say, They do not heed it, because we find that *to the principalities and powers is known by the church the manifold wisdom of God* (Eph. 3:10); but I will say, They do not need it, for they are continually praising God and there is no deficiency at all in their performances; and therefore when, in singing this psalm, we call upon the angels to praise God (as we did, Ps. 103:20), we mean that we desire God may be praised by the ablest hands and in the best manner, — that we are pleased to think he is so, — that we have a spiritual communion with those that dwell in his house above and are still praising him, — and that we have come by faith, and hope, and holy love, to the *innumerable company of angels*, Heb. 12:22.

II. That there is above us not only an assembly of blessed spirits, but a system of vast bodies too, and those bright ones, in which God is praised, that is, which may give us occasion (as far as we know any thing of them) to give to God the glory not only of their being, but of their beneficence to mankind. Observe,

1. What these creatures are that thus show us the way in praising God, and, whenever we look up and consider the heavens, furnish us with matter for his praises. (1.) There are the *sun, moon,* and *stars,* which continually, either day or night, present themselves to our view, as looking-glasses, in which we may see a faint shadow (for so I must call it, not a resemblance) of the glory of him that is *the Father of lights, v.* 3. The greater lights, the sun and moon, are not too great, too bright, to praise him; and the praises of the less lights, the stars, shall not be slighted. Idolaters made the sun, moon, and stars, their gods, and praised them, worshipping and serving the creature, because it is seen, more than the Creator, because he is not seen; but we, who worship the true God only, make them our fellow-worshippers, and call upon them to praise him with us, nay, as Levites to attend us, who, as priests, offer this spiritual sacrifice. (2.) There are the *heavens of heavens* above the sun and stars, the seat of the blessed; from the vastness and brightness of these unknown orbs abundance of glory redounds to God, for *the heavens of heavens are the Lord's* (Ps. 115:16) and yet *they cannot contain him,* 1 Ki. 8:27. The learned Dr. Hammond understands her, by *the heavens of heavens,* the upper regions of the air, or all the regions of it, as Ps. 68:33. We read of the heaven of heavens, whence *God sends forth his voice, and that a mighty voice,* meaning the thunder. (3.) There are *the waters that are above the heavens,* the clouds that hang above in the air, where they are reserved *against the day of battle and war,* Job 38:23. We have reason to praise God, not only that these waters do not drown the earth, but that they do water it and make it fruitful. The Chaldee paraphrase reads it, *Praise him, you heavens of heavens, and you waters that depend on the word of him who is above the heavens,* for the key of the clouds is one of the keys which God has in his hand, wherewith he opens and none can shut, he shuts and none can open.

2. Upon what account we are to give God the glory of them: *Let them praise the name of the Lord,* that is, let us praise the name of the Lord for them, and observe what constant and fresh matter for praise may be fetched from them. (1.) Because he made them, gave them their powers and assigned them their places: *He commanded* them (great as they are) out of nothing, *and they were created* at a word's speaking. God created, and therefore may command; for he commanded, and so created; his authority must always be acknowledged and acquiesced in, because he once spoke with such authority. (2.) Because he still upholds and preserves them in their beings and posts, their powers and motions (*v.* 6): *He hath established them for ever and ever,* that is, to the end of time, a short ever, but it is their ever; they shall last as long as there is occasion for them. *He hath made a decree,* the law of creation, *which shall not pass;* it was enacted by the wisdom of God, and therefore needs not be altered, by his sovereignty and inviolable fidelity, and therefore cannot be altered. All the creatures that praised God at first for their creation must praise him still for their continuance. And we have reason to praise him that they are kept within the bounds of a decree; for to that it is owing that the waters above the heavens have not a second time drowned the earth.

Verses 7–14

Considering that this earth, and the atmosphere that surrounds it, are the very sediment of the universe, it concerns us to enquire after those considerations that may be of use to reconcile us to our place in it; and I know none more likely than this (next to the visit which the Son of God once made to it), that even in this world, dark and as bad as it is, God is praised: *Praise you the Lord from the earth, v.* 7. As the rays of the sun, which are darted directly from heaven, reflect back (though more weakly) from the earth, so should the praises of God, with which this cold and infected world should be warmed and perfumed.

I. Even those creatures that are not dignified with the powers of reason are summoned into this concert, because God may be glorified in them, *v.* 7–10. Let the *dragons* or *whales,* that sport themselves in the mighty waters (Ps. 104:26), dance before the Lord, to his glory, who largely proves his own omnipotence by his dominion over the leviathan or whale, Job 41:1, etc. *All deeps,* and their inhabitants, praise God — the sea, and the animals there — the bowels of the earth, and the animals there. *Out of the depths* God may be praised as well as prayed unto. If we look up into the atmosphere we meet with a great variety of meteors, which, being a king of new productions (and some of them unaccountable), do in a special manner magnify the power of the great Creator. There are fiery meteors; lightning is fire, and there are other blazes sometimes kindled which may be so called. There are watery meteors, *hail,* and *snow,* and the *vapours* of which they are gendered. There are airy meteors, *stormy winds;* we know not whence they come nor whither they go, whence their mighty force comes nor how it is spent; but this we know, that, be they ever so strong, so stormy, they *fulfil God's word,* and do that, and no more than that, which he appoints them; and by *this* Christ showed himself to have a divine power, that he *commanded even the winds and the seas,* and *they obeyed him.* Those that will not fulfil God's word, but rise up in rebellion against it, show themselves to be more violent and headstrong than even the stormy winds, for they fulfil it. Take a view of the surface of the earth (*v.* 9), and there are presented to our view the exalted grounds, *mountains and all hills,* from the barren tops of some of which, and the fruitful tops of others, we may fetch matter for praise; there are the exalted plants, some that are exalted by their usefulness, as the *fruitful trees* of various kinds, for the fruits of which God is to be praised, others by their stateliness, as *all cedars,* those *trees of the Lord,* Ps. 104:16. Cedars, the high trees, are not the fruitful trees, yet they had their use even in God's temple. Pass we next to the animal kingdom, and there we find God glorified, even by the *beasts* that run wild, *and all cattle* that are tame and in the service of man, *v.* 10. Nay, even the *creeping things* have not sunk so low, nor do the *flying fowl* soar so high, as not to be called upon to *praise the Lord.* Much of the wisdom, power, and goodness of the Creator appears in the several capacities and instincts of the creatures, in the provision made for them and the use made of them. When we see all so very strange, and all so very good, surely we cannot but acknowledge God with wonder and thankfulness.

II. Much more those creatures that are dignified with the powers of reason ought to employ them in praising God: *Kings of the earth and all people, v.* 11, 12. 1. God is to be glorified in and for these, as in and for the inferior creatures, for their hearts are in the hand of the Lord and he makes what use he pleases of them. God is to be praised in the order and constitution of kingdoms, the *pars imperans — the part that commands,* and the *pars subdita — the part that is subject: Kings of the earth and all people.* It is by him that kings reign, and people are subject to them; the *princes and judges of the earth* have their wisdom and their commission from him, and we, to whom they are blessings, ought to bless God for them. God is to be praised also in the constitution of families, for he is the founder of them; and for all the comfort of relations, the comfort that parents and children, brothers and sisters, have in each other, God is to be praised. 2. God is to be glorified by these. Let all manner of persons praise God. (1.) Those of each rank, high and low. The praises of kings, and princes, and judges, are demanded; those on whom God has put honour must honour him with it, and the power they are entrusted with, and the figure they make in the world, put them in a capacity of bringing more glory to God and doing him more service than others. Yet the praises of the people are expected also, and God will graciously accept of them; Christ despised not the hosannas of the multitude. (2.) Those of each sex, *young men and maidens,* who are accustomed to make merry together; let them turn their mirth into this channel; let it be sacred, that it may be pure. (3.) Those of each age. *Old men* must still bring forth this fruit in old age, and not think that either the gravity or the infirmity of their age will excuse them from it; *and children* too must begin betimes to praise God; even *out of the mouth of babes and sucklings* this good work is perfected. A good reason is given (*v.* 13) why all these should *praise the name of the Lord,* because *his name alone is excellent* and worthy to be praised; it is a name above every name, no name, no nature, but his, has in it all excellency. *His glory is above* both *the earth and the heaven,* and let all inhabitants both of earth and heaven praise him and yet acknowledge his name to be exalted *far above all blessing and praise.*

III. Most of all his own people, who are dignified with peculiar privileges, must in a peculiar manner give glory to him, *v.* 14. Observe, 1. The dignity God has put upon *his people, even the children of Israel,* typical of the honour reserved for all true believers, who are God's spiritual Israel. *He exalts their horn,* their brightness, their plenty, their power. The people of Israel were, in many respects, honoured above any other nation, for *to them pertained the adoption, the glory, and the covenants,* Rom. 9:4. It was their own honour that they were *a people near unto God,* his *Segulla, his peculiar treasure;* they were admitted into his courts, when a stranger that came nigh must be put to death. They had him *nigh to them in all that which they called upon him for.* This blessing has not come upon the Gentiles, through Christ, for those that *were afar off are* by *his blood made nigh,* Eph. 2:13. It is the greatest honour that can be put upon a man to be brought near to god, the nearer the better; and it will be best of all when nearest of all in the kingdom of glory. 2. The duty God expects from them in consideration of this. Let those whom God honours honour him: *Praise you the Lord.* Let him be *the praise of all his saints,* the object of their praise; for he is a praise to them. *He is thy praise, and he is thy God,* Deu. 10:21. Some by the *horn of his people* understand David, as a type of Christ, whom God has exalted to be *a prince and a Saviour,* who is indeed the praise of all his saints and will be so for ever; for it is through him that they are *a people near to God.*

PSALM 149

The foregoing psalm was a hymn of praise to the Creator; this is a hymn of praise to the Redeemer. It is a psalm of triumph in the God of Israel, and over the enemies of Israel. Probably it was penned upon occasion of some victory which Israel was blessed and honoured with. Some conjecture that it was penned when David had taken the strong-hold of Zion, and settled his government there. But it looks further, to the kingdom of the Messiah, who, in the chariot of the everlasting gospel, goes forth conquering and to conquer. To him, and his graces and glories, we must have an eye, in singing this psalm, which proclaims, I. Abundance of joy to all the people of God (*v.* 1–5). II. Abundance of terror to the proudest of their enemies (*v.* 6–9).

Verses 1–5

We have here,

I. The calls given to God's Israel to praise. *All his works* were, in the foregoing psalm, excited to *praise him;* but here his saints in a particular manner are required to bless him. Observe then, 1. Who are called upon to praise God. *Israel* in general, the body of the church (*v.* 2), *the children of Zion* particularly, the inhabitants of that holy hill, who are nearer to God than other Israelites; those that have the word and ordinances of God near to them, that are not required to travel far to them, are justly expected to do more in praising God than others. All true Christians may call themselves *the children of Zion,* for in faith and hope *we have come unto Mount Zion,* Heb. 12:22. The saints must praise God, saints in profession, saints in power, for this is the intention of their sanctification; they are devoted to the glory of God, and renewed by the grace of God, that *they may be unto him for a name and a praise.* 2. What must be the principle of this praise, and that is holy joy in God: *Let Israel rejoice,* and *the children of Zion be joyful,* and *the saints be joyful in glory.* Our praises of God should flow from a heart filled with delight and triumph in God's attributes, and our relation to him. Much of the power of godliness in the heart consists in making God our chief joy and solacing ourselves in him; and our faith in Christ is described by our rejoicing in him. We then give honour to God when we take pleasure in him. We must *be joyful in glory,* that is, in him as our glory, and in the interest we have in him; and let us look upon it as our glory to be of those that rejoice in God. 3. What must be the expressions of this praise. We must by all proper ways show forth the praises of God: *Sing to the Lord.* We must entertain ourselves, and proclaim his name, by *singing praises to him* (*v.* 3), *singing aloud* (*v.* 5), for we should sing psalms with all our heart, as those that are not only not ashamed of it, but are enlarged in it. We must sing a *new song,* newly composed upon every special occasion, sing with new affections, which make the song new, though the words have been used before, and keep them from growing threadbare. Let God be *praised in the dance with timbrel and harp,* according to the usage of the Old-Testament church very early (Ex. 15:20), where we find God praised with *timbrels and dances.* Those who from this urge the use of music in religious worship must by the same rule introduce dancing, for they went together, as in David's dancing before the ark, and Jdg. 21:21. But, whereas many scriptures in the New Testament keep up singing as a gospel-ordinance, none provide for the keeping up of music and dancing; the gospel-canon for psalmody is to *sing with the spirit* and *with the understanding.* 4. What opportunities must be taken for praising God, none must be let slip, but particularly, (1.) We must praise God in public, in the *solemn assembly* (*v.* 1), *in the congregation of saints.* The more the better; it is the more like heaven. Thus God's name must be owned before the world; thus the service must have a solemnity put upon it, and we must mutually excite one another to it. The principle, end, and design of our coming together in religious assemblies is that we may join together in praising God. Other parts of the service must be in order to this. (2.) We must praise him in private. *Let the saints* be so transported with their joy in God as to *sing aloud upon their beds,* when they awake in the night, full of the praises of God, as David, Ps. 119:62. When God's Israel are brought to a quiet settlement, let them enjoy that, with thankfulness to God; much more may true believers, that have entered into God's rest, and find repose in Jesus Christ, sing aloud for joy of that. Upon their sick-beds, their death-beds, let them sing the praises of their God.

II. The cause given to God's Israel for praise. Consider, 1. God's doings for them. They have reason to rejoice inn God, to devote themselves to his honour and employ themselves in his service; for it is he that made them. He gave us our being as men, and we have reason to praise him for that, for it is a noble and excellent being. He gave Israel their being as a people, as a church, made them what they were, so very different from other nations. Let that people therefore praise him, for he formed them for himself, on purpose that they might *show forth his praise,* Isa. 43:21. Let Israel *rejoice in his Makers* (so it is in the original); for God said, *Let us make man;* and in this, some think, is the mystery of the Trinity. 2. God's dominion over them. This follows upon the former: if he made them, he is their King; he that gave being no doubt may give law; and this ought to be the matter of our joy and praise that we are under the conduct and protection of such a wise and powerful King. *Rejoice greatly, O daughter of Zion! for behold thy king comes,* the king Messiah, whom God has *set upon his holy hill of Zion;* let all the children of Zion *be joyful* in him, and go forth to meet him with their hosannas, Zec. 9:9. 3. God's delight in them. he is a king that rules by love, and therefore to be praised; for *the Lord takes pleasure in his people,* in their services, in their prosperity, in communion with them, and in the communications of his favour to them. He that is infinitely happy in the enjoyment of himself, and to whose felicity no accession can be made, yet graciously condescends to *take pleasure in his people,* Ps. 147:11. 4. God's designs concerning them. Besides the present complacency he has in them, he has prepared for their future glory: *He will beautify the meek,* the humble, and lowly, and contrite in heart, that tremble at his word and submit to it, that are patient under their afflictions and *show all meekness towards all men.* These men vilify and asperse, but God will justify them, and wipe off their reproach; nay, he will beautify them; they shall appear not only clear, but comely, before all the world, with the comeliness that he puts upon them. He will beautify them with salvation, with temporal salvations (when God works remarkable deliverances for his people those that had *been among the pots become as the wings of a dove covered with silver,* Ps. 68:13), but especially with eternal salvation. The righteous shall be beautified in that day when they *shine forth as the sun.* In the hopes of this, let them now, in the darkest day, *sing a new song.*

Verses 6–9

The Israel of God are here represented triumphing over their enemies, which is both the matter of their praise (let them give to God the glory of those triumphs) and the recompence of their praise; those that are truly thankful to God for their tranquillity shall be blessed with victory. Or it may be taken as a further expression of their praise (*v.* 6): *let the high praises of God be in their mouth,* and then, in a holy zeal for his honour, let them take a *two-edged sword in their hand,* to fight his battles against the enemies of his kingdom. Now this may be applied, 1. To the many victories which God blessed his people Israel with over the nations of Canaan and other nations that were devoted to destruction. These began in Moses and Joshua, who, when they taught Israel *the high praises of the Lord,* did withal put *a two-edged sword in their hand;* David did so too, for, as he was the sweet singer of Israel, so he was the captain of their hosts, and taught the children of Judah the use of the bow (2 Sa. 1:18), taught their hands to war, as God had taught his. Thus he and they went on victoriously, fighting the Lord's battles, and avenging Israel's quarrels on those that had oppressed them; then they *executed vengeance upon the heathen* (the Philistines, Moabites, Ammonites, and others, 2 Sa. 8:1, etc.) *and punishments upon the people,* for all the wrong they had done to God's people, *v.* 7. Their kings and nobles were taken prisoners (*v.* 8) and on some of them the judgment written was executed, as by Joshua on the kings of Canaan, by Gideon on the princes of Midian, by Samuel on Agag. The honour of this redounded to all the Israel of God; and to him who put it upon them they return it entirely in their hallelujahs. Jehoshaphat's army had at the same time *the high praises of God in their mouth and a two-edged sword in their hand,* for they went forth to war singing the praises of God, and then their sword did execution, 2 Chr. 20:23. Some apply it to the time of the Maccabees, when the Jews sometimes gained great advantages against their oppressors. And if it seem strange that the meek should, notwithstanding that character, be thus severe, and upon kings and nobles too, here is one word that justifies them in it; it is *the judgment written.* They do not do it from any personal malice and revenge, or any bloody politics that they govern themselves by, but by commission from God, according to his direction, and in obedience to his command; and Saul lost his kingdom for disobeying a command of this nature. Thus the kings of the earth that shall be employed in the destruction of the New-Testament Babylon will but *execute the judgment written,* Rev. 17:16, 17. But, since now no such special commissions can be produced, this will by no means justify the violence either of subjects against their princes or of princes against their subjects, or both against their neighbours, under pretence of religion; for Christ never intended that his gospel should be propagated by fire and sword or his righteousness wrought by the wrath of man. When the high praises of God are in our mouth with them we should have an olive-branch of peace in our hands. 2. To Christ's victories by the power of his gospel and grace over spiritual enemies, in which all believers are more than conquerors. The word of God is the *two-edged sword* (Heb. 4:12), the *sword of the Spirit* (Eph. 6:17), which it is not enough to have in our armoury, we must have it in our hand also, as our Master had, when he said, *It is written.* Now, (1.) With this two-edged sword the first preachers of the gospel obtained a glorious victory over the powers of darkness; vengeance was executed upon the gods of the heathen, by the conviction and conversion of those that had been long their worshippers, and by the consternation and confusion of those that would not repent (Rev. 6:15); the strongholds of Satan were cast down (2 Chr. 10:4, 5); great men were made to tremble at the word, as Felix; Satan, the god of this world, was cast out, according to the judgment given against him. *This* is the honour of all Christians, that their holy religion has been so victorious. (2.) With this two-edged sword believers fight against their own corruptions, and, through the grace of God, subdue and mortify them; the sin that had dominion over them is crucified; self, that once sat king, is bound with chains and brought into subjection to the yoke of Christ; the tempter is foiled and bruised under their feet. *This honour have all the saints.* (3.) The complete accomplishment of this will be in the judgment of the great day, when *the Lord* shall come *with ten thousands of his saints, to execute judgment upon all,* Jude 14, 15. Vengeance shall then be *executed upon the heathen* (Ps. 9:17), *and punishments,* everlasting punishments, *upon the people. Kings and nobles,* that cast away the bands and cords of Christ's government (Ps. 2:3), shall not be able to cast away the chains and fetters of his wrath and justice. Then shall be executed *the judgment written,* for *the secrets of men shall be judged according to the gospel. This* honour shall all the saints have, that, as assessors with Christ, they shall *judge the world,* 1 Co. 6:2. In the prospect of that let them praise the Lord, and continue Christ's faithful servants and soldiers to the end of their lives.

PSALM 150

The first and last of the psalms have both the same number of verses, are both short, and very memorable. But the scope of them is very different: the first psalm is an elaborate instruction in our duty, to prepare us for the comforts of our devotion; this is all rapture and transport, and perhaps was penned on purpose to be the conclusion of these sacred songs, to show what is the design of them all, and that is to assist us in praising God. The psalmist had been himself full of the praises of God, and here he would fain fill all the world with them: again and again he calls, "Praise the Lord, praise him, praise him," no less than thirteen times in these six short verses. He shows, I. For what, and upon what account, God is to be praised (*v.* 1, 2), II. How, and with what expressions of joy, God is to be praised (*v.* 3–5). III. Who must praise the Lord; it is every one's business (*v.* 6). In singing this psalm we should endeavour to get our hearts much affected with the perfections of God and the praises with which he is and shall be for ever attended, throughout all ages, world without end.

Verses 1–6

We are here, with the greatest earnestness imaginable, excited to praise God; if, as some suppose, this psalm was primarily intended for the Levites, to stir them up to do their office in the house of the Lord, as singers and players on instruments, yet we must take it as speaking to us, who are made to our God spiritual priests. And the repeated inculcating of the call thus intimates that it is a great and necessary duty, a duty which we should be much employed and much enlarged in, but which we are naturally backward to and cold in, and therefore need to be brought to, and held to, by precept upon precept, and line upon line. Observe here,

I. Whence this tribute of praise arises, and out of what part of his dominion it especially issues. It comes, 1. From *his sanctuary;* praise him there. Let his priests, let his people, that attend there, attend him with their praises. Where should he be praised, but there where he does, in a special manner, both manifest his glory and communicate his grace? *Praise God* upon the account of *his sanctuary,* and the privileges which we enjoy by having that among us, Eze. 37:26. *Praise God in his holy ones* (so some read it); we must take notice of the image of God as it appears on those that are sanctified, and love them for the sake of that image; and when we praise them we must praise God in them. 2. From *the firmament of his power. Praise him* because of his power and glory which appear in the firmament, its vastness, its brightness, and its splendid furniture; and because of the powerful influences it has upon this earth. Let those that have their dwelling *in the firmament of his power,* even the holy angels, lead in this good work. Some, by the *sanctuary,* as well as by *the firmament of his power,* understand the highest heavens, the residence of his glory; that is indeed his sanctuary, his holy temple, and there he is praised continually, in a far better manner than we can praise him. And it is a comfort to us, when we find we do it so poorly, that it is so well done there.

II. Upon what account this tribute of praise is due, upon many accounts, particularly, 1. The works of his power (*v.* 2): *Praise him for his mighty acts;* for *his mightinesses* (so the word is), for all the instances of his might, the power of his providence, the power of his grace, what he has done in the creation, government, and redemption of the world, for the children of men in general, for his own church and children in particular. 2. The glory and majesty of his being: *Praise him according to his excellent greatness, according to the multitude of his magnificence* (so Dr. Hammond reads it); not that our praises can bear any proportion to God's greatness, for it is infinite, but, since he is greater than we can express or conceive, we must raise our conceptions and expressions to the highest degree we can attain to. Be not afraid of saying too much in the praises of God, as we often do in praising even great and good men. *Deus non patitur hyperbolum — We cannot speak hyperbolically of God;* all the danger is of saying too little and therefore, when we have done our utmost, we must own that though we have praised him in consideration of, yet not in proportion to, *his excellent greatness.*

III. In what manner this tribute must be paid, with all the kinds of musical instruments that were then used in the temple-service, *v.* 3–5. It is well that we are not concerned to enquire what sort of instruments these were; it is enough that they were well known then. Our concern is to know, 1. That hereby is intimated how full the psalmist's heart was of the praises of God and how desirous he was that this good work might go on. 2. That in serving God we should spare no cost nor pains. 3. That the best music in God's ears is devout and pious affections, *non musica chordula, sed cor — not a melodious string, but a melodious heart.* Praise God with a strong faith; praise him with holy love and delight; praise him with an entire confidence in Christ; praise him with a believing triumph over the powers of darkness; praise him with an earnest desire towards him and a full satisfaction in him; praise him by a universal respect to all his commands; praise him by a cheerful submission to all his disposals; praise him by rejoicing in his love and solacing yourselves in his great goodness; praise him by promoting the interests of the kingdom of his grace; praise him by a lively hope and expectation of the kingdom of his glory. 4. That, various instruments being used in praising God, it should yet be done with an exact and perfect harmony; they must not hinder, but help one another. The New-Testament concert, instead of this, is *with one mind and one mouth to glorify God,* Rom. 15:6.

IV. Who must pay this tribute (*v.* 6): *Let every thing that has breath praise the Lord.* He began with a call to those that had a place in his sanctuary and were employed in the temple-service; but he concludes with a call to all the children of men, in prospect of the time when the Gentiles should be taken into the church, and *in every place,* as acceptably as at Jerusalem, *this incense should be offered,* Mal. 1:11. Some think that in *every thing that has breath* here we must include the inferior creatures (as Gen. 7:22), all *in whose nostrils was the breath of life.* They praise God according to their capacity. The singing of birds is a sort of praising God. The brutes do in effect say to man, "We would praise God if we could; do you do it for us." John in vision heard a song of praise from *every creature which is in heaven, and on the earth, and under the earth,* Rev. 5:13. Others think that only the children of men are meant; for into them God has in a more peculiar manner *breathed the breath of life,* and they have become *living souls,* Gen. 2:7. Now that the gospel is ordered to be preached *to every creature,* to every human creature, it is required that every human creature praise the Lord. What have we our breath, our spirit, for, but to spend it in praising God; and how can we spend it better? Prayers are called *our breathings,* Lam. 3:56. Let every one that breathes towards God in prayer, finding the benefit of that, breathe forth his praises too. Having breath, let the praises of God perfume our breath; let us be in this work as in our element; let it be to us as the air we breathe in, which we could not live without. Having our breath in our nostrils, let us consider that it is still going forth, and will shortly go and not return. Since therefore we must shortly breathe our last, while we have breath let us praise the Lord, and then we shall breathe our last with comfort, and, when death runs us out of breath, we shall remove to a better state to breathe God's praises in a freer better air.

The first three of the five books of psalms (according to the Hebrew division) concluded with *Amen and Amen,* the fourth with *Amen, Hallelujah,* but the last, and in it the whole book, concludes with only *Hallelujah,* because the last six psalms are wholly taken up in praising God and there is not a word of complaint or petition in them. The nearer good Christians come to their end the fuller they should be of the praises of God. Some think that this last psalm is designed to represent to us the work of glorified saints in heaven, who are there continually praising God, and that the musical instruments here said to be used are no more to be understood literally than the gold, and pearls, and precious stones, which are said to adorn the New Jerusalem, Rev. 21:18, 19. But, as those intimate that the glories of heaven are the most excellent glories, so these intimate that the praises the saints offer there are the most excellent praises. Prayers will there be swallowed up in everlasting praises; there will be no intermission in praising God, and yet no weariness — hallelujahs for ever repeated, and yet still new songs. Let us often take a pleasure in thinking what glorified saints are doing in heaven, what those are doing whom we have been acquainted with on earth, but who have gone before us thither; and let it not only make us long to be among them, but quicken us to do this part of the will of God on earth as those do it that are in heaven. And let us spend as much of our time as may be in this good work because in it we hope to spend a joyful eternity. *Hallelujah* is the word there (Rev. 19:1, 3); let us echo to it now, as those that hope to join in it shortly. *Hallelujah, praise you the Lord.*

AN EXPOSITION, WITH PRACTICAL OBSERVATIONS, OF

THE PROVERBS

We have now before us, I. A new author, or penman rather, or pen (if you will) made use of by the Holy Ghost for making known the mind of God to us, writing as moved by the *finger of God* (so the Spirit of God is called), and that is Solomon; through his hand came this book of Scripture and the two that follow it, Ecclesiastes and Canticles, a sermon and a song. Some think he wrote Canticles when he was very young, Proverbs in the midst of his days, and Ecclesiastes when he was old. In the title of his song he only writes himself *Solomon,* perhaps because he wrote it before his accession to the throne, being filled with the Holy Ghost when he was young. In the title of his Proverbs he writes himself *the son of David, king of Israel,* for then he ruled over all Israel. In the title of his Ecclesiastes he writes himself *the son of David, king of Jerusalem,* because then perhaps his influence had grown less upon the distant tribes, and he confined himself very much in Jerusalem. Concerning this author we may observe, 1. That he was a king, and a king's son. The penmen of scripture, hitherto, were most of them men of the first rank in the world, as Moses and Joshua, Samuel and David, and now Solomon; but, after him, the inspired writers were generally poor prophets, men of no figure in the world, because that dispensation was approaching in the which God would choose the *weak and foolish things of the world to confound the wise and mighty* and the poor should be employed to evangelize. Solomon was a very rich king, and his dominions were very large, a king of the first magnitude, and yet he addicted himself to the study of divine things, and was a prophet and a prophet's son. It is no disparagement to the greatest princes and potentates in the world to instruct those about them in religion and the laws of it. 2. That he was one whom God endued with extraordinary measures of wisdom and knowledge, in answer to his prayers at his accession to the throne. His prayer was exemplary: *Give me a wise and an understanding heart;* the answer to it was encouraging: he had what he desired and *all other things were added to him.* Now here we find what good use he made of the wisdom God gave him; he not only governed himself and his kingdom with it, but he gave rules of wisdom to others also, and transmitted them to posterity. Thus must we trade with the talents with which we are entrusted, according as they are. 3. That he was one who had his faults, and in his latter end turned aside from those good ways of God which in this book he had directed others in. We have the story of it 1 Ki. 11, and a sad story it is, that the penman of such a book as this should apostatize as he did. *Tell it not in Gath.* But let those who are most eminently useful take warning by this not to be proud or secure; and let us all learn not to think the worse of good instructions though we have them from those who do not themselves altogether live up to them.

II. A new way of writing, in which divine wisdom is taught us by Proverbs, or short sentences, which contain their whole design within themselves and are not connected with one another. We have had divine *laws, histories,* and *songs,* and how divine *proverbs;* such various methods has Infinite Wisdom used for our instruction, that, no stone being left unturned to do us good, we may be inexcusable if we perish in our folly. Teaching by proverbs was, 1. An ancient way of teaching. It was the most ancient way among the Greeks; each of the seven wise men of Greece had some one saying that he valued himself upon, and that made him famous. These sentences were inscribed on pillars, and had in great veneration as that which was said to come down from heaven. *A coelo descendit, Gnōthi seauton — Know thyself is a precept which came down from heaven.* 2. It was a plain and easy way of teaching, which cost neither the teachers nor the learners much pains, nor put their understandings nor their memories to the stretch. Long periods, and arguments far-fetched, must be laboured both by him that frames them and by him that would understand them, while a proverb, which carries both its sense and its evidence in a little compass, is quickly apprehended and subscribed to, and is easily retained. Both David's devotions and Solomon's instructions are sententious, which may recommend that way of expression to those who minister about holy things, both in praying and preaching. 3. It was a very profitable way of teaching, and served admirably well to answer the end. The word *Mashal,* here used for a proverb, comes from a word that signifies *to rule* or *have dominion,* because of the commanding power and influence which wise and weighty sayings have upon the children of men; he that teaches by them *dominatur in concionibus — rules his auditory.* It is easy to observe how the world is governed by proverbs. *As saith the proverb of the ancients* (1 Sa. 24:13), or (as we commonly express it) *As the old saying is,* goes very far with most men in forming their notions and fixing their resolves. Much of the wisdom of the ancients has been handed down to posterity by proverbs; and some think we may judge of the temper and character of a nation by the complexion of its vulgar proverbs. Proverbs in conversation are like axious in philosophy, maxims in law, and postulata in the mathematics, which nobody disputes, but every one endeavours to expound so as to have them on his side. Yet there are many corrupt proverbs, which tend to debauch men's minds and harden them in sin. The devil has his proverbs, and the world and the flesh have their proverbs, which reflect reproach on God and religion (as Eze. 12:22; 18:2), to guard us against the corrupt influences of which God has his proverbs, which are all wise and good, and tend to make us so. These proverbs of Solomon were not merely a collection of the wise sayings that had been formerly delivered, as some have imagined, but were the dictates of the Spirit of God in Solomon. The very first of them (*ch.* 1:7) agrees with what God said to man in the beginning (Job 28:28, *Behold, the fear of the Lord, that is wisdom*); so that though Solomon was great, and his name may serve as much as any man's to recommend his writings, yet, behold, *a greater than Solomon is here.* It is God, by Solomon, that here speaks to us: I say, to *us;* for these proverbs were *written for our learning,* and, when Solomon speaks to his son, the exhortation is said *to speak to us as unto children,* Heb. 12:5. And, as we have no book so useful to us in our devotions as David's psalms, so have we none so serviceable to us, for the right ordering of our conversations, as Solomon's proverbs, which as David says of the commandments, are *exceedingly broad,* containing, in a little compass, a complete body of divine ethics, politics, and economics, exposing every vice, recommending every virtue, and suggesting rules for the government of ourselves in every relation and condition, and every turn of the conversation. The learned bishop Hall has drawn up a system of moral philosophy out of Solomon's Proverbs and Ecclesiastes. The first nine chapters of this book are reckoned as a preface, by way of exhortation to the study and practice of wisdom's rules, and caution against those things that would hinder therein. We have then the first volume of Solomon's proverbs (*ch.* 10–24); after that a second volume (*ch.* 25–29); and then Agur's prophecy (*ch.* 30), and Lemuel's (*ch.* 31). The scope of all is one and the same, to direct us so to order our conversation aright as that in the end we may see the salvation of the Lord. The best comment on these rules is to be ruled by them.

CHAPTER 1

Those who read David's psalms, especially those towards the latter end, would be tempted to think that religion is all rapture and consists in nothing but the ecstasies and transports of devotion; and doubtless there is a time for them, and if there be a heaven upon earth it is in them: but, while we are on earth, we cannot be wholly taken up with them; we have a life to live in the flesh, must have a conversation in the world, and into that we must now be taught to carry our religion, which is a rational thing, and very serviceable to the government of human life, and tends as much to make us discreet as to make us devout, to make the face shine before men, in a prudent, honest, useful conversation, as to make the heart burn towards God in holy and pious affections. In this chapter we have, I. The title of the book, showing the general scope and design of it (*v.* 1–6). II. The first principle of it recommended to our serious consideration (*v.* 7–9). III. A necessary caution against bad company (*v.* 10–19). IV. A faithful and lively representation of wisdom's reasonings with the children of men, and the certain ruin of those who turn a deaf ear to those reasonings (*v.* 20–33).

Verses 1–6

We have here an introduction to this book, which some think was prefixed by the collector and publisher, as Ezra; but it is rather supposed to have been penned by Solomon himself, who, in the beginning of his book, proposes his end in writing it, that he might keep to his business, and closely pursue that end. We are here told,

I. Who wrote these wise sayings, *v.* 1. They are *the proverbs of Solomon.* 1. His name signifies *peaceable,* and the character both of his spirit and of his reign answered to it; both were peaceable. David, whose life was full of troubles, wrote a book of devotion; for *is any afflicted? let him pray.* Solomon, who lived quietly, wrote a book of instruction; for when the *churches had rest they were edified.* In times of peace we should learn ourselves, and teach others, that which in troublous times both they and we must practise. 2. He was *the son of David;* it was his honour to stand related to that good man, and he reckoned it so with good reason, for he fared the better for it, 1 Ki. 11:12. He had been blessed with a good education, and many a good prayer had been put up for him (Ps. 72:1), the effect of both which appeared in his wisdom and usefulness. The *generation of the upright* are sometimes thus blessed, that they are made blessings, eminent blessings, in their day. Christ is often called *the Son of David,* and Solomon was a type of him in this, as in other things, that he *opened his mouth in parables* or *proverbs.* 3. He was *king of Israel* — a king, and yet it was no disparagement to him to be an instructor of the ignorant, and a teacher of babes — king of Israel, that people among whom God was known and his name was great; among them he learned wisdom, and to them he communicated it. All the earth sought to Solomon *to hear his wisdom,* which excelled all men's (1 Ki. 4:30; 10:24); it was an honour to Israel that their king was such a dictator, such an oracle. Solomon was famous for apophthegms; every word he said had weight in it, and something that was surprising and edifying. His servants who attended him, and heard his wisdom, had, among them, collected 3000 proverbs of his which they wrote in their day-books; but these were of his own writing, and do not amount to nearly a thousand. In these he was divinely inspired. Some think that out of those other proverbs of his, which were not so inspired, the apocryphal books of *Ecclesiasticus* and the *Wisdom of Solomon* were compiled, in which are many excellent sayings, and of great use; but, take altogether, they are far short of this book. The Roman emperors had each of them his symbol or motto, as many now have with their coat of arms. But Solomon had many weighty sayings, not as theirs, borrowed from others, but all the product of that extraordinary wisdom which God had endued him with.

II. For what end they were written (*v.* 2–4), not to gain a reputation to the author, or strengthen his interest among his subjects, but for the use and benefit of all that in every age and place will govern themselves by these dictates and study them closely. This book will help us, 1. To form right notions of things, and to possess our minds with clear and distinct ideas of them, that we may *know wisdom and instruction,* that wisdom which is got by instruction, by divine revelation, may know both how to speak and act wisely ourselves and to give instruction to others. 2. To distinguish between truth and falsehood, good and evil — *to perceive the words of understanding,* to apprehend them, to judge of them, to guard against mistakes, and to accommodate what we are taught to ourselves and our own use, that we may *discern things that differ* and not be imposed upon, and may *approve things that are excellent* and not lose the benefit of them, as the apostle prays, Phil. 1:10. 3. To order our conversation aright in every things, *v.* 3. This book will give, that we may *receive, the instruction of wisdom,* that knowledge which will guide our practice in *justice, judgment, and equity* (*v.* 3), which will dispose us to render to all their due, to God the things that are God's, in all the exercises of religion, and to all men what is due to them, according to the obligations which by relation, office, contract, or upon any other account, we lie under to them. Note, Those are truly wise, and none but those, who are universally conscientious; and the design of the scripture is to teach us that wisdom, *justice* in the duties of the first table, *judgment* in those of the second table, *and equity* (that is sincerity) in both; so some distinguish them.

III. For whose use they were written, *v.* 4. They are of use to all, but are designed especially, 1. For *the simple, to give subtlety to* them. The instructions here given are plain and easy, and level to the meanest capacity, *the wayfaring men, though fools, shall not err therein;* and those are likely to receive benefit by them who are sensible of their own ignorance and their need to be taught, and are therefore desirous to receive instruction; and those who receive these instructions in their light and power, though they be simple, will hereby be made subtle, graciously crafty to know the sin they should avoid and the duty they should do, and to escape the tempter's wiles. He that is *harmless as* the *dove* by observing Solomon's rules may become *wise as* the *serpent;* and he that has been sinfully foolish when he begins to govern himself by the word of God becomes graciously wise. 2. For young people, to give them *knowledge and discretion.* Youth is the learning age, catches at instructions, receives impressions, and retains what is then received; it is therefore of great consequence that the mind be then seasoned well, nor can it receive a better tincture than from Solomon's proverbs. Youth is rash, and heady, and inconsiderate; *man is born like the wild ass's colt,* and therefore needs to be broken by the restraints and managed by the rules we find here. And, if young people will but take heed to their ways according to Solomon's proverbs, they will soon gain the knowledge and discretion of the ancients. Solomon had an eye to posterity in writing this book, hoping by it to season the minds of the rising generation with the generous principles of wisdom and virtue.

IV. What good use may be made of them, *v.* 5, 6. Those who are young and simple may by them be made wise, and are not excluded from Solomon's school, as they were from Plato's. But is it only for such? No; here is not only milk for babes, but strong meat for strong men. This book will not only make the foolish and bad wise and good, but the wise and good wiser and better; and though the simple and the young man may perhaps slight those instructions, and not be the better for them, yet the *wise man will hear.* Wisdom will be justified by her own children, though not by the children sitting in the market-place. Note, Even wise men must hear, and not think themselves too wise to learn. *A wise man* is sensible of his own defects *(Plurima ignoro, sed ignorantiam meam non ignoro — I am ignorant of many things, but not of my own ignorance),* and therefore is still pressing forward, that he may *increase* in *learning,* may know more and know it better, more clearly and distinctly, and may know better how to make use of it. As long as we live we should strive to increase in all useful learning. It was a saying of one of the greatest of the rabbim, *Qui non auget scientiam, amittit de ea — If our stock of knowledge by not increasing, it is wasting;* and those that would increase in learning must study the scriptures; these *perfect the man of God.* A wise man, by increasing in learning, is not only profitable to himself, but to others also, 1. As a counsellor. *A man of understanding* in these precepts of wisdom, by comparing them with one another and with his own observations, *shall* by degrees *attain unto wise counsels;* he stands fair for preferment, and will be consulted as an oracle, and entrusted with the management of public affairs; he shall come to *sit at the helm,* so the word signifies. Note, Industry is the way to honour; and those whom God has blessed with wisdom must study to do good with it, according as their sphere is. It is more dignity indeed to be counsellor to the prince, but it is more charity to be counsellor to the poor, as Job was with his wisdom. Job 29:15, *I was eyes to the blind.* 2. As an interpreter (*v.* 6) — *to understand a proverb.* Solomon was himself famous for expounding riddles and resolving hard questions, which was of old the celebrated entertainment of the eastern princes, witness the solutions he gave to the enquiries with which the queen of Sheba thought to puzzle him. Now here he undertakes to furnish his readers with that talent, as far as would be serviceable to the best purposes. "They shall *understand a proverb,* even *the interpretation,* without which the proverb is a nut uncracked; when they hear a wise saying, though it be figurative, they shall take the sense of it, and know how to make use of it." *The words of the wise* are sometimes *dark sayings.* In St. Paul's epistles there is that which is *hard to be understood;* but to those who, being well-versed in the scriptures, know how to *compare spiritual things with spiritual,* they will be easy and safe; so that, if you ask them, *Have you understood all these things?* they may answer, *Yea, Lord.* Note, It is a credit to religion when men of honesty are men of sense; all good people therefore should aim to be intelligent, and *run to and fro,* take pains in the use of means, that their *knowledge may be increased.*

Verses 7–9

Solomon, having undertaken to *teach a young man knowledge and discretion,* here lays down two general rules to be observed in order thereunto, and those are, to fear God and honour his parents, which two fundamental laws of morality Pythagoras begins his golden verses with, but the former of them in a wretchedly corrupted state. *Primum, deos immortales cole, parentesque honora — First worship the immortal gods, and honour your parents.* To make young people such as they should be,

I. Let them have regard to God as their supreme.

1. He lays down this truth, that *the fear of the Lord is the beginning of knowledge* (*v.* 7); it is *the principal part of knowledge* (so the margin); it is the head of knowledge; that is, (1.) Of all things that are to be known this is most evident, that *God is to be feared,* to be reverenced, served, and worshipped; this is so the beginning of knowledge that

those know nothing who do not know this. (2.) In order to the attaining of all useful knowledge this is most necessary, that we fear God; we are not qualified to profit by the instructions that are given us unless our minds be possessed with a holy reverence of God, and every thought within us be brought into obedience to him. *If any man will do his will, he shall know of his doctrine,* Jn. 7:17. (3.) As all our knowledge must take rise from the fear of God, so it must tend to it as its perfection and centre. Those know enough who know how to fear God, who are careful in every thing to please him and fearful of offending him in any thing; this is the Alpha and Omega of knowledge.

2. To confirm this truth, that an eye to God must both direct and quicken all our pursuits of knowledge, he *observes, Fools* (atheists, who have no regard to God) *despise wisdom and instruction;* having no dread at all of God's wrath, nor any desire of his favour, they will not give you thanks for telling them what they may do to escape his wrath and obtain his favour. Those who say to the Almighty, *Depart from us,* who are so far from fearing him that they set him at defiance, can excite no surprise if they desire not the knowledge of his ways, but despise that instruction. Note, Those are fools who do not fear God and value the scriptures; and though they may pretend to be admirers of wit they are really strangers and enemies to wisdom.

II. Let them have regard to their parents as their superiors (*v.* 8, 9): *My son, hear the instruction of thy father.* He means, not only that he would have his own children to be observant of him, and of what he said to them, nor only that he would have his pupils, and those who came to him to be taught, to look upon him as their father and attend to his precepts with the disposition of children, but that he would have all children to be dutiful and respectful to their parents, and to conform to the virtuous and religious education which they give them, according to the law of the fifth commandment.

1. He takes it for granted that parents will, with all the wisdom they have, instruct their children, and, with all the authority they have, give law to them for their good. They are reasonable creatures, and therefore we must not give them law without instruction; we must draw them with the cords of a man, and when we tell them what they must do we must tell them why. But they are corrupt and wilful, and therefore with the instruction there is need of a law. Abraham will not only catechize, but command, his household. Both the father and the mother must do all they can for the good education of their children, and all little enough.

2. He charges children both to receive and to retain the good lessons and laws their parents give them. (1.) To receive them with readiness: *"Hear the instruction of thy father;* hear it and heed it; hear it and bid it welcome, and be thankful for it, and subscribe to it." (2.) To retain them with resolution: *"Forsake not their law;* think not that when thou art grown up, and no longer under tutors and governors, thou mayest live at large; no, *the law of thy mother* was according to the law of thy God, and therefore it must never be forsaken; thou wast trained up in the way in which thou shouldst go, and therefore, when thou art old, thou must not depart from it." Some observe that whereas the Gentile ethics, and the laws of the Persians and Romans, provided only that children should pay respect to their father, the divine law secures the honour of the mother also.

3. He recommends this as that which is very graceful and will put an honour upon us: "The instructions and laws of thy parents, carefully observed and lived up to, *shall be an ornament of grace unto thy head* (*v.* 9), such an ornament as is, in the sight of God, of great price, and shall make thee look as great as those that wear gold *chains about their necks."* Let divine truths and commands be to us a coronet, or a collar of SS, which are badges of first-rate honours; let us value them, and be ambitious of them, and then they shall be so to us. Those are truly valuable, and shall be valued, who value themselves more by their virtue and piety than by their worldly wealth and dignity.

Verses 10–19

Here Solomon gives another general rule to young people, in order to their finding out, and keeping in, the paths of wisdom, and that is to take heed of the snare of bad company. David's psalms begin with this caution, and so do Solomon's proverbs; for nothing is more destructive, both to a lively devotion and to a regular conversation (*v.* 10): *"My son,* whom I love, and have a tender concern for, *if sinners entice thee, consent thou not."* This is good advice for parents to give their children when they send them abroad into the world; it is the same that St. Peter gave to his new converts, (Acts 2:40), *Save yourselves from this untoward generation.* Observe, 1. How industrious wicked people are to seduce others into the paths of the destroyer: they will entice. Sinners love company in sin; the angels that fell were tempters almost as soon as they were sinners. They do not threaten or argue, but entice with flattery and fair speech; with a bait they draw the unwary young man to the hook. But they mistake if they think that by bringing others to partake with them in their guilt, and to be bound, as it were, in the bond with them, they shall have the less to pay themselves; for they will have so much the more to answer for. 2. How cautious young people should be that they be not seduced by them: *"Consent thou not;* and then, though they entice thee, they cannot force thee. Do not say as they say, nor do as they do or would have thee to do; have no fellowship with them." To enforce this caution,

I. He represents the fallacious reasonings which sinners use in their enticements, and the arts of wheedling which they have for the beguiling of unstable souls. He specifies highwaymen, who do what they can to draw others into their gang, *v.* 11–14. See here what they would have the young man to do: *"Come with us* (*v.* 11); let us have thy company." At first they pretend to ask no more; but the courtship rises higher (*v.* 14): *"Cast in thy lot among us;* come in partner with us, join thy force to ours, and let us resolve to live and die together: thou shalt fare as we fare; and *let us all have one purse,* that what we get together we may spend merrily together," for that is it they aim it [at?]. Two unreasonable insatiable lusts they propose to themselves the gratification of, and therewith entice their pray into the snare: — 1. Their cruelty. They thirst after blood, and hate those that are innocent and never gave them any provocation, because by their honesty and industry they shame and condemn them: *"Let us* therefore *lay wait for* their *blood,* and *lurk privily* for them; they are conscious to themselves of no crime and consequently apprehensive of no danger, but travel unarmed; therefore we shall make the more easy prey of them. And, O how sweet it will be to *swallow them up alive!" v.* 12. These bloody men would do this as greedily as the hungry lion devours the lamb. If it be objected, "The remains of the murdered will betray the murderers;" they answer, "No danger of that; we will swallow them whole as those that are buried." Who could imagine that human nature should degenerate so far that it should ever be a pleasure to one man to destroy another! 2. Their covetousness. They hope to get a good booty by it (*v.* 13): "We shall *find all precious substance* by following this trade. What though we venture our necks by it? we shall *fill our houses with spoil."* See here, (1.) The idea they have of worldly wealth. They call it *precious substance;* whereas it is neither substance nor precious; it is a shadow; it is vanity, especially that which is got by robbery, Ps. 62:10. It is as that which is not, which will give a man no solid satisfaction. It is cheap, it is common, yet, in their account, it is precious, and therefore they will hazard their lives, and perhaps their souls, in pursuit of it. It is the ruining mistake of thousands that they over-value the wealth of this world and look on it as *precious substance.* (2.) The abundance of it which they promise themselves: We shall *fill our houses with it.* Those who trade with sin promise themselves mighty bargains, and that it will turn to a vast account (All this will I give thee, says the tempter); but they only *dream that they eat;* the housefuls dwindle into scarcely a handful, like the grass on the house-tops.

II. He shows the perniciousness of these ways, as a reason why we should dread them (*v.* 15): *"My son, walk not thou in the way with them;* do not associate with them; get, and keep, as far off from them as thou canst; *refrain thy foot from their path;* do not take example by them, not do as they do." Such is the corruption of our nature that our foot is very prone to step into the path of sin, so that we must use necessary violence upon ourselves to refrain our foot from it, and check ourselves if at any time we take the least step towards it. Consider, 1. How pernicious their way is in its own nature (*v.* 16): *Their feet run to evil,* to that which is displeasing to God and hurtful to mankind, for they *make haste to shed blood.* Note, The way of sin is down-hill; men not only cannot stop themselves, but, the longer they continue in it, the faster they run, and make haste in it, as if they were afraid they should not do mischief enough and were resolved to lose no time. They said they would proceed leisurely (Let us *lay wait for blood, v.* 11), but thou wilt find they are all in haste, so much has Satan *filled their hearts.* 2. How pernicious the consequences of it will be. They are plainly told that this wicked way will certainly end in their own destruction, and yet they persist in it. Herein, (1.) They are like the silly bird, that sees the net spread to take her, and yet it is in vain; she is decoyed into it by the bait, and will not take the warning which her own eyes gave her, *v.* 17. But we think ourselves *of more value than many sparrows,* and therefore should have more wit, and act with more caution. God has *made us wiser than the fowls of heaven* (Job 35:11), and shall we then be as stupid as they? (2.) They are worse than the birds, and have not the sense which we sometimes perceive them to have; for the fowler knows it is in vain to lay his snare *in the sight of the bird,* and therefore he has arts to conceal it. But the sinner sees ruin at the end of his way; the murderer, the thief, see the jail and the gallows before them, nay, they may see hell before them; their watchmen tell them they shall surely die, but it is to no purpose; they rush into sin, and rush on in it, like the horse into the battle. For really the stone they roll will turn upon themselves, *v.* 18, 19. They lay wait, and lurk privily, for the blood and lives of others, but it will prove, contrary to their intention, to be for *their own blood, their own lives;* they will come, at length, to a shameful end; and, if they escape the sword of the magistrate, yet there is a divine Nemesis that pursues them. *Vengeance suffers* them *not to live.* Their greediness of gain hurries them upon those practices which will not suffer them to live out half their days, but will cut off the number of their months in the midst. They have little reason to be proud of their property in that which *takes away the life of the owners* and then passes to other masters; and what is a man profited, though he gain the world, if he lose his life? For then he can enjoy the world no longer; much less if he lose his soul, and that be drowned in destruction and perdition, as multitudes are by the love of money.

Now, though Solomon specifies only the temptation to rob on the highway, yet he intends hereby to warn us against all other evils which sinners entice men to. Such are the ways of the drunkards and unclean; they are indulging themselves in those pleasures which tend to their ruin both here and for ever; and therefore consent not to them.

Verses 20–33

Solomon, having shown how dangerous it is to hearken to the temptations of Satan, here shows how dangerous it is not to hearken to the calls of God, which we shall for ever rue the neglect of. Observe,

I. By whom God calls to us — by *wisdom.* It is *wisdom* that *crieth without.* The word is plural — *wisdoms,* for, as there is infinite wisdom in God, so there is the *manifold wisdom of God,* Eph. 3:10. God speaks to the children of men by all the kinds of wisdom, and, as in every will, so in every word, of God there is a counsel. 1. Human understanding is wisdom, the light and law of nature, the powers and faculties of reason, and the office of conscience, Job 38:36. By these God speaks to the children of men, and reasons with them. *The spirit of a man is the candle of the Lord;* and, wherever men go, they may hear a voice behind them, saying, *This is the way;* and the voice of conscience is the voice of God, and not always a still small voice, but sometimes it cries. 2. Civil government is wisdom; it is God's ordinance; magistrates are his vicegerents [viceregents?]. God by David had *said to the fools, Deal not foolishly,* Ps. 75:4. *In the opening of the gates,* and in the *places of concourse,* where courts were kept, the judges, the wisdom of the nation, called to wicked people, in God's name, to repent and reform. 3. Divine revelation is wisdom; all its dictates, all its laws, are wise as wisdom itself. God does, by the written word, by the law of Moses, which sets before us the blessing and the curse, by the priests' lips which keep knowledge, by his servants the prophets, and all the ministers of this word, declare his mind to sinners, and give them warning as plainly as that which is proclaimed in the streets or courts of judicature by the criers. God, in his word, not only opens the case, but argues it with the children of men. *Come, now, and let us reason together,* Isa. 1:18. 4. Christ himself is Wisdom, is Wisdoms, for *in him are hidden all the treasures of wisdom and knowledge,* and he is the centre of all divine revelation, not only the *essential Wisdom,* but the *eternal Word,* by whom God speaks to us and to whom he has *committed all judgment;* he it is therefore who here both pleads with sinners and passes sentence on them. He calls himself *Wisdom,* Lu. 7:35.

II. How he calls to us, and in what manner. 1. Very publicly, that whosoever hath ears to hear may hear, since all are welcome to take the benefit of what is said and all are concerned to heed it. The rules of wisdom are published *without in the streets,* not in the schools only, or in the palaces of princes, but *in the chief places of concourse,* among the common people that pass and repass *in the opening of the gates* and *in the city.* It is comfortable casting the net of the gospel where there is a multitude of fish, in hopes that then some will be enclosed. This was fulfilled in our Lord Jesus, who taught openly in the temple, in crowds of people, and *in secret said nothing* (Jn. 18:20), and charged his ministers to *proclaim* his gospel *on the housetop,* Mt. 10:27. God says (Isa. 45:19), *I have not spoken in secret.* There is *no speech or language where* Wisdom's *voice is not heard.* Truth seeks not corners, nor is virtue ashamed of itself. 2. Very pathetically; she *cries,* and again she *cries,* as one in earnest. *Jesus stood and cried.* She *utters her voice,* she *utters her words* with all possible clearness and affection. God is desirous to be heard and heeded.

III. What the call of God and Christ is.

1. He reproves sinners for their folly and their obstinately persisting in it, *v.* 22. Observe, (1.) Who they are that Wisdom here reproves and expostulates with. In general, they are such as are *simple,* and therefore might justly be despised, such as *love simplicity,* and therefore might justly be despaired of; but we must use the means even with those that we have but little hopes of, because we know not what divine grace may do. Three sorts of persons are here called to: — [1.] *Simple ones that love simplicity.* Sin is simplicity, and sinners are simple ones; they do foolishly, very foolishly; and the condition of those is very bad who love simplicity, are fond of their simple notions of good and evil, their simple prejudices against the ways of God, and are in their element when they are doing a simple thing, sporting themselves in their own deceivings and flattering themselves in their wickedness. [2.] *Scorners that delight in scorning* — proud people that take a pleasure in hectoring all about them, jovial people that banter all mankind, and make a jest of every thing that comes in their way. But scoffers at religion are especially meant, the worst of sinners, that scorn to submit to the truths and laws of Christ, and to the reproofs and admonitions of his word, and take a pride in running down every thing that is sacred and serious. [3.] *Fools that hate knowledge.* None but fools hate knowledge. Those only are enemies to religion that do not understand it aright. And those are the worst of fools that hate to be instructed and reformed, and have a rooted antipathy to serious godliness. (2.) How the reproof is expressed: *"How long will you do so?"* This implies that the God of heaven desires the conversion and reformation of sinners and not their ruin, that he is much displeased with their obstinacy and dilatoriness, that he waits to be gracious, and is willing to reason the case with them.

2. He invites them to repent and become wise, *v.* 23. And here, (1.) The precept is plain: *Turn you at my reproof.* We do not make a right use of the reproofs that are given us for that which is evil if we do not turn from it to that which is good; for for this end the reproof was given. Turn, that is, return to your right mind, turn to God, turn to your duty, turn and live. (2.) The promises are very encouraging. Those that love simplicity find themselves under a moral impotency to change their own mind and way; they cannot turn by any power of their own. To this God answers, *"Behold, I will pour out my Spirit unto you;*

set yourselves to do what you can, and the grace of God shall set in with you, and work in you both to will and to do that good which, without that grace, you could not do." Help thyself, and God will help thee; *stretch forth thy withered hand,* and Christ will strengthen and heal it. [1.] The author of this grace is the Spirit, and that is promised: *I will pour out my Spirit unto you,* as oil, as water; you shall have the Spirit in abundance, *rivers of living water,* Jn. 7:38. Our heavenly Father *will give the Holy Spirit to those that ask him.* [2.] The means of this grace is the word, which, if we take it aright, will turn us; it is therefore promised, *"I will make known my words unto you,* not only speak them to you, but make them known, give you to understand them." Note, Special grace is necessary to a sincere conversion. But that grace shall never be denied to any that honestly seek it and submit to it.

3. He reads the doom of those that continue obstinate against all these means and methods of grace. It is large and very terrible, *v.* 24–32. Wisdom, having called sinners to return, pauses awhile, to see what effect the call has, *hearkens and hears; but they speak not aright* (Jer. 8:6), and therefore she goes on to tell them what will be in the end hereof.

(1.) The crime is recited and it is highly provoking. See what it is for which judgment will be given against impenitent sinners in the great day, and you will say they deserve it, and the Lord is righteous in it. It is, in short, rejecting Christ and the offers of his grace, and refusing to submit to the terms of his gospel, which would have saved them both from the curse of the *law of God* and from the dominion of the *law of sin.* [1.] Christ called to them, to warn them of their danger; he *stretched out his hand* to offer them mercy, nay, to help them out of their miserable condition, *stretched out his hand* for them to *take hold of,* but they *refused* and *no man regarded;* some were careless and never heeded it, nor took notice of what was said to them; others were wilful, and, though they could not avoid hearing the will of Christ, yet they gave him a flat denial, they refused, *v.* 24. They were in love with their folly, and would not be made wise. They were obstinate to all the methods that were taken to reclaim them. God *stretched out his hand* in mercies bestowed upon them, and, when those would not work upon them, in corrections, but all were in vain; they regarded the operations of his hand no more than the declarations of his mouth. [2.] Christ reproved and counselled them, not only reproved them for what they did amiss, but counselled them to do better (those are *reproofs of instruction* and evidences of love and good-will), but they *set at nought all his counsel* as not worth heeding, and *would none of his reproof,* as if it were below them to be reproved by him and as if they had never done any thing that deserved reproof, *v.* 25. This is repeated (*v.* 30): "They *would none of my counsel,* but rejected it with disdain; they called reproofs reproaches, and took them as an insult (Jer. 6:10); nay, *they despised all my reproof,* as if it were all a jest, and not worth taking notice of." Note, Those are marked for ruin that are deaf to reproof and good counsel. [3.] They were exhorted to submit to the government of right reason and religion, but they rebelled against both. *First,* Reason should not rule them, for *they hated knowledge* (*v.* 29), hated the light of divine truth because it discovered to them the evil of their deeds, Jn. 3:20. They hated to be told that which they could not bear to know. *Secondly,* Religion could not rule them, for they *did not choose the fear of the Lord,* but chose to walk in the way of *their heart and in the sight of their eyes.* They were pressed to *set God always before them,* but they chose rather to cast him and his fear *behind their backs.* Note, Those who do not *choose the fear of the Lord* show that they *have no knowledge.*

(2.) The sentence is pronounced, and it is certainly ruining. Those that will not submit to God's government will certainly perish under his wrath and curse, and the gospel itself will not relieve them. They would not take the benefit of God's mercy when it was offered them, and therefore justly fall as victims to his justice, *ch.* 29:1. The threatenings here will have their full accomplishment in the judgment of the great day and the eternal misery of the impenitent, of which yet there are some earnests in present judgments. [1.] Now sinners are in prosperity and secure; they live at ease, and set sorrow at defiance. But, *First,* Their *calamity will come* (*v.* 26); sickness will come,

and those diseases which they shall apprehend to be the very arrests and harbingers of death; other troubles will come, in mind, in estate, which will convince them of their folly in setting God at a distance. *Secondly,* Their calamity will put them into a great fright. Fear seizes them, and they apprehend that bad will be worse. When public judgments are abroad the *sinners in Zion are afraid, fearfulness surprises the hypocrites.* Death is the *king of terrors* to them (Job 15:21, etc.; 18:11, etc.); this fear will be their continual torment. *Thirdly,* According to their fright will it be to them. Their *fear shall come* (the thing they were afraid of shall befal them); it shall *come as desolation,* as a mighty deluge bearing down all before it; it shall be their *destruction,* their total and final destruction; and it shall come *as a whirlwind,* which suddenly and forcibly drives away all the chaff. Note, Those that will not admit the fear of God lay themselves open to all other fears, and their fears will not prove causeless. *Fourthly,* Their fright will then be turned into despair: *Distress and anguish shall come upon them,* for, having fallen into the pit they were afraid of, they shall see no way to escape, *v.* 27. Saul cries out (2 Sa. 1:9), *Anguish has come upon me;* and in hell there is *weeping, and wailing, and gnashing of teeth* for anguish, *tribulation and anguish to the soul* of the sinner, the fruit of the *indignation and wrath of the righteous God,* Rom. 2:8, 9. [2.] Now God pities their folly, but he will then *laugh at their calamity* (*v.* 26): "I also will laugh at your distress, even as you laughed at my counsel." Those that ridicule religion will thereby but make themselves ridiculous before all the world. The righteous will *laugh at them* (Ps. 52:6), for God himself will. It intimates that they shall be for ever shut out of God's compassions; they have so long sinned against mercy that they have now quite sinned it away. *His eye shall not spare, neither will he have pity.* Nay, his justice being glorified in their ruin, he will be pleased with it, though now he would rather they should *turn and live.* *Ah! I will ease me of my adversaries.* [3.] Now God is ready to hear their prayers and to meet them with mercy, if they would but seek to him for it; but then the door will be shut, and they shall cry in vain (*v.* 28): *"Then shall they call upon me* when it is too late, *Lord, Lord, open to us.* They would then gladly be beholden to that mercy which now they reject and make light of; but *I will not answer,* because, when I called, they would not answer;" all the answer then will be, *Depart from me, I know you not.* This has been the case of some even in this life, as of Saul, whom God answered not by *Urim* or *prophets;* but, ordinarily, while there is life there is room for prayer and hope of speeding, and therefore this must refer to the inexorable justice of the last judgment. Then those that slighted God will *seek him early* (that is, earnestly), but in vain; *they shall not find him,* because they sought him not when he might be found, Isa. 55:6. The rich man in hell begged, but was denied. [4.] Now they are eager upon their own way, and fond of their own devices; but then they will have enough of them (*v.* 31), according to the proverb, *Let men drink as they brew;* they shall *eat the fruit of their own way;* their wages shall be according to their work, and, as was their choice, *so shall their doom be,* Gal. 6:7, 8. Note, *First,* There is a natural tendency in sin to destruction, Jam. 1:15. Sinners are certainly miserable if they do but *eat the fruit of their own way. Secondly,* Those that perish must thank themselves, and can lay no blame upon any other. It is *their own device;* let them make their boast of it. God *chooses their delusions,* Isa. 66:4. [5.] Now they value themselves upon their worldly prosperity; but then that shall help to aggravate their ruin, *v.* 32. *First,* They are now proud that they can turn away from God and get clear of the restraints of religion; but that very thing shall slay them, the remembrance of it shall cut them to the heart. *Secondly,* They are now proud of their own security and sensuality; but *the ease of the simple* (so the margin reads it) *shall slay them;* the more secure they are the more certain and the more dreadful will their destruction be, *and the prosperity of fools shall* help to *destroy them,* by puffing them up with pride, gluing their hearts to the world, furnishing them with fuel for their lusts, and hardening their hearts in their evil ways.

4. He concludes with an assurance of safety and happiness to all those that submit to the instructions of wisdom (*v.* 33): *"Whoso hearkeneth unto me,* and will be ruled by me, he shall," (1.) "Be safe; he *shall dwell* under the

special protection of Heaven, so that nothing shall do him any real hurt." (2.) "He shall be easy, and have no disquieting apprehensions of danger; he shall not only be safe from evil, but *quiet from the fear of* it." *Though the earth be removed, yet shall not they fear.* Would we be safe from evil, and quiet from the fear of it? Let religion always rule us and the word of God be our counsellor. That is the way to *dwell safely* in this world, and to *be quiet from the fear of evil* in the other world.

CHAPTER 2

Solomon, having foretold the destruction of those who are obstinate in their impiety, in this chapter applies himself to those who are willing to be taught; and, I. He shows them that, if they would diligently use the means of knowledge and grace, they should obtain of God the knowledge and grace which they seek (*v.* 1–9). II. He shows them of what unspeakable advantage it would be to them. 1. It would preserve them from the snares of evil men (*v.* 10–15) and of evil women (*v.* 16–19). 2. It would direct them into, and keep them in, the way of good men (*v.* 20–22. So that in this chapter we are taught both how to get wisdom and how to use it when we have it, that we may neither seek it, nor receive it in vain.

Verses 1–9

Job had asked, long before this, *Where shall wisdom be found? Whence cometh wisdom?* (Job 28:12, 20) and he had given this general answer (*v.* 23), *God knoweth the place* of it; but Solomon here goes further, and tells us both where we may find it and how we may get it. We are here told,

I. What means we must use that we may obtain wisdom.

1. We must closely attend to the word of God, for that is the word of wisdom, *which is able to make us wise unto salvation, v.* 1, 2. (1.) We must be convinced that the words of God are the fountain and standard of wisdom and understanding, and that we need not desire to be wiser than they will make us. We must *incline our ear* and *apply our hearts* to them, as to *wisdom* or *understanding* itself. Many wise things may be found in human compositions, but divine revelation, and true religion built upon it, are all wisdom. (2.) We must, accordingly, receive the word of God with all readiness of mind, and bid it welcome, even the commandments as well as the promises, without murmuring or disputing. *Speak, Lord, for thy servant hears.* (3.) We must hide them with us, as we do our treasures, which we are afraid of being robbed of. We must not only receive, but retain, the word of God, and lodge it in our hearts, that it may be always ready to us. (4.) We must incline our ear to them; we must lay hold on all opportunities of hearing the word of God, and listen to it with attention and seriousness, as those that are afraid of letting it slip. (5.) We must apply our hearts to them, else inclining the ear to them will stand us in no stead.

2. We must be much in prayer, *v.* 3. We must *cry after knowledge,* as one that is ready to perish for hunger begs hard for bread. Faint desires will not prevail; we must be importunate, as those that know the worth of knowledge and our own want of it. We must cry, as new-born babes, after *the sincere milk of the word.* 1 Pt. 2:2. We must *lift our voice for understanding* lift it up to heaven; thence these good and perfect gifts must be expected, Jam. 1:17; Job 38:34. We must *give our voice to understanding* (so the word is), speak for it, vote for it, submit the tongue to the command of wisdom. We must consecrate our voice to it; having applied our heart to it, we must employ our voice in seeking for it. Solomon could write *probatum est — a tried remedy,* upon this method; he prayed for wisdom and so obtained it.

3. We must be willing to take pains (*v.* 4); we must *seek it as silver,* preferring it far before all the wealth of this world, and labouring in search of it as those who dig in the mines, who undergo great toil and run great hazards, with indefatigable industry and invincible constancy and resolution, in pursuit of the ore; or as those who will be rich rise up early, and sit up late, and turn every stone to get money and fill their treasures. Thus diligent must we be in the use of the means of knowledge, following on to know the Lord.

II. What success we may hope for in the use of these means. Our labour shall not be in vain; for, 1. We shall know how to maintain our acquaintance and communion with God: *"Thou shalt understand the fear of the Lord* (*v.* 5), that is, thou shalt know how to worship him aright, shalt be led into the meaning and mystery of every ordinance, and be enabled to answer the end of its institution." *Thou shalt find the knowledge of God,* which is necessary to our fearing him aright. It concerns us to understand how much it is our interest to know God, and to evidence it by agreeable affections towards him and adorations of him. 2. We shall know how to conduct ourselves aright towards all men (*v.* 9): *"Thou shalt understand,* by the word of God, *righteousness, and judgment, and equity,* shalt learn those principles of justice, and charity, and fair dealing, which shall guide and govern thee in the whole course of thy conversation, shall make thee fit for every relation, every business, and faithful to every trust. It shall give thee not only a right notion of justice, but a disposition to practise it, and to render to all their due; for those that do not do justly do not rightly understand it." This will lead them in *every good path,* for the scripture will *make the man of God perfect.* Note, Those have the best knowledge who know their duty, Ps. 111:10.

III. What ground we have to hope for this success in our pursuits of wisdom; we must take our encouragement herein from God only, *v.* 6–8.

1. God has wisdom to bestow, *v.* 6. *The Lord* not only is wise himself, but he *gives wisdom,* and that is more than the wisest men in the world can do, for it is God's prerogative to open the understanding. All the wisdom that is in any creature is his gift, his free gift, and he gives it liberally (Jam. 1:5), has given it to many, and is still giving it; to him therefore let us apply for it.

2. He has blessed the world with a revelation of his will. *Out of his mouth,* by the law and the prophets, by the written word and by his ministers, both which are his mouth to the children of men, *come knowledge and understanding,* such a discovery of truth and good as, if we admit and receive the impressions of it, will make us truly knowing and intelligent. It is both an engagement and encouragement to search after wisdom that we have the scriptures to search, in which we may find it if we seek it diligently.

3. He has particularly provided that good men, who are sincerely disposed to do his will, shall have that *knowledge and* that *understanding* which are necessary for them, Jn. 7:17. Let them seek wisdom, and they shall find it; let them ask, and it shall be given them, *v.* 7, 8. Observe here, (1.) Who those are that are thus favoured. They are *the righteous,* on whom the image of God is renewed, which consists in righteousness, and those who *walk uprightly,* who are honest in their dealings both with God and man and make conscience of doing their duty as far as they know it. They are *his saints,* devoted to his honour, and set apart for his service. (2.) What it is that is provided for them. [1.] Instruction. The means of wisdom are given to all, but wisdom itself, *sound wisdom,* is laid *up for the righteous,* laid up in Christ their head, in whom *are hidden all the treasures of wisdom and knowledge,* and who *is made of God to us wisdom.* The same that is the Spirit of revelation in the word is a Spirit of wisdom in the souls of those that are sanctified, that wisdom of the prudent which is to understand his way; and it is sound wisdom, its foundations firm, its principles solid, and its products of lasting advantage. [2.] Satisfaction. Some read it, He *lays up substance for the righteous,* not only substantial knowledge, but substantial happiness and comfort, Prov. 8:21. Riches are things that are not, and those that have them only fancy themselves happy; but what is laid up in the promises and in heaven for the righteous will make them truly, thoroughly, and eternally happy. [3.] Protection. Even those who *walk uprightly* may be brought into danger for the trial of their faith, but God is, and will be, *a buckler to them,* so that nothing that happens to them shall do them any real hurt, or possess them with any terrific apprehensions; they are safe, and they shall think themselves so. *Fear not, Abraham; I am thy shield.* It is their way, the paths of judgment in which they walk, that the Lord knows, and owns, and takes care of. [4.] Grace to persevere to the end. If we depend upon God, and seek to him for wisdom, he will uphold us in our integrity, will enable us to *keep the paths of judgment,* however we may be tempted to turn aside out of them; for he *preserves the way of his saints,* that it be not perverted, and so preserves them in it safe and blameless to his heavenly kingdom. The assurances God has given us of his grace, if duly improved, will excite and quicken our endeavours in doing our duty. *Work out your salvation,* for *God works in you.*

Verses 10–22

The scope of these verses is to show, 1. What great advantage true wisdom will be of to us; it will keep us from the paths of sin, which lead to ruin, and will therein do us a greater kindness than if it enriched us with all the wealth of the world. 2. What good use we should make of the wisdom God gives us; we must use it for our own guidance in the paths of virtue, and for the arming of us against temptations of every kind. 3. By what rules we may try ourselves whether we have this wisdom or no. This tree will be known by its fruits; if we be truly wise, it will appear by our care to avoid all evil company and evil practices.

This wisdom will be of use to us,

I. For our preservation from evil, from the evil of sin, and, consequently, from the evil of trouble that attends it.

1. In general (*v.* 10, 11), "When wisdom has entire possession of thee, it will *keep thee."* And when has it an entire possession of us? (1.) When it has dominion over us. When it not only fills the head with notions, but *enters into the heart* and has a commanding power and influence upon that, — when it is upon the throne there, and gives law to the affections and passions, — when it *enters into the heart* as the leaven into the dough, to diffuse its relish there, and to change it into its own image — then it is likely to do us good. (2.) When we have delight in it, when knowledge becomes *pleasant to the soul:* "When thou beginnest to relish it as the most agreeable entertainment, and art subject to its rules, of choice, and with satisfaction, — when thou callest the practice of virtue, not a slavery and a task, but *liberty* and *pleasure,* and a life of serious godliness the most comfortable life a man can live in this world, — then thou wilt find the benefit of it." Though its restraints should be in some respects unpleasant to the body, yet even those must be pleasant to the soul. When it has come to this, with us, *discretion shall preserve* us and keep us. God keeps *the way of his saints* (*v.* 8), by giving them discretion to keep out of harm's way, to keep themselves that the wicked one touch them not. Note, A principle of grace reigning in the heart will be a powerful preservative both against corruptions within and temptations without, Eccl. 9:16, 18.

2. More particularly, wisdom will preserve us,

(1.) From men of corrupt principles, atheistical profane men, who make it their business to debauch young men's judgments, and instil into their minds prejudices against religion and arguments for vice: "It will *deliver thee from the way of the evil man* (*v.* 12), and a blessed deliverance it will be, as from the very jaws of death, *from the way* in which he walks, and in which he would persuade thee to walk." The enemy is spoken of as one (*v.* 12), an *evil man,* but afterwards as many (*v.* 13); there is a club, a gang of them, that are in confederacy against religion, and join hand in hand for the support of the devil's kingdom and the interests of it. [1.] They have a spirit of contradiction to that which is good: They *speak froward things;* they say all they can against religion, both to show their own enmity to it and to dissuade others from it. They are advocates for Satan; they plead for Baal, and *pervert the right ways of the Lord.* How peevishly will profane wits argue for sin, and with what frowardness will they carp at the word of God! Wisdom will keep us either from conversing with such men or at least from being ensnared by them. [2.] They are themselves apostates from that which is good, and such are commonly the most malicious and dangerous enemies religion has, witness Julian (*v.* 13): *They leave the paths of uprightness,* which they were trained up in and had set out in, shake off the influences of their education, and break off the thread of their hopeful beginnings, *to walk in the ways of darkness,* in those wicked ways which hate the light, in which men are led blindfold by ignorance and error, and which lead men into utter darkness. The ways of sin are ways of darkness, uncomfortable and unsafe; what fools are those that leave the plain, pleasant, lightsome paths of uprightness, to walk in those ways! Ps. 82:5; 1 Jn. 2:11. [3.] They take a pleasure in sin, both in committing it themselves and in seeing others commit it (*v.* 14): They *rejoice* in an opportunity *to do evil,* and in the accomplishment and success of any wicked project. It is sport to fools to do mischief; nor is any sight more grateful to them than to see *the frowardness of the wicked,* to see those that are hopeful drawn into the ways of sin, and then to see them hardened and confirmed in those ways. They are pleased if they can discern that the devil's kingdom gets ground (see Rom. 1:32), such a height of impiety have they arrived at. [4.] They are resolute in sin (*v.* 15): Their *ways are crooked,* a great many windings and turnings to escape the pursuit of their convictions and break the force of them; some sly excuse, some subtle evasion or other, their deceitful hearts furnish them with, for the strengthening of their hands in their wickedness; and in the crooked mazes of that labyrinth they secure themselves from the arrests of God's word and their own consciences; for they are *froward in their paths,* that is, they are resolved to go on in them, whatever is said against it. Every wise man will shun the company of such as these.

(2.) From women of corrupt practices. The former lead to spiritual wickednesses, the lusts of the unsanctified mind; these lead to *fleshly lusts,* which defile the body, that living temple, but withal *war against the soul.* The adulteress is here called *the strange woman,* because no man that has any wisdom or goodness in him will have any acquaintance with her; she is to be shunned by every Israelite as if she were a heathen, and a stranger to that sacred commonwealth. A strange woman indeed! utterly estranged from all principles of reason, virtue, and honour. It is a great mercy to be delivered from the allurements of the adulteress, considering, [1.] How false she is. Who will have any dealings with those that are made up of treachery? She is a strange woman; for, *First,* She is false to him whom she entices. She speaks fair, tells him how much she admires him above any man, and what a kindness she has for him; but she *flatters with her words;* she has no true affection for him, nor any desire of his welfare, any more than Delilah had of Samson's. All she designs is to pick his pocket and gratify a base lust of her own. *Secondly,* She is false to her husband, and violates the sacred obligation she lies under to him. He was *the guide of her youth;* by marrying him she chose him to be so, and submitted herself to his guidance, with a promise to attend him only, and forsake all others. But she has *forsaken* him, and therefore it cannot be thought that she should be faithful to any one else; and whoever entertains her is partaker with her in her falsehood. *Thirdly,* She is false to God himself: She *forgets the covenant of her God,* the marriage-covenant (*v.* 17), to which God is not only a witness, but a party, for, he having instituted the ordinance, both sides vow to him to be true to each other. It is not her husband only that she sins against, but her God, who *will judge whoremongers and adulterers* because they despise the oath and break the covenant, Eze. 17:18; Mal. 2:14. [2.] How fatal it will prove to those that fall in league with her, *v.* 18, 19. Let the sufferings of others be our warnings. Take heed of the sin of whoredom; for, *First,* The ruin of those who are guilty of it is certain and unavoidable, if they do not repent. It is a sin that has a direct tendency to the killing of the soul, the extinguishing of all good affections and dispositions in it, and the exposing of it to the wrath and curse of God and the sword of his justice. Those that live in forbidden pleasures are dead while they live. Let discretion preserve every man, not only from the evil woman, but from the evil house, for the *house inclines to death;* it is in the road that leads directly to eternal death; *and her paths unto Rephaim,* to the *giants* (so some read it), the sinners of the old world, who, living in luxury and excess of riot, were cut down out of time, and their foundation was overthrown with a flood. Our Lord Jesus deters us from sinful pleasures with the consideration of everlasting torments which follow them. *Where the worm dies not, nor is the fire quenched.* See Mt. 5:28, 29. *Secondly,* Their repentance and recovery are extremely hazardous: *None,* or next to none, *that go unto her, return again.* It is very rare that any who are caught in this snare of the devil recover themselves, so much is the heart hardened, and the mind blinded, by the deceitfulness of this sin. Having once lost their *hold of the paths of life,* they know not how to take hold of them again, but are perfectly besotted and bewitched with those base lusts. Many learned interpreters think that this caution against the *strange woman,* besides the literal sense, is to be understood figuratively, as a caution, 1. Against idolatry, which is spir-

itual whoredom. Wisdom will keep thee from all familiarity with the worshippers of images, and all inclination to join with them, which had for many ages been of such pernicious consequence to Israel and proved so to Solomon himself. 2. Against the debauching of the intellectual powers and faculties of the soul by the lusts and appetites of the body. Wisdom will keep thee from being captivated by the carnal mind, and from subjecting the spirit to the dominion of the flesh, that notorious adulteress which *forsakes its guide,* violates the *covenant of our God,* which *inclines to death,* and which, when it has got an undisturbed dominion, makes the case of the soul desperate.

II. This wisdom will be of use to guide and direct us in that which is good (*v.* 20): *That thou mayest walk in the way of good men.* We must avoid the way of the *evil man,* and the *strange woman,* in order that we may walk in good ways; we must *cease to do evil,* in order that we may *learn to do well.* Note, 1. There is a way which is peculiarly the way of good men, the way in which good men, as such, and as far as they have really been such, have always walked. 2. It will be our wisdom to walk in that way, to ask for the good old way and walk therein, Jer. 6:16; Heb. 6:12; 12:1. And we must not only walk in that way awhile, but we must keep it, keep in it, and never turn aside out of it: *The paths of the righteous* are the paths of life, which all that are wise, having taken hold of, will keep their hold of. "That thou mayest imitate those excellent persons, the patriarchs and prophets (so bishop Patrick paraphrases it), and be preserved in *the paths of those righteous* men who followed after them." We must not only choose our way in general by the good examples of the saints, but must also take directions from them in the choice of our particular paths; observe the track, and go forth by the footsteps of the flock. Two reasons are here given why we should thus choose: — (1.) Because men's integrity will be their establishment, *v.* 21. It will be the establishment, [1.] Of their persons: *The upright shall dwell in the land,* peaceably and quietly, as long as they live; and their uprightness will contribute to it, as it settles their minds, guides their counsels, gains them the good-will of their neighbours, and entitles them to God's special favour. [2.] Of their families: *The perfect,* in their posterity, *shall remain in it.* They shall dwell and remain for ever in the heavenly Canaan, of which the earthly one was but a type. (2.) Because men's iniquity will be their destruction, *v.* 22. See what becomes of *the wicked,* who choose the way of *the evil man;* they *shall be cut off,* not only from heaven hereafter and all hopes of that, but *from the earth* now, on which they set their affections, and in which they lay up their treasure. They think to take root in it, but they and their families *shall be rooted out of it,* in judgment to them, but in mercy to the earth. There is a day coming which *shall leave them neither root nor branch,* Mal. 4:1. Let that wisdom then *enter into our hearts,* and be *pleasant to our souls,* which will keep us out of a way that will end thus.

CHAPTER 3

This chapter is one of the most excellent in all this book, both for argument to persuade us to be religious and for directions therein. I. We must be constant to our duty because that is the way to be happy (*v.* 1–4). II. We must live a life of dependence upon God because that is the way to be safe (*v.* 5). III. We must keep up the fear of God because that is the way to be healthful (*v.* 7, 8). IV. We must serve God with our estates because that is the way to be rich (*v.* 9, 10). V. We must hear afflictions well because that is the way to get good by them (*v.* 11, 12). VI. We must take pains to obtain wisdom because that is the way to gain her, and to gain by her (*v.* 13–20). VII. We must always govern ourselves by the rules of wisdom, of right reason and religion, because that is the way to be always easy (*v.* 21–26). VIII. We must do all the good we can, and no hurt, to our neighbours, because according as men are just or unjust, charitable or uncharitable, humble or haughty, accordingly they shall receive of God (*v.* 27–35). From all this it appears what a tendency religion has to make men both blessed and blessings.

Verses 1–6

We are here taught to live a life of communion with God; and without controversy great is this mystery of godliness, and of great consequence to us, and, as is here shown, will be of unspeakable advantage.

I. We must have a continual regard to God's precepts, *v.* 1, 2.

1. We must, (1.) Fix God's law, and his commandments, as our rule, by which we will in every thing be ruled and to which we will yield obedience. (2.) We must acquaint ourselves with them; for we cannot be said to forget that

which we never knew. (3.) We must remember them so that they may be ready to us whenever we have occasion to use them. (4.) Our wills and affections must be subject to them and must in every thing conform to them. Not only our heads, but our hearts, must *keep God's commandments;* in them, as in the ark of the testimony, both the tables of the law must be deposited.

2. To encourage us to submit ourselves to all the restraints and injunctions of the divine law, we are assured (*v.* 2) that it is the certain way to long life and prosperity. (1.) It is the way to be long-lived. God's commandments *shall add to us length of days;* to a good useful life on earth, they shall add an eternal life in heaven, *length of days for ever and ever,* Ps. 21:4. God shall be our life and the length of our days, and that will be indeed long life, with an addition. But, because length of days may possibly become a burden and a trouble, it is promised, (2.) That it shall prove the way to be easy too, so that even the days of old age shall not be evil days, but days in which thou shalt have pleasure: *Peace shall they be* continually *adding to thee.* As grace increases, peace shall increase; and *of the increase of Christ's government and peace,* in the heart as well as in the world, *there shall be no end. Great* and growing *peace have those that love the law.*

II. We must have a continual regard to God's promises, which go along with his precepts, and are to be received, and retained, with them (*v.* 3): "*Let not mercy and truth forsake thee,* God's mercy in promising, and his truth in performing. Do not forfeit these, but live up to them, and preserve thy interest in them; do not forget these, but live upon them, and take the comfort of them. *Bind them about thy neck,* as the most graceful ornament." It is the greatest honour we are capable of in this world to have an interest in the mercy and truth of God. "*Write to them upon the table of thy heart,* as dear to thee, thy portion, and most delightful entertainment; take a pleasure in applying them and thinking them over." Or it may be meant of the mercy and truth which are our duty, piety and sincerity, charity towards men, fidelity towards God. Let these be fixed and commanding principles in thee. To encourage us to do this we are assured (*v.* 4) that this is the way to recommend ourselves both to our Creator and fellow-creatures: *So shalt thou find favour and good understanding.* 1. A good man seeks the favour of God in the first place, is ambitious of the honour of being accepted of the Lord, and he shall find that favour, and with it a good understanding; God will make the best of him, and put a favourable construction upon what he says and does. He shall be owned as one of Wisdom's children, and shall have praise with God, as one having that *good understanding* which is ascribed to all those *that do his commandments.* 2. He wishes to have favour with men also (as Christ had, Lu. 2:52), to be *accepted of the multitude of his brethren* (Esth. 10:3), and that he shall have; they shall understand him aright, and in his dealings with them he shall appear to be prudent, shall act intelligently and with discretion. *He shall have good success* (so some translate it), the common effect of good understanding.

III. We must have a continual regard to God's providence, must own and depend upon it in all our affairs, both by faith and prayer. 1. By faith. We must repose an entire confidence in the wisdom, power, and goodness of God, assuring ourselves of the extent of his providence to all the creatures and all their actions. We must therefore *trust in the Lord with all our hearts* (*v.* 5); we must believe that he is able to do what he will, wise to do what is best, and good, according to his promise, to do what is best for us, if we love him, and serve him. We must, with an entire submission and satisfaction, depend upon him to perform all things for us, and not *lean to our own understanding,* as if we could, by any forecast of our own, without God, help ourselves, and bring our affairs to a good issue. Those who know themselves cannot but find their own understanding to be a broken reed, which, if they lean to, will certainly fail them. In all our conduct we must be diffident of our own judgment, and confident of God's wisdom, power, and goodness, and therefore must follow Providence and not force it. That often proves best which was least our own doing. 2. By prayer (*v.* 6): *In all thy ways acknowledge God.* We must not only in our judgment believe that there is an over-ruling hand of God ordering and disposing of us and all our affairs, but we must solemnly own it, and address ourselves to him accordingly. We must ask his leave, and not design any thing but what we are sure is lawful. We must ask his advice and beg direction from him, not only when the case is difficult (when we know not what to do, no thanks to us that we have our eyes up to him), but in every case, be it ever so plain, We must ask success of him, as those who know *the race is not to the swift.* We must refer ourselves to him as one from whom our judgment proceeds, and patiently, and with a holy indifferency, wait his award. *In all our ways* that prove direct, and fair, and pleasant, in which we gain our point to our satisfaction, we must acknowledge God with thankfulness. *In all our ways* that prove cross and uncomfortable, and that are hedged up with thorns, we must acknowledge God with submission. Our eye must be ever towards God; to him we must, in every thing, make our requests known, as Jephthah *uttered all his words before the Lord in Mizpeh,* Jdg. 11:11. For our encouragement to do this, it is promised, *"He shall direct thy paths,* so that thy way shall be safe and good and the issue happy at last." Note, Those that put themselves under a divine guidance shall always have the benefit of it. God will give them that wisdom which is profitable to direct, so that they shall not turn aside into the by-paths of sin, and then will himself so wisely order the event that it shall be to their mind, or (which is equivalent) for their good. Those that faithfully follow the pillar of cloud and fire shall find that though it may lead them about it leads them the right way and will bring them to Canaan at last.

Verses 7–12

We have here before us three exhortations, each of them enforced with a good reason: —

I. We must live in a humble and dutiful subjection to God and his government (*v.* 7): *"Fear the Lord,* as your sovereign Lord and Master; be ruled in every thing by your religion and subject to the divine will." This must be, 1. A humble subjection: *Be not wise in thy own eyes.* Note, There is not a greater enemy to the power of religion, and the fear of God in the heart, than conceitedness of our own wisdom. Those that have an opinion of their own sufficiency think it below them, and a disparagement to them, to take their measures from, much more to hamper themselves with, religion's rules. 2. A dutiful subjection: *Fear the Lord, and depart from evil;* take heed of doing any thing to offend him and to forfeit his care. To *fear the Lord,* so as to *depart from evil,* is true *wisdom* and *understanding* (Job 28:28); those that have it are truly wise, but self-denyingly so, and not *wise in their own eyes.* For our encouragement thus to live in the fear of God it is here promised (*v.* 8) that it shall be as serviceable even to the outward man as our necessary food. It will be nourishing: *It shall be health to thy navel.* It will be strengthening: It shall be *marrow to thy bones.* The prudence, temperance, and sobriety, the calmness and composure of mind, and the good government of the appetites and passions, which religion teaches, tend very much not only to the health of the soul, but to a good habit of body, which is very desirable, and without which our other enjoyments in this world are insipid. Envy is *the rottenness of the bones;* the sorrow of the world dries them; but hope and joy in God are marrow to them.

II. We must make a good use of our estates, and that is the way to increase them, *v.* 9, 10. Here is,

1. A precept which makes it our duty to serve God with our estates: *Honour the Lord with thy substance.* It is the end of our creation and redemption to honour God, to be to him for a name and a praise; we are no other way capable of serving him than in his honour. His honour we must show forth and the honour we have for him. We must honour him, not only *with our bodies and spirits which are his,* but with our estates too, for they also are his: we and all our appurtenances must be devoted to his glory. Worldly wealth is but poor substance, yet, such as it is, we must honour God with it, and then, if ever, it becomes substantial. We must honour God, (1.) *With our increase.* Where riches increase we are tempted to honour ourselves (Deu. 8:17) and to set our hearts upon the world (Ps. 62:10); but the more God gives us the more we should study to honour him. It is meant of the increase of the earth, for we live upon annual products, to keep us in constant dependence on God. (2.) *With all our increase.* As God has prospered us in every thing, we must honour him. Our law will allow a prescription for a *modus decimandi — a mode of tithing,* but none *de non decimando — for exemption from paying tithes.* (3.) *With the first-fruits of all,* as Abel, Gen. 4:4. This was the law (Ex. 23:19), and the prophets, Mal. 3:10. God, who is the first and best, must have the first and best of every thing; his right is prior to all other, and therefore he must be served first. Note, It is our duty to make our worldly estates serviceable to our religion, to use them and the interest we have by them for the promoting of religion, to do good to the poor with what we have and abound in all works of piety and charity, *devising liberal things.*

2. A promise, which makes it our interest to serve God with our estates. It is the way to make a little much, and much more; it is the surest and safest method of thriving: *So shall thy barns be filled with plenty.* He does not say thy bags, but thy barns, not thy wardrobe replenished, but thy presses: "God shall bless thee with an increase of that which is for use, not for show or ornament — for spending and laying out, not for hoarding and laying up." Those that do good with what they have shall have more to do more good with. Note, If we make our worldly estates serviceable to our religion we shall find our religion very serviceable to the prosperity of our worldly affairs. *Godliness has the promise of the life that now is* and most of the comfort of it. We mistake if we think that giving will undo us and make us poor. No, giving for God's honour will make us rich, Hag. 2:19. What we gave we have.

III. We must conduct ourselves aright under our afflictions, *v.* 11, 12. This the apostle quotes (Heb. 12:5), and calls it *an exhortation which speaks unto us as unto children,* with the authority and affection of a father. We are here in a world of troubles. Now observe,

1. What must be our care when we are in affliction. We must neither despise it nor be weary of it. His exhortation, before, was to those that are rich and in prosperity, here to those that are poor and in adversity. (1.) We must not despise an affliction, be it ever so light and short, as if it were not worth taking notice of, or as if it were not sent on an errand and therefore required no answer. We must not be stocks, and stones, and stoics, under our afflictions, insensible of them, hardening ourselves under them, and concluding we can easily get through them without God. (2.) We must not be weary of an affliction, be it ever so heavy and long, not *faint* under it, so the apostle renders it, not be dispirited, dispossessed of our own souls, or driven to despair, or to use any indirect means for our relief and the redress of our grievances. We must not think that the affliction either presses harder or continues longer than is meet, not conclude that deliverance will never come because it does not come so soon as we expect it.

2. What will be our comfort when we are in affliction. (1.) That it is a divine correction; it is *the chastening of the Lord,* which, as it is a reason why we should submit to it (for it is folly to contend with a God of incontestable sovereignty and irresistible power), so it is a reason why we should be satisfied in it; for we may be sure that a God of unspotted purity does us no wrong and that a God of infinite goodness means us no hurt. It is from God, and therefore must not be despised; for a slight put upon the messenger is an affront to him that sends him. It is from God, and therefore we must not be weary of it, for he knows our frame, both what we need and what we can bear. (2.) That it is a fatherly correction; it comes not from his vindictive justice as a Judge, but his wise affection as a Father. The father corrects *the son whom he* loves, nay, and because he loves him and desires he may be wise and good. He delights in that in his son which is amiable and agreeable, and therefore corrects him for the prevention and cure of that which would be a deformity to him, and an alloy to his delight in him. Thus God hath said, *As many as I love I rebuke and chasten,* Rev. 3:19. This is a great comfort to God's children, under their afflictions, [1.] That they not only consist with, but flow from, covenant-love. [2.] That they are so far from doing them any real hurt that, by the grace of God working with them, they do a great deal of good, and are happy means of their satisfaction.

Verses 13–20

Solomon had pressed us earnestly to seek diligently for wisdom (*ch.* 2:1, etc.), and had assured us that we should succeed in our sincere and constant pursuits. But the question is, What shall we get by it when we have found it? Prospect of advantage is the spring and spur of industry; he therefore shows us how much it will be to our profit, laying this down for an unquestionable truth, *Happy is the man that findeth wisdom,* that true wisdom which consists in the knowledge and love of God, and an entire conformity to all the intentions of his truths, providences, and laws. Now observe,

I. What it is to find wisdom so as to be made happy by it.

1. We must get it. He is the happy man who, having found it, makes it his own, gets both an interest in it and the possession of it, who *draws out understanding* (so the word it), that is, (1.) Who derives it from God. Having it not in himself, he draws it with the bucket of prayer from the fountain of all wisdom, *who gives liberally.* (2.) Who takes pains for it, as he does who draws ore out of the mine. It if do not come easily, we must put the more strength to draw it. (3.) Who improves in it, who, having some understanding, draws it out by growing in knowledge and making five talents ten. (4.) Who does good with it, who draws out from the stock he has, as wine from the vessel, and communicates to others, for their instruction, *things new and old.* That is well got, and to good purpose, that is thus used to good purpose.

2. We must trade for it. We read here of the merchandise of wisdom, which intimates, (1.) That we must make it our business, and not a by-business, as the merchant bestows the main of his thoughts and time upon his merchandise. (2.) That we must venture all in it, as a stock in trade, and be willing to part with all for it. This is that pearl of great price which, when we have found it, we must willingly sell all for the purchase of, Mt. 13:45, 46. *Buy the truth,* (Prov. 23:23); he does not say at what rate, because we must buy it at any rate rather than miss it.

3. We must lay hold on it as we lay hold on a good bargain when it is offered to us, which we do the more carefully if there be danger of having it taken out of our hands. We must apprehend with all our might, and put forth our utmost vigour in the pursuit of it, lay hold on all occasions to improve in it, and catch at the least of its dictates.

4. We must retain it. It is not enough to lay hold on wisdom, but we must keep our hold, hold it fast, with a resolution never to let it go, but to persevere in the ways of wisdom to the end. We must *sustain it* (so some read it), must embrace it with all our might, as we do that which we would sustain. We must do all we can to support the declining interests of religion in the places where we live.

II. What the happiness of those is who do find it.

1. It is a transcendent happiness, more than can be found in the wealth of this world, if we had ever so much of it, *v.* 14, 15. It is not only a surer, but a more gainful merchandise to trade for wisdom, for Christ, and grace, and spiritual blessings, than for silver, and gold, and rubies. Suppose a man to have got these in abundance, nay, to have all the things he can desire of this world (and who is it that ever had?), yet, (1.) All this would not purchase heavenly wisdom; no, it would *utterly be contemned;* it *cannot be gotten for gold,* Job 28:15, etc. (2.) All this would not countervail the want of heavenly wisdom nor be the ransom of a soul lost by its own folly. (3.) All this would not make a man half so happy, no, not in this world, as those are who have true wisdom, though they have none of all these things. (4.) Heavenly wisdom will procure that for us, and secure that to us, which silver, and gold, and rubies, will not be the purchase of.

2. It is a true happiness; for it is inclusive of, and equivalent to, all those things which are supposed to make men happy, *v.* 16, 17. Wisdom is here represented as a bright and bountiful queen, reaching forth gifts to her faithful and loving subjects, and offering them to all that will submit to her government. (1.) Is length of days a blessing? Yes, the most valuable; life includes all good, and therefore she offers that *in her right hand.* Religion puts us into the best methods of prolonging life, entitles us to the promises of it, and, though our days on earth should be no more than our neighbour's, yet it will secure to us everlasting life in a better world. (2.) Are riches and honour accounted bless-

ings? They are so, and them she reaches out with *her left hand*. For, as she is ready to embrace those that submit to her with both arms, so she is ready to give out to them with both hands. They shall have the wealth of this world as far as Infinite Wisdom sees good for them; while the true riches, by which men are rich towards God, are secured to them. Nor is there any honour, by birth or preferment, comparable to that which attends religion; it makes the *righteous more excellent than his neighbour*, recommends men to God, commands respect and veneration with all the sober part of mankind, and will in the other world make those that are now buried in obscurity to *shine forth as the sun*. (3.) Is pleasure courted as much as any thing? It is so, and it is certain that true piety has in it the greatest true pleasure. *Her ways are ways of pleasantness;* the ways in which she has directed us to walk are such as we shall find abundance of delight and satisfaction in. All the enjoyments and entertainments of sense are not comparable to the pleasure which gracious souls have in communion with God and doing good. That which is the only right way to bring us to our journey's end we must walk in, fair or foul, pleasant or unpleasant; but the way of religion, as it is the right way, so it is a pleasant way; it is smooth and clean, and strewed with roses: *All her paths are peace.* There is not only peace in the end, but peace in the way; not only in the way of religion in general, but in the particular paths of that way, in all her paths, all the several acts, instances, and duties of it. One does not embitter what the other sweetens, as it is with the allays of this world; but they are all peace, not only sweet, but safe. The saints enter into peace on this side heaven, and enjoy a present sabbatism.

3. It is the happiness of paradise (*v.* 18): *She is a tree of life.* True grace is that to the soul which the tree of life would have been, from which our first parents were shut out for eating of the forbidden tree. It is a seed of immortality, a *well of living waters, springing up to life eternal.* It is an earnest of the New Jerusalem, in the midst of which is *the tree of life*, Rev. 22:2; 2:7. Those that feed and feast on this heavenly wisdom shall not only be cured by it of every fatal malady, but shall find an antidote against age and death; they shall *eat and live for ever.*

4. It is a participation of the happiness of God himself, for wisdom is his everlasting glory and blessedness, *v.* 19, 20. This should make us in love with the wisdom and understanding which God gives, that *the Lord by wisdom founded the earth,* so that it cannot be removed, nor can ever fail of answering all the ends of its creation, to which it is admirably and unexceptionably fitted. *By understanding he has* likewise *established the heavens* and directed all the motions of them in the best manner. The heavenly bodies are vast, yet there is no flaw in them — numerous, yet no disorder in them — the motion rapid, yet no wear or tear; the depths of the sea are broken up, and thence come the waters beneath the firmament, and *the clouds drop down the dews,* the waters from above the firmament, and all this by the divine wisdom and knowledge; therefore *happy is the man that finds wisdom,* for he will thereby be *thoroughly furnished for every good word and work.* Christ is that Wisdom, by whom the worlds were made and still consist; happy therefore are those to whom he is *made of God wisdom,* for he has wherewithal to make good all the foregoing promises of long life, riches, and honour; for all the wealth of heaven, earth, and seas, is his.

Verses 21—26

Solomon, having pronounced those happy who not only lay hold on wisdom, but retain her, here exhorts us therefore to retain her, assuring us that we ourselves shall have the comfort of doing so.

I. The exhortation is, to have religion's rules always in view and always at heart, *v.* 21. 1. To have them always in view: "*My son, let them not depart from thy eyes;* let not thy eyes ever depart from them to wander after vanity. Have them always in mind, and do not forget them; be ever and anon thinking of them, and conversing with them, and never imagine that thou hast looked upon them long enough and that it is time now to lay them by; but, as long as thou livest, keep up and cultivate thy acquaintance with them." He who learns to write must always have his eye upon his copy, and not let that be out of his sight; and to the words of wisdom must those, in like manner,

have a constant respect, who will walk circumspectly. 2. To have them always at heart; for it is in that treasury, the hidden man of the heart, that we must *keep sound wisdom and discretion,* keep to the principles of it and keep in the ways of it. It is wealth that is worth keeping.

II. The argument to enforce this exhortation is taken from the unspeakable advantage which wisdom, thus kept, will be of to us. 1. In respect of strength and satisfaction: "It will be *life to thy soul* (*v.* 22); it will quicken thee to thy duty when thou beginnest to be slothful and remiss; it will revive thee under thy troubles when thou beginnest to droop and despond. It will be thy spiritual life, an earnest of life eternal." Life to the soul is life indeed. 2. In respect of honour and reputation: It shall be *grace to thy neck,* as a chain of gold, or a jewel. *Grace to thy jaws* (so the word is), grateful to thy *taste and relish* (so some); it shall infuse *grace into all thou sayest* (so others), shall furnish thee with acceptable words, which shall gain thee credit. 3. In respect of safety and security. This he insists upon in four verses, the scope of which is to show that *the effect of righteousness* (which is the same with *wisdom* here) is *quietness and assurance for ever,* Isa. 32:17. Good people are taken under God's special protection, and therein they may have an entire satisfaction. They are safe and may be easy, (1.) In their motions by day, *v.* 23. If our religion be our companion, it will be our convoy: "*Then shalt thou walk in thy way safely.* The natural life, and all that belongs to it, shall be under the protection of God's providence; the spiritual life, and all its interests, are under the protection of his grace; so that thou shalt be kept from falling into sin or trouble." Wisdom will direct us into, and keep us in, the safe way, as far as may be, from temptation, and will enable us to walk in it with holy security. The way of duty is the way of safety. "We are in danger of falling, but wisdom will keep thee, that *thy foot shall not stumble* at those things which are an offence and overthrow to many, but which thou shalt know how to get over." (2.) In their rest by night, *v.* 24. In our retirements we lie exposed and are most subject to frights. "But keep up communion with God, and keep a good conscience, and then *when thou liest down thou shalt not be afraid* of fire, or thieves, or specters, or any of the terrors of darkness, knowing that when we, and all our friends, are asleep, yet *he that keeps Israel and every true-born Israelite neither slumbers nor sleeps,* and to him thou hast committed thyself and taken shelter under the shadow of his wings. *Thou shalt lie down,* and not need to sit up to keep guard; having lain down, thou shalt sleep, and not have thy eyes held waking by care and fear; and *thy sleep shall be sweet* and refreshing to thee, being not disturbed by any alarms from without or from within," Ps. 4:8; 116:7. The way to have a good night is to keep a good conscience; and the sleep, as of the labouring man, so of the wise and godly man, is sweet. (3.) In their greatest straits and dangers. Integrity and uprightness will preserve us, so that we need *not be afraid of sudden fear, v.* 25. The harms that surprise us, unthought of, giving us no time to arm ourselves by consideration, are most likely to put us into confusion. But let not the wise and good man forget himself, and then he will not give way to any fear that has torment, be the alarm ever so sudden. Let him not fear the *desolation of the wicked, when it comes,* that is, [1.] The desolation which the wicked ones make of religion and the religious; though it comes, and seems to be just at the door, yet be not afraid of it; for, though God may make use of the wicked as instruments of his people's correction, yet he will never suffer them to be the authors of their desolation. Or rather, [2.] The desolation which wicked men will be brought into in a moment. It will come, and timorous saints may be apprehensive that they shall be involved in it; but let this be their comfort, that though judgments lay waste generally, at least promiscuously, yet God knows who are his and how to separate between the precious and the vile. Therefore be not afraid of that which appears most formidable, for (*v.* 26) "*the Lord shall be* not only thy protector to keep thee safe, but *thy confidence* to keep thee secure, so that thy foot *shall not be taken* by thy enemies nor ensnared by thy own fears." God has engaged to keep the feet of his saints.

Verses 27—35

True wisdom consists in the due discharge of our duty

towards man, as well as towards God, in honesty as well as piety, and therefore we have here divers excellent precepts of wisdom which relate to our neighbour.

I. We must render to all their due, both in justice and charity, and not delay to do it (*v.* 27, 28): "*Withhold not good from those to whom it is due* (either for want of love to them or through too much love to thy money) *when it is in the power of thy hand to do it,* for, if it be not, it cannot be expected; but it was thy great fault if thou didst, by thy extravagances, disable thyself to do justly and show mercy, and it ought to be the greatest of thy griefs if God had disabled thee, not so much that thou art straitened in thy own comforts and conveniences as that thou hast not wherewithal to give to those to whom it is due." *Withhold it not*; this implies that it is called for and expected, but that the hand is drawn in and the *bowels of compassion are shut up.* We must not hinder others from doing it, not be ourselves backward to it. "If thou hast it by thee to-day, hast it in the power of thy hand, say not to thy neighbour, *Go thy way for this time,* and come at a more convenient season, and I will then see what will be done; *to-morrow I will give;* whereas thou art not sure that thou shalt live till to-morrow, or that to-morrow thou shalt *have it by thee.* Be not thus loth to part with thy money upon a good account. Make not excuses to shift off a duty that must be done, nor delight to keep thy neighbour in pain and in suspense, nor to show the authority which the giver has over the beggar; but readily and cheerfully, and from a principle of conscience towards God, give good to *those to whom it is due,*" to the *lords and owners of it* (so the word is), to those who upon any account are entitled to it. This requires us, 1. To pay our just debts without fraud, covin, or delay. 2. To give wages to those who have earned them. 3. To provide for our relations, and those that have dependence on us, for to them it is due. 4. To render dues both to church and state, magistrates and ministers. 5. To be ready to all acts of friendship and humanity, and in every thing to be neighbourly; for these are things that are due by the law of doing as we would be done by. 6. To be charitable to the poor and necessitous. If others want the necessary supports of life, and we have wherewithal to supply them, we must look upon it as due to them and not withhold it. Alms are called *righteousness* because they are a debt to the poor, and a debt which we must not defer to pay, *Bis dat, qui cito dat — He gives twice who gives speedily.*

II. We must never design any hurt or harm to any body (*v.* 29): "*Devise not evil against thy neighbour;* do not contrive how to do him an ill-turn undiscovered, to prejudice him in his body, goods, or good name, and the rather because *he dwells securely by thee,* and, having given thee no provocation, entertains no jealousy or suspicion of thee, and therefore is off his guard." It is against the laws both of honour and friendship to do a man an ill-turn and give him no warning. *Cursed be he that smites his neighbour secretly.* It is a most base ungrateful thing, if our neighbours have a good opinion of us, that we will do them no harm, and we thence take advantage to cheat and injure them.

III. We must not be quarrelsome and litigious (*v.* 30): "*Do not strive with a man without cause;* contend not for that which thou hast no title to; resent not that as a provocation which peradventure was but an oversight. Never trouble thy neighbour with frivolous complaints and accusations, or vexatious law-suits, when either there is no harm done thee or none worth speaking of, or thou mightest right thyself in a friendly way." Law must be the last refuge; for it is not only our duty, but our interest, *as much as in us lies, to live peaceably with all men.* When accounts are balanced, it will be found there is little got by striving.

IV. We must not envy the prosperity of evil-doers, *v.* 31. This caution is the same with that which is so much insisted on, Ps. 37. "*Envy not the oppressor;* though he be rich and great, though he live in ease and pleasure, and make all about him to stand in awe of him, yet do not think him a happy man, nor wish thyself in his condition. *Choose none of his ways;* do not imitate him, nor take the courses he takes to enrich himself. Never think of doing as he does, though thou wert sure to get by it all that he has, for it would be dearly bought." Now, to show what little reason saints have to envy sinners, Solomon here, in the last four verses of the chapter, compares the condition of sinners and saints together (as his father David had done, Ps. 37), sets the one over against the other, that we may see how happy the saints are, though they be oppressed, and how miserable the wicked are, though they be oppressors. Men are to be judged of as they stand with God, and as he judges of them, not as they stand in the world's books. Those are in the right who are of God's mind; and, if we be of his mind, we shall see, whatever pretence one sinner may have to envy another, that saints are so happy themselves that they have no reason at all to envy any sinner, though his condition be ever so prosperous. For, 1. Sinners are hated of God, but saints are beloved, *v.* 32. The froward sinners, who are continually going from-ward him, whose lives are a perverse contradiction to his will, are *abomination to the Lord.* He that hates nothing that he has made yet abhors those who have thus marred themselves; they are not only abominable in his sight, but an abomination. The righteous therefore have no reason to envy them, for they have his secret with them; they are his favourites; he has that communion with them which is a secret to the world and in which they have a joy that a stranger does not intermeddle with; he communicates to them the secret tokens of his love; his covenant is with them; they know his mind, and the meanings and intentions of his providence, better than others can. *Shall I hide from Abraham the thing that I do?* 2. Sinners are under the curse of God, they and their houses; saints are under his blessing, they and their habitation, *v.* 33. The wicked has a house, a strong and stately dwelling perhaps, but *the curse of the Lord* is upon it, it is *in it,* and, though the affairs of the family may prosper, yet the very blessings are curses, Mal. 2:2. There is *leanness in the soul,* when the body is fed to the full, Ps. 106:15. The curse may work silently and slowly; but it is as a fretting leprosy; it will consume the *timber thereof and the stones thereof,* Zec. 5:4; Hab. 2:11. The just have a habitation, a poor cottage (the word is used for sheep-cotes), a very mean dwelling; but God blesses it; he is continually blessing it, from the beginning of the year to the end of it. The curse or blessing of God is upon the house according as the inhabitants are wicked or godly; and it is certain that a blessed family, though poor, has no reason to envy a cursed family, though rich. 3. God puts contempt upon sinners, but shows respect to saints, *v.* 34. (1.) Those who exalt themselves shall certainly be abased: *Surely he scorns the scorners.* Those who scorn to submit to the discipline of religion, scorn to take God's yoke upon them, scorn to be beholden to his grace, who scoff at godliness and godly people, and take a pleasure in bantering and exposing them, God will scorn them, and lay them open to scorn before all the world. He despises their impotent malice, *sits in heaven and laughs at them,* Ps. 2:4. He retaliates upon them (Ps. 18:26); he *resists the proud.* (2.) Those who humble themselves shall be exalted, for *he gives grace to the lowly;* he works that in them which puts honour upon them and for which they are *accepted of God and approved of men.* Those who patiently bear contempt from scornful men shall have respect from God and all good men, and then they have no reason to envy the scorners or to choose their ways. 4. The end of sinners will be everlasting shame, the end of saints endless honour, *v.* 35. (1.) Saints are wise men, and act wisely for themselves; for though their religion now wraps them up in obscurity, and lays them open to reproach, yet they are sure to inherit glory at last, the far more exceeding and eternal weight of glory. They shall have it, and have it by inheritance, the sweetest and surest tenure. God gives them grace (*v.* 34), and therefore they shall inherit glory, for grace is glory, 2 Co. 3:18. It is glory begun, the earnest of it, Ps. 84:11. (2.) Sinners are fools, for they are not only preparing disgrace for themselves, but at the same time flattering themselves with a prospect of honour, as if they only took the way to be great. Their end will manifest their folly: *Shame shall be their promotion.* And it will be so much the more their punishment as it will come instead of their promotion; it will be all the promotion they must ever expect, that God will be glorified in their everlasting confusion.

CHAPTER 4

When the things of God are to be taught precept must be upon precept, and line upon line, not only because the things themselves are of great worth and weight, but because men's minds, at the best, are unapt to admit them and commonly prejudiced against them; and therefore Solomon, in this chapter, with a great variety of expression and a pleasant powerful flood of divine eloquence, inculcates the same things that he had pressed upon us in the foregoing chapters. Here is, I. An earnest exhortation to the study of wisdom, that is, of true religion and godliness, borrowed from the good instructions which his father gave him, and enforced with many considerable arguments (*v.* 1–13). II. A necessary caution against bad company and all fellowship with the unfruitful works of darkness (*v.* 14–19). III. Particular directions for the attaining and preserving of wisdom, and bringing forth the fruits of it (*v.* 20–27). So plainly, so pressingly, is the case laid before us, that we shall be for ever inexcusable if we perish in our folly.

Verses 1–13

Here we have,

I. The invitation which Solomon gives to his children to come and receive instruction from him (*v.* 1, 2): *Hear, you children, the instruction of a father.* That is, 1. "Let my own children, in the first place, receive and give good heed to those instructions which I set down for the use of others also." Note, Magistrates and ministers, who are entrusted with the direction of larger societies, are concerned to take a more than ordinary care for the good instruction of their own families; from this duty their public work will by no means excuse them. This charity must begin at home, though it must not end there; for he that has not his children in subjection with all gravity, and does not take pains in their good education, how shall he do his duty as he ought *to the church of God?* 1 Tim. 3:4, 5. The children of those that are eminent for wisdom and public usefulness ought to improve in knowledge and grace in proportion to the advantages they derive from their relation to such parents. Yet it may be observed, to save both the credit and the comfort of those parents whose children do not answer the hopes that arose from their education, that Rehoboam, the son of Solomon, was far from being either one of the wisest or one of the best. We have reason to think that thousands have got more good by Solomon's proverbs than his own son did, to whom they seem to have been dedicated. 2. Let all young people, in the days of their childhood and youth, take pains to get knowledge and grace, for that is their learning age, and then their minds are formed and seasoned. He does not say, *My* children, but *You* children. We read but of one son that Solomon had of his own; but (would you think it?) he is willing to set up for a schoolmaster, and to teach other people's children! for at that age there is most hope of success; the branch is easily bent when it is young and tender. 3. Let all that would receive instruction come with the disposition of children, though they be grown persons. Let all prejudices be laid aside, and the mind be as white paper. let them be dutiful, tractable, and self-diffident, and take the word as the word of a father, which comes both with authority and with affection. We must see it coming from God as *our Father in heaven,* to whom we pray, from whom we expect blessings, the Father of our spirits, to whom we ought to be in subjection, that we may live. We must look upon our teachers as our fathers, who love us and seek our welfare; and therefore though the instruction carry in it reproof and correction, for so the word signifies, yet we must bid it welcome. Now, (1.) To recommend it to us, we are told, not only that it is the *instruction of a father,* but that it is *understanding,* and therefore should be welcome to intelligent creatures. Religion has reason on its side, and we are taught it by fair reasoning. It is a law indeed (*v.* 2), but that law is founded upon doctrine, upon unquestionable principles of truth, upon *good doctrine,* which is not only faithful, but worthy of all acceptation. If we admit the doctrine, we cannot but submit to the law. (2.) To rivet it in us, we are directed to receive it as a gift, to attend to it with all diligence, to attend so as to know it, for otherwise we cannot do it, and not to forsake it by disowning the doctrine or disobeying the law.

II. The instructions he gives them. Observe,

1. How he came by these instructions; he had them from his parents, and teaches his children the same that they taught him, *v.* 3, 4. Observe, (1.) His parents loved him, and therefore taught him: *I was my father's son.* David had many sons, but Solomon was his son *indeed,* as Isaac is called (Gen. 17:19) and for the same reason, because on him the covenant was entailed. He was his father's darling, above any of his children. God had a special kindness for Solomon (the prophet called him *Jedidiah,* because the Lord loved him, 2 Sa. 12:25), and for that reason David had a special kindness for him, for he was a man after God's own heart. If parents may ever love one child better than another, it must not be till it plainly appears that God does so. He was *tender, and only beloved, in the sight of his mother.* Surely there was a manifest reason for making such a distinction when both the parents made it. Now we see how they showed their love; they catechised him, kept him to his book, and held him to a strict discipline. Though he was a prince, and heir-apparent to the crown, yet they did not let him live at large; nay, therefore they tutored him thus. And perhaps David was the more strict with Solomon in his education because he had seen the ill effects of an undue indulgence in Adonijah, whom he had not *crossed in any thing* (1 Ki. 1:6), as also in Absalom. (2.) What his parents taught him he teaches others. Observe, [1.] When Solomon was grown up he not only remembered, but took a pleasure in repeating, the good lessons his parents taught him when he was a child. He did not forget them, so deep were the impressions they made upon him. He was not ashamed of them, such a high value had he for them, nor did he look upon them as the childish things, the mean things, which, when he became a man, a king, he should put away, as a disparagement to him; much less did he repeat them: as some wicked children have done, to ridicule them, and make his companions merry with them, priding himself that he had got clear from grave lessons and restraints. [2.] Though Solomon was a wise man himself, and divinely inspired, yet, when he was to teach wisdom, he did not think it below him to quote his father and to make use of his words. Those that would learn well, and teach well, in religion, must not affect new-found notions and new-coined phrases, so as to look with contempt upon the knowledge and language of their predecessors; if we must keep to the good old way, why should we scorn the good old words? Jer. 6:16. [3.] Solomon, having been well educated by his parents, thought himself thereby obliged to give his children a good education, the same that his parents had given him; and this is one way in which we must requite our parents for the pains they took with us, even by showing piety at home, 1 Tim. 5:4. They taught us, not only that we might learn ourselves, but that we might teach our children, the good knowledge of God, Ps. 78:6. And we are false to a trust if we do not; for the sacred deposit of religious doctrine and law was lodged in our hands with a charge to transmit it pure and entire to those that shall *come after us,* 2 Tim. 2:2. [4.] Solomon enforces his exhortations with the authority of his father David, a man famous in his generation upon all accounts. Be it taken notice of, to the honour of religion, that the wisest and best men in every age have been most zealous, not only for the practice of it themselves, but for the propagating of it to others; and we should therefore *continue in the things which we have learned, knowing of whom we have learned them,* 2 Tim. 3:14.

2. What these instructions were, *v.* 4–13.

(1.) By way of precept and exhortation. David, in teaching his son, though he was a child of great capacity and quick apprehension, yet to show that he was in good earnest, and to affect his child the more with what he said, expressed himself with great warmth and importunity, and inculcated the same thing again and again. So children must be taught. Deu. 6:7, *Thou shalt whet them diligently upon thy children.* David, though he was a man of public business, and had tutors for his son, took all this pains with him himself.

[1.] He recommends to him his Bible and his catechism, as the means, his father's *words* (*v.* 4), the *words of his mouth* (*v.* 5), his *sayings* (*v.* 10), all the good lessons he had taught him; and perhaps he means particularly the book of Psalms, many of which were *Maschils — psalms of instruction,* and two of them are expressly said to be *for Solomon.* These, and all his other words, Solomon must have an eye to. *First,* He must *hear and receive them* (*v.* 10), diligently attend to them, and imbibe them, *as the earth drinks in the rain that comes often upon it,* Heb. 6:7. God thus bespeaks our attention to his word: *Hear, O my son! and receive my sayings. Secondly,* He must *hold fast the form of sound words* which his father gave him (*v.* 4): *Let thy heart retain my words;* and except the word be hid in the heart, lodged in the will and affections, it will not be retained. *Thirdly,* He must govern himself by them: *Keep my commandments,* obey them, and that is the way to increase in the knowledge of them, Jn. 7:17. *Fourthly,* He must stick to them and abide by them: *"Decline not from the words of my mouth* (*v.* 5), as fearing they will be too great a check upon thee, but *take fast hold of instruction* (*v.* 13), as being resolved to keep thy hold and never let it go." Those that have a good education, though they strive to shake it off, will find it hang about them a great while, and, if it do not, their case is very sad.

[2.] He recommends to him wisdom and understanding as the end to be aimed at in the use of these means; that *wisdom* which is the *principal wisdom,* get that. *Quod caput est sapientia eam acquire sapientiam — Be sure to mind that branch of wisdom which is the top branch of it,* and that is the *fear of God, ch.* 1:7. Junius and Tremellius. A principle of religion in the heart is the one thing needful; therefore, *First,* Get this *wisdom,* get this *understanding, v.* 5. And again, *"Get wisdom,* and *with all thy getting, get understanding, v.* 7. Pray for it, take pains for it, give diligence in the use of all appointed means to attain it. *Wait at wisdom's gate,* Prov. 8:34. Get dominion over thy corruptions, which are thy follies: get possession of wise principles and the habits of wisdom. Get wisdom by experience, get it *above all thy getting;* be more in care and take more pains to get this than to get the wealth of this world; whatever thou forgettest, get this, reckon it a great achievement, and pursue it accordingly." True wisdom is God's gift, and yet we are here commanded to get it, because God gives it to those that labour for it; yet, after all, we must not say, *Our might and the power of our hand have gotten us this wealth. Secondly, Forget her not* (*v.* 5), *forsake her not* (*v.* 6), *let her not go* (*v.* 13), *but keep her.* Those that have got this wisdom must take heed of losing it again by returning to folly: it is indeed a good part, that shall not be *taken from us;* but then we must take heed lest we throw it from us, as those do that forget it first, and let it slip out of their minds, and then forsake it and turn out of its good ways. That good thing which is committed to us we must keep, and not let it drop, through carelessness, nor suffer it to be forced from us, nor suffer ourselves to be wheedled out of it; never let go such a jewel. *Thirdly, Love her* (*v.* 6), and *embrace her* (*v.* 8), as worldly men love their wealth and set their hearts upon it. Religion should be very dear to us, dearer than any thing in this world; and, if we cannot reach to be great masters of wisdom, yet let us be true lovers of it; and what grace we have let us embrace it with a sincere affection, as those that admire its beauty. *Fourthly, "Exalt her, v.* 8. Always keep up high thoughts of religion, and do all thou canst to bring it into reputation, and maintain the credit of it among men. Concur with God in his purpose, which is to magnify the law and make it honourable, and do what thou canst to serve that purpose." Let *Wisdom's* children not only justify her, but magnify her, and prefer her before that which is dearest to them in this world. In honouring those that fear the Lord, though they are low in the world, and in regarding a *poor wise man,* we exalt wisdom.

(2.) By way of motive and inducement thus to labour for wisdom, and submit to the guidance of it, consider, [1.] It is the main matter, and that which ought to be the chief and continual care of every man in this life (*v.* 7): *Wisdom is the principal thing;* other things which we are solicitous to get and keep are nothing to it. It is the *whole of man,* Eccl. 12:13. It is that which recommends us to God, which beautifies the soul, which enables us to answer the end of our creation, to live to some good purpose in the world, and to get to heaven at last; and therefore it is the principal thing. [2.] It has reason and equity on its side (*v.* 11): *"I have taught thee in the way of wisdom,* and so it will be found to be at last. *I have led thee,* not in the crooked ways of carnal policy, which does wrong under colour of wisdom, but *in right paths,* agreeable to the eternal rules and reasons of good and evil." The rectitude of the divine nature appears in the rectitude of all the divine laws. Observe, David not only taught his son by good instructions, but led him both by a good example and by applying general instructions to particular cases; so that nothing was wanting on his part to make him wise. [3.] It would be much for his own advantage: "If thou be wise and good, thou shalt be so for thyself." *First,* "It will be thy life, thy comfort, thy happiness; it is what thou canst not live without:" *Keep my commandments and live, v.* 4. That of our Saviour agrees with this, *If thou wilt enter into life, keep the commandments,* Mt. 19:17. It is upon pain of death, eternal death, and in prospect of life, eternal life, that we are required to be religious. "Receive wisdom's sayings, *and the years of thy life shall be many* (*v.* 10), as many in this world as Infinite Wisdom sees fit, and in the other world thou shalt live that life the years of which shall never be numbered. *Keep her* therefore, whatever it cost thee, *for she is thy life, v.* 13. All thy satisfaction will be found in this;" and a soul without true wisdom and grace is really a dead soul. *Secondly,* "It will be thy guard and guide, thy convoy and conductor, through all the dangers and difficulties of thy journey through this wilderness. Love wisdom, and cleave to her, and she shall *preserve thee, she shall keep thee* (*v.* 6) from sin, the worst of evils, the worst of enemies; she shall keep thee from hurting thyself, and then none else can hurt thee." As we say, "Keep thy shop, and thy shop will keep thee;" so, "Keep thy wisdom, and thy wisdom will keep thee." It will keep us from straits and stumbling-blocks in the management of ourselves and our affairs, *v.* 12. 1. That our steps be not straitened when we go, that we bring not ourselves into such straits as David was in, 2 Sa. 24:14. Those that make God's word their rule shall walk at liberty, and be at ease in themselves. 2. That our feet do not stumble when we run. If wise and good men be put upon sudden resolves, the certain rule of God's word which they go by will keep them even then from stumbling upon any thing that may be pernicious. Integrity and uprightness will preserve us. *Thirdly,* "It will be thy honour and reputation (*v.* 8): *Exalt* wisdom (do thou but show thy good-will to her advancement) and though she needs not thy service she will abundantly recompense it, *she shall promote thee, she shall bring thee to honour."* Solomon was to be a king, but his wisdom and virtue would be more his honour than his crown or purple; it was that for which all his neighbours had him so much in veneration; and no doubt, in his reign and David's, wise and good men stood fairest for preferment. However, religion will, first or last, bring all those *to honour* that cordially *embrace her;* they shall be accepted of God, respected by all wise men, owned in the great day, and shall inherit everlasting glory. This he insists on (*v.* 9): *"She shall give to thy head an ornament of grace* in this world, shall recommend thee both to God and man, and in the other world *a crown of glory shall she deliver to thee,* a crown that shall never totter, a crown of glory that shall never wither." That is the true honour which attends religion. *Nobilitas sola est atique unica virtus — Virtue is the only nobility!* David having thus recommended wisdom to his son, no marvel that when God bade him ask what he would he prayed, Lord, *give me a wise and an understanding heart.* We should make it appear by our prayers how well we are taught.

Verses 14–19

Some make David's instructions to Solomon, which began *v.* 4, to continue to the end of the chapter; nay, some continue them to the end of the ninth chapter; but it is more probable that Solomon begins here again, if not sooner. In these verses, having exhorted us to walk in the paths of wisdom, he cautions us against the path of the wicked. 1. We must take heed of the ways of sin and avoid them, every thing that looks like sin and leads to it. 2. In order to this we must keep out of the ways of sinners, and have no fellowship with them. For fear of falling into wicked courses, we must shun wicked company. Here is,

I. The caution itself, *v.* 14, 15. 1. We must take heed of falling in with sin and sinners: *Enter not into the paths of the wicked.* Our teacher, having like a faithful guide shown us the *right paths* (*v.* 11), here warns us of the by-paths into which we are in danger of being drawn aside. Those that have been well educated, and trained up in the way they should go, let them never turn aside into the way they should not go; let them not so much as enter into it, no, not to make trial of it, lest it prove a dangerous experiment and difficult to retreat with safety. "Venture not into the company of those that are infected with the plague, no, not though thou think thyself guarded with an antidote." 2. If at any time we are inveigled into an evil way, we must hasten out of it. "If, ere thou wast aware, thou didst enter in at the gate, because it was wide, *go not* on *in the way of evil men.* As soon as thou art made sensible of thy mistake, retire immediately, take not a step more, stay not a minute longer, in the way that certainly leads to destruction." 3. We must dread and detest the ways of sin and sinners, and decline them with the utmost care imaginable. *"The way of evil men* may seem a pleasant way and sociable, and the nearest way to the compassing of some secular end we may have in view; but it is an evil way, and will end ill, and therefore if thou love thy God and thy soul *avoid it, pass not by it,* that thou mayest not be tempted to enter into it; and, if thou find thyself near it, *turn from it and pass away,* and get as far off it as thou canst." The manner of expression intimates the imminent danger we are in, the need we have of this caution, and the great importance of it, and that our watchmen are, or should be, in good earnest, in giving us warning. It intimates likewise at what a distance we should keep from sin and sinners; he does not say, Keep at a due distance, but at a great distance, the further the better; never think you can get far enough from it. *Escape for thy life: look not behind thee.*

II. The reasons to enforce this caution.

1. "Consider the character of the men whose way thou art warned to shun." They are mischievous men (*v.* 16, 17); they not only care not what hurt they do to those that stand in their way, but it is their business to do mischief, and their delight, purely for mischief-sake. They are continually designing and endeavouring to *cause some to fall,* to ruin them body and soul. Wickedness and malice are in their nature, and violence is in all their actions. They are spiteful in the highest degree; for, (1.) Mischief is rest and sleep to them. As much satisfaction as a covetous man has when he has got money, an ambitious man when he has got preferment, and a good man when he has done good, so much have they when they have said or done that which is injurious and ill-natured; and they are extremely uneasy if they cannot get their envy and revenge gratified, as Haman, to whom every thing was unpleasant as long as Mordecai was unhanged. It intimates likewise how restless and unwearied they are in their mischievous pursuits; they will rather be deprived of sleep than of the pleasure of being vexatious. (2.) Mischief is meat and drink to them; they feed and feast upon it. *They eat the bread of the wickedness (they eat up my people as they eat bread,* Ps. 14:4) *and drink the wine of violence* (*v.* 17), *drink iniquity like water,* Job 15:16. All they eat and drink is got by rapine and oppression. Do wicked men think the time lost in which they are not doing hurt? Let good men make it as much their business and delight to do good. *Amici, diem perdidi — Friends, I have lost a day.* And let all that are wise, and wish well to themselves, avoid the society of the wicked; for, [1.] It is very scandalous; for there is no disposition of mind that is a greater reproach to human nature, a greater enemy to human society, a bolder defiance to God and conscience, that has more of the devil's image in it, or is more serviceable to his interests, than a delight to do mischief and to vex, and hurt, and ruin every body. [2.] It is very dangerous. "Shun those that delight to do mischief as thou tenderest thy own safety; for, whatever friendship they may pretend, one time or other they will do thee mischief; thou wilt ruin thyself if thou dost concur with them (*ch.* 1:18) and they will ruin thee if thou dost not."

2. "Consider the character of the way itself which thou art warned to shun, compared with the right way which thou art invited to walk in."

(1.) The way of righteousness is light (*v.* 18): *The path of the just,* which they have chosen, and in which they walk, *is as light;* the *light shines on their ways* (Job 22:28) and makes them both safe and pleasant. Christ is *their way* and he is *the light.* They are guided by the word of God and that is *a light to their feet;* they themselves are *light in the Lord* and they *walk in the light as he is in the light.* [1.] It is a *shining light.* Their way shines to themselves in the joy and comfort of it; it shines before others in the lustre and honour of it; *it shines before men, who see their good works,* Mt. 5:16. They go on in their way with a holy security and serenity of mind, as those that *walk in the light.* It is as the morning-light, which *shines out of obscurity* (Isa. 58:8, 10) and puts an end to the *works of darkness.* [2.] It is a growing light; it *shines more and more,* not like the light of a meteor, which soon disappears, or that of a candle, which burns dim and burns down, but like that of the rising sun, which goes forward shining, mounts upward shining. Grace, the guide of this way, is growing; *he that has clean hands shall be stronger and stronger.* That joy which is the pleasure of this way, that honour which is the brightness of it, and all that happiness which is indeed its light, shall be still increasing. [3.] It will arrive, in the end, at *the perfect day.* The light of the dayspring will at length be noon-day light, and it is this that the enlightened soul is pressing towards. The saints will not be perfect till they come to heaven, but there they shall themselves *shine as the sun when he goes forth in his strength,* Mt. 13:43. Their graces and joys shall be all consummate. Therefore it is our wisdom to keep close to *the path of the just.*

(2.) The *way of* sin *is as darkness, v.* 19. The works he had cautioned us not to have fellowship with are *works of darkness.* What true pleasure and satisfaction can those have who know no pleasure and satisfaction but what they have in doing mischief? What sure guide have those that cast God's word behind them? *The way of the wicked is dark,* and therefore dangerous; for they stumble and yet *know not at what they stumble.* They fall into sin, but are not aware which way the temptation came by which they were overthrown, and therefore know not how to avoid it the next time. They fall into trouble, but never enquire wherefore God contends with them; they *consider not that they do evil,* nor what will be in the end of it, Ps. 82:5; Job 18:5, 6. This is the way we are directed to shun.

Verses 20–27

Solomon, having warned us not to do evil, here teaches us how to do well. It is not enough for us to shun the occasions of sin, but we must study the methods of duty.

I. We must have a continual regard to the word of God and endeavour that it may be always ready to us.

1. The sayings of wisdom must be our principles by which we must govern ourselves, our monitors to warn us of duty and danger; and therefore, (1.) We must receive them readily: *"Incline thy ear to them* (*v.* 20); humbly bow to them; diligently listen to them." The attentive hearing of the word of God is a good sign of a work of grace begun in the heart and a good means of carrying it on. It is to be hoped that those are resolved to do their duty who are inclined to know it. (2.) We must retain them carefully (*v.* 21); we must lay them before us as our rule: *"Let them not depart from thy eyes;* view them, review them, and in every thing aim to conform to them." We must lodge them within us, as a commanding principle, the influences of which are diffused throughout the whole man: *"Keep them in the midst of thy heart,* as things dear to thee, and which thou art afraid of losing." Let the word of God be written in the heart, and that which is written there will remain.

2. The reason why we must thus make much of the words of wisdom is because they will be both food and physic to us, like *the tree of life,* Rev. 22:2; Eze. 47:12. Those that seek and find them, find and keep them, shall find in them, (1.) Food: *For they are life unto those that find them, v.* 22. As the spiritual life was begun by the word as the instrument of it, so by the same word it is still nourished and maintained. We could not live without it; we may by faith live upon it. (2.) Physic. They are *health to all their flesh,* to the whole man, both body and soul; they help to keep both in good plight. They are *health to all flesh,* so the Septuagint. There is enough to cure all the diseases of this distempered world. They are *a medicine to all their flesh* (so the word is), to all their corruptions, for they are called flesh, to all their grievances, which are as thorns in the flesh. There is in the word of God a proper remedy for all our spiritual maladies.

II. We must keep a watchful eye and a strict hand upon all the motions of our inward man, *v.* 23. Here is, 1. A great duty required by the laws of wisdom, and in order to our getting and preserving wisdom: *Keep thy heart with all diligence.* God, who gave us these souls, gave us a strict charge with them: Man, woman, *keep thy heart; take heed to thy spirit,* Deu. 4:9. We must maintain a holy jealousy of ourselves, and set a strict guard, accordingly, upon all the avenues of the soul; keep our hearts from doing hurt and getting hurt, from being defiled by sin and disturbed by trouble; keep them as our jewel, as our vineyard; keep a conscience void of offence; keep out bad thoughts; keep up good thoughts; keep the affections upon right objects and in due bounds. *Keep them with all keepings* (so the word is); there are many ways of keeping things — by care, by strength, by calling in help, and we must use them all in keeping our hearts; and all little enough, so deceitful are they, Jer. 17:9. Or *above all keepings;* we must keep our hearts with more care and diligence than we keep any thing else. We must keep our eyes (Job 31:1), keep our tongues (Ps. 34:13), keep our feet (Eccl. 5:1), but, above all, keep our hearts. 2. A good reason given for this care, because *out of it are the issues of life.* Out of a heart well kept will flow living issues, good products, to the glory of God and the edification of others. Or, in general, all the actions of the life flow from the heart, and therefore keeping that is making the tree good and healing the springs. Our lives will be regular or irregular, comfortable or uncomfortable, according as our hearts are kept or neglected.

III. We must set a *watch before the door of our lips,* that we offend not with out tongue (*v.* 24): *Put away from thee a froward mouth and perverse lips.* Our hearts being naturally corrupt, out of them a great deal of corrupt communication is apt to come, and therefore we must conceive a great dread and detestation of all manner of evil words, cursing, swearing, lying, slandering, brawling, filthiness, and foolish talking, all which come from a *froward mouth and perverse lips,* that will not be governed either by reason or religion, but contradict both, and which are as unsightly and ill-favoured before God as a crooked distorted mouth drawn awry is before men. All manner of tongue sins, we must, by constant watchfulness and stedfast resolution, *put from us,* put *far from us,* abstaining from all words that have an appearance of evil and fearing to learn any such words.

IV. We must make a covenant with our eyes: "Let them *look right on and straight before thee, v.* 25. Let the eye be fixed and not wandering; let it not rove after every thing that presents itself, for then it will be diverted form good and ensnared in evil. Turn it from beholding vanity; let thy eye be single and not divided; let thy intentions be sincere and uniform, and look not asquint at any by-end." We must keep our eye upon our Master, and be careful to approve ourselves to him; keep our eye upon our rule, and conform to that; keep our eye upon our mark, the *prize of the high calling,* and direct all towards that. *Oculum in metam — The eye upon the goal.*

V. We must act considerately in all we do (*v.* 26): *Ponder the path of thy feet, weigh it* (so the word is); "put the word of God in one scale, and what thou hast done, or art about to do, in the other, and see how they agree; be nice and critical in examining whether thy way be good before the Lord and whether it will end well." We must consider our past ways and examine what we have done, and our present ways, what we are doing, whither we are going, and *see that we walk circumspectly.* It concerns us to consider what are the duties and what the difficulties, what are the advantages and what the dangers, of our way, that we may act accordingly. "Do nothing rashly."

VI. We must act with steadiness, caution, and consistency: *"Let all thy ways be established* (*v.* 26) and be not unstable in them, as the double-minded man is; halt not between two, but go on in an even uniform course of obedience; *turn not to the right hand not to the left,* for there are errors on both hands, and Satan gains his point if he prevails to draw us aside either way. Be very careful to *remove thy foot from evil;* take heed of extremes, for in them there is evil, and *let thy eyes look right on,* that thou mayest keep the golden mean." Those that would approve themselves wise must always be watchful.

CHAPTER 5

The scope of this chapter is much the same with that of *ch.* 2. To write the same things, in other words, ought not to be grievous, for it is safe, Phil. 3:1. Here is, I. An exhortation to get acquaintance with and submit to the laws of wisdom in general (*v.* 2). II. A particular caution against the sin of whoredom (*v.* 3–14). III. Remedies prescribed against that sin. 1. Conjugal love (*v.* 15–20). 2. A regard to God's omniscience (*v.* 21). 3. A dread of the miserable end of wicked people (*v.* 22, 23). And all little enough to arm young people against those fleshly lusts which war against the soul.

Verses 1–14

Here we have,

I. A solemn preface, to introduce the caution which follows, *v.* 1, 2. Solomon here addresses himself to his son, that is, to all young men, as unto his children, whom he has an affection for and some influence upon. In God's name, he demands attention; for he writes by divine inspiration, and is a prophet, though he begins not with, *Thus saith the Lord. "Attend, and bow thy ear;* not only hear what is said, and read what is written, but apply thy mind to it and consider it diligently." To gain attention he urges, 1. The excellency of his discourse: "It is *my wisdom, my understanding;* if I undertake to teach thee wisdom I cannot prescribe any thing to be more properly called so; moral philosophy is my philosophy, and that which is to be learned in my school." 2. The usefulness of it: "Attend to what I say," (1.) "That thou mayest act wisely — *that thou mayest regard discretion."* Solomon's lectures are not designed to fill our heads with notions, with matters of nice speculation, or doubtful disputation, but to guide us in the government of ourselves, that we may act prudently, so as becomes us and so as will be for our true interest. (2.) "That thou mayest speak wisely — *that thy lips may keep knowledge,* and thou mayest have it ready at thy tongue's end" (as we say), "for the benefit of those with whom thou dost converse." The priest's lips are said to *keep knowledge* (Mal. 2:7); but those that are ready and mighty in the scriptures may not only in their devotions, but in their discourses, be spiritual priests.

II. The caution itself, and that is to abstain from fleshly lusts, from adultery, fornication, and all uncleanness. Some apply this figuratively, and by the adulterous woman here understand idolatry, or false doctrine, which tends to debauch men's minds and manners, or the sensual appetite, to which it may as fitly as any thing be applied; but the primary scope of it is plainly to warn us against seventh-commandment sins, which youth is so prone to, the temptations to which are so violent, the examples of which are so many, and which, where admitted, are so destructive to all the seeds of virtue in the soul that it is not strange that Solomon's cautions against it are so very pressing and so often repeated. Solomon here, as a faithful watchman, gives fair warning to all, as they regard their lives and comforts, to dread this sin, for it will certainly be their ruin. Two things we are here warned to take heed of: —

1. That we do not listen to the charms of this sin. It is true *the lips of a strange woman drop as a honey-comb* (*v.* 3); the pleasures of fleshly lust are very tempting (like the wine that *gives its colour in the cup* and *moves itself aright*); its mouth, the kisses of its mouth, the words of its mouth, are *smoother than oil,* that the poisonous pill may go down glibly and there may be no suspicion of harm in it. But consider, (1.) How fatal the consequences will be. What fruit will the sinner have of his honey and oil when the end will be, [1.] The terrors of conscience: It *is bitter as wormwood, v.* 4. What was luscious in the mouth rises in the stomach and turns sour there; it cuts, in the reflection, like *a two-edged sword;* take it which way you will, it wounds. Solomon could speak by experience, Eccl. 7:26. [2.] The torments of hell. If some that have been guilty of this sin have repented and been saved, yet the direct tendency of the sin is to destruction of body and soul; the *feet* of it *go down to death,* nay, they *take hold on hell,* to pull it to the sinner, as if the damnations slumbered too long, *v.* 5. Those that are entangled in this sin should be reminded that there is but a step between them and hell, and that they are ready to drop into it. (2.) Consider how false the charms are. The adulteress flatters and speaks fair, her words are honey and oil, but she will deceive those that hearken to her: *Her ways are movable, that thou canst not know them;* she often changes her disguise, and puts on a great variety of false colours, because, if she be rightly known, she is certainly hated. Proteus-like, she puts on many shapes, that she may keep in with those whom she has a design upon. And what does she aim at with all this art and management? Nothing but to keep them from *pondering the path of life,* for she knows that, if they once come to do that, she shall certainly lose them. Those are *ignorant of Satan's devices* who do not understand that the great thing he drives at in all his temptations is, [1.] To keep them from choosing the path of life, to prevent them from being religious and from going to heaven, that, being himself shut out from happiness, he may keep them out from it. [2.] In order hereunto, to keep them from pondering the path of life, from considering how reasonable it is that they should walk in that path, and how much it will be for their advantage. Be it observed, to the honour of religion, that it certainly gains its point with all those that will but allow themselves the liberty of a serious thought

and will weigh things impartially in an even balance, and that the devil has no way of securing men in his interests but by diverting them with continual amusements of one kind or another from the calm and sober consideration of the *things that belong to their peace.* And uncleanness is a sin that does as much as any thing blind the understanding, sear the conscience, and keep people from pondering the path of life. Whoredom *takes away the heart,* Hos. 4:11.

2. That we do not approach the borders of this sin, *v.* 7, 8.

(1.) This caution is introduced with a solemn preface: *"Hear me now therefore, O you children!* whoever you are that read or hear these lines, take notice of what I say, and mix faith with it, treasure it up, and *depart not from the words of my mouth,* as those will do that hearken to the words of the strange woman. Do not only receive what I say, for the present merely, but cleave to it, and let it be ready to thee, and of force with thee, when thou art most violently assaulted by the temptation."

(2.) The caution itself is very pressing: *"Remove thy way far from her;* if thy way should happen to lie near her, and thou shouldst have a fair pretence of being led by business within the reach of her charms, yet change thy way, and alter the course of it, rather than expose thyself to danger; *come not nigh the door of her house;* go on the other side of the street, nay, go through some other street, though it be about." This intimates, [1.] That we ought to have a very great dread and detestation of the sin. We must fear it as we would a place infected with the plague; we must loathe it as the odour of carrion, that we will not come near. *Then* we are likely to preserve our purity when we conceive a rooted antipathy to all fleshly lusts. [2.] That we ought industriously to avoid every thing that may be an occasion of this sin or a step towards it. Those that would be kept from harm must keep out of harm's way. Such tinder there is in the corrupt nature that it is madness, upon any pretence whatsoever, to come near the sparks. If we thrust ourselves into temptation, we mocked God when we prayed, *Lead us not into temptation.* [3.] That we ought to be jealous over ourselves with a godly jealousy, and not to be so confident of the strength of our own resolutions as to venture upon the brink of sin, with a promise to ourselves that *hitherto we will come and no further.* [4.] That whatever has become a snare to us and an occasion of sin, though it be as a *right eye* and a *right hand,* we must *pluck it out, cut it off, and cast it from us,* must part with that which is dearest to us rather than hazard our own souls; this is our Saviour's command, Mt. 5:28–30.

(3.) The arguments which Solomon here uses to enforce this caution are taken from the same topic with those before, the many mischiefs which attend this sin. [1.] It blasts the reputation. "Thou wilt *give thy honour unto others* (*v.* 9); thou wilt lose it thyself; thou wilt put into the hand of each of thy neighbours a stone to throw at thee, for they will all, with good reason, cry shame on thee, will despise thee, and trample on thee, as a foolish men." Whoredom is a sin that makes men contemptible and base, and no man of sense or virtue will care to keep company with one that keeps company with harlots. [2.] It wastes the time, gives *the years,* the years of youth, the flower of men's time, *unto the cruel,* "that base lust of thine, which with the utmost cruelty *wars against the soul,* that base harlot which pretends an affection for thee, but really hunts for the precious life." Those years that should be given to the honour of a gracious God are spent in the service of a cruel sin. [3.] It ruins the estate (*v.* 10): "*Strangers* will be *filled with thy wealth,* which thou art but entrusted with as a steward for thy family; and the fruit of *thy labours,* which should be provision for thy own house, will be in the *house of a stranger,* that neither has right to it nor will ever thank thee for it." [4.] It is destructive to the health, and shortens men's days: *Thy flesh and thy body* will be *consumed* by it, *v.* 11. The lusts of uncleanness not only *war against the soul,* which the sinner neglects and is in no care about, but they war against the body too, which he is so indulgent of and is in such care to please and pamper, such deceitful, such foolish, such hurtful lusts are they. Those that give themselves to work uncleanness with greediness waste their strength, throw themselves into weakness, and often have their bodies filled with loath-

some distempers, by which the number of their months is cut off in the midst and they fall unpitied sacrifices to a cruel lust. [5.] It will fill the mind with horror, if ever conscience be awakened. "Though thou art merry now, *sporting thyself in thy own deceivings,* yet thou wilt certainly *mourn at the last, v.* 11. Thou art all this while making work for repentance, and laying up matter for vexation and torment in the reflection, when the sin is set before thee in its own colours." Sooner or later it will bring sorrow, either when the soul is humbled and brought to repentance or when the *flesh and body are consumed,* either by sickness, when conscience flies in the sinner's face, or by the grave; when the body is rotting there, the soul is racking in the torments of hell, where the worm dies not, and *"Son, remember,"* is the constant peal [plea?]. Solomon here brings in the convinced sinner reproaching himself, and aggravating his own folly. He will then most bitterly lament it. *First,* That because he hated to be reformed he therefore hated to be informed, and could not endure either to be taught his duty (*How have I hated* not only the discipline of being instructed, but the *instruction* itself, though all true and good!) or to be told of his faults — *My heart despised reproof, v.* 12. He cannot but own that those who had the charge of him, parents, ministers, had done their part; they had been his teachers; they had instructed him, had given him good counsel and fair warning (*v.* 13); but to his own shame and confusion does he speak it, and therein justifies God in all the miseries that were brought upon him, he had not *obeyed their voice,* for indeed he *never inclined his ear to those that instructed him,* never minded what they said nor admitted the impressions of it. Note, Those who have had a good education and do not live up to it will have a great deal to answer for another day; and those who will not now remember what they were taught, to conform themselves to it, will be made to remember it as an aggravation of their sin, and consequently of their ruin. *Secondly,* That by the frequent acts of sin the habits of it were so rooted and confirmed that his heart was fully set in him to commit it (*v.* 14): *I was almost in all evil in the midst of the congregation and assembly.* When he came into the synagogue, or into the courts of the temple, to worship God with other Israelites, his unclean heart was full of wanton thoughts and desires and his eyes of adultery. Reverence of the place and company, and of the work that was doing, could not restrain him, but he was almost as wicked and vile there as any where. No sin will appear more frightful to an awakened conscience than the profanation of holy things; nor will any aggravation of sin render it more exceedingly sinful than the place we are honoured with in the congregation and assembly, and the advantages we enjoy thereby. Zimri and Cozbi avowed their villany *in the sight of Moses and all the congregation* (Num. 25:6), and heart-adultery is as open to God, and must needs be most offensive to him, when we draw nigh to him in religious exercises. *I was in all evil* in defiance of the magistrates and judges, and their assemblies; so some understand it. Others refer it to the evil of punishment, not to the evil of sin: "I was made an example, a spectacle to the world. I was under almost all God's sore judgments *in the midst of the congregation of Israel,* set up for a mark. *I stood up and cried in the congregation,*" Job 30:28. Let that be avoided which will be thus rued at last.

Verses 15–23

Solomon, having shown the great evil that there is in adultery and fornication, and all such lewd and filthy courses, here prescribes remedies against them.

I. Enjoy with satisfaction the comforts of lawful marriage, which was ordained for the prevention of uncleanness, and therefore ought to be made use of in time, lest it should not prove effectual for the cure of that which it might have prevented. Let none complain that God has dealt unkindly with them in forbidding them those pleasures which they have a natural desire of, for he has graciously provided for the regular gratification of them. "Thou mayest not indeed eat of every tree of the garden, but choose thee out one, which thou pleasest, and of that thou mayest freely eat; nature will be content with that, but lust with nothing." God, in thus confining men to one, has been so far from putting any hardship upon them that he has really consulted their true interest; for, as Mr. Her-

bert observes, *"If God had laid all common, certainly man would have been the encloser."* — Church-porch. Solomon here enlarges much upon this, not only prescribing it as an antidote, but urging it as an argument against fornication, that the allowed pleasures of marriage (however wicked wits may ridicule them, who are factors for the unclean spirit) far transcend all the false forbidden pleasures of whoredom.

1. Let young men marry, marry and not burn. Have *a cistern, a well of thy own* (*v.* 15), even the wife *of thy youth, v.* 18. *Wholly abstain, or wed.* — Herbert. "The world is wide, and there are varieties of accomplishments, among which thou mayest please thyself."

2. Let him that is married take delight in his wife, and let him be very fond of her, not only because she is the wife that he himself has chosen and he ought to be pleased with his own choice, but because she is the wife that God in his providence appointed for him and he ought much more to be pleased with the divine appointment, pleased with her because she is his own. *Let thy fountain be blessed* (*v.* 18); think thyself very happy in her, look upon her as a blessed wife, let her have thy blessing, pray daily for her, and then *rejoice with her.* Those comforts we are likely to have joy of that are sanctified to us by prayer and the blessing of God. It is not only allowed us, but commanded us, to be pleasant with our relations; and it particularly becomes yoke-fellows to rejoice together and in each other. Mutual delight is the bond of mutual fidelity. It is not only taken for granted that the *bridegroom rejoices over his bride* (Isa. 62:5), but given for law. Eccl. 9:9, *Live joyfully with the wife whom thou lovest all the days of thy life.* Those take not their comforts where God has appointed who are jovial and merry with their companions abroad, but sour and morose with their families at home.

3. Let him be fond of his wife and love her dearly (*v.* 19): *Let her be as the loving hind and the pleasant roe,* such as great men sometimes kept tame in their houses and played with. Desire no better diversion from severe study and business than the innocent and pleasant conversation of thy own wife; let her lie in thy bosom, as the poor man's ewe-lamb did in his (2 Sa. 12:3), and do thou repose thy head in hers, and let that *satisfy thee at all times;* and seek not for pleasure in any other. *"Err thou always in her love.* If thou wilt suffer thy love to run into an excess, and wilt be dotingly fond of any body, let it be only of thy own wife, where there is least danger of exceeding." This is *drinking waters,* to quench the thirst of thy appetite, *out of thy own cistern,* and *running waters,* which are clear, and sweet, and wholesome, *out of thy own well, v.* 15. 1 Co. 7:2, 3.

4. Let him take delight in his children and look upon them with pleasure (*v.* 16, 17): "Look upon them as streams from thy own pure fountains" (the Jews are said to *come forth out of the waters of Judah,* Isa. 48:1), "so that they are parts of thyself, as the streams are of the fountain. Keep to thy own wife, and thou shalt have," (1.) "A numerous offspring, like *rivers of water,* which run in abundance, and they shall be dispersed abroad, matched into other families, whereas those that *commit whoredom* shall *not increase,*" Hos. 4:10. (2.) "A peculiar offspring, which shall be *only thy own,* whereas the children of whoredom, that are fathered upon thee, are, probably, not so, but, for aught thou knowest, are the offspring of strangers, and yet thou must keep them." (3.) "A creditable offspring, which are an honour to thee, and which thou mayest send abroad, and appear with, in the streets, whereas a spurious brood is thy disgrace, and that which thou art ashamed to own." In this matter, virtue has all the pleasure and honour in it; justly therefore it is called *wisdom.*

5. Let him then scorn the offer of forbidden pleasures when he is *always ravished with the love* of a faithful virtuous wife; let him consider what an absurdity it will be for him to be *ravished with a strange woman* (*v.* 20), to be in love with a filthy harlot, and *embrace the bosom of a stranger,* which, if he had any sense of honour or virtue, he would loathe the thoughts of. "Why wilt thou be so sottish, such an enemy to thyself, as to prefer puddle-water, and that poisoned too and stolen, before pure living waters out of thy own well?" Note, If the dictates of reason may be heard, the laws of virtue will be obeyed.

II. "See the eye of God always upon thee and let his fear rule in thy heart," *v.* 21. Those that live in this sin promise themselves secresy (*the eye of the adulterer waits for the twilight*, Job 24:15); but to what purpose, when it cannot be hidden from God? For, 1. He sees it. *The ways of man*, all his motions, all his actions, are *before the eyes of the Lord*, all the workings of the heart and all the outgoings of the life, that which is done ever so secretly and disguised ever so artfully. God sees it in a true light, and knows it with all its causes, circumstances, and consequences. He does not cast an eye upon men's ways now and then, but they are always actually in his view and under his inspection; and darest thou sin against God in his sight, and do that wickedness under his eye which thou durst not do in the presence of a man like thyself? 2. He will call the sinner to an account for it; for he not only sees, but *ponders all his goings*, judges concerning them, as one that will shortly judge the sinner for them. Every action is *weighed*, and shall be *brought into judgment* (Eccl. 12:14), which is a good reason why we should *ponder the path of our feet* (*ch.* 4:26), and so *judge ourselves* that we *may not be judged*.

III. "Foresee the certain ruin of those that go on still in their trespasses." Those that live in this sin promise themselves impunity, but they deceive themselves; their sin will find them out, *v.* 22, 23. The apostle gives the sense of these verses in a few words. Heb. 13:4, *Whoremongers and adulterers God will judge*. 1. It is a sin which men with great difficulty shake off the power of. When the sinner is old and weak his lusts are strong and active, in *calling to remembrance the days of his youth*, Eze. 23:19. Thus *his own iniquities* having *seized the wicked himself* by his own consent, and he having voluntarily surrendered himself a captive to them, he is *held in the cords of his own sins*, and such full possession they have gained of him that he cannot extricate himself, but in the *greatness of his folly* (and what greater folly could there be than to yield himself a servant to such cruel task-masters?) he shall *go astray*, and wander endlessly. Uncleanness is a sin from which, when once men have plunged themselves into it, they very hardly and very rarely recover themselves. 2. It is a sin which, if it be not forsaken, men cannot possibly escape the punishment of; it will unavoidably be their ruin. As their own iniquities do arrest them in the reproaches of conscience and present rebukes (Jer. 7:19), so their own iniquities shall arrest them and bind them over to the judgments of God. There needs no prison, no chains; they shall be *holden in the cords of their own sins*, as the fallen angels, being incurably wicked, are thereby *reserved in chains of darkness*. The sinner, who, having been *often reproved, hardens his neck*, shall *die at length without instruction*. Having had general warnings sufficient given him already, he shall have no particular warnings, but he shall die without seeing his danger beforehand, shall die because he would not receive instruction, but *in the greatness of his folly* would *go astray;* and so shall his doom be, he shall never find the way home again. Those that are so foolish as to choose the way of sin are justly left of God to themselves to go in it till they come to that destruction which it leads to, which is a good reason why we should guard with watchfulness and resolution against the allurements of the sensual appetite.

CHAPTER 6

In this chapter we have, I. A caution against rash suretiship (*v.* 1–5). II. A rebuke to slothfulness (*v.* 6–11). III. The character and fate of a malicious mischievous man (*v.* 12–15). IV. An account of seven things which God hates (*v.* 16–19). V. An exhortation to make the word of God familiar to us (*v.* 20–23). VI. A repeated warning of the pernicious consequences of the sin of whoredom (*v.* 24–35). We are here dissuaded from sin very much by arguments borrowed from our secular interests, for it is not only represented as damning in the other world, but as impoverishing in this.

Verses 1–5

It is the excellency of the word of God that it teaches us not only divine wisdom for another world, but human prudence for this world, that we may order our affairs with discretion; and this is one good rule, To avoid suretiship, because by it poverty and ruin are often brought into families, which take away that comfort in relations which he had recommended in the foregoing chapter. 1. We must look upon suretiship as a snare and decline it accordingly, *v.* 1, 2. "It is dangerous enough for a man to be bound for his friend, though it be one whose circumstances he is well acquainted with, and well assured of his sufficiency, but much more to *strike the hands with a stranger*, to become surety for one whom thou dost not know to be either able or honest." Or the stranger here with whom the hand is stricken is the creditor, "the usurer to whom thou art become bound, and yet as to thee he is a stranger, that is, thou owest him nothing, nor hast had any dealings with him. If thou hast rashly entered into such engagements, either wheedled into them or in hopes to have the same kindness done for thee another time, know that *thou art snared with the words of thy mouth;* it was easily done, with a word's speaking; it was but setting thy hand to a paper, a bond is soon sealed and delivered, and a recognizance entered into. But it will not be so easily got clear of; thou art *in a snare* more than thou art aware of." See how little reason we have to make light of tongue-sins; if by a word of our mouth we may become indebted to men, and lie open to their actions, by the words of our mouth we may become obnoxious to God's justice, and even so may be snared. It is false that words are but wind: they are often snares. 2. If we have been drawn into this snare, it will be our wisdom by all means, with all speed, to get out of it, *v.* 3–5. It sleeps for the present; we hear nothing of it. The debt is not demanded; the principal says, "Never fear, we will take care of it." But still the bond is in force, interest is running on, the creditor may come upon thee when he will and perhaps may be hasty and severe, the principal may prove either knavish or insolvent, and then thou must rob thy wife and children, and ruin thy family, to pay that which thou didst neither nor drink for. And therefore *deliver thyself;* rest not till either the creditor give up the bond or the principal give thee counter-security; when *thou art come into the hand of thy friend*, and he has advantage against thee, it is no time to threaten or give ill language (that will provoke and make ill worse), but *humble thyself*, beg and pray to be discharged, go down on thy knees to him, and give him all the fair words thou canst; engage thy friends to speak for thee; leave no stone unturned till thou hast agreed with thy adversary and compromised the matter, so that thy bond may not come against thee or thine. This is a care which may well break thy sleep, and let it do so till thou hast got through. *"Give not sleep to thy eyes* till thou hast *delivered thyself*. Strive and struggle to the utmost, and hasten with all speed, *as a roe* or a *bird* delivers herself out of this snare of *the fowler* or hunter. Delays are dangerous, and feeble efforts will not serve." See what care God, in his word, has taken to make men good husbands of their estates, and to teach them prudence in the management of them. *Godliness* has precepts, as well as promises, relating to *the life that now is*.

But how are we to understand this? We are not to think it is unlawful in any case to become surety, or bail, for another; it may be a piece of justice or charity; he that has friends may see cause in this instance to show himself friendly, and it may be no piece of imprudence. Paul became bound for Onesimus, Philem. 19. We may help a young man into business that we know to be honest and diligent, and gain him credit by passing our word for him, and so do him a great kindness without any detriment to ourselves. But, 1. It is every man's wisdom to keep out of debt as much as may be, for it is an incumbrance upon him, entangles him in the world, puts him in danger of doing wrong or suffering wrong. The *borrower is servant to the lender*, and makes himself very much a slave to this world. Christians therefore, who are *bought with a price*, should not thus, without need, make themselves *the servants of men*, 1 Co. 7:23. 2. It is great folly to entangle ourselves with necessitous people, and to become bound for their debts, that are ever and anon taking up money, and lading, as we say, out of one hole into another, for it is ten to one but, some time or other, it will come upon us. A man ought never to be bound as surety for more than he is both able and willing to pay, and can afford to pay without wronging his family, in case the principal fail, for he ought to look upon it as his own debt. Ecclesiasticus 8:13, *Be not surety above thy power, for, if thou be surety, thou must take care to pay it*. 3. It is a necessary piece of after-wit, if we have foolishly entangled ourselves, to get out of the snare as fast as we can, to lose no time, spare no pains, and stick at no submission to make ourselves safe and easy, and get our affairs into a good posture. It is better to humble ourselves for an accommodation than to ruin ourselves by our stiffness and haughtiness. *Make sure thy friend* by getting clear from thy engagements from him; for rash suretiship is as much the bane of friendship as that which is prudent is sometimes the bond of it. Let us take heed lest we any way make ourselves guilty of other men's sins against God (1 Tim. 5:22), for that is worse, and much more dangerous, than being bound for other men's debts; and, if we must be in all this care to get our debts to men forgiven, much more to get our peace made with God. *"Humble thyself* to him; *make sure* of Christ *thy friend*, to intercede for thee; pray earnestly that thy sins may be pardoned, and thou mayest be delivered from going down to the pit, and it shall not be in vain. *Give not sleep to thy eyes nor slumber to thy eye lids*, till this be done."

Verses 6–11

Solomon, in these verses, addresses himself to the sluggard who loves his ease, lives in idleness, minds no business, sticks to nothing, brings nothing to pass, and in a particular manner is careless in the business of religion. Slothfulness is as sure a way to poverty, though not so short a way, as rash suretiship. He speaks here to the sluggard,

I. By way of instruction, *v.* 6–8. He sends him to school, for sluggards must be schooled. He is to take him to school himself, for, if the scholar will take no pains, the master must take the more; the sluggard is not willing to come to school to him (dreaming scholars will never love wakeful teachers) and therefore he has found him out another school, as low as he can desire. Observe,

1. The master he is sent to school to: *Go to the ant, to the bee*, so the Septuagint. Man is taught more than the beasts of the earth, and made wiser that the fowls of heaven, and yet is so degenerated that he may learn wisdom from the meanest insects and be shamed by them. When we observe the wonderful sagacities of the inferior creatures we must not only give glory to the God of nature, who has made them thus strangely, but receive instruction to ourselves; by spiritualizing common things, we may make the things of God both easy and ready to us, and converse with them daily.

2. The application of mind that is required in order to learn of this master: *Consider her ways*. The sluggard is so because he does not consider; nor shall we ever learn to any purpose, either by the word or the works of God, unless we set ourselves to consider. Particularly, if we would imitate others in that which is good, we must consider their ways, diligently observe what they do, that we may do likewise, Phil. 3:17.

3. The lesson that is to be learned. In general, learn wisdom, *consider, and be wise;* that is the thing we are to aim at in all our learning, not only to be knowing, but to be wise. In particular, learn to *provide meat in summer;* that is, (1.) We must prepare for hereafter, and not mind the present time only, not eat up all, and lay up nothing, but in gathering time treasure up for a spending time. Thus provident we must be in our worldly affairs, not with an anxious care, but with a prudent foresight; lay in for winter, for straits and wants that may happen, and for old age; much more in the affairs of our souls. We must provide meat and food, that which is substantial and will stand us in stead, and which we shall most need. In the enjoyment of the means of grace provide for the want of them, in life for death, in time for eternity; in the state of probation and preparation we must provide for the state of retribution. (2.) We must take pains, and labour in our business, yea, though we labour under inconveniences. Even *in summer*, when the weather is hot, the ant is busy in *gathering food* and laying it up, and does not indulge her ease, nor take her pleasure, as the grasshopper, that sings and sports in the summer and then perishes in the winter. The ants help one another; if one have a grain of corn too big for her to carry home, her neighbours will come in to her assistance. (3.) We must improve opportunities, we must gather when it is to be had, as the ant does in summer and harvest, in the proper time. It is our wisdom to improve the season while that favours us, because that may be done then which cannot be done at all, or not so well done, at another time. *Walk while you have the light*.

4. The advantages which we have of learning this lesson above what the ant has, which will aggravate our slothfulness and neglect if we idle away our time. She has *no guides, overseers*, and *rulers*, but does it of herself, following the instinct of nature; the more shame for us who do

not in like manner follow the dictates of our own reason and conscience, though besides them we have parents, masters, ministers, magistrates, to put us in mind of our duty, to check us for the neglect of it, to quicken us to it, to direct us in it, and to call us to an account about it. The greater helps we have for working out our salvation the more inexcusable shall we be if we neglect it.

II. By way of reproof, *v.* 9–11. In these verses,

1. He expostulates with the sluggard, rebuking him and reasoning with him, calling him to his work, as a master does his servant that has over-slept himself: *"How long wilt thou sleep, O sluggard? How long wouldst thou sleep if one would let thee alone? When wilt thou think it time to arise?"* Sluggards should be roused with a *How long?* This is applicable, (1.) To those that are slothful in the way of work and duty, in the duties of their particular calling as men or their general calling as Christians. *"How long wilt thou* waste thy time, and *when wilt thou* be a better husband of it? *How long wilt thou* love thy ease, and *when wilt thou* learn to deny thyself, and to take pains? *How long wilt thou* bury thy talents, and *when wilt thou* begin to trade with them? *How long wilt thou* delay, and put off, and trifle away thy opportunities, as one regardless of hereafter; and *when wilt thou* stir up thyself to do what thou hast to do, which, if it be not done, will leave thee for ever undone?"* (2.) To those that are secure in the way of sin and danger: "Hast thou not slept enough? Is it not far in the day? Does not thy Master call? Are not the Philistines upon thee? When then wilt thou arise?"

2. He exposes the frivolous excuses he makes for himself, and shows how ridiculous he makes himself. When he is roused he stretched himself, and begs, as for alms, for more *sleep,* more *slumber;* he is well in his warm bed, and cannot endure to think of rising, especially of rising to work. But, observe, he promises himself and his master that he will desire but *a little* more *sleep, a little* more *slumber,* and then he will get up and go to his business. But herein he deceives himself; the more a slothful temper is indulged the more it prevails; let him sleep awhile, and slumber awhile, and still he is in the same tune; still he asks for *a little* more *sleep, yet a little* more; he never thinks he has enough, and yet, when he is called, pretends he will come presently. Thus men's great work is left undone by being put off yet a little longer, *de die in diem — from day to day;* and they are cheated of all their time by being cheated of the present moments. A little more sleep proves an everlasting sleep. *Sleep on now, and take your rest.*

3. He gives him fair warning of the fatal consequences of his slothfulness, *v.* 11. (1.) *Poverty and want* will certainly come upon those that are slothful in their business. If men neglect their affairs, they not only will not go forward, but they will go backward. He that leaves his concerns at sixes and sevens will soon see them go to wreck and ruin, and bring his noble to nine-pence. Spiritual poverty comes upon those that are slothful in the service of God; those will want oil, when they should use it, that provide it not in their vessels. (2.) "It will come silently and insensibly, will grow upon thee, and come step by step, *as one that travels,* but will without fail come at last." *It will leave thee as naked as if thou wert stripped by a highwayman;* so bishop Patrick. (3.) "It will come irresistibly, *like an armed man,* whom thou canst not oppose nor make thy part good against."

Verses 12–19

Solomon here gives us,

I. The characters of one that is mischievous to man and dangerous to be dealt with. If the slothful are to be condemned, that do nothing, much more those that do ill, and contrive to do all the ill they can. It is a *naughty person* that is here spoken of, Heb. *A man of Belial;* I think it should have been so translated, because it is a term often used in scripture, and this is the explication of it. Observe,

1. How a man of Belial is here described. He is *a wicked man,* that makes a trade of doing evil, especially with his tongue, for he *walks* and works his designs *with a froward mouth* (*v.* 12), by lying and perverseness, and a direct opposition to God and man. He says and does every thing, (1.) Very artfully and with design. He has the subtlety of the serpent, and carries on his projects with a great deal of craft and management (*v.* 13), *with his eyes, with*

his feet, with his fingers. He expresses his malice *when he dares not speak out* (so some), or, rather, thus he carries on his plot; those about him, whom he makes use of as the tools of his wickedness, understand the ill meaning of a wink of his eye, a stamp of his feet, the least motion of his fingers. He gives orders for evil-doing, and yet would not be thought to do so, but has ways of concealing what he does, so that he may not be suspected. He is a close man, and upon the reserve; those only shall be let into the secret that would do any thing he would have them to do. He is a cunning man, and upon the trick; he has a language by himself, which an honest man is not acquainted with, nor desires to be. (2.) Very spitefully and with ill design. It is not so much ambition or covetousness that *is in his heart,* as downright *frowardness,* malice, and ill nature. He aims not so much to enrich and advance himself as to do an ill turn to those about him. He is *continually devising* one *mischief* or other, purely for mischief-sake — a man of Belial indeed, of the devil, resembling him not only in subtlety, but in malice.

2. What his doom is (*v.* 15): *His calamity shall come* and *he shall be broken;* he that devised mischief shall fall into mischief. His ruin shall come, (1.) Without warning. It shall come suddenly: *Suddenly shall he be broken,* to punish him for all the wicked arts he had to surprise people into his snares. (2.) Without relief. He shall be irreparably broken, and never able to piece again: *He shall be broken without remedy.* What relief can he expect that has disobliged all mankind? *He shall come to his end and none shall help him,* Dan. 11:45.

II. A catalogue of those things which are in a special manner odious to God, all which are generally to be found in those men of Belial whom he had described in the foregoing verses; and the last of them (which, being the seventh, seems especially to be intended, because he says they are six, yea, seven) is part of his character, that he *sows discord.* God hates sin; he hates every sin; he can never be reconciled to it; he hates nothing but sin. But there are some sins which he does in a special manner hate; and all those here mentioned are such as are injurious to our neighbour. It is an evidence of the good-will God bears to mankind that those sins are in a special manner provoking to him which are prejudicial to the comfort of human life and society. *Therefore* the men of Belial must expect their ruin to *come suddenly,* and *without remedy,* because their practices are such as the Lord hates and *are an abomination to him, v.* 16. Those things which God hates it is no thanks to us to hate in others, but we must hate them in ourselves. 1. Haughtiness, conceitedness of ourselves, and contempt of others — *a proud look.* There are seven things that God hates, and pride is the first, because it is at the bottom of much sin and gives rise to it. God sees the pride in the heart and hates it there; but, when it prevails to that degree that the show of men's countenance witnesses against them that they overvalue themselves and undervalue all about them, this is in a special manner hateful to him, for then pride is proud of itself and sets shame at defiance. 2. Falsehood, and fraud, and dissimulation. Next to a *proud look* nothing is more an abomination to God than *a lying tongue;* nothing more sacred than truth, nor more necessary to conversation than speaking truth. God and all good men hate and abhor lying. 3. Cruelty and blood-thirstiness. The devil was, from the beginning, a liar and a murderer (Jn. 8:44), and therefore, as *a lying tongue,* so *hands that shed innocent blood* are hateful to God, because they have in them the devil's image and do him service. 4. Subtlety in the contrivance of sin, wisdom to do evil, *a heart that* designs and a head that *devises wicked imaginations,* that is acquainted with the depths of Satan and knows how to carry on a covetous, envious, revengeful plot, most effectually. The more there is of craft and management in sin the more it is an abomination to God. 5. Vigour and diligence in the prosecution of sin — *feet that are swift in running to mischief,* as if they were afraid of losing time or were impatient of delay in a thing they are so greedy of. The policy and vigilance, the eagerness and industry, of sinners, in their sinful pursuits, may shame us who go about that which is good so awkwardly and so coldly. 6. False-witness bearing, which is one of the greatest mischiefs that the wicked imagination can devise, and against which there is least fence. There cannot be a greater affront to God (to whom in an oath appeal is

made) nor a greater injury to our neighbour (all whose interests in this world, even the dearest, lie open to an attack of this kind) than knowingly to give in a false testimony. There are seven things which God hates, and lying involves two of them; he hates it, and doubly hates it. 7. Making mischief between relations and neighbours, and using all wicked means possible, not only to alienate their affections one from another, but to irritate their passions one against another. The God of love and peace hates *him that sows discord among brethren,* for he delights in concord. Those that by tale-bearing and slandering, by carrying ill-natured stories, aggravating every thing that is said and done, and suggesting jealousies and evil surmises, blow the coals of contention, are but preparing for themselves a fire of the same nature.

Verses 20–35

Here is, I. A general exhortation faithfully to adhere to the word of God and to take it for our guide in all our actions.

1. We must look upon the word of God both as a light (*v.* 23) and as a law, *v.* 20, 23. (1.) By its arguments it is a light, which our understandings must subscribe to; *it is a lamp* to our eyes for discovery, and so to our feet for direction. The word of God reveals to us truths of eternal certainty, and is built upon the highest reason. Scripture-light is the sure light. (2.) By its authority it is a law, which our wills must submit to. As never such a light shone out of the schools of the philosophers, so never such a law issued from the throne of any prince, so well framed, and so binding. It is such a law as is a lamp and a light, for it carries with it the evidence of its own goodness.

2. We must receive it as *our father's commandment* and *the law of our mother, v.* 20. It is God's commandment and his law. But, (1.) Our parents directed us to it, put it into our hands, trained us up in the knowledge and observance of it, its original and obligation being most sacred. We believe indeed, not for their saying, for we have tried it ourselves and find it to be of God; but we were beholden to them for recommending it to us, and see all the reason in the world to *continue in the things we have learned, knowing of whom we have learned them.* (2.) The cautions, counsels, and commands which our parents gave us agree with the word of God, and therefore we must hold them fast. Children, when they are grown up, must remember *the law of* a good *mother,* as well as the *commandment* of a good *father,* Ecclesiasticus 3:2. *The Lord has given the father honour over the children and has confirmed the authority of the mother over the sons.*

3. We must retain the word of God and the good instructions which our parents gave us out of it. (1.) We must never cast them off, never think it a mighty achievement (as some do) to get clear of the restraints of a good education: *"Keep thy father's commandment,* keep it still, and never forsake it." (2.) We must never lay them by, no, not for a time (*v.* 21): *Bind them continually,* not only *upon thy hand* (as Moses had directed, Deu. 6:8) but *upon thy heart.* Phylacteries upon the hand were of no value at all, any further than they occasioned pious thoughts and affections in the heart. There the word must be written, there it must be hid, and laid close to the conscience. *Tie them about thy neck,* as an ornament, a bracelet, or gold chain, — *about thy throat* (so the word is); let them be a guard upon that pass; tie them about thy throat, that no forbidden fruit may be suffered to go in nor any evil word suffered to go out through the throat; and thus a great deal of sin would be prevented. Let the word of God be always ready to us, and let us feel the impressions of it, as of that which is bound upon our hearts and about our necks.

4. We must make use of the word of God and of the benefit that is designed us by it. If we bind it continually upon our hearts, (1.) It will be our guide, and we must follow its direction. *"When thou goest, it shall lead thee* (*v.* 22); it shall lead thee into, and lead thee in, the good and right way, shall lead thee from, and lead thee out of, every sinful dangerous path. It will say unto thee, when thou art ready to turn aside, *This is the way; walk in it.* It will be that to thee that the pillar of cloud and fire was to Israel in the wilderness. Be led by that, let it be thy rule, and then thou shalt be led by the Spirit; he will be thy monitor and support." (2.) It will be our guard, and we must put ourselves under the protection of it: *"When thou sleepest,*

and liest exposed to the malignant powers of darkness, *it shall keep thee;* thou shalt be safe, and shalt think thyself so." If we govern ourselves by the precepts of the word all day, and make conscience of the duty God has commanded to us, we may shelter ourselves under the promises of the word at night, and take the comfort of the deliverances God does and will command for us. (3.) It will be our companion, and we must converse with it: *"When thou awakest* in the night, and knowest not how to pass away thy waking minutes, if thou pleasest, *it shall talk with thee,* and entertain thee with pleasant meditations in the night-watch; *when thou awakest* in the morning, and art contriving the work of the day, *it shall talk with thee* about it, and help thee to contrive for the best," Ps. 1:2. The word of God has something to say to us upon all occasions, if we would but enter into discourse with it, would ask it what it has to say, and give it the hearing. And it would contribute to our close and comfortable walking with God all day if we would begin with him in the morning and let his word be the subject of our first thoughts. *When I awake I am still with thee;* we are so if the word be still with us. (4.) It will be our life; for, as the law *is a lamp* and *a light* for the present, so the *reproofs of instruction are the way of life.* Those reproofs of the word which not only show us our faults, but instruct us how to do better, are the way that leads to life, eternal life. Let not faithful reproofs therefore, which have such a direct tendency to make us happy, ever make us uneasy.

II. Here is a particular caution against the sin of uncleanness.

1. When we consider how much this iniquity abounds, how heinous it is in its own nature, of what pernicious consequence it is, and how certainly destructive to all the seeds of the spiritual life in the soul, we shall not wonder that the cautions against it are so often repeated and so largely inculcated. (1.) One great kindness God designed men, in giving them his law, was to preserve them from this sin, *v.* 24. "The reproofs of instruction are therefore *the way of life* to thee, because they are designed *to keep thee from the evil woman,* who will be certain death to thee, from being enticed by *the flattery of the tongue of a strange woman,* who pretends to love thee, but intends to ruin thee." Those that will be wrought upon by flattery make themselves a very easy prey to the tempter; and those who would avoid that snare must take well-instructed reproofs as great kindnesses and be thankful to those that will deal faithfully with them, Prov. 27:5, 6. (2.) The greatest kindness we can do ourselves is to keep at a distance from this sin, and to look upon it with the utmost dread and detestation (*v.* 25): *"Lust not after her beauty,* no, not *in thy heart,* for, if thou dost, thou hast *there* already *committed adultery with her.* Talk not of the charms in her face, neither be thou smitten with her amorous glances; they are all snares and nets; *let her* not *take thee with her eye-lids.* Her looks are arrows and fiery darts; they wound, they kill, in another sense than what lovers mean; they call it a pleasing captivity, but it is a destroying one, it is worse than Egyptian slavery."

2. Divers arguments Solomon here urges to enforce this caution against the sin of whoredom.

(1.) It is a sin that impoverishes men, wastes their estates, and reduces them to beggary (*v.* 26): *By means of a whorish woman a man is brought to a piece of bread;* many a man has been so, who has purchased the ruin of his body and soul at the expense of his wealth. The prodigal son spent his living on harlots, so that he brought himself to be fellow-commoner with the swine. And that poverty must needs lie heavily which men bring themselves into by their own folly, Job 31:12.

(2.) It threatens death; it kills men: *The adulteress will hunt for the precious life,* perhaps designedly, as Delilah for Samson's, at least, eventually, the sin strikes at the life. Adultery was punished by the law of Moses as a capital crime. *The adulterer and the adulteress shall surely be put to death.* Every one knew this. Those therefore who, for the gratifying of a base lust, would lay themselves open to the law, could be reckoned no better than self-murderers.

(3.) It brings guilt upon the conscience and debauches that. He that *touches his neighbour's wife,* with an immodest touch, cannot *be innocent, v.* 29. [1.] He is in imminent danger of adultery, as he that *takes fire in his bosom,* or *goes upon hot coals,* is in danger of being *burnt.* The way of this sin is down-hill, and those that venture upon the temptations to it hardly escape the sin itself. The fly fools away her life by playing the wanton with the flames. It is a deep pit, which it is madness to venture upon the brink of. He that keeps company with those of ill fame, that goes in with them, and touches them, cannot long preserve his innocency; he thrusts himself into temptation and so throws himself out of God's protection. [2.] He that commits adultery is in the high road to destruction. The bold presumptuous sinner says, "I may venture upon the sin and yet escape the punishment; I shall have peace though I go on." He might as well say, I will *take fire into my bosom and not burn my clothes,* or I will *go upon hot coals and not burn my feet. He that goes into his neighbour's wife,* however he holds himself, God will not hold him guiltless. The fire of lust kindles the fire of hell.

(4.) It ruins the reputation and entails perpetual infamy upon that. It is a much more scandalous sin than stealing is, *v.* 30–33. Perhaps it is not so in the account of men, at least not in our day. A thief is sent to the stocks, to the gaol, to Bridewell, to the gallows, while the vile adulterer goes unpunished, nay, with many, unblemished; he dares boast of his villanies, and they are made but a jest of. But, in the account of God and his law, adultery was much the more enormous crime; and, if God is the fountain of honour, his word must be the standard of it. [1.] As for the sin of stealing, if a man were brought to it by extreme necessity, if he stole meat for the *satisfying of his soul when he was hungry,* though that will not excuse him from guilt, yet it is such an extenuation of his crime that *men do not despise* him, do not expose him to ignominy, but pity him. Hunger will break through stone-walls, and blame will be laid upon those that brought him to poverty, or that did not relieve him. Nay, though he have not that to say in his excuse, *if he be found* stealing, and the evidence be ever so plain upon him, yet he shall only make restitution *seven-fold.* The law of Moses appointed that he who stole a sheep should restore four-fold, and an ox five-fold (Ex. 22:1); accordingly David adjudged, 2 Sa. 12:6. But we may suppose in those cases concerning which the law had not made provision the judges afterwards settled the penalties in proportion to the crimes, according to the equity of the law. Now, if he that stole an ox out of a man's field must restore five-fold, it was reasonable that he that stole a man's goods out of his house should *restore seven-fold;* for there was no law to put him to death, as with us, for burglary and robbery on the highway, and of this worst kind of theft Solomon here speaks; the greatest punishment was that a man might be forced to *give all the substance of his house* to satisfy the law and his blood was not attainted. But, [2.] Committing adultery is a more heinous crime; Job calls it so, and *an iniquity to be punished by the judge,* Job 31:11. When Nathan would convict David of the evil of his adultery he did it by a parable concerning the most aggravated theft, which, in David's judgment, deserved to be punished with death (2 Sa. 12:5), and then showed him that his sin was *more exceedingly sinful* than that. *First,* It is a greater reproach to a man's reason, for he cannot excuse it, as a thief may, by saying that it was to satisfy his hunger, but must own that it was to gratify a brutish lust which would break the hedge of God's law, not for want, but for wantonness. Therefore *whoso commits adultery with a woman lacks understanding,* and deserves to be stigmatized as an arrant fool. *Secondly,* It is more severely punished by the law of God. A thief suffered only a pecuniary mulct, but the adulterer suffered death. The thief *steals to satisfy his soul,* but the adulterer *destroys his own soul,* and falls an unpitied sacrifice to the justice both of God and man. "Sinner, thou hast destroyed thyself." This may be applied to the spiritual and eternal death which is the consequence of sin; *he that does it* wounds his conscience, corrupts his rational power, extinguishes all the sparks of the spiritual life, and exposes himself to the wrath of God for ever, and thus *destroys his own soul. Thirdly,* The infamy of it is indelible, *v.* 33. It will be *a wound* to his good name, a *dishonour* to his family, and, though the guilt of it may be done away by repentance, the *reproach* of it never will, but will stick to his memory when he is gone. David's sin in the matter of Uriah was not only a perpetual blemish upon his own character, but gave occasion to the enemies of the Lord to blaspheme his name too.

(5.) It exposes the adulterer to the rage of the jealous husband, whose honour he puts such an affront upon, *v.* 34, 35. He that touches his neighbour's wife, and is familiar with her, gives him occasion for jealousy, much more he that debauches her, which, if kept ever so secret, might then be *discovered by the waters of jealousy,* Num. 5:12. "When discovered, thou hadst better meet a bear robbed of her whelps than the injured husband, who, in the case of adultery, will be as severe an avenger of his own honour as, in the case of manslaughter, of his brother's blood. If thou art not afraid of the wrath of God, yet be afraid of the *rage of a man.* Such jealousy is; it is *strong as death* and *cruel as the grave.* In the *day of vengeance,* when the adulterer comes to be tried for his life, the prosecutor will not spare any pains or cost in the prosecution, will not relent towards thee, as he would perhaps towards one that had robbed him. He will not accept of any commutation, any composition; *he will not regard any ransom.* Though thou offer to bribe him, and *give him many gifts* to pacify him, he *will not rest content* with any thing less than the execution of the law. Thou must be *stoned to death.* If *a man would give all the substance of his house,* it would atone for a theft (*v.* 31), but not for adultery; in that case it would utterly be contemned. *Stand in awe therefore, and sin not;* expose not thyself to all this misery for a moment's sordid pleasure, which will be bitterness in the end."

CHAPTER 7

The scope of this chapter is, as of several before, to warn young men against the lusts of the flesh. Solomon remembered of what ill consequence it was to his father, perhaps found himself, and perceived his son, addicted to it, or at least had observed how many hopeful young men among his subjects had been ruined by those lusts; and therefore he thought he could never say enough to dissuade men from them, that "every one may possess his vessel in sanctification and honour, and not in the lusts of uncleanness." In this chapter we have, I. A general exhortation to get our minds principled and governed by the world of God, as a sovereign antidote against this sin (*v.* 1–5). II. A particular representation of the great danger which unwary young men are in of being inveigled into this snare (*v.* 6–23). III. A serious caution inferred thence, in the close, to take heed of all approaches towards this sin (*v.* 24–27). We should all pray, "Lord, lead us not into this temptation."

Verses 1–5

These verses are an introduction to his warning against fleshly lusts, much the same with that, *ch.* 6:20, etc., and ending (*v.* 5) as that did (*v.* 24), *To keep thee from the strange woman;* that is it he aims at; only there he had said, *Keep thy father's commandment,* here (which comes all to one), *Keep my commandments,* for he speaks to us as unto sons. He speaks in God's name; for it is God's *commandments* that we are to *keep,* his *words,* his *law.* The word of God must be to us, 1. As that which we are most careful of. We must keep it as our treasure; we must *lay up God's* commandments with us, lay them up safely, that we may not be robbed of them by the wicked one, *v.* 1. We must keep it as our life: *Keep my commandments and live* (*v.* 2), not only, "Keep them, and you shall live;" but, "Keep them as you would your life, as those that cannot live without them." It would be death to a good man to be deprived of the word of God, for by it he lives, and not *by bread alone.* 2. As that which we are most tender of: Keep *my law as the apple of thy eye.* A little thing offends the eye, and therefore nature has so well guarded it. We pray, with David, that God would keep us as the apple of his eye (Ps. 17:8), that our lives and comforts may be precious in his sight; and they shall be so (Zec. 2:8) if we be in like manner tender of his law and afraid of the least violation of it. Those who reproach strict and circumspect walking, as needless preciseness, consider not that the law is to be kept as the apple of the eye, for indeed it is the *apple of our eye;* the law is light; the law in the heart is the eye of the soul. 3. As that which we are proud of and would be ever mindful of (*v.* 3): *"Bind them upon thy fingers;* let them be precious to thee; look upon them as an ornament, as a diamond-ring, as the *signet on thy right hand;* wear them continually as thy wedding-ring, the badge of thy espousals to God. Look upon the word of God as putting an honour upon thee, as an ensign of thy dignity. *Bind them on thy fingers,* that they may be constant memorandums to thee of thy duty, that thou mayest have them always in view, as that which is *graven upon the palms of thy hands."* 4. As that which we are fond of and are ever thinking of: *Write them upon the table of thy heart,* as the names of the friends we dearly love, we say, are written in our hearts. *let the word of God dwell richly in us,* and be written there where it will be always at hand to be read. Where sin was written (Jer. 17:1) let the word of God be written. It is the matter of a promise (Heb. 8:10, *I will write my law in their hearts*), which makes the precept practicable and easy. 5. As that which we are intimately acquainted and conversant with (*v.* 4): *"Say unto wisdom, Thou art my sister,* whom I dearly love and take delight in; *and call understanding thy kinswoman,* to whom thou art nearly allied, and for whom thou hast a pure affection; call her thy friend, whom thou courtest." We must make the word of God familiar to us, consult it, and consult its honour, and take a pleasure in conversing with it. 6. As that which we make use of for our defence and armour, to keep us *from the strange woman,* from sin, that flattering but destroying thing, that adulteress; particularly from the sin of uncleanness, *v.* 5. Let the word of God confirm our dread of that sin and our resolutions against it; let it discover to us its fallacies and suggest to us answers to all its flatteries.

Verses 6–23

Solomon here, to enforce the caution he had given against the sin of whoredom, tells a story of a young man that was ruined to all intents and purposes by the enticements of an adulterous woman. Such a story as this would serve the lewd profane poets of our age to make a play of, and the harlot with them would be a heroine; nothing would be so entertaining to the audience, nor give them so much diversion, as her arts of beguiling the young gentleman and drawing in the country squire; her conquests would be celebrated as the triumphs of wit and love, and the comedy would conclude very pleasantly; and every young man that saw it acted would covet to be so picked up. Thus *fools make a mock at sin.* But Solomon here relates it, and all wise and good men read it, as a very melancholy story. The impudence of the adulterous woman is very justly looked upon, by all that have any sparks of virtue in them, with the highest indignation, and the easiness of the young man with the tenderest compassion; and the story concludes with sad reflections, enough to make all that read and hear it afraid of the snares of fleshly lusts and careful to keep at the utmost distance from them. It is supposed to be a parable, or imagined case, but I doubt it was too true, and, which is worse, that notwithstanding the warning it gives of the fatal consequences of such wicked courses it is still too often true, and the agents for hell are still playing the same game and with similar success.

Solomon was a magistrate, and, as such, inspected the manners of his subjects, looked often through his casement, that he might see with his own eyes, and made remarks upon those who little thought his eye was upon them, that he might know the better how to make the sword he bore a terror to evil-doers. But here he writes as a minister, a prophet, who is by office a watchman, to give warning of the approach of the enemies, and especially where they lie in ambush, that we may not be ignorant of Satan's devices, but may know where to double our guard. This Solomon does here, where we may observe the account he gives,

I. Of the person tempted, and how he laid himself open to the temptation, and therefore must thank himself if it end in his destruction. 1. He was a *young man, v.* 7. Fleshly lusts are called *youthful lusts* (2 Tim. 2:22), not to extenuate them as tricks of youth, and therefore excusable, but rather to aggravate them, as robbing God of the first and best of our time, and, by debauching the mind when it is tender, laying a foundation for a bad life ever after, and to intimate that young people ought in a special manner to fortify their resolutions against this sin. 2. He was a young man *void of understanding,* that went abroad into the world, not principled as he ought to have been with wisdom and the fear of God, and so ventured to sea without ballast, without pilot, cord, or compass; he knew not how to depart from evil, which is the best understanding, Job 28:28. Those become an easy prey to Satan who, when they have arrived to the stature of men, have scarcely the understanding of children. 3. He kept bad company. He was a *young man among the youths,* a silly young man *among the simple* ones. If, being conscious of his own weakness, he had associated with those that were older and wiser than himself, there would have been hopes of him. Christ, at twelve years old, conversed with the doctors, to set young people an example of this. But, if those that are simple choose such for their companions as are like themselves, simple they will still be, and hardened in their simplicity. 4. He was sauntering, and had nothing to do, but *passed through the street* as one that knew not how to dispose of himself. One of the sins of filthy Sodom was *abundance of idleness,* Eze. 16:49. He went in a starched stately manner, so (it is said) the word signifies. He appeared to be a nice formal fop, the top of whose accomplishments was to dress well and walk with a good air; fit game for that bird of prey to fly at. 5. He was a nightwalker, that hated and scorned the business that is to be done by day-light, from which the evening calls men in to their repose; and, having fellowship with the unfruitful works of darkness, he begins to move *in the twilight in the evening, v.* 9. And he chooses *the black and dark night* as fittest for his purpose, not the moonlight nights, when he might be discovered. 6. He steered his course towards the house of one that he thought would entertain him, and that he might be merry with; he went *near her corner,* the *way to her house* (*v.* 8), contrary to Solomon's advice (*ch.* 5:8), *Come not night the door of her house.* Perhaps he did not know it was the way to an infamous house, but, however, it was a way that he had no business in; and when we have nothing to do the devil will quickly find us something to do. We must take heed, not only of idle days, but of idle evenings, lest they prove inlets to temptation.

II. Of the person tempting, not a common prostitute, for she was a married wife (*v.* 19), and, for aught that appears, lived in reputation among her neighbours, not suspected of any such wickedness, and yet, in the *twilight of the evening,* when her husband was abroad, abominably impudent. She is here described, 1. By her dress. She had the *attire of a harlot* (*v.* 10), gaudy and flaunting, to set her off as a beauty; perhaps she was painted as Jezebel, and went with her neck and breasts bare, loose, and *en deshabille.* The purity of the heart will show itself in the modesty of the dress, which *becomes women professing godliness.* 2. By her craft and management. She is *subtle of heart,* mistress of all the arts of wheedling, and knowing how by all her caresses to serve her own base purposes. 3. By her temper and carriage. *She is loud and stubborn,* talkative and self-willed, noisy and troublesome, wilful and headstrong, all tongue, and will have her saying, right or wrong, impatient of check and control, and cannot bear to be counselled, much less reproved, by husband or parents, ministers or friends. She is a *daughter of Belial,* that will endure no yoke. 4. By her place, not her own house; she hates the confinement and employment of that; her *feet abide not there* any longer than needs must. She is all for gadding abroad, changing place and company. *Now is she without* in the country, under pretence of taking the air, now *in the streets* of the city, under pretence of seeing how the market goes. She is here, and there, and every where but where she should be. She *lies in wait at every corner,* to pick up such as she can make a prey of. Virtue is a penance to those to whom home is a prison.

III. Of the temptation itself and the management of it. She met the young spark. Perhaps she knew him; however she knew by his fashions that he was such a one as she wished for; so she *caught him about* the neck and *kissed* him, contrary to all the rules of modesty (*v.* 13), and waited not for his compliments or courtship, but *with an impudent face* invited him not only to *her house,* but to *her bed.*

1. She courted him to sup with her (*v.* 14, 15): *I have peace-offerings with me.* Hereby she gives him to understand, (1.) Her prosperity, that she was compassed about with so many blessings that she had occasion to offer peace-offerings, in token of joy and thankfulness; she was before-hand in the world, so that he needed not fear having his pocket picked. (2.) Her profession of piety. She had been to-day at the temple, and was as well respected there as any that worshipped in the courts of the Lord. She had paid her vows, and, as she thought, made all even with God Almighty, and therefore might venture upon a new score of sins. Note, The external performances of religion, if they do not harden men against sin, harden them in it, and embolden carnal hearts to venture upon it, in hopes that when they come to count and discount with God he will be found as much in debt to them for their peace-offerings and their vows as they to him for their sins. But it is sad that a show of piety should become the shelter of iniquity (which really doubles the shame of it, and makes it more exceedingly sinful) and that men should baffle their consciences with those very things that should startle them. The Pharisees made long prayers, that they might the more plausibly carry on their covetous and mischievous provisions. The greatest part of the flesh of the peace-offerings was by the law returned back to the offerers, to feast upon with their friends, which (if they were peace-offerings of thanksgiving) was to be all eaten *the same day* and *none of it left until the morning,* Lev. 7:15. This law of charity and generosity is abused to be a colour for gluttony and excess: "Come," says she, "come home with me, for I have good cheer enough, and only want good company to help me off with it." It was a pity that the peace-offerings should thus become, in a bad sense, sin-offerings, and that what was designed for the honour of God should become the food and fuel of a base lust. But this is not all. (4.) To strengthen the temptation, [1.] She pretends to have a very great affection for him above any man: *"Therefore,* because I have a good supper upon the table, *I came forth to meet thee,* for no friend in the world shall be so welcome to it as thou shalt, *v.* 15. Thou art he whom I came on purpose to seek, to *seek diligently,* came myself, and would not send a servant." Surely he cannot deny her his company when she put such a value upon it, and would take all this pains to obtain the favour of it. Sinners take pains to do mischief, and are as the roaring lion himself; they *go about seeking to devour,* and yet pretend they are seeking to oblige. [2.] She would have it thought that Providence itself countenanced her choice of him for her companion; for how quickly had she found him whom she sought!

2. She courted him to lie with her. They will sit down to eat and drink, and then rise up to play, to play the wanton, and there is a bed ready for them, where he shall find that which will be in all respects agreeable to him. To please his eye, it is *decked with coverings of tapestry* and *carved works,* exquisitely fine; he never saw the like. To please his touch, the sheets are not of home-spun cloth; they are far-fetched and dear bought; they are of *fine linen of Egypt, v.* 16. To gratify his smell, it is *perfumed* with the sweetest scents, *v.* 17. Come, therefore, and *let us take our fill of love, v.* 18. Of *love,* does she say? Of *lust* she means, brutish lust; but it is a pity that the name of love should be thus abused. True love is from heaven; this is from hell. How can those pretend to solace themselves and love one another who are really ruining themselves and one another?

3. She anticipated the objection which he might make of the danger of it. Is she not another man's wife, and what if her husband should catch them in adultery, in the very act? he will make them pay dearly for their sport, and where will the solace of their love be then? "Never fear," says she, "the *good man is not at home*" (*v.* 19); she does not call him her *husband,* for she *forsakes the guide of her youth* and *forgets the covenant of her God;* but "the *good man* of the house, whom I am weary of." Thus Potiphar's wife, when she spoke of her husband, would not call him so, but *he,* Gen. 39:14. It is therefore with good reason taken notice of, to Sarah's praise, that she spoke respectfully of her husband, calling him *lord.* She pleases herself with this that he is not at home, and therefore she is melancholy if she have not some company, and therefore whatever company she has she may be free with them, for she is from under his eye, and he shall never know. But will he not return quickly? No: "he has *gone a long journey,* and cannot return on a sudden; he *appointed the day* of his return, and he never comes home sooner than he says he will. *He has taken a bag of money with him,* either," (1.) "To trade with, to buy goods with and he will not return till he has laid it all out. It is a pity that an honest industrious man should be thus abused, and advantage taken of his absence, when it is upon business, for the good of his family." Or, (2.) "To spend and revel with." Whether justly or not, she insinuates that he was a bad husband; so she would represent him, because she was resolved to be a bad wife, and must have that for an excuse; it is often groundlessly suggested, but is never a sufficient excuse.

"He follows his pleasures, and wastes his estate abroad" (says she), "and why should not I do the same at home?"

IV. Of the success of the temptation. Promising the young man every thing that was pleasant, and impunity in the enjoyment, she gained her point, v. 21. It should seem, the youth, though very simple, had no ill design, else a word, a beck, a wink, would have served, and there would have been no need of all this harangue; but though he did not intend any such thing, nay, had something in his conscience that opposed it, yet *with her much fair speech she caused him to yield*. His corruptions at length triumphed over his convictions, and his resolutions were not strong enough to hold out against such artful attacks as these, but *with the flattery of her lips she forced him*; he could not stop his ear against such a charmer, but surrendered himself her captive. Wisdom's maidens, who plead her cause, and have reason on their side, and true and divine pleasures to invite men to, have a deaf ear turned to them, and with all their rhetoric cannot compel men to come in, but such is the dominion of sin in the hearts of men that its allurements soon prevail by falsehood and flattery. With what pity does Solomon here look upon this foolish young man, when he sees him follow the adulterous woman! (1.) He gives him up for gone; alas! he is undone. he goes to the slaughter (for houses of uncleanness are slaughter-houses to precious souls); a dart will presently *strike through his liver;* going without his breastplate, he will receive his death's wound, v. 23. It is his life, his precious life, that is thus irrecoverably thrown away, he is perfectly lost to all good; his conscience is debauched; a door is opened to all other vices, and this will certainly end in his endless damnation. (2.) That which makes his case the more piteous is that he is not himself aware of his misery and danger; he goes blindfold, nay, he goes laughing to his ruin. The ox thinks he is led to the pasture when he is led to the slaughter; *the fool* (that is, the drunkard, for, of all sinners, drunkards are the greatest fools) is led *to the correction of the stocks,* and is not sensible of the shame of it, but goes to it as if he were going to a play. The *bird* that *hastes to the snare* looks only at the bait, and promises herself a good bit from that, and considers not that *it is for her life.* Thus this unthinking unwary young man dreams of nothing but the pleasures he shall have in the embraces of the harlot, while really he is running headlong upon his ruin. Though Solomon does not here tell us that he put the law in execution against this base harlot, yet we have no reason to think but that he did, he was himself so affected with the mischief she did and had such an indignation at it.

Verses 24–27

We have here the application of the foregoing story: "*Hearken to me therefore,* and not to such seducers (v. 24); give ear to a father, and not to an enemy." 1. "Take good counsel when it is given you. *Let not thy heart decline to her ways* (v. 25); never leave the paths of virtue, though strait and narrow, solitary and up-hill, for the way of the adulteress, though green, and broad, and crowded with company. Do not only keep thy feet from those ways, but let not so much as thy heart incline to them; never harbour a disposition this way, nor think otherwise than with abhorrence of such wicked practices as these. Let reason, and conscience, and the fear of God ruling in the heart, check the inclinations of the sensual appetite. If thou goest in her paths, in any of the paths that lead to this sin, thou goest astray, thou art out of the right way, the safe way; therefore take heed, *go not astray,* lest thou wander endlessly." 2. "Take fair warning when it is given you." (1.) "Look back, and see what mischief this sin has done. The adulteress has been the ruin not of here and there one, but she has *cast down many wounded*." Thousands have been undone, now and for ever, by this sin; and those not only the weak and simple youths, such as he was of whom he had now spoken, but *many strong men have been slain by her, v.* 26. Herein, perhaps, he has an eye especially to Samson, who was slain by this sin, and perhaps to David too, who by this sin entailed a sword upon his house, though so far the Lord took it away that he himself should not die. These were men not only of great bodily strength, but of eminent wisdom and courage, and yet their fleshly lusts prevailed over them. *Howl, fir-trees, if the cedars be shaken. Let him that thinks he stands take heed lest he fall.*

(2.) "Look forward with an eye of faith, and see what will be in the end of it," v. 27. Her house, though richly decked and furnished, and called a *house of pleasure,* is the *way to hell;* and her chambers are the stair-case that goes down to the *chambers of death* and everlasting darkness. The cup of fornication must shortly be exchanged for the cup of trembling; and the flames of lust, if not quenched by repentance and mortification, will burn to the lowest hell. Therefore *stand in awe and sin not.*

CHAPTER 8

The word of God is two-fold, and, in both senses, is wisdom; for a word without wisdom is of little value, and wisdom without a word is of little use. Now, I. Divine revelation is the word and wisdom of God, and that pure religion and undefiled which is built upon it; and of that Solomon here speaks, recommending it to us as faithful, and well worthy of all acceptation (v. 1–2). God, by it, instructs, and governs, and blesses, the children of men. II. The redeemer is the eternal Word and wisdom, the Logos. He is the Wisdom that speaks to the children of men in the former part of the chapter. All divine revelation passes through his hand, and centres in him; but of him as the personal Wisdom, the second person in the Godhead, in the judgment of many of the ancients, Solomon here speaks (v. 22–31). He concludes with a repeated charge to the children of men diligently to attend to the voice of God in his word (v. 32–36).

Verses 1–11

The will of God revealed to us for our salvation is here largely represented to us as easy to be known and understood, that none may have an excuse for their ignorance or error, and as worthy to be embraced, that none may have an excuse for their carelessness and unbelief.

I. The things revealed are easy to be known, for they *belong to us and to our children* (Deu. 29:29), and we need not soar up to heaven, or dive into the depths, to get the knowledge of them (Deu. 30:11), for they are published and proclaimed in some measure by the works of the creation (Ps. 19:1), more fully by the consciences of men and the eternal reasons and rules of good and evil, but most clearly by Moses and the prophets; let them hear them. The precepts of wisdom may easily be known; for, 1. They are proclaimed aloud (v. 1): *Does not Wisdom cry?* Yes, she cries aloud, and does not spare (Isa. 58:1); she *puts forth her voice,* as one in earnest and desirous to be heard. *Jesus stood and cried,* Jn. 7:37. The curses and blessings were read with a loud voice by the Levites, Deu. 27:14. And men's own hearts sometimes speak aloud to them; there are clamours of conscience, as well as whispers. 2. They are proclaimed from on high (v. 2): *She stands in the top of high places;* it was from the top of Mount Sinai that the law was given, and Christ expounded it in a sermon upon the mount. Nay, if we slight divine revelation, we *turn away from him that speaks from heaven,* a high place indeed, Heb. 12:25. The adulterous woman spoke in secret, the oracles of the heathen muttered, but Wisdom speaks openly; truth seeks no corners, but gladly appeals to the light. 3. They are proclaimed *in the places of concourse,* where multitudes are gathered together, the more the better. Jesus spoke *in the synagogues and in the temple, whither the Jews always resorted,* Jn. 18:20. Every man that passes by on the road, of what rank or condition soever, may know what is good, and what the Lord requires of him, if it be not his own fault. There is no speech nor language where Wisdom's voice is not heard; her discoveries and directions are given to all promiscuously. *He that has ears to hear, let him hear.* 4. They are proclaimed where they are most needed. They are intended for the guide of our way, and therefore are published *in the places of the paths,* where many ways meet, that travellers may be shown, if they will but ask, which is the right way, just then when they are at a loss; thou shalt then *hear the word behind thee, saying, This is the way,* Isa. 30:21. The foolish man *known not how to go to the city* (Eccl. 10:15), and therefore Wisdom stands ready to direct him, stands *at the gates, at the entry of the city,* ready to tell him where the seer's house is, 1 Sa. 9:18. Nay, she follows men to their own houses, and cries to them *at the coming in at the doors,* saying, *Peace be to this house; and, if the son of peace be there,* it shall certainly abide upon it. God's ministers are appointed to testify to people both publicly and from house to house. Their own consciences follow them with admonitions wherever they go, which they cannot be out of the hearing of while they carry their own heads and hearts about with them, which are a law unto themselves. 5. They are directed to the children of men. We attend to that discourse in which

we hear ourselves named, though otherwise we should have neglected it; therefore Wisdom speaks to us: *"Unto you, O men! I call* (v. 4), not to angels (they need not these instructions), not to devils (they are past them), not to the brute-creatures (they are not capable of them), but *to you, O men!* who are taught more than the beasts of the earth and made wiser than the fowls of heaven. To you is this law given, to you is the word of this invitation, this exhortation sent. *My voice is to the sons of men,* who are concerned to receive instruction, and to whom, one would think, it should be very welcome. It is not, to you, O Jews! only, that Wisdom cries, nor to you, O gentlemen! not to you, O scholars! but *to you, O men! O sons of men!* even the meanest." 6. They are designed to make them wise (v. 5); they are calculated not only for men that are capable of wisdom, but for sinful men, fallen men, foolish men, that need it, and are undone without it: *"O you simple ones! understand wisdom.* Though you are ever so simple, Wisdom will take you for her scholars, and not only so, but, if you will be ruled by her, will undertake to give you *an understanding heart."* When sinners leave their sins, and become truly religious, then the *simple understand wisdom.*

II. The things revealed are worthy to be known, well worthy of all acceptation. We are concerned to hear; for, 1. They are of inestimable value. They are *excellent things* (v. 6), *princely things,* so the word is. Though they are level to the capacity of the meanest, yet there is that in them which will be entertainment for the greatest. They are divine and heavenly things, so excellent that, in comparison with them, all other learning is but children's play. Things which relate to an eternal God, an immortal soul, and an everlasting state, must needs be *excellent things.* 2. They are of incontestable equity, and carry along with them the evidence of their own goodness. They are *right things* (v. 6), *all in righteousness* (v. 8), and *nothing froward or perverse in them.* All the dictates and directions of revealed religion are consonant to, and perfective of, the light and law of nature, and there is nothing in them that puts any hardship upon us, that lays us under any undue restraints, unbecoming the dignity and liberty of the human nature, nothing that we have reason to complain of. *All God's precepts concerning all things are right.* 3. They are of unquestionable truth. Wisdom's doctrines, upon which her laws are founded, are such as we may venture our immortal souls upon: *My mouth shall speak truth* (v. 7), the whole truth, and nothing but the truth, for it is a testimony to the world. Every word of God is true; there are not so much as pious frauds in it, nor are we imposed upon in that which is told us for our good. Christ is a faithful witness, is the truth itself; *wickedness* (that is, lying) *is an abomination to his lips.* Note, Lying is wickedness, and we should not only refrain from it, but it should be an abomination to us, and as far from what we say as from what God says to us. His word to us is *yea, and amen;* never then let ours be *yea and nay.* 4. They are wonderfully acceptable and agreeable to those who take them aright, who understand themselves aright, who have not their judgments blinded and biassed by the world and the flesh, are not under the power of prejudice, are taught of God, and whose understanding he has opened, who impartially *seek knowledge,* take pains for it, and have found it in the enquiries they have hitherto made. To them, (1.) They are all *plain,* and not hard to be understood. If the book is sealed, it is to those who are willingly ignorant. *If our gospel is hidden, it is hidden to those who are lost;* but to those who *depart from evil,* which is *understanding,* who have that *good understanding* which those have who *do the commandments,* to them *they are all plain* and there is nothing difficult in them. The way of religion is a highway, and *the way-faring men, though fools, shall not err therein,* Isa. 35:8. Those therefore do a great wrong to the common people who deny them the use of the scripture under pretence that they cannot understand it, whereas it is plain for plain people. (2.) They are all *right,* and not hard to be submitted to. Those who discern things that differ, who know good and evil, readily subscribe to the rectitude of all Wisdom's dictates, and therefore, without murmuring or disputing, govern themselves by them.

III. From all this he infers that the right knowledge of those things, such as transforms us into the image of them, is to be preferred before all the wealth of this world (v. 10,

11): *Receive my instruction, and not silver.* Instruction must not only be heard, but received. We must bid it welcome, receive the impressions of it, and submit to the command of it; and this *rather than choice gold,* that is, 1. We must prefer religion before riches, and look upon it that, if we have the knowledge and fear of God in our hearts, we are really more happy and better provided for every condition of life than if we had ever so much silver and gold. *Wisdom is* in itself, and therefore must be in our account, *better than rubies.* It will bring us in a better price, be to us a better portion; show it forth, and it will be a better ornament than jewels and precious stones of the greatest value. Whatever we can sit down and wish for of the wealth of this world would, if we had it, be unworthy to be compared with the advantages that attend serious godliness. 2. We must be dead to the wealth of this world, that we may the more closely and earnestly apply ourselves to the business of religion. We must receive instruction as the main matter, and then be indifferent whether we receive silver or no; nay, we must not receive it as our portion and reward, as the rich man in his life-time *received his good things.*

Verses 12–21

Wisdom here is Christ, *in whom are hidden all the treasures of wisdom and knowledge;* it is Christ in the word and Christ in the heart, not only Christ revealed to us, but Christ revealed in us. It is the word of God, the whole compass of divine revelation; it is God the Word, in whom all divine revelation centres; it is the soul formed by the word; it is Christ formed in the soul; it is religion in the purity and power of it. Glorious things are here spoken of this excellent person, this excellent thing.

I. Divine wisdom gives men good heads (*v.* 12): *I Wisdom dwell with prudence,* not with carnal policy (the wisdom that is from above is contrary to that, 2 Co. 1:12), but with true discretion, which serves for the right ordering of the conversation, that wisdom of the prudent which is to *understand his way* and is in all cases *profitable to direct,* the wisdom of the serpent, not only to guard from harm, but to guide in doing food. *Wisdom dwells with prudence;* for prudence is the product of religion and an ornament to religion; and there are more *witty inventions* found out with the help of the scripture, both for the right understanding of God's providences and for the effectual countermining of Satan's devices and the doing of good in our generation, than were ever discovered by the learning of the philosophers or the politics of statesmen. We may apply it to Christ himself; he *dwells with prudence,* for his whole undertaking is the *wisdom of God in a mystery,* and in it God *abounds towards us in all wisdom and prudence.* Christ *found out the knowledge of* that great *invention,* and a costly one it was to him, man's salvation, by his satisfaction, an admirable expedient. We had found out many inventions for our ruin; he found out one for our recovery. The covenant of grace is so well ordered in all things that we must conclude that he who ordered it *dwelt with prudence.*

II. It gives men good hearts, *v.* 13. True religion, consisting in *the fear of the Lord,* which is the wisdom before recommended, teaches men, 1. To hate all sin, as displeasing to God and destructive to the soul: *The fear of the Lord is to hate evil, the evil way,* to hate sin as sin, and therefore to *hate every false way.* Wherever there is an awe of God there is a dread of sin, as an evil, as only evil. 2. Particularly to hate pride and passion, those two common and dangerous sins. Conceitedness of ourselves, *pride and arrogancy,* are sins which Christ hates, and so do all those who have the Spirit of Christ; every one hates them in others, but we must hate them in ourselves. *The froward mouth,* peevishness towards others, God hates, because it is such an enemy to the peace of mankind, and therefore we should hate it. Be it spoken to the honour of religion that, however it is unjustly accused, it is so far from making men conceited and sour that there is nothing more directly contrary to it than pride and passion, nor which it teaches us more to detest.

III. It has a great influence upon public affairs and the well-governing of all societies, *v.* 14. Christ, as God, has strength and wisdom; wisdom and might are his; as Redeemer, he is *the wisdom of God and the power of God.* To all that are his he is made of God both *strength* and *wisdom;* in him they are laid up for us, that we may both know and do our duty. He is the wonderful counsellor and gives that grace which alone is *sound wisdom.* He *is understanding* itself, and *has strength* for all those that strengthen themselves in him. True religion gives men the best counsel in all difficult cases, and helps to make their way plain. Wherever it is, it is *understanding,* it has *strength;* it will be all that to us that we need, both for services and sufferings. Where the word of God dwells richly it makes a man *perfect* and *furnishes him thoroughly for every good word and work.* Kings, princes, and judges, have of all men most need of wisdom and strength, of counsel and courage, for the faithful discharge of the trusts reposed in them, and that they may be blessings to the people over whom they are set. And therefore Wisdom says, *By me kings reign* (*v.* 15, 16), that is, 1. Civil government is a divine institution, and those that are entrusted with the administration of it have their commission from Christ; it is a branch of his kingly office that *by him kings reign;* from him to whom all judgment is committed their power is derived. They reign by him, and therefore ought to reign for him. 2. Whatever qualifications for government any kings or princes have they are indebted to the grace of Christ for them; he gives them the spirit of government, and they have nothing, no skill, no principles of justice, but what he endues them with. *A divine sentence is in the lips of the king;* and kings are to their subjects what he makes them. 3. Religion is very much the strength and support of the civil government; it teaches subjects their duty, and so *by it kings reign* over them the more easily; it teaches kings their duty, and so *by it kings reign* as they ought; they *decree justice,* while they *rule in the fear of God.* Those rule well whom religion rules.

IV. It will make all those happy, truly happy, that receive and embrace it.

1. They shall be happy in the love of Christ; for he it is that says, *I love those that love me, v.* 17. Those that *love the Lord Jesus Christ in sincerity* shall be beloved of him with a peculiar distinguishing love: he will *love them and manifest himself to them.*

2. They shall be happy in the success of their enquiries after him: *"Those that seek me early,* seek an acquaintance with me and an interest in me, seek me *early,* that is, seek me earnestly, seek me first before any thing else, that begin betimes in the days of their youth to seek me, they shall find what they seek." Christ shall be theirs, and they shall be his. He never said, *Seek in vain.*

3. They shall be happy in the wealth of the world, or in that which is infinitely better. (1.) They shall have as much riches and honour as Infinite Wisdom sees good for them (*v.* 18); they are *with Christ,* that is, he has them to give, and whether he will see fit to give them to us must be referred to him. Religion sometimes helps to make people rich and great in this world, gains them a reputation, and so increases their estates; and the riches which Wisdom gives to her favourites have these two advantages: — [1.] That they are *riches and righteousness,* riches honestly got, not by fraud and oppression, but in regular ways, and riches charitably used, for alms are called *righteousness.* Those that have their wealth from God's blessing on their industry, and that have a heart to do good with it, have *riches and righteousness.* [2.] That therefore they are *durable riches.* Wealth gotten by vanity will soon be diminished, but that which is well got will wear well and will be left to the children's children, and that which is well spent in works of piety and charity is put out to the best interest and so will be durable; for the friends made by *the mammon of unrighteousness when we fail will receive us into everlasting habitations,* Lu. 16:9. It will be found after many days, for the days of eternity. (2.) They shall have that which is infinitely better, if they have not riches and honour in this world (*v.* 19): *"My fruit is better than gold,* and will turn to a better account, will be of more value in less compass, *and my revenue better than* the *choicest silver,* will serve a better trade." We may assure ourselves that not only Wisdom's products at last, but her income in the mean time, not only her fruit, but her revenue, is more valuable than the best either of the possessions or of the reversions of this world.

4. They shall be happy in the grace of God now; that shall be their guide in the good way, *v.* 20. This is that fruit of wisdom which is *better than gold, than fine gold,* it *leads us in the way of righteousness,* shows us that way and goes before us in it, the way that God would have us walk in and which will certainly bring us to our desired end. It leads *in the midst of the paths of judgment,* and saves us from deviating on either hand. *In medio virtus — Virtue lies in the midst.* Christ by his Spirit guides believers into all truth, and so *leads them in the way of righteousness,* and they *walk after the Spirit.*

5. They shall be happy in the glory of God hereafter, *v.* 21. *Therefore* Wisdom *leads in the paths of righteousness,* not only that she may keep her friends in the way of duty and obedience, but that she may *cause them to inherit substance* and may *fill their treasures,* which cannot be done with the things of this world, nor with any thing less than God and heaven. The happiness of those that love God, and devote themselves to his service, is substantial and satisfactory. (1.) It is substantial; it is substance itself. It is a happiness which will subsist of itself, and stand alone, without the accidental supports of outward conveniences. Spiritual and eternal things are the only real and substantial things. Joy in God is substantial joy, solid and well-grounded. The promises are their bonds, Christ is their surety, and both substantial. They *inherit substance;* that is, their inheritance hereafter is substantial; it is a weight of glory; it is substance, Heb. 10:34. All their happiness they have as heirs; it is grounded upon their sonship. (2.) It is satisfying; it will not only fill their hands, but *fill their treasures,* not only maintain them, but make them rich. The things of this world may fill men's bellies (Ps. 17:14), but not their treasures, for they cannot in them secure to themselves *goods for many years;* perhaps they may be deprived of them *this night.* But let the treasures of the soul be ever so capacious there is enough in God, and Christ, and heaven, to fill them. In Wisdom's promises believers have goods laid up, not for days and years, but for eternity; her fruit therefore *is better than gold.*

Verses 22–31

That it is an intelligent and divine person that here speaks seems very plain, and that it is not meant of a mere essential property of the divine nature, for Wisdom here has personal properties and actions; and that intelligent divine person can be no other than the Son of God himself, to whom the principal things here spoken of wisdom are attributed in other scriptures, and we must explain scripture by itself. If Solomon himself designed only the praise of wisdom as it is an attribute of God, by which he made the world and governs it, so to recommend to men the study of that wisdom which belongs to them, yet the Spirit of God, who indited what he wrote, carried him, as David often, to such expressions as could agree to no other than the Son of God, and would lead us into the knowledge of great things concerning him. All divine revelation is *the revelation of Jesus Christ, which God gave unto him,* and here we are told who and what he is, as God, designed in the eternal counsels to be the Mediator between God and man. The best exposition of these verses we have in the first four verses of St. John's gospel. *In the beginning was the Word,* etc. Concerning the Son of God observe here,

I. His personality and distinct subsistence, one with the Father and of the same essence, and yet a person of himself, whom *the Lord possessed* (*v.* 22), *who was set up* (*v.* 23), *was brought forth* (*v.* 24, 25), *was by him* (*v.* 30), for he was *the express image of his person,* Heb. 1:3.

II. His eternity; he was begotten of the Father, for *the Lord possessed* him, as his own Son, his beloved Son, laid him in his bosom; he was *brought forth as the only-begotten of the Father,* and this *before all worlds,* which is most largely insisted upon here. The Word was eternal, and had a being before the world, before the beginning of time; and therefore it must follow that it was from eternity. *The Lord possessed him in the beginning of his way,* of his eternal counsels, for those were *before his works.* This way indeed had no beginning, for God's purposes in himself are eternal like himself, but God speaks to us in our own language. Wisdom explains herself (*v.* 23): *I was set up from everlasting.* The Son of God was, in the eternal counsels of God, designed and advanced to be the wisdom and power of the Father, light and life, and all in all both in the creation and in the redemption of the world. That he *was brought forth* as to his being, and *set up* as to the divine counsels concerning his office, before the world was made, is here set forth in a great variety of expressions, much the same with those by which the eternity of God himself is expressed. Ps. 90:2, *Before the mountains were brought forth.* 1. *Before the earth was,* and that was made *in the beginning,* before man was made; therefore the second Adam had a being before the first, for the first Adam was *made of the earth,* the second had a being *before the earth,* and therefore is *not of the earth,* Jn. 3:31. 2. Before the sea was (*v.* 24), *when there were no depths* in which the waters were gathered together, *no fountains* from which those waters might arise, none of that deep on which the Spirit of God moved for the production of the visible creation, Gen. 1:2. 3. Before the mountains were, the everlasting mountains, *v.* 25. Eliphaz, to convince Job of his inability to judge of the divine counsels, asks him (Job 15:7), *Wast thou made before the hills?* No, thou wast not. But *before the hills was* the eternal Word *brought forth.* 4. Before the habitable parts of the world, which men cultivate, and reap the profits of (*v.* 26), *the fields* in the valleys and plains, to which the mountains are as a wall, which are *the highest part of the dust of the world;* the *first part of the dust* (so some), the atoms which compose the several parts of the world; *the chief or principal part of the dust,* so it may be read, and understood of man, who was made of the dust of the ground and is dust, but is the principal part of the dust, dust enlivened, dust refined. The eternal Word had a being before man was made, for *in him was the life of men.*

III. His agency in making the world. He not only had a being before the world, but he was present, not as a spectator, but as the architect, when the world was made. God silenced and humbled Job by asking him, *"Where wast thou when I laid the foundations of the earth? Who hath laid the measures thereof?* (Job 38:4, etc.). Wast thou that eternal Word and wisdom, who was the prime manager of that great affair? No; thou art of yesterday." But here the Son of God, referring, as it should seem, to the discourse God had with Job, declares himself to have been engaged in that which Job could not pretend to be a witness of and a worker in, the creation of the world. *By him God made the worlds,* Eph. 3:9; Heb. 1:2; Col. 1:16. 1. When, on the first day of the creation, in the very beginning of time, God said, *Let there be light,* and with a word produced it, this eternal Wisdom was that almighty Word: Then *I was there, when he prepared the heavens,* the fountain of that light, which, whatever it is here, is there substantial. 2. He was no less active when, on the second day, he stretched out the firmament, the vast expanse, and *set* that as *a compass upon the face of the depth* (*v.* 27), surrounded it on all sides with that canopy, that curtain. Or it may refer to the exact order and method with which God framed all the parts of the universe, as the workman marks out his work with his line and compasses. The work in nothing varied from the plan of it formed in the eternal mind. 3. He was also employed in the third day's work, when the *waters above the heavens,* were gathered together by *establishing the clouds above,* and those under the heavens by *strengthening the fountains of the deep,* which send forth those waters (*v.* 28), and by preserving the bounds of the sea, which is the receptacle of those waters, *v.* 29. This speaks much the honour of this eternal Wisdom, for by this instance God proves himself a God greatly to be feared (Jer. 5:22) that *he has placed the sand for the bound of the sea,* that the dry land might continue to appear above water, fit to be a habitation for man; and thus he has *appointed the foundation of the earth.* How able, how fit, is the Son of God to be the Saviour of the world, who was the Creator of it!

IV. The infinite complacency which the Father had in him, and he in the Father (*v.* 30): *I was by him, as one brought up with him.* As by an eternal generation he was brought forth of the Father, so by an eternal counsel he was brought up with him, which intimates, not only the infinite love of the Father to the Son, who is therefore called *the Son of his love* (Col. 1:13), but the mutual consciousness and good understanding that were between them concerning the work of man's redemption, which the Son was to undertake, and about which the *counsel of peace was between them both,* Zec. 6:13. He was *alumnus patris — the Father's pupil,* as I may say, trained up from eternity for that service which in time, in the fulness of time, he was to go through with, and is therein taken under the special tuition and protection of the Father; he is *my servant whom I uphold,* Isa. 42:1. He did what he saw the Father do (Jn. 5:19), pleased his Father, sought his glory, did according to the commandment he received from his Father, and all this *as one brought up with him.* He was *daily his Father's delight (my elect, in whom my soul delighteth,* says God, Isa. 43:1), and he also *rejoiced always before him.* This may be understood either, 1. Of the infinite delight which the persons of the blessed Trinity have in each other, wherein consists much of the happiness of the divine nature. Or, 2. Of the pleasure which the Father took in the operations of the Son, when he *made the world;* God saw every thing that the Son made, *and, behold, it was very good,* it pleased him, and therefore his Son was *daily,* day by day, during the six days of the creation, upon that account, *his delight,* Ex. 39:43. And the Son also did himself *rejoice before him* in the beauty and harmony of the whole creation, Ps. 104:31. Or, 3. Of the satisfaction they had in each other, with reference to the great work of man's redemption. The Father delighted in the Son, as Mediator between him and man, was well-pleased with what he proposed (Mt. 3:17), and *therefore* loved him because he undertook to *lay down his life for the sheep;* he put a confidence in him that he would go through his work, and not fail nor fly off. The Son also *rejoiced always before him,* delighted to do his will (Ps. 40:8), adhered closely to his undertaking, as one that was well-satisfied in it, and, when it came to the setting to, expressed as much satisfaction in it as ever, saying, *Lo, I come,* to do *as in the volume of the book it is written of me.*

V. The gracious concern he had for mankind, *v.* 31. Wisdom *rejoiced,* not so much in the rich products of the earth, or the treasures hid in the bowels of it, as *in the habitable parts os* it, for her *delights were with the sons of men;* not only in the creation of man is it spoken with a particular air of pleasure (Gen. 1:26), *Let us make man,* but in the redemption and salvation of man. The Son of God was *ordained, before the world,* to that great work, 1 Pt. 1:20. A remnant of the sons of men were given him to be brought, through his grace, to his glory, and these were those in whom his delights were. His church was the habitable part of his earth, made habitable for him, *that the Lord God might dwell* even *among those* that had been rebellious; and this he rejoiced in, in the prospect of seeing his seed. Though he foresaw all the difficulties he was to meet with in his work, the services and sufferings he was to go through, yet, because it would issue in the glory of his Father and the salvation of those sons of men that were given him, he looked forward upon it with the greatest satisfaction imaginable, in which we have all the encouragement we can desire to come to him and rely upon him for all the benefits designed us by his glorious undertaking.

Verses 32–36

We have here the application of Wisdom's discourse; the design and tendency of it is to bring us all into an entire subjection to the laws of religion, to make us wise and good, not to fill our heads with speculations, or our tongues with disputes, but to rectify what is amiss in our hearts and lives. In order to this, here is,

I. An exhortation to hear and obey the voice of Wisdom, to attend and comply with the good instructions that the word of God gives us, and in them to discern the voice of Christ, as the sheep know the shepherd's voice.

1. We must be diligent *hearers of the word;* for how can we believe in him of whom we have not heart? *"Hearken unto me, O you children!" v.* 32. "Read the word written, sit under the word preached, bless God for both, and hear him in both speaking to you." Let children age, and what they hearken to then, it is likely, they will be so seasoned by as to be governed by all their days. Let Wisdom's children justify Wisdom by hearkening to her and show themselves to be indeed her children. We must hear Wisdom's words, (1.) Submissively, and with a willing heart (*v.* 33): *"Hear instruction, and refuse it not,* either as that which you need not or as that which you like not; it is offered you as a kindness, and it is at your peril if you refuse it." Those that reject the counsel of God reject it against themselves, Lu. 7:30. "Refuse it not now, lest you should not have another offer." (2.) Constantly, and with an attentive ear. We must hear Wisdom so as to *watch daily at her gates,* as beggars to receive an alms, as clients and patients to receive advice, and to wait as servants, with humility, and patience, and ready observance, *at the posts of her doors.* See here what a good house Wisdom keeps, for every day is dole-day; what a good school, for every day is lecture-day. While we have God's works before our eyes, and his word in our hand, we may be every day hearing Wisdom, and learning instruction from her. See here what a dutiful and diligent attendance is required of all Christ's disciples; they must *watch at the gates.* [1.] We must lay hold on all opportunities of getting knowledge and grace, and must get into, and keep in, a constant settled course of communion with God. [2.] We must be very humble in our attendance on divine instructions, and be glad of any place, even the meanest, so we may but be within hearing of them, as David, who would gladly be a door-keeper in the house of God. [3.] We must raise our expectations of these instructions, and hearken to them with care, and patience, and perseverance, must watch and wait, as Christ's hearers, that *hanged on him* to hear him, as the word in the original is (Lu. 19:48) and (*ch.* 21:38) *came early in the morning to hear him.*

2. We must be conscientious *doers of the work,* for we are *blessed only in our deed.* It is not enough to hearken unto Wisdom's words, but we must *keep her ways* (*v.* 32), do every thing that she prescribes, keep within the hedges of her ways, and not transgress them, keep in the tracks of her ways, proceed and persevere in them. *"Hear instruction and be wise;* let it be a means to make you wise in ordering your conversation." What we know is known in vain if it do not make us wise, *v.* 33.

II. An assurance of happiness to all those that do hearken to Wisdom. They are blessed, *v.* 32, and again *v.* 34. Those are blessed that watch and wait at Wisdom's gates; even their attendance there is their happiness; it is the best place they can be in. Those are blessed that wait there, for they shall not be put to wait long; let them continue to knock awhile and it shall be opened to them. They are seeking Wisdom, and they shall find what they seek. But will it make them amends if they do find it? Yes (*v.* 35): *Whoso finds me finds life,* that is, all happiness, all that good which he needs or can desire. He finds life in that grace which is the principle of spiritual life and the pledge of eternal life. He *finds life,* for he shall *obtain favour of the Lord,* and *in his favour is life.* If the king's favour is towards a wise son, much more the favour of the King of kings. Christ is Wisdom, and he that finds Christ, that obtains an interest in him, he *finds life;* for Christ is life to all believers. *He that has the Son of God has life,* eternal life, and he *shall obtain favour of the Lord,* who is well-pleased with all those that are in Christ; nor can we obtain God's favour, unless we find Christ and be found in him.

III. The doom passed upon all those that reject Wisdom and her proposals, *v.* 36. They are left to ruin themselves, and Wisdom will not hinder them, because they have set at nought all her counsel. 1. Their crime is very great; they *sin against Wisdom,* rebel against its light and laws, thwart its designs, and by their folly offend it. They *sin against Christ;* they act in contempt of his authority, and in contradiction to all the purposes of his life and death. This is construed into hating Wisdom, hating Christ; they are his enemies, who will not have him to reign over them. What can appear worse than hating him who is the centre of all beauty and fountain of all goodness, love itself? 2. Their punishment will be very just, for they wilfully bring it upon themselves. (1.) Those that offend Christ do the greatest wrong to themselves; they *wrong their own souls;* they wound their own consciences, bring a blot and stain upon their souls, which renders them odious in the eyes of God, and unfit for communion with him; they deceive themselves, disturb themselves, destroy themselves. Sin is a wrong to the soul. (2.) Those that are at variance with Christ are in love with their own ruin: *Those that hate me love death;* they love that which will be their death, and put that from them which would be their life. Sinners die because they will die, which leaves them inexcusable, makes their condemnation the more intolerable, and will for ever justify God when he judges. *O Israel! thou hast destroyed thyself.*

CHAPTER 9

Christ and sin are rivals for the soul of man, and here we are told how they both make their court to it, to have the innermost and uppermost place in it. The design of this representation is to set before us life and death, good and evil; and there needs no more than a fair stating of the case to determine us which of those to choose, and surrender our hearts to. They are both brought in making entertainment for the soul, and inviting it to accept of the entertainment; concerning both we are told what the issue will be; and, the matter being thus laid before us, let us consider, take advice, and speak our minds. And we are therefore concerned to put a value upon our own souls, because we see there is such striving for them. I. Christ, under the name of Wisdom, invites us to accept of his entertainment, and so to enter into acquaintance and communion with him (*v.* 1–6). And having foretold the different success of his invitation (*v.* 7–9) he shows, in short, what he requires from us (*v.* 10). and what he designs for us (*v.* 11), and then leaves it to our choice what we will do (*v.* 12). II. Sin, under the character of a foolish woman, courts us to accept of her entertainment, and (*v.* 13–16) pretends it is very charming (*v.* 17). But Solomon tells us what the reckoning will be (*v.* 18). And now choose you, this day, whom you will close with.

Verses 1–12

Wisdom is here introduced as a magnificent and munificent queen, very great and very generous; that Word of God is this Wisdom in which God makes known his goodwill towards men; God the Word is this Wisdom, to whom the Father has committed all judgment. He who, in the chapter before, showed his grandeur and glory as the Creator of the world, here shows his grace and goodness as the Redeemer of it. The word is plural, *Wisdoms;* for in Christ are hid treasures of wisdom, and in his undertaking appears the manifold wisdom of God in a mystery. Now observe here,

I. The rich provision which Wisdom has made for the reception of all those that will be her disciples. This is represented under the similitude of a sumptuous feast, whence it is probable, our Saviour borrowed those parables in which he compared the *kingdom of heaven* to a great supper, Mt. 22:2; Lu. 14:16. And so it was prophesied of, Isa. 25:6. It is such a feast as Ahasuerus made to *show the riches of his glorious kingdom.* The grace of the gospel is thus set before us in the ordinance of the Lord's supper. To bid her guests welcome, 1. Here is a stately palace provided, *v.* 1. Wisdom, not finding a house capacious enough for all her guests, has built one on purpose, and, both to strengthen it and to beautify it, she has *hewn out her seven pillars,* which make it to be very firm, and look very great. Heaven is the house which Wisdom has built to entertain all her guests that are called to the marriage-supper of the Lamb; that is her Father's house, where there are many mansions, and whither she has gone to prepare places for us. She has hanged the earth upon nothing, there in it we have no continuing city; but heaven is a city that has foundations, has pillars. The church is Wisdom's house, to which she invites her guests, supported by the power and promise of God, as by *seven pillars.* Probably, Solomon refers to the temple which he himself had lately built for the service of religion, and to which he would persuade people to resort, both to worship God and to receive the instructions of Wisdom. Some reckon the schools of the prophets to be here intended. 2. Here is a splendid feast got ready (*v.* 2): *She has killed her beasts; she has mingled her wine;* plenty of meat and drink are provided, and all of the best. *She has killed her sacrifice* (so the word is); it is a sumptuous, but a sacred feast, a feast upon a sacrifice. Christ has offered up himself a sacrifice for us, and it is *his flesh* that is *meat indeed* and *his blood* that is *drink indeed.* The Lord's supper is a feast of reconciliation and joy upon the sacrifice of atonement. The wine is *mingled* with something richer than itself, to give it a more than ordinary spirit and flavour. *She has* completely *furnished her table* with all the satisfactions that a soul can desire — righteousness and grace, peace and joy, the assurances of God's love, the consolations of the Spirit, and all the pledges and earnests of eternal life. Observe, It is all Wisdom's own doing; *she* has killed the beasts, *she* has mingled the wine, which denotes both the love of Christ, who makes the provision (he does not leave it to others, but takes the doing of it into his own hands), and the excellency of the preparation. That must needs be exactly fitted to answer the end which Wisdom herself has the fitting up of.

II. The gracious invitation she has given, not to some particular friends, but to all in general, to come and take part of these provisions. 1. She employs her servants to carry the invitation round about in the country: *She has sent forth her maidens, v.* 3. The ministers of the gospel are commissioned and commanded to give notice of the preparations which God has made, in the everlasting covenant, for all those that are willing to come up to the terms of it; and they, with maiden purity, not corrupting themselves or the word of God, and with an exact observance of their orders, are to call upon all they meet with, even in *the highways and hedges,* to come and feast with Wisdom, for *all things are now ready,* Lu. 14:23. 2. She herself *cries upon the highest places of the city,* as one earnestly desirous of the welfare of the children of men, and grieved to see them rejecting their own mercies for lying vanities. Our Lord Jesus was himself the publisher of his own gospel; when he had sent forth his disciples he followed them to confirm what they said; nay, it *began to be spoken by the Lord,* Heb. 2:3. He stood, and cried, *Come unto me.* We see who invited; now let us observe,

(1.) To whom the invitation is given: *Whoso is simple* and *wants understanding, v.* 4. If we were to make an entertainment, of all people we should not care for, much less court, the company of such, but rather of philosophers and learned men, that we might hear their wisdom, and whose table-talk would be improving. "Have I need of madmen?" But Wisdom invites such, because what she has to give is what they most need, and it is their welfare that she consults, and aims at, in the preparation and invitation. he that is simple is invited, that he may be made wise, and he that *wants a heart* (so the word is) let him come hither, and he shall have one. Her preparations are rather physic than food, designed for the most valuable and desirable cure, that of the mind. Whosoever he be, the invitation is general, and excludes none that do not exclude themselves; though they be ever so foolish, yet, [1.] They shall be welcome. [2.] They may be helped; they shall neither be despised nor despaired of. Our Saviour came, *not to call the righteous, but sinners,* not the wise in their own eyes, who say they see (Jn. 9:41), but the simple, those who are sensible of their simplicity and ashamed of it, and him that is willing to *become a fool, that he may be wise,* 1 Co. 3:18.

(2.) What the invitation is. [1.] We are invited to Wisdom's house: *Turn in hither.* I say *we* are, for which of us is there that must not own the character of the invited, that are *simple and want understanding?* Wisdom's doors stand open to such, and she is desirous to have some conversation with them, one word for their good, nor has she any other design upon them. [2.] We are invited to her table (*v.* 5): *Come, eat of my bread,* that is, taste of the true pleasures that are to be found in the knowledge and fear of God. By faith acted on the promises of the gospel, applying them to ourselves and taking the comfort of them, we feed, we feast, upon the provisions Christ has made for poor souls. What we eat and drink we make our own, we are nourished and refreshed by it, and so are our souls by the word of God; it has that in it which is *meat and drink* to those that have understanding.

(3.) What is required of those that may have the benefit of this invitation, *v.* 6. [1.] They must break off from all bad company: *"Forsake the foolish,* converse not with them, conform not to their ways, have no fellowship with the works of darkness, or with those that deal in such works." The first step towards virtue is to shun vice, and therefore to shun the vicious. *Depart from me, you evildoers.* [2.] They must awake and arise from the dead; they must live, not in pleasure (for those that do so are dead while they live), but in the service of God; for those only that do so live indeed, live to some purpose. "Live not a mere animal-life, as brutes, but now, at length, live the life of men. *Live* and you *shall live;* live spiritually, and you shall live eternally," Eph. 5:14. [3.] They must choose the paths of Wisdom, and keep to them: *"Go in the way of understanding;* govern thyself henceforward by the rules of religion and right reason." It is not enough to forsake the foolish, but we must join ourselves with those that walk in wisdom, and walk in the same spirit and steps.

III. The instructions which Wisdom gives to the maidens she sends to invite, to the ministers and others, who in their places are endeavouring tot serve her interests and designs. She tells them,

1. What their work must be, not only to tell in general what preparation is made for souls, and to give a general offer of it, but they must address themselves to particular persons, must tell them of their faults, *reprove, rebuke, v.* 7, 8. They must instruct them how to amend — *teach, v.* 9. The word of God is intended, and therefore so is the ministry of that word, *for reproof, for correction, and for instruction in righteousness.*

2. What different sorts of persons they would meet with, and what course they must take with them, and what success they might expect.

(1.) They would meet with some *scorners* and *wicked men* who would mock the messengers of the Lord, and misuse them, would *laugh those to scorn* that invite them to the feast of the Lord, as they did, 2 Chr. 30:10, would *treat them spitefully,* Mt. 22:6. And, though they are not forbidden to invite those simple ones to Wisdom's house, yet they are advised not to pursue the invitation by reproving and rebuking them. *Reprove not a scorner; cast not these pearls before swine,* Mt. 7:6. Thus Christ said of the Pharisees, *Let them alone,* Mt. 15:14. "Do not reprove them." [1.] "In justice to them, for those have forfeited the favour of further means who scorn the means they have had. Those that are thus *filthy, let them be filthy still;* those that are *joined to idols, let them alone; lo, we turn to the Gentiles."* [2.] "In prudence to yourselves; because, if you reprove them," *First,* "You lose your labour, and so *get to yourselves shame* for the disappointment." *Secondly,* "You exasperate them; do it ever so wisely and tenderly, if you do it faithfully, they will hate you, they will load you with reproaches, and say all the ill they can of you, and so you will get a blot; therefore you had better not meddle with them, for your reproofs will be likely to do more hurt than good."

(2.) They would meet with others, who are wise, and good, and just; thanks be to God, all are not scorners. We meet with some who are so wise for themselves, to just to themselves, as to be willing and glad to be taught; and when we meet with such, [1.] If there be occasion, we must reprove them; for wise men are not so perfectly wise but there is that in them which needs a reproof; and we must not connive at any man's faults because we have a veneration for his wisdom, nor must a *wise man* think that his wisdom exempts him from reproof when he says or does any thing foolishly; but the more wisdom a man has the more desirous he should be to have his weaknesses shown him, because a *little folly* is a great blemish to *him that is in reputation for wisdom and honour.* [2.] With our reproofs we must *give* them *instruction,* and must *teach* them, *v.* 9. [3.] We may expect that our doing so will be taken as a kindness, Ps. 141:5. A wise man will reckon those his friends who deal faithfully with him: "Rebuke such a one, and *he will love thee* for thy plain dealing, will thank thee, and desire thee to do him the same good turn another time, if there be occasion." It is as great an instance of wisdom to take a reproof well as to give it well, [4.] Being taken well, it will do good, and answer the intention. A *wise man* will be made wiser by the reproofs and instructions that are given him; he *will increase in learning,* will grow in knowledge, and so grow in grace. None must think themselves too wise to learn, nor so good that they need not be better and therefore need not be taught. We must still press forward, and follow on to know till we come to the perfect man. *Give to a wise man* (so it is in the original), give him advice, give him reproof, give him comfort, and *he will be yet wiser; give him occasion* (so the Septuagint), occasion to show his wisdom, and he will show it, and the acts of wisdom will strengthen the habits.

IV. The instructions she gives to those that are invited, which her maidens must inculcate upon them.

1. Let them know wherein true wisdom consists, and what will be their entertainment at Wisdom's table, *v.* 10 (1.) The heart must be principled with *the fear of God;* that *is the beginning of wisdom.* A reverence of God's majesty, and a dread of his wrath, are that fear of him which is the beginning, the first step towards true religion, whence all other instances of it take rise. This fear may, at first, have torment, but love will, by degrees, cast out the torment of it. (2.) The head must be filled with the knowledge of the things of God. *The knowledge of holy things* (the word is plural) *is understanding,* the things pertaining to the service of God (those are called *holy things*), that pertain to our own sanctification; reproof is called *that which is holy,* Mt. 7:6. Or the knowledge which holy men

have, which was taught by the holy prophets, of those things which *holy men spoke as they were moved by the holy Ghost,* this *is understanding;* it is the best and most useful understanding, will stand us in most stead and turn to the best account.

2. Let them know what will be advantages of this wisdom (*v.* 11): *"By me thy days shall be multiplied.* It will contribute to the health of thy body, and so *the years of thy life* on earth *shall be increased,* while men's folly and intemperance shorten their days. It will bring thee to heaven, and there thy days shall be multiplied *in infinitum — to infinity,* and the *years of thy life shall be increased without end."* There is no true wisdom but in the say of religion and no true life but in the end of that way.

3. Let them know what will be the consequence of their choosing or refusing this fair offer, *v.* 12. Here is, (1.) The happiness of those that embrace it: *"If thou be wise, thou shalt be wise for thyself;* thou wilt be the gainer by it, not Wisdom." A man cannot be profitable to God. It is to our own good that we are thus courted. "Thou wilt not leave the gain to others" (as we do our worldly wealth when we die, which is therefore called *another man's,* Lu. 16:12), "but thou shalt carry it with thee into another world." Those that are wise for their souls are wise for themselves, for the soul is the man; nor do any consult their own true interest but those that are truly religious. This recommends us to God, and recovers us from that which is our folly and degeneracy; it employs us in that which is most beneficial in this world, and entitles us to that which is much more so in the world to come. (2.) The shame and ruin of those that slight it: *"If thou scornest* Wisdom's proffer, *thou alone shalt bar it."* [1.] "Thou shalt bear the blame of it." Those that are good must thank God, but those that are wicked may thank themselves; it is not owing to God (he is not the author of sin); Satan can only tempt, he cannot force; and wicked companions are but his instruments; so that all the fault must lie on the sinner himself. [2.] "Thou shalt bear the loss of that which thou scornest; it will be to thy own destruction; thy blood will be upon thy own head, and the consideration of this will aggravate thy condemnation. *Son, remember,* that thou hadst this fair offer made thee, and thou wouldst not accept it; thou stoodest fair for life, but didst choose death rather."

Verses 13–18

We have heard what Christ has to say, to engage our affections to God and godliness, and one would think the whole world should go after him; but here we are told how industrious the tempter is to seduce unwary souls into the paths of sin, and with the most he gains his point, and Wisdom's courtship is not effectual. Now observe,

I. Who is the tempter — *a foolish woman,* Folly herself, in opposition to Wisdom. Carnal sensual pleasure I take to be especially meant by this *foolish woman* (*v.* 13); for that is the great enemy to virtue and inlet to vice; that defiles and debauches the mind, stupefies conscience, and puts out the sparks of conviction, more than any thing else. This tempter is here described to be, 1. Very ignorant: *She is simple and knows nothing,* that is, she has no sufficient solid reason to offer; where she gets dominion in a soul she works out all the knowledge of holy things; they are lost and forgotten. *Whoredom, and wine, and new wine, take away the heart;* they besot men, and make fools of them. (2.) Very importunate. The less she has to offer that is rational the more violent and pressing she is, and carries the day often by dint of impudence. She *is clamorous* and noisy (*v.* 13), continually haunting young people with her enticements. *She sits at the door of her house* (*v.* 14), watching for a prey; not as Abraham at his tent-door, seeking an opportunity to do good. *She sits on a seat (on a throne,* so the word signifies) *in the high places of the city,* as if she had authority to give law, and we were all *debtors to the flesh, to live after the flesh,* and as if she had reputation, and were in honour, and thought worthy of *the high places of the city;* and perhaps she gains upon many more by pretending to be fashionable than by pretending to be agreeable. "Do not all persons of rank and figure in the world" (says she) "give themselves a greater liberty than the strict laws of virtue allow; and why shouldst thou humble thyself so far as to be cramped by them?" Thus the tempter affects to seem both kind and great.

II. Who are the tempted — young people who have been well educated; these she will triumph most in being the ruin of. Observe, 1. What their real character is; they are *passengers that go right on their ways* (*v.* 15), that have been trained up in the paths of religion and virtue and set out very hopefully and well, that seemed determined and designed for good, and are not (as that young man, *ch.* 7:8) *going the way to her house.* Such as these she has a design upon, and lays snares for, and uses all her arts, all her charms, to pervert them; if they *go right on,* and will not look towards her, she will call after them, so urgent are these temptations. (2.) How she represents them. She calls them *simple* and *wanting understanding,* and therefore courts them to her school, that they may be cured of the restraints and formalities of their religion. This is the method of the stage (which is too close an exposition of this paragraph), where the sober young man, that has been virtuously educated, is the fool in the play, and the plot is to make him *seven times more a child of hell* than his profane companions, under colour of polishing and refining him, and setting him up for a wit and a beau. What is justly charged upon sin and impiety (*v.* 4), that it is folly, is here very unjustly retorted upon the ways of virtue; but the day will declare who are the fools.

III. What the temptation is (*v.* 17): *Stolen waters are sweet.* It is to water and bread, whereas Wisdom invites to the beasts she has killed and the wine she has mingled; however, bread and water are acceptable enough to those that are hungry and thirsty; and this is pretended to be more *sweet* and *pleasant* than common, for it is *stolen water and bread eaten in secret,* with a fear of being discovered. The pleasures of prohibited lusts are boasted of as more relishing than those of prescribed love; and dishonest gain is preferred to that which is justly gotten. Now this argues, not only a bold contempt, but an impudent defiance, 1. Of God's law, in that the waters are the sweeter for being stolen and come at by breaking through the hedge of the divine command. *Nitimur in vetitum — We are prone to what is forbidden.* This spirit of contradiction we have from our first parents, who thought the forbidden tree of all others *a tree to be desired.* 2. Of God's curse. The *bread is eaten in secret,* for fear of discovery and punishment, and the sinner takes a pride in having so far baffled his convictions, and triumphed over them, that, notwithstanding that fear, he dares commit the sin, and can make himself believe that, being eaten in secret, it shall never be discovered or reckoned for. Sweetness and pleasantness constitute the bait; but, by the tempter's own showing, even that is so absurd, and has such allays, that it is a wonder how it can have any influence upon men that pretend to reason.

IV. An effectual antidote against the temptation, in a few words, *v.* 18. He that so far wants understanding as to be drawn aside by these enticements is led on, ignorantly, to his own inevitable ruin: *He knows not,* will not believe, does not consider, the tempter will not let him know, *that the dead are there,* that those who live in pleasure are *dead while they live, dead in trespasses and sins.* Terrors attend these pleasures like the terrors of death itself. The giants are there — *Rephaim.* It was this that ruined the sinners of the old world, the giants that were *in the earth in those days. Her guests,* that are treated with those *stolen waters,* are not only in the highway to hell and at the brink of it, but they are already *in the depths of hell,* under the power of sin, led captive by Satan at his will, and ever and anon lashed by the terrors of their own consciences, which are a hell upon earth The depths of Satan are *the depths of hell.* Remorseless sin is remediless ruin; it is the bottomless pit already. Thus does Solomon show the hook; those that believe him will not meddle with the bait.

CHAPTER 10

Hitherto we have been in the porch or preface to the proverbs, here they begin. They are short but weighty sentences; most of them are distichs, two sentences in one verse, illustrating each other; but it is seldom that there is any coherence between the verses, much less any thread of discourse, and therefore in these chapters we need not attempt to reduce the contents to their proper heads, the several sentences will appear best in their own places. The scope of them all is to set before us good and evil, the blessing and the curse. Many of the proverbs in this chapter relate to the good government of the tongue, without which men's religion is vain.

Verse 1

Solomon, speaking to us as unto children, observes here how much the comfort of parents, natural, political, and ecclesiastical, depends upon the good behaviour of those under their charge, as a reason, 1. Why parents should be careful to give their children a good education, and to train them up in the ways of religion, which, if it obtain the desired effect, they themselves will have the comfort of it, or, if not, they will have for their support under their heaviness that they have done their duty, have done their endeavour. 2. Why children should conduct themselves wisely and well, and live up to their good education, that they may gladden the hearts of their parents, and not sadden them. Observe, (1.) It adds to the comfort of young people that are pious and discreet that thereby they do something towards recompensing their parents for all the care and pains they have taken with them, and occasion pleasure to them in the evil days of old age, when they most need it; and it is the duty of parents to rejoice in their children's wisdom and well-doing, yea, though it arrive at such an eminency as to eclipse them. (2.) It adds to the guilt of those that conduct themselves ill that thereby they grieve those whom they ought to be a joy to, and are a heaviness particularly to their poor mothers who bore them with sorrow, but with greater sorrow see them wicked and vile.

Verses 2–3

These two verses speak to the same purport, and the latter may be the reason of the former. 1. That wealth which men get unjustly will do them no good, because God will blast it: *Treasures of wickedness profit nothing, v.* 2. The treasures of wicked people, much more the treasure which they have made themselves masters of by any wicked people, by oppression of fraud, though it be ever so much, as a treasure, and laid up ever so safely, though it be hidden treasure, yet it *profits nothing;* when profit and loss come to be balanced the profit gained by the treasures will by no means countervail the loss sustained by the wickedness, Mt. 16:26. They do not profit the soul; they will not purchase any true comfort or happiness. They will stand a man in no stead at death, or in the judgment of the great day; and the reason is because God *casts away the substance of the wicked* (*v.* 3); he takes that from them which they have unjustly gotten; he rejects the consideration of it, not regarding the rich more than the poor. We often see that scattered by the justice of God which has been gathered together by the injustice of men. How can the treasures of wickedness profit, when, though it be counted substance, God casts it away and it vanishes as a shadow? 2. That which is honestly got will turn to a good account, for God will bless it. *Righteousness delivers from death,* that is, wealth gained, and kept, and used, in a right manner (righteousness signifies both honesty and charity); it answers the end of wealth, which is to keep us alive and be a defence to us. It will deliver from those judgments which men bring upon themselves by their wickedness. It will profit to such a degree as to deliver, though not from the stroke of death, yet from the sting of it, and consequently from the terror of it. For *the Lord will not suffer the soul of the righteous to famish* (*v.* 3), and so their *righteousness delivers from death,* purely by the favour of God to them, which is their life and livelihood, and which will keep them alive in famine. The soul of the righteous shall be kept alive by the word of God, and faith in his promise, when *young lions shall lack and suffer hunger.*

Verse 4

We are here told, 1. Who those are who, though rich, are in a fair way to *become poor* — those *who deal with a slack hand,* who are careless and remiss in their business, and never mind which end goes foremost, nor ever set their hands vigorously to their work or stick to it; those *who deal with a deceitful hand* (so it may be read); those who think to enrich themselves by fraud and tricking will, in the end, impoverish themselves, not only by bringing the curse of God on what they have, but by forfeiting their reputation with men; none will care to deal with those who deal with sleight of hand and are honest only with good looking to. 2. Who those are who, though poor, are in a fair way to become rich — those who are diligent and honest, who are careful about their affairs, and, what their hands find to do, do it with all their might, in a fair and honourable way, those are likely to increase what they have. *The hand of the acute* (so some), of those who are sharp, but not sharpers; *the hand of the active* (so others); the stirring hand gets a penny. This is true in the affairs of our souls as well as in our worldly affairs; slothfulness and hypocrisy lead to spiritual poverty, but those who are *fervent in spirit, serving the Lord,* are likely to be *rich in faith* and *rich in good works.*

Verse 5

Here is, 1. The just praise of those who improve their opportunities, who take pains to gather and increase what they have, both for soul and body, who provide for hereafter while provision is to be made, who *gather in summer,* which is gathering time. He who does so *is a wise son,* and it is his honour; he acts wisely for his parents, whom, if there be occasion, he ought to maintain, and he gives reputation to himself, his family, and his education. 2. The just reproach and blame of those who trifle away these opportunities: *He who sleeps,* loves his ease, idles away his time, and neglects his work, especially *who sleeps in harvest,* when he should be laying in for winter, who lets slip the season of furnishing himself with that which he will have occasion for, *is a son that causes shame;* for he is a foolish son; he prepares shame for himself when winter comes, and reflects shame upon all his friends. He who gets knowledge and wisdom in the days of his youth *gathers in summer,* and he will have the comfort and credit of his industry; but he who idles away the days of his youth will bear the shame of his indolence when he is old.

Verse 6

Here is, 1. *The head of the just* crowned with *blessings,* with the blessings both of God and man. Variety of blessings, abundance of blessings, shall descend from above, and visibly abide on the head of good men, real blessings; they shall not only be spoken well of, but done well to. Blessings shall be on their head as a coronet to adorn and dignify them and as a helmet to protect and secure them. 2. *The mouth of the wicked covered* with *violence.* Their mouths shall be stopped with shame for the violence which they have done; they shall not have a word to say in excuse for themselves (Job 5:16); their breath shall be stopped with the violence that shall be done to them, when their violent dealings shall return on their heads, shall be returned to their teeth.

Verse 7

Both the just and the wicked, when their days are fulfilled, must die. Between their bodies in the grave thee is no visible difference; between the souls of the one and the other, in the world of spirits, thee is a vast difference, and so there is, or ought to be, between their memories, which survive them.

I. Good men are and ought to be well spoken of when they are gone; it is one of the blessings that *comes upon the head of the just,* even when their head is laid. Blessed men leave behind them blessed memories. 1. It is part of the dignity of the saints, especially those who excel in virtue and are eminently useful, that they are remembered with respect when they are dead. Their good name, their name with good men, for good things, is then in a special manner as *precious ointment,* Eccl. 7:1. Those that honour God he will thus honour, Ps. 112:3, 6, 9. *The elders* by faith *obtained a good report* (Heb. 11:2), and, being dead, are yet spoken of. 2. It is part of the duty of the survivors: *Let the memory of the just be blessed,* so the Jews read it, and observe it as a precept, not naming an eminently just man that is dead without adding, *Let his memory be blessed.* We must delight in making an honourable mention of good men that are gone, bless God for them, and for his gifts and graces that appeared in them, and especially be followers of them in *that which is good.*

II. Bad men are and shall be forgotten, or spoken of with contempt. When their bodies are putrefying in the grave their *names* also *shall rot.* Either they shall not be preserved at all, but buried in oblivion (no good can be said of them, and therefore the greatest kindness that can be done them will be to say nothing of them), or they shall be loathsome, and mentioned with detestation, and that rule of honour, *De mortuis nil nisi bonum — Say nothing to the disadvantage of the dead,* will not protect them. Where the wickedness has been notorious, and cannot but be mentioned, it ought to be mentioned with abhorrence.

Verse 8

Here is, 1. The honour and happiness of the obedient. They *will receive commandments;* they will take it as a privilege, and really an ease to them, to be under government, which saves them the labour of deliberating and choosing for themselves; and they will take it as a favour to be told their duty and admonished concerning it. And this is their wisdom; those are *wise in heart* who are tractable, and those who thus bend, thus stoop, shall stand and be established, shall prosper, being well advised. 2. The shame and ruin of the disobedient, that will not be governed, nor endure any yoke, that will not be taught, nor take any advice. They are fools, for they act against themselves and their own interest; they are commonly *prating fools,* fools of lips, full of talk, but full of nonsense, boasting of themselves, prating spitefully against those that admonish them (3 Jn. 10), and pretending to give counsel and law to others. Of all fools, none more troublesome than the *prating fools,* nor that more expose themselves; but they *shall fall* into sin, into hell, because they received not commandments. Those that are full of tongue seldom look well to their feet, and therefore stumble and fall.

Verse 9

We are here told, and we may depend upon it, 1. That men's integrity will be their security: *He that walks uprightly* towards God and man, that is faithful to both, that designs as he ought and means as he says, *walks surely;* he is safe under a divine protection and easy in a holy security. He goes on his way with a humble boldness, being well armed against the temptations of Satan, the troubles of the world, and the reproaches of men. he knows what ground he stands on, what guide he follows, what guard he is surrounded with, and what glory he is going to, and therefore proceeds with assurance and *great peace,* Isa. 32:17; 33:15, 16. Some understand it as part of the character of an upright man, that he *walks surely,* in opposition to walking at all adventures. He will not dare to do that which he is not fully satisfied in his own conscience concerning the lawfulness of, but will see his way clear in every thing. 2. That men's dishonesty will be their shame: *He that perverts his way,* that turns aside into crooked paths, that dissembles with God and man, looks one way and rows another, though he may for a time disguise himself, and pass current, *shall be known* to be what he is. It is a thousand to one but some time or other he betrays himself; at least, God will discover him in the great day. *He that perverts his ways documento erit — shall be made an example of,* for warning to others; so some.

Verse 10

Mischief is here said to attend, 1. Politic, designing, self-disguising sinners: *He that winks with the eye,* as if he took no notice of you, when at the same time he is watching an opportunity to do you an ill turn, that makes signs to his accomplices when to come into assist him in executing his wicked projects, which are all carried on by trick and artifice, *causes sorrow* both to others and to himself. Ingenuity will be no excuse for iniquity, but the sinner must either repent or do worse, either rue it or be ruined by it. 2. Public, silly, self-exposing sinners: A *prating fool,* whose sins go before unto judgment, *shall fall,* as was said before, *v.* 8. But his case is less dangerous of the two, and, though he destroys himself, he does not create so much sorrow to others as *he that winks with his eyes.* The dog that bites is not always the dog that barks.

Verse 11

See here, 1. How industrious a good man is, by communicating his goodness, to do good with it: *His mouth,* the outlet of his mind, *is a well of life;* it is a constant spring, whence issues good discourse for the edification of others, like streams that water the ground and make it fruitful, and for their consolation, like streams that quench the thirst of the weary traveller. It is like *a well of life,* that is pure and clean, not only not poisoned, but not muddled, with any corrupt communication. 2. How industrious a bad man is, by concealing his badness, to do hurt with it: *The mouth of the wicked covers violence,* disguises the designed mischief with professions of friendship, that it may be carried on the more securely and effectually, as Joab kissed and killed, Judas kissed and betrayed; this is his sin, to which the punishment answers (*v.* 6): *Violence covers the mouth of the wicked;* what he got by violence shall by violence be taken from him, Job 5:4, 5.

Verse 12

Here is, 1. The great mischief-maker, and that is malice. Even where there is no manifest occasion of strife, yet *hatred* seeks occasion and so *stirs it up* and does the devil's work. Those are the most spiteful ill-natured people that can be who take a pleasure in setting their neighbours together by the ears, by tale-bearing, evil surmises, and misrepresentations, blowing up the sparks of contention, which had lain buried, into a flame, at which, with an unaccountable pleasure, they warm their hands. 2. The great peacemaker, and that is *love,* which *covers all sins,* that is, the offences among relations which occasion discord. Love, instead of proclaiming and aggravating the offence, conceals and extenuates it as far as it is capable of being concealed and extenuated. Love will excuse the offence which we give through mistake and unadvisedly; when we are able to say that there was no ill intended, but it was an oversight, and we love our friend notwithstanding, this covers it. It will also overlook the offence that is given us, and so cover it, and make the best of it: by this means strife is prevented, or, if begun, peace is recovered and restored quickly. The apostle quotes this, 1 Pt. 4:8. *Love will cover a multitude of sins.*

Verse 13

Observe, 1. Wisdom and grace are the honour of good men: He *that has understanding,* that good understanding which those have that do the commandments, *wisdom is found in his lips,* that is, it is discovered to be there, and consequently that he has within a good treasure of it, and it is derived thence for the benefit of others. It is a man's honour to have wisdom, but much more to be instrumental to make others wise. 2. Folly and sin are the shame of bad men: *A rod is for the back of him that is void of understanding — of him that wants a heart;* he exposes himself to the lashes of his own conscience, to the scourges of the tongue, to the censures of the magistrate, and to the righteous judgments of God. Those that foolishly and wilfully go on in wicked ways are preparing rods for themselves, the marks of which will be their perpetual disgrace.

Verse 14

Observe, 1. It is the wisdom of the wise that they treasure up a stock of useful knowledge, which will be their preservation: *Wisdom is* therefore *found in their lips* (*v.* 13), because it is laid up in their hearts, out of which store, like the good householder, they bring things new and old. Whatever knowledge may be at any time useful to us we must *lay it up,* because we know not but some time or other we may have occasion for it. We must continue laying up as long as we live; and be sure to lay it up safely, that it may not be to seek when we want it. 2. It is the folly of fools that they lay up mischief in their hearts, which is ready to them in all they say, and works terror and destruction both to others and to themselves. They *love devouring words* (Ps. 52:4), and these come uppermost. Their *mouth is near destruction,* having the *sharp arrows of bitter words* always at hand to throw about.

Verse 15

This may be taken two ways: — 1. As a reason why we should be diligent in our business, that we may avoid that sinking dispiriting uneasiness which attends poverty, and may enjoy the benefit and comfort which those have that are beforehand in the world. Taking pains is really the way to make ourselves and our families easy. Or, rather, 2. As a representation of the common mistakes both of rich and poor, concerning their outward condition. (1.) Rich people think themselves happy because they are rich; but it is their mistake: *The rich man's wealth is,* in his own conceit, *his strong city,* whereas the worst of evils it is too weak and utterly insufficient to protect them from. It will prove that they are not so safe as they imagine; nay, their wealth may perhaps expose them. (2.) Poor people think themselves undone because they are poor; but it is their mistake: *The destruction of the poor is their poverty;* it sinks their spirits, and ruins all their comforts; whereas a man may live very comfortably, though he has but a little to live on, if he be but content, and keep a good conscience, and live by faith.

Verse 16

Solomon here confirms what his father had said (Ps. 37:16), *A little that a righteous man has is better than the riches of many wicked.* 1. Perhaps a righteous man has no more than what he works hard for; he eats only *the labour of his hands,* but that *labour tends to life;* he aims at nothing but to get an honest livelihood, covets not to be rich and great, but is willing to live and maintain his family. Nor does it tend only to his own life, but he would enable himself to do good to others; he labours *that he may have to give* (Eph. 4:28); all his business turns to some good account or other. Or it may be meant of his labour in religion; he takes most pains in that which has a tendency to eternal life; he *sows to the Spirit,* that he may *reap life everlasting.* 2. Perhaps a wicked man's wealth is fruit which he did not labour for, but came easily by, but it tends *to sin.* He makes it the food and fuel of his lusts, his pride and luxury; he gets hurt with it and not good; he gets hurt by it and is hardened by it in his wicked ways. The things of this world are good or evil, life or death, as they are used, and as those are that have them.

Verse 17

See here, 1. That those are in the right that do not only receive instruction, but retain it, that do not let it slip through carelessness, as most do, nor let it go to those that would rob them of it, that *keep instruction* safely, keep it pure and entire, keep it for their own use, that they may govern themselves by it, keep it for the benefit of others, that they may instruct them; those that do so are *in the way of life,* the way that has true comfort in it and eternal life at the end of it. 2. That those are in the wrong that do not only not receive instruction, but wilfully and obstinately refuse it when it is offered them. They will not be taught their duty because it discovers their faults to them; that instruction which carries reproof in it they have a particular aversion to, and certainly they err; it is a sign that they err in judgment, and have false notions of good and evil; it is a cause of their erring in conversation. The traveller that has missed his way, and cannot bear to be told of it and shown the right way, must needs err still, err endlessly; he certainly misses *the way of life.*

Verse 18

Observe here, Malice is folly and wickedness. 1. It is so when it is concealed by flattery and dissimulation: He *is a fool,* though he may think himself a politician, *that hides hatred with lying lips,* lest, if it break out, he should be ashamed before men and should lose the opportunity of gratifying his malice. *Lying lips* are bad enough of themselves, but have a peculiar malignity in them when they are made *a cloak of maliciousness.* But he *is a fool* who thinks to hide any thing from God. 2. It is no better when it is vented in spiteful and mischievous language: He *that utters slander is a fool* too, for God will sooner or later bring forth that righteousness as the light which he endeavours to cloud, and will find an expedient to roll the reproach away.

Verse 19

We are here admonished concerning the government of the tongue, that necessary duty of a Christian. 1. It is good to say little, because *in the multitude of words there wanteth not sin,* or *sin doth not cease.* Usually, those that speak much speak much amiss, and among many words there cannot but be many idle words, which they must shortly give an account of. Those that love to hear themselves talk do not consider what work they are making for repentance; for that will be wanted, and first or last will be had, where *there wanteth not sin.* 2. It is therefore good to *keep our mouth as with a bridle: He that refrains his lips,* that often checks himself, suppresses what he has thought, and holds in that which would transpire, is a wise man; it is an evidence of his wisdom, and he therein consults his own peace. Little said is soon amended, Amos 5:13; Jam. 1:19.

Verses 20–21

We are here taught how to value men, not by their wealth and preferment in the world, but by their virtue.

I. Good men are good for something. Though they may be poor and low in the world, and may not have power and riches to do good with, yet, as long as they have a mouth to speak, that will make them valuable and useful, and upon that account we must honour those that fear the Lord, because *out of the good treasure of their heart they bring forth good things.* 1. This makes them valuable: *The tongue of the just is as choice silver;* they are sincere, freed from the dross of guile and evil design. God's words are compared to *silver purified* (Ps. 12:6), for they may be relied on; and such are the words of just men. They are of weight and worth, and will enrich those that hear them with wisdom, which is better than *choice silver.* 2. It makes them useful: *The lips of the righteous feed many;* for they are full of the word of God, which is the bread of life, and that sound doctrine wherewith souls are nourished up. Pious discourse is spiritual food to the needy, to the hungry.

II. Bad men are good for nothing. 1. One can get no good by them: *The heart of the wicked is little worth,* and therefore that which comes out of the abundance of his heart cannot be worth much. His principles, his notions, his thoughts, his purposes, and all the things that fill him, and affect him, are worldly and carnal, and therefore of no value. *He that is of the earth speaks of the earth,* and neither understands nor relishes the things of God, Jn. 3:31; 1 Co. 2:14. The wicked man pretends that, though he does not talk of religion as the just do, yet he has it within him, and thanks God that his heart is good; but he that searches the heart here says the contrary: *It is nothing worth.* 2. One can do no good to them. While many are fed by *the lips of the righteous, fools die for want of wisdom;* and fools indeed they are to die for want of that which they might so easily come by. *Fools die for want of a heart* (so the word is); they perish for want of consideration and resolution; they have no heart to do any thing for their own good. While the righteous feed others fools starve themselves.

Verse 22

Worldly wealth is that which most men have their hearts very much upon, but they generally mistake both in the nature of the thing they desire and in the way by which they hope to obtain it; we are therefore told here, 1. What that wealth is which is indeed desirable, not having abundance only, but having it and *no sorrow with it,* no disquieting care to get and keep it, no vexation of spirit in the enjoyment of it, no tormenting grief for the loss of it, no guilt contracted by the abuse of it — to have it and to have a heart to take the comfort of it, to do good with it and to serve God with joyfulness and gladness of heart in the use of it. 2. Whence this desirable wealth is to be expected, not by making ourselves drudges to the world (Ps. 127:2), but by *the blessing of God.* It is this that *makes rich and adds no sorrow;* what comes from the love of God has the grace of God for its companion, to preserve the soul from those turbulent lusts and passions of which, otherwise, the increase of riches if commonly the incentive. He had said (v. 4), *The hand of the diligent makes rich,* as a means; but here he ascribes it to *the blessing of the Lord;* but that blessing is upon *the hand of the diligent.* It is thus in spiritual riches. Diligence in getting them is our duty, but God's blessing and grace must have all the glory of that which is acquired, Deu. 8:17, 18.

Verse 23

Here is, 1. Sin exceedingly sinful: *It is as laughter to a fool to do mischief;* it is as natural to him, and as pleasant, as it is to a man to laugh. *Wickedness is his Isaac* (that is the word here); it is his delight, his darling, and that in which he pleases himself. He makes a laughing matter of sin. When he is warned not to sin, from the consideration of the law of God and the revelation of his wrath against sin, he makes a jest of the admonition, and laughs at the shaking of the spear; when he has sinned, instead of sorrowing for it, he boasts of it, ridicules reproofs, and laughs away the convictions of his own conscience, ch. 14:9. 2. Wisdom exceedingly wise, for it carries along with it the evidence of its own excellency; it may be predicated of itself, and this is encomium enough; you need say no more

in praise of *a man of understanding* than this, "He is an *understanding man; he has wisdom;* he is so wise as not to do mischief, or if he has, through oversight, offended, he is so wise as not to make a jest of it." Or, to pronounce wisdom wise indeed, read it thus: *As it is a sport to a fool to do mischief, so it is to a man of understanding to have wisdom and to show it.* Besides the future recompence, a good man has as much present pleasure in the restraints and exercises of religion as sinners can pretend to in the liberties and enjoyments of sin, and much more, and much better.

Verses 24–25

It is here said, and said again, to the righteous, that *it shall be well with them,* and to the wicked, *Woe to them;* and these are set the one over against the other, for their mutual illustration.

I. It shall be as ill with the wicked as they can fear, and as well with the righteous as they can desire. 1. The wicked, it is true, buoy themselves up sometimes in their wickedness with vain hopes which will deceive them, but at other times they cannot but be haunted with just fears, and those *fears shall come upon them;* the God they provoke will be every whit as terrible as they, when they are under their greatest damps, apprehend him to be. *As is thy fear, so is thy wrath,* Ps. 90:11. Wicked men fear the punishment of sin, but they have not wisdom to improve their fears by making their escape, and so the thing they feared comes upon them, and their present terrors are earnests of their future torments. 2. The righteous, it is true, sometimes have their fears, but their desire is towards the favour of God and a happiness in him, and that *desire shall be granted.* According to their faith, not according to their fear, it shall be *unto them,* Ps. 37:4.

II. The prosperity of the wicked shall quickly end, but the happiness of the righteous shall never end, v. 25. The wicked make a great noise, hurry themselves and others, like a *whirlwind,* which threatens to bear down all before it; but, like a *whirlwind,* they are presently gone, and they pass irrecoverably; they are *no more;* all about them are quiet and glad when the storm is over, Ps. 37:10, 36; Job 20:5. *The righteous,* on the contrary, make no show; they lie hid, like a *foundation,* which is low and out of sight, but they are fixed in their resolution to cleave to God, established in virtue, and they shall be an *everlasting foundation,* immovably good. He that is holy shall be holy still and immovably happy; his hope is built on a rock, and therefore not shocked by the storm, Mt. 7:24. *The righteous is the pillar of the world* (so some read it); the world stands for their sakes; the holy seed is the substance thereof.

Verse 26

Observe, 1. Those that are of a slothful disposition, that love their ease and cannot apply their minds to any business, are not fit to be employed, no, not so much as to be sent on an errand, for they will neither deliver a message with any care nor make any haste back. Such therefore are very unmeet to be ministers, Christ's messengers; he will not own the sending forth of sluggards into his harvest. 2. Those that are guilty of so great an oversight as to entrust such with any affair, and put confidence in them, will certainly have vexation with them. A slothful servant is to his master as uneasy and troublesome as *vinegar to the teeth* and *smoke to the eyes;* he provokes his passion, as vinegar sets the teeth on edge, and occasions him grief to see his business neglected and undone, as smoke sets the eyes a weeping.

Verses 27–28

Observe, 1. Religion lengthens men's lives and crowns their hopes. *What man is he that loves life?* Let him *fear God,* and that will secure him from many things that would prejudice his life, and secure to him life enough in this world and eternal life in the other; *the fear of the Lord* will add days more than was expected, will add them endlessly, will prolong them to the days of eternity. *What man is he that would see good days?* Let him be religious, and then his days shall not only be many, but happy, very happy as well as very many, for *the hope of the righteous shall be gladness;* they shall have what they hope for, to their unspeakable satisfaction. It is something future and unseen that they place their happiness in (Rom. 8:24, 25), not what they have in hand, but what they have in hope, and their hope will shortly be swallowed up in fruition, and it will be their everlasting *gladness. Enter thou into the joy of thy Lord.* 2. Wickedness shortens men's lives, and frustrates their hopes: *The years of the wicked,* that are spent in the pleasures of sin and the drudgery of the world, *shall be shortened.* Cut down the trees that cumber the ground. And whatever comfort or happiness a wicked man promises himself, in this world or the other, he will be frustrated; for *the expectation of the wicked shall perish;* his hope shall be turned into endless despair.

Verses 29–30

These two verses are to the same purport with those next before, intimating the happiness of the godly and the misery of the wicked; it is necessary that this be inculcated upon us, so loth are we to believe and consider it. 1. Strength and stability are entailed upon integrity: *The way of the Lord* (the providence of God, the way in which he walks towards us) *is strength to the upright,* confirms him in his uprightness. All God's dealings with him, merciful and afflictive, serve to quicken him to his duty and animate him against his discouragements. Or *the way of the Lord* (the way of godliness, in which he appoints us to walk) is *strength to the upright;* the closer we keep to that way, the more our hearts are enlarged to proceed in it, the better fitted we are both for services and sufferings. A good conscience, kept pure from sin, gives a man boldness in a dangerous time, and constant diligence in duty makes a man's work easy in a busy time. The more we do for God the more we may do, Job 17:9. That *joy of the Lord* which is to be found only in the *way of the Lord* will be our strength (Neh. 8:10), and therefore *the righteous shall never be removed.* Those that have an established virtue have an established peace and happiness which nothing can rob them of; they *have an everlasting foundation, v.* 25. 2. Ruin and destruction are the certain consequences of wickedness. *The wicked shall not* only not inherit the earth, though they lay up their treasure in it, but they shall not so much as *inhabit the earth;* God's judgments will root them out. *Destruction,* swift and sure destruction, *shall be to the workers of iniquity,* destruction from the presence of the Lord and the glory of his power. Nay, that way of the Lord which is the strength of the upright is consumption and terror *to the workers of iniquity;* the same gospel which to the one is a *savour of life unto life* to the other is a *savour of death unto death;* the same providence, like the same sun, softens the one and hardens the other, Hos. 14:9.

Verses 31–32

Here, as before, men are judged of, and, accordingly, are justified or condemned, by their words, Mt. 12:37. 1. It is both the proof and the praise of a man's wisdom and goodness that he speaks wisely and well. A good man, in his discourse, *brings forth wisdom* for the benefit of others. God gives him wisdom as a reward of his righteousness (Eccl. 2:26), and he, in gratitude for that gift and justice to the giver, does good with it, and with his wise and pious discourses edifies many. He *knows what is acceptable,* what discourse will be pleasing to God (for that is it that he studies more than to oblige the company), and what will be agreeable both to the speaker and to the hearers, what will become him and benefit them, and that he will speak. 2. It is the sin, and will be the ruin, of a wicked man, that he speaks wickedly like himself. *The mouth of the wicked speaks frowardness,* that which is displeasing to God and provoking to those he converses with; and what is the issue of it? Why, *the froward tongue shall be cut out,* as surely as the *flattering one,* Ps. 12:3.

CHAPTER 11

Verse 1

As religion towards God is a branch of universal righteousness (he is not an honest man that is not devout), so righteousness towards men is a branch of true religion, for he is not a godly man that is not honest, nor can he expect that his devotion should be accepted; for, 1. Nothing is more offensive to God than deceit in commerce. *A false balance* is here put for all manner of unjust and fraudulent practices in dealing with any person, which are all an *abomination to the Lord,* and render those abominable to him that allow themselves in the use of such accursed arts of thriving. It is an affront to justice, which God is the patron of, as well as a wrong to our neighbour, whom God is the protector of. Men make light of such frauds, and think there is no sin in that which there is money to be got by, and, while it passes undiscovered, they cannot blame themselves for it; a blot is no blot till it is hit, Hos. 12:7, 8. But they are not the less an abomination to God, who will be the avenger of those that are defrauded by their brethren. 2. Nothing is more pleasing to God than fair and honest dealing, nor more necessary to make us and our devotions acceptable to him: *A just weight is his delight.* He himself goes by a just weight, and holds the scale of judgment with an even hand, and therefore is pleased with those that are herein followers of him. A balance cheats, under pretence of doing right most exactly, and therefore is the greater abomination to God.

Verse 2

Observe, 1. How he that exalts himself is here abased, and contempt put upon him. *When pride comes then comes shame.* Pride is a sin which men have reason to be themselves ashamed of; it is a shame to a man who springs out of the earth, who lives upon alms, depends upon God, and has forfeited all he has, to be proud. It is a sin which others cry out shame on and look upon with disdain; he that is haughty makes himself contemptible; it is a sin for which God often brings men down, as he did Nebuchadnezzar and Herod, whose ignominy immediately attended their vain-glory; for God *resists the proud,* contradicts them, and counterworks them, in the thing they are proud of, Isa. 2:11, etc. 2. How he that humbles himself is here exalted, and a high character is given him. As with the proud there is folly, and will be shame, so *with the lowly there is wisdom,* and will be honour, for a man's wisdom gains him respect and makes his face to shine before men; or, if any be so base as to trample upon the humble, God will give them grace which will be their glory. Considering how safe, and quiet, and easy, those are that are of a humble spirit, what communion they have with God and comfort in themselves, we will say, *With the lowly is wisdom.*

Verse 3

It is not only promised that God will guide the upright, and threatened that he will destroy the transgressors, but, that we may be the more fully assured of both, it is here represented as if the nature of the thing were such on both sides that it would do it itself. 1. The integrity of an honest man will itself be his guide in the way of duty and the way of safety. His principles are fixed, his rule is certain, and therefore his way is plain; his sincerity keeps him steady, and he needs not tack about every time the wind turns, having no other end to drive at than to keep a good conscience. *Integrity and uprightness* will *preserve* men, Ps. 25:21. 2. The iniquity of a bad man will itself be his ruin. As the plainness of a good man will be his protection, though he is ever so much exposed, so the perverseness of sinners will be their destruction, though they think themselves eve so well fortified. They shall fall into pits of their own digging, *ch.* 5:22.

Verse 4

Note, 1. The *day of death* will be a *day of wrath.* It is a messenger of God's wrath; therefore when Moses had meditated on man's mortality he takes occasion thence to admire *the power of God's anger,* Ps. 110:11. It is a debt owing, not to nature, but to God's justice. *After death the judgment,* and that is a *day of wrath,* Rev. 6:17. 2. Riches will stand men in no stead that day. They will neither put by the stroke nor ease the pain, much less take out the sting; what profit will this world's birth-rights be of then? In the day of public judgments riches often expose men rather than protect them, Eze. 7:19. 3. It is righteousness only that will *deliver from* the evil of *death.* A good conscience will make death easy, and take off the terror of it; it is the privilege of the righteous only not to be hurt of the second death, and so not much hurt by the first.

Verses 5–6

These two verses are, in effect, the same, and both to the same purport with *v.* 3. For the truths are here of such certainty and weight that they cannot be too often inculcated. Let us govern ourselves by these principles.

I. That the ways of religion are plain and safe, and in them we may enjoy a holy security. A living principle of honesty and grace will be, 1. Our best direction in the right way, in every doubtful case to say to us, *This is the way, walk in it.* He that acts without a guide looks right on and sees his way before him. 2. Our best deliverance from every false way: *The righteousness of the upright* shall be armour of proof to them, to deliver them from the allurements of the devil and the world, and from their menaces.

The ways of wickedness are dangerous and destructive: *The wicked shall fail* into misery and ruin *by their own wickedness,* and be *taken in their own naughtiness* as in a snare. *O Israel! thou hast destroyed thyself.* Their sin will be their punishment; that very thing by which they contrived to shelter themselves will make against them.

Verse 7

Note, 1. Even wicked men, while they live, may keep up a confident expectation of a happiness when they die, or at least a happiness in this world. The hypocrite has his hope, in which he wraps himself as the spider in her web. The worldling expects great matters from his wealth; he calls it *goods laid up for many years,* and hopes to take his ease in it and to be merry; but in death their expectation will be frustrated: the worldling must leave this world which he expected to continue in and the hypocrite will come short of that world which he expected to remove to, Job 27:8. 2. It will be the great aggravation of the misery of wicked people that their hopes will sink into despair just when they expect them to be crowned with fruition. When a godly man dies his expectations are outdone, and all his fears vanish; but when a wicked man dies his expectations are dashed, dashed to pieces; in that very day his thoughts perish with which he had pleased himself, his hopes vanish.

Verse 8

As always in death, so sometimes in life, the righteous are remarkably favoured and the wicked crossed. 1. Good people are helped out of the distresses which they thought themselves lost in, and their feet are set in a large room, Ps. 66:12; 34:19. God has found out a way to deliver his people even when they have despaired and their enemies have triumphed, as if the wilderness had shut them in. 2. The wicked have fallen into the distresses which they thought themselves far from, nay, which they had been instrumental to bring the righteous into, so that they seem to come in their stead, as a ransom for the just. Mordecai is saved from the gallows, Daniel from the lion's den, and Peter from the prison; and their persecutors *come in their stead.* The Israelites are delivered out of the Red Sea and the Egyptians drowned in it. So precious are the saints in God's eye that he *gives men for them,* Isa. 43:3, 4.

Verse 9

Here is, 1. Hypocrisy designing ill. It is not only the murderer with his sword, but the *hypocrite with his mouth,* that *destroys his neighbour,* decoying him into sin, or into mischief, by the specious pretences of kindness and goodwill. *Death and life are in the power of the tongue,* but no tongue more fatal than the flattering tongue. 2. Honesty defeating the design and escaping the snare: *Through knowledge* of the devices of Satan *shall the just be delivered* from the snares which the hypocrite has laid for him; seducers shall not deceive the elect. By the knowledge of God, and the scriptures, and their own hearts, shall the just be delivered from those that lie in wait to deceive, and so to destroy, Rom. 16:18, 19.

Verses 10–11

It is here observed,

I. That good men are generally well-beloved by their neighbours, but nobody cares for wicked people. 1. It is true there are some few that are enemies to the righteous, that are prejudiced against God and godliness, and are therefore vexed to see good men in power and prosperity; but all indifferent persons, even those that have no great stock of religion themselves, have a good word for a good man; and therefore *when it goes well with the righteous,* when they are advanced and put into a capacity of doing good according to their desire, it is so much the better for all about them, and *the city rejoices.* For the honour and encouragement of virtue, and as it is the accomplishment of the promise of God, we should be glad to see virtuous men prosper in the world, and brought into reputation. 2. Wicked people may perhaps have here and there a well-wisher among those who are altogether such as themselves, but among the generality of their neighbours they get ill-will; they may be feared, but they are not loved, and therefore *when they perish there is shouting;* every body takes a pleasure in seeing them disgraced and disarmed, removed out of places of trust and power, chased out of the world, and wishes no greater loss may come to the town, the rather because they hope *the righteous may come in their stead,* as they into trouble instead of the righteous, *v.* 8. Let a sense of honour therefore keep us in the paths of virtue, that we may live desired and die lamented, and not be hissed off the stage, Job 27:23; Ps. 52:6.

II. That there is good reason for this, because those that are good do good, but *(as saith the proverb of the ancients) wickedness proceeds from the wicked.* 1. *Good men are public blessings — Vir bonus est commune bonum. By the blessing of the upright,* the blessings with which they are blessed, which enlarge their sphere of usefulness, — by the blessings with which they bless their neighbours, their advice, their example, their prayers, and all the instances of their serviceableness to the public interest, — by the blessings with which God blesses others for their sake, — by these *the city is exalted* and made more comfortable to the inhabitants, and more considerable among its neighbours. 2. Wicked men are public nuisances, not only the burdens, but the plagues of their generation. The city is *overthrown by the mouth of the wicked,* whose evil communications corrupt good manners, are enough to debauch a town, to ruin virtue in it, and bring down the judgments of God upon it.

Verses 12–13

I. Silence is here recommended as an instance of true friendship, and a preservative of it, and therefore an evidence, 1. Of wisdom: *A man of understanding,* that has rule over his own spirit, if he be provoked, *holds his peace,* that he may neither give vent to his passion nor kindle the passion of others by any opprobrious language or peevish reflections. 2. Of sincerity: *He that is of a faithful spirit,* that is true, not only to his own promise, but to the interest of his friend, *conceals every matter* which, if divulged, may turn to the prejudice of his neighbour.

II. This prudent friendly concealment is here opposed to two very bad vices of the tongue: — 1. Speaking scornfully of a man to his face: *He that is void of wisdom* discovers his folly by this; he *despises his neighbour,* calls him *Raca,* and *Thou fool,* upon the least provocation, and tramples upon him as not worthy to be set with the dogs of his flock. He undervalues himself who thus undervalues one that is made of the same mould. 2. Speaking spitefully of a man behind his back: *A tale-bearer,* that carries all the stories he can pick up, true or false, from house to house, to make mischief and sow discord, *reveals secrets* which he has been entrusted with, and so breaks the laws, and forfeits all the privileges, of friendship and conversation.

Verse 14

Here is, 1. The bad omen of a kingdom's ruin: *Where no counsel is,* no consultation at all, but every thing done rashly, or no prudent consultation for the common good, but only caballing for parties and divided interests, *the people fall,* crumble into factions, fall to pieces, fall together by the ears, and fall an easy prey to their common enemies. Councils of war are necessary to the operations of war; two eyes see more than one; and mutual advice is in order to mutual assistance. 2. The good presage of a kingdom's prosperity: *In the multitude of counsellors,* that see their need one of another, and act in concert and with concern for the public welfare, *there is safety;* for what prudent methods one discerns not another may. In our private affairs we shall often find it to our advantage to advise with many; if they agree in their advice, our way will be the more clear; if they differ, we shall hear what is to be said on all sides, and be the better able to determine.

Verse 15

Here we are taught, 1. In general, that we may not use our estates as we will (he that gave them to us has reserved to himself a power to direct us how we shall use them, for they are not our own; we are but stewards), and further that God in his law consults our interests and teaches us that charity which begins at home, as well as that which must not end there. There is a good husbandry which is good divinity, and a discretion in ordering our affairs which is part of the character of a good man, Ps. 112:5. Every man must be just to his family, else he is not true to his stewardship. 2. In particular, that we must not enter rashly into suretiship, (1.) Because there is danger of bringing ourselves into trouble by it, and our families too when we are gone: *He that is surety for a stranger,* for any one that asks him and promises him to be bound for him another time, for one whose person perhaps he knows, and thinks he knows his circumstances, but is mistaken, he *shall smart for it. Contritione conteretur — he shall be certainly and sadly crushed and broken by it,* and perhaps become a bankrupt. Our Lord Jesus was surety for us when we were strangers, nay, enemies, and he smarted for it; *it pleased the Lord to bruise him.* (2.) Because he that resolves against all such suretiship keeps upon sure grounds, which a man may do if he take care not to launch out any further into business than his own credit will carry him, so that he needs not ask others to be bound for him.

Verse 16

Here, 1. It is allowed that *strong men retain riches,* that those who bustle in the world, who are men of spirit and interest, and are able to make their part good against all who stand in their way, are likely to keep what they have and to get more, while those who are weak are preyed upon by all about them. 2. It is taken for granted that *a gracious woman* is as solicitous to preserve her reputation for wisdom and modesty, humility and courtesy, and all those other graces that are the true ornaments of her sex, as strong men are to secure their estates; and those women who are truly gracious will, in like manner, effectually secure their honour by their prudence and good conduct. *A gracious woman* is as honourable as a valiant man and her honour is as sure.

Verse 17

It is a common principle, Every one for himself. *Proximus egomet mihi — None so near to me as myself.* Now, if this be rightly understood, it will be a reason for the cherishing of gracious dispositions in ourselves and the crucifying of corrupt ones. We are friends or enemies to ourselves, even in respect of present comfort, according as we are or are not governed by religious principles. 1. A *merciful,* tender, good humoured *man, does good to his own soul,* makes and keeps himself easy. He has the pleasure of doing his duty, and contributing to the comfort of those that are to him as *his own soul;* for *we are members one of another.* He that waters others with his temporal good things shall find that God will water him with his spiritual blessings, which will do the best *good to his own soul.* See Isa. 58:7, etc. *If thou hide not thy eyes from thy own flesh,* but do good to others, as to thyself, if thou do good with thy own soul and *draw that out to the hungry,* thou wilt do good to thy own soul; for the Lord shall *satisfy thy soul* and *make fat thy bones.* Some make it part of the character of a *merciful man,* that he will make much of himself; that disposition which inclines him to be charitable to others will oblige him to allow himself also that which is convenient and to *enjoy the good of all his labour.* We may by the *soul* understand the *inward man,* as the apostle calls it, and then it teaches us that the first and great act of mercy is to provide well for our own souls the necessary supports of the spiritual life. 2. A *cruel,* froward, ill-natured man, *troubles his own flesh,* and so his sin becomes his punishment; he starves and dies for want of what he has, because he has not a heart to use it either for the good of others of for his own. He is vexatious to his nearest relations, that are, and should be, to him as his own flesh, Eph. 5:29. Envy, and malice, and greediness of the world, are the rottenness of the bones and the consumption of the flesh.

Verse 18

Note, 1. Sinners put a most fatal cheat upon themselves: *The wicked works a deceitful work,* builds himself a house upon the sand, which will deceive him when the storm comes, promises himself *that* by his sin which he will never gain; nay, it is cutting his throat when it smiles upon him. *Sin deceived me, and by it slew me.* 2. Saints lay up the best securities for themselves: He *that sows righteousness,* that is good, and makes it his business to do good, with an eye to a future recompence, he shall have *a sure reward;* it is made as sure to him as eternal truth can make it. If the seedness fail not, the harvest shall not, Gal. 6:8.

Verse 19

It is here shown that righteousness, not only by the divine judgment, will end in life, and wickedness in death, but that righteousness, in its own nature, has a direct tendency to life and wickedness to death. 1. True holiness is true happiness; it is a preparative for it, a pledge and earnest of it. *Righteousness* inclines, disposes, and leads, the soul *to life.* 2. In like manner, those that indulge themselves in sin are fitting themselves for destruction. The more violent a man is in sinful pursuits the more eagerly bent he is upon his own destruction; he awakens it when it seemed to slumber and hastens it when it seemed to linger.

Verse 20

It concerns us to know what God hates and what he loves, that we may govern ourselves accordingly, may avoid his displeasure and recommend ourselves to his favour. Now here we are told, 1. That nothing is more offensive to God than hypocrisy and double-dealing, for these are signified by the word which we translate *frowardness,* pretending justice, but intending wrong, walking in crooked ways, to avoid discovery. Those *are of a froward heart* who act in contradiction to that which is good, under a profession of that which is good, and such are, more than any sinners, an *abomination to the Lord,* Isa. 65:5. 2. That nothing is more pleasing to God than sincerity and plain-dealing: *Such as are upright in their way,* such as aim and act with integrity, such as have their conversation in the world *in simplicity and godly sincerity, not with fleshly wisdom,* these God delights in, these he even boasts of *(Hast thou considered my servant Job?)* and will have us to admire. *Behold an Israelite indeed!*

Verse 21

Observe, 1. That confederacies in sin shall certainly be broken, and shall not avail to protect the sinners: *Though hand join in hand,* though there are many that concur by their practice to keep wickedness in countenance, and engage to stand by one another in defending it against all the attacks of virtue and justice, — though they are in league for the support and propagation of it, — though wicked children tread in the steps of their wicked parents, and resolve to keep up the trade, in defiance of religion, — yet all this will not protect them from the justice of God; they shall not be held guiltless; it will not excuse them to say that they did as the most did and as their company did; they *shall not be unpunished;* witness the flood that was brought upon a whole world of ungodly men. Their number, and strength, and unanimity in sin will stand them in no stead when the day of vengeance comes. 2. That entails of religion shall certainly be blessed: *The seed of the righteous,* that follow the steps of their righteousness, though they may fall into trouble, shall, in due time, *be delivered.* Though justice may come slowly to punish the wicked, and mercy may come slowly to save the righteous, yet both will come surely. Sometimes *the seed of the righteous,* though they are not themselves righteous, are delivered for the sake of their godly ancestors, as Israel often, and the seed of David.

Verse 22

By *discretion* here we must understand *religion* and *grace,* a true taste and relish (so the word signifies) of the honours and pleasures that attend an unspotted virtue; so that *a woman without discretion* is a woman of a loose and dissolute conversation; and then observe, 1. It is taken for granted here that beauty or comeliness of body is *as a jewel of gold,* a thing very valuable, and, where there is wisdom and grace to guard against the temptations of it, it is a great ornament, *(Gratior est pulchro veniens de corpore virtus — Virtue appears peculiarly graceful when associated with beauty);* but a foolish wanton woman, of a light carriage, is fitly compared to a swine, though she be ever so handsome, wallowing in the mire of filthy lusts, with which the mind and conscience are defiled, and, though washed, returning to them. 2. It is lamented that beauty should be so abused as it is by those that have not modesty with it. It seems ill-bestowed upon them; it is quite misplaced, *as a jewel in a swine's snout,* with which he roots in the dunghill. If beauty be not guarded by virtue, the virtue is exposed by the beauty. It may be applied to all other bodily endowments and accomplishments; it is a pity that those should have them who have not discretion to use them well.

Verse 23

This tells us what *the desire* and *expectation of the righteous* and *of the wicked* are and how they will prove, what they would have and what they shall have. 1. *The righteous* would have *good, only good;* all they desire is that it may go well with all about them; they wish no hurt to any, but happiness to all; as to themselves, their desire is not to gratify any evil lust, but to obtain the favour of a good God and to preserve the peace of a good conscience; and good they shall have, that good which they desire, Ps. 37:4. 2. *The wicked* would have *wrath;* they desire the woeful day, that God's judgments may gratify their passion and revenge, may remove those that stand in their way, and that they may make an advantage to themselves by fishing in troubled waters; and wrath they shall have, so shall their doom be. They expect and desire mischief to others, but it shall return upon themselves; as they loved cursing, they shall have enough of it.

Verse 24

Note, 1. It is possible a man may grow rich by prudently spending what he has, may scatter in works of piety, charity, and generosity, and yet may increase; nay, by that means may increase, as the corn is increased by being sown. By cheerfully using what we have our spirits are exhilarated, and so fitted for the business we have to do, by minding which closely what we have is increased; it gains a reputation which contributes to the increase. But it is especially to be ascribed to God; he blesses the giving hand, and so makes it a getting hand, 2 Co. 9:20. *Give, and it shall be given you.* 2. It is possible a man may grow poor by meanly sparing what he has, *withholding more than is meet,* not paying just debts, not relieving the poor, not providing what is convenient for the family, not allowing necessary expenses for the preservation of the goods; this *tends to poverty;* it cramps men's ingenuity and industry, weakens their interest, destroys their credit, and forfeits the blessing of God: and, let men be ever so saving of what they have, if God blast it and blow upon it, it comes to nothing. *A fire not blown* shall *consume it,* Hag. 1:6, 9.

Verse 25

So backward we are to works of charity, and so ready to think that giving undoes us, that we need to have it very much pressed upon us how much it is for our own advantage to do good to others, as before, *v.* 17. 1. We shall have the comfort of it in our own bosoms: *The liberal soul,* the soul of blessing, that prays for the afflicted and provides for them, that scatters blessings with gracious lips and generous hands, that soul *shall be made fat* with true pleasure and enriched with more grace. 2. We shall have the recompence of it both from God and man: *He that waters* others with the streams of his bounty *shall be also watered himself;* God will certainly return it in the dews, in the plentiful showers, of his blessing, which he will *pour out, till there be not room enough to receive it,* Mal. 3:10. Men that have any sense of gratitude will return it if there be occasion; the *merciful shall find mercy* and the kind be kindly dealt with. 3. We shall be enabled still to do yet more good: *He that waters, even he shall be as rain* (so some read it); he shall be recruited as the clouds are which return after the rain, and shall be further useful and acceptable, as the rain to the new-mown grass. *he that teaches shall learn* (so the Chaldee reads it); he that uses his knowledge in teaching others shall himself be taught of God; to him that has, and uses what he has, more shall be given.

Verse 26

See here, 1. What use we are to make of the gifts of God's bounty; we must not hoard them up merely for our own advantage, that we may be enriched by them, but we must bring them forth for the benefit of others, that they may be supported and maintained by them. It is a sin, when corn is dear and scarce, to withhold it, in hopes that it will still grow dearer, so to keep up and advance the market, when it is already so high that the poor suffer by it; and at such a time it is the duty of those that have stocks of corn by them to consider the poor, and to be willing to sell at the market-price, to be content with moderate profit, and not aim to make a gain of God's judgments. It is a noble and extensive piece of charity for those that have stores wherewithal to do it to help to keep the markets low when the price of our commodities grows excessive. 2. What regard we are to have to the voice of the people. We are not to think it an indifferent thing, and not worth heeding, whether we have the ill will and word, or the good will and word, of our neighbours, their prayers or their curses; for here we are taught to dread their curses, and forego our own profit rather than incur them; and to court their blessings, and be at some expense to purchase them. Sometimes, *vox populi est vox Dei — the voice of the people is the voice of God.*

Verse 27

Observe, 1. Those that are industrious to do good in the world get themselves beloved both with God and man: *He that rises early to that which is good* (so the word is), that seeks opportunities of serving his friends and relieving the poor, and lays out himself therein, *procures favour.* All about him love him, and speak well of him, and will be ready to do him a kindness; and, which is better than that, better than life, he has God's lovingkindness. 2. Those that are industrious to do mischief are preparing ruin for themselves: *It shall come unto them;* some time or other they will be paid in their own coin. And, observe, *seeking mischief* is here set in opposition to *seeking good;* for those that are not doing good are doing hurt.

Verse 28

Observe, 1. Our riches will fail us when we are in the greatest need: *He that trusts in them,* as if they would secure him the favour of God and be his protection and portion, *shall fall,* as a man who lays his weight on a broken reed, which will not only disappoint him, but run into his hand and pierce him. 2. Our righteousness will stand us in stead when our riches fail us: *The righteous shall* then *flourish as a branch,* the branch of righteousness, like a tree whose leaf shall not wither, Ps. 1:3. Even in death, when riches fail men, the *bones* of the righteous *shall flourish as a herb,* Isa. 66:14. When those that take root in the world wither those that are grafted into Christ and partake of his root and fatness shall be fruitful and flourishing.

Verse 29

Two extremes in the management of family-affairs are here condemned and the ill consequences of them foretold: — 1. Carefulness and carnal policy, on the one hand. There are those that by their extreme earnestness in pursuit of the world, their anxiety about their business and fretfulness about their losses, their strictness with their servants and their niggardliness towards their families, *trouble their own houses* and give continual vexation to all about them; while others think, by supporting factions and feuds in their families, which are really a trouble to their houses, to serve some turn for themselves, and either to get or to save by it. But they will both be disappointed; they will *inherit the wind.* All they will get by these arts will not only be empty and worthless as the wind, but noisy and troublesome, vanity and vexation. 2. Carelessness and want of common prudence, on the other. He that is a fool in his business, that either minds it not or goes awkwardly about it, that has no contrivance and consideration, no only loses his reputation and interest, but becomes a *servant to the wise in heart.* He is impoverished, and forced to work for his living; while those that manage wisely raise themselves, and come to have dominion over him, and others like him. It is rational, and very fit, that *the fool* should *be servant to the wise in heart,* and upon that account, among others, we are bound to submit our wills to the will of God, and to be subject to him, because we are fools and he is infinitely wise.

Verse 30

This shows what great blessings good men are, especially those that are eminently wise, to the places where they live, and therefore how much to be valued. 1. The righteous are as *trees of life;* the fruits of their piety and charity, their instructions, reproofs, examples, and prayers, their interest in heaven, and their influence upon earth, are like the fruits of that tree, precious and useful, contributing to the support and nourishment of the spiritual life in many; they are the ornaments of paradise, God's church on earth, for whose sake it stands. 2. The wise are something more; they are as trees of knowledge, not forbidden, but commanded knowledge. *He that is wise,* by communicating his wisdom, *wins souls,* wins upon them to bring them in love with God and holiness, and so wins them over into the interests of God's kingdom among men. The wise are said to *turn many to righteousness,* and that is the same with winning souls here, Dan. 12:3. Abraham's proselytes are called *the souls that he had gotten,* Gen. 12:5. Those that would win souls have need of wisdom to know how to deal with them; and those that do win souls show that they are wise.

Verse 31

This, I think, is the only one of Solomon's proverbs that has that note of attention prefixed to it, *Behold!* which intimates that it contains not only an evident truth, which may be beheld, but an eminent truth, which must be considered. 1. Some understand both parts of a recompence in displeasure: *The righteous,* if they do amiss, shall be punished for their offences in this world; much more shall wicked people be punished for theirs, which are committed, not through infirmity, but with a high hand. If judgment begin at the house of God, what will become of the ungodly? 1 Pt. 4:17, 18; Lu. 23:31. 2. I rather understand it of a recompence of reward to the righteous and punishment to sinners. Let us behold providential retributions. There are some recompences *in the earth,* in this world, and in the things of this world, which prove that *verily there is a God that judges in the earth* (Ps. 58:11); but they are not universal; many sins go unpunished in the earth, and services unrewarded, which indicates that there is a judgment to come, and that there will be more exact and full retributions in the future state. Many times *the righteous* are *recompensed* for their righteousness here *in the earth,* though that is not the principal, much less the only reward either intended for them or intended by them; but whatever the word of God has promised them, or the wisdom of God sees good for them, they shall have *in the earth. The wicked* also, *and the sinner,* are sometimes remarkably punished in this life, nations, families, particular persons. And if the righteous, who do not deserve the least reward, yet have part of their recompence here on earth, much more shall the wicked, who deserve the greatest punishment, have part of their punishment on earth, as an earnest of worse to come. Therefore *stand in awe and sin not.* If those have two heavens that merit none, much more shall those have two hells that merit both.

CHAPTER 12

Verse 1

We are here taught to try whether we have grace or no by enquiring how we stand affected to the means of grace. 1. Those that have grace and love it will delight in all the instructions that are given them by way of counsel; admonition, or reproof, by the word or providence of God; they will value a good education, and think it not a hardship, but a happiness, to be under a strict and prudent discipline. Those that love a faithful ministry, that value it, and sit under it with pleasure, make it to appear that they *love knowledge.* 2. Those show themselves not only void of grace, but void of common sense, that take it as an affront to be told of their faults, and an imposition upon their liberty to be put in mind of their duty: *He that hates reproof is* not only foolish, but *brutish,* like the horse and the mule that have no understanding, or the ox that kicks against the goad. Those that desire to live in loose families and societies, where they may be under no check, that stifle the convictions of their own consciences, and count those their enemies that tell them the truth, are the *brutish* here meant.

Verse 2

Note, 1. We are really as we are with God. Those are happy, truly happy, for ever happy, that *obtain favour of the Lord,* though the world frown upon them, and they find little favour with men; for in God's favour is life, and that is the fountain of all good. On the other hand those are miserable whom *he condemns,* however men may applaud them, and cry them up; whom he condemns he condemns to the second death. 2. We are with God as we are with men, as we have our conversation in this world. Our Father judges of his children very much by their conduct one to another; and therefore *a good man,* that is merciful, and charitable, and does good, *draws out favour from the Lord* by his prayers; but a malicious man, that devises wickedness against his neighbours, *he will condemn,* as unworthy of a place in his kingdom.

Verse 3

Note, 1. Though men may advance themselves by sinful arts, they cannot by such arts settle and secure themselves; though they may get large estates they cannot get such as will abide: *A man shall not be established by wickedness;* it may set him in high places, but they are slippery places, Ps. 73:18. That prosperity which is raised by sin is built on the sand, and so it will soon appear. 2. Though good men may have but little of the world, yet that little will last, and what is honestly got will wear well: *The root of the righteous shall not be moved,* though their branches may be shaken. Those that by faith are rooted in Christ are firmly fixed; in him their comfort and happiness are so rooted as never to be rooted up.

Verse 4

Note, 1. He that is blessed with a good wife is as happy as if he were upon the throne, for she is no less than *a crown* to him. *A virtuous woman,* that is pious and prudent, ingenious and industrious, that is active for the good of her family and looks well to the ways of her household, that makes conscience of her duty in every relation, a woman of spirit, that can bear crosses without disturbance, such a one owns her husband for her head, and therefore she *is a crown* to him, not only a credit and honour to him, as *a crown* is an ornament, but supports and keeps up his authority in his family, as *a crown* is an ensign of power. She is submissive and faithful to him and by her example teaches his children and servants to be so too. 2. He that is plagued with a bad wife is as miserable as if he were upon the dunghill; for she is no better than *rottenness in his bones,* an incurable disease, besides that *she makes him ashamed.* She that is silly and slothful, wasteful and wanton, passionate and ill-tongued, ruins both the credit and comfort of her husband. If he go abroad, his head is hung down, for his wife's faults turn to his reproach. If he retire into himself, his heart is sunk; he is continually uneasy; it is an affliction that preys much upon the spirits.

Verse 5

Note, 1. The word of God is a discerner of the thoughts and intents of the heart, and judges them. We mistake if we imagine that thoughts are free. No, they are under the divine cognizance, and therefore under the divine command. 2. We ought to be observers of the thoughts and intents of our own hearts,, and to judge of ourselves by them; for they are the first-born of the soul, that have most of its image undisguised. Right thoughts are a righteous man's best evidences, as nothing more certainly proves a man wicked than wicked contrivances and designs. A good man may have in his mind bad suggestions, but he does not indulge them and harbour them till they are ripened into bad projects and resolutions. 3. It is a man's honour to mean honestly, and to have his thoughts right, though a word or action may be misplaced, or mistimed, or at least misinterpreted. But it is a man's shame to lie always at catch, to act with deceit, with trick and design, not only with a long reach, but with an overreach.

Verse 6

In the foregoing verse the *thoughts* of the wicked and righteous were compared; here their *words,* and those are as the abundance of the heart is. 1. Wicked people speak mischief to their neighbours; and wicked indeed those are whose *words* are to *lie in wait for blood;* their tongues are swords to those that stand in their way, to good men whom they hate and persecute. See an instance, Lu. 20:20, 21. 2. Good men speak help to their neighbours: The *mouth of the upright* is ready to be opened in the cause of those that are oppressed (*ch.* 31:8), to plead for them, to witness for them, and so to *deliver them,* particularly those whom the wicked *lie in wait* for. A man may sometimes do a very good work with one good word.

Verse 7

We are here taught as before (*v.* 3 and *ch.* 10:25, 30), 1. That the *triumphing of the wicked is short.* They may be exalted for a while, but in a little time they are *overthrown and are not;* their trouble proves their overthrow, and those who made a great show disappear, and their place knows them no more. *Turn the wicked, and they are not;* they stand in such a slippery place that the least touch of trouble brings them down, like the apples of Sodom, which look fair, but touch them and they go to dust. 2. That the prosperity of the righteous has a good bottom and will endure. Death will remove them, but their *house* shall *stand,* their families shall be kept up, and the generation of the upright shall be blessed.

Verse 8

We are here told whence to expect a good name. Reputation is what most have a high regard to and stand much upon. Now it is certain, 1. The best reputation is that which attends virtue and serious piety, and the prudent conduct of life: *A man shall be commended* by all that are wise and good, in conformity to the judgment of God himself, which we are sure is *according to truth,* not according to his riches or preferments, his craft and subtlety, but *according to his wisdom,* the honesty of his designs and the prudent choice of means to compass them. 2. The worst reproach is that which follows wickedness and an opposition to that which is good: *He that is of a perverse heart,* that turns aside to crooked ways, and goes on frowardly in them, *shall be despised.* Providence will bring him to poverty and contempt, and all that have a true sense of honour will despise him as unworthy to be dealt with and unfit to be trusted, as a blemish and scandal to mankind.

Verse 9

Note, 1. It is the folly of some that they covet to make a great figure abroad, take place, and take state, as persons of quality, and yet want necessaries at home, and, if their debts were paid, would not be worth a morsel of bread, nay, perhaps, pinch their bellies to put it on their backs, that they may appear very gay, because fine feathers make fine birds. 2. The condition and character of those is every way better who content themselves in a lower sphere, where they are despised for the plainness of their dress and the meanness of their post, that they may be able to afford themselves, not only necessaries, but conveniences, in their own houses, not only bread, but a servant to attend them and take some of their work off their hands. Those that contrive to live plentifully and comfortably at home are to be preferred before those that affect nothing so much as to appear splendid abroad, though they have not wherewithal to maintain their appearance, whose hearts are unhumbled when their condition is low.

Verse 10

See here, 1. To how great a degree a good man will be merciful; he has not only a compassion for the human nature under its greatest abasements, but he regards even *the life of his beast,* not only because it is his servant, but because it is God's creature, and in conformity to Providence, which *preserves man and beast.* The beasts that are under our care must be provided for, must have convenient food and rest, must in no case be abused or tyrannised over. Balaam was checked for beating his ass. The law took care for oxen. Those therefore are unrighteous men that are not just to the brute-creatures; those that are furious and barbarous to them evidence, and confirm in themselves, a habit of barbarity, and help to make the creation groan, Rom. 8:22. 2. To how great a degree a wicked man will be unmerciful; even his *tender mercies* are *cruel;* that natural compassion which is in him, as a man, is lost, and, by the power of corruption, is turned into hardheartedness; even that which they will have to pass for compassion is really cruel, as Pilate's resolution concerning Christ the innocent, *I will chastise him and let him go.* Their pretended kindnesses are only a cover for purposed cruelties.

Verse 11

Note, 1. It is men's wisdom to mind their business and follow an honest calling, for that is the way, by the blessing of God, to get a livelihood: *He that tills his land,* of which he is either the owner or the occupant, that keeps to his word and is willing to take pains, if he do not raise an estate by it (what need is there of that?), yet he *shall be satisfied with bread,* shall have food convenient for himself and his family, enough to bear his charges comfortably through the world. Even the sentence of wrath has this mercy in it, Thou shalt *eat bread,* though it be *in the sweat of thy face.* Cain was denied this, Gen. 4:12. Be busy, and that is the true way to be easy. Keep thy shop and thy shop will keep thee. *Thou shalt eat the labour of thy hands.* 2. It is men's folly to neglect their business. Those are *void of understanding* that do so, for then they fall in with idle companions and follow them in their evil courses, and so come to want bread, at least bread of their own, and make themselves burdensome to others, eating the bread out of other people's mouths.

Verse 12

See here, 1. What is the care and aim of a wicked man; he would do mischief: He *desires the net of evil men.* "Oh that I were but as cunning as such a man, to make a hand of those I deal with, that I had but his art of over-reaching, that I could but take my revenge on one I have spite to as effectually as he can!" He desires the *strong-hold, or fortress,* of evil men (so some read it), to act securely in doing mischief, that it may not turn upon him. 2. What is the care and aim of a good man: His *root yields fruit,* and is his strength and stability, and that is it that he desires, to do good and to be fixed and confirmed in doing good. The wicked desires only a net wherewith to fish for himself; the righteous desires to yield fruit for the benefit of others and God's glory, Rom. 14:6.

Verse 13

See here, 1. The wicked entangling themselves in trouble by their folly, when God in justice leaves them to themselves. They are often *snared by the transgression of their lips* and their throats are cut with their own tongues. By *speaking evil of dignities* they expose themselves to public justice; by giving ill language they become obnoxious to private resentments, are sued for defamation, and actions on the case for words are brought against them. Many a man has paid dearly in this world for the transgression of his lips, and has felt the lash on his back for want of a bridle upon his tongue, Ps. 64:8. 2. The righteous extricating themselves out of trouble by their own wisdom, when God in mercy comes in for their succour: *The just shall come out* of such troubles as the wicked throw themselves headlong into. It is intimated that the just may perhaps come into trouble; but, *though they fall, they shall not be utterly cast down,* Ps. 34:19.

Verse 14

We are here assured, for our quickening to every good word and work, 1. That even good words will turn to a good account (*v.* 14): *A man shall be satisfied with good* (that is, he shall gain present comfort, that inward pleasure which is truly satisfying) *by the fruit of his mouth,* by the good he does with his pious discourse and prudent advice. While we are teaching others we may ourselves learn, and feed on the bread of life we break to others. 2. That good works, much more, will be abundantly rewarded: The *recompence of a man's hands* for all his work and labour of love, all he has done for the glory of God and the good of his generation, *shall be rendered unto him,* and he shall reap as he has sown. Or it may be understood of the general rule of justice; God will *render to every man according to his work,* Rom. 2:6.

Verse 15

See here, 1. What it is that keeps a fool from being wise: *His way is right in his own eyes;* he thinks he is in the right in every thing he does, and *therefore* asks no advice, because he does not apprehend he needs it; he is confident he knows the way, and cannot miss it, and therefore never enquires the way. The rule he goes by is to do that which is *right in his own eyes,* to walk in the way of his heart. *Quicquid libet, licet — He makes his will his law.* He is a fool that is governed by his eye, and not by his conscience. 2. What it is that keeps a wise man from being a fool; he is willing to be advised, desires to have counsel given him, and *hearkens to counsel,* being diffident of his own judgment and having a value for the direction of those that are wise and good. He is wise (it is a sign he is so, and he is likely to continue so) whose ear is always open to good advice.

Verse 16

Note, 1. Passion is folly: *A fool is known by his anger* (so some read it); not but that a wise man may be angry when there is just cause for it, but then he has his anger under check and direction, is *lord of his anger,* whereas a fool's anger lords it over him. He that, when he is provoked, breaks out into indecent expressions, in words or behaviour, whose passion alters his countenance, makes him outrageous, and leads him to forget himself, *Nabal* certainly is his name and *folly is with him. A fool's indignation is known in the day;* he proclaims it openly, whatever company he is in. Or it is known in the day he is provoked; he cannot defer showing his resentments. Those that are soon angry, that are quickly put into a flame by the least spark, have not that rule which they ought to have over their own spirits. 2. Meekness is wisdom: *A prudent man covers shame.* (1.) He covers the passion that is in his own breast; when his *spirit is stirred,* and his *heart hot within him,* he keeps his mouth as with a bridle, and suppresses his resentments, by smothering and stifling them. Anger is shame, and, though a wise man be not perfectly free from it, yet he is ashamed of it, rebukes it, and suffers not the evil spirit to speak. (2.) He covers the provocation that is given him, the indignity that is done him, winks at it, covers it as much as may be from himself, that he may not carry his resentments of it too far. It is a kindness to ourselves, and contributes to the repose of our own minds, to extenuate and excuse the injuries and affronts that we receive, instead of aggravating them and making the worst of them, as we are apt to do.

Verse 17

Here is, 1. A faithful witness commended for an honest man. *He that* makes conscience of *speaking truth,* and representing every thing fairly, to the best of his knowledge, whether in judgment or in common conversation, whether he be upon his oath or no, he *shows forth righteousness;* he makes it to appear that he is governed and actuated by the principles and laws of righteousness, and he promotes justice by doing honour to it and serving the administration of it. 2. A false witness condemned for a cheat; he *shows forth deceit,* not only how little conscience he makes of deceiving those he deals with, but how much pleasure he takes in it, and that he is possessed by a lying spirit, Jer. 9:3–5. We are all concerned to possess ourselves with a dread and detestation of the sin of lying (Ps. 119:163) and with a reigning principle of honesty.

Verse 18

The tongue is death or life, poison or medicine, as it is used. 1. There are words that are cutting and killing, that are *like the piercings of a sword.* Opprobrious words grieve the spirits of those to whom they are spoken, and cut them to the heart. Slanders, like a sword, wound the reputation of those of whom they are uttered, and perhaps incurably. Whisperings and evil surmises, like a sword, divide and cut asunder the bounds of love and friendship, and separate those that have been dearest to each other. 2. There are words that are curing and healing: *The tongue of the wise is health,* closing up those wounds which the backbiting tongue had given, making all whole again, restoring peace, and accommodating matters in variance and persuading to reconciliation. Wisdom will find out proper remedies against the mischiefs that are made by detraction and evil-speaking.

Verse 19

Be it observed, to the honour of truth, that sacred thing, 1. That, if truth be spoken, it will hold good, and, whoever may be disobliged by it and angry at it, yet it will keep its ground. Great is the truth and will prevail. What is true will be always true; we may abide by it, and need not fear being disproved and put to shame. 2. That, if truth be denied, yet in time it will transpire. A *lying tongue,* that puts false colours upon things, *is but for a moment.* The lie will be disproved. The liar, when he comes to be examined, will be found in several stories, and not consistent with himself as he is that speaks truth; and, when he is found in a lie, he cannot gain his point, nor will he afterwards be credited. Truth may be eclipsed, but it will come to light. Those therefore that make a lie their refuge will find it a refuge of lies.

Verse 20

Note, 1. Those that devise mischief contrive, for the accomplishing of it, how to impose upon others; but it will prove, in the end, that they deceive themselves. Those that *imagine evil,* under colour of friendship, have their hearts full of this and the other advantage and satisfaction which they shall gain by it, but it is all a cheat. Let them imagine it ever so artfully, deceivers will be deceived. 2. Those that consult the good of their neighbours, that study the things which make for peace and give peaceable advice, promote healing attempts and contrive healing methods, and, according as their sphere is, further the public welfare, will have not only the credit, but the comfort of it. They will have joy and success, perhaps beyond their expectation. *Blessed are the peace-makers.*

Verse 21

Note, 1. Piety is a sure protection. If men be sincerely righteous, the righteous God has engaged that no evil shall happen to them. He will, by the power of his grace in them, that principle of justice, keep them from the evil of sin; so that, though they be tempted, yet they shall not be overcome by the temptation, and though they may come into trouble, into many troubles, yet to them those troubles shall have no evil in them, whatever they have to others (Ps. 91:10), for they shall be overruled to work for their good. 2. Wickedness is as sure a destruction. Those that live in contempt of God and man, that are set on mischief, with mischief they *shall be filled.* They shall be more mischievous, shall be *filled with all unrighteousness,* Rom. 1:29. Or they shall be made miserable with the mischiefs that shall come upon them. Those that delight in mischief shall have enough of it. Some read the whole verse thus, *There shall no evil happen to the just, though the wicked be filled with mischief* and spite against them. They shall be safe under the protection of Heaven, though hell itself break loose upon them.

Verse 22

We are here taught, 1. To hate lying, and to keep at the utmost distance from it, because it is an abomination to the Lord, and renders those abominable in his sight that allow themselves in it, not only because it is a breach of his law, but because it is destructive to human society. 2. To make conscience of truth, not only in our words, but in all our actions, because those that *deal truly* and sincerely in all their dealings are *his delight,* and he is well pleased with them. We delight to converse with, and make use of, those that are honest and that we may put a confidence in; such therefore let us be, that we may recommend ourselves to the favour both of God and man.

Verse 23

Note, 1. He that is wise does not affect to proclaim his wisdom, and it is his honour that he does not. He communicates his knowledge when it may turn to the edification of others, but he conceals it when the showing of it would only tend to his own commendation. Knowing men, if they be prudent men, will carefully avoid every thing that savours of ostentation, and not take all occasions to show their learning and reading, but only to use it for good purposes, and then let *their own works praise them. Ars est celare artem — The perfection of art is to conceal it.* 2. He that is foolish cannot avoid proclaiming his folly, and it is his shame that he cannot: *The heart of fools,* by their foolish words and actions, *proclaims foolishness;* either they do not desire to hide it, so little sense have they of good and evil, honour and dishonour, or they know not how to hide it, so little discretion have they in the management of themselves, Eccl. 10:3.

Verse 24

Note, 1. Industry is the way to preferment. Solomon advanced Jeroboam because he saw that he was an industrious young man, and minded his business, 1 Ki. 11:28. Men that take pains in study and serviceableness will thereby gain such an interest and reputation as will give them a dominion over all about them, by which means many have risen strangely. He that has been *faithful in a few things* shall be made *ruler over many things.* The elders, that *labour in the word and doctrine,* are *worthy of double honour;* and those that are diligent when they are young will get that which will enable them to rule, and so to rest, when they are old. 2. Knavery is the way to slavery: *The slothful* and careless, or rather the *deceitful* (for so the word signifies), *shall be under tribute.* Those that, because they will not take pains in an honest calling, live by their shifts and arts of dishonesty, are paltry and beggarly, and will be kept under. Those that are diligent and honest when they are apprentices will come to be masters; but those that are otherwise are the fools who, all their days, must be *servants to the wise in heart.*

Verse 25

Here is, 1. The cause and consequence of melancholy. It is *heaviness in the heart;* it is a load of care, and fear, and sorrow, upon the spirits, depressing them, and disabling them to exert themselves with any vigour on what is to be done or fortitude in what is to borne; it makes them stoop, prostrates and sinks them. Those that are thus oppressed can neither do the duty nor take the comfort of any relation, condition, or conversation. Those therefore that are inclined to it should watch and pray against it. 2. The cure of it: *A good word* from God, applied by faith, *makes it glad;* such a word is that (says one of the rabbin), *Cast thy burden upon the Lord, and he shall sustain thee;* the good word of God, particularly the gospel, is designed to make the hearts glad that are weary and heavy-laden, Mt. 11:28. Ministers are to be helpers of this joy.

Verse 26

See here, 1. That good men do well for themselves; for they have in themselves an excellent character, and they secure to themselves an excellent portion, and in both they excel other people: *The righteous is more abundant than his neighbour* (so the margin); he is richer, though not in this world's goods, yet in the graces and comforts of the Spirit, which are the true riches. There is a true excellency in religion; it ennobles men, inspires them with generous principles, makes them substantial; it is an excellency which is, in the sight of God, of great price, who is the true Judge of excellency. His neighbour may make a greater figure in the world, may be more applauded, but the righteous man has the intrinsic worth. 2. That wicked men do ill for themselves; they walk in a way which *seduces them.* It seems to them to be not only a pleasant way, but the right way; it is so agreeable to flesh and blood that they therefore flatter themselves with an opinion that it cannot be amiss, but they will not gain the point they aim at, nor enjoy the good they hope for. It is all a cheat; and therefore the righteous is wiser and happier than his neighbour, that yet despise him and trample upon him.

Verse 27

Here is, 1. That which may make us hate slothfulness and deceit, for the word here, as before, signifies both: *The slothful* deceitful *man* has roast meat, but that which he roasts is not what he himself *took in hunting,* no, it is what others took pains for, and he lives upon the fruit of their labours, like the drones in the hive. Or, if slothful deceitful men have taken any thing by hunting (as sportsmen are seldom men of business), yet they do not roast it when they have taken it; they have no comfort in the enjoyment of it; perhaps God in his providence cuts them short of it. 2. That which may make us in love with industry and honesty, that the *substance of a diligent man,* though it be not great perhaps, *is* yet *precious.* It comes from the blessing of God; he has comfort in it; it does him good, and his family. It is his own daily bread, not bread out of other people's mouths, and therefore he sees God gives it to him in answer to his prayer.

Verse 28

The way of religion is here recommended to us, 1. As a straight, plain, easy way; it is *the way of righteousness.* God's commands (the rule we are to walk by) are all holy, just, and good. Religion has right reason and equity on its side; it is a *path-way,* a way which God has cast up for us (Isa. 35:8); it is a highway, the king's highway, the King of kings' highway, a way which is tracked before us by all the saints, the good old way, full of the footsteps of the flock. 2. As a safe, pleasant, comfortable way. (1.) There is not only life at the end, but there is life in the way; all true comfort and satisfaction. The favour of God, which is better than life; the Spirit, who is life. (2.) There is not only life in it, but so as that in it *there is no death,* none of that sorrow of the world which works death and is an allay to our present joy and life. There is no end of that life that is in the way of righteousness. Here there is life, but there is death too. *In the way of righteousness* there *is life, and no death,* life and immortality.

CHAPTER 13

Verse 1

Among the children of the same parents it is no new thing for some to be hopeful and others the contrary; now here we are taught to distinguish. 1. There is great hope of those that have a reverence for their parents, and are willing to be advised and admonished by them. He is *a wise son,* and is in a far way to be wiser, that *hears his father's instruction,* desires to hear it, regards it, and complies with it, and does not merely give it the hearing. 2. There is little hope of those that will not so much as *hear rebuke* with any patience, but scorn to submit to government and scoff at those that deal faithfully with them. How can those mend a fault who will not be told of it, but count those their enemies who do them that kindness?

Verse 2

Note, 1. If that which comes from within, out of the heart, be good, and from a good treasure, it will return with advantage. Inward comfort and satisfaction will be daily bread; nay, it will be a continual feast to those who delight in that communication which is *to the use of edifying.* 2. Violence done will recoil in the face of him that does it: *The soul of the transgressors* that harbours and plots mischief, and vents it by word and deed, *shall eat violence;* they shall have their belly full of it. *Reward her as she has rewarded thee,* Rev. 18:6. Every man shall drink as he brews, eat as he speaks; for by our words we must be justified or condemned, Mt. 12:37. As our fruit is, so will our food be, Rom. 6:21, 22.

Verse 3

Note, 1. A guard upon the lips is a guard to the soul. He that is cautious, that thinks twice before he speaks once, that, if he have *thought evil, lays his hand upon his mouth* to suppress it, that keeps a strong bridle on his tongue and a strict hand on that bridle, he *keeps his soul* from a great deal both of guilt and grief and saves himself the trouble of many bitter reflections on himself and reflections of others upon him. 2. There is many a one ruined by an ungoverned tongue: *He that opens widely his lips,* to let our *quod in buccam venerit — whatever comes uppermost,* that loves to bawl, and bluster, and make a noise, and affects such a liberty of speech as bids defiance both to God and man, he *shall have destruction.* it will be the destruction of his reputation, his interest, his comfort, and his soul for ever, Jam. 3:6.

Verse 4

Here is, 1. The misery and shame of the slothful. See how foolish and absurd they are; they desire the gains which the diligent get, but they hate the pains which the diligent take; they covet every thing that is to be coveted, but will do nothing that is to be done; and therefore it follows, They have nothing; for he that will not labour let him hunger, and let him not *eat,* 2 Th. 3:10. *The desire of the slothful,* which should be his excitement, is his torment, which should make him busy, makes him always uneasy, and is really a greater toil to him than labour would be. 2. The happiness and honour of the diligent: Their *soul shall be made fat;* they shall have abundance, and shall have the comfortable enjoyment of it, and the more for its being the fruit of their diligence. This is especially true in spiritual affairs. Those that rest in idle wishes know not what the advantages of religion are; whereas those that take pains in the service of God find both the pleasure and profit of it.

Verse 5

Note, 1. Where grace reigns sin is loathsome. It is the undoubted character of every *righteous man* that he *hates lying* (that is, all sin, for every sin is a lie, and particularly all fraud and falsehood in commerce and conversation), not only that he will not tell a lie, but he abhors lying, from a rooted reigning principle of love to truth and justice, and conformity to God. 2. Where sin reigns the *man is loathsome.* If his eyes were opened, and his conscience awakened, he would be so to himself, he would *abhor himself and repent in dust and ashes;* however, he is so to God and all good men; particularly, he makes himself so by lying, than which there is nothing more detestable. And, though he may think to face it out awhile, yet he will *come to shame* and contempt at last and will blush to show his face, Dan. 12:2.

Verse 6

See here, 1. Saints secured from ruin. Those that are *upright in their way,* that mean honestly in all their actions, adhere conscientiously to the sacred and eternal rules of equity, and deal sincerely both with God and man, their integrity will keep them from the temptations of Satan, which shall not prevail over them, the reproaches and injuries of evil men, which shall not fasten upon them, to do them any real mischief, Ps. 25:21.

Hic murus aheneus esto, nil conscire sibi.
Be this thy brazen bulwark of defence,
Still to preserve thy conscious innocence.

2. Sinners secured for ruin. Those that are wicked, even their wickedness will be their overthrow at last, and they are held in the cords of it in the mean time. Are they corrected, destroyed? It is their own wickedness that corrects them, that destroys them; they alone shall bear it.

Verse 7

This observation is applicable,

I. To men's worldly estate. The world is a great cheat, not only the things of the world, but the men of the world. *All men are liars.* Here is an instance in two sore evils under the sun: — 1. Some that are really poor would be thought to be rich and are thought to be so; they trade and spend as if they were rich, make a great bustle and a great show as if they had hidden treasures, when perhaps, if all their debts were paid, they are not worth a groat. This is sin, and will be shame; many a one hereby ruins his family and brings reproach upon his profession of religion. Those that thus live above what they have choose to be subject to their own pride rather than to God's providence, and it will end accordingly. 2. Some that are really rich would be thought to be poor, and are thought to be so, because they sordidly and meanly live below what God has given them, and choose rather to bury it than to use it, Eccl. 6:1, 2. In this there is an ingratitude to God, injustice to the family and neighbourhood, and uncharitableness to the poor.

II. To their spiritual state. Grace is the riches of the soul; it is true riches; but men commonly misrepresent themselves, either designedly or through mistake and ignorance of themselves. 1. There are many presuming hypocrites, that are really poor and empty of grace and yet either think themselves rich, and will not be convinced of their poverty, or pretend themselves rich, and will not own their poverty. 2. There are many timorous trembling Christians, that are spiritually rich, and full of grace, and yet think themselves poor, and will not be persuaded that they are rich, or, at least, will not own it; by their doubts and fears, their complaints and griefs, they *make themselves poor.* The former mistake is destroying at last; this is disquieting in the mean time.

Verse 8

We are apt to judge of men's blessedness, at least in this world, by their wealth, and that they are more or less happy accordingly as they have more or less of this world's goods; but Solomon here shows what a gross mistake it is, that we may be reconciled to a poor condition, and may neither covet riches ourselves nor envy those that have abundance. 1. Those that are rich, if by some they are respected for their riches, yet, to balance that, by others they are envied and struck at, and brought in danger of their lives, which therefore they are forced to ransom with their riches. *Slay us not, for we have treasures in the field,* Jer. 41:8. Under some tyrants, it has been crime enough to be rich; and how little is a man beholden to his wealth when it only serves to redeem that life which otherwise would not have been exposed! 2. Those that are poor, if by some, that should be their friends, they are despised and overlooked, yet, to balance that, they are also despised and overlooked by others that would be their enemies if they had any thing to lose: *The poor hear not rebuke,* are not censured, reproached, accused, nor brought into trouble, as the rich are; for nobody thinks it worth while to take notice of them. When the rich Jews were carried captives to Babylon *the poor of the land were left,* 2 Ki. 25:12. Welcome nothing, once in seven years. *Cantabit vacuus coram latrone viator — When a traveller is met by a robber he will rejoice at not having much property about him.*

Verse 9

Here is, 1. The comfort of good men flourishing and lasting: *The light of the righteous rejoices,* that is, it increases, and makes them glad. Even their outward prosperity is their joy, and much more those gifts, graces, and comforts, with which their souls are illuminated; these *shine more and more, ch.* 4:18. The Spirit is their light, and he gives them a fulness of joy, and *rejoices to do them good.* 2. The comfort of bad men withering and dying: *The lamp of the wicked* burns dimly and faint; it looks melancholy, like a taper in an urn, and it will shortly *be put out* in utter darkness, Isa. 50:11. The light of the righteous is as that of the sun, which may be eclipsed and clouded, but will continue; that of the wicked is as a lamp of their own kindling, which will presently go out and is easily put out.

Verse 10

Note, 1. Foolish pride is the great make-bate. Would you know *whence come wars and fightings?* They come from this root of bitterness. Whatever hand other lusts may have in contention (passion, envy, covetousness), pride has the great hand; it is its pride that it will itself sow discord and needs no help. Pride makes men impatient of contradiction in either their opinions or their desires, impatient of competition and rivalship, impatient of contempt, or any thing that looks like a slight, and impatient of concession, and receding, from a conceit of certain right and truth on their side; and hence arise quarrels among relations and neighbours, quarrels in states and kingdoms, in churches and Christian societies. Men will be revenged, will not forgive, because they are proud. 2. Those that are humble and peaceable are wise and *well advised.* Those that will ask and take advice, that will consult their own consciences, their Bibles, their ministers, their friends, and will do nothing rashly, are wise, as in other things, so in this, that they will humble themselves, will stoop and yield, to preserve quietness and prevent quarrels.

Verse 11

This shows that riches wear as they are won and woven. 1. That which is won ill will never wear well, for a curse attends it which will waste it, and the same corrupt dispositions which incline men to the sinful ways of getting well incline them to the like sinful ways of spending: *Wealth gotten by vanity* will be bestowed upon vanity, and then it *will be diminished.* That which is got by such employments as are not lawful, or not becoming Christians, such as only serve to feed pride and luxury, that which is got by gaming or by the stage, may as truly be said to be *gotten by vanity* as that which is got by fraud and lying, and *will be diminished. De male quaesitis vix gaudet tertius haeres — Ill-gotten wealth will scarcely be enjoyed by the third generation.* 2. That which is got by industry and honesty will grow more, instead of growing less; it will be a maintenance; it will be an inheritance; it will be an abundance. *He that labours, working with his hands, shall so increase* as that he shall *have to give to him that needs* (Eph. 4:28); and, when it comes to that, it will increase yet more and more.

Verse 12

Note, 1. Nothing is more grievous than the disappointment of a raised expectation, though not in the thing itself by a denial, yet in the time of it by a delay: *Hope deferred makes the heart sick* and languishing, fretful and peevish; but hope quite dashed kills the heart, and the more high the expectation was raised the more cutting is the frustration of it. It is therefore our wisdom not to promise ourselves any great matters from the creature, not to feed ourselves with any vain hopes from this world, lest we lay up matter for our own vexation; and what we do hope for let us prepare to be disappointed in, that, if it should prove so, it may prove the easier; and let us not be hasty. 2. Nothing is more grateful than to enjoy that, at last, which we have long wished and waited for: *When the desire does come* it puts men into a sort of paradise, a garden of pleasure, for *it is a tree of life.* It will aggravate the eternal misery of the wicked that their hopes will be frustrated; and it will make the happiness of heaven the more welcome to the saints that it is what they have earnestly longed for as the crown of their hopes.

Verse 13

Here is, 1. The character of one that is marked for ruin: He that *despises the word* of God, and has no regard to it, no veneration for it, nor will be ruled by it, certainly he *shall be destroyed,* for he slights that which is the only means of curing a destructive disease and makes himself obnoxious to that divine wrath which will certainly be his destruction. Those that prefer the rules of carnal policy before divine precepts, and the allurements of the world and the flesh before God's promises and comforts, despise his word, giving the preference to those things that stand in competition with it; and it is to their own just destruction: they would not take warning. 2. The character of one that is sure to be happy: *He that fears the commandment,* that stands in awe of God, pays a deference to his authority, has a reverence for his word, is afraid of displeasing God and incurring the penalties annexed to the commandment, shall not only escape destruction, but *shall be rewarded* for his godly fear. *In keeping the commandment there is great reward.*

Verse 14

By *the law of the wise* and righteous, here, we may understand either the principles and rules by which they govern themselves or (which comes all to one) the instructions which they give to others, which ought to be as a law to all about them; and if they be so, 1. They will be constant springs of comfort and satisfaction, as *a fountain of life,* sending forth streams of living water; the closer we keep to those rules the more effectually we secure our own peace. 2. They will be constant preservatives from the temptations of Satan. Those that follow the dictates of this law will keep at a distance from the snares of sin, and so escape *the snares of death* which those run into that forsake *the law of the wise.*

Verse 15

If we compare not only the end, but the way, we shall find that religion has the advantage; for, 1. The way of saints is pleasant and agreeable: *Good understanding* gains *favour* with God and man; our Saviour grew in that favour when he *increased in wisdom.* Those that conduct themselves prudently, and order their conversation aright in every thing, that *serve Christ in righteousness, and peace, and joy in the Holy Ghost,* are *accepted of God and approved of men,* Rom. 14:17, 18. And how comfortably will that man pass through the world who is well understood and is therefore well accepted! 2. The way of sinners is rough and uneasy, and, for *this* reason, unpleasant to themselves, because unacceptable to others. It is *hard,* hard upon others, who complain of it, hard to the sinner himself, who can have little enjoyment of himself while he is doing that which is disobliging to all mankind. The service of sin is perfect slavery, and the road to hell is strewed with the thorns and thistles that are the products of the curse. Sinners labour in the very fire.

Verse 16

Note, 1. It is wisdom to be cautious. *Every prudent* discreet *man* does all *with knowledge* (considering with himself and consulting with others), acts with deliberation and is upon the reserve, is careful not to meddle with that which he has not some knowledge of, not to launch out into business which he has not acquainted himself with, will not *deal with* those that he has not some *knowledge* of, whether they may be confided in. He is still dealing in knowledge, that he may increase the stock he has. 2. It is folly to be rash, as the *fool* is, who is forward to talk of things he knows nothing of and undertake that which he is no way fit for, and so *lays open his folly* and makes himself ridiculous. He *began to build and was not able to finish.*

Verse 17

Here we have, 1. The ill consequences of betraying a trust. *A wicked messenger,* who, being sent to negotiate any business, is false to him that employed him, divulges his counsels, and so defeats his designs, cannot expect to prosper, but will certainly *fall into* some *mischief* or other, will be discovered and punished, since nothing is more hateful to God and man than the treachery of those that have a confidence reposed in them. 2. The happy effects of fidelity: An *ambassador* who *faithfully* discharges his trust, and serves the interests of those who employ him, *is health;* he is health to those by whom and for whom he is employed, heals differences that are between them, and preserves a good understanding; he is health to himself, for he secures his own interest. This is applicable to ministers, Christ's messengers and ambassadors; those that are wicked and false to Christ and the souls of men do mischief and *fall into mischief,* but those that are faithful will find sound words to be healing words to others and themselves.

Verse 18

Note, 1. He that is so proud that he scorns to be taught will certainly be abased. he that *refuses* the good *instruction* offered him, as if it were a reflection upon his honour and an abridgment of his liberty, *poverty and shame shall be to him:* he will become a beggar and live and die in disgrace; every one will despise him as foolish, and stubborn, and ungovernable. 2. He that is so humble that he takes it well to be told of his faults shall certainly be exalted: *He that regards a reproof,* whoever gives it to him, and will mend what is amiss when it is shown him, gains respect as wise and candid; he avoids that which would be a disgrace to him and is in a fair way to make himself considerable.

Verse 19

This shows the folly of those that refuse instruction, for they might be happy and will not. 1. They might be happy. There are in man strong desires of happiness; God has provided for the accomplishment of those desires, and that would be *sweet to the soul,* whereas the pleasures of sense are grateful only to the carnal appetite. *The desire* of good men towards the favour of God and spiritual blessings brings that which *is sweet to their souls;* we know those that can say so by experience, Ps. 4:6, 7. 2. Yet they will not be happy; for *it is an abomination to* them *to depart from evil,* which is necessary to their being happy. Never let those expect any thing truly sweet to their souls that will not be persuaded to leave their sins, but that roll them under their tongues as a sweet morsel.

Verse 20

Note, 1. Those that would be good must keep good company, which is an evidence for them that they would be good (men's character is known by the company they choose) and will be a means of making them good, of showing them the way and of quickening and encouraging them in it. He that would be himself wise must walk with those that are so, must choose such for his intimate acquaintance, and converse with them accordingly; must ask and receive instruction from them, and keep up pious and profitable talk with them. *Miss not the discourse of the elders, for they also learned of their fathers,* Ecclesiasticus 8:9. And (Ecclesiasticus 6:35), *Be willing to hear every godly discourse, and let not the parables of understanding escape thee.* 2. Multitudes are brought to ruin by bad company: *A companion of fools shall be broken* (so some), *shall be known* (so the Septuagint), known to be a fool; *noscitur ex socio — he is known by his company.* He *will be like them* (so some), *will be made wicked* (so others); it comes all to one, for all those, and those only, that make themselves wicked, will *be destroyed,* and those that associate with evil-doers are debauched, and so undone, and at last ascribe their death to it.

Verse 21

Here see, 1. How unavoidable the destruction of sinners is; the wrath of God pursues them, and all the terrors of that wrath: *Evil pursues* them closely wherever they go, as the avenger of blood pursued the manslayer, and they have no city of refuge to flee to; they attempt an escape, but in vain. Whom God pursues he is sure to overtake. They may prosper for a while and grow very secure, but their damnation slumbers not, though they do. 2. How indefeasible the happiness of the saints is; the God that cannot lie has engaged that *to the righteous good shall be repaid.* They shall be abundantly recompensed for all the good they have done, and all the ill they have suffered, in this world; so that, though many have been losers for their righteousness, they shall not be losers by it. Though the recompence do not come quickly, it will come in the day of payment, in the world of retribution; and it will be an abundant recompence.

Verse 22

See here, 1. How *a good man's* estate lasts: He *leaves an inheritance to his children's children.* It is part of his praise that he is thoughtful for posterity, that he does not lay all out upon himself, but is in care to do well for those that come after him, not by withholding more than is meet, but by a prudent and decent frugality. He trains up his children to this, that they may leave it to their children; and especially he is careful, both by justice and charity, to obtain the blessing of God upon what he has, and to entail that blessing upon his children, without which the greatest industry and frugality will be in vain: *A good man,* by being good and doing good, by honouring the Lord with his substance and spending it in his service, secures it to his posterity; or, if he should not leave them much of this world's goods, his prayers, his instructions, his good example, will be the best entail, and the promises of the covenant will be an inheritance to his *children's children,* Ps. 103:17. 2. How it increases by the accession of *the wealth of the sinner* to it, for that is *laid up for the just.* If it be asked, How should good men grow so rich, who are not so eager upon the world as others are and who commonly suffer for their well-doing? It is here answered, God, in his providence, often brings into their hands that which wicked people had laid up for themselves. *The innocent shall divide the silver,* Job 27:16, 17. The Israelites shall spoil the Egyptians (Ex. 12:36) and *eat the riches of the Gentiles,* Isa. 61:6.

Verse 23

See here, 1. How a small estate may be improved by industry, so that a man, by making the best of every thing, may live comfortably upon it: *Much food is in the tillage of the poor,* the poor farmers, that have but a little, but take pains with that little and husband it well. Many make it an excuse for their idleness that they have but a little to work on, a very little to be doing with; but the less compass the field is of the more let the skill and labour of the owner be employed about it, and it will turn to a very good account. Let him dig, and he needs not beg. 2. How a great estate may be ruined by indiscretion: *There is that* has a great deal, but it *is destroyed* and brought to nothing for *want of judgment,* that is, prudence in the management of it. Men over-build themselves or over-buy themselves, keep greater company, or a better table, or more servants, than they can afford, suffer what they have to go to decay and do not make the most of it; by taking up money themselves, or being bound for others, their estates are sunk, their families reduced, and all *for want of judgment.*

Verse 24

Note, 1. To the education of children in that which is good there is necessary a due correction of them for what is amiss; every child of ours is a child of Adam, and therefore has that foolishness bound up in its heart which calls for rebuke, more or less, the rod and reproof which give wisdom. Observe, It is *his* rod that must be used, the rod of a parent, directed by wisdom and love, and designed for good, not the rod of a servant. 2. It is good to begin betimes with the necessary restraints of children from that which is evil, before vicious habits are confirmed. The branch is easily bent when it is tender. 3. Those really hate their children, though they pretend to be fond of them, that do not keep them under a strict discipline, and by all proper methods, severe ones when gentle ones will not serve, make them sensible of their faults and afraid of offending. They abandon them to their worst enemy, to the most dangerous disease, and therefore hate them. Let this reconcile children to the correction their good parents give them; it is from love, and for their good, Heb. 12:7–9.

Verse 25

Note, 1. It is the happiness of the righteous that they shall have enough and that they know when they have enough. They desire not to be surfeited, but, being moderate in their desires, they are soon satisfied. nature is content with a little and grace with less; enough is as good as a feast. Those that feed on the bread of life, that feast on the promises, meet with abundant satisfaction of soul there, eat, and are filled. 2. It is the misery of the wicked that, through the insatiableness of their own desires, they are always needy; not only their souls shall not be satisfied with the world and the flesh, but even their *belly shall want;* their sensual appetite is always craving. In hell they shall be denied a drop of water.

CHAPTER 14

Verse 1

Note, 1. A good wife is a great blessing to a family. By a fruitful wife a family is multiplied and replenished with children, and so built up. But by a prudent wife, one that is pious, industrious, and considerate, the affairs of the family are made to prosper, debts are paid, portions raised, provision made, the children well educated and maintained, and the family has comfort within doors and credit without; thus is the house built. She looks upon it as her own to take care of, though she knows it is her husband's to bear rule in, Esth. 1:22. 2. Many a family is brought to ruin by ill housewifery, as well as by ill husbandry. A *foolish* woman, that has no fear of God nor regard to her business, that is wilful, and wasteful, and humoursome, that indulges her ease and appetite, and is all for jaunting and feasting, cards and the play-house, though she come to a plentiful estate, and to a family beforehand, she will impoverish and waste it, and will as certainly be the ruin of her house as if she *plucked it down with her hands;* and the husband himself, with all his care, can scarcely prevent it.

Verse 2

Here are, 1. Grace and sin in their true colours. Grace reigning is a reverence of God, and gives honour to him who is infinitely great and high, and to whom all honour is due, than which what is more becoming or should be more pleasing to the rational creature? Sin reigning is no less than a contempt of God. In *this,* more than in any thing, sin appears exceedingly sinful, that it despises God, whom angels adore. Those that despise God's precepts, and will not be ruled by them, his promises, and will not ac-

cept of them, despise God himself and all his attributes. 2. Grace and sin in their true light. By this we may know a man that has grace, and the fear of God, reigning in him, *he walks in his uprightness,* he makes conscience of his actions, is faithful both to God and man, and every stop he makes, as well as every step he takes, is by rule; here is one that honours God. But, on the contrary, *he that is perverse in his ways,* that wilfully follows his own appetites and passions, that is unjust and dishonest and contradicts his profession in his conversation, however he may pretend to devotion, he is a wicked man, and will be reckoned with as a despiser of God himself.

Verse 3

See here, 1. A proud fool exposing himself. Where there is pride in the heart, and no wisdom in the head to suppress it, it commonly shows itself in the words: *In the mouth there is pride,* proud boasting, proud censuring, proud scorning, proud commanding and giving law; this is the *rod,* or branch, *of pride;* the word is used only here and Isa. 11:1. It grows from that root of bitterness which is in the heart; it is a rod from that stem. The root must be plucked up, or we cannot conquer this branch, or it is meant of a smiting beating rod, a *rod of pride* which strikes others. The proud man with his tongue lays about him and deals blows at pleasure, but it will in the end be a rod to himself; the proud man shall come under an ignominious correction by the words of his own mouth, not cut as a soldier, but caned as a servant; and herein he will be beaten with his own rod, Ps. 64:8. 2. A humble wise man saving himself and consulting his own good: *The lips of the wise shall preserve them* from doing that mischief to others which proud men do with their tongues, and from bringing that mischief on themselves which haughty scorners are often involved in.

Verse 4

Note, 1. The neglect of husbandry is the way to poverty: *Where no oxen are,* to till the ground and tread out the corn, *the crib* is empty, *is clean;* there is no straw for the cattle, and consequently no bread for the service of man. Scarcity is represented by *cleanness of teeth,* Amos 4:6. *Where no oxen are* there is nothing to be done at the ground, and then nothing to be had out of it; *the crib* indeed *is clean* from dung, which pleases the neat and nice, that cannot endure husbandry because there is so much dirty work in it, and therefore will sell their oxen to keep the crib clean; but then not only the labour, but even the dung of the ox is wanted. This shows the folly of those who addict themselves to the pleasures of the country, but do not mind the business of it, who (as we say) keep more horses than kine, more dogs than swine; their families must needs suffer by it. 2. Those who take pains about their ground are likely to reap the profit of it. Those who keep that about them which is for use and service, not for state and show, more husbandmen than footmen, are likely to thrive. *Much increase is by the strength of the ox;* that is made for our service, and is profitable alive and dead.

Verse 5

In the administration of justice much depends upon the witnesses, and therefore it is necessary to the common good that witnesses be principled as they ought to be; for, 1. A witness that is conscientious will not dare to give in a testimony that is in the least untrue, nor, for good-will or ill-will, represent a thing otherwise than according to the best of his knowledge, whoever is pleased or displeased, and then judgment runs down like a river. 2. But a witness that will be bribed, and biassed, and browbeaten, *will utter lies* (and not stick nor startle at it), with as much readiness and assurance as if what he said were all true.

Verse 6

Note, 1. The reason why some people seek wisdom, and do not find it, is because they do not seek it from a right principle and in a right manner. They are scorners, and it is in scorn that they ask instruction, that they may ridicule what is told them and may cavil at it. Many put questions to Christ, tempting him, and that they might have whereof to accuse him, but they were never the wiser. No

marvel if those who seek wisdom, as Simon Magus sought the gifts of the Holy Ghost, to serve their pride and covetousness, do not find it, for they seek amiss. Herod desired to see a miracle, but he was a scorner, and therefore it was denied him, Lu. 23:8. Scorners speed not in prayer. 2. To those who understand aright, who *depart from evil* (for *that is understanding*), the *knowledge* of God and of his will *is easy.* The parables which harden scorners in their scorning, and make divine things more difficult to them, enlighten those who are willing to learn, and make the same things more plain, and intelligible, and familiar to them, Mt. 13:11, 15, 16. The same word which to the scornful *is a savour of death unto death* to the humble and serious *is a savour of life unto life.* He *that understands,* so as to *depart from evil* (for *that is understanding*), to quit his prejudices, to lay aside all corrupt dispositions and affections, will easily apprehend instruction and receive the impressions of it.

Verse 7

See here, 1. How we may discern a fool and discover him, a wicked man, for he is *a foolish man.* If we *perceive not in him the lips of knowledge,* if we find there is no relish or savour of piety in his discourse, that his communication is all corrupt and corrupting, and nothing in it *good and to the use of edifying,* we may conclude the treasure is bad. 2. How we must decline such a one and depart from him: *Go from his presence,* for *thou perceivest* there is no good to be gotten by his company, but danger of getting hurt by it. Sometimes the only way we have of reproving wicked discourse and witnessing against it is by leaving the company and going out of the hearing of it.

Verse 8

See here, 1. The good conduct of a wise and good man; he manages himself well. it is not the wisdom of the learned, which consists only in speculation, that is here recommended, but *the wisdom of the prudent,* which is practical, and is of use to direct our counsels and actions. Christian prudence consists in a right *understanding of our way;* for we are travellers, whose concern it is, not to spy wonders, but to get forward towards their journey's end. It *is to understand our own way,* not to be critics and busybodies in other men's matters, but to look well to ourselves and *ponder the path of our feet,* to understand the directions of our way, that we may observe them, the dangers of our way, that we may avoid them, the difficulties of our way, that we may break through them, and the advantages of our way, that we may improve them — to understand the rules we are to walk by and the ends we are to walk towards, and walk accordingly. 2. The bad conduct of a bad man; he puts a cheat upon himself. He does not rightly understand his way; he thinks he does, and so misses his way, and goes on in his mistake: *The folly of fools is deceit;* it cheats them into their own ruin. The folly of him that built on the sand was deceit.

Verse 9

See here, 1. How wicked people are hardened in their wickedness: they *make a mock at sin.* They make a laughing matter of the sins of others, making themselves and their companions merry with that for which they should mourn, and they make a light matter of their own sins, both when they are tempted to sin and when they have committed it; they *call evil good and good evil* (Isa. 5:20), turn it off with a jest, rush into sin (Jer. 8:6) and say they shall have peace though they go on. They care not what mischief they do by their sins, and laugh at those that tell them of it. They are advocates for sin, and are ingenious at framing excuses for it. *Fools make a mock at the sin-offering* (so some); those that make light of sin make light of Christ. Those are fools that make light of sin, for they make light of that which God complains of (Amos 2:13), which lay heavily upon Christ, and which they themselves will have other thoughts of shortly. 2. How good people are encouraged in their goodness: *Among the righteous there is favour;* if they in any thing offend, they presently repent and obtain the favour of God. They have a good-will one to another; and among them, in their societies, there is mutual charity and compassion in cases of offences, and no mocking.

Verse 10

This agrees with 1 Co. 2:11, *What man knows the things of a man,* and the changes of his temper, *save the spirit of a man?* 1. Every man feels most from his own burden, especially that which is a burden upon the spirits, for that is commonly concealed and the sufferer keeps it to himself. We must not censure the griefs of others, for we know not what they feel; their stroke perhaps is heavier than their groaning. 2. Many enjoy a secret pleasure, especially in divine consolations, which others are not aware of, much less are sharers in; and, as the sorrows of a penitent, so the joys of a believer are such as a *stranger does not intermeddle with* and therefore is no competent judge of.

Verse 11

Note, 1. Sin is the ruin of great families: *The house of the wicked,* though built ever so strong and high, *shall be overthrown,* shall be brought to poverty and disgrace, and at length be extinct. His hope for heaven, the house on which he leans, shall not stand, but fail in the storm; the deluge that comes will sweep it away. 2. Righteousness is the rise and stability even of mean families: Even *the tabernacle of the upright,* though movable and despicable as a tent, *shall flourish,* in outward prosperity if Infinite Wisdom see good, at all events in graces and comfort, which are true riches and honours.

Verse 12

We have here an account of the way and end of a great many self-deluded souls. 1. Their way is seemingly fair: It *seems right* to themselves; they please themselves with a fancy that they are as they should be, that their opinions and practices are good, and such as will bear them out. The way of ignorance and carelessness, the way of worldliness and earthly-mindedness, the way of sensuality and flesh-pleasing, seem right to those that walk in them, much more the way of hypocrisy in religion, external performances, partial reformations, and blind zeal; this they imagine will bring them to heaven; they flatter themselves in their own eyes that all will be well at last. 2. Their end is really fearful, and the more so for their mistake: It is *the ways of death,* eternal death; their iniquity will certainly be their ruin, and they will perish with a lie in their right hand. Self-deceivers will prove in the end self-destroyers.

Verse 13

This shows the vanity of carnal mirth, and proves what Solomon said of laughter, that *it is mad;* for, 1. There is sadness under it. Sometimes when sinners are under convictions, or some great trouble, they dissemble their grief by a forced mirth, and put a good face on it, because they will not seem to yield: they cry not when he binds them. Nay, when men really are merry, yet at the same time there is some alloy or other to their mirth, something that casts a damp upon it, which all their gaiety cannot keep from their heart. Their consciences tell them they have no reason to be merry (Hos. 9:1); they cannot but see the vanity of it. Spiritual joy is seated in the soul; the joy of the hypocrite is but from the teeth outward. See Jn. 16:22; 2 Co. 6:10. 2. There is worse after it: *The end of that mirth is heaviness.* It is soon over, like the crackling of thorns under a pot; and, if the conscience be awake, all sinful and profane mirth will be reflected upon with bitterness; if not, the heaviness will be so much the greater when *for all these things God shall bring the* sinner *into judgment.* The sorrows of the saints will end in everlasting joys (Ps. 126:5), but the laughter of fools will end in endless weeping and wailing.

Verse 14

Note, 1. The misery of sinners will be an eternal surfeit upon their sins: The *backslider in heart,* who for fear of suffering, or in hope of profit or pleasure, forsakes God and his duty, shall be *filled with his own ways;* God will give him enough of them. They would not leave their brutish lusts and passions, and therefore they shall stick by them, to their everlasting terror and torment. *He that is filthy shall be filthy still. "Son, remember,"* shall *fill them with their own ways,* and set their sins in order before them. Backsliding begins in the heart; it is the evil heart of unbelief that departs from God; and of all sinners backsliders will have most terror when they reflect on *their own ways,* Lu. 11:26. 2. The happiness of the saints will be an eternal satisfaction in their graces, as tokens of and qualifications for God's peculiar favour: *A good man shall be* abundantly *satisfied from himself,* from what God has wrought in him. He has *rejoicing in himself alone,* Gal. 6:3. As sinners never think they have sin enough till it brings them to hell, so saints never think they have grace enough till it brings them to heaven.

Verse 15

Note, 1. It is folly to be credulous, to heed every flying report, to give ear to every man's story, though ever so improbable, to take things upon trust from common fame, to depend upon every man's profession of friendship and give credit to every one that will promise payment; those are *simple* who thus *believe every word,* forgetting that all men, in some sense, are liars in comparison with God, all whose words we are to believe with an implicit faith, for he cannot lie. 2. It is wisdom to be cautious: *The prudent man* will try before he trusts, will weigh both the credibility of the witness and the probability of the testimony, and then give judgment as the thing appears or suspend his judgment till it appears. *Prove all things,* and *believe not every spirit.*

Verse 16

Note, 1. Holy fear is an excellent guard upon every holy thing, and against every thing that is unholy. It is wisdom to depart *from evil,* from the evil of sin, and thereby from all other evil; and therefore it is wisdom to fear, that is, to be jealous over ourselves with a godly jealousy, to keep up a dread of God's wrath, to be afraid of coming near the borders of sin or dallying with the beginnings of it. A wise man, for fear of harm, keeps out of harm's way, and starts back in a fright when he finds himself entering into temptation. 2. Presumption is folly. He who, when he is warned of his danger, *rages and is confident,* furiously pushes on, cannot bear to be checked, bids defiance to the wrath and curse of God, and, fearless of danger, persists in his rebellion, makes bold with the occasions of sin, and plays upon the precipice, he is a fool, for he acts against his reason and his interest, and his ruin will quickly be the proof of his folly.

Verse 17

Note, 1. Passionate men are justly laughed at. Men who are peevish and touchy, and are *soon angry* upon every the least provocation, *deal foolishly;* they say and do that which is ridiculous, and so expose themselves to contempt; they themselves cannot but be ashamed of it when the heat is over. The consideration of this should engage those especially who are in reputation for wisdom and honour with the utmost care to bridle their passion. 2. Malicious men are justly dreaded and detested, for they are much more dangerous and mischievous to all societies: *A man of wicked devices,* who stifles his resentments till he has an opportunity of being revenged, and is secretly plotting how to wrong his neighbour and to do him an ill turn, as Cain to kill Abel, such a man as this is hated by all mankind. The character of an angry man is pitiable; through the surprise of a temptation he disturbs and disgraces himself, but it is soon over, and he is sorry for it. But that of a spiteful revengeful man is odious; there is no fence against him nor cure for him.

Verse 18

Note, 1. Sin is the shame of sinners: *The simple,* who love simplicity, get nothing by it; they *inherit folly.* They have it *by inheritance,* so some. This corruption of nature is derived from our first parents, and all the calamities that attend it we have by kind; it was the inheritance they transmitted to their degenerate race, an hereditary disease. They are as fond of it as a man of his inheritance, hold it as fast, and are as loth to part with it. What they value themselves upon is really foolish; and what will be the issue of their simplicity but folly? They will for ever rue their own foolish choice. 2. Wisdom is the honour of the wise: *The prudent crown* themselves *with knowledge,* they look upon it as their brightest ornament, and there is nothing they are so ambitious of; they bind it to their heads as a crown, which they will by no means part with; they press towards the top and perfection of knowledge, which will crown their beginnings and progress. They shall have the praise of it; wise heads shall be respected as if they were crowned heads. They *crown knowledge* (so some read it); they are a credit to their profession. Wisdom is not only justified, but glorified, of all her children.

Verse 19

That is, 1. The wicked are oftentimes impoverished and brought low, so that they are forced to beg, their wickedness having reduced them to straits; while good men, by the blessing of God, are enriched, and enabled to give, and do give, even to the evil; for where God grants life we must not deny a livelihood. 2. Sometimes God extorts, even from bad men, an acknowledgement of the excellency of God's people. The evil ought always to *bow before the good,* and sometimes they are made to do it and *to know that God has loved them,* Rev. 3:9. They desire their favour (Esth. 7:7), their prayers, 2 Ki. 3:12. 3. There is a day coming when the upright shall have the dominion (Ps. 49:14), when the foolish virgins shall come begging to the wise for oil, and shall knock in vain at that gate of the Lord at which the righteous entered.

Verse 20

This shows, not what should be, but what is the common way of the world — to be shy of the poor and fond of the rich. 1. Few will give countenance to those whom the world frowns upon, though otherwise worthy of respect: *The poor,* who should be pitied, and encouraged, and relieved, *is hated,* looked strange upon, and kept at a distance, even *by his own neighbour,* who, before he fell into disgrace, was intimate with him and pretended to have a kindness for him. Most are swallow-friends, that are gone in winter. It is good having God our friend, for he will not desert us when we are poor. 2. Every one will make court to those whom the world smiles upon, though otherwise unworthy: *The rich have many friends,* friends to their riches, in hope to get something out of them. There is little friendship in the world but what is governed by self-interest, which is no true friendship at all, nor what a wise man will either value himself on or put any confidence in. Those that make the world their God idolize those that have most of its good things, and seek their favour as if indeed they were Heaven's favourites.

Verse 21

See here how men's character and condition are measured and judged of by their conduct towards their poor neighbours. 1. Those that look upon them with contempt have here assigned them a bad character, and their condition will be accordingly: *He that despises his neighbour* because he is low in the world, because he is of a mean extraction, rustic education, and makes but a mean figure, that thinks it below him to take notice of him, converse with him, or concern himself about him, and sets him with the dogs of his flock, *is a sinner,* is guilty of a sin, is in the way to worse, and shall be dealt with as a sinner; unhappy is he. 2. Those that look upon them with compassion are here said to be in a good condition, according to their character: *He that has mercy on the poor,* is ready to do all the good offices he can to him, and thereby puts an honour upon him, *happy is he;* he does that which is pleasing to God, which he himself will afterwards reflect upon with great satisfaction, for which the loins of the poor will bless him, and which will be abundantly recompensed in the resurrection of the just.

Verse 22

See here, 1. How miserably mistaken those are that not only do evil, but devise it: *Do they not err?* Yes, certainly they do; every one knows it. They think that by sinning with craft and contrivance, and carrying on their intrigues with more plot and artifice than others, they shall make a better hand of their sins than others do, and come off better. But they are mistaken. God's justice cannot be outwitted. Those that devise evil against their neighbours greatly err, for it will certainly turn upon themselves and end in their own ruin, a fatal error! 2. How wisely those consult their own interest that not only do good but devise it: *Mercy and truth* shall be to them, not a reward of debt (they will own that they merit nothing), but a reward of mercy, mere mercy, mercy according to the promise, mercy and truth, to which God is pleased to make himself a debtor. Those that are so liberal as to devise liberal things, that seek opportunities of doing good, and contrive how to make their charity most extensive and most acceptable to those that need it, *by liberal things they shall stand,* Isa. 32:8.

Verse 23

Note, 1. Working, without talking, will make men rich: *In all labour* of the head, or of the hand, *there is profit;* it will turn to some good account or other. Industrious people are generally thriving people, and where there is something done there is something to be had. *The stirring hand gets a penny.* It is good therefore to keep in business, and to keep in action, and what our hand finds to do to do it with all our might. 2. Talking, without working, will make men poor. Those that love to boast of their business and make a noise about it, and that waste their time in tittle-tattle, in telling and hearing new things, like the Athenians, and, under pretence of improving themselves by conversation, neglect the work of their place and day, they waste what they have, and the course they take *tends to penury,* and will end in it. It is true in the affairs of our souls; those that take pains in the service of God, that strive earnestly in prayer, will find profit in it. But if men's religion runs all out in talk and noise, and their praying is only the labour of the lips, they will be spiritually poor, and come to nothing.

Verse 24

Observe, 1. If men be wise and good, riches make them so much the more honourable and useful: *The crown of the wise is their riches;* their riches make them to be so much the more respected, and give them the more authority and influence upon others. Those that have wealth, and wisdom to use it, will have a great opportunity of honouring God and doing good in the world. *Wisdom is good* without *an inheritance,* but better *with* it. 2. If men be wicked and corrupt, their wealth will but the more expose them: *The foolishness of fools,* put them in what condition you will, *is folly,* and will show itself and shame them; if they have riches, they do mischief with them and are the more hardened in their foolish practices.

Verse 25

See here, 1. How much praise is due to a faithful witness: He *delivers the souls* of the innocent, who are falsely accused, and their good names, which are as dear to them as their lives. A man of integrity will venture the displeasure of the greatest, to bring truth to light and rescue those who are injured by falsehood. A faithful minister, who truly witnesses for God against sin, is thereby instrumental to deliver souls from eternal death. 2. How little regard is to be had to a false witness. He forges *lies,* and yet pours them out with the greatest assurance imaginable for the destruction of the innocent. It is therefore the interest of a nation by all means possible to detect and punish false-witness-bearing, yea, and lying in common conversation; for truth is the cement of society.

Verses 26–27

In these two verses we are invited and encouraged to live in the fear of God by the advantages which attend a religious life. The *fear of the Lord* is here put for all gracious principles, producing gracious practices. 1. Where this reigns it produces a holy security and serenity of mind. There is in it a *strong confidence;* it enables a man still to hold fast both his purity and his peace, whatever happens, and gives him boldness before God and the world. *I know that I shall be justified — None of these things move me;* such is the language of this confidence. 2. It entails a blessing upon posterity. The children of those that by faith make God their confidence shall be encouraged by the promise that God will be a God to believers and to their seed to flee to him as their refuge, and they shall find shelter in him. The children of religious parents often do the better for their parents' instructions and example and fare the better for their faith and prayers. "*Our fathers trusted in thee,* therefore we will." 3. It is an over-flowing ever-flowing spring of comfort and joy; it is *a fountain of life,* yielding constant pleasure and satisfaction to the soul, joys that are pure and fresh, are life to the soul, and quench

its thirst, and can never be drawn dry; it is a *well of living water,* that is springing up to, and is the earnest of, eternal life. 4. It is a sovereign antidote against sin and temptation. Those that have a true relish of the pleasures of serious godliness will not be allured by the baits of sin to swallow its hook; they know where to obtain better things than any it can pretend to offer, and therefore it is easy to them *to depart from the snares of death* and to keep their foot from being taken in them.

Verse 28

Here are two maxims in politics, which carry their own evidence with them: — 1. That it is much for the honour of a king to have a populous kingdom; it is a sign that he rules well, since strangers are hereby invited to come and settle under his protection and his own subjects live comfortably; it is a sign that he and his kingdom are under the blessing of God, the effect of which is being fruitful and multiplying. It is his strength, and makes him considerable and formidable; happy is the king, the father of his country, who has his *quiver full of arrows;* he *shall not be ashamed, but shall speak with his enemy in the gate,* Ps. 127:4, 5. It is therefore the wisdom of princes, by a mild and gentle government, by encouraging trade and husbandry, and by making all easy under them, to promote the increase of their people. And let all that wish well to the kingdom of Christ, and to his honour, do what they can in their places that many may be added to his church. 2. That when the people are lessened the prince is weakened: *In the want of people is the leanness of the prince* (so some read it); trade lies dead, the ground lies untilled, the army wants to be recruited, the navy to be manned, and all because there are not hands sufficient. See how much the honour and safety of kings depend upon their people, which is a reason why they should rule by love, and not with rigour. Princes are corrected by those judgments which abate the number of the people, as we find, 2 Sa. 24:13.

Verse 29

Note, 1. Meekness is wisdom. *He* rightly understands himself, and his duty and interest, the infirmities of human nature, and the constitution of human society, who *is slow to anger,* and knows how to excuse the faults of others as well as his own, how to adjourn his resentments, and moderate them, so as by no provocation to be put out of the possession of his own soul. A mild patient man is really to be accounted an intelligent man, one that learns of Christ, who is Wisdom itself. 2. Unbridled passion is folly proclaimed: *He that is hasty of spirit,* whose heart is tinder to every spark of provocation, that is all fire and tow, as we say, he thinks hereby to magnify himself and make those about stand in awe of him, whereas really he *exalts his own folly;* he makes it known, as that which is lifted up is visible to all, and he submits himself to it as to the government of one that is exalted.

Verse 30

The foregoing verse showed how much our reputation, this how much our health, depends on the good government of our passions and the preserving of the temper of the mind. 1. A healing spirit, made up of love and meekness, a hearty, friendly, cheerful disposition, is *the life of the flesh;* it contributes to a good constitution of body; people grow fat with good humour. 2. A fretful, envious, discontented spirit, is its own punishment; it consumes the flesh, preys upon the animal spirits, makes the countenance pale, and is the *rottenness of the bones.* Those that see the prosperity of others and are grieved, let them *gnash with their teeth and melt away,* Ps. 112:10.

> Rumpatur, quisquis rumpitur invidia.
> Whoever bursts for envy, let him burst.

Verse 31

God is here pleased to interest himself more than one would imagine in the treatment given to the poor. 1. He reckons himself affronted in the injuries that are done them. Whosoever he be that wrongs a poor man, taking advantage against him because he is poor and cannot help himself, let him know that he puts an affront upon his Maker. God made him, and gave him his being, the same that is the author of our being; we have all one Father,

one Maker; see how Job considered this, Job 31:15. God made him poor, and appointed him his lot, so that, if we deal hardly with any because they are poor, we reflect upon God as dealing hardly with them in laying them low, that they might be trampled upon. 2. He reckons himself honoured in the kindnesses that are done them; he takes them as done to himself, and will show himself accordingly pleased with them. *I was hungry, and you gave me meat.* Those therefore that have any true honour for God will show it by compassion to the poor, whom he has undertaken in a special manner to protect and patronise.

Verse 32

Here is, 1. The desperate condition of a wicked man when he goes out of the world: He *is driven away in his wickedness.* He cleaves so closely to the world that he cannot find in his heart to leave it, but is driven away out of it; his soul is required, is forced from him, And sin cleaves so closely to him that it is inseparable; it goes with him into another world; he *is driven away in his wickedness,* dies in his sins, under the guilt and power of them, unjustified, unsanctified. His wickedness is the storm in which he is hurried away, as chaff before the wind, chased out of the world. 2. The comfortable condition of a godly man when he finishes his course: He *has hope in his death* of a happiness on the other side death, of better things in another world than ever he had in this. *The righteous* then have the grace of hope in them; though they have pain, and some dread of death, yet they have hope. They have before them the good hoped for, even the blessed hope which God, who cannot lie, has promised.

Verse 33

Observe, 1. Modesty is the badge of wisdom. He that is truly wise hides his treasure, so as not to boast of it (Mt. 13:44), though he does not hide his talent, so as not to trade with it. His *wisdom rests in his heart;* he digests what he knows, and has it ready to him, but does not unseasonably talk of it and make a noise with it. The heart is the seat of the affections, and there wisdom must rest in the practical love of it, and not swim in the head. 2. Openness and ostentation are a mark of folly. If fools have a little smattering of knowledge, they take all occasions, though very foreign, to produce it, and bring it in by head and shoulders. Or the folly that *is in the midst of fools is made known* by their forwardness to talk. Many a foolish man takes more pains to show his folly than a wise man thinks it worth his while to take to show his wisdom.

Verse 34

Note, 1. Justice, reigning in a nation, puts an honour upon it. A righteous administration of the government, impartial equity between man and man, public countenance given to religion, the general practice and profession of virtue, the protecting and preserving of virtuous men, charity and compassion to strangers (*alms* are sometimes called *righteousness*), these *exalt a nation;* they uphold the throne, elevate the people's minds, and qualify a nation for the favour of God, which will make them high, as a *holy nation,* Deu. 26:19. 2. Vice, reigning in a nation, puts disgrace upon it: *Sin is a reproach to any* city or kingdom, and renders them despicable among their neighbours. The people of Israel were often instances of both parts of this observation; they were great when they were good, but when they forsook God all about them insulted them and trampled on them. It is therefore the interest and duty of princes to use their power for the suppression of vice and support of virtue.

Verse 35

This shows that in a well-ordered court and government smiles and favours are dispensed among those that are employed in public trusts according to their merits; Solomon lets them know he will go by that rule, 1. That those who behave themselves wisely shall be respected and preferred, whatever enemies they may have that seek to undermine them. No man's services shall be neglected to please a party or a favourite. 2. That those who are selfish and false, who betray their country, oppress the poor, and sow discord, and thus *cause shame,* shall be displaced and banished the court, whatever friends they may make to speak for them.

CHAPTER 15

Verse 1

Solomon, as conservator of the public peace, here tells us, 1. How the peace may be kept, that we may know how in our places to keep it; it is by soft words. If wrath be risen like a threatening cloud, pregnant with storms and thunder, *a soft answer* will disperse it and turn it away. When men are provoked, speak gently to them, and give them good words, and they will be pacified, as the Ephraimites were by Gideon's mildness (Jdg. 8:1–3); whereas, upon a like occasion, by Jephthah's roughness, they were exasperated, and the consequences were bad, Jdg. 12:1–3. Reason will be better spoken, and a righteous cause better pleaded, with meekness then with passion; hard arguments do best with soft words. 2. How the peace will be broken, that we, for our parts, may do nothing towards the breaking of it. Nothing stirs up anger, and sows discord, like *grievous words,* calling foul names, as *Raca,* and *Thou fool,* upbraiding men with their infirmities and infelicities, their extraction or education, or any thing that lessens them and makes them mean; scornful spiteful reflections, by which men affect to show their wit and malice, stir up the anger of others, which does but increase and inflame their own anger. Rather than lose a jest some will lose a friend and make an enemy.

Verse 2

Note, 1. A good heart by the tongue becomes very useful. He that has knowledge is not only to enjoy it, for his own entertainment, but to use it, to use it aright, for the edification of others; and it is *the tongue* that must make use of it in pious profitable discourse, in giving suitable and seasonable instructions, counsels, and comforts, with all possible expressions of humility and love, and then *knowledge is used aright;* and to him that has, and thus uses what he has, more shall be given. 2. A wicked heart by the tongue becomes very hurtful; for *the mouth of fools belches out foolishness,* which is very offensive; and the corrupt communication which proceeds from an evil treasure within (the filthiness, and foolish talking, and jesting) corrupts the good manners of some and debauches them, and grieves the good hearts of others and disturbs them.

Verse 3

The great truths of divinity are of great use to enforce the precepts of morality, and none more than this — That the eye of God is always upon the children of men. 1. An eye to discern all, not only from which nothing can be concealed, but by which every thing is actually inspected, and nothing overlooked or looked slightly upon: *The eyes of the Lord are in every place;* for he not only sees all from on high (Ps. 33:13), but he is every where present. Angels are *full of eyes* (Rev. 4:8), but God is all eye. It denotes not only his omniscience, that he sees all, but his universal providence, that he upholds and governs all. Secret sins, services, and sorrows, are under his eye. 2. An eye to distinguish both persons and actions. He *beholds the evil and the good,* is displeased with the evil and approves of the good, and will judge men according to the sight of his eyes, Ps. 1:6; 11:4. The wicked shall not go unpunished, nor the righteous unrewarded, for God has his eye upon both and knows their true character; this speaks as much comfort to saints as terror to sinners.

Verse 4

Note, 1. A good tongue is healing, healing to wounded consciences by comforting them, to sin-sick souls by convincing them, to peace and love when it is broken by accommodating differences, compromising matters in variance, and reconciling parties at variance; this is the healing of the tongue, which *is a tree of life,* the leaves of which have a sanative virtue, Rev. 22:2. He that knows how to discourse will make the place he lives in a paradise. 2. An evil tongue is wounding (*perverseness,* passion, falsehood, and filthiness *there, are a breach in the spirit*); it wounds the conscience of the evil speaker, and occasions either guilt or grief to the hearers, and both are to be reckoned *breaches in the spirit.* Hard words indeed break no bones, but many a heart has been broken by them.

Verse 5

Hence, 1. Let superiors be admonished to give instruction and reproof to those that are under their charge, as they will answer it in the day of account. They must not only instruct with the light of knowledge, but reprove with the heat of zeal; and both these must be done with the authority and affection of a father, and must be continued, though the desired effect be not immediately perceived. If the instruction be despised, give reproof, and rebuke sharply. It is indeed against the grain with good-humoured men to find fault, and make those about them uneasy; but better so than to suffer them to go on undisturbed in the way to ruin. 2. Let inferiors be admonished, not only to submit to instruction and reproof (even hardships must be submitted to), but to value them as favours and not despise them, to make use of them for their direction, and always to have a regard to them; this will be an evidence that they are wise and a means of making them so; whereas he that slights his good education is a fool and is likely to live and die one.

Verse 6

Note, 1. Where righteousness is riches are, and the comforts of them: *In the house of the righteous is much treasure.* Religion teaches men to be diligent, temperate, and just, and by these means, ordinarily, the estate is increased. But that is not all: God *blesses the habitation of the just,* and that blessing makes rich without trouble. Or, if there be not much of this world's goods, yet where there is grace there is true treasure; and those who have but little, if they have a heart to be therewith content, and to enjoy the comfort of that little, it is enough; it is all riches. The righteous perhaps are not themselves enriched, but there is treasure in their house, a blessing in store, which their children after them may reap the benefit of. A wicked worldly man is only for having his belly filled with those treasures, his own sensual appetite gratified (Ps. 17:14); but a righteous man's first care is for his soul and then for his seed, to have treasure in his heart and then in his house, which his relations and those about him may have the benefit of. 2. Where wickedness is, though there may be riches, yet there is vexation of spirit with them: *In the revenues of the wicked,* the great incomes they have, *there is trouble;* for there is guilt and a curse; there is pride and passion, and envy and contention; and those are troublesome lusts, which rob them of the joy of their revenues and make them troublesome to their neighbours.

Verse 7

This is to the same purport with *v.* 2, and shows what a blessing a wise man is and what a burden a fool is to those about him. Only here observe further, 1. That we then use knowledge aright when we disperse it, not confine it to a few of our intimates, and grudge it to others who would make as good use of it, but *give a portion of* this spiritual alms *to seven and also to eight,* not only be communicative, but diffusive, of this good, with humility and prudence. We must take pains to spread and propagate useful knowledge, must teach some that they may teach others, and so it is dispersed. 2. That it is not only a fault to *pour out foolishness,* but it is a shame not to *disperse knowledge,* at least not to drop some wise word or other: *The heart of the foolish does not so;* it has nothing to disperse that is good, or, if it had, has neither skill nor will to do good with it and therefore is little worth.

Verse 8

Note, 1. God so hates wicked people, whose hearts are malicious and their lives mischievous, that even their *sacrifices are an abomination* to him. God has sacrifices brought him even by wicked men, to stop the mouth of conscience and to keep up their reputation in the world, as malefactors come to a sanctuary, not because it is a holy place, but because it shelters them from justice; but their sacrifices, though ever so costly, are not accepted of God, because not offered in sincerity nor from a good principle; they dissemble with God, and in their conversations give the lie to their devotions, and for that reason they are *an abomination* to him, because they are made a cloak for sin, *ch.* 7:14. See Isa. 1:11. 2. God has such a love for upright good people that, though they are not at the expense of a sacrifice (he himself has provided that), their

prayer is a delight to him. Praying graces are his own gift, and the work of his own Spirit in them, with which he is well pleased. He not only answers their prayers, but delights in their addresses to him, and in doing them good.

Verse 9

This is a reason of what was said in the foregoing verse. 1. *The sacrifices of the wicked are an abomination to God,* not for want of some nice points of ceremony, but because *their way,* the whole course and tenour of their conversation, is wicked, and consequently an abomination to him. Sacrifices for sin were not accepted of those that resolved to go on in sin, and were to the highest degree abominable if intended to obtain a connivance at sin and a permission to go on in it. 2. Therefore *the prayer of the upright is his delight,* because he is a friend of God, and *he loves him who,* though he have not yet attained, is *following after righteousness,* aiming at it and pressing towards it, as St. Paul, Phil. 3:13.

Verse 10

This shows that those who cannot bear to be corrected must expect to be destroyed. 1. It is common for those who have known the way of righteousness, but have forsaken it, to reckon it a great affront to be reproved and admonished. They are very uneasy at reproof; they cannot, they will not, bear it; nay, because they hate to be reformed, they hate to be reproved, and hate those who deal faithfully and kindly with them. Of all sinners, reproofs are worst resented by apostates. 2. It is certain that those who will not be reproved will be ruined: *He that hates reproof,* and hardens his heart against it, is joined to his idols; let him alone. He *shall die,* and perish for ever, in his sins, since he would not be parted from his sins. 2 Chr. 25:15, *I know that God has determined to destroy thee,* because thou couldst not bear to be reproved; see also *ch.* 29:1.

Verse 11

This confirms what was said (*v.* 3) concerning God's omnipresence, in order to his judging of evil and good. 1. God knows all things, even those things that are hidden from the eyes of all living: *Hell and destruction are before the Lord,* not only the centre of the earth, and its subterraneous caverns, but the grave, and all the dead bodies which are there buried out of our sight; they are all *before the Lord,* all under his eye, so that none of them can be lost or be to seek when they are to be raised again. He knows where every man lies buried, even Moses, even those that are buried in the greatest obscurity; nor needs he any monument with a *Hic jacet — Here he lies,* to direct him. The place of the damned in particular, and all their torments, which are inexpressible, the state of separate souls in general, and all their circumstances, are under God's eye. The word here used for *destruction* is Abaddon, which is one of the devil's names, Rev. 9:11. That destroyer, though he deceives us, cannot evade or elude the divine cognizance. God examines him whence he comes (Job 1:7), and sees through all his disguises though he is sly, and subtle, and swift, Job 26:6. 2. He knows particularly *the hearts of the children of men.* If he sees through the depths and wiles of Satan himself, *much more* can he search men's hearts, though they be deceitful, since they learned all their fraudulent arts of Satan. *God is greater than our hearts,* and knows them better than we know them ourselves, and therefore is an infallible Judge of every man's character, Heb. 4:13.

Verse 12

A scorner is one that not only makes a jest of God and religion, but bids defiance to the methods employed for his conviction and reformation, and, as an evidence of that, 1. He cannot endure the checks of his own conscience, nor will he suffer it to deal plainly with him: *He loves not to reprove him* (so some read it); he cannot endure to retire into his own heart and commune seriously with that, will not admit of any free thought or fair reasoning with himself, nor let his own heart smite him, if he can help it. That man's case is sad who is afraid of being acquainted and of arguing with himself. 2. He cannot endure the advice and admonitions of his friends: *He will not go unto the wise,* lest they should give him wise counsel. We ought not only to bid the wise welcome when they come to us, but to go to them, as beggars to the rich man's door for an alms; but this the scorner will not do, for fear of being told of his faults and prevailed upon to reform.

Verse 13

Here, 1. Harmless mirth is recommended to us, as that which contributes to the health of the body, making men lively and fit for business, and to the acceptableness of the conversation, making the face to shine and rendering us pleasant one to another. A cheerful spirit, under the government of wisdom and grace, is a great ornament to religion, puts a further lustre upon the beauty of holiness, and makes men the more capable of doing good. 2. Hurtful melancholy is what we are cautioned against, as a great enemy to us, both in our devotion and in our conversation: *By sorrow of the heart,* when it has got dominion and plays the tyrant, as it will be apt to do it if be indulged awhile, *the spirit is broken* and sunk, and becomes unfit for the service of God. *The sorrow of the world works death.* Let us therefore *weep as though we wept not,* in justice to ourselves, as well as in conformity to God and his providence.

Verse 14

Here are two things to be wondered at: — 1. A wise man not satisfied with his wisdom, but still seeking the increase of it; the more he has the more he would have: *The heart of him that has understanding,* rejoices so in the knowledge it has attained to that it is still coveting more, and in the use of the means of knowledge is still labouring for more, *growing in grace, and in the knowledge of Christ. Si dixisti, Sufficit, periisti — If you say, I have enough, you are undone.* 2. A fool well satisfied with his folly and not seeking the cure of it. While a good man hungers after the solid satisfactions of grace, a carnal mind feasts on the gratifications of appetite and fancy. Vain mirth and sensual pleasures are its delight, and with these it can rest contented, flattering itself in these foolish ways.

Verse 15

See here what a great difference there is between the condition and temper of some and others of the children of men. 1. Some are much in affliction, and of a sorrowful spirit, and all their days are evil days, like those of old age, and days of which they say they *have no pleasure in them.* They *eat in darkness* (Eccl. 5:17) and never *eat with pleasure,* Job 21:25. How many are the afflictions of the afflicted in this world! Such are not to be censured or despised, but pitied and prayed for, succoured and comforted. It might have been our own lot, or may be yet, merry as we are at present. 2. Others enjoy great prosperity and are of a cheerful spirit; and they have not only good days, but have *a continual feast;* and if in the abundance of all things they serve God with gladness of heart, and it is oil to the wheels of their obedience (all this, and heaven too), then they serve a good Master. But let not such feast without fear; a sudden change may come; therefore *rejoice with trembling.*

Verses 16–17

Solomon had said in the foregoing verse that he who has not a large estate, or a great income, but a cheerful spirit, has *a continual feast;* Christian contentment, and joy in God, make the life easy and pleasant; now here he tells us what is necessary to that cheerfulness of spirit which will furnish a man with *a continual feast,* though he has but little in the world — holiness and love.

I. Holiness. *A little,* if we manage it and enjoy it in *the fear of the Lord,* if we keep a good conscience and go on in the way of duty, and serve God faithfully with the little we have, will be more comfortable, and turn to a better account, *than great treasure and trouble therewith.* Observe here, 1. It is often the lot of those that fear God to have but a little of this world. *The poor receive the gospel,* and poor they still are, Jam. 2:5. 2. Those that have *great treasure* have often great *trouble therewith;* it is so far from making them easy that it increases their care and hurry. *The abundance of the rich will not suffer them to sleep.* 3. If great treasure bring trouble with it, it is for want of the fear of God. If those that have great estates would do their duty with them, and then trust God with them, their treasure would not have so much trouble attending it. 4. It is

therefore far better, and more desirable, to have but a little of the world and to have it with a good conscience, to keep up communion with God, and enjoy him in it, and live by faith, than to have the greatest plenty and live without God in the world.

II. Love. Next to the fear of God, peace with all men is necessary to the comfort of this life. 1. If *brethren dwell together in unity,* if they are friendly, and hearty, and pleasant, both in their daily meals and in more solemn entertainments, that will make *a dinner of herbs* a feast sufficient; though the fare be coarse, and the estate so small that they can afford no better, yet love will sweeten it and they may be as merry over it as if they had all dainties. 2. If there be mutual enmity and strife, though there be a whole ox for dinner, a fat ox, there can be no comfort in it; the leaven of malice, of hating and being hated, is enough to sour it all. Some refer it to him that makes the entertainment; better have a slender dinner and be heartily welcome than a table richly spread with a grudging evil eye.

> Cum torvo vultu mihi conula nulla placebit,
> Cum placido vultu conula ulla placet.
>
> The most sumptuous entertainment, presented with a sullen brow, would offend me; while the plainest repast, presented kindly would delight me.

Verse 18

Here is, 1. Passion the great make-bate. Thence *come wars and fightings.* Anger strikes the fire which sets cities and churches into a flame: *A wrathful man,* with his peevish passionate reflections, *stirs up strife,* and sets people together by the ears; he gives occasion to others to quarrel, and takes the occasion that others give, though ever so trifling. When men carry their resentments too far, one quarrel still produces another. 2. Meekness the great peacemaker: *He that is slow to anger* not only *prevents* strife, that it be not kindled, but *appeases* it if it be already kindled, brings water to the flame, unites those again that have fallen out, and by gentle methods brings them to mutual concessions for peace-sake.

Verse 19

See here, 1. Whence those difficulties arise which men pretend to meet with in the way of their duty, and to be insuperable; they arise not from any thing in the nature of the duty, but from the slothfulness of those that have really no mind to it. Those that have no heart to their work pretend that their way is hedged up with thorns, and they cannot do their work at all (as if God were a hard Master, reaping where he had not sown), at least that their way is strewed with thorns, that they cannot do their work without a great deal of hardship and danger; and therefore they go about it with as much reluctance as if they were to go barefoot through a thorny hedge. 2. How these imaginary difficulties may be conquered. An honest desire and endeavour to do our duty will, by the grace of God, make it easy, and we shall find it strewed with roses: *The way of the righteous is made plain;* it is easy to be trodden and not rough, easy to be found, and not intricate.

Verse 20

Observe here, 1. To the praise of good children, that they are the joy of their parents, who ought to have joy of them, having taken so much care and pains about them. And it adds much to the satisfaction of those that are good if they have reason to think that they have been a comfort to their parents in their declining years, when evil days come. 2. To the shame of wicked children, that by their wickedness they put contempt upon their parents, slight their authority, and make an ill requital for their kindness: *A foolish son despises his mother,* that had most sorrow with him and perhaps had too much indulged him, which makes his sin in despising her the more sinful and her sorrow the more sorrowful.

Verse 21

Note, 1. It is the character of a wicked man that he takes pleasure in sin; he has an appetite to the bait, and swallows it greedily, and has no dread of the hook, nor feels from it when he has swallowed it: *Folly is joy to him;* the folly of others is so, and his own much more. He sins, not only without regret, but with delight, not only repents not

of it, but makes his boast of it. This is a certain sign of one that is graceless. 2. It is the character of a wise and good man that he makes conscience of his duty. A fool lives at large, walks at all adventures, by no rule, acts with no sincerity or steadiness; *but a man of understanding,* the eyes of whose understanding are enlightened by the Spirit (and those that have not a good understanding have no understanding), *walks uprightly,* lives a sober, orderly, regular life, and studies in every thing to conform himself to the will of God; and this is a constant pleasure and *joy to him.* But what foolishness remains in him, or proceeds from him at any time, is a grief to him, and he is ashamed of it. By these characters we may try ourselves.

Verse 22

See here, 1. Of what ill consequence it is to be precipitate and rash, and to act without advice: Men's *purposes are disappointed,* their measures broken, and they come short of their point, gain not their end, because they would not ask counsel about the way. If men will not take time and pains to deliberate with themselves, or are so confident of their own judgment that they scorn to consult with others, they are not likely to bring any thing considerable to pass; circumstances defeat them which, with a little consultation, might have been foreseen and obviated. It is a good rule, both in public and domestic affairs, to do nothing rashly and of one's own head. *Plus vident oculi quam oculus — Many eyes see more than one.* That often proves best which was least our own doing. 2. How much it will be for our advantage to ask the advice of our friends: *In the multitude of counsellors* (provided they be discreet and honest, and will not give counsel with a spirit of contradiction) *purposes are established.* Solomon's son made no good use of this proverb when he acquiesced not in the counsel of the old men, but because he would have a *multitude of counsellors,* regarding number more than weight, advised with the young men.

Verse 23

Note, 1. We speak wisely when we speak seasonably: *The answer of the mouth* will be our credit and joy when it is pertinent and to the purpose, and is *spoken in due season,* when it is needed and will be regarded, and, as we say, hits the joint. Many a good word comes short of doing the good it might have done, for want of being well-timed. Nor is any thing more the beauty of discourse than to have a proper answer ready off-hand, just when there is occasion for it, and it comes in well. 2. If we speak wisely and well, it will redound to our own comfort and to the advantage of others: *A man has joy by the answer of his mouth;* he may take a pleasure, but may by no means take a pride, in having spoken so acceptably and well that the hearers admire him and say, *"How good is it,* and how much good does it do!"

Verse 24

The way of wisdom and holiness is here recommended to us, 1. As very safe and comfortable: It is *the way of life,* the way that leads to eternal life, in which we shall find the joy and satisfaction which will be the life of the soul, and at the end of which we shall find the perfection of blessedness. Be wise and live. It is the way to escape that misery which we cannot but see ourselves exposed to, and in danger of. It is to *depart from hell beneath,* from the snares of hell, the temptations of Satan, and all his wiles, from the pains of hell, that everlasting destruction which our sins have deserved. 2. As very sublime and honourable: It *is above.* A good man sets his *affections on things above,* and deals in those things. His *conversation is in heaven;* his way leads directly thither; there his treasure is, *above,* out of the reach of enemies, above the changes of this lower world. A good man is truly noble and great; his desires and designs are high, and he lives above the common rate of other men. It is above the capacity and out of the sight of foolish men.

Verse 25

Note, 1. Those that are elevated God delights to abase, and commonly does it in the course of his providence: *The proud,* that magnify themselves, bid defiance to the God above them and trample on all about them, are such as God resists and *will destroy,* not them only, but *their houses,* which they are proud of and are confident of the continuance and perpetuity of. Pride is the ruin of multitudes. 2. Those that are dejected God delights to support, and often does it remarkably: *He will establish the border of the poor widow,* which proud injurious men break in upon, and which the poor widow is not herself able to defend and make good. It is the honour of God to protect the weak and appear for those that are oppressed.

Verse 26

The former part of this verse speaks of thoughts, the latter of words, but they come all to one; for thoughts are words to God, and words are judged of by the thoughts from which they proceed, so that, 1. *The thoughts and words of the wicked,* which are, like themselves, wicked, which aim at mischief, and have some ill tendency or other, *are an abomination to the Lord;* he is displeased at them and will reckon for them. The thoughts of wicked men, for the most part, are such as God hates, and are an offence to him, who not only knows the heart and all that passes and repasses there, but requires the innermost and uppermost place in it. 2. The thoughts and *words of the pure,* being pure like themselves, clean, honest, and sincere, *are pleasant words* and pleasant thoughts, well-pleasing to the holy God, who delights in purity. It may be understood both of their devotions to God (the *words of their mouth and the meditations of their heart,* in prayer and praise, are *acceptable to God,* Ps. 19:14; 69:13) and of their discourses with men, tending to edification. Both are pleasant when they come from a pure, a purified, heart.

Verse 27

Note, 1. Those that are covetous entail trouble upon their families: *He that is greedy of gain,* and therefore makes himself a slave to the world, rises up early, sits up late, and eats the bread of carefulness, in pursuit of it — he that hurries, and puts himself and all about him upon the stretch, in business, frets and vexes at every loss and disappointment, and quarrels with every body that stands in the way of his profit — he *troubles his own house,* is a burden and vexation to his children and servants. He that, in his greediness of gain, takes bribes, and uses unlawful ways of getting money, leaves a curse with what he gets to those that come after him, which sooner or later will bring trouble into the house, Hab. 2:9, 10. 2. Those that are generous as well as righteous entail a blessing upon their families: *He that hates gifts,* that shakes his hands from holding the bribes that are thrust into his hand to pervert justice and abhors all sinful indirect ways of getting money — that hates to be paltry and mercenary, and is willing, if there be occasion, to do good gratis — he shall live; he shall have the comfort of life, shall live in prosperity and reputation; his name and family shall live and continue.

Verse 28

Here is, 1. A good man proved to be a wise man by this, that he governs his tongue well; he that does so *the same is a perfect man,* Jam. 3:2. It is part of the character of a righteous man that being convinced of the account he must give of his words, and of the good and bad influence of them upon others, he makes conscience of speaking truly (it is his *heart that answers,* that is, he speaks as he thinks, and dares not do otherwise, he *speaks the truth in his heart,* Ps. 15:2), and of speaking pertinently and profitably, and therefore he *studies to answer,* that his speech may be with grace, Neh. 2:4; 5:7. 2. A wicked man is proved to be a fool by this, that he never heeds what he says, but his *mouth pours out evil things,* to the dishonour of God and religion, his own reproach, and the hurt of others. Doubtless that is an evil heart which thus overflows with evil.

Verse 29

Note, 1. God sets himself at a distance from those that set him at defiance: *The wicked say to the Almighty, Depart from us,* and he is, accordingly, *far from* them; he does not manifest himself to them, has no communion with them, will not hear them, will not help them, no, not in the time of their need. They shall be for ever banished from his presence and he will behold them afar off. *De-*

part from me, you cursed. 2. He will draw nigh to those in a way of mercy who draw nigh to him in a way of duty: *He hears the prayer of the righteous,* accepts it, is well pleased with it, and will grant an answer of peace to it. It is *the prayer of a righteous man* that *avails much,* Jam. 5:16. *He is nigh to them,* a present help, *in all that they call upon him for.*

Verse 30

Two things are here pronounced pleasant: — 1. It is pleasant to have a good prospect to see the light of the sun (Eccl. 11:7) and by it to see the wonderful works of God, with which this lower world is beautified and enriched. Those that want the mercy know how to value it; how would *the light of the eyes rejoice their hearts!* The consideration of this should make us thankful for our eyesight. 2. It is more pleasant to have *a good name,* a name for good things with God and good people; this *is as precious ointment,* Eccl. 7:1. *It makes the bones fat;* it gives a secret pleasure, and that which is strengthening. It is also very comfortable to hear (as some understand it) *a good report* concerning others; a good man has no greater joy than to hear that his friends walk in the truth.

Verse 31

Note, 1. It is the character of a wise man that he is very willing to be reproved, and therefore chooses to converse with those that, both by their words and example, will show him what is amiss in him: *The ear that* can take *the reproof* will love the reprover. Faithful friendly reproofs are here called *the reproofs of life,* not only because they are to be given in a lively manner, and with a prudent zeal (and we must reprove by our lives as well as by our doctrine), but because, where they are well-taken, they are means of spiritual life, and lead to eternal life, and (as some think) to distinguish them from rebukes and reproaches for well-doing, which are rather reproofs of death, which we must not regard nor be influenced by. 2. Those that are so wise as to bear reproof well will hereby be *made wiser* (*ch.* 9:9), and come at length to be numbered among the wise men of the age, and will have both ability and authority to reprove and instruct others. Those that learn well, and obey well, are likely in time to teach well and rule well.

Verse 32

See here, 1. The folly of those that will not be taught, that *refuse instruction,* that will not heed it, but turn their backs upon it, or will not hear it, but turn their hearts against it. They *refuse correction* (margin); they will not *take it,* no, not from God himself, but kick against the pricks. Those that do so *despise their own souls;* they show that they have a low and mean opinion of them, and are in little care and concern about them, considered as rational and immortal, instruction being designed to cultivate reason and prepare for the immortal state. The fundamental error of sinners is undervaluing their own souls; therefore they neglect to provide for them, abuse them, expose them, prefer the body before the soul, and wrong the soul to please the body. 2. The wisdom of those that are willing, not only to be taught, but to be reproved: *He that hears reproof,* and amends the faults he is reproved for, *gets understanding,* by which his soul is secured from bad ways and directed in good ways, and thereby he both evidences the value he has for his own soul and puts true honour upon it.

Verse 33

See here how much it is our interest, as well as duty, 1. To submit to our God, and keep up a reverence for him: *The fear of the Lord,* as it is *the beginning of wisdom,* so it is *the instruction* and correction *of wisdom;* the principles of religion, closely adhered to, will improve our knowledge, rectify our mistakes, and be the best and surest guide of our way. An awe of God upon our spirits will put us upon the wisest counsels and chastise us when we say or do unwisely. 2. To stoop to our brethren, and keep up a respect for them. Where there is humility there is a happy presage of honour and preparative for it. Those that humble themselves shall be exalted here and hereafter.

CHAPTER 16

Verse 1

As we read this, it teaches us a great truth, that we are not sufficient of ourselves to *think or speak any thing of ourselves* that is wise and good, but that all *our sufficiency is of God,* who is with the heart and with the mouth, and *works in us both to will and to do,* Phil. 2:13; Ps. 10:17. But most read it otherwise: *The preparation of the heart is in man* (he may contrive and design this and the other) but *the answer of the tongue,* not only the delivering of what he designed to speak, but the issue and success of what he designed to do, *is of the Lord.* That is, in short, 1. *Man purposes.* He has a freedom of thought and a freedom of will permitted him; let him form his projects, and lay his schemes, as he thinks best: but, after all, 1. *God disposes.* Man cannot go on with his business without the assistance and blessing of God, who *made man's mouth* and teaches us what we shall say. Nay, God easily can, and often does, cross men's purposes, and break their measures. It was a curse that was prepared in Balaam's heart, but the answer of the tongue was a blessing.

Verse 2

Note, 1. We are all apt to be partial in judging of ourselves: *All the ways of a man,* all his designs, all his doings, *are clean in his own eyes,* and he sees nothing amiss in them, nothing for which to condemn himself, or which should make his projects prove otherwise than well; and therefore he is confident of success, and that the answer of the tongue shall be according to the expectations of the heart; but there is a great deal of pollution cleaving to our ways, which we are not aware of, or do not think so ill of as we ought. 2. The judgment of God concerning us, we are sure, is according to truth: He *weighs the spirits* in a just and unerring balance, knows what is in us, and passes a judgment upon us accordingly, writing *Tekel* upon that which passed our scale with approbation — *weighed in the balance and found wanting;* and by his judgment we must stand or fall. He not only sees men's ways but tries their spirits, and we are as our spirits are.

Verse 3

Note, 1. It is a very desirable thing to have *our thoughts established,* and not tossed, and put into a hurry, by disquieting cares and fears, — to go on in an even steady course of honesty and piety, not disturbed, or put out of frame, by any event or change, — to be satisfied that all shall work for good and issue well at last, and therefore to be always easy and sedate. 2. The only way to have our *thoughts established* is to *commit our works to the Lord.* The great concerns of our souls must be committed to the grace of God, with a dependence upon and submission to the conduct of that grace (2 Tim. 1:12); all our outward concerns must be committed to the providence of God, and to the sovereign, wise, and gracious disposal of that providence. *Roll thy works upon the Lord* (so the word is); roll the burden of thy care from thyself upon God. Lay the matter before him by prayer. *Make known thy works unto the Lord* (so some read it), not only the works of thy hand, but the workings of thy heart; and then leave it with him, by faith and dependence upon him, submission and resignation to him. *The will of the Lord be done.* We may then be easy when we resolve that whatever pleases God shall please us.

Verse 4

Note, 1. That God is the first cause. He is the former of all things and all persons, the fountain of being; he gave every creature the being it has and appointed it its place. Even the wicked are his creatures, though they are rebels; he gave them those powers with which they fight against him, which aggravates their wickedness, that they will not let him that made them rule them, and therefore, though he made them, he will not save them. 2. That God is the last end. All is of him and from him, and therefore all is to him and for him. He made all according to his will and for his praise; he designed to serve his own purposes by all his creatures, and he will not fail of his designs; all are his servants. The wicked he is not glorified by, but he will be glorified upon. He makes no man wicked, but he made those who he foresaw would be wicked: yet he made them (Gen. 6:6), because he knew how to *get himself honour upon them.* See Rom. 9:22. Or (as some understand it) he made the wicked to be employed by him as the instruments of his wrath in the day of evil, when he brings judgments on the world. He makes some use even of wicked men, as of other things, to be his sword, his hand (Ps. 17:13, 14), *flagellum Dei — the scourge of God.* The king of Babylon is called his *servant.*

Verse 5

Note, 1. The pride of sinners sets God against them. He that, being high in estate is proud in heart, whose spirit is elevated with his condition, so that he becomes insolent in his conduct towards God and man, let him know that though he admires himself, and others caress him, yet he is *an abomination to the Lord.* The great God despises him; the holy God detest him. 2. The power of sinners cannot secure them against God, though they strengthen themselves with body hands. Though they may strengthen one another with their confederacies and combinations, joining forces against God, they shall not escape his righteous judgment. *Woe unto him that strives with his Maker, ch.* 11:21; Isa. 45:9.

Verse 6

See here, 1. How the guilt of sin is taken away from us — by the *mercy and truth* of God, mercy in promising, truth in performing, the mercy and truth which kiss each other in Jesus Christ the Mediator — by the covenant of grace, in which mercy and truth shine so brightly — by our mercy and truth, as the condition of the pardon and a necessary qualification for it — by these, and not by the legal sacrifices, Mic. 6:7, 8. 2. How the power of sin is broken in us. By the principles of *mercy and truth* commanding in us the corrupt inclinations are purged out (so we may take the former part); however, *by the fear of the Lord,* and the influence of that fear, *men depart from evil;* those will not dare to sin against God who keep up in their minds a holy dread and reverence of him.

Verse 7

Note, 1. God can turn foes into friends when he pleases. He that has all hearts in his hand has access to men's spirits and power over them, working insensibly, but irresistibly upon them, can make *a man's enemies to be at peace with him,* can change their minds, or force them into a feigned submission. He can slay all enemies, and bring those together that were at the greatest distance from each other. 2. He will do it for us when we please him. If we make it our care to be reconciled to God, and to keep ourselves in his love, he will incline those that have been envious towards us, and vexatious to us, to entertain a good opinion of us and to become our friends. God made Esau to be at peace with Jacob, Abimelech with Isaac, and David's enemies to court his favour and desire a league with Israel. The image of God appearing upon the righteous, and his particular loving-kindness to them, are enough to recommend them to the respect of all, even of those that have been most prejudiced against them.

Verse 8

Here, 1. It is supposed that an honest good man may have but a little of the wealth of this world (all the righteous are not rich), — that a man may have but little, and yet may be honest (though poverty is a temptation to dishonesty, *ch.* 30:9, yet not an invincible one), — and that a man may grow rich, for a while, by fraud and oppression, may have *great revenues,* and those got and kept *without right,* may have no good title to them nor make any good use of them. 2. It is maintained that a small estate, honestly come by, which a man is content with, enjoys comfortably, serves God with cheerfully, and puts to a right use, is much better and more valuable than a great estate ill-got, and then ill-kept or ill-spent. It carries with it more inward satisfaction, a better reputation with all that are wise and good; it will last longer, and will turn to a better account in the great day, when men will be judged, not according to what they had, but what they did.

Verse 9

Man is here represented to us, 1. As a reasonable creature, that has the faculty of contriving for himself: *His heart devises his way,* designs an end, and projects ways and means leading to that end, which the inferior creatures, who are governed by sense and natural instinct, cannot do. The more shame for him if he do not devise the way how to please God and provide for his everlasting state. 2. But as a depending creature, that is subject to the direction and dominion of his Maker. If men *devise their way,* so as to make God's glory their end and his will their rule, they may expect that he will *direct their steps* by his Spirit and grace, so that they shall not miss their way nor come short of their end. But let men devise their worldly affairs ever so politely, and with ever so great a probability of success, yet God has the ordering of the event, and sometimes *directs their steps* to that which they least intended. The design of this is to teach us to say, *If the Lord will, we shall live and do this or that* (Jam. 4:14, 15), and to have our eye to God, not only in the great turns of our lives, but in every step we take. *Lord, direct my way,* 1 Th. 3:11.

Verse 10

We wish this were always true as a proposition, and we ought to make it our prayer for kings, and all in authority, that a *divine sentence* may be in their lips, both in giving orders, that they may do that in wisdom, and in giving sentence, that they may do that in equity, both which are included in *judgment,* and that in neither *their mouth may transgress,* 1 Tim. 2:1. But it is often otherwise; and therefore, 1. it may be read as a precept to the kings and judges of the earth to be wise and instructed. Let them be just, and rule in the fear of God; let them act with such wisdom and conscience that there may appear a holy divination in all they say or do, and that they are guided by principles supernatural: let not their mouths transgress in judgment, for the judgment is God's. 2. It may be taken as a promise to all good kings, that if they sincerely aim at God's glory, and seek direction from him, he will qualify them with wisdom and grace above others, in proportion to the eminency of their station and the trusts lodged in their hands. When Saul himself was made king God gave him another spirit. 3. It was true concerning Solomon who wrote this; he had extraordinary wisdom, pursuant to the promise God made him, See 1 Ki. 3:28.

Verse 11

Note, 1. The administration of public justice by the magistrate is an ordinance of God; in it the scales are held, and ought to be held by a steady and impartial hand; and we ought to submit to it, for the Lord's sake, and to see his authority in that of the magistrate, Rom. 13:1; 1 Pt. 2:13. 2. The observance of justice in commerce between man and man is likewise a divine appointment. He taught men discretion to make scales and weights for the adjusting of right exactly between buyer and seller, that neither may be wronged; and all other useful inventions for the preserving of right are from him. He has also appointed by his law that they be just. It is therefore a great affront to him, and to his government, to falsify, and so to do wrong under colour and pretence of doing right, which is *wickedness in the place of judgment.*

Verse 12

Here is, 1. The character of a good king, which Solomon intended not for his own praise, but for instruction to his successors, his neighbours, and the viceroys under him. A good king not only does justice, but it is *an abomination* to him to do otherwise. He hates the thought of doing wrong and perverting justice; he not only abhors the wickedness done by others, but abhors the wickedness done by others, but abhors to do any himself, though, having power, he might easily and safety do it. 2. The comfort of a good king: His *throne is established by righteousness.* He that makes conscience of using his power aright shall find that to be the best security of his government, both as it will oblige people, make them easy, and keep them in the interest of it, and as it will obtain the blessing of God, which will be a firm basis to the throne and a strong guard about it.

Verse 13

Here is a further character of good kings, that they *love* and *delight* in those that *speak right.* 1. They hate parasites and those that flatter them, and are very willing that all about them should deal faithfully with them and tell them that which is true, whether it be pleasing or displeasing, both concerning persons and things, that every thing should be set in a true light and nothing disguised, *ch.* 29:12. 2. They not only do righteousness themselves, but take care to employ those under them that do righteousness too, which is of great consequence to the people, who must be subject not only to the king as supreme, but to the governors sent by him, 1 Pt. 2:14. A good king will therefore put those in power who are conscientious, and will say that which is righteous and discreet, and know how to speak aright and to the purpose.

Verses 14–15

These two verses show the power of kings, which is every where great, but was especially so in those eastern countries, where they were absolute and arbitrary. Whom they would they slew and whom they would they kept alive. Their will was a law. We have reason to bless God for the happy constitution of the government we live under, which maintains the prerogative of the prince without any injury to the liberty of the subject. But here it is intimated, 1. How formidable *the wrath of a king is:* It is *as messengers of death;* the wrath of Ahasuerus was so to Haman. An angry word from an incensed prince has been to many a *messenger of death,* and has struck so great a terror upon some as if a sentence of death had been pronounced upon them. He must be a very *wise man* that knows how to *pacify* the wrath of a king with a word fitly spoken, as Jonathan once pacified his father's rage against David, 1 Sa. 19:6. A prudent subject may sometimes suggest that to an angry prince which will cool his resentments. 2. How valuable and desirable the king's favour is to those that have incurred his displeasure; it is life from the dead if the king be reconciled to them. To others it is *as a cloud of the latter rain,* very refreshing to the ground. Solomon put his subjects in mind of this, that they might not do any thing to incur his wrath, but be careful to recommend themselves to his favour. We ought by it to be put in mind how much we are concerned to escape the wrath and obtain the favour of the King of kings. His frowns are worse than death, and his favour is better than life; and therefore those are fools who to escape the wrath, and obtain the favour, of an earthly prince, will throw themselves out of God's favour, and make themselves obnoxious to his wrath.

Verse 16

Solomon here not only asserts that it is better to get wisdom than gold (*ch.* 3:14, 8:19), but he speaks it with assurance, that it is much better, better beyond expression — with admiration *(How much better!)* as one amazed at the disproportion — with an appeal to men's consciences ("Judge in yourselves how much better it is") — and with an addition to the same purport, that understanding is *rather to be chosen than silver* and all the treasures of kings and their favourites. Note, 1. Heavenly wisdom is better than worldly wealth, and to be preferred before it. Grace is more valuable than gold. Grace is the gift of God's peculiar favour; gold only of common providence. Grace is for ourselves; gold for others. Grace is for the soul and eternity; gold only for the body and time. Grace will stand us in stead in a dying hour, when gold will do us no good. 2. The getting of this heavenly wisdom is better than the getting of worldly wealth. Many take care and pains to get wealth, and yet come short of it; but grace was never denied to any that sincerely sought it. There is vanity and vexation of spirit in getting wealth, but joy and satisfaction of spirit in getting wisdom. *Great peace have those that love it.*

Verse 17

Note, 1. It is *the way of the upright* to avoid sin, and every thing that looks like it and leads towards it; and this is a highway marked out by authority, tracked by many that have gone before us, and in which we meet with many that keep company with us; it is easy to find and safe to be travelled in, like a highway, Isa. 35:8. *To depart from evil is understanding.* 2. It is the care of the upright to preserve their own souls, that they be not polluted with sin, and that by the troubles of the world they may not be put out of the possession of them, especially that they may not perish for ever, Mt. 16:26. And it is therefore their care to keep their way, and not turn aside out of it, on either hand, but to press towards perfection. Those that adhere to their duty secure their felicity. Keep thy way and God will keep thee.

Verse 18

Note, 1. Pride will have a fall. Those that are of a *haughty spirit,* that think of themselves above what is meet, and look with contempt upon others, that with their pride affront God and disquiet others, will be brought down, either by repentance or by ruin. It is the honour of God to humble the proud, Job 40:11, 12. It is the act of justice that those who have lifted up themselves should be laid low. Pharaoh, Sennacherib, Nebuchadnezzar, were instances of this. Men cannot punish pride, but either admire it or fear it, and therefore God will take the punishing of it into his own hands. Let him alone to deal with proud men. 2. Proud men are frequently most proud, and insolent, and haughty, just before their destruction, so that it is a certain presage that they are upon the brink of it. When proud men set God's judgments at defiance, and think themselves at the greatest distance from them, it is a sign that they are at the door; witness the case of Benhadad and Herod. *While the word was in the king's mouth,* Dan. 4:31. Therefore let us not fear the pride of others, but greatly fear pride in ourselves.

Verse 19

This is a paradox which the children of this world cannot understand and will not subscribe to, that it is better to be poor and humble than to be rich and proud. 1. Those that *divide the spoil* are commonly proud; they value themselves and despise others, and their mind rises with their condition; those therefore that are *rich in this world* have need to be charged that they *be not high-minded,* 1 Tim. 6:17. Those that are proud and will put forth themselves, that thrust, and shove, and scramble, for preferment, are the men that commonly *divide the spoil* and share it among them; they have the world at will and the ball at their foot. 2. It is upon all accounts better to take our lot with those whose condition is low, and their minds brought to it, than to covet and aim to make a figure and a bustle in the world. Humility, though it should expose us to contempt in the world, yet while it recommends us to the favour of God, qualifies us for his gracious visits, prepares us for his glory, secures us from many temptations, and preserves the quiet and repose of our own souls, is much better than that high-spiritedness which, though it carry away the honour and wealth of the world, makes God a man's enemy and the devil his master.

Verse 20

Note, 1. Prudence gains men respect and success: *He that handles a matter wisely* (that is master of his trade and makes it to appear he understands what he undertakes, that is considerate in his affairs, and, when he speaks or writes on any subject, does it pertinently) shall *find good,* shall come into good repute, and perhaps may make a good hand of it. 2. But it is piety only that will secure men's true happiness: Those that *handle a matter wisely,* if they are proud and lean to their own understanding, though they may find some good, yet they will have no great satisfaction in it; but he that *trusts in the Lord,* and not in his own wisdom, *happy is he,* and shall speed better at last. Some read the former part of the verse so as to expound it of piety, which is indeed true wisdom: *He that attends to the word* (the word of God, ch. 13:13) shall *find good* in it and good by it. And whoso *trusts in the Lord,* in his word which he attends to, is happy.

Verse 21

Note, 1. Those that have solid wisdom will have the credit of it; it will gain them reputation, and they *shall be called prudent* grave men, and a deference will be paid to their judgment. *Do that which is wise and good and thou shalt have the praise of the same.* 2. Those that with their wisdom have a happy elocution, that deliver their sentiments easily and with a good grace, are communicative of their wisdom and have words at will, and good language as well as good sense, *increase learning;* they diffuse and propagate knowledge to others, and do good work with it, and by that means increase their own stock. They add doctrine, improve sciences, and do service to the commonwealth of learning. *To him that has,* and uses what he has, *more shall be given.*

Verse 22

Note, 1. There is always some good to be gotten by a wise and good man: His *understanding is a well-spring of life to him,* which always flows and can never be drawn dry; he has something to say upon all occasions that is instructive, and of use to those that will make use of it, things new and old to bring out of his treasure; at least, his understanding is a *spring of life* to himself, yielding him abundant satisfaction; within his own thoughts he entertains and edifies himself, if not others. 2. There is nothing that is good to be gotten by a fool. Even his instruction, his set and solemn discourses, are but folly, like himself, and tending to make others like him. When he does his best it is but folly, in comparison even with the common talk of a wise man, who speaks better at table than a fool in Moses's seat.

Verse 23

Solomon had commended eloquence, or *the sweetness of the lips* (v. 21), and seemed to prefer it before wisdom; but here he corrects himself, as it were, and shows that unless there be a good treasure within to support the eloquence it is worth little. Wisdom in *the heart* is the main matter. 1. It is this that directs us in speaking, that *teaches the mouth* what to speak, and when, and how, so that what is spoken may be proper, and pertinent, and seasonable; otherwise, though the language be ever so fine, it had better be unsaid. 2. It is this that gives weight to what we speak and *adds learning* to it, strength of reason and force of argument, without which, let a thing be ever so well worded, it will be rejected, when it comes to be considered, as trifling. Quaint expressions please the ear, and humour the fancy, but it is learning in the lips that must convince the judgment, and sway that, to which wisdom in the heart is necessary.

Verse 24

The *pleasant words* here commended must be those which *the heart of the wise teaches, and adds learning to* (v. 23), words of seasonable advice, instruction, and comfort, words taken from God's word, for that is it which Solomon had learned from his father to account *sweeter than honey and the honey-comb,* Ps. 19:10. These words, to those that know how to relish them, 1. Are pleasant. They are like the *honey-comb, sweet to the soul,* which tastes in them that *the Lord is gracious;* nothing more grateful and agreeable to the new man than the word of God, and those words which are borrowed from it, Ps. 119:103. 2. They are wholesome. Many things are pleasant that are not profitable, but these *pleasant words are health to the bones,* to the inward man, as well as *sweet to the soul.* They make *the bones,* which sin has broken and put out of joint, *to rejoice.* The bones are the strength of the body; and the good word of God is a means of spiritual strength, curing the diseases that weaken us.

Verse 25

This we had before (ch. 14:12), but here it is repeated, as that which is very necessary to be thought of, 1. By way of caution to us all to take heed of deceiving ourselves in the great concerns of our souls by resting in that which *seems right* and is not really so, and, for the preventing of a self-delusion, to be impartial in self-examination and keep up a jealousy over ourselves. 2. By way of terror to those whose way is not right, is not as it should be, however it may seem to themselves or others; the end of it will certainly be death; to that it has a direct and certain tendency.

Verse 26

This is designed to engage us to diligence, and quicken us, *what our hand finds to do, to do it with all our might,* both in our worldly business and in the work of religion; for in the original it is, *The soul that labours labours for itself.* It is heart-work which is here intended, the labour of the soul, which is here recommended to us, 1. As that which will be absolutely needful. Our mouth is continually craving it of us; the necessities both of soul and body are pressing, and require constant relief, so that we must either work or starve. Both call for daily bread, and therefore there must be daily labour; for in the sweat of our face we must eat, 2 Th. 3:10. 2. As that which will be unspeakably gainful. We know on whose errand we go: *He that labours* shall reap the fruit of his labour; it shall be *for himself;* he shall rejoice in his own work and *eat the labour of his hands.* If we make religion our business, God will make it our blessedness.

Verses 27–28

There are those that are not only vicious themselves, but spiteful and mischievous to others, and they are the worst of men; two sorts of such are here described: — 1. Such as envy a man the honour of his good name, and do all they can to blast that by calumnies and misrepresentations: They *dig up evil;* they take a great deal of pains to find out something or other on which to ground a slander, or which may give some colour to it. If none appear above ground, rather than want it they will dig for it, by diving into what is secret, or looking a great way back, or by evil suspicions and surmises, and forced innuendos. In the lips of a slanderer and backbiter *there is as a fire,* not only to brand his neighbour's reputation, to smoke and sully it, but *as a burning fire* to consume it. And how great a matter does a little of this fire kindle, and how hardly is it extinguished! James 3:5, 6. 2. Such as envy a man the comfort of his friendship, and do all they can to break that, by suggesting that on both sides which will set those at variance that are most nearly related and have been long intimate, or at least cool and alienate their affections one from another: A *froward man,* that cannot find in his heart to love any body but himself, is vexed to see others live in love, and therefore makes it is his business to *sow strife,* by giving men base characters one of another, telling lies, and carrying ill-natured stories between *chief friends,* so as to *separate* them one from another, and make them angry at or at least suspicious of one another. Those are bad men, and bad women too, that do such ill offices; they are doing the devil's work, and his will their wages be.

Verses 29–30

Here is another sort of evil men described to us, that we may neither do like them, nor have any thing to do with them. 1. Such as (like Satan) do all the mischief they can by force and violence, as roaring lions, and not only by fraud and insinuation, as subtle serpents: They are *violent men,* that do all by rapine and oppression, that *shut their eyes,* meditating with the closest intention and application of mind to *devise froward things,* to contrive how they may do the greatest mischief to their neighbour, to do it effectually and yet securely to themselves; and then *moving their lips,* giving the word of command to their agents, they *bring the evil to pass,* and accomplish the wicked device, *biting his lips* (so some read it) for vexation. When *the wicked plots against the just* he *gnasheth upon him with his teeth.* 2. Such as (like Satan still) do all they can to *entice* and draw in others to join with them in doing mischief, *leading them in a way that is not good,* that is not honest, nor honourable, nor safe, but offensive to God, and which will be in the end pernicious to the sinner. Thus he aims to ruin some in this world by bringing them into trouble, and others in the other world by bringing them into sin.

Verse 31

Note, 1. It ought to be the great care of old people to *be found in the way of righteousness,* the way of religion and serious godliness. Both God and man will look for them in that way; it will be expected that those that are old should be good, that the multitude of their years should teach them the best wisdom; let them therefore be found in that way. Death will come; the Judge is coming; *the Lord is at hand.* That they may *be found of him in peace,* let them *be found in the way of righteousness* (2 Pt. 3:14), *found so doing,* Mt. 24:46. Let old people be old disciples; let them persevere to the end *in the way of righteousness,* which they long since set out in, that they may then be found in it. 2. If old people *be found in the way of right-eousness,* their age will be their honour. Old age, as such, is honourable, and commands respect (*Thou shalt rise up before the hoary head,* Lev. 19:32); but, if it be found in the way of wickedness, its honour is forfeited, its crown profaned and laid in the dust, Isa. 65:20. Old people therefore, if they would preserve their honour, must still hold fast their integrity, and then their gray hairs are indeed *a crown* to them; they are *worthy of double honour.* Grace is the glory of old age.

Verse 32

This recommends the grace of meekness to us, which will well become us all, particularly *the hoary head, v.* 31. Observe, 1. The nature of it. it is to be *slow to anger,* not easily put into a passion, nor apt to resent provocation, taking time to consider before we suffer our passion to break out, that it may not transgress due bounds, so slow in our motions towards anger that we may be quickly stopped and pacified. It is to have the rule of our own spirits, our appetites and affections, and all our inclinations, but particularly our passions, our anger, keeping that under direction and check, and the strict government of religion and right reason. We must be *lords of our anger,* as God is, Nah. 1:3. *Aeolus sis, affectuum tuorum — Rule your passions, as Aeolus rules the winds.* 2. The honour of it. He that gets and keeps the mastery of his passions *is better than the mighty,* better *than he that* by a long siege *takes a city* or by a long war subdues a country. Behold, a greater than Alexander or Caesar is here. The conquest of ourselves, and our own unruly passions, requires more true wisdom, and a more steady, constant, and regular management, than the obtaining of a victory over the forces of an enemy. A rational conquest is more honourable to a rational creature than a brutal one. It is a victory that does nobody any harm; no lives or treasures are sacrificed to it, but only some base lusts. It is harder, and therefore more glorious, to quash an insurrection at home than to resist an invasion from a broad; nay, such are the gains of meekness that by it *we are more than conquerors.*

Verse 33

Note, 1. The divine Providence orders and directs those things which to us are perfectly casual and fortuitous. Nothing comes to pass by chance, nor is an event determined by a blind fortune, but every thing by the will and counsel of God. What man has neither eye nor hand in God is intimately concerned in. 2. When solemn appeals are made to Providence by the casting of lots, for the deciding of that matter of moment which could not otherwise be at all, or not so well, decided, God must be eyed in it, by prayer, that it may be disposed aright (*Give a perfect lot,* 1 Sa. 14:41; Acts 1:24), and by acquiescing in it when it is disposed, being satisfied that the hand of God is in it and that hand directed by infinite wisdom. All the disposals of Providence concerning our affairs we must look upon to be the directing of our lot, the determining of what we referred to God, and must be reconciled to them accordingly.

CHAPTER 17

Verse 1

These words recommend family-love and peace, as conducing very much to the comfort of human life. 1. Those that live in unity and quietness, not only free from jealousies and animosities, but vying in mutual endearments, and obliging to one another, live very comfortably, though they are low in the world, work hard and fare hard, though they have but each of them *a morsel,* and that *a dry morsel.* There may be peace and quietness where there are not three meals a day, provided there by a joint satisfaction in God's providence and a mutual satisfaction in each other's prudence. Holy love may be found in a cottage. 2. Those that live in contention, that are always jarring and brawling, and reflecting upon one another, though they have plenty of dainties, *a house full of sacrifices,* live uncomfortably; they cannot expect the blessing of God upon them and what they have, nor can they have any true relish of their enjoyments, much less any peace in their own consciences. Love will sweeten a *dry morsel,* but strife will

sour and embitter *a house full of sacrifices.* A little of the leaven of malice will leaven all the enjoyments.

Verse 2

Note, 1. True merit does not go by dignity. All agree that the son in the family is more worthy than the servant (Jn. 8:35), and yet sometimes it so happens that the servant is wise, and a blessing and credit to the family, when the son is a fool, and a burden and shame to the family. Eliezer of Damascus, though Abram could not bear to think that he should be his heir, was a stay to the family, when he obtained a wife for Isaac; whereas Ishmael, a son, was a shame to it, when he mocked Isaac. 2. True dignity will go by merit. If a servant be wise, and manage things well, he shall be further trusted, and not only *have rule* with, but *rule over a son that causes shame;* for God and nature have designed that *the fool shall be servant to the wise in heart.* Nay, a prudent servant may perhaps come to have such an interest in his master as to be taken in for a child's share of the estate and to *have part of the inheritance among the brethren.*

Verse 3

Note, 1. The hearts of the children of men are subject, not only to God's view, but to his judgment: As *the fining-pot is for silver,* both to prove it and to improve it so *the Lord tries the hearts;* he searches whether they are standard or no, and those that are he refines and makes purer, Jer. 17:10. God tries the heart by affliction (Ps. 66:10, 11), and often chooses his people in that furnace (Isa. 48:10) and makes them choice. 2. It is God only that *tries the hearts.* Men may try their *silver* and *gold* with *the fining-pot and the furnace,* but they have no such way of trying one another's hearts; God only does that, who is both the searcher and the sovereign of the heart.

Verse 4

Note, 1. Those that design to do ill support themselves by falsehood and lying: *A wicked doer gives* ear, with a great deal of pleasure, *to false lips,* that will justify him in the ill he does, to those that aim to make public disturbances, catch greedily at libels, and false stories, that defame the government and the administration. 2. Those that take the liberty to tell lies take a pleasure in hearing them told: *A liar gives* heed to a malicious backbiting tongue, that he may have something to graft his lies upon, and with which to give them some colour of truth and so to support them. Sinners will strengthen one another's hands; and those show that they are bad themselves who court the acquaintance and need the assistance of those that are bad.

Verse 5

See here, 1. What a great sin those are guilty of who trample upon the poor, who ridicule their wants and the meanness of their appearance, upbraid them with their poverty, and take advantage from their weakness to be abusive and injurious to them. They *reproach their Maker,* put a great contempt and affront upon him, who allotted the poor to the condition they are in, owns them, and takes care of them, and can, when he pleases, reduce us to that condition. Let those that thus reproach their Maker know that they shall be called to an account for it, Mt. 25:40, 41; Prov. 14:31. 2. What great danger those are in of falling into trouble themselves who are pleased to see and hear of the troubles of others: *He that is glad at calamities,* that he may be built up upon the ruins of others, and regales himself with the judgments of God when they are abroad, let him know that he *shall not go unpunished;* the cup shall be put into his hand, Eze. 25:6, 7.

Verse 6

They are so, that is, they should be so, and, if they conduct themselves worthily, they are so. 1. It is an honour to parents when they are old to leave children, and *children's children,* growing up, that tread in the steps of their virtues, and are likely to maintain and advance the reputation of their families. It is an honour to a man to live so long as to see his children's children (Ps. 128:6; Gen. 50:23), to see his house built up in them, and to see them likely to serve their generation according to the will of God. This crowns and completes their comfort in this

world. 2. It is an honour to children to have wise and godly parents, and to have them continued to them even after they have themselves grown up and settled in the world. Those are unnatural children who reckon their aged parents a burden to them, and think they live too long; whereas, if the children be wise and good, it is as much their honour as can be that thereby they are comforts to their parents in the unpleasant days of their old age.

Verse 7

Two things are here represented as very absurd: 1. That men of no repute should be dictators. What can be more unbecoming than for fools, who are known to have little sense and discretion, to pretend to that which is above them and which they were never cut out for? A fool, in Solomon's proverbs, signifies a wicked man, whom *excellent speech* does not become, because his conversation gives the lie to his excellent speech. What have those to do to declare God's statutes who *hate instruction?* Ps. 50:16. Christ would not suffer the unclean spirits to say that they knew him to be the Son of God. See Acts 16:17, 18. 2. That men of great repute should be deceivers. If it is unbecoming a despicable man to presume to speak as a philosopher or politician, and nobody heeds him, being prejudiced against his character, much more unbecoming is it for a prince, for a man of honour, to take advantage from his character and the confidence that is put in him to lie, and dissemble, and make no conscience of breaking his word. Lying ill becomes any man, but worst a prince, so corrupt is the modern policy, which insinuates that princes ought not to make themselves slaves to their words further than is for their interest, and *Qui nescit dissimulare nescit regnare — He who knows not how to dissemble knows not how to reign.*

Verse 8

The design of this observation is to show, 1. That those who have money in their hand think they can do any thing with it. Rich men value a little money as if it were a *precious stone,* and value themselves on it as if it gave them not only ornament, but power, and every one were bound to be at their beck, even justice itself. Whithersoever they turn this sparkling diamond they expect it should dazzle the eyes of all, and make them do just what they would have them do in hopes of it. The deepest bag will carry the cause. Fee high, and you may have what you will. 2. That those who have money in their eye, and set their hearts upon it, will do any thing for it: *A bribe is as a precious stone in the eyes of him that takes it;* it has a great influence upon him, and he will be sure to go the way that it leads him, hither and thither, though contrary to justice and not consistent with himself.

Verse 9

Note, 1. The way to preserve peace among relations and neighbours is to make the best of every thing, not to tell others what has been said or done against them when it is not at all necessary to their safety, nor to take notice of what has been said or done against them when it is not at all necessary to their safety, nor to take notice of what has been said or done against ourselves, but to excuse both, and put the best construction upon them. "It was an oversight; therefore overlook it. It was done through forgetfulness; therefore forget it. It perhaps made nothing of you; do you make nothing of it." 2. The ripping up of faults is the ripping out of love, and nothing tends more to the separating of friends, and setting them at variance, than the *repeating of matters* that have been in variance; for they commonly lose nothing in the repetition, but the things themselves are aggravated and the passions about them revived and exasperated. The best method of peace is by an amnesty or act of oblivion.

Verse 10

Note, 1. A word is enough to the wise. A gentle reproof will enter not only into the head, but into the heart of a wise man, so as to have a strong influence upon him; for, if but a hint be given to conscience, let it alone to carry it on and prosecute it. 2. Stripes are not enough for a fool, to make him sensible of his errors, that he may repent of them, and be more cautious for the future. He that is sottish and wilful is very rarely benefited by severity. David is softened with, *Thou art the man;* but Pharaoh remains hard under all the plagues of Egypt.

Verse 11

Here is the sin and punishment of an evil man. 1. His sin. He is an evil man indeed that seeks all occasions to rebel against God, and the government God has set over him, and to contradict and quarrel with those about him. *Quaerit jurgia — He picks quarrels;* so some. There are some that are actuated by a spirit of opposition, that will contradict for contradiction-sake, that will go on frowardly in their wicked ways in spite of all restraint and check. *A rebellious man seeks mischief* (so some read it), watches all opportunities to disturb the public peace. 2. His punishment. Because he will not be reclaimed by mild and gentle methods, *a cruel messenger shall be sent against him,* some dreadful judgment or other, as a messenger from God. Angels, God's messengers, shall be employed as ministers of his justice against him, Ps. 78:49. Satan, the angel of death, shall be let loose upon him, and the *messengers* of Satan. His prince shall send a sergeant to arrest him, an executioner to cut him off. He that *kicks against the pricks* is *waited for of the sword.*

Verse 12

Note, 1. A passionate man is a brutish man. However at other times he may have some wisdom, take him in his passion ungoverned, and he is a *fool in his folly;* those are fools in whose bosom anger rests and in whose countenance anger rages. He has put off man, and is become like a bear, a raging bear, *a bear robbed of her whelps;* he is as fond of the gratifications of his lusts and passions as a bear of her whelps (which, though ugly, are her own), as eager in the pursuit of them as she is in quest of her whelps when they are missing, and as full of indignation if crossed in the pursuit. 2. He is a dangerous man, falls foul of every one that stands in his way, though innocent, though his friend, as a bear robbed of her whelps sets upon the first man she meets as the robber. *Ira furor brevis est — Anger is temporary madness.* One may more easily stop, escape, or guard against an enraged bear, than an outrageous angry man. Let us therefore watch over our own passions (lest they get head and do mischief) and so consult our own honour; and let us avoid the company of furious men, and get out of their way when they are in their fury, and so consult our own safety. *Currenti cede furori — Give place unto wrath.*

Verse 13

A malicious mischievous man is here represented, 1. As ungrateful to his friends. He oftentimes is so absurd and insensible of kindnesses done him that he renders *evil for good.* David met with those that were his adversaries for his love, Ps. 109:4. To render evil for evil is brutish, but to render evil for good is devilish. He is an ill-natured man who, because he is resolved not to return a kindness, will revenge it. 2. As therein unkind to his family, for he entails a curse upon it. This is a crime so heinous that it shall be punished, not only in his person, but in his posterity, for whom he thus treasures up wrath. *The sword shall not depart from* David's *house* because he rewarded Uriah with evil for his good services. The Jews stoned Christ for his good works; therefore is his blood upon them and upon their children.

Verse 14

Here is, 1. The danger that there is in *the beginning of strife.* One hot word, one peevish reflection, one angry demand, one spiteful contradiction, begets another, and that a third, and so on, till it proves like the cutting of a dam; when the water has got a little passage it does itself widen the breach, bears down all before it, and there is then no stopping it, no reducing it. 2. A good caution inferred thence, to take heed of the first spark of contention and to put it out as soon as ever it appears. Dread the breaking of the ice, for, if once broken, it will break further; *therefore leave it off,* not only when you see the worst of it, for then it may be too late, but when you see the first of it. *Obsta principiis — Resist its earliest display.* Leave it off even *before it be meddled with;* leave it off, if it were possible, before you begin.

Verse 15

This shows what an offence it is to God, 1. When those that are entrusted with the administration of public justice, judges, juries, witnesses, prosecutors, counsel, do either acquit the guilty or condemn those that are not guilty, or in the least contribute to either; this defeats the end of government, which is to protect the good and punish the bad, Rom. 13:3, 4. It is equally provoking to God to *justify the wicked,* though it be in pity and *in favorem vitae — to safe life,* as to *condemn the just.* 2. When any private persons plead for sin and sinners, palliate and excuse wickedness, or argue against virtue and piety, and so *pervert the right ways of the Lord* and confound the eternal distinctions between good and evil.

Verse 16

Two things are here spoken of with astonishment: — 1. God's great goodness to foolish man, in putting *a price into his hand to get wisdom,* to get knowledge and grace to fit him for both worlds. We have rational souls, the means of grace, the strivings of the Spirit, access to God by prayer; we have time and opportunity. He that has a good estate (so some understand it) has advantages thereby of getting wisdom by purchasing instruction. Good parents, relations, ministers, friends, are helps to get wisdom. It is *a price,* therefore of value, a talent. It is *a price in the hand,* in possession; *the word is nigh thee.* It is a price for getting; it is for our own advantage; it is for getting wisdom, the very thing which, being fools, we have most need of. We have reason to wonder that God should so consider our necessity, and should entrust us with such advantages, though he foresaw we should not make a right improvement of them. 2. Man's great wickedness, his neglect of God's favour and his own interest, which is very absurd and unaccountable: *He has no heart to it,* not to the wisdom that is to be got, nor to the price in the use of which it may be got. *He has no heart,* no skill, nor will, nor courage, to improve his advantages. He has set his heart upon other things, so that he has no heart to his duty or the great concerns of his soul. Wherefore should a price be thrown away and lost upon one so undeserving of it?

Verse 17

This intimates the strength of those bonds by which we are bound to each other and which we ought to be sensible of. 1. Friends must be constant to each other *at all times.* That is not true friendship which is not constant; it will be so if it be sincere, and actuated by a good principle. Those that are fanciful or selfish in their friendship will love no longer than their humour is pleased and their interest served, and therefore their affections turn with the wind and change with the weather. Swallow-friends, that fly to you in summer, but are gone in winter; such friends there is no loss of. But if the friendship be prudent, generous, and cordial, if I love my friend because he is wise, and virtuous, and good, as long as he continues so, though he fall into poverty and disgrace, still I shall love him. Christ is a friend that loves at all times (Jn. 13:1) and we must so love him, Rom. 8:35. 2. Relations must in a special manner be careful and tender of one another in affliction: *A brother is born* to succour a brother or sister in distress, to whom he is joined so closely by nature that he may the more sensibly feel from their burdens, and be the more strongly inclined and engaged, as it were by instinct, to help them. We must often consider what we were *born for,* not only as men, but as in such a station and relation. *Who knows but we came* into such a family *for such a time as this?* We do not answer the end of our relations if we do not do the duty of them. Some take it thus: *A friend that loves at all times is born* (that is, becomes) *a brother in adversity,* and is so to be valued.

Verse 18

Though Solomon had commended friendship in adversity (*v.* 17), yet let not any, under pretence of being generous to their friends, be unjust to their families and wrong them; one part of our duty must be made to consist with another. Note, 1. It is a piece of wisdom to keep out of debt as much as may be, especially to dread suretiship. There may be a just occasion for a man to pass his word for his friend in his absence, till he come to engage himself; but to be *surety in the presence of his friend,* when he is upon the spot, supposes that his own word will not be taken, he being deemed insolvent or dishonest, and then who can with safety pass his word for him? 2. Those that are *void of understanding* are commonly taken in this snare, to the prejudice of their families, and therefore ought not to be trusted too far with their own affairs, but to be under direction.

Verse 19

Note, 1. Those that are quarrelsome involve themselves in a great deal of guilt: *He that loves strife,* that in his worldly business loves to go to law, in religion loves controversies, and in common conversation loves to thwart and fall out, that is never well but when he is in the fire, *he loves transgression;* for a great deal of sin attends that sin, and the way of it is down-hill. He pretends to stand up for truth, and for his honour and right, but really he loves sin, which God hates. 2. Those that are ambitious and aspiring expose themselves to a great deal of trouble, such as often ends in their ruin: *He that exalts his gate,* builds a stately house, at least a fine frontispiece, that he may overtop and outshine his neighbours, seeks his own destruction and takes a deal of pains to ruin himself; he makes his gate so large that his house and estate go out at it.

Verse 20

Note, 1. Framing ill designs will be of no advantage to us; there is nothing got by them: *He that has a froward heart,* that sows discord and is full of resentment, cannot promise himself to get by it sufficient to counterbalance the loss of his repose and reputation, nor can he take any rational satisfaction in it; he *finds no good.* 2. Giving ill language will be a great disadvantage to us: *He that has a perverse tongue,* spiteful and abusive, scurrilous or backbiting, *falls into* one *mischief* or other, loses his friends, provokes his enemies, and pulls trouble upon his own head. Many a one has paid dearly for an unbridled tongue.

Verse 21

This expresses that very emphatically which many wise and good men feel very sensibly, what a grievous vexatious thing it is to have a foolish wicked child. See here, 1. How uncertain all our creature-comforts are, so that we are often not only disappointed in them, but that proves the greatest cross in which we promised ourselves most satisfaction. There was *joy when a man-child was born into the world,* and yet, if he prove vicious, his own father will wish he had never been born. The name of Absalom signifies his *father's peace,* but he was his greatest trouble. It should moderate the desire of having children, and the delights of their parents in them, that they may prove a grief to them; yet it should silence the murmurings of the afflicted father in that case that if his son be a fool he is a fool of his own begetting, and therefore he must make the best of him, and take it up as his cross, the rather because Adam begets a son in his own likeness. 2. How unwise we are in suffering one affliction (and that of an untoward child as likely as any other) to drown the sense of a thousand mercies: *The father of a fool* lays that so much to heart that he *has no joy* of any thing else. For this he may thank himself; there are joys sufficient to counterbalance even that sorrow.

Verse 22

Note, 1. It is healthful to be cheerful. The Lord is for the body, and has provided for it, not only meat, but medicine, and has here told us that the best medicine is *a merry heart,* not a heart addicted to vain, carnal, sensual mirth; Solomon himself said of that mirth, It is not medicine, but madness; it is not food, but poison; *what doth it?* But he means a heart rejoicing in God, and serving him with gladness, and then taking the comfort of outward enjoyments and particularly that of pleasant conversation. It is a great mercy that God gives us leave to be cheerful and cause to be cheerful, especially if by his grace he gives us hearts to be cheerful. This *does good to a medicine* (so some read it); it will make physic more efficient. Or *it does good as a medicine* to the body, making it easy and fit for business. But, if mirth be a medicine (understand it of diversion and recreation), it must be used sparingly, only when there is occasion, not turned into food, and it must be used medicinally, *sub regimine — as a prescribed regimen,* and by rule. 2. The sorrows of the mind often contribute very much to the sickliness of the body: *A broken spirit,* sunk by the burden of afflictions, and especially a conscience wounded with the sense of guilt and fear of wrath, *dries the bones,* wastes the radical moisture, exhausts the very marrow, and makes the body a mere skeleton. We should therefore watch and pray against all melancholy dispositions, for they lead us into trouble as well as into temptation.

Verse 23

See here, 1. What an evil thing bribery is: He is *a wicked man* that will *take a gift* to engage him to give a false testimony, verdict, or judgment; when he does it he is ashamed of it, for he takes it, with all the secresy imaginable, *out of the bosom* where he knows it is laid ready for him; it is industriously concealed, and so slyly that, if he could, he would hide it from his own conscience. *A gift is taken out of the bosom of a wicked man* (so some read it); for he is a bad man that gives bribes, as well as he that takes them. 2. What a powerful thing it is. It is of such force that it *perverts the ways of judgment.* The course of justice is not only obstructed, but turned into injustice; and the greatest wrongs are done under colour of doing right.

Verse 24

Note, 1. He is to be reckoned an intelligent man that not only has wisdom, but has it ready when he has occasion for it. He lays his *wisdom before him,* as his card and compass which he steers by, has his eye always upon it, as he that writes has on his copy; and then he has it *before him;* it is not to seek, but still at hand. 2. He that has a giddy head, a roving rambling fancy, will never be fit for any solid business. He is a fool, and good for nothing, whose *eyes are in the ends of the earth,* here, and there and every where, any where but where they should be, who cannot fix his thoughts to one subject nor pursue any one purpose with any thing of steadiness. When his mind should be applied to his study and business it is filled with a thousand things foreign and impertinent.

Verse 25

Observe, 1. Wicked children are an affliction to both their parents. They are an occasion of *anger* to the father (so the word signifies), because they contemn his authority, but of sorrow and *bitterness* to the mother, because they abuse her tenderness. The parents, being jointsufferers, should therefore bring mutual comfort to bear them up under it, and strive to make it as easy as they can, the mother to mollify the father's anger, the father to alleviate the mother's grief. 2. That Solomon often repeats this remark, probably because it was his own case; however, it is a common case.

Verse 26

In differences that happen between magistrates and subjects, and such differences often arise, 1. Let magistrates see to it that they never *punish the just,* that they be in no case a *terror to good works,* for that is to abuse their power and betray that great trust which is reposed in them. It is *not good,* that is, it is a very evil thing, and will end ill, whatever end they may aim at in it. When princes become tyrants and persecutors their thrones will be neither easy nor firm. 2. Let subjects see to it that they do not find fault with the government for doing its duty, for it is a wicked thing *to strike princes for equity,* by defaming their administration or by any secret attempts against them to strike at them, as the ten tribes that revolted reflected upon Solomon for imposing necessary taxes. Some read it, *Nor to strike the ingenuous for equity.* Magistrates must take heed that none suffer under them for well doing; nor must parents *provoke their children to wrath* by unjust rebukes.

Verses 27–28

Two ways a man may show himself to be a wise man: — 1. By the good temper, the sweetness and the sedateness, of his mind: *A man of understanding is of an excellent spirit,* a *precious spirit* (so the word is); he is one that looks well to his spirit, that it be as it should be, and so keeps it in an even frame, easy to himself and pleasant to others. A gracious spirit is a precious spirit, and renders a man amiable and *more excellent than his neighbour.* He is of a *cool spirit* (so some read it), not heated with passion, nor put into any tumult or disorder by the *impetus* of any corrupt affection, but even and stayed. A cool head with a warm heart is an admirable composition. 2. By the good government of his tongue. (1.) A wise man will be *of few words,* as being afraid of speaking amiss: *He that has knowledge,* and aims to do good with it, is careful, when he does speak to speak to the purpose, and says little in order that he may take time to deliberate. He *spares his words,* because they are better spared than ill-spent. (2.) This is generally taken for such a sure indication of wisdom that a fool may gain the reputation of being a wise man if he have but wit enough to hold his tongue, to hear, and see, and say little. If a fool hold his peace, men of candour will think him wise, because nothing appears to the contrary, and because it will be thought that he is making observations on what others say, and gaining experience, and is consulting with himself what he shall say, that he may speak pertinently. See how easy it is to gain men's good opinion and to impose upon them. But when a *fool holds his peace* God knows his heart, and the folly that is bound up there; thoughts are words to him, and therefore he cannot be deceived in his judgment of men.

CHAPTER 18

Verse 1

The original here is difficult, and differently understood. 1. Some take it as a rebuke to an affected singularity. When men take a pride in *separating themselves* from the sentiments and society of others, in contradicting all that has been said before them and advancing new notions of their own, which, though ever so absurd, they are wedded to, it is to gratify a desire or lust of vain-glory, and they are seekers and meddlers with that which does not belong to them. He *seeks according to his desire, and intermeddles with every business,* pretends to pass a judgment upon every man's matter. He is morose and supercilious. Those generally are so that are opinionative and conceited, and they thus make themselves ridiculous, and are vexatious to others. 2. Our translation seems to take it as an excitement to diligence in the pursuit of wisdom. If we would get knowledge or grace, we must desire it, as that which we need and which will be of great advantage to us, 1 Co. 12:31. We must *separate ourselves* from all those things which would divert us from or retard us in the pursuit, retire out of the noise of this world's vanities, and then *seek and intermeddle with all* the means and instructions of *wisdom,* be willing to take pains and try all the methods of improving ourselves, be acquainted with a variety of opinions, that we may prove all things and hold fast that which is good.

Verse 2

A fool may pretend to understanding, and to seek and intermeddle with the means of it, but, 1. He has no true delight in it; it is only to please his friends or save his credit; he does not love his book, nor his business, nor his Bible, nor his prayers; he would rather be playing the fool with his sports. Those who take no pleasure in learning or religion will make nothing to purpose of either. No progress is made in them if they are a task and a drudgery. 2. He has no good design in it, only *that his heart may discover itself,* that he may have something to make a show with, something wherewith to varnish his folly, that that may pass off the better, because he loves to hear himself talk.

Verse 3

This may include a double sense: — 1. That wicked people are scornful people, and put *contempt* upon others. *When the wicked comes* into any company, comes into the schools of wisdom or into the assemblies for religious worship, *then comes contempt* of God, of his people and ministers, and of every thing that is said and done. You can expect no other from those that are profane than that they will be scoffers; they will be an *ignominy* and *reproach;* they will flout and jeer every thing that is serious and grave. But let not wise and good men regard it, for the proverb of the ancients says, such *wickedness proceeds from the wicked.* 2. That wicked people are shameful people, and bring *contempt* upon themselves, for God has said that those *who despise him shall be lightly esteemed.* As soon as ever sin entered shame followed it, and sinners make themselves despicable. Nor do they only draw contempt upon themselves, but they bring *ignominy* and *reproach* upon their families, their friends, their ministers, and all that are in any way related to them. Those therefore who would secure their honour must retain their virtue.

Verse 4

The similitudes here seem to be elegantly transposed. 1. The *well-spring of wisdom* is *as deep waters.* An intelligent knowing man has in him a good treasure of useful things, which furnishes him with something to say upon all occasions that is pertinent and profitable. This is as *deep waters,* which make no noise, but never run dry. 2. The words of such a *man's mouth are as a flowing brook.* What he sees cause to speak flows naturally from him and with a great deal of ease, and freedom, and natural fluency; it is clean and fresh, it is cleansing and refreshing; from his *deep waters* there flows what there is occasion for, to water those about him, as the brooks do the low grounds.

Verse 5

This justly condemns those who, being employed in the administration of justice, pervert judgment, 1. By conniving at men's crimes, and protecting and countenancing them in oppression and violence, because of their dignity, or wealth, or some personal kindness they have for them. Whatever excuses men may make for it, certainly *it is not good* thus to *accept the person of the wicked;* it is an offence to God, an affront to justice, a wrong to mankind, and a real service done to the kingdom of sin and Satan. The merits of the cause must be regarded, not the person. 2. By giving a cause against justice and equity, because the person is poor and low in the world, or not of the same party or persuasion, or a stranger of another country. This is *overthrowing the righteous in judgment,* who ought to be supported, and whom God will make to stand.

Verses 6–7

Solomon has often shown what mischief bad men do to others with their ungoverned tongues; here he shows what mischief they do to themselves. 1. They embroil themselves in quarrels: *A fool's lips,* without any cause or call, *enter into contention,* by advancing foolish notions which others find themselves obliged to oppose, and so a quarrel is begun, or by giving provoking language, which will be resented, and satisfaction demanded, or by setting men at defiance, and bidding them *do if they dare.* Proud, and passionate men, and drunkards, are fools, whose lips *enter into contention.* A wise man may, against his will, be drawn into a quarrel, but he is a fool that of choice enters into it when he might avoid it, and he will repent it when it is too late. 2. They expose themselves to correction: The *fool's mouth* does, in effect, *call for strokes;* he has said that which deserves to be punished with strokes, and is still saying that which needs to be checked, and restrained with strokes, as Ananias unjustly commanded that Paul should be *smitten on the mouth.* 3. They involve themselves in ruin: A *fool's mouth,* which has been, or would have been, the destruction of others, proves at length *his own destruction,* perhaps from men. Shimei's mouth was his own destruction, and Adonijah's, who spoke against his own head. And when a fool, by his foolish speaking, has run himself into a premunire, and thinks to bring himself off by justifying or excusing what he has said, his defence proves his offence, and his lips are still the snare of his soul, entangling him yet more and more. However, when men by their evil words shall be condemned at God's bar their mouths will be their destruction, and it will be such an aggravation of their ruin as will not admit one drop of water, one drop of comfort, to *cool their tongue,* which is their snare and will be their tormentor.

Verse 8

Tale-bearers are those who secretly carry stories from house to house, which perhaps have some truth in them, but are secrets not fit to be told, or are basely misrepresented, and false colours put upon them, and are all told with design to blast men's reputation, to break their friendship, to make mischief between relations and neighbours, and set them at variance. Now the words of such are here said to be, 1. *Like as when men are wounded* (so the margin reads it); they pretend to be very much affected with the miscarriages of such and such, and to be in pain for them, and pretend that it is with the greatest grief and reluctance imaginable that they speak of them. They look as if they themselves were wounded by it, whereas really they *rejoice in iniquity,* are fond of the story, and tell it with pride and pleasure. Thus their words seem; but they *go down as poison into the innermost parts of the belly,* the pill being thus gilded, thus sugared. 2. *As wounds* (so the text reads it), as deep wounds, deadly wounds, *wounds in the innermost parts of the belly;* the *venter medius vel infimus — the middle or lower belly,* the *thorax* or the *abdomen,* in either of which wounds are mortal. The words of the tale-bearer wound him of whom they are spoken, his credit and interest, and him to whom they are spoken, his love and charity. They occasion sin to him, which is a wound to the conscience. Perhaps he seems to slight them, but they would insensibly, by alienating his affections from one he ought to love.

Verse 9

Note, 1. Prodigality is very bad husbandry. Those are not only justly branded as fools among men, but will give an uncomfortable account to God of the talents they are entrusted with, who are wasters of their estates, who live above what they have, spend and give more than they can afford, and so, in effect, throw away what they have, and suffer it to run to waste. 2. Idleness is no better. He that is remiss in his work, whose *hands hang down* (so the word signifies), that stands, as we may, with his thumbs in his mouth, that neglects his business, does it not at all, or as if he did it not, he is own brother to him that is a prodigal, that is, he is as much a fool and in as sure and ready a way to poverty; one scatters what he has, the other lets it run through his fingers. The observation is too true in the affairs of religion; he that is trifling and careless in praying and hearing is brother to him that does not pray or hear at all; and omissions of duty and in duty are as fatal to the soul as commissions of sin.

Verse 10

Here is, 1. God's sufficiency for the saints: His *name is a strong tower* for them, in which they may take rest when they are weary and take sanctuary when they are pursued, where they may be lifted up above their enemies and fortified against them. There is enough in God, and in the discoveries which he has made of himself to us, to make us easy at all times. The wealth laid up in this tower is enough to enrich them, to be a continual feast and a continuing treasure to them. The strength of this tower is enough to protect them; *the name of the Lord* is all that whereby he has made himself known as God, and our God, not only his titles and attributes, but his covenant and all the promises of it; these make up a tower, a strong tower, impenetrable, impregnable, for all God's people. 2. The saints' security in God. It is a strong tower to those who know how to make use of it as such. *The righteous,* by faith and prayer, devotion towards God and dependence on him, *run into it,* as their city of refuge. Having made sure their interest in God's name, they take the comfort and benefit of it; they go out of themselves, retire from the world, live above, dwell in God and God in them, and so they are safe, they think themselves so, and they shall find themselves so.

Verse 11

Having described the firm and faithful defence of the righteous man (*v.* 10), Solomon here shows what is the false and deceitful defence of the rich man, that has his portion and treasure in the things of this world, and sets his heart upon them. His wealth is as much his confidence, and he expects as much from it, as a godly man from his God. See, 1. How he supports himself. He makes his *wealth his city,* where he dwells, where he rules, with a great deal of self-complacency, as if he had a whole city under his command. It *is his strong city,* in which he intrenches himself, and then sets danger at defiance, as if nothing could hurt him. *His scales are his pride;* his wealth is his wall in which he encloses himself, and he thinks it a *high wall,* which cannot be scaled or got over, Job 31:24; Rev. 18:7. 2. How herein he cheats himself. It is a *strong city,* and a *high wall,* but it is so only *in his own conceit;* it will not prove to be really so, but like the house built on the sand, which will fail the builder when he most needs it.

Verse 12

Note, 1. Pride is the presage of ruin, and ruin will at last be the punishment of pride; for *before destruction* men are commonly so infatuated by the just judgment of God that they are more haughty than ever, that their ruin may be the sorer and the more surprising. Of, if that do not always hold, yet after the heart has been lifted up with pride, a fall comes, *ch.* 16:18. 2. Humility is the presage of honour and prepares men for it, and honour shall at length be the reward of humility, as he had said before, *ch.* 15:33. That has need to be often said which men are so loth to believe.

Verse 13

See here how men often expose themselves by that very thing by which they hope to gain applause. 1. Some take a pride in being quick. They *answer a matter before they hear it,* hear it out, nay, as soon as they but hear of it. They think it is their honour to take up a cause suddenly; and, when they have heard one side, they think the matter so plain that they need not trouble themselves to hear the other; they are already apprized of it, and masters of all the merits of the cause. Whereas, though a ready wit is an agreeable thing to play with, it is solid judgment and sound wisdom that do business. 2. Those that take a pride in being quick commonly fall under the just reproach of being impertinent. It is folly for a man to go about to speak to a thing which he does not understand, or to pass sentence upon a matter which he is not truly and fully informed of, and has not patience to make a strict enquiry into; and, if it be folly, it is and will be shame.

Verse 14

Note, 1. Outward grievances are tolerable as long as the mind enjoys itself and is at ease. Many infirmities, many calamities, we are liable to in this world, in body, name, and estate, which a man may bear, and bear up under, if he have but good conduct and courage, and be able to act with reason and resolution, especially if he have a good conscience, and the testimony of that be for him; and, if the *spirit of a man* will *sustain the infirmity,* much more will the spirit of a Christian, or rather the Spirit of God witnessing and working with our spirits in a day of trouble. 2. The grievances of the spirit are of all others most heavy, and hardly to be borne; these make sore the shoulders which should sustain the other infirmities. If the spirit be wounded by the disturbance of the reason, dejection under the trouble, whatever it is, and despair of relief, if the spirit be wounded by the amazing apprehensions of God's wrath for sin, and the fearful expectations of judgment and fiery indignation, *who can bear* this? Wounded spirits cannot help themselves, nor do others know how to help them. It is therefore wisdom to keep conscience void of offence.

Verse 15

Note, 1. Those that are prudent will seek knowledge, and apply their ear and heart to the pursuit of it, their ear to attend to the means of knowledge and their heart to mix faith with what they hear and make a good improvement of it. Those that are prudent do not think they have prudence enough, but still see they have need of more; and the more prudent a man is the more inquisitive will he be after knowledge, the knowledge of God and his duty, and the way to heaven, for that is the best knowledge. 2. Those that prudently seek knowledge shall certainly get knowledge, for God never said to such, *Seek in vain,* but, *Seek and you shall find.* If the ear seeks it, the heart gets it, and keeps it, and is enriched by it. We must get knowledge, not only into our heads, but into our hearts, get the savour and relish of it, apply what we know to ourselves and experience the power and influence of it.

Verse 16

Of what great force gifts (that is, bribes) are he had intimated before, *ch.* 17:8, 23. Here he shows the power of gifts, that is, presents made even by inferiors to those that are above them and have much more than they have. A good present will go far, 1. Towards a man's liberty: *A man's gift,* if he be in prison, may procure his enlargement; there are courtiers, who, if they use their interest even for oppressed innocency, expect to receive a gratuity for it. Or, if a mean man know not how to get access to a great man, he may do it by a fee to his servants or a present to himself; those will make room for him. 2. Towards his preferment. It will bring him to sit among *great men,* in honour and power. See how corrupt the world is when men's gifts will not do, though ever so great; nay, will gain that for them which they are unworthy of and unfit for; and no wonder that those take bribes in their offices who gave bribes for them. *Vendere jura potest, emerat ille prius — He that bought law can sell it.*

Verse 17

This shows that one tale is good till another is told. 1. He that speaks first will be sure to tell a straight story, and relate that only which makes for him, and put the best colour he can upon it, so that his cause shall appear good, whether it really be so or no. 2. The plaintiff having done his evidence, it is fit that the defendant should be heard, should have leave to confront the witnesses and cross-examine them, and show the falsehood and fallacy of what has been alleged, which perhaps may make the matter appear quite otherwise than it did. We must therefore remember that we have two ears, to hear both sides before we give judgment.

Verse 18

Note, 1. Contentions commonly happen among the mighty, that are jealous for their honour and right and stand upon the punctilios of both, that are confident of their being able to make their part good and therefore will hardly condescend to the necessary terms of an accommodation; whereas those that are poor are forced to be peaceable, and sit down losers. 2. Even the contentions of the mighty may be ended by lot if they cannot otherwise be compromised, and sometimes better so than by arguments which are endless, or concessions which they are loth to stoop to, whereas it is no disparagement to a man to acquiesce in the determination of the lot when once it is referred to that. To prevent quarrels Canaan was divided by lot; and, if lusory lots had not profaned this way of appeal to Providence, perhaps it might be very well used now for the deciding of many controversies, both to the honour of God and the satisfaction of the parties, provided it were done with prayer and due solemnity, this and some other scriptures seeming to direct to it, especially Acts 1:26. If the law be a lottery (as some have called it), it were as well that a lottery were the law.

Verse 19

Note, 1. Great care must be taken to prevent quarrels among relations, and those that are under special obligation to each other, not only because they are most unnatural and unbecoming, but because between such things are commonly taken most unkindly, and resentments are apt to be carried too far. Wisdom and grace would indeed make it most easy to us to forgive our relations and friends if they offend us, but corruption makes it most difficult to forgive them; let us therefore take heed of disobliging a brother, or one that has been as a brother; ingratitude is very provoking. 2. Great pains must be taken to compromise matters in variance between relations, with all speed, because it is a work of so much difficulty, and consequently the more honourable if it be done. Esau was a *brother offended,* and seemed *harder to be won than a strong city,* yet by a work of God upon his heart, in answer to Jacob's prayer, he was won.

Verse 20

Note, 1. Our comfort depends very much upon the testimony of our own consciences, for us or against us. The *belly* is here put for the conscience, as *ch.* 20:27. Now it is of great consequence to us whether that be satisfied, and what that is filled with, for, accordingly, will our satisfaction be and our inward peace. 2. The testimony of our consciences will be for us, or against us, according as we have or have not governed our tongues well. According as *the fruit of the mouth* is good or bad, unto iniquity or unto righteousness, so the character of the man is, and consequently the testimony of his conscience concerning him. "We ought to take as great care about the words we speak as we do about the fruit of our trees or the increase of the earth, which we are to eat; for, according as they are wholesome or unwholesome, so will the pleasure or the pain be wherewith we shall be filled." So bishop Patrick.

Verse 21

Note, 1. A man may do a great deal of good, or a great deal of hurt, both to others and to himself, according to the use he makes of his tongue. Many a one has been his own death by a foul tongue, or the death of others by a false tongue; and, on the contrary, many a one has saved his own life, or procured the comfort of it, by a prudent gentle tongue, and saved the lives of others by a seasonable testimony or intercession for them. And, if by our words we must be justified or condemned, *death and life are,* no doubt, *in the power of the tongue.* Tongues were Aesop's best meat, and his worst. 2. Men's words will be judged of by the affections with which they speak; he that not only speaks aright (which a bad man may do to save his credit or please his company), but loves to speak so, speaks well of choice, and with delight, to him it will be life; and he that not only speaks amiss (which a good man may do through inadvertency), but loves to speak so (Ps. 52:4), to him it will be death. As men *love it* they shall *eat the fruit of it.*

Verse 22

Note, 1. A good wife is a great blessing to a man. He that *finds a wife* (that is, a wife indeed; a bad wife does not deserve to be called by a name of so much honour), that finds a help meet for him (that is a wife in the original acceptation of the word), that sought such a one with care and prayer and has found what he sought, he has found a *good thing,* a jewel of great value, a rare jewel; he has found that which will not only contribute more than any thing to his comfort in this life, but will forward him in the way to heaven. 2. God is to be acknowledged in it with thankfulness; it is a token of his favour, and a happy pledge of further favours; it is a sign that God delights in a man to do him good and has mercy in store for him; for this, therefore, God must be sought unto.

Verse 23

Note, 1. Poverty, though many inconveniences to the body attend it, has often a good effect upon the spirit, for it makes men humble and submissive, and mortifies their pride. It teaches them to *use entreaties.* When necessity forces men to beg it tells them they must not prescribe or demand, but take what is given them and be thankful. At the throne of God's grace we are all poor, and must use entreaties, not answer, but make application, must sue *sub forma pauperis — as a pauper.* 2. A prosperous condition, though it has many advantages, has often this mischief attending it, that it makes men proud, haughty, and imperious: *The rich answers the entreaties of the poor roughly,* as Nabal answered David's messengers with railing. It is a very foolish humour of some rich men, especially those who have risen from little, that they think their riches will warrant them to give hard words, and, even where they not design any rough dealing, that it becomes them to answer roughly, whereas gentlemen ought to be gentle, Jam. 3:17.

Verse 24

Solomon here recommends friendship to us, and shows, 1. What we must do that we may contract and cultivate friendship; we must *show ourselves friendly.* Would we have friends and keep them, we must not only not affront them, or quarrel with them, but we must love them, and make it appear that we do so by all expressions that are endearing, by being free with them, pleasing to them, visiting them and bidding them welcome, and especially by doing all the good offices we can and serving them in every thing that lies in our power; that is *showing ourselves friendly.*

Si vis amari, ama —
If you wish to gain affection, bestow it. — Sen.

Ut ameris, amabilis esto —
The way to be beloved is to be lovely. — Ovid.

2. That it is worth while to do so, for we may promise ourselves a great deal of comfort in a true friend. A *brother* indeed *is born for adversity,* as he had said, *ch.* 17:17. In our troubles we expect comfort and relief from our relations, but sometimes *there is a friend,* that is nothing akin to us, the bonds of whose esteem and love prove stronger than those of nature, and, when it comes to the trial, will do more for us than a brother will. Christ is a friend to all believers that *sticks closer than a brother;* to him therefore let them show themselves friendly.

CHAPTER 19

Verse 1

Here see, 1. What will be the credit and comfort of a poor man, and make him more excellent than his neighbour, though his poverty may expose him to contempt and may dispirit him. Let him be honest and *walk in integrity,* let him keep a good conscience and make it appear that he does so, let him always speak and act with sincerity when he is under the greatest temptations to dissemble and break his word, and then let him value himself upon that, for all wise and good men will value him. He is better, has a better character, is in a better condition, is better beloved, and lives to better purpose, than many a one that looks great and makes a figure. 2. What will be the shame of a rich man, notwithstanding all his pomp. If he have a shallow head and an evil tongue, if he is *perverse in his lips and is a fool,* if he is a wicked man and gets what he has by fraud and oppression, he *is a fool,* and an honest poor man is to be preferred far before him.

Verse 2

Two things are here declared to be of bad consequence: — 1. Ignorance: *To be without the knowledge of the soul is not good,* so some read it. Know we not our own selves, our own hearts? *A soul without knowledge is not good;* it is a great privilege that we have souls, but, if these souls have not knowledge, what the better are we? If man *has not understanding, he is as the beasts,* Ps. 49:20. An ignorant soul cannot be a good soul. That the soul be without knowledge is not safe, nor pleasant; what good can the soul do, of what is it good for, if it be without knowledge? 2. Rashness. *He that hastes with his feet* (that does things inconsiderately and with precipitation, and will not take time to ponder the path of his feet) *sins;* he cannot but often miss the mark and take many a false step, which those prevent that consider their ways. As good not know as not consider.

Verse 3

We have here two instances of men's folly: — 1. That they bring themselves into straits and troubles, and run themselves a-ground, and embarrass themselves: *The foolishness of man perverts his way.* Men meet with crosses and disappointments in their affairs, and things do not succeed as they expected and wished, and it is owing to themselves and their own folly; it is their own iniquity that corrects them. 2. That when they have done so they lay the blame upon God, and their hearts fret against him, as if he had done them wrong, whereas really they wrong themselves. In fretting, we are enemies to our own peace, and become self-tormentors; in *fretting against the Lord* we affront him, his justice, goodness, and sovereignty; and it is very absurd to take occasion from the trouble which we pull upon our own heads by our wilfulness, or neglect, to quarrel with him, when we ought to blame ourselves, for it is our own doing. See Isa. 50:1.

Verse 4

Here, 1. We may see how strong men's love of money is, that they will love any man, how undeserving soever he be otherwise, if he has but a deal of money and is free with it, so that they may hope to be the better for it. Wealth enables a man to send many presents, make many entertainments, and do many good offices, and so gains him many friends, who pretend to love him, for they flatter him and make their court to him, but really love what he has, or rather love themselves, hoping to get by him. 2. We may see how weak men's love of one another is. He who, while he prospered, was beloved and respected, if he fall into poverty is *separated from his neighbour,* is not owned nor looked upon, not visited nor regarded, is bidden to keep his distance and told he is troublesome. Even one that has been his neighbour and acquaintance will turn his face from him and pass by on the other side. Because men's consciences tell them they ought to relieve and succour such, they are willing to have this excuse, that they did not see them.

Verse 5

Here we have, 1. The sins threatened — bearing *false witness* in judgment and *speaking lies* in common conversation. Men could not arrive at such a pitch of impiety as to bear false witness (where to the guilt of a lie is added that of perjury and injury) if they had not advanced to it by allowing themselves to speak untruths in jest and banter, or under pretence of doing good. Thus men *teach their tongues to speak lies,* Jer. 9:5. Those that will take a liberty to tell lies in discourse are in a fair way to be guilty of the greater wickedness of false-witness-bearing, whenever they are tempted to it, though they seemed to detest it. Those that can swallow a false word debauch their consciences, so that a false oath will not choke them. 2. The threatening itself: They *shall not go unpunished;* they *shall not escape.* This intimates that that which emboldens them in the sin is the hope of impunity, it being a sin which commonly escapes punishment from men, though the law is strict, Deu. 19:18, 19. But it *shall not escape* the righteous judgment of God, who is jealous, and will not suffer his name to be profaned; we know where all liars will have their everlasting portion.

Verses 6–7

These two verses are a comment upon *v.* 4, and show, 1. How those that are rich and great are courted and caressed, and have suitors and servants in abundance. The prince that has power in his hand, and preferments at his disposal, has his gate and his ante-chamber thronged with petitioners, that are ready to adore him for what they can get. *Many will entreat his favour,* and think themselves happy in it. Even great men are humble suppliants to the prince. How earnest then should we be for the favour of God, which is far beyond that of any earthly prince. But, it should seem, liberality will go further than majesty itself to gain respect, for there are many that court the prince, but *every man is a friend to him that gives gifts;* not only those that have received, or do expect, gifts from him, will, as friends, be ready to serve him, but others also will, as friends, give him their good word. Prodigals, who are foolishly free of what they have, will have many hangers-on who will cry them up as long as it lasts, but will leave them when it is done. Those that are prudently generous make an interest by it which may stand them in good stead; those that are accounted benefactors exercise an authority which may give them an opportunity of doing good, Lu. 22:25. 2. How those that are poor and low are slighted and despised. Men may, if they please, court the prince, and the princely, but they may not trample upon the poor and look at them with disdain. Yet so it often is: *All the brethren of the poor do hate him;* even his own relations are shy of him, because he is needy and craving, and expects something from them, and because they look upon him as a blemish to their family; and then no marvel if others of his friends, that were nothing akin to him, *go far from him,* to get out of his way. *He pursues them with words,* hoping to prevail with them by his importunity to be kind to him, but all in vain; they have nothing for him. *They pursue him with words* (so some understand it), to excuse themselves from giving him any thing; they tell him that he is idle and impertinent, that he has brought himself into poverty, and therefore ought not to be relieved; as Nabal said to David's messengers: *"There are many servants now a days that run away from their masters;* and how do I know but that David may be one of them?" Let poor people therefore make God their friend, pursue him with their prayers, and he will not be wanting to them.

Verse 8

Those are here encouraged, 1. That take pains to *get*

wisdom, to get knowledge, and grace, and acquaintance with God; those that do so show that they *love their own souls,* and will be found to have done themselves the greatest kindness imaginable. No man ever *hated his own flesh,* but loves that, yet many are wanting in love to their own souls, for only those love their souls, and consequently love themselves, aright, that *get wisdom,* true wisdom. 2. That take care to keep it when they have got it; it is health, and wealth, and honour, and all, to the soul, and therefore he that *keeps understanding,* as he shows that he *loves his own soul,* so he shall certainly *find good,* all good. He that retains the good lessons he has learnt, and orders his conversation according to them, shall find the benefit and comfort of it in his own soul and shall be happy here and for ever.

Verse 9

Here is, 1. A repetition of what was said before (*v.* 5), for we have need to be again and again warned of the danger of the sin of lying and false-witness-bearing, since nothing is of more fatal consequence. 2. An addition to it in one word; there it was said, *He that speaks lies shall not escape,* and intimated that he shall be punished. Here it is said, His punishment shall be such as will be his destruction: he *shall perish;* the lies he forged against others will be his own ruin. It is a damning destroying sin.

Verse 10

Note, 1. Pleasure and liberty ill become a fool: *Delight is not seemly for* such a one. A man that has not wisdom and grace has no right nor title to true joy, and therefore it is unseemly. It ill becomes those that do not delight in God to delight in any thing, nor how to manage themselves, and therefore they do but expose themselves. It becomes ungracious fools to be afflicted, and mourn, and weep, not to laugh and be merry; rebukes are more proper for them than delights. Delight is seemly for a man of business, to refresh him when he is fatigued, but not *for a fool,* that lives an idle life and abuses his recreations. *The prosperity of fools* discovers their folly and *destroys them.* 2. Power and honour ill become a man of a servile spirit. Nothing is more unseemly than *for a servant to have rule over princes;* it is absurd in itself, and very preposterous, for none are so insolent and intolerable as a beggar on horseback, *a servant when he reigns,* ch. 30:22. It is very unseemly for one that is a servant to sin and his lusts to rule over and oppress those that are God's freemen and made kings and priests to him.

Verse 11

A wise man will observe these two rules about his anger: 1. Not to be over-hasty in his resentments: *Discretion* teaches us to *defer our anger,* to defer the admission of it till we have thoroughly considered all the merits of the provocation, seen them in a true light and weighed them in a just balance; and then to defer the prosecution of it till there be no danger of running into any indecencies. Plato said to his servant, "I would beat thee, but that I am angry." Give it time, and it will cool. 2. Not to be over-critical in his resentments. Whereas it is commonly looked upon as a piece of ingenuity to apprehend an affront quickly, it is here made a man's *glory to pass over a transgression,* to appear as if he did not see it (Ps. 38:13), or, if he sees fit to take notice of it, yet to forgive it and meditate no revenge.

Verse 12

This is to the same purport with what we had *ch.* 16:14, 15, and the design of it is, 1. To make kings wise and considerate in dispensing their frowns and smiles. They are not like those of common persons; their frowns are very terrible and their smiles very comfortable, and therefore it concerns them to be very careful that they never frighten a good man from doing well with their frowns, nor ever give countenance to a wicked man in doing ill with their smiles, for then they abuse their influence, Rom. 13:3. 2. To make subjects faithful and dutiful to their princes. Let them be restrained from all disloyalty by the consideration of the dreadful consequence of having the government against them; and let them be encouraged in all good services to the public by the hopes of the favour of their prince. Christ is a King whose wrath against his enemies

will be *as the roaring of a lion* (Rev. 10:3) and his favour to his own people as the refreshing dew, Ps. 72:6.

Verse 13

It is an instance of the vanity of the world that we are liable to the greatest grief in those things wherein we promise ourselves the greatest comfort. It is as it proves. What greater temporal comfort can a man have than a good wife and good children? Yet, 1. *A foolish son is* a great affliction, and may make a man wish a thousand times he had been written childless. A son that will apply himself to no study or business, that will take no advice, that lives a lewd, loose, rakish life, and spends what he has extravagantly, games it away and wastes it in the excess of riot, or that is proud, foppish, and conceited, such a one is the grief *of his father,* because he is the disgrace, and is likely to be the ruin, of his family. He hates all his labour, when he sees to whom he must leave the fruit of it. 2. A cross peevish wife is as great an affliction: Her *contentions are continual;* every day, and every hour in the day, she finds some occasion to make herself and those about her uneasy. Those that are accustomed to chide never want something or other to chide at; but it is a *continual dropping,* that is, a continual vexation, as it is to have a house so much out of repair that it rains in and a man cannot lie dry in it. That man has an uncomfortable life, and has need of a great deal of wisdom and grace to enable him to bear his affliction and do his duty, who has a sot for his son and a scold for his wife.

Verse 14

Note, 1. A discreet and virtuous wife is a choice gift of God's providence to a man — a wife that is *prudent,* in opposition to one that is contentious, *v.* 13. For, though a wife that is continually finding fault may think it is her wit and wisdom to be so, it is really her folly; *a prudent wife* is meek and quiet, and makes the best of every thing. If a man has such a wife, let him not ascribe it to the wisdom of his own choice or his own management (for the wisest have been deceived both in and by a woman), but let him ascribe it to the goodness of God, who made him a help meet for him, and perhaps by some hits and turns of providence that seemed casual brought her to him. Every creature is what he makes it. Happy marriages, we are sure, are made in heaven; Abraham's servant prayed in the belief of this, Gen. 24:12. 2. It is a more valuable gift than *house and riches,* contributes more to the comfort and credit of a man's life and the welfare of his family, is a greater token of God's favour, and about which the divine providence is in a more especial manner conversant. A good estate may be *the inheritance of fathers,* which, by the common direction of Providence, comes in course to a man; but no man has a good wife by descent or entail. Parents that are worldly, in disposing of their children, look no further than to match them to *house and riches,* but, if withal it be to *a prudent wife,* let God have the glory.

Verse 15

See here the evil of a sluggish slothful disposition. 1. It stupefies men, and makes them senseless, and mindless of their own affairs, as they were *cast into a deep sleep,* dreaming much, but doing nothing. Slothful people doze away their time, bury their talents, live a useless life, and are the unprofitable burdens of the earth; for any service they do when they are awake they might as well be always asleep. Even their souls are idle and lulled asleep, their rational powers chilled and frozen. 2. It impoverishes men and brings them to want. Those that will not labour cannot expect to eat, but must *suffer hunger: An idle soul,* one that is idle in the affairs of his soul, that takes no care or pains to work out his salvation, shall perish for want of that which is necessary to the life and happiness of the soul.

Verse 16

Here is, 1. The happiness of those that walk circumspectly. Those that make conscience of *keeping the commandment* in every thing, that live by rule, as becomes servants and patients, *keep their own souls;* they secure their present peace and future bliss, and provide every way well for themselves. If we keep God's word, God's word

will keep us from every thing really hurtful. 2. The misery of those that live at large and never mind what they do: Those *that despair their ways shall die,* shall perish eternally; they are in the high road to ruin. With respect to those that are careless about the end of their ways, and never consider whither they are going, and about the rule of their ways, that will walk in the way of their hearts and after the course of the world (Eccl. 11:9), that never consider what they have done nor what they are concerned to do, but *walk at all adventures* (Lev. 26:21), right or wrong, it is all one to them — what can come of this but the greatest mischief?

Verse 17

Here is, I. The duty of charity described. It includes two things: — 1. Compassion, which is the inward principle of charity in the heart; it is to *have pity on the poor.* Those that have not a penny for the poor, yet may have pity for them, a charitable concern and sympathy; and, if a man *give all his goods to feed the poor* and have not this charity in his heart, *it is nothing,* 1 Co. 13:3. We must *draw out our souls to the hungry,* Isa. 58:10. 2. Bounty and liberality. We must not only pity the poor, but give, according to their necessity and our ability, Jam. 2:15, 16. *That which he has given.* Margin, *His deed.* It is charity to do for the poor, as well as to give; and thus, if they have their limbs and senses, they may be charitable to one another.

II. The encouragement of charity. 1. A very kind construction shall be put upon it. What is given to the poor, or done for them, God will place it to account as lent to him, *lent upon interest* (so the word signifies); he takes it kindly, as if it were done to himself, and he would have us take the comfort of it and to be as well pleased as ever any usurer was when he had let out a sum of money into good hands. 2. A very rich recompence shall be made for it: *He will pay him again,* in temporal, spiritual, and eternal blessings. Almsgiving is the surest and safest way of thriving.

Verse 18

Parents are here cautioned against a foolish indulgence of their children that are untoward and viciously inclined, and that discover such an ill temper of mind as is not likely to be cured but by severity. 1. Do not say that it is all in good time to correct them; no, as soon as ever there appears a corrupt disposition in them check it immediately, before it gets head, and takes root, and is hardened into a habit: *Chasten thy son while there is hope,* for perhaps, if he be let alone awhile, he will be past hope, and a much greater chastening will not do that which now a less would effect. It is easiest plucking up weeds as soon as they spring up, and the bullock that is designed for the yoke should be betimes accustomed to it. 2. Do not say that it is a pity to correct them, and that, because they cry and beg to be forgiven, you cannot find in your heart to do it. If the point can be gained without correction, well and good; but if you find, as it often proves, that your forgiving them once, upon a dissembled repentance and promise of amendment, does but embolden them to offend again, especially if it be a thing that is in itself sinful (as lying, swearing, ribaldry, stealing, or the like), in such a case put on resolution, *and let not thy soul spare for his crying.* It is better that he should cry under thy rod than under the sword of the magistrate, or, which is more fearful, that of divine vengeance.

Verse 19

1. As we read this, it intimates, in short, that angry men never want woe. Those that are of strong, or rather headstrong, passions, commonly bring themselves and their families into trouble by vexatious suits and quarrels and the provocations they give; they are still smarting, in one instance or other, for their ungoverned heats; and, if their friends deliver them out of one trouble, they will quickly involve themselves in another, and they *must do it again,* all which troubles to themselves and others would be prevented if they would mortify their passions and get the rule of their own spirits. 2. It may as well be read, *He that is of great wrath* (meaning the child that is to be corrected and is impatient of rebuke, cries and makes a noise, even that wrath of his against the rod of correction) *deserves to be punished; for, if thou deliver him* for the sake of that,

thou wilt be forced to punish him so much the more next time. A stomachful high-spirited child must be subdued betimes, or it will be the worse for it.

Verse 20

Note, 1. It is well with those that are *wise in their latter end,* wise for their latter end, for their future state, wise for another world, that are found wise when their latter end comes, wise virgins, wise builders, wise stewards, that are wise at length, and *understand the things that belong to their peace, before they be hidden from their eyes.* A carnal worldling *at his end shall be a fool* (Jer. 17:11), but godliness will prove wisdom at last. 2. Those that would be *wise in their latter end* must *hear counsel* and *receive instruction,* in their beginnings must be willing to be taught and ruled, willing to be advised and reproved, when they are young. Those that would be stored in winter must gather in summer.

Verse 21

Here we have, 1. Men projecting. They keep their designs to themselves, but they cannot hide them from God; he knows the *many devices that are in men's hearts,* — devices against his counsels (as those, Ps. 2:1–3; Micah 4:11), — devices without his counsel (no regard had to his providence, as those Jam. 4:13, this and the other they will do, and not take God along with them), — devices unlike God's counsels; men are wavering in their devices, and often absurd and unjust, but God's counsels are wise and holy, steady and uniform. 2. God overruling. Various men have various designs, according as their inclination or interest leads them, but *the counsel of the Lord, that shall stand,* whatever becomes of the devices of men. His counsel often breaks men's measures and baffles their devices; but their devices cannot in the least alter his counsel, not disturb the proceedings of it, nor put him upon new counsels, Isa. 14:24; 46:11. What a check does this give to politic designing men, who think they can outwit all mankind, that there is a God in heaven that laughs at them! Ps. 2:4. What comfort does this speak to all God's people, that all God's purposes, which we are sure are right and good, shall be accomplished in due time!

Verse 22

Note, 1. The honour of doing good is what we may laudably be ambitious of. It cannot but be *the desire of man,* if he have any spark of virtue in him, to be kind; one would not covet an estate for any thing so much as thereby to be put into a capacity of relieving the poor and obliging our friends. 2. It is far better to have a heart to do good and want ability for it than have ability for it and want a heart to it: *The desire of a man* to be kind, and charitable, and generous, *is his kindness,* and shall be so construed; both God and man will accept his good-will, *according to what he has,* and will not expect more. *A poor man,* who wishes you well, but can promise you nothing, because he has nothing to be kind with, *is better than a liar,* than a rich man who makes you believe he will do mighty things, but, when it comes to the setting to, will do nothing. the character of the men of low degree, that they *are vanity,* from whom nothing is expected, is better than that of men of high degree, that they *are a lie,* they deceive those whose expectations they raised.

Verse 23

See what those that get by it that live in the fear of God, and always make conscience of their duty to him. 1. Safety: They *shall not be visited with evil;* they may be visited with sickness or other afflictions, but there shall be no evil in them, nothing to hurt them, because nothing to separate them *from the love of God,* or hurt to the soul. 2. Satisfaction: They *shall abide satisfied;* they shall have those comforts which are satisfying, and shall have a constant contentment and complacency in them. It is a satisfaction which will abide, whereas all the satisfactions of sense are transient and soon gone. *Satur pernoctabit, non cubabit incoenatus — He shall not go supperless to bed;* he shall have that which will make him easy and be an entertainment to him in his silent and solitary hours, Ps. 16:6, 7. 3. True and complete happiness. Serious godliness has a direct tendency *to life;* to all good, to eternal life; it is the sure and ready way to it; there is something in

the nature of it fitting men for heaven and so leading them to it.

Verse 24

A sluggard is here exposed as a fool, for, 1. All his care is to save himself from labour and cold. See his posture: He *hides his hand in his bosom,* pretends he is lame and cannot work; his hands are cold, and he must warm them in his bosom; and, when they are warm there, he must keep them so. He hugs himself in his own ease and is resolved against labour and hardship. Let those work that love it; for his part he thinks there is no such fine life as sitting still and doing nothing. 2. He will not be at the pains to feed himself, an elegant hyperbole; as we say, A man is so lazy that he would not shake fire off him, so here, He cannot find in his heart to take his hand out of his bosom, no, not to put meat into his own mouth. If the law be so that those that will not labour must not eat, he will rather starve than stir. Thus his sin is his punishment, and therefore is egregious folly.

Verse 25

Note, 1. The punishment of scorners will be a means of good to others. When men are so hardened in wickedness that they will not themselves be wrought upon by the severe methods that are used to reclaim and reform them, yet such methods must be used for the sake of others, that *they may hear and fear,* Deu. 19:20. If the *scorner* will not be recovered from his sin, the disease being inveterate, yet *the simple will beware* of venturing upon the sin which exposes men thus. If it cure not the infected, it may prevent the spreading of the infection. 2. The reproof of wise men will be a means of good to themselves. They need not be smitten; a word to the wise is enough. Do but *reprove one that has understanding and he will* so far understand himself and his own interest that he will *understand knowledge* by it, and not miss it again through ignorance and inadvertency when once he has been told of it; so kindly does he take reproof and so wisely improve it.

Verse 26

Here is, 1. The sin of a prodigal son. Besides the wrong he does to himself, he is injurious to his good parents, and basely ungrateful to those that were instruments of his being and have taken so much care and pains about him, which is a great aggravation of his sin and renders it exceedingly sinful in the eyes of God and man: *He wastes is father,* wastes his estate which he should have to support him in his old age, wastes his spirits, and breaks his heart, and brings his gray head *with sorrow to the grave.* He *chases away his mother,* alienates her affections from him, which cannot be done without a great deal of regret and uneasiness to her; he makes her weary of the house, with his rudeness and insolence, and glad to retire for a little quietness; and, when he has spent all, he turns her out of doors. 2. The shame of a prodigal son. It is a shame to himself that he should be so brutish and unnatural. He makes himself odious to all mankind. It is a shame to his parents and family, who are reflected upon, though, perhaps, without just cause, for teaching him no better, or being in some way wanting to him.

Verse 27

This is a good caution to those that have had a good education to take heed of hearkening to those who, under pretence of instructing them, draw them off from those good principles under the influence of which they were trained up. Observe, 1. There is that which seems designed for instruction, but really tends to the destruction of young men. The factors for vice will undertake to teach them free thoughts and a fashionable conversation, how to palliate the sins they have a mind to and stop the mouth of their own consciences, how to get clear of the restraints of their education, and to set up for wits and beaux. This is *the instruction* which *causes to err from the forms of sound words,* which should be held fast in faith and love. 2. It is the wisdom of young men to turn a deaf ear to such instructions, as the adder does to the charms that are designed to ensnare her. "Dread hearing such talk as tends top instil loose principles into the mind; and, if thou art linked in with such, break off from them; thou hast heard

enough, or too much, and therefore hear no more of the evil communication which corrupts good manners."

Verse 28

Here is a description of the worst of sinners, whose *hearts are fully set in them to do evil.* 1. They set that at defiance which would deter and detain them from sin: *An ungodly witness* is one that bears false witness against his neighbour, and will forswear himself to do another a mischief, in which there is not only great injustice, but great impiety; this is one of the worst of men. Or *an ungodly witness* is one that profanely and atheistically witnesses against religion and godliness, whose instructions seduce *from the words of knowledge* (v. 27); such a one *scorns judgment,* laughs at the terrors of the Lord, mocks at that fear, Job 15:26. Tell him of law and equity, that the scriptures and an oath are sacred things, and not to be jested with, that there will come a reckoning day; he laughs at it all, and scorns to heed it. 2. They are greedy, and glad of that which gives them an opportunity to sin: *The mouth of the wicked* eagerly *devours iniquity, drinks it in like water,* Job 15:16.

Verse 29

Note, 1. Scorners are fools. Those that ridicule things sacred and serious do but make themselves ridiculous. *Their folly shall be manifest unto all men.* 2. Those that scorn judgments cannot escape them, *v.* 28. The unbelief of man shall not make God's threatenings of no effect; those that *devour iniquity* swallow the hook with the bait. The civil magistrate has *judgments prepared for scorners,* for otherwise he would *bear the sword in vain;* but if he be remiss, and connive at sin, yet God's judgments slumber not; they are prepared, Mt. 25:41.

CHAPTER 20

Verse 1

Here is, 1. The mischief of drunkenness: *Wine is a mocker; strong drink is raging.* It is so to the sinner himself; it mocks him, makes a fool of him, promises him that satisfaction which it can never give him. It smiles upon him at first, but *at the last it bites.* In reflection upon it, it rages in his conscience. It is raging in the body, puts the humours into a ferment. *When the wine is in the wit is out,* and then the man, according as his natural temper is, either mocks like a fool or rages like a madman. Drunkenness, which pretends to be a sociable thing, renders men unfit for society, for it makes them abusive with their tongues and outrageous in their passions, ch. 23:29. 2. The folly of drunkards is easily inferred thence. He that is *deceived thereby,* that suffers himself to be drawn into this sin when he is so plainly warned of the consequences of it, *is not wise;* he shows that he has no right sense or consideration of things; and not only so, but he renders himself incapable of getting wisdom; for it is a sin that infatuates and besots men, and takes away their heart. A drunkard is a fool, and a fool he is likely to be.

Verse 2

See here, 1. How formidable kings are, and what a terror they strike upon those they are angry with. Their *fear,* with which (especially when they are absolute and their will is a law) they keep their subjects in awe, *is as the roaring of a lion,* which is very dreadful to the creatures he preys upon, and makes them tremble so that they cannot escape from him. Those princes that rule by wisdom and love rule like God himself, and bear his image; but those that rule merely by terror, and with a high hand, do but rule like a lion in the forest, with a brutal power. *Oderint, dum metuant — Let them hate, provided they fear.* 2. How unwise therefore those are that quarrel with them, that are angry at them, and so *provoke them to anger.* They *sin against their own lives.* Much more do those do so that provoke the King of kings to anger. *Nemo me impune lacesset — No one shall provoke me with impunity.*

Verse 3

This is designed to rectify men's mistakes concerning strife. 1. Men think it is their wisdom to engage in quarrels; whereas it is the greatest folly that can be. He thinks himself a wise man that is quick in resenting affronts, that stands upon every nicety of honour and right, and will not abate an ace of either, that prescribes, and imposes, and gives law, to every body; but he that thus meddles is a fool, and creates a great deal of needless vexation to himself. 2. Men think, when they are engaged in quarrels, that it would be a shame to them to go back and let fall the weapon; whereas really *it is an honour for a man to cease from strife*, an honour to withdraw an action, to drop a controversy, to forgive an injury, and to be friends with those that we have fallen out with. It is the honour of a man, a wise man, a man of spirit, to show the command he has of himself by *ceasing from strife*, yielding, and stooping, and receding from his just demands, for peace-sake, as Abraham, the better man, Gen. 13:8.

Verse 4

See here the evil of slothfulness and the love of ease. 1. It keeps men from the most necessary business, from ploughing and sowing when the season is: *The sluggard* has ground to occupy, and has ability for it; he can plough, but he *will not;* some excuse or other he has to shift it off, but the true reason is that it is *cold* weather. Though ploughing time is not in the depth of winter, it is in the borders of winter, when he thinks it too cold for him to be abroad. Those are scandalously sluggish who, in the way of their business, cannot find in their hearts to undergo so little toil as that of ploughing and so little hardship as that of a cold blast. Thus careless are many in the affairs of their souls; a trifling difficulty will frighten them from the most important duty; but good soldiers must endure hardness. 2. Thereby it deprives them of the most necessary supports: Those that *will not plough* in seedtime cannot expect to reap in harvest; and therefore they must beg their bread with astonishment when the diligent are bringing home their sheaves with joy. He that will not submit to the labour of ploughing must submit to the shame of begging. They *shall beg in harvest, and* yet *have nothing;* no, not then when there is great plenty. Though it may be charity to relieve sluggards, yet a man may, in justice, not relieve them; they deserve to be left to starve. Those that would not provide oil in their vessels begged when the bridegroom came, and were denied.

Verse 5

A man's wisdom is here said to be of use to him for the pumping of other people, and diving into them, 1. To get the knowledge of them. Though men's counsels and designs are ever so carefully concealed by them, so that they are as *deep water* which one cannot fathom, yet there are those who by sly insinuations, and questions that seem foreign, will get out of them both what they have done and what they intend to do. Those therefore who would keep counsel must not only put on resolution, but stand upon their guard. 2. To get knowledge by them. Some are very able and fit to give counsel, having an excellent faculty of cleaving a hair, hitting the joint of a difficulty, and advising pertinently, but they are modest, and reserved, and not communicative; they have a great deal in them, but it is loth to come out. In such a case *a man of understanding will draw it out*, as wine out of a vessel. We lose the benefit we might have by the conversation of wise men for want of the art of being inquisitive.

Verse 6

Note, 1. It is easy to find those that will pretend to be kind and liberal. Many a man will call himself a man of mercy, will boast what good he has done and what good he designs to do, or, at least, what an affection he has to well-doing. Most men will talk a great deal of their charity, generosity, hospitality, and piety, will sound a trumpet to themselves, as the Pharisees, and what little goodness they have will proclaim it and make a mighty matter of it. 2. But it is hard to find those that really are kind and liberal, that have done and will do more than either they speak of or care to hear spoken of, that will be true friends in a strait; such a one as one may trust to is like a black swan.

Verse 7

It is here observed to the honour of a good man, 1. That he does well for himself. He has a certain rule, which with

an even steady hand he governs himself by: He *walks in his integrity*; he keeps good conscience, and he has the comfort of it, for *it is his rejoicing.* He is not liable to those uneasinesses, either in contriving what he shall do or reflecting on what he has done, which those are liable to that walk in deceit. 2. That he does well for his family: *His children are blessed after him,* and fare the better for his sake. God has mercy in store for the seed of the faithful.

Verse 8

Here is, 1. The character of a good governor: He is *a king* that deserves to be called so who *sits in the throne,* not as a throne of honour, to take his ease, and take state upon him, and oblige men to keep their distance, but as a *throne of judgment,* that he may do justice, give redress to the injured and punish the injurious, who makes his business his delight and loves no pleasure comparably to it, who does not devolve the whole care and trouble upon others, but takes cognizance of affairs himself and sees with his own eyes as much as may be, 1 Ki. 10:9. 2. The happy effect of a good government. The presence of the prince goes far towards the putting of wickedness out of countenance; if he inspect his affairs himself, those that are employed under him will be kept in awe and restrained from doing wrong. If great men be good men, and will use their power as they may and ought, what good may they do and what evil may they prevent!

Verse 9

This question is not only a challenge to any man in the world to prove himself sinless, whatever he pretends, but a lamentation of the corruption of mankind, even that which remains in the best. Alas! *Who can say,* "I am sinless?" Observe, 1. Who the persons are that are excluded from these pretensions — all, one as well as another. Here, in this imperfect state, no person whatsoever can pretend to be without sin. Adam could say so in innocency, and saints can say so in heaven, but none in this life. Those that think themselves as good as they should be cannot, nay, and those that are really good will not, dare not, say this. 2. What the pretension is that is excluded. We cannot say, We *have made our hearts clean.* Though we can say, through grace, "We are cleaner than we have been," yet we cannot say, "We are clean and pure from all remainders of sin." Or, though we are clean from the gross acts of sin, yet we cannot say, "Our hearts are clean." Or, though we are washed and cleansed, yet we cannot say, "We ourselves made our own hearts clean;" it was the work of the Spirit. Or, though we are pure from the sins of many others, yet we cannot say, "We are *pure from our sin, the sin that easily besets us,* the body of death which Paul complained of," Rom. 7:24.

Verse 10

See here, 1. The various arts of deceiving that men have, all which evils the *love of money* is the root of. In paying and receiving money, which was then commonly done by the scale, they had *divers weights,* an under-weight for what they paid and an over-weight for what they received; in delivering out and taking in goods they had *divers measures,* a scanty measure to sell by and a large measure to buy by. This was done wrong with plot and contrivance, and under colour of doing right. Under these is included all manner of fraud and deceit in commerce and trade. 2. The displeasure of God against them. Whether they be about the money or the goods, in the buyer or in the seller, they are all *alike an abomination to the Lord.* He will not prosper the trade that is thus driven, nor bless what is thus got. He hates those that thus break the common faith by which justice is maintained, and will be *the avenger of all such.*

Verse 11

The tree is known by its fruits, a man *by his doings,* even a young tree by its first fruits, *a child by his* childish things, *whether his work be clean* only, appearing good (the word is used *ch.* 16:2), or *whether it be right,* that is, really good. This intimates, 1. That children will discover themselves. One may soon see what their temper is, and which way their inclination leads them, according as their constitution is. Children have not learned the art of dissembling and concealing their bent as grown people have.

2. That parents should observe their children, that they may discover their disposition and genius, and both manage and dispose of them accordingly, drive the nail that will go and draw out that which goes amiss. *Wisdom is* herein *profitable to direct.*

Verse 12

Note, 1. God is the God of nature, and all the powers and faculties of nature are derived from him and depend upon him, and therefore are to be employed for him. It was he that *formed the eye* and *planted the ear* (Ps. 94:9), and the structure of both is admirable; and it is he that preserves to us the use of both; to his providence we owe it that our eyes are *seeing eyes* and our ears *hearing ears.* Hearing and seeing are the learning senses, and must particularly own God's goodness in them. 2. God is the God of grace. It is he that gives the ear that hears God's voice, they eye that sees his beauty, for it is he that opens the understanding.

Verse 13

Note, 1. Those that indulge themselves in their ease may expect to want necessaries, which should have been gotten by honest labour. "Therefore, though thou must sleep (nature requires it), yet *love not sleep,* as those do that hate business. Love not sleep for its own sake, but only as it fits for further work. Love not much sleep, but rather grudge the time that is spent in it, and wish thou couldst live without it, that thou mightest always be employed in some good exercise." We must allow it to our bodies as men allow it to their servants, because they cannot help it and otherwise they shall have no good of them. Those that love sleep are likely to *come to poverty,* not only because they lose the time they spend in excess of sleep, but because they contract a listless careless disposition, and are still half asleep, never well awake. 2. Those that stir up themselves to their business may expect to have conveniences: "*Open thy eyes,* awake and shake off sleep, see how far in the day it is, how thy work wants thee, and how busy others are about thee! And, when thou art awake, look up, look to thy advantages, and do not let slip thy opportunities; apply thy mind closely to thy business and be in care about it. It is the easy condition of a great advantage: *Open thy eyes and thou shalt be satisfied with bread;* if thou dost not grow rich, yet though shalt have enough, and that is as good as a feast."

Verse 14

See here 1. What arts men use to get a good bargain and to buy cheap. They not only cheapen carelessly, as if they had no need, no mind for the commodity, when perhaps they cannot go without it (there may be prudence in that), but they vilify and run down that which yet they know to be of value; they cry, "*It is naught, it is naught;* it has this and the other fault, or perhaps may have; it is not good of the sort; and it is too dear; we can have better and cheaper elsewhere, or have bought better and cheaper." This is the common way of dealing; and after all, it may be, they know the contrary of what they affirm; but the buyer, who may think he has no other way of being even with the seller, does as extravagantly commend his goods and justify the price he sets on them, and so there is a fault on both sides; whereas the bargain would be made every jot as well if both buyer and seller would be modest and speak as they think. 2. What pride and pleasure men take in a good bargain when they have got it, though therein they contradict themselves, and own they dissembled when they were driving the bargain. When the buyer has beaten down the seller, who was content to lower his price rather than lose a customer (as many poor tradesmen are forced to do — small profit is better than none), then he goes his way, and boasts what excellent goods he has got at his own price, and takes it as an affront and a reflection upon his judgment if any body disparages his bargain. Perhaps he knew the worth of the good better than the seller himself did and knows how to get a great deal by them. See how apt men are to be pleased with their gettings and proud of their tricks; whereas a fraud and a lie are what a man ought to be ashamed of, though he have gained ever so much by them.

Verse 15

The *lips of knowledge* (a good understanding to guide the lips and a good elocution to diffuse the knowledge) are to be preferred far before gold, and pearl, and rubies; for, 1. They are more rare in themselves, more scarce and hard to be got. *There is gold* in many a man's pocket that has no grace in his heart. In Solomon's time there was plenty of gold (1 Ki. 10:21) and *abundance of rubies;* every body wore them; they were to be bought in every town. But wisdom is a rare thing, a precious jewel; few have it so as to do good with it, nor is it to be purchased of the merchants. 2. They are more enriching to us and more adorning. They make us rich towards God, rich in good works, 1 Tim. 2:9, 10. Most people are fond of gold, and a ruby or two will not serve, they must have a multitude of them, a cabinet of jewels; but he that has the lips of knowledge despises these, because he knows and possesses better things.

Verse 16

Two sorts of persons are here spoken of that are ruining their own estates, and will be beggars shortly, and therefore are not to be trusted with any good security: —1. Those that will be bound for any body that will ask them, that entangle themselves in rash suretiship to oblige their idle companions; they will break at last, nay, they cannot hold out long; these waste by wholesale. 2. Those that are in league with abandoned women, that treat them, and court them, and keep company with them. They will be beggars in a little time; never give them credit without good pledge. Strange women have strange ways of impoverishing men to enrich themselves.

Verse 17

Note, 1. Sin may possibly be pleasant in the commission: *Bread of deceit,* wealth gotten by fraud, by lying and oppression, may be *sweet to a man,* and the more sweet for its being ill-gotten, such pleasure does the carnal mind take in the success of its wicked projects. All the pleasures and profits of sin are *bread of deceit.* They are stolen, for they are forbidden fruit; and they will deceive men, for they are not what they promise. For a time, however, they are *rolled under the tongue as a sweet morsel,* and the sinner blesses himself in them. But, 2. It will be bitter in reflection. Afterwards the sinner's *mouth shall be filled with gravel.* When his conscience is awakened, when he sees himself cheated, and becomes apprehensive of the wrath of God against him for his sin, how painful and uneasy then is the thought of it! The pleasures of sin are but for a season, and are succeeded with sorrow. Some nations have punished malefactors by mingling gravel with their bread.

Verse 18

Note, 1. It is good in every thing to act with deliberation, and to consult with ourselves at least, and, in matters of moment, with our friends, too, before we determine, but especially to ask counsel of God, and beg direction from him, and observe the guidance of this eye. This is the way to have both our minds and our purposes established, and to succeed well in our affairs; whereas what is done hastily and with precipitation is repented of at leisure. Take time, and you will have done the sooner. *Deliberandum est diu, quod statuendum est semel — A final decision should be preceded by mature deliberation.* 2. It is especially our wisdom to be cautious in making war. Consider, and take advice, whether the war should be begun or no, whether it be just, whether it be prudent, whether we be a match for the enemy, and able to carry it on when it is too late to retreat (Lu. 14:31); and, when it is begun, consider how and by what arts it may be prosecuted, for management is as necessary as courage. Going to law is a kind of going to war, and therefore must be done with good advice, Prov. 25:8. The rule among the Romans was *nec sequi bellum, nec fugere — neither to urge war nor yet to shun it.*

Verse 19

Two sorts of people are dangerous to be conversed with: — 1. Tale-bearers, though they are commonly flatterers, and by fair speeches insinuate themselves into men's acquaintance. Those are unprincipled people that go about carrying stories, that make mischief among neighbours and relations, that sow in the minds of people jealousies of their governors, of their ministers, and of one another, that reveal secrets which they are entrusted with or which by unfair means they come to the knowledge of, under pretence of guessing at men's thoughts and intentions, tell that of them which is really false. "Be not familiar with such; do not give them the hearing when they tell their tales and reveal secrets, for you may be sure that they will betray your secrets too and tell tales of you." 2. Flatterers, for they are commonly tale-bearers. If a man fawn upon you, compliment and commend you, suspect him to have some design upon you, and stand upon your guard; he would pick that out of you which will serve him to make a story of to somebody else to your prejudice; therefore *meddle not with him that flatters with his lips.* Those too dearly love, and too dearly buy, their own praise, that will put confidence in a man and trust him with a secret or business because he flatters them.

Verse 20

Here is, 1. An undutiful child become very wicked by degrees. He began with despising his father and mother, slighting their instructions, disobeying their commands, and raging at their rebukes, but at length he arrives at such a pitch of impudence and impiety as to curse them, to give them scurrilous and opprobrious language, and to wish mischief to those that were instruments of his being and have taken so much care and pains about him, and this in defiance of God and his law, which had made this a capital crime (Ex. 21:17, Mt. 15:4), and in violation of all the bonds of duty, natural affection, and gratitude. 2. An undutiful child become very miserable at last: *His lamp shall be put out in obscure darkness;* all his honour shall be laid in the dust, and he shall for ever lose his reputation. Let him never expect any peace or comfort in his own mind, no, nor to prosper in this world. His days shall be shortened, and the lamp of his life extinguished, according to the reverse of the promise of the fifth commandment. His family shall be cut off and his posterity be a curse to him. And it will be his eternal ruin; the lamp of his happiness shall be *put out in the blackness of darkness* (so the word is), even that which is *for ever,* Jude 13, Mt. 22:13.

Verse 21

Note, 1. It is possible that an estate may be suddenly raised. There are those that will be rich, by right or wrong, who make no conscience of what they say or do if they can but get money by it, who, when it is in their power, will cheat their own father, and who sordidly spare and hoard up what they get, grudging themselves and their families food convenient and thinking all lost but what they buy land with or put out to interest. By such ways as these a man may grow rich, may grow very rich, in a little time, at his first setting out. 2. An estate that is suddenly raised is often as suddenly ruined. It was raised hastily, but, not being raised honestly, it proves *soon ripe and soon rotten: The end thereof shall not be blessed* of God, and, if he do not bless it, it can neither be comfortable nor of any continuance; so that he who got it at the end will be a fool. He had better have taken time and built firmly.

Verse 22

Those that live in this world must expect to have injuries done them, affronts given them, and trouble wrongfully created them, for we dwell among briers. Now here we are told what to do when we have wrong done us. 1. We must not avenge ourselves, no, nor so much as think of revenge, or design it: *"Say not thou,* no, not in thy heart, *I will recompense evil* for evil. Do not please thyself with the thought that some time or other thou shalt have an opportunity of being quits with him. Do not wish revenge, or hope for it, much less resolve upon it, no, not when the injury is fresh and the resentment of it most deep. Never say that thou wilt do a think which thou canst not in faith pray to God to assist thee in, and *that* thou canst not do in mediating revenge." 2. We must refer ourselves to God, and leave it to him to plead our cause, to maintain our right, and reckon with those that do us wrong in such a way and manner as he thinks fit and in his own due time: *"Wait on the Lord,* and attend his pleasure, acquiesce in his will, and he does not say that he will punish him that has injured thee (instead of desiring that thou must forgive him and pray for him), but *he will save thee,* and that is enough. He will protect thee, so that thy passing by one injury shall not (as is commonly feared) expose thee to another; nay, he will recompense good to thee, to balance thy trouble and encourage thy patience," as David hoped, when Shimei cursed him, 2 Sa. 16:12.

Verse 23

This is to the same purport with what was said *v.* 20. 1. It is here repeated, because it is a sin that God doubly hates (as lying, which is of the same nature with this sin, is mentioned twice among the seven things that God hates, *ch.* 6:17, 19), and because it was probably a sin very much practised at that time in Israel, and therefore made light of as if there were no harm in it, under pretence that, being commonly used, there was no trading without it. 2. It is here added, *A false balance is not good,* to intimate that it is not only abominable to God, but unprofitable to the sinner himself; there is really no good to be got by it, no, not a good bargain, for a bargain made by fraud will prove a losing bargain in the end.

Verse 24

We are here taught that in all our affairs, 1. We have a necessary and constant dependence upon God. All our natural actions depend upon his providence, all our spiritual actions upon his grace. The best man is no better than God makes him; and every creature is that to us which it is the will of God that it should be. Our enterprises succeed, not as we desire and design, but as God directs and disposes. The goings even of a strong man (so the word signifies) *are of the Lord,* for his strength is weakness without God, nor is the battle always to the strong. 2. We have no foresight of future events, and therefore know not how to forecast for them: *How can a man understand his own way?* How can he tell what will befal him, since God's counsels concerning him are secret, and therefore how can he of himself contrive what to do without divine direction? We so little understand our own way that we know not what is good for ourselves, and therefore we must make a virtue of necessity, and commit our way unto the Lord, in whose hand it is, follow the guidance and submit to the disposal of Providence.

Verse 25

Two things, by which God is greatly affronted, men are here said to be ensnared by, and entangled not only in guilt, but in trouble and ruin at length: — 1. Sacrilege, men's alienating holy things and converting them to their own use, which is here called *devouring* them. What is devoted in any way to the service and honour of God, for the support of religion and divine worship or the relief of the poor, ought to be conscientiously preserved to the purposes designed; and those that directly or indirectly embezzle it, or defeat the purpose for which it was given, will have a great deal to answer for. *Will a man rob God in tithes and offerings?* Mal. 3:8. Those that hurry over religious offices (their praying and preaching) and huddle them up in haste, as being impatient to get done, may be said to *devour that which is holy.* 2. Covenant-breaking. *It is a snare to a man, after* he has made *vows* to God, to *enquire* how he may evade them or get dispensed with, and to contrive excuses for the violating of them. If the matter of them was doubtful, and the expressions were ambiguous, that was his fault; he should have made them with more caution and consideration, for it will involve his conscience (if it be tender) in great perplexities, if he be to enquire concerning them afterwards (Eccl. 5:6); for, when we have opened our mouth to the Lord, it is too late to think of going back, Acts 5:4.

Verse 26

See here, 1. What is the business of magistrates. They are to be a terror to evil-doers. They must *scatter the wicked,* who are linked in confederacies to assist and embolden one another in doing mischief; and there is no doing this but by *bringing the wheel over them,* that is, putting the laws in execution against them, crushing their power and quashing their projects. Severity must sometimes be used to rid the country of those that are openly vicious and mischievous, debauched and debauching. 2.

What is the qualification of magistrates, which is necessary in order to do this. They have need to be both pious and prudent, for it is the wise king, who is both religious and discreet, that is likely to effect the suppression of vice and reformation of manners.

Verse 27

We have here the dignity of the soul, the great soul of man, that light which lighteth every man. 1. It is a divine light; it is the *candle of the Lord,* a candle of his lighting, for it is *the inspiration of the Almighty* that *gives us understanding.* He *forms the spirit of man within him.* It is after the image of God that man is created in knowledge. Conscience, that noble faculty, is God's deputy in the soul; it is a candle not only lighted by him, but lighted for him. The Father of spirits is therefore called the *Father of lights.* 2. It is a discovering light. By the help of reason we come to know men, to judge of their characters, and dive into their designs; by the help of conscience we come to know ourselves. The spirit of a man has a self-consciousness (1 Co. 2:11); it searches into the dispositions and affections of the soul, praises what is good, condemns what is otherwise, and judges of the thoughts and intents of the heart. This is the office, this the power, of conscience, which we are therefore concerned to get rightly informed and to keep void of offence.

Verse 28

Here we have, 1. The virtues of a good king. Those are *mercy and truth,* especially mercy, for that is mentioned twice here. He must be strictly faithful to his word, must be sincere, and abhor all dissimulation, must religiously discharge all the trusts reposed in him, must support and countenance truth. He must likewise rule with clemency, and by all acts of compassion gain the affections of his people. *Mercy and truth* are the glories of God's throne, and kings are called *gods.* 2. The advantages he gains thereby. These virtues will preserve his person and support his government, will make him easy and safe, beloved by his own people and feared by his enemies, if it be possible that he should have any.

Verse 29

This shows that both young and old have their advantages, and therefore must each of them be, according to their capacities, serviceable to the public, and neither of them despise nor envy the other. 1. Let not old people despise the young, for they are strong and fit for action, able to go through business and break through difficulties, which the aged and weak cannot grapple with. The *glory of young men is their strength,* provided they use it well (in the service of God and their country, not of their lusts), and that they be not proud of it nor trust to it. 2. Let not young people despise the old, for they are grave, and fit for counsel, and, though they have not the strength that young men have, yet they have more wisdom and experience. *Juniores ad labores, seniores ad honores — Labour is for the young, honour for the aged.* God has put honour upon the old man; for his *gray head* is his beauty. See Dan. 7:9.

Verse 30

Note, 1. Many need severe rebukes. Some children are so obstinate that their parents can do no good with them without sharp correction; some criminals must feel the rigour of the law and public justice; gentle methods will not work upon them; they must be beaten black and blue. And the wise God sees that his own children sometimes need very sharp afflictions. 2. Severe rebukes sometimes do a great deal of good, as corrosives contribute to the cure of a wound, eating out the proud flesh. The rod drives out even that foolishness which was bound up in the heart, and cleanses away the evil there. 3. Frequently those that most need severe rebukes can worse bear them. Such is the corruption of nature that men are as loth to be rebuked sharply for their sins as to be beaten till their bones ache. *Correction is grievous to him that forsakes the way,* and yet it is good for him, Heb. 12:11.

CHAPTER 21

Verse 1

Note, 1. Even the *hearts* of men are in God's hand, and not only their *goings,* as he had said, *ch.* 20:24. God can change men's minds, can, by a powerful insensible operation under their spirits, turn them from that which they seemed most intent upon, and incline them to that which they seemed most averse to, as the husbandman, by canals and gutters, turns the water through his grounds as he pleases, which does not alter the nature of the water, nor put any force upon it, any more than God's providence does upon the native freedom of man's will, but directs the course of it to serve his own purpose. 2. Even kings' hearts are so, notwithstanding their powers and prerogatives, as much as the hearts of common persons. The *hearts of kings are unsearchable* to us, much more unmanageable by us; as they have their *arcana imperii —state secrets,* so that they have great prerogatives of their crown; but the great God has them not only under his eye, but in his hand. Kings are what he makes them. Those that are most absolute are under God's government; he *puts things into their hearts,* Rev. 17:17; Ezra 7:27.

Verse 2

Note, 1. We are all apt to be partial in judging of ourselves and our own actions, and to think too favourably of our own character, as if there was nothing amiss in it: *Every way of a man,* even his by-way, *is right in his own eyes.* The proud heart is very ingenious in putting a fair face upon a foul matter, and in making that appear right to itself which is far from being so, to stop the mouth of conscience. 2. We are sure that the judgment of God concerning us is according to truth. Whatever our judgment is concerning ourselves, *the Lord ponders the heart.* God looks at the heart, and judges of men according to that, of their actions according to their principles and intentions; and his judgment of that is as exact as ours is of that which we ponder most, and more so; he weighs it in an unerring balance, *ch.* 16:2.

Verse 3

Here, 1. It is implied that many deceive themselves with a conceit that, if they offer sacrifice, that will excuse them from doing justice, and procure them a dispensation for their unrighteousness; and this makes their way *seem right, v.* 2. *We have fasted,* Isa. 58:3. *I have peace-offerings with me,* Prov. 7:14. 2. It is plainly declared that living a good life (doing justly and loving mercy) is more pleasing to God than the most pompous and expensive instances of devotion. Sacrifices were of divine institution, and were acceptable to God if they were offered in faith and with repentance, otherwise not, Is. 1:11, etc. But even then moral duties were preferred before them (1 Sa. 15:22), which intimates that their excellency was not innate nor the obligation to them perpetual, Mic. 6:6–8. Much of religion lies in doing judgment and justice from a principle of duty to God, contempt of the world, and love to our neighbour; and this is more pleasing to God than all burnt-offerings and sacrifices, Mk. 12:33.

Verse 4

This may be taken as showing us, 1. The marks of a wicked man. He that has a *high look and a proud heart,* that carries himself insolently and scornfully towards both God and man, and that is always ploughing and plotting, designing and devising some mischief or other, is indeed a wicked man. *The light of the wicked is sin.* Sin is *the pride, the ambition, the glory and joy,* and *the business of wicked men.* 2. The miseries of wicked man. His raised expectations, his high designs, and most elaborate contrivances and projects, are sin to him; he contracts guilt in them and so prepares trouble for himself. The very business of all wicked men, as well as their pleasure, is nothing but sin; so Bishop Patrick. They do all to serve their lusts, and have no regard to the glory of God in it, and therefore *their ploughing is sin,* and no marvel when their sacrificing is so, *ch.* 15:8.

Verse 5

Here is, 1. The way to be rich. If we would live plentifully and comfortably in the world, we must be diligent in our business, and not shrink from the toil and trouble of it, but prosecute it closely, improving all advantages and opportunities for it, and doing what we do with all our might; yet we must not be hasty in it, nor hurry ourselves and others with it, but keep doing fair and softly, which, we say, goes far in a day. With diligence there must be contrivance. The *thoughts of the diligent* are as necessary as the hand of the diligent. Forecast is as good as work. Seest thou a man thus prudent and diligent? He will have enough to live on. 2. The way to be poor. Those that are hasty, that are rash and inconsiderate in their affairs, and will not take time to think, that are greedy of gain, by right or wrong, and make haste to be rich by unjust practices or unwise projects, are in the ready road to poverty. Their thoughts and contrivances, by which they hope to raise themselves, will ruin them.

Verse 6

This shows the folly of those that hope to enrich themselves by dishonest practices, by oppressing and overreaching those with whom they deal, by false-witness-bearing, or by fraudulent contracts, of those that make no scruples of lying when there is any thing to be got by it. They may perhaps heap up treasures by these means, that which they make their treasure; but, 1. They will not meet with the satisfaction they expect. It is a *vanity tossed to and fro;* it will be disappointment and vexation of spirit to them; they will not have the comfort of it, nor can they put any confidence in it, but will be perpetually uneasy. It will be *tossed to and fro* by their own consciences, and by the censures of men; let them expect to be in a constant hurry. 2. They will meet with destruction they do not expect. While they are seeking wealth by such unlawful practices they are really seeking death; they lay themselves open to the envy and ill-will of men by the treasures they get, and to the wrath and curse of God, by the lying tongue wherewith they get them, which he will make to fall upon themselves and sink them to hell.

Verse 7

See here, 1. The nature of injustice. Getting money by lying (*v.* 6) is no better than downright robbery. Cheating is stealing; you might as well pick a man's pocket as impose upon him by a lie in making a bargain, which he had no fence against but by not believing you; and it will be no excuse from the guilt of robbery to say that he might choose whether he would believe you, for that is a debt we should owe to all men. 2. The cause of injustice. Men *refuse to do judgment;* they will not render to all their due, but withhold it, and omissions make way for commissions; they come at length to robbery itself. Those that refuse to do justice will choose to do wrong. 3. The effects of injustice; it will return upon the sinner's own head. The robbery of the wicked will *terrify them* (so some); their consciences will be filled with horror and amazement, will cut them, will *saw them asunder* (so others); it will *destroy them* here and for ever, therefore he had said (*v.* 6), *They seek death.*

Verse 8

This shows that as men are so is their way. 1. Evil men have evil ways. If the man be *froward,* his way also is *strange;* and this is the way of most men, such is the general corruption of mankind. *They have all gone aside* (Ps. 14:2, 3); all flesh have perverted their way. But the froward man, the man of deceit, that acts by craft and trick in all he does, his way is strange, contrary to all the rules of honour and honesty. It is strange, for you know not where to find him nor when you have him; it is strange, for it is alienated from all good and estranges men from God and his favour. It is what he behold afar off, and so do all honest men. 2. Men that are pure are proved to be such by their work, for it *is right,* it is just and regular; and they are accepted of God and approved of men. The way of mankind in their apostasy is froward and strange; but as for the pure, those that by the grace of God are recovered out of that state, of which there is here and there one, *their work is right,* as Noah's was in the old world, Gen. 7:1.

Verse 9

See here, 1. What a great affliction it is to a man to have a brawling scolding woman for his wife, who upon every occasion, and often upon no occasion, breaks out into a passion, and chides either him or those about her, is fretful to herself and furious to her children and servants, and, in both, vexatious to her husband. If a man has a wide house, spacious and pompous, this will embitter the comfort of it to him — *a house of society* (so the word is), in which a man may be sociable, and entertain his friends; this will make both him and his house unsociable, and unfit for enjoyments of true friendship. It makes a man ashamed of his choice and his management, and disturbs his company. 2. What many a man is forced to do under such an affliction. He cannot keep up his authority. He finds it to no purpose to contradict the most unreasonable passion, for it is unruly and rages so much the more; and his wisdom and grace will not suffer him to render railing for railing, nor his conjugal affection to use any severity, and therefore he finds it his best way to retire *into a corner of the house-top,* and sit alone there, out of the hearing of her clamour; and if he employ himself well there, as he may do, it is the wisest course he can take. Better do so than quit the house, and go into bad company, for diversion, as many, who, like Adam, make their wife's sin the excuse of their own.

Verse 10

See here the character of a very wicked man. 1. The strong inclination he has to do mischief. His very *soul desires evil,* desires that evil may be done and that he may have the pleasure, not only of seeing it, but of having a hand in it. The root of wickedness lies in the soul; the desire that men have to do evil, that is the lust which conceives and brings forth sin. 2. The strong aversion he has to do good: *His neighbour,* his friend, his nearest relation, *finds no favour in his eyes,* cannot gain from him the least kindness, though he be in the greatest need of it. And, when he is in the pursuit of the evil his heart is so much upon, he will spare no man that stands in his way; his next neighbour shall be used no better than a stranger, than an enemy.

Verse 11

This we had before (*ch.* 19:25), and it shows that there are two ways by which the simple may be made wise: —1. By the punishments that are inflicted on those that are incorrigibly wicked. Let the law be executed upon a scorner, and even he that is simple will be awakened and alarmed by it, and will discern, more than he did, the evil of sin, and will take warning by it and take heed. 2. By the instructions that are given to those that are wise and willing to be taught: *When the wise is instructed* by the preaching of the word *he* (not only the wise himself, but the simple that stands by) *receives knowledge.* It is no injustice at all to take a good lesson to ourselves which was designed for another.

Verse 12

1. As we read this verse, it shows why good men, when they come to understand things aright, will not envy the prosperity of evil-doers. When they see *the house of the wicked,* how full it is perhaps of all the good things of this life, they are tempted to envy; but when they *wisely consider* it, when they look upon it with an eye of faith, when they see *God overthrowing the wicked for their wickedness,* that there is a curse upon their habitation which will certainly be the ruin of it ere long, they see more reason to despise them, or pity them, than to fear or envy them. 2. Some give another sense of it: *The righteous man* (the judge or magistrate, that is entrusted with the execution of justice, and the preservation of public peace) *examines the house of the wicked,* searches it for arms or for stolen goods, makes a diligent enquiry concerning his family and the characters of those about him, that he may by his power *overthrow the wicked for their wickedness* and prevent their doing any further mischief, that he may fire the nests where the birds of prey are harboured or the unclean birds.

Verse 13

Here we have the description and doom of an uncharitable man. 1. His description: He *stops his ears at the cry of the poor,* at the cry of their wants and miseries (he resolves to take no cognizance of them), at the cry of their requests and supplications — he resolves he will not so much as give them the hearing, turns them away from his

door, and forbids them to come near him, or, if he cannot avoid hearing them, he will not need them, nor be moved by their complaints, no be prevailed with by their importunities; he *shuts up the bowels of his compassion,* and that is equivalent to the stopping of his ears, Acts 7:57. 2. His doom. He shall himself be reduced to straits, which will make him *cry,* and then *he shall not be heard.* Men will not hear him, but reward him as he has rewarded others. God will not hear him; for he that *showed no mercy shall have judgment without mercy* (Jam. 2:13), and he that on earth denied a crumb of bread in hell was denied a drop of water. God will be deaf to the prayers of those who are deaf to the cries of the poor, which, if they be not heard by us, will be heard against us, Ex. 22:23.

Verse 14

Here is, 1. The power that is commonly found to be in gifts. Nothing is more violent than *anger.* O the force of *strong wrath!* And yet a handsome present, prudently managed, will turn away some men's wrath when it seemed implacable, and disarm the keenest and most passionate resentments. Covetousness is commonly a master-sin and has the command of other lusts. *Pecuniae obediunt omnia — Money commands all things.* Thus Jacob pacified Esau and Abigail David. 2. The policy that is commonly used in giving and receiving bribes. It must be a *gift in secret and a reward in the bosom,* for he that takes it would not be thought to covet it, nor known to receive it, nor would he willingly be beholden to him whom he has been offended with; but, if it be done privately, all is well. No man should be too open in giving any gift, nor boast of the presents he sends; but, if it be a bribe to pervert justice, that is so scandalous that those who are fond of it are ashamed of it.

Verse 15

Note, 1. It is a pleasure and satisfaction to good men both to see justice administered by the government they live under, right taking place and iniquity suppressed, and also to practise it themselves, according as their sphere is. They no only do justice, but do it with pleasure, not only for fear of shame, but for love of virtue. 2. It is a terror to wicked men to see the laws put in execution against vice and profaneness. It is destruction to them; as it is also a vexation to them to be forced, either for the support of their credit or for fear of punishment, *to do judgment* themselves. Or, if we take it as we read it, the meaning is, There is true pleasure in the practice of religion, but certain destruction at the end of all vicious courses.

Verse 16

Here is, 1. The sinner upon his ramble: He *wanders out of the way of understanding,* and when once he has left that good way he wanders endlessly. The way of religion is *the way of understanding;* those that are not truly pious are not truly intelligent; those *that wander out of this way* break the hedge which God has set, and follow the conduct of the world and the flesh; and they go astray like lost sheep. 2. The sinner at his rest, or rather his ruin: He *shall remain* (quiescet — *he shall rest,* but not *in pace —in peace*) *in the congregation of the giants,* the sinners of the old world, that were swept away by the deluge; to that destruction the damnation of sinners is compared, as sometimes to the destruction of Sodom, when they are said to have their portion in fire and brimstone. Or *in the congregation of the damned,* that are under the power of the second death. There is a vast congregation of damned sinners, bound in bundles for the fire, and in that those shall remain, remain for ever, who are shut out from the congregation of the righteous. He that forsakes the way to heaven, if he return not to it, will certainly sink into the depths of hell.

Verse 17

Here is an argument against a voluptuous luxurious life, taken from the ruin it brings upon men's temporal interests. Here is 1. The description of an epicure: *He loves pleasure.* God allows us to use the delights of sense soberly and temperately, *wine to make glad the heart* and put vigour into the spirits, and *oil to make the face to shine* and beautify the countenance; but he that loves these, that sets his heart upon them, covets them earn-

estly, is solicitous to have all the delights of sense wound up to the height of pleasurableness, is impatient of every thing that crosses him in his pleasures, relishes these as the best pleasures, and has his mouth by them put out of taste for spiritual delights, he is an epicure, 2 Tim. 3:4. 2. The punishment of an epicure in this world: *He shall be a poor man;* for the lusts of sensuality are not maintained but at great expense, and there are instances of those who want necessaries, and live upon alms, who once could not live without dainties and varieties. Many a beau becomes a beggar.

Verse 18

This intimates, 1. What should be done by the justice of men: *The wicked,* that are the troublers of a land, ought to be punished, for the preventing and turning away of those national judgments which otherwise will be inflicted and in which even the righteous are many times involved. Thus when Achan was stoned he was *a ransom for the* camp of *righteous* Israel, and the seven sons of Saul, when they were hanged, were *a ransom for the* kingdom of *righteous* David. 2. What is often done by the providence of God: *The righteous is delivered out of trouble, and the wicked comes in his stead,* and so seems as if he were *a ransom for him,* ch. 11:8. God will rather leave many wicked people to be cut off than abandon his own people. *I will give men for thee,* Isa. 43:3, 4.

Verse 19

Note, 1. Unbridled passions embitter and spoil the comfort of all relations. A peevish angry wife makes her husband's life uneasy, to whom she should be a comfort and a meet help. Those cannot dwell in peace and happiness that cannot dwell in peace and love. Even those that are one flesh, if they be not withal one spirit, have no joy of their union. 2. It is better to have no company than bad company. The wife of thy covenant is thy companion, and yet, if she be peevish and provoking, *it is better to dwell in* a solitary *wilderness,* exposed to wind and weather, than in company with her. A man may better enjoy God and himself in a wilderness than among quarrelsome relations and neighbours. See *v.* 9.

Verse 20

Note, 1. Those that are wise will increase what they have and live plentifully; their wisdom will teach them to proportion their expenses to their income and to lay up for hereafter; so that *there is a treasure* of things *to be desired,* and as much as needs be desired, a good stock of all things convenient, laid up in season, and particularly of *oil,* one of the staple commodities of Canaan, Deu. 8:8. This is *in the habitation,* or cottage, *of the wise;* and it is better to have an old-fashioned house, and have it well furnished, than a fine modern one, with sorry housekeeping. God blesses the endeavors of the wise and then their houses are replenished. 2. Those that are foolish will misspend what they have upon their lusts, and so bring the stock they have to nothing. Those manage wretchedly that are in haste to spend what they had, but not in care which way to get more. Foolish children spend what their wise parents have laid up. *One sinner destroys much good,* as the prodigal son.

Verse 21

See here, 1. What it is to make religion our business; it is to *follow after righteousness and mercy,* not to content ourselves with easy performances, but to do our duty with the utmost care and pains, as those that are pressing forward and in fear of coming short. We must both do justly and love mercy, and must proceed and persevere therein; and, though we cannot attain to perfection, yet it will be a comfort to us if we aim at it and follow after it. 2. What will be the advantage of doing so: Those that do *follow after righteousness* shall *find righteousness;* God will give them grace to do good, and they shall have the pleasure and comfort of doing it; those that make conscience of being just to others shall have the pleasure and comfort of doing it; those that make conscience of being just to others shall be justly dealt with by others and others shall be kind to them. The Jews *followed after righteousness,* and did not find it, because they sought amiss, Rom. 9:31. Otherwise, *Seek and you shall find,* and with it shall find both *life and honour,* everlasting life and honour, the *crown of righteousness.*

Verse 22

Note, 1. Those that have power are apt to promise themselves great things from their power. *The city of the mighty* thinks itself impregnable, and therefore its strength is *the confidence thereof,* what it boasts of and trust in, bidding defiance to danger. 2. Those that have wisdom, though they are so modest as not to promise much, often perform great things, even against those that are so confident of their strength, by their wisdom. Good conduct will go far even against great force; and a stratagem, well managed, may effectually *scale the city of the mighty and cast down the strength* it had such a confidence in. *A wise man* will gain upon the affections of people and conquer them by strength of reason, which is a more noble conquest than that obtained by strength of arms. Those that understand their interest will willingly submit themselves to a wise and good man, and the strongest walls shall not hold out against him.

Verse 23

Note, 1. It is our great concern to keep our souls from straits, being entangled in snares and perplexities, and disquieted with troubles, that we may preserve the possession and enjoyment of ourselves and that our souls may be in frame for the service of God. 2. Those that would keep their souls must keep a watch before the door of their lips, must *keep the mouth* by temperance, that no forbidden fruit go into it, no stolen waters, that nothing be eaten or drunk to excess; they must *keep the tongue* also, that no forbidden word go out of the door of the lips, no corrupt communication. By a constant watchfulness over our words we shall prevent abundance of mischiefs which an ungoverned tongue runs men into. Keep thy heart, and that will keep thy tongue from sin; keep thy tongue, and that will keep thy heart from trouble.

Verse 24

See here the mischief of pride and haughtiness. 1. It exposes men to sin; it makes them passionate, and kindles in them the fire of *proud wrath.* They are continually dealing in it, as if it were their trade to be angry, and they had nothing so much to do as to barter passions and exchange bitter words. Most of the wrath that inflames the spirits and societies of men is *proud wrath.* Men cannot bear the least slight, nor in any thing to be crossed or contradicted, but they are out of humour, nay, in a heat, immediately. It likewise makes them scornful when they are angry, very abusive with their tongues, insolent towards those above them and imperious towards all about them. *Only by pride* comes all this. 2. It exposes men to shame. They get a bad name by it, and every one calls them *proud and haughty scorners,* and therefore nobody cares for having any thing to do with them. If men would but consult their reputation a little and the credit of their profession, which suffers with it, they would not indulge their pride and passion as they do.

Verses 25–26

Here we have, 1. The miseries of the slothful, whose *hands refuse to labour* in an honest calling, by which they might get an honest livelihood. They are as fit for labour as other men, and business offers itself, to which they might lay their hands and apply their minds, but they will not; herein they fondly think they do well for themselves, see ch. 26:16. Soul, take thy ease. But really they are enemies to themselves; for, besides that their slothfulness starves them, depriving them of their necessary supports, their desires at the same time stab them. Though their hands refuse to labour, their hearts cease not to covet riches, and pleasures, and honours, which yet cannot be obtained without labour. Their desires are impetuous and insatiable; they *covet greedily all the day long,* and cry, *Give, give;* they expect every body should do for them, though they will do nothing for themselves, much less for any body else. Now these *desires kill them;* they are a perpetual vexation to them, fret them to death, and perhaps put them upon such dangerous courses for the satisfying of their craving lusts as hasten them to an untimely end. Many that must have money with which to make provi-

sion for the flesh, and would not be at the pains to get it honestly, have turned highwaymen, and that has killed them. Those that are slothful in the affairs of their souls, and yet have desires towards that which would be the happiness of their souls, those *desires kill them,* will aggravate their condemnation and be witnesses against them that were convinced of the worth of spiritual blessings, but refused to be at the pains that were necessary to the obtaining of them. 2. The honours of the honest and diligent. The righteous and industrious have their desires satisfied, and enjoy not only that satisfaction, but the further satisfaction of doing good to others. The slothful are always craving and gaping to receive, *but the righteous* are always full and contriving to give; and *it is more blessed to give than to receive.* They *give and spare not,* give liberally and upbraid not; they *give a portion to seven and also to eight,* and do not spare for fear of wanting.

Verse 27

Sacrifices were of divine institution; and when they were offered in faith, and with repentance and reformation, God was greatly honoured by them and well-pleased in them. But they were often not only unacceptable, but an *abomination,* to God, and he declared so, which was an indication both that they were not required for their own sakes and that there were better things, and for effectual, in reserve, when sacrifice and offering should be done away. They were an *abomination,* 1. When they were brought by wicked men, who did not, according to the true intent and meaning of sacrificing, repent of their sins, mortify their lusts, and amend their lives. Cain brought his offering. Even wicked men may be found in the external performances of religious worship. Many can freely give God their beasts, their lips, their knees, who would not give him their hearts; the Pharisees gave alms. But when the person is an *abomination,* as every wicked man is to God, the performance cannot but be so; *even when he brings it diligently;* so some read the latter part of the verse. Though their offerings are continually before God (Ps. 50:8), yet they are an abomination to him. 2. *Much more when* they were brought with *wicked minds,* when their sacrifices were made, not only consistent with, but serviceable to, their wickedness, as Absalom's vow, Jezebel's fast, and the Pharisees' long prayers. When men make a show of devotion, that they may the more easily and effectually compass some covetous or malicious design, when holiness is pretended, but some wickedness intended, then especially the performance is an abomination, Isa. 66:5.

Verse 28

Here is, 1. The doom of *a false witness.* He who, for favour to one side or malice to the other, gives in a false evidence, or makes an affidavit of that which he knows to be false, or at least does not know to be true, if it be discovered, his reputation will be ruined. A man may tell a lie perhaps in his haste; but he that gives a false testimony does it with deliberation and solemnity, and it cannot but be a presumptuous sin, and a forfeiture of man's credit. But, though he should not be discovered, he himself shall be ruined; the vengeance he imprecated upon himself, when he took the false oath, will come upon him. 2. The praise of him that is conscientious: He *who hears* (that is, obeys) the command of God, which is to *speak every man truth with his neighbour,* he who testifies nothing but what he has heard and knows to be true, *speaks constantly* (that is, consistently with himself); he is always in the same story; he speaks *in finem — to the end;* people will give credit to him and hear him out; he speaks unto victory; he carries the cause, which the *false witness* shall lose; he shall speak to eternity. What is true is true eternally. *The lip of truth is established for ever.*

Verse 29

Here is, 1. The presumption and impudence of a wicked man: He *hardens his face* — brazens it, that he may not blush — steels it, that he may not tremble when he commits the greatest crimes; he bids defiance to the terrors of the law and the checks of his own conscience, the reproofs of the word and the rebukes of Providence; he will have his way and nothing shall hinder him, Isa. 57:17. 2. The caution and circumspection of a good man: *As for the upright,* he does not say, What *would* I do? What have I

a mind to? and that will I have; but, What *should* I do? What does God require of me? What is duty? What is prudence? What is for edification? And so he does not force his way, but *direct his way* by a safe and certain rule.

Verses 30–31

The designing busy part of mankind are directed, in all their counsels and undertakings, to have their eye to God, and to believe, 1. That there can be no success against God, and therefore they must never act in opposition to him, in contempt of his commands, or in contradiction to his counsels. Though they think they have *wisdom,* and *understanding,* and *counsel,* the best politics and politicians, on their side, yet, if it be *against the Lord,* it cannot prosper long; it shall not prevail at last. He that sits in heaven laughs at men's projects against him and his anointed, and will carry his point in spite of them, Ps. 2:1–6. Those that fight against God are preparing shame and ruin for themselves; whoever *make war with the Lamb,* he will certainly *overcome them,* Rev. 17:14. 2. That there can be no success without God, and therefore they must never act but in dependence on him. Be the cause ever so good, and the patrons of it ever so strong, and wise, and faithful, and the means of carrying it on, and gaining the point, ever so probable, still they must acknowledge God and take him along with them. Means indeed are to be used; *the horse* must be *prepared against the day of battle,* and the foot too; they must be armed and disciplined. In Solomon's time even Israel's kings used horses in war, though they were forbidden to multiply them. *But,* after all, *safety* and salvation *are of the Lord;* he can save without armies, but armies cannot save without him; and therefore he must be sought to and trusted in for success, and when success is obtained he must have all the glory. When we are preparing for *the day of battle* our great concern must be to make God our friend and secure his favour.

CHAPTER 22

Verse 1

Here are two things which are more valuable and which we should covet more than great riches: — 1. To be well spoken of: *A name* (that is, *a good name,* a name for good things with God and good people) *is rather to be chosen than great riches;* that is, we should be more careful to do that by which we may get and keep a good name than that by which we may raise and increase a great estate. Great riches bring great cares with them, expose men to danger, and add no real value to a man. A fool and a knave may have *great riches,* but *a good name* makes a man easy and safe, supposes a man wise and honest, redounds to the glory of God, and gives a man a greater opportunity of doing good. By great riches we may relieve the bodily wants of others, but by a good name we may recommend religion to them. 2. To be well beloved, to have an interest in the esteem and affections of all about us; this is better *than silver and gold.* Christ has neither silver nor gold, but he *grew in favour with God and man,* Lu. 2:52. This should teach us to look with a holy contempt upon the wealth of this world, not to set our hearts upon that, but with all possible care to *think of those things that are lovely and of good report,* Phil. 4:8.

Verse 2

Note, 1. Among the children of men divine Providence has so ordered it that some are *rich* and others *poor,* and these are intermixed in societies: *The Lord is the Maker of both,* both the author of their being and the disposer of their lot. The greatest man in the world must acknowledge God to be his Maker, and is under the same obligations to be subject to him that the meanest is; and the poorest has the honour to be the work of God's hands as much as the greatest. *Have they not all one Father?* Mal. 2:10; Job 31:15. God makes some rich, that they may be charitable to the poor, and others poor, that they may be serviceable to the rich; and they have need of one another, 1 Co. 12:21. He make some poor, to exercise their patience, and contentment, and dependence upon God, and others rich, to exercise their thankfulness and beneficence. Even *the poor* we *have always with* us; they shall never cease out of the land, nor the rich neither. 2. Notwithstanding the distance that is in many respects between *rich and poor,* yet in most things they *meet together,* especially before the *Lord,* who *is the Maker of them all,* and *regards not the rich more than the poor,* Job 34:19. *Rich and poor meet together* at the bar of God's justice, all guilty before God, concluded under sin, and shapen in iniquity, the rich as much as the poor; and they meet at the throne of God's grace; the poor are as welcome there as the rich. There is the same Christ, the same scripture, the same Spirit, the same covenant of promises, for them both. There is the same heaven for poor saints that there is for rich: Lazarus is in the bosom of Abraham. And there is the same hell for rich sinners that there is for poor. All stand upon the same level before God, as they do also in the grave. *The small and great are there.*

Verse 3

See here, 1. The benefit of wisdom and consideration: *A prudent man,* by the help of his prudence, will *foresee an evil,* before it comes, *and hide himself;* he will be aware when he is entering into a temptation and will put on his armour and stand on his guard. When the clouds are gathering for a storm he takes the warning, and flies to the name of the Lord as his strong tower. Noah foresaw the deluge, Joseph the years of famine, and provided accordingly. 2. The mischief of rashness and inconsideration. *The simple,* who believe every word that flatters them, will believe none that warns them, and so they *pass on and are punished.* They venture upon sin, though they are told what will be in the end thereof; they throw themselves into trouble, notwithstanding the fair warning given them, and they repent their presumption when it is too late. See an instance of both these, Ex. 9:20, 21. Nothing is so fatal to precious souls as this, they will not take warning.

Verse 4

See here, 1. Wherein religion does very much consist — in *humility and the fear of the Lord;* that is, walking humbly with God. We must so reverence God's majesty and authority as to submit with all humility to the commands of his word and the disposals of his providence. We must have such low thoughts of ourselves as to behave humbly towards God and man. Where the fear of God is there will be humility. 2. What is to be gotten by it — *riches, and honour,* and comfort, *and* long life, in this world, as far as God sees good, at least spiritual *riches and honour* in the favour of God, and the promises and privileges of the covenant of grace, *and* eternal *life* at last.

Verse 5

Note 1. The way of sin is vexatious and dangerous: *In the way of the froward,* that crooked way, which is contrary to the will and word of God, *thorns and snares are* found, thorns of grief for past sins and snares entangling them in further sin. He that makes no conscience of what he says and does will find himself hampered by that imaginary liberty, and tormented by his pleasures. Froward people, who are soon angry, expose themselves to trouble at every step. Every thing will fret and vex him that will fret and vex at every thing. 2. The way of duty is safe and easy: *He that keeps his soul,* that watches carefully over his own heart and ways, is *far from* those *thorns and snares,* for his way is both plain and pleasant.

Verse 6

Here is, 1. A great duty enjoined, particularly to those that are the parents and instructors of children, in order to the propagating of wisdom, that it may not die with them: *Train up children* in that age of vanity, to keep them from the sins and snares of it, in that learning age, to prepare them for what they are designed for. *Catechise* them; initiate them; keep them under discipline. *Train* them as soldiers, who are taught to handle their arms, keep rank, and observe the word of command. *Train* them up, not in the way they would go (the bias of their corrupt hearts would draw them aside), but *in the way they should go,* the way in which, if you love them, you would have them go. *Train up a child according as he is capable* (as some take it), with a gentle hand, as nurses feed children, little and often, Deu. 6:7. 2. A good reason for it, taken from the great advantage of this care and pains with children: When they *grow up,* when they *grow old,* it is to be hoped,

they *will not depart from it.* Good impressions made upon them then will abide upon them all their days. Ordinarily the vessel retains the savour with which it was first seasoned. Many indeed have departed from the good way in which they were trained up; Solomon himself did so. But early training may be a means of their recovering themselves, as it is supposed Solomon did. At least the parents will have the comfort of having done their duty and used the means.

Verse 7

He had said (*v.* 2.), *Rich and poor meet together;* but here he finds, here he shows, that, as to the things of this life, there is a great difference; for, 1. Those that have little will be in subjection to those that have much, because they have dependence upon them, they have received, and expect to receive, support from them: *The rich rule over the poor,* and too often more than becomes them, with pride and rigour, unlike to God, who, though he be great, yet despises not any. It is part of the affliction of the poor that they must expect to be trampled upon, and part of their duty to be serviceable, as far as they can, to those that are kind to them, and study to be grateful. 2. Those that are but going behindhand find themselves to lie much at the mercy of those that are before hand: *The borrower is servant to the lender,* is obliged to him, and must sometimes beg, *Have patience with me.* Therefore it is part of Israel's promised happiness that they should lend and borrow, Deu. 28:12. And it should be our endeavour to keep as much as may be out of debt. Some sell their liberty to gratify their luxury.

Verse 8

Note 1. Ill-gotten gains will not prosper: *He that sows iniquity,* that does an unjust thing in hopes to get by it, *shall reap vanity;* what he gets will never do him any good nor give him any satisfaction. He will meet nothing but disappointment. Those that create trouble to others do but prepare trouble for themselves. Men shall reap as they sow. 2. Abused power will not last. If the rod of authority turn into a *rod of anger,* if men rule by passion instead of prudence, and, instead of the public welfare, aim at nothing so much as the gratifying of their own resentments, it *shall fail* and be broken, and their power shall not bear them out in their exorbitances, Isa. 10:24, 25.

Verse 9

Here is, 1. The description of a charitable man; he has a *bountiful eye,* opposed to the evil eye (*ch.* 23:6) and the same with the *single eye* (Mt. 6:22), — an eye that seeks out objects of charity, besides those that offer themselves, — an eye that, upon the sight of one in want and misery, affects the heart with compassion, — an eye that with the alms gives a pleasant look, which makes the alms doubly acceptable. He has also a liberal hand: *He gives of his bread* to those that need — *his bread,* the bread appointed for his own eating. He will rather abridge himself than see the poor perish for want; yet he does not give all *his bread,* but *of his bread;* the poor shall have their share with his own family. 2. The blessedness of such a man. The loins of the poor will bless them, all about him will speak well of him, and God himself will bless him, in answer to many a good prayer put up for him, and he *shall be blessed.*

Verse 10

See here, 1. What *the scorner* does. It is implied that he sows discord and makes mischief wherever he comes. Much of the *strife and contention* which disturb the peace of all societies is owing to *the evil interpreter* (as some read it), that construes every thing into the worst, to those that despise and deride every one that comes in their way and take a pride in bantering and abusing all mankind. 2. What is to be done with the scorner that will not be reclaimed: *Cast* him *out* of your society, as Ishmael, when he mocked Isaac, was thrust out of Abraham's family. Those that would secure the peace must exclude the scorner.

Verse 11

Here is, 1. The qualification of an accomplished, a complete gentleman, that is fit to be employed in public business. He must be an honest man, a man *that loves pureness of heart* and hates all impurity, not only pure from

all fleshly lusts, but from all deceit and dissimulation, from all selfishness and sinister designs, that takes care to approve himself a man of sincerity, is just and fair from principle, and delights in nothing more than in keeping his own conscience clean and void of offence. He must also be able to speak with a good grace, not to daub and flatter, but to deliver his sentiments decently and ingeniously, in language clean and smooth as his spirit. 2. The preferment such a man stands fair for: *The king,* if he be wise and good, and understand his own and his people's interest, *will be his friend,* will make him of his cabinet-council, as there was one in David's court, and another in Solomon's, that was called the *king's friend;* or, in any business that he has, the king will befriend him. Some understand it of the King of kings. A man *in whose spirit there is no guile,* and whose speech is always with grace, God will be his friend, Messiah, the Prince, will be his friend. *This honour have all the saints.*

Verse 12

Here is, 1. The special care God takes to *preserve knowledge,* that is, to keep up religion in the world by keeping up among men the knowledge of himself and of good and evil, notwithstanding the corruption of mankind, and the artifices of Satan to blind men's minds and keep them in ignorance. It is a wonderful instance of the power and goodness of *the eyes of the Lord,* that is, his watchful providence. He preserves *men of knowledge,* wise and good men (2 Chr. 16:9), particularly faithful witnesses, who speak what they know; God protects such, and prospers their counsels. He does by his grace *preserve knowledge* in such, secures his own work and interest in them. See Prov. 2:7, 8. 2. The just vengeance God takes on those that speak and act against knowledge and against the interests of knowledge and religion in the world: *He overthrows the words of the transgressor,* and *preserves knowledge* in spite of him. He defeats all the counsels and designs of false and treacherous men, and turns them to their own confusion.

Verse 13

Note, 1. Those that have no love for their business will never want excuses to shake it off. Multitudes are ruined, both for soul and body, by their slothfulness, and yet still they have something or other to say for themselves, so ingenious are men in putting a cheat upon their own souls. And who, I pray, will be the gainer at last, when the pretences will be all rejected as vain and frivolous? 2. Many frighten themselves from real duties by imaginary difficulties: *The slothful man* has work to do *without* in the fields, but he fancies *there is a lion* there; nay, he pretends he dares not go along the streets for fear somebody or other should meet him and kill him. He does not himself think so; he only says so to those that call him up. He talks of *a lion without,* but considers not his real danger from the devil, that *roaring lion,* which is in bed with him, and from his own slothfulness, which kills him.

Verse 14

This is designed to warn all young men against the lusts of uncleanness. As they regard the welfare of their souls, let them take heed of *strange women,* lewd women, whom they ought to be strange to, of *the mouth of strange women,* of the kisses of their lips (*ch.* 7:13), of the words of their lips, their charms and enticements. Dread them; have nothing to do with them; for, 1. Those who abandon themselves to that sin give proof that they are abandoned of God: it *is a deep pit,* which those *fall* into that are *abhorred of the Lord,* who leaves them to themselves to enter into that temptation, and takes off the bridle of his restraining grace, to punish them for other sins. Value not thyself upon thy being in favour with such women, when it proclaims thee under the wrath of God. 2. It is seldom that they recover themselves, for it *is a deep pit;* it will be hard getting out of it, it so besots the mind and debauches the conscience, by pleasing the flesh.

Verse 15

We have here two very sad considerations: — 1. That corruption is woven into our nature. Sin is *foolishness;* it is contrary both to our right reason and to our true interest. It *is in the heart;* there is an inward inclination to sin, to speak and act foolishly. It *is in the heart of children;*

they bring it into the world with them; it is what they were shapen and conceived in. It is not only *found* there, but it is *bound* there; it is annexed to the heart (so some); vicious dispositions cleave closely to the soul, are bound to it as the cion to the stock into which it is grafted, which quite alters the property. There is a knot tied between the soul and sin, a true lover's knot; they two became one flesh. It is true of ourselves, it is true of our children, whom we have begotten in our own likeness. *O God! thou knowest* this *foolishness.* 2. That correction is necessary to the cure of it. It will not be got out by fair means and gentle methods; there must be strictness and severity, and that which will cause grief. Children need to be corrected, and kept under discipline, by their parents; and we all need to be corrected by our heavenly Father (Heb. 12:6, 7), and under the correction we must stroke down folly and kiss the rod.

Verse 16

This shows what evil courses rich men sometimes take, by which, in the end, they will impoverish themselves and provoke God, notwithstanding their abundance, to bring them to want; they *oppress the poor and give to the rich.* 1. They will not in charity relieve the poor, but withhold from them, that by saving that which is really the best, but which they think the most needless part of their expenses, they may *increase their riches;* but they will make presents *to the rich,* and give them great entertainments, either in pride and vain-glory, that they may look great, or in policy, that they may receive it again with advantage. Such *shall surely come to want.* Many have been beggared by a foolish generosity, but never any by a prudent charity. Christ bids us to invite the poor, Lu. 14:12, 13. 2. They not only will not relieve *the poor,* but they *oppress* them, rob the spital, extort from their poor tenants and neighbours, invade the rights of those who have not wherewithal to defend themselves, and then *give* bribes *to the rich,* to protect and countenance them in it. But it is all in vain; they *shall come to want.* Those that rob God, and so make him the enemy, cannot secure themselves by *giving to the rich,* to make them their friends.

Verses 17–21

Solomon here changes his style and manner of speaking. Hitherto, for the most part, since the beginning of *ch.* 10, he had laid down doctrinal truths, and but now and then dropped a word of exhortation, leaving us to make the application as we went along; but here, to the end of *ch.* 24, he directs his speech to his son, his pupil, his reader, his hearer, speaking as to a particular person. Hitherto, for the most part, his sense was comprised in one verse, but here usually it is drawn out further. See how Wisdom tries variety of methods with us, lest we should be cloyed with any one. To awaken attention and to assist our application the method of direct address is here adopted. Ministers must not think it enough to preach before their hearers, but must preach to them, nor enough to preach to them all in general, but should address themselves to particular persons, as here: Do *thou* do so and so. Here is,

I. An earnest exhortation to get wisdom and grace, by attending to *the words of the wise* men, both written and preached, the words of the prophets and priests, and particularly to that *knowledge* which Solomon in this book gives men of good and evil, sin and duty, rewards and punishments. To these *words,* to this *knowledge,* the ear must be *bowed down* in humility and serious attention and the heart *applied* by faith, and love, and close consideration. The ear will not serve without the heart.

II. Arguments to enforce this exhortation. Consider,

1. The worth and weight of the things themselves which Solomon in this book gives us the *knowledge* of. They are not trivial things, for amusements and diversion, not jocular proverbs, to be repeated in sport and in order to pass away time. No; they are *excellent things,* which concern the glory of God, the holiness and happiness of our souls, the welfare of mankind and all communities; they are *princely things* (so the word is), fit for kings to speak and senates to hear; they are things that concern *counsels and knowledge,* that is, wise counsels, relating to the most important concerns; things which will not only make us knowing ourselves, but enable us to advise others.

2. The clearness of the discovery of these things and the directing of them to us in particular. "They are *made known,* publicly known, that all may read, — plainly known, that he that runs may read, — *made known this day* more fully than ever before, in this day of light and knowledge, — *made known in this thy day.* But it is only a little while that this light is with thee; perhaps the things that are *this day made known to thee,* if thou improve not the day of thy visitation, may, before to-morrow, be *hidden from thy eyes.* They are *written,* for the greater certainty, and that they may be received and the more safely transmitted pure and entire to posterity. But that which the emphasis is here most laid upon is that they are *made known to thee, even to thee,* and *written to thee,* as if it were a letter directed to thee by name. It is suited to thee and to thy case; thou mayest in this glass see thy own face; it is intended for thee, to be a rule to thee, and by it thou must be judged." We cannot say of these things, "They are good things, but they are nothing to us;" no, they are of the greatest concern imaginable to us.

3. The agreeableness of these things to us, in respect both of comfort and credit. (1.) If we hide them in our hearts, they will be very pleasing and yield us an abundant satisfaction (*v.* 18): *"It is a pleasant thing,* and will be thy constant entertainment, *if thou keep them within thee;* if thou digest them, and be actuated and governed by them, and delivered into them as into a mould." The form of godliness, when that is rested in, is but a force put upon a man, and he does but do penance in that white clothing; those only that submit to the power of godliness, and make heart-work of it, find the pleasure of it, *ch.* 2:10. (2.) If we make use of them in our discourse, they will be very becoming, and gain us a good reputation. *They shall be fitted in thy lips.* "Speak of these things, and thou speakest like thyself, and as is fit for thee to speak considering thy character; thou wilt also have pleasure in speaking of these things as well as in thinking of them."

4. The advantage designed us by them. The *excellent things* which God has *written to* us are not like the commands which the master gives his servant, which are all intended for the benefit of the master, but like those which the master gives his scholar, which are all intended for the benefit of the scholar. These things must be kept by us, for they are written to us, (1.) That we may have a confidence in him and communion with him. *That thy trust may be in the Lord, v.* 19. We cannot trust in God except in the way of duty; we are *therefore* taught our duty, that we may have reason to trust in God. Nay, this is itself one great duty we are to learn, and a duty that is the foundation of all practical religion, to live a life of delight in God and dependence on him. (2.) That we may have a satisfaction in our own judgment: *"That I might make thee know the certainty of the words of truth;* that thou mayest know what is truth, mayest plainly distinguish between it and falsehood, and mayest know upon what grounds thou receivest and believest the truths of God." Note, [1.] It is a desirable thing to know, not only *the words of truth,* but *the certainty of* them, that our faith may be intelligent and rational, and may grow up to a full assurance. [2.] The way to *know the certainty of the words of truth* is to make conscience of our duty; for, *if any man do his will, he shall know* for certain that the doctrine is of God, Jn. 7:17. (3.) That we may be useful and serviceable to others for their instruction: *"That thou mayest* give a good account *of the words of truth to those that send to thee* to consult thee as an oracle," or (as the margin reads it) *"to those that send thee,* that employ thee as an agent or ambassador in any business." Knowledge is given us to do good with, that others may light their candle at our lamp, and that we may in our place serve our generation according to the will of God; and those who make conscience of keeping God's commandments will be best able to *give a reason of the hope that is in* them.

Verses 22–23

After this solemn preface, one would have expected something new and surprising; but no; here is a plain and common, but very needful caution against the barbarous and inhuman practices of oppressing poor people. Observe,

I. The sin itself, and that is *robbing the poor* and making them poorer, taking from those that have but little to lose and so leaving them nothing. It is bad to rob any man, but most absurd to rob the poor, whom we should relieve, — to squeeze those with our power whom we should water with our bounty, — *to oppress the afflicted,* and so to add affliction to them, — to give judgment against them, and so to patronise those that do rob them, which is as bad as if we robbed them ourselves. Rich men will not suffer themselves to be wronged; poor men cannot help themselves, and therefore we ought to be the more careful not to wrong them.

II. The aggravations of the sin. 1. If their inability, by reason of their poverty, to right themselves, embolden us to rob them, it is so much the worse; this is *robbing the poor because he is poor;* this is not only a base and cowardly thing, to take advantage against a man because he is helpless, but it is unnatural, and proves men worse than beasts. 2. Or, if it be done under the colour of law and justice, that is oppressing *the afflicted in the gate,* where they ought to be protected from wrong and to have justice done them against those that oppress them.

III. The danger that attends this sin. He that robs and oppresses the poor does it at his peril; for, 1. The oppressed will find God their powerful patron. He *will plead their cause,* and not suffer them to be run down and trampled upon. If men will not appear for them, God will. 2. The oppressors will find him a just avenger. He will make reprisals upon them, will *spoil the souls of those that spoil them;* he will repay them in spiritual judgments, in curses to their souls. He that robs the poor will be found in the end a murderer of himself.

Verses 24–25

Here is, 1. A good caution against being intimate with a passionate man. It is the law of friendship that we accommodate ourselves to our friends and be ready to serve them, and therefore we ought to be wise and wary in the choice of a friend, that we come not under the sacred tie to any one whom it would be our folly to accommodate ourselves to. Thought we must be civil to all, yet we must be careful whom we lay in our bosoms and contract a familiarity with. And, among others, a man who is easily provoked, touchy, and apt to resent affronts, who, when he is in a passion, cares not what he says or does, but grows outrageous, such a one is not fit to be made a friend or companion, for he will be ever and anon angry with us and that will be our trouble, and he will expect that we should, like him, be angry with others, and that will be our sin. 2. Good cause given for this caution: *Lest thou learn his way.* Those we go with we are apt to grow like. Our corrupt hearts have so much tinder in them that it is dangerous conversing with those that throw about the sparks of their passion. We shall thereby *get a snare to our souls,* for a disposition to anger is a great snare to any man, and an occasion of much sin. He does not say, "Lest thou have ill language given thee or get a broken head," but, which is must worse, "Lest thou imitate him, to humour him, and so contract an ill habit."

Verses 26–27

We have here, as often before, a caution against suretiship, as a thing both imprudent and unjust. 1. We must not associate ourselves, nor contract an intimacy, with men of broken fortunes, and reputations, who need and will urge their friends to be bound for them, that they may cheat their neighbours to feed their lusts, and by keeping up a little longer may do the more damage at last to those that give them credit. Have nothing to do with such; be not thou among them. 2. We must not cheat people of their money, by *striking hands* ourselves, or *becoming surety for others,* when we *have not to pay.* If a man by the divine providence is disabled to pay his debts, he ought to be pitied and helped; but he that takes up money or goods himself, or is bound for another, when he knows that he has not wherewithal to pay, or that what he has is so settled that the creditors cannot come at it, does in effect pick his neighbour's pocket, and though, in all cases, compassion is to be used, yet he may thank himself if the law have its course and his *bed* be *taken from under him,* which might be taken for a pledge to secure a debt, Ex. 22:26, 27. For, if a man appeared to be so poor that he had nothing else to give for security, he ought to be relieved, and it was honestly done to own it; but, for the recovery of a debt, it seems it might be taken by the *summum jus —the strict operation of law.* 3. We must not ruin our own estates and families. Every man ought to be just to himself and to his wife and children; those are not so who live above what they have, who by the mismanagement of their own affairs, or by encumbering themselves with debts of others, waste what they have and bring themselves to poverty. We may *take joyfully the spoiling of our goods* if it be for the testimony of a good conscience; but, if be for our own rashness and folly, we cannot but take it heavily.

Verse 28

1. We are here taught not to invade another man's right, though we can find ways of doing it ever so secretly and plausibly, clandestinely and by fraud, without any open force. Let not property in general be entrenched upon, by robbing men of their liberties and privileges, or of any just ways of maintaining them. Let not the property of particular persons be encroached upon. The land-marks, or meer-stones, are standing witnesses to every man's right; let not those be removed quite away, for thence come wars, and fightings, and endless disputes; let them not be removed so as to take from thy neighbour's lot to thy own, for that is downright robbing him and entailing the fraud upon posterity. 2. We may infer hence that a deference is to be paid, in all civil matters, to usages that have prevailed time out of mind and the settled constitutions of government, in which it becomes us to acquiesce, lest an attempt to change it, under pretence of changing it for the better, prove of dangerous consequence.

Verse 29

Here is, 1. A plain intimation what a hard thing it is to find a truly ingenious industrious man: *"Seest thou a man diligent in his business?* Thou wilt not see many such, so epidemical are dulness and slothfulness." He is here commended who lays out himself to get business, though it be but in a very low and narrow sphere, and is not easy when he is out of business, who loves business, is quick and active in it, and goes through it, not only with constancy and resolution, but with dexterity and expedition, a man of despatch, who knows how to bring a deal of business into a little compass. 2. A moral prognostication of the preferment of such a man; though now he *stands before mean men,* is employed by them and attends upon them, yet he will rise, and is likely enough to *stand before kings,* as an ambassador to foreign kings or prime-minister of state to his own. *Seest thou a man diligent* in the business of religion? He is likely to excel in virtue, and shall stand before the King of kings.

CHAPTER 23

Verses 1–3

The sin we are here warned against is luxury and sensuality, and the indulgence of the appetite in eating and drinking, a sin that most easily besets us. 1. We are here told when we enter into temptation, and are in most danger of falling into this sin: *"When thou sittest to eat with a ruler* thou has great plenty before thee, varieties and dainties, such a table spread as thou has seldom seen; thou are ready to think, as Haman did, of nothing but the honour hereby done thee (Esth. 5:12), and the opportunity thou hast of pleasing thy palate, and forgettest that there is a snare laid for thee." Perhaps the temptation may be stronger, and more dangerous, to one that is not used to such entertainments, than to one that always sits down to a good table. 2. We are here directed to double our guard at such a time. We must, (1.) Apprehend ourselves to be in danger: *"Consider diligently what is before thee,* what meat and drink are before thee, that thou mayest choose that which is safest for thee and which thou art least likely to eat and drink of to excess. Consider what company is before thee, the ruler himself, who, if he be wise and good, will take it as an affront for any of his guests to disorder themselves at his table." And, if when we sit to eat with a ruler, much more when we sit to eat with the ruler of rulers at the Lord's table, must we *consider diligently what is before us,* that we may not in any respect *eat and drink unworthily,* unbecomingly, lest that table become a snare. (2.) We must alarm ourselves into temperance and moderation: *"Put a knife to thy throat,* that is, restrain thyself, as it were with a sword hanging over thy head, from all excess. Let these words, *Take heed lest at any time your hearts be overcharged with surfeiting and drunkenness, and so that day come upon you unawares* — or those, *For all these things, God shall bring thee into judgment* — or those, *Drunkards, shall not inherit the kingdom of God,* be a knife to the throat." The Latins call luxury *gula — the throat.* "Take up arms against that sin. Rather be so abstemious that thy craving appetite will begin to think thy throat cut than indulge thyself in voluptuousness." We must never *feed ourselves without fear* (Jude 12), but we must in a special manner fear when temptation is before us. (3.) We must reason ourselves into a holy contempt of the gratifications of sense: *"If thou be a man given to appetite,* thou must, by a present solution, and an application of the terrors of the Lord, restrain thyself. When thou art in danger of falling into any excess *put a knife to thy throat;* that may serve for once. But that is not enough: lay the axe to the root; mortify that appetite which has such a power over thee: *Be not desirous of dainties."* Note, We ought to observe what is our own iniquity, and, if we find ourselves addicted to flesh-pleasing, we must not only stand upon our guard against temptations from without, but subdue the corruption within. Nature is desirous of food, and we are taught to pray for it, but it is lust that is desirous of dainties, and we cannot in faith pray for them, for frequently they are not food convenient for mind, body, or estate. They are deceitful meat, and therefore David, instead of praying for them, prays against them, Ps. 141:4. They are pleasant to the palate, but perhaps rise in the stomach, turn sour there, upbraid a man, and make him sick. They do not yield men the satisfaction they promised themselves from them; for those that are given to appetite, when they have that which is very dainty, are not pleased; they are soon weary of it; they must have something else more dainty. The more a luxurious appetite is humoured and indulged the more humoursome and troublesome it grows, and the more hard to please; dainties will surfeit, but never satisfy. But especially they are upon *this* account deceitful meat, that, while they please the body, they prejudice the soul, they overcharge the heart, and unfit it for the service of God, nay, they take away the heart, and alienate the mind from spiritual delights, and spoil its relish of them. Why then should we covet that which will certainly cheat us?

Verses 4–5

As some are given to appetite (*v.* 2) so others to covetousness, and those Solomon here takes to task. Men cheat themselves as much by setting their hearts on money (though it seems most substantial) as by setting them on dainties. Observe,

I. How he dissuades the covetous man from toiling and tormenting himself (*v.* 4). "Do not *aim to be rich,* to raise an estate, and to make what thou hast in abundance more than it is." We must endeavor to live comfortably, and provide for our children and families, according as our rank and condition are, but we must not seek great things. Be not of those that will be rich, that desire it as their chief good and design it as their highest end, 1 Tim. 6:9. Covetous men think it is their wisdom, imagining that if they be rich to such a degree they shall be completely happy. *Cease from that wisdom,* for it is a mistake; *a man's life consists not in the abundance of the things which he possesses,* Lu. 12:15. 1. Those that aim at great things fill their hands with business more than they can grasp, so that their life is both a perfect drudgery and a perpetual hurry; but be not thou such a fool; *labour not to be rich.* What thou hast, or doest, be master of it, and not a slave to it as those that *rise up early, sit up late,* and *eat the bread of carefulness,* and all to be rich. Moderate labour, *that we may have to give,* is our wisdom and duty, Eph. 4:28. Immoderate labour, that we may have to hoard, is our sin and folly. 2. They fill their heads with projects more than they understand, so that their life is a constant toss of care and fear; but do not thou thus vex thyself: *Cease from thy own wisdom;* go on quietly in the way of thy business, not contriving new ways and setting thy wits to work to find out new inventions. Acquiesce in God's wisdom, and cease from thy own, *ch.* 3:5, 6.

II. How he dissuades the covetous man from cheating and deceiving himself by an inordinate love and pursuit of that which is vanity and vexation of spirit; for,

1. It is not substantial and satisfying: *"Wilt thou* be such a fool as to *set thy eyes,* to cause thy eyes to fly with eagerness and violence, *upon that which is not?"* Note, (1.) The things of this world are things that are not. They have a real existence in nature and are the real gifts of Providence, but in the kingdom of grace they are things that are not; they are not a happiness and portion for a soul, are not what they promise to be nor what we expect them to be; they are a show, a shadow, a sham upon the soul that trusts to them. They are not, for in a little while they will not be, they will not be ours; they perish in the using; the fashion of them passes away. (2.) It is therefore folly for us to set our eyes upon them, to admire them as the best things, to appropriate them to ourselves as our good things, and to aim at them as our mark at which all our actions are levelled, to fly upon them as the eagle upon her prey. "Wilt thou do a thing so absurd in itself? What thou, a reasonable creature, wilt thou dote upon shadows? The eyes are put for rational and intellectual powers; wilt thou throw those away upon such undeserving objects? To set the hands and feet upon the world is well enough, but not the eyes, the eyes of the mind; those were made to contemplate better things. Wilt thou, my son, that professest religion, put such an affront upon God (towards whom the eyes should ever be) and such an abuse upon thy soul?"

2. It is not durable and abiding. Riches are very uncertain things; certainly they are so: *They make themselves wings, and fly away.* The more we cause our eyes to fly upon them the more likely they are to fly away from us. (1.) Riches will leave us. Those that hold them ever so fast cannot hold them long; either they must be taken from us or we must be taken from them. The goods are said to flow away as a stream (Job 20:28), here to flee as a bird. (2.) Perhaps they may leave us suddenly, when we have taken a great deal of pains for them and begin to take a great deal of pride and pleasure in them. The covetous man sits hatching upon his wealth, and brooding over it, till it is fledged, as the young ones under the hen, and then it is gone. Or, as if a man should be fond of a flight of wild-fowl that light in his field, and call them his own because they are upon his ground, whereas, if he offers to come near them, they take wing immediately and are gone to another man's field. (3.) The wings they fly away upon are of their own making. They have in themselves the principles of their own corruption, their own moth and rust. They are wasting in their own nature, and like a handful of dust, which, if it be grasped, slips through the fingers. Snow will last awhile, and look pretty, if it be left to lie on the ground where it fell, but, if gathered up and laid in the bosom, it is dissolved and gone immediately. (4.) They go irresistibly and irrecoverably, as *an eagle toward heaven,* that flies strongly (there is no stopping her), and flies out of sight and out of call (there is no bringing her back); thus do riches leave men, and leave them in grief and vexation if they set their hearts upon them.

Verses 6–8

Those that are voluptuous and given to appetite (*v.* 2) are glad to be where there is good cheer stirring, and those that are covetous and saving, that they may spare at home, will be glad to get a dinner at another man's table; and therefore both are here advised not to be forward to accept of every man's invitation, but especially not to thrust themselves in uninvited. Observe, 1. There are those that pretend to bid their friends welcome that are not hearty and sincere in it. They have a fair tongue, and know what they should say: *Eat and drink, saith he,* because it is expected that the master of the feast should so compliment his guests; but they have *an evil eye,* and grudge their guests every bit they eat, especially if the eat freely. They would seem to be liberal in making the entertainment, and would have the credit of it, but they have so great a love to their money, and so little to their friends, that they cannot have the comfort of it, nor any enjoyment of themselves or their friends. The miser's feast is his penance. If a man be so very selfish, and sordid, and mean that he cannot find in his heart to bid his friends welcome to what he has, he ought not to add to that the guilt of dissimulation by inviting them, but let him own himself to be what he is, that *the vile person may not be called liberal nor the churl bountiful,* Isa. 32:5. 2. One can have no comfort in accepting the entertainments that are given grudgingly: *"Eat not thou the bread* of such a man; let him keep it to himself. Do not sponge upon those that are bountiful, nor make thyself burdensome to any; but especially scorn to be beholden to those that are paltry and not sincere. Better have a dinner of herbs, and true welcome, than *dainty meats* without it. Therefore," (1.) "Judge of the man as his mind is. Thou thinkest to pay thy respect to him as a friend, so thou takest him to be, because he compliments thee, but *as he thinks in his heart so is he,* not as he speaks with his tongue." We are that really, both to God and man, which we are inwardly; and neither religion nor friendship is worth any thing further than as it is sincere. (2.) "Judge of the meat as the digestion is and as it agrees with thee. He bids thee eat freely, but, first or last, he will discover his sordid covetous humour, and *as he thinks in his heart* so will he look, and give thee to understand that thou art not welcome, and then *the morsel thou hast eaten thou shalt vomit up;* the very thought of that will make thee even to vomit the meat thou hast eaten, and eat the words thou has spoken in returning his compliments and giving him thanks for his civilities. Thou shalt *lose thy sweet words,* which he has given thee and thou has given him."

Verse 9

We are here directed not to *cast pearls before swine* (Mt. 7:6) and not to expose things sacred to the contempt and ridicule of profane scoffers. It is our duty to take all fit occasions to speak of divine things; but, 1. There are some that will make a jest of every thing, though it be ever so prudently and pertinently spoken, that will not only despise a wise man's words, but despise even the wisdom of them, that in them which is most improvable for their own edification; they will particularly reproach that, as if it had an ill design upon them, which they must guard against. 2. Those that do so forfeit the benefit of good advice and instruction, and a wise man is not only allowed, but advised, not to *speak in the ears* of such fools; let them be foolish still, and let not precious breath be thrown away upon them. If what a wise man says in his wisdom will not be heard, let him hold his peace, and try whether the wisdom of that will be regarded.

Verses 10–11

Note, 1. The fatherless are taken under God's special protection; with him they not only find mercy shown to them (Hos. 14:3) but justice done for them. He is *their Redeemer,* their *Goël,* their near kinsman, that will take their part and stand up for them with jealousy, as taking himself affronted in the injuries done to them. As their Redeemer *he will plead their cause* against those that do them any injury, and, one way or other, will not only defend their right, and recover it for them, but avenge the wrongs done to them. And he *is mighty,* almighty; his omnipotence is engaged and employed for their protection, and their proudest and most powerful oppressors will not only find themselves an unequal match for this, but will find that it is at their peril to contend with it. 2. Every man therefore must be careful not to injure them in any thing, or to invade their rights, either by a clandestine removal of the old land-marks or by a forcible entry into their fields. Being fatherless, they have none to redress their wrongs, and, being in their childhood, they do not so much as apprehend the wrong that is done them. Sense of honour, and much more the fear of God, would restrain men from offering injury to children, especially fatherless children.

Verses 12–16

Here is, 1. A parent instructing his child. He is here brought in persuading him to give his mind to his book, and especially to the scriptures and his catechism, to attend *to the words of knowledge,* by which he might come to know his duty, and danger, and interest, and not to think it enough to give them the hearing, but to apply his heart to them, to delight in them, and bow his will to the authority of them. The heart is *then* applied to the instruction when the instruction is applied to the heart. 2. A parent correcting his child. A tender parent can scarcely find in his heart to do this; it goes much against the grain. But he finds it is necessary; it is his duty, and therefore he dares not *withhold correction* when there is occasion for it *(spare the rod and spoil the child);* he *beats him with the rod,* gives him a gentle correction, the *stripes of the sons of men,* not such as we give to beasts. *Beat him with the rod and he shall not die.* The rod will not kill him; nay, it will prevent his killing himself by those vicious courses which the rod will be necessary to restrain him from. For the present *it is not joyous, but grievous,* both to the parent and to the child; but when it is given with wisdom, designed for good, accompanied with prayer, and blessed of God, it may prove a happy means of preventing his utter destruction and *delivering his soul from hell.* Our great care must be about our children's souls; we must not see them in danger of hell without using all possible means, with the utmost care and concern, to snatch them as brands out of everlasting burnings. Let the body smart, so that the spirit be *saved in the day of the Lord Jesus.* 3. A parent encouraging his child, telling him, (1.) What was all he expected, nothing but what would be for his own good, that *his heart be wise* and that his *lips speak right things,* that he be under the government of good principles, and that by those principles he particularly maintain a good environment of his tongue. It is to be hoped that those will do *right things* when they grow up who learn to *speak right things* when they are young, and dare not speak any bad words. (2.) What a comfort it would be to him if herein he answered his expectation: *"If thy heart be wise, my heart shall rejoice,* shall rejoice in thee, *even mine,* who have taken so much care and pains about thee, my heart, that has many a time ached for thee, for which thou shouldst study thus to make a grateful requital." Note, The wisdom of children will be the joy of their parents and teachers, who have no greater joy than to see them *walk in the truth,* 3 Jn. 4. "Children, if you be wise and good, devout and conscientious, God will be pleased with you, and that will be our joy: we shall think our labour in instructing you well bestowed; it will be a comfortable answer for the many prayers we have put up for you; we shall be eased of a great deal of care, shall not need to be so strict and severe in watching over you, and shall consequently be the easier both to you and to ourselves. We shall rejoice in hope that you will be a credit and comfort to us, if we should live to be old, that you will bear up the name of Christ in your generation, that you will live comfortably in this world and happily in another."

Verses 17–18

Here is, 1. A necessary caution against entertaining any favourable thoughts of prospering profaneness: *"Let not thy heart envy sinners;* do not grudge them either the liberty they take to sin or the success they are to be pitied rather than envied. Their prosperity is their portion (Ps. 12:14), nay, it is their poison," Prov. 1:32. We must not harbour in our hearts any secret discontent at the providence of God, though it seem to smile upon them, nor wish ourselves in their condition. *"Let not thy heart imitate sinners"* (so some read it); do not as they do; walk not in the way with them; use not the methods they take to enrich themselves, though they thrive by them. 2. An excellent direction to maintain high thoughts of God in our minds at all times: *Be thou in the fear of the Lord* every day and *all the day long.* We must be in the fear of the Lord as in our employment, exercising ourselves in holy adorings of God, in subjection to his precepts, submission to his providences, and a constant care to please him; we must be in it as in our element, taking a pleasure in contemplating God's glory and complying with his will. We must be *devoted to his fear* (Ps. 119:38); and governed by it as our commanding principle in all we say and do. All the days of our life we must constantly keep up an awe of God upon our spirits, must pay a deference to his authority, and have a dread of his wrath. We must be always so in his fear as never to be out of it. 3. A good reason for both of these (*v.* 18): *Surely there is an end,* an end and expectation, as Jer. 29:11. *There will be an end of the prosperity of the wicked,* therefore *do not envy them* (Ps. 73:17); there will be an end of thy afflictions, therefore be not weary of them, an end of thy services, thy work and warfare will be accomplished, *perfect love will shortly cast out fear,* and *thy expectation* of the reward not only will be *not cut off,* or disappointed, but it will be infinitely outdone. The consideration of the end will help to reconcile us to all the difficulties and discouragements of the way.

Verses 19–28

Here is good advice for parents to give to their children; words are put into their mouths, that they may *train them up in the way they should go.* Here we have,

I. An earnest call to young people to attend to the advice of their godly parents, not only to this that is here given, but to all other profitable instructions: *"Here, my son, and be wise, v.* 19. This will be an evidence that thou art wise and a means to make thee wiser." Wisdom, as *faith, comes by hearing.* And again (*v.* 22): *"Hearken unto thy father who begot thee,* and who therefore has an authority over thee and an affection for thee, and, thou mayest be sure, can have no other design than thy own good." We ought to *give reverence to the fathers of our flesh,* who begot us, and were the instruments of our being; much more ought we to obey and be in subjection to the *Father of our spirits,* who made us and is the author of our being. And since *the mother* also, from a sense of duty to God and from love to her child, gives him good instructions, let him not *despise her,* nor her advice, *when she is old.* When the mother was grown old we may suppose the children to be grown up; but let them not think themselves past being taught, even by her, but rather respect her the more for the multitude of her years and the wisdom which they teach. Scornful and insolent young men will make a jest, it may be, of the good advice of an aged mother, and think themselves not concerned to heed what an old woman says; but such will have a great deal to answer for another day, not only as having set at nought good counsel, but as having slighted and grieved a good mother, *ch.* 30:17.

II. An argument to enforce this call, taken from the great comfort which this will be to their parents, *v.* 24, 25. Note, 1. It is the duty of children to study how they may gladden the hearts of their good parents, and do it yet more and more, so that they may *greatly rejoice* in them, even when the *evil days come and the years of which they say they have no pleasure in them* but this, to see their children do well, as *Barzillai* to see *Chimham* preferred. 2. Children will be a joy to their parents if they be *righteous and wise.* Righteousness is true wisdom; those who do good so well for themselves. Those are completely such as they should be who are not only *wise* (that is, knowing and learned), but *righteous* (that is, honest and good), and not only *righteous* (that is, conscientious and well-meaning), but *wise* (that is, prudent and discreet) in the management of themselves. If such the children be, especially all the children, the father and mother will be glad, and think nothing too much that they have done, or do, for them; they will please themselves in them, and give God thanks for them; particularly she that bore them with pain, and nursed them with pains, will rejoice in them, and reckon herself well requited, and the sorrow more than forgotten, because a wise and good man is the product of it, who is a blessing to the world he was born into.

III. Some general precepts of wisdom and virtue.

1. *Guide thy heart in the way, v.* 19. It is the heart that must be taken care of and directed aright; the motions and affections of the soul must be towards right objects and under a steady guidance. If the heart be guided in the way, the steps will be guided and the conversation well ordered.

2. *Buy the truth and sell it not, v.* 23. Truth is that by which the heart must be guided and governed, for without truth there is no goodness; no regular practices without right principles. It is by the power of truth, known and believed, that we must be kept back from sin and constrained to duty. The understanding must be well-informed with wisdom and instruction, and therefore, (1.) We must buy it, that is, be willing to part with any thing for it. He does not say at what rate we must buy it, because we cannot buy it too dear, but must have it at any rate; whatever it costs us, we shall not repent the bargain. When we are at expense for the means of knowledge, and resolved not to starve so good a cause, then we *buy the truth.* Riches should be employed for the getting of knowledge, rather than knowledge for the getting of riches. When we are at pains in searching after truth, that we may come to the knowledge of it and may distinguish between it and error, then we buy it. *Dii laboribus omnia vendunt — Heaven concedes every thing to the laborious.* When we choose rather to suffer loss in our temporal interest than to deny or neglect the truth they we buy it; and it is a pearl of

such great price that we must be willing to part with all to purchase it, must make shipwreck of estate, trade, preferment, rather than of faith and a good conscience. (2.) We must not sell it. Do not part with it for pleasures, honours, riches, any things in this world. Do not neglect the study of it, nor throw off the profession of it, nor revolt from under the dominion of it, for the getting or saving of any secular interest whatsoever. *Hold fast the form of sound words,* and never let it go upon any terms.

3. *Give my thy heart, v.* 26. God in this exhortation, speaks to us as unto children: "Son, Daughter, *Give my thy heart."* The heart is that which the great God requires and calls for from every one of us; whatever we give, if we do not give him our hearts, it will not be accepted. We must set our love upon him. Our thoughts must converse much with him, and on him, as our highest end. *The intents of our hearts* must be fastened. We must make it our own act and deed to devote ourselves to the Lord, and we must be free and cheerful in it. We must not think to divide the heart between God and the world; he will have all or none. *Thou shalt love the Lord thy God with all thy heart.* To this call we must readily answer, *"My father, take my heart,* such as it is, and make it such as it should be; take possession of it, and set up thy throne in it."

4. *Let thy eyes observe my ways;* have an eye to the rule of God's word, the conduct of his providence, and the good examples of his people. Our eyes must observe these, as he that writes observes his copy, that we may keep in the right paths and may proceed and persevere in them.

IV. Some particular cautions against those sins which are, of all sins, the most destructive to the seeds of wisdom and grace in the soul, which impoverish and ruin it. 1. Gluttony and drunkenness, *v.* 20, 21. The world is full of examples of this sin and temptations to it, which all young people are concerned to stand upon their guard against and keep at a distance from *Be not a wine-bibber;* we are allowed to drink *a little wine* (1 Tim. 5:23), but not much, not to make a trade of it, never to drink to excess. *Be not a riotous eater of flesh,* as the Israelites were, who lusted exceedingly after it, saying, *Who will give us flesh to eat?* Whereas Paul, though he is free to eat flesh, yet resolves that *he will eat no flesh while the world stands rather than make his brother to offend;* so indifferent is he to it, 1 Co. 8:13. *Be not an* excessive *eater of flesh.* Intemperance must be avoided in meat as well as drink. *Be not a* luxurious *eater of flesh,* not pleased with any thing but what is very nice and delicate, savoury dishes, and forced meat. Some take not only a pleasure, but a pride, in being curious about their diet, and, as they call it, eating well; as if that were the ornament of a gentleman, which is really the shame of a Christian, making a God of the belly. *"Be not a wine bibber,* and *be not a riotous eater;* and therefore, *be not among wine-bibbers* nor *among riotous eaters;* do not give them countenance, lest thou learn their ways and insensibly fall into those sins, or at least lose the dread and detestation of them. They covet to have thee among them; for those that are debauched themselves are very desirous to debauch others; therefore do not gratify them, lest thou endanger thyself." He fetches an argument against this sin from the expensiveness of it and its tendency to impoverish men: and if men will not be deterred from it by the ruin it brings on their secular interests, which lie nearest their hearts, no marvel that they are not frightened from it by what they are told out of the word of God of the mischief it does them in their spiritual and eternal concerns. *The drunkard and the glutton* hate to be reformed, though they are told they *shall come to poverty,* nay, though they are told they shall come to hell. Drunkenness is the cause of *drowsiness;* it stupefies men, and makes them inattentive to business, and then all goes to wreck and ruin: thus men that have lived creditably come to be *clothed with rags.* 2. Whoredom. This is another sin which *takes away the heart* that should be given to God, Hos. 4:11. He shows the danger which attends that sin, *v.* 27, 28, (1.) It is a sin from which few recover themselves when once they are entangled in it. It is like *a deep ditch* and *a narrow pit,* which it is almost impossible to get out of; and therefore it is wisdom to keep far enough from the brink of it. Take heed of making any approaches towards this sin, because it is so hard to make a retreat from it, conscience, which should head the retreat, being debauched by it, and divine grace forfeited. (2.) It is a sin which bewitches men to their ruin: *The adulteress lies in wait as a robber,* pretending friendship, but designing the greatest mischief, to rob them of all they have that is valuable, to strip them both of their armour and of their ornaments. Even those who, being virtuously educated, endeavour to shun the adulteress, she will *lie in wait* for, that she may assault them when they are off their guard and she has them at an advantage. Let none therefore be at any time secure. (3.) It is a sin that contributes more than any other to the spreading of vice and immorality in a kingdom: It *increases the transgressors among men.* One adulteress may be the ruin of many a precious soul and may help to debauch a whole town. It increases the treacherous or perfidious ones; it not only occasions husbands to be false to their wives and servants to their masters, but many that have professed religion to throw off their profession and break their covenants with God. Houses of uncleanness are therefore such pest-houses as ought to be suppressed by those whose office it is to take care of the public welfare.

Verses 29–35

Solomon here gives fair warning against the sin of drunkenness, to confirm what he had said, *v.* 20.

I. He cautions all people to keep out of the way of temptations to this sin (*v.* 31): *Look not thou upon the wine when it is red.* Red wine was in Canaan looked upon as the best wine, it is therefore called *the blood of the grape.* Critics judge of wine, among other indications, by the colour of it; some wine, they say, looks charmingly, looks so well that it even says, "Come and drink me;" *it moves itself aright,* goes down very smoothly, or perhaps the roughness of it is grateful. It is said of generous strong-bodied wine that it even *causes the lips of those that are asleep to speak,* Cant. 7:9. But *look not thou upon it.* 1. "Be not ruled by sense, but by reason and religion. Covet not that which pleases the eye, in hopes that it will please the taste; but let thy serious thoughts correct the errors of thy senses and convince thee that that which seems delightful is really hurtful, and resolve against it accordingly. Let not the heart walk after the eye, for it is a deceitful guide." 2. "Be not too bold with the charms of this or any other sin; *look not,* lest thou lust, lest thou take the forbidden fruit." Note Those that would be kept from any sin must keep themselves from all the occasions and beginnings of it, and be afraid of coming within the reach of its allurements, lest they be overcome by them.

II. He shows the many pernicious consequences of the sin of drunkenness, for the enforcement of this caution. Take heed of the bait, for fear of the hook: *At the last it bites, v.* 32. All sin will be bitterness in the end, and this sin particularly. *It bites like a serpent,* when the drunkard is made sick by his surfeit, thrown by it into a dropsy or some fatal disease, beggared and ruined in his estate, especially when his conscience is awakened and he cannot reflect upon it without horror and indignation at himself, but worst of all, at last, when the cup of drunkenness shall be turned into a cup of trembling, the cup of the Lord's wrath, the dregs of which he must be for ever drinking, and shall not have a drop of water to cool his inflamed tongue. To take off the force of the temptation that there is in the pleasure of the sin, foresee the punishment of it, and what it will at last end in if repentance prevent not. In *its latter end it bites* (so the word is); think therefore what will be *in the end thereof.* But the inspired writer chooses to specify those pernicious consequences of this sin which are present and sensible.

1. It embroils men in quarrels, makes them quarrel with others, and say and do that which gives others occasion to quarrel with them, *v.* 29. He asks, *Who hath woe? Who hath sorrow?* Who has not, in this world? Many have woe and sorrow, and cannot help it; but drunkards wilfully create woe and sorrow to themselves. Those that have *contentions* have *woe and sorrow;* and drunkards are the fools whose *lips enter into contention.* When the wine is in the wit is out and the passions are up; and thence come drunken scuffles, and drunken frays, and drunken disputes over the cups; many a vexatious ruining law-suit has begun thus. There is *babbling,* quarrels in word and the exchanging of scurrilous language; yet it rests not there: you shall have *wounds without cause,* for causes are things which drunkards are in no capacity to judge of, and therefore they deal blows about without the least consideration why or wherefore, and must expect to be in like manner treated themselves. The wounds which men receive in defence of their country and its just rights are their honour; but *wounds without cause,* received in the service of their lusts, are marks of their infamy. Nay, drunkards wound themselves in a tender part, for they have *redness of eyes,* symptoms of an inward inflammation; their sight is weakened by it, and their looks are deformed. This comes, (1.) Of drinking long, *tarrying long at the wine,* and spending that time in drunken company which should be spent in useful business, or in sleep, which should fit for business, *v.* 30. O the precious hours which thousands throw away thus, every one of which will be brought into the account at the great day! (2.) Of drinking that which is strong and intoxicating. *They go* up and down *to seek wine* that will please them; their great enquiry is, "Where is the best liquor?" *They seek mixed wine,* which is most palatable, but most heady, so willingly do they sacrifice their reason to please their palate!

2. It makes men impure and insolent, *v.* 33. (1.) The *eyes* grow unruly and *behold strange women* to lust after them, and so let in adultery into the heart. *Est Venus in vinis — Wine is oil to the fire of lust. Thy eyes shall behold strange things* (so some read it); when men are drunk the house turns round with them, and every thing looks strange to them, so that them they cannot trust their own eyes. (2.) The tongue also grows unruly and talks extravagantly; by it the *heart utters perverse things,* things contrary to reason, religion, and common civility, which they would be ashamed to speak if they were sober. What ridiculous incoherent nonsense men will talk when they are drunk who at another time will speak admirably well and to the purpose!

3. It stupefies and besots men, *v.* 34. When men are drunk they know not where they are nor what they say and do. (1.) Their heads are giddy, and when they lie down to sleep they are as if they were tossed by the rolling waves *of the sea,* or *upon the top of a mast;* hence they complain that their heads swim; their sleep is commonly unquiet and not refreshing, and their dreams are tumultuous. (2.) Their judgments are clouded, and they have no more steadiness and consistency than he that sleeps *upon the top of a mast:* they *drink and forget the law* (*ch.* 31:5): *they err through wine* (Isa. 28:7), and think as extravagantly as they talk. (3.) They are heedless and fearless of danger, and senseless of the rebukes they are under either from God or man. They are in imminent danger of death, of damnation, lie as much exposed as if they slept *upon the top of a mast,* and yet are secure and sleep on. They fear no peril when the terrors of the Lord are laid before them; nay, they feel no pain when the judgments of God are actually upon them; they cry not when he binds them. Set a drunkard in the stocks, and he is not sensible of the punishment. *"They have stricken me, and I was not sick; I felt it not:* it made no impression at all upon me." Drunkenness turns me into stocks and stones; they are scarcely to be reckoned animals; they are dead while they live.

4. Worst of all, the heart is hardened in the sin, and the sinner, notwithstanding all these present mischiefs that attend it, obstinately persist in it, and hates to be reformed: *When shall I awake?* Much ado he has to shake off the chains of his drunken sleep; he can hardly get clear of the fumes of the wine, though he strives with them, that (being thirsty in the morning) he may return to it again. So perfectly lost is he to all sense of virtue and honour, and so wretchedly is his conscience seared, that he is not ashamed to say, *I will seek it yet again. There is no hope; no, they have loved* drunkards, and *after them they will go,* Jer. 2:25. This is *adding drunkenness to thirst,* and *following strong drink;* those that do so may read their doom Deu. 29:19, 20, their *woe* Isa. 5:11, and, if this be the end of the sin, with good reason were we directed to stop at the beginning of it: *Look not upon the wine when it is red.*

CHAPTER 24

Verses 1–2

Here, 1. The caution given is much the same with that which we had before (*ch.* 23:17), not to envy sinners, not to think them happy, nor to whish ourselves in their condition, though they prosper ever so much in this world, and are ever so marry and ever so secure. "Let not such a thought ever come into thy mind, O that I could shake off the restraints of religion and conscience, and take as great a liberty to indulge the sensual appetite, as I see such and such do! No; *desire not to be with them,* to do as they do and fare as they fare, and to *cast in thy lot among* them." 2. Here is another reason given for this caution: *"Be not envious against* them, not only because their end will be had, but because their way is so, *v.* 2. Do not think with them, *for their heart studies destruction* to others, but it will prove destruction to themselves. Do not speak like them, for *their lips talk of their mischief.* All they say has an ill tendency, to dishonour God, reproach religion, or wrong their neighbour; but it will be mischief to themselves at last. It is therefore thy wisdom to have nothing to do with them. Nor hast thou any reason to look upon them with envy, but with pity rather, or a just indignation at their wicked practices."

Verses 3–6

We are tempted to envy those that grow rich, and raise their estates and families, by such unjust courses as our consciences will by no means suffer us to use. But, to set aside that temptation, Solomon here shows that a man, with prudent management, may raise his estate and family by lawful and honest means, with a good conscience, and a good name, and the blessing of God upon his industry; and, if the other be raised a little sooner, yet these will last a great deal longer. 1. That which is here recommended to us as having the best influence upon our outward prosperity is *wisdom,* and *understanding,* and *knowledge;* that is, both piety towards God (for that is true wisdom) and prudence in the management of our outward affairs. We must govern ourselves in every thing by the rules of religion first and then of discretion. Some that are truly pious do not thrive in the world, for want of prudence; and some that are prudent enough, yet do not prosper, because they lean to their own understanding and do not acknowledge God in their ways; therefore both must go together to complete a wise man. 2. That which is here set before us as the advantage of true wisdom is that it will make men's outward affairs prosperous and successful. (1.) it will *build a house and establish it, v.* 3. Men may by unrighteous practices build their houses, but they cannot establish them, for the foundation is rotten (Hab. 2:9, 10); whereas what is honestly got will wear like steel and be an inheritance to children's children. (2.) It will enrich a house and furnish it, *v.* 4. Those that manage their affairs with wisdom and equity, that are diligent in the use of lawful means for increasing what they have that spare from luxury and spend in charity, are in a fair way to have their shops, their warehouses, their *chambers, filled with all precious and pleasant riches — precious* because got by honest labour, and *the substance of a diligent man is precious — pleasant* because enjoyed with holy cheerfulness. Some think this is to be understood chiefly of spiritual riches. *By knowledge the chambers* of the soul are filled with the graces and comforts of the Spirit, those *precious and pleasant riches;* for the Spirit, by enlightening the understanding, performs all his other operations on the soul. (3.) It will fortify a house and turn it into a castle: *Wisdom is better than weapons of war,* offensive or defensive. *A wise man is in strength,* is in a strong-hold, *yea, a man of knowledge strengthens might,* that is, increases it, *v.* 5. As we grow in knowledge we grow in all grace, 2 Pt. 3:18. Those that *increase in wisdom* are *strengthened with all might,* Col. 1:9, 11. A wise man will compass that by his wisdom which a strong man cannot effect by force of arms. The spirit is strengthened both for the spiritual work and the spiritual warfare by true wisdom. (4.) It will govern a house and a kingdom too, and the affairs of both, *v.* 6. Wisdom will erect a college, or council of state. Wisdom will be of use, [1.] For the managing of the public quarrels, so as not to engage in them but for an honest cause and with some probability of success, and, when they are engaged in, to manage them well, and so as to make either an advantageous peace or an honourable retreat: *By wise counsel thou shalt make war,* which is a thing that may prove of ill consequence if not done by wise counsel. [2.] For the securing of the public peace: *In the multitude of counsellors there is safety,* for one may foresee the danger, and discern the advantages, which another cannot. In our spiritual conflicts we need wisdom, for our enemy is subtle.

Verses 7–9

Here is the description, 1. Of a weak man: *Wisdom is too high* for him; he thinks it so, and therefore, despairing to attain it, he will take no pains in the pursuit of it, but sit down content without it. And really it is so; he has not capacity for it, and therefore the advantages he has for getting it are all in vain to him. It is no easy thing to get wisdom; those that have natural parts good enough, yet if they be foolish, that is, if they be slothful and will not take pains, if they be playful and trifling, and given to their pleasures, if they be viciously inclined and keep bad company, it *is too high* for them; they are not likely to reach it. And, for want of it, they are unfit for the service of their country: They *open not their mouth in the gate;* they are not admitted into the council or magistracy, or, if they are, they are dumb statues, and stand for cyphers; they say nothing, because they have nothing to say, and they know that if they should offer any thing it would not be heeded, nay, it would be hissed at. Let young men take pains to get wisdom, that they may be qualified for public business, and do it with reputation. 2. Of a wicked man, who is not only despised as a fool is, but detested. Two sorts of wicked men are so: — (1.) Such as are secretly malicious. Though they speak courteously and conduct themselves plausibly, they *devise to do evil,* are contriving to do an ill turn to those they bear a grudge to, or have an envious eye at. He that does so *shall be called a mischievous person,* or *a master of mischief,* which perhaps was then a common name of reproach; he shall be branded as an *inventor of evil things* (Rom. 1. 30), or if any mischief be done, he shall be suspected as the author of it, or at least accessory to it. This *devising evil is the thought of foolishness, v.* 9. It is made light of, and turned off with a jest, as only a foolish thing, but really it *is sin,* it is exceedingly sinful; you cannot call it by a worse name than to call it *sin.* It is bad to do evil, but it is worse to devise it; for that has in it the subtlety and poison of the old serpent. But it may be taken more generally. We contract guilt, not only by the act of foolishness, but by the thought of it, though it go no further; the first risings of sin in the heart are sin, offensive to God, and must be repented of or we are undone. Not only malicious, unclean, proud thoughts, but even foolish thoughts, are sinful thoughts. If *vain thoughts lodge in the heart,* they defile it (Jer. 4:14), which is a reason why we should *keep our hearts with all diligence,* and harbour no thoughts there which cannot give a good account of themselves, Gen. 6:5. (2.) Such as are openly abusive: *The scorner,* who gives ill-language to every body, takes a pleasure in affronting people and reflecting upon them, *is an abomination to men;* none that have any sense of honour and virtue will care to keep company with him. *The seat of the scornful* is the *pestilential chair* (as the Septuagint calls it, Ps. 1:1), which no wise man will come near, for fear of taking the infection. Those that strive to make others odious do but make themselves so.

Verse 10

Note, 1. In *the day of adversity* we are apt to *faint,* to droop and be discouraged, to desist from our work, and to despair of relief. Our spirits sink, and then our hands hang down and our knees grow feeble, and we become unfit for anything. And often those that are most cheerful when they are well droop most, and are most dejected, when any thing ails them. 2. This is an evidence that our *strength is small,* and is a means of weakening it more. "It is a sign that thou art not a man of any resolution, any firmness of thought, any consideration, any faith (for that is the strength of a soul), if thou canst not bear up under an afflictive change of thy condition." Some are so feeble that they can bear nothing; if a trouble does but *touch* them (Job 4:5), nay, if it does but threaten them, they faint immediately and are ready to give up all for gone; and by this means they render themselves unfit to grapple with their trouble and unable to help themselves. *Be of good courage* therefore, *and God shall strengthen thy heart.*

Verses 11–12

Here is, 1. A great duty required of us, and that is to appear for the relief of oppressed innocency. If we see the lives or livelihoods of any in danger of being taken away unjustly, we ought to bestir ourselves all we can to save them, by disproving the false accusations on which they are condemned and seeking out proofs of their innocency. Though the persons be not such as we are under any particular obligation to, we must help them, out of a general zeal for justice. If any be set upon by force and violence, and it be in our power to rescue them, we ought to do it. Nay, if we see any through ignorance exposing themselves to danger, or fallen in distress, as travellers upon the road, ships at sea, or any the like, it is our duty, though it be with peril to ourselves, to hasten with help to them and not *forbear to deliver them,* not to be slack, or remiss, or indifferent, in such a case. 2. An answer to the excuse that is commonly make for the omission of this duty. Thou wilt say, *"Behold, we knew it not;* we were not aware of the imminency of the danger the person was in; we could not be sure that he was innocent, nor did we know how to prove his innocence, nor which way to do any thing in favour of him, else we would have helped him." Now, (1.) It is easy to make such an excuse as this, sufficient to avoid the censures of men, for perhaps they cannot disprove us when we say, *We knew it not,* or, *We forgot;* and the temptation to tell a lie for the excusing of a fault is very strong when we know that it is impossible to be disproved, the truth lying wholly in our own breast, as when we say, *We thought so and so, and really designed it,* which no one is conscious of but ourselves. (2.) It is not so easy with such excuses to evade the judgment of God; and to the discovery of that we lie open and by the determination of that we must abide. Now, [1.] God *ponders the heart and keeps the soul;* he keeps an eye upon it, observes all the motions of it; its most secret thoughts and intents are all naked and open before him. It is his prerogative to do so, and that in which he glories. Jer. 17:10, *I the Lord search the heart.* He *keeps the soul,* holds it in life. This is a good reason why we should be tender of the lives of others, and do all we can to preserve them, because our lives have been precious in the sight of God and he has graciously kept them. [2.] He knows and considers whether the excuse we make be true or no, whether it was because we did not know it or whether the true reason was not because we did not love our neighbour as we ought, but were selfish, and regardless both of God and man. Let this serve to silence all our frivolous pleas, by which we think to stop the mouth of conscience when it charges us with the omission of plain duty: *Does not he that ponders the heart consider it?* [3.] He will judge us accordingly. As his knowledge cannot be imposed upon, so his justice cannot be biassed, but he will *render to every man according to his works,* not only the commission of evil works, but the omission of good works.

Verses 13–14

We are here quickened to the study of wisdom by the consideration both of the pleasure and the profit of it. 1. It will be very pleasant. We *eat honey because it is sweet to the taste,* and upon that account we call it *good,* especially that which runs first from the *honey-comb.* Canaan was said to flow with milk and honey, and honey was the common food of the country (Lu. 24:41, 42), even for children, Isa. 7:15. Thus should we feed upon wisdom, and relish the good instructions of it. Those that have tasted honey need no further proof that it is sweet, nor can they by any argument be convinced of the contrary; so those that have experienced the power of truth and godliness are abundantly satisfied of the pleasure of both; they have tasted the sweetness of them, and all the atheists in the world with their sophistry, and the profane with their banter, cannot alter their sentiments. 2. It will be very profitable. Honey may be *sweet to the taste* and yet not wholesome, but wisdom has a future recompence attending it, as well as a present sweetness in it. "Thou art permitted to *eat honey,* and the agreeableness of it to thy taste invites thee to it; but thou hast much more reason to relish and digest the precepts *of wisdom,* for *when thou hast found* that, *there shall be a reward;* thou shalt be paid for thy pleasure, while the servants of sin pay dearly for their pains. Wisdom does indeed set thee to work, but *there shall be a reward;* it does indeed raise great expectations in thee, but as thy labour, so thy hope, shall not be in vain; *thy expectation shall not be cut off* (*ch.* 23:18), nay, it shall be infinitely outdone."

Verses 15–16

This is spoken, not so much by way of counsel to wicked men (they will not receive instruction, *ch.* 23:9), but rather in defiance of them, for the encouragement of good people that are threatened by them. See here, 1. The designs of the wicked against the righteous, and the success they promise themselves in those designs. The plot is laid deeply: They *lay wait against the dwelling of the righteous,* thinking to charge some iniquity upon it, or compass dome design against it; they lie in wait at the door, to catch him when he stirs out, as David's persecutors, Ps. 59 *title.* The hope is raised high; they doubt not but to *spoil his dwelling-place* because he is weak and cannot support it, because his condition is low and distressed, and he is almost down already. All this is a fruit of the old enmity in the seed of the serpent against the seed of the woman. *The blood-thirsty hate the upright.* 2. The folly and frustration of these designs (1.) The righteous man, whose ruin was expected, recovers himself. He *falls seven times* into trouble, but, by the blessing of God upon his wisdom and integrity, he *rises again,* sees through his troubles and sees better times after them. The *just man falls,* sometimes *falls seven times* perhaps, into sin, sins of infirmity, through the surprise of temptation; but he *rises again* by repentance, finds mercy with God, and regains his peace. (2.) *The wicked* man, who expected to see his ruin and to help it forward, is undone. He *falls into mischief;* his sins and his troubles are his utter destruction.

Verses 17–18

Here, 1. The pleasure we are apt to take in the troubles of an enemy is forbidden us. If any have done us an ill turn, or if we bear them ill-will only because they stand in our light or in our way, when any damage comes to them (suppose they fall), or any danger (suppose they stumble), our corrupt hearts are too apt to conceive a secret delight and satisfaction in it — *Aha! so would we have it; they are entangled; the wilderness has shut them in* — or, as Tyrus said concerning Jerusalem (Eze. 26:2) *I shall be replenished, now she is laid waste.* "Men hope in the ruin of their enemies or rivals to wreak their revenge or to find their account; but be not thou so inhuman; *rejoice not when* the worst *enemy* thou hast *falls.*" There may be a holy joy in the destruction of God's enemies, as it tends to the glory of God and the welfare of the church (Ps. 58:10); but in the ruin of our enemies, as such, we must by no means rejoice; on the contrary, we must weep even with them when they weep (as David, Ps. 35:13, 14), and that in sincerity, not so much as letting our hearts be secretly glad at their calamities. 2. The provocation which that pleasure gives to God is assigned as the reason of that prohibition: *The Lord* will *see it,* though it be hidden in the heart only, *and it* will *displease him,* as it will displease a prudent father to see one child triumph in the correction of another, which he ought to tremble at, and take warning by, not knowing how soon it may be his own case, he having so often deserved it. Solomon adds an argument *ad hominem — addressed to the individual:* "Thou canst not do a greater kindness to *thy enemy,* when he has fallen, than to rejoice in it; for them, to cross thee and vex thee, God will *turn his wrath from him;* for, as *the wrath of man works not the righteousness of God,* so the righteousness of God was never intended to gratify the wrath of man, and humour his foolish passions; rather than seem to do that he will adjourn the execution of his wrath: nay, it is implied that when he *turns his wrath from him* he will turn it against thee and the cup of trembling shall be put into thy hand."

Verses 19–20

Here, 1. He repeats the caution he had before given against envying the pleasures and successes of wicked man in their wicked ways. This he quotes from his father David, Ps. 37:1. We must not in any case *fret* ourselves, or make ourselves uneasy, whatever God does in his providence how disagreeable soever it is to our sentiments, interests, and expectations, we must acquiesce in it. Even that which grieves us must not *fret* us; nor must our eye be evil against any because God is good. Are we more wise or just than he? If wicked people prosper, we must not therefore incline to do as they do. 2. He gives a reason for this caution, taken from the end of that way which wicked man walk in. Envy not their prosperity; for, (1.) There is no true happiness in it: *Thee shall be no reward to the evil man;* his prosperity only serves for his present subsistence; these are all the good things he must ever expect: there is none intended him in the world of retribution. *He has his reward,* Mt. 6:2. He shall have none. Those are not to be envied that have their portion in this life and must outlive it, Ps. 17:14. (2.) There is no continuance in it; their *candle* shines brightly, but it shall presently *be put out,* and a final period put to all their comforts, Job 21:14; Ps. 37:1, 2.

Verses 21–22

Note, 1. Religion and loyalty must go together. As men, it is our duty to honour our Creator, to worship and reverence him, and to be always in his fear; as members of a community, incorporated for mutual benefit, it is our duty to be faithful and dutiful to the government God has set over us, Rom. 13:1, 2. Those that are truly religious will be loyal, in conscience towards God; the godly in the land will be the *quite in the land;* and those are not truly loyal, or will be so no longer than is for their interest, that are not religious. How should he be true to his prince that is false to his God? And, if they come in competition, it is an adjudged case, we must *obey God rather than men.* 2. Innovations in both are to be dreaded. Have nothing to do, he does not say, with those that *change,* for there may be cause to change for the better, but *those that are given to change,* that affect change for change-sake, out of a peevish discontent with that which is and a fondness for novelty, or a desire to fish in troubled waters: *Meddle not with those that are given to change* either in religion or in a civil government; *come not into their secret;* join not with them in their cabals, nor enter into the mystery of their iniquity. 3. Those that are of restless, factious, turbulent spirits, commonly pull mischief upon their own heads ere they are aware: *Their calamity shall rise suddenly.* Though they carry on their designs with the utmost secresy, they will be discovered, and brought to condign punishment, when they little think of it. *Who knows* the time and manner of *the ruin* which both God and the king will bring on their contemners, *both* on them and those that meddle with them?

Verses 23–26

Here are lessons for *wise* men, that is, judges and princes. As subjects must do their duty, and be obedient to magistrates, so magistrates must do their duty in administering justice to their subjects, both in pleas of the crown and causes between party and party. These are lessons for them. 1. They must always weigh the merits of a cause, and not be swayed by any regard, one way or other, to the parties concerned: *It is not good* in itself, nor can it ever do well, *to have respect of persons in judgment;* the consequences of it cannot but be the perverting of justice and doing wrong under colour of law and equity. A good judge will know the truth, not know faces, so as to countenance a friend and help him out in a bad cause, or so much as omit any thing that can be said or done in favour of a righteous cause, when it is the cause of an enemy. 2. They must never connive at or encourage wicked people in their wicked practices. Magistrates in their places, and ministers in theirs, are to deal faithfully and the wicked man, though he be a great man or a particular friend, to convict him of his wickedness, to show him what will be in the end thereof, to discover him to others, that they may avoid him. But if those whose office it is thus to show people their transgressions palliate them and connive at them, if they excuse the wicked man, much more if they prefer him and associate with him (which is, in effect, to say, *Thou art righteous*), they shall justly be looked upon as enemies to the public peace and welfare, which they ought to advance, and *the people shall curse them* and cry out shame on them; and even those of other *nations shall abhor them,* as base betrayers of their trust. 3. They must discountenance and give check to all fraud, violence, injustice, and immorality; and, though thereby they may disoblige a particular person, yet they will recommend themselves to the favour of God and man. Let magistrates and ministers, and private persons too that are capable of doing it, *rebuke* the wicked, that they may bring them to repentance or put them to shame, and they shall have the comfort of it in their own bosoms: *To them shall be delight,* when their consciences witness for them that they have been witnesses for God; *and a good blessing shall come upon them,* the blessing of God and good men; they shall be deemed religion's patrons and their country's patriots. See *ch.* 28:23. 4. They must always give judgment according to equity (*v.* 26); they must *give a right answer,* that is, give their opinion and pass sentence according to law and them true merits of the cause; and *every one shall kiss his lips that* does so, that is, shall love and honour him, and be subject to his orders, for there is a kiss of allegiance as well as of affection. He that in common conversation likewise speaks pertinently and with sincerity recommends himself to his company and is beloved and respected by all.

Verse 27

This is a rule of prudence in the management of household affairs; for all good men should be good husbands, and manage with discretion, which would prevent a great deal of sin, and trouble, and disgrace to their profession. 1. We must prefer necessaries before conveniences, and not lay that out for show which should be expended for the support of the family. We must be contented with a mean cottage for a habitation, rather than want, or go in debt for, food convenient. 2. We must not think of building till we can afford it: "First apply thyself to *thy work without in the field;* let thy ground be put into good order; look after thy husbandry, for it is that by which thou must get; and, when thou hast got well by that, then, and not till then, thou mayest think of rebuilding and beautifying *thy house,* for that is it upon which, and in which, thou wilt have occasion to spend." Many have ruined their estates and families by laying out money on that which brings nothing in, beginning *to build* when they were *not able to finish.* Some understand it as advice to young men not to marry (for by that the house is built) till they have set up in the world, and not wherewith to maintain a wife and children comfortably. 3. When we have any great design on foot it is wisdom to take it before us, and make the necessary preparations, before we fall to work, that, when it is begun, it may not stand still for want of materials. Solomon observed this rule himself in building the house of God; all was made ready *before it was brought to the ground,* 1 Ki. 6:7.

Verses 28–29

We are here forbidden to be in any thing injurious to our neighbour, particularly in and by the forms of law, either, 1. As *a witness:* "Never bear a testimony against any man *without cause,* unless what thou sayest thou knowest to be punctually true and thou hast a clear call to testify it. Never bear a false testimony against any one;" for it follows, *"Deceive not with thy lips;* deceive not the judge and jury, deceive not those whom thou conversest with, into an ill opinion of thy neighbour. When thou speakest of thy neighbour do not only speak that which is true, but take heed lest, in the manner of thy speaking, thou insinuate any thing that is otherwise and so shouldst deceive by innuendos or hyperboles." Or, 2. As a plaintiff or prosecutor. If there be occasion to bring an action or information against thy neighbour, let it not be from a spirit of revenge. *"Say not,* I am resolved I will be even with him: *I will do so to him as he had done to me."* Even a righteous cause becomes unrighteous when it is thus prosecuted with malice. *Say not, I will render to the man according to his work,* and make him pay dearly for it; for it is God's prerogative to do so, and we must leave it to him, and not step into his throne, or take his work out of his hands. If we will needs be our own carvers, and judges in our own cause, we forfeit the benefit of an appeal to God's tribunal; therefore we must not avenge ourselves, because he has said, *Vengeance is mine.*

Verses 30–34

Here is, 1. The view which Solomon took of *the field and vineyard of the slothful* man. He did not go on purpose to see it, but, as he passed by, observing the fruitfulness of the ground, as it is very proper for travellers to do, and his subjects' management of their land, as it is very proper for magistrates to do, he cast his eye upon a *field* and a *vineyard* unlike all the rest; for, though the soil was good, yet there was nothing growing in them but *thorns and nettles,* not here and there one, but they were all over-run with weeds; and, if there had been any fruit, it would have been eaten up by the beasts, for there was no fence: *The stone-wall was broken down* See the effects of that curse upon the ground (Gen. 3:18), *"Thorns and thistles shall it bring forth unto thee,* and nothing else unless thou take pains with it." See what a blessing to the world the husbandman's calling is, and what a wilderness this earth, even Canaan itself, would be without it. *The king himself is served of the field,* but he would be ill served if God did not teach the husbandman discretion and diligence to clear the ground, plant it, sow it, and fence it. See what a great difference there is between some and others in the management even of their worldly affairs, and how little some consult their reputation, not caring though they proclaim their slothfulness, in the manifest effects of it, to all that pass by, shamed by their neighbour's diligence. 2. The reflections which he made upon it. He paused a little *and considered it, looked* again *upon it, and received instruction.* He did not break out into any passionate censures of the owner, did not call him any ill names, but he endeavoured himself to get good by the observation and to be quickened by it to diligence. Note, Those that are to give instruction to others must receive instruction themselves, and instruction may be received, not only from what we read and hear, but from what we see, not only from what we see of the works of God, but from what we see of the manners of man, not only from men's good manners, but from their evil manners. Plutarch relates a saying of Cato Major, "That wise men profit more by fools than fools by wise men; for wise men will avoid the faults of fools, but fools will not imitate the virtues of wise men." Solomon reckoned that he *received instruction* by this sight, though it did not suggest to him any new notion or lesson, but only put him in mind of an observation he himself had formerly made, both of the ridiculous folly of the sluggard (who, when he has needful work to do, lies dozing in bed and cries, *Yet a little sleep, a little slumber,* and still it will be a little more, till he has slept his eyes out, and, instead of being fitted by sleep for business, as wise men are, he is dulled, and stupefied, and made good for nothing) and of certain misery that attends him: his *poverty comes as one that travels;* it is constantly coming nearer and nearer to him, and will be upon him speedily, and want seizes him as irresistibly *as an armed man,* a highwayman that will strip him of all he has. Now this is applicable, not only to our worldly business, to show what a scandalous thing slothfulness in that is, and how injurious to the family, but to the affairs of our souls. Note, (1.) Our souls are our fields and vineyards, which we are every one of us to take care of, to dress, and to keep. They are capable of being improved with good husbandry; that may be got out of them which will be fruit abounding to our account. We are charged with them, to occupy them till our Lord come; and a great deal of care and pains it is requisite that we should take about them. (2.) These fields and vineyards are often in a very bad state, not only no fruit brought forth, but all overgrown with *thorns* and *nettles* (scratching, stinging, inordinate lusts and passions, pride, covetousness, sensuality, malice, those are the thorns and nettles, the wild grapes, which the unsanctified heart produces), no guard kept against the enemy, but the *stone-wall broken down,* and all lies in common, all exposed. (3.) Where it is thus it is owing to the sinner's own slothfulness and folly. He is a sluggard, loves sleep, hates labour; and he is void of understanding, understands neither his business nor his interest; he is perfectly besotted. (4.) The issue of it will certainly be the ruin of the soul and all its welfare. It is everlasting want that thus comes upon it as an armed man. We know the place assigned to the wicked and slothful servant.

CHAPTER 25

Verse 1

This verse is the title of this latter collection of Solomon's proverbs, for he *sought out and set in order many proverbs,* that by them he might be still *teaching the people*

knowledge, Eccl. 12:9. Observe, 1. The proverbs were Solomon's, who was divinely inspired to deliver, for the use of the church, these wise and weighty sentences; we have had many, but still there are more. Yet herein Christ is greater than Solomon, for if we had all upon record that Christ said, and did, that was instructive, *the world could not contain the books that would be written,* Jn. 21:25. 2. The publishers were Hezekiah's servants, who, it is likely, herein acted as his servants, being appointed by him to do this good service to the church, among other good offices that he did *in the law and in the commandments,* 2 Chr. 31:21. Whether he employed the prophets in this work, as Isaiah, Hosea, or Micah, who lived in his time, or some that were trained up in the schools of the prophets, or some of the priests and Levites, to whom we find him giving a charge concerning divine things (2 Chr. 29:4); or (as the Jews think) his princes and ministers of state, who were more properly called his *servants,* is not certain; if the work was done by Eliakim, and Joah, and Shebna, it was no diminution to their character. They copied out these proverbs from the records of Solomon's reign, and published them as an appendix to the former edition of this book. It may be a piece of very good service to the church to publish other man's works that have lain hidden in obscurity, perhaps a great while. Some think they culled these out of the 3000 proverbs which Solomon spoke (1 Ki. 4:32), leaving out those that were physical, and that pertained to natural philosophy, and preserving such only as were divine and moral; and in this collection some observe that special regard was had to those observations which concern kings and their administration.

Verses 2–3

Here is, 1. An instance given of the honour of God: *It is his glory to conceal a matter.* He needs not search into any thing, for he perfectly knows every thing by a clear and certain view, and nothing can be hidden from him; and yet his own *way is in the sea* and his *path in the great waters.* There is an unfathomable depth in his counsels, Rom. 11:33. It is but a little portion that is heard of him. *Clouds and darkness are round about him.* We see what he does, but we know not the reasons. Some refer it to the sins of men; it is his glory to pardon sin, which is covering it, not remembering it, not mentioning it; his forbearance, which he exercises towards sinners, is likewise his honour, in which he seems to keep silence and take no notice of the matter. 2. A double instance of the honour of kings: — (1.) It is God's glory that he needs not *search into a matter,* because he knows it without search; but it is the honour of kings, with a close application of mind, and by all the methods of enquiry, to search out the matters that are brought before them, to take pains in examining offenders, that they may discover their designs and bring to light the hidden works of darkness, not to give judgment hastily or till they have weighed things, nor to leave it wholly to others to examine things, but to see with their own eyes. (2.) It is God's glory that he cannot himself be found out by searching, and some of that honour is devolved upon kings, wise kings, that *search out matters;* their *hearts* are *unsearchable,* like the *height of heaven* or the *depth of the earth,* which we may guess at, but cannot measure. Princes have their *arcana imperii — state secrets,* designs which are kept private, and reasons of state, which private persons are not competent judges of, and therefore ought not to pry into. Wise princes, when they *search into a matter,* have reaches which one would not think of, as Solomon, when he called of a sword to divide the living child with, designing thereby to discover the true mother.

Verses 4–5

This shows that the vigorous endeavour of a prince to suppress vice, and reform the manners of his people, is the most effectual way to support his government. Observe, 1. what the duty of magistrates is: To *take away the wicked,* to use their power for the terror of evil works and evil workers, not only to banish those that are vicious and profane from their presence, and forbid them the court, but so to frighten them and restrain them that they may not spread the infection of their wickedness among their subjects. This is called *taking away the dross from the silver,* which is done by the force of fire. Wicked people are the

dross of a nation, the scum of the country, and, as such, to be taken away. If men will not take them away, God will, Ps. 119:119. If the *wicked be taken away from before the king,* if he abandon them and show his detestation of their wicked courses, it will go far towards the disabling of them to do mischief. The reformation of the court will promote the reformation of the kingdom, Ps. 101:3, 8. 2. What the advantage will be of their doing this duty. (1.) It will be the bettering of the subjects; they shall be made like silver refined, fit to be made *vessels of honour.* (2.) It will be the settling of the prince. *His throne shall be established in* this *righteousness,* for God will bless his government, the people will be pliable to it, and so it will become durable.

Verses 6–7

Here we see, 1. That religion is so far from destroying good manners that it reaches us to behave ourselves lowly and reverently towards our superiors, to keep our distance, and give place to those to whom it belongs: *"Put not forth thyself* rudely and carelessly *in the king's presence,* or in the presence of great men; do not *compare with them"* (so some understand it); "do not vie with them in apparel, furniture, gardens, house-keeping, or retinue, for that is an affront to them and will waste thy own estate." 2. That religion teaches us humility and self-denial, which is a better lesson than that of good manners: "Deny thyself the place thou art entitled to; covet not to make a fair show, nor air at preferment, nor thrust thyself into the company of those that are above thee; be content in a low sphere if that is it which God has allotted to thee." The reason he gives is because this is really the way to advancement, as our Saviour shows in a parable that seems to be borrowed from this, Lu. 14:9. Not that we must *therefore* pretend modesty and humility, and make a stratagem of it, for the courting of honour, but *therefore* we must really be modest and humble, because God will put honour on such and so will men too. It is better, more for a man's satisfaction and reputation, to be advanced above his pretensions and expectations, than to be thrust down below them, *in the presence of the prince,* whom it was a great piece of honour to be admitted to the sight of and a great piece of presumption to look upon without leave.

Verses 8–10

I. Here is good counsel given about going to law: —1. "Be not hasty in bringing an action, before thou hast thyself considered it, and consulted with thy friends about it: *Go not forth hastily to strive;* do not send for a writ in a passion, or upon the first appearance of right on thy side, but weigh the matter deliberately, because we are apt to be partial in our own cause; consider the certainty of the expenses and the uncertainty of the success, how much care and vexation it will be the occasion of, and, after all, the cause may go against thee; surely then thou shouldst not *go forth hastily to strive."* 2. "Bring not an action before thou hast tried to end the matter amicably (v. 9): *Debate thy cause with thy neighbour* privately, and perhaps you will understand one another better and see that there is no occasion to go to law." In public quarrels the war that must at length end might better have been prevented by a treaty of peace, and a great deal of blood and treasure spared. It is so in private quarrels: "Sue not thy neighbour as a *heathen man and a publican* until thou hast told him his fault between thee and him alone, and he has refused to refer the matter, or to come to an accommodation. Perhaps the matter in variance is a secret, not fit to be divulged to any, much less to be brought upon the stage before the country; and therefore end it privately, that it may not be discovered." *Reveal not the secret of another,* so some read it. "Do not, in revenge, to disgrace thy adversary, disclose that which should be kept private and which does not at all belong to the cause."

II. Two reasons he gives why we should be thus cautious in going to law: — 1. "Because otherwise the cause will be in danger of going against thee, and thou wilt *not know what to do* when the defendant has justified himself in what thou didst charge upon him, and made it out that thy complaint was frivolous and vexatious and that thou hadst no just cause of action, and so *put thee to shame,* non-suit thee, and force thee to pay costs, all which might have been prevented by a little consideration." 2.

"Because it will turn very much to thy reproach if thou fall under the character of being litigious. Not only the defendant himself (*v.* 8), but he that hears the cause tried will *put thee to shame,* will expose thee as a man of no principle, and *thy infamy will not turn away;* thou wilt never retrieve thy reputation."

Verses 11–12

Solomon here shows how much it becomes a man, 1. To speak pertinently: *A word upon the wheels,* that runs well, is well-circumstanced, in proper time and place —instruction, advice, or comfort, given seasonably, and in apt expressions, adapted to the case of the person spoken to and agreeing with the character of the person speaking — *is like golden balls* resembling *apples,* or like true apples of a golden colour (golden rennets), or perhaps gilded, as sometimes we have gilded laurels, and those embossed *in pictures of silver,* or rather brought to table in a silver network basket, or in a silver box of that which we call *filigree*-work, through which the golden apples might be seen. Doubtless in was some ornament of the table, then well known. As that was very pleasing to the eye, so is *a word fitly spoken* to the ear. 2. Especially to give a reproof with discretion, and so as to make it acceptable. If it be well given, by *a wise reprover,* and well taken, by an *obedient ear,* it is an *earring of gold* and an *ornament of fine gold,* very graceful and well becoming both the reprover and the reproved; both will have their praise, the reprover for giving it so prudently and the reproved for taking it so patiently and making a good use of it. Others will commend them both, and they will have satisfaction in each other; he who gave the reproof is pleased that it had the desired effect, and he to whom it was given has reason to be thankful for it as a kindness. *That is well given,* we say, *that is well taken;* yet it does not always prove that that is well taken which is well given. It were to be wished that a *wise reprover* should always meet with an *obedient ear,* but often it is not so.

Verse 13

See here, 1. What ought to be the care of a servant, the meanest that is sent on an errand and entrusted with any business, much more the greatest, the agent and ambassador of a prince; he ought to be *faithful to him that sends him,* and to see to it that he do not, by mistake or with design, falsify his trust, and that he be in nothing that lies in his power wanting to his master's interest. Those that act as factors, by commission, ought to act as carefully as for themselves. 2. How much this will be the satisfaction of the master; it will *refresh his soul* as much as ever the *cold of snow* (which is hot countries they preserve by art all the year round) refreshed the labourers in the harvest, that *bore the burden and heat of the day.* The more important the affair was, and the more fear of its miscarrying, the more acceptable is the messenger, if he have managed it successfully and well. A faithful minister, Christ's messenger, should be thus acceptable to us (Job 33:23); however, he will be a *sweet savour to God,* 2 Co. 2:15.

Verse 14

He may be said to boast of a false gift, 1. Who pretends to have received or given that which he never had, which he never gave, makes a noise of his great accomplishments and his good services, but it is all false; he is not what he pretends to be. Or, 2. Who promises what he will give and what he will do, but performs nothing, who raises people's expectations of the mighty things he will do for his country, for his friends, what noble legacies he will leave, but either he has not wherewithal to do what he says or he never designs it. Such a one is like the morning-cloud, that passes away, and disappoints those who looked for rain from it to water the parched ground (Jude 12), *clouds without water.*

Verse 15

Two things are here recommended to us, in dealing with others, as likely means to gain our point: — 1. Patience, to bear a present heat without being put into a heat by it, and to wait for a fit opportunity to offer our reasons and to give persons time to consider them. By this means even a *prince* may be *persuaded* to do a thing which he

seemed very averse to, much more a common person. That which is justice and reason now will be so another time, and therefore we need not urge them with violence now, but wait for a more convenient season. 2. Mildness, to speak without passion or provocation: *A soft tongue breaks the bone;* it mollifies the roughest spirits and overcomes those that are most morose, like lightning, which, they say, has sometimes broken the bone, and yet not pierced the flesh. Gideon with a soft tongue pacified the Ephraimites and Abigail turned away David's wrath. *Hard words,* we say, *break no bones,* and therefore we should bear them patiently; but, it seems, *soft words* do, and therefore we should, on all occasions, give them prudently.

Verse 16

Here, 1. We are allowed a sober and moderate use of the delights of sense: *Hast thou found honey?* It is not forbidden fruit to thee, as it was to Jonathan; thou mayest eat of it with thanksgiving to God, who, having created things grateful to our senses, has given us leave to make use of them. *Eat as much as is sufficient,* and no more. *Enough is as good as a feast.* 2. We are cautioned to take heed of excess. We must use all pleasures as we do honey, with a check upon our appetite, lest we take more than does us good and make ourselves sick with it. We are most in danger of surfeiting upon that which is most sweet, and therefore those that fare sumptuously every day have need to watch over themselves, *lest their hearts be at any time overcharged.* The pleasures of sense lose their sweetness by the excessive use of them and become nauseous, as honey, which turns sour in the stomach; it is therefore our interest, as well as our duty, to use them with sobriety.

Verse 17

Here he mentions another pleasure which we must not take too much of, that of visiting our friends, the former for fear of surfeiting ourselves, this for fear of surfeiting our neighbour. 1. It is a piece of civility to visit our neighbours sometimes, to show our respect to them and concern for them, and to cultivate and improve mutual acquaintance and love, and that we may have both the satisfaction and advantage of their conversation. 2. It is wisdom, as well as good manners, not to be troublesome to our friends in our visiting them, not to visit too often, nor stay too long, nor contrive to come at meal-time, nor make ourselves busy in the affairs of their families; hereby we make ourselves cheap, mean, and burdensome. Thy neighbour, who is thus plagued and haunted with thy visits, will be *weary of thee and hate thee,* and *that* will be the destruction of friendship which should have been the improvement of it. *Post tres saepe dies piscis vilescit et hospes — After the third day fish and company become distasteful.* Familiarity breeds contempt. *Nulli te facias nimis sodalem — Be not too intimate with any.* He that sponges upon his friend loses him. How much better a friend then is God than any other friend; for we need not withdraw our foot from his house, the throne of his grace (*ch.* 8:34); the oftener we come to him the better and the more welcome.

Verse 18

Here, 1. The sin condemned is *bearing false witness against our neighbour,* either in judgment or in common conversation, contrary to the law of the ninth commandment. 2. That which it is here condemned for is the mischievousness of it; it is in its power to ruin not only men's reputation, but their lives, estates, families, all that is dear to them. A false testimony is every thing that is dangerous; it *is a maul* (or *club* to knock a man's brains out with), a flail, which there is no fence against; it is a *sword* to wound near at hand and a *sharp arrow* to wound at a distance; we have therefore need to pray, *Deliver my soul, O Lord! from lying lips,* Ps. 120:2.

Verse 19

1. The *confidence of an unfaithful man* (so some read it) will be *like a broken tooth;* his policy, his power, his interest, all that which he trusted in to support him in his wickedness, will fail him in time of trouble, Ps. 52:7. 2. *Confidence in an unfaithful man* (so we read it), in a man whom we thought trusty and therefore depended on, but who proves otherwise; it proves not only unserviceable,

but painful and vexatious, like a *broken tooth, or a foot out of joint,* which, when we put any stress upon it, not only fails us, but makes us feel from it, especially *in time of trouble,* when we most expect help from it; it is like a broken reed, Isa. 36:6. Confidence in a faithful God, in time of trouble, will not prove thus; on him we may rest and in him dwell at ease.

Verse 20

1. The absurdity here censured is *singing songs to a heavy heart.* Those that are in great sorrow are to be comforted by sympathizing with them, condoling with them, and concurring in their lamentation. If we take that method, the *moving of our lips may assuage their grief* (Job 16:5); but we take a wrong course with them if we think to relieve them by being merry with them, and endeavouring to make them merry; for it adds to their grief to see their friends so little concerned for them; it puts them upon ripping up the causes of their grief, and aggravating them, and makes them harden themselves in sorrow against the assaults of mirth. 2. The absurdities this is compared to are, *taking away a garment* from a man in *cold weather,* which makes him colder, and pouring *vinegar upon nitre,* which, like water upon lime, puts it into a ferment; so improper, so incongruous, is it to sing pleasant songs to one that is of a sorrowful spirit. Some read it in a contrary sense: *As he that puts on a garment in cold weather* warms the body, or as *vinegar upon nitre* dissolves it, so he that *sings songs* of comfort to a person in sorrow refreshes him and dispels his grief.

Verses 21–22

By this it appears that, however the scribes and Pharisees had corrupted the law, not only the commandment of loving our brethren, but even that of loving our enemies, was not only a new, but also an old commandment, an Old-Testament commandment, though our Saviour has given it to us with the new enforcement of his own great example in loving us when we were enemies. Observe, 1. How we must express our love to our enemies by the real offices of kindness, even those that are expensive to ourselves and most acceptable to them: "If they be *hungry* and *thirsty,* instead of pleasing thyself with their distress and contriving how to cut off supplies from them, relieve them, as Elisha did the Syrians that came to apprehend him," 2 King 6:22. 2. What encouragement we have to do so. (1.) It will be a likely means to win upon them, and bring them over to be reconciled to us; we shall mollify them as the refiner melts the metal in the crucible, not only by putting it over the fire, but by heaping coals of fire upon it. The way to turn an enemy into a friend is, to act towards him in a friendly manner. If it do not gain him, it will aggravate his sin and punishment, and heap the burning coals of God's wrath upon his head, as rejoicing in his calamity may be an occasion of God's turning his wrath from him, *ch.* 24:17. (2.) However, we shall be no losers by our self-denial: "Whether he relent towards thee or no, *the Lord shall reward thee;* he shall forgive thee who thus showest thyself to be of a forgiving spirit. He shall provide for thee when thou art in distress (though thou hast been evil and ungrateful), as thou dost for thy enemy; at least it shall be recompensed in the resurrection of the just, when kindnesses done to our enemies shall be remembered as well as those shown to God's friends."

Verse 23

Here see, 1. How we must discourage sin and witness against it, and particularly the sin of slandering and backbiting; we must frown upon it, and, by giving it an angry countenance, endeavour to put it out of countenance. Slanders would not be so readily spoken as they are if they were not readily heard; but good manners would silence the slanderer if he saw that his tales displeased the company. We should show ourselves uneasy if we heard a dear friend, whom we value, evil-spoken of; the same dislike we should show of evil-speaking in general. If we cannot otherwise reprove, we may do it by our looks. 2. The good effect which this might probably have; who knows but it may silence and drive away a *backbiting tongue?* Sin, if it be countenanced, becomes daring, but, if it receive any check, it is so conscious of its own shame that it becomes cowardly, and this sin in particular, for many abuse those they speak of only in hopes to curry favour with those they speak to.

Verse 24

This is the same with what he had said, *ch.* 21:9. Observe, 1. How those are to be pitied that are unequally yoked, especially with such as are brawling and contentious, whether husband or wife; for it is equally true of both. It is better to be alone than to be joined to one who, instead of being a meet-help, is a great hindrance to the comfort of life. 2. How those may sometimes be envied that live in solitude; as they want the comfort of society, so they are free from the vexation of it. And as there are cases which give occasion to say, "Blessed is the womb that has not borne," so there are which give occasion to say, "Blessed is the man who was never married, but who lies like a servant in *a corner of the house-top.*"

Verse 25

See here, 1. How natural it is to us to desire to hear good news from our friends, and concerning our affairs at a distance. It is sometimes with impatience that we expect to hear from abroad; our souls thirst after it. But we should check the inordinateness of that desire; if it be bad news, it will come too soon, if good, it will be welcome at any time. 2. How acceptable such good news will be when it does come, as refreshing as cold water to one that is thirsty. Solomon himself had much trading abroad, as well as correspondence by his ambassadors with foreign courts; and how pleasant it was to hear of the good success of his negotiations abroad he well knew by experience. Heaven is a country afar off; how refreshing is it to hear good news thence, both in the everlasting gospel, which signified glad tidings, and in the witness of the Spirit with our spirits that we are God's children.

Verse 26

It is here represented as a very lamentable thing, and a public grievance, and of ill consequence to many, like the *troubling* of a *fountain* and the *corrupting* of a *spring,* for the righteous to *fall down before the wicked,* that is, 1. For the righteous to fall into sin in the sight of the wicked — for them to do any thing unbecoming their profession, which is *told in Gath,* and *published in the streets of Ashkelon,* and in which the *daughters of the Philistines rejoice.* For those that have been *in reputation for wisdom and honour* to fall from their excellency, this *troubles the fountains* by grieving some, and *corrupts the springs* by infecting others and emboldening them to do likewise. 2. For the righteous to be oppressed, and run down, and trampled upon, by the violence or subtlety of evil men, to be displaced and thrust into obscurity, this is the troubling of the fountains of justice and corrupting the very springs of government, *ch.* 28:12, 28; 29:2. 3. For the righteous to be cowardly, to truckle to the wicked, to be afraid of opposing his wickedness and basely to yield to him, this is a reflection upon religion, a discouragement to good men, and strengthens the hands of sinners in their sins, and so is like a *troubled fountain* and a *corrupt spring.*

Verse 27

I. Two things we must be graciously dead to: — 1. To the pleasures of sense, for *it is not good to eat much honey;* though it pleases the taste, and, if eaten with moderation, is very wholesome, yet, if eaten to excess, it becomes nauseous, creates bile, and is the occasion of many diseases. It is true of all the delights of the children of men that they will surfeit, but never satisfy, and they are dangerous to those that allow themselves the liberal use of them. 2. To the praise of man. We must not be greedy of that any more than of pleasure, because, *for men to search their own glory,* to court applause and covet to make themselves popular, is not their glory, but their shame; every one will laugh at them for it; and the glory which is so courted *is not glory* when it is got, for it is really no true honour to a man.

II. Some give another sense of this verse: *To eat much honey is not good,* but to search into glorious and excellent things is a great commendation, it is true glory; we cannot therein offend by excess. Others thus: "As honey, though pleasant to the taste, if used immoderately, oppresses the stomach, so an over-curious search into things sublime and glorious, though pleasant to us, if we pry too far, will overwhelm our capacities with a greater glory and lustre than they can bear." Or thus: "You may be surfeited with eating too much honey, but the last of glory, of their glory, the glory of the blessed, is glory; it will be ever fresh, and never pall the appetite."

Verse 28

Here is, 1. The good character of a wise and virtuous man implied. He is one that has *rule over his own spirit;* he maintains the government of himself, and of his own appetites and passions, and does not suffer them to rebel against reason and conscience. He has the rule of his own thoughts, his desires, his inclinations, his resentments, and keeps them all in good order. 2. The bad case of a vicious man, who has not this rule over his own spirit, who, when temptations to excess in eating or drinking are before him, has no government of himself, when he is provoked breaks out into exorbitant passions, such a one is *like a city that is broken down and without walls.* All that is good goes out, and forsakes him; all that is evil breaks in upon him. He lies exposed to all the temptations of Satan and becomes an easy prey to that enemy; he is also liable to many troubles and vexations; it is likewise as much a reproach to him as it is to a city to have its walls ruined, Neh. 1. 3.

CHAPTER 26

Verse 1

Note, 1. It is too common a thing for honour to be given to fools, who are utterly unworthy of it and unfit for it. Bad men, who have neither wit nor grace, are sometimes preferred by princes, and applauded and cried up by the people. *Folly is set in great dignity,* as Solomon observed, Eccl. 10:6. 2. It is very absurd and unbecoming when it is so. It is an incongruous *as snow in summer,* and as great a disorder in the commonwealth as that is in the course of nature and in the seasons of the year; nay, it is as injurious *as rain in harvest,* which hinders the labourers and spoils the fruits of the earth when they are ready to be gathered. When bad men are in power they commonly abuse their power, in discouraging virtue, and giving countenance to wickedness, for want of wisdom to discern it and grace to detest it.

Verse 2

Here is, 1. The folly of passion. It makes men scatter *causeless curses,* wishing ill to others upon presumption that they are bad and have done ill, when either they mistake the person or misunderstand the fact, or they call evil good and good evil. Give honour to a fool, and he thunders out his anathemas against all that he is disgusted with, right or wrong. Great men, when wicked, think they have a privilege to keep those about them in awe, by cursing them, and swearing at them, which yet is an expression of the most impotent malice and shows their weakness as much as their wickedness. 2. The safety of innocency. He that is cursed without cause, whether by furious imprecations or solemn anathemas, the curse shall do him no more harm than the bird that flies over his head, than Goliath's curses did to David, 1 Sa. 17:43. It will fly away like the sparrow or the wild dove, which go nobody knows where, till they return to their proper place, as the curse will at length return upon the head of him that uttered it.

Verse 3

Here, 1. Wicked men are compared to *the horse* and *the ass,* so brutish are they, so unreasonable, so unruly, and not to be governed but by force or fear, so low has sin sunk men, so much below themselves. Man indeed is *born like the wild ass's colt,* but as some by the grace of God are changed, and become rational, so others by custom in sin are hardened, and become more and more sottish, *as the horse and the mule,* Ps. 32:9. 2. Direction is given to use them accordingly. Princes, instead of giving *honour to a fool* (*v.* 1), must put disgrace upon him — instead of putting power into his hand, must exercise power over him. A *horse* unbroken needs *a whip* for correction, and an *ass a bridle* for direction and to check him when he would turn out of the way; so a vicious man, who will not be under the guidance and restraint of religion and reason, ought to be whipped and bridled, to be rebuked severely, and made to smart for what he has done amiss, and to be restrained from offending any more.

Verses 4–5

See here the noble security of the scripture-style, which seems to contradict itself, but really does not. Wise men have need to be directed how to deal with fools; and they have never more need of wisdom than in dealing with such, to know when to keep silence and when to speak, for there may be a time for both. 1. In some cases a wise man will not set his wit to that of a fool so far as to *answer him according to his folly* "If he boast of himself, do not answer him by boasting of thyself. If he rail and talk passionately, do not thou rail and talk passionately too. If he tell one great lie, do not thou tell another to match it. If he calumniate thy friends, do not thou calumniate his. If he banter, do not answer him in his own language, *lest thou be like him,* even thou, who knowest better things, who hast more sense, and hast been better taught." 2. Yet, in other cases, a wise man will use his wisdom for the conviction of a fool, when, by taking notice of what he says, there may be hopes of doing good, or at least preventing further, mischief, either to himself or others. "If thou have reason to think that thy silence will be deemed an evidence of the weakness of thy cause, or of thy own weakness, in such a case *answer him,* and let it be an answer *ad hominem — to the man,* beat him at his own weapons, and that will be an answer *ad rem — to the point,* or as good as one. If he offer any thing that looks like an argument, an answer that, and suit thy answer to his case. If he think, because thou dost not answer him, that what he says is unanswerable, then give him an answer, *lest he be wise in his own conceit* and boast of a victory." For (Lu. 7:35) Wisdom's children must justify her.

Verses 6–9

To recommend wisdom to us, and to quicken us to the diligent use of all the means for the getting of wisdom, Solomon here shows that fools are fit for nothing; they are either sottish men, who will never think and design at all, or vicious men, who will never think and design well. 1. They are not fit to be entrusted with any business, not fit to go on an errand (*v.* 6): *He that* does but *send a message by the hand of a fool,* of a careless heedless person, one who is so full of his jests and so given to his pleasures that he cannot apply his mind to any thing that is serious, will find his message misunderstood, the one half of it forgotten, the rest awkwardly delivered, and so many blunders made about it that he might as well have *cut off his legs,* that is, never have sent him. Nay, he will *drink damage;* it will be very much to his prejudice to have employed such a one, who, instead of bringing him a good account of his affairs, will abuse him and put a trick upon him; for, in Solomon's language, a knave and a fool are of the same signification. It will turn much to a man's disgrace to make use of the service of a fool, for people will be apt to judge of the master by his messenger. 2. They are not fit to have any honour put upon them. He had said (*v.* 1), *Honour is not seemly for a fool;* here he shows that it is lost and thrown away upon him, as if a man should throw a precious stone, or a stone fit to be used in weighing, into a heap of common stones, where it would be buried and of no use; it is as absurd as if a man should *dress up a stone in purple* (so others); nay, it is dangerous, it is like *a stone bound in a sling,* with which a man will be likely to do hurt. To *give honour to a fool* is to put a sword in a madman's hand, with which we know not what mischief he may do, even to those that put it into his hand. 3. They are not fit to deliver wise sayings, nor should they undertake to handle any matter of weight, though they should be instructed concerning it, and be able to say something to it. Wise sayings, as a foolish man delivers them and applies them (in such a manner that one may know he does not rightly understand them), lose their excellency and usefulness: *A parable in the mouth of fools* ceases to be a parable, and becomes a jest. If a man who lives a wicked life, yet speaks religiously and takes God's covenant into his mouth, (1.) He does but shame himself and his profession: As *the legs of the lame are not equal,* by reason of which their going is unseemly, so unseemly is it for a fool to pretend to speak apophthegms, and give advice, and for a man to talk devoutly whose conversation is a constant contradiction to his talk and gives him the lie. His good words raise him up, but then his bad life takes him down, and so his *legs are not equal.* "A wise saying," (says bishop Patrick) "doth as ill become a fool as dancing doth a cripple; for, as his lameness never so much appears as when he would seem nimble, so the other's folly is never so ridiculous as when he would seem wise." As therefore it is best for a lame man to keep his seat, so it is best for a silly man, or a bad man, to hold his tongue. (2.) He does but do mischief with it to himself and others, as a drunkard does with a thorn, or any other sharp thing which he takes in his hand, with which he tears himself and those about him, because he knows not how to manage it. Those that talk well and do not live well, their good words will aggravate their own condemnation and others will be hardened by their inconsistency with themselves. Some give this sense of it: The sharpest saying, by which a sinner, one would think, should be pricked to the heart, makes no more impression upon a fool, no, though it come out of his own mouth, than the scratch of a thorn does upon the hand of a man when he is drunk, who then feels it not nor complains of it, *ch.* 23:35.

Verse 10

Our translation gives this verse a different reading in the text and in the margin; and accordingly it expresses either, 1. The equity of a good God. The *Master,* or *Lord* (so *Rab* signifies), or, as we read it, *The great God that formed all things* at first, and still governs them in infinite wisdom, renders to every man according to his work. He *rewards the fool,* who sinned through ignorance, *who knew not his Lord's will, with few stripes;* and he *rewards the transgressor,* who sinned presumptuously and with a high hand, who *knew his Lord's will and would not do it, with many stripes.* Some understand it of the goodness of God's common providence even to fools and transgressors, on whom *he causes his sun to shine* and *his rain to fall.* Or, 2. The iniquity of a bad prince (so the margin reads it): *A great man grieves all, and he hires the fool; he hires also the transgressors.* When a wicked man gets power in his hand, by himself, and by the fools and knaves whom he employs under him, whom he hires and chooses to make use of, he grieves all who are under him and is vexatious to them. We should therefore *pray for kings and all in authority,* that, under them, our lives may be quiet and peaceable.

Verse 11

See here, 1. What an abominable thing sin is, and how hateful sometimes it is made to appear, even to the sinner himself. When his conscience is convinced, or he feels smart from his sin, he is sick of it, and vomits it up; he seems then to detest it and to be willing to part with it. It is in itself, and, first or last, will be to the sinner, more loathsome than the vomit of a dog, Ps. 36:2. 2. How apt sinners are to relapse into it notwithstanding. As the dog, after he has gained ease by vomiting that which burdened his stomach, yet goes and licks it up again, so sinners, who have been convinced only and not converted, return to sin again, forgetting how sick it made them. The apostle (2 Pt. 2:22) applies this proverb to those that *have known the way of righteousness* but are *turned from it;* but God will *spue them out of his mouth,* Rev. 3:16.

Verse 12

Here is, 1. A spiritual disease supposed, and that is self-conceit: *Seest thou a man?* Yes, we see many a one, *wise in his own conceit,* who has some little sense, but is proud of it, thinks it much more than it is, more than any of his neighbours, have, and enough, so that he needs no more, has such a conceit of his own abilities as makes him opinionative, dogmatical, and censorious; and all the use he makes of his knowledge is that it puffs him up. Or, if by a wise man we understand a religious man, it describes the character of those who, making some show of religion, conclude their spiritual state to be good when really it is very bad, like Laodicea, Rev. 3:17. 2. The danger of this disease. It is in a manner desperate: *There is more hope of a fool,* that knows and owns himself to be such, *than of* such a one. Solomon was not only a wise man himself, but a teacher of wisdom; and this observation he made upon his pupils, that he found his work most difficult and least successful with those that had a good opinion of themselves and were not sensible that they needed instruction. Therefore he that *seems* to himself *to be wise* must *become a fool, that he may be wise,* 1 Co. 3:18. There is more hope of a publican than of a proud Pharisee, Mt. 21:32. Many are hindered from being truly wise and religious by a false and groundless conceit that they are so, Jn. 9:40, 41.

Verse 13

When a man talks foolishly we say, He talks idly; for none betray their folly more than those who are idle and go about to excuse themselves in their idleness. As men's folly makes them slothful, so their slothfulness makes them foolish. Observe, 1. What *the slothful man* really dreads. He dreads *the way, the streets,* the place where work is to be done and a journey to be gone; he hates business, hates every thing that requires care and labour. 2. What he dreams of, and pretends to dread — *a lion in the way.* When he is pressed to be diligent, either in his worldly affairs or in the business of religion, this is his excuse (and a sorry excuse it is, as bad as none), *There is a lion in the way,* some insuperable difficulty or danger which he cannot pretend to grapple with. Lions frequent woods and deserts; and, in the day-time, when man has business to do, they are in their dens, Ps. 104:22, 23. But the sluggard fancies, or rather pretends to fancy, *a lion in the streets,* whereas the lion is only in his own fancy, nor is he so fierce as he is painted. Note, It is a foolish thing to frighten ourselves from real duties by fancied difficulties, Eccl. 11:4.

Verse 14

Having seen the slothful man in fear of his work, here we find him in love with his ease; he lies in his bed on one side till he is weary of that, and then turns to the other, but still in his bed, when it is far in the day and work is to be done, as the door is moved, but not removed; and so his business is neglected and his opportunities are let slip. See the sluggard's character. 1. He is one that does not care to get out of his bed, but seems to be hung upon it, *as the door upon the hinges.* Bodily ease, too much consulted, is the sad occasion of many a spiritual disease. Those that love sleep will prove in the end to have loved death. 2. He does not care to get forward with his business; in that he stirs to and fro a little, but to no purpose; he is where he was. Slothful professors turn, in profession, like *the door upon the hinges.* The world and the flesh are the two hinges on which they are hung, and though they move in a course of external services, have got into road of duties, and tread around in them like the horse in the mill, yet they get no good, they get no ground, they are never the nearer heaven — sinners unchanged, saints unimproved.

Verse 15

The sluggard has now, with much ado, got out of his bed, but he might as well have lain there still for any thing he is likely to bring to pass in his work, so awkwardly does he go about it. Observe, 1. The pretence he makes for his slothfulness: He *hides his hand in his bosom* for fear of cold; next to his warm bed in his warm bosom. Or he pretends that he is lame, as some do that make a trade of begging; something ails his hand; he would have it thought that it is blistered with yesterday's hard work. Or it intimates, in general, his aversion to business; he has tried, and his hands are not used to labour, and therefore he hugs himself in his own ease and cares for nobody. Note, It is common for those that will not do their duty to pretend they cannot. *I cannot dig,* Lu. 16:3. 2. The prejudice he sustains by his slothfulness. He himself is the loser by it, for he starves himself: *It grieves him to bring his hand to his mouth,* that is, he cannot find in his heart to feed himself, but dreads, as if it were a mighty toil, to lift his hand to his head. It is an elegant hyperbole, aggravating his sin, that he cannot endure to take the least pains, no, not for the greatest profit, and showing how his sin is his punishment. Those that are slothful in the business of religion will not be at the pains to feed their own souls with the word of God, the bread of life, nor to fetch in promised blessings by prayer, though they might have them for the fetching.

Verse 16

Observe, 1. The high opinion which the sluggard has of himself, notwithstanding the gross absurdity and folly of his slothfulness: He thinks himself *wiser than seven men,* than seven wise men, for they are such as *can render a reason.* It is the wisdom of a man to be able to *render a reason,* of a good man to be able to give *a reason of the hope that is in him,* 1 Pt. 3:15. What we do we should be able to *render a reason* for, though perhaps we may not have wit enough to show the fallacy of every objection against it. He that takes pains in religion can render a good reason for it; he knows that he is working for a good Master and that *his labour shall not be in vain.* But *the sluggard* thinks himself *wiser than seven* such; for let seven such persuade him to be diligent, with all the reasons they can render for it, it is to no purpose; his own determination, he thinks, answer enough to them and all their reasons. 2. The reference that this has to his slothfulness. It is *the sluggard,* above all men, that is thus self-conceited; for, (1.) His good opinion of himself is the cause of his slothfulness; he will not take pains to get wisdom because he thinks he is wise enough already. A conceit of the sufficiency of our attainments is a great enemy to our improvement. (2.) His slothfulness is the cause of his good opinion of himself. If he would but take pains to examine himself, and compare himself with the laws of wisdom, he would have other thoughts of himself. Indulged slothfulness is at the bottom of prevailing self-conceitedness. Nay, (3.) So wretchedly besotted is he that he takes his slothfulness to be his wisdom; he thinks it is his wisdom to make much of himself, and take all the ease he can get, and do no more in religion than he needs must, to avoid suffering, to sit still and see what other people do, that he may have the pleasure of finding fault with them. Of such sluggards, who are proud of that which is their shame, their is little hope, *v.* 12.

Verse 17

1. That which is here condemned is *meddling with strife that belongs not to us.* If we must not be hasty to strive in our own cause (*ch.* 25:8), much less in other people's, especially theirs that we are no way related to or concerned in, but light on accidentally as we pass by. If we can be instrumental to make peace between those that are at variance we must do it, though we should thereby get the ill-will of both sides, at least while they are in their heat; but to make ourselves busy in other men's matters, and parties in other men's quarrels, is not only to court our own trouble, but to thrust ourselves into temptation. *Who made* me *a judge?* Let them end it, as they began it, between themselves. 2. We are cautioned against it because of the danger it exposes us to; it is like taking a snarling cur *by the ears,* that will snap at you and bite you; you had better have let him alone, for you cannot get clear of him when you would, and must thank yourselves if you come off with a wound and dishonour. He that has got *a dog by the ears,* if he lets him go he flies at him, if he keeps his hold, he has his hands full, and can do nothing else. Let every one *with quietness work and mind his own business,* and not with unquietness quarrel and meddle with other people's business.

Verses 18–19

See here, 1. How mischievous those are that make no scruple of *deceiving their neighbours;* they are *as madmen that cast firebrands, arrows, and death,* so much hurt may they do by their deceits. They value themselves upon it as polite cunning men, but really they are *as madmen.* There is not a greater madness in the world than a wilful sin. It is not only the passionate furious man, but the malicious deceitful man, that is *a madman;* he does in effect *cast fire-brands, arrows, and death;* he does more mischief than he can imagine. Fraud and falsehood burn like firebrands, kill, even at a distance, like arrows. 2. See how frivolous the excuse is which men commonly make for the mischief they do, that they did it in a jest; with this they think to turn it off when they are reproved for it, *Am not I in sport?* But it will prove dangerous playing with fire and jesting with edge-tools. Not that those are to be commended who are captious, and can take no jest (those that themselves are *wise must suffer fools,* 2 Co. 11:19, 20), but those are certainly to be condemned who are any way abusive to their neighbours, impose upon their credulity, cheat them in their bargains with them, tell lies to them or tell lies of them, give them ill language, or sully their reputation, and then think to excuse it by saying that they did but jest. *Am not I in sport?* He that sins in just must repent in earnest, or his sin will be his ruin. Truth is too valuable a thing to be sold for a jest, and so is the reputation of our neighbour. By lying and slandering in jest men learn themselves, and teach others, to lie and slander in earnest; and a false report, raised in mirth, may be spread in malice; besides, if a man may tell a lie to make himself merry, why not to make himself rich, and so *truth quite perishes,* and men *teach their tongues to tell lies,* Jer. 9:5. If men would consider that a lie comes from the devil, and brings to hell-fire, surely that would spoil the sport of it; it is *casting arrows and death* to themselves.

Verses 20–22

Contention is as a fire; it heats the spirit, burns up all that is good, and puts families and societies into a flame. Now here we are told how that fire is commonly kindled and kept burning, that we may avoid the occasions of strife and so prevent the mischievous consequences of it. If then we would keep the peace, 1. We must not give ear to *tale-bearers,* for they feed the fire of contention with fuel; nay, they spread it with combustible matter; the tales they carry are fireballs. Those who by insinuating base characters, revealing secrets, and misrepresenting words and actions, do what they can to make relations, friends, and neighbours, jealous one of another, to alienate them one from another, and sow discord among them, are to be banished out of families and all societies, and then strife will as surely cease as the fire will go out when it has no fuel; the contenders will better understand one another and come to a better temper; old stories will soon be forgotten when there are no new ones told to keep up the remembrance of them, and both sides will see how they have been imposed upon by a common enemy. Whisperers and backbiters are incendiaries not to be suffered. To illustrate this, he repeats (*v.* 22) what he had said before (*ch.* 18:8), that *the words of a tale-bearer are as wounds,* deep and dangerous wounds, wounds in the vitals. They wound the reputation of him who is belied, and perhaps the wound proves incurable, and even the plaster of a recantation (which yet can seldom be obtained) may not prove wide enough for it. They wound the love and charity which he to whom they are spoken ought to have for his neighbour and give a fatal stab to friendship and Christian fellowship. We must therefore not only not be tale-bearers ourselves at any time, nor ever do any ill offices, but we should not give the least countenance to those that are. 2. We must not associate with peevish passionate people, that are exceptions, and apt to put the worst constructions upon everything, that pick quarrels upon the least occasion, and are quick, and high, and hot, in resenting affronts. These are *contentious men,* that *kindle strife, v.* 21. The less we have to do with such the better, for it will be very difficult to avoid quarrelling with those that are quarrelsome.

Verse 23

This may be meant either, 1. Of *a wicked heart* showing itself in *burning lips,* furious, passionate, outrageous words, burning in malice, and persecuting those to whom, or of whom, they are spoken; ill words and ill-will agree as well together as *a potsherd* and the *dross of silver,* which, now that the pot is broken and the dross separated from the silver, are fit to be thrown together to the dunghill. 2. Or of *a wicked heart* disguising itself with *burning lips,* burning with the professions of love and friendship, and even persecuting a man with flatteries; this is *like a potsherd covered with* the scum or *dross of silver,* with which one that is weak may be imposed upon, as if it were of some value, but a wise man is soon aware of the cheat. This sense agrees with the following verses.

Verses 24–26

There is cause to complain, not only of the want of sincerity in men's profession of friendship, and that they do not love so well as they pretend nor will serve their friends so much as they promise, but, which is much worse, of wicked designs in the profession of friendship, and the making of it subservient to the most malicious intentions. This is here spoken of as a common thing (*v.* 24): *He that hates* his neighbour, and is contriving to do him a mischief, yet *dissembles with his lips,* professes to have a respect for him and to be ready to serve him, talks kindly with him, as Cain with Abel, asks, *Art thou in health, my brother?* as Joab to Amasa, that his malice may not be suspected and guarded against, and so he may have the fairer opportunity to execute the purposes of it, this man *lays up deceit within him,* that is, he keeps in his mind the mischief he intends to do his neighbour till he catches him at an advantage. This is malice which has no less of the subtlety than it has of the venom of the old serpent in it. Now, as to this matter, we are here cautioned, 1. Not to be so foolish as to suffer ourselves to be imposed upon by the pretensions of friendship. Remember to distrust when a man *speaks fair;* be not too forward to *believe him* unless you know him well, for it is possible there may be *seven abominations in his heart,* a great many projects of mischief against you, which he is labouring so industriously to conceal with his fair speech. Satan is an enemy that hates us, and yet in his temptations speaks fair, as he did to Eve, but it is madness to give credit to him, *for there are seven abominations in his heart; seven other spirits* does one unclean spirit bring *more wicked than himself.* 2. Not to be so wicked as to impose upon any with a profession of friendship; for, though the fraud may be carried on plausibly awhile, it will be brought to light, *v.* 26. He *whose hatred is covered by deceit* will one time or other be discovered, and *his wickedness shown,* to his shame and confusion, *before the whole congregation;* and nothing will do more to make a man odious to all companies. Love (says one) is the best armour, but the worst cloak, and will serve dissemblers as the disguise which Ahab put on and perished in.

Verse 27

See here, 1. What pains men take to do mischief to others. As they put a force upon themselves by concealing their design with a profession of friendship, so they put themselves to a great deal of labour to bring it about; it is *digging a pit,* it is *rolling a stone,* hard work, and yet men will not stick at it to gratify their passion and revenge. 2. What preparation they hereby make of mischief to themselves. Their violent dealing will return upon their own heads; they shall themselves *fall into the pit they digged,* and the stone they rolled *will return upon them,* Ps. 7:15, 16; 9:15, 16. The righteous God will take the wise, not only *in their own craftiness,* but in their own cruelty. It is the plotter's doom. Haman is hanged on a gallows of his own preparing.

> — nec lex est justior ulla
> Quam necis artifices arte perire sua —
>
> Nor is there any law more just than that
> the contrivers of destruction should perish
> by their own arts.

Verse 28

There are two sorts of lies equally detestable: — 1. A slandering lie, which avowedly hates those it is spoken of: *A lying tongue hates those that are afflicted by it;* it afflicts them by calumnies and reproaches because it hates them, and can thus smite them secretly where they are without defence; and it hates them because it has afflicted them and made them its enemies. The mischief of this is open and obvious; it afflicts, it hates, and owns it, and every body sees it. 2. A flattering lie, which secretly works the ruin of those it is spoken to. In the former the mischief is plain, and men guard against it as well as they can, but in this it is little suspected, and men betray themselves by being credulous of their own praises and the compliments that are passed upon them. A wise man therefore will be more afraid of a flatterer that kisses and kills than of a slanderer that proclaims war.

CHAPTER 27

Verse 1

Here is, 1. A good caution against presuming upon time to come: *Boast not thyself,* no, not *of to-morrow,* much less of many days or years to come. This does not forbid preparing for to-morrow, but presuming upon to-morrow. We must not promise ourselves the continuance of our lives and comforts till to-morrow, but speak of it with submission to the will of God and as those who with good reason are kept at uncertainty about it. We must not *take thought for the morrow* (Mt. 6:34), but we must cast our care concerning it upon God. See James 4:13–15. We must not put off the great work of conversion, that one thing needful, till to-morrow, as if we were sure of it, *but to-day, while it is called to-day,* hear God's voice. 2. A good consideration, upon which this caution is grounded: *We know not what a day may bring forth,* what event may be in the teeming womb, of time; it is a secret till it is born, Eccl. 11:5. A little time may produce considerable changes, and such as we little think of. We *know not what* the present *day may bring forth;* the evening must commend it. *Nescis quid serus vesper vehat — Thou knowest not what the close of evening may bring with it.* God has wisely kept us in the dark concerning future events, and reserved to himself the knowledge of them, as a flower of the crown, that he may train us up in a dependence upon himself and a continued readiness for every event, Acts 1:7.

Verse 2

Note, 1. We must do that which is commendable, for which even strangers may praise us. Our *light* must *shine before men,* and we must do good works that may be seen, though we must not do them on purpose that they may be seen. Let our own works be such as will praise us, even *in the gates,* Phil. 4:8. 2. When we have done it we must not commend ourselves, for that is an evidence of pride, folly, and self-love, and a great lessening to a man's reputation. Every one will be forward to run him down that cries himself up. There may be a just occasion for us to vindicate ourselves, but it does not become us to applaud ourselves. *Proprio laus sordet in ore — Self-praise defiles the mouth.*

Verses 3–4

These two verses show the intolerable mischief, 1. Of ungoverned passion. The wrath of a fool, who when he is provoked cares not what he says and does, is more grievous than a great stone or a load of sand. It lies heavily upon himself. Those who have no command of their passions do themselves even sink under the load of them. The wrath of a fool lies heavily upon those he is enraged at, to whom, in his fury, he will be in danger of doing some mischief. It is therefore our wisdom not to give provocation to a fool, but, if he be in a passion, to get out of his way. 2. Of rooted malice, which is as much worse than the former as coals of juniper are worse than a fire of thorns. *Wrath* (it is true) *is cruel,* and does many a barbarous thing, *and anger is outrageous;* but a secret enmity at the person of another, an envy at his prosperity, and a desire of revenge for some injury or affront, are much more mischievous. One may avoid a sudden heat, as David escaped Saul's javelin, but when it grows, as Saul's did, to a settled envy, there is no *standing before it;* it will pursue; it will overtake. He that grieves at the good of another will be still contriving to do him hurt, and will keep his anger for ever.

Verses 5–6

Note, 1. It is good for us to be reproved, and told of our faults, by our friends. If true love in the heart has but zeal and courage enough to show itself in dealing plainly with our friends, and reproving them for what they say and do amiss, this is really *better,* not only than secret hatred (as Lev. 19:17), but *than secret love,* that love to our neighbours which does not show itself in this good fruit, which compliments them in their sins, to the prejudice of their souls. *Faithful are the reproofs of a friend,* though for the present they are painful as *wounds.* It is a sign that our friends are faithful indeed if, in love to our souls, they will not suffer sin upon us, nor let us alone in it. The physician's care is to cure the patient's disease, not to please his palate. 2. It is dangerous to be caressed and flattered by *an enemy,* whose *kisses are deceitful* We can take no pleasure in them because we can put no confidence in them (Joab's kiss and Judas's were deceitful), and therefore we have need to stand upon our guard, that we be not deluded by them; they are to be deprecated. Some read it: *The Lord deliver us from an enemy's kisses, from lying lips, and from a deceitful tongue.*

Verse 7

Solomon here, as often in this book, shows that the poor have in some respects the advantage of the rich; for, 1. They have a better relish of their enjoyments than the rich have. Hunger is the best sauce. Coarse fare, with a good appetite to it has a sensible pleasantness in it, which those are strangers to whose hearts are *overcharged with surfeiting.* Those that fare sumptuously every day nauseate even delicate food, as the Israelites did the quails; whereas those that have no more than their necessary food, though it be such as *the full soul* would call *bitter,* to them it *is sweet;* they eat it with pleasure, digest it, and are refreshed by it. 2. They are more thankful for their enjoyments: *The hungry* will bless God for bread and water, while those that are *full* think the greatest dainties and varieties scarcely worth giving thanks for. The virgin Mary seems to refer to this when she says (Lu. 1:53), *The hungry,* who know how to value God's blessings, *are filled with good things,* but *the rich,* who despise them, are justly *sent empty away.*

Verse 8

Note, 1. There are many that do not know when they are well off, but are uneasy with their present condition, and given to change. God, in his providence, has appointed them a place fit for them and has made it comfortable to them; but they affect unsettledness; they love to wander; they are glad of a pretence to go abroad, and do not care for staying long at a place; they needlessly absent themselves from their own work and care, and meddle with that which belongs not to them. 2. Those that thus desert the post assigned to them are like *a bird that wanders from her nest.* It is an instance of their folly; they are like a silly bird; they are always wavering, like the wandering bird that hops from bough to bough and rests nowhere. It is unsafe; the bird that wanders is exposed; a man's place is his castle; he that quits it makes himself an easy prey to the fowler. When the bird wanders from her nest the eggs and young ones there are neglected. Those that love to be abroad leave their work at home undone. *Let every man therefore, in the calling wherein he is called, therein abide,* therein abide *with God.*

Verses 9–10

Here is, 1. A charge given to be faithful and constant to our friends, our old friends, to keep up an intimacy with them, and to be ready to do them all the offices that lie in our power. It is good to have a friend, a bosom-friend, whom we can be free with, and with whom we may communicate counsels. It is not necessary that this friend should be a relation, or any way akin to us, though it is happiest when, among those who are so, we find one fit to make a friend of. Peter and Andrew were brethren, so were James and John; yet Solomon frequently distinguishes between a friend and a brother. But it is advisable to choose a friend among our neighbours who live near us, that acquaintance may be kept up and kindnesses the more frequently interchanged. It is good also to have a special respect to those who have been friends to our family: *"Thy own friend,* especially if he have been *thy father's friend, forsake not;* fail not both to serve him and to use him, as there is occasion. He is a tried friend; he knows thy affairs; he has a particular concern for thee; therefore be advised by him." It is a duty we owe to our parents, when they are gone, to love their friends and consult with them. Solomon's son undid himself by forsaking the counsel of his father's friends. 2. A good reason given why we should thus value true friendship and be choice of it. (1.) Because of the pleasure of it. There is a great deal of *sweetness* in conversing and consulting with a cordial friend. It is like *ointment and perfume,* which are very grateful to the smell, and exhilarate the spirits. It *rejoices the heart;* the burden of care is made lighter by unbosoming ourselves to our friend, and it is a great satisfaction to us to have his sentiments concerning our affairs. *The sweetness of* friendship lies not in hearty mirth, and hearty laughter, but in *hearty counsel,* faithful advice, sincerely given and without flattery, *by counsel of the soul* (so the word is), counsel which reaches the case, and comes to the heart,

counsel about soul-concerns, Ps. 66:16. We should reckon that the most pleasant conversation which is about spiritual things, and promotes the prosperity of the soul. (2.) Because of the profit and advantage of it, especially in a *day of calamity.* We are here advised not to go into a *brother's house,* not to expect relief from a kinsman merely for kindred-sake, for the obligation of that commonly goes little further than calling cousin and fails when it comes to the trial of a real kindness, but rather to apply ourselves to our neighbours, who are at hand, and will be ready to help us at an exigence. It is wisdom to oblige them by being neighbourly, and we shall have the benefit of it in distress, by finding them so to us, ch. 18:24.

Verse 11

Children are here exhorted to be wise and good, 1. That they may be a comfort to their parents and may *make their hearts glad,* even when *the evil days come,* and so recompense them for their care, ch. 23:15. 2. That they may be a credit to them: *"That I may answer him that reproaches me* with having been over-strict and severe in bringing up my children, and having taken a wrong method with them in restraining them from the liberties which other young people take. *My son, be wise,* and then it will appear, in the effect, that I went the wisest way to work with my children." Those that have been blessed with a religious education should in every thing conduct themselves so as to be a credit to their education and to silence those who say, *A young saint, an old devil;* and to prove the contrary, *A young saint, an old angel.*

Verse 12

This we had before, ch. 22:3. Note, 1. Evil may be foreseen. Where there is temptation, it is easy to foresee that if we thrust ourselves into it there will be sin, and as easy to foresee that if we venture upon the evil of sin there will follow the evil of punishment; and, commonly, God warns before he wounds, having *set watchmen over us,* Jer. 6:17. 2. It will be well or ill with us according as we do or do not improve the foresight we have of evil before us: The *prudent man, foreseeing the evil,* forecasts accordingly, *and hides himself, but the simple* is either so dull that he does not foresee it or so wilful and slothful that he will take no care to avoid it, and so he *passes on* securely *and is punished.* We do well for ourselves when we provide for hereafter.

Verse 13

This also we had before, ch. 20:16. 1. It shows who those are that are hastening to poverty, those that have so little consideration as to be bound for every body that will ask them and those that are given to women. Such as these will take up money as far as ever their credit will go, but they will certainly cheat their creditors at last, nay, they are cheating them all along. An honest man may be made a beggar, but he is not honest that makes himself one. 2. It advises us to be so discreet in ordering our affairs as not to lend money to those who are manifestly wasting their estates, unless they give very good security for it. Foolish lending is injustice to our families. He does not say, "Get another to be bound with him," for he that makes himself a common voucher will have those to be his security who are as insolvent as himself; therefore *take his garment.*

Verse 14

Note, 1. It is a great folly to be extravagant in praising even the best of our friends and benefactors. It is our duty to give every one his due praise, to applaud those who excel in knowledge, virtue, and usefulness, and to acknowledge the kindnesses we have received with thankfulness; but to do this *with a loud voice, rising early in the morning,* to be always harping on this string, in all companies, even to our friend's face, or so as that he may be sure to hear it, to do it studiously, as we do that which we rise early to, to magnify the merits of our friend above measure and with hyperboles, is fulsome, and nauseous, and savours of hypocrisy and design. Praising men for what they have done is only to get more out of them; and every body concludes the parasite hopes to be well paid for his panegyric or epistle dedicatory. We must not give that praise to our friend which is due to God only, as some think

is intimated in *rising early* to do it; for in the morning God is to be praised. We must not *make too much haste to praise men* (so some understand it), not cry up men too soon for their abilities and performances, but let them first be proved; lest they be lifted up with pride, and laid to sleep in idleness. 2. It is a greater folly to be fond of being ourselves extravagantly praised. A wise man rather counts it *a curse,* and a reflection upon him, not only designed to pick his pocket, but which may really turn to his prejudice. Modest praises (as a great man observes) invite such as are present to add to the commendation, but immodest immoderate praises tempt them to detract rather, and to censure one that they hear over-commended. And, besides, over-praising a man makes him the object of envy; every man puts in for a share of reputation, and therefore reckons himself injured if another monopolize it or have more given him than his share. And the greatest danger of all is that it is a temptation to pride; men are apt to think of themselves above what is meet when others speak of them above what is meet. See how careful blessed Paul was not to be over-valued, 2 Co. 12:6.

Verses 15–16

Here, as before, Solomon laments the case of him that has a peevish passionate wife, that is continually chiding, and making herself and all about her uneasy. 1. It is a grievance that there is no avoiding, for it is like *a continual dropping in a very rainy day.* The contentions of a neighbour may be like a sharp shower, troublesome for the time, yet, while it lasts, one may take shelter; but *the contentions of a wife* are like a constant soaking rain, for which there is no remedy but patience See ch. 19:13. 2. It is a grievance that there is no concealing. A wise man would hide it if he could, for the sake both of his own and his wife's reputation, but he cannot, any more than he can conceal the noise of the wind when it blows or the smell of a strong perfume. Those that are froward and brawling will proclaim their own shame, even when their friends, in kindness to them, would cover it.

Verse 17

This intimates both the pleasure and the advantage of conversation. One man is nobody; nor will poring upon a book in a corner accomplish a man as the reading and studying of men will. Wise and profitable discourse sharpens men's wits; and those that have ever so much knowledge may by conference have something added to them. It sharpens men's looks, and, by cheering the spirits, puts a briskness and liveliness into the countenance, and gives a man such an air as shows he is pleased himself and makes him pleasing to those about him. Good men's graces are sharpened by converse with those that are good, and bad men's lusts and passions are sharpened by converse with those that are bad, as iron is sharpened by its like, especially by the file. Men are filed, made smooth, and bright, and fit for business (who were rough, and dull, and inactive), by conversation. This is designed, 1. To recommend to us this expedient for sharpening ourselves, but with a caution to take heed whom we choose to converse with, because the influence upon us is so great either for the better or for the worse. 2. To direct us what we must have in our eye in conversation, namely to improve both others and ourselves, not to pass away time or banter one another, but to *provoke one another to love and to good works* and so to make one another wiser and better.

Verse 18

This is designed to encourage diligence, faithfulness, and constancy, even in mean employments. Though the calling be laborious and despicable, yet those who keep to it will find there is something to be got by it. 1. Let not a poor gardener, who *keeps the fig-tree,* be discouraged; though it require constant care and attendance to nurse up fig-trees, and, when they have grown to maturity, to keep them in good order, and gather the figs in their season, yet he shall be paid for his pains: He *shall eat the fruit* of it, 1 Co. 9:7. 2. Nay, let not a poor servant think himself incapable of thriving and being preferred; for if he be diligent in *waiting on his master,* observant of him and obedient to him, if *he keep his master* (so the word is), if he do all he can for the securing of his person and reputation and take care that his estate be not wasted or damaged, such a one *shall be honoured,* shall not only get a good word, but be preferred and rewarded. God is a Master who has engaged to put an honour on those that serve him faithfully, Jn. 12:26.

Verse 19

This shows us that there is a way, 1. Of knowing ourselves. As the water is a looking-glass in which we may see our faces by reflection, so there are mirrors by which the *heart of a man* is discovered to *a man,* that is, to himself. Let a man examine his own conscience, his thoughts, affections, and intentions. Let him behold his *natural face in the glass* of the divine law (Jam. 1:23), and he may discern what kind of man he is and what is his true character, which it will be of great use to every man rightly to know. 2. Of knowing one another by ourselves; for, as there is a similitude between the face of a man and the reflection of it in the water, so there is between one man's heart and another's for God has fashioned men's hearts alike; and in many cases we may judge of others by ourselves, which is one of the foundations on which that rule is built of doing to others as we would be done by, Ex. 23:9 *Nihil est unum uni tam simile, tam par, quam omnes inter nosmet ipsos sumus. Sui nemo ipse tam similis quam omnes sunt omnium — No one thing is so like another as man is to man. No person is so like himself as each person is to all besides. Cic. de Legib. lib.* 1. One corrupt heart is like another, and so is one sanctified heart, for the former bears the same image of the earthy, the latter the same image of the heavenly.

Verse 20

Two things are here said to be insatiable, and they are two things near of kin — death and sin. 1. Death is insatiable. The first death, the second death, both are so. The grave is not clogged with the multitude of dead bodies that are daily thrown into it, but is still an *open sepulchre,* and cries, *Give, give.* Hell also has enlarged itself, and still has room for the damned spirits that are committed to that prison. *Tophet is deep and large,* Isa. 30:33. 2. Sin is insatiable: *The eyes of man are never satisfied,* nor the appetites of the carnal mind towards profit or pleasure. The *eye is not satisfied with seeing,* nor is he the *loves silver satisfied with silver.* Men labour for that which surfeits, but satisfies not; nay, it is dissatisfying; but satisfies not; nay, it is dissatisfying; such a perpetual uneasiness have men justly been doomed to ever since our first parents were not satisfied with all the trees of Eden, but they must meddle with the forbidden tree. Those whose eyes are ever toward the Lord in him are satisfied, and shall for ever be so.

Verse 21

This gives us a touchstone by which we may try ourselves. Silver and gold are tried by putting them into the furnace and fining-pot; so is man tried by praising him. Let him be extolled and preferred, and then he will show himself what he is. 1. If a man be made, by the applause that is given him, proud, conceited, and scornful, — if he take the glory to himself which he should transmit to God, as Herod did, — if, the more he is praised, the more careless he is of what he says and does, — if he *lie in bed till noon* because *his name is up,* thereby it will appear that he is a vain foolish man, and a man who, though he be praised, has nothing in him truly praise-worthy. 2. If, on the contrary, a man is made by his praise more thankful to God, more respectful to his friends, more watchful against every thing that may blemish his reputation, more diligent to improve himself, and do good to others, that he may answer the expectations of his friends from him, by this it will appear that he is a wise and good man. He has a good temper of mind who knows how to pass by evil report and good report, and is still the same, 2 Co. 6:8.

Verse 22

Solomon had said (*ch.* 22:15), *The foolishness* which *is bound in the heart of a child may be driven out by the rod of correction,* for then the mind is to be moulded, the vicious habits not having taken root; but here he shows that, if it be not done then, it will be next to impossible to do it afterwards; if the disease be inveterate, there is a danger of its being incurable. *Can the Ethiopian change his skin?* Observe, 1. Some are so bad that rough and severe methods must be used with them, after gentle means have been tried in vain; they must be *brayed in a mortar.* God will take this way with them by his judgments; the magistrates must take this way with them by the rigour of the law. Force must be used with those that will not be ruled by reason, and love, and their own interest. 2. Some are so incorrigibly bad that even those rough and severe methods do not answer the end, their *foolishness will not depart from them,* so fully are their *hearts set in them to do evil;* they are often under the rod and yet not humbled, in the furnace and yet not refined, but, like Ahaz, trespass yet more (2 Chr. 28:22); and what remains then but that they should be rejected as reprobate silver?

Verses 23–27

Here is, I. A command given us to be diligent in our callings. It is directed to husbandmen and shepherds, and those that deal in cattle, but it is to be extended to all other lawful callings; whatever our business is, within doors or without, we must apply our minds to it. This command intimates, 1. That we ought to have some business to do in this world and not to live in idleness. 2. We ought rightly and fully to understand our business, and know what we have to do, and not meddle with that which we do not understand. 3. We ought to have an eye to it ourselves, and not turn over all the care of it to others. We should, with our own eyes, inspect the *state of our flocks,* it is the master's eye that makes them fat. 4. We must be discreet and considerate in the management of our business, *know the state* of things, and *look well* to them, that nothing may be lost, no opportunity let slip, but every thing done in proper time and order, and so as to turn to the best advantage. 5. We must be *diligent* and take pains; not only sit down and contrive, but be up and doing: "Set thy heart to thy herds, as one in care; lay thy hands, lay thy bones, to thy business."

II. The reasons to enforce this command. Consider,

1. The uncertainty of worldly wealth (*v.* 24): *Riches are not for ever.* (1.) Other riches are not so durable as these are: *"Look well to thy flocks and herds,* thy estate in the country and the stock upon that, for these are staple commodities, which, in a succession, will be for ever, whereas riches in trade and merchandise will not be so; the *crown* itself may perhaps not be so sure to thy family as thy flocks and herds." (2.) Even these riches will go to decay if they be not well looked after. If a man had *an abbey* (as we say), and were slothful and wasteful, he might make an end of it. Even the crown and the revenues of it, if care be not taken, will suffer damage, nor will it *continue to every generation* without very good management. Though David had the crown entailed on his family, yet he *looked well to his flocks,* 1 Chr. 27:29, 31.

2. The bounty and liberality of nature, or rather of the God of nature, and his providence (*v.* 25): *The hay appears.* In taking care of the *flocks and herds,* (1.) "There needs no great labour, no ploughing or sowing; the food for them is the spontaneous product of the ground; thou hast nothing to do but to turn them into it in the summer, *when the grass shows itself,* and to *gather the herbs of the mountains* for them against winter. God has done his part; thou art ungrateful to him, and unjustly refusest to serve his providence, if thou dost not do thine." (2.) "There is an opportunity to be observed and improved, a time when *the hay appears;* but, if thou let slip that time, thy flocks and herds will fare the worse for it. As for ourselves, so for our cattle, we ought, with the ant, to provide meat in summer."

3. The profit of good husbandry in a family: "Keep thy sheep, and thy sheep will help to keep thee; thou shalt have food for thy children and servants, *goats' milk enough* (*v.* 27); and *enough is as good as a feast.* Thou shalt have raiment likewise: the *lambs' wool shall be for thy clothing.* Thou shalt have money to pay thy rent; the goats thou shalt have to sell shall be *the price of thy field;"* nay, as some understand it, *"Thou shalt become a purchaser,* and buy land to leave to thy children," (*v.* 26). Note, (1.) If we have food and raiment, and wherewithal to give every body his own, we have enough, and ought to be not only content, but thankful. (2.) Masters of families must provide not only for themselves, but for their families, and see that their servants have a fitting maintenance. (3.) Plain food and plain clothing, if they be but competent, are all we should aim at. "Reckon thyself well done to if thou be clothed with home-spun cloth with the fleece of thy own lambs, and fed with goats' milk; let that serve for thy food which serves for the *food of thy household and the maintenance of thy maidens.* Be not desirous of dainties, *far-fetched and dear-bought."* (4.) This should encourage us to be careful and industrious about our business, that that will bring in a sufficient maintenance for our families; we shall *eat the labour of our hands.*

CHAPTER 28

Verse 1

See here, 1. What continual frights those are subject to that go on in wicked ways. Guilt in the conscience makes men a terror to themselves, so that they are ready *to flee when none pursues;* like one that absconds for debt, who thinks every one he meets a bailiff. Though they pretend to be easy, there are secret fears which haunt them wherever they go, so that they fear where no present or imminent danger is, Ps. 53:5. Those that have made God their enemy, and know it, cannot but see the whole creation at war with them, and therefore can have no true enjoyment of themselves, no confidence, no courage, but a *fearful looking for of judgment.* Sin makes men cowards.

> Degeneres animos timor arguit —
> Fear argues a degenerate soul. — Virgil
>
> Quos diri conscia facti mens habet attonitos —
> The consciousness of atrocious crimes astonishes
> and confounds. — Juvenal

If they flee when none pursues, what will they do when they shall see God himself pursuing them with his armies? Job 20:24; 15:24. See Deu. 28:25; Lev. 26:36. 2. What a holy security and serenity of mind those enjoy who *keep conscience void of offence* and so keep themselves in the love of God: *The righteous are bold as a lion,* as a young lion; in the greatest dangers they have a God of almighty power to trust to. *Therefore will not we fear though the earth be removed.* Whatever difficulties they meet with in the way of their duty, they are not daunted by them. *None of those things move me.*

> Hie murus aheneus esto, nil conscire sibi —
> Be this thy brazen bulwark of defence,
> Still to preserve thy conscious innocence. — Hon.

Verse 2

Note, 1. National sins bring national disorders and the disturbance of the public repose: *For the transgression of a land,* and a general defection from God and religion to idolatry, profaneness, or immorality, *many are the princes thereof,* many at the same time pretending to the sovereignty and contending for it, by which the people are crumbled into parties and factions, biting and devouring one another, or many successively, in a little time, one cutting off another, as 1 Ki. 16:8, etc., or soon cut off by the hand of God or of a foreign enemy, as 2 Ki. 24:5, etc. As the people suffer for the sins of the prince,

> Delirant reges, plectuntur Achivi —
> Kings play the madmen, and their people suffer for it,

so the government sometimes suffers for the sins of the people. 2. Wisdom will prevent or redress these grievances: *By a man,* that is, by a people, *of understanding,* that come again to themselves and their right mind, things are kept in a good order, or, if disturbed, brought back to the old channel again. Or, By a prince of *understanding and knowledge,* a privy-counsellor, or minister of state, that will restrain or suppress *the transgression of the land,* and take the right methods of healing the state thereof, the good estate of it will be prolonged. We cannot imagine what a great deal of service one wise man may do to a nation in a critical juncture.

Verse 3

See here, 1. How hard-hearted poor people frequently are to one another, not only not doing such good offices as they might do one to another, but imposing upon and over-reaching one another. Those who know by experience the miseries of poverty should be compassionate to those who suffer the like, but they are inexcusably barbarous if they be injurious to them. 2. How imperious and griping those commonly are who, being indigent and necessitous, get into power. If a prince prefer a poor man, he forgets that ever he was poor, and none shall be so oppressive to the poor as he, nor squeeze them so cruelly. The hungry leech and the dry sponge suck most. *Set a beggar on horseback, and he will ride* without mercy. He *is like a sweeping rain,* which washes away the corn in the ground, and lays and beats out that which has grown, so that it *leaves no food.* Princes therefore ought not to put those into places of trust who are poor, and in debt, and behind-hand in the world, nor any who make it their main business to enrich themselves.

Verse 4

Note, 1. Those that *praise the wicked* make it to appear that they do themselves *forsake the law,* and go contrary to it, for that curses and condemns the wicked. Wicked people will speak well of one another, and so strengthen one another's hands in their wicked ways, hoping thereby to silence the clamours of their own consciences and to serve the interests of the devil's kingdom, which is not done by any thing so effectually as by keeping vice in reputation. 2. Those that do indeed make conscience of the law of God themselves will, in their places, vigorously oppose sin, and bear their testimony against it, and do what they can to shame and suppress it. They will reprove the works of darkness, and silence the excuses which are made for those works, and do what they can to bring gross offenders to punishment, that others may hear and fear.

Verse 5

Note, I. As the prevalency of men's lusts is owing to the darkness of their understandings, so the darkness of their understandings is very much owing to the dominion of their lusts: *Men understand not judgment,* discern not between truth and falsehood, right and wrong; they understand not the law of God as the rule either of their duty or of their doom; and, 1. *Therefore* it is that they are *evil men;* their wickedness is the effect of their ignorance and error, Eph. 4:18. 2. *Therefore* they *understand not judgment,* because they are *evil men;* their corruptions blind their eyes, and fill them with prejudices, and because they do evil they *hate the light.* It is just with God also to *give them up to strong delusions.*

II. As men's *seeking the Lord* is a good sign that they do understand much, so it is a good means of their understanding more, even of their understanding all things needful for them. Those that set God's glory before them as their end, his favour as their felicity, and his word as their rule, and apply to him upon all occasions by prayer, *they seek the Lord,* and he will give them the spirit of wisdom. If a man *do his will,* he shall *know his doctrine,* Jn. 7:17. *A good understanding those have,* and a better they shall have, that *do his commandments,* Ps. 111:10; 1 Co. 2:12, 15.

Verse 6

Here, 1. It is supposed that a man may *walk in his uprightness* and yet be poor in this world, which is a temptation to dishonesty, and yet may resist the temptation and continue to *walk in his uprightness* — also that a man may be *perverse in his ways,* injurious to God and man, and yet be rich, and prosper in the world, for a while, may be rich, and so lie under great obligations and have great opportunities to do good, and yet be *perverse in his ways* and do a great deal of hurt. 2. It is maintained as a paradox to a blind world that an honest, godly, poor man, is better than a wicked, ungodly, rich man, has a better character, is in a better condition, has more comfort in himself, is a greater blessing to the world, and is worthy of much more honour and respect. It is not only certain that his case will be better at death, but it is better in life. When Aristides was by a rich man upbraided with his poverty he answered, *Thy riches do thee more hurt than my poverty does me.*

Verse 7

Note, 1. Religion is true wisdom, and it makes men wise in every relation. He that conscientiously *keeps the law* is wise, and he will be particularly *a wise son,* that is, will act discreetly towards his parents, for the law of God teaches him to do so. 2. Bad company is a great hindrance to religion. Those that are *companions of riotous men,* that

choose such for their companions and delight in their conversation, will certainly be drawn from *keeping the law of God* and drawn to transgress it, Ps. 119:115. 3. Wickedness is not only a reproach to the sinner himself, but to all that are akin to him. He that keeps rakish company, and spends his time and money with them, not only grieves his parents, but shames them; it turns to their disrepute, as if they had not done their duty to him. They are ashamed that a child of theirs should be scandalous and abusive to their neighbours.

Verse 8

Note, 1. That which is ill-got, though it may increase much, will not last long. A man may perhaps raise a great estate, in a little time, by usury and extortion, fraud, and oppression of the poor, but it will not continue; he gathers it for himself, but it shall prove to have been gathered for somebody else that he has no kindness for. His estate shall go to decay, and another man's shall be raised out of the ruins of it. 2. Sometimes God in his providence so orders it that that which one got unjustly another uses charitably; it is strangely turned into the hands of one *that will pity the poor* and do good with it, and so cut off the entail of the curse which he brought upon it who got it by deceit and violence. Thus the same Providence that punishes the cruel, and disables them to do any more hurt, rewards the merciful, and enables them to do so much the more good. *To him that has the ten pounds give the pound* which the wicked servant *hid in the napkin;* for *to him that has,* and uses it well, more *shall be given,* Lu. 19:24. Thus the poor are repaid, the charitable are encouraged, and God is glorified.

Verse 9

Note, 1. It is by the word and prayer that our communion with God is kept up. God speaks to us by his law, and expects we should hear him and heed him; *we* speak to him by prayer, to which we wait for an answer of peace. How reverent and serious should we be, whenever we are hearing from and speaking to the Lord of glory! 2. If God's word be not regarded by us, our prayers shall not only not be accepted of God, but they shall be an abomination to him, not only our sacrifices, which were ceremonial appointments, but even our prayers, which are moral duties, and which, when they are put up by the upright, are so much his delight. See Isa. 1:11, 15. The sinner whose prayers God is thus angry at is one who wilfully and obstinately refuses to obey God's commandments, who will not so much as give them the hearing, but causes his *ear to decline the law,* and refuses when God calls; God will therefore justly refuse him when he calls. See Prov. 1:24, 28.

Verse 10

Here is, 1. The doom of seducers, who attempt to draw good people, or those who profess to be such, into sin and mischief, who take pride in *causing the righteous to go astray in an evil way,* in drawing them into a snare, that they may insult over them. They shall not gain their point; it is impossible to deceive the elect. But they shall *fall themselves into their own pit;* and having been not only sinners, but tempters, not only unrighteous, but enemies to the righteous, their condemnation will be so much the greater, Mt. 23:14, 15. 2. The happiness of the sincere. They shall not only be preserved from the evil way which the wicked would decoy them into, but they shall *have good things,* the best things, *in possession,* the graces and comforts of God's Spirit, besides what they have in reversion.

Verse 11

Note, 1. Those that are rich are apt to think themselves wise, because, whatever else they are ignorant of, they know how to get and save; and those that are purse-proud expect that all they say should be regarded as an oracle and a law, and that none should dare to contradict them, but every sheaf bow to theirs; this humour is fed by flatterers, who, because (like Jezebel's prophets) they are fed at their table, cry up their wisdom. 2. Those that are poor often prove themselves wiser than they: A *poor man,* who has taken pains to get wisdom, having no other way (as the rich man has) to get a reputation, *searches him out,* and makes it to appear that he is not such a scholar, nor such a politician, as he is taken to be. See how variously

God dispenses his gifts; to some he gives wealth, to others wisdom, and it is easy to say which of these is the better gift, which we should *covet more earnestly.*

Verse 12

Note, 1. The comfort of the people of God is the honour of the nation in which they live. There is a *great glory* dwelling in the land when *the righteous do rejoice,* when they have their liberty, the free exercise of their religion, and are not persecuted, when the government countenances them and speaks comfortably to them, when they prosper and grow rich, and, much more, when they are preferred and employed and have power put into their hands. 2. The advancement of the wicked is the eclipsing of the beauty of a nation: *When the wicked rise* and get head they make head against all that is sacred, and then *a man is hidden,* a good man is thrust into obscurity, is necessitated to abscond for his own safety; corruptions prevail so generally that, as in Elijah's time, there seem to be no good men left, the *wicked walk* so thickly *on every side.*

Verse 13

Here is, 1. The folly of indulging sin, of palliating and excusing it, denying or extenuating it, diminishing it, dissembling it, or throwing the blame of it upon others: *He that* thus *covers his sins shall not prosper,* let him never expect it. He shall not succeed in his endeavour to cover his sin, for it will be discovered, sooner or later. *There is nothing hid which shall not be revealed.* A *bird of the air shall carry the voice.* Murder will out, and so will other sins. He *shall not prosper,* that is, he shall not obtain the pardon of his sin, nor can he have any true peace of conscience. David owns himself to have been in a constant agitation while he *covered his sins,* Ps. 32:3, 4. While the patient conceals his distemper he cannot expect a cure. 2. The benefit of parting with it, both by a penitent confession and a universal reformation: *He that confesses* his guilt to God, and is careful not to return to sin again, shall *find mercy* with God, and shall have the comfort of it in his own bosom. His conscience shall be eased and his ruin prevented. See 1 Jn. 1:9; Jer. 3:12, 13. When we set sin before our face (as David, *My sin is ever before me*) God casts it behind his back.

Verse 14

Here is, 1. The benefit of a holy caution. It sounds strangely, but it is very true: *Happy is the man that feareth always.* Most people think that those are happy who never fear; but there is a fear which is so far from having torment in it that it has in it the greatest satisfaction. Happy is the man who always keeps up in his mind a holy awe and reverence of God, his glory, goodness, and government, who is always afraid of offending God and incurring his displeasure, who keeps conscience tender and has a dread of the appearance of evil, who is always jealous of himself, distrustful of his own sufficiency, and lives in expectation of troubles and changes, so that, whenever they come, they are no surprise to him. He who keeps up such a fear as this will live a life of faith and watchfulness, and therefore happy is he, blessed and holy. 2. The danger of a sinful presumption: *He that hardens his heart,* that mocks at fear, and sets God and his judgments at defiance, and receives not the impressions of his word or rod, *shall fall into mischief;* his presumption will be his ruin, and whatever sin (which is the greatest mischief) he falls into it is owing to the hardness of his heart.

Verse 15

It is written indeed, *Thou shalt not speak evil of the ruler of thy people;* but if he be a wicked ruler, that oppresses the people, especially the poor people, robbing them of the little they have and making a prey of them, whatever we may call him, this scripture calls him *a roaring lion and a ranging bear.* 1. In respect of his character. He is brutish, barbarous, and blood-thirsty; he is rather to be put among the beasts of prey, the wildest and most savage, than to be reckoned of that noble rank of beings whose glory is reason and humanity. 2. In respect of the mischief he does to his subjects. He is dreadful as the *roaring lion,* who makes the forest tremble; he is devouring as a hungry *bear,* and the more necessitous he is the more mischief he does and the more greedy of gain he is.

Verse 16

Two things are here intimated to be the causes of the mal-administration of princes: — 1. The love of money, that *root of all evil;* for *hating covetousness* here stands opposed to *oppression,* according to Moses's character of good magistrates, *men fearing God and hating covetousness* (Ex. 18:21), not only not being covetous, but hating it, and shaking the hands from the holding of bribes. A ruler that is covetous will neither do justly nor love mercy, but the people under him shall be bought and sold. 2. Want of consideration: *He that hates covetousness shall prolong* his government and peace, shall be happy in the affections of his people and the blessing of his God. It is as much the interest as the duty of princes to reign in righteousness. Oppressors therefore and tyrants are the greatest fools in the world; they *want understanding;* they do not consult their own honour, ease, and safety, but sacrifice all to their ambition of an absolute and arbitrary power. They might be much happier in the hearts of their subjects than in their necks or estates.

Verse 17

This agrees with that ancient law, *Whoso sheddeth man's blood, by man shall his blood be shed* (Gen. 9:6), and proclaims, 1. The doom of the shedder of blood. He that has committed murder, though he flees for his life, shall be continually haunted with terrors, shall himself *flee to the pit,* betray himself, and torment himself, like Cain, who, when he had killed his brother, became a fugitive and a vagabond, and trembled continually. 2. The duty of the avenger of blood, whether the magistrate or the next of kin, or whoever are concerned in making inquisition for blood, let them be close and vigorous in the prosecution, and let it not be bought off. Those that acquit the murderer, or do any thing to help him off, come in sharers in the guilt of blood; nor can the land be purged from blood but by the blood of him that shed it, Num. 35:33.

Verse 18

Note, 1. Those that are honest are always safe. He that acts with sincerity, that speaks as he thinks, has a single eye, in every thing, to the glory of God and the good of his brethren, that would not, for a world, do an unjust thing if he knew it, that in all manner of conversation *walks uprightly,* he *shall be saved* hereafter. We find a glorious company of those *in whose mouth was found no guile,* Rev. 14:5. They shall be safe now. Integrity and uprightness will preserve men, will give them a holy security in the worst of times; for it will preserve their comfort, their reputation, and all their interests. They may be injured, but they cannot be hurt. 2. Those that are false and dishonest are never safe: *He that is perverse in his ways,* that thinks to secure himself by fraudulent practices, by dissimulation and treachery, or by an estate ill-got, he *shall fall,* nay, he *shall fall at once,* not gradually, and with warning given, but suddenly, without previous notice, for he is least safe when he is most secure. He *falls at once,* and so has neither time to guard against his ruin nor to provide for it; and, being a surprise upon him, it will be so much the greater terror to him.

Verse 19

Note, 1. Those that are diligent in their callings take the way to live comfortably: He that *tills his land,* and tends his shop, and minds his business, whatever it is, he *shall have plenty of bread,* of that which is necessary for himself and his family and with which he may be charitable to the poor; he shall *eat the labour of his hands.* 2. Those that are idle, and careless, and company-keepers, though they indulge themselves in living (as they think) easily and pleasantly, they take the way to live miserably. He that has land and values himself upon that, but does not till it, but *follows after vain persons,* drinks with them, joins with them in their frolics and vain sports, and idles away his time with him, he shall have *poverty enough,* shall be *satiated* or *replenished* with poverty (so the word is); he takes those courses which lead so directly to it that he seems to court it, and he shall have his fill of it.

Verse 20

Here, 1. We are directed in the true way to be happy, and that is to be holy and honest. He that is *faithful* to God and man shall be blessed of the Lord, and he *shall abound with blessings* of the upper and nether springs. Men shall praise him, and pray for him, and be ready to do him any kindness. He shall abound in doing good, and shall himself be a blessing to the place where he lives. Usefulness shall be the reward of faithfulness, and it is a good reward. 2. We are cautioned against a false and deceitful way to happiness, and that is, right or wrong, raising an estate suddenly. Say not, This is the way to *abound with blessings,* for *he that makes haste to be rich,* more haste than good speed, *shall not be innocent;* and, if he be not, he shall not be blessed of God, but rather bring a curse upon what he has; nor, if he be not innocent, can he long be easy to himself; he shall not be accounted innocent by his neighbours, but shall have their ill will and ill word. He does not say that he *cannot be innocent,* but there is all the probability in the world that he will not prove so: *He that hasteth with his feet sinneth,* stumbleth, falleth. *Sed quae reverentia legum, quis metus, aut pudor, est unquam properantis avari? — What reverence for law, what fear, what shame, was ever indicated by an avaricious man hasting to be rich?*

Verse 21

Note, 1. It is a fundamental error in the administration of justice, and that which cannot but lead men to abundance of transgression, to consider the parties concerned more than the merits of the cause, so as to favour one because he is a gentleman, a scholar, my countryman, my old acquaintance, has formerly done me a kindness, or may do me one, or is of my party and persuasion, and to bear hard on the other party because he is a stranger, a poor man, has done me an ill turn, is or has been my rival, or is not of my mind, or has voted against me. Judgment is perverted when any consideration of this kind is admitted into the scale, any thing but pure right. 2. Those that are partial will be paltry. Those that have once broken through the bonds of equity, though, at first, it must be some great bribe, some noble present, that would bias them, yet, when they have debauched their consciences, they will, at length, be so sordid that *for a piece of bread* they will give judgment against their consciences; they will rather play at small game than sit out.

Verse 22

Here again Solomon shows the sin and folly of those that will *be rich;* they are resolved that they will be so, *per fas, per nefas — right or wrong;* they will be so with all speed; they are getting hastily an estate. 1. They have no comfort in it: They *have an evil eye,* that is, they are always grieving at those that have more than they, and always grudging their necessary expenses, because they think the former keep them from seeming rich, the latter from being so, and between both they must needs be perpetually uneasy. 2. They have no assurance of the continuance of it, and yet take no thought to provide against the loss of it: *Poverty shall come upon* them, and the riches which they made wings for, that they might fly to them, will make themselves wings to fly from them; but they are secure and improvident, and do *not consider* this, that while they are making *haste to be rich* they are really making haste to be poor, else they would not *trust to uncertain riches.*

Verse 23

Note, 1. Flatterers may please those for a time who, upon second thoughts, will detest and despise them. If ever they come to be convinced of the evil of those sinful courses they were flattered in, and to be ashamed of the pride and vanity which were humoured and gratified by those flatteries, they will hate the fawning flatterers as having had an ill design upon them, and the fulsome flatteries as having had an ill effect upon them and become nauseous. 2. Reprovers may displease those at first who yet afterwards, when the passion is over and the bitter physic begins to work well, will love and respect them. He that deals faithfully with his friend, in telling him of his faults, though he may put him into some heat for the present, and perhaps have hard words, instead of thanks, for his pains, yet afterwards he will not only have the comfort in his own bosom of having done his duty, but he also whom he reproved will acknowledge that it was a kindness, will entertain a high opinion of his wisdom and faithfulness, and look upon him as fit to be a friend. He that cries out against his surgeon for hurting him when he is searching his wound will yet pay him well, and thank him too, when he has cured it.

Verse 24

As Christ shows the absurdity and wickedness of those children who think it is no duty, in some cases, to maintain their parents (Mt. 15:5), so Solomon here shows the absurdity and wickedness of those who think it is no sin to rob their parents, either by force or secretly, by wheedling them or threatening them, or by wasting what they have, and (which is no better than robbing them) running into debt and leaving them to pay it. Now, 1. This is commonly made light of by untoward children; they say, *"It is no transgression,* for it will be our own shortly, our parents can well enough spare it, we have occasion for it, we cannot live as gentlemen upon the allowance our parents give us, it is too strait for us." With such excuses as these they endeavour to shift off the conviction. But, 2. How lightly soever an ungoverned youth makes of it, it is really a very great sin; he that does it *is the companion of a destroyer,* no better than a robber on the highway. What wickedness will he scruple to commit who will rob his own parents?

Verse 25

Note, 1. Those make themselves lean, and continually unquiet, that are haughty and quarrelsome, for they are opposed to those that *shall be made fat: He that is of a proud heart,* that is conceited of himself and looks with a contempt upon all about him, that cannot bear either competition or contradiction, he *stirs up strife,* makes mischief, and creates disturbance to himself and every body else. 2. Those make themselves fat, and always easy, that live in a continual dependence upon God and his grace: *He who puts his trust in the Lord,* who, instead of struggling for himself, commits his cause to God, *shall be made fat.* He saves the money which others spend upon their pride and contentiousness; he enjoys himself, and has abundant satisfaction in his God; and thus his soul dwells at ease, and he is most likely to have plenty of outward good things. None live so easily, so pleasantly, as those who live by faith.

Verse 26

Here is, 1. The character of a fool: *He trusts to his own heart,* to his own wisdom and counsels, his own strength and sufficiency, his own merit and righteousness, and the good opinion he has of himself; he that does so *is a fool,* for he trusts to that, not only which *is deceitful above all things* (Jer. 17:9), but which has often deceived him. This implies that it is the character of a wise man (as before, *v.* 25) to *put his trust in the Lord,* and in his power and promise, and to follow his guidance, Prov. 3:5, 6. 2. The comfort of a wise man: He that *walks wisely,* that trusts not to his own heart, but is humble and self-diffident, and goes on in the strength of the Lord God, *he shall be delivered;* when the fool, *that trusts in his own heart,* shall be destroyed.

Verse 27

Here is, 1. A promise to the charitable: *He that gives to the poor* shall himself be never the poorer for so doing; he *shall not lack.* If he have but little, and so be in danger of lacking, let him give out of his little, and that will prevent it from coming to nothing; as the bounty of the widow of Sarepta to Elijah (for whom she made a little cake first) saved what she had, when it was reduced to a handful of meal. If he have much, let him give much out of it, and that will prevent its growing less; he and his shall not want what is given in pious charity. What we gave we have. 2. A threatening to the uncharitable: *He that hides his eyes,* that he may not see the miseries of the poor nor read their petitions, lest his eye should affect his heart and extort some relief from him, he *shall have many a curse,* both from God and man, and neither causeless, and therefore they shall come. Woeful is the condition of that man who has the word of God and the prayers of the poor against him.

Verse 28

This is to the same purport with what we had, *v.* 12. 1. When bad men are preferred, that which is good is clouded and run down. When power is put into the hands of *the wicked, men hide themselves;* wise men retire into privacy, and decline public business, not caring to be employed under them; rich men get out of the way, for fear of being squeezed for what they have; and, which is worst of all, good men abscond, despairing to do good and fearing to be persecuted and ill-treated. 2. When bad men are disgraced, degraded, and their power taken from them, then that which is good revives again, then *the righteous increase;* for, *when they perish,* good men will be put in their room, who will, by their example and interest, countenance religion and righteousness. It is well with a land when the number of good people increases in it; and it is therefore the policy of all princes, states, and potentates, to encourage them and to take special care of the good education of youth.

CHAPTER 29

Verse 1

Here, 1. The obstinacy of many wicked people in a wicked way is to be greatly lamented. They are *often reproved* by parents and friends, by magistrates and ministers, by the providence of God and by their own consciences, have had their sins set in order before them and fair warning given them of the consequences of them, but all in vain; they *harden their necks.* Perhaps they fling away, and will not so much as give the reproof a patient hearing; or, if they do, yet they go on in the sins for which they are reproved; they will not bow their necks to the yoke, but are children of Belial; they refuse reproof (*ch.* 10:17), despise it (*ch.* 5:12), hate it, *ch.* 12:1. 2. The issue of this obstinacy is to be greatly dreaded: Those that go on in sin, in spite of admonition, *shall be destroyed;* those that will not be reformed must expect to be ruined; if the rods answer not the end, expect the axes. They *shall be suddenly destroyed,* in the midst of their security, *and without remedy;* they have sinned against the preventing remedy, and therefore let them not expect any recovering remedy. Hell is remediless destruction. They *shall be destroyed, and no healing,* so the word is. If God wounds, who can heal?

Verse 2

This is what was said before, *ch.* 28:12, 28. 1. *The people* will have cause to *rejoice* or *mourn* according as their rulers are *righteous* or *wicked;* for, if *the righteous* be in *authority,* sin will be punished and restrained, religion and virtue will be supported and kept in reputation; *but,* if *the wicked* get power in their hands, wickedness will abound, religion and religious people will be persecuted, and so the ends of government will be perverted. 2. *The people* will actually *rejoice* or *mourn* according as their rulers are *righteous* or *wicked.* Such a conviction are even the common people under of the excellency of virtue and religion that they will rejoice when they see them preferred and countenanced; and, on the contrary, let men have ever so much honour or power, if they be wicked and vicious, and use it ill, they *make themselves contemptible and base before all the people* (as those priests, Mal. 2:9) and subjects will think themselves miserable under such a government.

Verse 3

Both the parts of this verse repeat what has been often said, but, on comparing them together, the sense of them will be enlarged from each other. 1. Be it observed, to the honour of a virtuous young man, that he *loves wisdom,* he is *a philosopher* (for that signifies *a lover of wisdom),* for religion is the best philosophy; he avoids bad company, and especially the company of lewd women. Hereby he *rejoices his* parents, and has the satisfaction of being a comfort to them, and increases his estate, and is likely to live comfortably. 2. Be it observed, to the reproach of a vicious young man, that he hates *wisdom; he keeps company with* scandalous women, who will be his ruin, both in soul and body; he grieves his parents, and, like the prodigal son, devours their living *with harlots.* Nothing will beggar men sooner than the lusts of uncleanness; and the best preservative from those ruinous lusts is *wisdom.*

Verse 4

Here is, 1. The happiness of a people under a good government. The care and business of a prince should be to *establish the land,* to maintain its fundamental laws, to settle the minds of his subjects and make them easy, to secure their liberties and properties from hostilities and for posterity, and to set in order the things that are wanting; this he must do *by judgment,* by wise counsels, and by the steady administration of justice, without respect of persons, which will have these good effects. 2. The misery of a people under a bad government: *A man of oblations* (so it is in the margin) *overthrows the land;* a man that is either sacrilegious or superstitious, or that invades the priest's office, as Saul and Uzziah — or a man that aims at nothing but getting money, and will, for a good bribe, connive at the most guilty, and, in hope of one, persecute the innocent — such governors as these will ruin a country.

Verse 5

Those may be said to *flatter their neighbours* who commend and applaud that good in them (the good they do or the good they have) which really either is not or is not such as they represent it, and who profess that esteem and that affection for them which really they have not; these *spread a net for their feet.* 1. For their neighbours' feet, whom they *flatter.* They have an ill design in it; they would not praise them as they do but that they hope to make an advantage of them; and it is therefore wisdom to suspect those who flatter us, that they are secretly laying a snare for us, and to stand on our guard accordingly. Or it has an ill effect on those who are flattered; it puffs them up with pride, and makes them conceited and confident of themselves, and so proves a net that entangles them in sin. 2. For their own feet; so some understand it. He that flatters others, in expectation that they will return his compliments and flatter him, does but make himself ridiculous and odious even to those he flatters.

Verse 6

Here is, 1. The peril of a sinful way. There is not only a punishment at the end of it, but *a snare* in it. One sin is a temptation to another, and there are troubles which, as *a snare,* come suddenly upon evil men in the midst of their transgressions; nay, their transgression itself often involves them in vexations; their sin is their punishment, and they are *holden in the cords of their own iniquity, ch.* 5:22. 2. The pleasantness of the way of holiness. The snare that is *in the transgression of evil men* spoils all their mirth, *but righteous* men are kept from those snares, or delivered out of them; they walk at liberty, walk in safety, and therefore they *sing and rejoice.* Those that make God their chief joy have him for their exceeding joy, and it is their own fault if they do not *rejoice evermore.* If there be any true joy on this side heaven, doubtless those have it whose conversation is in heaven.

Verse 7

It is a pity but that every one who sues *sub formâ pauperis — as a pauper,* should have an honest cause (they are of all others inexcusable if they have not), because the scripture has so well provided that it should have a fair hearing, and that the judge himself should be of counsel, as for the prisoner, so for the pauper. 1. It is here made the character of a *righteous* judge that he *considers the cause of the poor.* It is every man's duty to consider the poor (Ps. 41:1), but the judgment of the poor is to be considered by those that sit in judgment; they must take as much pains to find out the right in a poor man's cause as in a rich man's. Sense of justice must make both judge and advocate as solicitous and industrious in the poor man's cause as if they hoped for the greatest advantage. 2. It is made the character of a *wicked* man that because it is a poor man's cause, which there is nothing to be got by, he *regards not to know it,* in the true state of it, for he cares not which way it goes, right or wrong. See Job 29:16.

Verse 8

See here, 1. Who are the men that are dangerous to the public — *scornful men.* When such are employed in the business of the state they do things with precipitation, because they scorn to deliberate, and will not take time for consideration and consultation; they do things illegal and unjustifiable, because they scorn to be hampered by laws and constitutions; they break their faith, because they scorn to be bound by their word, and provoke the people, because they scorn to please them. Thus they *bring a city into a snare* by their ill conduct, or (as the margin reads it) they *set a city on fire;* they sow discord among the citizens and run them into confusion. Those are *scornful men* that mock at religion, the obligations of conscience, the fears of another world, and every thing that is sacred and serious. Such men are the plagues of their generation; they bring God's judgments upon a land, set men together by the ears, and so bring all to confusion. 2. Who are the men that are the blessings of a land — the *wise men* who by promoting religion, which is true wisdom, *turn away the wrath* of God, and who, by prudent counsels, reconcile contending parties and prevent the mischievous consequences of divisions. Proud and foolish men kindle the fires which wise and good men must extinguish.

Verse 9

A wise man is here advised not to set his wit to a fool's, not to dispute with him, or by contending with him to think either of fastening reason upon him or gaining right from him: *If a wise man contend with a wise man,* he may hope to be understood, and, as far as he has reason and equity on his side, to carry his point, at least to bring the controversy to a head and make it issue amicably; but, if he *contend with a foolish man, there is no rest;* he will see no end of it, nor will he have any satisfaction in it, but must expect to be always uneasy. 1. Whether the foolish man he contends with *rage or laugh,* whether he take angrily or scornfully what is said to him, whether he rail at it or mock at it, one of the two he will do, and so there will be *no rest.* However it is given, it will be ill-taken, and the wisest man must expect to be either scolded or ridiculed if he *contend with a fool.* He that fights with a dunghill, whether he be conqueror or conquered, is sure to be defiled. 2. Whether the wise man himself *rage or laugh,* whether he take the serious or the jocular way of dealing with the fool, whether he be severe or pleasant with him, whether he come with a rod or with *the spirit of meekness* (1 Co. 4:21), it is all alike, no good is done. *We have piped unto you, and you have not danced, mourned unto you, and you have not lamented.*

Verse 10

Note, 1. Bad men hate their best friends: *The blood-thirsty,* all the seed of the old serpent, who *was a murderer from the beginning,* all that inherit his enmity against the seed of the woman, *hate the upright;* they seek the ruin of good men because they condemn the wicked world and witness against it. Christ told his disciples that they should be *hated of all men.* Bloody men do especially *hate upright* magistrates, who would restrain and reform them, and put the laws in execution against them, and so really do them a kindness. 2. Good men love their worst enemies: *The just,* whom the bloody men hate, *seek their soul,* pray for their conversion, and would gladly do any thing for their salvation. This Christ taught us. *Father, forgive them. The just seek his soul,* that is, the soul of the upright, whom the bloody hate (so it is commonly understood), seek to protect it from violence, and save it from, or avenge it at, the hands of *the blood-thirsty.*

Verse 11

Note, 1. It is a piece of weakness to be very open: He is *a fool* who *utters all his mind,* — who tells every thing he knows, and has in his mouth instantly whatever he has in his thoughts, and can keep no counsel, — who, whatever is started in discourse, quickly shoots his bolt, — who, when he is provoked, will say any thing that comes uppermost, whoever is reflected upon by it, — who, when he is to speak of any business, will say all he thinks, and yet never thinks he says enough, whether choice or refuse, corn or chaff, pertinent or impertinent, you shall have it all. 2. It is a piece of wisdom to be upon the reserve: *A wise man* will not *utter all his mind* at once, but will take time for a second thought, or reserve the present thought for a fitter time, when it will be more pertinent and likely to answer his intention; he will not deliver himself in a continued speech, or starched discourse, but with pauses, that he may hear what is to be objected and answer it. *Non minus interdum oratorium est tacere quam dicere — True oratory requires an occasional pause.* Plin. Ep. 7.6.

Verse 12

Note, 1. It is a great sin in any, especially in rulers, to *hearken to lies;* for thereby they not only give a wrong judgment themselves of persons and things, according to the lies they give credit to, but they encourage others to give wrong informations. Lies will be told to those that will hearken to them; but the receiver, in this case, is as bad as the thief. 2. Those that do so will have *all their servants wicked.* All their servants will appear wicked, for they will have lies told of them; and they will be wicked, for they will tell lies to them. All that have their ear will fill their ear with slanders and false characters and representations; and so if princes, as well as people, will be deceived, they shall be deceived, and, instead of devolving the guilt of their own false judgments upon their servants that misinformed them, they must share in their servants' guilt, and on them will much of the blame lie for encouraging such misinformations and giving countenance and ear to them.

Verse 13

This shows how wisely the great God serves the designs of his providence by persons of very different tempers, capacities, and conditions in the world, even, 1. By those that are contrary the one to the other. Some are *poor* and forced to borrow; others are rich, have a great deal of *the mammon of unrighteousness (deceitful riches* they are called), and they are creditors, or *usurers,* as it is in the margin. Some are *poor,* and honest, and laborious; others are rich, slothful, and *deceitful.* They *meet together* in the business of this world, and have dealings with one another, and *the Lord enlightens both their eyes;* he causes his sun to shine upon both and gives them both the comforts of this life. To some of both sorts he gives his grace. He enlightens the eyes of the poor by giving them patience, and of the deceitful by giving them repentance, as Zaccheus. 2. By those that we think could best be spared. *The poor and the deceitful* we are ready to look upon as blemishes of Providence, but God makes even them to display the beauty of Providence; he has wise ends not only in leaving the poor always with us, but in permitting *the deceived and the deceiver,* for both *are his* (Job 12:16) and turn to his praise.

Verse 14

Here is, 1. The duty of magistrates, and that is, to judge faithfully between man and man, and to determine all causes brought before them, according to truth and equity, particularly to take care of *the poor,* not to countenance them in an unjust cause for the sake of their poverty (Ex. 23:3), but to see that their poverty do not turn to their prejudice if they have a just cause. The rich will look to themselves, but *the poor* and needy the prince must *defend* (Ps. 82:3) and plead for, Prov. 31:9. 2. The happiness of those magistrates that do their duty. Their *throne* of honour, their tribunal of judgment, *shall be established for ever.* This will secure to them the favour of God and strengthen their interest in the affections of their people, both which will be the establishment of their power, and help to transmit it to posterity and perpetuate it in the family.

Verse 15

Parents, in educating their children, must consider, 1. The benefit of due correction. They must not only tell their children what is good and evil, but they must chide them, and correct them too, if need be, when they either neglect that which is good or do that which is evil. If a *reproof* will serve without *the rod,* it is well, but *the rod* must never be used without a rational and grave *reproof;* and then, though it may be a present uneasiness both to the father and to the child, yet it will *give wisdom. Vexatio dat intellectum — Vexation sharpens the intellect.* The child will take warning, and so will get *wisdom.* 2. The mischief of undue indulgence: *A child* that is not restrained or reproved, but is *left to himself,* as Adonijah was, to follow his own inclinations, may do well if he will, but, if he take to ill courses, nobody will hinder him; it is a thousand to one but he proves a disgrace to his family, and *brings his mother,* who fondled him and humoured him in his licentiousness, *to shame,* to poverty, to reproach, and perhaps will himself be abusive to her and give her ill language.

Verse 16

Note, 1. The more sinners there are the more sin there is: *When the wicked,* being countenanced by authority, grow numerous, and walk on every side, no marvel if *transgression increases,* as a plague in the country is said to increase when still more and more are infected with it. *Transgression* grows more impudent and bold, more imperious and threatening, when there are many to keep it in countenance. In the old world, when *men began to multiply,* they began to degenerate and corrupt themselves and one another. 2. The more sin there is the nearer is the ruin threatened. Let not *the righteous* have their faith and hope shocked by the increase of sin and sinners. Let them not say that they have *cleansed their hands in vain,* or that *God has forsaken the earth,* but wait with patience; the transgressors shall fall, the measure of their iniquity will be full, and then they shall fall from their dignity and power, and fall into disgrace and destruction, and *the righteous shall* have the satisfaction of *seeing their fall* (Ps. 37:34), perhaps in this world, certainly in the judgment of the great day, when the fall of God's implacable enemies will be the joy and triumph of glorified saints. See Isa. 66:24; Gen. 19:28.

Verse 17

Note, 1. It is a very happy thing when children prove the comfort of their parents. Good children are so; they *give them rest,* make them easy, and free from the many cares they have had concerning them; *yea,* they *give delight unto their souls.* It is a pleasure to parents, which none know but those that are blessed with it, to see the happy fruit of the good education they have given their children, and to have a prospect of their well-doing for both worlds; it *gives delight* proportionable to the many thoughts of heart that have been concerning them. 2. In order to this, children must be trained up under a strict discipline, and not suffered to do what they will and to go without rebuke when they do amiss. The foolishness bound up in their hearts must by correction be driven out when they are young, or it will break out, to their own and their parents' shame, when they are grown up.

Verse 18

See here, I. The misery of the people that want a settled ministry: *Where there is no vision,* no prophet to expound the law, no priest or Levite to teach the good knowledge of the Lord, no means of grace, the word of the Lord is scarce, there is *no open vision* (1 Sa. 3:1), where it is so *the people perish;* the word has many significations, any of which will apply here. 1. *The people are made naked,* stripped of their ornaments and so exposed to shame, stripped of their armour and so exposed to danger. How bare does a place look without Bibles and ministers, and what an easy prey is it to the enemy of souls! 2. *The people rebel,* not only against God, but against their prince; good preaching would make people good subjects, but, for want of it, they are turbulent and factious, and *despise dominions,* because they know no better. 3. *The people are idle,* or *they play,* as the scholars are apt to do when the master is absent; they do nothing to any good purpose, but stand all the day idle, and sporting in the market-place, for want of instruction what to do and how to do it. 4. *They are scattered as sheep having no shepherd,* for want of the masters of assemblies to call them and keep them together, Mk. 6:34. They are scattered from God and their duty by apostasies, from one another by divisions; God is provoked to scatter them by his judgments, 2 Chr. 15:3, 5. 5. *They perish;* they are *destroyed for lack of knowledge,* Hos. 4:6. See what reason we have to be thankful to God for the plenty of *open vision* which we enjoy.

II. The felicity of a people that have not only a settled, but a successful ministry among them, the people that hear and *keep the law,* among whom religion is uppermost; *happy* are such a people and every particular person among them. It is not having the law, but obeying it, and living up to it, that will entitle us to blessedness.

Verse 19

Here is the description of an unprofitable, slothful, wicked servant, a slave that serves not from conscience, or love, but purely from fear. Let those that have such servants put on patience to bear the vexation and not disturb themselves at it. See their character. 1. No rational words will work upon them; they *will not be corrected* and reformed, not brought to their business, nor cured of their idleness and laziness, by fair means, no, nor by foul *words;* even the most gentle master will be forced to use severity with them; no reason will serve their turn, for they are unreasonable. 2. No rational words will be got from them. They are dogged and sullen; and, *though they understand* the questions you ask them, they *will not* give you an *answer;* though you make it ever so plain to them what you expect from them, they will not promise you to mend what is amiss nor to mind their business. See the folly of those servants whose mouth by their silence calls for strokes; they might *be corrected by words* and save blows, but they *will not.*

Verse 20

Solomon here shows that there is little hope of bringing a man to wisdom that is hasty either, 1. Through rashness and inconsideration: *Seest thou a man that is hasty in his matters,* that is of a light desultory wit, that seems to take a thing quickly, but takes it by the halves, gallops over a book or science, but takes no time to digest it, no time to pause or muse upon a business? *There is more hope of* making a scholar and a wise man of one that is dull and heavy, and slow in his studies, than of one that has such a mercurial genius and cannot fix. 2. Through pride and conceitedness: *Seest thou a man that is* forward to speak to every matter that is started, and affects to speak first to it, to open it, and speak last to it, to give judgment upon it, as if he were an oracle? *There is more hope of a* modest *fool,* who is sensible of his folly, than of such a self-conceited one.

Verse 21

Note, 1. It is an imprudent thing in a master to be too fond of a servant, to advance him too fast, and admit him to be too familiar with him, to suffer him to be over-nice and curious in his diet, and clothing, and lodging, and so to bring him up delicately, because he is a favourite, and an agreeable servant; it should be remembered that he is a servant, and, by being thus indulged, will be spoiled for any other place. Servants must endure hardness. 2. It is an ungrateful thing in a servant, but what is very common, to behave insolently because he has been used tenderly. The humble prodigal thinks himself unworthy *to be called a son,* and is content to be a servant; the pampered slave thinks himself too good to be called *a servant,* and will be *a son at the length,* will take his ease and liberty, will be on a par with his master, and perhaps pretend to the inheritance. Let masters *give their servants that which is equal* and fit for them, and neither more nor less. This is very applicable to the body, which is a servant to the soul; those that *delicately bring up* the body, that humour it, and are over-tender of it, will find that at length it will forget its place, and *become a son,* a master, a perfect tyrant.

Verse 22

See here the mischief that flows from an angry, passionate, furious disposition. 1. It makes men provoking to one another: *An angry man stirs up strife,* is troublesome and quarrelsome in the family and in the neighbourhood, blows the coals, and even forces those to fall out with him that would live peaceable and quietly by him. 2. It makes men provoking to God: *A furious man,* who is wedded to his humours and passions, cannot but *abound in transgressions.* Undue anger is a sin which is the cause of many sins; it not only hinders men from calling upon God's name, but it occasions their swearing, and cursing, and profaning God's name.

Verse 23

This agrees with what Christ said more than once, 1.

That those who *exalt themselves shall be abased.* Those that think to gain respect by lifting up themselves above their rank, by looking high, talking big, appearing fine, and applauding themselves, will on the contrary expose themselves to contempt, lose their reputation, and provoke God by humbling providences to bring them down and lay them *low.* 2. That those who *humble themselves shall be exalted,* and shall be established in their dignity: *Honour shall uphold the humble in spirit;* their humility is their honour, and that shall make them truly and safely great, and recommend them to the esteem of all that are wise and good.

Verse 24

See here what sin and ruin those involve themselves in who are drawn away by the enticement of sinners. 1. They incur a great deal of guilt: *He* does so that goes *partner with* such as rob and defraud, and *casts in his lot among them, ch.* 1:11, etc. The receiver is as bad as the thief; and, being drawn in to join with him in the commission of the sin, he cannot escape joining with him in the concealment of it, though it be with the most horrid perjuries and execrations. They *hear cursing* when they are sworn to tell the whole truth, but they will not confess. 2. They hasten to utter ruin: They even *hate their own souls,* for they wilfully do that which will be the inevitable destruction of them. See the absurdities sinners are guilty of; they love death, than which nothing is more dreadful, and *hate their own souls,* than which nothing is more dear.

Verse 25

Here, 1. We are cautioned not to dread the power of man, neither the power of a prince nor the power of the multitude; both are formidable enough, but the slavish fear of either *brings a snare,* that is, exposes men to many insults (some take a pride in terrifying the timorous), or rather exposes men to many temptations. Abraham, for *fear of man,* denied his wife, and Peter his Master, and many a one his God and religion. We must not shrink from duty, nor commit sin, to avoid the wrath of man, nor, though we see it coming upon us, be disquieted with fear, Dan. 3:16; Ps. 118:6. He must himself die (Isa. 51:12) and can but kill our body, Lu. 12:5. 2. We are encouraged to depend upon the power of God, which would keep us from all that *fear of man* which has either torment or temptation in it. *Whoso puts his trust in the Lord,* for protection and supply in the way of duty, *shall be* set on high, above the power of man and above the fear of that power. A holy confidence in God makes a man both great and easy, and enables him to look with a gracious contempt upon the most formidable designs of hell and earth against him. If God be my salvation, *I will trust and not be afraid.*

Verse 26

See here, 1. What is the common course men take to advance and enrich themselves, and make themselves great: they *seek the ruler's favour,* and, as if all their judgment proceeded from him, to him they make all their court. Solomon was himself a *ruler,* and knew with what sedulity men made their application to him, some on one errand, others on another, but all for his *favour.* It is the way of the world to make interest with great men, and expect much from the smiles of second causes, which yet are uncertain, and frequently disappoint them. *Many* take a great deal of pains in seeking the *ruler's favour* and yet cannot have it; many have it for a little while, but they cannot keep themselves in it, by some little turn or other they are brought under his displeasure; many have it, and keep it, and yet it does not answer their expectation, they cannot make that hand of it that they promised themselves they should. Haman had *the ruler's favour,* and yet it availed him nothing. 2. What is the wisest course men can take to be happy. Let them look up to God, and seek the favour of the Ruler of rulers; for *every man's judgment proceeds from the Lord.* It is not with us as the ruler pleases; his favour cannot make us happy, his frowns cannot make us miserable. But it is as God pleases; every creature is that to us that God makes it to be, no more and no other. He is the first Cause, on which all second causes depend; if he help not, they cannot, 2 Ki. 6:27; Job 34:29.

Verse 27

This expresses not only the innate contrariety that there is between virtue and vice, as between light and darkness, fire and water, but the old enmity that has always been between the seed of the woman and the seed of the serpent, Gen. 3:15. 1. All that are sanctified have a rooted antipathy to wickedness and wicked people. They have a good will to the souls of all (God has, and would have none perish); but they hate the ways and practices of those that are impious towards God and injurious towards men; they cannot hear of them nor speak of them without a holy indignation; they loathe the society of the ungodly and unjust, and dread the thought of giving them any countenance, but do all they can to bring the wickedness of the wicked to an end. Thus *an unjust* man makes himself odious *to the just,* and it is one part of his present shame and punishment that good men cannot endure him. 2. All that are unsanctified have a like rooted antipathy to godliness and godly people: *He that is upright in the way,* that makes conscience of what he says and does, *is an abomination to the wicked,* whose wickedness is restrained perhaps and suppressed, or, at least, shamed and condemned, by the uprightness of the upright. Thus Cain did, who was *of his father the devil.* And this is not only the wickedness of the wicked, that they hate those whom God loves, but their misery too, that they hate those whom them shall shortly see in everlasting bliss and honour, and who shall have *dominion over them in the morning,* Ps. 49:14.

CHAPTER 30

This and the following chapter are an appendix to Solomon's proverbs; but they are both expressly called prophecies in the first verses of both, by which it appears that the penmen of them, whoever they were, were divinely inspired. This chapter was penned by one that bears the name of "Agur Ben Jakeh." What tribe he was of, or when he lived, we are not told; what he wrote, being indited by the Holy Ghost, is here kept upon record. We have here, I. His confession of faith (*v.* 1–6). II. His prayer (*v.* 7–9). III. A caution against wronging servants (*v.* 10). IV. Four wicked generations (*v.* 11–14). V. Four things insatiable (*v.* 15, 16), to which is added fair warning to undutiful children (*v.* 17). VI. Four things unsearchable (*v.* 18–20). VII. Four things intolerable (*v.* 21–23). VIII. Four things little and wise (*v.* 24–28). IX. Four things stately (*v.* 29 to the end).

Verses 1–6

Some make *Agur* to be not the name of this author, but his character; he was a *collector* (so it signifies), a gatherer, one that did not compose things himself, but collected the wise sayings and observations of others, made abstracts of the writings of others, which some think is the reason why he says (*v.* 3), "*I have not learned wisdom* myself, but have been a scribe, or amanuensis, to other wise and learned men." Note, We must not bury our talent, though it be but one, but, as we have received the gift, so minister the same, if it be but to collect what others have written. But we rather suppose it to be his name, which, no doubt, was well known then, though not mentioned elsewhere in scripture. *Ithiel and Ucal* are mentioned, either, 1. As the names of his pupils, whom he instructed, or who consulted him as an oracle, having a great opinion of his wisdom and goodness. Probably they wrote from him what he dictated, as Baruch wrote from the mouth of Jeremiah, and by their means it was preserved, as they were ready to attest it to be his, for it was spoken to them; they were two witnesses of it. Or, 2. As the subject of his discourse. *Ithiel* signifies *God with me,* the application of *Immanuel, God with us.* The word calls him *God with us;* faith appropriates this, and calls him "*God with me,* who loved me, and gave himself for me, and into union and communion with whom I am admitted." *Ucal* signifies *the Mighty One,* for it is upon one that is mighty that help is laid for us. Many good interpreters therefore apply this to the Messiah, for to him all the prophecies bear witness, and why not this then? It is what Agur spoke concerning *Ithiel, even* concerning *Ithiel* (that is the name on which the stress is laid) *with us,* Isa. 7:14.

Three things the prophet here aims at: —

I. To abase himself. Before he makes confession of his faith he makes confession of his folly and the weakness and deficiency of reason, which make it so necessary that we be guided and governed by faith. Before he speaks concerning the Saviour he speaks of himself as needing a Saviour, and as nothing without him; we must go out of ourselves before we go into Jesus Christ. 1. He speaks of himself as wanting a righteousness, and having done foolish-

ly, very foolishly. When he reflects upon himself he owns, *Surely I am more brutish than any man. Every man has become brutish,* Jer. 10:14. But he that knows his own heart knows so much more evil of himself than he does of any other that he cries out, "*Surely* I cannot but think that *I am more brutish than any man;* surely no man has such a corrupt deceitful heart as I have. I have acted as one that has *not the understanding* of Adam, as one that is wretchedly degenerated from the knowledge and righteousness in which man was at first created; nay, I have not the common sense and reason of a man, else I should not have done as I have done." Agur, when he was applied to by others as wiser than most, acknowledged himself more foolish than any. Whatever high opinion others may have of us, it becomes us to have low thoughts of ourselves. 2. He speaks of himself as wanting a revelation to guide him in the ways of truth and wisdom. He owns (*v.* 3) "*I neither learned wisdom* by any power of my own (the depths of it cannot be fathomed by my line and plummet) *nor know I the knowledge of the holy* ones, the angels, our first parents in innocency, nor of the holy things of God; I can get no insight into them, nor make any judgment of them, further than God is pleased to make them known to me." The natural man, the natural powers, perceive not, nay, they *receive not, the things of the Spirit of God.* Some suppose Agur to be asked, as Apollo's oracle was of old, *Who was the wisest man?* The answer is, *He that is sensible of his own ignorance,* especially in divine things. *Hoc tantum scio, me nihil scire — All that I know is that I know nothing.*

II. To advance Jesus Christ, and the Father in him (*v.* 4): *Who ascended up into heaven,* etc. 1. Some understand this of God and of his works, which are both incomparable and unsearchable. He challenges all mankind to give an account of the heavens above, of the winds, the waters, the earth: "Who can pretend to have *ascended up to heaven,* to take a view of the orbs above, and then to have descended, to give us a description of them? Who can pretend to have had the command of the winds, to have grasped them in his hand and managed them, as God does, or to have bound the waves of the sea with a swaddling band, as God has done? Who has *established the ends of the earth,* or can describe the strength of its foundations or the extent of its limits? Tell me what is *the man's name* who can undertake to vie with God or to be of his cabinet-council, or, if he be dead, what is his name to whom he has bequeathed this great secret." 2. Others refer it to Christ, to Ithiel and Ucal, the Son of God, for it is the Son's name, as well as the Father's, that is here enquired after, and a challenge given to any to vie with him. We must now exalt Christ as one revealed; they then magnified him as one concealed, as one they had heard something of but had very dark and defective ideas of. *We have heard the fame of him with our ears,* but cannot describe him (Job 28:22); certainly it is God that has *gathered the wind in his fists* and *bound the waters as in a garment;* but *what is his name?* It is, *I am that I am* (Ex. 3:14), a name to be adored, not to be understood. What is *his Son's name,* by whom he does all these things? The Old-Testament saints expected the Messiah to be the *Son of the Blessed,* and he is here spoken of as a person distinct from the Father, but his name as yet secret. Note, The great Redeemer, in the glories of his providence and grace, can neither be paralleled nor found out to perfection. (1.) The glories of the kingdom of his grace are unsearchable and unparalleled; for who besides has *ascended into heaven and descended?* Who besides is perfectly acquainted with both worlds, and has himself a free correspondence with both, and is therefore fit to settle a correspondence between them, as Mediator, as Jacob's ladder? He was *in heaven* in the *Father's bosom* (Jn. 1:1, 18); thence he descended to take our nature upon him; and never was there such condescension. In that nature he again ascended (Eph. 4:9), to receive the promised glories of his exalted state; and who besides has done this? Rom. 10:6. (2.) The glories of the kingdom of his providence are likewise unsearchable and unparalleled. The same that reconciles heaven and earth was the Creator of both and governs and disposes of all. His government of the three lower elements of *air, water,* and *earth,* is here particularized. [1.] The motions of the air are of his directing. Satan pretends to be *the prince of the power of the air,* but even there Christ has *all power;* he *rebuked the winds* and they obeyed him. [2.] The bounds of the water are of his appointing: He *binds the waters as in a garment; hitherto they shall come, and no further,* Job 38:9–11. [3.] The foundations of the earth are of his establishing. He founded it at first; he upholds it still. If Christ had not interposed, the foundations of the earth would have sunk under the load of the curse upon the ground, for man's sin. Who and what is the mighty He that does all this? We cannot *find out God,* nor the *Son of God, unto perfection. Oh the depth of that knowledge!*

III. To assure us of the truth of the word of God, and to recommend it to us, *v.* 5, 6. Agur's pupils expect to be instructed by him in the things of God. "Alas!" says he, "I cannot undertake to instruct you; go to the word of God; see what he has there revealed of himself, and of his mind and will; you need know no more than what that will teach you, and that you may rely upon as sure and sufficient. *Every word of God is pure;* there is not the least mixture of falsehood and corruption in it." The words of men are to be heard and read with jealousy and with allowance, but there is not the least ground to suspect any deficiency in the word of God; it is *as silver purified seven times* (Ps. 12:6), without the least dross or alloy. *Thy word is very pure,* Ps. 119:140. 1. It is sure, and therefore we must trust to it and venture our souls upon it. God in his word, God in his promise, is *a shield,* a sure protection, to all those that put themselves under his protection and *put their trust in him.* The word of God, applied by faith, will make us easy in the midst of the greatest dangers, Ps. 46:1, 2. 2. It is sufficient, and therefore we must not add to it (*v.* 6): *Add thou not unto his words,* because they are pure and perfect. This forbids the advancing of any thing, not only in contradiction to the word of God, but in competition with it; though it be under the plausible pretence of explaining it, yet, if it pretend to be of equal authority with it, it is *adding to his words,* which is not only a reproach to them as insufficient, but opens a door to all manner of errors and corruptions; for, that one absurdity being granted, that the word of any man, or company of men, is to be received with the same faith and veneration as the word of God, a thousand follow. We must be content with what God has thought fit to make known to us of his mind, and not covet to be *wise above what is written;* for, (1.) God will resent it as a heinous affront: "*He* will *reprove thee,* will reckon with thee as a traitor against his crown and dignity, and lay thee under the heavy doom of those that add to his words, or diminish from them," Deu. 4:2; 12:32. (2.) We shall run ourselves into endless mistakes: "Thou wilt be found a liar, a corrupter of the word of truth, a broacher of heresies, and guilty of the worst of forgeries, counterfeiting the broad seal of heaven, and pretending a divine mission and inspiration, when it is all a cheat. Men may be thus deceived, but *God is not mocked.*"

Verses 7–9

After Agur's confession and creed, here follows his litany, where we may observe,

I. The preface to his prayer: *Two things have I required* (that is, *requested*) of thee, O God! Before we go to pray it is good to consider what we need, and what the things are which we have to ask of God. — What does our case require? What do our hearts desire? What would we that God should do for us? — that we may not have to seek for our petition and request when we should be presenting it. He begs, *Deny me not before I die.* In praying, we should think of dying, and pray accordingly. "Lord, give me pardon, and peace, and grace, before I die, *before I go hence and be no more;* for, if I be not renewed and sanctified before I die, the work will not be done after; if I do not prevail in prayer before I die, prayers afterwards will not prevail, no, not *Lord, Lord.* There is none of this wisdom or working in the grave. *Deny me not* thy grace, for, if thou do, I die, I perish; if thou be silent to me, *I am like those that go down to the pit,* Ps. 28:1. *Deny me not before I die;* as long as I continue in the land of the living, let me continue under the conduct of thy grace and good providence."

II. The prayer itself. The *two things* he requires are grace sufficient and food convenient. 1. Grace sufficient for his soul: "*Remove from me vanity and lies;* deliver me from sin, from all corrupt principles, practices, and affections, from error and mistake, which are at the bottom of all sin, from the love of the world and the things of it, which are

all *vanity and a lie.*" Some understand it as a prayer for the pardon of sin, for, when God forgives sin, he removes it, he takes it away. Or, rather, it is a prayer of the same import with that, *Lead us not into temptation.* Nothing is more mischievous to us than sin, and therefore there is nothing which we should more earnestly pray against than that we may *do no evil.* 2. Food convenient for his body. Having prayed for the operations of divine grace, he here begs the favours of the divine Providence, but such as may tend to the good and not to the prejudice of the soul. (1.) He prays that of God's free gift he might receive a competent portion of the good things of this life: "*Feed me with the bread of my allowance,* such bread as thou thinkest fit to allow me." As to all the gifts of the divine Providence, we must refer ourselves to the divine wisdom. Or, *"the bread that is fit for me,* as a man, a master of a family, that which is agreeable to my rank and condition in the world." For *as is the man so is his competency.* Our Saviour seems to refer to this when he teaches us to pray, *Give us this day our daily bread,* as this seems to refer to Jacob's vow, in which he wished for no more than *bread to eat and raiment to put on.* Food convenient for us is what we ought to be content with, though we have not dainties, varieties, and superfluities — what is for necessity, though we have not for delight and ornament; and it is what we may in faith pray for and depend upon God for. (2.) He prays that he may be kept from every condition of life that would be a temptation to him. [1.] He prays against the extremes of abundance and want: *Give me neither poverty nor riches.* He does not hereby prescribe to God, nor pretend to teach him what condition he shall allot to him, nor does he pray against poverty or riches absolutely, as in themselves evil, for either of them, by the grace of God, may be sanctified and be a means of good to us; but, *First,* He hereby intends to express the value which wise and good men have for a middle state of life, and, with submission to the will of God, desires that that might be his state, neither great honour nor great contempt. We must learn how to manage both (as St. Paul, Phil. 4:12), but rather wish to be always between both. *Optimus pecuniae modus qui nec in paupertatem cedit nec procul a paupertate discedit — The best condition is that which neither implies poverty nor yet recedes far from it.* Seneca. *Secondly,* He hereby intimates a holy jealousy he had of himself, that he could not keep his ground against the temptations either of an afflicted or a prosperous condition. Others may preserve their integrity in either, but he is afraid of both, and therefore grace teaches him to pray against riches as much as nature against poverty; but *the will of the Lord be done.* [2.] He gives a pious reason for his prayer, *v.* 9. He does not say, "*Lest I be rich,* and cumbered with care, and envied by my neighbours, and eaten up with a multitude of servants, or, *lest I be poor* and trampled on, and forced to work hard and fare hard;" but, "*Lest I be rich* and sin, or *poor* and sin." Sin is that which a good man is afraid of in every condition and under every event; witness Nehemiah (*ch.* 6:13), *that I should be afraid, and do so, and sin. First,* He dreads the temptations of a prosperous condition, and therefore even deprecates that: *Lest I be full and deny thee* (as Jeshurun, who *waxed fat and kicked,* and *forsook God who made him,* Deu. 32:15), and say, as Pharaoh in his pride, *Who is the Lord, that I should obey his voice?* Prosperity makes people proud and forgetful of God, as if they had no need of him and were therefore under no obligation to him. *What can the Almighty do for them?* Job 22:17. And therefore they will do nothing for him. Even good men are afraid of the worst sins, so deceitful do they think their own hearts to be; and they know that the greatest gains of the world will not balance the least guilt. *Secondly,* He dreads the temptations of a poor condition, and for that reason, and no other, deprecates that: *Lest I be poor and steal.* Poverty is a strong temptation to dishonesty, and such as many are overcome by, and they are ready to think it will be their excuse; but it will not bear them out at God's bar any more than at men's to say, "I stole because I was poor;" yet, if a man *steal for the satisfying of his soul when he is hungry,* it is a case of compassion (*ch.* 6:30) and what even those that have some principles of honesty in them may be drawn to. But observe why Agur dreads this, not because he should endanger himself by it, "Lest I steal, and be hanged for it, whipped or put in the stocks, or sold for a bond-

man," as among the Jews poor thieves were, who had not wherewithal to make restitution; but lest he should dishonour God by it: "*Lest I should steal, and take the name of my God in vain,* that is, discredit my profession of religion by practices disagreeable to it." Or, "Lest I steal, and, when I am charged with it, forswear myself." He *therefore* dreads one sin, because it would draw on another, for the way of sin is downhill. Observe, He calls God *his God,* and *therefore* he is afraid of doing any thing to offend him because of the relation he stands in to him.

Verses 10–14

Here is, I. A caution not to abuse other people's servants any more than our own, nor to make mischief between them and their masters, for it is an ill office, invidious, and what will make a man odious, *v.* 10. Consider, 1. It is an injury to the servant, whose poor condition makes him an object of pity, and therefore it is barbarous to add affliction to him that is afflicted: *Hurt not a servant with thy tongue* (so the margin reads it); for it argues a sordid disposition to smite any body secretly with the scourge of the tongue, especially a servant, who is not a match for us, and whom we should rather protect, if his master be severe with him, than exasperate him more. 2. "It will perhaps be an injury to thyself. If a servant be thus provoked, perhaps he will curse thee, will accuse thee and bring thee into trouble, or give thee an ill word and blemish thy reputation, or appeal to God against thee, and imprecate *his* wrath upon thee, who is the patron and protector of oppressed innocency."

II. An account, upon occasion of this caution, of some wicked generations of men, that are justly abominable to all that are virtuous and good. 1. Such as are abusive to their parents, give them bad language and wish them ill, call them bad names and actually injure them. *There is a generation* of such; young men of that black character commonly herd together, and irritate one another against their parents. A *generation of vipers* those are who curse their natural parents, or their magistrates, or their ministers, because they cannot endure the yoke; and those are near of kin to them who, though they have not yet arrived at such a pitch of wickedness as to curse their parents, yet do not bless them, cannot give them a good word, and will not pray for them. 2. Such as are conceited of themselves, and, under a show and pretence of sanctity, hide from others, and perhaps from themselves too, abundance of reigning wickedness in secret (*v.* 12); they are *pure in their own eyes,* as if they were in all respects such as they should be. They have a very good opinion of themselves and their own character, that they are not only righteous, but *rich and increased with goods* (Rev. 3:17), and yet *are not cleansed from their filthiness,* the filthiness of their hearts, which they pretend to be the best part of them. They are, it may be, swept and garnished, but they are not washed, nor sanctified; as the Pharisees that within were *full of all uncleanness,* Mt. 23:25, 26. 3. Such as are haughty and scornful to those about them, *v.* 13. He speaks of them with amazement at their intolerable pride and insolence: "*Oh how lofty are their eyes!* With what disdain do they look upon their neighbours, as not worthy to be set with the dogs of their flock! What a distance do they expect every body should keep; and, when they look upon themselves, how do they strut and vaunt like the peacock, thinking they make themselves illustrious when really they make themselves ridiculous!" There is a generation of such, on whom he that *resists the proud* will pour contempt. 4. Such as are cruel to the poor and barbarous to all that lie at their mercy (*v.* 14); their teeth are iron and steel, *swords and knives,* instruments of cruelty, with which they *devour the poor* with the greatest pleasure imaginable, and as greedily as hungry men cut their meat and eat it. God has so ordered it that the *poor we shall always have with us,* that they shall *never cease out of the land;* but there are those who, because they hate to relieve them, would, if they could, abolish them from the earth, from among men, especially God's poor. Some understand it of those who wound and ruin others by slanders and false accusations, and severe censures of their everlasting state; their tongues, and their teeth too (which are likewise organs of speech), are *as swords and knives,* Ps. 57:4.

Verses 15–17

He had spoken before of those that devoured the poor (v. 14), and had spoken of them last, as the worst of all the four generations there mentioned; now here he speaks of their insatiableness in doing this. The temper that puts them upon it is made up of cruelty and covetousness. Now those are *two daughters* of the *horse-leech*, its genuine offspring, that still cry, "*Give, give*, give more blood, give more money;" for the bloody are still blood-thirsty; being drunk with blood, they add thirst to their drunkenness, and will seek it yet again. Those also that *love silver* shall never *be satisfied with silver.* Thus, while from these two principles they are devouring the poor, they are continually uneasy to themselves, as David's enemies, Ps. 59:14, 15. Now, for the further illustration of this,

I. He specifies four other things which are insatiable, to which those devourers are compared, which say not, *It is enough,* or *It is wealth.* Those are never rich that are always coveting. Now these four things that are always craving are, 1. The grave, into which multitudes fall, and yet still more will fall, and it swallows them all up, and returns none, *Hell and destruction are never full, ch.* 27:20. When it comes to our turn we shall find the grave ready for us, Job 17:1. 2. The *barren womb,* which is impatient of its affliction in being barren, and cries, as Rachel did, *Give me children.* 3. The *parched ground* in time of drought (especially in those hot countries), which still soaks in the rain that comes in abundance upon it and in a little time wants more. 4. The *fire,* which, when it has consumed abundance of fuel, yet still devours all the combustible matter that is thrown into it. So insatiable are the corrupt desires of sinners, and so little satisfaction have they even in the gratification of them.

II. He adds a terrible threatening to disobedient children (v. 17), for warning to the first of those four wicked generations, that curse their parents (v. 11), and shows here,

1. Who they are that belong to that generation, not only those that curse their parents in heat and passion, but, (1.) Those that *mock* at them, though it be but with a scornful eye, looking with disdain upon them because of their bodily infirmities, or looking sour or dogged at them when they instruct or command, impatient at their checks and angry at them. God takes notice with what eye children look upon their parents, and will reckon for the leering look and the casts of the evil eye as well as for the bad language given them. (2.) Those that *despise to obey* them, that think it a thing below them to be dutiful to their parents, especially to the *mother,* they scorn to be controlled by her; and thus she that bore them in sorrow in greater sorrow bears their manners.

2. What their doom will be. Those that dishonour their parents shall be set up as monuments of God's vengeance; they shall be hanged in chains, as it were, for the birds of prey to pick out their eyes, those eyes with which they looked so scornfully on their good parents. The dead bodies of malefactors were not to hang all night, but before night the ravens would have picked out their eyes. If men do not punish undutiful children, God will, and will load those with the greatest infamy that conduct themselves haughtily towards their parents. Many who have come to an ignominious end have owned that the wicked courses that brought them to it began in a contempt of their parents' authority.

Verses 18–23

Here is, I. An account of four things that are unsearchable, *too wonderful* to be fully known. And here,

1. The first three are natural things, and are only designed as comparisons for the illustration of the last. We cannot trace, (1.) *An eagle in the air.* Which way she has flown cannot be discovered either by the footstep or by the scent, as the way of a beast may upon ground; nor can we account for the wonderful swiftness of her flight, how soon she has gone beyond our ken. (2.) *A serpent upon a rock.* The way of a serpent in the sand we may find by the track, but not of a serpent upon the hard rock; nor can we describe how a serpent will, without feet, in a little time creep to the top of a rock. (3.) *A ship in the midst of the sea.* The leviathan indeed *makes a path to shine after him, one would think the deep to be hoary* (Job 41:32), but a ship leaves no mark behind it, and sometimes it is so tossed upon the waves that one would wonder how

it lives at sea and gains its point. The kingdom of nature is full of wonders, marvellous things which the God of nature does, *past finding out.*

2. The fourth is a mystery of iniquity, more unaccountable than any of these; it belongs to the depths of Satan, that deceitfulness and that desperate wickedness of the heart which none can know, Jer. 17:9. It is twofold: — (1.) The cursed arts which a vile adulterer has to debauch a maid, and to persuade her to yield to his wicked and abominable lust. This is what a wanton poet wrote a whole book of, long since, *De arte amandi — On the art of love.* By what pretensions and protestations of love, and all its powerful charms, promises of marriage, assurances of secresy and reward, is many an unwary virgin brought to sell her virtue, and honour, and peace, and soul, and all to a base traitor; for so all sinful lust is in the kingdom of love. The more artfully the temptation is managed the more watchful and resolute ought every pure heart to be against it. (2.) The cursed arts which a vile adulteress has to conceal her wickedness, especially from her husband, from whom she treacherously departs; so close are her intrigues with her lewd companions, and so craftily disguised, that it is as impossible to discover her as to track an *eagle in the air.* She eats the forbidden fruit, after the similitude of Adam's transgression, and then *wipes her mouth,* that it may not betray itself, and with a bold and impudent face says, *I have done no wickedness.* [1.] To the world she denies the fact, and is ready to swear it that she is as chaste and modest as any woman, and never did the wickedness she is suspected of. Those are the works of darkness which are industriously kept from coming to the light. [2.] To her own conscience (if she have any left) she denies the fault, and will not own that that *great wickedness* is any wickedness at all, but an innocent entertainment. See Hos. 12:7, 8. Thus multitudes ruin their souls by calling evil good and out-facing their convictions with a self-justification.

II. An account of four things that are intolerable, that is, four sorts of persons that are very troublesome to the places where they live and the relations and companies they are in; the earth is *disquieted for them,* and groans under them as a burden it cannot bear, and they are all much alike: — 1. *A servant* when he is advanced, and entrusted with power, who is, of all others, most insolent and imperious; witness Tobiah the servant, the Ammonite, Neh. 2:10. 2. *A fool,* a silly, rude, boisterous, vicious man, who when he has grown rich, and is partaking of the pleasures of the table, will disturb all the company with his extravagant talk and the affronts he will put upon those about him. 3. An ill-natured, cross-grained, *woman,* when she gets a husband, one who, having made herself odious by her pride and sourness, so that one would not have thought any body would ever love her, yet, if at last she be married, that honourable estate makes her more intolerably scornful and spiteful than ever. It is a pity that that which should sweeten the disposition should have a contrary effect. A gracious woman, when she is married, will be yet more obliging. 4. An old maid-servant that has prevailed with her mistress, by humouring her, and, as we say, getting the length of her foot, to leave her what she has, or is as dear to her as if she was to be her heir, such a one likewise will be intolerably proud and malicious, and think all too little that her mistress gives her, and herself wronged if any thing be left from her. Let those therefore whom Providence has advanced to honour from mean beginnings carefully watch against that sin which will most easily beset them, pride and haughtiness, which will in them, of all others, be most insufferable and inexcusable; and let them humble themselves with the remembrance of the rock out of which they were hewn.

Verses 24–28

I. Agur, having specified four things that seem great and yet are really contemptible, here specifies four things that are little and yet are very admirable, great in miniature, in which, as bishop Patrick observes, he teaches us several good lessons; as, 1. Not to admire bodily bulk, or beauty, or strength, nor to value persons or think the better of them for such advantages, but to judge of men by their wisdom and conduct, their industry and application to business, which are characters that deserve respect. 2. To admire the wisdom and power of the Creator in the smallest and most despicable animals, in an ant as much as in an

elephant. 3. To blame ourselves who do not act so much for our own true interest as the meanest creatures do for theirs. 4. Not to despise the weak things of the world; there are those that are *little upon the earth,* poor in the world and of small account, and yet *are exceedingly wise,* wise for their souls and another world, and those *are exceedingly wise, wiser than their neighbours.* Margin, *They are wise, made wise* by the special instinct of nature. All that are wise to salvation are made wise by the grace of God.

II. Those he specifies are, 1. The *ants,* minute animals and very weak, and yet they are very industrious in gathering proper food, and have a strange sagacity to do it in the summer, the proper time. This is so great a piece of wisdom that we may learn of them to be wise for futurity, *ch.* 6:6. When the ravening *lions lack, and suffer hunger,* the laborious ants have plenty, and know no want. 2. The *conies,* or, as some rather understand it, the Arabian mice, field mice, weak creatures, and very timorous, yet they have so much wisdom as to *make their houses in the rocks,* where they are well guarded, and their feebleness makes them take shelter in those natural fastnesses and fortifications. Sense of our own indigence and weakness should drive us to him that is a *rock higher than we* for shelter and support; there let us make our habitation. 3. The *locusts;* they are little also, and *have no king,* as the bees have, but *they go forth all of them by bands,* like an army in battle-array; and, observing such good order among themselves, it is not any inconvenience to them that they *have no king.* They are called God's *great army* (Joel 2:25); for, when he pleases, he musters, he marshals them, and wages war by them, as he did upon Egypt. *They go forth all of them gathered together* (so the margin); sense of weakness should engage us to keep together, that we may strengthen the hands of one another. 4. The *spider,* an insect, but as great an instance of industry in our houses as the ants are in the field. Spiders are very ingenious in weaving their webs with a fineness and exactness such as no art can pretend to come near: They *take hold with their hands,* and spin a fine thread out of their own bowels, with a great deal of art; and they are not only in poor men's cottages, but in *kings' palaces,* notwithstanding all the care that is there taken to destroy them. Providence wonderfully keeps up those kinds of creatures, not only which men provide not for, but which every man's hand is against and seeks the destruction of. Those that will mind their business, and *take hold* of it *with their hands,* shall be *in kings' palaces;* sooner or later, they will get preferment, and may go on with it, notwithstanding the difficulties and discouragements they meet with. If one well-spun web be swept away, it is but making another.

Verses 29–33

Here is, I. An enumeration of four things which are majestic and stately in their going, which look great: — 1. *A lion,* the king of beasts, because *strongest among beasts.* Among beasts it is strength that gives the pre-eminence, but it is a pity that it should do so among men, whose *wisdom* is their honour, not their *strength* and *force.* The lion *turns not away,* nor alters his pace, for fear of any pursuers, since he knows he is too hard for them. Herein *the righteous are bold as a lion,* that they *turn not away* from their duty for fear of any difficulty they meet with in it. 2. *A greyhound* that is girt in the loins and fit for running; or (as the margin reads it) *a horse,* which ought not to be omitted among the creatures that *are comely in going,* for so he is, especially when he is dressed up in his harness or trappings. 3. *A he-goat,* the comeliness of whose going is when he goes first and leads the flock. It is the comeliness of a Christian's going to go first in a good work and to lead others in the right way. 4. *A king,* who, when he appears in his majesty, is looked upon with reverence and awe, and all agree that *there is no rising up against* him; none can vie with him, none can contend with him, whoever does it, it is at his peril. And, if *there is no rising up* against an earthly prince, *woe to him* then *that strives with his Maker.* It is intended that we should learn courage and fortitude in all virtuous actions from the *lion* and *not to turn away for any* difficulty we meet with; from the *greyhound* we may learn quickness and despatch, from the *he-goat* the care of our family and those under our charge, and from *a king* to have our children in subjection with all gravity, and from them all to *go well,* and to order the steps of our conversation so as that we may not only be safe, but *comely, in going.*

II. A caution to us to keep our temper at all times and under all provocations, and to take heed of carrying our resentments too far upon any occasion, especially when there is *a king* in the case, *against whom there is no rising up,* when it is a ruler, or one much our superior, that is offended; nay, the rule is always the same.

1. We must bridle and suppress our own passion, and take shame to ourselves, whenever we are justly charged with a fault, and not insist upon our own innocency: If we have *lifted up ourselves,* either in a proud conceit of ourselves or a peevish opposition to those that are over us, if we have transgressed the laws of our place and station, we have therein *done foolishly.* Those that magnify themselves over others or against others, that are haughty and insolent, do but shame themselves and betray their own weakness. Nay, if we have but *thought evil,* if we are conscious to ourselves that we have harboured an ill design in our minds, or it has been suggested to us, we must *lay our hand upon our mouth,* that is, (1.) We must humble ourselves for what we have done amiss, and even lie in the dust before God, in sorrow for it, as Job did, when he repented of what he had said foolishly (*ch.* 40:4, *I will lay my hand upon my mouth),* and as the convicted leper, who *put a covering upon his upper lip.* If we have *done foolishly,* we must not stand to it before men, but by silence own our guilt, which will be the best way of appeasing those we have offended. 2. We must keep the evil thought we have conceived in our minds from breaking out in any evil speeches. Do not give the evil thought an *imprimatur — a license;* allow it not to be published; but *lay thy hand upon thy mouth;* use a holy violence with thyself, if need be, and enjoin thyself silence; as Christ *suffered not the evil spirits to speak.* It is bad to think ill, but it is much worse to speak it, for that implies a consent to the evil thought and a willingness to infect others with it.

2. We must not irritate the passions of others. Some are so very provoking in their words and conduct that they even *force wrath,* they make those about them angry whether they will or no, and put those into a passion who are not only not inclined to it, but resolved against it. Now this *forcing of wrath brings forth strife,* and where that *is there is confusion and every evil work.* As the violent agitation of the cream fetches all the good out of the milk, and the hard *wringing of the nose* will extort blood from it, so this *forcing of wrath* wastes both the body and spirits of a man, and robs him of all the good that is in him. Or, as it is in *the churning of milk and the wringing of the nose, that* is done by force which otherwise would not be done, so the spirit is heated by degrees with strong passions; one angry word begets another, and that a third; one passionate debate makes work for another, and so it goes on till it ends at length in irreconcilable feuds. Let nothing therefore be said or done with violence, but every thing with softness and calmness.

CHAPTER 31

This chapter is added to Solomon's proverbs, some think because it is of the same author, supposing king Lemuel to be king Solomon; others only because it is of the same nature, though left in writing by another author, called Lemuel; however it be, it is a prophecy, and therefore given by inspiration and direction of God, which Lemuel was under in the writing of it, and putting it into this form, as his mother was in dictating to him the matter of it. Here is, I. An exhortation to Lemuel, a young prince, to take heed of the sins he would be tempted to and to do the duties of the place he was called to (*v.* 1–9). II. The description of a virtuous woman, especially in the relation of a wife and the mistress of a family, which Lemuel's mother drew up, not as an encomium of herself, though, no doubt, it was her own true picture, but either as an instruction to her daughters, as the foregoing verses were to her son, or as a direction to her son in the choice of a wife; she must be chaste and modest, diligent and frugal, dutiful to her husband, careful of her family, discreet in her discourse, and in the education of her children, and, above all, conscientious in her duty to God: such a one as this, if he can find her, will make him happy (*v.* 10–31).

Verses 1–9

Most interpreters are of opinion that Lemuel is Solomon; the name signifies one that is *for God,* or *devoted to God;* and so it agrees well enough with that honourable name which, by divine appointment, was given to Solomon (2 Sa. 12:25), *Jedediah — beloved of the Lord.* Lemuel is supposed to be a pretty, fond, endearing name, by which his mother used to call him; and so much did he value himself upon the interest he had in his mother's affections that he was not ashamed to call himself by it. One would the rather incline to think it is Solomon that here tells us what *his mother taught him* because he tells us (*ch.* 4:4) what his father taught him. But some think (and the conjecture is not improbable) that Lemuel was a prince of some neighbouring country, whose mother was a daughter of Israel, perhaps of the house of David, and taught him these good lessons. Note, 1. It is the duty of mothers, as well as fathers, to teach their children what is good, that they may do it, and what is evil, that they may avoid it; when they are young and tender they are most under the mother's eye, and she has then an opportunity of moulding and fashioning their minds well, which she ought not to let slip. 2. Even kings must be catechised; the greatest of men is less than the least of the ordinances of God. 3. Those that have grown up to maturity should often call to mind, and make mention of, the good instructions they received when they were children, for their own admonition, the edification of others, and the honour of those who were the guides of their youth.

Now, in this mother's (this queen mother's) catechism, observe,

I. Her expostulation with the young prince, by which she lays hold of him, claims an interest in him, and awakens his attention to what she is about to say (*v.* 2): *"What! my son?* What shall I say to thee?" She speaks as one considering what advice to give him, and choosing out words to reason with him; so full of concern is she for his welfare! Or, *What is it that thou doest?* It seems to be a chiding question. She observed, when he was young, that he was too much inclined to women and wine, and therefore she found it necessary to take him to task and deal roundly with him. *"What! my son?* Is this the course of life thou intendest to lead? Have I taught thee no better than thus? I must reprove thee, and reprove thee sharply, and thou must take it well, for," 1. "Thou art descended from me; thou art *the son of my womb,* and therefore what I say comes from the authority and affection of a parent and cannot be suspected to come from any ill-will. Thou art a piece of myself. I bore thee with sorrow, and I expect no other return for all the pains I have taken with thee, and undergone for thee, than this, Be wise and good, and then I am well paid." 2. "Thou art devoted to my God; thou art *the son of my vows,* the son I prayed to God to give me and promised to give back to God, and did so" (thus Samuel was the son of Hannah's vows); "Thou art the son I have often prayed to God to give his grace to (Ps. 72:1), and shall a child of so many prayers miscarry? And shall all my hopes concerning thee be disappointed?" Our children that by baptism are dedicated to God, for whom and in whose name we covenanted with God, may well be called *the children of our vows;* and, as this may be made a good plea with God in our prayers for them, so it may be made a good plea with them in the instructions we give them; we may tell them they are baptized, are *the children of our vows,* and it is at their peril if they break those bonds in sunder which in their infancy they were solemnly brought under.

II. The caution she gives him against those two destroying sins of *uncleanness* and *drunkenness,* which, if he allowed himself in them, would certainly be his ruin. 1. Against uncleanness (*v.* 3): *Give not thy strength unto women,* unto strange women. He must not be soft and effeminate, nor spend that time in a vain conversation with the ladies which should be spent in getting knowledge and despatching business, nor employ that wit (which is the strength of the soul) in courting and complimenting them which he should employ about the affairs of his government. "Especially shun all adultery, fornication, and lasciviousness, which waste the strength of the body, and bring into it dangerous diseases. *Give not thy ways,* thy affections, thy conversation, *to that which destroys kings,* which has destroyed many, which gave such a shock to the kingdom even of David himself, in the matter of Uriah. Let the sufferings of others be thy warnings." It lessens the honour of kings and makes them mean. Are those fit to govern others that are themselves slaves to their own lusts? It makes them unfit for business, and fills their court with the basest and worst of animals. Kings lie exposed to temptations of this kind, having wherewith both to please the humours and to bear the charges of the sin, and therefore they ought to double their guard; and, if they would preserve their people from the unclean spirit, they must themselves be patterns of purity. Meaner people may also apply it to themselves. Let none give their strength *to that which destroys souls.* 2. Against drunkenness, *v.* 4, 5. He must not *drink wine* or *strong drink* to excess; he must never sit to drink, as they used to do *in the day of their king,* when *the princes made him sick with bottles of wine,* Hos. 7:7. Whatever temptation he might be in from the excellency of the wine, or the charms of the company, he must deny himself, and be strictly sober, considering, (1.) The indecency of drunkenness in a king. However some may call it a fashionable accomplishment and entertainment, *it is not for kings, O Lemuel! it is not for kings, to* allow themselves that liberty; it is a disparagement to their dignity, and profanes their crown, by confusing the head that wears it; that which for the time unmans them does for the time unking them. Shall we say, *They are gods?* No, they are *worse than the beasts that perish.* All Christians are *made to our God kings and priests,* and must apply this to themselves. *It is not for* Christians, *it is not for* Christians, *to drink* to excess; they debase themselves if they do; it ill becomes the heirs of the kingdom and the spiritual priests, Lev. 10:9. (2.) The ill consequences of it (*v.* 5): *Lest they drink* away their understandings and memories, *drink and forget the law* by which they are to govern; and so, instead of doing good with their power, do hurt with it, *and pervert* or *alter the judgment of all the sons of affliction,* and, when they should right them, wrong them, and add to their affliction. It is a sad complaint which is made of the priests and prophets (Isa. 28:7), that *they have erred through wine, and through strong drink they are out of the way;* and the effect is as bad in kings, who when they are drunk, or intoxicated with the love of wine, cannot but stumble in judgment. Judges must have clear heads, which those cannot have who so often make themselves giddy, and incapacitate themselves to judge of the most common things.

III. The counsel she gives him to do good. 1. He must do good with his wealth. Great men must not think that they have their abundance only that out of it they may *made provision for the flesh, to fulfil the lusts of it,* and may the more freely indulge their own genius; no, but that with it they may relieve such as are in distress, *v.* 6, 7. "Thou hast wine or strong drink at command; instead of doing thyself hurt with it, do others good with it; let those have it that need it." Those that have wherewithal must not only give bread to the hungry and water to the thirsty, but they must *give strong drink to him that is ready to perish* through sickness or pain *and wine to those that* are melancholy and *of heavy heart;* for it was appointed to cheer and revive the spirits, and *make glad the heart* (as it does where there is need of it), not to burden and oppress the spirits, as it does where there is no need of it. We must deny ourselves in the gratifications of sense, that we may have to spare for the relief of the miseries of others, and be glad to see our superfluities and dainties better bestowed upon those whom they will be a real kindness to than upon ourselves whom they will be a real injury to. Let those that are *ready to perish* drink soberly, and it will be a means so to revive their drooping spirits that they will *forget their poverty* for the time *and remember their misery no more,* and so they will be the better able to bear it. The Jews say that upon this was grounded the practice of giving a stupifying drink to condemned prisoners when they were going to execution, as they did to our Saviour. But the scope of the place is to show that wine is a cordial, and therefore to be used for want and not for wantonness, by those only that need cordials, as Timothy, who is advised to *drink a little wine,* only *for his stomach's sake and his often infirmities,* 1 Tim. 5:23. 2. He must do good with his power, his knowledge, and interest, must administer justice with care, courage, and compassion, *v.* 8, 9. (1.) He must himself take cognizance of the causes his subjects have depending in his courts, and inspect what his judges and officers do, that he may support those that do their duty, and lay those aside that neglect it or are partial. (2.) He must, in all matters that come before him, *judge righteously,* and, without fear of the face of man, boldly pass sentence according to equity: *Open thy mouth,* which denotes the liberty of speech that princes and judges ought to use in passing sentence. Some observe that only wise men *open* their mouths, for fools have their mouths always open, are full of words. (3.) He must especially look upon himself as obliged to be the patron of oppressed innocency. The inferior magistrates perhaps had not zeal and tenderness enough to *plead the cause of the poor and needy;* therefore the king himself must interpose, and appear as an advocate, [1.] For those that were unjustly charged with capital crimes, as Naboth was, that were *appointed to destruction,* to gratify the malice either of a particular person or of a party. It is a case which it well befits a king to appear in, for the preserving of innocent blood. [2.] For those that had actions unjustly brought against them, to defraud them of their right, because they were *poor and needy,* and unable to defend it, not having wherewithal to fee counsel; in such a case also kings must be advocates for the poor. Especially, [3.] For those that were *dumb,* and knew not how to speak for themselves, either through weakness or fear, or being over-talked by the prosecutor or over-awed by the court. It is generous to speak for those that cannot speak for themselves, that are absent, or have not words at command, or are timorous. Our law appoints the judge to be of counsel for the prisoner.

Verses 10–31

This description of the *virtuous woman* is designed to show what wives the women should make and what wives the men should choose; it consists of twenty-two verses, each beginning with a letter of the Hebrew alphabet in order, as some of the *Psalms,* which makes some think it was no part of the lesson which Lemuel's mother taught him, but a poem by itself, written by some other hand, and perhaps had been commonly repeated among the pious Jews, for the ease of which it was made alphabetical. We have the abridgment of it in the New Testament (1 Tim. 2:9, 10, 1 Pt. 3:1–6), where the duty prescribed to wives agrees with this description of a good wife; and with good reason is so much stress laid upon it, since it contributes as much as any one thing to the keeping up of religion in families, and the entail of it upon posterity, that the mothers be wise and good; and of what consequence it is to the wealth and outward prosperity of a house every one is sensible. He that will thrive must ask his wife leave. Here is,

I. A general enquiry after such a one (v. 10), where observe, 1. The person enquired after, and that is *a virtuous woman — a woman of strength* (so the word is), though the weaker vessel, yet made strong by wisdom and grace, and the fear of God: it is the same word that is used in the character of good judges (Ex. 18:21), that they are *able men,* men qualified for the business to which they are called, *men of truth, fearing God.* So it follows, A *virtuous woman* is a woman of spirit, who has the command of her own spirit and knows how to manage other people's, one that is pious and industrious, and a help meet for a man. In opposition to this strength, we read of the weakness of the heart *of an imperious whorish woman,* Eze. 16:30. *A virtuous woman* is a woman of resolution, who, having espoused good principles, is firm and steady to them, and will not be frightened with winds and clouds from any part of her duty. 2. The difficulty of meeting with such a one: *Who can find* her? This intimates that good women are very scarce, and many that seem to be so do not prove so; he that thought he had found a *virtuous woman* was deceived; *Behold, it was Leah,* and not the Rachel he expected. But he that designs to marry ought to seek diligently for such a one, to have this principally in his eye, in all his enquiries, and to take heed that he be not biassed by beauty or gaiety, wealth or parentage, dressing well or dancing well; for all these may be and yet the woman not be virtuous, and there is many a woman truly virtuous who yet is not recommended by these advantages. 3. The unspeakable worth of such a one, and the value which he that has such a wife ought to put upon her, showing it by his thankfulness to God and his kindness and respect to her, whom he must never think he can do too much for. *Her price is far above rubies,* and all the rich ornaments with which vain women adorn themselves. The more rare such good wives are the more they are to be valued.

II. A particular description of her and of her excellent qualifications.

1. She is very industrious to recommend herself to her husband's esteem and affection. Those that are good really will be good relatively. A good woman, if she be brought into the marriage state, will be a good wife, and make it her business to *please her husband,* 1 Co. 7:34. Though she is a woman of spirit herself, yet *her desire is to her husband,* to know his mind, that she may accommodate herself to it, and she is willing that *he should rule over her.* (1.) She conducts herself so that he may repose an entire confidence in her. He trusts in her chastity, which she never gave him the least occasion to suspect or to entertain any jealousy of; she is not morose and reserved, but modest and grave, and has all the marks of virtue in her countenance and behaviour; her husband knows it, and therefore his *heart doth safely trust in her;* he is easy, and makes her so. He trusts in her conduct, that she will speak in all companies, and act in all affairs, with prudence and discretion, so as not to occasion him either damage or reproach. He trusts in her fidelity to his interests, and that she will never betray his counsels nor have any interest separate from that of his family. When he goes abroad, to attend the concerns of the public, he can confide in her to order all his affairs at home, as well as if he himself were there. She is a good wife that is fit to be trusted, and he is a good husband that will leave it to such a wife to manage for him. (2.) She contributes so much to his content and satisfaction *that he shall have no need of spoil;* he needs not be griping and scraping abroad, as those must be whose wives are proud and wasteful at home. She manages his affairs so that he is always before-hand, has such plenty of his own that he is in no temptation to prey upon his neighbours. He thinks himself so happy in her that he envies not those who have most of the wealth of this world; he needs it not, he has enough, having such a wife. Happy the couple that have such a satisfaction as this in each other! (3.) She makes it her constant business to *do him good,* and is afraid of doing any thing, even through inadvertency, that may turn to his prejudice, v. 12. She shows her love to him, not by a foolish fondness, but by prudent endearments, accommodating herself to his temper, and not crossing him, giving him good words, and not bad ones, no, not when he is out of humour, studying to make him easy, to provide what is fit for him both in health and sickness, and attending him with diligence and tenderness when any thing ails him; nor would she, no, not for the world, wilfully do any thing that might be a damage to his person, family, estate, or reputation. And this is her care *all the days of her life;* not at first only, or now and then, when she is in a good humour, but perpetually; and she is not weary of the good offices she does him: *She does him good,* not only all the days of *his* life, but *of her own* too; if she survive him, still she is doing him good in her care of his children, his estate, and good name, and all the concerns he left behind him. We read of kindness shown, not only *to the living,* but *to the dead,* Ruth 2:20. (4.) She adds to his reputation in the world (v. 23): *Her husband is known in the gates,* known to have a good wife. By his wise counsels, and prudent management of affairs, it appears that he has a discreet companion in his bosom, by conversation with whom he improves himself. By his cheerful countenance and pleasant humour it appears that he has an agreeable wife at home; for many that have not have their tempers strangely soured by it. Nay, by his appearing clean and neat in his dress, every thing about him decent and handsome, yet not gaudy, one may know he has a good wife at home, that takes care of his clothes.

2. She is one that takes pains in the duty of her place and takes pleasure in it. This part of her character is much enlarged upon here. (1.) She hates to sit still and do nothing: *She eats not the bread of idleness,* v. 27. Though she needs not work for her bread (she has an estate to live upon), yet she will not eat it in idleness, because she knows that we were none of us sent into this world to be idle, that when we have nothing to do the devil will soon find us something to do, and that it is not fit that those who *will not labour* should *eat.* Some eat and drink because they can find themselves nothing else to do, and needless visits must be received with fashionable entertainments; these are eating the bread of idleness, which she has no relish for, for she neither gives nor receives idle visits nor idle talk. (2.) She is careful to fill up time, that none of that be lost. When day-light is done, she does not then think it time to lay by her work, as those are forced to do whose business lies abroad in the fields (Ps. 104:23), but her business lying within-doors, and her work worth candle-light, with that she lengthens out the day; and *her candle goes not out by night,* v. 18. It is a mercy to have candle-light to supply the want of day-light, and a duty, having that advantage, to improve it. We say of an elaborate piece, It smells of the lamp. (3.) *She rises* early, *while it is yet night* (v. 15), to give her servants their breakfast, that they may be ready to go cheerfully about their work as soon as the day breaks. She is none of those who sit up playing at cards, or dancing, till midnight, till morning, and then lie in bed till noon. No; the *virtuous woman* loves her business better than her ease or her pleasure, is in care to be found in the way of her duty every hour of the day, and has more true satisfaction in having *given meat to her household* betimes in the morning than those can have in the money they have won, much more in what they have lost, who sat up all night at play. Those that have a family to take care of should not love their bed too well in a morning. (4.) She applies herself to the business that is proper for her. It is not in a scholar's business, or statesman's business, or husbandman's business, that she employs herself, but in women's business: *She seeks wool and flax,* where she may have the best of each at the best hand, and cheapest; she has a stock of both by her, and every thing that is necessary to the carrying on both of the woollen and the linen manufacture (v. 13), and with this she does not only set the poor on work, which is a very good office, but does herself work, *and work willingly, with her hands;* she *works with the counsel or delight of her hands* (so the word is); she goes about it cheerfully and dexterously, lays not only her hand, but her mind to it, and goes on in it without weariness in well-doing. *She lays her* own *hands to the spindle,* or spinning-wheel, *and her hands hold the distaff* (v. 19), and she does not reckon it either an abridgment of her liberty or a disparagement to her dignity, or at all inconsistent with her repose. The spindle and the distaff are here mentioned as her honour, while the ornaments of the daughters of Zion are reckoned up to their reproach, Isa. 2:18, etc. (5.) She does what she does with all her might, and does not trifle in it (v. 17); *She girds her loins with strength and strengthens her arms;* she does not employ herself in sitting work only, or in that which is only the nice performance of the fingers (there are works that are scarcely one remove from doing nothing); but, if there be occasion, she will go through with work that requires all the strength she has, which she will use as one that knows it is the way to have more.

3. She is one that makes what she does to turn to a good account, by her prudent management of it. She does not toil all night and catch nothing; no, she herself *perceives that her merchandise is good* (v. 18); she is sensible that *in all* her *labour there is profit,* and that encourages her to go on in it. She perceives that she can make things herself better and cheaper than she can buy them; she finds by observation what branch of her employment brings in the best returns, and to that she applies herself most closely. (1.) She brings in provisions of all things necessary and convenient for her family, v. 14. No *merchants' ships,* no, not Solomon's navy, ever made a more advantageous return than her employments do. Do they bring in foreign commodities with the effects they export? So does she with the fruit of her labours. What her own ground does not produce she can furnish herself with, if she have occasion for it, by exchanging her own goods for it; and so *she brings her food from afar.* Not that she values things the more for their being far-fetched, but, if they be ever so far off, if she must have them she knows how to come by them. (2.) She purchases lands, and enlarges the demesne of the family (v. 16): *She considers a field, and buys it.* She considers what an advantage it will be to the family and what a good account it will turn to, and therefore she buys it; or, rather, though she have ever so much mind to it she will not buy it till she has first considered it, whether it be worth her money, whether she can afford to take so much money out of her stock as must go to purchase it, whether the title be good, whether the ground will answer the character given of it, and whether she has money at command to pay for it. Many have undone themselves by buying without considering; but those who would make advantageous purchases must consider, and then buy. *She also plants a vineyard,* but it is *with the fruit of her hands;* she does not take up money, or run into debt, to do it, but she does it with what she can spare out

of the gains of her own housewifery. Men should not lay out any thing upon superfluities, till, by the blessing of God upon their industry, they have got before-hand, and can afford it; and *then* the fruit of the vineyard is likely to be doubly sweet, when it is the fruit of honest industry. (3.) She furnishes her house well and has good clothing for herself and her family (*v.* 22): *She makes herself coverings of tapestry* to hang her rooms, and she may be allowed to use them when they are of her own making. *Her* own *clothing* is rich and fine: it is *silk and purple,* according to her place and rank. Though she is not so vain as to spend much time in dressing herself, nor makes the putting on of apparel her adorning, nor values herself upon it, yet she has rich clothes and puts them on well. The senator's robes which her husband wears are of her own spinning, and they look better and wear better than any that are bought. She also gets good warm clothing for her children, and her servants' liveries. She needs not fear the cold of the most pinching winter, for she and her family are well provided with clothes, sufficient to keep out cold, which is the end chiefly to be aimed at in clothing: *All her household are clothed in scarlet,* strong cloth and fit for winter, and yet rich and making a good appearance. They are *all double clothed* (so some read it), have change of raiment, a winter suit and a summer suit. (4.) She trades abroad. She makes more than she and her household have occasion for; and therefore, when she has sufficiently stocked her family, *she sells fine linen and girdles to the merchants* (*v.* 24), who carry them to Tyre, the mart of the nations, or some other trading city. Those families are likely to thrive that sell more than they buy; as it is well with the kingdom when abundance of its home manufactures are exported. It is no disgrace to those of the best quality to sell what they can spare, nor to deal in trade and send ventures by sea. (5.) She lays up for hereafter: *She shall rejoice in time to come,* having laid in a good stock for her family, and having good portions for her children. Those that take pains when they are in their prime will have the pleasure and joy of it when they are old, both in reflecting upon it and in reaping the benefit of it.

4. She takes care of her family and all the affairs of it, *gives meat to her household* (*v.* 15), to every one *his portion of meat in due season,* so that none of her servants have reason to complain of being kept short or faring hard. She gives also *a portion* (an allotment of work, as well as meat) *to her maidens;* they shall all of them know their business and have their task. *She looks well to the ways of her household* (*v.* 27); she inspects the manners of all her servants, that she may check what is amiss among them, and oblige them all to behave properly and do their duty to God and one another, as well as to her; as Job, who put away iniquity far from his tabernacle, and David, who would suffer no wicked thing in his house. She does not intermeddle in the concerns of other people's houses; she thinks it enough for her to look well to her own.

5. She is charitable *to the poor, v.* 20. She is as intent upon giving as she is upon getting; she often serves the poor with her own hand, and she does if freely, cheerfully, and very liberally, with an out-stretched hand. Nor does she relieve her poor neighbours only, and those that are nigh at hand, but *she reaches forth her hands to the needy* that are at a distance, seeking opportunities *to do good and to communicate,* which is as good housewifery as any thing she does.

6. She is discreet and obliging in all her discourse, not talkative, censorious, nor peevish, as some are, that know how to take pains; no, *she opens her mouth with wisdom;* when she does speak, it is with a great deal of prudence and very much to the purpose; you may perceive by every word she says how much she governs herself by the rules of wisdom. She not only takes prudent measures herself, but gives prudent advice to others; and this not as assuming the authority of a dictator, but with the affection of a friend and an obliging air: *In her tongue is the law of kindness;* all she says is under the government of that law. The law of love and kindness is written in the heart, but it shows itself in the tongue; if we are *kindly affectioned one to another,* it will appear by affectionate expression. It is called a *law of kindness,* because it gives law to others, to all she converses with. Her wisdom and kindness together put a commanding power into all she says; they command respect, they command compliance. How forcible are right words! *In her tongue is the law of grace,* or *mercy* (so some read it), understanding it of the word and law of God, which she delights to talk of among her children and servants. She is full of pious religious discourse, and manages it prudently, which shows how full her heart is of another world even when her hands are most busy about this world.

7. That which completes and crowns her character is that she *fears the Lord, v.* 30. With all those good qualities she lacks not that *one thing needful;* she is truly pious, and, in all she does, is guided and governed by principles of conscience and a regard to God; this is that which is here preferred far before *beauty;* that *is vain and deceitful;* all that are wise and good account it so, and value neither themselves nor others on it. Beauty recommends none to God, nor is it any certain indication of wisdom and goodness, but it has deceived many a man who has made his choice of a wife by it. There may be an impure deformed soul lodged in a comely and beautiful body; nay, many have been exposed by their beauty to such temptations as have been the ruin of their virtue, their honour, and their precious souls. It is a fading thing at the best, and therefore *vain* and *deceitful.* A fit of sickness will stain and sully it in a little time; a thousand accidents may blast this flower in its prime; old age will certainly wither it and death and the grave consume it. But the fear of God reigning in the heart is the beauty of the soul; it recommends those that have it to the favour of God, and is, in his sight, of great price; it will last for ever, and bid defiance to death itself, which consumes the beauty of the body, but consummates the beauty of the soul.

III. The happiness of this virtuous woman.

1. She has the comfort and satisfaction of her virtue in her own mind (*v.* 25): *Strength and honour are her clothing,* in which she wraps herself, that is, enjoys herself, and in which she appears to the world, and so recommends herself. She enjoys a firmness and constancy of mind, has spirit to bear up under the many crosses and disappointments which even the wise and virtuous must expect to meet with in this world; and this is her clothing, for defence as well as decency. She deals honourably with all, and she has the pleasure of doing so, *and shall rejoice in time to come;* she shall reflect upon it with comfort, when she comes to be old, that she was not idle or useless when she was young. In the day of death it will be a pleasure to her to think that she has lived to some good purpose. Nay, *she shall rejoice in an eternity to come;* she shall be recompensed for her goodness with *fulness of joy and pleasures for evermore.*

2. She is a great blessing to her relations, *v.* 28. (1.) *Her children* grow up in her place, *and* they *call her blessed.* They give her their good word, they are themselves a commendation to her, and they are ready to give great commendations of her; they pray for her, and bless God that they had such a good mother. It is a debt which they owe her, a part of that honour which the fifth commandment requires to be paid to father and mother; and it is a double honour that is due to a good father and a good mother. (2.) *Her husband* thinks himself so happy in her that he takes all occasions to speak well of her, as one of the best of women. It is no indecency at all, but a laudable instance of conjugal love, for husbands and wives to give one another their due praises.

3. She gets the good word of all her neighbours, as Ruth did, whom *all the city of her people knew* to be *a virtuous woman,* Ruth 3:11. Virtue will have its praise, Phil. 4:8. A woman that fears the Lord, shall have praise *of God* (Rom. 2:29) and of men too. It is here shown, (1.) That she shall be highly praised (*v.* 29): *Many have done virtuously.* Virtuous women, it seems, are precious jewels, but not such rare jewels as was represented *v.* 10. There have been many, but such a one as this cannot be paralleled. *Who can find* her equal? *She excels them all.* Note, Those that are good should aim and covet to excel in virtue. *Many daughters,* in their father's house, and in the single state, *have done virtuously, but* a good wife, if she be virtuous, *excels them all,* and does more good in her place than they can do in theirs. Or, as some explain it, A man cannot have his house so well kept by good daughters, as by a good wife. (2.) That she shall be incontestably praised, without contradiction, *v.* 31. Some are praised above what is their due, but those that praise her do but *give her of the fruit of her hands;* they give her that which she has dearly earned and which is justly due to her; she is wronged if she have it not. Note, Those ought to be praised the fruit of whose hands is praise-worthy. The tree is known by its fruits, and therefore, if the fruit be good, the tree must have our good word. If her children be dutiful and respectful to her, and conduct themselves as they ought, they then *give her the fruit of her hands;* she reaps the benefit of all the care she has taken of them, and thinks herself well paid. Children must thus study to *requite their parents,* and this is *showing piety at home,* 1 Tim. 5:4. But, if men be unjust, the thing will speak itself, *her own works* will *praise her in the gates,* openly before all the people. [1.] She leaves it to her own works to praise her, and does not court the applause of men. Those are none of the truly virtuous women that love to hear themselves commended. [2.] *Her own works* will *praise her;* if her relations and neighbours altogether hold their peace, her good works will proclaim her praise. The widows gave the best encomium of Dorcas when they *showed the coats and garments she had made for the poor,* Acts 9:39. [3.] The least that can be expected from her neighbours is that they should *let her own works praise her,* and do nothing to hinder them. Those that *do that which is good,* let them *have praise of the same* (Rom. 13:3) and let us not enviously say, or do, any thing to the diminishing of it, but be provoked by it to a holy emulation. Let none have an ill report from us, that have *a good report* even *of the truth itself.* Thus is shut up this looking-glass for ladies, which they are desired to open and dress themselves by; and, if they do so, their adorning will be found to praise, and honour, and glory, at the appearing of Jesus Christ.

Twenty chapters of the book of *Proverbs* (beginning with *ch.* 10 and ending with *ch.* 29), consisting mostly of entire sentences in each verse, could not well be reduced to proper heads, and the contents of them gathered; I have therefore here put the contents of all these chapters together, which perhaps may be of some use to those who desire to see at once all that is said of any one head in these chapters. Some of the verses, perhaps, I have not put under the same heads that another would have put them under, but the most of them fall (I hope) naturally enough to the places I have assigned them.

1. Of the comfort, or grief, parents have in their children, according as they are wise or foolish, godly or ungodly, *ch.* 10:1; 15:20; 17:21, 25; 19:13, 26; 23:15, 16, 24, 25; 27:11; 29:3
2. Of the world's insufficiency, and religion's sufficiency, to make us happy (*ch.* 10:2, 3; 11:4) and the preference to be therefore given to the gains of virtue above those of this world, *ch.* 15:16, 17; 16:8, 16; 17:1; 19:1; 28:6, 11
3. Of slothfulness and diligence, *ch.* 10:4, 26; 12:11, 24, 27; 13:4, 23; 15:19; 16:26; 18:9; 19:15, 24; 20:4, 13; 21:5, 25, 26; 22:13, 29; 24:30–34; 26:13–16; 27:18, 23, 27; 28:19. Particularly the improving or neglecting opportunities, *ch.* 6:6; 10:5
4. The happiness of the righteous, and the misery of the wicked, *ch.* 10:6, 9, 16, 24, 25, 27–30; 11:3, 5–8, 18–21, 31; 12:2, 3, 7, 13, 14, 21, 26, 28; 13:6, 9, 14 15, 21, 22, 25; 14:11, 14, 19, 32; 15:6, 8, 9, 24, 26, 29; 20:7; 21:12, 15, 16, 18, 21; 22:12; 28:10, 18; 29:6
5. Of honour and dishonour, *ch.* 10:7; 12:8, 9; 18:3; 26:1; 27:21. And of vain-glory, *ch.* 25:14, 27; 27:2
6. The wisdom of obedience, and folly of disobedience, *ch.* 10:8, 17; 12:1, 15; 13:1, 13, 18; 15:5, 10, 12, 31, 32; 19:16; 28:4, 7, 9

AN EXPOSITION, WITH PRACTICAL OBSERVATIONS, OF
THE BOOK OF ECCLESIASTES

We are still among Solomon's happy men, his happy servants, that *stood continually before him to hear his wisdom;* and they are the choicest of all the dictates of his wisdom, such as were more immediately given by divine inspiration, that are here transmitted to us, not to be heard, as by them, but once, and then liable to be mistaken or forgotten, and by repetition to lose their beauty, but to be read, reviewed, revolved, and had in everlasting remembrance. The account we have of Solomon's apostasy from God, in the latter end of his reign (1 Ki. 11:1), is the tragical part of his story; we may suppose that he spoke his *Proverbs* in the prime of his time, while he kept his integrity, but delivered his *Ecclesiastes* when he had grown old (for of the burdens and decays of age he speaks feelingly *ch.* 12), and was, by the grace of God, recovered from his backslidings. There he dictated his observations; here he wrote his own experiences; this is what days speak, and wisdom which the multitude of years teaches. The title of the book and the penman we shall meet with in the first verse, and therefore shall here only observe,

I. That it is a sermon, a sermon in print; the text is (*ch.* 1:2), *Vanity of vanities, all is vanity;* that is the doctrine too; it is proved at large by many arguments and an induction of particulars, and divers objections are answered, and in the close we have the use and application of all, by way of exhortation, to *remember our Creator,* to *fear him,* and to *keep his commandments.* There are indeed many things in this book which are dark and hard to be understood, and some things which men of corrupt minds *wrest to their own destruction,* for want of distinguishing between Solomon's arguments and the objections of atheists and epicures; but there is enough easy and plain to convince us (if we will admit the conviction) of the vanity of the world, and its utter insufficiency to make us happy, the vileness of sin, and its certain tendency to make us miserable, and of the wisdom of being religious, and the solid comfort and satisfaction that are to be had in doing our duty both to God and man. This should be intended in every sermon, and that is a good sermon by which these points are in any measure gained. II. That it is a penitential sermon, as some of David's psalms are penitential psalms; it is a recantation-sermon, in which the preacher sadly laments his own folly and mistake, in promising himself satisfaction in the things of this world, and even in the forbidden pleasures of sense, which now he finds more bitter than death. His fall is a proof of the weakness of man's nature: *Let not the wise man glory in his wisdom,* nor say, "I shall never be such a fool as to do so

and so," when Solomon himself, the wisest of men, played the fool so egregiously; nor *let the rich man glory in his riches,* since Solomon's wealth was so great a snare to him, and did him a great deal more hurt than Job's poverty did him. His recovery is a proof of the power of God's grace, in bringing one back to God that has gone so far from him; it is a proof too of the riches of God's mercy in accepting him notwithstanding the many aggravations of his sin, pursuant to the promise made to David, that if his children should commit iniquity they should be corrected, but not abandoned and disinherited, 2 Sa. 7:14, 15. Let him therefore that thinks he stands take heed lest he fall; and let him that has fallen make haste to get up again, and not despair either of assistance or acceptance therein. III. That it is a practical profitable sermon. Solomon, being brought to repentance, resolves, like his father, to teach transgressors God's way (Ps. 51:13) and to give warning to all to take heed of splitting upon those rocks which had been fatal to him; and these were fruits meet for repentance. The fundamental error of the children of men, and that which is at the bottom of all their departures from God, is the same with that of our first parents, hoping to be as gods by entertaining themselves with that which seems good for food, pleasant to the eyes, and desirable to make one wise. Now the scope of this book is to show that this is a great mistake, that our happiness consists not in being as gods to ourselves, to have what we will and do what we will, but in having him that made us to be a God to us. The moral philosophers disputed much about man's felicity, or chief good. Various opinions they had about it; but Solomon, in this book, determines the question, and assures us that to fear God and to keep his commandments is the whole of man. He tried what satisfaction might be found in the wealth of the world and the pleasures of sense, and at last pronounced all vanity and vexation; yet multitudes will not take his word, but will make the same dangerous experiment, and it proves fatal to them. He, 1. Shows the vanity of those things in which men commonly look for happiness, as human learning and policy, sensual delight, honour and power, riches and great possessions. And then, 2. He prescribes remedies against the vexation of spirit that attends them. Though we cannot cure them of their vanity, we may prevent the trouble they give us, by sitting loose to them, enjoying them comfortable, but laying our expectations low from them, and acquiescing in the will of God concerning us in every event, especially by remembering God in the days of our youth, and continuing in his fear and service all our days, with an eye to the judgment to come.

CHAPTER 1

In this chapter we have, I. The inscription, or title of the book (*v.* 1). II. The general doctrine of the vanity of the creature laid down (*v.* 2) and explained (*v.* 3). III. The proof of this doctrine, taken, 1. From the shortness of human life and the multitude of births and burials in this life (*v.* 4). 2. From the inconstant nature, and constant revolutions, of all the creatures, and the perpetual flux and reflux they are in, the sun, wind, and water (*v.* 5–7). 3. From the abundant toil man has about them and the little satisfaction he has in them (*v.* 8). 4. From the return of the same things again, which shows the end of all perfection, and that the stock is exhausted (*v.* 9, 10). 5. From the oblivion to which all things are condemned (*v.* 11). IV. The first instance of the vanity of man's knowledge, and all the parts of learning, especially natural philosophy and politics. Observe, 1. The trial Solomon made of these (*v.* 12, 13, 16, 17). 2. His judgment of them, that all is vanity (*v.* 14). For, (1.) There is labour in getting knowledge (*v.* 13). (2.) There is little good to be done with it (*v.* 15). (3.) There is no satisfaction in it (*v.* 18). And, if this is vanity and vexation, all other things in this world, being much inferior to it in dignity and worth, must needs be so too. A great scholar cannot be happy unless he be a true saint.

Verses 1–3

Here is, I. An account of the penman of this book; it was Solomon, for no other son of David was king of Jerusalem; but he conceals his name *Solomon, peaceable,* because by his sin he had brought trouble upon himself and his kingdom, had broken his peace with God and lost the peace of his conscience, and therefore was no more worthy of that name. Call me not *Solomon,* call me *Marah,* for, *behold, for peace I had great bitterness.* But he calls himself,

1. *The preacher,* which intimates his present character. He is *Koheleth,* which comes from a word which signifies *to gather;* but it is of a feminine termination, by which perhaps Solomon intends to upbraid himself with his effeminacy, which contributed more than any thing to his apostasy; for it was to please his wives that he set up idols, Neh. 13:26. Or the word *soul* must be understood, and so *Koheleth* is,

(1.) A *penitent soul,* or one *gathered,* one that had rambled and gone astray like a lost sheep, but was now reduced, gathered in from his wanderings, gathered home to his duty, and come at length to himself. The spirit that was dissipated after a thousand vanities is now collected and made to centre in God. Divine grace can make great sinners great converts, and renew even those to repentance who, *after they had known the way of righteousness, turned aside from it,* and *heal their backslidings,* though it is a difficult case. It is only the penitent soul that God will accept, the heart that is broken, not the head that is bowed down like a bulrush only for a day, David's repentance, not Ahab's. And it is only the gathered soul that is the penitent soul, that comes back from its by-paths, that no longer *scatters its way to the strangers* (Jer. 3:13), but is *united to fear God's name. Out of the abundance of the heart the mouth will speak,* and therefore we have here the words of the penitent, and those published. If eminent professors of religion fall into gross sin, they are concerned, for the honour of God and the repairing of the damage they have done to his kingdom, openly to testify their repentance, that the antidote may be administered as extensively as the poison.

(2.) A *preaching soul,* or one *gathering.* Being himself *gathered* to the congregation of saints, out of which he had by his sin thrown himself, and being reconciled to the church, he endeavours to gather others to it that had gone astray like him, and perhaps were led astray by his example. He that has done any thing to seduce his brother ought to do all he can to restore him. Perhaps Solomon called together a congregation of his people, as he had done at the dedication of the temple (1 Ki. 8:2), so now at the rededicating of himself. In that assembly he presided as the people's mouth to God in prayer (*v.* 12); in this as God's mouth to them in preaching. God by his Spirit made him a preacher, in token of his being reconciled to him; a commission is a tacit pardon. Christ sufficiently testifies his forgiving Peter by committing his lambs and sheep to his trust. Observe, Penitents should be preachers; those that have taken warning themselves to turn and live should give warning to others not to go on and die. *When thou art converted strengthen thy brethren.* Preachers must be preaching *souls,* for that only is likely to reach to the heart that comes from the heart. Paul served God *with his spirit in the gospel of his Son,* Rom. 1:9.

2. *The son of David.* His taking this title intimates, (1.)

That he looked upon it as a great honour to be the son of so good a man, and valued himself very much upon it. (2.) That he also looked upon it as a great aggravation of his sin that he had such a father, who had given him a good education and put up many a good prayer for him; it cuts him to the heart to think that he should be a blemish and disgrace to the name and family of such a one as David. It aggravated the sin of Jehoiakim that he was the son of Josiah, Jer. 22:15–17. (3.) That his being the son of David encouraged him to repent and hope for mercy, for David had fallen into sin, by which he should have been warned not to sin, but was not; but David repented, and therein he took example from him and found mercy as he did. Yet this was not all; he was that son of David concerning whom God had said that though he would *chasten his transgression with the rod,* yet he would not *break his covenant* with him, Ps. 89:34. Christ, the great preacher, was the *Son of David.*

3. *King of Jerusalem.* This he mentions, (1.) As that which was a very great aggravation of his sin. He was a king. God had done much for him, in raising him to the throne, and yet he had so ill requited him; his dignity made the bad example and influence of his sin the more dangerous, and many would follow his pernicious ways; especially as he was king of Jerusalem, the holy city, where God's temple was, and of his own building too, where the priests, the Lord's ministers, were, and his prophets who had taught him better things. (2.) As that which might give some advantage to what he wrote, for *where the word of a king is there is power.* He thought it no disparagement to him, as a king, to be a preacher; but the people would regard him the more as a preacher because he was a king. If men of honour would lay out themselves to do good, what a great deal of good might they do! Solomon looked as great in the pulpit, preaching the vanity of the world, as in his throne of ivory, judging.

The Chaldee-paraphrase (which, in this book, makes very large additions to the text, or comments upon it, all along) gives this account of Solomon's writing this book, That by the spirit of prophecy he foresaw the revolt of the ten tribes from his son, and, in process of time, the destruction of Jerusalem and the house of the sanctuary, and the captivity of the people, in the foresight of which he said, *Vanity of vanities, all is vanity;* and to that he applies many passages in this book.

II. The general scope and design of the book. What is it that this royal preacher has to say? That which he aims at is, for the making of us truly religious, to take down our esteem of and expectation from the things of this world. In order to this, he shows,

1. That they are all vanity, *v.* 2. This is the proposition he lays down and undertakes to prove: *Vanity of vanities, all is vanity.* It was no new text; his father David had more than once spoken to the same purport. The truth itself here asserted is, that *all is vanity,* all besides God and considered as abstract from him, the *all* of this world, all worldly employments and enjoyments, the *all* that *is in the world* (1 Jn. 2:16), all that which is agreeable to our senses and to our fancies in this present state, which gains pleasure to ourselves or reputation with others. It is *all vanity,* not only in the abuse of it, when it is perverted by the sin of man, but even in the use of it. Man, considered with reference to these things, is vanity (Ps. 39:5, 6), and, if there were not another life after this, were made in vain (Ps. 89:47); and those things, considered in reference to man (whatever they are in themselves), are *vanity.* They are impertinent to the soul, foreign, and add nothing to it; they do not answer the end, nor yield any true satisfaction; they are uncertain in their continuance, are fading, and perishing, and passing away, and will certainly deceive and disappoint those that put a confidence in them. Let us not therefore *love vanity* (Ps. 4:2), nor *lift up our souls* to it (Ps. 24:4), for we shall but weary ourselves for it, Heb. 2:13. It is expressed here very emphatically; not only, *All is vain,* but in the abstract, *All is vanity;* as if vanity were the *proprium quarto modo — property in the fourth mode,* of the things of this world, that which enters into the nature of them. The are not only *vanity,* but *vanity of vanities,* the vainest vanity, vanity in the highest degree, nothing but vanity, such a vanity as is the cause of a great deal of vanity. And this is redoubled, because the thing is certain and past dispute, it is *vanity of vanities.* This intimates that the

wise man had his own heart fully convinced of and much affected with this truth, and that he was very desirous that others should be convinced of it and affected with it, as he was, but that he found the generality of men very loth to believe it and consider it (Job 33:14); it intimates likewise that we cannot comprehend and express the vanity of this world. But who is it that speaks thus slightly of the world? Is it one that will stand to what he says? Yes, he puts his name to it — *saith the preacher.* Is it one that was a competent judge? Yes, as much as ever any man was. Many speak contemptuously of the world because they are hermits, and know it not, or beggars, and have it not; but Solomon knew it. He had dived into nature's depths (1 Ki. 4:33), and he had it, more of it perhaps than ever any man had, his head filled with its notions and *his belly* with its *hidden treasures* (Ps. 17:14), and he passes this judgment on it. But did he speak as one having authority? Yes, not only that of a king, but that of a prophet, a preacher; he spoke in God's name, and was divinely inspired to say it. But did he not say it in his haste, or in a passion, upon occasion of some particular disappointment? No; he said it deliberately, said it and proved it, laid it down as a fundamental principle, on which he grounded the necessity of being religious. And, as some think, one main thing he designed was to show that the everlasting throne and kingdom which God had by Nathan promised to David and his seed must be of another world; for all things in this world are subject to vanity, and therefore have not in them sufficient to answer the extent of that promise. If Solomon find all to be vanity, then the kingdom of the Messiah must come, in which we shall inherit substance.

2. That they are insufficient to make us happy. And for this he appeals to men's consciences: *What profit has a man of all the pains he takes? v.* 3. Observe here, (1.) The business of this world described. It is *labour;* the word signifies both care and toil. It is work that wearies men. There is a constant fatigue in worldly business. It is *labour under the sun;* that is a phrase peculiar to this book, where we meet with it twenty-eight times. There is a world above the sun, a world which needs not the sun, for the glory of God is its light, where there is work without labour and with great profit, the work of angels; but he speaks of the work *under the sun,* the pains of which are great and the gains little. It is *under the sun,* under the influence of the sun, by its light and in its heat; as we have the benefit of the light of the day, so we have sometimes the burden and heat of the day (Mt. 20:12), and therefore *in the sweat of our face we eat bread.* In the dark and cold grave the weary are at rest. (2.) The benefit of that business enquired into: *What profit has a man of all that labour?* Solomon says (Prov. 14:23), *In all labour there is profit;* and yet here he denies that there is any profit. As to our present condition in the world, it is true that by labour we get that which we call *profit; we eat the labour of our hands;* but as the wealth of the world is commonly called *substance,* and yet it is *that which is not* (Prov. 22:5), so it is called *profit,* but the question is whether it be really so or no. And here he determines that it is not, that it is not a real benefit, that it is not a remaining benefit. In short, the wealth and pleasure of this world, if we had ever so much of them, are not sufficient to make us happy, nor will they be a portion for us. [1.] As to the body, and the life that now is, *What profit has a man of all his labour? A man's life consists not in an abundance,* Lu. 12:15. As goods are increased care about them is increased, and *those are increased that eat of them,* and a little thing will embitter all the comfort of them; and then *what profit has a man of all his labour?* Early up, and never the nearer. [2.] As to the soul, and the life that is to come, we may much more truly say, *What profit has a man of all his labour?* All he gets by it will not supply the wants of the soul, nor satisfy its desires, will not atone for the sin of the soul, nor cure its diseases, nor contervail the loss of it; what profit will they be of to the soul in death, in judgment, or in the everlasting state? The fruit of our labour in heavenly things is *meat that endures to eternal life,* but the fruit of our labour for the world is only *meat that perishes.*

Verses 4–8

To prove the vanity of all things under the sun, and their insufficiency to make us happy, Solomon here shows, 1. That the time of our enjoyment of these things is very short, and only while we *accomplish as a hireling his day.* We continue in the world but for one generation, which is continually passing away to make room for another, and we are passing with it. Our worldly possessions we very lately had from others, and must very shortly leave to others, and therefore to us they are vanity; they can be no more substantial than that life which is the *substratum* of them, and that is but a *vapour, which appears for a little while and then vanishes away.* While the stream of mankind is continually flowing, how little enjoyment has one drop of that stream of the pleasant banks between which it glides! We may give God the glory of that constant succession of generations, in which the world has hitherto had its existence, and will have to the end of time, admitting his patience in continuing that sinful species and his power in continuing that dying species. We may be also quickened to do the work of our generation diligently, and serve it faithfully, because it will be over shortly; and, in concern for mankind in general, we should consult the welfare of succeeding generations; but as to our own happiness, let us not expect it within such narrow limits, but in an eternal rest and consistency. 2. That when we leave this world we leave the earth behind us, that *abides for ever* where it is, and therefore the things of the earth can stand us in no stead in the future state. It is well for mankind in general that the earth endures to the end of time, when it and all the works in it shall be burnt up; but what is that to particular persons, when they remove to the world of spirits? 3. That the condition of man is, in this respect, worse than that even of the inferior creatures: *The earth abides for ever,* but man abides upon the earth but a little while. The sun sets indeed every night, yet it rises again in the morning, as bright and fresh as ever; the winds, though they shift their point, yet in some point or other still they are; the waters that go to the sea above ground come from it again under ground. *But man lies down and rises not,* Job 14:7, 12. 4. That all things in this world are movable and mutable, and subject to a continual toil and agitation, constant in nothing but inconstancy, still going, never resting; it was but once that the sun stood still; when it is risen it is hastening to set, and, when it is set, hastening to rise again (*v.* 5); the winds are ever and anon shifting (*v.* 6), and the waters in a continual circulation (*v.* 7), it would be of as bad consequence for them to stagnate as for the blood in the body to do so. And can we expect rest in a world where all things are thus full of labour (*v.* 8), on a sea that is always ebbing and flowing, and her waves continually working and rolling? 5. That though all things are still in motion, yet they are still where they were; The sun *parts* (as it is in the margin), but it is to the same place; the wind turns till it comes to the same place, and so the waters return to the place whence they came. Thus man, after all the pains he takes to find satisfaction and happiness in the creature, is but where he was, still as far to seek as ever. Man's mind is as restless in its pursuits as the sun, and wind, and rivers, but never satisfied, never contented; the more it has of the world the more it would have; and it would be no sooner filled with the streams of outward prosperity, the brooks of *honey and butter* (Job 20:17), than the sea is with *all the rivers that run into it;* it is still as it was, *a troubled sea that cannot rest.* 6. That *all things continue as they were from the beginning of the creation,* 2 Pt. 3:4. The earth is where it was; the sun, and winds, and rivers, keep the same course that ever they did; and therefore, if they have never yet been sufficient to make a happiness for man, they are never likely to be so, for they can but yield the same comfort that they have yielded. We must therefore look above the sun for satisfaction, and for a new world. 7. That this world is, at the best, a weary land: *All is vanity,* for all is *full of labour.* The whole creation is made subject to this vanity ever since man was sentenced to *eat bread in the sweat of his brows.* If we survey the whole creation, we shall see all busy; all have enough to do to mind their own business; none will be a portion or happiness for man; all labour to serve him, but none prove a *help-meet* for him. Man cannot express how full of labour all things are, can neither number the laborious nor measure the labours. 8. That our senses are unsatisfied, and the objects of them unsatisfying. He specifies those senses that perform their office with least toil, and are most capable of being pleased: *The eye is not satisfied with seeing,* but is weary of seeing

always the same sight, and covets novelty and variety. *The ear* is fond, at first, of a pleasant song or tune, but soon nauseates it, and must have another; both are surfeited, but neither satiated, and what was most grateful becomes ungrateful. Curiosity is still inquisitive, because still unsatisfied, and the more it is humoured the more nice and peevish it grows, crying, *Give, give.*

Verses 9–11

Two things we are apt to take a great deal of pleasure and satisfaction in, and value ourselves upon, with reference to our business and enjoyments in the world, as if they helped to save them from vanity. Solomon shows us our mistake in both.

1. The novelty of the invention, that it is such as was never known before. How grateful is it to think that none ever made such advances in knowledge, and such discoveries by it, as we, that none ever made such improvements of an estate or trade, and had the art of enjoying the gains of it, as we have. Their contrivances and compositions are all despised and run down, and we boast of new fashions, new hypotheses, new methods, new expressions, which jostle out the old, and put them down. But this is all a mistake: *The thing that* is, and *shall be, is* the same with *that which has been, and that which shall be done* will be but the same with *that which is done,* for *there is no new thing under the sun, v.* 9. It is repeated (*v.* 10) by way of question, *is there any thing* of which *it may be said,* with wonder, *See, this is new;* there never was the like? It is an appeal to observing men, and a challenge to those that cry up modern learning above that of the ancients. Let them name any thing which they take to be new, and though perhaps we cannot make it to appear, for want of the records of former times, yet we have reason to conclude *that it has been already of old time, which was before us.* What is there in the kingdom of nature of which we may say, *This is new? The works were finished from the foundation of the world* (Heb. 4:3); things which appear new to us, as they do to children, are not so in themselves. The heavens were *of old;* the earth abides for ever; the powers of nature and the links of natural causes are still the same that ever they were. In the kingdom of Providence, though the course and method of it have not such known and certain rules as that of nature, nor does it go always in the same track, yet, in the general, it is still the same thing over and over again. Men's hearts, and the corruptions of them, are still the same; their desires, and pursuits, and complaints, are still the same; and what God does in his dealings with men is according to the scripture, according to the manner, so that it is all repetition. What is surprising to us needs not be so, for there has been the like, the like strange revolutions and sudden turns, sudden turns of affairs; the miseries of human life have always been much the same, and mankind tread a perpetual round, and, as the sun and wind, are but where they were. Now the design of this is, (1.) To show the folly of the children of men in affecting things that are new, in imagining that they have discovered such things, and in pleasing and priding themselves in them. We are apt to nauseate old things, and to grow weary of what we have been long used to, as Israel of the manna, and covet, with the Athenians, still to tell and hear of some new thing, whereas it is all what has been. Tatianus the Assyrian, showing the Grecians how all the arts which they valued themselves upon owed their original to those nations which they counted barbarous, thus reasons with them: "For shame, do not call those things *eurēseis — inventions,* which are but *mimēseis — imitations.*" (2.) To take us off from expecting happiness or satisfaction in the creature. Why should we look for it there, where never any yet have found it? What reason have we to think that the world should be any kinder to us than it has been to those that have gone before us, since there is nothing in it that is new, and our predecessors have made as much of it as could be made? *Your fathers did eat manna, and* yet they are *dead.* See Jn. 8:8, 9; 6:49. (3.) To quicken us to secure spiritual and eternal blessings. If we would be entertained with new things, we must acquaint ourselves with the things of God, get a new nature; then *old things pass away, and all things become new,* 2 Co. 5:17. The gospel puts *a new song into our mouths.* In heaven *all is new* (Rev. 21:5), all new at first, wholly unlike the present state of things, a

new world indeed (Lu. 20:35), and all new to eternity, always fresh, always flourishing. This consideration should make us willing to die, That in this world there is nothing but the same over and over again, and we can expect nothing from it more or better than we have had.

2. The memorableness of the achievement, that it is such as will be known and talked of hereafter. Many think they have found satisfaction enough in this, that their names shall be perpetuated, that posterity will celebrate the actions they have performed, the honours they have won, and the estates they have raised, that *their houses shall continue for ever* (Ps. 49:11); but herein they deceive themselves. How many *former things* and persons were there, which in their day looked very great and made a mighty figure, and yet *there is no remembrance* of them; they are buried in oblivion. Here and there one person or action that was remarkable met with a kind historian, and had the good hap to be recorded, when at the same time there were others, no less remarkable, that were dropped: and therefore we may conclude that *neither shall there be any remembrance of things to come,* but that which we hope to be remembered by will be either lost or slighted.

Verses 12–18

Solomon, having asserted in general that *all is vanity,* and having given some general proofs of it, now takes the most effectual method to evince the truth of it, 1. By his own experience; he tried them all, and found them vanity. 2. By an induction of particulars; and here he begins with that which bids fairest of all to be the happiness of a reasonable creature, and that is knowledge and learning; if this be vanity, every thing else must needs be so. Now as to this,

I. Solomon tells us here what trial he had made of it, and that with such advantages that, if true satisfaction could have been found in it, he would have found it. 1. His high station gave him an opportunity of improving himself in all parts of learning, and particularly in politics and the conduct of human affairs, *v.* 12. He that is *the preacher* of this doctrine *was king over Israel,* whom all their neighbours admired as *a wise and understanding people,* Deu. 4:6. He had his royal seat *in Jerusalem,* which then deserved, better than Athens ever did, to be called *the eye of the world.* The heart of a king is unsearchable; he has reaches of his own, and *a divine sentence is often in his lips.* It is his honour, it is his business, to search out every matter. Solomon's great wealth and honour put him into a capacity of making his court the centre of learning and the rendezvous of learned men, of furnishing himself with the best of books, and either conversing or corresponding with all the wise and knowing part of mankind then in being, who made application to him to learn of him, by which he could not but improve himself; for it is in knowledge as it is in trade, all the profit is by barter and exchange; if we have that to say which will instruct others, they will have that to say which will instruct us. Some observe how slightly Solomon speaks of his dignity and honour. He does not say, *I the preacher am* king, but I *was king,* no matter what I am. He speaks of it as a thing past, because worldly honours are transitory. 2. He applied himself to the improvement of these advantages, and the opportunities he had of getting wisdom, which, though ever so great, will not make a man wise unless he give his mind to it. Solomon *gave his heart to seek and search out* all things to be known *by wisdom, v.* 13. He made it his business to acquaint himself with *all the things that are done under the sun,* that are done by the providence of God or by the art and prudence of man. He set himself to get all the insight he could into philosophy and mathematics, into husbandry and trade, merchandise and mechanics, into the history of former ages and the present state of other kingdoms, their laws, customs, and policies, into men's different tempers, capacities, and projects, and the methods of managing them; he set himself not only to seek, but to search, to pry into, that which is most intricate, and which requires the closes application of mind and the most vigorous and constant prosecution. Though he was a prince, he made himself a drudge to learning, was not discouraged by its knots, nor took up short of its depths. And this he did, not merely to gratify his own genius, but to qualify himself for the service of God, and his generation, and to make an experiment how far the enlargement of the knowledge would go towards the settlement and repose of the mind. 3. He made a very great progress in his studies, wonderfully improved all the parts of learning, and carried his discoveries much further than any that had been before him. He did not condemn learning, as many do, because they cannot conquer it and will not be at the pains to make themselves masters of it; no, what he aimed at he compassed; he *saw all the works that were done under the sun* (v. 14), works of nature in the upper and lower world, all within this vortex (to use the modern gibberish) which has the sun for its centre, works of art, the product of men's wit, in a personal or social capacity. he had as much satisfaction in the success of his searches as ever any man had; he *communed with his own heart* concerning his attainments in knowledge, with as much pleasure as ever any rich merchant had in taking account of his stock. He could say, *"Lo, I have magnified and increased wisdom,* have not only gotten more of it myself, but have done more to propagate it and bring it into reputation, than any, *than all that have been before me in Jerusalem."* Note, It becomes great men to be studious, and delight themselves most in intellectual pleasures. Where God gives great advantages of getting knowledge he expects improvements accordingly. It is happy with a people when their princes and noblemen study to excel others as much in wisdom and useful knowledge as they do in honour and estate; and they may do that service to the commonwealth of learning by applying themselves to the studies that are proper for them which meaner persons cannot do. Solomon must be acknowledged as competent judge of this matter, for he had not only got his head full of notions, but his *heart had great experience of wisdom and knowledge,* of the power and benefit of knowledge, as well as the amusement and entertainment of it; what he knew he had digested, and knew how to make use of. *Wisdom entered into his heart,* and so became *pleasant to his soul,* Prov. 2:10, 11; 22:18. 4. He applied his studies especially to that part of learning which is most serviceable to the conduct of human life, and consequently is the most valuable (v. 17): *"I gave my heart to know* the rules and dictates of *wisdom,* and how I might obtain it; *and to know madness and folly,* how I might prevent and cure it, to know the snares and insinuations of it, that I might avoid them, and guard against them, and discover its fallacies." So industrious was Solomon to improve himself in knowledge that he gained instruction both by the wisdom of prudent men and by the madness of foolish men, by *the field of the slothful,* as well as of *the diligent.*

II. He tells us what was the result of this trial, to confirm what he had said, that *all is vanity.*

1. He found that his searches after knowledge were very toilsome, and a weariness not only to the flesh, but to the mind (v. 13): *This sore travail,* this difficulty that there is in searching after truth and finding it, *God has given to the sons of men to be* afflicted *therewith,* as a punishment for our first parents' coveting forbidden knowledge. As bread for the body, so that for the soul, must be got and eaten *in the sweat of our face,* whereas both would have been had without labour if Adam had not sinned.

2. He found that the more he saw of *the works done under the sun* the more he saw of their vanity; nay, and the sight often occasioned him *vexation of spirit* (v. 14): *"I have seen all the works* of a world full of business, have observed what the children of men are doing; *and behold,* whatever men think of their own works, I see *all is vanity and vexation of spirit."* He had before pronounced all *vanity* (v. 2), needless and unprofitable, and that which does us no good; here he adds, It is all *vexation of spirit,* troublesome and prejudicial, and that which does us hurt. It is *feeding upon wind;* so some read it, Hos. 12:1. (1.) The works themselves which we see done are *vanity and vexation* to those that are employed in them. There is so much care in the contrivance of our worldly business, so much toil in the prosecution of it, and so much trouble in the disappointments we meet with in it, that we may well say, It is *vexation of spirit.* (2.) The sight of them is *vanity and vexation of spirit* to the wise observer of them. The more we see of the world the more we see to make us uneasy, and, with Heraclitus, to look upon all with weeping eyes. Solomon especially perceived that the knowledge of *wisdom and folly* was *vexation of spirit,* v. 17. It vexed him to see many that had wisdom not use it, and many that

had folly not strive against it. It vexed him when he knew wisdom to see how far off it stood from the children of men, and, when he saw folly, to see how fast it was bound in their hearts.

3. He found that when he had got some knowledge he could neither gain that satisfaction to himself nor do that good to others with it which he expected, v. 15. It would not avail, (1.) To redress the many grievances of human life: "After all, I find that *that which is crooked* will be crooked still and *cannot be made straight."* Our knowledge is itself intricate and perplexed; we must go far about and fetch a great compass to come at it. Solomon thought to find out a nearer way to it, but he could not. The paths of learning are as much a labyrinth as ever they were. The minds and manners of men are crooked and perverse. Solomon thought, with his wisdom and power together, thoroughly to reform his kingdom, and make that straight which he found crooked; but he was disappointed. All the philosophy and politics in the world will not restore the corrupt nature of man to its primitive rectitude; we find the insufficiency of them both in others and in ourselves. Learning will not alter men's natural tempers, nor cure them of their sinful distempers; nor will it change the constitution of things in this world; a vale of tears it is and so it will be when all is done. (2.) To make up the many deficiencies in the comfort of human life: *That which is wanting* there *cannot be numbered,* or counted out to us from the treasures of human learning, but what *is wanting* will still be so. All our enjoyments here, when we have done our utmost to bring them to perfection, are still lame and defective, and it cannot be helped; as they are, so they are likely to be. *That which is wanting* in our knowledge is so much that it *cannot be numbered.* The more we know the more we see of our own ignorance. *Who can understand his errors,* his defects?

4. Upon the whole, therefore, he concluded that great scholars do but make themselves great mourners; *for in much wisdom is much grief,* v. 18. There must be a great deal of pains taken to get it, and a great deal of care not to forget it; the more we know the more we see there is to be known, and consequently we perceive with greater clearness that our work is without end, and the more we see of our former mistakes and blunders, which occasions *much grief.* The more we see of men's different sentiments and opinions (and it is that which a great deal of our learning is conversant about) the more at a loss we are, it may be, which is in the right. Those *that increase knowledge* have so much the more quick and sensible perception of the calamities of this world, and for one discovery they make that is pleasing, perhaps, they make ten that are displeasing, and so they *increase sorrow.* Let us not therefore be driven off from the pursuit of any useful knowledge, but put on patience to break through the sorrow of it; but let us despair of finding true happiness in this knowledge, and expect it only in the knowledge of God and the careful discharge of our duty to him. *He that increases* in heavenly wisdom, and in an experimental acquaintance with the principles, powers, and pleasures of the spiritual and divine life, *increases* joy, such as will shortly be consummated in everlasting joy.

CHAPTER 2

Solomon having pronounced all vanity, and particularly knowledge and learning, which he was so far from giving himself joy of that he found the increase of it did but increase his sorrow, in this chapter he goes on to show what reason he has to be tired of this world, and with what little reason most men are fond of it. I. He shows that there is no true happiness and satisfaction to be had in mirth and pleasure, and the delights of sense (v. 1-11). II. He reconsiders the pretensions of wisdom, and allows it to be excellent and useful, and yet sees it clogged with such diminutions of its worth that it proves insufficient to make a man happy (v. 12-16). III. He enquires how far the business and wealth of this world will go towards making men happy, and concludes, from his own experience, that, to those who set their hearts upon it, "it is vanity and vexation of spirit," (v. 17-23), and that, if there be any good in it, it is only to those that sit loose to it (v. 24-26).

Verses 1–11

Solomon here, in pursuit of the *summum bonum — the felicity* of man, adjourns out of his study, his library, his elaboratory, his council-chamber, where he had in vain sought for it, into the park and the playhouse, his garden and his summer-house; he exchanges the company of the philosophers and grave senators for that of the wits and

gallants, and the beaux-esprits, of his court, to try if he could find true satisfaction and happiness among them. Here he takes a great step downward, from the noble pleasures of the intellect to the brutal ones of sense; yet, if he resolve to make a thorough trial, he must knock at this door, because here a great part of mankind imagine they have found that which he was in quest of.

I. He resolved to try what mirth would do and the pleasures of wit, whether he should be happy if he constantly entertained himself and others with merry stories and jests, banter and drollery; if he should furnish himself with all the pretty ingenious turns and repartees he could invent or pick up, fit to be laughed over, and all the bulls, and blunders, and foolish things, he could hear of, fit to be ridiculed and laughed at, so that he might be always in a merry humour. 1. This experiment made (v. 1): "Finding that *in much wisdom is much grief,* and that those who are serious are apt to be melancholy, *I said in my heart"* (to my heart), *"Go to now, I will prove thee with mirth;* I will try if that will give thee satisfaction." Neither the temper of his mind nor his outward condition had any thing in them to keep him from being merry, but both agreed, as did all other advantages, to further it; *therefore* he resolved to take a lease this way, and said, *"Enjoy pleasure,* and take thy fill of it; cast away care, and resolve to be merry." So a man may be, and yet have none of these fine things which he here got to entertain himself with; many that are poor are very merry; beggars in a barn are so to a proverb. Mirth is the entertainment of the fancy, and, though it comes short of the solid delights of the rational powers, yet it is to be preferred before those that are merely carnal and sensual. Some distinguish man from the brutes, not only as *animal rationale — a rational animal,* but as *animal risibile — a laughing animal;* therefore he that said to his soul, *Take thy ease, eat and drink,* added, *And be merry,* for it was in order to that that he would eat and drink. "Try therefore," says Solomon, "to laugh and be fat, to laugh and be happy." 2. The judgment he passed upon this experiment: *Behold, this also is vanity,* like all the rest; it yields no true satisfaction, v. 2. *I said of laughter, It is mad,* or, *Thou art mad,* and therefore I will have nothing to do with thee; *and of mirth* (of all sports and recreations, and whatever pretends to be diverting), *What doeth it?* or, *What doest thou?* Innocent mirth, soberly, seasonable, and moderately used, is a good thing, fits for business, and helps to soften the toils and chagrins of human life; but, when it is excessive and immoderate, it is foolish and fruitless. (1.) It does no good: *What doeth it? Cui bono — of what use is it?* It will not avail to quiet a guilty conscience; no, nor to ease a sorrowful spirit; nothing is more ungrateful than *singing songs to a heavy heart.* It will not satisfy the soul, nor ever yield it true content. It is but a palliative cure to the grievances of this present time. Great laughter commonly ends in a sigh. (2.) It does a great deal of hurt: *It is mad,* that is, it makes men mad, it transports men into many indecencies, which are a reproach to their reason and religion. They are mad that indulge themselves in it, for it estranges the heart from God and divine things, and insensibly eats out the power of religion. Those that love to be merry forget to be serious, and, while they take the timbrel and harp, they *say to the Almighty, Depart from us,* Job 21:12, 14. We may, as Solomon, *prove* ourselves, *with mirth,* and judge of the state of our souls by this: How do we stand affected to it? Can we be merry and wise? Can we use it as sauce, and not as food? But we need not try, as Solomon did, whether it will make a happiness for us, for we may take his word for it, *It is mad; and What does it?* Laughter and pleasure (says Sir William Temple) come from very different affections of the mind; for, as men have no disposition to laugh at things they are most pleased with, so they are very little pleased with many things they laugh at.

II. Finding himself not happy in that which pleased his fancy, he resolved next to try that which would please the palate, v. 3. Since the knowledge of the creature would not satisfy, he would see what the liberal use of it would do: *I sought in my heart to give myself unto wine,* that is, to good meat and good drink. Many give themselves to these without consulting their hearts at all, not looking any further than merely the gratification of the sensual appetite; but Solomon applied himself to it rationally, and as a man, critically, and only to make an experiment. Observe, 1. He did not allow himself any liberty in the use of the delights of sense till he had tired himself with his severe studies. Till his *increase* of *sorrow,* he never thought of giving himself *to wine.* When we have spent ourselves in doing good we may then most comfortably refresh ourselves with the gifts of God's bounty. *Then* the delights of sense are rightly used when they are used as we use cordials, only when we need them; as Timothy drank wine for his health's sake, 1 Tim. 5:23. *I thought to draw my flesh with wine* (so the margin reads it) or *to wine.* Those that have addicted themselves to drinking did at first put a force upon themselves; they drew their flesh to it, and with it; but they should remember to what miseries they hereby draw themselves. 2. He then looked upon it as folly, and it was with reluctance that he gave himself to it; as St. Paul, when he commended himself, called it a *weakness,* and desired to be borne with in his *foolishness,* 2 Co. 11:1. He sought *to lay hold on folly,* to see the utmost that that folly would do towards making men happy; but he had like to have carried the jest (as we say) too far. He resolved that the folly should not take hold of him, not get the mastery of him, but he would lay hold on it, and keep it at a distance; yet he found it too hard for him. 3. He took care at the same time to *acquaint* himself *with wisdom,* to manage himself wisely in the use of his pleasures, so that they should not do him any prejudice nor disfit him to be a competent judge of them. When he *drew his flesh with wine* he *led his heart with wisdom* (so the word is), kept up his pursuits after knowledge, did not make a sot of himself, nor become a slave to his pleasures, but his studies and his feasts were foils to each other, and he tried whether both mixed together would give him that satisfaction which he could not find in either separately. This Solomon proposed to himself, but he found it *vanity;* for those that think to give themselves to wine, and yet to acquaint their hearts with wisdom, will perhaps deceive themselves as much as those do that think to serve both God and mammon. *Wine is a mocker;* it is a great cheat; and it will be impossible for any man to say that thus far he will give himself to it and no further. 4. That which he aimed at was not to gratify his appetite, but to find out man's happiness, and this, because it pretended to be so, must be tried among the rest. Observe the description he gives of man's happiness — it is *that good for the sons of men which they should do under the heaven all their days.* (1.) That which we are to enquire after is not so much the good we must have (we may leave that to God), but the good we must do; that ought to be our care. *Good Master, what good thing shall I do?* Our happiness consists not in being idle, but in doing aright, in being well employed. If we *do that which is good,* no doubt we shall have comfort and *praise of the same.* (2.) It is good to be done *under the heaven,* while we are here in this world, while it is day, while our doing time lasts. This is our state of work and service; it is in the other world that we must expect the retribution. Thither our works will follow us. (3.) It is to be done *all the days of our life.* The good we are to do we must persevere in the doing of to the end, while our doing time lasts, *the number of the days of our life* (so it is in the margin); the days of our life are numbered to us by him in whose hand our times are and they are all to be spent as he directs. But that any man should give himself to wine, in hopes to find out in that the best way of living in this world, was an absurdity which Solomon here, in the reflection, condemns himself for. Is it possible that this should be the good that men should do? No; it is plainly very bad.

III. Perceiving quickly that it was folly to give himself to wine, he next tried the most costly entertainments and amusements of princes and great men. He had a vast income; the revenue of his crown was very great, and he laid it out so as might most please his own humour and make him look great.

1. He gave himself much to building, both in the city and in the country; and, having been at such vast expense in the beginning of his reign to build a house for God, he was the more excusable if afterwards he pleased his own fancy in building for himself; he began his work at the right end (Mt. 6:33), not as the people (Hag. 1:4), that *ceiled their own houses* while God's *lay waste,* and it prospered accordingly. In building, he had the pleasure of employing the poor and doing good to posterity. We read of Solomon's buildings (1 Ki. 9:15–19), and they were all *great works,* such as became his purse, and spirit, and great dignity. See his mistake; he enquired after the *good* works he should do (*v.* 3), and, in pursuit of the enquiry, applied himself to *great* works. *Good* works indeed are truly great, but many are reputed great works which are far from being good, wondrous works which are not gracious, Mt. 7:22.

2. He took to love a garden, which is to some as bewitching as building. He *planted himself vineyards,* which the soil and climate of the land of Canaan favoured; he *made himself* fine *gardens and orchards* (*v.* 5), and perhaps the art of gardening was no way inferior then to what it is now. He had not only forests of timber-trees, but *trees of all kinds of fruit,* which he himself had planted; and, if any worldly business would yield a man happiness, surely it must be that which Adam was employed in while he was in innocency.

3. He laid out a great deal of money in water-works, ponds, and canals, not for sport and diversion, but for use, *to water the wood that brings forth trees* (*v.* 6); he not only planted, but watered, and then left it to God to give the increase. *Springs of water* are great *blessings* (Jos. 15:19); but where nature has provided them art must direct them, to make them serviceable, Prov. 21:1.

4. He increased his family. When he proposed to himself to do *great works* he must employ many hands, and therefore procured *servants and maidens,* which were bought with his money, and of those he *had servants born in his house, v.* 7. Thus his retinue was enlarged and his court appeared more magnificent. See Ezra 2:58.

5. He did not neglect country business, but both entertained and enriched himself with that, and was not diverted from it either by his studies or by his pleasures. He *had large possessions of great and small cattle,* herds and flocks, as his father had before him (1 Chr. 27:29, 31), not forgetting that his father, in the beginning, was a keeper of sheep. Let those that deal in cattle neither despise their employment nor be weary of it, remembering that Solomon puts his having *possessions of cattle* among his *great works* and his pleasures.

6. He grew very rich, and was not at all impoverished by his building and gardening, as many are, who, for that reason only, repent it, and call it *vanity and vexation.* Solomon scattered and yet increased. He filled his exchequer with *silver and gold,* which yet did not stagnate there, but were made to circulate through his kingdom, so that he made *silver to be in Jerusalem as stones* (1 Ki. 10:27); nay, he had the *segullah, the peculiar treasure of kings and of the provinces,* which was, for richness and rarity, more accounted of than *silver and gold.* The neighbouring kings, and the distant provinces of his own empire, sent him the richest presents they had, to obtain his favour and the instructions of his wisdom.

7. He had every thing that was charming and diverting, all sorts of melody and music, vocal and instrumental, *men-singers and women-singers,* the best voices he could pick up, and all the wind and band-instruments that were then in use. His father had a genius for music, but it should seem he employed it more to serve his devotion than the son, who made it more for his diversion. These are called *the delights of the sons of men;* for the gratifications of sense are the things that the generality of people set their affections upon and take the greatest complacency in. The delights of the children of God are of quite another nature, pure, spiritual, and heavenly, and the delights of angels.

8. He enjoyed, more than ever any man did, a composition of rational and sensitive pleasures at the same time. He was, in this respect, *great, and increased more than all that were before him,* that he was wise amidst a thousand earthly enjoyments. It was strange, and the like was never met with, (1.) That his pleasures did not debauch his judgment and conscience. In the midst of these entertainments *his wisdom remained with him, v.* 9. In the midst of all these childish delights he preserved his spirit manly, kept the possession of his own soul, and maintained the dominion of reason over the appetites of sense; such a vast stock of wisdom had he that it was not wasted and impaired, as any other man's would have been, by this course of life. But let none be emboldened hereby to lay the reins on the neck of their appetites, presuming that they may do that and yet retain their wisdom, for they have not such a strength of wisdom as Solomon had; nay, and Solomon was deceived; for how did *his wisdom remain with him* when he lost his religion so far as to build altars to strange gods, for the humouring of his strange wives? But thus far *his wisdom remained with him* that he was master of his pleasures, and not a slave to them, and kept himself capable of making a judgment of them. He went over into the enemies' country, not as a deserter, but as a *spy, to discover the nakedness of their land.* (2.) Yet his judgment and conscience gave no check to his pleasures, nor hindered him from exacting the very quintessence of the delights of sense, *v.* 10. It might be objected against his judgment in this matter that if *his wisdom remained with him* he could not take the liberty that was necessary to a full experimental acquaintance with it: "Yea," said he, "I took as great a liberty as any man could take, for *whatsoever my eyes desired I kept not from them,* if it could be compassed by lawful means, though ever so difficult or costly; and as *I withheld not any joy from my heart* that I had a mind to, so *I withheld not my heart from any joy,* but, with a *non-obstante — with the full exercise* of my wisdom, I had a high gust of my pleasures, relished and enjoyed them as much as ever any Epicure did;" nor was there any thing either in the circumstances of his condition or in the temper of his spirit to sour or embitter them, or give them any alloy. In short, [1.] He had as much pleasure in his business as ever any man had: *My heart rejoiced in all my labour;* so that the toil and fatigue of that were no damp to his pleasures. [2.] He had no less profit by his business. He met with no disappointment in it to give him any disturbance: *This was my portion of all my labour;* he had this added to all the rest of his pleasures that in them he did not only see, but eat, the labour of his hands; and this was all he had, for indeed it was all he could expect, from his labours. It sweetened his business that he enjoyed the success of it, and it sweetened his enjoyments that they were the product of his business; so that, upon the whole, he was certainly as happy as the world could make him.

9. We have, at length, the judgment he deliberately gave of all this, *v.* 11. When the Creator had made his great works he reviewed them, and *behold, all was very good;* every thing pleased him. But when Solomon reviewed *all his works that his hands had wrought* with the utmost cost and care, *and the labour that he had laboured to do* in order to make himself easy and happy, nothing answered his expectation; *behold, all was vanity and vexation of spirit;* he had no satisfaction in it, no advantage by it; *there was no profit under the sun,* neither by the employments nor by the enjoyments of this world.

Verses 12–16

Solomon having tried what satisfaction was to be had in learning first, and then in the pleasures of sense, and having also put both together, here compares them one with another and passes a judgment upon them.

I. He sets himself to consider both wisdom and folly. He had considered these before (*ch.* 1:17); but lest it should be thought he was then too quick in passing a judgment upon them, he here turns himself again to behold them, to see if, upon a second view and second thoughts, he could gain more satisfaction in the search than he had done upon the first. He was sick of his pleasures, and, as nauseating them, he turned from them, that he might again apply himself to speculation; and if, upon this rehearing of the cause, the verdict be still the same, the judgment will surely be decisive; *for what can the man do that comes after the king?* especially such a king, who had so much of this world to make the experiment upon and so much wisdom to make it with. The baffled trial needs not be repeated. No man can expect to find more satisfaction in the world than Solomon did, nor to gain a greater insight into the principles of morality; when a man has done what he can still it is *that which has been already done.* Let us learn, 1. Not to indulge ourselves in a fond conceit that we can mend that which has been well done before us. Let us *esteem others better than ourselves,* and think how unfit we are to attempt the improvement of the performances of better heads and hands than ours, and rather own how much we are beholden to them, Jn. 4:37, 38. 2. To acquiesce in Solomon's judgment of the things of this world, and not to think of repeating the trial; for we can never think of having such advantages as he had to make the experiment nor of being able to make it with equal application of mind and so little danger to ourselves.

II. He gives the preference to wisdom far before folly. Let none mistake him, as if, when he speaks of the vanity of human lite-rapture, he designed only to amuse men with a paradox, or were about to write (as a great wit once did) *Encomium moriae — A panegyric in praise of folly.* No, he is maintaining sacred truths, and therefore is careful to guard against being misunderstood. I soon *saw* (says he) *that there is an excellency in wisdom more than in folly,* as much as there is in light above darkness. The pleasures of wisdom, though they suffice not to make men happy, yet vastly transcend the pleasures of wine. Wisdom enlightens the soul with surprising discoveries and necessary directions for the right government of itself; but sensuality (for that seems to be especially the folly here meant) clouds and eclipses the mind, and is as darkness to it; it puts out men's eyes, makes them to stumble in the way and wander out of it. Or, though wisdom and knowledge will not make a man happy (St Paul shows a *more excellent way* than gifts, and that is grace), yet it is much better to have them than to be without them, in respect of our present safety, comfort, and usefulness; for *the wise man's eyes are in his head* (v. 14), where they should be, ready to discover both the dangers that are to be avoided and the advantages that are to be improved; a wise man has not his reason to seek when he should use it, but looks about him and is quick-sighted, knows both where to step and where to stop; whereas *the fool walks in darkness,* and is ever and anon either at a loss, or at a plunge, either bewildered, that he knows not which way to go, or embarrassed, that he cannot go forward. A man that is discreet and considerate has the command of his business, and acts decently and safely, as those that walk in the day; but he that is rash, and ignorant, and sottish, is continually making blunders, running upon one precipice or other; his projects, his bargains, are all foolish, and ruin his affairs. Therefore *get wisdom, get understanding.*

III. Yet he maintains that, in respect of lasting happiness and satisfaction, the wisdom of this world gives a man very little advantage; for, 1. Wise men and fools fare alike. "It is true the wise man has very much the advantage of the fool in respect of foresight and insight, and yet the greatest probabilities do so often come short of success that *I myself perceived,* by my own experience, that *one event happens to them all* (v. 14); those that are most cautious of their health are as soon sick as those that are most careless of it, and the most suspicious are imposed upon." David had observed that *wise men die,* and are involved in the same common calamity with the fool and the brutish person, Ps. 49:12. See *ch.* 9:11. Nay, it has of old been observed that *Fortune favours fools,* and that half-witted men often thrive most, while the greatest projectors forecast worst for themselves. The same sickness, the same sword, devours wise men and fools. Solomon applies this mortifying observation to himself (v. 15), that though he was a wise man, he might not *glory in his wisdom; I said to my heart,* when it began to be proud or secure, *As it happens to the fool, so it happens to me, even to me;* for thus emphatically it is expressed in the original: "So, *as for me,* it happens to me. Am I rich? So is many a Nabal that fares as sumptuously as I do. Is a foolish man sick, does he get a fall? So do I, *even I;* and neither my wealth nor my wisdom will be my security. *And why was I then more wise?* Why should I take so much pains to get wisdom, when, as to this life, it will stand me in so little stead? *Then I said in my heart that this also is vanity."* Some make this a correction of what was said before, like that (Ps. 77:10), *"I said, This is my infirmity;* it is my folly to think that wise men and fools are upon a level;" but really they seem to be so, in respect of the event, and therefore it is rather a confirmation of what he had before said, That a man may be a profound philosopher and politician and yet not be a happy man. 2. Wise men and fools are forgotten alike (v. 16): *There is no remembrance of the wise more than of the fool.* It is promised to the righteous that they *shall be had in everlasting remembrance,* and their *memory shall be blessed,* and they shall shortly *shine as the stars;* but there is no such promise made concerning the wisdom of this world, that that shall perpetuate men's names, for those names only are perpetuated that are *written in heaven,* and otherwise the names of this world's wise

men are written with those of its fools in the dust. *That which now is in the days to come shall all be forgotten.* What was much talked of in one generation is, in the next, as if it had never been. New persons and new things jostle out the very remembrance of the old, which in a little time are looked upon with contempt and at length quite buried in oblivion. *Where is the wise? Where is the disputer of this world?* 1 Co. 1:20. And it is upon this account that he asks, *How dies the wise man? As the fool.* Between the death of a godly and a wicked man there is a great difference, but not between the death of a wise man and a fool; the fool is buried and forgotten (*ch.* 8:10), *and no one remembered the poor man that by his wisdom delivered the city* (*ch.* 9:15); so that to both the grave is a *land of forgetfulness;* and wise and learned men, when they have been awhile there out of sight, grow out of mind, a new generation arises that *knew them not.*

Verses 17–26

Business is a thing that wise men have pleasure in. They are in their element when they are in their business, and complain if they be out of business. They may sometimes be tired with their business, but they are not weary of it, nor willing to leave it off. Here therefore one would expect to have found the good that men should do, but Solomon tried this too; after a contemplative life and a voluptuous life, he betook himself to an active life, and found no more satisfaction in it than in the other; still it is all *vanity and vexation of spirit,* of which he gives an account in these verses, where observe,

I. What the business was which he made trial of; it was business *under the sun* (v. 17–20), about the things of this world, sublunary things, the riches, honours, and pleasures of this present time; it was the business of a king. There is business *above the sun,* perpetual business, which is perpetual blessedness; what we do in conformity to that business (doing *God's will as it is done in heaven*) and in pursuance of that blessedness, will turn to a good account; we shall have no reason to hate that labour, nor to despair of it. But it is *labour under the sun,* labour for the *meat that perishes* (Jn. 6:27; Isa. 55:2), that Solomon here speaks of with so little satisfaction. It was the better sort of business, not that of the *hewers of wood and drawers of water* (it is not so strange if men hate all that labour), but it was *in wisdom, and knowledge, and equity,* v. 21. It was rational business, which related to the government of his kingdom and the advancement of its interests. It was labour managed by the dictates of wisdom, of natural and acquired knowledge, and the directions of justice. It was labour at the council-board and in the courts of justice. It was labour wherein he *showed himself wise* (v. 19), which as much excels the labour wherein men only show themselves strong as the endowments of the mind, by which we are allied to angels, do those of the body, which we have in common with the brutes. That which many people have in their eye more than any thing else, in the prosecution of their worldly business, is to *show themselves wise,* to get the reputation of ingenious men and men of sense and application.

II. His falling out with this business. He soon grew weary of it. 1. He *hated all his labour,* because he did not meet with that satisfaction in which he expected. After he had had his fine houses, and gardens, and water-works, awhile, he began to nauseate them, and look upon them with contempt, as children, who are eager for a toy and fond of it at first, but, when they have played with it awhile, are weary of it, and throw it away, and must have another. This expresses not a gracious hatred of these things, which is our duty, to love them less than God and religion (Lu. 14:26), nor a sinful hatred of them, which is our folly, to be weary of the place God has assigned us and the work of it, but a natural hatred of them, arising from a surfeit upon them and a sense of disappointment in them. 2. He *caused his heart to despair of all his labour* (v. 20); he took pains to possess himself with a deep sense of the vanity of worldly business, that it would not bring in the advantage and satisfaction he had formerly flattered himself with the hopes of. Our hearts are very loth to quit their expectations of great things from the creature; we must go about, must fetch a compass, in arguing with them, to convince them that there is not that in the things of this world which we are apt to promise ourselves from them. Have

we so often bored and sunk into this earth for some rich mine of satisfaction, and found not the least sign or token of it, but been always frustrated in the search, and shall we not at length set our hearts at rest and despair of ever finding it? 3. He came to that, at length, that he *hated life itself* (v. 17), because it is subject to so many toils and troubles, and a constant series of disappointments. God had given Solomon such largeness of heart, and such vast capacities of mind, that he experienced more than other men of the unsatisfying nature of all the things of this life and their insufficiency to make him happy. Life itself, that is so precious to a man, and such a blessing to a good man, may become a burden to a man of business.

III. The reasons of this quarrel with his life and labours. Two things made him weary of them: —

1. That his business was so great a toil to himself: The *work that he had wrought under the sun was grievous unto him,* v. 17. His thoughts and cares about it, and that close and constant application of mind which was requisite to it, were a burden and fatigue to him, especially when he grew old. It is the effect of a curse on that we are to work upon. Our business is said to be the *work and toil of our hands, because of the ground which the Lord had cursed* (Gen. 5:29) and of the weakening of the faculties we are to work with, and of the sentence pronounced on us, that in *the sweat of our face we must eat bread.* Our labour is called *the vexation of our heart* (v. 22); it is to most a force upon themselves, so natural is it to us to love our ease. A man of business is described to be uneasy both in his *going out* and his *coming in,* v. 23. (1.) He is deprived of his pleasure by day, for *all his days are sorrow,* not only sorrowful, but sorrow itself, nay, many sorrows and various; his travail, or labour, all day, is grief. Men of business ever and anon meet with that which vexes them, and is an occasion of anger or sorrow to them. Those that are apt to fret find that the more dealings they have in the world the oftener they are made to fret. The world is a *vale of tears,* even to those that have much of it. Those that *labour* are said to be *heavy-laden,* and are therefore called to come to Christ for rest, Mt. 11:28. (2.) He is disturbed in his repose *by night.* When he is overcome with the hurries of the day, and hopes to find relief when he lays his head on his pillow, he is disappointed there; cares *hold his eyes waking,* or, if he sleep, yet his heart wakes, and that *takes no rest in the night.* See what fools those are that make themselves drudges to the world, and do not make God their rest; night and day they cannot but be uneasy. So that, upon the whole matter, it is *all vanity,* v. 17. *This is vanity* in particular (v. 19, 23), nay, it is *vanity and a great evil,* v. 21. It is a great affront to God and a great injury to themselves, therefore a *great evil;* it is a vain thing *to rise up early and sit up late* in pursuit of this world's goods, which were never designed to be our chief good.

2. That the gains of his business must all be left to others. Prospect of advantage is the spring of action and the spur of industry; *therefore* men labour, because they hope to get by it; if the hope fail, the labour flags; and *therefore* Solomon quarrelled with all the works, the great works, he had made, because they would not be of any lasting advantage to himself. (1.) He must leave them. He could not at death take them away with him, nor any share of them, nor should he return any more to them (Job 7:10), nor would the remembrance of them do him any good, Lu. 16:25. But I must *leave all to the man that shall be after me,* to the generation that comes up in the room of that which is passing away. As there were many before us, who built the houses that we live in, and into whose purchases and labours we have entered, so there shall be many after us, who shall live in the houses that we build, and enjoy the fruit of our purchases and labours. Never was land lost for want of an heir. To a gracious soul this is no uneasiness at all; why should we grudge others their turn in the enjoyments of this world, and not rather be pleased that, when we are gone, those that come after us shall fare the better for our wisdom and industry? But to a worldly mind, that seeks for its own happiness in the creature, it is a great vexation to think of leaving the beloved pelf behind, at this uncertainty. (2.) He must leave them to those that would never have taken so much pains for them, and will thereby excuse himself from taking any pains. He that raised the estate did it by *labouring in wisdom, and knowledge, and equity;* but he that enjoys it and spends it (it may

be) *has not laboured therein* (*v.* 21), and, more than that, never will. The bee toils to maintain the drone. Nay, it proves a snare to him: it is left him *for his portion,* which he rests in, and takes up with; and miserable he is in being put off with it for a portion. Whereas, if an estate had not come to him thus easily, who knows but he might have been both industrious and religious? Yet we ought not to perplex ourselves about this, since it may prove otherwise, that what is well got may come to one that will use it well and do good with it. (3.) He knows not whom he must leave it to (for God makes heirs), or at least what *he* will prove to whom he leaves it, whether *a wise man or a fool,* a wise man that will make it more or a fool that will bring it to nothing; *yet he shall have rule over all my labour,* and foolishly undo that which his father wisely did. It is probable that Solomon wrote this very feelingly, being afraid what Rehoboam would prove. St Jerome, in his commentary on this passage, applies this to the good books which Solomon wrote, in which he had shown himself wise, but he knew not into the hands of a fool, who, according to the perverseness of his heart, makes a bad use of what was well written. So that, upon the whole matter, he asks (*v.* 22), *What has man of all his labour?* What has he to himself and to his own use? What has he that will go with him into another world?

IV. The best use which is therefore to be made of the wealth of this world, and that is to use it cheerfully, to take the comfort of it, and do good with it. With this he concludes the chapter, *v.* 24–26. There is no true happiness to be found in these things. They are *vanity,* and, if happiness be expected from them, the disappointment will be *vexation of spirit.* But he will put us in a way to make the best of them, and to avoid the inconveniences he had observed. We must neither over-toil ourselves, so as, in pursuit of more, to rob ourselves of the comfort of what we have, nor must we over-hoard for hereafter, nor lose our own enjoyment of what we have to lay it up for those that shall come after us, but serve ourselves out of it first. Observe,

1. What that good is which is here recommended to us; and which is the utmost pleasure and profit we can expect or extract from the business and profit of this world, and the furthest we can go to rescue it from its *vanity* and the *vexation* that is in it. (1.) We must do our duty with them, and be more in care how to use an estate well, for the ends for which we were entrusted with it, than how to raise or increase an estate. This is intimated *v.* 26, where *those* only are said to have the comfort of this life who are good in *God's sight,* and again, *good before God,* truly good, as Noah, whom *God saw righteous before him.* We must set God always before us, and give diligence in every thing to approve ourselves to him. The Chaldee-paraphrase says, *A man* should *make his soul to enjoy good by keeping the commandments of God and walking in the ways that are right before him,* and (*v.* 25) by *studying the words of the law, and being in care about the day of the great judgment that is to come.* (2.) We must take the comfort of them. These things will not make a happiness for the soul; all the good we can have out of them is for the body, and if we make use of them for the comfortable support of that, so that it may be fit to serve the soul and able to keep pace with it in the service of God, then they turn to a good account. *There is* therefore *nothing better for a man,* as to these things, than to allow himself a sober cheerful use of them, according as his rank and condition are, to have meat and drink out of them for himself, his family, his friends, and so delight his senses and make his *soul enjoy good,* all the good that is to be had out of them; do not lose that, in pursuit of that good which is not to be had out of them. But observe, He would not have us to give up business, and take our ease, that we may *eat and drink;* no, we must *enjoy good in our labour;* we must use these things, not to excuse us from, but to make us diligent and cheerful in, our worldly business. (3.) We must herein *acknowledge God;* we must see that *it is from the hand of God,* that is, [1.] The *good things* themselves that we enjoy are so, not only the products of his creating power, but the gifts of his providential bounty to us. And *then* they are truly pleasant to us when we take them from the hand of God as a Father, when we eye his wisdom giving us that which is fittest for us, and acquiesce in it, and taste his love and goodness, relish them, and are thankful for them. [2.] A heart to enjoy them is so; this is the gift of God's grace. Unless he give us wisdom to make a right use of what he has, in his providence, bestowed upon us, and withal peace of conscience, that we may discern God's favour in the world's smiles, we cannot make our souls enjoy any good in them.

2. Why we should have this in our eye, in the management of ourselves as to this world, and look up to God for it. (1.) Because Solomon himself, with all his possessions, could aim at no more and desire no better (*v.* 25): *"Who can hasten to this more than I?* This is that which I was ambitious of: I wished for no more; and those that have but little, in comparison with what I have, may attain to this, to be content with what they have and enjoy the good of it." Yet Solomon could not obtain it by his own wisdom, without the special grace of God, and therefore directs us to expect it from the hand of God and pray to him for it. (2.) Because riches are a blessing or a curse to a man according as he has or has not a heart to make good use of them. [1.] God makes them a reward to a good man, if with them he give him *wisdom, and knowledge, and joy,* to enjoy them cheerfully himself and to communicate them charitably to others. To those who are *good in God's sight,* who are of a good spirit, honest and sincere, pay a deference to their God and have a tender concern for all mankind, *God will give wisdom and knowledge in this world, and joy with the righteous in the world to come;* so the Chaldee. Or he will give that wisdom and knowledge in things natural, moral, political, and divine, which will be a constant joy and pleasure to them. [2.] He makes them a punishment to a bad man if he denies him a heart to take the comfort of them, for they do but tantalize him and tyrannize over him: *To the sinner God gives by travail,* by leaving him to himself and his own foolish counsels, to *gather and to heap up* that, which, as to himself, will not only burden him like *thick clay* (Hab. 2:6), but be *a witness against him and eat his flesh as it were fire* (Jam. 5:3); while God designs, by an overruling providence, to give it to him that is *good before him;* for the *wealth of the sinner is laid up for the just,* and *gathered for him that will pity the poor.* Note, *First, Godliness, with contentment, is great gain;* and *those* only have true joy that are *good in God's sight,* and that have it from him and in him. *Secondly,* Ungodliness is commonly punished with discontent and an insatiable covetousness, which are sins that are their own punishment. *Thirdly,* When God gives abundance to wicked men it is with design to force them to a resignation in favour of his own children, when they are of age and ready for it, as the Canaanites kept possession of the good land till the time appointed for Israel's entering upon it. [3.] The burden of the song is still the same: *This is also vanity and vexation of spirit.* It is vanity, at the best, even to the good man; when he has all that the sinner has scraped together it will not make him happy without something else; but it is *vexation of spirit* to the sinner to see what he had laid up enjoyed by him that is *good in God's sight,* and therefore evil in his. So that, take it which way you will, the conclusion is firm, *All is vanity and vexation of spirit.*

CHAPTER 3

Solomon having shown the vanity of studies, pleasures, and business, and made it to appear that happiness is not to be found in the schools of the learned, nor in the gardens of Epicurus, nor upon the exchange, he proceeds, in this chapter, further to prove his doctrine, and the inference he had drawn from it, That therefore we should cheerfully content ourselves with, and make use of, what God has given us, by showing, I. The mutability of all human affairs (*v.* 1–10). II. The immutability of the divine counsels concerning them and the unsearchableness of those counsels (*v.* 11–15). III. The vanity of worldly honour and power, which are abused for the support of oppression and persecution if men be not governed by the fear of God in the use of them (*v.* 16). For a check to proud oppressors, and to show them their vanity, he reminds them, 1. That they will be called to account for it in the other world (*v.* 17). 2. That their condition, in reference to this world (for of that he speaks), is no better than that of the beasts (*v.* 18–21). And therefore he concludes that it is our wisdom to make use of what power we have for our own comfort, and not to oppress others with it.

Verses 1–10

The scope of these verses is to show, 1. That we live in a world of changes, that the several events of time, and conditions of human life, are vastly different from one another, and yet occur promiscuously, and we are continually passing and repassing between them, as in the revolutions of every day and every year. In the *wheel of nature* (Jam. 3:6) sometimes one spoke is uppermost and by and by the contrary; there is a constant ebbing and flowing, waxing and waning; from one extreme to the other does the *fashion of this world change,* ever did, and ever will. 2. That every change concerning us, with the time and season of it, is unalterably fixed and determined by a supreme power; and we must take things as they come, for it is not in our power to change what is appointed for us. And this comes in here as a reason why, when we are in prosperity, we should by easy, and yet not secure — not to be secure because we live in a world of changes and therefore have no reason to say, *To-morrow shall be as this day* (the lowest valleys join to the highest mountains), and yet to be easy, and, as he had advised (*ch.* 2:24), *to enjoy the good of our labour,* in a humble dependence upon God and his providence, neither lifted up with hopes, nor cast down with fears, but with evenness of mind expecting every event. Here we have,

I. A general proposition laid down: *To every thing there is a season, v.* 1. 1. Those things which seem most contrary the one to the other will, in the revolution of affairs, each take their turn and come into play. The day will give place to the night and the night again to the day. Is it summer? It will be winter. Is it winter? Stay a while, and it will be summer. Every purpose has its time. The clearest sky will be clouded, *Post gaudia luctus — Joy succeeds sorrow;* and the most clouded sky will clear up, *Post nubila Phoebus — The sun will burst from behind the cloud.* 2. Those things which to us seem most casual and contingent are, in the counsel and foreknowledge of God, punctually determined, and the very hour of them is fixed, and can neither be anticipated nor adjourned a moment.

II. The proof and illustration of it by the induction of particulars, twenty-eight in number, according to the days of the moon's revolution, which is always increasing or decreasing between its full and change. Some of these changes are purely the act of God, others depend more upon the will of man, but all are determined by the divine counsel. Every thing *under heaven* is thus changeable, but in heaven there is an unchangeable state, and an unchangeable counsel concerning these things. 1. There is *a time to be born and a time to die.* These are determined by the divine counsel; and, as we were born, so we must die, at the time appointed, Acts 17:26. Some observe that here is *a time to be born and a time to die,* but no time to live; that is so short that it is not worth mentioning; as soon as we are born we begin to die. But, as there is *a time to be born and a time to die,* so there will be a time to rise again, a set time when those that lie in the grave shall be remembered, Job 14:13. 2. *A time* for God *to plant* a nation, as that of Israel in Canaan, *and,* in order to that, *to pluck up* the seven nations *that were planted* there, to make room for them; and at length there was a time when God spoke concerning Israel too, to *pluck up and to destroy,* when the measure of their iniquity was full, Jer. 18:7, 9. There is *a time* for men *to plant,* a time of the year, a time of their lives; but, when *that which was planted* has grown fruitless and useless, it is *time to pluck it up.* 3. *A time to kill,* when the judgments of God are abroad in a land and lay all waste; but, when he returns in ways of mercy, then is *a time to heal* what *he has torn* (Hos. 6:1, 2), to comfort a people after the time that he has *afflicted them,* Ps. 90:15. There is a time when it is the wisdom of rulers to use severe methods, but there is a time when it is as much their wisdom to take a more gentle course, and to apply themselves to lenitives, not corrosives. 4. *A time to break down* a family, an estate, a kingdom, when it has ripened itself for destruction; but God will find *a time,* if they return and repent, to rebuild what he has broken down; there is *a time,* a set time, for the Lord *to build up Zion,* Ps. 102:13, 16. There is *a time* for men *to break up* house, and break off trade, and so *to break down,* which those that are busy in *building up* both must expect and prepare for. 5. *A time* when God's providence calls *to weep and mourn,* and when man's wisdom and grace will comply with the call, and will *weep and mourn,* as in times of common calamity and danger, and there it is very absurd to *laugh, and dance,* and make merry (Isa. 22:12, 13; Eze. 21:10); but then, on the other hand, there is a time when God calls to cheerfulness, *a time to laugh and dance,* and then he expects we should *serve him with joyfulness and gladness of heart.* Observe, The time of mourning and weeping is put first, before that of laughter and dancing, for we must first *sow in tears* and then *reap in joy.* 6. *A time to cast away stones,* by breaking down and demolishing fortifications, when God gives peace in the borders, and there is no more occasion for them; but there is *a time to gather stones together,* for the making of strong-holds, *v.* 5. A time for old towers to fall, as that in Siloam (Lu. 12:4), and for the temple itself to be so ruined as that *not one stone should be left upon another;* but also a time for towers and trophies too to be erected, when national affairs prosper. 7. *A time to embrace* a friend when we find him faithful, but *a time to refrain from embracing* when we find he is unfair or unfaithful, and that we have cause to suspect him; it is then our prudence to be shy and keep at a distance. It is commonly applied to conjugal embraces, and explained by 1 Co. 7:3–5; Joel 2:16. 8. *A time to get,* get money, get preferment, get good bargains and a good interest, when opportunity smiles, a time when a wise man will *seek* (so the word is); when he is setting out in the world and has a growing family, when he is in his prime, when he prospers and has a run of business, then it is time for him to be busy and make hay when the sun shines. There is *a time to get* wisdom, and knowledge, and grace, when a man has a price put into his hand; but then let him expect there will come a time to spend, when all he has will be little enough to serve his turn. Nay, there will come *a time to lose,* when what has been soon got will be soon scattered and cannot be held fast. 9. *A time to keep,* when we have use for what we have got, and can keep it without running the hazard of a good conscience; but there may come *a time to cast away,* when love to God may oblige us to cast away what we have, because we must deny Christ and wrong our consciences if we keep it (Mt. 10:37, 38), and rather to make shipwreck of all than of the faith; nay, when love to ourselves may oblige us to cast it away, when it is for the saving of our lives, as it was when Jonah's mariners heaved their cargo into the sea. 10. *A time to rend* the garments, as upon occasion of some great grief, *and a time to sew,* them again, in token that the grief is over. A time to undo what we have done and a time to do again what we have undone. Jerome applies this to the rending of the Jewish church and the sewing and making up of the gospel church thereupon. 11. *A time* when it becomes us, and is our wisdom and duty, *to keep silence,* when it is an *evil time* (Amos 5:13), when our speaking would be the *casting of pearl before swine,* or when we are in danger of speaking amiss (Ps. 39:2); but there is also *a time to speak* for the glory of God and the edification of others, when silence would be the betraying of a righteous cause, and when with the mouth confession is to be made to salvation; and it is a great part of Christian prudence to know when to speak and when to hold our peace. 12. *A time to love,* and to show ourselves friendly, to be free and cheerful, and it is a pleasant time; but there may come *a time to hate,* when we shall see cause to break off all familiarity with some that we have been fond of, and to be upon the reserve, as having found reason for a suspicion, which love is loth to admit. 13. *A time of war,* when God draws the sword for judgment and gives it commission to devour, when men draw the sword for justice and the maintaining of their rights, when there is in the nations a disposition to war; but we may hope for *a time of peace,* when the sword of the Lord shall be sheathed and he shall *make wars to cease* (Ps. 46:9), when the end of the war is obtained, and when there is on all sides a disposition to peace. War shall not last always, nor is there any peace to be called lasting on this side the everlasting peace. Thus in all these changes God has set the one over-against the other, that we may *rejoice as though we rejoiced not and weep as though we wept not.*

III. The inferences drawn from this observation. If our present state be subject to such vicissitude, 1. Then we must not expect our portion in it, for the good things of it are of no certainty, no continuance (*v.* 9): *What profit has he that works?* What can a man promise himself from planting and building, when that which he thinks is brought to perfection may so soon, and will so surely, be plucked up and broken down? All our pains and care will not alter either the mutable nature of the things themselves or the immutable counsel of God concerning them. 2. Then we must look upon ourselves as upon our probation in it. There is indeed no profit *in that wherein we labour;* the thing itself, when we have it, will do us little good; but, if we make a right use of the disposals of Providence about it, there will be profit in that (*v.* 10): *I have seen the travail which God has given to the sons of men,* not to make up a happiness by it, but *to be exercised in it,* to have various graces exercised by the variety of events, to have their dependence upon God tried by every change, and to be trained up to it, and taught both *how to want and how to abound,* Phil. 4:12. Note, (1.) There is a great deal of toil and trouble to be seen among the children of men. Labour and sorrow fill the world. (2.) This toil and this trouble are what God has allotted us. He never intended this world for our rest, and therefore never appointed us to take our ease in it. (3.) To many it proves a gift. God gives it to men, as the physician gives a medicine to his patient, to do him good. This travail is given to us to make us weary of the world and desirous of the remaining rest. It is given to us that we may be kept in action, and may always have something to do; for we were none of us sent into the world to be idle. Every change cuts us out some new work, which we should be more solicitous about, than about the event.

Verses 11–15

We have seen what changes there are in the world, and must not expect to find the world more sure to us than it has been to others. Now here Solomon shows the hand of God in all those changes; it is he that has made every creature to be that to us which it is, and therefore we must have our eye always upon him.

I. We must make the best of *that which is,* and must believe it best for the present, and accommodate ourselves to it: *He has made every thing beautiful in his time* (*v.* 11), and therefore, while its time lasts, we must be reconciled to it: nay, we must please ourselves with the beauty of it. Note, 1. Every thing is as God has made it; it is really as he appointed it to be, not as it appears to us. 2. That which to us seems most unpleasant is yet, in its proper time, altogether becoming. Cold is as becoming in winter as heat in summer; and the night, in its turn, is a black beauty, as the day, in its turn, is a bright one. 3. There is a wonderful harmony in the divine Providence and all its disposals, so that the events of it, when they come to be considered in their relations and tendencies, together with the seasons of them, will appear very beautiful, to the glory of God and the comfort of those that trust in him. Though we see not the complete beauty of Providence, yet we shall see it, and a glorious sight it will be, when the mystery of God shall be finished. Then every thing shall appear to have been done in the most proper time and it will be the wonder of eternity, Deu. 32:4. Eze. 1:18.

II. We must wait with patience for the full discovery of that which to us seems intricate and perplexed, acknowledging that we *cannot find out the work that God makes from the beginning to the end,* and therefore must judge nothing before the time. We are to believe that God has made all beautiful. Every thing is done well, as in creation, so in providence, and we shall see it when the end comes, but till then we are incompetent judges of it. While the picture is in drawing, and the house in building, we see not the beauty of either; but when the artist has put his last hand to them, and given them their finishing strokes, then all appears very good. We see but the middle of God's works, not from the beginning of them (then we should see how admirably the plan was laid in the divine counsels), nor to the end of them, which crowns the action (then we should see the product to be glorious), but we must wait till the veil be rent, and not arraign God's proceedings nor pretend to pass judgment on them. *Secret things belong not to us.* Those words, *He has set the world in their hearts,* are differently understood. 1. Some make them to be a reason why we may know more of God's works than we do; so Mr. Pemble: "God has not left himself without witness of his righteous, equal, and beautiful ordering of things, but has set it forth, to be observed in the book of *the world,* and this he has *set in men's hearts,* given man a large desire, and a power, in good measure, to comprehend and understand the history of nature, with the course of human affairs, so that, if men did but give themselves to the exact observation of things, they might in most of them perceive an admirable order and contrivance." 2. Others make them to be a reason why we do not know so much of God's works as we might; so bishop Reynolds: "We have the world so much in our hearts, are so taken up with thoughts and cares of worldly things, and are so exercised in our travail concerning them, that we have neither time nor spirit to eye God's hand in them." The world has not only gained possession of the heart, but has formed prejudices there against the beauty of God's works.

III. We must be pleased with our lot in this world, and cheerfully acquiesce in the will of God concerning us, and accommodate ourselves to it. *There is no* certain, lasting, *good in* these things; what good there is in them we are here told, *v.* 12, 13. We must make a good use of them, 1. For the benefit of others. All the *good* there is *in them* is *to do good* with them, to our families, to our neighbours, to the poor, to the public, to its civil and religious interests. What have we our beings, capacities, and estates for, but to be some way serviceable to our generation? We mistake if we think we were born for ourselves. No; it is our business *to do good;* it is in doing good that there is the truest pleasure, and what is so laid out is best laid up and will turn to the best account. Observe, It is *to do good in this life,* which is short and uncertain; we have but a little time to be doing good in, and therefore had need to redeem time. It is *in this life,* where we are in a state of trial and probation for another life. Every man's life is his opportunity of doing that which will make for him in eternity. 2. For our own comfort. Let us make ourselves easy, *rejoice, and enjoy the good of our labour,* as *it is the gift of God,* and so enjoy God in it, and taste his love, return him thanks, and make him the centre of our joy, *eat and drink* to his glory, and *serve him with joyfulness of heart, in the abundance of all things.* If all things in this world be so uncertain, it is a foolish thing for men sordidly to spare for the present, that they may hoard up all for hereafter; it is better to live cheerfully and usefully upon what we have, and let to-morrow *take thought for the things of itself.* Grace and wisdom to do this *is the gift of God,* and it is a good gift, which crowns the gifts of his providential bounty.

IV. We must be entirely satisfied in all the disposals of the divine Providence, both as to personal and public concerns, and bring our minds to them, because God, in all, performs the thing that is appointed for us, acts according to the counsel of his will; and we are here told, 1. That that counsel cannot be altered, and therefore it is our wisdom to make a virtue of necessity, by submitting to it. It must be as God wills: *I know* (and every one knows it that knows any thing of God) *that whatsoever God does it shall be for ever, v.* 14. *He is in one mind, and who can turn him?* His measures are never broken, nor is he ever put upon new counsels, but what he has purposed shall be effected, and all the world cannot defeat nor disannul it. It behoves us therefore to say, "Let it be as God wills," for, how cross soever it may be to our designs and interests, God's will is his wisdom. 2. That that counsel needs not to be altered, for there is nothing amiss in it, nothing that can be amended. If we could see it altogether at one view, we should see it so perfect that *nothing can be put to it,* for there is no deficiency in it, *nor any thing taken from it,* for there is nothing in it unnecessary, or that can be spared. As the word of God, so the works of God are every one of them perfect in its kind, and it is presumption for us either to add to them or to diminish from them, Deu. 4:2. It is therefore as much our interest, as our duty, to bring our wills to the will of God.

V. We must study to answer God's end in all his providences, which is in general to make us religious. *God does* all *that men should fear before him,* to convince them that there is a God above them that has a sovereign dominion over them, at whose disposal they are and all their ways, and in whose hands their times are and all events concerning them, and that therefore they ought to have their eyes ever towards him, to worship and adore him, to acknowledge him in all their ways, to be careful in every thing to please him, and afraid of offending him in any thing. God thus changes his disposals, and yet is unchangeable in his counsels, not to perplex us, much less to drive us to despair, but to teach us our duty to him and engage us to do it. That which God designs in the government of the world is the support and advancement of religion among men.

VI. Whatever changes we see or feel in this world, we must acknowledge the inviolable steadiness of God's government. The sun rises and sets, the moon increases and decreases, and yet both are where they were, and their revolutions are in the same method from the beginning according to *the ordinances of heaven;* so it is with the events of Providence (*v.* 15): *That which has been is now.* God has not of late begun to use this method. No; things were always as mutable and uncertain as they are now, and so they will be: *That which is to be has already been;* and therefore we speak inconsiderately when we say, "Surely the world was never so bad as it is now," or "None ever met with such disappointments as we meet with," or "The times will never mend;" they may mend with us, and after a time to mourn there may come a time to rejoice, but that will still be liable to the common character, to the common fate. The world, as it has been, is and will be constant in inconstancy; for *God requires that which is past,* that is, repeats what he has formerly done and deals with us no otherwise than as he has used to deal with good men; and *shall the earth be forsaken for us, or the rock removed out of his place?* There has no change befallen us, nor any temptation by it overtaken us, *but such as is common to men.* Let us not be proud and secure in prosperity, for God may recall a past trouble, and order that to seize us and spoil our mirth (Ps. 30:7); nor let us despond in adversity, for God may call back the comforts that are past, as he did to Job. We may apply this to our past actions, and our behaviour under the changes that have affected us. God will call us to account for *that which is past;* and therefore, when we enter into a new condition, we should judge ourselves for our sins in our former condition, prosperous or afflicted.

Verses 16–22

Solomon is still showing that every thing in this world, without piety and the fear of God, is vanity. Take away religion, and there is nothing valuable among men, nothing for the sake of which a wise man would think it worth while to live in this world. In these verses he shows that power (than which there is nothing men are more ambitious of) and life itself (than which there is nothing men are more fond, more jealous of) are nothing without the fear of God.

I. Here is the vanity of man as mighty, man in his best estate, man upon the throne, where his authority is submitted to, man upon the judgment-seat, where his wisdom and justice are appealed to, and where, if he be governed by the laws of religion, he is God's vicegerent; nay, he is of those to whom it is said, *You are gods;* but without the fear of God it *is vanity,* for, set that aside, and,

1. The judge will not judge aright, will not use his power well, but will abuse it; instead of doing good with it he will do hurt with it, and then it is not only vanity, but a lie, a cheat to himself and to all about him, *v.* 16. Solomon perceived, by what he had read of former times, what he heard of other countries, and what he had seen in some corrupt judges, even in the land of Israel, notwithstanding all his care to prefer good men, that there was *wickedness in the place of judgment.* It is not so above the sun: far be it from God that he should do iniquity, or pervert justice. But *under the sun* it is often found that that which should be the refuge, proves the prison, of oppressed innocency. *Man being in honour, and not understanding* what he ought to do, *becomes like the beasts that perish,* like the beasts of prey, even the most ravenous, Ps. 49:20. Not only from the persons that sat in judgment, but even *in the places* where judgment was, in pretence, administered, and righteousness was expected, *there was iniquity;* men met with the greatest wrongs in those courts to which they fled for justice. This is *vanity and vexation;* for, (1.) It would have been better for the people to have had no judges than to have had such. (2.) It would have been better for the judges to have had no power than to have had it and used it to such ill purposes; and so they will say another day.

2. The judge will himself be judged for not judging aright. When Solomon saw how judgment was perverted among men he looked up to God the Judge, and looked forward to the day of his judgment (*v.* 17): *"I said in my heart* that this unrighteous judgment is not so conclusive as both sides take it to be, for there will be a review of the judgment; *God shall judge* between *the righteous and the wicked,* shall judge for the righteous and plead their cause, though now it is run down, and judge against the wicked and reckon with them for all their *unrighteous decrees* and the *grievousness which they have prescribed,"* Isa. 10:1. With an eye of faith we may see, not only the period, but the punishment of the pride and cruelty of oppressors (Ps. 92:7), and it is an unspeakable comfort to the oppressed that their cause will be heard over again. Let them therefore wait with patience, for there is another *Judge* that *stands before the door.* And, though the day of affliction may last long, yet *there is a time,* a set time, for the examination of *every purpose, and every work* done under the sun. Men have their day now, but God's day is coming, Ps. 37:13. With God *there is a time* for the rehearing of causes, redressing of grievances, and reversing of unjust decrees, though as yet we see it not here, Job 24:1.

II. Here is the vanity of man as mortal. He now comes to speak more generally *concerning the estate of the sons of men* in this world, their life and being on earth, and shows that their reason, without religion and the fear of God, advances them but little above the beasts. Now observe,

1. What he aims at in this account of man's estate. (1.) That God may be honoured, may be justified, may be glorified — *that they might clear God* (so the margin reads it), that if men have an uneasy life in this world, full of vanity and vexation, they may thank themselves and lay no blame on God; let them clear him, and not say that he made this world to be man's prison and life to be his penance; no, God made man, in respect both of honour and comfort, *little lower than the angels;* if he be mean and miserable, it is his own fault. Or, *that God* (that is, the world of God) *might manifest them,* and discover them to themselves, and so appear to be *quick and powerful,* and a judge of men's characters; and we may be made sensible how open we lie to God's knowledge and judgment. (2.) That men may be humbled, may be vilified, may be mortified — *that they might see that they themselves are beasts.* It is no easy matter to convince proud men that *they are but men* (Ps. 9:20), much more to convince bad men *that they are beasts,* that, being destitute of religion, they are as *the beasts that perish,* as *the horse and the mule that have no understanding.* Proud oppressors are as beasts, as *roaring lions and ranging bears.* Nay, every man that minds his body only, and not his soul, makes himself no better than a brute, and must wish, at least, to die like one.

2. The manner in which he verifies this account. That which he undertakes to prove is that a worldly, carnal, earthly-minded *man, has no preeminence above the beast, for all* that which he sets his heart upon, places his confidence, and expects a happiness in, *is vanity, v.* 19. Some make this to be the language of an atheist, who justifies himself in his iniquity (*v.* 16) and evades the argument taken from the judgment to come (*v.* 17) by pleading that there is not another life after this, but that when man dies there is an end of him, and therefore while he lives he may live as he lists; but others rather think Solomon here speaks as he himself thinks, and that it is to be understood in the same sense with that of his father (Ps. 49:14), *Like sheep they are laid in the grave,* and that he intends to show the vanity of this world's wealth and honours "By the equal condition in mere outward respects (as bishop Reynolds expounds it) between men and beasts," (1.) The events concerning both seem much alike (*v.* 19); *That which befals the sons of men* is no other than that which *befals beasts;* a great deal of knowledge of human bodies is gained by the anatomy of the bodies of brutes. When the deluge swept away the old world the beasts perished with mankind. Horses and men are killed in battle with the same weapons of war. (2.) The end of both, to an eye of sense, seems alike too: *They have all one breath,* and breathe in the same air, and it is the general description of both that *in their nostrils is the breath of life* (Gen. 7:22), and therefore, *as the one dies, so dies the other;* in their expiring there is no visible difference, but death makes much the same change with a beast that it does with a man. [1.] As to their bodies, the change is altogether the same, except the different respects that are paid to them by the survivors. Let a man be *buried with the burial of an ass* (Jer. 22:19) and what *preëminence then has he above a beast?* The touch of the dead body of a man, by the law of Moses, contracted a greater ceremonial pollution than the touch of the carcase even of an unclean beast or fowl. And Solomon here observes that *all go unto one place;* the dead bodies of men and beasts putrefy alike; *all are of the dust,* in their original, for we see *all turn to dust again* in their corruption. What little reason then have we to be proud of our bodies, or any bodily accomplishments, when they must not only be reduced to the earth very shortly, but must be so in common with the beasts, and we must mingle our dust with theirs! [2.] As to their spirits there is indeed a vast difference, but not a visible one, *v.* 21. It is certain that *the spirit of* the sons of men at death is ascending; it *goes upwards* to the Father of spirits, who made it, to the world of spirits to which it is allied; it dies not with the body, but *is redeemed from the power of the grave,* Ps. 49:15. It *goes upwards* to be judged and determined to an unchangeable state. It is certain that *the spirit of the beast goes downwards to the earth;* it dies with the body; it perishes and is gone at death. The soul of a beast is, at death, like a candle blown out — there is an end of it; whereas the soul of a man is then like a candle taken out of a dark lantern, which leaves the lantern useless indeed, but does itself shine brighter. This great difference there is between the spirits of men and beasts; and a good reason it is why men should *set their affections on things above,* and lift up their souls to those things, not suffering them, as if they were the souls of brutes, to cleave to this earth. But *who knows* this difference? We cannot see the ascent of the one and the descent of the other with our bodily eyes; and therefore those that live by sense, as all carnal sensualists do, that *walk in the sight of their eyes* and will not admit any other discoveries, by their own rule of judgment have no *preëminence above the beasts. Who knows,* that is, who considers this? Isa. 53:1. Very few. Were it better considered, the world would be every way better; but most men live as if they were to be here always, or as if when they die there were an end of them; and it is not strange that those live like beasts who think they shall die like beasts, but on such the noble faculties of reason are perfectly lost and thrown away.

3. An inference drawn from it (*v.* 22): *There is nothing better,* as to this world, nothing better to be had out of our wealth and honour, *than that a man should rejoice in his own works,* that is, (1.) Keep a clear conscience, and never admit *iniquity* into *the place of righteousness. Let every man prove his own work,* and approve himself to God in it, *so shall he have rejoicing in himself alone,* Gal. 6:4. Let him not get nor keep any thing but what he can rejoice in. See 2 Co. 1:12. (2.) Live a cheerful life. If God have prospered the work of our hands unto us, let us rejoice in it, and take the comfort of it, and not make it a burden to ourselves and leave others the joy of it; *for that is our portion,* not the portion of our souls (miserable are those that have their portion in this life, Ps. 17:14, and fools are those that choose it and take up with it, Lu. 12:19), but it is the portion of the body; that only which we enjoy is ours out of this world; it is taking what is to be had and making the best of it, and the reason is because none can give us a sight of *what shall be after us,* either who shall have our estates or what use they will make of them. When we are gone it is likely we shall not see what is after us; there is no correspondence that we know of between the other world and this, Job 14:21. Those in the other world will be wholly taken up with that world, so that they will not care for seeing what is done in this; and while we are here we cannot foresee *what shall be after us,* either as to our families or the public. *It is not for us to know the times and seasons* that *shall be after* us, which, as it should be a restraint to our cares about this world, so it should be a reason for our concern about another. Since death is a final farewell to this life, let us look before us to another life.

CHAPTER 4

Solomon, having shown the vanity of this world in the temptation which those in power feel to oppress and trample upon their subjects, here further shows, I. The temptation which the oppressed feel to discontent and impatience (*v.* 1–3). II. The temptation which those that love their case feel to take their case and neglect business, for fear of being envied (*v.* 4–6). III. The folly of hoarding up abundance of worldly wealth (*v.* 7, 8). IV. A remedy against that folly, in being made sensible of the benefit of society and mutual assistance (*v.* 9–12). V. The mutability even of royal dignity, not only through the folly of the prince himself (*v.* 13, 14), but through the fickleness of the people, let the prince be ever so discreet (*v.* 15, 16). It is not the prerogative even of kings themselves to be exempted from the vanity and vexation that attend these things; let none else then expect it.

Verses 1–3

Solomon had a large soul (1 Ki. 4:29) and it appeared by this, among other things, that he had a very tender concern for the miserable part of mankind and took cognizance of the afflictions of the afflicted. He had taken the oppressors to task (*ch.* 3:16, 17) and put them in mind of the judgment to come, to be a curb to their insolence; now here he observes the oppressed. This he did, no doubt, as a prince, to do them justice and *avenge them of their adversaries,* for he both *feared God and regarded men;* but here he does it as a preacher, and shows,

I. The troubles of their condition (*v.* 1); of these he speaks very feelingly and with compassion. It grieved him, 1. To see might prevailing against right, to see so much *oppression done under the sun,* to see servants, and labourers, and poor workmen, oppressed by their masters, who take advantage of their necessity to impose what terms they please upon them, debtors oppressed by cruel creditors and creditors too by fraudulent debtors, tenants oppressed by hard landlords and orphans by treacherous guardians, and, worst of all, subjects oppressed by arbitrary princes and unjust judges. Such *oppressions are done under the sun;* above the sun righteousness reigns for ever. Wise men will *consider these oppressions,* and contrive to do something for the relief of those that are oppressed. *Blessed is he that considers the poor.* 2. To see how those that were wronged laid to heart the wrongs that were done them. He *beheld the tears of such as were oppressed,* and perhaps could not forbear weeping with them. The world is a place of weepers; look which way we will, we have a melancholy scene presented to us, *the tears of* those that are *oppressed* with one trouble or other. They find it is to no purpose to complain, and therefore mourn in secret (as Job, *ch.* 16:20; 30:28); but *Blessed are those that mourn.* 3. To see how unable they were to help themselves: *On the side of their oppressors there was power,* when they had done wrong, to stand to it and make good what they had done, so that the poor were borne down with a strong hand and had no way to obtain redress. It is sad to see power misplaced, and that which was given men to enable them to do good perverted to support them in doing wrong. 4. To see how they and their calamities were slighted by all about them. They wept and needed comfort, but there was none to do that friendly office: *They had no comforter;* their oppressors were powerful and threatening, and therefore *they had no comforter;* those that should have comforted them durst not, for fear of displeasing the oppressors and being made their companions for offering to be their comforters. It is sad to see so little humanity among men.

II. The temptations of their condition. Being thus hardly used, they are tempted to hate and despise life, and to envy those that are dead and in their graves, and to wish they had never been born (*v.* 2, 3); and Solomon is ready to agree with them, for it serves to prove that *all is vanity and vexation,* since life itself is often so; and if we disregard it, in comparison with the favour and fruition of God (as St. Paul, Acts 20:24, Phil. 1:23), it is our praise, but, if (as here) only for the sake of the miseries that attend it, it is our infirmity, and we judge therein after the flesh, as Job and Elijah did. 1. He here thinks those happy who have ended this miserable life, have done their part and quitted the stage; *"I praised the dead that are already dead,* slain outright, or that had a speedy passage through the world, made a short cut over the ocean of life, dead already, before they had well begun to live; I was pleased with their lot, and, had it been in their own choice, should have praised their wisdom for but looking into the world and then retiring, as not liking it. I concluded that it is better with them than with *the living that are yet alive* and that is all, dragging the long and heavy chain of life, and wearing out its tedious minutes." This may be compared not with Job 3:20, 21, but with Rev. 14:13, where, in times of persecution (and such Solomon is here describing), it is not the passion of man, but the Spirit of God, that says, *Blessed are the dead which die in the Lord from henceforth.* Note, The condition of the saints that are dead, and gone to rest with God, is upon many accounts better and more desirable than the condition of living saints that are yet continued in their work and warfare. 2. He thinks those happy who never began this miserable life; nay, they are happiest of all: *He that has not been is happier than both they.* Better never to have been born than be born to *see the evil work that is done under the sun,* to see so much wickedness committed, so much wrong done, and not only to be in no capacity to mend the matter, but to suffer ill for doing well. A good man, how calamitous a condition soever he is in in this world, cannot have cause to wish he had never been born, since he is glorifying the Lord even in the fires, and will be happy at last, for ever happy. Nor ought any to wish so while they are alive, for while there is life there is hope; a man is never undone till he is in hell.

Verses 4–6

Here Solomon returns to the observation and consideration of the vanity and vexation of spirit that attend the business of this world, which he had spoken of before, *ch.* 2:11.

I. If a man be acute, and dexterous, and successful in his business, he gets the ill-will of *his neighbours, v.* 4. Though he takes a great deal of pains, and goes through *all travail,* does not get his estate easily, but it costs him a great deal of hard labour, nor does he get it dishonestly, he wrongs no man, defrauds no man, but by *every right work,* by applying himself to his own proper business, and managing it by all the rules of equity and fair dealing, yet *for this he is envied of his neighbour,* and the more for the reputation he has got by his honesty. This shows, 1. What little conscience most men have, that they will bear a grudge to a neighbour, give him an ill word and do him an ill turn, only because he is more ingenious and industrious than themselves, and has more of the blessing of heaven. Cain envied Abel, Esau Jacob, and Saul David, and all for their right works. This is downright diabolism. 2. What little comfort wise and useful men must expect to have in this world. Let them behave themselves ever so cautiously, they cannot escape being envied; and *who can stand before envy?* Prov. 27:4. Those that excel in virtue will always be an eye-sore to those that exceed in vice, which should not discourage us from any right work, but drive us to expect the praise of it, not from men, but from God, and not to count upon satisfaction and happiness in the creature; for, if *right works* prove *vanity and vexation of spirit,* no works *under the sun* can prove otherwise. But for *every right work* a man shall be accepted of his God, and then he needs not mind though he be *envied of his neighbour,* only it may make him love the world the less.

II. If a man be stupid, and dull, and blundering in his business, he does ill for himself (*v.* 5): *The fool* that goes about his work as if *his hands* were muffled and *folded together,* that does every thing awkwardly, *the sluggard* (for he is a fool) that loves his ease and *folds his hands together* to keep them warm, because they refuse to labour, he *eats his own flesh,* is a cannibal to himself, brings himself into such a poor condition that he has nothing to eat but his own flesh, into such a desperate condition that he is ready to eat his own flesh for vexation. He has a dog's life — hunger and ease. Because he sees active men that thrive in the world envied, he runs into the other extreme; and, lest he should be envied for his right works, he does every thing wrong, and does not deserve to be pitied. Note, Idleness is a sin that is its own punishment. The following words (*v.* 6), *Better is a handful with quietness than both the hands full with travail and vexation of spirit,* may be taken either, 1. As the sluggard's argument for the excuse of himself in his idleness. He *folds his hands together,* and abuses and misapplies a good truth for his justification, as if, because *a little with quietness is better than* abundance with strife, therefore a little with idleness is better than abundance with honest labour: thus *wise in his own conceit* is he, Prov. 26:16. But, 2. I rather take it as Solomon's advice to keep the mean between that *travail* which will make *a man envied* and that slothfulness which will make a man *eat his own flesh.* Let us by honest industry lay hold on the handful, that we may not want necessaries, but not grasp at both the hands full, which will but create us vexation of spirit. Moderate pains and moderate gains will do best. A man may have but a handful of the world, and yet may enjoy it and himself with a great deal of *quietness,* with content of mind, peace of conscience, and the love and good-will of his neighbours, while many that have both their hands full, have more than heart could wish, have a great deal of travail and vexation with it. Those that cannot live on a little, it is to be feared, would not live as they should if they had ever so much.

Verses 7–12

Here Solomon fastens upon another instance of the vanity of this world, that frequently the more men have of it the more they would have; and on this they are so intent that they have no enjoyment of what they have. Now Solomon here shows,

I. That selfishness is the cause of this evil (*v.* 7, 8): *There is one alone,* that minds none but himself, cares for nobody, but would, if he could, be placed alone in the midst of the earth; *there is not a second,* nor does he desire there should be: one mouth he thinks enough in a house, and grudges every thing that goes beside him. See how this covetous muckworm is here described. 1. He makes himself a mere slave to his business. Though *he has* no charge, *neither child nor brother,* none to take care of but himself, none to hang upon him, or draw from him, no poor relations, nor dares he marry, for fear of the expense of a family, *yet is there no end of his labour;* he is at it night and day, early and late, and will scarcely allow necessary rest to himself and those he employs. He does not confine himself within the bounds of his own calling, but is for having a hand in any thing that he can get by. See Ps. 127:2. 2. He never thinks he has enough: *His eye is not satisfied with riches.* Covetousness is called *the lust of the eye* (1 Jn. 2:16) because the *beholding of it with his eyes* is all that the worldling seems to covet, Eccl. *v.* 11. He has enough for his back (as bishop Reynolds observes), for his belly, for his calling, for his family, for his living decently in the world, but he has not enough for his eyes. Though he can but see it, can but count his money, and not find in his heart to use it, yet he is not easy because he has not more to regale his eyes with. 3. He denies himself the comfort of what he has: he *bereaves his soul of good.* If our souls are bereaved of good, it is we ourselves that do bereave them. Others may bereave us of outward good, but cannot rob us of our graces and comforts, our spiritual good things. It is our own fault if we do not enjoy ourselves. Yet many are so set upon the world that, in pursuit of it, they *bereave their souls of good* here and for ever, make shipwreck of faith and of a good conscience, bereave themselves not only of the favour of God and eternal life, but of the pleasures of this world too and this present life. Worldly people, pretending to be wise for themselves, are really enemies to themselves. 4. He has no excuse for doing this: *He has neither child nor brother,* none that he is bound to, on whom he may lay out what he has to his satisfaction while he lives, none that he has a kindness for, for whom he may lay it up to his satisfaction and to whom he may leave it when he dies, none that are poor or dear to him. 5. He has not consideration enough to show himself the folly of this. He never puts this question to himself, *"For whom do I labour* thus? Do I labour, as I should, for the glory of God, and that I may have to give to those that need? Do I consider that it is but for the body that I am labouring, a dying body; it is for others, and I know not for whom — perhaps for a fool, that will scatter it as fast as I have gathered it — perhaps for a foe, that will be ungrateful to my memory?" Note, It is wisdom for those that take pains about this world to consider whom they take all this pains for, and whether it be really worth while to bereave themselves of good that they may bestow it on a stranger. If men do not consider this, it *is vanity, and a sore travail;* they shame and vex themselves to no purpose.

II. That sociableness is the cure of this evil. Men are thus sordid because they are all for themselves. Now Solomon shows here, by divers instances, that *it is not good for man to be alone* (Gen. 2:18); he designs hereby to recommend to us both marriage and friendship, two things which covetous misers decline, because of the charge of them; but such are the comfort and advantage of them both, if prudently contracted, that they will very well quit cost. Man, in paradise itself, could not be happy without a mate, and therefore is no sooner made than matched. 1. Solomon lays this down for a truth, That *two are better than one,* and more happy jointly than either of them could be separately, more pleased in one another than they could be in themselves only, mutually serviceable to each other's welfare, and by a united strength more likely to do good to others: *They have a good reward of their labour;* whatever service they do, it is returned to them another way. He that serves himself only has himself only for his paymaster, and commonly proves more unjust and ungrateful to himself than his friend, if he should serve him, would be to him; witness him that *labours endlessly* and yet *bereaves his soul of good;* he has no *reward of his labour.* But he that is kind to another has *a good reward;* the pleasure and advantage of holy love will be an abundant recompence for all the *work and labour of love.* Hence Solomon infers the mischief of solitude: *Woe to him that is alone.* He lies exposed to many temptations which good company and friendship would prevent and help him to guard against; he wants that advantage which a man has by the countenance of his friend, as iron has of being sharpened by iron. A monastic life then was surely never intended for a state of perfection, nor should those be reckoned the greatest lovers of God who cannot find in their hearts to love any one else. 2. He proves it by divers instances of the benefit of friendship and good conversation. (1.) Occasional succour in an exigency. It is good for two to travel together, *for if* one happen to *fall,* he may be lost for want of a little help. If a man fall *into sin,* his friend will help to *restore him with the spirit of meekness;* if he fall into trouble, his friend will help to comfort him and assuage his grief. (2.) Mutual warmth. As a fellow-traveller is of use *(amicus pro vehiculo — a friend is a good substitute for a carriage)* so is a bedfellow: *If two lie together, they have heat.* So virtuous and gracious affections are excited by good society, and Christians warm one another by *provoking one another to love and to good works.* (3.) United strength. If an enemy find a man alone, he is likely to *prevail against him;* with his own single strength he cannot make his part good, but, if he have a second, he may do well enough: *two shall withstand him.* "You shall help me against my enemy, and I will help you against yours;" according to the agreement between Joab and Abishai (2 Sa. 10:11), and so both are conquerors; whereas, acting separately, both would have been conquered; as was said of the ancient Britons, when the Romans invaded them, *Dum singuli pugnant, universi vincuntur — While they fight in detached parties, they sacrifice the general cause.* In our spiritual warfare we may be helpful to one another as well as in our spiritual work; next to the comfort of communion with God, is that of the communion of saints. He concludes with this proverb, *A threefold cord is not easily broken,* any more than a bundle of arrows, though each single thread, and each single arrow, is. Two together he compares to *a threefold cord;* for where two are closely joined in holy love and fellowship, Christ will by his Spirit come to them, and make the third, as he joined himself to the two disciples going to Emmaus, and then there is *a threefold cord* that can never be *broken. They that dwell in love, dwell in God, and God in them.*

Verses 13–16

Solomon was himself a king, and therefore may be allowed to speak more freely than another concerning the vanity of kingly state and dignity, which he shows here to be an uncertain thing; he had before said so (Prov. 27:24, *The crown doth not endure to every generation),* and his son found it so. Nothing is more slippery than the highest post of honour without wisdom and the people's love.

I. A king is not happy unless he have wisdom, *v.* 13, 14. He that is truly *wise,* prudent, and pious, though he be *poor* in the world, and very young, and upon both accounts despised and little taken notice of, *is better,* more truly valuable and worthy of respect, is likely to do better for himself and to be a greater blessing to his generation, *than a king, than an old king,* and therefore venerable both for his gravity and for his dignity, if he be *foolish,* and knows not how to manage public affairs himself nor *will be admonished* and advised by others — *who* knows not to *be admonished,* that is, will not suffer any counsel or admonition to be given him (no one about him dares contradict him) or will not hearken to the counsel and admonition that are given him. It is so far from being any part of the honour of kings that it is the greatest dishonour to them that can be not to be *admonished.* Folly and wilfulness commonly go together, and those that most need admonition can worst bear it; but neither age nor titles will secure men respect if they have not true wisdom and virtue to recommend them; while wisdom and virtue will gain men honour even under the disadvantages of youth and poverty. To prove the *wise child better than the foolish king* he shows what each of them comes to, *v.* 14. 1. *A poor* man by his wisdom comes to be preferred, as Joseph, who, when he was but young, was brought *out of prison* to be *the second* man in the kingdom, to which story Solomon seems here to refer. Providence sometimes *raises the poor out of the dust, to set them among princes,* Ps. 113:7, 8. Wisdom has wrought not only the liberty of men, but their dignity, raised them from the dunghill, from the dungeon, to the throne. 2. *A king* by his folly and wilfulness comes to be impoverished. Though he was *born in his kingdom,* came to it by inheritance, though he has lived to be old in it and has had time to fill his treasures, yet if he take ill courses, and *will no more be admonished* as he has been, thinking, because he is old, he is past it, he *becomes poor;* his treasure is exhausted, and perhaps he is forced to resign his crown and retire into privacy.

II. A king is not likely to continue if he have not a confirmed interest in the affections of the people; this is intimated, but somewhat obscurely, in the last two verses. 1. He that is king must have a successor, a *second,* a *child that shall stand up in his stead,* his own, suppose, or perhaps that *poor and wise child* spoken of, *v.* 13. Kings, when they grow old, must have the mortification of seeing those that are to jostle them out and stand up in their stead. 2. It is common with the people to adore the rising sun: *All the living who walk under the sun are with the second child,* are in his interests, are conversant with him, and make their court to him more than to the father, whom they look upon as going off, and despise because his best days are past. Solomon considered this; he saw this to be the disposition of his own people, which appeared immediately after his death, in their complaints of his government and their affectation of a change. 3. People are never long easy and satisfied: *There is no end,* no rest, *of all the people;* they are continually fond of changes, and know not what they would have. 4. This is no new thing, but it has been the way *of all that have been before them;* there have been instances of this in every age: even Samuel and David could not always please. 5. As it has been, so it is likely to be still: *Those that come after* will be of the same spirit, and *shall not* long *rejoice in him* whom at first they seemed extremely fond of. To-day, *Hosanna* — tomorrow, *Crucify.* 6. It cannot but be a great grief to princes to see themselves thus slighted by those they have studied to oblige and have depended upon; there is no faith in man, no stedfastness. *This is vanity and vexation of spirit.*

CHAPTER 5

Solomon, in this chapter, discourses, I. Concerning the worship of God, prescribing that as a remedy against all those vanities which he had already observed to be in wisdom, learning, pleasure, honour, power, and business. That we may not be deceived by those things, nor have our spirits vexed with the disappointments we meet with in them, let us make conscience of our duty to God and keep up our communion with him; but, withal, he gives a necessary caution against the vanities which are to often found in religious exercises, which deprive them of their excellency and render them unable to help against other vanities. If our religion be a vain religion, how great is that vanity! Let us therefore take heed of vanity, 1. In hearing the word, and offering sacrifice (*v.* 1). 2. In prayer (*v.* 2, 3). 3. In making vows (*v.* 4–6). 4. In pretending to divine dreams (*v.* 7). Now, (1.) For a remedy against those vanities, he prescribes the fear of God (*v.* 7). (2.) To prevent the offence that might arise from the present sufferings of good people, he directs us to look up to God (*v.* 8). II. Concerning the wealth of this world and the vanity and vexation that attend it. The fruits of the earth indeed are necessary to the support of life (*v.* 9), but as for silver, and gold, and riches, 1. They are unsatisfying (*v.* 10). 2. They are unprofitable (*v.* 11). 3. They are disquieting (*v.* 12). 4. They often prove hurtful and destroying (*v.* 13). 5. They are perishing (*v.* 14). 6. They must be left behind when we die (*v.* 15, 16). 7. If we have not a heart to make use of them, they occasion a great deal of uneasiness (*v.* 17). And therefore he recommends to us the comfortable use of that which God has given us, with an eye to him that is the giver, as the best way both to answer the end of our having it and to obviate the mischiefs that commonly attend great estates (*v.* 18–20). So that if we can but learn out of this chapter how to manage the business of religion, and the business of this world (which two take up most of our time), so that both may turn to a good account, and neither our sabbath days nor our week-days may be lost, we shall have reason to say, We have learned two good lessons.

Verses 1–3

Solomon's design, in driving us off from the world, by showing us its vanity, is to drive us to God and to our duty, that we may not walk in the way of the world, but by religious rules, nor depend upon the wealth of the world, but on religious advantages; and therefore,

I. He here sends us to *the house of God,* to the place of public worship, to the temple, which he himself had built at a vast expense. When he reflected with regret on all his other works (*ch.* 2:4), he did not repent of that, but reflected on it with pleasure, yet mentions it not, lest he should seem to reflect on it with pride; but he here sends those to it that would know more of the vanity of the world and would find that happiness which is in vain sought for in the creature. David, when he was perplexed, *went into the sanctuary of God,* Ps. 73:17. Let our disappointments in the creature turn our eyes to the Creator; let us have recourse to the word of God's grace and consult that, to the throne of his grace and solicit that. In the word and prayer there is a balm for every wound.

II. He charges us to behave ourselves well there, that we may not miss of our end in coming thither. Religious exercises are not vain things, but, if we mismanage them, they become vain to us. And therefore,

1. We must address ourselves to them with all possible seriousness and care: *"Keep thy foot,* not keep it back from the house of God (as Prov. 25:17), nor go slowly thither, as one unwilling to draw nigh to God, but *look well to thy goings, ponder the path of thy feet,* lest thou take a false step. Address thyself to the worship of God with a solemn pause, and take time to compose thyself for it, not going about it with precipitation, which is called *hasting with the feet,* Prov. 19:2. Keep thy thoughts from roving and wandering from the work; keep thy affections from running out towards wrong objects, for in the business of God's house there is work enough for the whole man, and all too little to be employed." Some think it alludes to the charge given to Moses and Joshua to *put off their shoes* (Ex. 3:5, Jos. 5:15,) in token of subjection and reverence. *Keep thy feet* clean, Ex. 30:19.

2. We must take heed that the sacrifice we bring be not *the sacrifice of fools* (of wicked men), for they are fools and their *sacrifice is an abomination to the Lord,* Prov. 15:8), that we bring not *the torn, and the lame, and the sick for sacrifice,* for we are plainly told that it will not be accepted, and therefore it is folly to bring it, — that we rest not in the sign and ceremony, and the outside of the performance, without regarding the sense and meaning of it, for that is the *sacrifice of fools.* Bodily exercise, if that be all, is a jest; none but fools will think thus to please him who is a Spirit and requires the heart, and they will see their folly when they find what a great deal of pains they have taken to no purpose for want of sincerity. They are *fools,* for they *consider not that they do evil;* they think they are doing God and themselves good service when really they are putting a great affront upon God and a great cheat upon their own souls by their hypocritical devotions. Men may be doing evil even when they profess to be doing good, and even when they do not know it, when they do not consider it. *They know not but to do evil,* so some read it. Wicked minds cannot choose but sin, even in the acts of devotion. Or, They *consider not that they do evil;* they act at a venture, right or wrong, pleasing to God or not, it is all one to them.

3. That we may not bring *the sacrifice of fools,* we must come to God's house with hearts disposed to know and do our duty. We must be *ready to hear,* that is, (1.) We must diligently *attend* to the word of God read and preached. *"Be swift to hear* the exposition which the priests give of the sacrifices, declaring the intent and meaning of them, and do not think it enough to gaze upon what they do, for it must be *a reasonable service,* otherwise it is *the sacrifice of fools."* (2.) We must resolve to comply with the will of God as it is made known to us. *Hearing* is often put for *obeying,* and that is it that is *better than sacrifice,* 1 Sa. 15:22; Isa. 1:15, 16. We come in a right frame to holy duties when we come with this upon our heart, *Speak, Lord, for thy servant hears. Let the word of the Lord come* (said a good man), *and if I had 600 necks I would bow them all to the authority of it.*

4. We must be very cautious and considerate in all our approaches and addresses to God (*v.* 2): *Be not rash with thy mouth,* in making prayers, or protestations, or promises; *let not thy heart be hasty to utter any thing before God.* Note, (1.) When we are in the *house of God,* in solemn

assemblies for religious worship, we are in a special manner before God and in his presence, there where he has promised to meet his people, where his eye is upon us and ours ought to be unto him. (2.) We have something to say, something to utter before God, when we *draw nigh to him* in holy duties; he is one *with whom we have to do,* with whom we have business of vast importance. If we come without an errand, we shall go away without any advantage. (3.) What we *utter before God* must come from *the heart,* and therefore we must not be *rash with our mouth,* never let our tongue outrun our thoughts in our devotions; the *words of our mouth,* must always be the product of the *meditation of our hearts.* Thoughts are words to God, and words are but wind if they be not copied from the thoughts. Lip-labour, though ever so well laboured, if that be all, is but lost labour in religion, Mt. 15:8, 9. (4.) It is not enough that what we say comes from the heart, but it must come from a composed heart, and not from a sudden heat or passion. As the mouth must not be rash, so the heart must not be hasty; we must not only think, but think twice, before we speak, when we are to speak either from God in preaching or to God in prayer, and not utter any thing indecent and undigested, 1 Co. 14:15.

5. We must be sparing of our words in the presence of God, that is, we must be reverent and deliberate, not talk to God as boldly and carelessly as we do to one another, not speak what comes uppermost, not repeat things over and over, as we do to one another, that what we say may be understood and remembered and may make impression; no, when we speak to God we must consider, (1.) That between him and us there is an infinite distance: *God is in heaven,* where he reigns in glory over us and all the children of men, where he is attended with an innumerable company of holy angels and is *far exalted above all our blessing and praise. We are on earth,* the footstool of his throne; we are mean and vile, unlike God, and utterly unworthy to receive any favour from him or to have any communion with him. Therefore we must be very grave, humble, and serious, and be reverent in speaking to him, as we are when we speak to a great man that is much our superior; and, in token of this, *let our words be few,* that they may be *well chosen,* Job 9:14. This does not condemn all long prayers; were they not good, the Pharisees would not have used them for a pretence; Christ prayed all night; and we are directed to *continue in prayer.* But it condemns careless heartless praying, *vain repetitions* (Mt. 6:7), repeating *Pater-nosters* by tale. Let us speak to God, and of him, in his own words, words which the scripture teaches; and let our words, words of our own invention, be few, lest, not speaking by rule, we speak amiss. (2.) That the multiplying of words in our devotions will make them the *sacrifices of fools, v.* 3. As confused dreams, frightful and perplexed, and such as disturb the sleep, are an evidence of a hurry of business which fills our head, so many words and hasty ones, used in prayer, are an evidence of folly reigning in the heart, ignorance of and unacquaintedness with both God and ourselves, low thoughts of God, and careless thoughts of our own souls. Even in common conversation *a fool is known by the multitude of words;* those that know least talk most (*ch.* 10:11), particularly in devotion; there, no doubt, *a prating fool shall fall* (Prov. 10:8, 10), shall fall short of acceptance. Those are fools indeed who think they *shall be heard,* in prayer, *for their much speaking.*

Verses 4–8

Four things we are exhorted to in these verses: —

I. To be conscientious in paying our vows.

1. A vow is a bond upon the soul (Num. 30:2), by which we solemnly oblige ourselves, not only, in general, to do that which we are already bound to do, but, in some particular instances, to do that to do which we were not under any antecedent obligation, whether it respects honouring God or serving the interests of his kingdom among men. When, under the sense of some affliction (Ps. 66:14), or in the pursuit of some mercy (1 Sa. 1:11), thou hast vowed such a vow as this *unto God,* know that *thou hast opened thy mouth unto the Lord and thou canst not go back;* therefore, (1.) Pay it; perform what thou hast promised; bring to God what thou hast dedicated and devoted to him: *Pay that which thou hast vowed;* pay it in full and *keep not back any part of the price;* pay it in kind, do not *alter it*

or *change it,* so the law was, Lev. 27:10. Have we vowed to *give our own selves unto the Lord?* Let us then be as good as our word, act in his service, to his glory, and not sacrilegiously alienate ourselves. (2.) *Defer not to pay it.* If it be in the power of thy hands to pay it to-day, leave it not till to-morrow; do not *beg a day,* nor put it off to a more convenient season. By delay the sense of the obligation slackens and cools, and is in danger of wearing off; we thereby discover a loathness and backwardness to perform our vow; and *qui non est hodie cras minus aptus erit — he who is not inclined to-day will be averse to-morrow.* The longer it is put off the more difficult it will be to bring ourselves to it; death may not only prevent the payment, but fetch thee to judgment, under the guilt of a broken vow, Ps. 76:11.

2. Two reasons are here given why we should speedily and cheerfully pay our vows: — (1.) Because otherwise we affront God; we play the fool with him, as if we designed to put a trick upon him; and *God has no pleasure in fools.* More is implied than is expressed; the meaning is, He greatly abhors such fools and such foolish dealings. *Has he need of fools?* No; *Be not deceived, God is not mocked,* but will surely and severely reckon with those that thus play fast and loose with him. (2.) Because otherwise we wrong ourselves, we lose the benefit of the making of the *vow,* nay, we incur the penalty for the breach of it; so that it would have been better a great deal *not to have vowed,* more safe and more to our advantage, than to *vow and not to pay.* Not to have *vowed* would have been but an omission, but to *vow and not pay* incurs the guilt of treachery and perjury; it is *lying to God,* Acts 5:4.

II. To be cautious in making our vows. This is necessary in order to our being conscientious in performing them, *v.* 6. 1. We must take heed that we never vow any thing that is sinful, or that may be an occasion of sin, for such a vow is ill-made and must be broken. *Suffer not thy mouth,* by such a vow, *to cause thy flesh to sin,* as Herod's rash promise caused him to cut off the head of John the Baptist. 2. We must not vow that which, through the frailty of the flesh, we have reason to fear we shall not be able to perform, as those that vow a single life and yet know not how to keep their vow. Hereby, (1.) They shame themselves; for they are forced to *say before the angel, It was an error,* that either they did not mean or did not consider what they said; and, take it which way you will, it is bad enough. "When thou hast made a *vow,* do not seek to evade it, nor find excuses to get clear of the obligation of it; *say not before the priest,* who is called the *angel or messenger of the Lord of hosts,* that, upon second thoughts, thou hast changed thy mind, and desirest to be absolved from the obligation of thy *vow;* but stick to it, and do not seek a hole to creep out at." Some by *the angel* understand the guardian angel which they suppose to attend every man and to inspect what he does. Others understand it of Christ, *the Angel of the covenant,* who is present with his people in their assemblies, who searches the heart, and cannot be imposed upon; *provoke him not, for God's name is in him,* and he is represented as strict and jealous, Ex. 23:20, 21. (2.) They expose themselves to the wrath of God, for he is *angry at the voice of* those that thus *lie unto him with their mouth and flatter him with their tongue,* and is displeased at their dissimulation, and *destroys the works of their hands,* that is, blasts their enterprises, and defeats those purposes which, when they made these vows, they were seeking to God for the success of. If we treacherously cancel the words of our mouths, and revoke our vows, God will justly overthrow our projects, and walk contrary, and at all adventures, with those that thus walk contrary, and at all adventures with him. It is *a snare to a man, after vows, to make enquiry.*

III. To keep up the fear of God, *v.* 7. Many, of old, pretended to know the mind of God by *dreams,* and were so full of them that they almost made God's people forget his name by their *dreams* (Jer. 23:25, 26); and many now perplex themselves with their frightful or odd dreams, or with other people's dreams, as if they foreboded this or the other disaster. Those that heed dreams shall have a multitude of them to fill their heads with; but in them all *there are divers vanities,* as there are in many words, and the more if we regard them. "They are but like the idle impertinent chat of children and fools, and therefore never heed them; forget them; instead of repeating them lay no stress upon

them, draw no disquieting conclusions from them, but *fear thou God;* have an eye to his sovereign dominion, set him before thee, keep thyself in his love, and be afraid of offending him, and then thou wilt not disturb thyself with foolish dreams." The way not to be dismayed at the signs of heaven, nor afraid of *the idols of the heathen,* is to *fear God as King of nations,* Jer. 10:2, 5, 7.

IV. With that to keep down the fear of man, *v.* 8. "Set God before thee, and then, if *thou seest the oppression of the poor,* thou wilt not *marvel at the matter,* nor find fault with divine Providence, nor think the worse of the institution of magistracy, when thou seest the ends of it thus perverted, nor of religion, when thou seest it will not secure men from suffering wrong." Observe here, 1. A melancholy sight on earth, and such as cannot but trouble every good man that has a sense of justice and a concern for mankind, to see *the oppression of the poor* because they are poor and cannot defend themselves, and the *violent perverting of judgment and justice in a province,* oppression under colour of law and backed with power. The kingdom in general may have a good government, and yet it may so happen that a particular province may be committed to a bad man, by whose mal-administration justice may be perverted; so hard it is for the wisest of kings, in giving preferments, to be sure of their men; they can but redress the grievance when it appears. 2. A comfortable sight in heaven. When things look thus dismal we may satisfy ourselves with this, (1.) That, though oppressors be high, God is *above them,* and in that very thing wherein *they deal proudly,* Ex. 18:11. God is *higher than the highest* of creatures, than the highest of princes, than the king that is *higher than Agag* (Num. 24:7), than the highest angels, the *thrones and dominions* of the upper world. God is the *Most High over all the earth,* and his *glory is above the heavens;* before him princes are worms, the brightest but glow-worms. (2.) That, though oppressors be secure, God has his eye upon them, takes notice of, and will reckon for, all their violent perverting of judgment; *he regards,* not only sees it but observes it, and keeps it on record, to be called over again; his *eyes are upon their ways.* See Job 24:23. (3.) That there is a world of angels, for there are *higher than they,* who are employed by the divine justice for protecting the injured and punishing the injurious. Sennacherib valued himself highly upon his potent army, but one angel proved too hard for him and all his forces. Some, by those *that are higher than they* understand the great council of the nation, the presidents to whom the *princes of the provinces are accountable* (Dan. 6:2), the senate that receive complaints against the proconsuls, the courts above to which appeals are made from the inferior courts, which are necessary to the good government of a kingdom. Let it be a check to oppressors that perhaps their superiors on earth may call them to an account; however, God the Supreme in heaven will.

Verses 9–17

Solomon had shown the vanity of pleasure, gaiety, and fine works, of honour, power, and royal dignity; and there is many a covetous worldling that will agree with him, and speak as slightly as he does of these things; but money, he thinks, is a substantial thing, and if he can but have enough of that he is happy. This is the mistake which Solomon attacks, and attempts to rectify, in these verses; he shows that there is as much vanity in great riches, and the *lust of the eye* about them, as there is in the *lusts of the flesh* and the *pride of life,* and a man can make himself no more happy by hoarding an estate than by spending it.

I. He grants that the products of the earth, for the support and comfort of human life, are valuable things (*v.* 9): *The profit of the earth is for all.* Man's body, being made of the earth, thence has its maintenance (Job 28:5), and that it has so, and that a *barren land is not made his dwelling* (as he has deserved for being rebellious, Ps. 68:6), is an instance of God's great bounty to him. There is *profit to be got out of the earth,* and it is *for all;* all need it; it is appointed for all; there is enough for all. It is not only for all men, but for all the inferior creatures; the same ground brings *grass for the cattle* that brings *herbs for the service of men.* Israel had *bread from heaven, angels' food,* but (which is a humbling consideration) the earth is our storehouse and the beasts are fellow-commoners with us. *The king himself is served of the field,* and would be ill served, would be quite starved, without its products. This puts a great honour upon the husbandman's calling, that it is the most necessary of all to the support of man's life. The many have the benefit of it; the mighty cannot live without it; it is *for all;* it is for the *king himself.* Those that have an abundance of the fruits of the earth must remember *they are for all,* and therefore must look upon themselves but as stewards of their abundance, out of which they must give to those that need. Dainty meats and soft clothing are only *for some,* but the *fruit of the earth is for all.* And even those that *suck the abundance of the seas* (Deu. 33:19) cannot be without the fruit of the earth, while those that have a competency of the *fruit of the earth* may despise the *abundance of the seas.*

II. He maintains that the riches that are more than these, that are for hoarding, not for use, are *vain things,* and will not make a man easy or happy. That which our Saviour has said (Lu. 12:15), *that a man's life consists not in the abundance of the things which he possesses,* is what Solomon here undertakes to prove by various arguments.

1. The more men have the more they would have, *v.* 10. A man may have but a little silver and be satisfied with it, may know when he has enough and covet no more. *Godliness, with contentment, is great gain. I have enough,* says Jacob; *I have all, and abound,* says St. Paul: but, (1.) He that *loves silver,* and sets his heart upon it, will never think he has enough, but *enlarges his desire as hell* (Hab. 2:5), *lays house to house and field to field* (Isa. 5:8), and, like *the daughters of the horse-leech, still cries, Give, give.* Natural desires are at rest when that which is desired is obtained, but corrupt desires are insatiable. Nature is content with little, grace with less, but lust with nothing. (2.) He that has silver in abundance, and has it increasing ever so fast upon him, yet does not find that it yields any solid satisfaction to his soul. There are bodily desires which silver itself will not satisfy; if a man be hungry, ingots of silver will do no more to satisfy his hunger than clods of clay. Much less will worldly abundance satisfy spiritual desires; he that has ever so much silver covets more, not only of that, but of something else, something of another nature. Those that make themselves drudges to the world are spending their *labour for that which satisfies not* (Isa. 55:2), which fills the belly, but will never fill the soul, Eze. 7:19.

2. The more men have the more occasion they have for it, and the more they have to do with it, so that it is as broad as it is long: *When goods increase, they are increased that eat them, v.* 11. *The more meat the more mouths.* Does the estate thrive? And does not the family at the same time grow more numerous and the children grow up to need more? The more men have the better house they must keep, the more servants they must employ, the more guests they must entertain, the more they must give to the poor, and the more they will have hanging on them, for where *the carcase is the eagles will be.* What we have more than food and raiment we have for *others;* and then *what good is there to the owners* themselves, but the pleasure of *beholding it with their eyes?* And a poor pleasure it is. An empty speculation is all the difference between the owners and the sharers; the owner sees that as his own which those about him enjoy as much of the real benefit of as he; only he has the satisfaction of doing good to others, which indeed is a satisfaction to one who believes what Christ said, that *it is more blessed to give than to receive;* but to a covetous man, who thinks all lost that goes beside himself, it is a constant vexation to see others eat of his increase.

3. The more men have the more care they have about it, which perplexes them and disturbs their repose, *v.* 12. Refreshing sleep is as much the support and comfort of this life as food is. Now, (1.) Those commonly sleep best that work hard and have but what they work for: *The sleep of the labouring man is sweet,* not only because he has tired himself with his labour, which makes his sleep the more welcome to him and makes him sleep soundly, but because he has little to fill his head with care about and so break his sleep. His sleep is sweet, though he eat but little and have but little to eat, for his weariness rocks him asleep; and, though he eat much, yet he can sleep well, for his labour gets him a good digestion. The sleep of the diligent Christian, and his long sleep, is sweet; for, having spent himself and his time in the service of God, he can cheerfully return to God and repose in him as his rest. (2.)

Those that have every thing else often fail to secure a good night's sleep. Either their eyes are held waking or their sleeps are unquiet and do not refresh them; and it is their abundance that breaks their sleep and disturbs it, both the abundance of their care (as the rich man's who, when his ground brought forth plentifully, thought within himself, *What shall I do?* Lu. 12:17) and the abundance of what they eat and drink which overcharges the heart, makes them sick, and so hinders their repose. Ahasuerus, after a banquet of wine, could not sleep; and perhaps consciousness of guilt, both in getting and using what they have, breaks their sleep as much as any thing. But *God gives his beloved sleep.*

4. The more men have the more danger they are in both of doing mischief and of having mischief done them (*v.* 13): *There is an evil, a sore evil,* which Solomon himself had *seen under the sun,* in this lower world, this theatre of sin and woe — *riches left for the owners thereof* (who have been industrious to hoard them and keep them safely) *to their hurt;* they would have been better without them. (1.) Their riches *do them hurt,* make them proud, secure, and in love with the world, draw away their hearts from God and duty, and make it very difficult for them to enter into the kingdom of heaven, nay, help to shut them out of it. (2.) They *do hurt with their riches,* which not only put them into a capacity of gratifying their own lusts and living luxuriously, but give them an opportunity of oppressing others and dealing hardly with them. (3.) Often they sustain *hurt by their riches.* They would not be envied, would not be robbed, if they were not rich. It is the fat beast that is led first to the slaughter. A very rich man (as one observes) has sometimes been excepted out of a general pardon, both as to life and estate, merely on account of his vast and overgrown estate; so riches *often take away the life of the owners thereof,* Prov. 1:19.

5. The more men have the more they have to lose, and perhaps they may lose it all, *v.* 14. Those riches that have been laid up with a great deal of pains, and kept with a great deal of care, *perish by evil travail,* by the very pains and care which they take to secure and increase them. Many a one has ruined his estate by being over-solicitous to advance it and make it more, and has lost all by catching at all. Riches are perishing things, and all our care about them cannot make them otherwise; they *make themselves wings and fly away.* He that thought he should have made his son a gentleman leaves him a beggar; he *begets a son,* and brings him up in the prospect of an estate, but, when he dies, leaves it under a charge of debt as much as it is worth, so that *there is nothing in his hand.* This is a common case; estates that made a great show do not prove what they seemed, but cheat the heir.

6. How much soever men have when they die, they must leave it all behind them (*v.* 15, 16): *As he came forth of his mother's womb naked, so shall he return;* only as his friends, when he came naked into the world, in pity to him, helped him with swaddling-clothes, so, when he goes out, they help him with grave-clothes, and that is all. See Job 1:21; Ps. 49:17. This is urged as a reason why we should be content with such things as we have, 1 Tim. 6:7. In respect of the body we must go as we came; the dust shall return to the earth as it was. But sad is our case if the soul return as it came, for we were born in sin, and if we die in sin, unsanctified, we had better never have been born; and that seems to be the case of the worldling here spoken of, for he is said to *return in all points as he came,* as sinful, as miserable, and much more so. This is a *sore evil; he* thinks it so whose heart is glued to the world, that he *shall take nothing of his labour which he may carry away in his hand;* his riches will not go with him into another world nor stand him in any stead there. If we labour in religion, the grace and comfort we get by that labour we may carry away in our hearts, and shall be the better for it to eternity; that is meat that endures. But if we labour only for the world, to fill our hands with that, we cannot take that away with us; we are born with our hands griping, but we die with them extended, letting go what we held fast. So that, upon the whole matter, he may well ask, *What profit has he that has laboured for the wind?* Note, Those that labour for the world labour for the wind, for that which has more sound than substance, which is uncertain, and always shifting its point, unsatisfying, and often hurtful, which we cannot hold fast, and which, if we

take up with it as our portion, will no more feed us than the *wind,* Hos. 12:1. Men will see that they have *laboured for the wind* when at death they find the profit of their labour is all gone, gone like the wind, they know not whither.

7. Those that have much, if they set their hearts upon it, have not only uncomfortable deaths, but uncomfortable lives too, *v.* 17. This covetous worldling, that is so bent upon raising an estate, *all his days eats in darkness and much sorrow, and it is his sickness and wrath;* he has not only no pleasure of his estate, nor any enjoyment of it himself, for he *eats the bread of sorrow* (Ps. 127:2), but a great deal of vexation to see others eat of it. His necessary expenses make him sick, make him fret, and he seems as if he were angry that himself and those about him cannot live without meat. As we read the last clause, it intimates how ill this covetous worldling can bear the common and unavoidable calamities of human life. When he is in health he *eats in darkness,* always dull with care and fear about what he has; but, if he be sick, *he has much sorrow and wrath with his sickness;* he is vexed that his sickness takes him off from his business and hinders him in his pursuits of the world, vexed that all his wealth will not give him any ease or relief, but especially terrified with the apprehensions of death (which his diseases are the harbingers of), of leaving this world and the things of it behind him, which he has set his affections upon, and removing to a world he has made no preparation for. He has not any *sorrow after a godly sort,* does not *sorrow to repentance,* but he has *sorrow and wrath,* is angry at the providence of God, angry at his sickness, angry at all about him, fretful and peevish, which doubles his affliction, which a good man lessens and lightens by patience and joy in his sickness.

Verses 18–20

Solomon, from the vanity of riches hoarded up, here infers that the best course we can take is to use well what we have, to serve God with it, to do good with it, and take the comfort of it to ourselves and our families; this he had pressed before, ch. 2:24; 3:22. Observe, 1. What it is that is here recommended to us, not to indulge the appetites of the flesh, or to take up with present pleasures or profits for our portion, but soberly and moderately to make use of what Providence has allotted for our comfortable passage through this world. We must not starve ourselves through covetousness, because we cannot afford ourselves food convenient, nor through eagerness in our worldly pursuits, nor through excessive care and grief, but *eat and drink* what is fit for us to keep our bodies in good plight for the serving of our souls in God's service. We must not kill ourselves with *labour,* and then leave others *to enjoy the good* of it, but take the comfort of that which our hands have laboured for, and that not now and then, but *all the days of our life which God gives us.* Life is God's gift, and he has appointed us *the number of the days* of our life (Job 14:5); let us therefore spend those days in *serving the Lord our God with joyfulness and gladness of heart.* We must not do the business of our calling as a drudgery, and make ourselves slaves to it, but we must *rejoice in our labour,* not grasp at more business than we can go through without perplexity and disquiet, but take a pleasure in the calling wherein God has put us, and go on in the business of it with cheerfulness. This it to *rejoice in our labour,* whatever it is, as *Zebulun in his going out and Issachar in his tents.* 2. What is urged to recommend it to us. (1.) That *it is good and comely* to do this. It is well, and it looks well. Those that cheerfully use what God has given them thereby honour the giver, answer the intention of the gift, act rationally and generously, do good in the world, and make what they have turn to the best account, and this is both their credit and their comfort; *it is good and comely;* there is duty and decency in it. (2.) That it is all the good we can have out of the things of this world: *It is our portion,* and in doing thus we take our portion, and make the best of bad. This is our part of our worldly possession. God must have his part, the poor theirs, and our families theirs, but this is ours; it is all that falls to our lot out of them. (3.) That a heart to do thus is such a gift of God's grace as crowns all the gifts of his providence. If God has given a man *riches and wealth,* he completes the favour, and makes that a blessing indeed, if withal he *gives him power to eat thereof,* wisdom and grace to take the good of it and to do good with it. If this *is God's gift,* we must *covet* it *earnestly* as *the best gift* relating to our enjoyments in this world. (4.) That this is the way to make our own lives easy and to relieve ourselves against the many toils and troubles which our lives on earth are incident to (*v.* 20): *He shall not much remember the days of his life,* the days of his sorrow and sore travail, his working days, his weeping days. He shall either forget them or remember them as waters that pass away; he shall not much lay to heart his crosses, nor long retain the bitter relish of them, *because God answers him in the joy of his heart,* balances all the grievances of his labour with the joy of it and recompenses him for it by giving him to *eat the labour of his hands.* If he does not answer all his desires and expectations, in the letter of them, yet he answers them with that which is more than equivalent, *in the joy of his heart.* A cheerful spirit is a great blessing; it makes the yoke of our employments easy and the burden of our afflictions light.

CHAPTER 6

In this chapter, I. The royal preacher goes on further to show the vanity of worldly wealth, when men place their happiness in it and are eager and inordinate in laying it up. Riches, in the hands of a man that is wise and generous, and good for something, but in the hands of a sordid, sneaking, covetous miser, they are good for nothing. 1. He takes an account of the possessions and enjoyments which such a man may have. He has wealth (*v.* 2), he has children to inherit it (*v.* 3), and lives long (*v.* 3, 6). 2. He describes his folly in not taking the comfort of it; he has no power to eat of it, lets strangers devour it, is never filled with good, and at last has no burial (*v.* 2, 3). 3. He condemns it as an evil, a common evil, vanity, and a disease (*v.* 1, 2). 4. He prefers the condition of a still-born child before the condition of such a one (*v.* 3). The still-born child's infelicity is only negative (*v.* 4, 5), but that of the covetous worldling is positive; he lives a great while to see himself miserable (*v.* 6). 5. He shows the vanity of riches as pertaining only to the body, and giving no satisfaction to the mind (*v.* 7, 8), and of those boundless desires with which covetous people vex themselves (*v.* 9), which, if they be gratified ever so fully, leave a man but a man still (*v.* 10). II. He concludes this discourse of the vanity of the creature with this plain inference from the whole, That it is folly to think of making up a happiness for ourselves in the things of this world (*v.* 11, 12). Our satisfaction must be in another life, not in this.

Verses 1–6

Solomon had shown, in the close of the foregoing chapter, how good it is to make a comfortable use of the gifts of God's providence; now here he shows the evil of the contrary, having and not using, gathering to lay up for I know not what contingent emergencies to come, not to lay out on the most urgent occasions present. This *is an evil which* Solomon himself saw *under the sun, v.* 1. A great deal of evil there is *under the sun.* There is a world above the sun where there is no evil, yet God *causes his sun to shine upon the evil* as well as upon *the good,* which is an aggravation of the evil. God has lighted up a candle for his servants to work by, but they bury their talent as slothful and unprofitable, and so waste the light and are unworthy of it. Solomon, as a king, inspected the manners of his subjects, and took notice of this evil as a prejudice to the public, who are damaged not only by men's prodigality on the one hand, but by their penuriousness on the other. As it is with the blood in the natural body, so it is with the wealth of the body politic, if, instead of circulating, it stagnates, it will be of ill consequence. Solomon as a preacher observed the evils that were done that he might reprove them and warn people against them. This evil was, in his days, *common,* and yet then there was great plenty of silver and gold, which, one would think, should have made people less fond of riches; the times also were peaceable, nor was there any prospect of trouble, which to some is a temptation to hoard. But no providence will of itself, unless the grace of God work with it, cure the corrupt affection that is in the carnal mind to the world and the things of it; nay, when *riches increase* we are most apt to set our *hearts upon them.* Now concerning this miser observe,

I. The abundant reason he has to serve God with joyfulness and gladness of heart; how well God has done for him.

1. He *has given* him *riches, wealth, and honour, v.* 2. Note, (1.) *Riches* and *wealth* commonly gain people *honour* among men. Though it be but an image, if it be a *golden* image, *all people, nations, and languages,* will *fall down and worship it.* (2.) *Riches, wealth, and honour,* are God's gifts, the gifts of his providence, and not given, as his rain and sunshine, alike to all, but to some, and not to others, as God sees fit. (3.) Yet they are given to many that do not make a good use of them, to many to whom God does not give wisdom and grace to take the comfort of them and serve God with them. The gifts of common providence are bestowed on many to whom are denied the gifts of a special grace, without which the gifts of providence often do more hurt than good.

2. *He wants nothing for his soul of all that he desires.* Providence has been so liberal to him that he has as much as *heart could wish,* and *more,* Ps. 73:7. He does not desire grace for his soul, the better part; all he desires is enough to gratify the sensual appetite, and that he has; his *belly* is *filled with* these *hidden treasures,* Ps. 17:14.

3. He is supposed to have a numerous family, to *beget a hundred children,* which are the stay and strength of his house and as a *quiver full of arrows* to him, which are the honour and credit of his house, and in whom he has the prospect of having his name built up and having all the immortality this world can give him. *They are full of children* (Ps. 17:14), while many of God's people are written childless and stripped of all.

4. To complete his happiness, he is supposed to *live many years,* or rather many *days,* for our life is to be reckoned rather by days than years: *The days of his years are many,* and so healthful is his constitution, and so slowly does age creep upon him, that they are likely to be many more. Nay, he is supposed to *live a thousand years* (which no man, that we know of, ever did), nay, *a thousand years twice told,* a small part of which time, one would think, were enough to convince men, by their own experience, of the folly both of those that expect to find all good in worldly wealth, and of those that expect to find any good in it but in using it.

II. The little heart he has to use this which God gives him, for the ends and purposes for which it was given him. This is his fault and folly that he *renders not again according to the benefit done unto him,* and *serves not the Lord God* his benefactor, *with joyfulness and gladness of heart, in the abundance of all things.* In the day of prosperity he is not joyful. *Tristis es, et felix? — Art thou happy, yet sad?* See his folly: 1. He cannot find in his heart to take the comfort of what he has himself. He has meat before him; he has wherewith to maintain himself and his family comfortably, but he has *not power to eat thereof.* His sordid niggardly temper will not suffer him to lay it out, no, not upon himself, no, not upon that which is most necessary for himself. He has not power to reason himself out of this absurdity, to conquer his covetous humour. He is weak indeed, who has not power to use what God gives him, for *God gives him not* that *power,* but withholds it from him, to punish him for his other abuses of his wealth. Because he has not the will to serve God with it, God denies him the power to serve himself with it. 2. He suffers those to prey upon him that he is under no obligation to: *A stranger eateth it.* This is the common fate of misers; they will not trust their own children perhaps, but retainers and hangers-on, that have the art of wheedling, insinuate themselves into them, and find ways of devouring what they have, or getting it to be left to them by their wills. God orders it so that *a stranger eats it. Strangers devour his strength,* Hos. 7:9; Prov. 5:10. This may be well called *vanity, and an evil disease.* What we have we have in vain if we do not use it; and that temper of mind is certainly a most wretched distemper which keeps us from using it. Our worst diseases are those that arise from the corruption of our own hearts. 3. He deprives himself of the good that he might have had of his worldly possessions, not only forfeits it, but robs himself of it and throws it from him: *His soul is not filled with good, v.* 3. He is still unsatisfied and uneasy. His hands are filled with riches, his barns filled, and his bags filled, but *his soul is not filled with good,* no, not with that good, for it is still craving more. Nay (*v.* 6), *he has not seen good;* he cannot so much as please his eye, for that is still looking further and looking with envy on those that have more. He has not even the sensible good of an estate. Though he looks not beyond the things that are seen, yet he looks not with any true pleasure even on them. 4. *He has no burial,* none agreeable to his rank, no decent burial, but *the burial of an ass.* Through the sordidness of his temper he will not allow himself a fashionable burial, but forbids it, or the strangers that have eaten him up leave him so poor, at last, that he has not wherewithal, or those to whom he leaves what he has have so little esteem for his memory, and are so greedy of what they are to have from him, that they will not be at the charges of burying him handsomely, which his own children, if he had left it to them, would not have grudged him.

III. The preference which the preacher gives to an untimely birth before him: *An untimely birth,* a child that is carried from the womb to the grave, *is better than he.* Better is the fruit that drops from the tree before it is ripe than that which is left to hang on till it is rotten. Job, in his passion, thinks the condition of *an untimely birth* better than his when he was in adversity (Job 3:16); but Solomon here pronounces it better than the condition of a worldling in his greatest prosperity, when the world smiles upon him. 1. He grants the condition of *an untimely birth,* upon many accounts, to be very sad (*v.* 4, 5): *He comes in with vanity* (for, as to this world, he that is born and dies immediately was born in vain), and he *departs in darkness;* little or no notice is taken of him; being an abortive, he has no *name,* or, if he had, it would soon be forgotten and buried in oblivion; it would *be covered with darkness,* as the body is with the earth. Nay (*v.* 5), *he has not seen the sun,* but from the darkness of the womb he is hurried immediately to that of the grave, and, which is worse than not being known to any, he has not *known any thing,* and therefore has come short of that which is the greatest pleasure and honour of man. Those that live in wilful ignorance, and know nothing to purpose, are no better than *an untimely birth* that *has not seen the sun nor known any thing.* 2. Yet he prefers it before that of a covetous miser. *This* untimely birth *has more rest than the other,* for *this* has some rest, but *the other* has none; *this* has no trouble and disquiet, but *the other* is in perpetual agitation, and has nothing but trouble, trouble of his own making. The shorter the life is the longer the rest; and the fewer the days, and the less we have to do with this troublesome world, the less trouble we know.

'Tis better die a child at four,
Than live, and die so at fourscore.

The reason he gives why *this has more rest* is because *all go to one place* to rest in, and this is sooner at his rest, *v.* 6. He that *lives a thousand years* goes to the same place with the child that does not live an hour, *ch.* 3:20. The grave is the place we shall all meet in. Whatever differences there may be in men's condition in this world, they must all die, are all under the same sentence, and, to outward appearance, their deaths are alike. The grave is to one, as well as another, a land of silence, of darkness, of separation from the living, and a sleeping-place. It is the common rendezvous of rich and poor, honourable and mean, learned and unlearned; the short-lived and long-lived meet in the grave, only one rides post thither, the other goes by a slower conveyance; the dust of both mingles, and lies undistinguished.

Verses 7–10

The preacher here further shows the vanity and folly of heaping up worldly wealth and expecting happiness in it.

I. How much soever we toil about the world, and get out of it, we can have for ourselves no more than a maintenance (*v.* 7): *All the labour of man is for his mouth,* which *craves it of him* (Prov. 16:26); it is but *food and raiment;* what is more others have, not we; it is all *for the mouth. Meats* are but *for the belly and the belly for meats;* there is nothing for the head and heart, nothing to nourish or enrich the soul. A little will serve to sustain us comfortably and a great deal can do no more.

II. Those that have ever so much are still craving; let a man labour ever so much *for his mouth, yet the appetite is not filled.* 1. Natural desires are still returning, still pressing; a man may be feasted to-day and yet hungry tomorrow. 2. Worldly sinful desires are insatiable, *ch.* 5:10. Wealth to a worldling is like drink to one in a dropsy, which does but increase the thirst. Some read the whole verse thus: *Though all a man's labour fall out to his own mind (ori ejus obveniat — so as to correspond with his views,* Juv.), just as himself would have it, *yet his desire is not satisfied,* still he has a mind to something more. 3. The desires of the soul find nothing in the wealth of the world to give them any satisfaction. *The soul is not filled,* so the word is. When God *gave* Israel *their request* he *sent leanness into their souls,* Ps. 106:15. He was a fool who, when his barns were full, said, *Soul, take thine ease.*

III. A fool may have as much worldly wealth, and may enjoy as much of the pleasure of it, as a wise man; nay, and perhaps not be so sensible of the vexation of it: *What has the wise more than the fool? v.* 8. Perhaps he has not so good an estate, so good a trade, nor such good preferment as the fool has. Nay, suppose them to be equal in their possessions, what can a wise man, a scholar, a wit, a politician, squeeze out of his estate more than needful supplies? and a half-witted man may do this. A fool can fare as well and relish it, can dress as well, and make as good a figure in any public appearance, as a wise man; so that if there were not pleasures and honour peculiar to the mind, which *the wise man has more than the fool,* as to this world they would be upon a level.

IV. Even a poor man, who has business, and is discreet, diligent, and dexterous, in the management of it, may get as comfortably through this world as he that is loaded with an overgrown estate. Consider *what the poor has* less than the rich, if he but *knows to walk before the living,* knows how to conduct himself decently, and do his duty to all, how to get an honest livelihood by his labour, how to spend his time well and improve his opportunities. *What has* he? Why, he is better beloved and more respected among his neighbours, and has a better interest than many a rich man that is griping and haughty. *What has* he? Why he has as much of the comfort of this life, has *food and raiment,* and is *therewith content,* and so is as truly rich as he that has abundance.

V. The enjoyment of what we have cannot but be acknowledged more rational than a greedy grasping at more (*v.* 9): *Better is the sight of the eyes,* making the best of that which is present, *than the wandering of the desire,* the uneasy walking of the soul after things at a distance, and the affecting of a variety of imaginary satisfactions. He is much happier that is always content, though he has ever so little, than he that is always coveting, though he has ever so much. We cannot say, *Better is the sight of the eyes than the* fixing *of the desire* upon God, and the resting of the soul in him; it is better to live by faith in things to come than to live by sense, which dwells only upon present things; but *better is the sight of the eyes than the* roving *of the desire* after the world, and the things of it, than which nothing is more uncertain nor more unsatisfying at the best. *This wandering of the desire is vanity and vexation of spirit.* It *is vanity* at the best; if what is desired, be obtained, it proves not what we promised ourselves from it, but commonly *the wandering desire* is crossed and disappointed, and then it turns to *vexation of spirit.*

VI. Our lot, whatever it is, is that which is appointed us by the counsel of God, which cannot be altered, and it is therefore our wisdom to reconcile ourselves to it and cheerfully to acquiesce in it (*v.* 10): *That which has been,* or (as some read it) *that which is,* and so likewise that which shall be, *is named already;* it is already determined in the divine foreknowledge, and all our care and pains cannot make it otherwise than as it is fixed. *Jacta est alea — The die is cast.* It is therefore folly to quarrel with that which will be as it is, and wisdom to make a virtue of necessity. We shall have what pleases God, and let that please us.

VII. Whatever we attain to in this world, still we are but men, and the greatest possessions and preferments cannot set us above the common accidents of human life: *That which has been,* and is, that busy animal that makes such a stir and such a noise in the world, *is named already.* He that made him gave him his name, *and it is known that it is man;* that is his name by which he must know himself, and it is a humbling name, Gen. 5:2. He *called their name Adam;* and all theirs have the same character, *red earth.* Though a man could make himself master of all the treasures of kings and provinces, yet he is a man still, mean, mutable, and mortal, and may at any time be involved in the calamities that are *common to men.* It is good for rich and great men to know and consider that they are *but men,* Ps. 9:20. *It is known that* they are but men; let them put what face they will upon it, and, like the king of Tyre, *set their heart as the heart of God,* yet the Egyptians are men, and not gods, and it is known that they are so.

VIII. How far soever our desires wander, and how closely soever our endeavours keep pace with them, we cannot strive with the divine Providence, but must submit to the disposals of it, whether we will or no. If *it is man, he may not contend with him that is mightier than he.* It is presumption to arraign God's proceedings, and to charge him with folly or iniquity; nor is it to any purpose to complain of him, for *he is in one mind and who can turn him?* Elihu pacifies Job with this incontestable principle, That *God is greater than man* (Job 33:12) and therefore *man may not contend with him,* nor resist his judgments, when they come with commission. A man cannot with the greatest riches make his part good against the arrests of sickness or death, but must yield to his fate.

Verses 11–12

Here, 1. Solomon lays down his conclusion which he had undertaken to prove, as that which was fully confirmed by the foregoing discourse: *There be many things that increase vanity;* the life of man is vain, at the best, and there are abundance of accidents that concur to make it more so; even that which pretends to increase the vanity and make it more vexatious. 2. He draws some inferences from it, which serve further to evince the truth of it. (1.) That a man is never the nearer to true happiness for the abundance that he has in this world: *What is man the better* for his wealth and pleasure, his honour and preferment? What remains to man? What residuum has he, what overplus, what real advantage, when he comes to balance his accounts? Nothing that will do him any good or turn to account. (2.) That we do not know what to wish for, because that which we promise ourselves most satisfaction in often proves most vexatious to us: *Who knows what is good for a man in this life,* where every thing is vanity, and any thing, even that which we most covet, may prove a calamity to us? Thoughtful people are in care to do every thing for the best, if they knew it; but as it is an instance of the corruption of our hearts that we are apt to desire that as good for us which is really hurtful, as children that cry for knives to cut their fingers with, so is it an instance of the vanity of this world that what, according to all probable conjectures, seems to be for the best, often proves otherwise; such is our shortsightedness concerning the issues and events of things, and such broken reeds are all our creature-confidences. We know not how to advise others for the best, nor how to act ourselves, because that which we apprehend likely to be for our welfare may become a trap. (3.) That therefore our life upon earth is what we have no reason to take any great complacency in, or to be confident of the continuance of. It is to be reckoned by *days;* it is but a *vain life,* and we spend it *as a shadow,* so little is there in it substantial, so fleeting, so uncertain, so transitory is it, and so little in it to be fond of or to be depended on. If all the comforts of life be vanity, life itself can have no great reality in it to constitute a happiness for us. (4.) That our expectations from this world are as uncertain and deceitful as our enjoyments are. Since every thing is vanity, *Who can tell a man what shall be after him under the sun?* He can no more please himself with the hopes of *what shall be after him,* to his children and family, than with the relish of what is with him, since he can neither foresee himself, nor can any one else foretel to him, *what shall be after him.* Nor shall he have any intelligence sent him of it when he is gone. *His sons come to honour, and he knows it not.* So that, look which way we will, *Vanity of vanity, all is vanity.*

CHAPTER 7

Solomon had given many proofs and instances of the vanity of this world and the things of it; now, in this chapter, I. He recommends to us some good means proper to be used for the redress of these grievances and the arming of ourselves against the mischief we are in danger of from them, that we may make the best of the bad, as 1. Care of our reputation (*v.* 1). 2. Seriousness (*v.* 2–6). 3. Calmness of spirit (*v.* 7–10). 4. Prudence in the management of all our affairs (*v.* 11, 12). 5. Submission to the will of God in all events, accommodating ourselves to every condition (*v.* 13–15). 6. A conscientious avoiding of all dangerous extremes (*v.* 16–18). 7. Mildness and tenderness towards those that have been injurious to us (*v.* 19–22). In short, the best way to save ourselves from the vexation which the vanity of the world creates us is to keep our temper and to maintain a strict government of our passions. II. He laments his own iniquity, as that which was more vexatious than any of these vanities, that mystery of iniquity, the having of many wives, by which he was drawn away from God and his duty (*v.* 23–29).

Verses 1–6

In these verses Solomon lays down some great truths which seem paradoxes to the unthinking part, that is, the far greatest part, of mankind.

I. That the honour of virtue is really more valuable and desirable than all the wealth and pleasure in this world (*v.* 1): *A good name is before good ointment* (so it may be read); it is preferable to it, and will be rather chosen by all that are wise. *Good ointment* is here put for all the profits of the earth (among the products of which oil was reckoned one of the most valuable), for all the delights of sense (for *ointment and perfume* which *rejoice the heart,* and it is called *the oil of gladness),* nay, and for the highest titles of honour with which men are dignified, for kings are anointed. *A good name is* better *than* all *riches* (Prov. 21:1), that is, a name for wisdom and goodness with those that are wise and good — *the memory of the just;* this is a good that will bring a more grateful pleasure to the mind, will give a man a larger opportunity of usefulness, and will go further, and last longer, than the most *precious box of ointment;* for Christ paid Mary for her ointment with a *good name,* a name in the gospels (Mt. 26:13), and we are sure he always pays with advantage.

II. That, all things considered, our going out of the world is a great kindness to us than our coming into the world was: *The day of death* is preferable to the *birth-day;* though, as to others, there was joy *when a child was born into the world,* and where there is death there is lamentation, yet, as to ourselves, if we have lived so as to merit a *good name, the day of our death,* which will put a period to our cares, and toils, and sorrows, and remove us to rest, and joy, and eternal satisfaction, *is better than the day of our birth,* which ushered us into a world of so much sin and trouble, vanity and vexation. We were born to uncertainty, but a good man does not die at uncertainty. *The day of our birth* clogged our souls with the burden of the flesh, but *the day of our death* will set them at liberty from that burden.

III. That it will do us more good to go to a funeral than to go to a festival (*v.* 2): *It is better to go to the house of mourning,* and there *weep with those that weep, than to go to the house of feasting,* to a wedding, or a wake, there to *rejoice with those that do rejoice.* It will do us more good, and make better impressions upon us. We may lawfully go to both, as there is occasion. Our Saviour both feasted at the wedding of his friend in Cana and wept at the grave of his friend in Bethany; and we may possibly glorify God, and do good, and get good, in the house of feasting; but, considering how apt we are to be vain and frothy, proud and secure, and indulgent of the flesh, *it is better* for us *to go to the house of mourning,* not to see the pomp of the funeral, but to share in the sorrow of it, and to learn good lessons, both from the dead, who is going thence to his long home, and from the mourners, who go about the streets.

1. The uses to be gathered from *the house of mourning* are, (1.) By way of information: *That is the end of all men.* It *is the end of man* as to this world, a final period to his state here; he shall return no more to his house. It *is the end of all men;* all *have sinned* and therefore *death passes upon all.* We must thus be left by our friends, as the mourners are, and thus leave, as the dead do. What is the lot of others will be ours; the cup is going round, and it will come to our turn to pledge it shortly. (2.) By way of admonition: *The living will lay it to his heart.* Will they? It were well if they would. Those that are spiritually alive *will lay it to heart,* and, as for all the survivors, one would think they should; it is their own fault if they do not, for nothing is more easy and natural than by the death of others to be put in mind of our own. Some perhaps *will lay that to heart,* and *consider their latter end,* who would not lay a good sermon to heart.

2. For the further proof of this (*v.* 4) he makes it the character, (1.) Of a wise man that his *heart is in the house of mourning;* he is much conversant with mournful subjects, and this is both an evidence and a furtherance of his wisdom. *The house of mourning* is the wise man's school, where he has learned many a good lesson, and there, where he is serious, he is in his element. When he *is in the house of mourning* his *heart* is there to improve the spectacles of mortality that are presented to him; nay, when he is in *the house of feasting,* his *heart is in the house of mourning,* by way of sympathy with those that are in

sorrow. (2.) It is the character of a fool that his *heart is in the house of mirth;* his heart is all upon it to be merry and jovial; his whole delight is in sport and gaiety, in merry stories, merry songs, and merry company, merry days and merry nights. If he be at any time in *the house of mourning,* he is under a restraint; his heart at the same time *is in the house of mirth;* this is his folly, and helps to make him more and more foolish.

IV. That gravity and seriousness better become us, and are better for us, than mirth and jollity, *v.* 3. The common proverb says, "An ounce of mirth is worth a pound of sorrow;" but the preacher teaches us a contrary lesson: *Sorrow is better than laughter,* more agreeable to our present state, where we are daily sinning and suffering ourselves, more or less, and daily seeing the sins and sufferings of others. While we are in a vale of tears, we should conform to the temper of the climate. It is also more for our advantage; *for, by the sadness* that appears in *the countenance, the heart is* often *made better.* Note, 1. That is best for us which is best for our souls, by which *the heart is made better,* though it be unpleasing to sense. 2. Sadness is often a happy means of seriousness, and that affliction which is impairing to the health, estate, and family, may be improving to the mind, and make such impressions upon that as may alter its temper very much for the better, may make it humble and meek, loose from the world, penitent for sin, and careful of duty. *Vexatio dat intellectum — Vexation sharpens the intellect. Periissem nisi periissem — I should have perished if I had not been made wretched.* It will follow, on the contrary, that by the mirth and frolicsomeness of the countenance the heart is made worse, more vain, carnal, sensual, and secure, more in love with the world and more estranged from God and spiritual things (Job 21:12, 14), till it become utterly unconcerned in *the afflictions of Joseph,* as those Amos 6:5, 6, and *the king and Haman,* Esth. 3:15.

V. That it is much better for us to have our corruptions mortified by the *rebuke of the wise* than to have them gratified by *the song of fools, v.* 5. Many that would be very well pleased to hear the information of the wise, and much more to have their commendations and consolations, yet do not care for *hearing their rebukes,* that is, care not for being told of their faults, though ever so wisely; but therein they are no friends to themselves, for *reproofs of instruction are the way of life* (Prov. 6:23), and, though they be not so pleasant as *the song of fools,* they are more wholesome. *To hear,* not only with patience, but with pleasure, *the rebuke of the wise,* is a sign and means of wisdom; but to be fond of *the song of fools* is a sign that the mind is vain and is the way to make it more so. And what an absurd thing is it for a man to dote so much upon such a transient pleasure as *the laughter of a fool* is, which may fitly be compared to the burning *of thorns under a pot,* which makes a great noise and a great blaze, for a little while, but is gone presently, scatters its ashes, and contributes scarcely any thing to the production of a boiling heat, for that requires a constant fire! *The laughter of a fool* is noisy and flashy, and is not an instance of true joy. *This is also vanity;* it deceives men to their destruction, for *the end of that mirth is heaviness.* Our blessed Saviour has read us our doom: *Blessed are you that weep now, for you shall laugh; woe to you that laugh now, for you shall mourn and weep,* Lu. 6:21, 25.

Verses 7–10

Solomon had often complained before of the *oppressions* which he saw *under the sun,* which gave occasion for many melancholy speculations and were a great discouragement to virtue and piety. Now here,

I. He grants the temptation to be strong (*v.* 7): *Surely* it is often too true that *oppression makes a wise man mad.* If a wise man be much and long oppressed, he is very apt to speak and act unlike himself, to lay the reins on the neck of his passions, and break out into indecent complaints against God and man, or to make use of unlawful dishonourable means of relieving himself. *The righteous,* when the *rod of the wicked rests* long *on their lot,* are in danger of *putting forth their hands to iniquity,* Ps. 125:3. When even wise men have unreasonable hardships put upon them they have much ado to keep their temper and to keep their place. *It destroys the heart of a gift* (so the latter clause may be read); even the generous heart that

is ready to give gifts, and a gracious heart that is endowed with many excellent gifts, is destroyed by being oppressed. We should therefore make great allowances to those that are abused and ill-dealt with, and not be severe in our censures of them, though they do not act so discreetly as they should; we know not what we should do if it were our own case.

II. He argues against it. Let us not fret at the power and success of oppressors, nor be envious at them, for, 1. The character of oppressors is very bad, so some understand *v.* 7. If he that had the reputation of *a wise man* becomes an *oppressor,* he becomes a *madman;* his reason has departed from him; he is no better than a roaring lion and a ranging bear, *and the gifts,* the bribes, he takes, the gains he seems to reap by his oppressions, do but *destroy his heart* and quite extinguish the poor remains of sense and virtue in him, and therefore he is rather to be pitied than envied; let him alone, and he will act so foolishly, and drive so furiously, that in a little time he will ruin himself. 2. The issue, at length, will be good: *Better is the end of a thing than the beginning thereof.* By faith see what the end will be, and with patience expect it. When proud men begin to oppress their poor honest neighbours they think their power will bear them out in it; they doubt not but to carry the day, and gain the point. But it will prove better in the end than it seemed at the beginning; their power will be broken, their wealth gotten by oppression will be wasted and gone, they will be humbled and brought down, and reckoned with for their injustice, and oppressed innocency will be both relieved and recompensed. *Better was the end of* Moses's treaty with Pharaoh, that proud oppressor, when Israel was brought forth with triumph, *than the beginning* of it, when the tale of bricks was doubled, and every thing looked discouraging.

III. He arms us against it with some necessary directions. If we would not be driven mad by oppression, but preserve the possession of our own souls,

1. We must be clothed with humility; *for the proud in spirit* are those that cannot bear to be trampled upon, but grow outrageous, and fret themselves, when they are hardly bestead. That will break a proud man's heart, which will not break a humble man's sleep. Mortify pride, therefore, and a lowly spirit will easily be reconciled to a low condition.

2. We must put on patience, *bearing* patience, to submit to the will of God in the affliction, and *waiting* patience, to expect the issue in God's due time. *The patient in spirit* are here opposed to *the proud in spirit,* for where there is humility there will be patience. Those will be thankful for any thing who own they deserve nothing at God's hand, *and the patient* are said to be *better than the proud;* they are more easy to themselves, more acceptable to others, and more likely to see a good issue of their troubles.

3. We must govern our passion with wisdom and grace (*v.* 9): *Be not hasty in thy spirit to be angry;* those that are hasty in their expectations, and cannot brook delays, are apt to be angry if they be not immediately gratified. "Be not angry at proud oppressors, or any that are the instruments of your trouble." (1.) "Be not soon angry, not quick in apprehending an affront and resenting it, nor forward to express your resentments of it." (2.) "Be not long angry;" for though anger may come into the bosom of a wise man, and pass through it as a wayfaring man, it *rests* only *in the bosom of fools;* there it resides, there it remains, there it has the innermost and uppermost place, there it is hugged as that which is dear, and laid in the bosom, and not easily parted with. He therefore that would approve himself so wise as not to *give place to the devil,* must not *let the sun go down upon his wrath,* Eph. 4:26, 27.

4. We must make the best of that which is (*v.* 10): "Take it not for granted *that the former days were better than these,* nor enquire *what is the cause* that they were so, for therein *thou dost not enquire wisely,* since thou enquirest into the reason of the thing before thou art sure that the thing itself is true; and, besides, thou art so much a stranger to the times past, and such an incompetent judge even of the present times, that thou canst not expect a satisfactory answer to the enquiry, and therefore *thou dost not enquire wisely;* nay, the supposition is a foolish reflection upon the providence of God in the government of the world." Note, (1.) It is folly to complain of the badness of our own times when we have more reason to complain

of the badness of our own hearts (if men's hearts were better, the times would mend) and when we have more reason to be thankful that they are not worse, but that even in the worst of times we enjoy many mercies, which help to make them not only tolerable, but comfortable. (2.) It is folly to cry up the goodness of former times, so as to derogate from the mercy of God to us in our own times; as if former ages had not the same things to complain of that we have, or if perhaps, in some respects, they had not, yet as if God had been unjust and unkind to us in casting our lot in an iron age, compared with the golden ages that went before us; this arises from nothing but fretfulness and discontent, and an aptness to pick quarrels with God himself. We are not to think there is any universal decay in nature, or degeneracy in morals. God has been always good, and men always bad; and if, in some respects, the times are now worse than they have been, perhaps in other respects they are better.

Verses 11–22

Solomon, in these verses, recommends wisdom to us as the best antidote against those distempers of mind which we are liable to, by reason of the vanity and vexation of spirit that there are in the things of this world. Here are some of the praises and the precepts of wisdom.

I. The praises of wisdom. Many things are here said in its commendation, to engage us to get and retain wisdom. 1. Wisdom is necessary to the right managing and improving of our worldly possessions: *Wisdom is good with an inheritance,* that is, an inheritance is good for little without wisdom. Though a man have a great estate, though it come easily to him, by descent from his ancestors, if he have not wisdom to use it for the end for which he has it, he had better have been without it. Wisdom is not only good for the poor, to make them content and easy, but it is good for the rich too, good with riches to keep a man from getting hurt by them, and to enable a man to do good with them. *Wisdom is good* of itself, and makes a man useful; but, if he have a good estate with it, that will put him into a greater capacity of being useful, and with his wealth he may be more serviceable to his generation than he could have been without it; he will also *make friends to himself,* Lu. 16:9. *Wisdom is as good as an inheritance, yea, better too* (so the margin reads it); it is more our own, more our honour, will make us greater blessings, will remain longer with us, and turn to a better account. 2. It is of great advantage to us throughout the whole course of our passage through this world: *By it there is* real *profit to those that see the sun,* both to those that have it and to their contemporaries. It is pleasant to *see the sun* (ch. 11:7), but that pleasure is not comparable to the pleasure of wisdom. The light of this world is an advantage to us in doing the business of this world (Jn. 11:9); but to those that have that advantage, unless withal they have wisdom wherewith to manage their business, that advantage is worth little to them. The clearness of the eye of the understanding is of greater use to us than bodily eye-sight. 3. It contributes much more to our safety, and is a shelter to us from the storms of trouble and its scorching heat; it *is a shadow* (so the word is), *as the shadow of a great rock in a weary land. Wisdom is a defence, and money* (that is, as *money) is a defence.* As a rich man makes his wealth, so a wise man makes his wisdom, a *strong city. In the shadow of wisdom* (so the words run) *and in the shadow of money* there is safety. He puts wisdom and money together, to confirm what he had said before, that *wisdom is good with an inheritance.* Wisdom is as a wall, and money may serve as a thorn hedge, which protects the field. 4. It is joy and true happiness to a man. This is *the excellency of knowledge,* divine knowledge, not only above money, but above wisdom too, human wisdom, *the wisdom of this world,* that it *gives life to those that have it. The fear of the Lord, that is wisdom,* and that is life; it prolongs life. Men's wealth exposes their lives, but their wisdom protects them. Nay, whereas wealth will not lengthen out the natural life, true wisdom will give spiritual life, the earnest of eternal life; so much *better is it to get wisdom than gold.* 5. It will put strength into a man, and be his stay and support (*v.* 19): *Wisdom strengthens the wise,* strengthens their spirits, and makes them bold and resolute, by keeping them always on sure grounds. It strengthens their interest, and gains them friends and reputation.

It strengthens them for their services under their sufferings, and against the attacks that are made upon them, *more than ten mighty men,* great commanders, strengthen *the city.* Those that are truly wise and good are taken under God's protection, and are safer there than if ten of the mightiest men in the city, men of the greatest power and interest, should undertake to secure them, and become their patrons.

II. Some of the precepts of wisdom, that wisdom which will be of so much advantage to us.

1. We must have an eye to God and to his hand in every thing that befals us (*v.* 13): *Consider the work of God.* To silence our complaints concerning cross events, let us consider the hand of God in them and not open our mouths against that which is his doing; let us look upon the disposal of our condition and all the circumstances of it as the *work of God,* and consider it as the product of his eternal counsel, which is fulfilled in every thing that befals us. Consider that every work of God is wise, just, and good, and there is an admirable beauty and harmony in his works, and all will appear at last to have been for the best. Let us therefore give him the glory of all his works concerning us, and study to answer his designs in them. *Consider the work of God* as that which we cannot make any alteration of. *Who can make that straight which he has made crooked?* Who can change the nature of things from what is settled by the God of nature? If he speak trouble, who can make peace? And, if he hedge up the way with thorns, who can get forward? If desolating judgments go forth with commission, who can put a stop to them? Since therefore we cannot mend God's work, we ought to make the best of it.

2. We must accommodate ourselves to the various dispensations of Providence that respect us, and do the work and duty of the day in its day, *v.* 14. Observe, (1.) How the appointments and events of Providence are counterchanged. In this world, at the same time, some are in prosperity, others are in adversity; the same persons at one time are in great prosperity, at another time in great adversity; nay, one event prosperous, and another grievous, may occur to the same person at the same time. Both come from the hand of God; *out of his mouth both evil and good proceed* (Isa. 14:7), and *he has set the one over against the other,* so that there is a very short and easy passage between them, and they are a foil to each other. Day and night, summer and winter, are set *the one over against the other,* that in prosperity we may rejoice *as though we rejoiced not,* and in adversity may weep *as though we wept not,* for we may plainly see the one from the other and quickly exchange the one for the other; and it is *to the end that man may find nothing after him,* that he may not be at any certainty concerning future events or the continuance of the present scene, but may live in a dependence upon Providence and be ready for whatever happens. Or that man may find nothing in the work of God which he can pretend to amend. (2.) How we must comply with the will of God in events of both kinds. Our religion, in general, must be the same in all conditions, but the particular instances and exercises of it must vary, as our outward condition does, that we may *walk after the Lord.* [1.] *In a day of prosperity* (and it is but a day), we must *be joyful,* be in good, be doing good, and getting good, maintain a holy cheerfulness, *and serve the Lord with gladness of heart in the abundance of all things.* "When the world smiles, *rejoice in God,* and praise him, and let *the joy of the Lord be thy strength.*" [2.] *In a day of adversity* (and that is but a day too) *consider.* Times of affliction are proper times for consideration, then God calls to *consider* (Hag. 1:5), then, if ever, we are disposed to it, and no good will be gotten by the affliction without it. We cannot answer God's end in afflicting us unless we consider why and wherefore he contends with us. And consideration is necessary also to our comfort and support under our afflictions.

3. We must not be offended at the greatest prosperity of wicked people, nor at the saddest calamities that may befal the godly in this life, *v.* 15. Wisdom will teach us how to construe those dark chapters of Providence so as to reconcile them with the wisdom, holiness, goodness, and faithfulness of God. We must not think it strange; Solomon tells us there were instances of this kind in his time: *"All things have I seen in the days of my vanity;* I have taken notice of all that passed, and this has been as surprising and perplexing to me as any thing." Observe, Though Solomon was so wise and great a man, yet he calls the days of his life *the days of his vanity,* for the best days on earth are so, in comparison with the days of eternity. Or perhaps he refers to the days of his apostasy from God (those were indeed the days of his vanity) and reflects upon this as one thing that tempted him to infidelity, or at least to indifferency in religion, that he saw *just men perishing in their righteousness,* that the greatest piety would not secure men from the greatest afflictions by the hand of God, nay, and sometimes did expose men to the greatest injuries from the hands of wicked and unreasonable men. Naboth perished in his righteousness, and Abel long before. He had also seen wicked men prolonging their lives in their wickedness; they *live, become old, yea, are mighty in power* (Job 21:7), yea, and by their fraud and violence they screen themselves from the sword of justice. "Now, in this, consider the work of God, and let it not be a stumbling-block to thee." The calamities of the righteous are preparing them for their future blessedness, and the wicked, while their days are prolonged, are but ripening for ruin. There is a judgment to come, which will rectify this seeming irregularity, to the glory of God and the full satisfaction of all his people, and we must wait with patience till then.

4. Wisdom will be of use both for caution to saints in their way, and for a check to sinners in their way. (1.) As to saints, it will engage them to proceed and persevere in their righteousness, and yet will be an admonition to them to take heed of running into extremes: *A just man may perish in his righteousness,* but let him not, by his own imprudence and rash zeal, pull trouble upon his own head, and then reflect upon Providence as dealing hardly with him. *"Be not righteous overmuch, v.* 16. In the acts of righteousness govern thyself by the rules of prudence, and be not transported, no, not by a zeal for God, into any intemperate heats or passions, or any practices unbecoming thy character or dangerous to thy interests." Note, There may be over-doing in well-doing. Self-denial and mortification of the flesh are good; but if we prejudice our health by them, and unfit ourselves for the service of God, we are *righteous overmuch.* To reprove those that offend is good, but to cast that pearl before swine, who will turn again and rend us, is to be *righteous overmuch. "Make not thyself over-wise.* Be not opinionative, and conceited of thy own abilities. Set not up for a dictator, nor pretend to give law to, and give judgment upon, all about thee. Set not up for a critic, to find fault with every thing that is said and done, nor busy thyself in other men's matters, as if thou knewest every thing and couldst do any thing. *Why shouldst thou destroy thyself,* as fools often do by meddling with strife that belongs not to them? Why shouldst thou provoke authority, and run thyself into the briers, by needless contradictions, and by going out of thy sphere to correct what is amiss? *Be wise as serpents;* beware of men." (2.) As to sinners, if it cannot prevail with them to forsake their sins, yet it may restrain them from growing very exorbitant. It is true *there is a wicked man that prolongs his life in his wickedness* (*v.* 15); but let none say that therefore they may safely be as wicked as they will; no, *be not overmuch wicked* (*v.* 17); do not run to an excess of riot. Many that will not be wrought upon by the fear of God, and a dread of the torments of hell, to avoid all sin, will yet, if they have ever so little consideration, avoid those sins that ruin their health and estate, and expose them to public justice. And Solomon here makes use of these considerations. *"The magistrate bears not the sword in vain,* has a quick eye and a heavy hand, and is *a terror to evildoers;* therefore be afraid of coming within his reach, be not so foolish as to lay thyself open to the law, *why shouldst thou die before thy time?"* Solomon, in these two cautions, had probably a special regard to some of his own subjects that were disaffected to his government and were meditating the revolt which they made immediately after his death. Some, it may be, quarrelled with the sins of their governor, and made them their pretence; to them he says, *Be not righteous overmuch.* Others were weary of the strictness of the government, and the temple-service, and that made them desirous to set up another king; but he frightens both from their seditious practices with the sword of justice, and others likewise from meddling *with those that were given to change.*

5. Wisdom will direct us in the mean between two extremes, and keep us always in the way of our duty, which we shall find a plain and safe way (*v.* 18): *"It is good that thou shouldst take hold of this,* this wisdom, this care, not to run thyself into snares. *Yea, also from this withdraw not thy hand;* never slacken thy diligence, nor abate thy resolution to maintain a due decorum, and a good government of thyself. Take hold of the bridle by which thy headstrong passions must be held in from hurrying thee into one mischief or other, as *the horse and mule that have no understanding;* and, having taken hold of it, keep thy hold, and withdraw not thy hand from it, for, it thou do, the liberty that they will take will be *as the letting forth of water,* and thou wilt not easily recover thy hold again. Be conscientious, and yet be cautious, and to this exercise thyself. Govern thyself steadily by the principles of religion, and thou shalt find that *he that fears God shall come forth out of all* those straits and difficulties which those run themselves into that cast off that fear." *The fear of the Lord* is that wisdom which will serve as a clue to extricate us out of the most intricate labyrinths. *Honesty is the best policy.* Those that truly fear God have but one end to serve, and therefore act steadily. God has likewise promised to direct those that fear him, and to order their steps not only in the right way, but out of every dangerous way, Ps. 37:23, 24.

6. Wisdom will teach us how to conduct ourselves in reference to the sins and offences of others, which commonly contribute more than any thing else to the disturbance of our repose, which contract both guilt and grief.

(1.) Wisdom teaches us not to expect that those we deal with should be faultless; we ourselves are not so, none are so, no, not the best. This *wisdom strengthens the wise* as much as any thing, and arms them against the danger that arises from provocation (*v.* 19), so that they are not put into any disorder by it. They consider that those they have dealings and conversation with are not incarnate angels, but sinful sons and daughters of Adam: even the best are so, insomuch that *there is not a just man upon earth, that doeth good and sinneth not, v.* 20. Solomon had this in his prayer (1 Ki. 8:46), in his proverbs (Prov. 20:9), and here in his preaching. Note, [1.] It is the character of just men that they *do good;* for the tree is known by its fruits. [2.] The best men, and those that do most good, yet cannot say that they are perfectly free from sin; even those that are sanctified are not sinless. None that live on this side of heaven live without sin. *If we say, We have not sinned, we deceive ourselves.* [3.] We sin even in our doing good; there is something defective, nay, something offensive, in our best performances. That which, for the substance of it, is good, and pleasing to God, is not so well done as it should be, and omissions in duty are sins, as well as omissions of duty. [4.] It is only just men upon earth that are subject thus to sin and infirmity; *the spirits of just men,* when they have got clear of the body, are made *perfect* in holiness (Heb. 12:23), and in heaven they *do good and sin not.*

(2.) Wisdom teaches us not to be quicksighted, or quickscented, in apprehending and resenting affronts, but to wink at many of the injuries that are done us, and act as if we did not see them (*v.* 21): *"Take no heed to all words that are spoken; set not thy heart to them.* Vex not thyself at men's peevish reflections upon thee, or suspicions of thee, but be *as a deaf man that hears not,* Ps. 38:13, 14. Be not solicitous or inquisitive to know what people say of thee; if they speak well of thee, it will feed thy pride, if ill, it will stir up thy passion. See therefore that thou approve thyself to God and thy own conscience, and then heed not what men say of thee. *Hearkeners,* we say, *seldom hear good of themselves;* if thou heed every word that is spoken, perhaps *thou wilt hear thy own servant curse thee* when he thinks thou dost not hear him; thou wilt be told that he does, and perhaps told falsely, if thou have thy ear open to tale-bearers, Prov. 29:12. Nay, perhaps it is true, and thou mayest stand behind the curtain and hear it thyself, mayest hear thyself not only blamed and despised, but cursed, the worst evil said of thee and wished to thee, and that by a servant, one of the meanest rank, of the abjects, nay, by thy own servant, who should be an advocate for thee, and protect thy good name as well as thy other interests. Perhaps it is a servant thou hast been kind to, and yet he requites thee thus ill, and this will vex thee; thou hadst better not have heard it. Perhaps it is a servant thou hast wronged and dealt unjustly with, and, though he dares not tell thee so, he tells others so, and tells God so, and then thy own conscience will join with him in the reproach, which will make it much more uneasy." The good names of the greatest lie much at the mercy even of the meanest. And perhaps there is a great deal more evil said of us than we think there is, and by those from whom we little expected it. But we do not consult our own repose, no, nor our credit, though we pretend to be jealous of it, if we take notice of every word that is spoken diminishingly of us; it is easier to pass by twenty such affronts than to avenge one.

(3.) Wisdom puts us in mind of our own faults (*v.* 22): "Be not enraged at those that speak ill of thee, or wish ill to thee, *for oftentimes,* in that case, if thou retire into thyself, thy own conscience will tell thee *that thou thyself hast cursed others,* spoken ill of them and wished ill to them, and thou art paid in thy own coin." Note, When any affront or injury is done us it is seasonable to examine our consciences whether we have not done the same, or as bad, to others; and if, upon reflection, we find we have, we must take that occasion to renew our repentance for it, must justify God, and make use of it to qualify our own resentments. If we be truly angry with ourselves, as we ought to be, for backbiting and censuring others, we shall be the less angry with others for backbiting and censuring us. We must show all meekness towards all men, for we ourselves *were sometimes foolish,* Tit. 3:2, 3; Mt. 7:1, 2; James 3:1, 2.

Verses 23–29

Solomon had hitherto been proving the vanity of the world and its utter insufficiency to make men happy; now here he comes to show the vileness of sin, and its certain tendency to make men miserable; and this, as the former, he proves from his own experience, and it was a dear-bought experience. He is here, more than any where in all this book, putting on the habit of a penitent. He reviews what he had been discoursing of already, and tells us that what he had said was what he knew and was well assured of, and what he resolved to stand by: *All this have I proved by wisdom, v.* 23. Now here,

I. He owns and laments the deficiencies of his wisdom. He had wisdom enough to see the vanity of the world and to experience that that would not make a portion for a soul. But, when he came to enquire further, he found himself at a loss; his eye was too dim, his line was too short, and, though he discovered this, there were many other things which he could not prove by wisdom.

1. His searches were industrious. God had given him a capacity for knowledge above any; he set up with a great stock of wisdom; he had the largest opportunities of improving himself that ever any man had; and, (1.) He resolved, if it were possible, to gain his point: *I said, I will be wise.* He earnestly desired it as highly valuable; he fully designed it as that which he looked upon to be attainable; he determined not to sit down short of it, Prov. 18:1. Many are not wise because they never said they would be so, being indifferent to it; but Solomon set it up for the mark he aimed at. When he made trial of sensual pleasures, he still thought *to acquaint his heart with wisdom* (*ch.* 2:3), and not to be diverted from the pursuits of that; but perhaps he did not find it so easy a thing as he imagined to keep up his correspondence with wisdom, while he addicted himself so much to his pleasures. However, his will was good; he said, *I will be wise.* And that was not all: (2.) He resolved to spare no pains (*v.* 25): *"I applied my heart;* I and my heart turned every way; I left no stone unturned, no means untried, to compass what I had in view. I set *myself to know, and to search, and to seek out wisdom,* to accomplish myself in all useful learning, philosophy, and divinity." If he had not thus closely applied himself to study, it would have been but a jest for him to say, *I will be wise,* for those that will attain the end must take the right way. Solomon was a man of great quickness, and yet, instead of using that (with many) as an excuse for slothfulness, he pressed it upon himself as an inducement to diligence, and the easier he found it to master a good notion the more intent he would be that he might be master of the more good notions. Those that have the best parts should take the greatest pains, as those that have the largest stock should trade most. He applied himself not only to know what lay on the surface, but to search what lay hidden out of the common view and road; nor did he search a little way, and then give it over because he did not presently find what he searched for, but he *sought it out,* went to the bottom of it; nor did he aim to know things only, but the reasons of things, that he might give an account of them.

2. Yet his success was not answerable or satisfying: *"I said, I will be wise, but it was far from me;* I could not compass it. After all, *This only I know that I know nothing,* and the more I know the more I see there is to be known, and the more sensible I am of my own ignorance. *That which is far off, and exceedingly deep, who can find it out?"* He means God himself, his counsels and his works; when he searched into these he presently found himself puzzled and run aground. He *could not order his speech by reason of darkness. It is higher than heaven, what can he do?* Job 11:8. Blessed be God, there is nothing which we have to do which is not plain and easy; *the word is nigh us* (Prov. 8:9); but there is a great deal which we would wish to know which is *far off, and exceedingly deep,* among the secret things which belong not to us. And probably it is a culpable ignorance and error that Solomon here laments, that his pleasures, and the many amusements of his court, had blinded his eyes and cast a mist before them, so that he could not attain to true wisdom as he designed.

II. He owns and laments the instances of his folly in which he had exceeded, as, in wisdom, he came short. Here is,

1. His enquiry concerning the evil of sin. He *applied his heart to know the wickedness of folly, even of foolishness and madness.* Observe, (1.) The knowledge of sin is a difficult knowledge, and hard to be attained; Solomon took pains for it. Sin has many disguises with which it palliates itself, as being loth to appear sin, and it is very hard to strip it of these and to see it in its true nature and colours. (2.) It is necessary to our repentance for sin that we be acquainted with the evil of it, as it is necessary to the cure of a disease to know its nature, causes, and malignity. St. Paul *therefore* valued the divine law, because it discovered sin to him, Rom. 7:7. Solomon, who, in the days of his folly, had set his wits on work to invent pleasures and sharpen them, and was ingenious in making provision for the flesh, now that God had opened his eyes is as industrious to find out the aggravations of sin and so to put an edge upon his repentance. Ingenious sinners should be ingenious penitents, and wit and learning, among the other spoils of the *strong man armed,* should be divided by the Lord Jesus. (3.) It well becomes penitents to say the worst they can of sin, for the truth is we can never speak ill enough of it. Solomon here, for his further humiliation, desired to see more, [1.] Of the sinfulness of sin; that is it which he lays the greatest stress upon in this inquiry, to *know the wickedness of folly,* by which perhaps he means his own iniquity, the sin of uncleanness, for that was commonly called *folly in Israel,* Gen. 34:7; Deu. 22:21; Jdg. 20:6; 2 Sa. 13:12. When he indulged himself in it, he made a light matter of it; but now he desires to see the *wickedness* of it, its *great wickedness,* so Joseph speaks of it, Gen. 39:9. Or it may be taken there generally for all sin. Many extenuate their sins with this, They were *folly;* but Solomon sees *wickedness* in those follies, an offence to God and a wrong to conscience. *This is wickedness,* Jer. 4:18; Zec. 5:8. [2.] Of the folly of sin; as there is a wickedness in folly, so there is a folly in wickedness, even foolishness and madness. Wilful sinners are fools and madmen; they act contrary both to right reason and to their true interest.

2. The result of this enquiry.

(1.) He now discovered more than ever of the evil of that great sin which he himself had been guilty of, the *loving of many strange women,* 1 Ki. 11:1. This is that which he here most feelingly laments, and in very pathetic expressions. [1.] He found the remembrance of the sin very grievous. O how heavily did it lie upon his conscience! what an agony was he in upon the thought of it — the wickedness, the foolishness, the madness, that he had been guilty of! *I find it more bitter than death.* As great a terror seized him, in reflection upon it, as if he had been under the arrest of death. Thus do those that have their sins set in order before them by a sound conviction cry out against them; they are bitter as gall, nay, bitter as death, to all true penitents. Uncleanness is a sin that is, in its own nature, more pernicious than death itself. Death may be made honourable and comfortable, but this sin can be no other than shame and pain, Prov. 5:9, 11. [2.] He found the temptation to the sin very dangerous, and that it was extremely difficult, and next to impossible, for those that ventured into the temptation to escape the sin, and for those that had fallen into the sin to recover themselves by repentance. The heart of the adulterous woman is *snares and nets;* she plays her game to ruin souls with as much art and subtlety as ever any fowler used to take a silly bird. The methods such sinners use are both deceiving and destroying, as snares and nets are. The unwary souls are enticed into them by the bait of pleasure, which they greedily catch at and promise themselves satisfaction in; but they are taken before they are aware, and taken irrecoverably. Her hands are as bands, with which, under colour of fond embraces, she holds those fast that she has seized; they are *held in the cords of their own sin,* Prov. 5:22. Lust gets strength by being gratified and its charms are more prevalent. [3.] He reckoned it a great instance of God's favour to any man if by his grace he has kept him from this sin: *He that pleases God shall escape from her,* shall be preserved either from being tempted to this sin or from being overcome by the temptation. Those that are kept from this sin must acknowledge it is God that keeps them, and not any strength or resolution of their own, must acknowledge it a great mercy; and those that would have grace sufficient for them to arm them against this sin must be careful to please God in every thing, by keeping his ordinances, Lev. 18:30. [4.] He reckoned it a sin that is as sore a punishment of other sins as a man can fall under in this life: *The sinner shall be taken by her. First,* Those that allow themselves in other sins, by which their minds are blinded and their consciences debauched, are the more easily drawn to this. *Secondly,* it is just with God to leave them to themselves to fall into it. See Rom. 1:26, 28; Eph. 4:18, 19. Thus does Solomon, as it were, with horror, bless himself from the sin in which he had plunged himself.

(2.) He now discovered more than ever of the general corruption of man's nature. He traces up that stream to the fountain, as his father had done before him, on a like occasion (Ps. 51:5): *Behold, I was shapen in iniquity.* [1.] He endeavoured to find out the number of his actual transgressions (*v.* 27): *"Behold, this have I found,* that is, this I hoped to find; I thought I could have understood my errors and have brought in a complete list, at least of the heads of them; I thought I could have counted them one by one, and have found out the account." He desired to find them out as a penitent, that he might the more particularly acknowledge them; and, generally, the more particular we are in the confession of sin the more comfort we have in the sense of the pardon; he desired it also as a preacher, that he might the more particularly give warning to others. Note, A sound conviction of one sin will put us upon enquiring into the whole confederacy; and the more we see amiss in ourselves the more diligently we should enquire further into our own faults, that what we see not may be discovered to us, Job 34:32. [2.] He soon found himself at a loss, and perceived that they were innumerable (*v.* 28): *"Which yet my soul seeks;* I am still counting, and still desirous to find out the account, but I find not, I cannot count them all, nor find out the account of them to perfection. I still make new and amazing discoveries of the desperate wickedness that there is in my own heart," Jer. 17:9, 10. *Who can know it? Who can understand his errors? Who can tell how often he offends?* Ps. 19:12. He finds that if God enters into judgment with him, or he with himself, for all his thoughts, words, and actions, he is *not able to answer for one of a thousand,* Job 9:3. This he illustrates by comparing the corruption of his own heart and life with the corruption of the world, where he scarcely found one good man among a thousand; nay, among all the thousand wives and concubines which he had, he did not find *one good woman.* "Even so," says he, "When I come to recollect and review my own thoughts, words, and actions, and all the passages of my life past, perhaps among those that were manly I might find one good among a thousand, and that was all; the rest even of those had some corruption or other in them." He found (*v.* 20) that he had sinned even in doing good. But for those that were effeminate, that passed in the indulgence of his pleasures, they were all naught; in that part of his life there did not appear so much as one of a thousand good. In our hearts and lives there appears little good, at the best, but sometimes none at all. Doubtless this is not intended as a censure of the female sex in general; it is probable that there have been and are more good women than good men (Acts 17:4, 12); he merely alludes to his own sad experience. And perhaps there may be this further in it: he does, in his proverbs, warn us against the snares both of the *evil man* and of the *strange woman* (Prov. 2:12, 16; 4:14; 5:3); now he had observed the ways of the *evil women* to be more deceitful and dangerous than those of the *evil men,* that it was more difficult to discover their frauds and elude their snares, and therefore he compares sin to an adulteress (Prov. 9:13), and perceives he can no more find out the deceitfulness of his own heart than he can that of a strange woman, whose ways are movable, that thou canst not know them. [3.] He therefore runs up all the streams of actual transgression to the fountain of original corruption. The source of all the folly and madness that are in the world is in man's apostasy from God and his degeneracy from his primitive rectitude (v. 20): "*Lo, this only have I found;* when I could not find out the particulars, yet the gross account was manifest enough; it is as clear as the sun that man is corrupted and revolted, and is not as he was made." Observe, *First,* How man was made by the wisdom and goodness of God: *God made man upright; Adam the first man,* so the Chaldee. God made him, and he made him *upright,* such a one as he should be; being made a rational creature, he was, in all respects, such a one as a rational creature should be, *upright,* without any irregularity; one could find no fault in him; he was *upright,* that is, determined to God only, in opposition to the *many inventions* which he afterwards turned aside to. Man, as he came out of God's hands, was (as we may say) a little picture of his Maker, who is *good and upright. Secondly,* How he was marred, and in effect unmade, by his own folly and badness: *They have sought out many inventions* — they, our first parents, or the whole race, all in general and every one in particular. *They have sought out great inventions* (so some), inventions to become great as gods (Gen. 3:5), or *the inventions of the great ones* (so some), of the angels that fell, the *Magnates,* or *many inventions.* Man, instead of resting in what God had found for him, was for seeking to better himself, like the prodigal that left his father's house to seek his fortune. Instead of being for one, he was for many; instead of being for God's institutions, he was for his own inventions. The law of his creation would not hold him, but he would be at his own disposal and follow his own sentiments and inclinations. *Vain man would be wise,* wiser than his Maker; he is giddy and unsettled in his pursuits, and therefore has *many inventions.* Those that forsake God wander endlessly. Men's actual transgressions are multiplied. Solomon could not find out how many they are (v. 28); but he found they were *very many.* Many kinds of sins, and those often repeated. *They are more than the hairs on our heads,* Ps. 40:12.

CHAPTER 8

Solomon, in this chapter, comes to recommend wisdom to us as the most powerful antidote against both the temptations and vexations that arise from the vanity of the world. Here is, I. The benefit and praise of wisdom (v. 1). II. Some particular instances of wisdom prescribed to us. 1. We must keep in due subjection to the government God has set over us (v. 2–5). 2. We must get ready for sudden evils, and especially for sudden death (v. 6–8). 3. We must arm ourselves against the temptation of an oppressive government and not think it strange (v. 9, 10). The impunity of oppressors makes them more daring (v. 11), but in the issue it will be well with the righteous and ill with the wicked (v. 12, 13), and therefore the present prosperity of the wicked and afflictions of the righteous ought not to be a stumbling-block to us (v. 14). 4. We must cheerfully use the gifts of God's providence (v. 15). 5. We must with an entire satisfaction acquiesce in the will of God, and, not pretending to find the bottom, we must humbly and silently adore the depth of his unsearchable counsels, being assured they are all wise, just, and good (v. 16, 17).

Verses 1–5

Here is, I. An encomium of *wisdom* (v. 1), that is, of true piety, guided in all its exercises by prudence and discretion. The wise man is the good man, that knows God and glorifies him, knows himself and does well for himself; his wisdom is a great happiness to him, for, 1. It advances him above his neighbours, and makes him more excellent than they: *Who is as the wise man?* Note, Heavenly wisdom will

make a man an incomparable man. No man without grace, though he be learned, or noble, or rich, is to be compared with a man that has true grace and is therefore accepted of God. 2. It makes him useful among his neighbours and very serviceable to them: *Who but the wise man knows the interpretation of a thing,* that is, understands the times and the events of them, and their critical junctures, so as to direct *what Israel ought to do,* 1 Chr. 12:32. 3. It beautifies a man in the eyes of his friends: *It makes his face to shine,* as Moses's did when he came down from the mount; it puts honour upon a man and a lustre on his whole conversation, makes him to be regarded and taken notice of, and gains him respect (as Job 29:7, etc.); it makes him lovely and amiable, and the darling and blessing of his country. *The strength of his face,* the sourness and severity of his countenance (so some understand the last clause), *shall be changed* by it into that which is sweet and obliging. Even those whose natural temper is rough and morose by *wisdom* are strangely altered; they become mild and gentle, and learn to look pleasant. 4. It emboldens a man against his adversaries, their attempts and their scorn: *The boldness of his face shall be* doubled by wisdom; it will add very much to his courage in maintaining his integrity when he not only has an honest cause to plead, but by his wisdom knows how to manage it and where to find *the interpretation of a thing. He shall not be ashamed, but shall speak with his enemy in the gate.*

II. A particular instance of wisdom pressed upon us, and that is subjection to authority, and a dutiful and peaceable perseverance in our allegiance to the government which Providence has set over us. Observe,

1. How the duty of subjects is here described. (1.) We must be observant of the laws. In all those things wherein the civil power is to interpose, whether legislative or judicial, we ought to submit to its order and constitutions: *I counsel thee;* it may as well be supplied, *I charge thee,* not only as a prince but as a preacher: he might do both; "I recommend it to thee as a piece of wisdom; I say, whatever those say that are given to change, *keep the king's commandment;* wherever the sovereign power is lodged, be subject to it. *Observe the mouth of a king"* (so the phrase is); "say as he says; do as he bids thee; let his word be a law, or rather let the law be his word." Some understand the following clause as a limitation of this obedience: "*Keep the king's commandment,* yet so as to have a *regard to the oath of God,* that is, so as to keep a good conscience and not to violate thy obligations to God, which are prior and superior to thy obligations to the king. *Render to Caesar the things that are Caesar's,* but so as to reserve pure and entire *to God the things that are* his." (2.) We must not be forward to find fault with the public administration, or quarrel with every thing that is not just according to our mind, nor quit our post of service under the government, and throw it up, upon every discontent (v. 3): "*Be not hasty to go out of his sight,* when he is displeased at thee (ch. 10:4), or when thou art displeased at him; fly not off in a passion, nor entertain such jealousies of him as will tempt thee to renounce the court or forsake the kingdom." Solomon's subjects, as soon as his head was laid low, went directly contrary to this rule, when upon the rough answer which Rehoboam gave them, they were *hasty to go out of his sight,* would not take time for second thoughts nor admit proposals of accommodation, but cried, *To your tents, O Israel!* "There may perhaps be a just cause *to go out of his sight;* but *be not hasty* to do it; act with great deliberation." (3.) We must not persist in a fault when it is shown us: "*Stand not in an evil thing;* in any offence thou hast given to thy prince humble thyself, and do not justify thyself, for that will make the offence much more offensive. In any ill design thou hast, upon some discontent, conceived against thy prince, do not proceed in it; but *if thou hast done foolishly in lifting up thyself, or hast thought evil, lay thy hand upon thy mouth,*" Prov. 30:32. Note, Though we may by surprise be drawn into an evil thing, yet we must not stand in it, but recede from it as soon as it appears to us to be evil. (4.) We must prudently accommodate ourselves to our opportunities, both for our own relief, if we think ourselves wronged, and for the redress of public grievances: *A wise man's heart discerns both time and judgment* (v. 5); it is the wisdom of subjects, in applying themselves to their princes, to enquire and consider both at what season and in what manner they may do

it best and most effectually, to pacify his anger, obtain his favour, or obtain the revocation of any grievous measure prescribed. Esther, in dealing with Ahasuerus, took a deal of pains to *discern both time and judgment,* and she sped accordingly. This may be taken as a general rule of wisdom, that every thing should be well timed; and our enterprises are *then* likely to succeed, when we embrace the exact opportunity for them.

2. What arguments are here used to engage us to be subject to the higher powers; they are much the same with those which St. Paul uses, Rom. 13:1, etc. (1.) We *must needs be subject, for conscience-sake,* and that is the most powerful principle of subjection. We must be subject because of the oath of God, the oath of allegiance which we have taken to be faithful to the government, *the covenant between the king and the people,* 2 Chr. 23:16. *David made a covenant,* or contract, *with the elders of Israel,* though he was king by divine designation, 1 Chr. 11:3. *"Keep the king's commandments,* for he has sworn to rule thee in the fear of God, and thou hast sworn, in that fear, to be faithful to him." It is called *the oath of God* because he is a witness to it and will avenge the violation of it. (2.) *For wrath's sake,* because of the sword which the prince bears and the power he is entrusted with, which make him formidable: *He does whatsoever pleases him;* he has a great authority and a great ability to support that authority (v. 4): *Where the word of a king is,* giving orders to seize a man, *there is power;* there are many that will execute his orders, which makes *the wrath of a king,* or supreme government, like *the roaring of a lion* and like *messengers of death. Who may say unto him, What doest thou?* He that contradicts him does it at his peril. Kings will not bear to have their orders disputed, but expect they should be obeyed. In short, it is dangerous contending with sovereignty, and what many have repented. A subject is an unequal match for a prince. *He* may command me who has legions at command. (3.) For the sake of our own comfort: *Whoso keeps the commandment,* and lives a quiet and peaceable life, *shall feel no evil thing,* to which that of the apostle answers (Rom. 13:3), *Wilt thou then not be afraid of the power* of the king? *Do that which is good,* as becomes a dutiful and loyal subject, *and thou shalt* ordinarily *have praise of the same.* He that does no ill shall feel no ill and needs fear none.

Verses 6–8

Solomon had said (v. 5) that *a wise man's heart discerns time and judgment,* that is, a man's wisdom will go a great way, by the blessing of God, in moral prognostications; but here he shows that few have that wisdom, and that even the wisest may yet be surprised by a calamity which they had not any foresight of, and therefore it is our wisdom to expect and prepare for sudden changes. Observe, 1. All the events concerning us, with the exact time of them, are determined and appointed in the counsel and foreknowledge of God, and all in wisdom: *To every purpose there is a time* prefixed, and it is the best time, for it *is time and judgment,* time appointed both in wisdom and righteousness; the appointment is not chargeable with folly or iniquity. 2. We are very much in the dark concerning future events and the time and season of them: Man *knows not that which shall be* himself; and *who can tell him when* or how *it shall be? v.* 7. It cannot either be foreseen by him or foretold him; the stars cannot foretel a man what shall be, nor any of the arts of divination. God has, in wisdom, concealed from us the knowledge of future events, that we may be always ready for changes. 3. It is our great unhappiness and misery that, because we cannot foresee an evil, we know not how to avoid it, or guard against it, and, because we are not aware of the proper successful season of actions, therefore we lose our opportunities and miss our way: *Because to every purpose there is* but one way, one method, one proper opportunity, *therefore the misery of man is great upon him;* because it is so hard to hit that, and it is a thousand to one but he misses it. Most of the miseries men labour under would have been prevented if they could have been foreseen and the happy time discovered to avoid them. Men are miserable because they are not sufficiently sagacious and attentive. 4. Whatever other evils may be avoided, we are all under a fatal necessity of dying, v. 8. (1.) When the soul is required it must be resigned, and it is to no purpose to dispute it, either by arms or arguments, by ourselves, or by any friend: *There is no man that has power over* his own *spirit, to retain it,* when it is summoned to return to God who gave it. It cannot fly any where out of the jurisdiction of death, nor find any place where its writs do not run. It cannot abscond so as to escape death's eye, though it is hidden from the eyes of all living. A man has no power to adjourn the day of his death, nor can he by prayers or bribes obtain a reprieve; no bail will be taken, no essoine [excuse], protection, or imparlance [conference], allowed. We have not *power over the spirit* of a friend, *to retain* that; the prince, with all his authority, cannot prolong the life of the most valuable of his subjects, nor the physician with his medicines and methods, nor the soldier with his force, not the orator with his eloquence, nor the best saint with his intercessions. The stroke of death can by no means be put by when our days are determined and the hour appointed us has come. (2.) Death is an enemy that we must all enter the lists with, sooner or later: *There is no discharge in that war,* no dismission from it, either of the men of business or of the faint-hearted, as there was among the Jews, Deu. 20:5, 8. While we live we are struggling with death, and we shall never put off the harness till we put off the body, never obtain a discharge till death has obtained the mastery; the youngest is not released as a freshwater soldier, nor the oldest as *miles emeritus — a soldier whose merits have entitled him to a discharge.* Death is a battle that must be fought, *There is no sending to that war* (so some read it), no substituting another to muster for us, no champion admitted to fight for us; we must ourselves engage, and are concerned to provide accordingly, as for a battle. (3.) Men's wickedness, by which they often evade or outface the justice of the prince, cannot secure them from the arrest of death, nor can the most obstinate sinner harden his heart against those terrors. Though he *strengthen himself* ever so much *in his wickedness* (Ps. 52:7), death will be too strong for him. The most subtle wickedness cannot outwit death, nor the most impudent wickedness outbrave death. Nay, the wickedness which men give themselves to will be so far from delivering them from death that it will deliver them up to death.

Verses 9–13

Solomon, in the beginning of the chapter, had warned us against having any thing to do with seditious subjects; here, in these verses, he encourages us, in reference to the mischief of tyrannical and oppressive rulers, such as he had complained of before, ch. 3:16; 4:1.

1. He had observed many such rulers, *v.* 9. In the serious views and reviews he had taken of the children of men and their state he had observed that many a time *one man rules over another to his hurt;* that is, (1.) To the hurt of the ruled (many understand it so); whereas they ought to be God's ministers unto their subjects *for their good* (Rom. 13:14), to administer justice, and to preserve the public peace and order, they use their power for their hurt, to invade their property, encroach upon their liberty, and patronise the acts of injustice. It is sad with a people when those that should protect their religion and rights aim at the destruction of both. (2.) To the hurt of the rulers (so we render it), *to their own hurt,* to the feeling of their pride and covetousness, the gratifying of their passion and revenge, and so to the filling up of the measure of their sins and the hastening and aggravating of their ruin. *Agens agendo repatitur — What hurt men do to others will return, in the end, to their own hurt.*

2. He had observed them to prosper and flourish in the abuse of their power (*v.* 10): *I saw* those *wicked* rulers *come and go from the place of the holy,* go in state to and return in pomp from the place of judicature (which is called *the place of the Holy One* because *the judgment is the Lord's,* Deu. 1:17, and he *judges among the gods,* Ps. 82:1, and *is with them in the judgment,* 2 Chr. 19:6), and they continued all their days in office, were never reckoned with for their mal-administration, but died in honour and were buried magnificently; their commissions were *durante vitâ — during life,* and not *quamdiu se bene gesserint — during good behaviour. And they were forgotten in the city where they had so done;* their wicked practices were not remembered against them to their reproach and infamy when they were gone. Or, rather, it denotes the vanity of their dignity and power, for that is his remark upon it in

the close of the verse: *This is also vanity.* They are proud of their wealth, and power, and honour, because they sit in *the place of the holy;* but all this cannot secure, (1.) Their bodies from being buried in the dust; *I saw* them laid in the grave; and their pomp, though it attended them thither, could *not descend after them,* Ps. 49:17. (2.) Nor their names from being buried in oblivion; for *they were forgotten,* as if they had never been.

3. He had observed that their prosperity hardened them in their wickedness, *v.* 11. It is true of all sinners in general, and particularly of wicked rulers, that, *because sentence against their evil works is not executed speedily,* they think it will never be executed, and therefore they set the law at defiance and *their hearts are full in them to do evil;* they venture to do so much the more mischief, fetch a greater compass in their wicked designs, and are secure and fearless in it, and commit iniquity with a high hand. Observe, (1.) Sentence is passed against evil works and evil workers by the righteous Judge of heaven and earth, even against the evil works of princes and great men, as well as of inferior persons. (2.) The execution of this sentence is often delayed a great while, and the sinner goes on, not only unpunished, but prosperous and successful. (3.) Impunity hardens sinners in impiety, and the patience of God is shamefully abused by many who, instead of being led by it to repentance, are confirmed by it in their impenitence. (4.) Sinners herein deceive themselves, for, though the *sentence* be *not executed speedily,* it will be executed the more severely at last. Vengeance comes slowly, but it comes surely, and wrath is in the mean time *treasured up against the day of wrath.*

4. He foresaw such an end of all these things as would be sufficient to keep us from quarrelling with the divine Providence upon account of them. He supposes a wicked ruler to do an unjust thing *a hundred times,* and that yet his punishment is deferred, and God's patience towards him *is prolonged,* much beyond what was expected, and the days of his power are lengthened out, so that he continues to oppress; yet he intimates that we should not be discouraged. (1.) God's people are certainly a happy people, though they be oppressed: *"It shall be well with those that fear God,* I say with all those, and those only, *who fear before him."* Note, [1.] It is the character of God's people that they *fear God,* have an awe of him upon their hearts and make conscience of their duty to him, and this because they see his eye always upon them and they know it is their concern to approve themselves to him. When they lie at the mercy of proud oppressors they fear God more then they fear them. They do not quarrel with the providence of God, but submit to it. [2.] It is the happiness of *all that fear God,* that in the worst of times *it shall be well with them;* their happiness in God's favour cannot be prejudiced, nor their communion with God interrupted, by their troubles; they are in a good case, for they are kept in a good frame under their troubles, and in the end they shall have a blessed deliverance from and an abundant recompence for their troubles. And therefore *"surely I know,* I know it by the promise of God, and the experience of all the saints, *that,* however it goes with others, *it shall go well with them."* All is well that ends well. (2.) Wicked people are certainly a miserable people; though they prosper, and prevail, for a time, the curse is as sure to them as the blessing is to the righteous: *It shall not be well with the wicked,* as others think it is, who judge by outward appearance, and as they themselves expect it will be; nay, *woe to the wicked; it shall be ill with them* (Isa. 3:10, 11); they shall be reckoned with for all the ill they have done; nothing that befals them shall be really well for them. *Nihil potest ad malos pervenire quod prosit, imo nihil quod non noceat — No event can occur to the wicked which will do them good, rather no event which will not do them harm.* Seneca. Note, [1.] The wicked man's days *are as a shadow,* not only uncertain and declining, as all men's days are, but altogether unprofitable. A good man's days have some substance in them; he lives to a good purpose. A wicked man's days are all *as a shadow,* empty and worthless. [2.] These days *shall not be prolonged* to what he promised himself; he *shall not live out half his days,* Ps. 55:23. Though they may be *prolonged* (*v.* 12) beyond what others expected, yet his day shall come to fall. He shall fall short of everlasting life, and then his long life on earth will be worth little. [3.] God's great quarrel with

wicked people is for their *not fearing before* him; that is at the bottom of their wickedness, and cuts them off from all happiness.

Verses 14–17

Wise and good men have, of old, been perplexed with this difficulty, how the prosperity of the wicked and the troubles of the righteous can be reconciled with the holiness and goodness of the God that governs the world. Concerning this Solomon here gives us his advice.

I. He would not have us to be surprised at it, as though some strange thing happened, for he himself saw it in his days, *v.* 14. 1. He saw *just men to whom it happened according to the work of the wicked,* who, notwithstanding their righteousness, suffered very hard things, and continued long to do so, as if they were to be punished for some great wickedness. 2. He saw *wicked men to whom it happened according to the work of the righteous,* who prospered as remarkably as if they had been rewarded for some good deed, and that from themselves, from God, from men. We see the just troubled and perplexed in their own minds, the wicked easy, fearless, and secure, — the just crossed and afflicted by the divine Providence, the wicked prosperous, successful, and smiled upon, — the just, censured, reproached, and run down, by the higher powers, the wicked applauded and preferred.

II. He would have us to take occasion hence, not to charge God with iniquity, but to charge the world with vanity. No fault is to be found with God; but, as to the world, This *is vanity upon the earth,* and again, *This is also vanity,* that is, it is a certain evidence that the things of this world are not the best things nor were ever designed to make a portion and happiness for us, for, if they had, God would not have allotted so much of this world's wealth to his worst enemies and so much of its troubles to his best friends; there must therefore be another life after this the joys and griefs of which must be real and substantial, and able to make men truly happy or truly miserable, for this world does neither.

III. He would have us not to fret and perplex ourselves about it, or make ourselves uneasy, but cheerfully to enjoy what God has given us in the world, to be content with it and make the best of it, though it be much better with others, and such as we think very unworthy (*v.* 15): *Then I commended joy,* a holy security and serenity of mind, arising from a confidence in God, and his power, providence, and promise, *because a man has no better thing under the sun* (though a good man has much better things *above the sun*) *than to eat and drink,* that is, soberly and thankfully to make use of the things of this life according as his rank is, *and to be cheerful,* whatever happens, *for that shall abide with him of his labour.* That is all the fruit he has for himself of the pains that he takes in the business of the world; let him therefore take it, and much good may it do him; and let him not deny himself that, out of a peevish discontent because the world does not go as he would have it. *That shall abide with him* during the *days of his life which God gives him under the sun.* Our present life is a life *under the sun,* but we look for *the life of the world to come,* which will commence and continue when *the sun shall be turned into darkness* and shine no more. This present life must be reckoned by days; this life is given us, and the days of it are allotted to us, by the counsel of God, and therefore while it does last we must accommodate ourselves to the will of God and study to answer the ends of life.

IV. He would not have us undertake to give a reason for that which God does, for *his way is in the sea and his path in the great waters,* past finding out, and therefore we must be contentedly and piously ignorant of the meaning of God's proceedings in the government of the world, *v.* 16, 17. Here he shows, 1. That both he himself and many others had very closely studied the point, and searched far into the reasons of the prosperity of the wicked and the afflictions of the righteous. He, for his part, had *applied his heart to know this wisdom, and to see the business that is done,* by the divine Providence, *upon the earth,* to find out if there were any certain scheme, any constant rule or method, by which the affairs of this lower world were administered, any course of government as sure and steady as the course of nature, so that by what is done now we might as certainly foretel what will be done next as by the moon's changing now we can foretel when it will be at the full; this he would fain have found out. Others had likewise set themselves to make this enquiry with so close an application that they could not find time for *sleep, either day or night,* nor find in their hearts to sleep, so full of anxiety were they about these things. Some think Solomon speaks of himself, that he was so eager in prosecuting this great enquiry that he could not sleep for thinking of it. 2. That it was all labour in vain, *v.* 17. When we look upon *all the works of God* and his providence, and compare one part with another, we *cannot find* that there is any such certain method by which *the work that is done under the sun* is directed; we cannot discover any key by which to decipher the character, nor by consulting precedents can we know the practice of this court, nor what the judgment will be. [1.] *Though a man* be ever so industrious, thou he *labour to seek it out.* [2.] Though he be ever so ingenious, *though* he be *a wise man* in other things, and can fathom the counsels of kings themselves and trace them by their footsteps. Nay, [3.] Though he be very confident of success, though he *think to know it, yet he shall not;* he cannot *find it out.* God's ways are above ours, nor is he tied to his own former ways, but *his judgments are a great deep.*

CHAPTER 9

Solomon, in this chapter, for a further proof of the vanity of this world, gives us four observations which he had made upon a survey of the state of the children of men in it: — I. He observed that commonly as to outward things, good and bad men fare much alike (*v.* 1–3). II. That death puts a final period to all our employments and enjoyments in this world (*v.* 4–6), whence he infers that it is our wisdom to enjoy the comforts of life and mind the business of life, while it lasts (*v.* 7–10). III. That God's providence often crosses the fairest and most hopeful probabilities of men's endeavour, and great calamities often surprise men ere they are aware (*v.* 11, 12). IV. That wisdom often makes men very useful, and yet gains them little respect, for that persons of great merit are slighted (*v.* 13–18). And what is there then in this world that should make us fond of it?

Verses 1–3

It has been observed concerning those who have pretended to search for the philosophers' stone that, though they could never find what they sought for, yet in the search they have hit upon many other useful discoveries and experiments. Thus Solomon, when, in the close of the foregoing chapter, he *applied his heart to know the work of God,* and took a great deal of pains to search into it, though he despaired of finding it out, yet he found out that which abundantly recompensed him for the search, and gave him some satisfaction, which he here gives us; *for* therefore he *considered all this in his heart,* and weighed it deliberately, that he might *declare* it for the good of others. Note, What we are *to declare* we should first *consider;* think twice before we speak once; and what we have *considered* we should then *declare. I believed, therefore have I spoken.*

The great difficulty which Solomon met with in studying the book of providence was the little difference that is made between good men and bad in the distribution of comforts and crosses, and the disposal of events. This has perplexed the minds of many wise and contemplative men. Solomon discourses of it in these verses, and, though he does not undertake to find out this *work of God,* yet he says that which may prevent its being a stumbling-block to us.

I. Before he describes the temptation in its strength he lays down a great and unquestionable truth, which he resolves to adhere to, and which, if firmly believed, will be sufficient to break the force of the temptation. This has been the way of God's people in grappling with this difficulty. Job, before he discourses of this matter, lays down the doctrine of God's omniscience (Job 24:1), Jeremiah the doctrine of his righteousness (Jer. 12:1), another prophet that of his holiness (Hab. 1:13), the psalmist that of his goodness and peculiar favour to his own people (Ps. 73:1), and that is it which Solomon here fastens upon and resolves to abide by, that, though good and evil seem to be dispensed promiscuously, yet God has a particular care of and concern for his own people: *The righteous and the wise, and their works, are in the hand of God,* under his special protection and guidance; all their affairs are managed by him for their good; all their wise and righteous actions *are in his hand,* to be recompensed in the other world, though not in this. They seem as if they were given up *into the*

hand of their enemies, but it is not so. Men have *no power against them but what is given them from above.* The events that affect them do not come to pass by chance, but all according to the will and counsel of God, which will turn that to be for them which seemed to be most against them. Let this make us easy, whatever happens, that all God's saints are in his hand, Deu. 33:3; Jn. 10:29; Ps. 31:15.

II. He lays this down for a rule, that the love and hatred of God are not to be measured and judged of by men's outward condition. If prosperity were a certain sign of God's love, and affliction of his hatred, then it might justly be an offence to us to see the wicked and godly fare alike. But the matter is not so: *No man knows either love or hatred by all that is before him* in this world, by those things that are the objects of sense. These we may know by that which is within us; if we love God with all our heart, thereby we may know that he loves us, as we may know likewise that we are under his wrath if we be governed by that carnal mind which is enmity to him. These will be known by that which shall be hereafter, by men's everlasting state; it is certain that men are happy or miserable according as they are under the love or hatred of God, but not according as they are under the smiles or frowns of the world; and therefore if God loves a righteous man (as certainly he does) he is happy, though the world frown upon him; and if he hates a wicked man (as certainly he does) he is miserable, though the world smile upon him. Then the offence of this promiscuous distribution of events has ceased.

III. Having laid down these principles, he acknowledges that *all things come alike to all;* so it has been formerly, and therefore we are not to think it strange if it be so now, if it be so with us and our families. Some make this, and all that follows to *v.* 13, to be the perverse reasoning of the atheists against the doctrine of God's providence; but I rather take it to be Solomon's concession, which he might the more freely make when he had fixed those truths which are sufficient to guard against any ill use that may be made of what he grants. Observe here (*v.* 2),

1. The great difference that there is between the characters of the righteous and the wicked, which, in several instances, are set the one over-against the other, to show that, though *all things come alike to all,* yet that does not in the least confound the eternal distinction between moral good and evil, but that remains immutable. (1.) The righteous are *clean,* have *clean hands and pure hearts;* the wicked are *unclean,* under the dominion of unclean lusts, *pure* perhaps *in their own eyes,* but not *cleansed from their filthiness,* God will certainly put a difference *between the clean and the unclean, the precious and the vile,* in the other world, though he does not seem to do so in this. (2.) The righteous *sacrifice,* that is, they make conscience of worshipping God according to his will, both with inward and outward worship; the wicked *sacrifice not,* that is, they live in the neglect of God's worship and grudge to part with any thing for his honour. *What is the Almighty, that they should serve him?* (3.) The righteous are *good,* good in God's sight, they do good in the world; the wicked are *sinners,* violating the laws of God and man, and provoking to both. (4.) The wicked man *swears,* has no veneration for the name of God, but profanes it by swearing rashly and falsely; but the righteous man *fears an oath,* swears not, but is sworn, and then with great reverence; he fears to take an oath, because it is a solemn appeal to God as a witness and judge; he fears, when he has taken a oath, to break it, because God is righteous who takes vengeance.

2. The little difference there is between the conditions of the righteous and the wicked in this world: *There is one event to* both. Is David rich? So is Nabal. Is Joseph favoured by his prince? So is Haman. Is Ahab killed in a battle? So is Josiah. Are the bad figs carried to Babylon? So are the good, Jer. 24:1. There is a vast difference between the original, the design, and the nature, of the same event to the one and to the other; the effects and issues of it are likewise vastly different; the same providence to the one is *a savour of life unto life,* to the other *of death unto death,* though, to outward appearance, it is the same.

IV. He owns this to be a very great grievance to those that are wise and good: "This is an evil, the greatest perplexity, *among all things that are done under the sun* (*v.* 3);

nothing has given me more disturbance than this, *that there is one event unto all.*" It hardens atheists, and strengthens the hands of evil-doers; for therefore it is that *the hearts of the sons of men are full of evil* and *fully set in them to do evil,* ch. 8:11. When they see that *there is one event to the righteous and the wicked* they wickedly infer thence that it is all one to God whether they are righteous or wicked, and therefore they stick at nothing to gratify their lusts.

V. For the further clearing of this great difficulty, as he began this discourse with the doctrine of the happiness of the righteous (whatever they may suffer, they *and their works are in the hands of God,* and therefore in good hands, they could not be in better), so he concludes with the doctrine of the misery of the wicked; however they may prosper, *madness is in their heart while they live, and after that they go to the dead.* Envy not the prosperity of evil-doers, for, 1. They are now madmen, and all the delights they seem to be blessed with are but like the pleasant dreams and fancies of a distracted man. They are *mad upon their idols* (Jer. 50:38), are mad against God's people, Acts 26:11. When the prodigal repented, it is said, *He came to himself* (Lu. 15:17), which intimates that he had been beside himself before. 2. They will shortly be dead men. They make a mighty noise and bustle *while they live,* but after awhile, *they go to the dead,* and there is an end of all their pomp and power; they will then be reckoned with for all their madness and outrage in sin. Though, on this side death, the righteous and the wicked seem alike, on the other side death there will be a vast difference between them.

Verses 4–10

Solomon, in a fret, had *praised the dead more than the living* (*ch.* 4:2); but here, considering the advantages of life to prepare for death and make sure the hope of a better life, he seems to be of another mind.

I. He shows the advantages which the living have above those that are dead, *v.* 4–6. 1. While there is life *there is hope. Dum spiro, spero — While I breathe, I hope.* It is the privilege of the living that they are *joined to the living,* in relation, commerce, and conversation, and, while they are so, *there is hope.* If a man's condition be, upon any account, bad, *there is hope* it will be amended. If *the heart be full of evil, and madness be in it,* yet while there is life *there is hope* that by the grace of God there may be a blessed change wrought; but after men *go to the dead* (*v.* 3) it is too late then; he that is then filthy will be filthy still, for ever filthy. If men be thrown aside as useless, yet, while they are *joined to the living, there is hope* that they may yet again take root and bear fruit; he that is alive is, or may be, good for something, but he that is dead, as to this world, is not capable of being any further serviceable. Therefore a *living dog is better than a dead lion;* the meanest beggar alive has that comfort of this world and does that service to it which the greatest prince, when he is dead, is utterly incapable of. 2. While there is life there is an opportunity of preparing for death: *The living know* that which the dead have no knowledge of, particularly they *know that they shall die,* and are, or may be, thereby influenced to prepare for that great change which will come certainly, and may come suddenly. Note, *The living* cannot but *know that they shall die,* that they must needs die. They know they are under a sentence of death; they are already taken into custody by its messengers, and feel themselves declining. This is a needful useful knowledge; for what is our business, while we live, but to get ready to die: *The living know they shall die;* it is a thing yet to come, and therefore provision may be made for it. The dead know they are dead, and it is too late; they are on the other side the great gulf fixed. 3. When life is gone all this world is gone with it, as to us. (1.) There is an end of all our acquaintance with this world and the things of it: *The dead know not any thing* of that which, while they lived, they were intimately conversant with. It does not appear that they know any thing of what is done by those they leave behind. Abraham is ignorant of us; they are removed *into darkness,* Job 10:22. (2.) There is an end of all our enjoyments in this world: *They have no more a reward* for their toils about the world, but all they got must be left to others; they have a reward for their holy actions, but not for their worldly ones. The meats and the belly will be destroyed together, Jn. 6:27; 1 Co. 6:13. It is explained *v.* 6. *Neither have they any more a portion for ever,* none of that which they imagined would be *a portion for ever,* of that which *is done* and got *under the sun.* The things of this world will not be a portion for the soul because they will not be a portion for ever; those that choose them, and have them for *their good things,* have only a *portion in this life,* Ps. 17:14. The world can only be an annuity for life, not a *portion for ever.* (3.) There is an end of their name. There are but few whose names survive them long; the grave is a land of forgetfulness, *for the memory of those* that are laid there *is* soon *forgotten;* their *place knows them no more,* nor the lands they called by their own names. (4.) There is an end of their affections, their friendships and enmities: *Their love, and their hatred, and their envy have now perished;* the good things they loved, the evil things they hated, the prosperity of others, which they envied, are now all at an end with them. Death parts those that loved one another, and puts an end to their friendship, and those that hated one another too, and puts an end to their quarrels. *Actio moritur cum personâ — The person and his actions die together.* There we shall be never the better for our friends (their love can do us no kindness), nor ever the worse for our enemies — their hatred and envy can do us no damage. *There the wicked cease from troubling.* Those things which now so affect us and fill us, which we are so concerned about and so jealous of, will there be at an end.

II. Hence he infers that it is our wisdom to make the best use of life that we can while it does last, and manage wisely what remains of it.

1. Let us relish the comforts of life while we live, and cheerfully take our share of the enjoyments of it. Solomon, having been himself ensnared by the abuse of sensitive delights, warns others of the danger, not by a total prohibition of them, but by directing to the sober and moderate use of them; we may use the world, but must not abuse it, take what is to be had out of it, and expect no more. Here we have,

(1.) The particular instances of this cheerfulness prescribed: "Thou art drooping and melancholy, *go thy way,* like a fool as thou art, and get into a better temper of mind." [1.] "Let thy spirit be easy and pleasant; then let there be *joy* and *a merry heart* within," *a good heart* (so the word is), which distinguishes this from carnal mirth and sensual pleasure, which are the evil of the heart, both a symptom and a cause of much evil there. We must enjoy ourselves, enjoy our friends, enjoy our God, and be careful to keep a good conscience, that nothing may disturb us in these enjoyments. We must serve God with gladness, in the use of what he gives us, and be liberal in communicating it to others, and not suffer ourselves to be oppressed with inordinate care and grief about the world. We must eat our bread as Israelites, *not in our mourning* (Deu. 26:14), as Christians, *with gladness and* liberality *of heart,* Acts 2:46. See Deu. 28:47. [2.] "Make use of the comforts and enjoyments which God has given thee: *Eat thy bread, drink thy wine,* thine, not another's, not *the bread of deceit,* nor *the wine of violence,* but that which is honestly got, else thou canst not eat it with any comfort nor expect a blessing upon it — *thy bread* and *thy wine,* such as are agreeable to thy place and station, not extravagantly above it nor sordidly below it; lay out what God has given thee for the ends for which thou art entrusted with it, as being but a steward." [3.] "Evidence thy cheerfulness (*v.* 8): *Let thy garments be always white.* Observe a proportion in thy expenses; reduce not thy food in order to gratify thy pride, nor thy clothing in order to gratify thy voluptuousness. Be neat, wear clean linen, and be not slovenly." Or, *"Let thy garments be white* in token of joy and cheerfulness," which were expressed by *white raiment* (Rev. 3:4); "and as a further token of joy, *let thy head lack no ointment* that is fit for it." Our Saviour admitted this piece of pleasure at a feast (Mt. 26:7), and David observes it among the gifts of God's bounty to him. Ps. 23:5, *Thou anointest my head with oil.* Not that we must place our happiness in any of the delights of sense, or set our hearts upon them, but what God has given us we must make as comfortable a use of as we can afford, under the limitations of sobriety and wisdom, and not forgetting the poor. [4.] "Make thyself agreeable to thy relations: *Live joyfully with the wife whom thou lovest.* Do not engross thy delights, making much of thyself only, and not caring what becomes of those about thee, but let them share with thee and make them easy too. Have a wife; for even in paradise *it was not good for man to be alone.* Keep to thy wife, to one, and do not multiply wives" (Solomon had found the mischief of that); "keep to her only, and have nothing to do with any other." How can a man live joyfully with one with whom he does not live honestly? "Love thy wife; and *the wife whom thou lovest* thou wilt be likely to *live joyfully with.*" When we do the duty of relations we may expect the comfort of them. See Prov. 5:19. "Live with thy wife, and delight in her society. *Live joyfully with her,* and be most cheerful when thou art with her. Take pleasure in thy family, thy vine and thy olive plants."

(2.) The qualifications necessary to this cheerfulness: "Rejoice and have *a merry heart,* if *God now accepts thy works.* If thou art reconciled to God, and recommended to him, then thou has reason to be cheerful, otherwise not." *Rejoice not, O Israel! for joy, as other people, for thou hast gone a whoring from thy God,* Hos. 9:1. Our first care must be to make our peace with God, and obtain his favour, to do that which he will accept of, and then, *Go thy way, eat thy bread with joy.* Note, Those whose works God has accepted have reason to be cheerful and ought to be so. 'Now that thou eatest the bread of thy sacrifices *with joy,* and partakest of the wine of thy drink-offerings *with a merry heart,* now *God accepts thy works.* Thy religious services, when performed with holy joy, are pleasing to God; he loves to have his servants sing at their work, it proclaims him a good Master.

(3.) The reasons for it. "Live joyfully, for," [1.] "It is all little enough to make thy passage through this world easy and comfortable: *The days of thy life* are the days *of thy vanity;* there is nothing here but trouble, and disappointment. Thou wilt have time enough for sorrow and grief when thou canst not help it, and therefore *live joyfully* while thou canst, and perplex not thyself with thoughts and cares about to-morrow; *sufficient to the day is the evil thereof.* Let a gracious serenity of mind be a powerful antidote against the vanity of the world." [2.] "It is all thou canst get from this world: *That is thy portion in* the things of *this life.* In God, and another life, thou shalt have a better portion, and a better recompence for thy labours in religion; but for thy pains *which thou takest* about the things *under the sun* this is all thou canst expect, and therefore do not deny this to thyself."

2. Let us apply ourselves to the business of life while life lasts, and so use the enjoyments of it as by them to be fitted for the employments: "Therefore *eat with joy* and *a merry heart,* not that thy soul may take its ease (as Lu. 12:19), but that thy soul may take the more pains and the joy of the Lord may be its strength and oil to its wheels," *v.* 10. *Whatsoever thy hand finds to do do it with thy might.* Observe here, (1.) There is not only something to be had, but something to be done, in this life, and the chief good we are to enquire after is *the good we should do,* Eccl. 2:3. This is the world of service; that to come is the world of recompence. This is the world of probation and preparation for eternity; we are here upon business, and upon our good behaviour. (2.) Opportunity is to direct and quicken duty. That is to be done which *our hand finds to do,* which occasion calls for; and an active hand will always find something to do that will turn to a good account. What must be done, of necessity, our hand will here find a price in it for the doing of, Prov. 17:16. (3.) What good we have an opportunity of doing we must do while we have the opportunity, and *do it with our might,* with care, vigour, and resolution, whatever difficulties and discouragements we may meet with in it. Harvest-days are busy days; and we must make hay while the sun shines. Serving God and working out our salvation must be done with *all that is within us,* and all little enough. (4.) There is good reason why we should *work the works of him that sent us while it is day, because the night comes, wherein no man can work,* Jn. 9:4. We must up and be doing now with all possible diligence, because our doing-time will be done shortly and we know not how soon. But this we know that, if the work of life be not done when our time is done, we are undone for ever: *"There is no work* to be done, *nor device* to do it, *no knowledge* for speculation, *nor wisdom* for practice, *in the grave whither thou goest."* We are all going towards the grave; every day brings us a step nearer to it; when we are *in the grave* it will be too late to mend the errors of life, too late to repent and make our peace with God, too late to lay up any thing in store for eternal life; it must be done now or never. The grave is a land of darkness and silence, and therefore there is no doing any thing for our souls there; it must be done now or never, Jn. 12:35.

Verses 11–12

The preacher here, for a further proof of the vanity of the world, and to convince us that *all our works are in the hand of God,* and not in our own hand, shows the uncertainty and contingency of future events, and how often they contradict the prospects we have of them. He had exhorted us (*v.* 10) to do what we have to do *with all our might;* but here he reminds us that, when we have done all, we must leave the issue with God, and not be confident of the success.

I. We are often disappointed of the good we had great hopes of, *v.* 11. Solomon had himself made the observation, and so has many a one since, that events, both in public and private affairs, do not always agree even with the most rational prospects and probabilities. *Nulli fortuna tam dedita est ut multa tentanti ubique respondeat — Fortune surrenders herself to no one so as to ensure him success, however numerous his undertakings.* Seneca. The issue of affairs is often unaccountably cross to every one's expectation, that the highest may not presume, nor the lowest despair, but all may live in a humble dependence upon God, from whom every man's judgment proceeds.

1. He gives instances of disappointment, even where means and instruments were most encouraging and promised fair. (1.) One would think that the lightest of foot should, in running, win the prize; and yet *the race is not* always *to the swift;* some accident happens to retard them, or they are too secure, and therefore remiss, and let those that are slower get the start of them. (2.) One would think that, in fighting, the most numerous and powerful army should be always victorious, and, in single combat, that the bold and mighty champion should win the laurel; but *the battle is not* always *to the strong;* a host of Philistines was once put to flight by Jonathan and his man; *one of you shall chase a thousand;* the goodness of the cause has often carried the day against the most formidable power. (3.) One would think that men of sense should always be men of substance, and that those who know how to live in the world should not only have a plentiful maintenance, but get great estates; and yet it does not always prove so; even *bread is not* always *to the wise,* much less *riches* always *to men of understanding.* Many ingenious men, and men of business, who were likely to thrive in the world, have strangely gone backward and come to nothing. (4.) One would think that those who understand men, and have the art of management, should always get preferment and obtain the smiles of great men; but many ingenious men have been disappointed, and have spent their days in obscurity, nay, have fallen into disgrace, and perhaps have ruined themselves by those very methods by which they hoped to raise themselves, for *favour is not* always *to men of skill,* but fools are favoured and wise men frowned upon.

2. He resolves all these disappointments into an overruling power and providence, the disposals of which to us seem casual, and we call them *chance,* but really they are according to the determinate counsel and foreknowledge of God, here called *time,* in the language of this book, *ch.* 3:1; Ps. 31:15. *Time and chance happen to them all.* A sovereign Providence breaks men's measures, and blasts their hopes, and teaches them that the way of man is not in himself, but subject to the divine will. We must use means, but not trust to them; if we succeed, we must give God the praise (Ps. 44:3); if we be crossed, we must acquiesce in his will and take our lot.

II. We are often surprised with the evils we were in little fear of (*v.* 12): *Man knows not his time,* the time of his calamity, his fall, his death, which, in scripture, is called *our day* and *our hour.* 1. We know not what troubles are before us, which will take us off our business, and take us out of the world, what *time and chance will happen to us,* nor what *one day,* or a night, *may bring forth.* It is *not for us to know the times,* no, not our own time, when or how we shall die. God has, in wisdom, kept us in the dark, that we may be always ready. 2. Perhaps we may meet with trouble in that very thing wherein we promise ourselves the greatest satisfaction and advantage; as the fishes and the birds are drawn into the snare and net by the bait laid to allure them, which they greedily catch at, so are the sons of men often *snared in an evil time,* when it falls suddenly upon them, before they are aware. And these things too *come alike to all.* Men often find their bane where they sought their bless, and catch their death where they thought to find a prize. Let us therefore never be secure, but always ready for changes, that, though they may be sudden, they may be no surprise or terror to us.

Verses 13–18

Solomon still recommends wisdom to us as necessary to the preserving of our peace and the perfecting of our business, notwithstanding the vanities and crosses which human affairs are subject to. He had said (*v.* 11), *Bread is not always to the wise;* yet he would not therefore be thought either to disparage, or to discourage, wisdom, no, he still retains his principle, that *wisdom excels folly as much as light excels darkness* (*ch.* 2:13), and we ought to love and embrace it, and be governed by it, for the sake of its own intrinsic worth, and the capacity it gives us of being serviceable to others, though we ourselves should not get wealth and preferment by it. This wisdom, that is, this which he here describes, wisdom which enables a man to serve his country out of pure affection to its interests, when he himself gains no advantage by it, no, not so much as thanks for his pains, or the reputation of it, this is the wisdom which, Solomon says, *seemed great unto him, v.* 13. A public spirit, in a private sphere, is wisdom which those who understand things that differ cannot but look upon as very magnificent.

I. Solomon here gives an instance, which probably was a case in fact, in some neighbouring country, of a *poor man* who with his wisdom did great service in a time of public distress and danger (*v.* 14): *There was a little city* (no great prize, whoever was master of it); there were but *few men within it,* to defend it, and men, if men of fortitude, are the best fortifications of a city; here were *few men,* and, because few, feeble, fearful, and ready to give up their city as not tenable. Against this little city a *great king* came with a numerous army, and besieged it, either in pride, or covetousness to possess it, or in revenge for some affront given him, to chastise and destroy it. Thinking it stronger than it was, he *built great bulwarks against it,* from which to batter it, and doubted not but in a little time to make himself master of it. What a great deal of unjust vexation do ambitious princes give to their harmless neighbours! This *great king* needed not fear this *little city;* why then should he frighten it? It would be little profit to him; why then should he put himself to such a great expense to gain it? But as unreasonable and insatiably greedy as little people sometimes are to *lay house to house, and field to field,* great kings often are to lay city to city, and province to province, *that they may be placed alone in the earth,* Isa. 5:8. Did victory and success attend the *strong?* No; there was found in this little city, among the few men that were in it, *one poor wise man* — a wise man, and yet poor, and not preferred to any place of profit or power in the city; places of trust were not given to men according to their merit, and meetness for them, else such a wise man as this would not have been a poor man. Now, 1. Being wise, he served the city, though he was poor. In their distress they found him out (Jdg. 11:7) and begged his advice and assistance; and *he by his wisdom delivered the city,* either by prudent instructions given to the besieged, directing them to some unthought-of stratagem for their own security, or by a prudent treaty with the besiegers, as the woman at Abel, 2 Sa. 20:16. He did not upbraid them with the contempt they had put upon him, in leaving him out of their council, nor tell them he was poor and had nothing to lose, and therefore cared not what became of the city; but he did his best for it, and was blessed with success. Note, Private interests and personal resentments must always be sacrificed to public good and forgotten when the common welfare is concerned. 2. Being poor, he was slighted by the city, though he was wise and had been an instrument to save them all from ruin: *No man remembered that same poor man;* his good services were not taken notice of, no recompence was made him, no marks of honour were put upon him, but he lived in as much poverty and obscurity as he had done before. *Riches were not* to this *man of understanding,* nor *favour to* this *man of skill.* Many who have well-merited of their prince and country have been ill-paid; such an ungrateful world do we live in. It is well that useful men have a God to trust to, who will be their bountiful rewarder; for, among men, great services are often envied and rewarded with evil for good.

II. From this instance he draws some useful inferences, looks upon it and receives instruction. 1. Hence he observes the great usefulness and excellency of wisdom, and what a blessing it makes men to their country: *Wisdom is better than strength, v.* 16. A prudent mind, which is the honour of a man, is to be preferred before a robust body, in which many of the brute creatures excel man. A man may by his wisdom effect that which he could never compass by his strength, and may overcome those by outwitting them who are able to overpower him. Nay, *wisdom is better than weapons of war,* offensive or defensive, *v.* 18. *Wisdom,* that is, religion and piety (for the wise man is here opposed to a sinner), is better than all military endowments or accoutrements, for it will engage God for us, and then we are safe in the greatest perils and successful in the greatest enterprises. *If God be for us, who can be against us* or stand before us? 2. Hence he observes the commanding force and power of wisdom, though it labour under external disadvantages (*v.* 17): *The words of wise men are heard in quiet;* what they speak, being spoken calmly and with deliberation (though, not being rich and in authority, they dare not speak aloud nor with any great assurance), will be hearkened to and regarded, will gain respect, nay, will gain the point, and sway with men more than the imperious clamour of him that *rules among fools,* who, like fools, chose him to be their ruler, for his noise and blustering, and, like fools, think he must by those methods carry the day with every body else. A few close arguments are worth a great many big words; and those will strike sail to fair reasoning who will answer those that hector and insult *according to their folly. How forcible are right words!* What is spoken wisely should be spoken calmly, and then it will be heard in quiet and calmly considered. But passion will lessen the force even of reason, instead of adding any force to it. 3. Hence he observes that wise and good men, notwithstanding this, must often content themselves with the satisfaction of having done good, or at least attempted it, and offered at it, when they cannot do the good they would do nor have the praise they should have. Wisdom capacitates a man to serve his neighbours, and he offers his service; but, alas! if he be poor his wisdom is despised and *his words are not heard, v.* 16. Many a man is buried alive in poverty and obscurity who, if he had but fit encouragement given him, might be a great blessing to the world; many a pearl is lost in its shell. But there is a day coming when wisdom and goodness shall be in honour, and the *righteous shall shine forth.*

4. From what he had observed of the great good which one wise and virtuous man may do he infers what a great deal of mischief one wicked man may do, and what a great deal of good he may be the hindrance of: *One sinner destroyeth much good.* (1.) As to himself, a sinful condition is a wasteful condition. How many of the good gifts both of nature and Providence does one sinner destroy and make waste of — good sense, good parts, good learning, a good disposition, a good estate, good meat, good drink, and abundance of God's good creatures, all made use of in the service of sin, and so destroyed and lost, and the end of giving them frustrated and perverted! He who destroys his own soul destroys much good. (2.) As to others, what a great deal of mischief may one wicked man do in a town or country! One sinner, who makes it his business to debauch others, may defeat and frustrate the intentions of a great many good laws and a great deal of good preaching, and draw many into his pernicious ways; one sinner may be the ruin of a town, as one Achan troubled the whole camp of Israel. The wise man who delivered the city would have had his due respect and recompence for it but that some one sinner hindered it, and invidiously diminished the service. And many a good project, well laid for the public welfare, had been destroyed by some one subtle adversary to it. The wisdom of some would have healed the nation, but, through the wickedness of a few, it would not be healed. See who are a kingdom's friends and enemies, if one saint does much good, and one sinner destroys much good.

CHAPTER 10

This chapter seems to be like Solomon's proverbs, a collection of wise sayings and observations, rather than a part of his sermon; but the preacher studied to be sententious, and "set in order many proverbs," to be brought in in his preaching. Yet the general scope of all the observations in this chapter is to recommend wisdom to us, and its precepts and rules, as of great use for the right ordering of our conversation and to caution us against folly. I. He recommends wisdom to private persons, who are in an inferior station. 1. It is our wisdom to preserve our reputation, in managing our affairs dexterously (*v.* 1–3). 2. To be submissive to our superiors if at any time we have offended them (*v.* 4). 3. To live quiet and peaceable lives, and not to meddle with those that are factious and seditious, and are endeavouring to disturb the government and the public repose, the folly and danger of which disloyal and turbulent practices he shows (*v.* 8–11). 4. To govern our tongues well (*v.* 12–15). 5. To be diligent in our business and provide well for our families (*v.* 18, 19). 6. Not to speak ill of our rulers, no, not in secret (*v.* 20). II. He recommends wisdom to rulers; let them not think that, because their subjects must be quiet under them, therefore they may do what they please; no, but, 1. Let them be careful whom they prefer to places of trust and power (*v.* 5–7). 2. Let them manage themselves discreetly, be generous and not childish, temperate and not luxurious (*v.* 16, 17). Happy the nation when princes and people make conscience of their duty according to these rules.

Verses 1–3

In these verses Solomon shows,

I. What great need wise men have to take heed of being guilty of any instance of folly; for *a little folly* is a great blemish to him that *is in reputation for wisdom and honour,* and is as hurtful to his good name as *dead flies* are to a sweet perfume, not only spoiling the sweetness of it, but making it *to send forth a stinking savour.* Note, 1. True wisdom is true honour, and will gain a man a reputation, which is like a box of precious ointment, pleasing and very valuable. 2. The reputation that is got with difficulty, and by a great deal of wisdom, may be easily lost, and by a *little folly,* because envy fastens upon eminency, and makes the worst of the mistakes and miscarriages of those who are cried up for wisdom, and improves them to their disadvantage; so that the folly which in another would not be taken notice of in them is severely censured. Those who make a great profession of religion have need to walk very circumspectly, to *abstain from all appearances of evil,* and approaches towards it, because many eyes are upon them, that watch for their halting; their character is soon sullied, and they have a great deal of reputation to lose.

II. What a deal of advantage a wise man has above a fool in the management of business (*v.* 2): *A wise man's heart is at his right hand,* so that he goes about his business with dexterity, turns his hand readily to it, and goes through it with despatch; his counsel and courage are ready to him, whenever he has occasion for them. But a *fool's heart is at his left hand;* it is always to seek when he has any thing to do that is of importance, and therefore he goes awkwardly about it, like a man that is left-handed; he is soon at a loss and at his wits' end.

III. How apt fools are at every turn to proclaim their own folly, and expose themselves; he that is either witless or graceless, either silly or wicked, if he be ever so little from under the check, and left to himself, if he but *walk by the way,* soon shows what he is; his *wisdom fails him,* and, by some impropriety or other, *he says to every one he meets that he is a fool* (*v.* 3), that is, he discovers his folly as plainly as if he had told them so. He cannot conceal it, and he is not ashamed of it. Sin is the reproach of sinners wherever they go.

Verses 4–11

The scope of these verses is to keep subjects loyal and dutiful to the government. In Solomon's reign the people were very rich, and lived in prosperity, which perhaps made them proud and petulant, and when the taxes were high, though they had enough to pay them with, it is probable that many conducted themselves insolently towards the government and threatened to rebel. To such Solomon here gives some necessary cautions.

I. Let not subjects carry on a quarrel with their prince upon any private personal disgust (*v.* 4): *"If the spirit of the ruler rise up against thee,* if upon some misinformation given him, or some mismanagement of thine, he is displeased at thee, and threaten thee, yet *leave not thy place,* forget not the duty of a subject, revolt not from thy allegiance, do not, in a passion, quit thy post in his service and throw up thy commission, as despairing ever to regain his favour. No, wait awhile, and thou wilt find he is not implacable, but that *yielding pacifies great offences."* Solomon speaks for himself, and for every wise and good man that is a master, or a magistrate, that he could easily forgive those, upon their submission, whom yet, upon their provocation, he had been very angry with. It is safer and better to yield to an angry prince than to contend with him.

II. Let not subjects commence a quarrel with their prince, though the public administration be not in every thing as they would have it. He grants *there is an evil often seen under the sun,* and it is a king's-evil, an evil which the king only can cure, for *it is an error which proceeds from the ruler* (*v.* 5); it is a mistake which rulers, consulting their personal affections more than the public interests, are too often guilty of, that men are not preferred according to their merit, but *folly is set in great dignity,* men of shattered brains, and broken fortunes, are put in places of power and trust, while the rich men of good sense and good estates, whose interest would oblige them to be true to the public, and whose abundance would be likely to set them above temptations to bribery and extortion, yet sit in low places, and can get no preferment (*v.* 6), either the ruler knows not how to value them or the terms of preferment are such as they cannot in conscience comply with. It is ill with a people when vicious men are advanced and men of worth are kept under hatches. This is illustrated *v.* 7. *"I have seen servants upon horses,* men not so much of mean extraction and education (if that were all, it were the more excusable, nay, there is many a wise servant who with good reason *has rule over a son that causes shame),* but of sordid, servile, mercenary dispositions. I have seen these riding in pomp and state as princes, while princes, men of noble birth and qualities, fit to rule a kingdom, have been forced to *walk as servants upon the earth,* poor and despised." Thus God, in his providence, punishes a wicked people; but, as far as it is the ruler's act and deed, it is certainly his *error,* and a *great evil,* a grievance to the subject and very provoking; but it is *an error under the sun,* which will certainly be rectified above the sun, and when it shall shine no more, for in heaven it is only wisdom and holiness that are set in great dignity. But, if the prince be guilty of his error, yet let not the subjects *leave their place,* nor rise up against the government, nor form any project for the alteration of it; nor let the prince carry on the humour too far, nor set such servants, such beggars, on horseback, as will ride furiously over the ancient land-marks of the constitution, and threaten the subversion of it.

1. Let neither prince nor people violently attempt any changes, nor make a forcible entry upon a national settlement, for they will both find it of dangerous consequence, which he shows here by four similitudes, the scope of which is to give us a caution not to meddle to our own hurt. Let not princes invade the rights and liberties of their subjects; let not subjects mutiny and rebel against their princes; for, (1.) *He that digs a pit* for another, it is ten to one but he *falls into it* himself, and his violent dealing returns upon his own head. If princes become tyrants, or subjects become rebels, all histories will tell both what is likely to be their fate and that it is at their utmost peril, and it were better for both to be content within their own bounds. (2.) *Whoso breaks a hedge,* an old hedge, that has long been a land-mark, let him expect that a *serpent,* or *adder,* such as harbour in rotten hedges, will *bite him;* some viper or other will fasten upon his hand, Acts 28:3. God, by his ordinance, as by a hedge, has inclosed the prerogatives and powers of princes; their persons are under his special protection; those therefore that form any treasonable designs against their peace, their crown, and dignity, are but twisting halters for themselves. (3.) *Whoso removes stones,* to pull down a wall or building, does but pluck them upon himself; he shall be *hurt therewith,* and will wish that he had let them alone. Those that go about to alter a well-modelled well-settled government, under colour of redressing some grievances and correcting some faults in it, will quickly perceive not only that it is easier to find fault than to mend, to demolish that which is good than to build up that which is better, but that they thrust their own fingers into the fire and overwhelm themselves in the ruin they occasion. (4.) *He that cleaves the wood,* especially if, as it follows, he has sorry tools (*v.* 10), *shall be endangered thereby;* the chips, or his own axe-head, will fly in his face. If we meet with knotty pieces of timber, and we think to master them by force and violence, and hew them to pieces, they may not only prove too hard for us, but the attempt may turn to our own damage.

2. Rather let both prince and people act towards each other with prudence, mildness, and good temper: *Wisdom is profitable to direct* the ruler how to manage a people that are inclined to be turbulent, so as neither, on the one hand, by a supine negligence to embolden and encourage them, nor, on the other hand, by rigour and severity to exasperate and provoke them to any seditious practices. It is likewise profitable to direct the subjects how to act towards a prince that is inclined to bear hard upon them, so as not to alienate his affections from them, but to win upon him by humble remonstrances (not insolent demands, such as the people made upon Rehoboam), by patient submissions and peaceable expedients. The same rule is to be observed in all relations, for the preserving of the comfort of them. Let wisdom direct to gentle methods and forbear violent ones. (1.) Wisdom will teach us to whet the tool we are to make use of, rather than, by leaving it blunt, oblige ourselves to exert so much the *more strength, v.* 10. We might save ourselves a great deal of labour, and prevent a great deal of danger, if we did whet before we cut, that is, consider and premeditate what is fit to be said and done in every difficult case, that we may accommodate ourselves to it and may do our work smoothly and easily both to others and to ourselves. Wisdom will direct how to sharpen and put an edge upon both ourselves and those we employ, not to *work deceitfully* (Ps. 52:2), but to work cleanly and cleverly. The mower loses no time when he is whetting his scythe. (2.) Wisdom will teach us to enchant the serpent we are to contend with, rather than think to out-hiss it (*v.* 11): *The serpent will bite* if he be not by singing and music charmed and enchanted, against which therefore he *stops his ears* (Ps. 58:4, 5); *and a babbler is no better* to all those who enter the lists with him, who therefore must not think by dint of words to out-talk him, but be prudent management to enchant him. *He that is lord of the tongue* (so the phrase is), a ruler that has liberty of speech and may say what he will, it is as dangerous dealing with him as with a serpent uncharmed; but, if you use the enchantment of a mild and humble submission, you may be safe and out of danger; herein *wisdom,* the meekness of wisdom, *is profitable to direct. By long forbearing is a prince persuaded,* Prov. 25:15. Jacob enchanted Esau with a present and Abigail David. To those that may say any thing it is wisdom to say nothing that is provoking.

Verses 12–15

Solomon, having shown the benefit of wisdom, and of what great advantage it is to us in the management of our affairs, here shows the mischief of folly and how it exposes men, which perhaps comes in as a reflection upon those rulers who *set folly in great dignity.*

I. Fools talk a great deal to no purpose, and they show their folly as much by the multitude, impertinence, and mischievousness of their words, as by any thing; whereas *the words of a wise man's mouth are gracious,* are grace, manifest grace in his heart and minister grace to the hearers, are good, and such as become him, and do good to all about him, *the lips of a fool* not only expose him to reproach and make him ridiculous, but *will swallow up himself* and bring him to ruin, by provoking the government to take cognizance of his seditious talk and call him to an account for it. Adonijah foolishly *spoke against his own life,* 1 Ki. 2:23. Many a man has been sunk by having *his own tongue fall upon him,* Ps. 64:8. See what a fool's talk is. 1. It takes rise from his own weakness and wickedness: *The beginning of the words of his mouth is foolishness,* the foolishness bound up in his heart, that is the corrupt spring out of which all these polluted streams flow, the evil treasure out of which evil things are brought. As soon as he begins to speak you may perceive his folly; at the very first he talks idly, and passionately, and like himself. 2. It rises up to fury, and tends to the hurt and injury of others: *The end of his talk,* the end it comes to, *is madness.* He will presently talk himself into an indecent heat, and break out into the wild extravagancies of a distracted man. The end he aims at is mischief; as, at first, he appeared to have little government of himself, so, at last, it appears he has a great deal of malice to his neighbours; that root of bitterness bears gall and wormwood. Note, It is not strange if those that begin foolishly end madly; for an ungoverned tongue, the more liberty is allowed, grows the more violent. 3. It is all the same over and over (*v.* 14): *A fool also is full of words,* a passionate fool especially, that runs on endlessly and never knows when to leave off. He will have the last word, though it be but the same with that which was the first. What is wanting in the weight and strength of his words he endeavours in vain to make up in the number of them; and they must be repeated, because otherwise there is nothing in them to make them regarded. Note, Many who are empty of sense are *full of words;* and the least solid are the most noisy. The following words may be taken either, (1.) As checking him for his vainglorious boasting in the multitude of his words, what he will do and what he will have, not considering that which every body knows that *a man cannot tell what shall be* in his own time, while he lives (Prov. 27:1), much less can one tell *what shall be after him,* when he is dead and gone. Would we duly consider our own ignorance of, and uncertainty about, future events, it would cut off a great many of the idle words we foolishly multiply. Or, (2.) As mocking him for his tautologies. He is *full of words,* for if he do but speak the most trite and common thing, *a man cannot tell what shall be,* because he loves to hear himself talk, he will say it again, *what shall be after him who can tell him?* like Battus in Ovid:

— Sub illis
Montibus (inquit) erant, et erant sub montibus illis —
Under those mountains were they,
They were under those mountains, I say —

whence vain repetitions are called *Battologies,* Mt. 6:7.

II. Fools toil a great deal to no purpose (*v.* 15); *The labour of the foolish,* to accomplish their designs, *wearies every one of them.* 1. They weary themselves in that labour which is very foolish and absurd. All their labour is for the world and the body, and the meat that perishes, and in this labour they spend their strength, and exhaust their spirits, and *weary themselves for very vanity,* Hab. 2:13; Isa. 55:2. They choose that service which is perfect drudgery rather than that which is perfect liberty. 2. That labour which is necessary, and would be profitable, and might be gone through with ease, wearies them, because they go about it awkwardly and foolishly, and so make their business a toil to them, which, if they applied themselves to it prudently, would be a pleasure to them. Many complain of the labours of religion as grievous, which they would have no reason to complain of if the exercises of Christian piety were always under the direction of Christian prudence. The foolish tire themselves in endless pursuits, and never bring any thing to pass, *because they know not how to go to the city,* that is, because they have not capacity to apprehend the plainest thing, such as the entrance into a great city is, where one would think it were impossible for a man to miss his road. Men's imprudent management of their business robs them both of the comfort and of the benefit of it. But it is the excellency of the way to the heavenly city that it is a high-way, in which the *wayfaring men, though fools, shall not err* (Isa. 35:8); yet sinful folly makes men miss that way.

Verses 16–20

Solomon here observes,

I. How much the happiness of a land depends upon the character of its rulers; it is well or ill with the people according as the princes are good or bad. 1. The people cannot be happy when their princes are childish and voluptuous (*v.* 16): *Woe unto thee, O land!* even the land of Canaan itself, though otherwise the glory of all lands, when *thy king is a child,* not so much in age (Solomon himself was young when his kingdom was happy in him) as in understanding; when the prince is weak and foolish as a child, fickle and fond of changes, fretful and humoursome, easily imposed upon, and hardly brought to business, it is ill with the people. The body staggers if the head be giddy. Perhaps Solomon wrote this with a foresight of his son Rehoboam's ill conduct (2 Chr. 13:7); he was a child all the days of his life and his family and kingdom fared the worse for it. Nor is it much better with a people when their princes *eat in the morning,* that is, make a god of their belly and make themselves slaves to their appetites. If the king himself be a child, yet if the princes and privy-counsellors are wise and faithful, and apply themselves to business, the land may do the better; but if they addict themselves to their pleasures, and prefer the gratifications of the flesh before the despatch of the public business, which they disfit themselves for by eating and drinking *in a morning,* when judges are epicures, and do not eat to live, but live to eat, what good can a nation expect! 2. The people cannot but be happy when their rulers are generous and active, sober and temperate, and men of business, *v.* 17. The land is then blessed, (1.) When the sovereign is governed by principles of honour, *when the king is the son of nobles,* actuated and animated by a noble spirit, which scorns to do any thing base and unbecoming so high a character, which is solicitous for the public welfare, and prefers that before any private interests. Wisdom, virtue, and the fear of God, beneficence, and a readiness to do good to all mankind, these ennoble the royal blood. 2. When the subordinate magistrates are more in care to discharge their trusts than to gratify their appetites; when they *eat in due season* (Ps. 145:15); let us not take ours unseasonable, lest we lose the comfort of seeing God give it to us. Magistrates should *eat for strength,* that their bodies may be fitted to serve their souls in the service of God and their country, *and not for drunkenness,* to make themselves unfit to do any thing either for God or man, and particularly to *sit in judgment,* for they will *err through wine* (Isa. 28:7), will *drink and forget the law,* Prov. 31:5. It is well with a people when their princes are examples of temperance, when those that have most to spend upon themselves know how to deny themselves.

II. Of what ill consequence slothfulness is both to private and public affairs (*v.* 18). *By much slothfulness and idleness of the hands,* the neglect of business, and the love of ease and pleasure, *the building decays, drops through* first, and by degrees drops down. If it be not kept well covered, and care be not taken to repair the breaches, as any happen, it will rain in, and the timber will rot, and the house will become unfit to dwell in. It is so with the family and the affairs of it; if men cannot find in their hearts to take pains in their callings, to tend their shops and look after their own business, they will soon run in debt and go behind-hand, and, instead of making what they have more for their children, will make it less. It is so with the public; if the king be *a child* and will take no care, if the *princes eat in the morning* and will take no pains, the affairs of the nation suffer loss, and its interests are prejudiced, its honour is sullied, its power is weakened, its borders are encroached upon, the course of justice is obstructed, the treasure is exhausted, and all its foundations are out of course, and all this through the slothfulness of self-seeking of those that should be the *repairers of its breaches and the restorers of paths to dwell in,* Isa. 58:12.

III. How industrious generally all are, both princes and people, to get money, because that serves for all purposes, *v.* 19. He seems to prefer money before mirth: *A feast is made for laughter,* not merely for eating, but chiefly for pleasant conversation and the society of friends, not the laughter of the fool, which is madness, but that of wise men, by which they fit themselves for business and severe studies. Spiritual feasts are made for spiritual laughter, holy joy in God. *Wine makes merry, makes glad the life, but money* is the measure of all things and *answers all things. Pecuniae obediunt omnia — Money commands all things.* Though *wine make merry,* it will not be a house for us, nor a bed, nor clothing, nor provisions and portions for children; *but money,* if men have enough of it, will be all these. The feast cannot be made without money, and, though men have wine, they are not so much disposed to be merry unless they have money for the necessary supports of life. Money of itself answers nothing; it will neither feed nor clothe; but, as it is the instrument of commerce, it answers all the occasions of this present life. What is to be had may be had for money. But it answers nothing to the soul; it will not procure the pardon of sin, the favour of God, the peace of conscience; the soul, as it is not redeemed, so it is not maintained, with *corruptible things as silver and gold.* Some refer this to rulers; it is ill with the people when they give up themselves to luxury and riot, feasting and making merry, not only

because their business is neglected, but because money must be had to *answer all* these *things,* and, in order to that, the people squeezed by heavy taxes.

IV. How cautious subjects have need to be that they harbour not any disloyal purposes in their minds, nor keep up any factious cabals or consultations against the government, because it is ten to one that they are discovered and brought to light, *v.* 20. "Though rulers should be guilty of some errors, yet be not, upon all occasions, arraigning their administration and running them down, but make the best of them." Here, 1. The command teaches us our duty "*Curse not the king, no, not in thy thought,* do not wish ill to the government in thy mind." All sin begins there, and therefore the first risings of it must be curbed and suppressed, and particularly that of treason and sedition. "*Curse not the rich,* the princes and governors, *in thy bed-chamber,* in a conclave or club of persons disaffected to the government; associate not with such; *come not into their secret;* join not with them in speaking ill of the government or plotting against it." 2. The reason consults our safety. "Though the design be carried on ever so closely, *a bird of the air shall carry the voice* to the king, who has more spies about than thou art aware of, *and that which has wings shall tell the matter,* to thy confusion and ruin." God sees what men do, and hears what they say, in secret; and, when he pleases, he can bring it to light by strange and unsuspected ways. Wouldst *thou then not be hurt by the powers* that be, nor *be afraid of* them? *Do that which is good and thou shalt have praise of the same; but, if thou do that which is evil, be afraid,* Rom. 13:3, 4.

CHAPTER 11

In this chapter we have, I. A pressing exhortation to works of charity and bounty to the poor, as the best cure of the vanity which our worldly riches are subject to and the only way of making them turn to a substantial good account (*v.* 1–6). II. A serious admonition to prepare for death and judgment, and to begin betimes, even in the days of our youth, to do so (*v.* 7–10).

Verses 1–6

Solomon had often, in this book, pressed it upon rich people to take the comfort of their riches themselves; here he presses it upon them to do good to others with them and to abound in liberality to the poor, which will, another day, abound to their account. Observe,

I. How the duty itself is recommended to us, *v.* 1. 1. *Cast thy bread upon the waters,* thy *bread-corn upon the low places* (so some understand it), alluding to the husbandman, who *goes forth, bearing precious seed,* sparing bread-corn from his family for the seedness, knowing that without that he can have no harvest another year; thus the charitable man takes from his bread-corn for seed-corn, abridges himself to supply the poor, that he may *sow beside all waters* (Isa. 32:20), because as he sows so he must *reap,* Gal. 6:7. We read of the *harvest of the river,* Isa. 23:3. Waters, in scripture, are put for multitudes (Rev. 16:5), and there are multitudes of poor (we do not want objects of charity); waters are put also for mourners: the poor are men of sorrows. Thou must give *bread,* the necessary supports of life, not only give good words but *good things,* Isa. 58:7. It must be *thy* bread, that which is honestly got; it is no charity, but injury, to give that which is none of our own to give; first *do justly,* and then *love mercy.* "*Thy* bread, which thou didst design for thyself, let the poor have a share with thee, as they had with Job, *ch.* 31:17. Give freely to the poor, as that which is *cast upon the waters.* Send it a voyage, send it as a venture, as merchants that trade by sea. Trust it *upon the waters;* it shall not sink."

2. "*Give a portion to seven and also to eight,* that is, be free and liberal in works of charity." (1.) "Give much if thou hast much to give, not a pittance, but *a portion,* not a bit or two, but a mess, a meal; give a large dole, not a paltry one; give *good measure* (Lu. 6:38); be generous in giving, as those were when, on festival days, they *sent portions to those for whom nothing was prepared* (Neh. 8:10), worthy portions." (2.) "Give to many, *to seven, and also to eight;* if thou meet with seven objects of charity, give to them all, and then, if thou meet with an eighth, give to that, and if with eight more, give to them all too. Excuse not thyself with the good thou hast done from the good thou hast further to do, but hold on, and mend. In hard times, when the number of the poor increases, let thy charity be proportionably enlarged." God is rich in mercy to all, to us, though unworthy; he *gives liberally, and*

upbraids *not* with former gifts, and we must be merciful as our heavenly Father is.

II. The reasons with which it is pressed upon us. Consider,

1. Our reward for well-doing is very certain. "Though thou *cast it upon the waters,* and it seem lost, thou thinkest thou hast given thy good word with it and art likely never to hear of it again, yet *thou shalt find it after many days,* as the husbandman finds his seed again in a plentiful harvest and the merchant his venture in a rich return. It is not lost, but well laid out, and well laid up; it brings in full interest in the present gifts of God's providence, and graces and comforts of his Spirit; and the principal is sure, laid up in heaven, for it is *lent to the Lord.*" Seneca, a heathen, could say, *Nihil magis possidere me credam, quam bene donata — I possess nothing so completely as that which I have given away. Hochabeo quodcunque dedi; hae sunt divitiae certae in quacunque sortis humanae levitate — Whatever I have imparted I still possess; these riches remain with me through all the vicissitudes of life.* "*Thou shalt find it,* perhaps not quickly, *but after many days;* the return may be slow, but it is sure and will be so much the more plentiful." Wheat, the most valuable grain, lies longest in the ground. Long voyages make the best returns.

2. Our opportunity for well-doing is very uncertain: "*Thou knowest not what evil may be upon the earth,* which may deprive thee of thy estate, and put thee out of a capacity to do good, and therefore, while thou hast wherewithal, be liberal with it, improve the present season, as the husbandman in sowing his ground, before the frost comes." We have reason to expect *evil upon the earth,* for we are born to trouble; what the evil may be we *know not,* but that we may be ready for it, whatever it is, it is our wisdom, in the day of prosperity, to be in good, to be doing good. Many make use of this as an argument against giving to the poor, because they know not what hard times may come when they may want themselves; whereas we should therefore the rather be charitable, that, when *evil days come,* we may have the comfort of having done good while we were able; we would then hope to find mercy both with God and man, and therefore should now show mercy. If by charity we trust God with what we have, we put it into good hands against bad times.

III. How he obviates the objections which might be made against this duty and the excuses of the uncharitable.

1. Some will say that what they have is their own and they have it for their own use, and will ask, Why should we *cast* it thus *upon the waters?* Why should I *take my bread, and my flesh, and give it to I know not* whom? So Nabal pleaded, 1 Sa. 25:11. "Look up, man, and consider how soon thou wouldest be starved in a barren ground, *if the clouds* over thy head should plead thus, that they have their waters for themselves; but thou seest, when they are *full of rain, they empty themselves upon the earth,* to make it fruitful, till they are wearied and spent with watering it, Job 37:11. Are the heavens thus bountiful to the poor earth, that is so far below them, and wilt thou grudge thy bounty to thy poor brother, who is *bone of thy bone?* Or thus: some will say, Though we give but little to the poor, yet, thank God, we have as charitable a heart as any." Nay, says Solomon, *if the clouds be full of rain, they will empty themselves;* if there be charity in the heart, it will show itself, Jam. 2:15, 16. He that *draws out his soul to the hungry* will reach forth his hand to them, as he has ability.

2. Some will say that their sphere of usefulness is low and narrow; they cannot do the good that they see others can, who are in more public stations, and therefore they will sit still and do nothing. Nay, says he, *in the place where the tree falls,* or happens to be, *there it shall be,* for the benefit of those to whom it belongs; every man must labour to be a blessing to that place, whatever it is, where the providence of God casts him; wherever we are we may find good work to do if we have but hearts to do it. Or thus: some will say, "Many present themselves as objects of charity who are unworthy, and I do not know whom it is fit to give it to." "Trouble not thyself about that" (says Solomon); "give as discreetly as thou canst, and then be satisfied that, though the person should prove undeserving of thy charity, yet, if thou give it with an honest heart, thou shalt not lose thy reward; which way soever the charity is directed, *north* or *south,* thine shall be the benefit

of it." This is commonly applied to death; *therefore* let us do good, and, as good trees, *bring forth the fruits of righteousness,* because death will shortly come and cut us down, and we shall then be determined to an unchangeable state of happiness or misery according to what was done in the body. As the tree falls at death, so it is likely to lie to all eternity.

3. Some will object the many discouragements they have met with in their charity. They have been reproached for it as proud and pharisaical; they have but little to give, and they shall be despised if they do not give as others do; they know not but their children may come to want it, and they had better lay it up for them; they have taxes to pay and purchases to make; they know not what use will be made of their charity, nor what construction will be put upon it; these, and a hundred such objections, he answers, in one word (*v.* 4): *He that observes the wind shall not sow,* which signifies doing good; *and he that regards the clouds shall not reap,* which signifies getting good. If we stand thus magnifying every little difficulty and making the worst of it, starting objections and fancying hardship and danger where there is none, we shall never go on, much less go through with our work, nor make any thing of it. If the husbandman should decline, or leave off, sowing for the sake of every flying cloud, and reaping for the sake of every blast of wind, he would make but an ill account of his husbandry at the year's end. the duties of religion are as necessary as sowing and reaping, and will turn as much to our own advantage. The discouragements we meet with in these duties are but as winds and clouds, which will do us no harm, and which those that put on a little courage and resolution will despise and easily break through. Note, Those that will be deterred and driven off by small and seeming difficulties from great and real duties will never bring any thing to pass in religion, for there will always arise some wind, some cloud or other, at least in our imagination, to discourage us. Winds and clouds are in God's hands, are designed to try us, and our Christianity obliges us to endure hardness.

4. Some will say, "We do not see in which way what we expend in charity should ever be made up to us; we do not find ourselves ever the richer; why should we depend upon the general promise of a blessing on the charitable, unless we saw which way to expect the operation of it?" To this he answers, *"Thou knowest not the work of God,* nor is it fit thou shouldst. Thou mayest be sure he will make good his word of promise, though he does not tell thee how, or which way, and though he works in a way by himself, according to the counsels of his unsearchable wisdom. He will work, and none shall hinder; but then he will work and none shall direct or prescribe to him. The blessing shall work insensibly but irresistibly. God's work shall certainly agree with his word, whether we see it or no." Our ignorance of the work of God he shows, in two instances: — (1.) We *know not what is the way of the Spirit, of the wind* (so some), we *know not whence it comes, or whither it goes,* or when it will turn; yet the seamen lie ready waiting for it, till it turns about in favour of them; so we must do our duty, in expectation of the time appointed for the blessing. Or it may be understood of the human soul; we know that God made us, and gave us these souls, but how they entered into these bodies, are united to them, animate them, and operate upon them, we know not; the soul is a mystery to itself, no marvel then that *the work of God* is so to us. (2.) We know not *how the bones are fashioned in the womb of her that is with child.* We cannot describe the manner either of the formation of the body or of its information with a soul; both, we know, are *the work of God,* and we acquiesce in his work, but cannot, in either, trace the process of the operation. We doubt not of the birth of the child that is conceived, though we know not how it is formed; nor need we doubt of the performance of the promise, though we perceive not how things work towards it. And we may well trust God to provide for us that which is convenient, without our anxious disquieting cares, and therein to recompense us for our charity, since it was without any knowledge or forecast of ours that our bodies were curiously wrought in secret and our souls found the way into them; and so the argument is the same, and urged to the same intent, with that of our Saviour (Mt. 6:25), *The life,* the living soul that God has given us, *is more than meat; the body,* that God has made us, *is more than raiment;* let him therefore that has done the greater for us be cheerfully depended upon to do the less.

5. Some say, "We have been charitable, have given a great deal to the poor, and never yet saw any return for it; many days are past, and we have not *found it again,"* to which he answers (*v.* 6), "Yet go on, proceed and persevere in well-doing; let slip no opportunity. *In the morning sow thy seed* upon the objects of charity that offer themselves early, *and in the evening do not withhold thy hand,* under pretence that thou art weary; as thou hast opportunity, be doing good, some way or other, all the day long, as the husbandman follows his seedness from morning till night. *In the morning* of youth lay out thyself to do good; give out of the little thou hast to begin the world with; *and in the evening* of old age yield not to the common temptation old people are in to be penurious; even then *withhold not thy hand,* and think not to excuse thyself from charitable works by purposing to make a charitable will, but do good to the last, *for thou knowest not* which work of charity and piety *shall prosper,* both as to others and as to thyself, *this or that,* but hast reason to hope that *both shall be alike good. Be not weary of well-doing, for in due season,* in God's time and that is the best time, *you shall reap,"* Gal. 6:9. This is applicable to spiritual charity, our pious endeavours for the good of the souls of others; let us continue them, for, though we have long laboured in vain, we may at length see the success of them. Let ministers, in the days of their seedness, sow both morning and evening; *for who* can tell *which shall prosper?*

Verses 7–10

Here is an admonition both to old people and to young people, to think of dying, and get ready for it. Having by many excellent precepts taught us how to live well, the preacher comes now, towards the close of his discourse, to teach us how to die well and to put us in mind of our latter end.

I. He applies himself to the aged, writes to them as fathers, to awaken them to think of death, *v.* 7, 8. Here is, 1. A rational concession of the sweetness of life, which old people find by experience: *Truly the light is sweet;* the light of *the sun* is so; it is *a pleasant thing for the eyes to behold* it. Light was the first thing made in the formation of the great world, as the eye is one of the first in the formation of the body, the little world. It is pleasant to see the light; the heathen were so charmed with the pleasure of it that they worshipped the sun. It is pleasant by it to see other things, the many agreeable prospects this world gives us. The light of life is so. Light is put for life, Job 3:20, 23. It cannot be denied that life is sweet. It is sweet to bad men because they have *their portion in this life;* it is sweet to good men because they have this life as the time of their preparation for a better life; it is sweet to all men; nature says it is so, and there is no disputing against it; nor can death be desired for its own sake, but dreaded, unless as a period to present evils or a passage to future good. Life is sweet, and therefore we have need to double a guard upon ourselves, lest we love it too well. 2. A caution to think of death, even in the midst of life, and of life when it is most sweet and we are most apt to forget death: *If a man live many years, yet let him remember the days of darkness* are coming. Here is, (1.) A summer's day supposed to be enjoyed — that life may continue long, even many years, and that, by the goodness of God, it may be made comfortable and a man may *rejoice in them all.* There are those that *live many years* in this world, escape many dangers, receive many mercies, and therefore are secure that they shall want no good, and that no evil shall befal them, that the pitcher which has come so often from the well safe and sound shall never come home broken. But who are those that *live many years and rejoice in them all?* Alas! none; we have but hours of joy for months of sorrow. However, some rejoice in their years, their many years, more than others; if these two things meet, a prosperous state and a cheerful spirit, these two indeed may do much towards enabling a man to *rejoice in them all,* and yet the most prosperous state has its alloys and the most cheerful spirit has its damps; jovial sinners have their melancholy qualms, and cheerful saints have their gracious sorrows; so that it is but a supposition, not a case in fact, that a man should *live many years and rejoice in them all.* But, (2.) Here is a winter's night proposed to be expected after this summer's day: *Yet let* this hearty old man *remember the days of darkness, for they shall be many.* Note, [1.] There are *days of darkness* coming, the days of our lying in the grave; there the body will lie in the dark; there the eyes see not, the sun shines not. The darkness of death is opposed to the light of life; the grave is a *land of darkness,* Job 10:21. [2.] Those *days of darkness* will *be many;* the days of our lying under ground will be more than the days of our living above ground. They are many, but they are not infinite; many as they are, they will be numbered and finished when *the heavens are no more,* Job 14:12. As the longest day will have its night, so the longest night will have its morning. [3.] It is good for us often to remember those *days of darkness,* that we may not be lifted up with pride, nor lulled asleep in carnal security, nor even transported into indecencies by vain mirth. [4.] Notwithstanding the long continuance of life, and the many comforts of it, *yet* we must *remember the days of darkness,* because those will certainly come, and they will come with much the less terror if we have thought of them before.

II. He applies himself to the young, and writes to them as children, to awaken them to think of death (*v.* 9, 10); here we have,

1. An ironical concession to the vanities and pleasures of youth: *Rejoice, O young man! in thy youth.* Some make this to be the counsel which the atheist and the epicure give to the young man, the poisonous suggestions against which Solomon, in the close of the verse, prescribes a powerful antidote. But it is more emphatic if we take it, as it is commonly understood, by way of irony, like that of Elijah to the priests of Baal *(Cry aloud, for he is a god),* or of Micaiah to Ahab *(Go to Ramoth-Gilead, and prosper),* or of Christ to his disciples, *Sleep on now. "Rejoice, O young man! in thy youth,* live a merry life, follow thy sports, and take thy pleasures; *let thy heart cheer thee in the days of thy youth,* cheer thee with its fancies and foolish hopes; entertain thyself with thy pleasing dreams; *walk in the ways of thy heart;* do whatever thou hast a mind to do, and stick at nothing that may gratify the sensual appetite. *Quicquid libet, licet — Make thy will thy law. Walk in the ways of thy heart, and* let thy heart walk after *thy eyes,* a rambling heart after a roving eye; what is pleasing in thy own eyes do it, whether it be pleasing in the eyes of God or no." Solomon speaks thus ironically to the young man to intimate, (1.) That this is that which he would do, and which he would fain have leave to do, in which he places his happiness and on which he sets his heart. (2.) That he wishes all about him would give him this counsel, would prophesy to him such smooth things as these, and cannot brook any advice to the contrary, but reckons those his enemies that bid him be sober and serious. (3.) To expose his folly, and the great absurdity of a voluptuous vicious course of life. The very description of it, if men would see things entirely, and judge of them impartially, is enough to show how contrary to reason those act that live such a life. The very opening of the cause is enough to determine it, without any argument. (4.) To show that if men give themselves to such a course of life as this it is just with God to give them up to it, to abandon them to their own heart's lusts, that they may *walk in their own counsels,* Hos. 4:7.

2. A powerful check given to these vanities and pleasures: *"Know thou that for all these things God shall bring thee into judgment,* and duly consider that, and then live such a luxurious life if thou canst, if thou darest." This is a *kolastērion — a corrective* to the foregoing concession, and plucks in the reins he had laid on the neck of the young man's lust. *"Know then,* for a certainty, that, if thou dost take such a liberty as this, it will be thy everlasting ruin; thou hast to do with a God who will not let it go unpunished." Note, (1.) There is a judgment to come. (2.) We must every one of us be brought into judgment, however we may now put far from us that evil day. (3.) We shall be reckoned with for all our carnal mirth and sensual pleasures in that day. (4.) It is good for all, but especially for young people, to know and consider this, that they may not, by the indulgence of their youthful lusts, *treasure up unto themselves wrath against that day of wrath,* the wrath of the Lamb.

3. A word of caution and exhortation inferred from all this, *v.* 10. Let young people look to themselves and man-

age well both their souls and their bodies, their heart and their flesh. (1.) Let them take care that their minds be not lifted up with pride, nor disturbed with anger, or any sinful passion: *Remove sorrow,* or anger, *from thy heart;* the word signifies any disorder or perturbation of the mind. Young people are apt to be impatient of check and control, to vex and fret at any thing that is humbling and mortifying to them, and their proud hearts rise against every thing that crosses and contradicts them. They are so set upon that which is pleasing to sense that they cannot bear any thing that is displeasing, but it goes with sorrow to their heart. Their pride often disquiets them, and makes them uneasy. "Put that away, and the love of the world, and lay thy expectations low from the creature, and then disappointments will not be occasions of sorrow and anger to thee." Some by sorrow here understand that carnal mirth described *v.* 9, the end of which will be bitterness and sorrow. Let them keep at a distance from every thing which will be sorrow in the reflection. (2.) Let them take care that their bodies be not defiled by intemperance, uncleanness, or any fleshly lusts: *"Put away evil from the flesh,* and let not the members of thy body be instruments of unrighteousness. The evil of sin will be the evil of punishment, and that which thou art fond of, as good for the flesh, because it gratifies the appetites of it, will prove evil, and hurtful to it, and therefore put it far from thee, the further the better."

III. The preacher, to enforce his admonition both to old and young, urges, as an effectual argument, that which is the great argument of his discourse, the vanity of all present things, their uncertainty and insufficiency. 1. He reminds old people of this (*v.* 8): *All that comes is vanity;* yea, though *a man live many years and rejoice in them all,* All that has come already, and all that is yet to come, how much soever men promise themselves from the concluding scenes, it is all *vanity.* What will be will do no more to make men happy than what has been. *All that come* into the world are *vanity;* they are altogether so, at their best estate. 2. He reminds young people of this: *Childhood and youth are vanity.* The dispositions and actions of childhood and youth have in them a great deal of impertinence and iniquity, sinful vanity, which young people have need to watch against and get cured. The pleasures and advantages of childhood and youth have in them no certainty, satisfaction, nor continuance. They are passing away; these flowers will soon wither, and these blossoms fall; let them therefore be knit into good fruit, which will continue and abound to a good account.

CHAPTER 12

The wise and penitent preacher is here closing his sermon; and he closes it, not only lie a good orator, but like a good preacher, with that which was likely to make the best impressions and which he wished might be powerful and lasting upon his hearers. Here is, I. An exhortation to young people to begin betimes to be religious and not to put it off to old age (*v.* 1), enforced with arguments taken from the calamities of old age (*v.* 1–5). and the great change that death will make upon us (*v.* 6, 7). II. A repetition of the great truth he had undertaken to prove in this discourse, the vanity of the world (*v.* 8). III. A confirmation and recommendation of what he had written in this and his other books, as worthy to be duly weighed and concluded, with a charge to all to be truly religious, in consideration of the judgment to come (*v.* 13, 14).

Verses 1–7

Here is, I. A call to young people to think of God, and mind their duty to him, when they are young: *Remember now thy Creator in the days of thy youth.* This is, 1. The royal preacher's application of his sermon concerning the vanity of the world and every thing in it. "You that are young flatter yourselves with expectations of great things from it, but believe those that have tried it; it yields no solid satisfaction to a soul; therefore, that you may not be deceived by this vanity, nor too much disturbed by it, *remember your Creator,* and so guard yourselves against the mischiefs that arise from the vanity of the creature." 2. It is the royal physician's antidote against the particular diseases of youth, the love of mirth, and the indulgence of sensual pleasures, the vanity which childhood and youth are subject to; to prevent and cure this, *remember thy Creator.* Here is, (1.) A great duty pressed upon us, to *remember* God as our *creator,* not only to remember that God is our Creator, that he *made us and not we ourselves,* and is therefore our rightful Lord and owner, but we must engage ourselves to him with the considerations which his being our Creator lay us under, and pay him the honour and duty which we owe him as our Creator. *Remember thy Creators;* the word is plural, as it is Job 35:10, *Where is God my Makers?* For God said, *Let us make man,* us, Father, Son, and Holy Ghost. (2.) The proper season for this duty — *in the days of thy youth,* the *days of thy choice* (so some), thy choice days, thy choosing days. "Begin in the beginning of thy days to remember him from whom thou hadst thy being, and go on according to that good beginning. Call him to mind when thou art young, and keep him in mind throughout all the days of thy youth, and never forget him. Guard thus against the temptations of youth, and thus improve the advantages of it."

II. A reason to enforce this command: *While the evil days come not, and the years of which thou shalt say I have no pleasure in them.*

1. Do it quickly, (1.) "Before sickness and death come. Do it while thou livest, for it will be too late to do it when death has removed thee from this state of trial and probation to that of recompence and retribution." The days of sickness and death are *the days of evil,* terrible to nature, *evil days* indeed to those that have forgotten their Creator. These *evil days* will *come* sooner or later; as yet they *come not,* for God is *long-suffering to us-ward,* and gives us *space to repent;* the continuing of life is but the deferring of death, and, while life is continued and death deferred, it concerns us to prepare, and get the property of death altered, that we may die comfortably. (2.) Before old age comes, which, if death prevent not, will come, and they will be *years of which we shall say, We have no pleasure in them,* — when we shall not relish the delights of sense, as Barzillai (2 Sa. 19:35), — when we shall be loaded with bodily infirmities, old and blind, or old and lame, — when we shall be taken off from our usefulness, and our *strength* shall be *labour and sorrow,* — when we shall either have parted with our relations, and all our old friends, or be afflicted in them and see them weary of us, — when we shall feel ourselves die by inches. These *years draw nigh,* when *all that comes* will be *vanity,* the remaining months all months of vanity, and there will be *no pleasure* but in the reflection of a good life on earth and the expectation of a better life in heaven.

2. These two arguments he enlarges upon in the following verses, only inverting the order, and shows,

(1.) How many are the calamities of old age, and that if we should live to be old, our days will be such as we shall *have no pleasure in,* which is a good reason why we should return to God, and make our peace with him, *in the days of our youth,* and not put it off till we come to be old; for it will be no thanks to us to leave the pleasures of sin when they have left us, nor to return to God when need forces us. It is the greatest absurdity and ingratitude imaginable to give the cream and flower of our days to the devil, and reserve the bran, and refuse, and dregs of them for God; this is offering *the torn, and the lame, and the sick for sacrifice;* and, besides, old age being thus clogged with infirmities, it is the greatest folly imaginable to put off that needful work till then, which requires the best of our strength, when our faculties are in their prime, and especially to make the work more difficult by a longer continuance in sin, and, laying up treasures of guilt in the conscience, to add to the burdens of age and make them much heavier. If the calamities of age will be such as are here represented, we shall have need of something to support and comfort us then, and nothing will be more effectual to do that than the testimony of our consciences for us that we begin betimes to remember our Creator and have not since laid aside the remembrance of him. How can we expect God should help us when we are old, if we will not serve him when we are young? See Ps. 71:17, 18.

[1.] The decays and infirmities of old age are here elegantly described in figurative expressions, which have some difficulty in them to us now, who are not acquainted with the common phrases and metaphors used in Solomon's age and language; but the general scope is plain — to show how uncomfortable, generally, the days of old age are. *First,* Then *the sun* and *the light* of it, *the moon* and *the stars,* and the light which they borrow from it, will *be darkened.* They look dim to old people, in consequence of the decay of their sight; their countenance is clouded, and the beauty and lustre of it are eclipsed; their intellectual powers and faculties, which are as lights in the soul, are weakened; their understanding and memory fail them, and their apprehension is not so quick nor their fancy so lively as it has been; the days of their mirth are over (light is often put for joy and prosperity) and they have not the pleasure either of the converse of the day or the repose of the night, for both *the sun* and *the moon* are darkened to them. *Secondly,* Then *the clouds return after the rain;* as, when the weather is disposed to wet, no sooner has one cloud blown over than another succeeds it, so it is with old people, when they have got free from one pain or ailment, they are seized with another, so that their distempers are *like a continual dropping in a very rainy day.* The end of one trouble is, in this world, but the beginning of another, and deep calls unto deep. Old people are often afflicted with defluxions of rheum, like soaking rain, after which still more clouds return, feeding the humour, so that it is continually grievous, and therein the body, as it were, melts away. *Thirdly,* Then *the keepers of the house tremble.* The head, which is as the watch-tower, shakes, and the arms and hands, which are ready for the preservation of the body, shake too, and grow feeble, upon every sudden approach and attack of danger. That vigour of the animal spirits which used to be exerted for self-defence fails and cannot do its office; old people are easily dispirited and discouraged. *Fourthly,* Then *the strong men shall bow themselves;* the legs and thighs, which used to support the body, and bear its weight, bend, and cannot serve for travelling as they have done, but are soon tired. Old men that have been in their time *strong men* become weak and stoop for *age,* Zec. 8:4. *God takes no pleasure in the legs of a man* (Ps. 147:10), for their strength will soon fail; but *in the Lord Jehovah there is everlasting strength;* he has everlasting arms. *Fifthly,* Then the *grinders cease because they are few;* the teeth, with which we grind our meat and prepare it for concoction, cease to do their part, *because they are few.* They are rotted and broken, and perhaps have been drawn because they ached. Some old people have lost all their teeth, and others have but few left; and this infirmity is the more considerable because the meat, not being well chewed, for want of teeth, is not well digested, which has as much influence as any thing upon the other decays of age. *Sixthly, Those that look out of the windows* are *darkened;* the eyes wax dim, as Isaac's (Gen. 27:1), and Ahijah's, 1 Ki. 14:4. Moses was a rare instance of one who, when 120 years old, had good eye-sight, but ordinarily the sight decays in old people as soon as any thing, and it is a mercy to them that art helps nature with spectacles. We have need to improve our sight well while we have it, because the light of the eyes may be gone before the light of life. *Seventhly, The doors are shut in the streets.* Old people keep within doors, and care not for going abroad to entertainments. The lips, the doors of the mouth, are shut in eating, because the teeth are gone and *the sound of the grinding* with them *is low,* so that they have not that command of their meat in their mouths which they used to have; they cannot digest their meat, and therefore little grist is brought to the mill. *Eightly,* Old people *rise up at the voice of the bird.* They have no sound sleep as young people have, but a little thing disturbs them, even the chirping of a bird; they cannot rest for coughing, and therefore rise up at cock-crowing, as soon as any body is stirring; or they are apt to be jealous, and timorous, and full of care, which breaks their sleep and makes them rise early; or they are apt to be superstitious, and *rise up* as in a fright, *at those voices of birds,* as of ravens, or screech-owls, which soothsayers call ominous. *Ninthly,* With them *all the daughters of music* are *brought low.* They have neither voice nor ear, can neither sing themselves nor take any pleasure, as Solomon had done in the days of his youth, in *singing men, and singing women, and musical instruments, ch.* 2:8. Old people grow hard of hearing, and unapt to distinguish sounds and voices. *Tenthly,* They are *afraid of that which is high,* afraid to go to the top of any high place, either because, for want of breath, they cannot reach it, or, their heads being giddy or their legs failing them, they dare not venture to it, or they frighten themselves with fancying that *that which is high* will fall upon them. *Fear* is *in the way;* they can neither ride nor walk with their former boldness, but are afraid of every thing that lies in their way, lest it throw them down. *Eleventhly, The almond-tree flourishes.* The old man's hair has grown white, so that his head looks like an almond-tree in the blossom. The almond-tree blossoms before any other tree, and therefore fitly shows what haste old age makes in seizing upon men; it prevents their expectations and comes faster upon them than they thought of. Gray hairs are here and there upon them, and they perceive it not. *Twelfthly, The grasshopper is a burden and desire fails.* Old men can bear nothing; the lightest thing sits heavily upon them, both on their bodies and on their minds, a little thing sinks and breaks them. Perhaps *the grasshopper* was some food that was looked upon to be very light of digestion (John Baptist's meat *was locusts),* but even that lies heavily upon an old man's stomach, and therefore *desire fails,* he has no appetite to his meat, neither shall he *regard the desire of woman,* as that king, Dan. 11:37. Old men become mindless and listless, and the pleasures of sense are to them tasteless and sapless.

[2.] It is probable that Solomon wrote this when he was himself old, and could speak feelingly of the infirmities of age, which perhaps grew the faster upon him for the indulgence he had given himself in sensual pleasures. Some old people bear up better than others under the decays of age, but, more or less, the days of old age are and will be *evil days* and of little pleasure. Great care therefore should be taken to pay respect and honour to old people, that they may have something to balance these grievances and nothing may be done to add to them. And all this, put together, makes up a good reason why we should *remember our Creator in the days of our youth,* that he may remember us with favour when these *evil days come,* and his comforts may delight our souls when the delights of sense are in a manner worn off.

(2.) He shows how great a change death will make with us, which will be either the prevention or the period of the miseries of old age. Nothing else will keep them off, nor any thing else cure them. "Therefore *remember thy Creator in the days of thy youth,* because death is certainly before thee, perhaps it is very near thee, and it is a serious thing to die, and thou shouldst feel concerned with the utmost care and diligence to prepare for it." [1.] Death will fix us in an unchangeable state: *Man* shall then *go to his long home,* and all these infirmities and decays of age are harbingers of and advances towards that awful remove. At death *man goes* from this world and all the employments and enjoyments of it. He has gone for good and all, as to his present state. He has gone *home,* for here he was a stranger and pilgrim; both soul and body go to the place whence they came, *v.* 7. He has gone to his rest, to the place where he is to fix. He has gone *to his home, to the house of his world* (so some), for this world is not his. He has gone *to his long home,* for the days of his lying in the grave will be many. He has gone *to his house of eternity,* not only to his house whence he shall never return to this world, but to the house where he must be for ever. This should make us willing to die, that, at death, we must *go home;* and why should we not long to go to our Father's house? And this should quicken us to get ready to die, that we must then go to our *long home,* to an *everlasting habitation.* [2.] Death will be an occasion of sorrow to our friends that love us. When *man goes to his long home the mourners go about the streets* — the real mourners, and those, as now with us, distinguished by their habits as they go along the streets, — the mourners for ceremony, that were hired to weep for the dead, both to express and to excite the real mourning. When we die we not only remove to a melancholy house before us, but we leave a melancholy house behind us. Tears are a tribute due to the dead, and this, among other circumstances, makes it a serious thing to die. But in vain do we *go to the house of mourning,* and see *the mourners go about the streets,* if it do not help to make us serious and pious mourners in the closet. [3.] Death will dissolve the frame of nature and take down the earthly house of this tabernacle, which is elegantly described, *v.* 6. Then shall *the silver cord,* by which soul and body were wonderfully fastened together, *be loosed,* that sacred knot untied, and those old friends be forced to part; then shall *the golden bowl,* which held the waters of life for us, *be broken;* then shall *the pitcher* with which we used to fetch up water, for the constant support of life and the repair of its decays, *be broken,* even *at the fountain,* so that it can fetch up no more; and *the wheel* (all those organs that serve for the collecting and distributing of nourishment) shall be *broken,* and disabled to do their office any more. The body shall become like a watch when the spring is broken, the motion of all the wheels is stopped and they all stand still; the machine is taken to pieces; the heart beats no more, nor does the blood circulate. Some apply this to the ornaments and utensils of life; rich people must, at death, leave behind them their clothing and furniture of *silver* and *gold,* and poor people their earthen *pitchers,* and the drawers of water will have their *wheel broken.* [4.] Death will resolve us into our first principles, *v.* 7. Man is a strange sort of creature, a ray of heaven united to a clod of earth; at death these are separated, and each goes to the place whence it came. *First,* The body, that clod of clay, *returns to* its own *earth.* It is made of *the earth;* Adam's body was so, and we are of the same mould; it is a house of clay. At death it is laid in *the earth,* and in a little time will be resolved into earth, not to be distinguished from common earth, according to the sentence (Gen. 3:19), *Dust thou art and* therefore *to dust thou shalt return.* Let us not therefore indulge the appetites of the body, nor pamper it (it will be worms' meat shortly), nor let *sin reign in our mortal bodies,* for they are mortal, Rom. 6:12. *Secondly,* The soul, that beam of light, *returns to* that *God* who, when he *made man of the dust of the ground, breathed into him the breath of life,* to make him *a living soul* (Gen. 2:7), and forms the spirit of every man within him. When the fire consumes the wood the flame ascends, and the ashes *return to the earth* out of which the wood grew. The soul does not die with the body; it is *redeemed from the power of the grave* (Ps. 49:15); it can subsist without it and will in a state of separation from it, as the candle burns, and burns brighter, when it is taken out of the dark lantern. It removes to the world of spirits, to which it is allied. It goes *to God* as a Judge, to give account of itself, and to be lodged either with *the spirits in prison* (1 Pt. 3:19) or with *the spirits in paradise* (Lu. 23:43), according to what was done in the body. This makes death terrible to the wicked, whose souls go to God as an avenger, and comfortable to the godly, whose souls go to God as a Father, into whose hands they cheerfully commit them, through a Mediator, out of whom sinners may justly dread to think of going *to God.*

Verses 8–12

Solomon is here drawing towards a close, and is loth to part till he has gained his point, and prevailed with his hearers, with his readers, to seek for that satisfaction in God only and in their duty to him which they can never find in the creature.

I. He repeats his text (*v.* 8), 1. As that which he had fully demonstrated the truth of, and so made good his undertaking in this sermon, wherein he had kept closely to his text, and both his reasons and his application were to the purpose. 2. As that which he desired to inculcate both upon others and upon himself, to have it ready, and to make use of it upon all occasions. We see it daily proved; let it therefore be daily improved: *Vanity of vanities, all is vanity.*

II. He recommends what he had written upon this subject by divine direction and inspiration to our serious consideration. The words of this book are faithful, and well worthy our acceptance, for,

1. They are the words of one that was a convert, a penitent, that could speak by dear-bought experience of the vanity of the world and the folly of expecting great things from it. He was *Coheleth,* one gathered in from his wanderings and gathered home to that God from whom he had revolted. *Vanity of vanities, saith the* penitent. All true penitents are convinced of the vanity of the world, for they find it can do nothing to ease them of the burden of sin, which they complain of.

2. They are the words of one that was wise, wiser than any, endued with extraordinary measures of wisdom, famous for it among his neighbours, who all sought unto him *to hear his wisdom,* and therefore a competent judge of this matter, not only wise as a prince, but wise as a preacher — and preachers have need of wisdom to win souls.

3. He was one that made it his business to do good, and to use wisdom aright. *Because* he *was* himself *wise,* but knew he had not his wisdom for himself, any more than he had it from himself, *he still taught the people* that *knowledge* which he had found useful to himself, and hoped might be so to them too. It is the interest of princes to have their people well taught in religion, and no disparagement to them to teach them themselves *the good knowledge of the Lord,* but their duty to encourage those whose office it is to teach them and to speak comfortably to them, 2 Chr. 30:22. Let not the people, the common people, be despised, no, not by the wisest and greatest, as either unworthy or incapable of good knowledge: even those that are well taught have need to be *still taught,* that they may grow in knowledge.

4. He took a great deal of pains and care to do good, designing to *teach the people knowledge.* He did not put them off with any thing that came next to hand, because they were inferior people, and he a very wise man, but considering the worth of the souls he preached to and the weight of the subject he preached on, he *gave good heed* to what he read and heard from others, that, having stocked himself well, he might *bring out of his treasury things new and old.* He *gave good heed* to what he spoke and wrote himself, and was choice and exact in it; all he did was elaborate. (1.) He chose the most profitable way of preaching, by proverbs or short sentences, which would be more easily apprehended and remembered than long and laboured periods. (2.) He did not content himself with a few parables, or wise sayings, and repeat them again and again, but he furnished himself with *many proverbs,* a great variety of grave discourses, that he might have something to say on every occasion. (3.) He did not only give them such observations as were obvious and trite, but he *sought out* such as were surprising and uncommon; he dug into the mines of knowledge, and did not merely pick up what lay on the surface. (4.) He did not deliver his heads and observations at random, as they came to mind, but methodized them, and *set them in order* that they might appear in more strength and lustre.

5. He put what he had to say in such a dress as he thought would be most pleasing: *He sought to find out acceptable words,* words of delight (*v.* 10); he took care that good matter might not be spoiled by a bad style, and by the ungratefulness and incongruity of the expression. Ministers should study, not for the big words, nor the fine words, but *acceptable words,* such as are likely to please men for their good, to edification, 1 Co. 10:33. Those that would win souls must contrive how to win upon them with *words fitly spoken.*

6. That which he wrote for our instruction is of unquestionable certainty, and what we may rely upon: *That which was written was upright* and sincere, according to the real sentiments of the penman, even *words of truth,* the exact representation of the thing as it is. Those are sure not to miss their way who are guided by these words. What good will *acceptable words* do us if they be not *upright and words of truth?* Most are for smooth things, that flatter them, rather than right things, that direct them (Isa. 30:10), but to those that understand themselves, and their own interest, *words of truth* will always be *acceptable words.*

7. That which he and other holy men wrote will be of great use and advantage to us, especially being inculcated upon us by the exposition of it, *v.* 11. Here observe, (1.) A double benefit accruing to us from divine truths if duly applied and improved; they are *profitable for doctrine, for reproof, for correction, and instruction in righteousness.* They are of use, [1.] To excite us to our duty. They are as goads to the ox that draws the plough, putting him forward when he is dull and quickening him, to amend his pace. The truths of God *prick men to the heart* (Acts 2:37) and put them upon bethinking themselves, when they trifle and grow remiss, and exerting themselves with more vigour in their work. While our good affections are so apt as they are to grow flat and cool, we have need of these *goads.* [2.] To engage us to persevere in our duty. They are *as nails* to those that are wavering and inconstant, to fix them to that which is good. They are *as goads* to such as are dull and draw back, and *nails* to such as are desultory and draw aside, means to establish the heart and confirm good resolutions, that we may not sit loose to our duty, nor even be taken off from it, but that what good there is in us may be *as a nail fastened in a sure place,* Ezra 9:8. (2.) A double way of communicating divine truths, in order to those benefits: — [1.] By the scriptures, as the standing rule, the *words of the wise,* that is, of the prophets, who are called *wise men,* Mt. 23:34. These we have in black and white, and may have recourse to them at any time, and make use of them *as goads and as nails.* By them

we may teach ourselves; let them but come with pungency and power to the soul, let the impressions of them be deep and durable, and the will *make us wise to salvation.* [2.] By the ministry. To make the *words of the wise* more profitable to us, it is appointed that they should be impressed and fastened by the *masters of assemblies.* Solemn assemblies for religious worship are an ancient divine institution, intended for the honour of God and the edification of his church, and are not only serviceable, but necessary, to those ends. There must be masters of these assemblies, who are Christ's ministers, and as such are to preside in them, to be God's mouth to the people and theirs to God. Their business is to fasten the *words of the wise,* and drive them as *nails* to the head, in order to which the word of God is likewise as *a hammer,* Jer. 23:29.

8. That which is written, and thus recommended to us, is of divine origin. Though it comes to us through various hands (many *wise men,* and many *masters of assemblies*), yet it is *given by one* and the same *shepherd,* the great *shepherd of Israel, that leads Joseph like a flock,* Ps. 80:1. God is that one Shepherd, whose good Spirit indited the scriptures, and assists the *masters of the assemblies* in opening and applying the scriptures. *These words of the wise* are the true sayings of God, on which we may rest our souls. From that one Shepherd all ministers must receive what they deliver, and speak according to the light of the written word.

9. The sacred inspired writings, if we will but make use of them, are sufficient to guide us in the way of true happiness, and we need not, in the pursuit of that, to fatigue ourselves with the search of other writings (*v.* 12): "*And further,* nothing now remains but to tell thee that that *of making many books there is no end,*" that is, (1.) Of *writing* many books. "If what I have written, serve not to convince thee of the vanity of the world, and the necessity of being religious, neither wouldst thou be convinced if I should write ever so much." If the end be not attained in the use of those books of scripture which God has blessed us with, neither should we obtain the end, if we had twice as many more; nay, if we had so many that the whole world could not contain them (Jn. 21:25), and much study of them would but confound us, and would rather be *a weariness to the flesh* than any advantage to the soul. We have as much as God saw fit to give us, saw fit for us, and saw us fit for. Much less can it be expected that those

who will not by these be admonished should be wrought upon by other writings. Let men write ever so many books for the conduct of human life, write till they have tired themselves with much study, they cannot give better instructions than those we have from the word of God. Or, (2.) Of *buying* many books, making ourselves master of them, and masters of what is in them, by much study; still the desire of learning would be unsatisfied. It will give a man indeed the best entertainment and the best accomplishment this world can afford him; but if we be not by these *admonished* of the vanity of the world, and human learning, among other things, and its insufficiency to make us happy without true piety, alas! there is no end of it, nor real benefit by it; it will weary the body, but never give the soul any true satisfaction. The great Mr. Selden subscribed to this when he owned that in all the books he had read he never found that on which he could rest his soul, but in the holy scripture, especially Tit. 2:11, 12. By these therefore let us be admonished.

Verses 13–14

The great enquiry which Solomon prosecutes in this book is, *What is that good which the sons of men should do? ch.* 2:3. What is the true way to true happiness, the certain means to attain our great end? He had in vain sought it among those things which most men are eager in pursuit of, but here, at length, he has found it, by the help of that discovery which God anciently made to man (Job 28:28), that serious godliness is the only way to true happiness: *Let us hear the conclusion of the whole matter,* the return entered upon the writ of enquiry, the result of this diligent search; you shall have all I have been driving at in two words. He does not say, *Do you hear it,* but *Let us hear it;* for preachers must themselves be hearers of that word which they preach to others, must hear it as from God; those are teachers by the halves who teach others and not themselves, Rom. 2:21. Every word of God is pure and precious, but some words are worthy of more special remark, as this; the Masorites begin it with a capital letter, as that Deu. 6:4. Solomon himself puts a *nota bene* before it, demanding attention in these words, *Let us hear the conclusion of the whole matter.* Observe here,

I. The summary of religion. Setting aside all matters of doubtful disputation, to be religious is to *fear God and keep his commandments.* 1. The root of religion is fear of God

reigning in the heart, and a reverence of his majesty, a deference to his authority, and a dread of his wrath. *Fear God,* that is, worship God, give him the honour due to his name, in all the instances of true devotion, inward and outward. See Rev. 14:7. 2. The rule of religion is the law of God revealed in the scriptures. Our fear towards God must be taught by his commandments (Isa. 29:13), and those we must keep and carefully observe. Wherever the fear of God is uppermost in the heart, there will be *a respect to all his commandments* and care to keep them. In vain do we pretend to fear God if we do not make conscience of our duty to him.

II. The vast importance of it: *This is the whole of man;* it is all his business and all his blessedness; our whole duty is summed up in this and our whole comfort is bound up in this. It is the concern of every man, and ought to be his chief and continual care; it is the common concern of all men, of their whole time. It is nothing to a man whether he be rich or poor, high or low, but it is the main matter, it is all in all to a man, to fear God and do as he bids him.

III. A powerful inducement to this, *v.* 14. We shall see of what vast consequence it is to us that we be religious if we consider the account we must every one of us shortly give of himself to God; thence he argued against a voluptuous and vicious life (*ch.* 11:9), and here for a religious life: *God shall bring every work into judgment.* Note, 1. There is a judgment to come, in which every man's eternal state will be finally determined. 2. God himself will be the Judge, God-man will, not only because he has a right to judge, but because he is perfectly fit for it, infinitely wise and just. 3. *Every work* will then be *brought into judgment,* will be enquired into and called over again. It will be a day to *bring to remembrance every thing done in the body.* 4. The great thing to be then judged of concerning *every work* is whether it be good or evil, conformable to the will of God or a violation of it. 5. Even *secret things,* both good and evil, will be brought to light, and brought to account, in the judgment of the great day (Rom. 2:16); there is no good work, no bad work, hid, but shall then be made manifest. 6. In consideration of the judgment to come, and the strictness of that judgment, it highly concerns us now to be very strict in our walking with God, that we may *give up our account with joy.*

AN EXPOSITION, WITH PRACTICAL OBSERVATIONS, OF

THE SONG OF SOLOMON

All *scripture,* we are sure, *is given by inspiration of God, and is profitable* for the support and advancement of the interests of his kingdom among men, and it is never the less so for there being found in it some things *dark and hard to be understood, which those that are unlearned and unstable wrest to their own destruction.* In our belief both of the divine extraction and of the spiritual exposition of this book we are confirmed by the ancient, constant, and concurring testimony both of the church of the Jews, to whom were *committed the oracles of God,* and who never made any doubt of the authority of this book, and of the Christian church, which happily succeeds them in that trust and honour. I. It must be confessed, on the one hand, that if he who barely reads this book be asked, as the eunuch was *Understandest thou what thou readest?* he will have more reason than he had to say, *How can I, except some man shall guide me?* The books of scripture-history and prophecy are very much like one another, but this *Song of Solomon's* is very much unlike the songs of his father David; here is not the name of God in it; it is never quoted in the New Testament; we find not in it any expressions of natural religion or pious devotion, no, nor is it introduced by vision, or any of the marks of immediate revelation. It seems as hard as any part of scripture to be made a *savour of life unto life,* nay, and to those who come to the reading of it with carnal minds and corrupt affections, it is in danger of being made a *savour of death unto death;* it is a flower out of which they extract poison; and therefore the Jewish doctors advised their young people not to read it till they were thirty years old, lest by the abuse of that which is most pure and sacred *(horrendum dictu — horrible to say!)* the flames of lust should be kindled with fire from heaven, which is intended for the altar only. But, II. It must be confessed, on the other hand, that with the help of the many faithful guides we have for the understanding of this book it appears to be a very bright and powerful ray of heavenly light, admirable fitted to excite pious and devout affections in holy souls, to draw out their desires towards God, to increase their delight in him, and improve their acquaintance and communion with him. It is an allegory, the letter of which kills those who rest in that and look no further, but the spirit of which gives life, 2 Co. 3:6; Jn. 6:63. It is a parable, which makes divine things more difficult to those who do not love them, but more plain and pleasant to those who do, Mt. 13:14, 16. Experienced Christians here find a coun-

terpart of their experiences, and to them it is intelligible, while *those* neither understand it nor relish it who have no part nor lot in the matter. It is a son, an *Epithalamium,* or nuptial song, wherein, by the expressions of love between a bridegroom and his bride, are set forth and illustrated the mutual affections that pass between God and a distinguished remnant of mankind. It is a pastoral; the bride and bridegroom, for the more lively representation of humility and innocence, are brought in as a shepherd and his shepherdess. Now, 1. This song might easily be taken in a spiritual sense by the Jewish church, for whose use it was first composed, and was so taken, as appears by the Chaldee-Paraphrase and the most ancient Jewish expositors. God betrothed the people of Israel to himself; he entered into covenant with them, and it was a marriage-covenant. He had given abundant proofs of his love to them, and required of them that they should love him with all their heart and soul. Idolatry was often spoken of as spiritual adultery, and doting upon idols, to prevent which this song was penned, representing the complacency which God took in Israel and which Israel ought to take in God, and encouraging them to continue faithful to him, though he might seem sometimes to withdraw and hide himself from them, and to wait for the further manifestation of himself in the promised Messiah. 2. It may more easily be taken in a spiritual sense by the Christian church, because the condescensions and communications of divine love appear more rich and free under the gospel than they did under the law, and the communion between heaven and earth more familiar. God sometimes spoke of himself as the husband of the Jewish church (Isa. 64:5, Hos. 2:16, 19), and rejoiced in it as his bride, Isa. 62:4, 5. But more frequently is Christ represented as the bridegroom of his church (Mt. 25:1; Rom. 7:4; 2 Co. 11:2; Eph. 5:32), and the church as the bride, the Lamb's wife, Rev. 19:7; 21:2, 9. Pursuant to this metaphor Christ and the church in general, Christ and particular believers, are here discoursing with abundance of mutual esteem and endearment. The best key to this book is the 45th Psalm, which we find applied to Christ in the New Testament, and therefore this ought to be so too. It requires some pains to find out what may, probably, be the meaning of the Holy Spirit in the several parts of this book; as David's songs are many of them level to the capacity of the meanest, and there are shallows in them learned, and there are depths in it in which an elephant may swim. But, when the meaning is found out, it will be of admirable use to excite pious and devout affections in us; and the same truths which are plainly laid down in other scriptures when they are extracted out of this come to the soul with a more pleasing power. When we apply ourselves to the study of this book we must not only, with Moses and Joshua, *put off our shoe from off our foot,* and even forget that we have bodies, because *the place where we stand is holy ground,* but we must, with John, *come up hither,* must spread our wings, take a noble flight, and soar upwards, till by faith and holy love we *enter into the holiest,* for *this is no other than the house of God and this is the gate of heaven.*

CHAPTER 1

In this chapter, after the title of the book (*v.* 1), we have Christ and his church, Christ and a believer, expressing their esteem for each other. I. The bride, the church, speaks to the bridegroom (*v.* 2–4), to the daughters of Jerusalem (*v.* 5, 6), and then to the bridegroom (*v.* 7). II. Christ, the bridegroom, speaks in answer to the complaints and requests of his spouse (*v.* 8–11). III. The church expresses the great value she has for Christ, and the delights she takes in communion with him (*v.* 12–14). IV. Christ commends the church's beauty (*v.* 15). V. The church returns the commendation (*v.* 16, 17). Where there is a fire of true love to Christ in the heart this will be of use to blow it up into a flame.

Verse 1

We have here the title of this book, showing, 1. The nature of it; it is a *song,* that it might the better answer the intention, which is to stir up the affections and to heat them, which poetry will be very instrumental to do. The subject is pleasing, and therefore fit to be treated of in a song, in singing which we may *make melody with our hearts unto the Lord.* It is evangelical; and gospel-times should be times of joy, for gospel-grace puts a *new song* into our mouths, Ps. 98:1. 2. The dignity of it; it is *the song of songs,* a most excellent song, not only above any human composition, or above all other songs which Solomon penned, but even above any other of the scripture-songs, as having more of Christ in it. 3. The penman of it; it is Solomon's. It is not the song of fools, as many of the songs of love are, but the song of the wisest of men; nor can any man give a better proof of his wisdom than to celebrate the love of God to mankind and to excite his own love to God and that of others with it. Solomon's songs were a thousand and five (1 Ki. 4:32); those that were of other subjects are lost, but this of seraphic love remains, and will to the end of time. Solomon, like his father, was addicted to poetry, and, which way soever a man's genius lies, he should endeavor to honour God and edify the church with it. One of Solomon's names was *Jedidiah — beloved of the Lord* (2 Sa. 12:25); and none so fit to write of the Lord's love as he that had himself so great an interest in it; none of all the apostles wrote so much of love as he that was himself the beloved disciple and lay in Christ's bosom. Solomon, as a king, had great affairs to mind and manage, which took up much of his thoughts and time, yet he found heart and leisure for this and other religious exercises. Men of business ought to be devout men, and not to think that business will excuse them from that which is every man's great business — to keep up communion with God. It is not certain when Solomon penned this sacred song. Some think that he penned it after he recovered himself by the grace of God from his backslidings, as a further proof of his repentance, and as if by doing good to many with this song he would atone for the hurt he had perhaps done with loose, vain, amorous songs, when he *loved many strange wives;* now he turned his wit the right way. It is more probable that he penned it in the beginning of his time, while he kept close to God and kept up his communion with him; and perhaps he put this song, with his father's psalms, into the hands of the chief musician, for the service of the temple, not without a key to it, for the right understanding of it. Some think that it was penned upon occasion of his marriage with Pharaoh's daughter, but that is uncertain; the tower of Lebanon, which is mentioned in this book (*ch.* 7:4), was not built, as is supposed, till long after the marriage. We may reasonably think that when in the height of his prosperity he *loved the Lord* (1 Ki. 3:3) he thus *served him with joyfulness and gladness of heart in the abundance of all things.* It may be rendered, *The song of songs, which is concerning Solomon,* who as the son and successor of David, on whom the covenant of royalty was entailed, as the founder of the temple, and as one that excelled in wisdom and wealth, was a type of Christ, in whom are *hidden all the treasures of wisdom and knowledge,* and yet is a greater than Solomon; this is therefore a song concerning him. It is here fitly placed after *Ecclesiastes;* for when by the book we are thoroughly convinced of the vanity of the creature, and its insufficiency to satisfy us and make a happiness for us, we shall be quickened to seek for happiness in the love of Christ, and that true transcendent pleasure which is to be found only in communion with God through him. The voice in the wilderness, that was to prepare Christ's way, cried, *All flesh is grass.*

Verses 2–6

The spouse, in this dramatic poem, is here first introduced addressing herself to the bridegroom and then to the daughters of Jerusalem.

I. To the bridegroom, not giving him any name or title, but beginning abruptly: *Let him kiss me;* like Mary Magdalen to the supposed gardener (Jn. 20:15), *If thou have borne him hence,* meaning Christ, but not naming him. The heart has been before taken up with the thoughts of him, and to this relative those thoughts were the antecedent, that good matter which the heart was inditing, Ps. 45:1. Those that are full of Christ themselves are ready to think that others should be so too. Two things the spouse desires, and pleases herself with the thoughts of: —

1. The bridegroom's friendship (*v.* 2): *"Let him kiss me with the kisses of his mouth,* that is, be reconciled to me, and let me know that he is so; let me have the token of his favour." Thus the Old-Testament church desired Christ's manifesting himself in the flesh, to be no longer under the law as a schoolmaster, under a dispensation of bondage and terror, but to receive the communications of divine grace in the gospel, in which God is reconciling the world unto himself, binding up and healing what by the law was torn and smitten; as the mother kisses the child that she has chidden. "Let him no longer send to me, but come himself, no longer speak by angels and prophets, but let me have the word of his own mouth, those *gracious words* (Lu. 4:22), which will be to me as the *kisses of the mouth,* sure tokens of reconciliation, as Esau's kissing Jacob was." All gospel duty is summed up in our kissing the Son (Ps. 2:12); so all gospel-grace is summed up in his kissing us, as the father of the prodigal kissed him when he returned a penitent. It is a kiss of peace. Kisses are opposed to wounds (Prov. 27:6), so are the kisses of grace to the wounds of the law. Thus all true believers earnestly desire the manifestations of Christ's love to their souls; they desire no more to make them happy than the assurance of his favour, the lifting up of the light of his countenance upon them (Ps. 4:6, 7), and the knowledge of that love of his which surpasses knowledge; this is the one thing they desire, Ps. 27:4. They are ready to welcome the manifestation of Christ's love to their souls by his Spirit, and to return them in the humble professions of love to him and complacency in him, above all. *The fruit of his lips is peace,* Isa. 57:19. "Let him give me ten thousand kisses whose very fruition makes me desire him more, and, whereas all other pleasures sour and wither by using, those of the Spirit become more delightful." So bishop Reynolds. She gives several reasons for this desire. (1.) Because of the great esteem she has for his love: *Thy love is better than wine.* Wine *makes glad the heart,* revives the drooping spirits, and exhilarates them, but gracious souls take more pleasure in loving Christ and being beloved of him, in the fruits and gifts of his love and in the pledges and assurances of it, than any man ever took in the most exquisite delights of sense, and it is more reviving to them than ever the richest cordial was to one ready to faint. Note, [1.] Christ's love is in itself, and in the account of all the saints, more valuable and desirable than the best entertainments this world can give. [2.] Those only may expect the kisses of Christ's mouth, and the comfortable tokens of his favour, who prefer his love before all delights of the children of men, who would rather forego those delights than forfeit his favour, and take more pleasure in spiritual joys than in any bodily refreshments whatsoever. Observe here the change of the person: *Let him kiss me;* there she speaks of him as absent, or as if she were afraid to speak to him; but, in the next words, she sees him near at hand, and therefore directs her speech to him: *"Thy love, thy loves"* (so the word is), "I so earnestly desire, because I highly esteem it." (2.) Because of the diffuse fragrancy of his love and the fruits of it (*v.* 3): *"Because of the savour of thy good ointment* (the agreeableness and acceptableness of thy graces and comforts to all that rightly understand both them and themselves), *thy name is as ointment poured forth,* thou art so, and all that whereby thou hast made thyself known; thy very name is precious to all the saints; it is an ointment and perfume which rejoice the heart." The unfolding of Christ's name is as the opening of a box of precious ointment, which the room is filled with the odour of. The preaching of his gospel was the *manifesting the savour of his knowledge in every place,* 2 Co. 2:14. The Spirit was the *oil of gladness* wherewith Christ was anointed (Heb. 1:9), and all true believers have that *unction* (1 Jn. 2:27), so that he is precious to them, and they to him and to one another. *A good name* is *as precious ointment,* but Christ's name is more fragrant than any other. Wisdom, like oil, *makes the face to shine;* but the Redeemer outshines, in beauty, all others. The name of Christ is not now like ointment sealed up, as it had been long *(Ask not after my name, for it is secret),* but like *ointment poured forth,* which denotes both the freeness and fulness of the communications of his grace by the gospel. (3.) Because of the general affection that all holy souls have to him: *Therefore do the virgins love thee.* It is *Christ's love shed abroad in our hearts* that draws them out in love to him; all that are pure from the corruptions of sin, that preserve the chastity of their own spirits, and are true to the vows by which they have devoted themselves to God, that not only suffer not their affections to be violated but cannot bear so much as to be solicited by the world and the flesh, those are the virgins that love Jesus Christ and *follow him whithersoever he goes,* Rev. 14:4. And, because Christ is the darling of all the *pure in heart,* let him be ours, and let our desires be towards him and towards the *kisses of his mouth.*

2. The bridegroom's fellowship, *v.* 4. Observe here,

(1.) Her petition for divine grace: *Draw me.* This implies sense of distance from him, desire of union with him. "Draw me to thyself, draw me nearer, draw me home to thee." She had prayed that he would draw nigh to her (*v.* 2); in order to that, she prays that he would draw her nigh to him. *"Draw me,* not only with the moral suasion which there is in the fragrancy of the good ointments, not only with the attractives of that name which is as ointment poured forth, but with supernatural grace, with the *cords of a man* and the *bands of love,"* Hos. 11:4. Christ has told us that none come to him but such as the Father draws, Jn. 6:44. We are not only weak, and cannot come of ourselves any further than we are helped, but we are naturally backward and averse to come, and therefore must pray for those influences and operations of the Spirit, by the power of which we are unwilling made willing, Ps. 110:3. *"Draw me,* else I move not; overpower the world and the flesh that would draw me from thee." We are not driven to Christ, but drawn in such a way as is agreeable to rational creatures.

(2.) Her promise to improve that grace: *Draw me,* and then *we will run after thee.* See how the doctrine of special and effectual grace consists with our duty, and is a powerful engagement and encouragement to it, and yet reserves all the glory of all the good that is in us to God only. Observe, [1.] The flowing forth of the soul after Christ, and its ready compliance with him, are the effect of his grace; we could not run after him if he did not draw us, 2 Co. 3:5; Phil. 4:13. [2.] The grace which God gives us we must diligently improve. When Christ by his Spirit draws us we must with our spirits run after him. As God says, *I will,* and *you shall* (Eze. 36:27), so we must say, *"Thou shalt* and *we will;* thou shalt *work in us both to will and to do,* and therefore we will work out our own salvation" (Phil. 2:12, 13); not only we will walk, but we will run after thee, which denotes eagerness of desire, readiness of affection, vigour of pursuit, and swiftness of motion. *When thou shalt enlarge my heart* then *I will run the way of thy* commandments (Ps. 119:32); when *thy right hand upholds me* then *my soul follows hard after thee* (Ps. 63:8); when with lovingkindness to us he draws us (Jer. 31:3) we with lovingkindness to him must run after him, Isa. 40:31. Observe the difference between the petition and the promise: "Draw me, and then we will run." When Christ pours out his Spirit upon the church in general, which is his bride, all the members of it do thence receive enlivening quickening influences, and are made to run to him with the more cheerfulness, Isa. 55:5. Or, "Draw me" (says the believing soul) "and then I will not only follow thee myself as fast as I can, but will bring all mine along with me: *We will run after thee,* I and the *virgins that love thee* (v. 3), I and all that I have any interest in or influence upon, *I and my house* (Jos. 24:15), I and the *transgressors whom I will teach thy ways,*" Ps. 51:13. Those that put themselves forth, in compliance with divine grace, shall find that their *zeal will provoke many,* 2 Co. 9:2. Those that are lively will be active; when Philip was drawn to Christ he drew Nathanael; and they will be exemplary, and so will win those that would not be won by the word.

(3.) The immediate answer that was given to this prayer: *The King has* drawn me, has *brought me into his chambers.* It is not so much an answer fetched by faith from the world of Christ's grace as an answer fetched by experience from the workings of his grace. If we observe, as we ought, the returns of prayer, we may find that sometimes, *while we are yet speaking,* Christ hears, Isa. 65:24. The bridegroom is a king; so much the more wonderful is his condescension in the invitations and entertainments that he gives us, and so much the greater reason have we to accept of them and to *run after him.* God is the King that has made the *marriage-supper* for his Son (Mt. 22:2) and brings in even *the poor and the maimed,* and even the most shy and bashful are *compelled to come in.* Those that are drawn to Christ are brought, not only into his courts, into his palaces (Ps. 45:15), but into his presence-chamber, where his secret is with them (Jn. 14:21), and where they are safe in his pavilion, Ps. 27:5; Isa. 26:20. Those that *wait at wisdom's gates* shall be *made to come* (so the word is) *into her chambers;* they shall be led into truth and comfort.

(4.) The wonderful complacency which the spouse takes in the honour which the king put upon her. Being *brought into the chamber,* [1.] "We have what we would have. Our desires are crowned with unspeakable delights; all our griefs vanish, and *we will be glad and rejoice.* If *a day in the courts,* much more an hour in the chambers, *is better than a thousand,* than ten thousand, elsewhere." Those that are, through grace, brought into covenant and communion with God, have reason to *go on their way rejoicing,* as the eunuch (Acts 8:39), and that joy will enlarge our hearts and be our strength, Neh. 8:10. [2.] All our joy shall centre in God: "*We will rejoice,* not in the ointments, or the chambers, but *in thee.* It is God only that is our *exceeding joy,* Ps. 43:4. We have no joy but in Christ, and which we are indebted to him for." *Gaudium in Domino — Joy in the Lord,* was the ancient salutation, and *Salus in Domino sempiterna — Eternal salvation in the Lord.* [3.] "We will retain the relish and savour of this kindness of thine and never forget it: *We will remember thy loves more than wine;* no only thy love itself (v. 2), but the very remembrance of it shall be more grateful to us than the strongest cordial to the spirits, or the most palatable liquor to the taste. We will remember to give thanks for thy love, and it shall make more durable impressions upon us than any thing in this world."

(5.) The communion which a gracious soul has with all the saints in this communion with Christ. In the chambers to which we are brought we not only meet with him, but meet with one another (1 Jn. 1:7); for *the upright love thee;* the congregation, the generation, of the *upright love thee.* Whatever others do, all that are Israelites indeed, and faithful to God, will love Jesus Christ. Whatever differences of apprehension and affection there may be among Christians in other things, this they are all agreed in, Jesus Christ is precious to them. *The upright* here are the same with the *virgins, v.* 3. All that *remember his love more than wine* will love him with a superlative love. Nor is any love acceptable to Christ but the love of *the upright,* love in sincerity, Eph. 6:24.

II. To *the daughters of Jerusalem, v.* 5, 6. The church

in general, being in distress, speaks to particular churches to guard them against the danger they were in of being offended at the church's sufferings, 1 Th. 3:3. Or the believer speaks to those that were professors at large in the church, but not of it, or to weak Christians, babes in Christ, that labour under much ignorance, infirmity, and mistake, not perfectly instructed, and yet willing to be taught in the things of God. She observed these by-standers look disdainfully upon her because of her blackness, in respect both of sins and sufferings, upon the account of which they though she had little reason to expect the kisses she wished for (v. 2) or to expect that they should join with her in her joys, v. 4. She therefore endeavors to remove this offence; she owns she is *black.* Guilt blackens; the heresies, scandals, and offences, that happen in the church, make her *black;* and the best saints have their failings. Sorrow blackens; that seems to be especially meant; the church is often in a low condition, mean, and poor, and in appearance despicable, her beauty sullied and her face foul with weeping; she is in mourning weeds, clothed with sackcloth, as the Nazarites that had become *blacker than a coal,* Lam. 4:8. Now, to take off this offence,

1. She asserts her own comeliness notwithstanding (v. 5): *I am black, but comely,* black *as the tents of Kedar,* in which the shepherds lived, which were very coarse, and never whitened, weather-beaten and discoloured by long use, but comely *as the curtains of Solomon,* the furniture of whose rooms, no doubt, was sumptuous and rich, in proportion to the stateliness of his houses. The church is sometimes *black* with persecution, *but comely* in patience, constancy, and consolation, and never the less amiable in the eyes of Christ, *black in the account of men, but comely* in God's esteem, *black* in some that are a scandal to her, *but comely* in others that are sincere and are an honour to her. True believers are *black* in themselves, *but comely* in Christ, with the comeliness that he puts upon them, *black* outwardly, for *the world knows them not,* but *all glorious within,* Ps. 45:13. St. Paul was *weak,* and yet *strong,* 2 Co. 12:10. And so the church is *black* and yet *comely;* a believer is a sinner and yet a saint; his own righteousnesses are *as filthy rags,* but he is clothed with the robe of Christ's righteousness. The Chaldee Paraphrase applies it to the people of Israel's blackness when they made the golden calf and their comeliness when they repented of it.

2. She gives an account how she came to be so black. The blackness was not natural, but contracted, and was owing to the hard usage that had been given her: *Look not upon me* so scornfully *because I am black.* We must take heed with what eye we look upon the church, especially when she is in black. *Thou shouldst not have looked upon the day of thy brother,* the day of his affliction, Obad. 12. Be not offended; for,

(1.) *I am black* by reason of my sufferings: *The sun has looked upon me.* She was fair and comely; whiteness was her proper colour; but she got this blackness by *the burden and heat of the day,* which she was forced to bear. She was sun-burnt, scorched with tribulation and persecution (Mt. 13:6, 21); and the greatest beauties, if exposed to the weather, are soonest tanned. Observe how she mitigates her troubles; she does not say, as Jacob (Gen. 31:40), *In the day the drought consumed me,* but, *The sun has looked upon me;* for it becomes not God's suffering people to make the worst of their sufferings. But what was the matter? [1.] She fell under the displeasure of those of her own house: *My mother's children were angry with me.* She was *in perils by false brethren;* her foes were *those of her own house* (Mt. 10:36), brethren by nature as men, by profession as members of the same sacred corporation, the children of the church her mother, but not of God her Father; they *were angry with* her. The Samaritans, who claimed kindred to the Jews, were vexed at any thing that tended to the prosperity of Jerusalem, Neh. 2:10. Note, It is no new thing for the people of God to fall under the anger of their own mother's children. *It was thou, a man, my equal,* Ps. 55:12, 13. This makes the trouble the more irksome and grievous; from such it is taken unkindly, and the anger of such is implacable. *A brother offended is hard to be won.* [2.] They dealt very hardly with her: *They made me the keeper of the vineyards,* that is, *First,* "They seduced me to sin, drew me into false worships, to serve their gods, which was like dressing the vineyards, *keeping the vine of Sodom;* and they would not let me *keep my own vine-*

yard, serve my own God, and observe those pure worships which he gave me in charge, and which I do and ever will own for mine." These are grievances which good people complain most of in a time of persecution, that their consciences are forced, and that those who rule them with rigour say *to their souls, Bow down, that we may go over,* Isa. 51:23. Or, *Secondly,* "They brought me into trouble, imposed that upon me which was toilsome, and burdensome, and very disgraceful." Keeping the vineyards was base servile work, and very laborious, Isa. 61:5. Her mother's children made her the drudge of the family. *Cursed be their anger, for it was fierce, and their wrath, for it was cruel.* The spouse of Christ has met with a great deal of hard usage.

(2.) "My sufferings are such as I have deserved; for *my own vineyard have I not kept.* How unrighteous soever my brethren are in persecuting me, God is righteous in permitting them to do so. I am justly made a slavish keeper of men's vineyards, because I have been a careless keeper of the vineyards God has entrusted me with." Slothful servants of God are justly made to serve their enemies, *that they may know his service, and the service of the kings of the countries,* 2 Chr. 12:8; Deu. 28:47, 48; Eze. 20:23, 24. "Think not the worse of the ways of God for my sufferings, for I smart for my own folly." Note, When God's people are oppressed and persecuted it becomes them to acknowledge their own sin to be the procuring cause of their troubles, especially their carelessness in keeping their vineyards, so that it has been like *the field of the slothful.*

Verses 7–11

Here is, I. The humble petition which the spouse presents to her beloved, the shepherdess to the shepherd, the church and every believer to Christ, for a more free and intimate communion with him. She turns from the *daughters of Jerusalem,* to whom she had complained both of her sins and of her troubles, and looks up to heaven for relief and succour against both, *v.* 7. Here observe, 1. The title she gives to Christ: *O thou whom my soul loveth.* Note, It is the undoubted character of all true believers that their souls love Jesus Christ, which intimates both the sincerity and the strength of their love; they *love him with all their hearts;* and those that do so may come to him boldly and may humbly plead it with him. 2. The opinion she has of him as the good shepherd of the sheep; she doubts not but he *feeds his flock* and *makes them rest at noon.* Jesus Christ graciously provides both repast and repose for his sheep; they are not starved, but well fed, not scattered upon the mountains, but fed together, fed *in green pastures* and in the hot time of the day *led by the still waters* and made to lie down under a cool refreshing shade. Is it with God's people a noon-time of outward troubles, inward conflicts? Christ has rest for them; he *carries them in his arms,* Isa. 40:11. 3. Her request to him that she might be admitted into his society: *Tell me where thou feedest.* Those that would be told, that would be taught, what they are concerned to know and do, must apply to Jesus Christ, and beg of him to teach them, to tell them. "Tell me where to find thee, where I may have conversation with thee, *where thou feedest* and tendest thy flock, that there I may have some of my company." Observe, by the way, We should not, in love to our friends and their company, tempt them or urge them to neglect their business, but desire such an enjoyment of them as will consist with it, and rather, if we can, to join with them in their business and help to forward it. "*Tell me where thou feedest,* and there I will sit with thee, walk with thee, feed my flocks with thine, and not hinder thee nor myself, but bring my work with me." Note, Those whose souls love Jesus Christ earnestly desire to have communion with him, by his word in which he speaks to us and by prayer in which we speak to him, and to share in the privileges of his flock; and we may learn from the care he takes of his church, to provide convenient food and rest for it, how to take care of our own souls, which are our charge. 4. The plea she uses for the enforcing of this request: "*For why should I be as one that turns aside by* (or after) *the flocks of thy companions,* that pretend to be so, but are really thy competitors, and rivals with thee." Note, Turning aside from Christ after other lovers is that which gracious souls dread, and deprecate, more than any thing else. "Thou wouldst not have me to *turn aside,* no, nor to *be as one that turns aside; tell me* then,

O tell me, where I may be near thee, and I will never leave thee." (1.) "*Why should I* lie under suspicion, and look as if I belonged to some other and not to thee? *Why should I be* thought *by the flocks of our companions* to be a deserter from thee, and a retainer to some other shepherd?" Good Christians will be afraid of giving any occasion to those about them to question their faith in Christ and their love to him; they would not do any thing that looks like unconcernedness about their souls; or uncharitableness towards their brethren, or that savours of indifference and disaffection to holy ordinances; and we should pray to God to direct us into and keep us in the way of our duty, that we may not so much as *seem to come short,* Heb. 4:1. (2.) "*Why should I* lie in temptation to *turn aside,* as I do while I am absent from thee?" We should be earnest with God for a settled peace in communion with God through Christ, that we may not be as waifs and strays, ready to be picked up by him that next passes by.

II. The gracious answer which the bridegroom gives to this request, *v.* 8. See how ready God is to answer prayer, especially prayers for instruction; even while she is yet speaking, he hears. Observe, 1. How affectionately he speaks to her: *O thou fairest among women!* Note, Believing souls are fair, in the eyes of the Lord Jesus, above any other. Christ sees a beauty in holiness, whether we do or no. The spouse has called herself black, but Christ calls her fair. Those that are low in their own eyes are so much the more amiable in the eyes of Jesus Christ. Blushing at their own deformity (says Mr. Durham) is a chief part of their beauty. 2. How mildly he checks her for her ignorance, in these words, *If thou know not,* intimating that she might have known it if it had not been her own fault. What! dost thou not know where to find me and my flock? Compare Christ's answer to a like address of Philip's (Jn. 14:9), *Have I been so long time with you, and yet hast thou not known me, Philip?* But, 3. With what tenderness he acquaints her where she might find him. If men say, *Lo, here is Christ, or, Lo, he is there, believe them not, go not after them,* Mt. 24:23, 26. But, (1.) *Walk in the way of good men* (Prov. 2:20), follow the track, ask for the good old way, observe *the footsteps of the flock,* and *go forth by* them. It will not serve to sit still and cry, "Lord, show me the way," but we must bestir ourselves to enquire out the way; and we may find it by looking which way *the footsteps of the flock* lead, what has been the practice of godly people all along; let that practice be ours, Heb. 6:12; 1 Co. 11:1. (2.) Sit under the direction of good ministers: "*Feed* thyself *and thy kids besides the tents of the under-shepherds.* Bring thy charge with thee" (it is probable that the custom was to commit the lambs and kids to the custody of the women, the shepherdesses); "they shall all be welcome; *the shepherds* will be no hindrance to thee, as they were to Reuel's daughters (Ex. 2:17), but helpers rather, and therefore abide by their tents." Note, Those that would have acquaintance and communion with Christ must closely and conscientiously adhere to holy ordinances, must join themselves to his people and attend his ministers. Those that have the charge of families must bring them with them to religious assemblies; let their *kids,* their children, their servants, have the benefit of *the shepherds' tents.*

III. The high encomiums which the bridegroom gives of his spouse. To be *given in marriage,* in the Hebrew dialect, is to be *praised* (Ps. 78:63, margin), so this spouse is here; her *husband praises* this *virtuous woman* (Prov. 31:28); he praises her, as is usual in poems, by similitudes. 1. He calls her his *love* (*v.* 9); it is an endearing compellation often used in this book: "My friend, my companion, my familiar." 2. He compares her to a set of strong and stately *horses in Pharaoh's chariots.* Egypt was famous for the best horses. Solomon had his thence; and Pharaoh, no doubt, had the choicest the country afforded for his own chariots. The church had complained of her own weakness, and the danger she was in of being made a prey of by her enemies: "Fear not," says Christ; "*I have made thee like a company of horses;* I have put strength into thee as I have done into *the horse* (Job 39:19), so that thou shalt with a gracious boldness *mock at fear, and not be affrighted,* like *the lion,* Prov. 28:1. *The Lord has made thee as his goodly horse in the day of battle,* Zec. 10:3. *I have compared thee to my company of horses* which triumphed over *Pharaoh's chariots,* the holy angels, *horses of fire.*" Hab. 3:15, *Thou didst walk through the sea with thy horses;* and see Isa. 63:13. We are weak in ourselves, but if Christ make us as horses, strong and bold, we need not fear what all the powers of darkness can do against us. 3. He admires the beauty and ornaments of her countenance (*v.* 10): *Thy cheeks are comely with rows of jewels,* the attire of the head, curls of hair, or favourites (so some), or knots of ribbons; *thy neck also with chains,* such as persons of the first rank wear, *chains of gold.* The ordinances of Christ are the ornaments of the church. The graces, gifts, and comforts of the Spirit, are the adorning of every believing soul, and beautify it; these render it, *in the sight of God, of great price.* The ornaments of the saints are many, but all orderly disposed in *rows* and *chains,* in which there is a mutual connexion with and dependence upon each other. The beauty is not from any thing in themselves, from the *neck* or from the *cheeks,* but from ornaments with which they are set off. It was *comeliness which I put upon thee, said the Lord God;* for we were born not only naked, but polluted, Eze. 16:14.

IV. His gracious purpose to add to her ornaments; for where God has given true grace he will give more grace; *to him that has shall be given.* Is the church courageous in her resistance of sin, as the *horses in Pharaoh's chariots?* Is she *comely* in the exercise of grace, as *with rows of jewels* and *chains of gold?* She shall be yet further beautified (*v.* 11): *We will make thee borders of gold,* inlaid, or enamelled, *with studs of silver.* Whatever is wanting shall be made up, till the church and every true believer come to be *perfect in beauty;* see Eze. 16:14. This is here undertaken to be done by the concurring power of the three persons in the Godhead: *We will* do it; like that (Gen. 1:26), "*Let us make man;* so let us new-make him, and perfect his beauty." The same that is the author will be the finisher of the good work; and it cannot miscarry.

Verses 12–17

Here the conference is carried on between Christ and his spouse, and endearments are mutually exchanged.

I. Believers take a great complacency in Christ, and in communion with him. *To you that believe he is precious,* above any thing in this world, 1 Pt. 2:7. Observe,

1. The humble reverence believers have for Christ as their Sovereign, *v.* 12. He is a *King* in respect both of dignity and dominion; he wears the crown of honour, he bears the sceptre of power, both which are the unspeakable satisfaction of all his people. This King has his royal table spread in the gospel, in which is *made for all nations a feast of fat things,* Isa. 25:6. Wisdom has *furnished her table,* Prov. 9:1. He *sits at this table* to *see his guests* (Mt. 22:11), to see that nothing be wanting that is fit for them; he *sups with them* and *they with him* (Rev. 3:20); he has fellowship with them and rejoices in them; he *sits at his table* to bid them welcome, and to carve for them, as Christ *broke the five loaves* and gave to his disciples, that they might distribute to the multitude. He sits there to receive petitions, as Ahasuerus admitted Esther's petition at *the banquet of wine.* He has promised to be present with his people in his ordinances always. Then believers do him all the honour they can, and study how to express their esteem of him and gratitude to him, as Mary did when she anointed his head with *the ointment of spikenard* that was *very costly,* one pound of it worth *three hundred pence,* and so fragrant that *the house was filled with the pleasing odour of it* (Jn. 12:3), which story seems as if it were designed to refer to this passage, for Christ was then *sitting at table.* When good Christians, in any religious duty, especially in the ordinance of the Lord's supper, where the King is pleased, as it were, to *sit* with us *at his* own *table,* have their graces exercised, their hearts broken by repentance, healed by faith, and inflamed with holy love and desires toward Christ, with joyful expectations of the glory to be revealed, then the *spikenard sends forth the smell thereof.* Christ is pleased to reckon himself honoured by it, and to accept of it as an instance of respect to him, as it was in the wise men of the east, who paid their homage to the new-born King of the Jews by presenting to him *frankincense and myrrh.* The graces of God's Spirit in the hearts of believers are exceedingly precious in themselves and pleasing to Christ, and his presence in ordinances draws them out into act and exercise. If he withdraw, graces wither and languish, as plants in the absence of the sun; if he approach, the face of the soul is renewed, as of the earth in the spring; and then it is time to bestir ourselves, that we may not lose the gleam, not lose the gale; for nothing is done acceptably but what grace does, Heb. 12:28.

2. The strong affection they have for Christ as their *beloved,* their *well-beloved, v.* 13. Christ is not only *beloved* by all believing souls, but is their *well-beloved,* their best-beloved, their only beloved; he has that place in their hearts which no rival can be admitted to, the innermost and uppermost place. Observe, (1.) How Christ is accounted of by all believers: He is *a bundle of myrrh* and *a cluster of camphire,* something, we may be sure, nay, every thing, that is pleasant and delightful. The doctrine of his gospel, and the comforts of his Spirit, are very refreshing to them, and they rest in his love; none of all the delights of sense are comparable to the spiritual pleasure they have in meditating on Christ and enjoying him. There is a complicated sweetness in Christ and an abundance of it; there is *a bundle of myrrh* and *a cluster of camphire.* We are not straitened in him whom there is *all fulness.* The word translated *camphire* is *copher,* the same word that signifies *atonement* or *propitiation.* Christ is *a cluster* of merit and righteousness to all believers; *therefore* he is dear to them because *he is the propitiation for their sins.* Observe what stress the spouse lays upon the application: He *is unto me,* and again *unto me,* all that is sweet; whatever he is to others, he is so *to me.* He *loved me, and gave himself for me.* He *is my Lord, and my God.* (2.) How he is accepted: *He shall lie all night between my breasts,* near my heart. Christ lays the beloved disciples in his bosom; why then should not they lay their beloved Saviour in their bosoms? Why should not they embrace him with both arms, and hold him fast, with a resolution never to let him go? Christ must *dwell in the heart* (Eph. 3:17), and, in order to that, the adulteries must be put from *between the breasts* (Hos. 2:2), no pretender must have his place in the soul. He shall be as *a bundle of myrrh,* or perfume bag, between *my breasts,* always sweet to me; or his effigies in miniature, his love-tokens, shall be hung between *my breasts,* according to the custom of those that are dear to each other. He shall not only be laid their for a while, but shall lie there, shall abide there.

II. Jesus Christ has a great complacency in his church and in every true believer; they are amiable in his eyes (*v.* 15): *Behold, thou art fair, my love;* and again, *Behold, thou art fair.* He says this, not to make her proud (humility is one principal ingredient in spiritual beauty), but, 1. To show that there is a real beauty in holiness, that all who are sanctified are thereby beautified; they are truly fair. 2. That he takes great delight in that good work which his grace has wrought on the souls of believers; so that though they have their infirmities, whatever they think of themselves, and the world thinks of them, he thinks them fair. He calls them friends. The *hidden man of the heart, in that which is not corruptible, is in the sight of God of great price,* 1 Pt. 3:4. 3. To comfort weak believers, who are discouraged by their own blackness; let them be told again and again that they are fair. 4. To engage all who are sanctified to be very thankful for that grace which has made them fair, who by nature were deformed, and changed the Ethiopian's skin. One instance of the beauty of the spouse is here mentioned, that she *has doves' eyes,* as *ch.* 4:1. Those are fair, in Christ's account, who have, not the piercing eye of the eagle, but the pure and chaste eye of the *dove,* not like the hawk, who, when he soars upwards, still has his eye upon the prey on earth, but a humble modest eye, such an eye as discovers a simplicity and godly sincerity and a dove-like innocency, eyes enlightened and guided by the Holy Spirit, that blessed Dove, weeping eyes. I did *mourn as a dove,* Eze. 7:16.

III. The church expresses her value for Christ, and returns esteem (*v.* 16): *Behold, thou art fair.* See how Christ and believers praise one another. Israel saith of God, *Who is like thee?* Ex. 15:11. And God saith of Israel, *Who is like thee?* Deu. 33:29. Lord, saith the church, "Dost thou call me *fair?* No; if we speak of strength, *thou art strong* (Job 9:19), so, if of beauty, *thou art fair.* I am fair no otherwise than as I have thy image stamped upon me. Thou art the great Original; I am but a faint and imperfect copy, I am but thy *umbra — the shadow of thee,* Jn. 1:16; 3:34. Thou art fair in thyself and (which is more) *pleasant* to all that are thine. Many are fair enough to look at, and yet the sourness of their temper renders them unpleasant; but *thou art fair, yea, pleasant.*" Christ is pleasant, as he is ours, in covenant with us, in relation to us. "Thou art pleasant now, when the *King sits at his table.*" Christ is always precious to believers, but in a special manner pleasant when they are admitted into communion with him, when they hear his voice, and see his face, and taste his love. *It is good to be here.* Having expressed her esteem of her husband's person, she next, like a loving spouse, that is transported with joy for having disposed of herself so well, applauds the accommodations he had for her entertainment, his *bed,* his *house,* his *rafters* or *galleries* (*v.* 16), which may be fitly applied to those holy ordinances in which believers have fellowship with Jesus Christ, receive the tokens of his love and return their pious and devout affections to him, increase their acquaintance with him and improve their advantages by him. Now, 1. These she calls *ours,* Christ and believers having a joint-interest in them. As husband and wife are *heirs together* (1 Pt. 3:7), so believers are *joint-heirs with Christ,* Rom. 8:17. They are his institutions and their privileges; in them Christ and believers meet. She does not call them *mine,* for a believer will own nothing as his but what Christ shall have an interest in, nor *thine,* for Christ has said, *All that I have is thine,* Lu. 15:31. All is *ours* if we are Christ's. Those that can by faith lay claim to Christ may lay claim to all that is his. 2. These are the best of the kind. Does the colour of the bed, and the furniture belonging to it, help to set it off? *Our bed is green,* a colour which, in a pastoral, is preferred before any other, because it is the colour of the fields and groves where the shepherd's business and delight are. It is a refreshing colour, good for the eyes; and it denotes fruitfulness. *I am like a green olive-tree,* Ps. 52:8. We are *married* to Christ, *that we should bring forth unto God,* Rom. 7:4. *The beams of our house are cedar* (*v.* 17), which probably refers to the temple Solomon had lately built for communion between God and Israel, which was of *cedar,* a strong sort of wood, sweet, durable, and which will never rot, typifying the firmness and continuance of the church, the gospel-temple. The galleries for walking are *of fir,* or *cypress,* some sort of wood that was pleasing both to the sight and to the smell, intimating the delight which the saints take in walking with Christ and conversing with him. Every thing in the covenant of grace (on which foot all their treaties are carried on) is very firm, very fine, and very fragrant.

CHAPTER 2

In this chapter, I. Christ speaks both concerning himself and concerning his church (*v.* 1, 2). II. The church speaks 1. Remembering the pleasure and satisfaction she has in communion with Christ (*v.* 3, 4). 2. Entertaining herself with the present tokens of his favour and taking care that nothing happen to intercept them (*v.* 5–7). 3. Triumphing in his approaches towards her (*v.* 8, 9). 4. Repeating the gracious calls he had given her to go along with him a walking, invited by the pleasures of the returning spring (*v.* 10–13), out of her obscurity (*v.* 14), and the charge he had given to the servants to destroy that which would be hurtful to his vineyard (*v.* 15). 5. Rejoicing in her interest in him (*v.* 16). 6. Longing for his arrival (*v.* 17). Those whose hearts are filled with love to Christ, and hope of heaven, know best what these things mean.

Verses 1–2

See here, I. What Christ is pleased to compare himself to; and he condescends very much in the comparison. He that is the Son of the Highest, the bright and morning star, calls and owns himself *the rose of Sharon, and the lily of the valleys,* to express his presence with his people in this world, the easiness of their access to him, and the beauty and sweetness which they find in him, and to teach them to adorn themselves with him, as shepherds and shepherdesses, when they appeared gay, were decked with roses and lilies, garlands and chaplets of flowers. *The rose,* for beauty and fragrance, is the chief of flowers, and our Saviour prefers the clothing of *the lily* before that of *Solomon in all his glory.* Christ is *the rose of Sharon,* where probably the best roses grew and in most plenty, *the rose of the field* (so some), denoting that the gospel salvation is a common salvation; it lies open to all; whoever will may come and gather the rose-buds of privileges and comforts that grow in the covenant of grace. He is not a rose locked up in a garden, but all may come and receive benefit by him and comfort in him. He is a *lily* for whiteness, a *lily of the valleys* for sweetness, for those which we call so yield a strong perfume. He is a *lily of the valleys,* or *low places,* in his humiliation, exposed to injury. Humble souls see most beauty in him. Whatever he is to others, to those that

are in the *valleys* he is a *lily.* He is the *rose, the lily;* there is none besides. Whatever excellence is in Christ, it is in him singularly and in the highest degree.

II. What he is pleased to compare his church to, *v.* 2. 1. She is *as a lily;* he himself is *the lily* (*v.* 1), she is *as the lily.* The beauty of believers consists in their conformity and resemblance to Jesus Christ. They are his love, and so they are as lilies, for those are made like Christ in whose hearts his *love is shed abroad.* 2. *As a lily among thorns, as a lily* compared with *thorns.* The church of Christ as far excels all other societies as a bed of roses excels a bush of thorns. *As a lily* compassed with *thorns.* The wicked, the *daughters* of this world, such as have no love to Christ, are as *thorns,* worthless and useless, good for nothing but to stop a gap; nay, they are noxious and hurtful; they came in with sin and are a fruit of the curse; they choke good seed, and hinder good fruit, and their *end is to be burned.* God's people are *as lilies among* them, scratched and torn, shaded and obscured, by them; they are dear to Christ, and yet exposed to hardships and troubles in the world; they must expect it, for they are planted *among thorns* (Eze. 2:6), but they are nevertheless dear to him; he does not overlook nor undervalue any of his lilies for their being *among thorns,* When they are *among thorns* they must still be *as lilies,* must maintain their innocency and purity, and, though they are *among thorns,* must not be turned into *thorns,* must *not render railing for railing,* and, if they thus preserve their character, they shall be still owned as conformable to Christ. Grace in the soul is a *lily among thorns;* corruptions are *thorns in the flesh* (2 Co. 12:7), are as Canaanites to God's Israel (Jos. 23:13); but *the lily* that is now *among thorns* shall shortly be transplanted out of this wilderness into that paradise where there is no *pricking brier* nor *grieving thorn,* Eze. 28:24.

Verses 3–7

Here, I. The spouse commends her beloved and prefers him before all others: *As the apple-tree among the trees of the wood,* which perhaps does not grow so high, nor spread so wide, as some other trees, yet is useful and serviceable to man, yielding pleasant and profitable fruit, while the other trees are of little use, no, not the cedars themselves, till they are cut down, *so is my beloved among the sons,* so far does he excel them all, — all *the sons of God,* the angels (that honour was put upon him which was never designed for them, Heb. 1:4), — all *the sons of* men; he is *fairer* than them all, fairer than the choicest of them, Ps. 45:2. Name what creature you will, and you will find Christ has the pre-eminence above them all. The world is a barren tree to a soul; Christ is a fruitful one.

II. She remembers the abundant comfort she has had in communion with him: She *sat down* by him *with great delight,* as shepherds sometimes repose themselves, sometimes converse with one another, under a tree. A double advantage she found in sitting down so near the Lord Jesus: — 1. A refreshing shade: *I sat down under his shadow,* to be sheltered by him from the scorching heat of the sun, to be cooled, and so to take some rest. Christ is to believers *as the shadow* of a great tree, nay, *of a great rock in a weary land,* Isa. 32:2; 25:4. When a poor soul is parched with convictions of sin and the terrors of the law, as David (Ps. 32:4), when fatigued with the troubles of this world, as Elijah when he *sat down under a juniper tree* (1 Ki. 19:4), they find that in Christ, in his name, his graces, his comforts, and his undertaking for poor sinners, which revives them and keeps them from fainting; those that *are weary and heavily laden* may find *rest* in Christ. It is not enough to pass by this shadow, but we must *sit down under it (here will I dwell, for I have desired it);* and we shall find it not like Jonah's gourd, that soon withered, and left him in a heat, both inward and outward, but like the tree of life, the leaves whereof were not only for shelter, but for the healing of the nations. We must *sit down under this shadow with delight,* must put an entire confidence in the protection of it (as Judges 9:15), and take an entire complacency in the refreshment of it. But that is not all: 2. Here is pleasing nourishing food. This tree drops its fruits to those that *sit down under its shadow,* and they are welcome to them, and will find them *sweet unto their taste,* whatever they are to others. Believers have tasted that the Lord Jesus is *gracious* (1 Pt. 2:3); his *fruits* are all the precious privileges of the new covenant, purchased by his

blood and communicated by his Spirit. Promises are sweet to a believer, yea, and precepts too. *I delight in the law of God after the inward man.* Pardons are sweet, and peace of conscience is sweet, assurances of God's love, joys of the Holy Ghost, the hopes of eternal life, and the present earnests and foretastes of it are sweet, all sweet to those that have their spiritual senses exercised. If our mouths be put out of taste for the pleasure of sin, divine consolations will be *sweet to our taste, sweeter than honey and the honeycomb.*

III. She owns herself obliged to Jesus Christ for all the benefit and comfort she had in communion with him (*v.* 4): "*I sat down under* the apple-tree, glad to be there, but he admitted me, nay, he pressed me, to a more intimate communion with him: *Come in, thou blessed of the Lord, why standest thou without? He brought me to the house of* wine, the place where he entertains his special friends, from lower to higher measures and degrees of comfort, from the fruit of the *apple tree* to the more generous fruit of the vine." *To him that* values the divine joys he *has more shall be given.* One of the rabbin by *the banqueting-house* understands the *tabernacle of the congregation, where the interpretation of the law was given;* surely we may apply it to Christian assemblies, where the gospel is preached and gospel-ordinances are administered, particularly the Lord's supper, that *banquet of wine,* especially to the inside of those ordinances, communion with God in them. Observe, 1. How she was introduced: "*He brought me,* wrought in me an inclination to draw nigh to God, helped me over my discouragements, took me by the hand, guided and led me, and gave me an *access* with boldness to God as a *Father,*" Eph. 2:18. We should never have come *into the banqueting-house,* never have been acquainted with spiritual pleasures, if Christ had not brought us, by opening for us a new and living way and opening in us a new and living fountain. 2. How she was entertained: *His banner over me was love; he brought me* in with a banner displayed over my head, not as one he triumphed over, but as one he triumphed in, and whom he always caused to triumph with him and in him, 2 Co. 2:14. The gospel is compared to a *banner* or *ensign* (Isa. 11:12), and that which is represented in the banner, written in it in letters of gold, letters of blood, is *love, love;* and this is the entertainment in *the banqueting-house.* Christ is the *captain of our salvation,* and he enlists all his soldiers under the *banner of love;* in that they centre; to that they must continually have an eye, and be animated by it. *The love of Christ* must *constrain* them to fight manfully. When a city was taken the conqueror set up his standard in it. "He has conquered me with his love, overcome me with kindness, and that is the *banner over me.*" This she speaks of as what she had formerly had experience of, and she remembers it with delight. Eaten bread must not be forgotten, but remembered with thankfulness to that God who has fed us with manna in this wilderness.

IV. She professes her strong affection and most passionate love to Jesus Christ (*v.* 5): *I am sick of love,* overcome, overpowered, by it. David explains this when he says (Ps. 119:20), *My soul breaks for the longing that it has unto thy judgments,* and (*v.* 81), *My soul faints for thy salvation,* languishing with care to make it sure and fear of coming short of it. The spouse was now absent perhaps from her beloved, waiting for his return, and cannot bear the grief of distance and delay. Oh how much better it is with the soul when it is *sick of love* to Christ than when it is surfeited with the love of this world! She cries out for cordials: "Oh *stay me with flagons,* or *ointments,* or *flowers,* any thing that is reviving; *comfort me with apples,* with the fruits of that *apple-tree,* Christ (*v.* 3), with the merit and meditation of Christ and the sense of his love to my soul." Note, Those that are *sick of love* to Christ shall not want spiritual supports, while they are yet waiting for spiritual comforts.

V. She experiences the power and tenderness of divine grace, relieving her in her present faintings, *v.* 6. Though he seemed to have withdrawn, yet he was even then a very present help, 1. To sustain the love-sick soul, and to keep it from fainting away: "*His left hand is under my head,* to bear it up, nay, as a pillow to lay it easy." David experienced God's hand upholding him then when *his soul was following hard after God* (Ps. 63:8), and Job in a state of desertion yet found that God *put strength* into him, Job

23:6. *All his saints are in his hand,* which tenderly holds their aching heads. 2. To encourage the love-sick soul to continue waiting till he returns: "For, in the mean time, *his right hand embraces me,* and thereby gives me an unquestionable assurance of his love." Believers owe all their strength and comfort to the supporting left hand and embracing right hand of the Lord Jesus.

VI. Finding her beloved thus nigh unto her she is in great care that her communion with him be not interrupted (*v.* 7): *I charge you, O you daughters of Jerusalem.* Jerusalem, the mother of us all, charges all her daughters, the church charges all her members, the believing soul charges all its powers and faculties, the spouse charges herself and all about her, not to *stir up, or awake, her love until he please,* now that he is asleep in her arms, as she was borne up in his, *v.* 6. She gives them this charge *by the roes and the hinds of the field,* that is, by every thing that is amiable in their eyes, and dear to them, *as the loving hind and the pleasant roe.* "My love is to me dearer than those can be to you, and will be disturbed, like them, with a very little noise." Note, 1. Those that experience the sweetness of communion with Christ, and the sensible manifestations of his love, cannot but desire the continuance of these blessed views, these blessed visits. Pester would make tabernacles upon the holy mount, Mt. 17:4. 2. Yet Christ will, when he pleases, withdraw those extraordinary communications of himself, for he is a free-agent, and the Spirit, as *the wind, blows where* and when *it listeth,* and in his pleasure it becomes us to acquiesce. But, 3. Our care must be that we do nothing to provoke him to withdraw and to hide his face, that we carefully watch over our own hearts and suppress every thought that may grieve his good Spirit. Let those that have comfort be afraid of sinning it away.

Verses 8–13

The church is here pleasing herself exceedingly with the thoughts of her further communion with Christ after she has recovered from her fainting fit.

I. She rejoices in his approach, *v.* 8. 1. She hears him speak: "It is *the voice of my beloved,* calling me to tell me he is coming." Like one of his own sheep, she *knows his voice* before she sees him, and can easily distinguish it from the *voice of a stranger* (Jn. 10:4, 5), and, like a faithful friend of the bridegroom, she *rejoices greatly because of the bridegroom's voice,* Jn. 3:29. With what an air of triumph and exultation does she cry out, *"It is the voice of my beloved,* it can be the voice of no other, for none besides can speak to the heart and make that burn." 2. She sees him come, sees the goings of *our God, our King,* Ps. 48:24. *Behold, he comes.* This may very well be applied to the prospect with the Old-Testament saints had of Christ's coming in the flesh. *Abraham saw his day* at a distance, *and was glad.* The nearer the time came the clearer discoveries were made of it; and those that waited for the consolation of Israel with an eye of faith saw him come, and triumphed in the sight: *Behold, he comes;* for they had heard him say (Ps. 40:7), *Lo, I come,* to which their faith here affixes its seal: *Behold, he comes* as he has promised. (1.) He comes cheerfully and with great alacrity; he comes leaping and skipping *like a roe* and like *a young hart* (*v.* 9), as one pleased with his own undertaking, and that had his heart upon it and his delights with the sons of men. When he came to be baptized with the baptism of blood, how was he *straitened till it was accomplished!* Lu. 12:50. (2.) He comes slighting and surmounting all the difficulties that lay in his way; he comes *leaping over the mountains, skipping over the hills* (so some read it), making nothing of the discouragements he was to break through; the curse of the law, the death of the cross, must be undergone, all the powers of darkness must be grappled with, but, before the resolutions of his love, these great mountains become plains. Whatever opposition is given at any time to the deliverance of God's church, Christ will break through it, will get over it. (3.) He comes speedily, *like a roe* or *a young hart;* they thought the time long (every day a year), but really he hastened; as now, so then, *surely he comes quickly; he that shall come will come, and will not tarry.* When he comes for the deliverance of his people he *flies upon a cloud,* and never stays beyond his time, which is the best time. We may apply it to particular believers, who find that even when Christ has withdrawn sensible comforts, and seems to forsake, yet it is but for a small moment, and he will soon return with everlasting loving-kindness.

II. She pleases herself with the glimpses she has of him, and the glances she has of his favour: "He *stands behind our wall;* I know he is there, for sometimes *he looks forth at the window,* or *looks in* at it, and displays *himself through the lattice."* Such was the state of the Old-Testament church while it was in expectation of the coming of the Messiah. The ceremonial law is called *a wall of partition* (Eph. 2:14), *a veil* (2 Co. 3:13); but Christ stood behind that wall. They had him near them; they had him with them, though they could not see him clearly. He that was the substance was not far off from the shadows, Col. 2:17. The saw him looking through the windows of the ceremonial institutions and smiling through those lattices; in their sacrifices and purifications Christ discovered himself to them, and gave them intimations and earnests of his grace, both to engage and to encourage their longings for his coming. Such is our present state in comparison with what it will be at Christ's second coming. We now *see him through a glass darkly* (the body is a wall between us and him, through the windows of which we now and then get a sight of him), but not *face to face,* as we hope to see him shortly. In the sacraments Christ is near us, but it is *behind the wall* of external signs, through *those lattices* he manifests himself to us; but we shall shortly *see him as he is.* Some understand this of the state of a believer when he is under a cloud; Christ is out of sight and yet not far off. See Job 34:14, and compare Job 23:8–10. She calls the wall that interposed between her and her beloved *our wall,* because it is sin, and nothing else, that separates between us and God, and that is a wall of our own erecting (Isa. 59:1); behind that he stands, as *waiting to be gracious,* and ready to be reconciled, upon our repentance. Then *he looks in at the window,* observes the frame of our hearts and the working of our souls; he looks forth at the window, and shows himself in giving them some comfort, that they may continue hoping for his return.

III. She repeats the gracious invitation he had given her to come a walking with him, *v.* 10–13. She remembers what her beloved said to her, for it had made a very pleasing and powerful impression upon her, and the *word that quickens us* we shall *never forget.* She relates it for the encouragement of others, telling them what he had said to her soul and *done for her soul,* Ps. 66:16.

1. He called her his love and his fair one. Whatever she is to others, to him she is acceptable, and in his eyes she is amiable. Those that take Christ for their beloved, he will own as his; never was any love lost that was bestowed upon Christ. Christ, by expressing his love to believers, invites and encourages them to follow him.

2. He called her to *rise and come away, v.* 10, and again *v.* 13. The repetition denotes backwardness in her (we have need to be often called to come away with Jesus Christ; *precept must be upon precept and line upon line*), but it denotes earnestness in him; so much is his heart set upon the welfare of precious souls that he importunes them most pressingly to that which is for their own good.

3. He gave for a reason the return of the spring, and the pleasantness of the weather.

(1.) The season is elegantly described in a great variety of expressions. [1.] *The winter is past,* the dark, cold, and barren winter. Long winters and hard ones pass away at last; they do no endure always. And the spring would not be so pleasant as it is if it did not succeed the winter, which is a foil to its beauty, Eccl. 7:14. Neither the face of the heavens nor that of the earth is always the same, but subject to continual vicissitudes, diurnal and annual. *The winter is past,* but has not passed away for ever; it will come again, and we must provide for it in summer, Prov. 6:6, 8. We must weep in winter, and rejoice in summer, as though we wept and rejoiced not, for both are passing. [2.] *The rain is over and gone,* the winter-rain, the cold stormy rain; it is over now, and *the dew is as the dew of herbs.* Even the rain that drowned the world was over and gone at last (Gen. 8:1–3), and God promised to drown the world no more, which was a type and figure of the covenant of grace, Isa. 54:9. [3.] *The flowers appear on the earth.* All winter they are dead and buried in their roots, and there is no sign of them; but in the spring they revive, and show themselves in a wonderful variety and verdure, and, like the dew that produces them, *tarry not for man,* Mic. 5:7. They appear, but they will soon disappear again, and man in herein like *the flower of the field,* Job 14:2. [4.] *The time of singing of birds has come.* The little birds, which all the winter lie hid in their retirements and scarcely live, when the spring returns forget all the calamities of the winter, and to the best of their capacity chant forth the praises of their Creator. Doubtless he who understands the birds that cry for want (Ps. 147:9) takes notice of those that *sing for joy* Ps. 104:12. The singing of the birds may shame our silence in God's praises, who are better fed (Mt. 6:26), and better taught (Job 35:11), and are of *more value than many sparrows.* They live without inordinate care (Mt. 6:26) and therefore they sing, while we murmur. [5.] *The voice of the turtle is heard in our land,* which is one of the season-birds mentioned Jer. 8:7, that observe the time of their coming and the time of their singing, and so shame us who *know not the judgment of the Lord,* understand not the times, nor do that which is *beautiful in its season,* do not sing in singing time. [6.] *The fig-tree puts forth her green figs,* by which *we know that summer is nigh* (Mt. 24:32), when the green figs will be ripe figs and fit for use; and the *vines with the tender grape give a good smell.* The earth produces not only *flowers* (*v.* 12), but *fruits;* and the smell of the fruits, which are profitable, is to be preferred far before that of the flowers, which are only for show and pleasure. Serpents, they say, are driven away by the smell of the vines; and who is the old serpent, and who the true vine, we know very well.

(2.) Now this description of the returning spring, as a reason for coming away with Christ, is applicable [1.] To the introducing of the gospel in the room of the Old-Testament dispensation, during which it had been winter time with the church. Christ's gospel warms that which was cold, makes that fruitful which before was dead and barren; when it comes to any place it puts a beauty and glory upon that place (2 Co. 3:7, 8) and furnishes occasion for joy. Spring-time is pleasant time, and so is gospel-time. *Aspice venturo laetentur ut omnia seclo — Behold what joy the dawning age inspires!* said Virgil, from the Sibyls, perhaps with more reference to the setting up of the Messiah's kingdom at that time than he himself thought of. See Ps. 96:11. *Arise then,* and improve this spring-time. *Come away* from the world and the flesh, come into *fellowship with Christ,* 1 Co. 1:9. [2.] To the delivering of the church from the power of persecuting enemies, and the restoring of liberty and peace to it, after a severe winter of suffering and restraint. When the storms of trouble are over and gone, when the *voice of the turtle,* the joyful sound of the gospel of Christ, is again heard, and ordinances are enjoyed with freedom, then *arise and come away* to improve the happy juncture. Walk in the light of the Lord; sing in the ways of the Lord. When the churches had rest, then were they edified, Acts 9:31. [3.] To the conversion of sinners from a state of nature to a state of grace. That blessed change is like the return of the spring, a universal change and a very comfortable one; it is a new creation; it is being born again. The soul that was hard, and cold, and frozen, and unprofitable, like the earth in winter, becomes fruitful, like the earth in spring, and by degrees, like it, brings its fruits to perfection. This blessed change is owing purely to the approaches and influences of the sun of righteousness, who calls to us from heaven to *arise and come away;* come, gather in summer. [4.] To the consolations of the saints after a state of inward dejection and despondency. A child of God, under doubts and fears, is like the earth in winter, its nights long, its days dark, good affections chilled, nothing done, nothing got, the hand sealed up. But comfort will return; the birds shall sing again, and the flowers appear. Arise therefore, poor drooping soul, and *come away* with thy beloved. *Arise, and shake thyself from the dust,* Isa. 52:2. *Arise, shine, for thy light has come* (Isa. 60:1); *walk in that light,* Isa. 2:5. [5.] To the resurrection of the body at the last day, and the glory to be revealed. The bones that lay in the grave, as the roots of the plants in the ground during the winter, shall then *flourish as a herb,* Isa. 66:14; 26:19. That will be an eternal farewell to winter and a joyful entrance upon an everlasting spring.

Verses 14–17

Here is, I. The encouraging invitation which Christ gives

to the church, and every believing soul, to come into communion with him, *v.* 14.

1. His love is now his *dove;* David had called the church God's *turtle-dove* (Ps. 84:19), and so she is here called; a dove for beauty, her *wings covered with silver* (Ps. 18:13), for innocence and inoffensiveness; a gracious spirit is a dove-like spirit, harmless, loving quietness and cleanliness, and faithful to Christ, as the turtle to her mate. The Spirit descended *like a dove* on Christ, and so he does on all Christians, making them of a *meek and quiet spirit.* She is Christ's *dove,* for he owns her and delights in her; she can find no rest but in him and his ark, and therefore to him, as her Noah, she returns.

2. This dove is *in the clefts of the rock and in the secret places of the stairs.* This speaks either, (1.) Her praise. Christ is the rock, to whom she flies for shelter and in whom alone she can think herself safe and find herself easy, as a dove in the hole of a rock, when struck at by the birds of prey, Jer. 48:28. Moses was hid in a cleft of the rock, that he might behold something of God's glory, which otherwise he could not have borne the brightness of. She retires *into the secret places of the stairs,* where she may be alone, undisturbed, and may the better commune with her own heart. Good Christians will find time to be private. Christ often withdrew to a mountain *himself alone, to pray.* Or, (2.) her blame. She crept into the *clefts of the rock,* and the *secret places,* for fear and shame, any where to hide her head, being heartless and discouraged, and shunning even the sight of her beloved. Being conscious to herself of her own unfitness and unworthiness to come into his presence, and speak to him, she drew back, and was *like a silly dove without heart,* Hos. 7:11.

3. Christ graciously calls her out of her retirements: Come, *let me see thy countenance, let me hear thy voice.* She was *mourning like a dove* (Isa. 38:14), bemoaning herself like the *doves of the valleys,* where they are near the clefts of the impending rocks, *mourning for her iniquities* (Eze. 7:16) and refusing to be comforted. But Christ calls her to *lift up her face without spot,* being purged from an evil conscience (Job 11:15; 22:26), to *come boldly to the throne of grace,* having a great *high priest* there (Heb. 4:16), to tell what her petition is and what her request: Let me *hear thy voice,* hear what thou hast to say; *what would you that I should do unto you?* Speak freely, speak up, and fear not a slight or repulse.

4. For her encouragement, he tells her the good thoughts he had of her, whatever she thought of herself: *Sweet is thy voice;* thy praying voice, though thou canst but *chatter like a crane or a swallow* (Isa. 38:14); it is music in God's ears. He has assured us that *the prayer of the upright is his delight;* he smelled a sweet savour from Noah's sacrifice, and the *spiritual sacrifices* are no less *acceptable,* 1 Pt. 2:5. This does not so much commend our services as God's gracious condescension in making the best of them, and the efficacy of the *much incense* which is *offered with the prayers of saints,* Rev. 8:3. "That countenance of thine, which thou art ashamed of, is comely, though now mournful, much more will it be so when it becomes cheerful." *Then* the voice of prayer is sweet and acceptable to God when the countenance, the conversation in which we show ourselves before men, is holy, and so comely, and agreeable to our profession. Those that are sanctified have the best comeliness.

II. The charge which Christ gives to his servants to oppose and suppress that which is a terror to his church and drives her, like a poor frightened dove, into the clefts of the rock, and which is an obstruction and prejudice to the interests of his kingdom in this world and in the heart (*v.* 15): *Take us the foxes* (take them for us, for it is good service both to Christ and the church), *the little foxes,* that creep in insensibly; for, though they are little, they do great mischief, they *spoil the vines,* which they must by no means be suffered to do at any time, especially now when our vines have *tender grapes* that must be preserved, or the vintage will fail. Believers are as vines, weak but useful plants; their fruits are as *tender crops* at first, which must have time to come to maturity. This charge to *take the foxes* is, 1. A charge to particular believers to mortify their own corruptions, their sinful appetites and passions, which are as *foxes, little foxes,* that destroy their graces and comforts, quash good motions, crush good beginnings, and prevent their coming to perfection. Seize the *little foxes,* the first risings of sin, the littles ones of Babylon (Ps. 137:9), those sins that seem little, for they often prove very dangerous. Whatever we find a hindrance to us in that which is good we must put away. 2. A charge to all in their places to oppose and prevent the spreading of all such opinions and practices as tend to corrupt men's judgments, debauch their consciences, perplex their minds, and discourage their inclinations to virtue and piety. Persecutors are foxes (Lu. 13:32); false prophets are foxes, Eze. 13:4. Those that sow the tares of heresy or schism, and, like Diotrephes, trouble the peace of the church and obstruct the progress of the gospel, they are the *foxes, the little foxes,* which must not be knocked on the head *(Christ came not to destroy men's lives),* but taken, that they may be tamed, or else restrained from doing mischief.

III. The believing profession which the church makes of her relation to Christ, and the satisfaction she take sin her interest in him and communion with him, *v.* 16. He had called her to *rise* and *come away* with him, to let him see her face and hear her voice; now this is her answer to that call, in which, though at present in the dark and at a distance,

1. She comforts herself with the thoughts of the mutual interest and relation that were between her and her beloved: *My beloved to me* and *I to him,* so the original reads it very emphatically; the conciseness of the language speaks the largeness of her affection: "What he is to me and I to him may better be conceived than expressed." Note, (1.) It is the unspeakable privilege of true believers that Christ is theirs: *My beloved is mine;* this denotes not only propriety ("I have a title to him") but possession and tenure — "I receive from his fulness." Believers are partakers of Christ; they have not only an interest in him, but the enjoyment of him, are taken not only in the covenant, but into communion with him. All the benefits of his glorious undertaking, as Mediator, are made over to them. He is that to them which the world neither is nor can be, all that which they need and desire, and which will make a complete happiness for them. All he is is theirs, and all he has, all he has done, and all he is doing; all he has promised in the gospel, all he has prepared in heaven, all is yours. (2.) It is the undoubted character of all true believers that they are Christ's, and then, and then only, he is theirs. They have given their own selves to him (2 Co. 8:5); they receive his doctrine and obey his laws; they bear his image and espouse his interest; they belong to Christ. If we be his, his wholly, his only, his for ever, we may take the comfort of his being ours.

2. She comforts herself with the thoughts of the communications of his grace to his people: *He feeds among the lilies.* When she wants the tokens of his favour to her in particular, she rejoices in the assurance of his presence with all believers in general, who are lilies in his eyes. He *feeds* among them, that is, he takes as much pleasure in them and their assemblies as a man does in his table or in his garden, for he *walks in the midst of the golden candlesticks;* he delights to converse with them, and to do them good.

IV. The church's hope and expectation of Christ's coming, and her prayer grounded thereupon. 1. She doubts not but that the *day will break* and the *shadows* will *flee away.* The gospel-day will dawn, and the shadows of the ceremonial law will flee away. This was the comfort of the Old-Testament church, that, after the long night of that dark dispensation, the *day-spring from on high would* at length *visit them,* to *give light to those that sit in darkness.* When the sun rises the shades of the night vanish, so do the shadows of the day when the substance comes. The day of comfort will come after a night of desertion. Or it may refer to the second coming of Christ, and the eternal happiness of the saints; the shadows of our present state will flee away, our darkness and doubts, our griefs and all our grievances, and a glorious day shall dawn, a morning when the *upright shall have dominion,* a day that shall have no night after it. 2. She begs the presence of her beloved, in the mean time, to support and comfort her: *"Turn, my beloved,* turn to me, come and visit me, come and relieve me, *be with me always to the end of the age.* In the day of my extremity, make haste to help me, *make no long tarrying.* Come over even *the mountains of division,* interposing time and days, with some gracious anticipations of that light and love." 3. She begs that he would not only turn to her for the present, but hasten his coming to fetch her to himself. *"Even so, come, Lord Jesus, come quickly.* Though there be mountains in the way, thou canst, *like a roe, or a young hart,* step over them with ease. *O show thyself to me, or take me up to thee."*

CHAPTER 3

In this chapter, I. The church gives an account of a sore trial wherewith she was exercised through the withdrawing of her beloved from her, the pains she was at before she recovered the comfortable sense of his favour again, and the resolution she took, when she did recover it, not to lose it again, as she had done through her own carelessness (*v.* 1–5). II. The daughters of Jerusalem admire the excellencies of the church (*v.* 6). III. The church admires Jesus Christ under the person of Solomon, his bed, and the life-guards about it (*v.* 7, 8), his chariot (*v.* 9, 10). She calls upon the daughters of Zion, who were admiring her, to admire him rather, especially as he appeared on his coronation day and the day of his nuptials (*v.* 11).

Verses 1–5

God is not wont to say to the seed of Jacob, *Seek you me in vain;* and yet here we have the spouse for a great while seeking her beloved in vain, but finding him at last, to her unspeakable satisfaction. It was hard to the Old-Testament church to find Christ in the ceremonial law, and the types and figures which then were *of good things to come.* Long was the consolation of Israel looked for before it came. The watchman of that church gave little assistance to those who enquired after him; but at length Simeon had *him* in his arms *whom his soul loved.* It is applicable to the case of particular believers, who often walk in darkness a great while, but *at even time it shall be light,* and those that seek Christ to the end shall find him at length. Observe,

I. How the spouse sought him in vain *upon her bed* (*v.* 1); when she was up and looking about her, grace in act and exercise, though her beloved was withdrawn, yet she could see him at a distance (*ch.* 2:8), but now it was otherwise. She still continued her affection to him, still it was *he whom her soul loved,* that bond of the covenant still continued firm. *"Though he slay me, I will trust in him;* though he leave me, I will love him. When I have him not in my arms, I have him in my heart." But she wanted the communion she used to have with him, as David when he *thirsted for God, for the living God.* She sought him, but, 1. It was *by night on her bed;* it was late and lazy seeking. Her understanding was clouded; it was by night, in the dark. Her affections were chilled, it was on her bed half asleep. The wise virgins slumbered in the absence of the bridegroom. It was a dark time with the believer; she saw not her signs, and yet she sought them. Those whose souls love Jesus Christ will continue to seek him even in silence and solitude: their *reins* instruct them to do so, even *in the night season.* 2. She failed in her endeavour. Sometimes he is *found of those that seek him not* (Isa. 65:1), but here he is not found of one that sought him, either for punishment of her corruptions, her slothfulness and security (we miss of comfort because we do not seek it aright), or for the exercises of grace, her faith and patience, to try whether she will continue seeking. The woman of Canaan sought Christ, and found him not at first, that she might find him, at length, so much the more to her honour and comfort.

II. How she had sought him in vain abroad, *v.* 2. She had made trial of secret worship, and had gone through the duties of the closet, had remembered him on her bed and meditated on him in the *night-watches* (Ps. 63:6), but she did not meet with comfort. *My sore ran in the night,* and then *I remembered God and was troubled,* Ps. 77:2, 3. And yet she is not driven off by the disappointment from the use of further means; she resolves, *"I will rise now;* I will not lie here if I cannot find my beloved here, nor be content if he be withdrawn. *I will rise now* without delay, and seek him immediately, lest he withdraw further from me." Those that would seek Christ so as to find him must lose no time. *"I will rise* out of a warm bed, and go out in a cold dark night, in quest of my beloved." Those that see Christ must not startle at difficulties. *"I will rise, and go about the city,* the holy city, in the streets, and the broad-ways;" for she knew he was not to be found in any blind by-ways. We must seek in the city, in Jerusalem, which was a type of the gospel-church. The likeliest place to find Christ is in the temple (Lu. 2:46), in the streets of the gospel-church, in holy ordinances, where the children of Zion pass and repass at all hours. She had a good purpose when she said, *I will arise now,* but the good performance was all in all. She arose, and *sought him* (those that are in pursuit of Christ, the knowledge of him and communion with him, must turn every stone, seek every where), and yet she *found him not;* she was still unsatisfied, uneasy, as Job, when he looked on all sides, but could not perceive any tokens of the divine favour (Job 23:8, 9), and the Psalmist often, when he complained that God hid his face from him, Ps. 88:14. We may be in the way of our duty and yet may miss the comfort, for *the wind bloweth where it listeth.* How heavy is the accent on this repeated complaint: *I sought him, but I found him not!* like that of Mary Magdalen, *They have taken away my Lord, and I know not where they have laid him,* Jn. 20:13.

III. How she enquired of the watchmen concerning him, *v.* 3. In the night the watchmen *go about the city,* for the preservation of its peace and safety, to guide and assist the honest and quiet, as well as to be a check upon those that are disorderly; these met her in her walks, and she asked them if they could give her any tidings of her beloved. In the streets and broad-ways of Jerusalem she might meet with enough to divert her from her pursuit and to entertain her, though she could not meet her beloved; but she regards none in comparison with him. Gracious souls press through crowds of other delights and contentments in pursuit of Christ, whom they prefer before their chief joy. Mary Magdalen sees angels in the sepulchre, but that will not do unless she see Jesus. *Saw you him whom my soul loveth?* Note, We must evince the sincerity of our love to Christ by our solicitous enquiries after him. *The children of the bride-chamber will mourn when the bridegroom is taken away* (Mt. 9:15), especially for the sin which provoked him to withdraw; and, if we do so, we shall be in care to recover the sense of his favour and diligent and constant in the use of proper means in order thereunto. We must search the scriptures, be much in prayer, keep close to ordinances, and all with this upon our heart, *Saw you him whom my soul loveth?* Those only who have seen Christ themselves are likely to direct others to a sight of him. When the Greeks came to worship at the feast they applied to Philip, with such an address as this of the spouse to the watchmen, *Sir, we would see Jesus,* Jn. 12:21.

IV. How she found him at last, *v.* 4. She *passed from* the watchmen as soon as she perceived they could give her no tidings of her beloved; she would not stay with them, because he was not among them, but went on seeking, for (as Ainsworth observes) the society neither of brethren, nor of the church, nor of ministers, can comfort the afflicted conscience unless Christ himself be apprehended by faith. But soon after she parted from the watchmen she found him whom she sought, and then called him *him whom my soul loveth,* with as much delight as before with desire. Note, Those that continue seeking Christ shall find him at last, and when perhaps they were almost ready to despair of finding him. See Ps. 42:7, 8; 77:9, 10; Isa. 54:7, 8. Disappointments must not drive us away from gracious pursuits. Hold out, faith and patience; *the vision is for an appointed time,* and, though the watchman can give us no account of it, *at the end* it shall itself *speak and not lie;* and the comfort that comes in after long waiting, in the use of means, will be so much the sweeter at last.

V. How close she kept to him when she had found him. She is now as much in fear of losing him as before she was in care to find him: *I held him,* held him fast, as the women, when they met with Christ after his resurrection, *held him by the feet, and worshipped him,* Mt. 28:9. "*I would not let him go.* Not only, I would never do any thing to provoke him to depart, but I would by faith and prayer prevail with him to stay, and by the exercise of grace preserve inward peace." Those that know how hard comfort is come by, and how dearly it is bought, will be afraid of forfeiting it and playing it away, and will think nothing too much to do to keep it safe. *Non minor est virtus quam quaerere parta tueri — As much is implied in securing our acquisitions as in making them.* Those that have laid hold on wisdom must *retain her,* Prov. 3:18. Those that hold Christ fast in the arms of faith and love shall *not let him go;* he will abide with them.

VI. How desirous she was to make others acquainted with him: "*I brought him to my mother's house,* that all my relations, all who are dear to me, might have the benefit of communion with him." When Zaccheus found Christ, or rather was found of him, *salvation came to his house,* Lu. 19:9. Wherever we find Christ we must take him home with us to our houses, especially to our hearts. The church is our mother, and we should be concerned for her interests, that she may have Christ present with her and be earnest in prayer for his presence with his people and ministers always. Those that enjoy the tokens of Christ's favour to their own souls should desire that the church, and all religious assemblies in their public capacity, might likewise enjoy the tokens of his favour.

VII. What care she was in that no disturbance might be given him (*v.* 5); she repeats the charge she had before given (*ch.* 2:7) to the *daughters of Jerusalem* not to *stir up or awake her love.* When she *had brought him into her mother's house,* among her sisters, she gives them a strict charge to keep all quiet and in good order, to be very observant of him, careful to please him, and afraid of offending him. The charge given to the church in the wilderness concerning the angel of the covenant, who was among them, explains this. Ex. 23:21, *Beware of him and obey his voice; provoke him not.* See that none of you stir out of your places, lest you disturb him, but *with quietness work and mind your own business;* make no noise; let all *clamour and bitterness be put* far *from you,* for that *grieves the Holy Spirit of God,* Eph. 4:30, 31. Some make this to be Christ's charge to the *daughters of Jerusalem* not to disturb or disquiet his church, nor trouble the minds of the disciples; for Christ is very tender of the peace of his church, and all the members of it, even the little ones; and those that trouble them *shall bear their judgment,* Gal. 5:10.

Verse 6

These are the words of the *daughters of Jerusalem,* to whom the charge was given, *v.* 5. They had looked shily upon the bride because she was black (*ch.* 1:6); but now they admire her, and speak of her with great respect: *Who is this?* How beautiful she looks! Who would have expected such a comely and magnificent person to *come out of the wilderness?* As, when Christ rode in triumph into Jerusalem, they said, *Who is this?* And of the accession of strangers to the church she herself says, with wonder (Isa. 49:21), *Who has begotten me these?* 1. This is applicable to the Jewish church, when, after forty years' wandering in the wilderness, they came out of it, to take a glorious possession of the land of promise; and this may very well be illustrated by what Balaam said of them at that time, when they ascended *out of the wilderness like pillars of smoke,* and he stood admiring them: *From the top of the rocks I see him. How goodly are thy tents, O Jacob!* Num. 23:9; 24:5. 2. It is applicable to any public deliverance of the church of God, as particularly of Babylon, the Old-Testament and the New-Testament Babylon; then the church is *like pillars of smoke,* ascending upwards in devout affections, the incense of praise, from which, as from Noah's sacrifice, God *smells a sweet savour;* then she is amiable in the eyes of her friends, and her enemies too cannot but have a veneration for her, and *worship at her feet, knowing that God has loved her,* Rev. 3:9. Sometimes the *fear of the Jews* was upon their neighbours, when they saw that *God was with them of a truth,* Esth. 8:17. 3. It is applicable to the recovery of a gracious soul out of a state of desertion and despondency. (1.) She ascends *out of the wilderness,* the dry and barren land, where there is *no way,* where there is *no water,* where travellers are still in want and ever at a loss; here a poor soul may long be left to wander, but shall come up, at last, under the conduct of the Comforter. (2.) She comes up *like pillars of smoke,* like a cloud of incense ascending from the altar or the smoke of the burnt-offerings. This intimates a fire of pious and devout affections in the soul, whence this smoke arises, and the mounting of the soul heaven-ward in this smoke (as Judges 13:20), the heart lifted up to God in the heavens, *as the sparks fly upward.* Christ's return to the soul gives life to its devotion, and its communion with God is most reviving when it ascends *out of a wilderness.* (3.) She is *perfumed with myrrh and frankincense.* She is replenished with the graces of God's Spirit, which are as sweet spices, or as the holy incense, which, being now kindled by his gracious returns, sends forth a very fragrant smell. Her devotions being now peculiarly lively, she is not only acceptable to God, but amiable in the eyes of others also, who are ready to cry out with admiration, *Who is this?* What a monument of mercy is this! The graces and comforts with which she is *perfumed* are called the *powders of the merchant,* for they are far-fetched and dear-bought, by our Lord Jesus, that blessed merchant, who took a long voyage, and was at vast expense, no less than that of his own blood, to purchase them for us. They are not the products of our own soil, nor the growth of our own country; no, they are imported from the heavenly Canaan, the better country.

Verses 7–11

The daughters of Jerusalem stood admiring the spouse and commending her, but she overlooks their praises, is not puffed up with them, but transfers all the glory to Christ, and directs them to look off from her to him, recommends him to their esteem, and sets herself to applaud him. Here he is three times called *Solomon,* and we have that name but three times besides in all this song, *ch.* 1:5; 8:11, 12. It is Christ that is here meant, who is greater than Solomon, and of whom Solomon was an illustrious type for his wisdom and wealth, and especially his building the temple.

Three things she admires him for: —

I. The safety of his bed (*v.* 7): *Behold his bed,* even *Solomon's,* very rich and fine; for such *the curtains of Solomon* were. *His bed, which is above Solomon's,* so some read it. Christ's bed, though he had *not where to lay his head,* is better than Solomon's best bed. The church is his bed, for he has said of it, *This is my rest for ever; here will I dwell.* The hearts of believers are his bed, for he lies all night between their breasts, Eph. 3:17. Heaven is his bed, the rest into which he entered when he had done his work. Or it may be meant of the sweet repose and satisfaction which gracious souls enjoy in communion with him; it is called *his bed,* because, though we are admitted to it, and therefore it is called *our bed* (*ch.* 1:16), yet it is his peace that is our rest, Jn. 14:27. *I will give you rest,* Mt. 11:28. It *is Solomon's bed,* whose name signifies *peace,* because in his days Judah and Israel *dwelt safely under their vines and fig-trees.* That which she admires his bed for is the guard that surrounded it. Those that rest in Christ not only dwell at ease (many do so who yet are in the greatest danger) but they dwell in safety. Their holy serenity is under the protection of a holy security. This bed had *threescore valiant men about it,* as yeomen of the guard, or the band of gentlemen-pensioners; they are *of the valiant of Israel,* and a great many bold and brave men David's reign had produced. The life-guard men are well armed: *They all hold swords,* and know how to hold them; they are *expert in war,* well skilled in all the arts of it. They are posted about the bed at a convenient distance. They are in a posture of defence, *every man* with *his sword upon his thigh* and his hand upon his sword, ready to draw upon the first alarm, and this *because of fear in the night,* because of the danger feared; for the lives of princes, even the wisest and best, as they are more precious, so they are more exposed, and require to be more guarded than the lives of common persons. Or, *because of the fear* of it, and the apprehension which the spouse may have of danger, these guards are set for her satisfaction, that she may be *quiet from the fear of evil,* which believers themselves are subject to, especially *in the night,* when they are under a cloud as to their spiritual state, or in any outward trouble more than ordinary. Christ himself was under the special protection of his Father in his whole undertaking. *In the shadow of his hand he hid me* (Isa. 49:2); he had legions of angels at his command. The church is well guarded; more are with her than against her. Lest any hurt this vineyard, God himself *keeps it night and day* (Isa. 27:2, 3); particular believers, when they repose themselves in Christ and with him, though it may be night-time with them, and they may have their *fears in the night,* and yet safe, as safe as Solomon himself in the midst of his guards; the angels have a charge concerning them, ministers are appointed to *watch for their souls,* and *they* ought to be *valiant* men, *expert in* the spiritual warfare, holding *the sword of the Spirit, which is the word of God,* and having that girt *upon their thigh,* always ready to them for the silencing *of the fears* of God's people *in the night.* All the attributes of God are engaged for the safety of believers; they are kept as in a strong-hold by his power (1 Pt. 1:5), are safe in *his name*

(Prov. 18:10), his peace protects those in whom it rules (Phil. 4:7), and the effect of righteousness in them is *quietness* and *assurance,* Isa. 32:17. Our danger is from *the rulers of the darkness of this world,* but we are safe in the *armour of light.*

II. The splendour of his chariot, *v.* 9, 10. As Christ and believers rest in safety under a sufficient guard, so when they appear publicly, as kings in their coaches of state, they appear in great magnificence. This chariot was of Solomon's own contriving and making, the materials very rich, *silver,* and *gold,* and *cedar,* and *purple.* He made it for himself, and yet made it *for the daughters of Jerusalem,* to oblige them. Some by this *chariot,* or *coach,* or *chaise* (the word is nowhere else used in scripture), understand the human nature of Christ, in which the divine nature rode as in an open chariot. It was a divine workmanship *(A body hast thou prepared me);* the structure was very fine, but that which was at the bottom of it was love, pure love to the children of men. Others make it to represent the everlasting gospel, in which, as in an open chariot, Christ shows himself, and as in a chariot of war rides forth triumphantly, *conquering and to conquer. The pillars,* the seven pillars (Prov. 9:1), are of *silver,* for the words of the Lord are *as silver tried* (Ps. 12:6), nay, they are better *than thousands of gold and silver.* It is hung with *purple,* a princely colour; all the adornings of it are dyed in the precious blood of Christ, and that gives them this colour. But that which completes the glory of it is *love; it is paved with love,* it is lined with love, not love of strangers, as Solomon's was in the days of his defection, but *love* of *the daughters of Jerusalem,* a holy *love.* Silver is better than cedar, gold than silver, but love is better than gold, better than all, and it is put last, for nothing can be better than that. The gospel is all *love.* Mr. Durham applies it to the covenant of redemption, the way of our salvation, as it is contrived in the eternal counsel of God, and manifested to us in the scriptures. This is that work of Christ himself wherein the glory of his grace and love to sinners most eminently appears, and which makes him amiable and admirable in the eyes of believers. In this covenant love is conveyed to them, and they are carried in it to the perfection of love, and, as it were, ride in triumph. It is admirably framed and contrived, both for the glory of Christ and for the comfort of believers. It is *well ordered in all things, and sure* (2 Sa. 23:5); it has *pillars* that cannot be shaken, it is *made of the wood of Lebanon,* which can never rot; the basis of it is *gold,* the most lasting metal; the blood of the covenant, that rich *purple,* is the cover of this chariot, by which believers are sheltered from the wind and storms of divine wrath, and the troubles of this world; but the midst of it, and that which is all in all in it, is *love,* that *love of Christ which surpasses knowledge* and the dimensions of which are immeasurable.

III. The lustre of his royal person, when he appears in his greatest pomp, *v.* 11. Here observe,

1. The call that is given to the *daughters of Zion* to acquaint themselves with the glories of *king Solomon: Go forth, and behold* him. The multitude of the spectators adds to the beauty of a splendid cavalcade. Christ, in his gospel, manifests himself. Let each of us add to the number of those that give honour to him, by giving themselves the satisfaction of looking upon him. Who should pay respects to Zion's king but Zion's daughters? They have reason to rejoice greatly when he comes, Zec. 9:9. (1.) *Behold him* then. Look with pleasure upon Christ in his glory. Look upon him with an eye of faith, with a fixed eye. Here is a sight worth seeing; *behold,* and admire him, *behold,* and love him; look upon him, and know him again. (2.) *Go forth and behold* him; go off from the world, as those that see no beauty and excellency in it in comparison with what is to be seen in the Lord Jesus. Go out of yourselves, and let the light of his transcendent beauty put you out of conceit with yourselves. *Go forth* to the place where he is to be seen, to the street through which he passes, as Zaccheus.

2. The direction that is given them to take special notice of that which they would not see every day, and that was his *crown,* either the crown of gold, adorned with jewels, which he wore on his coronation-day (Solomon's mother, Bathsheba, though she did not procure that for him, yet, by her seasonable interposal, she helped to secure it to him when Adonijah was catching at it), or the garland or crown of flowers and green tied with ribbons which his mother made for him, to adorn the solemnity of his nuptials. Perhaps Solomon's coronation day was his marriage-day, *the day of his espousals,* when the garland his mother crowned him with was added to the crown his people crowned him with. Applying this to Christ, it speaks, (1.) The many honours put upon him, and the power and dominion he is entrusted with: *Go forth,* and see king Jesus, *with the crown wherewith his* Father *crowned him,* when he declared him his *beloved Son, in whom* he was *well-pleased,* when he *set him as King upon his holy hill of Zion,* when he advanced him to his own right hand, and invested him with a sovereign authority, both *in heaven and in earth,* and *put all things under his feet.* (2.) The dishonour put upon him by his persecutors. Some apply it to the *crown of thorns* with which *his mother,* the Jewish church, *crowned him* on the day of his death, which was *the day of his espousals* to his church, when he *loved it, and gave himself for it* (Eph. 5:25); and it is observable that when he was *brought forth wearing the crown of thorns Pilate said,* and said it to the *daughters of Zion, Behold the man.* (3.) It seems especially to mean the honour done him by his church, as his mother, and by all true believers, in whose hearts he is formed, and of whom he has said, *These are my mother, my sister, and brother,* Mt. 12:50. They give him the glory of his undertaking; to him is glory *in the church,* Eph. 3:21. When believers accept of him as theirs, and join themselves to him in an everlasting covenant, [1.] It is his coronation-day in their souls. Before conversion they were crowning themselves, but then they begin to crown Christ, and continue to do so from that day forward. They appointed him their head; they bring *every thought into obedience to* him; they set up his throne in their hearts, and cast all their crowns at his feet. [2.] It is *the day of his espousals,* in which he betroths them to him for ever in lovingkindness and in mercies, joins them to himself in faith and love, and gives himself to them in the promises and all he has, to be theirs. *Thou shalt not be for another, so will I also be for thee,* Hos. 3:3. And to him they are presented as *chaste virgins.* [3.] It is *the day of the gladness of his heart;* he is pleased with the honour that his people do him, pleased with the progress of his interest among them. Does *Satan fall* before them? *In that hour Jesus rejoices in spirit,* Lu. 10:18, 21. There is joy in heaven over repenting sinners; the family is glad when the prodigal son returns. *Go forth and behold* Christ's grace toward sinners, as his *crown,* his brightest glory.

CHAPTER 4

In this chapter, I. Jesus Christ, having espoused his church to himself (*ch.* 3:11), highly commends her beauty in the several expressions of it, concluding her fair, all fair (*v.* 1–5 and again, *v.* 7). II. He retires himself, and invites her with him, from the mountains of terror to those of delight (*v.* 6, 8). III. He professes his love to her and his delight in her affection to him (*v.* 9–14). IV. She ascribes all she had that was valuable in her to him, and depends upon the continued influence of his grace to make her more and more acceptable to him (*v.* 15, 16).

Verses 1–7

Here is, I. A large and particular account of the beauties of the church, and of gracious souls on whom the image of God is renewed, consisting *in the beauty of holiness.* In general, he that is a competent judge of beauty, whose *judgment,* we are sure, *is according to truth,* and what all must subscribe to, he has said, *Behold, thou art fair.* She had commended him, and called all about her to take notice of his glories; and hereby she recommends herself to him, gains his favour, and, in return for her respects, he calls to all about him to take notice of her graces. Those that honour Christ he will honour, 1 Sa. 2:30.

1. He does not flatter her, nor design hereby either to make her proud of herself or to court her praises of him; but, (1.) It is to encourage her under her present dejections. Whatever others thought of her, she was amiable in his eyes. (2.) It is to teach her what to value herself upon, not any external advantages (which would add nothing to her, and the want of which would deprive her of nothing that was really excellent), but upon the comeliness of grace which he had put upon her. (3.) It is to invite others to think well of her too, and to join themselves to her: "Thou art *my love,* thou lovest me and art beloved of me, and therefore *thou art fair.*" All the beauty of the saints is derived from him, and they shine by reflecting his light; it is *the beauty of the Lord our God* that is *upon us,* Ps. 90:17. She was espoused to him, and that made her beautiful. *Uxor fulget radiis mariti — The spouse shines in her husband's rays.* It it repeated, *Thou art fair,* and again, *Thou art fair,* denoting not only the certainty of it, but the pleasure he took in speaking of it.

2. As to the representation here made of the beauty of the church, the images are certainly very bright, the shades are strong, and the comparisons bold, not proper indeed to represent any external beauty, for they were not designed to do so, but *the beauty of holiness, the new man, the hidden man of the heart, in that which is not corruptible.* Seven particulars are specified, a number of perfection, for the church is enriched with manifold graces by *the seven spirits* that *are before the throne,* Rev. 1:4; 1 Co. 1:5, 7.

(1.) Her *eyes.* A good eye contributes much to a beauty: *Thou hast doves' eyes,* clear and chaste, and often cast up towards heaven. It is not the eagle's eye, that can face the sun, but the *dove's eye,* a humble, modest, mournful eye, that is the praise of those whom Christ loves. Ministers are the church's eyes (Isa. 52:8, *thy watchmen shall see eye to eye*); they must be like *doves' eyes,* harmless and inoffensive (Mt. 10:16), having their *conversation in the world in simplicity and godly sincerity.* Wisdom and knowledge are the eyes of the new man; they must be clear, but not haughty, *not exercised in things too high for us.* When our aims and intentions are sincere and honest, then we have *doves' eyes,* when we look not unto *idols* (Eze. 18:6), but have *our eyes ever towards the Lord,* Ps. 25:15. The *doves' eyes are within the locks,* which area as a shade upon them, so that, [1.] They cannot fully see. As long as we are here in this world we *know but in part,* for a hair hangs in our eyes; *we cannot order our speech by reason of darkness;* death will shortly cut those locks, and then we shall see all things clearly. [2.] They cannot be fully seen, but as the stars through the thin clouds. Some make it to intimate the bashfulness of her looks; she suffers not her eyes to wander, but limits them with her locks.

(2.) Her *hair;* it is compared to *a flock of goats,* which looked white, and were, on the top of the mountains, like a fine head of hair; and the sight was more pleasant to the spectator because the goats have not only gravity from their beards, but they are *comely in going* (Prov. 30:29), but it was most pleasant of all to the owner, much of whose riches consisted in his flocks. Christ puts a value upon that in the church, and in believers, which others make no more account of than of their hair. He told his disciples that *the very hairs of their head were all numbered,* as carefully as men number their flocks (Mt. 10:30), and that *not a hair of their head should perish,* Lu. 21:18. Some by the *hair* here understand the outward conversation of a believer, which ought to be comely, and decent, and agreeable to the holiness of the heart. The apostle opposes good works, such as become the professors of godliness, to *the plaiting of the hair,* 1 Tim. 2:9, 10. Mary Magdalen's hair was beautiful when she wiped the feet of Christ with it.

(3.) Her *teeth, v.* 2. Ministers are the church's teeth; like nurses, they chew the meat for the babes of Christ. The Chaldee paraphrase applies it to the priests and Levites, who fed upon the sacrifices as the representatives of the people. Faith, by which we feed upon Christ, meditation, by which we ruminate on the word and chew the cud upon what we have heard, in order to the digesting of it, are the teeth of the new man. These are here compared to *a flock of sheep.* Christ called his disciples and ministers a *little flock.* It is the praise of teeth to be *even,* to be white, and kept clean, *like sheep from the washing,* and to be firm and well fixed in the gums, and not like sheep that cast their young; for so the word signifies which we translate *barren.* It is the praise of ministers to be even in mutual love and concord, to be pure and clean from all moral pollutions, and to be fruitful, bringing forth souls to Christ, and nursing his lambs.

(4.) Her *lips;* these are compared to *a thread of scarlet, v.* 3. Red lips are comely, and a sign of health, as the paleness of the lips is a sign of faintness and weakness; her *lips* were the colour *of scarlet,* but thin *lips, like a thread of scarlet.* The next words explain it: *Thy speech is comely,* always with grace, *good,* and *to the use of edifying,* which adds much to the beauty of a Christian. When we praise God with *our lips, and with the mouth make confession* of him *to salvation,* then they are as a *thread of scarlet.* All our good works and good words must be *washed in the blood of Christ,* dyed like the *scarlet thread,* and then, and not till then, they are acceptable to God. The Chaldee applies it to the chief priest, and his prayers for Israel on the day of atonement.

(5.) Her *temples,* or cheeks, which are here compared to *a piece of a pomegranate,* a fruit which, when cut in two, has rich veins or specks in it, like a blush in the face. Humility and modesty, blushing to lift up our faces before God, blushing at the remembrance of sin and in a sense of our unworthiness of the honour put upon us, will beautify us very much in the eyes of Christ. The blushes of Christ's bride are *within her locks,* which intimates (says Mr. Durham) that she blushes when no other sees, and for that which none sees but God and conscience; also that she seeks not to proclaim her humility, but modestly covers that too; yet the evidences of all these, in a tender walk, appear and are comely.

(6.) Her *neck;* this is here compared to *the tower of David, v.* 4. This is generally applied to the grace of faith, by which we are united to Christ, as the body is united to the head by the neck; this *is like the tower of David,* furnishing us with weapons of war, especially *bucklers* and *shields,* as the soldiers were supplied with them out of that tower, for *faith* is our *shield* (Eph. 6:16): those that have it never want a *buckler,* for God will compass them *with his favour as with a shield.* When this *neck is like a tower,* straight, and stately, and strong, a Christian goes on in his way, and works with courage and magnanimity, and does not hang a drooping head, and he does when faith fails. Some make the *shields of the mighty men,* that are here said to hang up in *the tower of David,* to be the monuments of the valour of David's worthies. Their shields were preserved, to keep in remembrance them and their heroic acts, intimating that it is a great encouragement to the saints to hold up their heads, to see what great things the saints in all ages have accomplished and won by faith. In Heb. 11 we have the *shields of* the *mighty men* hung up, the exploits of believers and the trophies of their victories.

(7.) Her *breasts;* these are *like two young roes that are twins, v.* 5. The church's breasts are both for ornament (Eze. 16:7) and for use; they are the *breasts of her consolation* (Isa. 66:11), as she is said to *suck the breasts of kings,* Isa. 60:16. Some apply these to the two Testaments; others to the two sacraments, the seals of the covenant of grace; others to ministers, who are to be spiritual nurses to the children of God and to give out to them the *sincere milk of the word, that they may grow thereby,* and, in order to that, are themselves to *feed among the lilies* where Christ feeds (*ch.* 2:16), that they may be to the babes of the church as full breasts. Or the breasts of a believer are his love to Christ, which he is pleased with, as a tender husband is with the affections of his wife, who is therefore said to be to him *as the loving hind and the pleasant roe,* because *her breasts satisfy him at all times,* Prov. 5:19. This includes also his edifying others and communicating grace to them, which adds much to a Christian's beauty.

II. The bridegroom's resolution hereupon to retire *to the mountain of myrrh* (*v.* 6) and there to make his residence. This *mountain of myrrh* is supposed to signify Mount Moriah, on which the temple was built, where incense was daily burnt to the honour of God. Christ was so pleased with the beauty of his church that he chose this to be his rest for ever; here he will dwell *till the day break and the shadows flee away.* Christ's parting promise to his disciples, as the representatives of the church, answer to this: *Lo, I am with you always, even to the end of the world.* Where the ordinances of God are duly administered there Christ will be, and there we must meet him at the door of the tabernacle of meeting. Some make these to be the words of the spouse, either modestly ashamed of the praises given her, and willing to get out of the hearing of them, or desirous to be constant to the holy hill, not doubting but there to find suitable and sufficient succour and relief in all her straits, and there to cast anchor, and wish for the day, which, at the time appointed, would *break and the shadows flee away.* The holy hill (as some observe) is here called both a *mountain of myrrh,* which is bitter, and a *hill of frankincense,* which is sweet, for there we have occasion both to mourn and rejoice; repentance is a bitter sweet. But in heaven it will be all frankincense, and no myrrh. Prayer is compared to incense, and Christ will meet his praying people and will bless them.

III. His repeated commendation of the beauty of the spouse (*v.* 7): *Thou art all fair, my love.* He had said (*v.* 1), *Thou art fair;* but here he goes further, and, in review of the particulars, as of those of the creation, he pronounces *all very good:* "*Thou art all fair, my love;* thou art all over beautiful, and there is nothing amiss in thee, and thou hast all beauties in thee; thou art *sanctified wholly* in every part; *all things have become new* (2 Co. 5:17); there is not only a new face and a new name, but a new man, a new nature; *there is no spot in thee,* as far as thou art renewed." The spiritual sacrifices must be without blemish. *There is no spot* but such as is often the spot of God's children, none of the leopard's spots. The church, when Christ shall present it to himself a glorious church, will be altogether *without spot or wrinkle,* Eph. 5:27.

Verses 8–14

These are still the words of Christ to his church, expressing his great esteem of her and affection to her, the opinion he had of her beauty and excellency, the desire he had of, and the delight he had in, her converse and society. And so ought men to love their wives as Christ loves the church, and takes pleasure in it as if it were spotless and had no fault, when yet it is compassed with infirmity. Now, observe here,

I. The endearing names and titles by which he calls her, to express his love to her, to assure her of it, and to engage and excite her love to him. Twice here he calls her *My spouse* (*v.* 8, 11) and three times *My sister, my spouse, v.* 9, 10, 12. Mention was made (*ch.* 3:11) of *the day of his espousals,* and, after that, she is called his *spouse,* not before. Note, There is a marriage-covenant between Christ and his church, between Christ and every true believer. Christ calls his church his *spouse,* and his calling her so makes her so. "I have betrothed thee unto me for ever; and, as the bridegroom rejoices over the bride, so shall thy God rejoice over thee." He is not ashamed to own the relation, but, as becomes a kind and tender husband, he speaks affectionately to her, and calls her his *spouse,* which cannot but strongly engage her to be faithful to him. Nay, because no one relation among men is sufficient to set forth Christ's love to his church, and to show that all this must be understood spiritually, he owns her in two relations, which among men are incompatible, *My sister, my spouse.* Abraham's saying of Sarah, *She is my sister,* was interpreted as a denying of her to be his wife; but Christ's church is to him both a *sister* and a *spouse,* as Mt. 12:50, a *sister and mother.* His calling her *sister* is grounded upon his taking our nature upon him in his incarnation, and his making us partakers of his nature in our sanctification. He clothed himself with a *body* (Heb. 2:14), and he clothes believers with his *Spirit* (1 Co. 6:17), and so they become his *sisters.* They are children of God his Father (2 Co. 6:18) and so they become his *sisters;* he that sanctifies, and those that are sanctified, are all of one (Heb. 2:11); and he owns them, and loves them, as his sisters.

II. The gracious call he gives her to come along with him as a faithful bride, that must forget her own people and her father's house, and leave all to cleave to him. *Ubi tu Caius, ibi ego Caia — Where thou Caius art, I Caia will be. Come with me from Lebanon, v.* 8.

1. It is a precept; so we take it, like that (*ch.* 2:10, 13), *Rise up, and come away.* All that have by faith come to Christ must come with Christ, in holy obedience to him and compliance with him. Being joined to him, we must walk with him. This is his command to us daily: *"Come with me, my spouse;* come with me to God as a Father; come with me onward, heavenward; come forward with me; come up with me; *come with me from Lebanon, from the top of Amana, from the lions' dens."* These mountains are to be considered, (1.) As seemingly delightful places. Lebanon is called *that goodly mountain,* Deu. 3:25. We read of the *glory of Lebanon* (Isa. 35:2) and its goodly smell, Hos. 14:6. We read of the pleasant *dew of Hermon* (Ps. 133:3) and the *joy of Hermon* (Ps. 89:12); and we may suppose the other mountains here mentioned to be pleasant ones, and so this is Christ's call to his spouse to come off from the world, all its products, all its pleasures, to sit loose to all the delights of sense. All those must do so that would come with Christ; they must take their affections off from all present things; yea, though they be placed at the upper end of the world, on *the top of Amana* and *the top of Shenir,* though they enjoy the highest satisfactions the creature can propose to give, yet they must *come away* from them all, and live above the tops of the highest hills on earth, that they may have *their conversation in heaven. Come from* those mountains, to go along with Christ to the holy mountain, the *mountain of myrrh, v.* 6. Even while we have our residence on these mountains, yet we must look for them, look above them. Shall we *lift up our eyes to the hills?* No; *our help comes from the Lord,* Ps. 121:1, 2. We must look beyond them, to *the things that are not seen* (as these high hills are), that *are eternal. From the tops of Shenir and Hermon,* which were on the other side Jordan, as from Pisgah, they could see the land of Canaan; from this world we must look forward to the better country. (2.) They are to be considered as really dangerous. These hills indeed are pleasant enough, but there are in them *lions' dens;* they are *mountains of the leopards,* mountains of prey, though they seem *glorious and excellent,* Ps. 76:4. Satan, that *roaring lion,* in the *prince of this world;* in the things of it he lies in wait to devour. On the tops of these mountains there are many dangerous temptations to those who would take up their residence in them; and therefore *come with me from* them; let us not set our hearts upon the things of this world, and then they can do us no hurt. *Come with me from* the temples of idolaters, and the societies of wicked people (so some understand it); *come out from among them, and be you separate. Come from* under the dominion of your own lusts, which are as *lions* and *leopards,* fierce upon us, and making us fierce.

2. It may be taken as a promise: Thou shalt *come with me from Lebanon, from the lions' dens;* that is, (1.) "Many shall be brought home to me, as living members of the church, from every point, from Lebanon in the north, Amana in the west, Hermon in the east, Shenir in the south, from all parts, to *sit down with Abraham, Isaac, and Jacob,*" Mt. 8:11. See Isa. 49:11, 12. Some *from the tops of* these mountains, some of the great men of this world, shall give themselves to Christ. (2.) The church shall be delivered from her persecutors, in due time; though now she *dwells among lions* (Ps. 57:4), Christ will take her with himself from among their dens.

III. The great delight Christ takes in his church and in all believers. He delights in them,

1. As in an agreeable bride, *adorned for her husband* (Rev. 21:2), who *greatly desires her beauty,* Ps. 45:11. No expressions of love can be more passionate than these here, in which Christ manifests his affection to his church; and yet that great proof of his love, his dying for it, that he might present it to himself a glorious church, goes far beyond them all. A spouse so dearly bought and paid for could not but be dearly loved. Such a price being given for her, a high value must needs be put upon her accordingly; and both together may well set us a wondering at *the height and depth, and length and breadth, of the love of Christ, which surpasses knowledge,* that love in which he *gave himself for us* and gives himself to us. Observe, (1.) How he is affected towards his spouse: *Thou hast ravished my heart;* the word is used only here. *Thou hast hearted me,* or *Thou has unhearted me.* New words are coined to express the inexpressibleness of Christ's surprising love to his church; and the strength of that love is set forth by that which is a weakness in men, the being so much in love with one object as to be heartless to every thing else. This may refer to that love which Christ had to the chosen remnant, before the worlds were, when *his delights were with the sons of men* (Prov. 8:31), that first love, which brought him from heaven to earth, to *seek and save* them at such vast expense, yet including the complacency he takes in them when he has brought them to himself. Note, Christ's heart is upon his church; so it has appeared all along. His treasure is in it; it is his *peculiar treasure* (Ex. 19:5); and therefore there his heart is also. "Never was love like unto the love of Christ, which made him even mindless of himself, when he emptied himself of his glory, and despised all shame and pain, for our sakes. The wound of love towards us, which he had from eternity in himself, made him neglect all the wounds and reproaches of the cross;" so Bishop Reynolds. Thus let us love him. (2.) What it is that thus affects him with delight. [1.]

The regard she has to him: *Thou hast ravished my heart with one of thy eyes,* those *doves' eyes,* clear and chaste (which were commended, *v.* 1), with one glance of those eyes. Christ is wonderfully pleased with those that look unto him as their Saviour, and through the eye of faith dart their affections to him, above any rival whatsoever, and whose *eyes are ever towards him;* he is soon aware of the first look of a soul towards him and meets it with his favours. [2.] The ornaments she has from him, that is, the obedience she yields to him, for that is the *chain of her neck,* the graces that enrich her soul, which are connected as links in chain, the exercise of these graces in a conversation which adorns both herself and the doctrine of Jesus Christ, which she professes to believe (as a gold chain is an ornament to persons of quality), and an entire submission to the commanding power of his love. Having shaken off the *bands of our neck,* by which we were tied to this world (Isa. 52:2), and *the yoke of our transgressions,* we are bound with the *cords of love,* as *chains of gold,* to Jesus Christ, and our necks are brought under his sweet and easy yoke, to drawn in it. This recommends us to Jesus Christ, for this is that true wisdom which, in his account, is *an ornament of grace unto the head and chains about the neck,* Prov. 1:9. [3.] The affection she has for him: *How fair is thy love!* how beautiful is it! Not only thy love itself, but all the fruits and products of it, its working in the heart, its works in the life. How well does it become a believer thus to love Christ, and what a pleasure does Christ take in it! Nothing recommends us to Christ as this does. *How much better is thy love than wine,* than all the wine that was poured out to the Lord in the drink-offerings! Hence the fruit of the vine is said to *cheer God and man,* Judges 9:13. She had said of Christ's love, *It is better than wine* (*ch.* 1:2), and now Christ says so of hers; there is nothing lost by praising Christ, nor will he be behindhand with his friends in kindness. [4.] The ointments, the odours wherewith she is perfumed, the gifts and graces of the Spirit, her good works, which are *an odour of a sweet smell, a sacrifice acceptable, well-pleasing to God,* Phil. 4:18. *The smell of thy ointment* is better *than all spices,* such as the queen of Sheba presented to Solomon, camel-loads of them (1 Ki. 10:2), or, rather, than all the spices that were used in compounding the holy incense which was burned daily on the golden altar. Love and obedience to God are more pleasing to Christ than sacrifice or incense. *The smell of her garments* too, the visible profession she makes of religion, and relation to Christ, before men, and wherein she appears to the world, this is very grateful to Christ, as *the smell of Lebanon.* Christ having put upon his spouse the *white raiment* of his own righteousness (Rev. 3:18), and *the righteousness of saints* (Rev. 19:8), and this perfumed with holy joy and comfort, he is well pleased with it. [5.] Her words, both in her devotion to God and her discourses with men (*v.* 11): *Thy lips O my spouse! drop as the honeycomb,* drop that which is very sweet, and drop it freely and plentifully. If what God speaks to us be *sweeter* to us *than the honey and the honeycomb* (Ps. 19:10), what we say to him in prayer and praise shall also be pleasing to him: *Sweet is thy voice.* And if *out of a good treasure* in the *heart* we *bring forth good things,* if our *speech be always with grace,* if our *lips use knowledge aright,* if they *disperse knowledge,* they then, in Christ's account, even *drop the honeycomb,* out-drop it. *Honey and milk* (the two staple commodities of Canaan) *are under thy tongue;* that is, in thy heart, not only reserved there for thy own use as a sweet morsel for thyself, but ready there for the use of others. In the word of God there is sweet and wholesome nourishment, milk for babes, honey for those that are grown up. Christ is well-pleased with those that are full of his word.

2. As in a pleasant garden. And well may a very great delight be compared to the delight taken in a garden, when the happiness of Adam in innocency was represented by the putting of him into a garden, a garden of pleasure. This comparison is pursued, *v.* 12–14. The church is fitly compared to a *garden,* to a garden which, as was usual, had *a fountain* in it. Where Solomon made himself *gardens* and *orchards* he made himself *pools of water* (Eccl. 2:5, 6), not only for curiosity and diversion, in water-works, but for use, to *water the gardens.* Eden was *well watered,* Gen. 2:10; 13:10. Observe, (1.) The peculiarity of this garden: It is *a garden enclosed,* a paradise separated from the common earth. It is appropriated to God; he has *set it apart for himself;* Israel is God's portion, the lot of his inheritance. It is enclosed for secresy; the saints are God's hidden ones, therefore *the world knows them not;* Christ walks in his garden unseen. It is enclosed for safety; a hedge of protection is made about it, which all the powers of darkness cannot either find or make a gap in. God's vineyard is *fenced* (Isa. 5:2); there is a wall about it, a wall of fire. It has a spring in it, and a fountain, but it is *a spring shut up* and *a fountain sealed,* which sends its streams *abroad* (Prov. 5:16), but is itself carefully locked up, that it may not by any injurious hand be muddied or polluted. The souls of believers are as *gardens enclosed;* grace in them is as *a spring shut up* there in *the hidden man of the heart,* where the water that Christ gives is *a well of living water,* Jn. 4:14; 7:38. The Old-Testament church was *a garden enclosed* by the partition wall of the ceremonial law. The Bible was then a *spring shut up* and *a fountain sealed;* it was confined to one nation; but now the wall of separation is removed, the gospel preached to every nation, and *in Jesus Christ there is neither Greek nor Jew.* (2.) The products of this garden. It is as the garden of Eden, where *the Lord God made to grow every tree that is pleasant to the sight and good for food,* Gen. 2:9. *Thy plants,* or plantations, *are an orchard of pomegranates with pleasant fruits, v.* 13. It is not like *the vineyard of the man void of understanding,* that was *all grown over with thorns and nettles;* but here are *fruits, pleasant fruits, all trees of frankincense,* and *all the chief spices, v.* 14. Here is a great plenty of fruits and great variety, nothing wanting which might either beautify or enrich this garden, might make it either delightful or serviceable to its great Lord. Every thing here is the best of the kind. Their *chief spices* were much more valuable, because much more durable, than the choicest of our flowers. Solomon was a great master in botany as well as other parts of natural philosophy; he treated largely of trees (1 Ki. 4:33), and perhaps had reference to some specific qualities of the fruits here specified, which made them very fit for the purpose for which he alludes to them; but we must be content to observe, in general, the saints in the church, and graces in the saints, are very fitly compared to these *fruits and spices;* for, [1.] They are planted, and do not grow of themselves; *the trees of righteousness* are the *planting of the Lord* (Isa. 61:3); grace springs from an incorruptible seed. [2.] They are precious and of high value; hence we read of the *precious sons of Zion* and their *precious faith;* they are *plants of renown.* [3.] They are pleasant, and of a sweet savour to God and man, and, as strong aromatics, diffuse their fragrancy. [4.] They are profitable and of great use. Saints are the blessings of this earth, and their graces are their riches, with which they trade as the merchants of the east with their spices. [5.] They are permanent, and will be preserved to good purpose, when flowers are withered and good for nothing. Grace, ripened into glory, will last for ever.

Verses 15–16

These seem to be the words of the spouse, the church, in answer to the commendations which Christ, the bridegroom, had given of her as a pleasant fruitful garden. Is she a garden?

I. She owns her dependence upon Christ himself to make this garden fruitful. To him she has an eye (*v.* 15) as the *fountain of gardens,* not only the founder of them, by whom they are planted and to whom they owe their being, but the fountain of them, by which they are watered and to which they own their continuance and well-being, and without whose constant supplies they would soon become like the dry and barren wilderness. To him she gives all the glory of her fruitfulness, as being nothing without him: *O fountain of gardens!* fountain of all good, of all grace, do not thou fail me. Does a believer say to the church, *All my springs are in thee,* in thee, O Zion? (Ps. 87:7), the church transmits the praise to Christ, and says to him, *All my springs are in thee;* thou art *the well of living waters* (Jer. 2:13), out of which flow the *streams of Lebanon,* the river Jordan, which had its rise at the foot of Mount Lebanon, and the waters of the sanctuary, which issued out *from under the threshold of the house,* Eze. 47:1. Those that are gardens to Christ must acknowledge him a fountain to them, from whose fulness they receive and to whom it is owing that their souls are as *a watered garden,* Jer. 31:12. *The city of God* on earth is made *glad* with the *river* that flows from this fountain (Ps. 46:4), and the new Jerusalem has its *pure river of water of life proceeding out of the throne of God and of the Lamb,* Rev. 22:1.

II. She implores the influences of the blessed Spirit to make this garden fragrant (*v.* 16): *Awake, O north wind! and come, thou south.* This is a prayer, 1. For the church in general, that there may be a plentiful effusion of the Spirit upon it, in order to its flourishing estate. Ministers' gifts are *the spices;* when the Spirit is poured out these flow forth, and then *the wilderness becomes a fruitful field,* Isa. 32:15. This prayer was answered in the pouring out of the Spirit on *the day of pentecost* (Acts 2:1), ushered in by a *mighty wind;* then the apostles, who were bound up before, flowed forth, and were *a sweet savour to God,* 2 Co. 2:15. 2. For particular believers. Note, (1.) Sanctified souls are as gardens, gardens of the Lord, enclosed for him. (2.) Graces in the soul are as spices in these gardens, that in them which is valuable and useful. (3.) It is very desirable that the spices of grace should flow forth both in pious and devout affections and in holy gracious actions, that with them we may honour God, adorn our profession, and do that which will be grateful to good men. (4.) The blessed Spirit, in his operations upon the soul, is as the *north and the south wind,* which *blows where it listeth,* and from several points, Jn. 3:8. There is the north wind of convictions, and the south wind of comforts; but all, like the wind, brought *out of God's treasuries* and *fulfilling his word.* (5.) The flowing forth of the spices of grace depends upon the gales of the Spirit; he stirs up good affections, and works in us both to will and to do that which is good; it is he that makes manifest the savour of his knowledge by us. (6.) We ought therefore to wait upon the Spirit of grace for his quickening influences, to pray for them, and to lay our souls under them. God has promised to give us his Spirit, but he will for this be enquired of.

III. She invites Christ to the best entertainment the garden affords: "*Let my beloved* then *come into his garden and eat his pleasant fruits;* let him have the honour of all the products of the garden (it is fit he should), and let me have the comfort of his acceptance of them, for that is the best account they can be made to turn to." Observe, 1. She calls it *his* garden; for those that are espoused to Christ call nothing their own, but what they have devoted to him and desire to be used for him. When the spices flow forth then it is fit to be called his garden, and not till then. The fruits of the garden are his pleasant fruits, for he planted them, watered them, and gave the increase. What can we pretend to merit at Christ's hands when we can invite him to nothing but what is his own already? 2. She begs he would visit it, and accept of what it produced. The believer can take little pleasure in his garden, unless Christ, the beloved of his soul, come to him, nor have any joy of the fruits of it, unless they redound some way or other to the glory of Christ, and he will think all he has well bestowed upon him.

CHAPTER 5

In this chapter we have, I. Christ's gracious acceptance of the invitation which his church had given him, and the kind visit which he made to her (*v.* 1). II. The account which the spouse gives of her own folly, in putting a slight upon her beloved, and the distress she was in by reason of his withdrawings (*v.* 2–8). III. The enquiry of the daughters of Jerusalem concerning the amiable perfections of her beloved (*v.* 9), and her particular answer to that enquiry (*v.* 10–16). "Unto you that believe he is thus precious."

Verse 1

These words are Christ's answer to the church's prayer in the close of the foregoing chapter, *Let my beloved come into his garden;* here he has come, and lets her know it. See how ready God is to hear prayer, how ready Christ is to accept the invitations that his people give him, though we are backward to hear his calls and accept his invitations. He is free in condescending to us, while we are shy of ascending to him. Observe how the return answered the request, and outdid it. 1. She called him *her beloved* (and really he was so), and invited him because she loved him; in return to this, he called her his *sister and spouse,* as several times before, *ch.* 4. Those that make Christ their best beloved shall be owned by him in the nearest and dearest relations. 2. She called the garden *his,* and the pleasant fruits of it *his,* and he acknowledges them to be so: It is *my garden,* it is *my spice.* When God was displeased with Israel he turned them off to Moses (They are *thy peo-*

ple, Ex. 32:7); and he called the appointed feasts of the Lord *their appointed feasts* (Isa. 1:14); but now that they are in his favour he owns them for his garden. "Though of small account, yet it is mine." Those that are in sincerity give up themselves and all they have and can do to Jesus Christ, he will do them the honour to stamp them, and what they have and do for him, with his own mark, and say, *It is mine.* 3. She invited him to *come into his garden,* and he says, *I have come.* Isa. 58:9, *Thou shalt cry, and he shall say, Here I am.* When Solomon prayed that God would come and take possession of the house he had built for him, he did come; *his glory filled the house* (2 Chr. 7:2), and (*v.* 16) he let him know that he had chosen and sanctified this house, that his *name might be there for ever.* Those that throw open the door of their souls to Jesus Christ shall find him ready to come in to them; and in every place where he records his name he will meet his people, and bless them, Ex. 20:24. 4. She desired him to *eat his pleasant fruits,* to accept of the sacrifices offered in his temple, which were as the fruits of his garden, and he does so, but finds they are not gathered and ready for eating, therefore he does himself gather them. As the fruits are his, so is the preparation of them; he finds his heart unready for his entertainment, but does himself draw out into exercise those gracious habits which he had planted there. What little good there is in us would be shed and lost if he did not gather it, and preserve it to himself. 5. She only desired him to *eat the fruits* of the garden, but he brought along with him something more, *honey,* and *wine,* and *milk,* which yield substantial nourishment, and which were the products of Canaan, Immanuel's land. Christ delights himself greatly in that which he has both conferred upon his people and wrought in them. Or we may suppose this to have been prepared by the spouse herself, as Esther prepared for the king her husband *a banquet of wine;* it is but plain fare, and what is natural, honey and milk, but, being kindly designed, it is kindly accepted; imperfections are overlooked; the honey-comb is eaten with the honey, and the weakness of the flesh passed by and pardoned, because the *spirit is willing.* When Christ appeared to his disciples after his resurrection he did eat with them a piece of a honey-comb (Lu. 24:42, 43), in which this scripture was fulfilled. He did not drink the wine only, which is liquor for men, for great men, but the milk too, which is liquor for children, little children, for he was to be the *holy child Jesus,* that had need of milk. 6. She only invited him to come himself, but he, bringing his own entertainment along with him, brings his friends too, and invites them to share in the provisions. *The more the merrier,* we say; and here, where there was so great a plenty, there was not the worse fare. When our Lord Jesus fed 5000 at once *they did all eat and were filled.* Christ invites all his friends to the *wine and milk* which he himself drinks of (Isa. 55:1), to the *feast of fat things* and *wines on the lees,* Isa. 25:6. The great work of man's redemption, and the riches of the covenant of grace, are a feast to the Lord Jesus and they ought to be so to us. The invitation is very free, and hearty, and loving: *Eat, O friends!* If Christ comes to sup with us, it is we that sup with him, Rev. 3:20. *Eat, O friends!* Those only that are Christ's friends are welcome to his table; his enemies, *that will not have him to reign over them,* have *no part nor lot in the matter. Drink, yea, drink abundantly.* Christ, in his gospel, has made plentiful provision for poor souls. *He fills the hungry with good things;* there is enough for all, there is enough for each; *we are not straitened in him* or in his grace, let us not therefore be straitened in our own bosoms. *Open the mouth widely, and Christ will fill it. Be not drunk with wine,* but *be filled with the Spirit,* Eph. 5:18. Those that entertain Christ must bid his friends welcome with him; Jesus and his disciples were called together to the marriage (Jn. 2:2), and Christ will have all his friends to rejoice with him in the day of his espousals to his church, and, in token of that, to feast with him. In spiritual and heavenly joys there is no danger of exceeding; there we may *drink abundantly, drink of the river of God's pleasures* (Ps. 36:8), and be *abundantly satisfied,* Ps. 65:4.

Verses 2–8

In this song of loves and joys we have here a very melancholy scene; the spouse here speaks, not to her beloved (as before, for he has withdrawn), but of him, and it is a sad story she tells of her own folly and ill conduct towards him, notwithstanding his kindness, and of the just rebukes she fell under for it. Perhaps it may refer to Solomon's own apostasy from God, and the sad effects of that apostasy after God had come into his garden, had taken possession of the temple he had built, and he had feasted with God upon the sacrifices (*v.* 1); however, it is applicable to the too common case both of the churches and particular believers, who by their carelessness and security provoke Christ to withdraw from them. Observe,

I. The indisposition that the spouse was under, and the listlessness that had seized her (*v.* 2): *I sleep, but my heart wakes.* Here is, 1. Corruption appearing in the actings of it: *I sleep.* The wise virgins slumbered. She *was on her bed* (*ch.* 3:1), but now she sleeps. Spiritual distempers, if not striven against at first, are apt to grow upon us and to get ground. *She slept,* that is, pious affections cooled, she neglected her duty and grew remiss in it, she indulged herself in her ease, was secure and off her watch. This is sometimes the bad effect of more than ordinary enlargements — a good cause. St. Paul himself was in danger of being puffed up with abundant revelations, and of saying, *Soul, take thy ease,* which made a *thorn in the flesh* necessary for him, to keep him from sleeping. Christ's disciples, when he had come into his garden, the garden of his agony, were heavy with sleep, and could not watch with him. True Christians are not always alike lively and vigorous in religion. 2. Grace remaining, notwithstanding, in the habit of it: *"My heart wakes;* my own conscience reproaches me for it, and ceases not to rouse me out of my sluggishness. *The spirit is willing,* and, *after the inner man, I delight in the law of God,* and *with my mind I serve that.* I am, for the present, overpowered by temptation, but all does not go one way in me. I sleep, but it is not a dead sleep; I strive against it; it is not a sound sleep; I cannot be easy under this indisposition." Note, (1.) We ought to take notice of our own spiritual slumbers and distempers, and to reflect upon it with sorrow and shame that we have fallen asleep when Christ has been nigh us in his garden. (2.) When we are lamenting what is amiss in us, we must not overlook the good that is wrought in us, and preserved alive: "My heart wakes in Christ, who is dear to me as my own heart, and is my life; when I sleep, *he neither slumbers nor sleeps."*

II. The call that Christ gave to her, when she was under this indisposition: *It is the voice of my beloved;* she knew it to be so, and was soon aware of it, which was a sign that her heart was awake. Like the child Samuel, she heard at the first call, but did not, like him, mistake the person; she knew it to be the voice of Christ. He knocks, to awaken us to come and let him in, knocks by his word and Spirit, knocks by afflictions and by our own consciences; though this is not expressly quoted, yet probably it is referred to (Rev. 3:20), *Behold, I stand at the door, and knock.* He calls sinners into covenant with him and saints into communion with him. Those whom he loves he will not let alone in their carelessness, but will find some way or other to awaken them, to rebuke and chasten them. When we are unmindful of Christ he thinks of us, and provides that our faith fail not. Peter denied Christ, but the Lord turned and looked upon him, and so brought him to himself again. Observe how moving the call is: *Open to me, my sister, my love.* 1. He sues for entrance who may demand it; he knocks who could easily knock the door down. 2. He gives her all the kind and most endearing titles imaginable: *My sister, my love, my dove, my undefiled;* he not only gives her no hard names, nor upbraids her with unkindness in not sitting up for him, but, on the contrary, studies how to express his tender affection to her still. *His loving-kindness he will not utterly take away.* Those that by faith are espoused to Christ he looks upon as his sisters, his loves, his doves, and all that is dear; and, being clothed with his righteousness, they are undefiled. This consideration should induce her to open to him. Christ's love to us should engage ours to him, even in the most self-denying instances. *Open to me.* Can we deny entrance to such a friend, to such a guest? Shall we not converse more with one that is infinitely worthy of our acquaintance, and so affectionately desirous of it, though we only can be gainers by it? 3. He pleads distress, and begs to be admitted *sub formâ pauperis — under the character of a poor traveller* that wants a lodging: *"My head is wet with the dew,* with the cold drops of the night; consider what hardships I have undergone, to merit thee, which surely may merit from thee so small a kindness as this." When Christ was crowned with thorns, which no doubt fetched blood from his blessed head, then was his head *wet with the dew.* "Consider what a grief it is to me to be thus unkindly used, as much as it would be to a tender husband to be kept out of doors by his wife in a rainy stormy night." Do we thus require him for his love? The slights which careless souls put upon Jesus Christ are him as a *continual dropping in a very rainy day.*

III. The excuse she made to put off her compliance with this call (*v.* 3): *I have put off my coat; how shall I put it on again?* She is half asleep; she knows the voice of her beloved; she knows his knock, but cannot find in her heart to open to him. She was undressed, and would not be at the pains to dress herself again; she had *washed her feet,* and would not have occasion to wash them again. She could not send another to open the door (it must be our own act and deed to let Christ into our hearts), and yet she was loth to go herself; she did not say, *I will not open,* but, *How shall I?* Note, Frivolous excuses are the language of prevailing slothfulness in religion; Christ calls to us to open to him, but we pretend we have no mind, or we have no strength, or we have no time, and therefore think we may be excused, as the *sluggard* that *will not plough by reason of cold.* And those who ought to *watch for the Lord's coming* with their *loins girt,* if they ungird themselves and put off their coat, will find it difficult to recover their former resolution and to put it on again; it is best therefore to keep tight. Making excuses (Lu. 14:18) is interpreted making light of Christ (Mt. 22:5), and so it is. Those put a great contempt upon Christ that cannot find in their hearts to bear a cold blast for him, or get out of a warm bed.

IV. The powerful influences of divine grace, by which she was made willing to rise and open to her beloved. When he could not prevail with her by persuasion he *put in his hand by the hole in the door,* to unbolt it, as one weary of waiting, *v.* 4. This intimates a work of the Spirit upon her soul, by which she was unwilling made willing, Ps. 110:3. The conversion of Lydia is represented by the *opening of her heart* (Acts 16:14) and Christ is said to open his disciples' understandings, Lu. 24:45. He that *formed the spirit of man within him* knows all the avenues to it, and which way to enter into it; he can find the *hole of the door* at which to put in his hand for the conquering of prejudices and the introducing of his own doctrine and law. He has the *key of David* (Rev. 3:7), with which he opens the door of the heart in such a way as is suited to it, as the key is fitted to the wards of the lock, in such a way as not to put a force upon its nature, but only upon its ill nature.

V. Her compliance with these methods of divine grace at last: *My bowels were moved for him.* The will was gained by a good work wrought upon the affections: *My bowels were moved for him,* as those of the two disciples were when Christ made their *hearts to burn within them.* She was moved with compassion to her beloved, because his *head was wet with dew.* Note, Tenderness of spirit, and a heart of flesh, prepare the soul for the reception of Christ into it; and therefore his love to us is represented in such a way as is most affecting. Did Christ redeem us in his pity? Let us in pity receive him, and, for his sake, those that are his, when at any time they are in distress. This good work, wrought upon her affections, raised her up, and made her ashamed of her dulness and slothfulness (*v.* 5, *I rose up, to open to my beloved*), his grace inclining her to do it and conquering the opposition of unbelief. It was her own act, and yet he wrought it in her. And now her *hands dropped with myrrh upon the handles of the lock.* Either, 1. She found it there when she applied her hand to the lock, to shoot it back; he that *put in his hand by the hole of the door* left it there as an evidence that he had been there. When Christ has wrought powerfully upon a soul he leaves a blessed sweetness in it, which is very delightful to it. With this he oiled the lock, to make it go easy. Note, When we apply ourselves to our duty, in the lively exercises of faith, under the influence of divine grace, we shall find it will go on much more readily and sweetly than we expected. If we will but rise up, to open to Christ, we shall find the difficulty we apprehended in it strangely overcome, and shall say with Daniel, *Now let my Lord speak, for thou hast strengthened me,* Dan. 10:19. Or, 2. She brought it thither. Her *bowels being moved for her beloved,* who had stood so long in the cold and wet, when she came to open to him she prepared to anoint his head, and so to refresh and comfort him, and perhaps to prevent his catching cold; she was in such haste to meet him that she would not stay to make the usual preparation, but dipped her hand in her box of ointment, that she might readily anoint his head at his first coming in. Those that open the doors of their hearts to Christ, those *everlasting doors,* must meet him with the lively exercises of faith and other graces, and with these must anoint him.

VI. Her said disappointment when she did open to her beloved. And here is the most melancholy part of the story: *I opened to my beloved,* as I intended, but, alas! *my beloved had withdrawn himself, and was gone. My beloved was gone, was gone,* so the word is.

1. She did not open to him at his first knock, and now she came too late, when afterwards she *would have inherited this blessing.* Christ will be sought while he may be found; if we slip our time, we may lose our passage. Note, (1.) Christ justly rebukes our delays with his denials, and suspends the communications of comfort from those that are remiss and drowsy in their duty. (2.) Christ's departures are matter of great grief and lamentation to believers. The royal psalmist never complains of any thing with such sorrowful accents as God's *hiding his face* from him, and *casting him off,* and *forsaking him.* The spouse here is ready to tear her hair, and rend her clothes, and wring her hands, crying, *He is gone, he is gone;* and that which cuts her to the heart is that she may thank herself, she provoked him to withdraw. If Christ departs, it is because he takes something unkindly.

2. Now observe what she does, in this case, and what befel her. (1.) She still calls him her *beloved,* being resolved, how cloudy and dark soever the day be, she will not quit her relation to him and interest in him. It is a weakness, upon every apprehension either of our own failings or of God's withdrawings, to conclude hardly as to our spiritual state. Every desertion is not despair. I will say, *Lord, I believe,* though I must say, *Lord, help my unbelief.* Though he leave me, I love him; he is mine. (2.) She now remembers the words he said to her when he called her, and what impressions they made upon her, reproaching herself for her folly in not complying sooner with her convictions: *"My soul failed when he spoke;* his words melted me when he said, *My head is wet with dew;* and yet, wretch that I was, I lay still, and made excuses, and did not open to him." The smothering and stifling of our convictions is a thing that will be very bitter in the reflection, when God opens our eyes. Sometimes the word has not its effect immediately upon the heart, but it melts it afterwards, upon second thoughts. *My soul* now *melted because of his words* which he had spoken before. (3.) She did not go to bed again, but went in pursuit of him: *I sought him; I called him.* She might have saved herself this labour if she would but have bestirred herself when he first called; but we cut ourselves out a great deal of work, and create ourselves a great deal of trouble, by our own slothfulness and carelessness in improving our opportunities. Yet it is her praise that, when her beloved has withdrawn, she continues seeking him; her desires toward him are made more strong, and her enquiries after him more solicitous, by his withdrawings. She calls him by prayer, calls after him, and begs of him to return; and she not only prays but uses means, she seeks him in the ways wherein she used to find him. (4.) Yet still she missed of him: *I could not find him; he gave me no answer.* She had no evidence of his favour, no sensible comforts, but was altogether in the dark, and in doubt concerning his love towards her. Note, There are those who have a true love for Christ, and yet have not immediate answers to their prayers for his smiles; but he gives them an equivalent if he strengthens them with the strength in their souls to continue seeking him, Ps. 138:3. St. Paul could not prevail for the removing of the *thorn in the flesh,* but was answered with grace sufficient for him. (5.) She was ill-treated by the watchmen; *They found me; they smote me; they wounded me, v.* 7. They took her for a lewd woman (because she went about the streets at that time of night, when they were walking their rounds), and beat her accordingly. Disconsolate saints are taken for sinners, and are censured and reproached as such. Thus Hannah, when she was praying in the *bitterness of her soul,* was wounded and smitten by Eli, one of the prime watchmen, when he said to her, *How long wilt thou be drunken?* so counting her a daughter of Belial, 1 Sa. 1:14, 15. It is no new thing for those that are of the loyal loving subjects of Zion's King to be misrepresented by the watchmen of Zion, as enemies or scandals to his kingdom; they could not abuse and persecute them but by putting them into an ill name. Some apply it to those ministers who, though watchmen by office, yet misapply the word to awakened consciences, and through unskillfulness, or contempt of their griefs, add affliction to the afflicted, and *make the hearts of the righteous sad whom God would not have made sad* (Eze. 13:22), discouraging those who ought to be encouraged and talking to the grief of those *whom God has wounded,* Ps. 59:26. Those watchmen were bad enough that could not, or would not, assist the spouse in her enquiries after her beloved (*ch.* 3:3); but these were much worse, that hindered her with their severe and uncharitable censures, *smote her* and *wounded her* with their reproaches, and though they were the *keepers of the wall of Jerusalem,* as if they had been the breakers of it, *took away her veil,* from her rudely and barbarously, as if it had been only a pretence of modesty, but a cover of the contrary. Those whose outward appearances are all good, and who yet are invidiously condemned and run down as hypocrites, have reason to complain, as the spouse here, of the *taking away of their veil* from them. (6.) When she was disabled by the abuses the watchmen gave her to prosecute her enquiry herself she gave charge to those about her to assist her in the enquiry (*v.* 8): *I charge you, O you daughters of Jerusalem!* all my friends and acquaintance, *if you find my beloved,* it may be you may meet with him before I shall, *what shall you tell him?* so some read. "Speak a good word for me; tell him that *I am sick of love."* Observe here, [1.] What her condition was. She loved Jesus Christ to such a degree that his absence made her sick, extremely sick, she could not bear it, and she was in pain for his return as a woman in travail, as Ahab for Naboth's vineyard, which he so passionately coveted. This is a sickness which is a sign of a healthy constitution of soul, and will certainly end well, a sickness that will not be death, but life. It is better to be sick of love to Christ than at ease in love to the world. (2.) What course she took in this condition. She did not sink into despair, and conclude that she should die of her disease, but she sent after her beloved; she asked the advice of her neighbours, and begged their prayers for her, that they would intercede with him on her behalf. "Tell him, though I was careless, and foolish, and slothful, and rose not up so soon as I should have done to open to him, yet I love him; he *knows all things,* he *knows that I do.* Represent me to him as sincere, though in many instances coming short of my duty; nay, represent me to him as sincere, though in many instances coming short of my duty; nay, represent me as an object of his pity, that he may have compassion on me and help me." She does not bid them tell him how the watchmen had abused her; how unrighteous soever they were in it, she acknowledges that *the Lord is righteous,* and therefore bears it patiently. "But tell him that I am wounded with love to him." Gracious souls are more sensible of Christ's withdrawings than of any other trouble whatsoever.

> Languet amaus, non languet amor —
> The lover languishes, but not his love.

Verses 9–16

Here is, I. The question which the daughters of Jerusalem put to the spouse concerning her beloved, in answer to the charge she had given them, *v.* 9. Observe, 1. The respectful title they give to the spouse: *O thou fairest among women!* Our Lord Jesus makes his spouse truly amiable, not only in his eyes, but in the eyes of all the daughters of Jerusalem. The church is the most excellent society in the world, the communion of saints the best communion, and the beauty of the sanctuary a transcendent beauty. The saints are the most excellent people; holiness is the symmetry of the soul; it is its agreement with itself; it recommends itself to all that are competent judges of it. Even those that have little acquaintance with Christ, as those daughters of Jerusalem here, cannot but see an amiable beauty in those that bear his image, which we should love wherever we see it, though in different dresses. 2. Their enquiry concerning her beloved: *"What is thy beloved more than another beloved?* If thou wilt have us to find him for thee, give us his marks, that we may know him when we see him." (1.) Some take it for a scornful question, blaming her for making such ado about him: "Why shouldst thou be so passionate in enquiring after thy beloved, more than others are after theirs? Why shouldst thou be so set upon him, more than others that yet have a kindness for him?" Those that are zealous in religion are men wondered at by such as are indifferent to it. The many careless ones laugh at the few that are solicitous and serious. "What is there in him that is so very charming, more than in another person? If he be gone, thou, who art the *fairest among women,* wilt soon have another with an equal flame." Note, Carnal hearts see nothing excellent or extraordinary in the Lord Jesus, in his person or offices, in his doctrine or in his favours; as if there were no more in the knowledge of Christ, and in communion with him, than in the knowledge of the world and in its conversation. (2.) Others rather take it for a serious question, and suppose that those who put it intended, [1.] To comfort the spouse, who, they knew, would recover new spirits if she did but talk awhile of her beloved; nothing would please her better, nor give a more powerful diversion to her grief, than to be put upon the pleasing task of describing the beauties of her beloved. [2.] To inform themselves; they had heard, in general, that he was excellent and glorious, but they desired to know more particularly. They wondered what moved the spouse to charge them concerning her beloved with so much vehemence and concern, and therefore concluded there must be something more in him than in another beloved, which they are willing to be convinced of. *Then* there begin to be some hopes of people when they begin to enquire concerning Christ and his transcendent perfections. And sometimes the extraordinary zeal of one, in enquiring after Christ, may be a means to provoke many (2 Co. 9:2), as the apostle, by the faith of the Gentiles, would stir up the Jews to a holy emulation, Rom. 11:14. See Jn. 4:10.

II. The account which the spouse gives of her beloved in answer to this question. We should always be ready to instruct and assist those that are enquiring after Christ. Experienced Christians, who are well acquainted with Christ themselves, should do all they can to make others acquainted with him.

1. She assures them, in general, that he is one of incomparable perfections and unparalleled worth (*v.* 10): "Do not you know my beloved? Can the daughters of Jerusalem be ignorant of him that is Jerusalem's crown and crowned head? Let me tell you then," (1.) That he has every thing in him that is lovely and amiable: *My beloved is white and ruddy,* the colours that make up a complete beauty. This points not at any extraordinary beauty of his body, when he should be incarnate (it was never said of the child Jesus, as of the child Moses, when he was born, that he was *exceedingly fair,* Acts 7:20; nay, *he had no form nor comeliness,* Isa. 53:2); but his divine glory, and the concurrence of every thing in him as Mediator, to make him truly lovely in the eyes of those that are enlightened to discern spiritual things. In him we may behold the *beauty of the Lord;* he was the *holy child Jesus;* that was his fairness. If we look upon him as made to us *wisdom, righteousness, sanctification, and redemption,* he appears, in all, very amiable. His love to us renders him lovely. He is *white* in the spotless innocency of his life, *ruddy* in the bloody sufferings he went through at his death, — *white* in his glory, as God (when he was transfigured *his raiment was white as the light*), *ruddy* in his assuming the nature of man, *Adam — red earth, — white* in his tenderness towards his people, *ruddy* in his terrible appearances against his and their enemies. His complexion is a very happy composition. (2.) That he has that loveliness in him which is not to be found in any other: He is *the chief among ten thousand,* a nonsuch for beauty, *fairer than the children of men,* than any of them, than all of them; there is none like him, nor any to be compared with him; every thing else is to be accounted *loss and dung in comparison of him,* Phil. 3:8. *He is higher than the kings of the earth* (Ps. 89:27) and has *obtained a more excellent name* than any of the principalities and powers of the upper or lower world, Phil. 2:9; Heb. 1, 4. He is a *standard-bearer among ten thousand* (so the word is), the tallest and comeliest of the com-

pany. He is himself *lifted up as an ensign* (Isa. 11:10), to whom we must be gathered and must always have an eye. And there is all the reason in the world why he should have the innermost and uppermost place in our souls who is the *fairest of ten thousands* in himself and the fittest of twenty thousands for us.

2. She gives a particular detail of his accomplishments, conceals not his power or comely proportion. Every thing in Christ is amiable. Ten instances she here gives of his beauty, which we need not be nice in the application of, lest the wringing of them bring forth blood and prove the wresting of them. The design, in general, is to show that he is every way qualified for his undertaking, and has all that in him which may recommend him to our esteem, love, and confidence. Christ's appearance to John (Rev. 1:13, etc.) may be compared with the description which the spouse gives of him here, the scope of both being to represent him transcendently glorious, that is, both great and gracious, made lovely in the eyes of believers and making them happy in himself. (1.) *His head is as the most fine gold. The head of Christ is God* (1 Co. 11:3), and it is promised to the saints that *the Almighty shall be their gold* (Job 22:25), their defence, their treasure; much more was he so to Christ, *in whom dwells all the fulness of the Godhead bodily,* Col. 2:9. Christ's head bespeaks his sovereign dominion over all and his vital influence upon his church and all its members. This is as *gold, gold;* the former word in the original signifies shining gold, the latter strong solid gold; Christ's sovereignty is both beautiful and powerful. Nebuchadnezzar's monarchy is compared to a *head of gold* (Dan. 2:38), because it excelled all the other monarchies, and so does Christ's government. (2.) *His locks are bushy and black,* not *black as the tents of Kedar,* whose blackness was their deformity, to which therefore the church compares herself (*ch.* 1:5), but *black as a raven,* whose blackness is his beauty. Sometimes Christ's hair is represented as *white* (Rev. 1:14), denoting his eternity, that he is *the ancient of days;* but here as *black and bushy,* denoting that he is ever young and that there is in him no decay, nothing that waxes old. Every thing that belongs to Christ is amiable in the eyes of a believer, even his hair is so; it was pity that it should be wet, as it was, *with the dew,* and these *locks with the drops of the night,* while he waited to be gracious, *v.* 2. (3.) *His eyes are as the eyes of doves,* fair and clear, and chaste and kind, *by the rivers of waters,* which doves delight in, and in which, as in a glass, they see themselves. They are washed, to make them clean, *washed with milk,* to make them white, and *fitly set,* neither starting out nor sunk in. Christ is *of purer eyes than to behold iniquity,* for they are doves' eyes, Hab. 1:13. All believers speak with pleasure of the omniscience of Christ, as the spouse here of *his eyes;* for, though it be terrible to his enemies *as a flame of fire* (Rev. 1:14), yet it is amiable and comfortable to his friends, as *doves' eyes,* for it is a witness to their integrity. *Thou knowest all things, thou knowest that I love thee.* Blessed and holy are those that walk always as under the eye of Christ. (4.) *His cheeks* (the rising of the face) *are as a bed of spices,* raised in the gardens, which are the beauty and wealth of them, and *as sweet flowers,* or towers of sweetness. There is that in Christ's countenance which is amiable in the eyes of all the saints, in the least glimpse of him, for the cheek is but a part of the face. The half discoveries Christ makes of himself to the soul are reviving and refreshing, fragrant above the richest flowers and perfumes. (5.) *His lips are like lilies,* not white like lilies, but sweet and pleasant. Such are *the words of his lips* to all that are sanctified, *sweeter than honey and the honey-comb;* such are the *kisses of his lips,* all the communications of his grace; *grace is poured into his lips,* and those that heard him *wondered at the gracious words which proceeded out of his mouth. His lips* are as *lilies, dropping sweet-smelling myrrh.* Never any lilies in nature dropped myrrh, but nothing in nature can fully set forth the beauty and excellence of Christ, and therefore, to do it by comparison, there must be a composition of images. (6.) *His hands are as gold rings set with the beryl,* a noted precious stone, *v.* 14. Great men had their hands adorned with gold rings on their fingers, set with diamonds or other precious stones, but, in her eye, *his hands* themselves were *as gold rings;* all the instances of his power, the works of his hands, all the performances of his providence and grace, are all rich, and pure, and precious, as gold, *as the precious onyx and the sapphire,* all fitted to the purpose for which they were designed *as gold rings* to the finger, and all beautiful and very becoming, *as rings set with beryl.* His hands, which are stretched forth both to receive his people and to give to them, are thus rich and comely. (7.) *His bowels are as bright ivory,* for so it should be rendered, rather than *his belly,* for it is the same word that was used for *bowels* (*v.* 4) and is often ascribed to God (as Isa. 63:15; Jer. 31:20), and so it denotes his tender compassion and affection for his spouse, and the love he has to her even in her desolate and deserted state. This love of his is like *bright ivory,* finely polished, and richly *overlaid with sapphires.* The love itself is strong and firm, and the instances and circumstances of it are bright and sparkling, and add much to the inestimable value of it. (8.) *His legs are as pillars of marble,* so strong, and stately, and no disgrace, no, not to the *sockets of fine gold upon* which they are *set, v.* 15. This bespeaks his stability and stedfastness; where he sets his foot he will fix it; he is able to bear all the weight of the government that is upon his shoulders, and his legs will never fail under him. This sets forth the stateliness and magnificence of *the goings of our God, our King, in his sanctuary* (Ps. 68:24), and the steadiness and evenness of all his dispensations towards his people. *The ways of the Lord are equal;* they are all *mercy and truth;* these are the *pillars of marble,* more lasting than the pillars of heaven. (9.) *His countenance* (his port and mien) *is as Lebanon,* that stately hill; his aspect beautiful and charming, like the prospect of that pleasant forest or park, *excellent as the cedars,* which, in height and strength, excel other trees, and are of excellent use. Christ is a goodly person; the more we look upon him the more beauty we shall see in him. (10.) *His mouth is most sweet;* it is sweetness itself; it is *sweetnesses* (so the word is); it is pure essence, nay, it is the quintessence of all delights, *v.* 16. The words of his mouth are all sweet to a believer, sweet as milk to babes (to whom it is agreeable), as honey to those that are grown up (Ps. 119:103), to whom it is delicious. The kisses of his mouth, all the tokens of his love, have a transcendent sweetness in them, and are most delightful to those who have their *spiritual senses exercised. To you that believe he is precious.*

3. She concludes with a full assurance both of faith and hope, and so gets the mastery of her trouble. (1.) Here is a full assurance of faith concerning the complete beauty of the Lord Jesus: *"He is altogether lovely.* Why should I stand to mention particulars, when throughout there is nothing amiss?" She is sensible she does him wrong in the particular descriptions of him, and comes far short of the dignity and merit of the subject, and therefore she breaks off with the general encomium: *He is* truly *lovely,* he is wholly so; there is nothing in him but what is amiable, and nothing amiable but what is in him. *He is all desires;* he has all in him that one can desire. And therefore all her desire is towards him, and she seeks him thus carefully and cannot rest contented in the want of him. Who can but love him who is so lovely? (2.) Here is a full assurance of hope concerning her own interest in him: *"This is my beloved, and this is my friend;* and therefore wonder not that I thus long after him." See with what a holy boldness she claims relation to him, and then with what a holy triumph she proclaims it. It is property that sweetens excellency. To see Christ, and not to see him as ours, would be rather a torture than a happiness; but to see one that is thus lovely, and to see him as ours, is a complete satisfaction. Here is a true believer, [1.] Giving an entire consent to Christ: "He is mine, *my Lord and my God* (Jn. 20:28), mine according to the tenour of the gospel-covenant, mine in all relations, bestowed upon me, to be all that to me that my poor soul stands in need of." [2.] Taking an entire complacency in Christ. It is spoken of here with an air of triumph: "This is he whom I have chosen, and to whom I have given up myself. None but Christ, none but Christ. This is he on whom my heart is, for he is my best-beloved; this is he in whom I trust, and from whom I expect all good, *for this is my friend."* Note, Those that make Christ their beloved shall have him their friend; he has been, is, and will be, a special friend to all believers. He loves those that love him; and those that have him their friend have reason to glory in him, and speak of him with delight. "Let others be governed by the love of the world, and seek their happiness in its friendship and favours, *This is my beloved and this is my friend.* Others may do as they please, but this is my soul's choice, my soul's rest, my life, my joy, my all; this is he whom I desire to live and die with."

CHAPTER 6

In this chapter, I. The daughters of Jerusalem, moved with the description which the church had given of Christ, enquire after him (*v.* 1). II. The church directs them where they may meet with him (*v.* 2, 3). III. Christ is now found of those that sought him, and very highly applauds the beauty of his spouse, as one extremely smitten with it (*v.* 4–7), preferring her before all others (*v.* 8, 9), recommending her to the love and esteem of all her neighbours (*v.* 10), and, lastly, acknowledging the impressions which her beauty had made upon him and the great delight he took in it (*v.* 11–13).

Verses 1–3

Here is, I. The enquiry which the daughters of Jerusalem made concerning Christ, *v.* 1. They still continue their high thoughts of the church, and call her, as before, the *fairest among women;* for true sanctity is true beauty. And now they raise their thoughts higher concerning Christ: *Whither has thy beloved gone, that we may seek him with thee?* This would be but an indecent, unacceptable, compliment, if the song were not to be understood spiritually; for love is jealous of a rival, would monopolize the beloved, and cares not that others should join in seeking him; but those that truly love Christ are desirous that others should love him too, and be joined to him; nay, the greatest instance of duty and respect that the church's children can show to their mother is to join with her in seeking Christ. The *daughters of Jerusalem,* who had asked (*ch.* 5:9), *What is thy beloved more than another beloved?* wondering that the spouse should be so passionately in love with him, are now of another mind, and are themselves in love with him; for, 1. The spouse had described him, and shown them his excellencies and perfections; and therefore, though they have not seen him, yet, believing, they love him. Those that undervalue Christ do so because they do not know him; when God, by his word and Spirit, discovers him to the soul, with that ray of light the fire of love to him will be kindled. 2. The spouse had expressed her own love to him, her rest in that love, and triumphed in it: *This is my beloved;* and that flame in her breast scattered sparks into theirs. As sinful lusts, when they break out, defile many, so the pious zeal of some may *provoke many,* 2 Co. 9:2. 3. The spouse had bespoken their help in seeking her beloved (*ch.* 5:8); but now they beg hers, for they perceive that now the cloud she had been under began to scatter, and the sky to clear up, and, while she was describing her beloved to them, she herself retrieved her comfort in him. Drooping Christians would find benefit themselves by talking of Christ, as well as do good to others. Now here, (1.) They enquire concerning him, *"Wither has thy beloved gone?* which may must we steer our course in pursuit of him?" Note, Those that are made acquainted with the excellencies of Christ, and the comfort of an interest in him, cannot but be inquisitive after him and desirous to know where they may meet with him. (2.) They offer their service to the spouse to accompany her in quest of him: *We will seek him with thee.* Those that would find Christ must seek him, seek him early, seek him diligently; and it is best seeking Christ in concert, to join with those that are seeking him. We must seek for communion with Christ in communion with saints. We know *whither our beloved has gone;* he has gone to heaven, *to his Father, and our Father.* He took care to send us notice of it, that we might know how to direct to him, Jn. 20:17. We must by faith see him there, and by prayer seek him there, with boldness *enter into the holiest,* and herein must join with *the generation of those that seek him* (Ps. 24:6), even with *all that in every place call upon him,* 1 Co. 1:2. We must pray with and for others.

II. The answer which the spouse gave to this enquiry, *v.* 2, 3. Now she complains not any more, as she had done (*ch.* 5:6), "He is gone, he is gone," that she knew not where to find him, or doubted she had lost him for ever; no,

1. Now she knows very well where he is (*v.* 2): *"My beloved* is not to be found in the streets of the city, and the crowd and noise that are there; there I have in vain looked for him" (as his parents *sought him among their kindred and acquaintance, and found him not*); "but he *has gone down to his garden,* a place of privacy and retirement." The more we withdraw from the hurry of the world the

more likely we are to have acquaintance with Christ, who took his disciples into a garden, there to be witnesses of the agonies of his love. Christ's church is a garden enclosed, and separated from the open common of the world; it is *his garden,* which he has planted as he did the garden of Eden, which he takes care of, and delights in. Though he had gone up to the paradise above, yet he comes down to his garden on earth; it lies low, but he condescends to visit it, and wonderful condescension it is. *Will God in very deed dwell with man upon the earth?* Those that would find Christ may expect to meet with him *in his garden* the church, for *there he records his name* (Ex. 20:24); they must attend upon him in the ordinances which he has instituted, the word, sacraments, and prayer, wherein he will be with us *always, even to the end of the world.* The spouse here refers to what Christ had said (ch. 5:1), *I have come into my garden.* It is as if she had said, "What a fool was I to fret and fatigue myself in seeking him where he was not, when he himself had told me where he was!" Words of direction and comfort are often out of the way when we have occasion to use them, till the blessed Spirit brings them to our remembrance, and then we wonder how we overlooked them. Christ has told us that he would *come into his garden;* thither therefore we must go to seek him. *The beds,* and smaller *gardens,* in this greater, are the particular churches, the *synagogues of God in the land* (Ps. 84:8); the *spices* and *lilies* are particular believers, the planting of the Lord, and pleasant in his eyes. When Christ comes down to his church it is, (1.) *To feed* among *the gardens,* to feed his flock, which he feeds not, as other shepherds, in the open fields, but in his garden, so well are they provided for, Ps. 23:2. He comes to feed his friends, and entertain them; there you may not only find him, but find his table richly furnished, and a hearty welcome to it. He comes to feed himself, that is, to please himself with the products of his own grace in his people; *for the Lord takes pleasure in those that fear him.* He has many gardens, many particular churches of different sizes and shapes; but, while they are his, he feeds in them all, manifests himself among them, and is well pleased with them. (2.) *To gather lilies,* wherewith he is pleased to entertain and adorn himself. He picks the lilies one by one, and gathers them to himself; and there will be a general harvest of them at the great day, when he will send forth his angels, to gather all his lilies, that he may be for ever glorified and admired in them.

2. She is very confident of her own interest in him (*v.* 3): *"I am my beloved's, and my beloved is mine;* the relation is mutual, and the knot is tied, which cannot be loosed; for *he feeds among the lilies,* and my communion with him is a certain token of my interest in him." She had said this before (ch. 2:16); but, (1.) Here she repeats it as that which she resolved to abide by, and which she took an unspeakable pleasure and satisfaction in; she liked her choice too well to change. Our communion with God is very much maintained and kept up by the frequent renewing of our covenant with him and rejoicing in it. (2.) She had occasion to repeat it, for she had acted unkindly to her beloved, and, for her so doing, he had justly withdrawn himself from her, and therefore there was occasion to take fresh hold of the covenant, which continues firm between Christ and believes, notwithstanding their failings and his frowns, Ps. 89:30–35. "I have been careless and wanting in my duty, and yet *I am my beloved's;"* for every transgression in the covenant does not throw us out of covenant. "He has justly hidden his face from me and denied me his comforts, and yet *my beloved is mine;"* for rebukes and chastenings are not only consistent with, but they flow from covenant-love. (3.) When we have not a full assurance of Christ's love we must live by a faithful adherence to him. "Though I have not the sensible consolation I used to have, yet I will cleave to this, *Christ is mine and I am his."* (4.) Though she had said the same before, yet now she inverts the order, and asserts her interest in her first: *I am my beloved's,* entirely devoted and dedicated to him; and then her interest in him and in his grace: *"My beloved is mine,* and I am happy, truly happy in him." If our own hearts can but witness for us that we are his, there is no room left to question his being ours; for the covenant never breaks on his side. (5.) It is now her comfort, as it was then, that *he feeds among the lilies,* that he takes delight in his people and converses freely with them, as we do with those with

whom we feed; and therefore, though at present he be withdrawn, "I shall meet with him again. *I shall yet praise him who is the health of my countenance, and my God."*

Verses 4–10

Now we must suppose Christ graciously returned to his spouse, from whom he had withdrawn himself, returned to converse with her (for he speaks to her and *makes her to hear joy and gladness),* returned to favour her, having forgiven and forgotten all her unkindness, for he speaks very tenderly and respectfully to her.

I. He pronounces her truly amiable (*v.* 4): *Thou art beautiful, O my love! as Tirzah,* a city in the tribe of Manasseh, whose name signifies *pleasant,* or *acceptable,* the situation, no doubt, being very happy and the building fine and uniform. *Thou art comely as Jerusalem,* a city *compact together* (Ps. 122:3), and which Solomon had built and beautified, *the joy of the whole earth;* it was an honour to the world (whether they thought so or no) that there was such a city in it. It was the holy city, and that was the greatest beauty of it; and fitly is the church compared to it, for it was figured and typified by it. The gospel-church is *the Jerusalem that is above* (Gal. 4:26), *the heavenly Jerusalem* (Heb. 12:22); in it God has *his sanctuary,* and is, in a special manner, present; thence he has the tribute of praise issuing; it is his rest for ever, and therefore it is *comely as Jerusalem,* and, being so, is *terrible as an army with banners.* Church-censures, duly administered, strike an awe upon men's consciences; the word (the weapons of her warfare) *casts down imaginations* (2 Co. 10:5), and even an unbeliever is convinced and judged by the solemnity of holy ordinances, 1 Co. 14:24, 25. The saints by faith *overcome the world* (1 Jn. 5:4); nay, like Jacob, they have *power with God and prevail,* Gen. 32:28.

II. He owns himself in love with her, *v.* 5. Though, for a small moment, and in a little wrath, he had hid his face from her, yet now he gathers her with very surprising instances of *everlasting lovingkindness,* Isa. 54:8. *Turn thy eyes towards me* (so some read it), "turn the eyes of faith and love towards me, *for they have lifted me up;* look unto me, and be comforted." When we are calling to God to turn the eye of his favour towards us he is calling to us to turn the eye of our obedience towards him. We read it as a strange expression of love, *"Turn away thy eyes from me, for* I cannot bear the brightness of them; *they have* quite *overcome me,* and I am prevailed with to overlook all that is past;" as God said to Moses, when he interceded for Israel, *"Let me alone,* or I must yield," Ex. 32:10. Christ is pleased to borrow these expressions of a passionate lover only to express the tenderness of a compassionate Redeemer, and the delight he takes in his redeemed and in the workings of his own grace in them.

III. He repeats, almost word for word, part of the description he had given of her beauty (ch. 4:1–3), her *hair,* her *teeth,* her *temples* (*v.* 5–7), not because he could not have described it in other words, and by other similitudes, but to show that he had still the same esteem for her since her unkindness to him, and his withdrawings from her, that he had before. Lest she should think that, though he would not quite cast her off, yet he would think the worse of her while he knew her, he says the same of her now that he had done; for those *to whom much is forgiven will love the more,* and, consequently, will be the more loved, for Christ has said, *I love those that love me.* He is pleased with his people, notwithstanding their weaknesses, when they sincerely repent of them and return to their duty, and commends them as if they had already arrived at perfection.

IV. He prefers her before all competitors, and sees all the beauties and perfections of others meeting and centering in her (*v.* 8, 9): *"There are,* it may be, *threescore queens,* who, like Esther, have by their beauty attained to the royal state and dignity, *and fourscore concubines,* whom kings have preferred before their own queens, as more charming, and these attended by their maids of honour, *virgins without number,* who, when there is a ball at court, appear in great splendour, with beauty that dazzles the eyes of the spectators; but *my dove, my undefiled, is but one,* a holy one." 1. She excels them all. Go through all the world, and view the societies of men that reckon themselves wise and happy, kingdoms, courts, senates, councils, or whatever incorporations you may think val-

uable, they are none of them to be compared with the church of Christ; their honours and beauties are nothing to hers. *Who is like unto thee, O Israel!* Deu. 33:29; 4:6, 7. There are particular persons, as *virgins without number,* who are famed for their accomplishments, the beauties of their address, language, and performances, but the beauty of holiness is beyond all other beauty: *"My dove, my undefiled, is one,* has that one beauty that she is a dove, an undefiled dove, and mine, and that makes her excel the queens and virgins, though they were ever so many." 2. She included them all. "Other kings have many queens, and concubines, and virgins, with whose conversation they entertain themselves, but *my dove, my undefiled,* is to me instead of all; in that one I have more than they have in all theirs." Or, "Though there are many particular churches, some of greater dignity, others of less, some of longer, others of shorter, standing, and many particular believers, of different gifts and attainments, some more eminent, others less so, yet they all constitute but one catholic church, are all but parts of that whole, and that is *my dove, my undefiled."* Christ is the centre of the church's unity; all the children of God that are scattered abroad are gathered by him (Jn. 11:52), and meet in him (Eph. 1:10), and are all his doves.

V. He shows how much she was esteemed, not by him only, but by all that had acquaintance with her and stood in relation to her. It would add to her praise to say, 1. That she was her mother's darling; she had that in her, from a child, which recommended her to the particular affection of her parents. As Solomon himself is said to have been *tender and an only one in the sight of his mother* (Prov. 4:3), so was she *the only one of her mother,* as dear as if she had been an only one, and, if there were many more, yet she was *the choice one of her that bore her,* more excellent than all the societies of men this world ever produced. All the kingdoms of the world, and the glory of them, are nothing, in Christ's account, compared with the church, which is made up of *the excellent ones of the earth,* the *precious sons of Zion, comparable to fine gold,* and *more excellent than their neighbours.* 2. That she was admired by all her acquaintance, not only *the daughters,* who were her juniors, but even *the queens and the concubines,* who might have reason to be jealous of her as a rival; *they* all *blessed her,* and wished well to her, *praised her,* and spoke well of her. *The daughters of Jerusalem* called her the *fairest among women;* all agreed to give her the pre-eminence for beauty, and every sheaf bowed to hers. Note, (1.) Those that have any correct sense of things cannot but be convinced in their consciences (whatever they say) that godly people are excellent people; many will give them their good word, and more their good-will. (2.) Jesus Christ takes notice what people think and speak of his church, and is well pleased with those that honour such as fear the Lord, and takes it ill of those that despise them, particularly when they are under a cloud, that *offend any of his little ones.*

VI. He produces the encomium that was given of her, and makes it his own (*v.* 10): *Who is she that looks forth as the morning?* This is applicable both to the church in the world and to grace in the heart.

1. They are amiable as the light, the most beautiful of all visible things. Christians are, or should be, the lights of the world. The patriarchal church *looked forth as the morning* when the promise of the Messiah was first made known, and *the day-spring from on high visited this dark world.* The Jewish church was *fair as the moon;* the ceremonial law was an imperfect light; it shone by reflection; it was changing as the moon, did not make day, nor had *the sun of righteousness yet risen.* But the Christian church is clear *as the sun,* exhibits a great *light to those that sat in darkness.* Or we may apply it to the kingdom of grace, the gospel-kingdom. (1.) In its rise, it *looks forth as the morning* after a dark night; it is discovering (Job 38:12, 13), and very acceptable, *looks forth* pleasantly as a clear morning; but it is small in its beginnings, and scarcely perceptible at first. (2.) It is, at the best, in this world, but *fair as the moon,* which shines with a borrowed light, which has her changes and eclipses, and her spots too, and, when at the full, does but rule by night. But, (3.) When it is perfected in the kingdom of glory then it will be *clear as the sun,* the church *clothed with the sun,* with Christ *the sun of righteousness,* Rev. 12:1. Those that love God will then

be *as the sun when he goes forth in his strength* (Jdg. 5:31; Mt. 13:43); they shall shine in inexpressible glory, and that which is perfect will then come; there shall be no darkness, no spots, Isa. 30:26.

2. The beauty of the church and of believers is not only amiable, but *awful as an army with banners.* The church, in this world, is *as an army,* as the camp of Israel in the wilderness; its state is militant; it is in the midst of enemies, and is engaged in a constant conflict with them. Believers are soldiers in this army. It has its *banners;* the gospel of Christ is an ensign (Isa. 11:12), the love of Christ, *ch.* 2:4. It is marshalled, and kept in order and under discipline. It is *terrible* to its enemies as Israel in the wilderness was, Ex. 15:14. When Balaam saw Israel encamped according to their tribes, by their standards, with colours displayed, he said, *How goodly are thy tents, O Jacob!* Num. 24:5. When the church preserves her purity she secures her honour and victory; when she is *fair as the moon,* and *clear as the sun,* she is truly great and formidable.

Verses 11–13

Christ having now returned to his spouse, and the breach being entirely made up, and the falling out of these lovers being the renewing of love, Christ here gives an account both of the distance and of the reconciliation.

I. That when he had withdrawn from his church as his spouse, and did not comfort her, yet even then he had his eye upon it as his garden, which he took care of (*v.* 11): *"I went down into the garden of nuts,* or nutmegs, *to see the fruits of the valley,* with complacency and concern, to see them as my own." When he was out of sight he was no further off than the garden, hid among the trees of the garden, in a low and dark valley; but then he was observing *how the vine flourished,* that he might do all that to it which was necessary to promote its flourishing, and might delight himself in it as a man does in a fruitful garden. He went to see whether *the pomegranates budded.* Christ observes the first beginnings of the good work of grace in the soul and the early buddings of devout affections and inclinations there, and is well pleased with them, as we are with the blossoms of the spring.

II. That yet he could not long content himself with this, but suddenly felt a powerful, irresistible, inclination in his own bosom to return to his church, as his spouse, being moved with her lamentations after him, and her languishing desire towards him (*v.* 12): *"Or ever I was aware, my soul made me like the chariots of Ammi-nadib;* I could not any longer keep at a distance; my repentings were kindled together, and I presently resolved to fly back to the arms of my love, my dove." Thus Joseph made himself strange to his brethren, for a while, to chastise them for their former unkindnesses, and make trial of their present temper, till he could no longer refrain himself, but, *or ever he was aware,* burst out into tears, and said, *I am Joseph,* Gen. 45:1, 3. And now the spouse perceives, as David did (Ps. 31:22), that though she *said in her haste, I am cut off from before thy eyes,* yet, at the same time, he *heard the voice of her supplications,* and became *like the chariots of Ammi-nadib,* which were noted for their beauty and swiftness. *My soul put me into the chariots of my willing people* (so some read it), "the chariots of their faith, and hope, and love, their desires, and prayers, and expectations, which they sent after me, to fetch me back, as chariots of fire with horses of fire." Note, 1. Christ's people are, and ought to be, a willing people. 2. If they continue seeking Christ and longing after him, even when he seems to withdraw from them, he will graciously return to them in due time, perhaps sooner than they think and with a pleasing surprise. No chariots sent for Christ shall return empty. 3. All Christ's gracious returns to his people take rise from himself. It is not they, it is his own soul, that puts him into the chariots of his people; for he is gracious because he will be gracious, and loves his Israel because he would love them; not for their sakes, be it known to them.

III. That he, having returned to her, kindly courted her return to him, notwithstanding the discouragements she laboured under. Let her not despair of obtaining as much comfort as ever she had before this distance happened, but take the comfort of the return of her beloved, *v.* 13. Here, 1. The church is called *Shulamite,* referring either to *Solomon,* the bridegroom in type, by whose name she is called, in token of her relation to him and union with

him (thus believers are called *Christians* from *Christ*), or referring to *Salem,* the place of her birth and residence, as the woman of *Shunem* is called the *Shunamite.* Heaven is the Salem whence the saints have their birth, and where they have their citizenship; those that belong to Christ, and are bound for heaven, shall be called *Shulamites.* 2. She is invited to return, and the invitation most earnestly pressed: *Return, return;* and again, *"Return, return;* recover the peace thou hast lost and forfeited; come back to thy former composedness and cheerfulness of spirit." Note, Good Christians, after they have had their comfort disturbed, are sometimes hard to be pacified, and need to be earnestly persuaded to return again to their rest. As revolting sinners have need to be called to again and again *(Turn you, turn you, why will you die?)* so disquieted saints have need to be called to again and again, *Turn you, turn you,* why will you droop; *Why art thou cast down, O my soul?* 3. Having returned, she is desired to show her face: *That we may look upon thee.* Go no longer with they face covered like a mourner. Let those that have made their peace with God *lift up their faces without spot* (Job 22:26); let them come boldly to his throne of grace. Christ is pleased with the cheerfulness and humble confidence of his people, and would have them look pleasant. "Let us *look upon thee,* not I only, but the holy angels, who rejoice in the consolation of saints as well as in the conversion of sinners; not I only, but all the daughters." Christ and believers are pleased with the beauty of the church. 4. A short account is given of what is to be seen in her. The question is asked, *What will you see in the Shulamite?* And it is answered, *As it were the company of two armies.* (1.) Some think she gives this account of herself; she is shy of appearing, unwilling to be looked upon, having, in her own account, no form or comeliness. Alas! says she, *What will you see in the Shulamite?* nothing that is worth your looking upon, nothing but *as it were the company of two armies* actually engaged, where nothing is to be seen but blood and slaughter. The watchmen had smitten her, and wounded her, and she carried in her face the marks of those wounds, looked as if she had been fighting. She had said (*ch.* 1:6), *Look not upon me because I am black;* here she says, "Look not upon me because I am bloody." Or it may denote the constant struggle that is between grace and corruption in the souls of believers; they are in them *as two armies* continually skirmishing, which makes her ashamed to show her face. (2.) Others think her beloved gives the account of her. "I will tell you what you shall *see in the Shulamite;* you shall see as noble a sight as that of two armies, or two parts of the same army, drawn out in rank and file; not only *as an army with banners,* but as *two armies,* with a majesty double to what was before spoken; she is as *Mahanaim,* as the two hosts which Jacob saw (Gen. 32:1, 2), a host of saints and a host of angels ministering to them; the church militant, the church triumphant." Behold *two armies;* in both the church appears beautiful.

CHAPTER 7

In this chapter, I. Christ, the royal bridegroom, goes on to describe the beauties of his spouse, the church, in many instances, and to express his love to her and the delight he has in her conversation (*v.* 1–9). II. The spouse, the church, expresses her great delight in him, and the desire that she had of communion and fellowship with him (*v.* 10–13). Such mutual esteem and endearment are there between Christ and believers. And what is heaven but an everlasting interchanging of loves between the holy God and holy souls!

Verses 1–9

The title which Jesus Christ here gives to the church is new: *O prince's daughter!* agreeing with Ps. 45:13, where she is called *the king's daughter.* She is so in respect of her new birth, born from above, begotten of God, and his workmanship, bearing the image of the King of kings, and guided by his Spirit. She is so by marriage; Christ, by betrothing her to himself, though he found her mean and despicable, has made her a *prince's daughter.* She has a princely disposition, something in her truly noble and generous; she is daughter and heir to the prince of the kings of the earth. *If children, then heirs.* Now here we have,

I. A copious description of the beauty of the spouse, which, some think, is given by the virgins her companions, and that those were they who called upon her to return; it seems rather to be given by Christ himself, and

to be designed to express his love to her and delight in her, as before, *ch.* 4:1, etc., and *ch.* 6:5, 6. The similitudes are here different from what they were before, to show that the beauty of holiness is such as nothing in nature can reach; you may still say more of it, and yet still come short of it. That commendation of the spouse, *ch.* 4, was immediately upon the espousals (*ch.* 3:11), this upon her return from a by-path (*ch.* 6:13); yet this exceeds that, to show the constancy of Christ's love to his people; *he loves them to the end,* since he made them *precious in his sight and honourable.* The spouse had described the beauty of her beloved in ten particulars (*ch.* 5:11, etc.); and now he describes her in as many, for he will not be behindhand with her in respects and endearments. Those that honour Christ he will certainly honour, and make honourable. As the prophet, in describing the corruptions of degenerate Israel, reckons *from the sole of the foot even unto the head* (Isa. 1:6), so here the beauties of the church are reckoned from foot to head, that, as the apostle speaks, when he is comparing the church, as here, to the natural body (1 Co. 12:23), *more abundant honour* might be bestowed on those parts *of the body which we think to be less honourable,* and which therefore *lacked honour, v.* 24. 1. Her *feet* are here praised; the feet of Christ's ministers are beautiful in the eyes of the church (Isa. 52:7), and her feet are here said to be beautiful in the eyes of Christ. *How beautiful are thy feet with shoes!* When believers, being made free from the captivity of sin (Acts 12:8), *stand fast in the liberty with which they are made free,* preserve the tokens of their enfranchisement, have *their feet shod with the preparation of the gospel of peace,* and walk steadily according to the rule of the gospel, then their *feet are beautiful with shoes;* they tread firmly, being well armed against the troubles they meet with in their way. When we rest not in good affections, but they are accompanied with sincere endeavors and resolutions, then our feet are beautified *with shoes.* See Eze. 16:10. 2. *The joint of the thighs are* here said to be *like jewels,* and those curiously wrought by *a cunning workman.* This is explained by Eph. 4:16 and Col. 2:19, where the mystical body of Christ is said to be held together by *joints and bands,* as the hips and knees (both which are *the joints of the thighs*) serve the natural body in its strength and motion. The church is *then* comely in Christ's eyes when those joints are kept firm by holy love and unity, and the communion of saints. When believers act in religion from good principles, and are steady and regular in their whole conversation, and turn themselves easily to every duty in its time and place, then *the joints are like jewels.* 3. The *navel* is here compared to a round cup or *goblet,* that *wants not* any of the agreeable *liquor* that one would wish to find in it, such as David's cup that ran over (Ps. 23:5), well shaped, and not as that miserable infant whose navel was not cut, Eze. 16:4. The fear of the Lord is said to be *health to the navel.* See Prov. 3:8. When the soul wants not that fear then the *navel wants not liquor.* 4. The *belly is like a heap of wheat* in the storechamber, which perhaps was sometimes, to make show, adorned with flowers. The *wheat* is useful, the *lilies* are beautiful; there is every thing in the church which may be to the members of that body either for use or for ornament. All the body is nourished from the *belly;* it denotes the spiritual prosperity of a believer and the healthful constitution of the soul all in good plight. 5. The *breasts are like two young roes that are twins, v.* 3. By the breasts of the church's consolations those are nourished who are born from its belly (Isa. 46:3), and by the navel received nourishment in the womb. This comparison we had before, *ch.* 4:5. 6. The *neck,* which before was compared to *the tower of David* (ch. 4:4), is here compared to *a tower of ivory,* so white, so precious; such is the faith of the saints, by which they are joined to Christ their head. The name of the Lord, improved by faith, is to the saints as a strong and impregnable tower. 7. The *eyes* are compared to *the fish-pools in Heshbon,* or the artificial fish-ponds, *by a gate,* either of Jerusalem or Heshbon, which is called *Bath-rabbim,* the daughter of a multitude, because a great thoroughfare. The understanding, the intentions of a believer, are clean and clear as these ponds. The eyes, weeping for sin, are as fountains (Jer. 9:1), and comely with Christ. 8. The *nose* is like *the tower of Lebanon,* the forehead or face set *like a flint* (Isa. 50:7), undaunted as that tower was impregnable. So it denotes the magnanimity and holy bravery of the church, or (as others) a spiritual sagacity to discern things that differ, as animals strangely distinguish by the smell. This tower *looks towards Damascus,* the head city of Syria, denoting the boldness of the church in facing its enemies and not fearing them. 9. The *head like Carmel,* a very high hill near the sea, *v.* 5. The head of a believer is *lifted up above his enemies* (Ps. 27:6), above the storms of the lower region, as the top of Carmel was, pointing heaven-ward. The more we get above this world, and the nearer to heaven, and the more secure and serene we become by that means, the more amiable we are in the eyes of the Lord Jesus. 10. *The hair of the head* is said to be *like purple.* This denotes the universal amiableness of a believer in the eyes of Christ, even to *the hair,* or (as some understand it) the pins with which *the hair* is dressed. Some by *the head and the hair* understand the governors of the church, who, if they be careful to do their duty, add much to her comeliness. *The head like crimson* (so some read it) *and the hair like purple,* the two colours worn by great men.

II. The complacency which Christ takes in his church thus beautified and adorned. She is lovely indeed if she be so in his eyes; as he puts the comeliness upon her, so it is his love that makes this comeliness truly valuable, for he is an unexceptionable judge. 1. He delighted to look upon his church, and to converse with it, rejoicing in that habitable part of his earth: *The king is held in the galleries,* and cannot leave them. This is explained by Ps. 132:13, 14, *The Lord has chosen Zion,* saying, *This is my rest for ever; here will I dwell;* and Ps. 147:11, *The Lord takes pleasure in those that fear him.* And, if Christ has such delight *in the galleries* of communion with his people, much more reason have they to delight in them, and to reckon *a day there better than a thousand.* 2. He was even struck with admiration at the beauty of his church (*v.* 6): *How fair and how pleasant art thou, O love! How art thou made fair!* (so the word is), "not born so, but made so with the comeliness which I have put upon thee." Holiness is a beauty beyond expression; the Lord Jesus is wonderfully pleased with it; the outward aspect of it is fair; the inward disposition of it is pleasant and highly agreeable, and the complacency he has in it is inexpressible. *O my dearest for delights!* so some read. 3. He determined to keep up communion with his church. (1.) To *take hold of her* as of *the boughs of a palm-tree.* He compares her *stature to a palm-tree* (*v.* 7), so straight, so strong, does she appear, when she is looked upon in her full proportion. The *palm-tree* is observed to flourish most when it is loaded; so the church, the more it has been afflicted, the more it has multiplied; and the branches of it are emblems of victory. Christ says, *"I will go up to the palm-tree,* to entertain myself with the shadow of it (*v.* 8) and *I will take hold of its boughs* and observe the beauty of them." What Christ has said he will do, in favour to his people; we may be sure he will do it, for his kind purposes are never suffered to fall to the ground; and if he *take hold of the boughs* of his church, take early hold of her branches, when they are young and tender, he will keep his hold and not let them go. (2.) To refresh himself with her fruits. He compares her *breasts* (her pious affections towards him) *to clusters of grapes,* a most pleasant fruit (*v.* 7), and he repeats it (*v.* 8): They *shall be* (that is, they shall be to me) *as clusters of the vine,* which *make glad the heart.* "Now that I come *up to the palm-tree* thy graces shall be exerted and excited." Christ's presence with his people kindles the holy heavenly fire in their souls, and then their *breasts shall be as clusters of the vine,* a cordial to themselves and acceptable to him. And since God, at first, *breathed into man's nostrils the breath of life,* and breathes the breath of the new life still, *the smell* of their nostrils is *like the smell of apples,* or oranges, which is pleasing and reviving. *The Lord smelt a sweet savour* from Noah's sacrifice, Gen. 8:21. And, *lastly, the roof of her mouth is like the best wine* (*v.* 9); her spiritual taste and relish, or the words she speaks of God and man, which come not from the teeth outward, but from *the roof of the mouth,* these are pleasing to God. *The prayer of the upright is his delight.* And, when *those that fear the Lord speak one to another* as becomes them, *the Lord hearkens, and hears* with pleasure, Mal. 3:16. It is like that wine which is, [1.] Very palatable and grateful to the taste. It *goes down sweetly;* it *goes straightly* (so the margin reads it); it *moves itself aright,* Prov. 23:31. The pleasures of sense seem right to the carnal appetite, and go down smoothly, but they are often wrong, and, compared with the pleasure of communion with God, they are harsh and rough. Nothing *goes down so sweetly* with a gracious soul as the wine of God's consolations. [2.] It is a great cordial. The presence of Christ by his Spirit with him people shall be reviving and refreshing to them, as that strong wine which makes *the lips* even *of those that are asleep* (that are ready to faint away in a deliquium), *to speak.* Unconverted sinners are asleep; saints are often drowsy, and listless, and half asleep; but the word and Spirit of Christ will put life and vigour into the soul, and *out of the abundance of the heart* that is thus filled*the mouth* will *speak.* When the apostles were filled with the Spirit they spoke *with tongues the wonderful works of God* (Acts 2:10, 12); and those who in opposition to being *drunk with wine, wherein is excess,* are *filled with the Spirit, speak to themselves in psalms and hymns,* Eph. 5:18, 19. When Christ is thus commending the sweetness of his spouse's love, excited by the manifestation of his, she seems to put in that word, *for my beloved,* as in a parenthesis. "Is there any thing in me that is pleasant or valuable? As it is from, so it is for my beloved." *Then* he delights in our good affections and services, when they are all for him and devoted to his glory.

Verses 10–13

These are the words of the spouse, the church, the believing soul, in answer to the kind expressions of Christ's love in the foregoing verses.

I. She here triumphs in her relation to Christ and her interest in him, and in his name will she boast all the day long. With what a transport of joy and holy exultation does she say (*v.* 10), *"I am my beloved's,* not my own, but entirely devoted to him and owned by him." If we can truly say that Christ is our *best beloved,* we may be confident that we are his and he *will save us,* Ps. 119:94. The gracious discoveries of Christ's love to us should engage us greatly to rejoice in the hold he has of us, his sovereignty over us and property in us, which is no less a spring of comfort than a bond of duty. Intimacy of communion with Christ should help clear up our interest in him. Glorying in this, that she is his, to serve him, and reckoning that her honour, she comforts herself with this, that his *desire is towards her,* that is, he is her husband; it is a periphrasis of the conjugal relation, Gen. 3:16. Christ's desire was strongly towards his chosen remnant, when he came from heaven to earth to seek and save them; and when, in pursuance of his undertaking, he was even straitened till the baptism of blood he was to pass through for them *was accomplished,* Lu. 12:50. He desired *Zion for a habitation;* this is a comfort to believers that, whosoever slights them, Christ has a desire towards them, such a desire as will again bring him from heaven to earth to receive them to himself; for he longs to have them all with him, Jn. 17:24; 14:3.

II. She humbly and earnestly desires communion with him (*v.* 11, 12): *"Come, my beloved,* let us take a walk together, that I may receive counsel, instruction, and comfort from thee, and may make known my wants and grievances to thee, with freedom, and without interruption." Thus Christ can walk with the two disciples that were going to the village called *Emmaus,* and talked with them, till he made their *hearts burn within them.* Observe here, 1. Having received fresh tokens of his love, and full assurances of her interest in him, she presses forward towards further acquaintance with him; as blessed Paul, who desired yet more and more of *the excellency of the knowledge of Christ Jesus,* Phil. 3:8. Christ has made it to appear how much his desire is towards us, and we are very ungrateful if ours be not towards him. Note, Communion with Christ is that which all that are sanctified earnestly breathe after; and the clearer discoveries he makes to them of his love the more earnestly do they desire it. Sensual pleasures pall the carnal appetite, and soon give it surfeit, but spiritual delights whet the desires, the language of which is, *Nothing more than God,* but still *more and more of him.* Christ had said, *I will go up to the palm-tree.* Come, saith she, *Let us go.* The promises Christ has made us of communion with him are not to supersede, but quicken and encourage, our prayers for that communion. 2. She desires to go forth into the fields and villages to have this communion with him. Those that would converse with Christ must go forth from the world and the amusements of it, must avoid every thing that would divert the mind and be a hindrance to it when it should be wholly taken up with Christ; we must contrive how to *attend upon the Lord without distraction* (1 Co. 7:35), for therefore the spouse here covets to get out of the noise of the town. *Let us go forth to him without the camp,* Heb. 14:13. Solitude and retirement befriend communion with God; therefore *Isaac went out into the field to meditate* and pray. *Enter into thy closet, and shut thy door.* A believer is never less alone than when alone with Christ, where no eye sees. 3. Having business to go abroad, to look after their grounds, she desires the company of her beloved. Note, Wherever we are, we may keep up our communion with God, if it be not our own fault, for he is always at our right hand, his eye always upon us, and both his word and his ear always nigh us. By going about our worldly affairs with heavenly holy hearts, mixing pious thoughts with common actions, and having our eyes ever towards the Lord, we may take Christ along with us whithersoever we go. Nor should we go any whither where we cannot in faith ask him to go along with us. 4. She is willing to rise betimes, to go along with her beloved: *Let us get up early to the vineyards.* It intimates her care to improve opportunities of conversing with her beloved; when the time appointed has come, we must lose no time, but, as the woman (Mk. 16:2), *go very early,* though it be to a *sepulchre,* if we be in hopes to meet him there. Those that will go abroad with Christ must begin betimes with him, early in the morning of their days, must begin every day with him, seek him early, seek him diligently. 5. She will be content to take up her lodging in the villages, the huts or cottages which the country people built for their shelter when they attended their business in the fields; there, in these mean and cold dwellings, she will gladly reside, if she may but have her beloved with her. His presence will make them fine and pleasant, and convert them into palaces. A gracious soul can reconcile itself to the poorest accommodations, if it may have communion with God in them. 6. The most pleasant delightful fields, even in the spring-time, when the country is most pleasant, will not satisfy her, unless she have her beloved with her. No delights on earth can make a believer easy, unless he enjoy God in all.

III. She desires to be better acquainted with the state of her own soul and the present posture of its affairs (*v.* 12): *Let us see if the vine flourish.* Our own souls are our vineyards; they are, or should be, planted with vines and pomegranates, choice and useful trees. We are made keepers of these vineyards, and therefore are concerned often to look into them, to examine the state of our own souls, to seek whether the *vine flourishes,* whether our graces be in act and exercise, whether we be fruitful in the fruits of righteousness, and whether our fruit abound. And especially let us enquire whether *the tender grape appear* and whether *the pomegranates bud forth,* what good motions and dispositions there are in us that are yet but young and tender, that they may be protected and cherished with a particular care, and may not be nipped, or blasted, or rubbed off, but cultivated, that they may bring forth fruit unto perfection. In this enquiry into our own spiritual state, it will be good to take Christ along with us, because his presence will make the *vine flourish* and the *tender grape appear,* as the returning sun revives the gardens, and because to him we are concerned to approve ourselves. If he sees the *vine flourish,* and the *tender grape appear* — if we can appeal to him, *Thou knowest all things, thou knowest that I love thee,* — if his Spirit witness with our spirit that our souls prosper, it is enough. And, if we would be acquainted with ourselves, we must beg of him to search and try us, to help us in the search, and discover us to ourselves.

IV. She promises to her beloved the best entertainment she can give him at her country seat; for he will come in to us, and sup with us, Rev. 3:20. 1. She promises him her best affections; and, whatever else she had for him, it would utterly be contemned if her heart were not entire for him: *"There* therefore *will I give thee my love;* I will repeat the professions of it, honour thee with the tokens of it; and the out-goings of my soul towards thee in adorations and desires shall be quickened and enlarged, and my heart offered up to thee in a holy fire." 2. She promises him her best provision, *v.* 13. "There we shall find pleasant odours, for *the mandrakes give a smell;"* the *love-flowers* or *lovely ones* (so the word signifies), or the *love-fruits;* it was something that was in all respects very grateful, so valuable that Rachel and Leah had like to have fallen out above it, Gen. 30:14. "We shall also find that which is good for food, as well as pleasant to the eye, all the rarities that the country affords: *At our gates are all manner of pleasant fruits."* Note, (1.) The fruits and exercises of grace are pleasant to the Lord Jesus. (2.) These must be carefully laid up for him, devoted to his service and honour, must be always ready to us when we have occasion for them, as that which is laid up at our gates, that, by our bringing forth much fruit, he may be glorified, Jn. 15:18. (3.) There is a great variety of these pleasant fruits, with which our souls should be well stocked; we must have all sorts of them, grace for all occasions, *new and old,* as the good householder has in his treasury, not only the products of this year, but remainders of the last, Mt. 13:52. We must not only have that ready to us, for the service of Christ, which we have heard, and learned, and experienced lately, but must retain that which we have formerly gathered; nor must we content ourselves only with what we have laid up in store in the days of old, but, as long as we live, must be still adding something new to it, that our stock may increase, and we may be *thoroughly furnished for every good work.* (4.) Those that truly love Christ will think all they have, even their most *pleasant fruits,* and what they have treasured up most carefully, too little to be bestowed upon him, and he is welcome to it all; if it were more and better, it should be at his service. It is all from him, and therefore it is fit it should be all for him.

CHAPTER 8

The affections between Christ and his spouse are as strong and lively here, in this closing chapter of the song, as ever, and rather more so. I. The spouse continues her importunity for a more intimate communion and fellowship with him (*v.* 1–3). II. She charges the daughters of Jerusalem not to interrupt her communion with her beloved (*v.* 4); and they, thereupon, admire her dependence on him (*v.* 5). III. She begs of her beloved, whom she raises up by her prayers (*v.* 5), that he would by his grace confirm that blessed union with him to which she was admitted (*v.* 6, 7). IV. She makes intercession for others also, that care might be taken of them (*v.* 8, 9), and pleases herself with the thoughts of her own interest in Christ and his affection to her (*v.* 10). V. She owns herself his tenant for a vineyard she held of him at Baal-hamon (*v.* 11, 12). VI. The song concludes with an interchanging of parting requests. Christ charges his spouse that she should often let him hear from her (*v.* 13), and she begs of him that he would hasten his return to her (*v.* 14).

Verses 1–4

Here, I. The spouse wishes for a constant intimacy and freedom with the Lord Jesus. She was already betrothed to him, but, the nuptials being yet not solemnized and published (the bride, the Lamb's wife, will not be completely ready till his second coming), she was obliged to be shy and to keep at some distance; she therefore wishes she may be taken for his sister, he having called her so (*ch.* 5:1), and that she might have the same chaste and innocent familiarity with him that a sister has with a brother, an own brother, that *sucked the breasts* of the same *mother* with her, who would therefore be exceedingly tender of her, as Joseph was of his brother Benjamin. Some make this to be the prayer of the Old-Testament saints for the hastening of Christ's incarnation, that the church might be the better acquainted with him, when, *forasmuch as the children are partakers of flesh and blood,* he should also himself likewise take part of the same, and not be ashamed to call them brethren. It is rather the wish of all believers for a more intimate communion with him, that they might *receive the Spirit of sanctification,* and so Christ must be as their brother, that is, that they might be as his brethren, which *then* they are when by grace they are made partakers of a divine nature, and *he that sanctifies, and those that are sanctified, are both of one,* Heb. 2:11, etc. It becomes brethren and sisters, the children of the same parents, that have been nursed at the same breast, to be very loving to and tender of one another; such a love the spouse desires might be between her and her beloved, that she might call him brother. 2. She promises herself then the satisfaction of making a more open profession of her relation to him than at present she could make: *"When I should find thee without,* any where, even before company, *I would kiss thee,* as a sister does her own brother, especially her little brother that is now *sucking the breasts of her mother"* (for so some understand it); "I would use all the decent freedom with thee that could be, and *should not be despised* for it, as doing any thing unbecoming the modesty of my sex." The church, since Christ's incarnation, can better own him than she could before, when she would have been laughed at for being so much in love with one that was not yet born. Christ has become as our brother; wherever we find him, therefore, let us be ready to own our relation to him and affection for him, and not fear being despised for it, nor regard that any more than David did when he danced before the ark. *If this be to be vile, I will be yet more vile.* Nay, let us hope that we shall not be despised so much as some imagine. *Of the maid-servants of whom thou hast spoken I shall be had in honour.* Wherever we find the image of Christ, though it be without, among those that do not follow him with us, we must love it, and testify that love, and we *shall not be despised* for it, but catholic charity will gain us respect. 3. She promises to improve the opportunity she should then have for cultivating an acquaintance with him (*v.* 2): *"I would lead thee,* as my brother, by the arm, and hang upon thee; I would show thee all the house of my precious things, would bring *thee into my mother's house,* into the church, into the solemn assemblies (*ch.* 3:4), into my closet" (for there the saints have most familiar communion with Christ), "and *there thou wouldst instruct me"* (so some read it), as brethren inform their sisters of what they desire to be instructed in. Those that know Christ shall be taught of him; and *therefore* we should desire communion with Christ that we may receive instruction from him. He has come that he might give us an understanding. Or, "My mother would instruct me when I have thee with me." It is the presence of Christ in and with his church that makes the word and ordinances instructive to her children, who shall all be taught of God. 4. She promises him to bid him welcome to the best she had; she would *cause him to drink of her spiced wine and the juice of her pomegranate,* and bid him welcome to it, wishing it better for his sake. The exercise of grace and the performance of duty are spiced wine to the Lord Jesus, very acceptable to him, as expressive of a grateful sense of his favours. Those that are pleased with Christ must study to be pleasing to him; and they will not find him hard to be pleased. He reckons hearty welcome his best entertainment; and, if he have that, he will bring his entertainment along with him. 5. She doubts not but to experience his tender care of her and affection to her (*v.* 3), that she should be supported by his power and kept from fainting in the hardest services and sufferings *(His left hand shall be under my head)* and that she should be comforted with his love — *His right hand should embrace me.* Thus Christ laid his right hand upon John when he was ready to die away, Rev. 1:17. See also Dan. 10:10, 18. It may be read as it is *ch.* 2:6, *His left hand is under my head* (for the words are the same in the original) and so it expresses an immediate answer to her prayer; she was answered with *strength in her soul,* Ps. 138:3. While we are following hard after Christ his *right hand sustains us,* Ps. 63:8. *Underneath are the everlasting arms.* 6. She charges those about her to take heed of doing any thing to interrupt the pleasing communion she now had with her beloved (*v.* 4), as she had done before, when he thus strengthened and comforted her with his presence (ch 2:7): Let me *charge you, O you daughters of Jerusalem,* and reason with you, *Why should you stir up, and why should you awake, my love, until he will?* The church, our common mother, charges all her children that they never do any thing to provoke Christ to withdraw, which we are very prone to do. Why should you put such an affront upon him? Why should you be such enemies to yourselves? We should thus reason with ourselves when we are tempted to do that which will grieve the Spirit. "What! Am I weary of Christ's presence, that I affront him and provoke him to depart from me? Why should I do that which he will take so unkindly and which I shall certainly repent of?"

Verses 5–7

Here, I. The spouse is much admired by those about her. It comes in in a parenthesis, but in it gospel-grace lies as plain, and as much above ground, as any where in this mystical song: *Who is this that comes up from the wilderness, leaning upon her beloved?* Some make these the words of the bridegroom, expressing himself well pleased with her reliance on him and resignation of herself to his guidance. They are rather the words of the daughters of Jerusalem, to whom she spoke (*v.* 4); they see her, and bless her. The angels in heaven, and all her friends on earth, are the joyful spectators of her bliss. The Jewish church came up from the wilderness supported by the divine power and favour, Deu. 32:10, 11. The Christian church was raised up from a low and desolate condition by the grace of Christ relied on, Gal. 4:27. Particular believers are amiable, nay, admirable, and divine grace is to be admired in them, when by the power of that grace they are brought *up from the wilderness, leaning* with a holy confidence and complacency *upon* Jesus Christ *their beloved.* This bespeaks the beauty of a soul, and the wonders of divine grace, 1. In the conversion of sinners. A sinful state is a *wilderness,* remote from communion with God, barren and dry, and in which there is no true comfort; it is a wandering wanting state. Out of this wilderness we are concerned to *come up,* by true repentance, in the strength of the grace of Christ, supported by our beloved and carried in his arms. 2. In the consolation of saints. A soul convinced of sin, and truly humbled for it, is in a *wilderness,* quite at a loss; and there is no coming out of this *wilderness* but *leaning* on Christ as our beloved, by faith, and not *leaning to our own understanding,* nor trusting to any righteousness or strength of our own as sufficient for us, but going forth, and going on, in the strength of the Lord God, and making mention of his righteousness, even his only, who is *the Lord our righteousness.* 3. In the salvation of those that belong to Christ. We must go up from the wilderness of this world having our conversation in heaven; and, at death, we must remove thither, *leaning* upon Christ, must live and die by faith in him. *To me to live is Christ,* and it is he that is gain in death.

II. She addresses herself to her beloved.

1. She puts him in mind of the former experience which she and others had had of comfort and success in applying to him. (1.) For her own part: *"I raised thee up under the apple tree,* that is, I have many a time wrestled with thee by prayer and have prevailed. When I was alone in the acts of devotion, retired in the orchard, under *the apple-tree"* (which Christ himself was compared to, *ch.* 2:3), as *Nathanael under the fig-tree* (Jn. 1:48), "meditating and praying, then *I raised thee up,* to help me and comfort me," as the disciples raised him up in the storm, saying, *Master, carest thou not that we perish?* (Mk. 4:38), and the church (Ps. 44:23), *Awake, why sleepest thou?* Note, The experience we have had of Christ's readiness to yield to the importunities of our faith and prayer should encourage us to continue instant in our addresses to him, to strive more earnestly, and not to faint. *I sought the Lord, and he heard me,* Ps. 34:4. (2.) Others also had like experience of comfort in Christ, as it follows there (Ps. 34:5), *They looked unto him,* as well as I, *and were lightened.* There *thy mother brought thee forth,* the universal church, or believing souls, in whom Christ was formed, Gal. 4:15. They were in pain for the comfort of an interest in thee, and *travailed in pain* with *great sorrow* (so the word here signifies); but they *brought thee forth;* the pangs did not continue always; those that had *travailed* in convictions at last *brought forth* in consolations, and the *pain was forgotten* for joy of the Saviour's birth. By this very similitude our Saviour illustrates the joy which his disciples would have in his return to them, after a mournful separation for a time, Jn. 16:21, 22. After the bitter pangs of repentance many a one has had the blessed birth of comfort; why then may not I?

2. She begs of him that her union with him might be confirmed, and her communion with him continued and made more intimate (*v.* 6): *Set me as a seal upon thy heart, as a seal upon thy arm.* (1.) "Let me have a place in thy heart, an interest in thy love." This is that which all those desire above any thing that know how much their happiness is bound up in the love of Christ. (2.) "Let me never lose the room I have in thy heart; let thy love to me be ensured, as that deed which is sealed up not to be robbed. Let nothing ever prevail either to separate me from thy love, or, by suspending the communications of it, to deprive me of the comfortable sense of it." (3.) "Let me be always near and dear to thee, as the *signet on thy right hand,* not to be parted with (Jer. 22:24), *engraven upon the palms of thy hands* (Isa. 49:14), be loved with a peculiar love." (4.) "Be thou my high priest; let my name be

written on thy breast-plate, nearer thy heart, as the names of all the tribes were engraven like the engravings of a signet in twelve precious stones on the breast-plate of Aaron, and also on two precious *stones* on the *two shoulders* or arms of the ephod," Ex. 28:11, 12, 21. (5.) "Let thy power be engaged for me, as an evidence of thy love to me; let me be not only a *seal upon thy heart,* but a *seal upon thy arm;* let me be ever borne up in thy arms, and know it to my comfort." Some make these to be the words of Christ to his spouse, commanding her to be ever mindful of him and of his love to her; however, if we desire and expect that Christ should set us as a *seal on his heart,* surely we cannot do less than set him as a seal on ours.

3. To enforce this petition, she pleads the power of love, of her love to him, which constrained her to be thus pressing for the tokens of his love to her.

(1.) Love is a violent vigorous passion. [1.] It is *strong as death.* The pains of a disappointed lover are like the pains of death; nay, the pains of death are slighted, and made nothing of, in pursuit of the beloved object. Christ's love to us was *strong as death,* for it broke through death itself. *He loved us, and gave himself for us.* The love of true believers to Christ is *strong as death,* for it makes them dead to every thing else; it even parts between soul and body, while the soul, upon the wings of devout affections, soars upward to heaven, an even forgets that it is yet clothed and clogged with flesh. Paul, in a rapture of this love, knew not whether he was in *the body or out of the body.* By it a believer is crucified to the world. [2.] *Jealousy is cruel as the grave,* which swallows up and devours all; those that truly love Christ are jealous of every thing that would draw them from him, and especially jealous of themselves, lest they should do any thing to provoke him to withdraw from them, and, rather than do so, would *pluck out a right eye* and *cut off a right hand,* than which what can be more cruel? Weak and trembling saints, who conceive a jealousy of Christ, doubting of his love to them, find that jealousy to prey upon them like the grave; nothing wastes the spirits more; but it is an evidence of the strength of their love to him. (3.) *The coals thereof,* its lamps, and flames, and beams, are very strong, and burn with incredible force, as the *coals of fire that have a most vehement flame, a flame of the Lord* (so some read it), a powerful piercing flame, as the lightning, Ps. 29:7. Holy love is a fire that begets a vehement heat in the soul, and consumes the dross and chaff that are in it, melts it down like wax into a new form, and carries it upwards as the sparks towards God and heaven.

(2.) Love is a valiant victorious passion. Holy love is so; the reigning love of God in the soul is constant and firm, and will not be drawn off from him either by fair means or foul, by *life or death* Rom. 8:38. [1.] Death, and all its terrors, will not frighten a believer from loving Christ: *Many waters,* though they will quench fire, *cannot quench this love,* no, nor the *floods drown it, v.* 7. The noise of these waters will strike no terror upon it; let them do their worst, Christ shall still be the best beloved. The overflowing of these waters will strike no damp upon it, but it will enable a man to rejoice in tribulation. *Though he slay me,* I will love him and *trust in him.* No waters could quench Christ's love to us, nor any floods drown it; he waded through the greatest difficulties, even seas of blood. Love sat king upon the floods; let nothing then abate our love to him. [2.] Life, and all its comforts, will not entice a believer from loving Christ: *If a man* could hire him with *all the substance of his house,* to take his love off from Christ and set it upon the world and the flesh again, he would reject the proposal with the utmost disdain; as Christ, when the kingdoms of this world and the glory of them were offered him, to buy him off from his undertaking, said, *Get thee hence, Satan.* It would utterly be contemned. Offer those things to those that know no better. Love will enable us to repel and triumph over temptations from the smiles of the world, as much as from its frowns. Some give this sense of it: *If a man would give all the substance of his house to* Christ, as an equivalent instead of love, to excuse it, *it would be contemned.* He seeks not ours, but us, the heart, not the wealth. *If I give all my goods to feed the poor, and have not love, it is nothing,* 1 Co. 13:1. Thus believers stand affected to Christ: the gifts of his providence cannot satisfy them without the assurances of his love.

Verses 8–12

Christ and his spouse having sufficiently confirmed their love to each other, and agreed it to be on both sides *strong as death* and inviolable, they are here, in these verses, like a loving husband and his wife, consulting together about their affairs, and considering what they should do. Yokefellows, having laid their hearts together, lay their heads together, to contrive about their relations and about their estates; and, accordingly, this happy pair are here advising with one another about a sister, and a vineyard.

I. They are here consulting about their sister, their little sister, and the disposing of her.

1. The spouse proposes her case with a compassionate concern (*v.* 8): *We have a little sister and she has no breasts* (she has not grown up to maturity); *what shall we do for* this *little sister* of *ours in the day that she shall be spoken for,* so as that we may do well for her? (1.) This may be understood as spoken by the Jewish church concerning the Gentile world. God has espoused the church of the Jews to himself, and she was richly endowed, but what shall become of the poor Gentiles, *the barren that has not borne,* and *the desolate?* Isa. 54:1. Their condition (say the pious Jews) is very deplorable and forlorn; they are *sisters,* children of the same fathers, God and Adam, but they are *little,* because not dignified with the knowledge of God; they *have no breasts,* no divine revelation, no scriptures, no ministers, no breasts of consolation drawn out to them, when they might suck, being *strangers to the covenants of promise,* no breasts of instruction themselves to draw out to their children, to nourish them, 1 Pt. 2:2. *What shall we do for* them? We can but pity them, and pray for them. Lord, what wilt thou do for them? The saints, in Solomon's time, might know, from David's psalms, that God had mercy in store for them, and they begged it might be hastened to them. Now the tables are turned; the Gentiles are betrothed to Christ, and ought to return the kindness by an equal concern for the bringing in of the Jews again, our eldest sister, that once had breasts, but now has none. If we take it in this sense, the unbelieving posterity of these pious Jews contradicted this prayer of their fathers; for, when the day came that the Gentiles should be *spoken for* and courted to Christ, instead of considering what to do for them they plotted to do all they could against them, which filled up the measure of their iniquity, 1 Th. 2:16. Or, (2.) It may be applied to any other that belong to the election of grace, but are yet uncalled. They are remotely related to Christ and his church, and sisters to them both, *other sheep that are not of this fold,* Jn. 10:16; Acts 18:10. They *have no breasts,* none yet fashioned (Eze. 16:7), no affection to Christ, no principle of grace. *The day* will come *when* they *shall be spoken for,* when the chosen shall be called, shall be courted for Christ, by the ministers, the friends of the bridegroom. A blessed day it will be, a day of visitation. What shall we do, in that day, to promote the match, to conquer their coyness, and persuade them to consent to Christ and present themselves chaste virgins to him? Note, Those that through grace are brought to Christ themselves should contrive what they may do to help others to him, to carry on the great design of his gospel, which is to espouse souls to Christ and convert sinners to him from whom they have departed.

2. Christ soon determines what to do in this case, and his spouse agrees with him in it (*v.* 9): *"If she be a wall,* if the good work be once begun with the Gentiles, with the souls that are to be called in, if the *little sister, when she shall be spoken for* by the gospel, will but receive the word, and build herself upon Christ the foundation, and frame her doings to turn to the Lord, as the wall is in order to the house, *we will build upon her a palace of silver,* or build her up into such a palace; we will carry on the good work that is begun, till the wall become a palace, the wall of stone a palace of silver," which goes beyond the boast of Augustus Caesar, that what he found brick he left marble. This *little sister,* when once she is joined to the Lord, shall be made to *grow into a holy temple, a habitation of God through the Spirit,* Eph. 2:21, 22. *If she be a door,* when this palace comes to be finished, and the doors of this wall set up, which was the last thing done (Neh. 7:1), then *we will enclose here with boards of cedar;* we will carefully and effectually protect her, that she shall receive no damage. *We will* do it; Father, Son, and Holy Ghost, all concur in contriving, carrying on, and crowning, the blessed work when the time comes. Whatever is wanting shall be set in order, and the work of faith shall be fulfilled with power. Though the beginnings of grace be small, the latter end shall greatly increase. The church is in care concerning those that are yet uncalled. "Let me alone," says Christ; "I will do all that which is necessary to be done for them. Trust me with it."

3. The spouse takes this occasion to acknowledge with thankfulness his kindness to her, *v.* 10. She is very willing to trust him with her *little sister,* for she herself had had great experience of his grace, and, for her part, she owed her all to him: *I am a wall, and my breasts like towers.* This she speaks, not as upbraiding her little sister that had no breasts, but comforting her concerning her, that he who had made her what she was, who had built her up upon himself and made her to grow up to maturity, could and would do the same kindness for those whose case she bore upon her heart. *Then was I in his eyes as one that found favour.* See, (1.) What she values herself upon, her having found favour in the eyes of Jesus Christ. Those are happy, truly happy, and for ever so, that have the favour of God and are accepted of him. (2.) How she ascribes the good work of God in her to the good-will of God towards her: "He has *made me a wall and my breasts as towers,* and then, in that instance more than in any thing, I experienced his love to me." *Hail, thou that art highly favoured,* for in thee Christ is formed. (3.) What pleasure God takes in the work of his own hands. When we are made as a *wall,* as a *brazen wall* (Jer. 1:18; 15:20), that stands firmly against *the blast of the terrible ones* (Isa. 25:4), then God takes delight in us to do us good. (4.) With what joy and triumph we ought to speak of God's grace towards us, and with what satisfaction we should look back upon the special times and seasons when *we were in his eyes as those that find favour;* these were days never to be forgotten.

II. They are here consulting about *a vineyard* they had in the country, the church of Christ on earth considered under the notion of *a vineyard* (*v.* 11, 12): *Solomon had a vineyard at Baal-hamon,* had a kingdom in the possession of a multitude, a numerous people. As he was a type of Christ, so his vineyard was a type of the church of Christ. Our Saviour has given us a key to these verses in the parable of the vineyard let out to the unthankful husbandmen, Mt. 21:33. The bargain was that, every one of the tenants having so much of the vineyard assigned him as would contain 1000 vines, he was to pay the annual rent of 1000 *pieces of silver;* for we read (Isa. 7:23) that in a fruitful soil there were 1000 *vines at* 1000 *silverlings.* Observe, 1. Christ's church is his vineyard, a pleasant and peculiar place, privileged with many honours; he delights to walk in it, as a man in his vineyard, and is pleased with its fruits. 2. He has entrusted each of us with his vineyard, as *keepers* of it. The privileges of the church are that good thing which he has committed to us, to be kept as a sacred trust. The service of the church is to be our business, according as our capacity is. *Son, go work to-day in my vineyard.* Adam, in innocency, was *to dress the garden, and to keep it.* 3. He expects rent from those that are employed in his vineyard and entrusted with it. *He comes, seeking fruit,* and requires gospel-duty of all those that enjoy gospel-privileges. Every one, of what rank or degree soever, must bring glory and honour to Christ, and do some service to the interest of his kingdom in the world, in consideration of what benefit and advantage they enjoy by their share of the privileges of the vineyard. 4. Though Christ has *let out his vineyard to keepers,* yet still it is his, and he has his eye always upon it for good; for, if he did not watch over it *night and day* (Isa. 27:1, 2), *the watchmen,* to whom he has let it out, would keep it *but in vain,* Ps. 127:1. Some take these for Christ's words (*v.* 12): *My vineyard, which is mine, is before me;* and they observe how he dwells upon his property in it: It is *my vineyard, which is mine;* so dear is his church to him, it is *his own in the world* (Jn. 13:1), and therefore he will always have it under his protection; it is his own, and he will look after it. 5. The church, that enjoys the privileges of the vineyard, must have them always before her. The keeping of the vineyard requires constant care and diligence. They are rather the words of the spouse: *My vineyard, which is mine, is before me.* She has lamented her fault and folly in not keeping her *own vineyard* (*ch.* 1:6), but now she resolves to reform. Our hearts are our vineyards, which we must *keep with all diligence;*

and therefore we must have a watchful jealous eye upon them at all times. 6. Our great care must be to pay our rent for what we hold of Christ's vineyard, and to see that we do not go behind-hand, nor disappoint the messengers he sends to *receive the fruits* (Mt. 21:34): *Thou, O Solomon! must have* 1000, and shalt have. The main of the profits belong to Christ; to him and his praise all our fruits must be dedicated. 7. If we be careful to give Christ the praise of our church-privileges, we may then take to ourselves the comfort and benefit of them. If the owner of the vineyard have had his due, the keepers of it shall be well paid for their cares and pains; they shall have 200, which sum, no doubt, was looked upon as a good profit. Those that work for Christ are working for themselves, and shall be unspeakable gainers by it.

Verses 13–14

Christ and his spouse are here parting for a while; she must stay below *in the gardens* on earth, where she has work to do for him; he must remove to *the mountains of spices* in heaven, where he has business to attend for her, as *an advocate with the Father.* Now observe with what mutual endearments they part.

I. He desires to hear often from her. She is ready at her pen; she must be sure to write to him; she knows how to direct (*v.* 13): *"Thou that,* for the present, *dwellest in the gardens,* dressing and keeping them till thou remove from the garden below to the paradise above — *thou,* O believer! whoever thou art, *that dwellest in the gardens* of solemn ordinances, *in the gardens* of church-fellowship and communion, *the companions* are so happy as to hear *thy voice, cause me to hear it* too." Observe, 1. Christ's friends should keep a good correspondence one with another, and, as dear companions, speak often to one another (Mal. 3:16) and hearken to one another's voice; they should edify, encourage, and respect one another. They are companions in the kingdom and patience of Christ, and, therefore, as fellow-travellers, should keep up mutual freedom, and not be shy of, nor strange to, one another. *The communion of saints* is an article of our covenant, as well as an article of our creed, *to exhort one another daily,* and be glad to be exhorted by another. *Hearken to the voice* of the church, as far as it agrees with the voice of Christ; his companions will do so. 2. In the midst of our communion with one another we must not neglect our communion with Christ, but let him see our countenance and hear our voice; he here bespeaks it: *"The companions hearken to thy voice;* it is a pleasure to them; *cause me to hear it.* Thou makest thy complaints to them when any thing grieves thee; why does thou not bring them to me, and let me hear them? Thou art free with them; be as free with me; pour out thy heart to me." Thus Christ, when he left his disciples, ordered them to send to him upon every occasion. *Ask, and you shall receive.* Note, Christ not only accepts and answers, but even courts his people's prayers, not reckoning them a trouble to him, but an honour and a *delight,* Prov. 15:8. We *cause him to hear* our prayers when we not only pray, but wrestle and strive in prayer. He loves to be pressingly importuned, which is not the manner of men. Some read it, *"Cause me to be heard;* thou hast often an opportunity of speaking to thy companions, and they hearken to what thou sayest; speak of me to them; let my name be heard among them; let me be the subject of thy discourse." "One word of Christ" (as archbishop Usher used to say) "before you part." No subject is more becoming, or should be more pleasing.

II. She desires his speedy return to her (*v.* 14): *Make haste, my beloved,* to come again, and receive me to thyself; *be thou like a roe, or a young hart, upon the mountains of spices;* let no time be lost; it is pleasant dwelling here *in the gardens, but to depart, and be with* thee, *is far better;* that therefore is what I wish, and wait, and long for. *Even so, come, Lord Jesus, come quickly.* Observe, 1. Though Jesus Christ be now retired, he will return. The heavens, those high *mountains* of sweet *spices,* must *contain him till the times of refreshing shall come;* and those times will come, *when every eye shall see him,* in all the pomp and power of the upper and better world, the mystery of God being finished and the mystical body completed. 2. True believers, as they are looking for, so they are hastening to, the coming of that *day of the Lord,* not that they would have him make more haste than good speed, but that the intermediate counsels may all be fulfilled, and then that the end may come — the sooner the better. Not that they think him *slack concerning his promise, as some men count slackness,* but thus they express the strength of their affections to him and the vastness of their expectations from him when he comes again. 3. Those only that can in sincerity call Christ their *beloved,* their *best beloved,* can, upon good grounds, desire him to hasten his second coming. As for those whose hearts go a whoring after the world, and who set their affections on the things of the earth, they cannot love his appearing, but dread it rather, because then the earth, and all the things of it which they have chosen for their portion, will be burnt up. But those that truly love Christ long for his second coming, because it will be the crown both of his glory and their bliss. 4. The comfort and satisfaction which we sometimes have in communion with God in grace here should make us breathe the more earnestly after the immediate vision and complete fruition of him in the kingdom of glory. The spouse, after an endearing conference with her beloved, finding it must break off, concludes with this affectionate request for the perfecting and perpetuating of this happiness in the future state. The clusters of grapes that meet us in this wilderness should make us long for the full vintage in Canaan. If a day in his courts be so sweet, what then will an eternity within the veil be! If this be heaven, O that I were there! 5. It is good to conclude our devotions with a joyful expectation of the glory to be revealed, and holy humble breathings towards it. We should not part but with the prospect of meeting again. It is good to conclude every sabbath with thoughts of the everlasting sabbath, which shall have no night at the end of it, nor any week-day to come after it. It is good to conclude every sacrament with thoughts of the everlasting feast, when we shall sit down with Christ at his table in his kingdom, to rise no more, and drink of the wine new there, and to break up every religious assembly in hopes of *the general assembly of the church of the first-born,* when time and days shall be no more: Let the blessed Jesus hasten that blessed day. *Why are his chariot-wheels so long a coming? Why tarry the wheels of his chariots?*

AN EXPOSITION, WITH PRACTICAL OBSERVATIONS, OF
THE BOOK OF THE PROPHET ISAIAH

Prophet is a title that sounds very great to those that understand it, though, in the eye of the world, many of those that were dignified with it appeared very mean. A prophet is one that has a great intimacy with Heaven and a great interest there, and consequently a commanding authority upon earth. Prophecy is put for all divine revelation (2 Pt. 1:20, 21), because that was most commonly by dreams, voices, or visions, communicated to prophets first, and by them to the children of men, Num. 12:6. Once indeed God himself spoke to all the thousands of Israel from the top of Mount Sinai; but the effect was so intolerably dreadful that they entreated God would for the future speak to them as he had done before, by men like themselves, *whose terror should not make them afraid, nor their hands be heavy upon them,* Job 33:7. God approved the motion *(they have well said,* says he, Deu. 5:27, 28), and the matter was then settled by consent of parties, that we must never expect to hear from God any more in that way, but by prophets, who received their instructions immediately from God, with a charge to deliver them to his church. Before the sacred canon of the Old Testament began to be written there were prophets, who were instead of Bibles to the church. Our Saviour seems to reckon Abel among the prophets, Mt. 23:31, 35. Enoch was a prophet; and by him *that* was first in prediction which is to be last in execution — the judgment of the great day. Jude 14, *Behold, the Lord comes with his holy myriads.* Noah was a preacher of righteousness. God said of Abraham, He *is a prophet,* Gen. 20:7. Jacob foretold things to come, Gen. 49:1. Nay, all the patriarchs are called *prophets.* Ps. 105:15, *Do my prophets no harm.* Moses was, beyond all comparison, the most illustrious of all the Old-Testament prophets, for with him the Lord spoke *face to face,* Deu. 34:10. He was the first writing prophet, and by his hand the first foundations of holy writ were laid. Even those that were called to be his assistants in the government had the spirit of prophecy, such a plentiful effusion was there of that spirit at that time, Num. 11:25. But after the death of Moses, for some ages, the Spirit of the Lord appeared and acted in the church of Israel more as a martial spirit than as a spirit of prophecy, and inspired men more for acting than speaking. I mean in the time of the judges. We find the Spirit of the Lord coming upon Othniel, Gideon, Samson, and others, for the service of their country, with their swords, not with their pens. Messages were then sent from heaven by angels, as to Gideon and Manoah, and to the people, Judges 2:1. In all the book of judges there is never once mention of a prophet, only Deborah is called a prophetess. Then the word of the Lord was precious; there was no open vision, 1 Sa. 3:1. They had the law of Moses, recently written; let them study that. But in Samuel prophecy revived, and in him a famous epocha, or period of the church began,

a time of great light in a constant uninterrupted succession of prophets, till some time after the captivity, when the canon of the Old Testament was completed in Malachi, and then prophecy ceased for nearly 400 years, till the coming of the great prophet and his forerunner. Some prophets were divinely inspired to write the histories of the church. But they did not put their names to their writings; they only referred for proof to the authentic records of those times, which were known to be drawn up by prophets, as Gad, Iddo, etc. David and others were prophets, to write sacred songs for the use of the church. After them we often read of prophets sent on particular errands, and raised up for special public services, among whom the most famous were Elijah and Elisha in the kingdom of Israel. But none of these put their prophecies in writing, nor have we any remains of them but some fragments in the histories of their times; there was nothing of their own writing (that I remember) but one epistle of Elijah's, 2 Chr. 21:12. But towards the latter end of the kingdoms of Judah and Israel, it pleased God to direct his servants the prophets to write and publish some of their sermons, or abstracts of them. The dates of many of their prophecies are uncertain, but the earliest of them was in the days of Uzziah king of Judah, and Jeroboam the second, his contemporary, king of Israel, about 200 years before the captivity, and not long after Joash had slain Zechariah the son of Jehoiada in the courts of the temple. If they begin to murder the prophets, yet they shall not murder their prophecies; these shall remain as witnesses against them. Hosea was the first of the writing prophets; and Joel, Amos, and Obadiah, published their prophecies about the same time. Isaiah began some time after, and not long; but his prophecy is placed first, because it is the largest of them all, and has most in it of him to whom all the prophets bore witness; and indeed so much of Christ that he is justly styled the *Evangelical Prophet,* and, by some of the ancients, a *fifth Evangelist.* We shall have the general title of this book (*v.* 1) and therefore shall here only observe some things,

I. Concerning the prophet himself. He was (if we may believe the tradition of the Jews) of the royal family, his father being (they say) brother to king Uzziah. He was certainly much at court, especially in Hezekiah's time, as we find in his story, to which many think it is owing that his style is more curious and polite than that of some other of the prophets, and, in some places, exceedingly lofty and soaring. The Spirit of God sometimes served his own purpose by the particular genius of the prophet; for prophets were not speaking trumpets, *through* which the Spirit spoke, but speaking men, *by* whom the Spirit spoke, making use of their natural powers, in respect both of light and flame, and advancing them above themselves.

II. Concerning the prophecy. It is transcendently excellent and useful; it was so to the church of God then, serving for conviction of sin, direction in duty, and consolation in trouble. Two great distresses of the church are here referred to, and comfort prescribed in reference to them, that by Sennacherib's invasion, which happened in his own time, and that of the captivity in Babylon, which happened long after; and in the supports and encouragements laid up for each of these times of need we find abundance of the grace of the gospel. There are not so many quotations in the gospels out of any, perhaps not out of all, the prophecies of the Old Testament, as out of this; nor such express testimonies concerning Christ, witness that of his being born of a virgin (*ch.* 7) and that of his sufferings, *ch.* 53. The beginning of this book abounds most with reproofs for sin and threatenings of judgment; the latter end of it is full of wood words and comfortable words. This method the Spirit of Christ took formerly in the prophets And does still, first to convince and then to comfort; and those that would be blessed with the comforts must submit to the convictions. Doubtless Isaiah preached many sermons, and delivered many messages to the people, which are not written in this book, as Christ did; and probably these sermons were delivered more largely and fully than they are here related, but so much is left on record as Infinite Wisdom thought fit to convey to us *on whom the ends of the world have come;* and these prophecies, as well as the histories of Christ, are written *that we might believe on the name of the Son of God, and that, believing, we might have life through his name; for to us is the gospel here preached as well as unto those* that lived then, and more clearly. O that it may be mixed with faith!

CHAPTER 1

The first verse of this chapter is intended for a title to the whole book, and it is probable that this was the first sermon that this prophet was appointed to publish and to affix in writing (as Calvin thinks the custom of the prophets was) to the door of the temple, as with us proclamations are fixed to public places, that all might read them (Hab. 2:2), and those that would might take out authentic copies of them, the original being, after some time, laid up by the priests among the records of the temple. The sermon which is contained in this chapter has in it, I. A high charge exhibited, in God's name, against the Jewish church and nation, 1. For their ingratitude (*v.* 2, 3). 2. For their incorrigibleness (*v.* 5). 3. For the universal corruption and degeneracy of the people (*v.* 4, 6, 21, 22). 4. For the perversion of justice by their rulers (*v.* 23). II. A sad complaint of the judgments of God, which they had brought upon themselves by their sins, and by which they were brought almost to utter ruin (*v.* 7–9). III. A just rejection of those shows and shadows of religion which they kept up among them, notwithstanding this general defection and apostasy (*v.* 10–15). IV. An earnest call to repentance and reformation, setting before them life and death, life if they compiled with the call and death if they did not (*v.* 16–20). V. A threatening of ruin to those that would not be reformed (*v.* 24, 28–31). VI. A promise of a happy reformation at last, and a return to their primitive purity and prosperity (*v.* 25–27). And all this is to be applied by us, not only to the communities we are members of, in their public interests, but to the state of our own souls.

Verse 1

Here is, I. The name of the prophet, *Isaiah,* or *Jesahiahu* (for so it is in the Hebrew), which, in the New Testament is read *Esaias.* His name signifies *the salvation of the Lord* — a proper name for a prophet by whom God *gives knowledge of salvation to his people,* especially for this prophet, who prophesies so much of Jesus the Saviour and of the great salvation wrought out by him. He is said to be *the son of Amoz,* not Amos the prophet (the two names in the Hebrew differ more than in the English), but, as the Jews think, of Amoz the brother, or son, of Amaziah king of Judah, a tradition as uncertain as that rule which they give, that, where a prophet's father is named, he also was himself a prophet. The prophets' pupils and successors are indeed often called their *sons,* but we have few instances, if any, of their own sons being their successors.

II. The nature of the prophecy. It is a vision, being revealed to him in a vision, when he was *awake, and heard the words of God, and saw the visions of the Almighty* (as Balaam speaks, Num. 24:4), though perhaps it was not so illustrious a vision at first as that afterwards, *ch.* 6:1. The prophets were called *seers,* or seeing men, and therefore their prophecies are fitly called *visions.* It was what he saw with the eyes of his mind, and foresaw as clearly by divine revelation, was as well assured of it, as fully apprised of it, and as much affected with it, as if he had seen it with his bodily eyes. Note 1. God's prophets saw what they spoke of, knew what they said, and require our belief of nothing but what they themselves believed and were sure of, Jn. 6:69; 1 Jn. 1:1. 2. They could not but speak what they saw, because they saw how much all about them were concerned in it, Acts 4:20; 2 Co. 4:13.

III. The subject of the prophecy. It was what *he saw concerning Judah and Jerusalem,* the country of the two tribes, and that city which was their metropolis; and there is little in it relating to Ephraim, or the ten tribes, of whom there is so much said in the prophecy of Hosea. Some chapters there are in this book which relate to Babylon, Egypt, Tyre, and some other neighbouring nations; but it takes its title from that which is the main substance of it, and is therefore said to be *concerning Judah and Jerusalem,* the other nations spoken of being such as the people of the Jews had concern with. Isaiah brings to them in a special manner, 1. Instruction; for it is the privilege of Judah and Jerusalem that to them pertain the oracles of God. 2. Reproof and threatening; for if in Judah, where God is known, if in Salem, where his name is great, iniquity be found, they, sooner than any other, shall be reckoned with for it. 3. Comfort and encouragement in evil times; for the children of Zion shall be joyful in their king.

IV. The date of the prophecy. Isaiah prophesied *in the days of Uzziah, Jotham, Ahaz, and Hezekiah.* By this it appears, 1. That he prophesied long, especially if (as the Jews say) he was at last put to death by Manasseh, to a cruel death, being sawn asunder, to which some suppose the apostle refers, Heb. 11:37. From the year that king Uzziah died (*ch.* 6:1) to Hezekiah's sickness and recovery was forty-seven years; how much before, and after, he prophesied, is not certain; some reckon sixty, others eighty years in all. It was an honour to him, and a happiness to his country, that he was continued so long in his usefulness; and we must suppose both that he began young and that he held out to old age; for the prophets were not tied, as the priests were, to a certain age, for the beginning or ending of their administration. 2. That he passed through variety of times. Jotham was a good king, and Hezekiah a better, and no doubt gave encouragement to and took advice from this prophet, were patrons to him, and he a privy-counsellor to them; but between them, and when Isaiah was in the prime of his time, the reign of Ahaz was very profane and wicked; then, no doubt, he was frowned upon at court, and, it is likely, forced to abscond. Good men and good ministers must expect bad times in this world, and prepare for them. Then religion was run down to such a degree that the *doors of the house of the Lord were shut up* and idolatrous *altars were erected in every corner of Jerusalem;* and Isaiah, with all his divine eloquence and messages immediately from God himself, could not help it. The best men, the best ministers, cannot do the good they would do in the world.

Verses 2–9

We will hope to meet with a brighter and more pleasant scene before we come to the end of this book; but truly here, in the beginning of it, every thing looks very bad, very black, with Judah and Jerusalem. What is the wilderness of the world, if the church, the vineyard, has such a dismal aspect as this?

I. The prophet, though he speaks in God's name, yet, despairing to gain audience with the children of his people, addresses himself to the heavens and the earth, and bespeaks their attention (*v.* 2): *Hear, O heavens! and give ear, O earth!* Sooner will the inanimate creatures hear, who observe the law and answer the end of their creation, than this stupid senseless people. Let the lights of the heaven shame their darkness, and the fruitfulness of the earth their barrenness, and the strictness of each to its time their irregularity. Moses begins thus in Deu. 32:1, to which the prophet here refers, intimating that now those times had come which Moses there foretold, Deu. 31:29. Or this is an appeal to heaven and earth, to angels and then to the inhabitants of the upper and lower world. Let them *judge between God and his vineyard;* can either produce such an instance of ingratitude? Note, God will be justified when he speaks, and both heaven and earth shall declare his righteousness, Mic. 6:1, 2; Ps. 50:6.

II. He charges them with base ingratitude, a crime of the highest nature. Call a man ungrateful, and you can call him no worse. Let heaven and earth hear and wonder at, 1. God's gracious dealings with such a peevish provoking people as they were: "I have nourished and brought them up as children; they have been well fed and well taught" (Deu. 32:6); "I have magnified and exalted them" (so some), "not only made them grow, but made them great — not only maintained them, but preferred them — not only trained them up, but raised them high." Note, We owe the continuance of our lives and comforts, and all our advancements, to God's fatherly care of us and kindness to us. 2. Their ill-natured conduct towards him, who was so tender of them: *"They have rebelled against me,"* or (as some read it) "they have revolted from me; they have been deserters, nay traitors, against my crown and dignity." Note, All the instances of God's favour to us, as the God both of our nature and of our nurture, aggravate our treacherous departures from him and all our presumptuous oppositions to him — children, and yet rebels!

III. He attributes this to their ignorance and inconsideration (*v.* 3): *The ox knows, but Israel does not.* Observe, 1. The sagacity of the ox and the ass, which are not only brute creatures, but of the dullest sort; yet the ox has such a sense of duty as to know his owner and to serve him, to submit to his yoke and to draw in it; the ass has such a sense of interest as to know has master's crib, or manger, where he is fed, and to abide by it; he will go to that of himself if he be turned loose. A fine pass man has come to when he is shamed even in knowledge and understanding by these silly animals, and is not only sent to school to them (Prov. 6:6, 7), but set in a form below them (Jer. 8:7), *taught more than the beasts of the earth* (Job 35:11) and yet knowing less. 2. The sottishness and stupidity of Israel. God is their owner and proprietor. He made us, and his we are more than our cattle are ours; he has provided well for us; providence is our Master's crib; yet many that are called the people of God do not know and will not consider this, but ask, *"What is the Almighty that we should serve him?* He is not our owner; and *what profit shall we have if we pray unto him?* He has no crib for us to feed at." He had complained (*v.* 2) of the obstinacy of their wills; *They have rebelled against me.* Here he runs it up to its cause: *"Therefore* they have rebelled because they do not know, they do not consider." The understanding is darkened, and therefore the whole soul is alienated from the life of God, Eph. 4:18. *"Israel does not know,* though their land is a land of light and knowledge; *in Judah is God known,* yet, because they do not live up to what they know, it is in effect as if they did not know. They know; but their knowledge does them no good, because they do not consider what they know; they do not apply it to their case, nor their minds to it." Note, (1.) Even among those that profess themselves God's people, that have the advantages and lie under the engagements of his people, there are many that are very careless in the affairs of their souls. (2.) Inconsideration of what we do know is as great an enemy to us in religion as ignorance of what we should know. (3.) *Therefore* men revolt from God, and rebel against him, because they do not know and consider their obligations to God in duty, gratitude, and interest.

IV. He laments the universal pravity and corruption of their church and kingdom. The disease of sin was epidemic, and all orders and degrees of men were infected with it; *Ah sinful nation! v.* 4. The prophet bemoans those that would not bemoan themselves: Alas for them! Woe to them! He speaks with holy indignation at their degeneracy, and a dread of the consequences of it. See here,

1. How he aggravates their sin, and shows the malignity that there was in it, *v.* 4. (1.) The wickedness was universal. They were a sinful nation; the generality of the people were vicious and profane. They were so in their national capacity. In the management of their public treaties abroad, and in the administration of public justice at home, they were corrupt. Note, It is ill with a people when sin becomes national. (2.) It was very great and heinous in its nature. They were *laden with iniquity;* the guilt of it, and the curse incurred by that guilt, lay very heavily upon them. It was a heavy charge that was exhibited against them, and one which they could never clear themselves from; their wickedness was upon them as *a talent of lead,* Zec. 5:7, 8. Their sin, as it did easily beset them

and they were prone to it, was a weight upon them, Heb. 12:1. (3.) They came of a bad stock, were a *seed of evil-doers.* Treachery ran in their blood; they had it by kind, which made the matter so much the worse, more provoking and less curable. They rose up in their fathers' stead, and trod in their fathers' steps, to *fill up the measure of their iniquity,* Num. 32:14. They were a race and family of rebels. (4.) Those that were themselves debauched did what they could to debauch others. They were not only corrupt children, born tainted, but *children that were corrupters,* that propagated vice, and infected others with it — not only sinners, but tempters — not only actuated by Satan, but agents for him. If those that are called *children, God's children,* that are looked upon as belonging to his family, be wicked and vile, their example is of the most malignant influence. (5.) Their sin was a treacherous departure from God. They were deserters from their allegiance: *"They have forsaken the Lord,* to whom they had joined themselves; *they have gone away backward,* are alienated or separated from God, have turned their back upon him, deserted their colours, and quitted their service." When they were urged forward, they ran backward, *as a bullock unaccustomed to the yoke, as a backsliding heifer,* Hos. 4:16. (6.) It was an impudent and daring defiance of him: *They have provoked the Holy One of Israel unto anger* wilfully and designedly; they knew what would anger him, and that they did. Note, The backslidings of those that have professed religion and relation to God are in a special manner provoking to him.

2. How he illustrates it by a comparison taken from a sick and diseased body, all overspread with leprosy, or, like Job's, with sore boils, *v.* 5, 6. (1.) The distemper has seized the vitals, and so threatens to be mortal. Diseases in the head and heart are most dangerous; now the head, the whole head, is sick — the heart, the whole heart, is faint. They had become corrupt in their judgment: the leprosy was in their head. They were utterly unclean; their affection to God and religion was cold and gone; the *things which remained were ready to die* away, Rev. 3:2. (2.) It has overspread the whole body, and so becomes exceedingly noisome; *From the sole of the foot even to the head,* from the meanest peasant to the greatest peer, there is *no soundness,* no good principles, no religion (for that is the health of the soul), nothing but *wounds and bruises,* guilt and corruption, the sad effects of Adam's fall, noisome to the holy God, painful to the sensible soul; they were so to David when he complained (Ps. 38:5), *My wounds stink, and are corrupt, because of my foolishness.* See Ps. 32:3, 4. No attempts were made for reformation, or, if they were, they proved ineffectual: The wounds *have not been closed, not bound up, nor mollified with ointment.* While sin remains unrepented of the wounds are unsearched, unwashed, the proud flesh in them not cut out, and while, consequently, it remains unpardoned, the wounds are not mollified or closed up, nor any thing done towards the healing of them and the preventing of their fatal consequences.

V. He sadly bewails the judgments of God which they had brought upon themselves by their sins, and their incorrigibleness under those judgments. 1. Their kingdom was almost ruined, *v.* 7. So miserable were they that both their towns and their lands were wasted, and yet so stupid that they needed to be told this, to have it shown to them. "Look and see how it is; *your country is desolate;* the ground is not cultivated, for want of inhabitants, the villages being deserted, Jdg. 5:7. And thus the fields and vineyards become like deserts, *all grown over with thorns,* Prov. 24:31. *Your cities are burned with fire,* by the enemies that invade you" (fire and sword commonly go together); "as for the fruits of your land, which should be food for your families, *strangers devour them;* and, to your greater vexation, it is *before your eyes,* and you cannot prevent it; you starve while your enemies surfeit on that which should be your maintenance. The overthrow of your country is as the overthrow of strangers; it is used by the invaders, as one might expect it should be used by strangers." Jerusalem itself, which was as the daughter of Zion (the temple built on Zion was a mother, a nursing mother, to Jerusalem), or Zion itself, the holy mountain, which had been dear to God as a daughter, was now lost, deserted, and exposed *as a cottage in a vineyard,* which, when the vintage is over, nobody dwells in or takes any care of, and looks as mean and despicable as *a lodge* or hut, *in a gar-*

den of cucumbers; and every person is afraid of coming near it, and solicitous to remove his effects out of it, as if it were *a besieged city, v.* 8. And some think, it is a calamitous state of the kingdom that is represented by a diseased body, *v.* 6. Probably this sermon was preached in the reign of Ahaz, when Judah was invaded by the kings of Syria and Israel, the Edomites and the Philistines, who slew many, and carried many away into captivity, 2 Chr. 28:5, 17, 18. Note, National impiety and immorality bring national desolation. Canaan, the glory of all lands, Mount Zion, the joy of the whole earth, both became a reproach and a ruin; and sin made them so, that great mischief-maker. 2. Yet they were not all reformed, and therefore God threatens to take another course with them (*v.* 5): *"Why should you be stricken any more,* with any expectation of doing you good by it, when you increase revolts as your rebukes are increased? *You will revolt more and more,* as you have done," as Ahaz particularly did, who, *in his distress, trespassed yet more against the Lord,* 2 Chr. 28:22. Thus the physician, when he sees the patient's case desperate, troubles him no more with physic; and the father resolves to correct his child no more when, finding him hardened, he determines to disinherit him. Note, (1.) There are those who are made worse by the methods God takes to make them better; the more they are stricken the more they revolt; their corruptions, instead of being mortified, are irritated and exasperated by their afflictions, and their hearts more hardened. (2.) God, sometimes, in a way of righteous judgment, ceases to correct those who have been long incorrigible, and whom therefore he designs to destroy. The reprobate silver shall be cast, not into the furnace, but to the dunghill, Jer. 6:29, 30. See Eze. 24:13; Hos. 4:14. He that is *filthy, let him be filthy still.*

VI. He comforts himself with the consideration of a remnant that should be the monuments of divine grace and mercy, notwithstanding this general corruption and desolation, *v.* 9. See here, 1. How near they were to an utter extirpation. They were almost like Sodom and Gomorrah in respect both of sin and ruin, had grown almost so bad that there could not have been found *ten righteous men among them,* and almost as miserable as if none had been left alive, but their country turned into a sulphureous lake. Divine Justice said, *Make them as Admah; set them as Zeboim;* but Mercy said, *How shall I do it?* Hos. 11:8, 9. 2. What it was that saved them from it: *The Lord of hosts left unto them a very small remnant,* that were kept pure from the common apostasy and kept safe and alive from the common calamity. This is quoted by the apostle (Rom. 9:27), and applied to those few of the Jewish nation who in his time embraced Christianity, when the body of the people rejected it, and in whom the promises made to the fathers were accomplished. Note, (1.) In the worst of times there is a remnant preserved from iniquity and reserved for mercy, as Noah and his family in the deluge, Lot and his in the destruction of Sodom. Divine grace triumphs in distinguishing by an act of sovereignty. (2.) This remnant is often a very small one in comparison with the vast number of revolting ruined sinners. Multitude is no mark of the true church. Christ's is a little flock. (3.) It is God's work to sanctify and save some, when others are left to perish in their impurity. It is the work of his power as the Lord of hosts. Except he had left us that remnant, there would have been none left; the corrupters (*v.* 4) did what they could to debauch all, and the devourers (*v.* 7) to destroy all, and they would have prevailed of God himself had not interposed to secure to himself a remnant, who are bound to give him all the glory. (4.) It is good for a people that have been saved from utter ruin to look back and see how near they were to it, just upon the brink of it, to see how much they owed to a few good men that stood in the gap, and that that was owing to a good God, who left them these good men. *It is of the Lord's mercies that we are not consumed.*

Verses 10–15

Here, I. God calls to them (but calls in vain) to hear his word, *v.* 10. 1. The title he gives them is very strange; *You rulers of Sodom,* and *people of Gomorrah.* This intimates what a righteous thing it would have been with God to make them like Sodom and Gomorrah in respect of ruin (*v.* 9), because that had made themselves like Sodom and Gomorrah in respect of sin. The men of Sodom were

wicked, and sinners before the Lord exceedingly (Gen. 13:13), and so were the men of Judah. When the rulers were bad, no wonder the people were so. Vice overpowered virtue, for it had the rulers, the men of figure, on its side; and it out-polled it, for it had the people, the men of number, on its side. The streams being thus strong, no less a power than that of the Lord of hosts could secure a remnant, *v.* 9. The rulers are boldly attacked here by the prophet as rulers of Sodom; for he knew not how to give flattering titles. The tradition of the Jews is that for this he was impeached long after, and put to death, as having cursed the gods and *spoken evil of the ruler of his people.* 2. His demand upon them is very reasonable: *"Hear the word of the Lord,* and *give ear to the law of our God;* attend to that which God has to say to you, and let his word be a law to you." The following declaration of dislike to their sacrifices would be a kind of new law to them, though really it was but an explication of the old law; but special regard is to be had to it, as is required to the like, Ps. 50:7, 8. "Hear this, and tremble; hear it, and take warning."

II. He justly refuses to hear their prayers and accept their services, their sacrifices and burnt-offerings, the fat and blood of them (*v.* 11), their attendance in his courts (*v.* 12), their oblations, their incense, and their solemn assemblies (*v.* 13), their new moons and their appointed feasts (*v.* 14), their devoutest addresses (*v.* 15); they are all rejected, because their hands were full of blood. Now observe,

1. There are many who are strangers, nay, enemies, to the power of religion, and yet seem very zealous for the show and shadow and form of it. This sinful nation, this seed of evil-doers, these rulers of Sodom and people of Gomorrah, brought, not to the altars of false gods (they are not here charged with that), but to the altar of the God of Israel, sacrifices, a multitude of them, as many as the law required and rather more — not only peace-offerings, which they themselves had their share of, but burnt-offerings, which were wholly consumed to the honour of God; nor did they bring the torn, and lame, and sick, but fed beasts, and the fat of them, the best of the kind. They did not send others to offer their sacrifices for them, but came themselves to appear before God. They observed the instituted *places* (not in high places or groves, but in God's own courts), and the instituted *time,* the new moons, and sabbaths, and appointed feasts, none of which they omitted. Nay, it should seem, they called extraordinary assemblies, and held solemn meetings for religious worship, besides those that God had appointed. Yet this was not all: they applied to God, not only with their ceremonial observances, but with the exercises of devotion. They prayed, prayed often, made many prayers, thinking they should be heard for their much speaking; nay, they were fervent and importunate in prayer, they spread forth their hands as men in earnest. Now we should have thought these, and, no doubt, they thought themselves, a pious religious people; and yet they were far from being so, for (1.) Their hearts were empty of true devotion. They came to *appear* before God (*v.* 12), *to be seen* before him (so the margin reads it); they rested in the outside of the duties; they looked no further than to be seen of men, and went no further than that which men see. (2.) Their hands were full of blood. They were guilty of murder, rapine, and oppression, under colour of law and justice. The people shed blood, and the rulers did not punish them for it; the rulers shed blood, and the people were aiding and abetting, as the elders of Jezreel were to Jezebel in shedding Naboth's blood. Malice is heart-murder in the account of God; he that hates his brother in his heart has, in effect, his hands full of blood.

2. When sinners are under the judgments of God they will more easily be brought to fly to their devotions than to forsake their sins and reform their lives. Their country was now desolate, and their cities were burnt (*v.* 7), which awakened them to bring their sacrifices and offerings to God more constantly than they had done, as if they would bribe God Almighty to remove the punishment and give them leave to go on in the sin. *When he slew them, then they sought him,* Ps. 78:34. Lord, *in trouble have they visited thee, ch.* 26:16. Many that will readily part with their sacrifices will not be persuaded to part with their sins.

3. The most pompous and costly devotions of wicked people, without a thorough reformation of the heart and life, are so far from being acceptable to God that really they are an abomination to him. It is here shown in a great

variety of expressions that *to obey is better than sacrifice;* nay, that sacrifice, without obedience, is a jest, an affront and provocation to God. The comparative neglect which God here expresses of ceremonial observance was a tacit intimation of what they would come to at last, when they would all be done away by the death of Christ. What was now made little of would in due time be made nothing of. *"Sacrifice and offering,* and prayer made in the virtue of them, *thou wouldest not; then said I, Lo, I come."* Their sacrifices are here represented,

(1.) As fruitless and insignificant; *To what purpose is the multitude of your sacrifices? v.* 11. They are *vain oblations, v.* 13. *In vain do they worship me,* Mt. 15:9. Their attention to God's institutions was all lost labour, and served not to answer any good intention; for, [1.] It was not looked upon as any act of duty or obedience to God: *Who has required these things at your hands? v.* 12. Not that God disowns his institutions, or refuses to stand by his own warrants; but in what they did they had not an eye to him that required it, nor indeed did he require it of those whose hands were full of blood and who continued impenitent. [2.] It did not recommend them to God's favour. He delighted not in the blood of their sacrifices, for he did not look upon himself as honoured by it. [3.] It would not obtain any relief for them. They pray, but God will not hear, because they regard iniquity (Ps. 66:18); he will not deliver them, for, though they make many prayers, none of them come from an upright heart. All their religious service turned to no account to them. Nay,

(2.) As odious and offensive. God did not only not accept them, but he did detest and abhor them. "They are *your* sacrifices, they are none of mine; I am full of them, even surfeited with them." He needed them not (Ps. 50:10), did not desire them, had had enough of them, and more than enough. Their coming into his courts he calls *treading them,* or trampling upon them; their very attendance on his ordinances was construed into a contempt of them. Their incense, though ever so fragrant, was an abomination to him, for it was burnt in hypocrisy and with an ill design. Their solemn assemblies he could not *away with,* could not see them with any patience, nor bear the affront they gave him. *The solemn meeting is iniquity;* though the thing itself was not, yet, as they managed it, it became so. It is a *vexation* (so some read it), a provocation, to God, to have ordinances thus prostituted, not only by wicked people, but to wicked purposes: *"My soul hates them; they are a trouble to me,* a burden, an incumbrance; I am perfectly sick of them, and *weary of bearing them."* God is never weary of hearing the prayers of the upright, but soon weary of the costly sacrifices of the wicked. He hides his eyes from their prayers, as that which he has an aversion to and is angry at. All this is to show, [1.] That sin is very hateful to God, so hateful that it makes even men's prayers and their religious services hateful to him. [2.] That dissembled piety is double iniquity. Hypocrisy in religion is of all things most abominable to the God of heaven. Jerome applies the passage to the Jews in Christ's time, who pretended a great zeal for the law and the temple, but made themselves and all their services abominable to God by filling their hands with the blood of Christ and his apostles, and so filling up the measure of their iniquities.

Verses 16–20

Though God had rejected their services as insufficient to atone for their sins while they persisted in them, yet he does not reject them as in a hopeless condition, but here calls upon them to forsake their sins, which hindered the acceptance of their services, and then all would be well. Let them not say that God picked quarrels with them; no, he proposes a method of reconciliation. Observe here,

I. A call to repentance and reformation: "If you would have your sacrifices accepted, and your prayers answered, you must begin your work at the right end: *Be converted to my law"* (so the Chaldee begins this exhortation), "make conscience of second-table duties, else expect not to be accepted in the acts of your devotion." As justice and charity will never atone for atheism and profaneness, so prayers and sacrifices will never atone for fraud and oppression; for righteousness towards men is as much a branch of pure religion as religion towards God is a branch of universal righteousness.

1. They must *cease to do evil,* must do no more wrong, shed no more innocent blood. This is the meaning of washing themselves and *making themselves clean, v.* 16. It is not only sorrowing for the sin they had committed, but breaking off the practice of it for the future, and mortifying all those vicious affections and dispositions which inclined them to it. Sin is defiling to the soul. Our business is to wash ourselves from it by repenting of it and turning from it to God. We must put away not only that evil of our doings which is before the eye of the world, by refraining from the gross acts of sin, but that which is before God's eyes, the roots and habits of sin, that are in our hearts; these must be crushed and mortified.

2. They must *learn to do well.* This was necessary to the completing of their repentance. Note, It is not enough that we cease to do evil, but we must learn to do well. (1.) We must be doing, not cease to do evil and then stand idle. (2.) We must be doing good, the good which the Lord our God requires and which will turn to a good account. (3.) We must do it well, in a right manner and for a right end; and, (4.) We must learn to do well; we must take pains to get the knowledge of our duty, be inquisitive concerning it, in care about it, and accustom ourselves to it, that we may readily turn our hands to our work and become masters of this holy art of doing well. He urges them particularly to those instances of well-doing wherein they had been defective, to second-table duties: *"Seek judgment;* enquire what is right, that you may do it; be solicitous to be found in the way of your duty, and do not walk carelessly. Seek opportunities of doing good: *Relieve the oppressed,* those whom you yourselves have oppressed; ease them of their burdens, *ch.* 58:6. You, that have power in your hands, use it for the relief of those whom others do oppress, for that is your business. Avenge those that suffer wrong, in a special manner concerning yourselves for the fatherless and the widow, whom, because they are weak and helpless, proud men trample upon and abuse; do you appear for them at the bar, on the bench, as there is occasion. Speak for those that know not how to speak for themselves and that have not wherewithal to gratify you for your kindness." Note, We are truly honouring God when we are doing good in the world; and acts of justice and charity are more pleasing to him than all burnt-offerings and sacrifices.

II. A demonstration, at the bar of right reason, of the equity of God's proceedings with them: *"Come now, and let us reason together* (*v.* 18); while your hands are full of blood I will have nothing to do with you, though you bring me a multitude of sacrifices; but if you wash, and make yourselves clean, you are welcome to draw nigh to me; come now, and let us talk the matter over." Note, Those, and those only, that break off their league with sin, shall be welcome into covenant and communion with God; he says, *Come now,* who before forbade them his courts. See Jam. 4:8. Or rather thus: There were those among them who looked upon themselves as affronted by the slights God put upon the multitude of their sacrifices, as *ch.* 58:3, *Wherefore have we fasted* (say they) *and thou seest not?* They represented God as a hard Master, whom it was impossible to please. "Come," says God, "let us debate the matter fairly, and I doubt not but to make it out that *my ways are equal, but yours are unequal,"* Eze. 18:25. Note, Religion has reason on its side; there is all the reason in the world why we should do as God would have us do. The God of heaven condescends to reason the case with those that contradict him and find fault with his proceedings; for *he will be justified when he speaks,* Ps. 51:4. The case needs only to be stated (as it is here very fairly) and it will determine itself. God shows here upon what terms they stood (as he does, Eze. 18:21–24; 33:18, 19) and then leaves it to them to judge whether these terms are not fair and reasonable.

1. They could not in reason expect any more then, if they repented and reformed. they should be restored to God's favour, notwithstanding their former provocations. "This you may expect," says God, and it is very kind; who could have the face to desire it upon any other terms? (1.) It is very little that is required, "only that you *be willing and obedient,* that you *consent to obey"* (so some read it), "that you subject your wills to the will of God, acquiesce in that, and give up yourselves in all things to be ruled by him who is infinitely wise and good" *Here is no penance imposed for their former stubbornness, nor the yoke made heavier or bound harder on their necks; only, "Whereas hitherto you have been perverse and refractory, and would not comply with that which was for your own good, now be tractable, be governable"* He does not say, "If you be *perfectly* obedient," but, "If you be *willingly* so;" for, if there be a willing mind, it is accepted. (2.) That is very great which is promised hereupon. [1.] That all their sins should be pardoned to them, and should not be mentioned against them. "Though they be as red as scarlet and crimson, though you lie under the guilt of blood, yet, upon your repentance, even that shall be forgiven you, and you shall appear in the sight of God as white as snow." Note, The greatest sinners, if they truly repent, shall have their sins forgiven them, and so have their consciences pacified and purified. Though our sins have been as scarlet and crimson, as deep dye, a double dye, first in the wool of original corruption and afterwards in the many threads of actual transgression — though we have been often dipped, by our many backslidings, into sin, and though we have lain long soaking in it, as the cloth does in the scarlet dye, yet pardoning mercy will thoroughly discharge the stain, and, being by it purged as *with hyssop, we shall be clean,* Ps. 51:7. If we make ourselves clean by repentance and reformation (*v.* 16), God will make us white by a full remission. [2.] That they should have all the happiness and comfort they could desire. "Be but willing and obedient, and *you shall eat the good of the land,* the land of promise; you shall have all the blessings of the new covenant, of the heavenly Canaan, all the good of the land." Those that go on in sin, though they may dwell in a good land, cannot with any comfort eat the good of it; guilt embitters all; but, if sin be pardoned, creature-comforts become comforts indeed.

2. They could not in reason expect any other than that, if they continued obstinate in their disobedience, they should be abandoned to ruin, and the sentence of the law should be executed upon them; what can be more just? (*v.* 20); *"If you refuse and rebel,* if you continue to rebel against the divine government and refuse the offers of the divine grace, *you shall be devoured with the sword,* with the sword of your enemies, which shall be commissioned to destroy you — with the sword of God's justice, his wrath, and vengeance, which shall be drawn against you; for this is that which *the mouth of the Lord has spoken,* and which he will make good, for the maintaining of his own honour." Note, Those that will not be governed by God's sceptre will certainly and justly be devoured by his sword.

"And now life and death, good and evil, are thus set before you. *Come, and let us reason together.* What have you to object against the equity of this, or against complying with God's terms?"

Verses 21–31

Here, I. The woeful degeneracy of Judah and Jerusalem is sadly lamented. See, 1. What the royal city had been, a faithful city, faithful to God and the interests of his kingdom among men, faithful to the nation and its public interests. *It was full of judgment;* justice was duly administered upon the thrones of judgment which were set there, the *thrones of the house of David,* Ps. 122:5. Men were generally honest in their dealings, and abhorred to do an unjust thing. *Righteousness lodged in it,* was constantly resident in their palaces and in all their dwellings, not called in now and then to serve a turn, but at home there. Note, Neither holy cities nor royal ones, neither places where religion is professed nor places where government is administered, are faithful to their trust if religion do not dwell in them. 2. What it had now become. That beauteous virtuous spouse was now debauched, and become an adulteress; righteousness no longer dwelt in Jerusalem *(terras Astraea reliquit — Astrea left the earth);* even murderers were unpunished and lived undisturbed there; nay, the princes themselves were so cruel and oppressive that they had become no better than murderers; an innocent man might better guard himself against a troop of banditti or assassins than against a bench of such judges. Note, It is a great aggravation of the wickedness of any family or people that their ancestors were famed for virtue and probity; and commonly those that thus degenerate prove the most wicked of all men. *Corruptio optimi est pessima — That which was originally the best becomes when corrupted the worst,* Lu. 11:26; Eccl. 3:16; See Jer. 22:15–17. The degeneracy of Jerusalem is illustrated, (1.) By similitudes (*v.* 22): *Thy silver has become dross.* This degeneracy of the magistrates, whose character is the reverse of that of their predecessors, is a great a reproach and injury to the kingdom as the debasing of their coin would be and the turning of their silver into dross. Righteous princes and righteous cities are as silver for the treasury, but unrighteous ones are as dross for the dunghill. *How has the gold become dim!* Lam. 4:1. *Thy wine is mixed with water,* and so has become flat and sour. Some understand both these literally: the wine they sold was adulterated, it was half water; the money they paid was counterfeit, and so they cheated all they dealt with. But it is rather to be taken figuratively: justice was perverted by their princes, and religion and the word of God were sophisticated by their priests, and made to serve what turn they pleased. Dross may shine like silver, and the wine that is mixed with water may retain the colour of wine, but neither is worth any thing. Thus they retained a show and pretence of virtue and justice, but had no true sense of either. (2.) By some instances (*v.* 23): "Thy princes, that should keep others in their allegiance to God and subjection to his law, are themselves rebellious, and set God and his law at defiance." Those that should restrain thieves (proud and rich oppressors, those worst of robbers, and those that designedly cheat their creditors, who are no better), are themselves companions of thieves, connive at them, do as they do, and with greater security and success, because they are princes, and have power in their hands; they share with the thieves they protect in their unlawful gain (Ps. 50:18) and *cast in their lot among them,* Prov. 1:13, 14. [1.] The profit of their places is all their aim, to make the best hand they can of them, right or wrong. They love gifts, and follow after rewards; they set their hearts upon their salary, the fees and perquisites of their offices, and are greedy of them, and never think they can get enough; nay, they will do any thing, though ever so contrary to law and justice, for a gift in secret. Presents and gratuities will blind their eyes at any time, and make them pervert judgment. These they love and are eager in the pursuit of, Hos. 9:18. [2.] The duty of their places is none of their care. They ought to protect those that are injured, and take cognizance of the appeals made to them; why else were they preferred? But *they judge not the fatherless,* take no care to guard the orphans, *nor does the cause of the widow come unto them,* because the poor widow has no bribe to give, with which to make way for her and to bring her cause on. Those will have a great deal to answer for who, when they should be the patrons of the oppressed, are their greatest oppressors.

II. A resolution is taken up to redress these grievances (*v.* 24): *Therefore saith the Lord, the Lord of hosts, the Mighty One of Israel* — who has power to make good what he says, who has hosts at command for the executing of his purposes, and whose power is engaged for his Israel — *Ah! I will ease me of my adversaries.* Observe,

1. Wicked people, especially wicked rulers that are cruel and oppressive, are God's enemies, his adversaries, and shall so be accounted and so dealt with. If the holy seed corrupt themselves, they are the foes of his own house.

2. They are a burden to the God of heaven, which is implied in his easing himself of them. The *Mighty One of Israel,* that can bear any thing, nay, that upholds all things, complains of his being *wearied with men's iniquities, ch.* 43:24. Amos 2:13.

3. God will find out a time and a way to ease himself of this burden, by avenging himself on those that thus bear hard upon his patience. He here speaks as one triumphing in the foresight of it: *Ah. I will ease me.* He will ease the earth of the burden under which it *groans* (Rom. 8:21, 22), will ease his own name of the reproaches with which it is loaded. He will be eased of his adversaries, by *taking vengeance on his enemies;* he will *spue them out of his mouth,* and so be eased of them, Rev. 3:16. He speaks with pleasure of the *day of vengeance* being *in his heart, ch.* 63:4. If God's professing people conform not to his image, as the Holy One of Israel (*v.* 4), they shall feel the weight of his hand as the Mighty One of Israel: his power, which was wont to be engaged for them, shall be armed against them. In two ways God will ease himself of this grievance:—

(1.) By reforming his church, and restoring good judges in the room of those corrupt ones. Though the church has a great deal of dross in it, yet it shall not be thrown away, but refined (*v.* 25): *"I will purely purge away thy dross.* I will amend what is amiss. Vice and profaneness shall be suppressed and put out of countenance, oppressors displaced, and deprived of their power to do mischief." When things are ever so bad God can set them to rights, and bring about a complete reformation; when he begins he will make an end, will take away all the tin. Observe, [1.] The reformation of a people is God's own work, and, if ever it be done, it is he that brings it about: *"I will turn my hand upon thee;* I will do that for the reviving of religion which I did at first for the planting of it." He can do it easily, with the turn of his hand; but he does it effectually, for what opposition can stand before the arm of the Lord revealed? [2.] He does it by blessing them with good magistrates and good ministers of state (*v.* 26): *"I will restore thy judges as at the first,* to put the laws in execution against evil-doers, *and thy counsellors,* to transact public affairs, *as at the beginning,"* either the same persons that had been turned out or others of the same character. [3.] He does it by restoring judgment and righteousness among them (*v.* 27), by planting in men's minds principles of justice and governing their lives by those principles. Men may do much by external restraints; but God does it effectually by the influences of *his Spirit,* as a *Spirit of judgment, ch.* 4:4; 28:6. See Ps. 85:10, 11. [4.] The reformation of a people will be the redemption of them and their converts, for sin is the worst captivity, the worst slavery, and the great and eternal redemption is that by which *Israel is redeemed from all his iniquities* (Ps. 130:8), and the *blessed Redeemer* is he that *turns away ungodliness from Jacob* (Rom. 11:26), and *saves his people from their sins,* Mt. 1:21. All the redeemed of the Lord shall be converts, and their conversion is their redemption: *"Her converts,* or *those that return of her* (so the margin), shall be redeemed with righteousness." God works deliverance for us by preparing us for it with judgment and righteousness. [5.] The reviving of a people's virtues is the restoring of their honour: *Afterwards thou shalt be called the city of righteousness, the faithful city;* that is, *First,* "Thou shalt *be* so;" the reforming of the magistracy is a good step towards the reforming of the city and the country too. *Secondly,* "Thou shalt have the *praise* of being so;" and a greater praise there cannot be to any city than to *be called the city of righteousness,* and to retrieve the ancient honour which was lost when *the faithful city became a harlot, v.* 21.

(2.) By cutting off those that hate to be reformed, that they may not remain either as snares or as scandals to the faithful city. [1.] it is an utter ruin that is here threatened. They shall be destroyed and consumed, and not chastened and corrected only. The extirpation of them will be necessary to the redemption of Zion. [2.] It is a universal ruin, which will involve the transgressors and the sinners together, that is, the openly profane that have quite cast of all religion, and the hypocrites that live wicked lives under the cloak of a religious profession — they shall both be destroyed together, for they are both alike an abomination to God, both those that contradict religion and those that contradict themselves in their pretensions to it. *And those that forsake the Lord,* to whom they had formerly joined themselves, *shall be consumed,* as the water in the conduit-pipe is soon consumed when it is cut off from the fountain. [3.] It is an inevitable ruin; there is no escaping it. *First,* Their idols shall not be able to help them, *the oaks which they have desired, and the gardens which they have chosen;* that is, the images, the dunghill-gods, which they had worshipped in their groves and under the green trees, which they were fond of and wedded to, for which they forsook the true God, and which they worshipped privately in their own garden even when idolatry was publicly discountenanced. "This was the practice of the transgressors and the sinners; but they shall be ashamed of it, not with a show of repentance, but of despair, *v.* 29. They shall have cause to be ashamed of their idols; for, after all the court they have made to them, they shall find no benefit by them; but the idols themselves *shall go into captivity," ch.* 46:1, 2. Note, Those that make creatures their confidence are but preparing confusion for themselves. You were fond of the oaks and the gardens, but you yourselves shall be, 1. *"Like an oak without leaves,* withered and blasted, and stripped of all its ornaments." Justly do those wear no leaves that bear no fruit; as the fig-tree that Christ cursed. 2. *"Like a garden without water,* that is neither rained upon nor *watered with the foot* (Deu. 11:10), that had no *fountain* (Cant. 4:15), and consequently is parched, and all the fruits of it gone to decay." Thus shall those be that trust in idols, or in an *arm of flesh,* Jer. 17:5, 6. But those that trust in God never find him as a wilderness, or as waters that fail, Jer. 2:31. *Secondly,* They shall not be able to help themselves (*v.* 31): *"Even the strong man shall be as tow* not only soon broken and pulled to pieces, but easily catching fire; and *his work* (so the margin reads it), that by which he hopes to fortify and secure himself, shall be as a spark to his own tow, shall set him on fire, and he and his work shall burn together. His counsels shall be his ruin; his own skin kindles the fire of God's wrath, which shall burn to the lowest hell, and none shall quench it." When the sinner has made himself as tow and stubble, and God makes himself to him as a consuming fore, what can prevent the utter ruin of the sinner?

Now all this is applicable, 1. To the blessed work of reformation which was wrought in Hezekiah's time after the abominable corruptions of the reign of Ahaz. Then good men came to be preferred, and the faces of the wicked were filled with shame. 2. To their return out of their captivity in Babylon, which had thoroughly cured them of idolatry. 3. To the gospel-kingdom and the pouring out of the Spirit, by which the New-Testament church should be made a new Jerusalem, a city of righteousness. 4. To the second coming of Christ, when he shall thoroughly purge his floor, his field, shall gather the wheat into his barn, into his garner, and burn the chaff, the tares, with unquenchable fire.

CHAPTER 2

With this chapter begins a new sermon, which is continued in the two following chapters. The subject of this discourse is Judah and Jerusalem (*v.* 1). In this chapter the prophet speaks, I. Of the glory of the Christians, Jerusalem, the gospel-church in the latter days, in the accession of many to it (*v.* 2, 3), and the great peace it should introduce into the world (*v.* 4), whence he infers the duty of the house of Jacob (*v.* 5). II. Of the shame of the Jews, Jerusalem, as it then was, and as it would be after its rejection of the gospel and being rejected of God. 1. Their sin was their shame (*v.* 6–9). 2. God by his judgments would humble them and put them to shame (*v.* 10–17). 3. They should themselves be ashamed of their confidence in their idols and in an arm of flesh (*v.* 18–22). And now which of these Jerusalems will we be the inhabitants of — that which is full of the knowledge of God, which will be our everlasting honour, or that which is full of horses and chariots, and silver and gold, and such idols, which will in the end be our shame?

Verses 1–5

The particular title of this sermon (*v.* 1) is the same with the general title of the book (*ch.* 1:1), only that what is there called the *vision* is here called *the word which Isaiah saw* (or the matter, or thing, which he saw), the truth of which he had as full an assurance of in his own mind as if he had seen it with his bodily eyes. Or this word was brought to him in a vision; something he saw when he received this message from God. John turned to *see the voice* that spoke with him. Rev. 1:12.

This sermon begins with the prophecy relating to the last days, the days of the Messiah, when his kingdom should be set up in the world, at the latter end of the Mosaic economy. In the last days of the earthly Jerusalem, just before the destruction of it, this heavenly Jerusalem should be erected, Heb. 12:22; Gal. 4:26. Note, Gospel times are the last days. For 1. They were long in coming, were a great while waited for by the Old-Testament saints, and came at last. 2. We are not to look for any dispensation of divine grace but what we have in the gospel, Gal. 1:8, 9. 3. We are to look for the second coming of Jesus Christ at the end of time, as the Old-Testament saints did for his first coming; *this is the last time,* 1 Jn. 2:18.

Now the prophet here foretels,

I. The setting up of the Christian church, and the planting of the Christian religion, in the world. Christianity shall then be the mountain of the Lord's house; where that is professed God will grant his presence, receive his people's homage, and grant instruction and blessing, as he did of old in the temple of Mount Zion. The gospel church, incorporated by Christ's charter, shall then be the rendezvous of all the spiritual seed of Abraham. Now it is here promised, I. That Christianity shall be openly preached and professed; it shall be *prepared* (so the margin reads it) in the top of the mountains, in the view and hearing of all. Hence Christ's disciples are compared to a city on a hill, which *cannot be hid,* Mt. 5:14. They had many eyes upon them. Christ himself *spoke openly to the world*, Jn. 18:20. What the apostles did was not *done in a corner*, Acts 26:26. It was the lighting of a beacon, the setting up of a standard. Its being every where spoken *against* supposes that it was every where spoken *of*. 2. That is shall be firmly fixed and rooted; it shall be established on the top of the everlasting mountains, built upon a *rock*, so that the *gates of hell shall not prevail against it*, unless they could pluck up mountains by the roots. He that dwells safely is said to *dwell on high*, ch. 33:16. *The Lord has founded the gospel Zion*. 3. That it shall not only overcome all opposition, but overtop all competition; it shall be *exalted above the hills*. This *wisdom of God in a mystery* shall outshine all the wisdom of this world, all its philosophy and all its politics. The spiritual worship which it shall introduce shall put down the idolatries of the heathen; and all other institutions in religion shall appear mean and despicable in comparison with this. See Ps. 68:16. *Why leap ye, ye high hills? This is the hill which God desires to dwell in.*

II. The bringing of the Gentiles into it. 1. The nations shall be admitted into it, even the uncircumcised, who were forbidden to come into the courts of the temple at Jerusalem. The partition wall, which kept them out, kept them off, shall be taken down. 2. *All nations shall flow into it;* having liberty of access, they shall improve their liberty, and multitudes shall embrace the Christian faith. They shall flow into it, as streams of water, which denotes the abundance of converts that the gospel should make and their speed and cheerfulness in coming into the church. They shall not be forced into it, but shall naturally flow into it. *Thy people shall be willing,* all volunteers, Ps. 110:3. To Christ shall the *gathering of the people be,* Gen. 49:10. See ch. 60:4, 5.

III. The mutual assistance and encouragement which this confluence of converts shall give to one another. Their pious affections and resolutions shall be so intermixed that they shall come in in one full stream. As, when the Jews from all parts of the country went up thrice a year to worship at Jerusalem, they called on their friends in the road and excited them to go along with them, so shall many of the Gentiles court their relations, friends, and neighbours, to join with them in embracing the Christian religion (*v.* 3): *"Come, and let us go up to the mountain of the Lord;* though it be uphill and against the heart, yet it is *the mountain of the Lord,* who will assist the assent of our souls towards him." Note, Those that are entering into covenant and communion with God themselves should bring as many as they can along with them; it becomes Christians to provoke one another to good works, and to further the communion of saints by inviting one another into it: not, "Do you *go up to the mountain of the Lord,* and pray for us, and we will stay at home;" nor, "We will go, and do you do as you will;" but, *"Come, and let us go,* let us go in concert, that we may strengthen one another's hands and support one another's reputation:" not, "We will consider of it, and advise about it, and go hereafter;" but, *Come, and let us go forthwith.* See Ps. 122:1. Many shall say this. Those that have had it said to them shall say it to others. The gospel church is here called, not only the *mountain of the Lord,* but *the house of the God of Jacob;* for in it God's covenant with Jacob and his praying seed is kept up and has its accomplishment; for to us now, as unto them, he never said, *Seek you me in vain,* ch. 45:19. Now see here, 1. What they promise themselves in going up to the *mountain of the Lord;* There *he will teach us of his ways.* Note, God's ways are to be learned in his church, in communion with his people, and in the use of instituted ordinances — the ways of duty which he requires us to walk in, the ways of grace in which he walks towards us. It is God that teaches his people, by his word and Spirit. It is worth while to take pains to go up to his holy mountain to be taught his ways, and those who are willing to take that pains shall never find it labour in vain. Then *shall we know if we follow on to know the Lord.* 2. What they *promise for themselves* and one another: "If he will *teach us his ways,* we will *walk in his paths;* is he will let us know our duty, we will by his grace make conscience of doing it." Those who attend God's word with this humble resolution shall not be sent away without their lesson.

IV. The means by which this shall be brought about: *Out of Zion shall go forth the law,* the New-Testament law, the law of Christ, as of old the law of Moses from Mount Sinai, even *the word of the Lord from Jerusalem.* The gospel is a law, a law of faith; it is the *word of the Lord;* it *went forth from Zion,* where the temple was built, and from Jerusalem. Christ himself began in Galilee, Mt. 4:23; Lu. 23:5. But, when he commissioned his apostles to preach the gospel to all nations, he appointed them to begin in Jerusalem, Lu. 24:47. See Rom. 15:19. Though most of them had their homes in Galilee, yet they must stay at Jerusalem, there to *receive the promise of the Spirit,* Acts 1:4. And in the temple on Mount Zion they preached the gospel, Acts 5:20. This honour was allowed to Jerusalem, even after Christ was crucified there, for the sake of what it had been. And it was by this gospel, which took rise from Jerusalem, that the gospel church was *established on the top of the mountains.* This was the rod of divine strength, that was *sent forth out of Zion,* Ps. 110:2.

V. The erecting of the kingdom of the Redeemer in the world: *He shall judge among the nations.* He whose word goes forth out of Zion shall by that word not only subdue souls to himself, but rule in them, *v.* 4. He shall, in wisdom and justice, order and overrule the affairs of the world for the good of his church, and rebuke and restrain those that oppose his interest. By his Spirit working on men's consciences he shall judge, and rebuke shall try men and check them; his kingdom is spiritual, *and not of this world.*

VI. The great peace which should be the effect of the success of the gospel in the world (*v.* 4): *They shall beat their swords into ploughshares;* their instruments of war shall be converted into implements of husbandry; as, on the contrary, when war is proclaimed, *ploughshares are beaten into swords,* Joel 3:10. *Nations shall then not lift up sword against nation,* as they now do, *neither shall they learn war any more,* for they shall have no more occasion for it. This does not make all war absolutely unlawful among Christians, nor is it a prophecy that in the days of the Messiah there shall be no wars. The Jews urge this against the Christians as an argument that Jesus is not the Messiah, because this promise is not fulfilled. But, 1. It was in part fulfilled in the peaceableness of the time in which Christ was born, when wars had in a great measure ceased, witness *the taxing,* Lu. 2:1. 2. The design and tendency of the gospel are to make peace and to slay all enmities. It has in it the most powerful obligations and inducements to peace; so that one might reasonably have expected it should have this effect, and it would have had it if it had not been for those lusts of men from which come wars and fightings. 3. Jew and Gentiles were reconciled and brought together by the gospel, and there were no more such wars between them as there had been; for they became *one sheepfold under one shepherd.* See Eph. 2:15. 4. The gospel of Christ, as far as it prevails, disposes men to be peaceable, softens men's spirits, and sweetens them; and the love of Christ, shed abroad in the heart, constrains men to love one another. 5. The primitive Christians were famous for brotherly love; their very adversaries took notice of it. 6. We have reason to hope that this promise shall yet have a more full accomplishment in the latter times of the Christian church, when the Spirit shall be poured out more plentifully from on high. Then there shall be on earth peace. *Who shall live when God doeth this?* But do it he will in due time, for *he is not a man that he should lie.*

Lastly, Here is a practical inference drawn from all this (*v.* 5): *O house of Jacob! come you, and let us walk in the light of the Lord.* By the house of Jacob is meant either, 1. Israel according to the flesh. Let them be provoked by this *to a holy emulation,* Rom. 11:14. "Seeing the Gentiles are thus ready and resolved for God, thus forward to go up to the house of the Lord, let us stir up ourselves to go too. Let is never be said that the sinners of the Gentiles were better friends to the holy mountain than the house of Jacob." Thus the zeal of some should provoke many. Or, 2. Spiritual Israel, all that are brought to the God of Jacob. Shall there be such great knowledge in gospel times (*v.* 3) and such grat peace (*v.* 4), and shall we share in these privileges? Come then, and let us live accordingly. What ever others do, *come, O come!* let us *walk in the light of the Lord.* (1.) Let us walk circumspectly in the light of this knowledge. Will God teach us his ways? Will he show us his glory in the face of Christ? Let us then *walk as children of the light and of the day,* Eph. 5:8; 1 Th. 5:8; Rom. 13:12 (2.) Let us walk comfortably in the light of this peace. Shall there be no more war? Let us then go on our way

rejoicing, and let this joy terminate in God, and be our strength, Neh. 8:10.. Thus shall we walk in the beams of the Sun of righteousness.

Verses 6–9

The calling in of the Gentiles was accompanied with the rejection of the Jews; it was their fall, and the *diminishing of them, that was the riches of the Gentiles;* and the *casting off of them* was *the reconciling of the world* (Rom. 11:12–15); and it should seem that these verses have reference to that, and are designed to justify God therein, and yet it is probable that they are primarily intended for the convincing and awakening of the men of that generation in which the prophet lived, it being usual with the prophets to speak of the things that then were, both in mercy and judgment, as types of the things that should be hereafter. Here is,

I. Israel's doom. This is set forth in two words, the first and the last of this paragraph; but they are two dreadful words, and which speak. 1. Their case sad, very sad (*v.* 6): *Therefore thou hast forsaken thy people.* Miserable is the condition of that people whom God has forsaken, and great certainly must the provocation be if he forsake those that have been his own people. This was the deplorable case of the Jewish church after they had rejected Christ. *Migremus hinc — Let us go hence. Your house is left unto you desolate,* Mt. 23:38. Whenever any sore calamity came upon the Jews thus far the Lord might be said to forsake them that he withdrew his help and succour from them, else they would not have fallen into the hands of their enemies. But God never leaves any till they first leave him. 2. Their case desperate, wholly desperate (*v.* 9): *Therefore forgive them not.* This prophetical prayer amounts to a threatening that they should not be forgiven, and some think it may be read: *And thou wilt not forgive them.* This refers not to particular persons (many of them repented and were pardoned), but to the body of that nation, against whom an irreversible doom was passed, that they should be wholly cut off and their church quite dismantled, never to be formed into such a body again, nor ever to have their old charter restored to them.

II. Israel's desert of this doom, and the reasons upon which it is grounded. In general, it is sin that brings destruction upon them; it is this, and nothing but this, that provokes God to forsake his people. The particular sins which the prophet specifies are such as abounded among them at that time, which he makes mention of for the conviction of those to whom he then preached, rather than that which afterwards proved the measure-filling sin, their crucifying Christ and persecuting his followers; for the sins of every age contributed towards the making up of the dreadful account at last. And there was a partial and temporary rejection of them by the captivity in Babylon hastening on, which was a type of their final destruction by the Romans, and which the sins here mentioned brought upon them. Their sins were such as directly contradicted all God's kind and gracious designs concerning them.

1. God set them apart for himself, as a peculiar people, distinguished from, and dignified above, all other people (Num. 23:9); but they were *replenished from the east;* they *naturalized* foreigners, not *proselyted,* and encouraged them to settle among them, and mingled with them, Hos. 7:8. Their country was peopled with Syrians and Chaldeans, Moabites and Ammonites, and other eastern nations, and with them they admitted the fashions and customs of those nations, and *pleased themselves in the children of strangers,* were fond of them, preferred their country before their own, and thought the more they conformed to them the more polite and refined they were; thus did they profane their crown and their covenant. Note, Those are in danger of being estranged from God who please themselves with those who are strangers to him, for we soon learn the ways of those whose company we love.

2. God gave them his oracles, which they might ask counsel of, not only the scriptures and the seers, but the breast-plate of judgment; but they slighted these, and became soothsayers like the Philistines, introduced their arts of divination, and hearkened to those who by the stars, or the clouds, or the flight of birds, or the entrails of beasts, or other magic superstitions, pretended to discover things secret or foretel things to come. The Philistines were noted

for diviners, 1 Sa. 6:2. Note, Those who slight true divinity are justly given up to lying divinations; and those will certainly be forsaken of God who thus forsake him and their own mercies for lying vanities.

3. God encouraged them to put their confidence in him, and assured them that he would be their wealth and strength; but, distrusting his power and promise, they made gold their hope, and furnished themselves with horses and chariots, and relied upon them for their safety, *v.* 7. God had expressly forbidden even their kings to multiply horses to themselves and *greatly to multiply silver and gold,* because he would have them to depend upon himself only; but they did not think their interest in God made them a match for their neighbours unless they had as full treasures of silver and gold, and as formidable hosts of chariots and horses, as they had. It is not having silver and gold, horses and chariots, that is a provocation to God, but, (1.) Desiring them insatiably, so that there is no end of the treasures, no end of the chariots, no bounds or limits set to the desire of them. Those shall never have enough in God (who alone is all-sufficient) that never know when they have enough of this world, which at the best is insufficient. (2.) Depending upon them, as if we could not be safe, and easy, and happy, without them, and could not but be so with them.

4. God himself was their God, the sole object of their worship, and he himself instituted ordinances of worship for them; but they slighted both him and his institutions, *v.* 8. Their land was full of idols; every city had its god (Jer. 11:13); and, according to the goodness of their lands, they made goodly images, Hos. 10:1. Those that think one God too little will find two too many, and yet hundreds were not sufficient; for those that love idols will multiply them; so sottish were they, and so wretchedly infatuated, that they *worshipped the work of their own hands,* as if that could be a god to them which was not only a creature, but *their* creature and that which their own fancies had devised and *their own fingers had made.* It was an aggravation of their idolatry that God had enriched them with silver and gold, and yet of that silver and gold they made idols; so it was, *Jeshurun waxed fat, and kicked,* see Hos. 2:8.

5. God had advanced them, and put honour upon them; but they basely diminished and disparaged themselves (*v.* 9): *The mean man boweth down to his idol,* a thing below the meanest that has any spark of reason left. Sin is a disparagement to the poorest and those of the lowest rank. It becomes the mean man to bow down to his superiors, but it ill becomes him to *bow down to the stock of a tree, ch.* 44:19. Nor is it only the illiterate and poor-spirited that do this, but even the *great men* forgets his grandeur and humbles himself to worship idols, deifies men no better than himself, and consecrates stones so much baser than himself. Idolaters are said to *debase themselves even to hell, ch.* 57:9. What a shame it is that great men think the service of the true God below them and will not stoop to it, and yet will humble themselves to bow down to an idol! Some make this a threatening that the mean men shall be brought down, and the great men humbled, by the judgements of God, when they come with commission.

Verses 10–22

The prophet here goes on to show what a desolation would be brought upon their land when God should have forsaken them. This may refer particularly to their destruction by the Chaldeans first, and afterwards by the Romans, or it may have a general respect to the method God takes to awaken and humble proud sinners, and to put them out of conceit with that which they delighted in and depended on more than God. We are here told that sooner or later God will find out a way,

I. To startle and awaken secure sinners, who cry peace to themselves, and bid defiance to God and his judgments (*v.* 10): *"Enter into the rock;* God will attack you with such terrible judgments, and strike you with such terrible apprehensions of them, that you shall be forced to *enter into the rock, and hide yourself in the dust, for fear of the Lord.* You shall lose all your courage, and tremble at the shaking of a leaf; your heart shall *fail you for fear* (Lu. 21:26), and you shall *flee when none pursues,"* Prov. 28:1. To the same purport, *v.* 19. *They shall go into the holes of the rocks, and into the caves of the earth,* the darkest the deepest places; they shall *call to the rocks and mountains to fall on them,* and rather crush them than not cover them, Hos. 10:8. It was so particularly at the destruction of Jerusalem by the Romans (Lu. 23:30) and of the persecuting pagan powers, Rev. 6:16. And all *for fear of the Lord, and of the glory of his majesty,* looking upon him then to be a consuming fire and themselves as stubble before him, *when he arises to shake terribly the earth,,* to *shake the wicked out of it* (Job 38:13), and to shake all those earthly props and supports with which they have buoyed themselves up, to shake them from under them. Note, 1. *With God is terrible majesty,* and the glory of it is such as sooner or later will oblige us all to flee before him. 2. Those that will not fear God and flee to him will be forced to fear him and flee from him to a refuge of lies. 3. It is folly for those that are pursued by the wrath of God to think to escape it, and to hide or shelter themselves from it. 4. The things of the earth are things that will be shaken; they are subject to concussions, and hastening towards a dissolution. 5. The shaking of the earth is, and will be, a terrible thing to those who set their affections wholly on things of the earth. 6. It will be in vain to think of finding refuge in the caves of the earth when the earth itself is shaken; there will be no shelter then but in God and in things above.

II. To humble and abase proud sinners, that look big, and think highly of themselves, and scornfully of all about them (*v.* 11): *The lofty looks of man shall be humbled.* The eyes that aim high, the countenance in which the pride of the heart shows itself, shall be cast down in shame and despair. And the *haughtiness of men shall be bowed down,* their spirits shall be broken, and they shall be crest-fallen, and those things which they were proud of they shall be ashamed of. It is repeated (*v.* 17), *The loftiness of man shall be bowed down.* Note, Pride will, one way or other, have a fall. Men's haughtiness will be brought down, either by the grace of God convincing them of the evil of their pride, and clothing them with humility, or by the providence of God depriving them of all those things they were proud of and laying them low. Our Saviour often laid it down for a maxim that *he who exalts himself shall be abased;* he shall either abase himself in true repentance or God will abase him and pour contempt upon him. Now here we are told,

1. Why this shall be done: because the *Lord alone will be exalted.* Note, Proud men shall be vilified because the Lord alone will be magnified. It is for the honour of God's power to humble the proud; by this he proves himself to be God, and disproves Job's pretensions to rival with him, Job 40:11–14. *Behold every one that is proud, and abase him; then will I also confess unto thee.* It is likewise for the honour of his justice. Proud men stand in competition with God, who is jealous for his own glory, and will not suffer men either to take to themselves or give to another that which is due to him only. They likewise stand in opposition to God; they resist him, and therefore he resists them; for he *will be exalted among the heathen* (Ps. 46:10), and there is a day coming in which he alone will be exalted, when he shall have put *down all opposing rule, principality, and power,* 1 Co. 15:24.

2. How this shall be done: by humbling judgments, that shall mortify men, and bring them down (*v.* 12): *The day of the Lord of hosts,* the day of his wrath and judgment, *shall be upon every one that is proud.* He now laughs at their insolence because he sees that his day is coming, this day, which will be upon them ere they are aware, Ps. 37:13. This day of the Lord is here said to be upon *all the cedars of Lebanon, that are high and lifted up.* Jerome observes that the cedars are said to praise God (Ps. 148:9) and are *trees of the Lord* (Ps. 104:16), *of his planting* (Isa. 41:19), and yet here God's wrath fastens upon the cedars, which denotes (says he) that some of every rank of men, some great men, will be saved, and some perish. It is brought in as an instance of the strength of God's voice that it *breaks the cedars* (Ps. 29:5), and here the day of the Lord is said to be *upon the cedars,* those of Lebanon, they were the straightest and statliest, — upon the oaks, those of Bashan, that were the strongest and sturdiest, — upon the natural elevations and fortresses, *the highest mountains and the hills that are lifted up* (*v.* 14), that overtop the valleys and seem to push the skies, — and upon the artificial fastnesses, *every high tower and every fenced wall, v.* 15. Understand these, (1.) As representing the proud people themselves, that are in their own apprehensions like the cedars and the oaks, firmly rooted, and not to be stirred by any storm, and looking on all around them as shrubs; these are the high mountains and the lofty hills that seem to fill the earth, that are gazed on by all, and think themselves immovable, but lie most obnoxious to God's thunderstrokes. *Feriuntique summos fulmina montes — The highest hills are most exposed to lightning.* And before the power of God's wrath these mountains are scattered and these hills bow and *melt like wax,* Hab. 3:6; Ps. 68:8. These vaunting men, who are as high towers in which the noisy bells are hung, on which the thundering murdering cannon are planted — these fenced walls, that fortify themselves with their native hardiness, and intrench themselves in their fastnesses — shall be brought down. (2.) As particularizing the things they are proud of, in which they trust, and of which they make their boast. The day of the Lord shall be upon those very things in which they put their confidence as their strength and security; he will *take from the all their armour wherein they trusted.* Did the inhabitants of Lebanon glory in their cedars, and those of Bashan in their oaks, such as no country could equal? The day of the Lord should rend those cedars, those oaks, and the houses built of them. Did Jerusalem glory in the mountains that were round about it, as its impregnable fortifications, or in its walls and bulwarks? These should be levelled and laid low in the day of the Lord. Besides those things that were for their strength and safety they were proud, [1.] Of their trade abroad; but the day of the Lord shall be *upon all the ships of Tarshish;* they shall be broken as Jehoshaphat's were, shall founder at sea or be shipwrecked in harbour. Zebulun was a haven of ships, but should now no more rejoice in his going out. When God is bringing ruin upon a people he can sink all the branches of their revenue. [2.] Of their ornaments at home; but the day of the Lord shall be *upon all pleasant pictures,* the painting of their ships (so some understand it) or the curious pieces of painting they brought home in their ships from other countries, perhaps from Greece, which afterwards was famous for painters. Upon *every thing that is beautiful to behold;* so some read it. Perhaps they were the pictures of their relations, and for that reason pleasant, or of their gods, which to the idolaters were delectable things; or they admired them for the fineness of their colours or strokes. There is no harm in making pictures, nor in adorning our rooms with them, provided they transgress not either the second or the seventh commandment. But to place our pictures among our pleasant things, to be fond of them and proud of them, to spend that upon them which should be laid out in charity, and to set out hearts upon them, as it ill becomes those who have so many substantial things to take pleasure in, so it tends to provoke God to strip us of all such vain ornaments.

III. To make idolaters ashamed of their idols, and of all the affection they have had for them and the respect they have paid to them (*v.* 18): *The idols he shall utterly abolish.* When the Lord alone shall be exalted (*v.* 17) he will not only pour contempt upon proud men, who like Pharaoh exalt themselves against him, but much more upon all pretended deities, who are rivals with him for divine honours. They shall be abolished, utterly abolished. Their friends shall desert them; their enemies shall destroy them; so that, one way or other, an utter riddance shall be made of them. See here, 1. The vanity of false gods; they cannot secure themselves, so far are they from being able to secure their worshippers. 2. The victory of the true God over them; for *great is the truth and will prevail.* Dagon fell before the ark, and Baal before the Lord God of Elijah. The gods of the heathen shall be famished (Zep. 2:11), and by degrees shall perish, Jer. 10:11. The rightful Sovereign will triumph over all pretenders. And, as God will abolish idols, so their worshippers shall abandon them, either from a gracious conviction of their vanity and falsehood (as Ephraim when he said, *What have I to do any more with idols?*) or from a late and sad experience of their inability to help them, and a woeful despair of relief by them, *v.* 20. When men are themselves frightened by the judgments of God into the holes of the rocks and caves of the earth, and find that they do thus in vain shift for their own safety, they shall cast their idols, which they have made their gods, and hoped to make their friends in the time of need, to the moles and to the bats, any where out of sight, that, being freed from the incumbrance of them, they may *go into the clefts of the rocks, for fear of the Lord, v.* 21. Note, (1.) Those that will not be reasoned out of their sins sooner or later shall be frightened out of them. (2.) God can make men sick of those idols that they have been most fond of, even the idols of silver and the idols of gold, the most precious. Covetous men make silver and gold their idols, money their god; but the time may come when they may feel it **as** much their burden as ever they made it their confidence, and may find themselves as much exposed by it as ever they hoped they should be guarded by it, when it tempts their enemy, sinks their ship, or retards their flight. There was a time when the mariners threw the wares, and even the *wheat into the sea* (Jonah 1:5; Acts 27:38), and the *Syrians cast away their garments for haste,* 2 Ki. 7:15. Or men may cast it away out of indignation at themselves for leaning upon such a broken reed. See Eze. 7:19. The idolaters here throw away their idols because they are ashamed of them and of their own folly in trusting to them, or because they are afraid of having them found in their possession when the judgments of God are abroad; as the thief throws away his stolen goods then he is searched for or pursued. (3.) The darkest holes, where the moles and the bats lodge, are the fittest places for idols, that have eyes and see not; and God can force men to cast their own idols there (*ch.* 30:22), when they are *ashamed of the oaks which they have desired, ch.* 1. 29. *Moab shall be ashamed of Chemosh, as the house of Israel was ashamed of Bethel,* Jer. 48:13. (4.) It is possible that sin may be both loathed and left and yet not truly repented of — loathed because surfeited on, left because there is no opportunity of committing it, yet not repented of out of any love to God, but only from a slavish fear of his wrath.

IV. To make those that have trusted in an arm of flesh ashamed of their confidence (*v.* 22): "*Cease from man.* The providences of God concerning you shall speak this aloud to you, and therefore take warning beforehand, that you may prevent the uneasiness and shame of disappointment; and consider, 1. How weak man is: *His breath is in his nostrils,* puffed out every moment, soon gone for good and all." Man is a dying creature, and may die quickly; our nostrils, in which our breath is, are of the outward parts of the body; what is there is like one standing at the door, ready to depart; nay the doors of the nostrils are always open, the breath in them may slip away ere we are aware, in a moment. Wherein then is man to be accounted of? Alas! no reckoning is to be made of him, for he is not what he seems to be, what he pretends to be, what we fancy him to be. Man is like vanity, nay, he is vanity, he is altogether vanity, he is less, he is lighter, than vanity, when weighed in the balance of the sanctuary. "2. How wise therefore those are that cease from man;" it is our duty, it is our interest, to do so. "*Put not your trust in man,* nor make even the greatest and mightiest of men your confidence; cease to do so. Let not your eye be to the power of man, for it is finite and limited, derived and depending; it is not from him that your judgment proceeds. Let not him be your fear, let not him be your hope; but look up to the power of God, to which all the powers of men are subject and subordinate; dread his wrath, secure his favour, take him for your help, and let your *hope be in the Lord your God.*"

CHAPTER 3

The prophet, in this chapter, goes on to foretel the desolations that were coming upon Judah and Jerusalem for their sins, both that by the Babylonians and that which completed their ruin by the Romans, with some of the grounds of God's controversy with them. God threatens, I. To deprive them of all the supports both of their life and of their government (*v.* 1–3). II. To leave them to fall into confusion and disorder (*v.* 4, 5, 12). III. To deny them the blessing of magistracy (*v.* 6–8). IV. To strip the daughters of Zion of their ornaments (*v.* 17–24). V. To lay all waste by the sword of war (*v.* 25, 26). The sins that provoked God to deal thus with them were, 1. Their defiance of God (*v.* 8). 2. Their impudence (*v.* 9). 3. The abuse of power to oppression and tyranny (*v.* 12–15). 4. The pride of the daughters of Zion (*v.* 16). In the midst of the chapter the prophet is directed how to address particular persons. (1.) To assure good people that it should be well with them, notwithstanding those general calamities (*v.* 10). (2.) To assure wicked people that, however God might, in judgment, remember mercy, yet it should go ill with them (*v.* 11). O that the nations of the earth, at this day, would hearken to rebukes and warnings which this chapter gives!

Verses 1–8

The prophet, in the close of the foregoing chapter, had given a necessary caution to all not to put confidence in

man, or any creature; he had also given a general reason for that caution, taken from the frailty of human life and the vanity and weakness of human powers. Here he gives a particular reason for it — God was now about to ruin all their creature-confidences, so that they should meet with nothing but disappointments in all their expectations from them (*v.* 1): *The stay and the staff* shall be taken away, all their supports, of what kind soever, all the things they trusted to and looked for help and relief from. Their church and kingdom had now grown old and were going to decay, and they were (after the manner of aged men, Zec. 8:4) leaning on a staff: now God threatens to take away their staff, and then they must fall of course, to take away the stays of both the city and the country, of Jerusalem and of Judah, which are indeed stays to one another, and, if one fail, the other feels from it. He that does this is the *Lord, the Lord of hosts — Adon,* the Lord that is himself the stay or foundation; if that stay depart, all other stays certainly break under us, for he is the strength of them all. He that is the Lord, the ruler, that has authority to do it, and the Lord of hosts, that has the ability to do it, he shall take away the stay and the staff. St. Jerome refers this to the sensible decay of the Jewish nation after they had crucified our Saviour, Rom. 11:9, 10. I rather take it as a warning to all nations not to provoke God; for if they make him their enemy, he can and will thus make them miserable. Let us view the particulars.

I. Was their plenty a support to them? It is so to any people; bread is the staff of life: but God can *take away the whole stay of bread, and the whole stay of water;* and it is just with him to do so when fulness of bread becomes an iniquity (Eze. 16:49), and that which was given to be provision for the life is made provision for the lusts. He can take away the bread and the water by withholding the rain, Deu. 28:23, 24. Or, if he allow them, he can take away the stay of bread and the stay of water by withholding his blessing, by which man lives, and not by bread only, and which is the staff of bread (Mt. 4:4.), and then the bread is not nourishing nor the water refreshing, Hag. 1:6. Christ is the bread of life and the water of life; if he be our stay, we shall find that this is a good part not to be taken away, Jn. 4:14; 6:27.

II. Was their army a support to them — their generals, and commanders, and military men? These shall be taken away, either cut off by the sword or so discouraged with the defeats they meet with that they shall throw up their commissions and resolve to act no more; or they shall be disabled by sickness, or dispirited, so as to be unfit for business; *The mighty men, and the man of war,* and even the inferior officer, *the captain of fifty,* shall be removed. It bodes ill with a people when their valiant men are lost. Let not the strong man therefore glory in his strength, nor any people trust too much to their mighty men; but let the strong *people glorify God* and the *city of the terrible nations fear him,* who can make them weak and despicable, *ch.* 25:3.

III. Were their ministers of state a support to them — their learned men, their politicians, their clergy, their wits and virtuoso? These also should be taken away — *the judges,* who were skilled in the laws, and expert in administering justice, — *the prophets,* whom they used to consult in difficult cases, — *the prudent,* who were celebrated as men of sense and sagacity above all others and were assistants to the judges, *the diviners* (so the word is), those who used unlawful arts, who, though rotten stays, yet were stayed on, (but it may be taken, as we read it, in a good sense), — *the ancients,* elders in age, in office, — *the honourable man,* the gravity of whose aspect commands reverence and whose age and experience make him fit to be a counsellor. Trade is one great support to a nation, even manufactures and handicraft trades; and therefore, when the whole stay is broken, *the cunning artificer* too shall be taken away; and the last is *the eloquent orator,* the man skilful of speech, who in some cases may do good service, though he be none of the prudent or the ancient, by putting the sense of others in good language. Moses cannot speak well, but Aaron can. God threatens to take these away, that is, 1. To disable them for the service of their country, *making judges fools, taking away the speech of the trusty and the understanding of the aged,* Job 12:17, etc. Every creature is that to us which God makes it to be; and we cannot be sure that those who have been serv-

iceable to us shall always be so. 2. To put an end to their days; for the reason why princes are not to be trusted in is because their *breath goeth forth,* Ps. 146:3, 4. Note, The removal of useful men by death, in the midst of their usefulness, is a very threatening symptom to any people.

IV. Was their government a support to them? It ought to have been so; it is the business of the sovereign to bear up the pillars of the land, Ps. 75:3. But it is here threatened that this stay should fail them. When the mighty men and the prudent are removed *children shall be their princes* — children in age, who must be under tutors and governors, who will be clashing with one another and making a prey of the young king and his kingdom — children in understanding and disposition, childish men, such as are babes in knowledge, no more fit to rule than a child in the cradle. These shall rule over them, with all the folly, fickleness, and frowardness, of a child. And *woe unto thee, O land! when thy king* is such a one! Eccl. 10:16.

V. Was the union of the subjects among themselves, their good order and the good understanding and correspondence that they kept with one another, a stay to them? Where this is the case a people may do better for it, though their princes be not such as they should be; but it is here threatened that God would send an evil spirit among them too (as Jdg. 9:23), which would make them, 1. Injurious and unneighbourly one towards another (*v.* 5): "*The people shall be oppressed every one by his neighbour,*" and their princes, being children, will take no care to restrain the oppressors or relieve the oppressed, nor is it to any purpose to appeal to them (which is a temptation to every man to be his own avenger), and therefore they bite and devour one another and will soon be consumed one of another. Then *homo homini lupus — man becomes a wolf to man; jusque datum sceleri — wickedness receives the stamp of law; nec hospes ab hospite tutus — the guest and the host are in danger from each other.* 2. Insolent and disorderly towards their superiors. It is as ill an omen to a people as can be when the rising generation among them are generally untractable, rude, and ungovernable, when *the child behaves himself proudly against the ancient,* whereas he should *rise up before the hoary head and honour the face of the old man,* Lev. 19:32. When young people are conceited and pert, and behave scornfully towards their superiors, their conduct is not only a reproach to themselves, but of ill consequence to the public; it slackens the reins of government and weakens the hands that hold them. It is likewise ill with a people when persons of honour cannot support their authority, but are affronted by the base and beggarly, when judges are insulted and their powers set at defiance by the mob. Those have a great deal to answer for who do this.

VI. It is some stay, some support, to hope that, though matters may be now ill-managed, yet other may be raised up, who may manage better? Yet this expectation also shall be frustrated, for the case shall be so desperate that no man of sense or substance will meddle with it.

1. The government shall go a begging, *v.* 6. Here, (1.) It is taken for granted that there is no way of redressing all these grievances, and bringing things into order again, but by good magistrates, who shall be invested with power by common consent, and shall exert that power for the good of the community. And it is probable that this was, in many places, the true origin of government; men found it necessary to unite in a subjection to one who was thought fit for such a trust, in order to the welfare and safety of them all, being aware that they must either be ruled or ruined. Here therefore is the original contract: "*Be thou our ruler,* and we will be subject to thee, and *let this ruin be under thy hand,* to be repaired and restored, and then to be preserved and established, and the interests of it advanced, *ch.* 58:12. Take care to protect us by the sword of war from being injured from abroad, and by the sword of justice from being injurious to another, and we will bear faith and true allegiance to thee." (2.) The case is represented as very deplorable, and things as having come to a sad pass; for, [1.] Children being their princes, every man will think himself fit to prescribe who shall be a magistrate, and will be for preferring his own relations; whereas, if the princes were as they should be, it would be left entirely to them to nominate the rulers, as it ought to be. [2.] Men will find themselves under a necessity even of forcing power into the hands of those that are thought to be

fit for it: *A man shall take hold* by violence of one to make him a ruler, perceiving him ready to resist the motion: nay, he shall urge it upon his brother; whereas, commonly, men are not willing that their equals should be their superiors, witness the envy of Joseph's brethren. [3.] It will be looked upon as ground sufficient for the preferring of a man to be a ruler that he has clothing better than his neighbours — a very poor qualification to recommend a man to a place of trust in the government. It was a sign that the country was much impoverished when it was a rare thing to find a man that had good clothes, or could afford to buy himself an alderman's gown or a judge's robes; and it was proof enough that the people were very unthinking when they had so much respect to a man in *gay clothing, with a gold ring* (Jam. 2:2, 3), that, for the sake thereof, they would make him their ruler. It would have been some sense to have said, "Thou hast wisdom, integrity, experience; be thou our ruler." But it was a jest to say, *Thou hast clothing; be thou our ruler.* A *poor wise man,* though in vile raiment, *delivered a city,* Eccl. 9:15. We may allude to this to show how desperate the case of fallen man was when our Lord Jesus was pleased to become our brother, and, though he was not courted, offered himself to be our ruler and Saviour, and to take this ruin under his hand.

2. Those who are thus pressed to come into office will swear themselves off, because, though they are taken to be men of some substance, yet they know themselves unable to bear the charges of the office and to answer the expectations of those that choose them (*v.* 7): *He shall swear* (shall lift up the hand, the ancient ceremony used in taking the oath) *I will not be a healer; make not me a ruler.* Note, Rulers must be healers, and good rulers will be so; they must study to unite their subjects, and not to widen the differences that are among them. Those only are fit for government that are of a meek, quiet, healing, spirit. They must also heal the wounds that are given to any of the interests of their people, by suitable applications. But why will he not be a ruler? Because *in my house is neither bread nor clothing.* (1.) If he said true, it was a sign that men's estates were sadly ruined when even those who made the best appearance really wanted necessaries — a common case, and a piteous one. Some who, having lived fashionably, are willing to put the best side outwards, are yet, if the truth were known, in great straits, and go with heavy hearts for want of bread and clothing. (2.) If he did not speak truth, it was a sign that men's consciences were sadly debauched, when, to avoid the expense of an office, they would load themselves with the guilt of perjury, and (which is the greatest madness in the world) would damn their souls to save their money, Mt. 16:26. (3.) However it was, it was a sign that the case of the nation was very bad when nobody was willing to accept a place in the government of it, as despairing to have either credit or profit by it, which are the two things aimed at in men's common ambition of preferment.

3. The reason why God brought things to this sad pass, even among his own people (which is given either by the prophet or by him that refused to be a ruler); it was not for want of good will to his country, but because he saw the case desperate and past relief, and it would be to no purpose to attempt it (*v.* 8): *Jerusalem is ruined* and *Judah is fallen;* and they may thank themselves. They have brought their destruction upon their own heads, for *their tongue and their doings are against the Lord;* in word and action they broke the law of God and therein designed an affront to him; they wilfully intended to offend him, in contempt of his authority and defiance of his justice. Their tongue was against the Lord, for they contradicted his prophets; and their doings were no better, for they acted as they talked. It was an aggravation of their sin that God's eye was upon them, and that his glory was manifested among them; but they provoked him to his face, as if the more they knew of his glory the greater pride they took in slighting it, and turning it into shame. And this, this, is it for which Jerusalem is ruined. Note, The ruin both of persons and people is owing to their sins. If they did not provoke God, he would *do them no hurt,* Jer. 25:6.

Verses 9–15

Here God proceeds in his controversy with his people. Observe,

I. The ground of his controversy. It was for sin that God

contended with them; if they vex themselves, let them look a little further and they will see that they must *thank* themselves: *Woe unto their souls! For they have rewarded evil unto themselves. Alas for their souls!* (so it may be read, in a way of lamentation), *for they have procured evil to themselves, v.* 9. Note, The condition of sinners is woeful and very deplorable. Note, also, It is the soul that is damaged and endangered by sin. Sinners may prosper in their outward estates, and yet at the same time there may be a woe to their souls. Note, further, Whatever evils befals sinners it is of their own procuring, Jer. 2:19. That which is here charged upon then is, 1. That the shame which should have restrained them from their sins was quite thrown off and they had grown impudent, *v.* 9. This hardens men against repentance, and ripens them for ruin, as much as anything: *The show of their countenance doth witness against them* that their minds are vain, and lewd, and malicious; their eyes declare plainly that they *cannot cease from sin,* 2 Pt. 2:14. One may look them in the face and guess at the desperate wickedness that there is in their hearts: *They declare their sin as Sodom,* so impetuous, so imperious, are their lusts, and so impatient of the least check, and so perfectly are all the remaining sparks of virtue extinguished in them. The Sodomites declared their sin, not only by the exceeding greatness of it (Gen. 13:13), so that it cried to heaven (Gen. 18:20), but by their shameless owning of that which was most shameful (Gen. 19:5); and thus Judah and Jerusalem did: they were so far from hiding it that they gloried in it, in the bold attempts they made upon virtue, and the victory they gained over their own convictions. They had a whore's forehead (Jer. 3:3) and could not blush, Jer. 6:15. Note, Those that have grown impudent in sin are ripe for ruin. Those that are past shame (we say) are past grace, and then past hope. 2. That their guides, who should direct them in the right way, put them out of the way (*v.* 12): *"Those who lead thee* (the princes, priests, and prophets) mislead thee; they *cause thee to err."* Either they preached to them that which was false and corrupt, or, if they preached that which was true and good, they contradicted it by their practices, and the people would soon follow a bad example than a good exhortation. Thus they *destroyed the ways of their paths,* pulling down with one hand what they built up with the other. *Que te beatificant — Those that call thee blessed* cause thee to err; so some read it. Their priests applauded them, as if nothing were amiss among them, cried *Peace, peace,* to them, as if they were in no danger; and thus they caused them to go on in their errors. 3. That their judges, who should have patronized and protected the oppressed, were themselves the greatest oppressors, *v.* 14, 15. The elders of the people, and the princes, who had learning and could not but know better things, who had great estates and were not under the temptation of necessity to encroach upon those about them, and who were men of honour and should have scorned to do a base thing, yet *they have eaten up the vineyard.* God's vineyard, which they were appointed to be the dressers and keepers of, they burnt (so the word signifies); they did as ill by it as its worst enemies could do, Ps. 80:16. Or the vineyards of the poor they wrested out of their possession, as Jezebel did Naboth's, or devoured the fruits of them, fed their lusts with that which should have been the necessary food of indigent families; the spoil of the poor was hoarded up in their houses; when God came to search for stolen goods there he found it, and it was a witness against them. It was to be had, and they might have made restitution, but would not. God reasons with these great men (*v.* 15): *"What mean you, that you beat my people into pieces?* What cause have you for it? What good does it do you?" Or, "What hurt have they done you? Do you think you had power given you for such a purpose as this?" Note, There is nothing more unaccountable, and yet nothing which must more certainly be accounted for, than the injuries and abuses that are done to God's people by their persecutors and oppressors. *"You grind the faces of the poor;* you put them to as much pain and terror as if they were ground in a mill, and as certainly reduce them to dust by one act of oppression after another." Or, "Their faces are bruised and crushed with the blows you have given them; you have not only ruined their estates, but have given them personal abuses." Our Lord Jesus was *smitten on the face,* Mt. 26:67.

II. The management of this controversy. 1. God himself is the prosecutor (*v.* 13): *The Lord stands up to plead,* or he sets himself to debate the matter, and he *stands to judge the people,* to judge for those that were oppressed and abused; and he will *enter into judgment with the princes, v.* 14. Note, The greatest of men cannot exempt or secure themselves from the scrutiny and sentence of God's judgment, nor demur to the jurisdiction of the court of heaven. 2. The indictment is proved by the notorious evidence of the fact: "Look upon the oppressors, and the *show of their countenance witnesses against them* (*v.* 9); look upon the oppressed, and you see how their faces are battered and abused," *v.* 15. 3. The controversy is already begun in the change of the ministry. To punish those that had abused their power to bad purposes God sets those over them that had not sense to use their power to any good purposes: *Children are their oppressors, and women rule over them* (*v.* 12), men that have as weak judgments and strong passions as women and children: this was their sin, that their rulers were such, and it became a judgment upon them.

III. The distinction that shall be made between particular persons, in the prosecution of this controversy (*v.* 10, 11): *Say to the righteous, It shall be well with thee. Woe to the wicked; it shall be ill with him.* He had said (*v.* 9), they *have rewarded evil to themselves,* in proof of which he here shows that God will *render to every man according to his works.* Had they been righteous, it would have been well with them; but, if it be ill with them, it is because they are wicked and will be so. Thus God stated the matter to Cain, to convince him that he had no reason to be angry, Gen. 4:7. Or it may be taken thus: God is threatening national judgments, which will ruin the public interests. Now, 1. Some good people might fear that they should be involved in that ruin, and therefore God bids the prophets comfort them against those fears: "Whatever becomes of the unrighteous nation, let *the righteous man* know that he shall not be lost in the crowd of sinners; the *Judge of all the earth will not slay the righteous with the wicked* (Gen. 18:25); no, assure him, in God's name, that *it shall be well with him.* The property of the trouble shall be altered to him, and he shall be *hidden in the day of the Lord's anger.* He shall have divine supports and comforts, which shall abound as afflictions abound, and so it shall be well with him." When the whole *stay of bread is taken away,* yet in the *day of famine the righteous shall be satisfied;* they *shall eat the fruit of their doings* — they shall have the testimony of their consciences for them that they kept themselves pure from the common iniquity, and therefore the common calamity is not the same thing to them that it is to others; they brought no fuel to the flame, and therefore are not themselves fuel for it. 2. Some wicked people might hope that they should escape that ruin, and therefore God bids the prophets shake their vain hopes: *"Woe to the wicked; it shall be ill with him, v.* 11. To him the judgments shall have sting, and there shall be *wormwood and gall* in the *affliction and misery."* There is a woe to wicked people, and, though they may think to shelter themselves from public judgments, yet it shall be ill with them; it will grow worse and worse with them if they repent not, and the worst of all will be at last; for the *reward of their hands shall be given them,* in the day when every man shall receive according to the things done in the body.

Verses 16–26

The prophet's business was to show all sorts of people what they had contributed to the national guilt and what share they must expect in the national judgments that were coming. Here he reproves and warns the daughters of Zion, tells the ladies of their faults; and Moses, in the law, having denounced God's wrath against *the tender and delicate woman* (the prophets being a comment upon the law, Deu. 28:56), he here tells them how they shall smart by the calamities that are coming upon them. Observe,

I. The sin charged upon the daughters of Zion, *v.* 16. The prophet expressly vouches God's authority for what he said. lest it should be thought it was unbecoming in him to take notice of such things, and should be resented by the ladies: *The Lord saith it.* "Whether they will hear, or whether they will forbear, let them know that God takes notice of, and is much displeased with, the folly and vanity of proud women, and his law takes cognizance even of their dress." Two things that here stand indicted for —

haughtiness and wantonness, directly contrary to that *modesty, shamefacedness, and sobriety, with which women ought to adorn themselves,* 1 Tim. 2:9. They discovered the disposition of their mind by their gait and gesture, and the lightness of their carriage. They are haughty, for they *walk with stretched-forth necks,* that they may seem tall, or, as thinking nobody good enough to speak to them or to receive a look or a smile from them. Their eyes are wanton, *deceiving* (so the word is); with their amorous glances they draw men into their snares. They affect a formal starched way of going, that people may look at them, and admire them, and know they have been at the dancing-school, and have learned the minuet-step. They go *mincing,* or nicely tripping, not willing to set so much as the sole of their foot to the ground, for tenderness and delicacy. They make a *tinkling with their feet,* having, as some think, chains, or little bells, upon their shoes, that made a noise: they go *as if they were fettered* (so some read it), like a horse trammelled, that he may learn to pace. Thus Agag came delicately, 1 Sa. 15:32. Such a nice affected mien is not only a force upon that which is natural, and ridiculous before men, men of sense; but as it is an evidence of a vain mind, it is offensive to God. And two things aggravated it here: 1. That these were the daughters of Zion, the holy mountain, who should have behaved with the gravity that becomes women professing godliness. 2. That it should seem, by the connexion, they were the wives and daughters of the princes who spoiled and oppressed the poor (*v.* 14, 15) that they might maintain the pride and luxury of their families.

II. The punishments threatened for this sin; and they answer the sin as face answers to face in a glass, *v.* 17, 18. 1. They *walked with stretched-forth necks,* but God will *smite with a scab the crown of their head,* which shall lower their crests, and make them ashamed to show their heads, being obliged by it to cut off their hair. Note, Loathsome diseases are often sent as the just punishment of pride, and are sometimes the immediate effect of lewdness, the flesh and the body being consumed by it. 2. They cared not what they laid out in furnishing themselves with great variety of fine clothes; but God will reduce them to such poverty and distress that they shall not have clothes sufficient to cover their nakedness, but their uncomeliness shall be exposed through their rags. 3. They were extremely fond and proud of their ornaments; but God will strip them of those ornaments, when their houses shall be plundered, their treasures rifled, and they themselves led into captivity. The prophet here specifies many of the ornaments which they used as particularly as if he had been the keeper of their wardrobe or had attended them in their dressing-room. It is not at all material to enquire what sort of ornaments these respectively were and whether the translations rightly express the original words; perhaps 100 years hence the names of some of the ornaments that are now in use in our own land will be as little understood as some of those here mentioned now are. Fashions alter, and so do the names of them; and yet the mention of them is not in vain, but is designed to expose the folly of the daughters of Zion; for, (1.) Many of these things, we may suppose, were very odd and ridiculous, and, if they had not been in fashion, would have been hooted at. They were fitter to be toys for children to play with than ornaments for grown people to go to Mount Zion in. (2.) Those things that were decent and convenient, as *the linen, the hoods, and the veils,* needed not be provided in such abundance and variety. It is necessary to have apparel and proper that all should have it according to their rank; but what occasion was there for so many changeable suits of apparel (*v.* 22), that they might not be seen two days together in the same suit? "They must have (as the homily against excess of apparel speaks) one gown for the day, another for the night — one long, another short — one for the working day, another for the holy-day — one of this colour, another of that colour — one of cloth, another of silk or damask — one dress afore dinner, another after — one of the Spanish fashion, another Turkey — and never content with sufficient." All this, as it is an evidence of pride and vain curiosity, so must needs spend a great deal in gratifying a base lust that ought to be laid out in works of piety and charity; and it is well if poor tenants be not racked, or poor creditors defrauded to support it. (3.) The enumeration of these things intimates what care they were in

about them, how much their hearts were upon them, what an exact account they kept of them, how nice and critical they were about them, how insatiable their desire was of them, and how much of their comfort was bound up in them. A maid could forget none of these ornaments, though they were ever so many (Jer. 2:32), but they would report them as readily, and talk of them with as much pleasure, as if they had been things of the greatest moment. The prophet did not speak of these things as in themselves sinful (they might lawfully be had and used), but as things which they were proud of and should therefore be deprived of.

III. They were very nice and curious about their clothes; but God would make those bodies of theirs, which were at such expense to beautify and make easy, a reproach and burden to them (*v.* 24): *Instead of sweet smell* (those tablets, or boxes, of perfume, *houses of the soul* or *breath,* as they are called, *v.* 20, *margin*) *there shall be stink,* garments grown filthy with being long worn, or from some loathsome disease or plasters for the cure of it. *Instead of a rich embroidered girdle* used to make the clothes sit tight, there shall be *a rent,* a rending of the clothes for grief, or old rotten clothes rent into rags. *Instead of well-set hair,* curiously plaited and powdered, there shall be *baldness,* the hair being plucked off or shaven, as was usual in times of great affliction (*ch.* 15:2; Jer. 16:6), or in great servitude, Eze. 29:18. *Instead of a stomacher,* or a scarf or sash, there shall be *a girding of sackcloth,* in token of deep humiliation; *and burning instead of beauty.* Those that had a good complexion, and were proud of it, when they are carried into captivity shall be tanned and sun-burnt; and it is observed that the best faces are soonest injured by the weather. From all this let us learn, 1. Not to be nice and curious about our apparel, not to affect that which is gay and costly, nor to be proud of it. 2. Not to be secure in the enjoyment of any of the delights of sense, because we know not how soon we may be stripped of them, nor what straits we may be reduced to.

IV. They designed by these ornaments to charm the gentlemen, and win their affections (Prov. 7:16, 17), but there shall be none to be charmed by them (*v.* 25): *Thy men shall fall by the sword, and the mighty in the war,* The *fire shall consume them,* and then the *maidens* shall *not be given in marriage;* as it is, Ps. 78:63. When the sword comes with commission the mighty commonly fall first by it, because they are most forward to venture. And, when Zion's guards are cut off, no marvel that Zion's gates *lament and mourn* (*v.* 26), the enemies having made themselves masters of them; and the city itself, being desolate, being emptied or swept, shall *sit upon the ground* like a disconsolate widow. If sin be harboured within the walls, lamentation and mourning are near the gates.

CHAPTER 4

In this chapter we have, I. A threatening of the paucity and scarceness of man (*v.* 1), which might fitly enough have been added to the close of the foregoing chapter, to which it has a plain reference. II. A promise of the restoration of Jerusalem's peace and purity, righteousness and safety, in the days of the Messiah (*v.* 2–6). Thus, in wrath, mercy is remembered, and gospel grace is a sovereign relief, in reference to the terrors of the law and the desolations made by sin.

Verse 1

It was threatened (*ch.* 3:25) that *the mighty men should fall by the sword in war,* and it was threatened as a punishment to the women that affected gaiety and a loose sort of conversation. Now here we have the effect and consequence of that great slaughter of men, 1. That though Providence has so wisely ordered that, *communibus annis — on an average of years,* there is nearly an equal number of males and females born into the world, yet, through the devastations made by war, there should scarcely be one man in seven left alive. As there are deaths attending the bringing forth of children, which are peculiar to the woman, who was first in transgression, so, to balance that, there are deaths peculiar to men, those by the sword in the high places of the field, which perhaps devour more than child-bed does. Here it is foretold that such multitudes of men should be cut off that there should be *seven women to one man.* 2. That by reason of the scarcity of men, though marriage should be kept up for the raising of recruits and the preserving of the race of mankind upon earth, yet the usual method of it should be quite altered,

— that, whereas men ordinarily make their court to the women, the women should now take hold of the men, foolishly fearing (as Lot's daughters did, when they saw the ruin of Sodom and perhaps thought it reached further than it did) that in a little time there would be none left (Gen. 19:31), — that whereas women naturally hate to come in sharers with others, seven should now, by consent, become the wives of one man, — and that whereas by the law the husband was obliged to provide food and raiment for his wife (Ex. 21:10), which with many would be the most powerful argument against multiplying wives, these women will be bound to support themselves; they will *eat bread of their own earning, and wear apparel of their own working,* and the man they court shall be at no expense upon them, only they desire to be called his wives, to *take away the reproach* of a single life. They are willing to be wives upon any terms, though ever so unreasonable; and perhaps the rather because in these troublesome times it would be a kindness to them to have a husband for their protector. Paul, on the contrary, thinks the single state preferable in a time of distress, 1 Co. 7:26. It were well if this were not introduced here partly as a reflection upon the daughters of Zion, that, notwithstanding the humbling providences they were under (*ch.* 3:18), they remained unhumbled, and, instead of repenting of their pride and vanity, when God was contending with them for them, all their care was to get husbands — that modesty, which is the greatest beauty of the fair sex, was forgotten, and with them the reproach of vice was nothing to the reproach of virginity, a sad symptom of the irrecoverable desolations of virtue.

Verses 2–6

By the foregoing threatenings Jerusalem is brought into a very deplorable condition: every thing looks melancholy. But here the sun breaks out from behind the cloud. Many exceedingly great and precious promises we have in these verses, giving assurance of comfort which may be discerned through the troubles, and of happy days which shall come after them, and these certainly point at the kingdom of the Messiah, and the great redemption to be wrought out by him, under the figure and type of the restoration of Judah and Jerusalem by the reforming reign of Hezekiah after Ahaz and the return out of their captivity in Babylon; to both these events the passage may have some reference, but chiefly to Christ. It is here promised, as the issue of all these troubles,

I. That God will raise up a righteous branch, which shall produce fruits of righteousness (*v.* 2): *In that day,* that same day, at that very time, when Jerusalem shall be destroyed and the Jewish nation extirpated and dispersed, the kingdom of the Messiah shall be set up; and then shall be the reviving of the church, when every one shall fear the utter ruin of it.

1. Christ himself shall be exalted. He is the *branch of the Lord,* the man the branch; it is one of prophetical names, *my servant the branch* (Zec. 3:8; 6:12), the *branch of righteousness* (Jer. 23:5; 33:15), a *rod out of the stem of Jesse and a branch out of his roots* (*ch.* 11:1), and this, as some think, is alluded to when he is called a *Nazarene,* Mt. 2:23. Here he is called *the branch of the Lord,* because planted by his power and flourishing to his praise. The ancient Chaldee paraphrase here reads it, *The Christ, or Messiah, of the Lord.* He shall be the beauty, and glory, and joy. (1.) He shall himself be advanced to the joy set before him and the glory which he had with the Father before the world was. He that was a reproach of men, whose visage was marred more than any man's, is now, in the upper world, beautiful and glorious, as the sun in his strength, admired and adored by angels. (2.) He shall be beautiful and glorious in the esteem of all believers, shall gain an interest in the world, and a name among men above every name. To those that believe he is precious, he is an honour (1 Pt. 2:7), the *fairest of ten thousand* (Cant. 5:10), and altogether glorious. Let us rejoice that he is so, and let him be so to us.

2. His gospel shall be embraced. The success of the gospel is the fruit of the branch of the Lord; all the graces and comforts of the gospel spring from Christ. But it is called *the fruit of the earth* because it sprang up in this world and was calculated for the present state. And Christ compares himself to a *grain of wheat,* that *falls into the ground and dies, and so brings forth much fruit,* Jn. 12:24.

The success of the gospel is represented by *the earth's yielding her increase* (Ps. 67:6), and the planting of the Christian church is God's *sowing it to himself in the earth,* Hos. 2:23. We may understand it of both the persons and the things that are the products of the gospel: they shall be excellent and comely, shall appear very agreeable and be very acceptable to those that have escaped of Israel, to that remnant of the Jews which was saved from perishing with the rest in unbelief, Rom. 11:5. Note, If Christ be precious to us, his gospel will be so and all its truths and promises — his church will be so, and all that belong to it. These are the good fruit of the earth, in comparison with which all other things are but weeds. It will be a good evidence to us that we are of the chosen remnant, distinguished from the rest that are called *Israel,* and marked for salvation, if we are brought to see a transcendent beauty in Christ, and in holiness, and in the saints, the excellent ones of the earth. As a type of this blessed day, Jerusalem, after Sennacherib's invasion and after the captivity in Babylon, should again flourish as a branch, and be blessed with the fruits of the earth. Compare *ch.* 37:31, 32. *The remnant shall again take root downward and bear fruit upward.* And if by the fruit of the earth here we understand the good things of this life, we may observe that these have peculiar sweetness in them to the chosen remnant, who, having a covenant-right to them, have the most comfortable use of them. If the branch of the Lord be beautiful and glorious in our eyes, even the fruit of the earth also will be excellent and comely, because then we may take it as the fruit of the promise, Ps. 37:16; 1 Tim. 4:8.

II. That God will reserve to himself a holy seed, *v.* 3. When the generality of those that have a place and a name in Zion and in Jerusalem shall be cut off as withered branches, by their own unbelief, yet some shall be left. Some shall remain, some shall still cleave to the church, when its property is altered and it has become Christian; for God will not quite *cast off his people,* Rom. 11:1. There is here and there one that is left. Now, 1. This is a remnant *according to the election of grace* (as the apostle speaks, Rom. 11:5), such as are written among the living, marked in the counsel and fore-knowledge of God for life and salvation, *written to life* (so the word is), designed and determined for it unalterably; for *"what I have written I have written."* Those that are kept alive in killing dying times were written for life in the book of divine Providence; and shall we not suppose those who are rescued from a greater death to be such as were *written in the Lamb's book of life?* Rev. 13:8. As many as were *ordained unto eternal life believed* to *the salvation of the soul,* Acts 13:48. Note, All that were *written among the living* shall be found among the living, every one; for of all that were given to Christ he will lose none. 2. It is a remnant *under the dominion of grace;* for every one that is *written among the living,* and is accordingly left, shall be called *holy,* shall be holy, and shall be accepted of God accordingly. Those only that are holy shall be left when the *Son of man shall gather out of his kingdom every thing that offends;* and all that are chosen to salvation are chosen to sanctification. See 2 Th. 2:13; Eph. 1:4.

III. That God will reform his church and will rectify and amend whatever is amiss in it, *v.* 4. Then the remnant shall be *called holy, when the Lord shall have washed away their filth,* washed it from among them by cutting off the wicked persons, washed it from within them by purging out the wicked thing. They shall not be called so till they are in some measure made so. Gospel times are times of reformation (Heb. 9:10), typified by the reformation in the days of Hezekiah and that after captivity, to which this promise refers. Observe, 1. The places and persons to be reformed. Jerusalem, though the holy city, needed reformation; and, being the holy city, the reformation of that would have a good influence upon the whole kingdom. The daughters of Zion also must be reformed, the women in a particular manner, whom he had reproved, *ch.* 3:16. When they were decked in their ornaments they thought themselves wondrously clean; but, being proud of them, the prophet call them their *filth,* for no sin is more abominable to God than pride. Or by the daughters of Zion may be meant the country towns and villages, which were related to Jerusalem as the mother-city, and which needed reformation. 2. The reformation itself. The filth shall be washed away; for wickedness is filthiness, particularly blood-shed, for which Jerusalem was infamous (2 Ki. 21:16), and which defiles the land more than any other sin. Note, The reforming of a city is the cleansing of it. When vicious customs and fashions are suppressed, and the open practice of wickedness is restrained, the place is made clean and sweet which before was a dunghill; and this is not only for its credit and reputation among strangers, but for the comfort and health of the inhabitants themselves. 3. The author of the reformation: *The Lord shall do it.* Reformation-work is God's work; if any thing be done to purpose in it, it is his doing. But how? By the judgment of his providence the sinners were destroyed and consumed; but it is by the Spirit of his grace that they are reformed and converted. This is the work that is done, not by might, nor by power, but by the *Spirit of the Lord of hosts* (Zec. 4:6), working both upon the sinners themselves that are to be reformed and upon magistrates, ministers, and others that are to be employed as instruments of reformation. The Spirit herein acts, (1.) As a spirit of judgment, enlightening the mind, convincing the conscience, — as a spirit of wisdom, guiding us to deal prudently, (Isa. 52:13), — as a discerning, distinguishing, Spirit, separating between the precious and the vile. (2.) As a Spirit of burning, quickening and invigorating the afflictions, and making men zealously affected in a good work. The Spirit works as fire, Mt. 3:11. An ardent love to Christ and souls, and a flaming zeal against sin, will carry men on with resolution in their endeavours to *turn away ungodliness from Jacob.* See Isa. 32:15, 16.

IV. That God will protect his church, and all that belong to it (*v.* 5, 6); when they are purified and reformed they shall no longer lie exposed, but God will take a particular care of them. Those that are sanctified are well fortified; for God will be to them a guide and a guard.

1. Their tabernacles shall be defended, *v.* 5.

(1.) This writ of protection refers to, [1.] Their dwelling places, the tabernacles of their rest, their own houses, where they worship God alone, and with their families. That blessing which is upon the *habitation of the just* shall be a protection to it, Prov. 3:33. In the *tabernacles of the righteous* shall the *voice of rejoicing and salvation be,* Ps. 118:15. Note, God takes particular cognizance and care of the dwelling-places of his people, of every one of them, the poorest cottage as well as the statliest palace. When iniquity is *put far from the tabernacle* the Almighty shall be its defence, Job 23:23, 26. [2.] Their assemblies or tabernacles of meeting for religious worship. No mention is made of the temple, for the promise points at a time when not one stone of that shall be left upon another; but all the congregations of Christians, though but two or three met together in Christ's name, shall be taken under the special protection of heaven; they shall be no more scattered, no more disturbed, nor shall *any weapon formed against them prosper.* Note, we ought to reckon it a great mercy if we have liberty to worship God in public, free from the alarms of the sword of war or persecution.

(2.) This writ of protection is drawn up, [1.] In a similitude taken from the safety of the camp of Israel when they marched through the wilderness. God will give to the Christian church as real proofs, though not so sensible, of his care of them, as he then gave to Israel. The Lord will again *create a cloud and smoke by day,* to screen them from the scorching heat of the sun, and the *shining of a flaming fire by night,* to enlighten and warm the air, which in the night is cold and dark. See Ex. 13:21; Neh. 9:19. This pillar of cloud and fire interposed between the Israelites and the Egyptians, Ex. 14:20. Note, Though miracles have ceased, yet God is the same to the New-Testament church that he was to Israel of old; the very same yesterday, to-day, and for ever. [2.] In a similitude taken from the outside cover of rams' skins and badgers' skins that was upon the curtains of the tabernacle, as if every dwelling place of Mount Zion and every assembly were as dear to God as that tabernacle was: *Upon all the glory shall be a defense,* to save it from wind and weather. Note, The church on earth has its glory. Gospel truths and ordinances, the scriptures and the ministry, are the church's glory; and upon all this glory there is a defence, and ever shall be, for the *gates of hell shall not prevail against the church.* If God himself be the glory in the midst of it, he will himself be a wall of fire around about it, impenetrable and impregnable. Grace in the soul is the glory of it, and those that have it are *kept by the power of God* as in a strong-hold, 1 Pt. 1:5.

2. Their tabernacle shall be a defence to them, *v.* 6. God's tabernacle was a pavilion to the saints (Ps. 27:5); but, when that is taken down, they shall not want a covert: the divine power and goodness shall be a tabernacle to all the saints. God himself will be their hiding-place (Ps. 32:7); they shall be at home in him, Ps. 91:9. He will himself be to them as the *shadow of a great rock* (*ch.* 32:2) and *his name a strong tower,* Prov. 18:10. He will be not only a shadow from the heat in the daytime, but a covert from storm and rain. Note, In this world we must expect change of weather and all the inconveniences that attend it; we shall meet with storm and rain in this lower region, and at other times the heat of the day no less burdensome; but God is a refuge to his people in all weathers.

CHAPTER 5

In this chapter the prophet, in God's name, shows the people of God their transgressions, even the house of Jacob their sins, and the judgments which were likely to be brought upon them for their sins, I. By a parable, under the similitude of an unfruitful vineyard, representing the great favours God had bestowed upon them, their disappointing his expectations from them, and the ruin they had thereby deserved (*v.* 1–7). II. By an enumeration of the sins that did abound among them, with a threatening of punishments that should answer to the sins. 1. Covetousness, and greediness of worldly wealth, which shall be punished with famine (*v.* 8–10) 2. Rioting, revelling, and drunkenness (*v.* 11, 12, 22, 23), which shall be punished with captivity and all the miseries that attend it (*v.* 13–17). 3. Presumption in sin, and defying the justice of God (*v.* 18, 19). 4. Confounding the distinctions between virtue and vice, and so undermining the principles of religion (*v.* 20). 5. Self-conceit (*v.* 21). 6. Perverting justice, for which, and the other instances of reigning wickedness among them, a great and general desolation in threatened, which should lay all waste (*v.* 24, 25), and which should be effected by a foreign invasion (*v.* 26–30), referring perhaps to the havoc made not long after by Sennacherib's army.

Verses 1–7

See what variety of methods the great God takes to awaken sinners to repentance by convincing them of sin, and showing them their misery and danger by reason of it. To this purport he speaks sometimes in plain terms and sometimes in parables, sometimes in prose and sometimes in verse, as here. "We have tried to *reason with you* (*ch.* 1:18); now let us put your case into a poem, inscribed to the honour of my well beloved." God the Father dictates it to the honour of Christ his well beloved Son, whom he has constituted Lord of the vineyard. The prophet sings it to the honour of Christ too, for he is his well beloved. The Old-Testament prophets were friends of the bridegroom. Christ is God's beloved Son and our beloved Saviour. Whatever is said or sung of the church must be intended to his praise, even that which (like this) tends to our shame. This parable was put into a song that it might be the more moving and affecting, might be the more easily learned and exactly remembered, and the better transmitted to posterity; and it is an exposition of he song of Moses (Deu. 32), showing that what he then foretold was now fulfilled. Jerome says, Christ the well-beloved did in effect sing this mournful song when he beheld Jerusalem *and wept over it* (Lu. 19:41), and had reference to it in the parable of the vineyard (Mt. 21:33, etc.), only here the fault was in the vines, there in the husbandmen. Here we have,

I. The great things which God had done for the Jewish church and nation. When all the rest of the world lay in common, not cultivated by divine revelation, that was his vineyard, they were his peculiar people. He acknowledged them as his own, set them apart for himself. The soil they were planted in was extraordinary; it was *a very fruitful hill, the horn of the son of oil;* so it is in the margin. There was plenty, a cornucopia; and there was dainty: they did there eat the fat and drink the sweet, and so were furnished with abundance of good things to honour God with in sacrifices and free-will offerings. The advantages of our situation will be brought into the account another day. Observe further what God did for this vineyard. 1. He fenced it, took it under his special protection, kept it night and day under his own eye, lest any should hurt it, *ch.* 27:2, 3. If they had not themselves thrown down their fence, no inroad could have been made upon them, Ps. 125:2; 131:4. 2. He gathered the stones out of it, that, as nothing from without might damage it, so nothing within might obstruct its fruitfulness. He proffered his grace to take away the stony heart. 3. He planted it with the choicest vine, set up a pure religion among them, gave them a most excellent law, instituted ordinances very proper for the keeping up of their acquaintance with God, Jer. 2:21. 4. He built a tower in the midst of it, either for defence against violence or for the dressers of the vineyard to lodge in; or rather it was for the owner of the vineyard to sit in, to take a view of the vines (Cant. 7:12) — a summer-house. The temple was this tower, about which the priests lodged, and where God promised to meet his people, and gave them the tokens of his presence among them and pleasure in them. 5. He made a wine-press therein, set up his altar, to which the sacrifices, as the fruits of the vineyard, should be brought.

II. The disappointment of his just expectations from them: *He looked that it should bring forth grapes*, and a great deal of reason he had for that expectation. Note, God expects vineyard-fruit from those that enjoy vineyard-privileges, not leaves only, as Mk. 11:12. A bare profession, though ever so green, will not serve: there must be more than buds and blossoms. Good purposes and good beginnings are good things, but not enough; there must be fruit, a good heart and a good life, vineyard fruit, thoughts and affections, words and actions, agreeable to the Spirit, which is the fatness of the vineyard (Gal. 5:22, 23), *answerable to the ordinances*, which are the dressings of the vineyard, acceptable to God, the Lord of the vineyard, and fruit according to the season. Such fruit as this God expects from us, grapes, the fruit of the vine, with which they honour God and man (Jdg. 9:13); and his expectations are neither high nor hard, but righteous and very reasonable. Yet see how his expectations are frustrated: *It brought forth wild grapes;* not only no fruit at all, but bad fruit, worse than none, grapes of Sodom, Deu. 32:32. 1. Wild grapes are the fruits of the corrupt nature, fruit according to the crab-stock, not according to the engrafted branch, from the root of bitterness, Heb. 12:15. Where grace does not work corruption will. 2. Wild grapes are hypocritical performances in religion, that look like grapes, but are sour or bitter, and are so far from being pleasing to God that they are provoking, as theirs mentioned in *ch.* 1:11. Counterfeit graces are wild grapes.

III. An appeal to themselves whether upon the whole matter God must not be justified and they condemned, *v.* 3, 4. And now the case is plainly stated: *O inhabitants of Jerusalem, and men of Judah! judge, I pray you, betwixt me and my vineyard.* This implies that God was blamed about them. There was a controversy between them and him; but the equity was so plain on his side that he could venture to put the decision of the controversy to their own consciences. "Let any inhabitant of Jerusalem, any man of Judah, that has but the use of his reason and a common sense of equity and justice, speak his mind impartially in this matter." Here is a challenge to any man to show, 1. Any instance wherein God had been wanting to them: *What could have been done more to my vineyard, that I have not done in it?* He speaks of the external means of fruitfulness, and such as might be expected from the dresser of a vineyard, from whom it is not required that he should change the nature of the vine. *What ought to have been done more?* so it may be read. They had everything requisite for instruction and direction in their duty, for quickening them to it and putting them in mind of it. No inducements were wanting to persuade them to it, but all arguments were used that were proper to work either upon hope or fear; and they had all the opportunities they could desire for the performance of their duty, the new moons, and the sabbaths, and solemn feasts; They had the scriptures, the lively oracles, a standing ministry in the priests and Levites, besides what was extraordinary in the prophets. No nation had statutes and judgments so righteous. 2. Nor could any tolerable excuse be offered for their walking thus contrary to God. "Wherefore, what reason can be given why it should bring forth wild grapes, when I looked for grapes?" Note, The wickedness of those that profess religion, and enjoy the means of grace, is the most unreasonable unaccountable thing in the world, and the whole blame of it must lie upon the sinners themselves. "*If thou scornest, thou alone shalt bear it,* and shalt not have a word to say for thyself in the judgment of the great day." God will prove his own ways equal and the sinner's ways unequal.

IV. Their doom read, and a righteous sentence passed upon them for their bad conduct towards God (*v.* 5, 6): "*And*

now go to, since nothing can be offered in excuse of the crime or arrest of the judgement, *I will tell you what I am now determined to do to my vineyard*. I will be vexed and troubled with it no more; since it will be good for nothing, it *shall* be good for nothing; in short, it shall cease to be a vineyard, and be turned into a wilderness: the church of the Jews shall be unchurched; their charter shall be taken away, and they shall become *lo-ammi — not my people*." 1. "They shall no longer be distinguished as a peculiar people, but be laid in common: *I will take away the hedge thereof*, and then it will soon be eaten up and become as bare as other ground." They mingled with the nations and therefore were justly scattered among them. 2. "They shall no longer be protected as God's people, but left exposed. God will not only suffer the wall to go to decay, but he will break it down, will remove all their defences from them, and then they will become an easy prey to their enemies, who have long waited for an opportunity to do them a mischief, and will now tread them down and trample upon them." 3. "They shall no longer have the face of a vineyard, and the form and shape of a church and commonwealth, but shall be levelled and laid waste." This was fulfilled when *Jerusalem for their sakes was ploughed as a field*, Mic. 3:12. 4. "No more pains shall be taken with them by magistrates or ministers, the dressers and keepers of their vineyard; it shall not be pruned nor digged, but every thing shall run wild, and nothing shall come up but briers and thorns, the products of sin and the curse," Gen. 3:18. When errors and corruptions, vice and immorality, go without check or control, no testimony borne against them, no rebuke given them or restraint put upon them, the vineyard is unpruned, is not dressed, or ridded; and then it will soon be like the vineyard of the man void of understanding, all grown over with thorns. 5. "That which completes its woe is that the dews of heaven shall be withheld; he that has the key of the clouds will command them that they rain no rain upon it, and that alone is sufficient to run it into a desert." Note, God in a way of righteous judgment, denies his grace to those that have long received it in vain. The sum of all is that those who would not bring forth good fruit should bring forth none. The curse of barrenness is the punishment of the sin of barrenness, as Mk. 11:14. This had its partial accomplishment in the destruction of Jerusalem by the Chaldeans, its full accomplishment in the final rejection of the Jews, and has its frequent accomplishment in the departure of God's Spirit from those persons who have long resisted him and striven against him, and the removal of his gospel from those places that have been long a reproach to it, while it has been an honour to them. It is no loss to God to lay his vineyard waste; for he can, when he please, turn a wilderness into a fruitful field; and when he does thus dismantle a vineyard, it is but as he did by the garden of Eden, which, when man had by sin forfeited his place in it, was soon levelled with common soil.

V. The explanation of this parable, or a key to it (*v.* 7), where we are told, 1. What is meant by the vineyard (it is *the house of Israel*, the body of the people, incorporated in one church and commonwealth), and what by the vines, the pleasant plants, the plants of God's pleasure, which he had been pleased in and delighted in doing good to; they are *the men of Judah;* these he had dealt graciously with, and from them he expected suitable returns. 2. What is meant by the grapes that were expected and the wild grapes that were produces: *He looked for judgment and righteousness,* that the people should be honest in all their dealings and the magistrates should strictly administer justice. This might reasonably be expected among a people that had such excellent laws and rules of justice given them (Deu. 4:8); but the fact was quite otherwise; instead of judgment there was the cruelty of the oppressors, and instead of righteousness the cry of the oppressed. Every thing was carried by clamour and noise, and not by equity and according to the merits of the cause. It is sad with a people when wickedness has usurped the place of judgment, Eccl. 3:16. It is very sad with a soul when instead of the grapes of humility, meekness, patience, love, and contempt of the world, which God looks for, there are the wild grapes of pride, passion, discontent, malice, and contempt of God — instead of the grapes of praying and praising, the wild grapes of cursing and swearing, which are a great offence to God. Some of the ancients apply this to the Jews in

Christ's time, among whom God looked for righteousness (that is, that they should receive and embrace Christ), but behold a cry, that cry, *Crucify him, crucify him.*

Verses 8–17

The world and the flesh are the two great enemies that we are in danger of being overpowered by; yet we are in no danger if we do not ourselves yield to them. Eagerness of the world, and indulgence of the flesh, are the two sins against which the prophet, in God's name, here denounces woes. These were sins which then abounded among the men of Judah, some of the wild grapes they brought forth (*v.* 4), and for which God threatens to bring ruin upon them. They are sins which we have all need to stand upon our guard against and dread the consequences of.

I. Here is a woe to those who set their hearts upon the wealth of the world, and place their happiness in that, and increase it to themselves by indirect and unlawful means (*v.* 8), who *join house to house and lay field to field, till there be no place,* no room for anybody to live by them.. If they could succeed, they would be placed alone in the midst of the earth, would monopolize possessions and preferments, and engross all profits and employments to themselves. Not that it is a sin for those who have a house and a field, of they have wherewithal, to purchase another; but

1. Their fault is, (1.) That they are inordinate in their desires to enrich themselves, and make it their whole care and business to raise an estate, as if they had nothing to mind, nothing to seek, nothing to do, in this world, but that. They never know when they have enough, but the more they have the more they would have; and, like the *daughters of the horseleech,* they cry, *Give, give.* They cannot enjoy what they have, nor do good with it, but are constantly contriving and studying to make it more. They must have variety of houses, a winter-house, and a summer-house, and if another man's house or field lie convenient to theirs, as Naboth's vineyard to Ahab's, they must have that too, or they cannot be easy. (2.) That they are herein careless of others, nay, and injurious to them. They would live so as to let nobody live but themselves. So that their insatiable covetings may be gratified, they care not what becomes of all about them, what encroachments they make upon their neighbours' rights, what hardships they put upon those that they have power over or advantage against, nor what base and wicked arts they use to heap up treasure to themselves. They would swell so big as to fill all space, and yet are still unsatisfied (Eccl. 5:10), as Alexander, who, when he fancied he had conquered the world, wept because he had not another world to conquer. *Deficiente terrâ, non impletur avaritia — If the whole earth were monopolized, avarice would thirst for more.* What! *will you be placed alone in the midst of the earth?* (so some read it); will you be so foolish as to desire it, when we have so much need of the service of others and so much comfort in their society? Will you be so foolish as to expect that the *earth shall be forsaken for us* (Job 18:4), when it is by multitudes that the earth is to be replenished? *An propter vos solos tanta terra creata est? — Was the wide world created merely for you?* Lyra.

2. That which is threatened as the punishment of this sin is that neither the houses nor the fields they were thus greedy of should turn to any account, *v.* 9, 10. God whispered it to the prophet in his ear, as he speaks in a like case (*ch.* 22:14): *It was revealed in my ears by the Lord of hosts* (as God told Samuel a thing *in his ear,* 1 Sa. 9:15); he thought he heard it still sounding in his ears; but he proclaimed it, as he ought, *upon the house-tops,* Mt. 10:27. (1.) That the houses they were so fond of should be untenanted, should stand long empty, and should yield them no rent, and go out of repair: *Many houses shall be desolate,* the people that should dwell in them, being cut off by sword, famine, or pestilence, or carried into captivity; or trade being dead, and poverty coming upon the country like an armed man, those that had been housekeepers were forced to become lodgers, or shift for themselves elsewhere. Even great and fair houses, that would invite tenants, and (there being a scarcity of tenants) might be taken at low rates, shall stand empty without inhabitants. God created not the earth in vain; he *formed it to be inhabited, ch.* 45:18. But men's projects are often frustrated, and what they frame answers not the intention. We have a say-

ing, That fools build houses for wise men to live in; but sometimes, as the event proves, they are built for no man to live in. God has many ways to empty the most populous cities. (2.) That the fields they were so fond of should be unfruitful (*v.* 10): *Ten acres of vineyard shall yield* only such a quantity of grapes as will make but *one bath* of wine (which was about eight gallons), *and the seed of a homer,* a bushel's sowing of ground, shall yield but an ephah, which was the tenth part of a homer; so that through the barrenness of the ground, or the unreasonableness of the weather, they should not have more than a tenth part of their seed again. Note, Those that set their hearts upon the world will justly be disappointed in their expectations from it.

II. Here is a woe to those that dote upon the pleasures and delights of sense, *v.* 11, 12. Sensuality ruins men as certainly as worldliness and oppression. As Christ pronounces a woe against those that are rich, so also against those that laugh now and are full (Lu. 6:24, 25), and fare sumptuously, Lu. 16:19. Observe,

1. Who the sinners are against whom this woe is denounced. (1.) They are such as are given to drink; they make their drinking their business, have their hearts upon it, and overcharge themselves with it. They rise early to follow strong drink, as husbandmen and tradesmen do to follow their employments; as if they were afraid of losing time from that which is the greatest misspending of time. Whereas commonly those that are drunken are drunken in the night, when they have despatched the business of the day, these neglect business, abandon it, and give up themselves to the service of the flesh; for they sit at their cups all day, *and continue till night, till wine inflame them* — inflame their lusts (chambering and wantonness follow upon rioting and drunkenness) — inflame their passions; for who but such have *contentions and wounds without cause?* Prov. 23:29–35. They make a perfect trade of drinking; nor do they seek the shelter of the night for this work of darkness, as men ashamed of it, but *count it a pleasure to riot in the day-time.* See 2 Pt. 2:13. (2.) They are such as are given to mirth. They have their feasts, and they are so merrily disposed that they cannot dine or sup without music, musical instruments of all sorts, like David (Amos 6:5), like Solomon (Eccl. 2:8); *the harp and the viol, the tarbet and pipe,* must accompany the wine, that every sense may be gratified to a nicety; they *take the timbrel and harp,* Job 21:12. The use of music is lawful in itself; but when it is excessive, when we set our hearts upon it, misspend time in it, so that it crowds our spiritual and divine pleasures and draws away the heart from God, then it turns into sin for us. (3.) They are such as never give their mind to any thing that is serious: *They regard not the work of the Lord;* they observe not his power, wisdom, and goodness, in those creatures which they abuse and subject to vanity, nor the bounty of his providence in giving them those good things which they make the food and fuel of their lusts. God's judgments have already seized them, and they are under the tokens of his displeasure, but they regard not; they consider not the hand of God in all these things; his hand is lifted up, but they will not see, because they will not disturb themselves in their pleasures nor think what God is doing with them.

2. What the judgments are which are denounced against them, and in part executed. It is here foretold, (1.) that they should be dislodged; the land should spue out these drunkards (*v.* 13): *My people* (so they call themselves, and were proud of it) have therefore *gone into captivity,* are as sure to go as if they were gone already, *because they have no knowledge;* how should they have knowledge when by their excessive drinking they make sots and fools of themselves? They set up for wits; but because they regard not God's controversy with them, nor take any care to make their peace with him, they may truly be said to have no knowledge; and the reason is because they will have none; they are inconsiderate and wilful, and are therefore destroyed for lack of knowledge. (2.) That they should be impoverished, and come to want that which they had wasted and abused to excess: Even *their glory are men of famine,* subject to it and slain by it; and *their multitude are dried up with thirst.* Both the great men and the common people are ready to perish for want of bread and water. This is the effect of the failure of the corn (*v.* 10), for *the king himself is served of the field,* Eccl. 5:9. And when the vintage fails the drunkards are called upon to weep, because *the new wine is cut off from their mouth* (Joel 1:5), and not so much because now they want it as because when they had it they abused it. It is just with God to make men want that for necessity which they have abused to excess. (3.) What multitudes should be cut off by famine and sword (*v.* 14): *Therefore hell has enlarged herself.* Tophet, the common burying-place, proves too little; so many are there to be buried that they shall be forced to enlarge it. The grave has opened her mouth without measure, *never saying, It is enough,* Prov. 30:15, 16. It may be understood of the place of the damned; luxury and sensuality fill these regions of darkness and horror; there those are tormented who made a god of their belly, Lu. 16:25; Phil. 3:19. (4.) That they should be humbled and abased, and all their honours laid in the dust. This will be done effectually by death and the grave: *Their glory shall descend,* not only to the earth, but into it; it shall not *descend after them* (Ps. 49:17), to stand them in any stead on the other side death, but it shall die and be buried with them — poor glory, which will thus wither! Did they glory in their numbers? Their multitude shall go down to the pit, Eze. 31:18; 32:32. Did they glory in the figure they made? Their pomp shall be at an end; their shouts with which they triumphed, and were attended. Did they glory in their mirth? Death will turn it into mourning; he that rejoices and revels, and never knows what it is to be serious, shall go thither where there are weeping and wailing. Thus the mean man and the mighty man meet together in the grave and under mortifying judgments. Let a man be ever so high, death will bring him low — ever so mean, death will bring him lower, in the prospect of which the eyes of the lofty should now be humbled, *v.* 15. It becomes those to look low that must shortly be laid low.

3. What the fruit of these judgments shall be.

(1.) God shall be glorified, *v.* 16. He that is the Lord of hosts, and the holy God, shall be exalted and sanctified in the judgment and righteousness of these dispensations. His justice must be owned in bringing those low what exalted themselves; and herein he is glorified, [1.] As a God is irresistible power. He will herein be exalted as the Lord of hosts, that is able to break the strongest, humble the proudest, and tame the most unruly. Power is not exalted but in judgment. It is the honour of God that, though he has a mighty arm, yet *judgment and justice are* always *the habitation of his throne,* Ps. 89:13, 14. [2.] As a God of unspotted purity. He that is holy, infinitely holy, shall be sanctified (that is, shall be owned and declared to be holy) in the righteous punishment of proud men. Note, When proud men are humbled the great God is honoured, and ought to be honoured by us.

(2.) Good people shall be relieved and succoured (*v.* 17): *Then shall the lambs feed after their manner;* the meek ones of the earth, who followed the Lamb, who were persecuted, and put into fear by those proud oppressors, shall feed quietly, feed in the green pastures, and there shall be none to make them afraid. See Eze. 34:14. When the enemies of the church are cut off then have the churches rest. *They shall feed at their pleasure;* so some read it. *Blessed are the meek, for they shall inherit the earth,* and delight themselves in abundant peace. *They shall feed according to their order or capacity* (so others read it), as they are able to hear the word, that bread of life.

(3.) The country shall be laid waste, and become a prey to the neighbours: *The waste places of the fats ones,* the possessions of those rich men that lived at their ease, shall be eaten by strangers that were nothing akin to them. In the captivity the poor of the land were left for *vine-dressers and husbandmen* (2 Ki. 25:12); these were the lambs that fed in the pastures of the fats ones, which were laid in common for strangers to eat. When the church of the Jews, those fat ones, was laid waste, their privileges were transferred to the Gentiles, who had been long strangers, and the lambs of Christ's flock were welcome to them.

Verses 18–30

Here are, I. Sins described which will bring judgments upon a people: and this perhaps is not only a charge drawn up against the men of Judah who lived at that time, and the particular articles of that charge, though it may relate primarily to them, but is rather intended for warning to all people, in all ages, to take heed of these sins, as destructive both to particular persons and to communities, and exposing men to God's wrath and his righteous judgments. Those are here said to be in a woeful condition,

1. Who are eagerly set upon sin, and violent in their sinful pursuits (*v.* 18), who *draw iniquity with cords of vanity,* who take as much pains to sin as the cattle do that draw a team, who put themselves to the stretch for the gratifying of their inordinate appetites, and, to humour a base lust, offer violence to nature itself. They think themselves as sure of compassing their wicked project as if they were pulling it towards them with strong cart-ropes; but they will find themselves disappointed, for they will prove cords of vanity, which will break when they come to any stress. For *the righteous Lord will cut in sunder the cords of the wicked,* Ps. 129:4; Job 4:8; Prov. 22:8. They are by long custom and confirmed habits so hardened in sin that they cannot get clear of it. Those that sin through infirmity are drawn away by sin; those that sin presumptuously draw iniquity to them, in spite of the oppositions of Providence and the checks of conscience. Some by sin understand the punishment of sin: they pull God's judgments upon their own heads as it were, with cart-ropes.

2. Who set the justice of God at defiance, and challenge the Almighty to do his worst (*v.* 19): *They say, Let him make speed, and hasten his work;* this is the same language with that of the scoffers of the last days, who say, *Where is the promise of his coming?* and therefore it is that, like them, they *draw iniquity with cords of vanity,* are violent and daring in sin, and walk after their own lusts, 2 Pt. 3:3, 4. (1.) They ridicule the prophets, and banter them. It is in scorn that they call God *the Holy One of Israel,* because the prophets used with great veneration to call him so. (2.) They will not believe the revelation of God's wrath from heaven against their ungodliness and unrighteousness; unless they see it executed, they will not know it, as if the curse were *brutum fulmen — a mere flash,* and all the threatenings of the word bugbears to frighten fools and children. (3.) If God should appear against them, as he has threatened, yet they think themselves able to make their part good with him, and provoke him to jealousy, as if they were stronger than he, 1 Co. 10:22. "We have heard his word, but it is all talk; let him hasten his work, we shall shift for ourselves well enough." Note, Those that wilfully persist in sin consider not the power of God's anger.

3. Who confound and overthrow the distinctions between moral good and evil, *who call evil good and moral evil* (*v.* 20), who not only live in the omission of that which is good, but condemn it, argue against it, and, because they will not practise it themselves, run it down in others, and fasten invidious epithets upon it — not only do that which is evil, but justify it, and applaud it, and recommend it to others as safe and good. Note, (1.) Virtue and piety are good, for they are light and sweet, they are pleasant and right; but sin and wickedness are evil; they are darkness, all the fruit of ignorance and mistake, and will be bitterness in the latter end. (2.) Those do a great deal of wrong to God, and religion, and conscience, to their own souls, and to the souls of others, who misrepresent these, and put false colours upon them — who call drunkenness good fellowship, and covetousness good husbandry, and, when they persecute the people of God, think they do him good service — and, on the other hand, who call seriousness ill-nature, and sober singularity ill-breeding, who say all manner of evil falsely concerning the ways of godliness, and do what they can to form in men's minds prejudices against them, and this in defiance of evidence as plain and convincing as that of sense, by which we distinguish, beyond contradiction, between light and darkness, and between that which to the taste is sweet and that which is bitter.

4. Who though they are guilty of such gross mistakes as these have a great opinion of their own judgments, and value themselves mightily upon their understanding (*v.* 21): They are *wise in their own eyes;* they think themselves able to disprove and baffle the reproofs and convictions of God's word, and to evade and elude both the searches and the reaches of his judgments; they think they can outwit Infinite Wisdom and countermine Providence itself. Or it may be taken more generally: God resists the proud, those particularly who are conceited of their own wisdom and lean to their own understanding; such must become fools, that

they may be truly wise, or else, at their end they shall appear to be fools before all the world.

5. Who glory in it as a great accomplishment that they are able to bear a great deal of strong liquor without being overcome by it (*v.* 22), *who are mighty to drink wine,* and use their strength and vigour, not in the service of their country, but in the service of their lusts. Let drunkards know from this scripture that, (1.) They ungratefully abuse their bodily strength, which God has given them for good purposes, and by degrees cannot but weaken it. (2.) It will not excuse them from the guilt of drunkenness that they can drink hard and yet keep their feet. (3.) Those who boast of their drinking down others glory in their shame. (4.) How light soever men make of their drunkenness, it is a sin which will certainly lay them open to the wrath and curse of God.

6. Who, as judges, pervert justice, and go counter to all rules of equity, *v.* 23. This follows upon the former; they *drink and forget the law* (Prov. 31:5), and *err through wine* (*ch.* 28:7), and take bribes, that they may have wherewithal to maintain their luxury. They *justify the wicked for reward,* and find some pretence or other to clear him from his guilt and shelter him from punishment; and they condemn the innocent, and *take away their righteousness from them,* that is, overrule their pleas, deprive them of the means of clearing up their innocency, and give judgment against them. In causes between man and man, might and money would at any time prevail against right and justice; and he who was ever so plainly in the wrong would with a small bribe carry the cause and recover the costs. In criminal causes, though the prisoner ever so plainly appeared to be guilty, yet for a reward they would acquit him; if he were innocent, yet if he did not fee them well, nay, if they were feed by the malicious prosecutor, or if they themselves had spleen against him, they would condemn him.

II. The judgments described, which these sins would bring upon them. Let not those expect to live easily who live thus wickedly; for the righteous God will take vengeance, *v.* 24–30. Here we may observe,

1. How complete this ruin will be, and how necessarily and unavoidably it will follow upon their sins. He had compared this people to a vine (*v.* 7), well fixed, and which, it was hoped, would be flourishing and fruitful; but the grace of God towards it was received in vain, and then the root became rottenness, being dried up from beneath, and the blossom would of course blow off as dust, as a light and worthless thing, Job 18:16. Sin weakens the strength, the root, of a people, so that they are easily rooted up; it defaces the beauty, the blossoms, of a people, and takes away the hopes of fruit. The sin of unfruitfulness is punished with the plague of unfruitfulness. Sinners make themselves as stubble and chaff, combustible matter, proper fuel to the fire of God's wrath, which then of course devours and consumes them, *as the fire devours the stubble,* and nobody can hinder it, or cares to hinder it. Chaff is consumed, unhelped and unpitied.

2. How just the ruin will be: *Because they have cast away the law of the Lord of hosts,* and would not have him to reign over them; and, as the law of Moses was rejected and thrown off, so *the word of the Holy One of Israel* by his servants the prophets, putting them in mind of his law and calling them to obedience, was despised and disregarded. God does not reject men for every transgression of his law and word; but, when his word is despised and his law cast away, what can they expect but that God should utterly abandon them?

3. Whence this ruin should come (*v.* 25): it is destruction from the Almighty. (1.) The justice of God appoints it; for that is *the anger of the Lord* which is *kindled against his people,* his necessary vindication of the honour of his holiness and authority. (2.) The power of God effects it: *He has stretched forth his hand against them.* That hand which had many a time been stretched out for them against their enemies is now stretched out against them at full length and in its full vigour; and *who knows the power of his anger?* Whether they are sensible of it or no, it is God that has smitten them, has blasted their vine and made it wither.

4. The consequences and continuance of this ruin. When God comes forth in wrath against a people the hills tremble, fear seizes even their great men, who are strong and high, the earth shakes under men and is ready to sink; and as this feels dreadful (what does more so than an earthquake?) so what sight can be more frightful than the carcases of men torn with dogs, or thrown *as dung* (so the margin reads it) *in the midst of the streets?* This intimates that great multitudes should be slain, not only soldiers in the field of battle, but the inhabitants of their cities put to the sword in cold blood, and that the survivors should neither have hands nor hearts to bury them. This is very dreadful, and yet such is the merit of sin that, *for all this, God's anger is not turned away;* that fire will burn as long as there remains any of the stubble and chaff to be fuel for it; *and his hand,* which he stretched forth against his people to smite them, because they do not by prayer take hold of it, nor by reformation submit themselves to it, *is stretched out still.*

5. The instruments that should be employed in bringing this ruin upon them: it should be done by the incursions of a foreign enemy, that should lay all waste. No particular enemy is named, and therefore we are to take it as a prediction of all the several judgments of this kind which God brought upon the Jews, Sennacherib's invasion soon after, and the destruction of Jerusalem by the Chaldeans first and at last by the Romans; and I think it is to be looked upon also as a threatening of the like desolation of those countries which harbour and countenance those sins mentioned in the foregoing verses; it is an exposition of those woes. When God designs the ruin of a provoking people,

(1.) He can send a great way off for instruments to be employed in effecting it; he can raise forces from afar, and summon them from the end of the earth to attend his service, *v.* 26. Those who know him not are made use of to fulfil his counsel, when, by reason of their distance, they can scarcely be supposed to have any ends of their own to serve. If God set up his standard, he can incline men's hearts to enlist themselves under it, though perhaps they know not why or wherefore. When the Lord of hosts is pleased to make a general muster of the forces he has at his command, he has a great army in an instant, Joel 2:2, 11. He needs not sound a trumpet, nor beat a drum, to give them notice or to animate them; no, he does but hiss to them, or rather whistle to them, and that is enough; they hear that, and that puts courage into them. Note, God has all the creatures at his beck.

(2.) He can make them come into the service with incredible expedition: *Behold, they shall come with speed swiftly.* Note, [1.] Those who will do God's work must not loiter, must not linger, nor shall they when his time has come. [2.] Those who defy God's judgments will be ashamed of their insolence when it is too late; they said scornfully (*v.* 19), *Let him make speed, let him hasten his work,* and they shall find, to their terror and confusion, that he will; *in one hour has the judgment come.*

(3.) He can carry them on in the service with amazing forwardness and fury. This is described here in very elegant and lofty expressions, *v.* 27–30. [1.] Though their marches be very long, yet *none among them shall be weary;* so desirous they be to engage that they shall forget their weariness, and make no complaints of it. [2.] Though the way be rough, and perhaps embarrassed by the usual policies of war, yet none among them shall *stumble,* but all the difficulties in their way shall easily be got over. [3.] Though they be forced to keep constant watch, yet *none shall slumber nor sleep,* so intent shall they be upon their work, in prospect of having the plunder of the city for their pains. [4.] They shall not desire any rest of relaxation; they shall not put off their clothes, nor *loose the girdle of their loins,* but shall always have their belts on and swords by their sides. [5.] They shall not meet with the least hindrance to retard their march or oblige them to halt; not a *latchet of their shoes shall be broken* which they must stay to mend, as Jos. 9:13. [6.] Their arms and ammunition shall all be fixed, and in good posture; *their arrows sharp,* to wound deep, *and all their bows bent,* none unstrung, for they expect to be soon in action. [7.] Their horses and chariots of war shall all be fit for service; their horses so strong, so hardy, that *their hoofs shall be like flint,* far from being beaten, or made tender, by their long march; and the wheels of their chariots not broken, or battered, or out of repair, but swift *like a whirlwind,* turning round so strongly upon their axle-trees. [8.] All the soldiers shall be bold and daring (*v.* 29): *Their roaring,* or shouting, before a battle, *shall be like a lion,* who with his roaring animates himself, and terrifies all about him. Those who would not hear the voice of God speaking to them by his prophets, but stopped their ears against their charms, shall be made to hear the voice of their enemies roaring against them and shall not be able to turn a deaf ear to it. *They shall roar like the roaring of the sea* in a storm; it roars and threatens to swallow up, as the lion roars and threatens to tear in pieces. [9.] There shall not be the least prospect of relief or succour. The enemy shall come in like a flood, and there shall be none to lift up a standard against him. He shall seize the prey, and none shall deliver it, none shall be able to deliver it, nay, none shall so much as dare to attempt the deliverance of it, but shall give it up for lost. Let the distressed look which way they will, every thing appears dismal; for, if God frowns upon us, how can any creature smile? *First,* Look round to the earth, to the land, to that land that used to be the land of light and the joy of the whole earth, and *behold darkness and sorrow,* all frightful, all mournful, nothing hopeful. *Secondly,* Look up to heaven, and there the light is darkened, where one would expect to have found it. If the light is darkened in the heavens, how great is that darkness! If God hide his face, no marvel the heavens hide theirs and appear gloomy, Job 34:29. It is our wisdom, by keeping a good conscience, to keep all clear between us and heaven, that we may have light from above even when clouds and darkness are round about us.

CHAPTER 6

Hitherto, it should seem, Isaiah had prophesied as a candidate, having only a virtual and tacit commission; but here we have him (if I may so speak) solemnly ordained and set apart to the prophetic office by a more express or explicit commission, as his work grew more upon his hands: or perhaps, having seen little success of his ministry, he began to think of giving it up; and therefore God saw fit to renew his commission here in this chapter, in such a manner as might excite and encourage his zeal and industry in the execution of it, though he seemed to labour in vain. In this chapter we have, I. A very awful vision which Isaiah saw of the glory of God (*v.* 1–4), the terror it put him into (*v.* 5), and the relief given him against that terror by an assurance of the pardon of his sins (*v.* 6, 7). II. A very awful commission which Isaiah received to go as a prophet, in God's name (*v.* 8), by his preaching to harden the impenitent in sin and ripen them for ruin (*v.* 9–12) yet with a reservation of mercy for a remnant, (*v.* 13). And it was as to an evangelical prophet that these things were shown him and said to him.

Verses 1–4

The vision which Isaiah saw when he was, as is said of Samuel, *established to be a prophet of the Lord* (1 Sa. 3:20), was intended, 1. To confirm his faith, that he might himself be abundantly satisfied of the truth of those things which should afterwards be made known to him. This God opened the communications of himself to him; but such visions needed not to be afterwards repeated upon every revelation. Thus God appeared at first as a God of glory to Abraham (Acts 7:2), and to Moses, Ex. 3:2. Ezekiel's prophecies and St. John's, begin with visions of the divine glory. 2. To work upon his affections, that he might be possessed with such a reverence of God as would both quicken him and fix him to his service. Those who are to teach others the knowledge of God ought to be well acquainted with him themselves.

The vision is dated, for the greater certainty of it. It was *in the year that king Uzziah died,* who had reigned, for the most part, as prosperously and well as any of the kings of Judah, and reigned very long, above fifty years. About the time that he died, Isaiah saw this vision of God upon a throne; for when the breath of princes goes forth, and they return to their earth, this is our comfort, that *the Lord shall reign for ever,* Ps. 146:3, 4, 10. Israel's king dies, but Israel's God still lives. From the mortality of great and good men we should take occasion to look up with an eye of faith to the King eternal, immortal. King Uzziah died under a cloud, for he was shut up as a leper till the day of his death. As the lives of princes have their periods, so their glory is often eclipsed; but, as God is everliving, so his glory is everlasting. King Uzziah dies in an hospital, but the King of kings still sits upon his throne.

What the prophet here saw is revealed to us, that we, mixing faith with that revelation, may in it, as in a glass, behold the glory of the Lord; let us turn aside therefore, and see this great sight with humble reverence.

I. See God upon his throne, and that throne *high and lifted up,* not only above other thrones, as it transcends them, but over other thrones, as it rules and commands them. Isaiah saw not *Jehovah* — the essence of God (no man has seen that, or can see it), but *Adonai* — his dominion. He saw the Lord Jesus; so this vision is explained Jn. 12:41, that Isaiah now saw Christ's glory and spoke of him, which is an incontestable proof of the divinity of our Saviour. He it is who when, after his resurrection, he sat down on the right hand of God, did but sit down where he was before, Jn. 17:5. See the rest of the Eternal Mind: Isaiah *saw the Lord sitting,* Ps. 29:10. See the sovereignty of the Eternal Monarch: he sits *upon a throne* — a throne of glory, before which we must worship, — a throne of government, under which we must be subject, — and a throne of grace, to which we may come boldly. This throne is high, and lifted up above all competition and contradiction.

II. See his temple, his church on earth, filled with the manifestations of his glory. His throne being erected at the door of the temple (as princes sat in judgment at the gates), *his train,* the skirts of his robes, *filled the temple,* the whole world (for it is all God's temple, and, as the heaven is his throne, so the earth is his footstool), or rather the church, which is filled enriched, and beautified with the tokens of God's special presence.

III. See the bright and blessed attendants on his throne, in and by whom his glory is celebrated and his government served (*v.* 2): *Above the throne,* as it were hovering about it, or nigh to the throne, bowing before it, with an eye to it, *the seraphim stood,* the holy angels, who are called *seraphim — burners;* for he *makes his ministers a flaming fire,* Ps. 104:4. They burn in love to God, and zeal for his glory and against sin, and he makes use of them as instruments of his wrath when he is a consuming fire to his enemies. Whether they were only two or four, or (as I rather think) an *innumerable company of angels,* that Isaiah saw, is uncertain; see Dan. 7:10.. Note, It is the glory of the angels that they are seraphim, have heat proportionable to their light, have abundance, not only of divine knowledge, but of holy love. Special notice is taken of their wings (and of no other part of their appearance), because of the use they made of them, which is designed for instruction to us. They had *each of them six wings,* not stretched upwards (as those whom Ezekiel saw, *ch.* 1:11), but, 1. Four were made use of for a covering, as the wings of a fowl, sitting, are; with the two upper wings, next to the head, they covered their faces, and with the two lowest wings they covered their feet, or lower parts. This bespeaks their great humility and reverence in their attendance upon God, for he is greatly feared in *the assembly of those saints,* Ps. 89:7. They not only cover their feet, those members of the body which are less honourable (1 Co. 12:23), but even their faces. Though angel's faces, doubtless, are much fairer than those of the children of men (Acts 6:15), yet in the presence of God, they cover them, because they cannot bear the dazzling lustre of the divine glory, and because, being conscious of an infinite distance from the divine perfection, they are ashamed to show their faces before the holy God, who *charges even his angels with folly* if they should offer to vie with him, Job 4:18. If angels be thus reverent in their attendance on God, with what godly fear should we approach his throne! Else we do not the will of God as the angels do it. Yet Moses, when he went into the mount with God, took the veil from off his face. See 2 Co. 3:18. 2. Two were made use of for flight; when they are sent on God's errands they fly swiftly (Dan. 9:21), more swiftly with their own wings than if they flew on the wings of the wind. This teaches us to do the work of God with cheerfulness and expedition.. Do angels come upon the wing from heaven to earth, to minister for our good, and shall not we soar upon the wing from earth to heaven, to share with them in their glory? Lu. 20:36.

IV. Hear the anthem, or song of praise, which the angels sing to the honour of him that sits on the throne, *v.* 3. Observe,

1. How this song was sung. With zeal and fervency — *they cried* aloud; and with unanimity — *they cried to another,* or one with another; they sang alternately, but in concert, and without the least jarring voice to interrupt the harmony.

2. What the song was; it is the same with that which is sung by the four living creatures, Rev. 4:8. Note, Praising God always was, and will be to eternity, the work of heaven, and the constant employment of blessed spirits above, Ps. 84:4. Note further, The church above is the same in its praises; there is no change of times or notes there. Two things the seraphim here give God the praise of: —

(1.) His infinite perfections in himself. Here is one of his most glorious titles praised: he is *the Lord of hosts,* of their hosts, of all hosts; and one of his most glorious attributes, his holiness, without which his being the Lord of hosts (or, as it is in the parallel place, Rev. 4:8, *the Lord God Almighty*) could not be so much as it is the matter of our joy and praise; for power, without purity to guide it, would be a terror to mankind. None of all the divine attributes is so celebrated in scripture as this is. God's power was spoken twice (Ps. 62:11), but his holiness thrice, *Holy, holy, holy.* This bespeaks, [1.] The zeal and fervency of the angels in praising God; they even want words to express themselves, and therefore repeat the same again. [2.] The particular pleasure they take in contemplating the holiness of God; this is a subject they love to dwell upon, to harp upon, and are loth to leave. [3.] The superlative excellency of God's holiness, above that of the purest creatures. He is holy, thrice holy, infinitely holy, originally, perfectly, and eternally so. [4.] It may refer to the three person in the Godhead, Holy Father, Holy Son, and Holy Spirit (for it follows, *v.* 8, *Who will go for us?*) or perhaps to *that which was, and is, and is to come;* for that title of God's honour is added to this song, Rev. 4:8. Some make the angels here to applaud the equity of that sentence which God was now about to pronounce upon the Jewish nation. Herein he was, and is, and will be, holy; his ways are equal.

(2.) The manifestation of these to the children of men: *The earth is full of his glory,* the glory of his power and purity; for he is holy in all his works, Ps. 145:17. The Jews thought the glory of God should be confined to their land; but it is here intimated that in the gospel times (which are pointed to in this chapter) the glory of God should fill all the earth, the glory of his holiness, which is indeed the glory of all his other attributes; this then *filled the temple* (*v.* 1), but, in the latter days, the earth shall be full of it.

V. Observe the marks and tokens of terror with which the temple was filled, upon this vision of the divine glory, *v.* 4. 1. The house was *shaken;* not only the door, but even *the posts of the door,* which were firmly fixed, *moved at the voice of him that cried,* at the voice of God, who called to judgment (Ps. 50:4), at the voice of the angel, who praised him. There are voices in heaven sufficient to drown all the noises of the many waters in this lower world, Ps. 93:3, 4. This violent concussion of the temple was an indication of God's wrath and displeasure against the people for their sins; it was an earnest of the destruction of it and the city by the Babylonians first, and afterwards by the Romans; and it was designed to strike an awe upon us. Shall walls and posts tremble before God, and shall we not tremble? 2. The house was *darkened;* it was *filled with smoke,* which was as a *cloud spread* upon *the face of his throne* (Job 26:9); we cannot take a full view of it, nor order our speech concerning it, by reason of darkness. In the temple above there will be no smoke, but everything will be seen clearly. There God dwells in light; here he *makes darkness his pavilion,* 2 Chron, 6:1.

Verses 5–8

Our curiosity would lead us to enquire further concerning the seraphim, their songs and their services; but here we leave them, and must attend to what passed between God and his prophet. *Secret things belong not to us,* the secret things of the world of angels, but things revealed to and by the prophets, which concern the administration of God's kingdom among men. Now here we have,

I. The consternation that the prophet was put into by the vision which he saw of the glory of God (*v.* 5): *Then said I, Woe is me!* I should have said, "Blessed art thou, who hast been thus highly favoured, highly honoured, and dignified, for a time, with the privilege of those glorious beings that *always behold the face of our Father.* Blessed were those eyes which saw the Lord sitting on his throne, and those ears which heard the angels' praises." And, one would think, he should have said, "Happy am I, for ever happy; nothing now shall trouble me, nothing make me blush or tremble;" but, on the contrary, he cries out, *"Woe is me! for I am undone.* Alas for me! I am a gone man; *I shall surely die* (Judges 13:22; 6:22); I am silenced; I am struck dumb, struck dead." Thus Daniel, when he heard the words of the angel, *became dumb,* and there was *no strength, no breath, left in him,* Dan. 10:15, 17. Observe,

1. What the prophet reflected upon in himself which terrified him: *"I am undone* if God deal with me in strict justice, for I have made myself obnoxious to his displeasure, *because I am a man of unclean lips."* Some think he refers particularly to some rash word he had spoken, or to his sinful silence in not reproving sin with the boldness and freedom that were necessary — a sin which God's ministers have too much cause to charge themselves with, and to blush at the remembrance of. But it may be taken more generally; *I am a sinner;* particularly, *I have offended in word;* and who is there that hath not? Jam. 3:2. We all have reason to bewail it before the Lord, (1.) That we are of unclean lips ourselves; our lips are not consecrated to God; he had not had the *first-fruits of our lips* (Heb. 13:15), and therefore they are counted common and unclean, *uncircumcised lips,* Ex. 6:30. Nay, they have been polluted with sin. We have spoken the language of an unclean heart, that evil communication which corrupts good manners, and whereby many have been defiled. We are unworthy and unmeet to take God's name into our lips. With what a pure lip did the angels praise God! "But," says the prophet, "I cannot praise him so, for *I am a man of unclean lips."* The best men in the world have reason to be ashamed of themselves, and the best of their services, when they come into comparison with the holy angels. The angels had celebrated the purity and holiness of God; and therefore the prophet, when he reflects upon sin, calls it *uncleanness;* for the sinfulness of sin is its contrariety to the holy nature of God, and upon that account especially it should appear both hateful and frightful to us. The impurity of our lips ought to be the grief of our souls, for by our words we shall be justified or condemned. (2.) That we dwell among those who are so too. We have reason to lament not only that we ourselves are polluted, but that the nature and race of mankind are so; the disease is hereditary and epidemic, which is so far from lessening our guilt that it should rather increase our grief, especially considering that we have not done what we might have done for the cleansing of the pollution of other people's lips; nay, we have rather learned their way and spoken their language, as Joseph in Egypt learned the courtier's oath, Gen. 42:16. *"I dwell in the midst of a people* who by their impudent sinnings are pulling down desolating judgments upon the land, which I, who am a sinner too, may justly expect to be involved in."

2. What gave occasion for these sad reflections at this time: *My eyes have seen the King, the Lord of hosts.* He saw God's sovereignty to be incontestable — he is the King; and his power irresistible — he is the Lord of hosts. These are comfortable truths to God's people, and yet they ought to strike an awe upon us. Note, A believing sight of God's glorious majesty should affect us all with reverence and godly fear. We have reason to be abased in the sense of that infinite distance that there is between us and God, and our own sinfulness and vileness before him, and to be afraid of his displeasure. We are undone if there be not a Mediator between us and this holy God, 1 Sa. 6:20. Isaiah was thus humbled, to prepare him for the honour he was now to be called to as a prophet. Note, Those are fittest to be employed for God who are low in their own eyes and are made deeply sensible of their own weakness and unworthiness.

II. The silencing of the prophet's fears by the good words, and comfortable words, with which the angel answered him, *v.* 6, 7. One of the seraphim immediately flew to him, to purify him, and so to pacify him. Note, God has strong consolations ready for holy mourners. Those that humble themselves in penitential shame and fear shall soon be encouraged and exalted; those that are struck down with the visions of God's glory shall soon be raised up again with the visits of his grace; he that tears will heal. Note, further, Angels are ministering spirits for the good of the saints, for their spiritual good. Here was one of the seraphim dismissed, for a time, from attending on the throne of God's glory, to be a messenger of his grace to a good man; and so well pleased was he with the office that he came flying to him. To our Lord Jesus himself, in his agony, there *appeared an angel from heaven, strength-*

ening him, Lu. 22:43. Here is, 1. A comfortable sign given to the prophet of the purging away of his sin. The seraph *brought a live coal from the altar,* and touched his lips with it, not to hurt them, but to heal them — not to cauterize, but to cleanse them; for there were purifications by fire, as well as by water, and the filth of Jerusalem was purged by the *spirit of burning,* ch. 4:4. The blessed Spirit works as fire, Mt. 3:11. The seraph, being himself kindled with a divine fire, put life into the prophet, to make him also zealously affected; for the way to purge the lips from the uncleanness of sin is to fire the soul with the love of God. This live coal was taken from off the altar, either the altar of incense or that of burnt-offerings, for they had both of them fire burning on them continually. Nothing is powerful to cleanse and comfort the soul but what is taken from Christ's satisfaction and the intercession he ever lives to make in the virtue of that satisfaction. It must be a coal from his altar that must put life into us and be our peace; it will not be done with strange fire. 2. An explication of this sign: *"Lo, this has touched thy lips,* to assure thee of this, that *thy iniquity is taken away and thy sin purged.* The guilt of thy sin is removed by pardoning mercy, the guilt of thy tongue-sins. Thy corrupt disposition to sin is removed by renewing grace; and therefore nothing can hinder thee from being accepted with God as a worshipper, in concert with the holy angels, or from being employed for God as a messenger to the children of men." Those only who are thus purged from an evil conscience are prepared *to serve the living God,* Heb. 9:14. The taking away of sin is necessary to our speaking with confidence and comfort either to God in prayer or from God in preaching; nor are any so fit to display to others the riches and power of gospel-grace as those who have themselves tasted the sweetness and felt the influence of that grace; and those shall have their sin taken away who complain of it as a burden and see themselves in danger of being undone by it.

III. The renewing of the prophet's mission, *v.* 8. Here is a communication between God and Isaiah about this matter. Those that would assist others in their correspondence with God must not themselves be strangers to it; for how can we expect that God should speak by us if we never heard him speaking to us, or that we should be accepted as the mouth of others to God if we never spoke to him heartily for ourselves? Observe here,

1. The counsel of God concerning Isaiah's mission. God is here brought in, after the manner of men, deliberating and advising with himself: *Whom shall I send? And who will go for us?* God needs not either to be counselled by others or to consult with himself; he knows what he will do, but thus he would show us that there is a counsel in his whole will, and teach us to consider our ways, and particularly that the sending forth of ministers is a work not to be done but upon mature deliberation. Observe, (1.) Who it is that is consulting. It is the Lord God in his glory, whom he saw upon the throne high and lifted up. It puts an honour upon the ministry that, when God would send a prophet to speak in his name, he appeared in all the glories of the upper world. Ministers are the ambassadors of the King of kings; how mean soever they are, he who sends them is great; it is God in three persons (Who will go for us? as Gen. 1:26, *Let us make man*), Father, Son, and Holy Ghost. They all concur, as in the creating, so in the redeeming and governing of man. Ministers are ordained in the same name into which all Christians are baptized. (2.) What the consultation is: *Whom shall I send? And who will go?* Some think this refers to the particular message of wrath against Israel, *v.* 9, 10. "Who will be willing to go on such a melancholy errand, on which they will go in the bitterness of their souls?" Eze. 3:14. But I rather take it more largely for all those messages which the prophet was entrusted to deliver, in God's name, to that people, in which that hardening work was by no means the primary intention, but a secondary effect of them, 2 Co. 2:16. *Whom shall I send?* intimating that the business was such as required a choice and well-accomplished messenger, Jer. 49:19. God now appeared, attended with holy angels, and yet asks, *Whom shall I send?* For he would send them a *prophet from among their brethren,* Heb. 2:17. Note, [1.] It is the unspeakable favour of God to us that he is pleased to send us his mind by men like ourselves, whose terror shall not make us afraid, and who are themselves con-

cerned in the messages they bring. Those who are workers together with God are sinners and sufferers together with us. [2.] It is a rare thing to find one who is fit to go for God, and carry his messages to the children of men: *Whom shall I send?* Who is sufficient? Such a degree of courage for God and concern for the souls of men as is necessary to make a man faithful, and withal such an insight into the mysteries of the kingdom of heaven as is necessary to make a man skilful, are seldom to be met with. Such an interpreter of the mind of God is one of a thousand, Job 33:23. [3.] None are allowed to go for God but those who are sent by him; he will own none but those whom he appoints, Rom. 10:15. It is Christ's work to put men into the ministry, 1 Tim. 1:12.

2. The consent of Isaiah to it: *Then said I, Here am I; send me.* He was to go on a melancholy errand; the office seemed to go a begging, and every body declined it, and yet Isaiah offered himself to the service. It is an honour to be singular in appearing for God, Judges 5:7. We must not say, "I would go if I thought I should have success;" but, "I will go, and leave the success to God. Here am I; send me." Isaiah had been himself in a melancholy frame (*v.* 5), full of doubts and fears; but now that he had the assurance of the pardon of his sin the clouds were blown over, and he was fit for service and forward to it. What he says denotes, (1.) His readiness: "Here am I, a volunteer, not pressed into the service." *Behold me;* so the word is. God says to us, *Behold me* (ch. 65:1), and, *Here I am* (ch. 58:9), even before we call; let us say so to him when he does call. (2.) His resolution; *"Here I am,* ready to encounter the greatest difficulties. *I have set my face as a flint."* Compare this with ch. 50:4–7. (3.) His referring himself to God: "Send me whither thou wilt; make what use thou pleasest of me. Send me, that is, Lord, give me commission and full instruction; send me, and then, no doubt, thou wilt stand by me." It is a great comfort to those whom God sends that they go for God, and may therefore speak in his name, as having authority, and be assured that he will bear them out.

Verses 9–13

God takes Isaiah at his word, and here sends him on a strange errand — to foretel the ruin of his people and even to ripen them for that ruin — to preach that which, by their abuse of it, would be to them a savour of death unto death. And this was to be a type and figure of the state of the Jewish church in the days of the Messiah, when they should obstinately reject the gospel, and should thereupon be rejected of God. These verses are quoted in part, or referred to, six times, in the New Testament, which intimates that in gospel time these spiritual judgments would be most frequently inflicted; and though they make the least noise, and come not with observation, yet they are of all judgments the most dreadful. Isaiah is here given to understand these four things: —

1. That the generality of the people to whom he was sent would turn a deaf ear to his preaching, and wilfully shut their eyes against all the discoveries of the mind and will of God which he had to make to them (*v.* 9): *"Go, and tell this people,* this foolish wretched people, tell them their own, tell them how stupid and sottish they are." Isaiah must preach to them, and they will *hear* him indeed, but that is all; they will not heed him; they will no *understand* him; they will not take any pains, nor use that application of mind which is necessary to the understanding of him; they are prejudiced against that which is the true intent and meaning of what he says, and therefore they will not understand him, or pretend they do not. They *see indeed* (for the vision is made plain on tables, so that he who runs may read it); *but they perceive not* their own concern in it; it is to them as a tale that is told. Note, There are many who hear the sound of God's word, but do not feel the power of it.

2. That, forasmuch as they would not be made better by his ministry, they should be made worse by it; those that were wilfully blind should be judicially blinded (*v.* 10): "They will not understand or perceive thee, and therefore thou shalt be instrumental to *make their heart fat,* senseless, and sensual, and so to *make their ears* yet more *heavy,* and to *shut their eyes* the closer; so that, at length, their recovery and repentance will become utterly impossible; they shall no more *see with their eyes* the danger they are

in, the ruin they are upon the brink of, nor the way of escape from it; they shall no more *hear with their ears* the warnings and instructions that are given them, nor *understand with their heart* the things that belong to their peace, so as to be converted from the error of their ways, and thus *be healed."* Note, (1.) The conversion of sinners is the healing of them. (2.) A right understanding is necessary to conversion. (3.) God sometimes, in a way of righteous judgment, gives men up to blindness of mind and strong delusions, because they would not *receive the truth in the love of it,* 2 Th. 2:10–12. *He that is filthy let him be filthy still.* (4.) Even the word of God oftentimes proves a means of hardening sinners. The evangelical prophet himself makes the heart of this people fat, not only as he foretels it, passing this sentence upon them in God's name, and seals them under it, but as his preaching had a tendency to it, rocking some asleep in security (to whom it was a lovely song), and making others more outrageous, to whom it was such a reproach that they were not able to bear it. Some looked upon the word as a privilege, and their convictions were smothered by it (Jer. 7:4); others looked upon it as a provocation, and their corruptions were exasperated by it.

3. That the consequence of this would be their *utter ruin,* v. 11, 12. The prophet had nothing to object against the justice of this sentence, nor does he refuse to go upon such an errand, but asks, *"Lord, how long?"* (an abrupt question): "Shall it always be thus? Must I and other prophets always labour in vain among them, and will things never be better?" Or, (as should seem by the answer) "Lord, what will it come to at last? What will be in the end hereof?" In answer to this he is told that it should issue in the final destruction of the Jewish church and nation. "When the word of God, especially the word of the gospel, had been thus abused by them, they shall be unchurched, and consequently undone. Their cities shall be uninhabited, and their country houses too; the land shall be untilled, *desolate with desolation* (as it is in the margin), the people who should replenish the houses and cultivate the ground being all cut off by sword, famine, or pestilence, and those who escape with their lives being removed far away into captivity, so that there shall be a great and general forsaking in the midst of the land; that populous country shall become desert, and that glory of all lands shall be abandoned." Note, Spiritual judgments often bring temporal judgments along with them upon persons and places. This was in part fulfilled in the destruction of Jerusalem by the Chaldeans, when the land, being left desolate, enjoyed her sabbaths seventy years; but, the foregoing predictions being so expressly applied in the New Testament to the Jews in our Saviour's time, doubtless this points at the final destruction of that people by the Romans, in which it had a complete accomplishment, and the effects of it that people and that land remain under to this day.

4. That yet a remnant should be reserved to be the monuments of mercy, v. 13. There was a remnant reserved in the last destruction of the Jewish nation (Rom. 11:5, *At this present time there is a remnant*); for so it was written here: *But in it shall be a tenth,* a certain number, but a very small number in comparison with the multitude that shall perish in their unbelief. It is that which, under the law, was God's proportion; they shall be consecrated to God as the tithes were, and shall be for his service and honour. Concerning this tithe, this saved remnant, we are here told, (1.) That they shall return (ch. 6:13; 10:21), shall return from sin to God and duty, shall return out of captivity to their own land. God will turn them, and they shall be turned. (2.) That they shall be eaten, that is, shall be accepted of God as the tithe was, which was meat in God's house, Mal. 3:10. The saving of this remnant shall be meat to the faith and hope of those that wish well to God's kingdom. (3.) That they shall be like a timber-tree in winter, which has life, though it has no leaves: *As a teil-tree and as an oak, whose substance is in them even when they cast their leaves,* so this remnant, though they may be stripped of their outward prosperity and share with others in common calamities, shall yet recover themselves, as a tree in the spring, and flourish again; though they fall, they shall not be utterly cast down. *There is hope of a tree, though it be cut down, that it will sprout again,* Job 14:7. (4.) That this distinguished remnant shall be the stay and support of the public interests. *The holy seed* in the soul is the sub-

stance of the man; a principle of grace reigning in the heart will keep life there; he that is *born of God* has *his seed remaining in him,* 1 Jn. 3:9. So the holy seed in the land is the substance of the land, keeps it from being quite dissolved, *and bears up the pillars of it,* Ps. 75:3. See *ch.* 1:9. Some read the foregoing clause with this, thus: *As the support at Shallecheth is in the elms and the oaks, so the holy seed is the substance thereof;* as the trees that grow on either side of the causeway (the raised way, or terrace-walk, that leads from the king's palace to the temple, 1 Ki. 10:5, at the gate of Shallecheth, 1 Chron, 26:16) support the causeway by keeping up the earth, which would otherwise be crumbling away, so the small residue of religious, serious, praying people, are the support of the state, and help to keep things together and save them from going to decay. Some make the holy seed to be Christ. The Jewish nation was *therefore* saved from utter ruin because *out of it, as concerning the flesh, Christ* was to come, Rom. 9:5. *Destroy it not, for that blessing is in it* (*ch.* 65:8); and when that blessing had come, it was soon destroyed. Now the consideration of this is designed for the support of the prophet in his work. Though far the greater part should perish in their unbelief, yet to some his word should be a savour of life unto life. Ministers do not wholly lose their labour if they be but instrumental to save one poor soul.

CHAPTER 7

This chapter is an occasional sermon, in which the prophet sings both of mercy and judgment to those that did not perceive or understand either; he piped unto them, but they danced not, mourned unto them, but they wept not. Here is, I. The consternation that Ahaz was in upon an attempt of the confederate forces of Syria and Israel against Jerusalem (*v.* 1, 2). II. The assurance which God, by the prophet, sent him for his encouragement, that the attempt should be defeated and Jerusalem should be preserved (*v.* 3–9). III. The confirmation of this by a sign which God gave to Ahaz, when he refused to ask one, referring to Christ, and our redemption by him (*v.* 10–16). IV. A threatening of the great desolation that God would bring upon Ahaz and his kingdom by the Assyrians, notwithstanding their escape from this present storm, because they went on still in their wickedness (*v.* 17–25). And this is written both for our comfort and for our admonition.

Verses 1–9

The prophet Isaiah had his commission renewed in the year that king Uzziah died, *ch.* 6:1. Jotham his son reigned, and reigned well, sixteen years. All that time, no doubt, Isaiah prophesied as he was commanded, and yet we have not in this book any of his prophecies dated in the reign of Jotham; but this, which is put first, was in the days of Ahaz the son of Jotham. Many excellent useful sermons he preached which were not published and left upon record; for, if all that was memorable had been written, *the world could not have contained the books,* Jn. 21:25. Perhaps in the reign of Ahaz, a wicked king, he had not opportunity to preach so much at court as in Jotham's time, and therefore then he wrote the more, for a testimony against them. Here is,

I. A very formidable design laid against Jerusalem by Rezin king of Syria and Pekah king of Israel, two neighbouring potentates, who had of late made descents upon Judah severally. At the end of the reign of Jotham, *the Lord began to send against Judah Rezin and Pekah,* 2 Ki. 15:37. But now, in the second or third year of the reign of Ahaz, encouraged by their former successes, they entered into an alliance against Judah. Because Ahaz, though he found the sword over his head, began his reign with idolatry, *God delivered him into the hand of the king of Syria and of the king of Israel* (2 Chr. 28:5), and a great slaughter they made in his kingdom, *v.* 6, 7. Flushed with this victory, they went up towards Jerusalem, the royal city, to war against it, to besiege it, and make themselves masters of it; but it proved in the issue that they could not gain their point. Note, The sin of a land brings foreign invasions upon it and betrays the most advantageous posts and passes to the enemy; and God sometimes makes one wicked nation a scourge to another; but judgment, ordinarily, begins at the house of God.

II. The great distress that Ahaz and his court were in when they received advice of this design: *It was told the house of David* that Syria and Ephraim had signed a league against Judah, *v.* 2. This degenerate royal family is called the *house of David,* to put us in mind of that article of God's covenant with David (Ps. 89:30–33), *If his children forsake my law, I will chasten their transgression with the rod; but my loving-kindness will I not utterly take away,* which is remarkably fulfilled in this chapter. News being brought that the two armies of Syria and Israel were joined, and had taken the field, the court, the city, and the country, were thrown into consternation; *The heart of Ahaz was moved with fear,* and then no wonder that *the heart of his people was so, as the trees of the wood are moved with the wind.* They were tossed and shaken, and put into a great disorder and confusion, were wavering and uncertain in their counsels, hurried hither and thither, and could not fix in any steady resolution. They yielded to the storm, and gave up all for gone, concluding it in vain to make any resistance. Now that which caused this fright was the sense of guilt and the weakness of their faith. They had made God their enemy, and knew not how to make him their friend, and therefore their fears tyrannised over them; while those whose consciences are kept *void of offence, and whose hearts are fixed, trusting in God, need not be afraid of evil tidings; though the earth be removed, yet will not they fear; but the wicked flee at the shaking of a leaf,* Lev. 26:36.

III. The orders and directions given to Isaiah to go and encourage Ahaz in his distress; not for his own sake (he deserved to hear nothing from God but words of terror, which might add affliction to his grief), but because he was a son of David and king of Judah. God had kindness for him for his father's sake, who must not be forgotten, and for his people's sake, who must not be abandoned, but would be encouraged if Ahaz were. Observe,

1. God appointed the prophet to meet Ahaz, though he did not send to the prophet to speak with him, nor desire him to enquire of the Lord for him (*v.* 3): *Go to meet Ahaz.* Note, God is often found of those who seek him not, much more will he be found of those who seek him diligently. He speaks comfort to many who not only are not worthy of it, but do not so much as enquire after it.

3. He ordered him to take his little son with him, because he carried a sermon in his name, *Shear-jashub — A remnant shall return.* The prophets sometimes recorded what they preached in the significant names of their children (as Hos. 1:4, 6, 9); therefore Isaiah's children are said to be *for signs, ch.* 8:18. This son was so called for the encouragement of those of God's people who were carried captive, assuring them that they should return, at least a remnant of them, which was more than they could pretend to merit; yet at this time God was better than his word; for he took care not only that a remnant should return, but the whole number of those whom the confederate forces of Syria and Israel had taken prisoners, 2 Chr. 28:15.

3. He directed him where he should find Ahaz. He was to meet with him not in the temple, or the synagogue, or royal chapel, but *at the end of the conduit of the upper pool,* where he was, probably with many of his servants about him, contriving how to order the water-works, so as to secure them to the city, or deprive the enemy of the benefits of them (*ch.* 22:9–11; 2 Chr. 32:3, 4), or giving some necessary directions for the fortifying of the city as well as they could; and perhaps finding every thing in a bad posture or defence, the conduit out of repair, as well as other things gone to decay, his fears increased, and he was now in greater perplexity than ever; therefore, *Go, meet him there.* Note, God sometimes sends comforts to his people very seasonably, and, what time they are most afraid, encourages them to trust in him.

4. He put words in his mouth, else the prophet would not have known how to bring a message of good to such a bad man, a sinner in Zion, that ought to be afraid; but God intended it for the support of faithful Israelites.

(1.) The prophet must rebuke their fears, and advise them by no means to yield to them, but keep their temper, and preserve the possession of their own souls (*v.* 4): *Take heed, and be quiet.* Note, In order to comfort there is need of caution; that we may be quiet, it is necessary that we take heed and watch against those things that threaten to disquiet us. "Fear not with this amazement, this fear, that weakens, and has torment; neither *let thy heart be tender,* so as to melt and fail within thee; but pluck up thy spirits, have a good heart on it, and be courageous; let not fear betray the succours which reason and religion offer for thy support." Note, Those who expect God should help them must help themselves, Ps. 27:14.

(2.) He must teach them to despise their enemies, not in pride, or security, or incogitancy (nothing more dangerous than so to despise an enemy), but in faith and dependence upon God. Ahaz's fear called them two powerful politic princes, for either of whom he was an unequal match, but, if united, he durst not look them in the face, nor make head against them. "No," says the prophet, "they are *two tails of smoking firebrands;* they are angry, they are fierce, they are furious, as firebrands, as fireballs; and they make one another worse by being in a confederacy, as sticks of fire put together burn the more violently. But they are only smoking firebrands: and where there is smoke there is some fire, but it may be not so much as was feared. Their threatenings will vanish into smoke. *Pharaoh king of Egypt is but a noise* (Jer. 46:17), and Rezin king of Syria but a smoke; and such are all the enemies of God's church, *smoking flax,* that will soon be quenched. Nay, they are but *tails* of smoking firebrands, in a manner burnt out already; their force is spent; they have consumed themselves with the heat of their own anger; you may put your foot on them, and tread them out." The two kingdoms of Syria and Israel were now near expiring. Note, The more we have an eye to God as a consuming fire the less reason we shall have to fear men, though they are ever so furious, nay, we shall be able to despise them as smoking firebrands.

(3.) He must assure them that the present design of these high allies (so they thought themselves) against Jerusalem should certainly be defeated and come to nothing, *v.* 5–7. [1.] That very thing which Ahaz thought most formidable is made the ground of their defeat — and that was the depth of their designs and the height of their hopes: *"Therefore* they shall be baffled and sent back with shame, *because they have taken evil counsel against thee,* which is an offence to God. These firebrands are a *smoke in his nose* (*ch.* 65:5), and therefore must be extinguished." *First,* They are very spiteful and malicious, and, therefore they shall not prosper. Judah had done them no wrong; they had no pretence to quarrel with Ahaz; but, without any reason, they said, *Let us go up against Judah, and vex it.* Note, Those that are vexatious cannot expect to be prosperous, those that love to do mischief cannot expect to do well. *Secondly,* They are very secure, and confident of success. They will vex Judah by going up against it; yet that is not all: they do not doubt but to make a breach in the wall of Jerusalem wide enough for them to march their army in at; or they count upon dissecting or dividing the kingdom into two parts, one for the king of Israel, the other for the king of Syria, who had agreed in one viceroy — *a king* to be *set in the midst of it, even the son of Tabeal,* some obscure person, it is uncertain whether a Syrian or an Israelite. So sure were they of gaining their point that they divided the prey before they had caught it. Note, Those that are most scornful are commonly least successful, for surely God scorns the scorners. [2.] God himself gives them his word that the attempt should not take effect (*v.* 7): *"Thus saith the Lord God,* the sovereign Lord of all, who *brings the counsel of the heathen to naught* (Ps. 33:10), *It shall not stand, neither shall it come to pass;* their measures shall all be broken, and they shall not be able to bring to pass their enterprise." Note, Whatever stands against God, or thinks to stand without him, cannot stand long. Man purposes, but God disposes; and *who is he that saith and it cometh to pass if the Lord commands it not or countermands it?* Lam. 3:37. See Prov. 19:21.

(4.) He must give them a prospect of the destruction of these enemies, at last, that were now such a terror to them. [1.] They should neither of them enlarge their dominions, nor push their conquests any further; *The head city of Syria is Damascus, and the head man of Damascus is Rezin;* this he glories in, and this let him be content with, *v.* 8. *The head city of Ephraim* has long been *Samaria, and the head man in Samaria is* now Pekah *the son of Remaliah.* These shall be made to know their own, their bounds are fixed, and they shall not pass them, to make themselves masters of the cities of Judah, much less to make Jerusalem their prey. Note, As God has appointed men the bounds of their habitation (Acts 17:26), so he has appointed princes the bounds of their dominion, within which they ought to confine themselves, and not encroach upon their neighbours' rights. [2.] Ephraim, which perhaps was the more malicious and forward enemy of the two, should shortly be quite rooted out, and should be so far from seizing other people's lands that they should not be able to hold their own. Interpreters are much at a loss how to compute the sixty-five years within which *Ephraim shall cease to be a people;* for the captivity of the ten tribes was but eleven years after this: and some make it a mistake of the transcriber, and think it should be read *within six and five years,* just eleven. But it is hard to allow that. Others make it to be sixty-five years from the time that the prophet Amos first foretold the ruin of the kingdom of the ten tribes; and some late interpreters make it to look as far forward as the last desolation of that country by Esarhaddon, which was about sixty-five years after this; then Ephraim was so broken that it was no more a people. Now it was the greatest folly in the world for those to be ruining their neighbours who were themselves marked for ruin, and so near to it. See what a prophet told them at this time, when they were triumphing over Judah, 2 Chr. 28:10. *Are there not with you, even with you, sins against the Lord your God?*

(5.) He must urge them to mix faith with those assurances which he had given them (*v.* 9): *"If you will not believe* what is said to you, *surely you shall not be established;* your shaken and disordered state shall not be established, your unquiet unsettled spirit shall not; though the things told you are very encouraging, yet they will not be so to you, unless you believe them, and be willing to take God's word." Note, The grace of faith is absolutely necessary to the quieting and composing of the mind in the midst of all the tosses of this present time, 2 Chr. 20:20.

Verses 10–16

Here, I. God, by the prophet, makes a gracious offer to Ahaz, to confirm the foregoing predictions, and his faith in them, by such sign or miracle as he should choose (*v.* 10, 11): *Ask thee a sign of the Lord thy God;* See here the divine faithfulness and veracity. God tells us nothing but what he is able and ready to prove. See his wonderful condescension to the children of men, in that he is so *willing to show to the heirs of promise the immutability of his counsel,* Heb. 6:17. He considers our frame, and that, living in a world of sense, we are apt to require sensible proofs, which therefore he has favoured us with in sacramental signs and seals. Ahaz was a bad man, yet God is called the Lord his God, because he was a child of Abraham and David, and of the covenants made with them. See how gracious God is even to the evil and unthankful; Ahaz is bidden to choose his sign, as Gideon about the fleece (Jdg. 6:37); let him ask for a sign in the air, or earth, or water, for God's power is the same in all.

II. Ahaz rudely refuses this gracious offer, and (which is not mannerly towards any superior) kicks at the courtesy, and puts a slight upon it (*v.* 12): *I will not ask.* The true reason why he would not ask for a sign was because, having a dependence upon the Assyrians, their forces, and their gods, for help, he would not thus far be beholden to the God of Israel, or lay himself under obligations to him. He would not ask a sign for the confirming of his faith because he resolved to persist in his unbelief, and would indulge his doubts and distrusts; yet he pretends a pious reason: *I will not tempt the Lord;* as if it would be a tempting of God to do that which God himself invited and directed him to do. Note, A secret disaffection to God is often disguised with the specious colours of respect to him; and those who are resolved that they will not trust God yet pretend that they will not tempt him.

III. The prophet reproves him and his court, him and the house of David, the whole royal family, for their contempt of prophecy, and the little value they had for divine revelation (*v.* 13) *"Is it a small thing for you to weary men* by your oppression and tyranny, with which you make yourselves burdensome and odious to all mankind? But *will you weary my God also* with the affronts you put upon him?" As the unjust judge that neither *feared God nor regarded man,* Lu. 18:2. *You have wearied the Lord with your words,* Mal. 2:17. Nothing is more grievous to the God of heaven than to be distrusted. *"Will you weary my God?* Will you suppose him to be tired and unable to help you, or to be weary of doing you good? Whereas *the youths may faint and be weary,* you may have tired all your friends, *the Creator of the ends of the earth faints not, neither is weary." ch.* 40:28–31. Or this: "In affronting the prophets, you think you put a slight only upon men like yourselves, and consider not that you affront God himself, whose messengers they are, and put a slight upon him, who will resent it accordingly." The prophet here calls God his God with a great deal of pleasure: Ahaz would not say, He is my God, though the prophet had invited him to say so (*v.* 11): *The Lord thy God;* but Isaiah will say, "He is mine." Note, Whatever others do, we must avouch the Lord for ours and abide by him.

IV. The prophet, in God's name, gives them a sign: "You will not ask a sign, but the unbelief of man shall not make the promise of God of no effect: *The Lord himself shall give you a sign* (*v.* 14), a double sign."

1. "A sign in general of his good-will to Israel and to the house of David. You may conclude it that he has mercy in store for you, and that you are not forsaken of your God, how great soever your present distress and danger are; for of your nation, of your family, the Messiah is to be born, and you cannot be destroyed while that blessing is in you, which shall be introduced," (1.) "In a glorious manner; for, whereas you have been often told that he should be born among you, I am now further to tell you that he shall be born of a virgin, which will signify both the divine power and the divine purity with which he shall be brought into the world, — that he shall be a extraordinary person, for he shall not be born by ordinary generation, — and that he shall be a holy thing, not stained with the common pollutions of the human nature, therefore incontestably fit to have the throne of his father David given him." Now this, though it was to be accomplished above 500 years after, was a most encouraging sign to the house of David (and to them, under that title, this prophecy is directed, *v.* 13) and an assurance that God would not cast them off. Ephraim did indeed envy Judah (*ch.* 11:13) and sought the ruin of that kingdom, but could not prevail; for the sceptre should never depart from Judah till the coming of Shiloh, Gen. 49:10. Those whom God designs for the great salvation may take that for a sign to them that they shall not be swallowed up by any trouble they meet with in the way. (2.) The Messiah shall be introduced on a glorious errand, wrapped up in his glorious name: They *shall call his name Immanuel — God with us,* God in our nature, God at peace with us, in covenant with us. This was fulfilled in their calling him *Jesus — a Saviour* (Mt. 1:21–25), for, if he had not been *Immanuel — God with us,* he could not have been *Jesus — a Saviour.* Now this was a further sign of God's favour to the house of David and the tribe of Judah; for he that intended to work this great salvation among them no doubt would work out for them all those other salvations which were to be the types and figures of this, and as it were preludes to this. "Here is a sign for you, not in the depth nor in the height, but in the prophecy, in the promise, in the covenant made with David, which you are no strangers to. The promised seed shall be Immanuel, *God with us;* let that word comfort you (*ch.* 8:10), that *God is with us,* and (*v.* 8) that your land is Immanuel's land. Let not *the heart of the house of David* be moved thus (*v.* 2), nor let Judah fear the setting up of the son of Tabeal (*v.* 6), for nothing can cut off the entail on the Son of David that shall be Immanuel." Note, The strongest consolations, in time of trouble, are those which are borrowed from Christ, our relation to him, our interest in him, and our expectations of him and from him. Of this child it is further foretold (*v.* 15) that though he shall not be born like other children, but of a virgin, yet he shall be really and truly man, and shall be nursed and brought up like other children: *Butter and honey shall he eat,* as other children do, particularly the children of that land which *flowed with milk and honey.* Though he be conceived by the power of the Holy Ghost, yet he shall not therefore be fed with angels' food, but, as it becomes him, shall be *in all things made like unto his brethren,* Heb. 2:17. Nor shall he, though born thus by extraordinary generation, be a man immediately, but, as other children, shall advance gradually through the several states of infancy, childhood, and youth, to that of manhood, and growing in wisdom and stature, shall at length wax strong in spirit, and come to maturity, so as to know how *to refuse the evil and choose the good.* See Lu. 2:40, 52. Note, Children are fed when they are little that they may be taught and instructed when they have grown up; they have their maintenance in order to their education.

2. Here is another sign in particular of the speedy destruction of these potent princes that were now a terror to Judah, *v.* 16. "Before *this* child (so it should be read), this child which I have now in my arms" (he means not Immanuel, but Shear-jashub his own son, whom he was ordered to take with him for a sign, *v.* 3), "before this *child shall know how to refuse the evil and choose the good"* (and those who saw what his present stature and forwardness were would easily conjecture how long that would be), "before this child be three or four years older, *the land that thou abhorrest,* these confederate forces of Israelites and Syrians, which thou hast such an enmity to and standest in such dread of, *shall be forsaken of both their kings,* both Pekah and Rezin," who were in so close an alliance that they seemed as if they were the kings of but one kingdom. This was fully accomplished; for within two or three years after this, Hoshea conspired against Pekah, and slew him (2 Ki. 15:30), and, before that, the king of Assyria took Damascus, and slew Rezin, 2 Ki. 16:9. Nay, there was a present event, which happened immediately, and when this child carried the prediction of in his name, which was a pledge and earnest of this future event. *Shear-jashub* signifies *The remnant shall return,* which doubtless points at the wonderful return of those 200,000 captives whom Pekah and Rezin had carried away, who were brought back, not by might or power, but by the Spirit of the Lord of hosts. Read the story, 2 Chr. 28:8–15. The prophetical naming of this child having thus had its accomplishment, no doubt this, which was further added concerning him, should have its accomplishment likewise, that Syria and Israel should be deprived of both their kings. One mercy from God encourages us to hope for another, if it engages us to prepare for another.

Verses 17–25

After the comfortable promises made to Ahaz as a branch of the house of David, here follow terrible threatenings against him, as a degenerate branch of that house; for though the loving-kindness of God shall not be utterly taken away, for the sake of David and the covenant made with him, yet his iniquity shall be *chastened with the rod,* and his sin with stripes. Let those that will not mix faith with the promises of God expect to hear the alarms of his threatenings.

I. The judgment threatened is very great, *v.* 17. It is very great, for it is general; it shall be brought upon the prince himself (high as he is, he shall not be out of the reach of it), and upon the people, the whole body of the nation, and upon the royal family, *upon* all *thy father's house;* it shall be a judgment entailed on posterity, and shall go along with the royal blood. It is very great, for it shall be unprecedented — *days that have not come;* so dark, so gloomy, so melancholy, as never were the like since the revolt of the ten tribes, when Ephraim departed from Judah, which was indeed a sad time to the house of David. Note, The longer men continue in sin the sorer punishments they have reason to expect. It is the Lord that will bring these days upon them, for our times are in his hand, and who can resist or escape the judgments he brings?

II. The enemy that should be employed as the instrument of this judgment is the king of Assyria. Ahaz reposed great confidence in that prince for help against the confederate powers of Israel and Syria, and minded the less what God said to him by his prophet for his encouragement because he built much upon his interest in the king of Assyria, and had meanly promised to be his servant if he would send him some succours; he had also, made him a present of gold and silver, for which he drained the treasures both of church and state, 2 Ki. 16:7, 8. Now God threatens that that king of Assyria whom he made his stay instead of God should become a scourge to him. He was so speedily; for, when he *came to him, he distressed him, but strengthened him not* (2 Chr. 28:20), the reed not only broke under him, but ran into his hand, and pierced it, and thenceforward the kings of Assyria were, for a long time, grieving thorns to Judah, and gave them a great deal of trouble. Note, The creature that we make our hope commonly proves our hurt. The king of Assyria, not long after this, made himself master of the ten tribes, carried them captive, and laid their country waste, so as fully to answer the prediction here; and perhaps it may refer to that, as an explication of *v.* 8, where it is foretold that Ephraim shall be broken, that it shall not be a people; and it is easy to suppose that the prophet (at *v.* 17) turns his speech to the king of Israel, denouncing God's judgments against him for invading Judah. But the expositors universally understand it of Ahaz and his kingdom. Now observe, 1. Summons given to the invaders (*v.* 18): *The Lord shall whistle for the fly and the bee.* See *ch.* 5:26. Enemies that seem as contemptible as a fly or a bee, and are as easily crushed, shall yet, when God pleases, do his work as effectually as lions and young lions. Though they are as far distant from one another as the rivers of Egypt and the land of Assyria, yet they shall punctually meet to join in this work when God commands their attendance; for, when God has work to do, he will not be at a loss for instruments to do it with. 2. Possession taken by them, *v.* 19. It should seem as if the country were in no condition to make resistance. They find no difficulties in forcing their way, but *come and rest all of them in the desolate valleys,* which the inhabitants had deserted upon the first alarm, and left them a cheap and easy prey to the invaders. They shall come and rest in the low grounds like swarms of flies and bees, and shall render themselves impregnable by taking shelter in the holes of the rocks, as bees often do, and showing themselves formidable by appearing openly upon all thorns and all bushes; so generally shall the land be overspread with them. These bees shall knit upon the thorns and bushes, and there rest undisturbed. 3. Great desolations made, and the country generally depopulated (*v.* 20): *The Lord shall shave the hair of the head, and beard, and feet;* he shall sweep all away, as the leper, when he was cleansed, *shaved off all his hair,* Lev. 14:8, 9. This is done with a razor which is hired, either which God has hired (as if he had none of his own; but what he hires, and whom he employs in any service for him, he will pay for. See Eze. 29:18, 19), or which Ahaz has hired for his assistance. God will make that to be an instrument of his destruction which he hired into his service. Note, Many are beaten with that arm of flesh which they trusted to rather than to the arm of the Lord, and which they were at a great expense upon, when by faith and prayer they might have found cheap and easy succour in God. 4. The consequences of this general depopulation. (1.) The flocks of cattle shall be all destroyed, so that a man who had herds and flocks in abundance shall be stripped of them all by the enemy, and shall with much ado save for his own use a young cow and two sheep — a poor stock (*v.* 21), yet he shall think himself happy in having any left. (2.) The few cattle that are left shall have such a large compass of ground to feed in that *they shall give abundance of milk,* and very good milk, such as shall produce butter enough, *v.* 22. There shall also be such want of men that the milk of one cow and two sheep shall serve a whole family, which used to keep abundance of servants and consume a great deal, but is now reduced. (3.) The breed of cattle shall be destroyed; so that those who used to eat flesh (as the Jews commonly did) shall be necessitated to confine themselves to butter and honey, for there shall be no flesh for them; and the country shall be so depopulated that there shall be butter and honey enough for the few that are left in it. (4.) Good land, that used to be let well, shall be all overrun with briers and thorns (*v.* 23); where there used to be a thousand vines planted, for which the tenants used to pay a thousand shekels, or pieces of silver, yearly rent, there shall be nothing now but briers and thorns, no profit either for landlord or tenant, all being laid waste by the army of the invaders. Note, God can soon turn a fruitful land into barrenness; and it is just with him to turn vines into briers if we, instead of bringing forth grapes to him, bring forth wild grapes, *ch.* 5:4. (5.) The implements of husbandry shall be turned into instruments of war, *v.* 24. The whole land having become briers and thorns, the grounds that men used to come to with sickles and pruning-hooks to gather in the fruits they shall now come to with arrows and bows, to hunt for wild beasts in the thickets, or to defend themselves from the robbers that lurk in the bushes, seeking for prey, or to kill the serpents and venomous beasts that are hid there. This denotes a very sad change of the face of that pleasant land. But what melancholy change is there which sin will not make with a people? (6.) Where briers and thorns were wont to be of use and to do good service, even in the hedges, for the defence of the enclosed grounds, they shall be plucked up, and all laid in common. There shall be briers and thorns in abundance where they should not be, but none where they should be, *v.* 25. *The hills that shall be digged with the mattock,* for special use, from which the cattle used to be kept off with the fear of briers and thorns, shall now be thrown open, the *hedges broken down for the boar out of the wood* to waste it, Ps. 80:12, 13. It shall be left at large for oxen to run in and less cattle. See the effect of sin and the curse; it has made the earth a forest of thorns and thistles, except as it is forced into some order by the constant care and labour of man. And see what folly it is to set our hearts upon possessions of lands, be they every so fruitful, ever so pleasant; if they lie ever so little neglected and uncultivated, or if they be abused by a wasteful careless heir or tenant, or the country be laid waste by war, they will soon become frightful deserts. Heaven is a paradise not subject to such changes.

CHAPTER 8

This chapter, and the four next that follow it (to chap. 13) are all one continued discourse or sermon, the scope of which is to show the great destruction that should now shortly be brought upon the kingdom of Israel, and the great disturbance that should be given to the kingdom of Judah by the king of Assyria, and that both were for their sins; but rich provision is made of comfort for those that feared God in those dark times, referring especially to the days of the Messiah. In this chapter we have, I. A prophecy of the destruction of the confederate kingdoms of Syria and Israel by the king of Assyria (*v.* 1–4). II. Of the desolations that should be made by that proud victorious prince in the land of Israel and Judah (*v.* 5–8). III. Great encouragement given to the people of God in the midst of those distractions; they are assured, 1. That the enemies shall not gain their point against them (*v.* 9, 10). 2. That if they kept up the fear of God, and kept down the fear of man, they should find God their refuge (*v.* 11–14), and while others stumbled, and fell into despair, they should be enabled to wait on God, and should see themselves reserved for better times (*v.* 15–18). Lastly, He gives a necessary caution to all, at their peril, not to consult with familiar spirits, for they would thereby throw themselves into despair, but to keep close to the word of God (*v.* 19–22). And these counsels and these comforts will still be of use to us in time of trouble.

Verses 1–8

In these verses we have a prophecy of the successes of the king of Assyria against Damascus, Samaria, and Judah, that the two former should be laid waste by him, and the last greatly frightened. Here we have,

I. Orders given to the prophet to write this prophecy, and publish it to be seen and read of all men, and to leave it upon record, that when the thing came to pass they might know that God had sent him; for that was one end of prophecy, Jn. 14:29. He must *take a great roll,* which would contain those five chapters fairly written in words at length; and he must write in it all that he had foretold concerning the king of Assyria's invading the country; he must *write it with a man's pen,* in the usual way and style of writing, so as that it might be legible and intelligible by all. See Hab. 2:2, *Write the vision, and make it plain.* Those that speak and write of the things of God should avoid obscurity, and study to speak and write so as to be understood, 1 Co. 14:19. Those that write for men should write with a man's pen, and not covet the pen or tongue of angels. And forasmuch as it is usual to put some short, but significant comprehensive title before books that are published, the prophet is directed to call his book *Maher-shalal-hash-baz — Make speed to the spoil, hasten to the prey,* intimating that the Assyrian army should come upon them with great speed and make great spoil. By this title the substance and meaning of the book would be enquired after by those that heard of it, and remembered by those that had read it or heard it read. It is sometimes a good help to memory to put much matter in few words, which serve as handles by which we take hold of more.

II. The care of the prophet to get this record well attested (*v.* 2): *I took unto me faithful witnesses to record;* he wrote the prophecy in their sight and presence, and made them subscribe their names to it, that they might be ready, if afterwards there should be occasion, to make oath of it, that the prophet had so long before foretold the descent which the Assyrians made upon that country. He names his witnesses for the greater certainty, that they might be appealed to by any. They were two in number (for *out of the mouth of two witnesses shall every word be established*); one was Uriah the priest; he is mentioned in the story of Ahaz, but for none of his good deeds, for he humoured Ahaz with an idolatrous altar (2 Ki. 16:10, 11); however, at this time, no exception lay against him, being a faithful witness. See what full satisfaction the prophets took care to give to all persons concerned of the sincerity of their intentions, that we might know with a full assurance the *certainty of the things wherein we have been instructed,* and that we have *not followed cunningly-devised fables.*

III. The making of the title of his book the name of his child, that it might be the more taken notice of and the more effectually perpetuated, *v.* 3. His wife (because the wife of a prophet) is called *the prophetess;* she *conceived and bore a son,* another son, who must carry a sermon in his name, as the former had done (*ch.* 7:3), but with this difference, that spoke mercy, *Shear-jashub — The remnant shall return;* but, that being slighted, this speaks judgment, *Maher-shalal-hash-baz — In making speed to the spoil he shall hasten, or he has hastened, to the prey.* The prophecy is doubled, even in this one name, for the thing was certain. *I will hasten my word,* Jer. 1:12. Every time the child was called by his name, or any part of it, it would serve as a memorandum of the judgments approaching. Note, It is good for us often to put ourselves in mind of the changes and troubles we are liable to in this world, and which perhaps are at the door. When we look with pleasure on our children it should be with the allay of this thought, We know not what they are yet reserved for.

IV. The prophecy itself, which explains this mystical name.

1. That Syria and Israel, who were now in confederacy against Judah, should in a very little time become an easy prey to the king of Assyria and his victorious army (*v.* 4): *"Before the child,* now newly born and named, shall have *knowledge to cry, My father, and My mother"* (which are usually some of the first things that children know and some of the first words that children speak), that is, "in about a year or two, *the riches of Damascus, and the spoil of Samaria,* those cities that are now so secure themselves and so formidable to their neighbours, *shall be taken away before the king of Assyria,* who shall plunder both city and country, and send the best effects of both into his own land, to enrich that, and as trophies of his victory." Note, Those that spoil others must expect to be themselves spoiled (*ch.* 33:1); for the Lord is righteous, and those that are troublesome shall be troubled.

2. That forasmuch as there were many in Judah that were secretly in the interests of Syria and Israel, and were disaffected to the house of David, God would chastise them also by the king of Assyria, who should create a great deal of vexation to Judah, as was foretold, *ch.* 7:17. Observe, (1.) What was the sin of the discontented party in Judah (*v.* 6): *This people,* whom the prophet here speaks to, *refuse the waters of Shiloah that go softly,* despise their own country and the government of it, and love to run it down, because it does not make so great a figure, and so great a noise, in the world, as some other kings and kingdoms do. They refuse the comforts which God's prophets offer them from the word of God, speaking to them in a still small voice, and make nothing of them; but *they rejoice in Rezin and Remaliah's son,* who were the enemies of their country, and were now actually invading it; they cried them up as brave men, magnified their policies and strength, applauded their conduct, were well pleased with their successes, and were hearty well-wishers to their designs, and resolved to desert and go over to them. Such vipers does many a state foster in its bosom, that eat its bread, and yet adhere to its enemies, and are ready to quit its interests if they but seem to totter. (2.) The judgment which God would bring upon them for this sin. The same king of Assyria that should lay Ephraim and Syria waste should be a scourge and terror to those of their party in Judah, *v.* 7, 8. Because they *refuse the waters of Shiloah,* and will not accommodate themselves to the government God has set over them, but are uneasy under it, *therefore the Lord brings upon them the waters of the river, strong and many,* the river Euphrates. They slighted the land of Judah, because it had no river to boast of comparable to that; the river at Jerusalem was a very inconsiderable one. "Well," says God, "if you be such admirers of Euphrates, you shall have enough of it; the king of Assyria, whose country lies upon that river, shall come with his glory, with his great army, which you cry up as his glory, despising your own king because he cannot bring such an army as that into the field; God shall bring that army upon you." If we value men, if we over-value them, for their worldly wealth and power, it is just with God to make them thereby a scourge to us. It is used as an argument against magnifying rich

men that *rich men oppress us,* Jam. 2:3, 5. Let us be best pleased with the waters of Shiloah, that go softly, for rapid streams are dangerous. It is threatened that the Assyrian army should break in upon them like a deluge, or inundation of waters, bearing down all before it, should come up over all his channels, and overflow all his banks. It would be to no purpose to oppose or withstand them. Sennacherib and his army should pass through Judah, and meet with so little resistance that it should look more like a march through the country than a descent upon it. *He shall reach even to the neck,* that is, he shall advance so far as to lay siege to Jerusalem, the head of the kingdom, and nothing but that shall be kept out of his hands; for that was the holy city. Note, In the greatest deluge of trouble God can and will keep the head of his people above water, and so preserve their comforts and spiritual lives; the waters that come into their souls may reach to the neck (Ps. 69:1), but there shall their proud waves be stayed. And here is another comfortable intimation that though the stretching out of the wings of the Assyrian, that bird of prey, though the right and left wing of his army, should fill the breadth of the land of Judah, yet still it was Immanuel's land. It is *thy land, O Immanuel!* It was to be Christ's land; for there he was to be born, and live, and preach, and work miracles. He was Zion's King, and therefore had a peculiar interest in and concern for that land. Note, The lands that Immanuel owns for his, as he does all those lands that own him, though they may be deluged, shall not be destroyed; *for, when the enemy shall come in like a flood,* Immanuel shall secure his own, and shall *lift up a standard against him, ch.* 59:19.

Verses 9–15

The prophet here returns to speak of the present distress that Ahaz and his court and kingdom were in upon account of the threatening confederacy of the ten tribes and the Syrians against them. And in these verses,

I. He triumphs over the invading enemies, and, in effect, sets them at defiance, and bids them do their worst (*v.* 9, 10): *"O you people, you of far countries,* give ear to what the prophet says to you in God's name." 1. "We doubt not but you will now make your utmost efforts against Judah and Jerusalem. You *associate yourselves* in a strict alliance. You *gird yourselves,* and again you *gird yourselves;* you prepare for action; you address yourselves to it with resolution; you gird on your swords; you gird up your loins. You animate and encourage yourselves and one another with all the considerations you can think of: you *take counsel together,* call councils of war, and all heads are at work about the proper methods for making yourselves masters of the land of Judah. *You speak the word;* you come to resolutions concerning it, and are not always deliberating; you determine what to do, and are very confident of the success of it, that the matter will be accomplished with a word's speaking." Note, It is with a great deal of policy, resolution, and assurance, that the church's enemies carry on their designs against it; and abundance of pains they take to roll a stone that will certainly return upon them. 2. "This is to let you know that all your efforts will be ineffectual. You cannot, you shall not, gain your point, nor carry the day: *You shall be broken in pieces.* Though you associate yourselves, though you gird yourselves, though you proceed with all the policy and precaution imaginable, yet, I tell you again and again, all your projects shall be baffled, *you shall be broken in pieces.* Nay, not only shall your attempts be ruined, but your attempts shall be your ruin; you shall be broken by those designs you have formed against Jerusalem: *Your counsels shall come to nought;* for there is no wisdom nor counsel against the Lord. Your resolves will not be put in execution; they shall not stand. You speak the word, but *who is he that saith, and it cometh to pass, if the Lord commandeth it not?* What sets up itself against God, and his cause and counsel, cannot stand, but must inevitably fall. *For God is with us"* (this refers to the name of *Immanuel — God with us*); "the Messiah is to be born among us, and a people designed for such an honour cannot be given up to utter ruin. We have now the special presence of God with us in his temple, his oracles, his promises, and these are our defence. God is with us; he is on our side, to take our part and fight for us; and, *if God be for us, who can be against us?"* Thus does the daughter of Zion despise them.

II. He comforts and encourages the people of God with the same comforts and encouragements which he himself had received. The attempt made upon them was very formidable; the house of David, the court and royal family, were at their wits' end (*ch.* 7:2), and then no marvel if the people were in a consternation. Now,

1. The prophet tells us how he was himself taught of God not to give way to such amazing fears as the people were disturbed with, nor to run into the same measures with them (*v.* 11): *"The Lord spoke to me with a strong hand not to walk in the way of this people,* not to say as they say nor do as they do, not to entertain the same frightful apprehensions of things nor to approve of their projects of making peace upon any terms, or calling in the help of the Assyrians." God instructed the prophet not to go down the stream. Note, (1.) There is a proneness in the best of men to be frightened at threatening clouds, especially when fears are epidemic. We are all too apt to walk in the way of the people we live among, though it be not a good way. (2.) Those whom God loves and owns he will instruct and enable to swim against the stream of common corruptions, particularly of common fears. He will find ways to teach his own people not to walk in the way of other people, but in a sober singularity. (3.) Corruption is sometimes so active in the hearts even of good men that they have need to be taught their duty with a strong hand, and it is God's prerogative to teach so, for he only can give an understanding and overpower the contradiction of unbelief and prejudice. He can teach the heart; and herein none teaches like him. (4.) Those that are to teach others have need to be themselves well instructed in their duty, and then they teach most powerfully when they teach experimentally. The word that comes from the heart is most likely to reach to the heart; and what we are ourselves by the grace of God instructed in we should, as we are able, teach others also.

2. Now what is it that he says to God's people?

(1.) He cautions them against a sinful fear, *v.* 12. It seems it was the way of this people at this time, and fear is catching. He whose heart fails him makes his brethren's heart to fail, like his heart (Deu. 20:8); therefore *Say you not, A confederacy, to all those to whom this people shall say, A confederacy;* that is, [1.] "Be not associated with them in the confederacies they are projecting and forecasting for. Do not join with those that, for the securing of themselves, are for making a league with the Assyrians, through unbelief, and distrust of God and their cause. Do not come into any such confederacy." Note, It concerns us, in time of trouble, to watch against all such fears as put us upon taking any indirect courses for our own security. [2.] "Be not afraid of the confederacies they frighten themselves and one another with. Do not distress yourselves with the apprehension of a confederacy upon every thing that stirs, nor, when any little thing is amiss, cry out presently, There is a plot, a plot. When they talk what dismal news there is, *Syria is joined with Ephraim,* what will become of us? must we fight, or must we flee, or must we yield? do not you fear their fear: *Be not afraid of the signs of heaven,* as the heathen are, Jer. 10:2. Be not afraid of evil tidings on earth, but let your hearts be fixed. Fear not that which they fear, nor be afraid as they are. Be not put into such a fright as causes trembling and shaking;" so the word signifies. Note, When the church's enemies have sinful confederacies on foot the church's friends should watch against the sinful fears of those confederacies.

(2.) He advises them to a gracious religious fear: *But sanctify the Lord of hosts himself, v.* 13. Note, The believing fear of God is a special preservative against the disquieting fear of man; see 1 Pt. 3:14, 15, where this is quoted, and applied to suffering Christians. [1.] We must look upon God as the Lord of hosts, that has all power in his hand and all creatures at his beck. [2.] We must sanctify him accordingly, give him the glory due to that name, and behave towards him as those that believe him to be a holy God. [3.] We must make him our fear, the object of our fear, and make him our dread, keep up a reverence of his providence and stand in awe of his sovereignty, be afraid of his displeasure and silently acquiesce in all his disposals. Were we but duly affected with the greatness and glory of God, we should see the pomp of our enemies eclipsed and clouded, and all their power restrained and under check; see Neh. 4:14. Those that are *afraid of the reproach*

of men forget the Lord their Maker, ch. 51:12, 13. Compare Lu. 12:4, 5.

(3.) He assures them of a holy security and serenity of mind in so doing (*v.* 14): *"He shall be for a sanctuary;* make him your fear, and you shall find him your hope, your help, your defence, and your mighty deliverer. He will sanctify and preserve you. He will be for a sanctuary," [1.] "To make you holy. He will be your sanctification;" so some read it. If we sanctify God by our praises, he will sanctify us by his grace. [2.] "To make you easy. He will be your sanctuary," to which you may flee for safety, and where you are privileged form all the arrests of fear; you shall find an inviolable refuge and security in him, and see yourselves our of the reach of danger. Those that truly fear God shall not need to fear any evil.

III. He threatens the ruin of the ungodly and unbelieving, both in Judah and Israel. They have no part nor lot in the foregoing comforts; that God who will be a sanctuary to those who trust in him will be a stone of stumbling, and a rock of offence, to those who *leave these waters of Shiloah, and rejoice in Rezin and Remaliah's son,* (*v.* 6), who make the creature their fear and their hope, *v.* 14, 15. The prophet foresees that the greatest part of both the houses of Israel would not *sanctify the Lord of hosts,* and to them he would be *for a gin and a snare;* he would be a terror to them, as he would be a support and stay to those that trusted in him. Instead of profiting by the word of God, they should be offended at it; and the providences of God, instead of leading them to him, would drive them from him. What was a savour of life unto life to others would be a savour of death unto death to them. "So that *many among them shall stumble and fall;* they shall fall both into sin and into ruin; they shall fall by the sword, shall be taken prisoners, and go into captivity." Note, If the things of God be an offence to us, they will be an undoing to us. Some apply this to the unbelieving Jews, who rejected Christ, and to whom he became a stone of stumbling; for the apostle quotes this scripture with application to all those who persisted in their unbelief of the gospel of Christ (1 Pt. 2:8); to them he is a rock of offence, because, being disobedient to the word, they stumble at it.

Verses 16–22

In these verses we have,

I. The unspeakable privilege which the people of God enjoy in having the oracles of God consigned over to them, and being entrusted with the sacred writings. That they may sanctify the Lord of hosts, may make him their fear and find him their sanctuary, *bind up the testimony, v.* 16. Note, It is a great instance of God's care of his church and love to it that he has lodged in it the invaluable treasure of divine revelation. 1. It is a *testimony* and a *law;* not only this prophecy is so, which must therefore be preserved safely for the comfort of God's people in the approaching times of trouble and distress, but the whole word of God is so; God has attested it, and he has enjoined it. As a testimony it directs our faith; as a law it directs our practice; and we ought both to subscribe to the truths of it and to submit to the precepts of it. 2. This testimony and this law are bound up and sealed, for we are not to add to them nor diminish from them; they are a letter from God to man, folded up and sealed, a proclamation under the broad seal. The binding up and sealing of the Old Testament signified that the full explication of many of the prophecies of it was reserved for the New-Testament times. Dan. 12:4, *Seal the book till the time of the end;* but what was then bound up and sealed is now open and unsealed, and *revealed unto babes,* Mt. 11:25. Yet with reference to the other world, and the future state, still the testimony is bound up and sealed, for we know but in part, and prophesy but in part. 3. They are lodged as a sacred deposit in the hands of the disciples of *the children of the prophets and the covenant,* Acts 3:25. This is the good thing which is committed to them, and which they are charged with the custody of, 2 Tim. 1:13, 14. Those that had prophets for their tutors must still keep close to the written word.

II. The good use which we ought to make of this privilege. This we are taught,

1. By the prophet's own practice and resolutions, *v.* 17, 18. He embraced the law ad the testimony, and he had the comfort of them, in the midst of the many discouragements he met with. Note, Those ministers can best rec-

ommend the word of God to others that have themselves found the satisfaction of relying upon it. Observe,

(1.) The discouragements which the prophet laboured under. He specifies two: — [1.] The frowns of God, not so much upon himself, but upon his people, whose interests lay very near his heart: "He *hides his face from the house of Jacob*, and seems at present to neglect them, and lay them under the tokens of his displeasure." The prophet was himself employed in revealing God's wrath against them, and yet grieved thus for it, as one that did not desire the woeful day. If the house of Jacob forsake the God of Jacob, let it not be thought strange that he hides his face from them. [2.] The contempt and reproaches of men, not only upon himself, but upon his disciples, among whom the law and the testimony were sealed: *I and the children whom the Lord has given me are for signs and wonders;* we are gazed at as monsters or outlandish people, pointed at as we go along the streets. Probably the prophetical names that were given to his children were ridiculed and bantered by the profane scoffers of the town. *I am as a wonder unto many,* Ps. 71:7. God's people are the world's wonder (Zec. 3:8) for their singularity, and because they run not with them to the same excess of riot, 1 Pt. 4:4. The prophet was herein a type of Christ; for this is quoted (Heb. 2:13) to prove that believers are Christ's children: *Behold, I and the children whom God has given me.* Parents must look upon their children as God's gifts, his gracious gifts; Jacob did so, Gen. 33:5. Ministers must look upon their converts as their children, and be tender of them accordingly (1 Th. 2:7), and as the children whom God has given them; for, whatever good we are instrumental of to others, it is owing to the grace of God. Christ looks upon believers as his children, whom the Father gave him (Jn. 17:6), and both he and they are for signs and wonders, spoken against (Lu. 2:34), every where spoken against, Acts 28:22.

(2.) The encouragement he took in reference to these discouragements. [1.] He saw the hand of God in all that which was discouraging to him, and kept his eye upon that. Whatever trouble the house of Jacob is in, it comes from God's hiding his face; nay, whatever contempt was put upon him or his friends, it is from the Lord of hosts; he has bidden Shimei curse David, Job 19:13; 30:11. [2.] He saw God dwelling in Mount Zion, manifesting himself to his people, and ready to hear their prayers and receive their homage. Though, for the present, he hide his face from the house of Jacob, yet they know where to find him and recover the sight of him; he dwells in Mount Zion. [3.] He therefore resolved to wait upon the Lord and to look for him; to attend his motions even while he hid his face, and to expect with a humble assurance his returns in a way of mercy. Those that wait upon God by faith and prayer may look for him with hope and joy. When we have not sensible comforts we must still keep up our observance of God and obedience to him, and then wait awhile; *at evening time it shall be light.*

2. By the counsel and advice which he gives to his disciples, among whom the law and the testimony were sealed, to whom were committed the lively oracles.

(1.) He supposes they would be tempted, in the day of their distress, to consult *those that had familiar spirits,* that dealt with the devil, asked his advice, and desired to be informed by him concerning things to come, that they might take their measures accordingly. Thus Saul, when he was in straits, made his application to the witch of Endor (1 Sa. 28:7, 15), and Ahaziah to the god of Ekron, 2 Ki. 1:2. These conjurors had strange fantastic gestures and tones: They *peeped and muttered;* they muffled their heads, that they could neither see nor be seen plainly, but peeped and were peeped at. Or both the words here used may refer to their voice and manner of speaking; they delivered what they had to say with a low, hollow, broken sound, scarcely articulate, and sometimes in a puling or mournful tone, like a crane, or a swallow, or a dove, *ch.* 38:14. They spoke not with that boldness and plainness which the prophets of the Lord spoke with, but as those who desire to amuse people rather than to instruct them; yet there were those who were so wretchedly sottish as to seek to them and to court others to do so, even the prophet's hearers, who knew better things, whom therefore the prophet warns not to say, *A confederacy* with such. There were express laws against this wickedness (Lev. 19:31; 20:27), and yet it was found in Israel, is found even in Christian nations; but let

all that have any sense of religion show it, by startling at the thought of it. *Get thee behind me, Satan.* Dread the use of spells and charms, and consulting those that by hidden arts pretend to tell fortunes, cure diseases, or discover things lost; for this is a heinous crime, and, in effect, denies the God that is above.

(2.) He furnishes them with an answer to this temptation, puts words into their mouths. "If any go about thus to ensnare you, give them this reply: *Should not a people seek to their God?* What! *for the living to the dead!*" [1.] "Tell them it is a principle of religion that a people ought to seek unto their God; now Jehovah is our God, and therefore to him we ought to seek, and to consult with him, and not with those that have familiar spirits. *All people will thus walk in the name of their God,* Mic. 4:5. Those that made the hosts of heaven their gods *sought unto them,* Jer. 8:2. Should not a people under guilt, and in trouble, seek to their God for pardon and peace? Should not a people in doubt, in want, and in danger, seek to their God for direction, supply, and protection? Since the Lord is our God, and we are his people, it is certainly our duty to seek him." [2.] "Tell them it is an instance of the greatest folly in the world to seek for living men to dead idols." What can be more absurd than to seek to lifeless images for life and living comforts, or to expect that our friends that are dead should do that for us, when we deify them and pray to them, which our living friends cannot do? The *dead know not any thing,* nor is there with them *any device or working,* Eccl. 9:5, 10. It is folly therefore for the living to make their court to them, with any expectation of relief from them. Necromancers consulted the dead, as the witch of Endor, and so proclaimed their own folly. We must live by the living, and not by the dead. What life or light can we look for from those that have no light or life themselves?

(3.) He directs them to consult the oracles of God. If the prophets that were among them did not speak directly to every case, yet they had the written word, and to that they must have recourse. Note, Those will never be drawn to consult wizards that know how to make a good use of their Bibles. Would we know how we may seek to our God, and come to the knowledge of his mind? *To the law and to the testimony.* There you will see what is good, and what the Lord requires of you. Make God's statutes your counsellors, and you will be counselled aright. Observe, [1.] What use we must make of the law and the testimony: we must *speak according to that word,* that is, we must make this our standard, conform to it, take advice from it, make our appeals to it, and in every thing be overruled and determined by it, consent to those wholesome healing words (1 Tim. 6:3), and speak of the things of God in the words which the Holy Ghost teaches. It is not enough to say nothing against it, but we must speak according to it. [2.] Why we must make this use of the law and the testimony: because we shall be convicted of the greatest folly imaginable if we do not. Those that concur not with the word of God do thereby evince that *there is no light,* no morning light (so the word is) *in them;* they have no right sense of things; they do not understand themselves, nor the difference between good and evil, truth and falsehood. Note, Those that reject divine revelation have not so much as human understanding; nor do those rightly admit the oracles of reason who will not admit the oracles of God. Some read it as a threatening: "If they speak not according to this word, there shall be no light to them, no good, no comfort or relief; but they shall be driven to darkness and despair;" as it follows here, *v.* 21, 22. What light had Saul when he consulted the witch? 1 Sa. 28:18, 20. Or what light can those expect that turn away from the Father of lights?

(4.) He reads the doom of those that seek to familiar spirits and regard not God's law and testimony; there shall not only be no light to them, no comfort or prosperity, but they may expect all horror and misery, *v.* 21, 22. [1.] The trouble they feared shall come upon them: They shall *pass through* the land, or pass to and fro in the land, unfixed, unsettled, and driven from place to place by the threatening power of an invading enemy; they shall be *hardly bestead* whither to go for the necessary supports of life, either because the country would be so impoverished that there would be nothing to be had, or at least themselves and their friends so impoverished that there

would be nothing to be had for them; so that those who used to be fed to the full shall be hungry. Note, Those that go away from God go out of the way of all good. [2.] They shall be very uneasy to themselves, by their discontent and impatience under their trouble. A good man may be in want, but then he quiets himself, and strives to make himself easy; but these people *when they shall be hungry shall fret themselves,* and when they have nothing to feed on their vexation shall prey upon their own spirits; for fretfulness is a sin that is its own punishment. [3.] They shall be very provoking to all about them, nay, to all above them; when they find all their measures broken, and themselves at their wits' end, they will forget all the rules of duty and decency, and will treasonably *curse their king* and blasphemously curse *their God,* and this more than *in their thought and in their bedchamber,* Eccl. 10:20. They begin with cursing their king for managing the public affairs no better, as if the fault were his, when the best and wisest kings cannot secure success; but, when they have broken the bonds of their allegiance, no marvel if those of their religion do not hold them long: they next curse their God, curse him, and die; they quarrel with his providence, and reproach that, as if he had done them wrong. *The foolishness of man perverts his way,* and then *his heart frets against the Lord,* Prov. 19:3. See what need we have to *keep our mouth as with a bridle* when our *heart is hot within us;* for the language of fretfulness is commonly very offensive. [4.] They shall abandon themselves to despair, and, which way soever they look, shall see no probability of relief. They shall look upward, but heaven shall frown upon them and look gloomy; and how can it be otherwise when they curse their God? They shall look to the earth, but what comfort can that yield to those with whom God is at war? There is nothing there but trouble, and darkness, and dimness of anguish, every thing threatening, and not one pleasant gleam, not one hopeful prospect; but they shall be driven to darkness by the violence of their own fears, which represent every thing about them black and frightful. This explains what he had said *v.* 20, that there shall be no light to them. Those that shut their eyes against the light of God's word will justly be abandoned to darkness, and left to wander endlessly, and the sparks of their own kindling will do them no kindness.

CHAPTER 9

The prophet in this chapter (according to the directions given him, *ch.* 3:10, 11) saith to the righteous, It shall be well with thee, but Woe to the wicked, it shall be ill with him. Here are, I. Gracious promises to those that adhere to the law and to the testimony; while those that seek to familiar spirits shall be driven into darkness and dimness, they shall see a great light, relief in the midst of their distresses, typical of gospel grace. 1. In the doctrine of the Messiah (*v.* 1–3). 2. His victories (*v.* 4, 5). 3. His government and dominion as Immanuel (*v.* 6, 7). II. Dreadful threatenings against the people of Israel, who had revolted from and were enemies to the house of David, that they should be brought to utter ruin, that their pride should bring them down (*v.* 8–10), that their neighbours should make a prey of them (*v.* 11, 12), that, for their impenitence and hypocrisy, all their ornaments and supports should be cut off (*v.* 13–17), and that by the wrath of God against them, and their wrath one against another, they should be brought to utter ruin (*v.* 18–21). And this is typical of the final destruction of all the enemies of the Son of David and his kingdom.

Verses 1–7

The first words of this chapter plainly refer to the close of the foregoing chapter, where every thing looked black and melancholy: *Behold, trouble, and darkness, and dimness* — very bad, yet not so bad but that *to the upright there shall arise light in the darkness* (Ps. 112:4) and *at evening time it shall be light,* Zec. 14:7. *Nevertheless it shall not be such dimness* (either not such for kind or not such for degree) as sometimes there has been. Note, In the worst of times God's people have a *nevertheless* to comfort themselves with, something to allay and balance their troubles; they are persecuted, but not forsaken (2 Co. 4:9), sorrowful yet always rejoicing, 2 Co. 6:10. And it is matter of comfort to us, when things are at the darkest, that he who *forms the light and creates the darkness* (*ch.* 45:7) has appointed to both their bounds and set the one over against the other, Gen. 4:4. He can say, "Hitherto the dimness shall go, so long it shall last, and no further, no longer."

I. Three things are here promised, and they all point ultimately at the grace of the gospel, which the saints then were to comfort themselves with the hopes of in every cloudy and dark day, as we now are to comfort ourselves in time of trouble with the hopes of Christ's second coming, though that be now, as his first coming then was, a thing at a great distance. The mercy likewise which God has in store for his church in the latter days may be a support to those that are mourning with her for her present calamities. We have here the promise.

1. Of a glorious light, which shall so qualify, and by degrees dispel, the dimness, that it shall not be as it sometimes has been: *Not such as was in her vexation;* there shall not be such dark times as were formerly, *when at first he lightly afflicted the land of Zebulun and Naphtali* (which lay remote and most exposed to the inroads of the neighbouring enemies), *and afterwards he more grievously afflicted the land by the way of the sea and beyond Jordan* (v. 1), referring probably to those days when *God began to cut Israel short* and to *smite them in all their coasts,* 2 Ki. 10:32. Note, God tries what less judgments will do with a people before he brings greater; but if a light affliction do not do its work with us, to humble and reform us, we must expect to be afflicted more grievously; for when God judges he will overcome. Well, those were dark times with the land of Zebulun and Naphtali, and there was *dimness of anguish in Galilee of the Gentiles,* both in respect of ignorance (they did not speak according *to the law and the testimony,* and then there was *no light in them,* ch. 8:20) and in respect of trouble, and the desperate posture of their outward affairs; we have both together, 2 Chr. 15:3, 5. *Israel has been without the true God and a teaching priest, and in those times there was no peace.* But the dimness threatened (ch. 8:22) shall not prevail to such a degree; for (*v.* 2) the *people that walked in darkness have seen a great light.* (1.) At this time when the prophet lived, there were many prophets in Judah and Israel, whose prophecies were a great light both for direction and comfort to the people of God, who adhered to the law and the testimony. Besides the written word, they had prophecy; there were those that had shown them how long (Ps. 74:9), which was a great satisfaction to them, when in respect of their outward troubles they *sat in darkness, and dwelt in the land of the shadow of death.* (2.) This was to have its full accomplishment when our Lord Jesus began to appear as a prophet, and to preach the gospel in the land of Zebulun and Naphtali, and in Galilee of the Gentiles. And the Old-Testament prophets, as they were witnesses to him, so they were types of him. When he came and dwelt in the borders of Zebulun and Naphtali, then this prophecy is said to have been fulfilled, Mt. 4:13–16. Note, [1.] Those that want the gospel walk in darkness, and know not what they do nor whither they go; and they dwell in the land of the shadow of death, in thick darkness, and in the utmost danger. [2.] When the gospel comes to any place, to any soul, light comes, a great light, a shining light, which will shine more and more. It should be welcome to us, as light is to those that sit in darkness, and we should readily entertain it, both because if is of such sovereign use to us and because it brings its own evidence with it. Truly this light is sweet.

2. Of a glorious increase, and a universal joy arising from it, (*v.* 3) *"Thou, O God! hast multiplied the nation,* the Jewish nation which thou hast mercy in store for; though it has been diminished by one sore judgment after another, yet now thou hast begun to multiply it again." The numbers of a nation are its strength and wealth if the numerous be industrious; and it is God that increases nations, Job 12:23. Yet it follows, *"Thou hast not increased the joy* — the carnal joy and mirth, and those things that are commonly the matter and occasion thereof. But, notwithstanding that, *they joy before thee;* there is a great deal of serious spiritual joy among them, joy in the presence of God, with an eye to him." This is very applicable to the times of gospel light, spoken of *v.* 2. Then God multiplied the nation, the gospel Israel. "And to him" (so the Masorites read it) "thou hast magnified the joy, to every one that receives the light." The following words favour this reading: *"They joy before thee;* they come before thee in holy ordinances with great joy'; their mirth is not like that of Israel under their vines and fig-trees (thou hast not increased that joy), but it is in the favour of God and in the tokens of his grace." Note, The gospel, when it comes in its light and power, brings joy along with it, and those who receive it aright do therein rejoice, yea, and will rejoice; therefor the conversion of the nations is prophesied of by this (Ps. 67:4), *Let the nations be glad, and sin for joy.* See Ps. 96:11.

(1.) It is holy joy: *They joy before thee;* they rejoice in spirit (as Christ did, Lu. 10:21), and that is before God. In the eye of the world they are always as sorrowful, and yet, in God's sight, *always rejoicing,* 2 Co. 6:10. (2.) It is great joy; it is *according to the joy in harvest,* when those who sowed in tears, and have with long patience waited for the precious fruits of the earth, reap in joy; and as in war men rejoice when, after a hazardous battle, *they divide the spoil.* The gospel brings with it plenty and victory; but those that would have the joy of it must expect to go through a hard work, as the husbandman before he has the joy of harvest, and a hard conflict, as the soldier before he has the joy of dividing the spoil; but the joy, when it comes, will be an abundant recompence for the toil. See Acts 8:8, 39.

3. Of a glorious liberty and enlargement (*v.* 4, 5): "They shall rejoice before thee, and with good reason, *for thou hast broken the yoke of his burden,* and made him easy, for he shall no longer be in servitude; and thou hast broken *the staff of his shoulder and the rod of his oppressor,* that rod of the wicked which rested long on the lot of the righteous," as the Midianites' yoke was broken from off the neck of Israel by the agency of Gideon. If God makes former deliverances his patterns in working for us, we ought to make them our encouragements to hope in him and to seek to him, Ps. 83:9. *Do unto them as to the Midianites.* What temporal deliverance this refers to is not clear, probably the preventing of Sennacherib from making himself master of Jerusalem, which was done, *as in the day of Midian,* by the immediate hand of God; and, whereas other battles were usually won with a great deal of noise and by the expense of much blood, this shall be done silently and without noise. *Under his glory God shall kindle a burning* (ch. 10:16); a *fire not blown shall consume him,* Job 20:26. But doubtless it looks further, to the blessed fruits and effects of that great light which should visit those that sat in darkness; it would bring liberty along with it, *deliverance to the captives,* Lu. 4:18. (1.) The design of the gospel, and the grace of it, is to break the yoke of sin and Satan, to remove the burden of guilt and corruption, and to free us from the rod of those oppressors, that we might be brought into the glorious liberty of the children of God. Christ broke the yoke of the ceremonial law (Acts 15:10; Gal. 5:1), and delivered us *out of the hand of our enemies,* that we might *serve him without fear,* Lu. 1:74, 75. (2.) This is done by the Spirit working like fire (Mt. 3:11), not as the battle of the warrior is fought, with confused noise; no, the weapons of our warfare are not carnal; but it is done with the Spirit of judgment and the Spirit of burning, ch. 4:4. It is done *as in the day of Midian,* by a work of God upon the hearts of men. Christ is our Gideon; it is his sword that doeth wonders.

II. But who, where, is he that shall undertake and accomplish these great things for the church? The prophet tells us (*v.* 6, 7) they shall be done by the Messiah, *Immanuel,* that son of a virgin whose birth he had foretold (ch. 7:14), and now speaks of, in the prophetic style, as a thing already done: the *child is born,* not only because it was as certain, and he was as certain of it as if it had been done already, but because the church before his incarnation reaped great benefit and advantage by his undertaking in virtue of that first promise concerning the *seed of the woman,* Gen. 3:15. As he was the Lamb slain, so he was the child born, *from the foundation of the world,* Rev. 13:8. All the great things that God did for the Old-Testament church were done by him as the eternal Word, and for his sake as the Mediator. He was the Anointed, to whom God had respect (Ps. 84:9), and it was for the Lord's sake, for the Lord Christ's sake, that God caused his face to shine upon his sanctuary, Dan. 9:17. The Jewish nation, and particularly the house of David, were preserved many a time from imminent ruin only because that blessing was in them. What greater security therefore could be given to the church of God then that it should be preserved, and be the special care of the divine Providence, than this, that God had so great a mercy in reserve for it? The Chaldee paraphrast understands it of the man that shall endure for ever, even Christ. And it is an illustrious prophecy of him and of his kingdom, which doubtless those that waited for the consolation of Israel built much upon, often turned to, and read with pleasure.

1. See him in his humiliation. The same that is *the mighty God* is *a child born;* the ancient of days becomes

an infant of a span long; the *everlasting Father* is *a Son given.* Such was his condescension in taking our nature upon him; thus did he humble and empty himself, to exalt and fill us. He is born into our world. *The Word was made flesh, and dwelt among us.* He is given, freely given, to be all that to us which our case, in our fallen state, calls for. God so loved the world that he gave him. He is born *to us,* he is given to us, us men, and not to the angels that sinned. It is spoken with an air of triumph, and the angel seems to refer to these words in the notice he gives to the shepherds of the Messiah's having come (Lu. 2:11), *Unto you is born, this day, a Saviour.* Note, Christ's being born and given to us is the great foundation of our hopes, and fountain of our joys, in times of greatest grief and fear.

2. See him in his exaltation. This child, this son, this Son of God, this Son of man, that is given to us, is in a capacity to do us a great deal of kindness; for he is invested with the highest honour and power, so that we cannot but be happy if he be our friend.

(1.) See the dignity he is advanced to, and the name he has above every name. He shall be called (and therefore we are sure he is and shall be) *Wonderful, Counsellor, etc.* His people shall know him and worship him by these names; and, as one that fully answers them, they shall submit to him and depend upon him. [1.] He is *wonderful, counsellor.* Justly is he called *wonderful,* for he is both God and man. His love is the wonder of angels and glorified saints; in his birth, life, death, resurrection, and ascension, he was wonderful. A constant series of wonders attended him, and, without controversy, great was the mystery of godliness concerning him. He is the *counsellor,* for he was intimately acquainted with the counsels of God from eternity, and he gives counsel to the children of men, in which he consults our welfare. It is by him that God has *given us counsel,* Ps. 16:7; Rev. 3:18. He is the wisdom of the Father, and is made of God to us wisdom. Some join these together: He is the wonderful counsellor, a wonder or miracle of a counsellor; in this, as in other things, he has the pre-eminence; none teaches like him. [2.] He is *the mighty God — God, the mighty One.* As he has wisdom, so he has strength, to go through with his undertaking: he is able to save to the utmost; and such is the work of the Mediator that no less a power than that of the mighty God could accomplish it. [3.] He is *the everlasting Father,* or *the Father of eternity;* he is God, one with the Father, who is from everlasting to everlasting. He is the author of everlasting life and happiness to them, and so is the Father of a blessed eternity to them. He is *the Father of the world to come* (so the Septuagint reads it), the father of the gospel-state, which is put in subjection to him, not to the angels, Heb. 2:5. He was, from eternity, Father of the great work of redemption: his heart was upon it; it was the product of his wisdom as *the counsellor,* of his love as *the everlasting Father.* [4.] He is *the prince of peace.* As a King, he preserves the peace, commands peace, nay, he creates peace, in his kingdom. He is our peace, and it is his peace that both keeps the hearts of his people and rules in them. He is not only a peaceable prince, and his reign peaceable, but he is the author and giver of all good, all that peace which is the present and future bliss of his subjects.

(2.) See the dominion he is advanced to, and the throne he has above every throne (*v.* 6): *The government shall be upon his shoulder* — his only. He shall not only wear the badge of it upon his shoulder (the *key of the house of David,* ch. 22:22), but he shall bear the burden of it. The Father shall devolve it upon him, so that he shall have an incontestable right to govern; and he shall undertake it, so that no doubt can be made of his governing well, for he shall set his shoulder to it, and will never complain, as Moses did, of his being overcharged. *I am not able to bear all this people,* Num. 11:11, 14. Glorious things are here spoken of Christ's government, *v.* 7. [1.] That it shall be an increasing government. It shall be multiplied; the bounds of his kingdom shall be more and more enlarged, and many shall be added to it daily. The lustre of it shall increase, and it shall shine more and more brightly in the world. The monarchies of the earth were each less illustrious than the other, so that what began in gold ended in iron and clay, and every monarchy dwindled by degrees; but the kingdom of Christ is a growing kingdom, and will come to perfection at last. [2.] That it shall be a peaceable government, agreeable to his character as the prince of peace. He shall rule by love, shall rule in men's hearts; so that wherever his government is there shall be peace, and as his government increases the peace shall increase. The more we are subject to Christ the more easy and safe we are. [3.] That it shall be a rightful government. He that is the Son of David shall reign upon the throne of David and over his kingdom, which he is entitled to. *God shall give him the throne of his father David,* Lu. 1:32, 33. The gospel church, in which Jew and Gentile are incorporated, is the holy hill of Zion, on which Christ reigns, Ps. 2:6. [4.] That it shall be administered with prudence and equity, and so as to answer the great end of government, which is the establishment of the kingdom: *He shall order it, and settle it, with justice and judgment.* Every thing is, and shall be, well managed, in the kingdom of Christ, and none of his subjects shall ever have cause to complain. [5.] That it shall be an everlasting kingdom: *There shall be no end of the increase of his government* (it shall be still growing), no end of the increase of the peace of it, for the happiness of the subjects of this kingdom shall last to eternity and perhaps shall be progressive *in infinitum — for ever.* He shall reign *henceforth even for ever;* not only throughout all generations of time, but, even when the kingdom shall be delivered up to God even the Father, the glory both of the Redeemer and the redeemed shall continue eternally. [6.] That God himself has undertaken to bring all this about: *"The Lord of hosts,* who has all power in his hand and all creatures at his beck, *shall perform this,* shall preserve the throne of David till this prince of peace is settled in it; his *zeal* shall do it, his jealousy for his own honour, and the truth of his promise, and the good of his church." Note, The heart of God is much upon the advancement of the kingdom of Christ among men, which is very comfortable to all those that wish well to it; *the zeal of the Lord of hosts* will overcome all opposition.

Verses 8–21

Here are terrible threatenings, which are directed primarily against Israel, the kingdom of the ten tribes, Ephraim and Samaria, the ruin of which is here foretold, with all the woeful confusions that were the prefaces to that ruin, all which came to pass within a few years after; but they look further, to all the enemies of the throne and kingdom of Christ the Son of David, and read the doom of all the nations that forget God, and will not have Christ to reign over them. Observe,

I. The preface to this prediction (*v.* 8): *The Lord sent a word into Jacob,* sent it by his servants the prophets. He warns before he wounds. He sent notice what he would do, that they might meet him in the way of his judgments; but they would not take the hint, took no care to turn away his wrath, and so it lighted upon Israel; for no word of God shall fall to the ground. It fell upon them as a storm of rain and hail from on high, which they could not avoid: *It has lighted upon them,* that is, it is as sure to come as if come already, and all the people shall know by feeling it what they would not know by hearing of it. Those that are willingly ignorant of the wrath of God revealed from heaven against sin and sinners shall be made to know it.

II. The sins charged upon the people of Israel, which provoked God to bring these judgments upon them. 1. Their insolent defiance of the justice of God, thinking themselves a match for him: "They *say, in the pride and stoutness of their heart,* Let God himself do his worst; we will hold our own, and make our part good with him. If he ruin our houses, we will repair them, and make them stronger and finer than they were before. our landlord shall not turn us out of doors, though we pay him no rent, but we will keep in possession. If the houses that were built of bricks be demolished in the war, we will rebuild them with hewn stones, that shall not so easily be thrown down. If the enemy cut down the sycamores, we will plant cedars in the room of them. we will make a hand of God's judgments, gain by them, and so outbrave them." Note, Those are ripening apace for ruin whose hearts are unhumbled under humbling providences; for God will walk contrary to those who thus walk contrary to him and provoke him to jealousy, as if they were stronger than he. 2. Their incorrigibleness under all the rebukes of Providence hitherto (*v.* 13); *The people turn not unto him that smiteth them* (they are not wrought upon to reform their lives, to forsake their sins, and to return to their duty), *neither do they seek the Lord of hosts;* either they are atheists, and have no religion, or idolaters, and seek to those gods that are the creatures of their own fancy and the works of their own hands. Note, That which God designs, in smiting us, is to turn us to himself and to set us a seeking him; and, if this point be not gained by less judgments, greater may be expected. God smites that he may not kill. 3. Their general corruption of manners and abounding profaneness. (1.) Those that should have reformed them helped to debauch them (*v.* 16): *The leaders of this people* mislead them, and *cause them to err,* by conniving at their wickedness and countenancing wicked people, and by setting them bad examples; and then no wonder if those that are led of them be deceived and so destroyed. But it is ill with a people when their physicians are their worst disease. *"Those that bless this people,* or *call them blessed* (so the margin reads it), that flatter them, and soothe them in their wickedness, and cry *Peace, peace, to them,* cause them to err; and those *that are called blessed of them are swallowed up* ere they are aware." We have reason to be afraid of those that speak well of us when we do ill; see Prov. 24:24; 29:5. (2.) Wickedness was universal, and all were infected with it (*v.* 17): *Every one is a hypocrite and an evil doer.* If there be any that are good, they do not, they dare not appear, for every mouth speaks folly and villany; every one is profane towards God (so the word properly signifies) and an evil doer towards man. These two commonly go together: those that fear not God regard not man; and then every mouth speaks folly, falsehood, and reproach, both against God and man; for *out of the abundance of the heart the mouth speaks.*

III. The judgments threatened against them for this wickedness of theirs; let them not think to go unpunished.

1. In general, hereby they exposed themselves to the wrath of God, which should both devour as fire and darken as smoke. (1.) It should devour as fire (*v.* 18): *Wickedness shall burn as the fire;* the displeasure of God, incurred by sin, shall consume the sinners, who have made themselves as briers and thorns before it, and as the thickets of the forest, combustible matter, which the wrath of the Lord of hosts, the mighty God, will go through and burn together. (2.) It should darken as smoke. The briers and thorns, when the fire consumes them, shall *mount up like the lifting up of smoke,* so that the whole land shall be darkened by it; they shall be in trouble, and see no way out (*v.* 19): *The people shall be as the fuel of the fire.* God's wrath fastens upon none but those that make themselves fuel for it, and then they mount up as the smoke of sacrifices, being made victims to divine justice.

2. God would arm the neighbouring powers against them, *v.* 11, 12. At this time the kingdom of Israel was in league with that of Syria against Judah; but the Assyrians, who were adversaries to the Syrians, when they had conquered them should invade Israel, and God would stir them up to do it, and join the enemies of Israel together in alliance against them, who yet had particular ends of their own to serve and were not aware of God's hand in their alliance. Note, When enemies are set up, and joined in confederacy against a people, God's hand must be acknowledged in it. Note further, Those that partake with each other in sin, as Syria and Israel in invading Judah, must expect to share in the punishment of sin. Nay, the Syrians themselves, whom they were now in league with, should be a scourge to them (for it is no unusual thing for those to fall out that have been united in sin), one attacking them in the front and the other flanking them or falling upon their rear; so that they should be surrounded with enemies on all sides, who should *devour them with open mouth, v.* 12. The Philistines were not now looked upon as formidable enemies, and the Syrians were looked upon as firm friends; and yet these shall devour Israel. When men's ways displease the Lord he makes even their friends to be at war with them.

3. God would take from the midst of them those they confided in and promised themselves help from, *v.* 14, 15. Because the people seek not God, those they seek to and depend upon shall stand them in no stead. *The Lord will cut off head and tail, branch and rush,* which is explained in the next verse. (1.) Their magistrates, who were honourable by birth and office and were the ancients of the people, these were *the head,* these were the branch which they promised themselves spirit and fruit from; but because these caused them to err they should be cut off, and their dignity and power should be no protection to them when the abuse of that dignity and power was the great provocation: and it was a judgment upon the people to have their princes cut off, though they were not such as they should have been. (2.) Their prophets, their false prophets, were *the tail* and the *rush,* the most despicable of all. A wicked minister is the worst of all. A wicked minister is the worst of men. *Corruptio optimi est pessima — The best things become when corrupted the worst.* The blind led the blind, and so both fell into the ditch; and the blind leaders fell first and fell undermost.

4. That the desolation should be as general as the corruption had been, and none should escape it, *v.* 17. (1.) Not those that were the objects of complacency. None shall be spared for love: *The Lord shall have no joy in their young men,* that were in the flower of their youth; nor will he say, *Deal gently with the young men for my sake;* no, "Let them fall with the rest, and with them let the seed of the next generation perish." (2.) Not those that were the objects of compassion. None shall be spared for pity: He *shall not have mercy on their fatherless and widows,* though he is, in a particular manner, the patron and protector of such. They had corrupted their way like all the rest; and, if the poverty and helplessness of their state was not an argument with them to keep them from sin, they could not expect it should be an argument with God to protect them from judgments.

5. That they should pull one another to pieces, that every one should help forward the common ruin, and they should be cannibals to themselves and one to another: *No man shall spare his brother,* if he come in the way of his ambition of covetousness, or if he have any colour to be revenged on him; and how can they expect God should spare them when they show no compassion one to another? Men's passion and cruelty one against another provoke God to be angry with them all and are an evidence that he is so. Civil wars soon bring a kingdom to desolation. Such there were in Israel, when, *for the transgression of the land, many were the princes thereof,* Prov. 28:2.

(1.) In these intestine broils, men *snatched on the right hand, and yet were hungry* still, and did eat the *flesh of their own arms,* preyed upon themselves for hunger or upon their nearest relations that were their own flesh, *v.* 20. This bespeaks, [1.] Great famine and scarcity; when men had pulled all they could to them it was so little that they were still hungry, at least God did not bless it to them, so that *they eat and have not enough,* Hag. 1:6. [2.] Great rapine and plunder. *Jusque datum sceleri — iniquity is established by law.* The hedge of property, which is a hedge of protection to men's estates, shall be plucked up, and every man shall think all that his own which he can lay his hands on *(vivitur ex rapto, non hospes ab hospite tutus — they live on the spoil, and the rites of hospitality are all violated);* and yet, when men thus catch at that which is none of their own, they are not satisfied. Covetous desires are insatiable, and this curse is entailed on that which is ill got, that it will never do well.

(2.) These intestine broils should be not only among particular persons and private families, but among the tribes (*v.* 21): *Manasseh shall devour Ephraim, and Ephraim Manasseh,* though they be combined against Judah. Those that could unite against Judah could not unite with one another; but that sinful confederacy of theirs against their neighbour *that dwelt securely by them* was justly punished by this separation of them one from another. Or Judah, having sinned like Manasseh and Ephraim, shall not only suffer with them, but suffer by them. Note, Mutual enmity and animosity among the tribes of God's Israel is a sin that ripens them for ruin, and a sad symptom of ruin hastening on apace. If Ephraim be against Manasseh, and Manasseh against Ephraim, and both against Judah, they will all soon become a very easy prey to the common enemy.

6. That, though they should be followed with all these judgments, yet God would not let fall his controversy with them. It is the heavy burden of this song (*v.* 12, 17, 21): *For all this his anger is not turned away, but his hand is stretched out still,* that is, (1.) They do nothing to turn away his anger; they do not repent and reform, do not humble themselves and pray, none stand in the gap, none answer God's calls nor comply with the designs of his providences, but they are hardened and secure. (2.) His anger therefore

continues to burn against them and *his hand is stretched out still.* The reason why the judgments of God are prolonged is because the point is not gained, sinners are not brought to repentance by them. *The people turn not to him that smites them,* and therefore he continues to smite them; for when God judges he will overcome, and the proudest stoutest sinner shall either bend or break.

CHAPTER 10

The prophet, in this chapter, is dealing, I. With the proud oppressors of his people at home, that abused their power, to pervert justice, whom he would reckon with for their tyranny (*v.* 1–4). II. With a threatening invader of his people from abroad, Sennacherib king of Assyria, concerning whom observe, 1. The commission given him to invade Judah (*v.* 5, 6). 2. His pride and insolence in the execution of that commission (*v.* 7–11, 13, 14). 3. A rebuke given to his haughtiness, and a threatening of his fall and ruin, when he had served the purposes for which God raised him up (*v.* 12, 15–19). 4. A promise of grace to the people of God, to enable them to bear up under the affliction, and to get good by it (*v.* 20–23). 5. Great encouragement given to them not to fear this threatening storm, but to hope that, though for the present all the country was put into a great consternation by it, yet it would end well, in the destruction of this formidable enemy (*v.* 24–34). And this is intended to quiet the minds of good people in reference to all the threatening efforts of the wrath of the church's enemies. If God be for us, who can be against us? None to do us any harm.

Verses 1–4

Whether they were the princes and judges of Israel of Judah, or both, that the prophet denounced this woe against, is not certain: if those of Israel, these verses are to be joined with the close of the foregoing chapter, which is probable enough, because the burden of that prophecy *(for all this his anger is not turned away)* is repeated here (*v.* 4); if those of Judah, they then show what was the particular design with which God brought the Assyrian army upon them — to punish their magistrates for maladministration, which they could not legally be called to account for. To them he speaks woes before he speaks comfort to God's own people. Here is,

I. The indictment drawn up against these oppressors, *v.* 1, 2. They are charged, 1. With making wicked laws and edicts: They *decree unrighteous decrees,* contrary to natural equity and the law of God: and what mischief they *prescribe* those under them *write* it, enrol it, and put it into the formality of a law. "Woe to the superior powers that devise and decree these decrees! they are not too high to be under the divine check. And woe to the inferior officers that draw them up, and enter them upon record — *the writers that write the grievousness,* they are not too mean to be within the divine cognizance. Principal and accessaries shall fall under the same woe." Note, It is bad to do hurt, but it is worse to do it with design and deliberation, to do wrong to many, and to involve many in the guilt of doing wrong. 2. With perverting justice in the execution of the laws that were made. No people had statutes and judgments to righteous as they had, and yet corrupt judges found ways to *turn aside the needy from judgment,* to hinder them from coming at their right and recovering what was their due, because they were needy and poor, and such as they could get nothing by nor expect any bribes from. 3. With enriching themselves by oppressing those that lay at their mercy, whom they ought to have protected. They make widows' houses and estates their prey, and they *rob the fatherless* of the little that is left them, because they have no friend to appear for them. Not to relieve them if they had wanted, not to right them if they were wronged, would have been crime enough in men that had wealth and power; but to rob them because on the side of the oppressors there was power, and the oppressed had no comforter (Eccl. 4:1), was such apiece of barbarity as one would think none could ever be guilty of that had either the nature of a man or the name of an Israelite.

II. A challenge given them with all their pride and power to outface the judgments of God (*v.* 3): *"What will you do? To whom will you flee?* You can trample upon the widows and fatherless; but *what will you do when God riseth up?"* Job 31:14. Great men, who tyrannise over the poor, think they shall never be called to account for their tyranny, shall never hear of it again, or fare the worse for it; but *shall not God visit for these things?* Jer. 5:29. Will there not come a desolation upon those that have made others desolate? Perhaps it may *come from far,* and therefore may be long in coming; but it will come at last (reprieves are not pardons), and coming from far, from a quarter whence it was least expected, it will be the greater surprise and the more terrible. What will then become of these unrighteous judges? Now they *see their help in the gate* (Job 31:21); but to whom will they then flee for help? Note, 1. There is a day of visitation coming, a day of enquiry and discovery, a searching day, which will bring to light, to a true light, every man, and every man's work. 2. The day of visitation will be a day of desolation to all wicked people, when all their comforts and hopes will be lost and gone, and buried in ruin, and themselves left desolate. 3. Impenitent sinners will be utterly at a loss, and will no know what to do in the day of visitation and desolation. They cannot fly and hide themselves, cannot fight it out and defend themselves; they have no refuge in which either to shelter themselves from the present evil *(to whom will you flee for help?)* or to secure to themselves better times hereafter: *"Where will you leave your glory,* to find it again when the storm is over?" The wealth they had got was their glory, and they had no place of safety in which to deposit that, but they should certainly see it flee away. If our souls be our glory, as they ought to be, and we make them our chief care, we know where to leave them, and into whose hands to commit them, even those of a faithful Creator. 4. It concerns us all seriously to consider what we shall do in the day of visitation, in a day of affliction, in the day of death and judgment, and to provide that we may do well.

III. Sentence passed upon them, by which they are doomed, some to imprisonment and captivity (*they shall bow down among the prisoners,* or *under them* — those that were most highly elevated in sin shall be most heavily loaded and most deeply sunk in trouble), others to death: they shall fall first, and so shall fall under the rest of the slain. Those that had trampled upon the widows and fatherless shall themselves be trodden down, *v.* 4. "This it will come to," says God, *"without me,* that is, because you have deserted me and driven me away from you." Nothing but utter ruin can be expected by those that live without God in the world, that cast him behind their back, and so cast themselves out of his protection.

And yet, *for all this, his anger is not turned away,* which intimates not only that God will proceed in his controversy with them, but that they shall be in a continual dread of it; they shall, to their unspeakable terror, see his hand still stretched out against them, and there shall remain nothing but *a fearful looking for of judgment.*

Verses 5–19

The destruction of the kingdom of Israel by Shalmaneser king of Assyria was foretold in the foregoing chapter, and it had its accomplishment in the sixth year of Hezekiah, 2 Ki. 18:10. It was total and final, head and tail were all cut off. Now the correction of the kingdom of Judah by Sennacherib king of Assyria is foretold in this chapter; and this prediction was fulfilled in the fourteenth year of Hezekiah, when that potent prince, encouraged by the successes of his predecessor against the ten tribes, *came up against all the fenced cities of Judah and took them, and laid siege to Jerusalem* (2 Ki. 18:13, 17), in consequence of which we may well suppose Hezekiah and his kingdom were greatly alarmed, though there was a good work of reformation lately begun among them: but it ended well, in the confusion of the Assyrians and the great encouragement of Hezekiah and his people in their return to God. Now let us see here,

I. How God, in his sovereignty, deputed the king of Assyria to be his servant, and made use of him as a mere tool to serve his own purposes with (*v.* 5, 6): *"O Assyrian!* know this, that thou art *the rod of my anger;* and I will send thee to be a scourge to *the people of my wrath."* Observe here, 1. How bad the character of the Jews was, though they appeared very good. They were *a hypocritical nation,* that made a profession of religion, and at this time particularly of reformation, but were not truly religious, not truly reformed, not so good as they pretended to be now that Hezekiah had brought goodness into fashion. When rulers are pious, and so religion is in reputation, it is common for nations to be hypocritical. They are *a profane nation;* so some read it. Hezekiah had in a great measure cured them of their idolatry, and now they ran into profaneness; nay, hypocrisy is profaneness: none profane the name of God so much as those who are called by that name and call upon it, and yet live in sin. Being a profane hypocritical nation, they are the people of God's wrath; they lie under his wrath, and are likely to be consumed by it. Note, Hypocritical nations are the people of God's wrath: nothing is more offensive to God than dissimulation in religion. See what a change sin made: those that had been God's chosen and hallowed people, above all people, had now become the *people of his wrath.* See Amos 3:2. 2. How mean the character of the Assyrian was, though he appeared very great. He was but *the rod of God's anger,* an instrument God was pleased to make use of for the chastening of his people, that, being thus *chastened of the Lord, they might not be condemned with the world.* Note, The tyrants of the world are but the tools of Providence. Men are God's hand, his sword sometimes, to kill and slay (Ps. 17:13, 14), at other times his rod to correct. *The staff in their hand,* wherewith they smite his people, *is his indignation;* it is his wrath that puts the staff into their hand and enables them to deal blows at pleasure among such as thought themselves a match for them. Sometimes God makes an idolatrous nation, that serves him not at all, a scourge to a hypocritical nation, that serves him not in sincerity and truth. The Assyrian is called the *rod of God's anger* because he is employed by him. (1.) From him his power is derived: *I will send him; I will give him a charge.* Note, All the power that wicked men have, though they often use it against God, they always receive from him. Pilate could have no power against Christ unless it were *given him from above,* Jn. 19:11. (2.) By him the exercise of that power is directed. The Assyrian is *to take the spoil and to take the prey,* not to shed any blood. We read not of any slain, but he is to plunder the country, rifle the houses, drive away the cattle, strip the people of all their wealth and ornaments, and *tread them down like the mire of the streets.* When God's professing people wallow in the mire of sin it is just with God to suffer their enemies to tread upon them like mire. But why must the Assyrian prevail thus against them? Not that they might be ruined, but that they might be thoroughly reformed.

II. See how the king of Assyria, in his pride, magnified himself as his own master, and pretended to be absolute and above all control, to act purely according to his own will and for his own honour. *God ordained him for judgment,* even the *mighty God established him for correction* (Hab. 1:12), to be an instrument of bringing his people to repentance, *howbeit he means not so, nor does his heart think so, v.* 7.

1. He does not think that he is either God's servant or Israel's friend, either that he *can* do no more than God will let him or that he *shall* do no more than God will make to work for the good of his people. God designs to correct his people for, and so to cure them of, their hypocrisy, and bring them nearer to himself; but was that Sennacherib's design? No, it was the furthest thing from his thoughts — *he means not so.* Note, (1.) The wise God often makes even the sinful passions and projects of men subservient to his own great and holy purposes. (2.) When God makes use of men as instruments in his hand to do his work it is very common for *him* to mean one thing and *them* to mean another, nay, for them to mean quite the contrary to what he intends. What Joseph's brethren designed for hurt God overruled for good, Gen. 50:20. See Mic. 4:11, 12. Men have their ends and God has his, but we are sure *the counsel of the Lord shall stand.* But what is it the proud Assyrian aims at? The heart of kings is unsearchable, but God knew what was in his heart.

2. He designs nothing but *to destroy and to cut off nations not a few,* and to make himself master of them. [1.] He designs to gratify his own cruelty; nothing will serve but to destroy and cut off. He hopes to regale himself with blood and slaughter; that of particular persons will not suffice, he must cut off nations. It is below him to deal by retail; he traffics in murders by wholesale. Nations, and those not a few, must have but one neck, which he will have the pleasure of cutting off. [2.] He designs to gratify his own covetousness and ambition, to set up for a universal monarch, *and to gather unto him all nations,* Hab. 2:5. An insatiable desire of wealth and dominion is that which carries him on in this undertaking.

3. The prophet here brings him in vaunting, and hectoring; and by his general's letter to Hezekiah, written in his name, vainglory and arrogance seem to have entered

very far into the spirit and genius of the man. His haughtiness and presumption are here described very largely, and his very language copied out, partly to represent him as ridiculous and partly to assure the people of God that he would be brought down; for that maxim generally holds true, that pride goes before destruction. It also intimates that God takes notice, and keeps an account, of all men's proud and haughty words, with which they set heaven and earth at defiance. Those that speak *great swelling words of vanity* shall hear of them again.

(1.) He boasts of the great things he had done to other nations. [1.] He had made their kings his courtiers (*v.* 8): *"My princes are altogether kings.* Those that are now my princes are such as have been kings." Or he means that he had raised his throng to such a degree that his servants, and those that were in command under him, were as great, and lived in as much pomp, as the kings of other countries. Or those that were absolute princes in their own dominions held their crowns under him, and did him homage. This was a vainglorious boast; but how great is our God whom we serve, who is indeed King of kings, and whose subjects are made to him kings! Rev. 1:6. [2.] He had made himself master of their cities. He names several (*v.* 9) that were all alike reduced by him. *Calno* soon yielded *as Carchemish* did, *Hamath* could not hold out any more than *Arpad,* and *Samaria* had become his as well as *Damascus.* To support his boasts he is obliged to bring the victories of his predecessor into the account; for it was he that conquered Samaria, not Sennacherib. [3.] He had been too hard for their idols, their tutelar gods, *had found out the kingdoms of the idols* and found out ways to make them his own, *v.* 10. Their kingdoms took denomination from the idols they worshipped; the Moabites are called *the people of Chemosh* (Jer. 48:46), because they imagined their gods were their patrons and protectors; and therefore Sennacherib vainly imagined that every conquest of a kingdom was the conquest of a god. [4.] He had enlarged his own dominions, and *removed the bounds of the people* (*v.* 13), enclosing many large territories within the limits of his own kingdom and shifting a great way further the ancient land-marks which his fathers had set; he could not bear to be hemmed in so closely, but must have more room to thrive. By his *removing the border of the people* Mr. White understands his arbitrarily transplanting colonies from place to place, which was the constant practice of the Assyrians in all their conquests; and this is a probable interpretation. [5.] He had enriched himself with their wealth, and brought it into his own exchequer: *I have robbed their treasures.* In this he said truly, Great conquerors are often no better than great robbers. [6.] He had mastered all the opposition he met with: *"I have put down the inhabitants as a valiant man.* Those that sat high, and thought they say firmly, I have humbled and made to come down."

(2.) He boasts of the manner in which he had done them. [1.] That he had done all this by his own policy and power (*v.* 13): *"By the strength of my hand,* for I am valiant; *and by my wisdom, for I am prudent;"* not by the permission of Providence and the blessing of God. He knows not that it is God that makes him what he is, and puts the staff into his hand, but *sacrifices to his own net,* Hab. 1:16. "This wealth is all gotten by *my might and the power of my hand,"* Deu. 8:17. Downright atheism and profaneness, as well as pride and vanity, are at the bottom of men's attributing their prosperity and success thus to themselves and their own conduct, and raising their own character upon it. [2.] That he had done all this with a great deal of ease, and had made but a sport and diversion of it, as if he had been taking birds' nests (*v.* 14): *my hand has found as a nest the riches of the people;* and when he had found them there was no more difficulty in taking them than in rifling a nest, nor any more reluctance or regret within his own breast in destroying families and cities than in destroying crows'-nests; killing children was no more to him than killing birds. *"As one gathers the eggs that are left* in the nest by the dam, so easily *have I gathered all the earth."* Like Alexander, he thought he had conquered the world; and whatever prey he seized there was none that *moved the wing, or opened the mouth, or peeped,* as birds do when their nests are rifled. They durst not make any opposition, no, nor any complaint; such awe did they stand in of this mighty conqueror. They were so weak that they knew it was to no purpose to resist, and he was so arbitrary that they knew it was to no purpose to complain. Strange that ever men who were made to do good should take a pride and a pleasure in doing wrong, and doing mischief to all about them without control, and should reckon that their glory which is their shame! But *their* day will come to fall who thus make themselves *the terror of thy mighty,* and much more of the feeble, *in the land of the living.*

(3.) He threatens what he will do to Jerusalem, which he was now about to lay siege to, *v.* 10, 11. He would master Jerusalem and her idols, as he had subdued other places and their idols, particularly Samaria. [1.] He blasphemously calls the God of Israel an *idol,* and sets him on a level with the false gods of other nations, as if none were the true God but Mithras, the sun, whom he worshipped. See how ignorant he was, and then we shall the less wonder that he was so proud. [2.] He prefers the graven images of other countries before those of Jerusalem and Samaria, when he might have known that the worshippers of the God of Israel were expressly forbidden to make any graven images, and if any did it must be by stealth, and therefore they could not be so rich and pompous as those of other nations. If he means the ark and the mercy-seat, he speaks like himself, very foolishly, and as one that judged by the sight of the eye, and might therefore be easily deceived in matters of spiritual concern. Those who make external pomp and splendour a mark of the true church go by the same rule. [3.] Because he had conquered Samaria, he concluded Jerusalem would fall of course: *"Shall not I do so to Jerusalem?* can I not as easily, and may I not as justly?" But it did not follow; for Jerusalem adhered to her God, whereas Samaria had forsaken him.

III. See how God, in his justice, rebukes his pride and reads his doom. We have heard what the great king, the king of Assyria, says, and how big he talks. Let us now hear what the great God has to say by his servant the prophet, and we shall find that, wherein he deals proudly, God is above him.

1. He shows the vanity of his insolent and audacious boasts (*v.* 15): *Shall the axe boast itself against him that hews therewith? or shall the saw magnify itself against him that draws it?* So absurd are the boasts of this proud man. "O what a dust do I make!" said the fly upon the cart-wheel in the fable. "What destruction do I make among the trees!" says the axe. Two ways the axe may be said to *boast itself against him that hews with it:* — (1.) By way of resistance and opposition. Sennacherib blasphemed God, insulted him, threatened to serve him as he had served the gods of the nations; now this was as if the axe should fly in the face of him that hews with it. The tool striving with the workman is no less absurd than the clay striving with the potter; and as it is a thing not to be justified that men should fight against God with the wit, and wealth, and power, which he gives them, so it is a thing not to be suffered. But if men will be thus proud and daring, and bid defiances to all that is just and sacred, let them expect that God will reckon with them; the more insolent they are the surer and sorer will their ruin be. (2.) By way of rivalship and competition. Shall the axe take to itself the praise of the work it is employed in? So senseless, so absurd was it for Sennacherib to say, *By the strength of my hand I have done it, and by my wisdom, v.* 13. It is as if the rod, when it is shaken, should boast that it guides the hand which shakes it; whereas, *when the staff is lifted up, is it not wood still?* so the last clause may be read. If it be an ensign of authority (as the nobles of the people carried staves, Num. 21:18), if it be an instrument of service, either to support a weak man or to correct a bad man, still it is wood, and can do nothing but as it is directed by him that uses it. The psalmist prays that God would make the nations to know that they *were but men* (Ps. 9:20), the staff to know that it is but wood

2. He foretels his fall and ruin.

(1.) That when God had done his work by him he would then do his work upon him, *v.* 12. For the comfort of the people of God in reference to Sennacherib's invasion, though it was a dismal time with them, let them know, [1.] That God designed to do good to Zion and Jerusalem by this providence. There is a work to be done upon them, which God intends, and which he will perform. Note, When God lets loose the enemies of his church and people, and suffers them for a time to prevail, it is in order to the performing of some great good work upon them; and, when that is done, then, and not till then, he will work deliverance for them. When God brings his people into trouble it is to try them (Dan. 11:35), to bring sin to their remembrance and humble them for it, and to awaken them to a sense of their duty, to teach them to pray and to love and help one another; and *this must be the fruit, even the taking away of sin, ch.* 27:9. When these points are, in some measure, gained by the affliction, it shall be removed, in mercy (Lev. 26:41, 42), otherwise not; for, as the word, so the rod shall *accomplish that for which God sends it.* [2.] That when God had wrought this work of grace for his people he would work a work of wrath and vengeance upon their invaders: *I will punish the fruit of the stout heart of the king of Assyria.* His big words are here said to come from his stout heart, and they are the fruit of it; for *out of the abundance of the heart the mouth speaks.* Notice is taken too of the *glory of his high looks,* for a proud look is the indication of a proud spirit. The enemies of the church are commonly very high and haughty; but, sooner or later, God will reckon for their haughtiness. He glories in it as an incontestable proof of his power and sovereignty that he *looks upon proud men and abases them,* Job 40:11, etc.

(2.) That, how threatening soever this attempt was upon Zion and Jerusalem, it should certainly be baffled, and broken, and come to nothing, and he should not be able to bring to pass his enterprise, *v.* 16, 19. Observe,

[1.] Who it is that undertakes his destruction, and will be the author of it; not Hezekiah, or his princes, or the militia of Judah and Jerusalem (what can they do against such a potent force?), but God himself will do it, as *the Lord of hosts,* and as *the light of Israel. First,* We are sure he can do it, for he is *the Lord of hosts,* of all the hosts of heaven and earth. All the creatures are at his command; he makes what use he pleases on them. He is the Lord of the hosts both of Judah and of Assyria, and can give the victory to which he pleases. Let us not fear the hosts of any enemy if we have the Lord of hosts for us. *Secondly,* We have reason to hope he will do it, for he is *the light of Israel, and his Holy One.* God is light; in him are perfect brightness, purity, and happiness. He is light, for he is the Holy One; his holiness is his glory. He is Israel's light, to direct and counsel his people, to favour and countenance them, and so to gladden and comfort them in the worst of times. He is their Holy One, for he is in covenant with them; his holiness is engaged and employed for them. God's holiness is the saints' comfort; they *give thanks at the remembrance* of it, and with a great deal of pleasure call him *their Holy One,* Hab. 1:12.

[2.] How this destruction is represented. It shall be, *First,* As a consumption of the body by a disease: *The Lord shall send leanness among his fatnesses,* or *his fat ones.* His numerous army, that was like a body covered with fatness, shall be diminished, and waste away, and become like a skeleton. *Secondly,* As a consumption of buildings, or trees and bushes, by fire: *Under his glory,* that very thing which he glories in, *he will kindle a burning, as the burning of a fire,* which shall lay his army in ruins as suddenly as a raging fire lays a stately house in ashes. Some make it an allusion to the fire kindled under the sacrifices; for proud sinners fall as sacrifices to divine justice. Observe, 1. How this fire shall be kindled, *v.* 17. The same God that is a rejoicing light to those that serve him faithfully will be a consuming fire to those that trifle with him or rebel against him. *The light of Israel shall be for a fire* to the Assyrians, as the same pillar of cloud was a light to the Israelites and a terror to the Egyptians in the Red Sea. What can oppose, what can extinguish, such a fire? 2. What desolation it shall make: *it shall burn and devour its thorns and briers,* his officers and soldiers, which are of little worth, and vexations to God's Israel, as thorns and briers, whose end is to be burned, and which are easily and quickly consumed by a devouring fire. *"Who would set the briers and thorns against me in battle?* They would be so far from stopping the fire that they would inflame it. *I would go through them and burn them together* (*ch.* 27:4); they shall be devoured in one day, all cut off in an instant." When they cried not only Peace and safety, but Victory and triumph, then sudden destruction came; it came surprisingly, and was completed in a little time. "Even *the glory of his forest* (*v.* 18), the choice troops of his army, the veterans, the troops of the household, the bravest regiments he had, that he was most proud of and depended most upon, that he valued as men do their timber-trees (the glory of their forest) or their fruit-trees (the glory of the Carmel), shall be put as briers and thorns before the fire; they shall be consumed both soul and body, entirely consumed, not only a limb burned, but life taken away." Note, God is able to destroy both soul and body, and therefore we should fear him more than man, who can but kill the body. Great armies before him are but as great woods, which he can fell or fire when he pleases.

[3.] What would be the effect of this great slaughter. The prophet tells us, *First,* That the army would hereby be reduced to a very small number: *The rest of the trees of his forest shall be few;* very few shall escape the sword of the destroying angel, so few that there needs no artist, no muster-master or secretary of war, to take an account of them, for even *a child may* soon reckon the numbers of them, and *write* the names of *them. Secondly,* That those few who remained should be quite dispirited: *They shall be as when a standard-bearer fainteth.* When he either falls or flees, and his colours are taken by the enemy, this discourages the whole army, and puts them all into confusion. Upon the whole matter we must say, *Who is able to stand before this great and holy Lord God?*

Verses 20–23

The prophet had said (*v.* 12) that *the Lord would perform his whole work upon Mount Zion and upon Jerusalem,* by Sennacherib's invading the land. Now here we are told what that work should be, a twofold work: —

I. The conversion of some, to whom this providence should be sanctified and yield the peaceable fruit of righteousness, though for the present it was not joyous, but grievous; these are but a remnant (*v.* 22), *the remnant of Israel* (*v.* 20), *the remnant of Jacob* (*v.* 21), but a very few in comparison with the vast numbers of the people of Israel, who were as the sand of the sea. Note, Converting work is wrought but on a remnant, who are distinguished from the rest and set apart for God. When we see how populous Israel is, how numerous the members of the visible church are, as the sand of the sea, and yet consider that of these a remnant only shall be saved, that of the many that are called there are but few chosen, we shall surely *strive to enter in at the strait gate* and fear lest we *seem to come short.* This remnant of Israel are said to be *such as had escaped of the house of Jacob,* such as escaped the corruptions of the house of Jacob, and kept their integrity in times of common apostasy; and that was a fair escape. And therefore they escape the desolations of that house, and shall be preserved in safety in times of common calamity; and that also will be a fair and narrow escape. Their *lives shall be given them for a prey,* Jer. 45:5. The *righteous scarcely are saved.* Now, 1. This remnant shall come off from all confidence in an arm of flesh, this providence shall cure them of that: "They *shall no more again stay upon him that smote them,* shall never depend upon the Assyrians, as they have done, for help against their other enemies, finding that they are themselves their worst enemies." *Ictus piscator sapit — sufferings teach caution.* "They have now learned by dear-bought experience the folly of leaning upon that staff as a stay to them which may perhaps prove a staff to beat them." It is part of the covenant of a returning people (Hos. 14:3), *Assyria shall not save us.* Note, By our afflictions we may learn not to make creatures our confidence. 2. They shall come home to God, to the mighty God (one of the names given to the Messiah, *ch.* 9:6), to the Holy One of Israel: *"The remnant shall return* (that was signified by the name of the prophet's son, *Shear-jashub, ch.* 7:3), *even the remnant of Jacob.* They shall return, after the raising of the siege of Jerusalem, not only to the quiet possession of their houses and lands, but to God and to their duty; they shall repent, and pray, and seek his face, and reform their lives." The remnant that escape are a returning remnant: they shall return to God, and shall stay upon him. Note, Those only may with comfort stay upon God that return to him; then may we have a humble confidence in God when we make conscience of our duty to him. They *shall stay upon the Holy One of Israel, in truth,* and not in pretence and profession only. This promise of the conversion and salvation of a remnant of Israel is applied by the apostle (Rom. 9:27) to the remnant of the Jews which at the first preaching of the gospel received and entertained it, and sufficiently proves that it was no new thing for God to abandon to ruin a great many of the seed of Abraham in full force and virtue; for so it was now. The number of the children of Israel was *as the sand of the sea* (according to the promise, Gen. 22:17), and yet only a remnant shall be saved.

II. The consumption of others: *The Lord God of hosts shall make a consumption, v.* 23. This is not meant (as that *v.* 18) of the consumption of the Assyrian army, but of the consumption of the estates and families of many of the Jews by the Assyrian army. This is taken notice of to magnify the power and goodness of God in the escape of the distinguished remnant, and to let us know what shall become of those that will not return to God; they shall be wasted away by this consumption, this general decay *in the midst of the land.* Observe, 1. It is a consumption of God's own making; he is the author of it. The Lord God of hosts, whom none can resist, shall make this consumption. 2. It is *decreed.* It is not the product of a sudden resolve, but was before ordained. It is *determined,* not only that there shall be such a consumption, but it is *cut out* (so the word is); it is particularly appointed how far it shall extend and how long it shall continue, who shall be consumed by it and who not. 3. It is an overflowing consumption, that shall overspread the land, and, like a mighty torrent or inundation, bear down all before it. 4. Though it overflows, it is not at random, but in *righteousness,* which signifies both wisdom and equity. God will justly bring this consumption upon a provoking people, but he will wisely and graciously set bounds to it. *Hitherto it shall come, and no further.*

Verses 24–34

The prophet, in his preaching, distinguishes between the precious and the vile; for God in his providence, even in the same providence, does so. He speaks terror, in Sennacherib's invasion, to the hypocrites, who were the *people of God's wrath, v.* 6. But here he speaks comfort to the sincere, who were the people of God's love. The judgment was sent for the sake of the former; the deliverance was wrought for the sake of the latter. Here we have,

I. An exhortation to God's people not to be frightened at this threatening calamity, nor to be put into any confusion or consternation by it. *Let the sinners in Zion be afraid* (*ch.* 33:14): but *O my people, that dwellest in Zion, be not afraid of the Assyrian, v.* 24. Note, It is against the mind and will of God that his people, whatever may happen, should give way to that fear which has torment and amazement. Those that dwell in Zion, where God dwells and where his people attend him, and are employed in his service, that are under the protection of the bulwarks that are *round about Zion* (Ps. 48:13), need not be afraid of any enemy. Let their souls dwell at ease in God.

II. Considerations offered for the silencing of their fear. 1. The Assyrian shall do nothing against them but what God has appointed and determined. They are here told before hand what he shall do, that it may be no surprise to them: *"He shall smite thee* by the divine permission, but it shall be only *with a rod* to correct thee, not with a sword to wound and kill; nay, *he shall but lift up his staff against thee,* threaten thee, and frighten thee, and shake the rod at thee, *after the manner of Egypt,* as the Egyptians shook their staff against your fathers at the Red Sea, when they said, *We will pursue, we will overtake* (Ex. 15:9), but could not reach to do them any hurt." Note, We should not be frightened at those enemies that can do no more than frighten us.

2. The storm shall soon blow over (*v.* 25): *Yet a very little while — a little, little while* (so the word is), *and the indignation shall cease, even my anger,* which is *the staff in their hand* (*v.* 5), so that when that ceases they are disarmed and disabled to do any further mischief. Note, God's anger against his people is but for a moment (Ps. 30:5), and when that ceases, and is turned away from us, we need not fear the fury of any man, for it is impotent passion.

3. The enemy that threatens them shall himself be reckoned with. God's anger against his people *shall cease in the destruction* of their enemies; when he turns away his wrath from Israel he shall turn it against the Assyrian; and the rod with which he corrected his people shall not only be laid aside, but thrown into the fire. He *lifted up his staff* against Zion, but God *shall stir up a scourge for him* (*v.* 26); he is a terror to God's people, but God will be a terror to him. The destroying angel shall be this scourge, which he can neither flee from nor contend with. The prophet, for the encouragement of God's people, quotes precedents, and puts them in mind of what God had done formerly against the enemies of his church, who were very strong and formidable, but were brought to ruin. The destruction of the Assyrian shall be, (1.) *According to the slaughter of Midian* (which was effected by an invisible power, but effected suddenly, and it was a total rout); and as, *at the rock of Oreb,* one of the princes of Midian, after the battle, was slain, so shall Sennacherib be in the temple of his god Nisroch, after the defeat of his forces, when he thinks the bitterness of death is past. Compare with this Ps. 83:11, *Make their nobles like Oreb and like Zeeb;* and see how God's promises and his people's prayers agree. (2.) *As his rod was upon the sea,* the Red Sea, as Moses' rod was upon that, to divide it first for the escape of Israel and then to close it again for the destruction of their pursuers, so shall his rod now be *lifted up, after the manner of Egypt,* for the deliverance of Jerusalem and the destruction of the Assyrian. Note, It is good to observe a resemblance between God's latter and former appearances for his people, and against his and their enemies.

4. They shall be wholly delivered from the power of the Assyrian, and from the fear of it, *v.* 27. "They shall not only be eased of the Assyrian army, which is now quartered upon them and which is a grievous yoke and burden to them, but they shall no more pay that tribute to the king of Assyria which before this invasion he exacted from them (2 Ki. 18:14), shall be no longer at his service, nor lie at his mercy, as they have done; nor shall he ever again put the country under contribution." Some think it looks further, to the deliverance of the Jews out of their captivity in Babylon; and further yet, to the redemption of believers from the tyranny of sin and Satan. The yoke shall not only be taken away, but it *shall be destroyed.* The enemy shall no more recover his strength, to do the mischief he has done; and this *because of the anointing,* for their sakes who were partakers of the anointing. (1.) For Hezekiah's sake, who was the anointed of the Lord, who had been an active reformer, and was dear to God. (2.) For David's sake. This is particularly given as the reason why God would defend Jerusalem from Sennacherib (*ch.* 37:35), *For my own sake, and for my servant David's sake.* (3.) For his people Israel's sake, the good people among them that had received the unction of divine grace. (4.) For the sake of the Messiah, the Anointed of God, whom God had an eye to in all the deliverances of the Old-Testament church, and hath still an eye to in all the favours he shows to his people. It is for his sake that the yoke is broken, and that we are made free indeed.

III. A description both of the terror of the enemy and the terror with which many were struck by it, and the folly of both exposed, *v.* 28, to the end. Here observe,

1. How formidable the Assyrians were and how daring and threatening they affected to appear. Here is a particular description of the march of Sennacherib, what course he steered, what swift advances he made: *He has come to Aiath,* etc. "This and the other place he has made himself master of, and has met with no opposition." *At Michmash he has laid up his carriages,* as if he had no further occasion for his heavy artillery, so easily was every place he came to reduced; or the store-cities of Judah, which were fortified for that purpose, had now become his magazines. Some remarkable pass, and an important one, he had taken: *They have gone over the passage.*

2. How cowardly the men of Judah were, the degenerate seed of that lion's whelp. They were *afraid;* they *fled* upon the first alarm, and did not offer to make any head against the enemy. Their apostasy from God had dispirited them, so that one chased a thousand of them. Instead of a valiant shout, to animate one another, nothing was heard by lamentation, to discourage and weaken one another. And *poor Anathoth,* a priests' city, that should have been a pattern of courage, shrieks louder than any, *v.* 30. With respect to those that *gathered themselves* together, it was not to fight, but to flee by consent, *v.* 31. This is designed either, (1.) To show how fast the news of the enemy's progress flew through the kingdom: *He has come to Aiath,*

says one; nay, says another, *He has passed to Migron*, etc. And yet, perhaps, it was not altogether so bad as common fame represented it. But we must watch against the fear, not only of evil things, but of evil tidings, which often make things worse than really they are, Ps. 112:7. Or, (2.) To show what imminent danger Jerusalem was in, when its enemies made so many bold advances towards it and its friends could not make one bold stand to defend it. Note, The more daring the church's enemies are, and the more dastardly those are that should appear for her, the more will God be exalted in his own strength, when, notwithstanding this, he works deliverance for her.

3. How impotent his attempt upon Jerusalem shall be: *he shall remain at Nob*, whence he may see Mount Zion, and there *he shall shake his hand* against it, *v.* 32. He shall threaten it, and that shall be all; it shall be safe, and shall set him at defiance. The daughter of Jerusalem, to be even with him, shall *shake her head* at him, *ch.* 37:22.

4. How fatal it would prove, in the issue, to himself. When he *shakes his hand at Jerusalem,* and is about to lay hands on it, then is God's time to appear against him; for Zion is the place of which God has said, *This is my rest for ever;* therefore those who threaten it affront God himself. Then *the Lord shall lop the bough with terror and cut down the thickets of the forest, v.* 33, 34. (1.) The pride of the enemy shall be humbled, the boughs that are lifted up on high shall be lopped off, the high and stately trees shall be hewn down; that is, the haughty shall be humbled. Those that lift up themselves in competition with God or opposition to him shall be abased. (2.) The power of the enemy shall be broken: *The thickets of the forest he shall cut down.* When the Assyrian soldiers were under their arms, and their spears erect, they looked like a forest, like Lebanon; but, when in one night they all became as dead corpses, the pikes were laid on the ground, and Lebanon was of a sudden cut down *by a mighty one,* by the destroying angel, who in a little time slew so many thousands of them: and, if this shall be the exit of that proud invader, let not God's people be afraid of him. *Who art thou, that thou shouldst be afraid of a man that shall die?*

CHAPTER 11

It is a very good transition in prophecy (whether it be so in rhetoric or no), and a very common one, to pass from the prediction of the temporal deliverances of the church to that of the great salvation, which in the fulness of time should be wrought out by Jesus Christ, of which the other were types and figures, to which all the prophets bore witness; and so the ancient Jews understood them. For what else was it that raised so great an expectation of the Messiah at the time he came. Upon occasion of the prophecy of the deliverance of Jerusalem from Sennacherib, here comes in a prophecy concerning Messiah the Prince. I. His rise out of the house of David (*v.* 1). II. His qualifications for his great undertaking (*v.* 2, 3). III. The justice and equity of his government (*v.* 3–5). IV. The peaceableness of his kingdom (*v.* 6–9). V. The accession of the Gentiles to it (*v.* 10), and with them the remnant of the Jews, that should be united with them in the Messiah's kingdom (*v.* 11–16) and of all this God would now shortly give them a type, and some dark representation, in the excellent government of Hezekiah, the great peace which the nation should enjoy under him, after the ruin of Sennacherib's design, and the return of many of the ten tribes out of their dispersion to their brethren of the land of Judah, when they enjoyed that great tranquility.

Verses 1–9

The prophet had before, in this sermon, spoken of a child that should be born, a son that should be given, on whose shoulders the government should be, intending this for the comfort of the people of God in times of trouble, as dying Jacob, many ages before, had intended the prospect of Shiloh for the comfort of his seed in their affliction in Egypt. He had said (*ch.* 10:27) that *the yoke should be destroyed because of the anointing;* now here he tells us on whom that anointing should rest. He foretels,

I. That the Messiah should, in due time, arise out of the house of David, as that *branch* of the Lord which he had said (*ch.* 4:2) should be excellent and glorious; the word is *Netzer,* which some think is referred to in Mt. 2:23, where it is said to be spoken by the prophets of the Messiah that he *should be called a Nazarene.* Observe here, 1. Whence this branch should arise — from *Jesse.* He should be the son of David, with whom the covenant of royalty was made, and to whom it was promised with an oath that *of the fruit of his loins God would raise of Christ,* Acts 2:30. David is often called *the son of Jesse,* and Christ is called so, because he was to be not only the Son of David, but David himself, Hos. 3:5. 2. The meanness of his appearance. (1.) He is called a *rod,* and a *branch;* both the words here used signify a weak, small, tender product, a *twig* and a *sprig* (so some render them), such as is easily broken off. The enemies of God's church were just before compared to strong and stately boughs (*ch.* 10:33), which will not, without great labour, be hewn down, but Christ to a tender branch (*ch.* 53:2); yet he shall be victorious over them. (2.) He is said to come out of Jesse rather than David, because Jesse lived and died in meanness and obscurity; his family was of small account (1 Sa. 18:18), and it was in a way of contempt and reproach that David was sometimes called the *son of Jesse,* 1 Sa. 22:7. (3.) He comes forth out of the *stem,* or *stump,* of Jesse. When the royal family, that had been as a cedar, was cut down, and only the stump of it left, almost levelled with the ground and lost in the grass of the field (Dan. 4:15), yet it shall sprout again (Job 14:7); nay, it *shall grow out of his roots,* which are quite buried in the earth, and, like the roots of flowers in the winter, have no stem appearing above ground. The house of David was reduced and brought very low at the time of Christ's birth, witness the obscurity and poverty of Joseph and Mary. The Messiah was thus to begin his estate of humiliation, for submitting to which he should be highly exalted, and would thus give early notice that his kingdom was not of this world. The Chaldee paraphrase reads this, *There shall come forth a King from the sons of Jesse, and the Messiah* (or Christ) *shall be anointed out of his sons' sons.*

II. That he should be every way qualified for that great work to which he was designed, that this tender branch should be so watered with the dews of heaven as to become a strong rod for a sceptre to rule, *v.* 2. 1. In general, *the Spirit of the Lord shall rest upon him.* The Holy Spirit, in all his gifts and graces, shall not only come, but rest and abide upon him; he shall have the Spirit not by measure, but without measure, the fulness of the Godhead dwelling in him, Col. 1:19; 2:9. He began his preaching with this (Lu. 4:18), *The Spirit of the Lord is upon me.* 2. In particular, the spirit of government, by which he should be every way fitted for that judgment which the Father has committed to him and *given him authority to execute* (Jn. 5:22, 27), and not only so, but should be made the fountain and treasury of all grace to believers, that from his fulness they might all receive the Spirit of grace, as all the members of the body derive animal spirits from the head. (1.) He shall have *the spirit of wisdom and understanding, of counsel and knowledge;* he shall thoroughly understand the business he is to be employed in. *No man knows the Father but the Son,* Mt. 11:27. What he is to make known to the children of men concerning God, and his mind and will, he shall be himself acquainted with and apprised of, Jn. 1:18. He shall know how to administer the affairs of his spiritual kingdom in all the branches of it, so as effectually to answer the two great intentions of it, the glory of God and the welfare of the children of men. The terms of the covenant shall be settled by him, and ordinances instituted, in wisdom: treasures of wisdom shall be hid in him; he shall be our counsellor, and shall be made of God to us wisdom. (2.) *The spirit of courage,* or *might,* or fortitude. The undertaking was very great, abundance of difficulty must be broken through, and therefore it was necessary that he should be so endowed that he *might not fail or be discouraged, ch.* 42:4. He was famed for courage in his teaching the way of God in truth, and not caring for any man, Mt. 22:16. (3.) The spirit of religion, or *the fear of the Lord;* not only he shall himself have a reverent affection for his Father, as his servant (*ch.* 42:1), and he was heard in *that he feared* (Heb. 5:7), but he shall have a zeal for religion, and shall design the advancement of it in his whole undertaking. Our faith in Christ was never designed to supersede and jostle out, but to increase and support, our fear of the Lord.

III. That he should be accurate, and critical, and very exact in the administration of his government and the exercise of the power committed to him (*v.* 3): The Spirit wherewith he shall be clothed *shall make him of quick understanding in the fear of the Lord* — of an acute smell or scent (so the word is), for the apprehensions of the mind are often expressed by the sensations of the body. Note, 1. Those are most truly and valuably intelligent that are so in the fear of the Lord, in the business of religion, for that is both the foundation and top-stone of wisdom. 2. By this it will appear that we have the Spirit of God, if we have spiritual senses exercised, and are of *quick understanding in the fear of the lord.* Those have divine illumination that know their duty and know how to go about it. 3. *Therefore* Jesus Christ had the spirit without measure, that he might perfectly understand his undertaking; and he did so, as appears not only in the admirable answers he gave to all that questioned with him, which proved him to be of *quick understanding in the fear of the Lord,* but in the management of his whole undertaking. He has settled the great affair of religion so unexpectedly well (so as effectually to secure both God's honour and man's happiness) that, it must be owned, he thoroughly understood it.

IV. That he should be just and righteous in all the acts of his government, and there should appear in it as much equity as wisdom. He shall judge as he expresses it himself, and as he himself would be judged of, Jn. 7:24. 1. Not according to outward appearance (*v.* 3): *he shall not judge after the sight of his eyes,* with respect of persons (Job 34:19) and according to outward shows and appearances, not *reprove after the hearing of his ears,* by common fame and report, and the representations of others, as men commonly do; nor does he judge of men by the fair words they speak, *calling him, Lord, Lord,* or their plausible actions before the eye of the world, which they do to be seen of men; but he will judge by the hidden man of the heart, and the inward principles men are governed by, of which he is an infallible witness. Christ will judge the secrets of men (Rom. 2:16), will determine concerning them, not according to their own pretensions and appearances (that were to *judge after the sight of the eyes*), not according to the opinion others have of them (that were to judge after the hearing of the ears), but we are sure that *his judgment is according to truth.* 2. He will judge righteous judgment (*v.* 5): *Righteousness shall be the girdle of his loins.* He shall be righteous in the administration of his government, and his righteousness shall be his girdle; it shall constantly compass him and cleave to him, shall be his ornament and honour; he shall gird himself for every action, shall gird on his sword for war in righteousness; his righteousness shall be his strength, and shall make him expeditious in his undertakings, as a man with his loins girt. In conformity to Christ, his followers must have the girdle of truth (Eph. 6:14) and it will be the stability of the times. Particularly, (1.) He shall in righteousness plead for the people that are poor and oppressed; he will be their protector (*v.* 4): *With righteousness shall he judge the poor;* he shall judge in favour and defence of those that have right on their side, though they are poor in the world, and because they are poor in spirit. It is the duty of princes to defend and deliver the poor (Ps. 82:3, 4), and the honour of Christ that he is the poor man's King, Ps. 72:2, 4. He shall *debate with evenness for the meek of the earth,* or of the land; those that bear the injuries done them with meekness and patience are in a special manner entitled to the divine care and protection. *I, as a deaf man, heard not, for thou wilt hear,* Ps. 38:13, 14. Some read it, *He shall reprove or correct the meek of the earth with equity.* If his own people, the meek of the land, do amiss, he will *visit their transgression with the rod.* (2.) He shall in righteousness plead against his enemies that are proud and oppressors (*v.* 4): *But he shall smite the earth,* the man of the earth, that doth oppress (see Ps. 10:18), the men of the world, that *mind earthly things* only (Ps. 17:14); these he shall smite *with the rod of his mouth,* the word of his mouth, speaking terror and ruin to them; his threatenings shall take hold of them, and be executed upon them. *With the breath of his lips,* by the operation of his Spirit, according to his word, and working with and by it, *he shall slay the wicked.* He will do it easily, with a word's speaking, as he laid those flat who came to seize him, by saying *I am he,* Jn. 18:6. Killing terrors shall arrest their consciences, killing judgments shall ruin them, their power, and all their interests; and in the other world everlasting tribulation will be recompensed to those that trouble his poor people. The apostle applies this to the destruction of the man of sin, whom he calls *that wicked one* (2 Th. 2:8) *whom the Lord will consume with the spirit of his mouth.* And the Chaldee here reads it, *He shall slay that wicked Romulus,* or Rome, as Mr. Hugh Broughton understands it.

V. That there should be great peace and tranquillity under his government; this is an explication of what was said in *ch.* 9:6, that he should be the Prince of peace. Peace signifies two things: —

1. Unity or concord, which is intimated in these figurative promises, that even *the wolf shall dwell* peaceably *with the lamb;* men of the most fierce and furious dispositions, who used to bite and devour all about them, shall have their temper so strangely altered by the efficacy of the gospel and grace of Christ that they shall live in love even with the weakest and such as formerly they would have made an easy prey of. So far shall the sheep be from hurting one another, as sometimes they have done (Eze. 34:20, 21), that even the wolves shall agree with them. Christ, who is our peace, came to slay all enmities and to settle lasting friendships among his followers, particularly between Jews and Gentiles: when multitudes of both, being converted to the faith of Christ, united in one sheep-fold, then the wolf and the lamb dwelt together; the wolf did not so much as threaten the lamb, nor was the lamb afraid of the wolf. *The leopard shall* not only not tear the kid, but shall *lie down with her:* even *their young ones shall lie down together,* and shall be trained up in a blessed amity, in order to the perpetuating of it. *The lion shall* cease to be ravenous and *shall eat straw like the ox,* as some think all the beasts of prey did before the fall. *The asp* and *the cockatrice* shall cease to be venomous, so that parents shall let their children *play* with them and *put their hands* among them. A generation of vipers shall become a seed of saints, and the old complaint of *homo homini lupus — man is a wolf to man,* shall be at an end. Those that inhabit the holy mountain shall live as amicably as the creatures did that were with Noah in the ark, and it shall be a means of their preservation, for *they shall not hurt nor destroy* one another as they have done. Now, (1.) This is fulfilled in the wonderful effect of the gospel upon the minds of those that sincerely embrace it; it changes the nature, and makes those that trampled on the meek of the earth, not only meek like them, but affectionate towards them. When Paul, who had persecuted the saints, joined himself to them, then the *wolf dwelt with the lamb.* (2.) Some are willing to hope it shall yet have a further accomplishment in the latter days, when *swords shall be beaten into ploughshares.*

2. Safety or security. Christ, the great Shepherd, shall take such care of the flock that those who would hurt them shall not; they shall not only not destroy one another, but no enemy from without shall be permitted to give them any molestation. The property of troubles, and of death itself, shall be so altered that they shall not do any real hurt to, much less shall they be the destruction of, any that *have their conversation in the holy mountain,* 1 Pt. 3:13. *Who,* or what, *can harm us, if we be followers of him that is good?* God's people shall be delivered, not only from evil, but from the fear of it. Even *the sucking child* shall without any terror *play upon the hole of the asp;* blessed Paul does so when he says, *Who shall separate us from the love of Christ?* and, *O death! where is thy sting?*

Lastly, Observe what shall be the effect, and what the cause, of this wonderful softening and sweetening of men's tempers by the grace of God. 1. The effect of it shall be tractableness, and a willingness to receive instruction: *A little child shall lead those* who formerly scorned to be controlled by the strongest man. Calvin understands it of their willing submission to the ministers of Christ, who are to instruct with meekness and not to use any coercive power, but to be as *little children,* Mt. 18:3. See 2 Co. 8:5. 2. The cause of it shall be the knowledge of God. The more there is of that the more there is of a disposition to peace. They shall thus live in love, *for the earth shall be full of the knowledge of the Lord,* which shall extinguish men's heats and animosities. The better acquainted we are with the God of love the more shall we be changed into the same image and the better affected shall we be to all those that bear his image. The earth shall be as full of this knowledge as the channels of the sea are of water — so broad and extensive shall this knowledge be and so far shall it spread — so deep and substantial shall this knowledge be, and so long shall it last. There is much more of the knowledge of God to be got by the gospel of Christ than could be got by the law of Moses; and, whereas *then* in *Judah* only was God known, now *all shall know him,* Heb. 8:11.

But that is knowledge falsely so called which sows discord among men; the right knowledge of God settles peace.

Verses 10–16

We have here a further prophecy of the enlargement and advancement of the kingdom of the Messiah, under the type and figure of the flourishing condition of the kingdom of Judah in the latter end of Hezekiah's reign, after the defeat of Sennacherib.

I. This prediction was in part accomplished when the great things God did for Hezekiah and his people proved as an ensign, inviting the neighbouring nations to them *to enquire of the wonders done in the land,* on which errand the king of Babylon's ambassadors came. To them the Gentiles sought; and Jerusalem, the rest or habitation of the Jews, was then glorious, *v.* 10. Then many of the Israelites who belonged to the kingdom of the ten tribes, who upon the destruction of that kingdom by the king of Assyria were forced to flee for shelter into all the countries about and to some that lay very remote, even to the islands of the sea, were encouraged to return to their own country and put themselves under the protection and government of the king of Judah, the rather because it was an Assyrian army by which their country had been ruined and that was not routed. This is said to be a recovery of them *the second time* (*v.* 11), such an instance of the power and goodness of God, and such a reviving to them, as their first deliverance out of Egypt was. Then the *outcasts of Israel* should be gathered in, and brought home, and those of Judah too, who, upon the approach of the Assyrian army, shifted for their own safety. Then the old feud between Ephraim and Judah shall be forgotten, and they shall join against the Philistines and their other common enemies, *v.* 13, 14. Note, Those who have been sharers with each other in afflictions and mercies, dangers and deliverances, ought in consideration thereof to unite for their joint and mutual safety and protection; and it is likely to be well with the church when Ephraim and Judah are one against the Philistines. Then, whatever difficulties there may be in the way of the return of the dispersed, the Lord shall find out some way or other to remove them, as when he brought Israel out of Egypt he dried up the Red Sea and Jordan (*v.* 15) and led them to Canaan through the invincible embarrassments of a vast howling wilderness, *v.* 16. The like will he do this second time, or that which shall be equivalent. When God's time has come for the deliverance of his people mountains of opposition shall become plain before him. Let us not despair therefore when the interests of the church seem to be brought very low; God can soon turn gloomy days into glorious ones.

II. It had a further reference to the days of the Messiah and the accession of the Gentiles to his kingdom; for to these the apostle applies *v.* 10, of which the following verses are a continuation. Rom. 15:12, *There shall be a root of Jesse; and he that shall rise to reign over the Gentiles, in him shall the Gentiles trust.* That is a key to this prophecy, which speaks of Christ as the root of Jesse, or *a branch out of his roots* (*v.* 1), *a root out of a dry ground, ch.* 53:2. He is the *root of David* (Rev. 5:5), the *root and offspring of David* Rev. 22:16.

1. *He shall stand,* or be set up, *for an ensign of the people.* When he was crucified he was *lifted up from the earth,* that, as an ensign of beacon, he might *draw* the eyes and the hearts of *all men unto him,* Jn. 12:32. He is set up as an ensign in the preaching of the everlasting gospel, in which the ministers, as standard-bearers, display the banner of his love, to allure us to him (Cant. 1:4), the banner of his truth, under which we may enlist ourselves, to engage in a holy war against sin and Satan. Christ is the ensign to which *the children of God that were scattered abroad are gathered together* (Jn. 11:51), and in him they meet as the centre of their unity.

2. *To him shall the Gentiles seek.* We read of Greeks that did so (Jn. 12:21, *We would see Jesus*), and upon that occasion Christ spoke of his being lifted up, to draw all men to him. The apostle, from the Septuagint (or perhaps the Septuagint from the apostle, in the editions after Christ) reads it (Rom. 15:12), *In him shall the Gentiles trust;* they shall seek to him with a dependence on him.

3. *His rest shall be glorious.* Some understand this of the death of Christ (the triumphs of the cross made even that glorious), others of his ascension, when he sat down

to rest at the right hand of God. Or rather it is meant of the gospel church, that Mount Zion of which Christ has said, *This is my rest,* and in which he resides. This, though despised by the world, having upon it the beauty of holiness, is truly glorious, a *glorious high throne,* Jer. 17:12.

4. Both Jews and Gentiles shall be gathered to him, *v.* 11. A remnant of both, a little remnant in comparison, which shall be recovered, as it were, with great difficulty and hazard. As formerly God delivered his people, and gathered them out of all the countries whither they were scattered (Ps. 106:47; Jer. 16:15, 16), so he will a second time, in another way, by the powerful working of the Spirit of grace with the word. He *shall set his hand* to do it; he shall exert his power, the *arm of the Lord shall be revealed* to do it. (1.) There shall be a remnant of the Jews gathered in: *The outcasts of Israel and the dispersed of Judah* (*v.* 12), many of whom, at the time of the bringing of them in to Christ, were *Jews of the dispersion, the twelve tribes that were scattered abroad* (James 1:1; 1 Pt. 1:1), shall flock to Christ; and probably more of those scattered Jews were brought into the church, in proportion, than of those which remained in their own land. (2.) Many of *the nations,* the Gentiles, shall be brought in by the lifting up of the ensign. Jacob foretold concerning Shiloh that *to him should the gathering of the people be.* Those that were strangers and foreigners shall be made nigh. The Jews were jealous of Christ's going to the dispersed among the Gentiles and of his *teaching the Gentiles,* Jn. 7:35.

5. There shall be a happy accommodation between Judah and Ephraim, and both shall be safe from their adversaries and have dominion over them, *v.* 13, 14. The coalescence between Judah and Israel at that time was a type and figure of the uniting of Jews and Gentiles, who had been so long at variance in the gospel church. *The house of Judah shall walk with the house of Israel* (Jer. 3:18) and become *one nation* (Eze. 37:22); so the Jews and Gentiles are made of *twain one new man* (Eph. 2:15), and, being at peace one with another, those that are adversaries to them both shall be cut off; for *they shall fly upon the shoulders of the Philistines,* as an eagle strikes at her prey, shall spoil those on the west side of them, and then they shall extend their conquests eastward over the Edomites, Moabites, and Ammonites. The gospel of Christ shall be successful in all parts, and some of all nations shall become obedient to the faith.

6. Every thing that might hinder the progress and success of the gospel shall be taken out of the way. As when God brought Israel out of Egypt he dried up the Red Sea and Jordan before them (*ch.* 63:11, 12), and as afterwards when he brought up the Jews out of Babylon he *prepared them their way* (*ch.* 62:10), so when Jews and Gentiles are to be brought together into the gospel church all obstructions shall be removed (*v.* 15, 16), difficulties that seemed insuperable shall be strangely got over, *the blind shall be led by a way that they knew not.* See *ch.* 42:15, 16; 43:19, 20. Converts shall be brought in chariots and in litters, *ch.* 66:20. Some think it is the further accession of multitudes to the church that is pointed at in that obscure prophecy of the drying up of the river Euphrates, that the way of the kings of the east may be prepared (Rev. 16:12), which seems to refer to this prophecy. Note, When God's time has come for the bringing of nations, or particular persons, home to himself, divine grace will be victorious over all opposition. At the presence of the Lord the sea shall flee and Jordan be driven back; and those who set their faces heavenward will find there are not such difficulties in the way as they thought there were, for there is a highway thither, *ch.* 35:8.

CHAPTER 12

The salvation promised in the foregoing chapter was compared to that of Israel "in the day that he came up out of the land of Egypt;" so that chapter ends. Now as Moses and the children of Israel then sang a song of praise to the glory of God (Ex. 15:1) so shall the people of God do in that day when the root of Jesse shall stand for an ensign of the people and shall be the desire and joy of all nations. In that day, I. Every particular believer shall sing a song of praise for his own interest in that salvation (*v.* 1, 3). "Thou shalt say, Lord, I will praise thee." Thanksgiving-work shall be closet-work. II. Many in concert shall join in praising God for the common benefit arising from this salvation (*v.* 4–6): "You shall say, Praise you the Lord." Thanksgiving-work shall be congregation-work; and the praises of God shall be publicly sung in the congregations of the upright.

Verses 1–3

This is the former part of the hymn of praise which is prepared for the use of the church, of the Jewish church when God would work great deliverances for them, and of the Christian church when the kingdom of the Messiah should be set up in the world in despite of the opposition of the powers of darkness: *In that day thou shalt say, O Lord! I will praise thee.* The scattered church, being united into one body, shall, as one man, with one mind and one mouth, thus praise God, who is one and his name one. *In that day,* when the Lord shall do these great things for thee, *thou shalt say, O Lord! I will praise thee.* That is,

I. "Thou shalt have cause to say so." The promise is sure, and the blessings contained in it are very rich, and, when they are bestowed, will furnish the church with abundant matter for rejoicing and therefore with abundant matter for thanksgiving. The Old-Testament prophecies of gospel times are often expressed by the joy and praise that shall then be excited; for the inestimable benefits we enjoy by Jesus Christ require the most elevated and enlarged thanksgivings.

II. "Thou shalt have a heart to say so." All God's other gifts to his people shall be crowned with this. He will give them grace to ascribe all the glory of them to him, and to speak of them upon all occasions with thankfulness to his praise. *Thou shalt say,* that is, thou oughtest to say so. *In that day,* when many are brought home to Jesus Christ and flock to him as doves to their windows, instead of envying the kind reception they find with Christ, as the Jews grudged the favour shown to the Gentiles, *thou shalt say, O Lord! I will praise thee.* Note, we ought to rejoice in, and give thanks for, the grace of God to others as well as to ourselves.

1. Believers are here taught to give thanks to God for the turning away of his displeasure from them and the return of his favour to them (*v.* 1): *O Lord! I will praise thee, though thou wast angry with me.* Note, Even God's frowns must not put us out of tune for praising him; though he be angry with us, though he slay us, yet we must put our trust in him and give him thanks. God has often just cause to be angry with us, but we have never any reason to be angry with him, nor to speak otherwise than well of him; even when he blames us we must praise him. *Thou was angry with us,* but *thy anger is turned away.* Note, (1.) God is sometimes angry with his own people and the fruits of his anger do appear, and they ought to take notice of this, that they may humble themselves under his mighty hand. (2.) Though God may for a time be angry with his people, yet his anger shall at length be turned away; it endures but for a moment, nor will he contend for ever. By Jesus Christ, the root of Jesse, God's anger against mankind was turned away; for *he is our peace.* (3.) Those whom God is reconciled to he comforts; even the turning away of his anger is a comfort to them; yet that is not all: those that are *at peace with God* may *rejoice in hope of the glory of God,* Rom. 5:1, 2. Nay, God sometimes brings his people into a wilderness that there he may *speak comfortably to them,* Hosea 2:14. (4.) The turning away of God's anger, and the return of his comforts to us, ought to be the matter of our joyful thankful praises.

2. They are taught to triumph in God and their interest in him (*v.* 2): *"Behold,* and wonder; *God is my salvation;* not only my Saviour, by whom I am saved, but my salvation, in whom I am safe. I depend upon him as my salvation, for I have found him to be so. He shall have the glory of all the salvations that have been wrought for me, and from him only will I expect the salvations I further need, and not from hills and mountains: and if God be my salvation, if he undertake my eternal salvation, *I will trust* in him to prepare me for it and preserve me to it. I will trust him with all my temporal concerns, not doubting but he will make all to work for my good. I will be confident, that is, I will be always easy in my own mind." Note, Those that have God for their salvation may enjoy themselves with a holy security and serenity of mind. Let faith in God as our salvation be effectual, (1.) To silence our fears. We must *trust, and not be afraid,* not be afraid that the God we trust in will fail us; no, there is no danger of that; not be afraid of any creature, though ever so formidable and threatening. Note, Faith in God is a sovereign remedy against disquieting tormenting fears. (2.) To support our hopes. Is the Lord Jehovah our salvation? Then he will be our *strength and song.* We have work to do and temptations to resist, and we may depend upon him to enable us for both, to *strengthen us with all might by his Spirit in the inner man,* for he is our strength; his grace is so, and that grace shall be sufficient for us. We have many troubles to undergo, and must expect griefs in a vale of tears; and we may depend upon him to comfort us in all our tribulations, for he is our song; he *giveth songs in the night.* If we make God our strength, and put our confidence in him, he will be our strength; if we make him our song, and place our comfort in him, he will be our song. Many good Christians have God for their strength who have him not for their song; they walk in darkness: but light is sown for them. And those that have God for their strength ought to make him their song, that is, to give him the glory of it (see Ps. 68:35) and to take to themselves the comfort of it, for he will become their salvation. Observe the title here given to God: *Jah, Jehovah.* Jah is the contraction of Jehovah, and both signify his eternity and unchangeableness, which are a great comfort to those that depend upon him as their strength and their song. Some make Jah to signify the Son of God made man; he is Jehovah, and in him we may glory as our strength, and song, and salvation.

3. They are aught to derive comfort to themselves from the love of God and all the tokens of that love (*v.* 3): *"Therefore,* because the Lord Jehovah is your strength and song and will be your salvation, *you shall draw water with joy."* Note, The assurances God has given us of his love, and the experiences we have had of the benefit and comfort of his grace, should greatly encourage our faith in him and our expectations from him: *"Out of the wells of salvation* in God, who is the fountain of all good to his people, *you shall draw water with joy.* God's favour shall flow forth to you, and you shall have the comfort of it and make use of the blessed fruits of it." Note, (1.) God's promises revealed, ratified, and given out to us, in his ordinances, are wells of salvation; wells of *the Saviour* (so some read it), for in them the Saviour and salvation are made known to us and made over to us. (2.) It is our duty by faith to draw water out of these wells, to take to ourselves the benefit and comfort that are treasured up for us in them, as those that acknowledge all our fresh springs to be there and all our fresh streams to be thence, Ps. 87:7. (3.) Water is to be drawn out of the wells of salvation with a great deal of pleasure and satisfaction. It is the will of God that we should rejoice before him and rejoice in him (Deu. 26:11), be joyful in his house of prayer (Isa. 56:7), and keep his feasts with gladness, Acts 2:46.

Verses 4–6

This is the second part of this evangelical song, and to the same purport with the former; there believers stir up themselves to praise God, here they invite and encourage one another to do it, and are contriving to spread his praise and draw in others to join with them in it. Observe,

I. Who are here called upon to praise God — *the inhabitants of Zion* and Jerusalem, whom God had in a particular manner protected from Sennacherib's violence, *v.* 6. Those that have received distinguishing favours from God ought to be most forward and zealous in praising him. The gospel church is Zion. Christ is Zion's King. Those that have a place and a name in the church should lay out themselves to diffuse the knowledge of Christ and to bring many to him. *Thou inhabitress of Zion;* the word is feminine. Let the weaker sex be strong in the Lord, and out of their mouth praise shall be perfected.

II. How they must praise the Lord. 1. By prayer: *Call upon his name.* As giving thanks for former mercy is a decent way of begging further mercy, so begging further mercy is graciously accepted as a thankful acknowledgment of the mercies we have received. In calling upon God's name we give unto him some of the glory that is due to his name as our powerful and bountiful benefactor. 2. By preaching and writing. We must not only speak to God, but speak to others concerning him, not only call upon his name, but (as the margin reads it) *proclaim his name;* let others know something more from us than they did before concerning God, and those things whereby he has made himself known. *Declare his doings,* his *counsels* (so some read it); the work of redemption is according to the counsel of his will, and in that and other wonderful works that he has done we must take notice of his *thoughts which are to us-ward,* Ps. 40:5. Declare these *among the people,* among the heathen, that they may be brought into communion with Israel and the God of Israel. When the apostles preached the gospel to all nations, beginning at Jerusalem, then this scripture was fulfilled, that his doings should be declared among the people and that what he has done should be known in all the earth. 3. By a holy exultation and transport of joy: *"Cry out and shout;* welcome the gospel to yourselves and publish it to others with huzzas and loud acclamations, as those that *shout for victory* (Ex. 32:18) or for the coronation of a king," Num. 23:21.

III. For what they must praise the Lord. 1. Because he has glorified himself. Remember it yourselves, and *make mention* of it to others, *that his name is exalted,* has become more illustrious and more conspicuous; in this every good man rejoices. 2. Because he has magnified his people: *He has done excellent things* for them, which make them look great and considerable. 3. Because he is, and will be, great among them: *Great is the Holy One,* for he is glorious in holiness; *therefore* great, because holy. True goodness is true greatness. He is great as *the Holy One of Israel,* and *in the midst of them,* praised by them (Ps. 76:1), manifesting himself among them, and appearing gloriously in their behalf. It is the honour and happiness of Israel that the God who is in covenant with them, and in the midst of them, is infinitely great.

CHAPTER 13

Hitherto the prophecies of this book related only to Judah and Israel, and Jerusalem especially; but now the prophet begins to look abroad, and to read the doom of divers of the neighbouring states and kingdoms: for he that is King of saints is King of nations, and rules in the affairs of the children of men as well as in those of his own children. But the nations to whom these prophecies do relate were all such as the people of God were in some way or other conversant and concerned with, such as had been kind or unkind to Israel, and accordingly God would deal with them, either in favour or in wrath; for the Lord's portion is his people, and to them he has an eye in all the dispensations of his providence concerning those about them, Deu. 32:8, 9. The threatenings we find here against Babylon, Moab, Damascus, Egypt, Tyre, etc., were intended for comfort to those in Israel that feared God, but were terrified and oppressed by those potent neighbours, and for alarm to those among them that were wicked. If God would thus severely reckon with those for their sins that knew him not, and made no profession of his name, how severe would he be with those that were called by his name and yet lived in rebellion against him! And perhaps the directing of particular prophecies to the neighbouring nations might invite some of those nations to the reading of the Jews' Bible, and so they might be brought to their religion. This chapter, and that which follows, contain what God had to say to Babylon and Babylon's king, who were at present little known to Israel, but would in process of time become a greater enemy to them than any other had been, for which God would at last reckon with them. In this chapter we have, I. A general rendezvous of the forces that were to be employed against Babylon (*v.* 1–5). II. The dreadfully bloody work that those forces should make in Babylon (*v.* 6–18). III. The utter ruin and desolation of Babylon, which this should end in (*v.* 19–22).

Verses 1–5

The general title of this book was, *The vision of Isaiah the son of Amoz, ch.* 1:1. Here we have that which Isaiah saw, which was represented to his mind as clearly and fully as if he had seen it with his bodily eyes; but the particular inscription of this sermon is *the burden of Babylon.* 1. It is a burden, a lesson they were to learn (so some understand it), but they would be loth to learn it, and it would be a burden to their memories, or a load which should lie heavily upon them and under which they should sink. Those that will not make the word of God their rest (*ch.* 28:12; Jer. 6:16) shall find it made a burden to them. 2. It is the burden of Babylon or Babel, which at this time was a dependent upon the Assyrian monarchy (the metropolis of which was Nineveh), but soon after revolted from it and became a monarchy of itself, and a very potent one, in Nebuchadnezzar. This prophet afterwards foretold the captivity of the Jews in Babylon, *ch.* 39:6. Here he foretels the reprisals God would make upon Babylon for the wrongs done to his people. In these verses a summons is given to those powerful and warlike nations whom God would make us of as the instruments of his wrath for the destruction of Babylon: he afterwards names them (*v.* 17) the *Medes,* who, in conjunction with the Persians, under the command of Darius and Cyrus, were the ruin of the Babylonian monarchy.

I. The place doomed to destruction is Babylon; it is here called *the gates of the nobles* (*v.* 2), because of the abundance of noblemen's houses that were in it, stately ones and richly furnished, which would invite the enemy to come, in hopes of a rich booty. The gates of nobles were strong and well guarded, and yet they would be no fence against those who came with commission to execute God's judgments. Before his power and wrath palaces are no more than cottages. Nor is it only the gates of the nobles, but *the whole land,* that is doomed to destruction (*v.* 5); for, though the nobles were the leaders in persecuting and oppressing God's people, yet the whole land concurred with them in it.

II. The persons brought together to lay Babylon waste are here called, 1. God's *sanctified ones* (*v.* 3), designed for this service and set apart to it by the purpose and providence of God, disengaged from other projects, that they might wholly apply themselves to this, such as were qualified for that to which they were called, for what work God employs men in he does in some measure fit them for. It intimates likewise that in God's intention, though not in theirs, it was a holy war; they designed only the enlargement of their own empire, but God designed the release of his people and a type of the destruction of the New-Testament Babylon. Cyrus, the person principally concerned, was justly called *a sanctified one,* for he was God's anointed (*ch.* 45:1) and a figure of him that was to come. It is a pity but all soldiers, especially those that fight the Lord's battles, should be in the strictest sense sanctified ones; and it is a wonder that those dare be profane ones who carry their lives in their hands. 2. They are called God's *mighty ones,* because they had their might from God and were now to use it for him. It is said of Cyrus that in this expedition *God held his right hand, ch.* 45:1. God's sanctified ones are his mighty ones. Those whom God calls he qualifies, and those whom he makes holy he makes strong in spirit. 3. They are said to rejoice in his highness, that is, to serve his glory and the purposes of it with great alacrity. Though Cyrus did not know God, nor actually design his honour in what he did, yet God used him as his servant (*ch.* 45:4, *I have surnamed thee* as my servant, though *thou hast not known me*), and he rejoiced in those successes by which God exalted his own name. 4. They are very numerous, *a multitude, a great people, kingdoms of nations* (*v.* 4), not rude and barbarous, but modelled and regular troops, such as are furnished out by well-ordered kingdoms. The great God has hosts at his command. 5. They are far-fetched: *They come from a far country, from the end of* heaven. The vast country of Assyria lay between Babylon and Persia. God can make those a scourge and ruin to his enemies that lie most remote from them and therefore are least dreaded.

III. The summons given them is effectual, their obedience ready, and they make a very formidable appearance: *A banner is lifted up upon the high mountain, v.* 2. God's standard is set up, a flag of defiance hung out against Babylon. It is erected on high, where all may see it; whoever will may come and enlist themselves under it, and they shall be taken immediately into God's pay. Those that beat up for volunteers must *exalt the voice* in making proclamation, to encourage soldiers to come in; they must *shake the hand,* to beckon those at a distance and to animate those that have enlisted themselves. And they shall not do this in vain; God has commanded and called those whom he designs to make use of (*v.* 3) and power goes along with his calls and commands, which cannot be resisted. He that makes men able to serve him can, when he pleases, make them willing too. It is the *Lord of hosts that musters the host of the battle, v.* 4. He raises them, brings them together, puts them in order, reviews them, has an exact account of them in his muster-roll, sees that they be all in their respective posts, and gives them their necessary orders. Note, All the hosts of war are under the command of the Lord of hosts; and that which makes them truly formidable is that, when they come against Babylon, the Lord comes, and brings them with him as *the weapons of his indignation, v.* 5. Note, Great princes and armies are but tools in God's hand, weapons that he is pleased to make use of in doing his work, and it is his wrath that arms them and gives them success.

Verses 6–18

We have here a very elegant and lively description of the terrible confusion and desolation which should be made in Babylon by the descent which the Medes and

Persians should make upon it. Those that were now secure and easy were bidden to *howl* and make sad lamentation; for,

I. God was about to appear in wrath against them, and it is a fearful thing to fall into his hands: *The day of the Lord is at hand* (*v.* 6), a little day of judgment, when God will act as a just avenger of his own and his people's injured cause. And there are those who will have reason to tremble when that day is at hand. *The day of the Lord cometh, v.* 9. Men have their day now, and they think to carry the day; but God laughs at them, for he sees that *his day is coming,* Ps. 37:13. Fury is not with God, and yet his day of reckoning with the Babylonians is said to be *cruel with wrath and fierce anger.* God will deal in severity with them for the severities they exercised upon God's people; with the froward, with the cruel, he will show himself froward, will show himself cruel, and give the bloodthirsty blood to drink.

II. Their hearts shall fail them, and they shall have neither courage nor comfort left; they shall not be able either to resist the judgment coming or to bear up under it, either to oppose the enemy or to support themselves, *v.* 7, 8. Those that in the day of their peace were *proud,* and *haughty,* and *terrible* (*v.* 11), shall, when trouble comes, be quite dispirited and at their wits' end: *All hands shall be faint,* and unable to hold a weapon, *and every man's heart shall melt,* so that they shall be ready to die for fear. The pangs of their fear shall be like those of a woman in hard labour, and *they shall be amazed one at another.* In frightening themselves, they shall frighten one another; they shall wonder to see those tremble that used to be bold and daring; or they shall be amazed looking one at another, as men at a loss, Gen. 42:1. *Their faces shall be as flames,* pale as flames, through fear (so some), or red as flames sometimes are, blushing at their own cowardice; or their faces shall be as faces scorched with the flame, or as theirs that labour in the fire, their *visage blacker than a coal,* or like *a bottle in the smoke,* Ps. 119:83.

III. All comfort and hope shall fail them (*v.* 10): *The stars of heaven shall not give their light,* but shall be clouded and overcast; *the sun shall be darkened in his going forth,* rising bright, but lost again, a certain sign of foul weather. They shall be as men in distress at sea, when neither sun nor stars appear, Acts 27:20. It shall be as dreadful a time with them as it would be with the earth if all the heavenly luminaries were turned into darkness, a resemblance of the day of judgment, when the sun shall be turned into darkness. The heavens frowning thus is an indication of the displeasure of the God of heaven. When things look dark on earth, yet it is well enough if all be clear upwards; but, if we have no comfort thence, wherewith shall we be comforted?

IV. God will visit them *for their iniquity;* and all this is intended for the punishment of sin, and particularly the sin of pride, *v.* 11. This puts wormwood and gall into the affliction and misery, 1. That sin must now have its punishment. Though Babylon be a little world, yet, being a wicked world, it shall not go unpunished. Sin brings desolation on the world of the ungodly; and when the kingdoms of the earth are quarrelling with one another it is the fruit of God's controversy with them all. 2. That pride must now have its fall: *The haughtiness of the terrible* must now be *laid low,* particularly of Nebuchadnezzar and his son Belshazzar, who had, in their pride, trampled upon, and made themselves very terrible to, the people of God. *A man's pride will bring him low.*

V. There shall be so great a slaughter as will produce a scarcity of men (*v.* 12): *I will make a man more precious than fine gold.* You could not have a man to be employed in any of the affairs of state, not a man to be enlisted in the army, not a man to match a daughter to, for the building up of a family, if you would give any money for one. The troops of the neighbouring nations would not be hired into the service of the king of Babylon, because they saw every thing go against him. Populous countries are soon depopulated by war. And God can soon make a kingdom that has been courted and admired to be dreaded and shunned by all, as a house that is falling, or a ship that is sinking.

VI. There shall be a universal confusion and consternation, such a confusion of their affairs that it shall be like the *shaking of the heavens* with dreadful thunders and the

removing of the earth by no less dreadful earthquakes. All shall go to rack and ruin *in the day of the wrath of the Lord of hosts, v.* 13. And such a consternation shall seize their spirits that Babylon, which used to be like a roaring lion and a raging bear to all about her, shall become *as a chased roe and as a sheep that no man takes up, v.* 14. The army they shall bring into the field, consisting of troops of divers nations (as great armies usually do), shall be so dispirited by their own apprehensions and so dispersed by their enemies' sword that they shall *turn every man to his own people;* each man shall shift for his own safety; the *men of might shall not find their hands* (Ps. 76:5), but take to their heels.

VII. There shall be a general scene of blood and horror, as is usual where the sword devours. No wonder that every one makes the best of his way, since the conqueror gives no quarter, but puts all to the sword, and not those only that are found in arms, as is usual with us even in the most cruel slaughters (*v.* 15): *Every one that is found alive shall be run through,* as soon as ever it appears that he is a Babylonian. Nay, because the sword devours one as well as another, *every one that is joined to them shall fall by the sword;* those of other nations that come in to their assistance shall be cut off with them. It is dangerous being in bad company, and helping those whom God is about to destroy. Those particularly that join themselves to Babylon must expect to share in her plagues, Rev. 18:4. And, since the most sacred laws of nature, and of humanity itself, are silenced by the fury of war (though they cannot be cancelled), the conquerors shall, in the most barbarous brutish manner, *dash the children to pieces, and ravish the wives. Jusque datum sceleri — Wickedness shall have free course, v.* 16. They had thus dealt with God's people (Lam. 5:11), and now they shall be paid in their own coin, Rev. 13:10. It was particularly foretold (Ps. 137:9) that the *little ones of Babylon should be dashed against the stones.* How cruel soever and unjust those were that did it, God was righteous who suffered it to be done, and to be done *before their eyes,* to their greater terror and vexation. It was just also that the houses which they had filled with the spoil of Israel should be spoiled and plundered. What is got by rapine is often lost in the same manner.

VIII. The enemy that God will send against them shall be inexorable, probably being by some provocation or other more than ordinarily exasperated against them; or, in whatever way it may be brought about, God himself will *stir up the Medes* to use this severity with the Babylonians. He will not only serve his own purposes by their dispositions and designs, but will put it into their hearts to make this attempt upon Babylon, and suffer them to prosecute it with all this fury. God is not the author of sin, but he would not permit it if he did not know how to bring glory to himself out of it. These Medes, in conjunction with the Persians, shall make thorough work of it; for, 1. They shall take no bribes, *v.* 17. All that men have they would give for their lives, but the Medes *shall not regard silver;* it is blood they thirst for, not gold; no man's riches shall with them be the ransom of his life. 2. They shall show no pity (*v.* 18), not to *the young men* that are in the prime of their time — they shall shoot them through with their bows, and then *dash them to pieces;* not to the age of innocency — *they shall have no pity on the fruit of the womb, nor spare little children,* whose cries and frights one would think should make even marble eyes to weep, and hearts of adamant to relent. Pause a little here and wonder, (1.) That men should be thus cruel and inhuman, and so utterly divested of all compassion; and in it see how corrupt and degenerate the nature of man has become. (2.) That the God of infinite mercy should suffer it, nay, and should make it to be the execution of his justice, which shows that, though he is gracious, yet he is the God to whom vengeance belongs. (3.) That little infants, who have never been guilty of any actual sin, should be thus abused, which shows that there is an original guilt by which life is forfeited as soon as it is had.

Verses 19–22

The great havoc and destruction which it was foretold should be made by the Medes and Persians in Babylon here end in the final destruction of it. 1. It is allowed that Babylon was a noble city. It was *the glory of kingdoms and the beauty of the Chaldees' excellency;* it was that *head of gold*

(Dan. 2:37, 38); it was called *the lady of kingdoms* (ch. 47:5), *the praise of the whole earth* (Jer. 51:41), *like a pleasant roe* (so the word signifies); but it shall be as a *chased roe, v.* 14. The Chaldeans gloried in the beauty and wealth of this their metropolis. 2. It is foretold that it should be wholly destroyed, like Sodom and Gomorrah; not so miraculously, nor so suddenly, but as effectually, though gradually; and the destruction should come upon them as that upon Sodom, when they were secure, eating and drinking, Lu. 17:28, 29. Babylon was taken when Belshazzar was in his revels; and, though Cyrus and Darius did not demolish it, yet by degrees it wasted away and in process of time it went all to ruin. It is foretold here (*v.* 20) *that it shall never be inhabited;* in Adrian's time nothing remained but the wall. And whereas it is prophesied concerning Nineveh, that great city, that when it should be deserted and left desolate yet flocks should lie down in the midst of it, it is here said concerning Babylon that *the Arabians,* who were *shepherds, should not make their folds there;* the country about should be so barren that there would be no grazing there; no, not for sheep. Nay, it shall be the receptacle of *wild beasts,* that affect solitude; the houses of Babylon, where the sons and daughters of pleasure used to rendezvous, *shall be full of doleful creatures, owls and satyrs,* that are themselves frightened thither, as to a place proper for them, and by whom all others are frightened thence. Historians say that this was fulfilled in the letter. Benjamin Bar-Jona, in his Itinerary, speaking of Babel, has these words: "This is that Babel which was of old thirty miles in breadth; it is now laid waste. There are yet to be seen the ruins of a palace of Nebuchadnezzar, but the sons of men dare not enter in, for fear of serpents and scorpions, which possess the place." Let none be proud of their pompous palaces, for they know not but they may become worse than cottages; nor let any think that *their houses shall endure for ever* (Ps. 49:11), when perhaps nothing may remain but the ruins and reproaches of them. 3. It is intimated that this destruction should come shortly (*v.* 22): *Her time is near to come.* This prophecy of the destruction of Babylon was intended for the support and comfort of the people of God when they were captives there and grievously oppressed; and the accomplishment of the prophecy was nearly 200 years after the time when it was delivered; yet it followed soon after the time for which it was calculated. When the people of Israel were groaning under the heavy yoke of Babylonish tyranny, sitting down in tears by the rivers of Babylon and upbraided with the songs of Zion, when their insolent oppressors were most haughty and arrogant (*v.* 11), then let them know, for their comfort, that Babylon's time, her day to fall, is near to come, and the days of her prosperity shall not be prolonged, as they have been. When God begins with her he will make an end. Thus it is said of the destruction of the New-Testament Babylon, whereof the former was a type, *In one hour has her judgment come.*

CHAPTER 14

In this chapter, I. More weight is added to the burden of Babylon, enough to sink it like a mill-stone; I. It is Israel's cause that is to be pleaded in this quarrel with Babylon (*v.* 1–3). 2. The king of Babylon, for the time being, shall be remarkably brought down and triumphed over (*v.* 4–20). 3. The whole race of the Babylonians shall be cut off and extirpated (*v.* 21–23). II. A confirmation of the prophecy of the destruction of Babylon, which was a thing at a distance, is here given in the prophecy of the destruction of the Assyrian army that invaded the land, which happened not long after (*v.* 24–27). III. The success of Hezekiah against the Philistines is here foretold, and the advantages which his people would gain thereby (*v.* 28–32).

Verses 1–3

This comes in here as the reason why Babylon must be overthrown and ruined, because God has mercy in store for his people, and therefore, 1. The injuries done to them must be reckoned for and revenged upon their persecutors. Mercy to Jacob will be wrath and ruin to Jacob's impenitent implacable adversaries, such as Babylon was. 2. The yoke of oppression which Babylon had long laid on their necks must be broken off, and they must be set at liberty; and, in order to this, the destruction of Babylon is as necessary as the destruction of Egypt and Pharaoh was to their deliverance out of that house of bondage. The same prediction is a promise to God's people and a threatening to their enemies, as the same providence has a bright side towards Israel and a black or dark side towards the Egyptians. Observe,

I. The ground of these favours to Jacob and Israel — the kindness God had for them and the choice he had made of them (*v.* 1): *"The Lord will have mercy on Jacob,* the seed of Jacob now captives in Babylon; he will make it to appear that he has compassion on them and has mercy in store for them, and that he will not contend for ever with them, but *will yet choose them,* will yet again return to them; though he has seemed for a time to refuse and reject them, he will show that they are his chosen people and that the election stands sure." However it may seem to us, God's mercy is not gone, nor does his promise fail, Ps. 77:8.

II. The particular favours he designed them. 1. He would bring them back to their native soil and air again: The *Lord will set them in their own land,* out of which they were driven. A settlement in the holy land, the land of promise, is a fruit of God's mercy, distinguishing mercy. 2. Many should be proselyted to their holy religion, and should return with them, induced to do so by the manifest tokens of God's favourable presence with them, the operations of God's grace in them, the operations of God's grace in them, and his providence for them: *Strangers shall be joined with them,* saying, *We will go with you, for we have heard that God is with you,* Zec. 8:23. It adds much to the honour and strength of Israel when strangers are joined with them and there are added to the church many from without, Acts 2:47. Let not the church's children be shy of strangers, but receive those whom God receives, and own those who cleave to the house of Jacob. 3. These proselytes should not only be a credit to their cause, but very helpful and serviceable to them in their return home: *The people among whom they live shall take them,* take care of them, take pity on them, and shall *bring them to their place —* as friends, loth to part with such good company — as servants, willing to do them all the good offices they could. God's people, wherever their lot is cast, should endeavour thus, by all the instances of an exemplary and winning conversation, to gain an interest in the affections of those about them, and recommend religion to their good opinion. This was fulfilled in the return of the captives from Babylon, when all that were about them, pursuant to Cyrus's proclamation, contributed to their removal (Ezra 1:4, 6), not as the Egyptians, because they were sick of them, but because they loved them. 4. They should have the benefit of their service when they had returned home, for many would of choice go with them in the meanest post, rather than not go with them: They *shall possess them in the land of the Lord for servants and handmaids;* and as the laws of that land saved it from being the purgatory of servants, providing that they should not be oppressed, so the advantages of that land made it the paradise of those servants that had been strangers to the covenants of promise, for there was *one law to the stranger and to those that were born in the land.* Those whose lot is cast in the land of the Lord, a land of light, should take care that their servants and handmaids may share in the benefit of it, who will then find it better to be possessed in the Lord's land than possessors in any other. 5. They should triumph over their enemies, and those that would not be reconciled to them should be reduced and humbled by them: *They shall take those captives whose captives they were and shall rule over their oppressors,* righteously, but not revengefully. The Jews perhaps bought Babylonian prisoners out of the hands of the Medes and Persians and made slaves of them. Or this might have its accomplishment in their victories over their enemies in the times of the Maccabees. It is applicable to the success of the gospel (when those were brought into obedience to it who had made the greatest opposition to it, as Paul) and to the interest believers have in Christ's victories over their spiritual enemies, when he led captivity captive, to the power they gain over their own corruptions, and to the dominion the upright shall have in the morning, Ps. 49:14. 6. They should see a happy termination of all their grievances (*v.* 3): *The Lord shall give thee rest from thy sorrow and thy fear, and from thy hard bondage.* God himself undertakes to work a blessed change, (1.) In their state. They shall have rest from their bondage; the days of their affliction, though many, shall have an end; and the rod of the wicked, though it lie long, shall not always lie on their lot. (2.) In their spirit. They shall have rest from their sorrow and fear, sense of their present burdens and dread of worse. Sometimes fear puts

the soul into a ferment as much as sorrow does, and those must needs feel themselves very easy to whom God has given rest from both. Those who are freed from the bondage of sin have a foundation laid for true rest from sorrow and fear.

Verses 4–23

The kings of Babylon, successively, were the great enemies and oppressors of God's people, and therefore the destruction of Babylon, the fall of the king, and the ruin of his family, are here particularly taken notice of and triumphed in. In the day that God has given Israel rest they shall *take up this proverb against the king of Babylon.* We must not rejoice when our enemy falls, as ours; but when Babylon, the common enemy of God and his Israel, sinks, then *rejoice over her, thou heaven, and you holy apostles and prophets,* Rev. 18:20. The Babylonian monarchy bade fair to be an absolute, universal, and perpetual one, and, in these pretensions, vied with the Almighty; it is therefore very justly, not only brought down, but insulted over when it is down; and it is not only the last monarch, Belshazzar, who *was slain on that night* that Babylon was taken (Dan. 5:30), who is here triumphed over, but the whole monarchy, which sunk in him; not without special reference to Nebuchadnezzar, in whom that monarchy was at its height. Now here,

I. The fall of the king of Babylon is rejoiced in; and a most curious and elegant composition is here prepared, not to adorn his hearse or monument, but to expose his memory and fix a lasting brand of infamy upon it. It gives us an account of the life and death of this mighty monarch, how he *went down slain to the pit,* though he had been *the terror of the mighty in the land of the living,* Eze. 32:27. In this parable we may observe,

1. The prodigious height of wealth and power at which this monarch and monarchy arrived. Babylon was a *golden city, v.* 4 (it is a Chaldee word in the original, which intimates that she used to call herself so), so much did she abound in riches and excel all other cities, as gold does all other metals. She is *gold-thirsty,* or an exactress of gold (so some read it); for how do men get wealth to themselves but by squeezing it out of others? The New Jerusalem is the only truly golden city, Rev. 21:18, 21. The king of Babylon, having so much wealth in his dominions and the absolute command of it, by the help of that *ruled the nations* (*v.* 6), gave them law, read them their doom, and at his pleasure *weakened the nations* (*v.* 12), that they might not be able to make head against him. Such vast and victorious armies did he bring into the field, that, which way soever he looked, he *made the earth to tremble, and shook kingdoms* (*v.* 16); all his neighbours were afraid of him, and were forced to submit to him. No one man could do this by his own personal strength, but by the numbers he has at his beck. Great tyrants, by making some do what they will, make others suffer what they will. How piteous is the case of mankind, which thus seems to be in a combination against itself, and its own rights and liberties, which could not be ruined but by its own strength!

2. The wretched abuse of all this wealth and power, which the king of Babylon was guilty of, in two instances:—

(1.) Great oppression and cruelty. He is known by the name of *the oppressor* (*v.* 4); he has *the sceptre of the rulers* (*v.* 5), has the command of all the princes about him; but it is *the staff of the wicked,* a staff with which he supports himself in his wickedness and wickedly strikes all about him. *He smote the people,* not in justice, for their correction and reformation, but *in wrath* (*v.* 6), to gratify his own peevish resentments, and that *with a continual stroke,* pursued them with his forces, and gave them no respite, no breathing time, no cessation of arms. He ruled the nations, but he ruled them *in anger,* every thing he said and did was in a passion; so that he who had the government of all about him had no government of himself. He *made the world as a wilderness,* as if he had taken a pride in being the plague of his generation and a curse to mankind, *v.* 17. Great princes usually glory in building cities, but he gloried in destroying them; see Ps. 9:6. Two particular instances, worse than all the rest, are here given of his tyranny: — [1.] That he was severe to his captives (*v.* 17): He *opened not the house of his prisoners;* he *did not let them loose homeward* (so the margin reads it); he kept them in close confinement, and never would suffer any to return to their own land. This refers especially to the people of the Jews, and it is that which fills up the measure of the king of Babylon's iniquity, that he had detained the people of God in captivity and would by no means release them; nay, and by profaning the vessels of God's temple at Jerusalem, did in effect say that they should never return to their former use, Dan. 5:3. For this he was quickly and justly turned out by one whose first act was to open the house of God's prisoners and send home the temple vessels. [2.] That he was oppressive to his own subjects (*v.* 20): *Thou hast destroyed thy land, and slain thy people;* and what did he get by that, when the wealth of the land and the multitude of the people are the strength and honour of the prince, who never rules so safely, so gloriously, as in the hearts and affections of the people? But tyrants sacrifice their interests to their lusts and passions; and God will reckon with them for their barbarous usage of those who are under their power, whom they think they may use as they please.

(2.) Great pride and haughtiness. Notice is here taken of his *pomp,* the extravagancy of his retinue, *v.* 11. He affected to appear in the utmost magnificence. But that was not the worst: it was the temper of his mind, and the elevation of that, that ripened him for ruin (*v.* 13, 14): *Thou has said in thy heart,* like Lucifer, *I will ascend into heaven.* Here is the language of his vainglory, borrowed perhaps from that of the angels who fell, who not content with their first estate, the post assigned them, would vie with God, and become not only independent of him, but equal with him. Or perhaps it refers to the story of Nebuchadnezzar, who, when he would be more than a man, was justly turned into a brute, Dan. 4:30. The king of Babylon here promises himself, [1.] That in pomp and power he shall surpass all his neighbours, and shall arrive at the very height of earthly glory and felicity, that he shall be as great and happy as this world can make him; that is the heaven of a carnal heart, and to that he hopes to ascend, and to be as far above those about him as the heaven is above the earth. Princes are the stars of God, which give some light to this dark world (Mt. 24:29); but he will exalt his throne above them all. [2.] That he shall particularly insult over God's Mount Zion, which Belshazzar, in his last drunken frolic, seems to have had a particular spite against when he called for the vessels of the temple at Jerusalem, to profane them; see Dan. 5:2. In the same humour he here said, *I will sit upon the mount of the congregation* (it is the same word that is used for the holy *convocations*), *in the sides of the north;* so Mount Zion is said to be situated, Ps. 48:2. Perhaps Belshazzar was projecting an expedition to Jerusalem, to triumph in the ruins of it, at the time when God cut him off. [3.] That he shall vie with the God of Israel, of whom he had indeed heard glorious things, that he had his residence *above the heights of the clouds.* "But thither," says he, "*will I ascend,* and be as great as he; I will be like him whom they call *the Most High.*" It is a gracious ambition to covet to be like the Most Holy, for he has said, *Be you holy, for I am holy;* but it is a sinful ambition to aim to be like the Most High, for he has said, *He that exalteth himself shall be abased,* and the devil drew our first parents in to eat forbidden fruit by promising them that they should be as gods. [4.] That he shall himself be deified after his death, as some of the first founders of the Assyrian monarchy were, and stars had even their names from them. "But," says he, "*I will exalt my throne above them all.*" Such as this was his pride, which was the undoubted omen of his destruction.

3. The utter ruin that should be brought upon him. It is foretold, (1.) That his wealth and power should be broken, and a final period put to his pomp and pleasure. He has been long an oppressor, but he shall cease to be so, *v.* 4. Had he ceased to be so by true repentance and reformation, according to the advice Daniel gave to Nebuchadnezzar, it might have been a lengthening of his life and tranquillity. But those that will not cease to sin God will make to cease. *"The golden city,* which one would have thought might continue for ever, *has ceased;* there is an end of that Babylon. *The Lord,* the righteous God, *has broken the staff of that wicked prince,* broken it over his head, in token of the divesting him of his office. God has taken his power from him, and rendered him incapable of doing any more mischief: he has broken the sceptres; for even these are brittle things, soon broken and often justly." (2.)

That he himself should be seized: *He is persecuted* (*v.* 6); violent hands are laid upon him, and none hinders. It is the common fate of tyrants, when they fall into the power of their enemies, to be deserted by their flatterers, whom they took for their friends. We read of another enemy like this, of whom it is foretold that *he shall come to his end and none shall help him,* Dan. 11:45. Tiberius and Nero thus saw themselves abandoned. (3.) That he should be slain, and *go down to the congregation of the dead,* to be *free among them, as the slain that are no more remembered,* Ps. 88:5. He shall be *weak as the dead* are, and *like unto them, v.* 10. His *pomp is brought down to the grave* (*v.* 11), that is, it perishes with him; the pomp of his life shall not, as usual, end in a funeral pomp. True glory (that is, true grace) will go up with the soul to heaven, but vain pomp will go down with the body to the grave: there is an end of it. *The noise of his viols* is now heard no more. Death is a farewell to the pleasures, as well as to the pomps, of this world. This mighty prince, that used to lie on a bed of down, to tread upon rich carpets, and to have coverings and canopies exquisitely fine, now shall have the *worms spread under him and the worms covering him,* worms bred out of his own putrefied body, which, though he fancied himself a god, proved him to be made of the same mould with other men. When we are pampering and decking our bodies it is good to remember they will be worms'-meat shortly. (4.) That he should not have the honour of a burial, much less of a decent one and in the sepulchres of his ancestors. *The kings of the nations lie in glory* (*v.* 18), either their dead bodies themselves so embalmed as to be preserved from putrefaction, as of old among the Egyptians, or their effigies (as with us) erected over their graves. Thus, as if they would defy the ignominy of death, they lay in a poor faint sort of glory, *every one in his own house,* that is, his own burying-place (for the grave is the house appointed for all living), a sleeping house, where the busy and troublesome will lie quiet and the troubled and weary lie at rest. But this king of Babylon is *cast out* and has no grave (*v.* 19); his dead body is thrown, like that of a beast, into the next ditch or upon the next dunghill, *like an abominable branch* of some noxious poisonous plant, which nobody will touch, or as the clothes of malefactors put to death and by the hand of justice *thrust through with a sword,* on whose dead bodies heaps of stones are raised, or they are thrown into some deep quarry among *the stones of the pit.* Nay, the king of Babylon's dead body shall be as the carcases of those who are slain in a battle, which are *trodden under feet* by the horses and soldiers and crushed to pieces. Thus he *shall not be joined with his ancestors in burial, v.* 20. To be denied decent burial is a disgrace, which, if it be inflicted for righteousness' sake (as Ps. 79:2), may, as other similar reproaches, be rejoiced in (Mt. 5:12); it is the lot of the two witnesses, Rev. 11:9. But if, as here, it be the just punishment of iniquity, it is an intimation that evil pursues impenitent sinners beyond death, greater evil than that, and that they shall *rise to everlasting shame and contempt.*

4. The many triumphs that should be in his fall.

(1.) Those whom he had been a great tyrant and terror to will be glad that they are rid of him, *v.* 7, 8. Now that he is gone the *whole earth is at rest and is quiet,* for he was the great disturber of the peace; now they all *break forth into singing,* for *when the wicked perish there is shouting* (Prov. 11:10); the fir-trees and cedars of Lebanon now think themselves safe; there is no danger now of their being cut down, to make way for his vast armies or to furnish him with timber. The neighbouring princes and great men, who are compared to fir-trees and cedars (Zec. 11:2), may now be easy, and out of fear of being dispossessed of their rights, for *the hammer of the whole earth is cut asunder and broken* (Jer. 50:23), the axe that *boasted itself against him that hewed with it, ch.* 10:15.

(2.) The congregation of the dead will bid him welcome to them, especially those whom he had barbarously hastened thither (*v.* 9, 10): *"Hell from beneath is moved for thee, to meet thee at thy coming,* and to compliment thee upon thy arrival at their dark and dreadful regions." *The chief ones of the earth,* who when they were alive were kept in awe by him and durst not come near him, but rose from their thrones, to resign them to him, shall upbraid him with it when he comes into the state of the dead. They shall go forth to meet him, as they used to do when he made

his public entry into cities he had become master of; with such a parade shall he be introduced into those regions of horror, to make his disgrace and torment the more grievous to him. They shall go forth to meet him, as they used to do when he made his public entry into cities he had become master of; with such a parade shall he be introduced into those regions of horror, to make his disgrace and torment the more grievous to him. They shall scoffingly rise from their thrones and seats there, and ask him if he will please to sit down in them, as he used to do in their thrones on earth? The confusion that will then cover him they shall make a jest of: *"Hast thou also become weak as we?* Who would have thought it? It is what thou thyself didst not expect it would ever come to when thou wast in every thing too hard for us. Thou that didst rank thyself among the immortal gods, art thou come to take thy fate among us poor mortal men? Where is thy pomp now, and where thy mirth? *How hast thou fallen from heaven, O Lucifer! son of the morning! v.* 11, 12. The king of Babylon shone as brightly as the morning star, and fancied that wherever he came he brought day along with him; and has such an illustrious prince as this fallen, such a star become a clod of clay? Did ever any man fall from such a height of honour and power into such an abyss of shame and misery?" This has been commonly alluded to (and it is a mere allusion) to illustrate the fall of the angels, who were as morning stars (Job 38:7), but *how have they fallen! How art thou cut down to the ground,* and levelled with it, that *didst weaken the nations!* God will reckon with those that invade the rights and disturb the peace of mankind, for he is King of nations as well as of saints. Now this reception of the king of Babylon into the regions of the dead, which is here described, surely is something more than a flight of fancy, and is designed to teach these solid truths: — [1.] That there is an invisible world, a world of spirits, to which the souls of men remove at death and in which they exist and act in a state of separation from the body. [2.] That separate souls have acquaintance and converse with each other, though we have none with them: the parable of the rich man and Lazarus intimates this. [3.] That death and hell will be death and hell indeed to those that fall unsanctified from the height of this world's pomps and the fulness of its pleasures. *Son, remember,* Lu. 16:25.

(3.) Spectators will stand amazed at his fall. When he shall be *brought down to hell, to the sides of the pit,* and be lodged there, *those that see him shall narrowly look upon him, and consider him* (*v.* 15, 16); they shall scarcely believe their own eyes. "Never was death so great a change to any man as it is to him. Is it possible that a man, who a few hours ago looked so great, so pleasant, and was so splendidly adorned and attended, should now look so ghastly, so despicable, and lie thus naked and neglected? *Is this the man that made the earth to tremble and shook kingdoms?* Who could have thought he should ever come to this?" Ps. 82:7.

5. Here is an inference drawn from all this (*v.* 20): *The seed of evil-doers shall never be renowned.* The princes of the Babylonian monarchy were all a seed of evil-doers, oppressors of the people of God, and therefore they had this infamy entailed upon them. *They shall not be renowned for ever* (so some read it); they may look big for a time, but all their pomp will only render their disgrace at last the more shameful. There is no credit in a sinful way.

II. The utter ruin of the royal family is here foretold, together with the desolation of The royal city.

1. The royal family is to be wholly extirpated. The Medes and Persians, that are to be employed in this destroying work, are ordered, when they have slain Belshazzar, to *prepare slaughter for his children* (*v.* 21) and not to spare them. The little ones of Babylon must be *dashed against the stones,* Ps. 137:9. These orders sound very harshly; but, (1.) They must suffer *for the iniquity of their fathers,* which is often *visited upon the children,* to show how much God hates sin and is displeased at it, and to deter sinners from it, which is the end of punishment. Nebuchadnezzar had slain Zedekiah's sons (Jer. 52:10), and, for that iniquity of his, his seed are paid in the same coin. (2.) They must be cut off now, that they *may not rise up to possess the land* and do as much mischief in their day as their fathers had done in theirs — that they may not be as vexatious to the world by building cities for the sup-

port of their tyranny (which was Nimrod's policy, Gen. 10:10, 11) as their ancestors had been by destroying cities. Pharaoh oppressed Israel in Egypt by setting them to build cities, Ex. 1:11. The providence of God consults the welfare of nations more than we are aware of by cutting off some who, if they had lived, would have done mischief. Justly may the enemies cut off the children: *For I will rise up against them, saith the Lord of hosts* (*v.* 22), and if God reveal it as his mind that he will have it done, as none can hinder it, so none need scruple to further it. Babylon perhaps was proud of the numbers of her royal family, but God had determined to *cut off the name and remnant* of it, so that none should be left, to have both the sons and grandsons of the king slain; and yet we are sure he never did, nor ever will do, any wrong to any of his creatures.

2. The royal city is to be demolished and deserted, *v.* 23. It shall be a possession for solitary frightful birds, particularly *the bittern,* joined with the cormorant and the owl, *ch.* 24:11. And thus the utter destruction of the New-Testament Babylon is illustrated, Rev. 18:2. It *has become a cage of every unclean and hateful bird.* Babylon lay low, so that when it was deserted, and no care taken to drain the land, it soon became *pools of water,* standing noisome puddles, as unhealthful as they were unpleasant: and thus God *will sweep it with the besom of destruction.* When a people have nothing among them but dirt and filth, and will not be made clean with the besom of reformation, what can they expect but to be swept off the face of the earth with the besom of destruction?

Verses 24–32

The destruction of Babylon and the Chaldean empire was a thing at a great distance; the empire had not risen to any considerable height when its fall was here foretold: it was almost 200 years from this prediction of Babylon's fall to the accomplishment of it. Now the people to whom Isaiah prophesied might ask, "What is this to us, or what shall we be the better for it, and what assurance shall we have of it?" To both questions he answers in these verses, by a prediction of the ruin both of the Assyrians and of the Philistines, the present enemies that infested them, which they should shortly be eye-witnesses of and have benefit by. These would be a present comfort to them, and a pledge of future deliverance, for the confirming of the faith of their posterity. God is to his people the same to day that he was yesterday and will be hereafter; and he will for ever be the same that he has been and is. Here is,

I. Assurance given of the destruction of the Assyrians (*v.* 25): *I will break the Assyrian in my land.* Sennacherib brought a very formidable army into the land of Judah, but there God broke it, broke all his regiments by the sword of a destroying angel. Note, Those who wrongfully invade God's land shall find that it is at their peril: and those who with unhallowed feet trample upon his holy mountains shall themselves there be trodden under foot. God undertakes to do this himself, his people having no might against the great company that came against them: *"I will break the Assyrian;* let me alone to do it who have angels, hosts of angels, at command." Now the breaking of the power of the Assyrian would be the breaking of the yoke from off the neck of God's people: *His burden shall depart from off their shoulders,* the burden of quartering that vast army and paying contribution; *therefore* the Assyrian must be broken, that Judah and Jerusalem may be eased. Let those that make themselves a yoke and a burden to God's people see what they are to expect. Now, 1. This prophecy is here ratified and confirmed by an oath (*v.* 24): *The Lord of hosts hath sworn,* that he might show the immutability of his counsel, and that his people may have strong consolation, Heb. 6:17, 18. What is here said of this particular intention is true of all God's purposes: *As I have thought, so shall it come to pass;* for *he is in one mind, and who can turn him?* Nor is he ever put upon new counsels, or obliged to take new measures, as men often are when things occur which they did not foresee. Let those who are *the called according to God's purpose* comfort themselves with this, that, *as God has purposed, so shall it stand,* and on that their stability depends. 2. The breaking of the Assyrian power is made a specimen of what God would do with all the powers of the nations that were engaged against him and his church (*v.* 26): *This is the purpose that is purposed upon the whole earth* (*the whole world,* so the Septuagint), *all the inhabitants of the earth* (so the Chaldee), not only upon the Assyrian empire (which was then reckoned to be in a manner all the world, as afterwards the Roman empire was, Lu. 2:1, and with it many nations fell that had dependence upon it), but upon all those states and potentates that should at any time attack his land, his mountains. The fate of the Assyrian shall be theirs; they shall soon find that they meddle to their own hurt. Jerusalem, as it was to the Assyrians, will be *to all people a burdensome stone; all that burden themselves with it shall infallibly be cut to pieces by it,* Zec. 12:3, 6. The same hand of power and justice that is now to be stretched out against the Assyrian for invading the people of God shall be *stretched out upon all the nations* that do likewise. It is still true, and will ever be so, *Cursed is he that curses God's Israel,* Num. 24:9. God will be an enemy to his people's enemies, Ex. 23:22. 3. All the powers on earth are defied to change God's counsel (*v.* 27): *"The Lord of hosts has purposed* to break the Assyrian's yoke, and every rod of the wicked laid upon the lot of the righteous; *and who shall disannul this purpose?* Who can persuade him to recall it, or find out a plea to evade it? *His hand is stretched out* to execute this purpose; *and who has power* enough *to turn it back* or to stay the course of his judgments?"

II. Assurance is likewise given of the destruction of the Philistines and their power. This burden, this prophecy, that lay as a load upon them, to sink their state, came *in the year that king Ahaz died,* which was the first year of Hezekiah's reign, *v.* 28. When a good king came in the room of a bad one then this acceptable message was sent among them. When we reform, then, and not till then, we may look for good news from heaven. Now here we have, 1. A rebuke to the Philistines for triumphing in the death of king Uzziah. He had been as a serpent to them (*v.* 29), had bitten them, had smitten them, had brought them very low, 2 Chr. 26:6. He *warred against the Philistines, broke down their walls, and built cities among them.* But when Uzziah died, or rather abdicated, it was told with joy in Gath and *published in the streets of Ashkelon.* It is inhuman thus to rejoice in our neighbour's fall. But let them not be secure; for though when Uzziah was dead they made reprisals upon Ahaz, and took many of the cities of Judah (2 Chr. 28:18), yet *out of the root* of Uzziah *should come a cockatrice,* a more formidable enemy than Uzziah was, even Hezekiah, the fruit of whose government should be to them *a fiery flying serpent,* for he should fall upon them with incredible swiftness and fury: we find he did so. 2 Ki. 18:8, *He smote the Philistines even to Gaza.* Note, If God remove one useful instrument in the midst of his usefulness, he can, and will, raise up others to carry on and complete the same work that they were employed in and left unfinished. 2. A prophecy of the destruction of the Philistines by famine and war. (1.) By famine, *v.* 30. "When the people of God, whom the Philistines has wasted, and distressed, and impoverished, shall enjoy plenty again," and *the first-born of their poor shall feed* (the poorest among them shall have food convenient), then, as for the Philistines, God will kill *their root with famine.* That which was their strength, and with which they thought themselves established as the tree is by the root, shall be starved and dried up by degrees, as those die that die by famine; and thus *he shall slay the remnant:* those that escape from one destruction are but reserved for another; and, when there are but a few left, those few shall at length be cut off, for God will make a full end. (2.) By war. When *the needy* of God's people *shall lie down in safety,* not terrified with the alarms of war, but delighting in the songs of peace, then every gate and every city of the Philistines shall be howling and crying (*v.* 31), and there shall be a total dissolution of their state; for from Judea, which lay north of the Philistines, *there shall come a smoke* (a vast army raising a great dust, a smoke that shall be the indication of a devouring fire at hand), *and none* of all that army *shall be alone in his appointed times;* none shall straggle or be missing when they are to engage; but they shall all be vigorous and unanimous in attacking the common enemy, when the time appointed for the doing of it comes. None of them shall decline the public service, as, in Deborah's time, Reuben abode among the sheepfolds and Asher on the sea-shore, Jdg. 5:16, 17. When God has work to do he will wonderfully endow and dispose men for it.

III. The good use that should be made of all these events for the encouragement of the people of God (*v.* 32): *What shall one then answer the messengers of the nations?*

1. This implies, (1.) That the great things God does for his people are, and cannot but be, taken notice of by their neighbours; those among the heathen make remarks upon them, Ps. 126:2. (2.) That messengers will be sent to enquire concerning them. Jacob and Israel had long been a people distinguished from all others and dignified with uncommon favours; and therefore some for good-will, others for ill-will, and all for curiosity, are inquisitive concerning them. (3.) That it concerns us always to be ready to give a reason of the hope that we have in the providence of God, as well as in his grace, in answer to every one that asks it, *with meekness and fear,* 1 Pt. 3:15. And we need go no further than the sacred truths of God's word for a reason; for God, in all he does, is fulfilling the scripture. (4.) The issue of God's dealings with his people shall be so clearly and manifestly glorious that any one, every one, shall be able to give an account of them to those that enquire concerning them. Now,

2. The answer which is to be given to the messengers of the nations is, (1.) That God is and will be a faithful friend to his church and people, and will secure and advance their interests. Tell them that *the Lord has founded Zion.* This gives an account both of the work itself that is done and of the reason of it. What is God doing in the world, and what is he designing in all the revolutions of states and kingdoms, in the ruin of some nations and the rise of others? He is, in all this, founding Zion; he is aiming at the advancement of his church's interests; and what he aims at he will accomplish. The messengers of the nations, when they sent to enquire concerning Hezekiah's successes against the Philistines, expected to learn by what politics, counsels, and arts of war he carried his point; but they are told that these successes were not owing to any thing of that nature, but to the care God took of his church and the interest he had in it. The Lord has founded Zion, and therefore the Philistines must fall. (2.) That his church has and will have a dependence upon him: *The poor of his people shall trust in it,* his poor people who have lately been brought very low, even the poorest of them; they more than others, for they have nothing else to trust to, Zep. 3:12, 13. The *poor receive the gospel,* Mt. 11:5. They shall trust to this, to this great truth, that the Lord has founded Zion; on this they shall build their hopes, and not on an arm of flesh. This ought to give us abundant satisfaction as to public affairs, that however it may go with particular persons, parties, and interests, the church, having God himself for its founder and Christ the rock for its foundation, cannot but stand firm. *The poor of his people shall betake themselves to it* (so some read it), shall join themselves to his church and embark in its interests; they shall concur with God in his designs to establish his people, and shall wind up all on the same plan, and make all their little concerns and projects bend to that. Those that take God's people for their people must be willing to take their lot with them and cast in their lot among them. Let the messengers of the nations know that the poor Israelites, who trust in God, having, like Zion, their foundation in the holy mountains (Ps. 87:1), are like Zion, which *cannot be removed, but abides for ever* (Ps. 125:1.), and therefore they will not fear what man can do unto them.

CHAPTER 15

This chapter, and that which follows it, are the burden of Moab — a prophecy of some great desolation that was coming upon that country, which bordered upon this land of Israel, and had often been injurious and vexatious to it, though the Moabites were descended from Lot, Abraham's kinsman and companion, and though the Israelites, by the appointment of God, had spared them when they might both easily and justly have cut them off with their neighbours. In this chapter we have, I. Great lamentation made by the Moabites, and by the prophet himself for them (*v.* 1–5). II. The great calamities which should occasion that lamentation and justify it (*v.* 6–9).

Verses 1–5

The country of Moab was of small extent, but very fruitful. It bordered upon the lot of Reuben on the other side Jordan and upon the Dead Sea. Naomi went to sojourn there when there was a famine in Canaan. This is the country which (it is here foretold) should be wasted and grievously harassed, not quite ruined, for we find another prophecy of its ruin (Jer. 48), which was accomplished by Nebuchadnezzar. This prophecy here was to be fulfilled *with-*

in three years (*ch.* 16:14), and therefore was fulfilled in the devastations made of that country by the army of the Assyrians, which for many years ravaged those parts, enriching themselves with spoil and plunder. It was done either by the army of Shalmaneser, about the time of the taking of Samaria, in the fourth year of Hezekiah (as is most probable), or by the army of Sennacherib, which, ten years after, invaded Judah. We cannot suppose that the prophet went among the Moabites to preach to them this sermon; but he delivered it to his own people, 1. To show them that, though judgment begins at the house of God, it shall not end there, — that there is a providence which governs the world and all the nations of it, — and that to the God of Israel the worshippers of false gods were accountable, and liable to his judgments. 2. To give them a proof of God's care of them and jealousy for them, and to convince them that God was an enemy to their enemies, for such the Moabites had often been. 3. That the accomplishment of this prophecy now shortly *(within three years)* might be a confirmation of the prophet's mission and of the truth of all his other prophecies, and might encourage the faithful to depend upon them.

Now concerning Moab it is here foretold,

I. That their chief cities should be surprised and taken in a night by the enemy, probably because the inhabitants, as the men of Laish, indulged themselves in ease and luxury, and dwelt securely (*v.* 1): Therefore there shall be great grief, *because in the night Air of Moab is laid waste and Kir of Moab,* the two principal cities of that kingdom. *In the night that they were taken,* or sacked, *Moab was cut off.* The seizing of them laid the whole country open, and made all the wealth of it an easy prey to the victorious army. Note, 1. Great changes and very dismal ones may be made in a very little time. Here are two cities lost in a night, though that is the time of quietness. Let us therefore lie down as those that know not what a night may bring forth. 2. As the country feeds the cities, so the cities protect the country, and neither can say to the other, *I have no need of thee.*

II. That the Moabites, being hereby put into the utmost consternation imaginable, should have recourse to their idols for relief, and pour out their tears before them (*v.* 2): *He* (that is, Moab, especially the king of Moab) *has gone up to Bajith* (or rather to the house or temple of Chemosh), *and Dibon,* the inhabitants of Dibon, *have gone up to the high places,* where they worshipped their idols, there to make their complaints. Note, It becomes a people in distress to seek to their God; and shall not we then thus *walk in the name of the Lord our God,* and call upon him in the time of trouble, before whom we shall not shed such useless profitless tears as they did before their gods?

III. That there should be the voice of universal grief all the country over. It is described here elegantly and very affectingly. Moab shall be a vale of tears — a little map of this world, *v.* 2. The Moabites shall lament the loss of Nebo and Medeba, two considerable cities, which, it is likely, were plundered and burnt. They shall tear their hair for grief to such a degree that *on all their heads shall be baldness, and they shall cut off their beards,* according to the customary expressions of mourning in those times and countries. When they go abroad they shall be so far from coveting to appear handsome that *in the streets they shall gird themselves with sackcloth* (*v.* 3), and perhaps being forced to use that poor clothing, the enemy having stripped them, and rifled their houses, and left them no other clothing. When they come home, instead of applying themselves to their business, they shall go up to *the tops of their houses* which were flat-roofed, and there they shall *weep abundantly,* nay, they shall *howl,* in crying to their gods. Those that *cry not to God with their hearts* do but *howl upon their beds,* Hos. 7:14; Amos 8:3. *They shall come down with weeping* (so the margin reads it); they shall come down from their high places and the tops of their houses weeping as much as they did when they went up. Prayer to the true God is heart's ease (1 Sa. 1:18), but prayers to false gods are not. Divers places are here named that should be full of lamentation (*v.* 4), and it is but a poor relief to have so many fellow-sufferers, fellow-mourners; to a public spirit it is rather an aggravation *socios habuisse doloris — to have associates in woe.*

IV. That the courage of their militia should fail them. Though they were bred soldiers, and were well armed, yet they *shall cry out* and shriek for fear, and every one of them shall have *his life become grievous to him,* though it is characteristic of a military life to delight in danger, *v.* 4. See how easily God can dispirit the stoutest of men, and deprive a nation of benefit by those whom it most depended upon for strength and defence. The Moabites shall generally be so overwhelmed with grief that life itself shall be a burden to them. God can easily make weary of life those that are fondest of it.

V. That the outcry for these calamities should propagate grief to all the adjacent parts, *v.* 5. 1. The prophet himself has very sensible impressions made upon his spirit by the prediction of it: *"My heart shall cry out for Moab;* though they are enemies to Israel, they are our fellow-creatures, of the same rank with us, and therefore it should grieve us to see them in such distress, the rather because we know not how soon it may be our own turn to drink of the same cup of trembling." Note, It becomes God's ministers to be of a tender spirit, not to desire the woeful day, but to be like their master, who wept over Jerusalem even when he gave her up to ruin, like their God, *who desires not the death of sinners.* 2. All the neighbouring cities shall echo to the lamentations of Moab. *The fugitives,* who are making the best of their way to shift for their own safety, shall carry the cry to *Zoar,* the city to which their ancestor Lot fled for shelter from Sodom's flames and which was spared for his sake. They shall make as great a noise with their cry *as a heifer of three years old* does when she goes *lowing* for her calf, as 1 Sa. 6:12. They shall go up the hill of *Luhith* (as David went up the ascent of Mount Olivet, many a weary step and all in tears, 2 Sa. 15:30), and *in the way of Horonaim* (a dual termination), the way that leads to the two Beth-horons, the upper and the nether, which we read of, Jos. 16:3, 5. Thither the cry shall be carried, there it shall be raised, even at that great distance: *A cry of destruction;* that shall be the cry, like, "Fire, fire! we are all undone." Grief is catching, so is fear, and justly, for trouble is spreading and when it begins who knows where it will end?

Verses 6–9

Here the prophet further describes the woeful and piteous lamentations that should be heard throughout all the country of Moab when it should become a prey to the Assyrian army. "By this time *the cry has gone round about* all *the borders of Moab,*" *v.* 8. Every corner of the country has received the alarm, and is in the utmost confusion upon it. It has reached to *Eglaim,* a city at one end of the country, and to *Beer-elim,* a city as far the other way. Where sin has been general, and all flesh have corrupted their way, what can be expected but a general desolation? Two things are here spoken of as causes of this lamentation: —

I. *The waters of Nimrim are desolate* (*v.* 6), that is, the country is plundered and impoverished, and all the wealth and substance of it swept away by the victorious army. Famine is usually the sad effect of war. Look into the fields that were well watered, the fruitful meadows that yielded delightful prospects and more delightful products, and there all is eaten up, or carried off by the enemy's foragers, and the remainder trodden to dirt by their horses. If an army encamp upon green fields, their greenness is soon gone. Look into the houses, and they are stripped too (*v.* 7): *The abundance* of wealth that *they had gotten* with a great deal of art and industry, and *that which they had laid up* with a great deal of care and confidence, *shall they carry away to the brook of the willows.* Either the owners shall carry it thither to hide it or the enemies shall carry it thither to pack it up and send it home, by water perhaps, to their own country. Note, 1. Those that are eager to get abundance of this world, and solicitous to lay up what they have gotten, little consider what may become of it and in how short a time it may be all taken from them. Great abundance, by tempting the robbers, exposes the owners; and those who depend upon it to protect them often find it does but betray them. 2. In times of distress great riches are often great burdens, and do but increase the owner's care or the enemies' strength. *Cantabit vacuus coram latrone viator — The penniless traveller will exult, when accosted by a robber, in having nothing about him.*

II. *The waters of Dimon are turned into blood* (*v.* 9), that is, the inhabitants of the country are slain in great numbers, so that the waters adjoining to the cities, whether rivers or pools, are discoloured with human gore, inhumanly shed like water. *Dimon* signifies *bloody;* the place shall answer to its name. Perhaps it was that place in the country of Moab where the waters seemed to the *Moabites as blood* (2 Ki. 3:22, 23), which occasioned their overthrow. But now, says God, *I will bring more upon Dimon,* more blood than was shed, or thought to be seen, at that time. *I will bring additions upon Dimon* (so the word is), additional plagues; I have yet more judgments in reserve for them. *For all this, God's anger is not turned away.* When he judges he will overcome; and to the roll of curses shall be *added many like words,* Jer. 36:32. See here what is the *yet more evil* to be brought upon Dimon, upon Moab, which is now to be made a land of blood. Some flee, and make their escape, others sit still, and are overlooked, and are as a remnant of the land; but upon both God *will bring lions,* beasts of prey (which are reckoned one of God's four judgments, Eze. 14:21), and these shall glean up those that have escaped the sword of the enemy. Those that continue impenitent in sin, when they are preserved from one judgment, are but reserved for another.

CHAPTER 16

This chapter continues and concludes the burden of Moab. In it, I. The prophet gives good counsel to the Moabites, to reform what was amiss among them, and particularly to be kind to God's people, as the likeliest way to prevent the judgments before threatened (*v.* 1–5). II. Fearing they would not take this counsel (they were so proud), he goes on to foretel the lamentable devastation of their country, and the confusion they should be brought to, and this within three years (*v.* 6–14).

Verses 1–5

God has made it to appear that he delights not in the ruin of sinners by telling them what they may do to prevent the ruin; so he does here to Moab.

I. He advises them to be just to the house of David, and to pay the tribute they had formerly covenanted to pay to the kings of his line (*v.* 1): *Send you the lamb to the ruler of the land.* David made the Moabites tributaries to him, 2 Sa. 8:2. They *became his servants, and brought gifts.* Afterwards they paid their tribute to the kings of Israel (2 Ki. 3:4), and paid it in lambs. Now the prophet requires them to pay it to Hezekiah. Let it be raised and levied from all parts of the country, *from Selah,* a frontier city of Moab on the one side, *to the wilderness,* a boundary of the kingdom on the other side: and let it be sent, where it should be sent, *to the mount of the daughter of Zion,* the city of David. Some take it as an advice to send a lamb for a sacrifice to God, *the ruler of the earth* (so it may be read), the Lord of the whole earth, ruler of all lands, the land of Moab as well as the land of Israel, "Send it to the temple built on Mount Zion." And some think it is in this sense spoken ironically, upbraiding the Moabites with their folly in delaying to repent and make their peace with God. "Now you would be glad to send a lamb to Mount Zion, to make the God of Israel your friend; but it is too late: the decree has gone forth, the consumption is determined, and the *daughters of Moab* shall be cast out *as a wandering bird,*" *v.* 2. I rather take it as good advice seriously given, like that of Daniel to Nebuchadnezzar when he was reading him his doom, Dan. 4:27. *Break off thy sins by righteousness, if it may be a lengthening of thy tranquillity.* And it is applicable to the great gospel duty of submission to Christ, as the ruler of the land, and our ruler: "Send him the lamb, the best you have, yourselves a living sacrifice. When you come to God, the great ruler, come in the name of the Lamb, the Lamb of God. *For else it shall be"* (so we may read it) *"that, as a wandering bird cast out of the nest, so shall the daughters of Moab be.* If you will not pay your quit-rent, your just tribute to the king of Judah, you shall be turned out of your houses: *The daughters of Moab* (the country villages, or the women of your country) shall flutter about the *fords of Arnon,* attempting that way to make their escape to some other land, *like a wandering bird thrown out of the nest* half-fledged." Those that will not submit to Christ, nor be gathered under the shadow of his wings, shall be *as a bird that wanders from her nest,* that shall either be snatched up by the next bird of prey or shall wander endlessly in continual frights. Those that will not yield to the fear of God shall be made to yield to the fear of every thing else.

II. He advises them to be *kind to the seed of Israel* (*v.* 3): "Take counsel, call a convention, and consult among yourselves what is fit to be done in the present critical juncture; and you will find it your best way to execute judgment, to reverse all the unrighteous decrees you have made, by which you have put hardships upon the people of God, and, in token of your repentance for them, study now how to oblige them, and this shall be accepted of God more than all burnt-offering and sacrifice."

1. The prophet foresaw some storm coming upon the people of God, perhaps the good people of the ten tribes, or of the two and a half on the other side Jordan, whose country joined to that of Moab, and who, by the merciful providence of God, escaped the fury of the Assyrian army, had their lives given them for a prey, and were reserved for better times, but were put to the utmost extremity to shift for their own safety. The danger and trouble they were in were like the scorching heat at noon; the face of the spoiler was very fierce upon them and the oppressor and extortioner were ready to swallow them up after stripping them of what they had.

2. He bespeaks a shelter for them in the land of Moab, when their own land was made too hot for them. This judgment they must execute; thus wisely must they do for themselves, and thus kindly must they deal with the people of God. If they would themselves continue in their habitations, let them now open their doors to the distressed dispersed members of God's church, and be to them like a cool shade to those that *bear the burden and heat of the day.* Let them not discover those that absconded among them, nor deliver them up to the pursuers that made search for them: *"Betray not him that wandereth,* nor deliver him up" (as the Edomites did, Obad. 13, 14), "but *hide the outcasts."* This was that good work by which Rahab's faith was justified, and proved to be sincere, Heb. 11:31. "Nay, do not only hide them for a time, but, if there be occasion, let them be naturalized: *Let my outcasts dwell with thee, Moab* (*v.* 4); find a lodging for them and *be thou a covert to them.* Let them be taken under the protection of the government, though they are but poor, and likely to be a charge to thee." Note, (1.) It is often the lot even of those who are Israelites indeed to be outcasts, driven out of house and harbour by persecution or war, Heb. 11:37. (2.) God owns them when men reject and disown them. They are *outcasts,* but they are *my outcasts.* The Lord knows those that are his wherever he finds them, even where no one else knows them. (3.) God will find a rest and shelter for his outcasts; for, though they are persecuted, they are not forsaken. He will himself be their dwelling-place if they have no other, and in him they shall be at home. (4.) God can, when he pleases, raise up friends for his people even among Moabites, when they can find none in all the land of Israel that can and dare shelter them. The earth often helps the woman, Rev. 12:16. (5.) Those that expect to find favour when they are in trouble themselves must show favour to those that are in trouble; and what service is done to God's outcasts shall no doubt be recompensed one way or other.

3. He assures them of the mercy God had in store for his people. (1.) That they should not long need their kindness, or be troublesome to them: *For the extortioner is almost at an end* already, *and the spoiler ceases.* God's people shall not be long outcasts; they *shall have tribulation ten days* (Rev. 2:10), and that is all. The spoiler would never cease spoiling if he might have his will; but God has him in a chain. *Hitherto he shall go, but no further.* (2.) That they should, ere long, be in a capacity to return their kindness (*v.* 5): "Though the throne of the ten tribes be sunk and overturned, yet *the throne of David shall be established in mercy,* by the mercy they receive from God and the mercy they show to others; and by the same methods may your throne be established if you please." It would engage great men to be kind to the people of God if they would but observe, as they easily might, how often such conduct brings the blessing of God upon kingdoms and families. "Make Hezekiah your friend, for you will find it your interest to do so upon the account both of the grace of God in him and the presence of God with him. He *shall sit upon the throne in truth,* and then he does indeed sit in honour and sit firmly. Then he shall sit *judging,* and will then be a protector to those that have been a shelter to the people of God." And see in him the character of a good magistrate. [1.] He shall *seek judgment;* that is, he shall seek occasions of doing right to those that are wronged, and shall punish the injurious even before they are complained of: or he shall diligently search into every cause brought before him, that he may find where the right lies. [2.] He shall *hasten righteousness,* and not delay to do justice, nor keep those long waiting that make application to him for the redress of their grievances. Though he seeks judgment, and deliberates upon it, yet he does not, under pretence of deliberation, stay the progress of the streams of justice. Let the Moabites take example by this, and then assure themselves that their state shall be established.

Verses 6–14

Here we have, I. The sins with which Moab is charged, *v.* 6. The prophet seems to check himself for going about to give good counsel to the Moabites, concluding they would not take the advice he gave them. He told them their duty (whether they would hear or whether they would forbear), but despairs of working any good upon them; he would have healed them, but they would not be healed. Those that will not be counselled cannot be helped. Their sins were, 1. Pride. This is most insisted upon; for perhaps there are more precious souls ruined by pride than by any one lust whatsoever. The Moabites were notorious for this: *"We have heard* in both ears *of the pride of Moab;* it is what all their neighbours cry out shame upon them for. *He is very proud;* the body of the nation is so, forgetting the baseness of their origin and the brand of infamy fastened upon them by that law of God which forbade a Moabite to *enter into the congregation of the Lord for ever,* Deu. 23:3. We have heard of *his haughtiness and his pride.* It is not the rash and rigid censure of one of two concerning them, but it is the character which all that know them will give of them. They are a proud people, and therefore they will not take good counsel when it is given them. They think themselves too wise to be advised; therefore they will not take example by Hezekiah to do justly and love mercy. They scorn to make him their pattern, for they think themselves able to teach him. They are proud, and therefore will not be subject to God himself nor regard the warnings he gives them. *The wicked, in the pride of his countenance, will not seek after God.* They are proud, and therefore will not entertain and protect God's outcasts; they scorn to have any thing to do with them." But this is not all: — 2. "We have heard of *his wrath* too (for those that are very proud are commonly very passionate), particularly his wrath against the people of God, whom therefore he will rather persecute than protect. 3. It is with *his lies* that he gains the gratifications of his pride and his passion; *but his lies shall not be so;* he shall not compass his proud and angry projects as he hoped he should." Some read it, *His haughtiness, his pride, and his wrath, are greater than his strength.* "We know that, if we lay at his mercy, we should find no mercy with him, but he has not power equal to his malice. His pride draws down ruin upon him; for it is the preface to destruction, and he has not strength to ward it off."

II. The sorrows with which Moab is threatened (*v.* 7): *Therefore shall Moab howl for Moab.* All the inhabitants shall bitterly lament the ruin of their country. They shall complain one to another: *Every one shall howl* in despair, and not one shall either see any cause or have any heart to encourage his friend. Observe,

1. The causes of this sorrow. (1.) The destruction of their cities: *For the foundations of Kir-haraseth shall you mourn.* That great and strong city, which had held out against a mighty force (2 Ki. 3:25), should now be levelled with the ground, either burnt or broken down, and its foundations *stricken,* bruised and broken (so the word signifies); they shall howl when they see their splendid cities turned into ruinous heaps. (2.) The desolation of their country. Moab was famous for its fields and vineyards; but those shall all be laid waste by the invading army, *v.* 8, 10. See, [1.] What a fruitful pleasant country they had, as the garden of the Lord, Gen. 13:10. It was planted with choice and noble vines, with *principal plants,* which reached *even to Jazer,* a city in the tribe of Gad. The luxuriant branches of their vines *wandered,* and wound themselves along the ranges on which they were spread, even *through the wilderness* of Moab. There were vineyards there. Nay, they were *stretched out,* and went even to *the sea,* the Dead Sea: the best grapes grew in their hedge-rows. [2.] How merry and pleasant they had been in it. Many a time they had shouted *for their summer fruits, and for their harvest,* as the country people sometimes do with us when they have cut down all their corn. They had had *joy and gladness* in their fields and vineyards, *singing* and *shouting at the treading of their grapes.* Nothing is said of their praising God for their abundance, and giving him the glory of it. If they had made it the matter of their thanksgiving, they might still have had it the food and fuel of their lusts; see therefore, [3.] How they should be stripped of all. "The fields shall *languish,* all the fruits of them being carried away or trodden down; they cannot now enrich their owners as they have done, and therefore they languish. The soldiers, called here *the lords of the heathen,* shall break down all the plants, though they were *principal plants,* the choicest that could be got. Now the shouting for the enjoyment of the summer fruits has fallen, and is turned into howling for the loss of them. The joy of harvest has ceased; there is no more singing, no more shouting, for the treading out of wine. They have not what they have had to rejoice in, nor have they a disposition to rejoice; the ruin of their country has marred their mirth." Note, *First,* God can easily change the note of those that are most addicted to mirth and pleasure, can soon turn their laughter into mourning and their joy into heaviness. *Secondly,* Joy in God is, upon this account, far better than the joy of harvest, that it is what we cannot be robbed of, Ps. 4:6, 7. Destroy the vines and the fig-trees, and you make all the mirth of a carnal heart to cease, Hos. 2:11, 12. But a gracious soul can rejoice in the Lord as the God of its salvation even when the fig-tree does not blossom and there is no fruit in the vine, Hab. 3:17, 18. In God therefore let us always rejoice with a holy triumph, and in other things let us always rejoice with a holy trembling, rejoice as though we rejoiced not.

2. The concurrence of the prophet with them in this sorrow: *"I will with weeping bewail Jazer, and the vine of Sibmah,* and look with a compassionate concern upon the desolations of such a pleasant country. *I will water thee with my tears, O Heshbon!* and mingle them with thy tears;" nay (*v.* 11), it appears to be an inward grief: *My bowels shall sound like a harp for Moab;* it should make such an impression upon him that he should feel an inward trembling, like that of the strings of a harp when it is played upon. It well becomes God's prophets to acquaint themselves with grief; the great prophet did so. The afflictions of the world, as well as those of the church, should be afflictions to us. See *ch.* 15:5.

III. In the close of the chapter we have, 1. The insufficiency of the gods of Moab, the false gods, to help them, *v.* 12. "Moab shall be soon *weary of the high place.* He shall spend his spirits and strength in vain in praying to his idols; they cannot help him, and he shall be convinced that they cannot." It is seen that it is to no purpose to expect any relief from the high places on earth; it must come from above the hills. Men are generally so stupid that they will not believe, till they are made to see, the vanity of idols and of all creature-confidences, nor will come off from them till they are made weary of them. But, when he is weary of his high places, he will not go, as he should, to God's sanctuary, but to *his* sanctuary, to the temple of Chemosh, the principal idol of Moab (so it is generally understood); and he shall pray there to as little purpose, and as little to his own case and satisfaction, as he did in his high places; for, whatever honours idolaters give to their idols, they do not thereby make them at all the better able to help them. Whether they are the *dii majorum gentium — gods of the higher order,* or *minorum — of the lower order,* they are alike the creatures of men's fancy and the work of men's hands. Perhaps it may be meant of their coming to God's sanctuary. When they found they could have no succours from their own high places some of them would come to the temple of God at Jerusalem, to pray there, but in vain; he will justly send them back to *the gods whom they have served,* Jdg. 10:14. 2. The sufficiency of the God of Israel, the only true God, to make good what he had spoken against them. (1.) The thing itself was long since determined (*v.* 13): *This is the word,* this is the thing, *that the Lord has spoken concerning Moab, since the time* that he began to be so proud, and insolent, and abusive to God's people. The country was long ago doomed to ruin; this was enough to give an assurance of it that *it is the word which the Lord has spoken;* and, as he will never unsay what he has spoken, so all the power of hell and earth cannot gainsay it, or obstruct the execution of it. (2.) Now it was made known when it should be done. The time was before fixed in the counsel of God, but now it was revealed: *The Lord has spoken* that it shall be *within three years, v.* 14. *It is not for us to know,* or covet to know, *the times and the seasons,* any further than God has thought fit to make them known, and so far we may and must take notice of them. See how God makes known his mind by degrees; the light of divine revelation shone more and more, and so does the light of divine grace in the heart. Observe, [1.] The sentence passed upon Moab: *The glory of Moab shall be contemned,* that is, it shall be contemptible, when all those things they have gloried in shall come to nothing. Such is the glory of this world, so fading and uncertain, admired awhile, but soon slighted. Let that therefore which will soon be contemptible in the eyes of others be always contemptible in our eyes in comparison with the *far more exceeding weight of glory.* It was the glory of Moab that their country was very populous and their forces were courageous; but where is her glory when all that great multitude is in a manner swept away, some by one judgment and some by another, and the little remnant that is left shall be *very small and feeble,* not able to bear up under their own griefs, much less to make head against their enemies' insults? Let not therefore the strong glory in their strength nor the many in their numbers. [2.] The time fixed for the execution of this sentence: *Within three years, as the years of a hireling,* that is, at the three years' end exactly, for a servant that is hired for a certain term keeps account to a day. Let Moab know that her ruin is very near, and prepare accordingly. Fair warning is given, and with it space to repent, which if they had improved, as Nineveh did, we have reason to think the judgments threatened would have been prevented.

CHAPTER 17

Syria and Ephriam were confederate against Judah (*ch.* 7:1, 2), and, they being so closely linked together in their counsels, this chapter, though it be entitled "the burden of Damascus" (which was the head city of Syria), reads the doom of Israel too. I. The destruction of the strong cities both of Syria and Israel is here foretold (*v.* 1–5 and *v.* 9–11). II. In the midst of judgment mercy is remembered to Israel, and a gracious promise made that a remnant should be preserved from the calamities and should get good by them (*v.* 6–8). III. The overthrow of the Assyrian army before Jerusalem is pointed at (*v.* 12–14). In order of time this chapter should be placed next after *ch.* 9, for the destruction of Damascus, here foretold, happened in the reign of Ahaz, 2 Ki. 16:9.

Verses 1–5

We have here the burden of Damascus; the Chaldee paraphrase reads it, *The burden of the cup of the curse to drink to Damascus in;* and, the ten tribes being in alliance, they must expect to pledge Damascus in this cup of trembling that is to go round. 1. Damascus itself, the head city of Syria, must be destroyed; the houses, it is likely, will be burnt, as least the walls, and gates, and fortifications demolished, and the inhabitants carried away captive, so that for the present it is *taken away from being a city,* and is reduced not only to a village, but to *a ruinous heap, v.* 1. Such desolating work as this does sin make with cities. 2. The country towns are abandoned by their inhabitants, frightened or forced away by the invaders: *The cities of Aroer* (a province of Syria so called) *are forsaken* (*v.* 2); the conquered dare not dwell in them, and the conquerors have no occasion for them, nor did they seize them for want, but wantonness; so that the places which should be for men to live in are for *flocks to lie down in,* which they may do, and none will disturb nor dislodge them. Stately houses are converted into sheep-cotes. It is strange that great conquerors should pride themselves in being common enemies to mankind. But, how unrighteous soever they are, God is righteous in causing those cities to spue out their inhabitants, who by their wickedness had made themselves vile; it is better that *flocks should lie down there* than that they should harbour such as are in open rebellion against God and virtue. 3. The strongholds of Israel, the kingdom of the ten tribes, will be brought to ruin: *The fortress shall cease from Ephraim* (*v.* 3), that in Samaria, and all the rest. They had joined with Syria in invading Judah very unnaturally; and now those that had been partakers in sin should be made partakers in ruin, and justly. When *the fortress shall cease from Ephraim,* by which Israel will be weakened, the kingdom will cease from Damascus, by which Syria will be ruined. The Syrians were the ring-leaders in that confederacy against Judah, and therefore they are punished first and sorest; and, because they boasted of their alliance with Israel, now that Israel is weakened they are upbraided with those boasts: *"The remnant of Syria shall be as the glory of the children of Israel;* those few that remain of the Syrians shall be in as mean and despicable a condition as the children of Israel are, and the glory of Israel shall be no relief or reputation to them." Sinful confederacies will be no strength, no stay, to the confederates, when God's judgments come upon them. See here what the glory of Jacob is when God contends with him, and what little reason Syria will have to be proud of resembling the glory of Jacob. (1.) It is wasted like a man in a consumption, *v.* 4. *The glory of Jacob* was their numbers, that they were as the sand of the sea for multitude; but this glory *shall be made thin,* when many are cut off, and few left. Then the *fatness of their flesh,* which was their pride and security, *shall was lean,* and the body of the people shall become a perfect skeleton, nothing but skin and bones. Israel died of a lingering disease; the kingdom of the ten tribes wasted gradually; God was to them *as a moth,* Hos. 5:12. Such is all the glory of this world: it soon withers, and is made thin; but thee is a far more exceeding and external weight of glory designed for the spiritual seed of Jacob, which is not subject to any such decay — fatness of God's house, which will not *wax lean.* (2.) It is all gathered and carried away by the Assyrian army, as the corn is carried out of the field by the husbandmen, *v.* 5. The corn is the glory of the fields (Ps. 65:13); but, when it is reaped and gone, where is the glory? The people had by their sins made themselves ripe for ruin, and their glory was as quickly, as easily, as justly, and as irresistibly, cut down and taken away, as the corn is out of the field by the husbandman. God's judgments are compared to the *thrusting in of the sickle when the harvest is ripe,* Rev. 14:15. And the victorious army, like the careful husbandmen in the valley of Rephaim, where the corn was extraordinary, would not, if they could help it, leave an ear behind, would lose nothing that they could lay their hands on.

Verses 6–8

Mercy is here reserved, in a parenthesis, in the midst of judgment, for a remnant that should escape the common ruin of the kingdom of the ten tribes. Though the Assyrians took all the care they could that none should slip out of their net, yet the meek of the earth were hidden in the day of the Lord's anger, and had their lives given them for a prey and made comfortable to them by their retirement to the land of Judah, where they had the liberty of God's courts. 1. They shall be but a small remnant, a very few, who shall be marked for preservation (*v.* 6): *Gleaning grapes shall be left in it.* The body of the people were carried into captivity, but here and there one was left behind, perhaps one of two in a bed when the other was taken, Lu. 17:34. The most desolating judgments in this world are short of the last judgment, which shall be universal and which none shall escape. In times of the greatest calamity some are kept safe, as in times of the greatest degeneracy some are kept pure. But the fewness of those that escape supposes the captivity of the far greatest part; those that are left are but like the poor remains of an olive tree when it has been carefully shaken by the owner; if there be *two or three berries in the top of the uppermost bough* (out of the reach of those that shook it), that is all. Such is the *remnant according to the election of grace,* very few in comparison with the multitudes that walk on in the broad way. 2. They shall be a sanctified remnant, *v.* 7, 8. These few that are preserved are such as, in the prospect of the judgment approaching, had repented of their sins and reformed their lives, and therefore were snatched thus as brands out of the burning, or such as having escaped, and becoming refugees in strange countries, were awakened, partly by a sense of the distinguishing mercy of their deliverance, and partly by the distresses they were still in, to return to God. (1.) They shall look up to their Creator, shall enquire, *Where is God my Maker, who giveth songs in the night,* in such a night of affliction as this? Job 35:10, 11. They shall acknowledge his hand in all the events concerning them, merciful and afflictive, and shall submit to his hand. They shall give him the glory due to his name, and be suitably affected with his providences. They shall expect relief and succour from him and depend upon him to help them. Their *eyes shall have respect* to him, *as the eyes of a servant to the hand of his master,* Ps. 123:2. Observe, It is our duty at all times to have respect to God, to have our eyes ever towards him, both as our Maker (the author of our being and the God of nature) and as the Holy One of Israel, a God in covenant with us and the God of grace; particularly, when we are in affliction, our eyes must be towards the Lord, to *pluck our feet out of the net* (Ps. 25:15); to bring us to this is the design of his providence as he is our Maker and the work of his grace as he is the Holy One of Israel. (2.) They shall look off from their idols, the creatures of their own fancy, shall no longer worship them, and seek to them, and expect relief from them. For God will be alone regarded, or he does not look upon himself as at all regarded. He that looks to his Maker must not *look to the altars, the work of his hands,* but disown them and cast them off, must not retain the least respect for *that which his fingers have made,* but break it to pieces, though it be his own workmanship — *the groves and the images;* the word signifies images made in honour of the sun and by which he was worshipped, the most ancient and most plausible idolatry, Deu. 4:19; Job 31:26. We have reason to account those happy afflictions which part between us and our sins, and by sensible convictions of the vanity of the world, that great idol, cool our affections to it and lower our expectations from it.

Verses 9–11

Here the prophet returns to foretel the woeful desolations that should be made in the land of Israel by the army of the Assyrians. 1. That the cities should be deserted. Even the strong cities, which should have protected the country, shall not be able to protect themselves: They *shall be as a forsaken bough and an uppermost branch* of an old tree, which has gone to decay, is forsaken of its leaves, and appears on the top of the tree, bare, and dry, and dead; so shall their strong cities look when the inhabitants have deserted them and the victorious army of the enemy pillaged and defaced them, *v.* 9. They shall be as the cities (so it may be supplied) which the Canaanites left, the old inhabitants of the land, because of the children of Israel, when God brought them in with a high hand, to take possession of that good land, cities which they built not. As the Canaanites then fled before Israel, so Israel should now flee before the Assyrians. And herein the word of God was fulfilled, that, if they committed the same abominations, *the land* should *spue them out, as it spued out the nations that were before them* (Lev. 18:28), and that as, while they had God on their side, *one of them chased a thousand,* so, when they had made him their enemy, *a thousand* of them should *flee at the rebuke of one;* so that in the cities should be desolation, according to the threatenings in the law, Lev. 26:31; Deu. 28:51. 2. That the country should be laid waste, *v.* 10, 11. Observe here, (1.) The sin that had provoked God to bring so great a destruction upon that pleasant land. It was *for the iniquity of those that dwelt therein.* "It is *because thou hast forgotten the God of thy salvation* and all the great salvations he has wrought for thee, hast forgotten thy dependence upon him and obligations to him, and *hast not been mindful of the rock of thy strength,* not only who is himself a strong rock, but who has been thy strength many a time, or thou wouldst have been sunk and broken long since." Note, The God of our salvation is the rock of our strength; and our forgetfulness and unmindfulness of him are at the bottom of all sin. *Therefore* have we *perverted our way, because we have forgotten the Lord our God,* and so we undo ourselves. (2.) The destruction itself, aggravated by the great care they took to improve their land and to make it yet more pleasant. [1.] Look upon it at the time of the seedness, and it was all like a garden and a vineyard; that pleasant land was replenished with pleasant plants, the choicest of its own growth; nay, so nice and curious were the inhabitants that, not content with them, they sent to all the neighbouring countries for strange slips, the more valuable for being strange, uncommon, far-fetched, and dear-bought, though perhaps they had of their own not inferior to them. This was an instance of their pride and vanity, and (that ruining error) their affection to be *like the nations. Wheat, and honey, and oil* were their staple commodities (Eze. 27:17); but, not content with these, they must have flowers and greens with strange names imported from other nations, and a great deal of care and pains must be taken by hot-beds to make these plants to grow; the soil must be forced, and they must be covered with glasses to shelter them, and early in the morning the gardeners must be up to make the seed to flourish, that it may excel those of their neighbours. The ornaments of nature are not to be altogether slighted, but it is a folly to be over-fond of them, and to bestow more time, and cost, and pains about them than they deserve, as many do. But here this instance seems to be put in general for their great industry in cultivating their ground, and their expectations from it accordingly; they doubt not but their plants will grow and flourish. But, [2.] Look upon the same ground at the time of harvest, and it is all like a wilderness, a dismal melancholy place, even to the spectators, much more to the owners; for *the harvest shall be a heap,* all in confusion, *in the day of grief and of desperate sorrow.* The harvest used to be a time of joy, of singing and shouting (*ch.* 16:10); but this harvest the hungry eat up (Job 5:5), which makes it a day of grief, and the more because the plants were pleasant and costly (*v.* 10) and their expectations proportionably raised. The harvest had sometimes been a day of grief, if the crop was thin and the weather unseasonable; and yet in that case there was hope that the next would be better. But this shall be desperate sorrow, for they shall see not only this year's products carried off, but the property of the ground altered and their conquerors lords of it. The margin reads it, *The harvest shall be removed* (into the enemy's country or camp, Deu. 28:33) *in the day of inheritance* (when thou thoughtest to inherit it), *and there shall be deadly sorrow.* This is a good reason why we should not lay up our treasure in those things which we may so quickly be despoiled of, but in that good part which shall never be taken away from us.

Verses 12–14

These verses read the doom of those that spoil and rob the people of God. If the Assyrians and Israelites invade and plunder Judah, if the Assyrian army take God's people captive and lay their country waste, let them know that ruin will be their lot and portion. They are here brought in, 1. Triumphing over the people of God. They relied upon their numbers. The Assyrian army was made up out of divers nations: it was *the multitude of many people* (*v.* 12), by which weight they hoped to carry the cause. They were very noisy, like the roaring of the seas; they talked big, hectored, and threatened, to frighten God's people from resisting them, and all their allies from sending in to their aid. Sennacherib and Rabshakeh, in their speeches and letters, made a mighty noise to strike a terror upon Hezekiah and his people; the nations that followed them *made a rushing like the rushing of many waters,* and those mighty ones, that threaten to bear down all before them and carry away every thing that stands in their way. *The floods have lifted up their voice, have lifted up their waves;* such is the tumult of the people, and the heathen, when they rage, Ps. 2:1; 93:3. 2. Triumphed over by the judgments of God. They thought to carry their point by dint of noise; but woe to them (*v.* 12), for he *shall rebuke them,* that is, God shall, one whom they little think of, have no regard to, stand in no awe of; he shall give them a check with an invisible hand, *and* then *they shall flee afar off.* Sennacherib, and Rabshakeh, and the remains of their forces, shall run away in a fright, and shall be chased by their own terrors, *as the chaff of the mountains* which stand bleak *before the wind, and like a rolling thing before the whirlwind,* like thistle-down (so the margin); they make themselves *as chaff before the wind* (Ps. 35:5) and then *the angel of the Lord* (as it follows there), the same angel that slew many of them, shall chase the rest. God will make *them like a wheel,* or rolling thing, and then *persecute them with his tempest* and *make them afraid with his storm,* Ps. 83:13, 15. Note, God can dispirit the enemies of his church when they are most courageous and confident, and dissipate them when they seem most closely consolidated. This shall be done suddenly (*v.* 14): *At evening-tide* they are very troublesome, and threaten trouble to the people of God; but *before the morning they are not.* At sleeping time they are cast into a deep sleep, Ps. 26:5, 6. It was in the night that the angel routed the Assyrian army. God can in a moment break the power of his church's enemies, even when it appears most formidable; and this is written for the encouragement of the people of God in all ages, when they find themselves an unequal match for their enemies; for *this is the portion of those that spoil us,* they shall themselves be spoiled. God will plead his church's cause, and those that meddle do it to their own hurt.

CHAPTER 18

Whatever country it is that is meant here by "the land shadowing with wings," here is a woe denounced against it, for God has, upon his people's account, a quarrel with it. I. They threaten God's people (*v.* 1, 2). II. All the neighbours are hereupon called to take notice what will be the issue (*v.* 3). III. Though God seem unconcerned in the distress of his people for a time, he will at length appear against their enemies and will remarkable cut them off (*v.* 4–6). IV. This shall redound very much to the glory of God (*v.* 7).

Verses 1–7

Interpreters are very much at a loss where to find this land that lies beyond the rivers of Cush. Some take it to be Egypt, a maritime country, and full of rivers, and which courted Israel to depend upon them, but proved broken reeds; but against this it is strongly objected that the next chapter is distinguished from this by the title of *the burden of Egypt.* Others take it to be Ethiopia, and read it, *which lies near,* or *about, the rivers of Ethiopia,* not that in Africa, which lay south of Egypt, but that which we call *Arabia,* which lay east of Canaan, which Tirhakah was now king of. He thought to protect the Jews, as it were, under *the shadow of his wings,* by giving a powerful diversion to the king of Assyria, when he made a descent upon his country, at the time that he was attacking Jerusalem, 2 Ki. 19:9. But though by his ambassadors he bade defiance to the king of Assyria, and encouraged the Jews to depend upon him, God by the prophet slights him, and will not go forth with him; he may take his own course, but God will take another course to protect Jerusalem, while he suffers the attempt of Tirhakah to miscarry and his Arabian army to be ruined; for the Assyrian army shall become a present or sacrifice to the Lord of hosts, and to the place of his name, by the hand of an angel, not by the hand of Tirhakah king of Ethiopia, *v.* 7. This is a very probable exposition of this chapter. But from a hint of Dr. Lightfoot's, in his Harmony of the Old Testament, I incline to understand this chapter as a prophecy against Assyria, and so a continuation of the prophecy in the last three verses of the foregoing chapter, with which therefore this should be joined. That was against the army of the Assyrians which rushed in upon Judah; this is against the land of Assyria itself, which lay beyond the rivers of Arabia, that is, the rivers Euphrates and Tigris, which bordered on *Arabia Deserta.* And in calling it *the land shadowing with wings* he seems to refer to what he himself had said of it (*ch.* 8:8), that *the stretching out of his wings shall fill the breadth of thy land, O Immanuel!* The prophet might perhaps describe the Assyrians by such dark expressions, not naming them, for the same reason that St. Paul, in his prophecy, speaks of the Roman empire by a periphrasis: *He who now letteth,* 2 Th. 2:7. Here is,

I. The attempt made by this land (whatever it is) upon *a nation scattered and peeled, v.* 2. Swift messengers are sent by water to proclaim war against them, as a nation marked by Providence, and *meted out,* to be trodden under foot. Whether this refer to the Ethiopians waging war with the Assyrians, or the Assyrians with Judah, it teaches us, 1. That a people which have been terrible from their beginning, have made a figure and borne a mighty sway, may yet become scattered and peeled, and may be spoiled even by their own rivers, that should enrich both the husbandman and the merchant. Nations which have been formidable, and have kept all in awe about them, may by a concurrence of accidents become despicable and an easy prey to their insulting neighbours. 2. Princes and states that are ambitious of enlarging their territories will always have some pretence or other to quarrel with those whose countries they have a mind to. "It is a nation that has been terrible, and therefore we must be revenged on it; it is now a nation scattered and peeled, meted out and trodden down, and therefore it will be an easy prey for us." Perhaps it was not brought so low as they represented it. God's people are trampled on as a nation scattered and peeled; but whoever think to swallow them up may find them still as terrible as they have been from their beginning; they are cast down, but not deserted, not destroyed.

II. The alarm sounded to the nations about, by which they are summoned to take notice of what God is about to do, *v.* 3. The Ethiopians and Assyrians have their counsels and designs, which they have laid deep, and promise themselves much from, and, in prosecution of them, send their ambassadors and messengers from place to place; but let us now enquire what the great God says to all this. 1. *He lifts up an ensign upon the mountains, and blows a trumpet,* by which he proclaims war against the enemies of his church, and calls in all her friends and well-wishers into her service, *v.* 3. He gives notice that he is about to do some great work, as *Lord of hosts.* 2. All the world is bidden to take notice of it; all the dwellers on earth must see the ensign and hear the trumpet, must observe the motions of the divine providence and attend the directions of the divine will. Let all enlist under God's banner, and be on his side, and hearken to the trumpet of his word, which gives not an uncertain sound.

III. The assurance God gives to his prophet, by him to be given to his people, that, though he might seem for a time to sit by as an unconcerned spectator, yet he would certainly and seasonably appear for the comfort of his people and the confusion of his and their enemies (*v.* 4): *So the Lord said unto me.* Men will have their saying, but God also will have his; and, as we may be sure his word shall stand, so he often whispers it in the ears of his servants the prophets. When he says, *I will take my rest,* it is not as if he were weary of governing the world, of as if he either needed or desired to retire from it and repose himself; but it intimates that the great God has a perfect, undisturbed, enjoyment of himself, in the midst of all the agitations and changes of this world (the Lord sits even upon the floods unshaken; the Eternal Mind is always easy), and, though he may sometimes seem to his people as if he took not wonted notice of what is done in this lower world (they are tempted to think he is *as one asleep,* or *as one astonished,* Ps. 44:23; Jer. 14:9), yet even then he knows very well what men are doing and what he himself will do.

1. He will take care of his people, and be a shelter to them. He will regard his *dwelling-place;* his eye and his heart are, and shall be, upon it for good continually. Zion is his rest for ever, where he will dwell; and he will *look after it* (so some read it); he will lift up the light of his countenance upon it, will consider over it what is to be done, and will be sure to do all for the best. He will adapt the comforts and refreshments he provides for his people to the exigencies of their case; and they will *therefore* be acceptable, because seasonable. (1.) Like a clear heat after rain (so the margin), which is very reviving and pleasant, and makes the herbs to flourish. (2.) Like a dew and *a cloud in the heat of harvest,* which are very welcome, the dew to the ground and the cloud to the labourers. Note, There is that in God which is a shelter and refreshment to his people in all weathers and arms them against the inconveniences of every change. Is the weather cool? There is that in his favour which will warm them. Is it hot? There is that in his favour which will cool them. Great men have their winter-house and their summer-house (Amos 3:15); but those that are at home with God have both in him.

2. He will reckon with his and their enemies, *v.* 5, 6. When the Assyrian army promises itself a plentiful harvest in the taking of Jerusalem and the plundering of that rich city, when the bud of that project is perfect, before the harvest is gathered in, while the sour grape of their enmity to Hezekiah and his people is ripening in the flower and the design is just ready to be put in execution, God shall destroy that army as easily as the husbandman cuts off the sprigs of the vine with pruning hooks, or because the grape is sour and good for nothing, and will not be cured, *takes away and cuts down the branches.* This seems to point at the overthrow of the Assyrian army by a destroying angel, when the dead bodies of the soldiers were scattered like the branches and sprigs of a wild vine, which the husbandman has cut to pieces. *And they shall be left to the fowls of the mountains, and the beasts of the earth,* to prey upon, both winter and summer; for as God's people are protected all seasons of the year, both in cold and heat (*v.* 4), so their enemies are at all seasons exposed; birds

and beasts of prey shall both summer and winter upon them, till they are quite ruined.

IV. The tribute of praise which should be brought to God from all this (*v.* 7): *In that time,* when this shall be accomplished, *shall the present be brought unto the Lord of hosts.* 1. Some understand this of the conversion of the Ethiopians to the faith of Christ in the latter days, of which we have the specimen and beginning in Philip's baptizing the Ethiopian eunuch, Acts 8:27, etc. Those that were *a people scattered and peeled, meted out, and trodden down* (*v.* 2), shall be a present to the Lord: and, though they seem useless and worthless, they shall be an acceptable present to him who judges of men by the sincerity of their faith and love, not by the pomp and prosperity of their outward condition. *Therefore* the gospel was ministered to the Gentiles that *the offering up of the Gentiles might be acceptable,* Rom. 15:16. It is prophesied (Ps. 68:31) that *Ethiopia shall soon stretch out her hands unto God.* 2. Others understand it of the spoil of Sennacherib's army, out of which, as usual, presents were brought to *the Lord of hosts,* Num. 31:50. It was the present of a people scattered and peeled. (1.) It was won from the Assyrians, who were now themselves reduced to such a condition as they scornfully described Judah to be in, *v.* 1. Those that unjustly trample upon others shall themselves be justly trampled upon. (2.) It was offered by the people of God, who were, in disdain, called *a people scattered and peeled.* God will put honour upon his people, though men put contempt upon them. *Lastly,* Observe, The present that is brought to the Lord of hosts must be brought *to the place of the name of the Lord of hosts;* what is offered to God must be offered in the way that he has appointed; we must be sure to attend him, and expect him to meet us, where he records his name.

CHAPTER 19

As Assyria was a breaking rod to Judah, with which it was smitten, so Egypt was a broken reed, with which it was cheated; and therefore God had a quarrel with them both. We have before read the doom of the Assyrians; now here we have the burden of Egypt, a prophecy concerning that nation, I. That it should be greatly weakened and brought low, and should be as contemptible among the nations as now it was considerable, rendered so by a complication of judgments which God would bring upon them (*v.* 1–17). II. That at length God's holy religion should be brought into Egypt, and set up there, in part by the Jews that should flee thither for refuge, but more fully by the preachers of the gospel of Christ, through whose ministry churches should be planted in Egypt in the says of the Messiah (*v.* 18–25), which would abundantly balance all the calamities here threatened.

Verses 1–17

Though the land of Egypt had of old been a house of bondage to the people of God, where they had been ruled with rigour, yet among the unbelieving Jews there still remained much of the humour of their fathers, who said, *Let us make us a captain and return into Egypt.* Upon all occasions they trusted to Egypt for help (*ch.* 30:2), and thither they fled, in disobedience to God's express command, when things were brought to the last extremity in their own country, Jer. 43:7. Rabshakeh upbraided Hezekiah with this, *ch.* 36:6. While they kept up an alliance with Egypt, and it was a powerful ally, they stood not in awe of the judgments of God; for against them they depended upon Egypt to protect them. Nor did they depend upon the power of God when at any time they were in distress; but Egypt was their confidence. To prevent all this mischief, Egypt must be mortified, and many ways God here tells them he will take to mortify them.

I. The gods of Egypt shall appear to them to be what they always really were, utterly unable to help them, *v.* 1. *"The Lord rides upon a cloud, a swift cloud, and shall come into Egypt.* As a judge goes in state to the bench to try and condemn the malefactors, or as a general takes the field with his troops to crush the rebels, so shall God come into Egypt with his judgments; and when he comes he will certainly overcome." In all this burden of Egypt here is no mention of any foreign enemy invading them; but God himself will come against them, and raise up the causes of their destruction from among themselves. He comes upon a cloud, above the reach of the opposition or resistance. He comes apace upon a swift cloud; for their judgment lingers not when the time has come. He *rides upon the wings of the wind,* with a majesty far excelling the greatest pomp and splendour of earthly princes. He *makes the clouds his chariots,* Ps. 18:9; 104:3. When he comes *the idols of Egypt shall be moved,* shall be removed at his presence, and perhaps be made to fall as Dagon did before the ark. Isis, Osiris, and Apis, those celebrated idols of Egypt, being found unable to relieve their worshippers, shall be disowned and rejected by them. Idolatry had got deeper rooting in Egypt than in any land besides, even the most absurd idolatries; and yet now the idols shall be moved and they shall be ashamed of them. When the Lord brought Israel out of Egypt he *executed judgments upon the gods of the Egyptians* (Num. 33:4); no marvel then if, when he comes, they begin to tremble. The Egyptians *shall seek to the idols,* when they are at their wits' end, and consult *the charmers and wizards* (*v.* 3); but all in vain; they see their ruin hastening on them notwithstanding.

II. The militia of Egypt, that had been famed for their valour, shall be quite dispirited and disheartened. No kingdom in the world was ever in a better method of keeping up a standing army than the Egyptians were; but now their heroes, that used to be celebrated for courage, shall be posted for cowards: *The heart of Egypt shall melt in the midst of it,* like wax before the fire (*v.* 1); *the spirit of Egypt shall fail, v.* 3. They shall have no inclination, no resolution, to stand up in defence of their country, their liberty, and property; but shall tamely and ingloriously yield all to the invader and oppressor. The Egyptians *shall be like women* (*v.* 16); they shall be frightened and put into confusion by the least alarm; even those that dwell in the heart of the country, in the midst of it, and therefore furthest from danger, will be as full of frights as those that are situate on the frontiers. Let not the bold and brave be proud or secure, for God can easily *cut off the spirit of princes* (Ps. 76:12) and *take away their hearts,* Job 12:24.

III. The Egyptians shall be embroiled in endless dissensions and quarrels among themselves. There shall be no occasion to bring a foreign force upon them to destroy them; they shall destroy one another (*v.* 2): *I will set the Egyptians against the Egyptians.* As these divisions and animosities are their sin, God is not the author of them, they come from men's lusts; but God, as a Judge, permits them for their punishment, and by their destroying differences corrects them for their sinful agreements. Instead of helping one another, and acting each in his place for the common good, *they shall fight every one against his brother and neighbour,* whom he ought to love as himself — *city against city, and kingdom against kingdom.* Egypt was then divided into twelve provinces, or dynasties; but Psammetichus, the governor of one of them, by setting them at variance with one another, at length made himself master of them all. A kingdom thus divided against itself would soon be brought to desolation. *En quo discordiâ cives perduxit miseros! — Oh the wretchedness brought upon a people by their disagreements among themselves!* It is brought to this by *a perverse spirit,* a spirit of contradiction, which the Lord would mingle, as an intoxicating draught made up of several ingredients, for the Egyptians, *v.* 14. One party shall be for a thing for no other reason than because the other is against it; that is a perverse spirit, which, if it mingle with the public counsels, tends directly to the ruin of the public interests.

IV. Their politics shall be all blasted, and turned into foolishness. When God will destroy the nation he will *destroy the counsel thereof* (*v.* 3), by taking away wisdom from the statesmen (Job 12:20), or setting them one against another (as Hushai and Ahithophel), or by his providence breaking their measures even when they seemed well laid; so that the *princes of Zoan are fools:* they make fools of one another, every one betrays his own folly, and divine Providence makes fools of them all, *v.* 11. Pharaoh had his wise counsellors. Egypt was famous for such. But their *counsel has all become brutish;* they have lost all their forecast; one would think they had become idiots, and were bereaved of common sense. Let no man glory then in his own wisdom, nor depend upon that, nor upon the wisdom of those about him; for he that gives understanding can when he please take it away. And from those it is most likely to be taken away that boast of their policy, as Pharaoh's counsellors here did, and, to recommend themselves to places of public trust, boast of their great understanding (*"I am the son of the wise,* of the God of wisdom, of wisdom itself," says one; "my father was an eminent privy-counsellor of note in his day for wisdom"), or of the antiquity and dignity of their families: "I am," says another, *"the son of ancient kings."* The nobles of Egypt boasted much of their antiquity, producing fabulous records of their succession for above 10,000 years. This humour prevailed much among them about this time, as appears by Herodotus, their common boast being that Egypt was some thousands of years more ancient than any other nation. "But *where are thy wise men? v.* 12. Let them now show their wisdom by foreseeing what ruin is coming upon their nation, and preventing it, if they can. Let them with all their skill *know what the Lord of hosts has purposed upon Egypt,* and arm themselves accordingly. Nay, so far are they from doing this that they themselves are, in effect, contriving the ruin of Egypt, and hastening it on, *v.* 13. *The princes of Noph* are not only deceived themselves, but they *have seduced Egypt,* by putting their kings upon arbitrary proceedings" (by which both themselves and their people were soon undone); "the governors of Egypt, that are the stay and cornerstones of the tribes thereof, are themselves undermining it." It is sad with a people when those that undertake for their safety are helping forward their destruction, and the physicians of the state are her worst disease, when the things that belong to the public peace are so far hidden from the eyes of those that are entrusted with the public counsels that in every thing they blunder and take wrong measures; so here (*v.* 14): *They have caused Egypt to err in every work thereof.* Every step they took was a false step. They always mistook either the end or the means, and their counsels were all unsteady and uncertain, like the staggerings and stammerings of a drunken man in his vomit, who knows not what he says nor where he goes. See what reason we have to pray for our privy-counsellors and ministers of state, who are the great supports and blessings of the state if God give them a spirit of wisdom, but quite the contrary if he hide their heart from understanding.

V. The rod of government shall be turned into the serpent of tyranny and oppression (*v.* 4): *"The Egyptians will I give over into the hand of a cruel lord,* not a foreigner, but one of their own, one that shall rule over them by an hereditary right, but shall be a fierce king and rule them with rigour," either the twelve tyrants that succeeded Sethon, or rather Psammetichus that recovered the monarchy again; for he speaks of one cruel lord. Now the barbarous usage which the Egyptian task masters gave to God's Israel long ago was remembered against them and they were paid in their own coin by another Pharaoh. It is sad with a people when the powers that should be for edification are for destruction, and they are ruined by those by whom they should be ruled, when such as this is the manner of the king, as it is described *(in terrorem — in order to impress alarm),* 1 Sa. 8:11.

VI. Egypt was famous for its river Nile, which was its wealth, and strength, and beauty, and was idolized by them. Now it is here threatened that *the waters shall fail from the sea* and the river shall be *wasted and dried up, v.* 5. Nature shall not herein favour them as she has done. Egypt was never watered with the rain of heaven (Zec. 14:18), and therefore the fruitfulness of their country depended wholly upon the overflowing of their river; if that therefore be dried up, their fruitful land will soon be turned into barrenness and their harvests cease: *Every thing sown by the brooks will wither* of course, will *be driven away, and be no more, v.* 7. If the paper-reeds by the brooks, at the very mouth of them, wither, much more the corn, which lies at a greater distance, but derives its moisture from them. Yet this is not all; the drying up of their rivers is the destruction, 1. Of their fortifications, for they are *brooks of defence* (*v.* 6), making the country difficult of access to an enemy. Deep rivers are the strongest lines, and most hardly forced. Pharaoh is said to be a *great dragon lying in the midst of his rivers,* and guarded by them, bidding defiance to all about him, Eze. 29:3. But these *shall be emptied and dried up,* not by an enemy, as Sennacherib with the *sole of his foot dried up mighty rivers* (*ch.* 37:25), and as Cyrus, who took Babylon by drawing Euphrates into many streams, but by the providence of God, which sometimes *turns water-springs into dry ground,* Ps. 107:33. 2. It is the destruction of their fish, which in Egypt was much of their food, witness that base reflection which the children of Israel made (Num. 11:5): *We remember the fish which we did eat in Egypt freely.* The drying up of the rivers will *kill the fish* (Ps. 105:29), and will thereby ruin those who make it their business, (1.) To catch fish, whether by angling or nets (*v.* 8); they shall *lament* and *languish,* for their trade is at an end. There is nothing which the children of this world do more heartily lament than the loss of that which they used to get money by. *Ploratur lachrymis amissa pecunia veris — Those are genuine tears which are shed over lost money.* (2.) To keep fish, that it may be ready when it is called for. There were those that *made sluices and ponds for fish* (*v.* 10), but *they shall be broken in the purposes thereof;* their business will fail, either for want of water to fill their ponds or for want of fish to replenish their waters. God can find ways to deprive a country even of that which is its staple commodity. The Egyptians may themselves remember *the fish they have formerly eaten freely,* but now cannot have for money. And that which aggravates the loss of these advantages by the river is that it is their own doing (*v.* 6): *They shall turn the rivers far away.* Their kings and great men, to gratify their own fancy, will drain water from the main river to their own houses and grounds at a distance, preferring their private convenience before the public good, and so by degrees the force of the river is sensibly weakened. Thus many do themselves a greater prejudice at last than they think of, [1.] Who pretend to be wiser than nature, and to do better for themselves than nature has done. [2.] Who consult their own particular interest more than the common good. Such may gratify themselves, but surely they can never satisfy themselves, who to serve a turn contribute to a public calamity, which they themselves, in the long run, cannot avoid sharing in. Herodotus tells us that Pharaoh-Necho (who reigned not long after this), projecting to cut a free passage by water from Nilus into the Red Sea, employed a vast number of men to make a ditch or channel for that purpose, in which attempt he impaired the river, lost 120,000 of his people, and yet left the work unaccomplished.

VII. Egypt was famous for the linen manufacture; but that trade shall be ruined. Solomon's merchants traded with Egypt for linen-yarn, 1 Ki. 10:28. Their country produced the best flax and the best hands to work it; but *those that work in fine flax shall be confounded* (*v.* 9), either for want of flax to work on or for want of a demand for that which they have worked or opportunity to export it. The decay of trade weakens and wastes a nation and by degrees brings it to ruin. The trade of Egypt must needs sink, for (*v.* 15) *there shall not be any work for Egypt* to be employed in; and where there is nothing to be done there is nothing to be got. There shall be a universal stop put to business, *no work which either head or tail, branch or rush, may do;* nothing for high or low, weak or strong, to do; *no hire,* Zec. 8:10. Note, The flourishing of a kingdom depends much upon the industry of the people; and *then* things are likely to do well when all hands are at work, when the head and top-branch do not disdain to labour, and the labour of the tail and rush is not disdained. But when the learned professions are unemployed, the principal merchants have no stocks, and the handicraft tradesmen nothing to do, poverty comes upon a people *as one that travaileth* and *as an armed man.*

VIII. A general consternation shall seize the Egyptians; they *shall be afraid and fear* (*v.* 16), which will be both an evidence of a universal decay and a means and presage of utter ruin. Two things will put them into this fright: — 1. What they hear from *the land of Judah;* that *shall be a terror to Egypt, v.* 17. When they hear of the desolations made in Judah by the army of Sennacherib, considering both the near neighbourhood and the strict alliance that was between them and Judah, they will conclude it must be their turn next to become a prey to that victorious army. When their neighbour's house was on fire they could not but see their own in danger; and therefore every one of the Egyptians that makes mention of Judah shall be afraid of himself, expecting the bitter cup shortly to be put into his hands. 2. What they see in their own land. They shall *fear* (*v.* 16) *because of the shaking of the hand of the Lord of hosts,* and (*v.* 17) *because of the counsel of the Lord of hosts,* which from the shaking of his hand they shall conclude *he has determined* against Egypt as well as Judah. For, if judgment begin at the house of God, where will it end? *If this be done in the green tree, what shall be done in the dry?* See here, (1.) How easily God can make those a terror to themselves that have been, not only secure, but a terror to all about them. It is but shaking his hand over them, or laying it upon some of their neighbours, and the stoutest hearts tremble immediately. (2.) How well it becomes us to fear before God when he does but shake his hand over us, and to humble ourselves under his mighty hand when it does but threaten us, especially when we see his counsel determined against us; for who can change his counsel?

Verses 18–25

Out of the thick and threatening clouds of the foregoing prophecy the sun of comfort here breaks forth, and it is the sun of righteousness. Still God has mercy in store for Egypt, and he will show it, not so much by reviving their trade and replenishing their river again as by bringing the true religion among them, calling them to, and accepting them in, the worship of the one only living and true God; and these blessings of grace were much more valuable than all the blessings of nature wherewith Egypt was enriched. We know not of any event in which this prophecy can be thought to have its full accomplishment short of the conversion of Egypt to the faith of Christ, by the preaching (as is supposed) of Mark the Evangelist, and the founding of many Christian churches there, which flourished for many ages. Many prophecies of this book point to the days of the Messiah; and why not this? It is no unusual thing to speak of gospel graces and ordinances in the language of the Old-Testament institutions. And, in these prophecies, those words, *in that day,* perhaps have not always a reference to what goes immediately before, but have a peculiar significancy pointing at that day which had been so long fixed, and so often spoken of, when the day-spring from on high should visit this dark world. Yet it is not improbable (which some conjecture) that this prophecy was in part fulfilled when those Jews who fled from their own country to take shelter in Egypt, when Sennacherib invaded their land, brought their religion along with them, and, being awakened to great seriousness by the troubles they were in, made an open and zealous profession of it there, and were instrumental to bring many of the Egyptians to embrace it, which was an earnest and specimen of the more plentiful harvest of souls that should be gathered in to God by the preaching of the gospel of Christ. Josephus indeed tells us that Onias the son of Onias the high priest, living an outlaw at Alexandria in Egypt, obtained leave of Ptolemy Philometer, then king, and Cleopatra his queen, to build a temple to the God of Israel, like that at Jerusalem, at Bubastis in Egypt, and pretended a warrant for doing it from this prophecy in Isaiah, that there shall be an *altar to the Lord in the land of Egypt;* and the service of God, Josephus affirms, continued in it about 333 years, when it was shut up by Paulinus soon after the destruction of Jerusalem by the Romans; see *Antiq.* 13.62–79, and *Jewish War* 7.426–436. But that temple was all along looked upon by the pious Jews as so great an irregularity, and an affront to the temple at Jerusalem, that we cannot suppose this prophecy to be fulfilled in it.

Observe how the conversion of Egypt is here described.

I. They shall *speak the language of Canaan,* the holy language, the scripture-language; they shall not only understand it, but use it (*v.* 18); they shall introduce that language among them, and converse freely with the people of God, and not, as they used to do, *by an interpreter,* Gen. 42:23. Note, Converting grace, by changing the heart, changes the language; *for out of the abundance of the heart the mouth speaks. Five cities in Egypt* shall speak this language; so many Jews shall come to reside in Egypt, and they shall so multiply there, that they shall soon replenish five cities, one of which shall be the city of Heres, or of the sun, Heliopolis, where the sun was worshipped, the most infamous of all the cities of Egypt for idolatry; even there shall be a wonderful reformation, they shall speak the language of Canaan. Or it may be taken thus, as we render it — That for every five cities that shall embrace religion there shall be one (a sixth part of the cities of Egypt) that shall reject it, and that shall be called *a city of destruction,* because it refuses the methods of salvation.

II. They shall swear to the Lord of hosts, not only swear by him, giving him the honour of appealing to him, as all nations did to the gods they worshipped; but they shall by a solemn oath and vow devote themselves to his honour and bind themselves to his service. They shall swear to cleave to him with purpose of heart, and shall worship him, not occasionally, but constantly. They shall swear allegiance to him as their King, to Christ, to whom all judgment is committed.

III. They shall set up the public worship of God in their land (*v.* 19): *There shall be an altar to the Lord* in the *midst of the land of Egypt,* an altar on which *they shall do sacrifice and oblation* (*v.* 21); therefore it must be understood spiritually. Christ, the great altar, who sanctifies every gift, shall be owned there, and the gospel sacrifices of prayer and praise shall be offered up; for by the law of Moses there was to be no altar for sacrifice but that at Jerusalem. In Christ Jesus all distinction of nations is taken away; and a spiritual altar, a gospel church, in the midst of the land of Egypt, is as acceptable to God as one in the midst of the land of Israel; and spiritual sacrifices of faith and love, and a contrite heart, *please the Lord better than an ox or bullock.*

IV. There shall be a face of religion upon the nation, and an open profession made of it, discernible to all who come among them. Not only in the heart of the country, but even in *the borders* of it, *there shall be a pillar,* or pillars, inscribed, *To Jehovah,* to his honour, as before there had been such pillars set up in honour of false gods. As soon as a stranger entered upon the borders of Egypt he might perceive what God they worshipped. Those that serve God must not be ashamed to own him, but be forward to do any thing that may be for a sign and for a witness to the Lord of hosts. Even in the land of Egypt he had some faithful worshippers, who boasted of their relation to him and made his name their strong tower, or bulwark, on their borders, with which their coasts were fortified against all assailants.

V. Being in distress, they shall seek to God, and he shall be found of them; and this *shall be a sign and a witness for the Lord of hosts* that he is a *God hearing prayer* to *all flesh* that *come to him, v.* 20. See Ps. 65:2. When they cry to God by reason of their oppressors, the cruel lords that shall *rule over them* (*v.* 4) he *shall be entreated of them* (*v.* 22); whereas he had told his people Israel, who had made it their own choice to have such a king, that they should *cry to him by reason of their king,* and he *would not hear them,* 1 Sa. 8:18.

VI. They shall have an interest in the great Redeemer. When they were under the oppression of cruel lords perhaps God sometimes raised them up mighty deliverers, as he did for Israel in the days of the judges; and by them, though he had smitten the land, he healed it again; and, upon their return to God in a way of duty, he returned to them in a way of mercy, and repaired the breaches of their tottering state. For repenting Egyptians shall find the same favour with God that repenting Ninevites did. But all these deliverances wrought for them, as those for Israel, were but figures of gospel salvation. Doubtless Jesus Christ is *the Saviour and the great one* here spoken of, whom God will send the glad tidings of to the Egyptians, and by whom he will *deliver them out of the hands of their enemies,* that they may *serve him without fear,* Lu. 1:74, 75. Jesus Christ delivered the Gentile nations from the service of dumb idols, and did himself both purchase and preach liberty to the captives.

VII. The knowledge of God shall prevail among them, *v.* 21. 1. They shall have the means of knowledge. For many ages in *Judah only was God known,* for there only were the lively oracles found; but now *the Lord,* and his name and will, *shall be known to Egypt.* Perhaps this may in part refer to the translation of the Old Testament out of Hebrew into Greek by the Septuagint, which was done at Alexandria in Egypt, by the command of Ptolemy king of Egypt; and it was the first time that the scriptures were translated into any other language. By the help of this (the Grecian monarchy having introduced their language into that country) *the Lord was known to Egypt,* and a happy omen and means it was of his being further known. 2. They shall have grace to improve those means. It is promised not only that the Lord shall be known to Egypt, but that *the Egyptians shall know the Lord;* they shall receive and entertain the light granted to them, and shall submit themselves to the power of it. The Lord is known to our nation, and yet I fear there are many of our nation that do not know the Lord. But the promise of the new covenant is that *all shall know the Lord, from the least even to the greatest,* which promise is sure to all the seed. The effect of this knowledge of God is that *they shall vow a vow to the Lord and perform it.* For those do not know God aright who either are not willing to come under binding obligations to the Lord or do not make good those obligations.

VIII. They shall come into the communion of saints. Being joined to the Lord, they shall be added to the church, and be incorporated with all the saints. 1. All enmities shall be slain. Mortal feuds there had been between Egypt and Assyria; they often made war upon one another; but now *there shall be a highway between Egypt and Assyria* (*v.* 23), a happy correspondence settled between he two nations; they shall trade with one another, and every thing that passes between them shall be friendly. *The Egyptians shall serve* (shall worship the true God) *with the Assyrians;* and therefore the Assyrians shall come into Egypt and the Egyptians into Assyria. Note, It becomes those who have communion with the same God, through the same Mediator, to keep up an amicable correspondence with one another. The consideration of our meeting at the same throne of grace, and our serving with each other in the same business of religion, should put an end to all heats and animosities, and knit our hearts to each other in holy love. 2. The Gentile nations shall not only unite with each other in the gospel fold under Christ the great shepherd, but they shall all be united with the Jews. When Egypt and Assyria become partners in serving God *Israel* shall *make a third with* them (*v.* 24); they shall become a *threefold cord, not easily broken.* The ceremonial law, which had long been the partition-wall between Jews and Gentiles, shall be taken down, and then they shall become *one sheep-fold under one shepherd.* Thus united, they shall be *a blessing in the midst of the land, whom the Lord of hosts shall bless, v.* 24, 25. (1.) Israel shall be a blessing to them all, because of *them, as concerning the flesh, Christ came,* and they were the natural branches of the good olive, to whom did originally pertain *its root and fatness,* and the Gentiles were but *grafted in among them,* Rom. 11:17. Israel lay between Egypt and Assyria, and was a blessing to them both by bringing them to meet in that word of the Lord which went forth from Jerusalem, and that church which was first set up in the land of Israel. *Qui conveniunt in aliquo tertio inter se conveniunt — Those who meet in a third meet in each other.* Israel is that third in whom Egypt and Assyria agree, and is therefore a blessing; for those are real and great blessings to their generation who are instrumental to unite those that have been at variance. (2.) They shall all be a blessing to the world: so the Christian church is, made up of Jews and Gentiles; it is the beauty, riches, and support of the world. (3.) They shall all be blessed of the Lord. [1.] They shall all be owned by him as his. Though Egypt was formerly a house of bondage to the people of God, and Assyria an unjust invader of them, all this shall now be forgiven and forgotten, and they shall be as welcome to God as Israel. They are all alike his people whom he takes under his protection. They are formed by him, for they are the *work of his hands;* not only as *a* people, but as *his* people. They are formed for him; for they are his inheritance, precious in his eyes, and dear to him, and from whom he has his rent of honour out of this lower world. [2.] They shall be owned together by him as jointly his, his in concert; they shall all share in one and the same blessing. Note, Those that are united in the love and blessing of God ought, for that reason, to be united to each other in charity.

CHAPTER 20

This chapter is a prediction of the carrying away of multitudes both of the Egyptians and the Ethiopians into captivity by the king of Assyria. Here is, I. the sign by which this was foretold, which was the prophet's going for some time barefoot and almost naked, like a poor captive (*v.* 1–2). II. The explication of that sign, with application to Egypt and Ethiopia (*v.* 3–5). III. The good use which the people of God should make of this, which is never to trust in an arm of flesh, because thus it will deceive them (*v.* 6).

Verses 1–6

God here, as King of nations, brings a sore calamity upon Egypt and Ethiopia, but, as King of saints, brings good to his people out of it. Observe,

I. The date of this prophecy. It was in the year that Ashdod, a strong city of the Philistines (but which some think was lately recovered from them by Hezekiah, when he smote the Philistines even unto Gaza, 2 Ki. 18:8), was besieged and taken by an army of the Assyrians. It is uncertain what year of Hezekiah that was, but the event was so remarkable that those who lived then could by that token fix the time to a year. He that was now king of Assyria is called *Sargon,* which some take to be the same with Sennacherib; others think he was his immediate predecessor, and succeeded Shalmaneser. Tartan, who was general, or commander-in-chief, in this expedition, was one of Sennacherib's officers, sent by him to bid defiance to Hezekiah, in concurrence with Rabshakeh, 2 Ki. 18:17.

II. The making of Isaiah a sign, by his unusual dress when he walked abroad. He had been a sign to his own people of the melancholy times that had come and were coming upon them, by the sackcloth which for some time he had worn, of which he had a gown made, which he girt about him. Some think he put himself into that habit of a mourner upon occasion of the captivity of the ten tribes. Others think sackcloth was what he commonly wore as a prophet, to show himself mortified to the world, and that he might learn to endure hardness; soft clothing better becomes those that attend in king's palaces (Mt. 11:8) than those that go on God's errands. Elijah wore hair-cloth (2 Ki. 1:8), and John Baptist (Mt. 3:4) and those that pretended to be prophets supported their pretension by wearing rough garments (Zec. 13:4); but Isaiah has orders given him to *loose his sackcloth from his loins,* not to exchange it for better clothing, but for none at all — no upper garment, no mantle, cloak, or coat, but only that which was next to him, we may suppose his shirt, waistcoat, and drawers; and he must *put off his shoes,* and go barefoot; so that compared with the dress of others, and what he himself usually wore, he might be said to go *naked.* This was a great hardship upon the prophet; it was a blemish to his reputation, and would expose him to contempt and ridicule; the boys in the streets would hoot at him, and those who sought occasion against him would say, *The prophet is* indeed *a fool, and the spiritual man is mad,* Hosea 9:7. It might likewise be a prejudice to his health; he was in danger of catching a cold, which might throw him into a fever, and cost him his life; but God bade him do it, that he might give a proof of his obedience to God in a most difficult command, and so shame the disobedience of his people to the most easy and reasonable precepts. When we are in the way of our duty we may trust God both with our credit and with our safety. The hearts of that people were strangely stupid, and would not be affected with what they only heard, but must be taught by signs, and therefore Isaiah must do this for their edification. If the dress was scandalous, yet the design was glorious, and what a prophet of the Lord needed not to be ashamed of.

III. The exposition of this sign, *v.* 3, 4. It was intended to signify that the Egyptians and the Ethiopians should be led away captive by the king of Assyria, thus stripped, or in rags, and very shabby clothing, as Isaiah was. God calls him his *servant Isaiah,* because in this matter particularly he had approved himself God's willing, faithful, obedient servant; and for this very thing, which perhaps others laughed at him for, God gloried in him. To obey is better than sacrifice; it pleases God and praises him more, and shall be more praised by him. Isaiah is said to have *walked naked and barefoot three years,* whenever in that time he appeared as a prophet. But some refer the three years, not to the sign, but to the thing signified: *He has walked naked and barefoot;* there is a stop in the original; provided he did so once that was enough to give occasion to all about him to enquire what was the meaning of his doing so; or, as some think, he did it three days, a day for a year; and this for a three years' sign and wonder, for a sign of that which should be done three years afterwards or which should be three years in the doing. Three campaigns successively shall the Assyrian army make, in spoiling the Egyptians and Ethiopians, and carrying them away captive in this barbarous manner, not only the soldiers taken in the field of battle, but the inhabitants, young and old; and it being a very piteous sight, and such as must needs move compassion in those that had the least degree of tenderness left them to see those who had gone all their days well dressed now stripped, and scarcely having rags to cover their nakedness, that circumstance of their captivity is particularly taken notice of, and foretold, the more to affect those to whom this prophecy was delivered. It is particularly said to be *to the shame of Egypt* (*v.* 4), because the Egyptians were a proud people, and therefore when they did fall into disgrace it was the more shameful to them; and the higher they had lifted up themselves the lower was their fall, both in their own eyes and in the eyes of others.

IV. The use and application of this, *v.* 5, 6. 1. All that had any dependence upon, or correspondence with, Egypt and Ethiopia, should now be ashamed of them, and afraid of having any thing to do with them. Those countries that were in danger of being overrun by the Assyrians expected that Tirhakah, king of Ethiopia, with his numerous forces, would put a stop to the progress of their victorious arms, and be a barrier to his neighbours; and with yet more assurance they gloried that Egypt, a kingdom so famous for policy and prowess, would do their business, would oblige them to raise the siege of Ashdod and retire with precipitation. But, instead of this, by attempting to oppose the king of Assyria they did but expose themselves and make their country a prey to him. Hereupon all about them were ashamed that ever they promised themselves any advantage from two such weak and cowardly nations, and were more afraid now than ever they were of the growing greatness of the king of Assyria, before whom Egypt and Ethiopia proved but as briers and thorns put to stop a consuming fire, which do but make it burn the more strongly. Note, Those who make any creature their expectation and glory, and so put it in the place of God, will sooner or later be ashamed of it, and their disappointment in it will but increase their fear. See Eze. 29:6, 7. 2. The Jews in particular should be convinced of their folly in resting upon such broken reeds, and should despair of any relief from them (*v.* 6): *The inhabitants of this isle* (the land of Judah, situated upon the sea, though not surrounded by it), of this country (so the margin); every one shall now have his eyes opened, and shall say, *"Behold, such is our expectation,* so vain, so foolish, and this is that which it will come to. We have fled for help to the Egyptians and Ethiopians, and have hoped by them to be delivered from the king of Assyria; but, now that they are broken thus, how shall we escape, that are not able to bring such armies into the field as they did?" Note, (1.) Those that confide in creatures will be disappointed, and will be made ashamed of their confidence; *for vain is the help of man, and in vain is salvation hoped for from the hills or the height and multitude of the mountains.* (2.) Disappointment in creature confidences, instead of driving us to despair, as here *(how shall we escape?),* should drive us to God; for, if we flee to him for help, our expectation shall not be frustrated.

CHAPTER 21

In this chapter we have a prophecy of sad times coming, and heavy burdens, I. Upon Babylon, here called "the desert of the sea," that it should be destroyed by the Medes and Persians with a terrible destruction, which yet God's people should have advantage by (*v.* 1–10). II. Upon Dumah, or Idumea (*v.* 11, 12). III. Upon Arabia, or Kedar, the desolation of which country was very near (*v.* 13–17). These and other nations which the princes and people of Israel had so much to do with the prophets of Israel could not but have something to say to. Foreign affairs must be taken notice of as well as domestic ones, and news from abroad enquired after as well as news at home.

Verses 1–10

We had one burden of Babylon before (*ch.* 13); here we have another prediction of its fall. God saw fit thus to possess his people with the belief of this event by line upon line, because Babylon sometimes pretended to be a friend to them (as *ch.* 39:1), and God would hereby warn them not to trust to that friendship, and sometimes was really an enemy to them, and God would hereby warn them not to be afraid of that enmity. Babylon is marked for ruin; and all that believe God's prophets can, through that glass, see it tottering, see it tumbling, even when with an eye of sense they see it flourishing and sitting as a queen. Babylon is here called the *desert* or *plain of the sea;* for it was a flat country, and full of lakes, or loughs (as they call them in Ireland), like little seas, and was abundantly watered with the many streams of the river Euphrates. Babylon did but lately begin to be famous, Nineveh having outshone it while the monarchy was in the Assyrian hands; but in a little time it became the lady of kingdoms; and, before it arrived at that pitch of eminency which it was at in Nebuchadnezzar's time, God by this prophet plainly foretold its fall, again and again, that his people might not be terrified at its rise, nor despair of relief in due time when they were its prisoners, Job 5:3; Ps. 37:35, 36. Some think it is here called a *desert* because, though it was now a populous city, it should in time be made a desert. And *therefore* the destruction of Babylon is so often prophesied of by this evangelical prophet, because it was typical of the destruction of the man of sin, the great enemy of the New-Testament church, which is foretold in the *Revelation* in many expressions borrowed from these prophecies, which therefore must be consulted and collated by those who would understand the prophecy of that book. Here is,

I. The powerful irruption and descent which the Medes and Persians should make upon Babylon (*v.* 1, 2): They will come *from the desert, from a terrible land.* The northern parts of Media and Persia, where their soldiers were mostly bred, was waste and mountainous, terrible to strangers that were to pass through it and producing soldiers that were very formidable. *Elam* (that is, Persia) is summoned to go up against Babylon, and, in conjunction with the forces of Media, to besiege it. When God has work of this kind to do he will find, though it be in a desert, in a terrible land, proper instruments to be employed in it. These forces come *as whirlwinds from the south,* so suddenly, so strongly, so terribly, such a mighty noise shall they make, and throw down every thing that stands in their way. As is usual in such a case, some deserters will go over to them: *The treacherous dealers will deal treacherously.* Historians tell us of Gadatas and Gobryas, two great officers of the king of Babylon, that went over to Cyrus, and, being well acquainted with all the avenues of the city, led a party directly to the palace, where Belshazzar was slain. Thus with the help of the *treacherous dealers the spoilers spoiled.* Some read it thus: *There shall be a deceiver of that deceiver, Babylon, and a spoiler of that spoiler,* or, which comes all to one, *The treacherous dealer has found one that deals treacherously, and the spoiler one that spoils,* as it is expounded, *ch.* 33:1. The Persians shall pay the Babylonians in their own coin; those that by fraud and violence, cheating and plundering, unrighteous wars and deceitful treaties, have made a prey of their neighbours, shall meet with their match, and by the same methods shall themselves be made a prey of.

II. The different impressions made hereby upon those concerned in Babylon. 1. To the poor oppressed captives it would be welcome news; for they had been told long ago that Babylon's destroyer would be their deliverer, and therefore, "when they hear that Elam and Media are coming up to besiege Babylon, *all their sighing will be made to cease;* they shall no longer mingle their tears with Euphrates' streams, but resume their harps, and smile when they remember Zion, which, before, they wept at the thought of." For the sighing of the needy the God of pity will arise in due time (Ps. 12:5); he will break the yoke from all their neck, will remove the rod of the wicked from off their lot, and so make their sighing to cease. 2. To the proud oppressors it would be a grievous vision (*v.* 2), particularly to the king of Babylon for the time being, and it should seem that he it is who is here brought in sadly lamenting his inevitable fate (*v.* 3, 4): *Therefore are my loins filled with pain; pangs have taken hold upon me, etc.,* which was literally fulfilled in Belshazzar, for that very night in which his city was taken, and himself slain, upon the sight of a hand writing mystic characters upon the wall *his countenance was changed and his thoughts troubled him, so that the joints of his loins were loosed and his knees smote one against another,* Dan. 5:6. And yet that was but the beginning of sorrows. Daniel's deciphering the writing could not but increase his terror, and the alarm which immediately followed of the executioners at the door would be the completing of it. And those words, *The night of my pleasure has he turned into fear to me,* plainly refer to that aggravating circumstance of Belshazzar's fall that he was slain on that night when he was in the height of his mirth and jollity, with his cups and concubines about him and a thousand of his lords revelling with him; that night of his pleasure, when he promised himself an undisturbed unallayed enjoyment of the most exquisite gratifications of sense, with a particular defiance of God and religion in the profanation of the temple vessels, was the night that was turned into all this fear. Let this give an effectual check to vain mirth and sensual pleasures, and forbid us ever to lay the reins on the neck of them — that we know not what heaviness the mirth may end in, nor how soon laughter may be turned into mourning; but this we know that for all these things God shall bring us into judgment; let us therefore mix trembling always with our joys.

III. A representation of the posture in which Babylon should be found when the enemy should surprise it — all in festival gaiety (*v.* 5): "Prepare the table with all manner of dainties. Set the guards; let them watch in the watch-tower while we eat and drink securely and make merry; and, if any alarm should be given, the princes shall arise and anoint the shield, and be in readiness to give the enemy a warm reception." Thus secure are they, and thus do they gird on the harness with as much joy as if they were putting it off.

IV. A description of the alarm which should be given to Babylon upon its being forced by Cyrus and Darius. The Lord, in vision, showed the prophet the watchman set in his watch-tower, near the watch-tower, near the palace, as is usual in times of danger; the king ordered those about him to post a sentinel in the most advantageous place for discovery, and, according to the duty of a watchman, let *him declare what he sees, v.* 6. We read of watchmen thus set to receive intelligence in the story of David (2 Sa. 18:24), and in the story of Jehu, 2 Ki. 9:17. This watchman here discovered a chariot with a couple of horsemen attending it, in which we may suppose the commander-in-chief to ride. He then saw another chariot drawn by asses or mules, which were much in use among the Persians, and a chariot drawn by camels, which were likewise much in use among the Medes; so that (as Grotius thinks) these two chariots signify the two nations combined against Babylon, or rather these chariots come to bring tidings to the palace; compare Jer. 51:31, 32. *One post shall run to meet another, and one messenger to meet another, to show the king of Babylon that his city is taken at one end* while he is revelling at the other end and knows nothing of the matter. The watchman, seeing these chariots at some distance, *hearkened diligently with much heed,* to receive the first tidings. And (*v.* 8) *he cried, A lion;* this word, coming out of a watchman's mouth, no doubt gave them a certain sound, and every body knew the meaning of it, though we do not know it now. It is likely that it was intended to raise attention: he that has an ear to hear, let him hear, as when a lion roars. *He cried as a lion,* very loud and in good earnest, the occasion being very urgent. And what has he to say? 1. He professes his constancy to the post assigned him: *"I stand, my lord, continually upon the watch-tower,* and have never discovered any thing material till just now; all seemed safe and quiet." Some make it to be a complaint of the people of God that they had long expected the downfall of Babylon, according to the prophecy, and it had not yet come; but withal a resolution to continue waiting; as Hab. 2:1, *I will stand upon my watch, and set me upon the tower,* to see what will be the issue of the present providences. 2. He gives notice of the discoveries he had made (*v.* 9): *Here comes a chariot of men with a couple of horsemen,* a vision representing the enemy's entry into the city with all their force or the tidings brought to the royal palace of it.

V. A certain account is at length given of the overthrow of Babylon. He in the chariot *answered and said* (when he heard the watchman speak), *Babylon has fallen, has fallen;* or God answered thus to the prophet enquiring concerning the issue of these affairs: "It has now come to this, Babylon has surely and irrecoverably fallen. Babylon's business is done now. *All the graven images of her gods he has broken unto the ground.*" Babylon was the mother of harlots (that is, of idolatry), which was one of the grounds of God's quarrel with her; but her idols should now be so far from protecting her that some of them should be broken down to the ground, and others of them, that were worth carrying way, should go into captivity, and be a burden to the beasts that carried them, *ch.* 46:1, 2.

VI. Notice is given to the people of God, who were then captives in Babylon, that this prophecy of the downfall of Babylon was particularly intended for their comfort and encouragement, and they might depend upon it that it should be accomplished in due season, *v.* 10. Observe,

1. The title the prophet gives them in God's name: *O my threshing, and the corn of my floor!* The prophet calls them *his,* because they were his countrymen, and such as he had a particular interest in and concern for; but he speaks it as from God, and directs his speech to those that were Israelites indeed, the faithful in the land. Note, (1.) The church is God's floor, in which the most valuable fruits and products of this earth are, as it were, gathered together and laid up. (2.) True believers are the corn of God's floor. Hypocrites are but as the chaff and straw, which take up a great deal of room, but are of small value, with which the wheat is now mixed, but from which it shall be shortly and for ever separated. (3.) The corn of God's floor must expect to be threshed by afflictions and persecutions. God's Israel of old was afflicted from her youth, often under the plougher's plough (Ps. 129:3) and the thresher's flail. (4.) Even then God owns it for his threshing; it is his still; nay, the threshing of it is by his appointment, and under his restraint and direction. The threshers could have no power against it *but what was given them from above.*

2. The assurance he gives them of the truth of what he had delivered to them, which therefore they might build their hopes upon: *That which I have heard of the Lord of hosts, the God of Israel* — that, and nothing else, that, and no fiction or fancy of my own — *have I declared unto you.* Note, In all events concerning the church, past, present, and to come, we must have an eye to God both as the Lord of hosts and as the God of Israel, who has power enough to do any thing for his church and grace enough to do every thing that is for her good, and to the words of his prophets, as words received from the Lord. As they dare not smother any thing which he has entrusted them to declare, so they dare not declare any thing as from him which he has not made known to them, 1 Co. 11:23.

Verses 11–12

This prophecy concerning Dumah is very short, and withal dark and hard to be understood. Some think that Dumah is a part of Arabia, and that the inhabitants descended from Dumah the sixth son of Ishmael, as those of Kedar (*v.* 16, 17) from Ishmael's second son, Gen. 25:13, 14. Others, because Mount Seir is here mentioned, by Dumah understand Idumea, the country of the Edomites. Some of Israel's neighbours are certainly meant, and their distress is foretold, not only for warning to them to prepare them for it, but for warning to Israel not to depend upon them, or any of the nations about them, for relief in a time of danger, but upon God only. We must see all creature confidences failing us, and feel them breaking under us, that we may not lay more weight upon them than they will bear. But though the explication of this prophecy be difficult, because we have no history in which we find the accomplishment of it, yet the application will be easy. We have here,

1. A question put by an Edomite to the watchman. Some one or other *called out of Seir,* somebody that was more concerned for the public safety and welfare than the rest, who were generally careless and secure. As the man of Macedonia, in a vision, desired Paul to come over and help them (Acts 16:9), so this man of Mount Seir, in a vision, desired the prophet to inform and instruct them. He calls not many; it is well there are any, that all are not alike unconcerned about the things that belong to the public peace. Some out of Seir ask advice of God's prophets, and are willing to be taught, when many of God's Israel heed nothing. The question is serious: *What of the night?* It is put to a proper person, the *watchman,* whose office it is to answer such enquiries. He repeats the question, as one in care, as one in earnest, and desirous to have an answer. Note, (1.) God's prophets and ministers are appointed to be watchmen, and we are to look upon them as such. They are as watchmen in the city in a time of peace, to see that all be safe, to knock at every door by personal enquiries ("Is it locked? Is the fire safe?"), to direct those that are at a loss, and check those that are disorderly, Cant. 3:3; 5:7. They are as watchmen in the camp in time of war, Eze. 33:7. They are to take notice of the motions of the enemy and to give notice of them, to make discoveries and then give warning; and in this they must deny themselves. (2.) It is our duty to enquire of the watchmen, especially to ask again and again, *What of the night?* for watchmen wake when other sleep. [1.] What time of the night? After a long sleep in sin and security, is it not time to rise, high time to awake out of sleep? Rom. 13:11. We have a great deal of work to do, a long journey to go; is it not time to be stirring? "Watchman, what o'clock is it? After

a long dark night is there any hope of the day dawning?" [2.] What tidings of the night? *What from the night?* (so some); "what vision has the prophet had to-night? We are ready to receive it." Or, rather, "What occurs to night? What weather is it? What news?" We must expect an alarm, and never be secure. The *day of the Lord will come as a thief in the night;* we must prepare to receive the alarm, and resolve to keep our ground, and then take the first hint of danger, and to our arms presently, to our spiritual weapons.

2. The watchman's answer to this question. The watchman was neither asleep nor dumb; though it was a man of Mount Seir that called to him, he was ready to give him an answer: *The morning comes.* He answers, (1.) By way of prediction: "There comes first a morning of light, and peace, and opportunity; you will enjoy one day of comfort more; but afterwards comes a night of trouble and calamity." Note, In the course of God's providence it is usual that morning and night are counterchanged and succeed each other. Is it night? Yet the morning comes, and the day-spring knows his place, Ps. 30:5. Is it day? Yet the night comes also. If there be a morning of youth and health, there will come a night of sickness and old age; if a morning of prosperity in the family, in the public, yet we must look for changes. But God usually gives a morning of opportunity before he sends a night of calamity, that his own people may be prepared for the storm and others left inexcusable. (2.) By way of excitement: *If you will enquire, enquire.* Note, It is our wisdom to improve the present morning in preparation for the night that is coming after it. "*Enquire, return, come.* Be inquisitive, be penitent, be willing and obedient." The manner of expression is very observable, for we are put to our choice what we will do: "*If you will enquire, enquire;* if not, it is at your peril; you cannot say but you have a fair offer made you." We are also urged to be at a point: "If you will, say so, and do not stand pausing; what you will do do quickly, for it is no time to trifle." Those that return and come to God will find they have a great deal of work to do and but a little time to do it in, and therefore they have need to be busy.

Verses 13–17

Arabia was a large country, that lay eastward and southward of the land of Canaan. Much of it was possessed by the posterity of Abraham. The *Dedanim,* here mentioned (*v.* 13), descended from Dedan, Abraham's son by Keturah; the inhabitants of Tema and Kedar descended from Ishmael, Gen. 25:3, 13, 15. The Arabians generally lived in tents, and kept cattle, were a hardy people, inured to labour; probably the Jews depended upon them as a sort of a wall between them and the more warlike eastern nations; and therefore, to alarm them, they shall hear *the burden of Arabia,* and see it sinking under its own burden.

I. A destroying army shall be brought upon them, with a sword, with *a drawn sword,* with *a bow* ready *bent,* and with all the *grievousness of war, v.* 15. It is probable that the king of Assyria, in some of the marches of his formidable and victorious army, took Arabia in his way, and, meeting with little resistance, made an easy prey of them. The consideration of the grievousness of war should make us thankful for the blessings of peace.

II. The poor country people will hereby be forced to flee for shelter wherever they can find a place; so that *the travelling companies of Dedanium,* which used to keep the high roads with their caravans, shall be obliged to quit them and *lodge in the forest in Arabia* (*v.* 13), and shall not have the wonted convenience of their own tents, poor and weather-beaten as they are.

III. They shall stand in need of refreshment, being ready to perish for want of it, in their flight from the invading army: "*O you inhabitants of the land of Tema!*" (who probably were next neighbours to the companies of Dedanim) "*bring you water*" (so the margin reads it) "*to him that is thirsty,* and *prevent with your bread those that flee,* for they are objects of your compassion; they do not wander for wandering sake, nor are they reduced to straits by any extravagance of their own, but *they flee from the sword.*" Tema was a country where water was sometimes a scarce commodity (as we find, Job 6:19), and we may conclude it would be in a particular manner acceptable to these poor distressed refugees. Let us learn hence. 1. To look for distress ourselves. We know not what straits we may be

brought into before we die. Those that live in cities may be forced to lodge in forests; and those may know the want of necessary food who now eat bread to the full. Our mountain stands not so strong but that it may be moved, rises not so high but that it may be scaled. These Arabians would the better bear these calamities because in their way of living they had used themselves to hardships. 2. To look with compassion upon those that are in distress, and with all cheerfulness to relieve them, not knowing how soon their case may be ours: "*Bring water to those that are thirsty,* and not only give bread to those that need and ask it, but prevent those with it that have need; give it to them unasked." Those that do so shall find it remembered to their praise, as (according to our reading) it is here remembered to the praise of the land of Tema that they did bring water to the thirsty and relieved even those that were on the falling side.

IV. All that which is the glory of Kedar shall vanish away and fail. Did they glory in their numerous herds and flocks? They shall all be driven away by the enemy. It seems they were famous about other nations for the use of the bow in battle; but their archers, instead of foiling the enemy, shall fall themselves; and *the residue of their number,* when they are reduced to a small number, *shall be diminished* (*v.* 17); their mighty able-bodied men, and men of spirit too, shall become very few; for they, being most forward in the defence of their country, were most exposed, and fell first, either by the enemies' sword or into the enemies' hand. Note, Neither the skill of archers (though they be ever so good marksmen) nor the courage of mighty men can protect a people from the judgments of God, when they come with commission; they rather expose the undertakers. That is poor glory which will thus quickly come to nothing.

V. All this shall be done in a little time: "*Within one year according to the years of a hireling* (within one year precisely reckoned) this judgment shall come upon Kedar." If this fixing of the time be of no great use to us now (because we find not either when the prophecy was delivered or when it was accomplished), yet it might be of great use to the Arabians then, to awaken them to repentance, that, like the men of Nineveh, they might prevent the judgment when they were thus told it was just at the door. Or, when it begins to be fulfilled, the business shall be done, be begun and ended in one year's time. God, when he please, can do a great work in a little time.

VI. It is all ratified by the truth of God (*v.* 16); "*Thus hath the Lord said to me;* you may take my word for it that it is his word;" and we may be sure no word of his shall fall to the ground. And again (*v.* 17): *The Lord God of Israel hath spoken it,* as the God of Israel, in pursuance of his gracious designs concerning them; and we may be sure *the strength of Israel will not lie.*

CHAPTER 22

We have now come nearer home, for this chapter is "the burden of the valley of vision," Jerusalem; other places had their burden for the sake of their being concerned in some way or other with Jerusalem, and were reckoned with either as spiteful enemies or deceitful friends to the people of God; but now let Jerusalem hear her own doom. This chapter concerns, I. The city of Jerusalem itself and the neighbourhood depending upon it. Here is, 1. A prophecy of the grievous distress they should shortly be brought into by Sennacherib's invasion of the country and laying siege to the city (*v.* 1–7). 2. A reproof given them for their misconduct in that distress, in two things: — (1.) Not having an eye to God in the use of the means of their preservation (*v.* 8–11). (2.) Not humbling themselves under his mighty hand (*v.* 12–14). II. The court of Hezekiah, and the officers of that court. 1. The displacing of Shebna, a bad man, and turning him out of the treasury (*v.* 15–19, 25). 2. The preferring of Eliakim, who should do his country better service, to his place (*v.* 20–24).

Verses 1–7

The title of this prophecy is very observable. It is *the burden of the valley of vision,* of Judah and Jerusalem; so all agree. Fitly enough is Jerusalem called a valley, for the mountains were round about it, and the land of Judah abounded with fruitful valleys; and by the judgments of God, though they had been as a towering mountain, they should be brought low, sunk and depressed, and become dark and dirty, as a valley. But most emphatically is it called a *valley of vision* because there God was known and his name was great, there the prophets were made acquainted with his mind by visions, and there the people saw the goings of their God and King in his sanctuary. Babylon, being a stranger to God, though rich and great, was called *the desert of the sea;* but Jerusalem, being entrusted with

his oracles, is *a valley of vision. Blessed are their eyes, for they see,* and they have seers by office among them. Where Bibles and ministers are there is a valley of vision, from which is expected fruit accordingly; but here is a *burden of the valley of vision,* and a heavy burden it is. Note, Church privileges, if they be not improved, will not secure men from the judgments of God. *You only have I known of all the families of the earth; therefore will I punish you.* The valley of vision has a particular burden. *Thou Capernaum,* Mt. 11:23. The higher any are lifted up in means and mercies the heavier will their doom be if they abuse them.

Now the *burden of the valley of vision* here is that which will not quite ruin it, but only frighten it; for it refers not to the destruction of Jerusalem by Nebuchadnezzar, but to the attempt made upon it by Sennacherib, which we had the prophecy of, *ch.* 10, and shall meet with the history of, *ch.* 36. It is here again prophesied of, because the desolations of many of the neighbouring countries, which were foretold in the foregoing chapters, were to be brought to pass by the Assyrian army. Now let Jerusalem know that when the cup is going round it will be put into her hand; and, although it will not be to her a fatal cup, yet it will be a cup of trembling. Here is foretold,

I. The consternation that the city should be in upon the approach of Sennacherib's army. It used to be full of stirs, a city of great trade, people hurrying to and fro about their business, a tumultuous city, populous and noisy. Where there is great trade there is great tumult. It used to be a joyous revelling city. What with the busy part and what with the merry part of mankind, places of concourse are places of noise. "But what ails thee now, that the shops are quitted, and there is no more walking in the streets and exchange, *but thou hast wholly gone up to the house-tops* (*v.* 1), to bemoan thyself in silence and solitude, or to secure thyself from the enemy, or to look abroad and see if any succours come to thy relief, or which way the enemies' motions are." Let both men of business and sportsmen *rejoice as though they rejoiced not,* for something may happen quickly, which they little think of, that will be a damp to their mirth and a stop to their business, and send them to *watch as a sparrow alone upon the house-top,* Ps. 102:7. But why is Jerusalem in such a fright? *Her slain men are not slain with the sword* (*v.* 2), but, 1. Slain with famine (so some); for Sennacherib's army having laid the country waste, and destroyed the fruits of the earth, provisions must needs be very scarce and dear in the city, which would be the death of many of the poorer sort of people, who would be constrained to feed on that which was unwholesome. 2. Slain with fear. They were put into this fright though they had not a man killed, but so disheartened themselves that they seemed as effectually stabbed with fear as if they had been run through with a sword.

II. The inglorious flight of the rulers of Judah, who fled from far, from all parts of the country, to Jerusalem (*v.* 3), fled together, as it were by consent, and were found in Jerusalem, having left their respective cities, which they should have taken care of, to be a prey to the Assyrian army, which, meeting with no opposition, when it *came up against all the defenced cities of Judah* easily *took them, ch.* 36:1. These rulers *were bound from the bow* (so the word is); they not only quitted their own cities like cowards, but, when they came to Jerusalem, were of no service there, but were as if their hands were tied from the use of the bow, by the extreme distraction and confusion they were in; they trembled, so that they could not draw a bow. See how easily God can dispirit men, and how certainly fear will dispirit them, when the tyranny of it is yielded to.

III. The great grief which this should occasion to all serious sensible people among them, which is represented by the prophet's laying the thing to heart himself; he lived to see it, and was resolved to share with the children of his people in their sorrows, *v.* 4, 5. He is not willing to proclaim his sorrow, and therefore bids those about him to look away from him; he will abandon himself to grief, and indulge himself in it, will weep secretly, but weep bitterly, and will have none go about to comfort him, for his grief is obstinate and he is pleased with his pain. But what is the occasion of his grief? A poor prophet had little to lose, and had been inured to hardship, when he walked naked and barefoot; but it is for *the spoiling of the daughter of* his people. It is *a day of trouble, and of treading down, and of perplexity.* Our enemies trouble us and tread us down, and our friends are perplexed and know not what course to take to do us a kindness. The Lord God of hosts is now contending with the valley of vision; the enemies with their battering rams are breaking down the walls, and we are in vain crying to the mountains (to keep off the enemy, or to fall on us and cover us) or looking for help to come to us over the mountains, or appealing, as God does, to the mountains, to hear our controversy (Mic. 6:1) and to judge between us and our injurious neighbours.

IV. The great numbers and strength of the enemy, that should invade their country and besiege their city, *v.* 6, 7. Elam (that is, the Persians) come with their quiver full of arrows, and with chariots of fighting men and horsemen. Kir (that is, the Medes) muster up their arms, unsheath the sword, and uncover the shield, and get every thing ready for battle, every thing ready for the besieging of Jerusalem. Then the choice valleys about Jerusalem, that used to be clothed with flocks and covered over with corn, shall be full of chariots of war, and at the gate of the city the *horsemen shall set themselves in array,* to cut off all provisions from going in, and to force their way in. What a condition must the city be in that was beset on all sides with such an army!

Verses 8–14

What is meant by *the covering of Judah,* which in the beginning of this paragraph is said to be *discovered,* is not agreed. The fenced cities of Judah were a covering to the country; but these, being taken by the army of the Assyrians, ceased to be a shelter, so that the whole country lay exposed to be plundered. The weakness of Judah, its nakedness, and inability to keep itself, now appeared more than ever; and thus the covering of Judah was discovered. Its magazines and stores, which had been locked up, were now laid open for the public use. Dr. Lightfoot gives another sense of it, that by this distress into which Judah should be brought God would discover their covering (that is, uncloak their hypocrisy), would show all that was in their heart, as is said of Hezekiah upon another occasion, 2 Chr. 32:31. Thus, by one means or other, *the iniquity of Ephraim will be discovered and the sin of Samaria,* Hos. 7:1.

They were now in a great fright, and in this fright they manifested two things much amiss: —

I. A great contempt of God's goodness, and his power to help them. They made use of all the means they could think of for their own preservation; and it is not for doing this that they are blamed, but, in doing this, they did not acknowledge God. Observe,

1. How careful they were to improve all advantages that might contribute to their safety. When Sennacherib had made himself master of all the defenced cities of Judah, and Jerusalem was left as a cottage in a vineyard, they thought it was time to look about them. A council was immediately called, a council of war; and it was resolved to stand upon their defence, and not tamely to surrender. Pursuant to this resolve, they took all the prudent measures they could for their own security. We tempt God if, in times of danger, we do not the best we can for ourselves. (1.) They inspected the magazines and stores, to see if they were well stocked with arms and ammunition: *They looked to the armour of the house of the forest,* which Solomon built in Jerusalem for an armoury (1 Ki. 10:17), and thence they delivered out what they had occasion for. It is the wisdom of princes, in time of peace, to provide for war, that they may not have arms to seek when they should use them, and perhaps upon a sudden emergency. (2.) They viewed the fortifications, the *breaches of the city of David;* they walked round the walls, and observed where they had gone to decay for want of seasonable repairs, or were broken by some former attempts made upon them. These breaches were many; the more shame for the house of David that they suffered the city of David to lie neglected. They had probably often seen those breaches; but now they saw them to consider what course to take about them. This good we should get by public distresses, we should be awakened by them to *repair our breaches,* and amend what is amiss. (3.) They made sure of water for the city, and did what they could to deprive the besiegers of it: *You gathered together the water of the lower pool,* of which there was probably no great store, and of which therefore

they were the more concerned to be good husbands. See what a mercy it is that, as nothing is more necessary to the support of human life than water, so nothing is more cheap and common; but it is bad indeed when that, as here, is a scarce commodity. (4.) They *numbered the houses of Jerusalem,* that every house might send in its quota of men for the public service, or contribute in money to it, which they raised by a poll, so much a head or so much a house. (5.) Because private property ought to give way to the public safety, those houses that stood in their way, when the wall was to be fortified, were broken down, which, in such a case of necessity, is no more an injury to the owner than blowing up houses in case of fire. (6.) They made a ditch between the outer and inner wall, for the greater security of the city; and they contrived to draw the water of the old pool to it, that they might have plenty of water themselves and might deprive the besiegers of it; for it seems that was the project, lest the Assyrian army *should come and find much water* (2 Chr. 32:4) and so should be the better able to prolong the siege. If it be lawful to destroy the forage of a country, much more to divert the streams of its waters, for the straitening and starving of an enemy.

2. How regardless they were of God in all these preparations: *But you have not looked unto the Maker thereof* (that is, of Jerusalem, the city you are so solicitous for the defence of) and of all the advantages which nature has furnished it with for its defence — the *mountains round about it* (Ps. 125:2), and the rivers, which were such as the inhabitants might turn which way soever they pleased for their convenience. Note, (1.) It is God that made his Jerusalem, and fashioned it long ago, in his counsels. The Jewish writers, upon this place, say, There were seven things which God made before the world (meaning which he had in his eye when he made the world): *the garden of Eden, the law, the just ones, Israel, the throne of glory, Jerusalem, and Messiah the Prince.* The gospel church has God for its Maker. (2.) Whatever service we do, or endeavour to do, at any time to God's Jerusalem, must be done with an eye to him as the Maker of it; and he takes it ill if it be done otherwise. It is here charged upon them that they did not look to God. [1.] They did not design his glory in what they did. They fortified Jerusalem because it was a rich city and their own houses were in it, not because it was the holy city and God's house was in it. In all our cares for the defence of the church we must look more at God's interest in it than at our own. [2.] They did not depend upon him for a blessing upon their endeavours, saw no need of it, and therefore sought not to him for it, but thought their own powers and policies sufficient for them. Of Hezekiah himself it is said that *he trusted in God* (2 Ki. 18:5), and particularly upon this occasion (2 Chr. 32:8); but there were those about him, it seems, who were great statesmen and soldiers, but had little religion in them. [3.] They did not give him thanks for the advantages they had, in fortifying their city, from *the waters of the old pool,* which were fashioned long ago, as Kishon is called *an ancient river,* Jdg. 5:21. Whatever in nature is at any time serviceable to us, we must therein acknowledge the goodness of the God of nature, who, when he fashioned it long ago, fitted it to be so, and *according to whose ordinance it continues to this day.* Every creature is that to us which God makes it to be; and therefore, whatever use it is of to us, we must *look at him that fashioned it,* bless him for it, and use it for him.

II. A great contempt of God's wrath and justice in contending with them, *v.* 12–14. Here observe,

1. What was God's design in bringing this calamity upon them: it was to humble them, bring them to repentance, and make them serious. In that day of trouble, and treading down, and perplexity, the Lord did thereby *call to weeping and mourning,* and all the expressions of sorrow, even *to baldness and girding with sackcloth;* and all this to lament their sins (by which they had brought those judgments upon their land), to enforce their prayers (by which they might hope to avert the judgments that were breaking in), and to dispose themselves to a reformation of their lives by a holy seriousness and a tenderness of heart under the word of God. To this God called them by his prophet's explaining his providences, and by his providences awakening them to regard what his prophets said. Note, When God threatens us with his judgments he expects and re-

quires that we humble ourselves under his mighty hand, that we tremble when the lion roars, and in a day of adversity consider.

2. How contrary they walked to this design of God (*v.* 13): *Behold, joy and gladness,* mirth and feasting, all the gaiety and all the jollity imaginable. They were as secure and cheerful as they used to be, as if they had had no enemy in their borders or were in no danger of falling into his hands. When they had taken the necessary precautions for their security, then they set all deaths and dangers at defiance, and resolved to be merry, let come on them what would. Those that should have been among the mourners were among the *wine-bibbers, the riotous eaters of flesh;* and observe what they said, *Let us eat and drink, for tomorrow we shall die.* This may refer either to the particular danger they were now in, and the fair warning which the prophet gave them of it, or to the general shortness and uncertainty of human life, and the nearness of death at all times. This was the language of the profane scoffers who *mocked the messengers of the Lord and misused his prophets.* (1.) They made a jest of dying. "The prophet tells us we must die shortly, perhaps to-morrow, and therefore we should mourn and repent to-day; no, rather *let us eat and drink,* that we may be fattened for the slaughter, and may be in good heart to meet our doom; if we must have a short life, let it be a merry one." (2.) They ridiculed the doctrine of a future state on the other side death; for, if there were no such state, the apostle grants there would be something of reason in what they said, 1 Co. 15:32. If, when we die, there were an end of us, it were good to make ourselves as easy and merry as we could while we live; but, if *for all these things God shall bring us into judgment,* it is at our peril if we walk *in the way of our heart and the sight of our eyes,* Eccl. 11:9. Note, A practical disbelief of another life after this is at the bottom of the carnal security and brutish sensuality which are the sin, and shame, and ruin of so great a part of mankind, as of the old world, who were *eating and drinking till the flood came.*

3. How much God was displeased at it. He signified his resentment of it to the prophet, *revealed it in his ears,* to be by him proclaimed upon the house-top: *Surely this iniquity shall not be purged from you till you die, v.* 14. It shall never be expiated with sacrifice and offering, any more than the iniquity of the house of Eli, 1 Sa. 3:14. It is a sin against the remedy, a baffling of the utmost means of conviction and rendering them ineffectual; and therefore it is not likely they should ever repent of it or have it pardoned. The Chaldee reads it, *It shall not be forgiven you till you die the second death.* Those that walk contrary to them; with the froward he will show himself froward.

Verses 15–25

We have here a prophecy concerning the displacing of Shebna, a great officer at court, and the preferring of Eliakim to the post of honour and trust that he was in. Such changes are common in the courts of princes; it is therefore strange that so much notice should be taken of it by the prophet here; but by the accomplishment of what was foretold concerning these particular persons God designed to confirm his word in the mouth of Isaiah concerning other and greater events; and it is likewise to show that, as God has burdens in store for those nations and kingdoms abroad that are open enemies to his church and people, so he has for those particular persons at home that are false friends to them and betray them. It is likewise a confirmation in general of the hand of divine Providence in all events of this kind, which to us seem contingent and to depend upon the wills and fancies of princes. *Promotion comes not from the east, nor from the west, nor from the south; but God is the Judge,* Ps. 25:6, 7. It is probable that this prophecy was delivered at the same time with that in the former part of the chapter, and began to be fulfilled before Sennacherib's invasion; for now Shebna was *over the house,* but then Eliakim was (ch. 36:3); and Shebna, coming down gradually, was only scribe. Here is,

I. The prophecy of Shebna's disgrace. He is called *this treasurer,* being entrusted with the management of the revenue; and he is likewise said to be *over the house,* for such was his boundless ambition and covetousness that less than two places, and those two of the greatest importance at court, would not satisfy him. It is common for self-seeking men thus to grasp at more than they can manage, and so the business of their places is neglected, while the pomp and profit of them wholly engage the mind. It does not appear what were the particular instances of Shebna's maladministration, for which Isaiah is here sent to prophesy against him; but the Jews say, "He kept up a traitorous correspondence with the king of Assyria, and was in treaty with him to deliver the city into his hands." However this was, it should seem that he was a foreigner (for we never read of the name of his father) and that he was an enemy to the true interests of Judah and Jerusalem: it is probable that he was first preferred by Ahaz. Hezekiah was himself an excellent prince; but the best masters cannot always be sure of good servants. We have need to pray for princes, that they may be wise and happy in the choice of those they trust. These were times of reformation, yet Shebna, a bad man, complied so far as to keep his places at court; and it is probable that many others did like him, for which reason Sennacherib is said to have been *sent against a hypocritical nation, ch.* 10:6. In this message to Shebna we have,

1. A reproof of his pride, vanity, and security (*v.* 16): *"What hast thou here, and whom hast thou here? What* a mighty noise and bustle dost thou make! What estate has thou here, that thou was born to? *Whom hast thou here,* what relations, that thou art allied to? Art thou not of mean and obscure original, *filius populi — a mere plebeian,* that comest we know not whence? What is the meaning of this then, that thou hast built thyself a fine house, *hast graved thyself a habitation?"* So very nice and curious was it that it seemed rather to be the work of an engraver than of a mason or carpenter; and it seemed engraven in a rock, so firmly was it founded and so impregnable was it. "Nay, *thou hast hewed thee out a sepulchre,"* as if he designed that his pomp should survive his funeral. Though Jerusalem was not *the place of his father's sepulchres* (as Nehemiah called it with a great deal of tenderness, Neh. 2:3), he designed it should be the place of his own, and therefore set up a monument for himself in his life-time, set it up on high. Those that make stately monuments for their pride forget that, how beautiful soever they appear outwardly, within *they are full of dead men's bones.* But it is a pity that the grave-stone should forget the grave.

2. A prophecy of his fall and the sullying of his glory. (1.) That he should not quickly be displaced and degraded (*v.* 19): *I will drive thee from thy station.* High places are slippery places; and those are justly deprived of their honour that are proud of it and puffed up with it, and deprived of their power that do hurt with it. God will do it, who shows himself to be God by *looking upon proud men and abasing them,* Job 40:11, 12. To this *v.* 25 refers. "The nail that is *now fastened in the sure place* (that is, Shebna, who thinks himself immovably fixed in his office) *shall be removed, and cut down, and fall."* Those are mistaken who think any place in this world a sure place, or themselves as nails fastened in it; for there is nothing here but uncertainty. When the nail falls the burden that was upon it is cut off; when Shebna was disgraced all that had a dependence upon him fell into contempt too. Those that are in high places will have many hanging upon them as favourites whom they are proud of and trust to; but they are burdens upon them, and perhaps with their weight break the nail, and both fall together, and by deceiving ruin one another — the common fate of great men and their flatterers, who expect more from each other than either performs. (2.) That after a while he should not only be driven from his station, but driven from his country: *The Lord will carry thee away with the captivity of a mighty man, v.* 17, 18. Some think the Assyrians seized him, and took him away, because he had promised to assist them and did not, but appeared against them: or perhaps Hezekiah, finding out his treachery, banished him, and forbade him ever to return; or he himself, finding that he had become obnoxious to the people, withdrew into some other country, and there spent the rest of his days in meanness and obscurity. Grotius thinks he was stricken with a leprosy, which was a disease commonly supposed to come from the immediate hand of God's displeasure, particularly for the punishment of the proud, as in the case of Miriam and Uzziah; and by reason of this disease he was *tossed*

like a ball out of Jerusalem. Those who, when they are in power, turn and toss others, will be justly turned and tossed themselves when their day shall come to fall. Many who have thought themselves fastened like a nail may come to be tossed like a ball; for here have we *no continuing city.* Shebna thought his place too strait for him, he had no room to thrive; God will therefore send him *into a large country,* where he shall have room to wander, but never find the way back again; for *there he shall die,* and lay his bones there, and not in the sepulchre he had hewn out for himself. And *there the chariots* which had been the chariots of his glory, in which he had rattled about the streets of Jerusalem, and which he took into banishment with him, should but serve to upbraid him with his former grandeur, *to the shame of his lord's house,* of the court of Ahaz, who had advanced him.

II. The prophecy of Eliakim's advancement, *v.* 20, etc. He is God's servant, has approved himself faithfully so in other employments, and therefore God will call him to this high station. Those that are diligent in doing the duty of a low sphere stand fairest for preferment in God's books. Eliakim does not undermine Shebna, nor make an interest against him, nor does he intrude into his office; but God calls him to it: and what God calls us to we may expect he will own us in. It is here foretold, 1. That Eliakim should be put into Shebna's place of lord-chamberlain of the household, lord-treasurer, and prime-minister of state. The prophet must tell Shebna this, *v.* 21. "He shall have *thy robe,* the badge of honour, and *thy girdle,* the badge of power; for he shall have *thy government."* To hear of it would be a great mortification to Shebna, much more to see it. Great men, especially if proud men, cannot endure their successors. God undertakes the doing of it, not only because he would put it into the heart of Hezekiah to do it, and his hand must be acknowledged guiding the hearts of princes in placing and displacing men (Prov. 21:1), but because the powers that are, subordinate as well as supreme, are ordained of God. It is God that clothes princes with their robes, and therefore we must submit ourselves to them for the Lord's sake and with an eye to him, 1 Pt. 2:13. and, since it is he that *commits the government into their hand,* they must administer it according to his will, for his glory; they must judge for him by whom they judge and *decree justice,* Prov. 8:15. And they may depend upon him to furnish them for what he calls them to, according to this promise: *I will clothe him;* and then it follows, *I will strengthen him.* Those that are called to places of trust and power should seek unto God for grace to enable them to do the duty of their places; for that ought to be their chief care. Eliakim's advancement is further described by the laying of the *key of the house of David upon his shoulders, v.* 22. Probably he carried a golden key upon his shoulder as a badge of his office, or had one embroidered upon his cloak or robe, to which this alludes. Being over the house, and having the key delivered to him, as the seals are to the lord-keeper, *he shall open and none shall shut, shut and none shall open.* He had access to *the house of the precious things, the silver, and the gold, and the spices;* and to the *house of the armour* and the *treasures* (ch. 39:2), and disposed of the stores there as he thought fit for the public service. He put whom he pleased into the inferior offices and turned out whom he pleased. Our Lord Jesus describes his own power as Mediator by an allusion to this (Rev. 3:7), that *he has the key of David,* wherewith he *opens and no man shuts,* he *shuts and no man opens.* His power in the kingdom of heaven, and in the ordering of all the affairs of that kingdom, is absolute, irresistible, and uncontrollable. 2. That he should be fixed and confirmed in that office. he shall have it for life, and not *durante bene placito — during pleasure* (*v.* 23): *I will fasten him as a nail in a sure place,* not to be removed or cut down. Thus lasting shall the honour be that comes from God to all those who use it for him. Our Lord Jesus is *as a nail in a sure place:* his kingdom cannot be shaken, and he himself is still the same. 3. That he should be a great blessing in his office; and it is this that crowns the favours here conferred upon him. God *makes his name great,* for he shall be a blessing, Gen. 12:2. (1.) He shall be a blessing to his country (*v.* 21): *He shall be a father to the inhabitants of Jerusalem and to the house of Judah.* he shall take care not only of the affairs of the king's household, but of all the public interests in Jerusalem and Judah. Note, Rulers

should be fathers to those that are under their government, to teach them with wisdom, rule them with love, and correct what is amiss with tenderness, to protect them and provide for them, and be solicitous about them as a man is for his own children and family. It is happy with a people when the court, the city, and the country, have no separate interests, but all centre in the same, so that the courtiers are true patriots, and whom the court blesses the country has reason to bless too; and when those who are fathers to Jerusalem, the royal city, are no less so to the house of Judah. (2.) He shall be a blessing to his family (*v.* 23, 24): *He shall be for a glorious throne to his father's house.* The consummate wisdom and virtue which recommended him to this great trust made him the honour of his family, which probably was very considerable before, but now became much more so. Children should aim to be a credit to their parents and relations. The honour men reflect upon their families by their piety and usefulness is more to be valued than that which they derive from their families by their names and titles. Eliakim being preferred, *all the glory of his father's house* was hung upon him; they all made their court to him, and his brethren's sheaves bowed to his. Observe, The glory of this world gives a man no intrinsic worth or excellency; it is but hung upon him as an appurtenance, and it will soon drop from him. Eliakim was compared to *a nail in a sure place,* in pursuance of which comparison all the relations of his family (which, it is likely, were numerous, and that was the glory of it) are said to have a dependence upon him, as in a house the vessels that have handles to them are hung up upon nails and pins. It intimates likewise that he shall generously take care of them all, and bear the weight of that care: *All the vessels,* not only *the flagons,* but *the cups, the vessels of small quantity,* the meanest that belong to his family, shall be provided for by him. See what a burden those bring upon themselves that undertake great trusts; they little think how many and how much will hand upon them if they resolve to be faithful in the discharge of their trust. Our Lord Jesus, having the key of the house of David, is as a *nail in a sure place,* and all *the glory of his father's house hangs* upon him, is derived from him, and depends upon him; even the meanest that belong to his church are welcome to him, and he is able to bear the stress of them all. That soul cannot perish, nor that concern fall to the ground, though ever so weighty, that is by faith hung upon Christ.

CHAPTER 23

This chapter is concerning Tyre, an ancient wealthy city, situated upon the sea, and for many ages one of the most celebrated cities for trade and merchandise in those parts of the world. The lot of the tribe of Asher bordered upon it. See Joshua 19:29, where it is called "the strong city Tyre." We seldom find it a dangerous enemy to Israel, but sometimes their faithful ally, as in the reigns of David and Solomon; for trading cities maintain their grandeur, not by the conquest of their neighbours, but by commerce with them. In this chapter is foretold, I. The lamentable desolation of Tyre, which was performed by Nebuchadnezzar and the Chaldean army, about the time that they destroyed Jerusalem; and a hard task they had of it, as appears Eze. 29:18, where they are said to have "served a hard service against Tyre," and yet to have no wages (*v.* 1–14). II. The restoration of Tyre after seventy years, and the return of the Tyrians out of their captivity to their trade again (*v.* 15–18).

Verses 1–14

Tyre being a sea-port town, this prophecy of its overthrow fitly begins and ends with, *Howl, you ships of Tarshish;* for all its business, wealth, and honour, depended upon its shipping; if that be ruined, they will be all undone. Observe,

I. Tyre flourishing. This is taken notice of that her fall may appear the more dismal. 1. *The merchants of Zidon,* who traded at sea, had at first *replenished her, v.* 2. Zidon was the more ancient city, situated upon the same seacost, a few leagues more to the north, and Tyre was at first only a colony of that; but the daughter had outgrown the mother, and become much more considerable. It may be a mortification to great cities to think how they were at first replenished. 2. Egypt had helped very much to raise her, *v.* 3. Sihor was the river of Egypt: by that river, and the ocean into which it ran, the Egyptians traded with Tyre; and the harvest of that river was her revenue. The riches of the sea, and the gains by goods exported and imported, are as much the harvest to trading towns as that of hay and corn is to the country; and sometimes *the har-*

vest of the river proves a better revenue than the harvest of the land. Or it may be meant of all the products of the Egyptian soil, which the men of Tyre traded in, and which were the harvest of the river Nile, owing themselves to the overflowing of that river. 3. She had become the mart of the nations, the great emporium of that part of the world. Some of every known nation might be found there, especially at certain times of the year, when there was a general rendezvous of merchants. This is enlarged upon by another prophet, Eze. 27:2, 3, etc. See how the hand of the diligent, by the blessing of God upon it, makes rich. Tyre became rich and great by industry, though she had no other ploughs going than those that plough the waters. 4. She was a *joyous city,* noted for mirth and jollity, *v.* 7. Those that were so disposed might find there all manner of sports and diversions, all the delights of the sons and daughters of men, balls, and plays, and operas, and every thing of that kind that a man had a fancy to. This made them secure and proud, and they despised the country people, who neither knew nor relished any joys of that nature. This also made them very loth to believe and consider what warnings God gave them by his servants; they were too merry to mind them. Her *antiquity* likewise was *of ancient days,* and she was proud of that, and that helped to make her secure; as if because she had been a city time out of mind, and her antiquity had been of ancient days, therefore she must continue a city time without end, and her continuance must be to the days of eternity. 5. She was *a crowning city* (*v.* 8), that crowned herself. Such were the power and pomp of her magistrates that they crowned those who had dependence on her and dealings with her. It is explained in the following words: *Her merchants are princes,* and live like princes for the ease and state they take; and *her traffickers,* whatever country they go to, *are the honourable of the earth,* who are respected by all. How slightly soever some now speak of tradesmen, it seems formerly, and among the wisest nations, there were merchants, and traders, and men of business, that were the honourable of the earth.

II. Here is Tyre falling. It does not appear that she brought trouble upon herself by provoking her neighbours with her quarrels, but rather by tempting them with her wealth; but, if it was this that induced Nebuchadnezzar to fall upon Tyre, he was disappointed; for after it had stood out a siege of thirteen years, and could hold out no longer, the inhabitants got away by sea, with their families and goods, to other places where they had an interest, and left Nebuchadnezzar nothing but the bare city. See a history of Tyre in Sir Walter Raleigh's History of the World, *lib.* 2. *cap.* 7. *sect.* 3, 43. *page.* 283, which will give much light to this prophecy and that in Ezekiel concerning Tyre.

1. See how the destruction of Tyre is here foretold. (1.) The haven shall be no convenient harbour for the reception of the ships of Tarshish, but all *laid waste* (1.), so that there shall be no house, no dock for the ships to ride in, no inns, or public houses for the seamen, no entering into the port. Perhaps it was choked with sand or blocked up by the enemy. Or, Tyre being destroyed and laid waste, the ships that used to come from Tarshish and Chittim into that port shall now no more enter in; for *it is revealed* or made known *to them,* they have received the dismal news, that Tyre is destroyed and laid waste; so that there is now no more business for them there. See how it is in this world; those that are spoiled by their enemies are commonly slighted by their old friends. (2.) The inhabitants are struck with astonishment. Tyre was an island. The inhabitants of it, who had made a mighty noise and bustle in the world, and revelled with loud huzzas, shall now be still and silent (*v.* 2); they shall sit down as mourners, so overwhelmed with grief that they shall not be able to express it. Their proud boasts of themselves, and defiances of their neighbours, shall be silenced. God can soon quiet those, and strike them dumb, that are the noisy busy people of the world. Be still; for God will do his work (Ps. 46:10; Zec. 2:13), and you cannot resist him. (3.) The neighbours are amazed, blush, and are in pain for them: *Zidon is ashamed* (*v.* 4), by whom Tyre was at first replenished; for the rolling waves of the sea brought to Zidon this news from Tyre; and there *the strength of the sea,* a high spring-tide, proclaimed saying, *"I travail not, nor bring forth children* now, as I have done. I do not now, as I used to do, bring shiploads of young people to Tyre, to be bred up there in trade and business," which was the thing that had made Tyre so rich and populous. Or the sea, that used to be loaded with fleets of ships about Tyre, shall not be as desolate as a sorrowful widow that is bereaved of all her children, and has none about her to nourish and bring up. Egypt indeed was a much larger and more considerable kingdom than Tyre was; and yet Tyre had so large a correspondence, upon the account of trade, that all the nations about shall be as much in pain, upon the report of the ruin of that one city, as they would have been, and not long after were, upon the report of the ruin of all Egypt, *v.* 5. Or, as some read it, *When the report shall reach to the Egyptians they shall be sorely pained to hear it of Tyre,* both because of the loss of their trade with that city and because it was a threatening step towards their own ruin; when their neighbour's house was on fire their own was in danger. (4.) The merchants, as many as could, should transmit their effects to other places, and abandon Tyre, where they had raised their estates, and thought they had made them sure (*v.* 6): *"You* that have long been *inhabitants of this isle"* (for it lay off in the sea about half a mile from the continent); "It is time to howl now, for you must pass over to Tarshish. The best course you can take is to make the best of your way to Tarshish, to the sea" (to Taressus, a city in Spain; so some), "or to some other of your plantations." Those that think their mountain stands strong, and cannot be moved, will find that here they have no continuing city. *The mountains shall depart and the hills be removed.* (5.) Those that could not make their escape must expect no other than to be carried into captivity; for it was the way of conquerors, in those times, to take those they conquered to be bondmen in their own country, and send of their own to be freemen in theirs (*v.* 7): *Her own feet shall carry her afar off to sojourn;* they shall be hurried away on foot into captivity, and many a weary step they shall take towards their own misery. Those that have lived in the greatest pomp and splendour know not what hardships they may be reduced to before they die. (6.) Many of those that attempted to escape should be pursued and fall into the hands of the enemy. Tyre shall *pass through her land as a river* (*v.* 10), running down, one company after another, into the ocean or abyss of misery. Or, though they hasten away as a river, with the greatest swiftness, hoping to outrun the danger, yet *there is no more strength;* they are quickly tired, and cannot get forward, but fall an easy prey into the hands of the enemy. And, as Tyre has no more strength, so her sister Zidon has no more comfort (*v.* 12): *"Thou shalt no more rejoice, O oppressed virgin, daughter of Zidon,* that art now ready to be overpowered by the victorious Chaldeans! Thy turn is next; therefore *arise; pass over to Chittim;* flee to Greece, to Italy, any where to shift for thy own safety; yet *there also shalt thou have no rest;* thy enemies shall disturb thee, and thy own fears shall disquiet thee, where thou hopedst to find some repose." Note, We deceive ourselves if we promise ourselves rest any where in this world. Those that are uneasy in one place will be so in another; and, when God's judgments pursue sinners, they will overtake them.

2. But whence shall all this trouble come?

(1.) God will be the author of it; it is a *destruction from the Almighty.* It will be asked (*v.* 8), *"Who has taken this counsel against Tyre?* Who has contrived it? Who has resolved it? Who can find in his heart to lay such a stately lovely city in ruins? And how is it possible that its ruin should be effected?" To this it will be answered, [1.] God has designed it, who is infinitely wise and just, and never did, nor ever will do, any wrong to any of his creatures (*v.* 9). *The Lord of hosts,* that has all things at his disposal and gives not account of any of his matters, he *has purposed it.* It shall be done according to the counsel of his will; and that which he aims at herein is *to stain the pride of all glory,* to pollute it, profane it, and throw it to be trodden upon; *and to bring into contempt* and make despicable *all the honourable ones of the earth,* that they may not admire themselves and be admired by others as usual. God did not bring those calamities upon Tyre in a way of sovereignty, to show an arbitrary and irresistible power; but he did it to punish the Tyrians for their pride. Many other sins, no doubt, reigned among them — idolatry, sensuality, and oppression; but the sin of pride is fastened upon as that which was the particular ground of God's controversy with Tyre; for he resists the proud. All the world observing and being surprised at the desolation of Tyre, we have here an exposition of it. God tells the world what he meant by it. *First,* He designed to convince men of the vanity and uncertainty of all earthly glory, to show them what a withering, fading, perishing thing it is even when it seems most substantial. It were well if men would be thoroughly taught this lesson, though it were at the expense of so great a destruction. Are men's learning and wealth, their pomp and power, their interest in, and influence upon, all about them, their glory? Are their stately houses, rich furniture, and splendid appearances, their glory? Look upon the ruins of Tyre, and see all this glory stained, and sullied, and buried in the dust. The honourable ones of heaven will be for ever such; but see the grandees of Tyre, some fled into banishment, others forced into captivity, and all impoverished, and you will conclude that the honourable of the earth, even the most honourable, know not how soon they may be brought into contempt. *Secondly,* He designed hereby to prevent their being proud of that glory, their being puffed up, and confident of the continuance of it. Let the ruin of Tyre be a warning to all places and persons to take heed of pride; for it proclaims to all the world that he who exalts himself shall be abased. [2.] God will do it, who has all power in his hand and can do it effectually (*v.* 11): *He stretched out his hand over the sea.* He has done so many a time, witness the dividing of the Red Sea and the drowning of Pharaoh in it. He has often shaken the kingdoms that were most secure; and he has now given commandment concerning this merchant-city, to destroy the strongholds thereof. As its beauty shall not intercede for it, but that shall be stained, so its strength shall not protect it, but that shall be broken. If any think it strange that a city so well fortified, and that has so many powerful allies, should be so totally ruined, let them know that it is the Lord of hosts that has given a commandment to destroy the strongholds thereof: and who can gainsay his orders or hinder the execution of them?

(2.) The Chaldeans shall be the instruments of it (*v.* 13): *Behold the land of the Chaldeans;* how easily they and their land were destroyed by the Assyrians. Though their own hands *founded it, set up the towers* of Babylon, and *raised up its palaces,* yet the Assyrians brought it to ruin, whence the Tyrians might infer that as easily as the old Chaldeans were subdued by the Assyrians so easily shall Tyre be vanquished by those new Chaldeans. Babel was built by the Assyrians for *those that dwelt in the wilderness.* It may be rendered *for the ships* (the Assyrians founded it for ships and shipmen that traffic upon those vast rivers Tigris and Euphrates to the Persian and Indian seas), *for men of the desert,* for Babylon is called the *desert of the sea, ch.* 21:1. Thus Tyrus was built upon the sea for the like purpose. But the Assyrians (says Dr. Lightfoot) brought that to ruin, now lately, in Hezekiah's time, and so shall Tyre hereafter be brought to ruin by Nebuchadnezzar. If we looked more upon the falling and withering of others, we should not be so confident as we commonly are of the continuance of our own flourishing and standing.

Verses 15–18

Here is, I. The time fixed for the continuance of the desolations of Tyre, which were not to be perpetual desolations: *Tyre shall be forgotten seventy years, v.* 15. So long it shall lie neglected and buried in obscurity. It was destroyed by Nebuchadnezzar much about the time that Jerusalem was, and lay as long as it did in its ruins. See the folly of that proud ambitious conqueror. What the richer, what the stronger, was he for making himself master of Tyre, when all the inhabitants were driven out of it and he had none of his own subjects to spare for the replenishing and fortifying of it? It is surprising to see what pleasure men could take in destroying cities and making *their memorial perish with them,* Ps. 9:6. He trampled on the pride of Tyre, and therein served God's purpose; but with greater pride, for which God soon after humbled him.

II. A prophecy of the restoration of Tyre to its glory again: *After the end of seventy years, according to the years of one king,* or one dynasty or family of kings, that of Nebuchadnezzar; when that expired, the desolations of Tyre came to an end. And we may presume that Cyrus at the same time when he released the Jews, and encouraged them to rebuild Jerusalem, released the Tyrians also, and encouraged them to rebuild Tyre. Thus the prosperity and adversity of places, as well as persons, are *set the one over against the other,* that the most glorious cities may not be secure nor the most ruinous despair. It is foretold, 1. That God's providence shall gain smile upon this ruined city (*v.* 17): *The Lord will visit Tyre* in mercy; for, though he contend, he will not contend for ever. It is not said, Her old acquaintance shall visit her, the colonies she has planted, and the trading cities she has had correspondence with (they have forgotten her); but, The Lord shall visit her by some unthought-of turn; he shall cause his indignation towards her to cease, and then things will run of course in their former channel. 2. That she shall use her best endeavours to recover her trade again. She shall sing as a harlot, that has been some time under correction for her lewdness; but, when she is set at liberty (so violent is the bent of corruption), she will use her old arts of temptation. The Tyrians having returned from their captivity, and those that remained recovering new spirits thereupon, they shall contrive how to force a trade, shall procure the best choice of goods, under-sell their neighbours, and be obliging to all customers; as a harlot that has been forgotten, when she comes to be spoken of again, recommends herself to company by singing and playing, *takes a harp, goes about the city,* perhaps in the night, serenading, *makes sweet melody, and sings many songs.* These are innocent and allowable diversions, if soberly, and moderately, and modestly used; but those that value themselves upon their virtue should not be over-fond of them, nor ambitious to excel in them, because, whatever they are now, anciently they were some of the baits with which harlots used to entice fools. Tyre shall now by degrees come to be the mart of nations again; she shall *return to her hire,* to her traffic, *and shall commit fornication* (that is, she shall have dealings in trade, for the prophet carries on the similitude of a harlot) *with all the kingdoms of the world* that she had formerly traded with in her prosperity. The love of worldly wealth is a spiritual whoredom, and therefore covetous people are called *adulterers and adulteresses* (James 4:4), and covetousness is spiritual idolatry. 3. That, having recovered her trade again, she shall make a better use of it than she had done formerly; and this good she should get by her calamities (*v.* 18): *Her merchandise, and her hire, shall be holiness to the Lord.* The trade of Tyre, and all the gains of her trade, shall be devoted to God and to his honour and employed in his service. It shall not be treasured and hoarded up, as formerly, to be the matter of their pride and the support of their carnal confidence; but it shall be laid out in acts of piety and charity. What they can spare from the maintenance of themselves and their families *shall be for those that dwell before the Lord,* for the priests, the Lord's ministers, that attend in his temple at Jerusalem; not to maintain them in pomp and grandeur, but that they and theirs may *eat sufficiently,* may have food convenient for them, with as little as may be of that care which would divert them from their ministration, and that they may have, not rich and fine clothing, but *durable clothing,* that which is strong and lasting, *clothing for old men* (so some read it), as if the priests, though they were young, must wear such plain grave clothing as old men used to wear. Now, (1.) This supposes that religion should be set up in New Tyre, that they should come to the knowledge of the true God and into communion with the Israel of God. Perhaps their being fellow-captives with the Jews in Babylon (who had prophets with them there) disposed them to join with them in their worship there, and turned them from idols, as it cured the Jews of their idolatry: and when they were released with them, and as they had reason to believe for their sakes, when they were settled again in Tyre, they would send gifts and offerings to the temple, and presents to the priests. We find men of Tyre then dwelling in the land of Judah, Neh. 13:16. Tyre and Sidon were better disposed to religion in Christ's time than the cities of Israel; for, if Christ had gone among them, *they would have repented,* Mt. 11:21. And we meet with Christians at Tyre (Acts 21:3, 4), and, many years after, did Christianity flourish there. Some of the rabbin refer this prophecy of the conversion of Tyre to the days of the Messiah. (2.) It directs those that have estates to make use of them in the service of God and religion, and to reckon that best laid up which is so laid out. Both the merchandise of the tradesmen and the hire of the day-labourers shall be devoted to God. Both the merchandise (the employment we fol-

low) and the hire (the gain of our employments) must *be holiness to the Lord,* alluding to the motto engraven on the frontlet of the high priest (Ex. 39:30), and to the separation of the tithe under the law, Lev. 27:30. See a promise like this referring to gospel times, Zec. 14:20, 21. We must first give up ourselves to be holiness to the Lord before what we do, or have, or get, can be so. When we abide with God in our particular callings, and do common actions after a godly sort — when we abound in works of piety and charity, are liberal in relieving the poor, and supporting the ministry, and encouraging the gospel — then our merchandise and our hire are holiness to the Lord, if we sincerely look at his glory in them. And our wealth need not be treasured and laid up on earth; for it is treasured and laid up in heaven, in *bags that wax not old,* Lu. 12:33.

CHAPTER 24

It is agreed that here begins a new sermon, which is continued to the end of chap. 27. And in it the prophet, according to the directions he had received, does, in many precious promises, "say to the righteous, It shall be well with them;" and, in many dreadful threatenings, he says, "Woe to the wicked, it shall be ill with them" (3:10, 11); and these are interwoven, that they may illustrate each other. This chapter is mostly threatening; and, as the judgments threatened are very sore and grievous ones, so the people threatened with those judgments are very many. It is not the burden of any particular city or kingdom, as those before, but the burden of the whole earth. The word indeed signifies only the land, because our own land is commonly to us as all the earth. But it is here explained by another word that is not so confined; it is the world (*v.* 4); so that it must at least take in a whole neighbourhood of nations. 1. Some think (and very probably) that it is a prophecy of the great havoc that Sennacherib and his Assyrian army should now shortly make of many of the nations in that part of the world. 2. Others make it to point at the like devastations which, about 100 years afterwards, Nebuchadnezzar and his armies should make in the same countries, going from one kingdom to another, not only to conquer them, but to ruin them and lay them waste; for that was the method which those eastern nations took in their wars. The promises that are mixed with the threatenings are intended for the support and comfort of the people of God in those very calamitous times. And, since here are no particular nations names either by whom or on whom those desolations should be brought, I see not but it may refer to both these events. Nay, the scripture has many fulfillings, and we ought to give it its full latitude; and therefore I incline to think that the prophet, from those and the like instances which he had a particular eye to, designs here to represent in general the calamitous state of mankind, and the many miseries which human life is liable to, especially those that attend the wars of the nations. Surely the prophets were sent, not only to foretel particular events, but to form the minds of men to virtue and piety, and for that end their prophecies were written and preserved even for our learning, and therefore ought not to be looked upon as of private interpretation. Now since a thorough conviction of the vanity of the world, and its insufficiency to make us happy, will go far towards bringing us to God, and drawing out our affections towards another world, the prophet here shows what vexation of spirit we must expect to meet with in these things, that we may never take up our rest in them, nor promise ourselves satisfaction any where short of the enjoyment of God. In this chapter we have, I. A threatening of desolating judgments for sin (*v.* 1–12), to which is added an assurance that in the midst of them good people should be comforted (*v.* 13–15). II. A further threatening of the like desolations (*v.* 16–22), to which is added an assurance that in the midst of all God should be glorified.

Verses 1–12

It is a very dark and melancholy scene that this prophecy presents to our view; turn our eyes which way we will, every thing looks dismal. The threatened desolations are here described in a great variety of expressions to the same purport, and all aggravating.

I. The earth is stripped of all its ornaments and looks as if it were taken off its basis; it is made *empty and waste* (*v.* 1), as if it were reduced to its first chaos, *Tohu* and *Bohu,* nothing but confusion and emptiness again (Gen. 1:2), *without form and void.* It is true earth sometimes signifies the *land,* and so the same word *eretz* is here translated (*v.* 3): *The land shall be utterly emptied and utterly spoiled;* but I see not why it should not there, as well as *v.* 1, be translated *the earth;* for most commonly, if not always, where it signifies some one particular land it has something joined to it, or at least not far from it, which does so appropriate it; as the land (or earth) of Egypt, or Canaan, or this land, or ours, or yours, or the like. It might indeed refer to some particular country, and an ambiguous word might be used to warrant such an application; for it is good to apply to ourselves, and our own hands, what the scripture says in general of the vanity and vexation of spirit that attend all things here below; but it should seem designed to speak what often happens to many countries, and will do while the world stands, and what may, we know not how soon, happen to our own, and what is the general character of all earthly things: they are empty of all solid comfort and

satisfaction; a little thing makes them waste. We often see numerous families, and plentiful estates, utterly emptied and utterly spoiled, by one judgment or other, or perhaps only by a gradual and insensible decay. Sin has turned the earth *upside down;* the earth has become quite a different thing to man from what it was when God made it to be his habitation. Sin has also *scattered abroad the inhabitants thereof.* The rebellion at Babel was the occasion of the dispersion there. How many ways are there in which the inhabitants both of towns and of private houses are scattered abroad, so that near relations and old neighbours know nothing of one another! To the same purport is *v.* 4. *The earth mourns, and fades away;* it disappoints those that placed their happiness in it and raised their expectations high from it, and proves not what they promised themselves it would be. *The* whole *world languishes and fades away,* as hastening towards a dissolution. It is, at the best, like a flower, which withers in the hands of those that please themselves too much with it, and lay it in their bosoms. And, as the earth itself grows old, so those that dwell therein are desolate; men carry crazy sickly bodies along with them, are often solitary, and confined by affliction, *v.* 6. When the earth languishes, and is not so fruitful as it used to be, then those that dwell therein, that make it their home, and rest, and portion, are desolate; whereas those that by faith dwell in God can rejoice in him even when the fir-tree does not blossom. If we look abroad, and see in how many places pestilences and burning fevers rage, and what multitudes are swept away by them in a little time, so that sometimes the living scarcely suffice to bury the dead, perhaps we shall understand what the prophet means when he says, *The inhabitants of the earth are burned,* or consumed, some by one disease, others by another, and there are but *few men left,* in comparison. Note, The world we live in is a world of disappointment, a vale of tears, and a dying world; and the children of men in it are but of few days, and full of trouble.

II. It is God that brings all these calamities upon the earth. *The Lord* that made the earth, and made it fruitful and beautiful, for the service and comfort of man, now *makes it empty and waste* (*v.* 1), for its Creator is and will be its Judge; he has an incontestable right to pass sentence upon it and an irresistible power to execute that sentence. It is *the Lord* that *has spoken this word,* and he will do the work (*v.* 3); it is his curse that has *devoured the earth* (*v.* 6), the general curse which sin brought upon *the ground for man's sake* (Gen. 3:17), and all the particular curses which families and countries bring upon themselves by their enormous wickedness. See the power of God's curse, how it makes all empty and lays all waste; those whom he curses are cursed indeed.

III. Persons of all ranks and conditions shall share in these calamities (*v.* 2): *It shall be as with the people, so with the priest,* etc. This is true of many of the common calamities of human life; all are subject to the same diseases of body, sorrows of mind, afflictions in relations, and the like. There is one event to those of very different stations; time and chance happen to them all. It is in a special manner true of the destroying judgments which God sometimes brings upon sinful nations; when he pleases he can make them universal, so that none shall escape them or be exempt from them; whether men have little or much, they shall lose it all. Those of the meaner rank smart first by famine; but those of the higher rank go first into captivity, while the poor of the land are left. It shall be all alike, 1. With high and low: *As with the people, so with the priest,* or prince. The dignity of magistrates and ministers, and the respect and reverence due to both, shall not secure them. *The faces of elders are not honoured,* Lam. 5:12. The priests had been as corrupt and wicked as the people; and, if their character served not to restrain them from sin, how can they expect it should serve to secure them from judgments? In both it is *like people, like priest,* Hosea 4:8, 9. 2. With bond and free: *As with the servant, so with his master; as with the maid, so with her mistress.* They have all corrupted their way, and therefore will all be made miserable when the earth is made waste. 3. With rich and poor. Those that have money before-hand, that are purchasing, and letting out money to interest, will fare no better than those that are so impoverished that they are forced to sell their estates and take up money at interest. There are judgments short of the great day of judgment in which rich and poor meet together. Let not those that are advanced in the world set their inferiors at too great a distance, because they know not how soon they may be set upon a level with them. *The rich man's wealth is his strong city* in his own conceit; but it does not always prove so.

IV. It is sin that brings these calamities upon the earth. The earth is made empty, and fades away, because it *is defiled under the inhabitants thereof* (v. 5); it is polluted by the sins of men, and therefore it is made desolate by the judgments of God. Such is the filthy nature of sin that it defiles the earth itself under the sinful inhabitants thereof, and it is rendered unpleasant in the eyes of God and good men. See Lev. 18:25, 27, 28. Blood, in particular, defiles the land, Num. 35:33. The earth never spues out its inhabitants till they have first defiled it by their sins. Why, what have they done? 1. They have transgressed the laws of their creation, not answered the ends of it. The bonds of the law of nature have been broken by them, and they have cast from them the cords of their obligations to the God of nature. 2. *They have changed the ordinances* of revealed religion, those of them that have had the benefit of that. *They have neglected the ordinances* (so some read it), and have made no conscience of observing them. They have passed over the laws, in the commission of sin, and have passed by the ordinance, in the omission of duty. 3. Herein they have *broken the everlasting covenant,* which is a perpetual bond and will be to those that keep it a perpetual blessing. It is God's wonderful condescension that he is pleased to deal with men in a covenant-way, to do them good, and thereby oblige them to do him service. Even those that had no benefit by God's covenant with Abraham had benefit by his covenant with Noah and his sons, which is called *an everlasting covenant,* his covenant with day and night; but they observe not the precepts of the sons of Noah, they acknowledge not God's goodness in the day and night, nor study to make him any grateful returns, and so break the everlasting covenant and defeat the gracious designs and intentions of it.

V. These judgments shall humble men's pride and mar their mirth. When the earth is made empty, 1. It is a great mortification to men's pride (v. 4): *The haughty people of the earth do languish;* for they have lost that which supported their pride, and for which they magnified themselves. As for those that have held their heads highest, God can make them hang the head. 2. It is a great damp to men's jollity. This is enlarged upon much (v. 7–9): *All the merry-hearted do sigh.* Such is the nature of carnal mirth, it is but *as the crackling of thorns under a pot,* Eccl. 7:6. Great laughters commonly end in a sigh. Those that make the world their chief joy cannot rejoice ever more. When God sends his judgments into the earth he designs thereby to make those serious that were wholly addicted to their pleasures. *Let your laughter be turned into mourning.* When the earth is emptied the *noise of those that rejoice in it ends.* Carnal joy is a noisy thing; but the noise of it will soon be at an end, and the end of it is heaviness. Two things are made use of to excite and express vain mirth, and the jovial crew is here deprived of both. — (1.) Drinking: *The new wine mourns;* it has grown sour for want of drinking; for, how proper soever it may be for the heavy heart (Prov. 31:6), it does not relish to them as it does to the merry-hearted. *The vine languishes,* and gives little hopes of a vintage, and therefore *the merry-hearted do sigh;* for they know no other gladness than that of their corn, and wine, and oil increasing (Ps. 4:7), and, if you *destroy their vines and their fig-trees, you make all their mirth to cease,* Hosea 2:11, 12. *They shall not* now *drink wine with a song* and with huzzas, as they used to, but rather drink it with a sigh; nay, *Strong drink shall be bitter to those that drink it,* because they cannot but mingle their tears with it; or, through sickness, they have lost the relish of it. God has many ways to embitter wine and strong drink to those that love them and have the highest gust of them: distemper of body, anguish of mind, the ruin of the estate or country, will make the strong drink bitter and all the delights of sense tasteless and insipid. (2.) Music: *The mirth of tabrets ceases, and the joy of the harp,* which used to be at their feasts, *ch.* 5:12. The captives in Babylon hang their harps on the willow trees. In short, *All joy is darkened;* there is not a pleasant look to be seen, nor has any one power to force a smile; all *the mirth of the land is gone*

(v. 11); and, if it was that mirth which Solomon calls *madness,* there is no great loss of it.

VI. The cities will in a particular manner feel from these desolations of the country (v. 10): *The city of confusion is broken, is broken down* (so we read it); it lies exposed to invading powers, not only by the breaking down of its walls, but by the confusion that the inhabitants are in. *Every house is shut up,* perhaps by reason of the plague, which has burned or consumed the inhabitants, so that there are *few men left, v.* 6. Houses infected are usually shut up that no man may come in. Or they are shut up because they are deserted and uninhabited. *There is a crying for wine,* that is, for the spoiling of the vintage, so that there is likely to be no wine. *In the city,* in Jerusalem itself, that had been so much frequented, there shall be left nothing but *desolation;* grass shall grow in the streets, and *the gate is smitten with destruction* (v. 12); all that used to pass and repass through the gate are smitten, and all the strength of the city is cut off. How soon can God make a city of order a city of confusion, and then it will soon be a city of desolation!

Verses 13–15

Here is mercy remembered in the midst of wrath. In Judah and Jerusalem, and the neighbouring countries, when they are overrun by the enemy, Sennacherib or Nebuchadnezzar, there shall be a remnant preserved from the general ruin, and it shall be a devout and pious remnant. And this method God usually observes when his judgments are abroad; he does not make a full end, *ch.* 6:13. Or we may take it thus: Though the greatest part of mankind have all their comfort ruined by the emptying of the earth, and the making of that desolate, yet there are some few who understand their interests better, who have laid up their treasure in heaven and not in things below, and therefore can keep up their comfort and joy in God even *when the earth mourns and fades away.* Observe,

I. The small number of this remnant, *v.* 13. When all goes to ruin *there shall be as the shaking of an olive-tree, and the gleaning grapes,* here and there one who shall escape the common calamity (as Noah and his family when the old world was drowned), that shall be able to sit down upon a heap of the ruins of all their creature comforts, and even then rejoice in the Lord (Hab. 3:16–18), who, when all faces gather blackness, can lift up their heads with joy, Lu. 21:26, 28. These few are dispersed, and at a distance from each other, like the gleanings of the olive-tree; and they are concealed, hid under the leaves. The Lord only knows those that are his; the world does not.

II. The great devotion of this remnant, which is the greater for their having so narrowly escaped this great destruction (v. 14): *They shall lift up their voice; they shall sing.* 1. They shall sing for joy in their deliverance. When the mirth of carnal worldlings ceases the joy of the saints is as lively as ever; when the merry-hearted do sigh because the vine languishes the upright-hearted do sing because the covenant of grace, the fountain of their comforts and the foundation of their hopes, never fails. Those that rejoice in the Lord can rejoice in tribulation, and by faith may be in triumphs when all about them are in tears. 2. They shall sing to the glory and praise of God, shall sing not only for the mercy but *for the majesty of the Lord.* Their songs are awful and serious, and in their spiritual joys they have a reverend regard to the greatness of God, and keep at a humble distance when they attend him with their praises. The majesty of the Lord, which is matter of terror to wicked people, furnishes the saints with songs of praise. They shall sing for the magnificence, or transcendent excellency, of the Lord, shown both in his judgments and in his mercies; for we must sing, and sing unto him, of both, Ps. 101:1. Those who have made, or are making, their escape from the land (that being emptied and made desolate) to the sea and the isles of the sea, shall thence cry aloud; their dispersion shall help to spread the knowledge of God, and they shall make even remote shores to ring with his praises. It is much for the honour of God if those who fear him rejoice in him, and praise him, even in the most melancholy times.

III. Their holy zeal to excite others to the same devotion (v. 15); they encourage their fellow-sufferers to do likewise. 1. Those who are *in the fires,* in the furnace of affliction, those fires by which the *inhabitants of the earth*

are burned, v. 6. Or in the valleys, the low, dark, dirty places. 2. Those who are *in the isles of the sea,* whither they are banished, or are forced to flee for shelter, and hide themselves remote from all their friends. They went *through fire and water* (Ps. 66:12); yet in both let them glorify the Lord, and glory him as the Lord God of Israel. Those who through grace can glory in tribulation ought to glorify God in tribulation, and give him thanks for their comforts, which abound as their afflictions do abound. We must in every fire, even the hottest, in every isle, even the remotest, keep up our good thoughts of God. When, though he slay us, yet we trust in him — when, though for his sake we are killed all the day long, yet none of these things move us — then we glorify the Lord in the fires. Thus the three children, and the martyrs that sang at the stake.

Verses 16–23

These verses, as those before, plainly speak,

I. Comfort to saints. They may be driven, by the common calamities of the places where they live, into *the uttermost parts of the earth,* or perhaps they are forced thither for their religion; but there they are singing, not sighing. Thence have we heard songs, and it is a comfort to us to hear them, to hear that good people carry their religion along with them even to the most distant regions, to hear that God visits them there and gives encouragement to hope that he will gather them thence, Deu. 30:4. And this is their song, *even glory to the righteous:* the word is singular, and may refer to *the righteous God,* who is just in all he has brought upon us. This is glorifying the Lord in the fires. Or the meaning may be, "These songs redound to the glory or beauty of the righteous that sing them." We do the greatest honour imaginable to ourselves when we employ ourselves in honouring and glorifying God. This may have reference to the sending of the gospel to the uttermost parts of the earth, as far as this island of ours, in the days of the Messiah, the glad tidings of which are echoed back in songs heard thence, from churches planted there, even glory to the righteous God, agreeing with the angels' song, *Glory be to God in the highest,* and glory to all righteous men; for the work of redemption was ordained before the world for our glory.

II. Terror to sinners. The prophet, having comforted himself and others with the prospect of a saved remnant, returns to lament the miseries he saw breaking in like a mighty torrent upon the earth: *"But I said, My leanness! my leanness! woe unto me!* The very thought of it frets me, and makes me lean," *v.* 16. He foresees,

1. The prevalency of sin, that iniquity should abound (v. 16): *The treacherous dealers have dealt treacherously;* this is itself a judgment, and that which provokes God to bring other judgments. (1.) Men are false to one another; there is no faith in man, but a universal dishonesty. Truth, that sacred bond of society, has departed, and there is nothing but treachery in men's dealings. See Jer. 9:1, 2. (2.) They are all false to their God; as to him, and their covenant with him, the children of men are all treacherous dealers, and have dealt very treacherously with their God, in departing from their allegiance to him. This is the original, and this the aggravation, of the sin of the world; and, when men have been false to their God, how should they be true to any other?

2. The prevalency of wrath and judgment for that sin. (2.) The inhabitants of the earth will be pursued from time to time, from place to place, by one mischief or other (v. 17, 18): *Fear, and the pit, and the snare* (fear of the pit and the snare) are upon them wherever they are; for the sons of men know not what evil they may suddenly be snared in, Eccl. 9:12. These three words seem to be chosen for the sake of an elegant paranomasia, or, as we now scornfully call it, a jungle of words: *Pachad,* and *Pachath,* and *Pach;* but the meaning is plain (v. 18), that *evil pursues sinners* (Prov. 13:21), that the curse shall overtake the disobedient (Deu. 28:15), that those who are secure because they have escaped one judgment know not how soon another may arrest them. What this prophet threatens all the inhabitants of the earth with another makes part of the judgment of Moab, Jer. 48:43, 44. But it is a common instance of the calamitous state of human life that when we seek to avoid one mischief we fall into a worse, and that the end of one trouble is often the beginning of another;

so that we are least safe when we are most secure. (2.) The earth itself will be shaken to pieces. It will be literally so at last, when all *the works therein shall be burnt up;* and it is often figuratively so before that period. *The windows from on high are open* to pour down wrath, as in the universal deluge. *Upon the wicked God shall rain snares* (Ps. 11:6); and, the fountains of the great deep being broken up, *the foundations of the earth do shake* of course, the frame of nature is unhinged, and all is in confusion. See how elegantly this is expressed (*v.* 19, 20): *The earth is utterly broken down; it is clean dissolved; it is moved exceedingly,* moved out of its place. *God shakes heaven and earth,* Hag. 2:6. See the misery of those who lay up their treasure in the things of the earth and mind those things; they place their confidence in that which will shortly be *utterly broken down and dissolved. The earth shall reel to and fro like a drunkard;* so unsteady, so uncertain, are all the motions of these things. Worldly men dwell in it as in a palace, as in a castle, as in an impregnable tower; but *it shall be removed like a cottage,* so easily, so suddenly, and with so little loss to the great landlord. The pulling down of the earth will be but like the pulling down of *a cottage,* which the country is willing to be rid of, because it does but harbour beggars; and therefore no care is taken to rebuild it: It *shall fall, and not rise again;* but there shall be new heavens and a new earth, in which shall dwell nothing but righteousness. But what is it that shakes the earth thus and sinks it? It is the transgression thereof that shall be heavy upon it. Note, Sin is a burden to the whole creation; it is a heavy burden, a burden under which it groans now and will sink at last. Sin is the ruin of states, and kingdoms, and families; they fall under the weight of that *talent of lead,* Zec. 5:7, 8. (3.) God will have a particular controversy with the kings and great men of the earth (*v.* 21): *He will punish the host of the high ones.* Hosts of princes are no more before God than hosts of common men; what can a host of high ones do with their combined force when the Most High, the Lord of hosts, contends with them to abase their height, and scatter their hosts, and break all their confederacies? The high ones, that are on high, that are puffed up with their height and grandeur, that think themselves so high that they are out of the reach of any danger, God will visit upon them all their pride and cruelty, with which they have oppressed and injured their neighbours and subjects, and it shall now return upon their own heads. *The kings of the earth* shall now be reckoned with *upon the earth,* to show that verily there is a God that judges in the earth and will render to the proudest of kings according to the fruit of their doings. Let those that are trampled upon by the high ones of the earth comfort themselves with this, that though they cannot, dare not, must not, resist them, yet there is a God that will call them to an account, that will triumph over them upon their own dunghill: for the earth they are kings of is in the eye of God no better. This is general only. It is particularly foretold (*v.* 22) that they shall be *gathered together as prisoners,* convicted condemned prisoners, are *gathered in the pit,* or dungeon, and there they shall *be shut up* under close confinement. The kings and high ones, who took all possible liberty themselves, and took a pride and pleasure in shutting up others, shall now be themselves shut up. Let not the free man glory in his freedom, any more than the strong man in his strength, for he knows not what restraints he is reserved for. But *after many days they shall be visited,* either, [1.] They shall be visited in wrath; it is the same word, in another form, that is used (*v.* 21), *the Lord shall punish* them; they shall be reserved to the day of execution, as condemned prisoners are, and as fallen angels are *reserved in chains of darkness to the judgment of the great day,* Jude 6. Let this account for the delays of divine vengeance; sentence is not executed speedily, because execution-day has not yet come, and perhaps will not come till after many days; but it is certain that the wicked is reserved for the day of destruction, and is therefore preserved in the mean time, but *shall be brought forth to the day of wrath,* Job 21:30. Let us therefore judge nothing before the time. [2.] They shall be visited in mercy, and be discharged from their imprisonment, and shall again obtain, if not their dignity, yet their liberty. Nebuchadnezzar, in his conquests, made many kings and princes his captives, and kept them in the dungeon in Babylon, and, among the rest, Jehoiachin King of Judah; but after many days, when Nebuchadnezzar's head was laid, his son visited them, and granted (as should seem) some reviving to them all in their bondage; for it is made an instance of his particular kindness to Jehoiachin that he *set his throne above the throne of the rest of the kings that were with him,* Jer. 52:32. If we apply this to the general state of mankind, it imports a revolution of conditions; those that were high are punished, those that were punished are relieved, after many days, that none in this world may be secure though their condition be ever so prosperous, nor any despair though their condition be ever so deplorable.

3. Glory to God in all this, *v.* 23. When all this comes to pass, when the proud enemies of God's church are humbled and brought down, (1.) Then it shall appear, beyond contradiction, that the Lord reigns, which is always true, but not always alike evident. When the kings of the earth are punished for their tyranny and oppression, then it is proclaimed and proved to all the world that God is King of kings — King above them, by whom they are accountable — that he reigns as *Lord of hosts,* of all hosts, of their hosts, — that he reigns *in Mount Zion, and in Jerusalem,* in his church, for the honour and welfare of that, pursuant to the promises on which that is founded, reigns in his word and ordinances, — that he reigns *before his ancients,* before all his saints, especially before his ministers, the elders of his church, who have their eye upon all the out-goings of his power and providence, and, in all these events, observe his hand. God's ancients, the old disciples, the experienced Christians, that have often, when they have been perplexed, gone into the sanctuary of God in Zion and Jerusalem, and acquainted themselves with his manifestations of himself there, shall see more than others of God's dominion and sovereignty in these operations of his providence. (2.) Then it shall appear, beyond comparison, that he reigns *gloriously,* in such brightness and lustre that *the moon shall be confounded and the sun ashamed,* as the smaller lights are eclipsed and extinguished by the greater. Great men, who thought themselves to have as bright a lustre and as vast a dominion as the sun and moon, shall be ashamed when God appears above them, much more when he appears against them. Then shall *their faces be filled with shame,* that they may seek God's name. The eastern nations worshipped the sun and moon; but, when God shall appear so gloriously for his people against his and their enemies, all these pretended deities shall be ashamed that ever they received the homage of their deluded worshippers. The glory of the Creator infinitely outshines the glory of the brightest creatures. In the great day, when the Judge of heaven and earth shall shine forth in his glory, *the sun shall* by his transcendent lustre *be turned into darkness and the moon into blood.*

CHAPTER 25

After the threatenings of wrath in the foregoing chapter we have here, I. Thankful praises for what God had done, which the prophet, in the name of the church, offers up to God, and teaches us to offer the like (*v.* 1–5). II. Precious promises of what God would yet further do for his church, especially in the grace of the gospel (*v.* 6–8). III. The church's triumph in God over her enemies thereupon (*v.* 9–12). This chapter looks as pleasantly upon the church as the former looked dreadfully upon the world.

Verses 1–5

It is said in the close of the foregoing chapter that the *Lord of hosts shall reign gloriously;* now, in compliance with this, the prophet here speaks of *the glorious majesty of his kingdom* (Ps. 145:12), and gives him the glory of it; and, however this prophecy might have an accomplishment in the destruction of Babylon and the deliverance of the Jews out of their captivity there, it seems to look further, to the praises that should be offered up to God by the gospel church for Christ's victories over our spiritual enemies and the comforts he has provided for all believers. Here,

I. The prophet determines to praise God himself; for those that would stir up others should in the first place stir up themselves to praise God (*v.* 1): *"O Lord! thou art my God,* a God in covenant with me." When God is punishing *the kings of the earth upon the earth,* and making them to tremble before him, a poor prophet can go to him, and, with a humble boldness, say, *O Lord! thou art my God,* and therefore *I will exalt thee, I will praise thy name.* Those that have the Lord for their God are bound to praise him; for *therefore* he took us to be his people *that we might be unto him for a name and for a praise,* Jer. 13:11. In praising God we exalt him; not that we can make him higher than he is, but we must make him to appear to ourselves and others than he does. See Ex. 15:2.

II. He pleases himself with the thought that others also shall be brought to praise God, *v.* 3. *"Therefore,* because of the *desolations thou hast made in the earth* by thy providence (Ps. 46:8) and the just vengeance thou hast taken on thy and thy church's enemies, *therefore shall the strong people glorify thee* in concert, *and the city* (the metropolis) *of the terrible nations fear thee."* This may be understood, 1. Of those people that have been strong and terrible against God. Those that have been enemies to God's kingdom, and have fought against the interests of it with a great deal of strength and terror, shall either be converted, and glorify God by joining with his people in his service, or at least convinced, so as to own themselves conquered. Those that have been the terror of the mighty shall be forced to tremble before the judgments of God and call in vain to rocks and mountains to hide them. Or, 2. Of those that shall be now made strong and terrible for God and by him, though before they were weak and trampled upon. God shall so visibly appear for and with those that fear him and glorify him that all shall acknowledge them a strong people and shall stand in awe of them. There was a time when *many of the people of the land became Jews, for the fear of the Jews fell upon them* (Esther 8:17), and when those that knew their God were strong and did exploits (Dan. 11:32), for which they glorified God.

III. He observes what is, and ought to be, the matter of this praise. We and others must exalt God and praise him; for, 1. He has done wonders, according to the counsel of his own will, *v.* 1. We exalt God by admiring what he has done as truly wonderful, wonderful proofs of his power beyond what any creature could perform, and wonderful proofs of his goodness beyond what such sinful creatures as we are could expect. These *wonderful things,* which are new and surprising to us, and altogether unthought of, are according to his *counsels of old,* devised by his wisdom and designed for his own glory and the comfort of his people. All the operations of providence are according to God's eternal counsels (and those faithfulness and truth itself), all consonant to his attributes, consistent with one another, and sure to be accomplished in their season. 2. He has in particular humbled the pride, and broken the power, of the mighty ones of the earth (*v.* 2): *"Thou hast made of a city,* of many a city, *a heap* of rubbish. Of many a defenced city, that thought itself well guarded by nature and art, and the multitude and courage of its militia, thou hast made a ruin." What created strength can hold out against Omnipotence? "Many a city so richly built that it might be called a *palace,* and so much frequented and visited by persons of the best rank from all parts that it might be called a *palace of strangers,* thou hast made to be no city; it is levelled with the ground, and not one stone left upon another, and it shall never be built again." This has been the case of many cities in divers parts of the world, and in our own nation particularly; cities that flourished once have gone to decay and are lost, and it is scarcely known (except by urns or coins digged up out of the earth) where they stood. How many of the cities of Israel have long since been heaps and ruins! God hereby teaches us that *here we have no continuing city* and must therefore seek one to come which will never be a ruin or go to decay. 3. He has seasonably relieved and succoured his necessitous and distressed people (*v.* 4): *Thou has been a strength to the poor, a strength to the needy.* As God weakens the strong that are proud and secure, so he strengthens the weak that are humble and serious, and stay themselves upon him. Nay, he not only makes them strong, but he is himself their strength; for in him they strengthen themselves, and it is his favour that is the *strength of their hearts.* He is a *strength to the needy in his distress,* when he needs strength, and when his distress drives him to God. And, as he strengthens them against their inward decays, so he shelters them from outward assaults. He is *a refuge from the storm* of rain or hail, and *a shadow from the* scorching *heat* of the sun in summer. God is a sufficient protection to his people in all weathers, hot and cold, wet and dry. The armour of righteousness serves both *on the right hand* and *on the left,* 2 Co. 6:7. Whatever dangers or troubles God's people may be in, effectual care is taken that they shall sustain no real hurt or damage. When perils are most threatening and alarming God will then appear for the safety of his people: *When the blast of the terrible ones is as a storm against the wall,* which makes a great noise, but cannot overthrow the wall. The enemies of God's poor are terrible ones; they do all they can to make themselves so to them. Their rage is like a blast of wind, loud, and blustering, and furious; but, like the wind, it is under a divine check; for God *holds the winds in his fist,* and God will be such a shelter to his people that they shall be able to stand the shock, keep their ground, and maintain their integrity and peace. A storm beating on a ship tosses it, but that which beats on a wall never stirs it, Ps. 76:10; 138:7. 4. That he does and will shelter those that trust in him from the insolence of their proud oppressors (*v.* 5): *Thou shalt,* or thou dost, *bring down the noise of strangers;* thou shalt abate and still it, as *the heat in a dry place* is abated and moderated *by the shadow of a cloud* interposing. *The branch,* or rather the son or triumph, *of the terrible ones shall be brought low,* and they shall be made to change their note and lower their voice. Observe here, (1.) The oppressors of God's people are called *strangers;* for they forget that those they oppress are made of the same mould, of the same blood, with them. They are called *terrible ones;* for so they affect to be, rather than amiable ones: they would rather be feared than loved. (2.) Their insolence towards the people of God is noisy and hot, and that is all; it is but the noise of strangers, who think to carry their point by hectoring and bullying all that stand in their way, and talking big. *Pharaoh king of Egypt is but a noise,* Jer. 46:17. It is like the heat of the sun scorching in the middle of the day; but where is it when the sun has set? (3.) Their noise, and heat, and all their triumph, will be humbled and brought low, when their hopes are baffled and all their honours laid in the dust. The branches, even the top branches, of the terrible ones, will be broken off, and thrown to the dunghill. (4.) If the labourers in God's vineyard be at any time called to *bear the burden and heat of the day,* he will find some way or other to refresh them, as with the shadow of a cloud, that they may not be pressed above measure.

Verses 6–8

If we suppose (as many do) that this refers to the great joy which there should be in Zion and Jerusalem when the army of the Assyrians was routed by an angel, or when the Jews were released out of their captivity in Babylon, or upon occasion of some other equally surprising deliverance, yet we cannot avoid making it to look further, to the grace of the gospel and the glory which is the crown and consummation of that grace; for it is at our resurrection through Christ that the saying here written *shall be brought to pass;* then, and not till then (if we may believe St. Paul), it shall have its full accomplishment: *Death is swallowed up in victory,* 1 Co. 15:54. This is a key to the rest of the promises here connected together. And so we have here a prophecy of the salvation and the grace brought unto us by Jesus Christ, into which *the prophets enquired and searched diligently,* 1 Pt. 1:10.

I. That the grace of the gospel should be a royal feast for all people; not like that of Ahasuerus, which was intended only to show the grandeur of the master of the feast (Esther 1:4); for this is intended to gratify the guests, and therefore, whereas all *there* was for show, all *here* is for substance. The preparations made in the gospel for the kind reception of penitents and supplicants with God are often in the New Testament set forth by the similitude of *a feast,* as Mt. 22:1, etc., which seems to be borrowed from this prophecy. 1. God himself is the Master of the feast, and we may be sure he prepares like himself, as becomes him to give, rather than as becomes us to receive. *The Lord of hosts* makes this feast. 2. The guests invited are *all people,* Gentiles as well as Jews. *Go preach the gospel to every creature.* There is enough for all, and whoever will may come, and partake freely, even those that are gathered out of the highways and the hedges. 3. The place is *Mount Zion.* Thence the preaching of the gospel takes rise: the preachers must begin at Jerusalem. The gospel church is the Jerusalem that is above; there this feast is made, and to it all the invited guests must go. 4. The provision is very rich, and every thing is of the best. It is a *feast,* which supposes abundance and variety; it is a continual feast to believers, it is their own fault if it be not. It is *a feast of fat things and full of marrow;* so relishing, so nourishing, are the comforts of the gospel to all those that feast upon them and digest them. The returning prodigal was entertained with the fatted calf; and David has that pleasure in communion with God with which his soul is satisfied as with marrow and fatness. It is a feast *of wines on the lees,* the strongest-bodied wines, that have been kept long upon the lees, and then are well refined from them, so that they are clear and fine. There is that in the gospel which, like wine soberly used, makes glad the heart and raises the spirits, and is fit for those that are of a heavy heart, being under convictions of sin and mourning for it, that they may drink and forget their misery (for that is the proper use of wine — it is a cordial for those that need it, Prov. 31:5, 6), may be of good cheer, knowing that their sins are forgiven, and may be vigorous in their spiritual work and warfare, as a strong man refreshed with wine.

II. That the world should be freed from that darkness of ignorance and mistake in the mists of which it had been so long lost and buried (*v.* 7): *He will destroy in this mountain the face of the covering* (the covering of the face) with which all people are covered (hood-winked or blind-folded) so that they cannot see their way nor go about their work, and by reason of which they wander endlessly. Their faces are covered as those of men condemned, or dead men. There is *a veil spread over all nations,* for they all sit in darkness; and no marvel, when the Jews themselves, among whom *God was known,* had a *veil upon their hearts,* 2 Co. 3:15. But this veil the Lord will destroy, by the light of his gospel shining in the world, and the power of his Spirit opening men's eyes to receive it. He will raise those to spiritual life that have long been dead in trespasses and sins.

III. That death should be conquered, the power of it broken, and the property of it altered: *He will swallow up death in victory, v.* 8. 1. Christ will himself, in his resurrection, triumph over death, will break its bands, its bars, asunder, and cast away all its cords. The grave seemed to swallow him up, but really he swallowed it up. 2. The happiness of the saints shall be out of the reach of death, which puts a period to all the enjoyments of this world, embitters them, and stains the beauty of them. 3. Believers may triumph over death, and look upon it as a conquered enemy: *O death! where is thy sting?* 4. When the dead bodies of the saints shall be raised at the great day, and their mortality swallowed up of life, then death will be for ever swallowed up of victory; and it is the last enemy.

IV. That grief shall be banished, and there shall be perfect and endless joy: *The Lord God will wipe away tears from off all faces.* Those that mourn for sin shall be comforted and have their consciences pacified. In the covenant of grace there shall be that provided which is sufficient to counterbalance all the sorrows of this present time, to wipe away our tears, and to refresh us. Those particularly that suffer for Christ shall have consolations abounding as their afflictions do abound. But in the joys of heaven, and nowhere short of them, will fully be *brought to pass this saying,* as that before, for there it is that God shall *wipe away all tears,* Rev. 7:17; 21:4. And *there shall be no more sorrow,* because *there shall be no more death.* The hope of this should now wipe away all excessive tears, all the weeping that hinders sowing.

V. That all the reproach cast upon religion and the serious professors of it shall be for ever rolled away: *The rebuke of his people,* which they have long lain under, the calumnies and misrepresentations by which they have been blackened, the insolence and cruelty with which their persecutors have trampled on them and trodden them down, *shall be taken away.* Their righteousness shall be brought forth as the light, in the view of all the world, who shall be convinced that they are not such as they have been invidiously characterized; and so their salvation from the injuries done them as such shall be wrought out. Sometimes in this world God does that for his people which *takes away their reproach from among men.* However, it will be done effectually at the great day; for the *Lord has spoken it,* who can, and will, make it good. Let us patiently bear sorrow and shame now, and improve both; for shortly both will be done away.

Verses 9–12

Here is, I. The welcome which the church shall give to these blessings promised in the foregoing verses (*v.* 9): *It shall be said in that day,* with a humble holy triumph and exultation, *Lo, this is our God; we have waited for him!* Thus will the deliverance of the church out of long and sore troubles be celebrated; thus will it be as life from the dead. With such transports of joy and praise will those entertain the glad tidings of the Redeemer who looked for him, and for redemption in Jerusalem by him; and with such a triumphant song as this will glorified saints *enter into the joy of their Lord.* 1. God himself must have the glory of all: *"Lo, this is our God, this is the Lord.* This which is done is his doing, and it is marvellous in our eyes. Herein he has done like himself, has magnified his own wisdom, power, and goodness. Herein he has done for us like our God, a God in covenant with us, and whom we serve." Note, Our triumphs must not terminate in what God does for us and gives to us, but must pass through them to himself, who is the author and giver of them: *This is our God.* Have any of the nations of the earth such a God to trust to? No, *their rock is not as our rock. There is none like unto the God of Jerusalem.* 2. The longer it has been expected the more welcome it is. "This is he whom we have waited for, in dependence upon his word of promise, and a full assurance that he would come in the set time, in due time, and therefore we were willing to tarry his time; and now we find it is not in vain to wait for him, for the mercy comes at last, with an abundant recompence for the delay." 3. It is matter of joy unspeakable: *"We will be glad and rejoice in his salvation.* We that share in the benefits of it will concur in the joyful thanksgivings for it." 4. It is an encouragement to hope for the continuance and perfection of this salvation: *We have waited for him, and he will save us,* will carry on what he has begun; for *as for God,* our God, *his work is perfect.*

II. A prospect of further blessings for the securing and perpetuating of these. 1. The power of God shall be engaged for them and shall continue to take their part: *In this mountain shall the hand of the Lord rest, v.* 10. The church and people of God shall have continued proofs of God's presence with them and residence among them: his hand shall be continually over them, to protect and guard them, and continually stretched out to them, for their supply. Mount Zion is *his rest for ever;* here he will dwell. 2. The power of their enemies, which is engaged against them, shall be broken. *Moab* is here put for all the adversaries of God's people, that are vexatious to them; they *shall* all *be trodden down* or threshed (for *then* they beat out the corn by treading it) and shall be thrown out as *straw to the dunghill,* being good for nothing else. God having *caused his hand to rest upon this mountain,* it shall not be a hand that hangs down, or is folded up, feeble and inactive; but he shall *spread forth his hands, in the midst* of his people, *like one that swims,* which intimates that he will employ and exert his power for them vigorously, — that he will be doing for them on all sides, — that he will easily and effectually put by the opposition that is given to his gracious intentions for them, and thereby further and push forward his good work among them, — and that on their behalf he will be continually active, for so the swimmer is. It is foretold, particularly, what he shall do for them. (1.) *He shall bring down the pride* of their enemies (and Moab was notoriously guilty of pride, *ch.* 16:6) by one humbling judgment after another, stripping them of that which they are proud of. (2.) He shall bring down *the spoils of their hands,* shall take from them that which they have got by spoil and rapine. He shall bring down the arms of their hands, which are lifted up against God's Israel; he shall quite break their power, and disable them to do mischief. (3.) He shall ruin all their fortifications, *v.* 12. Moab has his walls, and his high forts, with which he hopes to secure himself, and from which he designs to annoy the people of God; but God shall *bring them all down, lay them low, bring them to the ground, to the dust;* and so those who trusted to them will be left exposed. There is no fortress impregnable to Omnipotence, no fort so high but the arm of the Lord can overtop it and bring it down. This destruction of Moab is typical of Christ's victory over death (spoken of *v.* 8), his spoiling principalities and powers in his cross (Col. 2:15), his pulling down Satan's strong-holds by the preaching of his gospel (2 Co. 10:4), and his reigning till all his enemies be *made his footstool,* Ps. 110:1.

CHAPTER 26

This chapter is a song of holy joy and praise, in which the great things God had engaged, in the foregoing chapter, to do for his people against his enemies and their enemies are celebrated: it is prepared to be sung when that prophecy should be accomplished; for we must be forward to meet God with our thanksgivings when he is coming towards us with his mercies. Now the people of God are here taught, I. To triumph in the safety and holy security both of the church in general and of every particular member of it, under the divine protection (v. 1–4). II. To triumph over all opposing powers (v. 5, 6). III. To walk with God, and wait for him, in the worst and darkest times, v. 7–9. IV. To lament the stupidity of those who regarded not the providence of God, either merciful or afflictive (v. 10, 11). V. To encourage themselves, and one another, with hopes that God would still continue to do them good (v. 12, 14), and engage themselves to continue in his service (v. 13). VI. To recollect the kind providences of God towards them in their low and distressed condition, and their conduct under those providences (v. 15–18). VII. To rejoice in hope of a glorious deliverance, which should be as a resurrection to them (v. 19), and to retire in the expectation of it (v. 20, 21). And this is written for the support and assistance of the faith and hope of God's people in all ages, even those upon whom the ends of the world have come.

Verses 1–4

To the prophecies of gospel grace very fitly is a song annexed, in which we may give God the glory and take to ourselves the comfort of that grace: *In that day,* the gospel day, which the day of the victories and enlargements of the Old-Testament church was typical of (to some of which perhaps this has a primary reference), *in that day this song shall be sung;* there shall be persons to sing it, and cause and hearts to sing it; it shall be sung *in the land of Judah,* which was a figure of the gospel church; for the gospel covenant is said to be made *with the house of Judah,* Heb. 8:8. Glorious things are here said of the church of God.

I. That it is strongly fortified against those that are bad (v. 1): *We have a strong city.* It is a city incorporated by the charter of the everlasting covenant, fitted for the reception of all that are made free by that charter, for their employment and entertainment; it is a strong city, as Jerusalem was, while it was a city compact together, and had God himself a wall of fire round about it, so strong that none would have believed that an enemy could ever *enter into the gates of Jerusalem,* Lam. 4:12. The church is a strong city, for it has *walls and bulwarks,* or counterscarps, and those of God's own appointing; for he has, in his promise, appointed salvation itself to be its defence. Those that are designed for salvation will find that to be their protection, 1 Pt. 1:4.

II. That it is richly replenished with those that are good, and they are instead of fortifications to it; for the inhabitants of Jerusalem, if they are such as they should be, are its strength, Zec. 12:5. The gates are here ordered to be opened, *that the righteous nation, which keeps the truth, may enter in, v.* 2. They had been banished and driven out by the iniquity of the former times, but now the laws that were made against them are repealed, and they have liberty to enter in again. Or, There is an act for a general naturalization of all the righteous, whatever nation they are of, encouraging them to come and settle in Jerusalem. When God has done great things for any place or people he expects that thus they should render according to the benefit done unto them; they should be kind to his people, and take them under their protection and into their bosom. Note, 1. It is the character of righteous men that they keep the truths of God, a firm belief of which will have a commanding influence upon the regularity of the whole conversation. Good principles fixed in the head will produce good resolutions in the heart and good practices in the life. 2. It is the interest of states to countenance such, and court them among them, for they bring a blessing with them.

III. That all who belong to it are safe and easy, and have a holy security and serenity of mind in the assurance of God's favour. 1. This is here the matter of a promise (v. 3): *Thou wilt keep him in peace, peace,* in *perfect peace,* inward peace, outward peace, peace with God, peace of conscience, peace at all times, under all events; this peace shall *he* be put into, and kept in the possession of, *whose mind is stayed upon God, because it trusts in him.* It is the character of every good man that he trusts in God, puts himself under his guidance and government, and depends upon him that it shall be greatly to his advantage to do so. Those that trust in God must have their minds stayed upon him, must trust him at all times, under all events,

must firmly and faithfully adhere to him, with an entire satisfaction in him; and such as do so God will keep in perpetual peace, and that peace shall keep them. When evil tidings are abroad *those* shall calmly expect the event, and not be disturbed by frightful apprehensions arising from them, whose hearts are *fixed, trusting in the Lord,* Ps. 112:7. 2. It is the matter of a precept (v. 4): "Let us make ourselves easy by *trusting in the Lord for ever;* since God has promised peace to those that stay themselves upon him, let us not lose the benefit of that promise, but repose an entire confidence in him. Trust in him for ever, at all times, when you have nothing else to trust to; trust in him for that peace, that portion, which will be for ever." Whatever we trust to the world for, it will be but for a moment: all we expect from it is confined within the limits of time. But what we trust in God for will last as long as we shall last. For in the *Lord Jehovah — Jah, Jehovah,* in him who was, and is, and is to come, there is a rock of ages, a firm and lasting foundation for faith and hope to build upon; and the house built on that rock will stand in a storm. Those that trust in God shall not only find in him, but receive *from him, everlasting strength,* strength that will carry them to everlasting life, to that blessedness which is for ever; and therefore let them trust in him for ever, and never cast away nor change their confidence.

Verses 5–11

Here the prophet further encourages us to trust in the Lord for ever, and to continue waiting on him; for,

I. He will make humble souls that trust in him to triumph over their proud enemies, v. 5, 6. Those that exalt themselves shall be abased: For he *brings down those that dwell on high;* and wherein they deal proudly he is, and will be, above them. Even the lofty city Babylon itself, or Nineveh, he lays it low, *ch.* 25:12. He can do it, be it ever so well fortified. He has often done it. He will do it, for he resists the proud. It is his glory to do it, for he proves himself to be God by *looking on the proud and abasing them,* Job 40:12. But, on the contrary, those that humble themselves shall be exalted; for *the feet of the poor* shall tread upon the lofty cities, v. 6. He does not say, Great armies shall tread them down; but, When God will have it done, even the feet of the poor shall do it, Mal. 4:3. *You shall tread down the wicked. Come, set your feet on the necks of these kings.* See Ps. 147:6; Rom. 16:20.

II. He takes cognizance of the way of his people and has delight in it (v. 7): *The way of the just is evenness* (so it may be read): it is their endeavour and constant care to walk with God in an even steady course of obedience and holy conversation. *My foot stands in an even place,* goes in an even path, Ps. 26:12. And it is their happiness that God makes their way plain and easy before them: *Thou, most upright, dost level* (or *make even) the path of the just,* by preventing or removing those things that would be stumbling-blocks to them, so that nothing shall offend them, Ps. 119:165. God *weighs* it (so we read it); he considers it, and will give them grace sufficient for them, to help them over all the difficulties they may meet with in their way. Thus with the upright God will show himself upright.

III. It is our duty, and will be our comfort, to wait for God, and to keep up holy desires towards him in the darkest and most discouraging times, v. 8, 9. This has always been the practice of God's people, even when God has frowned upon them, 1. To keep up a constant dependence upon him: "*In the way of thy judgments we* have still *waited for thee;* when thou hast corrected us we have looked to no other hand than thine to relieve us," as the servant looks only *to the hand of his master, till he have mercy upon him,* Ps. 123:2. We cannot appeal from God's justice but to his mercy. If God's judgments continue long, if it be *a road of judgments* (so the word signifies), yet we must not be weary but continue waiting. 2. To send up holy desires towards him. Our troubles, how pressing soever, must never put us out of conceit with our religion, nor turn us away from God; but still *the desire of our soul must be to his name and to the remembrance of him;* and in the night, the darkest longest night of affliction, *with our souls must we desire him.* (1.) Our great concern must be for God's name, and our earnest desire must be that his name may be glorified, whatever becomes of us and our names. This is that which we must wait for, and pray for. "Father, glo-

rify *thy name,* and we are satisfied." (2.) Our great comfort must be in the remembrance of that name, of all that whereby God has made himself known. The remembrance of God must be our great support and pleasure; and, though sometimes we be unmindful of him, yet still our desire must be towards the remembrance of him and we must take pains with our own hearts to have him always in mind. (3.) Our desires towards God must be inward, fervent, and sincere. With our soul we must desire him, with our soul we must pant after him (Ps. 42:1), and with our spirits within us, with the innermost thought and the closest application of mind, we must seek him. We make nothing of our religion, whatever our profession be, if we do not make heart-work of it. (4.) Even in the darkest night of affliction our desires must be towards God, as our sun and shield; for, however God is pleased to deal with us, we must never think the worse of him, nor cool in our love to him. (5.) If our desires be indeed towards God,. we must give evidence that they are so by seeking him, and seeking him early, as those that desire to find him, and dread the thoughts of missing him. Those that would seek God and find him must seek betimes, and seek him earnestly. Though we come ever so early, we shall find him ready to receive us.

IV. It is God's gracious design, in sending abroad his judgments, thereby to bring men to seek him and serve him: *When thy judgments are upon the earth,* laying all waste, then we have reason to expect that not only God's professing people, but even *the inhabitants of the world, will learn righteousness,* will have their mistakes rectified and their lives reformed, will be brought to acknowledge God's righteousness in punishing them, will repent of their own unrighteousness in offending God, and so be brought to walk in right paths. They will do this; that is, judgments are designed to bring them to this, they have a natural tendency to produce this effect, and, though many continue obstinate, yet some even of the inhabitants of the world will profit by this discipline, and will learn righteousness; surely they will; they are strangely stupid if they do not. Note, The intention of afflictions is to teach us righteousness; and blessed is the man whom God chastens, and thus teaches, Ps. 94:12. *Discite justitiam, moniti, et non temnere divos — Let this rebuke teach you to cultivate righteousness, and cease from despising the gods.* — Virgil.

V. Those are wicked indeed that will not be wrought upon by the favourable methods God takes to subdue and reform them; and it is necessary that God should deal with them in a severe way by his judgments, which shall prevail to humble those that would not otherwise be humbled. Observe,

1. How sinners walk contrary to God, and refuse to comply with the means used for their reformation and to answer the intentions of them, v. 10. (1.) *Favour is shown* to them. They receive many mercies from God; he causes his sun to shine and his rain to fall upon them, nay, he prospers them, and into their hands he brings plentifully; they escape many of the strokes of God's judgments, which others less wicked than they have been cut off by; in some particular instances they seem to be remarkably favoured above their neighbours, and the design of all this is that they may be won upon to love and serve that God who thus favours them; and yet it is all in vain: *They will not learn righteousness,* will not be led to repentance by the goodness of God, and therefore it is requisite that God should send his judgments into the earth, to reckon with men for abused mercies. (2.) They live *in a land of uprightness,* where religion is professed and is in reputation, where the word of God is preached, and where they have many good examples set them, — in a land of *evenness,* where there are not so many stumbling-blocks as in other places, — in a land of *correction,* where vice and profaneness are discountenanced and punished; yet there they will *deal unjustly,* and go on frowardly in their evil ways. Those that do wickedly deal unjustly both with God and man, as well as with their own souls; and those that will not be reclaimed by the justice of the nation may expect the judgments of God upon them. Nor can those expect a place hereafter in the land of blessedness who now conform not to the laws and usages, nor improve the privileges and advantages, of the land of uprightness; and why do they not? It is because they *will not behold the majesty of the Lord,* will not believe, will not consider, what a God of terrible

majesty he is whose laws and justice they persist in the contempt of. God's majesty appears in all the dispensations of his providence; but they regard it not, and therefore study not to answer the ends of those dispensations. Even when we receive of the mercy of the Lord we must still behold the *majesty of the Lord and his goodness.* (3.) God lifts up his hand to give them warning, that they may, by repentance and prayer, make their peace with him; but they take no notice of it, are not aware that God is angry with them, or coming forth against them: *They will not see,* and none so blind as those who will not see, who shut their eyes against the clearest conviction of guilt and wrath, who ascribe that to chance, or common fate, which is manifestly a divine rebuke, who regard not the threatening symptoms of their own ruin, but cry Peace to themselves, when the righteous God is waging war with them.

2. How God will at length be too hard for them; for, when he judges, he will overcome: *They will not see, but they shall see,* shall be made to see, whether they will or no, that God is angry with them. Atheists, scorners, and the secure, will shortly feel what now they will not believe, that *it is a fearful thing to fall into the hands of the living God.* They will not see the evil of sin, and particularly the sin of hating and persecuting the people of God; but they shall see, by the tokens of God's displeasure against them for it and the deliverances in which God will plead his people's cause, that what is done against them he takes as done against himself and will reckon for it accordingly. They shall see that they have done God's people a great deal of wrong, and therefore shall be ashamed of their enmity and envy towards them, and their ill usage of such as deserved better treatment. Note, Those that bear ill-will to God's people have reason to be ashamed of it, so absurd and unreasonable is it; and, sooner or later, they shall be ashamed of it, and the remembrance of it shall fill them with confusion. Some read it, *They shall see and be confounded for the zeal of the people,* by the zeal God will show for his people; when they shall be made to know how jealous God is for the honour and welfare of his people they shall be confounded to think that they might have been of that people and would not. Their doom therefore is that, since they slighted the happiness of God's friends, *the fire of his enemies shall devour them,* that is, the fire which is prepared for his enemies and with which they shall be devoured, the fire designed for the devil and his angels. Note, Those that are enemies to God's people, and envy them, God looks upon as his enemies, and will deal with them accordingly.

Verses 12–19

The prophet in these verses looks back upon what God had done with them, both in mercy and judgment, and sings unto God of both, and then looks forward upon what he hoped God would do for them. Observe,

I. His reviews and reflections are mixed. When he looks back upon the state of the church he finds,

1. That God had in many instances been very gracious to them and had done great things for them. (1.) In general (*v.* 12): *Thou hast wrought all our works in us,* or for us. Whatever good work is done by us, it is owing to a good work wrought by the grace of God in us; it is he that puts good thoughts and affections into our hearts if at any time they be there, and that *works in us both to will and to do of his good pleasure. Acti, agimus — Being acted upon, we act.* And if any kindness be shown us, or any of our affairs be prosperous and successful, it is God that works it for us. Every creature, every business, that is in any way serviceable to our comfort, is made by him to be so; and sometimes he makes that to work for us which seemed to make against us. (2.) In particular (*v.* 15): *"Thou hast increased the nation, O Lord!* so that a little one has become a thousand (in Egypt they multiplied exceedingly, and afterwards in Canaan, so that they filled the land); and in this *thou art glorified,"* for the multitude of the people is the honour of the prince, and therein God was glorified as faithful to his covenant with Abraham, that he would make him a father of many nations. Note, God's nation is a growing nation, and it is the glory of God that it is so. The increase of the church, that holy nation, is *therefore* to be rejoiced in because it is the increase of those that make it their business to glorify God in this world.

2. That yet he had laid them under his rebukes.

(1.) The neighbouring nations had sometimes oppressed them and tyrannised over them (*v.* 13): *"O Lord our God!* thou who hast the sole right to rule us, whose subjects and servants we are, to thee we complain (for whither else should we go with our complaints?) that *other lords besides thee have had dominion over us."* Not only in the days of the Judges, but afterwards, God frequently sold them into the hand of their enemies, or rather, by their iniquities, they *sold themselves, ch.* 52:3–5. When they had been careless in the service of God, God suffered their enemies to have dominion over them, that they might know the difference between his service *and the service of the kingdoms of the countries.* It may be understood as a confession of sin, their serving other gods, and subjecting themselves to the superstitious laws and customs of their neighbours, by which other lords (for they called their idols *baals, lords*) had dominion over them, besides God. But now they promise that it shall be so no more: "Henceforth *by thee only will we make mention of thy name;* we will worship thee only, and in that way only which thou hast instituted and appointed." The same may be our penitent reflection: *Other lords, besides God, have had dominion over us;* every lust has been our lord, and we have been led captive by it; and it is has been long enough, and too long, that we have thus wronged both God and ourselves. The same therefore must be our pious resolution, that henceforth we will make mention of God's name only and by him only, that we will keep close to God and to our duty and never desert it.

(2.) They had sometimes been carried into captivity before their enemies (*v.* 15): "The nation which at first thou didst increase, and make to take root, thou hast now diminished, and plucked up, and *removed to all the ends of the earth, driven out to the utmost parts of heaven,"* as is threatened, Deu. 30:4; 28:64. But observe, Between the mention of the increasing of them and that of the removing of them it is said, *Thou art glorified;* for the judgments God inflicts upon his people for their sins are for his honour, as well as the mercies he bestows upon them in performance of his promise.

(3.) The prophet remembers that when they were thus oppressed and carried captive they cried unto God, which was a good evidence that they neither had quite forsaken him nor were quite forsaken of him, and that there were merciful intentions in the judgments they were under (*v.* 16): *Lord, in trouble have they visited thee.* This was usual with the people of Israel, as we find frequently in the story of the Judges. When *other lords had dominion over them* they *humbled themselves, and said, The Lord is righteous,* 2 Chr. 12:6. See here, [1.] The need we have of afflictions. They are necessary to stir up prayer; when it is said, *In trouble have they visited thee,* it is implied that in their peace and prosperity they were strangers to God, kept at a distance from him, and seldom came near him, as if, when the world smiled upon them, they had no occasion for his favours. [2.] The benefit we often have by afflictions. They bring us to God, quicken us to our duty, and show us our dependence upon him. Those that before seldom looked at God now visit him; they come frequently, they become friendly, and make their court to him. Before, prayer came drop by drop, but now they *pour out a prayer;* it comes now like water from a fountain, not like water from a still. They poured out *a secret speech;* so the margin. Praying is speaking to God, but it is a secret speech; for it is the language of the heart, otherwise it is not praying. Afflictions bring us to secret prayer, in which we may be more free and particular in our addresses to him than we can be in public. In affliction those will seek God early who before sought him slowly, Hos. 5:15. It will make men fervent and fluent in prayer. "They poured out a prayer, as the drink-offerings were poured out, when thy chastening was upon them." But it is to be feared, when the chastening is off them, they will by degrees return to their former carelessness, as they had often done.

(4.) He complains that their struggles for their own liberty had been very painful and perilous, but that they had not been successful, *v.* 17, 18. [1.] They had the throes and pangs they dreaded: "We have been like a woman in labour, that cries out in her pangs; we have with a great deal of anxiety and toil endeavoured to help ourselves, and our troubles have been increased by those attempts;" as when Moses came to deliver Israel the tale of bricks was dou-

bled. Their prayers were quickened by the acuteness of their pains, and became as strong and vehement as the cries of a woman in sore travail. *So have we been in thy sight, O Lord!* It was a comfort and satisfaction to them, in their distress, that God had his eye upon them, that all their miseries were in his sight; he was no stranger to their pangs or their prayers. *Lord, all my desire is before thee, and my groaning is not hidden from thee,* Ps. 38:9. Whenever they came to *present themselves before the Lord* with their complaints and petitions they were in agonies like those of a woman in travail. [2.] They came short of the issue and success they desired and hoped for: *"We have been with child;* we have had great expectation of a speedy and happy deliverance, have been big with hopes, and, when we have been in pain, have comforted ourselves with this, that the joyful birth would make us forget *our misery,* Jn. 16:21. But, alas! *we have as it were brought forth wind;* it has proved a false conception; our expectations have been frustrated, and our pains have been rather dying pains than travailing ones; we have had a miscarrying womb and dry breasts. All our efforts have proved abortive: *We have not wrought any deliverance in the earth,* for ourselves or for our friends and allies, but rather have made our own case and theirs worse; *neither have the inhabitants of the world,* whom we have been contesting with, *fallen* before us, either in their power or in their hopes; but they are still as high and arrogant as ever." Note, A righteous cause may be strenuously pleaded both by prayer and endeavour, both with God and man, and yet for a great while may be left under a cloud, and the point may not be gained.

II. His prospects and hopes are very pleasant. In general, *"Thou wilt ordain peace for us* (*v.* 12), that is, all that good which the necessity of our case calls for." What peace the church has, or hopes for, it is of God's ordaining; and we may comfort ourselves with this, that, what trouble soever may for a time be appointed to the people of God, peace will at length be ordained for them; for the *end of those men is peace.* And, if God by his Spirit *work all our works in us,* he will ordain peace for us (for the work of righteousness shall be peace), and that is true and lasting peace, such as the world can neither give nor take away, which God ordains; for, to those that have it, it shall be unchangeable as the ordinances *of the day and of the night.* Moreover, from what God has done for us, we may encourage ourselves to hope that he will yet further do us good. "Thou hast heard the desire of the humble, and therefore wilt (Ps. 10:17); and, when this peace is ordained for us, then *by thee only will we make mention of thy name* (*v.* 13); we will give the glory of it to thee only, and not to any other, and we will depend upon thy grace only to enable us to do so." We cannot praise God's name but by his strength. Two things in particular the prophet here comforts the church with the prospect of: — 1. The amazing ruin of her enemies (*v.* 14): *They are dead,* those *other lords* that *have had dominion over us;* their power is irrecoverably broken; they are quite cut off and extinguished: and *they shall not live,* shall never be able to hold up the head any more. Being *deceased, they shall not rise,* but, like Haman, when they have begun to fall before the seed of the Jews they shall sink like a stone. Because they are sentenced to this final ruin, therefore, in pursuance of that sentence, God himself has visited them in wrath, as a righteous Judge, and has cut off both the men themselves (*he has destroyed them*) and *the remembrance of them:* they and their names are buried together in the dust. He has *made all their memory to perish;* they are either forgotten or made mention of with detestation. Note, The cause that is maintained in opposition to God and his kingdom among men, though it may prosper awhile, will certainly sink at last, and all that adhere to it will perish with it. The Jewish doctors, comparing this with *v.* 19, infer that the resurrection of the dead belong to the Jews only, and that those of other nations shall not rise. But we know better; we know that *all who are in their graves shall hear the voice of the Son of God,* and that this speaks of the final destruction of Christ's enemies, which is the second death. 2. The surprising resurrection of her friends, *v.* 19. Though the church rejoices not in the birth of the man-child, of which she travailed in pain, *but has as it were brought forth wind* (*v.* 18), yet the disappointment shall be balanced in a way equivalent: *Thy dead men shall live;*

those who were thought to be dead, who had received a sentence of death within themselves, who were cast out as if they had been naturally dead, shall appear again in their former vigour. A spirit of life from God shall enter into the slain witnesses, and they shall prophesy again, Rev. 11:11. The *dry bones shall live,* and become an *exceedingly great army,* Eze. 37:10. *Together with my dead body shall they arise.* If we believe the resurrection of the dead, of our dead bodies at the last day, as Job did, and the prophet here, that will facilitate our belief of the promised restoration of the church's lustre and strength in this world. When God's time shall have come, how low soever she may be brought, they shall arise, even Jerusalem, the city of God, but now lying like a dead body, a carcase to which the eagles are gathered together. God owns it still for his, so does the prophet; but it shall arise, shall be rebuilt, and flourish again. And therefore let the poor, desolate, melancholy remains of its inhabitants, that dwell as in dust, *awake and sing;* for they shall see Jerusalem, the *city of their solemnities, a quiet habitation again, ch.* 33:20. The dew of God's favour shall be to it as the evening dew to the herbs that were parched with the heat of the sun all day, shall revive and refresh them. And as the spring-dews, that water the earth, and make the herbs that lay buried in it to put forth and bud, so shall they flourish again, and *the earth shall cast out the dead,* as it casts the herbs out of their roots. The earth, in which they seemed to be lost, shall contribute to their revival. When the church and her interests are to be restored neither the dew of heaven nor the fatness of the earth shall be wanting to do their part towards the restoration. Now this (as Ezekiel's vision, which is a comment upon it) may be fitly accommodated, (1.) To the spiritual resurrection of those that were dead in sin, by the power of Christ's gospel and grace. So Dr. Lightfoot applies it, *Hor. Hebr. in Joh.* 12.24. "The Gentiles shall live; with my body shall they arise; that is, they shall be called in after Christ's resurrection, shall rise with him, and sit with him in heavenly places; nay, they shall arise my body (says he); they shall become the mystical body of Christ, and shall arise as part of him." (2.) To the last resurrection, when dead saints shall live, and rise together with Christ's dead body; for he arose as the first-fruits, and believers shall arise by virtue of their union with him and their communion in his resurrection.

Verses 20–21

These two verses are supposed not to belong to the song which takes up the rest of the chapter, but to begin a new matter, and to be rather an introduction to the following chapter than the conclusion of this. Of whereas, in the foregoing song, the people of God had spoken to him, complaining of their grievances, here he returns an answer to their complaints, in which,

I. He invites them into their chambers (*v.* 20): *"Come, my people,* come to me, come with me" (he calls them nowhere but where he himself will accompany them); "let the storm that disperses others bring you nearer together. Come, and *enter into thy chambers;* stay not abroad, lest you be caught in the storm, as the Egyptians in the hail," Ex. 9:21. 1. "Come into chambers of *distinction;* come into your own apartments, and continue not any longer mixed with the children of Babylon. *Come out from among them, and be you separate,"* 2 Co. 6:17; Rev. 18:4. If God has set apart those that are godly for himself, they ought to set themselves apart. 2. "Into chambers of *defence,* in which by the secresy or the strength of them you may be safe in the worst of times." The attributes of God are the *secret of his tabernacle,* Ps. 27:5. His name is a strong tower, into which we may run for shelter, Prov. 18:10. We must be faith find a way into these chambers, and there hide ourselves; that is, with a holy security and serenity of mind, we must put ourselves under the divine protection. Come, as Noah into the ark, for he *shut the doors about him.* When dangers are threatening it is good to retire, and lie hid, as Elijah did by the brook Cherith. 3. Into chambers of *devotion.* "Enter into thy closet, and *shut thy door,* Mt. 6:6. Be private with God: *Enter into thy chamber,* to examine thyself, and commune with thy own heart, to pray, and humble thyself before God." This work is to be done in times of distress and danger; and thus we hide ourselves, that is, we recommend ourselves to God to hide us, and he will hide us either under heaven or in heaven. Israel must keep within doors when the destroying angel is slaying the first-born of Egypt, else the blood on the door-posts will not secure them. So must Rahab and her family when Jericho is being destroyed. Those are most safe that are least seen. *Qui bene latuit, benevixit — He has lived well who has sought a proper degree of concealment.*

II. He assures them that the trouble would be over in a very short time, that they should not long be in any fright or peril: *"Hide thyself for a moment,* the smallest part of time we can conceive, like an atom of matter; may, if you can imagine one moment shorter than another, it is but for a *little* moment, and that with a *quasi* too, *as it were for a little moment,* less than you think of. When it is over it will seem as nothing to you; you will wonder how soon it is gone. You shall not need to lie long in confinement, long in concealment. The indignation will presently be over-past; that is, the indignation of the enemies against you, their persecuting power and rage, which force you to abscond. *When the wicked rise, a man is hid.* This will soon be over; God will cut them off, will break their power, defeat their purposes, and find a way for your enlargement." When Athanasius was banished from Alexandria by an edict of Julian, and his friends greatly lamented it, he bade them be of good cheer. *Nubecula est quae cito pertransibit — It is a little cloud, that will soon blow over. You shall have tribulation ten days;* that is all, Rev. 2:10. This enables God's suffering people to call their afflictions light, that they are but for a moment.

III. He assures them that their enemies should be reckoned with for all the mischief they had done them by the sword, either of war or persecution, *v.* 21. The Lord will punish them for the blood they have shed. Here is, 1. The judgment set, and process issued out: *The Lord comes out of his place, to punish the inhabitants of the earth for their iniquity,* in giving such disturbance to all about them. There is a great deal of iniquity among the inhabitants of the earth; but though they all combine in it, though hand join in hand to carry it on, yet *it shall not go unpunished.* Besides the everlasting punishment into which the wicked shall go hereafter, there are often remarkable punishments of cruelty, oppression, and persecution, in this world. When men's indignation is over-past, and they have done their worst, let them then expect God's indignation, for *he sees that his day is coming,* Ps. 37:13. God *comes out of his place to punish.* He shows himself in an extraordinary manner from heaven, the firmament of his power, from the sanctuary, the residence of his grace. He is *raised up out of his holy habitation,* where he seemed before to conceal himself; and now he will do something great, the product of his wise, just, and secret counsels, as a prince that goes to take the chair or take the field, Zec. 2:13. Some observe that God's place is the mercy-seat; there he delights to be; when he punishes he comes out of his place, for he has no pleasure in the death of sinners. 2. The criminals convicted by the notorious evidence of the face: *The earth shall disclose her blood;* the innocent blood, the blood of the saints and martyrs, which has been shed upon the earth like water, and has soaked into it, and been concealed and covered by it, shall not be brought to light, and brought to account; for God will make inquisition for it, and will give those that shed it blood to drink, for they are worthy. Secret murders, and other secret wickednesses, shall be discovered, sooner or later. And the slain which the earth has long covered she shall no longer cover, but they shall be produced as evidence against the murderers. The voice of Abel's blood cries from the earth, Gen. 9:10, 11; Job 20:27. Those sins which seemed to be buried in oblivion will be called to mind, and called over again, when the day of reckoning comes. Let God's people therefore wait awhile with patience, for behold the Judge stands before the door.

CHAPTER 27

In this chapter the prophet goes on to show, I. What great things God would do for his church and people, which should now shortly be accomplished in the deliverance of Jerusalem from Sennacherib and the destruction of the Assyrian army; but it is expressed generally, for the encouragement of the church in after ages, with reference to the power and prevalency of her enemies. 1. That proud oppressors should be reckoned with (*v.* 1). 2. That care should be taken of the church, as of God's vineyard (*v.* 2, 3). 3. That God would let fall his controversy with the people, upon their return to him (*v.* 4, 5). 4. That he would greatly multiply and increase them (*v.* 6). 5. That, as to their afflictions, the property of them should be altered (*v.* 7), they should be mitigated and moderated (*v.* 8), and sanctified (*v.* 9). 6. That though the church might be laid waste, and made desolate, for a time (*v.* 10, 11), yet it should be restored, and the scattered members should be gathered together again (*v.* 12, 13). All this is applicable to the grace of the gospel, and God's promises to, and providences concerning, the Christian church, and such as belong to it.

Verses 1–6

The prophet is here singing of judgment and mercy,

I. Of judgment upon the enemies of God's church (*v.* 1), *tribulation to those that trouble it,* 2 Th. 1:6. When the Lord *comes out of his place, to punish the inhabitants of the earth* (*ch.* 26:21), he will be sure to punish *leviathan,* the *dragon that is in the sea,* every proud oppressing tyrant, that is the terror of the mighty, and, like the leviathan, is *so fierce that none dares stir him up,* and *his heart as hard as a stone,* and *when he raises up himself the mighty are afraid,* Job 41:10, 24, 25. The church has many enemies, but commonly some one that is more formidable than the rest. So Sennacherib was in his day, and Nebuchadnezzar in his, and Antiochus in his; so Pharaoh had been formerly, and is called *leviathan* and *the dragon, ch.* 51:9; Ps. 74:13, 14; Eze. 29:3. The New-Testament church has had its leviathans; we read of a great red dragon ready to devour it, Rev. 12:3. Those malignant persecuting powers are here compared to the leviathan for bulk, and strength, and the mighty bustle they make in the world, — to dragons for their rage and fury, — to serpents, *piercing serpents,* penetrating in their counsels, quick in their motions, and which, if they once get in their head, will soon wind in their whole body, — *crossing like a bar* (so the margin), standing in the way of all their neighbours and obstructing them, — to *crooked serpents,* subtle and insinuating, but perverse and mischievous. Great and mighty princes, if they oppose the people of God, are in God's account as dragons and serpents, the plagues of mankind; and the Lord will punish them in due time. They are too big for men to deal with and call to an account, and therefore the great God will take the matter into his own hands. He has a *sore, and great, and strong sword,* wherewith to do execution upon them when the *measure of their iniquity is full* and their *day has come to fall.* It is emphatically expressed in the original: *The Lord with his sword, that cruel one, and that great one, and that strong one, shall punish* this unwieldy, this unruly criminal; and it shall be capital punishment: *He shall slay the dragon that is in the sea;* for the wages of his sin is death. This shall not only be a prevention of his doing further mischief, as the slaying of a wild beast, but a just punishment for the mischief he has done, as the putting of a traitor or rebel to death. God has a strong sword for the doing of this, variety of judgments sufficient to humble the proudest and break the most powerful of his enemies; and he will do it when the day of execution comes: *In that day* he will punish, his day which is coming, Ps. 37:13. This is applicable to the spiritual victories obtained by our Lord Jesus over the powers of darkness. He not only disarmed, spoiled, and cast out, the prince of this world, but with his strong sword, the virtue of his death and the preaching of his gospel, he does and will *destroy him that had the power of death, that is, the devil,* that great leviathan, that old serpent, the dragon. He shall be bound, that he may not deceive the nations, and that is a punishment to him (Rev. 20:2, 3); and at length, for deceiving the nations, he shall be *cast into the lake of fire,* Rev. 20:10.

II. Of mercy to the church. In that same day, when God is punishing the leviathan, let the church and all her friends be easy and cheerful; let those that attend her sing to her for her comfort, sing her asleep with these assurances; let it be sung in her assemblies,

1. That she is God's vineyard, and is under his particular care, *v.* 2, 3. She is, in God's eye, *a vineyard of red wine.* The world is as a fruitless worthless wilderness; but the church is enclosed as a vineyard, a peculiar place, and of value, that has great care taken of it and great pains taken with it, and from which precious fruits are gathered, wherewith they honour God and man. It is a vineyard of *red wine,* yielding the best and choicest grapes, intimating the reformation of the church, that it now brings forth good fruit unto God, whereas before it brought forth fruit to itself, or brought forth wild grapes, *ch.* 5:4. Now God takes care, (1.) Of the safety of this vineyard: *I the Lord do keep it.* He speaks this as glorying in it that he is, and

has undertaken to be, the keeper of Israel. Those that bring forth fruit to God are and shall be always under his protection. He speaks this as assuring us that they shall be so: *I the Lord,* that can do every thing, but cannot lie nor deceive, *I do keep it; lest any hurt it, I will keep it night and day.* God's vineyard in this world lies much exposed to injury; there are many that would hurt it, would tread it down and lay it waste (Ps. 80:13); but God will suffer no real hurt or damage to be done it, but what he will bring good out of. He will keep it constantly, night and day, and not without need, for the enemies are restless in their designs and attempts against it, and, both night and day, seek an opportunity to do it a mischief. God will keep it in the night of affliction and persecution, and in the day of peace and prosperity, the temptations of which are no less dangerous. God's people shall be preserved, not only from the *pestilence that walketh in darkness,* but from the *destruction that wasteth at noon-day,* Ps. 91:6. This vineyard shall be well fenced. (2.) Of the fruitfulness of this vineyard: *I will water it every moment,* and yet it shall not be overwatered. The still and silent dews of God's grace and blessing shall continually descend upon it, that it may bring forth much fruit. We need the constant and continual waterings of the divine grace; for, if that be at any time withdrawn, we wither, and come to nothing. God waters his vineyard by the ministry of the word by his servants the prophets, whose doctrine shall drop as the dew. Paul plants, and Apollos waters, but God gives the increase; for without him the watchman wakes and the husbandman waters in vain.

2. That, though sometimes he contends with his people, yet, upon their submission, he will be reconciled to them, *v.* 4, 5. *Fury is not in him* towards his vineyard; though he meets with many things in it that are offensive to him, yet he does not seek advantages against it, nor is extreme to mark what is amiss in it. It is true if he find in it briers and thorns instead of vines, and they be set in battle against him (as indeed that in the vineyard which is not for him is against him), he will tread them down and burn them; but otherwise, "If I am angry with my people, they know what course to take; let them humble themselves, and pray, and seek my face, and so *take hold of my strength* with a sincere desire to make their peace with me, and I will soon be reconciled to them, and all shall be well." God sees the sins of his people and is displeased with them; but, upon their repentance, he turns away his wrath. This may very well be construed as a summary of the doctrine of the gospel, with which the church is to be watered every moment. (1.) Here is a quarrel supposed between God and man; for here is a battle fought, and peace to be made. It is an old quarrel, ever since sin first entered. It is, on God's part, a righteous quarrel, but, on man's part, most unrighteous. (2.) Here is a gracious invitation given us to make up this quarrel, and to get these matters in variance accommodated: "Let him that is desirous to be at peace with God take hold of his strength, of his strong arm, which is lifted up against the sinner to strike him dead; and let him by supplication keep back the stroke. Let him wrestle with me, as Jacob did, resolving not to let me go without a blessing; and he shall be *Israel — a prince with God.*" Pardoning mercy is called the power of our Lord; let him take hold of that. Christ is the *arm of the Lord, ch.* 53:1. Christ *crucified is the power of God* (1 Co. 1:24); let him by a lively faith take hold of him, as a man that is sinking catches hold of a bough, or cord, or plank, that is within his reach, or as the malefactor took hold of the horns of the altar, believing that there is no other name by which he can be saved, by which he can be reconciled. (3.) Here is a threefold cord of arguments to persuade us to do this. [1.] Time and space are given us to do it in; for *fury is not in God;* he does not carry it towards us as great men carry it towards their inferiors, when the one is in a fault and the other in a fury. Men in a fury will not take time for consideration; it is, with them, but a word and a blow. Furious men are soon angry, and implacable when they are angry; a little thing provokes them, and no little thing will pacify them. But it is not so with God; he considers our frame, is slow to anger, does not stir up all his wrath, nor always chide. [2.] It is in vain to think of contesting with him. If we persist in our quarrel with him, and think to make our part good, it is but like setting briers and thorns before a consuming fire, which will be so far from giving check to the progress of it that they will but make it burn the more outrageously. We are not an equal match for Omnipotence. *Woe unto him* therefore *that strives with his Maker!* He knows not the power of his anger. [3.] This is the only way, and it is a sure way, to reconciliation: "Let him take this course to make peace with me, *and he shall make peace;* and thereby good, all good, shall come unto him." God is willing to be reconciled to us if we be but willing to be reconciled to him.

3. That the church of God in the world shall be a growing body, and come at length to be a great body (*v.* 6): *In times to come* (so some read it), *in after-times,* when these calamities are overpast, or in the days of the gospel, the latter days, *he shall cause Jacob to take root,* deeper root than ever yet; for the gospel church shall be more firmly fixed than ever the Jewish church was, and shall spread further. Or, *He shall cause those of Jacob* that come back out of their captivity, or (as we read it) *those that come of Jacob, to take root downward, and bear fruit upward, ch.* 37:31. They shall be established in a prosperous state, and then they shall *blossom and bud,* and give hopeful prospects of a great increase; and so it shall prove, for *they shall fill the face of the world with fruit.* Many shall be brought into the church, proselytes shall be numerous, some out of all the nations about that shall be to the God of Israel for a name and a praise; and the converts shall be fruitful in the fruits of righteousness. The preaching of the gospel *brought forth fruit in all the world* (Col. 1:6), fruit that remains, Jn. 15:16.

Verses 7–13

Here is the prophet again singing of mercy and judgment, not, as before, judgment to the enemies and mercy to the church, but judgment to the church and mercy mixed with that judgment.

I. Here is judgment threatened even to Jacob and Israel. *They shall blossom and bud* (*v.* 6), but, 1. They shall be *smitten* and *slain* (*v.* 7), some of them shall. If God find any thing amiss among them, he will lay them under the tokens of his displeasure for it. Judgment shall begin at the house of God, and those whom God has known of all the families of the earth he will punish in the first place. 2. Jerusalem, their *defenced city, shall be desolate, v.* 10, 11. "God having tried a variety of methods with them for their reformation, which, as to many, have proved ineffectual, he will for a time lay their country waste," which was accomplished when Jerusalem was destroyed by the Chaldeans; then that *habitation* was for a long time *forsaken.* If less judgments do not do the work, God will send greater; for *when he judges he will overcome.* Jerusalem had been a defenced city, not so much by art or nature as by grace and the divine protection; but, when God was provoked to withdraw, her defence departed from her, and then she was left like a wilderness. "And in the pleasant gardens of Jerusalem cattle shall feed, shall lie down there, and there shall be none to disturb them or drive them away; there they shall be *levant and couchant,* and they shall eat the tender branches of the fruit-trees," which perhaps further signifies that the people should become an easy prey to their enemies. *"When the boughs thereof are withered* as they grow upon the tree, being blasted by winds and frosts and not pruned, *they shall be broken off* for fuel, and *the women* and children shall *come and set them on fire.* There shall be a total destruction, for the very trees shall be destroyed." And this is a figure of the deplorable state of the vineyard (*v.* 2) when it *brought forth wild grapes* (*ch.* 5:2); and our Saviour seems to refer to this when he says of the branches of the vine which *abide not in him* that they are *cast forth and withered, and men gather them, and cast them into the fire, and they are burned* (Jn. 15:6), which was in a particular manner fulfilled in the unbelieving Jews. The similitude is explained in the following words, *It is a people of no understanding,* brutish and sottish, and destitute of the knowledge of God, and that have no relish or savour of divine things, like a withered branch that has no sap in it; and this is at the bottom of all those sins for which God left them desolate, their idolatry first and afterwards their infidelity. Wicked people, however in other things they may be wits and politicians, in their greatest concerns are of no understanding; and their ignorance, being wilful, shall not only not be their excuse, but it shall be the ground of their condemnation; for therefore *he that made them,* that gave them their being, *will not have mercy on them,* nor save them from the ruin they bring upon themselves; and *he that formed them* into a people, formed them for himself, to show forth his praise, seeing they do not answer the end of their formation, but hate to be reformed, to be new-formed, will reject them, and *show them no favour;* and then they are undone: for, if he that made us by his power do not make us happy in his favour, we had better never have been made. Sinners flatter themselves with hopes of impunity, at least that they shall not be dealt with so severely as their ministers tell them, because God is merciful and because he is their Maker. But here we see how weak and insufficient those pleas will be; for, if they be of no understanding, he that made them, though he made them, and hates nothing that he has made, and though he has mercy in store for those who so far understand their interests as to apply to him for it, yet on them he will have no mercy, and will show them no favour.

II. Here is a great deal of mercy mixed with this judgment; for there are good people mixed with those that are corrupt and degenerate, *a remnant according to the election of grace,* on whom God will have mercy and to whom he will show favour: and these promises seem to point at all the calamities of the church, for which God would graciously provide these allays.

1. Though they shall be smitten and slain, yet not to that degree, and in that manner, in which their enemies shall be smitten and slain, *v.* 7. God has *smitten Jacob,* and he is slain. Many of those *that understand among the people shall fall by the sword and by flame many days,* Dan. 11:33. But it shall not be as those are smitten and slain, (1.) Who smote him formerly, who were the rod of God's anger and the staff in his hand, which he made us of for the correction of his people, and to whose turn it shall come to be reckoned with even for that: the child is spared, but the rod is burnt. (2.) Who shall afterwards be slain by him, when he shall get the dominion, and repay them in their own coin, or slain for his sake in the pleading of his cause. God's people and God's enemies are here represented, [1.] As struggling with each other; so the seed of the woman and the seed of the serpent have been, are, and will be. In this contest there are slain on both sides. God makes use of wicked men, not only to smite, but to slay his people; for they are his sword, Ps. 17:13. But, when the cup of trembling comes to be put into their hand, it will be much worse with them than ever it was with God's people in their greatest straits. The seed of the woman has only his heel bruised, but the serpent has his head crushed and broken. Note, Though God's persecuted people may be great losers, and great sufferers, for a while, yet those that oppress them will prove to be greater losers and greater sufferers at last, here or hereafter; for God will render double to them, Rev. 18:6. [2.] As sharing together in the calamities of this present time. They are both smitten, both slain, and both by the hand of God; for there is *one event to the righteous and to the wicked.* But is Jacob smitten as his enemies are? No, by no means; to him the property is altered, and it becomes quite another thing. Note, However it may seem to us, there is really a vast difference between the afflictions and deaths of good people and the afflictions and deaths of wicked people.

2. Though God will debate with them, yet it shall be in measure, and the affliction shall be mitigated, moderated, and proportioned to their strength, not to their deserts, *v.* 8. He will deal out afflictions to them as the wise physician prescribes medicines to his patients, just such a quantity of each ingredient, or orders how much blood shall be taken when a vein is opened: thus God orders the troubles of his people, not *suffering them to be tempted above what they are able,* 1 Co. 10:13. He measures out their afflictions by a little at a time, that they may not be pressed above measure; for he knows their frame, and corrects in judgment, and does not stir up all his wrath. When the affliction is shooting forth, when he is sending it out and giving it its commission, then he debates in measure, and not in extremity. He considers what we can bear when he begins to correct; and when he proceeds in his controversy, so that it is the *day of his east-wind,* which is not only blustering and noisy, but blasting and noxious, yet he stays his rough wind, checks it, and sets bounds to it, does not suffer it to blow so hard as was feared; when he

is winnowing his corn, it is with a gentle gale, that shall only blow away the chaff, but not the good corn. God has the winds at his command, and every affliction under his check. *Hitherto it shall go, but no further.* Let us not despair when things are at the worst; be the winds ever so rough, ever so high, God can say unto them, *Peace, be still.*

3. Though God will afflict them, yet he will make their afflictions to work for the good of their souls, and correct them as the father does the child, to drive out the foolishness that is bound up in their hearts (*v.* 9): *By this therefore shall the iniquity of Jacob be purged.* This is the design of the affliction, to this it is adapted as a proper means, and, by the grace of God working with it, it shall have this blessed effect. It shall mortify the habits of sin; by this those defilements of the soul shall be purged away. It shall break them off from the practice of sin: *This is all the fruit,* this is it that God intends, this is all the harm it will do them, *to take away their sin,* than which they could not have a greater kindness done them, though it be at the expense of an affliction. Therefore, because the affliction is mitigated and moderated, and the rough wind stayed, therefore we may conclude that he designs their reformation, not their destruction; and, because he deals thus gently with us, we should therefore study to answer his ends in afflicting us. The particular sin which the affliction was intended to cure them of was the sin of idolatry, the sin which did most easily beset that people and to which they were strangely addicted. *Ephraim is joined to idols.* But by the captivity in Babylon they were not only weaned from this sin, but set against it. *Ephraim shall say, What have I do to any more with idols?* Jacob has his sin taken away, his beloved sin, *when he makes all the stones of the altar,* of his idolatrous altar, the stones of which were precious and sacred to him, *as chalk-stones that are beaten asunder;* he not only has them in contempt, and values them no more than chalk-stones, but he conceives an indignation at them, and, in a holy revenge, beats them asunder as easily as chalk-stones are broken to pieces. *The groves and the images shall not* stand before this penitent, but they shall be thrown down too, never to be set up again. This was according to the law for the demolishing and destroying of all the monuments of idolatry (Deu. 7:5); and according to this promise, since the captivity in Babylon, no people in the world have such a rooted aversion to idols and idolatry as the people of the Jews. Note, The design of affliction is to separate between us and sin, especially that which has been *our own iniquity;* and then it appears that the affliction has done us good when we keep at a distance from the occasions of sin, and use all needful precaution that we may not only not relapse into it, but not so much as be tempted to it, Ps. 119:67.

4. Though Jerusalem shall be desolate and forsaken for a time, yet there will come a day when its scattered friends shall resort to it again out of all the countries whither they were dispersed (*v.* 12, 13); though the body of the nation is abandoned as a people of no understanding, yet those that are indeed children of Israel shall be gathered together again, as the sheep of the flock when the shepherds that scattered them are reckoned with, Eze. 34:10–19. Now observe concerning these scattered Israelites, (1.) Whence they shall be fetched: *The Lord shall beat them off* as fruit from the tree, or beat them out as corn out of the ear. He shall find them out, and separate them from those among whom they dwelt, and with whom they seemed to be incorporated, *from the channel of the river* Euphrates northeast, *unto* Nile, *the stream of Egypt,* which lay south-west — those that were driven into the land of Assyria, and were captives there in the land of their enemies, where they were ready to perish for want of necessaries, and ready to despair of deliverance — and those that were *outcasts in the land of Egypt,* whither many of those that were left behind, after the captivity in Babylon, went, contrary to God's express command (Jer. 43:6, 7), and there lived as outcasts: God has mercy in store for them all, and will make it to appear that, though they are cast out, they are not cast off. (2.) In what manner they shall be brought back: "*You shall be gathered one by one,* not in multitudes, not in troops forcing your way; but silently, and as it were by stealth, dropping in, first one, and then another." This intimates that the remnant that shall be saved consists but of few, and those saved with difficulty, and so as by fire, scarcely saved; they shall not come for company, but as God shall stir up every man's spirit. (3.) By what means they shall be gathered together: *The great trumpet shall be blown, and* then *they shall come.* Cyrus's proclamation of liberty to the captives is this great trumpet, which awakened the Jews that were asleep in their thraldom to bestir themselves; it was like the sounding of the jubilee-trumpet, which published the year of release. This is applicable both to the preaching of the gospel, by which sinners are gathered in to the grace of God, such as were outcasts and ready to perish (those that were afar off are made nigh; the gospel proclaims the acceptable year of the Lord), and also to the archangel's trumpet at the last day, by which saints shall be gathered to the glory of God, that lay as outcasts in their graves. (4.) For what end they shall be gathered together: *To worship the Lord in the holy mount at Jerusalem.* When the captives rallied again, and returned to their own land, the chief thing they had their eye upon, and the first thing they applied themselves to, was the worship of God. The holy temple was in ruins, but they had the holy mount, *the place of the altar,* Gen. 13:4. Liberty to worship God is the most valuable and desirable liberty; and, after restraints and dispersions, a free access to his house should be more welcome to us than a free access to our own houses. Those that are gathered by the sounding of the gospel trumpet are brought in to worship God and added to the church; and the great trumpet of all will gather the saints together, *to serve God day and night in his temple.*

CHAPTER 28

In this chapter, I. The Ephraimites are reproved and threatened for their pride and drunkenness, their security and sensuality (*v.* 1–8). But, in the midst of this, here is a gracious promise of God's favour to the remnant of his people (*v.* 5, 6). II. They are likewise reproved and threatened for their dulness and stupidity, and unaptness to profit by the instructions which the prophets gave them in God's name (*v.* 9–13). III. The rulers of Jerusalem are reproved and threatened for their insolent contempt of God's judgments, and setting them at defiance; and, after a gracious promise of Christ and his grace, they are made to know that the vain hopes of escaping the judgments of God with which they flattered themselves would certainly deceive them (*v.* 14–22). IV. All this is confirmed by a comparison borrowed from the method which the husbandman takes with his ground and grain, according to which they must expect God would proceed with his people, whom he had lately called his threshing and the corn of his floor (*ch.* 21:10) (*v.* 23–29). This is written for our admonition, and is profitable for reproof and warning to us.

Verses 1–8

Here, I. The prophet warns the kingdom of the ten tribes of the judgments that were coming upon them for their sins, which were soon after executed by the king of Assyria, who laid their country waste, and carried the people into captivity. Ephraim had his name from *fruitfulness,* their soil being very fertile and the products of it abundant and the best of the kind; they had a great many *fat valleys* (*v.* 1, 4), and Samaria, which was situated on a hill, was, as it were, *on the head of the fat valleys.* Their country was rich and pleasant, and as the garden of the Lord: it was the glory of Canaan, as that was the glory of all lands; their harvest and vintage were the *glorious beauty* on the head of their valleys, which were covered over with corn and vines. Now observe,

1. What an ill use they made of their plenty. What God gave them to serve him with they perverted, and abused, by making it the food and fuel of their lusts. (1.) They were puffed up with pride by it. The goodness with which God crowned their years, which should have been to him a crown of praise, was to them a *crown of pride.* Those that are rich in the world are apt to be high-minded, 1 Tim. 6:17. Their king, who wore the crown, was proud that he ruled over so rich a country; Samaria, their royal city, was notorious for pride. Perhaps it was usual at their festivals, or revels, to wear garlands made up of flowers and ears of corn, which they wore in honour of their fruitful country. Pride was a sin that generally prevailed among them, and therefore the prophet, in his name who resists the proud, boldly proclaims a *woe to the crown of pride.* If those who wear crowns be proud of them, let them not think to escape this woe. What men are proud of, be it ever so mean, is to them as a crown; he that is proud thinks himself as great as a king. But woe to those who thus exalt themselves, for they shall be abased; their pride is the preface to their destruction. (2.) They indulged themselves in sensuality. Ephraim was notorious for drunkenness, and excess of riot; Samaria, the head of the fat valleys, was full of those that were *overcome with wine,* were *broken with it,* so the margin. See how foolishly drunkards act, and no marvel when, in the very commission of the sin, they make fools and brutes of themselves; they yield, [1.] To be conquered by the sin; it overcomes them, and *brings them into bondage* (2 Pt. 2:19); they are led captive by it, and the captivity is the more shameful and inglorious because it is voluntary. Some of these wretched slaves have themselves owned that there is not a greater drudgery in the world than hard drinking. They are overcome not with the wine, but with the love of it. [2.] To be ruined by it. They are broken by wine. Their constitution is broken by it, and their health ruined. They are broken in the callings and estates, and their souls are in danger of being eternally undone, and all this for the gratification of a base lust. Woe to these *drunkards of Ephraim!* Ministers must bring the general woes of the word home to particular places and persons. We must say, *Woe to this or that person,* if he be a drunkard. There is a particular woe to the drunkards of Ephraim, for they are of God's professing people, and it becomes them worse than any other; they know better, and therefore should give a better example. Some make the *crown of pride* to belong to the drunkards, and to mean the garlands with which those were crowned that got the victory in their wicked drinking matches and drank down the rest of the company. They were proud of their being mighty to drink wine; but woe to those who thus glory in their shame.

2. The justice of God in taking away their plenty from them, which they thus abused. Their *glorious beauty,* the plenty they were proud of, *is but a fading flower;* it is meat that perishes. The most substantial fruits, if God blast them and blow upon them, are but fading flowers, *v.* 1. God can easily *take away their corn in the season thereof* (Hos. 2:9), and recover *locum vastatum — ground that has been alienated and has run to waste,* those goods of his which they prepared for Baal. God has an officer ready to make a seizure for him, has one at his beck, *a mighty and strong one,* who is able to do the business, even the king of Assyria, who *shall cast down to the earth with the hand,* shall easily and effectually, and with the turn of a hand, destroy all that which they are proud of and pleased with, *v.* 2. He shall throw it down to the ground, to be broken to pieces with a strong hand, with a hand that they cannot oppose. Then *the crown of pride,* and *the drunkards of Ephraim, shall be trodden under foot* (*v.* 3); they shall lie exposed to contempt, and shall not be able to recover themselves. Drunkards, in their folly, are apt to talk proudly, and vaunt themselves most when they most shame themselves; but they thereby render themselves the more ridiculous. The beauty of their valleys, which they gloried in, will be, (1.) Like *a fading flower* (as before, *v.* 1); it will wither of itself, and has in itself the principles of its own corruption; it will perish in time by its own moth and rust. (2.) Like *the hasty fruit,* which, as soon as it is discovered, is plucked and eaten up; so the wealth of this world, besides that it is apt to decay of itself, is subject to be devoured by others as greedily as the first-ripe fruit, which is earnestly desired, Mic. 7:1. *Thieves break through and steal.* The harvest which the worldling is proud of *the hungry eat up* (Job 5:5); no sooner do they see the prey but they catch at it, and swallow up all they can lay their hands on. It is likewise easily devoured, as that fruit which, being ripe before it has grown, is very small, and is soon eaten up; and there being little of it, and that of little worth, it is not reserved, but used immediately.

II. He next turns to the kingdom of Judah, whom he calls the *residue of his people* (*v.* 5), for they were but two tribes to the other ten.

1. He promises them God's favours, and that they shall be taken under his guidance and protection when the beauty of Ephraim shall be left exposed to be trodden down and eaten up, *v.* 5, 6. *In that day,* when the Assyrian army is laying Israel waste, and Judah might think that their neighbour's house being on fire their own was in danger, in that day of treading down and perplexity, then God will be to the residue of his people all they need and can desire; not only to the kingdom of Judah, but to those of Israel who had kept their integrity, and, as was probably the case with some, betook themselves to the land of Judah, to be sheltered by good king Hezekiah. When the Assyrian, that mighty one, was in Israel as *a tempest*

of hail, noisy and battering, as *a destroying storm* bearing down all before it, especially at sea, and *as a flood of mighty waters overflowing* the country (*v.* 2), then *in that day will the Lord of hosts,* of all hosts, distinguish by peculiar favours his people who have distinguished themselves by a steady and singular adherence to him, and that which they most need he will himself be to them. This very much enhances the worth of the promises that God, covenanting to be to his people a God all-sufficient, undertakes to be himself all that to them which they can desire. (1.) He will put all the credit and honour upon them which are requisite, not only to rescue them from contempt, but to gain them esteem and reputation. He will be to them *for a crown of glory and for a diadem of beauty.* Those that wore the crown of pride looked upon God's people with disdain, and trampled upon them, for they were the song of the drunkards of Ephraim; but God will so appear for them by his providence as to make it evident that they have his favour towards them, and that shall be to them a crown of glory; for what greater glory can any people have than for God to acknowledge them as his own? And he will so appear in them, by his grace, as to make it evident that they have his image renewed on them, and that shall be to them a diadem of beauty; for what greater beauty can any person have than the beauty of holiness? Note, Those that have God for their God have him for a crown of glory and a diadem of beauty; for they are made to him kings and priests. (2.) He will give them all the wisdom and grace necessary to the due discharge of the duty of their place. He will himself be *a spirit of judgment to those that sit in judgment;* the privy counsellors shall be guided by wisdom and discretion and the judges shall govern by justice and equity. It is a great mercy to any people when those that are called to places of power and public trust are qualified for their places, when those that sit in judgment have a spirit of judgment, a spirit of government. (3.) He will give them all the courage and boldness requisite to carry them resolutely through the difficulties and oppositions they are likely to meet with. He will be *for strength to those that turn the battle to the gate,* to the gates of the enemy whose cities they besiege, or to their own gates, when they sally out upon the enemies that besiege them. The strength of the soldiery depends as much upon God as the wisdom of the magistracy; and where God gives both these he is to that people a crown of glory. This may well be supposed to refer to Christ, and so the Chaldee paraphrast understands it: *In that day shall the Messiah be a crown of glory.* Simeon calls him the *glory of his people Israel;* and he is made of God to us wisdom, righteousness, and strength.

2. He complains of the corruptions that were found among them, and the many corrupt ones (*v.* 7): *But they also,* many of those of Judah, *have erred through wine.* There are drunkards of Jerusalem, as well as drunkards of Ephraim; and therefore the mercy of God is to be so much the more admired that he has not blasted the glory of Judah as he has done that of Ephraim. Sparing mercy lays us under peculiar obligations when it is thus distinguishing. Ephraim's sins are found in Judah, and yet not Ephraim's ruins. *They have erred through wine.* Their drinking to excess is itself a practical error; they think to raise their fancy by it, but they ruin their judgment, and so put a cheat upon themselves; they think to preserve their health by it and help digestion, but they spoil their constitution and hasten diseases and deaths. It is also the occasion of a great many errors in principle; their understanding is clouded and their conscience debauched by it; and therefore, to support themselves in it, they espouse corrupt notions, and form their minds in favour of their lusts. Probably some were drawn in to worship idols by their love of the wine and strong drink which there was plenty of at their idolatrous festivals; and so they erred through wine, as Israel, for love of the daughters of Moab, joined themselves to Baal-peor. Three things are here observed as aggravations of this sin: —(1.) That those were guilty of it whose business it was to warn others against it and to teach them better, and therefore who ought to have set a better example: *The priest and the prophet are swallowed up of wine;* their office is quite drowned and lost in it. The priests, as sacrificers, were obliged by a particular law to be temperate (Lev. 10:9), and, as rulers and magistrates, it was not for them to drink wine, Prov. 31:4. The prophets were a kind of Nazarites (as appears by Amos 2:11), and, as reprovers by office, were concerned to keep at the utmost distance from the sins they reproved in others; yet there were many of them ensnared in this sin. What! a priest, a prophet, a minister, and yet drunk! *Tell it not in Gath.* Such a scandal are they to their coat. (2.) That the consequences of it were very pernicious, not only by the ill influence of their example, but the prophet, when he was drunk, *erred in vision;* the false prophets plainly discovered themselves to be so when they were in drink. The priest *stumbled in judgment and forgot the law* (Prov. 31:5); he reeled and staggered as much in the operations of his mind as in the motions of his body. What wisdom or justice can be expected from those that sacrifice reason, and virtue, and conscience, and all that is valuable to such a base lust as the love of strong drink is? Happy art thou, O land! when *thy princes eat* and drink *for strength, and not for drunkenness,* Eccl. 10:17. (3.) That the disease was epidemic, and the generality of those that kept any thing of a table were infected with it: *All tables are full of vomit, v.* 8. See what an odious thing the sin of drunkenness is, what an affront it is to human society; it is rude and ill-mannered enough to sicken the beholders, for the tables where they eat their meat are filthily stained with the marks of this sin, which the sinners declare as Sodom. Their tables are full of vomit, so that the victor, instead of being proud of his crown, ought rather to be ashamed of it. It bodes ill to any people when so sottish a sin as drunkenness has become national.

Verses 9–13

The prophet here complains of the wretched stupidity of this people, that they were unteachable and made no improvement of the means of grace which they possessed; they still continued as they were, their mistakes not rectified, their hearts not renewed, nor their lives reformed. Observe,

I. What it was that their prophets and ministers designed and aimed at. It was to *teach* them *knowledge,* the knowledge of God and his will, and to *make them understand doctrine, v.* 9. This is God's way of dealing with men, to enlighten men's minds first with the knowledge of his truth, and thus to gain their affections, and bring their wills into a compliance with his laws; thus he enters in by the door, whereas the thief and the robber climb up another way.

II. What method they took, in pursuance of this design. They left no means untried to do them good, but taught them as children are taught, little children that are beginning to learn, that are taken from the breast to the book (*v.* 9), for among the Jews it was common for mothers to nurse their children till they were three years old, and almost ready to go to school. And it is good to begin betimes with children, to teach them, as they are capable, the good knowledge of the Lord, and to instruct them even when they are but newly weaned from the milk. The prophets taught them as children are taught; for, 1. They were constant and industrious in teaching them. They took great pains with them, and with great prudence, teaching them as they needed it and were able to bear it (*v.* 10): *Precept upon precept. It must be so,* or (as some read) *it has been so.* They have been taught, as children are taught to read, by *precept upon precept,* and taught to write by *line upon line, a little here* and *a little there,* a little of one thing and a little of another, that the variety of instructions might be pleasing and inviting, — a little at one time and a little at another, that they might not have their memories overcharged, — a little from one prophet and a little from another, that every one might be pleased with his friend and him whom he admired. Note, For our instruction in the things of God it is requisite that we have precept upon precept and line upon line, that one precept and line should be followed, and so enforced by another; the precept of justice must be upon the precept of piety, and the precept of charity upon that of justice. Nay, it is necessary that the same precept and the same line should be often repeated and inculcated upon us, that we may the better understand them and the more easily recollect them when we have occasion for them. Teachers should accommodate themselves to the capacity of the learners, give them what they most need and can best bear, and a little at a time, Deu. 6:6, 7. 2. They courted and persuaded them to learn, *v.* 12. God, by his prophets, said to them, *"This* way that we are directing you to, and directing you in, *is the rest,* the only rest, *wherewith you may cause the weary to rest; and this will be the refreshing* of your own souls, and will bring rest to your country from the wars and other calamities with which it has been long harassed." Note, God by his word calls us to nothing but what is really for our advantage; for the service of God is the only true rest for those that are weary of the service of sin and there is no refreshing but under the easy yoke of the Lord Jesus.

III. What little effect all this had upon the people. They were as unapt to learn as young children newly weaned from the milk, and it was as impossible to fasten any thing upon them (*v.* 9): nay, one would choose rather to teach a child of two years old than undertake to teach them; for they have not only (like such a child) no capacity to receive what is taught them, but they are prejudiced against it. As children, they have *need of milk,* and *cannot bear strong meat,* Heb. 5:12. 1. They *would not hear* (*v.* 12), no, not that which would be rest and refreshing to them. They had no mind to hear it. The word of God commanded their serious attention, but could not gain it; they were where it was preached, but they turned a deaf ear to it, or as it came in at one ear it went out at the other. 2. They would not heed. It was unto them *precept upon precept, and line upon line* (*v.* 13); they went on in a road of external performances; they kept up the old custom of attending upon the prophet's preaching and it was continually sounding in their ears, but that was all; it made no impression upon them; they had the letter of the precept, but no experience of the power and spirit of it; it was continually beating upon them, but it beat nothing into them. Nay, 3. It should seem, they ridiculed the prophet's preaching, and bantered it. The word of the Lord was unto them *Tsau latsau, kau lakau;* in the original it is in rhyme; they made a song of the prophet's words, and sang it when they were merry over their wine. David was the song of the drunkards. It is great impiety, and a high affront to God, thus to make a jest of sacred things, to speak of that vainly which should make us serious.

IV. How severely God would reckon with them for this. 1. He would deprive them of the privilege of plain preaching, and speak to them *with stammering lips and another tongue, v.* 11. Those that will not understand what is plain and level to their capacity, but despise it as mean and trifling, are justly amused with that which is above them. Or God will send foreign armies among them, whose language they understand not, to lay their country waste. Those that will not hear the comfortable voice of God's word shall be made to hear the dreadful voice of his rod. Or these words may be taken as denoting God's gracious condescension to their capacity in his dealing with them; he lisped to them in their own language, as nurses do to their children, with stammering lips, to humor them; he changed his voice, tried first one way and then another; the apostle quotes it as a favour (1 Co. 14:21), applying it to the gift of tongues, and complaining that yet for all this they would not hear. 2. He would bring utter ruin upon them. By their profane contempt of God and his word they are but hastening on their own ruin, and ripening themselves for it; it is *that they may go and fall backward,* may grow worse and worse, may depart further and further from God, and proceed from one sin to another, till they be quite *broken, and snared, and taken,* and ruined, *v.* 13. They have here a little and there a little of the word of God; they think it too much, and *say to the seers, See not;* but it proves too little to convert them, and will prove enough to condemn them. If it be not a *savour of life unto life,* it will be *a savour of death unto death.*

Verses 14–22

The prophet, having reproved those that made a jest of the word of God, here goes on to reprove those that made a jest of the judgments of God, and set them at defiance; for he is a jealous God, and will not suffer either his ordinances or his providences to be brought into contempt. He addressed himself to *the scornful men who ruled in Jerusalem,* who were the magistrates of the city, *v.* 14. It is bad with a people when their thrones of judgment become the seats of the scornful, when rulers are scorners; but that the rulers of Jerusalem should be men of such a character, that they should make light of God's judgments and scorn to take notice of the tokens of his displeasure, is very sad. Who will be mourners in Zion if they are scorners? Observe,

I. How these scornful men lulled themselves asleep in carnal security, and even challenged God Almighty to do his worst (*v.* 15) *You have said, We have made a covenant with death and the grave.* They thought themselves as sure of their lives, even when the most destroying judgments were abroad, as if they had made a bargain with death, upon a valuable consideration, not to come till they sent for him or not to take them away by any violence, but by old age. If we be at peace with God, and have made a covenant with him, we have in effect made a covenant with death that it shall come in the fittest time, that whenever it comes, it shall be no terror to us, nor do us any real damage; death is ours if we be Christ's (1 Co. 3:22, 23): but to think of making death our friend, or being in league with it, while by sin we are making God our enemy and are at war with him, is the greatest absurdity that can be. It was fond conceit which these scorners had, *"When the overflowing scourge shall pass through* our country, and others shall fall under it, yet *it shall not come to us,* not reach us, though it extend far, not bear us down, though it is an overflowing scourge." It is the greatest folly imaginable for impenitent sinners to think that either in this world or the other they shall fare better than their neighbours. But what is the ground of their confidence? Why, truly, *We have made lies our refuge.* Either, 1. Those things which the prophets told them would be lies and falsehood to them and would deceive, but which they themselves looked upon as substantial fences. The protection of their idols, the promises with which their false prophets soothed them, their policy, their wealth, their interest in the people; these they confided in, and not in God; nay, these they confided in against God. Or, 2. Those things which should be lies and falsehood to the enemy, who was *flagellum Dei* — *the scourge of God,* the overflowing scourge; they would secure themselves by imposing upon the enemy with their stratagems of war, or their feigned submissions in treaties of peace. The rest of the cities of Judah were taken because they made an obstinate defence; but the rulers of Jerusalem hope to succeed better. They think themselves greater politicians than those of the country towns; they will compliment the king of Assyria with a promise to surrender their city, or to become tributaries to him, with a purpose at the same time to shake off his yoke as soon as the danger is over, not caring though they be found liars to him, as the expression is, Deu. 33:29. Note, Those put a cheat upon themselves that think to gain their point by putting cheats upon those they deal with. Those that pursue their designs by trick and fraud, by mean and paltry shifts, may perhaps compasss them, but cannot expect comfort in them. Honesty is the best policy. But such refuges as these are those driven to that depart from God, and throw themselves out of his protection.

II. How God, by the prophet, awakens them out of this sleep, and shows them the folly of their security.

1. He tells them upon what grounds they might be secure. He does not disturb their false confidences, till he has first shown them a firm bottom on which they may repose themselves (*v.* 16): *Behold, I lay in Zion for a foundation a stone.* This foundation is, (1.) The promises of God in general — his word, upon which he has caused his people to hope — his covenant with Abraham, that he would be a God to him and his; this is a foundation, a foundation of stone, firm and lasting, for faith to build upon; it is *a tried stone,* for all the saints have stayed themselves upon it and it never failed them. (2.) The promise of Christ in particular; for to him this is expressly applied in the New Testament, 1 Pt. 2:6–8. He is that stone which has become *the head of the corner.* The great promise of the Messiah and his kingdom, which was to begin at Jerusalem, was sufficient to make God's people easy in the worst of times; for they knew well that till he came *the sceptre should not depart from Judah.* Zion shall continue while this foundation is yet to be laid there. *"Thus saith the Lord Jehovah,* for the comfort of those that dare not *make lies their refuge,* Behold, and look upon me as one that has undertaken to *lay in Zion a Stone,"* Jesus Christ is a foundation of God's laying. *This is the Lord's doing.* He is laid in Zion, in the church, in the holy hill. He is a tried stone, a trying stone (so some), a touch-stone, that shall distinguish between true and counterfeit. He is a precious stone, for such

are the foundations of the New Jerusalem (Rev. 21:19), a corner-stone, in whom the sides of the building are united, the *head-stone of the corner.* And *he that believes* these promises, and rests upon them, *shall not make haste,* shall not run to and fro in a hurry, as men at their wits' end, shall not be shifting hither and thither for his own safety, nor be driven to his feet by any terrors, as the wicked man is said to be (Job 18:11), but with a fixed heart shall quietly wait the event, saying, *Welcome the will of God.* He *shall not make haste* in his expectations, so as to anticipate the time set in the divine counsels, but, though it tarry, will wait the appointed hour, knowing that *he that shall come will come, and will not tarry.* He that believes will not make more haste than good speed, but be satisfied that God's time is the best time, and wait with patience for it. The apostle from the Septuagint explains this, 1 Pt. 2:6. *He that believes on him shall not be confounded;* his expectations shall not be frustrated, but far out-done.

2. He tells them that upon the grounds which they now built on they could not be safe, but their confidences would certainly fail them (*v.* 17): *Judgment will I lay to the line, and righteousness to the plummet.* This denotes,

(1.) The building up of his church; having laid the foundation (*v.* 16), he will raise the structure, as builders do, by line and plummet, Zec. 4:10. Righteousness shall be the line and judgment the plummet. The church, being grounded on Christ, shall be formed and reformed by the scripture, the standing rule of judgment and righteousness. *Judgment shall return unto righteousness,* Ps. 94:15. Or,

(2.) The punishing of the church's enemies, against whom he will proceed in strict justice, according to the threatenings of the law. He will give them their deserts, and bring upon them the judgments they have challenged, but in wisdom too, and by an exact rule, that the tares may not be plucked up with the wheat. And when God comes thus to execute judgment,

[1.] These scornful men will be made ashamed of the vain hopes with which they had deluded themselves. *First,* They designed to make lies their refuge; but it will indeed prove a refuge of lies, which *the hail shall sweep away,* that tempest of hail spoken of *v.* 2. Those that make lies their refuge build upon the sand, and the building will fall when the storm comes, and bury the builder in the ruins of it. Those that make any thing their hiding place but Christ shall find that the waters will overflow it, as every shelter but the ark was over-topped and overthrown by the waters of the deluge. Such is the hope of the hypocrite; this will come of all his confidences. *Secondly,* They boasted of a covenant with death, and an agreement with the grave; but it shall be *disannulled,* as made without his consent who has the keys and sovereign command of hell and death. Those do but delude themselves that think by any wiles to evade the judgments of God. *Thirdly,* They fancied that when the overflowing scourge should pass through the land it should not come near them; but the prophet tells them that then, when others were falling by the common calamity, they should not only share in it, but should be trodden down by it: "You shall be to it for a treading down; it shall triumph over you as much as over any other, and you shall become its easy prey." They are further told (*v.* 19), 1. That it shall begin with them; they shall be so far from escaping it that they shall be the first that shall fall by it: *"From the time it goes forth it shall take you,* as if it came on purpose to seize you." 2. That it shall pursue them closely: *"Morning by morning shall it pass over;* as duly as the day returns you shall hear of some desolation or other made by it; for divine justice will follow its blow; you shall never be safe nor easy by day nor by night; there shall be a pestilence walking in darkness and a destruction wasting at noonday." 3. That there shall be no avoiding it: "The understanding of the report of its approach shall not give you any opportunity to make your escape, for there shall be no way of escape open; but it shall be only a vexation, you shall see it coming, and not see how to help yourselves." Or, "The very report of it at a distance will be a terror to you; what then will the thing itself be?" Evil tidings are a terror and vexation to scorners, but he whose heart is fixed, *trusting in God, is not afraid of them;* whereas, when the *overflowing scourge* comes, then all the comforts and confidences of scorners fail them, *v.* 20. (1.) That in which they thought to repose themselves reaches not to the length of their expectations:

The bed is shorter than that a man can stretch himself upon it, so that he is forced to cramp and contract himself. (2.) That in which they thought to shelter themselves proves insufficient to answer the intention: *The covering is narrower than that a man can wrap himself in it.* Those that do not build upon Christ as their foundation, but rest in a righteousness of their own, will prove in the end thus to have deceived themselves; they can never be easy, safe, nor warm; the bed is too short, the covering is too narrow; like our first parents' fig-leaves, the shame of their nakedness will still appear.

[2.] God will be glorified in the accomplishment of his counsels, *v.* 21. When God comes to contend with these scorners, *First, He will do his work, and bring to pass his act,* he will work for his own honour and glory, according to his own purpose; the work shall appear to all that see it to be the work of God as the righteous Judge of the earth. *Secondly,* He will do it now against his people, as formerly he did it against their enemies, by which his justice will appear to be impartial; he will now *rise up against Jerusalem as,* in David's time, against the Philistines *in Mount Perazim* (2 Sa. 5:20), and as, in Joshua's time, against the Canaanites *in the valley of Gibeon.* If those that profess themselves members of God's church by their pride and scornfulness make themselves like Philistines and Canaanites, they must expect to be dealt with as such. *Thirdly,* This will be *his strange work, his strange act,* his foreign deed. It is work that he is backward to: he rather delights in showing mercy, and *does not afflict willingly.* It is work that he is not used to as to his own people; he protects and favours them. It is a strange work indeed if he *turn to be their enemy and fight against them, ch.* 63:10. It is a work that all the neighbours will stand amazed at (Deu. 29:24), and therefore the ruins of Jerusalem are said to be *an astonishment,* Jer. 25:18.

Lastly, We have the use and application of all this (*v.* 22): *"Therefore be you not mockers;* dare not to ridicule either the reproofs of God's word or the approaches of his judgments." *Mocking the messengers of the Lord* was Jerusalem's measure-filling sin. The consideration of the judgments of God that are coming upon hypocritical professors should effectually silence mockers, and make them serious: *"Be you not mockers, lest your bands be made strong,* both the bands by which you are bound under the dominion of sin" (for there is little hope of the conversion of mockers) "and the bands by which you are bound over to the judgments of God." God has bands of justice strong enough to hold those that break all the bonds of his law asunder and cast away all his cord from them. Let not these mockers make light of divine threatenings, for the prophet (who is one of those with whom the secret of the Lord is) assures them that the Lord God of hosts has, in his hearing, *determined a consumption upon the whole earth;* and can they think to escape? or shall their unbelief invalidate the threatening?

Verses 23–29

This parable, which (like many of our Saviour's parables) is borrowed from the husbandman's calling, is ushered in with a solemn preface demanding attention, *He that has ears to hear, let him hear,* hear and understand, *v.* 23.

I. The parable here is plain enough, that the husbandman applies himself to the business of his calling with a great deal of pains and prudence, *secundum artem* — *according to rule,* and, as his judgment directs him, observes a method and order in his work. 1. In his ploughing and sowing: *Does the ploughman plough all day to sow?* Yes, he does, and he *ploughs in hope* and *sows in hope,* 1 Co. 9:10. *Does he open and break the clods?* Yes, he does, that the land may be fit to receive the seed. And *when he has thus made plain the face thereof* does he not sow his seed, seed suitable to the soil? For the husbandman knows what grain is fit for clayey ground and what for sandy ground, and, accordingly, he sows each in its place — *wheat in the principal place* (so the margin reads it), for it is the principal grain, and was a staple commodity of Canaan (Eze. 27:17), *and barley in the appointed place.* The wisdom and goodness of the God of nature are to be observed in this, that, to oblige his creatures with a grateful variety of productions, he has suited to them an agreeable variety of earths. 2. In his threshing, *v.* 27, 28. This also he proportions to the grain that is to be threshed out. *The fitches and the cummin,* being easily got out of their husk or ear, are only threshed with *a staff and a rod;* but *the bread-corn* requires more force, and therefore that must be bruised with *a threshing instrument,* a sledge shod with iron, that was drawn to and fro over it, to beat out the corn; and yet *he will not be ever threshing it,* nor any longer than is necessary to loosen the corn from the chaff; *he will not break it,* or crush it, into the ground *with the wheel of his cart, nor bruise it* to pieces *with his horsemen;* the grinding of it is reserved for another operation. Observe, by the way, what pains are to be taken, not only for the earning, but for the preparing of our necessary food; and yet, after all, it is *meat that perishes.* Shall we then grudge to labour much more for the *meat which endures to everlasting life? Bread-corn is bruised.* Christ was so; *it pleased the Lord to bruise him,* that he might be the bread of life to us.

II. The interpretation of the parable is not so plain. Most interpreters make it a further answer to those who set the judgments of God at defiance: "Let them know that as the husbandman will not be always ploughing, but will at length sow his seed, so God will not be always threatening, but will at length execute his threatenings and bring upon sinners the judgments they have deserved; but in wisdom, and in proportion to their strength, not that they may be ruined, but that they may be reformed and brought to repentance by them." But I think we may give this parable a greater latitude in the exposition of it. 1. In general, that God who gives the husbandman this wisdom is, doubtless, himself infinitely wise. It is God that *instructs the husbandman to discretion, as his God, v.* 26. Husbandmen have need of discretion wherewith to order their affairs, and ought not undertake that business unless they do in some measure understand it; and they should by observation and experience endeavour to improve themselves in the knowledge of it. Since *the king himself is served of the field,* the advancing of the art of husbandry is a common service to mankind more than the cultivating of most other arts. The skill of the husbandman is from God, as every good and perfect gift is. This takes off somewhat of the weight and terror of the sentence passed on man for sin, that when God, in execution of it, sent man to till the ground, he taught him how to do it most to his advantage, otherwise, in the greatness of his folly, he might have been for ever *tilling the sand of the sea,* labouring to no purpose. It is he that gives men capacity for this business, an inclination to it, and a delight in it; and if some were not by Providence cut out for it, and mad to rejoice (as Issachar, that tribe of husbandmen) in their tents, notwithstanding the toil and fatigue of this business, we should soon want the supports of life. If some are more discreet and judicious in managing these or any other affairs than others are, God must be acknowledged in it; and to him husbandmen must seek for direction in their business, for they, above other men, have an immediate dependence upon the divine Providence. As to the other instance of the husbandman's conduct in threshing his corn, it is said, *This also comes forth from the Lord of hosts, v.* 29. Even the plainest dictate of sense and reason must be acknowledged to *come forth from the Lord of hosts.* And, if it is from him that men do things wisely and discreetly, we must needs acknowledge him to be *wise in counsel and excellent in working.* God's working is according to his will; he never acts against his own mind, as men often do, and there is a counsel in his whole will: he is *therefore* excellent in working, because he is wonderful in counsel. 2. God's church is his husbandry, 1 Co. 3. 9 If Christ is the true vine, his Father is the husbandman (Jn. 15:1), and he is continually by his word and ordinances cultivating it. *Does the ploughman plough all day,* and *break the clods* of his ground, that it may receive the seed, and does not God by his ministers break up the fallow ground? Does not the ploughman, when the ground is fitted for the seed, cast in the seed in its proper soil? He does so, and so the great God sows his word by the hand of his ministers (Mt. 13:19), who are to divide the word of truth and give every one his portion. Whatever the soil of the heart is, there is some seed or other in the word proper for it. And, as the word of God, so the rod of God is thus wisely made use of. Afflictions are God's threshing-instruments, designed to loosen us from the world, to separate between us and our chaff, and to prepare us for use. And, as to these, God will make use of them as there is occasion; but he will proportion them to our strength; they shall be no heavier than there is need. If the rod and the staff will answer the end, he will not make use of his cart-wheel and his horsemen. And where these are necessary, as for the bruising of the bread-corn (which will not otherwise be got clean from the straw), yet he will not be ever threshing it, will not always chide, but his anger shall endure but for a moment; nor will he *crush under his feet the prisoners of the earth.* And herein we must acknowledge him *wonderful in counsel and excellent in working.*

CHAPTER 29

This woe to Ariel, which we have in this chapter, is the same with the "burden of the valley of vision" (*ch.* 22:1), and (it is very probable) points at the same event — the besieging of Jerusalem by the Assyrian army, which was cut off there by an angel; yet it is applicable to the destruction of Jerusalem by the Chaldeans, and its last desolations by the Romans. Here is, I. The event itself foretold, that Jerusalem should be greatly distressed (*v.* 1–4, 6), but that their enemies, who distressed them, should be baffled and defeated (*v.* 5, 7, 8). II. A reproof to three sorts of sinners: — 1. Those that were stupid, and regardless of the warnings which the prophet gave them (*v.* 9–12). 2. Those that were formal and hypocritical in their religious performances (*v.* 13, 14). 3. Those politicians that atheistically and profanely despised God's providence, and set up their own projects in competition with it (*v.* 15, 16). III. Precious promises of grace and mercy to a distinguished remnant whom God would sanctify, and in whom he would be sanctified, when their enemies and persecutors should be cut off (*v.* 17–24).

Verses 1–8

That it is Jerusalem which is here called *Ariel* is agreed, for that was the city where David dwelt; that part of it which was called *Zion* was in a particular manner the city of David, in which both the temple and the palace were. But why it is so called is very uncertain: probably the name and the reason were then well known. Cities, as well as persons, get surnames and nicknames. *Ariel* signifies *the lion of God,* or *the strong lion:* as the lion is king among beasts, so was Jerusalem among the cities, giving law to all about her; it was *the city of the great King* (Ps. 48:1, 2); it was the head-city of Judah, who is called *a lion's whelp* (Gen. 49:9) and whose ensign was a lion; and he that is the lion of the tribe of Judah was the glory of it. Jerusalem was a terror sometimes to the neighbouring nations, and, while she was a righteous city, was bold as a lion. Some make *Ariel* to signify *the altar of burnt-offerings,* which devoured the beasts offered in sacrifice as the lion does his prey. Woe to that altar in the city where David dwelt; that was destroyed with the temple by the Chaldeans. I rather take it as a woe to Jerusalem, Jerusalem; it is repeated here, as it is Mt. 23:37, that it might be the more awakening. Here is,

I. The distress of Jerusalem foretold. Though Jerusalem be a strong city, as a lion, though a holy city, as a lion of God, yet, if iniquity be found there, woe be to it. It was *the city where David dwelt;* it was he that brought that to it which was its glory, and which made it a type of the gospel church, and his dwelling in it was typical of Christ's residence in his church. This mentioned as an aggravation of Jerusalem's sin, that in it were set both the testimony of Israel and the *thrones of the house of David.* 1. Let Jerusalem know that her external performance of religious services will not serve as an exemption from the judgments of God (*v.* 1): *"Add year to year;* go on in the road of your annual feasts, let all your males appear there three times a year before the Lord, and none empty, according to the law and custom, and let them never miss any of these solemnities: *let them kill the sacrifices,* as they used to do; but, as long as their lives are unreformed and their hearts unhumbled, let them not think thus to pacify an offended God and to turn away his wrath." Note, Hypocrites may be found in a constant track of devout exercises, and treading around in them, and with these they may flatter themselves, but can never please God nor make their peace with him. 2. Let her know that God is coming forth against her in displeasure, that she shall be *visited of the Lord of hosts* (*v.* 6); her sins shall be enquired into and punished: God will reckon for them with terrible judgments, with the frightful alarms and rueful desolations of war, which shall be like *thunder and earthquakes, storms and tempests, and devouring fire,* especially upon the account of the *great noise.* When a foreign enemy was not in the borders, but in the bowels of their country, roaring and ravaging, and laying all waste (especially such an army as that of the Assyrians, whose commanders being so very insolent, as appears by the conduct of Rabshakeh, the common soldiers, no doubt, were much more rude), they might see the Lord of those hosts visiting them with thunder and storm. Yet, this being here said to be *a great noise,* perhaps it is intimated that they shall be worse frightened than hurt. Particularly, (1.) Jerusalem shall be besieged, straitly besieged. He does not say, *I will destroy Ariel,* but I *will distress Ariel;* and she is *therefore* brought into distress, that, being thereby awakened to repent and reform, she may not be brought to destruction. *I will (v.* 3) encamp against thee round about. It was the enemy's army that encamped against it; but God says that he will do it, for they are his hand, he does it by them. God had often and long, by a host of angels, encamped for them round about them for their protection and deliverance; but now he was *turned to be their enemy* and fought against them. The siege laid against them was of his laying, and the forts raised against them were of his raising. Note, When men fight against us we must, in them, see God contending with us. (2.) She shall be in grief to see the country laid waste and all the fenced cities of Judah in the enemies' hand: *There shall be heaviness and sorrow* (*v.* 2), *mourning and lamentation* — so these two words are sometimes rendered. Those that are most merry and jovial are commonly, when they come to be in distress, most overwhelmed with heaviness and sorrow; their laughter is then turned into mourning. "All Jerusalem *shall* then *be unto me as Ariel,* as the altar, with fire upon it and slain victims about it:" so it was when Jerusalem was destroyed by the Chaldeans; and many, no doubt, were slain when it was besieged by the Assyrians. "the whole city shall be an altar, in which sinners, falling by the judgments that are abroad, shall be as victims to divine justice." Or thus: — *"There shall be heaviness and sorrow;* they shall repent, and reform, and return to God, and then it shall be to me as Ariel. Jerusalem shall be like itself, shall become to me a Jerusalem again, a holy city," *ch.* 1:26. (3.) She shall be humbled, and mortified, and made submissive (*v.* 4): *"Thou shalt be brought down* from the height of arrogancy and insolence to which thou hast arrived: the proud looks and the proud language shall be brought down by one humbling providence after another." Those that despise God's judgments shall be humbled by them; for the proudest sinners shall either bend or break before him. They had talked big, had *lifted up the horn on high,* and had *spoken with a stiff neck* (Ps. 75:5); but now *thou shalt speak out of the ground, out of the dust, as one that has a familiar spirit, whispering out of the dust.* This intimates, [1.] That they should be faint and feeble, not able to speak up, nor to say all they would say; but as those who are sick, or whose spirits are ready to fail, their speech shall be low and interrupted. [2.] That they should be fearful, and in consternation, forced to speak low as being afraid lest their enemies should overhear them and take advantage against them. [3.] That they should be tame, and obliged to submit to the conquerors. When Hezekiah submitted to the king of Assyria, saying, *I have offended, that which thou puttest on me I will bear* (2 Ki. 18:14), then his speech was low, out of the dust. God can make those to crouch that have been most daring, and quite dispirit them.

II. The destruction of Jerusalem's enemies is foretold, for the comfort of all that were her friends and well-wishers in this distress (*v.* 5, 7): *"Thou shalt be brought down* (*v.* 4), *to speak out of the dust;* so low thou shalt be reduced. *But"* (so it may be rendered) *"the multitude of thy strangers and thy terrible ones,* the numerous armies of the enemy, *shall* themselves *be like small dust,* not able to speak at all, or as much as whisper, but *as chaff that passes away.* Thou shalt be abased, but they shall be quite dispersed, smitten and slain after another manner (*ch.* 27:7); they shall pass away, *yea it shall be in an instant, suddenly:* the enemy shall be surprised with the destruction, and you with the salvation." The army of the Assyrians was by an angel laid dead upon the spot, in an instant, suddenly. Such will be the destruction of the enemies of the gospel Jerusalem. *In one hour shall their judgment come,* Rev. 18:10. Again (*v.* 6), *"Thou shalt be visited,* or (as it used to be rendered) *She shall be visited with thunder and a great noise.* Thou shalt be put into a fright which thou shalt soon recover. But (*v.* 7) *the multitude of the nations that fight against her shall be as a dream of a night-vision;* they and their prosperity and success shall soon vanish past recall." *The multitude of the nations that fight against Zion shall be as a hungry man who dreams that he eats,* but still is hungry; that is, 1. Whereas they hoped to make a prey of Jerusalem, and to enrich themselves with the plunder of that opulent city, their hopes shall prove vain dreams, with which their fancies may please and sport themselves for a while, but they shall be disappointed. They fancied themselves masters of Jerusalem, but shall never be so. 2. They themselves, and all their pomp, and power, and prosperity, shall vanish like a dream when one awakes, shall be of as little value and as short continuance. Ps. 73:20. He shall *fly away as a dream* Job 20:8. The army of Sennacherib vanished and was gone quickly, though it had filled the country as a dream fills a man's head, especially as a dream of meat fills the head of him that went to bed hungry. Many understand these verses as part of the threatening of wrath, when God comes to distress Jerusalem, and lay siege to her. (1.) The multitude of her friends, whom she relies upon for help shall do her no good; for, though they are terrible ones, they shall be like the small dust, and shall pass away. (2.) The multitude of her enemies shall never think they can do her mischief enough; but, when they have devoured her much, still they shall be but like a man who dreams he eats, hungry, and greedy to devour her more.

Verses 9–16

Here, I. The prophet stands amazed at the stupidity of the greatest part of the Jewish nation. They had Levites, who taught *the good knowledge of the Lord* and had encouragement from Hezekiah in doing so, 2 Chr. 30:22. They had prophets, who brought them messages immediately from God, and signified to them what were the causes and what would be the effects of God's displeasure against them. Now, one would think, *surely this great nation,* that has all the advantages of divine revelation, is *a wise and understanding people,* Deu. 4:6. But, alas! it was quite otherwise, *v.* 9. The prophet addresses himself to the sober thinking part of them, calling upon them to be affected with the general carelessness of their neighbours. It may be read, "They delay, they put off, their repentance, but wonder you that they should be so sottish. They sport themselves with their own deceivings; they riot and revel; but do you *cry out,* lament their folly, cry to God by prayer for them. The more insensible they are of the hand of God gone out against them the more do you lay to heart these things." Note, The security of sinners in their sinful way is just matter of lamentation and wonder to all serious people, who should think themselves concerned to pray for those that do not pray for themselves. But what is the matter? What are we thus to wonder at? 1. We may well wonder that the generality of the people should be so sottish and brutish, and so infatuated, as if they were intoxicated: *They are drunken, but not with wine* (not with wine only, though with that they were often drunk), and they *erred through wine, ch.* 28:7. They were drunk with the love of pleasures, with prejudices against religion, and with the corrupt principles they had imbibed. Like drunken men, they know not what they do or say, nor whither they go. They are not sensible of the divine rebukes they are under. *They have beaten me, and I felt it not,* says the drunkard, Prov. 23:35. God speaks to them once, yea, twice; but, like men drunk, they perceive it not, they understand it not, but forget the law. *They stagger* in their counsels, are unstable and unsteady, and stumble at every thing that lies in their way. There is such a thing as spiritual drunkenness. 2. It is yet more strange that God himself should have *poured out upon them a spirit of deep sleep, and closed their eyes* (*v.* 10), that he who bids them awake and open their eyes should yet lay them to sleep and shut their eyes; but it is in a way of righteous judgment, to punish them for their *loving darkness rather than light,* their loving sleep. When God by his prophets called them they said, *Yet a little sleep, a little slumber;* and therefore he gave them up to strong delusions, and said, *Sleep on now.* This is applied to the unbelieving Jews, who rejected the gospel of Christ, and were justly hardened in their infidelity, till wrath came upon them to the uttermost. Rom. 11:8, *God has given them the spirit of slumber.* And we have reason to fear it is the woeful case of many who live in the midst of gospel light. 3. It is very sad that this should be the case with those who were their prophets, and rulers, and seers, that those who should have been their guides were themselves blindfolded; and it is easy to tell what the fatal consequences will be when the blind lead the blind. This was fulfilled when, in the latter days of the Jewish church, the chief priests, and the scribes, and the elders of the people, were the great opposers of Christ and his gospel, and brought themselves under a judicial infatuation. 4. The sad effect of this was that all the means of conviction, knowledge, and grace, which they enjoyed, were ineffectual, and did not answer the end (*v.* 11, 12): "*The vision of all the* prophets, true and false, *has become to you as the words of a book,* or letter, *that is sealed up;* you cannot discern the truth of the real visions and the falsehood of the pretended ones." Or, every vision particularly that this prophet had seen for them, and published to them, had become unintelligible; they had it among them, but were never the wiser for it, any more than a man (though a good scholar) is for a book delivered to him sealed up, and which he must not open the seals of. He sees it is a book, and that is all; he knows nothing of what is in it. So they knew that what Isaiah said was a vision and prophecy, but the meaning of it was hidden from them; it was only a sound of words to them, which they were not at all alarmed by, nor affected with; it answered not the intention, for it made no impression at all upon them. Neither the learned nor the unlearned were the better for all the messages God sent them by his servants the prophets, nor desired to be so. The ordinary sort of people excused themselves from regarding what the prophets said with their want of learning and a liberal education, as if they were not concerned to know and do the will of God because they were not bred scholars: *It is nothing to me, I am not learned.* Those of better rank pretended that the prophet had a peculiar way of speaking, which was obscure to them, and which, though they were men of letters, they had not been used to; and, *Si non vis intelligi, debes negligi — If you wish not to be understood, you deserve to be neglected.* Both these are groundless pretences; for God's prophets have been no unfaithful debtors either to the wise or to the unwise, Rom. 1:14. Or we may take it thus: — The book of prophecy was given to them sealed, so that they could not read it, as a just judgment upon them; because it had often been delivered to them unsealed, and they would not take pains to learn the language of it, and then made excuse for their not reading it because they were not learned. But observe, "The vision has become thus to you whose minds the god of this world has blinded; but it is not so in itself, it is not so to all; the same vision which to you is a *savour of death unto death* to others is and shall be a *savour of life unto life.*" Knowledge is easy to him that understands.

II. The prophet, in God's name, threatens those that were formal and hypocritical in their exercises of devotion, *v.* 13, 14. Observe here,

1. The sin that is here charged upon them — dissembling with God in their religious performances, *v.* 13. He that knows the heart, and cannot be imposed upon with shows and pretences, charges it upon them, whether their hearts condemn them for it or no. He that is greater than the heart, and knows all things, knows that though they *draw nigh to him with their mouth,* and *honour him with their lips,* yet they are not sincere worshippers. To worship God is to make our approaches to him, and to present our adorations of him; it is to draw nigh to him as those that have business with him, with an intention therein to honour him. This we are to do with our mouth and our lips, in speaking of him and in speaking to him; we must *render to him the calves of our lips,* Hosea 14:2. And, if the heart be full of his love and fear, out of the abundance of that the mouth will speak. But there are many whose religion is lip-labour only. They say that which expresses an approach to God and an adoration of him, but it is only from the teeth outward. For, (1.) They do not apply their minds to the service. When they pretend to be speaking to God they are thinking of a thousand impertinences: *The have removed their hearts far from me,* that they might not be employed in prayer, nor come within reach of the word. When work was to be done for God, which required the heart, that was sent out of the way on purpose, with the fool's eyes, into the ends of the earth. (2.) They do not make the word of God the rule of their worship, nor his will their reason: *Their fear towards me is taught by the precept of men.* They worshipped the God of Israel, not according to his appointment, but their own inventions, the directions of their false prophets or their idolatrous kings, or the usages of the nations that were round about them. The tradition of the elders was of more value and validity with them than the laws which God commanded Moses. Or, if they did worship God in a way conformable to his institution in the days of Hezekiah, a great reformer, they had more an eye to the precept of the king than to God's command. This our Saviour applies to the Jews in his time, who were formal in their devotions and wedded to their own inventions, and pronounces concerning them that in vain they did worship God, Mt. 15:8, 9.

2. It is a spiritual judgment with which God threatens to punish them for their spiritual wickedness (*v.* 14): *I will proceed to do a marvellous work.* They did one strange thing; they removed all sincerity from their hearts. Now God will go on and do another; he will remove all sagacity from their heads. *The wisdom of their wise men shall perish.* They played the hypocrite, and thought to put a cheat upon God, and now they are left to themselves to play the fool, and not only to put a cheat upon themselves, but to be easily cheated by all about them. Those that make religion no more than a pretence, to serve a turn, are out in their politics; and it is just with God to deprive those of their understanding who part with their uprightness. This was fulfilled in the wretched infatuation which the Jewish nation were manifestly under, after they had rejected the gospel of Christ; they removed their hearts far from God, and therefore God justly removed wisdom far from them, and hid from their eyes the things that belonged even to their temporal peace. This is a marvelous work; it is surprising, it is astonishing, that wise men should of a sudden lose their wisdom and be given up to strong delusions. Judgments on the mind, though least taken notice of, are to be most wondered at.

III. He shows the folly of those that though to act separately and secretly from God, and were carrying on designs independent upon God and which they projected to conceal from his all-seeing eye. Here we have, 1. Their politics described (*v.* 15): They *seek deep to hide their counsel from the Lord,* that he may not know either what they do or what they design; they say, "Who sees us? No man, and therefore not God himself." The consultations they had about their own safety they kept to themselves, and never asked God's advice concerning them; nay, they knew they were displeasing to him, but thought they could conceal them from him; and, if he did not know them, he could not baffle and defeat them. See what foolish fruitless pains sinners take in their sinful ways; they seek deep, they sink deep, to hide their counsel from the Lord, who sits in heaven and laughs at them. Note, A practical disbelief of God's omniscience is at the bottom both of the carnal worships and of the carnal confidences of hypocrites; Ps. 94:7; Eze. 8:12; 9:9. 2. The absurdity of their politics demonstrated (*v.* 16): "*Surely your turning of things upside down* thus, your various projects, turning your affairs this and that way to make them shape as you would have them — or rather your inverting the order of things, and thinking to make God's providence give attendance to your projects, and that God must know no more than you think fit, which is perfectly turning things upside down and beginning at the wrong end — *shall be esteemed as the potter's clay.* God will turn and manage you, and all your counsels, with as much ease and as absolute a power as the potter forms and fashions his clay." See how God despises, and therefore what little reason we have to dread, those contrivances of men that are carried on without God, particularly those against him. (1.) Those that think to hide their counsels from God do in effect deny him to be their Creator. It is as if the work should say of him that made it, "He made me not; I made myself." If God made us, he certainly knows us as the Psalmist shows, (Ps. 139:1, 13–16); so that those who say that he does not see them might as well say that he did not make them. Much of the wickedness of the wicked arises from this, they forget that God formed them, Deu. 32:18. Or, (2.) Which comes to the same thing, they deny him to be a wise Creator: *The thing framed saith of him that framed it, He had no understanding;* for if he had understanding to make us so curiously, especially to make us intelligent beings and to *put understanding into the inward part* (Job 38:36), no doubt he has understanding to know us and all we say and do. As those that quarrel with God, so those that think to conceal themselves from him, do in effect charge him with folly; but *he that formed the eye, shall he not see?* Ps. 94:9.

Verses 17–24

Those that thought to hide their counsels from the Lord were said to turn things upside down (*v.* 16), and they intended to do it unknown to God; but God here tells them that he will turn things upside down his way; and let us see whose word shall stand, his or theirs. They disbelieve Providence: "Wait awhile," says God, "and you shall be convinced by ocular demonstration that there is a God who governs the world, and that he governs it and orders all the changes that are in it for the good of his church." The wonderful revolution here foretold may refer primarily to the happy settlement of the affairs of Judah and Jerusalem after the defeat of Sennacherib's attempt, and the repose which good people then enjoyed, when they were delivered from the alarms of the sword both of war and persecution. But it may look further, to the rejection of the Jews at the first planting of the gospel (for their hypocrisy and infidelity were here foretold, *v.* 13) and the admission of the Gentiles into the church.

I. In general, it is a great and surprising change that is here foretold, *v.* 17. *Lebanon,* that was a forest, *shall be turned into a fruitful field;* and Carmel, that was a fruitful field, shall become a forest. It is a counterchange. Note, Great changes, both for the better and for the worse, are often made in a very little while. It was a sign given them of the defeat of Sennacherib that the ground should be more than ordinarily fruitful (*ch.* 37:30): *You shall eat this year such as grows of itself;* food for man shall be (as food for beasts is) the spontaneous product of the soil. Then Lebanon became a fruitful field, so fruitful that that which used to be reckoned a fruitful field in comparison with it was looked upon but as a forest. When a great harvest of souls was gathered in to Christ from among the Gentiles then the wilderness was turned into a fruitful field; and the Jewish church, that had long been a fruitful field, became a desolate and deserted forest, *ch.* 54:1.

II. In particular,

1. Those that were ignorant shall become intelligent, *v.* 18. Those that understood not this prophecy (but it was to them as a sealed book, *v.* 11) shall, when it is accomplished, understand it, and shall acknowledge, not only the hand of God in the event, but the voice of God in the prediction of it: *The deaf shall then hear the words of the book.* The fulfilling of prophecy is the best exposition of it. The poor Gentiles shall then have divine revelation brought among them; and those that sat in darkness shall see a great light, those that were blind shall see out of obscurity; for the gospel was sent to them to *open their eyes,* Acts 26:18. Observe, In order to the making of men fruitful in good affections and actions, the course God's grace takes with them is to open their understandings and make them hear the words of God's book.

2. Those that were erroneous shall become orthodox (*v.* 24): *Those that erred in spirit,* that were under mistakes and misapprehensions concerning the words of the book and the meaning of them, shall come to understanding, to a right understanding of things; the Spirit of truth shall rectify their mistakes and lead them into all truth. This should encourage us to pray for *those that have erred and are deceived,* that God can, and often does, bring such to understanding. Those that murmured at the truths of God as hard sayings, and loved to pick quarrels with them, shall learn the true meaning of these doctrines, and then they will be better reconciled to them. Those that erred concerning the providence of God as to public affairs, and murmured at the disposals of it, when they shall see the issue of things shall better understand them and be aware of what God was designing in all, Hos. 14:9.

3. Those that were melancholy shall become cheerful and pleasant (*v.* 19): *The meek also shall increase their joy in the Lord.* Those who are poor in the world and poor in spirit, who, being in affliction, accommodate themselves to their affliction, are purely passive and not passionate, when they see God appearing for them, they shall *add,* or *repeat, joy in the Lord.* This intimates that even in their distress they kept up their joy in the Lord, but now they increased it. Note, Those who, when they are in trouble, can truly rejoice in God, shall soon have cause given them greatly to rejoice in him. When joy in the world is decreasing and fading joy in God is increasing and getting round. This shining light shall shine more and more; for that which is aimed at is that *this joy may be full.* Even *the poor among men* may rejoice in the Holy One of Israel, and their poverty needs not deprive them of that joy, Hab. 3:17, 18. And the meek, the humble, the patient, and dispassionate, shall grow in this joy. Note, The grace of meekness will contribute very much to the increase of our holy joy.

4. The enemies, that were formidable, shall become despicable. Sennacherib, that *terrible one,* and his great army, that put the country into such a consternation, shall be *brought to nought* (*v.* 20), shall be quite disabled to do any further mischief. The power of Satan, that terrible one indeed, shall be broken by the prevalency of Christ's gospel; and those that were subject to bondage through fear of him that had the power of death shall be delivered, Heb. 2:14, 15.

5. The persecutors, that were vexatious, shall be quieted, and so those they were troublesome to shall be quiet from the fear of them. To complete the repose of God's people, not only the terrible one from abroad shall be brought to nought, but the scorners at home too shall be consumed and cut off by Hezekiah's reformation. Those are a happy people, and likely to be so, who, when God gives them victory and success against their terrible enemies abroad, take care to suppress vice, and profaneness, and the spirit of persecution, those more dangerous enemies at home. Or, They shall be consumed and cut off by the judgments of God, shall be singled out to be made examples of. Or, They shall insensibly waste away, being put to confusion by the fulfilling of those predictions which they had made a jest of. Observe what had been the wickedness of these scorners, for which they should be cut off. They had been persecutors of God's people and prophets, probably of the prophet Isaiah particularly, and therefore he complains thus feelingly of them and of their subtle malice. Some as informers and persecutors, others as judges, did all they could to take away his life, or at least his liberty. And this is very applicable to the chief priests and Pharisees, who persecuted Christ and his apostles, and for that sin they and their nation of scorners were cut off and consumed. (1.) They ridiculed the prophets and the serious professors of religion; they despised them, and did their utmost to bring them into contempt; they were scorners, and sat in the seat of the scornful. (2.) They lay in wait for an occasion against them. By their spies they *watch for iniquity,* to see if they can lay hold of any thing that is said or done that may be called an iniquity. Or they themselves watch for an opportunity to do mischief, as Judas did to betray our Lord Jesus. (3.) They took advantage against them for the least slip of the tongue; and, if a thing were ever so little said amiss, it served them to ground an indictment upon. They *made a man,* though he were ever so wise and good a man, though he were a man of God, *an offender for a word,* a word mischosen or misplaced, when they could not but know that it was well meant, *v.* 21. They cavilled at every word that the prophets spoke to them by way of admonition, though ever so innocently spoken, and without any design to affront them. They put the worst construction upon what was said, and made it criminal by strained innuendoes. Those who consider how apt we all are to speak unadvisedly, and to mistake what we hear, will think it very unjust and unfair to *make a man an offender for a word.* (4.) They did all they could to bring those into trouble that dealt faithfully with them and told them of their faults. Those that *reprove in the gates,* reprovers by office, that were bound by the duty of their place, as prophets, as judges, and magistrates, to show people their transgressions, they hated these, and laid snares for them, as the Pharisees' emissaries, who were sent to watch our Saviour that they might *entangle him in his talk* (Mt. 22:15), that they might have something to lay to his charge which might render him odious to the people or obnoxious to the government. *So persecuted they the prophets;* and it is next to impossible for the most cautious to place their words so warily as to escape such snares. See how base wicked people are, who bear ill-will to those who, out of good-will to them, seek to save their souls from death; and see what need reprovers have both of courage to do their duty and of prudence to avoid the snare. (5.) They pervert judgment, and will never let an honest man carry an honest cause: *They turn aside the just for a thing of nought;* they condemn him, or give the cause against him, upon no evidence, no colour or pretence whatsoever. They run a man down, and misrepresent him, by all the little arts and tricks they can devise, as they did our Saviour. We must not think it strange if we see the best of men thus treated; *the disciple is not greater than his Master.* But wait awhile, and God will not only *bring forth their righteousness,* but cut off and consume these scorners.

6. Jacob, who was made to blush by the reproaches, and made to tremble by the threatenings, of his enemies, shall now be relieved both against his shame and against his fear, by the rolling away of those reproaches and the defeating of those threatenings (*v.* 22): *Thus the Lord saith who redeemed Abraham,* that is, called him out of Ur of the Chaldees, and so rescued him from the idolatry of his fathers and plucked him as a *brand out of the fire.* He that redeemed Abraham out of his snares and troubles will redeem all that are by faith his genuine seed out of theirs. He that began his care of his church in the redemption of Abraham, when it and its Redeemer were in his loins, will not now cast off the care of it. Because the enemies of his people are so industrious both to blacken them and to frighten them, therefore he will appear for the house of Jacob, and they shall not be ashamed as they have been, but shall have wherewith to answer those that reproach them, nor shall *their faces now wax pale;* but they shall gather courage, and look their enemies in the face without change of countenance, as those have reason to do who have the God of Abraham on their side.

7. Jacob, who thought his family would be extinct and the entail of religion quite cut off, shall have the satisfaction of seeing a numerous progeny devoted to God for a generation, *v.* 23. (1.) He shall see his children, multitudes of believers and praying people, the spiritual seed of faithful Abraham and wrestling Jacob. Having his quiver full of these arrows, he *shall not be ashamed* (*v.* 22) but shall speak with his enemy in the gate, Ps. 127:5. Christ shall *not be ashamed* (*ch.* 50:7), for *he shall see his seed* (*ch.* 53:10); he sees some, and foresees more, *in the midst of him,* flocking to the church, and residing there. (2.) His children are the work of God's hands; being formed by him, they are formed for him, his *workmanship, created unto good works.* It is some comfort to parents to think that their children are God's creatures, the work of the hands of his grace. (3.) He and his children shall sanctify the name of God as their God, as *the Holy One of Jacob,* and shall fear and worship the God of Israel. This is opposed to his being ashamed and waxing pale; when he is delivered from his contempts and dangers he shall not magnify himself, but *sanctify the Holy One of Jacob.* If God make our condition easy, we must endeavour to make his name glorious. Parents and children are ornaments and comforts indeed to each other when they join in sanctifying the name of God. When parents give up their children, and children give up themselves, to God, to be *to him for a name and a praise,* then the forest will soon become a fruitful field.

CHAPTER 30

The prophecy of this chapter seems to relate (as that in the foregoing chapter) to the approaching danger of Jerusalem and desolations of Judah by Sennacherib's invasion. Here is, I. A just reproof to those who, in that distress, trusted to the Egyptians for help, and were all in a hurry to fetch succors from Egypt (*v.* 1–7). II. A terrible threatening against those who slighted the good advice which God by his prophets gave them for the repose of their minds in that distress, assuring them that whatever became of others the judgment would certainly overtake them (*v.* 8–17). III. A gracious promise to those who trusted in God, that they should not only see through the trouble, but should see happy days after it, times of joy and reformation, plenty of the means of grace, and therewith plenty of outward good things and increasing joys and triumphs (*v.* 18–26), and many of these promises are very applicable to gospel grace. IV. A prophecy of the total rout and ruin of the Assyrian army, which should be an occasion of great joy and an introduction to those happy times (*v.* 27–33).

Verses 1–7

It was often the fault and folly of the people of the Jews that, when they were insulted by their neighbours on one side, they sought for succour from their neighbours on the other side, instead of looking up to God and putting their confidence in him. Against the Israelites they sought to the Syrians, 2 Chr. 16:2, 3. Against the Syrians they sought to the Assyrians, 2 Ki. 16:7. Against the Assyrians they here sought to the Egyptians, and Rabshakeh upbraided them with so doing, 2 Ki. 18:21. Now observe here,

I. How this sin of theirs is described, and what there was in it that was provoking to God. When they saw themselves in danger and distress, 1. They would not consult God. They would do things of their own heads, and not advise with God, though they had a ready and certain way of doing it by Urim or prophets. They were so confident of the prudence of their own measures that they thought it needless to consult the oracle; nay, they were not willing to put it to that issue: "They *take counsel* among themselves, and one from another; but they do not ask counsel, much less will they take counsel, of me. They *cover with a covering"* (they think to secure themselves with one shelter or other, which may serve to cover them from the violence of the storm), *"but not of my Spirit"* (not such as God by his Spirit, in the mouth of his prophets, directed them to), "and therefore it will prove too short a covering, and a refuge of lies." 2. They could not confide in God. They did not think it enough to have God on their side, nor were they at all solicitous to make him their friend, but they *strengthened themselves in the strength of Pharaoh;* they thought him a powerful ally, and doubted not but to be able to cope with the Assyrian while they had him for them. *The shadow of Egypt* (and it was but a shadow) was the covering in which they wrapped themselves.

II. What was the evil of this sin. 1. It bespoke them *rebellious children;* and a *woe* is here denounced against them under that character, *v.* 1. They were, in profession, God's children; but, not trusting in him, they were justly stigmatized as rebellious; for, if we distrust God's providence, we do in effect withdraw ourselves from our allegiance. 2. They added sin to sin. It was sin that brought them into distress; and then, instead of repenting, they *trespassed yet more against the Lord,* 2 Chr. 28:22. And those that had abused God's mercies to them, making them the fuel of their lusts, abused their afflictions too, making them an excuse for their distrust of God; and so they make bad worse, and add sin to sin; and those that do so, as they make their own chain heavy, so it is just with God to make their plagues wonderful. Now that which aggravated their sin was, (1.) That they took so much pains to secure the Egyptians for their allies: *They walk to go down to Egypt,* travel up and down to find an advantageous road thither; but they *have not asked at my mouth,* never considered whether God would allow and approve of it or no. (2.) That they were at such a vast expense to do it, *v.* 6. They load *the beasts of the south* (horses fetched from Egypt, which lay south from Judea) with their riches, fancying, as it is common with people in a fright, that they were safer any where than where they were. Or they sent their riches thither as bribes to Pharaoh's courtiers, to engage them in their interests, or as pay for their army. God would have helped them *gratis;* but, if they will have help from the Egyptians, they must pay dearly for it, and they seem willing to do so. The riches that are so spent will turn to a bad account. They carried their effects to Egypt through a land (so it may be read) of trouble and anguish, that vast howling wilderness which lay between Canaan and Egypt, *whence come the lion and fiery serpent,* Deu. 8:15. They would venture through that dangerous wilderness, to bring what they had to Egypt. Or it may be meant of Egypt itself, which had been to Israel a house of bondage and therefore a land of trouble and anguish, and which abounded in ravenous and venomous creatures. See what dangers men run into that forsake God, and what dangers they will run into in pursuance of their carnal confidences and their expectations from the creature.

III. What would be the consequence of it. 1. The Egyptians would receive their ambassadors, would address them very respectfully, and be willing to treat with them (*v.* 4): *His princes were at Zoan,* at Pharaoh's court there, and had their audience of the king, who encouraged them to depend upon his friendship and the succours he would send them. But, 2. They would not answer their expectation: They *could not profit them, v.* 5. For God says, *They shall not profit them* (*v.* 6), and every creature is that to us (and no more) which he makes it to be. The forces they were to furnish them with could not be raised in time; or, when they were raised, they were not fit for service, and they would not venture any of their veteran troops in the expedition; or the march was so long that they could not come up when they had occasion for them; or the Egyptians would not be cordial to Israel, but would secretly incline to the Assyrians, upon some account or other: *The Egyptians shall help in vain, and to no purpose, v.* 7. They shall hinder and hurt, instead of helping. And therefore, 3. These people, that were now so fond of the Egyptians, would at length be ashamed of them, and of all their expectations from them and confidence in them (*v.* 3): *"The strength of Pharaoh,* which was your pride, *shall be your shame;* all your neighbours will upbraid you, and you will upbraid yourselves, with your folly in trusting to it. And the *shadow of Egypt,* that *land shadowing with wings* (*ch.* 18:1), which was your confidence, shall be your confusion; it will not only disappoint you, and be the matter of your shame, but it will weaken all your other supports, and be an occasion of mischief to you." God afterwards threatens the ruin of Egypt for this very thing, because they had dealt treacherously with Israel and *been a staff of a reed* to them, Eze. 29:6, 7. The princes and ambassadors of Israel, who were so forward to court an alliance with them, when they come among them shall see so much of their weakness, or rather of their baseness, that *they shall all be ashamed of a people that could not be a help or profit to them,* but a *shame and reproach, v.* 5. Those that trust in God, in his power, providence, and promise, are never made ashamed of their hope; but those that put confidence in any creature will sooner or later find it a reproach to them. God is true, and may be trusted, but every man a liar, and must be suspected. The Creator is a rock of ages, the creature a broken reed. We cannot expect too little from man nor too much from God.

IV. The use and application of all this (*v.* 7): *"Therefore have I cried concerning this* matter, this project of theirs. I have published it, that all might take notice of it. I have pressed it as one in earnest. *Their strength is to sit still,* in a humble dependence upon God and his goodness and a quiet submission to his will, and not to wander about and put themselves to great trouble to seek help from this and the other creature." If we sit still in a day of distress, hoping and quietly waiting for the salvation of the Lord, and using only lawful regular methods for our own preservation, this will be the strength of our souls both for services and sufferings, and it will engage divine strength for us. We weaken ourselves, and provoke God to withdraw from us, when we make flesh our arm, for then our hearts depart from the Lord. When we have tired ourselves by seeking for help from creatures we shall find it the best way of recruiting ourselves to repose in the Creator. *Here I am, let him do with me as he pleases.*

Verses 8–17

Here, I. The preface is very awful. The prophet must not only preach this, but he must write it (*v.* 8), *write it in a table,* to be hung up and exposed to public view; he must carefully *note it,* not in loose papers which might be lost or torn, but *in a book,* to be preserved for posterity, *in perpetuam rei memoriam — for a standing testimony* against this wicked generation; let it remain not only to the next succeeding ages, but for ever and ever, while the world stands; and so it shall, for the book of the scriptures no doubt, shall continue, and be read, to the end of time. Let it be written, 1. To shame the men of the present age, who would not hear and heed it when it was spoken. Let it be written, that it may not be lost; their children may profit by it, though they will not. 2. To justify God in the judgments he was about to ring upon them; people will be tempted to think he was too hard upon them, and oversevere, unless they know how very bad they were, how very provoking, and what fair means God tried with them before he brought it to this extremity. 3. For warning to others not to do as they did, lest they should fare as they fared. It is designed for admonition to those of the remotest place and age, even those *upon whom the ends of the world have come,* 1 Co. 10:11. It may be of use for God's ministers not only to preach, but to write; for that which is written remains.

II. The character given of the profane and wicked Jews is very sad. He must, if he will draw them in their own colours, write this concerning them (and we are sure he does not bear false witness against them, nor make them worse than they were, for the judgment of God is according to truth), *That this is a rebellious people, v.* 9. The Jews were, for aught we know, the only professing people God had then in the world, and yet many of them were a rebellious people. 1. They rebelled against their own convictions and covenants: "They are *lying children,* that will not stand to what they say, that promise fair, but perform nothing;" when he took them into covenant with himself he said of them, *Surely they are my people, children that will not lie* (*ch.* 63:8); but they proved otherwise. 2. They rebelled against the divine authority: "They are *children that will not hear the law of the Lord,* nor heed it, but will do as they have a mind, let God himself say what he will to the contrary."

III. The charge drawn up against them is very high and the sentence passed upon them very dreadful. Two things they here stand charged with, and their doom is read for both, a fearful doom: —

1. They forbade the prophets to speak to them in God's name, and to deal faithfully with them.

(1.) This their sin is described, *v.* 10, 11. They set themselves so violently against the prophets to hinder them from preaching, or at least from dealing plainly with them in their preaching, did so banter them and browbeat them, that they did in effect *say to the seers, See not.* They had the light, but they loved darkness rather. It was their privilege that they had seers among them, but they did what they could to put out their eyes — that they had prophets among them, but they did what they could to stop their mouths; for they tormented them in their wicked ways, Rev. 11:10. Those that silence good ministers, and discountenance good preaching, are justly counted, and called, *rebels against God.* See what it was in the prophets' preaching with which they found themselves aggrieved. [1.] The prophets told them of their faults, and warned them of their misery and danger by reason of sin, and they could not bear that. They must speak to them smooth things, must flatter them in their sins, and say that they did well, and there was no harm, no peril, in the course of life they lived in. Let a thing be ever so right and true, if it be not smooth, they will not hear it. But if it be agreeable to the good opinion they have of themselves, and will confirm them in that, though it be ever so false and ever so great a cheat upon them, they will have it prophesied to them. Those deserve to be deceived that desire to be so. [2.] The prophets stopped them in their sinful pursuits, and stood in their way like the angel in Balaam's road, with the sword of God's wrath drawn in their hand; so that they could not proceed without terror. And this they took as a great insult. When they went on frowardly in the way of their hearts they said to the prophets, *"Get you out of the way, turn aside out of the paths.* What do you do in our way? Cannot you let us alone to do as we please?" Those have their hearts fully set in them to do evil that bid their faithful monitors to stand out of their way. *Forbear, why shouldst thou be smitten?* 2 Chr. 25:16. [3.] The prophets were continually telling them of the Holy One of Israel, what an enemy he is to sin ad how severely he will reckon with sinners; and this they could not endure to hear of. Both the thing itself and the expression of it were too serious for them; and therefore, if the prophets will speak to them, they will make it their bargain that they shall not call God *the Holy One of Israel;* for God's holiness is that attribute which wicked people most of all dread. Let us no more be troubled with that state-preface (as Mr. White calls it) to your impertinent harangues. Those have reason to fear perishing in their sins that cannot bear to be frightened out of them.

(2.) Now what is the doom passed upon them for this? We have it, *v.* 12, 13. Observe, [1.] Who it is that gives judgment upon them: *Thus saith the Holy One of Israel.* That title of God which they particularly excepted against the prophet makes use of. Faithful ministers will not be driven from using such expressions as are proper to awaken sinners, though they be displeasing. We must tell men that God is the *Holy One of Israel,* and so they shall find him, whether they will hear or whether they will forbear. [2.] What the ground of the judgment is: *Because they despise this word* — wither, in general, every word that the prophets said to them, or this word in particular, which declares

God to be *the Holy One of Israel:* "they despise this, and will neither make it their fear, to stand in awe of it, nor make it their hope, to put any confidence in it; but, rather than they will be beholden to *the Holy One of Israel,* they will *trust in oppression and perverseness,* in the wealth they have got and the interest they have made by fraud and violence, or in the sinful methods they have taken for their own security, in contradiction to God and his will. On these they lean, and therefore it is just that they should fall." [3.] What the judgment is that is passed upon them: *"This iniquity shall be to you as a breach ready to fall.* This confidence of yours will be like a house built upon the sand, which will fall in the storm and bury the builder in the ruins of it. Your contempt of that word of God which you might build upon will make every thing else you trust like a wall that bulges out, which, if any weight be laid upon it, comes down, nay, which often sinks with its own weight." The ruin they would hereby bring upon themselves should be, *First,* A surprising ruin: *The breaking shall come suddenly, at an instant,* when they do not expect it, which will make it the more frightful, and when they are not prepared or provided for it, which will make it the more fatal. *Secondly,* An utter ruin, universal and irreparable: "Your and all your confidences shall be not only weak as the potter's clay (*ch.* 29:16), but *broken to pieces as the potter's vessel.* He that has the rod of iron shall break it (Ps. 2:9) and he shall not spare, shall not have any regard to it, nor be in care to preserve or keep whole any part of it. But, when once it is broken so as to be unfit for use, let it be dashed, let it be crushed, all to pieces, so that there may not remain one *sherd* big enough *to take up* a little *fire or water"* — two things we have daily need of, and which poor people commonly fetch in a piece of a broken pitcher. They shall not only be as a *bowing wall* (Ps. 62:3), but as a broken mug or glass, which is good for nothing, nor can ever be made whole again.

2. They slighted the gracious directions God gave them, not only how to secure themselves and make themselves safe, but how to compose themselves and make themselves easy; they would take their own way, *v.* 15–17. Observe here,

(1.) The method God put them into for salvation and strength. The God that knew them, and knew what was proper for them, and desired their welfare, gave them this prescription; and it is recommended to us all. [1.] Would we be saved from the evil of every calamity, guarded against the temptation of it and secured from the curse of it, which are the only evil things in it? It must be *in returning and rest,* in returning to God and reposing in him as our rest. Let us return from our evil ways, into which we have gone aside, and rest and settle in the way of God and duty, and that is the way to be saved. "Return from this project of going down to Egypt, and rest satisfied in the will of God, and then you may trust him with your safety. *In returning* (in the thorough reformation of your hearts and lives) *and in rest* (in an entire submission of your souls to God and a complacency in him) *you shall be saved."* [2.] Would we be strengthened to do what is required of us and to bear what is laid upon us? It must be *in quietness and in confidence;* we must keep our spirits calm and sedate by a continual dependence upon God, and his power and goodness; we must retire into ourselves with a holy quietness, suppressing all turbulent and tumultuous passions, and keeping the peace in our own minds. And we must rely upon God with a holy confidence that he can do what he will and will do what is best for his people. And this will be our strength; it will inspire us with such a holy fortitude as will carry us with ease and courage through all the difficulties we may meet with.

(2.) The contempt they put upon this prescription; they would not take God's counsel, though it was so much for their own good. And justly will those die of their disease that will not take God for their physician. We are certainly enemies to ourselves if we will not be subjects to him. They would not so much as try the method prescribed: *"But you said, No* (*v.* 16), we will not compose ourselves, for *we will flee upon horses* and *we will ride upon the swift;* we will hurry hither and thither to fetch in foreign aids." They think themselves wiser than God, and that they know what is good for themselves better than he does. When Sennacherib took all the fenced cities of Judah, those rebellious children would not be persuaded to sit still and patiently to expect God's appearing for them, as he did wonderfully at last; but they would shift for their own safety, and thereby they exposed themselves to so much the more danger.

(3.) The sentence passed upon them for this. Their sin shall be their punishment: "You will flee, and therefore *you shall flee;* you will be upon the full speed, and therefore so shall those be that pursue you." The dogs are most apt to run barking after him that rides fast. The conquerors protected those that sat still, but pursued those that made their escape; and so that very project by which they hoped to save themselves was justly their ruin and the most guilty suffered most. It is foretold, *v.* 17, [1.] That they should be easily cut off; they should be so dispirited with their own fears, increased by their flight, that one of the enemy should defeat a thousand of them, and five put an army to flight, which could never be *unless their Rock had sold them* Deu. 32:30. [2.] That they should be generally cut off, and only here and there one should escape alone in a solitary place, and be left for a spectacle too, *as a beacon upon the top of a mountain,* a warning to others to avoid the like sinful courses and carnal confidences.

Verses 18–26

The closing words of the foregoing paragraph *(You shall be left as a beacon upon a mountain)* some understand as a promise that a remnant of them should be reserved as monuments of mercy; and here the prophet tells them what good times should succeed these calamities. Or the first words in this paragraph may be read by way of antithesis, *Notwithstanding this, yet will the Lord wait that he may be gracious.* The prophet, having shown that those who made Egypt their confidence would be ashamed of it, here shows that those who sat still and made God alone their confidence would have the comfort of it. It is matter of comfort to the people of God, when the times are very bad, that *all will be well yet,* well with those that fear God, when we say to the wicked, *It shall be ill with you.*

I. God will be gracious to them and will have mercy on them. This is the foundation of all good. If we find favour with God, and he have mercy upon us, we shall have comfort according to the time that we have been afflicted.

1. The mercy in store for them is very affectingly expressed. (1.) "He will *wait to be gracious* (*v.* 18); he will wait till you return to him and seek his face, and then he will be ready to meet you with mercy. He will wait, that he may do it in the best and fittest time, when it will be most for his glory, when it will come to you with the most pleasing surprise. He will continually follow you with his favours, and not let slip any opportunity of being gracious to you." (2.) "He will stir up himself to deliver you, will be exalted, will be *raised up out of his holy habitation* (Zec. 2:13), that he may appear for you in more than ordinary instances of power and goodness; *and thus he will be exalted,* that is, he will glorify his own name. This is what he aims at in having mercy on his people." (3.) *He will be very gracious* (*v.* 19), and this in answer to prayer, which makes his kindness doubly kind: *"He will be gracious to thee, at the voice of thy cry,* the cry of thy necessity, when that is most urgent — the cry of thy prayer, when that is most fervent. *When he shall hear it,* there needs no more; at the first word *he will answer thee,* and say, *Here I am."* Herein he is very gracious indeed. In particular, [1.] Those who were disturbed in the possession of their estates shall again enjoy them quietly. When the danger is over *the people shall dwell in Zion, at Jerusalem,* as they used to do; they shall dwell safely, free from the fear of evil. [2.] Those who were all in tears shall have cause to rejoice, and shall weep no more; and those who dwell in Zion, the holy city, will find enough there to wipe away tears from their eyes.

2. This is grounded upon two great truths: (1.) That *the Lord is a God of judgment;* he is both wise and just in all the disposals of his providence, true to his word and tender of his people. If he correct his children, it is *with judgment* (Jer. 10:24), with moderation and discretion, considering their frame. We think we may safely refer ourselves to a man of judgment; and shall we not commit our way to a God of judgment? (2.) That therefore all those are blessed who *wait for him,* who not only wait on him with their prayers, but wait for him with their hopes, who will not take any indirect course to extricate themselves out of their straits, or anticipate their deliverance, but patiently expect God's appearances for them in his own way and time. Because God is infinitely wise, those are truly happy who refer their cause to him.

II. They shall not again know the want of the means of grace, *v.* 20, 21. Here, 1. It is supposed that they might be brought into straits and troubles after this deliverance was wrought for them. It was promised (*v.* 19), that they should *weep no more* and that God would be *gracious to them;* and yet here it is taken for granted that God may give them the *bread of adversity and the water of affliction,* prisoners' fare (1 Ki. 22:27), coarse and sorry food, such as the poor use. When one trouble is over we know not how soon another may succeed; and we may have an interest in the favour of God, and such consolations as are sufficient to prohibit weeping, and yet may have bread of adversity given us to eat and water of affliction to drink. Let us therefore not judge of love or hatred by what is before us. 2. It is promised that their eyes should *see their teachers,* that is, that they should have faithful teachers among them, and should have hearts to regard them and not slight them as they had done; and then they might the better be reconciled to the bread of adversity and the water of affliction. It was a common saying among the old Puritans, *Brown bread and the gospel are good fare.* A famine of bread is not so great a judgment as a famine of the word of God, Amos 8:11, 12. It seems that their teachers had been removed into corners (probably being forced to shift for their safety in the reign of Ahaz), but it shall be so no more. *Veritas non quaerit angulos — Truth seeks no corners for concealment.* But the teachers of truth may sometimes be driven into corners for shelter; and it goes ill with the church when it is so, when the woman with her crown of twelve stars is forced to flee into the wilderness (Rev. 12:6), when the prophets are *hidden by fifty in a cave,* 1 Ki. 18:4. But God will find a time to call the teachers out of their corners again, and to replace them in their solemn assemblies, which shall *see their own teachers,* the *eyes of all the synagogue* being fastened on them, Lu. 4:20. And it will be the more pleasing because of the restraint they have been for some time under, as light out of darkness, as life from the dead. To all that love God and their own souls this return of faithful teachers out of their corners, especially with a promise that they *shall not be removed into corners any more,* is the most acceptable part of any deliverance, and has comfort enough in it to sweeten even the bread of adversity and the water of affliction. But this is not all: 3. It is promised that they shall have the benefit, not only of the public ministry, but of private and particular admonition and advice (*v.* 21): *"Thy ears shall hear a word behind thee,* calling after thee as a man calls after a traveller that he sees going out of his road." Observe, (1.) Whence this word shall come — from *behind thee,* from some one whom thou dost not see, but who sees thee. "Thy eyes see thy teachers; but this is a teacher out of sight, it is thy own conscience, which shall now by the grace of God be awakened to do its office." (2.) What the word shall be: *"This is the way, walk you in it.* When thou art doubting, conscience shall direct thee to the way of duty; when thou art dull and trifling, conscience shall quicken thee in that way." As God has not left himself without witness, so he has not left us without guides to show us our way. (3.) The seasonableness of this word: It shall come *when you turn to the right hand or to the left.* We are very apt to miss our way; there are turnings on both hands, and those so tracked and seemingly straight that they may easily be mistaken for the right way. There are right-hand and left-hand errors, extremes on each side virtue; the tempter is busy courting us into the by-paths. It is happy then if by the particular counsels of a faithful minister or friend, or the checks of conscience and the strivings of God's Spirit, we be set right and prevented from going wrong. (4.) The success of this word: "It shall not only be spoken, but thy ears shall hear it; whereas God has formerly *spoken once, yea, twice,* and thou *hast not perceived it* (Job 33:14), now thou shalt listen attentively to these secret whispers, and hear them with an obedient ear." If God gives us not only the word, but the hearing ear, not only the means of grace, but a heart to make a good use of those means, we have reason to say, He is very gracious to us, and reason to hope he has yet further mercy in store for us.

III. They shall be cured of their idolatry, shall fall out

with their idols, and never be reconciled to them again, *v.* 22. The deliverance God shall work for them shall convince them that it is their interest, as well as duty, to serve him only; and they shall own that, as their trouble was brought upon them for their idolatries, so it was removed upon condition that they should not return to them. This is also the good effect of their seeing their teachers and hearing the word behind them; by this it shall appear that they are the better for the means of grace they enjoy — they shall break off from their best-beloved sin. Observe, 1. How foolishly mad they had formerly been upon their idols, in the day of their apostasy. Idolaters are said to be *mad upon their idols* (Jer. 50:38), doatingly fond of them. They had *graven images of silver,* and *molten images of gold,* and, though gold needs no painting, they had coverings and ornaments on these; they spared no cost in doing honour to their idols. 2. How wisely mad (if I may so speak) they now were at their idols, what a holy indignation they conceived against them in the day of their repentance. They not only degraded their images, but defaced them, not only defaced them, but defiled them; they not only spoiled the shape of them, but in a pious fury threw away the gold and silver they were made of, though otherwise valuable and convertible to a good use. They could not find in their hearts to make any vessel of honour of them. The rich clothes wherewith their images were dressed up they cast away as a filthy cloth which rendered those that touched it *unclean until the evening,* Lev. 15:23. Note, To all true penitents sin has become very odious; they loathe it, and loathe themselves because of it; they cast it away to the dunghill, the fittest place for it, nay, to the cross, for they crucify the flesh; their cry against it is, *Crucify it, crucify it.* They say unto it, *Abi hinc in malam rem — Get thee hence.* They are resolved never to harbour it any more. They put as far from as they can all the occasions of sin and temptations to it, though they are as a right eye or a right hand, and protest against it as Ephraim did (Hos. 14:8), *What have I to do any more with idols?* Probably this was fulfilled in many particular persons, who, by the deliverance of Jerusalem from Sennacherib's army, were convinced of the folly of their idolatry and forsook it. It was fulfilled in the body of the Jewish nation at their return from their captivity in Babylon, for they abhorred idols ever after; and it is accomplished daily in the conversion of souls, by the power of divine grace, from spiritual idolatry to the fear and love of God. Those that join themselves to the Lord must abandon every sin, and say unto it, *Get thee hence.*

IV. God will then give them plenty of all good things. When he gives them their teachers, and they give him their hearts, so that they begin to seek the kingdom of God and the righteousness thereof, *then all other things shall be added to them* Mt. 6:33. And when the people are brought to praise God *then shall the earth yield her increase, and with it God, even our own God, shall bless us,* Ps. 67:5, 6. So it follows here: "When you shall have abandoned your idols, *then shall God give the rain of your seed," v.* 23. When we return to God in a way of duty he will meet us with his favours. 1. God will give you rain of your seed, rain to water the seed you sow, just at the time that it calls for it, as much as it needs and no more. Observe, How man's industry and God's blessing concur to the good things we enjoy relating to the life that now is: *Thou shalt sow the ground,* that is thy part, and then *God will give the rain of thy seed,* that is his part. It is so in spiritual fruit; we must take pains with our hearts and then wait on God for his grace. 2. The increase of the earth shall be rich and good, and every thing the best of the kind; it shall be *fat and fat,* very fat and very good, *fat and plenteous* (so we read it), good and enough of it. Your land shall be Canaan indeed; it was remarkably so after the defeat of Sennacherib, by the special blessing of God, *ch.* 37:30. God would thus repair the losses they sustained by that devastation. 3. Not only the tillage, but the pasture-ground should be remarkably fruitful: *The cattle shall feed in large pastures;* those that are at grass shall have room enough, and the oxen and asses that are kept up for use, to ear the ground, which must be the better fed for their being worked, *shall eat clean provender.* The corn shall not be given them in the chaff as usual, to make it go the further, but they shall have good clean corn fit for man's use, being *winnowed with the fan.* The brute-creatures shall share in the abundance; it is fit they should, for they groan under the burden of the curse which man's sin has brought upon the earth. 4. Even the tops of the mountains, that used to be barren, shall be so well watered with the rain of heaven that there shall be *rivers and streams* there, and running down thence to the valleys (*v.* 25), and this *in the day of the great slaughter* that should be made by the angel in the camp of the Assyrians, *when the towers* and batteries they had erected for the carrying on of the siege of Jerusalem, the army being slain, *should fall* of course. It is probable that this was fulfilled in the letter of it, and that about the same time that that army was cut off there were extraordinary rains in mercy to the land.

V. The effect of all this should be extraordinary comfort and joy to the people of God, *v.* 26. Light shall increase; that is, knowledge shall increase (when the prophecies are accomplished they shall be fully understood) or rather triumph shall: the light of the joy that is sown for the righteous shall now come up with a great increase. *The light of the moon shall become as* bright and as strong as *that of the sun, and that of the sun* shall increase proportionably and be *as the light of seven days;* every one shall be much more cheerful and appear much more pleasant than usual. There shall be a high spring-tide of joy in Judah and Jerusalem, upon occasion of the ruin of the Assyrian army, *when the Lord binds up the breach of his people,* not only saves them from being further wounded, but heals the wounds that have been given them by this invasion and makes up all their losses. The great distress they were reduced to, their despair of relief, and the suddenness of their deliverance, would much augment their joy. This is not unfitly applied by many to the light which the gospel brought into the world to those that sat in darkness, which has far exceeded the Old-Testament light as that of the sun does that of the moon, and which proclaims *healing to the broken-hearted, and the binding up of their wounds.*

Verses 27–33

This terrible prediction of the ruin of the Assyrian army, though it is a threatening to them, is part of the promise to the Israel of God, that God would not only punish the Assyrians for the mischief they had done to the Israel of God, but would disable and deter them from doing the like again; and this prediction, which would now shortly be accomplished, would ratify and confirm the foregoing promises, which should be accomplished in the latter days. Here is,

I. God Almighty angry, and coming forth in anger against the Assyrians. He is here introduced in all the power and all the terror of his wrath, *v.* 27. *The name of Jehovah,* which the Assyrians disdain and set at a distance from them, as if they were out of its reach and it could do them no harm, *behold, it comes from far.* A messenger in the name of the Lord comes from as far off as heaven itself. He is a messenger of wrath, *burning with his anger.* God's *lips are full of indignation* at the blasphemy of Rabshakeh, who compared the God of Israel with the gods of the heathen; *his tongue is as a devouring fire,* for he can speak his proud enemies to ruin; his very breath comes with as much force as an overflowing stream, and with it he shall slay the wicked, *ch.* 11:4. He does not stifle or smother his resentments, as men do theirs when they are either causeless or impotent; but he *shall cause his glorious voice to be heard* when he proclaims war with an enemy that sets him at defiance, *v.* 30. He shall display *the indignation of his anger,* anger in the highest degree; it shall be as *the flame of a devouring fire,* which carries and consumes all before it, with *lightning* or dissipation, and with *tempest and hailstones,* all which are the formidable phenomena of nature, and therefore expressive of the terror of the Almighty God of nature.

II. The execution done by this anger of the Lord. Men are often angry when they can only threaten and talk big; but when God causes his glorious voice to be heard that shall not be all: he will *show the lighting down of his arm* too, *v.* 30. The operations of his providence shall accomplish the menaces of his word. Those that *would not see the lifting up of his arm* (*ch.* 26:11) shall feel the lighting down of it, and find, to their cost, that the burden thereof is heavy (*v.* 27), so heavy that they cannot bear it, nor bear up against it, but must unavoidably sink and be crushed under it. *Who knows the power of his anger* or imagines what an offended God can do? Five things are here prepared for the execution: — 1. Here is *an overflowing stream,* that *shall reach to the midst of the neck,* shall quite overwhelm the whole body of the army, and Sennacherib only, the head of it, shall keep above water and escape this stroke, while yet he is reserved for another in the house of Nisroch his god. The Assyrian army had been to Judah *as an overflowing stream, reaching even to the neck* (*ch.* 8:7, 8), and now the breath of God's wrath will be so to it. 2. Here is *a sieve of vanity,* with which God would sift those nations of which the Assyrian army was composed, *v.* 28. The great God can sift nations, for they are all before him as the small dust of the balance; he will sift them, not to gather out of them any that should be preserved, but so as to shake them one against another, put them into great consternation, and shake them all away at last; for it is a sieve of vanity (which retains nothing) that they are shaken with, and they are found all chaff. 3. Here is *a bridle,* which God has in their jaws, to curb and restrain them from doing the mischief they would do, and to force and constrain them to serve his purposes against their own will, *ch.* 10:7. God particularly says of Sennacherib (*ch.* 37:29) that he will put a hook in his nose and a bridle in his lips. It is a *bridle causing them to err,* forcing them to such methods as will certainly be destructive to themselves and their interest and in which they will be infatuated. God with a word guides his people into the right way (*v.* 21), but with a bridle he turns his enemies headlong upon their own ruin. 4. Here is *a rod* and *a staff,* even *the voice of the Lord,* his word giving orders concerning it, with which *the Assyrian shall be beaten down, v.* 31. The Assyrian had been himself a rod in God's hand for the chastising of his people, and had smitten them, *ch.* 10:5. That was a transient rod; but against the Assyrian shall go forth *a grounded staff,* that shall give a steady blow, shall stick close to him and strike home, so as to leave an impression upon him. It is a staff with a foundation, founded upon the enemies' deserts and God's determinate counsel. It is a consumption determined (*ch.* 10:23), and therefore there is no escaping it, no getting out of the reach of it; it shall pass in every place where an Assyrian is found, and the Lord shall *lay it upon him,* and cause it to rest. *v.* 32. Such is the woeful case of those that persist in enmity to God: *the wrath of God abides on them.* 5. Here is *Tophet ordained* and *prepared* for them, *v.* 33. The valley of the son of Hinnom, adjoining to Jerusalem, was called *Tophet.* In that valley, it is supposed, many of the Assyrian regiments lay encamped, and were there slain by the destroying angel; or there the bodies of those that were so slain were burned. Hezekiah had *lately, and from yesterday* (so the word is) *ordained it;* that is, say some, he had cleared it of the images that were set up in it, to which they there burnt their children, and so prepared it to be a receptacle for the dead bodies of their enemies, *for the king of Assyria* (that is, for his army) *it is prepared,* and there is fuel enough ready to burn them all; and they shall be consumed as suddenly and effectually as if the fire were kept burning by a continual stream of brimstone, for such the breath of the Lord, his word and his wrath, will be to it. Now as the prophet, in the foregoing promises, slides insensibly into the promises of gospel graces and comforts, so here, in the threatening of the ruin of Sennacherib's army, he points at the final and everlasting destruction of all impenitent sinners. Our Saviour calls the future misery of the damned *Gehenna,* in allusion to the valley of Hinnom, which gives some countenance to the applying of this to that misery, as also that in the Apocalypse it is so often called the *lake that burns with fire and brimstone.* This is said to be prepared of old for the devil and his angels, for the greatest of sinners, the proudest, and that think themselves not accountable to any for what they say and do; even for kings it is prepared. It is *deep and large,* sufficient to receive the world of the ungodly; the *pile thereof is fire and much wood.* God's wrath is the fire, and sinners make themselves fuel to it; and *the breath of the Lord* (the power of his anger) *kindles it,* and will keep it ever burning. See *ch.* 66:24. Wherefore *stand in awe and sin not.*

III. The great joy which this should occasion to the people of God. The Assyrian's fall is Jerusalem's triumph (*v.* 29): *You shall have a song as in the night,* a psalm of praise such as those sing who *by night stand in the house of the Lord,* and sing to his glory who *gives songs in the night.*

It shall not be a song of vain mirth, but a sacred song, such as was sung when a holy solemnity was kept in a grave and religious manner. Our joy in the fall of the church's enemies must be a holy joy, *gladness of heart, as when one goes, with a pipe* (such as the sons of the prophets used when they prophesied, 1 Sa. 10:5), *to the mountain of the Lord,* there to celebrate the praises of *the Mighty One of Israel.* Nay, in every place where the divine vengeance shall pursue the Assyrians they shall not only fall unlamented, but all their neighbours shall attend their fall *with tabrets and harps,* pleased to see how God, *in battles of shaking,* such as shake them out of the world, fights with them (*v.* 32); for *when the wicked perish there is shouting;* and it is with a particular satisfaction that wise and good men see the ruin of those who, like the Assyrians, have insolently bidden defiance to God and trampled upon all mankind.

CHAPTER 31

This chapter is an abridgment of the foregoing chapter; the heads of it are much the same. Here is, I. A woe to those who, when the Assyrian army invaded them, trusted to the Egyptians, and not to God, for succour (*v.* 1–3). II. Assurance given of the care God would take of Jerusalem in that time of danger and distress (*v.* 4, 5). III. A call to repentance and reformation (*v.* 6, 7). IV. A prediction of the fall of the Assyrian army, and the fright which the Assyrian king should thereby be put into (*v.* 8, 9).

Verses 1–5

This is the last of four chapters together that begin with woe; and they are all woes to the sinners that were found among the professing people of God, to the *drunkards of Ephraim* (*ch.* 28:1), to *Ariel* (*ch.* 29:1), to the *rebellious children* (*ch.* 30:1), and here to *those that go down to Egypt for help;* for men's relation to the church will not secure them from divine woes if they live in contempt of divine laws. Observe,

I. What the sin was that is here reproved, *v.* 1. 1. Idolizing the Egyptians, and making court to them, as if happy were the people that had the Egyptians for their friends and allies. They *go down to Egypt for help* in every exigence, as if the worshippers of false gods had a better interest in heaven and were more likely to have success of earth than the servants of the living and true God. That which invited them to Egypt was that the Egyptians had many chariots to accommodate them with, and horses and horsemen that were strong; and, if they could get a good body of forces thence into their service, they would think themselves able to deal with the king of Assyria and his numerous army. Their kings were forbidden to multiply horses and chariots, and were told of the folly of trusting to them (Ps. 20:7); but they think themselves wiser than their Bible. 2. Slighting the God of Israel: *They look not to the Holy One of Israel,* as if he were not worth taking notice of in this distress. They advise not with him, seek not his favour, nor are in any care to make him their friend.

II. The gross absurdity and folly of this sin. 1. They neglected one whom, if they would not hope in him, they had reason to fear. They do not seek the Lord, nor make their application to him, *yet he also is wise, v.* 2. They are solicitous to get the Egyptians into an alliance with them, because they have the reputation of a politic people; and is not God wise too? and would not infinite wisdom, engaged on their side, stand them in more stead than all the policies of Egypt? They are at the pains of going down to Egypt, a tedious journey, when they might have had better advice, and better help, by looking up to heaven, and would not. But, if they will not court God's wisdom to act for them, they shall find it act against them. He is wise, too wise for them to outwit, and he will bring evil upon those who thus affront him. He will not call back his words as men do (because they are fickle and foolish), but he *will arise against the house of the evil-doers,* this cabal of them that go down to Egypt; God will appear to their confusion, according to the word that he has spoken, and will oppose the help they think to bring in from the workers of iniquity. Some think the Egyptians made it one condition of their coming into an alliance with him that they should worship the gods of Egypt, and they consented to it, and therefore they are both called *evil-doers* and *workers of iniquity.* 2. They trusted to those who were unable to help them and would soon appear to be so, *v.* 3. Let them know that *the Egyptians,* whom they depend so much upon, *are men and not God.* As it is good for men to *know themselves to be but men* (Ps. 9:20), so it is good for us to consider that those we love and trust to are but men. They therefore can do nothing without God, nothing against him, nothing in comparison with him. They are men, and therefore fickle and foolish, mutable and mortal, here to day and gone to morrow; they are men, and therefore let us not make gods of them, by making them our hope and confidence, and expecting that in them which is to be found in God only; they are not God, they cannot do that for us which God can do, and will, if we trust in him. Let us not then neglect him, to seek to them; let us not forsake the rock of ages for broken reeds, nor the fountain of living waters for broken cisterns. The Egyptians indeed have horses that are very strong; but *they are flesh, and not spirit,* and therefore, strong as they are, they may be wearied with a long march, and become unserviceable, or be wounded and slain in battle, and leave their riders to be ridden over. Every one knows this, that the Egyptians are not God and their horses are not spirit; but those that seek to them for help do not consider it, else they would not put such confidence in them. Sinners may be convicted of folly by the plainest and most self-evident truths, which they cannot deny, but will not believe. 3. They would certainly be ruined with the Egyptians they trusted in, *v.* 3. *When the Lord* does but *stretch out his hand* how easily, how effectually, will he make them ashamed of their confidence in Egypt, and the Egyptians ashamed of the encouragement they gave them to trust in them; for *he that helps and he that is helped shall fall together,* and their mutual alliance shall prove their joint ruin. The Egyptians were shortly to be reckoned with, as appears by the *burden of Egypt* (*ch.* 19), and then those who fled to them for shelter and succour should fall with them; for there is no escaping the judgments of God. *Evil pursues sinners,* and it is just with God to make that creature a scourge to us which we make an idol of. 4. They took God's work out of his hands. They pretended a great deal of care to preserve Jerusalem, in advising to an alliance with Egypt; and, when others would not fall in with their measures, they pleaded self preservation, and went to Egypt themselves. Now the prophet here tells them that Jerusalem should be preserved without aid from Egypt and that those who tarried there should be safe when those who fled to Egypt should be ruined. Jerusalem was under God's protection, and therefore there was no occasion to put it under the protection of Egypt. But a practical distrust of God's all-sufficiency is at the bottom of all our sinful departures from him to the creature. The prophet tells them he had it from God's own mouth: *Thus hath the Lord spoken to me.* They might depend upon it, (1.) That God would appear against Jerusalem's enemies with the boldness of a *lion over his prey, v.* 4. When the lion comes out to seize his prey *a multitude of shepherds come out against him;* for it becomes neighbours to help one another when persons or goods are in danger. These shepherds dare not come near the lion; all they can do is to make a *noise,* and with that they think to frighten him off. But does he regard it? *No: he will not be afraid of their voice,* nor abase himself so far as to be in the least moved by it either to quit his prey or to make any more haste than otherwise he would do in seizing it. *Thus will the Lord of hosts come down to fight for Mount Zion,* with such an unshaken undaunted resolution not to be moved by any opposition; and he will as easily and irresistibly destroy the Assyrian army as a lion tears a lamb in pieces. Whoever appear against God, they are but like a multitude of poor simple shepherds shouting at a lion, who scorns to take notice of them or so much as to alter his pace for them. Surely those that have such a protector need not go to Egypt for help. (2.) That God would appear for Jerusalem's friends with the tenderness of a bird over her young, *v.* 5. God was ready to *gather Jerusalem, as a hen gathers her brood under her wings* (Mt. 23:37); but those that trusted to the Egyptians would not be gathered. *As birds flying* to their nests with all possible speed, when they see them attacked, and fluttering about their nests with all possible concern, hovering over their young ones to protect them and drive away the assailants, with such compassion and affection *will the Lord of hosts defend Jerusalem.* As an eagle stirs up her young when they are in danger, *takes them and bears them on her wings,* so the Lord led Israel out of Egypt (Deu. 32:11, 12); and he has now the same tender concern for them that he had then, so that they need not flee into Egypt again for shelter. *Defending, he will deliver it;* he will so defend it as to secure the continuance of its safety, not defend it for a while and abandon it at last, but defend it so that it shall not fall into the enemies' hand. *I will defend this city to save it, ch.* 37:35. *Passing over he will preserve it;* the word for passing over is used in this sense only here and Ex. 12:12, 23, 27, concerning the destroying angel's passing over the houses of the Israelites when he slew all the first-born of the Egyptians, to which story this passage refers. The Assyrian army was to be routed by a destroying angel, who should pass over Jerusalem, though that deserved to be destroyed, and draw his sword only against the besiegers. They shall be slain by the pestilence, but none of the besieged shall take the infection. Thus he will again pass over the houses of his people and secure them.

Verses 6–9

This explains the foregoing promise of the deliverance of Jerusalem; she shall be fitted for deliverance, and then it shall be wrought for her; for in that method God delivers.

I. Jerusalem shall be reformed, and so she shall be delivered from her enemies within her walls, *v.* 6, 7. Here is, 1. A gracious call to repentance. This was the Lord's voice crying in the city, the voice of the rod, the voice of the sword, and the voice of the prophets interpreting the judgment: *"Turn you,* O turn you now, from your evil ways, *unto God,* return to your allegiance to him *from whom the children of Israel have deeply revolted,* from whom you, *O children of Israel!* have revolted." He reminds them of their birth and parentage, that they were *children of Israel,* and therefore under the highest obligations imaginable to the God of Israel, as an aggravation of their revolt from him and as an encouragement to them to return to him. "They have been backsliding children, yet children; therefore let them return, and their backslidings shall be healed. They have deeply revolted, with great address as they supposed (*the revolters are profound,* Hos. 5:2); but the issue will prove that they have revolted dangerously. The stain of their sins has gone deeply into their nature, not to be easily got out, like the blackness of the Ethiopian. *They have deeply corrupted themselves* (Hos. 9:9); they have sunk deep into misery, and cannot easily recover themselves; therefore you have need to hasten your return to God." 2. A gracious promise of the good success of this call (*v.* 7): *In that day every man shall cast away his idols,* in obedience to Hezekiah's orders, which, till they were alarmed by the Assyrian invasion, many refused to do. That is a happy fright which frightens us from our sins. (1.) It shall be a general reformation: every man shall cast away his own idols, shall begin with them before he undertakes to demolish other people's idols, which there will be no need of when every man reforms himself. (2.) It shall be a thorough reformation; for they shall part with their idolatry, their beloved sin, with their *idols of silver and gold,* their idols that they are most fond of. Many make an idol of their silver and gold, and by the love of that idol are drawn to revolt from God; but those that turn to God cast that away out of their hearts and will be ready to part with it when God calls. (3.) It shall be a reformation upon a right principle, a principle of piety, not of politics. They shall cast away their idols, because they have been unto them *for a sin,* an occasion of sin; therefore they will have nothing to do with them, though they had been the work of their *own hands,* and upon that account they had a particular fondness for them. Sin is the work of our own hands, but in working it we have been working our own ruin, and therefore we must cast it away; and those are strangely wedded to it who will not be prevailed upon to cast it away when they see that otherwise they themselves will be castaways. Some make this to be only a prediction that those who trust in idols, when they find they stand them in no stead, will cast them away in indignation. But it agrees so exactly with *ch.* 30:22 that I rather take it as a promise of a sincere reformation.

II. Jerusalem's besiegers shall be routed, and so she shall be delivered from the enemies about her walls. The former makes way for this. If a people return to God, they may leave it to him to plead their cause against their enemies. When they have cast away their idols, *then shall the Assyrian fall, v.* 8, 9. 1. The army of the Assyrians shall be laid dead upon the spot *by the sword, not of a mighty man, nor of a mean man,* not of any man at all, either Israelite or Egyptian, not forcibly by the sword of a mighty man nor surreptitiously by the sword of a mean man, but by the sword of an angel, who strikes more strongly than a mighty man and yet more secretly than a mean man, by the sword of the Lord, and his power and wrath in the hand of the angel. Thus the young men of the army shall melt, and be discomfited, and become tributaries to death. When God has work to do against the enemies of his church we expect it must be done by mighty men and mean men, officers and common soldiers; whereas God can, if he please, do it without either. *He* needs not armies of men who has legions of angels at command, Mt. 26:53. 2. The king of Assyria shall flee for the same, shall flee from that invisible sword, hoping to get out of the reach of it; and he shall make the best of his way to his own dominions, shall pass over to some strong-hold of his own, for fear lest the Jews should pursue him now that his army was routed. Sennacherib had been very confident that he should make himself master of Jerusalem, and in the most insolent manner had set both God and Hezekiah at defiance; yet now he is made to tremble for fear of both. God can strike a terror into the proudest of men, and make the stoutest heart to tremble. See Job 18:11; 20:24. *His princes* that accompany him *shall be afraid of the ensign,* shall be in a continual fright at the remembrance of the ensign in the air, which perhaps the destroying angel displayed before he gave the fatal bow. Or they shall be afraid of every ensign they see, suspecting it is a party of the Jews pursuing them. The banner that God displays for the encouragement of his people (Ps. 60:4) will be a terror to his and their enemies. Thus he *cuts off the spirit of princes and is terrible to the kings of the earth.* But who will do this? It is *the Lord, whose fire is in Zion and his furnace in Jerusalem.* (1.) Whose residence is there, and who there keeps house, as a man does where his fire and his oven are. It is the city of the great King, and let not the Assyrians think to turn him out of the possession of his own house. (2.) Who is there a consuming fire to all his enemies and will make them as a fiery oven in the day of his wrath, Ps. 21:9. He is himself *a wall of fire round about Jerusalem,* so that whoever assaults her does so at his peril, Zec. 2:5; Rev. 11:5. (3.) Who has his altar there, on which the holy fire is continually kept burning and sacrifices are daily offered to his honour, and with which he is well pleased; and therefore he will defend this city, especially having an eye to the great sacrifice which was there also to be offered, of which all the sacrifices were types. If we keep up the fire of holy love and devotion in our hearts and houses, we may depend upon God to be a protection to us and them.

CHAPTER 32

This chapter seems to be such a prophecy of the reign of Hezekiah as amounts to an abridgment of the history of it, and this with an eye to the kingdom of the Messiah, whose government was typified by the thrones of the house of David, for which reason he is so often called "the Son of David." Here is, I. A prophecy of that good work of reformation with which he should begin his reign, and the happy influence it should have upon the people, who had been wretchedly corrupted and debauched in the reign of his predecessor (*v.* 1–8). II. A prophecy of the great disturbance that would be given to the kingdom in the middle of his reign by the Assyrian invasion (*v.* 9–14). III. A promise of better times afterwards, towards the latter end of his reign, in respect both of piety and peace (*v.* 15–20), which promise may be supposed to look as far forward as the days of the Messiah.

Verses 1–8

We have here the description of a flourishing kingdom. "*Blessed art thou, O land!* when it is thus with thee, when kings, princes, and people, are in their places such as they should be." It may be taken as a directory both to magistrates and subjects, what both ought to do, or as a panegyric to Hezekiah, who ruled well and saw something of the happy effects of his good government, and it was designed to make the people sensible how happy they were under his administration and how careful they should be to improve the advantages of it, and withal to direct them to look for the kingdom of Christ, and the times of reformation which that kingdom should introduce. It is here promised and prescribed, for the comfort of the church,

I. That magistrates should do their duty in their places, and the powers answer the great ends for which they were ordained of God, *v.* 1, 2. 1. There shall be a king and princes that shall reign and rule; for it cannot go well when there is no king in Israel. The princes must have a king, a monarch over them as supreme, in whom they may unite; and the king must have princes under him as officers, by whom he may act, 1 Pt. 2:13, 14. They both shall know their place and fill it up. The king shall reign, and yet, without any diminution to his just prerogative, the princes shall rule in a lower sphere, and all for the public good. 2. They shall use their power according to law, and not against it. They shall reign in righteousness and in judgment, with wisdom and equity, protecting the good and punishing the bad; and those kings and princes Christ owns as reigning by him who decree justice, Prov. 8:15. Such a King, such a Prince, Christ himself is; he reigns by rule, and *in righteousness will he judge the world, ch.* 9:7; 11:4. 3. Thus they shall be great blessings to the people (*v.* 2): *A man,* that man, that king that reigns in righteousness, *shall be as a hiding-place.* When princes are as they should be people are as they would be. (1.) They are sheltered and protected from many mischiefs. This good magistrate is a covert to the subject from the tempest of injury and violence; he *defends the poor and fatherless,* that they be not made a prey of by the mighty. Whither should oppressed innocency flee, when blasted by reproach or borne down by violence, but to the magistrate as its hiding-place? To him it appeals, and by him it is righted. (2.) They are refreshed and comforted with many blessings. This good magistrate gives such countenance to those that are poor and in distress, and such encouragement to every thing that is praiseworthy, that he is *as rivers of water in a dry place,* cooling and cherishing the earth and making it fruitful, and *as the shadow of a great rock,* under which a poor traveller may shelter himself from the scorching heat of the sun *in a weary land.* It is a great reviving to a good man, who makes conscience of doing his duty, in the midst of contempt and contradiction, at length to be backed, and favoured, and smiled upon in it by a good magistrate. All this, and much more, the man Christ Jesus is to all the willing faithful subjects of his kingdom. When the greatest evils befal us, not only the wind, but the tempest, when storms of guilt and wrath beset us and beat upon us, they drive us to Christ, and in him we are not only safe, but satisfied that we are so; in him we find rivers of water for those that hunger and thirst after righteousness, all the refreshment and comfort that a needy soul can desire, and the shadow, not of a tree, which sun or rain may beat through, but of a rock, of a great rock, which reaches a great way for the shelter of the traveller. Some observe here that as the covert, and the hiding-place, and the rock, do themselves receive the battering of the wind and storm, to save those from it that take shelter in them, so Christ bore the storm himself to keep it off from us.

II. That subjects should do their duty in their places.

1. They shall be willing to be taught, and to understand things aright. They shall lay aside their prejudices against their rulers and teachers, and submit to the light and power of truth, *v.* 3. When this blessed work of reformation is set on foot, and men do their parts towards it, God will not be wanting to do his: Then *the eyes of those that see,* of the prophets, the seers, *shall not be dim;* but God will bless them with visions, to be by them communicated to the people; and those that read the word written shall no longer have a veil upon their hearts, but shall see things clearly. Then *the ears of those that hear* the word preached *shall hearken* diligently and readily receive what they hear, and not be so dull of hearing as they have been. This shall be done by the grace of God, especially gospel-grace; for *the hearing ear, and the seeing eyes, the Lord has made,* has new-made, even both of them.

2. There shall be a wonderful change wrought in them by that which is taught them, *v.* 4. (1.) They shall have a clear head, and be able to discern things that differ, and distinguish concerning them. *The heart of those that were* hasty and *rash,* and could not take time to digest and consider things, shall now be cured of their precipitation, and *shall understand knowledge;* for the Spirit of God will open their understanding. This blessed work Christ wrought in his disciples after his resurrection (Lu. 24:45), as a specimen of what he would do for all his people, in giving them an understanding, 1 Jn. 5:20. The pious designs of good princes are likely to take effect when their subjects allow themselves liberty to consider, and to think, so freely as to take things right. (2.) They shall have a ready utterance: *The tongue of the stammerers,* that used to blunder whenever they spoke of the things of God, *shall* now *be ready to speak plainly,* as those that understand what they speak of, that believe, and therefore speak. There shall be a great increase of such clear, distinct, and methodical knowledge in the things of God, that those from whom one would not have expected it shall speak intelligently of these things, very much to the honour of God and the edification of others. Their hearts being full of this good matter, their tongues shall be *as the pen of a ready writer,* Ps. 45:1.

3. The differences between good and evil, virtue and vice, shall be kept up, and no more confounded by those who put darkness for light and light for darkness (*v.* 5): *The vile shall no more be called liberal.*

(1.) Bad men shall no more be preferred by the prince. When a king reigns in justice he will not put those in places of honour and power that are ill-natured, and of base and sordid spirits, and care not what injury or mischief they do so they may but compass their own ends. Such as *vile* persons (as Antiochus is called, Dan. 11:21); when they are advanced they are called *liberal* and *bountiful;* they are called *benefactors* (Lu. 22:25): but it shall not always be thus; when the world grows wiser men shall be preferred according to their merit, and honour (which was never thought seemly for a fool, Prov. 26:1) shall no longer be thrown away upon such.

(2.) Bad men shall be no more had in reputation among the people, nor vice disguised with the colours of virtue. It shall no more be said to Nabal, *Thou art Nadib* (so the words are); such a covetous muck-worm as Nabal was, a fool but for his money, shall not be complimented with the title of a gentleman or a prince; nor shall they call a *churl,* that minds none but himself, does no good with what he has, but is an unprofitable burden of the earth, *My lord;* or, rather, they shall not say of him, *He is rich;* for so the word signifies. Those only are to be reckoned rich that are rich in good works; not those that have abundance, but those that use it well. In short, it is well with a people when men are generally valued by their virtue, and usefulness, and beneficence to mankind, and not by their wealth or titles of honour. Whether this was fulfilled in the reign of Hezekiah, and how far it refers to the kingdom of Christ (in which we are sure men are judged of by what they are, not by what they have, nor is any man's character mistaken), we will not say; but it prescribes an excellent rule both to prince and people, to respect men according to their personal merit. To enforce this rule, here is a description both of the vile person and of the liberal; and by it we shall see such a vast difference between them that we must quite forget ourselves if we pay that respect to the vile person and the churl which is due only to the liberal.

[1.] A vile person and a churl will do mischief, and the more if he be preferred and have power in his hand; his honours will make him worse and not better, *v.* 6, 7. See the character of these base ill-conditioned men. *First,* They are always plotting some unjust thing or other, designing ill either to particular persons or to the public, and contriving how to bring it about; and so many silly piques they have to gratify, and mean revenges, that there appears not in them the least spark of generosity. Their hearts will be still working some iniquity or other. Observe, There is the work of the heart, as well as the work of the hands. As thoughts are words to God, so designs are works in his account. See what pains sinners take in sin. They labour at it; their hearts are intent upon it, and with a great deal of art and application they *work iniquity.* They *devise wicked devices* with all the subtlety of the old serpent and a great deal of deliberation, which makes the sin exceedingly sinful; and the more there is of plot and management in a sin the more there is of Satan in it. *Secondly,* They carry on their plots by trick and dissimulation. When they are meditating iniquity, they *practise hypocrisy,* feign themselves just men, Lu. 20:20. The most abominable mischiefs shall be disguised with the most plausible pretences of devotion to God, regard to man, and concern for some common good. Those are the vilest of men that intend the worst mischiefs when they speak fair. *Thirdly,* They *speak villainy.* When they are in a passion you will see what they are by the base ill language they give to those about them, which no way becomes men of rank and honour; or, in giving verdict or judgment, they villainously put false colours upon things, to pervert justice. *Fourthly,* They affront God, who is a righteous God and loves righteousness: They *utter error against the Lord,* and therein they practise profaneness; for so the word which we translate *hypocrisy* signifies. They give an unjust sentence, and then profanely make use of the name of God for the ratification of it; as if, because the *judgment is God's* (Deu. 1:17), therefore their false and unjust judgment was his. This is *uttering error against the Lord,* under pretence of uttering truth and justice for him; and nothing can be more impudently done against God than to use his name to patronise wickedness. *Fifthly,* They abuse mankind, those particularly whom they are bound to protect and relieve. 1. Instead of supplying the wants of the poor, they impoverish them, they *make empty the souls of the hungry;* either taking away the food they have, or, which is almost equivalent, denying the supply which they want and which they have to give. And they *cause the drink of the thirsty to fail;* they cut off the relief they used to have, though they need it as much as ever. Those are vile persons indeed that rob the spital. 2. Instead of righting the poor, when they appeal to their judgment, they contrive to destroy the poor, to ruin them in their courts of judicature with lying words in favour of the rich, to whom they are plainly partial; yea, though the needy speak right, though the evidence be ever so full for them to make out the equity of their cause, it is the bribe that governs them, not the right. *Sixthly,* These churls and vile persons have always had instruments about them, that are ready to serve their villainous purposes: *All their servants are wicked.* There is no design so palpably unjust but there may be found those that would be employed as tools to put it in execution. *The instruments of the churl are evil,* and one cannot expect otherwise; but this is our comfort, that they can do no more mischief than God permits them.

[2.] One that is truly liberal, and deserves the honour of being called so, makes it his business to do good to every body according as his sphere is, *v.* 8. Observe, *First,* The care he takes, and the contrivances he has, to do good. He *devises liberal things.* As much as the churl or niggard projects how to save and lay up what he has for himself only, so much the good charitable man projects how to use and lay out what he has in the best manner for the good of others. Charity must be directed by wisdom, and liberal things done prudently and with device, that the good intention of them may be answered, that it may not be charity misplaced. The liberal man, when he has done all the liberal things that are in his own power, devises liberal things for others to do according to their power, and puts them upon doing them. *Secondly,* the comfort he takes, and the advantage he has, in doing good: *By liberal things he shall stand,* or be established. The providence of God will reward him for his liberality with a settled prosperity and an established reputation. The grace of God will give him abundance of satisfaction and confirmed peace in his own bosom. What disquiets others shall not disturb him; his heart is fixed. This is the recompence of charity, Ps. 112:5, 6. Some read it, *The prince, or honourable man, will take honourable courses; and by such honourable or ingenuous courses he shall stand or be established.* It is well with a land when the honourable of it are indeed men of honour and scorn to do a base thing, when its king is thus the son of nobles.

Verses 9–20

In these verses we have God rising up to judgment against the vile persons, to punish them for their villainy; but at length returning in mercy to the liberal, to reward them for their liberality.

I. When there was so great a corruption of manners, and so much provocation given to the holy God, bad times might well be expected, and here is a warning given of such times coming. The alarm is sounded to the *women that were at ease* (*v.* 9) and the *careless daughters,* to feed whose pride, vanity, and luxury, their husbands and fathers were tempted to starve the poor. Let them hear what the prophet has to say to them in God's name: *"Rise up, and hear* with reverence and attention."

1. Let them know that God was about to bring wasting desolating judgments upon the land in which they *lived in pleasure and were wanton.* This seems to refer primarily to the desolations made by Sennacherib's army when he seized all the fenced cities of Judah: but then those words, *many days and years,* must be rendered (as the margin reads them) *days above a year,* that is, something above a year shall this havock be in the making: so long it was from the first entrance of that army into the land of Judah to the overthrow of it. But it is applicable to the wretched disappointment which those will certainly meet with, first or last, that set their hearts upon the world and place their happiness in it: *You shall be troubled, you careless women.* It will not secure us from trouble to cast away care when we are at ease; nay, to those who affect to live carelessly even little troubles will be great vexations and press hard upon them. They were careless and at ease because they had money enough and mirth enough; but the prophet here tells them, (1.) That the country whence they had their tents and dainties should shortly be laid waste: *"The vintage shall fail;* and then what will you do for wine to make merry with? *The gathering* of fruit *shall not come,* for there shall be none to be gathered, and you will find the want of them, *v.* 10. You will want *the teats,* the good milk from the cows, *the pleasant fields* and their productions:" the useful fields that are serviceable to human life are the pleasant ones. "You will want the fruitful vine, and the grapes it used to yield you." The abuse of plenty is justly punished with scarcity; and those deserve to be deprived of the supports of life who make them the food and fuel of lust and prepare them for Baal. (2.) That the cities too, the cities of Judah, where they lived at ease, spent their rents, and made themselves merry with their dainties, should be laid waste (*v.* 13, 14): *Briers and thorns,* the fruits of sin and the curse, *shall come up,* not only *upon the land of my people,* which shall lie uncultivated, but upon *all the houses of joy* — the play-houses, the gaming-houses, the taverns — *in the joyous cities.* When a foreign army was ravaging the country the houses of joy, no doubt, became houses of mourning; then the palaces, or noblemen's houses, were forsaken by their owners, who perhaps fled to Egypt for refuge; the multitude of the city were left by their leaders to shift for themselves. Then the stately houses *shall be for dens for ever,* which had been as forts and towers for strength and magnificence. They shall be abandoned; the owners shall never return to them; every body shall look upon them to be like Jericho, an anathema; so that, even when peace returns, they shall not be rebuilt, but shall be thrown to the waste: *A joy of wild asses and a pasture of flocks.* Thus is many a house brought to ruin by sin. *Jam seges est ubi Troja fuit — Corn grows on the site of Troy.*

2. In the foresight of this let them *tremble* and *be troubled, strip themselves, and gird sackcloth upon their loins, v.* 11. This intimates not only that when the calamity comes they shall thus be made to tremble and be forced to strip themselves, that then God's judgments would strip them and make them bare, but, (1.) That the best prevention of the trouble would be to repent and humble themselves for their sin, and lie in the dust before God in true remorse and godly sorrow, which would be the lengthening out of their tranquillity. This is meeting God in the way of his judgments, and saving a correction by correcting our own mistakes. Those only shall break that will not bend. (2.) That the best preparation for the trouble would be to deny themselves and live a life of mortification, and to sit loose to all the delights of sense. Those that have already by a holy contempt of this world stripped themselves can easily bear to be stripped when trouble and death come.

II. While there was still a remnant that kept their integrity they had reason to hope for good times at length and such times the prophet here gives them a pleasant prospect of. Such times they saw in the latter end of the reign of Hezekiah; but the prophecy may well be supposed to look further, to the days of the Messiah, who is *King of righteousness* and *King of peace,* and to whom all the prophets bear witness. Now observe,

1. How those blessed times shall be introduced — by the *pouring out of the Spirit from on high* (*v.* 15), which speaks not only of the good-will of God towards us, but the good work of God in us; for then, and not till then, there will be good times, when God by his grace gives men good hearts; and therefore God's *giving his Holy Spirit to those that ask him* is in effect his giving them all good things, as appears by comparing Lu. 11:13 with Mt. 7:11. This is the great thing that God's people comfort themselves with the hopes of, that *the Spirit shall be poured out upon them,* that there shall be a more plentiful effusion of the Spirit of grace than formerly, according as the necessity of the church, in its desolate estate, calls for. This comes from on high, and therefore they look up to their Father in heaven for it. When God designs favours for his church he pours out his Spirit, both to prepare his people to receive his favours and to qualify and give success to those whom he designs to employ as instruments of his favour; for their endeavours to repair the desolations of the church are all fruitless *until the Spirit be poured out upon them* and then the work is done suddenly. The kingdom of the Messiah was brought in, and set up, by the pouring out of the Spirit (Acts 2), and so it is still kept up, and will be to the end.

2. What a wonderfully happy change shall then be made. That which was *a wilderness,* dry and barren, *shall become a fruitful field,* and that which we now reckon *a fruitful field,* in comparison with what it shall be then, *shall be counted for a forest. Then shall the earth yield her increase.* It is promised that in the days of the Messiah the *fruit of the earth shall shake like Lebanon,* Ps. 72:16. Some apply this to the admission of the Gentiles into the gospel church (which made the wilderness a fruitful field), and the rejection and exclusion of the Jews, which made that a forest which had been a fruitful field. On the Gentiles was poured out a spirit of life, but on the Jews a spirit of slumber. See what is the evidence and effect of the pouring out of the Spirit upon any soul; it is thereby made fruitful, and has its fruit unto holiness. Three things go to make these times happy: —

(1.) Judgment and righteousness, *v.* 16. When the Spirit is poured out upon a land, *then judgment shall dwell in the wilderness* and turn it into a fruitful field, and *righteousness shall remain in the fruitful field* and make it yet more fruitful. Ministers shall expound the law and magistrates execute it, and both so judiciously and faithfully that by both the bad shall be made good and the good made better. Among all sorts of people, the poor and low and unlearned, that are neglected as the wilderness, and the rich and great and learned, that are valued as the fruitful field, there shall be right thoughts of things, good principles commanding, and conscience made of good and evil, sin and duty. Or in all parts of the land, both champaign and enclosed, country and city, the ruder parts and those that are more cultivated and refined, justice shall be duly administered. The law of Christ introduces a judgment or rule by which we must be governed, and the gospel of Christ a righteousness by which we must be saved; and, wherever the Spirit is poured out, both these dwell and remain as an everlasting righteousness.

(2.) Peace and quietness, *v.* 17, 18. The peace here promised is of two kinds: —

[1.] Inward peace, *v.* 17. This follows upon the indwelling of righteousness, *v.* 16. Those in whom that work is wrought shall experience this blessed product of it. It is itself peace, and the effect of it is *quietness and assurance for ever,* that is, a holy serenity and security of mind, by which the soul enjoys itself and enjoys its God, and it is not in the power of this world to disturb it in those enjoyments. Note, Peace, and quietness, and everlasting assurance may be expected, and shall be found, in the way and work of righteousness. True satisfaction is to be had only in true religion, and there it is to be had without fail. Those are the quiet and peaceable lives that are spent *in all godliness and honesty,* 1 Tim. 2:2. *First,* Even *the work of righteousness shall be peace.* In the doing of our duty we shall find abundance of true pleasure, a present great reward of obedience in obedience. Though the work of righteousness may be toilsome and costly, and expose us to contempt, yet it is peace, such peace as is sufficient to bear our charges. *Secondly, The effect of righteousness shall be quietness and assurance,* not only to the end of time, of our time, and in the end, but to the endless ages of eternity. Real holiness is real happiness now and shall be perfect happiness, that is, perfect holiness, for ever.

[2.] Outward peace, *v.* 18. It is a great mercy when those who by the grace of God have quiet and peaceable spirits are by the providence of God made to *dwell in quiet and peaceable habitations*, not disturbed in their houses or solemn assemblies. When the terror of Sennacherib's invasion was over, the people, no doubt, were more sensible than ever of the mercy of a quiet habitation, not disturbed with the alarms of war. Let every family study to keep itself quiet from strifes and jars within, not two against three and three against two in the house, and then put itself under God's protection to dwell safely, and to be *quiet from the fear of evil* without. Jerusalem shall be a peaceable habitation; compare *ch.* 33:20. Even *when it shall hail*, and there shall be a violent battering storm *coming down on the forest* that lies bleak, then shall Jerusalem be *a quiet resting-place, for the city shall be low in a low place*, under the wind, not exposed (as those cities are that stand high) to the fury of the storm, but sheltered by the *mountains that are round about Jerusalem*, Ps. 125:2. The *high forts and towers are brought down* (*v.* 14), but the city that lies low shall be a quiet resting-place. Those are most safe, and may dwell most at ease, that are humble, and are willing to dwell low, *v.* 19. Those that would dwell in a peaceable habitation must be willing to dwell low, and in a low place. Some think here is an allusion to the preservation of the land of Goshen from the plague of hail, which made great destruction in the land of Egypt.

(3.) Plenty and abundance. There shall be such good crops gathered in every where, and every year, that the husbandmen shall be commended, and though happy, who *sow beside all water* (*v.* 20), who sow all the grounds that are fit for seedness, who *cast their bread*, or bread-corn, *upon the water*, Eccl. 11:1. God will give the increase, but then the husbandman must be industrious, and mind his business, and sow beside all waters; and, if he do this, the corn shall come up so thick and rank that he shall turn in his cattle, even the ox and the ass, to eat the tops of it and keep it under. This is applicable, [1.] To the preaching of the word. Some think it points at the ministry of the apostles, who, as husbandmen, went forth to sow their seed (Mt. 13:3); they sowed beside all waters; they preached the gospel wherever they came. Waters signify people, and they preached to multitudes. Wherever they found men's hearts softened, and moistened, and disposed to receive the word, they cast in the good seed. And whereas, by the law of Moses, the Jews were forbidden to *plough with an ox and an ass together* (Deu. 22:10), which intimated that Jews and Gentiles should not intermix, now that distinction shall be taken away, and both the ox and the ass, both Jews and Gentiles, shall be employed in, and enjoy the benefit of, the gospel husbandry. [2.] To works of charity. When God sends these happy times blessed are those that improve them in doing good with what they have, that sow beside all waters, that embrace all opportunities of relieving the necessitous; for in due season they shall reap.

CHAPTER 33

This chapter relates to the same events as the foregoing chapter, the distress of Judah and Jerusalem by Sennacherib's invasion and their deliverance out of that distress by the destruction of the Assyrian army. These are intermixed in the prophecy, in the way of a Pindaric. Observe, I. The great distress that Judah and Jerusalem should then be brought into (*v.* 7–9). II. The particular frights which the sinners in Zion should then be in (*v.* 13, 14). III. The prayers of good people to God in this distress (*v.* 2). IV. The holy security which they should enjoy in the midst of this trouble (*v.* 15, 16). V. The destruction of the army of the Assyrians (*v.* 1–3), in which God would be greatly glorified (*v.* 5, 10–12). VI. The enriching of the Jews with the spoil of the Assyrian camp (*v.* 4, 23, 24). VII. The happy settlement of Jerusalem, and the Jewish state, upon this. Religion shall be uppermost (*v.* 6), and their civil state shall flourish (*v.* 17–22). This was soon fulfilled, but is written for our learning.

Verses 1–12

Here we have,

I. The proud and false Assyrian justly reckoned with for all his fraud and violence, and laid under a woe, *v.* 1. Observe, 1. The sin which the enemy had been guilty of. He had spoiled the people of God, and made a prey of them, and herein had broken his treaty of peace with them, and dealt treacherously. Truth and mercy are two such sacred things, and have so much of God in them, that those cannot but be under the wrath of God that make conscience of neither, but are perfectly lost to both, that care not what mischief they do, what spoil they make, what dissimulations they are guilty of, nor what solemn engagements they violate, to compass their own wicked designs. Bloody and deceitful men are the worst of men. 2. The

aggravation of this sin. He spoiled those that had never done him any injury and that he had no pretence to quarrel with, and dealt treacherously with those that had always dealt faithfully with him. Note, The less provocation we have from men to do a wrong thing the more provocation we give to God by doing it. 3. The punishment he should fall under for this sin. He that spoiled the cities of Judah shall have his own army destroyed by an angel and his camp plundered by those whom he had made a prey of. The Chaldeans shall deal treacherously with the Assyrians and revolt from them. Two of Sennacherib's own sons shall deal treacherously with him and basely murder him at his devotions. Note, The righteous God often pays sinners in their own coin. *He that leads into captivity shall go into captivity*, Rev. 13:10; 18:6. 4. The time when he shall be thus dealt with. When he shall *make an end to spoil, and to deal treacherously*, not by repentance and reformation, which might prevent his ruin (Dan. 4:27), but when he shall have done his worst, when he shall have gone as far as God would permit him to go, to the utmost of his tether, then the cup of trembling shall be put into his hand. When he shall have arrived at his full stature in impiety, shall have filled up the measure of his iniquity, then all shall be called over again. When he has done God will begin, for his day is coming.

II. The praying people of God earnest at the throne of grace for mercy for the land now in its distress (*v.* 2): "*O Lord! be merciful to us.* Men are cruel; be thou gracious. We have deserved thy wrath, but we entreat thy favour; and, if we may find the propitious to us, we are happy; the trouble we are in cannot hurt us, shall not ruin us. It is in vain to expect relief from creatures; we have no confidence in the Egyptians, but *we have waited for thee* only, resolving to submit to thee, whatever the issue of the trouble be, and hoping that it shall be a comfortable issue." Those that by faith humbly wait for God shall certainly find him gracious to them. They prayed, 1. For those that were employed in military services for them: "*Be thou their arm every morning.* Hezekiah, and his princes, and all the men of war, need continual supplies of strength and courage from thee; supply their need therefore, and be to them a God all-sufficient. Every morning, when they go forth upon the business of the day, and perhaps have new work to do and new difficulties to encounter, let them be afresh animated and invigorated, and, *as the day, so let the strength be.*" In our spiritual warfare our own hands are not sufficient for us, nor can we bring any thing to pass unless God not only strengthen our arms (Gen. 49:24), but be himself our arm; so entirely do we depend upon him as our arm every morning, so constantly do we depend upon his power, as well as his compassions, which are new every morning, Lam. 3:23. If God leaves us to ourselves any morning, we are undone; we must therefore every morning commit ourselves to him, and go forth in his strength to do the work of the day in its day. 2. For the body of the people: "*Be thou our salvation also in the time of trouble*, ours who sit still, and do not venture into the high places of the field." They depend upon God not only as their Saviour, to work deliverance for them, but as their salvation itself; for, whatever becomes of their secular interests, they will reckon themselves safe and saved if they have him for their God. If he undertake to be their Saviour, he will be their salvation; for *as for God his work is perfect.* Some read it thus: "*Thou who wast their arm every morning*, who wast the continual strength and help of our fathers before us, *be thou our salvation also in time of trouble.* Help us as thou helpedst them; *they looked unto thee and were lightened* (Ps. 34:5); let us then not walk in darkness."

III. The Assyrian army ruined and their camp made a rich but cheap and easy prey to Judah and Jerusalem. No sooner is the prayer made (*v.* 2) than it is answered (*v.* 3), nay, it is outdone. They prayed that God would save them from their enemies; but he did more than that; he gave them victory over their enemies and abundant cause to triumph; for, 1. The strength of the Assyrian camp was broken (*v.* 3) when the destroying angel slew so many thousands of them: *At the noise of the tumult*, of the shrieks of the dying men (who, we may suppose, did not die silently), the rest of *the people fled*, and shifted every one for his own safety. When God did thus lift up himself the several nations, or clans, of which the army was composed,

were scattered. It was time to stir when such an unprecedented plague broke out among them. When God arises his enemies are scattered, Ps. 68:1. 2. The spoil of the Assyrian camp is seized, by way of reprisal, for all the desolations of the defenced cities of Judah (*v.* 4): *Your spoil shall be gathered* by the inhabitants of Jerusalem, *like the gathering of the caterpillar*, and *as the running to and fro of locusts*, that is, the spoilers shall as easily and as quickly make themselves masters of the riches of the Assyrians as a host of caterpillars, or locusts, make a field, or a tree, bare. Thus *the wealth of the sinner is laid up for the just* and Israel is enriched with the spoil of the Egyptians. Some make the Assyrians to be the caterpillars and locusts, which, when they are killed, are gathered together in heaps, as the frogs of Egypt, and are run upon, and trodden to dirt.

IV. God and his Israel glorified and exalted hereby. When the spoil of the enemy is thus gathered, 1. God will have the praise of it (*v.* 5): *The Lord is exalted.* It is his honour thus to abase proud men, and hide them in the dust, together; thus he magnifies his own name, and his people give him the glory of it, as Israel when the Egyptians were drowned, Ex. 15:1, 2, etc. He is exalted as one that dwells on high, out of the reach of their blasphemies, and that has an over-ruling power over them, and wherein they deal proudly delights to show himself above them — that does what he will, and they cannot resist him. 2. His people will have the blessing of it. When God lifts up himself to scatter the nations that are in confederacy against Jerusalem (*v.* 3) then, as a preparative for that, or as the fruit and product of it, *he has filled Zion with judgment and righteousness*, not only with a sense of justice, but with a zeal for it and a universal care that it be duly administered. It shall again be called, *The city of righteousness*, *ch.* 1:26. In this the grace of God is exalted, as much as his providence was in the destruction of the Assyrian army. We may conclude God has mercy in store for a people when he fills them with judgment and righteousness, when all sorts of people, and all their actions and affairs, are governed by them, and they are so full of them that no other considerations can crowd in to sway them against these. Hezekiah and his people are encouraged (*v.* 6) with an assurance that God would stand by them in their distress. Here is, (1.) A gracious promise of God for them to stay themselves upon: *Wisdom and knowledge shall be the stability of thy times, and strength of salvation.* Here is a desirable end proposed, and that is *the stability of our times*, that things be not disturbed and unhinged at home, and the *strength of salvation*, deliverance from, and success against, enemies abroad. The salvation that God ordains for his people has strength in it; it is a horn of salvation. And here are the way and means for obtaining this end — *wisdom and knowledge*, not only piety, but prudence. That is it which, by the blessing of God, will be the *stability of our times and the strength of salvation*, that wisdom which is first pure, then peaceable, and which sacrifices private interests to a public good; such prudence as this will establish truth and peace, and fortify the bulwarks in defence of them. (2.) A pious maxim of state for Hezekiah and his people to govern themselves by: *The fear of the Lord is his treasure.* It is God's treasure in the world, from which he receives his tribute; or, rather, it is the prince's treasure. A good prince accounts it so (that wisdom is better than gold) and he shall find it so. Note, True religion is the true treasure of any prince or people; it denominates them rich. Those places that have plenty of Bibles, and ministers, and serious good people, are really rich; and it contributes to that which makes a nation rich in this world. It is therefore the interest of a people to support religion among them and to take heed of every thing that threatens to hinder it.

V. The great distress that Jerusalem was brought into described, that those who believed the prophet might know beforehand what troubles were coming and might provide accordingly, and that when the foregoing promise of their deliverance should have its accomplishment the remembrance of the extremity of their case might help to magnify God in it and make them the more thankful, *v.* 7–9. It is here foretold, 1. That the enemy would be very insolent and abusive and there would be no dealing with him, either by treaties of peace (*for he has broken the covenant* without any hesitation, as if it were below him to be a servant to his word), or by the preparations of war, for *he has despised the cities;* he scorns to take notice either of their appeals to justice or of their petitions for mercy. He makes himself master of them so easily (though they are called *fenced cities*), and meets with so little resistance, that he despises them, and has no relentings when he puts all to the sword; for he regards no man, has no pity or concern, no, not for those that he is under particular obligations to. He neither fears God nor regards man, but is haughty and imperious to every one. There are those that take a pride in trampling upon all mankind, and have neither veneration for the honourable nor compassion for the miserable. 2. That therefore he would not be brought to any terms of reconciliation: *The valiant ones of Jerusalem,* being unable to make their parts good with him, must be contentedly run down with noise and insolence, which will make them cry without, because they cannot serve their country as they might have done against a fair adversary. *The ambassadors* sent by Hezekiah to treat *of peace,* finding him so haughty and unmanageable, *shall weep bitterly* for vexation at the disappointment they had met with in their negotiations; they shall weep like children, as despairing to find out any expedient to pacify him. 3. That the country should be made quite desolate for a time by his army. (1.) No man durst travel the roads; so that a stop was put to trade and commerce, and (which was worse) no man could safely go up to Jerusalem, to keep the solemn feasts: *The highways lie waste.* While the fields lie waste, trodden like the highways, the highways lie waste, untrodden like the fields, for *the traveller ceases.* (2.) No man had any profit from the grounds, *v.* 9. The earth used to rejoice in its own productions for the service of God's Israel, but now the enemies of Israel eat them up, or tread them down: it *mourns and languishes;* the country looks melancholy and the country people have misery in their countenances, wanting necessary food for themselves and their families; the wonted joy of harvest is turned into lamentation, so withering and uncertain are all worldly joys. The desolation is universal. That part of the country which belonged to the ten tribes was already laid waste: "*Lebanon* famed for cedars, *Sharon* for roses, *Bashan* for cattle, *Carmel* for corn, all very fruitful, have now become like wildernesses, *are ashamed* to be called by their old names, they are so unlike what they were. They *shake off their fruits* before their time into the hand of the spoiler, which used to be gathered seasonably by the hand of the owner."

VI. God appearing, at length, in his glory against his proud invader, *v.* 10–12. When things are brought thus to the last extremity, 1. God will magnify himself. He had seemed to sit by as an unconcerned spectator: "But *now will I arise, saith the Lord;* now will I appear and act, and therein I will be not only evidenced, but exalted." He will not only demonstrate that there is a God that judges in the earth, but that he is God over all, and higher than the highest. "Now *will I lift up myself,* will prepare for action, will act vigorously, and will be glorified in it." God's time to appear for his people is when their affairs are reduced to the lowest ebb, *when their strength is gone and there is none shut up nor left,* Deu. 32:36. When all other helpers fail, then is God's time to help. 2. He will bring down the Assyrian: "You, O Assyrians! are big with hopes that you shall have all the wealth of Jerusalem for your own, and are in pain till it be so; but all your hopes shall come to nothing: *You shall conceive chaff, and bring forth stubble,* which is not only worthless and good for nothing, but combustible and proper fuel for the fire, which it cannot escape, when *your* own *breath as fire shall devour you,* that is, the breath of God's wrath, provoked against you by the breath of your sins — your malignant breath, the threatenings and slaughter you breathe out against the people of God, this shall devour you, and your blasphemous breath against God and his name." God would make their own tongues to fall upon them, and their own breath to blow the fire that should consume them; and then no wonder that the people are *as the burnings of lime* in a lime-kiln, all on fire together, and *as thorns cut up,* which are dried and withered, and therefore easily take fire and are soon burnt up. Such was the destruction of the Assyrian army; it was like the burning up of thorns, which can well be spared, or the burning of lime, which makes it good for something. The burning of that army enlightened the world with the knowledge of God's power and made his name shine brightly.

Verses 13–24

Here is a preface that commands attention; and it is fit that all should attend, both near and afar off, to what God says and does (*v.* 13): *Hear, you that are afar off,* whether in place or time. Let distant regions and future ages hear what God has done. They do so; they will do so from the scripture, with as much assurance as those that were near, the neighbouring nations and those that lived at that time. But whoever hears what God has done, whether near or afar off, let them acknowledge his might, that it is irresistible, and that he can do every thing. Those are very stupid who hear what God has done and yet will not acknowledge his might. Now what is it that God has done which we must take notice of, and in which we must acknowledge his might?

I. He has struck a terror upon the sinners in Zion (*v.* 14): *Fearfulness has surprised the hypocrites.* There are sinners in Zion, hypocrites, that enjoy Zion's privileges and concur in Zion's services, but their hearts are not right in the sight of God; they keep up secret haunts of sin under the cloak of a visible profession, which convicts them of hypocrisy. Sinners in Zion will have a great deal to answer for above other sinners; and their place in Zion will be so far from being their security that it will aggravate both their sin and their punishment. Now those sinners in Zion, though always subject to secret frights and terrors, were struck with a more than ordinary consternation from the convictions of their own consciences. 1. When they saw the Assyrian army besieging Jerusalem, and ready to set fire to it and lay it in ashes, and burn the wasps in the nest. Finding they could not make their escape to Egypt, as some had done, and distrusting the promises God had made by his prophets that he would deliver them, they were at their wits' end, and ran about like men distracted, crying, *"Who among us shall dwell with devouring fire?* Let us therefore abandon the city, and shift for ourselves elsewhere; one had as good live in everlasting burnings as live here." *Who will stand up for us against this devouring fire?* so some read it. See here how the sinners in Zion are affected when the judgments of God are abroad; while they were only threatened they slighted them and made nothing of them; but, when they come to be executed, they run into the other extreme, then they magnify them, and make the worst of them; they call them *devouring fire* and *everlasting burnings,* and despair of relief and succour. Those that rebel against the commands of the word cannot take the comforts of it in a time of need. Or, rather, 2. When they saw the Assyrian army destroyed; for the destruction of that is the fire spoken of immediately before, *v.* 11, 2. When the sinners in Zion saw what dreadful execution the wrath of God made they were in a great fright, being conscious to themselves that they had provoked this God by their secretly worshipping other gods; and therefore they cry out, *Who among us shall dwell with this devouring fire,* before which so vast an army is as thorns? *Who among us shall dwell with* these *everlasting burnings,* which have made the Assyrians *as the burnings of lime? v.* 12. Thus they said, or should have said. Note, God's judgments upon the enemies of Zion should strike a terror upon the sinners in Zion, nay, David himself trembles at them, Ps. 119:120. God himself is this devouring fire, Heb. 12:29. Who is able to stand before him? 1 Sa. 6:20. His wrath will burn those everlastingly that have made themselves fuel for it. It is a fire that shall never be quenched, nor will ever go out of itself; for it is the wrath of an everlasting God preying upon the conscience of an immortal soul. Nor can the most daring sinners bear up against it, so as to bear either the execution of it or the fearful expectation of it. Let this awaken us all to flee from the wrath to come, by fleeing to Christ as our refuge.

II. He has graciously provided for the security of his people that trust in him: *Hear this, and acknowledge his* power in making those that *walk righteously,* and *speak uprightly,* to *dwell on high, v.* 15, 16. We have here,

1. The good man's character, which he preserves even in times of common iniquity, in divers instances. (1.) He walks righteously. In the whole course of his conversation he acts by rules of equity, and makes conscience of rendering to all their due, to God his due, as well as to men theirs. His walk is righteousness itself; he would not for a world wilfully do an unjust thing. (2.) He speaks uprightly, *uprightnesses* (so the word is); he speaks what is true and right, and with an honest intention. He cannot think one thing and speak another, nor look one way and row another. His word is to him as sacred as his oath, and is not yea and nay. (3.) He is so far from coveting ill-gotten gain that he despises it. He thinks it a mean and sordid thing, and unbecoming a man of honour, to enrich himself by any hardship put upon his neighbour. He scorns to do a wrong thing, nay, to do a severe thing, though he might get by it. He does not over-value gain itself, and therefore easily abhors the gain that is not honestly come by. (4.) If he have a bribe at any time thrust into his hand, to pervert justice, *he shakes his hands from holding* it, with the utmost detestation, taking it as an affront to have it offered him. (5.) *He stops his ears from hearing* any thing that tends to cruelty or bloodshed, or any suggestions stirring him up to revenge, Job 31:31. He turns a deaf ear to those that delight in war and entice him to *cast in his lot among them,* Prov. 1:14, 16. (6.) He *shuts his eyes from seeing evil.* He has such an abhorrence of sin that he cannot bear to see others commit it, and does himself watch against all the occasions of it. Those that would preserve the purity of their souls must keep a strict guard upon the senses of their bodies, must stop their ears to temptations, and turn away their eyes from beholding vanity.

2. The good man's comfort, which he may preserve even in times of common calamity, *v.* 16. (1.) He shall be safe; he shall escape the devouring fire and the everlasting burnings; he shall have access to, and communion with, that God who is a devouring fire, but shall be to him a rejoicing light. And, as to present troubles, *he shall dwell on high,* out of the reach of them, nay, out of the hearing of the noise of them; he shall not be really harmed by them, nay, he shall not be greatly frightened at them: *The floods of great waters shall not come nigh him;* or, if they should attack him, *his place of defence shall be the munitions of rocks,* strong and impregnable, fortified by nature as well as art. The divine power will keep him safe, and his faith in that power will keep him easy. God, the rock of ages, will be his high tower. (2.) He shall be supplied; he shall want nothing that is necessary for him: *Bread shall be given him,* even when the siege is straitest and provisions are cut off; and *his waters shall be sure,* that is, he shall be sure of the continuance of them, so that he shall not drink his water by measure and with astonishment. Those that fear the Lord shall not want any thing that is good for them.

III. He will protect Jerusalem, and deliver it out of the hands of the invaders. This storm that threatened them should blow over, and they should enjoy a prosperous state again. Many instances are here given of this prosperity.

1. Hezekiah shall put off his sackcloth and all the sadness of his countenance, and shall appear publicly in his beauty, in his royal robes and with a pleasing aspect (*v.* 17), to the great joy of all his loving subjects. Those that walk uprightly shall not only have bread given them, and their water sure, but they shall with an eye of faith see the King of kings in his beauty, the beauty of holiness, and that beauty shall be upon them.

2. The siege being raised, by which they were kept close within the walls of Jerusalem, they shall now be at liberty to go abroad upon business or pleasure without danger of falling into the enemies' hand: *They shall behold the land that is very far off;* they shall visit the utmost corners of the nation, and take a prospect of the adjacent countries, which will be the more pleasant after so long a confinement. Thus believers behold the heavenly Canaan, that land that is very far off, and comfort themselves with the prospect of it in evil times.

3. The remembrance of the fright they were in shall add to the pleasure of their deliverance (*v.* 18): *Thy heart shall meditate terror,* meditate it with pleasure when it is over. Thou shalt think thou still hearest the alarm in thy ears, when all the cry was, "Arm, arm, arm! every man to his post. *Where is the scribe* or secretary of war? Let him appear to draw up the muster-roll. *Where is the receiver* and pay-master of the army? Let him see what he had in bank, to defray the charge of a defence. *Where is he that counted the towers?* Let him bring in the account of them, that care may be taken to put a competent num-

ber of men in each." Or these words may be taken as Jerusalem's triumph over the vanquished army of the Assyrians, and the rather because the apostle alludes to them in his triumphs over the learning of this world, when it was baffled by the gospel of Christ, 1 Co. 1:20. The virgin, the daughter of Zion, despises all their military preparations. Where is the scribe or muster-master of the Assyrian army? Where is their weigher (or treasurer), and where are their engineers that counted the towers? They are all either dead or fled. There is an end of them.

4. They shall no more be terrified with the sight of the Assyrians, who were a fierce people naturally, and were particularly fierce against the people of the Jews, and were of a strange language, that could understand neither their petitions nor their complaints, and therefore had a pretence for being deaf to them, nor could themselves be understood: "They are *of a deeper speech than thou canst perceive,* which will make them the more formidable, *v.* 19. Thy eyes shall no more see them thus fierce, but their countenances changed when they shall all become dead corpses."

5. They shall no more be under apprehensions of the danger of Jerusalem — Zion, and the temple there (*v.* 20): *"Look upon Zion, the city of our solemnities,* the city where our solemn sacred feasts are kept, where we used to meet to worship God in religious assemblies." The good people among them, in the time of their distress, were most in pain for Zion upon this account, that it was the city of their solemnities, that the conquerors would burn their temple and they should not have that to keep their solemn feasts in any more. In times of public danger our concern should be most about our religion, and the cities of our solemnities should be dearer to us than either our strong cities or our store-cities. It is with an eye to this that God will work deliverance for Jerusalem, because it is the city of religious solemnities: let those be conscientiously kept up, as the glory of a people, and we may depend upon God to create a defence upon that glory. Two things are here promised to Jerusalem: — (1.) A well-grounded security. It shall be *a quiet habitation* for the people of God; they shall not be molested and disturbed, as they have been, by the alarms of the sword either of war or persecution, *ch.* 29:20. It shall be a quiet habitation, as it is the city of our solemnities. It is desirable to be quiet in our own houses, but much more so to be quiet in God's house and have none to make us afraid there. Thus it shall be with Jerusalem; and *the eyes shall see it,* which will be a great satisfaction to a good man, Ps. 128:5, 6. *"Thou shalt see the good of Jerusalem, and peace upon Israel;* thou shalt live to see it and share in it." (2.) An unmoved stability. Jerusalem, the city of our solemnities, is indeed but *a tabernacle,* in comparison with the New Jerusalem. The present manifestations of the divine glory and grace are nothing in comparison with those that are reserved for the future state. But it is such a tabernacle as *shall not be taken down.* After this trouble is over Jerusalem shall long enjoy a confirmed peace; and her sacred privileges, which are the stakes and cords of her tabernacle, shall not be removed from her, nor any disturbance given to the course and circle of her religious services. God's church on earth is a tabernacle, which, though it may be shifted from one place to another, shall not be taken down while the world stands; for in every age Christ will have a seed to serve him. The promises of the covenant are its stakes, which shall never be removed, and the ordinances and institutions of the gospel are its cords, which shall never be broken. They are things which cannot be shaken, though heaven and earth be, but shall remain.

6. God himself will be their protector and Saviour, *v.* 21, 22. This the principal ground of their confidence: "He that is himself *the glorious Lord* will display his glory for us and be a glory to us, such as shall eclipse the rival-glory of the enemy." God, in being a gracious Lord, is a glorious Lord; for his goodness is his glory. God will be the Saviour of Jerusalem and her glorious Lord, (1.) As a guard against their adversaries abroad. He will be *a place of broad rivers and streams.* Jerusalem had no considerable river running by it, as most great cities have, nothing but the brook Kidron, and so wanted one of the best natural fortifications, as well as one of the greatest advantages for trade and commerce, and upon this account their enemies despised them and doubted not but to make an easy prey of them; but the presence and power of God are sufficient at any time to make up to us the deficiencies of the creature and of its strength and beauty. We have all in God, all we need or can desire. Many external advantages Jerusalem has not which other places have, but in God there is more than an equivalent. But, if there be broad rivers and streams about Jerusalem, may not these yield an easy access to the fleet of an invader? No; these are rivers and streams *in which shall go no galley with oars,* no man of war or gallant ship. If God himself be the river, it must needs be inaccessible to the enemy; they can neither find nor force their way by it. (2.) As a guide to their affairs at home: *"For the Lord is our Judge,* to whom we are accountable, to whose judgment we refer ourselves, by whose judgment we abide, and who therefore (we hope) will judge for us. *He is our lawgiver;* his word is a law to us, and to him every thought within us is brought into obedience. *He is our King,* to whom we pay homage and tribute, and an inviolable allegiance, and therefore *he will save us."* For, as protection draws allegiance, so allegiance may expect protection, and shall have it with God. By faith we take Christ for our prince and Saviour, and as such depend upon him and devote ourselves to him. Observe with what an air of triumph, and with what an emphasis laid upon the glorious name of God, they comfort themselves with this: *Jehovah is our Judge, Jehovah is our Lawgiver, Jehovah is our King, who, being self-existent, is self-sufficient, and all-sufficient to us.*

7. The enemies shall be quite infatuated, and all their powers and projects broken, like a ship at sea in stress of weather, that cannot ride out the storm, but having her tackle torn, her masts split, and nothing wherewith to repair them, is given up for a wreck, *v.* 23. *The tacklings* of the Assyrian *are loosed;* they are like a ship whose tacklings are loose, or forsaken by the ship's crew, when they give it over for lost, finding that they cannot strengthen the mast, but it will come down. They thought themselves sure of Jerusalem; but when they were just entering the port as it were, and though all was their own, they were quite becalmed, and *could not spread their sail,* but lay wind-bound till God poured the fury of his wrath upon them. The enemies of God's church are often disarmed and unrigged when they think they have almost gained their point.

8. The wealth of their camp shall be a rich booty for the Jews: *Then is the prey of a great spoil divided.* When the greater part were slain the rest fled in confusion, and with such precipitation that (like the Syrians) they *left their tents as they were,* so that all the treasure in them fell into the hands of the besieged; and even *the lame take the prey.* Those that tarried at home did divide the spoil. It was so easy to come at that not only the strong man might make himself master of it, but even the lame man, whose hands were lame, that he could not fight, and his feet, that he could not pursue. As the victory shall cost them no peril, so the prey shall cost them no toil. And there was such abundance of it that when those who were forward, and came first, had carried off as much as they would, even the lame, who came late, found sufficient. Thus God brought good out of evil, and not only delivered Jerusalem, but enriched it, and abundantly recompensed the losses they had sustained. Thus comfortably and well do the frights and distresses of the people of God often end.

9. Both sickness and sin shall be taken away; and then sickness is taken away in mercy when this is all the fruit of it, and the recovery from it, even the taking away of sin. (1.) *The inhabitant shall not say, I am sick. As the lame shall take the prey,* so shall the sick, notwithstanding their weakness, make a shift to get to the abandoned camp and seize something for themselves; or there shall be such a universal transport of joy upon this occasion that even the sick shall, for the present, forget their sickness and the sorrows of it, and join with the public in its rejoicings; the deliverance of their city shall be their cure. Or it intimates that, whereas infectious diseases are commonly the effect of long sieges, it shall not be so with Jerusalem, but the inhabitants of it with their victory and peace shall have health also, and there shall be no complaining upon the account of sickness within their gates. Or those that are sick shall bear their sickness without complaining as long as they see it goes well with Jerusalem. Our sense of private grievances should be drowned in our thanksgivings for public mercies. (2.) *The people that dwell therein shall be forgiven their iniquity,* not only the body of the nation forgiven their national guilt in the removing of the national judgment, but particular persons, that dwell therein, shall repent, and reform, and have their sins pardoned. And this is promised as that which is at the bottom of all other favours; he will do so and so for them, *for he will be merciful to their unrighteousness,* Heb. 8:12. Sin is the sickness of the soul. When God pardons the sin he heals the disease; and, when the diseases of sin are healed by pardoning mercy, the sting of bodily sickness is taken out and the cause of it removed; so that either the inhabitant shall not be sick or at least shall not say, *I am sick.* If iniquity be taken away, we have little reason to complain of outward affliction. *Son, be of good cheer; thy sins are forgiven thee.*

CHAPTER 34

In this chapter we have the fatal doom of all the nations that are enemies to God's church and people, though Edom only is mentioned, because of the old enmity of Esau to Jacob, which was typical, as much as that more ancient enmity of Cain to Abel, and flowed from the original enmity of the serpent to the seed of the woman. It is probable that this prophecy had its accomplishment in the great desolations made by the Assyrian army first, or rather by Nebuchadnezzar's army some time after, among those nations that were neighbours to Israel and had been in some way or other injurious to them. That mighty conqueror took a pride in shedding blood, and laying countries waste, and therein, quite beyond his design, he was fulfilling what God here threatened against his and his people's enemies. But we have reason to think it is intended as a denunciation of the wrath of God against all those who fight against the interests of his kingdom among men, that it has its frequent accomplishment in the havoc made by the wars of the nations and other desolating judgments, and will have its full accomplishment in the final dissolution of all things at the day of judgment and perdition of ungodly men. Here is, I. A demand of universal attention (*v.* 1). II. A direful scene of blood and confusion presented (*v.* 2–7). III. The reason given for these judgments (*v.* 8). IV. The continuance of this desolation, the country being made like the lake of Sodom (*v.* 9, 10), and the cities abandoned to wild beasts and melancholy fowls (*v.* 11–15). V. The solemn ratification of all this (*v.* 16, 17). Let us hear, and fear.

Verses 1–8

Here we have a prophecy, as elsewhere we have a history, of the wars of the Lord, which we are sure are all both righteous and successful. This world, as it is his creature, he does good to; but as it is in the interest of Satan, who is called *the god of this world,* he fights against it.

I. Here is the trumpet sounded and the war proclaimed, *v.* 1. All nations must hear and hearken, not only because what God is about to do is well worthy their remark (as *ch.* 33:13), but because they are all concerned in it; it is with them that God has a quarrel; it is against them that God is coming forth in wrath. Let them all take notice that the great God is angry with them; his indignation is upon all nations, and therefore let all nations come near to hear. *The trumpet is blown in the city* (Amos 3:6), *and the watchmen on the walls cry, Hearken to the sound of the trumpet,* Jer. 6:17. *Let the earth hear, and the fulness thereof, for it is the Lord's* (Ps. 24:1) and ought to hearken to its Maker and Master. The world must hear, and *all things that come forth of it,* the children of men, that are of the earth earthy, come out of it, and must return to it; or the inanimate products of the earth are called to, as more likely to hearken than sinners, whose hearts are hardened against the calls of God. *Hear, O you mountains! the Lord's controversy,* Micah 6:2. It is so just a controversy that all the world may be safely appealed to concerning the equity of it.

II. Here is the manifesto published, setting forth,

1. Whom he makes war against (*v.* 2): *The indignation of the Lord is upon all nations;* they are all in confederacy against God and religion, all in the interests of the devil, and therefore he is angry with them all, even with all the nations that forget him. He has long *suffered all nations to walk in their own ways* (Acts 14:16), but now he will no longer keep silence. As they have all had the benefit of his patience, so they must all expect now to feel his resentments. *His fury is* in a special manner *upon all their armies,* (1.) Because with them they have done mischief to the people of God; those are they that have made bloody work with them, and therefore they must be sure to have blood given them to drink. (2.) Because with them they hope to make their part good against the justice and power of God they trust to them as their defence, and therefore on them, in the first place, God's fury will come. Armies

before God's fury are but as dry stubble before a consuming fire, though ever so numerous and courageous.

2. Whom he makes war for, and what are the grounds and reasons of the war (v. 8): *It is the day of the Lord's vengeance,* and he it is *to whom vengeance belongs,* and who is never *unrighteous in taking vengeance,* Rom. 3:5. As there is a day of the Lord's patience, so there will be a day of his vengeance; for, though he bear long, he will not bear always. It is *the year of recompences for the controversy of Zion.* Zion is the holy city, the city of our solemnities, a type and figure of the church of God in the world. Zion has a just quarrel with her neighbours for the wrongs they have done her, for all their treacherous and barbarous usage of her, profaning her holy things, laying waste her palaces, and slaying her sons. She has left it to God to plead her cause, and he will do so when the time, even the set time, to favour Zion shall have come; then he will recompense to her persecutors and oppressors all the mischiefs they have done her. The controversy will be decided, that Zion has been wronged, and therein Zion's God has been himself abused. Judgment will be given upon this decision, and execution done. Note, There is a time prefixed in the divine counsels for the deliverance of the church and the destruction of her enemies, a year of the redeemed, which will come, *a year of recompences for the controversy of Zion;* and we must patiently wait till then, and *judge nothing before the time.*

III. Here are the operations of the war, and the methods of it, settled, with an infallible assurance of success. 1. The sword of the Lord is *bathed in heaven;* this is all the preparation here made for the war, v. 5. It may probably allude to some custom they had then of bathing their swords in some liquor or other, to harden them or brighten them; it is the same with the furbishing of it, that it may glitter, Eze. 21:9–11. God's sword is bathed in heaven, in his counsel and decree, in his justice and power, and then there is not standing before it. 2. *It shall come down.* What he has determined shall without fail be put in execution. It shall come down from heaven, and the higher the place is, whence it comes, the heavier will it fall. It will come down *upon Idumea, the people of God's curse,* the people that lie under his curse and are by it doomed to destruction. Miserable, for ever miserable, are those that have by their sins made themselves the people of God's curse; for the sword of the Lord will infallibly attend the curse of the Lord and execute the sentences of it; and those whom he curses are cursed indeed. It shall come down *to judgment,* to execute judgment upon sinners. Note, God's sword of war is always a sword of justice. It is observed of him out of whose mouth goeth the sharp sword that *in righteousness he doth judge and make war,* Rev. 19:11, 15. 3. The nations and their armies shall be given up to the sword (v. 2): *God has delivered them to the slaughter,* and then they cannot deliver themselves, nor can all the friends they have deliver them from it. Those only are slain whom God delivers to the slaughter, for the keys of death are in his hand; and, in delivering them to the slaughter, he has *utterly destroyed* them; their destruction is as sure, when God has doomed them to it, as if they were destroyed already, utterly destroyed. God has, in effect, delivered all the cruel enemies of his church to the slaughter by that word (Rev. 13:10), *He that kills with the sword must be killed by the sword,* for the Lord is righteous. 4. Pursuant to the sentence, a terrible slaughter shall be made among them (v. 6): *The sword of the Lord,* when it comes down with commission, does vast execution; it *is filled,* satiated, surfeited, *with blood,* the blood of the slain, and *made fat with their fatness.* When the day of God's abused mercy and patience is over the sword of his justice gives no quarter, spares none. Men have by sin lost the honour of the human nature and made themselves like the beasts that perish; they are therefore justly denied the compassion and respect that are owing to the human nature and killed as beasts, and no more is made of slaying an army of men than of butchering a flock of lambs or goats and feeding on the fat of the kidneys of rams. Nay, the sword of the Lord shall not only dispatch the lambs and goats, the infantry of their armies, the poor common soldiers, but (v. 7) *the unicorns* too *shall* be made to *come down with them, and the bullocks with the bulls,* though they are ever so proud, and strong, and fierce (*the great men, and the mighty men, and the chief captains* Rev. 6:15), the sword

of the Lord will make as easy a prey of as of the lambs and the goats. The greatest of men are nothing before the wrath of the great God. See what bloody work will be made: *The land shall be soaked with blood,* as with the rain that comes often upon it and in great abundance; *and their dust,* their dry and barren land, shall be *made fat with the fatness* of men slain in their full strength, as with manure. Nay even *the mountains,* which are hard and rocky, *shall be melted with their blood,* v. 3. These expressions are hyperbolical (as St. John's vision of *blood to the horse-bridles,* Rev. 14:20), and are made use of because they sound very dreadful to sense (it makes us even shiver to think of such abundance of human gore), and are therefore proper to express the terror of God's wrath, which is dreadful beyond conception and expression. See what work sin and wrath make even in this world, and think how much more terrible the wrath to come is, which will bring down the unicorns themselves to the bars of the pit. 5. This great slaughter will be a great sacrifice to the justice of God (v. 6): *The Lord has a sacrifice in Bozrah;* there it is that the great Redeemer has his *garments dyed with blood,* ch. 63:1. Sacrifices were intended for the honour of God, to make it appear that he hates sin and demands satisfaction for it, and that nothing but blood will make atonement; and for these ends the slaughter is made, that in it *the wrath of God may be revealed from heaven against all the ungodliness and unrighteousness of men,* especially their ungodly unrighteous enmity to his people, which was the sin that the Edomites were notoriously guilty of. In great sacrifices abundance of beasts were killed, hecatombs offered, and their blood poured out before the altar; and so will it be in this day of the Lord's vengeance. And thus would the whole earth have been soaked with the blood of sinners if Jesus Christ, the great propitiation, had not shed his blood for us; but those who reject him, and will not make a covenant with God by that sacrifice, will themselves fall as victims to divine wrath. Damned sinners are everlasting sacrifices, Mk. 9:48, 49. Those that sacrifice not (which is the character of the ungodly, Eccl. 9:2) must be sacrificed. 6. These slain shall be detestable to mankind, and shall be as much their loathing as ever they were their terror (v. 3): *They shall be cast out,* and none shall pay them the respect of a decent burial; but *their stink shall come up out of their carcases,* that all people by the odious smell, as well as by the ghastly sight, may be made to conceive an indignation against sin and a dread of the wrath of God. They lie unburied, that they may remain monuments of divine justice. 7. The effect and consequence of this slaughter shall be universal confusion and desolation, as if the whole frame of nature were dissolved and melted down (v. 4): *All the host of heaven shall pine and waste away* (so the word is); the sun shall be darkened, and the moon look black, or be turned into blood; *the heavens* themselves *shall be rolled together as a scroll* or parchment when we have done with it, and lay it by, or as when it is shrivelled up by the heat of the fire. The stars shall fall as the leaves in autumn; all the beauty, joy, and comfort, of the vanquished nation shall be lost and done away, magistracy and government shall be abolished, and all dominion and rule, but that of the sword of war, shall fall. Conquerors, in those times, affected to lay waste the countries they conquered; and such a complete desolation is here described by such figurative expressions as will yet have a literal and full accomplishment in the dissolution of all things at the end of time, of which last day of judgment the judgments which God does now sometimes remarkably execute on sinful nations are figures, earnests, and forerunners; and by these we should be awakened to think of that, for which reason these expressions are used here and Rev. 6:12, 13. But they are used without a metaphor, 2 Pt. 3:10, where we are told that *the heavens shall pass away with a great noise and the earth shall be burnt up.*

Verses 9–17

This prophecy looks very black, but surely it looks so further than upon Edom and Bozrah. 1. It describes the melancholy changes that are often made by the divine Providence, in countries, cities, palaces, and families. Places that have flourished and been much frequented strangely go to decay. We know not where to find the places where many great towns, celebrated in history, once stood. Fruit-

ful countries, in process of time, are turned into barrenness, and pompous populous cities into ruinous heaps. Old decayed castles look frightful, and their ruins are almost as much dreaded as ever their garrisons were. 2. It describes the destroying judgments which are the effects of God's wrath and the just punishment of those that are enemies to his people, which God will inflict when *the year of the redeemed has come,* and *the year of recompences for the controversy of Zion.* Those that aim to ruin the church can never do that, but will infallibly ruin themselves. 3. It describes the final desolation of this wicked world, which is *reserved unto fire at the day of judgment,* 2 Pt. 3:7. The earth itself, when it, and all the works that are therein, shall be burnt up, will (for aught I know) be turned into a hell to all those that set their affections on earthly things. However, this prophecy shows us what will be the lot of the *generation of God's curse.*

I. The country shall become like the lake of Sodom, v. 9, 10. *The streams thereof,* that both watered the land and pleased and refreshed the inhabitants, *shall* now *be turned into pitch,* shall be congealed, shall look black, and shall move slowly, or not at all. *Their floods to lazy streams of pitch shall turn;* so Sir *R. Blackmore. The dust thereof shall be turned into brimstone;* so combustible has sin made their land that it shall take fire at the first spark of God's wrath struck upon it; and, when it has taken fire, it shall become burning pitch; the fire shall be universal, not a house, or town, on fire, but a whole country; and it shall not be in the power of any to suppress or extinguish it. It shall burn continually, burn perpetually, and *shall not be quenched night nor day.* The torment of those in hell, or that have a hell within them in their own consciences, is without interruption; the *smoke of this fire goes up for ever.* As long as there are provoking sinners on earth, *from one generation to another,* an increase of sinful men, to *augment the fierce anger of the Lord* (Num. 32:14), there will be a righteous God in heaven to punish them for it. And as long as a people keep up a succession of sinners God will have a succession of plagues for them; nor will any that fall under the wrath of God be ever able to recover themselves. It will be found, how light soever men make of it, that it is a *fearful thing to fall into the hands of the living God.* If the land be doomed to destruction, none shall pass through it, but travellers will choose rather to go a great way about than come within the smell of it.

II. The cities shall become like old decayed houses, which, being deserted by the owners, look very frightful, being commonly possessed by beasts of prey or birds of ill omen. See how dismally the palaces of the enemy look; the description is peculiarly elegant and fine. 1. God shall mark them for ruin and destruction. *He shall stretch out upon Bozrah the line of confusion with the stones* or plummets *of emptiness,* v. 11. This intimates the equity of the sentence passed upon it; it is given according to the rules of justice and the exact agreeableness of the execution with the sentence; the destruction is not wrought at random, but by line and level. The confusion and emptiness that shall overspread the face of the whole country shall be like that of the whole earth when it was *Tohu and Bohu* (the very words here used) — *without form and void.* Gen. 1:2. Sin will soon turn a paradise into a chaos, and sully the beauty of the whole creation. When there is confusion there will soon be emptiness; but both are appointed by the governor of the world, and in exact proportions. 2. Their great men shall be all cut off, and none of them shall dare to appear (v. 12): *They shall call the nobles of the kingdom* to take care of the arduous affairs which lie before them, but none shall be there to take this ruin under their hand, and all her princes, having the sad tidings brought them, shall be nothing, shall be at their wits' end, and not be able to stand them in stead, to shelter them from destruction.

III. Even the houses of state, and those of strength, shall become as wildernesses (v. 13); not only grass shall grow, but *thorns shall come up, in her palaces, nettles and brambles in the fortresses thereof,* and there shall be none to cut them up or tread them down. We sometimes see ruined buildings thus overgrown with rubbish. It intimates that the place shall not only be uninhabited and unfrequented where a full court used to be kept, but that it shall be under the curse of God; for thorns and thistles were the production of the curse, Gen. 3:18.

IV. They shall become the residence and rendezvous of fearful frightful beasts and birds, which usually frequent such melancholy places, because there they may be undisturbed, and, when they are frightened thither, they help to frighten men thence. This circumstance of the desolation, being apt to strike a horror upon the mind, is much enlarged upon here, *v.* 11. *The cormorant shall possess it,* or the pelican, which affects to be solitary (Ps. 102:6); and *the bittern,* which makes a hideous noise, *the owl,* a melancholy bird, *the raven,* a bird of prey, invited by the dead carcases, shall dwell there (*with all the ill-boding monsters of the air,* Sir *R. B.*), all the unclean birds, which were not for the service of man, *v.* 13. *It shall be a habitation for dragons,* which are poisonous and hurtful.

And in their lofty rooms of state,
Where cringing sycophants did wait,
Dragons shall hiss and hungry wolves shall howl;
In courts before by mighty lords possess'd
The serpent shall erect his speckled crest,
Or fold his circling spires to rest.
— Sir R. Blackmore

That which was a court for princes shall now be a court for owls or ostriches, *v.* 14. *The wild beasts of the desert,* the dry and sandy country, shall meet, as it were by appointment, with the wild beasts of the island, the wet marshy country, and shall regale themselves with such a perfect desolation as they shall find there.

Leopards, and all the rav'ning brotherhoods
That range the plains, or lurk in woods,
Each other shall invite to come,
And make this wilder place their home.
Fierce beasts of every frightful shape and size
Shall settle here their bloody colonies.
— Sir R. Blackmore

The satyr shall cry to his fellow to go with him to this desert place, or, being there, they shall please themselves that they have found such an agreeable habitation. There shall *the screech-owl rest,* a night-bird and an ominous one. *The great owl shall there make her nest* (*v.* 15) *and lay and hatch;* the breed of them shall be kept up to provide heirs for this desolate place. *The vultures* which feast on carcases, *shall be gathered there, every one with his mate.* Now observe, 1. How the places which men have deserted, and keep at a distance from, are proper receptacles for other animals, which the providence of God takes care of, and will not neglect. 2. Whom those resemble that are morose, unsociable, and unconversable, and affect a melancholy retirement; they are like these solitary creatures that take delight in desolations. 3. What a dismal change sin makes; it turns a fruitful land into barrenness, a frequented city into a wilderness.

V. Here is an assurance given of the full accomplishment of this prediction, even to the most minute circumstance of it (*v.* 16, 17): *"Seek you out of the book of the Lord and read.* When this destruction comes compare the event with the prediction, and you will find it to answer exactly." Note, The book of the prophets is the book of the Lord, and we ought to consult it and converse with it as of divine origin and authority. We must not only read it, but see out of it, search into it, turn first to one text and then to another and compare them together. Abundance of useful knowledge might thus be extracted, by a diligent search, out of the scriptures, which cannot be got by a superficial reading of them. When you have read the prediction out of the book of the Lord then observe, 1. That according to what you have read so you see; *not one of these shall fail,* either beast or fowl: and, it being foretold that they shall possess it *from generation to generation,* in order to that, that the species may be propagated, *none shall want her mate;* these marks of desolation shall be fruitful, and multiply, and replenish the land. 2. That God's mouth having commanded this direful muster *his Spirit shall gather them,* as the creatures by instinct were gathered to Adam to be named and to Noah to be housed. What God's word has appointed his Spirit will effect and bring about, for no word of God shall fall to the ground. The word of God's promise shall in like manner be accomplished by the operations of the Spirit. 3. That there is an exact order and proportion observed in the accomplishment of this threatening: *He has cast the lot* for these birds and beasts, so that each one shall know his place as readily as if it were marked by line. See the like, Joel 2:7, 8, *They shall not break their ranks, neither shall one thrust another.* The soothsayers among the heathen foretold events by the flight of birds, as if the fate of men depended on them. But here we find that the flight of birds is under the direction of the God of Israel: *he has cast the lot for them.* 4. That the desolation shall be perpetual: *They shall possess it for ever.* God's Jerusalem may be laid in ruins; but Jerusalem of old recovered itself out of its ruins, till it gave place to the gospel Jerusalem, which may be brought low, but shall be rebuilt, and shall continue till it give place to the heavenly Jerusalem. But the enemies of the church shall be for ever desolate, shall be punished with an everlasting destruction.

CHAPTER 35

As after a prediction of God's judgments upon the world (*ch.* 24) follows a promise of great mercy to be had in store for his church (*ch.* 25), so here after a black and dreadful scene of confusion in the foregoing chapter we have, in this, a bright and pleasant one, which, though it foretel the flourishing estate of Hezekiah's kingdom in the latter part of his reign, yet surely looks as far beyond that as the prophecy in the foregoing chapter does beyond the destruction of the Edomites; both were typical, and it concerns us most to look at those things which they were typical of, the kingdom of Christ and the kingdom of heaven. When the world, which lies in wickedness, shall be laid in ruins, and the Jewish church, which persisted in infidelity, shall become a desolation, then the gospel church shall be set up and made to flourish. I. The Gentiles shall be brought into it (*v.* 1, 2, 7). II. The well-wishers to it, who were weak and timorous, shall be encouraged (*v.* 3, 4). III. Miracles shall be wrought both on the souls and on the bodies of men (*v.* 5, 6). IV. The gospel church shall be conducted in the way of holiness (*v.* 8, 9). V. It shall be brought at last to endless joys (*v.* 10). Thus do we find more of Christ and heaven in this chapter than one would have expected in the Old Testament.

Verses 1–4

In these verses we have,

I. The desert land blooming. In the foregoing chapter we had a populous and fruitful country turned into a horrid wilderness; here we have in lieu of that, a wilderness turned into a good land. When the land of Judah was freed from the Assyrian army, those parts of the country that had been made as a wilderness by the ravages and outrages they committed began to recover themselves, and to look pleasantly again, and to blossom as the rose. When the Gentile nations, that had been long as a wilderness, bringing forth no fruit to God, received the gospel, joy came with it to them, Ps. 67:3, 4; 96:11, 12. When Christ was preached in Samaria there was *great joy in that city* (Acts 8:8); those that sat in darkness saw a great and joyful light, and then they blossomed, that is, gave hopes of abundance of fruit; for that was it which the preachers of the gospel aimed at (Jn. 15:16), to *go and bring forth fruit,* Rom. 1:13; Col. 1:6. Though blossoms are not fruit, and often miscarry and come to nothing, yet they are in order to fruit. Converting grace makes the soul that was *a wilderness to rejoice with joy and singing,* and to *blossom abundantly.* This flourishing desert shall have all *the glory of Lebanon* given to it, which consisted in the strength and stateliness of its cedars, together with *the excellency of Carmel and Sharon,* which consisted in corn and cattle. Whatever is valuable in any institution is brought into the gospel. All the beauty of the Jewish church was admitted into the Christian church, and appeared in its perfection, as the apostle shows at large in his epistle to the Hebrews. Whatever was excellent an desirable in the Mosaic economy is translated into the evangelical institutes.

II. The glory of God shining forth: *They shall see the glory of the Lord.* God will manifest himself more than ever in his grace and love to mankind (for that is his glory and excellency), and he shall give them eyes to see it, and hearts to be duly affected with it. This is that which will make the desert blossom. The more we see by faith of the glory of the Lord and the excellency of our God the more joyful and the more fruitful shall we be.

III. The feeble and faint-hearted encouraged, *v.* 3, 4. God's prophets and ministers are in a special manner charged, by virtue of their office, to *strengthen the weak hands,* to comfort those who could not yet recover the fright they had been put into by the Assyrian army with an assurance that God would now return in mercy to them. This is the design of the gospel, 1. To strengthen those that are weak and to confirm them — the weak hands, which are unable either to work or fight, and can hardly be lifted up in prayer, and the feeble knees, which are unable either to stand or walk and unfit for the race set before us. The gospel furnishes us with strengthening considerations, and shows us where strength is laid up for us. Among true Christians there are many that have weak hands and feeble knees, that are yet but babes in Christ; but it is our duty to strengthen our brethren (Lu. 22:32), not only to bear with the weak, but to do what we can to confirm them, Rom. 15:1; 1 Th. 5:14. It is our duty also to strengthen ourselves, to lift up *the hands which hang down* (Heb. 12:12), improving the strength God has given us, and exerting it. 2. To animate those that are timorous and discouraged: *Say to those that are of a fearful heart,* because of their own weakness and the strength of their enemies, that are *hasty* (so the word is), that are for betaking themselves to flight upon the first alarm, and giving up the cause, that say, in their haste, "We are cut off and undone" (Ps. 31:22), there is enough in the gospel to silence these fears; it says to them, and let them say it to themselves and one to another, *Be strong, fear not.* Fear is weakening; the more we strive against it the stronger we are both for doing and suffering; and, for our encouragement to strive, he that says to us, *Be strong* has laid help for us upon one that is mighty.

IV. Assurance given of the approach of a Saviour: *"Your God will come with vengeance.* God will appear for you against your enemies, will recompense both their injuries and your losses." The Messiah will come, in the fulness of time, to take vengeance on the powers of darkness, to spoil them, and make a show of them openly, to recompense those that mourn in Zion with abundant comforts. *He will come and save us.* With the hopes of this the Old-Testament saints strengthened their weak hands. He will come again at the end of time, will come in flaming fire, to recompense tribulation to those who have troubled his people, and, to those who were troubled, rest, such a rest as will be not only a final period to, but a full reward of, all their troubles, 2 Th. 1:6, 7. Those whose *hearts tremble for the ark of God,* and who are under a concern for his church in the world, may silence their fears with this, God will take the work into his own hands. Your God will come, who pleads your cause and owns your interest, even God himself, who is God alone.

Verses 5–10

"Then, when your God shall come, even Christ, to set up his kingdom in the world, to which all the prophets bore witness, especially towards the conclusion of their prophecies of the temporal deliverances of the church, and this evangelical prophet especially — then look for great things."

I. Wonders shall be wrought in the kingdoms both of nature and grace, wonders of mercy wrought upon the children of men, sufficient to evince that it is no less than a God that comes to us. 1. Wonders shall be wrought on men's bodies (*v.* 5, 6): *The eyes of the blind shall be opened;* this was often done by our Lord Jesus when he was here upon earth, with a word's speaking, and one he gave sight to that was *born* blind, Mt. 9:27; 12:22; 20:30; Jn. 9:6. By his power the ears of the deaf also were unstopped, with one word. *Ephphatha — Be opened,* Mk. 7:34. Many that were lame had the use of their limbs restored so perfectly that they could not only go, but *leap,* and with so much joy to them that they could not forbear leaping for joy, as that impotent man, Acts 3:8. The dumb also were enabled to speak, and then no marvel that they were disposed to sing for joy, Mt. 9:32, 33. These miracles Christ wrought to prove that he was sent of God (Jn. 3:2), nay, working them by his own power and in his own name, he proved that he was God, the same who at first made man's mouth, the hearing ear, and the seeing eye. When he would prove to John's disciples his divine mission he did it by miracles of this kind, in which this scripture was fulfilled. 2. Wonders, greater wonders, shall be wrought on men's souls. By the word and Spirit of Christ those that were spiritually blind were enlightened (Acts 26:18), those that were deaf to the calls of God were made to hear them readily, so Lydia, whose heart *the Lord opened,* so *that she attended,* Acts 16:14. Those that were impotent to every thing that is good by divine grace are made, not only able for it, but active in it, and run the way of God's commandments. Those also that were dumb, and knew not how to speak of God or to God, having their understandings opened to know him, shall thereby have their lips opened to show forth his praise. The tongue of the dumb shall sing for joy, the joy of God's salvation. Praise shall be perfected out of the mouth of babes and sucklings.

II. The Spirit shall be poured out from on high. There shall be *waters and streams,* rivers of living water; when our Saviour spoke of these as the fulfilling of the scripture, and most probably of this scripture, the evangelist tells us, *He spoke of the Spirit* (Jn. 7:38, 39), as does also this prophet (*ch.* 32:15); so here (*v.* 6), *in the wilderness,* where one would least expect it, *shall waters break out.* This was fulfilled when the *Holy Ghost fell upon the Gentiles* that *heard the word* (Acts 10:44); then were the fountains of life opened, whence streams flowed, that watered the earth abundantly. These waters are said to *break out,* which denotes a pleasing surprise to the Gentile world, such as brought them, as it were, into a new world. The blessed effect of this shall be that the *parched ground shall become a pool, v.* 7. Those that laboured and were heavily laden, under the burden of guilt, and were scorched with the sense of divine wrath, found rest, and refreshment, and abundant comforts in the gospel. In *the thirsty land,* where no water was, nor ordinances (Ps. 63:1), there shall be *springs of water,* a gospel ministry, and by that the administration of all gospel ordinances in their purity and plenty, which are *the river that makes glad the city of our God,* Ps. 46:4. *In the habitation of dragons,* who chose to dwell in the parched scorched ground (*ch.* 34:9, 13), these waters shall flow, and dispossess them, so that, *where each lay shall be grass with reeds and rushes,* great plenty of useful productions. Thus it was when Christian churches were planted, and flourished greatly, in the cities of the Gentiles, which, for many ages, had been habitations of dragons, or devils rather, as Babylon (Rev. 18:2); when the property of the idols' temples was altered, and they were converted to the service of Christianity, then the habitations of dragons became fruitful fields.

III. The way of religion and godliness shall be laid open: it is here called *the way of holiness* (*v.* 8) the way both of holy worship and a holy conversation. Holiness is the rectitude of the human nature and will, in conformity to the divine nature and will. The way of holiness is that course of religious duties in which men ought to walk and press forward, with an eye to the glory of God and their own felicity in the enjoyment of him. "When our God shall come to save us he shall chalk out to us this way by his gospel, so as it had never been before described." 1. It shall be an appointed way; not a way of sufferance, but *a highway,* a way into which we are directed by a divine authority and in which we are protected by a divine warrant. It is the King's highway, the King of Kings' highway, in which, though we may be waylaid, we cannot be stopped. The *way of holiness* is the way of God's commandments; it is (as highways usually are) the *good old way,* Jer. 6:16. 2. It shall be an appropriated way, the way in which God will bring his own chosen to himself, but *the unclean shall not pass over it,* either to defile it or to disturb those that walk in it. It is a way by itself, distinguished from the way of the world, for it is a way of separation from, and nonconformity to, this world. *It shall be for those* whom the Lord has *set apart for himself* (Ps. 4:3), shall be reserved for them: *The redeemed shall walk there,* and the satisfaction they take in these *ways of pleasantness* shall be out of the reach of molestation from an evil world. *The unclean shall not pass over it,* for it shall be a fair way; those that walk in it are the *undefiled in the way,* who *escape the pollution that is in the world.* 3. It shall be a straight way: *The wayfaring men,* who choose to travel in it, *though fools,* of weak capacity in other things, shall have such plain directions from the word and Spirit of God in this way that they *shall not err therein;* not that they shall be infallible even in their own conduct, or that they shall in nothing mistake, but they shall not be guilty of any fatal misconduct, shall not so miss their way but that they shall recover it again, and get well to their journey's end. Those that are in the narrow way, though some may fall into one path and others into another, not all equally right, but all meeting at last in the same end, shall yet never fall into the broad way again; the Spirit of truth shall lead them into all truth that is necessary for them. Note, The way to heaven is a plain way, and easy to hit. *God has chosen the foolish things of the world,* and made them wise to salvation. *Knowledge is easy to him that understands.* 4. It shall be a safe way: *No lion shall be there, nor any ravenous beast* (*v.* 9), none *to hurt or destroy.* Those that keep close to this way keep out of the reach of Satan the roaring lion, that wicked one touches them not. Those that walk in the way of holiness may proceed with a holy security and serenity of mind, knowing that nothing can do them any real hurt; they shall be quiet from the fear of evil. It was in Hezekiah's days, some time after the captivity of the ten tribes, that God, being displeased with the colonies settled there, *sent lions among them,* 2 Ki. 17:25. But Judah keeps her integrity, and therefore *no lions shall be there.* Those that walk in the *way of holiness* must separate themselves from the unclean and the ravenous, must *save themselves from an untoward generation;* hoping that they themselves are of the redeemed, let them walk *with the redeemed* who *shall walk there.*

IV. The end of this way shall be everlasting joy, *v.* 10. This precious promise of peace now will end shortly in endless joys and rest for the soul. Here is good news for the citizens of Zion, rest to the weary: *The ransomed of the Lord,* who therefore ought to follow him wherever he goes (Rev. 14:4), *shall return and come to Zion,* 1. To serve and worship God in the church militant: they shall deliver themselves out of Babylon (Zec. 2:7), shall *ask the way to Zion* (Jer. 50:5), and shall *find the way ch.* 52:12. God will open to them a door of escape out of their captivity, and it shall be an effectual door, though there be many adversaries. They shall join themselves to the gospel church, that *Mount Zion,* that *city of the living God,* Heb. 12:22. They shall come with songs of joy and praise for their deliverance out of Babylon, where they wept upon every *remembrance of Zion,* Ps. 137:1. Those that by faith are made citizens of the gospel Zion may *go on their way rejoicing* (Acts 8:39); they shall sing in the ways of the Lord, and be still praising him. They rejoice in Christ Jesus, and the sorrows and signs of their convictions are made to flee away by the power of divine consolations. Those that mourn are blessed, for they shall be comforted. 2. To see and enjoy God in the church triumphant; those that walk in *the way of holiness,* under guidance of their Redeemer, shall come to Zion at last, to the heavenly Zion, shall come in a body, shall all be presented together, *faultless, at the coming of Christ's glory with exceeding joy* (Jude 24; Rev. 7:17); they shall come with songs. When God's people returned out of Babylon to Zion they came *weeping* (Jer. 50:4); but they shall come to heaven singing a new song, which no man can learn, Rev. 14:3. When they shall *enter into the joy of their Lord* it shall be what the joys of this world never could be *everlasting joy,* without mixture, interruption, or period. It shall not only fill their hearts, to their own perfect and perpetual satisfaction, but it shall be *upon their heads,* as an ornament of grace and a crown of glory, as a garland worn in token of victory. Their joy shall be visible, and no longer a secret thing, as it is here in this world; it shall be proclaimed, to the glory of God and their mutual encouragement. They shall then obtain the joy and gladness which they could never expect on this side heaven; *and sorrow and sighing shall flee away* for ever, as the shadows of the night before the rising sun. Thus these prophecies, which relate to the Assyrian invasion, conclude, for the support of the people of God under that calamity, and to direct their joy, in their deliverance from it, to something higher. Our joyful hopes and prospects of eternal life should swallow up both all the sorrows and all the joys of this present time.

CHAPTER 36

The prophet Isaiah is, in this and the three following chapters, an historian; for the scripture history, as well as the scripture prophecy, is given by inspiration of God, and was dictated to holy men. Many of the prophecies of the foregoing chapters had their accomplishment in Sennacherib's invading Judah and besieging Jerusalem, and the miraculous defeat he met with there; and therefore the story of this is here inserted, both for the explication and for the confirmation of the prophecy. The key of prophecy is to be found in history; and here, that we might have the readier entrance, it is, as it were, hung at the door. The exact fulfilling of this prophecy might serve to confirm the faith of God's people in the other prophecies, the accomplishment of which was at a greater distance. Whether this story was taken from the book of the Kings and added here, or whether it was first written by Isaiah here and hence taken into the book of Kings, is not material. But the story is the same almost verbatim; and it was so memorable an event that it was well worthy to be twice recorded, 2 Ki. 18 and 19, and here, and an abridgment of it likewise, 2 Chr. 32. We shall be but short in our observations upon this story here, having largely explained it there. In this chapter we have, I. The descent which the king of Assyria made upon Judah, and his success against all the defenced cities (*v.* 1). II. The conference he desired to have with Hezekiah, and the managers on both sides (*v.* 2, 3). III. Rabshakeh's railing blasphemous speech, with which he designed to frighten Hezekiah into a submission, and persuade him to surrender at discretion (*v.* 4–10). IV. His appeal to the people, and his attempt to persuade them to desert Hezekiah, and so force him to surrender (*v.* 11–20). V. The report of this made to Hezekiah by his agents (*v.* 21, 22).

Verses 1–10

We shall here only observe some practical lessons. 1. A people may be in the way of their duty and yet meet with trouble and distress. Hezekiah was reforming, and his people were in some measure reformed; and yet their country is at that time invaded and a great part of it laid waste. Perhaps they began to grow remiss and cool in the work of reformation, were doing it by halves, and ready to sit down short of a thorough reformation; and then God visited them with this judgment, to put life into them and that good cause. We must not wonder if, when we are doing well, God sends afflictions to quicken us to do better, to do our best, and to press forward towards perfection. 2. That we must never be secure of the continuance of our peace in this world, nor think our mountain stands so strong that it cannot be moved. Hezekiah was not only a pious king, but prudent, both in his administration at home and in his treaties abroad. His affairs were in a good posture, and he seemed particularly to be upon good terms with the king of Assyria, for he had lately made his peace with him by a rich present (2 Ki. 18:14), and yet that perfidious prince pours an army into his country all of a sudden and lays it waste. It is good for us therefore always to keep up an expectation of trouble, that, when it comes, it may be no surprise to us, and then it will be the less a terror. 3. God sometimes permits the enemies of his people, even those that are most impious and treacherous, to prevail far against them. The king of Assyria took all, or most, of the defenced cities of Judah, and then the country would of course be an easy prey to him. Wickedness may prosper awhile, but cannot prosper always. 4. Proud men love to talk big, to boast of what they are, and have, and have done, nay and of what they will do, to insult over others, and set all mankind at defiance, though thereby they render themselves ridiculous to all wise men and obnoxious to the wrath of that God who resists the proud. But thus they think to make themselves feared, though they make themselves hated, and to carry their point by *great swelling words* of vanity, Jude 16. 5. The enemies of God's people endeavour to conquer them by frightening them, especially by frightening them from their confidence in God. Thus Rabshakeh here, with noise and banter, runs down Hezekiah as utterly unable to cope with his master, or in the least to make head against him. It concerns us therefore, that we may keep our ground against the enemies of our souls, to keep up our spirits by keeping up our hope in God. 6. It is acknowledged, on all hands, that those who forsake God's service forfeit his protection. If that had been true which Rabshakeh alleged, that Hezekiah had thrown down God's altars, he might justly infer that he could not with any assurance trust in him for succour and relief, *v.* 7, We may say thus to presuming sinners, who say that they trust in the Lord and in his mercy. Is not this he whose commandments they have lived in the contempt of, whose name they have dishonoured, and whose ordinances they have slighted? How then can they expect to find favour with him? 7. It is an easy thing, and very common, for those that persecute the church and people of God to pretend a commission from him for so doing. Rabshakeh could say, *Have I now come up without the Lord?* when really he had come up *against* the Lord, *ch.* 37:28. Those that kill the servants of the Lord think they do him service and say, *Let the Lord be glorified.* But, sooner or later, they will be made to know their error to their cost, to their confusion.

Verses 11–22

We may hence learn these lessons: — 1. That, while princes and counsellors have public matters under debate, it is not fair to appeal to the people. It was a reasonable motion which Hezekiah's plenipotentiaries made, that this parley should be held in a language which the people did not understand (*v.* 11), because reasons of state are secret things and ought to be kept secret, the vulgar being incompetent judges of them. It is therefore an unfair practice, and not doing as men would be done by, to incense subjects against their rulers by base insinuations. 2. Proud and haughty scorners, the fairer they are spoken to, commonly speak the fouler. Nothing could be said more mildly and respectfully than that which Hezekiah's agents said to Rabshakeh. Besides that the thing itself was just which they desired, they called themselves his *servants,* they petitioned for it: *Speak, we pray thee;* but this made him the more spiteful and imperious. To give rough answers to those who give us soft answers is one way of rendering evil for good; and those are wicked indeed, and it is to be feared incurable, with whom that which usually turns away wrath does but make bad worse. 3. When Satan would tempt men from trusting in God, and cleaving to him, he does so by insinuating that in yielding to him they may better their condition; but it is a false suggestion, and grossly absurd, and therefore to be rejected with the utmost abhorrence. When the world and the flesh say to us, *"Make an agreement* with us *and come out to us,* submit to our dominion and come into our interests, and *you shall eat every one of his own vine,"* they do but deceive us, promising liberty when they would lead us into the basest captivity and slavery. One might as well take Rabshakeh's word as theirs for kind usage and fair quarter; therefore, *when they speak fair, believe them not.* Let them say what they will, there is no land like the land of promise, the holy land. 4. Nothing can be more absurd in itself, nor a greater affront to the true and living God, than to compare him with the gods of the heathen; as if he could do no more for the protection of his worshippers than they can for the protection of theirs, and as if the God of Israel could as easily be mastered as the gods of Hamath and Arphad, whereas they are vanity and a lie. They are nothing; he is the great *I AM:* they are the creatures of men's fancy and the works of men's hands; he is the Creator of all things. 5. Presumptuous sinners are ready to think that, because they have been too hard for their fellow-creatures, they are therefore a match for their Creator. This and the other nation they have subdued, and therefore the Lord himself shall not deliver Jerusalem out of their hand. But, though the potsherds may strive with the potsherds of the earth, let them not strive with the potter. 6. It is sometimes prudent not to *answer a fool according to his folly.* Hezekiah's command was, *"Answer him not;* it will but provoke him to rail and blaspheme yet more and more; leave it to God to stop his mouth, for you cannot." They had reason enough on their side, but it would be hard to speak it to such an unreasonable adversary without a mixture of passion; and, if they should fall a railing like him, Rabshakeh would be much too hard for them at that weapon. 7. It becomes the people of God to lay to heart the dishonour done to God by the blasphemies of wicked men, though they do not think it prudent to reply to those blasphemies. Though they *answered him not a word,* yet they rent their clothes, in a holy zeal for the glory of God's name and a holy indignation at the contempt put upon it. They tore their garments when they heard blasphemy, as taking no pleasure in their own ornaments when God's honour suffered.

CHAPTER 37

In this chapter we have a further repetition of the story which we had before in the book of Kings concerning Sennacherib. In the foregoing chapter we had him conquering and threatening to conquer. In this chapter we have him falling, and at last fallen, in answer to prayer, and in fulfillment of many of the prophecies which we have met with in the foregoing chapters. Here we have, I. Hezekiah's pious reception of Rabshakeh's impious discourse (*v.* 1). II. The gracious message he sent to Isaiah to desire his prayers (*v.* 2–5). III. The encouraging answer which Isaiah sent to him from God, assuring him that God would plead his cause against the king of Assyria (*v.* 6, 7). IV. An abusive letter which the king of Assyria sent to Hezekiah, to the same purport with Rabshakeh's speech (*v.* 8–13). V. Hezekiah's humble prayer to God upon the receipt of this letter (*v.* 14–20). VI. The further full answer which God sent him by Isaiah, promising him that his affairs should shortly take a happy turn, that the storm should blow over and every thing should appear bright and serene (*v.* 21–35). VII. The immediate accomplishment of this prophecy in the ruin of his army (*v.* 36) and the murder of himself (*v.* 37, 38). All this was largely opened, 2 Ki. 19.

Verses 1–7

We may observe here, 1. That the best way to baffle the malicious designs of our enemies against us is to be driven by them to God and to our duty and so to fetch meat out of the eater. Rabshakeh intended to frighten Hezekiah from the Lord, but it proves that he frightens him to the Lord. The wind, instead of forcing the traveller's coat from him, makes him wrap it the closer about him. The more Rabshakeh reproaches God the more Hezekiah studies to honour him, by rending his clothes for the dishonour done to him and attending in his sanctuary to know his mind. 2. That it well becomes great men to desire the prayers of good men and good ministers. Hezekiah sent messengers, and honourable ones, those of the first rank, to Isaiah, to desire his prayers, remembering how much his prophecies of late had plainly looked towards the events of the present day, in dependence upon which, it is probable, he doubted not but that the issue would be comfortable, yet he would have it to be so in answer to prayer: *This is a day of trouble,* therefore let it be a day of prayer. 3. When we are most at a plunge we should be most earnest in prayer: Now that the *children are brought to the birth,* but *there is not strength to bring forth,* now let prayer come, and help at a dead lift. When pains are most strong let prayers be most lively; and, when we meet with the greatest difficulties, then is a time to stir up not ourselves only, but others also, to take hold on God. Prayer is the midwife of mercy, that helps to bring it forth. 4. It is an encouragement to pray though we have but some hopes of mercy (*v.* 4): *It may be the Lord thy God will hear; who knows but he will return and repent?* The *it may be* of the prospect of the haven of blessings should quicken us with double diligence to ply the oar of prayer. 5. When there is a remnant left, and but a remnant, it concerns us to lift up a prayer for that remnant, *v.* 4. The prayer that reaches heaven must be lifted up by a strong faith, earnest desires, and a direct intention to the glory of God, all which should be quickened when we come to the last stake. 6. Those that have made God their enemy we have no reason to be afraid of, for they are marked for ruin; and, though they may hiss, they cannot hurt. Rabshakeh has blasphemed God, and therefore let not Hezekiah be afraid of him, *v.* 6. He has made God a party to the cause by his invectives, and therefore judgment will certainly be given against him. God will certainly plead his own cause. 7. Sinners' fears are but prefaces to their falls. He shall *hear the rumour* of the slaughter of his army, which shall oblige him to retire to his own land, and there he shall be slain, *v.* 7. The terrors that pursue him shall bring him at last to the *king of terrors,* Job 18:11, 14. The curses that come upon sinners shall overtake them.

Verses 8–20

We may observe here, 1. That, if God give us inward satisfaction in his promise, this may confirm us in our silently bearing reproaches. God answered Hezekiah, but it does not appear that he, after deliberation, sent any answer to Rabshakeh; but, God having taken the work into his own hands, he quietly left the matter with him. *So Rabshakeh returned* to the king his master for fresh instructions. 2. Those that delight in war shall have enough of it. Sennacherib, without provocation given to him or warning given by him, went forth to war against Judah; and now with as little ceremony the king of Ethiopia goes forth to war against him, *v.* 9. Those that are quarrelsome may expect to be quarrelled with; and God sometimes checks the rage of his enemies by giving it a powerful diversion. 3. It is bad to talk proudly and profanely, but it is worse to write so, for this argues more deliberation and design, and what is written spreads further, lasts longer, and does the more mischief. Atheism and irreligion, written, will certainly be reckoned for another day. 4. Great successes often harden sinners' hearts in their sinful ways and make them the more daring. Because the kings of Assyria have destroyed all lands (though, in fact, they were but a few that fell within their reach), therefore they doubt not but to destroy God's land; because the gods of the nations were unable to help they conclude the God of Israel is so; because the idolatrous kings of Hamath and Arphad became an easy prey to them therefore they doubt not but to destroy God's land; because the idolatrous kings of Hamath and Arphad became an easy prey to them therefore the religious reforming king of Judah must needs be so too. Thus is this proud man ripened for ruin by the sunshine of prosperity. 5. Liberty of access to the throne of grace, and liberty of speech there, are the unspeakable privilege of the Lord's people at all times, especially in times of distress and danger. Hezekiah took Sennacherib's letter, and spread it before the Lord, not designing to make any complaints against him but those grounded upon his own handwriting. Let the thing speak itself; here it is in black and white: *Open thy eyes, O Lord! and see.* God allows his praying people to be humbly free with him, to utter all their words, as Jephthah did, before him, to spread the letter, whether of a friend or an enemy, before him, and leave the contents, the concern of it, with him. 6. The great and fundamental principles of our religion, applied by faith and improved in prayer, will be of sovereign use to us in our particular exigencies and distresses, whatever they are; to them therefore we must have recourse, and abide by them; so Hezekiah did here. He encouraged himself with this, that the God of Israel is *the Lord of hosts,* of all hosts, of the hosts of Israel, to animate him, of the hosts of their enemies, to dispirit and restrain them, — that he is God *alone,* and there is none that can stand in competition with him, — that he is the *God of all the kingdoms of the earth,* and disposes of them all as he pleases; for he made heaven and earth, and therefore both can do any thing and does every thing. 7. When we are afraid of men that are great destroyers we may with humble boldness appeal to God as the great Saviour. They have indeed destroyed the nations, who had thrown themselves out of the protection of the true God by worshipping false gods, but the Lord, the God alone, is our God, our King, our lawgiver, and he will save us, who is *the Saviour of those that believe.* 8. We have enough to take hold of, in our wrestling with God by prayer, if we can but plead that his glory is interested in our case, that his name will be profaned if we are run down and glorified if we are relieved. Thence therefore will our most prevailing pleas be drawn: "Do it for thy glory's sake."

Verses 21–38

We may here observe, 1. That those who receive messages of terror from men with patience, and send messages of faith to God by prayer, may expect messages of grace and peace from God for their comfort, even when they are most cast down. Isaiah sent a long answer to Hezekiah's prayer in God's name, sent it in writing (for it was too long to be sent by word of mouth), and sent it by way of return to his prayer, relation being thereunto had: *"Whereas thou hast prayed to me,* know, for thy comfort, that thy prayer is heard." Isaiah might have referred him to the prophecies he had delivered (particularly that *ch.* 10) and bid him pick out an answer from thence; but, that he might have abundant consolation, a message is sent him on purpose. The correspondence between earth and heaven is never let fall on God's side. 2. Those who magnify themselves, especially who magnify themselves against God and his people, do really vilify themselves, and made themselves contemptible, in the eyes of all wise men: *"The virgin, the daughter of Zion, has despised* Sennacherib, and all his impotent malice and menaces; she knows that, while she preserves her integrity, she is sure of the divine protection, and that though the enemy may bark he cannot bite. All his threats are a jest; it is all but *brutum fulmen — a mere flash,"* 3. Those who abuse the people of God affront God himself; and he takes what is said and done against them as said and done against himself: *"Whom hast thou reproached?* Even *the Holy One of Israel,* whom thou hast *therefore* reproached because he is a Holy One." And it aggravated the indignity Sennacherib did to God that he not only reproached him himself, but set his servants on to do the same: *By thy servants,* the abjects, *thou hast reproached me.* 4. Those who boast of themselves and their own achievements reflect upon God and his providence: *"Thou hast said, I have digged, and drunk water;* I have done mighty feats, and will do more; and wilt not own that *I have done it," v.* 24–26. The most active men are no more than God makes them, and God makes them no more than of old he designed to make them: *"What I have formed of ancient times,* in an eternal counsel, *now have I brought to pass"* (for God does all according to the counsel of his will), *"that thou shouldst be to lay waste defenced cities;* it is therefore intolerable arrogance to make it thy own doing." 5. All the malice, and all the motions and projects, of the church's enemies, are under the cognizance and check of the church's God. Sennacherib was active and quick, here, and there, and every where, but God knew his going out and coming in, and had always an eye upon him, *v.* 28. And that was not all; he had a hand upon him too, a strict hand, a strong hand, *a hook in his nose and a bridle in his lips,* with which, though he was very headstrong and unruly, he could and would *turn him back by the way which he came, v.* 29. *Hitherto he shall come and no further.* God had signed Sennacherib's commission against Judah (*ch.* 10:6); here he supersedes it. He has frightened them, but he must not hurt them, and therefore is discharged from going any further; nay, his commitment is here signed, by which he is clapped up, to answer for what he had done beyond his commission. 6. God is his people's bountiful benefactor, as well as their powerful protector, both a sun and a shield to those that trust in him. Jerusalem shall be defended (*v.* 35), the besiegers shall not come into it, no, nor come before it with any regular attack, but they shall be routed before they begin the siege, *v.* 33. But this is not all; God will return in mercy to his people, and will do them good. Their land shall be more than ordinarily fruitful, so that their losses shall be abundantly repaired; they shall not feel any of the ill effects either of the enemies' wasting the country or of their own being taken off from husbandry. But the earth, as at first, shall bring forth of itself, and they shall live and live plentifully upon its spontaneous productions. The blessing of the Lord can, when he pleases, make rich without the hand of the diligent. And let them not think that the desolations of their country would excuse them from observing the sabbatical year, which happened (as it should seem) the year after, and when they were not to plough or sow; no, though they had not now their usual stock beforehand for that year, yet they must religiously observe it, and depend upon God to provide for them. God must be trusted in the way of duty. 7. There is no standing before the judgments of God when they come with commission. (1.) The greatest numbers cannot stand before them: one angel shall, in one night, lay a vast army of men dead upon the spot, when God commissions him so to do, *v.* 36. Here are 185,000 brave soldiers in an instant turned into so many dead corpses. Many think the 76th Psalm was penned upon occasion of this defeat, where from *the spoiling of the stout-hearted,* and sending them to sleep their long sleep (*v.* 5), it is inferred that God is *more glorious and excellent than the mountains of prey* (*v.* 4), and that *he, even he, is to be feared, v.* 7. Angels are employed, more than we are aware of, as ministers of God's justice, to punish the pride and break the power of wicked men. (2.) The greatest men cannot stand before them: *The great king, the king of Assyria,* looks very little when he is forced to return, not only with shame, because he cannot accomplish what he had projected with so much assurance, but with terror and fear, lest the angel that had destroyed his army should destroy him; yet he is made to look less when his own sons, who should have guarded him, sacrificed him to his idol, whose protection he sought, *v.* 37, 38. God can quickly stop their breath who *breathe out threatenings and slaughter* against his people, and will do it when they have filled up the measure of their iniquity; and *the Lord is known by* these *judgments which he executes,* known to be a God that resists the proud. Many prophecies were fulfilled in this providence, which should encourage us, as far as they look further, and are designed as common and general assurances of the safety of the church and of all that trust in God, to depend upon God for the accomplishment of them. He that has delivered does and will deliver. Lord, forgive our enemies; but, *so let all thy enemies perish, O Lord!*

CHAPTER 38

This chapter proceeds in the history of Hezekiah. Here is, I. His sickness, and the sentence of death he received within himself (*v.* 1). II. His prayer in his sickness (*v.* 2, 3). III. The answer of peace which God gave to that prayer, assuring him that he should recover, that he should live fifteen years yet, that Jerusalem should be delivered from the king of Assyria, and that, for a sign to confirm his faith herein, the sun should go back ten degrees (*v.* 4–8). And this we read and opened before, 2 Ki. 20:1, etc. But, IV. Here is Hezekiah's thanksgiving for his recovery, which we had not before (*v.* 9–20). To which are added the means used (*v.* 21), and the end the good man aimed at in desiring to recover (*v.* 22). This is a chapter which will entertain the thoughts, direct the devotions, and encourage the faith and hopes of those that are confined by bodily distempers; it visits those that are visited with sickness.

Verses 1–8

We may hence observe, among others, these good lessons: — 1. That neither men's greatness nor their goodness will exempt them from the arrests of sickness and death. Hezekiah, a mighty potentate on earth and a mighty favourite of Heaven, is struck with a disease, which, without a miracle, will certainly be mortal; and this in the midst of his days, his comforts, and usefulness. *Lord, behold, he whom thou lovest is sick.* It should seem, this sickness seized him when he was in the midst of his triumphs over the ruined army of the Assyrians, to teach us always to rejoice with trembling. 2. It concerns us to prepare when we see death approaching: *"Set thy house in order,* and thy heart especially; put both thy affections and thy affairs into the best posture thou canst, that, when thy Lord comes, thou mayest be found of him in peace with God, with thy own conscience, and with all men, and mayest have nothing else to do but to die." Our being ready for death will make it come never the sooner, but much the easier: and those that are fit to die are most fit to live. 3. Is any afflicted with sickness? *Let him pray,* James 5:13. Prayer is a salve for every sore, personal or public. When Hezekiah was distressed by his enemies he prayed; now that he was sick he prayed. Whither should the child go, when any thing ails him, but to his Father? Afflictions are sent to bring us to our Bibles and to our knees. When Hezekiah was in health he *went up to the house of the Lord* to pray, for that was then the house of prayer. When he was sick in bed *he turned his face towards the wall,* probably towards the temple, which was a type of Christ, to whom we must look by faith in every prayer. 4. The testimony of our consciences for us that by the grace of God we have lived a good life, and have walked closely and humbly with God, will be a great support and comfort to us when we come to look death in the face. And though we may not depend upon it as our righteousness, by which to be justified before God, yet we may humbly plead it as an evidence of our interest in the righteousness of the Mediator. Hezekiah does not demand a reward from God for his good services, but modestly begs that God would remembers, not how he had reformed the kingdom, taken away the high places, cleansed the temple, and revived neglected ordinances, but, which was *better than all burnt-offerings and sacrifices,* how he had approved himself to God with a single eye and an honest heart, not only in these eminent performances, but in an even regular course of holy living: *I have walked before thee in truth* and sincerity, *and with a perfect,* that is, an upright, *heart;* for uprightness is our gospel perfection. 5. God has a gracious ear open to the prayers of his afflicted people. The same prophet that was sent to Hezekiah with warning to prepare for death is sent to him with a promise that he shall not only recover, but be restored to a confirmed state of health and live fifteen years yet. As Jerusalem was distressed, so Hezekiah was diseased, that God might have the glory of the deliverance of both, and that prayer too might have the honour of being instrumental in the deliverance. When we pray in our sickness, though God send not to us such an answer as he here sent to Hezekiah, yet, if by his Spirit he bids us be of good cheer, assures us that our sins are forgiven us, that his grace shall be sufficient for us, and that, whether we live or die, we shall be his, we have no reason to say that we pray in vain. God answers us if he *strengthens us with strength in our souls,* though not with bodily strength, Ps. 138:3. 6. A good man cannot take much comfort in his own health and prosperity unless withal he see the welfare and prosperity of the church of God. Therefore God, knowing what lay near Hezekiah's heart, promised him not only that he should live, but that he should *see the good of Jerusalem all the days of his life* (Ps. 128:5), otherwise he cannot live comfortably. Jerusalem, which is now delivered, shall still be defended from the Assyrians, who perhaps threatened to rally again and renew the attack. Thus does God graciously provide to make Hezekiah upon all accounts easy. 7. God is *willing to show to the heirs of promise the immutability of his counsel,* that they may have an unshaken faith in it, and therewith a strong consolation. God had given Hezekiah repeated assurances of his favour; and yet, as if all were thought too little, that he might expect from him uncommon favours, a sign is given him, an uncommon sign. None that we know of having had an absolute promise of living a certain number of years to come, as Hezekiah had, God thought fit to confirm this unprecedented favour with a miracle. The sign was the going back of the shadow upon the sun-dial. The sun is a faithful measurer of time, and *rejoices as a strong man to run a race;* but he that set that clock a going can set it back when he pleases, and make it to return; for the Father of all lights is the director of them.

Verses 9–22

We have here Hezekiah's thanksgiving-song, which he penned, by divine direction, after his recovery. He might have taken some of the psalms of his father David, and made use of them for his purpose; he might have found many very pertinent ones. He appointed *the Levites to praise the Lord with the words of David,* 2 Chr. 29:30. But the occasion here was extraordinary, and, his heart being full of devout affections, he would not confine himself to the compositions he had, though of divine inspiration, but would offer up his affections in his own words, which is most natural and genuine. He put this thanksgiving in writing, that he might review it himself afterwards, for the reviving of the good impressions made upon him by the providence, and that it might be recommended to others also for their use upon the like occasion. Note, There are writings which it is proper for us to draw up after we have been sick and have recovered. It is good to write a memorial of the affliction, and of the frame of our hearts under it, — to keep a record of the thoughts we had of things when we were sick, the affections that were then working in us, — to write a memorial of the mercies of a sick bed, and of our release from it, that they may never be forgotten, — to write a thanksgiving to God, write a sure covenant with him, and seal it, — to give it under our hands that we will never return again to folly. It is an excellent writing which Hezekiah here left, upon his recovery; and yet we find (2 Chr. 32:25) that *he rendered not again according to the benefit done to him.* The impressions, one would think, should never have worn off, and yet, it seems, they did. Thanksgiving is good, but thanksliving is better. Now in this writing he preserves upon record,

I. The deplorable condition he was in when his disease prevailed, and his despair of recovery, *v.* 10–13.

1. He tells us what his thoughts were of himself when he was at the worst; and these he keeps in remembrance, (1.) As blaming himself for his despondency, and that he gave up himself for gone; whereas while there is life there is hope, and room for our prayer and God's mercy. Though it is good to consider sickness as a summons to the grave, so as thereby to be quickened in our preparations for another world, yet we ought not to make the worse of our case, nor to think that every sick man must needs be a dead man presently. He that brings low can raise up. Or, (2.) As reminding himself of the apprehensions he had of death approaching, that he might always know and consider his own frailty and mortality, and that, though he had a reprieve for fifteen years, it was but a reprieve, and the fatal stroke he had now such a dread of would certainly come at last. Or, (3.) As magnifying the power of God in restoring him when his case was desperate, and his goodness in being so much better to him than his own fears. Thus David sometimes, when he was delivered out of trouble, reflected upon the black and melancholy conclusions he had made upon his own case when he was in trouble, and what he had then *said in his haste,* as Ps. 31:22; 77:7–9.

2. Let us see what Hezekiah's thoughts of himself were.

(1.) He reckoned that the number of his months was cut off in the midst. He was now about thirty-nine or forty years of age, and when he had a fair prospect of many years and happy ones, very happy, very many, before him. This distemper that suddenly seized him he concluded would be the *cutting off of his days,* that he should now be *deprived of the residue of his years,* which in a course of nature he might have lived (not which he could command as a debt due to him, but which he had reason to expect, considering the strength of his constitution), and with them he should be deprived not only of the comforts of life, but of all the opportunities he had of serving God and his generation. To the same purport (*v.* 12), *"My age has departed* and gone, and is removed from me as a shepherd's tent, out of which I am forcibly dislodged by the pulling of it down in an instant." Our present residence is but like that of a shepherd in his tent, a poor, mean, and cold lodging, where we are upon duty, and with a trust committed to our charge, as the shepherd has, of which we must give an account, and which will easily be taken down by the drawing of one pin or two. But observe, It is not the final period of our age, but only the removal of it to another world, where the tents of Kedar that are taken down, coarse, black, and weather-beaten, shall be set up again in the New Jerusalem, *comely as the curtains of Solomon.* He adds another similitude: *I have cut off, like a weaver, my life.* Not that he did by any act of his own cut off the thread of his life; but, being told that he must needs die, he was forced to cut off all his designs and projects, his *purposes were broken off,* even the *thoughts of his heart,* as Job's were, *ch.* 17:11. Our days are compared to the weaver's shuttle (Job 7:6), passing and repassing very swiftly, every throw leaving a thread behind it; and, when they are finished, the thread is cut off, and the piece taken out of the loom, and shown to our Master, to be judged of whether it be well woven or no, that we may *receive according to the things done in the body.* But as the weaver, when he has cut off his thread, has done his work, and the toil is over, so a good man, when his life is cut off, his cares and fatigues are cut off with it, and he rests from his labours. "But did I say, *I have cut off my life?* No, my times are not in my own hand; they are in God's hand, and it is he that *will cut me off from the thrum* (so the margin reads it); he has appointed what shall be the length of the piece, and, when it comes to that length, he will cut it off."

(2.) He reckoned that he should go to the gates of the grave — to the grave, the gates of which are always open; for it is still crying, *Give, give.* The grave is here put not only for the sepulchre of his fathers, in which his body would be deposited with a great deal of pomp and magnificence (for he was buried in the chief of the sepulchres of the kings, and all *Judah did him honour at his death,* 2 Chr. 32:33), which yet he himself took no care of, nor gave any order about, when he was sick; but for the state of the dead, that is, the *sheol,* the *hades,* the invisible world, to which he saw his soul going.

(3.) He reckoned that he was deprived of all the opportunities he might have had of worshipping God and doing good in the world (*v.* 1): *"I said,"* [1.] *"I shall not see the Lord,* as he manifests himself in his temple, in his oracles and ordinances, *even the Lord* here *in the land of the living."* He hopes to see him on the other side death, but he despairs of seeing him any more on this side death, as he had seen him in the sanctuary, Ps. 63:2. He shall no more see (that is, serve) the Lord in the land of the living, the land of conflict between his kingdom and the kingdom of Satan, this seat of war. He dwells much upon this: *I shall no more see the Lord, even the Lord;* for a good man wishes not to live for any other end than that he may serve God and have communion with him. [2.] *"I shall see man no more."* He shall see his subjects no more, whom he may protect and administer justice to, shall see no more objects of charity, whom he may relieve, shall see his friends no more, who were often sharpened by his countenance, as iron is by iron. Death puts an end to conversation, and removes our acquaintance into darkness, Ps. 88:18.

(4.) He reckoned that the agonies of death would be very sharp and severe: *"He will cut me off with pining sickness,* which will waste me, and wear me off, quickly." The distemper increased so fast, without intermission or remission, either day or night, morning or evening, that he concluded it would soon come to a crisis and make an end of him — that God, whose servants all diseases are, would by them, *as a lion, break all his bones* with grinding pain, *v.* 13. He thought that next morning was the utmost he could expect to live in such pain and misery; when he had outlived the first day's illness the second day he repeated his fears, and concluded that this must needs be his last night: *from day even to night wilt thou make an end of me.* When we are sick we are very apt to be thus calculating our time, and, after all, we are still at uncertainty. It should be more our care how we shall get safely to another world than how long we are likely to live in this world.

II. The complaints he made in this condition (*v.* 14): *"Like a crane, or swallow, so did I chatter;* I made a noise

as those birds do when they are frightened." See what a change sickness makes in a little time; he that, but the other day, spoke with so much freedom and majesty, nor, through the extremity of pain or deficiency of spirits, *chatters like a crane or a swallow.* Some think he refers to his praying in his affliction; it was so broken and interrupted with groanings which could not be uttered that it was more like the chattering of a crane or a swallow than what it used to be. Such mean thoughts had he of his own prayers, which yet were acceptable to God, and successful. He *mourned like a dove,* sadly, but silently and patiently. He had found God so ready to answer his prayers at other times that he could not but look upwards, in expectation of some relief now, but in vain: his *eyes failed,* and he saw no hopeful symptom, nor felt any abatement of his distemper; and therefore he prays, *"I am oppressed,* quite overpowered and ready to sink; *Lord, undertake for me;* bail me out of the hands of the serjeant that has arrested me; *be surety for thy servant for good,* Ps. 119:122. Come between me and the gates of the grave, to which I am ready to be hurried." When we recover from sickness, the divine pity does, as it were, beg a day for us, and undertakes we shall be forthcoming another time and answer the debt in full. And, when we receive the sentence of death within ourselves, we are undone if the divine grace do not undertake for us to carry us through the valley of the shadow of death, and to preserve us blameless to the heavenly kingdom on the other side of it — if Christ do not undertake for us, to bring us off in judgment, and present us to his Father, and to do all that for us which we need, and cannot do for ourselves. *I am oppressed, ease me* (so some read it); for, when we are agitated by a sense of guilt and the fear of wrath, nothing will make us easy but Christ's undertaking for us.

III. The grateful acknowledgment he makes of God's goodness to him in his recovery. He begins this part of the writing as one at a stand how to express himself (*v.* 15): *"What shall I say?* Why should I say so much by way of complaint when this is enough to silence all my complaints — *He has spoken unto me;* he has sent his prophet to tell me that I shall recover and live fifteen years yet; *and he himself has done it:* it is as sure to be done as if it were done already. What God has spoken he will himself do, for no word of his shall fall to the ground." God having spoken it, he is sure of it (*v.* 16): *"Thou wilt restore me, and make me to live;* not only restore me from this illness, but make me to live through the years assigned me." And, having this hope,

1. He promises himself always to retain the impressions of his affliction (*v.* 15): *"I will go softly all my years in the bitterness of my soul,* as one in sorrow for my sinful distrusts and murmurings under my affliction, as one in care to make suitable returns for God's favour to me and to make it appear that I have got good by the providences I have been under. *I will go softly,* gravely and considerately, and with thought and deliberation, not as many, who, when they have recovered, live as carelessly and as much at large as ever." Or, "I will go pleasantly" (so some understand it); "when God has delivered me I will walk cheerfully with him in all holy conversation, as having tasted that he is gracious." Or, "I will go softly, even *after the bitterness of my soul"* (so it may be read); "when the trouble is over I will endeavour to retain the impression of it, and to have the same thoughts of things that I had then."

2. He will encourage himself and others with the experiences he had had of the goodness of God (*v.* 16): *"By these things* which thou hast done for me *they live,* the kingdom lives" (for the life of such a king was the life of the kingdom); "all that hear of it shall live and be comforted; by the same power and goodness that have restored me all men have their souls held in life, and they ought to acknowledge it. *In all these things is the life of my spirit,* my spiritual life, that is supported and maintained by what God has done for the preservation of my natural life." The more we taste of the loving-kindness of God in every providence the more will our hearts be enlarged to love him and live to him, and that will be the life of our spirit. Thus our souls live, and they shall praise him.

3. He magnifies the mercy of his recovery, on several accounts.

(1.) That he was raised up from great extremity (*v.* 17): *Behold, for peace I had great bitterness.* When, upon the

defeat of Sennacherib, he expected nothing but an uninterrupted peace to himself and his government, he was suddenly seized with sickness, which embittered all his comforts to him, and went to such a height that it seemed to be the bitterness of death itself — *bitterness, bitterness,* nothing but gall and wormwood. This was his condition when God sent him seasonable relief.

(2.) That it came from the love of God, from love to his soul. Some are spared and reprieved in wrath, that they may be reserved for some greater judgment when they have filled up the measure of their iniquities; but temporal mercies are sweet indeed to us when we can taste the love of God in them. *He delivered me because he delighted in me* (Ps. 18:19); and the word here signifies a very affectionate love: *Thou hast loved my soul from the pit of corruption;* so it runs in the original. God's love is sufficient to bring a soul from the pit of corruption. This is applicable to our redemption by Christ; it was in love to our souls, our poor perishing souls, that he delivered them from the bottomless pit, snatched them as brands out of everlasting burnings. *In his love and in his pity he redeemed us.* And the preservation of our bodies, as well as the provision made for them, is doubly comfortable when it is in love to our souls — when God repairs the house because he has a kindness for the inhabitant.

(3.) That it was the effect of the pardon of sin: *"For thou hast cast all my sins behind thy back,* and thereby hast *delivered my soul from the pit of corruption,* in love to it." Note, [1.] When God pardons sin he casts it behind his back, as not designing to look upon it with an eye of justice and jealousy. He remembers it no more, to visit for it. The pardon does not make the sin not to have been, or not to have been sin, but not to be punished as it deserves. When we cast our sins behind our back, and take no care to repent of them, God sets them before his face, and is ready to reckon for them; but when we set them before our face in true repentance, as David did when his sin was ever before him, God casts them behind his back. [2.] When God pardons sins he pardons all, casts them all behind his back, though they have been as scarlet and crimson. [3.] The pardoning of the sin is the delivering of the soul from the pit of corruption. [4.] It is pleasant indeed to think of our recoveries from sickness when we see them flowing from the remission of sin; then the cause is removed, and then it is in love to the soul.

(4.) That it was the lengthening out of his opportunity to glorify God in this world, which he made the business, and pleasure, and end of life. [1.] If this sickness had been his death, it would have put a period to that course of service for the glory of God and the good of the church which he was now pursuing, *v.* 18. Heaven indeed praises God, and the souls of the faithful, when at death they remove thither, do that work of heaven as the angels, and with the angels, there; but what is this world the better for that? What does that contribute to the support and advancement of God's kingdom among men in this state of struggle? *The grave cannot praise God,* nor the dead bodies that lie there. *Death cannot celebrate him,* cannot proclaim his perfections and favours, to invite others into his service. *Those who go down to the pit,* being no longer in a state of probation, nor living by faith in his promises, cannot give him honour by hoping for his truth. Those that lie rotting in the grave, as they are not capable of receiving any further mercy from God, so neither are they capable of offering any more praises to him, till they shall be raised at the last day, and then they shall both receive and give glory. [2.] Having recovered from it, he resolves not only to proceed, but to abound, in praising and serving God (*v.* 19): *The living, the living, he shall praise thee.* They may do it; they have an opportunity of praising God, and that is the main thing that makes life valuable and desirable to a good man. Hezekiah was *therefore* glad to live, not that he might continue to enjoy his royal dignity and the honour and pleasure of his late successes, but that he might continue to praise God. The living must praise God; they live in vain if they do not. Those that have been dying and yet are living, whose life is from the dead, are in a special manner obliged to praise God, as being most sensibly affected with his goodness. Hezekiah, for his part, having recovered from this sickness, will make it his business to praise God: *"I do it this day;* let others do it in like manner." Those that give good exhortations should set good examples, and do themselves what they expect from others. "For my part," says Hezekiah, *"the Lord was ready to save me;* he not only did save me, but he was ready to do it just then when I was in the greatest extremity; his help came in seasonably; he showed himself willing and forward to save me. *The Lord was to save me,* was at hand to do it, saved me a the first word; and therefore," *First,* "I will publish and proclaim his praises. I and my family, I and my friends, I and my people, will have a concert of praise to his glory: *We will sing my songs to the stringed instruments,* that others may attend to them, and be affected with them, when they are in the most devout and serious frame in the house of the Lord." It is for the honour of God, and the edification of his church, that special mercies should be acknowledged in public praises, especially mercies to public persons, Ps. 116:18, 19. *Secondly,* "I will proceed and persevere in his praises." We should do so all the days of our life, because every day of our life is itself a fresh mercy and brings many fresh mercies along with it; and, as renewed mercies call for renewed praises, so former eminent mercies call for repeated praises. It is by the mercy of God that we live, and therefore, as long as we live, we must continue to praise him, while we have breath, nay, while we have being. *Thirdly,* "I will propagate and perpetuate his praises." We should not only praise him all the days of our life, but *the father to the children should make known his truth,* that the ages to come may give God the glory of his truth by trusting to it. It is the duty of parents to possess their children with a confidence in the truth of God, which will go far towards keeping them close to the ways of God. Hezekiah, doubtless, did this himself, and yet Manasseh his son walked not in his steps. Parents may give their children many good things, good instructions, good examples, good books, but they cannot give them grace.

IV. In the last two verses of this chapter we have two passages relating to this story which were omitted in the narrative of it here, but which we had 2 Ki. 20, and therefore shall here only observe two lessons from them: — 1. That God's promises are intended not to supersede, but to quicken and encourage, the use of means. Hezekiah is sure to recover, and yet he must *take a lump of figs and lay it on the boil, v.* 21. We do not trust God, but tempt him, if, when we pray to him for help, we do not second our prayers with our endeavours. We must not put physicians, or physic, in the place of God, but make use of them in subordination to God and to his providence; help thyself and God will help thee. 2. That the chief end we should aim at, in desiring life and health, is that we may glorify God, and do good, and improve ourselves in knowledge, and grace, and meetness for heaven. Hezekiah, when he meant, *What is the sign that I shall recover?* asked, *What is the sign that I shall go up to the house of the Lord,* there to honour God, to keep up acquaintance and communion with him, and to encourage others to serve him? *v.* 22. It is taken for granted that if God would restore him to health he would immediately go up to the temple with his thank-offerings. There Christ found the impotent man whom he had healed, Jn. 5:14. The exercises of religion are so much the business and delight of a good man that to be restrained from them is the greatest grievance of his afflictions, and to be restored to them is the greatest comfort of his deliverances. *Let my soul live, and it shall praise thee.*

CHAPTER 39

The story of this chapter likewise we had before, 2 Ki. 20:12, etc. It is here repeated, not only as a very memorable and improvable passage, but because it concludes with a prophecy of the captivity in Babylon; and as the former part of the prophecy of this book frequently referred to Sennacherib's invasion and the defeat of that, to which therefore the history of that was very fitly subjoined, so the latter part of this book speaks much of the Jews' captivity in Babylon and their deliverance out of that, to which therefore the first prediction of it, with the occasion thereof, is very fitly prefixed. We have here, I. The pride and folly of Hezekiah, in showing his treasures to the king of Babylon's ambassadors that were sent to congratulate him on his recovery (*v.* 1, 2). II. Isaiah's examination of him concerning it, in God's name, and his confession of it (*v.* 3, 4). III. The sentence passed upon him for it, that all his treasures should, in process of time, be carried to Babylon (*v.* 5–7). IV. Hezekiah's penitent and patient submission to this sentence (*v.* 8).

Verses 1–4

Hence we may learn these lessons: — 1. That humanity and common civility teach us to rejoice with our friends and neighbours when they rejoice, and to congratulate them on their deliverances, and particularly their recoveries from sickness. The king of Babylon, having heard that Hezekiah had been sick, and had recovered, sent to compliment him upon the occasion. If Christians be unneighbourly, heathens will shame them. 2. It becomes us to give honour to those whom our God puts honour upon. The sun was the Babylonians' god; and when they understood that it was with a respect to Hezekiah that the sun, to their great surprise, went back ten degrees, on such a day, they thought themselves obliged to do Hezekiah all the honour they could. Will all people thus walk in the name of their God, and shall not we? 3. Those that do not value good men for their goodness may yet be brought to pay them great respect by other inducements, and for the sake of their secular interests. The king of Babylon made his court to Hezekiah, not because he was pious, but because he was prosperous, as the Philistines coveted an alliance with Isaac because they saw the Lord was with him, Gen. 26:28. The king of Babylon was an enemy to the king of Assyria, and therefore was fond of Hezekiah, because the Assyrians were so much weakened by the power of his God. 4. It is a hard matter to keep the spirit low in the midst of great advancements. Hezekiah is an instance of it: he was a wise and good man, but, when one miracle after another was wrought in his favour, he found it hard to keep his heart from being lifted up, nay, a little thing then drew him into the snare of pride. Blessed Paul himself needed a thorn in the flesh, to keep him from being *lifted up with the abundance of revelations.* 5. We have need to watch over our own spirits when we are showing our friends our possessions, what we have done and what we have got, that we be not proud of them, as if our might or our merit had purchased and procured us this wealth. When we look upon our enjoyments, and have occasion to speak of them, it must be with humble acknowledgements of our own unworthiness and thankful acknowledgements of God's goodness, with a just value for the achievements of others and with an expectation of losses and changes, not dreaming that our mountain stands so strong but that it may soon be moved. 6. It is a great weakness for good men to value themselves much upon the civil respects that are paid them (yea, though there be something particular and uncommon in them) by the children of this world, and to be fond of their acquaintance. What a poor thing was it for Hezekiah, whom God has so dignified, to be thus over proud of the respect paid him by a heathen prince as if that added any thing to him! We ought to return the courtesies of such with interest, but not to be proud of them. 7. We must expect to be called to an account for the workings of our pride, though they are secret, and in such instances as we thought there was no harm in; and therefore we ought to call ourselves to an account for them; and when we have had company with us that have paid us respect, and been pleased with their entertainment, and commended every thing, we ought to be jealous over ourselves with a godly jealousy lest our hearts have been lifted up. As far as we see cause to suspect that this sly and subtle sin of pride has insinuated itself into our breasts, and mingled itself with our conversation, let us be ashamed of it, and, as Hezekiah here, ingenuously confess it and take shame to ourselves for it.

Verses 5–8

Hence let us observe, 1. That, if God love us, he will humble us, and will find some way or other to pull down our spirits when they are lifted up above measure. A mortifying message is sent to Hezekiah, that he might be humbled for the pride of his heart, and be convinced of the folly of it; for though God may suffer his people to fall into sin, as he did Hezekiah here, to *prove him, that he might know all that was in his heart,* yet he will not suffer them to lie still in it. 2. It is just with God to take that from us which we make the matter of our pride, and on which we build a carnal confidence. When David was proud of the numbers of his people God took a course to make them fewer; and when Hezekiah boasts of his treasures, and looks upon them with too great a complacency, he is told that he acts like the foolish traveller who shows his money and gold to one that proves a thief and is thereby tempted to rob him. 3. If we could but see things that will be, we should be ashamed of our thoughts of things that are. If Hezekiah had known that the seed and successors of this king of Babylon would hereafter be the ruin of his family and kingdom, he would not have complimented his ambassadors as he did; and, when the prophet told him that it would be so, we may well imagine how he was vexed at himself for what he had done. We cannot certainly foresee what will be, but are told, in general, *All is vanity,* and therefore it is vanity for us to take complacency and put confidence in any thing that goes under that character. 4. Those that are fond of an acquaintance or alliance with irreligious men will first or last have enough of it, and will have cause to repent it. Hezekiah thought himself very happy in the friendship of Babylon, though it was the mother of harlots and idolatries; but Babylon, who now courted Jerusalem, in process of time conquered her and carried her captive. Leagues with sinners, and leagues with sin too, will end thus; it is therefore our wisdom to keep at a distance from them. 5. Those that truly repent of their sins will take it well to be reproved for them and will be willing to be told of their faults. Hezekiah reckoned *that* word of the Lord good which discovered sin to him, and made him sensible that he had done amiss, which before he was not aware of. The language of true penitents is, *Let the righteous smite me; it shall be a kindness;* and the law is *therefore* good, because, being spiritual, in it sin appears sin, and exceedingly sinful. 6. True penitents will quietly submit, not only to the reproofs of the word, but to the rebukes of Providence for their sins. When Hezekiah was told of the punishment of his iniquity he said, *Good is the word of the Lord,* not only the mitigation of the sentence, but the sentence itself; he has nothing to object against the equity of it, but says *Amen* to the threatening. Those that see the evil of sin, and what it deserves, will justify God in all that is brought upon them for it, and own that he punishes them less than their iniquities deserve. 7. Though we must not be regardless of those that come after us, yet we must reckon ourselves well done by if there be *peace and truth in our days,* and better than we had reason to expect. If a storm be coming, we must reckon it a favour to get into the harbour before it comes, and be gathered to the grave in peace; yet we can never be secure of this, but must prepare for changes in our own time, that we may stand complete in all the will of God, and bid it welcome whatever it is.

CHAPTER 40

At this chapter begins the latter part of the prophecy of this book, which is not only divided from the former by the historical chapters that come between, but seems to be distinguished from it in the scope and style of it. In the former part the name of the prophet was frequently prefixed to the particular sermons, besides the general title (as 2:1; 7:3; 13:1); but this is all one continued discourse, and the prophet not so much as once named. That consisted of many burdens, many woes; this consists of many blessings. There the distress which the people of God were in by the Assyrian, and their deliverance out of that, were chiefly prophesied of; but that is here spoken of as a thing past (52:4); and the captivity in Babylon, and their deliverance out of that, which were much greater events, of more extensive and abiding concern, are here largely foretold. Before God sent his people into captivity he furnished them with precious promises for their support and comfort in their trouble; and we may well imagine of what great use to them the glorious, gracious, light of this prophecy was, in that cloudy and dark day, and how much it helped to dry up their tears by the rivers of Babylon. But it looks further yet, and to greater things; much of Christ and gospel grace we meet with in the foregoing part of this book, but in this latter part we shall find much more; and, as if it were designed for a prophetic summary of the New Testament, it begins with that which begins the gospels, "The voice of one crying in the wilderness" (40:3), and concludes with that which concludes the book of the Revelation, "The new heavens and the new earth," (66:22). Even Mr. White acknowledges that, as all the mercies of God to the Jewish nation bore some resemblance to those glorious things performed by our Saviour for man's redemption, so they are by the Spirit of God expressed in such terms as show plainly that while the prophet is speaking of the redemption of the Jews he had in his thoughts a more glorious deliverance. And we need not look for any further accomplishment of these prophecies yet to come; for if Jesus be he, and his kingdom be it, that should come, we are to look for no other, but the carrying on and completing of the same blessed work which was begun in the first preaching and planting of Christianity in the world.

Verses 1–2

We have here the commission and instructions given, not to this prophet only, but, with him, to all the Lord's prophets, nay, and to all Christ's ministers, to proclaim comfort to God's people. 1. This did not only warrant, but enjoin, this prophet himself to encourage the good people who lived in his own time, who could not but have very melancholy apprehensions of things when they saw Judah and Jerusalem by their daring impieties ripening apace for ruin, and God in his providence hastening ruin upon them. Let them be sure that, notwithstanding all this, God had mercy in store for them. 2. It was especially a direction to the prophets that should live in the time of captivity, when Jerusalem was in ruins; they must encourage the captives to hope for enlargement in due time. 3. Gospel ministers, being employed by the blessed Spirit as comforters, and as helpers of the joy of Christians, are here put in mind of their business. Here we have,

I. Comfortable words directed to God's people in general, *v.* 1. The prophets have instructions from their God (for he is the *Lord God of the holy prophets,* Rev. 22:6) to comfort the people of God; and the charge is doubled, *Comfort you, comfort you* — not because the prophets are unwilling to do it (no, it is the most pleasant part of their work), but because sometimes the souls of God's people refuse to be comforted, and their comforters must repeat things again and again, ere they can fasten any thing upon them. Observe here, 1. There are a people in the world that are God's people. 2. It is the will of God that his people should be a comforted people, even in the worst of times. 3. It is the work and business of ministers to do what they can for the comfort of God's people. 4. Words of conviction, such as we had in the former part of this book, must be followed with words of comfort, such as we have here; for he that has torn will heal us.

II. Comfortable words directed to Jerusalem in particular: *"Speak to the heart of Jerusalem* (*v.* 2); speak that which will revive her heart, and be a cordial to her and to all that belong to her and wish her well. Do not whisper it, but *cry unto her:* cry aloud, to show saints their comforts as well as to show sinners their transgressions; make her hear it:" 1. "That the days of her trouble are numbered and finished: *Her warfare is accomplished,* the set time of her servitude; the campaign is now at an end, and she shall retire into quarters of refreshment." Human life is a warfare (Job 7:1); the Christian life much more. But the struggle will not last always; the warfare will be accomplished, and then the good soldiers shall not only enter into rest, but be sure of their pay. 2. "That the cause of her trouble is removed, and, when that is taken away, the effect will cease. Tell her that *her iniquity is pardoned,* God is reconciled to her, and she shall no longer be treated as one guilty before him." Nothing can be spoken more comfortably than this, *Son, be of good cheer; thy sins be forgiven thee.* Troubles are *then* removed in love when sin is pardoned. 3. "That the end of her trouble is answered: *She has received of the Lord double for* the cure of *all her sins,* sufficient, and more than sufficient, to separate between her and her idols," the worship of which was the great sin for which God had a controversy with them, and from which he designed to reclaim them by their captivity in Babylon: and it had that effect upon them; it begat in them a rooted antipathy to idolatry, and was physic doubly strong for the purging out of that iniquity. Or it may be taken as the language of the divine compassion: *His soul was grieved for the misery of Israel* (Judges 10:16), and, like a tender father, *since he spoke against them he earnestly remembered them* (Jer. 31:20), and was ready to say that he had given them too much correction. They, being very penitent, acknowledged that God has *punished them less than their iniquities deserved;* but he, being very pitiful, owned, in a manner, that he had punished them more than they deserved. True penitents have indeed, in Christ and his sufferings, *received of the Lord's hand double for all their sins;* for the satisfaction Christ made by his death was of such an infinite value that it was more than double to the demerits of sin; *for God spared not his own Son.*

Verses 3–8

The time to favour Zion, yea, the set time, having come, the people of God must be prepared, by repentance and faith, for the favours designed them; and, in order to call them to both these, we have here *the voice of one crying in the wilderness,* which *may* be applied to those prophets who were with the captives in their wilderness-state, and who, when they saw the day of their deliverance dawn, called earnestly upon them to prepare for it, and assured them that all the difficulties which stood in the way of their deliverance should be got over. It is a good sign that mercy is preparing for us if we find God's grace preparing us for it, Ps. 10:17. But it *must* be applied to John

the Baptist; for, though God was the speaker, he was *the voice of one crying in the wilderness,* and his business was to *prepare the way of the Lord,* to dispose men's minds for the reception and entertainment of the gospel of Christ. The way of the Lord is prepared,

I. By repentance for sin; that was it which John Baptist preached to all Judah and Jerusalem (Mt. 3:2, 5), and thereby *made ready a people prepared for the Lord,* Lu. 1:17.

1. The alarm is given; let all take notice of it at their peril; God is coming in a way of mercy, and we must prepare for him, *v.* 3–5. If we apply it to their captivity, it may be taken as a promise that, whatever difficulties lie in their way, when they return they shall be removed. This voice in the wilderness (divine power going along with it) sets pioneers on work to level the roads. But it may be taken as a call to duty, and it is the same duty that we are called to, in preparation for Christ's entrance into our souls. (1.) We must get into such a frame of spirit as will dispose us to receive Christ and his gospel: *"Prepare you the way of the Lord;* prepare yourselves for him, and let all that be suppressed which would be an obstruction to his entrance. Make room for Christ: *Make straight a highway for him."* If he prepare the end for us, we ought surely to prepare the way for him. Prepare for the Saviour; *lift up your heads, O you gates!* Ps. 24:7, 9. Prepare for the salvation, the great salvation, and other minor deliverances. Let us get to be fit for them, and then God will work them out. Let us not stand in our own light, nor put a bar in our own door, but find, or make, a highway for him, even in that which was desert ground. This is that for which he waits to be gracious. (2.) We must get our hearts levelled by divine grace. Those that are hindered from comfort in Christ by their dejections and despondencies are the valleys that must be exalted. Those that are hindered from comfort in Christ by a proud conceit of their own merit and worth are the mountains and hills that must be made low. Those that have entertained prejudices against the word and ways of God, that are untractable, and disposed to thwart and contradict even that which is plain and easy because it agrees not with their corrupt inclinations and secular interests, are the crooked that must be made straight and the rough places that must be made plain. Let but the gospel of Christ have a fair hearing, and it cannot fail of acceptance. This prepares the way of the Lord; and thus God will by his grace prepare his own way in all the vessels of mercy, whose hearts he opens as he did Lydia's.

2. When this is done *the glory of the Lord shall be revealed, v.* 5. (1.) When the captives are prepared for deliverance Cyrus shall proclaim it, and those shall have the benefit of it, and those only, whose hearts the Lord shall stir up with courage and resolution to break through the discouragements that lay in their way, and to make nothing of the hills, and valleys, and all the rough places. (2.) When John Baptist has for some time preached repentance, mortification, and reformation, and so made ready a people prepared for the Lord (Lu. 1:17), then the Messiah himself shall be revealed in his glory, working miracles, which John did not, and by his grace, which is his glory, binding up and healing with consolations those whom John had wounded with convictions. And this revelation of divine glory shall be *a light to lighten the Gentiles. All flesh shall see it together,* and not the Jews only; they shall see and admire it, see it and bid it welcome; as the return out of captivity was taken notice of by the neighbouring nations, Ps. 126:2. And it shall be the accomplishment of the word of God, not one *iota* or tittle of which shall fall to the ground: *The mouth of the Lord has spoken it,* and therefore the hand of the Lord will effect it.

II. By confidence in the word of the Lord, and not in any creature. *The mouth of the Lord having spoken it,* the voice has this further to cry (he that has ears to hear let him hear it), *The word of our God shall stand for ever, v.* 8.

1. By this accomplishment of the prophecies and promises of salvation, and the performance of them to the utmost in due time, it appears that the word of the Lord is sure and what may be safely relied on. *Then* we are prepared for deliverance when we depend entirely upon the word of God, build our hopes on that, with an assurance that it will not make us ashamed: in a dependence upon this word we must be brought to own that *all flesh is grass,* withering and fading. (1.) The power of man, when it does appear against the deliverance, is not to be feared; for it

shall be as grass before the word of the Lord: it shall wither and be trodden down. The insulting Babylonians, who promise themselves that the desolations of Jerusalem shall be perpetual, are but as grass which the spirit of the Lord blows upon, makes nothing of, but blasts all its glory; for the word of the Lord, which promises their deliverance, shall stand for ever, and it is not in the power of their enemies to hinder the execution of it. (2.) The power of man, when it would appear for the deliverance, is not to be trusted to; for it is but as grass in comparison with the word of the Lord, which is the only firm foundation for us to build our hope upon. When God is about to work salvation for his people he will take them off from depending upon creatures, and looking for it from hills and mountains. They shall fail them, and their expectations from them shall be frustrated: *The Spirit of the Lord shall blow upon them;* for God will have no creature to be a rival with him for the hope and confidence of his people; and, as it is his word only that shall stand for ever, so in that word only our faith must stand. When we are brought to this, then, and not till then, we are fit for mercy.

2. The word of our God, that glory of the Lord which is now to be revealed, the gospel, and that grace which is brought with it to us and wrought by it in us, shall stand for ever; and this is the satisfaction of all believers, when they find all their creature-comforts withering and fading like grass. Thus the apostle applies it to the *word which by the gospel is preached unto us, and which lives and abides for ever as the incorruptible seed by which we are born again,* 1 Pt. 1:23–25. To prepare the way of the Lord we must be convinced, (1.) Of the vanity of the creature, that all flesh is grass, weak and withering. We ourselves are so, and therefore cannot save ourselves; all our friends are so, and therefore are unable to save us. All the beauty of the creature, which might render it amiable, is but as the flower of grass, soon blasted, and therefore cannot recommend us to God and to his acceptance. We are dying creatures; all our comforts in this word are dying comforts, and therefore cannot be the felicity of our immortal souls. We must look further for a salvation, look further for a portion. (2.) Of the validity of the promise of God. We must be convinced that the word of the Lord can do that for us which all flesh cannot — that, forasmuch as it stands for ever, it will furnish us with a happiness that will run parallel with the duration of our souls, which must live for ever; for the things that are not seen, but must be believed, are eternal.

Verses 9–11

It was promised (*v.* 5) *that the glory of the Lord shall be revealed;* that is it with the hopes of which God's people must be comforted. Now here we are told,

I. How it shall be revealed, *v.* 9. 1. It shall be revealed to Zion and Jerusalem; notice shall be given of it to the remnant that are left in Zion and Jerusalem, the poor of the land, who were vine-dressers and husbandmen; it shall be told them that their brethren shall return to them. This shall be told also to the captives who belonged to Zion and Jerusalem, and retained their affection for them. Zion is said to *dwell with the daughter of Babylon* (Zec. 2:7); and there she receives notice of Cyrus's gracious proclamation; and so the margin reads it, *O thou that tellest good tidings to Zion,* etc., meaning the persons who were employed in publishing that proclamation; let them do it with a good will, let them make the country ring of it, and let them tell it to the sons of Zion in their own language, *saying to them, Behold your God.* 2. It shall be published by Zion and Jerusalem (so the text reads it); those that remain there, or that have already returned, when they find the deliverance proceeding towards perfection, let them proclaim it in the most public places, whence they may be best heard by all the cities of Judah; let them proclaim it as loudly as they can: let them *lift up their voice with strength,* and not be afraid of overstraining themselves; let them not be afraid lest the enemy should hear it and quarrel with them, or lest it should not prove true, or not such good tidings as at first it appeared; let them say to the cities of Judah, and all the inhabitants of the country, *Behold your God.* When God is going on with the salvation of his people, let them industriously spread the news among their friends, let them tell them that it is God that has done it; whoever were the instruments, God was the author; it is *their* God, a God in covenant with them, and he does it as theirs, and they will reap the benefit and comfort of it. "Behold him, take notice of his hand in it, and look above second causes; behold, the God you have long looked for has come at last (*ch.* 25:9): *This is our God, we have waited for him."* This may refer to the invitation which was sent forth from Jerusalem to the cities of Judah, as soon as they had set up an altar, immediately upon their return out of captivity, to come and join with them in their sacrifices, Ezra 3:2–4. "When the worship of God is set up again, send notice of it to all your brethren, that they may share with you in the comfort of it." But this was to have its full accomplishment in the apostles' public and undaunted preaching of the gospel to all nations, beginning at Jerusalem. The voice crying in the wilderness gave notice that he was coming; but now notice is given that he has come. *Behold the Lamb of God;* take a full view of your Redeemer. Behold your King, behold your God.

II. What that glory is which shall be revealed. "Your God will come, will show himself,"

1. "With the power and greatness of a prince (*v.* 10): *He will come with strong hand,* too strong to be obstructed, though it may be opposed. His strong hand shall subdue his people to himself, and shall restrain and conquer his and their enemies. He will come who is strong enough to break through all the difficulties that lie in his way." Our Lord Jesus was full of power, a mighty Saviour. Some read it, *He will come against the mighty one,* and overpower him, overcome him. Satan is the strong man armed; but our Lord Jesus is stronger than he, and he shall make it to appear that he is so, for, (1.) He shall reign in defiance of all opposition: *His arm shall rule,* shall overrule *for him,* for the fulfilling of his counsels, to his own glory; for he is his own end. (2.) He shall recompense to all according to their works, as a righteous Judge: *His reward is with him;* he brings along with him, as a returning prince, punishments for the rebels and preferments for his loyal subjects. (3.) He shall proceed and accomplish his purpose: *His work is before him,* that is, he knows perfectly well what he has to do, which way to go about it, and how to compass it. *He himself knows what he will do.*

2. "With the pity and tenderness of a shepherd," *v.* 11. God is the *Shepherd of Israel* (Ps. 80:1); Christ is the good Shepherd, Jn. 10:11. The same that rules with the strong hand of a prince leads and feeds with the kind hand of a shepherd. (1.) He takes care of all his flock, the little flock: *He shall feed his flock like a shepherd.* His word is food for his flock to feed on; his ordinances are fields for them to feed in; his ministers are under-shepherds that are appointed to attend them. (2.) He takes particular care of those that most need his care, the lambs that are weak, and cannot help themselves, and are unaccustomed to hardship, and *those that are with young,* that are therefore heavy, and, if any harm be done them, are in danger of casting their young. He particularly takes care for a succession, that it may not fail or be cut off. The good Shepherd has tender care for children that are towardly and hopeful, for young converts, that are setting out in the way to heaven, for weak believers, and those that are of a sorrowful spirit. These are the lambs of his flock, that shall be sure to want nothing that their case requires. [1.] He will gather them in the arms of his power; his strength shall be made *perfect in their weakness,* 2 Co. 12:9. He will gather them in when they wander, gather them up when they fall, gather them together when they are dispersed, and gather them home to himself at last; and all this with his own arm, out of which none shall be able to pluck them, Jn. 10:28. [2.] He will carry them in the bosom of his love and cherish them there. When they tire or are weary, are sick and faint, when they meet with foul ways, he will carry them on, and take care they are not left behind. [3.] He will gently lead them. By his word he requires no more service, and by his providence he inflicts no more trouble, than he will fit them for; for he considers their frame.

Verses 12–17

The scope of these verses is to show what a great and glorious being the Lord Jehovah is, who is Israel's God and Saviour. It comes in here, 1. To encourage his people that were captives in Babylon to hope in him, and to depend upon him for deliverance, though they were ever so weak and their oppressors ever so strong. 2. To engage them

to cleave to him, and not to turn aside after other gods; for there are none to be compared with him. 3. To possess all those who receive the glad tidings of redemption by Christ with a holy awe and reverence of God. Though it was said (*v.* 9), *Behold your God,* and (*v.* 11) *He shall feed his flock like a shepherd,* yet these condescensions of his grace must not be thought of with any diminution to the transcendencies of his glory. Let us see how great our God is, and fear before him; for,

I. His power is unlimited, and what no creature can compare with, much less contend with, *v.* 12. 1. He has a vast reach. View the celestial globe, and you are astonished at the extent of it; but the great God *metes the heavens with a span;* to him they are but a hand-breadth, so large-handed is he. View the terraqueous globe, and he has the command of that too. All the waters in the world he can *measure in the hollow of his hand,* where we can hold but a little water; and the dry land he easily manages, for he *comprehends the dust of the earth in a measure,* or with his three fingers; it is no more to him than a *pugil,* or that which we take up between our thumb and two fingers. 2. He has a vast strength, and can as easily move mountains and hills as the tradesman heaves his goods into the scales and out of them again; he poises them with his hand as exactly as if he weighed them in a pair of balances. This may refer to the work of creation, when the heavens were stretched out as exactly as that which is spanned, and the earth and waters were put together in just proportions, as if they had been measured, and the mountains made of such a weight as to serve for ballast to the globe, and no more. Or it may refer to the work of providence (which is a continued creation) and the consistency of all the creatures with each other.

II. His wisdom is unsearchable, and what no creature can give either information or direction to, *v.* 13, 14. As none can do what God has done and does, so none can assist him in the doing of it or suggest any thing to him which he thought not of. When the Lord by his Spirit made the world (Job 26:13) there was none that directed his Spirit, or gave him any advice, either what to do or how to do it. Nor does he need any counsellor to direct him in the government of the world, nor is there any with whom he consults, as the wisest kings do with those that *know law and judgment,* Esther 1:13. God needs not to be told what is done, for he knows it perfectly; nor needs he be advised concerning what is to be done, for he knows both the right end and the proper means. This is much insisted upon here, because the poor captives had no politicians among them to manage their concerns at court or to put them in a way of gaining their liberty. "No matter," says the prophet, "you have a God to act for you, who needs not the assistance of statesmen." In the great work of our redemption by Christ matters were concerted *before the world was,* when there was one to *teach God in the path of judgment,* 1 Co. 2:7.

III. The nations of the world are nothing in comparison of him, *v.* 15, 17. Take them all together, all the great and mighty nations of the earth, kings the most pompous, kingdoms the most populous, both the most wealthy; take the isles, the multitude of them, the isles of the Gentiles: *Before him,* when they stand in competition with him or in opposition to him, they are *as a drop of the bucket* compared with the vast ocean, or *the small dust of the balance* (which does not serve to turn it, and therefore is not regarded, it is so small) in comparison with all the dust of the earth. *He takes them up,* and throws them away from him, *as a very little thing,* not worth speaking of. They are all in his eye *as nothing,* as if they had no being at all; for they add nothing to his perfection and all-sufficiency. *They are counted by him,* and are to be counted by us in comparison of him, *less than nothing, and vanity.* When he pleases, he can as easily bring them all into nothing as at first he brought them out of nothing. When God has work to do he values not either the assistance or the resistance of any creature. They are all *vanity;* the word that is used for the chaos (Gen. 1:2), to which they will at last be reduced. Let this beget in us high thoughts of God and low thoughts of this world, and engage us to make God, and not man, both our fear and our hope. This magnifies God's love to the world, that, though it is of such small account and value with him, yet, for the redemption of it, he *gave his only-begotten Son,* Jn. 3:16.

IV. The services of the church can make no addition to him nor do they bear any proportion to his infinite perfections (*v.* 16): *Lebanon is not sufficient to burn;* not the wood of it, to be for the fuel of the altar, though it be so well stocked with cedars; not the beasts of it, to be for sacrifices, though it be so well stocked with cattle, *v.* 16. Whatever we honour God with, it falls infinitely short of the merit of his perfection; for he is exalted *far above all blessing and praise,* all burnt-offerings and sacrifices.

Verses 18–26

The prophet here reproves those, 1. Who represented God by creatures, and so changed his truth into a lie and his glory into shame, who made images and then said that they resembled God, and paid their homage to them accordingly. 2. Who put creatures in the place of God, who feared them more than God, as if they were a match for him, or loved them more than God, as if they were fit to be rivals with him. Twice the challenge is here made, *To whom will you liken God? v.* 18, and again *v.* 25. The Holy One himself says, *To whom will you liken me?* This shows the folly and absurdity, (1.) Of corporal idolatry, making visible images of him who is invisible, imagining the image to be animated by the deity, and the deity to be presentiated by the image, which, as it was an instance of the corruption of the human nature, so it was an intolerable injury to the honour of the divine nature. (2.) Of spiritual idolatry, making creatures equal with God in our affections. Proud people make themselves equal with God; covetous people make their money equal with God; and whatever we esteem or love, fear or hope in, more than God, that creature we equal with God, which is the highest affront imaginable to him who is *God over all.* Now, to show the absurdity of this,

I. The prophet describes idols as despicable things and worthy of the greatest contempt (*v.* 19, 20): "Look upon the better sort of them, which rich people set up, and worship; they are made of some base metal, cast into what shape the founder pleases, and that is gilded, or overlaid with plates of gold, that it may pass for a golden image. It is a creature; for the workman made it; *therefore it is not God,* Hos. 8:6. It depended upon his will whether it should be a god at all, and of what shape it should be. It is a cheat; for it is gold on the outside, but within it is lead or copper, in this indeed representing the deities, that they were not what they seemed to be, and deceived their admirers. How despicable then are the worst sort of them — the poor men's gods! *He that is so impoverished* that he has scarcely a sacrifice to offer to his god when he has made him will yet not be without an enshrined deity of his own; and, though he cannot procure one of brass or stone, he will have a wooden one rather than none, and for that purpose *chooses a tree that will not soon rot,* and of that he will have his graven image made. Both agree to have their image well fastened, that they may not be robbed of it. The better sort have silver chains to fix theirs with; and, though it be but a wooden image, care is taken that it *shall not be moved."* Let us pause a little and see, 1. How these idolaters shame themselves, and what a reproach they put upon their own reason, in dreaming that gods of their own making (*Nehushtans,* pieces of brass or logs of wood) should be able to do them any kindness. Thus vain were they in their imaginations; and how was their foolish heart darkened! 2. See how these idolaters shame us, who worship the only living and true God. They spared no cost upon their idols; we grudge that as waste which is spent in the service of our God. They took care that their idols should not be moved; we wilfully provoke our God to depart from us.

II. He describes God as infinitely great, and worthy of the highest veneration; so that between him and idols, whatever competition there may be, there is no comparison. To prove the greatness of God he appeals,

1. To what they had *heard of him by the hearing of the ear,* and the consent of all ages and nations concerning him (*v.* 21): *"Have you not known* by the very light of nature? *Has it not been told you* by your fathers and teachers, according to the constant tradition received from their ancestors and predecessors, even from the beginning?" (Those notices of God are as ancient as the world.) *"Have you not understood* it as always acknowledged *from the foundation of the earth,* that God is a great God, and a

great King above all gods?" It has been a truth universally admitted that there is an infinite Being who is the fountain of all being. This is understood not only ever since the beginning of the world, but from and by the origin of the universe. It is founded upon the foundation of the earth. The invisible things of God are *clearly seen from the creation of the world,* Rom. 1:20. Thou mayest not only ask thy father, and he shall tell thee this, and thy elders (Deu. 32:7); but *ask those that go by the way* (Job 21:29), ask the first man you meet, and he will say the same. Some read it, *Will you not know? Will you not hear it?* For those that are ignorant of this are willingly ignorant; the light shines in their faces, but they shut their eyes against it. Now that which is here said of God is, (1.) That he has the command of all the creatures. The heaven and the earth themselves are under his management: *He sits upon the circle,* or globe, *of the earth, v.* 22. He that has the special residence of his glory in the upper world maintains a dominion over this lower world, gives law to it, and directs all the motions of it to his own glory. He sits undisturbed upon the earth, and so establishes it. He is still stretching out the heavens, his power and providence keep them still stretched out, and will do so till the day comes that they shall be rolled together like a scroll. He spreads them out as easily as we draw a curtain to and fro, opening these curtains in the morning and drawing them close again at night. And the heaven is to this earth *as a tent to dwell in;* it is a canopy drawn over our heads, *et quod tegit omnia coelum — and it encircles all. —* Ovid. See Ps. 104:2. (2.) That the children of men, even the greatest and mightiest, are as nothing before him. The numerous inhabitants of this earth are in his eye as grasshoppers in ours, so little and inconsiderable, of such small value, of such little use, and so easily crushed. Proud men's lifting up themselves is but like the grasshopper's leap; in an instant they must stoop down to the earth again. If the spies thought themselves grasshoppers before the sons of Anak (Num. 13:33), what are we before the great God? Grasshoppers live but awhile, and live carelessly, not like the ant; so do the most of men. (3.) That those who appear and act against him, how formidable soever they may be to their fellow-creatures, will certainly be humble and brought down by the mighty hand of God, *v.* 23, 24. Princes and judges, who have great authority, and abuse it to the support of oppression and injustice, make nothing of those about them; *as for all their enemies they puff at them* (Ps. 10:5; 12:5); but, when the great God takes them to task, he brings them to nothing; he humbles them, and tames them, and makes them as vanity, little regarded, neither feared nor loved. He makes them utterly unable to stand before his judgments, which shall either, [1.] Prevent their settlement in their authority: *They shall not be planted; they shall not be sown;* and those are the two ways of propagating plants, either by seed or slips. Nay, if they should gain a little interest, and so be planted or sown, yet *their stock shall not take root in the earth,* they shall not continue long in power. Eliphaz saw the foolish taking root, but *suddenly cursed their habitation.* And then how soon is the fig-tree withered away! Or, [2.] He will blast them when they think they are settled. He does but *blow upon them,* and then *they shall wither,* and come to nothing, and *the whirlwind shall take them away as stubble.* For God's wrath, though it seem at first to blow slightly upon them, will soon become a mighty whirlwind. When God judges he will overcome. Those that will not bow before him cannot stand before him.

2. He appeals to what *their eyes saw of him* (v. 26): "*Lift up your eyes on high;* be not always poring on this earth" (*O curvae in terras animae et coelestium inanes! — Degenerate minds, that can bend so towards the earth, having nothing celestial in them!),* "but sometimes look up" (*Os homini sublime dedit, coelumque tueri jussit — Heaven gave to man an erect countenance, and bade him gaze on the stars);* "behold the glorious lights of heaven, consider who has created them. They neither made nor marshalled themselves; doubtless, therefore, there is a God that gave them their being, power, and motion." What we see of the creature should lead us to the Creator. The idolaters, when they lifted up their eyes and beheld the hosts of heaven, being wholly immerged in sense, looked no further, but worshipped them, Deu. 4:19; Job 31:26. Therefore the prophet here directs us to make use of our reason

as well as our senses, and to consider who created them, and to pay our homage to him. Give him the glory of his sovereignty over them — He *brings out their host by number,* as a general draws out the squadrons and battalions of his army; of the knowledge he has of them — *He calls them all by names,* proper names, according as their place and influence are (Ps. 147:4); and of the use he makes of them; when he calls them out to any service, so obsequious are they that, *by the greatness of his might, not one of them fails,* but, as when *the stars in their courses fought against Sisera,* every one does that to which he is appointed. To make these creatures therefore rivals with God, which are such ready servants to him, is an injury to them as well as an affront to him.

Verses 27–31

Here, I. The prophet reproves the people of God, who are now supposed to be captives in Babylon for their unbelief and distrust of God, and the dejections and despondencies of their spirit under their affliction (v. 27): "*Why sayest thou, O Jacob!* to thyself and to those about thee, *My way is hidden from the Lord?* Why dost thou make hard and melancholy conclusions concerning thyself and thy present case as if the latter were desperate?" 1. The titles he here gives them were enough to shame them out of their distrusts: *O Jacob! O Israel!* Let them remember whence they took these names — from one who had found God faithful to him and kind in all his straits; and why they bore these names — as God's professing people, a people in covenant with him. 2. The way of reproving them is by reasoning with them: "Why? Consider whether thou hast any ground to say so." Many of our foolish frets and foolish fears would vanish before a strict enquiry into the causes of them. 3. That which they are reproved for is an ill-natured, ill-favoured, word they spoke of God, as if he had cast them off. There seems to be an emphasis laid upon their saying it: Why *sayest* thou and *speakest* thou? It is bad to have evil thoughts rise in our mind, but it is worse to put an *imprimatur — a sanction* to them, and turn them into evil words. David reflects with regret upon what he said in his haste, when he was in distress. 4. The ill word they said was a word of despair concerning their present calamitous condition. They were ready to conclude, (1.) That God would not heed them: "*My way is hidden from the Lord;* he takes no notice of our straits, nor concerns himself any more in our concernments. There are such difficulties in our case that even divine wisdom and power will be nonplussed." A man *whose way is hidden* is one whom *God has hedged in,* Job 3:23. (2.) That God could not help them: "*My judgment is passed over from my God;* my case is past relief, so far past it that God himself cannot redress the grievances of it. *Our bones are dried.*" Eze. 37:11.

II. He reminds them of that which, if duly considered, was sufficient to silence all those fears and distrust. For their conviction, as before for the conviction of idolaters (v. 21), he appeals to what they had known and what they had heard. Jacob and Israel were a knowing people, or might have been, and their knowledge came by hearing; for Wisdom cried in their chief places of concourse. Now, among other things, they had heard that *God had spoken once, twice,* yea, many a time they had *heard it, That power belongs unto God* (Ps. 62:11), That is,

1. He is himself an almighty God. He must needs be so, for he is *the everlasting God, even Jehovah.* He was from eternity; he will be to eternity; and therefore with him there is no deficiency, no decay. He has his being of himself, and therefore all his perfections must needs be boundless. He is without beginning of days or end of life, and therefore with him there is no change. He is also the *Creator of the ends of the earth,* that is, of the whole earth and all that is in it from end to end. He therefore is the rightful owner and ruler of all, and must be concluded to have an absolute power over all and an all-sufficiency to help his people in their greatest straits. Doubtless he is still as able to save his church as he was at first to make the world. (1.) He has wisdom to contrive the salvation, and that wisdom is never at a loss: *There is no searching of his understanding,* so as to countermine the counsels of it and defeat its intentions; no, nor so as to determine what he will do, for he has ways by himself, ways in the sea. None can say, "Thus far God's wisdom can go, and no fur-

ther;" for, when we know not what to do, he knows. (2.) He has power to bring about the salvation, and that power is never exhausted: *He faints not, nor is weary;* he upholds the whole creation, and governs all the creatures, and is neither tired nor toiled; and therefore, no doubt, he has power to relieve his church, when it is brought ever so low, without weakness or weariness.

2. He gives strength and power to his people, and helps them by enabling them to help themselves. He that is the strong God is the strength of Israel. (1.) He can help the weak, *v.* 29. Many a time *he gives power to the faint,* to those that are ready to faint away; and *to those that have no might he* not only gives, but *increases strength,* as there is more and more occasion for it. Many out of bodily weakness are wonderfully recovered, and made strong, by the providence of God: and many that are feeble in spirit, timorous and faint-hearted, unfit for services and sufferings, are yet strengthened by the grace of God *with all might in the inward man.* To those who are sensible of their weakness, and ready to acknowledge they have no might, God does in a special manner increase strength; for, *when we are weak* in ourselves, *then are we strong in the Lord.* (2.) He will help the willing, will help those who, in a humble dependence upon him, help themselves, and will do well for those who do their best, *v.* 30, 31. Those who trust to their own sufficiency, and are so confident of it that they neither exert themselves to the utmost nor seek unto God for his grace, are *the youth* and *the young men,* who are strong, but are apt to think themselves stronger than they are. And they *shall faint and be weary,* yea, they *shall utterly fail* in their services, in their conflicts, and under their burdens; they shall soon be made to see the folly of trusting to themselves. *But those that wait on the Lord,* who make conscience of their duty to him, and by faith rely upon him and commit themselves to his guidance, shall find that God will not fail them. [1.] They shall have grace sufficient for them: They *shall renew their strength* as their work is renewed, as there is new occasion; they shall be anointed, and their lamps supplied, with fresh oil. God will be their *arm every morning, ch.* 33:2. If at any time they have been foiled and weakened they shall recover themselves, and so renew their strength. Heb. *They shall change their strength,* as their work is changed — doing work, suffering work; they shall have strength to labour, strength to wrestle, strength to resist, strength to bear. As the day so shall the strength be. [2.] They shall use this grace for the best purposes. Being strengthened, *First,* They shall soar upward, upward towards God: *They shall mount up with wings like eagles,* so strongly, so swiftly, so high and heaven-ward. In the strength of divine grace, their souls shall ascend above the world, and even enter into the holiest. Pious and devout affections are the eagles' wings on which gracious souls mount up, Ps. 25:1. *Secondly,* They shall press forward, forward towards heaven. They shall walk, they shall run, the way of God's commandments, cheerfully and with alacrity (they *shall not be weary*), constantly and with perseverance (they *shall not faint*); and therefore in due season they shall reap. Let Jacob and Israel therefore, in their greatest distresses, continue waiting upon God, and not despair of timely and effectual relief and succour from him.

In this chapter we have, I. Orders given to preach and publish the glad tidings of redemption (v. 1, 2). II. These glad tidings introduced by a voice in the wilderness, which gives assurance that all obstructions shall be removed (v. 3–5), and that, though all creatures fail and fade, the word of God shall be established and accomplished (v. 6–8). III. A joyful prospect given to the people of God of the happiness which this redemption should bring along with it (v. 9–11). IV. The sovereignty and power of that God magnified who undertakes to work out this redemption (v. 12–17). V. Idols therefore triumphed over and idolaters upbraided with their folly (v. 18–26). VI. A reproof given to the people of God for their fears and despondencies, and enough said, in a few words, to silence those fears (v. 27–31). And we, through patience and comfort of this scripture, may have hope.

CHAPTER 41

This chapter, as the former, in intended both for the conviction of idolaters and for the consolation of all God's faithful worshippers; for the Spirit is sent, and ministers are employed by him, both to convince and to comfort. And however this might be primarily intended for the conviction of

Babylonians, and the comfort of Israelites, or for the conviction of those in Israel that were addicted to idolatry, as multitudes were, and the comfort of those that kept their integrity, doubtless it was intended both for admonition and encouragement to us, admonition to keep ourselves from idols and encouragement to trust in God. Here, I. God by the prophet shows the folly of those that worshipped idols, especially that thought their idols able to contest with him and control him (*v.* 1–9). II. He encourages his faithful ones to trust in him, with an assurance that he would take their part against their enemies, make them victorious over them, and bring about a happy change of their affairs (*v.* 10–20). III. He challenges the idols, that were rivals with him for men's adoration, to vie with him either for knowledge or power, either to show things to come or to do good or evil (*v.* 21–29). So that the chapter may be summed up in those words of Elijah, "If Jehovah be God, then follow him; but, if Baal be God, then follow him;" and in the people's acknowledgment, upon the issue of the trial, "Jehovah he is the God, Jehovah he is the God."

Verses 1–9

That particular instance of God's care for his people Israel in raising up Cyrus to be their deliverer is here insisted upon as a great proof both of his sovereignty above all idols and of his power to protect his people. Here is,

I. A general challenge to the worshippers and admirers of idols to make good their pretensions, in competition with God and opposition to him, *v.* 1. Is is renewed (*v.* 21): *Produce your cause.* The court is set, summonses are sent to the islands that lay most remote, but not out of God's jurisdiction, for he is the *Creator and possessor of the ends of the earth,* to make their appearance and give their attendance. Silence (as usual) is proclaimed while the cause is in trying: *"Keep silence before me,* and judge nothing before the time"; while the cause is in trying between the kingdom of God and the kingdom of Satan it becomes all people silently to expect the issue, not to object against God's proceedings, but to be confident that he will carry the day. The defenders of idolatry are called to say what they can in defence of it: *"Let them renew their strength,* in opposition to God, and see whether it be equal to the strength which those renew that wait upon him (*ch.* 40:31); let them try their utmost efforts, whether by force of arms or force of argument. *Let them come near;* they shall not complain that God's *dread makes them afraid* (Job 13:21), so that they cannot say what they have to say, in vindication and honour of their idols; no, *let them speak* freely: *Let us come near together to judgment."* Note. 1. The cause of God and his kingdom is not afraid of a fair trial; if the case be but fairly stated, it will be surely carried in favour of religion. 2. The enemies of God's church and his holy religion may safely be challenged to say and do their worst for the support of their unrighteous cause. He that *sits in heaven laughs at them,* and the *daughter of Zion despises them;* for *great is the truth and will prevail.*

II. He particularly challenges the idols to do that for their worshippers, and against his, which he had done and would do for his worshippers, and against theirs. Different senses are given of *v.* 2, concerning *the righteous man raised up from the east;* and, since we cannot determine which is the true, we will make use of each as good.

1. That which is to be proved is, (1.) That *the Lord is God* alone, *the first and with the last* (*v.* 4), that he is infinite, eternal, and unchangeable, that he governed the world from the beginning, and will to the end of time. He has reigned of old, and will reign for ever; the counsels of his kingdom were from eternity, and the continuance of it will be to eternity. (2.) That *Israel* is *his servant* (*v.* 8), whom he owns, and protects, and employs, and in whom he is and will be glorified. As there is a God in heaven, so there is a church on earth that is his particular care. Elijah prays (1 Ki. 18:36), *Let it be known that thou art God, and that I am thy servant.* Now,

2. To prove this he shows,

(1.) That it was he who called Abraham, the father of this despised nation, out of an idolatrous country, and by many instances of his favour *made his name great,* Gen. 12:2. He is *the righteous man whom God raised up from the east.* Of him the Chaldee paraphrast expressly understands it: *Who brought Abraham publicly from the east?* To maintain the honour of the people of Israel, it was very proper to show what a figure this great ancestor of theirs made in his day; and *v.* 8 seems to be the explication of it, where God calls Israel the *seed of Abraham my friend;* and (*v.* 4) he *calls the generations* (namely, the generations of Israel) *from the beginning.* Also, to put contempt upon idolatry, and particularly the Chaldean idolatry, it was proper to show how Abraham was called from serving other gods (Jos. 24:2, 3, etc.), so that an early testimony was borne against that idolatry which boasted so much of its antiquity. Also, to encourage the captives in Babylon to hope that God would find a way for their return to their own land, it was proper to remind them how at first he brought their father Abraham out of the same country into this land, to give it to him for an inheritance, Gen. 15:7. Now observe what is here said concerning him. [1.] That he was a *righteous man,* or *righteousness,* a *man of righteousness,* that *believed God, and it was counted to him for righteousness;* and so he became the father of all those who by faith in Christ are made the *righteousness of God through him,* Rom. 4:3, 11; 2 Co. 5:21. He was a great example of righteousness in his day, and *taught his household to do judgment and justice,* Gen. 18:19. [2.] That God *raised him up from the east,* from Ur first and afterwards from Haran, which lay east from Canaan. God would not let him settle in either of those places, but did by him as the eagle by her young, when she stirs up her nest: he raised him out of iniquity and made him pious, out of obscurity and made him famous. [3.] He *called him to his foot,* to follow him with an implicit faith; for he *went out, not knowing whither he went,* but whom he followed, Heb. 11:8. Those whom God effectually calls he calls to his foot, to be subject to him, to attend him, and *follow the Lamb whithersoever he goes;* and we must all either come to his foot or be made his footstool. [4.] *He gave nations before him,* the nations of Canaan, which he promised to make him master of, and thus far gave him an interest in that the Hittites acknowledged him a mighty prince among them, Gen. 23:6. He *made him rule over* those *kings* whom he conquered for the rescue of his brother Lot, Gen. 14. And when God *gave them as dust to his sword, and as driven stubble to his bow* (that is, made them an easy prey to his catechised servants), *he* then *pursued them, and passed safely,* or in peace, under the divine protection, though it was in a way he was altogether unacquainted with; and so considerable was this victory that Melchizedec himself appeared to celebrate it. Now who did this but the great Jehovah? Can any of the gods of the heathen do so?

(2.) That it is he who will, ere long, raise up Cyrus from the east. It is spoken of according to the language of prophecy as a thing past, because as sure to be done in its season as if it were already done. *God will raise him up in righteousness* (so it may be read, *ch.* 45:13), *will call him to his foot,* make what use of him he pleases, and make him victorious over the nations that oppose his coming to the crown, and give him success in all his wars; and he shall be a type of Christ, who is righteousness itself, the Lord our righteousness, whom God will, in the fulness of time, raise up and make victorious over the powers of darkness; so that he shall spoil them and make a show of them openly.

III. He exposes the folly of idolaters, who, notwithstanding the convincing proofs which the God of Israel had given of his being God alone, obstinately persisted in their idolatry, nay, were so much the more hardened in it (*v.* 5): *The isles of the Gentiles saw this,* not only what God did for Abraham himself, but what he did for his seed, for his sake, how he brought them out of Egypt, and made them *rule over kings,* and *they feared,* Ex. 15:14–16. They were afraid, and, according to the summons (*v.* 1), they *drew near, and came;* they could not avoid taking notice of what God did for Abraham and his seed; but, instead of helping to reason one another out of their sottish idolatries, they helped to confirm one another in them, *v.* 6, 7. 1. They looked upon it as a dangerous design upon their religion, which they were jealous for the honour of, and were resolved, right or wrong, to adhere to, and therefore were alarmed to appear vigorously for the support of it, as the Ephesians for their Diana. When God, by his wonderful appearances on the behalf of his people, went about to wrest their idols from them, they held them so much the faster, and said one to another, *"Be of good courage;* let us unanimously agree to keep up the reputation of our gods. Though Dagon fall before the ark, he shall be set up again in his place." One tradesman encourages another to come into a confederacy for the keeping up of the noble craft of god-making. Thus men's convictions often exasperate their corruptions, and they are made worse both by the word and the works of God, which should make them better. 2. They looked upon it as a dangerous design upon themselves. They thought themselves in danger from the growing greatness both of Abraham that was a convert from idolatry, and of the people of Israel that were separatists from it; and therefore they not only had recourse to their old gods for protection, but made *new* ones, Deu. 32:17. *So the carpenter,* having done his part to the timberwork, *encouraged the goldsmith* to do his part in gilding or overlaying it; and, when it came into the goldsmith's hand, *he that smooths with the hammer* that polishes it, or beats it thin, quickened *him that smote the anvil,* bade him be expeditious, and told him it was *ready for the soldering,* which perhaps was the last operation about it, and then it is *fastened with nails,* and you have a god of it presently. Do sinners thus animate and quicken one another in the ways of sin? And shall not the servants of the living God both stir up one another to, and strengthen one another in, his service? Some read all this ironically, and by way of permission: *Let them help every one his neighbour; let the carpenter encourage the goldsmith;* but all in vain; idols shall fall for all this.

IV. He encourages his own people to trust in him (*v.* 8, 9): *"But thou, Israel, art my servant.* They know me not, but thou knowest me, and knowest better than to join with such ignorant besotted people as these" (for it is intended for a warning to the people of God not to *walk in the way of the heathen*); "they put themselves under the protection of these impotent deities, but thou art under my protection. *Those that make them are like unto them, and so is every one that trusts in them; but thou, O Israel!* art the servant of a better Master." Observe what is suggested here for the encouragement of God's people when they are threatened and insulted over. 1. They are God's servants, and he will not see them abused, especially for what they do in his service: *Thou art my servant* (*v.* 8), and (*v.* 9) *"I have said unto thee, Thou art my servant;* and I will not go back from my word." 2. He has *chosen* them to be a peculiar people to himself. They were not forced upon him, but of his own good-will he set them apart. 3. They were the seed of Abraham his friend. It was the honour of Abraham that he was *called the friend of God* (James 2:23), whom God covenanted and conversed with as a friend, and the *man of his counsel;* and *this honour have all the saints,* Jn. 15:15. And for the father's sake the people of Israel were beloved. God was pleased to look upon them as the posterity of an old friend of his, and therefore to be kind to them; for the covenant of friendship was made with Abraham and his seed. 4. He had sometimes, when they had been scattered among the heathen, fetched them from the ends of the earth and taken them out of the hands of the chief ones thereof, and therefore he would not now abandon them. Abraham their father was fetched from a place at a great distance, and they in his loins; and those who had been thus far-fetched and dear-bought he could not easily part with. 5. He had not yet cast them away, though they had often provoked him, and therefore he would not now abandon them. What God has done for his people, and what he has further engaged to do, should encourage them to trust in him at all times.

Verses 10–20

The scope of these verses is to silence the fears, and encourage the faith, of the servants of God in their distresses. Perhaps it is intended, in the first place, for the support of God's Israel, in captivity; but all that faithfully serve God *through patience and comfort of this scripture may have hope.* And it is addressed to Israel as a single person, that it might the more easily and readily be accommodated and applied by every Israelite indeed to himself. That is a word of caution, counsel, and comfort, which is so often repeated, *Fear thou not;* and again (*v.* 13), *Fear not;* and (*v.* 14), *"Fear not, thou worm Jacob;* fear not the threatenings of the enemy, doubt not the promise of thy God; fear not that thou shalt perish in thy affliction or that the promise of thy deliverance shall fail." It is against the mind of God that his people should be a timorous people. For the suppressing of fear he assures them,

I. That they may depend upon his presence with them as their God, and a God all-sufficient for them in the worst of times. Observe with what tenderness God speaks, and how willing he is to let the heirs of promise know the immutability of his counsel, and how desirous to make them easy: *"Fear thou not, for I am with thee,* not only within call, but present with thee; *be not dismayed* at the power of those that are against thee, for *I am thy God,* and engaged for thee. Art thou weak? *I will strengthen thee.* Art thou destitute of friends? *I will help thee* in the time of need. Art thou ready to sink, ready to fall? *I will uphold thee with the right hand of my righteousness,* that right hand which is full of righteousness, in dispensing rewards and punishments," Ps. 48:10. And again (*v.* 13) it is promised, 1. That God will strengthen their hands, that is, will help them: *"I will hold thy right hand,* go hand in hand with thee" (so some): he will take us by the hand as our guide, to lead us in our way, will help us up when we are fallen or prevent our falls; when we are weak he will hold us up — wavering, he will fix us — trembling, he will encourage us, and so *hold us by the right hand,* Ps. 73:23. 2. That he will silence their fears: *Saying unto thee, Fear not.* He has said it again and again in his word, and has there provided sovereign antidotes against fear: but he will go further; he will by his Spirit say it to their hearts, and make them to hear it, and so will help them.

II. That though their enemies be now very formidable, insolent, and severe, yet the day is coming when God will reckon with them and they shall triumph over them. There are those that are incensed against God's people, that *strive with them* (*v.* 11), that war against them (*v.* 12), that hate them, that seek their ruin, and are continually picking quarrels with them. But let not God's people be incensed at them, nor strive with them, nor render evil for evil; but wait God's time, and believe, 1. That they shall be convinced of the folly, at least, if not of the sin of striving with God's people; and, finding it to no purpose, *they shall be ashamed and confounded,* which might bring them to repentance, but will rather fill them with rage. 2. That they shall be quite ruined and undone (*v.* 11): *They shall be as nothing* before the justice and power of God. When God comes to deal with his proud enemies he makes nothing of them. Or they shall be brought to nothing, shall be as if they had never been. This is repeated (*v.* 12): They *shall be as nothing and as a thing of nought,* or as that which is gone and has failed. Those that were formidable shall become despicable; those that fancied they could do any thing shall be able to bring nothing to pass; those that made a figure in the world, and a mighty noise, shall become mere ciphers and be buried in silence. They shall perish, not only be nothing, but be miserable: *Thou shalt seek them,* shalt enquire what has become of them, that they do not appear as usual, but thou *shalt not find them* as David, Ps. 37:36. *I sought him, but he could not be found.*

III. That they themselves should become a terror to those who were now a terror to them, and victory should turn on their side, *v.* 14–16. See here, 1. How Jacob and Israel are reduced and brought very low. It is the *worm Jacob,* so little, so weak, and so defenceless, despised and trampled on by every body, forced to creep even into the earth for safety; and we must not wonder that Jacob has become a worm, when even Jacob's King calls himself *a worm and no man,* Ps. 22:6. God's people are sometimes as worms, in their humble thoughts of themselves and their enemies' haughty thoughts of them — worms, but not vipers, as their enemies are, not of the serpent's seed. God regards Jacob's low estate, and says, *"Fear not, thou worm Jacob;* fear not that thou shalt be crushed; and *you men of Israel"* (*you few men,* so some read it, *you dead men,* so others) "do not give up yourselves for gone notwithstanding." Note, The grace of God will silence fears even when there seems to be the greatest cause for them. *Perplexed but not in despair.* 2. How Jacob and Israel are advanced from this low estate, and made as formidable as ever they have been despicable. But *by whom shall Jacob arise, for he is small?* We are here told: *I will help thee, saith the Lord;* and it is the honour of God to help the weak. He will help them, for he is their Redeemer, who is wont to redeem them, who has undertaken to do it. Christ is the Redeemer, from him is our help found. He will help them, for he is the *Holy One of Israel,* worshipped among them in the beauty of holiness and engaged by promise to them. The Lord will help them by enabling them to help themselves and making Jacob to become *a threshing instrument.* Observe, He is but an instrument, a tool in God's hand, that he is pleased to make use of; and he is an instrument of God's making and is no more than God makes

him. But, if God make him a threshing instrument, he will make use of him, and therefore will make him fit for use, *new* and *sharp,* and *having teeth,* or sharp spikes; and then, by divine direction and strength, *thou shalt thresh the mountains,* the highest, and strongest, and most stubborn of thy enemies: thou shalt not only beat them, but *beat them small;* they shall not be a corn threshed out, which is valuable, and is carefully preserved (such God's people are when they are under the flail, *ch.* 21:10: *O my threshing!* yet *the corn of my floor,* that shall not be lost); but these are made *as chaff,* which is good for nothing, and which the husbandman is glad to get rid of. He pursues the metaphor, *v.* 16. Having threshed them, *thou shalt winnow them, and the wind shall scatter them.* This perhaps had its accomplishment, in part, in the victories of the Jews over their enemies in the times of the Maccabees; but it seems in general designed to read the final doom of all the implacable enemies of the church of God, and to have its accomplishment likewise in the triumphs of the cross of Christ, the gospel of Christ, and all the faithful followers of Christ, over the powers of darkness, which, first or last, shall all be dissipated, and in Christ all believers shall be more than conquerors, and *he that overcomes shall have power over the nations,* Rev. 2:26.

IV. That, hereupon, they shall have abundance of comfort in God, and God shall have abundance of honour from them: *Thou shalt rejoice in the Lord, v.* 16. When we are freed from that which hindered our joy, and are blessed with that which is the matter of it, we ought to remember that God is our exceeding joy and in him all our joys must terminate. When we rejoice over our enemies we must rejoice in the Lord, for to him alone we owe our liberties and victories. "Thou shalt also *glory in the Holy One of Israel,* in thy interest in him and relation to him, and what he has done for thee." And, if thus we make God our praise and glory, we become to him for a praise and a glory.

V. That they shall have seasonable and suitable supplies of every thing that is proper for them in the time of need; and, if there be occasion, God will again do for them as he did for Israel in their march from Egypt to Canaan, *v.* 17–19. When the captives, either in Babylon or in their return thence, are in distress for want of water or shelter, God will take care of them, and, one way or other, make their journey, even through a wilderness, comfortable to them. But doubtless this promise has more than such a private interpretation. Their return out of Babylon was typical of our redemption by Christ; and so the contents of these promises, 1. Were provided by the gospel of Christ. That glorious discovery of his love has given full assurance to all those who hear this joyful sound that God has provided inestimable comforts for them, sufficient for the supply of all their wants, the balancing of all their griefs, and the answering of all their prayers. 2. They are applied by the grace and Spirit of Christ to all believers, that they may have strong consolation in their way and a complete happiness in their end. Our way to heaven lies through the wilderness of this world. Now, (1.) It is here supposed that the people of God, in their passage through this world, are often in straits: *The poor and needy seek water, and there is none; the poor in spirit hunger and thirst after righteousness.* The soul of man, finding itself empty and necessitous, seeks for satisfaction somewhere, but soon despairs of finding it in the world, that has nothing in it to make it easy: creatures are *broken cisterns, that can hold no water;* so that *their tongue fails for thirst,* they are weary of seeking that satisfaction in the world which is not to be had in it. Their sorrow makes them thirsty; so does their toil. (2.) It is here promised that, one way or other, all their grievances shall be redressed and they shall be made easy. [1.] God himself will be nigh unto them in all that which they call upon him for. Let all the praying people of God take notice of this, and take comfort of it; he has said, *"I the Lord will hear them,* will answer them; *I, the God of Israel, will not forsake them;* I will be with them, as I have always been, in their distresses." While we are in the wilderness of this world this promise is to us what the pillar of cloud and fire was to Israel, an assurance of God's gracious presence. [2.] They shall have a constant supply of fresh water, as Israel had in the wilderness, even where one would least expect it (*v.* 18): *I will open rivers in high places,* rivers of grace, rivers of pleasure, *rivers of living water,* which he spoke of the Spirit (Jn. 7:38, 39), that Spir-

it which should be poured out upon the Gentiles, who had been as high places, dry and barren, and lifted up on their own conceit above the necessity of that gift. And there shall be *fountains in the midst of the valleys,* the valleys of Baca (Ps. 84:6), that are sandy and wearisome; or among the Jews, who had been as fruitful valleys in comparison with the Gentile mountains. The preaching of the gospel to the world turned that wilderness into a pool of water, yielding fruit to the owner of it and relief to the travellers through it. [3.] They shall have a pleasant shade to screen them from the scorching heat of the sun, as Israel when they pitched at Elim, where they had not only wells of water, but palm-trees (Ex. 15:27): *"I will plant in the wilderness the cedar, v.* 19. I will turn the wilderness into an orchard or garden, such as used to be planted with these pleasant trees, so that they shall pass through the wilderness with as much ease and delight as a man walks in his grove. These trees shall be to them what the pillar of cloud was to Israel in the wilderness, a shelter from the heat." Christ and his grace are so to believers, *as the shadow of a great rock, ch.* 32:2. When God sets up his church in the Gentile wilderness there shall be as great a change made by it in men's characters as if thorns and briers were turned into cedars, and fir-trees, and myrtles; and by this a blessed change is described, *ch.* 55:13. [4.] They shall see and acknowledge the hand of God, his power and his favour, in this, *v.* 20. God will do these strange and surprising things on purpose to awaken them to a conviction and consideration of his hand in all: *That they may see* this wonderful change, *and knowing* that it is above the ordinary course and power of nature may consider that therefore it comes from a superior power, and, comparing notes upon it, *may understand together,* and concur in the acknowledgment of it, *that the hand of the Lord,* that mighty hand of his which is stretched out for his people and stretched out to them, *has done this,* and *the Holy One of Israel has created it,* made it anew, made it out of nothing, made it for the comfort of his people. Note, God does great things for his people, that he may be taken notice of.

Verses 21–29

The Lord, by the prophet, here repeats the challenge to idolaters to make out the pretentions of their idols: *"Produce your cause* (*v.* 21) and make your best of it; *bring forth the strongest reasons* you have to prove that your idols are gods, and worthy of your adoration."* Note, There needs no more to show the absurdity of sin than to produce the reasons that are given in defence of it, for they carry with them their own confutation.

I. The idols are here challenged to bring proofs of their knowledge and power. Let us see what they can inform us of, and what they can do. Understanding and active power are the accomplishments of a man. Whoever pretends to be a god must have these in perfection; and have the idols made it to appear that they have? No;

1. "They can tell us nothing that we did not know before, so ignorant are they. We challenge them to inform us," (1.) "What has been formerly: *Let them show the former things,* and raise them out of the oblivion in which they were buried" (God inspired Moses to write such a history of the creation as the gods of the heathen could never have dictated to any of their enthusiasts); or "let the defenders of idols tell us what mighty achievements they can boast of as performed by their gods in former times. What did they ever do that was worth taking notice of? Let them specify any thing, and it shall be considered, its due weight shall be given it, and it shall be compared with the latter end of it; and if, in the issue, it prove to be as great as it pretended to be, they shall have the credit of it." (2.) "We challenge them to tell us what shall happen, to declare to us *things to come* (*v.* 22), and again (*v.* 23), *show the things that are to come hereafter.* Give this evidence of your omniscience, that nothing can be hidden from you, and of your sovereignty and dominion. Make it to appear that you have the doing of all, by letting us know beforehand what you deign to do. Do this kindness to the world; let them know what is to come, that they may provide accordingly. Do this, and we will own that you are gods above us, and gods to us, and worthy of our adoration." No creature can foretel things to come, otherwise than by divine information, with any certainty.

2. "They can do nothing that we cannot do ourselves,

so impotent are they." He challenges them to do either *good or evil,* good to their friends or evil to their enemies: "Let them do, if they can, any thing extraordinary, that people will admire and be affected with. Let them either bless or curse, with power. Let us see them either inflict such plagues such as God brought on Egypt or bestow such blessings as God bestowed on Israel. Let them do some great thing, and we shall be amazed when we see it, and frightened into a veneration of them, as many have been into a veneration of the true God." That which is charged upon these idols, and let them disprove it if they can, is that *they are of nothing, v.* 24. Their claims have no foundation at all, nor is there any ground or reason in the least for men's paying them the respect they do; there is nothing in them worthy our regard. "They are less than nothing, worse than nothing;" so some read it. *"The work they do is of nought,* and so is the ado that is made about them. There is no pretence or colour for it; it is all a jest; it is all a sham put upon the world; and therefore *he that chooses you,* and so give you your deity, and" (as some read it) "that delights in you, *is an abomination;"* so some take it. A servant is at liberty to choose his master, but a man is not at liberty to choose his God. He that chooses any other than the true God chooses an abomination; his choosing it makes it so.

II. God here produces proofs that he is the true God, and that there is none besides him. Let him produce his strong reasons.

1. He has an irresistible power. This he will shortly make to appear in the raising up of Cyrus and making him a type of Christ (*v.* 25): *He will raise him up from the north* and *from the rising of the sun.* Cyrus by his father was a Mede, by his mother a Persian; and his army consisted of Medes, whose country lay north, and Persians, whose country lay east, from Babylon. God will raise him up to great power, and he shall come against Babylon with ends of his own to serve. But, (1.) *He shall proclaim God's name;* so it may be read. He shall publish the honour of the God of Israel; so he did remarkably when, in his proclamation for the release of the Jews out of their captivity, he acknowledged that the Lord God of Israel was the Lord God of heaven, and *the God:* and he might be said to call on his name when he encouraged the building of his temple, and very probably did himself call upon him and pray to him, Ezra 1:2, 3. (2.) All opposition shall fall before him: *He shall come upon the princes of Babylon,* and all others that stood in his way, *as mortar,* and trample upon them *as the potter treads clay,* to serve his own purposes with it. Christ, as man, was raised up from the north, for Nazareth lay in the northern parts of Canaan; as the angel of the covenant, he ascends from the east. He maintained the honour of heaven *(he shall call upon my name),* and broke the powers of hell, came upon the prince of darkness as mortar and trod him down.

2. He has an infallible foresight. He would not only do this, but he did now, by his prophet, foretel it. Now the false gods not only could not do it, but they could not foresee it. (1.) He challenges them to produce any of their pretended deities, or their diviners, that had given notice of this, or could (*v.* 26): *"Who has declared from the beginning* any thing of this kind, or has told it before-time? Tell us if there be any that you know of, for we know not any; if there be any, *we will say, He is righteous,* he is true, his cause is just, his claims are proved, and he is in the right in demanding to be worshipped." This agrees with *v.* 22, 23. (2.) He challenges to himself the sole honour of doing it and foretelling it (*v.* 27): *I am the first* (so it may be read) *that will say to Zion, Behold, behold them,* that will let the people of Israel know their deliverers are at hand (for there were those who understood by books, God's books, the approach of the time, Dan. 9:2), and I am he that *will give to Jerusalem one that brings good tidings,* these good tidings of their enlargement. This is applicable to the work of redemption, in which the Lord showed himself much more than in the release of the Jews out of Babylon: he it was that contrived our salvation, and he brought it about, and he has given to us the glad tidings of reconciliation.

III. Judgment is here given upon this trial. 1. None of all the idols had foretold, or could foresee, this work of wonder. Other nations besides the Jews were released out of captivity in Babylon by Cyrus, or at least were greatly concerned in the revolution of the monarchy and there transferring of it to the Persians; and yet none of them had any intelligence given them of it beforehand, by any of their gods or prophets: *"There is none that shows* (*v.* 26), *none that declares,* none that gives the least intimation of it; *there is none* of the nations *that hears your words,* that can pretend to have heard from their gods such words as you, O Israelites! have heard from your God, by your prophets," Ps. 147:20. None of all the gods of the nations have shown their worshippers the way of salvation, which God will show by the Messiah. The good tidings which the Lord will send in the gospel is a mystery hidden from ages and generations, Rom. 16:25, 26. 2. None of those who pleaded for them could produce any instance of their knowledge or power that had in it any colour of proof that they were gods. All their advocates were struck dumb with this challenge (*v.* 28): *"I beheld, and there was no man* that could give evidence for them, even among those that were their most zealous admirers; *and there was no counsellor,* none that could offer any thing for the support of their cause. Even among the idols themselves there was none fit to give counsel in the most trivial matters, and yet there were those that asked counsel of them in the most important and difficult affairs. When I asked them what they had to say for themselves they stood mute; the case was so plain against them that there was *none who could answer a word."* Judgment must therefore be given against the defendant upon *Nihil dicit — He is mute.* He has nothing to say for himself. *He was speechless,* Mt. 22:12. 3. Sentence is therefore given according to the charge exhibited against them (*v.* 24): *"Behold, they are all vanity* (*v.* 29); they are a lie and a cheat; they are not in themselves what they pretend to be, nor will their worshippers find that in them which they promise themselves. *Their works are nothing,* of no force, of no worth; their enemies need fear no hurt from them; their worshippers can hope for no good from them. *Their molten images,* and indeed all their images, *are wind and confusion,* vanity and vexation; those that worship them will be deceived in them, and will reflect upon their own folly with the greatest bitterness. Therefore, *dearly beloved, flee from idolatry,"* 1 Co. 10:14.

CHAPTER 42

The prophet seems here to launch out yet further into the prophecy of the Messiah and his kingdom under the type of Cyrus; and, having the great work of man's salvation by him yet more in view, he almost forgets the occasion that led him into it and drops the return out of Babylon; for indeed the prospect of this would be a greater comfort and support to the believing pious Jews, in their captivity, than the hope of that. And (as Mr. Gataker well observes) in this and similar prophecies of Christ, that are couched in types, as of David and Solomon, some passages agree to the type and not to the truth, other to the truth and not to the type, and many to the type in one sense and the truth in another. Here is, I. A prophecy of the Messiah's coming with meekness, and yet with power, to do the Redeemer's work (*v.* 1–4). II. His commission opened, which he received from the Father (*v.* 5–9). III. The joy and rejoicing with which the glad tidings of this should be received (*v.* 10–12). IV. The wonderful success of the gospel, for the overthrow of the devil's kingdom (*v.* 13–17). V. The rejection and ruin of the Jews for their unbelief (*v.* 18–25).

Verses 1–4

We are sure that these verses are to be understood of Christ, for the evangelist tells us expressly that in him this prophecy was fulfilled, Mt. 12:17–21. *Behold* with an eye of faith, behold and observe, behold and admire, *my servant, whom I uphold.* Let the Old-Testament saints behold and remember him. Now what must we behold and consider concerning him?

I. The Father's concern for him and relation to him, the confidence he put and the complacency he took in him. This put an honour upon him, and made him remarkable, above any other circumstance, *v.* 1. 1. God owns him as one employed for him: He is *my servant.* Though he was a Son, yet, as a Mediator, he *took upon him the form of a servant,* learned obedience to the will of God and practised it, and laid out himself to advance the interests of God's kingdom, and so he was God's servant. 2. As one chosen by him: He is *my elect.* He did not thrust himself into the service, but was called of God, and pitched upon as the fittest person for it. Infinite Wisdom made the choice and then avowed it. 3. As one he put a confidence in: He is *my servant on whom I lean;* so some read it. The Father put a confidence in him that he would go through with his undertaking, and, in that confidence, brought many sons to glory. It was a great trust which the Father reposed in the Son, but he knew him to be *par negotio — equal to it,* both able and faithful. 4. As one he took care of: He is *my servant whom I uphold;* so we read it. The Father bore him up, and bore him out, in his upholding him; he stood by him and strengthened him. 5. As one whom he took an entire complacency in: *My elect, in whom my soul delights.* His delight was in him from eternity, when he was *by him as one brought up with him,* Prov. 8:30. He had a particular satisfaction in his undertaking: he declared himself *well pleased in him* (Mt. 3:17; 17:5), and *therefore* loved him, because he laid down his life for the sheep. Let our souls delight in Christ, rely on him, and rejoice in him; and thus let us be united to him, and then, for his sake, the Father will be well pleased with us.

II. The qualification of him for his office: *I have put my Spirit upon him,* to enable him to go through his undertaking, *ch.* 61:1. The Spirit did not only come, but rest, upon him (*ch.* 11:2), not by measure, as on others of God's servants, but without measure. Those whom God employs as his servants; as he will uphold them and be well pleased with them, so he will put his Spirit upon them.

III. The work to which he is appointed; it is to *bring forth judgment to the Gentiles,* that is, in infinite wisdom, holiness, and equity, to set up a religion in the world under the bonds of which the Gentiles should come and the blessings of which they should enjoy. The judgments of the Lord, which had been hidden from the Gentiles (Ps. 147:20), he came to bring forth to the Gentiles, for he was *to be a light to lighten them.*

IV. The mildness and tenderness with which he should pursue this undertaking, *v.* 2, 3. He shall carry it on, 1. In silence, and without noise: *He shall not strive nor cry.* It shall not be proclaimed, *Lo, here, is Christ* or *Lo, he is there;* as when great princes ride in progress or make a public entry. He shall have no trumpet sounded before him, nor any noisy retinue to follow him. The opposition he meets with he shall not strive against, but patiently *endure the contradiction of sinners against himself.* His kingdom is spiritual, and therefore its weapons are not carnal, nor is its appearance pompous; it comes not with observation. 2. Gently, and without rigour. Those that are wicked he will be patient with; when he has begun to crush them, so that they are as bruised reeds, he will give them space to repent and not immediately break them; though they are very offensive, as smoking flax (*ch.* 65:5), yet he will bear with them, as he did with Jerusalem. Those that are weak he will be tender of; those that have but a little life, a little heat, that are weak as a reed, oppressed with doubts and fears, *as a bruised reed,* that are as *smoking flax,* as the wick of a candle newly lighted, which is ready to go out again, he will not despise them, will not plead against them with his great power, nor lay upon them more work or more suffering than they can bear, which would break and quench them, but will graciously consider their frame. More is implied than is expressed. *He will not break the bruised reed,* but will strengthen it, that it may become a cedar in the courts of our God. *He will not quench the smoking flax,* but blow it up into a flame. Note, Jesus Christ is very tender toward those that have true grace, though they are but weak in it, and accepts the willingness of the spirit, pardoning and passing by the weakness of the flesh.

V. The courage and constancy with which he should persevere in this undertaking, so as to carry his point at last (*v.* 4): *He shall not fail nor be discouraged.* Though he meets with hard service and much opposition, and foresees how ungrateful the world will be, yet he goes on with his part of the work, till he is able to say, *Is is finished;* and he enables his apostles and ministers to go on with theirs too, and not to fail nor be discouraged, till they also have finished their testimony. And thus he accomplishes what he undertook. 1. *He brings forth judgment unto truth.* By a long course of miracles, and his resurrection at last, he shall fully evince the truth of his doctrine and the divine origin and authority of that holy religion which he came to establish. 2. He *sets judgment in the earth.* He erects his government in the world, a church for himself among men, reforms the world, and by the power of his gospel and grace fixes such principles in the minds of men as tend to make them wise and just. 3. *The isles* of the Gentiles *wait for his law,* wait for his gospel, that is, bid it welcome as if it had been a thing they had long waited for. They shall become his disciples, shall sit at his feet, and be ready to receive the law from his mouth. *What wilt thou have us to do?*

Verses 5–12

Here is I. The covenant God made with and the commission he gave to the Messiah, *v.* 5–7, which are an exposition of *v.* 1, *Behold my servant, whom I uphold.*

1. The royal titles by which the great God here makes himself known, and distinguishes himself from all pretenders, speak very much his glory (*v.* 5): *Thus saith God the Lord.* And who are thou, Lord? Why, he is the fountain of all being and therefore the fountain of all power. He is the fountain of being, 1. In the upper world; for *he created the heavens and stretched them out* (*ch.* 40:22), and keeps the vast expanse still upon the stretch. 2. In the lower world: for *he spread forth the earth,* and made it a capacious habitation, *and that which comes out of it* is produced by his power. 3. In the world of mankind: *He gives breath to the people upon it,* not only air to breathe in, but the breath of life itself and organs to breathe with; nay, he gives *spirit,* the powers and faculties of a rational soul, to those that walk therein. Now this is prefixed to God's covenant with the Messiah, and the commission given him, not only to show that he has authority to make such a covenant and give such a commission, and had power sufficient to bear him out, but that the design of the work of redemption was to maintain the honour of the Creator, and to restore man to the allegiance he owes to God as his Maker.

2. The assurances which he gives to the Messiah of his presence with him in all he did pursuant to his undertaking speak much encouragement to him, *v.* 6. (1.) God owns that the Messiah did not take the honour of being Mediator to himself, but was called of God, that he was no intruder, no usurper, but was fairly brought to it (Heb. 5:4): *I have called thee in righteousness.* God not only did him no wrong in calling him to this hard service, he having voluntarily offered himself to it, but did himself right in providing for his own honour and performing the word which he had spoken. (2.) He promises to stand by him and strengthen him in it, to hold his hand, not only to his work, but in it, to hold his hand, that it might not shake, that it might not fail, and so to keep him. When an angel was sent from heaven to strengthen him in his agonies, and the Father himself was with him, then this promise was fulfilled. Note, Those whom God calls he will own and help, and will hold their hands.

3. The great intentions of this commission speak abundance of comfort to the children of men. He was given *for a covenant of the people,* for a mediator, or guarantee, of the covenant of grace, which is all summed up in him. God, in giving us Christ, has with him freely given us all the blessings of the new covenant. Two glorious blessings Christ, in his gospel, brings with him to the Gentile world — light and liberty. (1.) He is given *for a light to the Gentiles,* not only to reveal to them what they were concerned to know, and which otherwise they could not have known, but to open the blind eyes, that they might know it. By his Spirit in the word he presents the object; by his Spirit in the heart he prepared the organ. When the gospel came light came, a great light, to those that sat in darkness, Mt. 4:16; Jn. 3:19. And St. Paul was sent to the Gentiles *to open their eyes,* Acts 26:18. Christ is the light of the world. (2.) He is sent to proclaim liberty to the captives, as Cyrus did, *to bring out the prisoners;* not only to open the prison-doors, and give them leave to go out, which was all that Cyrus could do, but to bring them out, to induce and enable them to make use of their liberty, which none did but those whose spirits God stirred up. This Christ does by his grace.

II. The ratification and confirmation of this grant. That we may be assured of the validity of it consider, 1. The authority of him that makes the promise (*v.* 8): *I am the Lord, Jehovah, that is my name,* and that was the name by which he made himself known when he began to perform the promise made to the patriarchs; whereas, before, he manifested himself by the name of God Almighty, Ex. 6:3. If he is the Lord that gives being and birth to all things, he will give being and birth to this promise. If his name be *Jehovah,* which speaks him God alone, we may be sure his name is *jealous,* and he *will not give his glory to another,* whoever it is that stands in competition with him, especially not to *graven images.* He will send the Messiah to open men's eyes, that so he may turn them from the service of dumb idols to serve the living God, because, though he has long winked at the times of ignorance, he will now maintain his prerogative, and will not give his glory to graven images. He will perform his word because he will not lose the honour of being true to it, nor be ever charged with falsehood by the worshippers of false gods. He will deliver his people from under the power of idolaters because it looks as if he had given his praise to graven images when he gives up his own worshippers to be worshippers of images. 2. The accomplishment of the promises he had formerly made concerning his church, which are proofs of the truth of his word and the kindness he bears to his people (*v.* 9): *"Behold, the former things have come to pass;* hitherto the Lord has helped his church, has supported her under former burdens, relieved her in former staits; and this in performance of the promises made to the fathers. *There has not failed one word,* 1 Ki. 8:56. *And* now *new things do I declare.* Now I will make new promises, which shall as certainly be fulfilled in their season as old ones were; now I will bestow new favours, such as have not been conferred formerly. Old-Testament blessings you have had abundantly; now I declare New-Testament blessings, not a fruitful country and dominion over your neighbours, but *spiritual blessings in heavenly things. Before they spring forth* in the preaching of the gospel *I tell you of them,* under the type and figure of the former things." Note, The receipt of former mercies may encourage us to hope for further mercies; for God is constant in his care for his people, and his compassions are still new.

III. The song of joy and praise which should be sung hereupon to the glory of God (*v.* 10): *Sing unto the Lord a new song,* a New-Testament song. The giving of Christ for *a light to the Gentiles* (*v.* 6) was a new thing, and very surprising. The apostle speaks of it as a mystery which, in other ages, was not made known, as it is now revealed, *that the Gentiles should be fellow-heirs,* Eph. 3:5, 6. Now, this being the new thing which God declares, the newness of the song which is to be sung on this occasion is this, that whereas, before, the songs of the Lord were very much confined to the temple at Jerusalem (David's psalms were in the language of the Jews only, and sung by them in their own country only; for, when they were in a strange land, they hung their harps on the willow-trees and could not sing the Lord's song, as we find, Ps. 137:2–4), now the songs of holy joy and praise shall be sung all the world over. The Gentile nations shall share equally with the Jews in New-Testament blessings, and therefore shall join in New-Testament praises and acts of worship. There shall be churches set up in Gentile nations and they shall sing a new song. The conversion of the Gentiles is often foretold under this notion, as appears, Rom. 15:9–11. It is here promised that the praises of God's grace shall be sung with joy and thankfulness, 1. By those that live in *the end of the earth,* in countries that lie most remote from Jerusalem. *From the uttermost parts of the earth have we heard songs, ch.* 24:16. This was fulfilled when Christianity was planted in our land. 2. By mariners and merchants, and those that *go down to the sea,* that do business in great waters, and suck the riches of the sea, and so make themselves masters of the fulness thereof and all that is therein, with which they shall praise God, and justly, for it is his, Ps. 24:1; 95:5. The Jews traded little at sea; if therefore God's praises be sung by those that go down to the sea, it must be by Gentiles. Sea-faring men are called upon to praise God, Ps. 107:23. 3. By *the islands and the inhabitants thereof, v.* 10, and again. *v.* 12. Let them *declare his praise in the islands,* the isles of the Gentiles, probably referring to the islands of Greece. 4. *By the wilderness and the cities thereof, and the villages of Kedar.* These lay east from Jerusalem, as the islands lay west, so that the gospel songs should be sung from the rising of the sun to the going down of the same. The whole Gentile world had been like an island, cut off from communication with God's church, and like a wilderness, uncultivated and bringing forth no fruit to God; but now the islands and the wilderness shall praise God. 5. By *the inhabitants of the rock,* and those that dwell *on the tops of the mountains,* not only the Gentiles, but the poorest and meanest and most despicable, those that dwell in cottages, as well as those that inhabit cities and villages. The rude and most barbarous, as the mountaineers commonly are, shall be civilized by the gospel. Or by the inhabitants of the rock may be meant the inhabitants of that part of Arabia which is called *Petraea — the rocky.* Perhaps the neighbouring countries shared in the joy of the Israelites when they returned out of Babylon and some of them came and joined with them in their praises; but we find not that it was to any such degree as might fully answer this illustrious prophecy, and must conclude that it reaches further, and was fulfilled in that which many other prophecies of the joy of the nations are said in the New-Testament to be fulfilled in, the conversion of the Gentiles to the faith of Christ. When they are brought into the church they are brought to give glory to the Lord; then they are to him for a name and a praise, and they make it their business to praise him. He is glorified in them and by them.

Verses 13–17

It comes all to one whether we make these verses (as some do) the song itself that is to be sung by the Gentile world or a prophecy of what God will do to make way for the singing of that song, that evangelical new song.

I. He will appear in his power and glory more than ever. So he did in the preaching of his gospel, in the divine power and energy which went along with it, and in the wonderful success it had in the *pulling down of Satan's stronghold, v.* 13, 14. *He had long held his peace, and been still, and refrained himself, while he winked at the times of the ignorance of the Gentile world* (Acts 17:30), and *suffered all nations to walk in their own ways* (Acts 14:16); but now *he shall go forth as a mighty man, as a man of war,* to attack the devil's kingdom and give it a fatal blow. The going forth of the gospel is thus represented, Rev. 6:2. Christ, in it, went forth conquering and to conquer. The ministry of the apostles is called their *warfare;* and they were the soldiers of Jesus Christ. *He shall stir up jealousy,* shall appear more jealous than ever for the glory of his own name and against idolatry. 1. *He shall cry,* in the preaching of his word, *cry like a travailing woman;* for the ministers of Christ preached as men in earnest, and that travailed in birth again till they saw Christ formed in the souls of the people, Gal. 4:19. *He shall cry, yea, roar,* in the gospel woes, which are more terrible than the roaring of a lion, and which must be preached along with gospel blessings to awaken a sleeping world. 2. He shall conquer by the power of his Spirit: *He shall prevail against his enemies,* shall prevail to make them friends, Col. 1:21. Those that contradict and blaspheme his gospel, he shall prevail to put them to silence and shame. He will destroy and devour at once all the oppositions of the powers of darkness. Satan shall fall as lightning from heaven, and he that had the power of death shall be destroyed. As a type and figure of this, to make way for the redemption of the Jews out of Babylon, God will humble the pride, and break the power, of their oppressors, and *will at once destroy and devour* the Babylonian monarchy. In accomplishing this destruction of Babylon by the Persian army under the command of Cyrus, *he will make waste mountains and hills,* level the country, and *dry up all their herbs.* The army, as usual, shall either carry off the forage or destroy it, and by laying bridges of boats over rivers shall turn them into islands, and so drain the fens and low grounds, to make way for the march of their army, that the pools shall be dried up. Thus, when the gospel shall be preached, it shall have a free course, and that which hinders the progress of it shall be taken out of the way.

II. He will manifest his favour and grace towards those whose spirits he had stirred up to follow him, as Ezra 1:5. Those who ask the way to Zion he will show the way, and lead in it, *v.* 16. Those who by nature were blind, and those who, being under convictions of sin and wrath are quite at a loss and know not what to do with themselves, God will *lead by a way that they knew not,* will show them the way to life and happiness by Jesus Christ, who is the way, and will conduct and carry them on in that way, which before they were strangers to. Thus, in the conversion of Paul, he was struck blind first, and then God revealed his Son in him, and made the scales to fall from his eyes. They are weak in knowledge, and the truths of God at first seem unintelligible; but God will *make darkness light before them,* and knowledge shall be easy to them. They are weak in duty, the commands of God seem impracticable, and insuperable difficulties are in the way of their obedience; but God will make *crooked things straight;* their way shall be plain, and the yoke easy. Those whom God brings into the right way he will guide in it. As a type of this, he will lead the Jews, when they return out of captivity, in a ready road to their own land again, and nothing shall occur to perplex or embarrass them in their journey. These are great things, and kind things, very great and very kind; but lest any should say, "They are too great, too kind, to be expected from God by such an undeserving people as that of the Jews, such an undeserving world as that of the Gentiles," he adds, *These things will I do unto them,* take my word for it I will, and *I will not forsake them;* he that begins to show this great mercy will go on to do them good.

III. He will particularly put those to confusion who adhere to idols notwithstanding the attempts made by the preaching of the gospel to turn them from idols (*v.* 17): *They shall be turned back, and greatly ashamed, that trust in graven images.* The Babylonians shall when they see how the Jews, who despise their images, are owned and delivered by the God they worship without images, and the Gentiles when they see how idolatry falls before the preaching of the gospel, is scattered like darkness before the light of the sun, and melts like snow before its heat. They shall be ashamed that ever they said to these molten images, *You are our gods;* for how can those help their worshippers who cannot help themselves, nor save themselves from falling into contempt? In times of reformation, when many turn from iniquity, and sin, being generally deserted, becomes unfashionable, it may be hoped that those who will not otherwise be reclaimed will be wrought upon by that consideration to be ashamed of it.

Verses 18–25

The prophet, having spoken by way of comfort and encouragement to the believing Jews who waited for the consolation of Israel, here turns to those among them who were unbelieving, for their conviction and humiliation. Among those who were in captivity in Babylon there were some who were as the evil figs in Jeremiah's vision, who were sent thither *for their hurt, to be removed into all the kingdoms of the earth, for a reproach and a proverb,* Jer. 24:9. In them there was a type of the Jews who rejected Christ and were rejected by him, and then fell more than ever under the curse, when those who believed were inheriting the blessing; for they were broken, and ruined, and remain dispersed unto this day. Observe,

I. The call that is given to this people (*v.* 18): *"Hear, you deaf,* and attend to the joyful sound, *and look you blind, that you may see* the joyful light." There is no absurdity in this command, nor is it unbecoming the wisdom and goodness of God to call us to do that good which yet of ourselves we are not sufficient for; for those have natural powers which they may employ so as to do better than they do, and may have supernatural grace if it be not their own fault, who yet labour under a moral impotency to that which is good. This call to the deaf to hear and the blind to see is like the command given to the man that had the withered hand to stretch it forth; though he could not do this, because it was withered, yet, if he had not attempted to do it, he would not have been healed, and his being healed thereupon was owing, not to his act, but to the divine power.

II. The character that is given of them (*v.* 19, 20): *Who is blind, but my servant, or deaf as my messenger?* The people of the Jews were in profession God's servants, and their priests and elders his messengers (Mal. 2:7); but they were deaf and blind. The verse before may be understood as spoken to the Gentile idolaters, whom he calls *deaf* and *blind,* because they worshipped gods that were so. "But," says he, "no wonder you are deaf and blind when my own people are as bad as you, and many of them as much set upon idolatry."

1. He complains of their sottishness — they are blind; and of their stubbornness — they are deaf. They were even worse than the Gentiles themselves. *Corruptio optimi est pessima — What is best becomes, when corrupted, the worst.* "Who is so wilfully, so scandalously, blind and deaf as my servant and my messenger, as Jacob who is my servant (*ch.* 41:8), and as their prophets and teachers who are my messengers? Who is blind as he that in profession and pretension is perfect, that should come nearer to perfection than other people, their priests and prophets? The one prophesies falsely, and the other bears rule by their means; and who so blind as those that will not see when they have the light shining in their faces?" Note, (1.) It is a common thing, but a very sad thing, for those that in profession are God's servants and messengers to be themselves blind and deaf in spiritual things, ignorant, erroneous, and very careless. (2.) Blindness and deafness in spiritual things are worse in those that profess themselves to be God's servants and messengers than in others. It is in them the greater sin and shame, the greater dishonour to God, and to themselves a greater damnation.

2. The prophet goes on (*v.* 20) to describe the blindness and obstinacy of the Jewish nation, just as our Saviour describes it in his time (Mt. 13:14, 15): *Seeing many things, but thou observest not.* Multitudes are ruined for want of observing that which they cannot but see; they perish, not through ignorance, but mere carelessness. The Jews in our Saviour's time saw many proofs of his divine mission, but they did not observe them; they seemed to open their ears to him, but they did not hear, that is, they did not heed, did not understand, or believe, or obey, and then it was all one as if they had not heard.

III. The care God will take of the honour of his own name, notwithstanding their blindness and deafness, especially of his word, which he has magnified above all his name. *Shall the unbelief and obstinacy of men make the promise of God of no effect? God forbid,* Rom. 3:3, 4. No, though they are blind and deaf, God will be no loser in his glory (*v.* 21): *The Lord is well pleased for his righteousness' sake;* not well pleased with their sin, but well pleased in the manifestation of his own righteousness, in rejecting them for rejecting the great salvation. He speaks as one well pleased, *ch.* 1:24: *Ah! I will ease me of my adversaries;* and Eze. 5:13, *I will be comforted.* The scripture was fulfilled in the casting off of the Jews as well as in the calling in of the Gentiles, and therein the Lord will be well pleased. *He will magnify the law* (divine revelation in all the parts of it) *and will make it honourable.* The law is truly honourable, and the things of it are great things; and, if men will not magnify it by their obedience to it, God will magnify it himself by punishing them for their disobedience. He will magnify the law by accomplishing what is written in it, will magnify its authority, its efficacy, its equity. He will do it at last, when all men shall be judged by the law of liberty, James 2:12. He is doing it every day. What is it that God is doing in the world, but magnifying the law and making it honourable?

IV. The calamities God will bring upon the Jewish nation for their wilful blindness and deafness, *v.* 22. They are *robbed and spoiled.* Those that were impenitent and unreformed in Babylon were sentenced to perpetual captivity. It was for their sins that they were spoiled of all their possessions, not only in their own land, but in the land of their enemies. They were some of them *snared in holes,* and others *hidden in prison-houses.* They cannot help themselves, for they are snared. Their friends cannot help them, for they are hidden; and their enemies have forgotten them in their prisons. They, and all they have, are for a prey and for a spoil; and there is none that delivers either by force or ransom, nor any that dares say to the proud oppressors, *Restore.* There they lie, and there they are likely to lie. This had its full accomplishment in the final destruction of the Jewish nation by the Romans, which God brought upon them for rejecting the gospel of Christ.

V. The counsel given them in order to their relief; for, though their case be sad, it is not desperate.

1. The generality of them are deaf; they will not hearken to the voice of God's word. He will therefore try his rod, and see *who among them will give ear to that, v.* 23. We must not despair concerning those who have been long reasoned with in vain; some of them may, at length, give ear and hearken. If one method not take effect, another may, and sinners shall be left inexcusable. Observe, (1.) We may all of us, if we will, hear the voice of God, and we are called and invited to hear it. (2.) It is worth while to enquire who they are that perceive God speaking to them and are willing to hear him. (3.) Of the many that hear the voice of God there are very few that hearken to it or heed it, that hear it with attention and application. (4.) In hearing the word we must have an eye to the time to come. We must hear for hereafter, for what may occur between us and the grave; we must especially hear for eternity. We must hear the word with another world in our eye.

2. The counsel is, (1.) To acknowledge the hand of God in their afflictions, and, whoever were the instruments, to have an eye to him as the principal agent (*v.* 24): *"Who gave Jacob and Israel,* that people that used to have such an interest in heaven and such a dominion on earth, who gave them *for a spoil to the robbers,* as they are now to the Babylonians and to the Romans? *Did not the Lord?* You know he did; consider it then, and hear his voice in these judgments." (2.) To acknowledge that they had provoked God thus to abandon them, and had brought all these calamities upon themselves. [1.] These punishments were first inflicted on them for their disobedience to the laws of God: It is he *against whom we have sinned;* the prophet puts himself into the number of the sinners, As Dan. 9:7, 8. *"We have sinned;* we have all brought fuel to the fire; and there are those among us that have wilfully refused to walk in his ways." Jacob and Israel would never have been given up to the robbers if they had not by their iniquities sold themselves. *Therefore* it is, because they have violated the commands of the law, that God has brought upon them the curses of the law; he has not dropped, but *poured upon him the fury of his anger and the strength of battle,* all the desolations of war, which have *set him on fire round about;* for God surrounds the wicked with his favours. See the power of God's anger; there is no resisting it, no escaping it. See the mischief that sin makes; it provokes God to anger against a people, and so kindles a universal conflagration, sets all on fire. [2.] These judgments were continued upon them for their senselessness and incorrigibleness under the rod of God. The fire of God's wrath kindled upon him, and *he knew it not,* was not aware of it, took no notice of the judgments, at least not of the hand of God in them. Nay, *it burned him,* and, though he could not then but know it and feel it, yet he *laid it not to heart,* was not awakened by the fiery rebukes he was under nor at all affected with them. Those who are not humbled by less judgments must expect greater; for when God judges he will overcome.

CHAPTER 43

The contents of this chapter are much the same with those of the foregoing chapter, looking at the release of the Jews out of their captivity, but looking through that, and beyond that, to the great work of man's redemption by Jesus Christ, and the grace of the gospel, which through him believers partake of. Here are, I. Precious promises made to God's people in their affliction, of his presence with them, for their support under it, and their deliverance out of it (*v.* 1–7). II. A challenge to idols to vie with the omniscience and omnipotence of God (*v.* 8–13). III. Encouragement given to the people of God to hope for their deliverance out of Babylon, from the consideration of what God did for their fathers when he brought them out of Egypt (*v.* 14–21). IV. A method taken to prepare the people for their deliverance, by putting them in mind of their sins, by which they had provoked God to send them into captivity and continue them there, that they might repent and seek to God for pardoning mercy (*v.* 22–28).

Verses 1–7

This chapter has a plain connexion with the close of the foregoing chapter, but a very surprising one. It was there said that Jacob and Israel would not walk in God's ways, and that when he corrected them for their disobedience they were stubborn and laid it not to heart; and now one would think it should have followed that God would utterly abandon and destroy them; but no, the next words are, *But now, fear not, O Jacob! O Israel! I have redeemed thee, and thou art mine.* Though many among them were untractable and incorrigible, yet God would continue his love and care for his people, and the body of that nation should still be reserved for mercy. God's goodness takes occasion from man's badness to appear so much the more illustrious. *Where sin abounded, grace did much more abound* (Rom. 5:20), and mercy *rejoices against judgment,* as having prevailed and carried the day, Jam. 2:13. Now the sun, breaking out thus of a sudden from behind a thick and dark cloud, shines the brighter, and with a pleasing surprise. The expressions of God's favour and good-will to his people here are very high, and speak abundance of comfort to all the spiritual seed of upright Jacob and praying Israel; for *to us is this gospel preached as well as unto those* that were captives in Babylon, Heb. 4:2. Here we have,

I. The grounds of God's care and concern for his people and the interests of his church and kingdom among men. Jacob and Israel, though in a sinful miserable condition, shall be looked after; for, 1. They are God's *workmanship, created by him unto good works,* Eph. 2:10. He has created them and formed them, not only given them a being, but this being, formed them into a people, constituted their government, and incorporated them by the charter of his covenant. The new creature, wherever it is, is of God's forming, and *he will not forsake the work of his own hands.* 2. They are the people of his purchase: he has redeemed them. Out of the land of Egypt he first redeemed them, and out of many another bondage, *in his love, and in his pity* (*ch.* 63:9); much more will he take care of those who are redeemed with the blood of his Son. 3. They are his peculiar people, whom he has distinguished from others, and set apart for himself: he has called them by name, as those he has a particular intimacy with and concern for, and they are his, are appropriated to him and he has a special interest in them. 4. He is their God in covenant (*v.* 3): *I am the Lord thy God,* worshipped by thee and engaged by promise to thee, *the Holy One of Israel,* the God of Israel; for the true God is a holy one, and holiness becomes his house. And upon all these accounts he might justly say, *Fear not* (*v.* 1), and again *v.* 5, *Fear not.* Those that have God for them need not fear who or what can be against them.

II. The former instances of this care. 1. God has purchased them dearly: *I gave Egypt for thy ransom;* for Egypt was quite laid waste by one plague after another, all their first-born were slain and all their men of war drowned; and all this to force a way for Israel's deliverance from them. Egypt shall be sacrificed rather than Israel shall continue in slavery, when the time has come for their release. The Ethiopians had invaded them in Asa's time; but they shall be destroyed rather than Israel shall be disturbed. And if this was reckoned so great a thing, to give Egypt for their ransom, what reason have we to admire God's love to us in giving his own Son to be a *ransom for us!* 1 Jn. 4:10. What are Ethiopia and Seba, all their lives and all their treasures, compared with the blood of Christ? 2. He had prized them accordingly, and they were very dear to him (*v.* 4): *Since thou hast been precious in my sight thou hast been honourable.* Note, True believers are precious in God's sight; they are his jewels, his peculiar treasure (Ex. 19:5); he loves them, his delight is in them, above any people. His church is his vineyard. And this makes God's people truly honourable, and their name great; for men are really what they are in God's eye. When the forces of Sennacherib, that they might be diverted from falling upon Israel, were directed by Providence to fall upon Egypt, Ethiopia, and Seba, then God gave those countries for Israel, and showed how precious his people were in his sight. So some understand it.

III. The further instances God would yet give them of his care and kindness. 1. He would be present with them in their greatest difficulties and dangers (*v.* 2): *"When thou passest* through the waters and the rivers, through the fire and the flame, *I will be with thee,* and that shall be thy security; when dangers are very imminent and threatening, thou shalt be delivered out of them." Did they, in their journey, pass through deep water? They should not perish in them: *"The rivers shall not overflow thee."* Should they by their persecutors be cast into a fiery furnace, for their constant adherence to their God, yet then the flame should not kindle upon them, which was fulfilled in the letter in the wonderful preservation of the three children, Dan. 3. Though they went through fire and water, which would be to them as the *valley of the shadow of death,* yet, while they had God with them, they need fear no evil, they should be borne up, and *brought out into a wealthy place,* Ps. 66:12. 2. He would still, when there was occasion, make all the interests of the children of men give way to the interests of his own children: *"I will give men for thee,* great men, mighty men, and men of war, *and people* (men by wholesale) *for thy life.* Nations shall be sacrificed to thy welfare." All shall be cut off rather than God's Israel shall, so precious are they in his sight. The affairs of the world shall all be ordered and directed so as to be most for the good of the church, 2 Chr. 16:9. 3. Those of them that were scattered and dispersed in other nations should all be gathered in and share in the blessings of the public, *v.* 5–7. Some of the seed of Israel were dispersed into all countries, east, west, north, and south, or into all the parts of the country of Babylon; but those whose spirits God stirred up to go to Jerusalem should be fetched in from all parts; divine grace should reach those that lay most remote, and at the greatest distance from each other; and, when the time should come, nothing should prevent their coming together to return in a body, in answer to that prayer (Ps. 106:47), *Gather us from among the heathen,* and in performance of that promise (Deu. 30:4), *If any of thine be driven to the utmost parts of heaven, thence will the Lord thy God gather thee,* which we find pleaded on behalf of the children of the captivity, Neh. 1:9. But who are the seed of Israel that shall be thus carefully gathered in? He tells us (*v.* 7) they are such as God has marked for mercy; for, (1.) They are called by his name; they make profession of religion, and are distinguished from the rest of the world by their covenant-relation to God and denomination from him. (2.) They are created for his glory; the spirit of Israelites is created in them, and they are formed according to the will of God, and these shall be gathered in. Note, Those only are fit to be called by the name of God that are created by his grace for his glory; and those whom God has created and called shall be gathered in now to Christ as their head and hereafter to heaven as their home. *He shall gather in his elect from the four winds.* This promise points at the gathering in of the dispersed of the Gentiles, and the strangers scattered, by the gospel of Christ, who died to *gather together in one* the children of God that were scattered abroad; for the promise was to all that were afar off, even as many as the Lord our God shall call and create. God is with the church, and therefore let her not fear; none that belong to her shall be lost.

Verses 8–13

God here challenges the worshippers of idols to produce such proofs of the divinity of their false gods as even this very instance (to go no further) of the redemption of the Jews out of Babylon furnished the people of Israel with, to prove that their God is the true and living God, and he only.

I. The patrons of idolatry are here called to appear, and say what they have to say in defence of their idols, *v.* 8, 9. Their gods have *eyes and see not, ears and hear not,* and those that make them and trust in them are like unto them; so David had said (Ps. 115:8), to which the prophet seems here to refer when he calls idolaters *blind people that have eyes, and deaf people that have ears.* They have the shape, capacities, and faculties, of men; but they are, in effect, destitute of reason and common sense, or they would never worship gods of their own making. *"Let all the nations therefore be gathered together,* let them help one another, and with a combined force plead the cause of their dunghill gods; and, if they have nothing to say in their own justification, let them hear what the God of Israel has to say for their conviction and confutation."

II. God's witnesses are subpoenaed, or summoned to appear, and give in evidence for him (*v.* 10): *"You, O Israelites!* all you that are *called by my name,* you *are all my witnesses, and so is my servant whom I have chosen."* It was Christ himself that was so described (*ch.* 42:1), *My servant and my elect.* Observe,

1. All the prophets that testified to Christ, and Christ himself, the great prophet, are here appealed to as God's witnesses. (1.) God's people are witnesses for him, and can attest, upon their own knowledge and experience, concerning the power of his grace, the sweetness of his comforts, the tenderness of his providence, and the truth of his promise. They will be forward to witness for him that he is gracious and that no word of his has fallen to the ground. (2.) His prophets are in a particular manner witnesses for him, with whom his secret is, and who know more of him than others do. But the Messiah especially is given to be a witness for him to the people; having lain in his bosom from eternity, he has declared him. Now,

2. Let us see what the point is which these witnesses are called to prove (*v.* 12): *You are my witnesses, saith the Lord, that I am God.* Note, Those who do themselves acknowledge that the Lord is God should be ready to testify what they know of him to others, that they also may be brought to the acknowledgement of it. *I believed, therefore have I spoken.* Particularly, "Since you cannot but know, and believe, and understand, you must be ready to bear record, (1.) That I am he, the only true God, that I am a being self-existent and self-sufficient; I am he whom you are to fear, and worship, and trust in. Nay (*v.* 13), *before the day was* (before the first day of time, before the creation of the light, and, consequently, from eternity) *I am he."* The idols were but of yesterday, *new gods that came newly up* (Deu. 32:17); but the God of Israel was from everlasting. (2.) That *there was no God formed before me, nor shall be after me.* The idols were gods formed (*dii facti — made gods,* or rather *fictitii — fictitious*); *by nature they were no gods,* Gal. 4:8. But God has a being from eternity, yea, and a religion in this world before there were either idols or idolaters (truth is more ancient than error); and he will have a being to eternity, and will be worshipped and glorified when idols are famished and abolished and idolatry shall be no more. True religion will keep its ground, and survive all opposition and competition. *Great is the truth, and will prevail.* (3.) That *I, even I, am the Lord,* the great Jehovah, who is, and was, and is to come; and *besides me there is no Saviour, v.* 11. See what it is that the great God glories in, not so much that he is the only ruler as that he is the only Saviour; for he *delights to do good:* he is the *Saviour of all men,* 1 Tim. 4:10.

3. Let us see what the proofs are which are produced for the confirmation of this point. It appears,

(1.) That the Lord is God, by two proofs: [1.] He has an infinite and infallible knowledge, as is evident from *the predictions of his word* (*v.* 12): *"I have declared and I have shown* that which has without fail come to pass; nay, I never declared nor showed any thing but it has been accomplished. *I showed when there was no strange god among you,* that is, when you pretended not to consult any oracles but mine, nor to have any prophets but mine." It is said, when they came out of Egypt, that *the Lord alone did lead him, and there was no strange god with him.* [2.] He has an infinite and irresistible power, as is evident from the performances of his providence. He pleads not only, I have *shown,* but, I have *saved,* not only foretold what none else could foresee, but done what none else could do; for (*v.* 13), *"None can deliver out of my hand* those whom I will punish; not only no man can, but none of all the gods of the heathen can protect." It is therefore a *fearful thing to fall into the hands of the living God,* because there is no getting out of them again. "I will work what I have designed, both in mercy and judgment, and who shall either oppose or retard it?"

(2.) That the gods of the heathen, who are rivals with him, are not only inferior to him, but no gods at all, which is proved (*v.* 9) by a challenge: *Who among them can declare this* that I now declare? Who can foretel things to come? Nay, which of them can *show us former things? ch.* 41:22. They cannot so much as inspire an historian, much less a prophet. They are challenged to join issue upon this: *Let them bring forth their witnesses,* to prove their omniscience and omnipotence. And, [1.] If they do prove them, they shall be justified, the idols in demanding homage and the idolaters in paying it. [2.] If they do not prove them, *let them say, It is truth;* let them own the true God, and receive the truth concerning him, that he is God alone. The cause of God is not afraid to stand a fair trial; but it may reasonably be expected that those who cannot justify themselves in their irreligion should submit to the power of the truth and true religion.

Verses 14–21

To so low an ebb were the faith and hope of God's people in Babylon brought that there needed line upon line to assure them that they should be released out of their captivity; and therefore, that they might have strong consolation, the assurances of it are often repeated, and here very expressly and encouragingly.

I. God here takes to himself such titles of his honour as were very encouraging to them. He is *the Lord their Redeemer,* not only he will redeem them, but will take it upon him as his office and make it his business to do so. If he be their God, he will be all that to them which they need, and therefore, when they are in bondage, he will be their Redeemer. He is the *Holy One of Israel* (*v.* 14), and again (*v.* 15), *their Holy One,* and therefore will make good every word he has spoken to them. He is *the Creator of Israel,* that made them a people out of nothing (for that is creation), nay, worse than nothing; and he is their *King,* that owns them as his people and presides among them.

II. He assures them he will find out a way to break the power of their oppressors that held them captives and filled up the measure of their own iniquity by their resolution never to let them go, *ch.* 14:17. God will take care to send a victorious prince and army to Babylon, that shall *bring down all their nobles,* and lay their honour in the dust, and all their people too, even *the Chaldeans, whose cry is in the ships* (for seamen are apt to be noisy), or whose cry is *to the ships,* as their refuge when the city is taken, that they may escape by the benefit of their great river. Note, The destruction of Babylon must make way for the enlargement of God's people. And in the prediction of the fall of the New-Testament Babylon we meet with the cries and lamentations of the sailors, Rev. 18:17, 18. And observe, It is for Israel's sake that Babylon is ruined, to make way for their deliverance.

III. He reminds them of the great things he did for their fathers when he brought them out of the land of Egypt; for so it may be read (*v.* 16, 17): *"Thus saith the Lord, who did make a way in the sea,* the Red Sea, and did *bring forth* Pharaoh's *chariot and horse,* that they might lie down together in the bottom of the sea, and never rise, but be extinct. He that did this can, if he please, make a way for you in the sea when you return out of Babylon, and will do so rather than leave you there." Note, For the encouragement of our faith and hope, it is good for us often to remember what God has done formerly for his people against his and their enemies. Think particularly what he did at the Red Sea, how he made it, 1. A road to his people, a straight way, a near way, nay, a refuge to them, into which they fled and were safe the waters being a wall unto them. 2. A grave to his enemies. The chariot and horse were drawn out by him who is Lord of all hosts, on purpose that they might fall together; howbeit, *they meant not so,* Mic. 4:11, 12.

IV. He promises to do yet greater things for them than he had done in the days of old; so that they should not have reason to ask, in a way of complaint, as Gideon did, *Where are all the wonders that our fathers told us of?* for they should see them repeated, nay, they should see them outdone (*v.* 18): *"Remember not the former things,* from them to take occasion, as some do, to undervalue the present things, as if *the former days were better than these;* no, you may, if you will, comparatively forget them, and yet know enough by the events of your own day to convince you that the Lord is God alone; for, *behold, the Lord will do a new thing,* no way inferior, both for the wonder and the worth of the mercy, to the things of old." The best exposition of this is, Jer. 16:14, 15; 23:7, 8. *It shall no more be said, The Lord liveth that brought up the children of Israel out of the land of Egypt;* that is an old thing, the remembrance of which will be in a manner lost in the new thing, in the new proof that the Lord liveth, for he *brought up the children of Israel out of the land of the north.* Though former mercies must not be forgotten, fresh mercies must in a special manner be improved. *Now it springs forth,* as it were a surprise upon you; you are like those that dream. *Shall you now know it?* And will you not own God's hand in it?

V. He promises not only to deliver them out of Babylon, but to conduct them safely and comfortably to their own land (*v.* 19, 20): *I will make a way in the wilderness and rivers in the desert;* for, it seems, the way from Babylon to Canaan, as well as from Egypt, lay through a desert land, which, while the returning captives passed through, God would provide for them, that their camp should be both well victualled and under a good conduct. The same power that made *a way in the sea* (*v.* 16) can make *a way in the wilderness,* and will force its passage through the greatest difficulties. And he that made dry land in the waters can produce waters in the dryest land, in such abundance as not only to *give drink to his people, his chosen,* but to the *beasts of the field,* also *the dragons and the ostriches,* who are therefore said to honour God for it; it is such a sensible refreshment, and yields them so much satisfaction, that, if they were capable of doing it, they would praise God for it, and shame man, who is made capable of praising his benefactor and does not. Now, 1. This looks back to what God did for Israel when he led them through the wilderness from Egypt to Canaan, and fetched water out of a rock to follow them; what God did for them formerly he would do again, for he is still the same. And, though we do not find that the miracle was repeated in their return out of Babylon, yet the mercy was, in the common course of Providence, for which it became them to be no less thankful to God. 2. It looks forward, not only to all the instances of God's care of the Jewish church in the latter ages of it, between their return from Babylon and the coming of Christ, but to the grace of the gospel, especially as it is manifested to the Gentile world, by which a way is opened in the wilderness and rivers in the desert; the world, which lay like a desert, in ignorance and unfruitfulness, was blessed with divine direction and divine comforts, and, in order to both, with a plentiful effusion of the Spirit. The sinners of the Gentiles, who had been as the beasts of the field, running wild, fierce as the dragons, stupid as the owls or ostriches, shall be brought to honour God for the extent of his grace to his chosen among them.

VI. He traces up all these promised blessings to their great original, the purposes and designs of his own glory (*v.* 21): *This people have I formed for myself,* and therefore I do all this for them, that they may *show forth my praise.* Note, 1. The church is of God's forming, and so are all the living members of it. The new heaven, the new earth, the new man, are the work of God's hand, and are no more, no better, than he makes them; they are fashioned according to his will. 2. He forms it for himself. He that is the first cause is the highest end both of the first and of the new creation. *The Lord has made all things for himself,* his Israel especially, to be to him for *a people, and for a name, and for a praise;* and no otherwise can they be for him, or serviceable to him, than as his grace is glorified in them, Jer. 13:11; Eph. 1:6, 12, 14. 3. It is therefore our duty to show forth his praise, not only with our lips, but in our lives, by giving up ourselves to his service. As he formed us, so he feeds us, and keeps us, and leads us, and all for himself; for every instance therefore of his goodness we must praise him, else we answer not the end of the beings and blessings we have.

Verses 22–28

This charge (and a high charge it is which is here exhibited against Jacob and Israel, God's professing people) comes in here, 1. To clear God's justice in bringing them into captivity, and to vindicate that. Were they not in covenant with him? Had they not his sanctuary among them? *Why then did the Lord deal thus with his land?* Deu. 29:24. Here is a good reason given: they had neglected God and had cast him off, and therefore he justly rejected them and *gave them to the curse* (*v.* 28); and they must be brought to own this before they are prepared for deliverance; and they did so, Dan. 9:5; Neh. 9:33. 2. To advance God's mercy in their deliverance and to make that appear more glorious. Many things are before observed to magnify the power of God in it; but this magnifies his goodness, that he should do such great and kind things for a people that had been so very provoking to him and were now suffering the just punishment of their iniquity. The pardoning of their sin was as great an instance of God's power (for so Moses reckons it, Num. 14:17, etc.) as the breaking of the yoke of their captivity. Now observe here,

I. What the sins are which they are here charged with.

1. Omissions of the good which God had commanded; and this part of the charge is here much insisted upon. Observe how it comes in with a *but;* compare *v.* 21, where God tells them what favours he had bestowed upon them and what his just expectations were from them. He had formed them for himself, intending they should show forth his praise. But they had not done so; they had frustrated God's expectations from them, and made very ill returns to him for his favours. For, (1.) They had cast off prayer: *Thou hast not called upon me, O Jacob!* Jacob was a man famous for prayer (Hosea 12:4); his seed bore his name, but did not tread in his steps, and therefore are justly upbraided with it. God takes it ill when children degenerate from the virtue and devotion of their pious ancestors. To boast of the name of Jacob, and yet live without prayer, is to mock God and deceive ourselves. If Jacob does not call upon God, who will? (2.) They had grown weary of their religion: "Thou art Israel, the seed not only of a praying but of a prevailing father, that was a prince with God; and yet, not valuing his experiences any more than his example, *thou hast been weary of me."* They had been in relation to God, employed in his service and in communion with him; but they began to snuff at it, and to say, *Behold, what a weariness is it!* Note, Those who neglect to call upon God do in effect tell him they are weary of him and have a mind to change their Master. (3.) They grudged the expense of their devotion, and were niggardly and penurious in it. They were for a cheap religion; and in those acts of devotion that were costly they desired to be excused. They had *not brought,* no, not their *small cattle,* the lambs and kids, which God required for *burnt-offerings* (*v.* 23), much less did they bring their greater cattle, pretending they could not spare them, they must have them for the maintenance of their families. So little sense had they of the greatness of God and their obligations to him that they could not find in their hearts to part with a lamb out of their flock for his honour, though he called for it and would graciously have accepted it. *Sweet cane,* or *calamus,* was used for the holy oil, incense, and perfume; but they were not willing to be at the charge of that, *v.* 24. What they had must serve, though it was old and good for nothing; they would not buy fresh. Perhaps it was usual for devout pious persons to bring free-will incense as well as other free-will offerings; but they were not so generous, nor did they fill the altar of God, nor moisten it abundantly, as they should have done, *with the fat of their sacrifices;* what sacrifices they did bring were of the lean and refuse of their cattle, that had no fat in them to regale the altar with. (4.) What sacrifices they did offer they did not honour God with them, and so they were, in effect, as no sacrifices (*v.* 23): *Neither hast thou honoured me with thy sacrifices.* Some of them offered their sacrifices to false gods; others, who offered them to the true God, were either careless in the manner of offering them or hypocritical in their intentions, so that they might be truly said not to honour God with them, but rather to dishonour him. (5.) That which aggravated their neglect of sacrificing was that, as God had appointed it, it was no burdensome thing; it was not a service that they had any reason at all to complain of: *"I have not caused thee to serve with an offering;* I have not made it a task and drudgery to you, whatever you, through the corruption of your natures, have made it yourselves. I have *not wearied thee with incense."* None of God's commandments are grievous, no, not those concerning sacrifice and incense. They were not more costly than might be afforded by those that lived in such a plentiful country, nor did their attendance on them require any more time than they could well spare. But that which especially forbade them to call it *a wearisome service* was that they were required to be cheerful and pleasant, and to rejoice before God in all their approaches to him, Deu. 12:12. They had many feasts and good days, but only one day in all the year in which they were to afflict their souls. The ordinances of the ceremonial law, though, in comparison with Christ's easy yoke, they are spoken of as heavy (Acts 15:10), yet, in comparison with the service that idolaters did to their false gods, they were light, and not to be called *services* nor found fault with as wearisome. God did not require them to sacrifice their children, as Moloch did.

2. Commissions of the evil which God had forbidden; and omissions commonly make way for commissions: *Thou hast made me to serve with thy sins.* When we make God's gifts the food and fuel for our lusts, and his providence the patron of our wicked projects, especially when we encourage ourselves to continue in sin because grace has abounded, then we make God to serve with our sins. Or it may denote what a grief and burden sin is to God; it not only wearies men and makes the creation groan, but it *wearies my God also* (*ch.* 7:13) and makes the Creator complain that he is *grieved* (Ps. 95:10), that he is *broken* (Eze. 6:9), that he is pressed with sinners *as a cart is pressed that is full of sheaves* (Amos 2:13), and to cry out, *Ah! I will ease me of my adversaries, ch.* 1:24. The antithesis is observable: God had not made them to serve with their sacrifices, but they had made him to serve with their sins. The master had not tired the servants with his commands, but they had tired him with their disobedience. Those are wicked servants indeed that behave so ill to so good a Master. God is tender of our comfort, but we are careless of his honour. Let *this* engage us to keep close

to our duty, that it is easy and reasonable, and no disparagement to us, nor too hard for us.

II. What were the aggravations of their sin, *v.* 27. 1. That they were children of disobedience; for their *first father* (that is, their forefathers) *had sinned;* and they had not only sinned in their loins, but sinned like them. Ezra confesses this: *Since the days of our fathers have we been in a great trespass, ch.* 9:7. But their forefathers are called their *first father* to put us in mind of the apostasy and rebellion of our first father Adam, to which corrupt fountain we must trace up the streams of all our transgressions. 2. That they were scholars of disobedience too: for *their teachers had transgressed against God,* were guilty of gross scandalous sins, and the people, no doubt, would learn to do as they did. It is ill with a people when their leaders cause them to err, and their teachers, who should reform them, corrupt them.

III. What were the tokens of God's displeasure against them for their sins, *v.* 23. He brought ruin both upon church and state. 1. The honour of their church was laid in the dust and trampled on: *I have profaned the princes of the sanctuary,* that is, the priests and Levites who presided with great dignity and power in the temple-service; they profaned themselves, and made themselves vile, by their enormities, and then God profaned them and made them vile, by their calamities and the contempt they fell into, Mal. 2:9. 2. The honour of their state was ruined likewise: *"I have given Jacob to the curse,* that is, to be cursed, and hated, and abused by all their neighbours, *and Israel to reproach,* to be insulted, ridiculed, and triumphed over by their enemies." They reproached them perhaps for that in them that was good; they *mocked at their sabbaths* (Lam. 1:7); but God gave them up to reproach, to correct them for what was amiss. Note, The dishonour which men at any time do us should humble us for the dishonour we have done to God; and we must bear it patiently because we suffer it justly, and must acknowledge that to us belongs confusion.

IV. What were the riches of God's mercy towards them notwithstanding (*v.* 25): *I even I, am he who* notwithstanding all this *blotteth out thy transgressions.*

1. This gracious declaration of God's readiness to pardon sin comes in very strangely. The charge ran very high: *Thou hast wearied me with thy iniquities, v.* 24. Now one would think it would follow: *"I, even I, am he* that will destroy thee, and burden myself no longer with care about thee." No, *I, even I, am he that will forgive thee;* as if the great God would teach us that forgiving injuries is the best way to make ourselves easy and to keep ourselves from being wearied with them. This comes in here to encourage them to repent, because there is forgiveness with God, and to show the freeness of divine mercy; where sin has been exceedingly sinful grace appears exceedingly gracious. Apply this, (1.) To the forgiving of the sins of Israel as a people, in their national capacity. When God stopped the course of threatening judgments, and saved them from utter ruin, even then when he had them under severe rebukes, then he might be said to *blot out their transgressions.* Though he corrected them, he was reconciled to them again, and did not cut them off from being a people. This he did many a time, till they rejected Christ and his gospel, which was a sin against the remedy, and then he would forgive them no more as a nation, but utterly destroyed them. (2.) To the forgiving of the sins of every particular believing penitent — *transgressions and sins,* infirmities though ever so numerous, backslidings though ever so heinous. Observe here, [1.] How the pardon is expressed; he will *blot them out,* as a cloud is blotted out by the beams of the sun (*ch.* 44:22), as a debt is blotted out not to appear against the debtor (the book is crossed as if the debt were paid, because it is pardoned upon the payment which the surety has made), or as a sentence is blotted out when it is reversed, as the curse was blotted out with the waters of jealousy, which made it of no effect to the innocent, Num. 5:23. He *will not remember* the sin, which intimates not only that he will remit the punishment of what is past, but that it shall be no diminution to his love for the future. When God forgives he forgets. [2.] What is the ground and reason of the pardon. It is not for the sake of any thing in us, but for his own sake, for his mercies'sake, his promise-sake, and especially for his Son's sake, and that he may himself be glorified in it. [3.] How God glories in it: *I, even I, am he.* He glories in it as his prerogative. None can forgive sin but God only, and he will do it; it is his settled resolution. He will do it willingly and with delight; it is his pleasure; it is his honour; so he is pleased to reckon it.

2. Those words (*v.* 26), *Put me in remembrance,* may be understood either (1.) As a rebuke to a proud Pharisee, that stands upon his own justification before God, and expects to find favour for his merits and not to be beholden to free grace: "If you have any thing to say in your own justification, any thing to offer for the sake of which you should be pardoned, and not for my sake, put me in remembrance of it. I will give you leave to plead your own cause with me; declare what your merits are, that you may be justified by them:" but those who are thus challenged will be speechless. Or, (2.) As a publican. Is God thus ready to pardon sin, and, when he pardons it, will he remember it no more? Let us then put him in remembrance, mention before him those sins which he has forgiven; for they must be ever before us, to humble us, though they are pardoned, Ps. 51:3. Put him in remembrance of the promises he has made to penitents, and the satisfaction his Son has made for them. Plead these with him in wrestling for pardon, and declare these things, in order that thou mayest be justified freely by his grace. This is the only way, and it is a sure way, to peace. *Only acknowledge thy transgression.*

CHAPTER 44

God, by the prophet, goes on in this chapter, as before, I. To encourage his people with the assurance of great blessings he had in store for them at their return out of captivity, and those typical of much greater which the gospel church, his spiritual Israel, should partake of in the days of the Messiah; and hereby he proves himself to be God alone against all pretenders (*v.* 1–8). II. To expose the sottishness and amazing folly of idol-makers and idol-worshippers (*v.* 9–20). III. To ratify and confirm the assurances he had given to his people of those great blessings, and to raise their joyful and believing expectations of them (*v.* 21–28).

Verses 1–8

Two great truths are abundantly made out in these verses: —

I. That the people of God are a happy people, especially upon account of the covenant that is between them and God. The people of Israel were so as a figure of the gospel Israel. Three things complete their happiness: —

1. The covenant-relations wherein they stand to God, *v.* 1, 2. Israel is here called *Jeshurun — the upright one;* for those only, like Nathanael, are Israelites indeed, in whom is no guile, and those only shall have the everlasting benefit of these promises. Jacob and Israel had been represented, in the close of the foregoing chapter, as very provoking and obnoxious to God's wrath, and already given to the curse and to reproaches; but, as if God's bowels yearned towards him and his repentings were kindled together, mercy steps in with a *non-obstante — notwithstanding,* to all these quarrels: *"Yet now, hear, O Jacob my servant!* thou and I will be friends again for all this." God had said (*ch.* 43:25), *I am he that blotteth out thy transgression,* which is the only thing that creates this distance; and when that is taken away the streams of mercy run again in their former channel. The pardon of sin is the inlet of all the other blessings of the covenant. So and so I will do for them, says God (Heb. 8:12), *for I will be merciful to their unrighteousness.* Therefore *hear, O Jacob!* hear these comfortable words; therefore *fear not, O Jacob!* fear not thy troubles, for by the pardon of sin the property of them too is altered. Now the relations wherein they stand to him are very encouraging. (1.) They are his *servants;* and those that serve him he will own and stand by and see that they be not wronged. (2.) They are his *chosen,* and he will abide by his choice; he knows those that are his, and those whom he has chosen he takes under special protection. (3.) They are his creatures. He *made them,* and brought them into being; he *formed them,* and cast them into shape; he began betimes with them, for he *formed them from the womb;* and therefore he will help them over their difficulties and help them in their services.

2. The covenant-blessings which he has secured to them and theirs, *v.* 3, 4. (1.) Those that are sensible of their spiritual wants, and the insufficiency of the creature to supply them, shall have abundant satisfaction in God: *I will pour water upon him that is thirsty,* that thirsts after righteousness; he shall be filled. Water shall be poured out to those who truly desire spiritual blessings above all the delights of sense. (2.) Those that are barren as the dry ground shall be watered with the grace of God, with floods of that grace, and God will himself give the increase. If the ground be ever so dry, God has floods of grace to water it with. (3.) The water God will pour out is *his Spirit* (Jn. 7:39), which God will pour out without measure upon the seed, that is, Christ (Gal. 3:16), and by measure upon all the seed of the faithful, upon all the praying wrestling seed of Jacob, Lu. 11:13. This is the great New-Testament promise, that God, having sent his servant Christ, and upheld him, will send his Spirit to uphold us. (4.) This gift of the Holy Ghost is the great blessing God had reserved the plentiful effusion of for the latter days: *I will pour my Spirit,* that is, *my blessing;* for where God gives his Spirit he will give all other blessings. (5.) This is reserved for the seed and offspring of the church; for so the covenant of grace runs: *I will be a God to thee and to thy seed.* To all who are thus made to partake of the privileges of adoption God will give the spirit of adoption. (6.) Hereby there shall be a great increase of the church. Thus it shall be spread to distant places. Thus it shall be propagated and perpetuated to after-times: *They shall spring up* and grow as fast *as willows by the watercourses,* and in every thing that is virtuous and praiseworthy shall be eminent and excel all about them, as the willows overtop the grass among which they grow, *v.* 4. Note, It is a great happiness to the church, and a great pleasure to good men, to see the rising generation hopeful and promising. And it will be so if God pour his Spirit upon them, that blessing, that blessing of blessings.

3. The consent they cheerfully give to their part of the covenant, *v.* 5. When the Jews returned out of captivity they renewed their covenant with God (Jer. 50:5), particularly that they would have no more to do with idols, Hos. 14:2, 3, 8. Backsliders must thus repent and do their first works. Many of those that were without did at that time join themselves to them, invited by that glorious appearance of God for them, Zec. 8:23; Esth. 8:17. And they say, *We are the Lord's* and *call themselves by the name of Jacob;* for there was one law, one covenant, *for the stranger and for those that were born in the land.* And doubtless it looks further yet, to the conversion of the Gentiles, and the multitudes of them who, upon the effusion of the Spirit, after Christ's ascension, should be *joined to the Lord* and *added to the church.* These converts are *one and another,* very many, of different ranks and nations, and all welcome to God, Col. 3:11. When one does it another shall by his example be invited to do it, and then another; thus the zeal of one may provoke many. (1.) They shall resign themselves to God: not one in the name of the rest, but every one for himself shall say, *"I am the Lord's;* he has an incontestable right to rule me, and I submit to him, to all his commands, to all his disposal. I am, and will be, his only, his wholly, his for ever, will be for his interests, will be for his praise; living and dying I will be his." (2.) They shall incorporate themselves with the people of God, *call themselves by the name of Jacob,* forgetting their own people and their fathers' house, and desirous to wear the character and livery of God's family. They shall love all God's people, shall associate with them, give them the right hand of fellowship, espouse their cause, seek the good of the church in general and of all the particular members of it, and be willing to take their lot with them in all conditions. (3.) They shall do this very solemnly. Some of them shall *subscribe with their hand unto the Lord,* as, for the confirming of a bargain, a man sets his hand to it, and delivers it as his act and deed. The more express we are in our covenanting with God the better, Ex. 24:7; Jos. 24:26, 27; Neh. 9:38. Fast bind, fast find.

II. That, as the Israel of God are a happy people, so the God of Israel is a great God, and he is God alone. This also, as the former, speaks abundant satisfaction to all that trust in him, *v.* 6–8. Observe here, to God's glory and our comfort, 1. That the God we trust in is a God of incontestable sovereignty and irresistible power. He is *the Lord,* Jehovah, self-existent and self-sufficient; and he is *the Lord of hosts,* of all the hosts of heaven and earth, of angels and men. 2. That he stands in relation to, and has a particular concern for, his church. He is *the King of Israel and his Redeemer; therefore* his Redeemer because his King; and those that take God for their King shall have him for their

Redeemer. When God would assert himself God alone he proclaims himself Israel's God, that his people may be encouraged both to adhere to him and to triumph in him. 3. That he is eternal — *the first and the last.* He is God from everlasting, before the worlds were, and will be so to everlasting, when the world shall be no more. If there were not a God to create, nothing would ever have been; and, if there were not a God to uphold, all would soon come to nothing again. He is all in all, is the first cause, from whom are all things, and the last end, to and for whom are all things (Rom. 11:36), the *Alpha and the Omega,* Rev. 1:11. 4. That he is God alone (*v.* 6): *Besides me there is no God. Is there a God besides me? v.* 8. We will appeal to the greatest scholars. Did they ever in all their reading meet with any other? To those that have had the largest acquaintance with the world. Did they ever meet with any other? There are *gods many* (1 Co. 8:5, 6), *called gods,* and counterfeit gods: but is there any besides our God that is infinite and eternal, any besides him that is the creator of the world and the protector and benefactor of the whole creation, any besides him that can do that for their worshippers which he can and will do for his? *"You are my witnesses.* I have been a nonsuch to you. You have tried other gods; have you found any of them all-sufficient to you, or any of them like me? *Yea, there is no god,"* no rock (so the word is), none besides Jehovah that can be a rock for a foundation to build on, a rock for shelter to flee to. God is the rock, and *their rock is not as ours,* Deu. 32:4, 31. *I know not any;* as if he had said, "I never met with any that offered to stand in competition with me, or that durst bring their pretensions to a fair trial; if I did know of any that could befriend you better than I can, I would recommend you to them; but I know not any." There is no God besides Jehovah. He is infinite, and therefore there can be no other; he is all-sufficient, and therefore there needs no other. This is designed for the confirming of the hopes of God's people in the promise of their deliverance out of Babylon, and, in order to that, for the curing of them of their idolatry; when the affliction had done its work it should be removed. They are reminded of the first and great article of their creed, that *the Lord their God is one Lord,* Deu. 6:4. And therefore, (1.) They needed not to hope in any other god. Those on whom the sun shines need neither moon nor stars, nor the light of their own fire. (2.) They needed not to fear any other god. Their own God was more able to do them good than all the false and counterfeit gods of their enemies were to do them hurt. 5. That none besides could foretel these things to come, which God now by his prophet gave notice of to the world, above 200 years before they came to pass (*v.* 7): *"Who, as I, shall call,* shall call Cyrus to Babylon? Is there any but God that can call effectually, and has every creature, every heart, at his beck? Who *shall declare it,* how it shall be, and by whom, as I do?" Nay, God goes further; he not only sees it in order, as having the foreknowledge of it, but *sets it in order,* as having the sole management and direction of it. Can any other pretend to this? He has always set things in order according to the counsel of his own will, ever *since he appointed the ancient people,* the people of Israel, who could give a truer and fuller account of the antiquities of their own nation than any other kingdom in the world could give of theirs. Ever since he appointed that people to be his peculiar people his providence was particularly conversant about them, and he told them beforehand the events that should occur respecting them — their bondage in Egypt, their deliverance from it, and their settlement in Canaan. All was set in order in the divine predictions as well as in the divine purposes. Could any other have done so? Would any other have been so far concerned for them? He challenges the pretenders to show the things that shall come hereafter: "Let them, if they can, tell us the name of the man that shall destroy Babylon ad deliver Israel? Nay, if they cannot pretend to tell us *the things that shall come* hereafter, let them tell us the things that *are coming,* that are nigh at hand and at the door. Let them tell us what shall come to pass tomorrow; but they cannot do that; fear them not therefore, nor be afraid of them. What harm can they do you? What hindrance can they give to your deliverance, when I have told thee it shall be accomplished in its season, and I have solemnly declared it?" Note, Those who have

the word of God's promise to depend upon need not be afraid of any adverse powers or policies whatsoever.

Verses 9–20

Often before, God, by the prophet, had mentioned the folly and strange sottishness of idolaters; but here he enlarges upon that head, and very fully and particularly exposes them to contempt and ridicule. This discourse is intended, 1. To arm the people of Israel against the strong temptation they would be in to worship idols when they were captives in Babylon, in compliance with the custom of the country (they being far from the city of their own solemnities) and to humour those who were now their lords and masters. 2. To cure them of their inclination to idolatry, which was the sin that did most easily beset them and to reform them from which they were sent into Babylon. As the rod of God is of use to enforce the word, so the word of God is of use to explain the rod, that the voice of both together may be heard and answered. 3. To furnish them with something to say to their Chaldean taskmasters. When they insulted over them, when they asked, *Where is your God?* they might hence ask them, *What are your gods?* 4. To take off their fear of the gods of their enemies, and to encourage their hope in their own God that he would certainly appear against those who set up such scandalous competitors as these with him for the throne.

Now here, for the conviction of idolaters, we have,

I. A challenge given to them to clear themselves, if they can, from the imputation of the most shameful folly and senselessness imaginable, *v.* 9–11. They set their wits on work to contrive, and their hands on work to frame, graven images, and they call them *their delectable things;* extremely fond they are of them, and mighty things they expect from them. Note, Through the corruption of men's nature, those things that should be detestable to them are desirable and delectable; but those are far gone in a distemper to whom that which is the food and fuel of it is most agreeable. Now, 1. We tell them that those that do so are all vanity; they deceive themselves and one another, and put a great cheat upon those for whom they make these images. 2. We tell them that *their delectable things shall not profit* them, nor make them any return for the pleasure they take in them; they can neither supply them with good nor protect them from evil. The *graven images* are *profitable for nothing* at all, nor will they ever get any thing by the devoirs they pay to them. 3. We appeal to themselves whether it be not a silly sottish thing to expect any good from gods of their own making: *They are their own witnesses,* witnesses against themselves, if they would but give their own consciences leave to deal faithfully with them, that they are blind and ignorant in doing thus. *They see not nor know,* and let them own it, *that they may be ashamed.* If men would but be true to their own convictions, ordinarily we might be sure of their conversion, particularly idolaters; for *who has formed a god?* Who but a mad-man, or one out of his wits, would think of forming a god, of making that which, if he make it a god, he must suppose to be his maker? 4. We challenge them to plead their own cause with any confidence or assurance. If any one has the front to say that he has formed a god, when all his fellows come together to declare what each of them has done towards the making of this god, they will all be ashamed of the cheat they have put upon themselves, and laugh in their sleeves at those whom they have imposed upon; for *the workmen* that formed this god *are of men,* weak and impotent, and therefore cannot possibly make a being that shall be omnipotent, nor can they without blushing pretend to do so. *Let them all be gathered together,* as Demetrius and the craftsmen were, to support their sinking trade; *let them stand up* to plead their own cause, and make the best they can of it, with hand joined in hand; *yet they shall fear* to undertake it when it comes to the setting to, as conscious to themselves of the weakness and badness of their cause, *and they shall be ashamed* of it, not only when they appear singly, but when by appearing together they hope to keep one another in countenance. Note, Idolatry and impiety are things which men may justly both tremble and blush to appear in the defence of.

II. A particular narrative of the whole proceeding in making a god; and there needs no more to expose it than to describe it and tell the story of it.

1. The persons employed about it are handicraft tradesmen, the meanest of them, the very same that you would employ in making the common utensils of your husbandry, a cart or a plough. You must have a *smith,* a blacksmith, who *with the tongs works in the coals;* and it is hard work, for he *works with the strength of his arms,* till *he is hungry* and his strength fails, so eager is he, and so hasty are those who set him at the work to get it despatched. He cannot allow himself time to eat or drink, for *he drinks no water, and* therefore *is faint, v.* 12. Perhaps it was a piece of superstition among them for the workman not to eat or drink while he was making a god. The plates with which the smith was to cover the image, or whatever iron-work was to be done about it, *he fashioned with hammers,* and made it all very exact, according to the model given him. Then comes *the carpenter,* and he takes as much care and pains about the timber-work, *v.* 13. He brings his box of tools, for he has occasion for them all: *He stretches out his rule* upon the piece of wood, *marks it with a line,* where it must be sawed or cut of; *he fits it,* or polishes it, *with planes,* the greater first and then the less; *he marks out with the compasses* what must be the size and shape of it; and it is just what he pleases.

2. The form in which it is made is that of a man, a poor, weak, dying creature; but it is the noblest form and figure that he is acquainted with, and, being his own, he has a peculiar fondness for it and is willing to put all the reputation he can upon it. He makes it *according to the beauty of a man,* in comely proportion, with those limbs and lineaments that are the beauty of a man, but are altogether unfit to represent the beauty of the Lord. God put a great honour upon man when, in respect of the powers and faculties of his souls, he made him after the image of God; but man does a great dishonour to God when he makes him, in respect of bodily parts and members, after the image of man. Nor will it at all atone for the affront so far to compliment his god as to take the fairest of the children of men for his original whence to take his copy, and to give him all the beauty of a man that he can think of; for all the *beauty of the body of a man,* when pretended to be put upon him who is an infinite Spirit, is a deformity and diminution to him. And, when the goodly piece is finished, it must *remain in the house,* in the temple or shrine prepared for it, or perhaps in the dwelling house if it be one of the *lares* or *penates* — the household gods.

3. The matter of which it is mostly made is sorry stuff to make a god of; it is the stock of a tree.

(1.) The tree itself was fetched out *of the forest,* where it grew among other trees, of no more virtue or value than its neighbours. It was a *cedar,* it may be, or a *cypress,* or an *oak, v.* 14. Perhaps he had an eye upon it some time before for this use, and *strengthened it for himself,* used some art or other to make it stronger and better-grown than other trees were. Or, as some read it, *which hath strengthened or lifted up itself among the trees of the forest,* the tallest and strongest he can pick out. Or, it may be, it pleases his fancy better to take *an ash,* which is of a quicker growth, and which was of his own planting for this use, and which has been nourished with rain from heaven. See what a fallacy he puts upon himself, in making that his refuge which was of his own planting, and which he not only gave the form to, but prepared the matter for; and what an affront he puts upon the God of heaven in setting up that a rival with him which was nourished by his rain, that rain which falls upon the just and unjust.

(2.) The boughs of this tree were good for nothing but for fuel; to that use were they put, and so were the chips that were cut off from it in the working of it; they are *for a man to burn, v.* 15, 16. To show that that tree has no innate virtue in it for its own protection, it is as capable of being burnt as any other tree; and, to show that he who chose it had no more antecedent value for it than for any other tree, he makes no difficulty of throwing part of it into the fire as common rubbish, asking no question for conscience' sake. [1.] It serves him for his parlour-fire: *He will take thereof and warm himself* (*v.* 15), and he finds the comfort of it, and is so far from having any regret in his mind for it that he saith, *Aha! I am warm; I have seen the fire;* and certainly that part of the tree which served him for fuel, the use for which God and nature designed it, does him a much greater kindness and yields him more satisfaction than ever that will which he makes a god of. [2.]

It serves him for his kitchen-fire: *He eats flesh* with it, that is, he dresses the flesh with it which he is to eat; he *roasteth roast, and is satisfied* that he has not done amiss to put it to this use. Nay, [3.] It serves him to heat the oven with, in which we use that fuel which is of least value: *He kindles it and bakes bread* with the heat of it, and none charges him with doing wrong.

(3.) Yet, after all, the stock or body of the tree shall serve to make a god of, when it might as well have served to make a bench, as one of themselves, even a poet of their own, upbraids them, *Horat. Sat.* 1.8:

> Olim truncus eram ficulnus, inutile lignum,
> Quum faber, incertus scamnum faceretne Priapum,
> Maluit esse deum; deus inde ego —
>
> In days of yore our godship stood
> A very worthless log of wood,
> The joiner, doubting or to shape us
> Into a stool or a Priapus,
> At length resolved, for reasons wise,
> Into a god to bid me rise. — Francis

And another of them threatens the idol to whom he had committed the custody of his woods that, if he did not preserve them to be fuel for his fire, he should himself be made use of for that purpose:

> Furaces moneo manus repellas,
> Et silvam domini focis reserves,
> Si defecerit haec, et ipse lignum es.
>
> Drive the plunderers away, and preserve the wood
> for thy master's hearth, or thou thyself shalt
> be converted into fuel. — Martial

When the besotted idolater has thus served the meanest purposes with part of his tree, and the rest has had time to season (he makes that a god in his imagination while that is in the doing, *and worships it*): He *makes it a graven image, and falls down thereto* (v. 15), that is (v. 17), *The residue thereof he makes a god, even his graven image,* according to his fancy and intention; he *falls down to it, and worships it,* gives divine honours to it, prostrates himself before it in the most humble reverent posture, as a servant, as a suppliant; *he prays to it,* as having a dependence upon it, and great expectations from it; *he saith, Deliver me, for thou art my god.* There where he pays his homage and allegiance he justly looks for protection and deliverance. What a strange infatuation is this, to expect help from gods that cannot help themselves! But it is this praying to them that makes them gods, not what the smith or the carpenter did to them. What we place our confidence in for deliverance that we make a god of.

> Qui fingit sacros, auro vel marmore, vultus
> Non facit ille deos; qui rogat, ille facit.
>
> He who supplicates the figure, whether it be
> of gold or of marble, makes it a god, and not
> he who merely constructs it. — Martial

III. Here is judgment given upon this whole matter, *v.* 18–20. In short, it is the effect and evidence of the greatest stupidity and sottishness that one could ever imagine rational beings to be guilty of, and shows that man has become worse than the beasts that perish; for they act according to the dictates of sense, but man acts not according to the dictates of reason (v. 18): *They have not known nor understood* common sense; men that act rationally in other things in this act most absurdly. Though they have some knowledge and understanding, yet they are strangers to, nay, they are rebels against the great law of consideration (v. 12): *None considers in his heart,* nor has so much application of mind as to reason thus with himself, which one would think he might easily do, though there were none to reason with him: "*I have burnt part of this tree in the fire,* for baking and roasting; *and now shall I make the residue thereof an abomination?*" (that is, *an idol,* for that is an abomination to God and all wise and good men); "shall I ungratefully choose to do, or presumptuously dare to do, what the Lord hates? shall I be such a fool as to fall down to the stock of a tree — a senseless, lifeless, helpless thing? shall I so far disparage myself, and make myself like that I bow down to?" A growing tree may be a beautiful stately thing, but the stock of a tree has lost its glory, and he has lost his that gives glory to it. Upon the whole, the sad character given of these idolaters is, 1. That they put a cheat upon themselves (v. 20): *They feed on ashes;* they feed themselves with hopes of advantage by worshipping these idols, but they will be disappointed

as much as a man that would expect nourishment by feeding on ashes. Feeding on ashes is an evidence of a depraved appetite and a distempered body; and it is a sign that the soul is overpowered by very bad habits when men, in their worship, go no further than the sight of their eyes will carry them. They are wretchedly deluded, and it is their own fault: *A deceived heart* of their own, more than the deceiving tongue of others, *has turned them aside* from the faith and worship of the living God to dumb idols. They are *drawn away of their own lusts and enticed.* The apostasy of sinners from God is owing entirely to themselves and to the evil heart of unbelief that is in their own bosom. A revolting and rebellious heart is a deceived heart. 2. That they wilfully persist in their self-delusion and will not be undeceived. There is none of them that can be persuaded so far to suspect himself as to say, *Is there not a lie in my right hand?* and so to think of delivering his soul. Note, (1.) Idolaters have a lie in their right hand; for an idol is a lie, is not what it pretends, performs not what it promises, and it is a *teacher of lies,* Hab. 2:18. (2.) It highly concerns those that are secure in an evil way seriously to consider whether there be not a lie in their right hand. Is not that a lie which with complacency we hold fast as our chief good? Are our hearts set upon the wealth of the world and the pleasures of sense? They will certainly prove a lie in our right hand. And is not that a lie which with confidence we hold fast by, as the ground on which we build our hopes for heaven? If we trust to our external professions and performances, as if those would save us, we deceive ourselves with a lie in our right hand, with a house built on the sand. (3.) Self-suspicion is the first step towards self-deliverance. We cannot be faithful to ourselves unless we are jealous of ourselves. He that would deliver his soul must begin with putting this question to his own conscience. *Is there not a lie in my right hand?* (4.) Those that are given up to believe in a lie are under the power of strong delusions, which it is hard to get clear of, 2 Th. 2:11.

Verses 21–28

In these verses we have,

I. The duty which Jacob and Israel, now in captivity, were called to, that they might be qualified and prepared for the deliverance designed them. Our first care must be to get good by our afflictions, and then we may hope to get out of them. The duty is expressed in two words: *Remember* and *return,* as in the counsel to Ephesus, Rev. 2:4, 5. 1. "*Remember these, O Jacob!* Remember what thou hast been told of the folly of idolatry, and let the convictions thou art now under be ready to thee whenever thou art tempted to that sin. Remember that *thou art my servant,* and therefore must not serve other masters." 2. *Return unto me, v.* 22. It is the great concern of those who have backslidden from God to hasten their return to him; and this is that which he calls them to when they are in affliction, and when he is returning to them in a way of mercy.

II. The favours which Jacob and Israel, now in captivity, were assured of; and what is here promised to them upon their remembering and returning to God is in a spiritual sense promised to all that in like manner return to God. It is a very comfortable word, for more is implied in it than is expressed (v. 21): "*O Israel! thou shalt not be forgotten of me,* though for the present thou seemest to be so." When we begin to remember God he will begin to remember us; nay, it is he that remembers us first. Now observe here,

1. The grounds upon which God's favourable intentions to his people were built and on which they might build their expectations from him. He will deliver them out of captivity; for, (1.) They are his servants, and therefore he has a just quarrel with those that detain them. *Let my people go, that they may serve me.* The servants of the King of kings are under special protection. (2.) He formed them into a people, formed them *from the womb, v.* 24. From the first beginning of their increase into a nation they were under his particular care and government, more than any other people; their national constitution was of his framing, and his covenant with them was the charter by which they were incorporated. They are his, and he will save them. (3.) He has redeemed them formerly, has many a time redeemed them out of great distress, and he is still the same, in the same relation to them, has the same con-

cern for them. "Therefore *return unto me, for I have redeemed thee, v.* 22. Whither wilt thou go, but to me?" Having redeemed them, as well as formed them, he has acquired a further title to them and propriety in them, which is a good reason why they should dutifully return to him and why he will graciously return to them. The *Lord has redeemed Jacob;* he is about to do it (v. 23); he has determined to do it; for he is the Lord their Redeemer, *v.* 24. Note, The work of redemption which God has by his Son wrought for us encourages us to hope for all promised blessings from him. He that has redeemed us at so vast an expense will not lose his purchase. (4.) He has *glorified himself in them* (v. 23), and therefore will do so still, Jn. 12:28. It is matter of comfort to us to see God's glory interested in the deliverances of the church; for *therefore* he will certainly redeem Jacob, because thus he will glorify himself. And *this* assures us that he will perfect the redemption of his saints by Jesus Christ, because there is a day set when he will be glorified and admired in them all. (5.) He has pardoned their sins, which were the cause of their calamity and the only obstruction to their deliverance, *v.* 22. *Therefore* he will break the yoke of captivity from off their necks, because he has *blotted out, as a thick cloud, their transgressions.* Note, [1.] Our transgressions and our sins are as a cloud, a thick cloud; they interpose between heaven and earth, and for a time suspend and intercept the correspondence between the upper and lower world (sin *separates between us and God,* ch. 59:2); they threaten a storm, a deluge of wrath, as thick clouds do, which God will rain upon sinners. Ps. 11:6. [2.] When God pardons sin he blots out this cloud, this thick cloud, so that the intercourse with heaven is laid open again. God looks down upon the soul with favour; the soul looks up to him with pleasure. The cloud is scattered by the influence of the Sun of righteousness. It is only through Christ that sin is pardoned. When sin is pardoned, like a cloud that is scattered, it appears no more, it is quite gone. The *iniquity of Jacob shall be sought for, and not found,* Jer. 50:20. And the comforts that flow into the soul when sin is pardoned are like the *clear shining after clouds and rain.*

2. The universal joy which the deliverance of God's people should bring along with it (v. 23): *Sing, O you heavens!* This intimates, (1.) That the whole creation shall have cause for joy and rejoicing in the redemption of God's people; to that it is owing that it subsists (that it is rescued from the curse which the sin of man brought upon the ground) and that it is again put into a capacity of answering the ends of its being, and is assured that though now it groans, being burdened, it shall at last be delivered from the bondage of corruption. The greatest establishment of the world is the kingdom of God in it, Ps. 96:11–13; 98:7–9. (2.) That the angels shall rejoice in it, and the inhabitants of the upper world. The heavens shall sing, for the Lord has done it. And there is joy in heaven when God and man are reconciled (Lu. 15:7), joy when Babylon falls, Rev. 18:20. (3.) That those who lay at the greatest distance, even the inhabitants of the Gentile world, should join in these praises, as sharing in these joys. The *lower parts of the earth,* the forest and the trees there, shall bring in the tribute of thanksgiving for the redemption of Israel.

3. The encouragement we have to hope that though great difficulties, and such as have been thought insuperable, lie in the way of the church's deliverance, yet, when the time for it shall come, they shall all be got over with ease; for *thus saith Israel's Redeemer, I am the Lord that maketh all things,* did make them at first and am still making them; for providence is a continued creation. All being, power, life, emotion, and perfection, are from God. He *stretches forth the heavens alone,* has no help nor needs any; and the earth too he *spreads abroad by himself,* and by his own power. Man was not by him when he did it (Job 38:4), nor did any creature advise or assist; only his own eternal wisdom and Word was by him then as *one brought up with him,* Prov. 8:30. His stretching out the heavens by himself denotes the boundless extent of his power. The strongest man, if he has to stretch a thing out, must get somebody or other to lend a hand; but God stretched out the vast expanse and keeps it still upon the stretch, himself, by his own power. Let not Israel be discouraged then; nothing is too hard for him to do that made the world, Ps. 124:8. And, having made all things, he can

make what use he pleases of all, and has it in his power to serve his own purposes by them.

4. The confusion which this would put upon the oracles of Babylon, by the confutation it would give them, *v.* 25. God, by delivering his people out of Babylon, would *frustrate the tokens of the liars,* of all the lying prophets, that said the Babylonian monarchy had many ages yet to live, and pretended to ground their predictions upon some token, some sign or other, which, according to the rules of their arts, foreboded its prosperity. How mad will these conjurors grow with vexation when they see that their skill fails them, and that the contrary happens to that which they so coveted and were so confident of. Nor would it only baffle their pretended prophets, but their celebrated politicians too: He *turns the wise men backward.* Finding they cannot go on with their projects, they are forced to quit them; and so he makes the judges fools, *and makes their knowledge foolish.* Those that are made acquainted with Christ see all the knowledge they had before to be foolishness in comparison with the knowledge of him. And those that are adversaries to him will find all their counsels, like Ahitophel's, turned into foolishness, and themselves *taken in their own craftiness,* 1 Co. 3:19.

5. The confirmation which this would give to the oracles of God, which the Jews had distrusted and their enemies despised: God *confirms the word of his servant* (*v.* 26); he confirms it by accomplishing it in its season; and *performs the counsel of the messengers* whom he hath many a time sent to his people, to tell them what great blessings he had in store for them. Note, The exact fulfilling of the prophecies of scripture is a confirmation of the truth of the whole book and an incontestable evidence of its divine origin and authority.

6. The particular favours God designed for his people, that were now in captivity, *v.* 26–28. These were foretold long before they went into captivity, that they might see reason to expect a correction, but no reason to fear a final destruction. (1.) It is here supposed that Jerusalem, and the cities of Judah, should for a time lie in ruins, dispeopled and uninhabited; but it is promised that they shall be rebuilt and repeopled. When Isaiah lived, Jerusalem and the cities of Judah were full of inhabitants; but they will be emptied, burnt, and destroyed. It was then hard to believe that concerning such strong and populous cities. But the justice of God will do that; and, when that is done, it will be hard to believe that ever they will recover themselves again, and yet the zeal of the Lord of hosts will do that to. God has said to Jerusalem, *Thou shalt be inhabited;* for, while the world stands, God will have a church in it, and therefore he will raise up those who *shall say to Jerusalem, Thou shalt be built;* for, if it be not built, it cannot be inhabited, Ps. 69:35, 36. When God's time shall have come for the building up of his church, let him alone to find both houses for his people (for they shall not lie exposed) and people for his houses, for they shall not stand empty. The cities of Judah too shall again be built. The Assyrian army under Sennacherib only took them, and then, upon the defeat of that army, they returned undamaged to the right owners; but the Chaldean army demolished them, and by carrying away the inhabitants left them to go to decay of themselves; for, if less judgments prevail not to humble and reform men, God will send greater. Yet these desolations shall not be perpetual. God will *raise up the* wastes and *decayed places thereof;* for he will not contend for ever. The city of strangers, when it is ruined, shall never be built (*ch.* 25:2), but the city of God's own children is but discontinued for a time. (2.) It is here supposed that the temple too should be destroyed, and lie for a time rased to the foundations; but it is promised that the foundation of it shall again be laid, and no doubt built upon. As the desolation of the sanctuary was to all the pious Jews the most mournful part of the destruction, so the restoration and re-establishment of it would be the most joyful part of the deliverance. What joy can they have in the rebuilding of Jerusalem if the temple there be not rebuilt? for it is that which makes it a holy city and truly beautiful. This therefore was the chief thing that the Jews had at heart and had in view in their return; therefore they would go back to Jerusalem, to *build the house of the Lord God of Israel there,* Ezra 1:3. (3.) It is here supposed that very great difficulties would lie in the way of this deliverance, which it would be impossible for them to wade

through; but it is promised that by a divine power they shall all be removed (*v.* 27): *God saith to the deep, Be dry;* so he did when he brought Israel out of Egypt, and so he will again when he brings them out of Babylon, if there be occasion. *Who art thou, O great mountain?* Dost thou stand in the way? Before Zerubbabel, the commander-in-chief of the returning captives, *thou shalt become a plain,* Zec. 4:7. So, *Who art thou, O great deep?* Dost thou retard their passage and think to block it up? Thou shalt be dry, and thy rivers that supply thee shall be dried up. When Cyrus took Babylon by draining the river Euphrates into many channels, and so making it passable for his army, this was fulfilled. Note, Whatever obstructions lie in the way of Israel's redemption, God can remove them with a word's speaking. (4.) It is here supposed that none of the Jews themselves would be able by might and power to force their way out of Babylon but it is promised that God will raise up a stranger from afar off, that shall fairly open the way for them, and now at length he names the very man, many scores of years before he was born or thought of (*v.* 28): *That saith of Cyrus, He is my shepherd.* Israel is his people, and the sheep of his pasture. These sheep are now in the midst of wolves, in the hands of the thief and robber; they are impounded for trespass. Now Cyrus shall be his shepherd, employed by him to release these sheep, and to take care of their return to their own green pasture again. "In this *he shall perform all my pleasure,* shall bring about what is purposed by me and will be highly pleasing to me." Note, [1.] The most contingent things are certain to the divine prescience. He knew who was the person, and what was his name, that should be the deliverer of his people, and, when he pleased, he could let his church know it, that, when they heard of such a name beginning to be talked of in the world, they might *lift up their heads with joy, knowing that their redemption drew nigh.* [2.] It is the greatest honour of the greatest men to be employed for God as instruments of his favour to his people. It was more the praise of Cyrus to be God's shepherd than to be emperor of Persia. [3.] God makes what use he pleases of men, of mighty men, of those that act with the greatest freedom; and, when they think to do as they please, he can overrule them, and make them do as he pleases. Nay, in those very things wherein they are serving themselves, and look no further than that, God is serving his own purposes by them and making them to perform all his pleasure. Rich princes shall do what poor prophets have foretold.

CHAPTER 45

Cyrus was nominated, in the foregoing chapter, to be God's shepherd; more is said to him and more of him in this chapter, not only because he was to be instrumental in the release of the Jews out of their captivity, but because he was to be therein a type of the great Redeemer, and that release was to be typical of the great redemption from sin and death; for that was the salvation of which all the prophets witnessed. We have here, I. The great things which God would do for Cyrus, that he might be put into a capacity to release God's people (*v.* 1–4). II. The proof God would hereby give of his eternal power and godhead, and his universal, incontestable, sovereignty (*v.* 5–7). III. A prayer for the hastening of this deliverance (*v.* 8). IV. A check to the unbelieving Jews, who quarrelled with God for the lengthening out of their captivity (*v.* 9, 10). V. Encouragement given to the believing Jews, who trusted in God and continued instant in prayer, assuring them that God would in due time accomplish this work by the hand of Cyrus (*v.* 11–15). VI. A challenge given to the worshippers of idols and their doom read, and satisfaction given to the worshippers of the true God and their comfort secured, with an eye to the Mediator, who is made of God to us both righteousness and sanctification (*v.* 16–25). And here, as in many other parts of this prophecy, there is much of Christ and of gospel grace.

Verses 1–4

Cyrus was a Mede, descended (as some say) from Astyages king of Media. The pagan writers are not agreed in their accounts of his origin. Some tell us that in his infancy he was an outcast, left exposed, and was saved from perishing by a herdsman's wife. However, it is agreed that, being a man of an active genius, he soon made himself very considerable, especially when Croesus king of Lydia made a descent upon his country, which he not only repulsed, but revenged, prosecuting the advantages he had gained against Croesus with such vigour that in a little time he took Sardis and made himself master of the rich kingdom of Lydia and the many provinces that then belonged to it. This made him very great (for Croesus was rich to a proverb) and enabled him to pursue his victories in many countries; but it was nearly ten years afterwards that, in

conjunction with his uncle Darius and with the forces of Persia, he made this famous attack upon Babylon, which is here foretold, and which we have the history of Dan. 5. Babylon had now grown exorbitantly rich and strong. It was forty-five miles in compass (some say more): the walls were thirty-two feet thick and 100 cubits high. Some say, They were so thick that six chariots might drive abreast upon them; others say, They were fifty cubits thick and 200 high. Cyrus seems to have had a great ambition to make himself master of this place, and to have projected it long; and at last he performed it. Now here, 210 years before it came to pass, we are told,

I. What great things God would do for him, that he might put it into his power to release his people. In order to this he shall be a mighty conqueror and a wealthy monarch and nations shall become tributaries to him and help him both with men and money. Now that which God here promised to do for Cyrus he could have done for Zerubbabel, or some of the Jews themselves; but the wealth and power of this world God has seldom seen fit to entrust his own people with much of, so many are the snares and temptations that attend them; but if here has been occasion, for the god of the church, to make use of them, God has been pleased rather to put them into the hands of others, to be employed for them, than to venture them in their own hands. Cyrus is here called God's *anointed,* because he was both designed and qualified for this great service by the counsel of God, and was to be herein a type of the Messiah. God engages to hold his right hand, not only to strengthen and sustain him, but to direct his motions and intentions, as Elisha put his hands upon the king's hands when he was to shoot his arrow against Syria, 2 Ki. 13:16. Being under such direction,

1. He shall extend his conquests very far and shall make nothing of the opposition that will be given him. Babylon is too strong a place for a young hero to begin with; and therefore, that he may be able to deal with that, great additions shall be made to his strength by other conquests. (1.) Populous kingdoms shall yield to him. God will *subdue nations before him;* when he is in the full career of his successes he shall make nothing of a nation's being born to him at once: yet it is not he that subdues them; it is God that subdues them for him; the battle is his, and therefore his is the victory. (2.) Potent kings shall fall before him: *I will loose the loins of kings,* either the girdle of their loins (divesting them of their power and dignity) or the strength of their loins, and then it was literally fulfilled in Belshazzar, for, when he was terrified by the handwriting on the wall, *the joints of his loins were loosed,* Dan. 5:6. (3.) Great cities shall surrender themselves into his hands, without giving him or themselves any trouble. God will incline the keepers of the city to *open before him the two-leaved gates,* not treacherously nor timorously, but from a full conviction that it is to no purpose to contend with him; and therefore the gates shall not be shut to keep him out as an enemy, but thrown open to admit him as a friend. (4.) The longest and most dangerous marches shall be made easy and ready to him: *I will go before thee,* to clear the way, and to conduct thee in it, and then the *crooked places,* shall be made *straight;* or, as some read it, the hilly places shall be levelled and made even. Those will find a ready road that have God going before them. (5.) No opposition shall stand before him. He that gives him his commission *will break in pieces the gates of brass* that are shut against him, *and cut asunder the bars of iron* wherewith they are fastened. This was fulfilled in the letter, if that be true which Herodotus reports, that the city of Babylon had 100 gates all of brass, with posts and hooks of the same metal.

2. He shall replenish his coffers very much (*v.* 3): *I will give thee the treasures of darkness,* treasures of gold and silver, that have been long kept close under lock and key and had not seen the light of many years, or had been buried under ground by the inhabitants, in their fright, upon the taking of the city. The riches of many nations had been brought to Babylon, and Cyrus seized all together. *The hidden riches of secret places,* which belonged either to the crown or to private persons, shall all be a prey to Cyrus. Thus God, designing him to do a piece of service to his church, paid him richly for it beforehand; and Cyrus very honestly owned God's goodness to him, and, in consideration of that, released the captives. Ezra 1:2,

God has given me all the kingdoms of the earth and thereby has obliged *me to build him a house at Jerusalem.*

II. We are here told what God designed in doing all this for Cyrus. What Cyrus aimed at in undertaking his wars we may easily guess; but what God aimed at in giving him such wonderful success in his wars we are here told.

1. It was that the God of Israel might be glorified: *"That thou mayest know* by all this *that I the Lord am the God of Israel;* for I have *called thee by thy name* long before thou wast born." When Cyrus should have this prophecy of Isaiah shown to him, and should there find his own name and his own achievements particularly described so long before, he should thereby be brought to acknowledge that the God of Israel was the Lord, Jehovah, the only living and true God, and that he continued to own his Israel though now in captivity. It is well when thus men's prosperity brings them to the knowledge of God, for too often it makes them forget him.

2. It was that the Israel of God might be released, *v.* 4. Cyrus knew not God as the God of Israel. Having been trained up in the worship of idols, the true God was to him an unknown God. But, though he knew not God, God not only knew him when he came into being, but foreknew him, and bespoke him for his shepherd. He called him by his name, *Cyrus,* nay, which was yet great honour, he surnamed him and called him his *anointed.* And why did God do all this for Cyrus? Not for his own sake, be it known to him; whether he was a man of virtue or no is questioned. Xenophon indeed, when he would describe the heroic virtues of an excellent prince, made use of Cyrus's name, and many of the particulars of his story, in his Cyropaedia; but other historians represent him as haughty, cruel, and bloodthirsty. The reason why God preferred him was *for Jacob his servant's sake.* Note, (1.) In all the revolutions of states and kingdoms, the sudden falls of the great and strong, and the surprising advancements of the weak and obscure, God is designing the good of his church. (2.) It is therefore the wisdom of those to whom God has given wealth and power to use them for his glory, by showing kindness to his people. Cyrus is preferred that Israel may be released. He shall have a kingdom, only that God's people may have their liberty; for their kingdom is not of this world, it is yet to come. In all this Cyrus was a type of Christ, who was made victorious over principalities and powers, and entrusted with unsearchable riches, for the use and benefit of God's servants, his elect. *When he ascended on high he led captivity captive,* took those captives that had taken others captives, and *opened the prison to those that were bound.*

Verses 5–10

God here asserts his sole and sovereign dominion, as that which he designed to prove and manifest to the world in all the great things he did for Cyrus and by him. Observe,

I. How this doctrine is here laid down concerning the sovereignty of the great Jehovah, in two things: — 1. That he is God alone, and there is no God besides him. This is here inculcated as a fundamental truth, which, if it were firmly believed, would abolish idolatry out of the world. With what an awful, commanding, air of majesty and authority, bidding defiance, as it were, to all pretenders, does the great God here proclaim it to the world: *I am the Lord, I the Lord, Jehovah,* and *there is none else, there is no God besides me,* no other self-existent, self-sufficient, being, none infinite and eternal. And again (*v.* 6), *There is none besides me;* all that are set up in competition with me are counterfeits; they are all vanity and a lie, for *I am the Lord, and there is none else.* This is here said to Cyrus, not only to cure him of the sin of his ancestors, which was the worshipping of idols, but to prevent his falling into the sin of some of his predecessors in victory and universal monarchy, which was the setting up of themselves for gods and being idolized, to which some attribute much of the origin of idolatry. Let Cyrus, when he becomes thus rich and great, remember that still he is but a man, and there is no God but one. 2. That he is Lord of all, and there is nothing done without him (*v.* 7): *I form the light,* which is grateful and pleasing, and *I create darkness,* which is grievous and unpleasing. *I make peace* (put here for all good) and *I create evil,* not the evil of sin (God is not the author of that), but the evil of punishment. *I the Lord* order, and direct, and *do all these things.* Observe, (1.) The very different events that befal the children of men. Light and darkness are opposite to each other, and yet, in the course of providence, they are sometimes intermixed, like the morning and evening twilights, *neither day nor night,* Zec. 14:6. There is a mixture of joys and sorrows in the same cup, allays to each other. Sometimes they are counterchanged, as noonday light and midnight darkness. In the revolution of every day each takes its turn, and there are short transitions from the one to the other, witness Job's case. (2.) The self-same cause of both, and that is he that is the first Cause of all: *I the Lord,* the fountain of all being, am the fountain of all power. He who formed the natural light (Gen. 1:3) still forms the providential light. He who at first made peace among the jarring seeds and principles of nature makes peace in the affairs of men. He who allowed the natural darkness, which was a mere privation, creates the providential darkness; for concerning troubles and afflictions he gives positive orders. Note, The wise God has the ordering and disposing of all our comforts, and all our crosses, in this world.

II. How this doctrine is here proved and published. 1. It is proved by that which God did for Cyrus: *"There is no God besides me,* for (*v.* 5) *I girded thee, though thou hast not known me.* It was not thy own idol, which thou didst know and worship, that girded thee for this expedition, that gave thee authority and ability for it. No, it was I that girded thee, I whom thou didst not know, nor seek to." By *this* it appears that the God of Israel is the only true God, that he manages and makes what use he pleases even of those that are strangers to him and pay their homage to other gods. 2. It is published to all the world by the word of God, by his providence, and by the testimony of the suffering Jews in Babylon, that all may know from the east and from the west, sunrise and sun-set, that the Lord is God and there is none else. The wonderful deliverance of the Israel of God proclaimed to all the world that *there is none like unto the God of Jeshurun, that rides on the heavens for their help.*

III. How this doctrine is here improved and applied.

1. For the comfort of those that earnestly longed, and yet quietly waited, for the redemption of Israel (*v.* 8): *Drop down, you heavens, from above.* Some take this as the saints' prayer for the deliverance. I rather take it as God's precept concerning it; for he is said to *command deliverances,* Ps. 44:4. Now the precept is directed to heaven and earth, and all the hosts of both, as royal precepts commonly run — *To all officers, civil and military.* All the creatures shall be made in their places to contribute to the carrying on of this great work, when God will have it done. If men will not be aiding and assisting, God will produce it without them, as he does the dews of heaven and the grass of the earth, which *tarry not for man, nor wait for the sons of men,* Mic. 5:7. Observe, (1.) The method of this great deliverance that is to be wrought for Israel. *Righteousness* must first be wrought in them; they must be brought to repent of their sins, to renounce their idolatries, to return to God, and reform their lives, and then the salvation shall be wrought for them, and not till then. We must not expect salvation without righteousness, for they spring up together and together the Lord hath created them; what he has joined together, let not us therefore put asunder. See Ps. 85:9–11. Christ died to save us from our sins, not in our sins, and is made redemption to us by being made to us righteousness and sanctification. (2.) The means of this great deliverance. Rather than it shall fail, when the set time for it shall come, the *heavens shall drop down righteousness, and the earth shall open to bring forth salvation,* and both concur to the reformation, and so to the restoration, of God's Israel. It is from heaven, from above the skies, that righteousness drops down, for every grace and good gift is from above; nay, since the more plentiful effusion of the Spirit it is now *poured* down, and, if our hearts be open to receive it, the product will be the fruits of righteousness and the great salvation.

2. For reproof to those of the church's enemies that opposed this salvation, or those of her friends that despaired of it (*v.* 9): *Woe unto him that strives with his Maker!* God is the Maker of all things, and therefore our Maker, which is a reason why we should always submit to him and never contend with him. (1.) Let not the proud oppressors, in the elevation of their spirits, oppose God's designs concerning the deliverance of his people, nor think to detain them any longer when the time shall come for their release. Woe to the insulting Babylonians that set God at defiance, as Pharaoh did, and will not let his people go! (2.) Let not the poor oppressed, in the dejection of their spirits, murmur and quarrel with God for the prolonging of their captivity, as if he dealt unjustly or unkindly with them, or think to force their way out before God's time shall come. Note, Those will find themselves in a woeful condition that strive with their Maker; for none ever hardened his heart against God and prospered. Sinful man is indeed a quarrelsome creature; but *let the potsherds strive with the potsherds of the earth.* Men are but earthen pots, nay, they are broken potsherds, and are made so very much by their mutual contentions. They are dashed in pieces one against another; and, if they are disposed to strive, let them strive with one another, let them meddle with their match; but let them not dare to contend with him that is infinitely above them, which is as senseless and absurd as, [1.] For the clay to find fault with the potter: *Shall the clay say to him that forms it, "What makest thou?* Why dost thou make me of this shape and not that?" Nay, it is as if the clay should be in such a heat and passion with the potter as to tell him that *he has no hands,* or that he works as awkwardly as if he had none. "Shall the clay pretend to be wiser than the potter and therefore to advise him, or mightier than the potter and therefore to control him?" He that gave us being, that gave us this being, may design concerning us, and dispose of us, as he pleases; and it is impudent presumption for us to prescribe to him. Shall we impeach God's wisdom, or question his power, who are ourselves so curiously, so wonderfully, made? Shall we say, *He has no hands,* whose hands made us and in whose hands we are? The doctrine of God's sovereignty has enough in it to silence all our discontents and objections against the methods of his providence and grace, Rom. 9:20, 21. [2.] It is as unnatural as for the child to find fault with the parents, to say to the father, *What begettest thou?* or to the mother, *"What hast thou brought forth?* Why was I not begotten and born an angel, exempt from the infirmities of human nature and the calamities of human life?" Must not those who are children of men expect to share in the common lot and to fare as others fare? If God is our Father, where is the honour we owe to him by submitting to his will?

Verses 11–19

The people of God in captivity, who reconciled themselves to the will of God in their affliction and were content to wait his time for their deliverance, are here assured that they should not wait in vain.

I. They are invited to enquire concerning the issue of their troubles, *v.* 11. *The Holy One of Israel, and his Maker,* though he does not allow them to strive with him, yet encourages them, 1. To consult his word: *"Ask of me things to come;* have recourse to the prophets and their prophecies, and see what they say concerning these things. Ask the watchmen, What of the night? Ask them, How long?" Things to come, as far as they are revealed, belong to us and to our children, and we must not be strangers to them. 2. To seek unto him by prayer: *"Concerning my sons and concerning the work of my hands,* which as becomes them submit to the will of their Father, the will of their potter, *command you me,* not by way of prescription, but by way of petition. Be earnest in your requests, and confident in your expectations, as far as both are guided by and grounded upon the promise." We may not strive with our Maker by passionate complaints, but we may wrestle with him by faithful and fervent prayer. *My sons, and the work of my hands, commend to me* (so some read it), bring them to me and leave them with me. See the power of prayer, and its prevalency with God: *Thou shalt cry, and he shall say, Here I am; what would you that I should do unto you?* Some read it with an interrogation, as carrying on the reproof (*v.* 9, 10): *Do you question me concerning things to come?* and am I bound to give you an account? *And concerning my children, even concerning the work of my hands, will you command me,* or prescribe to me? Dare you do so? *Shall any teach God knowledge,* or give law to him? Those that complain of God do in effect assume an authority over him.

II. They are encouraged to depend upon the power of God when they are brought very low and are utterly incapable of helping themselves, *v.* 12. Their *help stands in the name of the Lord, who made heaven and earth,* which he mentions here, not only for his own glory, but for their comfort. The heavens and earth shall contribute, if he please, to the deliverance of the church (*v.* 8), for he created both, and therefore has both at command. 1. He *made the earth, and created man upon it,* for it was intended to be a habitation for man, Ps. 115:16. He has therefore not only authority, but wisdom and power sufficient to govern man here on this earth and to make what use he pleases of him. 2. His *hands have stretched out the heavens, and all their hosts he commanded* into being at first, and therefore still governs all their motions and influences. It is good news to God's Israel that their God is the creator and governor of the world.

III. They are particularly told what God would do for them, that they might know what to depend upon; and this shall lead them to expect a more glorious Redeemer and redemption, of whom, and of which, Cyrus and their deliverance by him were types and figures.

1. Liberty shall be proclaimed to them, *v.* 13. Cyrus is the man that shall proclaim it; and, in order hereunto, God will put power into his hands: *I have raised him up in righteousness,* that is, in pursuance and performance of my promises and to plead my people's just but injured cause. He will give him success in all his enterprises, particularly that against Babylon: *I will direct all his ways;* and then it follows that he will prosper him, for those must needs speed well that are under a divine direction. God will make plain the way of those whom he designs to employ for him. Two things Cyrus must do for God: — (1.) Jerusalem is God's city, but it is now in ruins, and he must rebuild it, that is, he must give orders for the rebuilding of it, and give wherewithal to do it. (2.) Israel is God's people, but they are now captives, and he must release them freely and generously, not demanding any ransom, nor compounding with them for price or reward. And Christ is anointed to do that for poor captive souls which Cyrus was to do for the captive Jews, to proclaim the *opening of the prison to those that were bound* (*ch.* 61:1), enlargement from a worse bondage than that in Babylon.

2. Provision shall be made for them. They went out poor, and unable to bear the expenses of their return and re-establishment; and therefore it is promised that the labour of Egypt and other nations should *come over to them and be theirs, v.* 14. Cyrus, having conquered those countries, out of their spoils provided for the returning Jews; and he ordered his subjects to furnish them with necessaries (Ezra 1:4), so that they did not go out empty from Babylon any more than from Egypt. Those that are redeemed by Christ shall be not only provided for, but enriched. Those whose spirits God stirs up to go to the heavenly Zion may depend upon him to bear their charges. The world is theirs as far as is good for them.

3. Proselytes shall be brought over to them: *Men of stature shall come after thee in chains; they shall fall down to thee, saying, Surely God is in thee.* This was in part fulfilled when many of the people of the land became Jews (Esther 8:17), *and said, We will go with you,* humbly begging leave to do so, *for we have heard that God is with you,* Zec. 8:23. The restoration would be a means of the conviction of many and the conversion of some. Perhaps many of the Chaldeans who were now themselves conquered by Cyrus, when they saw the Jews going back in triumph, came and begged pardon for the affronts and abuses they had given them, owned that God was among them and that he was God alone, and therefore desired to join themselves to them. But this promise was to have its full accomplishment in the gospel church, — when the Gentiles shall become obedient by word and deed to the faith of Christ (Rom. 15:18), as willing captives to the church (Ps. 110:3), glad to wear her chains, — when an infidel, beholding the public worship of Christians, shall own himself convinced that *God is with them of a truth* (1 Co. 14:24, 25) and shall assay to join himself to them, — and when those that had been *of the synagogue of Satan shall come and worship before the church's feet,* and be made to *know that God has loved her* (Rev. 3:9), and the *kings of the earth and the nations shall bring their glory into the gospel Jerusalem,* Rev. 21:24. Note, It is good to be with those, though it be in chains, that have God with them.

IV. They are taught to trust God further than they can see him. The prophet puts this word into their mouths, and goes before them in saying it (*v.* 15): *Verily, thou art a God that hidest thyself.* 1. God hid himself when he brought them into the trouble, *hid himself and was wroth, ch.* 57:17. Note, Though God be his people's God and Saviour, yet sometimes, when they provoke him, he hides himself from them in displeasure, suspends his favours, and lays them under his frowns: but let them *wait upon the Lord that hides his face, ch.* 8:17. 2. He hid himself when he was bringing them out of the trouble. Note, When God is acting as Israel's God and Saviour commonly *his way is in the sea,* Ps. 77:19. The salvation of the church is carried on in a mysterious way, by the Spirit of the Lord of hosts working on men's spirits (Zec. 4:6), by weak and unlikely instruments, small and accidental occurrences, and not wrought till the last extremity; but this is our comfort, though God hide himself, we are sure he is *the God of Israel,* the *Saviour.* See Job 35:14.

V. They are instructed to triumph over idolaters and all the worshippers of other gods (*v.* 16): *Those who are makers of idols,* not only who frame them, but who make gods of them by praying to them, *shall be ashamed and confounded,* when they shall be convinced of their mistakes and shall be forced to acknowledged that the God of Israel is the only true God, and when they shall be disappointed in their expectations from their idols, under whose protection they had put themselves. They shall go to confusion when they shall find that they can neither excuse the sin nor escape the punishment of it, Ps. 97:7. It is not here and there one more timorous than the rest that shall thus shrink, and give up the cause, but *all of them;* nay, though they appear in a body, though hand join in hand, and they do all they can to keep one another in countenance, yet *they shall go to confusion together.* Bind them in bundles, to burn them.

VI. They are assured that those who trust in God shall never be made ashamed of their confidence in him, *v.* 17. Now that God was about to deliver them out of Babylon he directed them by his prophet, 1. To look up to him as the author of their salvation: *Israel shall be saved in the Lord.* Not only their salvation shall be wrought out by his power, but it shall be treasured up for them in his grace and promise, and so secured to them. They shall be saved in him; for his name shall be their strong tower, into which they shall run, and in which they shall be safe. 2. To look beyond this temporal deliverance to that which is spiritual and has reference to another world, to think of that salvation by the Messiah which is an everlasting salvation, the salvation of the soul, a rescue from everlasting misery and a restoration to everlasting bliss. "Give diligence to make that sure, for it may be made sure, so sure that *you shall not be ashamed nor confounded world with out end.* You shall not only be delivered from the *everlasting shame and contempt* which will be the portion of idolaters (Dan. 12:2), but you shall have everlasting honour and glory." [1.] There is a world without end; and it will be well or ill with us according as it will be with us in that world. [2.] Those who are saved with the everlasting salvation shall never be ashamed of what they did or suffered in the hopes of it; for it will so far outdo their expectations as to be a more abundant reimbursement. The returning captives owned that to them did *belong confusion of face* (Dan. 9:7, 8); yet God tells them that they shall not be confounded, but shall have assurance for ever. Those who are confounded as penitents for their own sin shall not be confounded as believers in God's promise and power.

VII. They are engaged for ever to cleave to God, and never to desert him, never to distrust him. What had been often inculcated before is here again repeated, for the encouragement of his people to continue faithful to him, and to hope that he would be so to them: *I am the Lord, and there is none else.* That the Lord we serve and trust in is God alone appears by the two great lights, that of nature and that of revelation.

1. It appears by the light of nature; for he made the world, and therefore may justly demand its homage (*v.* 18): *"Thus saith the Lord, that created the heavens and formed the earth, I am the Lord,* the sovereign Lord of all, *and there is none else."* The gods of the heathen did not do this, nay, they did not pretend to do it. He here mentions the creation of the heavens, but enlarges more upon that of the earth, because that is the part of the creation which we have the nearest view of and are most conversant with. It is here observed, (1.) That he formed it. It is not a rude and indigested chaos, but cast into the most proper shape and size by Infinite Wisdom. (2.) That he fixed it. When he had made it he established it, *founded it on the seas,* (Ps. 24:2), *hung it on nothing* (Job 26:7) as at first he made it of nothing, and yet made it substantial an hung it fast, *ponderibus librata suis — poised by its own weight.* (3.) That he fitted it for use, and for the service of man, to whom he designed to give it. *He created it not in vain,* merely to be a proof of his power; but *he formed it to be inhabited* by the children of men, and for that end he drew the waters off from it, with which it was at first covered, and made the *dry land appear,* Ps. 104:6, 7. Be it observed here, to the honour of God's wisdom, that he made nothing in vain, but intended every thing for some end and fitted it to answer the intention. If any man prove to have been made in vain, it is his own fault. It should also be observed, to the honour of God's goodness and his favour to man, that he reckoned that not made in vain which serves for his use and benefit, to be a habitation and maintenance for him.

2. It appears by the light of revelation. As the works of God abundantly prove that he is God alone, so does his word, and the discovery he has made of himself and of his mind and will by it. His oracles far exceed those of the Pagan deities, as well as his operations, *v.* 19. The preference is here placed in three things: — All that God has said is plain, satisfactory, and just. (1.) In the manner of the delivery of it it is plain and open: *I have not spoken in secret, in a dark place of the earth.* The Pagan deities delivered their oracles out of dens and caverns, with a low and hollow voice, and in ambiguous expressions; those that had familiar spirits whispered and muttered (*ch.* 8:19); but God delivered his law from the top of Mount Sinai before all the thousands of Israel, in distinct, audible, and intelligible sounds. Wisdom *cries in the chief places of concourse,* Prov. 1:20, 21; 8:1–3. The vision is written, and made plain, so that he who runs may read it; if he be obscure to any, they may thank themselves. Christ pleaded in his own defence what God says here, *In secret have I said nothing,* Jn. 18:20. (2.) In the use and benefit of it it was highly satisfactory: *I said not unto the seed of Jacob,* who consulted these oracles and governed themselves by them, *Seek you me in vain,* as the false gods did to their worshippers, who sought *for the living to the dead, ch.* 8:19. This includes all the gracious answers that God gave both to those who consulted him (his word is to them a faithful guide) and to those that prayed to him. The seed of Jacob are a praying people; it is the *generation of those that seek him,* Ps. 24:6. And, as he has in his word invited them to seek him, so he never denied their believing prayers nor disappointed their believing expectations. He said not to them, to any of them, *Seek you me in vain;* for, if he did not think fit to give them the particular thing they prayed for, yet he gave them such a sufficiency of grace and such comfort and satisfaction of soul as were equivalent. What we say of winter is true of prayer, It never rots in the skies. God not only gives a gracious answer to those that diligently seek him, but will be their bountiful rewarder. (3.) In the matter of it it was incontestably just, and there was no iniquity in it: *I the Lord speak righteousness, I declare things that are right,* and consonant to the eternal rules and reasons of good and evil. The heathen deities dictated those things to their worshippers which were the reproach of human nature and tended to the extirpation of virtue; but God speaks righteousness, dictates that which is right in itself and tends to make men righteous; and therefore he is God, and there is none else.

Verses 20–25

What here is said is intended, as before,

I. For the conviction of idolators, to show them their folly in worshipping gods that cannot help them, and neglecting a God that can. Let all *that have escaped of the nations,* not only the people of the Jews, but those of other nations that were by Cyrus released out of captivity in Babylon, let them come, and hear what is to be said against the worshipping of idols, that they may be cured of it as well as the Jews, that Babylon, which had of old been the womb of idolatry, might now become the grave of it. Let the refugees assemble themselves and come together; God has something to say to them for their own good, and it is this, that idolatry is a foolish sottish thing, upon two accounts: —

1. It is setting up a refuge of lies for themselves: *They set up the wood of their graven image;* for that is the *substratum.* Though they overlay it with gold, deck it with ornaments, and make a god of it, yet still it is but wood. They *pray to a god that cannot save;* for he cannot hear, he cannot help, he can do nothing. How do those disparage themselves who give honour to that as a god which cannot, as a god, give good to them! How do those deceive themselves who pray for relief to that which is in no capacity at all to relieve them! Certainly those have no knowledge, or are brutish in their knowledge, who take so much pains, and do so much penance, in seeking the favour of a god that has no power.

2. It is setting up a rival with God, the only living and true God (*v.* 21): "Summon them all; tell them that the great cause shall again be tried, though once adjudged, between God and Baal. *Bring them near, and let them take counsel together* what to say in defence of themselves and their idols. It shall, as before, be put upon this issue: let them show when any of their gods did with any certainty foretel future events, as the God of Israel has done, and it shall be acknowledged that they have some colour for their pretensions. But None of them ever did; their prophets were lying prophets; but *I the Lord have told it from that time,* long before it came to pass; therefore you must own *thee is no other God besides me."* (1.) None besides is fit to rule. He is *a just God,* and rules in justice, and will execute justice for those that are oppressed. (2.) None besides is able to help. As he is a just God, so he is *the Saviour,* who can save without the assistance of any, but without whom none can save. Those therefore have no sense of truth and falsehood, good and evil, no, nor of their own interest, that set up any in competition with him.

II. For the comfort and encouragement of all God's faithful worshippers, whoever they are, *v.* 22. Those that worship idols pray to gods that cannot save; but the God of Israel says it to all the ends of the earth, to his people, though they are scattered into the utmost corners of the world and seem to be lost and forgotten in their dispersion, "Let them but *look to me* by faith and prayer, look above instruments and second causes, look off from all pretenders, and look up to me, and they shall *be saved."* It seems to refer further to the conversion of the Gentiles that live in the ends of the earth, the most distant nations, when the standard of the gospel is set up. *To it shall the Gentiles seek.* When Christ is lifted up from the earth, as the brazen serpent upon the pole, he shall draw the eyes of all men to him. They shall all be invited to look unto him, as the stung Israelites did to the brazen serpent; and so strong is the eye of faith that by divine grace it will reach the Saviour and fetch in salvation by him even from the ends of the earth; for *he is God, and the is none else.* Two things are here promised, for the abundant satisfaction of all that by faith look to the Saviour: —

1. That the glory of the God they serve shall be greatly advanced; and this will be good news to all the Lord's people, that, how much soever they and their names are depressed, God will be exalted, *v.* 23. This is confirmed by an oath, that we might have strong consolation: *I have sworn by myself* (and God can swear by no greater, Heb. 6:13); *the word has gone out of my mouth,* and shall neither be recalled nor return empty; it has gone forth *in righteousness,* for it is the most reasonable equitable thing in the world that he who made all should be Lord of all, that, since all beings are derived from him, they should all be devoted to him. He has said it, and it shall be made good, *I will be exalted,* Ps. 46:10. He has assured us, (1.) That he will be universally submitted to, that the kingdoms of the world shall become his kingdom. They shall do him homage — *Unto me every knee shall bow;* and they shall bind themselves by an oath of allegiance to him — *Unto me every tongue shall swear.* This is applied to the dominion of our Lord Jesus, Rom. 14:10, 11. *We shall all stand before the judgment-seat of Christ* and give account to him, for it is written, *As I live, saith the Lord, every knee shall bow to me and every tongue shall confess to God;* and it seems to be referred to, Ps. 2:9, 10. If the heart be brought into obedience to Christ, and made willing in the day of his power, the knee will bow to him in humble adorations and addresses, and in cheerful obedience to his commands, submission to his disposals, and compliance with his will in both; and the tongue will swear to him, will lay a bond upon the soul to engage it for ever to him; for he that bears an honest mind never startles at assurances. (2.) That he will be universally sought unto, and application shall be made to him from all parts of the world: *Unto him shall men of distant countries come,* to implore his favour. *Unto thee shall all flesh come* with their request, Ps. 65:2. And, when Christ was *lifted up from the earth, he drew all men to him.* (3.) That it will be to no purpose to make opposition to him. *All that are incensed against him,* that rage at his bonds and cords — the nations that are angry because he has taken to himself his great power and has reigned, that have been incensed at the strictness of his laws, the success of his gospel, and the spiritual nature of his kingdom — they *shall be ashamed;* some shall be brought to a penitential shame for it, others to a remediless ruin. One way or other, sooner or later, all that are uneasy at Christ's government and victories will be made ashamed of their folly and obstinacy. Blessed be God for the assurance here given us that, whatever becomes of us and our interests, *the Lord will reign for ever!*

2. That the welfare of the souls they are concerned for shall be effectually secured: *Surely shall one say,* and another shall learn by his example to say the same, so that all the seed of Israel, according to the Spirit, shall say, and stand to it, (1.) That God has a sufficiency for them and that in Christ there is enough to supply all their needs: *In the Lord is all righteousness and strength* (so the margin reads it); he is himself righteous and strong. He can do every thing, and yet will do nothing but what is unquestionably just and equitable. He has also wherewithal to supply the needs of those that seek to him and depend upon him, upon the equity of his providence and the treasures of his grace; nay, we may say, not only *"He* has it," but, "In him *we* have it," because he has said that he will be to us a God. In the Lord the captive Jews had righteousness (that is, grace both to sanctify their afflictions to them and to qualify them for deliverance) and strength for their support and escape. In the Lord Jesus we have righteousness to recommend us to the goodwill of God towards us, and strength to begin and carry on the good work of God in us. He is the fountain of both, and on him we must depend for both, must *go forth in his strength, and make mention of his righteousness,* Ps. 71:16. (2.) That they shall have an abundant bliss and satisfaction in this. [1.] The people of the Jews shall in the Lord be justified before men and openly glory in their God. The oppressors reproached them, loaded them with calumny, and boasted even of a right to oppress them, as abandoned by their God; but, when God shall work out their deliverance, that shall be their justification from these hard censures, and therefore they shall glory in it. [2.] All true Christians, that depend upon Christ for strength and righteousness, in him shall be justified and shall glory in that. Observe, *First,* All believers are the seed of Israel, an upright praying seed. *Secondly,* The great privilege they enjoy by Jesus Christ is that in him, and for his sake, they are justified before God, Christ being made of God to them righteousness. All that are justified will own it is in Christ that they are justified, nor could they be justified by any other; and those who are justified shall be glorified. And therefore, *Thirdly,* The great duty believers owe to Christ is to glory in him, and to make their boast of him. *Therefore* he is made all in all to us, that *whose glories may glory in the Lord;* and let us comply with this intention.

CHAPTER 46

God, by the prophet here, designing shortly to deliver them out of their captivity, prepared them for that deliverance by possessing them with a detestation of idols and with a believing confidence in God, even their own God. I. Let them not be afraid of the idols of Babylon, as if they could in any way obstruct their deliverance, for they should be defaced (*v.* 1, 2); but let them trust in that God who had often delivered them to do it still, to do it now (*v.* 3, 4). II. Let them not think to make idols of their own, images of the God of Israel, by them to worship him, as the Babylonians worship their gods (*v.* 5–7). Let them not be so sottish (*v.* 8), but have an eye to God in his word, not in an image; let them depend upon that, and upon the promises and predictions of it, and God's power to accomplish them all (*v.* 9–11). And let them know that the unbelief of man shall not make the word of God of no effect (*v.* 12, 13).

Verses 1–4

We are here told,

I. That the false gods will certainly fail their worshippers when they have most need of them, *v.* 1, 2. Bel and Nebo were two celebrated idols of Babylon. Some make Bel to be a contraction of Baal; others rather think not, but that it was Belus, one of their first kings, who after his death was deified. As Bel was a deified prince, so (some think) Nebo was a deified prophet, for so Nebo signifies; so that Bel and Nebo were their Jupiter and their Mercury or Apollo. Barnabas and Paul passed at Lystra for Jupiter and Mercury. The names of these idols were taken into the names of their princes, Bel into Belshazzar's, Nebo into Nebuchadnezzar's and Nebuzaradan's. These gods they had long worshipped, and in their revels praised them for their successes (as appears, Dan. 5:4); and they insulted over Israel as if Bel and Nebo were too hard for Jehovah and could detain them in captivity in defiance of their God. Now, that this might be no discouragement to the poor captives, God here tells them what shall become of these idols, which they threaten them with. When Cyrus takes Babylon, down go the idols. It was usual then with conquerors to destroy the gods of the places and people they conquered, and to put the gods of their own nation in the room of them, *ch.* 37:19. Cyrus will do so; and then Bel and Nebo, that were set up on high, and looked great, bold, and erect, shall *stoop and bow down* at the feet of the soldiers that plunder their temples. And because there is a great deal of gold and silver upon them, which was intended to adorn them, but serves to expose them, they carry them away with the rest of the spoil. The carriers' horses, or mules, are laden with them and their other idols, to be sent among other lumber (for so it seems they accounted them rather than treasure) into Persia. So far are they from being able to support their worshippers that they are themselves a heavy load in the wagons, and *a burden to the weary beast.* The idols cannot help one another (*v.* 2): *They stoop, they bow down together.* They are all alike, tottering things, and their day has come to fall. Their worshippers cannot help them: *They could not deliver the burden* out of the enemy's hand, *but themselves* (both the idols and the idolaters) *have gone into captivity.* Let not therefore God's people be afraid of either. When God's ark was taken prisoner by the Philistines it proved a burden, not to the beasts, but to the conquerors, who were forced to return it; but, when Bel and Nebo have gone into captivity, their worshippers may even give their good word with them: they will never recover themselves.

II. That the true God will never fail his worshippers: "You hear what has become of Bel and Nebo, now *hearken to me, O house of Jacob! v.* 3, 4. Am I such a god as these? No; though you are brought low, and the house of Israel is but a remnant, your God has been, is, and ever will be, your powerful and faithful protector."

1. Let God's Israel do him the justice to own that he has hitherto been kind to them, careful of them, tender over them, and has all along done well for them. Let them own, (1.) That he bore them at first: *I have made.* Out of what womb came they, but that of his mercy, and grace, and promise? He formed them into a people and gave them their constitution. Every good man is what God makes him. (2.) That he bore them up all along: You have been *borne by me from the belly,* and *carried from the womb.* God began betimes to do them good, as soon as ever they were formed into a nation, nay, when as yet they were very few, and strangers. God took them under a special protection, and *suffered no man to do them wrong,* Ps. 105:12–14. In the infancy of their state, when they were not only foolish and helpless, as children, but forward and peevish, God carried them in the arms of his power and love, bore them *as upon eagles' wings,* Ex. 19:4; Deu. 32:11. Moses had not patience *to carry them as the nursing father does the sucking child* (Num. 11:12), but God bore them, and *bore their manners,* Acts 13:18. And as God began early to do them good (when *Israel was a child, then I loved him),* so he had constantly continued to do them good: he had carried them from the womb to this day. And we may all witness for God that he has been thus gracious to us. We have been borne by him from the belly, from the womb, else we should have died from the womb and given up the ghost when we came out of the belly. We have been the constant care of his kind provi-

dence, carried in the arms of his power and in the bosom of his love and pity. The new man is so; all that in us which is born of God is borne up by him, else it would soon fail. Our spiritual life is sustained by his grace as necessarily and constantly as our natural life by his providence. The saints have acknowledged that God has carried them from the womb, and have encouraged themselves with the consideration of it in their greatest straits, Ps. 22:9, 10; 71:5, 6, 17.

2. He will then do them the kindness to promise that he will never leave them. He that was their first will be their last; he that was the author will be the finisher of their well-being (*v.* 4): "You have been *borne by me from the belly,* nursed when you were children; and *even to your old age I am he,* when, by reason of your decays and infirmities, you will need help as much as in your infancy." Israel were now growing old, so was their covenant by which they were incorporated, Heb. 8:13. *Gray hairs were here and there upon them,* Hos. 7:9. And they had hastened their old age, and the calamities of it, by their irregularities. But God will not cast them off now, will not fail them when their strength fails; he is still their God, will still carry them in the same everlasting arms that were laid under them in Moses's time, Deu. 33:27. He has made them and owns his interest in them, and therefore he will bear them, will bear with their infirmities, and bear them up under their afflictions: "Even *I will carry and will deliver* them; I will now bear them upon eagles' wings out of Babylon, as in their infancy I bore them out of Egypt." This promise to aged Israel is applicable to every aged Israelite. God has graciously engaged to support and comfort his faithful servants, even in their old age: *"Even to your old age,* when you grow unfit for business, when you are compassed with infirmities, and perhaps your relations begin to grow weary of you, yet *I am he* — he that I am, he that I have been — the very same by whom you have been borne from the belly and carried from the womb. You change, but I am the same. I am he that I have promised to be, he that you have found me, and he that you would have me to be. *I will carry you, I will bear,* will bear you up and bear you out, and will carry you on in your way and carry you home at last."

Verses 5–13

The deliverance of Israel by the destruction of Babylon (the general subject of all these chapters) is here insisted upon, and again promised, for the conviction both of idolaters who set up as rivals with God, and of oppressors who were enemies to the people of God.

I. For the conviction of those who made and worshipped idols, especially those of Israel who did so, who would have images of their God, as the Babylonians had of theirs,

1. He challenges them either to frame an image that should be thought a resemblance of him or to set up any being that should stand in competition with him (*v.* 5): *To whom will you liken me?* It is absurd to think of representing an infinite and eternal Spirit by the figure of any creature whatsoever. It is to change his truth into a lie and to turn his glory into shame. None ever saw any similitude of him, nor can see his face and live. *To whom then can we liken God? ch.* 40:18, 25. It is likewise absurd to think of making any creature equal with the Creator, who is infinitely above the noblest creatures, yea, or to make any comparison between the creature and the Creator, since between infinite and finite there is no proportion.

2. He exposes the folly of those who made idols and then prayed to them, *v.* 6, 7. (1.) They were at great charge upon their idols and spared no cost to fit them for their purpose: *They lavish gold out of the bag;* no little will serve, and they do not care how much goes, though they pinch their families and weaken their estates by it. How does the profuseness of idolaters shame the niggardliness of many who call themselves God's servants but are for a religion that will cost them nothing! Some *lavish gold out of the bag* to make an idol of it in the house, while others *hoard up gold in the bag* to make an idol of it in the heart; for *covetousness is idolatry,* as dangerous, though not as scandalous, as the other. *They weigh silver in the balance,* either to be the matter of their idol (for even those that were most sottish had so much sense as to think that God should be served with the best they had, the best they could possibly afford; those that represented him by a calf made it a golden one) or to pay the workmen's wages. The service of sin often proves very expensive. (2.) They were in great care about their idols and took no little pains about them (*v.* 7): *They bear him upon their* own *shoulders,* and do not hire porters to do it; they *carry him, and set him in his place,* more like a dead corpse than a living God. They set him on a pedestal, *and he stands.* They take a great deal of pains to fasten him, and *from his place he shall not remove,* that they may know where to find him, though at the same time they know he can neither move a hand nor stir a step to do them any kindness. (3.) After all, they paid great respect to their idols, though they were but the works of their own hands and the creatures of their own fancies. When the goldsmith has made it that which they please to call a god *they fall down, yea, they worship it.* If they magnified themselves too much in pretending to make a god, as if they would atone for that, they vilified themselves as much in prostrating themselves to a god that they knew the original of. And, if they were deceived by the custom of their country in making such gods as these, they did no less deceive themselves when they cried unto them, though they knew they could not answer them, could not understand what they said to them, nor so much as reply Yea, or No, much less could they *save them out of their trouble.* Now shall any that have some knowledge of, and interest in, the true and living God, thus make fools of themselves?

3. He puts it to themselves, and their own reason, let that judge in the case (*v.* 8): *"Remember this,* that has been often told you, what senseless helpless things idols are, *and show yourselves men* — men and not brutes, men and not babes. Act with reason; act with resolution; act for your own interest. Do a wise thing; do a brave thing; and scorn to disparage your own judgment as you do when you worship idols." Note, Sinners would become saints if they would but show themselves men, if they would but support the dignity of their nature and use aright its powers and capacities. "Many things you have been reminded of; *bring them again to mind,* recall them into you memories, and revolve them there. *O! you transgressors, consider your ways; remember whence you have fallen, and repent,* and so recover yourselves."

4. He again produces incontestable proofs that he is God, that he and none besides is so (*v.* 9): *I am God, and there is none like me.* This is that which we have need to be reminded of again and again; for proof of it he refers, (1.) To the sacred history: *"Remember the former things of old,* what the God of Israel did for his people in their beginnings, whether he did not that for them which no one else could, and which the false gods did not, nor could do, for their worshippers. Remember those things, and you will own that *I am God and there is none else."* This is a good reason why we should give glory to him as a nonsuch, and why we should not give that glory to any other which is due to him alone, Ex. 15:11. (2.) To the sacred prophecy. He is God alone, for it is he only that *declares the end from the beginning, v.* 10. From the beginning of time he declared the end of time, and end of all things. Enoch prophesied, *Behold, the Lord comes.* From the beginning of a nation he declares what the end of it will be. He told Israel what should befal them in *the latter days,* what *their end should be,* and wished they were so wise as to consider it, Deu. 32:20, 20. From the beginning of an event he declares what the end of it will be. *Known unto God are all his works,* and, when he pleases, he makes them known. Further than prophecy guides us it is impossible for us to *find out the work that God makes from the beginning to the end,* Eccl. 3:11. He *declares from ancient times the things that are not yet done.* Many scripture prophecies which were delivered long ago are not yet accomplished; but the accomplishment of some in the mean time is an earnest of the accomplishment of the rest in due time. By this it appears that he is *God, and none else;* it is he, and none besides, that can say, and make his words good, *"My counsel shall stand,* and all the powers of hell and earth cannot control or disannul it nor all their policies correct or countermine it." As God's operations are all according to his counsels, so his counsels shall all be fulfilled in his operations, and none of his measures shall be broken, none of his designs shall miscarry. This yields abundant satisfaction to those who have bound up all their comforts in God's counsels, that his counsel shall undoubtedly stand; and, if we are brought to this, that whatever pleases God pleases us, nothing can contribute more to make us easy than to be assured of this, that *God will do all his pleasure,* Ps. 135:6. The accomplishment of this particular prophecy, which relates to the elevation of Cyrus and his agency in the deliverance of God's people out of their captivity, is mentioned for the confirmation of this truth, that the Lord is God and there is none else; and this is a thing which shall shortly come to pass, *v.* 11. God by his counsel *calls a ravenous bird from the east,* a bird of prey, *Cyrus,* who (they say) had a nose like the beak of a hawk or eagle, to which some think this alludes, or (as others say) to the eagle which was his standard, as it was afterwards that of the Romans, to which there is supposed to be a reference, Mt. 24:28. Cyrus came from the east at God's call: for God is Lord of hosts and of those that have hosts at command. And, if God give him a call, he will give him success. He is the man that shall *execute God's counsel,* though he comes *from a far country* and knows nothing of the matter. Note, Even those that know not, and mind not, God's revealed will, are made use of to fulfil the counsels of his secret will, which shall all be punctually accomplished in their season by what hand he pleases. That which is here added, to ratify this particular prediction, may abundantly show to the heirs of promise the immutability of his counsel: *"I have spoken of it* by my servants the prophets, and what I have spoken is just the same with what *I have purposed."* For, though God has many things in his purposes which are not in his prophecies, he has nothing in his prophecies but what are in his purposes. And he *will do it,* for he will never change his mind; he *will bring it to pass,* for it is not in the power of any creature to control him. Observe with what majesty he says it, as one having authority: *I have spoken it, I will also bring it to pass. Dictum, factum — no sooner said than done. I have purposed it,* and he does not say, "I will take care it shall be done," but, *"I will do it."* Heaven and earth shall pass away sooner than one tittle of the word of God.

II. For the conviction of those that daringly opposed the counsels of God assurance is here given not only that they shall be accomplished, but that they shall be accomplished very shortly, *v.* 12, 13.

1. This is addressed to the *stout-hearted,* that is, either, (1.) The proud and obstinate Babylonians, *that are far from righteousness,* far from doing justice or showing mercy to those they have power over, that say they will never let the oppressed go free, but will still detain them in spite of their petitions or God's predictions, that are far from any thing of clemency or compassion to the miserable. Or, (2.) The unhumbled Jews, that have been long under the hammer, long in the furnace, but are not broken are not melted, that, like the unbelieving murmuring Israelites in the wilderness, think themselves far from God's righteousness (that is, from the performance of his promise, and his appearing to judge for them), and by their distrusts set themselves at a yet further distance from it, and keep good things from themselves, as their fathers, who could not enter into the land of promise because of unbelief. This is applicable to the Jewish nation when they rejected the gospel of Christ; though they *followed after the law of righteousness,* they *attained not to righteousness, because they sought it not by faith,* Rom. 9:31, 32. They perished far from righteousness; and it was because they were *stout-hearted,* Rom. 10:3.

2. Now to them God says that, whatever they think, the one in presumption, the other in despair, (1.) Salvation shall be certainly wrought for God's people. If men will not do them justice, God will, and his righteousness shall effect that for them which men's righteousness would not reach to. He *will place salvation in Zion,* that is, he will make Jerusalem a place of safety and defence to all those who will plant themselves there; thence shall salvation go forth *for Israel his glory.* God glories in his Israel; and he will be glorified in the salvation he designs to work out for them; it shall redound greatly to his honour. This salvation shall be in Zion; for thence the gospel shall take rise (*ch.* 2:3), thither the Redeemer comes (*ch.* 59:20, Rom. 11:26), and it is Zion's King that has salvation, Zec. 9:9. (2.) It shall be very shortly wrought. This is especially insisted on with those who thought it at a distance: *"I bring near*

my righteousness, nearer than you think of; perhaps it is nearest of all when your straits are greatest and your enemies most injurious; it shall not be far off when there is occasion for it, Ps. 85:9. *Behold, the Judge stands before the door.* My salvation shall not tarry any longer than till it is ripe and you are ready for it; and therefore, *though it tarry, wait for it;* wait patiently, for *he that shall come will come, and will not tarry."*

CHAPTER 47

Infinite Wisdom could have ordered things so that Israel might have been released and yet Babylon unhurt; but if they will harden their hearts, and will not let the people go, they must thank themselves that their ruin is made to pave the way to Israel's release. That ruin is here, in this chapter, largely foretold, not to gratify a spirit of revenge in the people of God, who had been used barbarously by them, but to encourage their faith and hope concerning their own deliverance, and to be a type of the downfall of that great enemy of the New-Testament church which, in the Revelation, goes under the name of "Babylon." In this chapter we have, I. The greatness of the ruin threatened, that Babylon should be brought down to the dust, and made completely miserable, should fall from the height of prosperity into the depth of adversity (*v.* 1–5). II. The sins that provoked God to bring this ruin upon them. 1. Their cruelty to the people of God (*v.* 6). 2. Their pride and carnal security (*v.* 7–9). 3. Their confidence in themselves and contempt of God (*v.* 10). 4. Their use of magic arts and their dependence upon enchantments and sorceries, which should be so far from standing them in any stead that they should but hasten their ruin (*v.* 11–15).

Verses 1–6

In these verses God by the prophet sends a messenger even to Babylon, like that of Jonah to Nineveh: "The time is at hand when Babylon shall be destroyed." Fair warning is thus given her, that she may by repentance prevent the ruin and there may be a lengthening of her tranquility. We may observe here,

I. God's controversy with Babylon. We will begin with that, for there all the calamity begins; she has made God her enemy, and then who can befriend her: Let her know that the righteous Judge, to whom vengeance belongs, has said (*v.* 3), *I will take vengeance.* She has provoked God, and shall be reckoned with for it when the measure of her iniquities is full. Woe to those on whom God comes to take vengeance; for who knows the power of his anger and what a fearful thing it is to fall into his hands? Were it a man like ourselves who would be revenged on us, we might hope to be a match for him, either to make our escape from him or to make our part good with him. But he says, *"I will not meet thee as a man,* not with the compassions of a man, but I will be to the as a lion, and a *young lion"* (Hos. 5:14); or, rather, not with the strength of a man, which is easily resisted, but with the power of a God, which cannot be resisted. Not with the justice of a man, which may be bribed, or biassed, or mollified by a foolish pity, but with the justice of a God, which is strict and severe, and can never be evaded. As in pardoning the penitent, so in punishing the impenitent, he is *God and not man,* Hos. 11:9.

II. The particular ground of this controversy. We are sure that there is cause for it, and it is a just cause; it is the *vengeance of his temple* (Jer. 50:28); it is for *violence done to Zion,* Jer. 51:35. God will plead his people's cause against them. It is acknowledged (*v.* 6) that God had, in wrath, delivered his people into the hands of the Babylonians, had made use of them for the correction of his children, and had by their means *polluted his inheritance,* had left his peculiar people exposed to suffer in common with the rest of the nations, had suffered the heathen, who should have been kept at a distance, to *come into his sanctuary* and *defile his temple,* Ps. 79:1. Herein God was righteous; but the Babylonians carried the matter too far, and, when they had them in their hands (triumphing to see a people that had been so much in reputation for wisdom, holiness, and honour, brought thus low), with a base and servile spirit they trampled upon them, *and showed them no mercy,* no, not the common instances of humanity which the miserable are entitled to purely by their misery. They used them barbarously, and with an air of contempt, nay, and of complacency in their calamities. They were brought under the yoke; but, as if that were not enough, they *laid the yoke on very heavily,* adding affliction to the afflicted. Nay, they laid it *on the ancient* — the elders in years, who were past their labour, and must sink under a yoke which those in their youthful strength would easily bear — the elders in office, those that had been judges and magistrates, and persons of the first rank. They took a pride in putting these to the meanest hardest drudgery. Jeremiah laments this, that the *faces of elders were not honoured,* Lam. 5:12. Nothing brings a surer or a sorer ruin upon any people than cruelty, especially to God's Israel.

III. The terror of this controversy. She has reason to tremble when she is told who it is that has this quarrel with her (*v.* 4): *"As for our Redeemer,* our *Goël,* that undertakes to plead our cause as the avenger of our blood, he has two names which speak not only comfort to us, but terror to our adversaries." 1. "He is *the Lord of hosts,* that has all the creatures at his command, and therefore has *all power both in heaven and in earth."* Woe to those against whom the Lord fights, for the whole creation is at war with them. 2. "He is the *Holy One of Israel,* a God in covenant with us, who has his residence among us, and will faithfully perform all the promises he has made to us." God's power and holiness are engaged against Babylon and for Zion. This may fitly be applied to Christ, our great Redeemer. He is both Lord of hosts and the Holy One of Israel.

IV. The consequences of it to Babylon. She is called a *virgin,* because so she thought herself, though she was the mother of harlots. She was beautiful as a virgin, and courted by all about her; she had been called *tender and delicate* (*v.* 1), and *the lady of kingdoms* (*v.* 5); but now the case is altered. 1. Her honour is gone, and she must bid farewell to all her dignity. She that had sat at the upper end of the world, sat in state and sat at ease, must now *come down and sit in the dust,* as very mean and a deep mourner, must *sit on the ground,* for she shall be so emptied and impoverished that she shall not have a seat left her to sit upon. 2. Her power is gone, and she must bid farewell to all her dominion. She shall rule no more as she has done, nor give law as she has done to her neighbours: *There is no throne,* none for thee, *O daughter of the Chaldeans!* Note, Those that abuse their honour or power provoke God to deprive them of it, and to make them *come down and sit in the dust.* 3. Her ease and pleasure are gone: "She shall *no more be called tender and delicate* as she has been, for she shall not only be deprived of all those things with which she pampered herself, but shall be put to hard service and made to feel both want and pain, which will be more than doubly grievous to her who formerly *would not venture to set* so much as *the sole of her foot to the ground for tenderness and for delicacy,"* Deu. 28:56. It is our wisdom not to use ourselves to be tender and delicate, because we know not how hardly others may use us before we die not what straits we may be reduced to. 4. Her liberty is gone, and she is brought into a state of servitude and as sore a bondage as she in her prosperity had brought others to. Even the great men of Babylon must now receive the same law from the conquerors that they used to give to the conquered: *"Take the mill-stones and grind meal* (*v.* 2), set to work, to hard labour" (like beating hemp in Bridewell), "which will make thee sweat so that thou must throw off all thy head-dresses, and *uncover thy locks."* When they were driven from one place to another, at the capricious humours of their masters, they must be forced to wade up to the middle through the waters, to *make bare the leg* and *uncover the thigh,* that they might *pass over the rivers,* which would be a great mortification to those that used to ride in state. But let them not complain, for just thus they had formerly used their captives; and *with what measure they* then *meted* it is now *measured to them again.* Let those that have power use it with temper and moderation, considering that the spoke which is uppermost will be under. 5. All her glory, and all her glorying, are gone. Instead of glory, she has ignominy (*v.* 3): *Thy nakedness shall be uncovered and thy shame shall be seen,* according to the base and barbarous usage they commonly gave their captives, to whom, for covetousness of their clothes, they did not leave rags sufficient to cover their nakedness, so void were they of the modesty as well as of the pity due to the human nature. Instead of glorying she *sits silently, and gets into darkness* (*v.* 5), ashamed to show her face, for she has quite lost her credit and *shall no more be called the lady of kingdoms.* Note, God can make those sit silently that used to make the greatest noise in the world, and send those into darkness that used to make the greatest figure. Let him that glories, therefore, glory in a God that changes not, and not in any worldly wealth, pleasure, or honour, which are subject to change.

Verses 7–15

Babylon, now doomed to ruin, is here justly upbraided with her pride, luxury, and security, in the day of her prosperity, and the confidence she had in her own wisdom and forecast, and particularly in the prognostications and counsels of the astrologers. These things are mentioned both to justify God in bringing these judgments upon her and to mortify her, and put her to so much the greater shame, under these judgments; for, when God comes forth to take vengeance, glory belongs to him, but confusion to the sinner.

I. The Babylonians are here upbraided with their pride and haughtiness, and the great conceit they had of themselves, because of their wealth and power, and the vast extent of their dominion; it was the language both of the government and of the body of the people: *Thou sayest in thy heart* (and God, who searches all hearts, can tell men what they say there, though they never speak it out) *I am, and none else besides me, v.* 8, 10. The repetition of this part of the charge intimates that they said it often, and that it was very offensive to God. It is the very word that God has often said concerning himself, *I am, and none else besides me,* denoting his self-existence, his infinite and incomparable perfections, and his sole supremacy. All this Babylon pretends to; and no wonder if she that assumed a power to make what gods and goddesses she pleased for the people to worship made herself one among the rest. It is presumption to say of any creature, "It is, and there is not its like, there is none besides it" (for creatures stand very nearly upon a level with one another); but it is insufferable arrogance for any to say so of themselves, and an evidence of their self-ignorance.

II. They are upbraided with their luxury and love of ease (*v.* 8): *"Thou that art given to pleasures,* art a slave to them, art in them as in thy element, and, that thou mayest enjoy them without disturbance or interruption, *dwellest carelessly* and layest nothing to heart." Great wealth and plenty are great temptations to sensuality, and, where there is fulness of bread, there is commonly abundance of idleness. But if those that are given to pleasures, and dwell carelessly, would but hear this, that *for all these things God will bring them into judgment,* it would be a damp to their mirth, an allay to their pleasure, and would find them something to be in care about.

III. They are upbraided with their carnal security and their vain confidence of the perpetuity of their pomps and pleasures. This is much insisted on here. Observe,

1. The cause of their security. They thought themselves safe and out of danger, not because they were ignorant of the uncertainty of all earthly enjoyments and the inevitable fate that attends states and kingdoms as well as particular persons, but *because they did not lay this to heart,* did not apply it to themselves, nor give it a due consideration. They lulled themselves asleep in ease and pleasure, and dreamt of nothing else but that *to-morrow should be as this day, and much more abundant.* They did not *remember the latter end of it* — the latter end of their prosperity, that it is a fading flower, and will wither — the latter end of their iniquity, that it will be bitterness, that they day will come when their injustice and oppression must be reckoned for and punished. *She did not remember her latter end* (so some read it); she forgot that her day would come to fall and what would be in the end hereof. It was the ruin of Jerusalem (Lam. 1:9) that *she remembered not her last end, therefore she came down wonderfully;* and it was Babylon's ruin too. The children of men are easy, and think themselves safe, in their sinful ways, only because they never think of death, and judgment, and their future state.

2. The ground of their security. They trusted in their wickedness and in their wisdom, *v.* 10. (1.) Their power and wealth, which they had gotten by fraud and oppression, were their confidence: *Thou hast trusted in thy wickedness,* As Doeg. Ps. 52:7. Many have so debauched their own consciences, and have got to such a pitch of daring wickedness, that they stick at nothing; and this they trust to carry them through those difficulties which embarrass men who make conscience of what they say and do. They doubt not but they shall be too hard for all their enemies, be-

cause they dare lie, and kill, and forswear themselves, and do any thing for their interest. Thus they trust in their wickedness to secure them, which is the only thing that will ruin them. (2.) Their policy and craft, which they called their *wisdom,* were their confidence. They thought they could outwit all mankind, and therefore might set all their enemies at defiance. But their *wisdom and knowledge perverted them,* and turned them out of the way, made them forget themselves, and the preparation necessary to be made for hereafter.

3. The expressions of their security. Three things this proud and haughty monarchy said, in her security: — (1.) *"I shall be a lady for ever,"* v. 7. She looked upon the patent of her honour to be not merely during the pleasure of the sovereign Lord, the fountain of honour, or during her own good behaviour, but to be perpetual to the present generation and their heirs and successors for ever. She was not only proud that she was a lady, but confident that she should be a lady for ever. Thus the New-Testament Babylon says, *I sit as a queen, and shall see no sorrow,* Rev. 18:7. Those ladies mistake themselves, and consider not their latter end, who think they shall be ladies for ever; for death will shortly lay their honour with them in the dust. Saints will be saints for ever, but lords and ladies will not be so for ever. (2.) *"I shall not sit as a widow,* in solitude and sorrow, shall never lose the power and wealth I am thus wedded to; the monarchy shall never want a monarch to espouse and protect it, and be a husband to the state; *nor shall I know the loss of children,"* v. 8. She was as confident of the continuance of the numbers of her people as of the dignity of her prince, and had no fear of being either deposed or depopulated. Those that are in the height of prosperity are apt to fancy themselves out of the reach of adverse fate. (3.) *"No one sees me* when I do amiss, and therefore there will be none to call me to an account,"* v. 10. It is common for sinners to promise themselves impunity, because they promise themselves secrecy, in their wicked ways. They trust to their wicked arts and designs to stand them in stead, because they think they have carried them on so plausibly that none can discern the wickedness and deceit of them.

4. The punishment of their security. It shall be their ruin; and it will be, (1.) A complete ruin; and it will be, (1.) A complete ruin, the ruin of all their comforts and confidences: *"These two things shall come upon thee* (the very two things that thou didst set at defiance), *loss of children and widowhood,* v. 9. Both thy princes and thy people shall be cut off, so that thou shalt be no more a government, no more a nation." Note, God often brings upon secure sinners those very mischiefs which they least feared and thought themselves in least danger of. *"They shall come upon thee in their perfection,* with all their aggravating circumstances and without any thing to allay or mitigate them." Afflictions to God's children are not afflictions in perfection. Widowhood is not to them a calamity in perfection, for they have this to comfort themselves with, that their Maker is their husband; loss of children is not, for he is better to them than ten sons. But on his enemies they come in perfection. Widowhood and loss of children are either of them great griefs, but both together great indeed. Naomi thinks she may well be called *Marah* when she is *left both of her sons and of her husband* (Ruth 1:5); and yet on her these evils did not come in perfection, for she had two daughters-in-law left, that were comforts to her. But on Babylon they come in perfection; she has no comfort remaining. (2.) It will be a sudden and surprising ruin. The evil shall come *in one day,* nay, *in a moment,* which will make it much the more terrible, especially to those that were so very secure. *"Evil shall come upon thee* (v. 11) and thou shalt have neither time nor way to provide against it, or to prepare for it; for *thou shalt not know whence it rises,* and therefore shalt not know where to stand upon thy guard." *Thou shalt not know the morning thereof;* so the Hebrew phrase is. We know just when and where the day will break and the sun rise, but we know not what the day, when it comes, will bring forth, nor when or where trouble will arise; perhaps the storm may come from that point of the compass which we little thought of. Babylon pretended to great wisdom and knowledge (v. 10), but with all her knowledge she cannot foresee, nor with all her wisdom prevent, the ruin threatened: *"Desolation shall come upon thee suddenly,* as a thief in the night,

which thou shalt not know, that is, which thou little thoughtest of." Fair warning was indeed given them, by Isaiah and other prophets of the Lord, of this desolation; but they slighted that notice, and would give no credit to it, and therefore justly is it so ordered that they should have no other notice of it, but that partly through their own security, and partly through the swiftness and subtlety of the enemy, when it came it should be a perfect surprise to them. Those that slight the warnings of the written word, let them not expect any other premonitions. (3.) It will be an irresistible ruin, and such as they will have no fence against: *"Mischief shall come upon thee* so suddenly that thou shalt have no time to turn thee in, so strongly that thou shalt not be able to make head against it and to put it off and save thyself." There is no opposing the judgments of God when they come with commission. Babylon herself, with all her wealth, and power, and multitude, is not able to put off the mischief that comes.

IV. They are upbraided with their divinations, their magical and astrological arts and sciences, which the Chaldeans, above any other nation, were notorious for, and from them other nations borrowed all their learning of that kind.

1. This is here spoken of as one of their provoking sins, which would bring the judgments of God upon them, v. 9. "These evils shall come upon thee to punish thee *for the multitude of thy sorceries, and the great abundance of thy enchantments."* Witchcraft is a sin in its own nature exceedingly heinous; it is giving that honour to the devil which is due to God only, making God's enemy our guide and the father of lies our oracle. In Babylon it was a national sin, and had the protection and countenance of the government; conjurors, for aught that appears, were their privy counsellors and prime ministers of state. And shall not God visit for these things? Observe what a multitude, what a great abundance, of sorceries and enchantments there were among them. Such a bewitching sin this was that when it was once admitted it spread like wildfire, and they never knew any end of it; the deceived and the deceivers both increased strangely.

2. It is here spoken of as one of their vain confidences, which they relied much upon, but should be deceived in, for it would not serve so much as to give them notice of the judgments coming, much less to guard against them. (1.) They are here upbraided with the mighty pains they had taken about their sorceries and enchantments: Thou hast *laboured in them from thy youth,* v. 12. They trained up their young men in these studies, and those that applied themselves to them were indefatigable in their labours about them — reading books, making observations, trying experiments. Well, let them stand up now with their enchantments, and try their skill in the critical moment. Let them make a stand, if they can, in opposition to the invading enemy; let them stand to offer their service to their country; but to what purpose? *"Thou art wearied in the multitude of thy counsels* of this kind (v. 13); thou hast advised with them all, but hast received no satisfaction from them; the different schemes they have erected, and the different judgments they have given, have but increased thy perplexity and tired thee out." In the multitude of such counsellors there is no safety. (2.) They are upbraided with the variety they had of such kinds of people among them, v. 13. They had their *astrologers,* or viewers of the heavens, that did not consider them, as David, to behold the wisdom and power of God in them; but, under pretence of foretelling future events by them, they viewed the heavens and forgot him that made them and set *their dominion on the earth* (Job 38:33), and has himself dominion over them, for he rides on the heavens. They had their *star-gazers,* who by the motions of the stars, their conjunctions and oppositions, read the doom of states and kingdoms. They had their *monthly prognosticators,* their almanac-makers, that told what weather it should be or what news they should have each month. The great stock they had of these was what they valued themselves much upon; but they were all cheats, and their art was a sham. I confess I see not how the judicial astrology which some now pretend to, by the rules of which they undertake to prophecy concerning things to come, can be distinguished from that of the Chaldeans, nor therefore how it can escape the censure and contempt which this text lays that under; yet I fear there are some who study their almanacs, and regard

them and their prognostications, more than their Bibles and the prophecies there. (3.) They are upbraided with the utter inability and insufficiency of all these pretenders to do them any kindness in the day of their distress. Let them see whether with the help of their enchantments they can prevail against their enemies, or profit themselves, inspirit their own forces or dispirit those that come against them, v. 12. Let them see what service those can do them who make a trade of divination: *"Let them stand up,* and either by their power save thee from these evils that are coming upon thee or by their foresight make such a discovery of them beforehand that thou mayest by needful precautions save thyself;" as Elisha, by notifying to the king of Israel the motions of the Syrian army, enabled him to *save himself, not once nor twice,* 2 Ki. 6:10. This baffling of the diviners was literally fulfilled when, the night that Babylon was taken and Belshazzar slain, all his astrologers, soothsayers, and wise men, were quite nonplussed with the handwriting on the wall that pronounced the fatal sentence, Dan. 5:8. (4.) They are upbraided with the fall of the wise men themselves in the common ruin, v. 14. Those are unlikely to stand their friends in any stead who cannot secure themselves; they are as stubble at the best, worthless and useless, and *they shall be as stubble* before a consuming fire. The Persians, to make room for their own wise men, will cut off those of Babylon; that *fire shall burn them,* and *they shall not deliver themselves from the power of the flame.* Those can expect no other than to be devoured by their sins make themselves fuel to a devouring fire. When God kindles a fire among them it *shall not be a coal to warm at,* and *a fire to sit before,* but a coal to burn them. Or, rather, it denotes that they shall be utterly consumed by the judgments of God, burnt quite to ashes, and there shall not remain one live coal to do any body any service; for *when God judges he will overcome.* (5.) They are upbraided with their merchants, and those they dealt with (v. 15), such as they dealt with from their youth, either, [1.] In a way of consultation. These astrologers, that dealt in the black art, they always loved to be dealing with, and they were in effect their merchants; fortune-telling was one of the best trades in Babylon, and those that followed that trade probably lived as splendidly and got as much money as the richest merchants; yet, when some of them were devoured, others fled their country, *every one to his quarter,* and there was none to save Babylon. Miserable comforters are they all. Or, [2.] In a way of commerce. As their astrologers, with whom they had laboured, failed them, so did their merchants; they took care to secure their own effects, and then valued not what became of Babylon. They *wandered every one to his own quarter;* each man shifted for his own safety, but none would offer to lend a helping hand, no, not to a city by which they had got so much money. Every one was for himself, but few for his friends. The New-Testament Babylon is lamented by the merchants that were made rich by her, but they very prudently stand afar off to lament her (Rev. 18:15), not willing to attempt any thing for her succour. Happy are those who by faith and prayer deal with one that will be a *very present help in time of trouble!*

CHAPTER 48

God, having in the foregoing chapter reckoned with the Babylonians, and shown them their sins and the desolation that was coming upon them for their sins, to show that he hates sin wherever he finds it and will not connive at it in his own people, comes, in this chapter, to show the house of Jacob their sins, but, withal, the mercy God had in store for them notwithstanding; and he therefore sets their sins in order before them, that by their repentance and reformation they might be prepared for that mercy. I. He charges them with hypocrisy in that which is good and obstinacy in that which is evil, especially in their idolatry, notwithstanding the many convincing proofs God had given them that he is God alone, (v. 1–8). II. He assures them that their deliverance would be wrought purely for the sake of God's own name and not for any merit of theirs (v. 9–11). III. He encourages them to depend purely upon God's power and promise for this deliverance (v. 12–15). IV. He shows them that, as it was by their own sin that they brought themselves into captivity, so it would be only by the grace of God that they would obtain the necessary preparatives for their enlargement (v. 16–19). V. He proclaims their release, yet with a proviso that the wicked shall have no benefit by it (v. 20–22).

Verses 1–8

We may observe here,

I. The hypocritical profession which many of the Jews made of religion and relation to God. To those who made such a profession the prophet is here ordered to address himself, for their conviction and humiliation, that they might own God's justice in what he had brought upon them. Now observe here,

1. How high their profession of religion soared, what a fair show they made in the flesh and how far they went towards heaven, what a good livery they wore and what a good face they put upon a very bad heart. (1.) They were the *house of Jacob;* they had a place and a name in the visible church. *Jacob have I loved.* Jacob is God's chosen; and they are not only retainers to his family, but descendants from him. (2.) They were *called by the name of Israel,* an honourable name; they were of that people to whom pertained both the giving of the law and the promises. *Israel* signifies *a prince with God;* and they prided themselves in being of that princely race. (3.) *They came forth out of the waters of Judah,* and thence were called *Jews;* they were of the royal tribe, the tribe of which Shiloh was to come, the tribe that adhered to God when the rest revolted. (4.) They *swore by the name of the Lord,* and thereby owned him to be the true God, and their God, and gave glory to him as the righteous Judge of all. They *swore to the name of the Lord* (so it may be read); they took an oath of allegiance to him as their King and joined themselves to him in covenant. (5.) They *made mention of the God of Israel* in their prayers and praises; they often spoke of him, observed his memorials, and pretended to be very mindful of him. (6.) They *called themselves of the holy city,* and, when they were captives in Babylon, purely from a principle of honour, and jealousy for their native country, they valued themselves upon their interest in it. Many, who are themselves unholy, are proud of their relation to the church, the holy city. (7.) They *stayed themselves upon the God of Israel,* and boasted of his promises and his covenant with them; they *leaned on the Lord,* Mic. 3:11. And, if they were asked concerning their God, they could say, *"The Lord of hosts is his name,* the Lord of all;" happy are we therefore, and very great, who have relation to him!

2. How low their profession of religion sunk, notwithstanding all this. It was all in vain; for it was all a jest; it was *not in truth and righteousness.* Their hearts were not true nor right in these professions. Note, All our religious professions avail nothing further than they are made in truth and righteousness. If we be not sincere in them, we do but *take the name of the Lord our God in vain.*

II. The means God used, and the method he took, to keep them close to himself, and to prevent their turning aside to idolatry. The many excellent laws he gave them, with their sanctions, and the hedges about them, it seems, would not serve to restrain them from that sin which did most easily beset them, and therefore to those God added remarkable prophecies, and remarkable providences in pursuance of those prophecies, which were all designed to convince them that their God was the only true God and that it was therefore both their duty and interest to adhere to him. 1. He both dignified and favoured them with remarkable prophecies (*v.* 3): *I have declared the former things from the beginning.* Nothing material happened to their nation from its original which was not prophesied of before — their bondage in Egypt, their deliverance thence, the situation of their tribes in Canaan, etc. All these things *went forth out of God's mouth and he showed them.* Herein they were honoured above any nation, and even their curiosity was gratified. Their prophecies were such as they could rely upon, and such as concerned themselves and their own nation; and they were all verified by the accomplishment of them. *I did them suddenly,* when they were least expected by themselves or others, and therefore could not be foreseen by any but a divine prescience. *I did them and they came to pass;* for what God does he does effectually. The very calamities they were now groaning under in Babylon God did from the beginning declare to them by Moses, as the certain consequences of their apostasy from God, Lev. 26:31, etc.; Deu. 28:36, etc.; 29:28. He also declared to them their return to God, and to their own land again, Deu. 30:4, etc.; Lev. 26:44, 45. Thus he showed them how he would deal with them long before it came to pass. Let them compare their present state together with the deliverance they had now in prospect with what was written in the law, and they would find the scripture exactly fulfilled. 2. He both dignified and favoured them with remarkable providence (*v.* 6): *I have shown thee new things from this time.* Besides the general view given from the beginning of God's proceedings with them, he showed them new things by the prophets of their own day, and created them. They were *hidden things,* which they could not otherwise know, as the prophecy concerning Cyrus and the exact time of their release out of Babylon. These things God *created now, v.* 7. Their restoration was in effect their creation, and they had a promise of it not from the beginning, but of late; for to prevent their apostasy from God, or to recover them, prophecy was kept up among them. Yet it was told them when they could not come to the knowledge of it in any other way than by divine revelation. "Consider," says God, "how much soever it is talked of now among you and expected, it was told you by the prophets, when it was the furthest thing from your thoughts, when you had not heard it, when you had not known it, nor had any reason to expect it, and when your ear was not opened concerning it (*v.* 7, 8), when the thing seemed utterly impossible, and you would scarcely have given any one the hearing who should have told you of it." God had shown them hidden things which were out of the reach of their knowledge, and done for them great things, out of the reach of their power: "Now," says he (*v.* 6), *"thou hast heard; see all this.* Thou hast heard the prophecy; see the accomplishment of it, and observe whether the word and works of God do not exactly agree; *and will you not declare it,* that as you have heard so you have seen? Will you not own that the Lord is the true God, the only true God, that he has the knowledge and power which no creature has and which none of the gods of the nations can pretend to? Will you not own that your God has been a good God to you? Declare this to his honour, and your own shame, who have dealt so deceitfully with him and preferred others before him."

III. The reasons why God would take this method with them.

1. Because he would anticipate their boastings of themselves and their idols. (1.) God by his prophets told them beforehand of their deliverance, lest they should attribute the accomplishment of it to their idols. Thus he saw it necessary to secure the glory of it to himself, which otherwise would have been given by some of them to their graven images: "I spoke of it," says God, *"lest thou shouldst say, My idol has done it or has commanded it to be done," v.* 5. There were those that would be apt to say so, and so would be confirmed in their idolatry by that which was intended to cure them of it. But they would now be for ever precluded from saying this; for, if the idols had done it, the prophets of the idols would have foretold it; but, the prophets of the Lord having foretold it, it was no doubt the power of the Lord that effected it. (2.) God foretold it by his prophets, lest they should assume the foresight of it to themselves. Those that were not so profane as to have ascribed the thing itself to an idol were yet so proud as to have pretended that by their own sagacity they foresaw it, if God had not been beforehand with them and spoken first: *Lest thou shouldst say, Behold, I knew them, v.* 7. Thus vain men, who would be thought wise, commonly undervalue a thing which is really great and surprising with this suggestion, that it was no more than they expected and they knew it would come to this. To anticipate this, and that this boasting might for ever be excluded, God told them of it before the day, when as yet they dreamed not of it. God has said and done enough to prevent men's boastings of themselves, and that *no flesh may glory in his presence,* and, if it have not the intended effect, it will aggravate the sin and ruin of the proud; and, sooner, or later, *every mouth shall be stopped, and all flesh shall become silent before God.*

2. Because he would leave them inexcusable in their obstinacy. *Therefore* he took this pains with them, because he knew they were obstinate, *v.* 4. He knew they were so obstinate and perverse that, if he had not supported the doctrine of providence by prophecy, they would have had the impudence to deny it, and would have said that their idol had done that which God did. He knew very well, (1.) How wilful they would be, and how fully bent they would be upon that which is evil: *I knew that thou wast hard;* so the word is. There were prophecies as well as precepts which God gave them because of the hardness of their hearts: *"Thy neck is an iron sinew,* unapt to yield and submit to the yoke of God' commandments, unapt to turn and look back upon his dealings with thee or look up to his displeasure against thee; not flexible to the will of God, nor pliable to his intentions, nor manageable by his word or providence. *Thy brow is brass;* thou art impudent and canst not blush, insolent and wilt not fear or give back, but wilt thrust on in the way of thy heart." God uses means to bring sinners to comply with him, though he knows they are obstinate. (2.) How deceitful they would be and how insincere in that which is good, *v.* 8. God sent his prophets to them, but they did not hear, they would not know, and it was no more than was expected, considering what they had been. Thou *wast called,* and not miscalled, *a transgressor from the womb.* Ever since they were first formed into a people they were prone to idolatry; they brought with them out of Egypt a strange addictedness to that sin; and they were murmurers as soon as ever they began their march to Canaan. They were justly upbraided with it then, Deu. 9:7, 24. Therefore *I knew that thou wouldst deal very treacherously.* God foresaw their apostasy, and gave this reason for it, that he had always found them false and fickle, Deu. 31:16, 27, 29. This is applicable to particular persons. We are all born children of disobedience; we were called *transgressors from the womb,* and therefore it is easy to foresee that we shall deal treacherously, very treacherously. Where original sin is actual sin will follow of course. God knows it, and yet deals not with us according to our deserts.

Verses 9–15

The deliverance of God's people out of their captivity in Babylon was a thing upon many accounts so improbable that there was need of line upon line for the encouragement of the faith and hope of God's people concerning it. Two things were discouraging to them — their own unworthiness that God should do it for them and the many difficulties in the thing itself; now, in these verses, both these discouragements are removed, for here is,

I. A reason why God would do it for them, though they were unworthy; not for their sake, be it known to them, but *for his name's sake, for his own sake, v.* 9–11. 1. It is true they had been very provoking, and God had been justly angry with them. Their captivity was the punishment of their iniquity; and if, when he had them in Babylon, he had left them to pine away and perish there, and made the desolations of their country perpetual, he would only have dealt with them according to their sins, and it was what such a sinful people might expect from an angry God. "But," says God, *"I will defer my anger"* (or, rather, *stifle and suppress it);* "I will make it appear that I am slow to wrath, and will refrain from thee, not pour upon thee what I justly might, that I should cut thee off from being a people." And why will God thus stay his hand? *For my name's sake;* because this people was called by his name, and made profession of his name, and, if they were cut off, the enemies would blaspheme his name. *It is for my praise;* because it would redound to the honour of his mercy to spare and reprieve them, and, if he continued them to be to him a people, they might be to him for a name and a praise. 1. It is true they were very corrupt and ill-disposed, but God would himself refine them, and make them fit for the mercy he intended for them: *"I have refined thee,* that thou mightest be made a vessel of honour." Though he does not find them meet for his favour, he will make them so. And this accounts for his bringing them into the trouble, and continuing them in it so long as he did. It was not to cut them off, but to do them good. It was to refine them, *but not as silver,* or *with silver,* not so thoroughly as men refine their silver, which they continue in the furnace till all the dross is separated from it; if God should take that course with them, they would be always in the furnace, for they are all dross, and, as such, might justly be put away (Ps. 119:119) as reprobate silver, Jer. 6:30. He therefore takes them as they are, refined in part only, and not thoroughly. *"I have chosen thee in the furnace of affliction,* that is, I have made thee a choice one by the good which the affliction has done thee, and then designed thee for great things." Many have been brought home to God as chosen vessels and a good work of grace has been begun in them in the furnace of affliction. Affliction is no bar to God's choice, but subservient to his purpose. 3. It is true they could not pretend to merit at God's hand so great a favour as their deliverance out of Babylon, which would put such an honour upon them and bring them so much joy; therefore, says God, *For my own sake, even for my own sake, will I do it, v.* 11. See how the emphasis is laid upon that; for it is a reason that cannot fail, and therefore the resolution grounded upon it cannot fall to the ground. God will do it, not because he owes them such a favour, but to save the honour of his own name, that that may not be polluted by the insolent triumphs of the heathen, who, in triumphing over Israel, thought they triumphed over the God of Israel and imagined their gods too hard for him. This was plainly the language of Belshazzar's revels, when he profaned the holy vessels of God's temple at the same time that he praised his idols (Dan. 5:2, 4), and of the Babylonians' demand (Ps. 137:3), *Sing us one of the songs of Zion.* God will *therefore* deliver his people, because he will not suffer his glory to be thus given to another. Moses pleaded this often with God: Lord, *what will the Egyptians say?* Note, God is jealous for the honour of his own name, and will not suffer the wrath of man to proceed any further than he will make it turn to his praise. And it is matter of comfort to God's people that, whatever becomes of them, God will secure his own honour; and, as far as is necessary to that, God will work deliverance for them.

II. Here is a proof that God could do it for them, though they were unable to help themselves and the thing seemed altogether impracticable. Let Jacob and Israel hearken to this, and believe it, and take the comfort of it. They are God's called, *called according to his purpose,* called by him out of Egypt (Hos. 11:1) and now out of Babylon, a people whom with a distinguishing favour he calls by name, and to whom he calls. They are his called, for they are called to him, called by his name, and called his; and therefore he will look after them, and they may be assured that, as he will deliver them for his own sake, so he will deliver them by his own strength. They need not fear them, for, 1. He is God alone, and the eternal God (*v.* 12): *"I am he who can do what I will and will do what is best, he whom none can compare with, much less contend with. I am the first; I also am the last."* Who can be too quick for him that is the first, or anticipate him? Who can be too hard for him that is the last, and will keep the field against all opposers, and will reign till they are all made his footstool? What room then is left to doubt of their deliverance when *he* undertakes it whose designs cannot but be well laid, for he is the first, and well executed, for he is the last. As for this God, his work is perfect. 2. He is the God that made the world, and he that did that can do any thing, *v.* 13. Look we down? We see the earth firm under us, and feel it so; it was his hand that *laid the foundation of it.* Look we up? We see the heavens spread out as a canopy over our heads, and it was his hand that spread them, that *spanned* them, that stretched them out, and did it by an exact measure, as the workman sometimes metes out his work by spans. This intimates that God has a vast reach and can compass designs of the greatest extent. *If the palm of his right hand* (so the margin reads it) has gone so far as to stretch out the heavens, what will he do with his outstretched arm? Yet this is not all: he has not only made the heavens and the earth, and therefore he in whom our hope and help is omnipotent (Ps. 124:8), but he has the command of all the hosts of both; when he calls them into his service, to go on his errands, they stand up together, they come at the call, they answer to their names: "Here we are; what wilt thou have us to do?" They stand up, not only in reverence to their Creator, but in a readiness to execute his orders: *They stand up together,* unanimously concurring, and helping one another in the service of their Maker. If God therefore will deliver his people, he cannot be at a loss for instruments to be employed in effecting their deliverance. 3. He has already foretold it, and, having infinite knowledge, so that he foresaw it, no doubt he has almighty power to effect it: "*All you* of the house of Jacob, *assemble yourselves, and hear* this for your comfort, *Which among them,* among the gods of the heathen, or their wise men, *has declared these things,* or could declare them?" *v.* 14. They had no foresight of them at all, but those who consulted them were very confident that Babylon should be a lady for ever and Israel perpetual slave; and their oracles did not give them the least hint to the contrary, to undeceive them; whereas God by his prophets had given notice to the Jews, long before, of their captivity and the destruction of Jerusalem, as he had now likewise given them notice of their release (*v.* 15): *I, even*

I, have spoken; and he would not have spoken it if he could not have made it good: none could out-see him, and therefore we may be sure that none could outdo him. 4. The person is pitched upon who is to be employed in this service, and the measures are concerted in the divine counsels, which are unalterable. Cyrus is the man who must do it; and it tends much to strengthen our assurance that a thing shall be done when we are particularly informed how and by whom. It is not left at uncertainty who shall do it, but the matter is fixed. (1.) It is one whom God is well pleased in, upon this account, because he is designed for this service: *The Lord has loved him* (*v.* 14); he has done him this favour, this honour, to make him an instrument in the redemption of his people and therein a type of the great Redeemer, God's beloved Son, *in whom he was well pleased.* Those God does a great kindness to, and has a great kindness for, whom he makes serviceable to his church. (2.) It is one to whom God will give authority and commission: *I have called him,* have given him a sufficient warrant, and therefore will bear him out. (3.) It is one whom God will by a series of providences lead to this service: "*I have brought him from a far* country, brought him to engage against Babylon, brought him step by step, quite beyond his own intentions." Whom God calls he will bring, will *cause them to come* (so the word is), to come at the call. (4.) It is one whom God will own and give success to. Cyrus will *do God's pleasure on Babylon,* that which it is his pleasure should be done and which he will be pleased with the doing of, though Cyrus has ends of his own to serve and has no regard either to the will of God or to his favour in the doing of it. *His arm* (Cyrus's army, and in it God's arm) *shall* come, and *be upon the Chaldeans,* to bring them down (*v.* 14); for, if God call him and bring him, he will certainly *make his way prosperous, v.* 15. *Then* we may hope to prosper in our way when we follow a divine call and guidance.

Verses 16–22

Here, as before, Jacob and Israel are summoned to hearken to the prophet speaking in God's name, or rather to God speaking in and by the prophet, and that as a type of the great prophet by whom God has in these last days spoken unto us, and that is sufficient: *Come near* therefore, *and hear this.* Note, Those that would hear and understand what God says must come near, and approach to him; let them come as near as they can. Let those that have hearkened to the tempter now come near, and hear this, that they may be confirmed in their resolutions to serve God. Those that draw nigh to God may depend upon this, that his secret shall be with them. Here,

I. God refers them to what he hath both said to them and done for them formerly, which if they would reflect upon, they might thence fetch great encouragement to trust in God at this time. 1. He had always spoken plainly to them *from the beginning,* by Moses and all the prophets: *I have not spoken in secret,* but publicly, from the top of Mount Sinai, and in the chief places of concourse, the solemn assemblies of their tribes; he did not deliver his oracles obscurely and ambiguously, but so that they might be understood, Hab. 2:2. 2. He had always acted wonderfully for them: "*From the time* that they were first formed into a people *there I am,* there have I been resident among them and presiding in their affairs (he sent them prophets, raised them up judges, and frequently appeared for them), and therefore there I will be still." He that has been with his people hitherto will be to the end.

II. The prophet himself, as a type of the great prophet, asserts his own commission to deliver this message: *Now the Lord God* (the same that spoke from the beginning and did not speak in secret) *has by his Spirit sent me, v.* 16. The Spirit of God is here spoken of as a person distinct from the Father and the Son, and having a divine authority to send prophets. Note, Whom God sends the Spirit sends. Those whom God commissions for any service the Spirit in some measure qualifies for it; and those may speak boldly, and must be heard obediently, whom God and his Spirit send. As that which the prophet says to the same purport with this (*ch.* 61:1) is applied to Christ (Lu. 4:21), so may this be; the Lord God sent him, and he had the Spirit without measure.

III. God by the prophet sends them a gracious message for their support and comfort under their affliction. The

preface to this message is both awful and encouraging (*v.* 17): *Thus saith Jehovah,* the eternal God, *thy Redeemer,* that has often been so, that has engaged to be so, and will be faithful to the engagement, for he is *the Holy One,* that cannot deceive, *the Holy One of Israel,* that will not deceive them. The same words that introduce the law, and give authority to that, introduce the promise, and give validity to that: *"I am the Lord thy God,* whom thou mayest depend upon as in relation to thee and in covenant with thee."

1. Here is the good work which God undertakes to fulfil in them. He that is their Redeemer, in order to that, will be, (1.) Their instructor: *"I am thy God that teaches thee to profit,* that is, teaches thee such things as are profitable for thee, things that belong to thy peace." By *this* God shows himself to be a God in covenant with us, by his *teaching us* (Heb. 8:10, 11); and none teaches like him, for he gives an understanding. Whom God redeems he teaches; whom he designs to deliver out of their afflictions he first teaches to profit by their afflictions, makes them partakers of his holiness, for that is the *profit for which he chastens us,* Heb. 12:10. (2.) Their guide: *He leads them* to the way and *in the way by which they should go.* He not only enlightens their eyes, but directs their steps. By his grace he leads them in the way of duty, by his providence he leads them in the way of deliverance. Happy are those that are under such a guidance!

2. Here is the good-will which God declares he had for them by his good wishes concerning them, *v.* 18, 19. He had indeed brought them into captivity, but it was owing to themselves, nor did he afflict them willingly. (1.) As when he gave them his law he earnestly wished they might be obedient (*O that there were such a heart in them!* Deu. 5:29. *O that they were wise!* Deu. 32:29), so, when he had punished them for the breach of his law, he wished they had been obedient: *O that thou hadst hearkened to my commandments! v.* 18. *O that my people had hearkened unto me!* Ps. 81:13. This confirms what God had said and sworn, that he has *no pleasure in the death of sinners.* (2.) He assures them that, if they had been obedient, that would not only have prevented their captivity, but would have advanced and perpetuated their prosperity. He had abundance of good things ready to bestow upon them if their sins had not *turned them away, ch.* 59:1, 2. [1.] They should have been carried on in a constant uninterrupted stream of prosperity: *"Thy peace should have been as a river;* thou shouldst have enjoyed a series of mercies, one continually following another, as the waters of a river, which always last." *Labitur, et labetur in omne volubilis aevum — It flows, and will for ever flow;* not like the waters of a land-flood, which are soon gone. [2.] Their virtue and honour, and the justice of their cause, should in all cases have borne down opposition by their own strength, *as the waves of the sea.* Such should their righteousness have been that nothing should have stood before it; whereas, now they had been disobedient, the current of their prosperity was interrupted, and their righteousness overpowered. [3.] The rising generation should have been very numerous and very prosperous; whereas they were now very few, as appears by the small number of the returning captives (Ezra 2:64), not so many as of one tribe when they came out of Egypt. They should have been *numberless as the sand,* according to the promise (Gen. 22:17), which they had forfeited the benefit of: "*The offspring of thy bowels* would have been innumerable, *like the gravel of the sea,* if thy righteousness had been irresistible and unconquerable as the waves of the sea." [4.] The honour of Israel should still have been unstained, untouched: *His name should not have been cut off,* as now it is in the land of Israel, which is either desolate or inhabited by strangers; nor should it have *been destroyed from before God.* We cannot reckon the name either of a family or of a kingdom destroyed till it is destroyed from before God, till it ceases to be a name in his holy place. Now God tells them thus what he would have done for them if they had persevered in their obedience, *First,* That they might be the more humbled for their sins, by which they had forfeited such rich mercies. Note, *This* should engage us (I might say, enrage us) against sin, that it has not only deprived us of the good things we have enjoyed, but prevented the good things God had in store for us. It will make the misery of the disobedient the more intolerable to think how happy they might have been.

Secondly, That his mercy might appear the more illustrious in working deliverance for them, though they had forfeited it and rendered themselves unworthy of it. Nothing but a prerogative of mercy would have saved them.

3. Here is assurance given of the great work which God designed to work for them, even their salvation out of their captivity, when he had accomplished his work in them.

(1.) Here is a commission granted them to leave Babylon. God proclaimed, long before Cyrus did, that whoever would might return to his own land (*v.* 20): "You have a full discharge sent you: *Go you forth out of Babylon;* the prison-doors are thrown open, and the trumpet sounds, proclaiming a release." Perhaps with this word, as a means, the Spirit of the Lord stirred up the spirits of those that did take the benefit of Cyrus's proclamation (Ezra 1:5): *Flee you from the Chaldeans,* not with an ignominious stolen flight, as Jacob fled from Laban, but with a holy disdain, as scorning to stay any longer among them; flee you, not silently and sorrowfully, but with a voice, with a voice of singing, as they fled of old out of Egypt, Ex. 15:1.

(2.) Here is the news of this sent to all parts: "Let it be declared; let it be told; let it be uttered; make it to be heard by the most remote, by the most remiss; send the tidings of it by word of mouth; send it by writing, from city to city, from kingdom to kingdom, even to the utmost regions, *to the ends of the earth."* This was a figure of the publishing of the gospel to all the world; but that brings glad tidings which all the world is concerned in, this only that which it is fit all should take notice of, that they may be invited by it to forsake their idols and come into the service of the God of Israel. Let them all know then, [1.] That those whom God owns for his are such as he has dearly bought and paid for: *The Lord has redeemed his servant Jacob;* he has done it formerly, when he brought them out of Egypt, and now he is about to do it again. Jacob was God's servant, and therefore he redeemed him; for what had other masters to do with God's servants? Israel is God's son, therefore Pharaoh must let him go. God redeemed Jacob, and therefore it was fit that he should be his servant (Ps. 116:16); the bonds God had loosed tied them the faster to him. He that redeemed us has an unquestionable right to us. [2.] That those whom God designs to bring home to himself he will take care of, that they want not for the necessary expenses of their journey. When he brought them out of Egypt, and *led them through the deserts,* they *thirsted not* (*v.* 21), for in all their removals the water out of the rock followed them; thence *he caused the waters to flow,* and, since rock-water is the clearest and finest, God *clave the rock, and the waters gushed out;* for he can fetch in necessary supplies for his people in a way that they think the least likely. This refers to what he did for them when he brought them out of Egypt; when all this was literally true. But it should now be in effect done again, in their return out of Babylon, so well provided for should they and theirs be in their return. God does his work as effectually by marvellous providences as by miracles, though perhaps they are not so much taken notice of. This is applicable to those treasures of grace laid up for us in Jesus Christ, from which all good flows to us as the water did to Israel out of the rock, for that rock is Christ.

(3.) Here is a caveat put in against the wicked who go on still in their trespasses. Let not them think to have any benefit among God's people. Though in show and profession they herd themselves among them, let them not expect to come in sharers; no (*v.* 22), though God's thoughts concerning the body of that people were thoughts of peace, yet to those among them that were *wicked* and hated to be reformed *there is no peace,* no peace with God or their own consciences, no real good, whatever is pretended to. What have those to do with peace who are enemies to God? Their false prophets cried Peace to those to whom it did not belong; but God tells them that there shall be no peace, nor any think like it, to the wicked. The quarrel sinners have commenced with God, if not taken up in time by repentance, will be an everlasting quarrel.

CHAPTER 49

Glorious things had been spoken in the previous chapters concerning the deliverance of the Jews out of Babylon; but lest any should think, when it was accomplished, that it looked much greater and brighter in the prophecy than in the performance, and that the return of about 40,000 Jews in a poor condition out of Babylon to Jerusalem was not an event sufficiently answering to the height and grandeur of the expressions used in the prophecy, he here comes to show that the prophecy had a further intention, and was to have its full accomplishment in a redemption that should as far outdo these expressions as the other seemed to come short of them, even the redemption of the world by Jesus Christ, of whom not only Cyrus, who was God's servant in foretelling it, was a type. In this chapter we have, I. The designation of Christ, under the type of Isaiah, to his office as Mediator (*v.* 1–3). II. The assurance given him of the success of his undertaking among the Gentiles (*v.* 4–8). III. The redemption that should be wrought by him, and the progress of that redemption (*v.* 9–12). IV. The encouragement given hence to the afflicted church (*v.* 13–17). V. The addition of many to it, and the setting up of a church among the Gentiles (*v.* 18–23). VI. A ratification of the prophecy of the Jews' release out of Babylon, which was to be the figure and type of all these blessings, (*v.* 24–26). If this chapter be rightly understood, we shall see ourselves to be more concerned in the prophecies relating to the Jews' deliverance out of Babylon than we thought we were.

Verses 1–6

Here, I. An auditory is summoned together and attention demanded. The sermon in the foregoing chapter was directed to the house of Jacob and the people of Israel, *v.* 1, 12. But this is directed to the isles (that is, the Gentiles, for they are called *the isles of the Gentiles,* Gen. 10:5) and to *the people from far,* that were *strangers to the commonwealth of Israel,* and afar off. Let these listen (*v.* 1) as to a thing at a distance, which yet they are to hear with desire and attention. Note, 1. The tidings of a Redeemer are sent to the Gentiles, and to those that lie most remote; and they are concerned to listen to them. 2. The Gentiles listened to the gospel when the Jews were deaf to it.

II. The great author and publisher of the redemption produces his authority from heaven for the work he had undertaken. 1. God had appointed him and set him apart for it: *The Lord has called me from the womb* to this office and *made mention of my name,* nominated me to be the Saviour. By an angel he called him *Jesus — a Saviour,* who *should save his people from their sins,* Mt. 1:21. Nay, from the womb of the divine counsels, before all worlds, he was called to this service, and help was laid upon him; and he came at the call, for he said, *Lo, I come,* with an eye to what was written of him *in the volume of the book.* This was said of some of the prophets, as types of him, Jer. 1:5. Paul was separated to the apostleship from his mother's womb, Gal. 1:15. 2. God had fitted and qualified him for the service to which he designed him. He *made his mouth like a sharp sword,* and *made him* like *a polished shaft,* or a bright arrow, furnished him with every thing necessary to fight God's battles against the powers of darkness, to conquer Satan, and bring back God's revolted subjects to their allegiance, by his word: that is the *two-edged sword* (Heb. 4:12) which comes out of his mouth, Rev. 19:15. The convictions of the word are the arrows that shall be sharp in the hearts of sinners, Ps. 45:5. 3. God had preferred him to the service for which he had reserved him: *He has hidden me in the shadow of his hand* and in his quiver, which denotes, (1.) Concealment. The gospel of Christ, and the calling in of the Gentiles by it, were long hidden from ages and generations, hidden in God (Eph. 3:5, Rom. 16:25), hidden in the shadow of the ceremonial law and the Old-Testament types. (2.) Protection. The house of David was the particular care of the divine Providence, because that blessing was in it. Christ in his infancy was sheltered from the rage of Herod. 4. God had owned him, had said unto him, *"Thou art my servant,* whom I have employed and will prosper; thou art Israel, in effect, *the prince with God,* that hast wrestled and prevailed; and in thee I will be glorified." The people of God are *Israel,* and they are all gathered together, summed up, as it were, in Christ, the great representative of all Israel, as the high priest who had the names of all the tribes on his breastplate; and in him God is and will be glorified; so he said by a voice from heaven, Jn. 12:27, 28. Some read the words in two clauses: *Thou art my servant* (so Christ is, *ch.* 42:1); *it is Israel in whom I will be glorified by thee;* it is the spiritual Israel, the elect, in the salvation of whom by Jesus Christ God will be glorified, and his free grace for ever admired.

III. He is assured of the good success of his undertaking; for whom God calls he will prosper. And as to this,

1. He objects the discouragement he had met with at his first setting out (*v.* 4): "Then I said, with a sad heart, *I have laboured in vain;* those that were ignorant, and careless, and strangers to God, are so still: *I have called, and they have refused;* I have *stretched out my hands to a gainsaying people."* This was Isaiah's complaint, but it was no more than he was told to expect, *ch.* 6:9. The same was a temptation to Jeremiah to resolve he would labour no more, Jer. 20:9. It is the complaint of many a faithful minister, that has not loitered, but laboured, not spared, but spent, his strength, and himself with it, and yet, as to many, it is all in vain and for nought; they will not be prevailed with to repent and believe. But here it seems to point at the obstinacy of the Jews, among whom Christ went in person preaching the gospel of the kingdom, laboured and spent his strength, and yet the rulers and the body of the nation rejected him and his doctrine; so very few were brought in, when one would think none should have stood out, that he might well say, *"I have laboured in vain,* preached so many sermons, wrought so many miracles, in vain." Let not the ministers think it strange that they are slighted when the Master himself was.

2. He comforts himself under this discouragement with this consideration, that it was the cause of God in which he was engaged and the call of God that engaged him in it: *Yet surely my judgment is with the Lord,* who is the Judge of all, *and my work with my God,* whose servant I am. His comfort is, and it may be the comfort of all faithful ministers, when they see little success of their labours, (1.) That, however it be, it is a righteous cause that they are pleading. They are with God, and for God; they are on his side, and workers together with him. They like not their judgment, the rule they go by, nor their work, the business they are employed in, ever the worse for this. The unbelief of men gives them no cause to suspect the truth of their doctrine, Rom. 3:3. (2.) That their management of this cause, and their prosecution of this work, were known to God, and they could appeal to him concerning their sincerity, and that it was not through any neglect of theirs that they laboured in vain. *"He knows the way that I take; my judgment is with the Lord,* to determine whether I have not delivered my soul and left the blood of those that perish on their own heads." (3.) Though the labour be in vain as to those that are laboured with, yet not as to the labourer himself, if he be faithful: his judgment is with the Lord, who will justify him and bear him out, though men condemn him and run him down; and his work (the reward of his work) is with his God, who will take care he shall be no loser, no, not by his lost labour. (4.) Though the judgment be not yet brought forth unto victory, nor the work to perfection, yet both are with the Lord, to carry them on and give them success, according to his purpose, in his own way and time.

3. He receives from God a further answer to this objection, *v.* 5, 6. He knew very well that God had set him on work, had *formed him from the womb to be his servant,* had not only called him so early to it (*v.* 1), but begun so early to fit him for it and dispose him to it. Those whom God designs to employ as his servants he is fashioning and preparing to be so long before, when perhaps neither themselves nor others are aware of it. It is he that forms the spirit of man within him. Christ was to be *his servant, to bring Jacob again to him,* that had treacherously departed from him. The seed of Jacob therefore, according to the flesh, must first be dealt with, and means used to bring them back. Christ, and the word of salvation by him, are sent to them first; nay, Christ comes in person to them only, *to the lost sheep of the house of Israel.* But what if Jacob will not be brought back to God and Israel will not be gathered? So it proved; but this is a satisfaction in that case, (1.) Christ will be glorious in the eyes of the Lord; and those are truly glorious that are so in God's eyes. Though few of the Jewish nation were converted by Christ's preaching and miracles, and many of them loaded him with ignominy and disgrace, yet God put honour upon him, and made him glorious, at his baptism, and in his transfiguration, spoke to him from heaven, sent angels to minister to him, made even his shameful death glorious by the many prodigies that attended it, much more his resurrection. In his sufferings God was his strength, so that though he met with all the discouragement imaginable, by the contempts of a people whom he had done so much to oblige, yet he *did not fail nor was discouraged.* An angel was sent from heaven to *strengthen* him, Lu. 22:43. Faithful ministers, though they see not the fruit of their labours, shall yet be accepted of God, and in that they shall be truly glorious, for his favour is our honour; and they shall be assisted to proceed and persevere in their labours

notwithstanding. This weakens their hands, but their God will be their strength. (2.) The gospel shall be glorious in the eyes of the world; though it be not so in the eyes of the Jews, yet it shall be entertained by the nations, *v.* 6. The Messiah seemed as if he had been primarily designed to *bring Jacob back, v.* 5. But he is here told that it is comparatively but a small matter; a higher orb of honour than that, and a larger sphere of usefulness, are designed him: *"It is a light thing that thou shouldst be my servant, to raise up the tribes of Jacob* to the dignity and dominion they expect by the Messiah, and to *restore the preserved of Israel,* and make them a flourishing church and state as formerly" (nay, considering what a little handful of people they are, it would be but a small matter, in comparison, for the Messiah to be the Saviour of them only); "and therefore *I will give thee for a light to the Gentiles* (many great and mighty nations by the gospel of Christ shall be brought to the knowledge and worship of the true God), *that thou mayest be my salvation,* the author of that salvation which I have designed for lost man, and this *to the end of the earth,* to nations at the greatest distance." Hence Simeon learned to call Christ *a light to lighten the Gentiles* (Lu. 2:32), and St. Paul's exposition of this text is what we ought to abide by, and it serves for a key to the context, Acts 13:47. *Therefore,* says he, we turn to the Gentiles, to preach the gospel to them, *because so has the Lord commanded us, saying, I have set thee to be a light to the Gentiles.* In this the Redeemer was truly glorious, though Israel was not gathered; the setting up of his kingdom in the Gentile world was more his honour than if he had raised up all the tribes of Jacob. This promise is in part fulfilled already, and will have a further accomplishment, if that time be yet to come which the apostle speaks of, when the fulness of the Gentiles shall be brought in. Observe, God calls it his salvation, which some think intimates how well pleased he was with it, how he gloried in it, and (if I may so say) how much his heart was upon it. They further observe that Christ is given for a light to all those to whom he is given for salvation. It is in darkness that men perish. Christ enlightens men's eyes, and so makes them holy and happy.

Verses 7–12

In these verses we have,

I. The humiliation and exaltation of the Messiah (*v.* 7): *The Lord, the Redeemer of Israel, and Israel's Holy One,* who had always taken care of the Jewish church and wrought out for them those deliverances that were typical of the great salvation, speaks here to him, who was the undertaker of that salvation. And, 1. He takes notice of his humiliation, the instances of which were uncommon, nay, unparalleled. He was one *whom man despised.* He is *despised and rejected of men, ch.* 53:3. To be despised by so mean a creature (man, who is himself a worm) bespeaks the lowest and most contemptible condition imaginable. Man, whom he came to save and to put honour upon, yet despised him and put contempt upon him; so wretchedly ungrateful were his persecutors. The ignominy he underwent was not the least of his sufferings. They not only made him despicable, but odious. He was *one whom the nation abhorred;* they treated him as the worst of men, and cried out, *Crucify him, crucify him.* The nation did it, the Gentiles as well as Jews, and the Jews herein worse than Gentiles; for his cross was *to the one a stumbling-block* and *to the other foolishness.* He was *a servant of rulers;* he was trampled upon, abused, scourged, and crucified as a slave. Pilate boasted of his power over him, Jn. 19:10. This he submitted to for our salvation. 2. He promises him his exaltation. Honour was done him even in the depth of his humiliation. Herod the king stood in awe of him, saying, *I it John the Baptist;* noblemen, rulers, centurions came and kneeled to him. But this was more fully accomplished when kings received his gospel, and submitted to his yoke, and joined in the worship of him, and called themselves the vassals of Christ. Not that Christ values the rich more than the poor (they stand upon a level with him), but it is for the honour of his kingdom among men when the great ones of the earth appear for him and do homage to him. This shall be the accomplishment of God's promise, and he will give him the heathen for his inheritance, and *therefore* it shall be done, *because of the Lord who is faithful* and true to his promise; and this shall be an evidence that Christ had a commission for what he did, and that God had chosen him, and would own the choice he had made.

II. The blessings he has in store for all those to whom he is made salvation.

1. God will own and stand by him in his undertaking (*v.* 8): *In an acceptable time have I heard thee,* that is, I will hear thee. Christ, *in the days of his flesh, offered up strong cries, and was heard,* Heb. 5:7. He knew that the *Father heard him always* (Jn. 11:42), heard him for himself (for, though the cup might not pass from him, yet he was enabled to drink it), heard him for all that are his, and therefore he interceded for them as one having authority. *Father, I will,* Jn. 17:24. All our happiness results from the Son's interest in the Father and the prevalency of his intercession, that he always heard him; and this makes the gospel time an acceptable time, welcome to us, because we are accepted of God, both reconciled and recommended to him, that God hears the Redeemer for us, Heb. 7:25. Nor will he hear him only, but help him to go through with his undertaking. The Father was always with him at his right hand, and did not leave him when his disciples did. Violent attacks were made upon our Lord Jesus by the powers of darkness, when it was their hour, to drive him off from his undertakings, but God promises to preserve him and enable him to persevere in it; on that *one stone were seven eyes,* Zec. 3:9. God would preserve him, would preserve his interest, his kingdom among men, though fought against on all sides. Christ is preserved while Christianity is.

2. God will authorize him to apply to his church the benefits of the redemption he is to work out. God's preserving and helping him was to make the day of his gospel a day of salvation. And so the apostle understands it: *Behold, now is the day of salvation,* now the word of reconciliation by Christ is preached, 2 Co. 6:2.

(1.) He shall be guarantee of the treaty of peace between God and man: I will *give thee for a covenant of the people.* This we had before (*ch.* 42:6), and it is here repeated as faithful, and well worthy of all acceptation and observation. He is given for a covenant, that is, for a pledge of all the blessings of the covenant. It was in him that God was *reconciling the world to himself;* and he that *spared not his own Son* will deny us nothing. He is given for a covenant, not only as he is the Mediator of the covenant, the blessed *days-man who has laid his hand upon us both,* but as he is all in all in the covenant. All the duty of the covenant is summed up in our being his; and all the privilege and happiness of the covenant are summed up in his being ours.

(2.) He shall repair the decays of the church and build it upon a rock. He shall *establish the earth,* or rather the *land,* the land of Judea, a type of the church. He shall *cause the desolate heritages to be inherited;* so the cities of Judah were after the return out of captivity, and so the church, which in the last and degenerate ages of the Jewish nation had been as a country laid waste, but was again replenished by the fruits of the preaching of the gospel.

(3.) He shall free the souls of men from the bondage of guilt and corruption and bring them into the glorious liberty of God's children. He shall *say to the prisoners* that were bound over to the justice of God, and bound under the power of Satan, *Go forth, v.* 9. Pardoning mercy is a release from the curse of the law, and renewing grace is a release from the dominion of sin. Both are from Christ, and are branches of the great salvation. It is he that says, *Go forth;* it is the Son that makes us free, and then we are free indeed. He saith *to those that are in darkness, Show yourselves;* "not only *see,* but *be seen,* to the glory of God and your own comfort." When he discharged the lepers from their confinement, he said, *Go show yourselves to the priest.* When we see the light, let our light shine.

(4.) He shall provide for the comfortable passage of those whom he sets at liberty to the place of their rest and happy settlement, *v.* 9–11. These verses refer to the provision made for the Jews' return out of their captivity, who were taken under the particular care of the divine Providence, as favourites of Heaven, and now so in a special manner; but they are applicable to that guidance of divine grace which all God's spiritual Israel are under, from their release out of bondage to their settlement in the heavenly Canaan. [1.] They shall have their charges borne and shall be fed at free cost with food convenient: *They shall feed in the ways,* as sheep; for now, as formerly, God *leads Joseph like a flock.* When God pleases even highway ground shall be good ground for the sheep of his pasture to feed in. Their pastures shall be not only in the valleys, but *in all high places,* which are commonly dry and barren. Wherever God brings his people he will take care they shall want nothing that is good for them, Ps. 34:10. And so well shall they be provided for that they shall not hunger nor thirst, for what they need they shall have seasonably, before their need of it comes to an extremity. [2.] They shall be sheltered and protected from every thing that would incommode them: *Neither shall the heat nor sun smite them,* or God causes *his flock to rest at noon,* Cant. 1:7. No evil thing shall befal those that put themselves under a divine protection; they shall be enabled to *bear the burden and heat of the day.* [3.] They shall be under God's gracious guidance: *He that has mercy on them,* in bringing them out of their captivity, *shall lead them,* as he did their fathers in the wilderness, by a pillar of cloud and fire. *Even by springs of water,* which will be ready to them in their march, *shall he guide them.* God will furnish them with suitable and seasonable comforts, not like the pools of rainwater in the valley of Baca, but like the water out of the rock which followed Israel. Those who are under a divine guidance, and follow that closely, while they do so, may, upon good grounds, hope for divine comforts and cordials. The world leads its followers by broken cisterns, or brooks that fail in summer; but God leads those that are his by springs of water. And those whom God guides shall find a ready road and all obstacles removed (*v.* 11): *I will make all my mountains a way.* He that in times past made the sea a way, now with as much ease will make the mountains a way, though they seemed impassable. The highway, or causeway, shall be raised, to make it both the plainer and the fairer. Note, The ways in which God leads his people he himself will be the overseer of, and will take care that they be well mended and kept in repair, as of old the ways that led to the cities of refuge. The levelling of the roads from Babylon, as it was foretold (*ch.* 40:2, 3), was applied to gospel work, and so may this be. Though there be difficulties in the way to heaven, which we cannot by our own strength get over, yet the grace of God shall be sufficient to help us over them and to make even the mountains a way, *ch.* 35:8.

(5.) He shall bring them all together from all parts, that they may return in a body, that they may encourage one another and be the more taken notice of. They were dispersed into several parts of the country of Babylon, as their enemies pleased, to prevent any combination among themselves. But, when God's time shall come to bring them home together, one spirit shall animate them all, all that lie at the greatest distance from each other, and those also that had taken shelter in other countries shall meet them in the land of Judah, *v.* 12. Here shall a party *come from far,* some *from the north,* some *from the west,* some *from the land of Sinim,* which probably is some province of Babylon not elsewhere named in scripture, but some make it to be a country belonging to one of the chief cities of Egypt, called *Sin,* of which we read, Eze. 30:15, 16. Now this promise was to have a further accomplishment in the great confluence of converts to the gospel church, and its full accomplishment when God's chosen shall come from the east and from the west to sit down with the patriarchs in the kingdom of God, Mt. 8:11.

Verses 13–17

The scope of these verses is to show that the return of the people of God out of their captivity, and the eternal redemption to be wrought out by Christ (of which that was a type), would be great occasions of joy to the church and great proofs of the tender care God has of the church.

I. Nothing can furnish us with better matter for songs of praise and thanksgiving, *v.* 13. Let the whole creation join with us in songs of joy, for it shares with us in the benefits of the redemption, and all they can contribute to this sacred melody is little enough in return for such inestimable favours, Ps. 96:11. Let there be joy in heaven, and let the angels of God celebrate the praises of the great Redeemer; let the earth and the mountains, particularly the great ones of the earth, *be joyful,* and *break forth into singing, for the earnest expectation of the creature* that *waits for the glorious liberty of the children of God* (Rom. 8:19, 21) shall now be *abundantly answered.* God's people are the blessings and ornaments of the world, and therefore let there be universal joy, for *God has comforted his people* that were in sorrow and *he will have mercy upon the afflicted* because of his compassion, upon *his* afflicted because of his covenant.

II. Nothing can furnish us with more convincing arguments to prove the most tender and affectionate concern God has for his church, and her interests and comforts.

1. The troubles of the church have given some occasion to question God's care and concern for it, *v.* 14. *Zion,* in distress, *said, The Lord has forsaken me,* and looks after me no more; *my Lord has forgotten me,* and *will* look after me no more. See how deplorable the case of God's people may be sometimes, such that they may seem to be forsaken and forgotten of their God; and at such a time their temptations may be alarmingly violent. Infidels, in their presumption, say *God has forsaken the earth* (Eze. 8:12), and has *forgotten their sins,* Ps. 10:11. Weak believers, in their despondency, are ready to say, "God has forsaken his church and forgotten the sorrows of his people." But we have no more reason to question his promise and grace than we have to question his providence and justice. He is as sure a rewarder as he is a revenger. Away therefore with these distrusts and jealousies, which are the bane of friendship.

2. The triumphs of the church, after her troubles, will in due time put the matter out of question.

(1.) What God will do for Zion we are told, *v.* 17. [1.] Her friends, who had deserted her, shall be gathered to her, and shall contribute their utmost to her assistance and comfort: *Thy children shall make haste.* Converts to the faith of Christ are the children of the church; they shall join themselves to her with great readiness and cheerfulness, and flock into the communion of saints, as doves to their windows. *"Thy builders shall make haste"* (so some read it), "who shall build up thy houses, thy walls, especially thy temple; they shall do it with expedition." Church work is usually slow work; but, when God's time shall come, it shall be done suddenly. [2.] Her enemies, who had threatened and assaulted her, shall be forced to withdraw from her: *Thy destroyers, and those who made thee waste,* who had made themselves masters of the country and ravaged it, *shall go forth of thee.* By Christ the prince of this world, the great destroyer, is cast out, is dispossessed, has his power broken and his attempts quite baffled.

(2.) Now by this it will appear that Zion's suggestions were altogether groundless, that God has not forsaken her, nor forgotten her, nor ever will. Be assured, [1.] That God has a tender affection for his church and people, *v.* 15. In answer to Zion's fears, God speaks as one concerned for his own glory (he takes himself to be reflected upon if Zion say, *The Lord has forsaken me,* and he will clear himself), as one concerned also for his people's comfort; he would not have them droop, and be discouraged, and give way to any uneasy thoughts. "You think that I have forgotten you. *Can a woman forget her sucking child?" First,* It is not likely that she should. A woman, whose honour it is to be of the tender sex as well as the fair one, cannot but have compassion for a child, which, being both harmless and helpless, is a proper object of compassion. A mother, especially, cannot but be concerned for her own child; for it is her own, a piece of herself, and very lately one with her. A nursing mother, most of all, cannot but be tender of her sucking child; her own breasts will soon put her in mind of it if she should forget it. But, *Secondly,* It is possible that she may forget. A woman may perhaps be so unhappy as not to be able to remember her sucking child (she may be sick, and dying, and going to the land of forgetfulness), or she may be so unnatural as not to have *compassion on the son of her womb,* as those who, to conceal their shame, are the death of their children as soon as they are their life, Lam. 4:10; Deu. 28:57. But, says God, *I will not forget thee.* Note, God's compassions to his people infinitely exceed those of the tenderest parents towards their children. What are the affections of nature to those of the God of nature! [2.] That he has a constant care of his church and people (*v.* 16): *I have engraven thee upon the palms of my hands.* This does not allude to the foolish art of palmistry, which imagines every man's fate to be engraved in the palms of his hands and to be legible in the lines there, but to the custom of those who tie a string upon their hands or fingers to put them in mind of things which they are afraid they shall forget, or to the wearing of signet or locket-rings in remembrance of some dear friend. His setting them thus as a seal upon his arm denotes his setting them as a seal upon his heart, and his being ever mindful of them and their interests, Cant. 8:6. If we *bind God's law as a sign upon our hand* (Deu. 6:8, 11, 18), he will engrave our interests as a sign on his hand, and will look upon that and remember the covenant. He adds, *"Thy walls shall be continually before me;* thy ruined walls, though no pleasing spectacle, shall be in my thoughts of compassion." Do Zions' friends *favour her dust?* Ps. 102:14. So does her God. Or, "The plan and model of thy walls, that are to be rebuilt, is before me, and they shall certainly be built according to it." Or, "Thy walls (that is, thy safety) are my continual care; so are the watchmen on thy walls." Some apply his engraving his church on the palms of his hands to the wounds in Christ's hands when he was crucified; he will look on the marks of them, and remember those for whom he suffered and died.

Verses 18–23

Two things are here promised, which were to be in part accomplished in the reviving of the Jewish church after its return out of captivity, but more fully in the planting of the Christian church by the preaching of the gospel of Christ; and we may take the comfort of these promises.

I. That the church shall be replenished with great numbers added to it. It was promised (*v.* 17) that *her children should make haste;* that promise is here enlarged upon, and is made very encouraging. It is promised,

1. That multitudes shall flock to the church from all parts. *Look round, and see how they gather themselves to thee* (*v.* 18), by a local accession to the Jewish church. They come to Jerusalem from all the adjacent countries, for that was then the centre of their unity; but, under the gospel, it is by a spiritual accession to the mystical body of Christ in faith and love. Those that *come to Jesus as the Mediator of the new covenant* do thereby *come to the Mount Zion,* the *church of the first-born,* Heb. 12:22, 23. *Lift up thy eyes, and behold* how *the fields are white unto the harvest,* Jn. 4:35. Note, It is matter of joy to the church to see a multitude of converts to Christ.

2. That such as are added to the church shall not be a burden and blemish to her, but her strength and ornament. This part of the promise is confirmed with an oath: *As I live, saith the Lord, thou shalt surely clothe thyself with them all.* The addition of such numbers to the church shall complete her clothing; and, when all that were chosen are effectually called, then the bride, the Lamb's wife, shall have made herself ready, shall be quite dressed, Rev. 19:7. They shall make her to appear comely and considerable; and she shall therefore bind them on with as much care and complacency as a bride does her ornaments. When those that are added to the church are serious, and holy, and exemplary in their conversation, they are an ornament to it.

3. That thus the country which was waste and desolate, and *without inhabitant* (*ch.* 5:9; 6:11), shall be again peopled, nay, it shall be over-peopled (*v.* 19): *"Thy waste and thy desolate places,* that have long lain so, *and the land of thy destruction,* that land of thine which was destroyed with thee and which nobody cared for dwelling in, shall now be so full of people that there shall be no room for the inhabitants." Here is blessing poured out till there be not *room enough to receive it,* Mal. 3:10. Not that they shall be crowded by their enemies, or straitened for room, as Abraham and Lot were, because of the Canaanite in the land. "No, *those that swallow thee up,* and took possession of thy land when thy possession of it was discontinued, *shall be far away.* Thy people shall be numerous, and there shall be no stranger, no enemy, among them." Thus the *kingdom of God among men,* which had been impoverished and almost depopulated, partly by the corruptions of the Jewish church and partly by the abominations of the Gentile world, was again peopled and enriched by the setting up of the Christian church, and by its graces and glories.

4. That the new converts shall strangely increase and multiply. Jerusalem, after she has lost abundance of her children by the sword, famine, and captivity, shall have a new family growing up instead of them, children which she *shall have after she has lost the other* (*v.* 20), as Seth, who was *appointed another seed instead of Abel,* and Job's children, which God blessed him with instead of those that were killed in the ruins of the house. God will repair his church's losses and secure to himself a seed to serve him in it. It is promised to the Jews, after their return, that *Jerusalem shall be full of boys and girls playing in the streets,* Zec. 8:5. The church, after it has lost the Jews, who will be cut off by their own infidelity, shall have abundance of children still, more than she had when the Jews belonged to her. See Gal. 4:27. They shall be so numerous that, (1.) The Children shall complain for want of room; they shall say (and it is a good hearing), "Our numbers increase so fast that *the place is too strait for us;"* as the sons of the prophets complained, 2 Ki. 6:1. But, strait as the place is, still more shall desire to be admitted, and the church shall gladly admit them, and the inconvenient straitness of the place shall be no hindrance to either; for it will be found, whatever we think, that even when the *poor and the maimed, the halt and the blind,* are brought in, *yet still there is room,* room enough for those that are in and room for more, Lu. 14:21, 22. (2.) The mother shall stand amazed at the increase of her family, *v.* 21. She shall say, *Who has begotten me these?* and, *Who has brought up these?* They come to her with all the duty, affection, and submission of children; and yet she never bore any pain for them, nor took any pains with them, but has them ready reared to her hand. This gives her a pleasing surprise, and she cannot but be astonished at it, considering what her condition had been very lately and very long. The Jewish nation had left her children; they were cut off. She had been desolate, without ark, and altar, and temple-service, those tokens of God's espousals to them; nay, she had been a captive, and continually removing to and fro, in an unsettled condition, and not likely to bring up children either for God or herself. She was left alone in obscurity *(this is Zion whom no man seeks after),* left in all the solitude and sorrow of a widowed state. How then came she to be thus replenished? See here, [1.] That the church is not perpetually visible, but there are times when it is desolate, and left alone, and made few in number. [2.] That yet on the other hand its desolations shall not be perpetual, nor will it be found too hard for God to repair them, and out of stones to raise up children unto Abraham. [3.] That sometimes this is done in a very surprising way, as when a nation is born at once, *ch.* 66:8.

5. That this shall be done with the help of the Gentiles, *v.* 22. The Jews were cast off, among whom it was expected that the church should be built up; but God will *sow it to himself in the earth,* and will thence reap a plentiful crop, Hos. 2:23. Observe, (1.) How the Gentiles shall be called in. God will *lift up his hand to them,* to invite or beckon them, having all the day stretched it out in vain to the Jews, *ch.* 65:2. Or it denotes the exerting of an almighty power, that of his Spirit and grace, to compel them to come in, to make them willing. And he will *set up his standard to them,* the preaching of the everlasting gospel, to which they shall gather, and under which they shall enlist themselves. (2.) How they shall come: *They shall bring thy sons in their arms.* They shall assist the sons of Zion, which are found among them, in their return to their own country, and shall forward them with as much tenderness as ever any parent carried a child that was weak and helpless. God can raise up friends for returning Israelites even among Gentiles. *The earth helped the woman,* Rev. 12:16. Or, "When they come themselves, they shall bring their children, and make them thy children;" compare *ch.* 60:4. "Dost thou ask, *Who has begotten and brought up these?* Know that they were begotten and brought up among the Gentiles, but they are now brought into thy family." Let all that are concerned about young converts, and young beginners in religion, learn hence to deal very tenderly and carefully with them, as Christ does with the lambs which he *gathers with his arms and carries in his bosom.*

II. That the church shall have a great and prevailing interest in the nations, *v.* 22, 23. 1. Some of the princes of the nations shall become patrons and protectors to the church: *King shall be thy nursing fathers,* to carry thy sons in their arms (as Moses, Num. 11:12); and, because women are the most proper nurses, *their queens shall be thy nursing mothers.* This promise was in part fulfilled to the Jews, after their return out of captivity. Several of the kings of Persia were very tender of their interests, countenanced and encouraged them, as Cyrus, Darius, and Artaxerxes; Esther the queen was a nursing mother to the Jews that remained in their captivity, putting her life in her hand to snatch the child out of the flames. The Christian church, after a long captivity, was happy in some such kings and queens as Constantine and his mother Helena, and afterwards Theodosius, and others, who nursed the church with all possible care and tenderness. Whenever the sceptre of government is put into the hands of religious princes, then this promise is fulfilled. The church in this world is in an infant state, and it is in the power of princes and magistrates to do it a great deal of service; it is happy when they do so, when their power is a praise to those that do well. 2. Others of them, who stand it out against the church's interests, will be forced to yield and to repent of their opposition: *They shall bow down to thee and lick the dust.* The promise to the church of Philadelphia seems to be borrowed from this (Rev. 3:9): *I will make those of the synagogue of Satan to come and worship before thy feet.* Or it may be meant of the willing subjection which kings and kingdoms shall pay to Christ the church's King, as he manifests himself in the church (Ps. 72:11): *All kings shall fall down before him.* And by all this it shall be made to appear, (1.) That God is the Lord, the sovereign Lord of all, against whom there is no standing out nor rising up. (2.) That those who wait for him, in a dependence upon his promise and a resignation to his will, shall not be made ashamed of their hope; for the vision of peace is for an appointed time, and at the end *it shall speak and shall not lie.*

Verses 24–26

Here is, I. An objection started against the promise of the Jews' release out of their captivity in Babylon, suggesting that it was a thing not to be expected; for (*v.* 24) they were a prey in the hand of the mighty, of such as were then the greatest potentates on earth, and therefore it was not likely they should be rescued by force. Yet that was not all: they were lawful captives; by the law of God, having offended, they were justly delivered into captivity; and by the law of nations, being taken in war, they were justly detained in captivity till they should be ransomed or exchanged. Now this is spoken either, 1. By the enemies, as justifying themselves in their refusal to let them go. They plead both might and right. Proud men think all their own that they can lay their hands on and their title good if they have but the longest sword. Or, 2. By their friends, either in a way of distrust, despairing of the deliverance ("for who is able to deal with those that detain us, either by force of arms or a treaty of peace?"), or in a way of thankfulness, admiring the deliverance. "Who would have thought that ever the prey should be *taken from the mighty?* Yet it is done." This is applicable to our redemption by Christ. As to Satan, we were a prey in the hand of the mighty, and yet delivered even from him that had the power of death, by him that had the power of life. As to the justice of God, we were lawful captives, and yet delivered by a price of inestimable value.

II. This objection answered by an express promise, and a further promise; for God's promises being all yea, and amen, they may well serve to corroborate one another. 1. Here is an express promise with a *non-obstante — notwithstanding* to the strength of the enemy (*v.* 25): *"Even the captives of the mighty,* though they are mighty, shall be taken away, and it is to no purpose for them to oppose it; *and the prey of the terrible,* though they are terrible, shall be delivered; and, as they cannot with all their strength outforce, so they cannot with all their impudence outface, the deliverance, and the counsels of God concerning it." *The Lord saith thus,* who, having all power and all hearts in his hands is able to make his words good. 2. Here is a further promise, showing how, and in what way, God will bring about the deliverance. He will bring judgments upon the oppressors, and so will work salvation for the oppressed: *"I will contend with him that contends with thee,* will plead thy cause against those that justify themselves in oppressing thee; whoever it be, though but a single person, that contends with thee, he shall know that it is at his peril, and thus *I will save thy children."* The captives shall be delivered by *leading captivity captive,* that is, sending those into captivity that had held God's people captive, Rev. 13:10. Nay, they shall have blood for blood (*v.* 26): *"I will feed those that oppress thee with their own flesh,* and *they shall be drunken with their own blood.* The proud Babylonians shall become not only an easy, but an acceptable, prey to one another. God will send a dividing spirit among them, and their ruin, which was begun by a foreign invasion, shall be completed by their intestine divisions. They shall *bite and devour one another,* till they are *consumed one of another.* They shall greedily and with delight prey upon those that are their own flesh and blood." God can make the oppressors of his church to be their own tormentors and their own destroyers. The New-Testament Babylon, having made herself drunk with the blood of the saints, shall have *blood given her to drink, for she is worthy.* See how cruel men sometimes are to themselves and to one another: indeed those who are so to others are so to themselves, for God's justice and men's revenge will mete to them what they have measured to others. They not only thirst after blood, but drink it so greedily that they are drunken with it, and with as much pleasure as if it were sweet wine. If God had not more mercy on sinners than they would have one upon another were their passions let loose, the world would be soon an *Aceldama,* nay, a desolation.

III. See what will be the effect of Babylon's ruin: *All flesh shall know that I the Lord am thy Saviour.* God will make it to appear, to the conviction of all the world, that, though Israel seem lost and cast off, they have a Redeemer, and, though they are made a prey to the mighty, Jacob has a mighty One, who is able to deal with all his enemies. God intends, by the deliverances of his church, both to notify and to magnify his own name.

CHAPTER 50

In this chapter, I. Those to whom God sends are justly charged with bringing all the troubles they were in upon themselves, by their own wilfulness and obstinacy, it being made to appear that God was able and ready to help them if they had been fit for deliverance (*v.* 1–3). II. He by whom God sends produces his commission (*v.* 4), alleges his own readiness to submit to all the services and sufferings he was called to in the execution of it (*v.* 5, 6), and assures himself that God, who sent him, would stand by him and bear him out against all opposition (*v.* 7–9). III. The message that is sent is life and death, good and evil, the blessing and the curse, comfort to desponding saints and terror to presuming sinners (*v.* 10, 11). Now all this seems to have a double reference, 1. To the unbelieving Jews in Babylon, who quarrelled with God for his dealings with them, and to the prophet Isaiah, who, though dead long before the captivity, yet, prophesying so plainly and fully of it, saw fit to produce his credentials, to justify what he had said. 2. To the unbelieving Jews in our Saviour's time, whose own fault it was that they were rejected, Christ having preached much to them, and suffered much from them, and being herein borne up by a divine power. The "contents" of this chapter, in our Bibles, give this sense of it, very concisely, thus: — "Christ shows that the dereliction of the Jews is not to be imputed to him, by his ability to save, by his obedience in that work, and by his confidence in divine assistance." The prophet concludes with an exhortation to trust in God and not in ourselves.

Verses 1–3

Those who have professed to be the people of God, and yet seem to be dealt severely with, are apt to complain of God, and to lay the fault upon him, as if he had been hard with them. But, in answer to their murmurings, we have here,

I. A challenge given them to prove, or produce any evidence, that the quarrel began on God's side, *v.* 1. They could not say that he had done them any wrong or had acted arbitrarily. 1. He had been a husband to them; and husbands were then allowed a power to put away their wives upon any little disgust: if their wives found not favour in their eyes, they made nothing of giving them a bill of divorce, Deu. 24:1; Mt. 19:7. But they could not say that God had dealt so with them. It is true they were now separated from him, and had abode many days without ephod, altar, or sacrifice; but whose fault was that? They could not say that God had given their mother a bill of divorce; let them produce it if they can, for a bill of divorce was given into the hand of her that was divorced. 2. He had been a father to them; and fathers had then a power to sell their children for slaves to their creditors, in satisfaction for the debts they were not otherwise able to pay. Now it is true the Jews were sold to the Babylonians then, and afterwards to the Romans; but did God sell them for payment of his debts? No, he was not indebted to any of those to whom they were sold, or, if he had sold them, he *did not increase his wealth by their price,* Ps. 44:12. When God chastens his children, it is neither for his pleasure (Heb. 12:10) nor for his profit. All that are saved are saved by a prerogative of grace, but those that perish are cut off by an act of divine holiness and justice, not of absolute sovereignty.

II. A charge exhibited against them, showing them that they were themselves the authors of their own ruin: *"Behold, for your iniquities,* for the pleasure of them and the gratification of your own base lusts, *you have sold yourselves, for your iniquities you are sold;* not as children are sold by their parents, to pay their debts, but as malefactors are sold by the judges, to punish them for their crimes. You sold yourselves to work wickedness, and therefore God justly sold you into the hands of your enemies, 2 Chr. 12:5, 8. It is for your transgressions that your mother is put away, for her whoredoms and adulteries," which were always allowed to be a just cause of divorce. The Jews were sent into Babylon for their idolatry, a sin which broke the marriage covenant, and were at last rejected for crucifying the Lord of glory; these were the iniquities for which they were sold and put away.

III. The confirmation of this challenge and this charge. 1. It is plain that it was owing to themselves that they were cast off; for God came and offered them his favour, offered them his helping hand, either to prevent their trouble or to deliver them out of it, but they slighted him and all the tenders of his grace. "Do you lay it upon me?" (says God); "tell me, then, wherefore, *when I came, was there no man* to meet me, *when I called, was there none to answer me?" v.* 2. God came to them by his servants the prophets, demanding the fruits of his vineyard (Mt. 21:34); he sent them his messengers, *rising up betimes and sending them* (Jer. 35:15); he called to them to leave their sins, and so prevent their own ruin: but *was there* no man, or next to none, that had any regard to the warnings which the prophets gave them, none that answered the calls of God, or complied with the messages he sent them; and this was it for which they were sold and put away. Because they *mocked the messengers of the Lord,* therefore, *God brought upon them the king of the Chaldeans,* 2 Chr. 36:16, 17. Last of all *he sent unto them his Son.* He *came to his own,* but *his own received him not;* he called them to himself, but there were none that answered; he would have gathered Jerusalem's children together, but they would not; they knew not, because they would not know, the things that belonged to their peace, nor the day of their visitation, and for that transgression it was that they were put away and their house was left desolate, Mt. 21:41; 23:37, 38; Lu. 19:41, 42. When God calls men to happiness, and they will not answer, they are justly left to be miserable. 2. It is plain that it was not owing to a want of power in God, for he is almighty, and could have recovered them from so great a death; nor was it owing to a want of power in Christ, for he is *able to save to the uttermost.* The unbelieving Jews in Babylon thought they were not delivered because their God was not able to deliver them; and those in Christ's time were ready to ask, in scorn, *Can this man save us?* For *himself he cannot save.* "But" (says God) *"is my hand shortened at all,* or is it weakened?" Can any limits be set to Omnipotence? Cannot he redeem who is the great Redeemer? Has he no *power to deliver* whose all power is? To put to silence, and for ever to put to shame, their doubts concerning his power, he here gives unquestionable proofs of it. (1.) He can, when he pleases, *dry up the seas,* and make the rivers a wilderness. He did so for Israel when he redeemed them out of Egypt, and he can do so again for their redemption out of Babylon. It is done at his *rebuke,* as easily as with a word's speaking. He can so dry up the rivers as to leave the fish to die for want of water, and to putrefy. When God *turned the waters of Egypt into blood* he *slew the fish,* Ps. 105:29. The expression our Saviour sometimes used concerning the power of faith, that it will *remove mountains and plant sycamores in the sea,* is not unlike this; if their faith could do that, no doubt their faith would save them, and therefore they were inexcusable if they perished in unbelief. (2.) He can, when he pleases, eclipse the lights of heaven, *clothe then with blackness, and make sackcloth their covering* (*v.* 3) by thick and dark clouds interposing, which he balances, Job 36:32; 37:16.

Verses 4–9

Our Lord Jesus, having proved himself able to save, here shows himself as willing as he is able to save, here shows himself as willing as he is able. We suppose the prophet Isaiah to say something of himself in these verses, engaging and encouraging himself to go on in his work as a prophet, notwithstanding the many hardships he met with, not doubting but that God would stand by him and strengthen him; but, like David, he speaks of himself as a type of Christ, who is here prophesied of and promised to be the Saviour.

I. As an acceptable preacher. Isaiah, a a prophet, was qualified for the work to which he was called, so were the rest of God's prophets, and others whom he employed as his messengers; but Christ was anointed with the Spirit above his fellows. To make the man of God perfect, he has, 1. *The tongue of the learned,* to know how to give instruction, *how to speak a word in season to him that is weary, v.* 4. God, who made man's mouth, gave Moses the tongue of the learned, to speak for the terror and conviction of Pharaoh, Ex. 4:11, 12. He gave to Christ the tongue of the learned, to speak a word in season for the comfort of those that are weary and heavily laden under the burden of sin, Mt. 11:28. *Grace was poured into his lips,* and they are said to *drop sweet-smelling myrrh.* See what is the best learning of a minister, to know how to comfort troubled consciences, and to speak pertinently, properly, and plainly, to the various cases of poor souls. An ability to do this is God's gift, and it is one of the best gifts, which we should covet earnestly. Let us repose ourselves in the many comfortable words which Christ has spoken to the weary. 2. The ear of the learned, to receive instruction. Prophets have as much need of this as of the tongue of the learned; for they must deliver what they are taught and no other, must hear the word from God's mouth diligently and attentively, that they may speak it exactly, Eze. 3:17. Christ himself received that he might give. None must undertake to be teachers who have not first been learners. Christ's apostles were first disciples, *scribes instructed unto the kingdom of heaven,* Mt. 13:52. Nor is it enough to hear, but we must *hear as the learned,* hear and understand, hear and remember, hear as those that would learn by what we hear. Those that would hear as the learned must be awake, and wakeful; for we are naturally drowsy and sleepy, and unapt to hear at all, or we hear by the halves, hear and do not heed. Our ears need to be wakened; we need to have something said to rouse us, to awaken us out of our spiritual slumbers, that we may hear as for our lives. We need to be awakened *morning by morning,* as duly as the day returns, to be awakened to do the work of the day in its day. Our case calls for continual fresh supplies of divine grace, to free us from the dulness we contract daily. The morning, when our spirits are most lively, is a proper time for communion with God; then we are in the best frame both to speak to him *(my voice shalt thou hear in the morning)* and to hear from him. The people came *early in the morning* to hear Christ in the temple (Lu. 21:38), for, it seems, his were morning lectures. And it is God that wakens us morning by morning. If we do any thing to purpose in his service, it is he who, as our Master, calls us up; and we should doze perpetually if he did not waken us morning by morning.

II. As a patient sufferer, *v.* 5, 6. One would think that he who was commissioned and qualified to speak comfort to the weary should meet with no difficulty in his work, but universal acceptance. It is however quite otherwise; he has both hard work to do and hard usage to undergo; and here he tells us with what undaunted constancy he went through with it. We have no reason to question but that the prophet Isaiah went on resolutely in the work to which God had called him, though we read not of his undergoing any such hardships as are here supposed; but we are sure that the prediction was abundantly verified in Jesus Christ: and here we have, 1. His patient obedience in his doing work. "The Lord God has not only wakened my ear to hear what he says, but has opened my ear to receive it, and comply with it" (Ps. 40:6, 7, *My ear hast thou opened; then said I, Lo, I come);* for when he adds, *I was not rebellious, neither turned away back,* more is implied than expressed — that he was willing, that though he foresaw a great deal of difficulty and discouragement, though he was to take pains and give constant attendance as a servant, though he was to empty himself of that which was very great and humble himself to that which was very mean, yet he did not fly off, did not fail, nor was discouraged. He continued very free and forward to his work even when he came to the hardest part of it. Note, As a good understanding in the truths of God, so a good will to the work and service of God, is from the grace of God. 2. His obedient patience in his suffering work. I call it obedient patience because he was patient with an eye to his Father's will, thus pleading with himself, *This commandment have I received of my Father,* and thus submitting to God, *Not as I will, but as thou wilt.* In this submission he resigned himself, (1.) To be scourged: *I gave my back to the smiters;* and that not only by submitting to the indignity when he was smitten, but by permitting it (or admitting it rather) among the other instances of pain and shame which he would voluntarily undergo for us. (2.) To be buffeted: *I gave my cheeks to those that* not only smote them, but *plucked off the hair* of the beard, which was a greater degree both of pain and of ignominy. (3.) To be spit upon: *I hid not my face from shame and spitting.* He could have hidden his face from it, could have avoided it, but he would not, because he was made a reproach of men, and thus he would answer to the type of Job, that man of sorrows, of whom it is said that they *smote him on the cheek reproachfully* (Job 16:10), which was an expression not only of contempt, but of abhorrence and indignation. All this Christ underwent for us, and voluntarily, to convince us of his willingness to save us.

III. As a courageous champion, *v.* 7–9. The Redeemer is as famous for his boldness as for his humility and patience, and, though he yields, yet he is more than a conqueror. Observe, 1. The dependence he has upon God. What was the prophet Isaiah's support was the support of Christ himself (*v.* 7): *The Lord God will help me;* and again, *v.* 9. Those whom God employs he will assist, and will take care they want not any help that they or their work call for. God, having laid help upon his Son for us, gave help to him, and his hand was all along *with the man of his right hand.* Nor will he only assist him in his work, but accept of him (*v.* 8): *He is near that justifieth.* Isaiah, no doubt, was falsely accused and loaded with reproach and calumny, as other prophets were; but he despised the reproach, knowing that God would roll it away and bring forth his righteousness as the light, perhaps in this world (Ps. 37:6), at furthest in the great day, when there will be a resurrection of names as well as bodies, and the righteous shall shine forth as the morning sun. And so it was verified in Christ; by his resurrection he was proved to be not the man that he was represented, not a blasphemer, not a deceiver, not an enemy to Caesar. The judge that condemned him owned he found no fault in him; the centurion, or sheriff, that had charge of his execution, declared him a righteous man: so near was he that justified him. But it was true of him in a further and more peculiar sense: the Father justified him when he accepted the satisfaction he made for the sin of man, and constituted him *the Lord our righteousness,* who was made sin for us. He was *justified in the Spirit,* 1 Tim. 3:16. He was near who did it; for his resurrection, by which he was justified, soon followed his condemnation and crucifixion. He was straightway glorified, Jn. 13:32. 2. He was straightway glorified, Jn. 13:32. 2. The confidence he thereupon has of success in his undertaking: "If God will help me, if he will justify me, will stand by me and bear me out, *I shall not be confounded,* as those are that come short of the end they aimed at and the satisfaction they promised themselves: *I know that I shall not be ashamed."* Though his enemies did all they could to put him to shame, yet he kept his ground, he kept his countenance, and was not ashamed of the work he had undertaken. Note, Work for God is work that we should not be ashamed of; and hope in God is hope that we shall not be ashamed of. Those that trust in God for help shall not be disappointed; they know whom they have trusted, and therefore know they shall not be ashamed. 3. The defiance which in this confidence he bids to all opposers and opposition: "God will help me, and *therefore have I set my face like a flint."* The prophet did so; he was bold in reproving sin, in warning sinners (Eze. 3:8, 9), and in asserting the truth of his predictions. Christ did so; he went on in his work, as Mediator, with unshaken constancy and undaunted resolution; he did not fail nor was discouraged; and here he challenges all his opposers, (1.) To enter the lists with him: *Who will contend with me,* either in law or by the sword? *Let us stand together* as combatants, or as the plaintiff and defendant. *Who is my adversary?* Who is *the master of my cause?* so the word is, "Who will pretend to enter an action against me? Let him appear, and *come near to me,* for I will not abscond." Many offered to dispute with Christ, but he put them to silence. The prophet speaks this in the name of all faithful ministers; those who keep close to the pure word of God, in delivering their message, need not fear contradiction; the scriptures will bear them out, whoever contends with them. *Great is the truth and will prevail.* Christ speaks this in the name of all believers, speaks it as their champion. Who dares be an enemy to those whom he is a friend to, or contend with those for whom he is an advocate? Thus St. Paul applies it (Rom. 8:33): *Who shall lay any thing to the charge of God's elect?* (2.) He challenges them to prove any crime upon him (*v.* 9): *Who is he that shall condemn me?* The prophet perhaps was condemned to die; Christ we are sure was; and yet both could say, *Who is he that shall condemn?* For there is no condemnation to those whom God justifies. There were those that did condemn them, but what became of them? *They all shall wax old as a garment.* The righteous cause of Christ and his prophets shall outlive all opposition. The *moth shall eat them up* silently and insensibly; a little thing will serve to destroy them. But the roaring lion himself shall not prevail against God's witnesses. All believers are enabled to make this challenge, *Who is he that shall condemn? It is Christ that died.*

Verses 10–11

The prophet, having the tongue of the learned given him, that he might give to every one his portion, here makes use of it, rightly dividing the word of truth. It is the summary of the gospel. *He that believes shall be saved* (he that trusts in the name of the Lord shall be comforted, though for a while he walk in darkness and have no light), but *he that believes not shall be damned;* though for a while he walk in the light of his own fire, yet he shall lie down in sorrow.

I. Comfort is here spoken to disconsolate saints, and they are encouraged to trust in God's grace, *v.* 10. Here observe, 1. What is always the character of a child of God. He is one that fears the Lord with a filial fear, that stands in awe of his majesty and is afraid of incurring his displeasure. This is a grace that usually appears most in good people when they walk in darkness, when other graces appear not. They then *tremble at his word* (*ch.* 66:2) and are *afraid of his judgments,* Ps. 119:120. He is one that obeys the voice of God's servant, is willing to be ruled by the Lord Jesus, as God's servant in the great work of man's redemption, one that yields a sincere obedience to the law of Christ and cheerfully comes up to the terms of his covenant. Those that truly fear God will obey the voice of Christ. 2. What is sometimes the case of a child of God. It is supposed that though he has in his heart the fear of God, and faith in Christ, yet for a time he walks in darkness and has no light, is disquieted and has little or no comfort. Who is there that does so? This intimates that it is a case which sometimes happens among the professors of religion, yet not very often; but, whenever it happens, God takes notice of it. It is no new thing for the children and heirs of light sometimes to walk in darkness, and for a time not to have any glimpse or gleam of light. This is not meant so much of the comforts of this life (those that fear God, when they have ever so great an abundance of them, do not walk in them as their light) as of their spiritual comforts, which relate to their souls. They walk in darkness when their evidences for heaven are clouded, their joy in God is interrupted, the testimony of the Spirit is suspended, and the light of God's countenance is eclipsed. Pensive Christians are apt to be melancholy, and those who fear always are apt to fear too much. 3. What is likely to be an effectual cure in this sad case. He that is thus in the dark, (1.) *Let him trust in the name of the Lord,* in the goodness of his nature, and that which he has made known of himself, his wisdom, power, and goodness. *The name of the Lord is a strong tower,* let his run into that. Let him depend upon it that if he walk before God, which a man may do though he walk in the dark, he shall find God all-sufficient to him. (2.) Let him *stay himself upon his God,* his in covenant; let him keep hold of his covenant-relation to God, and call God *his God,* as Christ on the cross, *My God, My God.* Let him stay himself upon the promises of the covenant, and build his hopes on them. When a child of God is ready to sink he will find enough in God to stay himself upon. Let him trust in Christ, for God's *name is in him* (Ex. 23:21), trust in that name of his, *The Lord our righteousness,* and stay himself upon God as his God, in and through a Mediator.

II. Conviction is here spoken to presuming sinners, and they are warned not to trust in themselves, *v.* 11. Observe, 1. The description given of them. They *kindle a fire,* and *walk in the light of that fire.* They depend upon their own righteousness, offer all their sacrifices, and burn all their incense, with that fire (as Nadab and Abihu) and not with the fire from heaven. In their hope of acceptance with God they have no regard to the righteousness of Christ. They refresh and please themselves with a conceit of their own merit and sufficiency, and warm themselves with that. It is both light and heat to them. They *compass themselves about with sparks of their own kindling.* As they trust in their own righteousness, and not in the righteousness of Christ, so they place their happiness in their worldly possessions and enjoyments, and not in the favour of God. Creature-comforts are as sparks, short-lived and soon gone; yet the children of this world, while they last, warm themselves by them, and walk with pride and pleasure in the light of them. 2. The doom passed upon them. They are ironically told to *walk in the light of their own fire.* "Make your best of it, while it lasts. But what will be in the end thereof, what will it come to at last? This shall you have of my hand (says Christ, for to him the judgment is committed), *you shall lie down in sorrow,* shall go to bed in the dark." See Job 18:5, 6. *His candle shall be put out with him.* Those that make the world their comfort, and their own righteousness their confidence, will certainly meet with a fatal disappointment, which will be bitterness in the end. A godly man's way may be melancholy, but his end shall be peace and everlasting light. A wicked man's way may be pleasant, but his end and endless abode will be utter darkness.

CHAPTER 51

This chapter is designed for the comfort and encouragement of those that fear God and keep his commandments, even when they walk in darkness and have no light. Whether it was intended primarily for the support of the captives in Babylon is not certain, probably it was; but comforts thus generally expressed ought not to be so confined. Whenever the church of God is in distress her friends and well-wishers may comfort themselves and one another with these words, I. That God, who raised his church at first out of nothing, will take care that it shall not perish (*v.* 1–3). II. That the righteousness and salvation he designs for his church are sure and near, very near and very sure (*v.* 4–6). III. That the persecutors of the church are weak and dying creatures (*v.* 7, 8). IV. That the same power which did wonders for the church formerly is now engaged and employed for her protection and deliverance (*v.* 9–11). V. That God himself, the Maker of the world, had undertaken both to deliver his people out of their distress and to comfort them under it, and sent his prophet to assure them of it (*v.* 12–16). VI. That, deplorable as the condition of the church now was (*v.* 17–20), to the same woeful circumstances her persecutors and oppressors should shortly be reduced, and worse (*v.* 21–23). The first three paragraphs of this chapter begin with, "Hearken unto me," and they are God's people that are all along called to hearken; for even when comforts are spoken to them sometimes they "hearken not, through anguish of spirit" (Ex. 6:9); therefore they are again and again called to hearken (*v.* 1, 4, 7). The two other paragraphs of this chapter begin with "Awake, awake;" in the former (*v.* 9) God's people call upon him to awake and help them; in the latter (*v.* 17) God calls upon them to awake and help themselves.

Verses 1–3

Observe, 1. How the people of God are here described, to whom the word of this consolation is sent and who are called upon to hearken to it, *v.* 1. They are such as *follow after righteousness,* such as are very desirous and solicitous both to be justified and to be sanctified, are pressing hard after this, to have the favour of God restored to them and the image of God renewed on them. These are those *that seek the Lord,* for it is only in the say of righteousness that we can seek him with any hope of finding him. 2. How they are here directed to look back to their original, and the smallness of their beginning: *"Look unto the rock whence you were hewn"* (the idolatrous family in Ur of the Chaldees, out of which Abraham was taken, the generation of slaves which the heads and fathers of their tribes were in Egypt); "look unto *the hole of the pit out of which you were digged,* as clay, when God formed you into a people." Note, It is good for those that are privileged by a new birth to consider what they were by their first birth, how they were *conceived in iniquity and shapen in sin.* That which is *born of the flesh is flesh.* How hard was that rock out of which we were hewn, unapt to receive impressions, and how miserable *the hole of that pit out of which we were digged!* The consideration of this should fill us with low thoughts of ourselves and high thoughts of divine grace. Those that are now advanced would do well to remember how low they began (*v.* 2): *"Look unto Abraham your father,* the father of all the faithful, of all that follow after the righteousness of faith as he did (Rom. 4:11), *and unto Sarah that bore you,* and whose daughters you all are as long as you do well. Think how Abraham was *called alone,* and yet was *blessed* and *multiplied;* and let that encourage you to depend upon the promise of God even when a sentence of death seems to be upon all the means that lead to the performance of it. Particularly let it encourage the captives in Babylon, though they are reduced to a small number, and few of them left, to hope that yet they shall increase so as to replenish their own land again." When Jacob is very small, yet he is not so small as Abraham was, who yet became father of many nations. "Look unto Abraham, and see what he got by trusting in the promise of God, and take example by him to follow God with an implicit faith." 3. How they are here assured that their present seedness of tears should at length end in a harvest of joys, *v.* 3. The church of God on earth, even the gospel Zion, has sometimes had her deserts and waste places, many parts of the church, through either corruption or persecution, made like a wilderness, unfruitful to God or uncomfortable to the inhabitants; but God will find out a time and way to *comfort Zion,* not only by speaking comfortably to her, but by acting graciously for her. God has comforts in store even for the *waste places* of his church, for those parts of it that seem not regarded or valued. (1.) He will make them fruitful, and so give them cause to rejoice; her wildernesses shall put on a new face, and look pleasant as Eden, and abound in all good fruits, *as the garden of the Lord.* Note, It is the greatest comfort of the church to be made serviceable to the glory of God, and to be as his garden in which he delights. (2.) He will make them cheerful, and so give them hearts to rejoice. With the *fruits of righteousness, joy and gladness shall be found therein;* for the more holiness men have, and the more good they do, the more gladness they have. And where there is gladness, to their satisfaction, it is fit that there should be thanksgiving, to God's honour; for whatever is the matter of our rejoicing ought to be the matter of our thanksgiving; and the returns of God's favour ought to be celebrated with the voice of melody, which will be the more melodious when God gives *songs in the night,* songs in the desert.

Verses 4–8

Both these proclamations, as I may call them, end alike with an assurance of the perpetuity of God's righteousness and his salvation; and therefore we put them together, both being designed for the comfort of God's people. Observe,

I. Who they are to whom this comfort belongs: *"My people,* and *my nation,* that I have set apart for myself, that own me and are owned by me." Those are God's people and his nation who are subject to him as their King and their God, pay allegiance to him, and put themselves under his protection accordingly. They are a people who *know righteousness,* who not only have the means of knowledge, and to whom righteousness is made known, but who improve those means, and are able to form a right judgment of truth and falsehood, good and evil. And, as they have good heads, so they have good hearts, for they have the law of God in them, written and ruling there. Those God owns for his people *in whose hearts his law is.* Even those who know righteousness, and have the law of God in their hearts, may yet be in great distress and sorrow, and loaded with reproach and contempt; but their God will comfort them with the righteousness they know and the law they have in their hearts.

II. What the comfort is that belongs to God's people. 1. That the gospel of Christ shall be preached and published to the world: *A law shall proceed from me,* an evangelical law, the law of Christ, the law of faith, *ch.* 2:3. This law is his judgment; for it is that law of liberty by which the world shall be governed and judged. This shall not only go forth, but shall continue and rest, it shall take firm footing and deep root in the world. It shall rest, not only for the benefit of the Jews, who had the first notice of it, but *for a light of the people* of other nations. It is this law, this judgment, that we are required to hearken and give ear to, at our peril; for how shall we escape if we neglect it and turn a deaf ear to it? When a law proceeds from God, *he that has ears to hear, let him hear.* 2. That this law and judgment shall bring with them righteousness and salvation, shall open a ready way to the children of men, that they may be justified and saved, *v.* 5. These are called *God's righteousness* and *his* salvation, because of his contriving and bringing them about. The former is a righteousness which he will accept for us and accept us for, and a righteousness which he will work in us and graciously accept of. The latter is the *salvation of the Lord,* for it arises from him and terminates in him. Observe, There is no salvation without righteousness; and, wherever there is the *righteousness of God,* there shall be his salvation. All those, and those only, that are justified and sanctified shall be glorified. 3. That this righteousness and salvation shall very shortly appear: *My righteousness is near.* It is near in time; behold, all things are now ready. It is near in place, not far to seek, but the word is nigh us, and Christ in the word, righteousness in the word, Rom. 10:8. *My salvation has gone forth.* The decree has gone forth concerning it; it shall as certainly be introduced as if it had gone forth already, and the time for it is at hand. 4. That this evangelical righteousness and salvation shall not be confined to the Jewish nation, but shall be extended to the Gentiles; *My arms shall judge the people.* Those that will not yield to the judgments of God's mouth shall be crushed by the judgments of his hand. Some shall thus be judged by the gospel, for *for judgment Christ came into this world;* but others, and those of *the isles, shall wait upon him,* and bid his gospel, and the commands as well as the comforts of it, welcome. It was a comfort to God's people, to his nation, that multitudes should be added to them, and the increase of their number should be the increase of their strength and beauty. It is added, *And on my arm shall they trust,* that *arm of the Lord* which is revealed in Christ, *ch.* 53:1. Observe, God's arm shall judge the people that are impenitent, and yet on his arm shall others trust and be saved by it; for it is to us as we make it, a savour of life or of death. 5. That this righteousness and salvation *shall be for ever,* and shall never be abolished, *v.* 8. It is an everlasting righteousness that the Messiah brings in (Dan. 9:24), an eternal redemption that he is the author of, Heb. 5:9. As it shall spread through all the nations of the earth, so it shall last through all the ages of the world. We must never expect any other way of salvation, any other covenant of peace or rule of righteousness, than what we have in the gospel, and what we have there shall continue to the end, Mt. 28:20. It is for ever; for the consequences of it shall be to eternity, and by this law of liberty men's everlasting state will be determined. This perpetuity of the gospel and the blessed things it brings in is illustrated by the fading and perishing of this world and all things in it. Look up to the visible heavens above, which have continued hitherto, and seem likely to continue, but they shall *vanish like smoke* that soon spends itself and disappears; they shall be rolled like a scroll, and their lights shall fall like leaves in autumn. Look down to the earth beneath; that abides too for a short *ever* (Eccl. 1:4), but it shall *wax old like a garment* that will be the worse for wearing; *and those that dwell therein,* all the inhabitants of the earth, even those that seem to have the best settlement in it, *shall die in like manner:* the soul shall, as to this world, vanish like smoke, and the body be thrown by like a garment waxen old. They shall be easily crushed (Job 4:19), and no loss of them. But when *heaven and earth pass away,* when all flesh and the glory of it wither as grass, the *word of the Lord endures for ever,* and *not one iota or tittle of that shall fall to the ground.* Those whose happiness is bound up in Christ's righteousness and salvation will have the comfort of it when time and days shall be no more.

III. What use they are to make of this comfort. If God's righteousness and salvation are near to them, then let them *not fear the reproach of men,* of mortal miserable men, nor be *afraid of their revilings* or spiteful taunts, theirs who bid you sing them the songs of Zion, or who ask you, in scorn, *Where is now your God?* Let not those who embrace the gospel righteousness be afraid of those who will call them *Beelzebub,* and will say all manner of evil against them falsely. Let them not be afraid of them; let them not be disturbed by these opprobrious speeches, nor made uneasy by them, as if they would be the ruin of their reputation and honour and they must for ever lie under the load of them. Let them not be afraid of their executing their menaces, nor be deterred thereby from their duty, nor frightened into any sinful compliances, nor driven to take any indirect courses for their own safety. Those can bear but little for Christ that cannot bear a hard word for him. Let us not fear the reproach of men; for, 1. They will be quickly silenced (*v.* 8): *The moth shall eat them up like a garment, ch.* 50:9. *The worm shall eat them like wool,* or woollen cloth. If we have the approbation of a living God, we may despise the censure of dying men; the matter is not great what those say of us who must shortly be food for worms. Or it intimates the judgments of God with which they shall be visited, with which they shall be consumed, for their malice against the people of God; they shall be slowly and silently, but effectually destroyed, when God shall come to reckon with them *for all their hard speeches,* Jude 14, 15. 2. The cause we suffer for cannot be run down. The falsehood of their reproaches will be detected, but truth shall triumph, and the righteousness of religion's injured cause shall be for ever plain. Clouds darken the sun, but give no obstruction to his progress.

Verses 9–16

In these verses we have,

I. A prayer that God would, in his providence, appear and act for the deliverance of his people and the mortification of his and their enemies. *Awake, awake! put on strength, O arm of the Lord! v.* 9. The arm of the Lord is Christ, or it is put for God himself, as Ps. 44:23. *Awake! why sleepest thou?* He that keeps Israel neither slumbers nor sleeps; but, when we pray that he would awake, we mean that he would make it to appear that he watches over his people and is always awake to do them good. The arm of the Lord is said to awake when the power of God exerts itself with more than ordinary vigour on his people's behalf. When a hand or arm is benumbed we say, It is asleep; when it is stretched forth for action, It awakes. God needs not to be reminded nor excited by us, but he gives us leave thus to be humbly earnest with him for such appearances of his power as will be for his own praise. *"Put on strength,"* that is, "put forth strength: appear in thy strength, as we appear in the clothes we put on," Ps. 21:13. The church sees her case bad, her enemies many and mighty, her friends few and feeble; and therefore she depends purely upon the strength of God's arm for her relief. *"Awake, as in the ancient days,"* that is, "do for us now as thou didst for our fathers formerly, repeat *the wonders they told us of,"* Jdg. 6:13.

II. The pleas to enforce this prayer. 1. They plead precedents, the experiences of their ancestors, and the great things God had done for them. "Let the arm of the Lord be made bare on our behalf; for it has done great things formerly in defence of the same cause, and we are sure it is neither shortened nor weakened. It did wonders against the Egyptians, who enslaved and oppressed God's son, his first-born; it *cut Rahab* to pieces with one direful plague after another, *and wounded* Pharaoh, *the dragon,* the Leviathan (as he is called, Ps. 74:13, 14); it gave him his death's wound. It did wonders for Israel. *It dried up the sea,* even *the waters of the great deep,* as far as was requisite to open *a way* through the sea *for the ransomed to pass over," v.* 10. God is never at a loss for a way to accomplish his purposes concerning his people, but will either find one or make one. Past experiences, as they are great supports to faith and hope, so they are good pleas in prayer. *Thou hast; wilt thou not?* Ps. 85:1–6. 2. They plead promises (*v.* 11): *And the redeemed of the Lord shall return,* that is (as it may be supplied), *thou hast said, They shall,* referring to *ch.* 35:10, where we find this promise, that *the redeemed of the Lord,* when they are released out of their captivity in Babylon, *shall come with singing unto* Zion. Sinners, when they are brought out of the slavery of sin into the glorious liberty of God's children, may come singing, as a bird got loose out of the cage. The souls of

believers, when they are delivered out of the prison of the body, come to the heavenly Zion with singing. Then this promise will have its full accomplishment, and we may plead it in the mean time. He that designs such joy for us at last will he not work such deliverances for us in the mean time as our case requires? When the saints come to heaven they *enter into the joy of their Lord;* it crowns their heads with immortal honour; it fills their hearts with complete satisfaction. *They shall obtain* that *joy and gladness* which they could never obtain in this vale of tears. In this world of changes it is a short step from joy to sorrow, but in that world *sorrow and mourning shall flee away,* never to return or come in view again.

III. The answer immediately given to this prayer (*v.* 12): *I, even, I, am he that comforteth you.* They prayed for the operations of his power; he answers them with the consolations of his grace, which may well be accepted as an equivalent. If God do not wound the dragon, and dry the sea, as formerly, yet, if he comfort us in soul under our afflictions, we have no reason to complain. If God do not answer immediately *with the saving strength of his right hand,* we must be thankful if he answer us, as an angel himself was answered (Zec. 1:13), *with good words and comfortable words.* See how God resolves to comfort his people: *I, even I,* will do it. He had ordered his ministers to do it (*ch.* 40:1); but, because they cannot reach the heart, he takes the work into his own hands: *I, even I,* will do it. See how he glories in it; he takes it among the titles of his honour to be *the God that comforts those that are cast down;* he delights in being so. Those whom God comforts are comforted indeed; nay, his undertaking to comfort them is comfort enough to them.

1. He comforts those that were in fear; and fear has torment, which calls for comfort. The fear of man has a snare in it which we have need of comfort to preserve us from. He comforts the timorous by chiding them, and that is no improper way of comforting either others or ourselves: *Why art thou cast down, and why disquieted? v.* 12, 13. God, who comforts his people, would not have them disquiet themselves with amazing perplexing fears of the reproach of men (*v.* 7), or of their growing threatening power and greatness, or of any mischief they may intend against us or our people. Observe,

(1.) The absurdity of those fears. It is a disparagement to us to give way to them: *Who art thou, that thou shouldst be afraid?* In the original, the pronoun is feminine, *Who art thou, O woman!* unworthy the name of a man? Such a weak and womanish thing it is to give way to perplexing fears. [1.] It is absurd to be in such dread of a dying man. What! *afraid of a man that shall die,* shall certainly and shortly die, *of the son of man who shall be made as grass,* shall wither and be trodden down or eaten up? The greatest men, and the most formidable, that are *the terror of the mighty in the land of the living,* are *but men* (Ps. 9:20) and shall *die like men* (Ps. 81:7), are but grass sprung out of the earth, cleaving to it, and retiring again into it. Note, We ought to look upon every man as a man that shall die. Those we admire, and love, and trust to, are men that shall die; let us not therefore delight too much in them nor depend too much upon them. Those we fear we must look upon as frail and mortal, and consider what a foolish thing it is for the servants of the living God to be afraid of dying men, that are here to-day and gone to-morrow. [2.] It is absurd to *fear continually every day* (*v.* 13), to put ourselves upon a constant rack, so as never to be easy, nor to have any enjoyment of ourselves. Now and then a danger may be imminent and threatening, and it may be prudent to fear it; but to be always in a toss, jealous of dangers at every step, and to tremble at the shaking of every leaf, is to make ourselves all our lifetime *subject to bondage* (Heb. 2:15), and to bring upon ourselves that sore judgment which is threatened, Deu. 28:66, 67. *Thou shalt fear, day and night.* [3.] It is absurd to fear beyond what there is cause: "Thou art *afraid of the fury of the oppressor.* It is true, there is an oppressor, and he is furious, and he designs, it may be, when he has an opportunity, to do thee a mischief, and it will be thy wisdom therefore to stand upon thy guard; but thou art afraid of him, *as if he were ready to destroy,* as if he were just now going to cut thy throat, and as if there were no possibility of preventing it." A timorous spirit is thus apt to make the worst of every thing, and to apprehend the danger greater and nearer

than really it is. Sometimes God is pleased at once to show us the folly of so doing: *"Where is the fury of the oppressor?* It is gone in an instant, and the danger is over ere thou art aware." His heart is turned, or his hands are tied. *Pharaoh king of Egypt is but a noise,* and the king of Babylon no more. What has become of all the furious oppressors of God's Israel, that hectored them, and threatened them, and were a terror to them? they passed away, and, lo, they were not; and so shall these.

(2.) The impiety of those fears: "Thou art *afraid of a man that shall die, and forgettest the Lord thy Maker,* who is also the Maker of all the world, who *has stretched forth the heavens and laid the foundations of the earth,* and therefore has all the hosts and all the powers of both at his command and disposal." Note, Our inordinate fear of man is a tacit forgetfulness of God. When we disquiet ourselves with the fear of man we forget that there is a God above him, and that the greatest of men have no power but what is given them from above; we forget the providence of God, by which he orders and overrules all events according to the counsel of his own will; we forget the promises he has made to protect his people, and the experiences we have had of his care concerning us, and his seasonable interposition for our relief many a time, when we thought the oppressor ready to destroy; we forget our Jehovah-jirehs, monuments of mercy in the mount of the Lord. Did we remember to make God our fear and our dread, we should not be so much afraid as we are of the frowns of men, *ch.* 8:12, 13. Happy is the man that fears God always, Prov. 28:14; Lu. 12:4, 5.

2. He comforts those that were in bonds, *v.* 14, 15. See here, (1.) What they do for themselves: *The captives exile hastens that he may be loosed* and may return to his own country, from which he is banished; his care is *that he may not die in the pit* (not die a prisoner, through the inconveniences of his confinement), and that *his bread should not fail,* either the bread he should have to keep him alive in prison or that which should bear his charges home; his stock is low, and therefore he hastens to be loosed. Now some understand this as his fault. He is distrustfully impatient of delays, cannot wait God's time, but thinks he is undone and must die in the pit if he be not released immediately. Others take it to be his praise, that when the doors are thrown open he does not linger, but applies himself with all diligence to procure his discharge. And then it follows, *But I am the Lord thy God,* which intimates, (2.) What God will do for them, even that which they cannot do for themselves. God has all power in his hand to help the captive exiles; for he has *divided the sea,* when the roaring of its waves was more frightful than any of the impotent menaces of proud oppressors. He has *stilled or quieted the sea,* so some think it should be read, Ps. 65:7; 89:9. This is not only a proof of what God can do, but a resemblance of what he has done, and will do, for his people; he will find out a way to still the threatening storm, and bring them safely into the harbour. *The Lord of hosts is his name,* his name for ever, the name by which his people have long known him. And, as he is able to help them, so he is willing and engaged to do it; for he is *thy God,* O captive-exile! thine in covenant. This is a check to the desponding captives. Let them not conclude that they must either be loosed immediately or die in the pit; for he that is the Lord of hosts can relieve them when they are brought ever so low. It is also an encouragement to the diligent captives, who, when liberty is proclaimed, are willing to lose no time; let them know that the Lord is their God, and, while they thus strive to help themselves, they may be sure he will help them.

3. He comforts all his people who depended upon what the prophets said to them in the name of the Lord, and built their hopes upon it. When the deliverances which the prophets spoke of either did not come so soon as they looked for them or did not come up to the height of their expectation they began to be cast down in their own eyes; but, as to this, they are encouraged (*v.* 16) by what God says to his prophet, not to this only, but to all his prophets, nor to this, or them, principally, but to Christ, the great prophet. It is a great satisfaction to those to whom the message is sent to hear the God of truth and power say to his messenger, as he does here, *I have put my words in thy mouth, that* by them *I may plant the heavens.* God undertook to comfort his people (*v.* 12); but still he does it by

his prophets, by his gospel; and, that he may do it by these, he here tells us, (1.) That his word in them is very true. He owns what they have said to be what he had directed and enjoined them to say: *"I have put my words in thy mouth,* and therefore he that receives thee and them receives me." This is a great stay to our faith, that Christ's doctrine was not his, but his that sent him, and that the words of the prophets and apostles were God's own words, which he put into their mouths. God's Spirit not only revealed to them the things themselves they spoke of, but dictated to them the words they should speak (2 Pt. 1:21; 1 Co. 2:13); so that these are the true sayings of God, of a God that cannot lie. (2.) That it is very safe: I have *covered thee in the shadow of my hand* (as before, *ch.* 49:2), which speaks the special protection not only of the prophets, but of their prophecies, not only of Christ, but of Christianity, of the gospel of Christ; it is not only the faithful word of God which the prophets deliver to us, but it shall be carefully preserved till it have its accomplishment for the use of the church, notwithstanding the restless endeavours of the powers of darkness to extinguish this light. They shall *prophesy again* (Rev. 10:11), though not in their persons, yet in their writings, which God has always *covered in the shadow of his hand,* preserved by a special providence, else they would have been lost ere this. (3.) That this word, when it comes to be accomplished, will be very great and will not fall short of the pomp and grandeur of the prophecy: *"I have put my words in thy mouth,* not that by the performance of them I may plant a nation, or found a city, but *that I may plant the heavens and lay the foundations of the earth,* may do that for my people which will be a new creation." This must look as far forward as to the great work done by the gospel of Christ and the setting up of his holy religion in the world. As God by Christ made the world at first (Heb. 1:2), and by him formed the Old-Testament church (Zec. 6:12), so by him, and the words put into his mouth, he will set up, [1.] A new world, will again plant the heavens and found the earth. Sin having put the whole creation into disorder, Christ's taking away the sin of the world put all into order again. *Old things have passed away, all things have become new;* things in heaven and things on earth are reconciled, and so put into a new posture, Col. 1:20. Through him, according to the promise, *we look for new heavens and a new earth* (2 Pt. 3:13), and to this the prophets bear witness. [2.] He will set up a new church, a New-Testament church: *He will say unto Zion, Thou art my people.* The gospel church is called *Zion* (Heb. 12:22) and *Jerusalem* (Gal. 4:26); and, when the Gentiles are brought into it, it shall be said unto them, *You are my people.* When God works great deliverances for his church, and especially when he shall complete the salvation of it in the great day, he will thereby own that poor despised handful to be his people, whom he has chosen and loved.

Verses 17–23

God, having awoke for the comfort of his people, here calls upon them to awake, as afterwards, *ch.* 52:1. It is a call to awake not so much out of the sleep of sin (though that also is necessary in order to their being ready for deliverance) as out of the stupor of despair. When the inhabitants of Jerusalem were in captivity they, as well as those who remained upon the spot, were so overwhelmed with the sense of their troubles that they had no heart or spirit to mind any thing that tended to their comfort or relief; they were as the disciples in the garden, *sleeping for sorrow* (Lu. 22:45), and therefore, when the deliverance came, they are said to have been *like those that dream,* Ps. 136:1. Nay, it is a call to awake, not only from sleep, but from death, like that to the dry bones to live, Eze. 37:9. "Awake, and look about thee, that thou mayest see the day of thy deliverance dawn, and mayest be ready to bid it welcome. Recover thy senses; sink not under thy load, but stand up, and bestir thyself for thy own help." This may be applied to the Jerusalem that was in the apostle's time, which is said to have been *in bondage with her children* (Gal. 4:25), and to have been under the power of *a spirit of slumber* (Rom. 11:8); they are called to awake, and mind the things that belonged to their everlasting peace, and then the cup of trembling should be taken out of their hands, peace should be spoken to them, and they should triumph over Satan, who had blinded their eyes and lulled them asleep. Now,

I. It is owned that Jerusalem had long been in a very deplorable condition, and sunk into the depths of misery.

1. She had lain under the tokens of God's displeasure. He had put into her hand *the cup of his fury,* that is, her share of his displeasure. The dispensations of his providence concerning her had been such that she had reason to think he was angry with her. She had provoked him to anger most bitterly, and was made to taste the bitter fruits of it. The cup of God's fury is, and will be, a *cup of trembling* to all those that have it put into their hands: damned sinners will find it so to eternity. It is said (Ps. 75:8) that *the dregs of the cup,* the loathsome sediments in the bottom of it, *all the wicked of the earth shall wring them out, and drink them;* but here Jerusalem, having made herself as the wicked of the earth, is compelled to wring them out and drink them; for wherever there has been a cup of fornication, as there had been in Jerusalem's hand when she was idolatrous, sooner or later there will be a cup of fury, a cup of trembling. Therefore *stand in awe and sin not.*

2. Those that should have helped her in her distress failed her, and were either unable or unwilling to help her, as might have been expected, *v.* 18. She is intoxicated with the cup of God's fury, and, being so, staggers, and is very unsteady in her counsels and attempts. She knows not what she says or does, much less knows she what to say or do; and, in this unhappy condition, *of all the sons that she has brought forth* and brought up, that she was borne and educated (and there were many famous ones, for of Zion it was said *that this and that man were born there,* Ps. 87:5), *there is none to guide her,* none to take her by the hand to keep her either from falling or from shaming herself, to lend either a hand to help her out of her trouble or a tongue to comfort her under it. Think it not strange if wise and good men are disappointed in their children, and have not that succour from them which they expected, but those that were arrows in their hand prove arrows in their heart, when Jerusalem herself has none of all her sons, prince, priest, nor prophet, that has such a sense either of duty or gratitude as to help her when she has most need of help. Thus they complain, Ps. 74:9. There is *none to tell us how long.* Now that which aggravated this disappointment was, (1.) That her trouble was very great, and yet there was none to pity or help her: *These two things have come unto thee* (*v.* 19), to complete thy desolation and destruction, even *the famine and the sword,* two sore judgments, and very terrible. Or the two things were the *desolation and destruction* by which the city was wasted and the famine and sword by which the citizens perished. Or the two things were the trouble itself (made up of desolation, destruction, famine, and sword) and her being helpless, forlorn, and comfortless, under it. "Two sad things indeed, to be in this woeful case, and to have none to pity thee, to sympathize with thee in thy griefs, or to help to bear the burden of thy cares, to have none to comfort thee, by suggesting that to thee which might help to alleviate thy grief or doing that for thee which might help to redress thy grievances." Or these two things that had come upon Jerusalem are the same with the two things that were afterwards to come upon Babylon (*ch.* 47:9), *loss of children and widowhood* — piteous case, and yet, "when thou hast brought it upon thyself by thy own sin and folly, *who shall be sorry for thee?* — a case that calls for comfort, and yet, when thou art froward under thy trouble, frettest, and makest thyself uneasy, *by whom shall I comfort thee?"* Those that will not be counselled cannot be helped. (2.) That those who should have been her comforters were their own tormentors (*v.* 20): *They have fainted,* as quite dispirited and driven to despair; they have no patience in which to keep possession of their own souls and the enjoyment of themselves, nor any confidence in God's promise, by which to keep possession of the comfort of that. They throw themselves upon the ground, in vexation at their troubles, and there *they lie at the head of all the streets,* complaining to all that pass by (Lam. 1:12), pining away for want of necessary food; there they lie like *a wild bull in a net,* fretting and raging, struggling and pulling, to help themselves, but entangling themselves so much the more, and making their condition the worse by their own passions and discontents. Those that are of a meek and quiet spirit are, under affliction, like a dove in a net, mourning indeed, but silent and patient. Those that are of a froward peevish spirit are like a wild bull in a net, uneasy to themselves, vexatious to their friends, and provoking to their God: *They are full of the fury of the Lord, the rebuke of our God.* God is angry with them, and contends with them, and they are full of that only, and take no notice of his wise and gracious designs in afflicting them, never enquire wherefore he contends with them, and therefore nothing appears in them but anger at God and quarrelling with him. They are displeased at God for the dispensations of his providence concerning them, and so they do but make bad worse. This had long been Jerusalem's woeful case, and God took cognizance of it. But,

II. It is promised that Jerusalem's troubles shall at length come to an end, and be transferred to her persecutors (*v.* 21): *Nevertheless hear this, thou afflicted.* It is often the lot of God's church to be afflicted, and God has always something to say to her then which she will do well to hearken to. "Thou art *drunken, not* as formerly *with wine,* not with the intoxicating cup of Babylon's whoredoms and idolatries, but with the cup of affliction. Know then, for thy comfort," 1. "That the Lord Jehovah is thy Lord and thy God, for all this." It is expressed emphatically (*v.* 22): *"Thus saith thy Lord, the Lord, and thy God* — the Lord, who is able to help thee, and has wherewithal to relieve thee, — *thy* Lord, who has an incontestable right to thee, and will not alienate it, — thy God, in covenant with thee, and who has undertaken to make thee happy." Whatever the distresses of God's people may be, he will not disown his relation to them, nor have they lost their interest in him and in his promise. 2. "That he is the God *who pleads the cause of his people,* as their patron and protector, who takes what is done against them a done against himself." The cause of God's people, and of that holy religion which they profess, is a righteous cause, otherwise the righteous God would not appear for it; yet it may for a time be run down, and seem as if it were lost. But God will plead it, either by convincing the consciences or confounding the mischievous projects of those that fight against it. He will plead it by clearing up the equity and excellency of it to the world and by giving success to those that act in defence of it. It is his own cause; he has espoused it, and therefore will plead it with jealousy. 3. That they should shortly take leave of their troubles and bid a final farewell to them: *"I will take out of thy hand the cup of trembling,* that bitter cup; it shall pass from thee." Throwing away the cup of trembling will not do, nor saying, "We will not, we cannot, drink it;" but, if we patiently submit, he that put it into out hands will himself take it out of our hands. Nay, it is promised, *"Thou shalt no more drink it again.* God has let fall his controversy with thee, and will not revive the judgment." 4. That their persecutors and oppressors should be made to drink of the same bitter cup of which they had drunk so deeply, *v.* 23. See here, (1.) How insolently they had abused and trampled upon the people of God: *They have said to thy soul,* to thee, to thy life, *Bow down, that we may go over.* Nay, they have said it to thy conscience, taking a pride and pleasure in forcing thee to worship idols. Herein the New-Testament Babylon treads in the steps of that old oppressor, tyrannizing over men's consciences, giving law to them, putting them upon the rack, and compelling them to sinful compliances. Those that set up an infallible head and judge, requiring an implicit faith in his dictates and obedience to his commands, do in effect say to men's souls, *Bow down, that we may go over,* and they say it with delight. (2.) How meanly the people of God (having by their sin lost much of their courage and sense of honour) truckled to them: *Thou hast laid thy body as the ground.* Observe, The oppressors required souls to be subjected to them, that every man should believe and worship just as they would have them. But all they could gain by their threats and violence was that people laid their bodies on the ground; they brought them to an external and hypocritical conformity, but conscience cannot be forced, nor is it mentioned to their praise that they yielded thus far. But observe, (3.) How justly God will reckon with those who have carried it so imperiously towards his people: *The cup of trembling shall be put into their hand.* Babylon's case shall be as bad as ever Jerusalem's was. Daniel's persecutors shall be thrown into

Daniel's den; let them see how they like it. And the Lord is known by these judgments which he executes.

CHAPTER 52

The greater part of this chapter is on the same subject with the chapter before, concerning the deliverance of the Jews out of Babylon, which yet is applicable to the great salvation Christ has wrought out for us; but the last three verses are on the same subject with the following chapter, concerning the person of the Redeemer, his humiliation and exaltation. Observe, I. The encouragement that is given to the Jews in captivity to hope that God would deliver them in his own way and time (*v.* 1–6). II. The great joy and rejoicing that shall be both with ministers and people upon that occasion (*v.* 7–10). III. The call given to those that remained in captivity to shift for their own enlargement when liberty was proclaimed (*v.* 11, 12). IV. A short idea given here of the Messiah, which is enlarged upon in the next chapter (*v.* 13–15).

Verses 1–6

Here, I. God's people are stirred up to appear vigorous for their own deliverance, *v.* 1, 2. They had desired that God would *awake* and *put on his strength, ch.* 51:9. Here he calls upon them to *awake* and *put on their strength,* to bestir themselves; let them awake from their despondency, and pluck up their spirits, encourage themselves and one another with the hope that all will be well yet, and no longer succumb and sink under their burden. Let them awake from their distrust, look above them, look about them, look into the promises, look into the providences of God that were working for them, and let them raise their expectations of great things from God. Let them awake from their dullness, sluggishness, and incogitancy, and raise up their endeavours, not to take any irregular courses for their own relief, contrary to the law of nations concerning captives, but to use all likely means to recommend themselves to the favour of the conqueror and make an interest with him. God here gives them an assurance, 1. That they should be reformed by their captivity: *There shall no more come into thee the uncircumcised and the unclean* (*v.* 1); their idolatrous customs should be no more introduced, or at least not harboured; for when by the marriage of strange wives, in Ezra's time and Nehemiah's, the unclean crept in, they were soon by the vigilance and zeal of the magistrates expelled again, and care was taken that Jerusalem should be a holy city. Thus the gospel Jerusalem is purified by the blood of Christ and the grace of God, and made indeed a holy city. 2. That they should be relieved and rescued out of their captivity, that the bands of their necks should be loosed, that they should not now be any longer oppressed, nay, that they should not be any more invaded, as they had been: *There shall no more come against thee* (so it may be read) *the uncircumcised and the clean.* The heathen shall not again enter into God's sanctuary and profane his temple, Ps. 79:1. This must be understood with a condition. If they keep close to God, and keep in with him, God will keep off, will keep out of the enemy; but, if they again corrupt themselves, Antiochus will profane their temple and the Romans will destroy it. However, for some time they shall have peace. And to this happy change, now approaching, they are here called to accommodate themselves. (1.) Let them prepare for joy: *"Put on thy beautiful garments,* no longer to appear in mourning weeds and the habit of thy widowhood. Put on a new face, a smiling countenance, now that a new and pleasant scene begins to open." The beautiful garments were laid up then, when the harps were hung on the willow trees; but, now there is occasion for both, let both be resumed together. "Put on thy strength, and, in order to that, put on thy beautiful garments, in token of triumph and rejoicing." Note, *The joy of the Lord will be our strength* (Neh. 8:10), and our beautiful garments will serve for armour of proof against the darts of temptation and trouble. And observe, Jerusalem must put on her beautiful garments when she becomes a holy city, for the beauty of holiness is the most amiable beauty, and the more holy we are the more cause we have to rejoice. (2.) Let them prepare for liberty: *"Shake thyself from the dust* in which thou hast lain, and into which thy proud oppressors have trodden thee (*ch.* 51:23), or into which thou hast in thy extreme sorrow rolled thyself." *Arise, and set up;* so it may be read. "O Jerusalem! prepare to get clear of all the marks of servitude thou hast been under and to shift thy quarters: *Loose thyself from the bands of thy neck;* be inspired with generous principles and resolutions to assert thy own liberty." The gospel proclaims liberty to those who were bound with fears and makes it their duty to take hold of their liberty. Let those who have been weary and heavily laden under the burden of sin, finding relief in Christ, shake themselves from the dust of their doubts and fears and loose themselves from those bands; for, *if the Son make them free, they shall be free indeed.*

II. God stirs up himself to appear jealous for the deliverance of his people. He here pleads their cause with himself, and even stirs up himself to come and save them, for his reasons of mercy are fetched from himself. Several things he here considers.

1. That the Chaldeans who oppressed them never acknowledged God in the power they gained over his people, any more than Sennacherib did, who, when God made use of him as an instrument for the correction and reformation of his people, meant not so, *ch.* 10:6, 7. *"You have sold yourselves for nought;* you got nothing by it, nor did I," *v.* 3. (God considers that when they by sin had sold themselves he himself, who had the prior, nay, the sole, title to them, *did not increase his wealth by their price,* Ps. 44:12. They did not so much as pay their debts to him with it; the Babylonians gave him no thanks for them, but rather reproached and blasphemed his name upon that account.) "And therefore they, having so long had you for nothing, shall at last restore you for nothing: *You shall be redeemed without price,"* as was promised, *ch.* 45:13. Those that give nothing must expect to get nothing; however, God is a debtor to no man.

2. That they had been often before in similar distress, had often smarted for a time under the tyranny of their task-masters, and therefore it was a pity that they should now be left always in the hand of these oppressors (*v.* 4): *"My people went down into Egypt,* in an amicable way to settle there; but they enslaved them, and ruled them with rigour." And then they were delivered, notwithstanding the pride, and power, and policies of Pharaoh. And why may we not think God will deliver his people now? At other times *the Assyrian oppressed* the people of God *without cause,* as when the ten tribes were carried away captive by the king of Assyria; soon afterwards Sennacherib, another Assyrian, with a destroying army oppressed and made himself master of all the defenced cities of Judah. The Babylonians might not unfitly be called *Assyrians,* their monarchy being a branch of the Assyrians; and they now oppressed them without cause. Though God was righteous in delivering them into their hands, they were unrighteous in using them as they did, and could not pretend a dominion over them as their subjects, as Pharaoh might when they were settled in Goshen, part of his kingdom. When we suffer by the hands of wicked and unreasonable men it is some comfort to be able to say that as to them it is without cause, that we have not given them any provocation, Ps. 7:3–5, etc.

3. That God's glory suffered by the injuries that were done to his people (*v.* 5): *What have I here,* what do I get by it, *that my people are taken away for nought?* God is not worshipped as he used to be in Jerusalem, his altar there is gone and his temple in ruins; but if, in lieu of that, he were more and better worshipped in Babylon, either by the captives or by the natives, it were another matter — God might be looked upon as in some respects a gainer in his honour by it; but, alas! it is not so. (1.) The captives are so dispirited that they cannot praise him; instead of this they are continually howling, which grieves him and moves his pity; *Those that rule over them make them to howl,* as the Egyptians of old made them to sigh, Ex. 2:23. So the Babylonians now, using them more hardly, extorted from them louder complaints and made them to howl. This gives us no pleasing idea of the temper the captives were now in; their complaints were not so rational and pious as they should have been, but brutish rather; they *howled,* Hos. 7:14. However God heard them, and came down to deliver them, as he did out of Egypt, Ex. 3:7, 8. (2.) The natives are so insolent that they will not praise him, but, instead of that, they are continually blaspheming, which affronts him and moves his anger. They boasted that they were too hard for God because they were too hard for his people, and set him at defiance, as unable to deliver them, and thus his *name continually every day was blasphemed among them.* When they praised their own idols they *lifted up themselves against the Lord of heaven,* Dan. 5:23. "Now," says God, "this is not to be suffered. I will go down to deliver them; for what honour, what rent, what tribute of praise have I from the world, when my people, who should be to me for a name and praise, are to me for a reproach? For their oppressors will neither praise God themselves nor let them do it." The apostle quotes this with application to the wicked lives of the Jews, by which God was dishonoured among the Gentiles then, as much as now he was by their sufferings, Rom. 2:23, 24.

4. That his glory would be greatly manifested by their deliverance (*v.* 6): *"Therefore,* because my name is thus blasphemed, I will arise, and *my people shall know my name,* my name Jehovah." By this name he had made himself known in delivering them out of Egypt, Ex. 6:3. God will do something to vindicate his own honour, something for his great name; and his people, who have almost lost the knowledge of it, shall know it to their comfort and shall find it their strong tower. They shall know that God's providence governs the world, and all the affairs of it, that it is he who speaks deliverance for them by the word of his power, that it is he who speaks deliverance for them by the word of his power, that it is he only, who at first spoke and it was done. They shall know that God's word, which Israel is blessed with above other nations, shall without fail have its accomplishment in due season, that it is he who speaks by the prophet; it is he, and they do not speak of themselves; for not one iota or tittle of what they say shall fall to the ground.

Verses 7–12

The removal of the Jews from Babylon to their own land again is here spoken of both as a mercy and as a duty; and the application of *v.* 7 to the preaching of the gospel (by the apostle, Rom. 10:15) plainly intimates that that deliverance was a type and figure of the redemption of mankind by Jesus Christ, to which what is here said of their redemption out of Babylon ought to be accommodated.

I. It is here spoken of as a great blessing, which ought to be welcomed with abundance of joy and thankfulness. 1. Those that bring the tidings of their release shall be very acceptable (*v.* 7): *"How beautiful upon the mountains,* the mountains round about Jerusalem, over which these messengers are seen coming at a distance, *how beautiful are their feet,* when it is known what tidings they bring!" It is not meant so much of the common posts, or the messengers sent express by the government to disperse the proclamation, but rather of some of the Jews themselves, who, being at the fountain-head of intelligence, had early notice of it, and immediately went themselves, or sent their own messengers, to all parts, to disperse the news, and even to Jerusalem itself, to tell the few who remained there that their brethren would be with them shortly; for it is published not merely as matter of news, but as a proof that Zion's God reigns, for in that language it is published: they say unto Zion, *Thy God reigns.* Those who bring the tidings of peace and salvation, that Cyrus has given orders for the release of the Jews, tidings which were so long expected by those that waited for the consolation of Israel, those *good tidings* (so the original reads it, without the tautology of our translation, *good tidings of good),* put this construction upon it, *O Zion! thy God reigns.* Note, When bad news is abroad this is good news, and when good news is abroad this is the best news, that Zion's God reigns, that God is Zion's God, in covenant with her, and as such he reigns, Ps. 146:10; Zec. 9:9. *The Lord has founded Zion, ch.* 14:32. All events have their rise in the disposals of the kingdom of his providence and their tendency to the advancement of the kingdom of his grace. This must be applied to the preaching of the gospel, which is a proclamation of peace and salvation; it is gospel indeed, good news, glad tidings, tidings of victory over our spiritual enemies and liberty from our spiritual bondage. The good news is that the Lord Jesus reigns and all power is given to him. Christ himself brought these tidings first (Lu. 4:18, Heb. 2:3), and of him the text speaks: *How beautiful are his feet!* his feet that were nailed to the cross, how beautiful upon Mount Calvary! his feet when he came *leaping upon the mountains* (Cant. 2:8), how beautiful were they to those who knew his voice and knew it to be the voice of their beloved! His ministers proclaim these good tidings; they ought to keep their feet clean from the pollutions of the world, and then they ought to be beautiful in the eyes of those to whom they are sent, who sit at their feet, or rather at

Christ's in them, to hear his word. They must be *esteemed in love* for *their work's sake* (1 Th. 5:13), for their message sake, which is well worthy of all acceptation. 2. Those to whom the tidings are brought shall be put thereby into a transport of joy. (1.) Zion's watchmen shall then rejoice because they are surprisingly illuminated, *v.* 8. The watchmen on Jerusalem's walls shall lead the chorus in this triumph. Who they were we are told, *ch.* 62:6. They were such as God set on the walls of Jerusalem, to make mention of his name, and to continue instant in prayer to him, till he again *made Jerusalem a praise in the earth.* These watchmen stand upon their watch-tower, waiting for an answer to their prayers (Hab. 2:1); and therefore when the good news comes they have it first, and the longer they have continued and the more importunate they have been in praying for it the more will they be elevated when it comes: They shall *lift up the voice, with the voice together shall they sing* in concert, to invite others to join with them in their praises. And that which above all things will transport them with pleasure is that *they shall see eye to eye,* that is, face to face. Whereas God had been a God hiding himself, and they could scarcely discern any thing of his favour through the dark cloud of their afflictions, now that the cloud is scattered they shall plainly see it. They shall see *Zion's king eye to eye;* so it was fulfilled when the Word was made flesh and dwelt among us, and there were those that *saw his glory* (Jn. 1:14) *and looked upon it,* 1 Jn. 1:1. They shall see an exact agreement and correspondence between the prophecy and the event, the promise and the performance; they shall see how they look one upon another eye to eye, and be satisfied that the same God spoke the one and did the other. When the Lord shall bring again Zion out of her captivity the prophets shall thence receive and give fuller discoveries than ever of God's good-will to his people. Applying this also, as the foregoing verse, to gospel times, it is a promise of the pouring out of the Spirit upon gospel ministers, as a spirit of wisdom and revelation, to lead them into all truth, so that they shall see eye to eye, shall see God's grace more clearly than the Old-Testament saints could see it: and they shall herein be unanimous; in these great things concerning the common salvation they shall concur in their sentiments as well as their songs. Nay, St. Paul seems to allude to this when he makes it the privilege of our future state that *we shall see face to face.* (2.) Zion's waste places shall then rejoice because they shall be surprisingly comforted (*v.* 9): *Break forth into joy, sing together, you waste places of Jerusalem;* that is, all parts of Jerusalem, for it was all in ruins, and even those parts that seemed to lie most desolate shall share in the joy; and they, having little expected it, shall break forth into joy, as men that dream, Ps. 126:1, 2. Let them sing together. Note, Those that share in mercies ought to join in praises. Here is matter for joy and praise. [1.] God's people will have the comfort of this salvation; and what is the matter of our rejoicing ought to be the matter of our thanksgiving. *He has redeemed Jerusalem* (the inhabitants of Jerusalem that were sold into the hands of their enemies) and thereby he has *comforted his people* that were in sorrow. The redemption of Jerusalem is the joy of all God's people, whose character it is that they look for that redemption, Lu. 2:38. [2.] God will have the glory of it, *v.* 10. He *has made bare his holy arm* (manifested and displayed his power) *in the eyes of all the nations.* God's arm is a holy arm, stretched out in purity and justice, in defence of holiness and in pursuance of his promise. [3.] All the world will have the benefit of it. In the great salvation wrought out by our Lord Jesus the *arm of the Lord was revealed and all the ends of the earth were made to see the great salvation,* not as spectators of it only, as they saw the deliverance of the Jews out of Babylon, but as sharers in it; some of all nations, the most remote, shall partake of the benefits of the redemption. This is applied to our salvation by Christ. Lu. 3:6, *All flesh shall see the salvation of God,* that *great salvation.*

II. It is here spoken of as a great business, which ought to be managed with abundance of care and circumcision. When the liberty is proclaimed, 1. Let the people of God hasten out of Babylon with all convenient speed; though they are ever so well settled there, let them not think of taking root in Babylon, but *Depart, depart* (*v.* 11), *go out from the midst of her;* not only those that are in the borders, but those that are in the midst, in the heart of the country, let them be gone. Babylon is no place for Israelites. As soon as they have leave to let go, let them lose no time. With this word God stirred up the spirits of those that were moved to go up, Ezra 1:5. And it is a call to all those who are yet in the bondage of sin and Satan to make use of the liberty which Christ has proclaimed to them. And, if the Son *make them free, they shall be free indeed.* 2. Let them take heed of carrying away with them any of the pollutions of Babylon: *Touch no unclean thing.* Now that God makes bare his holy arm for you, *be you holy as he is, and keep yourselves from every wicked thing.* When they came out of Egypt they brought with them the idolatrous customs of Egypt (Eze. 23:3), which were their ruin; let them take heed of doing so now that they come out of Babylon. Note, When we are receiving any special mercy from God we ought more carefully than ever to watch against all impurity. But especially let those be *clean* who *bear the vessels of the Lord,* that is, the priests, who had the charge of the vessels of the sanctuary (when they were restored by a particular grant) to carry them to Jerusalem, Ezra 1:7; 8:24, etc. Let them not only avoid touching any unclean thing, but be very careful to *cleanse themselves according to the purification of the sanctuary.* Christians are made to our God spiritual priests, Rev. 1:6. They are to bear the vessels of the Lord, are entrusted to keep the ordinances of God pure and entire; it is a good thing that is committed to them, and they ought to be clean, to wash their hands in innocency and so to compass God's altars and carry his vessels, and keep themselves pure. 3. Let them depend upon the presence of God with them and his protection in their removal (*v.* 12): *You shall not go out with haste.* They were to go with a diligent haste, not to lose time nor linger as Lot in Sodom, but they were not to go with a diffident distrustful haste, as if they were afraid of being pursued (as when they came out of Egypt) or of having the orders for their release recalled and countermanded: no, they shall find that, as for God, his work is perfect, and therefore they need not make more haste than good speed. Cyrus shall give them an honourable discharge, and they shall have an honourable return, and not steal away; *for the Lord will go before them* as their general and commander-in-chief, *and the God of Israel will be their rearward,* or he that will gather up those that are left behind. God will both lead their van and bring up their rear; he will secure them from enemies that either meet them or follow them, for with his favour will he compass them. The pillar of cloud and fire, when they came out of Egypt, sometimes went behind them, to secure their rear (Ex. 14:19), and God's presence with them would now be that to them which that pillar was a visible token of. Those that are in the way of their duty are under God's special protection; and he that believes this will not make haste.

Verses 13–15

Here, as in other places, for the confirming of the faith of God's people and the encouraging of their hope in the promises of temporal deliverances, the prophet passes from them to speak of the great salvation which should in the fulness of time be wrought out by the Messiah. As the prophecy of Christ's incarnation was intended for the ratification of the promise of their deliverance from the Assyrian army, so this of Christ's death and resurrection is to confirm the promise of their return out of Babylon; for both these salvations were typical of the great redemption and the prophecies of them had a reference to that. This prophecy, which begins here and is continued to the end of the next chapter, points as plainly as can be at Jesus Christ; the ancient Jews understood it of the Messiah, though the modern Jews take a great deal of pains to pervert it, and some of ours (no friends therein to the Christian religion) will have it understood of Jeremiah; but Philip, who hence preached Christ to the eunuch, has put it past dispute that *of him speaks the prophet this,* of him and of no other man, Acts 8:34, 35. Here,

I. God owns Christ to be both commissioned and qualified for his undertaking. 1. He is appointed to it. "He is *my servant,* whom I employ and therefore will uphold." In his undertaking he does his Father's will, seeks his Father's honour, and serves the interests of his Father's kingdom. 2. He is qualified for it. He *shall deal prudently,* for the *spirit of wisdom and understanding shall rest upon him, ch.* 11:2. The word is used concerning David when he *behaved himself wisely,* 1 Sa. 18:14. Christ is wisdom itself, and, in the contriving and carrying on the work of our redemption, there appeared much of *the wisdom of God in a mystery,* 1 Co. 2:7. Christ, when he was here upon earth, dealt very prudently, to the admiration of all.

II. He gives a short prospect both of his humiliation and his exaltation. See here, 1. How he humbled himself: *Many were astonished at him,* as they were at David when by reason of his sorrows and troubles he became a *wonder unto many,* Ps. 71:7. Many wondered to see what base usage he met with, how inveterate people were against him, how inhuman, and what indignities were done him: *His visage was marred more than any man's* when he was buffeted, smitten on the cheek, and crowned with thorns, and *hid not his face from shame and spitting. His face was foul with weeping,* for he was *a man of sorrows;* he that really was *fairer than the children of men* had his face spoiled with the abuses that were done him. Never was man used so barbarously; his form, when he took upon him *the form of a servant,* was more mean and abject than that of any of the sons of men. Those that saw him said, "Surely never man looked so miserably, *a worm and no man,*" Ps. 22:6. The *nation abhorred him* (*ch.* 49:7), treated him as the *off-scouring of all things. Never was sorrow like unto his sorrow.* 2. How highly God exalted him, and exalted him because he humbled himself. Three words are used for this (*v.* 13): *He shalt be exalted and extolled and be very high.* God shall exalt him, men shall extol him, and with both he shall be very high, higher than the highest, higher than the heavens. He shall prosper in his work, and succeed in it, and that shall raise him very high. (1.) Many nations shall be the better for him, for *he shall sprinkle them,* and not the Jews only; the blood of sprinkling shall be applied to their consciences, to purify them. He suffered, and died, and so sprinkled many nations; for in his death there was *a fountain opened,* Zec. 13:1. He shall sprinkle many nations by his heavenly doctrine, which shall drop as the rain and distil as the dew. Moses's did so only on one nation (Deu. 32:2), but Christ's on many nations. He shall do it by baptism, which is the washing of the body with pure water, Heb. 10:22. So that this promise had its accomplishment when Christ sent his apostles to disciple all nations, by baptizing or sprinkling them. (2.) The great ones of the nation shall show him respect: *Kings shall shut their mouths at him,* that is, they shall not open their mouths against him, as they have done, to contradict and blaspheme his sacred oracles; nay, they shall acquiesce in, and be well pleased with, the methods he takes of setting up his kingdom in the world; they shall with great humility and reverence receive his oracles and laws, as those who, when they heard Job's wisdom, *after his speech spoke not again,* Job 29:9, 22. *Kings shall see and arise, ch.* 49:7. (3.) The mystery which was kept secret from the beginning of the world shall by him be *made known to all nations for the obedience of faith,* as the apostle speaks, Rom. 16:25, 26. *That which had not been told them shall they see;* the gospel brings to light things new and unheard of, which will awaken the attention and engage the reverence of kings and kingdoms. This is applied to the preaching of the gospel in the Gentile world, Rom. 15:21. These words are there quoted according to the Septuagint translation: *To whom he was not spoken of they shall see, and those that have not heard shall understand.* As the things revealed had long been kept secret, so the persons to whom they were revealed had long been kept in the dark; but now they shall see and consider the glory of God shining in the face of Christ, which before they had not been told of — *they had not heard.* That shall be discovered to them by the gospel of Christ which could never be told them by all the learning of their philosophers, or the art of their diviners, or any of their pagan oracles. Much had been said in the Old Testament concerning the Messiah; much had been told them, and they had heard it. But, as the queen of Sheba found concerning Solomon, what they shall see in him, when he comes, shall far exceed what had been told them. Christ disappointed the expectations of those who looked for a Messiah according to their fancies, as the carnal Jews, but outdid theirs who looked for such a Messiah as was promised. According to their faith, nay, and beyond it, it was to them.

CHAPTER 53

The two great things which the Spirit of Christ in the Old-Testament prophets testified beforehand were the sufferings of Christ and the glory that should follow, 1 Pt. 1:11. And that which Christ himself, when he expounded Moses and all the prophets, showed to be the drift and scope of them all was that Christ ought to suffer and then to enter into his glory, Lu. 24:26, 27. But nowhere in all the Old-Testament are these two so plainly and fully prophesied of as here in this chapter, out of which divers passages are quoted with application to Christ in the New-Testament. This chapter is so replenished with the unsearchable riches of Christ that it may be called rather the gospel of the evangelist Isaiah than the prophecy of the prophet Isaiah. We may observe here, I. The reproach of Christ's sufferings — the meanness of his appearance, the greatness of his grief, and the prejudices which many conceived in consequences against his doctrine (*v.* 1–3). II. The rolling away of this reproach, and the stamping of immortal honour upon his sufferings, notwithstanding the disgrace and ignominy of them, by four considerations: — 1. That therein he did his Father's will (*v.* 4, 6, 10). 2. That thereby he made atonement for the sin of man (*v.* 4–6, 8, 11, 12), for it was not for any sin of his own that he suffered (*v.* 9). 3. That he bore his sufferings with an invincible and exemplary patience (*v.* 7). 4. That he should prosper in his undertaking, and his sufferings should end in his immortal honour (*v.* 10–12). By mixing faith with the prophecy of this chapter we may improve our acquaintance with Jesus Christ and him crucified, with Jesus Christ and him glorified, dying for our sins and rising again for our justification.

Verses 1–3

The prophet, in the close of the former chapter, had foreseen and foretold the kind reception which the gospel of Christ should find among the Gentiles, that nations and their kings should bid it welcome, that those who had not seen him should believe in him; and though they had not any prophecies among them of gospel grace, which might raise their expectations, and dispose them to entertain it, yet upon the first notice of it they should give it its due weight and consideration. Now here he foretels, with wonder, the unbelief of the Jews, notwithstanding the previous notices they had of the coming of the Messiah in the Old Testament and the opportunity they had of being personally acquainted with him. Observe here,

I. The contempt they put upon the gospel of Christ, *v.* 1. The unbelief of the Jews in our Saviour's time is expressly said to be the fulfilling of this word, Jn. 12:38. And it is applied likewise to the little success which the apostles' preaching met with among Jews and Gentiles, Rom. 10:16. Note, 1. Of the many that hear the report of the gospel there are few, very few, that believe it. It is reported openly and publicly, not whispered in a corner, or confined to the schools, but proclaimed to all; and it is so faithful a saying, and so well worthy of all acceptation, that one would think it should be universally received and believed. But it is quite otherwise; few believed the prophets who spoke before of Christ; when he came himself none of the rulers nor of the Pharisees followed him, and but here and there one of the common people; and, when the apostles carried this report all the world over, some in every place believed, but comparatively very few. To this day, of the many that profess to believe this report, there are few that cordially embrace it and submit to the power of it. 2. *Therefore* people believe not the report of the gospel, because *the arm of the Lord is not revealed* to them; they do not discern, nor will be brought to acknowledge, that divine power which goes along with the word. The *arm of the Lord is made bare* (as was said, *ch.* 52:10) in the miracles that were wrought to confirm Christ's doctrine, in the wonderful success of it, and its energy upon the conscience; though it is a still voice, it is a strong one; but they do not perceive this, nor do they experience in themselves that working of the Spirit which makes the word effectual. They believe not the gospel because, by rebelling against the light they had, they had forfeited the grace of God, which therefore he justly denied them and withheld from them, and for want of that they believed not. 3. This is a thing we ought to be much affected with; it is to be wondered at, and greatly lamented, and ministers may go to God and complain of it to him, as the prophet here. What a pity is it that such rich grace should be received in vain, that precious souls should perish at the pool's side, because they will not step in and be healed!

II. The contempt they put upon the person of Christ because of the meanness of his appearance, *v.* 2, 3. This seems to come in as a reason why they rejected his doctrine, because they were prejudiced against his person. When he was on earth many that heard him preach, and could not but approve of what they heard, would not give it any regard or entertainment, because it came from one that made so small a figure and had no external advantages to recommend him. Observe here,

1. The low condition he submitted to, and how he abased and emptied himself. The entry he made into the world, and the character he wore in it, were no way agreeable to the ideas which the Jews had formed of the Messiah and their expectations concerning him, but quite the reverse. (1.) It was expected that his extraction would be very great and noble. He was to be the Son of David, of a family that had *a name like to the names of the great men that were in the earth,* 2 Sa. 7:9. But he sprang out of this royal and illustrious family when it was reduced and sunk, and Joseph, that son of David, who was his supposed father, was but a poor carpenter, perhaps a ship-carpenter, for most of his relations were fishermen. This is here meant by his being *a root out of a dry ground,* his being born of a mean and despicable family, in the north, in Galilee, of a family out of which, like a dry and desert ground, nothing green, nothing great, was expected, in a country of such small repute that it was thought no good thing could come out of it. His mother, being a virgin, was as dry ground, yet from her *he* sprang who is not only fruit, but root. The seed on the stony ground had no root; but, though Christ grew out of a dry ground, he is both *the root and the offspring of David,* the root of the good olive. (2.) It was expected that he should make a public entry, and come in pomp and with observation; but, instead of that, he grew up before God, not before men. God had his eye upon him, but men regarded him not: *He grew up as a tender plant,* silently and insensibly, and without any noise, as the corn, that tender plant, grows up, *we know not how,* Mk. 4:27. Christ rose as a tender plant, which, one would have thought, might easily be crushed, or might be nipped in one frosty night. The gospel of Christ, in its beginning, was as a grain of mustard-seed, so inconsiderable did it seem, Mt. 13:31, 32. (3.) It was expected that he should have some uncommon beauty in his face and person, which should charm the eye, attract the heart, and raise the expectations of all that saw him. But there was nothing of this kind in him; not that he was in the least deformed or misshapen, but *he had no form nor comeliness,* nothing extraordinary, which one might have thought to meet with in the countenance of an incarnate deity. Those who saw him could not see that there was any beauty in him *that they should desire him, nothing in him more than in another beloved,* Cant. 5:9. Moses, when he was born, was exceedingly fair, to such a degree that it was looked upon as a happy presage, Acts 7:20; Heb. 11:23. David, when he was anointed, was *of a beautiful countenance, and goodly to look to,* 1 Sa. 16:12. But our Lord Jesus had nothing of that to recommend him. Or it may refer not so much to his person as to the manner of his appearing in the world, which had nothing in it of sensible glory. His gospel is preached, *not with the enticing words of man's wisdom,* but with all plainness, agreeable to the subject. (4.) It was expected that he should live a pleasant life, and have a full enjoyment of all the delights of the sons and daughters of men, which would have invited all sorts to him; but, on the contrary, he was *a man of sorrows and acquainted with grief.* It was not only his last scene that was tragical, but his whole life was so, not only mean, but miserable,

> — but one continued chain
> Of labour, sorrow, and consuming pain.
> — Sir R. Blackmore

Thus, being *made sin for us,* he underwent the sentence sin had subjected us to, that we should *eat in sorrow all the days of our life* (Gen. 3:17), and thereby relaxed much of the rigour and extremity of the sentence as to us. His condition was, upon many accounts, sorrowful. He was unsettled, had not where to lay his head, lived upon alms, was opposed and menaced, and *endured the contradiction of sinners against himself.* His spirit was tender, and he admitted the impressions of sorrow. We never read that he laughed, but often that he wept. Lentulus, in his epistle to the Roman senate concerning Jesus, says, *"he was never seen to laugh;"* and so worn and macerated was he with continual grief that when he was but a little above thirty years of age he was taken to be nearly fifty, Jn. 8:57. Grief was his intimate acquaintance; for he acquainted himself with the grievances of others, and sympathized with them, and he never set his own at a distance; for in his transfiguration he talked of his own decease, and in his triumph he wept over Jerusalem. Let us look unto him and mourn.

2. The low opinion that men had of him, upon this account. Being generally apt to judge of persons and things by the sight of the eye, and according to outward appearance, they saw no beauty in him that they should desire him. There was a great deal of true beauty in him, the beauty of holiness and the beauty of goodness, enough to render him *the desire of all nations;* but the far greater part of those among whom he lived, and conversed, saw none of this beauty, for it was spiritually discerned. Carnal hearts see no excellency in the Lord Jesus, nothing that should induce them to desire an acquaintance with him or interest in him. Nay, he is not only not desired, but *he is despised and rejected,* abandoned and abhorred, a reproach of men, an abject, one that men were shy of keeping company with and had not any esteem for, a worm and no man. He was despised as a mean man, rejected as a bad man. He was the stone which the builders refused; they would not have him to reign over them. Men, who should have had so much reason as to understand things better, so much tenderness as not to trample upon a man in misery — men whom he came to seek and save rejected him: *"We hid as it were our faces from him,* looked another way, and his sufferings were as nothing to us; though *never sorrow was like unto his sorrow.* Nay, we not only behaved as having no concern for him, but as loathing him, and having him in detestation." It may be read, *He hid as it were his face from us,* concealed the glory of his majesty, and drew a veil over it, and therefore *he was despised and we esteemed him not,* because we could not see through that veil. Christ having undertaken to make satisfaction to the justice of God for the injury man had done him in his honour by sin (and God cannot be injured except in his honour), he did it not only by divesting himself of the glories due to an incarnate deity, but by submitting himself to the disgraces due to the worst of men and malefactors; and thus by vilifying himself he glorified his Father: but this is a good reason why we should esteem him highly, and study to do him honour; let *him* be received by us whom men rejected.

Verses 4–9

In these verses we have,

I. A further account of the sufferings of Christ. Much was said before, but more is said here, of the very low condition to which he abased and humbled himself, to which he became obedient even to the death of the cross. 1. He had griefs and sorrows; being acquainted with them, he kept up the acquaintance, and did not grow shy, no, not of such melancholy acquaintance. Were griefs and sorrows allotted him? He bore them, and blamed not his lot; he carried them, and did neither shrink from them, nor sink under them. The load was heavy and the way long, and yet he did not tire, but persevered to the end, till he said, *It is finished.* 2. He had blows and bruises; he was *stricken, smitten, and afflicted.* His sorrows bruised him; he felt pain and smart from them; they touched him in the most tender part, especially when God was dishonoured, and when he forsook him upon the cross. All along he was smitten with the tongue, when he was cavilled at and contradicted, put under the worst of characters, and had all manner of evil said against him. At last he was smitten with the hand, with blow after blow. 3. He had wounds and stripes. He was scourged, not under the merciful restriction of the Jewish law, which allowed not above forty stripes to be given to the worst of male factors, but according to the usage of the Romans. And his scourging, doubtless, was the more severe because Pilate intended it as an equivalent for his crucifixion, and yet it proved a preface to it. He was wounded in his hands, and feet, and side. Though it was so ordered that not a bone of him should be broken, yet he had scarcely in any part a whole skin (how fond soever we are to sleep in one, even when we are called out to suffer for him), but from the crown of his head, which was crowned with thorns, to the soles of his feet, which were nailed to the cross, nothing appeared but wounds and bruises. 4. He was wronged and abused (*v.* 7): *He was oppressed,* injuriously treated and hardly dealt with. That was laid to his charge which he was perfectly innocent of, that laid upon him which he did not deserve, and in both he was oppressed and injured. *He was afflicted* both in mind and body; being oppressed, he laid it to heart, and, though, he was patient, was not stupid under it, but mingled his tears with those of the oppressed, that have no comforter, because *on the side of the oppressors there is power,* Eccl. 4:1. Oppression is a sore affliction; it has made many a wise man mad (Eccl. 7:7); but our Lord Jesus, though, when he was oppressed, he was afflicted, kept possession of his own soul. 5. he was judged and imprisoned, as is implied in his being *taken from prison and judgment, v.* 8. God having made him sin for us, he was proceeded against as a malefactor; he was apprehended and taken into custody, and made a prisoner; he was judge, accused, tried, and condemned, according to the usual forms of law: God filed a process against him, judged him in pursuance of that process, and confined him in the prison of the grave, at the door of which a stone was rolled and sealed. 6. He was *cut off* by an untimely death *from the land of the living,* though he lived a most useful life, did so many good works, and they were all such that one would be apt to think it was for some of them that they stoned him. He was stricken to death, to the grave which he made *with the wicked* (for he was crucified between two thieves, as if he had been the worst of the three) and yet *with the rich,* for he was buried in a sepulchre that belonged to Joseph, an honourable counsellor. Though he died with the wicked, and according to the common course of dealing with criminals should have been buried with them in the place where he was crucified, yet God here foretold, and Providence so ordered it, that he should make his grave with the innocent, with the rich, as a mark of distinction put between him and those that really deserved to die, even in his sufferings.

II. A full account of the meaning of his sufferings. It was a very great mystery that so excellent a person should suffer such hard things; and it is natural to ask with amazement, "How came it about? What evil had he done?" His enemies indeed looked upon him as suffering justly for his crimes; and, though they could lay nothing to his charge, they *esteemed him stricken, smitten of God, and afflicted, v.* 4. Because they hated him, and persecuted him, they thought that God did, that he was his enemy and fought against him; and therefore they were the more enraged against him, saying, *God has forsaken him; persecute and take him,* Ps. 71:11. Those that are justly smitten are smitten of God, for by him princes decree justice; and so they looked upon him to be smitten, justly put to death as a blasphemer, a deceiver, and an enemy to Caesar. Those that saw him hanging on the cross enquired not into the merits of his cause, but took it for granted that he was guilty of every thing laid to his charge and that therefore vengeance suffered him not to live. Thus Job's friends esteemed him smitten of God, because there was something uncommon in his sufferings. It is true he was *smitten of God, v.* 10 (or, as some read it, *he was God's smitten and afflicted,* the Son of God, though smitten and afflicted), but not in the sense in which they meant it; for, though he suffered all these things,

1. He never did any thing in the least to deserve this hard usage. Whereas he was charged with perverting the nation, and sowing sedition, it was utterly false; he had *done no violence,* but went about doing good. And, whereas he was called *that deceiver,* he never deserved that character; for *there was no deceit in his mouth* (*v.* 9), to which the apostle refers, 1 Pt. 2:22. *He did no sin, neither was guile found in his mouth.* He never offended either in word or deed, nor could any of his enemies take up that challenge of his, *Which of you convinceth me of sin?* The judge that condemned owned he found no fault in him, and the centurion that executed him professed that certainly he was a righteous man.

2. He conducted himself under his sufferings so as to make it appear that he did not suffer as an evil-doer; for, though he was *oppressed and afflicted,* yet he *opened not his mouth* (*v.* 7), no, not so much as to plead his own innocency, but freely offered himself to suffer and die for us, and objected nothing against it. This takes away the scandal of the cross, that he voluntarily submitted to it, for great and holy ends. By his wisdom he could have evaded the sentence, and by his power have resisted the execution; but *thus it was written, and thus it behoved him to suffer. This commandment he received from his Father,* and therefore he was led *as a lamb to the slaughter,* without any difficulty or reluctance (he is the *Lamb of God);* and as *a sheep is dumb before the shearers,* nay, before the butchers, so he *opened not his mouth,* which denotes not only his exemplary patience under affliction (Ps. 39:9), and his meekness under reproach (Ps. 38:13), but his cheerful compliance with his Father's will. *Not my will, but thine be done. Lo, I come.* By this will we are sanctified, his making his own soul, his own life, an offering for our sin.

3. It was for our good, and in our stead, that Jesus Christ suffered. This is asserted here plainly and fully, and in a very great variety of emphatical expressions.

(1.) It is certain that we are all guilty before God. We have all sinned, and have come short of the glory of God (*v.* 6): *All we like sheep have gone astray,* one as well as another. The whole race of mankind lies under the stain of original corruption, and every particular person stands charged with many actual transgressions. We have all gone astray from God our rightful owner, alienated ourselves from him, from the ends he designed us to move towards and the way he appointed us to move in. We have gone astray like sheep, which are apt to wander, and are unapt, when they have gone astray, to find the way home again. That is our true character; we are bent to backslide from God, but altogether unable of ourselves to return to him. This is mentioned not only as our infelicity (that we go astray from the green pastures and expose ourselves to the beasts of prey), but as our iniquity. We affront God in going astray from him, for we turn aside every one to his own way, and thereby set up ourselves, and our own will, in competition with God and his will, which is the malignity of sin. Instead of walking obediently in God's way, we have turned wilfully and stubbornly to our own way, the way of our own heart, the way that our own corrupt appetites and passions lead us to. We have set up for ourselves, to be our own masters, our own carvers, to do what we will and have what we will. Some think it intimates our own evil way, in distinction from the evil way of others. Sinners have their own iniquity, their beloved sin, which does most easily beset them, their own evil way, that they are particularly fond of and bless themselves in.

(2.) Our sins are our sorrows and our griefs (*v.* 4), or, as it may be read, *our sicknesses and our wounds:* the Septuagint reads it, *our sins;* and so the apostle, 1 Pt. 2:24. Our original corruptions are the sickness and disease of the soul, an habitual indisposition; our actual transgressions are the wounds of the soul, which put conscience to pain, if it be not seared and senseless. Or our sins are called our *griefs and sorrows* because all our griefs and sorrows are owing to our sins and our sins deserve all our griefs and sorrows, even those that are most extreme and everlasting.

(3.) Our Lord Jesus was appointed and did undertake to make satisfaction for our sins and so to save us from the penal consequences of them. [1.] He was appointed to do it, by the will of his Father; for *the Lord has laid on him the iniquity of us all.* God chose him to be the Saviour of poor sinners and would have him to save them in this way, by bearing their sins and the punishment of them; not the *idem — the same* that we should have suffered, but the *tantundem* — that which was more than equivalent for the maintaining of the honour of the holiness and justice of God in the government of the world. Observe here, *First,* In what way we are saved from the ruin to which by sin we had become liable — by laying our sins on Christ, as the sins of the offerer were laid upon the sacrifice and those of all Israel upon the head of the scapegoat. Our sins were *made to meet upon him* (so the margin reads it); the sins of all that he was to save, from every place and every age, met upon him, and he was met with for them. They were made to fall upon him (so some read it) as those rushed upon him that came with swords and staves to take him. The laying of our sins upon Christ implies the taking of them off from us; we shall not fall under the curse of the law if we submit to the grace of the gospel. They were laid upon Christ when he was *made sin* (that is, a sin-offering) *for us,* and redeemed us from the curse of the law by *being made a curse for us;* thus he put himself into a capacity to make those easy that come to him heavily laden under the burden of sin. See Ps. 40:6–12. *Secondly,* By whom this was appointed. It was the Lord that laid our iniquities on Christ; he contrived this way of reconciliation and salvation, and he accepted of the vicarious satisfaction Christ was to make. Christ was delivered to death *by the determinate counsel and foreknowledge of God.* None but God had power to lay our sins upon Christ, both because the sin was committed against him and to him the satisfaction was to be made, and because Christ, on whom the iniquity was to be laid, was his own Son, the Son of his love, and his holy child Jesus, who himself knew no sin. *Thirdly,* For whom this atonement was to be made. It was *the iniquity of us all* that was laid on Christ; for in Christ there is a sufficiency of merit for the salvation of all, and a serious offer made of that salvation to all, which excludes none that do not exclude themselves. It intimates that this is the one only way of salvation. All that are justified are justified by having their sins laid on Jesus Christ, and, though they were ever so many, he is able to bear the weight of them all. [2.] He undertook to do it. God laid upon him our iniquity; but did he consent to it? Yes, he did; for some think that the true reading of the next words (*v.* 7) is, *It was exacted, and he answered;* divine justice demanded satisfaction for our sins, and he engaged to make the satisfaction. He became our surety, not as originally bound with us, but as bail to the action: "Upon me be the curse, my Father." And therefore, when he was seized, he stipulated with those into whose hands he surrendered himself that that should be his disciples' discharge: *If you seek me, let these go their way,* Jn. 18:8. By his own voluntary undertaking he made himself responsible for our debt, and it is well for us that he was responsible. Thus *he restored that which he took not away.*

(4.) Having undertaken our debt, he underwent the penalty. Solomon says: *He that is surety for a stranger shall smart for it.* Christ, being surety for us, did smart for it. [1.] *He bore our griefs and carried our sorrows, v.* 4. He not only submitted to the common infirmities of human nature, and the common calamities of human life, which sin had introduced, but he underwent the extremities of grief, when he said, *My soul is exceedingly sorrowful.* He made the sorrows of this present time heavy to himself, that he might make them light and easy for us. Sin is the wormwood and the fall in the affliction and the misery. Christ bore our sins, and so *bore our griefs,* bore them off us, that we should never be pressed above measure. This is quoted (Mt. 8:17) with application to the compassion Christ had for the sick that came to him to be cured and the power he put forth to cure them. [2.] He did this by suffering for our sins (*v.* 5): *He was wounded for our transgressions,* to make atonement for them and to purchase for us the pardon of them. Our sins were the thorns in his head, the nails in his hands and feet, the spear in his side. Wounds and bruises were the consequences of sin, what we deserved and what we had brought upon ourselves, *ch.* 1:6. That these wounds and bruises, though they are painful, may not be mortal, *Christ was wounded for our transgressions,* was tormented or pained (the word is used for the pains of a woman in travail) for our revolts and rebellions. *He was bruised,* or crushed, *for our iniquities;* they were the procuring cause of his death. To the same purport is *v.* 8, *for the transgression of my people was he smitten, the stroke* was *upon him* that should have been upon us; and so some read it, *He was cut off for the iniquity of my people, unto whom the stroke belonged,* or *was due. He was delivered* to death *for our offences,* Rom. 4:25. Hence it is said to be *according to the scriptures,* according to this scripture, that Christ *died for our sins,* 1 Co. 15:3. Some read this, *by the transgressions of my people;* that is, by the wicked hands of the Jews, who were, in profession, God's people, he was stricken, was crucified and slain, Acts 2:23. But, doubtless, we are to take it in the former sense, which is abundantly confirmed by the angel's prediction of the Messiah's undertaking, solemnly delivered to Daniel, that he shall *finish transgression, make an end of sin, and make reconciliation for iniquity,* Dan. 9:24.

(5.) The consequence of this to us is our peace and healing, *v.* 5. [1.] Hereby we have peace: *The chastisement of our peace was upon him;* he, by submitting to these chastisements, slew the enmity, and settled an amity, between God and man; he *made peace by the blood of his cross.* Whereas by sin we had become odious to God's holiness and obnoxious to his justice, through Christ God is reconciled to us, and not only forgives our sins and saves us from ruin, but takes us into friendship and fellowship with himself, and thereby *peace* (that is, all good) *comes unto us,* Col. 1:20. *He is our peace,* Eph. 2:14. Christ was in pain that we might be at ease; he gave satisfaction to the justice of God that we might have satisfaction in our own minds, might be of good cheer, knowing that through him our sins are forgiven us. [2.] Hereby we have healing; for *by his stripes we are healed.* Sin is not only a crime, for which we were condemned to die and which Christ purchased for us the pardon of, but it is a disease, which tends directly to the death of our souls and which Christ provided for the cure of. By his stripes (that is, the sufferings he underwent) he purchased for us the Spirit and grace of God to mortify our corruptions, which are the distempers of our souls, and to put our souls in a good state of health, that they may be fit to serve God and prepared to enjoy him. And by the doctrine of Christ's cross, and the powerful arguments it furnishes us with against sin, the dominion of sin is broken in us and we are fortified against that which feeds the disease.

(6.) The consequence of this to Christ was his resurrection and advancement to perpetual honour. This makes the offence of the cross perfectly to cease; he yielded himself to die as a sacrifice, as a lamb, and, to make it evident that the sacrifice he offered of himself was accepted, we are told here, *v.* 8, [1.] That he was discharged: *He was taken from prison and from judgment;* whereas he was imprisoned in the grave under a judicial process, lay there under an arrest for our debt, and judgment seemed to be given against him, he was by an express order from heaven taken out of the prison of the grave, an angel was sent on purpose to roll away the stone and set him at liberty, by which the judgment given against him was reversed and taken off; this redounds not only to his honour, but to our comfort; for, being *delivered for our offences,* he was *raised again for our justification.* That discharge of the bail amounted to a release of the debt. [2.] That he was preferred: *Who shall declare his generation?* his *age,* or *continuance* (so the word signifies), the time of his life? He rose *to die no more; death had no more dominion over him.* He that *was dead is alive,* and *lives for evermore;* and who can describe that immortality to which he rose, or number the years and ages of it? And he is advanced to this eternal life because for the transgression of his people he became obedient to death. We may take it as denoting the time of his usefulness, as David is said to *serve his generation,* and so to answer the end of living. Who can declare how great a blessing Christ by his death and resurrection will be to the world? Some by *his generation* understand his spiritual seed: Who can count the vast numbers of converts that shall by the gospel be begotten to him, like the dew of the morning?

When thus exalted he shall live to see
A numberless believing progeny
Of his adopted sons; the godlike race
Exceed the stars that heav'n's high arches grace.
— Sir R. Blackmore

Of this generation of his let us pray, as Moses did for Israel, *The Lord God of our fathers make them a thousand times so many more as they are, and bless them as he has promised them,* Deu. 1:11.

Verses 10–12

In the foregoing verses the prophet had testified very particularly of the sufferings of Christ, yet mixing some hints of the happy issue of them; here he again mentions his sufferings, but largely foretels the glory that should follow. We may observe, in these verses,

I. The services and sufferings of Christ's state of humiliation. Come, and see how he loved us, see what he did for us.

1. He submitted to the frowns of Heaven (*v.* 10): *Yet it pleased the Lord to bruise him, to put him to* pain, or torment, or *grief.* The scripture nowhere says that Christ is his sufferings underwent the wrath of God; but it says here, (1.) That the Lord bruised him, not only permitted men to bruise him, but awakened his own sword against him, Zec. 13:7. They esteemed him smitten of God for some very great sin of his own (*v.* 4); now it was true that he was smitten of God, but it was for our sin; the Lord bruised him, for he *did not spare him, but delivered him up for us all,* Rom. 8:32. He it was that put the bitter cup into his hand, and obliged him to drink it (Jn. 18:11), having laid upon him our iniquity. He it was that made him sin and a curse for us, and turned to ashes all his burnt-offering, in token of the acceptance of it, Ps. 20:3. (2.) That he bruised him so as to put him to grief. Christ accommodated himself to this dispensation, and received the impressions of grief from his Father's delivering him up; and he was troubled to such a degree that it put him into an agony, and he began to be amazed and very heavy. (3.) It pleased the Lord to do this. He determined to do it; it was the result of an eternal counsel; and he delighted in it, as it was an effectual method for the salvation of man and the securing and advancing of the honour of God.

2. He substituted himself in the room of sinners, as a sacrifice. He *made his soul an offering for sin;* he himself explains this (Mt. 20:28), that *he came to give his life a ransom for many.* When men brought bulls and goats as sacrifices for sin they made them offerings, for they had an interest in them, God having put them under the feet of man. But Christ made himself an offering; it was his own act and deed. We could not put him in our stead, but he put himself, and said, *Father, into thy hands I commit my spirit,* in a higher sense than David said, or could say it. "Father, *I commit my soul to thee,* I deposit it in thy hands, as the life of a sacrifice and the price of pardons." Thus he shall bear the iniquities of the many that he designed to justify (*v.* 11), shall take away the sin of the world by taking it upon himself, Jn. 1:29. This mentioned again (*v.* 12): *He bore the sin of many,* who, if they had borne it themselves, would have been sunk by it to the lowest hell. See how this dwelt upon; for, whenever we think of the sufferings of Christ, we must see him in them bearing our sin.

3. He subjected himself to that which to us is the wages of sin (*v.* 12): *He has poured out his soul unto death,* poured it out as water, so little account did he make of it, when the laying of it down was the appointed means of our redemption and salvation. He *loved not his life unto the death,* and his followers, the martyrs, did likewise, Rev. 12:11. Or, rather, he poured it out as a drink-offering, to make his sacrifice complete, poured it out as wine, that his blood might be drink indeed, as his flesh is meat indeed to all believers. There was not only a colliquation of his body in his sufferings (Ps. 22:14, *I am poured out like water),* but a surrender of his spirit; he poured out that, even unto death, though he is the Lord of life.

4. He suffered himself to be ranked with sinners, and yet offered himself to be an intercessor for sinners, *v.* 12. (1.) It was a great aggravation of his sufferings that he was *numbered with transgressors,* that he was not only condemned as a malefactor, but executed in company with two notorious malefactors, and he in the midst, as if he had been the worst of the three, in which circumstance of his suffering, the evangelist tells us, this prophecy was fulfilled, Mk. 15:27, 28. Nay, the vilest malefactor of all, Barabbas, who was a traitor, a thief, and a murderer, was put in election with him for the favour of the people, and carried it; for they would not have Jesus released, but Barabbas. In his whole life he was numbered among the transgressors; for he was called and accounted a sabbath-breaker, a drunkard, and a friend to publicans and sinners. (2.) It was a great commendation of his sufferings, and redounded very much to his honour, that in his sufferings he *made intercession for the transgressors,* for those that reviled and crucified him; for he prayed, *Father, forgive them,* thereby showing, not only that he forgave them, but that he was now doing that upon which their forgiveness, and the forgiveness of all other transgressors, were to be founded. That prayer was the language of his blood, crying, not for vengeance, but for mercy, and therein it speaks better things than that of Abel, even for those who with wicked hands shed it.

II. The grace and glories of his state of exaltation; and the graces he confers on us are not the least of the glories conferred on him. These are secured to him by the covenant of redemption, which these verses give us some idea of. He promises to make his soul an offering for sin, consents that the Father shall deliver him up, and undertakes to bear the sin of many, in consideration of which the Father promises to glorify him, not only with the glory he had, as God, before the world was (Jn. 17:5), but with the glories of the Mediator.

1. He shall have the glory of an everlasting Father. Under this title he was *brought into the world* (*ch.* 9:6), and he shall not fail to answer the title when he goes out of the world. This was the promise made to Abraham (who herein was a type of Christ), that he should be *the father of many nations* and so be *the heir of the world,* Rom. 4:13, 17. As he was the root of the Jewish church, and the covenant was made with him and his seed, so is Christ of the universal church and with him and his spiritual seed is the covenant of grace made, which is grounded upon and grafted in the covenant of redemption, which here we have some of the glorious promises of. It is promised,

(1.) That the Redeemer shall have a seed to serve him and to bear up his name, Ps. 22:30. True believers are the seed of Christ; the Father gave them to him to be so, Jn. 17:6. He died to purchase and purify them to himself, fell to the ground as a corn of wheat, that he might *bring forth much fruit,* Jn. 12:24. The word, that incorruptible see, of which they are born again, is his word; the Spirit, the great author of their regeneration, is his Spirit; and it is his image that is impressed upon them.

(2.) That he shall live to see his seed. Christ's children have a living Father, and because he lives they shall live also, for he is their life. Though he died, he rose again, and left not his children orphans, but took effectual care to secure to them the spirit, the blessing, and the inheritance of sons. He shall see a great increase of them; the word is plural, *He shall see his seeds,* multitudes of them, so many that they cannot be numbered.

(3.) That he shall himself continue to take care of the affairs of this numerous family: *He shall prolong his days.* Many, when they see their seed, their seed's seed, wish to depart in peace; but Christ will not commit the care of his family to any other, no, he shall himself live long, and *of the increase of his government and peace there shall be no end,* for he ever lives. Some refer it to believers: *He shall see a seed that shall prolong its days,* agreeing with Ps. 89:29, 36, *His seed shall endure for ever.* While the world stands Christ will have a church in it, which he himself will be the life of.

(4.) That his great undertaking shall be successful and shall answer expectation: *The pleasure of the Lord shall prosper in his hand.* God's purposes shall take effect, and not one iota or tittle of them shall fail. Note, [1.] The work of man's redemption is in the hands of the Lord Jesus, and it is in good hands. It is well for us that it is in his, for our own hands are not sufficient for us, but he is able to save to the uttermost. It is in his hands who upholds all things. [2.] It is the good pleasure of the Lord, which denotes not only his counsel concerning it, but his complacency in it; and *therefore* God loved him, and was well pleased in him, because he undertook to lay down his life for the sheep. [3.] It has prospered hitherto, and shall prosper, whatever obstructions or difficulties have been, or may be, in the way of it. Whatever is undertaken according to God's pleasure shall prosper, *ch.* 46:10. Cyrus, a type of Christ, shall perform all God's pleasure (*ch.* 44:28), and therefore, no doubt, Christ shall. Christ was so perfectly well qualified for his undertaking, and prosecuted it with so much vigour, and it was from first to last so well devised, that it could not fail to prosper, to the honour of his Father and the salvation of all his seed.

(5.) That he shall himself have abundant satisfaction in it (*v.* 11): *He shall see of the travail of his sous, and shall be satisfied.* He shall see it beforehand (so it may be understood); he shall with the prospect of his sufferings have a prospect of the fruit, and he shall be satisfied with the bargain. He shall see it when it is accomplished in the conversion and salvation of poor sinners. Note, [1.] Our Lord Jesus was in travail of soul for our redemption and salvation, in great pain, but with longing desire to be delivered, and all the pains and throes he underwent were in order to it and hastened it on. [2.] Christ does and will see the blessed fruit of the travail of his soul in the founding and building up of his church and the eternal salvation of all that were given him. He will not come short of his end in any part of his work, but will himself see that he has not laboured in vain. [3.] The salvation of souls is a great satisfaction to the Lord Jesus. He will reckon all his pains well bestowed, and himself abundantly recompensed, if the many sons be by him brought through grace to glory. Let him have this, and he has enough. God will be glorified, penitent believers will be justified, and then Christ will be satisfied. Thus, in conformity to Christ, it should be a satisfaction to us if we can do any thing to serve the interests of God's kingdom in the world. Let it always be our meat and drink, as it was Christ's, to do God's will.

2. He shall have the glory of bringing in an everlasting righteousness; for so it was foretold concerning him, Dan. 9:24. And here, to the same purport, *By his knowledge* (the knowledge of him, and faith in him) *shall my righteous servant justify many;* for he shall bear the sins of many, and so lay a foundation for our justification from sin. Note, (1.) The great privilege that flows to us from the death of Christ is justification from sin, our being acquitted from that guilt which alone can ruin us, and accepted into God's favour, which alone can make us happy. (2.) Christ, who purchased our justification for us, applies it to us, by his intercession made for us, his gospel preached to us, and his Spirit witnessing in us. The Son of man had power even on earth to forgive sin. (3.) There are many whom Christ justifies, not all (multitudes perish in their sins), yet many, even as many as he gave his life a ransom for, as many as the Lord our God shall call. He shall justify not here and there one that is eminent and remarkable, but those of the many, the despised multitude. (4.) It is by faith that we are justified, by our consent to Christ and the covenant of grace; in this way we are saved, because thus God is most glorified, free grace most advanced, self most abased, and our happiness most effectually secured. (5.) Faith is the knowledge of Christ, and without knowledge there can be no true faith. Christ's way of gaining the will and affections is by enlightening the understanding and bringing that unfeignedly to assent to divine truths. (6.) That knowledge of Christ, and that faith in him, by which we are justified, have reference to him both as a servant to God and as a surety for us. [1.] As one that is employed for God to pursue his designs and secure and advance the interests of his glory. "He is my righteous servant, and as such justifies men." God has authorized and appointed him to do it; it is according to God's will and for his honour that he does it. He is himself righteous, and of his righteousness have all we received. He that is himself righteous (for he could not have made atonement for our sin if he had had any sin of his own to answer for) is *made of God to us righteousness, the Lord our righteousness.* [2.] As one that has undertaken for us. We must know him, and believe in him, as one that bore our iniquities — saved us from sinking under the load by taking it upon himself.

3. He shall have the glory of obtaining an incontestable victory and universal dominion, *v.* 12. Because he has done all these good services, *therefore will I divide him a portion with the great,* and, according to the will of the Father, *he shall divide the spoil with the strong,* as a great general, when he has driven the enemy out of the field, takes the plunder of it for himself and his army, which is both an unquestionable evidence of the victory and a recompense for all the toils and perils of the battle. Note, (1.) God the Father has engaged to reward the services and sufferings of Christ with great glory: "I will set him among the great, highly exalt him, and give him a name above every name." Great riches are also assigned to him: *He shall divide the spoil,* shall have abundance of graces and comforts to bestow upon all his faithful soldiers. (2.) Christ comes at his glory by conquest. He has set upon the strong man armed, dispossessed him, and divided the spoil. He has vanquished principalities and powers, sin and Satan, death and hell, the world and the flesh; these are the strong that he has disarmed and taken the spoil of. (3.) Much of the glory with which Christ is recompensed, and the spoil which he has divided, consists in the vast multitudes of willing, faithful, loyal subjects, that shall be brought in to him; for so some read it: *I will give many to him, and he shall obtain many for a spoil.* God will *give him the heathen for his inheritance and the uttermost parts of the earth for his possession,* Ps. 2:8. *His dominion shall be from sea to sea.* Many shall be wrought upon by the grace of God to give up themselves to him to be ruled, and taught, and saved by him, and hereby he shall reckon himself honoured, and enriched, and abundantly recompensed for all he did and all he suffered. (4.) What God designed for the Redeemer he shall certainly gain the possession of: "I will divide it to him," and immediately it follows, *He shall divide it,* notwithstanding the opposition that is given to him; for, as Christ finished the work that was given him to do, so God completed the recompence that was promised him for it; for he is both able and faithful. (5.) The spoil which God divided to Christ he divides (it is the same word), he distributes, among his followers; for, when he *led captivity captive,* he received gifts for men, that he might give gifts to men; for as he has told us (Acts 20:35) he did himself reckon it more blessed and honourable to give than to receive. Christ conquered for us, and through him we are more than conquerors. He has divided the spoils, the fruits of his conquest, to all that are his: let us therefore cast in our lot among them.

CHAPTER 54

The death of Christ is the life of the church and of all that truly belong to it; and therefore very fitly, after the prophet had foretold the sufferings of Christ, he foretels the flourishing of the church, which is a part of his glory, and that exaltation of him which was the reward of his humiliation: it was promised him that he should see his seed, and this chapter is an explication of that promise. It may easily be granted that it has a primary reference to the welfare and prosperity of the Jewish church after their return out of Babylon, which (as other things that happened to them) was typical of the glorious liberty of the children of God, which through Christ we are brought into; yet it cannot be denied but that it has a further and principal reference to the gospel church, into which the Gentiles were to be admitted. And the first words being understood by the apostle Paul of the New-Testament Jerusalem (Gal. 4:26, 27) may serve as a key to the whole chapter and that which follows. It is here promised concerning the Christian church, I. That, though the beginnings of it were small, it should be greatly enlarged by the accession of many to it among the Gentiles, who had been wholly destitute of church privileges (*v.* 1–5). II. That though sometimes God might seem to withdraw from her, and suspend the tokens of his favour, he would return in mercy and would not return to contend with them any more (*v.* 6–10). III. That, though for a while she was in sorrow and under oppression, she should at length be advanced to greater honour and splendour than ever (*v.* 11, 12). IV. That knowledge, righteousness, and peace, should flourish and prevail (*v.* 13, 14). V. That all attempts against the church should be baffled, and she should be secured from the malice of her enemies (*v.* 14–17).

Verses 1–5

If we apply this to the state of the Jews after their return out of captivity, it is a prophecy of the increase of their nation after they were settled in their own land. Jerusalem had been in the condition of a wife written childless, or a desolate solitary widow; but now it is promised that the city should be replenished and the country peopled again, that not only the ruins of Jerusalem should be repaired, but the suburbs of it extended on all sides and a great many buildings erected upon new foundations, — that those estates which had for many years been wrongfully held by the Babylonian Gentiles should now return to the right owners. God will again be a husband to them, and the reproach of their captivity, and the small number to which they were then reduced, shall be forgotten. And it is to be observed that, by virtue of the ancient promise made to Abraham of the increase of his seed, when they were restored to God's favour they multiplied greatly. Those that first came out of Babylon were but 42,000 (Ezra 2:64), about a fifteenth part of their number when they came out of Egypt; many came dropping to them afterwards, but we may suppose that to be the greatest number that ever came in a body; and yet above 500 years after, a little before their destruction by the Romans, a calculation was made by the number of the paschal lambs, and the lowest computation by that rule (allowing only ten to a lamb, whereas they might be twenty) made the nation to be nearly three millions. Josephus says, seven and twenty hundred thousand and odd, *Jewish War* 6.425. But we must apply it to the church of God in general; I mean the kingdom of God among men, God's city in the world, the children of God incorporated. Now observe,

I. The low and languishing state of religion in the world for a long time before Christianity was brought in. It was like one *barren, that did not bear,* or travail with child, was like one desolate, that had lost husband and children; the church lay in a little compass, and brought forth little fruit. The Jews were indeed by profession married to God, but few proselytes were added to them, the rising generations were unpromising, and serious godliness manifestly lost ground among them. The Gentiles had less religion among them than the Jews; their proselytes were in a dispersion; and the children of God, like the children of a broken, reduced family, were *scattered abroad* (Jn. 11:52), did not appear nor make any figure.

II. Its recovery from this low condition by the preaching of the gospel and the planting of the Christian church.

1. Multitudes were converted from idols to the living God. Those were the church's children that were born again, were partakers of a new and divine nature, by the word. *More were the children of the desolate than of the married wife;* there were more good people found in the Gentile church (when that was set up) that had long been afar off, and without God in the world, than ever were found in the Jewish church. God's sealed ones out of the tribes of Israel are numbered (Rev. 7:4), and they were but a remnant compared with the thousands of Israel; but those of other nations were so many, and crowded in so thickly, and lay so much scattered in all parts, that no man could number them, *v.* 9. Sometimes more of the power of religion is found in those places and families that have made little show of it, and have enjoyed but little of the means of grace, than in others that have distinguished themselves by a flourishing profession; and then more are the children of the desolate, more the fruits of their righteousness, than those of the married wife; so the last shall be first. Now this is spoken of as matter of great rejoicing to the church, which is called upon to break forth into singing upon this account. The increase of the church is the joy of all its friends and strengthens their hands. The longer the church has lain desolate the greater will the transports of joy be when it begins to recover the ground it has lost and to gain more. Even in heaven, among the angels of God, there is an uncommon joy for a sinner that repents, much more for a nation that does so. If the barren fig-tree at length bring forth fruit, it is well; it shall rejoice, and others with it.

2. The bounds of the church were extended much further than ever before, *v.* 2, 3. (1.) It is here supposed that the present state of the church is a tabernacle state; it dwells in tents, like the heirs of promise of old (Heb. 11:9); its dwelling is mean and movable, and of no strength against a storm. The city, the continuing city, is reserved for hereafter. A tent is soon taken down and shifted, so the candlestick of church privileges is soon *removed out of its place* (Rev. 2:5), and, when God pleases, it is as soon fixed elsewhere. (2.) Though it be a tabernacle state, it is sometimes very remarkably a growing state; and, if this family increase, no matter though it be in a tent. Thus it was in the first preaching of the gospel; it was the business of the apostles to disciple all nations, to stretch forth the curtains of the church's habitation, to preach the gospel where Christ had not yet been named (Rom. 15:20), to leaven with the gospel those towns and countries that had hitherto been strangers to it, and so to lengthen the cords of this tabernacle, that more might be enclosed, which would make it necessary to strengthen the stakes proportionably, that they might bear the weight of the enlarged curtains. The more numerous the church grows the more cautious she must be to fortify herself against errors and corruptions, and to support her seven pillars, Prov. 9:1. (3.) It was a proof of divine power going along with the gospel that in all places it *grew and prevailed mightily,* Acts 19:20. It broke forth, as the breaking forth of waters — *on the right hand and on the left,* that is, on all hands. The gospel spread itself into all parts of the world; there were eastern and western churches. The church's seed inherited the Gentiles, and the cities that had been desolate (that is, destitute of the knowledge and worship of the true God) came to be inhabited, that is, to have religion set up in them and the name of Christ professed.

3. This was the comfort and honour of the church (*v.* 4): *"Fear not, for thou shalt not be ashamed,* as formerly, of the straitness of thy borders, and the fewness of thy children, which thy enemies upbraided thee with, but shalt *forget the reproach of thy youth,* because there shall be no more ground for that reproach." It was the reproach of the Christian religion, in its youth, that none of the rulers or princes of this world embraced it and that it was entertained and professed by a despicable handful of men; but, after awhile, nations were discipled, the empire became Christian, and then this *reproach of its youth was forgotten.*

4. This was owing to the relation in which God stood to his church, as her husband (*v.* 5): *Thy maker is thy husband.* Believers are said to be married to Christ, that they may *bring forth fruit unto God* (Rom. 7:4); so the church is married to him, that she may bear and bring up a holy seed to God, that shall be accounted to him for a generation. Jesus Christ is the church's Maker, by whom she

is formed into a people — her Redeemer, by whom she is brought out of captivity, the bondage of sin, the worst of slaveries. This is he that espoused her to himself; and, (1.) He is *the Lord of hosts,* who has an irresistible power, an absolute sovereignty, and a universal dominion! Kings who are lords of some hosts, find there are others who are lords of other hosts, as many and mighty as theirs; but God is the Lord of all hosts. (2.) He is *the Holy One of Israel,* the same that presided in the affairs of the Old-Testament church and was the Mediator of the covenant made with it. The promises made to the New-Testament Israel are as rich and sure as those made to the Old-Testament Israel; for he that is our Redeemer is the Holy One of Israel. (3.) He is and shall be called *the Lord of the whole earth,* as God, and as Mediator, for he is the heir of all things; but *then* he shall be called so, when the ends of the earth shall be made to see his salvation, when all the earth shall call him their God and have an interest in him. Long he had been called, in a peculiar manner, *the God of Israel;* but now, the partition wall between Jew and Gentile being taken down, he shall be called *the God of the whole earth* even where he has been, as at Athens itself, an *unknown God.*

Verses 6–10

The seasonable succour and relief which God sent to his captives in Babylon, when they had a discharge from their bondage there, are here foretold, as a type and figure of all those consolations of God which are treasured up for the church in general and all believers in particular, in the covenant of grace.

I. Look back to former troubles, and in comparison with them God's favours to his people appear very comfortable, *v.* 6–8. Observe, 1. How sorrowful the church's condition had been. She had been as a woman forsaken, whose husband was dead, or had fallen out with her, though she was *a wife of youth,* upon which account she is grieved in spirit, takes it very ill, frets, and grows melancholy upon it; or she had been as one refused and rejected, and therefore full of discontent. Note, Even those that are espoused to God may yet seem to be refused and forsaken, and may be grieved in spirit under the apprehensions of being so. Those that shall never be forsaken and left in despair may yet for a time be perplexed and in distress. The similitude is explained (*v.* 7, 8): *For a small moment have I forsaken thee. In a little wrath I hid my face from thee.* When God continues his people long in trouble he seems to forsake them; so their enemies construe it (Ps. 71:11); so they themselves misinterpret it, *ch.* 49:14. When they are comfortless under their troubles, because their prayers and expectations are not answered, God hides his face from them, as if he regarded them not nor designed them any kindness. God owns that he had done this; for he keeps an account of the afflictions of his people, and, though he never turned his face against them (as against the wicked, Ps. 34:16), he remembers how often he turned his back upon them. This arose indeed from his displeasure. It was in wrath that he forsook them and hid his face from them (*ch.* 57:17); yet it was but in a little wrath: not that God's wrath ever is a little thing, or to be made light of *(Who knows the power of his anger?),* but little in comparison with what they had deserved, and what others justly suffer, on whom the full vials of his wrath are poured out. He did not stir up all his wrath. But God's people, though they be sensible of ever so small a degree of God's displeasure, cannot but be grieved in spirit because of it. As for the continuance of it, it was but *for a moment,* a *small* moment; for God does not keep his anger against his people for ever; no, it is soon over. As he is slow to anger, so he is swift to show mercy. The afflictions of God's people, as they are light, so they are but for a moment, a cloud that presently blows over. 2. How sweet the returns of mercy would be to them when God should come and comfort them according to the time that he had afflicted them. God called them into covenant with himself when they were forsaken and grieved; he called them out of their afflictions when they were most pressing, *v.* 6. God's anger endures for a moment, but he will gather his people when they think themselves neglected, will gather them out of their dispersions, that they may return in a body to their own land, — will gather them into his arms, to protect them, embrace them, and bear them up, — and will gather them at last to himself, *will gather the wheat into the barn.* He will have mercy on them. This supposes the turning away of his anger and the admitting of them again into his favour. God's gathering his people takes rise from his mercy, not any merit of others; and it is with *great mercies* (*v.* 7), *with everlasting kindness, v.* 8. The wrath is little, but the mercies are great; the wrath is for a moment, but the kindness everlasting. See how one is set over against the other, that we may neither despond under our afflictions nor despair of relief.

II. Look forward to future dangers, and in defiance of them God's favours to his people appear very constant, and his kindness everlasting; for it is formed into a covenant, here called a *covenant of peace,* because it is founded in reconciliation and is inclusive of all good. Now,

1. This is as firm as the covenant of providence. It is *as the waters of Noah,* that is, as that promise which was made concerning the deluge that there should never be the like again to disturb the course of summer and winter, seed-time and harvest, *v.* 9. God then contended with the world in great wrath, and for a full year, and yet at length returned in mercy, everlasting mercy; for he gave his word, which was as inviolable as his oath, that Noah's flood should never return, that he would never drown the world again; see Gen. 8:21, 22; 9:11. And God has ever since kept his word, though the world has been very provoking; and he will keep it to the end; for the world that now is is reserved unto fire. And thus inviolable is the covenant of grace: *I have sworn that I would not be wroth with thee,* as I have been, *and rebuke thee,* as I have done. He will not be so angry with them as to cast them off and break his covenant with them (Ps. 89:34), nor rebuke them as he has rebuked the heathen, to destroy them, and *put out their name for ever and ever,* Ps. 9:5.

2. It is more firm than the strongest parts of the visible creation (*v.* 10): The *mountains shall depart,* which are called *everlasting mountains,* and *the hills be removed,* though they are called *perpetual hills,* Hab. 3:6. Sooner shall they remove than God's covenant with his people be broken. Mountains have sometimes been shaken by earthquakes, and removed; but the promises of God were never broken by the shock of any event. The day will come when all *the mountains shall depart* and all *the hills be removed,* not only the tops of them covered, as they were by the waters of Noah, but the roots of them torn up; for the earth and all the works that are therein shall be burned up; but then the covenant of peace between God and believers shall continue in the everlasting bliss of all those who are the children of that covenant. Mountains and hills signify great men, men of bulk and figure. Do these mountains seem to support the skies (as Atlas) and bear them up? They shall depart and be removed. Creature-confidences shall fail us. *In vain is salvation hoped for from those hills and mountains.* But the firmament is firm, and answers to its name, when those who seem to prop it are gone. When our friends fail us our God does not, nor does his kindness depart? Do these mountains threaten, and seem to top the skies, and bid defiance to them, as Pelion and Ossa? Do the kings of the earth, and the rulers, set themselves against the Lord? They shall depart and be removed. Great mountains, that stand in the way of the salvation of the church, shall be *made plain* (Zec. 4:7); but God's kindness shall never depart from his people, for whom he loves he loves to the end; nor shall the covenant of his peace ever be removed, for he is the Lord that has mercy on his people. *Therefore* the covenant is immovable and inviolable, because it is built not on our merit, which is a mutable uncertain thing, but on God's mercy, which is from everlasting to everlasting.

Verses 11–17

Very precious promises are here made to the church in her low condition, that God would not only continue his love to his people under their troubles as before, but that he would restore them to their former prosperity, nay, that he would raise them to greater prosperity than any they had yet enjoyed. In the foregoing chapter we had the humiliation and exaltation of Christ; here we have the humiliation and exaltation of the church; for, if we suffer with him, we shall reign with him. Observe,

I. The distressed state the church is here reduced to by the providence of God (*v.* 11): *"O thou afflicted,* poor, and indigent society, that art *tossed with tempests,* like a ship driven from her anchors by a storm and hurried into the ocean, where she is ready to be swallowed up by the waves, and in this condition *not comforted* by any compassionate friend that will sympathize with thee, or suggest to thee any encouraging considerations (Eccl. 4:1), not comforted by any allay to thy trouble, or prospect of deliverance out of it." This was the condition of the Jews in Babylon, and afterwards, for a time, under Antiochus. It is often the condition of Christian churches and of particular believers; without are fightings, within are fears; they are like the disciples in a storm, ready to perish; and where is their faith?

II. The glorious state the church is here advanced to by the promise of God. God takes notice of the afflicted distressed state of his church, and comforts her, when she is most disconsolate and has no other comforter. Let the people of God, when they are afflicted and tossed, think they hear God speaking comfortably to them by these words, taking notice of their griefs and fears, what afflictions they are under, what distresses they are in, and what comforts their case calls for. When they bemoan themselves, God bemoans them, and speaks to them with pity: *O thou afflicted, tossed with tempests, and not comforted;* for in all their afflictions he is afflicted. But this is not all; he engages to raise her up out of her affliction, and encourages her with the assurance of the great things he would do for her, both for her prosperity and for the securing of that prosperity to her.

1. Whereas now she lay in disgrace, God promises that which would be her beauty and honour, which would make her easy to herself and amiable in the eyes of others.

(1.) This is here promised by a similitude taken from a city, and it is an apt similitude, for the church is the city of the living God, the heavenly Jerusalem. Whereas now Jerusalem lay in ruins, a heap of rubbish, it shall be not only rebuilt, but beautified, and appear more splendid than ever; the stones shall be laid not only firm, but fine, laid with fair colours; they shall be *glistering stones,* 1 Chr. 29:2. The foundations shall be laid or garnished with *sapphires,* the most precious of the precious stones here mentioned; for Christ (the church's foundation), and the foundation of the apostles and prophets, are precious above any thing else. The windows of this house, city, or temple, shall be made of *agates,* the gates of *carbuncles,* and all the *borders* (the walls that enclose the courts, or the boundaries by which her limits are marked, the mere-stones) shall be *of pleasant stones, v.* 12. Never was this literally true; but it intimates, [1.] That, God having graciously undertaken to build his church, we may expect that to be done for it, that to be wrought in it, which is very great and uncommon. [2.] That the glory of the New-Testament church shall far exceed that of the Jewish church, not in external pomp and splendour, but in those gifts and graces of the Spirit which are infinitely more valuable, that wisdom which is *more precious than rubies* (Prov. 3:15), than the precious onyx and the sapphire, and which the *topaz of Ethiopia cannot equal,* Job 28:16, 19. [3.] That the wealth of this world, and those things of it that are accounted most precious, shall be despised by all the true living members of the church, as having no value, no glory, in comparison with that which far excels. That which the children of this world lay up among their treasures, and too often in their hearts, the children of God make pavements of, and put under their feet, the fittest place of it.

(2.) It is here promised in the particular instances of those things that shall be the beauty and honour of the church, which are knowledge, holiness, and love, the very image of God, in which man was created, renewed, and restored. And these are the sapphires and carbuncles, the precious and pleasant stones, with which the gospel temple shall be enriched and beautified, and these wrought by the power and efficacy of those doctrines which the apostle compares to gold or silver, and precious stones, that are to be *built upon the foundation,* 1 Co. 3:12. Then the church is all glorious, [1.] When it is full of the knowledge of God, and that is promised here (*v.* 13): *All thy children shall be taught of the Lord.* The church's children, being born of God, shall be taught of God; being his children by adoption, he will take care of their education. It was promised (*v.* 1) that the church's children should be many; but lest we should think that being many, as sometimes it happens in numerous families, they will be neglected, and not have instruction given them so carefully as if they were but few, God here takes that work into his own hand: *They shall all be taught of the Lord;* and none teaches like him. *First,* It is a promise of the means of instruction and those means authorized by a divine institution: *They shall all be taught of God,* that is, they shall be taught by those whom God shall appoint and whose labours shall be under his direction and blessing. He will ordain the methods of instruction, and by his word and ordinances will diffuse a much greater light than the Old-Testament church had. Care shall be taken for the teaching of the church's children, that knowledge may be transmitted from generation to generation, and that all may be enriched with it, from the least even to the greatest. *Secondly,* It is a promise of the Spirit of illumination. Our Saviour quotes it with application to gospel grace, and makes it to have its accomplishment in all those that were brought to believe in him (Jn. 6:45): *It is written in the prophets, They shall be all taught of God,* whence he infers that those, and those only, come to him by faith that have heard and learned of the Father, that are *taught by him as the truth is in Jesus,* Eph. 4:21. There shall be a plentiful effusion of the Spirit of grace upon Christians, to *teach them all things,* Jn. 14:26. [2.] When the members of it live in love and unity among themselves: *Great shall be the peace of thy children.* Peace may be taken here for all good. As where no knowledge of God is no good can be expected, so those that are taught of God to know him are in a fair way to prosper for both worlds. *Great peace have those that* know and *love God's law,* Ps. 119:165. But it is often put for love and unity; and so we may take it. All that are taught of God are taught to *love one another* (1 Th. 4:9) and that will keep peace among the church's children and prevent their falling out by the way. [3.] When holiness reigns; for that above any thing is the beauty of the church (*v.* 14): *In righteousness shall thou be established.* The reformation of manners, the restoration of purity, the due administration of public justice, and the prevailing of honesty and fair dealing among men, are the strength and stability of any church or state. The kingdom of God, set up by the gospel of Christ, is not meat and drink, but this righteousness and peace, holiness and love.

2. Whereas now she lay in danger, God promises that which would be her protection and security.

(1.) God engages here that though, in the day of her distress, without were fightings and within were fears, now she shall be safe from both. [1.] There shall be no fears within (*v.* 14): *"Thou shalt be far from oppression.* Those that have oppressed thee shall be removed, those that would oppress thee shall be restrained, and therefore thou shalt not fear, but mayest look upon it as a thing at a great distance, that thou art now in no danger of. Thou shalt be far from terror, not only from evil, but from the fear of evil, for it shall not come near thee so as to do thee any hurt or to put thee in any fright." Note, Those are far from terror that are far from oppression; for it is as great a terror as can fall on a people to have the rod of government turned into the serpent of oppression, because against this there is no fence, nor is there any flight from it. [2.] There shall be no fightings without. Though attempts should be made upon them to insult them, to invade their country, or besiege their towns, they should all be in vain, and none of them succeed, *v.* 15. It is granted, *"They shall surely gather together against thee;* thou must expect it." The confederate force of hell and earth will be renewing their assaults. As long as there is a devil in hell, and a persecutor out of it, God's people must expect frequent alarms; but, *First,* God will not own them, will not give them either commission or countenance; they gather together, hand joins in hand, but it is *not by me.* God gave them no such order as he did to Sennacherib, to *take the spoil, and to take the prey, ch.* 10:6. And therefore, *Secondly,* Their attempt will end in their own ruin: *"Whosoever shall gather together against thee,* be they ever so many and ever so mighty, they shall not only be baffled, but they *shall fall for thy sake,* or they shall fall before thee, which shall be the just punishment of their enmity to thee." God will make them to fall for the sake of the love he bears to his church and the care he has of it, in answer to the prayers made by his people, and in pursuance of the promises made to them. "They shall fall, that thou mayest stand," Ps. 27:2.

(2.) That we may with the greatest assurance depend upon God for the safety of his church, we have here, [1.] The power of God over the church's enemies asserted, *v.* 16. The truth is they have *no power but what is given them from above,* and he that gave them their power can limit and restrain them. *Hitherto they shall go, and no further. First,* They cannot carry on their design without arms and weapons of war; and the smith that makes those weapons is God's creature, and he gave him his skill to work in iron and brass (Ex. 31:3, 4) and particularly to make proper instruments for warlike purposes. It is melancholy to think, as if men did not die fast enough of themselves, how ingenious and industrious they are to make instruments of death and to find out ways and means to kill one another. *The smith blows the coals in the fire,* to make his iron malleable, to soften it first, that it may be hardened into steel, and so *he may bring forth an instrument proper for the work of those that seek to destroy.* It is the iron age that is the age of war. But *God has created the smith,* and therefore can tie his hands, so that the project of the enemy shall miscarry (as many a project has done) for want of arms and ammunition. Or the smith that forges the weapons is perhaps put here for the council of war that forms the design, blows the coals of contention, and brings forth the plan of the war; these can do no more than God will let them. *Secondly,* They cannot carry it on without men, they must have soldiers, and it is *God that created the waster to destroy.* Military men value themselves upon their great offices and splendid titles, and even the common soldiers call themselves *gentlemen;* but God calls them *wasters made to destroy,* for wasting and destruction are their business. They think their own ingenuity, labour, and experience, made them soldiers; but it was God that created them, and gave them strength and spirit for that hazardous employment; and therefore he not only can restrain them, but will serve his own purposes and designs by them. [2.] The promise of God concerning the church's safety solemnly laid down, as *the heritage of the servants of the Lord* (*v.* 17), as that which they may depend upon and be confident of, that God will protect them from their adversaries both in camps and courts. *First,* From their field-adversaries, that think to destroy them by force and violence, and dint of sword: *"No weapon that is formed against thee* (though ever so artfully formed by the smith that blows the coals, *v.* 16, though ever so skilfully managed by the waster that seeks to destroy) *shall prosper;* it shall not prove strong enough to do any harm to the people of God; it shall miss its mark, shall fall out of the hand or perhaps recoil in the face of him that uses it against thee." It is the happiness of the church that *no weapons formed against it shall prosper* long, and therefore the folly of its enemies will at length be made manifest to all, for they are but preparing instruments of ruin for themselves. *Secondly,* From their law-adversaries, that think to run them down under colour of right and justice. When the weapons of war do not prosper there are tongues that rise in judgment. Both are included in the gates of hell, that seek to destroy the church; for they had their courts of justice, as well as their magazines and military stores, in their gates. The tongues that rise in judgment against the church are as such as either demand a dominion over it, as if God's children were their lawful captives, pretending an authority to oppress their consciences, or they are such as misrepresent them, and falsely accuse them, and by slanders and calumnies endeavour to make them odious to the people and obnoxious to the government. This the enemies of the Jews did, to incense the kings of Persia against them, Ezra 4:12; Esth. 3:8. "But these insulting threatening tongues thou shalt condemn; thou shalt have wherewith to answer their insolent demands, and to put to silence their malicious reflections. Thou shalt do it *by well-doing* (1 Pt. 2:15), by doing that which will make thee manifest in the consciences even of thy adversaries, that thou art not what thou art represented to be. *Thou shalt condemn them,* that is, God shall condemn them for thee. *He shall bring forth thy righteousness as the light,* Ps. 37:6. Thou shalt condemn them as Noah condemned the old world that reproached him, by building the ark, and so saving his house, in contempt of their contempts." The day is coming when God will reckon with the wicked men for all their hard speeches which they have spoken against him, Jude 15.

The last words refer not only to this promise, but to all that go before: *This is the heritage of the servants of the Lord.* God's servants are his sons, for he has provided an inheritance for them, rich, sure, and indefeasible. God's promises are their *heritage for ever* (Ps. 119:111); *and their righteousness is of me, saith the Lord.* God will clear up the righteousness of their cause before men. It is with him, for he knows it; it is with him, for he will plead it. Or their reward for their righteousness, and for all that which they have suffered unrighteously, is of God, that God who judges in the earth, and with whom *verily there is a reward for the righteous.* Or their righteousness itself, all that in them which is good and right, is of God, who works it in them; it is of Christ who is made righteousness to them. In those for whom God designs a heritage hereafter he will work righteousness now.

CHAPTER 55

As we had much of Christ in the 53rd chapter, and much of the church of Christ in the 54th chapter, so in this chapter we have much of the covenant of grace made with us in Christ. The "sure mercies of David," which are promised here (*v.* 3), are applied by the apostle to the benefits which flow to us from the resurrection of Christ (Acts 13:34), which may serve as a key to this chapter; not but that it was intended for the comfort of the people of God that lived then, especially of the captives in Babylon, and others of the dispersed of Israel; but unto us was this gospel preached as well as unto them, and much more clearly and fully in the New Testament. Here is, I. A free and gracious invitation to all to come and take the benefit of gospel grace (*v.* 1). II. Pressing arguments to enforce this invitation (*v.* 2–4). III. A promise of the success of this invitation among the Gentiles (*v.* 5). IV. An exhortation to repentance and reformation, with great encouragement given to hope for pardon thereupon (*v.* 6–9). V. The ratification of all this, with the certain efficacy of the word of God (*v.* 10, 11). And a particular instance of the accomplishment of it in the return of the Jews out of their captivity, which was intended for a sign of the accomplishment of all these other promises.

Verses 1–5

Here, I. We are all invited to come and take the benefit of that provision which the grace of God has made for poor souls in the new covenant, of that which is the *heritage of the servants of the Lord* (*ch.* 54:17), and not only their heritage hereafter, but their cup now, *v.* 1. Observe,

1. Who are invited: *Ho, every one.* Not the Jews only, to whom first the word of salvation was sent, but the Gentiles, the poor and the maimed, the halt and the blind, are called to this marriage supper, whoever can be picked up out of the highways and the hedges. It intimates that in Christ there is enough for all and enough for each, that ministers are to make a general offer of life and salvation to all, that in gospel times the invitation should be more largely made than it had been and should be sent to the Gentiles, and that the gospel covenant excludes none that do not exclude themselves. The invitation is published with an *Oyez — Ho,* take notice of it. *He that has ears to hear let him hear.*

2. What is the qualification required in those that shall be welcome — they must thirst. All shall be welcome to gospel grace upon those terms only that gospel grace be welcome to them. Those that are satisfied with the world and its enjoyments for a portion, and seek not for a happiness in the favour of God, — those that depend upon the merit of their own works for a righteousness, and see no need they have of Christ and his righteousness, — these do not thirst; they have no sense of their need, are in no pain or uneasiness about their souls, and therefore will not condescend so far as to be beholden to Christ. But those that thirst are invited to the waters, as those that labour, and are heavy-laden, are invited to Christ for rest. Note, Where God gives grace he first gives a thirsting after it; and, where he has given a thirsting after it, he will give it, Ps. 81:10.

3. Whither they are invited: *Come you to the waters.* Come to the water-side, to the ports, and quays, and wharfs, on the navigable rivers, into which goods are imported; thither come and buy, for that is the market-place of foreign commodities; and to us they would have been for ever foreign if Christ had not brought in an everlasting righteousness. Come to Christ; for he is the fountain opened; he is the rock smitten. Come to holy ordinances, to those streams that make glad the city of our God; come to them, and though they may seem to you plain and common things, like waters, yet to those who believe in Christ the

things signified will be as wine and mile, abundantly refreshing. Come to the healing waters; come to the living waters. Whoever will, let him come, and *partake of the waters of life,* Rev. 22:17. Our Saviour referred to it, Jn. 7:37. *If any man thirst, let him come to me and drink.*

4. What they are invited to do. (1.) *Come, and buy.* Never did any tradesman court customers that he hoped to get by as Christ courts us to that which we only are to be gainers by. "Come and buy, and we can assure you you shall have a good bargain, which you will never repent of nor lose by. Come and buy; make it your own by an application of the grace of the gospel to yourselves; make it your own upon Christ's terms, nay, your own upon any terms, nor deliberating whether you shall agree to them." (2.) *"Come, and eat;* make it still more your own, as that which we eat is more our own than that which we only buy." We must buy the truth, not that we may lay it by to be looked at, but that we may feed and feast upon it, and that the spiritual life may be nourished and strengthened by it. We must buy necessary provisions for our souls, be willing to part with any thing, though ever so dear to us, so that we may but have Christ and his graces and comforts. We must part with sin, because it is an opposition to Christ, part with all opinion of our own righteousness, as standing in competition with Christ, and part with life itself, and its most necessary supports, rather than quit our interest in Christ. And, when we have bought what we need, let us not deny ourselves the comfortable use of it, but enjoy it, and eat the labour of our hands: *Buy, and eat.*

5. What is the provision they are invited to: *"Come, and buy wine and milk,* which will not only quench the thirst" (fair water would do that), "but nourish the body, and revive the spirits." The world comes short of our expectations. We promise ourselves, at least, water in it, but we are disappointed of that, as *the troops of Tema,* Job 6:19. But Christ outdoes our expectations. We come to the waters, and would be glad of them, but we find there wine and milk, which were the staple commodities of the tribe of Judah, and which the Shiloh of that tribe is furnished with to entertain the *gathering of the people to him,* Gen. 49:10, 12. *His eyes shall be red with wine and his teeth white with milk.* We must come to Christ, to have milk for babes, to nourish and cherish those that are but lately born again; and with him strong men shall find that which will be a cordial to them: they shall have wine to make glad their hearts. We must part with our puddle-water, nay, with our poison, that we may procure this wine and milk.

6. The free communication of this provision: *Buy it without money, and without price.* A strange way of buying, not only without ready money (that is common enough), but without any money, or the promise of any; yet it seems not so strange to those who have observed Christ's counsel to Laodicea, that was wretchedly poor, to *come and buy,* Rev. 3:17, 18. Our buying without money intimates, (1.) That the gifts offered us are invaluable and such as no price can be set upon. Wisdom is that which cannot be gotten for gold. (2.) That he who offers them has no need of us, nor of any returns we can make him. He makes us these proposals, not because he has occasion to sell, but because he has a disposition to give. (3.) That the things offered are already bought and paid for. Christ purchased them at the full value, with price, not with money, but with *his own blood,* 1 Pt. 1:19. (4.) That we shall be welcome to the benefits of the promise, though we are utterly unworthy of them, and cannot make a tender of any thing that looks like a valuable consideration. We ourselves are not of any value, nor is any thing we have or can do, and we must own it, that, if Christ and heaven be ours, we may see ourselves for ever indebted to free grace.

II. We are earnestly pressed and persuaded (and O that we would be prevailed with!) to accept this invitation, and make this good bargain for ourselves.

1. That which we are persuaded to is to hearken to God and to his proposals: *"Hearken diligently unto me, v.* 2. Not only give me the hearing, but approve of what I say, and apply it to yourselves (*v.* 3): *Incline your ear,* as you do to that which you find yourselves concerned in and pleased with; bow the ear, and let the proud heart stoop to the humbling methods of the gospel; bend the ear this way, that you may hear with attention and remark; hear, *and come unto me;* not only come and treat with me, but comply with me, come up to my terms;" accept God's offers

as very advantageous; answer his demands as very fit and reasonable.

2. The arguments used to persuade us to this are taken, (1.) From the unspeakable wrong we do to ourselves if we neglect and refuse this invitation: *"Wherefore do you spend money for that which is not bread,* which will not yield you, no, not beggar's food, dry bread, when with me you may have wine and milk without money? *Wherefore do you spend your labour* and toil *for that which* will not be so much as dry bread to you, for it *satisfies not?"* See here, [1.] The vanity of the things of this world. They are not bread, not proper food for a soul; they afford no suitable nourishment or refreshment. Bread is the staff of the natural life, but it affords no support at all to the spiritual life. All the wealth and pleasure in the world will not make one meal's meat for a soul. Eternal truth and eternal good are the only food for a rational and immortal soul, the life of which consists in reconciliation and conformity to God, and in union and communion with him, which the things of the world will not at all befriend. *They satisfy not;* they yield not any solid comfort and content to the soul, nor enable it to say, "Now I have what I would have." Nay, they do not satisfy even the appetites of the body. The more men have the more they would have, Eccl. 1:8. Haman was unsatisfied in the midst of his abundance. They flatter, but they do not fill; they please for a while, like the dream of a hungry man, who awakes and his soul is empty. They soon surfeit, but they never satisfy; they cloy a man, but do not content him, or make him truly easy. It is all vanity and vexation. [2.] The folly of the children of this world. They spend their money and labour for these uncertain unsatisfying things. Rich people live by their money, poor people by their labour; but both mistake their truest interest, while the one is trading, the other toiling, for the world, both promising themselves satisfaction and happiness in it, but both miserably disappointed. God vouchsafes compassionately to reason with them: "Wherefore do you thus act against your own interest? Why do you suffer yourselves to be thus imposed upon?" Let us reason with ourselves, and let the result of these reasonings be a holy resolution not to *labour for the meat that perishes, but for that which endures to everlasting life,* Jn. 6:27. Let all the disappointments we meet with in the world help to drive us to Christ, and lead us to seek for satisfaction in him only. This is the way to make sure which will be made sure.

(2.) From the unspeakable kindness we do to ourselves if we accept this invitation and comply with it. [1.] hereby we secure to ourselves present pleasure and satisfaction: "If you hearken to Christ, you *eat that which is good,* which is both wholesome and pleasant, good in itself and good for you." God's good word and promise, a good conscience, and the comforts of God's good Spirit, are a continual feast to those that hearken diligently and obediently to Christ. Their souls shall *delight themselves in fatness,* that is, in the riches and most grateful delights. Here the invitation is not, "Come, and *buy,"* lest that should discourage, but, "Come, and *eat;* come and entertain yourselves with that which will be abundantly pleasing; eat, O friends!" It is sad to think that men should need to be courted thus to their own bliss. [2.] Hereby we secure to ourselves lasting happiness: *"Hear, and your soul shall live;* you shall not only be saved from perishing eternally, but you shall be eternally blessed:" for less than that cannot be the life of an immortal soul. The words of Christ are spirit and life, life to spirits (Jn. 6:33, 63), the words of this life, Acts 5:20. On what easy terms is happiness offered to us! It is but "Hear, and you shall live." [3.] The great God graciously secures all this to us: "Come to me, *and I will make an everlasting covenant with you,* will put myself into covenant-relations and under covenant-engagements to you, and thereby settle upon you *the sure mercies of David."* Note, *First,* If we come to God to serve him, he will covenant with us to do us good and make us happy; such are his condescension to us and concern for us. *Secondly,* God's covenant with us is an everlasting covenant — its contrivance from everlasting, its continuance to everlasting. *Thirdly,* The benefits of this covenant are mercies suited to our case, who, being miserable, are the proper objects of mercy. They come from God's mercy, and are ordered every way in kindness to us. *Fourthly,* They are the mercies of David, such mercies as God promised to David (Ps. 89:28, 29, etc.),

which are called *the mercies of David his servant,* and are appealed to by Solomon, 2 Chr. 6:42. It shall be a covenant as sure as that with David, Jer. 33:25, 26. The covenant of royalty was a figure of the covenant of grace, 2 Sa. 23:5. Or, rather, by David here we are to understand the Messiah. Covenant-mercies are all *his* mercies; they are purchased by him; they are promised in him; they are treasured up in his hand, and out of his hand they are dispensed to us. He is the Mediator and trustee of the covenant; to him this is applied, Acts 13:34. They are the *ta hosia* (the word used there, and by the Septuagint here) — *the holy things* of David, for they are confirmed by the holiness of God (Ps. 89:35) and are intended to advance holiness among men. *Fifthly,* They are sure mercies. The covenant, being well-ordered in all things, is sure. It is sure in the general proposal of it; God is real and sincere, serious and in earnest, in the offer of these mercies. It is sure in the particular application of it to believers; God's gifts and callings are without repentance. They are the mercies of David, and therefore sure, for in Christ the promises are all yea and amen.

III. Jesus Christ is promised for the making good of all the other promises which we are here invited to accept of, *v.* 4. He is that David whose sure mercies all the blessings and benefits of the covenant are. "And God has *given him* in his purpose and promise, has constituted and appointed him, and in the fulness of time will as surely send him as if he had already come, to be all that to us which is necessary to our having the benefit of these preparations." He has given him freely; for what more free than a gift? There was nothing in us to merit such a favour, but Christ is the gift of God. We want one, 1. To attest the truth of the promises which we are invited to take the benefit of; and Christ is given *for a witness* that God is willing to receive us into his favour upon gospel terms, to confirm the promises made unto the fathers, that we may venture our souls upon those promises with entire satisfaction. Christ is a faithful witness, we may take his word — a competent witness, for he lay in the bosom of the Father from eternity, and was perfectly apprised of the whole matter. Christ, as a prophet, testifies the will of God to the world; and to believe is to receive his testimony. 2. To assist us in closing with the invitation, and coming up to the terms of it. We know not how to find the way to the waters where we are to be supplied, but Christ is given to be *a leader.* We know not what to do that we may be qualified or it, and become sharers in it, but he is given for *a commander,* to show us what to do and enable us to do it. Much difficulty and opposition lie in our way to Christ; we have spiritual enemies to grapple with, but, to animate us for the conflict, we have a good captain, like Joshua, a leader and commander to tread our enemies under our feet and to put us in possession of the land of promise. Christ is a commander by his precept and a leader by his example; our business is to obey him and follow him.

IV. The Master of the feast being fixed, it is next to be furnished with guests, for the provision shall not be lost, nor made in vain, *v.* 5. 1. The Gentiles shall be called to this feast, shall be invited out of the highways and the hedges: *"Thou shalt call a nation that thou knowest not,* that is, that was not formerly called and owned as thy nation, that thou didst not send prophets to as to Israel, the people whom God knew above all the families of the earth." The Gentiles shall now be favoured as they never were before; their knowing God is said to be rather their *being known of God,* Gal. 4:9. 2. They shall come at the call: *Nations that knew not thee shall run unto thee;* those that had long been afar off from Christ shall be made nigh; those that had been running from him shall run to him, with the greatest speed and alacrity imaginable. There shall be a concourse of believing Gentiles to Christ, who, being lifted up from the earth, will draw all men to him. Now see the reason, (1.) Why the Gentiles will thus flock to Christ; it is *because of the Lord his God,* because he is the Son of God, and is declared to be so with power, because they now see his God is one with whom they have to do, and there is no coming to him as their God but by making an interest in his Son. Those that are brought to be acquainted with God, and understand how the concern lies between them and him, cannot but run to Jesus Christ, who is the only Mediator between God and Man, and there is no coming to God but by him. (2.) Why God will bring them to him; it is because he is the Holy One of Israel, true to his promises, and he has promised to glorify him by giving him the heathen for his inheritance. When Greeks began to enquire after Christ he said, *The hour has come that the Son of man should be glorified,* Jn. 12:22, 23. And his being glorified in his resurrection and ascension was the great argument by which multitudes were wrought upon to run to him.

Verses 6–13

We have here a further account of that covenant of grace which is made with us in Jesus Christ, both what is required and what is promised in the covenant, and of those considerations that are sufficient abundantly to confirm our believing compliance with and reliance on that covenant. This gracious discovery of God's good-will to the children of men is not to be confined either to the Jew or to the Gentile, to the Old Testament or to the New, much less to the captives in Babylon. No, both the precepts and the promises are here given to all, to *every one that thirsts after happiness, v.* 1. And who does not? Hear this, and live.

I. Here is a gracious offer made of pardon, and peace, and all happiness, to poor sinners, upon gospel terms, *v.* 6, 7.

1. Let them pray, and their prayers shall be heard and answered (*v.* 6): "*Seek the Lord while he may be found.* Seek him whom you have left by revolting from your allegiance to him and whom you have lost by provoking him to withdraw his favour from you. *Call upon him* now *while he is near,* and within call." Observe here,

(1.) The duties required. [1.] "Seek the Lord. Seek to him, and enquire of him, as your oracle. *Ask the law at his mouth. What wilt thou have me to do?* Seek for him, and enquire after him, as your portion and happiness; seek to be reconciled to him and acquainted with him, and to be happy in his favour. Be sorry that you have lost him; be solicitous to find him; take the appointed method of finding him, making use of Christ as your way, the Spirit as your guide, and the word as your rule." [2.] "Call upon him. Pray to him, to be reconciled, and, being reconciled, pray to him for every thing else you have need of."

(2.) The motives made use of to press these duties upon us: *While he may be found — while he is near.* [1.] It is implied that now God is near and will be found, so that it shall not be in vain to seek him and to call upon him. Now his patience is waiting on us, his word is calling to us, and his Spirit striving with us. Let us now improve our advantages and opportunities; for now is the accepted time. But, [2.] There is a day coming when he will be afar off, and will not be found, when the day of his patience is over, and his Spirit will strive no more. There may come such a time in this life, when the heart is incurably hardened; it is certain that at death and judgment the door will be *shut,* Lu. 16:26; 13:25, 26. Mercy is now offered, but then judgment without mercy will take place.

2. Let them repent and reform, and their sins shall be pardoned, *v.* 7. Here is a call to the unconverted, to *the wicked and the unrighteous* — to the wicked, who live in known gross sins, to the unrighteous, who live in the neglect of plain duties: to them is the word of this salvation sent, and all possible assurance given that penitent sinners shall find God a pardoning God. Observe here,

(1.) What it is to repent. There are two things involved in repentance: — [1.] It is to turn from sin; it is to forsake it. It is to leave it, and to leave it with loathing and abhorrence, never to return to it again. The wicked must *forsake his way,* his evil way, as we would forsake a false way that will never bring us to the happiness we aim at, and a dangerous way, that leads to destruction. Let him not take one step more in that way. Nay, there must be not only a change of the way, but a change of the mind; the unrighteous must *forsake his thoughts.* Repentance, if it be true, strikes at the root, and washes the heart from wickedness. We must alter our judgments concerning persons and things, dislodge the corrupt imaginations and quit the vain pretences under which an unsanctified heart shelters itself. Note, It is not enough to break off from evil practices, but we must enter a caveat against evil thoughts. Yet this is not all: [2.] To repent is to *return to the Lord;* to return to him as our God, our sovereign Lord, against whom we have rebelled, and to whom we are concerned to reconcile ourselves; it is to return to the Lord as the fountain

of life and living waters, which we had forsaken for broken cisterns.

(2.) What encouragement we have thus to repent. If we do so, [1.] God *will have mercy.* He will not deal with us as our sins have deserved, but will have compassion on us. Misery is the object of mercy. Now both the consequences of sin, by which we have become truly miserable (Eze. 16:5, 6), and the nature of repentance, by which we are made sensible of our misery and are brought to bemoan ourselves (Jer. 31:18), both these make us objects of pity, and with God there are tender mercies. [2.] *He will abundantly pardon. He will multiply to pardon* (so the word is), as we have multiplied to offend. Though our sins have been very great and very many, and though we have often backslidden and are still prone to offend, yet God will repeat his pardon, and welcome even backsliding children that return to him in sincerity.

II. Here are encouragements given us to accept this offer and to venture our souls upon it. For, look which way we will, we find enough to confirm us in our belief of its validity and value.

1. If we look up to heaven, we find God's counsels there high and transcendent, his thoughts and ways infinitely above ours, *v.* 8, 9. The wicked are urged to forsake their evil ways and thoughts (*v.* 7) and to return to God, that is, to bring their ways and thoughts to concur and comply with his; "for" (says he) "my thoughts and ways are not as yours. Yours are conversant only about things beneath; they are of the earth earthy: but mine are above, *as the heaven is high above the earth;* and, if you would approve yourselves true penitents, yours must be so too, and your affections must be set on things above." Or, rather, it is to be understood as an encouragement to us to depend upon God's promise to pardon sin, upon repentance. Sinners may be ready to fear that God will not be reconciled to them, because they could not find in their hearts to be reconciled to one who should have so basely and so frequently offended them. "But" (says God) "my thoughts in this matter are not as yours, but as far above them as the heaven is above the earth." They are so in other things. Men's sentiments concerning sin, and Christ, and holiness, concerning this world and the other, are vastly different from God's; but in nothing more than in the matter of reconciliation. We think God apt to take offence and backward to forgive — that, if he forgives once, he will not forgive a second time. Peter thought it a great deal to *forgive seven times* (Mt. 18:21), and a hundred pence go far with us; but God meets returning sinners with pardoning mercy; he forgives freely, and as he gives: it is without upbraiding. We forgive and cannot forget; but, when God forgives sin, he remembers it no more. Thus God invites sinners to return to him, by possessing them with good thoughts of him, as Jer. 31:20.

2. If we look down to this earth, we find God's word there powerful and effectual, and answering all its great intentions, *v.* 10, 11. Observe here, (1.) The efficacy of God's word in the kingdom of nature. He saith to the snow, Be thou on the earth; he appoints when it shall come, to what degree, and how long it shall lie there; he saith so *to the small rain and the great rain of his strength,* Job 37:6. And according to his order they come down from heaven, and do *whatsoever he commands them upon the face of the world, whether it be for correction, or for his land, or for mercy, v.* 12, 13. It returns not *re infectâ — without having accomplished its end,* but waters the earth, which he is therefore said to do *from his chambers,* Ps. 104:13. And the watering of the earth is in order to its fruitfulness. Thus he makes it to *bring forth and bud,* for the products of the earth depend upon the dews of heaven; and thus it gives not only *bread to the eater,* present maintenance to the owner and his family, but *seed* likewise *to the sower,* that he may have food for another year. The husbandman must be a sower as well as an eater, else he will soon see the end of what he has. (2.) The efficacy of his word in the kingdom of providence and grace, which is as certain as the former: "*So shall my word be,* as powerful in the mouth of prophets as it is in the hand of providence; *it shall not return unto me void,* as unable to effect what it was sent for, or meeting with an insuperable opposition; no, *it shall accomplish that which I please*" (for it is the declaration of his will, according to the counsel of which he works all things) *"and it shall prosper in the thing for*

which I sent it." This assures us, [1.] That the promises of God shall all have their full accomplishment in due time, and not one iota or tittle of them shall fail, 1 Ki. 8:56. These promises of mercy and grace shall have as real an effect upon the souls of believers, for their sanctification and comfort, as ever the rain had upon the earth, to make it fruitful. [2.] That according to the different errands on which the word is sent it will have its different effects. If it be not a savour of life unto life, it will be a savour of death unto death; if it do not convince the conscience and soften the heart, it will sear the conscience and harden the heart; if it do not ripen for heaven, it will ripen for hell. See *ch.* 6:9. One way or other, it will take effect. [3.] That Christ's coming into the world, as the dew from heaven (Hos. 14:5), will not be in vain. For, if Israel be not gathered, he will be glorious in the conversion of the Gentiles; to them therefore the tenders of grace must be made when the Jews refuse them, that the wedding may be furnished with guests and the gospel not return void.

3. If we take a special view of the church, we shall find what great things God has done, and will do, for it (*v.* 12, 13): *You shall go out with joy, and be led forth with peace.* This refers, (1.) To the deliverance and return of the Jews out of Babylon. They shall go out of their captivity, and be led forth towards their own land again. God will go before them as surely, though not as sensibly, as before their fathers in the pillar of cloud and fire. They shall go out, not with trembling, but with triumph, not with any regret to part with Babylon, or any fear of being fetched back, but *with joy* and *peace.* Their journey home over the mountains shall be pleasant, and they shall have the good-will and good wishes of all the countries they pass through. *The hills* and their inhabitants shall, as in a transport of joy, *break forth into singing;* and, if the people should altogether hold their peace, even *the trees of the field* would attend them with their applauses and acclamations. And, when they come to their own land, it shall be ready to bid them welcome; for, whereas they expected to find it all overgrown with briers and thorns, it shall be set with *fir-trees and myrtle-trees:* for, though it lay desolate, yet it *enjoyed its sabbaths* (Lev. 26:34), which, when they were over, like the land after the sabbatical year, it was the better for. And this shall redound much to the honour of God and be to him *for a name.* But, (2.) Without doubt it looks further. This shall be *for an everlasting sign,* that it, [1.] The redemption of the Jews out of Babylon shall be a ratification of those promises that relate to gospel times. The accomplishment of the predictions relating to that great deliverance would be a pledge and earnest of the performance of all the other promises; for thereby it shall appear that *he is faithful who has promised.* [2.] It shall be a representation of the blessings promised and a type and figure of them. *First,* Gospel grace will set those at liberty that were in bondage to sin and Satan. They *shall go out and be led forth.* Christ shall make them free, and then they shall be free indeed. *Secondly,* It will fill those with joy that were melancholy. Ps. 14:7, *Jacob shall rejoice, and Israel shall be glad.* The earth and the inferior part of the creation shall share in the joy of this salvation, Ps. 94:11, 12. *Thirdly,* It will make a great change in men's characters. Those that were as thorns and briers, good for nothing but the fire, nay, hurtful and vexatious, shall become graceful and useful as the fir-tree and the myrtle-tree. Thorns and briers came in with sin and were the fruits of the curse, Gen. 3:18. The raising of pleasant trees in the room of them signifies the removal of the curse of the law and the introduction of gospel blessings. The church's enemies were as thorns and briers; but, instead of them, God will raise up friends to be her protection and ornament. Or it may denote the world's growing better; instead of a generation of thorns and briers, there shall come up a generation of fir-trees and myrtles; the children shall be wiser and better than the parents. And, *fourthly,* in all this God shall be glorified. It shall be to him for a name, by which he will be made known and praised, and by it the people of God shall be encouraged. It shall be for an everlasting sign of God's favour to them, assuring them that, though it may for a time be clouded, it shall never *be cut off.* The covenant of grace is an everlasting covenant; for the present blessings of it are signs of everlasting ones.

CHAPTER 56

After the exceedingly great and precious promises of gospel grace, typified by temporal deliverances, which we had in the foregoing chapter, we have here, I. A solemn charge given to us all to make conscience of our duty, as we hope to have the benefit of those promises (v. 1, 2). II. Great encouragement given to strangers that were wiling to come under the bonds of the covenant, assuring them of the blessings of the covenant (v. 3–8). III. A high charge drawn up against the watchmen of Israel, that were careless and unfaithful in the discharge of their duty (v. 9–12), which seems to be the beginning of a new sermon, by way of reproof and threatening, which is continued in the following chapters. And the word of God was intended for conviction, as well as for comfort and instruction in righteousness.

Verses 1–2

The scope of these verses is to show that when God is coming towards us in a way of mercy we must go forth to meet him in a way of duty.

I. God here tells us what are his intentions of mercy to us (v. 1): *My salvation is near to come* — the great salvation wrought out by Jesus Christ (for that was the salvation of which the *prophets enquired and searched diligently,* 1 Pt. 1:10), typified by the salvation of the Jews from Sennacherib or out of Babylon. Observe, 1. The gospel salvation is the salvation of the Lord. It was contrived and brought about by him; he glories in it as his. 2. In that salvation God's righteousness is revealed, which is so much the beauty of the gospel that St. Paul makes this the ground of his glorying in it. (Rom. 1:17), *because therein is the righteousness of God revealed from faith to faith.* The law revealed that righteousness of God by which all sinners stand condemned, but the gospel reveals that by which all believers stand acquitted. 3. The Old-Testament saints saw this salvation coming, and drawing near to them, long before it came; and they had notice by the prophets of its approach. As Daniel understood by Jeremiah's books the approach of the redemption out of Babylon, at the end of seventy years, so others understood by Daniel's books the approach of our redemption by Christ at the end of seventy weeks of years.

II. He tells us what are his expectations of duty from us, in consideration thereof. Say not, "We see the salvation near, and therefore we may live as we list, for there is no danger now of missing it or coming short of it;" that is turning the grace of God into wantonness. But, on the contrary, when the salvation is near double your guard against sin. Note, The fuller assurances God gives us of the performance of his promises the stronger obligations he lays us under to obedience. The salvation here spoken of has now come; yet, there being still a further salvation in view, the apostle presses duty upon us Christians with the same argument. Rom. 3:11, *Now is our salvation nearer than when we believed.* That which is here required to qualify and prepare us for the approaching salvation is,

1. That we be honest and just in all our dealings: *Keep you judgment and do justice.* Walk by rule, and make conscience of what you say and do, that you do no wrong to any. Render to all their dues exactly, and, in exacting what is due to you, keep up a court of equity in your own bosom, to moderate the rigours of the law. Be ruled by that golden rule, "Do as you would be done by." Magistrates must administer justice wisely and faithfully. This is required to evidence the sincerity of our faith and repentance, and to open the way of mercy. *Repent for the kingdom of heaven is at hand.* God is true to us; let us be so to one another.

2. That we religiously observe the sabbath day, v. 2. We are not just if we rob God of his time. Sabbath-sanctification is here put for all the duties of the first table, the fruits of our love to God, as justice and judgment are put for all those of the second table, the fruits of our love to our neighbour. Observe, (1.) The duty required, which is to *keep the sabbath,* to keep it as a talent we are to trade with, as a treasure we are entrusted with. "Keep it holy; keep it safe; keep it with care and caution; keep it from polluting it. Allow neither yourselves nor others either to violate the holy rest or omit the holy work of that day." If this be intended primarily for the Jews in Babylon, it was fit that they should be particularly put in mind of this, because when, by reason of their distance from the temple, they could not observe the other institutions of their law, yet they might distinguish themselves from the heathen by putting a difference between God's day and other days. But

it being required more generally of man, and *the son of man,* it intimates that sabbath-sanctification should be a duty in gospel times, when the bounds of the church should be enlarged and other rites and ceremonies abolished. Observe, Those that would keep the sabbath from polluting it must put on resolution, must not only do this, but lay hold on it, for sabbath time is precious, but is very apt to slip away if we take not great care; and therefore we must lay hold on it and keep our hold, must do it and persevere in it. (2.) The encouragement we have to do this duty: *Blessed is he that doeth it.* The way to have the blessing of God upon our employments all the week is to make conscience, and make a business, of sabbath-sanctification; and in doing so we shall be the better qualified to do judgment and justice. The more godliness the more honesty, 1 Tim. 2:2.

3. That we have nothing to do with sin: *Blessed is the man* that *keeps his hand from doing evil,* any wrong to his neighbour, in body, goods, or good name — or, more generally, any thing that is displeasing to God and hurtful to his own soul. Note, The best evidence of our having kept the sabbath well will be a care to keep a good conscience all the week. By this it will appear that we have been in the mount with God if our faces shine in a holy conversation before men.

Verses 3–8

The prophet is here, in God's name, encouraging those that were hearty in joining themselves to God and yet laboured under great discouragements. 1. Some were discouraged because they were not of the seed of Abraham. They had *joined themselves to the Lord,* and bound their souls with a bond to be his for ever (this is the root and life of religion, to break off from the world and the flesh, and devote ourselves entirely to the service and honour of God); but they questioned whether God would accept them, because they were of *the sons of the stranger,* v. 3. They were Gentiles, strangers to the commonwealth of Israel and aliens from the covenants of promise, and therefore feared they had no part nor lot in the matter. They said, "*The Lord has utterly separated me from his people,* and will not own me as one of them, nor admit me to their privileges." It was often said that there should be *one law for the stranger and for him that was born in the land* (Ex. 12:49), and yet they came to this melancholy conclusion. Note, Unbelief often suggests things to the discouragement of good people which are directly contrary to what God himself has said, things which he has expressly guarded against. Let not the *sons of the stranger* therefore say thus, for they have no reason to say it. Note, Ministers must have answers ready for the disquieting fears and jealousies of weak Christians, which, how unreasonable soever, they must take notice of. 2. Others were discouraged because they were not fathers in Israel. The eunuch said, *Behold, I am a dry tree.* So he looked upon himself, and it was his grief; so others looked upon him, and it was his reproach. He was thought to be of no use because he had no children, nor was ever likely to have any. This was then the more grievous because eunuchs were not admitted to be priests (Lev. 21:20), nor to *enter into the congregation* (Deu. 23:1), and because the promise of a numerous posterity was the particular blessing of Israel and the more valuable because from among them the Messiah was to come. Yet God would not have the eunuchs to make the worst of their case, nor to think that they should be excluded from the gospel church, and from being spiritual priests, because they were shut out from the congregation of Israel and the Levitical priesthood; no, as the taking down of the partition wall, contained in ordinances, admitted the Gentiles, so it let in likewise those that had been kept out by ceremonial pollutions. Yet, by the reply here given to this suggestion, it should seem the chief thing which the eunuch laments in his case is his being written childless.

Now suitable encouragements are given to each of these.

I. To those who have no children of their own, who, though they had the honour to be the children of the church and the covenant themselves, yet had none to whom they might transmit that honour, none to receive the sign of circumcision and the privileges secured by that sign. Now observe,

1. What a good character they have, though they lie under this ignominy and affliction; and those only are entitled to the following comforts who in some measure answer to these characters. (1.) They *keep God's sabbaths* as he has appointed them to be kept. In the primitive times, if a Christian were asked, "Hast thou kept holy the Lord's day?" He would readily answer, "I am a Christian, and dare not do otherwise." (2.) In their whole conversation they *choose those things that please God.* They do that which is good; they do it with a sincere design to please God in it; they do it of choice, and with delight. If sometimes, through infirmity, they come short in doing that which pleases God, yet they choose it, they endeavour after it, and aim at it. Note, Whatever is God's pleasure should without dispute be our choice. (3.) They *take hold of his covenant,* and that is a thing that pleases God as much as any thing. The covenant of grace is proposed and proffered to us in the gospel; to take hold of it is to consent to it, to accept the offer and come up to the terms, deliberately and sincerely to take God to be to us a God and to give up ourselves to him to be to him a people. Taking hold of the covenant denotes an entire and resolute consent to it, taking hold as those that are afraid of coming short, catching at it as a good bargain, and as those that are resolved never to let it go, for it is our life: and we take hold of it as a criminal took hold of the horns of the altar to which he fled for refuge.

2. What a great deal of comfort they may have if they answer to this character, though they are not built up into families (v. 5): *Unto them will I give a better place and name.* It is supposed that there is a place and a name, which we have from sons and daughters, that is valuable and desirable. It is a pleasing notion we have that we live in our children when we are dead. But there is a better place, and a better name, which those have that are in covenant with God, and it is sufficient to counterbalance the want of the former. A place and a name denote rest and reputation; a place to live comfortably in themselves, and a name to live creditably with among their neighbours; they shall be happy, and may be easy both at home and abroad. Though they have not children to be the music of their house, or arrows in their quiver, to keep them in countenance when they speak with their enemies in the gate, yet they shall have a place and a name more than equivalent. For, (1.) God will give it to them, will give it to them by promise; he will himself be both their habitation and their glory, their place and their name. (2.) He will give it to them in his house, and within his walls; there they shall have a place, shall be planted so as to take root (Ps. 92:13), shall *dwell all the days of their life,* Ps. 27:4. They shall be at home in communion with God, as Anna, that *departed not from the temple night nor day.* There they shall have a name. A name for the good things with God and good people is a name *better than that of sons and daughters.* Our relation to God, our interest in Christ, our title to the blessings of the covenant, and our hopes of eternal life, are things that give us in God's house a blessed place and a blessed name. (3.) It shall be *an everlasting name, that shall never* be extinct, shall never be *cut off;* like the place and name of angels, who *therefore* marry not, because they die not. Spiritual blessings are unspeakably better than those of sons and daughters; for children are a certain care and may prove the greatest grief and shame of a man's life, but the blessings we partake of in God's house are a sure and constant joy and honour, comforts which cannot be embittered.

II. To those that are themselves the children of strangers.

1. It is here promised that they shall now be welcome to the church, v. 6, 7. When God's Israel come out of Babylon, let them bring as many of their neighbours along with them as they can persuade to come, and God will find room enough for them all in his house. And here, (as before) we may observe,

(1.) Upon what terms they shall be welcome. Let them know that God's Israel, when they come out of Babylon, will not be plagued, as they were when they came out of Egypt, with a mixed multitude, that went with them, but were not cordially for them; no, the sons of the strangers shall have a place and a name in God's house provided, [1.] That they forsake other gods, all rivals and pretenders whatsoever, and *join themselves to the Lord,* so as to become *one spirit,* 1 Co. 6:17. [2.] That they join themselves to him as subjects to their prince and soldiers to their general, by an oath of fidelity and obedience, *to serve him,* not occasionally, as one would serve a turn, but to be constantly his servants, entirely subject to his command, and devoted to his interest. [3.] That they join themselves to him as friends to his honour and the interests of his kingdom in the world, *to love the name of the Lord,* to be well pleased with all the discoveries he has made of himself and all the memorials they make of him. Observe, Serving him and loving him go together; for those that love him truly will serve him faithfully, and that obedience is most acceptable to him, as well as most pleasant to us, which flows from a principle of love, for then *his commandments are not grievous,* 1 Jn. 5:3. [4.] That they keep the sabbath from polluting it; for the stranger that is within thy gates is particularly required to do that. [5.] That they take hold of the covenant, that is, that they come under the bonds of it, and put in for the benefits of it.

(2.) To what privileges they shall be welcome, *v.* 7. Three things are here promised them, in their coming to God: — [1.] Assistance: *"I will bring them to my holy mountain,* not only bid them welcome when they come, but incline them to come, will show them the way, and lead them in it." David himself prays that God by his light and truth would bring them to his *holy hill,* Ps. 43:3. And the sons of the stranger shall be under the same guidance. The church is God's holy hill, on which he hath set his King, and, in bringing them to Zion Hill, he brings them to be subjects to Zion's King, as well as worshippers in Zion's holy temple. [2.] Acceptance: *"Their burnt-offerings and their sacrifices shall be accepted on my altar,* and be never the less acceptable for being theirs, though they are sons of the stranger." The prayers and praises (those spiritual sacrifices) of devout Gentiles shall be as pleasing to God as those of the pious Jews, and no difference shall be made between them; for, though they are Gentiles by birth, yet through grace they shall be looked upon as the believing seed of faithful Abraham and the praying seed of wrestling Jacob, for in Christ Jesus there is neither Greek nor Jew, circumcision nor uncircumcision. [3.] Comfort. They shall not only be accepted, but they themselves shall have the pleasure of it: *I will make them joyful in my house of prayer.* They shall have grace, not only to serve God, but to serve him cheerfully and with gladness, and that shall make the service the more acceptable to him; for, when we sing in the ways of the Lord, then great is the glory of our God. They shall go away and *eat their bread with joy,* because *God now accepts their works,* Eccl. 9:7. Nay, though they came mourning to the house of prayer, they shall go away rejoicing, for they shall there find such ease, by casting their cares and burdens upon God, and referring themselves to him, that, like Hannah, they shall go away and their countenance shall be no more sad. Many a sorrowful spirit has been made joyful in the house of prayer.

2. It is here promised that multitudes of the Gentiles shall come to the church, not only that the few who come dropping in shall be made welcome, but that great numbers shall come in, and the door be thrown open to them: *My house shall be called a house of prayer for all people.* The temple was then God's house, and to that Christ applies these words (Mt. 21:13), but with an eye to it as a type of the gospel church, Heb. 9:8, 9. For Christ calls it *his house,* Heb. 3:6. Now concerning this house it is promised, (1.) That it shall not be a house of sacrifice, but a house of prayer. The religious meetings of God's people shall be meetings for prayer, in which they shall join together, as a token of their united faith and mutual love. (2.) That it shall be a house of prayer, not for the people of the Jews only, but for all people. This was fulfilled when Peter was made, not only to perceive it himself, but to tell it to the world, that *in every nation he that fears God and works righteousness is accepted of him,* Acts 10:35. It had been declared again and again that *the stranger that comes nigh shall be put to death,* but Gentiles shall now be looked upon no longer as strangers and foreigners, Eph. 2:19. And it appears by Solomon's prayer, at the dedication of the temple, both that it was primarily intended for a house of prayer and that strangers should be welcome to it, 1 Ki. 8:30, 41, 43. And it is intimated here (*v.* 8) that when the Gentiles are called in they shall be incorporated into one body with the Jews, that (as Christ says, Jn. 10:16) there may be *one fold and one Shepherd;* for, [1.] God will *gather the outcasts of Israel.* Many of the Jews that had by their unbelief cast themselves out shall by faith be brought in again, *a remnant according to the election of grace,* Rom. 11:5. Christ came to the *lost sheep of the house of Israel* (Mt. 15:24), to *gather their outcasts* (Ps. 147:2), to *restore their preserved* (*ch.* 49:6), and *to be their glory,* Lu. 2:32. [2.] He will gather others also to him, besides his own outcasts that are gathered to him. Or, though some of the Gentiles have come over now and then into the church, that shall not serve (as some may think) to answer the extent of these promises; no, there are still more and more to be brought in: *"I will gather others to him besides these;* these are but the first-fruits in comparison with the harvest that shall be gathered for Christ in the nations of the earth, when the fulness of the Gentiles shall come in." Note, The church is a growing body: when some are gathered to it we may still hope there shall be more, till the mystical body be completed. *Other sheep I have.*

Verses 9–12

From words of comfort the prophet here, by a very sudden change of his style, passes to words of reproof and conviction, and goes on in that strain, for the most part, in the three following chapters; and therefore some here begin a new sermon. He had assured the people that in due time God would deliver them out of captivity, which was designed for the comfort of those that should live when God would do this. Now here he shows what their sins and provocations were, for which God would send them into captivity, and this was designed for the conviction of those that lived in his own time, nearly a hundred years before the captivity, who were now filling up the measure of the nation's sin, and to justify God in what he brought upon them. God will lay them waste by the fierceness of their enemies, for the falseness of their friends.

I. Desolating judgments are here summoned, *v.* 9. The sheep of God's pasture are now to be made the sheep of his slaughter, to fall as victims to his justice, and therefore *the beasts of the field and the forest* are called to come and devour. They are beasts of prey, and do it from their own ravenous disposition; but God permits them to do it, nay, he employs them as his servants in doing it, the ministers of his justice, though they mean not so, neither does their heart think so. If this refers primarily to the descent made upon them by the Babylonians, and their devouring them, yet it may look further, to the destruction of Jerusalem and the Jewish nation by the Romans, after these outcasts of them (mentioned *v.* 8) were gathered in to the Christian church. The Roman armies came upon them as beasts of the forest to devour them, and they quite *took away their place and nation.* Note, When God has bloody work to do he has beasts of prey within call, to be employed in doing it.

II. The reason of these judgments is here given. The shepherds, who should have been the watchmen of the flock, to discover the approaches of the beasts of prey, to keep them off, and protect the sheep, were treacherous and careless, minded not their business, nor made any conscience of the trust reposed in them, and so the sheep became an easy prey to the wild beasts. Now this may refer to the false prophets that lived in Isaiah's, Jeremiah's, and Ezekiel's time (who flattered the people in their wicked ways, and told them they should have peace though they went on) and to the priests that bore rule by their means. Or it may refer to the wicked princes, the sons of Josiah, that *did evil in the sight of the Lord,* and other wicked magistrates under them, who betrayed their trust, were vicious and profane, and, instead of making up the breach at which the judgments of God were breaking in upon them, made it wider, and augmented the fierce anger of the Lord instead of doing any thing to turn it away. They should have kept judgment and justice (*v.* 1), but they abandoned both, Jer. 5:1. Or it may refer to those who were the nation's watchmen in our Saviour's time, the chief priests and the scribes, who should have discerned the signs of the times and have given notice to the people of the approach of the Messiah, but who, instead of that, opposed him, and did all they could to keep people from coming to the knowledge of him and to prejudice them against him. It is a very sad character that is here given of these watchmen. *Woe unto thee, O land!* when thy guides are such. 1. They had no sense or knowledge of their business. They were wretchedly ignorant of their work, and very unfit to teach, being so ill-taught themselves: *His watchmen are blind,* and therefore utterly unfit to be watchmen. If the seers see not, who shall see for us? *If the light that is in us be darkness, how great is that darkness!* Christ describes the Pharisees to be *blind leaders of the blind,* Mt. 15:14. The beasts of the field come to devour, and the watchmen are blind, and are not aware of them. *They are all ignorant* (*v.* 10), *shepherds that cannot understand* (*v.* 11), that know not what is to be done about the sheep, nor can *feed them with understanding,* Jer. 3:15. 2. What little knowledge they had they made no use of it; no one was the better for it. As they were blind watchmen, that could not discern the danger, so they were *dumb dogs,* that would not give warning of it. And why are the dogs set to guard the sheep if they cannot bark to waken the shepherd and frighten the wolf? Such were these; those that had the charge of souls never reproved men for their faults, nor told them what would be in the end thereof, never gave them notice of the judgments of God that were breaking in upon them. They barked at God's prophets, and bit them too, and worried the sheep, but made no opposition to the wolf or thief. 3. They were very lazy, and would take no pains. They loved their ease, and hated business, were always *sleeping, lying down* and *loving to slumber.* They were not overcome and overpowered by sleep, as the disciples, through grief and fatigue, but they lay down on purpose to invite sleep, and said, *Soul, take thy ease. Yet a little sleep.* It is bad with a people when their shepherds slumber (Nah. 3:18), and it is well for God's people that their shepherd, the keeper of Israel, neither slumbers nor sleeps. 4. They were very covetous and eager after the world — *greedy dogs that can never have enough.* If they had ever so much, they would think it too little. They so love silver as never to be satisfied with silver, Eccl. 5:10. All their enquiry is what they shall get, not what they shall do. Let them have the wages, and they care not whether the work be done or no; they feed not the flock, but fleece it. They are every one looking to his *own way,* minding his own private interests, and have no regard at all to the public welfare. It was St. Paul's complaint of the watchmen in his time (Phil. 2:21), *All seek their own, not the things that are Jesus Christ's.* Every one is for propagating his own opinion, advancing his own party, raising his own family, and having every thing to his own mind, while the common concerns of the public are wretchedly neglected and postponed. They look *every one to his gain from his quarter,* from his end or part of the work. They are for fain from every quarter *(Rem rem quocunque modo rem — Money, money, by fair means or by foul we must have money),* but especially from their own quarter, where they will be sure to take care that they lose nothing, nor miss any thing that is to be got. If any one put not into their mouths they not only will do him no service, but they *prepare war against him,* Mic. 3:5. 5. They were perfect epicures, given to their pleasures, never so much in their element as in their drunken revels (*v.* 12): *Come* (say they), *I will fetch wine* (they have that at command; their cellars are better furnished than their closets) *and we will fill ourselves,* or be drunk, *with strong drink.* They were often drunk, not overseen (as we say) or overtaken in drink, but designedly. The watchmen did thus invite and encourage one another to drink to excess, or they courted the people to sit and drink with them, and so confirmed those in their wicked ways, and hardened their hearts, whom they should have reproved. How could they think it any harm to be drunk when the watchmen themselves joined with them and led them to it! 6. They were very secure and confident of the continuance of their prosperity and ease; they said, *"To-morrow shall be as this day and much more abundant;* we shall have as much to spend upon our lusts to-morrow as we have to-day." They had no thought at all of their own frailty and mortality, though they were shortening their days and hastening their deaths by their excesses. They had no dread of the judgments of God, though they were daily provoking him and making themselves liable to his wrath and curse. They never considered the uncertainty of all the delights and enjoyments of sense, how they perish in the using and pass away with the lusts of them. They resolved to continue in this wicked course, whatever their consciences said to the contrary, to be as merry to-morrow as they are to-day. *But boast not thyself of to-morrow* when perhaps *this night thy soul shall be required of thee.*

CHAPTER 57

The prophet, in this chapter, makes his observations, I. Upon the deaths of good men, comforting those that were taken away in their integrity and reproving those that did not make a due improvement of such providences (*v.* 1, 2). II. Upon the gross idolatries and spiritual whoredoms which the Jews were guilty of, and the destroying judgments they were thereby bringing upon themselves (*v.* 3–12). III. Upon the gracious returns of God to his people to put an end to their captivity and re-establish their prosperity (*v.* 13–21).

Verses 1–2

The prophet, in the close of the foregoing chapter, had condemned the watchmen for their ignorance and sottishness; here he shows the general stupidity and senselessness of the people likewise. No wonder they were inconsiderate when their watchmen were so, who should have awakened them to consideration. We may observe here,

I. The providence of God removing good men apace out of this world. *The righteous,* as to this world, *perish;* they are gone and their place knows them no more. Piety exempts none from the arrests of death, nay, in persecuting times, the most righteous are most exposed to the violences of bloody men. The first that died died a martyr. Righteousness delivers from the sting of death, but not from the stroke of it. They are said to *perish* because they are utterly removed from us, and to express the great loss which this world sustains by the removal of them, not that their death is their undoing, but it often proves an undoing to the places where they lived and were useful. Nay, even *merciful men are taken away,* those good men that are distinguished from the righteous, for whom *some would even dare to die,* Rom. 5:7. Those are often removed that could be worst spared; the fruitful trees are cut down by death and the barren left still to cumber the ground. Merciful men are often taken away by the hands of men's malice. Many good works they have done, and for some of them they are stoned. Before the captivity in Babylon perhaps there was a more than ordinary mortality of good men, so that there were scarcely any left, Jer. 5:1. The godly ceased, and the faithful failed, Ps. 12:1.

II. The careless world slighting these providences, and disregarding them: *No man lays it to heart, none considers it.* There are very few that lament it as a public loss, very few that take notice of it as a public warning. The death of good men is a thing to be laid to heart and considered more than common deaths. Serious enquiries ought to be made, wherefore God contends with us, what good lessons are to be learned by such providences, what we may do to help to make up the breach and to fill up the room of those that are removed. God is justly displeased when such events are not laid to heart, when the voice of the rod is not heard nor the intentions of it answered, much more when it is rejoiced in, as the slaying of the witnesses is, Rev. 11:10. Some of God's choicest blessings to mankind, being thus easily parted with, are really undervalued; and it is an evidence of very great incogitancy. Little children, when they are little, least lament the death of their parents, because they know not what a loss it is to them.

III. The happiness of the righteous in their removal.

1. They *are taken away from the evil to come,* then when it is just coming, (1.) In compassion to them, that they may not *see the evil* (2 Ki. 22:20), nor share in it, nor be in temptation by it. When the deluge is coming they are called into the ark, and have a hiding-place and rest in heaven when there was none for them under heaven. (2.) In wrath to the world, to punish them for all the injuries they have done to the righteous and merciful ones; those are taken away that stood in the gap to turn away the judgments of God, and then what can be expected but a deluge of them? It is a sign that God intends war when he calls home his ambassadors.

2. They go to be easy out of the reach of that evil. The righteous man, who while he lived walked in his uprightness, when he dies *enters into peace* and *rests in his bed.* Note, (1.) Death is gain, and rest, and bliss, to those only who walked in their uprightness, and who, when they die, can appeal to God concerning it, as Hezekiah (2 Ki. 20:3). *Now, Lord, remember it.* (2.) Those that practised uprightness, and persevered in it to the end, shall find it well with them when they die. Their souls then enter into peace, into the world of peace, where peace is in perfection and where there is no trouble. *Enter thou into the joy of the Lord.* Their bodies rest in their beds. Note, The grave is a bed of rest to all the Lord's people; there they rest from all their labours, Rev. 14:13. And the more weary they were the more welcome will that rest be to them, Job 3:17. This bed is made in the darkness, but that makes it the more quiet; it is a bed out of which they shall rise refreshed in the morning of the resurrection.

Verses 3–12

We have here a high charge, but a just one no doubt, drawn up against that wicked generation out of which God's righteous ones were removed, because the world was not worthy of them. Observe,

I. The general character here given of them, or the name and title by which they stand indicted, *v.* 3. They are told to draw near and hear the charge, are set to the bar, and arraigned there as *sons of the sorceress,* or of a witch, *the seed of an adulterer and a whore,* that is, they were such themselves, they were strongly inclined to be such, and their ancestors were such before them. Sin is sorcery and adultery, for it is departing from God and dealing with the devil. They were *children of disobedience.* "Come," says the prophet, "draw near hither, and I will read you your doom; to the righteous death will bring peace and rest, but not to you; you are *children of transgression* and *a seed of falsehood* (*v.* 4), that have it by kind, and have it woven into your very nature, to backslide from God and to deal treacherously with him," *ch.* 48:8.

II. The particular crimes laid to their charge.

1. Scoffing at God and his word. They were a generation of scorners (*v.* 4): *"Against whom do you sport yourselves?* You think it is only against the poor prophets whom you trample upon as contemptible men, but really it is against God himself, who sends them, and whose message they deliver." Mocking the messengers of the Lord was Jerusalem's measure-filling sin, for what was done to them God took as done to himself. When they were reproved for their sins, and threatened with the judgments of God, they ridiculed the word of God with the rudest and most indecent gestures and expressions of disdain. They sported themselves, and made themselves merry, with that which should have made them serious, and under which they should have humbled themselves. They made wry mouths at the prophets, and drew out the tongue, contrary to all the laws of good breeding; nor did they treat God's prophets with the common civility with which they would have treated a gentleman's servant that had been sent to them on an errand. Note, Those who mock at God, and bid defiance to his judgments, had best consider who it is towards whom they conduct themselves so insolently.

2. Idolatry. This was that sin which the people of the Jews were most notoriously guilty of before the captivity; but that affliction cured them of it. In Isaiah's time it abounded, witness the abominable idolatries of Ahaz (which some think are particularly referred to here) and of Manasseh. (1.) They were dotingly fond of their idols, were inflamed with them, as those that burn in unlawful unnatural lusts, Rom. 1:27. They were *mad upon their idols,* Jer. 50:38. They inflamed themselves with them by their violent passions in the worship of them, as those of Baal's prophets that *leaped upon the altar, and cut themselves,* 1 Ki. 18:26, 28. Note, Vile corruptions, the more they are gratified the more they are inflamed. They worshipped their idols *under every green tree,* in the open air, and in the shade; yet that did not cool the heat of their impetuous lusts, but rather the charming beauty of the green trees made them the more fond of their idols which they worshipped there. Thus that in nature which is pleasing, instead of drawing them to the God of nature, drew them from him. The flame of their zeal in the worship of false gods may shame us for our coldness and indifference in the worship of the true God. They strove to inflame themselves, but we distract and deaden ourselves. (2.) They were barbarous and unnaturally cruel in the worship of their idols. They slew their children, and offered them in sacrifice to their idols, not only in the valley of the son of Hinnom, the headquarters of that monstrous idolatry, but in other valleys, in imitation of that, and *under the cliffs of the rock,* in dark and solitary places, the fittest for such works of darkness. (3.) They were abundant and insatiable in their idolatries. They never thought they could have idols enough, nor could spend enough upon them and do enough in their service. The Syrians had once a notion of the God of Israel that he was a God of the hills, but not a *God of the valleys* (1 Ki. 20:28); but these idolaters, to make sure work, had both. [1.] They had gods of the valleys, which they worshipped in the low places by the water side (*v.* 6): *Among the smooth stones of the valley,* or brook, *is thy portion.* If they saw a smooth carved stone, though set up but for a way-mark or a mere-stone, they were ready to worship it, as the papists do crosses. Or in stony valleys they set up their gods, which they called their *portion,* and took for their lot, as God's people take him for their lot and portion. But these gods of stone would really be no better a portion for them, no better a lot, than the smooth stones of the stream near which they were set up, for sometimes they worshipped their rivers. *"They, they, are the lot* which thou trustest to and art pleased with, but thou shalt be put off with it for thy lot, and miserable will thy case be." See the folly of sinners, who take the smooth stones of the stream for their portion, when they might have the precious stones of God's Jerusalem, and the high priest's ephod, to portion themselves with. Having taken these idols for their lot and portion, they stick at no charge in doing honour to them: *"To them hast thou poured a drink-offering, and offered a meat-offering,* as if they had given thee thy meat and drink." They loved their idols better than their children, for their own tables must be robbed to replenish the altars of their idols. Have we taken the true God for our portion? Is he, even he, our lot? Let us then serve him with our meat and drink, not, as they did, by depriving ourselves of the use of them, but by eating and drinking to his glory. Here, in a parenthesis, comes in an expression of God's just resentment of this wickedness of theirs: *Should I receive comfort in these* — in such a people as this? Can those expect that God will take any pleasure in them, or accept their devotions at his altar, who thus serve Baal with the gifts of his providence? God takes comfort in his people, while they are faithful to him; but what comfort can he take in them when those that should be his witnesses against the idolatries of the world do themselves fall in with them? *Should I have compassion on these?* (so some), or *should I repent me concerning these?* so others. "How can they expect that I should spare them, and either adjourn or abate their punishment, when they are so very provoking? *Shall I not visit for these things?"* Jer. 5:7, 9. [2.] They had gods of the hills too (*v.* 7): *"Upon a lofty and high mountain* (as if thou wouldst vie with the high and lofty One himself, *v.* 15) *hast thou set thy bed,* thy idol, thy idol's temple and altar, the bed of thy uncleanness, where thou committest spiritual whoredom, with all the wantonness of an idolatrous fancy, and in direct violation of the covenant of thy God. *Thither wentest thou up* readily enough, though it was up-hill, *to offer sacrifice."* Some think this bespeaks the impudence they arrived at in their idolatries; at first they had some sense of shame, when they worshipped their idols in the valleys, in obscure places; but they soon conquered that, and came to do it upon the lofty high mountains. They were not ashamed, neither could they blush. [3.] As if these were not enough, they had household-gods too, their *lares* and *penates. Behind the doors and the posts* (*v.* 8), where the law of God should be written for a memorandum to them of their duty, they set up the remembrance of their idols, not so much to keep up their own remembrance of them (they were so fond of them that they could not forget them), but to show to others how mindful they were of them, and to put their children in mind of them, and possess them betimes with a veneration for these dunghill deities. [4.] As they were insatiable in their idolatries, so they were inseparable from them. They were hardened in their wickedness; they worshipped their idols openly and in public view, as being neither ashamed of the sin nor afraid of the punishment; they went as publicly, and in as great crowds, to the idol-temples, as ever they had gone to God's house. This was like an impudent harlot, *discovering themselves to another than God,* making profession of another than the true religion. They took a pride in making proselytes to their idolatries, and not only went up themselves to their high places, but *enlarged their bed,* that is, their idol-temples,

and (as the margin reads the following words) *thou hewedst it for thyself larger than theirs,* than theirs from whom thou copiedst it, and tookest the platform of it, as Ahaz of his altar from that which he saw at Damascus, 2 Ki. 16:10. And being thus involved over head and ears, as it were, in their idolatries, there is no parting them from them. Ephraim is now joined to idols both in love and league. *First,* In league: *"Thou hast made a covenant with them,* with the idols, with the idol-worshippers, to live and die together." This was a complete renunciation of their covenant with God and an avowed resolution to persist in their apostasy from him. *Secondly,* In love: *"Thou lovedst their bed,* that is, the temple of an idol, wherever thou sawest it." Justly therefore were they given up to their own hearts' lusts.

3. Another sin charged upon them is their trusting in and seeking to foreign aids and succours, and contracting a communion with the Gentile powers (*v.* 9): *Thou wentest to the king,* which some understand of the idol they worshipped, particularly *Moloch,* which signifies *a king.* "Thou didst every thing to ingratiate thyself with those idols, didst offer incense and sweet ointments at their altars." Or it may be meant of the king of Assyria, whom Ahaz made his court to, or of the king of Babylon, whose ambassadors Hezekiah caressed, or of other kings of the nations whose idolatrous usages they admired and were desirous to learn and imitate, and for that end went and sent to cultivate an acquaintance and correspondence with them, that they might be like them and strengthen themselves by an alliance with them. See here, (1.) What an expense they were at in forming and procuring this grand alliance. They went *with ointments and perfumes,* either bestowed upon themselves, to beautify their own faces and so make themselves considerable and worthy the friendship of the greatest king, or to be presented to those whose favour they were ambitious of, because a man's gift makes room for him and brings him before great men. "When the first present of rich perfumes was thought too little, thou didst increase them;" and thus many seek the ruler's favour, forgetting that, after all, every man's judgment proceeds from the Lord. So fond were they of those heathen princes that they not only went themselves, in all their airs, to those that were near them, but sent messengers to those that were afar off, *ch.* 18:2. (2.) How much they hereby disparaged themselves and laid the honour of their crown and nation in the dust: *Thou didst debase thyself even unto hell.* They did so by their idolatries. It is a dishonour to the children of men, who are endued with the powers of reason, to worship that as their god which is the creature of their own fancy and the work of their own hands, to bow down to the stock of a tree. It is much more a dishonour to the children of God, who are blessed with the privilege of divine revelation, to forsake such a God as they know theirs to be for a thing of nought, their own mercies for lying vanities. They likewise debased themselves by truckling to their heathen neighbours, and depending upon them, when they had a God to go to who is all-sufficient and in covenant with them. How did those shame themselves to the highest degree, and sink themselves to the lowest, that forsook the fountain of life for broken cisterns and the rock of ages for broken reeds! Note, Sinners disparage and debase themselves; the service of sin is an ignominious slavery; and those who thus debase themselves to hell will justly have their portion there.

III. The aggravations of their sin. 1. They had been tired with disappointments in their wicked courses, and yet they would not be convinced of the folly of them (*v.* 10): *"Thou art wearied in the greatness of thy way;* thou hast undertaken a mighty task, to find out true satisfaction and happiness in that which is vanity and a lie." Those that set up idols, instead of God, for the object of their worship, and princes, instead of God, for the object of their hope and confidence, and think thus to better themselves and make themselves easy, go a great way about, and will never come to their journey's end: *Thou art wearied in the multitude,* or *multiplicity, of thy ways* (so some read it): those that forsake the only right way wander endlessly in a thousand by-paths, and lose themselves in the many inventions which they have sought out. They weary themselves with fresh chases and fierce ones, but never gain their point, like the Sodomites, that *wearied themselves to find the door* (Gen. 19:11) and could not find it at last. The pleasures of sin will soon surfeit, but never satisfy; a man may quickly tire himself in the pursuit of them, but can never repose himself in the enjoyment of them. They found this by experience. The idols they had often worshipped never did them any kindness; the kings they courted distressed them, and helped them not; and yet they were so wretchedly besotted that they could not say, *"There is no hope;* it is in vain any longer to expect that satisfaction in creature-confidences, and in the worship of idols, which we have so often looked for, and never met with." Note, Despair of happiness in the creature, and of satisfaction in the service of sin, is the first step towards a well-grounded hope of happiness in God and a well-fixed resolution to keep to his service; and those are inexcusable who have had sensible convictions of the vanity of the creature, and yet will not be brought to say, "There is no hope to be happy short of the Creator." 2. Though they were convinced that the way they were in was a sinful way, yet, because they had found some present sensual pleasure and worldly profit by it, they could not persuade themselves to be sorry for it: *"Thou hast found the life of thy hand"* (or *the living of it*); thou boastest how fortune smiles upon thee, and therefore thou art not grieved, any more than Ephraim when he said (Hos. 12:8), *"I have become rich; I have found out substance."* Note, Prosperity in sin is a great bar to conversion from sin. Those that live at ease in their sinful projects, are tempted to think God favours them, and therefore they have nothing to repent of. Some read it ironically, or by way of question: "Thou hast found the life of thy hand, hast found true satisfaction and happiness, no doubt thou hast; hast thou not? And therefore thou art so far from being grieved that thou blessest thyself in thy own evil way; but review thy gains once more, and come to a balance of profit and loss, and then say, What fruit hast thou of those things whereof thou art ashamed and for which *God shall bring thee into judgment?"* Rom. 6:21. 3. They had dealt very unworthily with God by their sin; for, (1.) It should seem they pretended that the reason why they left God was because he was too terrible a majesty for them to deal with; they must have gods that they could be more free and familiar with. "But," says God, *"of whom hast thou been afraid or feared, that thou hast lied,* that thou hast dealt falsely and treacherously with me, and dissembled in thy covenants with me and prayers to me? What did I ever do to frighten thee from me? What occasion have I given thee to think hardly of me, that thou hast gone to seek a kinder master?" (2.) However, it is certain that they had no true reverence of God nor any serious regard to him. So that question is commonly understood, *"Of whom hast thou been afraid, or feared?* Of none; for thou hast not feared me whom thou shouldst fear; for thou hast lied to me." Those that dissemble with God make it to appear they stand in no awe of him. "Thou *hast not remembered me,* neither what I have said nor what I have done, neither the promises nor the threatenings, nor the performances of either; thou hast *not laid them to thy heart,* as thou wouldst have done if thou hadst feared me." Note, Those who lay not the word of God and his providences to their hearts do thereby show that they have not the fear of God before their eyes. And multitudes are ruined by fearlessness, forgetfulness, and mere carelessness; they do not aright nor to good purpose fear any thing, remember any thing, nor lay any thing to heart. Nay, (3.) They were hardened in their sin by the patience and forbearance of God. *"Have not I held my peace of old,* and for a long time? These things thou hast done and I kept silence. And therefore, as it follows here, thou fearest me not;" as if because God had spared long he would never punish, Eccl. 8:11. Because he kept silence the sinner thought him altogether such a one as himself, and stood in no awe of him.

IV. Here is God's resolution to call them to an account, though he had long borne with them (*v.* 12): *"I will declare* (like that, Ps. 50:21, *But I will reprove thee), I will declare thy righteousness,* which thou makest thy boast of, and let the world see, and thyself too, to thy confusion, that it is all a sham, all a cheat, it is not what it pretends to be. When thy righteousness comes to be examined it will be found that it was unrighteousness, and that there was no sincerity in all thy pretensions. I will declare *thy works,* what they have been and what the gain thou pretendest to have gotten by them, and it will appear that at long-run *they shall not profit thee,* nor turn to any account." Note, Sinful works, as they are works of darkness, and there is no reason nor righteousness in them, so they are unfruitful works and there is nothing got by them; and, however they look now, it will be made to appear so another day. Sin profits not, nay, it ruins and destroys.

Verses 13–16

Here, I. God shows how insufficient idols and creatures were to relieve and succour those that worshipped them and confided in them (*v.* 13): *"When thou criest* in thy distress and anguish, lamentest thy misery and callest for help, *let thy companies deliver thee,* thy idol-gods which thou hast heaped to thyself companies of, the troops of the confederate forces which thou hast relied so much upon, let them deliver thee if they can; expect no other relief than what they can give." Thus God said to Israel, when in their trouble they called upon him (Jdg. 10:14), *Go, and cry to the gods which you have chosen, let them deliver you.* But in vain is salvation hoped for from them: *The wind shall carry them all away,* the wind of God's wrath, that breath of his mouth which shall slay the wicked; they have made themselves as chaff, and therefore the wind will of course hurry them away. Vanity they are, and *vanity shall take them* away, to vanity they shall be reduced, and vanity shall be their recompence. Both the idols and their worshippers shall come to nothing.

II. He shows that there was a sufficiency, an all-sufficiency, in him for the comfort and deliverance of all those that put their confidence in him and made their application to him. Their safety and satisfaction appear the more comfortable because their hopes are crowned with fruition, when those that seek to other helpers have their hopes frustrated: *"He that puts his trust in me,* and in me only, he shall be happy, both for soul and body, for this world and the other."

1. Observe, in general, (1.) Those that trust in God's providence take the best course to secure their secular interests. They *shall possess the land,* as much of it as is good for them, and what they have they shall have it from a good hand and hold it by a good title. Ps. 37:3, *They shall dwell in the land, and verily they shall be fed.* (2.) Those that trust in God's grace take the best course to secure their sacred interests. They *shall inherit my holy mountain.* They shall enjoy the privileges of the church on earth, and be brought at length to the joys of heaven; and no wind shall carry them away.

2. More particularly,

(1.) The captives, that trust in God, shall be released (*v.* 14): *They shall say* (that is, the messengers of his providence, in that great event shall say), *Cast you up, cast you up, prepare the way.* When God's time shall have come for their deliverance the way of bringing it about shall be made plain and easy, obstacles shall be removed, difficulties that seemed insuperable shall be speedily got over, and all things shall concur both to accelerate and facilitate their return. See *ch.* 40:3, 4. This refers to the provision which the gospel, and the grace of it, have made for our ready passage through this world to a better. The way of religion is now cast up; it is a highway; ministers' business is to direct people in it, and to help them over the discouragements they meet with, that nothing may offend them.

(2.) The contrite, that trust in God, shall be *revived, v.* 15. Those that trusted to idols and creatures for help went with their *ointments and perfumes* (*v.* 9); but here God shows that those who may expect help from him are such as are destitute of, and set themselves at a distance from, the gaieties of the world and the delights of sense. God's glory appears here very bright, [1.] In his greatness and majesty: He is *the high and lofty One that inhabits eternity.* Let this inspire us with very high and honourable thoughts of the God with whom we have to do, *First,* That his being and perfections are exalted infinitely above every creature, not only above what they have themselves, but above what they can conceive concerning him, *far above all their blessing and praise,* Neh. 9:5. *He is the high and lofty One,* and there is no creature like him, nor any to be compared with him. The language likewise intimates his sovereign dominion over all and the incontestable right he has to give both law and judgment to all. He is *higher than the highest* (Eccl. 5:8), than the *highest heavens,* Ps. 113:4. *Secondly,* That with him there is neither beginning of days nor end of life, nor change of time; he is both immortal and immutable. He only *has immortality,* 1 Tim. 6:16. He has it of himself, and he has it constantly; he inhabits it, and cannot be dispossessed of it. We must shortly remove into eternity, but God always inhabits it. *Thirdly,* That there is an infinite rectitude in his nature, and an exact conformity with himself and a steady design of his own glory in all that he does; and this appears in every thing by which he has made himself known, for his name is *holy,* and all that desire to be acquainted with him must know him as a holy God. *Fourthly,* That the peculiar residence and manifestation of his glory are in the mansions of light and bliss above: *"I dwell in the high and holy place,* and will have all the world to know it." Whoever have any business with God must direct to him as their Father in heaven, for there he dwells. These great things are here said of God to inspire us with a holy reverence of him, to encourage our confidence in him, and to magnify his compassion and condescension to us, that though he is thus high yet he has respect unto the lowly; he that rides on the heavens by his name JAH stoops to concern himself for poor *widows* and *fatherless,* Ps. 68:4, 5. [2.] In his grace and mercy. He has a tender pity for the humble and contrite, for those that are so in respect of their state. If they be his people, he will not overlook them though they are poor and low in the world, and despised and trampled upon by men; but he here refers to the temper of their mind; he will have a tender regard to those who, being in affliction, accommodate themselves to their affliction, and bring their mind to their condition, be it ever so low and ever so sad and sorely broken — those that are truly penitent for sin, who mourn in secret for it, and have a dread of the wrath of God, which they have made themselves obnoxious to, and are submissive under all his rebukes. Now, *First,* With these God will dwell. He will visit them graciously, will converse familiarly with them by his word and Spirit, as a man does with those of his own family; he will be always nigh to them and present with them. He that dwells in the highest heavens dwells in the lowest hearts and inhabits sincerity as surely as he inhabits eternity. In these he delights. *Secondly,* He will revive their heart and spirit, will speak that to them, and work that in them by the word and Spirit of his grace, which will be reviving to them, as a cordial to one that is ready to faint. He will give them reviving joys and hopes sufficient to counterbalance all the griefs and fears that break their spirits. He dwells with them, and his presence is reviving.

(3.) Those with whom he contends, if they trust in him, shall be relieved, and received into favour, *v.* 16. He will *revive the heart of the contrite ones,* for he will not contend for ever. Nothing makes a soul contrite so much as God's contending, and therefore nothing revives it so much as his ceasing his controversy. Here is, [1.] A gracious promise. It is not promised that he will never be angry with his people, for their sins are displeasing to him, or that he will never contend with them, for they must expect the rod; but he *will not contend for ever,* nor be always wroth. As he is not soon angry, so he is not long angry. He will not always chide. Though he contend with them by convictions of sin, he will not contend for ever; but, instead of the spirit of bondage, they shall receive the Spirit of adoption. He has torn, but he will heal. Though eh contend with them by the rebukes of providence, yet the correction shall not last always, shall not last long, shall last no longer than there is need (1 Pt. 1:6), no longer than they can bear, no longer than till it has done its work. Though their whole life be calamitous, yet their end will be peace, and so will their eternity be. [2.] A very compassionate consideration, upon which this promise is grounded: "If I should contend for ever, *the spirit would fail before me, ever the souls which I have made."* Note, *First,* God is the Father of spirits, Heb. 12:9. Those with whom he will not always contend are the souls that he has made, that he gave being to by creation and a new being to by regeneration. *Secondly,* Though the Lord is for the body, yet he concerns himself chiefly for the souls of his people, that the spirit do not fail, and its graces and comforts. *Thirdly,* When troubles last long, the spirit even of good men is apt to fail. They are tempted to entertain hard thoughts of God, to think it in vain to serve him; they are ready to put comfort away from them, and to despair of relief, and then the spirit fails. *Fourthly,* It is in consideration of this that God will not contend for ever; for he will not forsake the work of his own hands nor defeat the purchase of his Son's blood. The reason is taken not from our merit, but from our weakness and infirmity; for *he remembers that we are flesh* (Ps. 78:39) and that flesh is weak.

Verses 17–21

The body of the people of Israel, in this account of God's dealings with them, is spoken of as a particular person (*v.* 17, 18), but divided into two sorts, differently dealt with — some who were sons of peace, to whom peace is spoken (*v.* 19), and others who were not, who have nothing to do with peace, *v.* 20, 21. Observe here,

I. The just rebukes which that people were brought under for their sin: *For the iniquity of his covetousness I was wroth, and smote him.* Covetousness was a sin that abounded very much among that people. Jer. 6:13, *From the least to the greatest of them, every one is given to covetousness.* Those that did not worship images were yet carried away by this spiritual idolatry: for such is covetousness; it is making money the god, Col. 3:5. No marvel that the people were covetous when their watchmen themselves were notoriously so, *ch.* 56:11, Yet, covetous as they were, in the service of their idols they were prodigal, *v.* 6. And it is hard to say whether their profuseness in that or their covetousness in every thing else was more provoking. But for this iniquity, among others, God was angry with them, and brought one judgment after another upon them, and their destruction at last by the Chaldeans. 1. God was wroth. He resented it, took it very ill that a people who were devoted to himself, and portioned in himself, should be so entirely given up to the world and choose that for their portion. Note, Covetousness is an iniquity that is very displeasing to the God of heaven. It is a heart-sin, but he sees it, and *therefore* hates it, and looks upon it with jealousy, because it sets up a rival with him in the soul. It is a sin which men *bless themselves in* (Ps. 49:18) and in which their neighbours *bless them* (Ps. 10:3); but God abhors it. 2. He motes him, reproved him for it by his prophets, corrected him by his providence, punished him in those very things he so doted upon and was covetous of. Note, Sinners shall be made to feel from the anger of God. Those whom he is wroth with he smites; and covetousness particularly lays men under the tokens of God's displeasure. Those that set their hearts upon the wealth of this world are disappointed of it or it is embittered to them; it is either clogged with a cross or turned into a curse. 3. God hid himself from him when he was under these rebukes, and continued wroth with him. When we are under the rod, if God manifest himself to us, we may bear it the better; but if he both smite us and hide himself from us, send us no prophets, speak to us no comfortable word, show us no token for good, if he *tear and go away* (Hos. 5:14), we are very miserable.

II. Their obstinacy and incorrigibleness under these rebukes: *He went on frowardly in the way of his heart,* in his evil way. He was not sensible of the displeasure of God that he was under. He felt the smart of the rod, but had no regard at all to the hand; the more he was crossed in his worldly pursuits the more eager he was in them. He either would not see his error or if he saw it would not amend it. Covetousness was the way of his heart; it was what he was inclined to and intent upon, and he would not be reclaimed, but *in his distress he trespassed yet more,* 2 Chr. 28:22. See the strength of the corruption of men's hearts, and the sinfulness of sin, which will take its course in despite of God himself and all the flames of his wrath. See also how insufficient afflictions of themselves are to reform men, unless God's grace work with them.

III. God's wonderful return in mercy to them, notwithstanding the obstinacy of the generality of them.

1. The greater part of them went on frowardly, but there were some among them that were mourners for the obstinacy of the rest; and with an eye to them, or rather for his own name's sake, God determines not to contend for ever with them. *With the froward* God may justly *show himself froward* (Ps. 18:26), and *walk contrary* to those that *walk contrary* to him, Lev. 26:24. When this sinner here went on frowardly in the way of his heart, one would think it should have followed, "I have seen his ways and will destroy him, will abandon him, will never have any thing more to do with him." But such are the riches of divine mercy and grace, and so do they rejoice against judgment, that it follows, *I have seen his ways and will heal him.* See how God's goodness takes occasion from man's badness to appear so much the more illustrious; and where sin has abounded grace much more abounds. God's reasons of mercy are fetched from within himself, for in us there appears nothing but what is provoking: "I have seen his ways, and yet I will heal him for my own name's sake." God knew how bad the people were, and yet would not cast them off. But observe the method. God will first give him grace, and then, and not till then, give him peace: "I have seen his way, that he will never turn to me of himself, and therefore I will turn him." Those whom God has mercy in store for he has grace in readiness for, to prepare and qualify them for that mercy which they were running from as fast as they could. (1.) God will heal him of his corrupt and vicious disposition, will cure him of his covetousness, though it be ever so deeply rooted in him and his heart have been long exercised to covetous practices. There is no spiritual disease so inveterate, but almighty grace can conquer it. (2.) God *will lead him also;* not only amend what was amiss in him, that he may cease to do evil, but direct him into the way of duty, that he may learn to do well. He goes on frowardly, as Saul, yet breathing out threatenings and slaughter, but God will lead him into a better mind, a better path. And them, (3.) He will restore those comforts to him which he had forfeited and lost, and for the return of which he had thus prepared him. There was a wonderful reformation wrought upon captives in Babylon, and then a wonderful redemption wrought for them, which brought comfort to them, to their mourners, to those among them that mourned for their own sins, the sins of their people, and the desolations of the sanctuary. To those mourners the mercy would be most comfortable, and to them God had an eye in working it out. Blessed are those that mourn, for to them comfort belongs, and they shall have it.

2. Now, as when that people went into captivity some of them were good figs, very good, others of them bad figs, very bad, and accordingly their captivity was to them for their good or for *their hurt* (Jer. 24:8, 9), so, when they came out of captivity, still some of them were good, others bad, and the deliverance was to them accordingly.

(1.) To those among them that were good their return out of captivity was peace, such peace as was a type and earnest of the peace which should be preached by Jesus Christ (*v.* 19): *I create the fruit of the lips, peace.* [1.] God designed to give them matter for praise and thanksgiving, for that is the *fruit of the lips* (Heb. 13:15), the *calves of the lips,* Hos. 14:2. *I create this.* Creation is out of nothing, and this is surely out of worse than nothing, when God creates matter of praise for those that went on frowardly in the way of their heart. [2.] In order to this, peace shall be published: *Peace, peace* (perfect peace, all kinds of peace) *to him that is afar off* from the general rendezvous, or from the head-quarters, as well as *to him that is near.* Peace with God; though he has contended with them, he will be reconciled and will let fall his controversy. Peace of conscience, a holy security and serenity of mind, after the many reproaches of conscience and agitations of spirit they had been under their captivity. Thus God creates the fruit of the lips, fresh matter for thanksgiving; for, when he speaks peace to us, we must speak praises to him. This peace is itself of God's creating. He, and he only, can work it; it is the fruit of the lips, of his lips — he commands it, of the minister's lips — he speaks it by them, *ch.* 40:1. It is the fruit of preaching lips and praying lips; it is the fruit of Christ's lips, whose lips drop as a honeycomb; for to him this is applied, Eph. 2:17: *He came and preached peace to you who were afar off,* you Gentiles as well as to the Jews, who were nigh — to after-ages, who were afar off in time, as well as to those of the present age.

(2.) To those among them that were wicked, though they might return with the rest, their return was no peace, *v.* 20. The wicked, wherever he is, in Babylon or in Jerusalem, carries about with him the principle of his own uneasiness, and is like the troubled sea. God healed those to whom he spoke peace (*v.* 19): *I will heal them;* all shall be well again and set to rights; but the wicked would not be healed by the grace of God and therefore shall not be healed by his comforts. They are always like the sea in a storm, for they carry about with them, [1.] Unmortified corruptions. They are not cured and conquered, and their ungoverned lusts and passions make them like the troubled sea when it cannot rest, vexatious to all about them and therefore uneasy to themselves, noisy and dangerous. When the intemperate heats of the spirit break out in scurrilous and abusive language, then the troubled sea casts forth mire and dirt. [2.] Unpacified consciences. They are under a frightful apprehension of guilt and wrath, that they cannot enjoy themselves; when they seem settled they are in disquietude, when they seem merry they are in heaviness; like Cain, who always dwelt in the land of shaking. The terrors of conscience disturb all their enjoyments, and cast forth such mire and dirt as make them a burden to themselves. Though this does not appear (it may be) at present, yet it is a certain truth, what this prophet had said before (*ch.* 48:22), and here repeats (*v.* 21), *There is no peace to the wicked,* no reconciliation to God (nor can they be upon good terms with him, while they go on still in their trespasses), no quietness or satisfaction in their own mind, no real good, no peace in death, because no hope. *My God hath said it,* and all the world cannot unsay it, That there is no peace to those that allow themselves in any sin. What have they to do with peace?

CHAPTER 58

The prophet, in this chapter, has his commission and charge renewed to reprove the sinners in Zion, particularly the hypocrites, to show them their transgressions (*v.* 1). It is intended for admonition and warning to all hypocrites, and is not to be confined to those of any one age. Some refer it primarily to those at that time when Isaiah prophesied; see 33:14; 29:13. Others to the captives in Babylon, the wicked among them, to whom the prophet had declared there was no peace 57:21. Against the terror of that word they thought to shelter themselves with their external performances, particularly their fastings, which they kept up in Babylon, and for some time after their return to their own land, Zec. 7:3, etc. The prophet therefore here shows them that their devotions would not entitle them to peace while their conversations were not at all of a piece with them. Others think it is principally intended against the hypocrisy of the Jews, especially the Pharisees before and in our Saviour's time: they boasted of their fastings, but Christ (as the prophet here) showed them their transgressions (Mt. 23), much the same with those they are here charged with. Observe, I. The plausible profession of religion which they made (*v.* 2). II. The boasts they made of that profession, and the blame they laid upon God for taking no more notice of it (*v.* 3). III. The sins they are charged with, which spoiled the acceptableness of their fasts (*v.* 4, 5). IV. Instructions given them how to keep fasts aright (*v.* 6, 7). V. Precious promises made to those who do so keep fasts (*v.* 8–12). VI. The like precious promises made to those that sanctify sabbaths aright (*v.* 13, 14).

Verses 1–2

When our Lord Jesus promised to send the Comforter he added, *When he shall come he shall convince* (Jn. 16:7, 8); for conviction must prepare for comfort, and must also separate between the precious and the vile, and mark out those to whom comfort does not belong. God had appointed this prophet to comfort his people (*ch.* 40:1); here he appoints him to convince them, and show them their sins.

I. He must tell them how very bad they really were, *v.* 1. 1. He must deal faithfully and plainly with them. "Though they are called *the people of God* and *the house of Jacob,* though they wear an honourable title and character, by which they are interested in many glorious privileges, yet do not flatter them, but show them their transgressions and their sins, be particular in telling them their faults, what sins are committed among them, which they do not know of, nay, what sins are committed by them which they do not acknowledge to be sins; though in some things they are reformed, let them know that in other things they are still as bad as ever. Show them their transgressions and their sins, that is, all their transgressions in their sins, their sins and all the aggravations of them," Lev. 16:21. Note, (1.) God sees sin in his people, in the house of Jacob, and is displeased with it. (2.) They are often unapt and unwilling to see their own sins, and need to have them shown them, and to be told, *Thus and thus thou hast done.* 2. He must be vehement and in good earnest herein, must *cry aloud, and not spare,* not spare them (not touch them with his reproofs as if he were afraid of hurting them, but search the wound to the bottom, lay it bare to the bone), not spare himself or his own pains, but cry as loud as he can; though he spend his strength and waste his spirits, though he get their ill-will by it and get himself into an ill name, yet he must not spare. He must lift up his voice like a trumpet, to make those hear of their faults that were apt to be deaf when admonition was addressed to them. He must give his reproofs in the most powerful and pressing manner possible, as one who desired to be heeded. The trumpet does not give an uncertain sound, but, though loud and shrill, is intelligible; so must his alarms be, giving them warning of the fatal consequences of sin, Eze. 33:3.

II. He must acknowledge how very good they seemed to be, notwithstanding (*v.* 2): *Yet they seek me daily.* When the prophet went about to show them their transgressions they pleaded that they could see no transgressions which they were guilty of; for they were diligent and constant in attending on God's worship — and what more would he have of them? Now,

1. He owns the matter of fact to be true. As far as hypocrites do that which is good, they shall not be denied the praise of it; let them make their best of it. It is owned that they have a form of godliness. (1.) They go to church, and observe their hours of prayer: *They seek me daily;* they are very constant in their devotions and never omit them nor suffer any thing to put them by. (2.) They love to hear good preaching; *They delight to know my ways,* as Herod, who heard John gladly, and the stony ground, that received the seed of the word with joy; it is to them *as a lovely song,* Eze. 33:32. (3.) They seem to take great pleasure in the exercises of religion and to be in their element when they are at their devotions: *They delight in approaching to God,* not for his sake to whom they approach, but for the sake of some pleasing circumstance, the company, or the festival. (4.) They are inquisitive concerning their duty and seem desirous only to know it, making no question but that then they should do it: *They ask of me the ordinances of justice,* the rules of piety in the worship of God, the rules of equity in their dealings with men, both which are ordinances of justice. (5.) They appear to the eye of the world as if they made conscience of doing their duty: *They are as a nation that did righteousness and forsook not the ordinances of their God;* others took them for such, and they themselves pretended to be such. Nothing lay open to view that was a contradiction to their profession, but they seemed to be such as they should be. Note, Men may go a great way towards heaven and yet come short; nay, may go to hell with a good reputation. But,

2. He intimates that this was so far from being a cover or excuse for their sin that really it was an aggravation of it: "Show them their sins which they go on in notwithstanding their knowledge of good and evil, sin and duty, and the convictions of their consciences concerning them."

Verses 3–7

Here we have, I. The displeasure which these hypocrites conceived against God for not accepting the services which they themselves had a mighty opinion of (*v.* 3): *Wherefore have we fasted, say they, and thou seest not?* Thus they went in the way of Cain, who was angry at God, and resented it as a gross affront that his offering was not accepted. Having gone about to put a cheat upon God by their external services, here they go about to pick a quarrel with God for not being pleased with their services, as if he had not done fairly or justly by them. Observe, 1. How they boast of themselves, and magnify their own performances: *"We have fasted, and afflicted our souls;* we have not only sought God daily (*v.* 2), but have kept some certain times of more solemn devotion." Some think this refers to the yearly fast (which was called *the day of atonement),* others to their arbitrary occasional fasts. Note, It is common for unhumbled hearts to be proud of their professions of humiliation, as the Pharisee (Lu. 18:12), *I fast twice in the week.* 2. What they expected from their performances. They thought God should take great notice of them, and own himself a debtor to them for their services. Note, It is a common thing for hypocrites, while they perform the external services of religion, to promise themselves that acceptance with God which he has promised only to the sincere; as if they must be accepted of course, or for a compliment. 3. How heinously they take it that God had not put some particular marks of his favour upon them, that he had not immediately delivered them out of their troubles and advanced them to honour and prosperity. They charge God with injustice and partiality, and seem resolved to throw up their religion, and justify themselves in doing so with this, that they had found no *profit in praying* to God, Job 21:14, 15; Mal. 3:14. Note, Reigning hypocrisy often breaks out in daring impiety and an open contempt and reproach of God and religion for that which the hypocrisy itself must bear all the blame of. Sinners reflect upon religion as a hard and melancholy service, and on which there is nothing to be got by, when really it is owing to themselves that it seems so to them, because they are not sincere in it.

II. The true reason assigned why God did not accept their fastings, nor answer the prayers they made on their fast-days; it was because they did not fast aright — *to God, even to him,* Zec. 7:5. They fasted indeed, but they persisted in their sins, and did not, as the Ninevites, turn every one from his evil way; but *in the day of their fast,* notwithstanding the professed humiliations and covenants of that day, they went on to *find pleasure,* that is, to do whatsoever seemed right in their own eyes, lawful or unlawful, *quicquid libet, licet — making their inclinations their law;* though they seemed to afflict their souls, they still gratified their lusts as much as ever. 1. They were as covetous and unmerciful as ever: *"You exact all your labours* from your servants, and will neither release them according to the law nor relax the rigour of their servitude." This was their fault before the captivity, Jer. 34:8, 9. It was no less their fault after their captivity, notwithstanding all their solemn fasts, Neh. 5:5. *"You exact all your dues,* your *debts"* (so some read it); "you are as rigorous and severe in extorting what you demand from those that are poor as ever you were, though it was at the close of the yearly fast that the release was proclaimed." 2. They were contentious and spiteful (*v.* 4): *Behold, you fast for strife and debate.* When they proclaimed a fast to deprecate God's judgments, they pretended to search for those sins which provoked God to threaten them with his judgments, and under that pretence perhaps particular persons were falsely accused, as Naboth in the day of Jezebel's fast, 1 Ki. 21:12. Or the contending parties among them upon those occasions were bitter and severe in their reflections one upon another, one side crying out, "It is owing to you," and the other, "It is owing to you, that our deliverance is not wrought." Thus, instead of judging themselves, which is the proper work of a fast-day, they condemned one another. They *fasted for strife,* with emulation which should make the most plausible appearance on a fast-day and humour the matter best. Nor was it only tongue-quarrels that were fomented in the times of their fasting, but they came to blows too: *You smite with the fist of wickedness.* The cruel task-masters beat their servants, and the creditors their insolvent debtors, whom they delivered to the tormentors; they abused poor innocents *with wicked hands.* Now while they thus *continued in sin,* in those very sins which were directly contrary to the intention of a fasting day, (1.) God would not allow them the use of such solemnities: *"You shall not fast* at all if you fast *as you do this day, causing your voice to be heard on high,* in the heat of your clamours one against another, or in your devotions, which you perform so as to make them to be taken notice of for ostentation. *Bring me no more* of these empty, noisy, *vain oblations," ch.* 1:13. Note, Those are justly forbidden the honour of a profession of religion that will not submit to the power of it. (2.) He would not accept of them in the use of them: *"You shall not fast,* that is, it shall not be looked upon as a fast, nor shall the voice of your prayers on those days be heard on high in heaven." Note, Those that fast and pray, and yet go on in their wicked ways, do but mock God and deceive themselves.

III. Plain instructions given concerning the true nature of a religious fast.

1. In general, a fast is intended, (1.) For the honouring and pleasing of God. It must be such a performance as he has chosen (*v.* 5); it must be *an acceptable day to the Lord,* in the duties of which we must study to approve ourselves to him and obtain his favour, else it is not a fast, else there is nothing done to any purpose. (2.) For the humbling and abasing of ourselves. A fast is *a day to afflict the soul;* if it do not express a genuine sorrow for sin, and do not promote a real mortification of sin, it is not a fast; the law of the day of atonement was that on that day they should *afflict their souls,* Lev. 16:29. That must be done on a fast-day which is a real affliction to the soul, as far as it is yet unregenerate and unsanctified, though a real pleasure and advantage to the soul as far as it is itself.

2. It concerns us therefore to enquire, on a fast-day, what

it is that will be acceptable to God, and afflictive to our corrupt nature, and tending to its mortification.

(1.) We are here told negatively what is not the fast that God has chosen, and which does not amount to the afflicting of the soul. [1.] It is not enough to look demure, to put on a grave and melancholy aspect, to bow down the head like a bulrush that is withered and broken: as the hypocrites, that were *of a sad countenance, and disfigured their faces, that they might appear unto men to fast,* Mt. 6:16. Hanging down the head did indeed well enough become the publican, whose heart was truly humbled and broken for sin, and who therefore, in token of that, *would not so much as lift up his eyes to heaven* (Lu. 18:13); but when it was only mimicked, as here, it was justly ridiculed: it is but *hanging down the head like a bulrush,* which nobody regards or takes any notice of. As the hypocrite's humiliations are but like the hanging down of a bulrush, so his elevations in his hopes are but like the *flourishing of a bulrush* (Job 8:11, 12), which, *while it is yet in its greenness, withers before any other herb.* [2.] It is not enough to do penance, to mortify the body a little, while the body of sin is untouched. It is not enough for a man *to spread sackcloth and ashes under him,* which may indeed give him some uneasiness for the present, but will soon be forgotten when he returns to *stretch himself upon his beds of ivory,* Amos 6:4. *Wilt thou call this a fast?* No, it is but the shadow and carcase of a fast. *Wilt thou call this an acceptable day to the Lord?* No, it is so far from being so that the hypocrisy of it is an abomination to him. Note, The shows of religion, though they show ever so fair in the eye of the world, will not be accepted of God without the substance of it.

(2.) We are here told positively what is the fast that God has chosen, what that is which will recommend a fast-day to the divine acceptance, and what is indeed afflicting the soul, that is, crushing and subduing the corrupt nature. It *is not afflicting the soul for a day* (as some read it, *v.* 5) that will serve; no, it must be the business of our whole lives. It is here required, [1.] That we be just to those with whom we have dealt hardly. The fast that God has chosen consists in reforming our lives and undoing what we have done amiss (*v.* 6): *To loose the bands of wickedness,* the bands which we have wickedly tied, and by which others are bound out from their right or bound down under severe usage. Those which perhaps were at first bands of justice, tying men to pay a due debt, become, when the debt is exacted with rigour from those whom Providence has reduced and emptied, *bands of wickedness,* and they must be loosed, or they will bring us into bonds of guilt much more terrible. It is *to undo the heavy burden* laid on the back of the poor servant, under which he is ready to sink. It is *to let the oppressed go free* from the oppression which makes his life bitter to him. "Let the prisoner for debt that has nothing to pay be discharged, let the vexatious action be quashed, let the servant that is forcibly detained beyond the time of his servitude be released, and thus *break every yoke;* not only let go those that are wrongfully kept under the yoke, but break the yoke of slavery itself, that it may not serve again another time nor any by made again to serve under it." [2.] That we be charitable to those that stand in need of charity, *v.* 7. The particulars in the former verse *may* be taken as acts of charity, that we not only release those whom we have unjustly oppressed — that is justice, but that we contribute to the rescue and ransom of those that are oppressed by others, to the release of captives and the payment of the debts of the poor; but those in this verse are *plainly* acts of charity. This then is the fast that God has chosen. *First,* To provide food for those that want it. This is put first, as the most necessary, and which the poor can but a little while live without. It is *to break thy bread to the hungry.* Observe, "It must be *thy* bread, that which is honestly got (not that which thou hast robbed others of), the bread which thou thyself hast occasion for, the bread of thy allowance." We must deny ourselves, that we may have to give to him that needeth. "Thy bread which thou hast spared from thyself and thy family, on the fast-day, if that, or the value of it, be not given to the poor, it is the miser's fast, which he makes a hand of; it is fasting for the world, not for God. This is the true fast, to break thy bread to the hungry, not only to give them that which is already broken meat, but to break bread on purpose for them, to give them loaves and not to put them off with scraps." *Secondly,* To provide lodging for those that want it: It is *to take care of the poor that are cast out,* that are forced from their dwelling, turned out of house and harbour, *are cast out as rebels* (so some critics render it), that are attainted, and whom therefore it is highly penal to protect. "If they suffer unjustly, make no difficulty of sheltering them; do not only find out quarters for them and pay for their lodging elsewhere, but, which is a greater act of kindness, bring them to thy own house, make them thy own guests. Be not forgetful to entertain strangers: for though thou mayest not, as some have done, thereby entertain angels, thou mayest entertain Christ himself, who will recompense it in the resurrection of the just. *I was a stranger and you took me in.*" *Thirdly,* To provide clothing for those that want it: *"When thou seest the naked, that thou cover him,* both to shelter him from the injuries of the weather and to enable him to appear decently among his neighbours; give him clothes to come to church in, and in these and other instances *hide not thyself from thy own flesh."* Some understand it more strictly of a man's own kindred and relations: "If those of thy own house and family fall into decay, thou art *worse than an infidel* if thou dost not *provide* for them." 1 Tim. 5:8. Others understand it more generally; all that partake of the human nature are to be looked upon as our own flesh, for have we not all one Father? And for this reason we must not hide ourselves from them, not contrive to be out of the way when a poor petitioner enquires for us, not look another way when a moving object of charity and compassion presents itself; let us remember that they are flesh of our flesh and therefore we ought to sympathize with them, and in doing good to them we really do good to our own flesh and spirit too in the issue; for thus *we lay up for ourselves a good foundation,* a good bond, *for the time to come.*

Verses 8–12

Here are precious promises for those to feast freely and cheerfully upon by faith who keep the fast that God has chosen; let them know that God will make it up to them. Here is,

I. A further account of the duty to be done in order to our interest in these promises (*v.* 9, 10); and here, as before, it is required that we both do justly and love mercy, that we cease to do evil and learn to do well. 1. We must abstain from all acts of violence and fraud. "Those must be *taken away from the midst of thee,* from the midst of *thy person,* out of *thy heart"* (so some); "thou must not only refrain from the practice of injury, but mortify in thee all inclination and disposition towards it." Or *from the midst of thy people.* Those in authority must not only not be oppressive themselves, but must do all they can to prevent and restrain oppression in all within their jurisdiction. They must not only *break the yoke* (*v.* 6), but take away the yoke, that those who have been oppressed may never be re-enslaved (as they were Jer. 34:10, 11); they must likewise *forbear threatening* (Eph. 6:9) and take away the *putting forth of the finger,* which seems to have been then, as sometimes with us, a sign of displeasure and the indication of a purpose to correct. Let not the finger be put forth to point at those that are poor and in misery, and so to expose them to contempt; such expressions of contumely as are provoking, and the products of ill-nature, ought to be banished from all societies. And let them not *speak vanity,* flattery or fraud, to one another, but let all conversation be governed by sincerity. Perhaps that dissimulation which is the bane of friendship is meant by the putting forth of the finger (as Prov. 6:13 by *teaching with the finger),* or it is putting forth the finger with the ring on it, which was the badge of authority, and which therefore they produced when they spoke iniquity, that is, gave unrighteous sentences. 2. We must abound in all acts of charity and beneficence. We must not only give alms according as the necessities of the poor require, but, (1.) We must give freely and cheerfully, and from a principle of charity. We must *draw out our soul to the hungry* (*v.* 10), not only draw out the money and reach forth the hand, but do this from the heart, heartily, and without grudging, from a principle of compassion and with a tender affection to such as we see to be in misery. Let the heart go along with the gift; for God loves a cheerful giver, and so does a poor man too. When our Lord Jesus healed and fed the multitude it was as having compassion on them. (2.) We must give plentifully and largely, so as not to tantalize, but to *satisfy, the afflicted soul:* "Do not only feed the hungry, but gratify the desire of the afflicted, and, if it lies in your power, make them easy." What are we born for, and what have we our abilities of body, mind, and estate for, but to do all the good we can in this world with them? And the poor we have always with us.

II. Here is a full account of the blessings and benefits which attend the performance of this duty. If a person, a family, a people, be thus disposed to every thing that is good, let them know for their comfort that they shall find God their bountiful rewarder and what they lay out in works of charity shall be abundantly made up to them. 1. God will surprise them with the return of mercy after great affliction, which shall be as welcome as the light of the morning after a long and dark night (*v.* 8): *"Then shall thy light break forth as the morning* and (*v.* 10) *thy light shall rise in obscurity.* Though thou hast been long buried alive thou shalt recover thy eminency; though long overwhelmed with grief, thou shalt again look pleasant as the dawning day." Those that are cheerful in doing good God will make cheerful in enjoying good; and this also is a special *gift of God,* Eccl. 2:24. Those that have shown mercy shall find mercy. Job, who in his prosperity had done a great deal of good, had friends raised up for him by the Lord when he was reduced, who helped him with their substance, so that his light rose in obscurity. "Not only thy light, which is sweet, but thy health too, or the healing of the wounds thou hast long complained of, shall spring forth speedily; all thy grievances shall be redressed, and thou shalt renew thy youth and recover thy vigour." Those that have helped others out of trouble will obtain help of God when it is their turn. 2. God will put honour upon them. Good works shall be recompensed with a good name; this is included in that *light which rises out of obscurity.* Though a man's extraction be mean, his family obscure, and he has no external advantages to gain him honour, yet, if he do good in his place, that will procure him respect and veneration, and his darkness shall by this means become *as the noon-day,* that is, he shall become very eminent and shine brightly in his generation. See here what is the surest way for a man to make himself illustrious; let him study to do good. He that would be the greatest of all, and best-loved, let him by humility and industry make himself a servant of all. *"Thy righteousness shall answer for thee* (as Jacob says, Gen. 30:33), that is, it shall silence reproaches, nay, it shall bespeak thee more praises than thy humility can be pleased with." He that has *given to the poor, his righteousness* (that is, the honour of it) *endures for ever,* Ps. 112:9. 3. They shall always be safe under the divine protection: *"Thy righteousness shall go before* thee as thy vanguard, to secure thee from enemies that charge thee in the front, and *the glory of the Lord shall be thy rearward,* the gathering host, to bring up those of thee that are weary and are left behind, and to secure thee from the enemies, that, like Amalek, fall upon thy rear." Observe, How good people are safe on all sides. Let them look which way they will, behind them or before them; let them look backward or forward; they see themselves safe, and find themselves easy and quiet from the fear of evil. And observe what it is that is their defence; it is their righteousness, and the glory of the Lord, that is, as some suppose, Christ; for it is by him that we are justified, and God is glorified. He it is that goes before us, and is the captain of our salvation, as he is the Lord our righteousness; he it is that is our rearward, on whom alone we can depend for safety when our sins pursue us and are ready to take hold on us. Or, "God himself in his providence and grace shall both go before thee as thy guide to conduct thee, and attend thee as thy rearward to protect thee, and this shall be the reward of thy righteousness and so shall be for the glory of the Lord as the rewarder of it." 4. God will be always nigh unto them, to hear their prayers, *v.* 9. As, on the one hand, he that shuts his ears to the cry of the poor shall himself cry and God will not hear him; so, on the other hand, he that is liberal to the poor, his prayers shall come up with his alms for a memorial before God, as Cornelius's did (Acts 10:4): *"Then shalt thou call,* on thy fast-days, which ought to be days of prayer, *and the Lord shall answer,* shall give thee the things thou callest to him for; *thou shalt cry* when thou art in any distress or sudden fright, *and he shall say, Here I am."* This is a very condescending expression of God's readiness to hear prayer. When God calls to us by his word it becomes us to say, *Here we are; what saith our Lord unto his servants?* But that God should say to us, *Behold me, here I am,* is strange. When we cry to him, as if he were at a distance, he will let us know that he is near, even at our right hand, nearer than we thought he was. *It is I, be not afraid.* When danger is near our protector is nearer, *a very present help.* "Here I am, ready to give you what you want, and do for you what you desire; what have you to say to me?" God is attentive to the prayers of the upright, Ps. 130:2. No sooner do they call to him than he answers, *Ready, ready.* Wherever they are praying, God says, "Here I am hearing; I am *in the midst of you."* He is *nigh unto them in all things,* Deu. 4:7. 6. God will direct them in all difficult and doubtful cases (*v.* 11): *The Lord shall guide thee continually.* While we are here, in the wilderness of this world, we have need of continual direction from heaven; for, if at any time we be left to ourselves, we shall certainly miss our way; and therefore it is to those who are good in God's sight that he gives the wisdom which in all cases is profitable to direct, and he will be to them *instead of eyes,* Eccl. 2:26. His providence will make their way plain to them, both what is their duty and what will be most for their comfort. 6. God will give them abundance of satisfaction in their own minds. As the world is a wilderness in respect of wanderings, so that they need to be guided continually, so also is it in respect of wants, which makes it necessary that they should have continual supplies, as Israel in the wilderness had not only the pillar of cloud to guide them continually, but manna and water out of the rock to satisfy their souls in drought, *in a dry and thirsty land where no water is,* Ps. 63:1. To a good man God gives not only wisdom and knowledge, but joy; he is satisfied in himself with the testimony of his conscience and the assurances of God's favour. "These will *satisfy thy soul,* will put gladness into thy heart, even *in the drought* of affliction; *these will make fat thy bones,* and fill them with marrow, will give thee that pleasure which will be a support to thee as the bones to the body, that joy of the Lord which will be thy strength. *He shall give thy bones rest"* (so some read it), "rest from the pain and sickness which they have laboured under and been chastened with;" so it agrees with that promise made to the merciful. The Lord will *make all his bed in his sickness,* Ps. 41:3. *"Thou shalt be like a watered garden,* so flourishing and fruitful in graces and comforts, *and like a spring of water,* like a garden that has a spring of water in it, *whose waters fail not* either in droughts or in frosts." The principle of holy love in those that are good shall be a *well of living water,* Jn. 4:14. As a spring of water, though it is continually sending forth its streams, is yet always full, so the charitable man abounds in good as he abounds in doing good and is never the poorer for his liberality. He that waters shall himself be watered. 7. They and their families shall be public blessings. It is a good reward to those that are fruitful and useful to be rendered more so, and especially to have those who descend from them to be so too. This is here promised (*v.* 12): "Those that now are of thee, thy princes, and nobles, and great men, shall have such authority and influence as they never had;" or, *"Those that* hereafter *shall be of thee,* thy posterity, shall be serviceable to their generation, as thou art to thine." It completes the satisfaction of a good man, as to this world, to think that those that come after him shall be doing good when he is gone. 1. They shall re-edify cities that have been long in ruins, *shall build the old waste places,* which had lain so long desolate that the rebuilding of them was quite despaired of. This was fulfilled when the captives, after their return, repaired the cities of Judah, and dwelt in them, and many of those in Israel too, which had lain waste ever since the carrying away of the ten tribes. 2. They shall carry on and finish that good work which was begun long before, and shall be helped over the obstructions which had retarded the progress of it: *They shall raise up* to the top that building *the foundation of* which was laid long since and has been for *many generations* in the rearing. This was fulfilled when the building of the temple was revived after it had stood still for many years, Ezra 5:2. Or, "They shall raise up foundations which shall continue for many generations yet to come;" they shall do that good which shall be of lasting consequence. 3. They shall have the blessing and praise of all about them: *"Thou shalt be called* (and it shall be to thy honour) *the repairer of the breach,* the breach made by the enemy in the wall of a besieged city, which whoso has the courage and dexterity to make up, or make good, gains great applause." Happy are those who make up the breach at which virtue is running out and judgments are breaking in. "Thou shalt be *the restorer of paths,* safe and quiet paths, not only to travel in, but *to dwell in,* so safe and quiet that people shall make no difficulty of building their houses by the road-side." The sum is that, if they keep such fasts as God has chosen, he will settle them again in their former peace and prosperity, and there shall be none to make them afraid. See Zec. 7:5, 9; 8:3–5. It teaches us that those who do justly and love mercy shall have the comfort thereof in this world.

Verses 13–14

Great stress was always laid upon the due observance of the sabbath day, and it was particularly required from the Jews when they were captives in Babylon, because by keeping that day, in honour of the Creator, they distinguished themselves from the worshippers of the gods that have not made the heavens and the earth. See *ch.* 56:1, 2, where keeping the sabbath is joined, as here, with *keeping judgment* and *doing justice.* Some, indeed, understand this of the day of atonement, which they think is the fast spoken of in the former part of the chapter, and which is called a *sabbath of rest,* Lev. 23:32. But, as the fasts before spoken of seem to be those that were occasional, so this sabbath is doubtless the weekly sabbath, that great sign between God and his professing people — his appointing it a sign of his favour to them and their observing it a sign of their obedience to him. Now observe here,

I. How the sabbath is to be sanctified (*v.* 13); and, there remaining still a sabbatism for the people of God, this law of the sabbath is still binding to us on our Lord's day.

1. Nothing must be done that puts contempt upon the sabbath day, or looks like having mean thoughts of it, when God has so highly dignified it. We must *turn away our foot from the sabbath,* from trampling upon it, as profane atheistical people do, from travelling on that day (so some); we must turn away our foot *from doing out pleasure on that holy day,* that is, from living at large, and taking a liberty to do what we please on sabbath days, without the control and restraint of conscience, or from indulging ourselves in the pleasures of sense, in which the modern Jews wickedly place the sanctification of the sabbath, though it is as great a profanation of it as any thing. On sabbath days we must not walk in *our own ways* (that is, not follow our callings), not *find our own pleasure* (that is, not follow our sports and recreations); nay, we must not *speak our own words,* words that concern either our callings or our pleasures; we must not allow ourselves a liberty of speech on that day as on other days, for we must then mind God's ways, make religion the business of the day; we must choose the things that please him; and speak his words, speak of divine things as we sit in the house and walk by the way. In all we say and do we must put a difference between this day and other days.

2. Every thing must be done that puts an honour on the day and is expressive of our high thoughts of it. We must call it *a delight,* not a *task and a burden;* we must delight ourselves in it, in the restraints it lays upon us and the services it obliges us to. We must be in our element when we are worshipping God, and in communion with him. *How amiable are thy tabernacles, O Lord of hosts!* We must not only count it a delight, but call it so, must openly profess the complacency we take in the day and the duties of it. We must call it so to God, in thanksgiving for it and earnest desire of his grace to enable us to do the work of the day in its day, because we delight in it. We must call it so to others, to invite them to come and share in the pleasure of it; and we must call it so to ourselves, that we may not entertain the least thought of wishing the sabbath gone that we may sell corn. We must call it *the Lord's holy day, and honourable.* We must call it - *holy,* separated from common use and devoted to God and to his service, must call it *the holy of the Lord,* the day which he has sanctified to himself. Even in Old-Testament times the sabbath was called *the Lord's day,* and therefore it is fitly called so still, and for a further reason, because it is the *Lord Christ's day,* Rev. 1:10. It is holy because it is the Lord's day, and upon both accounts it is honourable. It is a beauty of holiness that is upon it; it is ancient, and its antiquity is its honour; and we must make it appear that we look upon it as honourable by honouring God on that day. We put honour upon the day when we give honour to him that instituted it, and to whose honour it is dedicated.

II. What the reward is of the sabbath-sanctification, *v.* 14. If we thus *remember the sabbath day to keep it holy,*

1. We shall have the comfort of it; the work will be its own wages. *If we call the sabbath a delight, then shall we delight ourselves in the Lord;* he will more and more manifest himself to us as the delightful subject of our thoughts and meditations and the delightful object of our best affections. Note, The more pleasure we take in serving God the more pleasure we shall find in it. If we go about duty with cheerfulness, we shall go from it with satisfaction and shall have reason to say, "It is good to be here, good to draw near to God."

2. We shall have the honour of it: *I will cause thee to ride upon the high places of the earth,* which denotes not only a great security (as that, *ch.* 32:16, *He shall dwell on high),* but great dignity and advancement. "Thou shalt ride in state, shalt appear conspicuous, and the eyes of all thy neighbours shall be upon thee." It was said of Israel, when God led them triumphantly out of Egypt, that *he made them to ride on the high places of the earth,* Deu. 32:12, 13. Those that honour God and his sabbath he will thus honour. If God by his grace enable us to live above the world, and so to manage it as not only not to be hindered by it, but to be furthered and carried on by it in our journey towards heaven, then he makes us *to ride on the high places of the earth.*

3. We shall have the profit of it: I will *feed thee with the heritage of Jacob thy father,* that is, with all the blessings of the covenant and all the precious products of Canaan (which was a type of heaven), for these were the heritage of Jacob. Observe, The heritage of believers is what they shall not only be portioned with hereafter, but fed with now, fed with the hopes of it, and not flattered, fed with the earnests and foretastes of it; and those that are so fed have reason to say that they are well fed. In order that we may depend upon it, it is added, *"The mouth of the Lord has spoken it;* you may take God's word for it, for he cannot lie nor deceive; what his mouth has spoken his hand will give, his hand will do, and not one iota or tittle of his good promise shall fall to the ground." *Blessed, therefore,* thrice blessed, *is he that doeth this, and lays hold on it, that keeps the sabbath from polluting it.*

CHAPTER 59

In this chapter we have sin appearing exceedingly sinful, and grace appearing exceedingly gracious; and, as what is here said of the sinner's sin (*v.* 7, 8) is applied to the general corruption of mankind (Rom. 3:15), so what is here said of a Redeemer (*v.* 20) is applied to Christ, Rom. 11:26. I. It is here charged upon this people that they had themselves stopped the current of God's favours to them, and the particular sins are specified which kept good things from them (*v.* 1–8). II. It is here charged upon them that they had themselves procured the judgments of God upon them, and they are told both what the judgments were which they had brought upon their own heads (*v.* 9–11) and what the sins were which provoked God to send those judgments (*v.* 12–15). III. It is here promised that, notwithstanding this, God would work deliverance for them, purely for his own name's sake (*v.* 16–19), and would reserve mercy in store for them and entail it upon them (*v.* 20, 21).

Verses 1–8

The prophet here rectifies the mistake of those who had been quarrelling with God because they had not the deliverances wrought for them which they had been often fasting and praying for, *ch.* 58:3. Now here he shows,

I. That it was not owing to God. They had no reason to lay the fault upon him that they were not saved out of the hands of their enemies; for, 1. He was still as able to help as ever: *His hand is not shortened,* his power is not at all lessened, straitened, or abridged. Whether we consider the extent of his power or the efficacy of it, God can reach as far as ever and with as strong a hand as ever. Note, The church's salvation comes from the hand of God, and that has not waxed weak nor is it at all shortened. *Has the Lord's hand waxed short?* (says God to Moses, Num. 11:23). No, it has not; he will not have it thought so. Neither length of time nor strength of enemies, no, nor weakness of instruments, can shorten or straiten the power of

God, with which it is all one to save by many or by few. 2. He was still as ready and willing to help as ever in answer to prayer: *His ear is not heavy, that it cannot hear.* Though he has many prayers to hear and answer, and though he has been long hearing prayer, yet he is still as ready to hear prayer as ever. The prayer of the upright is as much his delight as ever it was, and the promises which are pleaded and put in suit in prayer are still yea and amen, inviolably sure. More is implied than is expressed; not only his ear is not heavy, but he is quick of hearing. *Even before they call he answers*, ch. 65:24. If your prayers be not answered, and the salvation we wait for be not wrought for us, it is not because God is weary of hearing prayer, but because we are weary of praying, not because his ear is heavy when we speak to him, but because our ears are heavy when he speaks to us.

II. That it was owing to themselves; they stood in their own light and put a bar in their own door. God was coming towards them in ways of mercy and they hindered him. *Your iniquities have kept good things from you*, Jer. 5:25.

1. See what mischief sin does. (1.) It hinders God's mercies from coming down upon us; it is a partition wall that separates between us and God. Notwithstanding the infinite distance that is between God and man by nature, there was a correspondence settled between them, till sin set them at variance, justly provoked God against man and unjustly alienated man from God; thus it *separates between them and God.* "He is your God, yours in profession, and therefore there is so much the more malignity and mischievousness in sin, which separates between you and him." Sin *hides his face from us* (which denotes great displeasure, Deu. 31:17); it provokes him in anger to withdraw his gracious presence, to suspend the tokens of his favour and the instances of his help; he hides his face, as refusing to be seen or spoken with. See here sin in its colours, sin exceedingly sinful, withdrawing the creature from his allegiance to his Creator; and see sin in its consequences, sin exceedingly hurtful, separating us from God, and so separating us not only *from all good*, but *to all evil* (Deu. 29:21), which is the very quintessence of the curse. (2.) It hinders our prayers from coming up unto God; it provokes him to hide his face, that he will not hear, as he has said, ch. 1:15. If we *regard iniquity in our heart*, if we indulge it and allow ourselves in it, God *will not hear our prayers*, Ps. 66:18. We cannot expect that he should countenance us while we go on to affront him.

2. Now, to justify God in hiding his face from them, and proceeding in his controversy with them, the prophet shows very largely, in the following verses, how many and great their iniquities were, according to the charge given him (ch. 58:1), *to show God's people their transgressions;* and it is a black bill of indictment that is here drawn up against them, consisting of many particulars, any one of which was enough to separate between them and a just and a holy God. Let us endeavour to reduce these articles of impeachment to proper heads.

(1.) We must begin with their thoughts, for there all sin begins, and thence it takes its rise: *Their thoughts are thoughts of iniquity, v.* 7. Their imaginations are so, only evil continually. Their projects and designs are so; they are continually contriving some mischief or other, and how to compass the gratification of some base lust (v. 4): *They conceive mischief* in their fancy, purpose, counsel, and resolution (thus the embryo receives its shape and life), and then they *bring forth iniquity*, put it in execution when it is ripened for it. Though it is in pain perhaps that the iniquity is brought forth, through the oppositions of Providences and the checks of their own consciences, yet, when they have compassed their wicked purpose, they look upon it with as much pride and pleasure as if it were a *man-child born into the world;* thus, *when lust has conceived, it bringeth forth sin*, Jam. 1:15. This is called (v. 5) *hatching the cockatrice' egg and weaving the spider's web.* See how the thoughts and contrivances of wicked men are employed, and about what they set their wits on work. [1.] At the best it is about that which is foolish and frivolous. Their thoughts are vain, like weaving the spider's web, which the poor silly animal takes a great deal of pains about, and, when all is done, it is a weak insignificant thing, a reproach to the place where it is, and which the besom sweeps away in an instant: such are the thoughts which worldly men entertain themselves with, building castles

in the air, and pleasing themselves with imaginary satisfaction, like the *spider*, which *takes hold with her hands* very finely (Prov. 30:28), but cannot keep her hold. [2.] Too often it is about that which is malicious and spiteful. They hatch the eggs of the cockatrice or adder, which are poisonous and produce venomous creatures; such are the thoughts of the wicked who delight in doing mischief. *He that eats of their eggs* (that is, he is in danger of having some mischief or other done him), *and that which is crushed* in order to be eaten of, or which begins to be hatched and you promise yourself some useful fowl from it, *breaks out into a viper*, which you meddle with at your peril. Happy are those that have least to do with such men. Even the spider's web which they wove was woven with a spiteful design to catch flies in and make a prey of them; for, rather than not be doing mischief, they will play at small game.

(2.) Out of this abundance of wickedness in the heart their mouth speaks, and yet it does not always speak out the wickedness that is within, but, for the more effectually compassing the mischievous design, it is dissembled and covered *with much fair speech* (v. 3): *Your lips have spoken lies;* and again (v. 4), *They speak lies*, pretending kindness where they intend the greatest mischief; or by slanders and false accusations they blasted the credit and reputation of those they had a spite to and so did them a real mischief unseen, and perhaps by suborning witnesses against them took from them their estates and lives; for a false tongue is sharp arrows, and coals of juniper, and every thing that is mischievous. *Your tongue has muttered perverseness.* When they could not, for shame, speak their malice against their neighbours aloud, or durst not, for fear of being disproved and put to confusion, they muttered it secretly. Backbiters are called *whisperers.*

(3.) Their actions were all of a piece with their thoughts and words. They were guilty of shedding innocent blood, a crime of the most heinous nature: *Your hands are defiled with blood* (v. 3); for blood is defiling; it leaves an indelible stain of guilt upon the conscience, which nothing but the blood of Christ can cleanse it from. Now was this a case of surprise, or one that occurred when there was something of a force put upon them; but (v. 7) *their feet ran to this evil*, naturally and eagerly, and, hurried on by the *impetus* of their malice and revenge, *they made haste to shed innocent blood*, as if they were afraid of losing an opportunity to do a barbarous thing, Prov. 1:16; Jer. 22:17. *Wasting and destruction are in their paths.* Wherever they go they carry mischief along with them, and the tendency of their way is to lay waste and destroy, nor do they care what havoc they make. Nor do they only thirst after blood, but with other iniquities are their *fingers defiled* (v. 3); they wrong people in their estates and make every thing their own that they can lay their hands on. *They trust in vanity* (v. 4); they depend upon their arts of cozenage to enrich themselves with, which will prove vanity to them, and their deceiving others will but deceive themselves. *Their works*, which they take so much pains about and have their hearts so much upon, *are all works of iniquity;* their whole business is one continued course of oppressions and vexations, *and the act of violence is in their hands*, according to the arts of violence that are in their heads and the thoughts of violence in their hearts.

(4.) No methods are taken to redress these grievances and reform these abuses (v. 4): *None calls for justice*, none complains of the violation of the sacred laws of justice, nor seeks to right those that suffer wrong or to get the laws put in execution against vice and profaneness, and those lewd practices which are the shame, and threaten to be the bane, of the nation. Note, When justice is not done there is blame to be laid not only upon the magistrates that should administer justice, but upon the people that should call for it. Private persons ought to contribute to the public good by discovering secret wickedness, and giving those an opportunity to punish it that have the power of doing so in their hands; but it is ill with a state when princes rule ill and the people love to have it so. Truth is opposed, and there is not any that *pleads for it*, not any that has the conscience and courage to appear in defence of an honest cause, and confront a prosperous fraud and wrong. *The way of peace* is as little regarded as the way of truth; they *know it not*, that is, they never study the things that make for peace, no care is taken to prevent

or punish the breaches of the peace and to accommodate matters in difference among neighbours; they are utter strangers to every thing that looks quiet and peaceable, and affect that which is blustering and turbulent. *There is no judgment in their goings;* they have not any sense of justice in their dealings; it is a thing they make no account of at all, but can easily break through all its fences if they stand in the way of their malicious covetous designs.

(5.) In all this they act foolishly, very foolishly, and as much against their interest as against reason and equity. Those that practise iniquity *trust in vanity*, which will certainly deceive them, *v.* 4. *Their webs*, which they weave with so much art and industry, *shall not become garments, neither shall they cover themselves*, either for shelter or for ornament, *with their works, v.* 6. They may do hurt to others with their projects, but can never do any real service or kindness to themselves by them. There is nothing to be got by sin, and so it will appear when profit and loss come to be compared. Those paths of iniquity are *crooked paths* (v. 8), which will perplex them, but will never bring them to their journey's end; whoever go therein, though they say that they shall have peace notwithstanding they go on, deceive themselves; for they shall not know peace, as appears by the following verses.

Verses 9–15

The scope of this paragraph is the same with that of the last, to show that sin is the great mischief-maker; as it is that which keeps good things from us, so it is that which brings evil things upon us. But as there it is spoken by the prophet, in God's name, to the people, for their conviction and humiliation, and that God might be justified when he speaks and clear when he judges, so *here* it seems to be spoken by the people to God, as an acknowledgment of that which was there told them and an expression of their humble submission and subscription to the justice and equity of God's proceedings against them. Their uncircumcised hearts here seem to be humbled in some measure, and they are brought to confess (the confession is at least extorted from them), that God had justly walked contrary to them, because they had walked contrary to him.

I. They acknowledge that God had contended with them and had walked contrary to them. Their case was very deplorable, *v.* 9–11. 1. They were in distress, trampled upon and oppressed by their enemies, unjustly dealt with, and ruled with rigour; and God did not appear for them, to plead their just and injured cause: *"Judgment is far from us, neither does justice overtake us, v.* 9. Though, as to our persecutors, we are sure that we have right on our side; and they are the wrong-doers, yet we are not relieved, we are not righted. We have not done justice to one another, and therefore God suffers our enemies to deal thus unjustly with us, and we are as far as ever from being restored to our right and recovering our property again. Oppression is near us, and judgment is far from us. Our enemies are far from giving our case its due consideration, but still hurry us on with the violence of their oppressions, and justice does not overtake us, to rescue us out of their hands." 2. Herein their expectations were sadly disappointed, which made their case the more sad: "We *wait for light* as those that wait for the morning, but *behold obscurity;* we cannot discern the least dawning of the day of our deliverance. We *look for judgment, but there is none* (v. 11); neither God nor man appears for our succour; we look for salvation, because God (we think) has promised it, and we have prayed for it with fasting; we look for it as for brightness, but it is far off from us, as far off as ever for aught we can perceive, and still *we walk in darkness;* and the higher our expectations have been raised the sorer is the disappointment." 3. They were quite at a loss what to do to help themselves and were at their wits' end (v. 10): *"We grope for the wall like the blind;* we see no way open for our relief, nor know which way to expect it, or what to do in order to it." If we shut our eyes against the light of divine truth, it is just with God to hide from our eyes the things that belong to our peace; and, if we use not our eyes as we should, it is just with him to let us be as if we had no eyes. Those that will not see their duty shall not see their interest. Those whom God has given up to a judicial blindness are strangely infatuated; they stumble at noon-day as in the night; they see not either those dangers, or those advantages, which all about them see. *Quos Deus vult perdere, eos dementat — God infatuates those whom he means to destroy.* Those that love darkness rather than light shall have their doom accordingly. 4. They sunk into despair and were quite overwhelmed with grief, the marks of which appeared in every man's countenance; they grew melancholy upon it, shunned conversation, and affected solitude: *We are in desolate places as dead men.* The state of the Jews in Babylon is represented by *dead and dry bones* (Eze. 37:12) and the explanation of the comparison there (*v.* 11) explains this text: *Our hope is lost; we are cut off for our parts.* In this despair the sorrow and anguish of some were loud and noisy: *We roar like bears;* the sorrow of others was silent, and preyed more upon their spirits: *"We mourn sore like doves,* like doves of the valleys; we mourn both *for our iniquities* (Eze. 7:16) and *for our calamities."* Thus they owned that *the hand of the Lord had gone out against them.*

II. They acknowledge that they had provoked God thus to contend with them, that he had done right, for they had done wickedly, *v.* 12–15. 1. They owned that they had sinned, and that to this day they were in a great trespass, as Ezra speaks (Ezra 10:10): *"Our transgressions are with us;* the guilt of them is upon us, the power of them prevails among us, we are not yet reformed, nor have we parted with our sins, though they have done so much mischief. Nay, *our transgressions are multiplied;* they are more numerous and more heinous than they have been formerly. Look which way we will, we cannot look off them; all places, all orders and degrees of men, are infected. The sense of our transgression is with us, as David said, *My sin is ever before me;* it is too plain to be denied or concealed, too bad to be excused or palliated. God is a witness to them: *They are multiplied before thee,* in thy sight, under thy eye. We are witnesses against ourselves: *As for our iniquities, we know them,* though we may have foolishly endeavoured to cover them. Nay, they themselves are witnesses: *Our sins* stare us in the face and *testify against us,* so many have they been and so deeply aggravated." 2. They owned the great evil and malignity of sin, of their sin; it is *transgressing and lying against the Lord, v.* 13. The sins of those that profess themselves God's people, and bear his name, are upon *this* account worse than the sins of others, that in transgressing they *lie against the Lord,* they falsely accuse him, they misrepresent and belie him, as if he had dealt hardly and unfairly with them; or they perfidiously break covenant with him and falsify their most sacred and solemn engagements to him, which is *lying against him: it is departing away from our God,* to whom we are bound as our God and to whom we ought to cleave with purpose of heart; from him we have departed, as the rebellious subject from his allegiance to his rightful prince, and the adulterous wife from the guide of her youth and the covenant of her God. 3. They owned that there was a general decay of moral honesty; and it is not strange that those who were false to their God were unfaithful to one another. They *spoke oppression,* declared openly for that, though it was a revolt from their God and a revolt from the truth, by the sacred bonds of which we should always be tied and held fast. They *conceived and uttered words of falsehood.* Many ill thing is conceived in the mind, yet is prudently stifled there, and not suffered to go any further; but these sinners were so impudent, so daring, that whatever wickedness they conceived, they gave it an *imprimatur — a sanction,* and made no difficulty of publishing it. To think an ill thing is bad, but to say it is much worse. Many a word of falsehood is uttered in haste, for want of consideration; but these were conceived and uttered, were uttered-deliberately and of malice prepense. They were words of falsehood, and yet they are said to be uttered *from the heart,* because, though they differed from the real sentiments of the heart and therefore were words of falsehood, yet they agreed with the malice and wickedness of the heart, and were the natural language of that; it was a *double heart,* Ps. 12:2. Those who by the grace of God kept themselves free from these enormous crimes yet put themselves into the confession of sin, because members of that nation which was generally thus corrupted. 4. They owned that that was not done which might have been done to reform the land and to amend what was amiss, *v.* 14. "*Judgment,* that should go forward,

and bear down the opposition that is made to it, that should run in its course like a river, like a mighty stream, *is turned away backward,* a contrary course. The administration of justice has become but a cover to the greatest injustice. Judgment, that should check the proceedings of fraud and violence, is driven back, and so they go on triumphantly. *Justice stands afar off,* even from our courts of judicature, which are so crowded with the patrons of oppression that *equity cannot enter,* cannot have admission into the court, cannot be heard, or at least will not be heeded. Equity enters not into the unrighteous decrees which they decree, *ch.* 10:1. *Truth is fallen in the street,* and there she may lie to be trampled upon by every foot of pride, and she has never a friend that will lend a hand to help her up; *yea, truth fails* in common conversation, and in dealings between man and man, so that one knows not whom to believe nor whom to trust." 5. They owned that there was a prevailing enmity in men's minds to those that were good: *He that does evil goes unpunished,* but *he that departs from evil makes himself a prey* to those beasts of prey that were before described. It is crime enough with them for a man not to do as they do, and they treat *him* as an enemy who will not partake with them in their wickedness. *He that departs from evil is accounted mad;* so the margin reads. Sober singularity is branded as folly, and he is thought next door to a madman who swims against the stream that runs so strongly. 6. They owned that all this could not but be very displeasing to the God of heaven. The evil was done in his sight. They knew very well, though they were not willing to acknowledge it, that the Lord saw it; though it was done secretly, and gilded over with specious pretences, yet it could not be concealed from his all-seeing eye. All the wickedness that is in the world is naked and open before the eyes of God; and, as he is of quicker eyes than not to see iniquity, so he is of purer eyes than to behold it with the least approbation or allowance. *He saw it, and it displeased him,* though it was among his own professing people that he saw it. It was evil in his eyes; he saw the sinfulness of all this sin, and that which was most offensive to him was *that there was no judgment,* no reformation; had he seen any signs of repentance, though the sin displeased him, he would soon have been reconciled to the sinners upon their returning from their evil way. *Then* the sin of a nation becomes national, and brings public judgments, when it is not restrained by public justice.

Verses 16–21

How sin abounded we have read, to our great amazement, in the former part of the chapter; how grace does much more abound we read in these verses. And, as sin took occasion from the commandment to become more exceedingly sinful, so grace took occasion from the transgression of the commandment to appear more exceedingly gracious. Observe,

I. Why God wrought salvation for this provoking people, notwithstanding their provocations. It was purely for his own name's sake; because there was nothing in them either to bring it about, or to induce him to bring it about for them, no merit to deserve it, no might to effect it, he would do it himself, would be exalted in his own strength, for his own glory.

1. He took notice of their weakness and wickedness: *He saw that there was no man* that would do any thing for the support of the bleeding cause of religion and virtue among them, not a man that would execute judgment (Jer. 5:1), that would bestir himself in a work of reformation; those that complained of the badness of the times had not zeal and courage enough to appear and act against it; there was a universal corruption of manners, and nothing done to stem the tide; most were wicked, and those that were not so were yet weak, and durst not attempt any thing in opposition to the wickedness of the wicked. *There was no intercessor,* either none to intercede with God, to stand in the gap by prayer to turn away his wrath (it would have pleased him to be thus met, and he wondered that he was not), or, rather, none to interpose for the support of justice and truth, which were trampled upon and run down (*v.* 14), no advocate to speak a good word for those who were made a prey of because they kept their integrity, *v.* 15. They complained that God did not appear for them (*ch.* 58:3); but God with much more reason com-

plains that they did nothing for themselves, intimating how ready he would have been to do them good if he had found among them the least motion towards a reformation.

2. He engaged his own strength and righteousness for them. They shall be saved, notwithstanding all this; and, (1.) Because they have no strength of their own, nor any active men that will set to it in good earnest to redress the grievances either of their iniquities or of their calamities, therefore *his own arm shall bring salvation to him,* to his people, or to him whom he would raise up to be the deliverer, Christ, the power of God and arm of the Lord, that man of his right hand whom he made strong for himself. The work of reformation (that is the first and principal article of the salvation) shall be wrought by the immediate influences of the divine grace on men's consciences. Since magistrates and societies for reformation fail of doing their part, one will not do justice nor the other call for it, God will let them know that he can do it without them when his time shall come thus to prepare his people for mercy, and then the work of deliverance shall be wrought by the immediate operations of the divine Providence on men's affections and affairs. When God stirred up the spirit of Cyrus, and brought his people out of Babylon, *not by might, nor by power, but by the Spirit of the Lord of hosts,* then his own arm, which is never shortened, brought salvation. (2.) Because they have no righteousness of their own to merit these favours, and to which God might have an eye in working for them, therefore *his own righteousness sustained him* and bore him out in it. Divine justice, which by their sins they had armed against them, through grace appears for them. Though they can expect no favour as due to them, yet he will be just to himself, to his own purpose and promise, and covenant with his people: he will, in righteousness, punish the enemies of his people; see Deu. 9:5. *Not for thy righteousness, but for the wickedness of these nations* they are driven out. In our redemption by Christ, since we had no righteousness of our own to produce, on which God might proceed in favour to us, he brought in a righteousness by the merit and meditation of his own Son (it is called *the righteousness which is of God by faith,* Phil. 3:9), and this righteousness sustained him, and bore him out in all his favours to us, notwithstanding our provocations. *He put on righteousness as a breast-plate,* securing his own honour, as a breast-plate does the vitals, in all his proceedings, by the justice and equity of them; and then he put *a helmet of salvation upon his head;* so sure is he to effect the salvation he intends that he takes salvation itself for his helmet, which therefore must needs be impenetrable, and in which he appears very illustrious, formidable in the eyes of his enemies and amiable in the eyes of his friends. When righteousness is his coat of arms, salvation is his crest. In allusion to this, among the pieces of a Christian's armour we find *the breast-plate of righteousness,* and for a helmet *the hope of salvation* (Eph. 6:14–17; 1 Th. 5:8), and it is called *the armour of God,* because he wore it first and so fitted it for us. (3.) Because they have no spirit or zeal to do any thing for themselves, God will put *on the garments of vengeance for clothing, and clothe himself with zeal as a cloak;* he will make his justice upon the enemies of his church and people, and his jealousy for his own glory and the honour of religion and virtue among men, to appear evident and conspicuous in the eye of the world; and in these he will show himself great, as a man shows himself in his rich attire or in the distinguishing habit of his office. If men be not zealous against sin, God will, and will take vengeance on it for all the injury it has done to his honour and his people's welfare; and this was the business of Christ in the world, to take away sin and be revenged on it.

II. What the salvation is that shall be wrought out by the righteousness and strength of God himself.

1. There shall be a present temporal salvation wrought out for the Jews in Babylon, or elsewhere in distress and captivity. This is promised (*v.* 18, 19) as a type of something further. When God's time shall come he will do his own work, though those fail that should forward it. It is here promised, (1.) That God will reckon with his enemies and will render to them according to their deeds, to the enemies of his people abroad, that have oppressed them, to the enemies of justice and truth at home, that have oppressed them, for they also are God's enemies; and, when the day of vengeance shall have come, he will deal with

both as they have deserved, *according to retribution* (so the word is), the law of retributions (Rev. 13:10), or *according to former retributions;* as he has rendered to his enemies formerly, accordingly he will now repay, *fury to his adversaries, recompence to his enemies;* his fury shall not exceed the rules of justice, as men's fury commonly does. Even *to the islands,* that lie most remote, if they have appeared against him, *he will repay recompence;* for *his hand shall find out all his enemies* (Ps. 21:8), and his arrows reach them. Though God's people have behaved so ill that they do not deserve to be delivered, yet his enemies behave so much worse that they do deserve to be destroyed. (2.) That, whatever attempts the enemies of God's people may afterwards make upon them to disturb their peace, they shall be baffled and brought to nought: *When the enemy shall come in like a flood,* like a high spring-tide, or a landflood, which threaten to bear down all before them without control, then *the Spirit of the Lord* by some secret undiscerned power *shall lift up a standard against him,* and so (as the margin reads it) *put him to flight.* He that has delivered will still deliver. When God's people are weak and helpless, and have no standard to lift up against the invading power, God will *give a banner to those that fear him* (Ps. 60:4), will by his Spirit lift up a standard, which will draw multitudes together to appear on the church's behalf. Some read it, *He shall come* (the name of the Lord, and his glory, before foreseen of the Messiah promised) *like a straight river, the Spirit of the Lord lifting him up for an ensign.* Christ by the preaching of his gospel shall cover the earth with the knowledge of God as with the waters of a flood, the *Spirit of the Lord* setting up Christ as a *standard* to the *Gentiles, ch.* 11:10. (3.) That all this should redound to the glory of God and the advancement of religion in the world (*v.* 19): *So shall they fear the name of the Lord and his glory* in all nations that lie eastward or westward. The deliverance of the Jews out of captivity, and the destruction brought on their oppressors, would awaken multitudes to enquire concerning the God of Israel, and induce them to serve and worship him and enlist themselves under the standard which the Spirit of the Lord shall lift up. God's appearances for his church shall occasion the accession of many to it. This had its full accomplishment in gospel times, when many came *from the east and west,* to fill up the places of *the children of the kingdom* that were *cast out,* when there were set up eastern and western churches, Mt. 8:11.

2. There shall be a more glorious salvation wrought out by the Messiah in the fulness of time, which salvation all the prophets, upon all occasions, had in view. We have here the two great promises relating to that salvation: —

(1.) That the Son of God shall come to us to be our Redeemer (*v.* 20): *Thy Redeemer shall come;* it is applied to Christ, Rom. 9:26. *There shall come the deliverer.* The coming of Christ as the Redeemer is the summary of all the promises both of the Old and New Testament, and this was the redemption in Jerusalem which the believing Jews looked for, Lu. 2:38. Christ is our *Goël,* our next kinsman, that redeems both the person and the estate of the poor debtor. Observe, [1.] The place where this Redeemer shall appear: He *shall come to Zion,* for there, on that holy hill, the Lord would set him up as his King, Ps. 2:6. In Zion the chief corner-stone was to be laid, 1 Pt. 2:6. He came to his temple there, Mal. 3:1. There salvation was to be placed (*ch.* 46:13), for thence the law was to go forth, *ch.* 2:3. Zion was a type of the gospel church, for which the Redeemer acts in all his appearances: *The Redeemer shall come for the sake of Zion;* so the Septuagint reads it. [2.] The persons that shall have the comfort of the Redeemer's coming, that shall then lift up their heads, knowing that their redemption draws nigh. He shall come *to those that turn from the ungodliness in Jacob,* to those that are in Jacob, to the praying seed of Jacob, in answer to their prayers; yet not to all that are in Jacob, that are within the pale of the visible church, but to those only that turn from transgression, that repent, and reform, and forsake those sins which Christ came to redeem them from. The sinners in Zion will fare never the better for the Redeemer's coming to Zion if they go on still in their trespasses.

(2.) That the Spirit of God shall come to us to be our sanctifier, *v.* 21. In the Redeemer there was a new covenant made with us a covenant of promises; and this is the great and comprehensive promise of that covenant, that God will give and continue his word and Spirit to his church and people throughout all generations. God's giving the *Spirit to those that ask him* includes the giving of them all *good things,* Lu. 11:13; Mt. 7:11. This covenant is here said to *be made with them,* that is, with those that turn from transgression; for those that cease to do evil shall be taught to do well. But the promise is made to a single person — *My Spirit that is upon thee,* being directed either, [1.] To Christ as the head of the church, who received that he might give. The Spirit promised to the church was first upon him, and from his head that precious ointment descended to the skirts of his garments; and the word of the gospel was first put into his mouth; for *it began to be spoken by the Lord.* And all believers are his seed, in whom he prolongs his days, *ch.* 53:10. Or, [2.] To the church; and so it is a promise of the continuance and perpetuity of the church in the world to the end of time, parallel to those promises that the throne and seed of Christ shall endure for ever, Ps. 89:29, 36; 22:30. Observe, *First,* How the church shall be kept up, in a succession, as the world of mankind is kept up, by the seed and the seed's seed. As one generation passes away another generation shall come. *Instead of the fathers shall be the children. Secondly,* How long it shall be kept up — *henceforth and for ever,* always, even *unto the end of the world;* for, the world being left to stand for the sake of the church, we may be sure that as long as it does stand Christ will have a church in it, though no always visible. *Thirdly,* By what means it shall be kept up; by the constant residence of the word and Spirit in it. 1. The Spirit that was upon Christ shall always continue in the hearts of the faithful; there shall be some in every age on whom he shall work, and in whom he shall dwell, and thus the Comforter shall abide with the church for ever, Jn. 14:16. 2. The word of Christ shall always continue in the mouths of the faithful; there shall be some in every age who, *believing with the heart* unto righteousness, shall *with the tongue make confession unto salvation.* The word shall never depart out of the mouth of the church; for there shall still be a seed to speak Christ's holy language and profess his holy religion. Observe, The Spirit and the word go together, and by them the church is kept up. For the word in the mouths of our ministers, nay, the word in our own mouths, will not profit us, unless the Spirit work with the word, and give us an understanding. But the Spirit does his work by the word and in concurrence with it; and whatever is pretended to be a dictate of the Spirit must be tried by the scriptures. On these foundations the church is built, stands firmly, and shall stand for ever, Christ himself being the chief corner-stone.

CHAPTER 60

This whole chapter is all to the same purport, all in the same strain; it is a part of God's covenant with his church, which is spoken of in the last verse of the foregoing chapter, and the blessings here promised are the fruits of the word and Spirit there promised. The long continuance of the church, even unto the utmost ages of time, was there promised, and here the large extent of the church, even unto the utmost regions of the earth; and both these tend to the honour of the Redeemer. It is here promised, I. That the church shall be enlightened and shone upon (*v.* 1, 2). II. That it shall be enlarged and great additions made to it, to join in the service of God (*v.* 3–8). III. That the new converts shall be greatly serviceable to the church and to the interests of it (*v.* 9–13). IV. That the church shall be in great honour and reputation among men (*v.* 14–16). V. That it shall enjoy a profound peace and tranquility (*v.* 17, 18). VI. That, the members of it being all righteous, the glory and joy of it shall be everlasting (*v.* 19–22). Now this has some reference to the peaceable and prosperous condition which the Jews were sometimes in after their return out of captivity into their own land; but it certainly looks further, and was to have its full accomplishment in the kingdom of the Messiah, the enlargement of that kingdom by the bringing in of the Gentiles into it, and the spiritual blessings in heavenly things by Christ Jesus with which it should be enriched, and all these earnests of eternal joy and glory.

Verses 1–8

It is here promised that the gospel temple shall be very lightsome and very large.

I. It shall be very lightsome: *Thy light has come.* When the Jews returned out of captivity they had *light and gladness, and joy and honour;* they then were made to *know the Lord* and to *rejoice in his great goodness;* and upon both accounts their light came. When the Redeemer came to Zion he brought light with him, he himself came to be a light. Now observe, 1. What this light is, and whence it springs: *The Lord shall arise upon thee* (*v.* 2), *the glory of the Lord* (*v.* 1) *shall be seen upon thee.* God is the father and fountain of lights, and it is in his light that we shall see light. As far as we have the knowledge of God in us, and the favour of God towards us, our light has come. When God appears to us, and we have the comfort of his favour, then *the glory of the Lord rises upon us* as the morning light; when he appears for us, and we have the credit of his favour, when he shows us some token for good and proclaims his favour to us, then his glory is seen upon us, as it was upon Israel in the *pillar of cloud and fire.* When Christ arose as the sun of righteousness, and in him *the day-spring from on high visited us,* then *the glory of the Lord was* seen upon us, the glory *as of the first-begotten of the Father.* 2. What a foil there shall be to this light: *Darkness shall cover the earth;* but, though it be gross darkness, darkness that might be felt, like that of Egypt, that shall overspread the people, yet the church, like Goshen, shall have light at the same time. When the case of the nations that have not the gospel shall be very melancholy, those *dark corners of the earth* being *full of the habitations of cruelty* to poor souls, the state of the church shall be very pleasant. 3. What is the duty which the rising of this light calls for: *"Arise, shine;* not only receive this light, and" (as the margin reads it) *"be enlightened by it,* but reflect this light; *arise and shine* with rays borrowed from it." The children of light ought to shine as lights in the world. If God's glory be seen upon us to our honour, we ought not only with our lips, but in our lives, to return the praise of it *to his honour,* Mt. 5:16; Phil. 2:15.

II. It shall be very large. When the Jews were settled again in their own land, after their captivity, many of the people of the land joined themselves to them; but it does not appear that there ever was any such numerous accession to them as would answer the fulness of this prophecy; and therefore we must conclude that this looks further, to the bringing of the Gentiles into the gospel church, not their flocking to one particular place, though under that type it is here described. There is no place now that is the centre of the church's unity; but the promise respects their flocking to Christ, and coming by faith, and hope, and holy love, into that society which is incorporated by the charter of his gospel, and of the unity of which he only is the centre — that family which is named from him, Eph. 3:15. The gospel church is expressly called *Zion* and *Jerusalem,* and under that notion all believers are said to *come* to it (Heb. 12:22. *You have come unto Mount Zion, to the city of the living God, the heavenly Jerusalem),* which serves for a key to this prophecy, Eph. 2:19. Observe,

1. What shall invite such multitudes to the church: "They shall *come to thy light and to the brightness of thy rising, v.* 3. They shall be allured to join themselves to thee," (1.) "By the light that shines upon thee," the light of the glorious gospel, which the churches hold forth, in consequence of which they are called *golden candlesticks.* This light which discovers so much of God and his good will to man, by which life and immortality are brought to light, this shall invite all the serious well-affected part of mankind to come and join themselves to the church, that they may have the benefit of this light to inform them concerning truth and duty. (2.) "By the light with which thou shinest." The purity and love of the primitive Christians, their heavenly-mindedness, contempt of the world, and patient sufferings, were the brightness of the church's rising, which drew many into it. The beauty of holiness was the powerful attractive by which Christ had a willing people brought to him in *the day of his power,* Ps. 110:3.

2. What multitudes shall come to the church. Great numbers *shall come, Gentiles* (or *nations*) *of those that are saved,* as it is expressed with allusion to this, Rev. 21:24. *Nations* shall be *discipled* (Mt. 28:19), and even kings, men of figure, power, and influence, shall be *added to the church.* They come from all parts (*v.* 4): *Lift up thy eyes round about, and see* them coming, *devout men out of every nation under heaven,* Acts 2:5. See how *white the fields are already to the harvest,* Jn. 4:35. See them coming in a body, as one man, and with one consent: They *gather themselves together,* that they may strengthen one another's hands, and encourage one another. *Come, and let us go, ch.* 2:3. "They come from the remotest parts: *They come to thee from far,* having *heard the report* of thee, as the queen of Sheba, or *seen thy star in the east,* as the wise men, and they will not be discouraged by the length of the journey from coming to thee. There shall come some of both sexes. Sons and daughters shall come in the most

dutiful manner, as thy sons and thy daughters, resolved to be of thy family, to submit to the laws of thy family and put themselves under the tuition of it. They shall come *to be nursed at thy side,* to have their education with thee from their cradle." The church's children must be nursed at her side, not sent out to be nursed among strangers; there, where alone the unadulterated milk of the word is to be had, must the church's new-born babes be nursed, *that they may grow thereby,* 1 Pt. 2:1, 2. Those that would enjoy the dignities and privileges of Christ's family must submit to the discipline of it.

3. What they shall bring with them and what advantage shall accrue to the church by their accession to it. Those that are brought into the church by the grace of God will be sure to bring all they are worth in with them, which with themselves they will devote to the honour and service of God and do good with in their places. (1.) The merchants shall write *holiness to the Lord* upon their merchandise and their hire, as *ch.* 23:18. *"The abundance of the sea,* either the wealth that is fetched out of the sea (the fish, the pearls) or that which is imported by sea, *shall* all *be converted to thee* and to thy use." The wealth of the rich merchants shall be laid out in works of piety and charity. (2.) The mighty men of the nations shall employ their might in the service of the church: *"The forces,* or troops, *of the Gentiles shall come unto thee,* to guard thy coasts, strengthen thy interests, and, if occasion be, to fight thy battles." The forces of the Gentiles had often been against the church, but now they shall be for it; for as God, when he pleases, can, and, when we please him, will, make even *our enemies to be at peace with us* (Prov. 16:7), so, when Christ overcomes the strong man armed, he divides his spoils, and makes that to serve his interests which had been used against them, Lu. 11:22. (3.) The wealth imported by land-carriage, as well as that by sea, shall be made use of in the service of God and the church (*v.* 6): *The camels and dromedaries that bring gold and incense* (gold to make the golden altar of and incense and sweet perfumes to burn upon it), *those of Midian and Sheba,* shall bring the richest commodities of their country, not to trade with, but to honour God with, and not in small quantities, but camel-loads of them. This was in part fulfilled when the *wise men of the east* (perhaps some of the countries here mentioned), drawn by the brightness of the star, came to Christ, and presented to him treasures of *gold, frankincense, and myrrh,* Mt. 2:11. (4.) Great numbers of sacrifices shall be brought to God's altar, acceptable sacrifices, and, though brought by Gentiles, they shall find acceptance, *v.* 7. *Kedar* was famous for flocks, and probably the fattest rams were those of *Nebaioth;* these shall come up with acceptance on God's altar. God must be served and honoured with what we have, according as he has blessed us, and with the best we have. This was fulfilled when by the decree of Darius the governors beyond the rivers (perhaps of some of these countries) were ordered to furnish the temple at Jerusalem *with bullocks, rams, and lambs, for the burnt-offering of the God of heaven,* Ezra 6:9. It had a further accomplishment, and we trust will have, in the bringing in of the fulness of the Gentiles to the church, which is called the *sacrificing* or *offering up of the Gentiles* unto God, Rom. 15:16. The flocks and rams are precious souls; for they are said to minister to the church, and to come up as living sacrifices, presenting themselves to God by a *reasonable service* on *his altar,* Rom. 12:1.

4. How God shall be honoured by the increase of the church and the accession of such numbers to it. (1.) They shall intend the honour of God's name in it. When they bring their gold and incense it shall not be to show the riches of their country, nor to gain applause to themselves for piety and devotion, but to *show forth the praises of the Lord, v.* 6. Our greatest services and gifts to the church are not acceptable further than we have an eye to the glory of God in them. And this must be our business in our attendance on public ordinances, to *give unto the Lord the glory due to his name;* for *therefore,* as these here, we are called out of darkness into light, that we should *show forth the praises of him that called us,* 1 Pt. 2:9. (2.) God will advance the honour of his own name by it; so he has said (*v.* 7): *I will glorify the house of my glory.* The church is the house of God's glory, where he manifests his glory to his people and receives that homage by which they do honour to him. And it is for the glory of this house, and of him that keeps house there, both that the Gentiles shall bring their offerings to it and that they shall be accepted therein.

5. How the church shall herself be affected with this increase of her numbers, *v.* 5. (1.) She shall be in a transport of joy upon this account: *"Thou shalt see* and *flow together"* (or flow to and fro), "as in a pleasing agitation about it, surprised at it, but extremely glad of it." (2.) There shall be a mixture of fear with this joy: *"Thy heart shall fear,* doubting whether it be lawful to *go in to the uncircumcised* and *eat with them."* Peter was so impressed with this fear that he needed a vision and voice from heaven to help him over it, Acts 10:28. But, (3.) "When this fear is conquered thy heart shall be enlarged in holy love, so enlarged that thou shalt have room in it for all the Gentile converts; thou shalt not have such a narrow soul as thou hast had nor affections so confined within the Jewish pale." When God intends the beauty and prosperity of his church he gives this largeness of heart and an extensive charity. (4.) These converts flocking to the church shall be greatly admired (*v.* 8): *Who are these that fly as a cloud?* Observe, [1.] How the conversion of souls is here described. It is flying to Christ and to his church, for thither we are directed; it is flying like a cloud, though in great multitudes, so as to overspread the heavens, yet with great unanimity, all as one cloud. They shall come with speed, as a cloud flying on the wings of the wind, and come openly, and in the view of all, *their* very *enemies beholding them* (Rev. 11:12), and yet not able to hinder them. They shall *fly as doves to their windows,* in great flights, many together; they fly on the wings of the harmless dove, which flies low, denoting their innocency and humility. They fly to Christ, to the church, to the word and ordinances, as doves, by instinct, to their own windows, to their own home; thither they fly for refuge and shelter when they are pursued by the birds of prey, and thither they fly for rest when they have been wandering and are weary, as Noah's dove to the ark. [2.] How the conversion of souls is here admired. It is spoken of with wonder and pleasure: *Who are these?* We have reason to wonder that so many flock to Christ: when we see them all together we shall wonder whence they all came. And we have reason to admire with pleasure and affection those that do flock to him: *Who are these?* How excellent, how amiable are they! What a pleasant sight is it to see poor souls hastening to Christ, with a full resolution to abide with him!

Verses 9–14

The promises made to the church in the foregoing verses are here repeated, ratified, and enlarged upon, designed still for the comfort and encouragement of the Jews after their return out of captivity, but certainly looking further, to the enlargement and advancement of the gospel church and the abundance of spiritual blessings with which it shall be enriched.

I. God will be very gracious and propitious to them. We must begin with that promise, because thence all the rest take rise. The sanctuary that was desolate begins to be repaired when God *causes his face to shine upon it,* Dan. 9:17. All the favour that the people of God find with men is owing to the light of God's countenance and his favour to them (*v.* 10): "All shall now make court to thee, *for in my wrath I smote thee,* while thou wast in captivity" (and the sufferings of the church, especially by its corruptions, decays, and divisions, against which these promises will be its relief, are sad tokens of God's displeasure), "But now *in my favour have I had mercy on thee,* and therefore have all this mercy in store for thee."

II. Many shall be brought into the church, even from far countries (*v.* 9): *Surely the isles shall wait for me,* shall welcome the gospel, and shall attend God with their praises for it and their ready subjection to it. *The ships of Tarshish,* transport-ships, shall lie ready to carry members from far distant regions to the church, or (which is equivalent) to carry the ministers of the church to remote parts, to preach the gospel and to bring in souls to join themselves to the Lord. Observe, 1. Who are brought — *thy sons,* that is, such as are designed to be so, those *children of God that are scattered abroad,* Jn. 11:52. 2. What they shall bring with them. They live at such a distance that they cannot bring their flocks and their rams; but, like those who lived remote from Jerusalem (who, when they came up to worship at the feast, because they could not bring their tithes in kind, turned them into money), they shall *bring their silver and gold with them.* Note, When we give up ourselves to God we must with ourselves give up all we have to him. If we honour him with our spirits, we shall honour him with our substance. 3. To whom they shall devote and dedicate themselves and all they are worth — *to the name of the Lord thy God,* to God as the Lord of all and the church's God and King, even to the *Holy One of Israel* (whom Israel worships as a Holy One, in the beauty of holiness), *because he has glorified thee.* Note, The honour God puts upon his church and people should not only engage us to honour them, but invite us to join ourselves to them. *We will go with you, for God is with you,* Zec. 8:23.

III. Those that come into the church shall be welcome; for so spacious is the holy city that though, *Lord, it is done as thou hast commanded, yet still there is room. "Therefore thy gates shall be open continually* (*v.* 11), not only because thou hast no reason to fear thy enemies, but because thou hast reason to expect thy friends." It is usual with us to leave our doors open, or leave some one ready to open them, all night, if we look for a child or a guest to come in late. Note, Christ is always ready to entertain those that come to him, is never out of the way, nor can they ever come unseasonably; the gate of mercy is always open, night and day, or shall soon be opened to those that knock. Ministers, the door-keepers, must be always ready to admit those that offer themselves to the Lord. God not only keeps a good house in his church, but he keeps open house, that at any time, by the preaching of the word, *in season and out of season, the forces of the Gentiles,* and the kings or commanders of those forces, *may be brought* into the church. *Lift up your heads, O you gates!* and let such welcome guests as these come in.

IV. All that are about the church shall be made in some way or other serviceable to it. Though dominion is far from being founded in men's grace, it is founded in God's; and he that made the inferior creatures useful to man will make the nations of men useful to the church. The earth helped the woman. *All things are for your sakes.* So here (*v.* 10), "Even *the sons of strangers,* that have neither knowledge of thee nor kindness for thee, that have always been *aliens to the commonwealth of Israel,* even they *shall build up thy wall, and their kings shall* in that and other things *ministers unto thee* and not think it any disparagement to them to do so." This was fulfilled when the king of Persia, and the governors of the provinces by his order, were aiding and assisting Nehemiah in building the wall about Jerusalem. Rather than Jerusalem's walls shall lie still in ruins, the *sons of the stranger* shall be raised up to build them. Even those that do not belong to the church may be a protection to it. And the greatest of men should not think it below them to minister to the church, but rejoice that they are in a capacity, and have a heart, to do it any service. Nay, it is the duty of all to do what they can in their places to advance the interests of God's kingdom among men; it is at their peril if they do not; for (*v.* 12), *The nation and kingdom that will not serve thee shall perish;* not that they must perish by the sword or by human anathemas, or as if this gave any countenance to the using of external force for the propagating of the gospel, or as if men might be compelled by penalties and punishments to come into the church; by no means. But those who will not by faith submit to Jesus Christ, the King of the church, and serve him, shall perish eternally, Ps. 2:12. Those that will not be subject to Christ's golden sceptre, to the government of his word and Spirit, that will not be brought under, or kept in, by the discipline of his family, shall be broken in pieces by his iron rod. *Bring them forth and slay them before me,* Lu. 19:27. Nations of such shall be utterly and eternally wasted, when Christ shall come to take vengeance on those that *obey not his gospel,* 2 Th. 1:8.

V. There shall be abundance of beauty added to the ordinances of divine worship (*v.* 13): *The glory of Lebanon,* the strong and stately cedars that grow there, *shall come unto thee,* as of old to Solomon, when he built the temple (2 Chr. 2:16), and with them shall be brought other timber, proper for the carved work thereof, which the enemy had broken down, Ps. 74:5, 6. The temple, the *place of God's sanctuary,* shall be not only rebuilt, but beautified. It is the *place of his feet,* where he rests and resides,

Eze. 43:7. The ark is called his *footstool,* because it was under the mercy-seat, Ps. 132:7. This he will make glorious in the eyes of his people and of all their neighbours. *The glory of the latter house,* to which this refers, though in many instances inferior, was yet really *greater than the glory of the former,* because Christ came to that temple, Mal. 3:1. It was likewise *adorned with goodly stones and gifts* (Lu. 21:5), to which this promise may have some reference; yet so slightly did Christ speak of them there that we must suppose it to have its full accomplishment in the beauties of holiness, and the graces and comforts of the Spirit, with which gospel ordinances are adorned and enriched.

VI. The church shall appear truly great and honourable, *v.* 14. The people of the Jews, after their return out of captivity, by degrees became more considerable, and made a better figure than one would have expected, after they had been so much reduced, and than any of the other nations recovered that had been in like manner humbled by the Chaldeans. It is probable that many of those who had oppressed them in Babylon, when they were themselves driven out by the Persians, made their court to the Jews for shelter and supply and were willing to scrape acquaintance with them. This prophecy is further fulfilled when those that have been enemies to the church are wrought upon by the grace of God to see their error, and come, and join themselves to it: *"The sons of those that afflicted thee,* if not they themselves, yet their children, shall crouch to thee, shall beg pardon for their folly and beg an interest in thy favour and admission into thy family," 1 Sa. 2:36. A promise like this is made to the church of Philadelphia, Rev. 3:9. And it is intended to be, 1. A mortification to the proud oppressors of the church, that have afflicted her, and despised her, and taken a pleasure in doing so; they shall be brought down; their spirits shall be broken, and their condition shall be so mean and miserable that they shall be glad to be obliged to those whom they have most studied to disoblige. Note, Sooner or later God will pour contempt upon those that put contempt upon his people. 2. An exaltation to the poor oppressed ones of the church; and this is the honour that shall be done to them, they shall have an opportunity of doing good to those who have done evil to them and saving those alive who have afflicted and despised them. It is a pleasure to a good man, and he accounts it an honour, to show mercy to those with whom he has found no mercy. Yet this is not all. "They shall not only become suppliants to thee for their own interest, but they shall give honour to thee: *They shall call thee, The city of the Lord;* they shall at length be convinced that thou art a favourite of heaven, and the particular care of the divine providence." That city is truly great and honourable, it is strong, it is rich, it is safe, it is beautiful, it is the most desirable place that can be to live in, which is *the city of the Lord,* which he owns, in which he dwells, in which religion is uppermost. Such a one is Zion; it is the place which God has chosen to put his name there; it is *the Zion of the Holy One of Israel;* therefore, we may be sure, it is a holy city, else the Holy One of Israel would never be called the patron of it.

Verses 15–22

The happy and glorious state of the church is here further foretold, referring principally and ultimately to the Christian church and the spiritual peace of that, but under the type of that little gleam of outward peace which the Jews sometimes enjoyed after their return out of captivity. This is here spoken of,

I. As compared with what it had been. *This* made her peace and honour the more pleasant, that her condition had been much otherwise.

1. She had been despised, but now she should be honoured, *v.* 15, 16. Jerusalem had been forsaken and hated, abandoned by her friends, abhorred by her enemies; no man went through that desolate city, but declined it as a rueful spectacle; it was an *astonishment and a hissing.* But now it shall be made an eternal excellency, being reformed from idolatry and having recovered the tokens of God's favour, and it shall be *the joy* of good people for *many generations.* Yet considering how short Jerusalem's excellency was, and how short it came of the vast compass of this promise, we must look for the full accomplishment of it in the perpetual excellencies of the gospel church, far exceeding those of the Old-Testament church, and the glorious privileges and advantages of the Christian religion, which are indeed the joy of many generations. Two things are here spoken of as her excellency and joy, in opposition to her having been forsaken and hated: — (1.) She shall find herself countenanced by her neighbours. The nations, and their kings, that are brought to embrace Christianity, shall lay themselves out for the good of the church, and maintain its interests with the tenderness and affection that the nurse shows to the child at her breasts (*v.* 16): *"Thou shalt suck the milk of the Gentiles,* not suck their blood (that is not the spirit of the gospel); thou *shalt suck the breast of kings,* who shall be to thee as nursing fathers." (2.) She shall find herself countenanced by her God: *"Thou shalt know that I the Lord am thy Saviour and thy Redeemer,* shalt know it by experience; for such a salvation, such a redemption, shall be wrought out for thee as plainly discovers itself to be the work of the Lord, the work of a mighty one, for it is a great salvation, of the *Mighty One of Jacob,* for it secures the welfare of all those that are Israelites indeed." They before knew the Lord to be their God; now they know him to be their Saviour, their Redeemer. Their Holy One now appears their Mighty One.

2. She had been impoverished, but now she shall be enriched, and every thing shall be changed for the better with her, *v.* 17. When those who were raised out of the dust are set among princes, instead of brass money in their purses they have bold, and instead of iron vessels in their houses they have silver ones, and other improvements agreeable: so much shall the spiritual glory of the New-Testament church exceed the external pomp and splendour of the Jewish economy, which had no glory in comparison with that which quite excels it, 2 Co. 3:10. When we had baptism in the room of circumcision, the Lord's supper in the room of the passover, and a gospel ministry in the room of a Levitical priesthood, we had gold instead of brass. Sin turned gold into brass when Rehoboam made brazen shields instead of the golden ones he had pawned; but God's favour, when that returns, will turn brass again into gold.

3. She had been oppressed by her own princes, which was sadly complained of, not only as her sin, but as her misery (*ch.* 59:14); but now all the grievances of that kind shall be redressed (*v.* 17): *"I will make thy officers peace;* men of peace shall be made officers, and shall be indeed justices, not patrons of injustice, and justices of peace, not instruments of trouble and vexation. They shall *be peace,* that is, they shall sincerely seek thy welfare and by their means thou shalt enjoy good." They shall be *peace,* for they shall be righteousness; and *then* the peace is as a river, when the righteousness is as the waves of the sea. Even *exactors,* whose business it is to demand the public tribute, though they be exact, must not be exacting, but must be just to the subject as well as to the prince, and, according to the instructions John Baptist gave to the publicans must *exact no more than is appointed them,* Lu. 3:13.

4. She had been insulted by her neighbours, invaded, spoiled, and plundered; but now it shall be so no more (*v.* 18): *"Violence shall no more be heard in thy land;* neither the threats and triumphs of those that do violence nor the outcries and complaints of those that suffer violence shall again be heard, but every man shall peaceably enjoy his own. There shall be no *wasting nor destruction,* either of persons of possessions, any where *within thy borders;* but *thy walls shall be called salvation* (they shall be safe, and means of safety to thee) *and thy gates shall be praise,* praise to thee (every one shall commend thee for the good condition they are kept in), and praise to thy God, *who strengthens the bars of thy gates,"* Ps. 147:13. When God's salvation is upon the walls it is fit that his praises should be in the gates, the places of concourse.

II. As completed in what it shall be. It should seem that in the close of this chapter we are directed to look further yet, as far forward as to the glory and happiness of heaven, under the type and figure of the flourishing state of the church on earth, which yet was never such as to come any thing near to what is here foretold; and several of the images and expressions here made use of we find in the description of the *new Jerusalem,* Rev. 21:23; 22:5. As the prophets sometimes insensibly pass from the blessings of the Jewish church to the spiritual blessings of the Christian church, which are eternal, so sometimes they rise from the church militant to the church triumphant, where, and where only, all the promised peace, and joy, and honour will be in perfection. 1. God shall be all in all in the happiness here promised; so he is always to true believers (*v.* 19): *The sun and the moon shall be no more thy light.* God's people, when they enjoy his favour, and walk in the light of his countenance, make little account of sun and moon, and the other lights of this world, but could walk comfortably in the light of the Lord though they should withdraw their shining. In heaven there shall be no occasion for sun or moon, for it is the inheritance of the saints in light, such light as will swallow up the light of the sun as easily as the sun does that of a candle. "Idolaters worshipped the sun and moon (which some have thought the most ancient and plausible idolatry); but these *shall be no more thy light,* shall no more be idolized, but the Lord shall be to thee a constant light, both day and night, in the night of adversity as well as in the day of prosperity." Those that make God their only light shall have him their all-sufficient light, their *sun and shield. Thy God shall be thy glory.* Note, God is the glory of those whose God he is and will be so to eternity. It is their glory that they have him for their God, and they glory in it; it is to them instead of beauty. God's people are, upon *this* account, an honourable people, that they have an interest in God as their sin covenant. 2. The happiness here promised shall know no change, period, or allay (*v.* 20): *"Thy sun shall no more go down,* but it shall be eternal day, eternal sunshine, with thee; that shall not be thy sun which is sometimes eclipsed, often clouded, and, though it shine ever so bright, ever so warm, will certainly set and leave thee in the dark, in the cold, in a few hours; but *he* shall be a sun, a fountain of light to thee, who is himself the *Father of all lights,* with whom there is *no variableness,* nor *shadow of turning,"* James 1:17. We read of the sun's standing still once, and not hasting to go down for the space of a day, and it was a glorious day, never was the like; but what was that to the day that shall never have a night? Or, if it had, it should be a light night; for *neither shall thy moon withdraw itself;* it shall never wane, shall never change, but be always at the full. The comforts and joys that are in heaven, the glories provided for the soul, as the light of the sun, and those prepared for the glorified body too, as the light of the moon, shall never know the least cessation or interruption; how should they when *the Lord shall* himself *be thy everlasting light* — a light which never wastes nor can ever be extinguished? *And the days of thy mourning shall be ended,* so as never to return; for *all tears shall be wiped away,* and the fountains of them, sin and affliction, dried up, so that *sorrow and sighing shall flee away* for ever. 3. Those that are entitled to this happiness, being duly prepared and qualified for it, shall never be put out of the possession of it (*v.* 21): *Thy people,* that shall inhabit this New Jerusalem, *shall all be righteous,* all justified by the righteousness of the Messiah, all sanctified by his Spirit; all that people, that Jerusalem, must be righteous, must have that *holiness without which no man shall see the Lord.* They are all righteous, for we know that *the unrighteous shall not inherit the kingdom of God.* There are no people on earth that are all righteous; there is a mixture of some bad in the best societies on this side heaven; but there are no mixtures there. They shall be *all righteous,* that is, they shall be entirely righteous; as there shall be none corrupt among them, so there shall be no corruption in them; the *spirits of just men* shall there be *made perfect.* And they shall be *all the righteous* together who shall replenish the New Jerusalem; it is called the *congregation of the righteous,* Ps. 1:5. And, because they are *all righteous,* therefore *they shall inherit the land for ever,* for nothing but sin can turn them out of it. The perfection of the saints' holiness secures the perpetuity of their happiness. 4. The glory of the church shall redound to the honour of the church's God: "They shall appear to be the *branch of my planting, the work of my hands,* and I will own them as such." It was by the grace of God that they were designed to this happiness; they are *the branch of his planting,* or of his plantations; he broke them off from the wild olive and grafted them into the good olive, transplanted them out of the field, when they were as tender branches, into his nursery, that, being now planted in his *garden on earth,* they might shortly be removed to his *paradise in heaven.* It was by his grace likewise that they were prepared and fitted for this happiness; they *are the work of his hands* (Eph. 2:10), are *wrought to the self-same thing,* 2 Co. 5:5. It is a work of time, and, when it shall be finished, will appear a work of wonder; and God will be glorified, who began it, and carried it on; for the Lord Jesus will then be *admired in all those that believe.* God will glorify himself in glorifying his chosen. 5. They will appear the more glorious, and God will be the more glorified in them, if we compare what they are with what they were, the happiness they have arrived at with the smallness of their beginnings (*v.* 22): *"A little one shall become a thousand and a small one a strong nation."* The captives that returned out of Babylon strangely multiplied, and became a strong nation. The Christian church was a little one, a very small one at first — the number of their names was once but 120; yet it became a thousand. The stone cut out of the mountain without hands swelled so as to fill the earth. The triumphant church, and every glorified saint, will be a thousand out of a little one, a strong nation out of a small one. The grace and peace of the saints were at first like a *grain of mustard-seed,* but they increase and multiply, and make a little one to become a thousand, the weak to be as David. When they come to heaven, and look back upon the smallness of their beginning, they will wonder how they got thither. And so wonderful is all this promise that it needed the ratification with which it is closed: *I the Lord will hasten it in his time* — all that is here said relating to the Jewish and Christian church, to the militant and triumphant church, and to every particular believer. (1.) It may seem too difficult to be brought about, and therefore may be despaired of; but the God of almighty power has undertaken it: *"I the Lord will do it,* who can do it, and who have determined to do it." It will be done by him whose power is irresistible and his purposes unalterable. (2.) It may seem to be delayed and put off so long that we are out of hopes of it; but, as the Lord will do it, so he will *hasten it,* will do it with all convenient speed; though much time may pass before it is done, no time shall be lost; he will *hasten it in its time,* in the proper time, in the season wherein it will be beautiful; he will do it in the time appointed by his wisdom, though not in the time prescribed by our folly. And this is really hastening it; for, though it seem to tarry, it does not tarry if it come in God's time, for we are sure that that is the best time, which he that believes will patiently wait for.

CHAPTER 61

In this chapter, I. We are sure to find the grace of Christ, published by himself to a lost world in the everlasting gospel, under the type and figure of Isaiah's province, which was to foretel the deliverance of the Jews out of Babylon (*v.* 1–3). II. We think we find the glories of the church of Christ, its spiritual glories, described under the type and figure of the Jews' prosperity after their return out of their captivity 1. It is promised that they decays of the church shall be repaired (*v.* 4). 2. That those from without shall be made serviceable to the church (*v.* 5). 3. That the church shall be a royal priesthood, maintained by the riches of the Gentiles (*v.* 6). 4. That she shall have honour and joy in lieu of all her shame and sorrow (*v.* 7). 5. That her affairs shall prosper (*v.* 8). 6. That prosperity shall enjoy these blessings (*v.* 9). 7. That righteousness and salvation shall be the eternal matter of the church's rejoicing and thanksgiving (*v.* 10, 11). If the Jewish church was ever thus blessed, much more shall the Christian church be so, and all that belong to it.

Verses 1–3

He that is the best expositor of scripture has no doubt given us the best exposition of these verses, even our Lord Jesus himself, who read this in the synagogue at Nazareth (perhaps it was the lesson for the day) and applied it entirely to himself, saying, *This day is this scripture fulfilled in your ears* (Lu. 4:17, 18, 21); and the gracious words which proceeded out of his mouth, in the opening of this text, were admired by all that heard them. As Isaiah was authorized and directed to proclaim liberty to the Jews in Babylon, so was Christ, God's messenger, to publish a more joyful jubilee to a lost world. And here we are told,

I. How he was fitted and qualified for this work: *The Spirit of the Lord God is upon me, v.* 1. The prophets had the Spirit of God moving them at times, both instructing them what to say and exciting them to say it. Christ had the Spirit always resting on him without measure; but to the same intent that the prophets had, as a Spirit of counsel and a Spirit of courage, *ch.* 11:1–3. When he entered upon the execution of his prophetical office the Spirit, as a dove, *descended upon him,* Mt. 3:16. This Spirit which was upon him he communicated to those whom he sent to proclaim the same glad tidings, saying to them, when he gave them their commission, *Receive you the Holy Ghost,* thereby ratifying it.

II. How he was appointed and ordained to it: *The Spirit of God is upon me, because the Lord God has anointed me.* What service God called him to he furnished him for; *therefore* he gave him his Spirit, because he had by a sacred and solemn unction set him apart to this great office, as kings and priests were of old destined to their offices by anointing. Hence the Redeemer was called the *Messiah,* the *Christ,* because he was *anointed with the oil of gladness above his fellows. He has sent me;* our Lord Jesus did not go unsent; he had a commission from him that is the fountain of power; *the Father sent him* and *gave him commandment.* This is a great satisfaction to us, that, whatever Christ said, he had a warrant from heaven for; his doctrine was not his, but his that sent him.

III. What the work was to which he was appointed and ordained.

1. He was to be a preacher, was to execute the office of a prophet. So well pleased was he with the good-will God showed towards men through him that he would himself be the preacher of it, that an honour might thereby be put upon the ministry of the gospel and the faith of the saints might be confirmed and encouraged. He must preach *good tidings* (so *gospel* signified) *to the meek,* to the penitent, and humble, and poor in spirit; to them the tidings of a Redeemer will be indeed good tidings, pure gospel, *faithful sayings, and worthy of all acceptation.* The poor are commonly best disposed to receive the gospel (Jam. 2:5), and it is likely to profit us when it is received with meekness, as it ought to be; to such Christ preached good tidings when he said, *Blessed are the meek.*

2. He was to be a healer. He was sent to *bind up the broken-hearted,* as pained limbs are rolled to give them ease, as broken bones and bleeding wounds are bound up, that they may knit and close again. Those whose hearts are broken for sin, who are truly humbled under the sense of guilt and dread of wrath, are furnished in the gospel of Christ with that which will make them easy and silence their fears. Those only who have experienced the pains of a penitential contrition may expect the pleasure of divine cordials and consolations.

3. He was to be a deliverer. He was sent as a prophet to preach, as a priest to heal, and as a king to issue out proclamations and those of two kinds: — (1.) Proclamations of peace to his friends: He shall *proclaim liberty to the captives* (as Cyrus did to the Jews in captivity) and the *opening of the prison to those that were bound.* Whereas, by the guilt of sin, we are bound over to the justice of God, are his lawful captives, sold for sin till payment be made of that great debt, Christ lets us know that he has made satisfaction to divine justice for that debt, that his satisfaction is accepted, and if we will plead that, and depend upon it, and make over ourselves and all we have to him, in a grateful sense of the kindness he has done us, we may be faith sue out our pardon and take the comfort of it; there is, and shall be, *no condemnation to us.* And whereas, by the dominion of sin in us, we are bound under the power of Satan, sold under sin, Christ lets us know that he has conquered Satan, has *destroyed him that had the power of death and his works,* and provided for us grace sufficient to enable us to shake off the yoke of sin and to loose ourselves from *those bands of our neck. The Son* is ready by his Spirit to *make us free;* and then we shall be *free indeed,* not only discharged from the miseries of captivity, but advanced to all the immunities and dignities of citizens. This is the gospel proclamation, and it is like the blowing of the jubilee-trumpet, which proclaimed the great year of release (Lev. 25:9, 40), in allusion to which it is here called *the acceptable year of the Lord,* the time of our acceptance with God, which is the origin of our liberties; or it is called the *year of the Lord* because it publishes his free grace, to his own glory, and an *acceptable year* because it brings glad tidings to us, and what cannot but be very acceptable to those who know the capacities and necessities of their own souls. (2.) Proclamations of war against his enemies. Christ proclaims *the day of vengeance of our God,* the vengeance he takes, [1.] On sin and Satan, death and hell, and all the powers of darkness, that were to be destroyed in order to our deliverances; these Christ triumphed over in his cross, having spoiled and weakened them, shamed them, and *made a show of them openly,* therein taking vengeance on them for all the injury they had done both to God and man, Col. 2:15. [2.] On those of the children of men that stand it out against those fair offers. They shall not only be left, as they deserve, in their captivity, but be dealt with as enemies; we have the gospel summed up, Mk. 16:16, where that part of it, *He that believes shall be saved,* proclaims *the acceptable year of the Lord* to those that will accept of it; but the other part, *He that believes not shall be damned,* proclaims *the day of vengeance of our God,* that vengeance which he will take on those that *obey not the gospel of Jesus Christ,* 2 Th. 1:8.

4. He was to be a comforter, and so he is as preacher, healer, and deliverer; he is sent to *comfort all who mourn,* and who, mourning, seek to him, and not to the world, for comfort. Christ not only provides comfort for them, and proclaims it, but he applies it to them; he does by his Spirit comfort them. There is enough in him to *comfort all who mourn,* whatever their sore or sorrow is; but this comfort is sure to those who *mourn in Zion,* who sorrow *after a godly sort,* according to God, for his residence is in Zion, — who *mourn because of Zion's* calamities and desolations, and mingle their tears by a holy sympathy with those of all God's suffering people, though they themselves are not in trouble; such tears God has *a bottle* for (Ps. 56:8), such mourners he has comfort in store for. As *blessings out of Zion* are spiritual blessings, so *mourners in Zion* are holy mourners, such as carry their sorrows to the throne of grace (for in Zion was the mercy-seat) and pour them out as Hannah did before the Lord. To such as these Christ has appointed by his gospel, and will give by his Spirit (*v.* 3), those consolations which will not only support them under their sorrows, but turn them into songs of praise. He will give them, (1.) *Beauty for ashes.* Whereas they lay in ashes, as was usual in times of great mourning, they shall not only be raised out of their dust, but made to look pleasant. Note, The holy cheerfulness of Christians is their beauty and a great ornament to their profession. Here is an elegant *paronomasia* in the original: He will give them *pheer — beauty,* for *epher — ashes;* he will turn their sorrow into joy as quickly and as easily as you can transpose a letter; for he speaks, and it is done. (2.) *The oil of joy,* which *make the face to shine,* instead of *mourning,* which *disfigures the countenance* and makes it unlovely. this *oil of joy* the saints have from that *oil of gladness* with which Christ himself was *anointed above his fellows,* Heb. 1:9. (3.) *The garments of praise,* such beautiful garments as were worn on thanksgiving-days, instead of the *spirit of heaviness, dimness,* or *contraction* — open joys for secret mournings. The *spirit of heaviness* they keep to themselves (Zion's mourners *weep in secret);* but the joy they are recompensed with they are clothed with as with a garment in the eye of others. Observe, Where God gives the oil of joy he gives the garment of praise. Those comforts which come from God dispose the heart to, and enlarge the heart in, thanksgivings to God. Whatever we have the joy of God must have the praise and glory of.

5. He was to be a planter; for the church is God's husbandry. *Therefore* he will do all this for his people, will cure their wounds, release them out of bondage, and comfort them in their sorrows, *that they may be called trees of righteousness, the planting of the Lord,* that they may be such, and be acknowledged to be such, that they may be ornaments to God's vineyard and may be *fruitful in the fruits of righteousness,* as the branches of *God's planting, ch.* 60:21. All that Christ does for us is to make us God's people, and some way serviceable to him as living trees, *planted in the house of the Lord,* and *flourishing in the courts of our God;* and all this *that he may be glorified* — that we may be brought to glorify him by a sincere devotion and an exemplary conversation (for *herein is our Father glorified, that we bring broth much fruit*), that others also may take occasion from God's favour shining on his people, and his grace shining in them, to praise him, and that he may be for ever *glorified in his saints.*

Verses 4–9

Promises are here made to the Jews now returned out of captivity, and settled again in their own land, which are to be extended to the gospel church, and all believers, who through grace are delivered out of spiritual thraldom; for they are capable of being spiritually applied.

I. It is promised that their houses shall be rebuilt (*v.* 4), that their cities shall be raised out of the ruins in which they had long lain, and be fitted up for their use again: *They shall build the old wastes;* the *old wastes* shall be built, the *waste cities shall be repaired,* the *former desolations,* even *the desolations of many generations,* which it was feared would never be repaired, shall be *raised up.* The setting up of Christianity in the world repaired the decays of natural religion and raised up those desolations both of piety and honesty which had been for many generations the reproach of mankind. An unsanctified soul is like a city that is broken down and has no walls, like a house in ruins; but by the power of Christ's gospel and grace it is repaired, it is put in order again, and fitted to be a habitation of God through the Spirit. And *they* shall do this, those that are released out of captivity; for we are brought out of the house of bondage that we may serve God, both in building up ourselves to his glory and in helping to build up his church on earth.

II. Those that were so lately servants themselves, working for their oppressors and lying at their mercy, shall now have servants to do their work for them and be at their command, not of their brethren (they are all the Lord's freemen), but of *the strangers, and the sons of the alien,* who shall *keep their sheep, till their ground,* and *dress their gardens,* the ancient employments of Abel, Cain, and Adam: *Strangers shall feed your flocks, v.* 5. When, by the grace of God, we attain to a holy indifference as to all the affairs of this world, *buying as though we possessed not* — when, though our hands are employed about them, our hearts are not entangled with them, but reserved entire for God and his service — then *the sons of the alien are our ploughmen and vine-dressers.*

III. They shall not only be released out of their captivity, but highly preferred and honourably employed (*v.* 6): "While the strangers are *keeping your flocks,* you shall be keeping *the charge of the sanctuary;* instead of being slaves to your task-masters, *you shall be named the priests of the Lord,* a high and holy calling." Priests were princes' peers, and in Hebrew were called by the same name. You *shall be the ministers of our God,* as the Levites were. Note, Those whom God sets at liberty he sets to work; he *delivers them out of the hands of their enemies* that they may *serve him,* Lu. 1:74, 75; Ps. 116:16. But his service is perfect freedom, nay, it is the greatest honour. When God brought Israel out of Egypt he took them to be to him a *kingdom of priests,* Ex. 19:6. And the gospel church is a *royal priesthood,* 1 Pt. 2:9. All believers are made to our God kings and priests; and they ought to conduct themselves as such in their devotions and in their whole conversation, with *holiness to the Lord* written upon their foreheads, that men may *call them the priests of the Lord.*

IV. The wealth and honour of the Gentile converts shall redound to the benefit and credit of the church, *v.* 6. *The Gentiles* shall be brought into the church. Those that were strangers shall become *fellow-citizens with the saints;* and with themselves they shall bring all they have, to be devoted to the glory of God and used in his service; and the priests, the Lord's ministers, shall have the advantage of it. It will be a great strengthening and quickening, as well as a comfort and encouragement, to all good Christians, to see the Gentiles serving the interests of God's kingdom. 1. They shall *eat the riches of the Gentiles,* not which they have themselves seized by violence, but which are fairly and honourably presented to them, as *gifts brought to the altar,* which the priests and their families lived comfortably upon. It is not said, "You shall *hoard the riches of the Gentiles,* and treasure them," but, "You shall *eat them;"* for there is nothing better in riches than to use them and to do good with them. 2. They shall *boast themselves in their glory.* Whatever was the honour of the Gentiles converts before their conversion — their nobility, estates, learning, virtue, or places of trust and power — it shall all turn to the reputation of the church to which they have joined themselves; and whatever is their glory after their conversion — their holy zeal and strictness of conversation, their usefulness, their patient suffering, and all the displays of that blessed change which divine grace has made in them — shall be very much for the glory of God and therefore all good men shall glory in it.

V. They shall have abundance of comfort and satisfaction in their own bosoms, *v.* 7. The Jews no doubt were thus privileged after their return; they were in a new world, and now knew how to value their liberty and property, the pleasures of which were continually fresh and blooming. Much more do all those rejoice whom Christ has brought into the glorious liberty of God's children, especially when the privileges of their adoption shall be completed in the resurrection of the body. 1. *They shall rejoice in their portion;* they shall not only have their own again, but (which is a further gift of God) they shall have the comfort of it, and a heart to rejoice in it, Eccl. 3:13. Though the houses of the returned Jews, as well as their temple, be much inferior to what they were before the captivity, yet they shall be well pleased with them and thankful for them. It is a portion *in their land,* their own land, the holy land, Immanuel's land, and therefore they shall rejoice in it, having so lately known what it was to be *strangers in a strange land.* Those that have God and heaven for their portion have reason to say that they have a worthy portion and to rejoice in it. 2. *Everlasting joy shall be unto them,* that is, a joyful state of their people, which shall last long, much longer than the captivity had lasted. Yet that joy of the Jewish nation was so much allayed, so often interrupted, and so soon brought to an end, that we must look for the accomplishment of this promise in the spiritual joy which believers have in God and the eternal joy they hope for in heaven. 3. This shall be a double recompence to them, and more than double, for all the reproach and vexation they have lain under in the land of their captivity: *"For your shame you shall have double* honour, and *in your land* you *shall possess double* wealth, to what you lost; the blessing of God upon it, and the comfort you shall have in it, shall make an abundant reparation for all the damages you have received. You shall be owned not only as *God's sons,* but as his *first-born* (Ex. 4:22), and therefore entitled to a double portion." As the miseries of their captivity were so great that in them they are said to have received *double for all their sins* (*ch.* 40:2), so the joys of their return shall be so great that in them they shall receive *double for all their shame.* The former is applicable to the fulness of Christ's satisfaction, in which God received *double for all our sins;* the latter to the fulness of heaven's joys, in which we shall receive more than *double for all our services* and sufferings. Job's case illustrates this: when God *turned again his captivity,* he gave him *twice as much as he had before.*

VI. God will be their faithful guide and a God in covenant with them (*v.* 8): *I will direct their work in truth.* God by his providence will order their affairs for the best, according to the word of his truth. He will guide them in the ways of true prosperity, by the rules of true policy. He will by his grace direct the works of good people in the right way, the true way that leads to happiness; he will direct them to be done in sincerity and then they are pleasing to him. God *desires truth in the inward parts;* and, if we do our works in truth, he will *make an everlasting covenant with us;* for to those that *walk before him* and *are upright* he will certainly be a *God all-sufficient.* Now, as a reason both of this and of the foregoing promise, that God will recompense to them *double for their shame,* those words come in, in the former part of the verse, *I the Lord love judgment.* He loves that judgment should be done among men, both between magistrates and subjects and between neighbour and neighbour, and therefore he hates all injustice; and, when wrongs are done to his people by their oppressors and persecutors, he is displeased with them, not only because they are done to his people, but because they are wrongs, and against the eternal rules of equity. If men do not do justice, he loves to do judgment himself in giving redress to those that suffer wrong and punishing those that do wrong. God pleads his people's injured cause, not only because he is jealous for them, but because he is jealous for justice. To illustrate this, it is added that he *hates robbery for burnt-offering.* He hates injustice even in his own people, who honour him with what they have in their burnt-offerings, much more does he hate it when it is against his own people; if he hates robbery when it is for burnt-offerings to himself, much more when it is for burnt-offerings to idols, and when not only his people are robbed of their estates, but he is robbed of his offerings. It is a truth much to the honour of God that ritual services will never atone for the violation of moral precepts, nor will it justify any man's robbery to say, "It was for burnt-offerings," or *Corban — It is a gift.* Behold, *to obey is better than sacrifice,* to *do justly and love mercy* better than *thousands of rams;* nay, that robbery is most of all hateful to God which is covered with this pretence, for it makes the righteous God to be the patron of unrighteousness. Some make this a reason of the rejection of the Jews upon the bringing in of the Gentiles (*v.* 6), because they were so corrupt in their morals, and, while they tithed mint and cummin, made nothing of *judgment and mercy* (Mt. 23:23), whereas *God loves judgment* and insists upon that, and he hates both *robbery for burnt offerings* and *burnt-offerings for robbery* too, as that of the Pharisees, who made long prayers that they might the more plausibly devour widows' houses. Others read these words thus: *I hate rapine by iniquity,* that is, the spoil which the enemies of God's people had unjustly made of them; God hated this, and therefore would reckon with them for it.

VII. God will entail a blessing upon their posterity after them (*v.* 9): *Their seed* (the children of those persons themselves that are now the blessed of the Lord, or their successors in profession, the church's seed) shall be *accounted to the Lord for a generation,* Ps. 22:30. 1. They shall signalize themselves and make their neighbours to take notice of them: *They shall be known among the Gentiles,* shall distinguish themselves by the gravity, seriousness, humility, and cheerfulness of their conversation, especially by that brotherly love by which all men shall know them to be Christ's disciples. And, they thus distinguishing themselves, God shall dignify them, by making them the blessings of their age and instruments of his glory, and by giving them remarkable tokens of his favour, which shall make them eminent and gain them respect from all about them. Let the children of godly parents love in such a manner that they may be known to be such, that all who observe them may see in them the fruits of a good education, and an answer to the prayers that were put up for them; and then they may expect that God will make them known, by the fulfilling of that promise to them, that *the generation of the upright shall be blessed.* 2. God shall have the glory of this, for every one shall attribute it to the blessing of God; all that see them shall see so much of the grace of God in them, and his favour towards them, that they shall *acknowledge them to be the seed which the Lord has blessed* and doth bless, for it includes both. See what it is to be blessed of God. Whatever good appears in any it must be taken notice of as the fruit of God's blessing and he must be glorified in it.

Verses 10–11

Some make this the song of joy and praise to be sung by the prophet in the name of Jerusalem, congratulating her on the happy change of her circumstances in the accomplishment of the foregoing promises; others make it to be spoken by Christ in the name of the New-Testament church triumphing in gospel grace. We may take in both, the former as a type of the latter. We are here taught to rejoice with holy joy, to God's honour, 1. In the beginning of this good work, the clothing of the church *with righteousness and salvation, v.* 10. Upon this account *I will greatly rejoice in the Lord.* Those that rejoice in God have cause to rejoice greatly, and we need not fear running into an extreme in the greatness of our joy when we make God the gladness of our joy. The first gospel song begins like this, *My soul doth magnify the Lord, and my spirit hath rejoiced in God my Saviour,* Lu. 1:46, 47. There is just matter for this joy, and all the reason in the world why it should terminate in God; for salvation and righteousness are wrought out and brought in, and the church is clothed with them. The salvation God wrought for the Jews, and that righteousness of his in which he appeared for them, and that reformation which appeared among them, made them look as glorious in the eyes of all wise men as if they had been clothed in robes of state or nuptial garments. Christ has clothed his church with an eternal salvation (and that is truly great) by clothing it with the righteousness both of justification and sanctification. The *clean linen is the righteousness of saints,* Rev. 19:8. Observe how these tow are put together; those, and those only, shall be clothed with the garments of salvation hereafter that are covered with the robe of righteousness now: and those garments are rich and splendid clothing, like the priestly garments (for so the word signifies) with which the *bridegroom decks himself*. The brightness of the sun itself is compared to them. Ps. 19:5, *He is as a bridegroom* coming out of his chamber, completely dressed. Such is the beauty of God's grace in those that are clothed with the robe of righteousness, that by the righteousness of Christ are recommended to God's favour and by the sanctification of the Spirit have God's image renewed upon them; they are decked as a bride to be espoused to God, and taken into covenant with him; they are decked as a priest to be employed for God, and taken into communion with him. 2. In the progress and continuance of this good work, *v.* 11. It is not like a day of triumph, which is glorious for the present, but is soon over. No; the righteousness and salvation with which the church is clothed are durable clothing; so they are said to be, *ch.* 23:18. The church, when she is pleasing herself with the righteousness and salvation that Jesus Christ has clothed her with, rejoices to think that these inestimable blessings shall both spring for future ages and spread to distant regions. (1.) They shall spring forth for ages to come, as the fruits of the earth which are produced very year, from generation to generation. *As the earth,* even that which lies common, *brings forth her bud,* the tender grass at the return of the year, and as *the garden* enclosed *causes the things that are sown in it to spring forth* in their season, so duly, so constantly, so powerfully, and with such advantage to mankind *will the Lord God cause righteousness and praise to spring forth,* by virtue of the covenant of grace, as, in the former case, by virtue of the covenant of providence. See what the promised blessings are — *righteousness and praise* (for those that are clothed with righteousness *show forth the praises* of him that clothed them); these shall spring forth under the influence of the dew of divine grace. Though it may sometimes be winter with the church, when those blessings seem to wither and do not appear, yet the root of them is fixed, a spring-time will come, when through the reviving beams of the approaching Sun of righteousness they shall flourish again. (2.) They shall spread far, and *spring forth before all the nations;* the great salvation shall be published and proclaimed to all the world and the ends of the earth shall see it.

CHAPTER 62

The business of prophets was both to preach and pray. In this chapter, I. The prophet determines to apply closely and constantly to this business (*v.* 1). II. God appoints him and others of his prophets to continue to do so, for the encouragement of his people during the delays of their deliverance (*v.* 6, 7). III. The promises are here repeated and ratified of the great things God would do for his church, for the Jews after their return out of captivity and for the Christian church when it shall be set up in the world. 1. The church shall be made honourable in the eyes of the world (*v.* 2). 2. It shall appear to be very dear to God, precious and honourable in his sight (*v.* 3–5). 3. It shall enjoy great plenty (*v.* 8, 9). 4. It shall be released out of captivity and grow up again into a considerable nation, particularly owned and favoured by heaven (*v.* 10–12).

Verses 1–5

The prophet here tells us,

I. What he will do for the church. A prophet, as he is a seer, so he is a spokesman. This prophet resolves to perform that office faithfully, *v.* 1. He *will not hold his peace; he will not rest;* he will mind his business, will take pains, and never desire to take his ease; and herein he was a type of Christ, who was indefatigable in executing the office of a prophet and made it his meat and drink till he had finished his work. Observe here, 1. What the prophet's resolution is: *He will not hold his peace.* He will continue instant in preaching, will not only faithfully deliver, but frequently repeat, the messages he has *received from the Lord.* If people receive not the precepts and promises at first, he will inculcate them and give them line upon line. And he will continue instant in prayer; he will never hold his peace at the throne of grace till he has prevailed with God for the mercies promised; he will *give himself to prayer and to the ministry of the word,* as Christ's ministers must (Acts 6:4), who must labour frequently in both and never be weary of this well-doing. The business of ministers is to speak from God to his people and to God for his people; and in neither of these must they be silent. 2. What is the principle of this resolution — *for Zion's sake, and for Jerusalem's,* not for the sake of any private interest of his own, but for the church's sake, because he has an af-

fection and concern for Zion, and it lies near his heart. Whatever becomes of his own house and family, he desires to *see the good of Jerusalem* and resolves to seek it all the days of his life, Ps. 122:8, 9; 118:5. It is God's Zion and his Jerusalem, and it is *therefore* dear to him, because it is so to God and because God's glory is interested in its prosperity. 3. How long he resolves to continue this importunity — till the promise of the church's righteousness and salvation, given in the foregoing chapter, be accomplished. Isaiah will not himself live to see the release of the captives out of Babylon, much less the bringing in of the gospel, in which *grace reigns through righteousness unto life* and salvation; yet he will *not hold his peace till* these be accomplished, even the utmost of them, because his prophecies will continue speaking of these things, and there shall in every age be a remnant that shall continue to pray for them, as successors to him, till the promises be performed, and so the prayers answered that were grounded upon them. Then the church's *righteousness* and *salvation* will *go forth as brightness,* and *as a lamp that burns,* so plainly that it will carry its own evidence along with it. It will bring honour and comfort to the church, which will hereupon both look pleasant and appear illustrious; and it will bring instruction and direction to the world, a light not only to the eyes but to the feet, and to *the paths* of those who before *sat in darkness and in the shadow of death.*

II. What God will do for the church. The prophet can but pray and preach, but God will confirm the word and answer the prayers. 1. The church shall be greatly admired. When that righteousness which is her salvation, her praise, and her glory, shall be *brought forth,* the *Gentiles shall see* it. The tidings of it shall be carried to the Gentiles, and a tender of it made to them; they may so see this righteousness as to share in it if it be not their own fault. "Even kings shall see and be in love with the *glory of thy righteousness"* (*v.* 2), shall overlook the glory of their own courts and kingdoms, and look at, and look after, the spiritual glory of the church as that which excels. 2. She shall be truly admirable. Great names make men considerable in the world, and great respect is paid them thereupon; now it is agreed that *honor est in honorante* — *honour derives its value from the dignity of him who confers it.* God is the fountain of honour and from him the church's honour comes: *"Thou shalt be called by a new name,* a pleasant name, such as thou wast never called by before, no, not in the day of thy greatest prosperity, and the reverse of that which thou wast called by in the day of thy affliction; thou shalt have a new character, be advanced to a new dignity, and those about thee shall have new thoughts of thee." This seems to be alluded to in that promise (Rev. 2:17) of the *white stone and in the stone a new name,* and that (Rev. 3:12) of the *name of the city of my God* and my *new name.* It is a name *which the mouth of the Lord shall name,* who, we are sure, miscalls nothing, and who will oblige others to call her by the name he has given her; for his judgment is according to truth and all shall concur with it sooner or later. Two names God shall give her: — (1.) He shall call her his crown (*v.* 3): *Thou shalt be a crown of glory in the hand of the Lord,* not on his head (as adding any real honour or power to him, as crowns do to those that are crowned with them), but in his hand. He is pleased to account them, and show them forth, as a glory and beauty to him. When he took them to be his people it was that they might be *unto him for a name, and for a praise, and for a glory* (Jer. 13:11): "Thou shalt be a *crown of glory* and a *royal diadem,* through the hand, the good hand, of thy God upon thee; he shall make thee so, for he shall be *to thee a crown of glory, ch.* 28:5. Thou shalt be so *in his hand,* that is, under his protection; he that shall put glory upon thee shall *create a defence upon all that glory,* so that the flowers of thy crown shall never wither nor shall its jewels be lost." (2.) He shall call her his spouse, *v.* 4, 5. This is a yet greater honour, especially considering what a forlorn condition she had been in. [1.] Her case had been very melancholy. She was called *forsaken* and her land *desolate* during the captivity, like a woman reproachfully divorced or left a disconsolate widow. Such as the state of religion in the world before the preaching of the gospel — it was in a manner forsaken and desolate, a thing that no man looked after nor had any real concern for. [2.] It should now be very pleasant,

for God would return in mercy to her. Instead of those two names of reproach, she shall be called by two honourable names. *First,* She shall be called *Hephzi-bah,* which signifies, *My delight is in her;* it was the name of Hezekiah's queen, Manasseh's mother (2 Ki. 21:1), a proper name for a wife, who ought to be her husband's delight, Prov. 5:19. And here it is the church's Maker that is her husband: *The Lord delights in thee.* God by his grace has wrought that in his church which makes her his delight, she being refined, and reformed, and brought home to him; and then by his providence he does that for her which makes it appear that she is his delight and that he delights to do her good. *Secondly,* She shall be called *Beulah,* which signifies *married,* whereas she had been desolate, a condition opposed to that of the *married wife, ch.* 54:1. "*Thy land shall be married,* that is, it shall become fruitful again, and be replenished." Though she has long been barren, she shall again be peopled, shall again be made to keep house and to be a joyful mother of children, Ps. 113:9. *She shall be married,* for, 1. Her sons shall heartily espouse the land of their nativity and its interests, which they had for a long time neglected, as despairing ever to have any comfortable enjoyment of it: *Thy sons shall marry thee,* that is, they shall live with thee and take delight in thee. When they were in Babylon, they seemed to have espoused that land, for they were appointed to settle, and to seek the peace of it, Jer. 29:5–7. But now they shall again marry their own land, *as a young man marries a virgin* that he takes great delight in, is extremely fond of, and is likely to have many children by. It bodes well to a land when its own natives and inhabitants are pleased with it, prefer it before other lands, when its princes marry their country and resolve to take their lot with it. 2. *Her God* (which is much better) shall *betroth her to himself in righteousness,* Hosea 2:19, 20. He will take pleasure in his church: *As the bridegroom rejoices over the bride,* is pleased with his relation to her and her affection to him, *so shall thy God rejoice over thee:* he shall rest in his love to thee (Zep. 3:17); *he shall take pleasure in thee* (Ps. 147:11), and shall *delight to do thee good with his whole heart and his whole soul,* Jer. 32:41. This is very applicable to the love Christ has for his church and the complacency he takes in it, which appears so brightly in Solomon's Song, and which will be complete in heaven.

Verses 6–9

Two things are here promised to Jerusalem: —

I. Plenty of the means of grace — abundance of good preaching and good praying (*v.* 6, 7), and this shows the method God takes when he designs mercy for a people; he first brings them to their duty and pours out a spirit of prayer upon them, and then brings salvation to them. Provision is made,

1. That ministers may do their duty as watchmen. It is here spoken of as a token for good, as a step towards further mercy and an earnest of it, that, in order to what he designed for them, he would set *watchmen on their walls who should never hold their peace.* Note, (1.) Ministers are watchmen on the church's walls, for it is as a city besieged, whose concern it is to have sentinels on the walls, to take notice and give notice of the motions of the enemy. It is necessary that, as watchmen, they be wakeful, and faithful, and willing to endure hardness. (2.) They are concerned to stand upon their guard day and night; they must never be off their watch as long as those for whose souls they watch are not out of danger. (3.) They must never hold their peace; they must take all opportunities to give warning to sinners, in season, out of season, and must never betray the cause of Christ by a treacherous or cowardly silence. They must never hold their peace at the throne of grace; they must *pray, and not faint,* as Moses lifted up his hands and kept them steady, till Israel had obtained the victory over Amalek, Ex. 17:10, 12.

2. That people may do their duty. As those that make mention of the Lord, let not them keep silence neither, let not them think it enough that their watchmen pray for them, but let them pray for themselves; all will be little enough to meet the approaching mercy with due solemnity. Note, (1.) It is the character of God's professing people that they make mention of the Lord, and continue to do so even in bad times, when the land is termed *forsaken* and *desolate.* They are *the Lord's remembrancers* (so

the margin reads it); they remember the Lord themselves and put one another in mind of him. (2.) God's professing people must be a praying people, must be public-spirited in prayer, must wrestle with God in prayer, and continue to do so: *"Keep not silence;* never grow remiss in the duty nor weary of it." *Give him no rest* — alluding to an importunate beggar, to the widow that with her continual coming wearied the judge into a compliance. God said to *Moses, Let me alone* (Ex. 32:10), and Jacob to Christ, *I will not let thee go except thou bless me,* Gen. 32:26. (3.) God is so far from being displeased with our pressing importunity, as men commonly are, that he invites and encourages it; he bids us to cry after him; he is not like those disciples who discouraged a petitioner, Mt. 15:23. He bids us make pressing applications at the throne of grace, and *give him no rest,* Lu. 11:5, 8. He suffers himself not only to be reasoned with, but to be wrestled with. (4.) The public welfare or prosperity of God's Jerusalem is that which we should be most importunate for at the throne of grace; we should pray for the good of the church. [1.] That it may be safe, that he would *establish* it, that the interests of the church may be firm, may be settled for the present and secured to posterity. [2.] That it may be great, may be *a praise in the earth,* that it may be praised, and God may be praised for it. When gospel truths are cleared and vindicated, when gospel ordinances are duly administered in their purity and power, when the church becomes eminent for holiness and love, then Jerusalem is a praise in the earth, then it is in reputation. (5.) We must persevere in our prayers for mercy to the church till the mercy come; we must do as the prophet's servant did, go yet seven times, till the promising cloud appear, 1 Ki. 18:44. (6.) It is a good sign that God is coming towards a people in ways of mercy when he pours out a spirit of prayer upon them and stirs them up to be fervent and constant in their intercessions.

II. Plenty of all other good things, *v.* 8. This follows upon the former; when the people praise God, when *all the people praise him, then shall the earth yield her increase* (Ps. 67:5, 6), and outward prosperity, crowning its piety, shall help to make Jerusalem a praise in the earth. Observe,

1. The great distress they had been in, and the losses they had sustained. Their corn had been meat for their enemies, which they hoped would be meat for themselves and their families. Here was a double grievance, that they themselves wanted that which was necessary to the support of life and were in danger of perishing for want of it, and that their enemies were strengthened by it, had their camp victualled with it, and so were the better able to do them a mischief. God is said to give their corn to their enemies, because he not only permitted it, but ordered it, to be the just punishment both of their abuse of plenty and of their symbolizing with strangers, *ch.* 1:7. The wine which they had laboured for, and which in their affliction they needed for the relief of those among them that were of a heavy heart, strangers drank it, to gratify their lusts with; this sore judgment was threatened for their sins, Lev. 26:16; Deu. 28:33. See how uncertain our creature-comforts are, and how much it is our wisdom to labour for that meat which we can never be robbed of.

2. The great fulness and satisfaction they should now be restored to (*v.* 9): *Those that have gathered it shall eat it, and praise the Lord.* See here, (1.) God's mercy in giving plenty, and peace to enjoy it, — that the earth yields her increase, that there are hands to be employed in gathering it in, and that they are not taken off by plague and sickness, or otherwise employed in war, — that strangers and enemies do not come and gather it for themselves, or take it from us when we have gathered it, — that we eat the labour of our hands and the bread is not eaten out of our mouths, — and especially that we have opportunity and a heart to honour God with it, and that his courts are open to us and we are not restrained from attending on him in them. (2.) Our duty in the enjoyment of this mercy. We must gather what God gives, with care and industry; we must eat it freely and cheerfully, not bury the gifts of God's bounty, but make use of them. We must, when we have eaten and are full, *bless the Lord,* and give him thanks for his bounty to us; and we must serve him with our abundance, use it in works of piety and charity, eat it and *drink it in the courts of his holiness,* where the altar, the priest, and the poor must all have their share. The greatest comfort that a good man has in his meat and

drink is that it furnishes him with a meat-offering and a drink-offering for the Lord his God (Joel 2:14); the greatest comfort that he has in an estate is that it gives him an opportunity of honouring God and doing good. This wine is to be *drunk in the courts of God's holiness,* and therefore moderately and with sobriety, as before the Lord.

3. The solemn ratification of this promise: *The Lord has sworn by his right hand, and by the arm of his strength,* that he will do this for his people. God confirms it by an oath, that his people, who trust in him and his word, may have *strong consolation,* Heb. 6:17, 18. And, since he can swear by no greater, he swears by himself, sometimes by his being *(As I live,* Eze. 33:11), sometimes by his holiness (Ps. 89:35), here by his power, his right hand (which was lifted up in swearing, Deu. 32:40), and his arm of power; for it is a great satisfaction to those who build their hopes on God's promise to be sure that *what he has promised he is able to perform,* Rom. 4:21. To assure us of this he has sworn by his strength, pawning the reputation of his omnipotence upon it; if he do not do it, let it be said, *It was because he could not,* which the Egyptians shall never say (Num. 14:16) nor any other. It is the comfort of God's people that his power is engaged for them, his right hand, where the Mediator sits.

Verses 10–12

This, as many like passages before, refers to the deliverance of the Jews out of Babylon, and, under the type and figure of that, to the great redemption wrought out by Jesus Christ, and the proclaiming of gospel grace and liberty through him. 1. Way shall be made for this salvation; all difficulties shall be removed, and whatever might obstruct it shall be taken out of the way, *v.* 10. The gates of Babylon shall be thrown open, that they may with freedom go through them; the way from Babylon to the land of Israel shall be prepared; causeways shall be made and cast up through wet and miry places, and the stones gathered out from places rough and rocky; in the convenient places appointed for their rendezvous standards shall be set up for their direction and encouragement, that they may embody for their greater safety. Thus John Baptist was sent to *prepare the way of the Lord,* Mt. 3:3. And, before Christ by his graces and comforts comes to any for salvation, preparation is made for him by repentance, which is called the *preparation of the gospel of peace,* Eph. 6:15. Here the way is levelled by it, there the feet are shod with it, which comes all to one, for both are in order to a journey. 2. Notice shall be given of this salvation, *v.* 11, 12. It shall be proclaimed to the captives that they are set at liberty and may go if they please; it shall be proclaimed to their neighbours, to all about them, *to the end of the world,* that God has pleaded Zion's just, injured, and despised cause. Let is be said to Zion, for her comfort, *Behold, thy salvation comes* (that is, thy Saviour, who brings salvation); he will bring such a work, such a reward, in this salvation, as shall be admired by all, a reward of comfort and peace with him; but a work of humiliation and reformation before him, to prepare his people for that recompence of their sufferings; and then, with reference to each, it follows, they shall be called, *The holy people,* and the *redeemed of the Lord. The work before him,* which shall be wrought in them and upon them, shall denominate them a holy people, cured of their inclination to idolatry and consecrated to God only; and the *reward with him,* the deliverance wrought for them, shall denominate them the *redeemed of the Lord,* so redeemed as none but God could redeem them, and redeemed to be his, their bonds loosed, that they might be his servants. Jerusalem shall then be called, *Sought out, a city not forsaken.* She had been forsaken for many years; there were neither traders nor worshippers that enquired the way to Jerusalem as formerly, when it was frequented by both. But now God will again make her considerable. She shall be sought out, visited, resorted to, and court made to her, as much as ever. When Jerusalem is called a *holy city,* then it is called *sought out;* for holiness puts an honour and beauty upon any place or person, which draws respect, and makes them to be admired, beloved, and enquired after. But this being proclaimed to the end of the world must have a reference to the gospel of Christ, which was to be preached to every creature; and it intimates, (1.) The glory of Christ. It is published immediately to the church, but is thence echoed to

every nation: *Behold, thy salvation cometh.* Christ is not only the Saviour, but the salvation itself; for the happiness of believers is not only from him, but in him, *ch.* 12:2. His salvation consists both in the work and in the reward which he brings with him; for those that are his shall neither be idle nor lose their labour. (2.) The beauty of the church. Christians shall be called *saints* (1 Co. 1:2), *the holy people,* for they are chosen and called *to salvation through sanctification.* They shall be called *the redeemed of the Lord;* to him they owe their liberty, and therefore to him they owe their service, and they shall not be ashamed to own both. None are to be *called the redeemed of the Lord* but those that are the *holy people;* the people of God's purchase are a holy nation. And they shall be called, *Sought out.* God shall seek them out, and find them, wherever they are dispersed, eclipsed, or lost in a crowd; men shall seek them out, that they may join themselves to them, and not forsake them. It is good to associate with *the holy people,* that we may learn their ways, and with *the redeemed of the Lord,* that we may share in the blessings of the redemption.

CHAPTER 63

In this chapter we have, I. God coming towards his people in ways of mercy and deliverance, and this is to be joined to the close of the foregoing chapter, where it was said to Zion, "Behold, thy salvation comes;" for here it is shown how it comes (*v.* 1–6). II. God's people meeting him with their devotions, and addressing themselves to him with suitable affections; and this part of the chapter is carried on to the close of the next. In this we have, 1. A thankful acknowledgment of the great favours God had bestowed upon them (*v.* 7). 2. The magnifying of these favours, from the consideration of God's relation to them (*v.* 8), his compassionate concern for them (*v.* 9), their unworthiness (*v.* 10), and the occasion which it gave both him and them to call to mind former mercies (*v.* 11–14). 3. A very humble and earnest prayer to God to appear for them in their present distress, pleading God's mercy (*v.* 15), their relation to him (*v.* 16), their desire towards him (*v.* 17), and the insolence of their enemies (*v.* 18, 19). So that, upon the whole, we learn to embrace God's promises with an active faith, and then to improve them, and make use of them, both in prayers and praises.

Verses 1–6

It is a glorious victory that is here enquired into first and then accounted for. 1. It is a victory obtained by the providence of God over the enemies of Israel; over the Babylonians (say some), whom Cyrus conquered and God by him, and they will have the prophet to make the first discovery of him in his triumphant return when he is in the country of Edom: but this can by no means be admitted, because the country of Babylon is always spoken of as the land of the north, whereas Edom lay south from Jerusalem, so that the conqueror would not return through that country; the victory therefore is obtained over the Edomites themselves, who had triumphed in the destruction of Jerusalem by the Chaldeans (Ps. 137:7) and cut off those who, making their way as far as they could from the enemy, escaped to the Edomites (Obad. 12, 13), and were therefore reckoned with when Babylon was; for no doubt that prophecy was accomplished, though we do not meet in history with the accomplishment of it (Jer. 49:13), *Bozrah shall become a desolation.* Yet this victory over Edom is put as an instance or specimen of the like victories obtained over other nations that had been enemies to Israel. This over the Edomites is named for the sake of the old enmity of Esau against Jacob (Gen. 27:41) and perhaps with an allusion to David's glorious triumphs over the Edomites, by which it should seem, more than by any other of his victories, he *got himself a name,* Ps. 60, *title,* 2 Sa. 8:13, 14. But this is not all: 2. It is a victory obtained by the grace of God in Christ over our spiritual enemies. We find the garments dipped in blood adorning him whose name is called *The Word of God,* Rev. 19:13. And who that is we know very well; for it is through him that we are more than conquerors over those principalities and powers which on the cross he spoiled and triumphed over.

In this representation of the victory we have,

I. An admiring question put to the conqueror, *v.* 1, 2. It is put by the church, or by the prophet in the name of the church. He sees a mighty hero returning in triumph from a bloody engagement, and makes bold to ask him two questions: — 1. Who he is. He observes him to come from the country of Edom, to come in such apparel as was glorious to a soldier, not embroidered or laced, but besmeared with blood and dirt. He observes that he does not come as one either frightened or fatigued, but that he *travels in the greatness of his strength,* altogether unbroken.

> Triumphant and victorious he appears,
> And honour in his looks and habit wears.
> How strong he treads! how stately doth he go!
> Pompous and solemn is his pace,
> And full of majesty, as is his face;
> Who is this mighty hero — who!
> — Mr. Norris

The question, *Who is this?* perhaps means the same with that which Joshua put to the same person when he appeared to him with his sword drawn (Jos. 5:13): *Art thou for us or for our adversaries?* Or, rather, the same with that which Israel put in a way of adoration (Ex. 15:11): *Who is a God like unto thee?* 2. The other question it, *"Wherefore art thou red in thy apparel?* What hard service hast thou been engaged in, that thou carriest with thee these marks of toil and danger?" Is it possible that one who has such majesty and terror in his countenance should be employed in the mean and servile work of *treading the wine-press?* Surely it is not. That which is really the glory of the Redeemer seems, *primâ facie — at first,* a disparagement to him, as it would be to a mighty prince to do the work of the wine-dressers and husbandmen; for he *took upon him the form of a servant,* and carried with him the marks of servitude.

II. An admirable answer returned by him.

1. He tells who he is: *I that speak in righteousness, mighty to save.* He is the Saviour. God was Israel's Saviour out of the hand of their oppressors; the Lord Jesus is ours; his name, *Jesus,* signifies a *Saviour,* for he *saves his people from their sins.* In the salvation wrought he will have us to take notice, (1.) Of the truth of his promise, which is therein performed: He speaks *in righteousness,* and will therefore make good every word that he has spoken with which he will have us to compare what he does, that, setting the word and the work the one over against the other, what he does may ratify what he has said and what he has said may justify what he does. (2.) Of the efficacy of his power, which is therein exerted: He is *mighty to save,* able to bring about the promised redemption, whatever difficulties and oppositions may lie in the way of it.

> 'Tis I who to my promise faithful stand,
> I, who the powers of death, hell, and the grave,
> Have foil'd with this all-conquering hand,
> I, who most ready am, and mighty too, to save.
> — Mr. Norris

2. He tells how he came to appear in this hue (*v.* 3): *I have trodden the wine-press alone.* Being compared to one that treads in the wine-fat, such is his condescension, in the midst of his triumphs, that he does not scorn the comparison, but admits it and carries it on. He does indeed *tread the wine-press,* but it is *the great wine-press of the wrath of God* (Rev. 14:19), in which we sinners deserved to be cast; but Christ was pleased to cast our enemies into it, and to *destroy him that had the power of death,* that he might deliver us. And of this the bloody work which God sometimes made among the enemies of the Jews, and which is here foretold, was a type and figure. Observe the account the conqueror gives of his victory.

(1.) He gains the victory purely by his own strength: *I have trodden the wine-press alone, v.* 3. When God delivered his people and destroyed their enemies, if he made use of instruments, he did not need them. But among his people, for whom the salvation was to be wrought, no assistance offered itself; they were weak and helpless, and had no ability to do any thing for their own relief; they were desponding and listless, and had no heart to do any thing; they were not disposed to give the least stroke or struggle for liberty, neither the captives themselves nor any of their friends for them (*v.* 5): *"I looked, and there was none to help,* as one would have expected, nothing of a bold active spirit appeared among them; nay, there was not only none to lead, but, which was more strange, *there was none to uphold,* none that would come in as a second, that had the courage to join with Cyrus against their oppressors; *therefore my arm brought* about *the salvation; not by* created *might or power,* but *by the Spirit of the Lord of hosts,* my own arm." Note, God can help when all other helpers fail; nay, that is his time to help, and therefore for that very reason he will put forth his own power so much the more gloriously. But this is most fully applicable to Christ's victories over our spiritual enemies, which he obtained by a single combat. He trod the wine-press of his Father's wrath alone, and triumphed over principalities and powers *in himself,* Col. 2:15. *Of the people there was none with him;* for, when he entered the lists with the powers of darkness, *all his disciples forsook him and fled.* There was *non to help,* none that could, none that durst; and he might well wonder that among the children of men, whose concern it was, there was not only *none to uphold,* but that there were so many to oppose and hinder it if they could.

(2.) He undertakes the war purely out of his own zeal. It is *in his anger,* it is *in his fury,* that he *treads down* his enemies (*v.* 3), and that *fury upholds him* and carries him on in this enterprise, *v.* 5. God wrought salvation for the oppressed Jews purely because he was very angry with the oppressing Babylonians, angry at their idolatries and sorceries, their pride and cruelty, and the injuries they did to his people, and, as they increased their abominations and grew more insolent and outrageous, his anger increased to fury. Our Lord Jesus wrought out our redemption in a holy zeal for the honour of his Father and the happiness of mankind, and a holy indignation at the daring attempts Satan had made upon both; this zeal and indignation upheld him throughout his whole undertaking. Two branches there were of this zeal that animated him: — [1.] He had a zeal against his and his people's enemies: *The day of vengeance is in my heart* (*v.* 4), the day fixed in the eternal counsels for taking vengeance on them; this was written in his heart, so that he could not forget it, could not let it slip; his heart was full of it, and it lay as a charge, as a weight, upon him, which made him push on this holy war with so much vigour. Note, There is a day fixed for divine vengeance, which may be long deferred, but will come at last; and we may be content to wait for it, for the Redeemer himself does so, though his heart is upon it. [2.] He had a zeal for his people, and for all that he designed to make sharers in the intended salvation: *"The year of my redeemed has come,* the year appointed for their redemption." There was a year fixed for the deliverance of Israel out of Egypt, and God kept time to a day (Ex. 12:41); so there was for their release out of Babylon (Dan. 9:2); so there was for Christ's coming to destroy the works of the devil; so there is for all the deliverances of the church, and the deliverer has an eye to it. Observe, *First,* With what pleasure he speaks of his people; they are his *redeemed;* they are his own, dear to him. Though their redemption is not yet wrought out, yet he calls them *his redeemed,* because it shall as surely be done as if it were done already. *Secondly,* With what pleasure he speaks of his people's redemption; how glad he is that *the time has come,* though he is likely to meet with a sharp encounter. "Now that the year of my redeemed has come, *Lo, I come;* delay shall be no longer. *Now will I arise,* saith the Lord. *Now thou shalt see what I will do to Pharaoh."* Note, The promised salvation must be patiently waited for till the time appointed comes; yet we must attend the promises with our prayers. Does Christ say, *Surely I come quickly;* let our hearts reply, *Even so come;* let the *year of the redeemed come.*

(3.) He will obtain a complete victory over them all. [1.] Much is already done; for he now appears *red in his apparel;* such abundance of blood is shed that the conqueror's garments are all stained with it. This was predicted, long before, by dying Jacob, concerning *Shiloh* (that is, *Christ),* that he should *wash his garments in wine and his clothes in the blood of grapes,* which perhaps this alludes to, Gen. 49:11.

> With ornamental drops bedeck'd I stood,
> And wrote my vict'ry with my en'my's blood.
> — Mr. Norris

In the destruction of the antichristian powers we meet with abundance of blood shed (Rev. 14:20, 19:13), which yet, according to the dialect of prophecy, may be understood spiritually, and doubtless so may this here. [2.] More shall yet be done (*v.* 6): *I will tread down the people* that yet stand it out against me, *in my anger;* for the victorious Redeemer, when the *year of the redeemed shall have come,* will go on *conquering and to conquer,* Rev. 6:2. When he begins he will also make an end. Observe how he will complete his victories over the enemies of his church. *First,* He will infatuate them; he will make them drunk, so that there shall be neither sense nor steadiness in their counsels; they shall drink of the cup of his fury, and that shall intoxicate them: or he will make them *drunk with their own blood,* Rev. 17:6. Let those that make themselves drunk with the cup of riot (and then they are in their fury) repent and reform, lest God make them drunk with the *cup of trembling,* the cup of his fury. *Secondly,* He will enfeeble them; he will *bring down their strength,* and so bring them down *to the earth;* for what strength can hold out against Omnipotence?

Verses 7–14

The prophet is here, in the name of the church, taking a review, and making a thankful recognition, of God's dealings with his church all along, ever since he founded it, before he comes, in the latter end of this chapter and in the next, as a watchman upon the walls, earnestly to pray to God for his compassion towards her in her present deplorable state; and it was usual for God's people, in their prayers, thus to look back.

I. Here is a general acknowledgment of God's goodness to them all along, *v.* 7. It was said, in general, of God's prophets and people (*ch.* 62:6) that they *made mention of the Lord;* now here we are told what it is in God that they do especially delight to make mention of, and that is his goodness, which the prophet here so makes mention of as if he thought he could never say enough of it. He mentions the *kindness of God* (which never appeared so evident, so eminent, as in his love to mankind in *sending his Son* to save us, Tit. 3:4), his loving-kindness, kindness that shows itself in every thing that is endearing; nay, so plenteous are the springs, and so various the streams, of divine mercy, that he speaks of it in the plural number — *his loving-kindnesses;* for, if we would count the fruits of his loving-kindness, they are *more in number than the sand.* With his loving-kindnesses he mentions his *praises,* that is, the thankful acknowledgments which the saints make of his loving-kindness, and the angels too. It must be mentioned, to God's honour, what a tribute of praise is paid to him by all his creatures in consideration of his loving-kindness. See how copiously he speaks, 1. Of the goodness that is from God, the gifts of his loving-kindness — *all that the Lord has bestowed* on us in particular, relating to life and godliness, in our personal and family capacity. Let every man speak for himself, speak as he has found, and he must own that he has had a great deal bestowed upon him by the divine bounty. But we must also mention the favours bestowed upon his church, his *great goodness towards the house of Israel, which he has bestowed on them.* Note, We must bless God for the mercies enjoyed by others as well as for those enjoyed by ourselves, and reckon that bestowed on ourselves which is bestowed on *the house of Israel.* 2. Of the goodness that is in God. God does good because he is good; what he bestowed upon us must be traced up to the original; it is *according to his mercies* (not according to our merits) and *according to the multitude of his loving-kindnesses,* which can never be spent. Thus we should magnify God's goodness, and speak honourably of it, not only when we plead it (as David, Ps. 51:1), but when we praise it.

II. Here is particular notice taken of the steps of God's mercy to Israel ever since it was formed into a nation.

1. The expectations God had concerning them that they would conduct themselves well, *v.* 8. When he brought them out of Egypt and took them into covenant with himself he said, *"Surely they are my people,* I take them as such, and am willing to hope they will approve themselves so, *children that will not lie,"* that will not *dissemble with God* in their covenantings with him, nor treacherously depart from him by breaking their covenant and starting aside like a broken bow. They said, more than once, *All that the Lord shall say unto us we will do and will be obedient;* and thereupon he took them to be his peculiar people, saying, *Surely they will not lie.* God deals fairly and faithfully with them, and therefore expects they should deal so with him. They are *children of the covenant* (Acts 3:25), children of those that clave unto the Lord, and therefore it may be hoped that they will tread in the steps of their fathers' constancy. Note, God's people are *children that will not lie;* for those that will are not his children but the devil's.

2. The favour he showed them with an eye to these expectations: *So he was their Saviour* out of the bondage of

Egypt and all the calamities of their wilderness-state, and many a time since he had been their Saviour. See particularly (*v.* 9) what he did for them as their Saviour. (1.) The principle that moved him to work salvation for them; it was *in his love and in his pity,* out of mere compassion to them and a tender affection for them, not because he either needed them or could be benefited by them. This is strangely expressed here: *In all their affliction he was afflicted;* not that the Eternal Mind is capable of grieving or God's infinite blessedness of suffering the least damage or diminution (God cannot be afflicted); but thus he is pleased to show forth the love and concern he has for his people in their affliction; thus far he sympathizes with them, that he takes what injury is done to them as done to himself and will reckon for it accordingly. Their cries move him (Ex. 3:7), and he appears for them as vigorously as if he were pained in their pain. *Saul, Saul, why persecutest thou me?* This is matter of great comfort to God's people in their affliction that God is so far from *afflicting willingly* (Lam. 3:33) that, if they humble themselves under his hand, he is *afflicted in their affliction,* as the tender parents are in the severe operations which the case of a sick child calls for. There is another reading of these words in the original: *In all their affliction there was no affliction;* though they were in great affliction, yet the property of it was so altered by the grace of God sanctifying it to them for their good, the rigour of it was so mitigated and it was so allayed and balanced with mercies, they were so wonderfully supported and comforted under it, and it proved so short, and ended so well, that it was in effect no affliction. The troubles of the saints are not that to them which they are to others; they are not afflictions, but medicines; saints are enabled to call them *light,* and *but for a moment,* and, with an eye to heaven as all in all, to make nothing of them. (2.) The person employed in their salvation — *the angel of his face,* or presence. Some understand it of a created angel. The highest angel in heaven, even the angel of his presence, that attends next the throne of his glory, is not thought too great, too good, to be sent on this errand. Thus the little ones' angels are said to be those that *always behold the face of our Father,* Mt. 18:10. But this is rather to be understood of Jesus Christ, the eternal Word, that angel of whom God spoke to Moses (Ex. 23:20, 21), whose *voice Israel was to obey.* He is called *Jehovah,* Ex. 13:21; 14:21, 24. He is the angel of the covenant, God's messenger to the world, Mal. 3:1. He is the *angel of God's face,* for he is the *express image of his person;* and the glory of God shines in the face of Christ. He that was to work out the eternal salvation, as an earnest of that, wrought out the temporal salvations that were typical of it. (3.) The progress and perseverance of this favour. He not only redeemed them out of their bondage, but *he bore them and carried them all the days of old;* they were weak, but he supported them by his power, sustained them by his bounty; when they were burdened, and ready to sink, he bore them up; in the wars they made upon the nations he stood by them and bore them out; though they were peevish, he bore with them and suffered their manners, Acts 13:18. He carried them as the nursing father does the child, though they would have tired any arms but his; he carried them as the eagle her young upon her wings, Deu. 32:11. And it was a long time that he was *troubled with them* (if we may so speak): it was *all the days of old;* his care of them was not at an end even when they had grown up and were settled in Canaan. All this was *in his love and pity, ex mero motu — of his mere good-will;* he loved them because he would love them, as he says, Deu. 7:7, 8.

3. Their disingenuous conduct towards him, and the trouble they thereby brought upon themselves (*v.* 10): *But they rebelled.* Things looked very hopeful and promising; one would have thought that they should have continued dutiful children to God, and then there was no doubt but he would have continued a gracious Father to them; but here is a sad change on both sides, and *on them be the breach.* (1.) They revolted from their allegiance to God and took up arms against him: *They rebelled, and vexed his Holy Spirit* with their unbelief and murmuring, besides the iniquity of the golden calf; and this had been their way and manner ever since. Though he was ready to say of them, *They will not lie,* though he had done so much for them, *borne them and carried them,* yet they thus ill requited him, like *foolish people and unwise,* Deu. 32:6. This grieved him, Ps. 95:10. The ungrateful rebellions of God's children against him are a vexation to his Holy Spirit. (2.) Thereupon he justly withdrew his protection, and not only so, but made war upon them, as a prince justly does upon the rebels. He who had been so much their friend was *turned to be their enemy and fought against them,* by one judgment after another, both in the wilderness and after their settlement in Canaan. See the malignity and mischievousness of sin; it makes God an enemy even to those for whom he has done the part of a good friend, and makes him angry who was all love and pity. See the folly of sinners; they wilfully lose him for a friend who is the most desirable friend, and make him their enemy who is the most formidable enemy. This refers especially to those calamities that were of late brought upon them by their captivity in Babylon for their idolatries and other sins. That which is both the original and the great aggravation of their troubles was that God was *turned to be their enemy.*

4. A particular reflection made, on this occasion, upon what God did for them when he first formed them into a people: *Then he remembered the days of old, v.* 11.

(1.) This may be understood either of the people or of God. [1.] We may understand it of the people. Israel then (spoken of as a single person) *remembered the days of old,* looked into their Bibles, read the story of God's bringing their fathers out of Egypt, considered it more closely than ever they did before, and reasoned upon it, as Gideon did (Jdg. 6:13), *Where are all the wonders that our fathers told us of? "Where is he that brought them up* out of Egypt? Is he not as able to bring us up out of Babylon? *Where is the Lord God of Elijah? Where is the Lord God of our fathers?"* This they consider as an inducement and an encouragement to them to repent and return to him; their fathers were a provoking people and yet found him a pardoning God; and why may not they find him so if they return to him? They also use it as a plea with God in prayer for the turning again of their captivity, like that *ch.* 51:9, 10. Note, When the present days are dark and cloudy it is good to *remember the days of old,* to recollect our own and others' experiences of the divine power and goodness and make use of them, to look back upon *the years of the right hand of the Most High* (Ps. 77:5, 10), and remember that he is *God, and changes not.* [2.] We may understand it of God; he put himself in mind of the days of old, of his covenant with Abraham (Lev. 26:42); he said, *Where is he that brought Israel up out of the sea?* stirring up himself to come and save them with this consideration, "Why should not I appear for them now as I did for their fathers, who were as undeserving, as ill-deserving, as they are?" See how far off divine mercy will go, how far back it will look, to find out a reason for doing good to his people, when ho present considerations appear but what make against them. Nay, it makes that a reason for relieving them which might have been used as a reason for abandoning them. He might have said, "I have delivered them formerly, but they have again brought trouble upon themselves (Prov. 19:19); there *I will deliver them no more,"* Jdg. 10:13. But no; mercy rejoices against judgment, and turns the argument the other way: "I have formerly delivered them and therefore will now."

(2.) Which way soever we take it, whether the people plead it with God or God with himself, let us view the particulars, and they agree very much with the confession and prayer which the children of the captivity made upon a solemn fast-day (Neh. 9:5. etc.), which may serve as a comment on these verses which call to mind *Moses and his people,* that is, what God did by Moses for his people, especially in bringing them through the Red Sea, for that is it that is here most insisted on; for it was a work which he much gloried in and which his people therefore may in a particular manner encourage themselves with the remembrance of. [1.] God *led them by the right hand of Moses* (*v.* 12) and the wonder-working rod in his hand. Ps. 77:20, *Thou leddest thy people like a flock by the hand of Moses.* It was not Moses that led them, any more than it was Moses that fed them (Jn. 6:32), but God by Moses; for it was he that qualified Moses for, called him to, assisted and prospered him in that great undertaking. Moses is here called *the shepherd of his flock;* God was the owner of the flock and the chief shepherd of Israel (Ps. 80:1); but Moses was a shepherd under him, and he was inured to labour and patience, and so fitted for this pastoral care, by his being trained up to *keep the flock of his father Jethro.* Herein he was a type of Christ the good shepherd, that *lays down his life for the sheep,* which was more than Moses did for Israel, though he did a great deal for them. [2.] He *put his holy Spirit within him; the Spirit of God was among them,* and not only his providence, but his grace, did work for them. Neh. 9:20, *Thou gavest thy good Spirit to instruct them.* The spirit of wisdom and courage, as well as the Spirit of prophecy, was put into Moses, to qualify him for that service among them to which he was called; and some of his spirit was put upon the seventy elders, Num. 11:17. This was a great blessing to Israel, that they had among them not only inspired writings, but inspired men. [3.] He carried them safely through the Red Sea, and thereby saved them out of the hands of Pharaoh. *First, He divided the water before them* (*v.* 12), so that it gave them not only passage, but protection, not only opened them a lane, but erected them a wall on either side. *Secondly, He led them through the deep as a horse in the wilderness,* or *in the plain* (*v.* 13); they and their wives and children, with all their baggage, went as easily and readily through the bottom of the sea (though we may suppose it muddy or stony, or both) as a horse goes along upon even ground; so that they did not stumble, though it was an untrodden path, which neither they nor any one else ever went before. If God make us a way, he will make it plain and level; the road he opens to his people he will lead them in. *Thirdly,* To complete the mercy, he *brought them up out of the sea, v.* 11. Though the ascent, it is likely, was very steep, dirty, slippery, and unconquerable (at least by the women and children, and the men, considering how they were loaded, Ex. 12:34, and how fatigued), yet God by his power brought them up from the depths of the earth; and it was a kind of resurrection to them; it was as *life from the dead.* [4.] He brought them safely to a place of rest: *As a beast goes down into the valley,* carefully and gradually, so *the Spirit of the Lord caused him to rest.* Many a time in their march through the wilderness they had resting-places provided for them by the direction of the Spirit of the Lord in Moses, *v.* 11. And at length they were made to rest finally in Canaan, and the Spirit of the Lord gave them that rest according to the promise. It is by the Spirit of the Lord that God's Israel are caused to return to God and repose in him as their rest. [5.] All this he did for them by his own power, for his own praise. *First,* It was by his own power, as the God of nature, that has all the powers of nature at his command; he did it with his glorious arm, *the arm of his gallantry,* or *bravery;* so the word signifies. It was not Moses's rod, but God's glorious arm, that did it. *Secondly,* It was for his own praise, to *make himself an everlasting name* (*v.* 12), *a glorious name* (*v.* 14), that he might be glorified, everlastingly glorified, upon this account. This is that which God is doing in the world with his glorious arm, he is making to himself a glorious name, and it shall last to endless ages, when the most celebrated names of the great ones of the earth shall be written in the dust.

Verses 15–19

The foregoing praises were intended as an introduction to this prayer, which is continued to the end of the next chapter, and it is an affectionate, importunate, pleading prayer. It is calculated for the time of the captivity. As they had promises, so they had prayers, prepared for them against that time of need, that they might take with them words in turning to the Lord, and say unto him what he himself taught them to say, in which they might the better hope to prevail, the words being of God's own inditing. Some good interpreters think this prayer looks further, and that it expresses the complaints of the Jews under their last and final rejection from God and destruction by the Romans; for there is one passage in it (*ch.* 64:4) which is applied to the grace of the gospel by the apostle (1 Co. 2:9), that grace for the rejecting of which they were rejected. In these verses we may observe,

I. The petitions they put up to God. 1. That he would take cognizance of their case and of the desires of their souls towards him: *Look down from heaven, and behold, v.* 15. They knew very well that God sees all, but they prayed that he would regard them, would condescend to favour them, would look upon them with an eye of compassion and concern, as he looked upon the affliction of his people in Egypt when he was about to appear for their deliverance. In begging that he would only look down upon them and behold them they did in effect appeal to his justice against their enemies, and pray for judgment against them (as Jehoshaphat, 2 Chr. 20:11, 12, *Behold, how they reward us. Wilt thou not judge them?),* implicitly confiding in his mercy and wisdom as to the way in which he will relieve them (Ps. 25:18, *Look upon my affliction and my pain): Look down from the habitation of thy holiness and of thy glory.* God's holiness is his glory. Heaven is his habitation, the throne of his glory, where he most manifests his glory, and whence he is said to look down upon the earth, Ps. 33:14. His holiness is in a special manner celebrated there by the blessed angels (*ch.* 6:3; Rev. 4:8); there his holy ones attend him, and are continually about him; so that it is the *habitation of his holiness.* It is an encouragement to all his praying people, who desire to be holy as he is holy, that he *dwells in a holy place.* 2. That he would take a course for their relief (*v.* 17): *"Return;* change thy way towards us, and proceed not in thy controversy with us; return in mercy, and let us have not only a gracious look towards us, but thy gracious presence with us." God's people dread nothing more than his departures from them and desire nothing more than his returns to them.

II. The complaints they made to God. Two things they complained of: — 1. That they were given up to themselves, and God's grace did not recover them, *v.* 17. It is a strange expostulation, *"Why hast thou made us to err from thy ways,* that is, many among us, the generality of us; and this complaint we have all of us some cause to make that *thou hast hardened our heart from thy fear."* Some make it to be the language of those among them that were impious and profane; when the prophets reproved them for the *error of their ways,* their *hardness of heart,* and *contempt of God's word and commandments,* they with a daring impudence charged their sin upon God, made him the author of it, and asked *why doth he then find fault?* Note, Those are wicked indeed that lay the blame of their wickedness upon God. But I rather take it to be the language of those among them that lamented the unbelief and impenitence of their people, not accusing God of being the author of their wickedness, but complaining of it to him. They owned that they had *erred from God's ways,* that their *hearts* had been *hardened from his fear,* that they had not received the impressions which the fear of God ought to make upon them and this was the cause of all their errors from his ways; or *from his fear* may mean from the true worship of God, and that is a hard heart indeed which is alienated from the service of a God so incontestably great and good. Now this they complain of, as their great misery and burden, that God had for their sins left them to this, had permitted them to *err from his ways* and had justly withheld his grace, so that their *hearts were hardened from his fear.* When they ask, *Why hast thou done this?* it is not as charging him with wrong, but lamenting it as a sore judgment. God had *caused them to err and hardened their hearts,* not only by withdrawing his Spirit from them, because they had grieved, and vexed, and quenched him (*v.* 10), but by a judicial sentence upon them *(Go, make the heart of this people fat, ch.* 6:9, 10) and by his providences concerning them, which had proved sad occasions for their departure from him. David complains of his banishment, because in it he was in effect bidden to *go and serve other gods,* 1 Sa. 26:19. Their troubles had alienated many of them from God, and prejudiced them against his service; and, because the *rod of the wicked had lain long on their lot,* they were ready to *put forth their hand unto iniquity* (Ps. 125:3), and this was the thing they complained most of; their afflictions were their temptations, and to many of them invincible ones. Note, Convinced consciences complain most of spiritual judgments and dread that most in an affliction which draws them from God and duty. 2. That they were given up to their enemies, and God's providence did not rescue and relieve them (*v.* 18): *Our adversaries have trodden down thy sanctuary.* As it was a grief to them that in their captivity the generality of them had lost their affection to God's worship, and had their hearts hardened from it by their affliction, so it was a further grief that they were deprived of their opportunities of worshipping God in solemn assemblies. They complained not so much of the adversaries treading down their houses and cities as of their treading down God's sanctuary, because thereby God was immediately affronted, and they were robbed of the comforts they valued most and took most pleasure in.

III. The pleas they urged with God for mercy and deliverance. 1. They pleaded the tender compassion God used to show to his people and his ability and readiness to appear for them, *v.* 15. The most prevailing arguments in prayer are those that are taken *from God himself;* such these are. *Where is thy zeal and thy strength?* God has a zeal for his own glory, and for the comfort of his people; his name is *Jealous;* and he is a jealous God; and he has strength proportionable to secure his own glory and the interest of his people, in despite of all opposition. Now where are these? Have they not formerly appeared? Why do they not appear now? It cannot be that divine zeal, which is infinitely wise and just, should be cooled, that divine strength, which is infinite, should be weakened. Nay, his people had experienced not only *his zeal and his strength, but the sounding of his bowels,* or rather the yearning of them, such a degree of compassion to them as in men causes a commotion and agitation within them, as Hos. 11:8, *My heart is turned within me, my repentings are kindled together;* and Jer. 31:20, *My bowels are troubled* (or sound) *for him.* "Thus God used to be affected towards his people, and to express a *multitude of mercies towards them;* but where are they now? *Are they restrained?* Ps. 77:9. Has God, who so often remembered to be gracious, now forgotten to be so? *Has he in anger shut up his tender mercies?* It can never be." Note, We may ground good expectations of further mercy upon our experiences of former mercy. 2. They pleaded God's relation to them as their Father (*v.* 16): "Thy tender mercies are not restrained, for they are the tender mercies of a father, who, though he may be for a time displeased with his child, will yet, through the force of natural affection, soon be reconciled. *Doubtless thou art our Father,* and therefore thy bowels will years towards us." Such good thoughts of God as these we should always keep up in our hearts. *However it be, yet God is good;* for he is our Father. They own themselves fatherless if he be not their Father, and so cast themselves upon him with whom *the fatherless findeth mercy,* Hos. 14:3. It was the honour of their nation that *they had Abraham to their father* (Mt. 3:9), who was the friend of God, and Israel, who was a prince with God; but what the better were they for that unless they had God himself for their Father? "Abraham and Israel cannot help us; they have not the power that God has; they are dead long since, and are *ignorant of us, and acknowledge us not;* they know not what our case is, nor what our wants are, and therefore know not which way to do us a kindness. If Abraham and Israel were alive with us, they would intercede for us and advise us; but they have gone to the other world, and we know not that they have any communication at all with this world, and therefore they are not capable of doing us any kindness any further than that we have the honour of being called their children." When the father is dead *his sons come to honour and he knows it not,* Job 14:21. "But *thou, O Lord! art our Father still* (the fathers of our flesh may call themselves *ever-loving;* but they are not *ever-living;* it is God only that is the immortal Father, that always knows us, and is never at a distance from us), and therefore *our Redeemer from everlasting is thy name,* the name by which we will know and own thee. It is the name by which from of old thou hast been known; thy people have always looked upon thee as the God to whom they might appeal to redress their grievances and plead their cause. Nay" (according to the sense some give of this place), "though Abraham and Israel not only cannot, but would not, help us, thou wilt. They have not the pity thou hast. We are so degenerate and corrupt that Abraham and Israel would not own us for their children, yet we fly to thee as our Father. Abraham cast out his son Ishmael; Jacob disinherited his son Reuben and cursed Simeon and Levi; but our heavenly Father, in pardoning sin, is *God, and not man,"* Hos. 11:9. 3. They pleaded God's interest in them, that he was their Lord, their owner and proprietor: "We are thy servants; what service we can do thou art entitled to, and therefore we ought not to serve strange kings and strange gods: *Return for thy servants' sake."* As a father finds himself obliged by natural affection to relieve and protect his child, so a master thinks himself obliged in honour to rescue and protect his servant: *"We are thine* by the strongest engagements, as well as the highest endearments. Thou hast borne rule over us; therefore, Lord, assert thy own interest, maintain thy own right; for *we are called by thy name,* and therefore whither shall we go but to thee, to be righted and protected? *We are thine, save us* (Ps. 119:94), thy own, acknowledge us. We are the *tribes of thy inheritance,* not only thy servants, but thy tenants; we are thine, not only to do work for thee, but to pay rent to thee. The tribes of Israel are God's inheritance, whence issue the little praise and worship that he receives from this lower world; and wilt thou suffer thy own servants and tenants to be thus abused?" 4. They pleaded that they had had but a short enjoyment of the land of promise and the privileges of the sanctuary (*v.* 18): *The people of thy holiness have possessed it but a little while.* From Abraham to David were but fourteen generations, and from David to the captivity but fourteen more (Mt. 1:17), and that was but a little while in comparison with what might have been expected from the promise of the *land of Canaan for an everlasting possession* (Gen. 17:8) and from the power that was put forth to bring them into that land and settle them in it. "Though we are *the people of thy holiness,* distinguished from other people and consecrated to thee, yet we are soon dislodged." But this they might thank themselves for; they were, in profession, the *people of God's holiness,* but it was their wickedness that turned them out of the possession of that land. 5. They pleaded that those who had and kept possession of their land were such as were strangers to God, such as he had no service or honour from: *"Thou never didst bear rule over them,* nor did they ever yield thee any obedience; they *were not called by thy name,* but professed relation to other gods and were the worshippers of them. Will God suffer those that do not stand in any relation to him to trample upon those that do?" Some give another reading of this: *"We have become as those over whom thou didst never bear rule and who were never called by thy name;* we are rejected and abandoned, despised and trampled upon, as if we never had been in thy service nor had thy name called upon us." Thus the shield of *Saul was vilely cast away, as though he had not been anointed with oil.* But the covenant that seems to be forgotten shall be remembered again.

CHAPTER 64

This chapter goes on with that pathetic pleading prayer which the church offered up to God in the latter part of the foregoing chapter. They had argued from their covenant-relation to God and his interest and concern in them; now here, I. They pray that God would appear in some remarkable and surprising manner for them against his and their enemies (*v.* 1, 2). II. They plead what God had formerly done, and was always ready to do, for his people (*v.* 3–5). III. They confess themselves to be sinful and unworthy of God's favour, and that they had deserved the judgments they were now under (*v.* 6, 7). IV. They refer themselves to the mercy of God as a Father, and submit themselves to his sovereignty (*v.* 8). V. They represent the very deplorable condition they were in, and earnestly pray for the pardon of sin and the turning away of God's anger (*v.* 9–12). And this was not only intended for the use of the captive Jews, but may serve for direction to the church in other times of distress, what to ask of God and how to plead with him. Are God's people at any time in affliction, in great affliction? Let them pray, let them thus pray.

Verses 1–5

Here, I. The petition is that God would appear wonderfully for them now, *v.* 1, 2. Their case was represented in the close of the foregoing chapter as very sad and very hard, and in this case it was time to cry, "Help, Lord; O that God would manifest his zeal and his strength!" They had prayed (*ch.* 63:15) that God would *look down from heaven;* here they pray that he would come down to deliver them, as he had said, Ex. 3:8. 1. They desire that God would in his providence manifest himself both to them and for them. When God works some extraordinary deliverance for his people he is said to *shine forth,* to show himself strong; so, here, they pray that he would *rend the heavens and come down,* as when he delivered David he is said to *bow the heavens, and come down* (Ps. 18:9), to display his power, and justice, and goodness, in an extraordinary manner, so that all may take notice of them and acknowledge them. This God's people desire and pray for, that they themselves having the satisfaction of seeing him though his way be in the sea, others may be made to see him when his way is in the clouds. This is applicable to the second coming of Christ, when *the Lord himself shall descend from heaven with a shout. Come, Lord Jesus, come quickly.* 2.

They desire that he would vanquish all opposition and that it might be made to give way before him: *That the mountains might flow down at thy presence,* that the fire of thy wrath may burn so fiercely against thy enemies as even to dissolve the rockiest mountains and melt them down before it, as metal in the furnace, which is made liquid and cast into what shape the operator pleases; so *the melting fire burns, v.* 2. Let things be put into a ferment, in order to a glorious revolution in favour of the church: *As the fire causes the waters to boil.* There is an allusion here, some think, to the *volcanoes,* or burning mountains, which sometimes send forth such sulphureous streams as make the adjacent rivers and seas to boil, which, perhaps, are left as sensible intimations of the power of God's wrath and warning-pieces of the final conflagration. 3. They desire that this may tend very much to the glory and honour of God, *may make his name known,* not only to his friends (they knew it before, and trusted in his power), but to his adversaries likewise, that they may know it and *tremble at his presence,* and may say, with the men of Bethshemesh, *Who is able to stand before this holy Lord God? Who knows the power of his anger?* Note, Sooner or later God will make his name known to his adversaries and force those to *tremble at his presence* that would not come and worship in his presence. God's name, if it be not a strong-hold for us, into which we may run and be safe, will be a strong-hold against us, out of the reach of which we cannot run and be safe. The day will come when nations shall be made to tremble at the presence of God, though they be ever so numerous and strong.

II. The plea is that God had appeared wonderfully for his people formerly; and *thou hast,* therefore *thou wilt,* is good arguing at the throne of grace, Ps. 10:17.

1. They plead what he had done for his people Israel in particular when he brought them out of Egypt, *v.* 3. He then *did terrible things* in the plagues of Egypt, *which they looked not for;* they despaired of deliverance, so far were they from any thought of being delivered with such a high hand and outstretched arm. Then he came down upon Mount Sinai in such terror as made that and the adjacent mountains to *flow down at his presence,* to *skip like rams* (Ps. 114:4), to tremble, so that they were scattered and the perpetual hills were made to bow, Hab. 3:6. In the many great salvations God wrought for that people he did *terrible things which they looked not for,* made great men, that seemed as stately and strong as mountains, to fall before him, and great opposition to give way. See Jdg. 5:4, 5; Ps. 68:7, 8. Some refer this to the defeat of Sennacherib's powerful army, which was as surprising an instance of the divine power as the melting down of rocks and mountains would be.

2. They plead what God had been used to do, and had declared his gracious purpose to do, for his people in general. The provision he has made for the safety and happiness of his people, even of all those that seek him, and serve him, and trust in him, is very rich and very ready, so that they need not fear being either disappointed of it, for it is sure, or disappointed in it, for it is sufficient.

(1.) It is very rich, *v.* 4. Men have not heard nor seen what God has *prepared for those that wait for him.* Observe the character of God's people; they are such as wait for him in the way of duty, wait for the salvation he has promised and designed for them. Observe where the happiness of this people is bound up; it is *what God has prepared for them,* what he has designed for them in his counsel and is in his providence and grace preparing for them and preparing them for, what he has *done* or *will* do, so it may be read. Some of the Jewish doctors have understood this of the blessings reserved for the days of the Messiah, and to them the apostle applies these words; and others extend them to the glories of the world to come. It is all that goodness which God has *laid up for those that fear him, and wrought for those that trust in him,* Ps. 31:19. Of this it is here said that *since the beginning of the world,* in the most prying and inquisitive ages of it, men have not, either by hearing or seeing, the two learning senses, come to the full knowledge of it. None have seen, nor heaard, nor can understand, but God himself, what the provision is that is made for the present and future felicity of holy souls. For, [1.] Much of it was concealed in former ages; they knew it not, because the *unsearchable riches of Christ* were *hidden in God,* were *hidden from the wise and prudent;* but in latter ages they were revealed by the gospel; so the apostle applies this (1 Co. 2:9), for it follows (*v.* 10), *But God has revealed them unto us by his Spirit;* compare Rom. 16:25, 26, with Eph. 3:9. That which men had not heard *since the beginning of the world* they should hear before the end of it, and at the end of it should see, when the veil shall be rent to introduce the glory that is yet to be revealed. God himself knew what he had in store for believers, but none knew besides him. [2.] It cannot be fully comprehended by the human understanding, no, not when it is revealed; it is spiritual, and refined from those ideas which our minds are most apt to receive in this world of sense; it is very great, and will far outdo the utmost of our expectations. Even the present peace of believers, much more their future bliss, is such as surpasses all conception and expression, Phil. 4:7. None can comprehend it but God himself, whose understanding is infinite. Some give another reading of these words, referring the transcendency, not so much to the work itself as to the author of it: *Neither has the eye seen a god besides thee, who doth so* (or has done or can do so) *for him that waits for him.* We must infer from God's works of wonderous grace, as well as from his works of wondrous power, from the kind things, as well as from the great things, he does, that there is *no god like him,* nor any among the sons of the mighty to be compared with him.

(2.) It is very ready (*v.* 5): *"Thou meetest him that rejoices and works righteousness,* meetest him with that good which thou hast prepared for him (*v.* 4), and dost not forget *those that remember thee in thy ways."* See here what communion there is between a gracious God and a gracious soul. [1.] What God expects from us, in order to our having communion with him. *First,* We must make conscience of doing our duty in every thing, we must *work righteousness,* must do that which is good and which the Lord our God requires of us, and must do it well. *Secondly,* We must be cheerful in doing our duty, we must *rejoice and work righteousness,* must delight ourselves in God and in his law, must be cheerful in his service and sing at our work. God loves a cheerful giver, a cheerful worshipper. We must *serve the Lord with gladness. Thirdly,* We must conform ourselves to all the methods of his providence concerning us and be suitably affected with them, must *remember him in his ways,* in all the ways wherein he walks, whether he walks towards us or walks contrary to us. We must mind him and make mention of him with thanksgiving when his ways are ways of mercy *(in a day of prosperity be joyful),* with patience and submission when he contends with us. *In the way of thy judgments we have waited for thee;* for *in a day of adversity* we must *consider.* [2.] We are here told what we may expect from God if we thus attend him in the way of duty: *Thou meetest him.* This intimates the friendship, fellowship, and familiarity to which God admits his people; he meets them, to converse with them, to manifest himself to them, and to receive their addresses, Ex. 20:24; 29:43. It likewise intimates his freeness and forwardness in doing them good; he will *anticipate them with the blessings of his goodness,* will *rejoice to do good* to those that *rejoice in working righteousness,* and wait to be gracious to those that *wait for him.* He meets his penitent people with a pardon, as the father of the prodigal met his returning son, Lu. 15:20. He meets his praying people with an answer of peace, while they are yet speaking, *ch.* 65:24.

3. They plead the unchangeableness of God's favour and the stability of his promise, notwithstanding the sins of his people and his displeasure against them for their sins: *"Behold, thou hast* many a time *been wroth with us because we have sinned,* and we have been under the tokens of thy wrath; *but in those,* those ways of thine, the ways of mercy in which we have *remembered thee, in those is continuance,"* or *"in those thou art ever"* (his mercy endures for ever), *"and* therefore *we shall* at last *be saved,* though thou art wroth, and we have sinned." This agrees with the tenour of God's covenant, that, if we *forsake the law,* he will *visit our transgression with a rod,* but *his lovingkindness* he *will not utterly take away, his covenant he will not break* (Ps. 89:30, etc.), and by this his people have been many a time saved from ruin when they were just upon the brink of it; see Ps. 78:38. And by this continuance of the covenant we hope to be saved, for its being an everlasting covenant is all our salvation. Though God has been angry with us for our sins, and justly, yet his anger has endured but for a moment and has been soon over; but *in his favour is life,* because *in it is continuance;* in the ways of his favour he proceeds and perseveres, and on that we depend for our salvation, see *ch.* 54:7, 8. It is well for us that our hopes of salvation are built not upon any merit or sufficiency of our own (for in that there is no certainty, even Adam in innocency did not abide), but upon God's mercies and promises, for *in those,* we are sure, *is continuance.*

Verses 6–12

As we have the Lamentations of Jeremiah, so here we have the Lamentations of Isaiah; the subject of both is the same — the destruction of Jerusalem by the Chaldeans and the sin of Israel that brought that destruction — only with this difference, Isaiah sees it at a distance and laments it by the Spirit of prophecy, Jeremiah saw it accomplished. In these verses,

I. The people of God in their affliction confess and bewail their sins, thereby justifying God in their afflictions, owning themselves unworthy of his mercy, and thereby both improving their troubles and preparing for deliverance. Now that they were under divine rebukes for sin they had nothing to trust to but the mere mercy of God and the continuance of that; for among themselves there is none to help, none to uphold, none to stand in the gap and make intercession, for they are all polluted with sin and therefore unworthy to intercede, all careless and remiss in duty and therefore unable and unfit to intercede.

1. There was a general corruption of manners among them (*v.* 6): *We are all as an unclean thing,* or as an unclean *person,* as one overspread with a leprosy, who was to be shut out of the camp. The body of the people were like one under a ceremonial pollution, who was not admitted into the courts of the tabernacle, or like one labouring under some loathsome disease, from the crown of the head to the sole of the foot *nothing but wounds and bruises, ch.* 1:6. We have all by sin become not only obnoxious to God's justice, but odious to his holiness; for sin is that *abominable thing which the Lord hates,* and cannot endure to look upon. *Even all our righteousnesses are as filthy rags.* (1.) "The best of our persons are so; we are all so corrupt and polluted that even those among us who pass for righteous men, in comparison with what our fathers were who *rejoiced and wrought righteousness* (*v.* 5), are but as filthy rags, fit to be case to the dunghill. *The best of them is as a brier."* (2.) "The best of our performances are so. There is not only a general corruption of manners, but a general defection in the exercises of devotion too; those which pass for the *sacrifices of righteousness,* when they come to be enquired into, are *the torn, and the lame, and the sick,* and therefore are provoking to God, as nauseous as filthy rags." Our performances, though they be ever so plausible, if we depend upon them as our righteousness and think to merit by them at God's hand, are as filthy rags — rags, and will not cover us — filthy rags, and will but defile us. True penitents cast away their idols as filthy rags (*ch.* 30:22), odious in their sight; here they acknowledge even their righteousness to be so in God's sight if he should deal with them in strict justice. Our best duties are so defective, and so far short of the rule, that they are as rags, and so full of sin and corruption cleaving to them that they are as filthy rags. When we would do good evil is present with us; and the iniquity of our holy things would be our ruin if we were under the law.

2. There was a general coldness of devotion among them, *v.* 7. The measure was filled by the abounding iniquity of the people, and nothing was done to empty it. (1.) Prayer was in a manner neglected: *"There is none that calls on thy name,* none that seeks to thee for grace to reform us and take away sin, or for mercy to relieve us and take away the judgments which our sins have brought upon us." *Therefore* people are so bad, because they do not pray; compare Ps. 14:3, 4, *They have altogether become filthy, for they call not upon the Lord.* It bodes ill to a people when prayer is restrained among them. (2.) It was very negligently performed. If there was here and there one that called on God's name, it was with a great deal of indifferency: *There is none that stirs up himself to take hold of God.* Note, [1.] To pray is to *take hold of God,* by

faith to take hold of the promises and the declarations God has made of his good-will to us and to plead them with him, — to take hold of him as of one who is about to depart from us, earnestly begging of him not to leave us, or of one that has departed, soliciting his return, — to take hold of him as he that wrestles takes hold of him he wrestles with; for the seed of Jacob wrestle with him and so prevail. But when we *take hold of God* it is as the boatman with his hook takes hold on the shore, as if he would pull the shore to him, but really it is to pull himself to the shore; so we pray, not to bring God to our mind, but to bring ourselves to him. [2.] Those that would take hold of God in prayer so as to prevail with him must stir up themselves to do it; all that is within us must be employed in the duty (and all little enough), our thoughts fixed and our affections flaming. In order hereunto all that is within us must be engaged and summoned into the service; we must *stir up the gift that is in us* by an actual consideration of the importance of the work that is before us and a close application of mind to it; but how can we expect that God should come to us in ways of mercy when there are none that do this, when those that profess to be intercessors are mere triflers?

II. They acknowledge their afflictions to be the fruit and product of their own sins and God's wrath. 1. They brought their troubles upon themselves by their own folly: *"We are all as an unclean thing, and* therefore *we do all fade away as a leaf* (*v.* 6), we not only wither and lose our beauty, but we fall and drop off" (so the word signifies) "as leaves in autumn; our profession of religion withers, and we grow dry and sapless; our prosperity withers and comes to nothing; we fall to the ground, as despicable and contemptible; and then *our iniquities like the wind have taken us away* and hurried us into captivity, as the winds in autumn blow off, and then blow away, the faded withered leaves," Ps. 1:3, 4. Sinners are blasted, and then carried away, by the malignant and violent wind of their own iniquity; it withers them and then ruins them. 2. God brought their troubles upon them by his wrath (*v.* 7): *Thou hast hidden thy face from us;* hast been displeased with us and refused to afford us any succour. When they made themselves *as an unclean thing* no wonder that God turned his face away from them, as loathing them. Yet this was not all: *Thou hast consumed us because of our iniquities.* This is the same complaint with that (Ps. 90:7, 8), *We are consumed by thy anger;* thou hast *melted us,* so the word is. God had put them in the furnace, not to consume them as dross, but to melt them as gold, that they might be refined and new-cast.

III. They claim relation to God as their God, and humbly plead it with him, and in consideration of it cheerfully refer themselves to him (*v.* 8): *"But now, O Lord! thou art our Father:* though we have conducted ourselves very undutifully and ungratefully towards thee, yet still we have owned thee as our Father; and, though thou hast corrected us, yet thou hast not cast us off. Foolish and careless as we are, poor and despised and trampled upon as we are by our enemies, yet still *thou art our Father;* to thee therefore we return in our repentance, as the prodigal arose and came to his father; to thee we address ourselves by prayer; from whom should we expect relief and succour but from our Father? It is the wrath of a Father that we are under, who will be reconciled and not *keep his anger for ever."* God is their Father, 1. By creation; he gave them their being, formed them into a people, shaped them as he pleased: *"We are the clay and thou our potter,* therefore we will not quarrel with thee, however thou art pleased to deal with us, Jer. 18:6. Nay, therefore we will hope that thou wilt deal well with us, that thou who madest us wilt new-make us, new-form us, though we have unmade and deformed ourselves: *We are all as an unclean thing,* but *we are all the work of thy hands,* therefore do away our uncleanness, that we may be fit for thy use, the use we were made for. We are the *work of thy hands,* therefore *forsake us not,"* Ps. 138:8. 2. By covenant; this is pleaded (*v.* 9): *"Behold, see, we beseech thee, we are all thy people,* all the people thou hast in the world, that make open profession of thy name. We are called *thy people,* our neighbours look upon us as such, and therefore what we suffer reflects upon thee, and the relief that our case requires is expected from thee. *We are thy people;* and *should not a people seek unto their God? ch.* 8:19. *We are thine; save us,"* Ps. 119:94. Note, When we are under providential rebukes from God it is good to keep fast hold of our covenant-relation to him.

IV. They are importunate with God for the turning away of his anger and the pardoning of their sins (*v.* 9): *"Be not wroth very sore, O Lord!* though we have deserved that thou shouldst, *neither remember iniquity for ever* against us." They do not expressly pray for the removal of the judgment they were under; as to that, they refer themselves to God. But, 1. They pray that God would be reconciled to them, and then they can be easy whether the affliction be continued or removed: *"Be not wroth to extremity,* but let thy anger be mitigated by the clemency and compassion of a father." They do not say, *Lord, rebuke us not,* for that may be necessary, but *Not in thy anger, not in thy hot displeasure.* It is but *in a little wrath* that God *hides his face.* 2. They pray that they may not be dealt with according to the desert of their sin: *Neither remember iniquity for ever.* Such is the evil of sin that it deserves to be remembered for ever; and this is that which they deprecate, that consequence of sin, which is for ever. Those make it to appear that they are truly humbled under the hand of God who are more afraid of the terror of God's wrath, and the fatal consequences of their own sin, than of any judgment whatsoever, looking upon these as the sting of death.

V. They lodge in the court of heaven a very melancholy representation, or memorial, of the lamentable condition they were in and the ruins they were groaning under. 1. Their own houses were in ruins, *v.* 10. The cities of Judah were destroyed by the Chaldeans and the inhabitants of them were carried away, so that there was none to repair them or take any notice of them, which would in a few years make them look like perfect deserts: *Thy holy cities are a wilderness.* The cities of Judah are called *holy cities,* for the people were unto God a kingdom of priests. The cities had synagogues in them, in which God was served; and therefore they lamented the ruins of them, and insisted upon this in pleading with God for them, not so much that they were stately cities, rich or ancient ones, but that they were holy cities, cities in which God's name was known, professed, and called upon. "These cities are a wilderness; the beauty of them is sullied; they are neither inhabited nor visited, as formerly. *They have burnt up all the synagogues of God in the land,"* Ps. 74:8. Nor was it only the smaller cities that were thus left as a wilderness unfrequented, but even *"Zion is a wilderness;* the city of David itself lies in ruins; Jerusalem, that was *beautiful for situation* and *the joy of the whole earth,* is now deformed, and has become the scorn and scandal of the whole earth; that noble city is a desolation, a heap of rubbish." See what devastations sin brings upon a people; and an external profession of sanctity will be no fence against them; *holy cities,* if they become wicked cities, will be soonest of all turned into a wilderness, Amos 3:2. 2. God's house was in ruins, *v.* 11. This they lament most of all, that *the temple was burnt with fire;* but, as soon as it was built, they were told what their sin would bring it to. 2 Chr. 7:21, *This house, which is high, shall be an astonishment.* Observe how pathetically they bewail the ruins of the temple. (1.) It was *their holy and beautiful house;* it was a most sumptuous building, but the holiness of it was in their eye the greatest beauty of it, and consequently the profanation of it was the saddest part of its desolation and that which grieved them most, that the sacred services which used to be performed there were discontinued. (2.) It was the place *where their fathers praised God* with their sacrifices and songs; what a pity is it that that should lie in ashes which had been for so many ages the glory of their nation! It aggravated their present disuse of the songs of Zion that their fathers had so often praised God with them. They interest God in the cause when they plead that it was the house where *he had been praised,* and put him in mind too of his covenant with their fathers by taking notice of their fathers' praising him. (3.) With it *all their pleasant things were laid waste,* all their desires and delights, all those things which were employed by them in the service of God, which they had a great delight in; not only the furniture of the temple, the altars and table, but especially the sabbaths and new moons, and all their religious feasts, which they used to keep with gladness, their ministers and solemn assemblies, these were all a desolation. Note, God's people reckon their sacred things their most delectable things; rob them of holy ordinances and the means of grace, and you *lay waste all their pleasant things.* What have they more? Observe here how God and his people have their interest twisted and interchanged; when they speak of the cities for their own habitation they call them *thy holy cities,* for to God they were dedicated; when they speak of the temple wherein God dwelt they call it *our beautiful* house and its furniture *our pleasant things,* for they had heartily espoused it and all the interests of it. If thus we interest God in all our concerns by devoting them to his service, and interest ourselves in all his concerns by laying them near our hearts, we may with satisfaction leave both with him, for he will perfect both.

VI. They conclude with an affectionate expostulation, humbly arguing with God concerning their present desolations (*v.* 12): *"Wilt thou refrain thyself for these things?* Or, *Canst thou contain thyself at these things?* Canst thou see thy temple ruined and not resent it, not revenge it? Has the jealous God forgotten to be jealous? Ps. 74:22, *Arise, O God! plead thy own cause.* Lord, thou art insulted, thou art blasphemed; and *wilt thou hold thy peace* and take no notice of it? Shall the highest affronts that can be done to Heaven pass unrebuked?" When we are abused we hold our peace, because vengeance does not belong to us, and because we have a God to refer our cause to. When God is injured in his honour it may justly be expected that he should speak in the vindication of it; his people prescribe not to him what he shall say, but their prayer is (as here) Ps. 83:1, *Keep not thou silence, O God!* and Ps. 109:1, *"Hold not thy peace, O God of my praise!* Speak for the conviction of thy enemies, speak for the comfort and relief of thy people; for *wilt thou afflict us very grievously,* or *afflict us for ever?"* It is a sore affliction to good people to see God's sanctuary laid waste and nothing done towards the raising of it out of its ruins. But God has said that he *will not contend for ever,* and therefore his people may depend upon it that their afflictions shall be neither to extremity nor to eternity, but *light* and *for a moment.*

CHAPTER 65

We are now drawing towards the conclusion of this evangelical prophecy, the last two chapters of which direct us to look as far forward as the new heavens and the new earth, the new world which the gospel dispensation should bring in, and the separation that should by it be made between the precious and the vile. "For judgment" (says Christ) "have I come into this world." And why should it seem absurd that the prophet here should speak of that to which all the prophets bore witness? 1 Pt. 1:10, 11. The rejection of the Jews, and the calling in of the Gentiles, are often mentioned in the New Testament as that which was foreseen and foretold by the prophets, Acts 10:43; 13:40; Rom. 16:26. In this chapter we have, I. The anticipating of the Gentiles with the gospel call (*v.* 10). II. The rejection of the Jews for their obstinacy and unbelief (*v.* 2–7). III. The saving of a remnant of them by bringing them into the gospel church (*v.* 8–10). IV. The judgments of God that should pursue the rejected Jews (*v.* 11–16). V. The blessings reserved for the Christian church, which should be its joy and glory (*v.* 17–25). But these things are here prophesied of under the type and figure of the difference God would make between some and others of the Jews after their return out of captivity, between those that feared God and those that did not, with reproofs of the sins then found among them and promises of the blessings then in reserve for them.

Verses 1–7

The apostle Paul (an expositor we may depend upon) has given us the true sense of these verses, and told us what was the event they pointed at and were fulfilled in, namely, the calling in of the Gentiles and the rejection of the Jews, by the preaching of the gospel, Rom. 10:20, 21. And he observes that herein *Esaias is very bold,* not only in foretelling a thing so improbable ever to be brought about, but in foretelling it to the Jews, who would take it as a gross affront to their nation, and therein Moses's words would be made good (Deu. 32:21), *I will provoke you to jealousy by those that are no people.*

I. It is here foretold that the Gentiles, who had been afar off, should be made nigh, *v.* 1. Paul reads it thus: *I was found of those that sought me not; I was made manifest to those that asked not for me.* Observe what a wonderful and blessed change was made with them and how they were surprised into it. 1. Those who had long been without God in the world shall now be set a seeking him; those who had not said, *Where is God my maker?* shall now begin to enquire after him. Neither they nor their fathers had called upon his name, but either lived without prayer or prayed to stocks and stones, the work of men's hands.

But now they shall *be baptized and call on the name of the Lord,* Acts 2:21. With what pleasure does the great God here speak of his being sought unto, and how does he glory in it, especially by those who in time past had not asked for him! For there is joy in heaven over great sinners who repent. 2. God shall anticipate their prayers with his blessings: *I am found of those that sought me not.* This happy acquaintance and correspondence between God and the Gentile world began on his side; they came to know God because they were *known of him* (Gal. 4:9), to seek God and find him because they were first sought and found of him. Though in after-communion God is found of those that seek him (Prov. 8:17), yet in the first conversion he is found of those that seek him not; for *therefore we love him because he first loved us.* The design of the bounty of common providence to them was *that they might seek the Lord, if haply they might feel after him and find him,* Acts 17:27. But they sought him not; still he was to them *an unknown God,* and yet God was found of them. 3. God gave the advantages of a divine revelation to those who had never made a profession of religion: *I said, Behold me, behold me* (gave them a sight of me and invited them to take the comfort and benefit of it) to those who *were not called by my name,* as the Jews for many ages had been. When the apostles went about from place to place, preaching the gospel, this was the substance of what they preached: *"Behold God, behold him,* turn towards him, fix the eyes of your minds upon him, acquaint yourselves with him, admire him, adore him; look off from your idols that you have made, and look upon the living God who made you." Christ in them said, *Behold me, behold me* with an eye of faith; *look unto me, and be you saved.* And this was said to those that had long been *lo-ammi,* and *lo-ruhamah* (Hos. 1:8, 9), *not a people,* and that *had not obtained mercy,* Rom. 9:25, 26.

II. It is here foretold that the Jews, who had long been a people near to God, should be cast off and set at a distance *v.* 2. The apostle applies this to the Jews in his time, as a seed of evil-doers. Rom. 10:21, *But to Israel he saith, All day long I have stretched forth my hands unto a disobedient and gainsaying people.* Here observe,

1. How the Jews were courted to the divine grace. God himself, by his prophets, by his Son, by his apostles, *stretched forth his hands to them,* as Wisdom did, Prov. 1:24. God *spread out his hands to them,* as one reasoning and expostulating with them, not only beckoned to them with the finger, but *spread out his hands,* as being ready to embrace and entertain them, reaching forth the tokens of his favour to them, and importuning them to accept them. When Christ was crucified his hands were *spread out and stretched forth,* as if he were preparing to receive returning sinners into his bosom; and this *all the day,* all the gospel-day. He waited to be gracious, and was not weary of waiting; even those that came in at the eleventh hour of the day were not rejected.

2. How they contemned the invitation; it was given to a rebellious and gainsaying people; they were invited to the wedding-supper, and would not come, but *rejected the counsel of God against themselves.* Now here we have,

(1.) The bad character of this people. The world shall see that it was not for nothing that they were rejected of God; no, it was for their whoredoms that they were put away.

[1.] Their character in general was such as one would not expect of those who had been so much the favourites of Heaven. *First,* They were very wilful. Right or wrong they would do as they had a mind. "They generally *walk* on *in a way that is not good,* not the right way, not a safe way, for they *walk after their own thought,* their own devices and desires." If our guide be our own thoughts, our way is not likely to be good; for *every imagination of the thought of our hearts is only evil.* God had told them his thoughts, what his mind and will were, but they would walk *after their own thoughts,* would do what they thought best. *Secondly,* They were very provoking. This was God's complaint of them all along — they grieved him, they *vexed his Holy Spirit,* as if they would contrive how to make him their enemy: They *provoke me to anger continually to my face.* They cared not what affront they gave to God, though it were in his sight and presence, in a downright contempt of his authority and defiance of his justice; and this *continually;* it had been their way and manner ever since they were a people, witness the *day of temptation in the wilderness.*

[2.] The prophet speaks more particularly of *their iniquities and the iniquities of their fathers,* as the ground of God's casting them off, *v.* 7. Now he gives instances of both.

First, The most provoking iniquity of their fathers was idolatry; this, the prophet tells them, was provoking God to his face; and it is an iniquity which, as appears by the second commandment, God often *visits upon the children.* This was the sin that brought them into captivity, and, though the captivity pretty well cured them of it, yet, when the final ruin of that nation came, that was again brought into the account against them; for in the day when God visits he will visit that, Ex. 32:34. Perhaps there were many, long after the captivity, who, though they did not worship other gods, were yet guilty of the disorders here mentioned; for they married strange wives. 1. They forsook God's temple, and *sacrificed in gardens or groves,* that they might have the satisfaction of doing it in their own way, for they liked not God's institutions. 2. They forsook God's altar, and *burnt incense upon bricks,* altars of their own contriving (they burnt incense according to their own inventions, which were of no more value, in comparison with God's institution, than an altar of bricks in comparison with the golden altar which God appointed them to burn incense on), or *upon tiles* (so some read it), such as they covered their flat-roofed houses with, and on them sometimes they burnt incense to their idols, as appears, 2 Ki. 23:12, where we read of altars *on the top of the upper chamber of Ahaz,* and Jer. 19:13, of their burning incense to the host of heaven upon the roofs of their houses. 3. "They used necromancy, or consulting with the dead, and, in order to that, they *remained among the graves,* and *lodged in the monuments,"* to seek for the living to the dead (*ch.* 8:19), as the witch of Endor. Or they used to consult the evil spirits that haunted the sepulchres. 4. They violated the laws of God about their meat, and broke through the distinction between clean and unclean before it was taken away by the gospel. They *ate swine's flesh.* Some indeed chose rather to die than to eat swine's flesh, as Eleazar and the seven brethren in the story of the Maccabees; but it is probable that many ate of it, especially when it came to be a condition of life. In our Saviour's time we read of a vast herd of swine among them, which gives us cause to suspect that there were many then who made so little conscience of the law as to eat swine's flesh, for which they were justly punished in the destruction of the swine. *And the broth,* or *pieces,* of other forbidden meats, called here *abominable things,* was *in their vessels,* and was made use of for food. The forbidden meat is called *an abomination,* and those that meddle with it are said to *make themselves abominable,* Lev. 11:42, 43. Those that durst not eat the meat yet made bold with the broth, because they would come as near as might be to that which was forbidden, to show how they coveted the forbidden fruit. Perhaps this is here put figuratively for all forbidden pleasures and profits which are obtained by sin, that *abominable thing which the Lord hates;* they loved to be dallying with it, to be tasting of its broth. But those who thus take a pride in venturing upon the borders of sin, and the brink of it, are in danger of falling into the depths of it. But,

Secondly, The most provoking iniquity of the Jews in our Saviour's time was their pride and hypocrisy, that sin of the scribes and Pharisees against which Christ denounced so many woes, *v.* 5. They say, *"Stand by thyself,* keep off" *(get thee to thine,* so the original is); "keep to thy own companions, but *come not near to me,* lest thou pollute me; *touch me not;* I will not allow thee any familiarity with me, *for I am holier than thou,* and therefore thou art not good enough to converse with me; *I am not as other men are, nor even as this publican."* This they were ready to say to every one they met with, so that, in saying, *I am holier than thou,* they thought themselves holier than any, not only very good, as good as they should be, as good as they needed to be, but better than any of their neighbours. *These are a smoke in my nose* (says God), such a smoke as comes not from a quick fire, which soon becomes glowing and pleasant, but from a fire of wet wood, which *burns all the day,* and is nothing but smoke. Note, Nothing in men is more odious and offensive to God than a proud conceit of themselves and contempt of others; for commonly those are most unholy of all that think themselves holier than any.

(2.) The controversy God had with them for this. The proof against them is plain: *Behold, it is written before me, v.* 6. It is written, to be remembered against them in time to come; for they may not perhaps be immediately reckoned with. The sins of sinners, and particularly the vainglorious boasts and scorns of hypocrites, are *laid up in store* with God, Deu. 32:34. And what is written shall be read and proceeded upon: *"I will not keep silence* always, though I may keep silence long." They shall not think him altogether such a one as themselves, as sometimes they have done; but *he will recompense, even recompense into their bosom.* Those basely abuse religion, that honourable and sacred thing, who make their profession of it the matter of their pride, and the jealous God will reckon with them for it; the profession they boast of shall but serve to aggravate their condemnation. [1.] The *iniquity of their fathers* shall come against them; not but that their own sin deserved whatever judgments God brought upon them, and much heavier; and this they owned, Ezra 9:13. But God would not have wrought so great a desolation upon them if he had not therein had an eye to the sins of their fathers. Therefore in the last destruction of Jerusalem God is said to bring upon them the blood of the Old-Testament martyrs, even that of *Abel,* Mt. 23:35. God will reckon with them, not only for their fathers' idols, but for their *high places,* their *burning incense upon the mountains and the hills,* though perhaps it was to the true God only. This was blaspheming or reproaching God; it was a reflection upon the choice he had made of the place where he would record his name, and the promise he had made that there he would meet them and bless them. [2.] Their own with that shall bring ruin upon them: *Your iniquities and the iniquities of your fathers* together, the one aggravating the other, constitute the former work, which, though it may seem to be overlooked and forgotten, shall be *measured into their bosom.* God will render into the bosom, not only of his open enemies (Ps. 79:12), but of his false and treacherous friends, *the reproach wherewith they have reproached him.*

Verses 8–10

This is expounded by St. *Paul,* Rom. 11:1–5, where, when, upon occasion of the rejection of the Jews, it is asked, *Hath God then cast away his people?* he answers, No; for *at this time there is a remnant according to the election of grace.* This prophecy has reference to that distinguished remnant. When that hypocritical nation is to be destroyed God will separate and secure to himself some from among them; some of the Jews shall be brought to embrace the Christian faith, shall be added to the church, and so be saved. And our Saviour has told us that *for the sake of these elect* the days of the destruction of the Jews should be shortened, and a stop put to the desolation, which otherwise would have proceeded to such a degree that *no flesh should be saved,* Mt. 24:22. Now,

I. This is illustrated here by a comparison, *v.* 8. When a vine is so blasted and withered that there seems to be no sap nor life in it, and therefore the dresser of the vineyard is inclined to pluck it up or cut it down, yet, if ever so little of the juice of the grape, fit to make new wine, be found, though but in one cluster, a stander-by interposes, and says, *Destroy it not, for a blessing is in it;* there is life in the root, and hope that yet it may become good for something. Good men are blessings to the places where they live; and sometimes God spares whole cities and nations for the sake of a few such in them. How ambitious should we be of this honor, not only to be distinguished from others, but serviceable to others!

II. Here is a description of those that shall make up this saved saving remnant. 1. They are such as serve God. It is *for my servants' sake* (*v.* 8), and they are *my servants* that *shall dwell there, v.* 9. God's faithful servants, however they are looked upon, are the best friends their country has; and those who serve him do therein *serve their generation.* 2. They are such as seek God, make it the end of their lives to glorify God and the business of their lives to call upon him. It is *for my people that have sought me.* Those that seek God shall find him, and shall find him their bountiful rewarder.

III. Here is an account of the mercy God has in store

for them. The remnant that shall return out of captivity shall have a happy settlement again in their own land, and that by an hereditary right, as *a seed out of Jacob,* in whom the family is kept up and the entail preserved, and from whom, as from the seed sown, shall spring a numerous increase; and these typify the remnant of Jacob that shall be incorporated into the gospel church by faith. 1. They shall have a good portion for themselves. They shall inherit *my mountains,* the holy mountains on which Jerusalem and the temple were built, or the mountains of Canaan, *the land of promise,* typifying the covenant of grace, which all God's servants, his elect, both inhabit and inherit; they make it their refuge, their rest and residence, so they dwell in it, are at home in it; and they have taken it to be their heritage for ever, and it shall be to them an inheritance incorruptible. God's chosen, the spiritual seed of praying Jacob, shall be the inheritors of his mountains of bliss and joy, and shall be carried safely to them through the vale of tears. 2. They shall have a green pasture for their flocks, *v.* 10. *Sharon and the valley of Achor* shall again be as well replenished as ever they were with cattle. Sharon lay westward, near Joppa; Achor lay eastward, near Jordan. It is therefore intimated that they shall recover the possession of the whole land, that they shall have wherewith to stock it all, and that they shall peaceably enjoy it and there shall be none to disturb them nor make them afraid. Gospel-ordinances are the fields and valleys where the sheep of Christ *shall go in and out and find pasture* (Jn. 10:9), and where they are *made to lie down* (Ps. 23:2), as Israel's herds in *the valley of Achor,* Hos. 2:15.

Verses 11–16

Here the different states of the godly and wicked, of the Jews that believed and of those that still persisted in unbelief, are set the one over-against the other, as life and death, good and evil, the blessing and the curse.

I. Here is the fearful doom of those that persisted in their idolatry after the deliverance out of Babylon, and in infidelity after the preaching of the gospel of Christ. Observe,

1. What the doom is that is here threatened: "*I will number you to the sword* as sheep for the slaughter, and there shall be no escaping, no standing out; *you shall all bow down to it,*" *v.* 12. God's judgments come, (1.) Regularly, and are executed according to the commission. Those fall by the sword that are numbered or counted out to it, and none besides. Though the sword seems to devour promiscuously *one as well as another,* yet it is made to know its number and shall not exceed. (2.) Irresistibly. The strongest and most stout-hearted sinners shall be forced to bow before them; for none ever hardened their hearts against God and prospered.

2. What the sins are that number them to the sword. (1.) Idolatry was the ancient sin (*v.* 11): "*You are those who,* instead of seeking me and serving me as my people, *forsake the Lord,* disown him, and cast him off to embrace other gods, who *forget my holy mountain* (the privileges it confers and the obligations it lays you under) to burn incense upon the mountains of your idols (*v.* 7), and have deserted the one only living and true God." They *prepared a table for that troop of* deities which the heathen worship and *poured out drink-offerings to that* numberless number of them; for those that thought one God too little never thought scores and hundreds sufficient, but were still adding to the number of them, till they had as many gods as cities and their altars were as thick as *heaps in the furrows of the field,* Hos. 12:11. Some take *Gad* and *Meni,* which we translate *a troop* and *a number,* to be the proper names of two of their idols, answering to Jupiter and Mercury. Whatever they were, their worshippers spared no cost to do them honour; they prepared a table for them, and filled out mixed wine for drink-offerings to them; they would pinch their families rather than stint their devotions, which should shame the worshippers of the true God out of their niggardliness. (2.) Infidelity was the sin of the later Jews (*v.* 12): *When I called, you did not answer,* which refers to the same that *v.* 2 did *(I have stretched out my hands to a rebellious people),* and that is applied to those who rejected the gospel. Our Lord Jesus himself called (he *stood and cried,* Jn. 7:37), but they did not hear, they would not answer; they were not convinced by his reasonings nor moved by his expostulations; both the fair warnings he

gave them of death and ruin and the fair offers he made them of life and happiness were slighted and made no impression upon them. Yet this was not all: *You did evil before my eyes,* not by surprise, or through inadvertency, but with deliberation: *You did choose that wherein I delighted not;* he means that which he utterly detested and abhorred. It is not strange that those who will not be persuaded to choose that which is good persist in their choice and pursuit of that which is evil. See the malignity of sin; it is evil in God's eyes, highly offensive to him, and yet it is committed before his eyes, in his sight and presence, and in contempt of him; it is likewise a contradiction to the will of God; it is doing that, of choice, which we know will displease him.

II. The aggravation of this doom, from the consideration of the happy state of those that were brought to repentance and faith.

1. The blessedness of those that serve God, and the woeful condition of those that rebel against him, are here set the *one over-against the other,* that they may serve as a foil to each other, *v.* 13–16. (1.) God's servants may well think themselves happy, and for ever indebted to that free grace which made them so, when they see how miserable some of their neighbours are for want of that grace, who are hardened, and likely to perish for ever in unbelief, and what a narrow escape they had of being among them. See *ch.* 66:24. (2.) It will add to the grief of those that perish to see the happiness of God's servants (whom they had hated, and vilified, and looked upon with the utmost disdain), and especially to think that they might have shared in their bliss if it had not been their own fault. It made the torment of the rich man in hell the more grievous that he *saw Abraham afar off and Lazarus in his bosom,* Lu. 16:23. See Lu. 13:28. Sometimes the providence of God makes such a difference as this between good and bad in this world, and the prosperity of the righteous becomes a grievous eye-sore and vexation of heart to the wicked (Ps. 112:10), and it will certainly be so in the great day. *We fools counted his life madness and his end without honour; but now how is he numbered with the saints and his lot is among the chosen.* Now,

2. The difference of their states lies in two things: —

(1.) In point of comfort and satisfaction. [1.] God's servants shall eat and drink; they shall have the bread of life to feed, to feast upon, continually, shall be abundantly replenished with the goodness of his house, and shall want nothing that is good for them. Heaven's happiness will be to them an everlasting feast; they shall be filled with that which now they hunger and thirst after. But those who set their hearts upon the world, and place their happiness in that, shall be hungry and thirsty, always empty, always craving; for it is not bread; it surfeits, but it satisfies not. In communion with God, and dependence upon him, there is full satisfaction; but in sinful pursuits there is nothing but disappointment. [2.] God's servants *shall rejoice* and sing for joy of heart. They have constant cause for joy, and there is nothing that may be an occasion of grief to them but they have an allay sufficient for it; and, as far as faith is in act and exercise, they have a heart to rejoice, and their joy is their strength. They shall rejoice in their hope, because it shall not make them ashamed. Heaven will be a world of everlasting joy to all that are now sowing in tears. But, on the other hand, those that forsake the Lord shut themselves out from all true joy, for *they shall be ashamed* of their vain confidence in themselves, and their own righteousness, and the hopes they had built thereon. When the expectations of bliss wherewith they had flattered themselves are frustrated, O what confusion will fill their faces! Then shall they *cry for sorrow of heart,* and *howl for vexation of spirit,* perhaps in this world, when their laughter shall be turned into mourning and their joy into heaviness, and certainly in that world where the torment will be endless, easeless, and remediless — nothing but weeping, and wailing, and gnashing of teeth, to eternity. Let these two be compared, *Now he is comforted* and *thou art tormented,* and which of the two will we choose to take our lot with?

(2.) In point of honour and reputation, *v.* 15, 16. *The memory of the just is,* and shall be, *blessed, but the name of the wicked shall rot.* [1.] The name of the idolaters and unbelievers shall be left *for a curse,* shall be loaded with ignominy and made for ever infamous. It shall be used in

giving bad characters — *Thou art as cruel as a Jew;* and in imprecation — *God make thee as miserable as a Jew.* It shall be *for a curse to God's chosen,* that is, for a warning to them; they shall be afraid of falling under the curse upon the Jewish nation, of perishing after the *same example of unbelief.* The curse of those whom God rejects should make his chosen stand in awe. *The Lord God shall slay thee;* he shall quite extirpate the Jews and cut them off from being a people; they shall no longer live as a nation, nor ever be incorporated again. [2.] The name of God's chosen shall become a blessing: *He shall call his servants by another name.* The children of the covenant shall no longer be called *Jews,* but *Christians;* and to them, under that name, all the promises and privileges of the new covenant shall be secured. This other name shall be an honourable name; it shall not be confined to one nation, but with it men shall *bless themselves in the earth,* all the world over. God shall have servants out of all nations who shall all be dignified with this new name. They shall bless themselves *in the God of truth. First,* They shall give honour to God both in their prayers and in their solemn oaths, in their addresses for his favour as their felicity and their appeals to his justice as their Judge. This is a part of the homage we owe to God; we must bless ourselves in him, that is, we must reckon that we have enough to make us happy, that we need no more, and can desire no more, if we have him for our God. It is of great consequence what we bless ourselves in, what we most please ourselves with and value ourselves by our interest in. Worldly people bless themselves in the abundance they have of this world's goods (Ps. 49:18; Lu. 12:19); but God's servants bless themselves in him, as a God all-sufficient for them. He is their crown of glory and diadem of beauty, their strength and portion. By him also *they shall swear,* and not by any creature or any false god. To his judgment they shall refer their cause, from whom every man's judgment doth proceed. *Secondly,* They shall give honour to him as *the God of truth, the God of the Amen* (so the word is); some understand it of Christ who is himself the *Amen,* the *faithful witness* (Rev. 3:14), and in whom all the promises are *yea and amen,* 2 Co. 1:20. In him we must bless ourselves, and by him we must swear unto the Lord and covenant with him. He that is *blessed in the earth* (so some read it) *shall be blessed in the true God,* for Christ is *the true God and eternal life,* 1 Jn. 5:20. And it was promised of old that *in him all the families of the earth should be blessed,* Gen. 12:3. Some read it, *He shall bless himself in the God of the faithful people,* in God as the God of all believers, desiring no more than to share in the blessings wherewith they are blessed, to be dealt with as he deals with them. *Thirdly,* They shall give him honour as the author of this blessed change which they have the experience of; they shall think themselves happy in having him for their God who has made them to forget their former troubles, the remembrance of them being swallowed up in their present comforts: *Because they are hidden from God's eyes,* that is, they are quite taken away; for, if there were any remainder of their troubles, God would be sure to have his eye upon it, in compassion to them and concern for them. They shall no longer feel them; for God will no longer see them. He is pleased to speak as if he would make himself easy by making them easy; and therefore they shall with a great deal of satisfaction bless themselves in him.

Verses 17–25

If these promises were in part fulfilled when the Jews, after their return out of captivity, were settled in peace in their own land and brought as it were into a new world, yet they were to have their full accomplishment in the gospel church, militant first and at length triumphant. *The Jerusalem that is from above is free and is the mother of us all.* In the graces and comforts which believers have in and from Christ we are to look for this new heaven and new earth. It is in the gospel that *old things have passed away and all things have become new,* and by it that those who are in Christ are *new creatures,* 2 Co. 5:17. It was a mighty and happy change that was described *v.* 16, that *the former troubles were forgotten;* but here it rises much higher: even the *former world* shall be *forgotten* and *shall no more come into mind.* Those that were converted to the Christian faith were so transported with the comforts of it that all the comforts they were before acquainted with became as nothing to them; not only their foregoing griefs, but their foregoing joys, were lost and swallowed up in this. The glorified saints will *therefore* have forgotten this world, because they will be entirely taken up with the other: *For, behold, I create new heavens and a new earth.* See how inexhaustible the divine power is; the same God that created one heaven and earth can create another. See how entire the happiness of the saints is; it shall be all of a piece; with the new heavens God will create them (if they have occasion for it to make them happy) a new earth too. *The world is yours* if you be Christ's, 1 Co. 3:22. When God is reconciled to us, which gives us a new heaven, the creatures too are reconciled to us, which gives us a new earth. The future glory of the saints will be so entirely different from what they ever knew before that it may well be called *new heavens and a new earth,* 2 Pt. 3:13. *Behold, I make all things new,* Rev. 21:5.

I. There shall be new joys. For, 1. All the church's friends, and all that belong to her, shall rejoice (*v.* 18): You shall *be glad and rejoice for ever in that which I create.* The new things which God creates in and by his gospel are and shall be matter of everlasting joy to all believers. *My servants shall rejoice* (*v.* 13), at last they shall, though now they mourn. *Enter thou into the joy of thy Lord.* 2. The church shall be the matter of their joy, so pleasant, so prosperous, shall her condition be: *I create Jerusalem a rejoicing and her people a joy.* The church shall not only rejoice but be rejoiced in. Those that have sorrowed with the church shall rejoice with her. 3. The prosperity of the church shall be a rejoicing to God himself, who has pleasure in the prosperity of his servants (*v.* 19): *I will rejoice in Jerusalem's* joy, and will *joy in my people;* for *in all their affliction he was afflicted.* God will not only rejoice in the church's welldoing, but will himself *rejoice to do her good* and *rest in his love* to her, Zep. 3:17. What God rejoices in it becomes us to rejoice in. 4. There shall be no allay of this joy, nor any alteration of this happy condition of the church: *The voice of weeping shall be no more heard in her.* If this relate to any state of the church in this life, it means no more than that the former occasions of grief shall not return, but God's people shall long enjoy an uninterrupted tranquillity. But in heaven it shall have a full accomplishment, in respect both of the perfection and the perpetuity of the promised joy; there *all tears shall be wiped away.*

II. There shall be new life, *v.* 20. Untimely deaths by the sword or sickness shall be no more known as they have been, and by this means there shall be *no more the voice of crying, v.* 19. When there shall be *no more death* there shall be *no more sorrow,* Rev. 21:4. As death has reigned by sin, so life shall reign by righteousness, Rom. 5:14, 21. 1. Believers through Christ shall be satisfied with life, though it be ever so short on earth. If an infant end its days quickly, yet it shall not be reckoned to die untimely; for the shorter its life is the longer will its rest be. Though *death reign over those that have not sinned after the similitude of Adam's transgression,* yet they, dying in the arms of Christ, the second Adam, and belonging to his kingdom, are not to be called *infants of days,* but even the child shall be reckoned to *die a hundred years old,* for he shall rise again at full age, shall rise to eternal life. Some understand it of children who in their childhood are so eminent for wisdom and grace, and by death nipped in the blossom, that they may be said to die a hundred years old. And, as for old men, it is promised that *they shall fill their days* with the *fruits of righteousness,* which they shall *still bring forth in old age, to show that the Lord is upright,* and then it is a good old age. An old man who is wise, and good, and useful, may truly be said to have *filled his days.* Old men who have their hearts upon the world have never filled their days, never have enough of this world, but would still continue longer in it. But that man dies old, and *satur dierum — full of days,* who, with Simeon, having seen God's salvation, desires now to depart in peace. 2. Unbelievers shall be unsatisfied and unhappy in life, though it be ever so long. The sinner, though he live to *a hundred years old, shall be accursed.* His living so long shall be no token to him of the divine favour and blessing, nor shall it be any shelter to him from the divine wrath and curse. The sentence he lies under will certainly be executed, and his long life is but a long reprieve; nay, it is itself a curse to him, for the longer he lives the more wrath he treasures up against the day of wrath and the more sins he will have to answer for. So that the matter is not great whether our lives on earth be long or short, but whether we live the lives of saints or the lives of sinners.

III. There shall be a new enjoyment of the comforts of life. Whereas before it was very uncertain and precarious, their enemies *inhabited the houses* which *they built* and *ate the fruit* of the trees which *they planted,* now it shall be otherwise; they shall *build houses and inhabit them,* shall *plant vineyards* and *eat the fruit of them, v.* 21, 22. Their intimates that the labour of their hands shall be blessed and be made to prosper; they shall gain what they aimed at, and what they have gained shall be preserved and secured to them; they shall enjoy it comfortably, and nothing shall embitter it to them, and they shall live to enjoy it long. Strangers shall not break in upon them, to expel them, and plant themselves in their room, as sometimes they have done: *My elect shall wear out,* or *long enjoy, the work of their hands;* it is honestly got, and it will wear well; it is *the work of their hands,* which they themselves have laboured for, and it is most comfortable to enjoy that, and not to eat the *bread of idleness,* or *bread of deceit.* If we have a heart to enjoy it, that is the gift of God's grace (Eccl. 3:13); and, if we live to enjoy it long, it is the gift of God's providence, for that is here promised: *As the days of a tree are the days of my people;* as the *days of an oak* (*ch.* 6:13), *whose substance is in it, though it cast its leaves;* though it be stripped every winter, it recovers itself again, and lasts many ages; as the days *of the tree of life;* so the Septuagint. Christ is to them the tree of life, and in him believers enjoy all those spiritual comforts which are typified by the abundance of temporal blessings here promised; and it shall not be in the power of their enemies to deprive them of these blessings or disturb them in the enjoyment of them.

IV. There shall be a new generation rising up in their stead to inherit and enjoy these blessings (*v.* 23): *They shall not labour in vain,* for they shall not only enjoy the work of their hands themselves, but they shall leave it with satisfaction to those that shall come after them, and not with such a melancholy prospect as Solomon did, Eccl. 2:18, 19. They shall not beget and *bring forth* children *for trouble; for they are* themselves *the seed of the blessed of the Lord,* and there is a blessing entailed upon them by descent from their ancestors which *their offspring with them* shall partake of, and shall be, as well as they, *the seed of the blessed of the Lord.* They shall not bring forth for trouble; for, 1. God will make their children that rise up comforts to them; they shall have the joy of seeing them *walk in the truth.* 2. He will make the times that come after comfortable to their children. As they shall be good, so it shall be well with them; they shall not be brought forth to days of trouble; nor shall it ever be said, *Blessed is the womb that bore not.* In the gospel church Christ's name shall be borne up by a succession. *A seed shall serve him* (Ps. 22:30), *the seed of the blessed of the Lord.*

V. There shall be a good correspondence between them and their God (*v.* 24): *Even before they call, I will answer.* God will anticipate their prayers with the blessings of his goodness. David did but say, *I will confess,* and *God forgave,* Ps. 32:5. The father of the prodigal met him in his return. *While they are yet speaking,* before they have finished their prayer, I will give them the thing they pray for, or the assurances and earnests of it. These are high expressions of God's readiness to hear prayer; and this appears much more in the grace of the gospel than it did under the law; we owe the comfort of it to the mediation of Christ as our advocate with the Father and are obliged in gratitude to give a ready ear to God's calls.

VI. There shall be a good correspondence between them and their neighbours (*v.* 25): *The wolf and the lamb shall feed together,* as they did in Noah's ark. God's people, though they are as sheep in the midst of wolves, shall be safe and unhurt; for God will not so much break the power and tie the hands of their enemies as formerly, but he will turn their hearts, will alter their dispositions by his grace. When Paul, who had been a persecutor of the disciples (and who, being of the tribe of Benjamin, ravened *as a wolf,* Gen. 49:27) joined himself to them and became one of them, then *the wolf and the lamb fed together.* So also when the enmity between Jews and Gentiles was slain, all hostilities ceased, and they fed together as one sheepfold under Christ the great Shepherd, Jn. 10:16. The enemies of the church ceased to do the mischief they had done, and its members ceased to be so quarrelsome with and injurious to one another as they had been, so that there was none either from without or from within to hurt or destroy, none to disturb it, much less to ruin it, *in all the holy mountain;* as was promised, *ch.* 11:9. For, 1. Men shall be changed: *The lion* shall no more be a beast of prey, as perhaps he never would have been if sin had not entered, but *shall eat straw like the bullock,* shall *know his owner,* and *his master's crib,* as *the ox* does. When those that lived by spoil and rapine, and coveted to enrich themselves, right or wrong, are brought by the grace of God to accommodate themselves to their condition, to live by honest labour, and to be content with such things as they have — when those that stole steal no more, but work with their hands the thing that is good — then this is fulfilled, that *the lion shall eat straw like the bullock.* 2. Satan shall be chained, the dragon bound; for *dust shall be the serpent's meat again.* That great enemy, when he has been let loose, has glutted and regaled himself with the precious blood of saints, who by his instigation have been persecuted, and with the precious souls of sinners, who by his instigation have become persecutors and have ruined themselves for ever; but now he shall be confined to dust, according to the sentence, *On thy belly shalt thou go, and dust shalt thou eat,* Gen. 3:14. All the enemies of God's church, that are subtle and venomous as serpents, shall be conquered and subdued, and be made to lick the dust, Christ shall reign as Zion's King till all the enemies of his kingdom be made his footstool, and theirs too. In the holy mountain above, and there only, shall this promise have its full accomplishment, that there shall be none to hurt nor destroy.

CHAPTER 66

The scope of this chapter is much the same as that of the foregoing chapter and many expressions of it are the same; it therefore looks the same way, to the different state of the good and bad among the Jews at their return out of captivity, but that typifying the rejection of the Jews in the days of the Messiah, the conversion of the Gentiles, and the setting up of the gospel-kingdom in the world. The first verse of this chapter is applied by Stephen to the dismantling of the temple by the planting of the Christian church (Acts 7:49, 50), which may serve as a key to the whole chapter. We have here, I. The contempt God puts upon ceremonial services in comparison with moral duties, and an intimation therein of his purpose shortly to put an end to the temple, and sacrifice and reject those that adhered to them (*v.* 1–4). II. The salvation God will in due time work for his people out of the hands of their oppressors (*v.* 5), speaking terror to the persecutors (*v.* 6) and comfort to the persecuted, a speedy and complete deliverance (*v.* 7–9), a joyful settlement (*v.* 10, 11), the accession of the Gentiles to them, and abundance of satisfaction therein (*v.* 12–14). III. The terrible vengeance which God will bring upon the enemies of his church and people (*v.* 15–18). IV. The happy establishment of the church upon large and sure foundations, its constant attendance on God and triumph over its enemies (*v.* 19–24). And we may well expect that this evangelical prophet, here, in the close of his prophecy, should (as he does) look as far forward as to the latter days, to the last day, to the days of eternity.

Verses 1–4

Here, I. The temple is slighted in comparison with a gracious soul, *v.* 1, 2. The Jews in the prophet's time, and afterwards in Christ's time, gloried much in the temple and promised themselves great things from it; to humble them therefore, and to shake their vain confidence, both the prophets and Christ foretold the ruin of the temple, that God would leave it and then it would soon be desolate. After it was destroyed by the Chaldeans it soon recovered itself and the ceremonial services were revived with it; but by the Romans it was made a perpetual desolation, and the ceremonial law was abolished with it. That the world might be prepared for this, they were often told, as here, of what little account the temple was with God. 1. That he did not need it. Heaven is the throne of his glory and government; there he sits, infinitely exalted in the highest dignity and dominion, above all blessing and praise. The earth is his footstool, on which he stands, over-ruling all the affairs of it according to his will. If God has so bright a throne, so large a footstool, *where then is the house they can build* unto God, that can be the residence of his glory, or *where is the place of his rest?* What satisfaction can the Eternal Mind take in a house made with men's hands? What occasion has he, as we have, for a house to repose himself in, who *faints not neither is weary,* who neither slumbers nor sleeps? Or, if he had occasion, he *would not tell us* (Ps. 50:12), for *all these things hath his hand made,* heaven and all its courts, earth and all its borders, and all the hosts of both. All *these things have been,* have had their beginning, by the power of God, who was happy from eternity before they were, and therefore could not be benefited by them. *All these things are* (so some read it); they still continue, upheld by the same power that made them; so that *our goodness extends not to him.* If he required a house for himself to dwell in, he would have made one himself when he made the world; and, if he had made one, it would have continued to this day, as other creatures do, according to his ordinance; so that he had no need of a temple made with hands. 2. That he would not heed it as he would a humble, penitent, gracious heart. He has a heaven and earth of his own making, and a temple of man's making; but he overlooks them all, that he may look with favour to him that is poor in spirit, humble and serious, self-abasing and self-denying, whose heart is truly contrite for sin, penitent for it, and in pain to get it pardoned, and who *trembles at God's word,* not as Felix did, with a transient qualm that was over when the sermon was done, but with an habitual awe of God's majesty and purity and an habitual dread of his justice and wrath. Such a heart is a living temple for God; he dwells there, and it is the place of his rest; it is like heaven and earth, his throne and his footstool.

II. Sacrifices are slighted when they come from ungracious hands. *The sacrifice of the wicked* is not only unacceptable, but it *is an abomination to the Lord* (Prov. 15:8); this is largely shown here, *v.* 3, 4. Observe, 1. How detestable their sacrifices were to God. The carnal Jews, after their return out of captivity, though they relapsed not to idolatry, grew very careless and loose in the service of God; they brought the *torn, and the lame, and the sick* for *sacrifice* (Mal. 1:8, 13), and this made their services abominable to God; they had no regard to their sacrifices, and therefore how could they think God would have any regard to them? The unbelieving Jews, after the gospel was preached and in it notice given of the offering up of the great sacrifice, which put an end to all the ceremonial services, continued to offer sacrifices, as if the law of Moses had been still in force and could *make the comers thereunto perfect:* this was an abomination. *He that kills an ox* for his own table is welcome to do it; but he that now kills it, that thus kills it, for God's altar, *is as if he slew a man;* it is as great an offence to God as murder itself; he that does it does in effect set aside Christ's sacrifice, *treads under foot the blood of the covenant,* and makes himself accessory to the guilt of *the body and blood of the Lord,* setting up what Christ died to abolish. *He that sacrifices a lamb,* if it be a corrupt thing, and not the male in his flock, the best he has, if he think to put God off with any thing, he affronts him, instead of pleasing him; it is *as if he cut off a dog's neck,* a creature in the eye of the law so vile that, whereas an ass might be redeemed, the price of a dog was never to be brought into the treasury, Deu. 23:18. *He that offers an oblation,* a meat offering or drink-offering, is as if he thought to make atonement with *swine's blood,* a creature that must not be eaten nor touched, the *broth of it* was abominable (*ch.* 65:4), much more the blood of it. *He that burns incense to God,* and so puts contempt upon the incense of Christ's intercession, is *as if he blessed an idol;* it was as great an affront to God as if they had paid their devotions to a false god. Hypocrisy and profaneness are as provoking as idolatry. 2. What their wickedness was which made their sacrifices thus detestable. It was *because they had chosen their own ways,* the ways of their own wicked hearts, and not only their hands did but *their souls delighted in their abominations.* They were vicious and immoral in their conversations, chose the way of sin rather than the way of God's commandments, and took pleasure in that which was provoking to God; this made their sacrifices so offensive to God, *ch.* 1:11–15. Those that pretend to honour God by a profession of religion, and yet live wicked lives, put an affront upon him, as if he were the patron of sin. And that which was an aggravation of their wickedness was that they persisted in it, notwithstanding the frequent calls given them to repent and reform; they turned a deaf ear to all the warnings of divine justice and all the offers of divine grace: *When I called, none did answer,* as before, *ch.* 65:12. And the same follows here that did there: *They did evil before my eyes.* Being deaf to what he said, they cared not what he saw, but *chose that in*

which they knew *he delighted not.* How could those expect to please him in their devotions who took no care to please him in their conversations, but, on the contrary, designed to provoke him? 3. The doom passed upon them for this. They *chose their own ways,* therefore, says God, I also will *choose their delusions. They have made their choice* (as Mr. Gataker paraphrases it), *and now I will make mine; they have taken what course they pleased with me, and I will take what course I please with them.* I will choose their *illusions,* or *mockeries* (so some); as they have mocked God and dishonoured him by their wickedness, so God will give them up to their enemies, to be trampled upon and insulted by them. Or they shall be deceived by those vain confidences with which they have deceived themselves. God will make their sin their punishment; they shall be beaten with their own rod and hurried into ruin by their own delusions. God will *bring their fears upon them,* that is, will bring upon them that which shall be a great terror to them, or that which they themselves have been afraid of and thought to escape by sinful shifts. Unbelieving hearts, and unpurified unpacified consciences, need no more to make them miserable than to have their own fears brought upon them.

Verses 5–14

The prophet, having denounced God's judgments against a hypocritical nation, that made a jest of God's word and would not answer him when he called to them, here turns his speech to those that *trembled at his word,* to comfort and encourage them; they shall not be involved in the judgments that are coming upon their unbelieving nation. Ministers must distinguish thus, that, when they speak terror to the wicked, they may not *make the hearts of the righteous sad. Bone Christiane, hoc nihil ad te — Good Christian, this is nothing to thee.* The prophet, having assured those that tremble at God's word of a gracious look from him (*v.* 2), here brings them a gracious message from him. The word of God has comforts in store for those that by true humiliation for sin are prepared to receive them. There were those (*v.* 4) who, when *God spoke, would not hear;* but, if some will not, others sill. If the heart *tremble at the word,* the ear will be open to it. Now what is here said to them?

I. Let them know that God will plead their just but injured cause against their persecutors (*v.* 5): *Your brethren that hated you said, Let the Lord be glorified. But he shall appear to your joy.* This perhaps might have reference to the case of some of the Jews at their return out of captivity; but nothing like it appears in the history, and therefore it is rather to be referred to the first preachers and professors of the gospel among the Jews, to whose case it is very applicable. Observe, 1. How the faithful servants of God were persecuted: *Their brethren hated them.* The apostles were Jews by birth, and yet even in the cities of the Gentiles the Jews they met with there were their most bitter and implacable enemies and *stirred up the Gentiles* against them. The spouse complains (Cant. 1:6) that her *mother's children were angry with her.* Pilate upbraided our Lord Jesus with this, *Thy own nation have delivered thee unto me,* Jn. 18:35. Their brethren, who should have loved them and encouraged them for their work's sake hated them, and cast them out of their synagogues, excommunicated them as if they had been the greatest blemishes, when they were really the greatest blessings, of their church and nation. This was a fruit of the old enmity in the *seed of the serpent* against the *seed of the woman.* Those that hated Christ hated his disciples, because they supported his kingdom and interest (Jn. 15:18), and they *cast them out for his name's sake,* because they were called by his name, and called upon his name, and laid out themselves to advance his name. Note, It is no new thing for church censures to be misapplied, and for her artillery, which was intended for her defence, to be turned against her best friends, by the treachery of her governors. And those that did this *said, Let the Lord be glorified;* they pretended conscience and a zeal for the honour of God and the church in it, and did it with all the formalities of devotion. Our Saviour explains this, and seems to have reference to it, Jn. 16:2. *They shall put you out of their synagogues,* and *whosoever kills you will think that he does God service. In nomine Domini incipit omne malum — In the name of the Lord commences evil of every kind.* Or

we may understand it as spoken in defiance of God: "You say God will be glorified in your deliverance; *let him be glorified then; let him make speed and hasten his work* (*ch.* 5:19); *let him deliver him, seeing he delighted in him.*" Some take it to be the language of the profane Jews in captivity, bantering their brethren that hoped for deliverance, and ridiculing the expectations they often comforted themselves with, that God would shortly be glorified in it. They thus did what they could to *shame the counsel of the poor,* Ps. 14:6. 2. How they were encouraged under these persecutions: "Let your faith and patience hold out yet a little while; your enemies hate you and oppress you, your brethren hate you and cast you out, but your Father in heaven loves you, and will appear for you when no one else will or dare. His providence shall order things so as shall be for comfort to you; he shall appear *for your joy* and for the confusion of those that abuse you and trample on you; they *shall be ashamed* of their enmity to you." This was fulfilled when, upon the signals given of Jerusalem's approaching ruin, the *Jews' hearts failed them for fear;* but the disciples of Christ, whom they had hated and persecuted, *lifted up their heads with joy, knowing that their redemption drew nigh,* Lu. 21:26, 28. Though God seem to hide himself, he will in due time show himself.

II. Let them know that God's appearances for them will be such as will make a great noise in the world (*v.* 6): There shall be *a voice of noise from the city, from the temple.* Some make it the joyful and triumphant voice of the church's friends, others the frightful lamenting voice of her enemies, surprised in the city, and fleeing in vain to the temple for shelter. These voices do but echo to the *voice of the Lord,* who is now rendering a *recompence to his enemies;* and those that will not hear him speaking this terror shall hear them returning the alarms of it in doleful shrieks. We may well think what a confused noise there was in the city and temple when Jerusalem, after a long siege, was at last taken by the Romans. Some think this prophecy was fulfilled in the prodigies that went before that destruction of Jerusalem, related by Josephus in his *History of the Wars of the Jews* (4.388 and 6.311), that the temple-doors flew open suddenly of their own accord, and the priests heard a noise of motion or shifting in the most holy place, and presently a voice, saying, *Let us depart hence.* And, some time after, one Jesus Bar-Annas went up and down the city, at the feast of tabernacles, continually crying, *A voice from the east, a voice from the west, a voice from the four winds, a voice against Jerusalem and the temple, a voice against all this people.*

III. Let them know that God will set up a church for himself in the world, which shall be abundantly replenished in a little time (*v.* 7): *Before she travailed she brought forth.* This is to be applied in the type to the deliverance of the Jews out of their captivity in Babylon, which was brought about very easily and silently, without any pain or struggle, such as was when they were brought out of Egypt; that was done *by might and power* (Deu. 4:34), but this by *the Spirit of the Lord of hosts,* Zec. 4:6. The man-child of the deliverance is rejoiced in, and yet the mother was never in labour for it; *before her pain came she was delivered.* This is altogether surprising, uncommon, and without precedent, unless in the story which the Egyptian midwives told of the Hebrew women (Ex. 1:19), that *they were lively and were delivered ere the midwives came in unto them.* But *shall the earth be made to bring forth her fruits in one day?* No, it is the work of some weeks in the spring to *renew the face of the earth* and cover it with its products. Some read this to the same purport with the next clause, *Shall a land be brought forth in one day,* or *shall a nation be born at once?* Is it to be imagined that a woman at one birth should bring children sufficient to people a country and that they should in an instant grow up to maturity? No; something like this was done in the creation; but God has since rested from all such works, and leaves second causes to produce their effects gradually. *Nihil facit per saltum — He does nothing abruptly.* Yet, in this case, *as soon as Zion travailed she brought forth.* Cyrus's proclamation was no sooner issued out than the captives were formed into a body and were ready to make the best of their way to their own land. And the reason is given (*v.* 9), because *it is the Lord's doing; he* undertakes it whose work is perfect. If he *bring to the birth* in preparing his people for deliverance, he will *cause to bring forth* in the accomplishment of the deliverance. When every thing is ripe and ready for their release, and the number of their months is accomplished, so that *the children are brought to the birth,* shall not I then *give strength to bring forth,* but leave mother and babe to perish together in the most miserable case? How will this agree with the divine pity? Shall I begin a work and not go through with it? How will that agree with the divine power and perfection? *Am I he that causes to bring forth* (so the following clause may be read) *and shall I restrain her?* Does God cause mankind, and all the species of living creatures, to propagate, and *replenish the earth,* and *will he restrain Zion?* Will he not make her fruitful in a blessed offspring to replenish the church? Or, *Am I he that begat, and should I restrain from bringing forth?* Did God beget the deliverance in his purpose and promise, and will he not bring it forth in the accomplishment and performance of it? But this was a figure of the setting up of the Christian church in the world, and the replenishing of that family with children which was to be named from Jesus Christ. When the Spirit was poured out, and the gospel went forth from Zion, multitudes were converted in a little time and with little pains compared with the vast product. The apostles, even before they travailed, brought forth, and the children born to Christ were so numerous, and so suddenly and easily produced, that they were rather like the dew from the morning's womb than like the son from the mother's womb, Ps. 110:3. The success of the gospel was astonishing; that light, like the morning, strangely diffused itself till it took hold even of *the ends of the earth.* Cities and nations were born at once to Christ. The same day that the Spirit was poured out there were 3000 souls added to the church. And, when this glorious work was once begun, it was carried on wonderfully, beyond what could be imagined, *so mightily grew the word of God and prevailed.* He that brought to the birth in conviction of sin caused to bring forth in a thorough conversion to God.

IV. Let them know that their present sorrows shall shortly be turned into abundant joys, *v.* 10, 11. Observe, 1. How the church's friends are described; they are such as *love her, and mourn* with her and *for her.* Note, All that love God love Jerusalem; they love the church of God, and lay its interest very near their heart. They admire the beauty of the church, take pleasure in communion with it, and heartily espouse its cause. And those that have a sincere affection for the church have a cordial sympathy with her in all the cares and sorrows of her militant state. They mourn for her; all her grievances are their griefs; if Jerusalem be in distress, their harps are hung on the willow-trees. 2. How they are encouraged: *Rejoice with her,* and again and again *I say, Rejoice.* This intimates that Jerusalem shall have cause to rejoice; the days of her mourning shall be at an end, and she shall be comforted according to the time that she has been afflicted. It is the will of God that all her friends should join with her in her joys, for they shall share with her in those blessings that will be the matter of her joy. If *we suffer with Christ* and sorrow with his church, *we shall reign with him* and rejoice with her. We are here called, (1.) To bear our part in the church's praises: "Come, *rejoice with her, rejoice for joy with her,* rejoice greatly, rejoice and know why you rejoice, rejoice on the days appointed for public thanksgiving. You that mourned for her in her sorrows cannot but from the same principle rejoice with her in her joys." (2.) To take our part in the church's comforts. We must *suck and be satisfied with the breasts of her consolation.* The word of God, the covenant of grace (especially the promises of that covenant), the ordinances of God, and all the opportunities of attending on him and conversing with him, are the breasts, which the church calls and counts the *breasts of her consolations,* where her comforts are laid up, and whence by faith and prayer they are drawn. With her therefore we must suck from these breasts, by an application of the promises of God to ourselves and a diligent attendance on his ordinances; and with the consolations which are drawn hence we must be satisfied, and not be dissatisfied though we have ever so little of earthly comforts. It is the glory of the church that she has the Lord for her God, that to her *pertain the adoption and the service of God;* and with *the abundance of* this *glory* we must be *delighted.* We must take more pleasure in our relation to God and communion with him than in all the delights of the sons and daughters of men. Whatever is the glory of the church must be *our glory and joy,* particularly her purity, unity, and increase.

V. Let them know that he who gives them this call to rejoice will give them cause to do so and hearts to do so, *v.* 12–14.

1. He will give them cause to do so. For, (1.) They shall enjoy a long uninterrupted course of prosperity: *I will extend,* or am extending, *peace to her* (that is, all good to her) *like a river* that runs in a constant stream, still increasing till it be swallowed up in the ocean. The gospel brings with it, wherever it is received in its power, such peace as this, which shall go on *like a river,* supplying souls with all good and making them fruitful, as a river does the lands it passes through, such a *river of peace* as the springs of the world's comforts cannot send forth and the dams of the world's troubles cannot stop nor drive back nor its sand rack up, such a river of peace as will carry us to the ocean of boundless and endless bliss. (2.) There shall be large and advantageous additions made to them: *The glory of the Gentiles* shall come to them *like a flowing stream.* Gentiles converts shall come pouring into the church, and swell the river of her peace and prosperity; for they shall *bring their glory* with them; their wealth and honour, their power and interest, shall all be devoted to the service of God and employed for the good of the church: *"Then shall you suck* from the breasts of her consolations. When you see such crowding for a share in those comforts you shall be the more solicitous and the more vigorous to secure your share, not for fear of having the less for others coming in to partake of Christ" (there is no danger of that; he has enough for all and enough for each), "but *their zeal* shall *provoke you to a holy jealousy."* It is well when it does so, Rom. 11:14; 2 Co. 9:2. (3.) God shall be glorified in all, and that ought to be more the matter of our joy than any thing else (*v.* 14): *The hand of the Lord shall be known towards his servants,* the protecting supporting hand of his almighty power, the supplying enriching hand of his inexhaustible goodness; the benefit which his servants have by both these *shall be known* to his glory as well as theirs. And, to make this the more illustrious, he will at the same time make known *his indignation towards his enemies.* God's mercy and justice shall both be manifested and for ever magnified

2. God will not only give them cause to rejoice, but will speak comfort to them, will speak it *to their hearts;* and it is he only that can do that, and make it fasten there. See what he will do for the comfort of all the sons of Zion. (1.) Their country shall be their tender nurse: You shall be *carried on her sides,* under her arms, as little children are, and shall be *dangled upon her knees,* as darlings are, especially when they are weary and out of humour, and must be got to sleep. Those that are joined to the church must be treated thus affectionately. The great Shepherd *gathers the lambs in his arms and carries them in his bosom,* and so must the under-shepherds, that they may not be discouraged. Proselytes should be favourites. (2.) God will himself be their powerful comforter: *As one whom his mother comforts,* when he is sick or sore, or upon any account in sorrow, *so will I comfort you;* not only with the rational arguments which a prudent father uses, but with the tender affections and compassions of a loving mother, that bemoans her afflicted child when it has fallen and hurt itself, that she may quiet it and make it easy, or endeavours to pacify it after she has chidden it and fallen out with it (Jer. 31:20): *Since I spoke against him, my bowels are troubled for him;* he is a dear son, he is a pleasant child. Thus the mother comforts. Thus *you shall be comforted in Jerusalem,* in the favours bestowed on the church, which you shall partake of, and in the thanksgivings offered by the church, which you shall concur with. (3.) They shall feel the blessed effects of this comfort in their own souls (*v.* 13): *When you see this,* what a happy state the church is restored to, not only your tongues and your countenances, but *your hearts shall rejoice.* This was fulfilled in the wonderful satisfaction which Christ's disciples had in the success of their ministry. Christ, with an eye to that, tells them (Jn. 16:22), *Your heart shall rejoice and your joy no man taketh from you.* Then *your bones,* that were dried and withered (the marrow of them quite exhausted), shall recover a youthful strength and vigour and *shall flourish like a herb.* Divine comforts reach the inward man; *they are marrow* and moistening to the bones, Prov. 3:8. The bones are the strength of the body; those shall be made to flourish with these comforts. *The joy of the Lord* will be *your strength,* Neh. 8:10.

Verses 15–24

These verses, like the pillar of cloud and fire, have a dark side towards the enemies of God's kingdom and all that are rebels against his crown, and a bright side towards his faithful loyal subjects. Probably they refer to the Jews in captivity in Babylon, of whom some are said to have been sent thither for their hurt, and with them God here threatens to proceed in his controversy; they hated to be reformed, and therefore should be ruined by the calamity (Jer. 24:9); others were sent thither for their good, and they should have the trouble sanctified to them, should in due time get well through it and see many a good day after it. Many of the expressions here used are accommodated to that glorious dispensation; but doubtless the prophecy looks further, to the judgment for which Christ did come once, and will come again, into this world, and to the distinction which his word in both makes *between the precious and the vile.*

I. Christ will appear to the confusion and terror of all those that stand it out against him. Sometimes he will appear in temporal judgments. The Jews that persisted in infidelity were cut off *by fire* and *by his sword.* The ruin was very extensive; *the Lord* then *pleaded with all flesh;* and, it being his sword with which they are cut off, they are called *his slain,* sacrificed to his justice, and they *shall be many.* In the great day the wrath of God will be his fire and sword, with which he will cut off and consume all the impenitent; and his word, when it takes hold of sinners' consciences, burns like fire, and is sharper *than any two-edged sword.* Idolaters will especially be contended with in the day of wrath, *v.* 17. Perhaps some of those who returned out of Babylon retained such instances of idolatry and superstition as are here mentioned, had their *idols in their gardens* (not daring to set them up publicly in the high places) and there *purified themselves* (as the worshippers of the true God used to do) when they went about their idolatrous rites, *one after another,* or, as we read it, *behind one tree in the midst,* behind *Ahad* or *Ehad,* some idol that they worshipped by that name and in honour of which they *ate swine's flesh* (which was expressly forbidden by the law of God), *and other abominations,* as *the mouse,* or some other like animal. But the prophecy may refer to all those judgments which the wrath of God, according to the word of God, will bring upon provoking sinners, that live in contempt of God and are devoted to the world and the flesh: They *shall be consumed together.* From the happiness of heaven we find expressly excluded all *idolaters, and whosoever worketh abomination,* Rev. 21:27; 22:15. In the day of vengeance secret wickedness will be brought to light and brought to the account; for (*v.* 18), *I know their works and their thoughts.* God knows both what men do and from what principle and with what design they do it; and therefore is fit to judge the world, because he can *judge the secrets of men,* Rom. 2:16.

II. He will appear to the comfort and joy of all that are faithful to him in the setting up of his kingdom in this world, the kingdom of grace, the earnest and first-fruits of the kingdom of glory. The time shall come that he will *gather all nations and tongues to himself,* that they may *come and see his glory* as it shines in the face of Jesus Christ, *v.* 18. This was fulfilled when all nations were to be discipled and the gift of tongues was bestowed in order thereunto. The church had hitherto been confined to one nation and in one tongue only God was worshipped; but in the days of the Messiah the partition-wall should be taken down, and those that had been strangers to God should be brought acquainted with him and should *see his glory* in the gospel, as the Jews had seen it *in the sanctuary.* As to this, it is here promised,

1. That some of the Jewish nation should, by the grace of God, be distinguished form the rest, and marked for salvation: I will not only set up a *gathering ensign* among them, to which the Gentiles shall seek (as is promised, *ch.* 11:12), but there shall be those among them on whom *I will set a differencing sign;* for so the word signifies. Though they are a corrupt degenerate nation, yet God will set apart a remnant of them, that shall be devoted to him and em-

ployed for him, and a mark shall be set upon them, with such certainty will God own them, Eze. 9:4. The *servants of God* shall be *sealed in their foreheads,* Rev. 7:3. The Lord knows those that are his. Christ's sheep are marked.

2. That those who are themselves distinguished thus by the grace of God shall be commissioned to invite others to come and take the benefit of that grace. Those that escape the power of those prejudices by which the generality of that nation is kept in unbelief shall be *sent to the nations* to carry the gospel among them, and preach it to every creature. Note, Those who themselves have escaped the wrath to come should do all they can to snatch others also as brands out of the burning. God chooses to send those on his errands that can deliver their message feelingly and experimentally, and warn people of their danger by sin as those who have themselves narrowly escaped the danger. (1.) They shall be sent *to the nations,* several of which are here named, Tarshish, and Pul, and Lud, etc. It is uncertain, nor are interpreters agreed, what countries are here intended. *Tarshish* signifies in general *the sea,* yet some take it for Tarsus in Cilicia. *Pul* is mentioned sometimes as the name of one of the kings of Assyria; perhaps some part of that country might likewise bear that name. *Lud* is supposed to be Lydia, a warlike nation, famed for archers: the Lydians are said to *handle* and *bend the bow,* Jer. 46:9. *Tubal,* some think, is Italy or Spain; and *Javan* most agree to be Greece, the Iones; and the *isles of the Gentiles,* that were peopled by the posterity of Japhet (Gen. 10:5), probably are here meant by the *isles afar off, that have not heard my name, neither have seen my glory.* In Judah only was God known, and there only his name was great for many ages. Other countries sat in darkness, heard no the joyful sound, saw not the joyful light. This deplorable state of theirs seems to be spoken of here with compassion; for it is a pity that any of the children of men should be at such a distance from their Maker as not to hear his name and see his glory. In consideration of this, (2.) Those that are sent to the nations shall go upon God's errand, to *declare his glory among the Gentiles.* The Jews that shall be dispersed among the nations shall declare the glory of God's providence concerning their nation all along, by which many shall be invited to join with them, as also by the appearances of God's glory among them in his ordinances. Some out of all languages of the nations shall *take hold of the skirt of him that is a Jew,* entreating him to take notice of them, to admit them into his company, and to stay a little while for them, till they are ready, "for *we will go with you, having heard that God is with you,*" Zec. 8:23. Thus the glory of God was in part declared among the Gentiles; but more clearly and fully by the apostles and early preachers of the gospel, who were sent into all the world, even to the isles afar off, to publish the glorious gospel of the blessed God. They *went forth and preached every where, the Lord working with them,* Mk. 16:20.

3. That many converts shall hereby be made, *v.* 20. (1.) *They shall bring all your brethren* (for proselytes ought to be owned and embraced as brethren) *for an offering unto the Lord.* God's glory shall not be in vain declared to them, but they shall be both invited and directed to join themselves to the Lord. Those that are sent to them shall succeed so well in their negotiation that thereupon there shall be as great flocking to Jerusalem as used to be at the time of a solemn feast, when all the males from all parts of the country were to attend there, and not to appear empty. Observe, [1.] The conveniences that they shall be furnished with for their coming. Some shall come *upon horses,* because they came from far and the journey was too long to travel on foot, as the Jews usually did to their feasts. Persons of quality shall come *in chariots,* and the aged, and sickly, and little children, shall be brought *in litters* or covered wagons, and the young men *on mules and swift beasts.* This intimates their zeal and forwardness to come. They shall spare no trouble nor charge to get to Jerusalem. Those that cannot ride on horseback shall come in litters; and in such haste shall they be, and so impatient of delay, that those that can shall ride upon mules and swift beasts. These expressions are figurative, and these various means of conveyance are heaped up to intimate (says the learned Mr. Gataker) the abundant provision of all those gracious helps requisite for the bringing of God's elect home to Christ. All shall be welcome, and nothing shall be wanting for their assistance and encouragement. [2.] The character under which they shall be brought. They shall come, not as formerly they used to come to Jerusalem, to be offerers, but to be themselves *an offering unto the Lord,* which must be understood spiritually, of their being presented to God as *living sacrifices,* Rom. 12:1. The apostle explains this, and perhaps refers to it, Rom. 15:16, where he speaks of his *ministering the gospel to the Gentiles,* that the *offering up,* or *sacrificing, of the Gentiles might be acceptable.* They shall offer themselves, and those who are the instruments of their conversion shall offer them, as the spoils which they have taken for Christ and which are devoted to his service and honour. They shall be brought *as the children of Israel bring an offering in a clean vessel,* with great care that they be holy, purified from sin, and sanctified to God. It is said of the converted Gentiles (Acts 15:9) that *their hearts were purified by faith.* Whatever was brought to God was brought in a clean vessel, a vessel appropriated to religious uses. God will be served and honoured in the way that he has appointed, in the ordinances of his own institution, which are the proper vehicles for these spiritual offerings. When the soul is offered up to God the body must be a clean vessel for it, possessed *in sanctification and honour, and not in the lusts of uncleanness* (1 Th. 4:4, 5); and converts to Christ are not only *purged from an evil conscience,* but have their *bodies also washed with pure water,* Heb. 10:22. Now,

(2.) This may refer, [1.] To the Jews, devout men, and proselytes out of every nation under heaven, that flocked together to Jerusalem, expecting the kingdom of the Messiah to appear, Acts 2:5, 6, 10. They came from all parts to the holy *mountain of Jerusalem,* as an *offering to the Lord,* and there many of them were brought to the faith of Christ by the gift of tongues poured out on the apostles. Methinks there is some correspondence between that history and this prophecy. The eunuch some time after came to worship at Jerusalem in his chariot and took home with him the knowledge of Christ and his holy religion. [2.] To the Gentiles, some of all nations, that should be converted to Christ, and so added to his church, which, though a spiritual accession, is often in prophecy represented by a local motion. The apostle says of all true Christians that they *have come to Mount Zion, and the heavenly Jerusalem* (Heb. 12:22), which explains this passage, and shows that the meaning of all this parade is only that they shall be brought into the church by the grace of God, and in the use of the means of that grace, as carefully, safely, and comfortably, as if they were carried in chariots and litters. Thus God shall *persuade Japhet* and he shall *dwell in the tents of Shem,* Gen. 9:27.

4. That a gospel ministry shall be set up in the church, it being thus enlarged by the addition of such a multitude of members to it (*v.* 21): *I will take of them* (of the proselytes, of the Gentile converts) *for priests and for Levites,* to minister in holy things and to preside in their religious assemblies, which is very necessary for doctrine, worship, and discipline. Hitherto the priests and Levites were all taken from among the Jews and were all of one tribe; but in gospel times God will take of the converted Gentiles to minister to him in holy things, to teach the people, to bless them in the name of the Lord, to be the stewards of the mysteries of God as the priests and Levites were under the law, to be pastors and teachers (or bishops), to *give themselves to the word and prayer,* and deacons to *serve tables,* and, as the Levites, to take care of the *outward business of the house of God,* Phil. 1:1; Acts 6:2–4. The apostles were all Jews, and so were the seventy disciples; the great apostle of the Gentiles was himself *a Hebrew of the Hebrews;* but, when churches were planted among the Gentiles, they had ministers settled who were *of themselves, elders in every church* (Acts 14:23, Tit. 1:5), which made the ministry to spread the more easily, and to be the more familiar, and, if not the more venerable, yet the more acceptable; gospel grace, it might be hoped, would cure people of those corruptions which kept a prophet from having *honour in his own country.* God says, *I will take,* not *all of them,* though they are all in a spiritual sense made to our God kings and priests, but *of them,* some of them. It is God's work originally to choose ministers by qualifying them for and inclining them to the service, as well as to make ministers by giving them their commission. *I will take them,* that is, I will admit them, though Gentiles, and will accept of them and their ministrations. This is a great honour and advantage to the Gentile church, as it was to the Jewish church that God *raised up of their sons for prophets* and *their young men for Nazarites,* Amos 2:11.

5. That the church and ministry, being thus settled, shall continue and be kept up in a succession from one generation to another, *v.* 22. The change that will be made by the setting up of the kingdom of the Messiah is here described to be, (1.) A very great and universal change; it shall be a new world, *the new heavens and the new earth* promised before, *ch.* 65:17. *Old things have passed away,* behold *all things have become new* (2 Co. 5:17), the old covenant of peculiarity is set aside, and a new covenant, a covenant of grace, established, Heb. 8:13. We are now to serve *in newness of the spirit,* and *not in the oldness of the letter,* Rom. 7:6. New commandments are given relating both to heaven and earth, and new promises relating to both, and both together make a New Testament; so that they are new heavens and a new earth that God will create, and these a preparative for the new heavens and new earth designed at the end of time, 2 Pt. 3:13. (2.) A change of God's own making; he will create the new heavens and the new earth. The change was made by him that had authority to make new ordinances, as well as power to make new worlds. (3.) It will be an abiding lasting change, a change never to be changed, a new world that will be always new, and never wax old, as that does which is ready to vanish away: *It shall remain before me* unalterable; for the gospel dispensation is to continue to the end of time and not to be succeeded by any other. The kingdom of Christ is a *kingdom that cannot be moved;* the laws and privileges of it *are things that cannot be shaken,* but shall *for ever remain,* Heb. 12:27, 28. It shall *therefore* remain, because it is before God; it is under his eye, and care, and special protection. (4.) It will be maintained in a seed that shall serve Christ: *Your seed,* and in them *your name, shall remain* — a seed of ministers, a seed of Christians; as one generation of both passes away, another generation shall come; and thus the name of Christ, with that of Christians, shall continue on earth while the earth remains, and his throne as the days of heaven. The gates of hell, though they fight against the church, shall not *prevail,* nor *wear out the saints of the Most High.*

6. That the public worship of God in religious assemblies shall be carefully and constantly attended upon by all that are thus brought *as an offering to the Lord, v.* 23. This is described in expressions suited to the Old-Testament dispensation, to show that though the ceremonial law should be abolished, and the temple service should come to an end, yet God should be still as regularly, constantly, and acceptably worshipped as ever. Heretofore only Jews went up to appear before God, and they were bound to attend only three times a year, and the males only; but now all flesh, Gentiles as well as Jews, women as well as men, shall *come and worship before God,* in his presence, though not in his temple at Jerusalem, but in religious assemblies dispersed all the world over, which shall be to them as the tabernacle of meeting was to the Jews. God will in them record his name, and, though but two or three come together, he will be among them, will meet them, and bless them. And they shall have the benefit of these holy convocations frequently, every new moon and every sabbath, not, as formerly, at the three annual feasts only. There is no necessity of one certain place, as the temple was of old. Christ is our temple, in whom by faith all believers meet, and now that the church is so far extended it is impossible that all should meet at one place; but it is fit that there should be a certain time appointed, that the service may be done certainly and frequently, and a token thereby given of the spiritual communion which all Christian assemblies have with each other by faith, hope, and holy love. The *new moons* and the *sabbaths* are mentioned because, under the law, though the yearly feasts were to be celebrated at Jerusalem, yet the new moons and the sabbaths were religiously observed all the country over, in the *schools of the prophets* first and afterwards *in the synagogues* (2 Ki. 4:23, Amos 8:5, Acts 15:21), according to the model of which Christian assemblies seem to be formed. Where the Lord's day is weekly sanctified, and the Lord's supper monthly celebrated, and both are duly attended on, there this promise is fulfilled, there the

Christian new moons and sabbaths are observed. See, here, (1.) That God is to be worshipped in solemn assemblies, and that it is the duty of all, as they have opportunity, to wait upon God in those assemblies: *All flesh must come;* though flesh, weak, corrupt, and sinful, let them come that the flesh may be mortified. (2.) In worshipping God we present ourselves before him, and are in a special manner in his presence. (3.) For doing this there ought to be stated times, and are so; and we must see that it is our interest as well as our duty constantly and conscientiously to observe these times.

7. That their thankful sense of God's distinguishing favour to them should be very much increased by the consideration of the fearful doom and destruction of those that persist and perish in their infidelity and impiety, *v.* 24. Those that have been worshipping the Lord of hosts, and rejoicing before him in the goodness of his house, shall, in order to affect themselves the more with their own happiness, take a view of the misery of the wicked. Observe, (1.) Who they are whose misery is here described. They are men that have *transgressed against God,* not only broken his laws, but broken covenant with him, and thought themselves able to contend with him. It may be meant especially of the unbelieving Jews that rejected the gospel of Christ. (2.) What their misery is. It is here represented by the frightful spectacle of a field of battle, covered with the *carcases* of the slain, that lie rotting above ground, full of *worms* crawling about them and feeding on them; and, if you go to burn them, they are so scattered, and it is such a noisome piece of work to get them together, that it would be endless, and the *fire would never be quenched;* so that they are an *abhorring to all flesh,* nobody cares to come near them. Now this is sometimes accomplished in temporal judgments, and perhaps never nearer the letter than in the destruction of Jerusalem and the Jewish nation by the Romans, in which destruction it is computed that above two millions, first and last, were cut off by the sword, besides what perished by famine and pestilence. It may refer likewise to the spiritual judgments that came upon the unbelieving Jews, which St. Paul looks upon, and shows us, Rom. 11:8, etc. They became dead in sins, twice dead. The church of the Jews was a *carcase* of a church; all its members were putrid carcases; *their worm died not,* their own consciences made them continually uneasy, and the fire of their rage against the gospel was not quenched, which was their punishment as well as their sin; and they became, more than ever any nation under the sun, *an abhorring to all flesh.* But our Saviour applies it to the everlasting misery and torment of impenitent sinners in the future state, where their *worm dies not, and their fire is not quenched* (Mk. 9:44); for the soul, whose conscience is its constant tormentor, is immortal, and God, whose wrath is its constant terror, is eternal. (3.) What notice shall be taken of it. Those that worship God shall *go forth and look upon them,* to affect their own hearts with the love of their Redeemer, when they see what misery they are redeemed from. As it will aggravate the miseries of the damned to see others in the kingdom of heaven and *themselves thrust out* (Lu. 13:28), so it will illustrate the joys and glories of the blessed to see what becomes of those that died in their transgression, and it will elevate their praises to think that they were themselves as brands plucked out of that burning. To the honour of that free grace which thus distinguished them let the redeemed of the Lord with all humility, and not without a holy trembling, sing their triumphant songs.

AN EXPOSITION, WITH PRACTICAL OBSERVATIONS, OF

THE BOOK OF THE PROPHET JEREMIAH

The Prophecies of the Old Testament, as the Epistles of the New, are placed rather according to their bulk than their seniority — the longest first, not the oldest. There were several prophets, and writing ones, that were contemporaries with Isaiah, as Micah, or a little before him, as Hosea, and Joel, and Amos, or soon after him, as Habakkuk and Nahum are supposed to have been; and yet the prophecy of Jeremiah, who began many years after Isaiah finished, is placed next to his, because there is so much in it. Where we meet with most of God's word, there let the preference be given; and yet those of less gifts are not to be despised nor excluded. Nothing now occurs to be observed further concerning prophecy in general; but concerning this prophet Jeremiah we may observe, I. That he was betimes a prophet; he began young, and therefore could say, from his own experience, that it is good for a man to *bear the yoke in his youth,* the yoke both of service and of affliction, Lam. 3:27. Jerome observes that Isaiah, who had more years over his head, had his tongue touched with a coal of fire, to purge away his iniquity (6:7), but that when God touched Jeremiah's mouth, who was yet but young, nothing was said of the purging of his iniquity (1:9), because, by reason of his tender years, he had not so much sin to answer for. II. That he continued long a prophet, some reckon fifty years, others above forty. He began in the thirteenth year of Josiah, when things went well under that good king, but he continued through all the wicked reigns that followed; for when we set out for the service of God, though the wind may then be fair and favourable, we know not how soon it may turn and be tempestuous. III. That he was a reproving prophet, was sent in God's name to tell Jacob of their sins and to warn them of the judgments of God that were coming upon them; and the critics observe that therefore his style or manner of speaking is more plain and rough, and less polite, than that of Isaiah and some others of the prophets. Those that are sent to discover sin ought to lay aside the enticing words of man's wisdom. Plain-dealing is best when we are dealing with sinners to bring them to repentance. IV. That he was a weeping prophet; so he is commonly called, not only because he penned the Lamentations, but because he was all along a mournful spectator of the sins of his people and of the desolating judgments that were coming upon them. And for this reason, perhaps, those who imagined our Saviour to be one of the prophets thought him of any of them to be most like to Jeremiah (Mt. 16:14), because he was *a man of sorrows and acquainted with grief.* V. That he was a suffering prophet. He was persecuted by his own people more than any of them, as we shall find in the story of this book; for he lived and preached just before the Jews' destruction by the Chaldeans, when their character seems to have been the same as it was just before their destruction by the Romans, when they *killed the Lord Jesus, and persecuted* his *disciples, pleased not God, and were contrary to all men, for wrath had come upon them to the uttermost,* 1 Th. 2:15, 16. The last account we have of him in his history is that the remaining Jews forced him to go down with them into Egypt; whereas the current tradition is, among Jews and Christians, that he suffered martyrdom. Hottinger, out of Elmakin, an Arabic historian, relates that, continuing to prophesy in Egypt against the Egyptians and other nations, he was stoned to death; and that long after, when Alexander entered Egypt, he took up the bones of Jeremiah where they were buried in obscurity, and carried them to Alexandria, and buried them there. The prophecies of this book which we have in the first nineteen chapters seem to be the heads of the sermons he preached in a way of general reproof for sin and denunciation of judgment; afterwards they are more particular and occasional, and mixed with the history of his day, but not placed in due order of time. With the threatenings are intermixed many gracious promises of mercy to the penitent, of the deliverance of the Jews out of their captivity, and some that have a plain reference to the kingdom of the Messiah. Among the Apocryphal writings an epistle is extant said to be written by Jeremiah to the captives in Babylon, warning them against the worship of idols, by exposing the vanity of idols and the folly of idolaters. It is in Baruch, *ch.* 6. But it is supposed not to be authentic; nor has it, I think, any thing like the life and spirit of Jeremiah's writings. It is also related concerning Jeremiah (2 Mac. 2:4) that, when Jerusalem was destroyed by the Chaldeans, he, by direction from God, took the ark and the altar of incense, and, carrying them to Mount Nebo lodged them in a hollow cave there and stopped the door; but some that followed him, and thought that they had marked the place, could not find it. He blamed them for seeking it, telling them that the place should be unknown till the time that God should gather his people together again. But I know not what credit is to be given to that story, though it is there said to be found in the records. We cannot but be concerned, in the reading of Jeremiah's prophecies, to find that they were so little regarded by the men of that generation; but let us make use of that as a reason why we should regard them the more; for they are written for our learning too, and for warning to us and to our land.

CHAPTER 1

In this chapter we have, I. The general inscription or title of this book, with the time of the continuance of Jeremiah's public ministry (*v.* 1–3). II. The call of Jeremiah to the prophetic office, his modest objection against it answered, and an ample commission given him for the execution of it (*v.* 4–10). III. The visions of an almond-rod and a seething-pot, signifying the approaching ruin of Judah and Jerusalem by the Chaldeans (*v.* 11–16). IV. Encouragement given to the prophet to go on undauntedly in his work, in an assurance of God's presence with him (*v.* 17–19). Thus is he set to work by one that will be sure to bear him out.

Verses 1–3

We have here as much as it was thought fit we should know of the genealogy of this prophet and the chronology of this prophecy. 1. We are told what family the prophet was of. He was *the son of Hilkiah,* not that Hilkiah, it is supposed, who was high priest in Josiah's time (for then he would have been called so, and not, as here, one *of the priests that were in Anathoth),* but another of the same name. Jeremiah signifies one *raised up by the Lord.* It is said of Christ that he is a prophet whom the Lord our God *raised up unto us,* Deu. 18:15, 18. He was *of the priests,* and, as a priest, was authorized and appointed to teach the people; but to that authority and appointment God added the extraordinary commission of a prophet. Ezekiel also was a priest. Thus God would support the honour of the priesthood at a time when, by their sins and God's judgments upon them, it was sadly eclipsed. He was of the priests in Anathoth, a city of priests, which lay about three miles from Jerusalem. Abiathar had his country house there, 1 Ki. 2:26. 2. We have the general date of his prophecies, the knowledge of which is requisite to the understanding of them. (1.) He began to prophesy in the thirteenth year of Josiah's reign, *v.* 2. Josiah, in the twelfth year of his reign, began a work of reformation, applied himself with all sincerity to purge Judah and Jerusalem from the *high places, and the groves, and the images,* 2 Chr. 34:3. And very seasonably then was this young prophet raised up to assist and encourage the young king in that good work. Then *the word of the Lord* came to him, not only a charge and commission to him to prophesy, but a revelation of the things themselves which he was to deliver. As it is an encouragement to ministers to be countenanced and protected by such pious magistrates as Josiah was, so it is a great help to magistrates, in any good work of reformation, to be advised and animated, and to have a great deal of their work done for them, by such faithful zealous ministers as Jeremiah was. Now, one would have expected when these two joined forces, such a prince, and such a prophet (as in a like case, Ezra 5:1, 2), and both young, such a complete reformation would be brought about and settled as would prevent the ruin of the church and state; but it proved quite otherwise. In the eighteenth year of Josiah we find there were a great many of the relics of idolatry that were not purged out; for what can the best princes and prophets do to prevent the ruin of a people that hate to be reformed? And therefore, though it was a time of reformation, Jeremiah continued to foretel the destroying judgments that were coming upon them; for there is no symptom more threatening to any people than fruitless attempts of reformation. Josiah and Jeremiah would have healed them, but they would not be healed. (2.) He continued to prophesy through the reigns of Jehoiakim and Zedekiah, each of whom reigned eleven years. He prophesied *to the carrying away of Jerusalem captive* (*v.* 3), that great event which he had so often prophesied of. He continued to prophesy after that, *ch.* 40:1. But the computation here is made to end with that because it was the accomplishment of many of his predictions; and from the thirteenth of Josiah to the captivity was just forty years. Dr. Lightfoot observes that as Moses was so long with the people, a teacher in the wilderness, till they entered into their own land, Jeremiah was so long in their own land a teacher, before they went into the wilderness of the heathen: and he thinks that *therefore* a special mark is set upon the last forty years of the iniquity of Judah, which Ezekiel bore forty days, a day for a year, because during all that time they had Jeremiah prophesying among them, which was a great aggravation of their impenitency. God, in this prophet, suffered their manners, their ill manners, forty years, and at length swore in his wrath that they should not continue in his rest.

Verses 4–10

Here is, I. Jeremiah's early designation to the work and office of a prophet, which God gives him notice of as a reason for his early application to that business (*v.* 4, 5): *The word of the Lord came to him,* with a satisfying assurance to himself that it was the word of the Lord and not a delusion; and God told him, 1. That he had *ordained him a prophet to the nations,* or *against the nations,* the nation of the Jews in the first place, who are now *reckoned among the nations* because they had learned their works and mingled with them in their idolatries, for otherwise they would not have been numbered with them, Num. 23:9. Yet he was given to be a prophet, not to the Jews only, but to the neighbouring nations, to whom he was to *send yokes* (*ch.* 27:2, 3) and whom he must make to *drink of the cup* of the Lord's anger, *ch.* 25:17. He is still in his writings a prophet to the nations (to our nation among the rest), to tell them what the national judgments are which may be expected for national sins. It would be well for the nations would they take Jeremiah for their prophet and attend to the warnings he gives them. 2. That before he was born, even in his eternal counsel, he had designed him to be so. Let him know that he who gave him his commission is the same that gave him his being, that *formed him in the belly* and brought him *forth out of the womb,* that therefore he was his rightful owner and might employ him and make use of him as he pleased, and that this commission was given him in pursuance of the purpose God had purposed in himself concerning him, before he was born: *"I knew thee, and I sanctified thee,"* that is, "I determined that thou shouldst be a prophet and set thee apart for the office." Thus St. Paul says of himself that God had *separated him from his mother's womb* to be a Christian and an apostle, Gal. 1:15. Observe, (1.) The great Creator knows what use to make of every man before he makes him. He has *made all for himself,* and of the same lumps of clay designs *a vessel of honour or dishonour,* as he pleases, Rom. 9:21. (2.) What God has designed men for he will call them to; for his purposes cannot be frustrated. Known unto God are all his own works beforehand, and his knowledge is infallible and his purpose unchangeable. (3.) There is a particular purpose and providence of God conversant about his prophets and ministers; they are by special counsel designed for their work, and what they are designed for they are fitted for: I that *knew thee, sanctified thee.* God destines them to it, and forms them for it, when he first forms the spirit of man within him. *Propheta nascitur, non fit — Original endowment, not education, makes a prophet.*

II. His modestly declining this honourable employment, *v.* 6. Though God had predestinated him to it, yet it was news to him, and a mighty surprise, to hear that he should be *a prophet to the nations.* We know not what God intends us for, but he knows. One would have thought he would catch at it as a piece of preferment, for so it was; but he objects against it, as a work for which he is unqualified: *"Ah, Lord God! behold, I cannot speak* to great men and multitudes, as prophets must; I cannot speak finely nor fluently, cannot word things well, as a message from God should be worded; I cannot speak with any authority, nor can expect to be heeded, *for I am a child* and my youth will be despised." Note, It becomes us, when we have any service to do for God, to be afraid lest we mismanage it, and lest it suffer through our weakness and unfitness for it; it becomes us likewise to have low thoughts of ourselves and to be diffident of our own sufficiency. Those that are young should consider that they are so, should be afraid, as Elihu was, and not venture beyond their length.

III. The assurance God graciously gave him that he would stand by him and carry him on in his work.

1. Let him not object that he is a child; he shall be a prophet for all that (*v.* 7): *"Say no* any more, *I am a child.* It is true thou art; but," (1.) "Thou hast God's precept, and let not thy being young hinder thee from obeying it. Go to all *to whom I shall send thee and speak whatsoever I command thee."* Note, Though a sense of our own weakness and insufficiency should make us go humbly about our work, yet it should not make us draw back from it when God calls us to it. God was angry with Moses even for his modest excuses, Ex. 4:14. (2.) "Thou hast God's presence, and let not thy being young discourage thee from depending upon it. Though thou art a child, thou shalt be *enabled to go to all to whom I shall send thee,* though they are ever so great and ever so many. And *whatsoever I command thee* thou shalt have judgment, memory, and language, wherewith to speak it as it should be spoken." Samuel delivered a message from God to Eli, when he was a little child. Note, God can, when he pleases, make children prophets, and *ordain strength out of the mouth of babes and sucklings.*

2. Let him not object that he shall meet with many enemies and much opposition; God will be his protector (*v.* 8): *"Be not afraid of their races;* though they look big, and so think to outface thee and put thee out of countenance, yet *be not afraid to speak to them;* no, not to speak that to them which is most unpleasing. Thou speakest in the name of the King of kings, and by authority from him, and with that thou mayest *face them down.* Though they look angry, be not afraid of their displeasure nor disturbed with apprehensions of the consequences of it." Those that have messages to deliver from God must not be *afraid of the face of man,* Eze. 3:9. "And thou hast cause both to be bold and easy; for *I am with thee,* not only to assist thee in thy work, but to deliver thee out of the hands of the persecutors; and, *if God be for thee, who can be against thee?"* If God do not deliver his ministers from trouble, it is to the same effect if he support them under their trouble. Mr. Gataker well observes here, That earthly princes are not wont to go along with their ambassadors; but God goes along with those whom he sends, and is, by his powerful protection, at all times and in all places present with them; and with this they ought to animate themselves, Acts 18:10.

3. Let him not object that he cannot speak as becomes him — God will enable him to speak.

(1.) To speak intelligently, and as one that had acquaintance with God, *v.* 9. He having now a vision of the divine glory, the Lord *put forth his hand,* and by a sensible sign conferred upon him so much of the gift of the tongue as was necessary for him: *He touched his mouth,* and with that touch *opened his lips,* that his mouth should show forth God's praise, with that touch sweetly conveyed *his words into his mouth,* to be ready to him upon all occasions, so that he could never want words who was thus furnished by him that *made man's mouth.* God not only put knowledge into his head, but *words into his mouth;* for there are *words which the Holy Ghost teaches,* 1 Co. 2:13. It is fit God's message should be delivered in his own words, that it may be delivered accurately. Eze. 3:4, *Speak with my words.* And those that faithfully do so shall not want instructions as the case requires; God will give them a mouth and wisdom *in that same hour,* Mt. 10:19.

(2.) To speak powerfully, and as one that had authority from God, *v.* 10. It is a strange commission that is here given him: *See, I have this day set thee over the nations and over the kingdoms.* This sounds very great, and yet Jeremiah is a poor despicable priest still; he is not set over the kingdoms as a prince to rule them by the sword, but as a prophet by the power of the word of God. Those that would hence prove the pope's supremacy over kings, and his authority to depose them and dispose of their kingdoms at his pleasure, must prove that he has the same extraordinary spirit of prophecy that Jeremiah had, else how can be have the power that Jeremiah had by virtue of that spirit? And yet the power that Jeremiah had (who, notwithstanding his power, lived in meanness and contempt, and under oppression) would not content these proud men. Jeremiah was *set over the nations,* the Jewish nation in the first place, and other nations, some great ones besides, against whom he prophesied; he was set over them, not to demand tribute from them nor to enrich himself with their spoils, but to *root out, and pull down, and destroy,* and yet withal *to build and plant.* [1.] He must attempt to reform the nations, to *root out, and pull down, and destroy* idolatry and other wickednesses among them, to extirpate those vicious habits and customs which had long taken root, to *throw down* the kingdom of sin, that religion and virtue might be *planted* and *built* among them. And, to the introducing and establishing of that which is good, it is necessary that that which is evil be removed. [2.] He must tell them that it would be well or ill with them according as they were, or were not, reformed. He must set before them *life and death, good and evil,* according to God's declaration of the method he takes with kingdoms and nations, *ch.* 18:9–10. He must assure those who persisted in their wickedness that they should be *rooted out and destroyed,* and those who repented that they should be *built and planted.* He was authorized to read the doom of nations, and God would *ratify it* and *fulfil it* (Isa. 44:26), would do it according to his word, and therefore is said to do it *by* his word. It is thus expressed partly to show how sure the word of prophecy is — it will as certainly be accomplished as if it were done already, and partly to put an honour upon the prophetic office and make it look truly great, that others may not despise the prophets nor they disparage themselves. And yet more honourable does the gospel ministry look, in that declarative power Christ gave his apostles to *remit and retain sin* (Jn. 20:23), *to bind and loose,* Mt. 18:18.

Verses 11–19

Here, I. God gives Jeremiah, in vision, a view of the principal errand he was to go upon, which was to foretel the destruction of Judah and Jerusalem by the Chaldeans, for their sins, especially their idolatry. This was at first represented to him in a way proper to make an impression upon him, that he might have it upon his heart in all his dealings with this people.

1. He intimates to him that the people were ripening apace for ruin and that ruin was hastening apace towards them. God, having answered his objection, that he was *a child,* goes on to initiate him in the prophetical learning and language; and, having promised to enable him to speak intelligibly to the people, he here teaches him to understand what God says to him; for prophets must have eyes in their heads as well as tongues, must be seers as well as speakers. He therefore asks him, *"Jeremiah, what seest thou?* Look about thee, and observe now." And he was soon aware of what was presented to him: *"I see a rod,* denoting affliction and chastisement, a correcting rod hanging over us; and it is a *rod of an almond-tree,* which is one of the forwardest trees in the spring, is in the bud and blossom quickly, when other trees are scarcely broken out;" it flourishes, says Pliny, in the month of January, and by March has ripe fruits; hence it is called in the Hebrew, *Shakedh,* the *hasty tree.* Whether this rod that Jeremiah saw had already budded, as some think, or whether it was stripped and dry, as others think, and yet Jeremiah knew it to be of an almond-tree, as Aaron's rod was, is uncertain; but God explained it in the next words (*v.* 12): *Thou hast well seen.* God commended him that he was so observant, and so quick of apprehension, as to be aware, though it was the first vision he ever saw, that it was *a rod of an almond-tree,* that his mind was so composed as to be able to distinguish. Prophets have need of good eyes; and those that see well shall be commended, and not those only that speak well. "Thou hast seen a *hasty tree,* which signifies that *I will hasten my word to perform it."* Jeremiah shall prophesy that which he himself shall live to see accomplished. We have the explication of this, Eze. 7:10, 11, *"The rod hath blossomed, pride hath budded, violence*

has risen up into a rod of wickedness. The measure of Jerusalem's iniquity fills very fast; and, as if their destruction slumbered too long, they waken it, they hasten it, and I will hasten to perform what I have spoken against them."

2. He intimates to him whence the intended ruin should arise. Jeremiah is a second time asked: *What seest thou?* and he sees *a seething-pot* upon the fire (*v.* 13), representing Jerusalem and Judah in great commotion, like boiling water, by reason of the descent which the Chaldean army made upon them; made *like a fiery oven* (Ps. 21:9), all in a heat, wasting away as boiling water does and sensibly evaporating and growing less and less, ready to boil over, to be thrown out of their own city and land, as out of the pan into the fire, from bad to worse. Some think that those scoffers referred to this who said (Eze. 11:3), *This city is the cauldron, and we are the flesh.* Now the mouth or face of the furnace or hearth, over which this pot boiled, was *towards the north,* for thence the fire and the fuel were to come that must *make the pot boil thus.* So the vision is explained (*v.* 14): *Out of the north an evil shall break forth,* or *shall be opened.* It had been long designed by the justice of God, and long deserved by the sin of the people, and yet hitherto the divine patience had restrained it, and held it in, as it were; the enemies had intended it, and God had checked them; but now all restraints shall be taken off, and the *evil shall break forth;* the direful scene shall open, and the enemy shall come in like a flood. It shall be a universal calamity; it shall come *upon all the inhabitants of the land,* from the highest to the lowest, for they have all corrupted their way. Look for this storm to arise *out of the north, whence fair weather usually comes,* Job 37:22. When there was friendship between Hezekiah and the king of Babylon they promised themselves many advantages *out of the north;* but it proved quite otherwise: *out of the north* their trouble arose. Thence sometimes the fiercest tempests come whence we expected fair weather. This is further explained *v.* 15, where we may observe, (1.) The raising of the army that shall invade Judah and lay it waste: *I will call all the families of the kingdoms of the north, saith the Lord.* All the northern crowns shall unite under Nebuchadnezzar, and join with him in this expedition. They lie dispersed, but God, who has all men's hearts in his hand, will bring them together; they lie at a distance from Judah, but God, who directs all men's steps, will call them, and they shall come, though they be ever so far off. God's summons shall be obeyed; those whom he calls shall come. When he has work to do of any kind he will find instruments to do it, though he send to the utmost parts of the earth for them. And, that the armies brought into the field may be sufficiently numerous and strong, he will call not only the *kingdoms of the north, but all the families* of those kingdoms, into the service; not one able-bodied man shall be left behind. (2.) The advance of this army. The commanders of the troops of the several nations shall take their post in carrying on the siege of Jerusalem and the other cities of Judah. They shall set *every one his throne,* or seat. When a city is besieged we say, The enemy sits down before it. They shall encamp some at the *entering of the gates, others against the walls round about,* to cut off both the going out of the mouths and the coming in of the meat, and so to starve them.

3. He tells him plainly what was the procuring cause of all these judgments; it was the *sin of Jerusalem* and of the *cities of Judah* (*v.* 16): *I will pass sentence upon them* (so it may be read) or *give judgment against them* (this sentence, this judgment) *because of all their wickedness;* it is this that plucks up the flood-gates and lets in this inundation of calamities. They *have forsaken God* and revolted from their allegiance to him, and have *burnt incense to other gods,* new gods, strange gods, and all false gods, pretenders, usurpers, the creatures of their own fancy, and *they have worshipped the works of their own hands.* Jeremiah was young, had looked but little abroad into the world, and perhaps did not know, nor could have believed, what abominable idolatries the children of his people were guilty of; but God tells him, that he might know what to level his reproofs against and what to ground his threatenings upon, and that he might himself be satisfied in the equity of the sentence which in God's name he was to pass upon them.

II. God excites and encourages Jeremiah to apply himself with all diligence and seriousness to his business. A great trust is committed to him. He is sent in God's name as a herald at arms, to proclaim war against his rebellious subjects; for God is pleased to give warning of his judgments beforehand, that sinners may be awakened to meet him by repentance, and so *turn away his wrath,* and that, if they do not, they may be left inexcusable. With this trust Jeremiah has a charge given him (*v.* 17): *"Thou, therefore, gird up thy loins;* free thyself from all those things that would unfit thee for or hinder thee in this service; buckle to it with readiness and resolution, and be not entangled with doubts about it." He must be quick: *Arise,* and lose no time. He must be busy: *Arise, and speak unto them* in season, out of season. He must be bold: *Be not dismayed at their faces,* as before, *v.* 8. In a word, he must be faithful; it is required of ambassadors that they be so.

1. In two things he must be faithful: — (1.) He must speak all that he is charged with: *Speak all that I command thee.* He must forget nothing as minute, or foreign, or not worth mentioning; every word of God is weighty. He must conceal nothing for fear of offending; he must alter nothing under pretence of making it more fashionable or more palatable, but, without addition or diminution, *declare the whole counsel of God.* (2.) He must speak to all that he is charged against; he must not whisper it in a corner to a few particular friends that will take it well, but he must appear *against the kings of Judah,* if they be wicked kings, and bear his testimony against the sins even *of the princes thereof;* for the greatest of men are not exempt from the judgments either of God's hand or of his mouth. Nay, he must not spare *the priests thereof;* though he himself was a priest, and was concerned to maintain the dignity of his order, yet he must not therefore flatter them in their sins. He must appear against the *people of the land,* though they were his own people, as far as they were against the Lord.

2. Two reasons are here given why he should do thus: — (1.) Because he had reason to fear the wrath of God if he should be false: *"Be not dismayed at their faces,* so as to ??desert thy office, or shrink from the duty of it, *lest I confound and dismay thee before them,* lest I give thee up to thy faintheartedness." Those that consult their own credit, ease, and safety, more than their work and duty, are justly left of God to themselves, and to bring upon themselves the shame of their own cowardliness. Nay, *lest I reckon with thee for thy faintheartedness, and break thee to pieces;* so some read it. Therefore this prophet says (*ch.* 17:17), Lord, *be not thou a terror to me.* Note, The fear of God is the best antidote against the fear of man. Let us always be afraid of offending God, who after he has killed has power to cast into hell, and then we shall be in little danger of fearing the faces of men that can but kill the body, Lu. 12:4, 5. See Neh. 4:14. It is better to have all the men in the world our enemies than God our enemy. (2.) Because he had no reason to fear the wrath of men if he were faithful; for the God whom he served would protect him, and bear him out, so that they should neither sink his spirits nor drive him off from his work, should neither stop his mouth nor take away his life, till he had finished his testimony, *v.* 18. This young stripling of a prophet is made by the power of God as an impregnable city, fortified with iron pillars and surrounded with walls of brass; he sallies out upon the enemy in reproofs and threatenings, and *keeps them in awe.* They set upon him on every side; the kings and princes batter him with their power, the priests thunder against him with their church-censures, and *the people of the land* shoot their arrows at him, even slanderous and bitter words; but he shall keep his ground and make his part good with them; he shall still be a curb upon them (*v.* 19): *They shall fight against thee, but they shall not prevail to destroy thee, for I am with thee to deliver thee* out of their hands; nor shall they prevail to defeat the word that God sends them by Jeremiah, nor to deliver themselves; it shall take hold of them, for God is against them to destroy them. Note, Those who are sure that they have God with them (as he is if they be with him) need not, ought not, to be afraid, whoever is against them.

CHAPTER 2

It is probable that this chapter was Jeremiah's first sermon after his ordination; and a most lively pathetic sermon it is as any we have is all the books of the prophets. Let him not say, "I cannot speak, for I am a child;" for, God having touched his mouth and put his words into it, none can speak better. The scope of the chapter is to show God's people their transgressions, even the house of Jacob their sins; it is all by way of reproof and conviction, that they might be brought to repent of their sins and so prevent the ruin that was coming upon them. The charge drawn up against them is very high, the aggravations are black, the arguments used for their conviction very close and pressing, and the expostulations very pungent and affecting. The sin which they are most particularly charged with here is idolatry, forsaking the true God, their own God, for other false gods. Now they are told, I. That this was ungrateful to God, who had been so kind to them (*v.* 1–8). II. That it was without precedent, that a nation should change their god (*v.* 9–13). III. That hereby they had disparaged and ruined themselves (*v.* 14–19). IV. That they had broken their covenants and degenerated from their good beginnings (*v.* 20, 21). V. That their wickedness was too plain to be concealed and too bad to be excused (*v.* 22, 23, 35). VI. That they persisted wilfully and obstinately in it, and were irreclaimable and indefatigable in their idolatries (*v.* 24, 25, 33, 36). VII. That they shamed themselves by their idolatry and should shortly be made ashamed of it when they should find their idols unable to help them (*v.* 26–29, 37). VIII. That they had not been convinced and reformed by the rebukes of Providence that had been under (*v.* 30). IX. That they had put a great contempt upon God (v 31, 32). X. That with their idolatries they had mixed the most unnatural murders, shedding the blood of the poor innocents (*v.* 34). Those hearts were hard indeed that were untouched and unhumbled when their sins were thus set in order before them. O that by meditating on this chapter we might be brought to repent of our spiritual idolatries, giving that place in our souls to the world and the flesh which should have been reserved for God only!

Verses 1–8

Here is, I. A command given to Jeremiah to go and carry a message from God to the inhabitants of Jerusalem. He was charged in general (*ch.* 1:17) to go and *speak to them;* here he is particularly charged to go and speak *this* to them. Note, It is good for ministers by faith and prayer to take out a fresh commission when they address themselves solemnly to any part of their work. Let a minister carefully compare what he has to deliver with the word of God, and see that it agrees with it, that he may be able to say, not only, *The Lord sent me,* but, He sent me to *speak this.* He must go from Anathoth, where he lived in a pleasant retirement, spending his time (it is likely) among a few friends and in the study of the law, and must make his appearance at Jerusalem, that noisy tumultuous city, and *cry in their ears,* as a man in earnest and that would be heard: "Cry aloud, that all may hear, and none may plead ignorance. Go close to them, and *cry in the ears* of those that have stopped their ears."

II. The message he was commanded to deliver. He must upbraid them with their horrid ingratitude in forsaking a God who had been of old so kind to them, that this might either make them ashamed and bring them to repentance, or might justify God in turning his hand against them.

1. God here puts them in mind of the favours he had of old bestowed upon them, when they were first formed into a people (*v.* 2): *"I remember for thy sake,* and I would have thee to remember it, and improve the remembrance of it for thy good; I cannot forget *the kindness of thy youth and the love of thy espousals."*

(1.) This may be understood of the kindness they had for God; it was not such indeed as they had any reason to boast of, or to plead with God for favour to be shown them (for many of them were very unkind and provoking, and, when they did return and enquire early after God, they did but flatter him), yet God is pleased to mention it, and plead it with them; for, though it was but little love that they showed him, he took it kindly. When *they believed the Lord and his servant Moses,* when they *sang God's praise at the Red Sea,* when at the foot of Mount Sinai they promised, *All that the Lord shall say unto us we will do and will be obedient,* then was the *kindness of their youth and the love of their espousals.* When they seemed so forward for God he said, *Surely they are my people,* and will be faithful to me, *children that will not lie.* Note, Those that begin well and promise fair, but do not perform and persevere, will justly be upbraided with their hopeful and promising beginnings. God remembers the *kindness of our youth and the love of our espousals,* the zeal we then seemed to have for him and the affection wherewith we made our covenants with him, the buds and blossoms that never came to perfection; and it is good for us to remember them, that we may remember whence we have fallen, and return to our first love, Rev. 2:4, 5; Gal. 4:15. In two things appeared the *kindness of their youth:* — [1.] That they followed the direction of the pillar of cloud and fire in the wilderness; and though sometimes they spoke of returning into Egypt, or pushing forward into Canaan, yet they did neither, but for forty years together *went after God in the wilderness,* and trusted him to provide for them, though it was *a land that was not sown.* This God took kindly, and took notice of it to their praise long after, that, though much was amiss among them, yet they never forsook the guidance they were under. Thus, though Christ often chid his disciples, yet he commended them, at parting, for continuing with him, Lu. 22:28. It must be the strong affection of the youth, and the espousals, that will carry us on to follow God in a wilderness, with an implicit faith and an entire resignation; and it is a pity that those who have so followed him should ever leave him. [2.] That they entertained divine institutions, set up the tabernacle among them, and attended the service of it. Israel *was then holiness to the Lord;* they joined themselves to him in covenant as a peculiar people. Thus they began in the spirit, and God puts them in mind of it, that they might be ashamed of ending *in the flesh.*

(2.) Or it may be understood of God's kindness to them; of that he afterwards speaks largely. *When Israel was a child, then I loved him,* Hos. 11:1. He then espoused that people to himself with all the affection with which a *young man marries a virgin* (Isaiah 62:5), for the time was *a time of love,* Eze. 16:8. [1.] God appropriated them to himself. Though they were a sinful people, yet, by virtue of the covenant made with them and the church set up among them, they were *holiness to the Lord,* dedicated to his honour and taken under his special tuition; they were the *first fruits of his increase,* the first constituted church he had in the world; they were the first-fruits, but the full harvest was to be gathered from among the Gentiles. The *first-fruits of the increase* were God's part of it, were offered to him, and he was honoured with them; so were the people of the Jews; what little tribute, rent, and homage, God had from the world, he had it chiefly from them; and it was their honour to be thus set apart for God. This honour have all the saints; they are the *first-fruits of his creatures,* Jam. 1:18. [2.] Having espoused them, he espoused their cause, and became an *enemy to their enemies,* Ex. 23:22. Being the *first-fruits of his increase, all that devoured him* (so it should be read) *did offend;* they *trespassed,* they contracted guilt, and evil befel them, as those were reckoned *offenders* that *devoured the first-fruits,* or any thing else that was *holy to the Lord,* that embezzled them, or converted them to their own use, Lev. 5:15. Whoever offered any injury to the people of God did so at their peril; their God was ready to avenge their quarrel, and said to the proudest of kings, *Touch not my anointed,* Ps. 105:14, 15; Ex. 17:14. He had in a special manner a controversy with those that attempted to debauch them and draw them off from being *holiness to the Lord;* witness his *quarrel with the Midianites about the matter of Peor,* Num. 25:17, 18. [3.] He *brought them out of Egypt* with a high hand and great terror (Deu. 4:34), and yet with a kind hand and great tenderness led them through a vast howling wilderness (*v.* 6), *a land of deserts and pits,* or of *graves, terram sepulchralem — a sepulchral land,* where there was ground, not to feed them, but to bury them, where there was no good to be expected, for it was a *land of drought,* but all manner of evil to be feared, for it was *the shadow of death.* In that darksome valley they walked forty years; but *God was with them; his rod,* in Moses's hand, *and his staff, comforted them,* and even there God *prepared a table for them* (Ps. 23:4, 5), gave them bread out of the clouds and drink out of the rocks. It was a land abandoned by all mankind, as yielding neither road nor rest. It was no thoroughfare, for *no man passed through it* — no settlement, for *no man dwelt there.* For God will teach his people to tread untrodden paths, to dwell alone, and to be singular. The difficulties of the journey are thus insisted on, to magnify the power and goodness of God in bringing them, through all, safely to their journey's end at last. All God's spiritual Israel must own their obligations to him for a safe conduct through the wilderness of this world, no less dangerous to the soul than that was to the body. [4.] At length he settled them in Canaan (*v.* 7): *I brought you into a plentiful country,* which would be the more acceptable after they had been for so many years in *a land of drought.* They did *eat the fruit thereof* and the *goodness thereof,* and were allowed so to do. I brought you *into a land of Carmel* (so the word is); Carmel was a place of extraordinary fruitfulness, and Canaan was as one great fruitful field, Deu. 8:7. [5.] God gave them the means of knowledge and grace, and communion with him; this is implied, *v.* 8. They had priests that *handled the law,* read it, and expounded it to them; that was part of their business, Deu. 33:8. They had pastors, to guide them and take care of their affairs, magistrates and judges; they had prophets to consult God for them and to make known his mind to them.

2. He upbraids them with their horrid ingratitude, and the ill returns they had made him for these favours; let them all come and answer to this charge (*v.* 4); it is exhibited in the name of God against *all the families of the house of* Israel, for they can none of them plead, *Not guilty.* (1.) He challenges them to produce any instance of his being unjust and unkind to them. Though he had conferred favours upon them in some things, yet, if in other things he had dealt hardly with them, they would not have been altogether without excuse. He therefore puts it fairly to them to show cause for their deserting him (*v.* 5): *"What iniquity have your fathers found in me,* or you either? Have you, upon trial, found God a hard master? Have his commands put any hardship upon you or obliged you to any thing unfit, unfair, or unbecoming you? Have his promises put any cheats upon you, or raised your expectations of things which you were afterwards disappointed of? You that have renounced your covenant with God, can you say that it was a hard bargain and that which you could not live upon? You that have forsaken the ordinances of God, can you say that it was because they were a wearisome service, or work that there was nothing to be got by? No; the disappointments you have met with were owing to yourselves, not to God. The yoke of his commandments if easy, and in the *keeping of them there is great reward."* Note, Those that forsake God cannot say that he has ever given them any provocation to do so: for this we may safely appeal to the consciences of sinners; the slothful servant that offered such a plea as this had it overruled *out of his own mouth,* Lu. 19:22. Though he afflicts us, we cannot say that there is iniquity in him; he does us no wrong. The ways of the Lord are undoubtedly equal; all the iniquity is in our ways. (2.) He charges them with being very unjust and unkind to him notwithstanding. [1.] They had quitted his service: *"They have gone from me,* nay, they have gone *far from me."* They studied how to estrange themselves from God and their duty, and got as far as they could out of the reach of his commandments and their own convictions. Those that have deserted religion commonly set themselves at a greater distance from it, and in a greater opposition to it, than those that never knew it. [2.] They had quitted it for the service of idols, which was so much the greater reproach to God and his service; they went from him, not to better themselves, but to cheat themselves: *They have walked after vanity,* that is, idolatry; for an idol is a vain thing; it is *nothing in the world,* 1 Co. 8:4; Deu. 32:21; Jer. 14:22. Idolatrous worships are vanities, Acts 14:15. Idolaters are vain, for those that make idols *are like unto them* (Ps. 115:8), as much stocks and stones as the images they worship, and good for as little. [3.] They had with idolatry introduced all manner of wickedness. When they entered into the good land which God gave them they defiled it (*v.* 7), by defiling themselves and disfitting themselves for the service of God. It was God's land; they were but tenants to him, sojourners in it, Lev. 25:23. It was his heritage, for it was a holy land, Immanuel's land; but they *made it an abomination,* even to God himself, who was wroth, and greatly abhorred Israel. [4.] Having forsaken God, though they soon found that they had changed for the worse, yet they had no thoughts of returning to him again, nor took any steps towards it. Neither the people nor the priests made any enquiry after him, took any thought about their duty to him, nor expressed any desire to recover his favour. *First,* The *people* said not, *Where is the Lord? v.* 6. Though they were trained up in an observance of him as their God, and had been often told that he *brought them out of the land of Egypt,* to be a people peculiar to himself, yet they never asked after him nor desired the *knowledge of his ways. Secondly,* The *priests* said not, *Where is the Lord? v.* 8. Those whose office it was to attend immediately upon him were in no concern to acquaint themselves with him, or approve themselves to him. Those who should have instructed the people in the knowledge of God took no care to get the knowledge of him themselves. The scribes, who *handled the law,* did not know God nor his will, could not expound the scriptures at all, or not aright. The pastors, who should have kept the flock from transgressing, were themselves ringleaders in transgression: *They have transgressed against me.* The pretenders to prophecy prophesied by Baal, in his name, to his honour, being backed and supported by the wicked kings to confront the Lord's prophets. Baal's prophets joined with Baal's priests, and walked after the *things which do not profit,* that is, after the idols which can be no way helpful to their worshippers. See how the best characters are usurped, and the best offices liable to corruption; and wonder not at the sin and ruin of a people when the *blind* are *leaders of the blind.*

Verses 9–13

The prophet, having shown their base ingratitude in forsaking God, here shows their unparalleled fickleness and folly (*v.* 9): *I will yet plead with you.* Note, Before God punishes sinners he pleads with them, to bring them to repentance. Note, further, When much has been said of the evil of sin, still there is more to be said; when one article of the charge is made good, there is another to be urged; when we have said a great deal, still *we have yet to speak on God's behalf,* Job 36:2. Those that deal with sinners, for their conviction, must urge a variety of arguments and follow their blow. God had before pleaded with their fathers, and asked why they *walked after vanity* and became vain, *v.* 5. Now he pleads with those who persisted in that *vain conversation received by tradition from their fathers,* and *with their children's children,* that is, with all that in every age tread in their steps. Let those that forsake God know that he is willing to argue the case fairly with them, that he may be *justified when he speaks.* He pleads that with us which we should plead with ourselves.

I. He shows that they acted contrary to the usage of all nations. Their neighbours were more firm and faithful to their false gods than they were to the true God. They were ambitious of being *like the nations,* and yet in this they were unlike them. He challenges them to produce an instance of any nation that had *changed their gods* (*v.* 10, 11) or were apt to change them. Let them survey either the old records or the present state of the isles of Chittim, Greece, and the European islands, the countries that were more polite and learned, and of Kedar, that lay south-east (as the other north-west from them), which were more rude and barbarous; and they should not find an instance of a nation that had *changed their gods,* though they had never done them any kindness, nor could do, for *they were no gods.* Such a veneration had they for their gods, so good an opinion of them, and such a respect for the choice their fathers had made, that though they were gods of wood and stone they would not change them for gods of silver and gold, no, not for the living and true God. *Shall we praise them for this? We praise them not.* But it may well be urged, to the reproach of Israel, that they, who were the only people that had no cause to change their God, were yet the only people that had changed him. Note, Men are with difficulty brought off from that religion which they have been brought up in, though ever so absurd and grossly false. The zeal and constancy of idolaters should shame Christians out of their coldness and inconstancy.

II. He shows that they acted contrary to the dictates of common sense, in that they not only changed (it may sometimes be our duty and wisdom to do so), but that they changed for the worse, and made a bad bargain for themselves. 1. They parted from a God who was their glory, who made them truly glorious and every way put honour upon them, one whom they might with a humble confidence glory in as theirs, who is himself a glorious God and the glory of those whose God he is; he was particularly the glory of his people Israel, for his glory had often appeared on their tabernacle. 2. They closed with gods that could do them no good, gods that *do not profit* their worshippers. Idolaters change God's glory into shame (Rom. 1:23) and so they do their own; in dishonouring him, they disgrace and disparage themselves, and are enemies to their own interest. Note, Whatever those turn to who forsake God, it will never do them any good; it will flatter them and please them, but it *cannot profit them.* Heaven itself is here called upon to stand amazed at the sin and folly of these apostates from God (*v.* 12, 13): *Be astonished, O you heavens! at this.* The earth is so universally corrupt that it will take no notice of it; but let the heavens and heavenly bodies be astonished at it. Let the sun blush to see such ingratitude and be afraid to shine upon such ungrateful wretches. Those that forsook God worshipped *the host of heaven,* the sun, moon, and stars; but these, instead of being pleased with the adorations that were paid to them, *were astonished and horribly afraid;* and would rather have been *very desolate, utterly exhausted* (as the word is) and deprived of their light, than that it should have given occasion to any to worship them. Some refer it to the *angels of heaven;* if they rejoice at the return of souls to God, we may suppose that they are astonished and horribly afraid at the revolt of souls from him. The meaning is that the conduct of this people towards God was, (1.) Such as we may well be astonished and wonder at, that ever men, who pretend to reason, should do a thing so very absurd. (2.) Such as we ought to have a holy indignation at as impious, and a high affront to our Maker, whose honour every good man is jealous for. (3.) Such as we may tremble to think of the consequences of. What will be in the end hereof? Be horribly afraid to think of the wrath and curse which will be the portion of those who thus throw themselves out of God's grace and favour. Now what is it that is to be thought of with all this horror? It is this: *"My people,* whom I have taught and should have ruled, *have committed two* great evils, ingratitude and folly; they have acted contrary both to their duty and to their interest." [1.] They have *affronted their God,* by turning their back upon him, as if he were not worthy their notice: *"They have forsaken me, the fountain of living waters,* in whom they have an abundant and constant supply of all the comfort and relief they stand in need of, and have it freely." God is their *fountain of life,* Ps. 36:9. There is in him an all-sufficiency of grace and strength; all our springs are in him and our streams from him; to forsake him is, in effect, to deny this. He has been to us a bountiful benefactor, a *fountain of living waters,* over-flowing, ever-flowing, in the gifts of his favour; to forsake him is to refuse to acknowledge his kindness and to withhold that tribute of love and praise which his kindness calls for. [2.] They have cheated themselves, they forsook *their own mercies,* but it was for lying vanities. They took a great deal of pains to *hew themselves out cisterns,* to dig pits or pools in the earth or rock which they would carry water to, or which should receive the rain; but they proved *broken cisterns,* false at the bottom, so that they could *hold no water.* When they came to quench their thirst there they found nothing but mud and mire, and the filthy sediments of a standing lake. Such idols were to their worshippers, and such a change did those experience who turned from God to them. If we make an idol of any creature — wealth, or pleasure, or honour, — if we place our happiness in it, and promise ourselves the comfort and satisfaction in it which are to be had in God only, — if we make it our joy and love, our hope and confidence, we shall find it a cistern, which we take a great deal of pains to hew out and fill, and at the best it will hold but a little water, and that dead and flat, and soon corrupting and becoming nauseous. Nay, it is a broken cistern, that cracks and cleaves in hot weather, so that the water is lost when we have most need of it, Job 6:15. Let us therefore with purpose of heart cleave to the Lord only, for whither else *shall we go?* He has *the words of eternal life.*

Verses 14–19

The prophet, further to evince the folly of their forsaking God, shows them what mischiefs they had already brought upon themselves by so doing; it had already cost them dear, for to this were owing all the calamities their country was now groaning under, which were but an earnest of more and greater if they repented not. See how they smarted for their folly.

I. Their neighbours, who were their professed enemies, prevailed against them, and this was owing to their sin. 1. They were enslaved and lost their liberty (*v.* 14): *Is Israel a servant?* No; *Israel is my son, my first-born,* Ex. 4:22. They are children; they are heirs. Nay, their extraction is noble; they are the seed of Abraham, God's friend, and of Jacob his chosen. *Is he a home-born slave?* No; he is not the *son of the bond-woman,* but of the free. They were designed for dominion, not for servitude. Every thing in their constitution carried about it the marks of freedom and honour. *Why then is he spoiled* of his liberty? Why is he used as a servant, as a *home-born slave?* Why does he *make himself a slave* to his lusts, to his idols, to that which does not profit? *v.* 11. What a thing is this, that such a birthright should be sold for a mess of pottage, such a crown profaned and laid in the dust! Why is he made a slave to the oppressor? God provided that a Hebrew servant should be free the seventh year, and that their slaves should be *of the heathen,* not *of their brethren,* Lev. 25:44, 46. But, notwithstanding this, the princes made slaves of their subjects, and masters made slaves of their servants (*ch.* 34:11), and so made their country mean and miserable, which God had made happy and honourable. The neighbouring princes and powers broke in upon them, and made some of them slaves even in their own country, and perhaps sold others for slaves into foreign countries. And how came they thus to lose their liberties? For *their iniquities they sold themselves,* Isa. 50:1. We may apply this spiritually. Is the soul of man a *servant? Is it a home-born slave?* No, it is not. Why then is it spoiled? It is because it has sold its own liberty and enslaved itself to divers lusts and passions, which is a lamentation, and should be for a lamentation. 2. They were impoverished and had lost their wealth. God brought them into a plentiful country (*v.* 7), but all their neighbours made a prey of it (*v.* 15): *Young lions roar aloud over him and yell;* they are a continual terror to him. Sometimes one potent enemy, and sometimes another, and sometimes many in confederacy, fall upon him, and triumph over him. They carry off the fruits of his land, and make that *waste,* and *burn his cities,* when first they have plundered them, so that they remain *without inhabitant,* either because there are no houses to dwell in or because those that should dwell in them are carried into captivity. 3. They were abused, and insulted over, and beaten by every body (*v.* 16): "Even *the children of Noph and Tahapanes,* despicable people, not famed for military courage nor strength, *have broken the crown of thy head,* or fed upon it. In all their struggles with thee they have been too hard for thee, and thou hast always come off with a broken head. The principal part of thy country, that which lay next Jerusalem, has been and is a prey to them." How calamitous the condition of Judah had been of late in the reign of Manasseh we find, 2 Chr. 33:11, and perhaps it had not now much recovered itself. 4. All this was owing to their sin (*v.* 17): *Hast thou not procured this unto thyself?* By their sinful confederacies with the nations, and especially their conformity to them in their idolatrous customs and usages, they had made themselves very mean and contemptible, as all those do that have made a profession of religion and afterwards throw it off. Nothing now appeared of that which, by their constitution, made them both honourable and formidable, and therefore nobody either respected them or feared them. But this was not all; they had provoked God to give them up into the hands of their enemies, and to make them a scourge to them and give them success against them; and "thus thou hast *procured it to thyself, in that thou hast forsaken the Lord thy God,* revolted from thy allegiance to him and so thrown thyself out of his protection; for protection and allegiance go together." Whatever trouble we are in at any time we may thank ourselves for it; for we bring it upon our own head by our forsaking God: *"Thou hast forsaken thy God at the time that he was leading thee by the way"* (so it should be read); "Then when he was leading thee on to a happy peace and settlement, and thou wast within a step of it, then thou forsookest him, and so didst put a bar in thy own door."

II. Their neighbours, that were their pretended friends, deceived them, distressed them, and helped them not, and this also was owing to their sin. 1. They did in vain seek to Egypt and Assyria for help (*v.* 18): *"What hast thou to do in the way of Egypt?* When thou art under apprehensions of danger thou art running to Egypt for help, Isa. 30:1, 2; 31:1. Thou art for *drinking the waters of Sihor,"* that is, *Nilus.* "Thou reliest upon their multitude, and refreshest thy self with the fair promises they make thee. At other times thou art *in the way of Assyria,* sending or going with all speed to fetch recruits thence, and thinkest to satisfy thyself with the *waters of the river Euphrates;* what *hast thou to do* there? What wilt thou get by applying to them? They shall *help in vain,* shall be broken reeds to thee, and what thou thoughtest would be to thee as a river will be but a broken cistern." 2. This also was because of their sin. The judgment shall unavoidably come upon them which their sin has deserved; and then to what purpose is it to call in help against it? *v.* 19. *"Thy own wickedness shall correct thee,* and then it is impossible for them to save thee; *know and see* therefore, upon the whole matter, *that it is an evil thing that thou hast forsaken God,* for it is that which makes thy enemies enemies indeed, and thy friends friends in vain." Observe here, (1.) The nature of sin; it is *forsaking the Lord* as our God; it is the soul's alienation from him and aversion to him. Cleaving to sin is leaving God. (2.) The cause of sin; it is because *his fear is not in us.* It is for want of a good principle in us, particularly for want of the fear of God; this is at the bottom of our apostasy from him; men forsake their duty to God because they stand in no awe of him nor have any dread of his displeasure. (3.) The malignity of sin; it is *an evil thing and a bitter.* Sin is an evil thing, only evil, an evil that has no good in it, an evil that is the root and cause of all other evil; it is evil indeed, for it is not only the greatest contrariety to the divine nature, but the greatest corruption of the human nature. It is *bitter;* a state of sin is the *gall of bitterness,* and every sinful way will be *bitterness in the latter end;* the wages of it is death, and death is bitter. (4.) The fatal consequences of sin; as it is in itself evil and bitter, so it has a direct tendency to make us miserable: *"Thy own wickedness shall correct thee, and thy backslidings shall reprove thee,* not only destroy and ruin thee hereafter, but correct and reprove thee now; they will certainly bring trouble upon thee; and punishment will so inevitably follow the sin that the sin shall itself be said to punish thee. Nay, the punishment, in its kind and circumstances, shall so directly answer to the sin, that thou mayest read the sin in the punishment; and the justice of the punishment shall be so plain that thou shalt not have a word to say for thyself; thy own wickedness shall convince thee and stop thy mouth for ever and thou shalt be forced to own that *the Lord is righteous."* (5.) The use and application of all this: *"Know therefore,* and see it, and repent of thy sin, that so the iniquity which is thy correction *may not be thy ruin."*

Verses 20–28

In these verses the prophet goes on with his charge against this backsliding people. Observe here,

I. The sin itself that he charges them with — idolatry, that great provocation which they were so notoriously guilty of. 1. They frequented the places of idol-worship (*v.* 20): *"Upon every high hill and under every green tree,* in the high places and the groves, such as the heathen had a foolish fondness and veneration for, *thou wanderest,* first to one and then to another, like one unsettled, and still uneasy and unsatisfied; but in all *playing the harlot,"* worshipping false gods, which is spiritual whoredom, and was commonly accompanied with corporal whoredom too. Note, Those that leave God wander endlessly, and a vagrant lust is insatiable. 2. They made images for themselves, and gave divine honour to them (*v.* 26, 27); not only the common people, but even the kings and princes, who should have restrained the people from doing ill, and the priests and prophets, who should have taught them to do well, were themselves so wretchedly sottish and stupid, and under the power of such a strong delusion, as to *say to a stock, "Thou art my father* (that is, Thou art my god, the author of my being, to whom I owe duty and on whom I have a dependence)," and *to a stone,* to an idol made of stone, *"Thou hast* begotten me, or *brought me forth;* therefore protect me, provide for me, and bring me up." What greater affront could men put upon God, who is our Father that has made us? It was a downright disowning of their obligations to him. What greater affront could men put upon themselves and their own reason than to acknowledge that which is in itself absurd and impossible, and, by making stocks and stones their parents, to make themselves no better than stocks and stones? When these were first made the objects of worship they were supposed to be animated by some celestial power or spirit; but by degrees the thought of this was lost, and so vain did idolaters become *in their imagination,* even the princes and priests themselves, that the very idol, though made of wood and stone, was supposed to be their father, and adored accordingly. 3. They multiplied these dunghill deities endlessly (v. 28): *According to the number of thy cities are thy gods, O Judah!* When they had forsaken that God who is one, and all-sufficient for all, (1.) They were not satisfied with any gods they had, but still desired more, that idolatry being in this respect of the same nature with covetousness, which is spiritual idolatry (for the more men have the more they would have), which is a plain evidence that what men make an idol of they find to be insufficient and unsatisfying, and that it cannot *make the comers thereunto perfect.* (2.) They could not agree in the same god. Having left the centre of unity, they fell into endless discord; one city fancied one deity and another another, and each was anxious to have one of its own to be near them and to take special care of them. Thus did they in vain seek that in many gods which is to be found in one God only.

II. The proof of this. No witnesses need be called; it is proved by the notorious evidence of the facts. 1. They went about to deny it, and were ready to plead, *Not guilty.* They pretended that they would acquit themselves from this guilt, they *washed themselves with nitre,* and *took much soap,* offered many things in excuse and extenuation of it, v. 22. They pretended that they did not worship these as gods, but as demons, and mediators between the immortal God and mortal men, or that it was not divine honour that they gave them, but civil respect; thus they sought to evade the convictions of God's word and to screen themselves from the dread of his wrath. Nay, some of them had the impudence to deny the thing itself; they said, *I am not polluted, I have not gone after Baalim,* v. 23. Because it was done secretly, and industriously concealed (Eze. 8:12), they thought it could never be proved upon them, and they had impudence enough to deny it. In this, as in other things, their way was like that of *the adulterous woman, that says, I have done no wickedness,* Prov. 30:20. 2. Notwithstanding all their evasions, they are convicted of it and found guilty: *"How canst thou* deny the fact, and say, *I have not gone after Baalim?* How canst thou deny the fault, and say, *I am not polluted?"* The prophet speaks with wonder at their impudence: "How canst thou put on a face to say so, when it is certain?" (1.) "God's omniscience is a witness against thee: *Thy iniquity is marked before me, saith the Lord God;* it is laid up and hidden, to be produced against thee in the day of judgment, *sealed up among his treasures,"* Deu. 32:34; Job 21:19; Hos. 13:12. "It is *imprinted deeply* and *stained* before me;" so some read it. "Though thou endeavour to wash it out, as murderers to get the stain of the blood of the person slain out of their clothes, yet it will never be got out." God's eye is upon it, and we are sure that his judgment is according to truth. (2.) "Thy own conscience is a witness against thee. *See thy way in the valley"* (they had worshipped idols, not only on the high hills, but in the valleys, Isa. 57:5, 6), in the *valley overagainst Beth-peor* (so some), where they worshipped Baalpeor (Deu. 34:6, Num. 25:3), as if the prophet looked as far back as the *iniquity of Peor;* but, if it mean any particular valley, surely it is the *valley of the son of Hinnom,* for that was the place where they sacrificed their children to Moloch and which therefore witnessed against them more than any other: "look into that valley, and thou canst not but *know what thou hast done."*

III. The aggravations of this sin with which they are charged, which made it exceedingly sinful.

1. God had done great things for them, and yet they revolted from him and rebelled against him (v. 20): *Of old time I have broken thy yoke and burst thy bonds;* this refers to the bringing of them out of the *land of Egypt* and the *house of bondage,* which they would not remember (v. 6), but God did; for, when he told them that they should have no other gods before him, he prefixed this as a reason: *I am the Lord thy God that brought thee out of the land of Egypt!* These bonds of theirs which God had loosed should have bound them for ever to him; but they had ungratefully broken the bonds of duty to that God who had broken the bonds of their slavery.

2. They had promised fair, but had not made good their promise: *"Thou saidst, I will not transgress;* then, when the mercy of thy deliverance was fresh, thou wast so sensible of it that thou wast willing to lay thyself under the most sacred ties to continue faithful to thy God and never to forsake him." Then they said, *Nay, but we will serve the Lord,* Jos. 24:21. How often have we said that we *would*

not transgress, we would not offend any more, and yet we have *started aside, like a deceitful bow,* and repeated and multiplied our transgressions!

3. They had wretchedly degenerated from what they were when God first formed them into a people (v. 21). *I had planted thee a noble vine.* The constitution of their government both in church and state was excellent, their laws were righteous, and all the ordinances instructive and very significant; and a generation of good men there was among them when they first settled in Canaan. *Israel served the Lord,* and kept close to him *all the days of Joshua, and the elders that out-lived Joshua,* Jos. 24:31. They were then *wholly a right seed,* likely to replenish the vineyard they were planted in with choice vines. But it proved otherwise; they very next generation *knew not the Lord, nor the works which he had done* (Jdg. 2:10), and so they were worse and worse till they became the *degenerate plants of a strange vine.* They were now the reverse of what they were at first. Their constitution was quite broken, and there was nothing in them of that good which one might have expected from a people so happily formed, nothing of the purity and piety of their ancestors. *Their vine is as the vine of Sodom,* Deu. 32:32. This may fitly be applied to the nature of man; it was planted by its great author *a noble vine,* a *right seed* (God made man upright); but it is so universally corrupt that it has become the *degenerate plant of a strange vine,* that *bears gall and wormwood,* and it is so to God, it is highly distasteful and offensive to him.

4. They were violent and eager in the pursuit of their idolatries, doted on their idols, and were fond of new ones, and they would not be restrained form them either by the word of God or by his providence, so strong was the *impetus* with which they were carried out after this sin. They are here compared to a *swift dromedary traversing her ways,* a female of that species of creatures hunting about for a male (v. 23), and, to the same purport, *a wild ass used to the wilderness* (v. 24), not tamed by labour, and therefore very wanton, *snuffing up the wind at her pleasure* when she comes near the he-ass, and on such an *occasion who can turn her away?* Who can hinder her from that which she lusts after? *Those that seek her* then *will not weary themselves for her,* for they know it is to no purpose; but will have a little patience till she is big with young, till that month comes which is the last of *the months that she fulfils* (Job 39:2), when she is heavy and unwieldy, and then *they shall find her,* and she cannot outrun them. Note, (1.) Eager lust is a brutish thing, and those that will not be turned away from the gratifying and indulging of it by reason, and conscience, and honour, are to be reckoned as brute-beasts and no better, such as were born, and still are, *like the wild ass's colt;* let them not be looked upon as rational creatures. (2.) Idolatry is strangely intoxicating, and those that are addicted to it will with great difficulty be cured of it. That lust is as headstrong as any. (3.) There are some so violently set upon the prosecution of their lusts that it is to no purpose to attempt to give check to them: those that do so weary themselves in vain. *Ephraim is joined to idols; let him alone.* (4.) The time will come when the most fierce will be tamed and the most wanton will be manageable; when distress and anguish come upon them, then their ears will be open to discipline, that is the month in which you may find them, Ps. 141:5, 6.

5. They were obstinate in their sin, and, as they could not be restrained, so they would not be reformed, v. 25. Here is, (1.) Fair warning given them of the ruin that this wicked course of life would certainly bring them to at last, with a caution therefore not to persist in it, but to break off from it. He would certainly bring them into a miserable captivity, when their feet should be unshod, and they should be forced to travel barefoot, and when they would be denied fair water by their oppressors, so that their throat should be dried with thirst; this will be in the end hereof. Those that affect strange gods, and strange ways of worship, will justly be made prisoners to a strange king in a strange land. "Take up in time therefore; thy running after thy idols will run the *shoes off thy feet,* and thy panting after them will bring thy throat to thirst; withhold therefore thy foot from these violent pursuits, and thy throat from these violent desires." One would think that it should effectually check us in the career of sin to consider what

it will bring us to at last. (2.) Their rejecting this fair warning. They said to those that would have persuaded them to repent and reform, *"There is no hope; no,* never expect to work upon us, or prevail with us to cast away our idols, for *we have loved strangers, and after them we will go;* we are resolved we will, and therefore trouble not yourselves nor us any more with your admonitions; it is to no purpose. There is no hope that we should ever break the corrupt habit and disposition we have got, and therefore we may as well yield to it as go about to get the mastery of it." Note, Their case is very miserable who have brought themselves to such a pass that their corruptions triumph over their convictions; they know they should reform, but own they cannot, and therefore resolve they will not. But, as we must not despair of the mercy of God, but believe that sufficient for the pardon of our sins, though ever so heinous, if we repent and sue for that mercy, so neither must we despair of the grace of God, but believe that able to subdue our corruptions, though ever so strong, if we pray for and improve that grace. A man must never say *There is no hope,* as long as he is on this side hell.

6. They had shamed themselves by their sin, in putting confidence in that which would certainly deceive them in the day of their distress, and putting him away that would have helped them, v. 26–28. *As the thief is ashamed* when, notwithstanding all his arts and tricks to conceal his theft, he is found, and brought to punishment, *so are the house of Israel ashamed,* not with a penitent shame for the sin they had been guilty of, but with a penal shame for the disappointment they met with in that sin. They will be ashamed when they find, (1.) That they are forced to cry to the God whom they had put contempt upon. In their prosperity they had turned the back to God and not the face; they had slighted him, acted as if they had forgotten him, or did what they could to forget him, would not look towards him, but looked another way; they went from him as fast and as far as they could; but in the time of their trouble they will find no satisfaction but in applying to him; then *they will say, Arise, and save us.* Their fathers had many a time taken this shame to themselves (Jdg. 3:9, 4:3, 10:10), yet they would not be persuaded to cleave to God, that they might come to him in their trouble with the more confidence. (2.) That they have no relief from the gods they have made their court to. They will be ashamed when they perceive that the gods they have made cannot serve them, and that the God who made them will not serve them. To bring them to this shame, if so be they might hereby be brought to repentance, they are here sent *to the gods whom they served,* Jdg. 10:14. They cried to God, *Arise, and save us.* God says of the idols, *"Let them arise, and save thee,* for thou hast no reason to expect that I should Let them arise, if they can, from the places where they are fixed; let them try whether they can save thee: but thou wilt be ashamed when thou findest that they can do thee no good, for, though thou hadst a god for every city, yet *thy cities are burnt without inhabitant,"* v. 15. Thus it is the folly of sinners to please themselves with that which will certainly be their grief, and pride themselves in that which will certainly be their shame.

Verses 29–37

The prophet here goes on in the same strain, aiming to bring a sinful people to repentance, that their destruction might be prevented.

I. He avers the truth of the charge. It was evident beyond contradiction; it was the greatest absurdity imaginable in them to think of denying it (v. 29): *"Wherefore will you plead with me,* and put me upon the proof of it, or wherefore will you go about to plead any thing in excuse of the crime or to obtain a mitigation of the sentence? Your plea will certainly be overruled, and judgment given against you: you know *you have all transgressed,* one as well as another; why then to you *quarrel with me* for contending with you?"

II. He heightens it from the consideration both of their incorrigibleness and of their ingratitude. 1. They had not been wrought upon by the judgments of God which they had been under (v. 30): *In vain have I smitten your children,* that is, the children or people of Judah. They had been under divine rebukes of many kinds. God therein designed to bring them to repentance; but it was *in vain.* They did not answer God's end in afflicting them; their consciences were not awakened, nor their hearts softened and humbled, nor were they driven to seek unto God; *they received no instruction* by the *correction,* were not made the better by it; and it is a great loss thus to lose an affliction. They *did not receive,* they did not submit to, or comply with, the correction, but their hearts fretted against the Lord, and so they were *smitten in vain.* Even *the children,* the *young people,* among them (so it may be taken), were *smitten in vain;* they were so soon prejudiced against repentance that they were as untractable as the old ones that had been long *accustomed to do evil.* 2. They had not been wrought upon by the word of God which he had sent them in the mouth of his servants the prophets; nay, they had killed the messengers for the sake of the message: "*Your own sword has devoured your prophets like a destroying lion;* you have put them to death for their faithfulness with as much rage and fury, and with as much greediness and pleasure, as a lion devours his prey." Their prophets, who were their greatest blessings, were treated by them as if they had been the plagues of their generation, and this was their measure-filling sin, 2 Chr. 36:16. They *killed their own prophets,* 1 Th. 2:15. 3. They had not been wrought upon by the favours God had bestowed upon them (*v.* 31): "*O generation!*" (he does not call them, as he might, *O faithless* and *perverse* generation! *O generation of vipers!* but speaks gently, O you men of this generation!) "*see the word of the Lord,* do not only hear it, but consider it diligently, apply your minds closely to it." As we are bidden to *hear the rod* (Micah 6:9), for that has its voice, so we are bidden to *see the word,* for that has its visions, its views. It intimates that what is here said is plain and undeniable; you may see it to be very evident; it is written as with a sun-beam, so that he that runs may read it: *Have I been a wilderness to Israel, a land of darkness.* Note, None of those who have had any dealings with God ever had reason to complain of him as *a wilderness* or a *land of darkness.* He has blessed us with the fruits of the earth, and therefore we cannot say that he has been a wilderness to us, a dry and barren land, that (as Mr. Gataker expresses it) he has held us to *hard meat,* as cattle fed upon the common. No; his sheep have been led into green pastures. He has also blessed us with the lights of heaven, and has not withheld them, so that we cannot say, He has been to us a land of darkness. He has caused his sun to shine, as well as his rain to fall, upon the evil and unthankful. Or the meaning is, in general, that the service of God has not been to any either an unpleasant or an unprofitable service. God sometimes has led his people *through a wilderness* and a *land of darkness,* but he himself was then to them all that which they needed; he so fed them with manna, and led them by a pillar of fire, that it was to them a fruitful field and a land of light. The world is, to those who make it their home and their portion, a wilderness and a land of darkness, vanity and vexation of spirit; but those that dwell in God have the *lines fallen to them in pleasant places.* 4. Instead of being wrought upon by these, they had grown intolerably insolent and imperious. They say, *We are lords; we will come no more unto thee.* Now that they had become a potent kingdom, or thought themselves such, they set up for themselves, and shook off their dependence upon God. This is the language of presumptuous sinners, and it is not only very impious and profane, but very unreasonable and foolish. (1.) It is absurd for us who are subjects to say, *We are lords* (that is, *rulers)* and we will come no more to *God* to receive commands form him; for, as he is King of old, so he is King for ever, and we can never pretend to be from under his authority. (2.) It is absurd for us who are beggars to say, *We are lords,* that is, We are rich, and we will come no more to God, to receive favours from him, as if we could live without him and need not be beholden to him. God justly takes it ill when those to whom he has been a bountiful benefactor care not either for hearing from him or speaking to him.

III. He lays the blame of all their wickedness upon their forgetting God (*v.* 32): *They have forgotten me;* they have industriously banished the thoughts of God out of their minds, jostled those thoughts out with thoughts of their idols, and avoided all those things that would put them in mind of God. 1. Though they were his own people, in covenant with him and professing relation to him, and had the tokens of his presence in the midst of them and of his

favour to them, yet they forgot him. 2. They had long neglected him, *days without number,* time out of mind, as we say. They had not for a great while entertained any serious thoughts of him; so that they seem quite to have forgotten him, and resolved never to remember him again. How many days of our lives have passed without suitable remembrance of God! Who can number those empty days? 3. They had not had such a regard and affection to him as young ladies generally have to their fine clothes: *Can a maid forget her ornaments or a bride her attire?* No; their hearts are upon them; they value them so much, and themselves upon them, that they are ever and anon thinking and speaking of them. When they are to appear in public they do not forget any of *their ornaments,* but put every one in its place, as they are described, Isa. 3:18, etc. And *yet my people have forgotten me.* It is sad that any should be more in love with their fine clothes than with their God, and should rather leave their religion behind them, or part with that, than leave any of their ornaments behind them, or part with them. Is not God our ornament? Is he not *a crown of glory* and a *diadem of beauty* to his people? Did we look upon him to be so, and upon our religion as an *ornament of grace to our head* and *chains about our neck* (Prov. 1:9), we should be as mindful of them as ever any maid was of her ornaments, or a bride of her attire, we should be as careful to preserve them and as fond to appear in them.

IV. He shows them what a bad influence their sins had had upon others. The sins of God's professing people harden and encourage those about them in their evil ways, especially when they appear forward and ringleaders in sin (*v.* 33): *Why trimmest thou thy way to seek love?* There is an allusion here to the practice of lewd women who strive to recommend themselves by their ogling looks and gay dress, as Jezebel, who *painted her face and tired her head.* Thus had they courted their neighbours into sinful confederacies with them and communion in their idolatries, and had *taught the wicked ones their ways,* their ways of mixing God's institutions with their idolatrous customs and usages, which was a great profanation of that which was sacred and made the ways of their idolatry worse than that of others. Those have a great deal to answer for who, by their fellowship with the unfruitful works of darkness, make wicked ones more wicked than otherwise they would be.

V. He charges them with the guilt of murder added to the guilt of their idolatry (*v.* 34): *Also in thy skirts is found the blood of the souls,* the life-blood of the poor innocents, which cried to heaven, and for which God was now *making inquisition.* The reference is to the children that were offered in sacrifice to Moloch; or it may be taken more generally for all the *innocent blood* which Manasseh shed, and with which he had *filled Jerusalem* (2 Ki. 21:16), the *righteous blood,* especially the blood of the prophets and others that witnessed against their impieties. This blood was found *not by secret search,* not *by diggings* (so the word is), but *upon all these;* it was above ground. This intimates that the guilt of this kind which they had contracted was certain and evident, not doubtful or which would bear a dispute; and that it was avowed and barefaced, and which they had not so much sense either of shame or fear as to endeavour to conceal, which was a great aggravation of it.

VI. He overrules their plea of, *Not guilty.* Though this matter be so plain, yet thou sayest, *Because I am innocent, surely his anger shall turn from me;* and again, *Thou sayest, I have not sinned* (*v.* 35); therefore *I will plead with thee,* and will convince thee of thy mistake. Because they deny the charge, and stand upon their own justification, therefore God will join issue with them and plead with them, both by his word and by his rod. Those shall be made to know how much they deceive themselves, 1. Who say that they have not offended God, that they are innocent, though they have been guilty of the grossest enormities. 2. Who expect that God will be reconciled to them though they do not repent and reform. They own that they had been under the tokens of God's anger, but they think that it was causeless, and that they by pleading innocency had proved it to be so, and therefore they conclude that God will immediately let fall his action and *his anger shall be turned from them.* This is very provoking, and God will plead with them, and convince them that his anger is just,

for they have sinned, and he will never cease his controversy till they, instead of justifying themselves thus, humble, and judge, and condemn themselves.

VII. He upbraids them with the shameful disappointments they met with, in making creatures their confidence, while they made God their enemy, *v.* 36, 37. It was a piece of spiritual idolatry they were often guilty of that they trusted in *an arm of flesh* and their hearts therein *departed from the Lord.* Now here he shows them the folly of it. 1. They were restless, and unsatisfied in the choice of their confidences: "*Why gaddest thou about so much to change thy way?* Doubtless it is because thou meetest not with that in those thou didst confide in which thou promisedst thyself." Those that make God their hope, and walk in a continual dependence upon him, need not *gad about to change their way;* for their souls may return to him, and repose in him, as their rest: but those that trust in creatures will be perpetually uneasy, like Noah's dove, that found no rest for the sole of her foot. Every thing they trust to fails them, and then they think to change for the better, but they will be still disappointed. They first trusted to Assyria, and, when that proved a broken reed, they depended upon Egypt, and that proved no better. Creatures being vanity, they will be vexation of spirit to all those that put their confidence in them; they *gad about, seeking rest* and finding none. 2. They were quite disappointed in the confidences they made choice of; so the prophet tells them they should be: *Thou shalt be ashamed of Egypt,* which thou now trustest in, as formerly *thou wast of Assyria, who distressed them and helped them not,* 2 Chr. 28:20. The Jews were a peculiar people in their profession of religion, and for that reason none of the neighbouring nations cared for them, nor could heartily love them; and yet the Jews were still courting them, and confiding in them, and were well enough served when deceived by them. See what will come of it (*v.* 37): *Thou shalt go forth from him,* thy ambassadors or envoys shall return from Egypt *re infectâ — disappointed,* and therefore *with their hands upon their heads,* lamenting the desperate condition of their people. Or, *Thou shalt go forth hence,* that is, into captivity in a strange land, *with thy hands upon thy head,* holding it because it aches (*ubi dolor ibi digitus — where the pain is the finger will be applied),* or as people ashamed, for Tamar, in the height of her confusion, *laid her hand on her head,* 2 Sa. 13:19. "And Egypt, that thou reliest on, shall not be able to prevent it nor to rescue thee out of captivity." Those that will not lay their hand on their heart in godly sorrow, which works life, shall be made to lay their hand on their head in the sorrow of the world, which works death. And no wonder that Egypt cannot help them, when God will not, If the Lord do not help thee, whence should I? The Egyptians are broken reeds, for *the Lord has rejected thy confidences;* he will not make use of them for thy relief, will neither so far honour them, nor so far give countenance to thy confidence in them, as to appoint them to be the instruments of any good to thee, and therefore *thou shalt not prosper in them;* they shall not stand thee in any stead nor give thee any satisfaction. As *there is no counsel or wisdom* that can prevail against the Lord, so there is none that can prevail without him. Some read it, *The Lord has rejected thee for thy confidences;* because thou hast dealt so unfaithfully with him as to trust in his creatures, nay, in his enemies when thou shouldst have trusted in him only, he has abandoned thee to that destruction from which thou thoughtest thus to shelter thyself; and then thou *canst not prosper,* for none ever either hardened himself against God or estranged himself from God and prospered.

CHAPTER 3

The foregoing chapter was wholly taken up with reproofs and threatenings against the people of God, for their apostasies from him; but in this chapter gracious invitations and encouragements are given them to return and repent, notwithstanding the multitude and greatness of their provocations, which are here specified, to magnify the mercy of God, and to show that as sin abounded grace did much more abound. Here, I. It is further shown how bad they had been and how well they deserved to be quite abandoned, and yet how ready God was to receive them into his favour upon their repentance (*v.* 1–5) II. The impenitence of Judah, and their persisting in sin, are aggravated from the judgments of God upon Israel, which they should have taken warning by (*v.* 6–11). III. Great encouragements are given to these backsliders to return and repent, and promises made of great mercy which God had in store for them, and which he would prepare them for by bringing them home to himself (*v.* 12–19) IV. The charge renewed against them for their apostasy from God, and the invitation repeated to return and repent, to which are here added the words that are put in their mouth, which they should make use of in their return to God (*v.* 20–25).

Verses 1–5

These verses some make to belong to the sermon in the foregoing chapter, and they open a door of hope to those who receive the conviction of the reproofs we had there; God wounds that he may heal. Now observe here,

I. How basely this people had forsaken God and gone a whoring from him. The charge runs very high here. 1. They had multiplied their idols and their idolatries. To have admitted one strange God among them would have been bad enough, but they were insatiable in their lustings after false worships: *Thou hast played the harlot with many lovers, v.* 1. She had become a common prostitute to idols; not a foolish deity was set up in all the neighbourhood but the Jews would have it quickly. Where was a high place in the country but they had had an idol in it? *v.* 2. Note, In repentance it is good to make sorrowful reflections upon the particular acts of sin we have been guilty of, and the several places and companies where it has been committed, that we may give glory to God and take shame to ourselves by a particular confession of it. 2. They had sought opportunity for their idolatries, and had sent about to enquire for new gods: *In the high-ways hast thou sat for them,* as Tamar when she put on the disguise of *a harlot* (Gen. 38:14), and as the *foolish woman,* that sits to *call passengers, who go right on their way,* Prov. 9:14, 15. *As the Arabian in the wilderness* — the *Arabian huckster* (so some), that courts customers, or waits for the merchants to get a good bargain and forestal the market — or the *Arabian thief* (so others), that watches for his prey; so had they waited either to court new gods to come among them (the newer the better, and the more fond they were of them) or to court others to join with them in their idolatries. They were not only sinners, but Satans, not only traitors themselves, but tempters to others. 3. They had grown very impudent in sin. They not only polluted themselves, but *their land, with their whoredoms and with their wickedness* (*v.* 2); for it was universal and unpunished, and so became a national sin. And yet (*v.* 3), *"Thou hadst a whore's forehead,* a brazen face of thy own. *Thou refusedst to be ashamed;* thou didst enough to shame thee for ever, and yet wouldst not take shame to thyself." Blushing is the colour of virtue, or at least a relic of it; but those that are past shame (we say) are past hope. Those that have an adulterer's heart, if they indulge that, will come at length to have a whore's forehead, void of all shame and modesty. 4. They abounded in all manner of sin. They polluted the land not only with *their whoredoms* (that is, their idolatries), but with *their wickedness,* or malice (*v.* 2), sins against the second table: for how can we think that those will be true to their neighbour that are false to their God? "Nay (*v.* 5), *thou hast spoken and done evil things as thou couldst,* and wouldst have spoken and done worse if thou hadst known how; thy will was to do it, but thou lackedst opportunity." Note, Those are wicked indeed that sin to the utmost of their power, that never refuse to comply with a temptation because they should not, but because they cannot.

II. How gently God had corrected them for their sins. Instead of raining fire and brimstone upon them, because, like Sodom, they had *avowed their sin* and had gone after strange gods as Sodom after strange flesh, he only *withheld the showers from them,* and that only one part of the year: *There has been no latter rain,* which might serve as an intimation to them of their continual dependence upon God; when they had the former rain, that was no security to them for the latter, but they must still look up to God. But it had not this effect.

III. How justly God might have abandoned them utterly, and refused ever to receive them again, though they should return; this would have been but according to the known rule of divorces, *v.* 1. *They say* (it is an adjudged case, nay, it is a case in which the law is very express, and it is what every body knows and speaks of, Deu. 24:4), that if a woman be once put away for whoredom, and be joined to *another man,* her first husband shall never, upon any pretence whatsoever, take her again to be his wife; such playing fast and loose with the marriage-bond would be a horrid profanation of that ordinance and would *greatly pollute that land.* Observe, What the law says in this case — *They say,* that is, every one will say, and subscribe to the equity of the law in it; for every man finds something in himself that forbids him to entertain one that is *another man's.* And in like manner they had reason to expect that God would refuse ever to take them to be his people again, who had not only been joined to one strange god, but had *played the harlot with many lovers.* If we had to do with a man like ourselves, after such provocations as we have been guilty of, he would be implacable, and we might have despaired of his being reconciled to us.

IV. How graciously he not only invites them, but directs them, to return to him.

1. He encourages them to hope that they shall find favour with him, upon their repentance: "Thou thou hast been bad, *yet return again to me," v.* 1. This implies a promise that he will receive them: "Return, and thou shalt be welcome." God has not tied himself by the laws which he made for us, nor has he the peevish resentment that men have; he will be more kind to Israel, for the sake of his covenant with them, than ever any injured husband was to an adulterous wife; for in receiving penitents, as much as in any thing, he is *God and not man.*

2. He therefore kindly expects that they will repent and return to him, and he directs them what to say to him (*v.* 4): *"Wilt thou not from this time cry unto me?* Wilt not *thou,* who hast been in such relation to me, and on whom I have laid such obligations, *wilt not thou cry to me?* Though thou hast gone a whoring from me, yet, when thou findest the folly of it, surely thou wilt think of returning to me, now at least, now at last, in this thy day. Wilt thou not *at this time,* nay, wilt thou not *from this time* and forward, *cry unto me?* Whatever thou hast said or done hitherto, wilt thou not *from this time* apply to me? *From this time* of conviction and correction, now that thou hast been made to see thy sins (*v.* 2) and to smart for them (*v.* 3), wilt thou not now forsake them and return to me, saying, *I will go and return to my first husband, for then it was better with me than now?"* Hos. 2:7. Or *"from this time* that thou hast had so kind an invitation to return, and assurance that thou shalt be well received: will not this grace of God overcome thee? Now that pardon is proclaimed wilt thou not come in and take the benefit of it? Surely thou wilt."

(1.) He expects that they will claim relation to God, as theirs: *Wilt thou not cry unto me, My Father, thou art the guide of my youth?* [1.] They will surely come towards him as a father, to beg his pardon for their undutiful behaviour to him *(Father, I have sinned)* and will hope to find in him the tender compassions of a father towards a returning prodigal. They will come to him as a father, to whom they will make their complaints, and in whom they will put their confidence for relief and succour. They will now own him as their father, and themselves fatherless without him; and therefore, hoping to find mercy with him (as those penitents, Hos. 14:3), [2.] They will come to him as *the guide of their youth,* that is, as their husband, for so that relation is described, Mal. 2:14. "Though thou hast gone after many lovers, surely thou wilt at length remember the love of thy espousals, and return to the *husband of thy youth."* Or it may be taken more generally: "As *my Father,* thou *art the guide of my youth."* Youth needs a guide. In our return to God we must thankfully remember that he *was the guide of our youth* in the way of comfort; and we must faithfully covenant that he shall be our guide henceforward in the way of duty, and that we will follow his guidance, and give up ourselves entirely to it, that in all doubtful cases we will be determined by our religion.

(2.) He expects that they will appeal to the mercy of God and crave the benefit of that mercy (*v.* 5), that they will reason thus with themselves for their encouragement to return to him: *"Will he reserve his anger for ever?* Surely he will not, for he has proclaimed his name *gracious and merciful."* Repenting sinners may encourage themselves with this, that, though God chide, he will not always chide, though he be angry, he will not keep his anger to the end, but, *though he cause grief, he will have compassion,* and may thus plead for reconciliation. Some understand this as describing their hypocrisy, and the impudence of it: "Though thou hast *a whore's forehead* (*v.* 3) and art still *doing evil as thou canst* (*v.* 5), yet art thou not ever and anon *crying to me, My Father?"* Even when they were most addicted to idols they pretended a regard to God and his service and kept up the forms of godliness and devotion. It is a shameful thing for men thus to call God father, and yet to do the *works of the devil* (as the Jews, Jn. 8:44), to call him the *guide of their youth,* and yet give up themselves to *walk after the flesh,* and to flatter themselves with the expectation that *his anger shall have an end,* while they are continually *treasuring up to themselves wrath against the day of wrath.*

Verses 6–11

The date of this sermon must be observed, in order to the right understanding of it; it was *in the days of Josiah,* who set on foot a blessed work of reformation, in which he was hearty, but the people were not sincere in their compliance with it; to reprove them for that, and warn them of the consequences of their hypocrisy, is the scope of that which God here said to the prophet, and which he *delivered to them.* The case of the two kingdoms of Israel and Judah is here compared, the *ten tribes* that revolted from the throne of David and the temple of Jerusalem and the *two tribes* that adhered to both. The distinct history of those two kingdoms we have in the two books of the Kings, and here we have an abstract of both, as far as relates to this matter.

I. Here is a short account of Israel, the ten tribes. Perhaps the prophet had been just reading the history of that kingdom when God came to him, and said, *Hast thou seen what backsliding Israel has done? v.* 6. For he could not see it otherwise than in history, they having been carried into captivity long before he was born. But what we read in the histories of scripture should instruct us and affect us, as if we ourselves had been eye-witnesses of it. She is called *backsliding Israel* because that kingdom was first founded in an apostasy from the divine institutions, both in church and state. Now he had seen concerning them, 1. That they were wretchedly addicted to idolatry. They had *played the harlot upon every high mountain and under every green tree* (*v.* 6), that is, they had worshipped other gods in their high places and groves; and no marvel, when from the first they had worshipped God by the images of the *golden calves* at Dan and Bethel. The way of idolatry is down-hill: those that are in love with images, and will have them, soon become in love with other gods, and will have them too; for how should those stick at the breach of the first commandment who make no conscience of the second? 2. That God by his prophets had invited and encouraged them to repent and reform (*v.* 7): *"After she had done all these things,* for which she might justly have been abandoned, yet *I said* unto her, *Turn thou unto me* and I will receive thee." Though they had forsaken both the house of David and the house of Aaron, who both had their authority *jure divino — from God,* without dispute, yet God sent his prophets among them, to call them to *return to him,* to the worship of him only, not insisting so much as one would have expected upon their return to the house of David, but pressing their return to the house of Aaron. We read not that Elijah, that great reformer, ever mentioned their return to the house of David, while he was anxious for their return to the faithful service of the true God according as they had it among them. It is serious piety that God stands upon more than even his own rituals. 3. That, notwithstanding this, they had persisted in their idolatries: *But she returned not,* and God *saw it;* he took notice of it, and was much displeased with it, *v.* 7, 8. Note, God keeps account, whether we do or no, how often he has called to us to turn to him and we have refused. 4. That he had therefore cast them off, and given them up into the hands of their enemies (*v.* 8): *When I saw* (so it may be read) *that for all the actions wherein she had committed adultery I must dismiss her, I gave her a bill of divorce.* God divorced them when he threw them out of his protection and left them an easy prey to any that would lay hands on them, when he scattered all their synagogues and the schools of the prophets and excluded them from laying any further claim to the covenant made with their fathers. Note, Those will justly be divorced from God that join themselves to such as are rivals with him. For proof of this go and see what God did to Israel.

II. Let us now see what was the case of Judah, the kingdom of the two tribes. She is called *treacherous sister Judah,* a sister because descended from the same common stock, Abraham and Jacob; but, as Israel had the character of a *backslider,* So Judah is called *treacherous,* because, though she professed to keep close to God when Israel had backslidden (she adhered to the kings and priests that were of God's own appointing, and did not withdraw from her allegiance, so that it was expected she should deal faithfully), yet she proved treacherous, and false, and unfaithful to her professions and promises. Note, The treachery of those who pretend to cleave to God will be reckoned for, as well as the apostasy of those who openly revolt from him. Judah saw what Israel did, and what came of it, and should have taken warning. Israel's captivity was intended for Judah's admonition; but it had not the designed effect. Judah feared not, but thought herself safe because she had Levites to be her priests and sons of David to be her kings. Note, It is an evidence of great stupidity and security when we are not awakened to a holy fear by the judgments of God upon others. It is here charged on Judah, 1. That when they had a wicked king that debauched them they heartily concurred with him in his debaucheries. Judah was forward enough to *play the harlot,* to worship any idol that was introduced among them and to join in any idolatrous usage; so that *through the lightness* (or, as some read it, the *vileness and baseness) of her whoredom,* or (as the margin reads it) by the fame and *report* of her whoredom, her *notorious* whoredom, for which she had become infamous, she *defiled the land,* and made it an abomination to God; for she *committed adultery with stones and stocks,* with the basest idols, those made of *wood and stone.* In the reigns of Manasseh and Amon, when they were disposed to idolatry, the people were so too, and all the country was corrupted with it, and none feared the ruin which Israel by this means had brought upon themselves. 2. That when they had a good king, that reformed them, they did not heartily concur with him in the reformation. This was the present case. God tried whether they would be good in a good reign, but the evil disposition was still the same: *They returned not to me with their whole heart, but feignedly, v.* 10. Josiah went further in destroying idolatry than the best of his predecessors had done, and for his own part he *turned to the Lord with all his heart and with all his soul;* so it is said of him, 2 Ki. 23:25. The people were forced to an external compliance with him, and joined with him in keeping a very solemn passover and in renewing their covenants with God (2 Chr. 34:32, 35:17); but they were not sincere in it, nor were their *hearts right with God.* For this reason God at that very time said, *I will remove Judah out of my sight, as I removed Israel* (2 Ki. 23:27), because Judah was not removed from their sin by the sight of Israel's removal from their land. Hypocritical and ineffectual reformations bode ill to a people. We deceive ourselves if we think to deceive God by a feigned return to him. I know no religion without sincerity.

III. The case of these sister kingdoms is compared, and judgment given upon the comparison, that of the two Judah was the worse (*v.* 11): *Israel has justified herself more than Judah,* that is, she is not so bad as Judah is. This comparative justification will stand Israel in little stead; what will it avail us to say, *We are not so bad as others,* when yet we are not really good ourselves? But it will serve as an aggravation of the sin of Judah, which was in two respects worse than that of Israel: — 1. More was expected from Judah than from Israel; so that Judah dealt treacherously, they vilified a more sacred profession, and falsified a more solemn promise, than Israel did. 2. Judah might have taken warning by the ruin of Israel for their idolatry, and would not. God's judgments upon others, if they be not means of our reformation, will help to aggravate our destruction. The prophet Ezekiel (*ch.* 23:11) makes the same comparison between Jerusalem and Samaria that this prophet here makes between Judah and Israel, nay, and (Eze. 16:48) between Jerusalem and Sodom, and Jerusalem is made the worst of the three.

Verses 12–19

Here is a great deal of gospel in these verses, both that which was always gospel, God's readiness to pardon sin and to receive and entertain returning repenting sinners, and those blessings which were in a special manner reserved for gospel times, the forming and founding of the gospel church by bringing into it the *children of God that were scattered abroad,* the superseding of the ceremonial law, and the uniting of Jews and Gentiles, typified by the uniting of Israel and Judah in their return out of captivity. The prophet is directed to *proclaim these words towards the north,* for they are a call to backsliding Israel, the ten tribes that were carried captive into Assyria, which lay north from Jerusalem. That way he must look, to show that God had not forgotten them, though their brethren had, and to upbraid the men of Judah with their obstinacy in refusing to answer the calls given them. One might as well call to those who lay many hundred miles off in the land of the north; they would as soon hear as these unbelieving and disobedient people; *backsliding Israel* will sooner accept of mercy, and have the benefit of it, than *treacherous Judah.* And perhaps the proclaiming of these words towards the north looks as far forward as the *preaching of repentance and remission of sins unto all nations, beginning at Jerusalem,* Lu. 24:47. A call to Israel in the land of the north is a call to others in that land, even as many as belong to the election of grace. When it was suspected that Christ would *go to the dispersed* Jews among the Gentiles, it was concluded that he would *teach the Gentiles,* Jn. 7:35. So here.

I. Here is an invitation given to *backsliding Israel,* and in them to the backsliding Gentiles, to *return unto God,* the God from whom they had revolted (*v.* 12): *Return, thou backsliding Israel.* And again (*v.* 14): "*Turn, O backsliding children!* repent of your backslidings, return to your allegiance, come back to that good way which you have missed and out of which you have turned aside." Pursuant to this invitation, 1. They are encouraged to return. "*Repent, and be converted, and your sins shall be blotted out,* Acts 3:19. You have incurred God's displeasure, but return to me, and *I will not cause my anger to fall upon you.*" God's anger is ready to fall upon sinners, as a lion falls on his prey, and there is none to deliver, as a mountain of lead falling on them, to sink them past recovery into the lowest hell. But if they repent it shall be turned away, Isa. 12:1. *I will not keep my anger for ever,* but will be reconciled, *for I am merciful.* We that are sinful were for ever undone if God were not merciful; but the goodness of his nature encourages us to hope that, if we by repentance undo what we have done against him, he will by a pardon unsay what he has said against us. 2. They are directed how to return (*v.* 13): "*Only acknowledge thy iniquity,* own thyself in a fault and thereby take shame to thyself and give glory to God." *I will not keep my anger for ever* (that is a previous promise); you shall be delivered form that anger of God which is everlasting, from the wrath to come; but upon what terms? Very easy and reasonable ones. *Only acknowledge thy sins. If we confess our sins, he is faithful and just to forgive them.* This will aggravate the condemnation of sinners, that the terms of pardon and peace were brought so low, and yet they would not come up to them. *If the prophet had told thee to do some great thing wouldst thou not have done it? How much more when he says, Only acknowledge thy iniquity?* 2 Ki. 5:13. In confessing sin, (1.) We must own the corruption of our nature: *Acknowledge thy iniquity,* the perverseness and irregularity of thy nature. (2.) We must own our actual sins: "*That thou hast transgressed against the Lord thy God,* hast affronted him and offended him." (3.) We must own the multitude of our transgressions: "*That thou hast scattered thy ways to the strangers,* run hither and thither in pursuit of thy idols, *under every green tree.* Wherever thou hast rambled thou hast left behind thee the marks of thy folly." (4.) We must aggravate our sin from the disobedience that there is in it to the divine law. The sinfulness of sin is the worst thing in it: "*You have not obeyed my voice;* acknowledge that, and let that humble you more than any thing else."

II. Here are precious promises made to these backsliding children, if they do return, which were in part fulfilled in the return of the Jews out of their captivity, many that belonged to the ten tribes having perhaps joined themselves to those of the two tribes, in the prospect of their deliverance, and returning with them; but the prophecy is to have its full accomplishment in the gospel church, and the gathering together of *the children of God that were scattered abroad* to that: "Return, for, though you are backsliders, yet you are children; nay, though a treacherous wife, yet a wife, for *I am married to you* (*v.* 14) and will not disown the relation." Thus God remembers his covenant with their fathers, that marriage covenant, and in consideration of that he *remembers their land,* Lev. 26:42.

1. He promises to gather them together from all places whither they are dispersed and scattered abroad, Jn. 11:52, *I will take you, one of a city, and two of a family,* or clan; *and I will bring you to Zion, v.* 14. All those that by repentance return to their duty shall return to their former comfort. Observe, (1.) God will graciously receive those that return to him, nay, it is he that by his distinguishing grace takes them out from among the rest that persist in their backslidings; if he had left them, they would have been undone. (2.) Of the many that have backslidden from God there are but few, very few in comparison, that return to him, like the gleanings of the vintage — *one of a city and two of a country;* Christ's flock is a little flock, and *few there are that find the strait gate.* (3.) Of those few, though dispersed, yet not one shall be lost. Though there be but *one in a city,* God will find out that one; he shall not be overlooked in a crowd, but shall be brought safely to Zion, safely to heaven. The scattered Jews shall be brought to Jerusalem, and those of the ten tribes shall be as welcome there as those of the two. God's chosen, scattered all the world over, shall be brought to *the gospel church,* that Mount Zion, the heavenly Jerusalem, that holy hill on which Christ reigns.

2. He promises to set those over them that shall be every way blessings to them (*v.* 15): *I will give you pastors after my heart,* alluding to the character given of David when God pitched upon him to be king. 1 Sa. 13:14, *The Lord hath sought him a man after his own heart.* Observe, (1.) When a church is gathered it must be governed. "*I will bring them to Zion,* not to live as they list, but to be under discipline, not as wild beasts, that range at pleasure, but as sheep that are under the direction of a shepherd." *I will give them pastors,* that is, both magistrates and ministers; both are God's ordinance for the support of his kingdom. (2.) It is well with a people when their pastors are *after God's own heart,* such as they should be, such as we would have them be, who shall make his will their rule in all their administrations, and such as endeavour in some measure to conform to his example, who rule for him, and, as they are capable, rule like him. (3.) Those are pastors after God's own heart who make it their business to feed the flock, not to *feed themselves and fleece the flocks,* but to do all they can for the good of those that are under their charge, who *feed them with wisdom and understanding* (that is, wisely and understandingly), as David fed them, in the *integrity of his heart* and by the *skilfulness of his hand,* Ps. 78:72. Those who are not only pastors, but teachers, must feed them with the word of God, which is wisdom and understanding, which is able to make us wise to salvation.

3. He promises that there shall be no more occasion for the *ark of the covenant,* which had been so much the glory of the tabernacle first and afterwards of the temple, and was the token of God's presence with them; that shall be set aside, and there shall be no more enquiry after, nor enquiring of, it (*v.* 16): *When you shall be multiplied and increased in the land,* when the kingdom of the Messiah shall be set up, which by the accession of the Gentiles will bring in to the church a vast increase (and the days of the Messiah the Jewish masters themselves acknowledge to be here intended), then *they shall say no more, The ark of the covenant of the Lord,* they shall have it no more among them to value, or value themselves upon, because they shall have a pure spiritual way of worship set up, in which there shall be no occasion for any of those external ordinances; with the *ark of the covenant* the whole ceremonial law shall be set aside, and all the institutions of it, for Christ, the truth of all those types, exhibited to us in the word and sacraments of the New Testament, will be to us instead of all. It is very likely (whatever the Jews suggest to the contrary) that *the ark of the covenant* was in the second temple, being restored by Cyrus with the other *vessels of the house of the Lord,* Ezra 1:7. But in the gospel temple Christ *is the ark;* he is the propitiatory, or mercy-seat; and it is the spiritual presence of God in his ordinances that we are now to expect. Many expressions are here used concerning the setting aside of the ark, that it shall not *come to mind,* that they *shall not remember it,* that they shall *not visit it,* that none of these things shall be *any more done;* for the *true worshippers shall worship the Father in spirit and in truth,* Jn. 4:24. But this variety

of expressions is used to show that the ceremonies of the law of Moses should be totally and finally abolished, never to be used any more, but that it would be with difficulty that those who had been so long wedded to them should be weaned from them; and that they would not quite let them go till their holy city and holy house should both be levelled with the ground.

4. He promises that the gospel church, here called *Jerusalem,* shall become eminent and conspicuous, *v.* 17. Two things shall make it famous: — (1.) God's special residence and dominion in it. It shall be called, *The throne of the Lord* — the throne of *his glory,* for that shines forth in the church — the throne of *his government,* for that also is erected there; there he rules his willing people by his word and Spirit, and brings every thought into obedience to himself. As the gospel got ground this *throne of the Lord* was set up even where *Satan's seat* had been. It is especially the throne of *his grace;* for those that by faith come to this Jerusalem come to *God the judge of all,* and to *Jesus the mediator of the new covenant,* Heb. 12:22–24. (2.) The accession of the Gentiles to it. *All the nations shall be* discipled, and so *gathered* to the church, and shall become subjects to that *throne of the Lord* which is there set up, and devoted to the honour of that *name of the Lord* which is there both manifested and called upon.

5. He promises that there shall be a wonderful reformation wrought in those that are gathered to the church: *They shall not walk any more after the imagination of their evil hearts.* They shall not live as they list, but live by rules, not do according to their own corrupt appetites, but according to the will of God. See what leads in sin — *the imagination of our own evil hearts;* and what sin is — it is *walking after* that imagination, being governed by fancy and humour; and what converting grace does — it takes us off from walking after *our own inventions* and brings us to be governed by religion and right reason.

6. That Judah and Israel shall be happily united in one body, *v.* 18. They were so in their return out of captivity and their settlement again in Canaan: *The house of Judah shall walk with the house of Israel,* as being perfectly agreed, and become *one stick in the hand of the Lord,* as Ezekiel also foretold, *ch.* 37:16, 17. Both Assyria and Chaldea fell into the hands of Cyrus, and his proclamation extended to all the Jews in all his dominions. And therefore we have reason to think that many of *the house of Israel* came with those of Judah out of *the land of the north;* though at first there returned but 42,000 (whom we have an account of, Ezra 2) yet Josephus says (*Antiq.* 11.68) that some few years after, under Darius, Zerubbabel went and fetched up above 4,000,000 of souls, *to the land that was given for an inheritance to their fathers.* And we never read of such animosities and enmities between Israel and Judah as had been formerly. This happy coalescence between Israel and Judah in Canaan was a type of the uniting of Jews and Gentiles in the gospel church, when, all enmities being slain, they should become one *sheepfold under one shepherd.*

III. Here is some difficulty started, that lies in the way of all this mercy; but an expedient is found to get over it.

1. God asks, *How shall I* do this for thee? Not as if God showed favour with reluctancy, as he punishes with a *How shall I give thee up?* Hos. 11:8, 9. No, though he is slow to anger, he is swift to show mercy. But it intimates that we are utterly unworthy of his favours, that we have no reason to expect them, that there is nothing in us to deserve them, that we can lay no claim to them, and that he contrives how to do it in such a way as may save the honour of his justice and holiness in the government of the world. *Means* must be *devised that his banished be not for ever expelled from him,* 2 Sa. 14:14. How shall I do it? (1.) Even backsliders, if they return and repent, shall be *put among the children;* and who could ever have expected that? *Behold what manner of love is this!* 1 Jn. 3:1. How should we who are so mean and weak, so worthless and unworthy, and so provoking, ever be *put among the children.* (2.) To those whom God puts among the children he will *give the pleasant land,* the land of Canaan, that glory of all lands, *that goodly heritage of the hosts of nations,* which nations and their hosts wish for and prefer to their own country, or which the hosts of the nations have now got possession of. It was a type of heaven, where there are *pleasures for evermore.* Now who could expect a place in that *pleasant land* that has so often *despised it* (Ps. 106:24) and is so unworthy of it and unfit for it? Is this the manner of men?

2. He does himself return answer to this question: *But I said, Thou shalt call me, My Father.* God does himself answer all the objections that are taken from our unworthiness, or they would never be got over. (1.) That he may put returning penitents *among the children,* he will give them the *Spirit of adoption,* teaching them *to cry, Abba, Father,* Gal. 4:6. *"Thou shalt call me, My Father;* thou shalt return to me, and resign thyself to me as a father, and that shall recommend thee to my favour." (2.) That he may *give them the pleasant land,* he will *put his fear in their hearts,* that they may never *turn from him,* but may persevere to the end.

Verses 20–25

Here is, I. The charge God exhibits against Israel for their treacherous departures from him, *v.* 20. As an adulterous wife elopes from her husband, so have they gone a whoring from God. They were joined to God by a marriage-covenant, but they broke that covenant, they *dealt treacherously* with God, who had always dealt kindly and faithfully with them. Treacherous dealing with men like ourselves is bad enough, but to deal treacherously with God is to deal treasonably.

II. Their conviction and confession of the truth of this charge, *v.* 21. When God reproved them for their apostasy, there were some among them, even such as God would take and *bring to Zion,* whose *voice was heard upon the high places weeping and praying,* humbling themselves before the God of their fathers, lamenting their calamities, and their sins, the procuring cause of them; for this is that which they lament, for this they bemoan themselves, that *they have perverted their way and forgotten the Lord their God.* Note, 1. Sin is the perverting of our way, it is turning aside to crooked ways and *perverting that which is right.* 2. Forgetting the Lord our God is at the bottom of all sin. If men would remember God, his eye upon them and their obligation to him, they would not transgress as they do. 3. By sin we embarrass ourselves, and bring ourselves into trouble, for that also is the perverting of our way, Lam. 3:9. 4. Prayers and tears well become those whose consciences tell them that they have *perverted their way and forgotten their God.* When the *foolishness of man perverts his way his heart* is apt to *fret against the Lord* (Prov. 19:3), whereas it should be melted and poured out before him.

III. The invitation God gives them to return to him (*v.* 22): *Return, you backsliding children.* He calls them *children* in tenderness and compassion to them, foolish and froward as children, yet *his sons,* whom though he corrects he will not disinherit; for, though they are *refractory children* (so some render it), yet they are *children.* God bears with such children, and so much parents. When they are convinced of sin (*v.* 21), and humbled for that, then they are prepared and then they are *invited* to *return,* as Christ invites those to him that are *weary* and *heavy-laden.* The promise to those that return is, *"I will heal your backslidings;* I will comfort you under the grief you are in for your backslidings, deliver you out of the troubles you have brought yourselves into by your backslidings, and cure you of your refractoriness and tendency to backslide." God will *heal our backslidings* by his pardoning mercy, his quieting peace, and his renewing grace.

IV. The ready consent they give to this invitation, and their cheerful compliance with it: *Behold, we come unto thee.* This is an echo to God's call; as a voice returned from broken walls, so this from broken hearts. God says, *Return;* they answer, *Behold, we come.* It is an immediate speedy answer, without delay, not, "We will come hereafter," but, "We do come now; we need not take time to consider of it;" not, "We come towards thee," but, "We come to thee, we will make a thorough turn of it." Observe how unanimous they are: *We come,* one and all. 1. They come devoting themselves to God as theirs: *"Thou art the Lord our God;* we take thee to be ours, we give up ourselves to thee to be thine; whither shall we go but to thee? It is our sin and folly that we have gone from thee." It is very comfortable, in our returns to God after our backslidings, to look up to him as ours in covenant. 2. They come disclaiming all expectations of relief and succour but from God only: *"In vain is salvation hoped for from the hills and from the multitude of the mountains;* we now see our folly in relying upon creature-confidences, and will never so deceive ourselves any more." They worshipped their idols upon hills and mountains (*v.* 6), and they had a multitude of idols upon their mountains, which they had sought unto and put a confidence in; but now they will have no more to do with them. In vain do we look for any thing that is good from them, while from God we may look for every thing that is good, even salvation itself. Therefore, 3. They come depending upon God only as their God: *In the Lord our God is the salvation of Israel.* He is *the Lord,* and he only can save; he can save when all other succours and saviours fail; and he is *our God,* and will in his own way and time work salvation for us. It is very applicable to the great salvation from sin, which Jesus Christ wrought out for us; that is the *salvation of the Lord,* his *great salvation.* 4. They come justifying God in their troubles and judging themselves for their sins, *v.* 24, 25. (1.) They impute all the calamities they had been under to their idols, which had not only done them no good, but had done them abundance of mischief, all the mischief that had been done them: *Shame* (the idol, that shameful thing) *has devoured the labour of our fathers.* Note, [1.] True penitents have learned to call sin *shame;* even the beloved sin which has been as an idol to them, which they have been most pleased with and proud of, even that they shall call a scandalous thing, shall put contempt upon it and be ashamed of it. [2.] True penitents have learned to call sin death and ruin, and to charge upon it all the mischiefs they suffer: "It has *devoured* all those good things which our fathers *laboured for* and left to us; we have found *from our youth* that our idolatry has been the destruction of our prosperity." Children often throw away upon their lusts that which their fathers took a great deal of pains for; and it is well if at length they are brought (as these here) to see the folly of it, and to call those vices their shame which have wasted their estates and *devoured the labour of their fathers.* Of the labour of their fathers, which their idols had devoured, they mention particularly *their flocks and their herds, their sons and their daughters. First,* their idolatries had provoked God to bring these desolating judgments upon them, which had ruined their country and families, and made their estates a prey and their children captives to the conquering enemy. They had *procured these things to themselves.* Or, rather, *Secondly,* These had been sacrificed to their idols, had been *separated unto that shame* (Hos. 9:10), and they had devoured them without mercy; they did *eat the fat of their sacrifices* (Deu. 32:38), even their human sacrifices. (2.) They take to themselves the shame of their sin and folly (*v.* 25): *"We lie down in our shame,* being unable to bear up under it; *our confusion covers us,* that is, both our penal and our penitential shame. Sin has laid us under such rebukes of God's providence, and such reproaches of our own consciences, as surround us and fill us with shame. For *we have sinned,* and shame came in with sin and still attends upon it. We are sinners by descent; guilt and corruption are entailed upon us: *We and our fathers have sinned.* We were sinners betimes; we began early in a course of sin: We have sinned *from our youth;* we have continued in sin, have sinned *even unto this day,* though often called to repent and forsake our sins. That which is the malignity of sin, the worst thing in it, is the affront we have put upon God by it: *We have not obeyed the voice of the Lord our God,* forbidding us to sin and commanding us, when we have sinned, to repent." Now all this seems to be the language of the penitents of *the house of Israel* (*v.* 20), of the ten tribes, either of those that were in captivity or those of them that remained in their own land. And the prophet takes notice of their repentance to provoke the men of Judah to a holy emulation. David used it as an argument with the elders of Judah that it would be a shame for those that were *his bone and his flesh* to be *the last in bringing the king back,* when the men of Israel appeared forward in it, 2 Sa. 19:11, 12. So the prophet excites Judah to repent because Israel did: and well it were if the zeal of others less likely would provoke us to strive to get before them and go beyond them in that which is good.

CHAPTER 4

It should seem that the first two verses of this chapter might better have been joined to the close of the foregoing chapter, for they are directed to

Israel, the ten tribes, by way of reply to their compliance with God's call, directing and encouraging them to hold their resolution (*v.* 1, 2). The rest of the chapter concerns Judah and Jerusalem. I. They are called to repent and reform (*v.* 3, 4). II. They are warned of the advance of Nebuchadnezzar and his forces against them, and are told that it is for their sins, from which they are again exhorted to wash themselves (*v.* 5–18). III. To affect them the more with the greatness of the desolation that was coming, the prophet does himself bitterly lament it, and sympathize with his people in the calamities it brought upon them, and the plunge it brought them to, representing it as a reduction of the world to its first chaos (*v.* 19–31).

Verses 1–2

When God called to backsliding Israel to return (*ch.* 3:22) they immediately answered, *Lord, we return;* now God here takes notice of their answer, and, by way of reply to it,

I. He directs them how to pursue their good resolutions: "Dost thou say, *I will return?*" 1. "Then thou must *return unto me;* make a thorough work of it. Do not only turn from thy idolatries, but return to the instituted worship of the God of Israel." Or, "Thou must return speedily and not delay (as Isa. 21:12, *If you will enquire, enquire you);* if you will return unto me, return you: do not talk of it, but do it." 2. "Thou must utterly abandon all sin, and not retain any of the relics of idolatry: *Put away thy abominations out of my sight,"* that is, out of all places (for every place is under the eye of God), especially out of the temple, the house which he had in a particular manner his eye upon, to see that it was kept clean. It intimates that their idolatries were not only obvious, but offensive, to the eye of God. They were abominations which he could not endure the sight of; therefore they must be *put away out of his sight,* because they were a provocation to the pure eyes of God's glory. Sin must be put away out of the heart, else it is not put away out of God's sight, for the heart and all that is in it lie open before his eye. 3. They must not return to sin again; so some understand that, *Thou shalt not remove,* reading it, *Thou shalt not,* or *must not, wander. "If thou wilt put away thy abominations, and wilt not wander* after them again, as thou hast done, all shall be well." 4. They must give unto God the glory due unto his name (*v.* 2): *"Thou shalt sear, The Lord liveth.* His existence shall be with thee the most sacred fact, than which nothing can be more sure, and his judgment the supreme court to which thou shalt appeal, than which nothing can be more awful." Swearing is an act of religious worship, in which we are to give honour to God three ways: — (1.) We must swear by the true God only, and not by creatures, or any false gods, — by the God that liveth, not by the gods that are deaf and dumb and dead, — by him only, and not *by the Lord and by Malcham,* as Zec. 1:5. (2.) We must swear that only which is true, *in truth and in righteousness,* not daring to assert that which is false, or which we do not know to be true, nor to assert that as certain which is doubtful, nor to promise that which we mean not to perform, nor to violate the promise we have made. To say that which is untrue, or to do that which is unrighteous, is bad, but to back either with an oath is much worse. (3.) We must do it solemnly, swear *in judgment,* that is, when judicially called to it, and not in common conversation. Rash swearing is as great a profanation of God's name as solemn swearing is an honour to it. See Deu. 10:20; Mt. 5:34, 37.

II. He encourages them to keep in this good mind and adhere to their resolutions. If the scattered Israelites will thus return to God, 1. They shall be blessed themselves; for to that sense the first words may be read: *"If thou wilt return to me,* then *thou shalt return,* that is, thou shalt be brought back out of thy captivity into thy own land again, as was of old promised," Deu. 4:29; 30:2. Or, "Then *thou shalt rest in me,* shalt return to me as thy rest, even while thou art in the land of thy captivity." 2. They shall be blessings to others; for their returning to God again will be a means of others turning to him who never new him. If thou wilt own the living Lord, thou wilt thereby influence the nations among whom thou art to bless themselves in him, to place their happiness in his favour and to think themselves happy in being brought to the fear of him. See Isa. 65:16. They shall bless themselves *in the God of truth,* and not in false gods, shall do themselves the honour, and give themselves the satisfaction, to join themselves to him; and then *in him shall they glory;* they shall make him their glory, and shall please, nay, shall pride, themselves in the blessed change they have made. Those that part with their sins to return to God, however they scrupled at the bargain at first, *when they go away, then they boast.*

Verses 3–4

The prophet here turns his speech, in God's name, to the men of the place where he lived. We have heard what words he proclaimed *towards the north* (*ch.* 3:12), for the comfort of those that were now in captivity and were humbled under the hand of God; let us now see what he says to the *men of Judah and Jerusalem,* who were now in prosperity, for their conviction and awakening. In these two verses he exhorts them to repentance and reformation, as the only way left them to prevent the desolating judgments that were ready to break in upon them. Observe,

I. The duties required of them, which they are concerned to do.

1. They must do by their hearts as they do by their ground that they expect any good of; they must plough it up (*v.* 3): *"Break up your fallow-ground. Plough to yourselves a ploughing* (or *plough up your plough land*), that you *sow not among thorns,* that you may not labour in vain, for your own safety and welfare, as those do that sow good seed among thorns and as you have been doing a great while. Put yourselves into a frame fit to receive mercy from God, and put away all that which keeps it from you, and then you may expect to receive mercy and to prosper in your endeavours to help yourselves." Note, (1.) An unconvinced unhumbled heart is like fallow-ground, ground untilled, unoccupied. It is ground capable of improvement; it is our ground, let out to us, and we must be accountable for it; but it is fallow; it is unfenced and lies common; it is unfruitful and of no advantage to the owner, and (which is principally intended) it is overgrown with thorns and weeds, which are the natural product of the corrupt heart; and, if it be not renewed with grace, rain and sunshine are lost upon it, Heb. 6:7, 8. (2.) We are concerned to get this fallow-ground ploughed up. We must search into our own hearts, let the word of God divide (as the plough does) *between the joints and the marrow,* Heb. 4:12. We must *rend our hearts,* Joel 2:13. We must pluck up by the roots those corruptions which, as thorns, choke both our endeavours and our expectations, Hos. 10:12.

2. They must do that to their souls which was done to their bodies when they were taken into covenant with God (*v.* 4): *"Circumcise yourselves to the Lord, and take away the foreskin of your heart.* Mortify the flesh and the lusts of it. Pare off that *superfluity of naughtiness* which hinders your *receiving with meekness the engrafted word,* Jam. 1:21. Boast not of, and rest not in, the circumcision of the body, for that is but a sign, and will not serve without the thing signified. It is a dedicating sign. Do that in sincerity which was done in profession by your circumcision; devote and consecrate yourselves unto the Lord, to be to him a peculiar people. Circumcision is an *obligation to keep the law;* lay yourselves afresh under that obligation. It is a *seal of the righteousness of faith;* lay hold then of that righteousness, and so *circumcise yourselves to the Lord."*

II. The danger they are threatened with, which they are concerned to avoid. Repent and reform, *lest my fury come forth like fire,* which it is now ready to do, as that fire which came forth from the Lord and consumed the sacrifices, and which was always kept burning upon the altar and none might quench it; such is God's wrath against impenitent sinners, *because of the evil of their doings.* Note, 1. That which is to be dreaded by us more than any thing else is the wrath of God; for that is the spring and bitterness of all present miseries and will be the quintessence and perfection of everlasting misery. 2. It is the *evil of our doings* that kindles the fire of God's wrath against us. 3. The consideration of the imminent danger we are in of falling and perishing under this wrath should awaken us with all possible care to *sanctify ourselves to God's glory* and to see to it that we be *sanctified by his grace.*

Verses 5–18

God's usual method is to warn before he wounds. In these verses, accordingly, God gives notice to the Jews of the general desolation that would shortly be brought upon them by a foreign invasion. This must be declared and published in all the cities of Judah and streets of Jerusalem, that all might hear and fear, and by this loud alarm be either brought to repentance or left inexcusable. The prediction of this calamity is here given very largely, and in lively expressions, which one would think should have awakened and affected the most stupid. Observe,

I. The war proclaimed, and general notice given of the advance of the enemy. It is published now, some years before, by the prophet; but, since this will be slighted, it shall be published after another manner when the judgment is actually breaking in, *v.* 5, 6. The *trumpet* must be *blown,* the *standard* must be *set up,* a summons must be issued out to the people to *gather together* and to draw *towards Zion,* either to guard it or expecting to be guarded by it. There must be a general rendezvous. The militia must be raised and all the forces mustered. Those that are able men, and fit for service, must *go into the defenced cities,* to garrison them; those that are weak, and would lessen their provisions, but not increase their strength, must *retire,* and *not stay.*

II. An express arrived with intelligence of the approach of the king of Babylon and his army. It is an evil that God will *bring from the north* (as he had said, *ch.* 1:15), *even a great destruction,* beyond all that had yet come upon the nation of the Jews. The enemy is here compared, 1. To *a lion* that *comes up from his thicket,* when he is hungry, to seek his prey, *v.* 7. The helpless beasts are so terrified with his roaring (as some report) that they cannot flee from him, and so become an easy prey to him. Nebuchadnezzar is this roaring tearing lion, *the destroyer of the nations,* that has laid many countries waste, and now is *on his way* in full speed towards the land of Judah. The *destroyer of the Gentiles* shall be the *destroyer of the Jews* too, when they have by their idolatry made themselves like the Gentiles. "He has *gone forth from his place,* from Babylon, or the place of the rendezvous of his army, on purpose against *this land;* that is the prey he has now his eye upon, not to plunder it only, but to make it desolate, and herein he shall succeed to such a degree that the cities shall be *laid waste, without inhabitants,* shall be *overgrown with grass* as a field;" so some read it. 2. To a *drying* blasting *wind* (*v.* 11), a parching scorching wind, which spoils the fruits of the earth and withers them, not a wind which brings rain, but such as comes *out of the north,* which *drives away rain* (Prov. 25:23), but brings something worse instead of it; such shall this evil out of the north be to this people, a *black* freezing wind, which they can neither fence against nor flee from, but, wherever they go, it shall surround and pursue them; and they cannot see it before it comes, but, when it comes, they shall feel it. It is a *wind of the high places in the wilderness,* or *plain,* that beats upon the tops of the hills or that carries all before it in the plain, where there is no shelter, but the ground is all champaign. It shall come in its full force *towards the daughters of my people,* that have been brought up so tenderly and delicately that they could not endure to have the wind blow upon them. Now this fierce wind shall come against them, *not to fan, nor cleanse* them, not such a gentle wind as is used in winnowing corn, but a *full wind* (*v.* 12), a strong and violent wind, blowing full upon them. This shall come *to me,* or rather *for me;* it shall come with commission from God and shall accomplish that for which he sends it; for this, as other *stormy winds, fulfills his word.* 3. To clouds and whirlwinds for swiftness, *v.* 13. The Chaldean army shall *come up as clouds* driven with the wind, so thick shall they stand, so fast shall they march, and it shall be to no purpose to offer to stop them or make head against them, any more than to arrest a cloud or give check to a whirlwind. The horses are *swifter than eagles* when they fly upon their prey; it is in vain to think either of opposing them or of outrunning them. 4. To watchers and the keepers of a field, *v.* 15–17. *The voice declares from Dan,* a city which lay furthest north of all the cities of Canaan, and therefore received the first tidings of this *evil from the north* and hastened it to Mount Ephrain, that part of the land of Israel which lay next to Judea; they received the news of the affliction and transmitted it to Jerusalem. Ill news flies apace; and an impenitent people, that hates to be reformed, can expect no other that ill news. Now, what is the news? *"Tell the nations,* those mixed nations that now inhabit the cities of the ten tribes, mention it to them, that they may provide for their own safety; but publish it *against Jerusalem,* that is the place aimed at, the game shot at, let them know that *watchers have come from a far country,* that is, soldiers, that will watch all opportunities to do mischief." Private soldiers we call *private sentinels*, or *watchmen*. "They are coming in full career, and *give out their voice against the cities of Judah;* they design to invest them, to make themselves masters of them, and to attack them with loud shouts, as sure of victory. As *keepers of a field* surround it, to keep all out from it, so shall they surround the cities of Judah, to keep all in them, till they be constrained to surrender at discretion; they are *against her round about, compassing her in on every side.*" See Lu. 19:43. As formerly the good angels, *those watchers,* and *holy ones,* were like *keepers of a field* to Jerusalem, watching about it, that nothing might go in to its prejudice, so now their enemies were as watchers and keepers of a field, surrounding it that nothing might go in to its relief and succour.

III. The lamentable cause of this judgment. How is it that Judah and Jerusalem come to be thus abandoned to ruin? See how it came to this. 1. They sinned against God; it was all owing to themselves: *She has been rebellious against me, saith the Lord, v.* 17. Their enemies surrounded them as keepers of a field, because they had taken up arms against their rightful Lord and sovereign, and were to be seized as rebels. The Chaldeans were breaking in upon them, and it was sin that opened the gap at which they entered: *Thy way and thy doings have procured these things unto thee* (v. 18), thy evil way and thy doings that have not been good. It was not a false step or two that did them this mischief, but their way and course of living were bad. Note, Sin is the procuring cause of all our troubles. Those that go on in sin while they are endeavouring to ward off mischiefs with one hand are at the same time pulling them upon their own heads with the other. 2. God was angry with them for their sin. It is the *fierce anger of the Lord* that makes the army of the Chaldeans thus fierce, thus furious; that is kindled against us, and is *not turned back from us, v.* 8. Note, In men's anger against us, and the violence of that, we must see and own God's anger and the power of that. If that were turned back from us, our enemies could not come forward against us. 3. In his just and holy anger he condemned them to this dreadful punishment: *Now also will I give sentence against them, v.* 12. The execution was done, not in a heat, but in pursuance of a sentence solemnly passed, according to equity, and upon mature deliberation. Some read it, *Now will I do execution upon them,* according to the doom formerly passed; and *we are sure that the judgment of God is according to the truth,* and the execution of that judgment.

IV. The lamentable effects of this judgment, upon the first alarm given of it. 1. The people that should fight shall quite despair and shall not have a heart to make the least stand against the enemy (v. 8): *"For this gird yourself with sackcloth, lament and howl,"* that is, "you will do so. When the cry is made through the kingdom, *Arm, arm!* all will be seized with a consternation, and all put into confusion. Instead of girding on the sword, they will gird on the sackcloth; instead of animating one another to a vigorous resistance, they will *lament and howl,* and so dishearten one another. While the enemy is yet at a distance they will give up all for gone, and cry, *Woe unto us! for we are spoiled, v.* 13. We are all undone, the spoilers will certainly carry the day, and it is in vain to make head against them." Judah and Jerusalem had been famed for valiant men; but see what is the effect of sin: by depriving men of their confidence towards God, it deprives them of their courage towards men. 2. Their great men, who should contrive for the public safety, shall be at their wits' end (v. 9): *At that day the heart of the king shall perish,* both his wisdom and his courage. Despairing of success, he shall have no spirit to do any thing, and, if he had, he will not know what to do. His princes and privy-counselors, who should animate and advise him, shall be as much at a loss and as much in despair as he. See how easily, how effectually, God can bring ruin upon a people that are doomed to it, merely by dispiriting them, *taking away the heart of the chief* of them (Job 12:20, 24), *cutting off the spirit of princes,* Ps. 76:12. The business of the priests was to encourage the people in the time of war; they were to say to the people, *Fear not, and let not your hearts faint,* Deu. 20:2, 3. They were to blow the trumpets, for an assurance to them that in the day of battle they should be *remembered before the Lord their God,* Num. 10:9. But now *the priests* themselves *shall be astonished,* and shall have no heart themselves

to do their office, and therefore shall not be likely to put spirit into the people. *The prophets* too, the false prophets, who had cried *peace* to them, shall be put into the greatest amazement imaginable, seeing their own guilty blood ready to be shed by that sword which they had often told the people there was no danger of. Note, God's judgments come with the greatest terror upon those that have been most secure. Our Saviour foretels that at the last destruction of Jerusalem *men's hearts* should *fail them for fear,* Lu. 21:26. And it is common for those who have cheated and flattered people into a carnal security not only to fail them, but to discourage them, when the trouble comes.

V. The prophet's complaint of the people's being deceived, v. 10. It is expressed strangely, as we read it: *Ah! Lord God, surely thou hast greatly deceived this people, saying, You shall have peace.* We are sure that God deceives none. *Let no man say, when he is tempted* or deluded, that God has tempted or deluded him. But, 1. The people deceived themselves with the promises that God had made in general of his favour to that nation, and the many peculiar privileges with which they were dignified, building upon them, though they took no care to perform the conditions on which the accomplishment of those promises and the continuance of those privileges did depend; and they had no regard to the threatenings which in the law were set over-against those promises. Thus they cheated themselves and then wickedly complained that God had cheated them. 2. The false prophets deceived them with promises of peace, which they made them in God's name. *ch.* 23:17; 27:9. If God had sent them, he had indeed greatly deceived the people, but he had not. It was the people's fault that they gave them credit; and here also they deceived themselves. 3. God had permitted the false prophets to deceive, and the people to be deceived by them, giving both up to *strong delusions,* to punish them *for not receiving the truth in the love of it.* Herein the Lord was righteous; but the prophet complains of it as the sorest judgment of all, for by this means they had been hardened in their sins. 4. It may be read with an interrogation, *"Hast thou indeed thus deceived this people?* It is plain that they are greatly deceived, for they expect *peace,* whereas *the sword reaches unto the soul;* that is, it is a killing sword, abundance of lives are lost, and more likely to be." Now, was it God that deceived them? No, he had often given them warning of judgments in general and of this in particular; but their own prophets deceive them, and cry peace to those to whom the God of heaven does not speak peace. It is a pitiable thing, and that which every good man greatly laments, to see people flattered into their own ruin, and promising themselves peace when war is at the door; and this we should complain of to God, who alone can prevent such a fatal delusion.

VI. The prophet's endeavour to undeceive them. When the prophets they loved and caressed dealt falsely with them, he whom they hated and persecuted dealt faithfully. 1. He shows them their wound. They were loth to see it, very loth to have it searched into; but, if they will allow themselves the liberty of a free thought, they might discover their punishment in their sin (v. 18): *"This is thy wickedness because it is bitter.* Now thou seest that it is a bitter thing to depart from God, and will certainly be *bitterness in the latter end, ch.* 2:19. It produces bitter effects, and grief that *reaches unto the heart,* touches to the quick, and in the most tender part; the sword *reaches to the soul," v.* 10. God can make trouble reach the heart even of those that would lay nothing to heart. "And by this thou mayest see *what is thy wickedness,* that it is a bitter thing, *a root of bitterness, that bears gall and wormwood,* and that it has *reached to the heart;* it is the corruption of the soul, of the *imagination of the thought of the heart.*" If the heart were not polluted with sin, it would not be disturbed and disquieted as it is with trouble. 2. He shows them the cure, v. 14. "Since *thy wickedness reaches to the heart,* there the application must be made. *O Jerusalem! wash thy heart from wickedness, that thou mayest be saved.*" By Jerusalem he means each one of the inhabitants of Jerusalem; for every man has a heart of his own to take care of, and it is personal reformation that must help the public. Every one must return from *his own evil way,* and, in order to that, cleanse *his own evil heart.* "And let *the heart of the city* too be purified, not the suburbs only, the outskirts of it." The vitals of a state must be amended by the refor-

mation of those that have the commanding influence upon it. Note, (1.) Reformation is absolutely necessary to salvation. There is no other way of preventing judgments, or turning them away when we are threatened with them, but taking away the sin by which we have procured them to ourselves. (2.) No reformation is saving but that which reaches the heart. There is heart-wickedness that is defiling to the soul, from which we must wash ourselves. By repentance and faith we must wash our hearts from the guilt we have contracted by spiritual wickedness, by those sins which begin and end in the heart and go no further; and by mortification and watchfulness we must suppress and prevent this heart-wickedness for the future. The tree must be made good, else the fruit will not. Jerusalem was all overspread with the leprosy of sin. Now as the physicians agree with respect to the body when afflicted with leprosy that external applications will do no good, unless physic be taken inwardly to carry off the humours that lurk there and to change the mass of the blood, so it is with the soul, so it is with the state: there will be no effectual reformation of the manners without a reformation of the mind; the mistakes there must be rectified, the corruptions there must be mortified, and the evil dispositions there changed. "Though thou art Jerusalem, called a *holy city,* that will not save thee, unless thou *wash thy heart from wickedness.*" In the latter part of the verse he reasons with them: *How long shall thy vain thoughts lodge within thee?* He complains here [1.] Of the delays of their reformation: *"How long* shall that filthy heart of thine continue unwashed? When shall it once be?" Note, The God of heaven thinks the time long that his room is usurped, and his interest opposed, in our souls, ch. 13:27. [2.] Of the root of their corruption, the *vain thoughts that lodged within them* and defiled their hearts, from which they must wash their hearts. *Thoughts of iniquity* or *mischief,* these are the evil thoughts that are the spawn of the evil *heart,* from which all other wickedness is produced, Mt. 15:19. These are our own, the conceptions of our own lusts (Jam. 1:15), and they are the most dangerous when they lodge within us, when they are admitted and entertained as guests, and are suffered to continue. Some read it *thoughts of affliction,* such thoughts as will bring nothing but affliction and misery. Some by the vain thoughts here understand all those frivolous pleas and excuses with which they turned off the reproofs and calls of the word and rendered them ineffectual, and bolstered themselves up in their wickedness. *Wash thy heart from wickedness,* and think not to say, *We are not polluted* (ch. 2:23), or, "We are Jerusalem; *we have Abraham to our father,*" Mt. 3:8, 9.

Verses 19–31

The prophet is here in an agony, and cries out like one upon the rack of pain with some acute distemper, or as a woman in travail. The expressions are very pathetic and moving, enough to melt a heart of stone into compassion: *My bowels! my bowels! I am pained at my very heart;* and yet well, and in health himself, and nothing ails him. Note, A good man, in such a bad world as this is, cannot but be a *man of sorrows. My heart makes a noise in me,* through the tumult of my spirits, and *I cannot hold my peace.* Note, The grievance and the grief sometimes may be such that the most prudent patient man cannot forbear complaining.

Now, what is the matter? What is it that puts the good man into such agitation? It is not for himself, or any affliction in his family that he grieves thus; but it is purely upon the public account, it is his people's case that he lays to heart thus.

I. They are very sinful and will not be reformed, v. 22. These are the words of God himself, for so the prophet chose to give this character of the people, rather than in his own words, or as from himself: *My people are foolish.* God calls them his people, though they are foolish. They have cast him off, but he has not cast them off, Rom. 11:1. "They are *my people,* whom I have been in covenant with, and still have mercy in store for. They are *foolish,* for *they have not known me.*" Note, Those are foolish indeed that have not known God, especially that call themselves his people, and have the advantages of coming into acquaintance with him, and yet have not known him. They are *sottish children,* stupid and senseless, and have *no understanding.* They cannot distinguish between truth and falsehood, good and evil; they cannot discern the mind of God either in his word or in his providence; they do not understand what their true interest is, nor on which side it lies. They are *wise to do evil,* to plot mischief against the quiet in the land, wise to contrive the gratification of their lusts, and then to conceal and palliate them. But *to do good they have no knowledge,* no contrivance, no application of mind; they know not how to make a good use either of the ordinances or of the providences of God, nor how to bring about any design for the good of their country. Contrary to this should be our character. Rom. 16:19, *I would have you wise unto that which is good, and simple concerning evil.*

II. They are miserable, and cannot be relieved.

1. He cries out, *Because thou hast heard, O my soul! the sound of the trumpet,* and *seen the standard,* both giving *the alarm of war, v.* 19, 21. He does not say, *Thou hast heard,* O my *ear!* but, O my *soul!* because the event was yet future, and it is by the spirit of prophecy that he see it and receives the impression of it. His *soul* heard it from the words of God, and therefore he was as well assured of it, and as much affected with it, as if he had heard it with his bodily ears. He expresses this deep concern, (1.) To show that, though he foretold this calamity, yet he was far from *desiring the woeful day;* for a woeful day it would be to him. It becomes us to tremble at the thought of the misery that sinners are running themselves into, though we have good hopes, through grace, that we ourselves are *delivered from the wrath to come.* (2.) To awaken them to a holy fear, and so to a care to prevent so great a judgment by a true and timely repentance. Note, Those that would affect other with the word of God should evidence that they are themselves affected with it. Now,

2. Let us see what there is in the destruction here foreseen and foretold that is so very affecting.

(1.) It is a swift and *sudden* destruction; it comes upon Judah and Jerusalem ere they are aware, and pours in so fast upon them that they have not the east breathing time. They have no time to recollect their thoughts, much less to recruit or recover their strength: *Destruction upon destruction is cried* (*v.* 20), *breach upon breach,* one sad calamity, like Job's messengers, treading upon the heels of another. The death of Josiah breaks the ice, and plucks up the flood-gates; within three months after that his son and successor Jehoahaz is deposed by the king of Egypt; within two or three years after Nebuchadnezzar besieged Jerusalem and took it, and thenceforward he was continually making descents upon the land of Judah with his armies during the reigns of Jehoiakim, Jeconiah, and Zedekiah, till about nineteen years after he completed their ruin in the destruction of Jerusalem: but *suddenly were their tents spoiled and their curtains in a moment.* Though the cities held out for some time, the country was laid waste at the very first. The shepherds and all that lived in tents were plundered immediately; they and their effects fell into the enemies' hands; therefore we find the Rechabites, who dwelt in tents, upon the first coming of the army of the Chaldees into the land retiring to Jerusalem, Jer. 35:11. The inhabitants of the villages soon ceased: *Suddenly were the tents spoiled.* The plain men that dwelt in tents were first made a prey of.

(2.) This dreadful war continued a great while, not in the borders, but in the bowels of the country; for the people were very obstinate, and would not submit to the king of Babylon, but took all opportunities to rebel against him, which did but lengthen out the calamity; they might as well have yielded at first as at last. This is complained of (*v.* 21): *How long shall I see the standard?* Shall the sword devour for ever? Good men are none of those that *delight in war,* for they know not how to fish in troubled waters; they are *for peace* (Ps. 120:7), and will heartily say *Amen* to that prayer, "Give peace in out time, O Lord!" *O thou sword of the Lord! when wilt thou be quiet?*

(3.) The desolations made by it in the land were general and universal: *The whole land is spoiled,* or plundered (*v.* 20); so it was at first, and at length it became a perfect chaos. It was such a desolation as amounted in a manner to a dissolution; not only the superstructure, but even the foundations, were all *out of course.* The prophet in vision saw the extent and extremity of this destruction, and he here gives a most lively description of it, which one would think might have made those uneasy in their sins who dwelt in a land doomed to such a ruin, which might yet have been prevented by their repentance. [1.] The earth is *without form, and void* (*v.* 23), as it was Gen. 1:2. It is *Tohu* and *Bohu,* the words there used, as far as the land of Judea goes. It is *confusion* and *emptiness,* stripped of all its beauty, void of all its wealth, and, compared with what it was, every thing out of place and out of shape. To a worse chaos than this will the earth be reduced at the end of time, when it, *and all the works that are therein, shall be burnt up.* [2.] The *heavens* too are *without light,* as the earth is without fruits. This alludes to the *darkness* that was *upon the face of the deep* (Gen. 1:2), and represents God's displeasure against them, as the eclipse of the sun did at our Saviour's death. It was not only the earth that failed them, but heaven also frowned upon them; and with their trouble they had darkness, for they could not see through their troubles. The smoke of their houses and cities which the enemy burnt, and the dust which their army raised in its march, even darkened the sun, so that *the heavens had no light.* Or it may be taken figuratively: *The earth* (that is, the common people) was impoverished and in confusion; and the *heavens* (that is, the princes and rulers) *had no light,* no wisdom in themselves, nor were any comfort to the people, nor a guide to them. Comp. Mt. 24:29. [3.] The *mountains trembled, and the hills moved lightly, v.* 24. So formidable were the appearances of God against his people, as in the days of old they had been for them, that *the mountains skipped like rams and the little hills like lambs,* Ps. 114:4. The *everlasting mountains* seemed to be *scattered,* Hab. 3:6. The mountains on which they had worshipped their idols, the mountains over which they had looked for succours, all trembled, as if they had been conscious of the people's guilt. The mountains, those among them that seemed to the highest and strongest, and of the firmest resolution, trembled at the approach of the Chaldean army. The hills moved lightly, as being eased of the burden of a sinful nation, Isa. 1:24. [4.] Not the earth only, but the air, was dispeopled, and left uninhabited (*v.* 25): *I beheld* the cities, the countries that used to be populous, *and, lo, there was no man* to be seen; all the inhabitants were either killed, or fled, or taken captives, such a ruining depopulating thing is sin: nay, even *the birds of the heavens,* that used to fly about and *sing among the branches,* had now *fled* away, and were no more to be seen or heard. The *land of Judah* had now become like the *lake of Sodom,* over which (they say) no bird flies; see Deu. 29:23. The enemies shall make such havoc of the country that they shall not so much as leave a bird alive in it. [5.] Both the ground and the houses shall be laid waste (*v.* 26): *Lo, the fruitful place was a wilderness,* being deserted by the inhabitants that should cultivate it, and then soon overgrown with thorns and briers, or being trodden down by the destroying army of the enemy. The *cities* also and their gates and walls are *broken down* and levelled with the ground. Those that look no further than second causes impute it to the policy and fury of the invaders; but the prophet, who looks to the first cause, says that it is *at the presence of the Lord,* at *his face* (that is, the anger of his countenance), even *by his fierce anger,* that this was done. Even angry men cannot do us any real hurt, unless God be angry with us. If our *ways please him,* all is well. [6.] The meaning of all this is that the nation shall be entirely ruined, and every part of it shall share in the destruction; neither town nor country shall escape. *First,* Not the country, for *the whole land shall be desolate,* corn land and pasture land, both common and enclosed, it shall be laid waste (*v.* 27); the conquerors will have occasion for it all. *Secondly,* Not the men, for (*v.* 29) *the whole city shall flee,* all the inhabitants of the town shall quit their habitations by consent, *for fear of the horsemen and bowmen.* Rather than lie exposed to their fury, they shall *go into the thickets,* where they are in danger of being torn by briers, nay, to be torn in pieces by wild beasts; and they shall *climb up upon the rocks,* where their lodging will be hard and cold, and the precipice dangerous. Let us not be over-fond of our houses and cities; for the time may come when rocks and thickets may be preferable, and chosen rather. This shall be the common case, for *every city shall be forsaken,* and *not a man* shall be left that dares *dwell therein.* Both government and trade shall be at an end, and all civil societies and incorporations dissolved. It is a very dismal idea which this gives of the approaching desolation; but in the midst of all these threatenings comes in one comfortable word (*v.* 27): *Yet will not I make a full end* — not a total consumption, for God will reserve a remnant to himself, that shall be hidden in the day of the Lord's anger — not a final consumption, for Jerusalem shall again be built and the land inhabited. This comes in here, in the midst of the threatenings, for the comfort of those that *trembled at God's word;* and it intimates to us the changeableness of God's providence; as it breaks down, so it raises up again; every end of our comforts is not a full end, however we may be ready to think it so. It also intimates the unchangeableness of God's covenant, which stands so firmly, that, though he may correct his people severely, yet he will not *cast them off, ch.* 30:11.

(4.) Their case was helpless and without remedy. [1.] God would not help them; so he tells them plainly, *v.* 28. And, if the Lord do not help them, who can? This is that which makes their case deplorable. *"For this the earth mourns and the heavens above are black* (there are no prospects but what are very dismal), *because I have spoken it;* I have given the word which shall not be called back; *I have purposed it* (it is a consumption decreed, determined) *and I will not repent,* not change this way, but proceed in it, and will not *turn back from it."* They would not repent and turn back from the way of their sins (*ch.* 2:25), and therefore God will not repent and turn back from the way of his judgments. [2.] They could not help themselves, *v.* 30, 31. When the thing appeared at a distance they flattered themselves with hopes that, though God should not appear for them as he had done for Hezekiah against the Assyrian army, yet they should find some means or other to secure themselves and give check to the forces of the enemy. But the prophet tells them that, when it comes to the setting to, they will be quite at a loss: *"When thou art spoiled, what wilt thou do?* What course wilt thou take? Sit down now, and consider this in time." He assures them that, whatever were now their contrivances and confidences, *First,* They will then be despised by their allies whom they depended upon for assistance. He had often compared the sin of Jerusalem to whoredom, not only her idolatry, but her trust in creatures, in the neighbouring powers. Now here he compares her to a harlot abandoned by all the lewd ones that used to make court to her. She is supposed to do all she can to keep up her interest in their affections. She does what she can to make herself appear considerable among the nations, and a valuable ally. She compliments them by her ambassadors to the highest degree, to engage them to stand by her now in her distress. She *clothes herself with crimson,* as if she were rich, and *decks herself with ornaments of gold,* as if her treasuries were still as full as ever they had been. She *rents her face with painting,* puts the best colours she can upon her present distresses and does her utmost to palliate and extenuate her losses, sets a good face upon them. But this painting, though it beautifies the face for the present, really rends it; the frequent use of paint spoils the skin, cracks it, and makes it rough; so the case which by false colours has been made to appear better than really it was, when truth comes to light, will look so much the worse. "And, after all, *in vain shalt thou make thyself fair;* all thy neighbours are sensible how low thou art brought; the Chaldeans will strip thee of thy crimson and ornaments, and then thy confederates will not only slight thee and refuse to give thee any succour, but they will join with those that *seek thy life,* that they may come in for a share in the prey of so rich a country." Here seems to be an allusion to the story of Jezebel, who thought, by making herself look fair and fine, to outface her doom, but in vain, 2 Ki. 9:30, 33. See what creatures prove when we confide in them, how treacherous they are; instead of saving the life, they seek the life; they often change, so that they will sooner do us an ill turn than any service. And see to how little purpose it is for those that have by sin deformed themselves in God's eyes to think by any arts they can use to beautify themselves in the eye of the world. *Secondly,* They will then be themselves in despair; they will find their troubles to be like the pains of a woman in travail, which she cannot escape: *I have heard the voice of the daughter of Zion,* her groans echoing to the triumphal shouts of the Chaldean army, which he heard, *v.* 15. It is like the *voice of a woman in travail,* whose pain is exquisite, and the fruit of sin and the curse too (Gen. 3:16), and exhorts lamentable outcries, especially of a *woman in travail of her first child,* who, having never known before what that pain is, is the more terrified by it. Troubles are most grievous to those that have not been used to them. Zion, in this distress, since her neighbours refuse to pity her, *bewails herself,* fetching *deep sighs* (so the word signifies), and she *spreads her hands,* either wringing them for grief or reaching them forth for succour. All the cry is, *Woe is me now!* (now that the decree has gone forth against her and is past recall), for *my soul is wearied because of murderers.* The Chaldean soldiers put all to the sword that gave them any opposition, so that the land was full of murders. Zion was weary of hearing tragical stories from all parts of the country, and cried out, *Woe is me!* It was well if their sufferings put them in mind of their sins, the murders committed upon them of the murders committed by them; for God was now making inquisition for the *innocent blood* shed in Jerusalem, *which the Lord would not pardon,* 2 Ki. 24:4. Note, As sin will find out the sinner, so sorrow will, sooner or later, find out the secure.

CHAPTER 5

Reproof for sin and threatenings of judgment are intermixed in this chapter, and are set the one over against the other: judgments are threatened, that the reproofs of sin might be the more effectual to bring them to repentance; sin is discovered, that God might be justified in the judgments threatened. I. The sins they are charged with are very great: — Injustice (*v.* 1), hypocrisy in religion (*v.* 2), incorrigibleness (*v.* 3), the corruption and debauchery of both poor and rich (*v.* 4, 5), idolatry and adultery (*v.* 7, 8), treacherous departures from God (*v.* 11), and impudent defiance of him (*v.* 12, 13), and, that which is at the bottom of all this, want of the fear of God, notwithstanding the frequent calls given them to fear him (*v.* 20–24). In the close of the chapter they are charged with violence and oppression (*v.* 26–28), and a combination of those to debauch the nation who should have been active to reform it (*v.* 30, 31). II. The judgments they are threatened with are very terrible. In general, they shall be reckoned with (*v.* 9, 29). A foreign enemy shall be brought in upon them (*v.* 15–17), shall set guards upon them (*v.* 6), shall destroy their fortification (*v.* 10), shall carry them away into captivity (*v.* 19), and keep all good things from them (*v.* 25). Herein the words of God's prophets shall be fulfilled (*v.* 14). But, III. Here is an intimation twice given that God would in the midst of wrath remember mercy, and not utterly destroy them (*v.* 10, 18). This was the scope and purport of Jeremiah's preaching in the latter end of Josiah's reign and the beginning of Jehoiakim's; but the success of it did not answer expectation.

Verses 1–9

Here is, I. A challenge to produce any one right honest man, or at least any considerable number of such, in Jerusalem, *v.* 1. Jerusalem had become like the old world, in which *all flesh had corrupted their way.* There were some perhaps who flattered themselves with hopes that there were yet many good men in Jerusalem, who would stand in the gap to turn away the wrath of God; and there might be others who boasted of its being the holy city and thought that this would save it. But God bids them search the town, and intimates that they should scarcely find a man in it who executed judgment and made conscience of what he said and did: "Look in *the streets,* where they make their appearance and converse together, and in *the broad places,* where they keep their markets; *see if you can find a man, a magistrate* (so some), *that executes judgment,* and administers justice impartially, that will put the laws in execution against vice and profaneness." When the faithful thus cease and fail it is time to cry *Woe is me!* (Mic. 7:1, 2), high time to cry, *Help Lord,* Ps. 12:1. "If there be here and there a man that is truly conscientious, and does at least *speak the truth,* yet you shall not find him in *the streets and broad places;* he dares not appear publicly, lest he should be abused and run down. *Truth has fallen in the street* (Isa. 59:14), and is forced to *seek for corners.*" So pleasing would it be to God to find any such that for their sake he would pardon the city; if there were but ten righteous men in Sodom, if but one of a thousand, of ten thousand, in Jerusalem, it should be spared. See how ready God is to forgive, how swift to show mercy. But it might be said, "What do you make of those in Jerusalem that continue to make profession of religion and relation to God? Are not they men for whose sakes Jerusalem may be spared?" No, for they are not sincere in their profession (*v.* 2): *They say, The Lord liveth,* and will swear by his name only, but they *swear falsely,* that is, 1. They are not sincere in the profession they make of respect to God, but are false to him; they *honour him with their lips, but their hearts are far from him.* 2. Though they appeal to God only, they make no conscience of calling him to witness

to a lie. Though they do not swear by idols, they forswear themselves, which is no less an affront to God, as the God of truth, than the other is as the only true God.

II. A complaint which the prophet makes to God of the obstinacy and wilfulness of these people. God had appealed to their eyes (*v.* 1); but here the prophet appeals to his eyes (*v.* 3): "*Are not thy eyes upon the truth?* Dost thou not see every man's true character? And is not this the truth of their character, that *they have made their faces harder than a rock?*" Or, "*Behold, thou desirest truth in the inward part;* but where is it to be found among the men of this generation? For though they say, *The Lord liveth,* yet they never regard him; *thou hast stricken them* with one affliction after another, *but they have not grieved* for the affliction, they have been as stocks and stones under it, much less have they grieved for the sin by which they have brought it upon themselves. *Thou* hast gone further yet, *hast consumed them,* hast corrected them yet more severely; *but they have refused to receive correction,* to accommodate themselves to thy design in correcting them and to answer to it. They would not receive instruction by the correction. The have set themselves to outface the divine sentence and to outbrave the execution of it, for *they have made their faces harder than a rock;* they cannot change countenance, neither blush for shame nor look pale for fear, cannot be beaten back from the pursuit of their lusts, whatever check is given them; for, though often called to it, *they have refused to return,* and would go forward, right or wrong, as *the horse into the battle.*"

III. The trial made both of rich and poor, and the bad character given of both.

1. The poor were ignorant, and therefore they were wicked. He found many that *refused to return,* for whom he was willing to make the best excuse their case would bear, and it was this (*v.* 4): "*Surely, these are poor, they are foolish.*" They never had the advantage of a good education, nor have they wherewithal to help themselves now with the means of instruction. They are forced to work hard for their living, and have no time nor capacity for reading or hearing, so that *they know not the way of the Lord, nor the judgments of their God;* they understand neither the way in which God by his precepts will have them to walk towards him nor the way in which he by his providence is walking towards them." Note, (1.) Prevailing ignorance is the lamentable cause of abounding impiety and iniquity. What can one expect but works of darkness from brutish sottish people that know nothing of God and religion, but choose to *sit in darkness?* (2.) This is commonly a reigning sin among poor people. There are the devil's poor as well as God's, who, notwithstanding their poverty, might *know the way of the Lord,* so as to walk in it and do their duty, without being book-learned; but they are willingly ignorant, and therefore their ignorance will not be their excuse.

2. The rich were insolent and haughty, and therefore they were wicked (*v.* 5): "*I will get me to the great men,* and see if I can find them more pliable to the word and providence of God. I will *speak to them,* preach at court, in hopes to make some impression upon men of polite literature. But all in vain; for, though *they know the way of the Lord and the judgment of their God,* yet they are too stiff to stoop to his government: *These have altogether broken the yoke and burst the bonds.* They know their Master's will, but are resolved to have their own will, to *walk in the way of their heart and in the sight of their eyes.* They think themselves too goodly to be controlled, too big to be corrected, even by the sovereign Lord of all himself. They are for breaking even *his bands asunder,* Ps. 2:3. The poor are weak, the rich are wilful, and so neither do their duty."

IV. Some particular sins specified, which they were notoriously guilty of, and which cried most loudly to heaven for vengeance. *Their transgressions* indeed *were many,* of many kinds and often repeated, *and their backslidings were increased;* they added to the number of them and grew more and more impudent in them, *v.* 6. But two sins especially were justly to be looked upon as unpardonable crimes: — 1. Their spiritual whoredom, giving that honour to idols which is due to God only. "*Thy children have forsaken me,* to whom they were born and dedicated and under whom they have been brought up, *and they have sworn by those that are no gods,* have made their appeal

to them as if they had been omniscient and their proper judges." This is here put for all acts of religious worship due to God only, but with which they had honoured their idols. *They have sworn to them* (so it may be read), have joined themselves to them and covenanted with them. Those that forsake God make a bad change for those that are no gods. 2. Their corporal whoredom. Because they had forsaken God and served idols, he gave them up to vile affections; and those that dishonoured him were left to dishonour themselves and their own families. They *committed adultery* most scandalously, without sense of shame or fear of punishment, for they *assembled themselves by troops in the harlots' houses* and did not blush to be seen by one another in the most scandalous places. So impudent and violent was their lust, so impatient of check, and so eager to be gratified, that they became perfect beasts (*v.* 8); like high-fed horses, they *neighed every one after his neighbour's wife, v.* 8. Unbridled lusts make men *like natural brute beasts,* such monstrous odious things are they. And that which aggravated their sin was that it was the abuse of God's favours to them: *When they were fed to the full,* then their lusts grew thus furious. Fulness of bread was fuel to the fire of Sodom's lusts. *Sine Cerere et Bacchio friget Venu — Luxurious living feeds the flames of lust.* Fasting would help to tame the unruly evil that is so *full of deadly poison,* and bring the body into subjection.

V. A threatening of God's wrath against them for their wickedness and the universal debauchery of their land.

1. The particular judgment that is threatened, *v.* 6. A foreign enemy shall break in upon them, get dominion over them, and shall lay waste: their country shall be as if it were overrun and perfectly mastered by wild beasts. This enemy shall be, (1.) Like *a lion of the forest;* so strong, so furious, so irresistible; and he *shall slay them.* (2.) Like *a wolf of the evening,* which comes out at night, when he is hungry, to seek his prey, and is very fierce and ravenous; and the noise both of the lions' roaring and of the wolves' howling is very hideous. (3.) Like *a leopard,* which is very swift and very cruel, and withal careful not to miss his prey. The army of the enemy shall *watch over their cities* so strictly as to put the inhabitants to this sad dilemma — if they stay in, they are starved; if they stir out, they are stabbed; *Every one that goeth out thence shall be torn in pieces,* which intimates that in many places the enemy gave no quarter. And all this bloody work is owing to the *multitude of their transgressions.* It is sin that makes the great slaughter.

2. An appeal to themselves concerning the equity of it (*v.* 9); "*Shall I not visit for these things?* Can you yourselves think that the God whose name is *Jealous* will let such idolatries go unpunished, or that a God of infinite purity will connive at such abominable uncleanness?" These are things that must be reckoned for, else the honour of God's government cannot be maintained, nor his laws saved from contempt; but sinners will be tempted to think him *altogether such a one as themselves,* contrary to that conviction of their own consciences concerning the judgment of God which is necessary to be supported, That *those who do such things are worthy of death,* Rom. 1:32. Observe, when God punishes sin, he is said to *visit* for it, or enquire into it; for he weighs the cause before he passes sentence. Sinners have reason to expect punishment upon the account of God's holiness, to which sin is highly offensive, as well as upon the account of his justice, to which it renders us obnoxious; this is intimated in that, *Shall not my soul be avenged on such a nation as this?* It is not only the word of God, but his soul, that takes vengeance. And he has national judgments wherewith to take vengeance for national sins. *Such nations as this* was cannot long go unpunished. *How shall I pardon thee for this? v.* 7. Not but that those who have been guilty of these sins have found mercy with God, as to their eternal state (Manasseh himself did, though so much accessory to the iniquity of these times); but nations, *as such,* being rewardable and punishable only in this life, it would not be for the glory of God to let a nation so very wicked as this pass without some manifest tokens of his displeasure.

Verses 10–19

We may observe in these verses, as before,

I. The sin of this people, upon which the commission signed against them is grounded. God disowns them and dooms them to destruction, *v.* 10. But *is there not a cause?* Yes; for, 1. They have deserted the law of God (*v.* 11): *The house of Israel and the house of Judah,* though at variance with one another, yet both agreed to *deal very treacherously against God.* They forsook the worship of him, and therein violated their covenants with him; they revolted from him, and played the hypocrite with him. 2. They have defied the judgments of God and given the lie to his threatenings in the mouth of his prophets, *v.* 12, 13. They were often told that evil would certainly come upon them; they must expect some desolating judgment, *sword or famine;* but they were secure and said, *We shall have peace, though we go on.* For, (1.) They did not fear what God is. They belied him, and confronted the dictates even of natural light concerning him; for they said, *"It is not he,* that is, he is not such a one as we have been made to believe he is; he does not see, or not regard, or will not require it; and therefore *no evil shall come upon us."* Multitudes are ruined by being made to believe that God will not be so strict with them as his word says he will; nay, by this artifice Satan undid us all: *You shall not surely die.* So here: *Neither shall we see sword nor famine.* Vain hopes of impunity are the deceitful support of all impiety. (2.) They did not fear what God said. The prophets gave them fair warning, but they turned it off with a jest: "They do but talk so, because it is their trade; they are words of course, and words are but wind. It is not the word of the Lord that is in them; it is only the language of their melancholy fancy or their ill-will to their country, because they are not preferred." Note, Impenitent sinners are not willing to own any thing to be the word of God that makes against them, that tends either to part them from, or disquiet them in, their sins. They threaten the prophets: *"They shall become wind,* shall pass away unregarded, and *thus shall it be done unto them;* what they threaten against us we will inflict upon them. Do they frighten us with famine? Let them be *fed with the bread of affliction."* So Micaiah was, 1 Ki. 22:27. "Do they tell us of the sword? Let them perish by the sword," *ch.* 2:30. Thus their mocking and misusing God's messengers filled the measure of their iniquity.

II. The punishment of this people for their sin. 1. The threatenings they laughed at shall be executed (*v.* 14): *Because you speak this word* of contempt concerning the prophets, and the word in their mouths, therefore God will put honour upon them and their words, for not one iota or tittle of them shall *fall to the ground,* 1 Sa. 3:19. Here God turns to the prophet Jeremiah, who had been thus bantered, and perhaps had been a little uneasy at it: *Behold, I will make my words in thy mouth fire.* God owns them for his words, though men denied them, and will as surely make them to take effect as the fire consumes combustible material that is in its way. *The word shall be fire and the people wood.* Sinners by sin make themselves fuel to that wrath of God which is *revealed from heaven against all ungodliness and unrighteousness of men* in the scripture. The word of God will certainly be too hard for those that contend with it. Those shall break who will not bow before it. 2. The enemy they thought themselves in no danger of shall be brought upon them. God gives them their commission (*v.* 10): *"Go you up upon her walls,* mount them, trample upon them, tread them down. Walls of stone, before the divine commission, shall be but mud walls. Having made yourselves masters of the walls, you may *destroy* at pleasure. You may *take away her battlements,* and leave the fenced fortified cities to lie open; for her battlements *are not the Lord's* he does not own them and therefore will not protect and fortify them." They were not erected in his fear, nor with a dependence upon him; the people have trusted to them more than to God, and therefore they are not his. When the city is filled with sin God will not patronise the fortifications of it, and then they are paper walls. What can defend us when he who is our defence, and the defender of all our defences, has *departed from us?* Num. 14:9. What is not of God cannot stand, not stand long, nor stand us in any stead. What dreadful work these invaders should make is here described (*v.* 15): *Lo, I will bring a nation upon you, O house of Israel!* Note, God has all nations at his command, does what he pleases with them and makes what use he pleases of them. And sometimes he is pleased to make the nations of the earth, the heathen nations, a scourge to the house of Israel, when that has become a *hypocritical nation.* This nation of the Chaldeans is here said to be a remote nation; it is *brought upon them from afar,* and therefore will make the greater spoil and the longer stay, that the soldiers may pay themselves well for so long a march. "It is a nation that thou hast had no commerce with, by reason of their distance, and therefore canst not expect to find favour with." God can bring trouble upon us from places and causes very remote. It is a *mighty nation,* that there is no making head against, an *ancient nation,* that value themselves upon their antiquity and will therefore be the more haughty and imperious. It is *a nation whose language thou knowest not;* they spoke the Syriac tongue, which the Jews at that time were not acquainted with, as appears, 2 Ki. 18:26. The difference of language would make it the more difficult to treat with them of peace. Compare this with the threatening, Deu. 28:49, which it seems to have a reference to, for the law and the prophets exactly agree. They are well armed: *Their quiver is as an open sepulchre;* their arrows shall fly so thick, hit so sure, and wound so deep, that they shall be reckoned to breathe nothing but death and slaughter: they are able-bodied, all effective, *mighty men, v.* 16. And, when they have made themselves masters of the country, they shall devour all before them, and reckon all their own that they can lay their hands on, *v.* 17. (1.) They shall strip the country, shall not only sustain, but surfeit, their soldiers with the rich products of this fruitful land. "They shall not store up (then it might possibly by retrieved), but *eat up thy harvest* in the field *and thy bread* in the house, *which thy sons and thy daughters should eat."* Note, What we have we have for our families, and it is a comfort to see our sons and daughters eating that which we have taken care and pains for. But it is a grievous vexation to see it devoured by strangers and enemies, to see their camps victualled with our stores, while those that are dear to us are perishing for want of it: this also is according to the curse of the law, Deu. 28:33. *"They shall eat up thy flocks and herds,* out of which thou hast taken sacrifices for thy idols; they shall not leave thee the fruit of *thy vines and fig-trees."* (2.) They shall starve the towns: "They *shall impoverish thy fenced cities"* (and what fence is there against poverty, when it comes like an armed man?), "those cities *wherein thou trustedst* to be a protection to the country." Note, It is just with God to impoverish that which we make our confidence. They shall impoverish them *with the sword,* cutting off all provisions from coming to them and intercepting trade and commerce, which will impoverish even fenced cities.

III. An intimation of the tender compassion God has yet for them. The enemy is commissioned to destroy and lay waste, but must not *make a full end, v.* 10. Though they make a great slaughter, yet some must be left to live; though they make a great spoil, yet something must be left to live upon, for God has said it (*v.* 18) with a *non obstante — a nevertheless* to the present desolation: "Even *in those days,* dismal as they are, *I will not make a full end with you;"* and, if God will not, the enemy shall not. God has mercy in store for his people, and therefore will set bounds to this desolating judgment. *Hitherto it shall come, and no further.*

IV. The justification of God in these proceedings against them. As he will appear to be gracious in not making a full end with them, so he will appear to be righteous in coming so near it, and will have it acknowledged that he has done them no wrong, *v.* 19. Observe, 1. A reason demanded, insolently demanded, by the people for these judgments. They *will say "Wherefore doth the Lord our God do all this unto us?* What provocation have we given him, or what quarrel has he with us?" As if against such a sinful nation there did not appear cause enough of action. Note, Unhumbled hearts are ready to charge God with injustice in their afflictions, and pretend they have to seek for the cause of them when it is written in the forehead of them. But, 2. Here is a reason immediately assigned. The prophet is instructed what answer to give them; for God *will be justified when he speaks,* though he speaks with ever so much terror. He must tell them that God does this against them for what they have done against him, and that they may, if they please, read their sin in their punishment. Do not they know very well that they have *forsaken God,* and therefore can they think it strange if he has forsaken them? Have they forgotten how often they *served gods in their own land,* that good land, in the abundance of the fruits of which they ought to have served God with gladness of heart? and therefore is it not just with God to make them *serve strangers* in a strange land, where they can call nothing their own, as he has threatened to do? Deu. 28:47, 48. Those that are fond of strangers, to strangers let them go.

Verses 20–24

The prophet, having reproved them for sin and threatened the judgments of God against them, is here sent to them again upon another errand, which he must *publish in Judah;* the purport of it is to persuade them to fear God, which would be an effectual principle of their reformation, as the want of that fear had been at the bottom of their apostasy.

I. He complains of the shameful stupidity of this people, and their bent to backslide from God, speaking as if he knew not what course to take with them. For,

1. Their understandings were darkened and unapt to admit the rays of the divine light: They are a *foolish people and without understanding;* they apprehend not the mind of God, though ever so plainly declared to them by the written word, by his prophets, and by his providence (*v.* 21): *They have eyes, but they see not, ears, but they hear not,* like the idols which they made and worshipped, Ps. 115:5, 6, 8. One would have thought that they took notice of things, but really they did not; they had intellectual faculties and capacities, but they did not employ and improve them as they ought. Herein they disappointed the expectations of all their neighbours, who, observing what excellent means of knowledge they had, concluded, *Surely they are a wise and an understanding people* (Deu. 4:6), and yet really they are a *foolish people and without understanding.* Note, We cannot judge of men by the advantages and opportunities they enjoy: there are those that sit in darkness in a land of light, that live in sin even in a holy land, that are bad in the best places. 2. Their wills were stubborn and unapt to submit to the rules of the divine law (*v.* 23): *This people has a revolting and a rebellious heart;* and no wonder when they were *foolish and without understanding,* Ps. 82:5. Nay, it is the corrupt bias of the will that bribes and besots the understanding: none so blind as those that will not see. The character of this people is the true character of all people by nature, till the grace of God has wrought a change. We are *foolish,* slow of understanding, and apt to mistake and forget; yet that is not the worst. We have *a revolting and a rebellious heart,* a carnal mind, that is enmity against God, and is not in subjection to his law, not only revolting from him by a rooted aversion to that which is good, but rebellious against him by a strong inclination to that which is evil. Observe, The revolting heart is a rebellious one: those that withdraw from their allegiance to God do not stop there, but by siding in with sin and Satan take up arms against him. *They have revolted and gone.* The revolting heart will produce a revolting life. *They are gone,* and they *will go* (so it may be read); now *nothing will be restrained from them,* Gen. 11:6.

II. He ascribed this to the want of the fear of God. When he observes them to be without understanding he asks, *"Fear you not me, saith the Lord, and will you not tremble at my presence? v.* 22. If you would but keep up an awe of God, you would be more observant of what he says to you: and, did you but understand your own interest better, you would be more under the commanding rule of God's fear." When he observes that *they have revolted and gone* he adds this, as the root and cause of their apostasy (*v.* 24), *Neither say they in their hearts, Let us now fear the Lord our God.* Therefore so many bad thoughts come into their mind, and hurry them to that which is evil, because they will not admit and entertain good thoughts, and particularly not this good thought, *Let us now fear the Lord our God.* It is true it is God's work to put his fear into our hearts; but it is our work to stir up ourselves to fear him, and to fasten upon those considerations which are proper to affect us with a holy awe of him; and it is because we do not do this that our hearts are so destitute of his fear as they are, and so apt to revolt and rebel.

III. He suggests some of those things which are proper to possess us with a holy fear of God.

1. We must fear the Lord and his greatness, *v.* 22. Upon this account he demands our fear: *Shall we not tremble*

at his presence, and not be afraid of affronting him, or trifling with him, who in the kingdom of nature and providence gives such incontestable proofs of his almighty power and sovereign dominion? Here is one instance given of very many that might be given: he keeps the sea within compass. Though the tides flow with a mighty strength twice every day, and if they should flow on awhile would drown the world, though in a storm the billows rise high and dash to the shore with incredible force and fury, yet they are under check, they return, they retire, and no harm is done. *This is the Lord's doing,* and, if it were not common, it would be *marvellous in our eyes.* He has *placed the sand for the bound of the sea,* not only for a *meerstone,* to mark out how far it may come and where it must stop, but as a *mound,* or fence, to put a stop to it. A wall of sand shall be as effectual as a wall of brass to check the flowing waves, when God is pleased to make it so; nay, that is chosen rather, to teach us that a *soft answer,* like the soft sand, *turns away wrath,* and quiets a foaming rage, when *grievous words,* like hard rocks, do but exasperate, and make *the waters cast forth* so much the more *mire and dirt.* This bound is placed *by a perpetual decree,* by an ordinance *of antiquity* (so some read it), and then it sends us as far back as to the creation of the world, when God divided between the sea and dry land, and fixed marches between them, Gen. 1:9, 10 (which is elegantly described, Ps. 104:6, etc., and Job 38:8, etc.), or to the period of Noah's flood, when God promised that he would never drown the world again, Gen. 9:11. An ordinance of *perpetuity* — so our translation takes it. It is a *perpetual decree;* it has had its effect all along to this day and shall still continue till day and night come to an end. This *perpetual decree* the waters of the sea *cannot pass over* nor break through. *Though the waves thereof toss themselves,* as the *troubled sea* does *when it cannot rest,* yet *can they not prevail; though they roar* and rage as if they were vexed at the check given them, *yet can they not pass over.* Now this is a good reason why we should fear God; for, (1.) By this we see that he is a God of almighty power and universal sovereignty, and therefore to be feared and had in reverence. (2.) This shows us how easily he could drown the world again and how much we continually lie at his mercy, and therefore we should be afraid of making him our enemy. (3.) Even the unruly waves of the sea observe his decree and retreat at his check, and shall not we then? Why are our hearts revolting and rebellious, when the sea neither revolts nor rebels?

2. We must fear the Lord and his goodness, Hos. 3:5. The instances of this, as of the former, are fetched from God's common providence, *v.* 24. We must *fear the Lord our God,* that is, we must worship him, and give him glory, and be always in care to keep ourselves in his love, because he is continually doing us good: he gives us both *the former and the latter rain,* the former a little after seedtime, the latter a little before harvest, and both *in their season;* and by this means *he reserves to us the appointed weeks of harvest.* Harvest is reckoned by weeks, because in a few weeks enough is gathered to serve for sustenance the year round. The weeks of the harvest are appointed us by the promise of God, that *seed-time and harvest shall not fail.* And in performance of that promise they are reserved to us by the divine providence, otherwise we should come short of them. In harvest mercies therefore God is to be acknowledged, his power, and goodness, and faithfulness, for they all come from him. And it is good reason why we should fear him, that we may keep ourselves in his love, because we have such a necessary dependence upon him. The fruitful seasons were witnesses for God, even to the heathen world, sufficient to leave them inexcusable in their contempt of him (Acts 14:17); and yet the Jews, who had the written word to explain their testimony by, were not wrought upon to fear the Lord, though it appears how much it is our interest to do so.

Verses 25–31

Here, I. The prophet shows them what mischief their sins had done them: They *have turned away these things* (*v.* 25), the *former and the latter rain,* which they used to have *in due season* (*v.* 24), but which had of late been withheld (*ch.* 3:3), by reason of which the appointed weeks of harvest had sometimes disappointed them. "It is *your sin* that *has withholden good from you,* when God was ready to bestow it upon you." Note, It is sin that stops the current of God's favour to us, and deprives us of the blessings we used to receive. It is that which makes the heavens as brass and the earth as iron.

II. He shows them how great their sins were, how heinous and provoking. When they had forsaken the worship of the true God, even moral honesty was lost among them: *Among my people are found wicked men* (*v.* 26), some of the worst of men, and so much the worse they were for being found among God's people. 1. They were spiteful and malicious. Such are properly *wicked men,* men that delight in doing mischief. They were *found* (that is, caught) in the very act of their wickedness. As hunters or fowlers lay snares for their game, so did they *lie in wait* to *catch men,* and made a sport of it, and took as much pleasure in it as if they had been entrapping beasts or birds. They contrives ways of doing mischief to good people (whom they hated for their goodness), especially to those that faithfully reproved them (Isa. 29:21), or to those that stood in the way of their preferment or whom they supposed to have affronted them or done them a diskindness, or to those whose estates they coveted; so Jezebel ensnared Naboth for his vineyard. Nay, they did mischief for mischief's sake. 2. They were false and treacherous (*v.* 27): *"As a cage,* or *coop,* is *full of birds,* and of food for them to fatten them for the table, so are *their houses full of deceit,* of wealth obtained by fraudulent practices or of arts and methods of defrauding. All the business of their families is done with deceit; whoever deals with them, they will cheat him if they can, which is easily done by those who make no conscience of what they say and do. Herein *they overpass the deed of the wicked, v.* 28. Those that act by deceit, with a colour of law and justice, do more mischief perhaps than those wicked men (*v.* 26) that carry all before them by open force and violence; or they are worse than the heathen themselves, yea, the worst of them. And (would you think it?) they prosper in these wicked courses and therefore their hearts are hardened in them. They are greedy of the world, because they find it flows in upon them, and they stick not at any wickedness in pursuit of it, because they find that it is so far from hindering their prosperity that it furthers it: *They have become great* in the world; *they have waxen rich,* and thrive upon it. They have wherewithal to make provision for the flesh to fulfill all the lusts of it, to which they are very indulgent, so that *they have waxen fat* with living at ease and bathing themselves in all the delights of sense. They are sleek and smooth: *The shine;* they look fair and gay; every body admires them. And they *pass by matters of evil* (so some read the following words); they escape the evils which one would expect their sins should bring upon them; *they are not in trouble as other men,* much less as we might expect bad men," Ps. 73:5, etc. 3. When they had grown great, and had got power in their hands, they did not do that good with it which they ought to have done: *They judge not the cause, the cause of the fatherless, and the right of the needy.* The fatherless are often needy, always need assistance and advice, and advantage is taken of their helpless condition to do them an injury. Who should succour them then but the great and rich? What have men wealth for but to do good with it? But these would take no cognizance of any such distressed cases: they had not so much sense of justice, or compassion for the injured; or, if they did concern themselves in the cause, it was not to do right, but to protect those that did wrong. And *yet they prosper* still; *God layeth not folly to them.* Certainly then the things of this world are not the best things, for often-times the worst men have the most of them; yet we are not to think that, because they prosper, God allows of their practices. No; *though sentence against* their *evil works be not executed speedily,* it will be executed. 4. There was a general corruption of all orders and degrees of men among them (*v.* 30, 31); *A wonderful and horrible thing is committed in the land.* The degeneracy of such a people, so privileged and advanced, was a wonderful thing, and to be viewed with amazement. How could they ever break through so many obligations? It was a horrible thing, a thing to be detested and the consequences of it dreaded. To frighten ourselves from sin, let us call it a horrible thing. What was the matter? In short, this: (1.) The leaders misled the people: *The prophets prophesy falsely,* counterfeit a commission from heaven when they are factors for hell. Religion is never more dangerously attacked than under colour and pretence of divine revelation. But why did not the priests, who had power in their hands for that purpose, restrain these false prophets? Alas! instead of doing that they made use of them as the tools of their ambition and tyranny: *The priests bear rule by their means;* they supported themselves in their grandeur and wealth, their laziness and luxury, their impositions and oppressions, by the help of the false prophets and their interest in the people. Thus they were in a combination against every thing that was good, and strengthened one another's hands in evil. (2.) The people were well enough pleased to be so misled: "They are *my people,"* says God, "and should have stood up for me, and borne their testimony against the wickedness of their priests and prophets; but they *love to have it so."* If the priests and prophets will let them alone in their sins, they will give them no disturbance in theirs. They love to be ridden with a loose rein, and like those rulers very well that will not restrain their lusts and those teachers that will not reprove them.

III. He shows them how fatal the consequences of this would certainly be. Let them consider,

1. What the reckoning would be for their wickedness (*v.* 29): *Shall not I visit for these things?* as before, *v.* 9. Sometimes mercy rejoices against judgment: *How shall I give thee up, Ephraim?* Here, judgment is reasoning against mercy: *Shall I not visit?* We are sure that Infinite Wisdom knows how to accommodate the matter between them. The manner of expression is very emphatic, and denotes, (1.) The certainty and necessity of God's judgments: *Shall not my soul be avenged?* Yes, without doubt, vengeance will come, it must come, if the sinner repent not. (2.) The justice and equity of God's judgments; he appeals to the sinner's own conscience, Do not those deserve to be punished that have been guilty of such abominations? Shall he not be avenged on *such a nation,* such a wicked provoking nation as this?

2. What the direct tendency of their wickedness was: *What will you do in the end thereof?* That is, (1.) "What a pitch of wickedness will you come to at last! *What will you do?* What will you not do that is base and wicked. What will this grow to? You will certainly grow worse and worse, till you have filled up the measure of your iniquity." (2.) "What a pit of destruction will you come to at last! When things are brought to such a pass as this, nothing can be expected from you but a deluge of sin, so nothing can be expected from God but a deluge of wrath; and what will you do when that shall come?" Note, Those that walk in bad ways would do well to consider the tendency of them both to greater sin and utter ruin. An end will come; the end of a wicked life will come, when it will be all called over again, and without doubt will be bitterness in the latter end.

CHAPTER 6

In this chapter, as before, we have, I. A prophecy of the invading of the land of Judah and the besieging of Jerusalem by the Chaldean army (*v.* 1–6), with the spoils they should make of the country (*v.* 9) and the terror which all should be seized with on that occasion (*v.* 22–26). II. An account of those sins of Judah and Jerusalem which provoked God to bring this desolating judgment upon them. Their oppression (*v.* 7), their contempt of the word of God (*v.* 10–12), their worldliness (*v.* 13), the treachery of their prophets (*v.* 14), their impudence in sin (*v.* 15), their obstinacy against reproofs (*v.* 18, 19), which made their sacrifices unacceptable to him (*v.* 20), and for which he gave them up to ruin (*v.* 21), but tried them first (*v.* 27) and then rejected them as irreclaimable (*v.* 28–30). III. Good counsel given them in the midst of all this, but in vain (*v.* 8, 16, 17).

Verses 1–8

Here is I. Judgment threatened against Judah and Jerusalem. The city and the country were at this time secure and under no apprehension of danger; they saw no cloud gathering, but every thing looked safe and serene: but the prophet tells them that they shall shortly be invaded by a foreign power, an army shall be brought against them *from the north,* which shall lay all waste, and shall cause not only a general consternation, but a general desolation. It is here foretold,

1. That the alarm of this should be loud and terrible. This is represented, *v.* 1. The children of Benjamin, in which tribe part of Jerusalem lay, are here called to shift for their own safety in the country; for the city (to which it was first thought advisable for them to flee, *ch.* 4:5, 6) would soon be made too hot for them, and they would find it

the wisest course to flee out of the midst of it. It is common, in public frights, for the people to think any place safer than that in which they are; and therefore those in the city are for shifting into the country, in hopes there to escape out of danger, and those in the country are for shifting into the city, in hopes there to make head against the danger; but it is all in vain when evil pursues sinners with commission. They are told to send the alarm into the country, and to do what they can for their own safety: *Blow the trumpet in Tekoa,* a city which lay twelve miles north from Jerusalem. Let them be stirred up to stand upon their guard: *Set up a sign of fire* (that is, kindle the beacons) *in Beth-haccerem,* the *house of the vineyard,* which lay on a hill between Jerusalem and Tekoa. Prepare to make a vigorous resistance, *for the evil appears out of the north.* This may be taken ironically: "Betake yourselves to the best methods you can think of for your own preservation, but all shall be in vain; for, when you have done your best, it will be a great destruction, for it is in vain to contend with God's judgments."

2. That the attempt upon them should be bold and formidable and such as they should be a very unequal match for. (1.) See what *the daughter of Zion* is, on whom the assault is made. She is compared *to a comely and delicate woman* (*v.* 2), bred up in every thing that is nice and soft, that will not set so much as the sole *of her foot to the ground for tenderness and delicacy* (Deu. 28:56), nor suffer the wind to blow upon her; and, not being accustomed to hardship, she will be the less able either to resist the enemy (for those that make war must *endure hardness)* or to bear the destruction with that patience which is necessary to make it tolerable. The more we indulge ourselves in the pleasures of this life the more we disfit ourselves for the troubles of this life. (2.) See what the daughter of Babylon is, by whom the assault is made. The generals and their armies are compared to *shepherds* and *their flocks* (*v.* 3), in such numbers and in such order did they come, the soldiers following their leaders as the sheep their shepherds. The daughter of *Zion dwelt at home* (so some read it), expecting to be courted with love, but was invaded with fury. This comparing of the enemies to shepherds inclines me to embrace another reading, which some give of *v.* 2, *The daughter of Zion is like a comely pasture-ground and a delicate land,* which invite the shepherds to bring their flocks thither to graze; and as the shepherds easily make themselves masters of an open field, which (as was then usual in some parts) lies common, owned by none, *pitch their tents* in it, and their flocks quickly eat it bare, so shall the Chaldean army easily break in upon the land of Judah, force for themselves a free quarter where they please, and in a little time devour all. For the further illustration of this he shows, [1.] How God shall commission them to make this destruction even of the holy land and the holy city, which were his own possession. It is he that says (*v.* 4), *Prepare you war against her;* for he is the *Lord of hosts,* that has all hosts at his command, and he has said (*v.* 6), *Hew you down trees, and cast a mount against Jerusalem,* in order to the attacking of it. The Chaldeans have great power against Judah and Jerusalem, and yet they have no power but what is *given them from above.* God has marked out Jerusalem for destruction. He has said, *"This is the city to be visited,* visited in wrath, visited by the divine justice, and this is the time of her visitation." The day is coming when those that are careless and secure in sinful ways will certainly be visited. [2.] How they shall animate themselves and one another to execute that commission. God's counsels being against Jerusalem, which cannot be altered or disannulled, the councils of war which the enemies held are made to agree with his counsels. God having said, *Prepare war against her,* their determinations are made subservient to his; and, notwithstanding the distance of place and the many difficulties that lay in the way, it is soon resolved, *nemine contradicente — unanimously. Arise, and let us go.* Note, It is good to see how the counsel and decree of God are pursued and executed in the devices and designs of men, even theirs that know him not, Isa. 10:6, 7. In this campaign, *First,* They resolve to be very expeditious. They have no sooner resolved upon it than they address themselves to it; it shall never be said that they left any thing to be done towards it to-morrow which they could do to-day: *Arise, let us go up at noon,* though it be in the heat of the day; nay, (*v.* 5), *Arise, let us go up at night,* though it be in the dark. Nothing shall hinder them; they are resolved to *lose no time.* They are described as men in care to make despatch (*v.* 4): *"Woe unto us, for the day goes away,* and we are not going on with our work; *the shadows of the evening are stretched out,* and we sit still, and let slip the opportunity." O that we were thus eager in our spiritual work and warfare, thus afraid of losing time, or any opportunity, in taking the *kingdom of heaven by violence!* It is folly to trifle when we have an eternal salvation to work out, and the enemies of that salvation to fight against. *Secondly,* They confidently expect to be very successful: *"Let us go up,* and let us destroy her palaces and make ourselves masters of the wealth that is in them." It was not that they might fulfill God's counsels, but that they might fill their own treasures, that they were thus eager; yet God thereby served his own purposes.

II. The cause of this judgment assigned. It is all for their wickedness; they have brought it upon themselves; they must bear it, for they must bear the blame of it. They are thus oppressed because they have been oppressors; they have dealt hardly with one another, each in his turn, as they have had power and advantage, and now the enemy shall come and deal hardly with them all. This sin of oppression, and violence, and wrong-doing, is here charged upon them, 1. As a national sin (*v.* 6): *Therefore* This city *is to be visited,* it is time to make inquisition, for *she is wholly oppression in the midst of her.* All orders and degrees of men, from the prince on the throne to the meanest master of a shop, were oppressive to those that were under them. Look which way you might, there were causes for complaints of this kind. 2. As a sin that had become in a manner natural to them (*v.* 7): She *casts out wickedness,* in all the instances of malice and mischievousness, *as a fountain casts out her waters,* so plentifully and constantly, the streams bitter and poisonous, like the fountain. The waters out of the fountain will not be restrained, but will find or force their way, nor will they be checked by laws or conscience in their violent proceedings. This is fitly applied to the corrupt heart of man in his natural state; it *casts out wickedness,* one evil imagination or other, as a fountain *casts out her waters,* naturally and easily; it is always flowing, and yet always full. 3. As that which had become a constant practice with them; *Violence and spoil are heard in her.* The cry of it had come up before God as that of Sodom: *Before me continually are grief and wounds* — the complaint of those that find themselves aggrieved, being unjustly wounded in their bodies or spirits, in their estates or reputation. Note, He that is the common Parent of mankind regards and resents, and sooner or later will revenge, the mischiefs and wrongs that men do to one another.

III. The counsel given them how to prevent this judgment. Fair warning is given now upon the whole matter: *"Be thou instructed, O Jerusalem! v.* 8. Receive the instruction given thee both by the law of God and by the prophets; be wise at length for thyself." They knew very well what they had been instructed to do; nothing remained but to do it, for till then they could not be said to be instructed. The reason for this counsel is taken from the inevitable ruin they ran upon if they refused to comply with the instructions given them: *Lest my soul depart,* or *be disjoined, from thee.* This intimates what a tender affection and concern God had had for them; his very soul had been joined to them, and nothing but sin could disjoin it. Note, 1. The God of mercy is loth to depart even from a provoking people, and is earnest with them by true repentance and reformation to prevent things coming to that extremity. 2. Their case is very miserable from whom God's soul is disjoined; it intimates the loss not only of their outward blessings, but of those comforts and favours which are the more immediate and peculiar tokens of his love and presence. Compare this with that dreadful word (Heb. 10:38), *If any man draw back, my soul shall have no pleasure in him.* 3. Those whom God forsakes are certainly undone; when God's soul departs from Jerusalem she soon becomes desolate and uninhabited, Mt. 23:38.

Verses 9–17

The heads of this paragraph are the very same with those of the last; for precept must be upon precept and line upon line.

I. The ruin of Judah and Jerusalem is here threatened. We had before the haste which the Chaldea army made to the war (*v.* 4, 5); now here we have the havoc made by the war. How lamentable are the desolations here described! The enemy shall so long quarter among them, and be so insatiable in their thirst after blood and treasure, that they shall seize all they can meet with, and what escapes them at one time shall fall into their hands another (*v.* 9): *They shall thoroughly glean the remnant of Israel as a vine;* as the *grape-gatherer,* who is resolved to leave none behind, still *turns back his hand into the baskets,* to put more in, till he has gathered all, so that they be picked up by the enemy, though dispersed, though hid, and none of them shall escape their eye and hand. Perhaps the people, being *given to covetousness* (*v.* 13), had not observed that law of God which forbade them to *glean all their grapes* (Lev. 19:10), and now they themselves shall be in like manner *thoroughly gleaned* and shall either fall by the sword or go into captivity. This is explained *v.* 11, 12, where God's *fury* and his *hand* are said to be *poured out* and *stretched out,* in the fury and by the hand of the Chaldeans; for even wicked men are often made use of as God's hand (Ps. 17:14), and in their anger we may see God angry. Now see on whom the fury is poured out in full vials — *upon the children abroad,* or *in the streets,* where they are playing (Zec. 8:5) or whither they run out innocently to look about them: the sword of the merciless Chaldeans shall not spare them, *ch.* 9:21. The children perish in the calamity which the fathers' sins have procured. The execution shall likewise reach *the assembly of young men,* their merry meetings, their clubs which they keep up to strengthen one another's hands in wickedness; they shall be *cut off together.* Nor shall those only fall into the enemies' hands who meet for lewdness (*ch.* 5:7), but *even the husband with the wife shall be taken,* these two in bed together, and neither left, but both taken prisoners. And, as they have no compassion for the weak but fair sex, so they have none for the decrepit but venerable age: *The old with the full of days,* whose deaths can contribute no more to their safety than their lives to their service, who are not in a capacity to do them either good or harm, shall be either cut off or carried off. *Their houses shall then be turned to others* (*v.* 12); the conquerors shall dwell in their habitations, use their goods, and live upon their stores; their *fields and vines* shall fall *together* into their hands, as was threatened, Deu. 28:30, etc. For God *stretches out his hand upon the inhabitants of the land,* and none can go out of the reach of it. Now as to this denunciation of God's wrath, 1. The prophet justifies himself in preaching thus terribly, for herein he dealt faithfully (*v.* 11): *"I am full of the fury of the Lord,* full of the thoughts and apprehensions of it, and am carried out with a powerful impulse, by the spirit of prophecy, to speak of it thus vehemently." He took no delight in threatening, nor was it any pleasure to him with such sermons as these to make those about him uneasy; but he could not contain himself; he was *weary with holding in;* he suppressed it as long as he could, as long as he durst, but he was so *full of power by the Spirit of the Lord of hosts* that he must speak, whether they will hear or whether they will forbear. Note, When ministers preach the terrors of the Lord according to the scripture we have no reason to be displeased at them; for they are but messengers, and must deliver their message, pleasing or unpleasing. 2. He condemns the false prophets who preached plausibly, for therein they flattered people and dealt unfaithfully (*v.* 13, 14): *The priest and the prophet,* who should be their watchmen and monitors, have *dealt falsely,* have not been true to their trust not told the people their faults and the danger they were in; they should have been their physicians, but they murdered their patients by letting them have their will, by giving them every thing that had a mind to, and flattering them into an opinion that they were in no danger (*v.* 14): They have *healed the hurt of the daughter of my people slightly,* or *according to the cure of some slight hurt,* skinning over the wound and never searching it to the bottom, applying lenitives only, when there was need of corrosives, soothing people in their sins, and giving them opiates to make them easy for the present, while the disease was preying upon the vitals. They said, *"Peace peace* — all shall be well." (if there were some thinking people among them, who were awake, and apprehensive of danger, they soon stopped their mouths with their priestly and prophetical authority, boldly averring that neither church nor state was in any danger), when *there is no peace,* because they went on in their idolatries and daring impieties. Note, Those are to be reckoned our false friends (that is, our worst and most dangerous enemies) who flatter us in a sinful way.

II. The sin of Judah and Jerusalem, which provoked God to bring this ruin upon them and justified him in it, is here declared. 1. They would by no means bear to be told of their faults, nor of the danger they were in. God bids the prophet give them warning of the judgment coming (*v.* 9), "but," says he, *"to whom shall I speak and give warning?* I cannot find out any that will so much as give me a patient hearing. I may give warning long enough, but these is nobody that will take warning. I cannot speak *that they may hear,* cannot speak to any purpose, or with any hope of success; for *their ear is uncircumcised,* it is carnal and fleshly, indisposed to receive the voice of God, so that *they cannot hearken.* They have, as it were, a thick skin grown over the organs of hearing, so that divine things might to as much purpose be spoken to a stone as to them. Nay, they are not only deaf to it, but prejudiced against it; therefore they cannot hear, because they are resolved that they will not: The *word of the Lord is unto them a reproach;* both the reproofs and the threatenings of the word are so;" they reckoned themselves wronged and affronted by both, and resented the prophet's plain-dealing with them as they would the most causeless slander and calumny. This was *kicking against the pricks* (Acts 9:5), as the lawyers against the word of Christ, Lu. 11:45, *Thus saying, thou repoachest us also.* Note, Those reproofs that are counted reproaches, and hated as such, will certainly be turned into the heaviest woes. When it is here said, *They have no delight in the word,* more is implied than is expressed; "they have an antipathy to it; their hearts rise at it; it exasperates them, and enrages their corruptions, and they are ready to fly in the face and pull out the eyes of their reprovers." And how can those expect that the word of the Lord should speak any comfort to them who have no delight in it, but would rather be any where than within hearing of it? 2. They were inordinately set upon the world, and wholly carried away by the love of it (*v.* 13): *"From the least of them even to the greatest,* old and young, rich and poor, high and low, those of all ranks, professions, and employments, *every one is given to covetousness,* greedy of filthy lucre, all for what they can get, *per fas per nefas — right or wrong;"* and this made them oppressive and violent (*v.* 6, 7), for of those evils, as well as others, the love of money is the bitter root. Nay, and this hardened their hearts against the word of God and his prophets. It was the covetous Pharisees that derided Christ, Lu. 16:14. 3. They had become impudent in sin and were past shame. After such a high charge of flagrant crimes proved upon them, it was very proper to ask (*v.* 15), *Were they ashamed when they had committed* all these *abominations,* which are such a reproach to their reason and religion? Did they blush at the conviction, and acknowledge that confusion of face belonged to them? If so, there is some hope of them yet. But, alas! there did not appear so much as this colour of virtue among them; their hearts were so hardened that *they were not at all ashamed, neither could they blush,* they had so brazened their faces. They even gloried in their wickedness, and openly confronted the convictions which should have humbled them and brought them to repentance. They resolved to face it out against God himself and not to own their guilt. Some refer this to the priests and prophets, who had healed the people slightly and told them that they should have peace, and yet were not ashamed of their treachery and falsehood, no, not when the event disproved them and gave them the lie. Those that are shameless are graceless and their case is hopeless. But those that will not submit to a penitential shame, nor take that to themselves as their due, shall not escape an utter ruin; for so it follows: *Therefore they shall fall among* those *that fall;* they shall have their portion with those that are quite undone; and, when God visits the nation in wrath, they shall be sure to be cast down and be made to tremble, because they would not blush. Note, Those that sin and cannot blush for it are in an evil case now, and it will be worse with them shortly. At first they hardened themselves and would not blush, afterwards they were so hardened that they could not. *Quod unum habebant in malis bonum perdunt, peccandi verecundiam — they have lost the only good property which once blended itself with many bad ones, that is, shame for having done amiss.* — Senec. De Vit. Beat.

III. They are put in mind of the good counsel which had been often given them, but in vain. They had a great deal said to them to little purpose,

1. By way of advice concerning their duty, *v.* 16. God had been used to say to them, *Stand in the ways and see.* That is, (1.) He would have them to consider, not to proceed rashly, but to do as travellers in the road, who are in care to find the right way which will bring them to their journey's end, and therefore pause and enquire for it. If they have any reason to think that they have missed their way, they are not easy till they have obtained satisfaction. O that men would be thus *wise for their souls,* and would ponder the path of their feet, as those that believe lawful and unlawful are of no less consequence to us than the right way and the wrong are to a traveller! (2.) He would have them to consult antiquity, the observations and experiences of those that went before them: *"Ask for the old paths, enquire of the former age* (Job 8:8), *ask thy father, thy elders* (Deu. 32:7), and thou wilt find that the way of godliness and righteousness has always been the way which God has owned and blessed and in which men have prospered. Ask for the *old paths,* the paths prescribed by the law of God, the written word, that true standard of antiquity. Ask for the paths that the patriarchs travelled in before you, Abraham, and Isaac, and Jacob; and, as you hope to inherit the promises made to them, tread in their steps. *Ask for the old paths, Where is the good way?"* We must not be guided merely by antiquity, as if the plea of prescription and long usage were alone sufficient to justify our path. No; there is an *old way which wicked men have trodden,* Job 22:15. But, when we ask for the old paths, it is only in order to find out the *good way,* the highway of the upright. Note, The way of religion and godliness is a good old way, the way that all the saints in all ages have walked in. (3.) He would have them to resolve to act according to the result of these enquiries: "When you have found out which is the good way, *walk therein,* practise accordingly, keep closely to that way, proceed, and persevere in it." Some make this counsel to be given them with reference to the struggles that were between the true and false prophets, between those that said they should have peace and those that told them trouble was at the door; they pretended they knew not which to believe: *"Stand in the way,"* says God, "and see, and enquire, which of these two agrees with the written word and the usual methods of God's providence, which of these directs you to the good way, and do accordingly." (4.) He assures them that, if they do thus, it will secure the welfare and satisfaction of their own souls: *"Walk in the good old way* and you will find your walking in that way will be easy and pleasant; you will enjoy both your God and yourselves, and the way will lead you to true rest. Though it cost you some pains to walk in that way, you will find an abundant recompence at your journey's end." (5.) He laments that this good counsel, which was so rational in itself and so proper for them, could not find acceptance: *"But they said, We will not walk therein,* not only we will not be at the pains to enquire *which is the good way,* the *good old way;* but when it is told us, and we have nothing to say to the contrary but that it is the right way, yet we will not deny ourselves and our humours so far as to *walk in it."* Thus multitudes are ruined for ever by downright wilfulness.

2. By way of admonition concerning their danger. Because they would not be ruled by fair reasoning, God takes another method with them; by less judgments he threatens greater, and sends his prophets to give them this explication of them, and to frighten them with an apprehension of the danger they were in (*v.* 17); *Also I set watchmen over you.* God's ministers are watchmen, and it is a great mercy to have them set over us in the Lord. Now observe here, (1.) The fair warning given by these watchmen. This was the burden of their song; they cried again and again, *Hearken to the sound of the trumpet.* God, in his providence, sounds the trumpet (Zec. 9:14); the watchmen hear it themselves and are affected with it (Jer. 4:19), and they are to call upon others to hearken to it too, to hear the Lord's controversy, to observe the voice of Providence, to improve it, and answer the intentions of it. (2.) This fair warning slighted: *"But they said, We will not hearken;* we will not hear, we will not heed, we will not believe; the prophets may as well save themselves and us the trouble." The reason why sinners perish is because they *do not hearken to the sound of the trumpet;* and the reason why they do not is because they will not; and they have no reason to give why they will not but because they will not, that is, they are herein most unreasonable. One may more easily deal with ten men's reasons than one man's will.

Verses 18–30

Here, I. God appeals to all the neighbours, nay, to the whole world, concerning the equity of his proceedings against Judah and Jerusalem (*v.* 18, 19): *"Hear, you nations, and know* particularly, *O congregation* of the mighty, the great men of the nations, that take cognizance of the affairs of states about you and make remarks upon them. Observe now what is doing among those of Judah and Jerusalem; you hear of the desolations brought upon them, the earth rings of it, trembles under it; you all wonder that *I* should *bring evil upon this people,* that are in covenant with me, that profess relation to me, that have worshipped me, and been highly favoured by me; you are ready to ask, *Wherefore has the Lord done thus to this land?* Deu. 29:24. Know then," 1. "That it is the natural product of their devices. The evil brought upon them is *the fruit of their thought.* They thought to strengthen themselves by their alliance with foreigners, and by that very thing they weakened and diminished themselves, they betrayed and exposed themselves." 2. "That it is the just punishment of their disobedience and rebellion. God does but execute upon them the curse of the law for their violation of its commands. It is because *they have not hearkened to my words nor to my law,* nor regarded a word I have said to them, but rejected it all. They would never have been ruined thus by the judgments of God's hand if they had not refused to be ruled by the judgments of his mouth: therefore you cannot say that they have any wrong done them."

II. God rejects their plea, by which they insisted upon their external services as sufficient to atone for all their sins. Alas! it is a frivolous plea (*v.* 20): *"To what purpose come there to me incense and sweet cane,* to be burnt for a perfume on the golden altar, though it was the best of the kind, and far-fetched? What care I for *your burnt-offerings* and *your sacrifices?"* They not only cannot profit God (no sacrifice does, Ps. 50:9), but they do not please him, for none does this but the sacrifice of the upright; that of the wicked is an *abomination to him.* Sacrifice and incense were appointed to excite their repentance, and to direct them to a Mediator, and assist their faith in him. Where this good use was made of them they were acceptable, God had respect to them and to those that offered them. But when they were offered with an opinion that thereby they made God their debtor, and purchased a license to go on in sin, they were so far from being pleasing to God that they were a provocation to him.

III. He foretels the desolation that was now coming upon them. 1. God designs their ruin because they hate to be reformed (*v.* 21): *I will lay stumbling-blocks before this people,* occasions of falling not into sin, but into trouble. Those whom God has marked for destruction he perplexes and embarrasses in their counsels, and obstructs and retards all the methods they take for their own safety. The parties of the enemy, which they met with wherever they went, were stumbling-blocks to them; in ever corner they stumbled upon them and were dashed to pieces by them: *The fathers and the sons together shall fall upon them;* neither the fathers with their wisdom, nor the sons with their strength and courage, shall escape them, or get over them. The sons that sinned with their fathers fall with them. Even the *neighbour and his friend shall perish* and not be able to help either themselves or one another. 2. He will make use of the Chaldeans as instruments of it; for whatever work God has to do he will find out proper instruments for the doing of it. This is a people fetched *from the north, from the sides of the earth.* Babylon itself lay a great way off northward; and some of the countries that were subject to the king of Babylon, out of which his army was levied, lay much further. These must be employed in this service, *v.* 22, 23. For, (1.) It is a people very numerous, *a great nation,* which will make their invasion the more formidable. (2.) It is a warlike people. *They lay hold on bow and spear,* and at this time know how to use them, for they are used to them. *They ride upon horses,* and therefore they march the more swiftly, and in battle press the harder. No nation had yet brought into the field a better cavalry that the Chaldeans. (3.) It is a barbarous people. They *are cruel and have no mercy,* being greedy of prey and flushed with victory. They take a pride in frightening all about them; their voice *roars like the sea.* And, (4.) They have a particular design upon Judah and Jerusalem, in hopes greatly to enrich themselves with the spoil of that famous country. They are *set in array against thee, O daughter of Zion!* The sins of God's professing people make them an easy prey to those that are God's enemies as well as theirs.

IV. He describes the very great consternation which Judah and Jerusalem should be in upon the approach of this formidable enemy, *v.* 24–26. 1. They own themselves in a fright, upon the first intelligence brought them of the approach of the enemy: "When *we have but heard the fame thereof our hands wax feeble,* and we have no heart to make any resistance; *anguish has taken hold of us,* and we are immediately in an extremity of pain, like that of *a woman in travail."* Note, Sense of guilt quite dispirits men, upon the approach of any threatening trouble. What can those hope to do for themselves who have made God their enemy? 2. They confine themselves by consent to their houses, not daring to show their heads abroad; for, though they could not but expect that the sword of the enemy would at last find them out there, yet they would rather die tamely and meanly there than run any venture, either by fight or flight, to help themselves. Thus they say one to another, *"Go not forth into the field,* no, not to fetch in your provision thence, *nor walk by the way;* dare not to go to church or market, it is at your peril if you do, for the *sword of the enemy,* and the fear of it, are *on every side;* the *highways are unoccupied,* as in Jael's time," Jdg. 5:6. Let this remind us, when we travel the roads in safety and there is none to make us afraid, to bless God for our share in the public tranquillity. 3. The prophet calls upon them sadly to lament the desolations that were coming upon them. He was himself the lamenting prophet, and called upon his people to join with him in his lamentations: *"O daughter of my people,* hear they God calling thee to weeping and mourning, and answer his call: do not only put on sackcloth for a day, but gird it on for thy constant wear; do not only put ashes on thy head, but *wallow thyself in ashes,* put thyself into close mourning, and use all the tokens of bitter lamentation, not forced and for show only, but with the greatest sincerity, as parents *mourn for an only son,* and think themselves comfortless because they are childless. Thus do thou lament for *the spoiler that suddenly comes upon us.* Though he has not come yet, he is *coming,* the decree has *gone forth:* let us therefore meet the execution of it with a suitable sadness." As saints may rejoice in hope of God's mercies, though they see them only in the promise, so sinners must mourn for fear of God's judgments, though they see them only in the threatenings.

V. He constitutes the prophet a judge over this people that now stand upon their trial: as *ch.* 1:10, *I have set thee over the nations;* so here, *I have set thee for a tower,* or as a sentinel, or a watchman, upon a tower, *among my people,* as an inspector of their actions, *that thou mayest know, and try their way, v.* 27. Not that God needed any to inform him concerning them; on the contrary, the prophet knew little of them in comparison but by the spirit of prophecy. But thus God appeals to the prophet himself, and his own observation concerning their character, that he might be fully satisfied in the equity of God's proceedings against them and with the more assurance give them warning of the judgments coming. God set him for a tower, conspicuous to all and attacked by many, but made him a *fortress,* a *strong tower,* gave him courage to stem the tide and bear the shock of their displeasure. Those that will be faithful reprovers have need to be firm as fortresses. Now in trying their way he will find two things: — 1. That they are wretchedly debauched (*v.* 28): *They are all grievous revolters, revolters of revolters* (so the word is), the worst of revolters, as a *servant of servants* is the meanest servant. They have a revolting heart, have deeply revolted, and revolt more and more. They seemed to start fair, but they revolt and start back. They *walk with slanders;* they make nothing of belying and backbiting one another, nay, they make a perfect trade of it; it is their constant course,

and they govern themselves by the slanders they hear, hating those that they hear ill-spoken of, though ever so unjustly. They are *brass and iron,* base metals, and there is nothing in them that is valuable. They were as silver and gold, but they have degenerated. Nay, as *they are all revolters,* so *they are all corrupters,* not only debauched themselves, but industrious to debauch others, to corrupt them as they themselves are corrupt; nay, to make them seven times more the children of hell than themselves. It is often so; sinners soon become tempters. 2. That they would never be reclaimed and reformed; it was in vain to think of reforming them, for various methods had been tried with them, and all to no purpose, *v.* 29, 30. He compares them to ore that was supposed to have some good metal in it, and was therefore put into the furnace by the refiner, who used all his art, and took abundance of pains, about it, but it proved all dross, nothing of any value could be extracted out of it. God by his prophets and by his providences had used the most proper means to refine this people and to purify them from their wickedness; but it was all in vain. By the continual preaching of the word, and in a series of afflictions, they had been kept in a constant fire, but all to no purpose. *The bellows* have been still kept so near the fire, to blow it, that they *are burnt* with the heat of it, or they are quite worn out with long use and thrown into the fire as good for nothing. The prophets have preached their throats sore with crying aloud against the sins of Israel, and yet they are not convinced and humbled. The *lead,* which was then used in refining silver, as quicksilver is now, *is consumed of the fire,* and has not done its work. *The founder melts in vain;* his labour is lost, *for the wicked are not plucked away,* no care is taken to separate between the precious and the vile, to purge out the old leaven, to cast out of communion those who, being corrupt themselves, are in danger of infecting others. Or, *Their wickednesses are not removed* (so some read it); they are still as bad as ever, and nothing will prevail to part between them and their sins. They will not be brought off from their idolatries and immoralities by all they have heard, and all they have felt, of the wrath of God against them; and therefore that doom is passed upon them (*v.* 30): *Reprobate silver shall they be called,* useless and worthless; they glitter as if they had some silver in them, but there is nothing of real virtue or goodness to be found among them; and for this reason the *Lord has rejected them.* He will no more own them as his people, nor look for any good from them; he will *take them away like dross* (Ps. 119:119), and prepare a consuming fire for those that would not be purified by a refining fire. By this it appears, (1.) That God has *no pleasure in the death* and ruin of sinners, for he tries all ways and methods with them to prevent their destruction and qualify them for salvation. Both his ordinances and his providences have a tendency this way, to part between them and their sins; and yet with many it is all lost labour. *We have piped unto you, and you have not danced; we have mourned unto you, and you have not wept.* Therefore, (2.) God will be justified in the death of sinners and all the blame will lie upon themselves. He did not reject them till he had used all proper means to reform them; did not cast them off so long as there was any hope of them, nor abandon them as dross till it appeared that they were *reprobate silver.*

CHAPTER 7

The prophet having in God's name reproved the people for their sins, and given them warning of the judgments of God that were coming upon them, in this chapter prosecutes the same intention for their humiliation and awakening. I. He shows them the invalidity of the plea they so much relied on, that they had the temple of God among them and constantly attended the service of it, and endeavours to take them off from their confidence in their external privileges and performances (*v.* 1–11). II. He reminds them of the desolations of Shiloh, and foretels that such should be the desolations of Jerusalem (*v.* 12–16). III. He represents to the prophet their abominable idolatries, for which he was thus incensed against them (*v.* 17–20). IV. He sets before the people that fundamental maxim of religion that "to obey is better than sacrifice" (1 Sa. 15:22), and that God would not accept the sacrifices of those that obstinately persisted in disobedience (*v.* 21–28). V. He threatens to lay the land utterly waste for their idolatry and impiety, and to multiply their slain as they had multiplied their sin (*v.* 29–34).

Verses 1–15

These verses begin another sermon, which is continued in this and the two following chapters, much to the same effect with those before, to reason them to repentance. Observe,

I. The orders given to the prophet to preach this sermon; for he had not only a general commission, but particular directions and instructions for every message he delivered. This was *a word* that *came to him from the Lord, v.* 1. We are not told when this sermon was to be preached; but are told, 1. Where it must be preached — *in the gate of the Lord's house,* through which they entered into the outer court, or the *court of the people.* It would affront the priests, and expose the prophet to their rage, to have such a message as this delivered within their precincts; but the prophet must not fear the face of man, he cannot be faithful to his God if he do. 2. To whom it must be preached — to the men of *Judah, that enter in at these gates to worship the Lord;* probably it was at one of three feasts, when all the males from all parts of the country were to appear before the Lord in the courts of his house, and not to *appear empty:* then he had many together to preach to, and that was the most seasonable time to admonish them not to trust to their privileges. Note, (1.) Even those that profess religion have need to be preached to as well as those that are without. (2.) It is desirable to have opportunity of preaching to many together. Wisdom chooses to cry *in the chief place of concourse,* and, as Jeremiah here, *in the opening of the gates,* the temple-gates. (3.) When we are going to worship God we have need to be admonished to *worship him in the spirit,* and *to have no confidence in the flesh,* Phil. 3:3.

II. The contents and scope of the sermon itself. It is delivered in the name of *the Lord of hosts, the God of Israel,* who commands the world, but covenants with his people. As creatures we are bound to regard the *Lord of hosts,* as Christians *the God of Israel;* what he said to them he says to us, and it is much the same with that which John Baptist said to those whom he baptized (Mt. 3:8, 9), *Bring forth fruits meet for repentance; and think not to say within yourselves, We have Abraham to our father.* The prophet here tells them,

1. What were the true words of God, which they might trust to. In short, they might depend upon it that if they would repent and reform their lives, and return to God in a way of duty, he would restore and confirm their peace, would redress their grievances, and return to them in a way of mercy (*v.* 3): *Amend your ways and your doings.* This implies that there had been much amiss in their ways and doings, many faults and errors. But it is a great instance of the favour of God to them that he gives them liberty to amend, shows them where and how they must amend, and promises to accept them upon their amendment: *"I will cause you to dwell* quietly and peaceably *in this place,* and a stop shall be put to that which threatens your expulsion." Reformation is the only way, and a sure way to ruin. He explains himself (*v.* 5–7), and tells them particularly,

(1.) What the amendment was which he expected from them. They must *thoroughly amend;* in *making good,* they must *make good their ways and doings;* they must reform with resolution, and it must be a universal, constant, preserving reformation — not partial, but entire — not hypocritical, but sincere — not wavering, but constant. They must make the tree good, and so make the fruit good, must amend their hearts and thoughts, and so amend their ways and doings. In particular, [1.] They must be honest and just in all their dealings. Those that had power in their hands must *thoroughly execute judgment between a man and his neighbour,* without partiality, and according as the merits of the cause appeared. They must not either in judgment or in contract *oppress the stranger, the fatherless, or the widow,* nor countenance or protect those that did oppress, nor refuse to do them justice when they sought for it. They must *not shed innocent blood,* and with it defile *this place* and the land wherein they dwelt. [2.] They must keep closely to the worship of the true God only: *"Neither walk after other gods;* do not hanker after them, nor hearken to those that would draw you into communion with idolaters; for it is, and will be, *to your own hurt.* Be not only so just to your God, but so wise for yourselves, as not to throw away your adorations upon those who are not able to help you, and thereby provoke him who is able to destroy you." Well, this is all that God insists upon.

(2.) He tells them what the establishment is which, upon this amendment, they may expect from him (*v.* 7): "Set about such a work of reformation as this with all speed, go through with it, and abide by it; *and I will cause you to dwell in this place,* this temple; it shall continue your place of resort and refuge, the place of your comfortable meeting with God and one another; and you shall dwell *in the land that I gave to your fathers for ever and ever,* and it shall never be turned out either from God's house or from your own." It is promised that they shall still enjoy their civil and sacred privileges, that they shall have a comfortable enjoyment of them: *I will cause you to dwell here;* and those dwell at ease to whom God gives a settlement. They shall enjoy it by covenant, by virtue of the grant made of it to their fathers, not by providence, but by promise. They shall continue in the enjoyment of it without eviction or molestation; they shall not be disturbed, much less dispossessed, *for ever and ever;* nothing but sin could throw them out. An everlasting inheritance in the heavenly Canaan is hereby secured to all that live in godliness and honesty. And the vulgar Latin reads a further privilege here, *v.* 3, 7. *Habitabo vobiscum — I will dwell with you in this place;* and we should find Canaan itself but an uncomfortable place to dwell in if God did not dwell with us there.

2. What were the lying words of their own hearts, which they must not trust to. He cautions them against this self-deceit (*v.* 4): *"Trust no in lying words.* You are told in what way, and upon what terms, you may be easy safe, and happy; now do not flatter yourselves with an opinion that you may be so on any other terms, or in any other way." Yet he charges them with this self-deceit arising from vanity (*v.* 8): *"Behold,* it is plain that *you* do *trust in lying words,* notwithstanding what is said to you; you trust in *words that cannot profit;* you rely upon a plea that will stand you in no stead." Those that slight the words of truth, which would profit them, take shelter in words of falsehood, which cannot profit them. Now these lying words were, *"The temple of the Lord, the temple of the Lord, the temple of the Lord are these.* These buildings, the courts, the holy place, and the holy of holies, are the *temple of the Lord,* built by his appointment, to his glory; here he resides, here he is worshipped, here we meet three times a year to pay our homage to him as our King in his palace." This they thought was security enough to them to keep God and his favours from leaving them, God and his judgments from breaking in upon them. When the prophets told them how sinful they were, and how miserable they were likely to be, still they appealed to the temple: "How can we be either so or so, as long as we have that holy happy place among us?" The prophet repeats it because they repeated it upon all occasions. It was the cant of the times; it was in their mouths upon all occasions. If they heard an awakening sermon, if any startling piece of news was brought to them, they lulled themselves asleep again with this, "We cannot but do well, for we have *the temple of the Lord among us."* Note, The privileges of a *form of godliness* are often the pride and confidence of those that are strangers and enemies to the power of it. It is common for those that are furthest from God to boast themselves most of their being near to the church. They are *haughty because of the holy mountain* (Zep. 3:11), as if God's mercy were so tied to them that they might defy his justice. Now to convince them what a frivolous plea this was, and what little stead it would stand them in,

(1.) He shows them the gross absurdity of it in itself. If they knew any thing either of the *temple of the Lord* or of the *Lord of the temple,* they must think that to plead that, either in excuse of their sin against God or in arrest of God's judgment against them, was the most ridiculous unreasonable thing that could be. [1.] God is a holy God; but this plea made him the patron of sin, of the worst of sins, which even the light of nature condemns, *v.* 9, 10. "What," says he, *"will you steal, murder, and commit adultery,* be guilty of the vilest immoralities, and which the common interest, as well as the common sense, of mankind witness against? *Will you swear falsely,* a crime which all nations (who with the belief of a God have had a veneration for an oath) have always had a horror of? Will *you burn incense to Baal,* a dunghill-deity, that sets up as a rival with the great Jehovah, and, not content with that, *will you walk after other gods* too, *whom you know not,* and by all these crimes put a daring affront upon God, both as *the Lord of hosts* and as the *God of Israel?* Will you exchange a God of whose power and goodness you have had such a long experience for gods of whose ability and willingness to help you you know nothing? And, when you have thus done the worst you can against God, will you brazen your faces so far as to come and *stand before him in this house which is called by his name* and in which his name is called upon — stand before him as servants waiting his commands, as supplicants expecting his favour? Will you act in open rebellion against him, and yet herd among his subjects, among the best of them? By this, it should seem, you think that either he does not discover or does not dislike your wicked practices, to imagine either of which is to put the highest indignity possible upon him. It is as if you should say, *We are delivered to do all these abominations."* If they had not the front to say this, *totidem verbis — in so many words,* yet their actions spoke it aloud. They could not but own that God, even their own God, had many a time delivered them, and been a present help to them, when otherwise they must have perished. He, in delivering them, designed to reduce them to himself, and by his goodness to lead them to repentance; but they resolved to persist in their abominations notwithstanding. As soon as they were delivered (as of old in the days of the Judges) they *did evil again in the sight of the Lord,* which was in effect to say, in direct contradiction to the true intent and meaning of the providences which had affected them, that God had delivered them in order to put them again into a capacity of rebelling against him, by sacrificing the more profusely to their idols. Note, Those who continue in sin because grace has abounded, or that grace may abound, do in effect their idols. Note, Those who continue in sin because grace has abounded, or that grace may abound, do in effect make Christ the minister of sin. Some take it thus: "You present yourselves before God with your sacrifices and sin-offerings, and then say, *We are delivered,* we are discharged from our guilt, now it shall do us no hurt; when all this is but to blind the world, and stop the mouth of conscience, that you may, the more easily to yourselves and the more plausibly before others, *do all these abominations."* [2.] His temple was a holy place; but this plea made it a protection to the most unholy persons: *"Has this house, which is called by my name* and is a standing sign of God's kingdom of sin and Satan — *has this become a den of robbers in your eyes?* Do you think it was built to be not only a rendezvous of, but a refuge and shelter to, the vilest of malefactors?" No; though the horns of the altar were a sanctuary to him that slew a man unawares, yet they were not so to a wilful murderer, nor to one that did aught presumptuously, Ex. 21:14; 1 Ki. 2:29. Those that think to excuse themselves in unchristian practices with the Christian name, and sin the more boldly and securely because there is a sin-offering provided, do, in effect, make God's house of prayer a den of thieves, as the priests in Christ's time, Mt. 21:13. But could they thus impose upon God? No: *Behold, I have seen it, saith the Lord,* have seen the real iniquity through the counterfeit and dissembled piety. Note, Though men may deceive one another with the appearances of devotion, yet they cannot deceive God.

(2.) He shows them the insufficiency of this plea adjudged long since in the case of Shiloh. [1.] It is certain that Shiloh was ruined, though it had God's sanctuary in it, when by its wickedness it profaned that sanctuary (*v.* 12): *Go you now to my place which was in Shiloh.* It is probable that the ruins of that once flourishing city were yet remaining; they might, at least, read the history of it, which ought to affect them as if they saw the place. There God *set his name at the first,* there the tabernacle was set up when Israel first took possession of Canaan (Jn. 18:1), and thither the tribes went up; but those that attended the service of the tabernacle there corrupted both themselves and others, and from them arose the *wickedness of his people Israel;* that fountain was poisoned, and sent forth malignant streams; and what came of it? No; God *forsook* it (Ps. 78:60), sent his ark into captivity, cut off the house of Eli that presided there; and it is very probable that the city was quite destroyed, for we never read any more of it but as a monument of divine vengeance upon holy places when they harbour wicked people. Note, God's judgments upon others, who have really revolted from God while they have kept up a profession of nearness to him, should be a warning to us not to *trust in lying words.* It is good to consult precedents, and make use of them. *Remember Lot's wife;* remember Shiloh and the seven churches of Asia; and know that the ark and candlestick are moveable things, Rev. 2:5; Mt. 21:43. [2.] It is as certain that Shiloh's fate will be Jerusalem's doom if a speedy and sincere repentance prevent it not. *First,* Jerusalem was now as sinful as ever Shiloh was; that is proved by the unerring testimony of God himself against them (*v.* 13): *"You have done all these works,* you cannot deny it:" and they continued obstinate in their sin; that is proved by the testimony of God's return and repent, *rising up early and speaking,* as one in care, as one in earnest, as one who would lose no time in dealing with them, nay, who would take the fittest opportunity for speaking to them early *in the morning,* when, if ever, they were sober, and had their thoughts free and clear; but it was all in vain. God spoke, but they *heard not,* they heeded not, they never minded; he *called them,* but they *answered not;* they would not come at his call. Note, What God has spoken to us greatly aggravates what we have done against him. *Secondly,* Jerusalem shall shortly be as miserable as ever Shiloh was: *Therefore I will do unto this house as I did to Shiloh,* ruin it, and lay it waste, *v.* 14. Those that tread in the steps of the wickedness of those that went before them must expect to fall by the like judgments, for all these things *happened to them for ensamples.* The temple at Jerusalem, though ever so strongly built, if wickedness was found in it, would be as unable to keep its ground and as easily conquered as even the tabernacle in Shiloh was, when God's day of vengeance had come. "This house" (says God) "is *called by my name,* and therefore you may think that I should protect it; it is the house *in which you trust,* and you think that it will protect you; this land is *the place,* this city *the place, which I gave to you and your fathers,* and therefore you are secure of the continuance of it, and think that nothing can turn you out of it; but the men of Shiloh thus flattered themselves and did but deceive themselves." He quotes another precedent (*v.* 15), the ruin of the kingdom of the ten tribes, who were the seed of Abraham, and had the covenant of circumcision, and possessed the land which God gave to them and their fathers, and yet the idolatries threw them out and extirpated them: "And can you think but that the same evil courses will be as fatal to you?" Doubtless they will be so; for God is uniform and of a piece with himself in his judicial proceedings. It is a rule of justice, *ut parium par sit ratio — that in similar cases the same judgment should proceed.* "You have corrupted *yourselves as your brethren* the *seed of Ephraim* did, and have become their brethren in iniquity, and therefore I will *cast you out of my sight, as I have cast them."* The interpretation here given of the judgment makes it a terrible one indeed; the casting of them out of their land signified God's casting them out of his sight, as if he would never look upon them, never look after them, more. Whenever we are cast, it is well enough, if we be kept in the love of God; but, if we are thrown out of his favour, our case is miserable though we dwell in our own land. This threatening, that God would make this house like Shiloh, we shall meet with again, and find Jeremiah indicted for it, *ch.* 26:6.

Verses 16–20

God had shown them, in the foregoing verses, that the temple and the service of it, of which they boasted and in which they trusted, should not avail to prevent the judgment threatened. But there was another thing which might stand them in some stead, and which yet they had no value for, and that was the prophet's intercession for them; his prayers would do them more good than their own pleas: now here that support is taken from them; and their case is said indeed who have lost their interest in the prayers of God's ministers and people.

I. God here forbids the prophet to pray for them (*v.* 16): "The decree has gone forth, their ruin is resolved on, therefore *pray not thou for this people,* that is, pray not for the preventing of this judgment threatened; they have *sinned unto death,* and therefore pray not for their life, but for the life of their souls," 1 Jn. 5:16. See here, 1. That God's prophets are praying men; Jeremiah foretold the destruction of Judah and Jerusalem, and yet prayed for their preservation, not knowing that the decree was absolute; and it is the will of God that we *pray for the peace of Jerusalem.* Even when we threaten sinners with damnation we must pray for their salvation, that they may *turn and live.* Jeremiah was hated, and persecuted, and reproached, by the children of his people, and yet he prayed for them; for it becomes us to render good for evil. 2. That God's praying prophets have a great interest in heaven, how little soever they have on earth. When God has determined to destroy this people, he bespeaks the prophet not to pray for them, because he would not have his prayers to lie (as prophets' prayers seldom did) unanswered. God said to Moses, *Let me alone,* Ex. 22:10. 3. It is an ill omen to a people when God restrains the spirits of his ministers and people from praying for them, and gives them to see their case so desperate that they have no heart to speak a good word for them. 4. Those that will not regard good ministers' preaching cannot expect any benefit by their praying. If you will not hear us when we speak from God to you, God will not hear us when we speak to him for you.

II. He gives him a reason for this prohibition. Praying breath is too precious a thing to be lost and thrown away upon a people hardened in sin and marked for ruin.

1. They are resolved to persist in their rebellion against God, and will not be turned back by the prophet's preaching. For this he appeals to the prophet himself, and his own inspection and observation (*v.* 17): *Seest thou not what they do openly and publicly,* without either shame or fear, *in the cities of Judah and in the streets of Jerusalem?* This intimates both that the sin was evident and could not be denied and that the sinners were impudent and would not be reclaimed; they committed their wickedness even in the prophet's presence and under his eye; he saw what they did, and yet they did it, which was an affront to his office, and to him whose officer he was, and bade defiance to both. Now observe,

(1.) What the sin is with which they are here charged — it is idolatry, *v.* 18. Their idolatrous respects are paid to the *queen of heaven,* the moon, either in an image or in the original, or both. They worshipped it probably under the name of *Ashtaroth,* or some other of their goddesses, being in love with the brightness in which they saw the moon walk, and thinking themselves indebted to her for her benign influences or fearing her malignant ones, Job 31:26. The worshipping of the moon was much in use among the heathen nations, *ch.* 44:17, 19. Some read it the *frame* or *workmanship of heaven.* The whole celestial globe with all its ornaments and powers was the object of their adoration. They *worshipped the host of heaven,* Acts 7:42. The homage they should have paid to their Prince they paid to the statues that beautified the frontispiece of his palace; they worshipped the creatures instead of him that made them, the servants instead of him that commands them, and the gifts instead of him that gave them. *With the queen of heaven* they worshipped *other gods,* images of things not only in *heaven above, but in earth beneath, and in the waters under the earth;* for those that forsake the true God wander endlessly after false ones. To these deities of their own making they offer *cakes* for meat-offerings, and *pour out drink-offerings,* as if they had their meat and drink from them and were obliged to make to them their acknowledgments: and see how busy they are, and how every hand is employed in the service of these idols, according as they used to be employed in their domestic services. *The children* were sent to *gather wood; the fathers kindled the fire* to heat the oven, being of the poorer sort that could not afford to keep servants to do it, yet they would rather do it themselves than it should be undone; *the women kneaded the dough* with their own hands, for perhaps, though they had servants to do it, they took a pride in showing their zeal for their idols by doing it themselves. Let us be instructed, even by this bad example, in the service of our God. [1.] Let us *honour him with our substance,* as those that have our subsistence from him, and eat and drink to the glory of him from whom we have our meat and drink. [2.] Let us not decline the hardest services, nor disdain to stoop to the meanest, by which God may be honoured; for none shall *kindle a fire on God's altar for nought.* Let us think it an honour to be employed in any work for God. [3.] Let us bring up our children in the acts of devotion; let them, as they are capable, be employed in doing something towards the keeping up of religious exercises.

(2.) What is the direct tendency of this sin: "It is *that they may provoke me to anger;* they cannot design any thing else in it. But (*v.* 19) *do they provoke me to anger?* Is it because I am hard to be pleased, or easily provoked? Or am I to bear the blame of the resentment? No; it is their

own doing; they may thank themselves, and they alone shall bear it." *Is it against God that they provoke him to wrath?* Is he the worse for it? Does it do him any real damage? No; is *it not against themselves,* to the *confusion of their own faces?* It is malice against God, but it is impotent malice; it cannot hurt him: nay, it is foolish malice; it will hurt themselves. They show their spite against God, but they do the spite to themselves. Canst thou think any other than that a people, thus desperately set upon their own ruin, should be abandoned?

2. God is resolved to proceed in his judgments against them, and will not be turned back by the prophet's prayers (*v.* 20): *Thus saith the Lord God,* and what he saith he will not unsay, nor can all the world gainsay it; hear it therefore, and tremble. *"Behold, my anger and my fury shall be poured out upon this place,* as the flood of waters was upon the old world or the shower of fire and brimstone upon Sodom; since they will anger me, let them see what will come of it." They shall soon find, (1.) That there is no escaping this deluge of fire, either by flying from it or fencing against it; it shall be poured out on *this place,* though it be a holy place, the Lord's house. It shall reach both *man and beast,* like the plagues of Egypt, and, like some of them, shall destroy the *trees of the field and the fruit of the ground,* which they had designed and *prepared for Baal,* and of which they had made *cakes to the queen of heaven.* (2.) There is no extinguishing it: *It shall burn and shall not be quenched;* prayers and tears shall then avail nothing. When *his wrath is kindled but a little,* much more when it is kindled to such a degree, there shall be no quenching it. God's wrath is that fire unquenchable which eternity itself will not see the period of. *Depart, you cursed, into everlasting fire.*

Verses 21–28

God, having shown the people that the temple would not protect them while they polluted it with their wickedness, here shows them that their sacrifices would not atone for them, nor be accepted, while they went on in disobedience. See with what contempt he here speaks of their ceremonial service (*v.* 21). *"Put your burnt-offerings to your sacrifices;* go on in them as long as you please; add one sort of sacrifice to another; turn your *burntofferings* (which were to be wholly burnt to the honour of God) into *peace-offerings"* (which the offerer himself had a considerable share of), "that you may *eat flesh,* for that is all the good you are likely to have from your sacrifices, a good meal's meat or two; but expect not any other benefit by them while you live at this loose rate. *Keep your sacrifices to yourselves"* (so some understand it); "let them be served up at your own table, for they are no way acceptable at God's altars." For the opening of this,

I. He shows them that obedience was the only thing he required of them, *v.* 22, 23. He appeals to the original contract, by which they were first formed into a people, when they were brought out of Egypt. God made them a *kingdom of priests* to himself, not that he might be regaled with their sacrifices, as the devils, whom the heathen worshipped, which are represented as eating with pleasure the fat of their sacrifices and drinking the wine of their drink-offerings, Deu. 32:38. No: *Will God eat the flesh of bulls?* Ps. 50:13. *I spoke not to your fathers concerning burnt-offerings or sacrifices,* not of them *at first.* The precepts of the moral law were given before the ceremonial institutions; and those came afterwards, as trials of their obedience and assistances to their repentance and faith. The Levitical law begins thus: *If any man of you will bring an offering,* he must do so and so (Lev. 1:2, 2:1), as if it were intended rather to regulate sacrifice than to require it. But that which God commanded, which he bound them to by his supreme authority and which he insisted upon as the condition of the covenant, was, *Obey my voice;* see Ex. 15:26, where this was the statute and the ordinance by which God proved them: *Hearken diligently to the voice of the Lord thy God.* The condition of their being God's peculiar people was this (Ex. 19:5), *If you will obey my voice indeed.* "Make conscience of the duties of natural religion, observe positive institutions from a principle of obedience, and then *I will be your God and you shall be my people,"* which is the greatest honour, happiness, and satisfaction, that any of the children of men are capable of. "Let your conversation be regular, and in every thing study to com-

ply with the will and word of God; *walk* within the bounds that I have set you, and *in all the ways that I have commanded you,* and then you may assure yourselves that *it shall be well with you."* The demand here is very reasonable, that we should be directed by Infinite Wisdom to that which is fit, that he that made us should command us, and that he should give us law who gives us our being and all the supports of it; and the promise is very encouraging: Let God's will be your rule and his favour shall be your felicity.

II. He shows them that disobedience was the only thing for which he had a quarrel with them. *He would not reprove them for their sacrifices,* for the omission of them; they had been *continually before him* (Ps. 50:8); with them they hoped to bribe God, and purchase a license to go on in sin. That therefore which God had all along laid to their charge was breaking his commandments in the course of their conversation, while they observed them, in some instances, in the course of their devotion, *v.* 24, 25, etc. 1. They set up their own will in competition with the will of God: *They hearkened not* to God and to his law; they never heeded that; it was to them as if it had never been given or were of no force; they *inclined not their ear* to attend to it, much less their hearts to comply with it. But they would have their own way, would do as they chose, and not as they were bidden. *Their own counsels* were their guide, and not the dictates of divine wisdom; that shall be lawful and good with them which they think so, though the word of God says quite contrary. *The imagination of their evil heart,* the appetites and passions of it, shall be a law to them, and they will walk in the way of it, and in the sight of their eyes. 2. If they began well, yet they did not proceed, but soon flew off. They *went backward,* when they talked of making a captain, and returning to Egypt again, and would not go forward under God's conduct. They promised fair: *All that the Lord shall say unto us we well do;* and, if they would but have kept in that good mind, all would have been well; but, instead of going on in the way of duty, they drew back into the way of sin, and were worse than ever. 3. When God sent to them by word of mouth to put them in mind of the written word, which was the business of the prophets, it was all one; still they were disobedient. God had servants of his among them in every age, *since they came out of Egypt unto this day,* some or other to tell them of their faults and put them in mind of their duty, whom he *rose up early to send* (as before, *v.* 13), as men rise up early to call servants to their work; but they were as deaf to the prophets as they were to the law (*v.* 26): *Yet they hearkened not, nor inclined their ear.* This had been their way and manner all along; they were of the same stubborn refractory disposition with those that went before them; it had all along been the genius of the nation, and an evil genius it was, that continually haunted them till it ruined them at last. 4. Their practice and character were still the same. They are worse, and not better, *than their fathers.* (1.) Jeremiah can himself witness against them that they were disobedient, or he shall soon find it so (*v.* 27): *"Thou shalt speak all these words to them,* shalt particularly charge them with disobedience and obstinacy. But even that will not work upon them: *They will not hearken to thee,* nor heed thee. Thou shalt go, and *call to them* with all the plainness and earnestness imaginable, but *they will not answer thee;* they will either give thee no answer at all or not an obedient answer; they will not come at thy call." (2.) He must therefore own that they deserved the character of a disobedient people, that were ripe for destruction, and must go to them and tell them so to their faces (*v.* 28): *"Say unto them,* This is a nation that obeys not the voice of the Lord their God.* They are notorious for their obstinacy; they sacrifice to the Lord as their God, but they will not be ruled by him as their God; they will not receive either the instruction of his word or the correction of his rod; they will not be reclaimed or reformed by either. *Truth has perished* among them; they cannot receive it; they will not submit to it nor be governed by it. They will not speak truth; there is no believing a word they say, for it is *cut off from their mouth,* and lying comes in the room of it. They are false both to God and man."

Verses 29–34

Here is, I. A loud call to weeping and mourning. Jerusalem, that had been a joyous city, the joy of the whole earth, must now *take up a lamentation on high places* (v. 29), the high places where they had served their idols; there must they now bemoan their misery. In token both of sorrow and slavery, Jerusalem must now *cut off her hair and cast it away;* the word is peculiar to the hair of the Nazarites, which was the badge and token of their dedication to God, and it is called *their crown.* Jerusalem had been a city which was a Nazarite to God, but now must *cut off her hair,* must be profaned, degraded, and separated from God, as she had been separated to him. It is time for those that have lost their holiness to lay aside their joy.

II. Just cause given for this great lamentation.

1. The sin of Jerusalem appears here very heinous, nowhere worse, or more exceedingly sinful (v. 30): "*The children of Judah*" (God's profession people, that *came forth out of the waters of Judah,* Isa. 48:1) "*have done evil in my sight,* under my eye, in my presence; they have affronted me to my face, which very much aggravates the affront:" or, "They have done that which they know to be *evil in my sight,* and in the highest degree offensive to me." Idolatry was the sin which was above all other sins evil in God's sight. Now here are two things charged upon them in their idolatry, which were very provoking: (1.) That they were very impudent in it towards God and set him at defiance: *They have set their abominations* (their abominable idols and the altars erected to them) *in the house that is called by my name,* in the very courts of the temple, *to pollute it* (Manasseh did so, 2 Ki. 21:7, 23:12), as if they thought God would connive at it, or cared not though he was ever so much displeased with it, or as if they would reconcile heaven and hell, God and Baal. The heart is the place which God has chosen to *put his name there;* if sin have the innermost and uppermost place there, we pollute the temple of the Lord, and therefore he resents nothing more than *setting up idols in the heart,* Eze. 14:4. (2.) That they were very barbarous in it towards their own children, v. 31. They have particularly *built the high places of Tophet,* where the image of Moloch was set up, *in the valley of the son of Hinnom,* adjoining to Jerusalem; and there *they burnt their sons and their daughters in the fire,* burnt them alive, killed them, and killed them in the most cruel manner imaginable, to honour or appease those idols that were devils and not gods. This was surely the greatest instance that ever was of the power of Satan in the children of disobedience, and of the degeneracy and corruption of the human nature. One would willingly hope that there were not many instances of such a barbarous idolatry; but it is amazing that there should be any, that men could be so perfectly void of natural affection as to do a thing so inhuman as to burn little innocent children, and their own too, that they should be so perfectly void of natural religion as to think it lawful to do this, nay, to think it acceptable. Surely it was in a way of righteous judgment, because they had changed the glory of God into the similitude of a beast, that God gave them up to such vile affections that changed them into worse than beasts. God says of this that it was *what he commanded them not, neither cam it into his heart,* which is not meant of his not commanding them thus to worship Moloch (this he had expressly *forbidden* them), but he had never commanded that his worshippers should be at such an expense, nor put such a force upon their natural affection, in honouring him; it never came into his heart to have children offered to him, yet they had forsaken his service for the service of such gods as, by commanding this, showed themselves to be indeed enemies to mankind.

2. The destruction of Jerusalem appears here very terrible. That speaks misery enough in general (v. 29), *The Lord hath rejected and forsaken the generation of his wrath.* Sin makes those the generation of God's wrath that had ben the generation of his love. And God will reject and quite forsake those who have thus made themselves *vessels of wrath fitted to destruction.* He will disown them for his. "Verily, I say unto you, I know you not." And he will give them up to the terrors of their own guilt, and leave them in those hands. (1.) Death shall triumph over them, v. 32. 33. Sin reigns unto death; for that is the wages of it, the end of those things. *Tophet,* the valley adjoining to Jerusalem, *shall be called the valley of slaughter,* for there multitudes shall be slain, when, in their sallies out of the

city and their attempts to escape, they fall into the hands of the besiegers. Or it shall be called *the valley of slaughtered ones,* because thither the corpses of those that are slain shall be brought to be buried, all other burying places being full; and there they shall bury *until there be no more place* to make a grave. This intimates the multitude of those that shall die by the sword, pestilence, and famine. Death shall ride on prosperously, with dreadful pomp and power, *conquering and to conquer. The slain of the Lord shall be many.* This valley of Tophet was a place where the citizens of Jerusalem walked to take the air; but it shall now be spoiled for that use, for it shall be so full of graves that there shall be no walking there, because of the danger of contracting a ceremonial pollution by the touch of a grave. There it was that they sacrificed some of their children, and dedicated others to Moloch, and there they should fall as victims to divine justice. Tophet had formerly been the burying place, or burning place, of the dead bodies of the besiegers, when the Assyrian army was routed by an angel; and for this it was *ordained of old,* Isa. 30:33. But they having forgotten this mercy, and made it the place of their sin, God will now turn it into a burying place for the besieged. In allusion to this valley, hell is in the New Testament called *Gehenna — the valley of Hinnom,* for there were buried both the invading Assyrians and the revolting Jews; so hell is a receptacle after death both for infidels and hypocrites, the open enemies of God's church and its treacherous friends; it is *the congregation of the dead;* it is prepared for the *generation of God's wrath.* But so great shall that slaughter be that even the spacious valley of Tophet shall not be able to contain the slain; and at length there shall not be enough left alive to bury the dead, so that *the carcases of the people shall be meat* for the birds and beasts of prey, that shall feed upon them like carrion, and none shall have the concern or courage to frighten them away, as Rizpah did from the dead bodies of Saul's sons, 2 Sa. 28:26, *Thy carcase shall be meat to the fowls and beasts, and no man shall drive them away.* Thus do the law and the prophets agree, and the execution with both. The decent burying of the dead is a piece of humanity, in remembrance of what the dead body has been — the tabernacle of a reasonable soul. Nay, it is a piece of divinity, in expectation of what the dead body shall be at the resurrection. The want of it has sometimes been an instance of the rage of men against God's witnesses, Rev. 11:9. Here it is threatened as an instance of the wrath of God against his enemies, and is an intimation that *evil pursues sinners* even after death. (2.) Joy shall depart from them (v. 34): *Then will I cause to cease the voice of mirth.* God had *called* by his prophets, and by less judgments, *to weeping and mourning;* but they walked contrary to him, and would hear of nothing but joy and gladness, Isa. 22:12, 13. And what came of it? Now God *called* to lamentation (v. 29), and he made his call effectual, leaving them neither cause nor heart for joy and gladness. Those that will not weep shall weep; those that will not by the grace of God be cured of their vain mirth shall by the justice of God be deprived of all mirth; for *when God judges he will overcome.* It is threatened here that there shall be nothing to rejoice in. There shall be none of the joy of weddings; no mirth, for there shall be no marriages. The comforts of life shall be abandoned, and all care to keep up mankind upon earth cast off; there shall be none of *the voice of the bridegroom* and the *bride,* no music, no nuptial songs. Nor shall there be any more of the joy of the harvest, *for the land shall be desolate,* uncultivated and unimproved. Both *the cities of Judah and the streets of Jerusalem* shall look thus melancholy; and when they thus look about them, and see no cause to rejoice, no marvel if they retire into themselves and find no heart to rejoice. Note, God can soon mar the mirth of the most jovial, and make it to cease, which is a reason why we should always rejoice with trembling, be merry and wise.

CHAPTER 8

The prophet proceeds, in this chapter, both to magnify and to justify the destruction that God was bringing upon this people, to show how grievous it would be and yet how righteous. I. He represents the judgments coming as so very terrible that death should appear so as most to be dreaded and yet should be desired (v. 1–3) II. He aggravates the wretched stupidity and wilfulness of this people as that which brought this ruin upon them

(v. 4–12). III. He describes the great confusion and consternation that the whole land should be in upon the alarm of it (v. 13–17). IV. The prophet is himself deeply affected with it and lays it very much to heart (v. 18–22).

Verses 1–3

These verses might fitly have been joined to the close of the foregoing chapter, as giving a further description of the dreadful desolation which the army of the Chaldeans should make in the land. It shall strangely alter the property of death itself, and for the worse too.

I. Death shall not now be, as it always used to be — the repose of the dead. When Job makes his court to the grave it is in hope of this, that *there he shall rest with kings and counsellors of the earth;* but now the ashes of the dead, even of *kings* and *princes,* shall be disturbed, and their *bones scattered at the grave's mouth,* Ps. 141:7. It was threatened in the close of the former chapter that the slain should be unburied; that might be through neglect, and was not so strange; but here we find the graves of those that were buried industriously and maliciously opened by the victorious enemy, who either for covetousness, hoping to find treasure in the graves, or for spite to the nation and in a rage against it, *brought out the bones of the kings of Judah and the princes.* The dignity of their sepulchres could not secure them, nay, did the more expose them to be rifled; but it was base and barbarous thus to trample upon royal dust. We will hope that the bones of good Josiah were not disturbed, because he piously protected the bones of the man of God when he burnt the bones of the idolatrous priests, 2 Ki. 23:18. The bones of the priests and prophets too were digged up and thrown about. Some think the false prophets and the idol-priests, God putting this mark of ignominy upon them: but, if they were God's prophets and his priests, it is what the Psalmist complains of as the fruit of the outrage of the enemies, Ps. 79:1, 2. Nay, those of the spiteful Chaldeans that could not reach to violate the sepulchres of princes and priests would rather play at small game than sit out, and therefore pulled the bones of the ordinary *inhabitants of Jerusalem out of their graves.* The barbarous nations were sometimes guilty of these absurd and inhuman triumphs over those they had conquered, and God permitted it here, for a mark of his displeasure against the generation of his wrath, and for terror to those that survived. The bones, being dug out of the graves, were spread abroad upon the face of the earth in contempt, and to make the reproach the more spreading and lasting. They spread them to be dried that they might carry them about in triumph, or might make fuel of them, or make some superstitious use of them. *They shall be spread before the sun* (for they shall not be ashamed openly to avow the fact at noon day) and before *the moon and stars,* even *all the host of heaven,* whom they have made idols of, v. 2. From the mention of the *sun, moon, and stars,* which should be the unconcerned spectators of this tragedy, the prophet takes occasion to show how they had idolized them, and paid those respects to them which they should have paid to God only, that it might be observed how little they got by worshipping the creature, for the creatures they worshipped when they were in distress saw it, but regarded it not, nor gave them any relief, but were rather pleased to see those abused in being vilified by whom they had been abused in being deified. See how their respects to their idols are enumerated, to show how we ought to behave towards our God. 1. They *loved* them. As amiable being and bountiful benefactors they esteemed them and delighted in them, and therefore did all that follows. 2. They *served* them, did all they could in honour of them, and thought nothing too much; they conformed to all the laws of their superstition, without disputing. 3. They *walked after* them, strove to imitate and resemble them, according to the characters and accounts of them they had received, which gave rise and countenance to much of the abominable wickedness of the heathen. 4. They *sought* them, consulted them as oracles, appealed to them as judges, implored their favour, and prayed to them as their benefactors. 5. They *worshipped* them, gave them divine honour, as having a sovereign dominion over them. Before these light of heaven, which they had courted, shall their dead bodies be cast, and left to putrefy, and to be *as dung upon the face of the earth;* and the sun's shining upon them will but make them the more noisome and offensive. Whatever we make a god of but the true God only, it will stand us in no stead on the other side death and the grave, nor for the body, much less for the soul.

II. Death shall now be what it never used to be — the choice of the living, not because there appears in it any thing delightsome; on the contrary, death never appeared in more horrid frightful shapes than now, when they cannot promise themselves either a comfortable death or a human burial; and yet every thing in this world shall become so irksome, and all the prospects so black and dismal, that *death shall be chosen rather than life* (v. 3), not in a believing hope of happiness in the other life, but in an utter despair of any ease in this life. The nation is now reduced to a *family,* so small is the *residue of those that remain* in it; and it is an *evil family,* still as bad as ever, their hearts unhumbled and their lusts unmortified. These *remain* alive (and that is all) in the many *places whither they were driven* by the judgments of God, some prisoners in the country of their enemies, others beggars in their neighbour's country, and others fugitives and vagabonds there and in their own country. And, though those that died died very miserably, yet those that survived and were thus driven out should live yet more miserably, so that they should *choose death rather than life,* and wish a thousand times that they had fallen with those that fell by the sword. Let this cure us of the inordinate love of life, that the case may be such that it may become a burden and terror, and we may be strongly tempted to *choose strangling* and death rather.

Verses 4–12

The prophet here is instructed to set before this people the folly of their impenitence, which was it that brought this ruin upon them. They are here represented as the most stupid senseless people in the world, that would not be made wise by all the methods that Infinite Wisdom took to bring them to themselves and their right mind, and so to prevent the ruin that was coming upon them.

I. They would not attend to the dictates of reason. They would not act in the affairs of their souls with the same common prudence with which they acted in other things. Sinners would become saints if they would but show themselves men, and religion would soon rule them if right reason might. Observe it here. *Come, and let us reason together, saith the Lord* (v. 4, 5): *Shall men fall and not arise?* If men happen to fall to the ground, to fall into the dirt, will they not get up again as fast as they can? They are not such fools as to lie still when they are down. Shall *a man turn aside* out of the right way? Yes, the most careful traveller may miss his way; but then, as soon as he is aware of it, *will he not return?* Yes, certainly he will, with all speed, and will thank him that showed him his mistake. Thus men do in other things. *Why then has this people of Jerusalem slidden back by a perpetual backsliding?* Why do not they, when they have fallen into sin, hasten to get up again by repentance? Why do not they, when they see they have missed their way, correct their error and reform? No man in his wits will go on in a way that he knows will never bring him to his journey's end; *why then has this people slidden back by a perpetual backsliding?* See the nature of sin — it is a *backsliding* it is going back from the right way, not only into a by-path, but into a contrary path, back from the way that leads to life to that which leads to utter destruction. And this backsliding, if almighty grace do not interpose to prevent it, will be a perpetual backsliding. The sinner not only wanders endlessly, but proceeds end-ways towards ruin. The same subtlety of the tempter that brings men to sin holds them fast in it, and they contribute to their own captivity: *They hold fast deceit.* Sin is a great cheat, and they *hold it fast;* they love it dearly, and resolve to stick to it, and baffle all the methods God takes to separate between them and their sins. The excuses they make for their sins are deceits, and so are all their hopes of impunity; yet they hold fast these, and will not be undeceived, and therefore *they refuse to return.* Note, There is some deceit or other which those hold fast that go on wilfully in sinful ways, some *lie in their right hand,* by which they keep hold of their sins.

II. They would not attend to the dictates of conscience, which is our reason reflecting upon ourselves and our own actions, *v.* 6. Observe, 1. What expectations there were from them, that they would bethink themselves: *I heark-*

ened and heard. The prophet listened to see what effect his preaching had upon them; God himself listened, as one that desires not the death of sinners, that would have been glad to hear any thing that promised repentance, that would certainly have heard it if there had been any thing said of that tendency, and would soon have answered it with comfort, as he did David when he said, *I will confess,* Ps. 32:5. God *looks upon men* when they have done amiss (Job 33:27), to see what they will do next; he *hearkens and hears.* 2. How these expectations were disappointed: *They spoke not aright,* as I thought they would have done. They did not only not *do right,* but not so much as *speak right;* God could not get a good word from them, nothing on which to ground any favour to them or hopes concerning them. There was *none of them* that *spoke aright,* none that *repented him of his wickedness.* those that have sinned then, and then only, speak aright when they speak of repenting; and it is sad when those that have made so much work for repentance do not say a word of repenting. Not only did God not find any repenting of the national wickedness, which might have helped to empty the measure of public guilt, but none repented of that particular wickedness which he knew himself guilty of. (1.) They did not so much as take the first step towards repentance; they did not so much as say, *What have I done?* There was no motion towards it, not the least sign or token of it. Note, True repentance beings in a serious and impartial inquiry into ourselves, *what have we done,* arising from a conviction that we have done amiss. (2.) They were so far from repenting of their sins that they went on resolutely in their sins: *Every one turned to his course,* his wicked course, that course of sin which he had chosen and accustomed himself to, *as the horse rushes into the battle,* eager upon action, and scorning to be curbed. How the horse rushes into the battle is elegantly described, Job 39:21, etc. *He mocks at fear and is not affrighted.* Thus the daring sinner laughs at the threatenings of the word as bugbears, and runs violently upon the instruments of death and slaughter, and nothing will be restrained from him.

III. They would not attend to the dictates of providence, nor understand the voice of God in them, *v.* 7. It is an instance of their sottishness that, though they are God's people, and therefore should readily understand his mind upon every intimation of it, yet they *know not the judgment of the Lord;* they apprehend not the meaning either of a mercy or an affliction, not how to accommodate themselves to either, nor to answer God's intention in either. They know not how to improve the seasons of grave that God affords them when he sends them his prophets, nor how to make use of the rebukes they are under when *his voice cries in the city.* They *discern not the signs of the times* (Mt. 16:3), nor are aware how God is dealing with them. They know not that way of duty which God had prescribed them, though it be written both in their hearts and in their books. 2. It is an aggravation of their sottishness that there is so much sagacity in the inferior creatures. *The stork in the heaven knows her appointed times* of coming and continuing; so do other season-birds, *the turtle, the crane, and the swallow.* These by a natural instinct change their quarters, as the temper of the air alters; they come when the spring comes, and go, we know not whither, when the winter approaches, probably into warmer climates, as some birds come with winter and go when that is over.

IV. They would not attend to the dictates of the written word. They say, *We are wise,* but *how* can they say so? *v.* 8. With what face can they pretend to any thing of wisdom, when they do not understand themselves so well as the brute-creatures? Why, truly, they think they are wise because *the law of the Lord is with them,* the book of the law and the interpreters of it; and their neighbours, for the same reason, conclude they are wise, Deu. 4:6. But their pretensions are groundless for all this: *Lo, certainly in vain made he it;* surely never any people had Bibles to so little purpose as they have. They might as well have been without the law, unless they had made a better use of it. God has indeed made it able to make men wise to salvation, but as to them it is made so in vain, for they are never the wiser for it: *The pen of the scribes,* of those that first wrote the law and of those that now write expositions of it, *is in vain.* Both the favour of their God and the labour of their scribes are lost upon them; they receive the grace

of God therein in vain. Note, There are many that enjoy abundance of the means of grace, that have great plenty of Bibles and ministers, but they have them in vain; they do not answer the end of their having them. But it might be said, They have some wise men among them, to whom the law and the pen of the scribes are not in vain. To this it is answered (v. 9): *The wise men are ashamed,* that is, they have reasons to be so, that they have not made a better use of their wisdom, and lived more up to it. *They are confounded and taken;* all their wisdom has not served to keep them from those courses that tend to their ruin. They are taken in the same snares that others of their neighbours, who have not pretended to so much wisdom, are taken in, and filled with the same confusion. Those that have more knowledge than others, and yet do no better than others for their own souls, have reason to be ashamed. They talk of their wisdom, but, *Lo, they have rejected the word of the Lord;* they would not be governed by it, would not follow its direction, would not do what they knew; *and then what wisdom is in them?* None to any purpose; none that will be found to their praise at the great day, how much soever it is found to their pride now. The pretenders to wisdom, who said, *"We are wise and the law of the Lord is with us,"* were the priests and the false prophets; with them the prophet here deals plainly. 1. He threatens the judgments of God against them. Their families and estates shall be ruined (v. 10): *Their wives shall be given to others,* when they are taken captives, *and their fields.* shall be taken from them by their victorious enemy and shall be given *to those that shall inherit them,* not only strip them for once, but take possession of them as their own and acquire a property in them as their own and acquire a property in them, which they shall transmit to their posterity. And (v. 12), notwithstanding all their pretensions to wisdom and sanctity, *they shall fall among those that fall;* for, *if the blind lead the blind, both shall fall together into the ditch. In the time of their visitation,* when the wickedness of the land comes to be enquired into, it will be found that they have contributed to it more than any, and therefore *they shall be* sure to be *cast down* and cast out. 2. He gives a reason for these judgments (v. 10–12) even the same account of their badness which we meet with before (*ch.* 6:13–15), where it was opened at large. (1.) They were greedy of the wealth of this world, which is bad enough in any, but worst in prophets and priests, who should be best acquainted with another world and therefore should be most dead to this. But these, *from the least to the greatest,* were *given to covetousness.* The *priests teach for hire* and the *prophets divine for money,* Mic. 3:11. (2.) They made no conscience of speaking truth, no, not when they spoke as priests and prophets: *Every one deals falsely,* looks one way and rows another. There is no such thing as sincerity among them. (3.) They flattered people in their sins, and so flattered them into destruction. They pretended to be the physicians of the state, but knew not how to apply proper remedies to its growing maladies; they *healed them slightly,* killed the patient with palliative cures, silencing their fears and complaints with, *"Peace, peace, all is well, and there is no danger,"* when the God of heaven was proceeding in his controversy with them, so that there could be no peace to them. (4.) When it was made to appear how basely they prevaricated *they* were not at all ashamed of it, but rather gloried in it, (v. 12): *They could not blush,* so perfectly lost were they to all sense of virtue and honour. When they were convicted of the grossest forgeries they would justify what they had done, and laugh at those whom they had imposed upon. Such as these were ripe for ruin.

Verses 13–22

In these verses we have,

I. God threatening the destruction of a sinful people. He has borne long with them, but they are still more and more provoking, and therefore now their ruin is resolved on: *I will surely consume them* (v. 13), consuming I will consume them, not only surely, but utterly, consume them, will follow them with one judgment after another, till they are quite consumed; it is a *consumption determined,* Isa. 10:23. 1. They shall be quite stripped of all their comforts (v. 13): *There shall be no grapes on the vine.* Some understand this as intimating their sin; God came looking for grapes from this vineyard, seeking fruit upon this fig-tree, but he *found none* (as Isa. 5:2, Lu. 13:6); nay, they had not so much as leaves, Mt. 21:19. But it is rather to be understood of God's judgments upon them, and may be meant literally — The enemy shall seize the fruits of the earth, shall pluck the grapes and figs for themselves and beat down the very leaves with them; or, rather, figuratively — They shall be deprived of all their comforts and shall have nothing left them wherewith to *make glad their hearts.* It is expounded in the last clause: *The things that I have given them shall pass away from them.* Note, God's gifts are upon condition, and revocable upon non-performance of the condition. Mercies abused are forfeited, and it is just with God to take the forfeiture. 2. They shall be set upon by all manner of grievances, and surrounded with calamities (*v.* 17): *I will send serpents among you,* the Chaldean army, fiery serpents, flying serpents, cockatrices; these shall bite them with their venomous teeth, give them wounds that shall be mortal; and they *shall not be charmed,* as some serpents used to be, with music. These are serpents of another nature, that are not so wrought upon, or they are as *the deaf adder, that stops her ear, and will not hear the voice of the charmer.* The enemies are so intent upon making slaughter that it will be to no purpose to accost them gently, or offer any thing to pacify them, or mollify them, or to bring them to a better temper. No peace with God, therefore none with them.

II. The people sinking into despair under the pressure of those calamities. Those that were void of fear (when the trouble was at a distance) and set it at defiance, are void of hope now that it breaks in upon them, and have no heart either to make head against it or to bear up under it, *v.* 14. They cannot think themselves safe in the open villages: *Why do we sit still here?* Let us *assemble, and go* into a body *into the defenced cities.* Though they could expect no other than to be surely cut off there at last, yet not so soon as in the country, and therefore, *"Let us go, and be silent there;* let us attempt nothing, nor so much as make a complaint; for to what purpose?" It is not a submissive, but a sullen silence, that they here condemn themselves to. Those that are most jovial in their prosperity commonly despond most, and are most melancholy, in trouble. Now observe what it is that sinks them.

1. They are sensible that God is angry with them: "*'The Lord our God has put us to silence,* has struck us with astonishment, and *given us water of gall to drink,* which is both bitter and stupifying, or intoxicating. Ps. 60:3, *Thou hast made us to drink the wine of astonishment.* We had better sit still than rise up and fall; better say nothing than say nothing to the purpose. To what purpose is it to contend with our fate when God himself has become our enemy and fights against us? *Because we have sinned against the Lord,* therefore we are brought to the plunge." This may be taken as the language, (1.) Of their indignation. They seem to quarrel with God as if he had dealt hardly with them in putting them to silence, not permitting them to speak for themselves, and then telling them that it was because they had sinned against him. Thus men's foolishness *perverts their way, and* then *their hearts fret against the Lord.* Or rather, (2.) Of their convictions. At length they begin to see the hand of God lifted up against them, and stretched out in the calamities under which they are now groaning, and to own that they have provoked him to contend with them. Note, Sooner or later God will bring the most obstinate to acknowledge both his providence and his justice in all the troubles they are brought into, to see and say both that it is his hand and that he is righteous.

2. They are sensible that the enemy is likely to be too hard for them, *v.* 16. They are soon apprehensive that it is to no purpose to make head against such a mighty force; they and their people are quite dispirited; and, when the courage of a nation is gone, their numbers will stand them in little stead. *The snorting of the horses was heard from Dan,* that is, the report of the formidable strength of their cavalry was soon carried all the nation over and every body *trembled at the sound of the neighing of his steeds;* for *they have devoured the land and all that is in the city;* both town and country are laid waste before them, not only the wealth, but the inhabitants, of both, *those that dwell therein.* Note, When God appears against us, every thing else that is against us appears very formidable; whereas, if he be for us, every thing appears very despicable, Rom. 8:31.

3. They are disappointed in their expectations of deliverance out of their troubles, as they had been surprised when their troubles came upon them; and this double disappointment very much aggravated their calamity. (1.) The trouble came when they little expected it (*v.* 15): *We looked for peace,* the continuance of our peace, *but no good came,* no good news from abroad; we looked *for a time of health* and prosperity to our nation, but, *behold, trouble,* the alarms of war; for, as it follows (*v.* 16), *the noise of the* enemies' *horses was heard from Dan.* Their false prophets had cried *Peace, peace,* to them, which made it the more terrible when the scene of war opened on a sudden. This complaint will occur again, *ch.* 14:19. (2.) The deliverance did not come when they had long expected it (*v.* 20): *The harvest is past, the summer is ended;* that is, there is a great deal of time gone. Harvest and summer are parts of the year, and when they are gone the year draws towards a conclusion; so the meaning is, "One year passes after another, one campaign after another, and yet our affairs are in as bad a posture as ever they were; no relief comes, nor is any thing done towards it: *We are not saved."* Nay, there is a great deal of opportunity lost, the season of action is over and slipped, the summer and harvest are gone, and a cold and melancholy winter succeeds. Note, The salvation of God's church and people often goes on very slowly, and God keeps his people long in the expectation of it, for wise and holy ends. Nay, they stand in their own light, and put a bar in their own door, and are not saved because they are not ready for salvation.

4. They are deceived in those things which were their confidence and which they thought would have secured their peace to them (*v.* 19): *The daughter of my people* cries, cries aloud, *because of those that dwell in a far country,* because of the foreign enemy that invades them, that comes from a far country to take possession of ours; this occasions the cry; and what is the cry? It is this: *Is not the Lord in Zion? Is not her king in her?* These were the two things that they had all along buoyed up themselves with and depended upon, (1.) That they had among them the temple of God, and the tokens of his special presence with them. The common cant was, *"Is not the Lord in Zion?* What danger then need we fear?" And they held by this when the trouble was breaking in upon them. "Surely we shall do well enough, for have we not God among us?" But, when it grew to an extremity, it was an aggravation of their misery that they had thus flattered themselves. (2.) That they had the throne of the house of David. As they had a temple, so they had a monarchy, *jure divino — by divine right: Is not Zion's king in her?* And will not Zion's God protect Zion's king and his kingdom? Surely he will; but why does he not? "What" (say they) "has Zion neither a God nor a king to stand by her and help her, that she is thus run down and likely to be ruined?" This outcry of theirs reflects upon God, as if his power and promise were broken or weakened; and therefore he returns an answer to it immediately: *Why have they provoked me to anger with their graven images?* They quarrel with God as if he had dealt unkindly by them in forsaking them, whereas they by their idolatry had driven him from them; they have withdrawn from their allegiance to him, and so have thrown themselves out of this protection. They *fret themselves, and curse their king and their God* (Isa. 8:21), when it is their own sin that *separates between them and God* (Isa. 59:2); they *feared not the Lord,* and then *what can a king do for them?* Hos. 10:3.

III. We have here the prophet himself bewailing the calamity and ruin of his people; for there were more of the lamentations of Jeremiah than those we find in the book that bears that title. Observe here, 1. How great his griefs were. He was an eyewitness of the desolations of his country, and saw those things which by the spirit of prophecy he had foreseen. In the foresight, much more in the sight, of them, he cries out, *"My heart is faint in me,* I sink, I die away at the consideration of it, *v.* 18. *When I would comfort myself against my sorrow,* I do but labour in vain; nay, every attempt to alleviate the grief does but aggravate it." It is our wisdom and duty, under mournful events, to do what we can to *comfort ourselves against our sorrow,* by suggesting to ourselves such considerations as are proper to allay the grief and balance the grievance. But sometimes the sorrow is such that the more it is repressed the more strongly it recoils. This may sometimes be the case of very good men, as of the prophet here, whose soul refused to be comforted and fainted at the cordial, Ps. 77:2, 3. He tells us (*v.* 21) what was the matter: "It is *for the hurt of the daughter of my people* that *I am* thus *hurt;* it is for their sin, and the miseries they have brought upon themselves by it; it is for this that *I am black,* that I look black, that I go in black as mourners do, and that *astonishment has taken hold on me,* so that I know not what to do nor which way to turn." Note, The miseries of our country ought to be very much the grief of our souls. A gracious spirit will be a public spirit, a tender spirit, a mourning spirit. It becomes us to lament the miseries of our fellow-creatures, much more to lay to heart the calamities of our country, and especially of the church of God, to *grieve for the affliction of Joseph.* Jeremiah had prophesied the destruction of Jerusalem, and, though the truth of his prophecy was questioned, yet he did not rejoice in the proof of the truth of his prophecy was questioned, yet he did not rejoice in the proof of the truth of it by the accomplishment of it, preferring the welfare of his country before his own reputation. If Jerusalem had repented and been spared, he would have been far from fretting as Jonah did. Jeremiah had many enemies in Judah and Jerusalem, that hated, and reproached, and persecuted him; and in the judgments brought upon them God reckoned with them for it and pleaded his prophet's cause; yet he was far from rejoicing in it, so truly did he forgive his enemies and desire that God would forgive them. 2. How small his hopes were (*v.* 22): *"Is there no balm in Gilead* — no medicine proper for a sick and dying kingdom? *Is there no physician there* — no skilful faithful hand to apply the medicine?" He looks upon the case to be deplorable and past relief. There is no balm in Gilead that can cure the disease of sin, no physician there that can restore the health of a nation quite overrun by such a foreign army as that of the Chaldeans. The desolations made are irreparable, and the disease has presently come to such a height that there is no checking it. Or this verse may be understood as laying all the blame of the incurableness of their disease upon themselves; and so the question must be answered affirmatively: *Is there no balm in Gilead — no physician there?* Yes, certainly there is; God is able to help and heal them, there is a sufficiency in him to redress all their grievances. Gilead was a place in their own land, not far off. They had among themselves God's law and his prophets, with the help of which they might have been brought to repentance, and their ruin might have been prevented. They had princes and priests, whose business it was to reform the nation and redress their grievances. What could have been done more than had been done for their recovery? *Why then was not* their health restored? Certainly it was not owing to God, but to themselves; it was not for want of balm and a physician, but because they would not admit the application nor submit to the methods of cure. The physician and physic were both ready, but the patient was wilful and irregular, would not be tied to rules, but must be humoured. Note, If sinners die of their wounds, their blood is upon their own heads. The blood of Christ is balm in Gilead, his Spirit is the physician there, both sufficient, all-sufficient, so that they might have been healed, but would not.

CHAPTER 9

In this chapter the prophet goes on faithfully to reprove sin and to threaten God's judgments for it, and yet bitterly to lament both, as one that neither rejoiced at iniquity nor was glad at calamities. I. He here expresses his great grief for the miseries of Judah and Jerusalem, and his detestation of their sins, which brought those miseries upon them (*v.* 1–11). II. He justifies God in the greatness of the destruction brought upon them (*v.* 9–16). III. He calls upon others to bewail the woeful case of Judah and Jerusalem (*v.* 17–22). IV. He shows them the folly and vanity of trusting in their own strength or wisdom, or the privileges of their circumcision, or any thing but God only (*v.* 23–26).

Verses 1–11

The prophet, being commissioned both to foretel the destruction coming upon Judah and Jerusalem and to point out the sin for which that destruction was brought upon them, here, as elsewhere, speaks of both very feelingly: what he said of both came from the heart, and therefore one would have thought it would reach to the heart.

I. He abandons himself to sorrow in consideration of

the calamitous condition of his people, which he sadly laments, a one that preferred Jerusalem before his chief joy and her grievances before his chief sorrows.

1. He laments the slaughter of the persons, the blood shed and the lives lost (v. 1): "O that my head were waters, quite melted and dissolved with grief, that so my eyes might be fountains of tears, weeping abundantly, continually, and without intermission, still sending forth fresh floods of tears as there still occur fresh occasions for them!" The same word in Hebrew signifies both the eye and a fountain, as if in this land of sorrows our eyes were designed rather for weeping than seeing. Jeremiah wept much, and yet wished he could weep more, that he might affect a stupid people and rouse them to a due sense of the hand of God gone out against them. Note, It becomes us, while we are here in this vale of tears, to conform to the temper of the climate and to sow in tears. Blessed are those that mourn, for they shall be comforted hereafter; but let them expect that while they are here the clouds will still return after the rain. While we find our hearts such fountains of sin, it is fit that our eyes should be fountains of tears. But Jeremiah's grief here is upon the public account: he would weep day and night, not so much for the death of his own near relations, but for the slain of the daughter of his people, the multitudes of his countrymen that fell by the sword of war. Note, When we hear of the numbers of the slain in great battles and sieges we ought to be much affected with the intelligence, and not to make a light matter of it; yea, though they be not of the daughter of our people, for, whatever people they are of, they are of the same human nature with us, and there are so many precious lives lost, as dear to them as ours to us, and so many precious souls gone into eternity.

2. He laments the desolations of the country. This he brings in (v. 10), for impassioned mourners are not often very methodical in their discourses: "Not only for the towns and cities, but for the mountains, will I take up a weeping and wailing" (not barren mountains, but the fruitful hills with which Judea abounded), and for the habitations of the wilderness, or rather the pastures of the plain, that used to be clothed with flocks or covered over with corn, and a goodly sight it was; but now they are burnt up by the Chaldean army (which, according to the custom of war, destroyed to the custom of war, destroyed the forage and carried off all the cattle), so that no one dares to pass through them, for fear of meeting with some parties of the enemy, no one cares to pass through them, every thing looks so melancholy and frightful, no one has any business to pass through them, for they hear not the voice of the cattle there as usual, the bleating of the sheep and the lowing of the oxen, that grateful music to the owners; nay, both the fowl of the heavens and the beasts have fled. either frightened away by the rude noises and terrible fires which the enemies make, or forced away because there is no subsistence for them. Note, God has many ways of turning a fruitful land into barrenness for the wickedness of those that dwell therein; and the havoc war makes in a country cannot but be for a lamentation to all tender spirits, for it is a tragedy which destroys the stage it is acted on.

II. He abandons himself to solitude, in consideration of the scandalous character and conduct of his people. Though he dwells in Judah where God is known, in Salem where his tabernacle is, yet he is ready to cry out, Woe is me that I sojourn in Mesech! Ps. 120:5. While all his neighbours are fleeing to the defenced cities, and Jerusalem especially, in dread of the enemies' rage (ch. 4:5, 6) he is contriving to retire into some desert, in detestation of his people's sin (v. 2): "O that I had in the wilderness a lodging-place of wayfaring men, such a lonely cottage to dwell in as they have in the deserts of Arabia, which are uninhabited, for travellers to repose themselves in, that I might leave my people and go from them!" Not only because of the ill usage they gave him (he would rather venture himself among the wild beasts of the desert than among such treacherous barbarous people), but principally because his righteous soul was vexed from day to day, as Lot's was in Sodom, with the wickedness of their conversation, 2 Pt. 2:7, 8. This does not imply any intention or resolution that he had thus to retire. God had cut him out work among them, which he must not quit for his own ease. We must not go out of the world, bad as it is, before our time. If he could

not reform them, he could bear a testimony against them; if he could not do good to many, yet he might to some. but it intimates the temptation he was in to leave them, involves a threatening that they should be deprived of his ministry, and especially expresses the holy indignation he had against their abominable wickedness, which continued notwithstanding all the pains he had taken with them to reclaim them. It made him even weary of his life to see them dishonouring God as they did and destroying themselves. Time was when the place which God had chosen to put his name there was the desire and delight of good men. David, in a wilderness, longed to be again in the courts of God's house; but now Jeremiah, in the courts of God's house (for there he was when he said this), wishes himself in a wilderness. Those have made themselves very miserable that have made God's people and ministers weary of them and willing to get from them. Now, to justify his willingness to leave them, he shows,

1. What he himself had observed among them.

(1.) He would not think of leaving them because they were poor and in distress, but because they were wicked. [1.] They were filthy: They are all adulterers, that is, the generality of them are, ch. v. 8. They all either practised this sin or connived at those that did. Lewdness and uncleanness constituted that crying sin of Sodom at which righteous Lot was vexed in soul, and it is a sin that renders men loathsome in the eyes of God and all good men; it makes men an abomination. [2.] They were false. This is the sin that is most enlarged upon here. Those that had been unfaithful to their God were so to one another, and it was a part of their punishment as well as their sin, for even those that love to cheat, yet hate to be cheated. First, Go into their solemn meetings for the exercises of religion, for the administration of justice, or for commerce — to church, to court, or to the exchange — and they are an assembly of treacherous men; they are so by consent, they strengthen one another's hands in doing any thing that is perfidious. There they will cheat deliberately and industriously, with design, with a malicious design, for (v. 3) they bend their tongues, like their bow, for lies, with a great deal of craft; their tongues are fitted for lying, as a bow that is bent is for shooting, and are as constantly used for that purpose. Their tongue turns as naturally to a lie as the bow to the strong. But they are not valiant for the truth upon the earth. Their tongues are like a bow strung, with which they might do good service if they would use the art and resolution which they are so much masters of in the cause of truth; but they will not do so. They appear not in defence of the truths of God, which were delivered to them by the prophets; but even those that could not deny them to be truths were content to see them run down. In the administration of justice they have not courage to stand by an honest cause that has truth on its side, if greatness and power be on the other side. Those that will be faithful to the truth must be valiant for it, and not be daunted by the opposition given to it, nor fear the face of man. They are not valiant for the truth in the land, the land which has truth for the glory of it. Truth has fallen in the land, and they dare not lend a hand to help it up, Isa. 59:14, 15. We must answer, another day, not only for our enmity in opposing truth, but for our cowardice in defending it. Secondly, Go into their families, and you will find they will cheat their own brethren (every brother will utterly supplant); they will trip up one another's heels if they can, for they lie at the catch to seek all advantages against those they hope to make a hand of. Jacob had his name from supplanting; it is the word here used; they followed him in his name, but not in his true character, without guile. So very false are they that you cannot trust in a brother, but must stand as much upon your guard as if you were dealing with a stranger, with a Canaanite that has balances of deceit in his hand. Things have come to an ill pass indeed when a man cannot put confidence in his own brother. Thirdly, Go into company and observe both their commerce and their conversation, and you will find there is nothing of sincerity or common honesty among them. Nec hospes ab hospite tutus — The host and the guest are in danger from each other. The best advice a wise man can give you is to take heed every one of his neighbour, nay, of his friend (so some read it), of him whom he has befriended and who pretends friendship to him. No man thinks himself bound to be either grateful or sincere. Take

them in their conversation and every neighbour will walk with slander; they care not what ill they say one of another, though ever so false; that way that the slander goes they will go; they will walk with it. They will walk about from house to house too, carrying slanders along with them, all the ill-natured stories they can pick up or invent to make mischief. Take them in their trading and bargaining, and they will deceive every one his neighbour, will say any thing, though they know it to be false, for their own advantage. Nay, they will lie for lying sake, to keep their tongues in use to it, for they will not speak the truth, but will tell a deliberate lie and laugh at it when they have done.

(2.) That which aggravates the sin on this false and lying generation is, [1.] That they are ingenious to sin: They have taught their tongue to speak lies, implying that through the reluctances of natural conscience they found it difficult to bring themselves to it. Their tongue would have spoken truth, but they taught it to speak lies, and by degrees have made themselves masters of the art of lying, and have got such a habit of it that use has made it a second nature to them. They learnt it when they were young (for the wicked are estranged from the womb, speaking lies, Ps. 58:3), and now they have grown dexterous at it. [2.] That they are industrious to sin: They weary themselves to commit iniquity; they put a force upon their consciences to bring themselves to it; they tire out their convictions by offering them continual violence, and they take a great deal of pains, till they have even spent themselves in bringing about their malicious designs. They are wearied with their sinful pursuits and yet not weary of them. The service of sin is a perfect drudgery; men run themselves out of breath in it, and put themselves to a great deal of toil to damn their own souls. [3.] That they grow worse and worse (v. 3): They proceed from evil to evil, from one sin to another, from one degree of sin to another. They began with less sins. Nemo repente fit turpissimus — No one reaches the height of vice at once. They began with equivocating and bantering, but at last came to downright lying. And they are now proceeding to greater sins yet, for they know not me, saith the Lord; and where men have no knowledge of God, or no consideration of what they have known of him, what good can be expected from them? Men's ignorance of God is the cause of all their ill conduct one towards another.

2. The prophet shows what God had informed him of their wickedness, and what he had determined against them.

(1.) God had marked their sin. He could tell the prophet (and he speaks of it with compassion) what sort of people they were that he had to deal with. I know thy works, and where thou dwellest, Rev. 2:13. So here (v. 6): "Thy habitation is in the midst of deceit, all about thee are addicted to it; therefore stand upon thy guard." If all men are liars, it concerns us to beware of men,. and to be wise as serpents. They are deceitful men; therefore there is little hope of thy doing any good among them; for, make things ever so plain, they have some trick or other wherewith to shuffle off their convictions. This charge is enlarged upon, v. 8. Their tongue was a bow bent (v. 3), plotting and preparing mischief; here it is an arrow shot out, putting in execution what they had projected. It is as a slaying arrow (so some readings of the original have it); their tongue has been to many an instrument of death. They speak peaceably to their neighbours, against whom they are at the same time lying in wait; as Joab kissed Abner when he was about to kill him, and Cain, that he might not be suspected of any ill design, talked with his brother, freely and familiarly. Note, Fair words, when they are not attended with good intentions, are despicable, but, when they are intended as a cloak and cover for wicked intentions they are abominable. While they did all this injury to one another they put a great contempt upon God: "Not only they know not me, but (v. 6) through deceit, through the delusions of the false prophets, they refuse to know me; they are so cheated into a good opinion of their own ways, the ways of their own heart, that they desire not the knowledge of my ways." Or, "They are so wedded to this sinful course which they are in, and so bewitched with that, and its gains, that they will by no means admit the knowledge of God, because that would be a check upon them in their sins." This is the ruin of sinners: they might be taught the good knowledge of the Lord and they will not learn it; and where no knowledge of God is, what good can be expected? Hos. 4:1.

(2.) He had marked them for ruin, v. 7, 9, 11. Those that will not know God as their lawgiver shall be made to know him as their judge. God determines here to bring his judgments upon them, for the refining of some and the ruining of the rest. [1.] Some shall be refined (v. 7): "Because they are thus corrupt, *behold I will melt them and try them,* will bring them into trouble and see what that will do towards bringing them to repentance, whether the furnace of affliction will purify them from their dross, and whether, when they are melted, they will be new-cast in a better mould." He will make trial of less afflictions before he brings upon them utter destruction; for he *desires not the death of sinners.* They shall not be *rejected as reprobate silver* till the founder has melted in vain, ch. 6:29, 30. *For how shall I do for the daughter of my people?* He speaks as one consulting with himself what to do with them that might be for the best, and as one that could not find in his heart to cast them off and give them up to ruin till he had first tried all means likely to bring them to repentance. Or, "*How else shall I do for them?* They have grown so very corrupt that there is no other way with them but to put them into the furnace; what other course can I take with them? Isa. v. 4, 5. It is *the daughter of my people,* and I must do something to vindicate my own honour, which will be reflected upon if I connive at their wickedness. I must do something to reduce and reform them." A parent corrects his own children because they are his own. Note, When God afflicts his people, it is with a gracious design to mollify and reform them; it is but when need is and when he knows it is the best method he can use. [2.] The rest shall be ruined (v. 9): *Shall I not visit for these things?* Fraud and falsehood are sins which God hates and which he will reckon for. "*Shall not my soul be avenged on such a nation as this,* that is so universally corrupt, and, by its impudence in sin, even dares and defies divine vengeance?" The sentence is passed, the decree has gone forth (v. 11): *I will make Jerusalem heaps* of rubbish, and lay it in such ruins that it shall be fit for nothing but to be *a den of dragons; and the cities of Judah shall be a desolation.*" God makes them so, for he gives the enemy warrant and power to do it: but why is the holy city made a heap? The answer is ready, Because it has become an unholy one?

Verses 12–22

Two things the prophet designs, in these verses, with reference to the approaching destruction of Judah and Jerusalem: — 1. To convince people of the justice of God in it, that they had by sin brought it upon themselves and that therefore they had no reason to quarrel with God, who did them no wrong at all, but a great deal of reason to fall out with their sins, which did them all this mischief. 2. To affect people with the greatness of the desolation that was coming, and the miserable effects of it, that by a terrible prospect of it they might be awakened to repentance and reformation, which was the only way to prevent it, or, at least, mitigate their own share in it. This being designed,

I. He calls for the thinking men, by them to show people the equity of God's proceedings, though they seemed harsh and severe (v. 12): "*Who,* where, *is the wise man,* or the prophet, *to whom the mouth of the Lord hath spoken?* You boast of your wisdom, and of the prophets you have among you; produce me any one that has but the free use of human reason or any acquaintance with divine revelation, and he will soon understand this himself, and it will be so clear to him that he will be ready to declare it to others, that there is a just ground of God's controversy with this people." Do these wise men enquire, *For what does the land perish?* What is the matter, that such a change is made with this land? It used to be a land that God cared for, and he had his eyes upon it for good (Deu. 11:12), but it is now a land that he has forsaken and that his face is against. It used to flourish as the garden of the Lord and to be replenished with inhabitants; but now it is burnt up like a wilderness, that *none passeth through* it, much less cares to settle in it. It was supposed, long ago, that it would be asked, when it came to this, *Wherefore has the Lord done thus unto this land? What means the heat of this great anger?* (Deu. 29:24), to which question God here gives a

full answer, before which all flesh must be silent. He produces out of the record,

1. The indictment preferred and proved against them, upon which they had been found guilty, v. 13, 14. It is charged upon them, and it cannot be denied, (1.) That they have revolted from their allegiance to their rightful Sovereign. *Therefore.* God has *forsaken their land,* and justly, because they have *forsaken his law,* which he had so plainly, so fully, so frequently *set before them,* and had not observed his orders, not *obeyed his voice,* nor *walked in* the ways that he had appointed. Here their wickedness began, in the omission of their duty to their God and a contempt of his authority. But it did not end here. It is further charged upon them, (2.) That they have entered themselves into the service of pretenders and usurpers, have not only withdrawn themselves from their obedience to their prince, but have taken up arms against him. For, [1.] They have acted according to the dictates of their own lusts, have set up their own will, the wills of the flesh, and the carnal mind, in competition with, and contradiction to the will of God: *They have walked after the imagination of their own hearts;* they would do as they pleased, whatever God and conscience said to the contrary. [2.] They have worshipped the creatures of their own fancy, the work of their own hands, according to the tradition received from their fathers: *They have walked after Baalim:* the word is plural; they had many Baals, Baal-peor and Baal-berith, the Baal of this place and the Baal of the other place; for they had *lords many,* which *their fathers taught them* to worship, but which the God of their fathers had again and again forbidden. This was it for which *the land perished.* The King of kings never makes war thus upon his own subjects but when they treacherously depart from him and rebel against him, and it has become necessary by this means to chastise their rebellion and reduce them to their allegiance; and they themselves shall at length acknowledge that he is just in all that is brought upon them.

2. The judgment given upon this indictment, the sentence upon the convicted rebels, which must now be executed, for it was righteous and nothing could be moved in arrest of it: *The Lord of hosts, the God of Israel, hath said it* (v. 15, 16), and who can reverse it? (1.) That all their comforts at home shall be poisoned and embittered to them: *I will feed this people with wormwood* (or rather with *wolf's-bane,* for it signifies a herb that is not wholesome, as wormwood is though it be bitter, but some herb that is both nauseous and noxious), *and I will give them water of gall* (or *juice of hemlock* or some other herb that is poisonous) *to drink.* Every thing about them, till it comes to their very meat and drink, shall be a terror and torment to them. God will *curse their blessings,* Mal. 2:2. (2.) That their dispersion abroad shall be their destruction (v. 16): *I will scatter them among the heathen.* They were corrupted and debauched by their intimacy with the heathen, with whom they *mingled* and *learned their works;* and now they shall lose themselves, where they lost their virtue, *among the heathen.* They set up gods which *neither they nor their fathers had known,* strange gods, new gods (Deu. 32:17); and now God will put them among neighbours whom *neither they nor their fathers have known,* whom they can claim no acquaintance with, and therefore can expect no favour from. And yet, though they are scattered so as that they will not know where to find one another. God will know where to find them all out (Ps. 21:8) with that evil which still pursues impenitent sinners: *I will send a sword after them,* some killing judgment or other, *till I have consumed them;* for when God judges he will overcome, when he pursues he will overtake. And now we see for what the land perishes; all this desolation is the desert of their deeds and the performance of God's words.

II. He calls for the mourning women, and engages them, with the arts they practise to affect people and move their passions, to lament these sad calamities that had come or were coming upon them, that the nation might be alarmed to prepare for them: *The Lord of hosts* himself says, *Call for the mourning women, that they may come,* v. 17. the scope of this is to show how very woeful and lamentable the condition of this people was likely to be. 1. Here is work for the counterfeit mourners: *Send for cunning women,* that know how to compose mournful ditties, or at least to sing them in mournful tunes and accents, and therefore are made use of at funerals to supply the want

of true mourners. Let these *take up a wailing* for us, v. 18. The deaths and funerals were so many that people wept for them till they *had no power to weep,* as those, 1 Sa. 30:4. Let those therefore do it now whose trade it is. Or, rather, it intimates the extreme sottishness and stupidity of the people, that laid not to heart the judgments they were under, nor, even when there was so much blood shed, could find in their hearts to shed a tear. *They cry not when God binds them,* Job 36:13. God sent his mourning prophets to them, to call them to weeping and mourning, but his word in their mouths did not work upon their faith; rather therefore than they shall go laughing to their ruin, let the mourning women come, and try to work upon their fancy, *that their eyes may* at length *run down with tears, and their eyelids gush out with waters.* First or last, sinners must be weepers. 2. Here is work for the real mourners. (1.) There is that which is a lamentation. The present scene is very tragical (v. 19): *A voice of wailing is heard out of Zion.* Some make this to be the song of the mourning women: it is rather an echo to it, returned by those whose affections were moved by their wailings. In Zion the voice of joy and praise used to be heard, while the people kept closely to God. But sin has altered the note; it is now the *voice of lamentation.* It should seem to be the voice of those who fled from all parts of the country to the castle of Zion for protection. Instead of rejoicing that they had got safely thither, they lamented that they were forced to seek for shelter there: "*How are we spoiled!* How are we stripped of all our possessions! *We are greatly confounded,* ashamed of ourselves and our poverty;" for that is it that they complain of, that is it that they blush at the thoughts of, rather than of their sin: *We are confounded because we have forsaken the land* (forced so to do by the enemy), not because we *have* forsaken the Lord, being drawn aside of *our own lust and enticed — because our dwellings have cast us out,* not because our God has cast us off. Thus unhumbled hearts lament their calamity, but not their iniquity, the procuring cause of it. (2.) There is more still to come which shall be for a lamentation. Things are bad, but they are likely to be worse. Those whose land has *spued them out* (as it did their predecessors the Canaanites, and justly, because they trod in their steps, Lev. 18:28) complain that they are driven into the city, but, after a while, those of the city, and they with them, shall be forced thence too: *Yet hear the word of the Lord;* he has something more to say to you (v. 20); let *the women* hear it, whose tender spirits are apt to receive the impressions of grief and fear, for the men will not heed it, will not give it a patient hearing. The prophets will be glad to preach to a congregation of women that *tremble at God's word. Let your ear receive the word of God's mouth,* and bid it welcome, though it be a word of terror. Let the women *teach their daughters wailing;* this intimates that the trouble shall last long, grief shall be entailed upon the generation to come. Young people are apt to love mirth, and expect mirth, and are disposed to be gay and airy; but let the elder women teach the younger to be serious, tell them what a vale of tears they must expect to find this world, and train them up among the mourners in Zion, Tit. 2:4, 5. Let *every one teach her neighbour lamentation;* this intimates that the trouble shall spread far, shall go from house to house. People shall not need to sympathize with their friends; they shall all have cause enough to mourn for themselves. Note, Those that are themselves affected with the terrors of the Lord should endeavour to affect others with them. The judgment here threatened is made to look terrible. [1.] Multitudes shall be slain, v. 21. Death shall ride in triumph, and there shall be no escaping his arrests when he comes with commission, neither within doors nor without. Not within doors, for let the doors be shut ever so fast, let them be ever so firmly locked and bolted, *death comes up into our windows,* like a thief in the night; it steals upon us ere we are aware. Nor does it thus boldly attack the cottages only, but it has *entered into our palaces,* the palaces of our princes and great men, though ever so stately, ever so strongly built and guarded. Note, No palaces can keep out death. Nor are those more safe that are abroad; death *cuts off* even *the children from without and the young men from the streets.* The children who might have been spared by the enemy in pity, because they had never been hurtful to them, and the young men who might have been spared in policy, because capable of being serviceable to them, shall fall together by the sword. It is usual now, even in the severest military executions, to put none to the sword. It is usual now, even in the severest military executions, to put none to the sword but those that are found in arms; but then even the boys and girls playing in the streets were sacrificed to the fury of the conqueror. [2.] Those that are slain shall be left unburied (*v.* 22): *Speak, Thus saith the Lord* (for the confirmation and aggravation of what was before said), *Even the carcases of men shall fall as dung,* neglected, and left to be offensive to the smell, as dung is. Common humanity obliges the survivors to bury the dead, even for their own sake; but here such numbers shall be slain, and those so dispersed all the country over, that it shall be an endless thing to bury them all, nor shall there be hands enough to do it, nor shall the conquerors permit it, and those that should do it shall be overwhelmed with grief, so that they shall have no heart to do it. The dead bodies even of the fairest and strongest, when they have lain awhile, become dung, such vile bodies have we. And here such multitudes shall fall that their bodies shall lie as thick as heaps of dung *in the furrows of the field,* and no more notice shall be taken of them than of the *handfuls* which *the harvestman* drops for the gleaners, for *none shall gather them,* but they shall remain in sight, monuments of divine vengeance, that the eye of the impenitent survivors may affect their heart. *Slay them not,* bury them not, *lest my people forget,* Ps. 59:11.

Verses 23–26

The prophet had been endeavouring to possess this people with a holy fear of God and his judgments, to convince them both of sin and wrath; but still they had recourse to some sorry subterfuge or other, under which to shelter themselves from the conviction and with which to excuse themselves in the obstinacy and carelessness. He therefore sets himself here to drive them from these refuges of lies and to show them the insufficiency of them.

I. When they were told how inevitable the judgment would be they pleaded the defence of their politics and powers, which, with the help of their wealth and treasure, they thought made their city impregnable. In answer to this he shows them the folly of trusting to and boasting of all these stays, while they have not a God in covenant to stay themselves upon, *v.* 23, 24. Here he shows, 1. What we may not depend upon in a day of distress: *Let not the wise man glory in his wisdom,* as if with the help of that he could outwit or countermine the enemy, or in the greatest extremity find out some evasion or other; for a man's wisdom may fail him when he needs it most, and he may fail him when he needs it most, and he may be taken in his own craftiness. Ahithophel was befooled, and counsellors are often *led away spoiled.* But, if a man's policies fail him, yet surely he may gain his point by might and dint of courage. No: *Let not the strong man glory in his strength,* for the battle is not always to the strong. David the stripling proves too hard for Goliath the giant. All human force is nothing without God, worse than nothing against him. But may not the *rich man's wealth be his strong city?* (money answers all things) No: *Let not the rich man glory in his riches,* for they may prove so far from sheltering him that they may expose him and make him the fairer mark. Let not the people boast of the *wise men, and mighty men, and rich men* that they have among them, as if they could make their part good against the Chaldeans because they have wise men to advise concerning the war, mighty men to fight their battles, and rich men to bear the charges of the war. Let not particular persons think to escape the common calamity by their wisdom, might, or money; for all these will prove but *vain things for safety.* 2. He shows what we may depend upon in a day of distress. (1.) Our only comfort in trouble will be that we have done our duty. Those that *refused to know God* (*v.* 6) will boast in vain of their wisdom and wealth; but those that *know God,* intelligently, that *understand* aright *that he is the Lord,* that have not only right apprehensions concerning his nature, and attributes, and relations to man, but receive and retain the impressions of them, may *glory in this* it will be their rejoicing in the day of evil. (2.) Our only confidence in trouble will be that, having through grace in some measure done our duty, we shall find God a God all-sufficient to us. We may *glory in this,* that, wherever we are, we have an acquaintance with an interest in a God that *exercises lovingkindness, and judgment, and righteousness in the earth,* that is not only just to all his creatures and will do no wrong to any of them, but kind to all his children and will protect them and provide for them. *For in these things I delight.* God delights to show kindness and to execute judgment himself, and is pleased with those who herein are *followers of him as dear children.* Those that have such knowledge of the glory of God as to be changed into the same image, and to partake of his holiness, find it to be their perfection and glory; and the God they thus faithfully conform to they may cheerfully confide in, in their greatest straits. But the prophet intimates that the generality of this people took no care about this. Their wisdom, and might, and riches, were their joy and hope, which would end in grief and despair. But those few among them that had the knowledge of God might please themselves with it, and boast themselves of it; it would stand them in better stead than *thousands of gold and silver.*

II. When they were told how provoking their sins were to God they vainly pleaded the covenant of their circumcision. They were undoubtedly the people of God; as they had the temple of the Lord in their city, so they had the mark of his children in their flesh. "It is true that Chaldean army has laid such and such nations waste, because they were uncircumcised, and therefore not under the protection of the divine providence, as we are." To this the prophet answers, That the days of visitation were now at hand, in which God would punish all wicked people, without making any distinction between the circumcised and uncircumcised, *v.* 25, 26. They had by sin profaned the crown of their peculiarity, and lived in common with the uncircumcised nations, and so had forfeited the benefit of that peculiarity and must expect to fare never the better for it. God will *punish the circumcised with the uncircumcised.* As the ignorance of the uncircumcised shall not excuse their wickedness, so neither shall the privileges of the circumcised excuse theirs, but they shall be punished together. Note, The Judge of all the earth is impartial, and none shall fare the better at his bar for any external advantages, but he will render to every man, circumcised or uncircumcised, according to his works. The condemnation of impenitent sinners that are baptized will be as sure as, nay, and more severe than, that of impenitent sinners that are unbaptized. It would affect one to find here Judah industriously put between Egypt and Edom, as standing upon a level with them and under the same doom, *v.* 26. These nations were forbidden a share in the Jews' privileges (Deu. 23:3); but the Jews are here told that they shall share in their punishments. Those *in the utmost corners, that dwell in the wilderness,* are supposed to be the Kedarenes and those of the kingdoms of Hazor, as appears by comparing *ch.* 49:28–32. Some think they are so called because they dwelt as it were in a corner of the world, others because they had *the hair of their head polled into corners.* However that was, they were of those nations that were uncircumcised in flesh, and the Jews are ranked with them and are as near to ruin for their sins as they; for *all the house of Israel are uncircumcised in the heart:* they have the sign, but not the thing signified, *ch.* 4:4. They are heathens in their hearts, strangers to God, and enemies in their minds by wicked works. Their hearts are disposed to idols, as the hearts of the uncircumcised Gentiles are. Note, The seals of the covenant, though they dignify us, and lay us under obligations, will not save us, unless the temper of our minds and the tenour of our lives agree with the covenant. That only is circumcision, and that baptism, which is *of the heart,* Rom. 2:28, 29.

CHAPTER 10

We may conjecture that the prophecy of this chapter was delivered after the first captivity, in the time of Jeconiah or Jehoiachin, when many were carried away to Babylon; for it has a double reference: — I. To those that were carried away into the land of the Chaldeans, a country notorious above any other for idolatry and superstition; and they are here cautioned against the infection of the place, not to learn the way of the heathen (*v.* 1, 2), for their astrology and idolatry are both foolish things (*v.* 3–5), and the worshippers of idols brutish (*v.* 8, 9). So it will appear in the day of their visitation (*v.* 14, 15). They are likewise exhorted to adhere firmly to the God of Israel, for there is none like him (*v.* 6, 7). He is the true God, lives for ever, and has the government of the world (*v.* 10–13), and his people are happy in him (*v.* 16). II. To those that yet remained in their own land. They are cautioned against security, and told to expect distress (*v.* 17, 18) and that by a foreign enemy, which God would bring upon them for their sin (*v.* 20–22). This calamity the prophet laments (*v.* 19) and prays for the mitigation of it (*v.* 23–25).

Verses 1–16

The prophet Isaiah, when he prophesied of the captivity in Babylon, added warnings against idolatry and largely exposed the sottishness of idolaters, not only because the temptations in Babylon would be in danger of drawing the Jews there to idolatry, but because the afflictions in Babylon were designed to cure them of their idolatry. Thus the prophet Jeremiah here arms people against the idolatrous usages and customs of the heathen, not only for the use of those that had gone to Babylon, but of those also that staid behind, that being convinced and reclaimed, by the word of God, the rod might be prevented; and it is *written for our learning.* Observe here,

I. A solemn charge given to the people of God not to conform themselves to the ways and customs of the heathen. Let the house of Israel hear and receive this word from the God of Israel: *"Learn not the way of the heathen,* do not approve of it, no, nor think indifferently concerning it, much less imitate it or accustom yourselves to it. Let not any of their customs steal in among you (as they are apt to do insensibly) nor mingle themselves with your religion." Note, It ill becomes those that are taught of God to *learn the way of the heathen,* and to think of worshipping the true God with such rites and ceremonies as they used in the worship of their false gods. See Deu. 12:29–31. It was the way of the heathen to worship the host of heaven, the sun, moon, and stars; to them they gave divine honours, and from them they expected divine favours, and therefore, according as *the signs of heaven* were, whether they were auspicious or ominous, they thought themselves countenanced or discountenanced by their deities, which made them observe those signs, the eclipses of the sun and moon, the conjunctions and oppositions of the planets, and all the unusual phenomena of the celestial globe, with a great deal of anxiety and trembling. Business was stopped if any thing occurred that was thought to bode ill; if it did but thunder on their left hand, they were almost as if they had been thunderstruck. Now God would not have his people to be *dismayed at the signs of heaven,* to reverence the stars as deities, nor to frighten themselves with any prognostications grounded upon them. Let them fear the God of heaven, and keep up a reverence of his providence, and then they need not be *dismayed at the signs of heaven,* for the *stars in their courses* fight not against any that are at peace with God. The heathen are dismayed at these signs, for they know no better; but let not the *house of Israel,* that are taught of God, be so.

II. Divers good reasons given to enforce this charge.

1. The way of the heathen is very ridiculous and absurd, and is condemned even by the dictates of right reason, *v.* 3. The statutes and ordinances of the heathen are vanity itself; they cannot stand the test of a rational disquisition. This is again and again insisted upon here, as it was by Isaiah. The Chaldeans valued themselves upon their wisdom, in which they thought that they excelled all their neighbours; but the prophet here shows that they, and all others that worshipped idols and expected help and relief from them, were brutish and sottish, and had not common sense. (1.) Consider what the idol is that is worshipped. It was a *tree cut out of the forest* originally. It was fitted up by *the hands of the workman,* squared, and sawed, and worked into shape; see Isa. 44:12, etc. But, after all, it was but the stock of a tree, fitter to make a gate-post of than any thing else. But, to hide the wood, *they deck it with silver and gold,* they gild or lacquer it, or they deck it with gold and silver lace, or cloth of tissue. *They fasten it* to its place, which they themselves have assigned it, *with nails and hammers,* that it fall not, nor be thrown down, nor stolen away, *v.* 4. The image is made straight enough, and it cannot be denied but that the workman did his part, for it *is upright as the palm-tree* (*v.* 5); it looks stately, and stands up as if it were going to speak to you, but it *cannot speak;* it is a poor dumb creature; nor can it take one step towards your relief. If there be any occasion for it to shift its place, it must be carried in procession, for it *cannot go.* Very fitly does the admonition come in here, *"Be not afraid of them,* any more than of the signs of heaven; be not afraid of incurring their displeasure, for *they can do no evil;* be not afraid of forfeiting their favour, *for neither is it in them to do good.* If you think to mend the matter by mending the materials of which the idol is made, you deceive yourselves. Idols of gold and silver are an unworthy to be wor-

shipped as wooden gods. *The stock is a doctrine of vanities, v.* 8. It teaches lies, teaches lies concerning God. It is *an instruction of vanities; it is wood."* It is probable that the idols of gold and silver had wood underneath for the substratum, and then *silver spread into plates is brought from Tarshish,* imported from beyond sea, *and gold from Uphaz,* or *Phaz,* which is sometimes rendered the *fine* or *pure gold,* Ps. 21:3. A great deal of art is used, and pains taken, about it. They are not such ordinary mechanics that are employed about these as about the wooden gods, *v.* 3. these are cunning men; it is *the work of the workman;* the graver must do his part when it has passed through *the hands of the founder.* Those were but decked here and there with silver and gold; these are silver and gold all over. And, that these gods might be reverenced as kings, *blue and purple are their clothing,* the colour of royal robes (*v.* 9), which amuses ignorant worshippers, but makes the matter no better. For what is the idol when it is made and when they have made the best they can of it? He tells us (*v.* 14): *They are falsehood;* they are not what they pretend to be, but a great cheat put upon the world. They are worshipped as the gods that give us breath and life and sense, whereas they are lifeless senseless things themselves, and *there is no breath in them;* there is *no spirit in them* (so the word is); they are not animated, or inhabited, as they are supposed to be, by any *divine spirit* or *numen — divinity.* They are so far from being gods that they have not so much as the *spirit of a beast that goes downward. They are vanity, and the work of errors, v.* 15. Enquire into the use of them and you will find they are vanity; they are good for nothing; no help is to be expected from them nor any confidence put in them. They are a *deceitful work, works of illusions,* or *mere mockeries;* so some read the following clause. They *delude* those that put their trust in them, make fools of them, or, rather, they make fools of themselves. Enquire into the use of them and you will find they are *the work of errors,* grounded upon the grossest mistakes that ever men who pretended to reason were guilty of. They are the creatures of a deluded fancy; and the errors by which they were produced they propagate among their worshippers. (2.) Infer hence what the idolaters are that worship these idols. (*v.* 8): *They are altogether brutish and foolish.* Those that make them are like unto them, senseless and stupid, and there is no spirit in them — no use of reason, else they would never stoop to them, *v.* 14. *Every man* that makes or worships idols has become *brutish in his knowledge,* that is, brutish for want of knowledge, or brutish in that very thing which one would think they should be fully acquainted with; compare Jude 10, *What they know naturally,* what they cannot but know by the light of nature, *in those things as brute beasts they corrupt themselves.* Though in the works of creation they cannot but see the eternal power and godhead of the Creator, yet they have become *vain in their imaginations, not liking to retain God in their knowledge.* See Rom. 1:21, 18. Nay, whereas they thought it a piece of wisdom thus to multiply gods, it really was the greatest folly they could be guilty of. *The world by wisdom knew not God,* 1 Co. 1:21; Rom. 1:22. *Every founder* is himself *confounded by the graven image;* when he has made it by a mistake he is more and more confirmed in his mistake by it; he is bewildered, bewitched, and cannot disentangle himself from the snare; or it is what he will one time or other be ashamed of.

2. The God of Israel is the one only living and true God, and those that have him for their God need not make their application to any other; nay, to set up any other in competition with him is the greatest affront and injury that can be done him. Let the house of Israel cleave to the God of Israel and serve and worship him only, for,

(1.) He is a non-such. Whatever men may set in competition with him, there is none to be compared with him. The prophet turns from speaking with the utmost disdain of the idols of the heathen (as well he might) to speak with the most profound and awful reverence of the God of Israel (*v.* 6, 7): *"Forasmuch as there is none like unto thee, O Lord!* none of all the heroes which the heathen have deified and make such ado about," the dead men of whom they made dead images, and whom they worshipped. "Some were deified and adored for their wisdom; but, *among all the wise men of the nations,* the greatest philosophers or statesmen, as Apollo or Hermes, *there is none like thee.* Others were deified and adored for their dominion; but, *in all their royalty"* (so it may be read), "among all their kings, as Saturn and Jupiter, *there is none like unto thee."* What is the glory of a man that invented a useful art or founded a flourishing kingdom (and these were grounds sufficient among the heathen to entitle a man to an apotheosis) compared with the glory of him that is the Creator of the world and that *forms the spirit of man within him?* What is the glory of the greatest prince or potentate, compared with the glory of him whose *kingdom rules over all?* He acknowledges (*v.* 6), *O Lord! thou art great,* infinite and immense, and *thy name is great in might;* thou hast all power, and art known to have it. Men's name is often beyond their might; they are thought to be greater than they are; but God's *name is great,* and no greater than he really is. And therefore *who would not fear thee, O King of nations?* Who would not choose to worship such a God as this, that can do every thing, rather than such dead idols as the heathen worship, that can do nothing? Who would not be afraid of offending or forsaking a God whose name is so *great in might?* Which of all the nations, if they understood their interests aright, *would not fear him* who is the *King of nations?* Note, There is an admirable decency and congruity in the worshipping of God only. It is fit that he who is God alone should alone be served, that he who is Lord of all should be served by all, that he who is great should be greatly feared and greatly praised.

(2.) His verity is as evident as the idol's vanity, *v.* 10. They are the work of men's hands, and therefore nothing is more plain than that it is a jest to worship them, if that may be called a jest which is so great an indignity to him that made us: *But the Lord is the true God,* the God of truth; he is God in truth. *God Jehovah is truth;* he is not a counterfeit and pretender, as they are, but is really what he has revealed himself to be; he is one we may depend upon, in whom and by whom we cannot be deceived. [1.] Look upon him as he is in himself, and he is *the living God.* He is life itself, has life in himself, and is the fountain of life to all the creatures. The gods of the heathen are dead things, worthless and useless, but ours is a living God, and hath immortality. [2.] Look upon him with relation to his creatures, he is a *King,* and absolute monarch, over them all, is their owner and ruler, has an incontestable right both to command them and dispose of them. As a king, he protects the creatures, provides for their welfare, and preserves peace among them. He is *an everlasting king.* The counsels of his kingdom were from everlasting and the continuance of it will be to everlasting. He is a *King of eternity.* The idols whom they call their kings are but of yesterday, and will soon be abolished; and the kings of the earth, that set them up to be worshipped, will themselves be in the dust shortly; but *the Lord shall reign for ever, thy God, O Zion! unto all generations.*

(3.) None knows the power of his anger. Let us stand in awe, and not dare to provoke him by giving that glory to another which is due to him alone; for *at his wrath the earth shall tremble,* even the strongest and stoutest of the kings of the earth; nay, the earth, firmly as it is fixed, when he pleases is made to quake and the rocks to tremble, Ps. 104:32; Hab. 3:6, 10. Though the nations should join together to contend with him, and unite their force, yet they would be found utterly unable not only to resist, but even *to abide his indignation.* Not only can they not make head against it, for it would overcome them, but they cannot bear up under it, for it would overload them, Ps. 76:7, 8; Nah. 1:6.

(4.) He is the God of nature, the fountain of all being; and all the powers of nature are at his command and disposal, *v.* 12, 13. The God we worship is he that made the heavens and the earth, and has a sovereign dominion over both; so that his *invisible things* are manifested and proved in the *things that are seen.* [1.] If we look back, we find that the whole world owed its origin to him as its first cause. It was a common saying even among the Greeks — *He that sets up to be another god ought first to make another world.* While the heathen worship gods that they made, we worship the God that made us and all things. *First, The earth* is a body of vast bulk, has valuable treasures in its bowels and more valuable fruit on its surface. It and them he has *made by his power;* and it is by no less than an infinite power that it *hangs upon nothing,* as it does (Job 26:7) — *ponderibus librata suis — poised by its own weight. Secondly, The world,* the habitable part of the earth, is admirably fitted for the use and service of man, and *he hath established it* so *by his wisdom,* so that it continues serviceable in constant changes and yet a continual stability from one generation to another. Therefore both the earth and the world are his, Ps. 24:1. *Thirdly, The heavens* are wonderfully *stretched out* to an incredible extent, and it is *by his discretion* that they are so, and that the motions of the heavenly bodies are directed for the benefit of this lower world. These *declare his glory* (Ps. 19:1), and oblige us to declare it, and not give that glory to the heavens which is due to him that made them. [2.] If we look up, we see his providence to be a continued creation (*v.* 13): *When he uttereth his voice* (gives the word of command) *there is a multitude of waters in the heavens,* which are poured out on the earth, whether for judgment or mercy, as he intends them. When he utters his voice in the thunder, immediately there follow thunder-showers, in which there are a multitude of waters; and those come with *a noise,* as the margin reads it; and we read of the *noise of abundance of rain,* 1 Ki. 18:41. Nay, there are wonders done daily in the kingdom of nature without noise: *He causes the vapours to ascend from the ends of the earth,* from all parts of the earth, even the most remote, and chiefly those that lie next the sea. All the earth pays the tribute of vapours, because all the earth receives the blessing of rain. And thus the moisture in the universe, like the money in a kingdom and the blood in the body, is continually circulating for the good of the whole. Those vapours produce wonders, for of them are formed *lightnings for the rain,* and *the winds* which God from time to time *brings forth out of his treasures,* as there is occasion for them, directing them all in such measure and for such use as he thinks fit, as payments are made out of the treasury. All the meteors are so ready to serve God's purposes that he seems to have treasures of them, that cannot be exhausted and may at any time be drawn from, Ps. 135:7. God glories in the treasures he has of these, Job 38:22, 23. This God can do; but which of the idols of the heathen can do the like? Note, There is no sort of weather but what furnishes us with a proof and instance of the wisdom and power of the great Creator.

(5.) This God is Israel's God in covenant, and the felicity of every Israelite indeed. Therefore let the house of Israel cleave to him, and not forsake him to embrace idols; for, if they do, they certainly change for the worse, for (*v.* 16) *the portion of Jacob is not like them;* their rock is not as our rock (Deu. 32:31), nor ours like their mole-hills. Note, [1.] Those that have the Lord for their God have a full and complete happiness in him. The *God of Jacob* is the *portion of Jacob;* he is his all, and in him he has enough and needs no more in this world nor the other. In him we have a worthy portion, Ps. 16:5. [2.] If we have entire satisfaction and complacency in God as our portion, he will have a gracious delight in us as his people, whom he owns as *the rod of his inheritance,* his possession and treasure, with whom he dwells and by whom he is served and honoured. [3.] It is the unspeakable comfort of all the Lord's people that he who is their God is *the former of all things,* and therefore is able to do all that for them, and give all that to them, which they stand in need of. Their *help stands in his name who made heaven and earth.* And he is the *Lord of hosts,* of all the hosts in heaven and earth, has them all at his command, and will command them into the service of his people when there is occasion. This is the name by which they know him, which they first give him the glory of and then take to themselves the comfort of. [4.] Herein God's people are happy above all other people, happy indeed, *bona si sua norint — did they but know their blessedness.* The gods which the heathen pride, and please, and so portion themselves in, are vanity and a lie; but *the portion of Jacob is not like them.*

3. The prophet, having thus compared the gods of the heathen with the God of Israel (between whom there is no comparison), reads the doom, the certain doom, of all those pretenders, and directs the Jews, in God's name, to read it to the worshippers of idols, though they were their lords and masters (*v.* 11): *Thus shall you say unto them* (and the God you serve will bear you out in saying it), *The gods which have not made the heavens and the earth* (and therefore are no gods, but usurpers of the honour due to him only who did make heaven and earth) *shall perish,* perish

of course, because they are vanity — perish by his righteous sentence, because they are rivals with him. As gods they shall perish *from off the earth* (even all those things *on earth beneath* which they make gods of) *and from under these heavens,* even all those things in the firmament of heaven, under the highest heavens, which are deified, according to the distribution in the second commandment. These words in the original are not in the Hebrew, like all the rest, but in the Chaldee dialect, that the Jews in captivity might have this ready to say to the Chaldeans in their own language when they tempted them to idolatry: "Do you press us to worship your gods? We will never do that; for," (1.) "They are counterfeit deities; they are no gods, for they *have not made the heavens and the earth,* and therefore are not entitled to our homage, nor are we indebted to them either for the products of the earth or the influences of heaven, as we are to the God of Israel." The primitive Christians would say, when they were urged to worship such a god, *Let him make a world and he shall be my god.* While we have him to worship who made heaven and earth, it is very absurd to worship any other. (2.) "They are condemned deities. They *shall perish;* the time shall come when they shall be no more respected as they are now, but shall be buried in oblivion, and they and their worshippers shall sink together. The earth shall no longer bear them; the heavens shall no longer cover them; but both shall abandon them." It is repeated (*v.* 15), *In the time of their visitation* they shall perish. When God comes to reckon with idolaters he will make them weary of their idols, and glad to be rid of them. They shall *cast them to the moles and to the bats,* Isa. 2:20. Whatever runs against God and religion will be run down at last.

Verses 17–25

In these verses,

I. The prophet threatens, in God's name, the approaching ruin of Judah and Jerusalem, *v.* 17, 18. The Jews that continued in their own land, after some were carried into captivity, were very secure; they thought themselves *inhabitants of a fortress;* their country was their strong hold, and, in their own conceit, impregnable; but they are here told to think of leaving it: they must prepare to go after their brethren, and pack up their effects in expectation of it: *"Gather up thy wares out of the land;* contract your affairs, and bring them into as small a compass as you can. *Arise, depart, this is not your rest,"* Mic. 2:10. Let not what you have lie scattered, for the Chaldeans will be upon you again, to be the executioners of the sentence God has passed upon you (*v.* 18): *"Behold, I will sling out the inhabitants of the land at this once;* they have hitherto dropped out, by a few at a time, but one captivity more shall make a thorough riddance, and they shall be slung out as a stone out of a sling, so easily, so thoroughly shall they be cast out; nothing of them shall remain. they shall be thrown out with violence, and driven to a place at a great distance off, in a little time." See this comparison used to signify an utter destruction, 1 Sa. 25:29. *Yet once more* God will shake their land, and *shake the wicked out of it,* Heb. 12:26. He adds, *And I will distress them, that they may find it so.* He will not only throw them out hence (that he may do and yet they may be easy elsewhere); but, whithersoever they go, trouble shall follow them; they shall be continually perplexed and straitened, and at a loss within themselves: and who or what can make those easy whom God *will distress,* whom he will distress *that they may find it so,* that they may feel that which they would not believe? They were often told of the weight of God's wrath and their utter inability to make head against it, or bear up under it. They were told that their sin would be their ruin, and they would not regard nor credit what was told them; but now *they shall find it so;* and *therefore* God will pursue them with his judgments, *that they may find it so,* and be forced to acknowledge it. Note, sooner or later sinners will find it just as the word of God has represented things to them, and no better, and that the threatenings were not bugbears.

II. He brings in the people sadly lamenting their calamities (*v.* 19): *Woe is me for my hurt!* Some make this the prophet's own lamentation, not for himself, but for the calamities and desolations of his country. He mourned for those that would not be persuaded to mourn for themselves; and, since there were none that had so much sense as to join with them, he weeps in secret, and cries out, *Woe is me!* In mournful times it becomes us to be of a mournful spirit. But it may be taken as the language of the people, considered as a body, and therefore speaking as a single person. The prophet puts into their mouths the words they *should* say; whether they would say them or no, they should have cause to say them. Some among them would thus bemoan themselves, and all of them, at last, would be forced to do it. 1. They lament that the affliction is very great, and it is very hard to them to bear it, the more hard because they had not been used to trouble and now did not expect it: *"Woe is me for my hurt,* not for what I fear, but for what I feel;" for they are not, as some are, worse frightened than hurt. Nor is it a slight hurt, but *a wound,* a wound that is *grievous,* very painful, and very threatening. 2. That there is no remedy but patience. They cannot help themselves, but must sit still, and abide it: *But I said,* when I was about to complain of my wound, To what purpose is it to complain? *This is a grief, and I must bear it* as well as I can. This is the language rather of a sullen than of a gracious submission, of a patience per force, not a patience by principle. When I am in affliction I should say, "This is an evil, and I will bear it, because it is the will of God that I should, because his wisdom has appointed this for me and his grace will make it work for good to me." This is *receiving evil* at the hand of God, Job 2:10. But to say, "This is an evil, *and I must bear it,* because I cannot help it," is but a brutal patience, and argues a want of those good thoughts of God which we should always have, even under our afflictions, saying, not only, God can and will do what he pleases, but, *Let him do what he pleases.* 3. That the country was quite ruined and wasted (*v.* 20): *My tabernacle is spoiled.* Jerusalem, though a strong city, now proves as weak and moveable as a tabernacle or tent, when it is taken down, and *all its cords,* that should keep it together, are *broken.* Or by the tabernacle here may be meant the temple, the sanctuary, which at first was but a tabernacle, and is now called so, as then it was sometimes called a temple. Their church is ruined, and all the supports of it fail. It was a general destruction of church and state, city and country, and there were none to repair these desolations. *"My children have gone forth of me;* some have fled, others are slain, others carried into captivity, so that as to me, *they are not;* I am likely to be an outcast, and to perish for want of shelter; for *there is none to stretch forth my tent any more,* none of my children that used to do it for me, *none to set up my curtains,* none to do me any service." *Jerusalem has none to guide her of all her sons,* Isa. 51:18. 4. That the rulers took no care, nor any proper measures, for the redress of their grievances and the re-establishing of heir ruined state (*v.* 21): *The pastors have become brutish.* When the tents, the shepherds' tents, were spoiled (*v.* 20), it concerned the shepherds to look after them; but they were foolish shepherds. Their kings and princes had no regard at all for the public welfare, seemed to have no sense of the desolations of the land, but were quite besotted and infatuated. The priests, the pastors of God's tabernacle, did a great deal towards the ruin of religion, but nothing towards the repair of it. They are *brutish* indeed, for *they have not sought the Lord;* they have neither made their peace with him nor their prayer to him; they had no eye to him and his providence, in their management of affairs; they neither acknowledged the judgment, nor expected the deliverance, to come from his hand. Note, Those are brutish people that do not seek the Lord, that live without prayer, and live without God in the world. Every man is either a saint or a brute. But it is sad indeed with a people when their pastors, that should *feed them with knowledge and understanding,* are themselves thus brutish. And what comes of it? *Therefore they shall not prosper;* none of their attempts for the public safety shall succeed. Note, Those cannot expect to prosper who do not by faith and prayer take God along with them in all their ways. And, when the pastors are brutish, what else can be expected but that *all their flocks* should be *scattered? For, if the blind lead the blind, both will fall into the ditch.* The ruin of a people is often owing to the brutishness of their pastors. 5. That the report of the enemy's approach was very dreadful (*v.* 22): *The noise of the bruit has come,* of the report which at first was but whispered and bruited abroad, as wanting confirmation. It now proves too true: *A great commotion* arises *out of the north country,* which threatens to make all *the cities of Judah desolate and a den of dragons;* for they must all expect to be sacrificed to the avarice and fury of the Chaldean army. And what else can that place expect but to be made a den of dragons which has by sin made itself a den of thieves?

III. He turns to God, and addresses himself to him, finding it to little purpose to speak to the people. It is some comfort to poor ministers that, if men will not hear them, God will; and to him they have liberty of access at all times. Let them close their preaching with prayer, as the prophet, and then they shall have no reason to say that they have laboured in vain.

1. The prophet here acknowledges the sovereignty and dominion of the divine Providence, that by it, and not by their own will and wisdom, the affairs both of nations and particular persons are directed and determined, *v.* 23. This is an article of our faith which it is very proper for us to make confession of at the throne of grace when we are complaining of an affliction or suing for a mercy: *"O Lord, I know,* and believe, *that the way of man is not in himself;* Nebuchadnezzar did not come of himself against our land, but by the direction of a divine Providence." We cannot of ourselves do any thing for our own relief, unless God work with us and command deliverance for us; for *it is not in man that walketh to direct his steps,* though he seem in his walking to be perfectly at liberty and to choose his own way. Those that had promised themselves a long enjoyment of their estates and possessions were made to know, by sad experience, when they were thrown out by the Chaldeans, that *the way of man is not in himself;* he designs which men lay deep, and think well-formed, are dashed to pieces in a moment. We must all apply this to ourselves, and mix faith with it, that we are not at our own disposal, but under a divine direction; the event is often overruled so as to be quite contrary to our intention and expectation. We are not masters of our own way, nor can we think that every thing should be according to our mind; we must therefore refer ourselves to God and acquiesce in his will. Some think that the prophet here mentions this with a design to make this comfortable use of it, that, the way of the Chaldean army being not in themselves, they can do no more than God permits them; he can set bounds to thee proud waves, and say, *Hitherto they shall come, and no further.* And a quieting consideration it is that the most formidable enemies have *no power against us but what is given them from above.*

2. He deprecates the divine wrath, that it might not fall upon God's Israel, *v.* 24. He speaks not for himself only, but on the behalf of his people: *O Lord, correct me, but with judgment* (in measure and with moderation, and in wisdom, no more than is necessary for driving out of the foolishness that is bound up in our hearts), *not in thy anger* (how severe soever the correction be, let it come from thy love, and be designed for our good and made to work for good), not to *bring us to nothing,* but to bring us home to thyself. Let it not be according to the desert of our sins, but according to the design of thy grace. Note, (1.) We cannot pray in faith that we may never be corrected, while we are conscious to ourselves that we need correction and deserve it, and know that as many as God loves he chastens. (2.) The great thing we should dread in affliction is the wrath of God. Say not, Lord, *do not correct* me, but, Lord, do not correct me *in anger;* for that will infuse wormwood and gall into the affliction and misery that will *bring us to nothing.* We may bear the smart of his rod, but we cannot bear the weight of his wrath.

3. He imprecates the divine wrath against the oppressors and persecutors of Israel (*v.* 25): *Pour out thy fury upon the heathen that know thee not.* This prayer does not come from a spirit of malice or revenge, nor is it intended to prescribe to God whom he should execute his judgments upon, or in what order; but, (1.) It is an appeal to his justice. As if he had said, "Lord, we are a provoking people; but are there not other nations that are more so? And shall we only be punished? We are thy children, and may expect a fatherly correction; but they are thy enemies, and against them we have reason to think thy indignation should be, not against us." This is God's usual method. The *cup put into the hands* of God's people is *full of mixtures,* mixtures of mercy; but the *dregs of the cup* are reserved for *the wicked of the earth,* let them *wring them out,* Ps.

75:8. (2.) It is a prediction of God's judgments upon all the impenitent enemies of his church and kingdom. If *judgment begin* thus *at the house of God,* what shall be *the end of those that obey not his gospel?* 1 Pt. 4:17. See how the heathen are described, on whom God's fury shall be poured out. [1.] They are strangers to God, and are content to be so. they *know him not,* nor desire to know him. They are families that live without prayer, that have nothing of religion among them; they *call not on God's name.* Those that restrain prayer prove that they know not God; for those that know him will seek to him and entreat his favour. [2.] They are persecutors of the people of God and are resolved to be so. *They have eaten up Jacob* with as much greediness as those that are hungry eat their necessary food; nay, with more, they have *devoured him, and consumed him, and made his habitation desolate,* that is, the land in which he lives, or the temple of God, which is his habitation among them. Note, What the heathen, in their rage and malice, do against the people of God, though therein he makes use of them as the instruments of his correction, yet he will, for that, make them the objects of his indignation. This prayer is taken from Ps. 79:6, 7.

CHAPTER 11

In this chapter, I. God by the prophet puts the people in mind of the covenant he had made with their fathers, and how much he had insisted upon it, as the condition of the covenant, that they should be obedient to him (*v.* 1–7). II. He charges it upon them that they, in succession to their fathers, and in confederacy among themselves, had obstinately refused to obey him (*v.* 8–10). III. He threatens to punish them with utter ruin for their disobedience, especially for their idolatry (*v.* 11, 13), and tells them that their idols should not save them (*v.* 12), that their prophets should not pray for them (*v.* 14); he also justifies his proceedings herein, they having brought all this mischief upon themselves by their own folly and wilfulness (*v.* 15–17). IV. Here is an account of a conspiracy formed against Jeremiah by his fellow-citizens, the men of Anathoth; God's discovery of it to him (*v.* 18, 19), his prayer against them (*v.* 20), and a prediction of God's judgments upon them for it (*v.* 21–23).

Verses 1–10

The prophet here, as prosecutor in God's name, draws up an indictment against the Jews for wilful disobedience to the commands of their rightful Sovereign. For the more solemn management of this charge,

I. He produces the commission he had to draw up the charge against them. He did not take pleasure in accusing the children of his people, but God commanded him to *speak it to the men of Judah, v.* 1, 2. In the original it is plural: *Speak you this.* For what he said to Jeremiah was the same that he gave in charge to all his servants the prophets. They none of them said any other than what Moses, in the law, had said; to that therefore they must refer themselves, and direct the people: *"Hear the words of this covenant;* turn to your Bibles, be judged by them." Jeremiah must now proclaim this in the cities *of Judah and the streets of Jerusalem,* that all may hear, for all are concerned. All the words of reproof and conviction which the prophets spoke were grounded upon the *words of the covenant,* and agreed with that; and therefore *"hear these words,* and understand by them upon what terms you stood with God at first; and then, by comparing yourselves with the covenant, you will soon be aware upon what terms you now stand with him."

II. He opens the charter upon which their state was founded and by which they held their privileges. They had forgotten the tenour of it, and lived as if they thought that the grant was absolute and that they might do what they pleased and yet have what God had promised, or as if they thought that the keeping up of the ceremonial observances was all that God required of them. He therefore shows them, with all possible plainness, that the thing God insisted upon was *obedience,* which was *better than sacrifice.* He said, *Obey my voice, v.* 4 and again *v.* 7. "Own God for your Master; give up yourselves to him as his subjects and servants; attend to all the declarations of his mind and will, and make conscience of complying with them. *Do my commandments,* not only in some things, but *according to all which I command you;* make conscience of moral duties especially, and rest not in those that are merely ritual; hear the words of the covenant, and do them." 1. This was the original contract between God and them, when he first formed them into a people. It was what he *commanded their fathers* when he first *brought them forth out*

of the land of Egypt, v. 4 and *v.* 7. He never intended to take them under his guidance and protection upon any other terms. This was what he required from them in gratitude for the great things he did for them when he brought them *from the iron furnace.* He redeemed them out of the service of the Egyptians, which was perfect slavery, that he might take them into his own service, which is perfect freedom, Lu. 1:74, 75. 2. This was not only laid before them then, but it was with the greatest importunity imaginable pressed upon them, *v.* 7. God not only commanded it, but *earnestly protested it to their fathers,* when he brought them into covenant with himself. Moses inculcated it again and again, by precept upon precept and line upon line. 3. This was made the condition of the relation between and God, which was so much their honour and privilege: *"So shall you be my people and I will be your God;* I will own you for mine, and you may call upon me as yours;" this intimates that, if they refused to obey, they could no longer claim the benefit of the relation. 4. It was upon these terms that the land of Canaan was given them for a possession: *Obey my voice, that I may perform the oath sworn to your fathers, to give them a land flowing with milk and honey, v.* 5. God was ready to fulfil the promise, but then they must fulfil the condition; if not, the promise is void, and it is just with God to turn them out of possession. Being brought in upon their good behaviour, they had no wrong done them if they were turned out upon their ill behaviour. Obedience was the rent reserved by the lease, with a power to re-enter for non-payment. 5. This obedience was not only made a condition of the blessing, but was required under the penalty of a curse. This is mentioned first here (*v.* 3), that they might, if possible, be awakened by the terrors of the Lord: *Cursed be the man,* though it were but a single person, *that obeys not the words of this covenant,* much more when it is the body of the nation that rebels. There are curses of the covenant as well as blessings: and Moses set before them not only *life and good,* but *death and evil* (Deu. 30:15), so that they had fair warning given them of the fatal consequences of disobedience. 6. Lest this covenant should be forgotten, and, because out of mind, should be thought out of date, God had from time to time called to them to remember it, and by his servants the prophets had made a continual claim of this rent, so that they could not plead, in excuse of their non-payment, that it had never been demanded; *from the day when he brought them out of Egypt to this day* (and that was nearly 1000 years) he had been, in one way or other, *at sundry times and in divers manners,* protesting to them the necessity of obedience. God keeps an account how long we have enjoyed the means of grace and how powerful those means have been, how often we have been not only spoken to, but protested to, concerning our duty. 7. This covenant was consented to (*v.* 5): *Then answered I, and said, So be it, O Lord!* These are the words of the prophet, expressing either, (1.) His own consent to the covenant for himself, and his desire to have the benefit of it. God promised Canaan to the obedient: "Lord," says he, "I take thee at thy word, I will be obedient; let me have my inheritance in the land of promise, of which Canaan is a type." Or, (2.) His good will, and good wish, that his people might have the benefit of it. *"Amen;* Lord, let them still be kept in possession of this good land, and not turned out of it; make good the promise to them." Or, (3.) His people's consent to the covenant: *"Then answered I,* in the name of the people, *So be it."* Taking it in this sense, it refers to the declared consent which the people gave to the covenant, not only to the precepts of it when they said, *All that the Lord shall say unto us we will do and will be obedient,* but to the penalties when they said *Amen* to all the curses upon Mount Ebal. The more solemnly we have engaged ourselves to God the more reason we have to hope that the engagement will be perpetual; and yet here it did not prove so.

III. He charges them with breach of covenant, such a breach as amounted to a forfeiture of their charter, *v.* 8. God had said again and again, by his law and by his prophets, *"Obey my voice,* do as you are bidden, and all shall be well;" *yet they obeyed not;* and, because they were resolved not to submit their souls to God's commandments, they would not so much as incline their ears to them, but got as far as they could out of call: *They walked every one in the imagination of their evil heart,* followed their own

inventions; every man did as his fancy and humour led him, right or wrong, lawful or unlawful, both in their devotions and in their conversations; see *ch.* 7:24. What then could they expect, but to fall under the curse of the covenant, since they would not comply with the commands and conditions of it? *Therefore I will bring upon them all the words of this covenant,* that is, all the threatenings contained in it, because *they did not what they were commanded.* Note, The words of the covenant shall not fall to the ground. If we do not by our obedience qualify ourselves for the blessings of it, we shall by our disobedience bring ourselves under the curses of it. That which aggravated their defection from God, and rebellion against him, was that it was general, and as it were *by consent, v.* 9, 10. Jeremiah himself saw that many lived in open disobedience to God, but the Lord told him that the matter was worse than he thought of: *A conspiracy is found among them,* by him whose eye is upon the hidden works of darkness. There is a combination against God and religion, a dangerous design formed to overthrow God's government and bring in the pretenders, the counterfeit deities. This intimates that they were wilful and deliberate in wickedness (they rebelled against God, not through incogitancy, but presumptuously, and with a high hand), — that they were subtle and ingenious in wickedness, and carried on their plot against religion with a great deal of art and contrivance, — that they were linked together in the design, and, as is usual among conspirators, engaged to stand by one another in it and to live and die together; they were resolved to go through with it. A cursed conspiracy! O that there were not the like in our day! Observe, 1. What the conspiracy was. They designed to overthrow divine revelation, and set that aside, and persuade people not to hear, not to heed, the words of God. They did all they could to derogate from the authority of the scriptures and to lessen the value of them; they designed to draw people *after other gods to serve them,* to consult them as their oracles and make court to them as their benefactors. Human reason shall be their god, a light within their god, an infallible judge their god, saints and angels their gods, the god of this or the other nation shall be theirs; thus, under several disguises, they are in the same confederacy *against the Lord and against his anointed.* 2. Who were in conspiracy. One would have expected find some foreigners ring-leaders in it; but no, (1.) *The inhabitants of Jerusalem* are in conspiracy with *the men of Judah;* city and country agree in this, however they may differ in other things. (2.) Those of this generation seem to be in conspiracy with those of the foregoing generation, to carry on the war from age to age against religion: *They are turned back to the iniquities of their forefathers,* and have risen up in their stead, *a seed of evil-doers,* and *increase of sinful men,* Num. 32:14. In Josiah's time there had been a reformation, but after this death the people returned to the idolatries which then they had renounced. (3.) Judah and Israel, the kingdom of the ten tribes and that of the two, that were often at daggers-drawing one with another, were yet *in a conspiracy to break the covenant God had made with their fathers,* even with the heads of all the twelve tribes. The house of Israel began the revolt, but the house of Judah soon came into the conspiracy. Now what else could be expected but that god should take severe methods, both for the chastising of the conspirators and the crushing of this conspiracy; for none ever hardened his heart thus against God and prospered? He that rolls this stone will find it return upon him.

Verses 11–17

This paragraph, which contains so much of God's wrath, might very well be expected to follow upon that which goes next before, which contained so much of his people's sin. When God found so much evil among them we cannot think it strange if it follows, *Therefore I will bring evil upon them* (*v.* 11), the evil of punishment for the evil of sin; and there is no remedy, no relief: the decree has gone forth and the sentence will be executed.

I. They cannot help themselves, but will be found too weak to contest with God's judgments: it is *evil which they shall not be able to escape,* or to *go forth out of,* by any evasion whatsoever. Note, Those that will not submit to God's government shall not be able to escape his wrath. There is no fleeing from his justice, no avoiding his cognizance. Evil pursues sinners and entangles them in snares out of which they cannot extricate themselves.

II. Their God will not help them; his providence shall no way favour them: *Though they shall cry unto me, I will not hearken to them.* In their affliction they will seek the God whom before they slighted, and cry to him whom before they would not vouchsafe to speak to. But how can they expect to speed? For he has plainly told us that he that *turns away his ears from hearing the law,* as they did, for they *inclined not their ear* (*v.* 8), even his prayer shall be an abomination to him, as the word of the Lord was now to them a reproach.

III. Their idols shall not help them, *v.* 12. They shall *go, and cry to the gods to whom they* now *offer incense,* and put them in mind of the costly services wherewith they had honoured them, expecting they should now have relief from them, but in vain. They shall be sent to the *gods whom they served* (Jdg. 10:14; Deu. 32:37, 38), and what the better? *They shall not save them at all,* shall do nothing towards their salvation, nor give them any prospect of it; they shall not afford them the least comfort, nor relief, nor mitigation of their trouble. It is God only that is a friend at need, *a present* powerful *help in time of trouble.* The idols cannot help themselves; how then should they help their worshippers? Those that make idols of the world and the flesh will in vain have recourse to them in a day of distress. If the idols could have done any real kindness to their worshippers, they would have done it for this people, who had renounced the true God to embrace them, had multiplied them *according to the number of their cities* (*v.* 13), nay, in Jerusalem, *according to the number of their streets.* Suspecting both their sufficiency and their readiness to help them, they must have many, lest a few would not serve; they must have them dispersed in every corner, lest they should be out of the way when they had occasion for them. In *Jerusalem,* the city which God had chosen to put his name there, publicly in the streets of Jerusalem, in every street, they had *altars to that shameful thing,* that *shame,* even to Baal, which they ought to have been ashamed of, with which they did reproach the Lord and bring confusion upon themselves. But now in their distress their many gods, and many altars, should stand them in stead. Note, Those that will not be ashamed of their commission of sin as a wicked thing will be ashamed of their expectations from sin as a fruitless thing.

IV. Jeremiah's prayers shall not help them, *v.* 14. What God had said to him before (*ch.* 7:16) he here says again, *Pray not thou for this people.* This is not designed for a command to the prophet, so much as for a threatening to the people, that they should have no benefit by the prayers of their friends for them. God would give no encouragement to the prophets to pray for them, would not stir up the spirit of prayer, but cast a damp upon it, would put it into their hearts to pray, not for the body of the people, but for the remnant among them, to pray for their eternal salvation, not for their deliverance from the temporal judgments that were coming upon them; and what other prayers were put up for them should not be heard. Those are in a sad case indeed that are cut off from the benefit of prayer. *"I will not hear them when they cry,* and therefore to not thou pray for them." Note, Those that have so far thrown themselves out of God's favour that he will not hear their prayers cannot expect benefit by the prayers of others for them.

V. The profession they make of religion shall stand them in no stead, *v.* 15. They were originally God's *beloved,* his spouse, he was married to them by the covenant of peculiarity; even the unbelieving Jews are said to be *beloved for the fathers' sake,* Rom. 11:28. As such they had a place *in God's house;* they were admitted to worship in the courts of his temple; they partook of God's altar; they ate of the flesh of their peace-offerings here called the *holy flesh,* which God had the honour of and they had the comfort of. This they gloried in, and trusted to. What harm could come to those who were God's beloved, who were under the protection of his house? Even when they *did evil* yet *they rejoiced* and gloried in this, made a mighty noise of this. And *when their evil was* (so the margin reads it), when trouble came upon them, *they rejoiced in this,* and made this their confidence; but their confidence would deceive them, for God has rejected it, they themselves having forfeited the privileges they so much boasted of. They have

wrought lewdness with many, have been guilty of spiritual whoredom, have worshipped many idols; and therefore, 1. God's temple will *yield them no protection;* it is fit that the adulteress, especially when she has so often repeated her whoredoms and has grown so impudent in them and irreclaimable, should be *put away,* and turned out of doors: *"What has my beloved to do in my house?* She is a scandal to it, and therefore it shall no longer be a shelter to her." 2. God's altar will yield them no satisfaction, nor can they expect any comfort from that: *"The holy flesh has passed from thee,* that is, an end will soon be put to thy sacrifices, when the temple shall be laid in ruins; and where then will the holy flesh be, that thou art so proud of?" A holy heart will be a comfort to us when the holy flesh has passed from us; an inward principle of grace will make up the want of the outward means of grace. But woe unto us if the departure of the holy flesh be accompanied with the departure of the Holy Spirit.

VI. God's former favours to them shall stand them in no stead, *v.* 16, 17. Their remembrance of them shall be no comfort to them under their troubles, and God's remembrance of them shall be no argument for their relief. 1. It is true God had done great things for them; that people had been favourites above any people under the sun; they had been the darlings of heaven. God had *called Israel's name a green olive-tree,* and had made them so, for he miscalls nothing; he had *planted* them (*v.* 17), had formed them into a people, with all the advantages they could have to make them a fruitful and flourishing people, so good was their law and so good was their land. One would think no other than that a people so planted, so watered, so cultivated, should be, as the olive-tree is, ever green, in respect both of piety and prosperity, Ps. 52:8. God called them *fair and of goodly fruit,* both good for food and pleasant to the eye, both amiable and serviceable to God and man, for which the greenness and fatness of the olive both are honoured, Jdg. 9:9. 2. It is as true that they have done evil things against God. He had planted them a green olive, a good olive, but they had degenerated into a *wild olive,* Rom. 11:17. Both *the house of Israel.* and the *house of Judah* had *done evil,* had *provoked God to anger in burning incense unto Baal,* setting up other mediators between them and the supreme God besides the promised Messiah; nay, setting up other gods in competition with the true and living God, for they had *gods many,* as well as *lords many.* 3. When they have conducted themselves so ill they can expect no other than that, notwithstanding what good he has done to them and designed for them, he should now bring upon them the evil he has *pronounced against them.* He that planted this green olive-tree, and expected fruit from it, finding it barren and grown wild, *has kindled fire upon it,* to burn it as it stands; for, being without fruit, it is *twice dead, plucked up by the roots* (Jude 12), it is *cut down and cast into the fire,* the fittest place for trees that cumber the ground, Mt. 3:10. The *branches of it,* the *high and lofty boughs* (so the word signifies), are *broken* are *broken down,* both princes and priests cut off. And thus it proves that the evil done against God, to *provoke him to anger,* is really done *against themselves;* they *wrong their own souls;* God is out of their reach, but they ruin themselves. See *ch.* 7:19. Note, Every sin against God is a sin against ourselves, and so it will be found sooner or later.

Verses 18–23

The prophet Jeremiah has much in his writings concerning himself, much more than Isaiah had, the times he lived in being very troublesome. Here we have (as it should seem) the beginning of his sorrows, which arose from the people of his own city, Anathoth, a priest's city, and yet a malignant one. Observe here,

I. Their plot against him, *v.* 19. They *devised devices against him,* laid their heads together to contrive how they might be in the most plausible and effectual manner the death of him. Malice is ingenious in its devices, as well as industrious in its prosecutions. They said concerning Jeremiah, *Let us destroy the tree with the fruit thereof* — a proverbial expression, meaning, "Let us utterly destroy him root and branch. Let us destroy both the father and the family" (as, when Naboth was put to death for treason, his sons were put to death with him), or rather "both the prophet and the prophecy; let us kill the one and defeat

the other. *Let us cut him off from the land of the living,* as a false prophet, and load him with ignominy and disgrace, *that his name may be no more remembered* with respect. Let us sink his reputation, and so spoil the credit of his predictions." This was their plot; and 1. It was a cruel one; but so cruel have the persecutors of God's prophets been. They *hunt for* no less than *the precious life,* and very precious the lives are that they hunt for. But, (2.) It was a baffled one. They thought to put an end to his days, but he survived most of his enemies; they thought to blast his memory, but it lives to this day, and will be blessed while time lasts.

II. The information which God gave him of this conspiracy against him. He knew nothing of it himself, so artfully had they concealed it; he came to Anathoth, meaning no harm to them and therefore fearing no harm from them, *like a lamb or an ox,* that thinks he is driven as usual to the field, *when he is brought to the slaughter;* so little did poor Jeremiah dream of the design his citizens that hated him had upon him. None of his friends could, and none of his enemies would, give him any notice of his danger, that he might shift for his own safety, as Paul's sister's son gave him intelligence of the Jews that were lying in wait for him. There is but a step between Jeremiah and death; but then *the Lord gave him knowledge of it,* by dream or vision, or impression upon his spirit, that he might save himself, as the king of Israel did upon the notice Elisha gave him, 2 Ki. 6:10. Thus he came to *know it.* God *showed him their doings;* and such were their devices that the discovering of them was the defeating of them. If God had not let him know his own danger, it would have been improved by unreasonable men against the reputation of his predictions, that he who foretold the ruin of his country could not foresee his own peril and avoid it. See what care God takes of his prophets: He *suffers no man to do them wrong;* all the rage of their enemies cannot prevail to take them off till they have finished their testimony. God knows all the secret designs of his and his people's enemies, and can, when he pleases, make them know. *A bird of the air shall carry the voice.*

III. His appeal to God hereupon, *v.* 20. His eye is to God as *the Lord of hosts, that judges righteously.* It is a matter of comfort to us, when men deal unjustly with us, that we have a God to go to who does and will plead the cause of injured innocency and appear against the injurious. God's justice, which is a terror to the wicked, is a comfort to the godly. His eye is towards him as the God that *tries the reins and the heart,* that perfectly sees what is in man, what are his thoughts and intents. He knew the integrity that was in Jeremiah's heart, and that he was not the man they represented him to be. He knew the wickedness that was in their hearts, though ever so cunningly concealed and disguised. Now, 1. Jeremiah prays judgment against them: *"Let me see thy vengeance on them,* that is, do justice between me and them in such a way as thou pleasest." Some think there was something of human frailty in this prayer; at least Christ has taught us another lesson, both by precept and by pattern, which is to pray for our persecutors. Others think it comes from a pure zeal for the glory of God and a pious and prophetic indignation against men that were by profession priests, the Lord's ministers, and yet were so desperately wicked as to fly out against one that did them no harm, merely for the service he did to God. This petition was a prediction that he should see God's vengeance on them. 2. He refers his cause entirely to the judgment of God: *"Unto thee have I revealed my cause;* to thee I have committed it, not desiring nor expecting to interest any other in it." Note, It is our comfort, when we are wronged, that we have a God to commit our cause to, and our duty to commit it to him, with a resolution to acquiesce in his definitive sentence, to subscribe, and not prescribe, to him.

IV. Judgment given against his persecutors, *the men of Anathoth.* It was to no purpose for him to appeal to the courts at Jerusalem, he could not have justice done him there: the priests there would stand by the priests at Anathoth, and rather second them than discountenance them; but God will *therefore* take cognizance of the cause himself, and we are sure that *his judgment is according to truth.* Here is, 1. Their crime recited, on which the sentence is grounded, *v.* 21. They sought the prophet's life, for they forbad him to prophesy upon pain of death; they were resolved either to silence him or to slay him. The provocation he gave them was his prophesying *in the name of the Lord* without license from those that were the governors of the city which he was a member of, and not prophesying such smooth things as they always bespoke. Their forbidding him to prophesy was in effect seeking his life, for it was seeking to defeat the end and business of his life and to rob him of the comfort of it. It is as bad to God's faithful ministers to have their mouth stopped as to have their breath stopped. But especially when it was resolved that if he did prophesy, as certainly he would notwithstanding their inhibition, he should *die by their hand;* they would be accusers, judges, executioners, and all. It used to be said that *a prophet could not perish but at Jerusalem,* for there the great council sat; but so bitter were the men of Anathoth against Jeremiah that they would undertake to be the death of him themselves. A prophet then shall find not only no honour, but no favour, in his own country. 2. The sentence passed upon them for this crime, *v.* 22, 23. God says, *I will punish them;* let me alone to deal with them. *I will visit* this *upon them;* so the word is. God will enquire into it and reckon for it. Two of God's four sore judgments shall serve to ruin their town: — *The sword* shall devour their *young men,* though they were young priests, not men of war (their character shall not be their protection), and *famine* shall destroy the children, *sons and daughters,* that tarry at home, which is a more grievous death than that by the sword, Lam. 4:9. The destruction shall be final (*v.* 23): *There shall be no remnant of them left,* none to be the seed of another generation. They sought Jeremiah's life, and therefore they shall die; they would destroy him *root and branch,* that *his name* might be *no more remembered,* and therefore *there shall be no remnant of them;* and herein the Lord is righteous. Thus *evil is brought upon them, even the year of their visitation,* and that is evil enough, a recompence according to their deserts. Then shall Jeremiah *see his desire upon his enemies.* Note, Their condition is sad who have the prayers of good ministers and good people against them.

CHAPTER 12

In this chapter we have, I. The prophet's humble complaint to God of the success that wicked people had in their wicked practices (*v.* 1, 2) and his appeal to God concerning his own integrity (*v.* 3), with a prayer that God would, for the sake of the public, bring the wickedness of the wicked to an end (*v.* 3, 4). II. God's rebuke to the prophet for his uneasiness at his present troubles, bidding him prepare for greater (*v.* 5, 6). III. A sad lamentation of the present deplorable state of the Israel of God (*v.* 7–13). IV. An intimation of mercy to God's people, in a denunciation of wrath against their neighbours that helped forward their affliction, that they should be plucked out; but with a promise that if they would at last join themselves with the people of God they should come in sharers with them in their privileges (*v.* 14–17).

Verses 1–6

The prophet doubts not but it would be of use to others to know what had passed between God and his soul, what temptations he had been assaulted with and how he had got over them; and therefore he here tells us,

I. What liberty he humbly took, and was graciously allowed him, to reason with God concerning his judgments, *v.* 1. He is about to *plead* with God, not to quarrel with him, or find fault with his proceedings, but to enquire into the meaning of them, that he might more and more see reason to be satisfied in them, and might have wherewith to answer both his own and others' objections against them. The works of the Lord, and the reasons of them, are *sought out* even *of those that have pleasure therein.* Ps. 111:2. We may not *strive with our Maker,* but we may reason with him. The prophet lays down a truth of unquestionable certainty, which he resolves to abide by in managing this argument: *Righteous art thou, O Lord! when I plead with thee.* Thus he arms himself against the temptation wherewith he was assaulted, to envy the prosperity of the wicked, before he entered into a parley with it. Note, When we are most in the dark concerning the meaning of God's dispensations we must still resolve to keep up right thoughts of God, and must be confident of this, that he never did, nor ever will do, the least wrong to any of his creatures; even when his *judgments are* unsearchable as *a great deep,* and altogether unaccountable, yet *his righteousness* is as conspicuous and immovable as *the great mountains,* Ps. 36:6. Though sometimes *clouds and darkness are round about him,* yet *justice and judgment are* always *the habitation of his throne,* Ps. 97:2. When we find it hard to understand particular providences we must have recourse to general truths as our first principles, and abide by them; however dark the providence may be, *the Lord is righteous;* see Ps. 73:1. And we must acknowledge it to him, as the prophet here, even when we *plead with him,* as those that have no thoughts of contending but of learning, being fully assured that he will be *justified when he speaks.* Note, However we may see cause for our own information to plead with God, yet it becomes us to own that, whatever he says or does, he is in the right.

II. What it was in the dispensations of divine Providence that he stumbled at and that he thought would bear a debate. It was that which has been a temptation to many wise and good men, and such a one as they have with difficulty got over. They see the designs and projects of wicked people successful: *The way of the wicked prospers;* they compass their malicious designs and gain their point. They see their affairs and concerns in a good posture: *They are happy,* happy as the world can make them, though *they deal* treacherously, *very treacherously,* both with God and man. Hypocrites are chiefly meant (as appears, *v.* 2), who dissemble in their good professions, and depart from their good beginnings and good promises, and in both they deal treacherously, very treacherously. It has been said that men cannot expect to prosper who are unjust and dishonest in their dealings; but these deal treacherously, and yet *they are happy.* The prophet shows (*v.* 2) both their prosperity and their abuse of their prosperity. 1. God had been very indulgent to them and they were got beforehand in the world: "They are planted in a good land, a land flowing with milk and honey, and *thou hast planted them!* nay, thou didst cast out the heathen to plant them," Ps. 44:2, 80:8. Many a tree is planted that yet never grows nor comes to any thing; but *they have taken root;* their prosperity seems to be confirmed and settled. They take root in the earth, for there they fix themselves, and thence they draw the sap of all their satisfaction. Many trees however take root which yet never come on; but these *grow, yea they bring forth fruit;* their families are built up, they live high, and spend at a great rate; and all this was owing to the benignity of the divine Providence, which smiled upon them, Ps. 73:7. 2. Thus God had favoured them, though they had dealt treacherously with him: *Thou art near in their mouth and far from their reins.* This was no uncharitable censure, for he spoke by the Spirit of prophecy, without which it is not safe to charge men with hypocrisy whose appearances are plausible. Observe, (1.) Thought they cared not for thinking of God, nor had any sincere affection to him, yet they could easily persuade themselves to speak of him frequently and with an air of seriousness. Piety from the teeth outward is no difficult thing. Many speak the language of Israel that are not Israelites indeed. (2.) Though they had on all occasions the name of God ready in their mouth, and accustomed themselves to those forms of speech that savoured of piety, yet they could not persuade themselves to keep up the fear of God in their hearts. The form of godliness should engage us to keep up the power of it; but with them it did not do so.

III. What comfort he had in appealing to God concerning his own integrity (*v.* 3): *But thou, O Lord! knowest me.* Probably the wicked men he complains of were forward to reproach and censure him (*ch.* 18:18), in reference to which this was his comfort, that God was a witness of his integrity. God knew he was not such a one as they were (who had God *near in their mouths, but far from their reins),* nor such a one as they took him to be, and represented him, a deceiver and a false prophet; those that thus abused him did not know him, 1 Co. 2:8. *"But thou, O Lord! knowest me,* though they think me not worth their notice." 1. Observe what the matter is concerning which he appeals to God: Thou knowest *my heart towards thee.* Note, We are as our hearts are, and our hearts are good or bad according as they are, or are not, towards God; and this is that therefore concerning which we should examine ourselves, that we may approve ourselves to God. 2. The cognizance to which he appeals: *"Thou knowest me* better than I know myself, not by hearsay or report, for *thou hast seen me,* not with a transient glance, but thou hast *tried my heart."* God's knowledge of us is as clear and exact and certain as if he had made the most strict scrutiny. Note, The God with whom we have to do perfectly knows how our hearts are towards him. He knows both the guile of the hypocrite and the sincerity of the upright.

IV. He prays that God would turn his hand against these wicked people, and not suffer them to prosper always, though they had prospered long: "Let some judgment come to *pull them out* of this fat pasture *as sheep for the slaughter,* that it may appear their long prosperity was but like the feeding of lambs in a large place, to *prepare them for the day of slaughter,"* Hos. 4:16. God suffered them to prosper that by their pride and luxury they might fill up the measure of their iniquity and so be ripened for destruction; and therefore he thinks it a piece of necessary justice that they should fall into mischief themselves, because they had done so much mischief to others, that they should be pulled out of their land, because they had brought ruin upon the land, and the longer they continued in it the more hurt they did, as the plagues of their generation (*v.* 4): *"How long shall the land mourn.* (as it does under the judgments of God inflicted upon it) *for the wickedness of those that dwell therein?* Lord, shall those prosper themselves that ruin all about them?" 1. See here what the judgment was which the land was now groaning under: *The herbs of every field wither* (the grass is burnt up and all the products of the earth fail), and then it follows of course, the beasts are consumed, and the birds, 1 Ki. 18:5. This was the effect of a long drought, or want of rain, which happened, as it should seem, at the latter end of Josiah's reign and the beginning of Jehoiakim's; it is mentioned *ch.* 3:3, 8:13, 9:10, 12, and more fully afterwards, *ch.* 14. If they would have been brought to repentance by this less judgment, the greater would have been prevented. Now why was it that this *fruitful land* was *turned into barrenness,* but *for the wickedness of those that dwelt therein?* Ps. 17:34. Therefore the prophet prays that these wicked people might *die for their own sin,* and that the whole nation might not suffer for it. 2. See here what was the language of their wickedness: *They said, He shall not see our last end,* either, (1.) God himself shall not. Atheism is the root of hypocrisy. God is *far from their reins,* though *near in their mouth,* because they say, *How doth God know?* Ps. 73:11; Job 22:13. He knows not what way we take nor what it will end in. Or, (2.) Jeremiah *shall not see our last end;* whatever he pretends, when he asks us what shall be in the end hereof he cannot himself foresee it. They look upon him as a false prophet. Or, "whatever it is, he shall not live to see it, for we will be the death of him," *ch.* 11:21. Note, [1.] Men's setting their latter end at a great distance, or looking upon it as uncertain, is at the bottom of all their wickedness, Lam. 1:9. [2.] The whole creation groans under the burden of the sin of man, Rom. 8:22. It is for this that *the earth mourns* (so it may be read); *cursed is the ground for thy sake.*

V. He acquaints us with the answer God gave to those complaints of his, *v.* 5, 6. We often find the prophets admonished, whose business it was to admonish others, as Isa. 8:11. Ministers have lessons to learn as well as lessons to teach, and must themselves hear God's voice and preach to themselves. Jeremiah complained much of the wickedness of the men of Anathoth, and that, notwithstanding that, they prospered. Now, this seems to be an answer to that complaint. 1. It is allowed that he had cause to complain (*v.* 6): *"Thy brethren,* the priests of Anathoth, who are of *the house of thy father,* who ought to have protected thee and pretended to do so, *even they have dealt treacherously with thee,* have been false to thee, and, under colour of friendship, have designedly done thee all the mischief they could; they *have called a multitude after thee,* raised the mob upon thee, to whom they have endeavoured, by all arts possible, to render thee despicable or odious, while at the same time they pretended that they had no design to persecute thee nor to deprive thee of thy liberty. They are indeed such as thou canst *not believe, though they speak fair words to thee.* They seem to be thy friends, but are really thy enemies." Note, God's faithful servants must not think it at all strange if their foes be *those of their own house* (Mt. 10:36), and if those they expect kindness from prove such as they can put no confidence in, Mic. 7:5. 2. Yet he is told that he carried the matter too far. (1.) He laid the unkindness of his countrymen too much to heart. *They wearied* him, because it was *in a land of peace wherein he trusted, v.* 5. It was very grievous to him to be thus hated and abused by his own kindred. He was disturbed in his mind by it; his spirit was sunk and overwhelmed with it, so that he was in great agitation and distress about it. Nay, he was discouraged in his work by it, began to be weary of prophesying, and to think of giving it up. (2.) He did not consider that this was but the beginning of his sorrow, and that he had sorer trials yet before him; and, whereas he should endeavour by a patient bearing of this trouble to prepare himself for greater, by his uneasiness under this he did but unfit himself for what further lay before him: *If thou hast run with the footmen and they have wearied thee,* and run thee quite out of breath,*then how wilt thou contend with horses?* If the injuries done him by the men of Anathoth made such an impression upon him, what would he do when the princes and chief priests at Jerusalem should set upon him with their power, as they did afterwards? *ch.* 20:2; 32:2. If he was so soon tired *in a land of peace,* where there was little noise or peril, *what would he do in the swellings of Jordan,* when that overflows all its banks and frightens even lions out of their thickets? *ch.* 49:19. Note, [1.] While we are in this world we must expect troubles and difficulties. Our life is a race, a warfare; we are in danger of being run down. [2.] God's usual method being to begin with smaller trials, it is our wisdom to expect greater than any we have yet met with. We may be called out to *contend with horsemen,* and the sons of Anak may perhaps be reserved for the last encounter. [3.] It highly concerns us to prepare for such trials and to consider what we should do in them. How shall we preserve our integrity and peace when we come to *the swellings of Jordan?* [4.] In order to our preparation for further and greater trials, we are concerned to approve ourselves well in present smaller trials, to keep up our spirits, keep hold of the promise, keep in our way, with our eye upon the prize, so run that we may obtain it. Some good interpreters understand this as spoken to the people, who were very secure and fearless of the threatened judgments. If they have been so humbled and impoverished by smaller calamities, so wasted by the Assyrians, — if the Ammonites and Moabites, who were their brethren, and with whom they were in league, proved false to them (as undoubtedly they would), — then how would they be able to deal with such a powerful adversary as the Chaldeans would be? How would they bear up their head against that invasion which should come like *the swelling of Jordan?*

Verses 7–13

The people of the Jews are here marked for ruin.

I. God is here brought in falling out with them and leaving them desolate; and they could never have been undone if they had not provoked God to desert them. It is a terrible word that God here says (*v.* 7): *I have forsaken my house* — the temple, which had been his palace; they had polluted it, and so forced him out of it: *I have left my heritage,* and will look after it no more. His people that he has taken such delight in, and care of, are now thrown out of his protection. They had been *the dearly beloved of his soul,* precious in his sight and honorable above any people, which is mentioned to aggravate their sin in returning him hatred for his love and their misery in throwing themselves out of the favour of one that had such a kindness for them, and to justify God in his dealings with them. He sought not occasion against them, but, if they would have conducted themselves with any tolerable propriety, he would have made the best of them, for they were *the beloved of his soul;* but they had conducted themselves so that they had provoked him to *give them into the hand of their enemies,* to leave them unguarded, an easy prey to those that bore them ill-will. But what was the quarrel God had with a people that had been so long dear to him? Why, truly, they had degenerated. 1. They had become like *beasts of prey,* which nobody loves, but every body avoids and gets as far off from as he can (*v.* 8): *My heritage is unto me as a lion in the forest.* Their sins cry to heaven for vengeance as loud as a lion roars. Nay, they *cry out against God* in the threatenings and slaughter which they breathe against his prophets that speak to them in his name; and what is said and done against them God takes as said and done against himself. They blaspheme his name, oppose his authority, and bid defiance to his justice, and so *cry out against him as a lion in the forest.* Those that were the *sheep of God's pasture* had become barbarous and rav-

enous, and as ungovernable as lions in the forest; *therefore he hated them;* for what delight could the God of love take in a people that had now become as roaring lions and raging beasts, fit to be taken and shot at, as a vexation and torment to all about them? 2. They had become like *birds of prey,* and therefore also unworthy a place in God's house, where neither beasts nor birds of prey were admitted to be offered in sacrifice (*v.* 9): *My heritage is unto me as a bird with talons* (so some read it, and so the margin); they are continually pulling and pecking at one another; they have by their unnatural contentions made their country a cock-pit. Or *as a speckled bird,* dyed, or sprinkled, or bedewed with the blood of her prey. The shedding of innocent blood was Jerusalem's measure-filling sin, and hastened their ruin, not only as it provoked their neighbours likewise; for those that have *their hand against every man* shall have *every man's hand against them* (Gen. 16:12), and so it follows here: *The birds round about are against her.* Some make her a *speckled, pied,* or *motley bird,* upon the account of their mixing the superstitious customs and usages of the heathen with divine institutions in the worship of God; they were fond of a party-coloured religion, and thought it made them fine, when really it made them odious. God's turtle-dove is no speckled bird.

II. The enemies are here brought in falling upon them and laying them desolate. And some think it is upon this account that they are compared to a speckled bird, because fowls usually make a noise about a bird of an odd unusual colour. God's people are, among the children of this world, as *men wondered at,* as a *speckled bird;* but this people had by their own folly made themselves so; and the beasts and birds are called and commissioned to prey upon them. Let *all the birds round* be *against her,* for God has forsaken her, and with them let *all the beasts of the field come to devour.* Those that have made a prey of others shall themselves be preyed upon. It did not lessen the sin of the nations, but very much increased the misery of Judah and Jerusalem, that the desolation brought upon them was by order from heaven. The birds and beasts are perhaps called to feast upon the bodies of the slain, as in St. John's vision, Rev. 19:17, 18. The utter desolation of the land by the Chaldean army is here spoken of as a thing done, so sure, so near, was it. God speaks of it as a thing which he had appointed to be done, and yet which he had no pleasure in, any more than in the death of other sinners.

1. See with what a tender affection he speaks of this land, notwithstanding the sinfulness of it, in remembrance of his covenant, and the tribute of honour and glory he had formerly had from it: It is *my vineyard, my portion, my pleasant portion, v.* 10. Note, God has a kindness and concern for his church, though there be much amiss in it; and his correcting it will every way consist with his complacency in it.

2. See with what a tender compassion he speaks of the desolations of this land: *Many pastors* (the Chaldean generals that made themselves masters of the country and ate it up with their armies as easily as the Arabian shepherds with their flocks eat up the fruits of a piece of ground that lies common) *have destroyed my vineyard,* without any consideration had either of the value of it or of my interest in it; they have with the greatest insolence and indignation *trodden it under foot,* and that which was a pleasant land they have made *a desolate wilderness.* The destruction was universal: *The whole land is made desolate, v.* 11. It is made so by the sword of war: *The spoilers,* the Chaldean soldiers,*have come through the plain upon all high places;* they have made themselves masters of all the natural fastnesses and artificial fortresses, *v.* 12. *The sword devours from one end of the land to the other;* all places lie exposed, and the numerous army of the invaders disperse themselves into every corner of that fruitful country, so that *no flesh shall have peace,* none shall be exempt from the calamity nor be able to enjoy any tranquillity. When all flesh have corrupted their way, no flesh shall have peace; those only have peace that walk after the Spirit.

3. See whence all this misery comes. (1.) It comes from the displeasure of God. It is *the sword of the Lord* that *devours, v.* 12. While God's people keep close to him the sword of their protectors and deliverers is the sword of the Lord, witness that of Gideon; but when they have forsaken him, so that he has become their enemy and fights

against them, then the sword of their invaders and destroyers becomes the *sword of the Lord;* witness this of the Chaldeans. It is *because of the fierce anger of the Lord* (*v.* 13); it was this that kindled this fire among them and made their enemies so furious. And *who may stand before him when he is angry?* (2.) It is their sin that has made God their enemy, particularly their incorrigibleness under former rebukes (*v.* 11): The land *mourns unto me;* the country that lies desolate does, as it were, pour out its complaint before God and humble itself under his hand; but the inhabitants are so senseless and stupid that *none of them lays it to heart;* they do not mourn to God, but are unaffected with his displeasure, while the very ground they go upon shames them. Note, When God's hand is lifted up, and men will not see, it shall be laid on, and they shall be made to feel, Isa. 26:11.

4. See how unable they should be to guard against it (*v.* 13): *"They have sown wheat,* that is, they have taken a great deal of pains for their own security and promised themselves great matters from their endeavors, but it is all in vain; *they shall reap thorns,* that is, that which shall prove very grievous and vexatious to them. Instead of helping themselves, they shall but make themselves more uneasy. *They have put themselves to pain,* both with their labour and with their expectations, *but it shall not profit;* they shall not prevail to extricate themselves out of the difficulties into which they have plunged themselves. *They shall be ashamed of your revenues,* ashamed that they have depended so much upon their preparations for war and particularly upon their ability to bear the charges of it." Money constitutes the sinews of war; they thought they had enough of that, but shall be ashamed of it; for their silver and gold shall not profit them in the day of the Lord's anger.

Verses 14–17

The prophets sometimes, in God's name, delivered messages both of judgment and mercy to the nations that bordered on the land of Israel: but here is a message to all those in general who had in their turns been one way or other injurious to God's people, had either oppressed them or triumphed in their being oppressed. Observe,

I. What the quarrel was that God had with them. They were *his evil neighbours* (*v.* 14), evil neighbours to his church, and what they did against it he took as done against himself, and therefore called them *his evil neighbours,* that should have been neighbourly to Israel, but were quite otherwise. Note, It is often the lot of good people to live among bad neighbours, that are unkind and provoking to them; and it is bad indeed when they are all so. These evil neighbours were the Moabites, Ammonites, Syrians, Edomites, Egyptians, that had been evil neighbours to Israel in helping to debauch them and draw them from God (therefore God calls them his evil neighbours), and now they helped to make them desolate, and joined with the Chaldeans against them. It is just with God to make those the instruments of trouble to us whom we have made instruments of sin. That which God lays to their charge is: They have *meddled with the inheritance which I have caused my people Israel to inherit;* they unjustly seized that which was none of their own: nay, they sacrilegiously turned that to their own use which was given to God's peculiar people. He that said, *Touch not my anointed,* said also, *"Touch not their inheritance;* it is at your peril if you do." Not only the persons but the estates of God's people are under his protection.

II. What course he would take with them. 1. He would break the power they had got over his people, and force them to make restitution: *I will pluck out the house of Judah from among them.* This would be a great favour to God's people, who had either been taken captive by them, or, when they fled to them for shelter, had been detained and made prisoners; but it would be a great mortification to their enemies, who would be like a lion disappointed of his prey. The house of Judah either cannot or will not make any bold struggles towards their own liberty; but God will with a gracious violence pluck them out, will by his Spirit compel them to come out and by his power compel their task-masters to let them go, as he plucked Israel out of Egypt. 2. He would bring upon them the same calamities that they had been instrumental to bring upon his people: *I will pluck them out of their land.*

Judgment began at the house of God, but it did not end there. Nebuchadnezzar, when he had wasted the land of Israel, turned his hand against their evil neighbours and was a scourge to them.

III. What mercy God had in store for such of them as would join themselves to him and become his people, *v.* 15, 16. They had drawn in God's backsliding people to join with them in the service of idols. If now they would be drawn by a returning people to join with them in the service of the true and living God, they should not only have their enmity to the people of God forgiven them, but the distance which they had been kept at before should be removed, and they should be received to stand upon the same level with the Israel of God. This had its accomplishment in part when, after the return out of captivity, many of the people of the lands that had been evil neighbours to Israel became Jews; and it was to have its accomplishment in the conversion of the Gentiles to the faith of Christ. Let not Israel, though injured by them, be implacable towards them, for God is not: *After that I have plucked them out,* in justice for their sins and in jealousy for the honour of Israel, *I will return,* will change my way, *and have compassion on them.* Though, being heathen, they can lay no claim to the mercies of the covenant, yet they shall have benefit by the compassions of the Creator, who will notwithstanding look upon them as the work of his hands. Note, God's controversies with his creatures, though they cannot be disputed, may be accommodated. Those who (as these) have been not only strangers, but *enemies in their minds by wicked works,* may be *reconciled,* Col. 1:21. Observe here,

1. What were the terms on which God would show favour to them. It is always provided *that they will diligently learn the ways of my people,* that is, in general, the ways that they walk in when they conduct themselves as *my people* (not the crooked ways into which they have turned aside), the ways which my people are directed to take. Note, (1.) There are good ways that are peculiarly *the ways of God's people,* which however they may differ in the choice of their paths, they are all agreed to walk in. The ways of holiness and heavenly-mindedness, of love and peaceableness, the ways of prayer and sabbath-sanctification, and diligent attendance on instituted ordinances — these, and the like, are *the ways of God's people.* (2.) Those that would have their lot with God's people, and their last end like theirs, must learn their ways and walk in them, must observe the rule they walk by and conform to that rule they walk by and conform to that rule and go forth by those footsteps. By an intimate conversation with God's people they must learn to do as they do. (3.) It is impossible to learn the ways of God's people as they should be learnt, without a great deal of care and pains. We must diligently observe these ways and diligently obliges ourselves to walk in them, must look diligently (Heb. 12:15), and work diligently, Lu. 13:24. In particular, they must learn to give honour to God's name by making all their solemn appeals to him. They must learn to say, *The Lord liveth* (to own him, to adore him, and to abide by his judgment), *as they taught my people to swear by Baal.* It was bad enough that they did themselves swear by Baal, worse that they taught God's own people, who had been better taught; and yet, if they will at length reform, they shall be accepted. observe, [1.] We must not despair of the conversion of the worst; no, not of those who have been instrumental to pervert and debauch others; even they may be brought to repentance, and, if they be, shall find mercy. [2.] Those whom we have been industrious to draw to that which is evil, when God opens their eyes and ours, we should be as industrious to follow in that which is good. It will be a holy revenge upon ourselves to become pupils to those in the way of duty to whom we have been tutors in the was of sin. [3.] The conversion of the deceived may prove a happy occasion of the conversion even of the deceivers. Thus those who fall together into the ditch are sometimes plucked together out of it.

2. What should be the tokens and fruits of this favour when they return to God and God to them. (1.) They shall be restored to and re-established in their own land (*v.* 15): *I will bring them again every man to his heritage.* The same hand that plucked them up shall plant them again. (2.) They shall become entitled to the spiritual privileges of God's Israel: "If they will be towardly, and *learn the ways of my people,* will conform to the rules and confine themselves to the restraints of my family, *then shall they be built in the midst of my people.* They shall not only be brought among them, to have a name and a place in the house of the Lord, where there was a court for the Gentiles, but they shall be built among them; they shall unite with them; the former enmities shall be slain; they shall be both edified and settled among them." See Isa. 56:5–7. Note, Those that diligently learn the ways of God's people shall enjoy the privileges and comforts of his people.

IV. What should become of those that were still wedded to their own evil ways, yea, though many of those about them turned to the Lord (*v.* 17): *If there will not obey,* if any of them continue to stand it out, *I will utterly pluck up and destroy that nation,* that family, that particular person, *saith the Lord.* Those that will not be ruled by the grace of God shall be ruined by the justice of God. And, if disobedient nations shall be destroyed, much more disobedient churches from whom better things are expected.

CHAPTER 13

Still the prophet is attempting to awaken this secure and stubborn people to repentance, by the consideration of the judgments of God that were coming upon them. He is to tell them, I. By the sign of a girdle spoiled that their pride should be stained (*v.* 1–11). II. By the sign of bottles filled with wine that their counsels should be blasted (*v.* 12–14). III. In consideration hereof he is to call them to repent and humble themselves (*v.* 15–21). IV. He is to convince them that it is for their obstinacy and incorrigibleness that the judgments of God are so prolonged and brought to extremity (*v.* 22–27).

Verses 1–11

Here is, I. A sign, the marring of a girdle, which the prophet had worn for some time, by hiding it in a hole of a rock near the river Euphrates. It was usual with the prophets to teach by signs, that a stupid unthinking people might be brought to consider, and believe, and be affected with what was thus set before them. 1. He was to wear a linen girdle for some time, *v.* 1, 2. Some think he wore it under his clothes, because it was linen, and it is said to *cleave to his loins, v.* 11. It should rather seem to be worn upon his clothes, for it was worn for a name and a praise, and probably was a fine sash, such as officers wear and such as are commonly worn at this day in the eastern nations. He must *not put it in water,* but wear it as it was, that it might be the stronger, and less likely to rot: linen wastes almost as much with washing as with wearing. Being not wet, it was the more stiff and less apt to bend, yet he must make a shift to wear it. Probably it was very fine linen which will wear long without washing. The prophet, like John Baptist, was none of those that wore soft clothing, and therefore it would be the more strange to see him with a linen girdle on, who probably used to wear a leathern one. 2. After he had worn this linen girdle for some time, he must go, and *hide it in a hole of a rock* (*v.* 4) by the water's side, where, when the water was high, it would be wet, and when it fell would grow dry again, and by that means would soon rot, sooner than if it were always wet or always dry. 3. After many days, he must look for it, and he should find it quite spoiled, gone all to rags and good for nothing, *v.* 7. It has been of old a question among interpreters whether this was really done, so as to be seen and observed by the people, or only in a dream or vision, so as to go no further than the prophet's own mind. It seems hard to imagine that the prophet should be sent on two such long journeys as to the river Euphrates, each of which would take him up some week's time, when he could so ill be spared at home. For this reason most incline to think the journey, at least, was only in vision, like that of Ezekiel, from the captivity in Chaldea to Jerusalem (Eze. 8:3) and thence back to Chaldea (*ch.* 11:24); and the explanation of this sign is given only to the prophet himself (*v.* 8), not to the people, the sign not being public. But there being, it is probable, at that time, great conveniences of travelling between Jerusalem and Babylon, and some part of Euphrates being not so far off but that it was made the utmost border of the land of promise (Jos. 1:4), I see no inconvenience in supposing the prophet to have made two journeys thither; for it is expressly said, *He did as the Lord commanded him;* and thus gave a signal proof of his obsequiousness to his God, to shame the stubbornness of a disobedient people: the toil of his journey would be very proper to signify both the pains they took to corrupt themselves with their idolatries and the sad fatigue of their captivity; and Euphrates being the river of Babylon, which was to be the place of their bondage, was a material circumstance in this sign.

II. The thing signified by this sign. The prophet was willing to be at any cost and pains to affect this people with the word of the Lord. Ministers must spend, and be spent, for the good of souls. We have the explanation of this sign, *v.* 9–11.

1. The people of Israel had been to God as this girdle in two respects: — (1.) He had taken them into covenant and communion with himself: *As the girdle cleaves* very closely *to the loins of a man* and surrounds him, *so have I caused to cleave to me the houses of Israel and Judah.* They were a people near to God (Ps. 148:14); they were his own, a peculiar people to him, a kingdom of priests that had access to him above other nations. He *caused them to cleave* to him by the law he gave them, the prophets he sent among them, and the favours which in his providence he showed them. He required their stated attendance in the courts of his house, and the frequent ratification of their covenant with him by sacrifices. Thus they were made so as to cleave to him that one would think they could never have been parted. (2.) He had herein designed his own honour. When he took them to be *to him for a people,* it was that they might be to him *for a name, and for a praise, and for a glory,* as a girdle is an ornament to a man, and particularly the *curious girdle of the ephod* was to the high-priest *for glory and for beauty.* Note, Those whom God takes to be to him for a people he intends to be to him for a praise. [1.] It is their duty to honour him, by observing his institutions and aiming therein at his glory, and thus adorning their profession. [2.] It is their happiness that he reckons himself honoured in them and by them. He is pleased with them, and glories in his relation to them, while they behave themselves as become his people. He was pleased to take it among the titles of his honour to be *the God of Israel,* even *a God to Israel,* 1 Chr. 17:24. In vain do we pretend to be to God for a people if we be not to him for a praise.

2. They had by their idolatries and other iniquities loosed themselves from him, thrown themselves at a distance, robbed him of the honour they owed him, buried themselves in the earth, and foreign earth too, mingled among the nations, and were so spoiled and corrupted that they were *good for nothing:* they could no more be to God, as they were designed, *for a name and a praise,* for they would not hear either their duty to do it or their privilege to value it: *They refused to hear the words of God,* by which they might have been kept still cleaving closely to him. *They walked in the imagination of their heart,* wherever their fancy led them; and denied themselves no gratification they had a mind to, particularly in their worship. They would not *cleave to God,* but *walked after other gods, to serve them,* and *to worship them;* they doted upon the gods of the heathen nations that lay towards Euphrates, so that they were quite spoiled for the service of their own God, and were as *this girdle,* this rotten girdle, a disgrace to their profession and not an ornament. A thousand pities it was that such a girdle should be so spoiled, that such a people should so wretchedly degenerate.

3. God would by his judgments separate them from him, send them into captivity, deface all their beauty and ruin their excellency, so that they should be like a fine girdle gone to rags, a worthless, useless, despicable people. God will after this manner *mar the pride of Judah, and the great pride of Jerusalem.* He would strip them of all that which was the matter of their pride, of which they boasted and in which they trusted; it should not only be sullied and stained, but quite destroyed, like this linen girdle. Observe, He speaks of *the pride of Judah* (the country people were proud of their holy land, their good land), but of *the great pride of Jerusalem;* there the temple was, and the royal palace, and therefore those citizens were more proud than the inhabitants of other cities. God takes notice of the degrees of men's pride, the pride of some and the great pride of others; and he will mar it, he will stain it. Pride will have a fall, for God resists the proud. He will either mar the pride that is in us (that is, mortify it by his grace, make us ashamed of it, and, like Hezekiah, humble us for the pride of our hearts, the great pride, and cure us of it, great as it is; and this marring of the pride will be making of

the soul; happy for us if the humbling providences our hearts be humbled) or else he will mar the thing we are proud of. Parts, gifts, learning, power, external privileges, if we are proud of these, it is just with God to blast them; even the temple, when it became Jerusalem's pride, was marred and laid in ashes. It is the honour of God to *took upon every one that is proud and abase him.*

Verses 12–21

Here is, I. A judgment threatened against this people that would quite intoxicate them. This doom is pronounced against them in a figure, to make it the more taken notice of and the more affecting (v. 12): *Thus saith the Lord God of Israel, every bottle shall be filled with wine;* that is, those that by their sins have made themselves *vessels of wrath fitted to destruction* shall be filled with the wrath of God as a bottle is with wine; and, as every vessel of mercy prepared for glory shall be filled with mercy and glory, so they shall *be full of the fury of the Lord* (Isa. 51:20); and they shall be brittle as bottles; and, like old bottles into which new wine is put, they shall burst and be broken to pieces, Mt. 9:17. Or, They shall have their heads as full of wine as bottle are; for so it is explained, v. 13, *They shall be filled with drunkenness;* compare Isa. 51:17. It is probable that this was a common proverb among them, applied in various ways; but they, not being aware of the prophet's meaning in it, ridiculed him for it: *"Do we not certainly know that every bottle shall be filled with wine? What strange thing is there in that? Tell us something that we did not know before."* Perhaps they were thus touchy with the prophet because they apprehended this to be a reflection upon them for their drunkenness, and probably it was in part so intended. They *loved flagons of wine,* Hos. 3:1. Their watchmen were all *for wine,* Isa. 56:12. They loved their false prophets *that prophesied to them of wine* (Mic. 2:11), that bade them be merry, for that they should never want their bottle to make them so. "Well," says the prophet, "you shall have your *bottles full of wine,* but not such wine as you desire." They suspected that he had some mystical meaning in it which prophesied no good concerning them, but evil; and he owns that so he had. What he meant was this,

1. That they should be a giddy as men in drink. A drunken man is fitly compared to a bottle or cask full of wine; for, when the wine is in, the wit, and wisdom, and virtue, and all that is good for any thing, are out. Now God threatens (v. 13) that shall they shall all be *filled with drunkenness;* they shall be full of confusion in their counsels, shall falter in all their talk and stagger in all their motions; they shall not know what they say or do, much less what they should say or do. They shall be sick of all their enjoyments and throw them up as drunken men do, Job 20:15. They shall fall into a slumber, and be utterly unable to help themselves, and, like men that have drunk away their reason, shall lie at the mercy and expose themselves to the contempt of all about them. And this shall be the condition not of some among them (if any had been sober, they might have helped the rest), but *even the kings that sit upon the throne of David,* that should have been like their father David, who was *wise as an angel of God,* shall be thus intoxicated. Their priests and prophets too, their false prophets, that pretended to guide them, were as indulgent of their lusts, and therefore were justly as much deprived of their senses, as any other. Nay, *all the inhabitants,* both *of the land* and *of Jerusalem* were as far gone as they. Whom God will destroy he infatuates.

2. That, being giddy, they should run upon one another. The cup of the wine of the Lord's fury shall throw them not only into a lethargy, so that they shall not be able to help themselves or one another, but into a perfect frenzy, so that they shall do mischief to themselves and one another (v. 14): *I will dash a man against his brother.* Not only their drunken follies, but their drunken frays, shall help to ruin them. Drunken men are often quarrelsome, and upon that account they have *woe and sorrow* (Prov. 23:29, 30); so their sin is their punishment; it was so here. God sent an evil spirit into families and neighbourhoods (as Jdg. 9:23), which made them jealous of, and spiteful towards, one another; so that the *fathers and sons* went *together* by the ears, and were ready to pull one another to pieces, which made them all an easy prey to the common enemy. This decree against them having gone forth, God says, *I* will not pity, nor spare, nor have mercy, but destroy them; for they *will not pity, nor spare, nor have mercy,* but destroy one another; see Hab. 2:15, 16.

II. Here is good counsel given, which, if taken, would prevent this desolation. It is, in short, to *humble themselves under the mighty hand of God.* If they will *hearken and give ear,* this is that which God has to say to them, *Be not proud, v.* 15. This was one of the sins for which God had a controversy with them (v. 9); let them mortify and forsake this sin, and God will let fall his controversy. *"Be not proud.; when* God speaks to you by his prophets do not think yourselves too good to be taught; be not scornful, be not wilful, let not your hearts rise against the word, nor slight the messengers that bring it to you. When God is coming forth against you in his providence (and by them he speaks) be not secure when he threatens, be not impatient when he strikes, for pride is at the bottom of both." It is the great God that has spoken, whose authority is incontestable, whose power is irresistible; therefore bow to what he says, and *be not proud,* as you have been. They must not be proud, for,

1. They must advance God, and study how to do him honour: "Give *glory to the Lord your God,* and not to your idols, not to other gods. Give him glory by confessing your sins, owning yourselves guilty before him, and accepting the punishment of your iniquity, v. 16. Give him glory by confessing your sins, owning yourselves guilty before him, and accepting the punishment of your iniquity, v. 16. Give him glory by a sincere repentance and reformation." The and not till then, we begin to live as we should, and to some good purpose, when we begin to *give glory to the Lord our God,* to make his honour our chief end and to seek it accordingly. "Do this quickly, while your space to repent is continued to you; *before he cause darkness,* before you will see no way of escaping." Note, Darkness will be the portion of those that will not repent to *give glory to God.* When those that by the fourth vial were scorched with heat *repented not, to give glory to God.* When those that by the fourth vial were scorched with heat *repented not, to give glory to God,* the next vial filled them with *darkness,* Rev. 16:9, 10. The aggravation of the darkness here threatened is, (1.) That their attempts to escape shall hasten their ruin: *Their feet shall stumble* when they are making all the haste they can over *the dark mountains,* and they shall fall, and be unable to get up again. Note, Those that think to out-run the judgments of God will find their road impassable; let them make the best of their way, they can make nothing of it, the judgments that pursue them will overtake them; their way is dark and slippery, Ps. 35:6. And therefore, before it comes to that extremity, it is our wisdom to give glory to him, and so make our peace with him, to fly to his mercy, and then there will be no occasion to fly from his justice. (2.) That their hopes of a better state of things will be disappointed: *While you look for light,* for comfort and relief, he will *turn it into the shadow of death,* which is very dismal and terrible, and make it *gross darkness,* like that of Egypt, when Pharaoh continued to harden his heart, which was darkness that might be felt. The expectation of impenitent sinners perishes when they die and think to have it satisfied.

2. They must abase themselves, and take shame to themselves; the prerogative of the king and queen will not exempt them from this (v. 18): *Say to the king and queen,* that, great as they are, they must *humble themselves* by true repentance, and so give both glory to God and a good example to their subjects." Note, Those that are exalted above others in the world must humble themselves before God, who is higher than the highest, and to whom kings and queens are accountable. They must *humble themselves,* and *sit down* — sit down, and consider what is coming — sit down in the dust, and lament themselves. Let them humble themselves, for God will otherwise take an effectual course to humble them: "Your principalities shall *come down,* the honour and power on which you value yourselves and in which you confide, *even the crown of your glory,* your goodly or glorious crown: when you are led away captives, where will your principality and all the badges of it be then?" Blessed be God there is a crown of glory, which those shall inherit who do humble themselves, that shall never *come down.*

III. This counsel is enforced by some arguments if they continue proud and unhumbled.

1. It will be the prophet's unspeakable grief (v. 17): *"If you will not hear it,* will not submit to the word, but continue refractory, not only my eye, but *my soul shall weep in secret places."* Note, The obstinacy of people, in refusing to hear the word of God, will be heart-breaking to the poor ministers, who know something of the terrors of the Lord and the worth of souls, and are so far from desiring that they tremble at the thoughts of the death of sinners. His grief for it was undissembled (his *soul wept*) and void of affectation, for he chose to weep *in secret places,* where no eye saw him but his who is all eye. He would mingle his tears not only with his public preaching, but with his private devotions. Nay, thoughts of their case would make him melancholy, and he would become a perfect recluse. It would grieve him, (1.) To see their sins unrepented of: *"My soul shall weep for your pride,* your haughtiness, and stubbornness, and vain confidence." Note, The sins of others should be matter of sorrow to us. We must mourn for that which we cannot mend, and mourn the more for it because we cannot mend it. (2.) To see their calamity past redress and remedy: *"My eyes shall weep sorely,* not so much because my relations, friends, and neighbours are in distress, but *because the Lord's flock,* his people and the sheep of his pasture, *are carried away captive."* That should always grieve us most by which God's honour suffers and the interest of his kingdom is weakened.

2. It will be their own inevitable ruin, v. 19–21. (1.) The land shall be laid waste: *The cities of the south shall be shut up.* The cities of Judah lay in the southern part of the land of Canaan; these shall be straitly besieged by the enemy, so that there shall be no going in or out, or they shall be deserted by the inhabitants, that there shall be none to go in and out. Some understand it of the cities of Egypt, which was south from Judah; the places there whence they expected succours shall fail them, and they shall find no access to them. (2.) The inhabitants shall be hurried away into a foreign country, there to live in slavery: *Judah shall be carried away captive.* Some were already carried off, which they hoped might serve to answer the prediction, and that the residue should still be left; but no: *It shall be carried away all of it.* God will make a full end with them: *It shall be wholly carried away.* So it was in the last captivity under Zedekiah, because they repented not. (3.) The enemy was now at hand that should do this (v. 20): "Lift up your eyes. I see upon their march, and you may if you will *behold, those that come from the north,* from the land of the Chaldeans; see how fast they advance, how fierce they appear." Upon this he addresses himself to the king, or rather (because the pronouns are feminine) to the city or state. [1.] "What will you do now with the people who are committed to your charge, and whom you ought to protect? *Where is the flock that was given thee, thy beautiful flock?* Whither canst thou take them now for shelter? How can they escape these ravening wolves?" Magistrates must look upon themselves as shepherds, and those that are under their charge as their flock, which they are entrusted with the care of and must give an account of; they must take delight in them as their beautiful flock, and consider what to do for their safety in times of public danger. Masters of families, who neglect their children and suffer them to perish for want of a good education, and ministers who neglect their people, should think they hear God putting this question to them: *Where is the flock that was given thee* to feed, *that beauteous flock?* It is starved; it is left exposed to the beasts of prey. What account wilt thou give of them when the chief shepherd shall appear? [2.] "What have you to object against the equity of God's proceedings? *What will thou say when he shall visit upon thee* the former days? v.* 21. Thou canst say nothing, but that *God is just in all that is brought upon thee."* Those that flatter themselves with hopes of impunity, what will they say? What confusion will cover their faces when they shall find themselves deceived and that God punishes them! [3.] "What thoughts will you now have of your own folly, in giving the Chaldeans such power over you, by seeking to them for assistance, and joining in league with them? Thus *thou hast taught them against thyself to be captains* and to *become the head."* Hezekiah began when he showed his treasures to the ambassadors of the king of Babylon, tempting him thereby to come and plunder him. Those who, having a God to trust to, court foreign alliances and confide in them, do but make rods

for themselves and teach their neighbours how to become their masters. [4.] "How will you bear the trouble that is at the door? *Shall not sorrows take thee as a woman in travail?* Sorrows which thou canst not escape nor put off, extremity of sorrows; and in these respects more grievous than those of a woman in travail that they were not expected before, and that there is no manchild to be born, the joy of which shall make them afterwards to be forgotten."

Verses 22–27

Here is, I. Ruin threatened as before, that the Jews shall go into captivity, and fall under all the miseries of beggary and bondage, shall be stripped of their clothes, *their skirts discovered* for want of upper garments to cover them, and their *heels made bare* for want of shoes, *v.* 22. Thus they used to deal with prisoners taken in war, when they drove them into captivity, *naked and barefoot,* Isa. 20:4. Being thus carried off into a strange country, they shall be scattered there, *as the stubble that is blown away by the wind of the wilderness,* and nobody is concerned to bring it together again, *v.* 24. If the stubble escape the fire, it shall be carried away by the wind. If one judgment do not do the work, another shall, with those that by sin have made themselves as stubble. They shall be stripped of all their ornaments and exposed to shame, as harlots that are carted, *v.* 26. They made their pride appear, but God will *make their shame appear;* so that those who have doted on them shall be ashamed of them.

II. An enquiry made by the people into the cause of this ruin, *v.* 22. Thou wilt *say in thy heart* (and God knows how to give a proper answer to what men say in their hearts, though they do not speak it out; *Jesus, knowing their thoughts,* replied to *them,* Mt. 9:4), *Wherefore came these things upon me?* The question is supposed to come into the heart, 1. Of a sinner quarrelling with God and refusing to receive correction. They could not see that they had done any thing which might justly provoke God to be thus angry with them. They durst not speak it out; but in their hearts they thus charged God with unrighteousness, if he had *laid upon them more than was meet.* They seek for the cause of their calamities, when, if they had not been willfully blind, they might easily have seen it. Or, 2. Of a sinner returning to God. If there come but a penitent thought into the heart at any time (saying, *What have I done? ch.* 8:6, wherefore am I in affliction? why doth God contend with me?) God takes notice of it, and is ready by his Spirit to impress the conviction, that, sin being discovered, it may be repented of.

III. An answer to this enquiry. God will be justified when he speaks and will oblige us to justify him, and therefore will set the sin of sinners in order before them. Do they ask, *Wherefore come these things upon us?* Let them know it is all owing to themselves.

1. It is for the greatness of their iniquities, *v.* 22. God does not take advantage against them for small faults; no, the sins for which he now punishes them are of the first rate, very heinous in their own nature and highly aggravated — for *the multitude of thy iniquity* (so it may be read), sins of every kind and often repeated and relapsed into. Some think we are more in danger from the multitude of our smaller sins than from the heinousness of our greater sins; of both we may say, *Who can understand his errors?*

2. It is for their obstinacy in sin, their being so long accustomed to it that there was little hope left of their being reclaimed from it (*v.* 23): *Can the Ethiopian change his skin,* that is by nature black, or the *leopard his spots,* that are even woven into the skin? Dirt contracted may be washed off, but we cannot alter the natural colour of a hair (Mt. *v.* 36), much less of the skin; and so impossible is it, morally impossible, to reclaim and reform these people. (1.) They had been long *accustomed to do evil.* They were taught to do evil; they had been educated and brought up in sin; they had served an apprenticeship to it, and had all their days made a trade of it. It was so much their constant practice that it had become a second nature to them. (2.) Their prophets therefore despaired of ever bring them to do good. This was what they aimed at; they persuaded them to cease to do evil and learn to do well, but could not prevail. They had so long been used to do evil that it was next to impossible for them to repent, and amend, and begin to do good. Note, Custom in sin is a very great hindrance to conversion from sin. The disease that is inveterate is generally thought incurable. Those that have been long accustomed to sin have shaken off the restraint of fear and shame; their consciences are seared; the habits of sin are confirmed; it pleads prescription; and it is just with God to give those up to their own hearts' lusts that have long refused to give themselves up to his grace. Sin is the blackness of the soul, the deformity of it; it is its spot, the discolouring of it; it is natural to us, we were shapen in it, so that we cannot get clear of it by any power of our own. But there is an almighty grace that is able to change the Ethiopian's skin, and that grace shall not be wanting to those who in a sense of their need of it seek it earnestly and improve it faithfully.

3. It is for their treacherous departures from the God of truth and dependence on lying vanities (*v.* 25): *"This is thy lot,* to be scattered and driven away; this is *the portion of thy measures from me,* the punishment assigned thee as by line and measure; this shall be thy share of the miseries of this world; expect it, and think not to escape it: it is *because thou hast forgotten me,* the favours I have bestowed upon thee and the obligations thou art under to me; thou hast no sense, no remembrance, of these." Forgetfulness of God is at the bottom of all sin, as the remembrance of our Creator betimes is the happy and hopeful beginning of a holy life. "Having *forgotten me, thou hast trusted in falsehood,* in idols, in an arm of flesh in Egypt and Assyria, in the self-flatteries of a deceitful heart." Whatever those trust to that forsake God, they will find it a *broken reed,* a *broken cistern.*

4. It is for their idolatry, their spiritual whoredom, that sin which is of all sins most provoking to the *jealous God.* They are exposed to a shameful calamity (*v.* 26) because they have been guilty of a shameful iniquity and yet are shameless in it (*v.* 27): *"I have seen thy adulteries* (thy inordinate fancy for strange gods, which thou hast been impatient for the gratification of, and hast even *neighed* after it), even the *lewdness of thy whoredoms,* thy impudence and insatiableness in them, thy eager worshipping of idols *on the hills in the fields,* upon the high places. This is that for which a *woe* is denounced against thee, *O Jerusalem!* nay, and many woes."

IV. Here is an affectionate expostulation with them, in the close, upon the whole matter. Though it was adjudged next to impossible for them to be brought to do good (*v.* 23), yet while there is life there is hope, and therefore still he reasons with them to bring them to repentance, *v.* 27. 1. He reasons with them concerning the thing itself: *Wilt thou not be made clean?* Note, It is the great concern of those who are polluted by sin to be made clean by repentance, and faith, and a universal reformation. The reason why sinners are not made clean is because they will not be made clean; and herein they act most unreasonably: *"Wilt thou not be made clean?* Surely thou wilt at length be persuaded to *wash thee, and make thee clean,* and so be wise for thyself." 2. Concerning the time of it: *When shall it once be?* Note, It is an instance of the wonderful grace of God that he desires the repentance and conversion of sinners, and thinks the time long till they are brought to relent; but it is an instance of the wonderful folly of sinners that they put that off from time to time which is of such absolute necessity that, if it be not done some time, they are certainly undone for ever. They do not say that they will never be cleansed, but not yet; they will defer it to a more convenient season, but cannot tell us when it shall once be.

CHAPTER 14

This chapter was penned upon occasion of a great drought, for want of rain. This judgment began in the latter end of Josiah's reign, but, as it should seem, continued in the beginning of Jehoiakim's: for less judgments are sent to give warning of greater coming, if not prevented by repentance. This calamity was mentioned several times before, but here, in this chapter, more fully. Here is, I. A melancholy description of it (*v.* 1–6). II. A prayer to God to put an end to this calamity and to return in mercy to their land (*v.* 7–9). III. A severe threatening that God would proceed in his controversy, because they proceeded in their iniquity (*v.* 10–12). IV. The prophet's excusing the people, by laying the blame on their false prophets; and the doom passed both on the deceivers and the deceived (*v.* 13–16). V. Directions given to the prophet, instead of interceding for them, to lament them; but his continuing notwithstanding to intercede for them (*v.* 17–22).

Verses 1–9

The first verse is the title of the whole chapter: it does indeed all *concern the dearth,* but much of it consists of the prophet's prayers concerning it; yet these are not unfitly said to be, *The word of the Lord which came to him* concerning it, for every acceptable prayer is that which God puts into our hearts; nothing is our word that comes to him but what is first his word that comes from him. In these verses we have,

I. The language of nature lamenting the calamity. When the heavens were as brass, and distilled no dews, the earth was as iron, and produced no fruits; and then the grief and confusion were universal. 1. The people of the land were all in tears. Destroy their vines and their fig-trees and you cause all their mirth to cease, Hos. 2:11, 12. All their joy fails with the joy of harvest, with that of their corn and wine. *Judah mourns* (*v.* 2), not for the sin, but for the trouble — for the withholding of the rain, not for the withdrawing of God's favour. *The gates thereof,* all that go in and out at their gates, *languish,* look pale, and grow feeble, for want of the necessary supports of life and for fear of the further fatal consequences of this judgment. *The gates,* through which supplies of corn formerly used to be brought into their cities, now look melancholy, when, instead of that, the inhabitants are departing through them to seek for bread in other countries. Even those that sit in the gates languish; *they are black unto the ground,* they go in black as mourners and sit on the ground, a the poor beggars at the gates are *black in the face* for want of food, *blacker than a coal,* Lam. 4:8. Famine is represented by a black horse, Rev. 6:5. They fall to the ground through weakness, not being able to go along the streets. *The cry of Jerusalem has gone up;* that is, of the citizens (for the city is *served by the field*), or of people from all parts of the country met at Jerusalem to pray for rain; so some. But I fear it was rather the cry of their trouble, and the cry of their prayer. 2. The great men of the land felt from this judgment (*v.* 3): *The nobles sent their little ones to the water,* perhaps their own children, having been forced to part with their servants because they had not wherewithal to keep them, and being willing to train up their children, when they were little, to labour, especially in a case of necessity, as this was. We find Ahab and Obadiah, the king and the lord chamberlain of his household, in their own persons, seeking for water in such a time of distress as this was, 1 Ki. 18:5, 6. Or, rather, *their meaner ones,* their servants and inferior officers; these they sent to seek for water, which there is no living without; but there was none to be found: They *returned with their vessels empty;* the springs were dried up when there was no rain to feed them; and then *they* (their masters that sent them) *were ashamed and confounded* at the disappointment. They would not be ashamed of their sins, nor confounded at the sense of them, but were unhumbled under the reproofs of the word, thinking their wealth and dignity set them above repentance; but God took a course to make them ashamed of that which they were so proud of, when they found that even on this side hell their nobility would not purchase them a drop of water to cool their tongue. Let our reading the account of this calamity make us thankful for the mercy of water, that we may not by the feeling of the calamity be taught to value it. What is most needful is most plentiful. 3. The husbandmen felt most sensibly and immediately from it (*v.* 4): *The ploughmen were ashamed,* for the ground was so parched and hard that it would not admit the plough even when it was so *chapt* and cleft that it seemed as if it did not need the plough. They were ashamed to be idle, for there was nothing to be done, and therefore nothing to be expected. The *sluggard, that will not plough by reason of cold,* is not ashamed of his own folly; but the diligent husbandman, that cannot plough by reason of heat, is ashamed of his own affliction. See what an immediate dependence husbandmen have upon the divine Providence, which therefore they should always have an eye to, for they cannot plough nor sow in hope unless God *water their furrows,* Ps. 65:10. 4. The case even of the wild beasts was very pitiable, *v.* 5, 6. Man's sin brings those judgments upon the earth which make even the inferior creatures groan: and the prophet takes notice of this as a plea with God for mercy. Judah and Jerusalem have sinned, but the hinds and the wild asses, what have they done? The hinds are pleasant creatures, lovely and loving, and particularly tender of their young; and yet such is the extremity of the case that, contrary to the instinct of the nature, they leave their young, even when they are newly calved and most need them, to seek for grass elsewhere; and, if they can find none, they *abandon* them, because not able to suckle them. It grieved not the hind so much that she had no grass herself as that she had none for her young, which will shame those who spend that upon their lusts which they should preserve for their families. The hind, when she has brought forth her young, is said to have *cast forth her sorrows* (Job 39:3), and yet she continues her cares; but, as it follows there, she soon sees the good effect of them, for *her young ones* in a little while *grow up,* and trouble her no more, *v.* 4. But here the great trouble of all is that she has nothing for them. Nay, one would be sorry even for the *wild asses* (though they are creatures that none have any great affection for); for, though the *barren land* is made *their dwelling* at the best (Job 39:5, 6), yet even that is now made too hot for them, so hot that they cannot breathe in it, but they get to the *highest places* they can reach, where the air is coolest, and *snuff up the wind like dragons,* like those creatures which, being very hot, are continually panting for breath. *Their eyes fail,* and so does their strength, *because there is no grass* to support them. The tame ass, that serves her owner, is welcome to *his crib* (Isa. 1:3) and has her keeping for her labour, when the *wild ass,* that *scorns the crying of the driver,* is forced to *live upon air,* and is well enough served for not serving. *He that will not labour, let him not eat.*

II. Here is the language of grace, lamenting the iniquity, and complaining to God of the calamity. The people are not forward to pray, but the prophet here prays for them, and so excites them to pray for themselves, and puts words into their mouths, which they may make use of, in hopes to speed, *v.* 7–9. In this prayer, 1. Sin is humbly confessed. When we come to pray for the preventing or removing of any judgment we must always acknowledge that our *iniquities testify against us.* Our sins are witnesses against us, and true penitents see them to be such. They testify, for they are plain and evident; we cannot deny the charge. They testify against us, for our conviction, which tends to our present shame and confusion, and our future condemnation. They disprove and overthrow all our pleas for ourselves; and so not only accuse us, but answer against us. If we boast of our own excellencies, and trust to our own righteousness, our iniquities testify against us, and prove us perverse. If we quarrel with God as dealing unjustly or unkindly with us in afflicting us, our iniquities testify against us that we do him wrong; "for *our backslidings are many* and our revolts are great, whereby *we have sinned against thee* — too numerous to be concealed, for they are many, too heinous to be excused, for they are against thee." 2. Mercy is earnestly begged: *"Though our iniquities testify against us,* and against the granting of the favour which the necessity of our case calls for, yet *do thou it."* They do not say particularly what they would have done; but, as becomes penitents and beggars, they refer the matter to God: "Do with us as thou thinkest fit," Jdg. 10:15. Not, *Do thou it* in this way or at this time, but *"Do thou it for thy name's sake;* do that which will be most for the glory of thy name." Note, Our best pleas in prayer are those that are fetched from the glory of God's own name. "Lord, do it, that they mercy may be magnified, thy promise fulfilled, and thy interest in the world kept up; we have nothing to plead in ourselves, but every thing in thee." There is another petition in this prayer, and it is a very modest one (*v.* 9): *"Leave us not,* withdraw not thy favour and presence." Note, We should dread and deprecate God's departure from us more than the removal of any or all our creature-comforts. 3. Their relation to God, their interest in him, and their expectations from him grounded thereupon, are most pathetically pleaded with him, *v.* 8, 9. (1.) They look upon him as one they have reason to think should deliver them when they are in distress, yea, though their iniquities testify against them; for in him mercy has often rejoiced against judgment. The prophet, like Moses of old, is willing to make the best he can of the case of his people, and therefore, though he must own that they have sinned many a great sin (Ex. 32:31), yet he pleads, *Thou art the hope of Israel.* God has encouraged his peo- to hope in him; in calling himself so often the *God of* the *rock of Israel,* and the *Holy One of Israel,* he [illegible]e himself the *hope of Israel.* He has given Israel [illegible]o hope in, and caused them to hope in it; and there are those yet in Israel that make God alone their hope, and expect he will be *their Saviour in time of trouble,* and they look not for salvation in any other; "Thou hast many a time been such, in the time of their extremity." Note, Since God is his people's all-sufficient Saviour, they ought to hope in him in their greatest straits; and, since he is their only Saviour, they ought to hope in him alone. They plead likewise, *"Thou art in the midst of us;* we have the special tokens of thy presence with us, thy temple, thy ark, thy oracles, and *we are called by the name,* the *Israel* of God; and therefore we have reason to hope thou wilt not leave us; *we are thine, save us.* Thy name is called upon us, and therefore what evils we are under reflect dishonour upon thee, as if thou wert not able to relieve thy own." The prophet had often told the people that their profession of religion would not protect them from the judgments of God; yet here he pleads it with God, as Moses, Ex. 32:11. Even this may go far as to temporal punishments with a God of mercy. *Valeat quantum valere potest — Let the plea avail as far as is proper.* (2.) It therefore grieves them to think that he does not appear for their deliverance; and, though they do not charge it upon him as unrighteous, they humbly plead it with him why he should be gracious, for the glory of his own name. For otherwise he will seem, [1.] Unconcerned for his own people: *What will the Egyptians say?* they will say, "Israel's hope and Saviour does not mind them; he has become *as a stranger in the land,* that does not at all interest himself in its interests; his temple, which he called *his rest for ever,* is no more so, but he is in it *as a wayfaring man, that turns aside to tarry but for a night* in an inn, which he never enquires into the affairs of, nor is in any care about." Though God never is, yet he sometimes seems to be, as if he cared not what became of his church: Christ slept when his disciples were in storm. [2.] Incapable of giving them any relief. The enemies once said, Because the Lord *was not able to bring* his people to Canaan, he let them *perish in the wilderness* (Num. 14:16); so now they will say, "Either his wisdom or his power fails him; either he is *as a man astonished* (who, though he has the reason of a man, yet, being astonished, is quite at a loss and at his wits' end) or as a *mighty man* who is overpowered by such as are more mighty, and therefore *cannot save;* though mighty, yet a man, and therefore having his power limited." Either of these would be a most insufferable reproach to the divine perfections; and therefore, why has the God that we are sure *is in the midst of us* become *as a stranger?* Why does the almighty God seem as if he were no more than a mighty man, who, when he is astonished, though he would, yet cannot save? It becomes us in prayer to show ourselves concerned more for God's glory than for our own comfort. Lord, *what wilt thou do unto thy great name?*

Verses 10–16

The dispute between God and his prophet, in this chapter, seems to be like that between the owner and the dresser of the vineyard concerning the barren fig-tree, Lu. 13:7. The justice of the owner condemns it to be cut down; the clemency of the dresser intercedes for a reprieve. Jeremiah had been earnest with God, in prayer, to return in mercy to this people. Now here,

I. God overrules the plea which he had offered in their favour, and shows him that it would not hold. In answer to it thus he says concerning *this people, v.* 10. He does not say, concerning *my people,* for he disowns them, because they had broken covenant with him. It is true they were *called by his name,* and had the tokens of his presence among them; but they had sinned, and provoked God to withdraw. This the prophet had owned, and had hoped to obtain mercy for them, notwithstanding this, through intercession and sacrifice; therefore God here tells him, 1. That they were not duly qualified for a pardon. The prophet had owned that *their backslidings were many;* and, though they were so, yet there was hope for them if they returned. But *this people* show no disposition at all to return; they have wandered, and *they have loved to wander;* their backslidings have been their choice and their pleasure, which should have been their shame and pain, and therefore they will be their ruin. They cannot expect God should take up his rest with them when they take such delight in going astray from him after their idols. It is not through necessity or inadvertency that they wander, but they love to wander. Sinners are wanderers from God; their wanderings forfeit God's favour, but it is their loving to wander that quite cuts them off from it. They were told what their wanderings would come to that one sin would hurry them on to another, and all to ruin; and yet they have not taken warning and *refrained their feet.* So far were they from returning to their God that neither his prophets nor his judgments could prevail upon them to give themselves the least check in a sinful pursuit. This is that for which God is now reckoning with them. When he denies them rain from heaven he is *remembering their iniquity* and *visiting their sin;* that is it for which their *fruitful land* is thus *turned into barrenness.* 2. That they had no reason to expect that the God they had rejected should accept them; no, not though they betook themselves to fasting and prayer and put themselves to the expense of burnt-offerings and sacrifice: *The Lord doth not accept them, v.* 10. *He takes no pleasure in them* (so the word is); for what pleasure can the holy God take in those that take pleasure in his rivals, in any service, in any society, rather than his? *"When they fast* (*v.* 12), which is a proper expression of repentance and reformation, — *when they offer a burnt offering and an oblation,* which was designed to be an expression of faith in a Mediator, — though their prayers be thus enforced, and offered up in those vehicles that used to be acceptable, yet, because they do not proceed from humble, penitent, and renewed hearts, but still they *love to wander,* therefore *I will not hear their cry,* be it ever so loud; *nor will I accept them,* neither their persons nor their performances." It had been long since declared, *The sacrifice of the wicked is an abomination to the Lord;* and those only are *accepted* that *do well,* Gen. 4:7. 3. That they had forfeited all benefit by the prophet's prayers for them because they had not regarded his preaching to them. This is the meaning of that repeated prohibition given to the prophet (*v.* 11): *Pray not thou for this people for their good,* as before, *ch.* 7:15; 11:14. This did not forbid him thus to express his *good-will* to them (Moses continued to intercede for Israel after God had said, *Let me alone,* Ex. 32:10), but it forbade them to expect any good effect from it as long as they *turned away their ear from hearing the law.* Thus was the doom of the impenitent ratified, as that of Saul's rejection was by that word to Samuel, *When wilt thou cease to mourn for Saul?* It therefore follows (*v.* 12), *I will consume them,* not only by this famine, but by the further sore judgments of sword and pestilence; for God has many arrows in his quiver, and those that will not be convinced and reclaimed by one shall be consumed by another.

II. The prophet offers another plea in excuse for the people's obstinacy, and it is but an excuse, but he was willing to say whatever their case would bear; it is this, That the prophets, who pretended a commission from heaven, imposed upon them, and flattered them with assurances of peace though they went on in their sinful way, *v.* 13. He speaks of it with lamentation: *"Ah! Lord God,* the poor people seem willing to take notice of what comes in thy name, and there are those who in thy name tell them that they *shall not see the sword nor famine;* and they say it as from thee, with all the gravity and confidence of prophets: *I will* continue you *in this place,* and will *give you assured peace* here, peace of truth. I tell them the contrary; but I am one against many, and every one is apt to credit that which makes for them; therefore, Lord, pity and spare them, for *their leaders cause them to err."* This excuse would have been of some weight if they had not had warning given them, before, of false prophets, and rules by which to distinguish them; so that if they were deceived it was entirely their own fault. But this teaches us, as far as we can with truth, to make the best of bad, and judge as charitably of others as their case will bear.

III. God not only overrules this plea, but condemns both the blind leaders and the blind followers to fall together into the ditch. 1. God disowns the flatteries (*v.* 14): *They prophesy lies in my name.* They had no commission from God to prophesy at all: *I neither sent them, nor commanded them, nor spoke unto them.* They never were employed to go on any errand at all from God; he never made himself known to them, much less by them to the people; never any word of the Lord came to them, no call, no warrant, no instruction, much less did he send them on this errand, to rock them asleep in security. No; men may flatter themselves, and Satan may flatter them, but God never does. It is *a false vision, and a thing of nought.* Note, What is false and groundless in vain and worthless. The vision that is not true, be it ever so pleasing, is good for nothing; it is the *deceit of their heart,* a spider's web spun out of their own bowels, and in it they think to shelter themselves, but it will be swept away in a moment and prove a great cheat. Those that oppose their own thoughts of God's word (God indeed says so, but they think otherwise) walk in the *deceit of their heart,* and it will be their ruin. 2. He passes sentence upon the flatterers, *v.* 15. As for the prophets, who put this abuse upon the people by telling them they shall have peace, and this affront upon God by telling them so in God's name, let them know that they shall have no peace themselves. They shall fall first by those very judgments which they have flattered others with the hopes of an exemption from. They undertook to warrant people that *sword and famine* should *not be in the land;* but it shall soon appear how little their warrants are good for, when they themselves shall be cut off by sword and famine. How should they secure others or foretel peace to them when they cannot secure themselves, nor have such a foresight of their own calamities as to get out of the way of them? Note, The sorest punishment await those who promise sinners impunity in their sinful ways. 3. He lays the flattered under the same doom: The *people to whom they prophesy lies,* and who willingly suffer themselves to be thus imposed upon, *shall die by sword and famine, v.* 16. Note, The unbelief of the deceived, with all the falsehood of the deceivers, shall not make the divine threatenings of no effect; sword and famine will come, whatever they say to the contrary; and those will be least safe that are most secure. Impenitent sinners will not escape the damnation of hell by saying that they can never believe there is such a thing, but will feel what they will not fear. It is threatened that this people shall not only fall by *sword and famine,* but that they shall be as it were hanged up in chains, as monuments of that divine justice which they set at defiance; their bodies shall be *cast out,* even *in the streets of Jerusalem,* which of all places, one would think, should be kept clear from such nuisances: there they shall lie unburied; their nearest relations, who should do them that last office of love, being so poor that they cannot afford it, or so weakened with hunger that they are not able to attend it, or so overwhelmed with grief that they have no heart to it, or so destitute of natural affection that they will not pay them so much respect. Thus will God *pour their wickedness upon them,* that is, the punishment of their wickedness; the full vials of God's wrath shall be poured upon them, to which they have made themselves obnoxious. Note, When sinners are overwhelmed with trouble they must in it see their own wickedness poured upon them. This refers to the wickedness both of the false prophets and of the people; the blind lead the blind, and both fall together into the ditch, where they will be miserable comforters one to another.

Verses 17–22

The present deplorable state of Judah and Jerusalem is here made the matter of the prophet's lamentation (*v.* 17, 18) and the occasion of his prayer and intercession for them (*v.* 19), and I am willing to hope that the latter, as well as the former, was by divine direction, and that these words (*v.* 17), *Thus shalt thou say unto them* (or *concerning them,* or *in their hearing*), refer to the intercession, as well as to the lamentation, and then it amounts to a revocation of the directions given to the prophet not to pray for them, *v.* 11. However, it is plain, by the prayers we find in these verses, that the prophet did not understand it as a prohibition, but only as a discouragement, like that 1 Jn. 5:16, *I do not say he shall pray for that.* Here,

I. The prophet stands weeping over the ruins of his country; God directs him to do so, that, showing himself affected, he might, if possible, affect them with the foresight of the calamities that were coming upon them. Jeremiah must say it not only to himself, but to them too: *Let my eyes run down with tears, v.* 17. Thus he must signify to them that he certainly foresaw *the sword* coming, and another sort of famine, more grievous even than this which they were now groaning under; this was in the country for want of rain, that would be in the city through the straitness of the siege. The prophet speaks as if he already

saw the miseries attending the descent which the Chaldeans made upon them: *The virgin daughter of my people,* that is as dear to me as a daughter to her father, *is broken with a great breach, with a very grievous blow,* much greater and more grievous than any she has yet sustained; for (*v.* 18) *in the field* multitudes lie dead that were *slain by the sword,* and in the city multitudes lie dying for want of food. Doleful spectacles! *"The prophets and the priests,* the false prophets that flattered them with their lies and the wicked priests that persecuted the true prophets, are now expelled their country, and *go about* either as prisoners and captives, whithersoever their conquerors lead them, or as fugitives and vagabonds, wherever they can find shelter and relief, *in a land that they know not."* Some understand this of the true prophets, Ezekiel and Daniel, that were carried to Babylon with the rest. The prophet's eyes must run down *with tears day and night,* in prospect of this, that the people might be convinced, not only that this woeful day would infallibly come, and would be a very woeful day indeed, but that he was far from desiring it, and would as gladly have brought them messages of peace as their false prophets, if he might have had warrant from heaven to do it. Note, Because God, though he inflicts death on sinners, yet delights not in it, it becomes his ministers, though in his name they pronounce the death of sinners, yet sadly to lament it.

II. He stands up to make intercession for them; for who knows but God will yet return and repent? While there is life there is hope, and room for prayer. And, though there were many among them who neither prayed themselves nor valued the prophet's prayers, yet there were some who were better affected, would join with him in his devotions, and set the seal of their *Amen* to them.

1. He humbly expostulates with God concerning the present deplorableness of their case, *v.* 19. It was very sad, for, (1.) Their expectations from their God failed them; they thought he had avouched Judah to be his, but now, it seems, he has *utterly rejected* it, and cast it off, will not own any relation to it nor concern for it. They thought Zion was the beloved of his soul, was his rest for ever; but now *his soul* even *loathes Zion,* loathes even the services there performed, for the sake of the sins there committed. (2.) Then no marvel that all their other expectations failed them: *They were smitten,* and their wounds were multiplied, but there was *no healing* for them; they *looked for peace,* because after a storm there usually comes a calm and fair weather, after a long fit of wet; but *there was no good,* things went still worse and worse. They looked for a *healing time,* but could not gain so much as a *breathing time.* *"Behold, trouble* at the door, by which we hoped peace would enter. And is it so then? *Hast thou* indeed *rejected Judah?* Justly thou mightest. *Hath thy soul loathed Zion?* We deserve it should. But wilt thou not at length in wrath remember mercy?"

2. He makes a penitent confession of sin, speaking that language which they all should have spoken, though but few did (*v.* 20): *"We acknowledge our wickedness,* the abounding wickedness of our land *and the iniquity of our fathers,* which we have imitated, and therefore justly smart for. *We know, we acknowledge,* that *we have sinned against thee,* and therefore thou art just in all that is brought upon us; but, because we confess our sins, we hope to find thee faithful and just in forgiving our sins."

3. He deprecates God's displeasure, and by faith appeals to his honour and promise, *v.* 21. His petition is, *"Do not abhor us;* though thou afflict us, *do not abhor us;* though thy hand by turned *against* us, let not thy heart be so, nor let thy mind be alienated from us." They own God might justly abhor them, they had rendered themselves odious in his eyes; yet, when they pray, *Do not abhor us,* they mean, "Receive us into favour again. *Let not thy soul loathe Zion, v.* 19. Let not our incense be an abomination." They appeal, (1.) To the honour of God, the honour of his scriptures, by which he has made himself known — his *word,* which he has *magnified above all his name:* *"Do not abhor us, for thy name's sake,* that the name of thine by which we are called and which we call upon." The honour of his sanctuary is pleaded: "Lord, do not abhor us, for that will *disgrace the throne of thy glory"* (the temple, which is called *a glorious high throne from the beginning, ch.* 17:12); let not that which has been the *joy of the whole earth* be made a *hissing* and an *astonishment.*

We deserve to have disgrace put upon us, but let it not be so as to reflect upon thyself; let not the desolations of the temple give occasion to the heathen to reproach him that used to be worshipped there, as if he could not, or would not, protect it, or as if the gods of the Chaldeans had been too hard for him. Note, Good men lay the credit of religion, and its profession in the world, nearer their hearts than any private interest or concern of their own; and those are powerful pleas in prayer which are fetched thence and great supports to faith. We may be sure that God will not *disgrace the throne of his glory* on earth; nor will he eclipse the glory of his throne by one providence without soon making it shine forth, and more brightly than before, by another. God will be no loser in his honour at the long-run. (2.) To the promise of God; of this they are humbly bold to put him in mind: *Remember thy covenant with us, and break not* that covenant. Not that they had any distrust of his fidelity, or that they thought he needed to be put in mind of his promise to them, but what he had said he would plead with himself they take the liberty to plead with him. *Then will I remember my covenant,* Lev. 26:42.

4. He professes a dependence upon God for the mercy of rain, which they were now in want of, *v.* 22. If they have forfeited their interest in him as their God in covenant, yet they will not let go their hold on him as the God of nature. (1.) They will never make application to the idols of the heathen, for that would be foolish and fruitless: *Are there any among the vanities of the Gentiles that can cause rain?* No; in a time of great drought in Israel, Baal, though all Israel presented their prayers to him in the days of Ahab, could not relieve them; it was that God only who *answered by fire* that could answer *by water* too. (2.) They will not terminate their regards in second causes, nor expect supply from nature only: *Can the heavens give showers?* No, not without orders from the God of heaven; for it is he that has the key of the clouds, that *opens the bottles of heaven* and *waters the earth from his chambers.* But, (3.) All their expectation therefore is from him and their confidence in him: *"Art not thou he, O Lord our God!* from whom we may expect succour and to whom we must apply? Art thou not he that *causest rain* and *givest showers?* For *thou hast made all these things;* thou gavest them being, and therefore thou givest them law and hast them all at thy command; thou madest that moisture in nature which is in a constant circulation to serve the intentions of Providence, and thou directest it, and makest what use thou pleasest of it; *therefore we will wait upon thee,* and upon thee only; we will *ask of the Lord rain,* Zec. 10:1. We will trust in him to give it to us in due time, and be willing to tarry his time; it is fit that we should, and it will not be in vain to do so." Note, The sovereignty of God should engage, and his all-sufficiency encourage, our attendance on him and our expectations from him at all times.

CHAPTER 15

When we left the prophet, in the close of the foregoing chapter, so pathetically poring out his prayers before God, we had reason to hope that in this chapter we should find God reconciled to the land and the prophet brought into a quiet composed frame; but, to our great surprise, we find it much otherwise as to both. I. Notwithstanding the prophet's prayers, God here ratifies the sentence given against the people, and abandons them to ruin turning a deaf ear to all the intercessions made for them (*v.* 1–9). II. The prophet himself, notwithstanding the satisfaction he had in communion with God, still finds himself uneasy and out of temper. 1. He complains to God of his continual struggle with his persecutors (*v.* 10). 2. God assures him that he shall be taken under special protection, though there was a general desolation coming upon the land (*v.* 11–14). 3. He appeals to God concerning his sincerity in the discharge of his prophetic office and thinks it hard that he should not have more of the comfort of it (*v.* 15–18). 4. Fresh security is given him, that, upon condition he continue faithful, God will continue his care of him and his favour to him (*v.* 19–21). And thus, at length, we hope he regained the possession of his own soul.

Verses 1–9

We scarcely find any where more pathetic expressions of divine wrath against a provoking people than we have here in these verses. The prophet had prayed earnestly for them, and found some among them to join with him; and yet not so much as a reprieve was gained, nor the least mitigation of the judgment; but this answer is given to the prophet's prayers, that the decree had gone forth, was irreversible, and would shortly be executed. Observe here,

I. What the sin was upon which this severe sentenc

was grounded. 1. It is in remembrance of a former iniquity; it is because of Manasseh, for that which he did in Jerusalem, *v.* 4. What that was we are told, and that it was for it that Jerusalem was destroyed, 2 Ki. 24:3, 4. It was for his idolatry, and *the innocent blood which he shed, which the Lord would not pardon.* He is called *the son of Hezekiah* because his relation to so good a father was a great aggravation of his sin, so far was it from being an excuse of it. The greatest part of a generation was worn off since Manasseh's time, yet his sin is brought into the account; as in Jerusalem's last ruin God brought upon it all *the righteous blood shed on the earth,* to show how heavy the guilt of blood will light and lie somewhere, sooner or later, and that reprieves are not pardons. 2. It is in consideration of their present impenitence. See how their sin is described (*v.* 6): "*Thou hast forsaken me,* my service and thy duty to me; *thou hast gone backward* into the ways of contradiction, art become the reverse of what thou shouldst have been and of what God by his law would have led thee forward to." See how the impenitence is described (*v.* 7): *They return not from their ways,* the ways of their own hearts, into the ways of God's commandments again. There is mercy for those who have turned aside if they will return; but what favour can those expect that persist in their apostasy?

II. What the sentence is. It is such as denotes no less than an utter ruin.

1. God himself abandons and abhors them: *My mind cannot be towards them.* How can it be thought that the holy God should have any remaining complacency in those that have such a rooted antipathy to him? It is not in a passion, but with a just and holy indignation, that he says, "*Cast them out of my sight,* as that which is in the highest degree odious and offensive, and *let them go forth,* for I will be troubled with them no more."

2. He will not admit any intercession to be made for them (*v.* 1): "*Though Moses and Samuel stood before me,* by prayer or sacrifice to reconcile me to them, yet I could not be prevailed with to admit them into favour." Moses and Samuel were two as great favourites of Heaven as ever were the blessings of this earth, and were particularly famed for the success of their mediation between God and his offending people; many a time they would have been destroyed if Moses had not stood before him in the breach; and to Samuel's prayers they owed their lives (1 Sa. 12:19); yet even their intercessions should not prevail, no, not though they were now in a state of perfection, much less Jeremiah's who was now *a man subject to like passions* as others. The putting of this as a case, *Though they should stand before me,* supposes that they do not, and is an intimation that saints in heaven are not intercessors for saints on earth. It is the prerogative of the Eternal Word to be the only Mediator in *the other world,* whatever Moses, and Samuel, and others were in this.

3. He condemns them all to one destroying judgment or other. When God casts them out of his presence, *whither shall they go forth? v.* 2. Certainly nowhere to be safe or easy, but to be met by one judgment while they are pursued by another, till they find themselves surrounded with mischiefs on all hands, so that they cannot escape; *Such as are for death to death.* By death here is meant the pestilence (Rev. 6:8), for it is death without visible means. *Such as are for death to death,* or *for the sword to the sword;* every man shall perish in that way that God has appointed: the law that appoints the malefactor's death determines what death he shall die. Or, He that is by his own choice for this judgment, let him take it, or for that, let him take it, but by the one or the other they shall all fall and none shall escape. It is a choice like that which David was put to, and was thereby put into a *great strait,* 2 Sa. 24:14. *Captivity* is mentioned last, some think, because the sorest judgment of all, it being both a complication and continuance of miseries. That of *the sword* is again repeated (*v.* 3), and is made the first of another four frightful set of destroyers, which God will *appoint over them,* as officers over the soldiers, to do what they please with them. As those that escape *the sword* shall be cut off by pestilence, famine, or captivity, so those that fall by the sword shall be cut off by divine vengeance, which pursues sinners on the other side death; there shall be *dogs* in the field to devour. And, if there be any that think to escape justice, they shall be made the most public monuments of it: *They shall be removed into all kingdoms of the earth* (*v.* 4), like Cain, who, that he might be made a spectacle of horror to all, became *a fugitive and a vagabond* in the earth.

4. They shall fall without being relieved. Who can do any thing to help them? for (1.) God, even their own God (so he had been) appears against them: *I will stretch out my hand against thee,* which denotes a deliberate determined stroke, which will reach far and wound deeply. *I am weary with repenting* (*v.* 6); it is a strange expression; they had behaved so provokingly, especially by their treacherous professions of repentance, that they had put even infinite patience itself to the stretch. God had often turned away his wrath when it was ready to break forth against them; but now he will grant no more reprieves. Miserable is the case of those who have sinned so long against God's mercy that at length they have sinned it away. (2.) Their own country expels them, and is ready to *spue them out,* as it had done the Canaanites that were before them; for so it was threatened (Lev. 18:28): *I will fan them with a fan in the gates of the land,* in their own gates, through which they shall be scattered, or *into the gates of the earth,* into the cities of all the nations about them, *v.* 7. (3.) Their own children, that should assist them when they speak with the enemy in the gate, shall be cut off from them: *I will bereave them of children,* so that they shall have little hopes that the next generation will retrieve their affairs, for *I will destroy my people;* and, when the inhabitants are slain, the land will soon be desolate. This melancholy article is enlarged upon, *v.* 8, 9, where we have, [1.] The destroyer brought upon them. When God has bloody work to do he will find out bloody instruments to do it with. Nebuchadnezzar is here called *a spoiler at noon-day,* not a thief in the night, that is afraid of being discovered, but one that without fear shall break through and destroy all the fences of rights and properties, and this in the face of the sun and in defiance of its light: *I have brought against the mother a young man, a spoiler* (so some read it); for Nebuchadnezzar, when he first invaded Judah, was but a *young man,* in the first year of his reign. We read it, *I have brought upon them,* even *against the mother of the young men, a spoiler,* that is, against Jerusalem, a mother city, that had a very numerous family of young men: or that invasion was in a particular manner terrible to those mothers who had many sons fit for war, who must now hazard their lives in the high places of the field, and, being an unequal match for the enemy, would be likely to fall there, to the inexpressible grief of their poor mothers, who had nursed them up with a great deal of tenderness. The same God that brought the spoiler upon them *caused him to fall upon it,* that is, upon the spoil delivered to him, *suddenly* and by surprise; and then *terrors* came *upon the city.* the original is very abrupt — *the city and terrors. O the city!* what a consternation will it then be in! *O the terrors* that shall then seize it! Then the city and terrors shall be brought together, that seemed at a distance from each other. *I will cause to fall suddenly upon her* (upon Jerusalem) *a watcher and terrors;* so Mr. Gataker reads it, for the word is used for a watcher (Dan. 4:13, 23), and the Chaldean soldiers were called watchers, *ch.* 4:16. [2.] The destruction made by this destroyer. A dreadful slaughter is here described. *First,* The wives are deprived of their husbands: *Their widows are increased above the sand of the seas,* so numerous have they now grown. It was promised that the men of Israel (for those only were numbered) should be *as the sand of the sea for multitude;* but now *they* shall be all cut off, and their widows shall be so. But observe, God says, *They are increased to me.* Though the husbands were cut off by the sword of his justice, their poor widows were gathered in the arms of his mercy, who has taken it among the titles of his honour to be *the God of the widows.* Widows are said to be *taken into the number,* the number of those whom God has a particular compassion and concern for. *Secondly,* The parents are deprived of their children: *She that has borne seven* sons, whom she expected to be the support and joy of her age, now *languishes,* when she has seen them all cut off by the sword in one day, who had been many years her burden and care. *She that had many children has waxed feeble,* 1 Sa. 2:5. See what uncertain comforts children are; and let us therefore rejoice in them *as though we rejoiced not.* When the children are slain the mother *gives up the ghost,* for her life was bound up in theirs: *Her sun has gone down while it was yet day;* she is bereaved of all her comforts just when she thought herself in the midst of the enjoyment of them. She is now *ashamed and confounded* to think how proud she was of her sons, how fond of them, and how much she promised herself from them. Some understand, by this languishing mother, Jerusalem lamenting the death of her inhabitants as passionately as ever poor mother bewailed her children. Many are cut off already, *and the residue of them,* who have yet escaped, and, as was hoped, were reserved to be the seed of another generation, even these *will I deliver to the sword before their enemies* (as the condemned malefactor is delivered to the sheriff to be executed), *saith the Lord,* the Judge of heaven and earth, who, we are sure, herein judges according to truth, though the judgment seem severe.

5. They shall fall without being pitied (*v.* 5): "*For who shall have pity on thee, O Jerusalem?* When thy God has *cast thee out of his sight,* and his compassions fail and are shut up from thee, neither thy enemies nor thy friends shall have any compassion for thee. They shall have no sympathy with thee; they shall not *bemoan thee* nor be sorry for thee; they shall have no concern for thee, shall not go a step out of their way to *ask how thou dost.*" For, (1.) Their friends, who were expected to do these friendly offices, were all involved with them in the calamities, and had enough to do to bemoan themselves. (2.) It was plain to all their neighbours that they had brought all this misery upon themselves by their obstinacy in sin, and that they might easily have prevented it by repentance and reformation, which they were often in vain called to; and therefore *who can pity them? O Israel! thou hast destroyed thyself.* Those will perish for ever unpitied that might have been saved upon such easy terms and would not. (3.) God will thus complete their misery. He will set their acquaintance, as he did Job's at a distance from them; and his hand, his righteous hand, is to be acknowledged in all the unkindnesses of our friends, as well as in all the injuries done us by our foes.

Verses 10–14

Jeremiah has now returned from his public work and retired into his closet; what passed between him and his God there we have an account of in these and the following verses, which he published afterwards, to affect the people with the weight and importance of his messages to them. Here is,

I. The complaint which the prophet makes to God of the many discouragements he met with in his work, *v.* 10.

1. He met with a great deal of contradiction and opposition. He was a *man of strife and contention to the whole land* (so it might be read, rather than to *the whole earth,* for his business lay only in that land); both city and country quarrelled with him, and set themselves against him, and said and did all they could to thwart him. He was a peaceable man, gave no provocation to any, nor was apt to resent the provocations given him, and yet *a man of strife,* not a man striving, but a man striven with; he was for peace, but, when he spoke, they were for war. And, whatever they pretended, that which was the real cause of their quarrels with him was his faithfulness to God and to their souls. He showed them their sins that were working their ruin, and put them into a way to prevent that ruin, which was the greatest kindness he could do them; and yet this was it for which they were incensed against him and looked upon him as their enemy. Even the prince of peace himself was thus a man of strife, a sign spoken against, continually *enduring the contradiction of sinners against himself.* And the gospel of peace brings division, even to fire and sword, Mt. 10:34, 35; Lu. 12:49, 51. Now this made Jeremiah very uneasy, even to a degree of impatience. He cried out, *Woe is me, my mother, that thou hast borne me,* as if it were his mother's fault that she bore him, and he had better never have been born than be born to such an uncomfortable life; nay, he is angry that she had *borne him a man of strife,* as if he had been fatally determined to this by the stars that were in the ascendant at his birth. If he had any meaning of this kind, doubtless it was very much his infirmity; we rather hope it was intended for no more than a pathetic lamentation of his own case. Note, (1.) Even those who are most quiet and peaceable, if they serve God faithfully, are often made men of

strife. We can but *follow peace;* we have the making only of one side of the bargain, and therefore can but, *as much as in us lies, live peaceably.* (2.) It is very uncomfortable to those who are of a peaceable disposition to live among those who are continually picking quarrels with them. (3.) Yet, if we cannot live so peaceably as we desire with our neighbours, we must not be so disturbed at it as thereby to lose the repose of our own minds and put ourselves upon the fret.

2. He met with a great deal of contempt, contumely, and reproach. They every one of them cursed him; they branded him as a turbulent factious man, as an incendiary and a sower of discord and sedition. They ought to have blessed him, and to have blessed God for him; but they had arrived at such a pitch of enmity against God and his word that for his sake they cursed his messenger, spoke ill of him, wished ill to him, did all they could to make him odious. They all did so; he had scarcely one friend in Judah or Jerusalem that would give him a good word. Note, It is often the lot of the best of men to have the worst of characters ascribed to them. *So persecuted they the prophets.* But one would be apt to suspect that surely Jeremiah had given them some provocation, else he could not have lost himself thus: no, not the least: *I have neither lent* money *nor borrowed* money, have been neither creditor nor debtor; for so general is the signification of the words here. (1.) It is implied here that those who deal much in the business of this world are often involved thereby in strife and contention; *meum et tuum — mine and thine* are the great make-bates; lenders and borrowers sue and are sued, and great dealers often get a great deal of ill-will. (2.) it was an instance of Jeremiah's great prudence, and it is written for our learning, that, being called to be a prophet, he *entangled not himself in the affairs of this life,* but kept clear from them, that he might apply the more closely to the business of his profession and might not give the least shadow of suspicion that he aimed at secular advantages in it nor any occasion to his neighbours to contend with him. He *put out* no money, for he was no usurer, nor indeed had he any money to lend: he *took up* no money, for he was no purchaser, no merchant, no spendthrift. He was perfectly dead to this world and the things of it: a very little served to keep him, and we find (*ch.* 16:2) that he had neither wife nor children to keep. And yet, (3.) Though he behaved thus discreetly, and so as one would think should have gained him universal esteem, yet he lay under a general odium, through the iniquity of the times. Blessed be God, bad as things are with us, they are not so bad but that there are those with whom virtue has its praise; yet let not those who behave most prudently think it strange if they have not the respect and esteem they deserve. *Marvel not, my brethren, if the world hate you.*

II. The answer which God gave to this complaint. Though there was in it a mixture of passion and infirmity, yet God graciously took cognizance of it, because it was *for his sake* that the prophet suffered reproach. In this answer, 1. God assures him that he should weather the storm and be made easy at last, *v.* 11. Though his neighbours quarrelled with him for what he did in the discharge of his office, yet God accepted him and promised to stand by him. It is in the original expressed in the form of an oath: *"If I* take not care of thee, let me never be counted faithful; *verily it shall go well with thy remnant,* with the remainder of thy life" (for so the word signifies); "the residue of thy days shall be more comfortable to thee than those hitherto have been." *Thy end shall be good;* so the Chaldee reads it. Note, It is a great and sufficient support to the people of God that, how troublesome soever their way may be, it shall be well with them in their latter end, Ps. 37:37. They have still a *remnant,* a *residue,* something behind and left in reserve, which will be sufficient to counterbalance all their grievances, and the hope of it may serve to make them easy. It should seem that Jeremiah, besides the vexation that his people gave him, was uneasy at the apprehension he had of sharing largely in the public judgments which he foresaw coming; and, though he mentioned not this, God replied to his thought of it, as to Moses, Ex. 4:19. Jeremiah thought, "If my friends are thus abusive to me, what will my enemies be?" And God had thought fit to awaken in him an expectation of this kind, *ch.* 12:5. But here he quiets his mind with this promise: *"Verily I will cause the enemy to entreat thee well in the time of evil,* when all about thee shall be laid waste." Note, God has all men's hearts in his hand, and can turn those to favour his servants whom they were most afraid of. And the prophets of the Lord have often met with fairer and better treatment among open enemies than among those that call themselves his people. When we see trouble coming, and it looks very threatening, let us not despair, but hope in God, because it may prove better than we expect. This promise was accomplished when Nebuchadnezzar, having taken the city, charged the captain of the guard to be kind to Jeremiah, and let him have every thing he had a mind to, *ch.* 39:11, 12. The following words, *Shall iron break the northern iron, and the steel,* or *brass?* (*v.* 12), being compared with the promise of God made to Jeremiah (*ch.* 1:18), that he would make him an *iron pillar* and *brazen walls,* seem intended for his comfort. They were continually clashing with him, and were rough and hard as iron; but Jeremiah, being armed with power and courage from on high, is as northern iron, which is naturally stronger, and as steel, which is hardened by art; and therefore they shall not prevail against him; compare this with Eze. 2:6; 3:8, 9. He might the better bear their quarrelling with him when he was sure of the victory. 2. God assures him that his enemies and persecutors should be lost in the storm, should be ruined at last, and that therein the word of God in his mouth should be accomplished and he proved a true prophet, *v.* 13, 14. God here turns his speech from the prophet to the people. To them also *v.* 12 may be applied: *Shall iron break the northern iron, and the steel?* Shall their courage and strength, and the most hardly and vigorous of their efforts, be able to contest either with the counsel of God or with the army of the Chaldeans, which are as inflexible, as invincible, as the northern iron and steel. Let them therefore hear their doom: *Thy substance and thy treasure will I give to the spoil,* and that *without price;* the spoilers shall have it *gratis;* it shall be to them a cheap and easy prey. Observe, The prophet was poor; he neither lent nor borrowed; he had nothing to lose, neither *substance.* nor *treasure,* and therefore the enemy will treat him well, *Cantabit vacuus coram latrone viator — The traveller that has no property about him will congratulate himself when accosted by a robber.* But the people that had great estates in money and land would be slain for what they had, or the enemy, finding they had much, would use them hardly, to make them confess more. And it is their own iniquity that herein corrects them: It is *for all thy sins, even in all thy borders.* All parts of the country, even those which lay most remote, had contributed to the national guilt, and all shall now be brought to account. Let not one tribe lay the blame upon another, but each take shame to itself: It is for *all thy sins in all thy borders.* Thus shall they stay at home till they see their estates ruined, and then they shall be carried into captivity, to spend the sad remains of a miserable life in slavery: *"I will make thee to pass with thy enemies,* who shall lead thee in triumph *into a land that thou knowest not,* and therefore canst expect to find no comfort in it." All this is the fruit of God's wrath: "It is *a fire kindled in my anger, which shall burn upon you,* and, if not extinguished in time, will burn eternally."

Verses 15–21

Here, as before, we have,

I. The prophet's humble address to God, containing a representation both of his integrity and of the hardships he underwent notwithstanding. It is a matter of comfort to us that, whatever ails us, we have a God to go to, before whom we may spread our case and to whose omniscience we may appeal, as the prophet here, *"O Lord! thou knowest;* thou knowest my sincerity, which men are resolved they will not acknowledge; thou knowest my distress, which men disdain to take notice of." Observe here,

1. What it is that the prophet prays for, *v.* 15. (1.) That God would consider his case and be mindful of him: *"O Lord! remember me;* think upon me for good." (2.) That God would communicate strength and comfort to him: *"Visit me;* not only remember me, but let me know that thou rememberest me, that thou art nigh unto me." (3.) That he would appear for him against those that did him wrong: *Revenge me of my persecutors,* or rather, *Vindicate me from my persecutors;* give judgment against them, and let that judgment be executed so far as is necessary for my vindication and to compel them to acknowledge that they have done me wrong. Further than this a good man will not desire that God should avenge him. Let something be done to convince the world that (whatever blasphemers say to the contrary) Jeremiah is a righteous man and the God whom he serves is a righteous God. (4.) That he would yet spare him and continue him in the land of the living: *"Take me not away* by a sudden stroke, but *in thy long-suffering* lengthen out my days." The best men will own themselves so obnoxious to God's wrath that they are indebted to his patience for the continuance of their lives. Or, "While thou exercisest long-suffering towards my persecutors, let not them prevail to take me away." Though in a passion he complained of his birth (*v.* 10), yet he desires here that his death might not be hastened; for life is sweet to nature, and the life of a useful man is so to grace. *I pray not that thou shouldst take them out of the world.*

2. What it is that he pleads with God for mercy and relief against his enemies, persecutors, and slanderers.

(1.) That God's honour was interested in this case: *Know,* and make it known, *that for thy sake I have suffered rebuke.* Those that lay themselves open to reproach by their own fault and folly have great reason to bear it patiently, but no reason to expect that God should appear for them. But if it is for doing well that we suffer ill, and for righteousness' sake that we have all manner of evil said against us, we may hope that God will vindicate our honour with his own. To the same purport (*v.* 16), *I am called by thy name, O Lord of hosts!* It was for that reason that his enemies hated him, and therefore for that reason he promised himself that God would own him and stand by him.

(2.) That the word of God, which he was employed to preach to others, he had experienced the power and pleasure of in his own soul, and therefore had the graces of the Spirit to qualify him for the divine favour, as well as his gifts. We find some rejected of God who yet could say, *Lord, we have prophesied in thy name.* But Jeremiah could say more (*v.* 16): *"Thy words were found,* found *by me"* (he searched the scripture, diligently studied the law, and found that in it which was reviving to him: if we seek we shall find), "found *for me"* (the words which he was to deliver to others were laid ready to his hand, were brought to him by inspiration), *"and I did* not only taste them, but *eat them,* received them entirely, conversed with them intimately; they were welcome to me, as food to one that is hungry; I entertained them, digested them, turned them *in succum et sanguinem — into blood and spirits,* and was myself delivered into the mould of those truths which I was to deliver to others." The prophet was told to *eat the roll,* Eze. 2:8; Rev. 10:9. *I did eat it* — that is, as it follows, it *was to me the joy and rejoicing of my heart,* nothing could be more agreeable. Understand it, [1.] Of the message itself which he was to deliver. Though he was to foretel the ruin of his country, which was dear to him, and in the ruin of which he could not but have a deep share, yet all natural affections were swallowed up in zeal for God's glory, and even these messages of wrath, being divine messages, were a satisfaction to him. He also rejoiced, at first, in hope that the people would take warning and prevent the judgment. Or, [2.] Of the commission he received to deliver this message. Though the work he was called to was not attended with any secular advantages, but, on the contrary, exposed him to contempt and persecution, yet, because it put him in a way to serve God and do good, he took pleasure in it, was glad to be so employed, and it was his *meat and drink to do the will of him that sent him,* Jn. 4:34. Or, [3.] Of the promise God gave him that he would assist and own him in his work (*ch.* 1:8); he was satisfied in that, and depended upon it, and therefore hoped it should not fail him.

(3.) That he had applied himself to the duty of his office with all possible gravity, seriousness, and self-den[illegible] though he had had of late but little satisfaction in it[illegible] [1.] It was his comfort that he had given up him[illegible] ly to the business of his office and had done [illegible] ther to divert himself from it or disfit himsel[illegible] no unsuitable company, denied himself th[illegible] ful recreations, abstained from every [illegible] levity, lest thereby he should make [illegible] regarded. He *sat alone,* spent a grea[illegible] closet, *because of the hand* of the L[illegible] upon him to carry him on his work, Eze. 3:14. *"For thou hast filled me with indignation,* with such messages of wrath against this people as have made me always pensive." Note, It will be a comfort to God's ministers, when men despise them, if they have the testimony of their consciences for them that they have not by any vain foolish behaviour made themselves despicable, that they have been dead not only to the wealth of the world, as this prophet was (*v.* 10), but to the pleasures of it too, as here. But, [2.] It is his complaint that he had had but little pleasure in his work. It was at first the rejoicing of his heart, but of late it had made him melancholy, so that he had no heart to *sit in the meeting of those that make merry.* He cared not for company, for indeed no company cared for him. He *sat alone,* fretting at the people's obstinacy and the little success of his labours among them. This filled him with a holy *indignation.* Note, It is the folly and infirmity of some good people that they lose much of the pleasantness of their religion by the fretfulness and uneasiness of their natural temper, which they humour and indulge, instead of mortifying it.

(4.) He throws himself upon God's pity and promise in a very passionate expostulation (*v.* 18): *"Why is my pain perpetual,* and nothing done to ease it? Why are the wounds which my enemies are continually giving both to my peace and to my reputation incurable, and nothing done to retrieve either my comfort or my credit? I once little thought that I should be thus neglected; will the God that has promised me his presence *be to me as a liar,* the God on whom I depend to be me *as waters that fail?"* We are willing to make the best we can of it, and to take it as an appeal, [1.] To the mercy of God: "I know he will not let the pain of his servant be perpetual, but he will ease it, will not let his wound be incurable, but he will heal it; and therefore I will not despair." [2.] To his faithfulness: *"Wilt thou be to me as a liar?* No; I know thou wilt not. God is not a man that he should lie. The fountain of life will never be to his people as *waters that fail."*

II. God's gracious answer to this address, *v.* 19–21. Though the prophet betrayed much human frailty in his address, yet God vouchsafed to answer him with good words and comfortable words; for he knows our frame. Observe,

1. What God here requires of him as the condition of the further favours he designed him. Jeremiah had done and suffered much for God, yet God is no debtor to him, but he is still upon his good behaviour. God will own him. But, (1.) He must recover his temper, and be reconciled to his work, and friends with it again, and not quarrel with it any more as he had done. He must *return,* must shake off these distrustful discontented thoughts and passions, and not give way to them, must regain the peaceable possession and enjoyment of himself, and resolve to be easy. Note, When we have stepped aside into any disagreeable frame or way our care must be to return and compose ourselves into a right temper of mind again; and *then* we may expect God will help us, if thus we endeavour to help ourselves. (2.) He must resolve to be faithful in his work, for he could not expect the divine protection any longer than he did approve himself so. Though there was no cause at all to charge Jeremiah with unfaithfulness, and God knew his heart to be sincere, yet God saw fit to give him this caution. Those that do their duty must not take it ill to be told their duty. In two things he must be faithful: — [1.] He must distinguish between some and others of those he preached to: Thou must *take forth the precious from the vile.* The righteous are the precious be they ever so mean and poor; the wicked are the vile be they ever so rich and great. In our congregations these are mixed, wheat and chaff in the same floor; we cannot distinguish them by name, but we must by character, and must give to each a portion, speaking comfort to precious saints and terror to vile sinners, neither *making the heart of the righteous sad* nor *strengthening the hands of the wicked* (Eze. 13:22), ut *rightly dividing the word of truth.* Ministers must take se whom they see to be precious into their bosoms, and *sit alone* as Jeremiah did, but keep up conversation ose they may do good to and get good by. [2.] He sely adhere to his instructions, and not in the least them: *Let them return to thee, but return not* , that is, he must do the utmost he can, in to bring people up to the mind of God; he must tell them they must, at their peril, comply with that. Those that had flown off from him, that did not like the terms upon which God's favour was offered to them, *"Let them return to thee,* and, upon second thoughts, come up to the terms and strike the bargain; but do not thou *return to them,* do not compliment them, nor comply with them, nor think to make the matter easier to them than the word of God has made it." Men's hearts and lives must come up to God's law and comply with that, for God's law will never come down to them nor comply with them.

2. What God here promises to him upon the performance of these conditions. If he approve himself well, (1.) God will tranquilize his mind and pacify the present tumult of his spirits: *If thou return, I will bring thee again,* will *restore thy soul,* as Ps. 23:3. The best and strongest saints, if at any time they have gone aside out of the right way, and are determined to return, need the grace of God to bring them again. (2.) God will employ him in his service as a prophet, whose work, even in those bad times, had comfort and honour enough in it to be its own wages: *"Thou shalt stand before me,* to receive instructions from me, as a servant from his master; and *thou shalt be as my mouth* to deliver my messages to the people, as an ambassador is the mouth of the prince that sends him." Note, Faithful ministers are God's mouth to us; they are so to look upon themselves, and to speak God's mind and *as becomes the oracles of God;* and we are so to look upon them, and to hear God speaking to us by them. Observe, If thou keep close to thy instructions, *thou shalt be as my mouth,* not otherwise; so far, and no further, God will stand by ministers, as they go by the written word. *"Thou shalt be as my mouth,* that is, what thou sayest shall be made good, as if I myself had said it." See Isa. 44:26; 1 Sa. 3:19. (3.) He shall have strength and courage to face the many difficulties he meets with in his work, and his spirit shall not fail again as now it does (*v.* 20): *"I will make thee unto this people as a fenced brazen wall,* which the storm batters and beats violently upon, but cannot shake. *Return not thou to them* by any sinful compliances, and then trust thy God to arm thee by his grace with holy resolutions. Be not cowardly, and God will make thee daring." He had complained that he was made a *man of strife.* "Expect to be so (says God); they will *fight against thee,* they will still continue their opposition, *but they shall not prevail against thee* to drive thee off from thy work nor to cut thee off from the land of the living." (4.) He shall have God for his protector and mighty deliverer: *I am with thee to save thee.* Those that have God with them have a Saviour with them who has wisdom and strength enough to deal with the most formidable enemy; and those that are with God, and faithful to him, he will deliver (*v.* 21) either from trouble or through it. They may perhaps fall *into the hand of the wicked,* and they may appear terrible to them, but God will rescue them *out of their hands.* They shall not be able to kill them till they have finished their testimony; they shall not prevent their happiness. God will so deliver them as to *preserve them to his heavenly kingdom* (2 Tim. 4:18), and that is deliverance enough. There are many tings that appear very frightful that yet do not prove at all hurtful to a good man.

CHAPTER 16

In this chapter, I. The greatness of the calamity that was coming upon the Jewish nation is illustrated by prohibitions given to the prophet neither to set up a house of his own (*v.* 1–4) nor to go into the house of mourning (*v.* 5–7) nor into the house of feasting (*v.* 8, 9). II. God is justified in these severe proceedings against them by an account of their great wickedness (*v.* 10–13). III. An intimation is given of mercy in reserve (*v.* 14, 15). IV. Some hopes are given that the punishment of the sin should prove the reformation of the sinners, and that they should return to God at length in a way of duty, and so be qualified for his returns to them in a way of favour (*v.* 16–21).

Verses 1–9

The prophet is here for a sign to the people. They would not regard what he said; let it be tried whether they will regard what he *does.* In general, he must conduct himself so, in every thing, as became one that expected to see his country in ruins very shortly. This he foretold, but few regarded the prediction; therefore he is to show that he is himself fully satisfied in the truth of it. Others go on in their usual course, but he, in the prospect of these sad times, is forbidden and therefore forbears marriage, mourning for the dead, and mirth. Note, Those that would convince others of and affect them with the word of God must make it appear, even in the most self-denying instances, that they do believe it themselves and are affected with it. If we would rouse others out of their security, and persuade them to sit loose to the world, we must ourselves be mortified to present things and show that we expect the dissolution of them.

I. Jeremiah must not marry, nor think of having a family and being a housekeeper (*v.* 2): *Thou shalt not take thee a wife,* nor think of *having sons and daughters in this place,* not in the land of Judah, not in Jerusalem, not in Anathoth. The Jews, more than any people, valued themselves on their early marriages and their numerous offspring. But Jeremiah must live a bachelor, not so much in honour of virginity as in diminution of it. By this it appears that it was advisable and seasonable only in calamitous times, and times of *present distress,* 1 Co. 7:26. That it is so is a part of the calamity. There may be a time when it will be said, *Blessed is the womb that bears not,* Lu. 23:29. When we see such times at hand it is wisdom for all, especially for prophets, to keep themselves as much as may be from being *entangled with the affairs of this life* and encumbered with that which, the dearer it is to them, the more it will be the matter of their care, and fear, and grief, at such a time. The reason here given is because the *fathers* and *mothers, the sons and the daughters, shall die of grievous deaths, v.* 3, 4. As for those that have wives and children, 1. They will have such a clog upon them that they cannot flee from those deaths. A single man may make his escape and shift for his own safety, when he that has a wife and children can neither find means to convey with them nor find in his heart to go and leave them behind him. 2. They will be in continual terror for fear of those deaths; and the more they have to lose by them the greater will the terror and consternation be when death appears every where in its triumphant pomp and power. 3. The death of every child, and the aggravating circumstances of it, will be a new death to the parent. Better have no children than have them brought forth and bred up *for the murderer* (Hos. 9:13, 14), than see them live and die in misery. Death is grievous, but some deaths are more grievous than others, both to those that die and to their relations that survive them; hence we read of *so great a death,* 2 Co. 1:10. Two things are used a little to palliate and alleviate the terror of death as to this world, and to sugar the bitter pill — bewailing the dead and burying them; but, to make those deaths grievous indeed, these are denied: *They shall not be lamented,* but shall be carried off, as if all the world were weary of them; nay, they *shall not be buried,* but left exposed, as if they were designed to be monuments of justice. *They shall be a dung upon the face of the earth,* not only despicable, but detestable, as if they were good for nothing but to manure the ground; being *consumed,* some *by the sword* and some *by famine, their carcases shall be meat for the fowls of heaven and the beasts of the earth.* Will not any one say, "Better be without children than live to see them come to this?" What reason have we to say,*All is vanity and vexation of spirit,* when those creatures that we expect to be our greatest comforts may prove not only our heaviest cares, but our sorest crosses!

II. Jeremiah must not go to the house of mourning upon occasion of the death of any of his neighbours or relations (*v.* 5): *Enter thou not into the house of mourning.* It was usual to condole with those whose relations were dead, to *bemoan them,* to *cut themselves,* and *make themselves bald,* which, it seems, was commonly practised as an expression of mourning, though forbidden by the law, Deu. 14:1. Nay, sometimes, in a passion of grief, they did *tear themselves for them* (*v.* 6, 7), partly in honour of the deceased, thus signifying that they thought there was a great loss of them, and partly in compassion to the surviving relations, to whom the burden will be made the lighter by their having sharers with them in their grief. They used to mourn with them, and so *to comfort them for the dead,* as Job's friends with him and the Jews with Martha and Mary; and it was a friendly office to *give them a cup of consolation to drink,* to provide cordials for them and press them earnestly to drink of them for the support of their spirits, give wine to those that are of heavy heart *for their father or mother,* that it may be some comfort to them to find that, though they have lost their parents, yet they have some friends left that have a concern for them. Thus the usage stood, and it was a laudable usage. It is a good work to others, as well as of good use to ourselves, to *go to the house of mourning.* It seems, the prophet Jeremiah had been wont to abound in good offices of this kind, and it well became his character both as a pious man and as a prophet; and one would think it should have made him better beloved among his people than it should seem he was. But now God bids him not lament the death of his friends as usual, for 1. His sorrow for the destruction of his country in general must swallow up his sorrow for particular deaths. His tears must now be turned into another channel; and there is occasion enough for them all. 2. He had little reason to lament those who died now just before the judgments entered which he saw at the door, but rather to think those happy who were seasonable *taken away from the evil to come.* 3. This was to be a type of what was coming, when there should be such universal confusion that all neighbourly friendly offices should be neglected. Men shall be in deaths so often, and even dying daily, that they shall have no time, no room, no heart, for the ceremonies that used to attend death. The sorrows shall be so ponderous as not to admit relief, and every one so full of grief for his own troubles that he shall have no thought of his neighbours. All shall be mourners then, and no comforters; every one will find it enough to bear his own burden; for (*v.* 5), *"I have taken away my peace from this people,* put a full period to their prosperity, deprived them of health, wealth, and quiet, and friends, and every thing wherewith they might comfort themselves and one another." Whatever peace we enjoy, it is God's peace; it is his gift, and, *if he give quietness, who then can make trouble?* But, if we make not a good use of his peace, he can and will take it away; and where are we then? Job 34:29. "I will take away my peace, *even my loving-kindness and mercies;"* these shall be shut up and restrained, which are the fresh springs from which all their fresh streams flow, and then farewell all good. Note, Those have cut themselves off from all true peace that have thrown themselves out of the favour of God. All is gone when God takes away from us his lovingkindness and his mercies. Then it follows (*v.* 6), *Both the great and the small shall die,* even *in this land,* the land of Canaan, that used to be called the *land of the living.* God's favour is our life; take away that, and *we die, we perish, we all perish.*

III. Jeremiah must not go to the house of mirth, any more than to the house of mourning, *v.* 8. It had been his custom, and it was innocent enough, when any of his friends made entertainments at their houses and invited him to them, to *go and sit with them,* not merely to drink, but *to eat and to drink,* soberly and cheerfully. But now he must not take that liberty, 1. Because it was unseasonable, and inconsistent with the providences of God in reference to that land and nation. God called aloud to *weeping, and mourning, and fasting;* he was coming forth against them in his judgments; and it was time for them to *humble themselves;* and it well became the prophet who gave them the warning to give them an example of taking the warning, and complying with it, and so to make it appear that he did himself believe it. Ministers ought to be examples of self-denial and mortification, and to show themselves affected with those terrors of the Lord with which they desire to affect others. And it becomes all the sons of Zion to sympathize with her in her afflictions, and not to be merry when she is perplexed, Amos 6:6. 2. Because he must thus show the people what sad times were coming upon them. His friends wondered that he would not meet them, as he used to do, in the house of feasting. But he lets them know it was to intimate to them that all their feasting would be at an end shortly (*v.* 9): *"I will cause to cease the voice of mirth.* You shall have nothing to feast on, nothing to rejoice in, but be surrounded with calamities that shall mar your mirth and cast a damp upon it." God can find ways to tame the most jovial. "This shall be done *in this place,* in Jerusalem, that used to be the *joyous city* and thought her joys were all secure to her. It shall be done *in your eyes,* in your sight, to be a vexation to you, who now look so haughty and so merry. It shall be done *in your days;* you yourselves shall live to see it." The voice of praise they had made to cease by their iniquities and idolatries, and therefore justly God made to cease among them *the voice of mirth and gladness.* The voice of God's prophets was not heard, was not heeded, among them, and therefore no longer shall *the voice of the bridegroom and of the bride,* of the songs that used to grace the nuptials, be heard among them. See *ch.* 7:34.

Verses 10–13

Here is, 1. An enquiry made into the reasons why God would bring those judgments upon them (*v.* 10): *When thou shalt show this people all these words,* the words of this curse, they will say unto thee, *Wherefore has the Lord pronounced all this great evil against us?* One would hope that there were some among them that asked this question with a humble penitent heart, desiring to know what was the sin for which God contended with them, that they might cast it away and prevent the judgment: "Show us the Jonah that raises the storm and we will throw it overboard." But it seems here to be the language of those who quarrelled at the word of God, and challenged him to show what they had done which might deserve so severe a punishment: *"What is our iniquity? Or what is our sin?* What crime have we even been guilty of, proportionable to such a sentence?" Instead of humbling and condemning themselves, they stand upon their own justification and insinuate that God did them wrong in pronouncing this evil against them, that he *laid upon them more than was right,* and that they had reason to *enter into judgment with God,* Job 34:23. Note, It is amazing to see how hardly sinners are brought to justify God and judge themselves when they are in trouble, and to own the iniquity and the sin that have procured them the trouble. 2. A plain and full answer given to this enquiry. Do they ask the prophet why, and for what reason, God is thus angry with them? He shall not stop their mouths by telling them that they may be sure there is a sufficient reason, the righteous God is never *angry without cause,* without good cause; but he must tell them particularly what is the cause, that they may be convinced and humbled, or at least that God may be justified. Let them know then, (1.) That God visited upon them the iniquities of their fathers (*v.* 11): *Your fathers have forsaken me, and have not kept my law.* They shook off divine institutions and grew weary of them (they thought them too plain, too mean), and then they *walked after other gods,* whose worship was more gay and pompous; and, being fond of variety and novelty, they *served them and worshipped them;* and this was the sin which God had said, in the second commandment, he would *visit upon their children,* who kept up these idolatrous usages, because they received them *by tradition from their fathers,* 1 Pt. 1:18. (2.) That God reckoned with them for their own iniquities (*v.* 12): "You have made your fathers' sin your own, and have become obnoxious to the punishment which in their days was deferred, for *you have done worse than your fathers."* If they had made a good use of their fathers' reprieve, and had been led by the patience of God to repentance, they would have fared the better for it and the judgment would have been prevented, the reprieve turned into a national pardon; but, making an ill use of it, and being hardened by it in their sins, they fared the worse for it, and, the reprieve having expired, an addition was made to the sentence and it was executed with the more severity. They were more impudent and obstinate in sin than their fathers, *walked every one after the imagination of his own heart,* made that their guide and rule and were resolved to follow that, on purpose *that they might not hearken to God* and his prophets. They designedly suffered their own lusts and passions to be noisy, that they might drown the voice of their consciences. No wonder then that God has taken up this resolution concerning them (*v.* 13): *"I will cast you out of this land,* this land of light, this valley of vision. Since you will not hearken to me, you shall not hear me; you shall be hurried away, not into a neighbouring country which you have formerly had some acquaintance and correspondence with, but into a far country, *a land that you know not, neither you nor your fathers,* in which you have no interest, nor can expect to meet with any comfortable society, to be an allay to your misery." Justly were those banished into a strange land who doted upon strange gods, which neither they nor their fathers knew, Deu. 32:17. Two things would make their case there very miserable, and both of them relate to the soul, the better part; the greatest calamities of their captivity were those which affected that and debarred that from its bliss. [1.] "It is the happiness of the soul to be employed in the service of God; but *there shall you serve other gods day and night;* that is, you shall be in continual temptation to serve them and perhaps compelled to do it by your cruel task-masters; and, when you are forced to worship idols, you will be as sick of such worship as ever you were fond of it when it was forbidden you by your godly kings." See how God often makes men's sin their punishment, and *fills the backslider in heart with his own ways.* "You shall have no public worship at all but the worship of idols, and then you will think with regret how you slighted the worship of the true God." [2.] "It is the happiness of the soul to have some tokens of the lovingkindness of God, but you shall go to a strange land, *where I will not show you favour."* If they had had God's favour, that would have made even the land of their captivity a pleasant land; but, if they lie under his wrath, the yoke of their oppression will be intolerable to them.

Verses 14–21

There is a mixture of mercy and judgment in these verses, and it is hard to know to which to apply some of the passages here — they are so interwoven, and some seem to look as far forward as the times of the gospel.

I. God will certainly execute judgment upon them for their idolatries. Let them expect it, for the decree has gone forth. 1. God sees all their sins, though they commit them ever so secretly and palliate them ever so artfully (*v.* 17): *My eyes are upon all their ways.* They have not their eye upon God, have no regard to him, stand in no awe of him; but he has his eye upon them; neither they nor their sins are *hidden from his face, from his eyes.* Note, None of the sins of sinners either can be concealed from God or shall be overlooked by him, Prov. 5:21; Job 34:21; Ps. 90:8. 2. God is highly displeased, particularly at their idolatries, *v.* 18. As his omniscience convicts them, so his justice condemns them: *I will recompense their iniquity and their sin double,* not double to what it deserves, but double to what they expect and to what I have done formerly. Or I will recompense it *abundantly;* they shall now pay for their long reprieve and the divine patience they have abused. The sin for which God has a controversy with them is their having *defiled God's land* with their idolatries, and not only alienated that which he was entitled to as his inheritance, but polluted that which he dwelt in with delight as his inheritance, and made it offensive to him *with the carcases of their detestable things,* the gods themselves which they worshipped, the images of which, though they were of gold and silver, were as loathsome to God as the putrid carcases of men or beasts are to us. Idols are *carcases of detestable things.* God hates them, and so should we. Or he might refer to the sacrifices which they offered to these idols, with which *the land was filled;* for they had high places in all the coasts and corners of it. This was the sin which, above any other, incensed God against them. 3. He will find out and raise up instruments of his wrath, that shall *cast them out of their land,* according to the sentence passed upon them (*v.* 16): *I will send for many fishers and many hunters* — the Chaldean army, that shall have many ways of ensnaring and destroying them, by fraud as fishers, by force as hunters. They shall find them out wherever they are, and shall chase and closely pursue them, to their ruin. They shall discover them wherever they are hid, in *hills* or *mountains,* or *holes of the rocks,* and shall drive them out. God has various ways of prosecuting a people with his judgments that avoid the convictions of his word. He has men at command fit for his purpose; he has them within call, and can send for them when he pleases. 4. Their bondage in Babylon shall be sorer and much more grievous than that in Egypt, their task-masters more cruel, and their lives made more bitter. This is implied in the promise (*v.* 14, 15), that their deliverance out of Babylon shall be more illustrious in itself, and more welcome to them, than that out of Egypt. Their slavery in Egypt came upon them gradually and almost insensibly; that in Babylon came upon them at once and with all the aggravating circumstances of terror. In Egypt they had a Goshen of their own, but none such in Babylon. In Egypt they were used as servants that were useful, in Babylon as captives that had been hateful. 5. They shall be warned, and God shall be glorified, by these judgments brought upon them. These judgments have a voice, and speak aloud, (1.) Instruction to them. When God chastens them he teaches them. By this rod God expostulates with them (*v.* 20): *"Shall a man make gods to himself?* Will any man be so perfectly void of all reason and consideration as to think that a god of his own making can stand him in any stead? Will you ever again be such fools as you have been, to make to yourselves gods which are no gods, when you have a God whom you may call your own, who made you, and is himself the true and living God?" (2.) Honour to God; for he will be known by the judgments which he executes. He will first recompense their iniquity (*v.* 18), and then he will *this once* (*v.* 21) — this once for all, not by many interruptions of their peace, but this one desolation and destruction of it. "For *this once,* and no more, *I will cause them to know my hand,* the length and weight of my punishing hand, how far it can reach and how deeply it can wound. *And they shall know that my name is Jehovah,* a God with whom there is no contending, who gives being to threatenings and puts life into them as well as promises."

II. Yet he has mercy in store for them, intimations of which come in here for the encouragement of the prophet himself and of those few among them that tremble at God's word. It was said, with an air of severity (*v.* 13), that God would banish them into a strange land; but, that thereby they might not be driven to despair, there follow immediately words of comfort.

1. *The days will come,* the joyful days, when the same hand that dispersed them shall gather them again, *v.* 14, 15. They are cast out, but they are not cast off, they are not cast away. They shall be *brought up from the land of the north,* the land of their captivity, where they are held with a strong hand, *and from all the lands whither they are driven,* and where they seemed to be lost and buried in the crowd; nay, *I will bring them again into their own land,* and settle them there. As he foregoing threatenings agreed with what was written in this law, so does this promise. *Yet will I not cast them away,* Lev. 26:44. *Thence will the Lord thy God gather thee,* Deu. 30:4. And the following words (*v.* 16) may be understood as a promise; God will send for fishers and hunters, the Medes and Persians, that shall find them out in the countries where they are scattered, and send them back to their own land; or Zerubbabel, and others of their own nation, who should fish them out and hunt after them, to persuade them to return; or whatever instruments the Spirit of God made use of to *stir up their spirits to go up,* which at first they were backward to do. They began to nestle in Babylon; but, *as an eagle stirs up her nest and flutters over her young,* so God did by them, Zec. 2:7.

2. Their deliverance out of Babylon should, upon some accounts, be more illustrious and memorable than their deliverance out of Egypt was. Both were the Lord's doing and marvellous in their eyes; both were proofs that the Lord liveth and were to be kept in everlasting remembrance, to his honour, as the living God; but the fresh mercy shall be so surprising, so welcome, that it shall even abolish the memory of the former. Not but that new mercies should put us in mind of old ones, and give us occasion to renew our thanksgivings for them; yet because we are tempted to think that the former days were better than these, and to ask, *Where are all the wonders that our fathers told us of?* as if God's *arm* had *waxed short,* and to cry up the age of miracles above the later ages, when mercies are wrought in a way of common providence, therefore we are allowed here comparatively to forget the bringing of Israel out of Egypt as a deliverance outdone by that out of Babylon. That was done *by might and power,* this *by the Spirit of the Lord of hosts,* Zec. 4:6. In this there was more of pardoning mercy (the most glorious branch of divine mercy) than in that; for their captivity in Babylon had more in it of the punishment of sin than their bondage in Egypt; and therefore that which comforts Zion in her deliverance out of Babylon is this, that *her iniquity is pardoned,* Isa. 40:2. Note, God glorifies himself, and we must glorify him, in those mercies that have no miracles in them, as well as in those that have. And, though the favours of God to our fathers must not be forgotten, yet those to ourselves in our own day we must especially give thanks for.

3. Their deliverance out of captivity shall be accompanied with a blessed reformation, and they shall return effectually cured of their inclination to idolatry, which will complete their deliverance and make it a mercy indeed. They had defiled their own land with their *detestable things, v.* 18. But, when they have smarted for so doing, they shall come and humble themselves before God, *v.* 19–21. (1.) They shall be brought to acknowledge that their God only is God indeed, for he is a God in need — *"My strength* to support and comfort me, *my fortress* to protect and shelter me, *and my refuge* to whom I may flee *in the day of affliction."* Note, Need drives many to God who had set themselves at a distance from him. Those that slighted him in the day of their prosperity will be glad to flee to him in the day of their affliction. (2.) They shall be quickened to return to him by the conversion of the Gentiles: *The Gentiles shall come to thee from the ends of the earth;* and therefore shall not we come? Or, "The Jews, who had by their idolatries made themselves as Gentiles (so I rather understand it), *shall come to thee* by repentance and reformation, shall return to their duty and allegiance, even *from the ends of the earth,* from all the countries whither they were driven." The prophet comforts himself with the hope of this, and in a transport of joy returns to God the notice he had given him of it: *"O Lord! my strength and my fortress,* I am now easy, since thou hast given me a prospect of multitudes that shall *come to thee from the ends of the earth,* both of Jewish converts and of Gentile proselytes." Note, Those that are brought to God themselves cannot but rejoice greatly to see others coming to him, coming back to him. (3.) They shall acknowledge the folly of their ancestors, which it becomes them to do, when they were smarting for the sins of their ancestors: *"Surely our fathers have inherited,* not the satisfaction they promised themselves and their children, but *lies, vanity, and things wherein there is no profit.* We are now sensible that our fathers were cheated in their idolatrous worship; it did not prove what it promised, and therefore what have we to do any more with it?" Note, It were well if the disappointment which some have met with in the service of sin, and the pernicious consequences of it to them, might prevail to deter others from treading in their steps. (4.) They shall reason themselves out of their idolatry; and that reformation is likely to be sincere and durable which results from a rational conviction of the gross absurdity there is in sin. They shall argue thus with themselves (and it is well argued), *Should a man* be such a fool, so perfectly void of the reason of a man, as to *make gods to himself,* the creatures of his own fancy, the work of his own hands, when they are really *no gods? v.* 20. Can a man be so besotted, so perfectly lost to human understanding, as to expect any divine blessing or favour from that which pretends to no divinity but what it first received from him? (5.) They shall herein give honour to God, and make it to appear that they know both his hand in his providence and his name in his word, and that they are brought to know his name by what they are made to know of his hand, *v.* 21. *This once,* now at length, they shall be made to know that which they would not be brought to know by all the pains the prophets took with them. Note, So stupid are we that nothing less than the mighty hand of divine grace, known experimentally, can make us know rightly the name of God as it is revealed to us.

4. Their deliverance out of captivity shall be a type and figure of this great salvation to be wrought out by the Messiah, who shall *gather together in one the children of God that were scattered abroad.* And this is that which so far outshines the deliverance out of Egypt as even to eclipse the lustre of it, and make it even to be forgotten. To this some apply that of the *many fishers* and *hunters,* the preachers of the gospel, who were *fishers of men,* to enclose souls with the gospel net, to find them out *in every mountain* and *hill,* and secure them for Christ. Then the Gentiles came to God, some *from the ends of the earth,* and turned to the worship of him from the service of dumb idols.

CHAPTER 17

In this chapter, I. God convicts the Jews of the sin of idolatry by the notorious evidence of the fact, and condemns them to captivity for it (*v.* 1–4). II. He shows them the folly of all their carnal confidences, which should stand them in no stead when God's time came to contend with them, and that this was one of the sins upon which his controversy with them was grounded (*v.* 5–11). III. The prophet makes his appeal and address to God upon occasion of the malice of his enemies against him, committing himself to the divine protection, and begging of God to appear for him (*v.* 12–18). IV. God, by the prophet, warns the people to keep holy the sabbath day, assuring them that, if they did, it should be the lengthening out of their tranquility, but that, if not, God would by some desolating judgment assert the honour of his sabbaths (*v.* 19–27).

Verses 1–4

The people had asked (*ch.* 16:10), *What is our iniquity, and what is our sin?* as if they could not be charged with any thing worth speaking of, for which God should enter into judgment with them; their challenge was answered there, but here we have a further reply to it, in which,

I. The indictment is fully proved upon the prisoners, both the fact and the fault; their sin is too plain to be denied and too bad to be excused, and they have nothing to plead either in extenuation of the crime or in arrest and mitigation of the judgment. 1. They cannot plead, *Not guilty,* for their sins are upon record in the book of God's omniscience and their own conscience; nay, and they are obvious to the eye and observation of the world, *v.* 1, 2. They are *written* before God in the most legible and indelible characters, and *sealed among his treasures,* never to be forgotten, Deu. 32:34. They are written there with *a pen of iron and with the point of a diamond;* what is so written will not be worn out by time, but is, as Job speaks, *graven in the rock for ever.* Note, The sin of sinners is never forgotten till it is forgiven. It is ever before God, till by repentance it comes to be ever before us. *It is graven upon the table of their heart;* their own consciences witness against them, and are instead of a thousand witnesses. What is *graven on the heart,* though it may be covered and closed up for a time, yet, being graven, it cannot be erased, but will be produced in evidence when the books shall be opened. Nay, we need not appeal to the tables of the heart, perhaps they will not own the convictions of their consciences. We need go no further, for proof of the charge, than *the horns of their altars,* on which the blood of their idolatrous sacrifices was sprinkled, and perhaps the names of the idols to whose honour they were erected were inscribed. Their neighbours will witness against them, and all the creatures they have abused by using them in the service of their lusts. To complete the evidence, their own children shall be witnesses against them; they will tell truth when their fathers dissemble and prevaricate; they *remember the altars and the groves* to which their parents took them when they were little, *v.* 2. It appears that they were full of them, and acquainted with them betimes, they talked of them so frequently, so familiarly, and with so much delight. 2. They cannot plead that they repent, or are brought to a better mind. No, as the guilt of their sin is undeniable, so their inclination to sin is invincible and incurable. In this sense many understand *v.* 1, 2. Their sin is deeply *engraven* as with *a pen of iron in the tables of their hearts.* They have a rooted affection to it; it is woven into their very nature; their sin is dear to them, as that is dear to us of which we say, It is *engraven on our hearts.* The bias of their minds is still as strong as ever towards their idols, and they are not wrought upon either by the word or rod of God to forget them and abate their affection to them. It is written *upon the horns of their altars,* for they have given up their names to their idols and resolve to abide by what they have done; they have bound themselves, as with cords, to the horns of their altars. And *v.* 2 may be read fully to this sense: *As they remember their children, so remember they their altars and their groves;* they are as fond of them and take as much pleasure in them as men do in their own children, and are as loth to part with them; they will live and die with their idols, and can no more forget them than *a woman* can *forget her sucking child.*

II. The indictment being thus fully proved, the judgment is affirmed and the sentence ratified, *v.* 3, 4. Forasmuch as they are thus wedded to their sins, and will not part with them, 1. They shall be made to part with their treasures, and those shall be given into the hands of strangers. Jerusalem is God's *mountain in the field;* it was built on a hill in the midst of a plain. *All the treasures* of that wealthy city will God *give to the spoil.* Or, *My mountains with the fields, thy wealth and all thy treasures will I expose to spoil;* both the products of the country and the stores of the city shall be seized by the Chaldeans. Justly are men stripped of that which they have served their idols with and have made the food and the fuel of their lusts.

My mountain (so the whole land was, Ps. 78:54, Deu. 11:11) you have turned into *your high places for sin,* have worshipped your idols upon *the high hills* (*v.* 2), and now they shall be *give for a spoil in all your borders.* What we make for a sin God will make for a spoil; for what comfort can we expect in that wherewith God is dishonoured? 2. They shall be made to part with their inheritance, and shall be carried captives into a strange land (*v.* 4): *Thou, even thyself* (or *thou thyself and those that are in thee,* all the inhabitants), *shall discontinue from thy heritage that I gave thee.* God owns that it was their heritage, and that he gave it to them; they had an unquestionable title to it, which was an aggravation of their folly in throwing themselves out of the possession of it. It is *through thyself* (so some read it), through thy own default, that thou art disseised. *Thou shalt discontinue,* or *intermit,* the occupation of thy land. The law appointed them to *let their land rest* (it is the word here used) one year in seven, Ex. 23:11. They did not observe that law, and now God would compel them to *let it rest* (the land shall *enjoy her sabbaths,* Lev. 26:34); and yet it shall be not rest to them; they shall *serve their enemies in a land they know not.* Observe, (1.) Sin works a discontinuance of our comforts and deprives us of the enjoyment of that which God has given us. Yet, (2.) A discontinuance of the possession is not a defeasance of the right, but it is intimated that upon their repentance they shall recover possession again. For the present, *you have kindled a fire in my anger,* which burns so fiercely that it seems as if it would burn *for ever;* and so it will unless you repent, for it is the anger of an everlasting God fastening upon the immortal souls, and *who knows the power of that anger?*

Verses 5–11

It is excellent doctrine that is preached in these verses, and of general concern and use to us all, and it does not appear to have any particular reference to the present state of Judah and Jerusalem. The prophet's sermons were not all prophetical, but some of them practical; yet this discourse, which probably we have here only the heads of, would be of singular use to them by way of caution not to misplace their confidence in the day of their distress. Let us all learn what we are taught here,

I. Concerning the disappointment and vexation those will certainly meet with who depend upon creatures for success and relief when they are in trouble (*v.* 5, 6): *Cursed be the man that trusts in man.* God pronounces him cursed for the affront that he thereby puts upon him. Or, *Cursed* (that is, miserable) *is the man* that does so, for he leans upon a broken reed, which will not only fail him, but will *run into his hand and pierce it.* Observe, 1. The sin here condemned; it is *trusting in man,* putting that confidence in the wisdom and power, the kindness and faithfulness, of men, which should be placed in those attributes of God only, making our applications to men and raising our expectations from them as principal agents, whereas they are but instruments in the hand of Providence. It is *making flesh the arm* we stay upon, the arm we work with and with which we hope to work our point, the arm under which we shelter ourselves and on which we depend for protection. God is his people's *arm,* Isa. 32:2. We must not think to make any creature to be that to us which God has undertaken to be. Man is called *flesh,* to show the folly of those that make him their confidence; he is flesh, weak and feeble as flesh without bones or sinews, that has no strength at all in it; he is inactive as flesh without spirit, which is a dead thing; he is mortal and dying as flesh, which soon putrefies and corrupts, and is continually wasting. Nay, he is false and sinful, and has lost his integrity; so his being flesh signifies, Gen. 6:3. The great malignity there is in this sin; it is the *departure of the evil heart of unbelief from the living God.* Those that trust in man perhaps draw nigh to God with their mouth and honour him with their lips, they call him their hope and say that they trust in him, but really *their heart departs from him;* they distrust him, despise him, and decline a correspondence with him. Cleaving to the cistern is leaving the fountain, and is resented accordingly. 3. The fatal consequences of this sin. He that puts a confidence in man puts a cheat upon himself; for (*v.* 6) *he shall be like the heath in the desert,* a sorry shrub, the product of barren ground, sapless, useless, and worthless; his comforts shall all fail him and his hopes be blasted; he shall wither, be dejected in himself and trampled on by all about him. *When good comes* he *shall not see it,* he shall not share in it; when the times mend they shall not mend with him, but he shall *inhabit the parched places in the wilderness;* his expectation shall be continually frustrated; when others have a harvest he shall have none. Those that trust to their own righteousness and strength, and think they can do well enough without the merit and grace of Christ, thus *make flesh their arm,* and their souls cannot prosper in graces or comforts; they can neither produce the fruits of acceptable services to God nor reap the fruits of saving blessings from him; they *dwell in a dry land.*

II. Concerning the abundant satisfaction which those have, and will have, who make God their confidence, who live by faith in his providence and promise, who refer themselves to him and his guidance at all times and repose themselves in him and his love in the most unquiet times, *v.* 7, 8. Observe, 1. The duty required of us — to *trust in the Lord,* to do our duty to him and then depend upon him to bear us out in doing it — when creatures and second causes either deceive or threaten us, either are false to us or fierce against us, to commit ourselves to God as all-sufficient both to fill up the place of those who fail us and to protect us from those who set upon us. It is to *make the Lord our hope,* his favour the good we hope for and his power the strength we hope in. 2. The comfort that attends the doing of this duty. He that does so shall be *as a tree planted by the waters,* a choice tree, about which great care has been taken to set it in the best soil, so far from being like *the heath in the wilderness;* he shall be like a tree that *spreads out its roots,* and thereby is firmly fixed, spreads them out *by the rivers,* whence it draws abundance of sap, which denotes both the establishment and the comfort which those have who make God their hope; they are easy, they are pleasant, and enjoy a continual security and serenity of mind. A tree thus planted, thus watered, shall *not see when heat comes,* shall not sustain any damage from the most scorching heats of summer; it is so well moistened from its roots that it shall be sufficiently guarded against drought. Those that make God their hope, (1.) They shall flourish in credit and comfort, like a tree that is *always green,* whose leaf does not wither; they shall be cheerful to themselves and beautiful in the eyes of others. Those who thus give honour to God by giving him credit God will put honour upon, and make them the ornament and delight of the places where they live, as green trees are. (2.) They shall be fixed in an inward peace and satisfaction: They *shall not be careful in a year of drought,* when there is want of rain; for, as the tree has *seed in itself,* so it has *its moisture.* Those who make God their hope have enough in him to make up the want of all creature-comforts. We need not be solicitous about the breaking of a cistern as long as we have the fountain. (3.) They shall be fruitful in holiness, and in all good works. Those who trust in God, and by faith derive strength and grace from him, *shall not cease from yielding fruit;* they shall still be enabled to do that which will redound to the glory of God, the benefit of others, and their own account.

III. Concerning the sinfulness of man's heart, and the divine inspection it is always under, *v.* 9, 10. It is folly to trust in man, for he is not only frail, but false and deceitful. We are apt to think that we trust in God, and are entitled to the blessings here promised to those who do so. But this is a thing about which our own hearts deceive us as much as any thing. We think that we trust in God when really we do not, as appears by this, that our hopes and fears rise or fall according as second causes smile or frown.

1. It is true in general. (1.) There is that wickedness in our hearts which we ourselves are not aware of and do not suspect to be there; nay, it is a common mistake among the children of men to think themselves, their own hearts at least, a great deal better than they really are. *The heart,* the conscience of man, in his corrupt and fallen state, *is deceitful above all things.* It is subtle and false; it is apt to *supplant* (so the word properly signifies); it is that from which Jacob had his name, a *supplanter.* It calls evil good and good evil, puts false colours upon things, and cries peace to those to whom peace does not belong. When men say in their hearts (that is, suffer their hearts to whisper to them) that there is no God, or he does not see, or he will not require, or they shall have peace though they go on; in these, and a thousand similar suggestions the heart is deceitful. It cheats men into their own ruin; and this will be the aggravation of it, that they are self-deceivers, self-destroyers. Herein the heart is *desperately wicked;* it is deadly, it is desperate. The case is bad indeed, and in a manner deplorable and past relief, if the conscience which should rectify the errors of the other faculties is itself a mother of falsehood and a ring-leader in the delusion. What will become of a man if that in him which should be *the candle of the Lord* give a false light, if God's deputy in the soul, that is entrusted to support his interests, betrays them? Such is the deceitfulness of the heart that we may truly say, *Who can know it?* Who can describe how bad the heart is? We cannot know our own hearts, not what they will do in an hour of temptation (Hezekiah did not, Peter did not), not what corrupt dispositions there are in them, nor in how many things they have turned aside; who can understand his errors? Much less can we know the hearts of others, or have any dependence upon them. But, (2.) Whatever wickedness there is in the heart God sees it, and knows it, is perfectly acquainted with it and apprised of it: *I the Lord search the heart.* This is true of all that is in the heart, all the thoughts of it, the quickest, and those that are most carelessly overlooked by ourselves — all the intents of it, the closest, and those that are most artfully disguised, and industriously concealed from others. Men may be imposed upon, but God cannot. He not only searches the heart with a piercing eye, but he tries the reins, to pass a judgment upon what he discovers, to give every thing its true character and due weight. He tries it, as the gold is tried whether it be standard or no, as the prisoner is tried whether he be guilty or no. And this judgment which he makes of the heart is in order to his passing judgment upon the man; it is *to give to every man according to his ways* (according to the desert and the tendency of them, life to those that walked in the ways of life, and death to those that persisted in *the paths of the destroyer) and according to the fruit of his doings,* the effect and influence his doings have had upon others, or according to what is settled by the word of God to be the fruit of men's doings, blessings to the obedient and curses to the disobedient. Note, *Therefore* God is *Judge himself,* and he alone, because he, and none besides, knows the hearts of the children of men.

2. It is true especially of all the deceitfulness and wickedness of the heart, all its corrupt devices, desires, and designs. God observes and discerns them; and (which is more than any man can do) he judges of the overt act by the heart. Note, God knows more evil of us than we do of ourselves, which is a good reason why we should not flatter ourselves, but always stand in awe of the judgment of God.

IV. Concerning the curse that attends wealth unjustly gotten. Fraud and violence had been reigning crying sins in Judah and Jerusalem; now the prophet would have those who had been guilty of these sins, and were now stripped of all they had, to read their sin in their punishment (*v.* 11): *He that gets riches and not by right,* though he may make them his hope, shall never have joy of them. Observe, It is possible that those who use unlawful means to get wealth may succeed therein and prosper for a time; and it is a temptation to many to defraud and oppress their neighbours when there is money to be got by it. He who has got *treasures* by *vanity* and a *lying tongue* may hug himself in his success, and say, *I am rich;* nay, and I am innocent too (Hos. 12:8), but *he shall leave them in the midst of his days;* they shall be taken from him, or he from them; God shall cut him off with some surprising stroke then when he says, *Soul, take thy ease, thou hast goods laid up for many years,* Lu. 12:19, 20. He shall leave them to he knows not whom, and shall not be able to take any of his riches away with him. It intimates what a great vexation it is to a worldly man at death that he must leave his riches behind him; and justly may it be a terror to those who got them unjustly, for, though the wealth will not follow them to another world, the guilt will, and the torment of an everlasting, *Son, remember,* Lu. 16:25. Thus, *at his end, he shall be a fool,* a Nabal, whose wealth did him no good, which he had so sordidly hoarded, when *his heart* became *dead as a stone.* He was a fool all along; sometimes perhaps his own conscience told him so, but *at his end* he will appear to be so. Those are fools indeed who are fools in *their latter end;* and such multitudes will prove who were applauded as *wise men,* that did *well for themselves,* Ps. 49:13, 18. Those that get grace will be wise *in the latter end,* will have the comfort of it in death and the benefit of it to eternity (Prov. 19:20); but those that place their happiness in the wealth of the world, and, right or wrong, *will be rich,* will rue the folly of it when it is too late to rectify the fatal mistake. This is like *the partridge that sits on eggs and hatches them not,* but they are broken (as Job 39:15), or stolen (as Isa. 10:14), or they become addle: some sort of fowl there was, well known among the Jews, whose case this commonly was. The rich man takes a great deal of pains to get an estate together, and sits brooding upon it, but never has any comfort nor satisfaction in it; his projects to enrich himself by sinful courses miscarry and come to nothing. Let us therefore be wise in time — what we get to get it honestly, and what we have to use it charitably, that we may lay up in store a good foundation and be wise for eternity.

Verses 12–18

Here, as often before, we have the prophet retired for private meditation, and *alone with God.* Those ministers that would have comfort in their work must be much so. In his converse here with God and his own heart he takes the liberty which devout souls sometimes use in their soliloquies, to pass from one thing to another, without tying themselves too strictly to the laws of method and coherence.

I. He acknowledges the great favour of God to his people in setting up a revealed religion among them, and dignifying them with divine institutions (*v.* 12): *A glorious high throne from the beginning is the place of our sanctuary.* The temple at Jerusalem, where God manifested his special presence, where the lively oracles were lodged, where the people paid their homage to their Sovereign, and whither they fled for refuge in distress, was the *place of their sanctuary.* That was a *glorious high throne.* It was a throne of holiness, which made it truly glorious; it was God's throne, which made it truly high. Jerusalem is called *the city of the great King,* not only Israel's King, but the King of the whole earth, so that it might justly be deemed the metropolis, or royal city, of the world. It was *from the beginning,* so, from the first projecting of it by David and building of it by Solomon, 2 Chr. 2:9. It was the honour of Israel that God set up such a glorious throne among them. *As the glorious and high throne* (that is, heaven) *is the place of our sanctuary;* so some read it. Note, All good men have a high value and veneration for the ordinances of God, and reckon the place of the sanctuary a glorious high throne. Jeremiah here mentions this either as a plea with God for mercy to their land, in honour of the *throne of his glory* (*ch.* 14:21), or as an aggravation of the sin of his people in forsaking God though his throne was among them, and so profaning his crown and the place of his sanctuary.

II. He acknowledges the righteousness of God in abandoning those to ruin that forsook him and revolted from their allegiance to him, *v.* 13. He speaks it to God, as subscribing both to the certainty and to the equity of it: *O Lord! the hope of* those in Israel that adhere to thee, *all that forsake thee shall be ashamed.* They must of necessity be so, for they forsake thee for lying vanities, which will deceive them and make them ashamed. They will be ashamed, for they shame themselves. They will justly be put to shame, for they have forsaken him who alone can keep them in countenance when troubles come. *Let them be ashamed* (so some read it); and so it is a pious imprecation of the wrath of God upon them, or a petition for his grace, to make them penitently ashamed. *"Those that depart from me,* from the word of God which I have preached, do in effect depart from God;" as those that return to God are said to return to the prophet, *ch.* 15:19. *Those that depart from thee* (so some read it) shall be *written in the earth.* They shall soon be blotted out, as that is which is written in the dust. They shall be trampled upon and exposed to contempt. They belong to the earth, and shall be numbered among earthly people, who lay up their treasure on earth and whose names are not *written in heaven.* And they deserve to be thus written with the fools in Israel, that their folly may be made manifest unto all, because they have *forsaken the Lord, the fountain of living waters* (that is, spring waters), and that for broken cisterns. Note, God is to all that are his a *fountain of living waters.* There is a fulness of comfort in him, an over-flowing ever-flowing fulness, like that of a fountain; it is always fresh, and clear, and clean, like spring water, while the pleasures of sin are puddle-waters. They are free to it; it is not a *fountain sealed.* They deserve therefore to be condemned, as Adam, to *red earth,* to which by the corruption of their nature they are allied, because they have forsaken the *garden of the Lord,* which is so well-watered. Those that depart from God are *written in the earth.*

III. He prays to God for healing saving mercy for himself. "If the case of those that depart from God be so miserable, let me always draw nigh to him (Ps. 73:27, 28), and, in order to do that, Lord, *heal me,* and *save me, v.* 14. Heal my backslidings, my bent to backslide, and save me from being carried away by the strength of the stream to forsake thee." He was wounded in spirit with grief upon many accounts. "Lord, *heal me* with thy comforts, and make me easy." He was continually exposed to the malice of unreasonable men. "Lord, *save me* from them, and let me not fall into their wicked hands. *Heal me,* that is, sanctify me by thy grace; *save me,* that is, bring me to thy glory." All that shall be saved hereafter are sanctified now; unless the disease of sin be purged out the soul cannot live. To enforce this petition he pleads, 1. The firm belief he had of God's power: *Heal thou me, and then I shall be healed;* the cure will certainly be wrought if thou undertake it; it will be a thorough cure and not a palliative one. Those that come to God to be healed ought to be abundantly satisfied in the all-sufficiency of their physician. *Save me,* and *then I shall* certainly *be saved,* be my dangers and enemies ever so threatening. If God hold us up, we shall live; if he protect us, we shall be safe. 2. The sincere regard he had to God's glory: *"For thou art my praise,* and for that reason I desire to be healed and saved, *that I may live and praise thee,* Ps. 119:175. Thou art he whom I praise, and the praise due to thee I never gave to another. Thou art he whom I glory in, and boast of, for on thee do I depend. Thou art he that furnishes me with continual matter for praise, and I have given thee the praise of the favours already bestowed upon me. *Thou shalt be my praise"* (so some read it); "heal me, and save me, and thou shalt have the glory of it. *My praise shall be continually of thee,"* Ps. 71:6; 79:13.

IV. He complains of the infidelity and daring impiety of the people to whom he preached. It greatly troubled him, and he shows before God this trouble, as the servant that had slights put upon him by the guests he was sent to invite *came and showed his Lord these things.* He had faithfully delivered God's message to them; and what answer has he to return to him that sent him? *Behold, they say unto me, Where is the word of the Lord? Let it come now, v.* 15, Isa. 5:19. They bantered the prophet, and made a jest of that which he delivered with the greatest seriousness. 1. They denied the truth of what he said: "If that be the *word of the Lord* which thou speakest to us, *where is it?* Why is it not fulfilled?" Thus the patience of God was impudently abused as a ground to question his veracity. 2. They defied the terror of what he said. "Let God Almighty do his worst; let all he has said come to pass; we shall do well enough; the lion is not so fierce as he is painted," Amos 5:18. "Lord, to what purpose is it to speak to men that will neither believe nor fear?"

V. He appeals to God concerning his faithful discharge of the duty to which he was called, *v.* 16. The people did all they could to make him weary of his work, to exasperate him and make him uneasy, and to tempt him to prevaricate and alter his message for fear of displeasing them; but, "Lord," says he, *"thou knowest* I have not yielded to them." 1. He continued constant to his work. His office, instead of being his credit and protection, exposed him to reproach, contempt, and injury. "Yet," says he, *"I have not hastened from being a pastor after thee;* I have not left my work, nor sued for a discharge or a *quietus."* Prophets were pastors to the people, to feed them with the good word of God; but they were to be *pastors after God,* and all ministers must be so, *according to his heart* (*ch.* 3:15), to follow him and the directions and instructions he gives. Such a pastor Jeremiah was; and, though he met with as much difficulty and discouragement as ever any man did, yet he did not fly off as Jonah did, nor desire to be excused from going any more on God's errands. Note, Those that are employed for God, though their success answer nor their expectations, must not therefore throw up their commission. but continue to follow God, though the storm be in their faces. 2. He kept up his affection to the people. Though they were very abusive to him, he was compassionate to them: *I have not desired the woeful day.* The day of the accomplishment of his prophecies would be a woeful day indeed to Jerusalem, and therefore he deprecated it, and wished it might never come, though, as to himself, it would be the avenging of him upon his persecutors and the proving of him a true prophet (which they had questioned, *v.* 15), and upon those accounts he might be tempted to desire it. Note, God does not, and therefore ministers must not, desire the death of sinners, but rather that they may turn and live. Though we warn of the woeful day, we must not wish for it, but rather weep because of it, as Jeremiah did. 3. He kept closely to his instructions. Though he might have curried favour with the people, or at least have avoided their displeasure, if he had not been so sharp in his reproofs and severe in his threatenings, yet he would deliver his message faithfully; and that he had done so was a comfort to him. "Lord, *thou knowest that that which came out of my lips was right before thee;* it exactly agreed with what I received from thee, and therefore thou art reflected upon in their quarrelling with me." Note, If what we say and do be right before God, we may easily despise the reproaches and censures of men. *It is a small thing to be judged of their judgment.*

VI. He humbly begs of God that he would own him, and protect him, and carry him on cheerfully in that work to which God had so plainly called him and to which he had so sincerely devoted himself. Two things he here desires: — 1. That he might have comfort in serving the God that sent him (*v.* 17): *Be not thou a terror to me.* Surely more is implied than is expressed. "Be thou a comfort to me, and let thy favour rejoice my heart and encourage me, when my enemies do all they can to terrify me and either to drive me from my work or to make me drive on heavily in it." Note, The best have that in them which might justly make God a terror to them, as he was for some time to Job (*ch.* 6:4), to Asaph (Ps. 77:3), to Heman, Ps. 88:15. And this is that which good men, *knowing the terrors of the Lord,* dread and deprecate more than any thing; nay, whatever frightful accidents may befal them, or how formidable soever their enemies may appear to them, they can do well enough so long as God is not a terror to them. He pleads, *"Thou art my hope;* and then nothing else is my fear, no, not *in the day of evil,* when it is most threatening, most pressing. My dependence is upon thee; and therefore *be not a terror to me."* Note, Those that by faith make God their confidence shall have him for their comfort in the worst of times, if it be not their own fault: if we make him our trust, we shall not find him our terror. 2. That he might have courage in dealing with the people to whom he was sent, *v.* 18. Those persecuted him who should have entertained and encouraged him. "Lord," says he, *"let them be confounded* (let them be overpowered by the convictions of the word and made ashamed of their obstinacy, or else let the judgments threatened be at length executed upon them), *but let not me confounded,* let not me be terrified by their menaces, so as to betray my trust." Note, God's ministers have work to do which they need not be either ashamed or afraid to go on in, but they do need to be helped by the divine grace to go on in it without shame or fear. Jeremiah had not desired the woeful day upon his country in general; but as to his persecutors, in a just and holy indignation at their malice, he prays, *Bring upon them the day of evil,* in hope that the bringing of it upon them might prevent the bringing of it upon the country; if they were taken away, the people would be better; "therefore *destroy them with a double destruction;* let them be utterly destroyed, root and branch, and let the prospect of that destruction be their present confusion." This the prophet prays, not at all that he might be avenged, nor so much that he might be eased, but that *the Lord* may be *known by the judgments which he executes.*

Verses 19–27

These verses are a sermon concerning sabbath-sanctification. It is a word which the prophet *received from* the Lord, and was ordered to deliver in the most solemn and public manner to the people; for they were sent not only to reprove sin, and to press obedience, in general, but they must descend to particulars. This message concerning the sabbath was probably sent in the days of Josiah, for the furtherance of that work of reformation which he set on foot; for the promises here (*v.* 25, 26) are such as I think we scarcely find when things come nearer to the extremity. This message must be proclaimed in all the places of concourse, and therefore in *the gates,* not only because through them people were continually passing and repassing, but because in them they kept their courts and laid up their stores. It must be proclaimed (as the king or queen is usually proclaimed) at the court-gate first, the gate *by which the kings of Judah come in and go out, v.* 19. Let them be told their duty first, particularly this duty; for, if sabbaths be not sanctified as they should be, *the rulers of Judah are to be contended with* (so they were, Neh. 13:17), for they are certainly wanting in their duty. He must also preach it *in all the gates of Jerusalem.* It is a matter of great and general concern; therefore let all take notice of it. Let the *kings of Judah* hear the *word of the Lord* (for, high as they are, he is above them), *and all the inhabitants of Jerusalem,* for, mean as they are, he takes notice of them, and of what they say and do on sabbath days. Observe,

I. How the sabbath is to be sanctified, and what is the law concerning it, *v.* 21, 11. 1. They must rest from their worldly employment on the sabbath day, must do no servile work. They must *bear no burden* into the city nor out of it, into their houses nor out of them; husbandmen's burdens of corn must not be carried in, nor manure carried out; nor must tradesmen's burdens of wares or merchandises be imported or exported. There must not a loaded horse, or cart, or wagon, be seen on the sabbath day either in the streets or in the roads; the porters must not ply on that day, nor must the servants be suffered to fetch in provisions or fuel. It is a day of rest, and must not be made a day of labour, unless in case of necessity. 2. They must apply themselves to that which is the proper work and business of the day: "*Hallow you the sabbath,* that is, consecrate it to the honour of God and spend it in his service and worship." It is in order to this that worldly business must be laid aside, that we may be entire for, and intent upon, that work, which requires and deserves the whole man. 3. They must herein be very circumspect: "*Take heed to yourselves,* watch against every thing that borders upon the profanation of the sabbath." Where God is jealous we must be cautious. "*Take heed to yourselves,* for it is at your peril if you rob God of that part of your time which he has reserved to himself." *Take heed to your souls* (so the word is); in order to the right sanctifying of sabbaths, we must look well to the frame of our spirits and have a watchful eye upon all the motions of the inward man. Let not the soul be burdened with the cares of this world on sabbath days, but let that be employed, even all that is within us, in the work of the day. And, 4. He refers them to the law, the statute in this case made and provided: "This is no new imposition upon you, but is what *I commanded your fathers;* it is an ancient law; it was an article of the original contract; nay, it was a command to the patriarchs."

II. How the sabbath had been profaned (*v.* 23): "Your fathers were required to keep holy the sabbath day, *but they obeyed not;* they *hardened their necks* against this as well as other commands that were given them." This is mentioned to show that there needed a reformation in this matter, and that God had a just controversy with them for the long transgression of this law which they had been guilty of. They hardened their necks against this command, that they might not hear and receive instruction concerning other commands. Where sabbaths are neglected all religion sensibly goes to decay.

III. What blessings God had in store for them if they would make conscience of sabbath-sanctification. Though their fathers had been guilty of the profanation of the sabbath they should not only not smart for it, but their city and nation should recover its ancient glory, if they would keep sabbaths better, *v.* 24–26. Let them take care to *hallow the sabbath* and *do no work therein;* and then, 1. The court shall flourish. *Kings* in succession, or the many branches of the royal family at the same time, all as great

as kings, with the other *princes* that *sit upon the thrones* of judgment, *the thrones of the house of David* (Ps. 122:5), shall ride in great pomp *through the gates of Jerusalem,* some in chariots and some on horses, attended with a numerous retinue of the men of Judah. Note, The honour of the government is the joy of the kingdom; and the support of religion would contribute greatly to both. 2. The city shall flourish. Let there be a face of religion kept up in Jerusalem, by sabbath-sanctification, that it may answer to its title, *the holy city,* and then it *shall remain for ever, shall for ever be inhabited* (so the word may be rendered); it shall not be destroyed and dispeopled, as it is threatened to be. Whatever supports religion tends to establish the civil interests of a land. 3. The country shall flourish: *The cities of Judah and the land of Benjamin* shall be replenished with vast numbers of inhabitants, and those abounding in plenty and living in peace, which will appear by the multitude and value of their offerings, which they shall present to God. By this the flourishing of a country may be judged of, What does it do for the honour of God? Those that starve their religion either are poor or are in a fair way to be so. 4. The church shall flourish: *Meat-offerings, and incense, and sacrifices of praise,* shall be brought *to the house of the Lord,* for the maintenance of the service of that house and the servants that attend it. God's institutions shall be conscientiously observed; no sacrifice nor incense shall be offered to idols, nor alienated from God, but every thing shall go in the right channel. They shall have both occasion and hearts to bring sacrifices of praise to God. This is made an instance of their prosperity. Then a people truly flourish when religion flourishes among them. And this is the effect of sabbath-sanctification; when that branch of religion is kept up other instances of it are kept up likewise; but, when that is lost, devotion is lost either in superstition or in profaneness. It is a true observation, which some have made, that the streams of all religion run either deep or shallow according as the banks of the sabbath are kept up or neglected.

IV. What judgments they must expect would come upon them if they persisted in the profanation of the sabbath (*v.* 27): "*If you will not hearken to me* in this matter, to keep the gates shut on sabbath days, so that there may be no unnecessary *entering in,* or going out, on that day — if you will break through the enclosure of the divine law, and lay that day in common with other days — know that God will *kindle a fire in the gates* of your city," intimating that it shall be kindled by an enemy besieging the city and assaulting the gates, who shall take this course to force an entrance. Justly shall those gates be fired that are not used as they ought to be to shut out sin and to keep people in to an attendance on their duty. This fire shall devour even *the palaces of Jerusalem,* where the princes and nobles dwelt, who did not use their power and interest as they ought to have done to keep up the honour of God's sabbaths; but *it shall not be quenched* until it has laid the whole city in ruins. This was fulfilled by the army of the Chaldeans, *ch.* 52:13. The profanation of the sabbath is a sin for which God has often contended with a people by fire.

CHAPTER 18

In this chapter we have, I. A general declaration of God's ways in dealing with nations and kingdoms, that he can easily do what he will with them, as easily as the potter can with the clay (*v.* 1–6), but that he certainly will do what is just and fair with them. If he threaten their ruin, yet upon their repentance he will return in mercy to them, and, when he is coming towards them in mercy, nothing but their sin will stop the progress of his favours (*v.* 7–10). II. A particular demonstration of the folly of the men of Judah and Jerusalem in departing from their God to idols, and so bringing ruin upon themselves notwithstanding the fair warnings given them and God's kind intentions towards them (*v.* 11–17). III. The prophet's complaint to God of the base ingratitude and unreasonable malice of his enemies, persecutors, and slanderers, and his prayers against them (*v.* 18–23).

Verses 1–10

The prophet is here sent to *the potter's house* (he knew where to find it), not to preach a sermon as before to the gates of Jerusalem, but to prepare a sermon, or rather to receive it ready prepared. Those needed not to study their sermons that had them, as he had this, by immediate inspiration. "*Go to the potter's house,* and observe how he manages his work, and there *I will cause thee,* by silent whispers, *to hear my words.* There thou shalt receive a message, to be delivered to the people." Note, Those that

would know God's mind must observe his appointments, and attend where they may hear his words. The prophet was never *disobedient to the heavenly vision,* and therefore went to the potter's house (*v.* 3) and took notice how he *wrought his work upon the wheels,* just as he pleased, with a great deal of ease, and in a little time. And (*v.* 4) when a lump of clay that he designed to form into one shape either proved too stiff, or had a stone in it, or some way or other came to be *marred in his hand,* he presently turned it into another shape; if it will not serve for a vessel of honour, it will serve for a vessel of dishonour, just *as seems good to the potter.* It is probable that Jeremiah knew well enough how the potter wrought his work, and how easily he threw it into what form he pleased; but he must go and observe it *now,* that, having the idea of it fresh in his mind, he might the more readily and distinctly apprehend that truth which God designed thereby to represent to him, and might the more intelligently explain it to the people. God *used similitudes by his servants the prophets* (Hos. 12:10), and it was requisite that they should themselves understand the similitudes they used. Ministers will make a good use of their converse with the business and affairs of this life if they learn thereby to speak more plainly and familiarly to people about the things of God, and to expound scripture comparisons. For they ought to make all their knowledge some way or other serviceable to their profession.

Now let us see what the message is which Jeremiah receives, and is entrusted with the delivery of, at the potter's house. While he looks carefully upon the potter's work, God darts into his mind these two great truths, which he must preach to *the house of Israel:* —

I. That God has both an incontestable authority and an irresistible ability to form and fashion kingdoms and nations as he pleases, so as to serve his own purposes: "*Cannot I do with you as this potter, saith the Lord? v.* 6. Have not I as absolute a power over you in respect both of might and of right?" Nay, God has a clearer title to a dominion over us than the potter has over the clay; for the potter only gives it its form, whereas we have both matter and form from God. *As the clay is in the potter's hand* to be moulded and shaped as he pleases, *so are you in my hand.* This intimates, 1. That God has an incontestable sovereignty over us, is not debtor to us, may dispose of us as he thinks fit, and is not accountable to us, and that it would be as absurd for us to dispute this as for the clay to quarrel with the potter. 2. That it is a very easy thing with God to make what use he pleases of us and what changes he pleases with us, and that we cannot resist him. One turn of the hand, one turn of the wheel, quite alters the shape of the clay, makes it a vessel, unmakes it, new-makes it. Thus are our times in God's hand, and not in our own, and it is in vain for us to strive with him. It is spoken here of nations; the most politic, the most potent, are what God is pleased to make them, and no other. See this explained by Job (*ch.* 12:23), *He increaseth the nations and destroyeth them; he enlargeth the nations and straiteneth them again.* See Ps. 107:33 etc., and compare Job 34:29. *All nations before God are as the drop of the bucket,* soon wiped away, *or the small dust of the balance,* soon blown away (Isa. 40:15), and therefore, no doubt, as easily managed as the clay by the potter. 3. That God will not be a loser by any in his glory, at long run, but, if he be not glorified by them, he will be glorified upon them. If the potter's vessel be marred for one use, it shall serve for another; those that will not be monuments of mercy shall be monuments of justice. *The Lord has made all things for himself, yea, even the wicked for the day of evil,* Prov. 16:4. God formed us out of the clay (Job 33:6), nay, and we are still as clay in his hands (Isa. 64:8); and has not he the same power over us that the potter has over the clay? (Rom. 9:21), and are not we bound to submit, as the clay to the potter's wisdom and will? Isa. 29:15, 16; 45:9.

II. That, in the exercise of this authority and ability, he always goes by fixed rules of equity and goodness. He dispenses favours indeed in a way of sovereignty, but never punishes by arbitrary power. *High is his right hand,* yet he rules not with a *high hand,* but, as it follows there, *Justice and judgment are the habitation of his throne,* Ps. 89:13, 14. God asserts his despotic power, and tells us what he might do, but at the same time assures us that he will act as a righteous and merciful Judge. 1. When God is coming against us in ways of judgment we may be sure that it is for our sins, which shall appear by this, that national repentance will stop the progress of the judgments (*v.* 7,8): *If God speak concerning a nation to pluck up* its fences that secure it, and so lay it open, its fruit-trees that adorn and enrich it, and so leave it desolate — to pull down its fortifications, that the enemy may have liberty to enter in, its habitations, that the inhabitants may be under a necessity of going out, and so *destroy it* as either a vineyard or a city is destroyed — in this case, if *that nation* take the alarm, repent of their sins and reform their lives, turn every one from his evil way and return to God, God will graciously accept them, will not proceed in his controversy, will return in mercy to them, and, though he cannot change his mind, he will change his way, so that it may be said, He *repents him of the evil he said he would do to them.* Thus often in the time of the Judges, when the oppressed people were penitent people, still God raised them up saviours; and, when they turned to God, their affairs immediately took a new turn. It was Nineveh's case, and we wish it had oftener been Jerusalem's; see 2 Chr. 7:14. It is an undoubted truth that a sincere conversion from the evil of sin will be an effectual prevention of the evil of punishment; and God can as easily raise up a penitent people from their ruins as the potter can make anew the vessel of clay when it was *marred in his hand.* 2. When God is coming towards us in ways of mercy, if any stop be given to the progress of that mercy, it is nothing but sin that gives it (*v.* 9, 10): *If God speak concerning a nation to build and to plant it,* to advance and establish all the true interests of it, it is *his husbandly* and *his building* (1 Co. 3:9), and, if he speak in favour of it, it is done, it is increased, it is enriched, it is enlarged, its trade flourishes, its government is settled in good hands, and all its affairs prosper and its enterprises succeed. but if this nation, which God is thus loading with benefits, *do evil in his sight* and *obey not his voice,* — if it lose its virtue, and become debauched and profane, — if religion grow into contempt, and vice to get to be fashionable, and so be kept in countenance and reputation, and there be a general decay of serious godliness among them, — then God will turn his hand against them, will pluck up what he was planting, and pull down what he was building (*ch.* 45:4); the good work that was in the doing shall stand still and be let fall, and what favours were further designed shall be withheld; and this is called his *repenting of the good wherewith he said he would benefit them,* as he changed his purpose concerning Eli's house (1 Sa. 2:30) and hurried Israel back into the wilderness when he had brought them within sight of Canaan. Note, Sin is the great mischief-maker between God and a people; it forfeits the benefit of his promises and spoils the success of their prayers. It defeats his kind intentions concerning them (Hos. 7:1) and baffles their pleasing expectations from him. It ruins their comforts, prolongs their grievances, brings them into straits, and retards their deliverances, Isa. 59:1, 2.

Verses 11–17

These verses seem to be the application of the general truths laid down in the foregoing part of the chapter to the nation of the Jews and their present state.

I. God was now speaking concerning them *to pluck up,* and *to pull down,* and *to destroy;* for it is that part of the rule of judgment that their case agrees with (*v.* 11): *"Go, and tell* them" (saith God), *"Behold I frame evil against you and devise against you.* Providence in all its operations is plainly working towards your ruin. Look upon your conduct towards God, and you cannot but see that you deserve it; look upon his dealings with you, and you cannot but see that he designs it." He frames evil, as the potter frames the vessel, so as to answer the end.

II. He invites them by repentance and reformation to meet him in the way of his judgments and so to prevent his further proceedings against them: *"Return you now every one from his evil ways,* that so (according to the rule before laid down) God may turn from the evil he had purported to do unto you, and that providence which seemed to be framed like a vessel on the wheel against you shall immediately be thrown into a new shape, and the issue shall be in favour of you." Note, The warnings of God's word, and the threatenings of his providence, should be improved by us as strong inducements to us to reform our lives, in which it is not enough to *turn from our evil ways,* but we must *make our ways and our doings good,* conformable to the rule, to the law.

III. He foresees their obstinacy, and their perverse refusal to comply with this invitation, though it tended so much to their own benefit (*v.* 12): *They said, "There is no hope.* If we must not be delivered unless we return from our evil ways, we may even despair of ever being delivered, for we are resolved that *we will walk after our own devices.* It is to no purpose for the prophets to say any more to us, to use any more arguments, or to press the matter any further; we will have our way, whatever it cost us; *we will do every one the imagination of his* own *evil heart,* and will not be under the restraint of the divine law." Note, That which ruins sinners is affecting to live as they list. They call it liberty to live at large; whereas for a man to be a slave to his lusts is the worst of slaveries. See how strangely some men's hearts are hardened by the deceitfulness of sin that they will not so much as promise amendment; nay, they set the judgments of God at defiance: "We will go on with *our own devices,* and let God go on with his; and we will venture the issue."

IV. He upbraids them with the monstrous folly of their obstinacy, and their hating to be reformed. Surely never were people guilty of such an absurdity, never any that pretended to reason acted so unreasonably (*v.* 13): *Ask you among the heathen,* even those that had not the benefit of divine revelation, no oracles, no prophets, as Judah and Jerusalem had, yet, even among them, *who hath heart such a thing?* The Ninevites, when thus warned, turned from their evil ways. Some of the worst of men, when they are told of their faults, especially when they begin to smart for them, will at least promise reformation and say that they will endeavour to mend. But *the virgin of Israel* bids defiance to repentance, is resolved to go on frowardly, whatever conscience and Providence say to the contrary, and thus *has done a horrible thing.* She should have preserved herself pure and chaste for God, who had espoused her to himself; but she has alienated herself from him, and refuses to return to him. Note, It is *a horrible thing,* enough to make one tremble to think of it, that those who have made their condition sad by sinning should make it desperate by refusing to reform. Wilful impenitence is the grossest self-murder; and that is *a horrible thing,* which we should abhor the thought of.

V. He shows their folly in two things: —

1. In the nature of the sin itself that they were guilty of. They forsook God for idols, which was the most horrible thing that could be, for they put a most dangerous cheat upon themselves (*v.* 14, 15): *Will a* thirsty traveller *leave the snow,* which, being melted, runs down from the mountains *of Lebanon,* and, passing over *the rock of the field,* flows in clear, clean, crystal streams? Will he leave these, pass these by, and think to better himself with some dirty puddle-water? *Or shall the cold flowing waters that come from any other place be forsaken* in the heat of summer? No; when men are parched with heat and drought, and meet with cooling refreshing streams, they will make use of them, and not turn their backs upon them. The margin reads it, *"Will a man* that is travelling the road *leave my fields,* which are plain and level, *for a rock,* which is rough and hard, *or for the snow of Lebanon,* which, lying in great drifts, makes the road impassable? *Or shall the running waters be forsaken for the strange cold waters?* No; in these things men know when they are well off, and will keep so; they will not leave a certainty for an uncertainty. But *my people have forgotten me* (*v.* 15), have quitted *a fountain of living waters for broken cisterns. They have burnt incense to* idols, that are as vain as *vanity* itself, that are not what they pretend to be nor can perform what is expected from them." They had not the common wit of travellers, but even their leaders caused them to err, and they were content to be misled. (1.) They left *the ancient paths,* which were appointed by the divine law, which had been walked in by all the saints, which were therefore the right way to their journey's end, a safe way, and, being well-tracked, were both easy to hit and easy to walk in. But, when they were advised to keep to the good old way, they positively said that they would not, *ch.* 6:16. (2.) They chose by-paths; they walked *in a way not cast up,* not in the highway, the King's highway, in which they might travel safely, and which would certainly lead them to their right end, but in a dirty way, a rough way, a way in which they could not but *stumble;* such was the way of idolatry (such is the way of all iniquity — it is a false way, it is a way full of stumbling-blocks) and yet this way they chose to walk in and lead others in.

2. In the mischievous consequences of it. Though the thing itself were bad, they might have had some excuse for it if they could have promised themselves any good out of it. But the direct tendency of it was *to make their land desolate, and,* consequently, themselves miserable (for so the inhabitants must needs be if their country be laid waste), and both themselves and their land *a perpetual hissing.* Those deserve to be hissed that have fair warning given them and will not take it. *Every one that passes by* their land shall make his remarks upon it, and *shall be astonished, and way his head,* some wondering, others commiserating, others triumphing in the desolations of a country that had been *the glory of all lands.* They shall wag their heads in derision, upbraiding them with their folly in forsaking God and their duty, and so pulling this misery upon their own heads. Note, Those that revolt from God will justly be made the scorn of all about them, and, having reproached the Lord, will themselves be a reproach. *Their land* being made *desolate,* in pursuance of their destruction, it is threatened (*v.* 17), *I will scatter them as with an east wind,* which is fierce and violent; by it they shall be hurried to and fro *before the enemy,* and find no way open to escape. They shall not only flee before the enemy (that they might do and yet make an orderly retreat), but they shall be scattered, some one way and some another. That which completes their misery is, *I will show them the back, and not the face, in the day of their calamity.* Our calamities may be easily borne if God look towards us, and smile upon us, when we are under them, if he countenance us and show us favour; but if he turn *the back* upon us, if he show himself displeased, if he be deaf to our prayers and refuse us his help, if he forsake us, leave us to ourselves, and stand at a distance from us, we are quite undone. *If he hide his face, who then can behold him?* Job 34:29. herein God would deal with them as they had dealt with him (*ch.* 2:27), *They have turned their back unto me, and not their face.* It is a righteous thing with God to show himself strange to those in the day of their trouble who have shown themselves rude and undutiful to him in their prosperity. This will have its full accomplishment in that day when God will say to those who, though they have been professors of piety, were yet workers of iniquity, *Depart from me, I know you not,* nay, *I never knew you.*

Verses 18–23

The prophet here, as sometimes before, brings in his own affairs, but very much for instruction to us.

I. See here what are the common methods of the persecutors. We may see this in Jeremiah's enemies, *v.* 18.

1. They laid their heads together to consult what they should do against him, both to be revenged on him for what he had said and to stop his mouth for the future: *They said, Come and let us devise devices against Jeremiah.* The enemies of God's people and ministers have been often very crafty themselves, and confederate with one another, to do them mischief. What they cannot act to the prejudice of religion separately they will try to do in concert. *The wicked plots against the just.* Caiaphas, and the chief priests and elders, did so against our blessed Saviour himself. The opposition which the gates of hell give to the kingdom of heaven is carried on with a great deal of cursed policy. God had said (*v.* 11), *I devise a device against you;* and now, as if they resolved to be quits with him and to outwit Infinite Wisdom itself, they resolve to *devise devices against* God's prophet, not only against his person, but against the word he delivered to them, which they thought by their subtle management to defeat. O the prodigious madness of those that hope to disannul God's counsel!

2. Herein they pretended a mighty zeal for the church, which, they suggested, was in danger if Jeremiah was tolerated to preach as he did: *"Come,"* say they, "let us silence and crush him, *for the law shall not perish from the priest; the law of truth is in their mouths* (Mal. 2:6) and there we will seek it; the administration of ordinances according to

the law is in their hands, and neither the one nor the other shall be wrested from them. *Counsel shall not perish from the wise;* the administration of public affairs shall always be lodged with the privy-counsellors and ministers of state, to whom it belongs; *nor* shall *the word* perish *from the prophets"* — they mean those of their own choosing, who prophesied to them smooth things, and flattered them with visions of peace. Two things they insinuated: — (1.) That Jeremiah could not be himself a true prophet, but was a pretender and a usurper, because he neither was commissioned by the priests, nor concurred with the other prophets, whose authority therefore will be despised if he be suffered to go on. "If Jeremiah be regarded as an oracle, farewell the reputation of our priests, our wise men, and prophets; but *that* must be supported, which is reason enough why he must be suppressed." (2.) That the matter of his prophecies could not be from God, because it reflected sometimes upon the prophets and priests; he had charged them with being the ringleaders of all the mischief (*ch.* 5:31) and deceiving the people (*ch.* 14:14); he had foretold that their *heart should perish,* and *be astonished* (*ch.* 4:9), that *the wise men should be dismayed* (*ch.* 8:9, 10), that the priests and prophets should be intoxicated, *ch.* 13:13. Now this galled them more than any thing else. Presuming upon the promise of God's presence with their priests and prophets, they could not believe that he would ever leave them. The guides of the church must needs be infallible, and therefore he who foretold their being infatuated must be condemned as a false prophet. Thus, under colour of zeal for the church, have its best friends been run down.

3. They agreed to do all they could to blast his reputation: *"Come, let us smite him with the tongue,* put him into an ill name, fasten a bad character upon him, represent him to some as despicable and fit to be prosecuted, to all as odious and not fit to be tolerated." This was their device, *fortiter calumniari, aliquid adhaerebit — to throw the vilest calumnies at him, in hopes that some would adhere to him.* to dress him up in bearskins, otherwise they could not bait him. Those who projected this, it is likely, were men of figure, whose tongue was no small slander, whose representations, though ever so false, would be credited both by princes and people, to make him obnoxious to the justice of the one and the fury of the other. The scourge of such tongues will give not only smart lashes, but deep wounds; it is a great mercy therefore to be *hidden from it,* Job 5:21.

4. To set others an example, they resolved that they would not themselves regard any thing he said, though it appeared ever so weighty and ever so well confirmed as a message from God: *Let us not give heed to any of his words;* for, right or wrong, they will look upon them to be *his words,* and not the words of God. What good can be done with those who hear the word of God with a resolution not to heed it or believe it? Nay,

5. That they may effectually silence him, they resolve to be the death of him (*v.* 23): *All their counsel against me is to slay me.* They *hunt for the precious life;* and a precious life indeed it was that they hunted for. Long was this Jerusalem's wretched character, *Thou that killedst* many of *the prophets,* and wouldst have killed them all.

II. See here what is the common relief of the persecuted. This we may see in the course that Jeremiah took when he met with this hard usage. He immediately applied to his God by prayer, and so gave himself ease.

1. He referred himself and his cause to God's cognizance, *v.* 19. They would not regard a word he said, would not admit his complaints, nor take any notice of his grievances; but, *Lord* (says he), *do thou give heed to me.* It is matter of comfort to faithful ministers that, if men will not give heed to their praying. He appeals to God as an impartial Judge, that will hear both sides, as every judge ought to do. "Do not only *give heed to me,* but *hearken to the voice of those that contend with me;* hear what they have to say against me and for themselves, and then make it to appear that thou *sittest in the throne, judging right.* Hear the voice of my contenders, how noisy and clamorous they are, how false and malicious all they say is, and let them be *judged out of their own mouth; cause their own tongues to fall upon them."*

2. He complains of their base ingratitude to him (*v.* 20): *"Shall evil be recompensed for good,* and shall it go unpunished? Wilt not thou recompense me good for that evil?" 2 Sa. 16:12. To render good for good is human, evil for evil is brutish, good for evil is Christian, but evil for good is devilish; it is so very absurd and wicked a thing that we cannot think but God will avenge it. See how great the evil was that they did against him: *They have dug a pit for my soul;* they aimed to take away his life (no less would satisfy them), and that not in a generous way, by an open assault, against which he might have an opportunity of defending himself, but in a base, cowardly, clandestine way: *they dug pits for* him, which there was no fence against, Ps. 119:85. But see how great the good was which he had done for them: *Remember that I stood before thee to speak good for them;* he had been an intercessor with God for them, had used his interest in heaven on their behalf, which was the greatest kindness they could expect from one of his character. *He is a prophet and he shall pray for thee,* Gen. 20:7. Moses often did this for Israel, and yet they quarrelled with him, and sometimes *spoke of stoning him.* He did them this kindness when they were in imminent danger of destruction and most needed it. They had themselves provoked God's wrath against them, and it was ready to break in upon them, but he stood in the gap (as Moses, Ps. 106:23) *and turned away* that *wrath.* Now, (1.) This was very base in them. Call a man ungrateful and you can call him no worse. But it was not strange that those who had forgotten their God did not know their best friends. (2.) It was very grievous to him, as the like was to David. Ps. 35:13; 109:4, *For my love they are my adversaries.* Thus disingenuously do sinners deal with the great intercessor, crucifying him afresh, and speaking against him on earth, while his blood is speaking for them in heaven. See Jn. 10:32. But, (3.) It was a comfort to the prophet that, when they were so spiteful against him, he had the testimony of his conscience for him that he had done his duty to them; and the same will be our rejoicing in such a day of evil. *The blood-thirsty hate the upright, but the just seek his soul,* Prov. 29:10.

3. He imprecates the judgments of God upon them, not from a revengeful disposition, but in a prophetical indignation against their horrid wickedness, *v.* 21–23. He prays, (1.) That their families might be starved for want of bread: *"Deliver up the children to the famine,* to the famine in the country for want of rain, and that in the city through the straitness of the siege. Thus let this iniquity of the fathers be visited upon the children." (2.) That they might be cut off *by the sword* of war, which, whatever it was in the enemy's hand, would be, in God's hand, a sword of justice: *"Pour them out* (so the word is) *by the hands of the sword;* let *their blood* be shed as profusely as water, that *their wives* may be left childless *and widows,* their husbands being taken away by *death"* (some think that the prophet refers to *pestilence*); *let their young men,* that are the strength of this generation and the hope of the next, *be slain by the sword in battle.* (3.) That the terrors and desolations of war might seize them suddenly and by surprise, that thus their punishment might answer to their sin (*v.* 22): *"Let a cry be heard from their houses,* loud shrieks, *when thou shalt bring a troop* of the Chaldeans *suddenly upon them,* to seize them and all they have, to make them prisoners and their estates a prey;" for thus they would have done by Jeremiah; they aimed to ruin him at once ere he was aware: *"They have dug a pit* for *me,* as for a wild beast, *and* have *hid snares for* me, as for some ravenous noxious fowl." Note, Those that think to ensnare others will justly be themselves ensnared in an evil time. (4.) That they might be dealt with according to the desert of this sin, which was without excuse: *"Forgive not their iniquity, neither blot out their sin from thy sight;* that is, let them not escape the just punishment of it; let them lie under all the miseries of those whose sins are unpardoned." (5.) That God's wrath against them might be their ruin: *Let them be overthrown before thee.* This intimates that justice was in pursuit of them, that they endeavoured to make their escape from it, but in vain; "they shall be made to stumble in their flight, and being overthrown they will certainly be overtaken." And then, Lord, *in the time of thy anger,* do to them (he does not say what he would have done to them, but) do to them as thou thinkest fit, as thou usest to do with those whom thou art angry with — *deal thus with them.* Now this is not written for our imitation. Jeremiah was a prophet, and by the impulse of the spirit of prophecy, in the foresight of the ruin certainly coming upon his persecutors, might pray such prayers as we may not; and, if we think by this example to justify ourselves in such imprecations, we *know not what manner of spirit we are of;* our Master has taught us, by his precept and pattern, to *bless those that curse us and pray for those that despitefully use us.* Yet it is written for our instruction, and is of use to teach us, [1.] That those who have forfeited the benefit of the prayers of God's prophets for them may justly expect to have their prayers against them. [2.] That persecution is a sin that fills the measure of a people's iniquity very fast, and will bring as sure and sore a destruction upon them as any thing. [3.] Those who will not be won upon by the kindness of God and his prophets will certainly at length feel the just resentments of both.

CHAPTER 19

The same melancholy theme is the subject of this chapter that was of those foregoing — the approaching ruin of Judah and Jerusalem for their sins. This Jeremiah had often foretold; here he has particularly full orders to foretel it again. I. He must set their sins in order before them, as he had often done, especially their idolatry (*v.* 4, 5). II. He must describe the particular judgments which were now coming apace upon them for these sins (*v.* 6–9). III. He must do this in the valley of Tophet, with great solemnity, and for some particular reasons (*v.* 2, 3). IV. He must summon a company of the elders together to be witnesses of this (*v.* 1). V. He must confirm this, and endeavour to affect his hearers with it, by a sign, which was the breaking of an earthen bottle, signifying that they should be dashed to pieces like a potter's vessel (*v.* 10–13). VI. When he had done this in the valley of Tophet he ratified it in the court of the temple (*v.* 14, 15). Thus were all likely means tried to awaken this stupid senseless people to repentance, that their ruin might be prevented; but all in vain.

Verses 1–9

The corruption of man having made it necessary that *precept* should be *upon precept, and line upon line* (so unapt are we to receive, and so very apt to let slip, the things of God), the grace of God has provided that there shall be, accordingly, *precept upon precept, and line upon line,* that those who are irreclaimable may be inexcusable. For this reason the prophet is here sent with a message to the same purport with what he had often delivered, but with some circumstances that might make it the more taken notice of, a thing which ministers should study, for a little circumstance may sometimes be a great advantage, and those that would win souls must be wise.

I. He must take of the elders and chief men, both in church and state, to be his auditors and witnesses to what he said — *the ancients of the people and the ancients of the priests,* the most eminent men both in the magistracy and in the ministry, that they might be *faithful witnesses to record,* as those Isa. 8:2. It is strange that these great men should be at the beck of a poor prophet, and obey his summons to attend him out of the city, they know not whither and they knew not why. But, though the generality of the elders were disaffected to him, yet it is likely that there were some few among them who looked upon him as a prophet of the Lord, and would pay this respect to the heavenly vision. Note, Persons of rank and figure have an opportunity of honouring God, by a diligent attendance on the ministry of the word and other divine institutions; and they ought to think it an honour, and no disparagement to themselves, yea, though the circumstances be mean and despicable. It is certain that the greatest of men is less than the least of the ordinances of God.

II. He must *go to the valley of the son of Hinnom,* and deliver this message there; for *the word of the Lord* is not bound to any one place; as good a sermon may be preached in the valley of Tophet as in the gate of the temple. Christ preached on a mountain and out of a ship. This valley lay partly on the south side of Jerusalem, but the prophet's way to it was *by the entry on the east gate — the sun gate* (*v.* 2), so some render it, and suppose it to look not towards the sun-rising, but the noon sun — *the potter's gate,* so some. This sermon must be preached in that place, in *the valley of the son of Hinnom,* 1. Because there they had been guilty of the vilest of their idolatries, the sacrificing of their children to Moloch, a horrid piece of impiety, which the sight of the place might serve to remind them of and upbraid them with. 2. Because there they should feel the sorest of their calamities; there the greatest slaughter should be made among them; and, it being the common sink of the city, let them look upon it and see what a miserable spectacle this magnificent city would be when it should be all like the valley of Tophet.

God bids him go thither, *and proclaim there the words that I shall tell thee,* when thou comest thither; whereby it appears (as Mr. Gataker well observed) that God's messages were frequently not revealed to the prophets before the very instant of time wherein they were to deliver them.

III. He must give general notice of a general ruin now shortly coming upon Judah and Jerusalem, *v.* 3. He must, as those that make proclamation, begin with an *Oyes: Hear you the word of the Lord,* though it be a terrible word, for you may thank yourselves if it be so. Both rulers and ruled must attend to it, at their peril; the *kings of Judah,* the king and his sons, the king and his princes and privy-counsellors, must hear the word of the King of kings, for, high as they are, he is above them. The *inhabitants of Jerusalem* also must hear what God has to say to them. Both princes and people have contributed to the national guilt and must concur in the national repentance, or they will both share in the national ruin. Let them all know that *the Lord of hosts,* who is therefore able to do what he threatens, though he is *the God of Israel,* nay, because he is so, will therefore punish them in the first place for their iniquities (Amos 3:2): *He will bring evil upon this place* (upon *Judah and Jerusalem)* so surprising, and so dreadful, that *whosoever hears* it, *his ears shall tingle;* whosoever hears the prediction of it, hears the report and representation of it, it shall make such an impression of terror upon him that he shall still think he hears it sounding in his ears and shall not be able to get it out of his mind. The ruin of Eli's house is thus described (1 Sa. 3:11), and of Jerusalem, 2 Ki. 21:12.

IV. He must plainly tell them what their sins were for which God had this controversy with them, *v.* 4, 5. They are charged with apostasy from God *(They have forsaken me)* and abuse of the privileges of the visible church, and which they had been dignified — *They have estranged this place.* Jerusalem (the holy city), the temple (the holy house), which was designed for the honour of God and the support of his kingdom among men, they had alienated from those purposes, and (as some render the word) *they had strangely abused.* They had so polluted both with their wickedness that God had disowned both, and abandoned them to ruin. He charges them with an affection for and the adoration of false *gods,* such as *neither they nor their fathers have known,* such as never had recommended themselves to their belief and esteem by any acts of power or goodness done for them or their ancestors, as that God had abundantly done whom they forsook; yet they took them at a venture for their gods; nay, being fond of change and novelty, they liked them the better for their being upstarts, and new fashions in religion were as grateful to their fancies as in other things. They also stand charged with murder, wilful murder, from malice prepense: *They have filled this place with the blood of innocents.* It was Manasseh's sin (2 Ki. 24:4), *which the Lord would not pardon.* Nay, as if idolatry and murder, committed separately, were not bad enough and affront enough to God and man, they have put them together, have consolidated them into one complicated crime, that of burning their children in the fire to Baal (*v.* 5), which was the most insolent defiance to all the laws both of natural and revealed religion that ever mankind was guilty of; and by it they openly declared that they loved their new gods better than ever they loved the true God, though they were such cruel task-masters that they required human sacrifices (inhuman I should call them), which the Lord Jehovah, whose all lives and souls are, never demanded from his worshippers; he never *spoke* of such a thing, nor *came it into his mind.* See *ch.* 7:31.

V. He must endeavour to affect them with the greatness of the desolation that was coming upon them. He must tell them (as he had done before, *ch.* 7:32) that this *valley of the son of Hinnom* shall acquire a new name, *the valley of slaughter* (*v.* 6), for (*v.* 7) multitudes shall *fall* there *by the sword,* when either they sally out upon the besiegers and are repulsed or attempt to make their escape and are seized: *They* shall *fall before their enemies,* who not only endeavour to make themselves masters of their houses and estates, but have such an implacable enmity to them that they *seek their lives;* they thirst after their blood, and, when they are dead, will not allow a cartel for the burying of the slain, but *their carcases* shall *be meat for the fowls of the heaven and beasts of the earth.* What a dismal place will the valley of Tophet be then! And as for those that remain within the city, and will not capitulate with the besiegers, they shall perish for want of food, when first they have eaten *the flesh of their sons and daughters,* and dearest *friends,* through the *straitness wherewith their enemies shall straiten them, v.* 9. This was threatened in the law as an instance of the extremity to which the judgments of God should reduce them (Lev. 26:29, Deu. 28:53) and was accomplished, Lam. 4:10. And, *lastly,* the whole *city* shall be *desolate,* the houses laid in ashes, the inhabitants slain or taken prisoners; there shall be no resort to it, nor any thing in it but what looks rueful and horrid; so that *every one that passes by shall be astonished* (*v.* 8), as he had said before, *ch.* 18:16. That place which holiness had made *the joy of the whole earth* sin had made the reproach and shame of the whole earth.

VI. He must assure them that all their attempts to prevent and avoid this ruin, so long as they continued impenitent and unreformed, would be fruitless and vain (*v.* 7): *I will make void the counsel of Judah and Jerusalem* (of the princes and senators of Judah and Jerusalem) *in this place,* in the royal palace, which lay on the south side of the city, not far from the place where the prophet now stood. Note, There is no fleeing from God's justice but by fleeing to his mercy. Those that will not make good God's counsel, by humbling themselves under his mighty hand, shall find that God will make void their counsel and blast their projects, which they think ever so well concerted for their own preservation. There is *no counsel* or strength *against the Lord.*

Verses 10–15

The message of wrath delivered in the foregoing verses is here enforced, that it might gain credit, two ways: —

I. By a visible sign. The prophet was to take along with him an *earthen bottle* (*v.* 1), and, when he had delivered his message, he was to *break the bottle* to pieces (*v.* 10), and the same that were auditors of the sermon must be spectators of the sign. He had compared this people, in the chapter before, to the potter's clay, which is easily marred in the making. But some might say, "It is past that with us; we have been made and hardened long since." "And what though you be," says he, "the potter's vessel is as soon broken in the hand of any man as the vessel while it is soft clay is marred in the potter's hand, and its case is, in this respect, much worse, that the vessel while it is soft clay, though it be marred, may be moulded again, but, after it is hardened, when it is broken it can never be pieced again." Perhaps what they see will affect them more than what they only hear talk of; that is the intention of sacramental signs, and teaching by symbols was anciently used. In the explication of this sign he must inculcate what he had before said, with a further reference to the place where this was done, in the valley of Tophet. 1. As the bottle was easily, irresistibly, and irrecoverably broken by the Chaldean army, *v.* 11. They depended much upon the firmness of their constitution, and the fixedness of their courage, which they thought hardened them like a vessel of brass; but the prophet shows that all that did but harden them like a vessel of earth, which, though hard, is brittle and sooner broken than that which is not so hard. Though they were made vessels of honour, still they were vessels of earth, and so they shall be made to know if they dishonour God and themselves, and serve not the purposes for which they were made. It is God himself, who made them, that resolves to unmake them: *I will break this people and this city,* dash them in pieces like *a potter's vessel;* the doom of the heathen (Ps. 2:9, Rev. 2:27), but now Jerusalem's doom, Isa. 30:14. *A potter's vessel,* when once broken, *cannot be made whole again, cannot be cured,* so the word is. The ruin of Jerusalem shall be an utter ruin; no hand can repair it but his that broke it; and if they return to him, though he has torn, he will heal. 2. This was done in Tolphet, to signify two things: — (1.) That Tophet should be the receptacle of the slain: *They shall bury in Tophet till there be no place to bury* any more there; they shall jostle for room to lay their dead, and a very little room will then serve those who, while they lived, *laid house to house and field to field.* Those that would be *placed alone in the midst of the earth* while they were above ground, and obliged all about them to keep their distance, must lie with the multitude when they are underground, for there are innumerable before them. (2.) That Tophet should be a resemblance of the whole city (*v.* 12): *I will make this city as Tophet.* As they had filled the valley of Tophet with the slain which they sacrificed to their idols, so God will fill the whole city with the slain that shall fall as sacrifices to the justice of God. We read (2 Ki. 23:10) of Josiah's defiling Tophet, because it had been abused to idolatry, which he did (as should seem, *v.* 14) by *filling it with the bones of men;* and, whatever it was before, thenceforward it was looked upon as a detestable place. Dead carcases, and other filth of the city, were carried thither, and a fire was continually kept there for the burning of it. This was the posture of that valley when Jeremiah was sent thither to prophesy; and so execrable a place was it looked upon to be that, in the language of our Saviour's time, hell was called, in allusion to it, *Gehenna, the valley of Hinnom.* "Now" (says God) "since that blessed reformation, when Tophet was defiled, did not proceed as it ought to have done, nor prove a thorough reformation, but though the idols in Tophet were abolished and made odious those in Jerusalem remained, therefore will I do with the city as Josiah did by Tophet, fill it with the bodies of men, and make it a heap of rubbish." Even *the houses of Jerusalem, and* those *of the kings of Judah,* the royal palaces not excepted, *shall be defiled as the place of Tophet* (*v.* 13), and for the same reason, because of the idolatries that have been committed there; since they will not defile them by a reformation, God will defile them by a destruction, *because* upon the *roofs of their houses they have burnt incense unto the host of heaven.* The flat roofs of their houses were sometimes used by devout people as convenient places for prayer (Acts 10:9), and by idolaters they were used as high places, on which they sacrificed to strange gods, especially to *the host of heaven,* the sun, moon, and stars, that there they might be so much nearer to them and have a clearer and fuller view of them. We read of those that *worshipped the host of heaven upon the house-tops* (Zep. 1:5), and of *altars on the top of the upper chamber of Ahaz,* 2 Ki. 23:12. This sin upon the house-tops brought a curse into the house, which consumed it, and made it a dunghill like Tophet.

II. By a solemn recognition and ratification of what he had said *in the court of the Lord's house, v.* 14, 15. The prophet returned from Tophet to the temple, which stood upon the hill over that valley, and there confirmed, and probably repeated, what he had said in the valley of Tophet, for the benefit of those who had not heard it; what he had said he would stand to. Here, as often before, he both assures them of judgments coming upon them and assigns the cause of them, which was their sin. Both these are here put together in a little compass, with a reference to all that had gone before. 1. The accomplishment of the prophecies is here the judgment threatened. The people flattered themselves with a conceit that God would be better than his word, that the threatening was but to frighten them and keep them in awe a little; but the prophet tells them that they deceive themselves if they think so: *For thus saith the Lord of hosts,* who is able to make his words good, *I will bring upon this city, and upon all her towns,* all the smaller cities that belong to Jerusalem the metropolis, *all the evil that I have pronounced against it.* Note, Whatever men may think to the contrary, the executions of Providence will fully answer the predictions of the word, and God will appear as terrible against sin and sinners as the scripture makes him; nor shall the unbelief of men make either his promises or his threatenings of no effect or of less effect than they were thought to be of. 2. The contempt of the prophecies is here the sin charged upon them, as the procuring cause of this judgment. It is *because they have hardened their necks,* and would not bow and bend them to the yoke of God's commands, would *not hear my words,* that is, would not heed them and yield obedience to them. Note, The obstinacy of sinners in their sinful ways is altogether their own fault; if their necks are hardened, it is their own act and deed, they have hardened them; if they are deaf to the word of God, it is because they have stopped their own ears. We have need therefore to pray that God, by his grace, would deliver us *from hardness of heart and contempt of his word and commandments.*

CHAPTER 20

Such plain dealing as Jeremiah used in the foregoing chapter, one might easily foresee, if it did not convince and humble men, would provoke and exasperate them; and so it did; for here we find, I. Jeremiah persecuted by Pashur for preaching that sermon (*v.* 1, 2). II. Pashur threatened for so doing, and the word which Jeremiah had preached confirmed (*v.* 3–6). III. Jeremiah complaining to God concerning it, and the other instances of hard measure that he had since he began to be a prophet, and the grievous temptations he had struggled with (*v.* 7–10), encouraging himself in God, lodging his appeal with him, not doubting but that he shall yet praise him, by which it appears that he had much grace (*v.* 11–13) and yet peevishly cursing the day of his birth (*v.* 14–18), by which it appears that he had sad remainders of corruption in him too, and was a man subject to like passions as we are.

Verses 1–6

Here is, I. Pashur's unjust displeasure against Jeremiah, and the fruits of that displeasure, *v.* 1, 2. This Pashur was a priest, and therefore, one would think, should have protected Jeremiah, who was of his own order, a priest too, and the more because he was a prophet of the Lord, whose interests the priests, his ministers, ought to consult. But this priest was a persecutor of him whom he should have patronized. He was *the son of Immer;* that is, he was of the sixteenth course of the priests, of which Immer, when these courses were first settled by David, was father (1 Chr. 24:14), as Zechariah was of the order of Abiah, Lu. 1:5. Thus this Pashur is distinguished from another of the same name mentioned *ch.* 21:1, who was of the fifth course. This Pashur was *chief governor in the temple;* perhaps he was only so *pro tempore — for a short period,* the course he was head of being now in waiting, or he was suffragan to the high priest, or perhaps captain of the temple or of the guards about it. Acts 4:1. This was Jeremiah's great enemy. The greatest malignity to God's prophets was found among those that professed sanctity and concern for God and the church. We cannot suppose that Pashur was one of those ancients of the priests that went with Jeremiah to the valley of Tophet to hear him prophesy, unless it were with a malicious design to take advantage against him; but, when he came into the courts of the Lord's house, it is probable that he was himself a witness of what he said, and so it may be read (*v.* 1), *He heard Jeremiah prophesying these things.* As we read it, the information was brought to him by others, whose examinations he took: *He heard that Jeremiah prophesied these things,* and could not bear it, especially that he should dare to preach in the courts of the Lord's house, where he was *chief governor,* without his leave. When power in the church is abused, it is the most dangerous power that can be employed against it. Being incensed at Jeremiah, 1. He *smote* him, struck him with his hand or staff of authority. Perhaps it was a blow intended only to disgrace him, like that which the high priest ordered to be given to Paul (Acts 23:2), he struck him on the mouth, and bade him hold his prating. Or perhaps he gave him many blows intended to hurt him; he beat him severely, as a malefactor. It is charged upon the husbandmen (Mt. 21:35) that they beat the servants. The method of proceeding here was illegal; the high priest, and the rest of the priests, ought to have been consulted, Jeremiah's credentials examined, and the matter enquired into, whether he had an authority to say what he said. But these rules of justice are set aside and despised, as mere formalities; right or wrong, Jeremiah must be run down. The enemies of piety would never suffer themselves to be bound by the laws of equity. 2. He *put him in the stocks.* Some make it only a place of confinement; he imprisoned him. It rather seems to be an instrument of closer restraint, and intended to put him both to pain and shame. Some think it was a pillory for his neck and arms; others (as we) a pair of stocks for his legs: whatever engine it was, he continued in it all night, and in a public place too, *in the high gate of Benjamin, which was* in, or *by, the house of the Lord,* probably a gate through which they passed between the city and the temple. Pashur intended thus to chastise him, that he might deter him from prophesying; and thus to expose him to contempt and render him odious, that he might not be regarded if he did prophesy. Thus have the best men met with the worst treatment from this ungracious ungrateful world; and the greatest blessings of their age have been counted as the *off-scouring of all things.* Would it not raise a pious indignation to see such a man as Pashur upon the bench and such a man as Jer-

emiah in the stocks? It is well that there is another life after this, when persons and things will appear with another face.

II. God's just displeasure against Pashur, and the tokens of it. *On the morrow Pashur* gave Jeremiah his discharge, *brought him out of the stocks* (*v.* 3); it is probable that he continued him there, in little-ease, as long as was usual to continue any in that punishment. And now Jeremiah has a message from God to him. We do not find that, when Pashur put Jeremiah in the stocks, the latter gave him any check for which he did; he appears to have quietly and silently submitted to the abuse; *when he suffered, he threatened not.* But, when he brought him out of the stocks, then God put a word into the prophet's mouth, which would awaken his conscience, if he had any. For, when the prophet of the Lord was bound, *the word of the Lord was not.* What can we think Pashur aimed at in smiting and abusing Jeremiah? Whatever it is, we shall see by what God says to him that he is disappointed.

1. Did he aim to establish himself, and make himself easy, by silencing one that told him of his faults and would be likely to lessen his reputation with the people? He shall not gain this point; for, (1.) Though the prophet should be silent, his own conscience shall fly in his face and make him always uneasy. To confirm this he shall have a name given him, *Magor-missabib — Terror round about,* or *Fear on every side.* God himself shall give him this name, whose calling him so will make him so. It seems to be a proverbial expression, bespeaking a man not only in distress but in despair, not only in danger on every side (that a man may be and yet by faith may be in no terror, as David, Ps. 3:6, 27:3), but in fear on every side, and that a man may be when there appears no danger. *The wicked flee when no man pursues,* are in *great gear where no fear is.* This shall be Pashur's case (*v.* 4): *"Behold, I will make thee a terror to thyself;* that is, thou shalt be subject to continual frights, and thy own fancy and imagination shall create thee a constant uneasiness." Note, God can make the most daring sinner a terror to himself, and will find out a way to frighten those that frighten his people from doing their duty. And those that will not hear of their faults from God's prophets, that are reprovers in the gate, shall be made to hear of them from conscience, which is a reprover in their own bosoms that will not be daunted nor silenced. And miserable is the man that is thus made a terror to himself. Yet this is not all; some are very much a terror to themselves, but they conceal it and seem to others to be pleasant; but, *"I will make thee a terror to all thy friends;* thou shalt, upon all occasions, express thyself with so much horror and amazement that all thy friends shall be afraid of conversing with thee and shall choose to stand aloof from thy torment." Persons in deep melancholy and distraction are a terror to themselves and all about them, which is a good reason why we should be very thankful, so long as God continues to us the use of our reason and the peace of our consciences. (2.) His friends, whom he put a confidence in and perhaps studied to oblige in what he did against Jeremiah, shall all fail him. God does not presently strike him dead for what he did against Jeremiah, but lets him live miserably, like Cain in the *land of shaking,* in such a continual consternation that wherever he goes he shall be a monument of divine justice; and, when it is asked, "What makes this man in such a continual terror?" it shall be answered, "It is God's hand upon him for putting Jeremiah in the stocks." His friends, who should encourage him, shall all be cut off; they shall *fall by the sword of the enemy,* and *his eyes shall behold it,* which dreadful sight shall increase his terror. (3.) He shall find, in the issue, that his terror is not causeless, but that divine vengeance is waiting for him (*v.* 6); he and his family shall *go into captivity,* even to *Babylon;* he shall neither die before the evil comes, as Josiah, nor live to survive it, as some did, but he shall die a captive, and shall in effect be buried in his chains, he *and all his friends.* Thus far is the doom of Pashur. Let persecutors read it, and tremble; tremble to repentance before they be made to tremble to their ruin.

2. Did he aim to keep the people easy, to prevent the destruction that Jeremiah prophesied of, and by sinking his reputation to make his words fall to the ground? It is probable that he did; for it appears by *v.* 6 that he did himself set up for a prophet, and told the people that they should have peace. He *prophesied lies to them;* and be-

cause Jeremiah's prophecy contradicted his, and tended to awaken those whom he endeavoured to rock asleep in their sins, therefore he set himself against him. But could he gain his point? No; Jeremiah stands to what he has said against Judah and Jerusalem, and God by his mouth repeats it. Men get nothing by silencing those who reprove and warn them, for the word will have its course; so it had here. (1.) The country shall be ruined (*v.* 4): *I will give all Judah into the hand of the king of Babylon.* It had long been God's own land, but he will now transfer his title to it to Nebuchadnezzar, he shall be master of the country and dispose of the inhabitants some to the sword and some to captivity, as he pleases, but none shall escape him. (2.) The city shall be ruined too, *v.* 5. The king of Babylon shall spoil that, and carry all that is valuable in it to Babylon. [1.] He shall seize their magazines and military stores (here called *the strength of this city*) and turn them against them. These they trusted to as their strength; but what stead could they stand them in when they had thrown themselves out of God's protection, and when he who was indeed their strength had departed from them? [2.] He shall carry off all their stock in trade, their wares and merchandises, here called *their labours,* because it was what they laboured about and got by their labour. [3.] He shall plunder their fine houses, and take away their rich furniture, here called their *precious things,* because they valued them and set their hearts so much upon them. Happy are those who have secured to themselves precious things in God's precious promises, which are out of the reach of soldiers. [4.] He shall rifle the exchequer, and take away the jewels of the crown and *all the treasures of the kings of Judah.* This was that instance of the calamity which was first of all threatened to Hezekiah long ago as his punishment for showing his treasures to the king of Babylon's ambassadors, Isa. 39:6. The treasury, they thought, was their defence; but that betrayed them, and became an easy prey to the enemy.

Verses 7–13

Pashur's doom was to be a *terror to himself;* Jeremiah, even now, in this hour of temptation, is far from being so; and yet it cannot be denied but that he is here, through the infirmity of the flesh, strangely agitated within himself. Good men are but men at the best. God is not extreme to mark what they say and do amiss, and therefore we must not be so, but make the best of it. In these verses it appears that, upon occasion of the great indignation and injury that Pashur did to Jeremiah, there was a struggle in his breast between his graces and his corruptions. His discourse with himself and with his God, upon this occasion, was somewhat perplexed; let us try to methodize it.

I. Here is a sad representation of the wrong that was done him and the affronts that were put upon him; and this representation, no doubt, was according to truth, and deserves no blame, but was very justly and very fitly made to him that sent him, and no doubt would bear him out. He complains,

1. That he was ridiculed and laughed at; they made a jest of every thing he said and did; and this cannot but be a great grievance to an ingenuous mind (*v.* 7, 8): *I am in derision; I am mocked.* They played upon him, and made themselves and one another merry with him, as if he had been a fool, good for nothing but to make sport. Thus he was continually: *I was in derision daily.* Thus he was universally: *Every one mocks me;* the greatest so far forget their own gravity, and the meanest so far forget mine. Thus our Lord Jesus, on the cross, was reviled both by priests and people; and the revilings of each had their peculiar aggravation. And what was it that thus exposed him to contempt and scorn? It was nothing but his faithful and zealous discharge of the duty of his office, *v.* 8. They could find nothing for which to deride him but his preaching; it was *the word of the Lord* that *was made a reproach.* That for which they should have honoured and respected him — that he was entrusted to deliver the *word of the Lord* to them was the very thing for which they reproached and reviled him. He never preached a sermon, but, though he kept as closely as possible to his instructions, they found something or other in it for which to banter and abuse him. Note, It is sad to think that, though divine revelation be one of the greatest blessings and honours that ever was bestowed upon the world, yet it has been turned very

much to the reproach of the most zealous preachers and believers of it. Two things they derided him for: — (1.) The manner of his preaching: *Since he spoke, he cried out.* He had always been a lively affectionate preacher, and since he began to speak in God's name he always spoke as a man in earnest; he *cried aloud and did not spare,* spared neither himself nor those to whom he preached; and this was enough for those to laugh at who hated to be serious. It is common for those that are unaffected with and disaffected to, the things of God themselves, to ridicule those that are much affected with them. Lively preachers are the scorn of careless unbelieving hearers. (2.) The matter of his preaching: He *cried violence and spoil.* He reproved them for the violence and spoil which they were guilty of towards one another; and he prophesied of the violence and spoil which should be brought upon them as the punishment of that sin; for the former they ridiculed him as over-precise, for the latter as over-credulous; in both he was provoking to them, and therefore they resolved to run him down. This was bad enough, yet he complains further.

2. That he was plotted against and his ruin contrived; he was not only ridiculed as a weak man, but reproached and misrepresented as a bad man and dangerous to the government. This he laments as his grievance, *v.* 10. Being laughed at, though it touches a man in point of honour, is yet a thing that may be easily laughed at again; for, as it has been well observed, it is no shame to be laughed at, but to deserve to be so. But there were those that acted a more spiteful part, and with more subtlety. (1.) They spoke ill of him behind his back, when he had no opportunity of clearing himself, and were industrious to spread false reports concerning him: *I heard,* at second hand, *the defaming of many, fear on every side* (*of many Magor-missabibs,* so some read it), of many such men as Pashur was, and who may therefore expect his doom. Or this was the matter of their defamation; they represented Jeremiah as a man that instilled fears and jealousies on every side into the minds of the people, and so made them uneasy under the government, and disposed them to a rebellion. Or he perceived them to be so malicious against him that he could not but be *afraid on every side;* wherever he was he had reason to fear informers; so that they made him almost a *Magor-missabib.* These words are found in the original, *verbatim,* the same, Ps. 31:13, *I have heard the slander* or *defaming of many, fear on every side.* Jeremiah, in his complaint, chooses to make use of the same words that David had made use of before him, that it might be a comfort to him to think that other good men had suffered similar abuses before him, and to teach us to make use of David's psalms with application to ourselves, as there is occasion. Whatever we have to say, we may thence take with us words. See how Jeremiah's enemies contrived the matter: *Report, say they, and we will report it.* They resolve to cast an odium upon him, and this is the method they take: "Let some very bad thing be said of him, which may render him obnoxious to the government, and, though it be ever so false, we will second it, and spread it, and add to it." (For the reproaches of good men lose nothing by the carriage.) "Do you that frame a story plausibly, or you that can pretend to some acquaintance with him, report it once, and we will all report it from you, in all companies, that we come into. Do you say it, and we will swear it; do you set it a going, and we will follow it." And thus both are equally guilty, those that raise and those that propagate the false report. The receiver is as bad as the thief. (2.) They flattered him to his face, that they might get something from him on which to ground an accusation, as the spies that came to Christ feigning themselves to be just men, Lu. 20:20; 11:53, 54. His familiars, that he conversed freely with and put a confidence in, *watched for his halting,* observed what he said, which they could by any strained *innuendo* put a bad construction upon, and carried it to his enemies. His case was very sad when those betrayed him whom he took to be his friends. They said among themselves, "If we accost him kindly, and insinuate ourselves into his acquaintance, per-adventure he will be enticed to own that he is in confederacy with the enemy and a pensioner to the king of Babylon, or we shall wheedle him to speak some treasonable words; and then *we shall prevail against him,* and *take our revenge upon him* for telling us of our faults and threatening us with the judgments of God." Note, Neither the innocence of the dove, no, nor the prudence of the serpent to help it, can secure men from unjust censure and false accusation.

II. Here is an account of the temptation he was in under this affliction; his *feet were almost gone,* as the psalmist's, Ps. 73:2. And this is that which is most to be dreaded in affliction, being driven by it to sin, Neh. 6:13. 1. He was tempted to quarrel with God for making him a prophet. This he begins with (*v.* 7): *O Lord! thou hast deceived me, and I was deceived.* This as we read it, sounds very harshly. God's servants have been always ready to own that he is a faithful Master and never cheated them; and therefore this is the language of Jeremiah's folly and corruption. If, when God called him to be a prophet and told him he would *set him over the kingdoms* (*ch.* 1:10) and *make him a defenced city,* he flattered himself with an expectation of having universal respect paid to him as a messenger from heaven, and living safe and easy, and afterwards it proved otherwise, he must not say that God had deceived him, but that he had deceived himself; for he knew how the prophets before him had been persecuted, and had no reason to expect better treatment. Nay, God had expressly told him that all the *princes, priests, and people of the land would fight against him* (*ch.* 1:18, 19), which he had forgotten, else he would not have laid the blame on God thus. Christ thus told his disciples what opposition they should meet with, *that they might not be offended,* Jn. 16:1, 2. But the words may very well be read thus: *Thou hast persuaded me, and I was persuaded;* it is the same word that was used, Gen. 9:27, margin, *God shall persuade Japhet.* And Prov. 25:15, *By much forbearance is a prince persuaded.* And Hos. 2:14, *I will allure her.* And this agrees best with what follows: *"Thou wast stronger than I,* didst over-persuade me with argument; nay, didst overpower me, by the influence of thy Spirit upon me, and *thou hast prevailed."* Jeremiah was very backward to undertake the prophetic office; he pleaded that he was under age and unfit for the service; but God over-ruled his pleas, and told him that *he must go, ch.* 1:6, 7. "Now, Lord," says he, "since thou hast put this office upon me, why dost thou not stand by me in it? Had I thrust myself upon it, I might justly have been in derision; but why am I so when thou didst thrust me into it?" It was Jeremiah's infirmity to complain thus of God as putting a hardship upon him in calling him to be a prophet, which he would not have done had he considered the lasting honour thereby done him, sufficient to counterbalance the present contempt he was under. Note, As long as we see ourselves in the way of God and duty it is weakness and folly, when we meet with difficulties and discouragements in it, to wish we had never set out in it. 2. He was tempted to quit his work and give it over, partly because he himself met with so much hardship in it and partly because those to whom he was sent, instead of being edified and made better, were exasperated and made worse (*v.* 9): *"Then I said,* Since by prophesying in the name of the Lord I gain nothing to him or myself but dishonour and disgrace, *I will not make mention of him* as my author for any thing I say, nor *speak any more in his name;* since my enemies do all they can to silence me, I will even silence myself, and speak no more, for I may as well speak to the stones as to them." Note, It is a strong temptation to poor ministers to resolve that they will preach no more when they see their preaching slighted and wholly ineffectual. But let people dread putting their ministers into this temptation. Let not their labour be in vain with us, lest we provoke them to say that they will take no more pains with us, and provoke God to say, They shall take no more. Yet let not ministers hearken to this temptation, but go on in their duty, notwithstanding their discouragements, for this is the more thankworthy; and, *though Israel be not gathered,* yet they *shall be glorious.*

III. Here is an account of his faithful adherence to his work and cheerful dependence on his God notwithstanding.

1. He found the grace of God mighty in him to keep him to this business, notwithstanding the temptation he was in to throw it up: *"I said,* in my haste, *I will speak no more in his name;* what I have in my heart to deliver I will stifle and suppress. But I soon found it was *in my heart as a burning fire shut up in my bones,* which glowed inwardly, and must have vent; it was impossible to smother it; I was like a man in a burning fever, uneasy and in a continual agitation; while *I kept silence from good my heart was hot within me,* it was *pain and grief to me,* and I must speak, that I might be refreshed;" Ps. 29:2, 3; Job 32:20. *While I kept silence, my bones waxed old,* Ps. 32:3. See the power of the spirit of prophecy in those that were actuated by it; and thus will a holy zeal for God even eat men up, and make them forget themselves. *I believed, therefore have I spoken.* Jeremiah was soon weary with forbearing to preach, and could not contain himself; nothing puts faithful ministers to pain so much as being silenced, nor to terror so much as silencing themselves. Their convictions will soon triumph over temptations of that kind; for *woe is unto me if I preach not the gospel,* whatever it cost me, 1 Co. 9:16. And it is really a mercy to have the word of God thus mighty in us to overpower our corruptions.

2. He was assured of God's presence with him, which would be sufficient to baffle all the attempts of his enemies against him (*v.* 11): "They say, *We shall prevail against him;* the day will undoubtedly be our own. But I am sure that *they shall not prevail, they shall not prosper.* I can safely set them all at defiance, for *the Lord is with me,* is on my side, to take my part against them (Rom. 8:31), to protect me from all their malicious designs upon me. He is with me to support me and bear me up under the burden which now presses me down. He is with me to make the word I preach answer the end he designs, though not the end I desire. He is with me as a mighty terrible one, to strike a terror upon them, and so to overcome them." Note, Even that in God which is terrible is really comfortable to his servants that trust in him, for it shall be turned against those that seek to terrify his people. God's being a mighty God bespeaks him a terrible God to all those that take up arms against him or any one that, like Jeremiah, was commissioned by him. How terrible will the wrath of God be to those that think to daunt all about them and will themselves be daunted by nothing! The most formidable enemies that act against us appear despicable when we see the Lord for us as a *mighty terrible one,* Neh. 4:14. Jeremiah speaks now with a good assurance: "If *the Lord be with me, my persecutors shall stumble,* so that, when they pursue me, they shall not overtake me (Ps. 27:2), and then *they shall be greatly ashamed* of their impotent malice and fruitless attempts. Nay, *their everlasting confusion* and infamy *shall never be forgotten;* they shall not forget it themselves, but it shall be to them a constant and lasting vexation, whenever they think of it; others shall not forget it, but it shall leave upon them an indelible reproach."

3. He appeals to God against them as a righteous Judge, and prays judgment upon his cause, *v.* 12. He looks upon God as the God that *tries the righteous,* takes cognizance of them, and of every cause that they are interested in. He does not judge in favour of them with partiality, but *tries them,* and finding that they have right on their side, and that their persecutors wrong them and are injurious to them, he gives sentence for them. He that tries the righteous tries the unrighteous too, and he is very well qualified to do both; for he *sees the reins and the heart,* he certainly knows men's thoughts and affections, their aims and intentions, and therefore can pass an unerring judgment on their words and actions. Now this is the God, (1.) To whom the prophet here refers himself, and in whose court he lodges his appeal: *Unto thee have I opened my cause.* Not but that God perfectly knew his cause, and all the merits of it, without his opening; but the cause we commit to God we must spread before him. He knows it, but he will know it from us, and allows us to be particular in the opening of it, not to affect him, but to affect ourselves. Note, It will be an ease to our spirits, when we are oppressed and burdened, to open our cause to God and pour out our complaints before him. (2.) By whom he expects to be righted; *"Let me see thy vengeance on them,* such vengeance as thou thinkest fit to take for their conviction and my vindication, the vengeance thou usest to take on persecutors." Note, Whatever injuries are done us, we must not study to avenge ourselves, but must leave it to that God to do it *to whom vengeance belongs,* and who hath said, *I will repay.*

4. He greatly rejoices and praises God, in a full confidence that God would appear for his deliverance, *v.* 13. So full is he of the comfort of God's presence with him, the divine protection he is under, and the divine promise he has to depend upon, that in a transport of joy he stirs up himself and others to give God the glory of it: *Sing unto*

the Lord, praise you the Lord. Here appears a great change with him since he began this discourse; the clouds are blown over, his complaints all silenced and turned into thanksgivings. He has now an entire confidence in that God whom (*v.* 7) he was distrusting; he stirs up himself to praise that name which (*v.* 9) he was resolving no more to make mention of. It was the lively exercise of faith that made this happy change, that turned his sighs into songs and his tremblings into triumphs. It is proper to express our hope in God by our praising him, and our praising God by our singing to him. That which is the matter of the praise is, *He hath delivered the soul of the poor from the hand of the evil-doers;* he means especially himself, his own poor soul. "He hath delivered me formerly when I was in distress, and now of late out of the hand of Pashur, and he will continue to deliver me, 2 Co. 1:10. He will deliver my soul from the sin that I am in danger of falling into when I am thus persecuted. He hath *delivered me from the hand of evil-doers,* so that they have not gained their point, nor had their will." Note, Those that are faithful in well-doing need not fear those that are spiteful in evil-doing, for they have a God to trust to who has well-doers under the hand of his protection and evil-doers under the hand of his restraint.

Verses 14–18

What is the meaning of this? Does there *proceed out of the same mouth blessing and cursing?* Could he that said so cheerfully (*v.* 13), *Sing unto the Lord, praise you the Lord,* say so passionately (*v.* 14), *Cursed be the day wherein I was born?* How shall we reconcile these? What we have in these verses the prophet records, I suppose, to his own shame, as he had recorded that in the foregoing verses to God's glory. It seems to be a relation of the ferment he had been in while he was in the stocks, out of which by faith and hope he had recovered himself, rather than a new temptation which he afterwards fell into, and it should come in like that of David (Ps. 31:22), *I said in my haste, I am cut off;* this is also implied, Ps. 77:7. When grace has got the victory it is good to remember the struggles of corruption, that we may be ashamed of ourselves and our own folly, may admire the goodness of God in not taking us at our word, and may be warned by it to double our guard upon our spirits another time. See here how strong the temptation was which the prophet, by divine assistance, got the victory over, and how far he yielded to it, that we may not despair if we through the weakness of the flesh be at any time thus tempted. Let us see here,

I. What the prophet's language was in this temptation. 1. He fastened a brand of infamy upon his birth-day, as Job did in a heat (*ch.* 3:1): *"Cursed be the day wherein I was born.* It was an ill day to me (*v.* 14), because it was the beginning of sorrows, and an inlet to all this misery." It is a wish that he had never been born. Judas in hell has reason to wish so (Mt. 26:24), but no man on earth has reason to wish so, because he knows not but he may yet become a vessel of mercy, much less has any good man reason to wish so. Whereas some keep their birth-day, at the return of the year with gladness, he will look upon his birth-day as a melancholy day, and will solemnize it with sorrow, and will have it looked upon as an ominous day. 2. He wished ill to the messenger that brought his father the news of his birth, *v.* 15. It made his father very glad to hear that he had a child born (perhaps it was his first-born), especially that it was a man-child, for then, being of the family of the priests, he might live to have the honour of serving God's altar; and yet he is ready to curse the man that brought him the tidings, when perhaps the father to whom they were brought gave him a gratuity for it. Here Mr. Gataker well observes, "That parents are often much rejoiced at the birth of their children when, if they did but foresee what misery they are born to, they would rather lament over them than rejoice in them." He is very free and very fierce in the curses he pronounces upon the messenger of his birth (*v.* 16): *"Let him be at the cities of Sodom and Gomorrah, which the Lord utterly overthrew, and repented not,* did not in the least mitigate or alleviate their misery. *Let him hear the cry* of the invading besieging enemy *in the morning,* as soon as he is stirring; then let him take the alarm, and by noon let him hear their *shouting* for victory. And thus let him live in constant terror." 3. He is angry that the fate of the Hebrews' children in Egypt was not his, that he was not *slain from the womb,* that his first breath was not his last, and that he was not strangled as soon as he came into the world, *v.* 17. He wishes the messenger of his birth had been better employed and had been his murderer; nay, that his mother of whom he was born had been, to her great misery, always with child of him, and so the womb in which he was conceived would have served, without more ado, as a grave for him to be buried in. Job intimates a near alliance and resemblance between the womb and the grave, Job 1:21. *Naked came I out of my mother's womb, and naked shall I return thither.* 4. He thinks his present calamities sufficient to justify these passionate wishes (*v.* 18): *"Wherefore came I forth out of the womb,* where I lay hid, was not seen, was not hated, where I lay safely and knew no evil, to see all this *labour and sorrow,* nay to have my *days consumed with shame,* to be continually vexed and abused, to have my life not only spent in trouble, but wasted and worn away by trouble?"

II. What use we may make of this. It is not recorded for our imitation, and yet we may learn good lessons from it. 1. See the vanity of human life and the vexation of spirit that attends it. If there were not another life after this, we should be tempted many a time to wish that we have never known this; for our few days here are full of trouble. 2. See the folly and absurdity of sinful passion, how unreasonably it talks when it is suffered to ramble. What nonsense is it to curse a day — to curse a messenger for the sake of his message! What a brutish barbarous thing for a child to wish his own mother had never been delivered of him! See Isa. 45:10. We can easily see the folly of it in others, and should take warning thence to suppress all such intemperate heats and passions in ourselves, to stifle them at first and not to suffer these evil spirits to speak. When the heart is hot, let the tongue be bridled, Ps. 39:1, 2. 3. See the weakness even of good men, who are but men at the best. See how much those who think they stand are concerned to take heed lest they fall, and to pray daily, Father in heaven, *lead us not into temptation!*

CHAPTER 21

It is plain that the prophecies of this book are not placed here in the same order in which they were preached; for there are chapters after this which concern Jehoahaz, Jehoiakim, and Jeconiah, who all reigned before Zedekiah, in whose reign the prophecy of this chapter bears date. Here is, I. The message which Zedekiah sent to the prophet, to desire him to enquire of the Lord for them (*v.* 1, 2). II. The answer which Jeremiah, in God's name, sent to that message, in which, 1. He foretels the certain and inevitable ruin of the city, and the fruitlessness of their attempts for its preservation (*v.* 3–7). 2. He advises the people to make the best of bad, by going over to the king of Babylon (*v.* 8–10). 3. He advises the king and his family to repent and reform (*v.* 11, 12), and not to trust to the strength of their city and grow secure (*v.* 13, 14).

Verses 1–7

Here is, I. A very humble decent message which king Zedekiah, when he was in distress, sent to Jeremiah the prophet. It is indeed charged upon this Zedekiah that he *humbled not himself before Jeremiah the prophet, speaking from the mouth of the Lord* (2 Chr. 36:12); he did not always humble himself as he did sometimes; he never humbled himself till necessity forced him to it; he humbled himself so far as to desire the prophet's assistance, but not so far as to take his advice, or to be ruled by him. Observe,

1. The distress which king Zedekiah was now in: *Nebuchadrezzar made war upon him,* not only invaded the land, but besieged the city, and had now actually invested it. Note, Those that put the evil day far from them will be the more terrified when it comes upon them; and those who before slighted God's ministers may then perhaps be glad to court an acquaintance with them.

2. The messengers he sent — *Pashur and Zephaniah,* one belonging to the fifth course of the priests, the other to the twenty-fourth, 1 Chr. 24:9, 18. It was well that he sent, and that he sent persons of rank; but it would have been better if he had desired a personal conference with the prophet, which no doubt he might easily have had if he would so far have humbled himself. Perhaps these priests were no better than the rest, and yet, when they were commanded by the king, they must carry a respectful message to the prophet, which was both a mortification to them and an honour to Jeremiah. he had rashly said (*ch.* 20:18), *My days are consumed with shame;* and yet here we find that he lived to see better days than those were when he made that complaint; now he appears in reputation. Note, It is folly to say, when things are bad with us, "They will always be so." It is possible that those who are despised may come to be respected; and it is promised that those who *honour God he will honour,* and that those who have *afflicted his people shall bow to them,* Isa. 60:14.

3. The message itself: *Enquire, I pray thee, of the Lord for us, v.* 2. Now that the Chaldean army had got into their borders, into their bowels, they were at length convinced that Jeremiah was a true prophet, though loth to own it and brought too late to it. Under this conviction they desire him to stand their friend with God, believing him to have that interest in heaven which none of their other prophets had, who had flattered them with hopes of peace. They now employ Jeremiah, (1.) To consult the mind of God for them: *"Enquire of the Lord for us;* ask him what course we shall take in our present strait, for the measures we have hitherto taken are all broken." Note, Those that will not take the direction of God's grace how to get clear of their sins would yet be glad of the directions of his providence how to get clear of their troubles. (2.) To seek the favour of God for them (so some read it): *"Entreat the Lord for us;* be an intercessor for us with God." Note, Those that slight the prayers of God's people and ministers when they are in prosperity may perhaps be glad of an interest in them when they come to be in distress. *Give us of your oil.* The benefit they promise themselves is, *It may be the Lord will deal with us* now *according to the wondrous works he wrought for our fathers,* that the enemy may raise the siege and *go up from us.* Observe, [1.] All their care is to get rid of their trouble, not to make their peace with God and be reconciled to him — "That our enemy may *go up from us,"* not, "That our God may return to us." Thus Pharaoh (Ex. 10:17): *Entreat the Lord that he may take away this death.* [2.] All their hope is that God had done wondrous works formerly in the deliverance of Jerusalem when Sennacherib besieged it, at the prayer of Isaiah (so we are told, 2 Chr. 32:20, 21), and who can tell but he may destroy these besiegers (as he did those) at the prayer of Jeremiah? But they did not consider how different the character of Zedekiah and his people was from that of Hezekiah and his people: those were days of general reformation and piety, these of general corruption and apostasy. Jerusalem is now the reverse of what it was then. Note, It is folly to think that God should do for us while we hold fast our iniquity as he did for those that held fast their integrity.

II. A very startling cutting reply which God, by the prophet, sent to that message. If Jeremiah had been to have answered the message of himself we have reason to think that he would have returned a comfortable answer, in hope that their sending such a message was an indication of some good purposes in them, which he would be glad to make the best of, for he did not desire the woeful day. But God knows their hearts better than Jeremiah does, and sends them an answer which has scarcely one word of comfort in it. He sends it to them in the name of *the Lord God of Israel* (*v.* 3), to intimate to them that though God allowed himself to be called the *God of Israel,* and had done great things for Israel formerly, and had still great things in store for Israel, pursuant to his covenants with them, yet this should stand the present generation in no stead, who were Israelites in name only, and not in deed, any more than God's dealings with them should cut off his relation to Israel as their God. It is here foretold,

1. That God will render all their endeavours for their own security fruitless and ineffectual (*v.* 4): "I will be so far from teaching your hands to war, and putting an edge upon your swords, that I will *turn back the weapons of war that are in your hand,* when you sally out upon the besiegers to beat them off, so that they shall not give the stroke you design; nay, they shall recoil into your own faces, and be turned upon yourselves." Nothing can make for those who have God against them.

2. That the besiegers shall in a little time make themselves masters of Jerusalem, and of all its wealth and strength: *I will assemble* those *in the midst of this city* who are now surrounding it. Note, If that place which should have been a centre of devotion be made a centre of wick-

edness, it is not strange if God make it a rendezvous of destroyers.

3. That God himself will be their enemy; and then I know not who can befriend them, no, not Jeremiah himself (*v.* 5): "I will be so far from protecting you, as I have done formerly in a like case, that *I myself will fight against you.*" Note, Those who rebel against God may justly expect that he will make war upon them, and that, (1.) With the power of a God who is irresistibly victorious: *I will fight against you with an outstretched hand,* which will reach far, and *with a strong arm,* which will strike home and wound deeply. (2.) With the displeasure of a God who is indisputably righteous. It is not a correction in love, but an execution *in anger, in fury, and in great wrath;* it is upon a sentence sworn in wrath, against which there will lie no exception, and it will soon be found what a fearful thing it is to fall into the hands of the living God.

4. That those who, for their own safety, decline sallying out upon the besiegers, and so avoid their sword, shall yet not escape the sword of God's justice (*v.* 6): *I will smite those that abide in the city* (so it may be read), *both man and beast,* both the beasts that are for food and those that are for service in war, foot and horse; *they shall, die of a great pestilence,* which shall rage within the walls, while the enemies are encamped about them. Though Jerusalem's gates and walls may for a time keep out the Chaldeans, they cannot keep out God's judgments. His arrows of pestilence can reach those that think themselves safe from other arrows.

5. That the king himself, and people that escape the *sword, famine,* and *pestilence,* shall fall *into the hands* of the Chaldeans, who shall cut them off in cold blood (*v.* 7): They *shall not spare them,* nor *have pity* on them. Let not those expect to find mercy with men who have forfeited God's compassions, and shut themselves out from his mercy. Thus had the decree gone forth; and then to what purpose was it for Jeremiah to *enquire of the Lord for them?*

Verses 8–14

By the civil message which the king sent to Jeremiah it appeared that both he and the people began to have a respect for him, which it would have been Jeremiah's policy to make some advantage of for himself; but the reply which God obliges him to make is enough to crush the little respect they begin to have for him, and to exasperate them against him more than ever. Not only the predictions in the foregoing verses, but the prescriptions in these, were provoking; for here,

I. He advises the people to surrender and ??desert to the Chaldeans, as the only means left them to save their lives, *v.* 8–10. This counsel was very displeasing to those who were flattered by their false prophets into a desperate resolution to hold out to the last extremity, trusting to the strength of their walls and the courage of their soldiery to keep out the enemy, or to their foreign aids to raise the siege. The prophet assures them, *"The city shall be given into the hand of the king of Babylon,* and he shall not only plunder it, but *burn it with fire,* for God himself hath *set his face against this city for evil and not for good,* to lay it waste and not to protect it, *for evil* which shall have no good mixed with it, no mitigation or merciful allay; and therefore, if you would make the best of bad, you must beg quarter of the Chaldeans, and surrender prisoners of war." In vain did Rabshakeh persuade the Jews to do this while they had God for them (Isa. 36:16), but it was the best course they could take now that God was against them. Both the law and the prophets had often set before them life and death in another sense — life if they obey the voice of God, death if they persist in disobedience, Deu. 30:19. But they had slighted that life which would have made them truly happy, to upbraid them with which the prophet here uses the same expression (*v.* 8): *Behold, I set before you the way of life and the way of death,* which denotes not, as that, a fair proposal, but a melancholy dilemma, advising them of two evils to choose the less; and that less evil, a shameful and wretched captivity, is all the life now left for them to propose to themselves. *He that abides in the city,* and trusts to that to secure him, shall certainly die either by *the sword* without the walls or *famine* or *pestilence* within. But he that can so far bring down his spirit, and quit his vain hopes, as to go out, and

fall *to the Chaldeans, his life shall be given him for a prey;* he shall save his life, but with much difficulty and hazard, as a prey is taken from the mighty. It is an expression like that, *He shall be saved, yet so as by fire.* He shall escape but very narrowly, or he shall have such surprising joy and satisfaction in escaping with his life from such a universal destruction as shall equal theirs that divide the spoil. They thought to make a prey of the camp of the Chaldeans, as their ancestors did that of the Assyrians (Isa. 33:23), but they will be sadly disappointed; if by yielding at discretion they can but save their lives, that is all the prey they must promise themselves. Now one would think this advice from a prophet, in God's name, should have gained some credit with them and been universally followed; but, for aught that appears, there were few or none that took it; so wretchedly were their hearts hardened, to their destruction.

II. He advises the king and princes to reform, and make conscience of the duty of their place. Because it was the king that sent the message to him, in the reply there shall be a particular word for *the house of the king,* not to compliment or court them (that was no part of the prophet's business, no, not when they did him the honour to send to him), but to give them wholesome counsel (*v.* 11, 12): *"Execute judgment in the morning;* do it carefully and diligently. Those magistrates that would fill up their place with duty had need rise betimes. Do it quickly, and do not delay to do justice upon appeals made to you, and tire out poor petitioners as you have done. Do not lie in your beds in a morning to sleep away the debauch of the night before, nor spend the morning in pampering the body (as those princes, Eccl. 10:16), but spend it in the despatch of business. You would be delivered out of the hand of those that distress you, and expect that therein God should do you justice; see then that you do justice to those that apply to you, and *deliver them out of the hand of their oppressors, lest my fury go out like fire* against you in a particular manner, and you fare worst who think to escape best, *because of the evil of your doings."* Now, 1. This intimates that it was their neglect to do their duty that brought all this desolation upon the people. It was the *evil of their doings* that kindled the fire of God's wrath. Thus plainly does he deal even with the *house of the king;* for those that would have the benefit of a prophet's prayers must thankfully take a prophet's reproofs. 2. This directs them to take the right method for a national reformation. The princes must begin, and set a good example, and then the people will be invited to reform. They must use their power for the punishment of wrong, and then the people will be obliged to reform. He reminds them that they are *the house of David,* and therefore should tread in his steps, who executed judgment and justice to his people. 3. This gives them some encouragement to hope that there may yet be a lengthening of their tranquillity, Dan. 4:27. If any thing will recover their state from the brink of ruin, this will.

III. He shows them the vanity of all their hopes so long as they continued unreformed, *v.* 13, 14. Jerusalem is an *inhabitant of the valley,* guarded with mountains on all sides, which were their natural fortifications, making it difficult for an army to approach them. It is a *rock of the plain,* which made it difficult for an enemy to undermine them. These advantages of their situation they trusted to more than to the power and promise of God; and, thinking their city by these means to be impregnable, they set the judgments of God at defiance, saying, *"Who shall come down against us?"* None of our neighbours dare make a descent upon us, or, if they do, *who shall enter into our habitations?"* They had some colour for this confidence; for it appears to have been the sense of all their neighbours that no enemy could force his way into Jerusalem, Lam. 4:12. But those are least safe that are most secure. God soon shows the vanity of that challenge, *Who shall come down against us?* when he says (*v.* 13), *Behold, I am against thee.* They had indeed by the wickedness driven God out of their city when he would have tarried with them as a friend; but they could not by their bulwarks keep them out of their city when he came against them as an enemy. If God be for us, who can be against us? But, if he be against us, who can be for us, to stand us in any stead? Nay, he comes against them not as an enemy that may lawfully and with some hope of success be resisted, but as a judge that cannot be resisted; for he says (*v.* 14), *I will punish you,* by due

course of law, *according to the fruit of your doings,* that is, according to the merit of them and the direct tendency of them. That shall be brought upon you which is the natural product of sin. Nay, he will not only come with the anger of an enemy and the justice of a judge, but with the force of a consuming fire, which has no compassion, as a judge sometimes has, nor spares any thing combustible that comes in its way. Jerusalem has become a forest, in which God will *kindle a fire* that shall consume all before it; for our God is himself *a consuming fire;* and *who is able to stand in his sight* when once he is angry?

CHAPTER 22

Upon occasion of the message sent in the foregoing chapter to the house of the king, we have here recorded some sermons which Jeremiah preached at court, in some preceding reigns, that it might appear they had had fair warning long before that fatal sentence was pronounced upon them, and were put in a way to prevent it. Here is, I. A message sent to the royal family, as it should seem in the reign of Jehoiakim, relating partly to Jehoahaz, who was carried away captive into Egypt, and partly to Jehoiakim, who succeeded him and was now upon the throne. The king and princes are exhorted to execute judgment, and are assured that, if they did so, the royal family should flourish, but otherwise it should be ruined (*v.* 1–9). Jehoahaz, called here Shallum, is lamented (*v.* 10–12). Jehoiakim is reproved and threatened (*v.* 13–19). II. Another message sent them in the reign of Jehoiachin (alias, Jeconiah) the son of Jehoiakim. He is charged with an obstinate refusal to hear, and is threatened with destruction, and it is foretold that in him Solomon's house should fail (*v.* 20–30).

Verses 1–9

Here we have,

I. Orders given to Jeremiah to go and preach before the king. In the foregoing chapter we are told that Zedekiah sent messengers to the prophet, but here the prophet is bidden to go, in his own proper person, *to the house of the king,* and demand his attention to the word of the King of kings (*v.* 2): *Hear the word of the Lord, O king of Judah!* Subjects must own that where the word of the king is there is power over them, but kings must own that where the word of the Lord is there is power over them. The *king of Judah* is here spoken to as *sitting upon the throne of David,* who was a man after God's own heart, as holding his dignity and power by the covenant made with David; let him therefore conform to his example, that he may have the benefit of the promises made to him. With the king his *servants* are spoken to, because a good government depends upon a good ministry as well as a good king.

II. Instructions given him what to preach.

1. He must tell them what was their duty, what was the good which the Lord their God required of them, *v.* 3. They must take care, (1.) That they do all the good they can with the power they have. They must do justice in defence of those that were injured, and must *deliver the spoiled out of the hand of their oppressors.* This was the duty of their place, Ps. 82:3. Herein they must be ministers of God for good. (2.) That they do no hurt with it, *no wrong, no violence.* That is the greatest wrong and violence which is done under colour of law and justice, and by those whose business it is to punish and protect from wrong and violence. They must *do no wrong to the stranger, fatherless, and widow;* for these God does in a particular matter patronise and take under his tuition, Ex. 22:21, 22.

2. He must assure them that the faithful discharge of their duty would advance and secure their prosperity, *v.* 4. There shall then be a succession of kings, an uninterrupted succession, *upon the throne of David* and of his line, these enjoying a perfect tranquillity, and living in great state and dignity, *riding in chariots and on horses,* as before, *ch.* 17:25. Note, the most effectual way to preserve the dignity of the government is to do the duty of it.

3. He must likewise assure them that the iniquity of their family, if they persisted in it, would be the ruin of their family, though it was a royal family (*v.* 5): *If you will not hear,* will not obey, *this house shall become a desolation,* the palace of the kings of Judah shall fare no better than other habitations in Jerusalem. Sin has often been the ruin of royal palaces, though ever so stately, ever so strong. This sentence is ratified by an oath: *I swear by myself* (and God can swear by no greater, Heb. 6:13) that this house shall be laid in ruins. Note, Sin will be the ruin of the houses of princes as well as of mean men.

4. He must show how fatal their wickedness would be to their kingdom as well as to themselves, to Jerusalem especially, the royal city, *v.* 6–9. (1.) It is confessed that

Judah and Jerusalem had been valuable in God's eyes and considerable in their own: *thou art Gilead unto me and the head of Lebanon.* Their lot was cast in a place that was rich and pleasant as Gilead; Zion was a stronghold, as stately as Lebanon: this they trusted to as their security. But, (2.) This shall not protect them; the country that is now fruitful as Gilead shall be made *a wilderness.* The cities that are now strong as Lebanon shall be cities *not inhabited;* and, when the country is laid waste, the cities must be dispeopled. See how easily God's judgments can ruin a nation, and how certainly sin will do it. When this desolating work is to be done, [1.] There shall be those that shall do it effectually (*v.* 7): *"I will prepare destroyers against thee;* I will *sanctify* them" (so the word is); "I will appoint them to this service and use them in it." Note, When destruction is designed destroyers are prepared, and perhaps are in the preparing, and things are working towards the designed destruction, and are getting ready for it, long before. And who can contend with destroyers of God's preparing? They shall destroy cities as easily as men fell trees in a forest: *They shall cut down thy choice cedars;* and yet, when they are down, shall value them no more than thorns and briers; they shall *cast them into the fire,* for their choicest cedars have become rotten ones and good for nothing else. [2.] There shall be those who shall be ready to justify God in the doing of it (*v.* 8, 9); persons of *many nations,* when they *pass by* the ruins of *this city* in their travels, will ask, *"Wherefore hath the Lord done thus unto this city?* How came so strong a city to be overpowered? so rich a city to be impoverished? so populous a city to be depopulated? so holy a city to be profaned? and a city that had been so dear to God to be abandoned by him?" The reason is so obvious that it shall be ready in every man's mouth. Ask those *that go by the way,* Job 21:29. Ask the next man you meet, and he will tell you it was because they changed their gods, which other nations never used to do. They forsook *the covenant* of Jehovah their own God, revolted from their allegiance to him and from the duty which their covenant with him bound them to, and they *worshipped other gods and served them,* in contempt of him; and therefore he gave them up to this destruction. Note, God never casts any off until they first cast him off. "Go," says God to the prophet, "and preach this to the royal family."

Verses 10–19

Kings, though they are gods to us, are men to God, and shall *die like men;* so it appears in these verses, where we have a sentence of death passed upon two kings who reigned successively in Jerusalem, two brothers, and both the ungracious sons of a very pious father.

I. Here is the doom of Shallum, who doubtless is the same with Jehoahaz, for he is that son of Josiah king of Judah who reigned *in the stead of Josiah his father* (*v.* 11), which Jehoahaz did by the act of the people, who made him king though he was not the eldest son, 2 Ki. 23:30; 2 Chr. 36:1. Among the sons of Josiah (1 Chr. 3:15) there is one Shallum mentioned, and not Jehoahaz. Perhaps the people preferred him before his elder brother because they thought him a more active daring young man, and fitter to rule; but God soon showed them the folly of their injustice, and that it could not prosper, for within three months the king of Egypt came upon him, deposed him, and carried him away prisoner into Egypt, as God had threatened, Deu. 28:68. It does not appear that any of the people were taken into captivity with him. We have the story 2 Ki. 23:34; 2 Chr. 36:4. Now here, 1. The people are directed to lament him rather than his father Josiah: *"Weep not for the dead,* weep not any more for Josiah." Jeremiah had been himself a true mourner for hm, and had stirred up the people to mourn for him (2 Chr. 35:25): yet now he will have them go out of mourning for him, though it was but three months after his death, and to turn their tears into another channel. They must weep sorely for Jehoahaz, who had gone into Egypt; not that there was any great loss of him to the public, as there was of his father, but that his case was much more deplorable. Josiah went to the grave in peace and honour, was prevented from seeing the evil to come in this world and removed to see the good to come in the other world; and therefore, *Weep not for him,* but for his unhappy son, who is likely to live and die in disgrace and misery, a wretched captive. Note, Dying saints may be justly envied, while living sinners are justly pitied. And so dismal perhaps the prospect of the times may be that tears even for a Josiah, even for a Jesus, must be restrained, that they may be reserved for *ourselves and for our children,* Lu. 23:28. 2. The reason given is because he shall never return out of captivity, as he and his people expected, but shall die there. They were loth to believe this, therefore it is repeated here again and again, He shall *return no more, v.* 10. He shall never have the pleasure of seeing *his native country,* but shall have the continual grief of hearing of the desolations of it. He has gone *forth out of this place,* and shall *never return, v.* 11. *He shall die in the place whither they have led him captive, v.* 12. This came of his forsaking the good example of his father, and usurping the right of his elder brother. In Ezekiel's lamentation for the princes of Israel this Jehoahaz is represented as a young lion, that soon learned to *catch the prey,* but was taken, and brought in chains to Egypt, and was long expected to return, but in vain. See Eze. 19:3–5.

II. Here is the doom of Jehoiakim, who succeeded him. Whether he had any better right to the crown than Shallum we know not; for, though he was older than his predecessor, there seems to be another son of Josiah, older than he, called *Johanan,* 1 Chr. 3:15. But this we know he ruled no better, and fared no better at last. Here we have,

1. His sins faithfully reproved. It is not fit for a private person to say to a king, *Thou art wicked;* but a prophet, who has a message from God, betrays his trust if he does not deliver it, be it ever so unpleasing, even to kings themselves. Jehoiakim is not here charged with idolatry, and probably he had not yet put Urijah the prophet to death (as we find afterwards he did, *ch.* 26:22, 23), for then he would have been told of it here; but the crimes for which he is here reproved are, (1.) Pride and affection of pomp and splendour; as if all the business of a king were to look great, and to do good were to be the least of his care. He must build himself a stately palace, a *wide house,* and *large chambers, v.* 14. He must have *windows cut out* after the newest fashion, perhaps like sash-windows with us. The rooms must be *ceiled with cedar,* the richest sort of wood. His house must be as well-roofed and wainscoted as the temple itself, or else it will not please him, 1 Ki. 6:15, 16. Nay, it must exceed that, for it must be painted with *minium,* or *vermilion,* which dyes red, or, as some read it, with *indigo,* which dyes blue. No doubt it is lawful for princes and great men to build, and beautify, and furnish their houses so as is agreeable to their dignity; but he that knows what is in man knew that Jehoiakim did this in the pride of his heart, which makes that to be sinful, exceedingly sinful, which is in itself lawful. Those therefore that are enlarging their houses, and making them more sumptuous, have need to look well to the frame of their own spirits in the doing of it, and carefully to watch against all the workings of vain-glory. But that which was particularly amiss in Jehoiakim's case was that he did this when he could not but perceive, both by the word of God and by his providence, that divine judgments were breaking in upon him. He reigned his first three years by the permission and allowance of the king of Egypt, and all the rest by the permission and allowance of the king of Babylon; and yet he that was no better than a viceroy will covet to vie with the greatest monarchs in building and furniture. Observe how peremptory he is in this resolution: *"I will build myself a wide house;* I am resolved *I will,* whoever advises me to the contrary." Note, It is the common folly of those that are sinking in their estates to covet to make a fair show. Many have unhumbled hearts under humbling providences, and look most haughty when God is bringing them down. This is striving with our Maker. (2.) Carnal security and confidence in his wealth, depending upon the continuance of his prosperity, as if his mountain now stood so strong that it could never be moved. He thought he must reign without any disturbance or interruption because he had *enclosed himself in cedar* (*v.* 15), as if that were too fine to be assaulted and too strong to be broken through, and as if God himself could not, for pity, give up such a stately house as that to be burned. Thus when Christ spoke of the destruction of the temple his disciples came to him, to show him what a magnificent structure it was, Mt. 23:38; 24:1. Note, Those wretchedly deceive themselves who think their present prosperity is a lasting security, and dream of reigning because they are *enclosed in cedar.* It is but in his own conceit that *the rich man's wealth is his strong city.* (3.) Some think he is here charged with sacrilege, and robbing the house of God to beautify and adorn his own house. He *cuts him out* my *windows* (so it is in the margin), which some understand as if he had taken windows out of the temple to put into his own palace and then *painted them* (as it follows) *with vermilion,* that it might not be discovered, but might look of a piece with his own buildings. Note, Those cheat themselves, and ruin themselves at last, who think to enrich themselves by robbing God and his house; and, however they may disguise it, God discovers it. (4.) He is here charged with extortion and oppression, violence and injustice. He *built his house by unrighteousness,* with money unjustly got and materials which were not honestly come by, and perhaps upon ground obtained as Ahab obtained Naboth's vineyard. And, because he went beyond what he could afford, he defrauded his workmen of their wages, which is one of the sins that *cries in the ears of the Lord of hosts,* Jam. 5:4. God takes notice of the wrong done by the greatest of men to their poor servants and labourers, and will repay those, in justice, that will not in justice pay those whom they employ, but *use their neighbour's service without wages.* Observe, The greatest of men must look upon the meanest as their neighbours, and be just to them accordingly, and love them as themselves. Jehoiakim was oppressive, not only in his buildings, but in the administration of his government. He did not do justice, made no conscience of shedding innocent blood, when it was to serve the purposes of his ambition, avarice, and revenge. He was all for *oppression* and *violence,* not to threaten it only, but to do it; and, when he was set upon any act of injustice, nothing should stop him, but he would go through with it. And that which was at the bottom of all was covetousness, that love of *money which is the root of all evil. Thy eyes and thy heart are not but for covetousness;* they were for that, and nothing else. Observe, In covetousness the heart walks after the eyes: it is therefore called *the lust of the eye,* 1 Jn. 2:16; Job 31:7. It is *setting the eyes upon that which is not,* Prov. 23:5. The eyes and the heart are then for covetousness when the aims and affections are wholly set upon the wealth of this world; and, where they are so, the temptation is strong to murder, oppression, and all manner of violence and villany. (5.) That which aggravated all his sins was that he was the son of a good father, who had left him a good example, if he would but have followed it (*v.* 15, 16): *Did not thy father eat and drink?* When Jehoiakim enlarged and enlightened his house it is probable that he spoke scornfully of his father for contenting himself with such a mean and inconvenient dwelling, below the grandeur of a sovereign prince, and ridiculed him as one that had a dull fancy, a low spirit, and could not find in his heart to lay out his money, nor cared for what was fashionable; that should not serve him which served his father: but God, by the prophet, tells him that his father, though he had not the spirit of building, was a man of an excellent spirit, a better man than he, and did better for himself and his family. Those children that despise their parents' old fashions commonly come short of their real excellences. Jeremiah tells him, [1.] That he was directed to do his duty by his father's practice: He *did judgment and justice;* he never did wrong to any of his subjects, never oppressed them, nor put any hardship upon them, but was careful to preserve all their just rights and properties. Nay, he not only did not abuse his power for the support of wrong, but he used it for the maintaining of right. He *judged the cause of the poor and needy,* was ready to hear the cause of the meanest of his subjects and do them justice. Note, The care of magistrates must be, not to support their grandeur and take their ease, but to do good, not only not to oppress the poor themselves, but to defend those that are oppressed. [2.] That he was encouraged to do his duty by his father's prosperity. *First,* God accepted him: *"Was not this to know me, saith the Lord?* Did he not hereby make it to appear that he rightly knew his God, and worshipped him, and consequently was known and owned of him?" Note, The right knowledge of God consists in doing our duty, particularly that which is the duty of our place and station in the world. *Secondly,* He himself had the comfort of it: *Did he not eat and drink* soberly and cheerfully, so as to fit himself for his business, *for strength and not for drunkenness?* Eccl. 10:17.

He did *eat, and drink, and do judgment;* he did not (as perhaps Jehoiakim and his princes did) *drink, and forget the law, and pervert the judgment of the afflicted,* Prov. 31:5. He did *eat and drink;* that is, God blessed him with great plenty, and he had the comfortable enjoyment of it himself and gave handsome entertainments to his friends, was very hospitable and very charitable. It was Jehoiakim's pride that he had built a fine house, but Josiah's true praise that he kept a good house. Many times those have least in them of true generosity that have the greatest affection for pomp and grandeur; for, to support the extravagant expense of that, hospitality, bounty to the poor, yea, and justice itself, will be pinched. It is better to live with Josiah in an old-fashioned house, and do good, than live with Jehoiakim in a stately house, and leave debts unpaid. Josiah did *justice and judgment,* and then *it was well with him, v.* 15, and it is repeated again, *v.* 16. He lived very comfortably; his own subjects, and all his neighbours, respected him; and whatever he put his hand to prospered. Note, While we do well we may expect it will be well with us. This Jehoiakim knew, that his father found the way of duty to be the way of comfort, and yet he would not tread in his steps. Note, It should engage us to keep up religion in our day that our godly parents kept it up in theirs and recommended it to us from their own experience of the benefit of it. They told us that they had found the promises which godliness has of the *life that now* is made good to them, and that religion and piety are friendly to outward prosperity. So that we are inexcusable if we turn aside from that good way.

2. Here we have Jehoiakim's doom faithfully read, *v.* 18, 19. We may suppose that it was in the utmost peril of his own life that Jeremiah here foretold the shameful death of Jehoiakim; but *thus saith the Lord concerning* him, and therefore thus saith he. (1.) He shall die unlamented; he shall make himself so odious by his oppression and cruelty that all about him shall be glad to part with him, and none shall do him the honour of dropping one tear for him, whereas his father, who *did judgment and justice,* was universally lamented; and it is promised to Zedekiah that he should be lamented at his death, for he conducted himself better than Jehoiakim had done, *ch.* 34:5. His relations shall not *lament him,* no, not with the common expressions of grief used at the funeral of the meanest, where they cried, *Ah, my brother!* or, *Ah, sister!* His subjects shall not lament him, nor cry out, as they used to do at the graves of their princes, *Ah, lord!* or *Ah his glory!* It is sad for any to live so that, when they die, none will be sorry to part with them. Nay, (2.) He shall lie unburied. This is worse than the former. Even those that have no tears to grace the funerals of the dead with would willingly have them buried out of their sight; but Jehoiakim shall be *buried with the burial of an ass,* that is, he shall have no burial at all, but his dead body shall be cast into a ditch or upon a dunghill; it shall be *drawn,* or dragged, ignominiously, and *cast forth beyond the gates of Jerusalem.* It is said, in the story of Jehoiakim (2 Chr. 36:6), that Nebuchadnezzar *bound him in fetters, to carry him to Babylon,* and (Eze. 19:9) that he was *brought in chains to the king of Babylon.* But it is probable that he died a prisoner, before he was carried away to Babylon as was intended; perhaps he died for grief, or, in the pride of his heart, hastened his own end, and, for that reason, was denied a decent burial, as self-murderers usually are with us. Josephus says that Nebuchadnezzar slew him at Jerusalem, and left his body thus exposed, somewhere at a grat distance from the *gates of Jerusalem.* And it is said (2 Ki. 24:6) *he slept with his fathers.* When he built himself a stately house, no doubt he designed himself a stately sepulchre; but see how he was disappointed. Note, Those that are lifted up with great pride are commonly reserved for some great disgrace in life or death.

Verses 20–30

This prophecy seems to have been calculated for the ungracious inglorious reign of Jeconiah, or Jehoiachin, the son of Jehoiakim, who succeeded him in the government, reigned but three months, and was then carried captive to Babylon, where he lived many years, *ch.* 52:31. We have, in these verses, a prophecy,

I. Of the desolations of the kingdom, which were now hastening on apace, *v.* 20–23. Jerusalem and Judah are here spoken to, or the Jewish state as a single person, and we have it here under a threefold character: — 1. Very haughty in a day of peace and safety (*v.* 21): *"I spoke unto thee in thy prosperity,* spoke by my servants the prophets, reproofs, admonitions, counsels, *but thou saidst, I will not hear,* I will not heed, *thou obeyedst not my voice,* and wast resolved that thou wouldst not, and hadst the front to tell me so." It is common for those that live at ease to live in contempt of the word of God. *Jeshurun waxed fat, and kicked.* This is so much the worse that they had it by kind: *This has been thy manner from thy youth.* They were called *transgressors from the womb,* Isa. 48:8. 2. Very timorous upon the alarms of trouble (*v.* 20): "When thou seest *all thy lovers destroyed,* when thou findest thy idols unable to help thee and thy foreign alliances failing thee, thou wilt then go up to Lebanon, and cry, as one undone and giving up all for lost, cry with a bitter cry; thou wilt cry, *Help, help, or we are lost;* thou wilt *lift up thy voice* in fearful shrieks upon *Lebanon and Bashan,* two high hills, in hope to be heard thence by the advantage of the rising ground. Thou wilt *cry from the passages,* from the roads, where thou wilt ever and anon be in distress." Thou wilt cry from *Abarim* (so some read it, as a proper name), a famous mountain in the border of Moab. "Thou wilt cry, as those that are in great consternation use to do, to all about thee; but in vain, for (*v.* 22) *the wind shall eat up all thy pastors,* or *rulers,* that should protect and lead thee, and provide for thy safety; they shall be blasted, and withered, and brought to nothing, as buds and blossoms are by a bleak or freezing wind; they shall be devoured suddenly, insensibly, and irresistibly, as fruits by the wind. *Thy lovers,* that thou dependest upon and hast an affection for, shall *go into captivity,* and shall be so far from saving thee that they shall not be able to save themselves." 3. Very tame under the heavy and lasting pressures of trouble: "When there appears no relief from any of thy confederates, and thy own priests are at a loss, *then shalt thou be ashamed and confounded for all thy wickedness," v.* 22. Note, Many will never be ashamed of their sins till they are brought by them to the last extremity; and it is well if we get this good by our straits to be brought by them to confusion for our sins. The Jewish state is here called *an inhabitant of Lebanon,* because that famous forest was within their border (*v.* 23), and all their country was wealthy, and well-guarded as with Lebanon's natural fastnesses; but so proud and haughty were they that they are said to *make their nest in the cedars,* where they thought themselves out of the reach of all danger, and whence they looked with contempt upon all about them. "But, *how gracious wilt thou be when pangs come upon thee!* Then thou wilt humble thyself before God and promise amendment. When thou art overthrown in stony places thou wilt be glad to *hear those words* which in thy prosperity *thou wouldst not hear,* Ps. 141:6. Then thou wilt endeavour to make thyself acceptable with that God whom, before, thou madest light of." Note, Many have their pangs of piety who, when the pangs are over, show that they have no true piety. Some give another sense of it: "What will all thy pomp, and state, and wealth avail thee? What will become of it all, or what comfort shalt thou have of it, when thou shalt be in these distresses? No more than *a woman in travail,* full of pains and fears, can take comfort in her ornaments while she is in that condition." So Mr. Gataker. Note, Those that are proud of their worldly advantages would do well to consider how they will look when pangs come upon them, and how they will then have lost all their beauty.

II. Here is a prophecy of the disgrace of the king; his name was *Jeconiah,* but he is here once and again called *Coniah,* in contempt. The prophet shortens or nicks his name, and gives him, as we say, a nickname, perhaps to denote that he should be despoiled of his dignity, that his reign should be shortened, and the number of his months cut off in the midst. Two instances of dishonour are here put upon him: —

1. He shall be carried away *into captivity* and shall spend and end his days in bondage. He was born to a crown, but it should quickly fall from his head, and he should exchange it for fetters. Observe the steps of this judgment. (1.) God will abandon him, *v.* 24. The God of truth says it, and confirms it with an oath: *"Though he were the signet upon my right hand* (his predecessors have been so, and he might have been so if he had conducted himself well, but he being degenerated) *I will pluck him thence."* The godly kings of Judah had been as signets on God's right hand, near and dear to him; he had gloried in them, and made use of them as instruments of his government, as the prince does of his signet-ring, or sign manual; but Coniah has made himself utterly unworthy of the honour, and therefore the privilege of his birth shall be no security to him; notwithstanding that, he shall be thrown off. Answerable to this threatening against Jeconiah is God's promise to Zerubbabel, when he made him his people's guide in their return out of captivity (Hag. 2:23): *I will take thee, O Zerubbabel! my servant, and make thee as a signet.* Those that think themselves as signets on God's right hand must not be secure, but fear lest they be plucked thence. (2.) The king of Babylon shall seize him. *Those* know not what enemies and mischiefs they lie exposed to who have thrown themselves out of God's protection, *v.* 25. The Chaldeans are here said to be such as had a spite to *Coniah;* they *sought his life;* no less than that, they thought, would satisfy their rage; they were such as he had a dread of (they are those *whose face thou fearest*) which would make it the more terrible to him to fall into their hands, especially when it was God himself that gave *him into their hands.* And, if God deliver him to them, who can deliver him from them? (3.) He and his family shall be carried to Babylon, where they shall wear out many tedious years of their lives in a miserable captivity — *he and his mother* (*v.* 26), *he and his seed* (*v.* 28), that is, he and all the royal family (for he had no children of his own when he went into captivity), or he and the children in his loins; they shall all be cast out to another country, to a strange country, *a country where they were not born,* nor such a country as that where they were born, *a land which they know not,* in which they have no acquaintance with whom to converse or from whom to expect any kindness. Thither they shall be carried, from a land where they were entitled to dominion, into a land where they shall be compelled to servitude. But have they no hopes of seeing their own country again? No: *To the land whereunto they desire to return, thither shall they not return, v.* 27. They conducted themselves ill in it when they were in it, and therefore they shall never see it more. Jehoahaz was carried to Egypt, the land of the south, Jeconiah to Babylon, the land of the north, both far remote, the quite contrary way, and must never expect to meet again, nor either of them to breathe their native air again. Those that had abused the dominion they had over others were justly brought thus under the dominion of others. Those that had indulged and gratified their sinful desires, by their oppression, luxury, and cruelty, were justly denied the gratification of their innocent desire to see their own native country again. We may observe something very emphatic in that part of this threatening (*v.* 26), *In the country where you were not born, there shall you die.* As there is a *time to be born* and a *time to die,* so there is a place to be born in and a place to die in. We know where we were born, but where we shall die we know not; it is enough that our God knows. Let it be our care that we die in Christ, and then it will be well with us, wherever we die, though it should be in a far country. (4.) This shall render him very mean and despicable in the eyes of all his neighbours. They shall be ready to say (*v.* 28), *"This is Coniah a despised broken idol?* Yes, certainly he is, and much debased from what he was." [1.] Time was when he was dignified, nay, when he was almost deified. The people who had seen his father lately deposed were ready to adore him when they saw him upon the throne, but now *he is a despised broken idol,* which, when it was whole, was worshipped, but, when it is rotten and broken, is thrown by and despised, and nobody regards it, or remembers what it has been. Note, What is idolized will, first or last, be despised and broken; what is unjustly honoured will be justly contemned, and rivals with God will be the scorn of man. Whatever we idolize we shall be disappointed in and then shall despise. [2.] Time was when he was delighted in; but now he is *a vessel in which is not pleasure,* or to which there is no desire, either because grown out of fashion or because cracked or dirtied, and so rendered unserviceable. Those whom God has no pleasure in will, some time or other, be so mortified that men will have no pleasure in them.

2. He shall leave no posterity to inherit his honour. The prediction of this is ushered in with a solemn preface (*v.* 29):

O earth, earth, earth! hear the word of the Lord. Let all the inhabitants of the world take notice of these judgments of God upon a nation and a family that had been near and dear to him, and thence infer that God is impartial in the administration of justice. Or it is an appeal to the earth itself on which we tread, since those that dwell on earth are so deaf and careless, like that (Isa. 1:2), *Hear, O heavens! and give ear, O earth!* God's word, however slighted, will be heard; the earth itself will be made to hear it, and yield to it, when it, and all the works that are therein, shall be burnt up. Or it is a call to men that *mind earthly things,* that are swallowed up in those things and are inordinate in the pursuit of them; such have need to be called upon again and again, and a third time, to *hear the word of the Lord.* Or it is a call to men considered as mortal, of the earth, and hastening to the earth again. We all are so; earth we are, *dust we are,* and, in consideration of that, are concerned to hear and regard *the word of the Lord,* that, though we are earth, we may be found among those whose names are written in heaven. Now that which is here to be taken notice of is that Jeconiah is *written childless* (*v.* 30), that is, as it follows, *No man of his seed shall prosper, sitting upon the throne of David.* In him the line of David was extinct as a royal line. Some think that he had children born in Babylon because mention is made of his seed being cast out there (*v.* 28) and that they died before him. We read in the genealogy (1 Chr. 3:17) of seven sons of Jeconiah Assir (that is, Jeconiah the captive) of whom Salathiel is the first. Some think that they were only his adopted sons, and that when it is said (Mt. 1:12), *Jeconiah begat Salathiel,* no more is meant than that he bequeathed to him what claims and pretensions he had to the government, the rather because Salathiel is called the *son of Neri* of *the house of Nathan,* Lu. 3:27, 31. Whether he had children begotten, or only adopted, thus far he was childless that none of his seed ruled as kings in Judah. He was the *Augustulus* of that empire, in whom it determined. Whoever are childless, it is God that writes them so; and those who take no care to do good in their days cannot expect to prosper in their days.

CHAPTER 23

In this chapter the prophet, in God's name, is dealing his reproofs and threatenings, I. Among the careless princes, or pastors of the people (*v.* 1, 2), yet promising to take care of the flock, which they had been wanting in their duty to (*v.* 3–8). II. Among the wicked prophets and priests, whose bad character is here given at large in divers instances, especially their imposing upon the people with their pretended inspirations, at which the prophet is astonished, and for which they must expect to be punished (*v.* 9–32). III. Among the profane people, who ridiculed God's prophets and bantered them (*v.* 33–40). When all have thus corrupted their way they must all expect to be told faithfully of it.

Verses 1–8

I. Here is a word of terror to the negligent shepherds. The day is at hand when God will reckon with them concerning the trust and charge committed to them: *Woe be to the pastors* (to the *rulers,* both in church and state) who should be to those they are set over as pastors to lead them, feed them, protect them, and take care of them. They are not owners of the sheep. God here calls them *the sheep of my pasture,* whom I am interested in, and have provided good pasture for. Woe be to those therefore who are commanded to feed God's people, and pretend to do it, but who, instead of that, *scatter the flock,* and *drive them away* by their violence and oppression, and *have not visited them,* nor taken any care for their welfare, nor concerned themselves at all to do them good. In not visiting them, and doing their duty to them, they did in effect scatter them and drive them away. The beasts of prey scattered them, and the shepherds are in the fault, who should have kept them together. *Woe be to them* when God will visit upon them the evil of their doings and deal with them as they deserve. They would not visit the flock in a way of duty, and therefore God will visit them in a way of vengeance.

II. Here is a word of comfort to the neglected sheep. Though the under-shepherds take no care of them, no pains with them, but betray them, the chief Shepherd will look after them. *When my father and my mother forsake me, then the Lord taketh me up.* Though the interests of God's church in the world are neglected by those who should take care of them, and postponed to their own private secular interests, yet they shall not therefore sink. God will perform his promise, though those he employs do not perform their duty.

1. The dispersed Jews shall at length return to their own land, and be happily settled there under a good government, *v.* 3, 4. Though there be but a remnant of God's flock left, a little remnant, that has narrowly escaped destruction, he will gather that remnant, will find them out wherever they are and find out ways and means to bring them back out of all countries *whither he had driven them.* It was the justice of God, for the sin of their shepherds, that dispersed them; but the mercy of God shall gather in the sheep, when the shepherds that betrayed them are cut off. *They shall be brought* to their former habitations, as sheep to their folds, and there *they shall be fruitful, and increase* in numbers. And, though their former shepherds took no care of them, it does not therefore follow that they shall have no more. If some have abused a sacred office, that is no good reason why it should be abolished. "They destroyed the sheep, but I will set shepherds over them who shall make it their business to feed them." Formerly they were continually exposed and disturbed with some alarm or other; but now *they shall fear no more, nor be dismayed;* they shall be in no danger from without, in no fright from within. Formerly some or other of them were ever and anon picked up by the beasts of prey; but now *none of them shall be lacking,* none of them missing. Though the times may have been long bad with the church, it does not follow that they will be ever so. Such pastors as Zerubbabel and Nehemiah, though they lived not in the pomp that Jehoiakim and Jeconiah did, nor made such a figure, were as great blessings to the people as the others were plagues to them. The church's peace is not bound up in the pomp of her rulers.

2. Messiah the Prince, that great and good Shepherd of the sheep, shall in the latter days be raised up to bless his church, and to be *the glory of his people Israel, v.* 5, 6. The house of David seemed to be quite sunk and ruined by that threatening against Jeconiah (*ch.* 22:30), that none of his seed should ever *sit upon the throne of David.* But here is a promise which effectually secures the honour of the covenant made with David notwithstanding; for by it the house will be raised out of its ruins to a greater lustre than ever, and shine brighter far than it did in Solomon himself. We have not so many prophecies of Christ in this book as we had in that of the prophet Isaiah; but here we have one, and a very illustrious one; of him doubtless the prophet here speaks, of him, and of no other man. The first words intimate that it would be long ere this promise should have its accomplishment: *The days come,* but they are not yet. *I shall see him, but not now.* But all the rest intimate that the accomplishment of it will be glorious. (1.) Christ is here spoken of as a *branch from David,* the *man the branch* (Zec. 3:8), his appearance mean, his beginnings small, like those of a bud or sprout, and his rise seemingly out of the earth, but growing to be green, to be great, to be loaded with fruits. A branch from David's family, when it seemed to be a *root in a dry ground,* buried, and not likely to revive. Christ is the *root and offspring of David,* Rev. 22:16. In him doth the *horn of David bud,* Ps. 132:17, 18. He is a branch of God's raising up; he sanctified him, and sent him into the world, gave him his commission and qualifications. He is *a righteous branch,* for he is righteous himself, and through him many, even all that are his, are made righteous. As an advocate, he is *Jesus Christ the righteous.* (2.) He is here spoken of as his church's King. This branch shall be raised as high as the throne of his father David, and there *he shall reign and prosper,* not as the kings that now were of the house of David, who went backward in all their affairs. No; he shall set up a kingdom in the world that shall be victorious over all opposition. In the chariot of the everlasting gospel he shall go forth, he shall go on *conquering and to conquer.* If God raise him up, he will prosper him, for he will own the work of his own hands; what is *the good pleasure of the Lord* shall *prosper in the hands* of those to whom it is committed. He shall prosper; for *he shall execute judgment and justice in the earth,* all the world over, Ps. 96:13. The present kings of the house of David were unjust and oppressive, and therefore it is no wonder that they did not prosper. But Christ shall, by his gospel, break the usurped power of Satan, institute a perfect rule of holy living, and, as far as it prevails, make all the world righteous. The effect of this shall be a holy security and serenity of mind in all his faithful loyal subjects. *In his days,* under his dominion, *Judah shall be saved and Israel shall dwell safely;* that is, all the spiritual seed of believing Abraham and praying Jacob shall be protected from the curse of heaven and the malice of hell, shall be privileged from the arrests of God's law and delivered from the attempts of Satan's power, shall be saved from sin, the guilt and dominion of it, and then shall *dwell safely,* and be quiet from the fear of all evil. See Lu. 1:74, 75. Those that shall be saved hereafter from the wrath to come may dwell safely now; for, *if God be for us, who can be against us?* In the days of Christ's government in the soul, when he is uppermost there, the soul *dwells at ease.* (3.) He is here spoken of as *The Lord our righteousness.* Observe, [1.] Who and what he is. As God, he is *Jehovah,* the incommunicable name of God, denoting his eternity and self-existence. As Mediator, he is *our righteousness.* By making satisfaction to the justice of God for the sin of man, he has brought in an everlasting righteousness, and so made it over to us in the covenant of grace that, upon our believing consent to that covenant, it becomes ours. His being *Jehovah our righteousness* implies that he is so our righteousness as no creature could be. He is a sovereign, all-sufficient, eternal righteousness. All our righteousness has its being from him, and by him it subsists, and we are made *the righteousness of God in him.* [2.] The profession and declaration of this: *This is the name whereby he shall be called,* not only he shall be so, but he shall be known to be so. God shall call him by this name, for he shall appoint him to be *our righteousness.* By this name Israel shall call him, every true believer shall call him, and call upon him. That is our righteousness by which, as an allowed plea, we are justified before God, acquitted from guilt, and accepted into favour; and nothing else have we to plead but this, "Christ has died, yea, rather has risen again;" and we have taken him for our Lord.

3. This great salvation, which will come to the Jews in the latter days of their state, after their return out of Babylon, shall be so illustrious as far to outshine the deliverance of Israel out of Egypt (*v.* 7, 8): *They shall no more say, The Lord liveth that brought up Israel out of Egypt; but, The Lord liveth that brought them up out of the north.* This we had before, *ch.* 16:14, 15. But here it seems to point more plainly than it did there to the days of the Messiah, and to compare not so much the two deliverances themselves (giving the preference to the latter) as the two states to which the church by degrees grew after those deliverances. Observe the proportion: Just 480 years after they had come out of Egypt Solomon's temple was built (1 Ki. 6:1); and at that time that nation, which was so wonderfully brought up out of Egypt, had gradually arrived to its height, to its zenith. Just 490 years (70 weeks) after they came out of Babylon Messiah the Prince set up the gospel temple, which was the greatest glory of that nation that was so wonderfully brought out of Babylon; see Dan. 9:24, 25. Now the spiritual glory of the second part of that nation, especially as transferred to the gospel church, is much more admirable and illustrious than all the temporal glory of the first part of it in the days of Solomon; for that was no glory compared with the glory which excelleth.

Verses 9–32

Here is a long lesson for the false prophets. As none were more bitter and spiteful against God's true prophets than they, so there were none on whom the true prophets were more severe, and justly. The prophet had complained to God of those false prophets (*ch.* 14:13), and had often foretold that they should be involved in the common ruin; but here they have woes of their own.

I. He expresses the deep concern that he was under upon this account, and what a trouble it was to him to see men who pretended to a divine commission and inspiration ruining themselves, and the people among whom they dwelt, by their falsehood and treachery (*v.* 9): *My heart within me is broken; I am like a drunken man.* His head was in confusion with wonder and astonishment; his heart was under oppression with grief and vexation. Jeremiah was a man that laid things much to heart, and what was any way threatening to his country made a deep impression upon his spirits. He is here in trouble, 1. *Because of the prophets* and their sin, the false doctrine they preached, the wicked lives they lived; especially it filled him with horror to hear them making use of God's name and pretending to have their instruction from him. Never was the Lord so abused, and *the words of his holiness,* as by these men. Note, The dishonour done to God's name, and the profanation of his holy word, are the greatest grief imaginable to a gracious soul. 2. *"Because of the Lord,* and his judgments, which by this means are brought in upon us like a deluge." He trembled to think of the ruin and desolation which were coming *from the face of the Lord* (so the word is) *and from the face of the word of his holiness,* which will be inflicted by the power of God's wrath, according to the threatenings of his word, confirmed by *his holiness.* Note, Even those that have God for them cannot but tremble to think of the misery of those that have God against them.

II. He laments the abounding abominable wickedness of the land and the present tokens of God's displeasure they were under for it (*v.* 10): *The land is full of adulterers;* it is full both of spiritual and corporal whoredom. They go a whoring from God, and, having cast off the fear of him, no marvel that they abandon themselves to all manner of lewdness; and, having dishonoured themselves and their own bodies, they dishonour God and his name by rash and false swearing, *because of which the land mourns.* Both perjury and common swearing are sins for which a land must mourn in true repentance or it will be made to mourn under the judgments of God. Their land mourned now under the judgment of famine; the *pleasant places,* or rather *the pastures,* or (as some read it) *the habitations of the wilderness,* are dried up for want of rain, and yet we see no signs of repentance. They answer not the end of the correction. The tenour and tendency of men's conversations are sinful, *their course continues evil,* as bad as ever, and they will not be diverted from it. They have a great deal of resolution, but it is turned the wrong way; they are *zealously affected,* but not *in a good thing: Their force is not right;* their *heart is fully set in them to do evil,* and they are not valiant for the truth, have not courage enough to break off their evil courses, though they see God thus contending with them.

III. He charges it all upon the prophets and priests, especially the prophets. They are *both profane* (*v.* 11); the priests profane the ordinances of God they pretend to administer; the prophets profane the word of God they pretend to deliver; their converse and all their conversation are profane, and then it is not strange that the people are so debauched. They both *play the hypocrite* (so some read it); under sacred pretensions they carry on the vilest designs; yea, not only in their own houses, and the bad houses they frequent, but *in my house have I found their wickedness;* in the temple, where the priests ministered, where the prophets prophesied, there were they guilty both of idolatry and immorality. See a woeful instance in Hophni and Phinehas, 1 Sa. 2:22. God searches his house, and what wickedness is there he will find it out; and the nearer it is to him the more offensive it is. Two things are charged upon them: — 1. That they taught people to sin by their examples. He compares them with the prophets of Samaria, the head city of the kingdom of the ten tribes, which had been long since laid waste. It was the folly of the prophets of Samaria that *they prophesied in Baal,* in Baal's name; so Ahab's prophets did, and so *they caused my people Israel to err,* to forsake the service of the true God and to worship Baal, *v.* 13. Now the prophets of Jerusalem did not do so; they prophesied in the name of the true God, and valued themselves upon that, that they were not like the prophets of Samaria, who prophesied in Baal; but what the better, when they debauched the nation as much by their immoralities as the other had done by their idolatries? It is a horrible thing in the prophets of Jerusalem that they make use of the name of the holy God, and yet wallow in all manner of impurity; they make nothing of committing adultery. They make use of the name of the God of truth, and yet *walk in lies;* they not only prophesy lies, but in their common conversation one cannot believe a word they say. It is all either jest and banter or fraud and design. Thus they encourage sinners to go on in their wicked ways; for every one will say, "Surely we may do as the prophets do; who can expect that we should be better than our teachers?" By this means it is that none returns from his wickedness; but they all say that they shall have *peace,* though they go on, for their prophets tell them so. By this means Judah and Jerusalem have become *as Sodom and Gomorrah,* that were wicked, *and sinners before the Lord exceedingly;* and God looked upon them accordingly as fit for nothing but to be destroyed, as they were, with fire and brimstone. 2. That they encouraged people in sin by their false prophecies. They made themselves believe that there was no harm, no danger in sin, and practiced accordingly; and then no marvel that they made others believe so too (*v.* 16): *They speak a vision of their own heart;* it is the product of their own invention, and agrees with their own inclination, but it is *not out of the mouth of the Lord;* he never dictated it to them, nor did it agree either with the law of Moses or with what God has spoken by other prophets. They tell sinners that it shall be well with them though they persist in their sins, *v.* 17. See here who those are that they encourage — those that *despise God,* that slight his authority, and have low and mean thoughts of his institutions, and those that *walk after the imagination of their own heart,* that are worshippers of idols and slaves to their own lusts; those that are devoted to their pleasures put contempt upon their God. Yet see how these prophets caressed and flattered them: they should have been still saying, There is no peace to those that go on in their evil ways — *Those that despise God shall be lightly esteemed* — Woe, and a thousand woes, to them; but they still said, *You shall have peace; no evil shall come upon you.* And, which was worst of all, they told them, *God has said so,* so making him to patronize sin, and to contradict himself. Note, Those that are resolved to go on in their evil ways will justly be given up to believe the strong delusions of those who tell them that they shall have peace though they go on.

IV. God disowns all that these false prophets said to sooth people up in their sins (*v.* 21): *I have not sent these prophets;* they never had any mission from God. They were not only not sent by him on this errand, but they were never sent by him on any errand; he never had employed them in any service or business for him; and, as to this matter, whereas they pretended to have instructions from him to assure this people of peace, he declares that he never gave them any such instructions. Yet they were very forward — *they ran;* they were very bold — *they prophesied* without any of that difficulty with which the true prophets sometimes struggled. They said to sinners, *You shall have peace.* But (*v.* 18): *"Who hath stood in the counsel of the Lord?* Who of you has, that are so confident of this? You deliver this message with a great deal of assurance; but have you consulted God about it? No; you never considered whether it be agreeable to the discoveries God has made of himself, whether it will consist with the honour of his holiness and justice, to let sinners go unpunished. You have not *perceived and heard his word,* nor *marked* that; you have not compared this with the scripture; if you had taken notice of that, and of the constant tenour of it, you would never have delivered such a message." The prophets themselves must try the spirits by the touchstone of the law and of the testimony, as well as those to whom they prophesy; but which of those did so that prophesied of peace? That they did not *stand in God's counsel* nor *hear his word* is proved afterwards, *v.* 22. *If they had stood in my counsel,* as they pretend, 1. They would have made the scriptures their standard: *They would have caused my people to hear my words,* and would have conscientiously kept closely to them. But, not speaking according to that rule, it is a plain evidence that there is no light in them. 2. They would have made the conversion of souls their business, and would have aimed at that in all their preaching. They would have done all they could to *turn* people *from their evil way* in general and from all the particular *evil of their doings.* They would have encouraged and assisted the reformation of manners, would have made this their scope in all their preaching, to part between men and their sins; but it appeared that this was a thing they never aimed at, but, on the contrary, to encourage sinners in their sins. 3. They would have had some seals of their ministry. This sense our translation gives it: *If they had stood in my counsel,* and the words they had preached had been *my words,* then they should *have turned them from their evil way;* a divine power should have gone along with the word for the conviction of sinners. God will bless his own institutions. Yet this is no certain rule; Jeremiah himself, though God sent him, prevailed with but few to *turn from their evil way.*

V. God threatens to punish these prophets for their wickedness. They promised the people *peace;* and to show them the folly of that God tells them that they should have no peace themselves. They were very unfit to warrant the people, and pass their word to them that no evil shall come upon them, when all evil is coming upon themselves and they are not aware of it, *v.* 12. Because the prophets and priests are profane, *therefore their ways shall be unto them as slippery ways in the darkness.* Those that undertake to lead others, because they mislead them, and know they do so, shall themselves have no comfort in their way. 1. They pretend to show others the way, but they shall themselves be in the dark, or in a mist; their light or sight shall fail, so that they shall not be able to look before them, shall have no forecast for themselves. 2. They pretend to give assurances to others, but they themselves shall find no firm footing: *Their ways shall be to them as slippery ways,* in which they shall not go with any steadiness, safety, or satisfaction. 3. They pretend to make the people easy with their flatteries, but they shall themselves be uneasy: *They shall be driven,* forced forward as captives, or making their escape as those that are pursued, and *they shall fall in the way* by which they hoped to escape, and so fall into the enemies' hands. 4. They pretend to prevent the evil that threatens others, but God will *bring evil upon them, even the year of their visitation,* the time fixed for calling them to an account; such a time is fixed concerning all that do not judge themselves, and it will be an evil time. *The year of visitation* is the year of recompenses. It is further threatened (*v.* 15), *I will feed them with wormwood,* or poison, with that which is not only nauseous, but noxious, and *make them drink waters of gall,* or (as some read it) *juice of hemlock;* see *ch.* 9:15. Justly is the cup of trembling put into their hand first, for *from the prophets of Jerusalem,* who should have been patterns of piety and every thing that is praiseworthy, even *from them has profaneness gone forth into all the lands.* Nothing more effectually debauches a nation than the debauchery of ministers.

VI. The people are here warned not to give any credit to these false prophets; for, though they flattered them with hopes of impunity, the judgments of God would certainly break out against them, unless they repented (*v.* 16): "Take notice of what God says, and *hearken not to the words of these prophets;* for you will find, in the issue, that God's word shall stand, and not theirs. God's word will make you serious, but *they make you vain,* feed you with vain hopes, which will fail you at last. They tell you, *No evil shall come upon you;* but hear what God says (*v.* 19), *Behold, a whirlwind of the Lord has gone forth in fury.* They tell you, All shall be calm and serene; but God tells you, There is a storm coming, a *whirlwind of the Lord,* of his sending, and therefore there is no standing before it. It is a whirlwind raised by divine wrath; it has *gone forth in fury,* a wind that is brought forth out of the treasuries of divine vengeance; and therefore it is a *grievous whirlwind,* and shall light heavily, with rain and hail, *upon the head of the wicked,* which they cannot avoid nor find any shelter from." It shall *fall upon the wicked* prophets themselves who deceived the people, and the wicked people who suffered themselves to be deceived. A *horrible tempest* shall be *the portion of their cup,* Ps. 11:6. This sentence is bound on as irreversible (*v.* 20): *The anger of the Lord shall not return,* for the decree has gone forth. God will not alter his mind, nor suffer his anger to be turned away, *till he have executed* the sentence and *performed the thoughts of his heart.* God's whirlwind, when it comes *down from heaven, returns not thither, but accomplishes that for which he sent it,* Isa. 55:11. This they will not consider now; but *in the latter days you shall consider it perfectly,* consider it *with understanding* (so the word is) or *with consideration.* Note, Those that will not fear the threatenings shall feel the execution of them, and will then perfectly understand what they will not now admit the evidence of, what a *fearful thing it is to fall into the hands of* a just and jealous God. Those that will not consider in time will be made to consider when it is too late. *Son, remember.*

VII. Several things are here offered to the consideration of these false prophets for their conviction, that, if possible, they might be brought to recant their error and acknowledge the cheat they had put upon God's people.

1. Let them consider that though they may impose upon men God is too wise to be imposed upon. Men cannot see through their fallacies, but God can and does. Here,

(1.) God asserts his own omnipresence and omniscience in general, *v.* 23, 24. When they told the people that no evil should befall them though they went on in their evil ways they went upon atheistical principles, that the Lord doth not see their sin, that he cannot judge through the dark cloud, that he will not require it; and therefore they must be taught the first principles of their religion, and confronted with the most incontestable self-evident truths. [1.] That though God's throne is prepared in the heavens, and this earth seems to be at a distance from him, yet he is a God here in this lower world, which seems to be afar off, as well as in the upper world, which seems to be at hand, *v.* 23. The eye of God is the same on earth that it is in heaven. Here it *runs to and fro* as well as there (2 Chr. 16:9); and what is in the minds of men, whose spirits are veiled in flesh, is as clearly seen by him as what is in the mind of angels, those unveiled spirits above that surround his throne. The power of God is the same on earth among its inhabitants that it is in heaven among its armies. With us nearness and distance make a great difference both in our observations and in our operations, but it is not so with God; to him darkness and light, at hand and afar off, are both alike. [2.] That, how ingenious and industrious soever men are to disguise themselves and their own characters and counsels, they cannot possibly be concealed from God's all-seeing eye (*v.* 24): *"Can any hide himself in the secret places* of the earth, *that I shall not see him?* Can any hide his projects and intentions in the secret places of the heart, that I shall not see them?" No arts of concealment can hide men from the eye of God, nor deceive his judgment of them. [3.] That he is every where present; he does not only rule heaven and earth, and uphold both by his universal providence, but he *fills heaven and earth* by his essential presence, Ps. 139:7, 8, etc. No place can either include him or exclude him.

(2.) He applies this to these prophets, who had a notable art of disguising themselves (*v.* 25, 26): *I have heard what the prophets said that prophesy lies in my name.* They thought that he was so wholly taken up with the other world that he had no leisure to take cognizance of what passed in this. But God will make them know that he knows all their impostures, all the shams they have put upon the world, under colour of divine revelation. What they intended to humour the people with they pretended to have had from God in a dream, when there was no such thing. This they could not discover. If a man tell me that he dreamed so and so, I cannot contradict him; he knows I cannot. But God discovered the fraud. Perhaps the false prophets whispered what they had to say in the ears of such as were their confidants, saying, So and so *I have dreamed;* but God overheard them. The heart-searching eye of God traced them in all the methods they took to deceive the people, and he cries out, *How long?* Shall I always bear with them? *Is it in the hearts of those prophets* (so some read it) *to be ever prophesying lies and prophesying the deceits of their own hearts?* Will they never see what an affront they put upon God, what an abuse they put upon the people, and what judgments they are preparing for themselves?

2. Let them consider that their palming upon people counterfeit revelations, and fathering their own fancies upon divine inspiration, was the ready way to bring all religion into contempt and make men turn atheists and infidels; and this was the thing they really intended, though they frequently made mention of the name of God, and prefaced all they said with, *Thus saith the Lord.* Yet, says God, *They think to cause my people to forget my name by their dreams.* They designed to draw people off from the worship of God, from all regard to God's laws and ordinances and the true prophets, as their fathers *forgot God's name for Baal.* Note, The great thing Satan aims at is to make people forget God, and all that whereby he has made himself known; and he has many subtle methods to bring them to this. Sometimes he does it by setting up false gods (bring men in love with Baal, and they soon forget the name of God), sometimes by misrepresenting the true God, as if he were altogether such a one as ourselves. Pretenses

to new revelation may prove as dangerous to religion as the denying of all revelation; and false prophets in God's name may perhaps do more mischief to the power of godliness than false prophets in Baal's name, as being less guarded against.

3. Let them consider what a vast difference there was between their prophecies and those that were delivered by the true prophets of the Lord (*v.* 28): *The prophet that has a dream,* which was the way of inspiration that the false prophets most pretended to, if he has a dream, *let him tell it as a dream;* so Mr. Gataker reads it. "Let him lay no more stress upon it than men do upon their dreams, nor expect any more regard to be had to it. Let them not say that it is from God, nor call their foolish dreams divine oracles. But let the true prophet, that *has my word, speak my word faithfully,* speak it *as a truth"* (so some read it): "let him keep closely to his instructions, and you will soon perceive a vast difference between the dreams that the false prophets tell and the divine dictates which the true prophets deliver. He that pretends to have a message from God, whether by dream or voice, let him declare it, and it will easily appear which is of God and which is not. Those that have spiritual senses exercised will be able to distinguish; for *what is the chaff to the wheat?* The promises of peace which these prophets make to you are no more to be compared to God's promises than chaff to wheat." Men's fancies are light, and vain, and worthless, as the chaff *which the wind drives away.* But the word of God has substance in it; it is of value, is food for the soul, the bread of life. Wheat was the staple commodity of Canaan, that valley of vision, Deu. 8:8; Eze. 27:17. There is as much difference between the vain fancies of men and the pure word of God as between the chaff and the wheat. It follows (*v.* 29), *Is not my word like a fire, saith the Lord?* Is their word so? Has it the power and efficacy that the word of God has? No; nothing like it; there is no more comparison than between painted fire and real fire. Theirs is like an *ignis fatuus — a deceiving meteor,* leading men into by-paths and dangerous precipices. Note, The word of God is like fire. The law was a fiery law (Deu. 33:2), and of the gospel Christ says, *I have come to send fire on the earth,* Lu. 12:49. Fire has different effects, according as the matter is on which it works; it hardens clay, but softens wax; it consumes the dross, but purifies the gold. So the word of God is to some *a savour of life unto life, to others of death unto death.* God appeals here to the consciences of those to whom the word was sent: *"Is not my word like fire?* Has it not been so to you? Zec. 1:6. Speak as you have found." It is compared likewise to a *hammer breaking the rock in pieces.* The unhumbled heart of man is like a rock; if it will not be melted by the word of God as the fire, it will be broken to pieces by it as the hammer. Whatever opposition is given to the word, it will be borne down and broken to pieces.

4. Let them consider that while they went on in this course God was against them. Three times they are told this, *v.* 30, 31, 32. *Behold, I am against the prophets.* They pretended to be for God, and made use of his name, but were really against him; he looks upon them as they were really, and is against them. How can they be long safe, or at all easy, that have a God of almighty power against them? While these prophets were promising peace to the people God was proclaiming war against them. They stand indicted here, (1.) For robbery: *They steal my word every one from his neighbour.* Some understand it of that word of God which the good prophets preached; they stole their sermons, their expressions, and mingled them with their own, as hucksters mingle bad wares with some that are good, to make them vendible. Those that were strangers to the spirit of the true prophets mimicked their language, picked up some good sayings of theirs, and delivered them to the people as if they had been their own, but with an ill grace; they were not of a piece with the rest of their discourses. *The legs of the lame are not equal, so is a parable in the mouth of fools,* Prov. 26:7. Others understand it of the word of God as it was received and entertained by some of the people; they stole it out of their hearts, as the wicked one in the parable is said to steal the good seed of the word, Mt. 13:19. By their insinuations they diminished the authority, and so weakened the efficacy, of the word of God upon the minds of those that seemed to be under convictions by it. (2.) They stand indicted for

counterfeiting the broad seal. *Therefore* God is against them (*v.* 31), because they *use their tongues* at their pleasure in their discourses to the people; they say what they themselves think fit, and then father it upon God, pretend they had it from him, and say, He saith it. Some read it, *They smooth their tongues;* they are very complaisant to the people, and say nothing but what is pleasing and plausible; they never reprove them nor threaten them, but *their words are smoother than butter.* Thus they ingratiate themselves with them, and get money by them; and they have the impudence and impiety to make God the patron of their lies; they say, "He saith so." What greater indignity can be done to the God of truth than to lay the brats of the father of lies at his door? (3.) They stand indicted as common cheats (*v.* 32): *I am against them,* for they *prophesy false dreams,* pretending that to be a divine inspiration which is but an invention of their own. This is a horrid fraud; nor will it excuse them to say, *Caveat emptor — Let the buyer take care of himself,* and *Si populus vult decipi, decipiatur — If people will be deceived, let them.* No; it is the people's fault that they err, that they take things upon trust, and do not try the spirits; but it is much more the prophets' fault that they cause God's people *to err by their lies and by their lightness,* by the flatteries of their preaching soothing them up in their sins, and by the looseness and lewdness of their conversation encouraging them to persist in them. [1.] God disowns their having any commission from him: *I sent them not, nor commanded them;* they are not God's messengers, nor is what they say his message. [2.] He therefore justly denies his blessing with them: *Therefore they shall not profit this people at all.* All the profit they aim at is to make them easy; but they shall not so much as do that, for God's providences will at the same time be making them uneasy. They *do not profit this people* (so some read it); and more is implied than is expressed; they not only do them no good, but do them a great deal of hurt. Note, Those that corrupt the word of God, while they pretend to preach it, are so far from edifying the church that they do it the greatest mischief imaginable.

Verses 33–40

The profaneness of the people, with that of the priests and prophets, is here reproved in a particular instance, which may seem of small moment in comparison of their greater crimes; but profaneness in common discourse, and the debauching of the language of a nation, being a notorious evidence of the prevalency of wickedness in it, we are not to think it strange that this matter was so largely and warmly insisted upon here. Observe,

I. The sin here charged upon them is bantering God's prophets and dialect they used, and jesting with sacred things. They asked, *What is the burden of the Lord? v.* 33 and *v.* 34. They say, *The burden of the Lord, v.* 38. This was the word that gave great offence to God, that, whenever they spoke of *the word of the Lord,* they called it, in scorn and derision, *the burden of the Lord.* Now, 1. This was a word that the prophets much used, and used it seriously, to show what a weight the word of God was upon their spirits, of what importance it was, and how pressingly it should come upon those that heard it. The words of the false prophets had nothing ponderous in them, but God's words had; those were as chaff, these as wheat. Now the profane scoffers took this word, and made a jest and a by-word of it; they made people merry with it, that so, when the prophets used it, they might not make people serious with it. Note, It has been the artifice of Satan, in all ages, to obstruct the efficacy of sacred things by turning them into matter of sport and ridicule, the mocking of God's messengers was the baffling of his messages. 2. Perhaps this word was caught at and reproached by the scoffers as an improper word, newly-coined by the prophets, and not used in that sense by any classic author. It was only in this and the last age that the *word of the Lord* was called the *burden of the Lord,* and it could not be found in their lexicons to have that signification. But if men take a liberty, as we see they do, to form new phrases which they think more expressive and significant in other parts of learning, why not in divinity? But especially we must observe it as a rule that the Spirit of God is not tied to our rules of speaking. 3. Some think that because when the *word of the Lord* is called a *burden* it signifies some word of reproof and threatening, which would lay a load upon the hearers (yet I know not whether that observation will always hold), therefore in using this word *the burden of the Lord* in a canting way they reflected upon God as always bearing hard upon them, always teasing them, always frightening them, and so making the word of God a perpetual uneasiness to them. They make the word of God a burden to themselves, and then quarrel with the ministers for making it a burden to them. Thus the scoffers of the latter days, while they slight heaven and salvation, reproach faithful ministers for preaching hell and damnation. Upon the whole we may observe that, how light soever men may make of it, the great God takes notice of, and is much displeased with, those who burlesque sacred things, and who, that they may make a jest of scripture truths and laws, put jests upon scripture language. In such wit as this I am sure there is no wisdom, and so it will appear at last. *Be you not mockers, lest your bands be made strong.* Those that were here guilty of this sin were some of the false prophets, who perhaps came to steal the word of God from the true prophets, some of the priests, who perhaps came to seek occasions against them on which to ground an information, and some of the people, who had learned of the profane priests and prophets to play with the things of God. The people would not have affronted the prophet and his God thus if the priests and the prophets, those ringleaders of mischief, had not shown them the way.

II. When they are reproved for this profane way of speaking they are directed how to express themselves more decently. We do not find that the prophets are directed to make no more use of this word; we find it used long after this (Zec. 9:1; Mal. 1:1; Nah. 1:1; Hab. 1:1); and we do not find it once used in this sense by Jeremiah either before or after. It is true indeed that in many cases it is advisable to make no use of such words and things as some have made a bad use of, and it may be prudent to avoid such phrases as, though innocent enough, are in danger of being perverted and made stumbling-blocks. But here God will have the prophet keep to his rule (*ch.* 15:19), *Let them return unto thee, but return not thou unto them.* Do not thou leave off using this word, but let them leave off abusing it. You *shall not mention the burden of the Lord any more* in this profane careless manner (*v.* 36), for it is *perverting the words of the living God* and making a bad use of them, which is an impious dangerous thing; for, consider, he is *the Lord of hosts our God.* Note, If we will but look upon God as we ought to do in his greatness and goodness, and be but duly sensible of our relation and obligation to him, it may be hoped that we shall not dare to affront him by making a jest of his words. It is an impudent thing to abuse him that is the *living God,* the *Lord of hosts,* and *our God.* How then must they express themselves? He tells them (*v.* 37): *Thus shalt thou say to the prophet,* when thou art enquiring of him, *What hath the Lord answered thee? And what hath the Lord spoken?* And they must say thus when they enquire of *their neighbours, v.* 35. Note, We must always speak of the things of God reverently and seriously, and as becomes the oracles of God. It is a commendable practice to enquire after the mind of God, to enquire of our brethren what they have heard, to enquire of our prophets what they have to say from God; but then, to show that we enquire for a right end, we must do it after a right manner. Ministers may learn here, when they reprove people for what they say and do amiss, to teach them how to say and do better.

III. Because they would not leave off this bad way of speaking, though they were admonished of it, God threatens them here with utter ruin. They would still say, *The burden of the Lord,* though God had sent to them to forbid them, *v.* 38. What little regard have those to the divine authority that will not be persuaded by it to leave an idle word! But see what will come of it. 1. Those shall be severely reckoned with that thus *pervert the words of God,* that put a wrong construction on them and make a bad use of them; and it shall be made to appear that it is a great provocation to God to mock his messengers: *I will even punish that man and his house;* whether he be prophet or priest, or one of the common people, it shall be visited upon him, *v.* 34. Perverting God's word, and ridiculing the preachers of it, are sins that bring ruining judgments upon families and entail a curse upon a house. Another threatening we have *v.* 36. *Every man's word shall be his own burden;* that is, the guilt of this sin shall be so heavy upon him as to sink him into the pit of destruction. God *shall make their own tongue to fall upon them,* Ps. 64:8. God will give them enough of their jest, so that *the burden of the Lord* they shall have no heart to mention any more; it will be too heavy to make a jest of. They are as *the madman that casts firebrands, arrows, and death,* while they pretend to be *in sport.* 2. The words of God, though thus perverted, shall be accomplished. Do they ask, *What is the burden of the Lord?* Let the prophet ask them, *What burden* do you mean? Is it this: *I will even forsake you? v.* 33. This is the burden that shall be laid and bound upon them (*v.* 39, 40): *"Behold I, even I, will utterly forget you, and I will forsake you.* I will leave you, and have no thoughts of returning to you." Those are miserable indeed that are forsaken and forgotten of God; and men's bantering God's judgments will not baffle them. Jerusalem was the city God had taken to himself as a holy city, and then *given to them and their fathers;* but that shall now be forsaken and forgotten. God had taken them to be a people near to him; but they shall now be *cast out of his presence.* They had been great and honourable among the nations; but now God will bring upon them an *everlasting reproach* and a *perpetual shame.* Both their sin and their punishment shall be their lasting disgrace. It is here upon record, to their infamy, and will remain so to the world's end. Note, God's word will be magnified and made honourable when those that mock at it shall be vilified and made contemptible. *Those that despise me shall be lightly esteemed.*

CHAPTER 24

In the close of the foregoing chapter we had a general prediction of the utter ruin of Jerusalem, that it should be forsaken and forgotten, which, whatever effect it had upon others, we have reason to think made the prophet himself very melancholy. Now, in this chapter, God encourages him, by showing him that, though the desolation seemed to be universal, yet all were not equally involved in it, but God knew how to distinguish, how to separate, between the precious and the vile. Some had gone into captivity already with Jeconiah; over them Jeremiah lamented, but God tells him that it should turn to their good. Others yet remained hardened in their sins, against whom Jeremiah had a just indignation; but those, God tells him, should go into captivity, and it should prove to their hurt. To inform the prophet of this, and affect him with it, here is, I. A vision of two baskets of figs, one very good and the other very bad (*v.* 1–3). II. The explication of this vision, applying the good figs to those that were already sent into captivity for their good (*v.* 4–7), the bad figs to those that should hereafter be sent into captivity for their hurt (*v.* 8–10).

Verses 1–10

This short chapter helps us to put a very comfortable construction upon a great many long ones, by showing us that the same providence which to some is a *savour of death unto death* may by the grace and blessing of God be made to others a *savour of life unto life;* and that, though God's people share with others in the same calamity, yet it is not the same to them that it is to others, but is designed for their good and shall issue in their good; to them it is a correcting rod in the hand of a tender Father, while to others it is an avenging sword in the hand of a righteous Judge. Observe,

I. The date of this sermon. It was after, a little after, Jeconiah's captivity, *v.* 1. Jeconiah was himself a *despised broken vessel,* but with him were carried away some very valuable persons, Ezekiel for one (Eze. 1:12); many of the *princes of Judah* then went into captivity, Daniel and his fellows were carried off a little before; of the people only *the carpenters and the smiths* were forced away, either because the Chaldeans needed some ingenious men of those trades (they had a great plenty of astrologers and stargazers, but a great scarcity of smiths and carpenters) or because the Jews would severely feel the loss of them, and would, for want of them, be unable to fortify their cities and furnish themselves with weapons of war. Now, it should seem, there were many good people carried away in that captivity, which the pious prophet laid much to heart, while there were those that triumphed in it, and insulted over those to whose lot it fell to go into captivity. Note, We must not conclude concerning the first and greatest sufferers that they were the worst and greatest sinners; for perhaps it may appear quite otherwise, as it did here.

II. The vision by which this distinction of the captives was represented to the prophet's mind. He saw *two baskets of figs, set before the temple,* there ready to be offered as first-fruits to the honour of God. Perhaps the priests, being remiss in their duty, were not ready to receive them and dispose of them according to the law, and therefore Jeremiah sees them standing *before the temple.* But that which was the significancy of the vision was that the figs in one basket were extraordinarily good, those in the other basket extremely bad. The children of men are all as the fruits of the fig-tree, capable of being made serviceable to God and man (Jdg. 9:11); but some are as good figs, than which nothing is more pleasant, others as damaged rotten figs, than which nothing is more nauseous. What creature viler than a wicked man, and what more valuable than a godly man! The good figs were like those that are first ripe, which are most acceptable (Mic. 7:1) and most prized when newly come into season. The bad figs are such as could *not be eaten, they were so evil;* they could not answer the end of their creation, were neither pleasant nor good for food; and what then were they good for? If God has no honour from men, nor their generation any service, they are even like the bad figs, that cannot be eaten, that will not answer any good purpose. *If the salt have lost its savour, it is thenceforth* fit for nothing but *the dunghill.* Of the persons that are presented to the Lord at the door of his tabernacle, some are sincere, and they are very good; others dissemble with God, and they are very bad. Sinners are the worst of men, hypocrites the worst of sinners. *Corruptio optimi est pessima — That which is best becomes, when corrupted, the worst.*

III. The exposition and application of this vision. God intended by it to raise the dejected spirit of those that had gone into captivity, by assuring them of a happy return, and to humble and awaken the proud and secure spirits of those who continued yet in Jerusalem, by assuring them of a miserable captivity.

1. Here is the moral of the good figs, that were very good, the first ripe. These represented the pious captives, that seemed first ripe for ruin, for they went first into captivity, but should prove first ripe for mercy, and their captivity should help to ripen them; these are pleasing to God, as good figs are to us, and shall be carefully preserved for use. Now observe here,

(1.) Those that were already carried into captivity were the good figs that God would own. This shows, [1.] That we cannot determine of God's love or hatred *by all that is before us.* When God's judgments are abroad those are not always the worst that are first seized by them. [2.] That early suffering sometimes proves for the best to us. The sooner the child is corrected the better effect the correction is likely to have. Those that went first into captivity were as the son whom the *father loves, and chastens betimes,* chastens while there is hope; and it did well. But those that staid behind were like a child long *left to himself,* who, when afterwards corrected, is stubborn, and made worse by it, Lam. 3:27.

(2.) God owns their captivity to be his doing. Whoever were the instruments of it, he ordered and directed it (*v.* 5): *I have sent them out of this place into the land of the Chaldeans.* It is God that puts his gold into the furnace, to be tried; his hand is, in a special manner, to be eyed in the afflictions of good people. The judge orders the malefactor into the hand of an executioner, but the father corrects the child with his own hand.

(3.) Even this disgraceful uncomfortable captivity God intended for their benefit; and we are sure that his intentions are never frustrated: *I have sent them into the land of the Chaldeans for their good.* It seemed to be every way for their hurt, not only as it was the ruin of their estates, honours, and liberties, separated them from their relations and friends, and put them under the power of their enemies and oppressors, but as it sunk their spirits, discouraged their faith, deprived them of the benefit of God's oracles and ordinances, and exposed them to temptations; and yet it was designed for their good, and proved so, in the issue, as to many of them. *Out of the eater came forth meat.* By their afflictions they were convinced of sin, humbled under the hand of God, weaned from the world, made serious, taught to pray, and turned from their iniquity; particularly they were cured of their inclination to idolatry; and thus it was *good for them that they were afflicted,* Ps. 119:67, 71.

(4.) God promises them that he will own them in their captivity. Though they seem abandoned, they shall be acknowledged; the scornful relations they left behind will scarcely own them, or their kindred to them, but God says,

I will acknowledge them. Note, *The Lord knows those that are his,* and will own them in all conditions; nakedness and sword shall not separate them from his love.

(5.) God assures them of his protection in their trouble, and a glorious deliverance out of it in due time, *v.* 6. Being sent into captivity *for their good,* they shall not be lost there; but it shall be with them as it is with gold which the refiner puts into the furnace. [1.] He has his eye upon it while it is there, and it is a careful eye, to see that it sustain no damage: *"I will set my eyes upon them for good,* to order every thing for the best, that all the circumstances of the affliction may concur to the answering of the great intention of it." [2.] He will be sure to take it out of the furnace again as soon as the work designed upon it is done: *I will bring them again to this land.* They were sent abroad for improvement awhile, under a severe discipline; but they shall be fetched back, when they have gone through their trial there, to their Father's house. [3.] He will fashion his gold when he has refined it, will make it a vessel of honour fit for his use; so, when God has brought them back from their trial, he *will build them* and make them a habitation for himself, will *plant them* and make them a vineyard for himself. Their captivity was to square the rough stones and make them fit for his building, to prune up the young trees and make them fit for his planting.

(6.) He engages to prepare them for these temporal mercies which he designed for them by bestowing spiritual mercies upon them, *v.* 7. It is this that will make their captivity be for their good; this shall be both the improvement of their affliction and their qualification for deliverance. When our troubles are sanctified to us, then we may be sure that they will end well. Now that which is promised is, [1.] That they should be better acquainted with God; they should learn more of God by his providences in Babylon than they had learned by all his oracles and ordinances in Jerusalem, thanks to divine grace, for, if that had not wrought mightily upon them in Babylon, they would for ever have forgotten God. It is here promised, *I will give them,* not so much a head to know me, but *a heart to know me,* for the right knowledge of God consists not in notion and speculation, but in the convictions of the practical judgment directing and governing the will and affections. *A good understanding have all those that do his commandments,* Ps. 111:10. Where God gives a sincere desire and inclination to know him he will give that knowledge. It is God himself that gives a heart to know him, else we should perish for ever in our ignorance. [2.] That they should be entirely converted to God, to his will as their rule, his service as their business, and his glory as their end: *They shall return to me with their whole heart.* God himself undertakes for them that they shall; and, if he turn us, we shall be turned. This follows upon the former; for those that have a heart to know God aright will not only turn to him, but turn with their whole heart; for those that are either obstinate in their rebellion, or hypocritical in their religion, may truly be said to be ignorant of God. [3.] That thus they should be again taken into covenant with God, as much to their comfort as ever: *They shall be my people, and I will be their God.* God will own them, as formerly, for his people, in the discoveries of himself to them, in his acceptance of their services, and in his gracious appearances on their behalf; and they shall have liberty to own him for their God in their prayers to him and their expectations from him. Note, Those that have backslidden from God, if they do in sincerity return to him, are admitted as freely as any to all the privileges and comforts of the everlasting covenant, which is herein well-ordered, that every transgression in the covenant does not throw us out of covenant, and that afflictions are not only consistent with, but flowing from, covenant-love.

2. Here is the moral of the bad figs. *Zedekiah and his princes* and partizans *yet remain in the land,* proud and secure enough, Eze. 11:3. Many had fled into Egypt for shelter, and they thought they had shifted well for themselves and their own safety, and boasted that though therein they had gone contrary to the command of God yet they had acted prudently for themselves. Now as to both these, that looked so scornfully upon those that had gone into captivity, it is here threatened, (1.) That, whereas those who were already carried away were settled in one country, where they had the comfort of one another's society, though in captivity, these should be dispersed *and removed into all the kingdoms of the earth,* where they should have no joy one of another. (2.) That, whereas those were carried captives for their good, these should be removed into all countries *for their hurt.* Their afflictions should be so far from humbling them that they should harden them, not bring them nearer to God, but set them at a greater distance from him. (3.) That, whereas those should have the honour of being owned of God in their troubles, these should have the shame of being abandoned by all mankind: *In all places whither I shall drive them they shall be a reproach and a proverb.* "Such a one is as false and proud as a Jew" — "Such a one is as poor and miserable as a Jew." All their neighbours shall make a jest of them, and of the calamities brought upon them. (4.) That, whereas those should *return to their own land,* never to see it more, and it shall be of no avail to them to plead that it was the land God gave to their fathers, for they had it from God, and he gave it to them upon condition of their obedience. (5.) That, whereas those were reserved for better times, these were reserved for worse; wherever they are removed *the sword, and famine, and pestilence,* shall be sent after them, shall soon overtake them, and, coming with commission so to do, shall overcome them. God has variety of judgments wherewith to prosecute those that fly from justice; and those that have escaped one may expect another, till they are brought to repent and reform.

Doubtless this prophecy had its accomplishment in the men of that generation yet, because we read not of any such remarkable difference between those of Jeconiah's captivity and those of Zedekiah's, it is probable that this has a typical reference to the last destruction of the Jews by the Romans, in which those of them that believed were taken care of, but those that continued obstinate in unbelief were driven into all countries for *a taunt and a curse,* and so they remain to this day.

CHAPTER 25

The prophecy of this chapter bears date some time before those prophecies in the chapters next foregoing, for they are not placed in the exact order of time in which they were delivered. This is dated in the first year of Nebuchadrezzar, that remarkable year when the sword of the Lord began to be drawn and furbished. Here is, I. A review of the prophecies that had been delivered to Judah and Jerusalem for many years past, by Jeremiah himself and other prophets, with the little regard given to them and the little success of them (*v.* 1–7). II. A very express threatening of the destruction of Judah and Jerusalem, by the king of Babylon, for their contempt of God, and their continuance in sin (*v.* 8–11), to which is annexed a promise of their deliverance out of their captivity in Babylon, after 70 years (*v.* 12–14). III. A prediction of the devastation of divers other nations about, by Nebuchadrezzar, represented by a "cup of fury" put into their hands (*v.* 15–28), by a sword sent among them (*v.* 29–33), and a desolation made among the shepherds and their flocks and pastures (*v.* 34–38); so that we have here judgment beginning at the house of God, but not ending there.

Verses 1–7

We have here a message from God concerning all the people of Judah (*v.* 1), which Jeremiah delivered, in his name, unto all the people of Judah, *v.* 2. Note, That which is of universal concern ought to be of universal cognizance. It is fit that the word which concerns all the people, as the word of God does, the word of the gospel particularly, should be divulged to all in general, and, as far as may be, addressed to each in particular. Jeremiah had been sent to the *house of the king* (*ch.* 22:1), and he took courage to deliver his message to them, probably when they had all come up to Jerusalem to worship at one of the solemn feasts; then he had them together, and it was to be hoped then, if ever, they would be well disposed to hear counsel and receive instruction.

This prophecy is dated in the fourth year of Jehoiakim and the first of Nebuchadrezzar. It was in the latter end of Jehoiakim's third year that Nebuchadrezzar began to reign by himself alone (having reigned some time before in conjunction with his father), as appears, Dan. 1:1. But Jehoiakim's fourth year was begun before Nebuchadrezzar's first was completed. Now that that active, daring, martial prince began to set up for the world's master, God, by his prophet, gives notice that he is his servant, and intimates what work he intends to employ him in, that his growing greatness, which was so formidable to the nations, might not be construed as any reflection upon the power and providence of God in the government of the world. Nebuchadrezzar should not bid so fair for universal monarchy (I should have said universal tyranny) but that God had purposes of his own to serve by him, in the execution of which the world shall see the meaning of God's permitting and ordering a thing that seemed such a reflection on his sovereignty and goodness.

Now in this message we may observe the great pains that had been taken with the people to bring them to repentance, which they are here put in mind of, as an aggravation of their sin and a justification of God in his proceedings against them.

I. Jeremiah, for his part, had been a constant preacher among them twenty-three years; he began in the thirteenth year of Josiah, who reigned thirty-one years, so that he prophesied about eighteen or nineteen years in his reign, then in the reign of Jehoahaz, and now four years of Jehoiakim's reign. Note, God keeps an account, whether we do or no, how long we have enjoyed the means of grace; and the longer we have enjoyed them the heavier will our account be if we have not improved them. *These three years* (these three and twenty years) *have I come seeking fruit on this fig-tree.* All this while, 1. God had been constant in sending messages to them, as there was occasion for them: "From that time *to this very day the word of the Lord has come into me,* for your use." Though they had the substance of the warning sent them already in the books of Moses, yet, because those were not duly regarded and applied, God sent to enforce them and make them more particular, that they might be without excuse. Thus God's Spirit was striving with them, as with the old world, Gen. 6:3. 2. Jeremiah had been faithful and industrious in delivering those messages. He could appeal to themselves, as well as to God and his own conscience, concerning this: *I have spoken to you, rising early and speaking.* He had declared to them *the whole counsel of God;* he had taken a great deal of care and pains to discharge his thrust in such a manner as might be most likely to win and work upon them. What men are solicitous about and intent upon they rise up early to prosecute. It intimates that his head was so full of thoughts about it, and his heart so intent upon doing good, that it broke his sleep, and made him get up betimes to project which way he might take that would be most likely to do them good. He rose early, both because he would lose no time and because he would lay hold on and improve the best time to work upon them, when, if ever, they were sober and sedate. Christ came *early in the morning* to preach in the temple, and the people as early to hear him, Lu. 21:38. Morning lectures have their advantages. *My voice shalt thou hear in the morning.*

II. Besides him, God had sent them other prophets, on the same errand, *v.* 4. Of the writing prophets Micah, Nahum, and Habakkuk, were a little before him, and Zephaniah contemporary with him. But, besides those, there were many other of God's *servants the prophets* who preached awakening sermons, which were never published. And here God himself is said to *rise early* and *send them,* intimating how much his heart also was upon it, that this people should *turn and live,* and not *go on and die,* Eze. 33:11.

III. All the messages sent them were to the purpose, and much to the same purport, *v.* 5, 6. 1. They all told them of their faults, *their evil way,* and the *evil of their doings.* Those were not of God's sending who flattered them as if there were nothing amiss among them. 2. They all reproved them particularly for their idolatry, as a sin that was in a special manner provoking to God, their *going after other gods, to serve them and to worship them,* gods that were *the work of their own hands.* 3. They all called on them to repent of their sins and to reform their lives. This was the burden of every song, *Turn you now every one from his evil way.* Note, Personal and particular reformation must be insisted on as necessary to a national deliverance: *every one* must *turn from his* own *evil way.* The street will not be clean unless every one sweep before his own door. 4. They all assured them that, if they did so, it would certainly be the *lengthening out of their tranquillity.* The mercies they enjoyed should be continued to them: *"You shall dwell in the land,* dwell at ease, dwell in peace, in this good land, *which the Lord has given you and your fathers.* Nothing but sin will turn you out of it, and that shall not if you turn from it." The judgments they feared should be prevented: *Provoke me not, and I will do you no hurt.* Note, We should never receive from God the evil punishment if we did not provoke him by the evil of sin.

God deals fairly with us, never corrects his children without cause, nor causes grief to us unless we give offence to him.

IV. Yet all was to no purpose. They were not wrought upon to take the right and only method to turn away the wrath of God. Jeremiah was a very lively affectionate preacher, yet *they hearkened not* to him, *v.* 3. The other prophets dealt faithfully with them, but neither did they *hearken to them,* nor *incline their ear, v.* 4. That very particular sin which they were told, of all others, was most offensive to God, and made them obnoxious to his justice, they wilfully persisted in: You *provoke me with the works of your hands to your own hurt.* Note, What is a provocation to God will prove, in the end, hurt to ourselves, and we must bear the blame of it. *O Israel! thou hast destroyed thyself.*

Verses 8–14

Here is the sentence grounded upon the foregoing charge: *"Because you have not heard my words,* I must take another course with you," *v.* 8. Note, When men will not regard the judgments of God's mouth they may expect to feel the judgments of his hands, to hear the rod, since they would not hear the word; for the sinner must either be parted from his sin or perish in it. Wrath comes without remedy against those only that sin without repentance. It is not so much men's turning aside that ruins them as their not returning.

I. The ruin of the land of Judah by the king of Babylon's armies is here decreed, *v.* 9. God sent to them *his servants the prophets,* and they were not heeded, and therefore God will send for *his servant the king of Babylon,* whom they cannot mock, and despise, and persecute, as they did his servants the prophets. Note, The messengers of God's wrath will be sent against those that would not receive the messengers of his mercy. One way or other God will be heeded, and will make men know that *he is the Lord.* Nebuchadrezzar, though a stranger to the true God, the God of Israel, nay, an enemy to him and afterwards a rival with him, was yet, in the descent he made upon his country. *God's servant,* accomplished his purpose, was employed by him, and was an instrument in his hand for the correction of his people. He was really serving God's designs when he thought he was serving his own ends. Justly therefore does God here call himself *The Lord of hosts* (*v.* 8), for here is an instance of his sovereign dominion, not only over the inhabitants, but over the armies of this earth, of which he makes what use he pleases. He has them all at his command. The most potent and absolute monarchs are his servants. Nebuchadrezzar, who is an instrument of his wrath, is as truly his servant as Cyrus, who is an instrument of his mercy. The land of Judah being to be made desolate, God here musters his army that is to make it so, gathers it together, takes *all the families of the north,* if there be occasion for them, leads them on as their commander-in-chief, *brings them against this land,* gives them success, not only against Judah and Jerusalem, but against *all the nations round about,* that there might be no dependence upon them as allies or assistants against that threatening force. The utter destruction of this and all the neighbouring lands is here described, *v.* 9–11. It shall be total: *The whole land shall be a desolation,* not only desolate, but a desolation itself; both city and country shall be laid waste, and all the wealth of both be made a prey of. It shall be lasting, even *perpetual desolations;* they shall continue so long in ruins, and after long waiting there shall appear so little prospect of relief, that every one shall call it perpetual. This desolation shall be the ruin of their credit among their neighbours; it shall bury their honour in the dust, shall *make them an astonishment and a hissing;* every one will be amazed at them, and hiss them off the stage of action with just disgrace for deserting a God who would have been their protection for impostors who would certainly be their destruction. It will likewise be the ruin of all their comfort among themselves; it shall be a final period of all their joy: *I will take from them the voice of mirth,* hang their harps on the willow-trees, and put them out of tune for songs. *I will take from them the voice of mirth;* they shall neither have cause for it nor hearts for it. They would not hear the voice of God's word and therefore the voice of mirth shall no more be heard among them. They shall be deprived of food: *The sound of the mill-stones shall not be heard;* for, when the enemy has seized their stores, the sound of the grinding must needs be low, Eccl. 12:4. An end shall be put to all business; there shall not be seen *the light of a candle,* for there shall be no work to be done worth candle-light. And, *lastly,* they shall be deprived of their liberty: *Those nations shall serve the king of Babylon seventy years.* The fixing of time during which the captivity should last would be of great use, not only for the confirmation of the prophecy, when the event (which in this particular could by no human sagacity be foreseen) should exactly answer the prediction, but for the comfort of the people of God in their calamity and the encouragement of faith and prayer. Daniel, who was himself a prophet, had an eye to it, Dan. 9:2. Nay, God himself had an eye to it (2 Chr. 36:22); for *therefore* he *stirred up the spirit of Cyrus,* that the word spoken by the mouth of Jeremiah might be accomplished. *Known unto God are all his works from the beginning of the world,* which appears by this, that, when he has thought fit, some of them have been made known to his servants the prophets and by them to his church.

II. The ruin of Babylon, at last, is here likewise foretold, as it had been, long before, by Isaiah, *v.* 12–14. The destroyers must themselves be destroyed, and the rod thrown into the fire, when the correcting work is done with it. This shall be done when *seventy years are accomplished;* for the destruction of Babylon must make way for the deliverance of the captives. It is a great doubt when these *seventy years* commence; some date them from the captivity in the fourth year of Jehoiakim and first of Nebuchadrezzar, others from the captivity of Jehoiachin eight years after. I rather incline to the former, because then these nations began *to serve the king of Babylon,* and because usually God has taken the earliest time from which to reckon the accomplishment of a promise of mercy, as will appear in computing the 400 years' servitude in Egypt. And, if so, eighteen or nineteen years of the seventy had run out before Jerusalem and the temple were quite destroyed in the eleventh year of Zedekiah. However that be, when the time, the set time, to favour Zion, has come, the king of Babylon must be visited, and all the instances of his tyranny reckoned for; then that nation shall be punished *for their iniquity,* as the other nations have been punished for theirs. That land must then be a *perpetual desolation,* such as they had made other lands; for the *Judge of all the earth* will both *do right* and *avenge wrong,* as King of nations and King of saints. Let proud conquerors and oppressors be moderate in the use of their power and success, for it will come at last to their own turn to suffer; their day will come to fall. In this destruction of Babylon, which was to be brought about by the Medes and Persians, reference shall be had, 1. To what God had said: *I will bring upon that land all my words;* for all the wealth and honour of Babylon shall be sacrificed to the truth of the divine predictions, and all its power broken, rather than one iota or tittle of God's word shall fall to the ground. The same Jeremiah that prophesied the destruction of other nations by the Chaldeans foretold also the destruction of the Chaldeans themselves; and this must be brought upon them, *v.* 13. It is with reference to this very event that God says, I will *confirm the word of my servant,* and *perform the counsel of my messengers,* Isa. 44:26. 2. Two what they had done (*v.* 14): *I will recompense them according to their deeds,* by which they transgressed the law of God, even then when they were made to serve his purposes. They had made many nations to serve them, and trampled upon them with the greatest insolence imaginable; but not that the measure of their iniquity is full *many nations and great kings,* that are in alliance with and come in to the assistance of Cyrus king of Persia, shall *serve themselves of them* also, shall make themselves masters of their country, enrich themselves with their spoils, and make them the footstool by which to mount the throne of universal monarchy. They shall make use of them for servants and soldiers. *He that leads into captivity shall go into captivity.*

Verses 15–29

Under the similitude of a cup going round, which all the company must drink of, is here represented the universal desolation that was now coming upon that part of the world which Nebuchadrezzar, who just now began to reign and act, was to be the instrument of, and which should at length recoil upon his own country. The cup in the vision is to be a sword in the accomplishment of it: so it is explained, *v.* 16. It is *the sword that I will send among them,* the sword of war, that should be irresistibly strong and implacably cruel.

I. As to the circumstances of this judgment, observe,

1. Whence this destroying sword should come — *from the hand of God.* It is the *sword of the Lord* (*ch.* 47:6), *bathed in heaven,* Isa. 34:5. Wicked men are made use of as his sword, Ps. 17:13. It is *the wine-cup of his fury.* It is the just anger of God that sends this judgment. The nations have provoked him by their sins, and they must fall under the tokens of his wrath. These are compared to some intoxicating liquor, which they shall be forced to drink of, as, formerly, condemned malefactors were sometimes executed by being compelled to drink poison. The wicked are said to *drink the wrath of the Almighty,* Job 21:20; Rev. 14:10. Their share of troubles in his world is represented by the dregs of a cup of red wine full of mixture, Ps. 75:8. See Ps. 11:6. The wrath of God in this world is but as a cup, in comparison of the full streams of it in the other world.

2. By whose hand it should be sent to them — by the hand of Jeremiah as the judge *set over the nations* (*ch.* 1:10), to pass his sentence upon them, and by the hand of Nebuchadrezzar as the executioner. What a much greater figure then does the poor prophet make than what the potent prince makes, if we look upon their relation to God, though in the eye of the world it was the reverse of it! Jeremiah must *take the cup at God's hand,* and compel the nations *to drink it.* He foretells no hurt to them but what God appoints him to foretell; and what is foretold by a divine authority will certainly be fulfilled by a divine power.

3. On whom it should be sent — on all the nations within the verge of Israel's acquaintance and the lines of their communication. Jeremiah took the cup, and *made all the nations to drink of it,* that is, he prophesied concerning each of the nations here mentioned that they should share in this great desolation that was coming. *Jerusalem and the cities of Judah* are put first (*v.* 18); for *judgment begins at the house of God* (1 Pt. 4:17), at the sanctuary, Eze. 9:6. Whether Nebuchadrezzar had his eye principally upon Jerusalem and Judah in this expedition or no does not appear; probably he had; for it was as considerable as any of the nations here mentioned. However God had his eye principally to them. And this part of the prophecy was already begun to be accomplished; this is denoted by that melancholy parenthesis *(as it is this day),* for in the fourth year of Jehoiakim things had come into a very bad posture, and all the foundations were out of course. *Pharaoh king of Egypt* comes next, because the Jews trusted to that broken reed (*v.* 19); the remains of them fled to Egypt, and there Jeremiah particularly foretold the destruction of that country, *ch.* 43:10, 11. All the other nations that bordered upon Canaan must pledge Jerusalem in this bitter cup, this cup of trembling. The *mingled people,* the Arabians (so some), some rovers of divers nations that lived by rapine (so others); *the kings of the land of Uz,* joined to the country of the Edomites. The Philistines had been vexatious to Israel, but now their cities and their lords become a prey to this mighty conqueror. Edom, Moab, Ammon, Tyre, and Zidon, are places well known to border upon Israel; the *Isles beyond,* or *beside, the sea,* are supposed to be those parts of Phoenicia and Syria that lay upon the coast of the Mediterranean Sea. Dedan and the other countries mentioned (*v.* 23, 24) seem to have lain upon the confines of Idumea and Arabia the desert. Those of Elam are the Persians, with whom the Medes are joined, now looked upon as inconsiderable and yet afterwards able to make reprisals upon Babylon for themselves and all their neighbours. The *kings of the north,* that lay nearer to Babylon, and others that lay at some distance, will be sure to be seized on and made a prey of by the victorious sword of Nebuchadrezzar. Nay, he shall push on his victories with such incredible fury and success that all the kingdoms of the world that were then and there known should become sacrifices to his ambition. Thus Alexander is said to have conquered *the world,* and the Roman empire is called *the world,* Lu. 2:1. Or it may be taken as reading the doom of *all the kingdoms* of the earth; one time or other, they shall feel the dreadful effects of war. The world has been, and will be, a great cockpit, while men's lusts war as they do *in their members,* Jam. 4:1. But, that the conquerors

may see their fate with the conquered, it concludes, *The king of Sheshach shall drink after them,* that is, the king of Babylon himself, who has given his neighbours all this trouble and vexation, shall at length have it return upon his own head. That by Sheshach is meant Babylon is plain from *ch.* 51:41; but whether it was another name of the same city or the name of another city of the same kingdom is uncertain. Babylon's ruin was foretold, *v.* 12, 13. Upon this prophecy of its being the author of the ruin of so many nations it is very fitly repeated here again.

4. What should be the effect of it. The desolations which the sword should make in all these kingdoms are represented by the consequences of excessive drinking (*v.* 16): *They shall drink, and be moved, and be mad. They shall be drunken, and spue, and fall and rise no more, v.* 27. Now this may serve, (1.) To make us loathe the sin of drunkenness, that the consequences of it are made use of to set forth a most woeful and miserable condition. Drunkenness deprives men, for the present, of the use of their reason, makes them mad. It takes from them likewise that which, next to reason, is the most valuable blessing, and that is health; it makes them sick, and endangers the bones and the life. Men in drink often *fall and rise no more;* it is a sin that is its own punishment. How wretchedly are those intoxicated and besotted that suffer themselves at any time to be intoxicated, especially to be by the frequent commission of the sin besotted with wine or strong drink! (2.) To make us dread the judgments of war. When God sends the sword upon a nation, with warrant to make it desolate, it soon becomes like a drunken man, filled with confusion at the alarms of war, put into a hurry; its counsellors *mad,* and at their wits' end, staggering in all the measures they take, all the motions they make, sick at heart with continual vexation, *vomiting up the riches* they have greedily *swallowed down* (Job 20:15), *falling* down before the enemy, and as unable to get up again, or do any thing to help themselves, as a man *dead drunk is,* Hab. 2:16.

5. The undoubted certainty of it, with the reason given for it, *v.* 28, 29. They will *refuse to take the cup at thy hand;* not only they will be loth that the judgment should come, but they will be loth to believe that ever it will come; they will not give credit to the prediction of so despicable a man as Jeremiah. But he must tell them that it is *the word of the Lord of hosts,* he hath said it; and it is in vain for them to struggle with Omnipotence: *You shall certainly drink.* And he must give them this reason, It is a time of visitation, it is a reckoning day, and Jerusalem has been called to an account already: *I begin to bring evil on the city that is called by my name;* its relation to me will not exempt it from punishment, and *should you be utterly unpunished?* No; *If this be done in the green tree, what shall be done in the dry?* If those who have some good in them smart so severely for the evil that is found in them, can those expect to escape who have worse evils, and no good, found among them? If Jerusalem be punished for learning idolatry of the nations, shall not the nations be punished, of whom they learned it? No doubt they shall: *I will call for a sword upon all the inhabitants of the earth,* for they have helped to debauch the inhabitants of Jerusalem.

II. Upon this whole matter we may observe, 1. That there is a God that judges in the earth, to whom all the nations of the earth are accountable, and by whose judgment they must abide. 2. That God can easily bring to ruin the greatest nations, the most numerous and powerful, and such as have been most secure. 3. That those who have been vexatious and mischievous to the people of God will be reckoned with for it at last. Many of these nations had in their turns given disturbance to Israel, but now comes destruction on them. The year of the redeemer will come, even the *year of recompenses* for the controversy of Zion. 4. That the *burden of the word of the Lord* will at last become the burden of his judgments. Isaiah had prophesied long since against most of these nations (*ch.* 13, etc.) and now at length all his prophecies will have their complete fulfilling. 5. That those who are ambitious of power and dominion commonly become the troublers of the earth and the plagues of their generation. Nebuchadrezzar was so proud of his might that he had no sense of right. These are the men that turn the world upside down, and yet expect to be admired and adored. Alexander thought himself a great prince when others thought him no better than a great pirate. 6. That the greatest pomp and power in this world are of very uncertain continuance. Before Nebuchadrezzar's greater force kings themselves must yield and become captives.

Verses 30–38

We have, in these verses, a further description of those terrible desolations which the king of Babylon with his armies should make in all the countries and nations round about Jerusalem. In Jerusalem God had erected his temple; there were his oracles and ordinances, which the neighbouring nations should have attended to and might have received benefit by; thither they should have applied for the knowledge of God and their duty, and then they might have had reason to bless God for their neighbourhood to Jerusalem; but they, instead of that, taking all opportunities either to debauch or to disturb that holy city, when God came to reckon with Jerusalem because it learned so much of the *way of the nations,* he reckoned with the nations because they learned so little of the way of Jerusalem.

They will soon be aware of Nebuchadrezzar's making war upon them; but the prophet is here directed to tell them that it is God himself that makes war upon them, a God with whom there is no contending. 1. The war is here proclaimed (*v.* 30): *The Lord shall roar from on high;* not *from Mount Zion and Jerusalem* (as Joel 3:16, Amos 1:2), but from *heaven,* from *his holy habitation* there; for now Jerusalem is one of the places against which he roars. *He shall mightily roar upon his habitation* on earth from that above. He has been long silent, and seemed not to take notice of the wickedness of the nations; the times of this ignorance God winked at; but now *he shall give a shout,* as the assailants in battle do, *against all the inhabitants of the earth,* to whom it shall be a shout of terror, and yet a shout of joy in heaven, as theirs that *tread the grapes;* for, when God is reckoning with the proud enemies of his kingdom among men, there is a *great voice of much people heard in heaven, saying, Hallelujah,* Rev. 19:1. He *roars as a lion* (Amos 3:4, 8), as a lion that has *forsaken his covert* (*v.* 38), and is going abroad to seek his prey, upon which he roars, that he may the more easily seize it. 2. The manifesto is here published, showing the causes and reasons why God proclaims this war (*v.* 31): *The Lord has a controversy with the nations;* he has just cause to contend with them, and he will take this way of pleading with them. His quarrel with them is, in one word, for their wickedness, their contempt of him, and his authority over them and kindness to them. *He will give those that are wicked to the sword.* They have provoked God to anger, and thence comes all this destruction; it is *because of the fierce anger of the Lord* (*v.* 37 and again *v.* 38), the *fierceness of the oppressor,* or (as it might better be read) *the fierceness of the oppressing sword* (for the word is feminine) is *because of his fierce anger;* and we are sure that he is never angry without cause; but *who knows the power of his anger?* 3. The alarm is here given and taken: *A noise will come even to the ends of the earth,* so loud shall it roar, so far shall it reach, *v.* 31. The alarm is not given by sound of trumpet, or beat of drum, but by a *whirlwind, a great whirlwind, storm,* or *tempest,* which shall be *raised up from the coasts,* the remote coasts *of the earth, v.* 32. The Chaldean army shall be like a hurricane raised in the north, but thence carried on with incredible fierceness and swiftness, bearing down all before it. It is like the whirlwind out of which God answered Job, which was exceedingly terrible, Job 37:1; 38:1. And, when the wrath of God thus roars like a lion from heaven, no marvel if it be echoed with shrieks from earth; for who can choose but tremble when God thus speaks in displeasure? See Hosea 11:10. Now the shepherds shall *howl and cry,* the kings, and princes, and the great ones of the earth, the *principal of the flock.* They used to be the most courageous and secure, but now their hearts shall fail them; *they shall wallow themselves in the ashes, v.* 34. Seeing themselves utterly unable to make head against the enemy, and seeing their country, which they have the charge of and a concern for, inevitably ruined, they shall abandon themselves to sorrow. There shall be *a voice of the cry of the shepherds,* and a *howling of the principal of the flock shall be heard, v.* 36. Those are great calamities indeed that strike such a terror upon the great men, and put them into this consternation. *The Lord hath spoiled their pasture,* in which they fed their flock, and out of which they fed themselves; the spoiling of that makes them cry-out thus. Perhaps, carrying on the metaphor of a lion roaring, it alludes to the great fright that shepherds are in when they hear a roaring lion coming towards their flocks, and find they have *no way to flee* (*v.* 35) for their own safety, neither can the *principal of their flock escape.* The enemy will be so numerous, so furious, so sedulous, and the extent of their armies so vast, that it will be impossible to avoid falling into their hands. Note, As we cannot out-face, so we cannot out-run, the judgments of God. This is that for which the shepherds *howl and cry.* 4. The progress of this war is here described (*v.* 32): *Behold, evil shall go forth from nation to nation;* as the cup goes round, every nation shall have its share and take warning by the calamities of another to repent and reform. Nay, as if this ere to be a little representation of the last and general judgment, it shall reach *from one end of the earth even unto the other end of the earth, v.* 33. The day of vengeance is in his heart, and now *his hand shall find out all his enemies,* wherever they are, Ps. 21:8. Note, When our neighbour's house is on fire it is time to be concerned for our own. When one nation is a seat of war every neighbouring nation should hear, and fear, and make its peace with God. 5. The dismal consequences of this war are here foretold: *The days of slaughter and dispersions are accomplished,* that is, they are fully come (*v.* 34), the time fixed in the divine counsel for the slaughter of some and the dispersion of the rest, which will make the nations completely desolate. Multitudes shall fall by the sword of the merciless Chaldeans, so that *the slain of the Lord* shall be every where found: they are slain by commission from him, and are sacrificed to his justice. The slain for sin are the *slain of the Lord.* To complete the misery of their slaughter, *they shall not be lamented* in particular, so general shall the matter of lamentation be. Nay, they shall not *be gathered* up, nor *buried,* for they shall have no friends left to bury them, and the enemies shall not have so much humanity in them as to do it; and then they shall be *as dung upon the earth,* so vile and noisome: and it is well if, as dung manures the earth and makes it fruitful, so these horrid spectacles, which lie as monuments of divine justice, might be a means to awaken the inhabitants of the earth to *learn righteousness.* The effect of this war will be the *desolation of the whole land* that is the seat of it (*v.* 38), one land after another. But here are two expressions more that seem to make the case in a particular manner piteous. (1.) *You shall fall like a pleasant vessel, v.* 34. The most desirable persons among them, who most valued themselves and were most valued, who were looked upon as *vessels of honour,* shall fall by the sword. You shall fall as a Venice glass or a China dish, which is soon broken all to pieces. Even the tender and delicate shall share in the common calamity; the sword devours one as well as another. (2.) Even *the peaceable habitations are cut down.* Those that used to be quiet, and not molested, the habitations in which you have long dwelt in peace, shall now be no longer such, but *cut down* by the war. Or, Those who used to be quiet, and not molesting any of their neighbours, those who lived in peace, easily, and gave no provocation to any, even those shall not escape. This is one of the direful effects of war, that even those who were most harmless and inoffensive suffer hard things. Blessed be God, there is a *peaceable habitation* above for all the sons of peace, which is out of the reach of fire and sword.

CHAPTER 26

As in the history of the Acts of the Apostles that of their preaching and that of their suffering are interwoven, so it is in the account we have of the prophet Jeremiah; witness this chapter, where we are told, I. How faithfully he preached (*v.* 1–6). II. How spitefully he was persecuted for so doing by the priests and the prophets (*v.* 7–11). III. How bravely he stood to his doctrine, in the face of his persecutors (*v.* 12–15). IV. How wonderfully he was protected and delivered by the prudence of the princes and elders (*v.* 16–19). Though Urijah, another prophet, was about the same time put to death by Jehoiakim (*v.* 20–23), yet Jeremiah met with those that sheltered him (*v.* 24).

Verses 1–6

We have here the sermon that Jeremiah preached, which gave such offence that he was in danger of losing his life for it. It is here left upon record, as it were, by way of appeal to the judgment of impartial men in all ages, whether Jeremiah was worthy to die for delivering such a message as this from God, and whether his persecutors were not very wicked and unreasonable men.

I. God directed him where to preach this sermon, and when, and to what auditory, *v.* 2. Let not any censure Jeremiah as indiscreet in the choice of place and time, nor say that he might have delivered his message more privately, in a corner, among his friends that he could confide in, and that he deserved to smart for not acting more cautiously; for God gave him orders to preach *in the court of the Lord's house,* which was within the peculiar jurisdiction of his sworn enemies the priests, and who would therefore take themselves to be in a particular manner affronted. He must preach this, as it should seem, at the time of one of the most solemn festivals, when persons had come from all the *cities of Judah* to *worship in the Lord's house.* These worshippers, we may suppose, had a great veneration for their priests, would credit the character they gave of men, and be exasperated against those whom they defamed, and would, consequently, side with them and strengthen their hands against Jeremiah. But none of these things must move him or daunt him; in the face of all this danger he must preach this sermon, which, if it were not convincing, would be very provoking. And because the prophet might be in some temptation to palliate the matter, and make it better to his hearers than God had made it to him, to exchange an offensive expression for one more plausible, therefore God charges him particularly *not to diminish a word,* but to speak all the things, nay, *all the words,* that he had commanded him. Note, God's ambassadors must keep closely to their instructions, and not in the least vary from them, either to please men or to save themselves from harm. They must neither *add* nor *diminish,* Deu. 4:2.

II. God directed him what to preach, and it is that which could not give offence to any but such as were resolved to go on still in their trespasses. 1. He must assure them that if they would *repent of their sins,* and turn from them, though they were in imminent danger of ruin and desolating judgments were just at the door, yet a stop should be put to them, and God would proceed no further in his controversy with them, *v.* 3. This was the main thing God intended in sending him to them, to try if they would return from their sins, that so God might turn from his anger and turn away the judgments that threatened them, which he was not only willing, but very desirous to do, as soon as he could do it without prejudice to the honour of his justice and holiness. See how God *waits to be gracious,* waits till we are duly qualified, till we are fit for him to be gracious to, and in the mean time tries a variety of methods to bring us to be so. 2. He must, on the other hand, assure them that if they continued obstinate to all the calls God gave them, and would persist in their disobedience, it would certainly end in the ruin of their city and temple, *v.* 4–6. (1.) That which God required of them was that they should be observant of what he had said to them, both by the written word and by his ministers, that they should *walk in all his law which he set before them,* the law of Moses and the ordinances and commandments of it, and that they should *hearken to the words of his servants the prophets,* who pressed nothing upon them but what was agreeable to the law of Moses, which was *set before them* as a touchstone to try the spirits by; and by this they were distinguished from the false prophets, who drew them from the law, instead of drawing them to it. The law was what God himself set before them. The prophets were his own servants, and were immediately sent by him to them, and sent with a great deal of care and concern, *rising early to send them,* lest they should come too late, when their prejudices had got possession and become invincible. They had hitherto been deaf both to the law and to the prophets: *You have not hearkened.* All he expects now is that at length they should heed what he said, and make his word their rule — a reasonable demand. (2.) That which is threatened in case of refusal is that this city, and the temple in it, shall fare as their predecessors did, Shiloh and the tabernacle there, for a like refusal to walk in God's law and hearken to his prophets, then when the present dispensation of prophecy just began in Samuel. Now could a sentence be expressed more unexceptionably? Is it not a rule of justice *ut parium par sit ratio — that those whose cases are the same be dealt with alike?* If Jerusalem be

like Shiloh in respect of sin, why should it not be like Shiloh in respect of punishment? Can any other be expected? This was not the first time he had given them warning to this effect; see *ch.* 7:12–14. When the temple, which was the glory of Jerusalem, was destroyed, the city was thereby *made a curse;* for the temple was that which made it a blessing. *If the salt lose that savour, it is thenceforth good for nothing.* It shall be *a curse,* that is, it shall be the pattern of a curse; if a man would curse any city, he would say, *God make it like Jerusalem!* Note, Those that will not be subject to the commands of God make themselves subject to the curse of God.

Verses 7–15

One would have hoped that such a sermon as that in the foregoing verses, so plain and practical, so rational and pathetic, and delivered in God's name, would work upon even this people, especially meeting them now at their devotions, and would prevail with them to repent and reform; but, instead of awakening their convictions, it did but exasperate their corruptions, as appears by this account of the effect of it.

I. Jeremiah is charged with it as a crime that he had preached such a sermon, and is apprehended for it as a criminal. The *priests,* and *false prophets,* and *people,* heard him speak these words, *v.* 7. They had patience, it seems, to hear him out, did not disturb him when he was preaching, nor give him any interruption till he had *made an end of speaking all that the Lord commanded him to speak, v.* 8. So far they dealt more fairly with him than some of the persecutors of God's ministers have done; they let him say all he had to say, and yet perhaps with a bad design, in hopes to have something worse yet to lay to his charge; but, having no worse, this shall suffice to ground an indictment upon: He hath said, *This house shall be like Shiloh, v.* 9. See how unfair they are in representing his words. He had said, in God's name, *If you will not hearken to me, then will I make this house like Shiloh;* but they leave out God's hand in the desolation (*I will make* it so) and their own hand in it in not hearkening to the voice of God, and charge it upon him that he blasphemed *this holy place,* the crime charged both on our Lord Jesus and on Stephen: He said, *This house shall be like Shiloh.* Well might he complain, as David does (Ps. 56:5), *Every day they wrest my words;* and we must not think it strange if we, and what we say and do, be thus misrepresented. When the accusation was so weakly grounded, no marvel that the sentence passed upon it was unjust: *Thou shalt surely die.* What he had said agreed with what God had said when he took possession of the temple (1 Ki. 9:6–8), *If you shall at all turn from following after me, then this house shall be abandoned;* and yet he is condemned to die for saying it. It is not out of any concern for the honour of the temple that they appear thus warm, but because they are resolved not to part with their sins, in which they flatter themselves with a conceit that the *temple of the Lord* will protect them; therefore, right or wrong, *Thou shalt surely die.* This outcry of the priests and prophets raised the mob, and *all the people were gathered together against Jeremiah* in a popular tumult, ready to pull him to pieces, were *gathered about him* (so some read it); they flocked together, some crying one thing and some another. The people that were at first present were hot against him (*v.* 8), but their clamours drew more together, only to see what the matter was.

II. He is arraigned and indicted for it before the highest court of judicature they had. Here, 1. The *princes of Judah* were his judges, *v.* 10. Those that filled the thrones of judgment, *the thrones of the house of David,* the elders of Israel, they, hearing of this tumult in the temple, *came up from the king's house,* where they usually sat near the court, *to the house of the Lord,* to enquire into this matter, and to see that nothing was done disorderly. They *sat down in the entry of the new gate of the Lord's house,* and held a court, as it were, by a special commission of *Oyer and Terminer.* 2. The *priests and prophets* were his prosecutors and accusers, and were violently set against him. They appealed to *the princes,* and *to all the people,* to the court and the jury, whether *this man* were not *worthy to die, v.* 11. The corrupt priests and counterfeit prophets have always been the most bitter enemies of the prophets of the Lord; they had ends of their own to serve, which they

thought such preaching as this would be an obstruction to. When Jeremiah prophesied in the house of the king concerning the fall of the royal family (*ch.* 22:1, etc.), the court, though very corrupt, bore it patiently, and we do not find that they persecuted him for it; but when he comes into the *house of the Lord,* and touches the copyhold of the priests, and contradicts the lies and flatteries of the false prophets, then he is adjudged *worthy to die.* For the prophets *prophesied falsely,* and the *priests bore rule by their means, ch.* 5:31. Observe, When Jeremiah is indicted before the princes the stress of his accusation is laid upon what he said concerning the city, because they thought the princes would be most concerned about that. But concerning the words spoken they appeal to the people, *"You have heard* what he hath said; let it be given in evidence."

III. Jeremiah makes his defence before the princes and the people. He does not go about to deny the words, nor to diminish aught from them; what he has said he will stand to, though it cost him his life; he owns that he had prophesied against *this house* and *this city,* but, 1. He asserts that he did this by good authority, not maliciously nor seditiously, not out of any ill-will to his country nor any disaffection to the government in church or state, but, *The Lord sent me* to prophesy thus: so he begins his apology (*v.* 12), and so he concludes it, for this is that which he resolves to abide by as sufficient to bear him out (*v.* 15): *Of a truth the Lord hath sent me unto you, to speak all these words.* As long as ministers keep closely to the instructions they have from heaven they need not fear the opposition they may meet with from hell or earth. He pleads that he is but a messenger, and, if he faithfully deliver his message, he must bear no blame; but he is a messenger from the Lord, to whom they were accountable as well as he, and therefore might demand regard. If he speak but what God appointed him to speak, he is under the divine protection, and whatever affront they offer to the ambassador will be resented by the Prince that sent him. 2. He shows them that he did it with a good design, and that it was their fault if they did not make a good use of it. It was said, not by way of fatal sentence, but of fair warning; if they would take the warning, they might prevent the execution of the sentence, *v.* 13. Shall I take it ill of a man that tells me of my danger, while I have an opportunity of avoiding it, and not rather return him thanks for it, as the greatest kindness he could do me? *"I have indeed* (says Jeremiah) prophesied *against this city;* but, *if you will now amend your ways and your doings,* the threatened ruin shall be prevented, which was the thing I aimed at in giving you the warning." Those are very unjust who complain of ministers for preaching hell and damnation, when it is only to keep them from that place of torment and to bring them to heaven and salvation. 3. He therefore warns them of their danger if they proceed against him (*v.* 14): *"As for me,* the matter is not great what become of me; *behold, I am in your hand;* you know I am; I neither have any power, nor can make any interest, to oppose you, nor is it so much my concern to save my own life: *do with me as seems meet unto you;* if I be led to the slaughter, it shall be as a lamb." Note, It becomes God's ministers, that are warm in preaching, to be calm in suffering and to behave submissively to the powers that are over them, though they be persecuting powers. But, for themselves, he tells them that it is at their peril if they put him to death: *You shall surely bring innocent blood upon yourselves, v.* 15. They might think that killing the prophet would help to defeat the prophecy, but they would prove wretchedly deceived; it would but add to their guilt and aggravate their ruin. Their own consciences could not but tell them that, if Jeremiah was (as certainly he was) sent of God to bring them this message, it was at their utmost peril if they treated him for it as a malefactor. Those that persecute God's ministers hurt not them so much as themselves.

Verses 16–24

Here is, I. The acquitting of Jeremiah from the charge exhibited against him. He had indeed spoken the words as they were laid in the indictment, but they are not looked upon to be seditious or treasonable, ill-intended or of any bad tendency, and therefore the court and country agree to find him not guilty. The priests and prophets, notwithstanding his rational plea for himself, continued to demand judgment against him; but the princes, and all the people, are clear in it that *this man is not worthy to die* (*v.* 16); for (say they) *he hath spoken to us,* not of himself, but *in the name of the Lord our God.* And are they willing to own that he did indeed speak to them *in the name of the Lord* and that that Lord is their God? Why then did they not amend their ways and doings, and take the method he prescribed to prevent the ruin of their country? If they say, His prophecy is *from heaven,* it may justly be asked, *Why did you not then believe him?* Mt. 21:25. Note, It is a pity that those who are so far convinced of the divine original of gospel preaching as to protect it from the malice of others do not submit to the power and influence of it themselves.

II. A precedent quoted to justify them in acquitting Jeremiah. Some of the *elders of the land,* either the princes before mentioned or the more intelligent men of the people, stood up, and put the assembly in mind of a former case, as is usual with us in giving judgment; for the wisdom of our predecessors is a direction to us. The case referred to is that of Micah. We have extant the book of his prophecy among the minor prophets. 1. Was it thought strange that Jeremiah prophesied against this city and the temple? Micah did so before him, even in the reign of Hezekiah, that reign of reformation, *v.* 18. Micah said it as publicly as Jeremiah had now spoken to the same purport, *Zion shall be ploughed like a field,* the building shall be all destroyed, so that nothing shall hinder but it may be ploughed; *Jerusalem shall become heaps* of ruins, and *the mountain of the house* on which the temple is built shall be *as the high places of the forest,* overrun with briers and thorns. That prophet not only spoke this, but wrote it, and left it on record; we find it, Mic. 3:12. By this it appears that a man may be, as Micah was, a true prophet of the Lord, and yet may prophesy the destruction of Zion and Jerusalem. When we threaten secure sinners with the taking away of the Spirit of God and the kingdom of God from them, and declining churches with the removal of the candlestick, we say no more than what has been said many a time, and what we have warrant from the word of God to say. 2. Was it thought fit by the princes to justify Jeremiah in what he had done? It was what Hezekiah did before them in a like case. Did Hezekiah, and the people of Judah (that is, the representatives of the people, the commons in parliament), did they complain of Micah the prophet? Did they impeach him, or make an act to silence him and put him to death? No; on the contrary, they took the warning he gave them. Hezekiah, that renowned prince, of blessed memory, set a good example before his successors, for he *feared the Lord* (*v.* 19), as Noah, who, being *warned of God of things not seen as yet,* was *moved with fear.* Micah's preaching drove him to his knees; he *besought the Lord* to turn away the judgment threatened and to be reconciled to them, and he found it was not in vain to do so, for *the Lord repented him of the evil* and returned in mercy to them; he sent an angel, who routed the army of the Assyrians, that threatened to plough *Zion like a field.* Hezekiah got good by the preaching, and then you may be sure he would do no harm to the preacher. These elders conclude that it would be of dangerous consequence to the state if they should gratify the importunity of the priests and prophets in putting Jeremiah to death: *Thus might we procure great evil against our souls.* Note, It is good to deter ourselves from sin with the consideration of the mischief we shall certainly do to ourselves by it and the irreparable damage it will be to our own souls.

III. Here is an instance of another prophet that was put to death by Jehoiakim for prophesying as Jeremiah had done, *v.* 20, etc. Some make this to be urged by the prosecutors, as a case that favoured the prosecution, a modern case, in which speaking such words as Jeremiah had spoken was adjudged treason. Others think that the elders, who were advocates for Jeremiah, alleged this to show that thus they might *procure great evil against their souls,* for it would be adding sin to sin. Jehoiakim, the present king, had slain one prophet already; let them not fill up the measure by slaying another. Hezekiah, who protected Micah, prospered; but did Jehoiakim prosper who slew Urijah? No; they all saw the contrary. As good examples, and the good consequences of them, should encourage us in that which is good, so the examples of bad men, and the bad consequences of them, should deter us from that which is evil. But some good interpreters take this narrative from the historian that penned the book, Jeremiah himself, or Baruch, who, to make Jeremiah's deliverance by means of the princes the more wonderful, takes notice of this that happened about the same time; for both were in the reign of Jehoiakim, and this *in the beginning of his reign, v.* 1. Observe, 1. Urijah's prophecy. It was *against this city, and this land, according to all the words of Jeremiah.* The prophets of the Lord agreed in their testimony, and one would have thought that out of the mouth of so many witnesses the word would be regarded. 2. The prosecution of him for it, *v.* 21. Jehoiakim and his courtiers were exasperated against him, and *sought to put him to death;* in this wicked design the king himself was principally concerned. 3. His absconding thereupon: *When he heard* that the king had become his enemy, and sought his life, *he was afraid, and fled, and went in to Egypt.* This was certainly his fault, and an effect of the weakness of his faith, and it sped accordingly. He distrusted God, and his power to protect him and bear him out; he was too much under the power of that *fear of man* which *brings a snare.* It looked as if he durst not stand to what he had said or was ashamed of his Master. It was especially unbecoming him to flee *into Egypt,* and so in effect to abandon the land of Israel and to throw himself quite out of the way of being useful. Note, There are many that have much grace, but they have little courage, that are very honest, but withal very timorous. 4. His execution notwithstanding. Jehoiakim's malice, one would think, might have contented itself with his banishment, and it might suffice to have driven him out of the country; but those are *bloodthirsty* that *hate the upright,* Prov. 29:10. It was the life, that precious life, that he hunted after, and nothing else would satisfy him. So implacable is his revenge that he sends a party of soldiers into Egypt, some hundreds of miles, and they bring him back by force of arms. It would not sufficiently gratify him to have him slain in Egypt, but he must feed his eyes with the bloody spectacle. They *brought him to Jehoiakim,* and he *slew him with the sword,* for aught I know with his own hands. Yet neither did this satisfy his insatiable malice, but he loads the dead body of the good man with infamy, would not allow it the decent respects usually and justly paid to the remains of men of distinction, but cast it into *the graves of the common people,* as if he had not been a prophet of the Lord; thus was the *shield of Saul vilely cast away, as though he had not been anointed with oil.* Thus Jehoiakim hoped both to ruin his reputation with the people, that no heed might be given to his predictions, and to deter others from prophesying in like manner; but in vain; Jeremiah says the same. There is no contending with the word of God. Herod thought he had gained his point when he had cut off John Baptist's head, but found himself deceived when, soon after, he heard of Jesus Christ, and said, in a fright, *This is John the Baptist.*

IV. Here is Jeremiah's deliverance. Though Urijah was lately put to death, and persecutors, when they have tasted the blood of saints, are apt to thirst after more (as Herod, Acts 12:2, 3), yet God wonderfully preserved Jeremiah, though he did not flee, as Urijah did, but stood his ground. Ordinary ministers may use ordinary means, provided they be lawful ones, for their own preservation; but those that had an extraordinary protection. God raised up a friend for Jeremiah, whose hand was with him; he took him by the hand in a friendly way, encouraged him, assisted him, appeared for him. It was *Ahikam the son of Shaphan,* one that was a minister of state in Josiah's time; we read of him, 2 Ki. 22:12. Some think Gedaliah was the son of this Ahikam. He had a great interest, it should seem, among the princes, and he used it in favour of Jeremiah, to prevent the further designs of the priests and prophets against him, who would have had him turned over *into the hand of the people,* not those people (*v.* 16) that had adjudged him innocent, but the rude and insolent mob, whom they could persuade by their cursed insinuations not only to cry, *Crucify him, crucify him,* but to *stone him to death* in a popular tumult; for perhaps Jehoiakim had been so reproached by his own conscience for slaying Urijah that they despaired of making him the tool of their malice. Note, God can, when he pleases, raise up great men to patronize good men; and it is an encouragement to us to trust him in the way of duty that he has all men's hearts in his hands.

CHAPTER 27

Jeremiah the prophet, since he cannot persuade people to submit to God's precept, and so to prevent the destruction of their country by the king of Babylon, is here persuading them to submit to God's providence, by yielding tamely to the king of Babylon, and becoming tributaries to him, which was the wisest course they could now take, and would be a mitigation of the calamity, and prevent the laying of their country waste by fire and sword; the sacrificing of their liberties would be the saving of their lives. I. He gives this counsel, in God's name, to the kings of the neighbouring nations, that they might make the best of bad, assuring them that there was no remedy, but they must serve the king of Babylon; and yet in time there should be relief, for his dominion should last but 70 years (*v.* 1–11). II. He gives this counsel to Zedekiah king of Judah particularly (*v.* 12–15) and to the priests and people, assuring them that the king of Babylon should still proceed against them till things were brought to the last extremity, and a patient submission would be the only way to mitigate the calamity and make it easy (*v.* 16–22). Thus the prophet, if they would but have hearkened to him, would have directed them in the paths of true policy as well as of true piety.

Verses 1–11

Some difficulty occurs in the date of this prophecy. This word is said to come to Jeremiah *in the beginning of the reign of Jehoiakim* (*v.* 1), and yet the messengers, to whom he is to deliver the badges of servitude, are said (*v.* 3) to come to *Zedekiah king of Judah,* who reigned not till eleven years after the beginning of Jehoiakim's reign. Some make it an error of the copy, and think that it should be read (*v.* 1), *In the beginning of the reign of Zedekiah,* for which some negligent scribe, having his eye on the title of the foregoing chapter, wrote *Jehoiakim.* And, if one would admit a mistake any where, it should be here, for Zedekiah is mentioned again (*v.* 12), and the next prophecy is dated the same year, and said to be in the *beginning of the reign of Zedekiah, ch.* 28:1. Dr. Lightfoot solves it thus: In the beginning of Jehoiakim's reign Jeremiah is to make these bonds and yokes, and to put them upon his own neck, in token of Judah's subjection to the king of Babylon, which began at that time; but he is to send them to the neighbouring kings afterwards in the reign of Zedekiah, of whose succession to Jehoiakim, and the ambassadors sent to him, mention is made by way of prediction.

I. Jeremiah is to prepare a sign of the general reduction of all these countries into subjection to the king of Babylon (*v.* 2): *Make thee bonds and yokes,* yokes with bonds to fasten them, that the beast may not slip his neck out of the yoke. Into these the prophet must put his own neck to make them taken notice of as a prophetic representation; for every one would enquire, What is the meaning of Jeremiah's yokes? We find him with one on, *ch.* 28:10. Hereby he intimated that he advised them to nothing but what he was resolved to do himself; for he was not one of those that *bind heavy burdens* on others, which they themselves will not *touch with one of their fingers.* Ministers must thus lay themselves under the weight and obligation of what they preach to others.

II. He is to send this, with a sermon annexed to it, to all the neighbouring princes; those are mentioned (*v.* 3) that lay next to the land of Canaan. It should seem, there was a treaty of alliance on foot between the king of Judah and all those other kings. Jerusalem was the place appointed for the treaty. Thither they all sent their plenipotentiaries; and it was agreed that they should bind themselves in a league offensive and defensive, to stand by one another, in opposition to the growing threatening greatness of the king of Babylon, and to reduce his exorbitant power. They had great confidence in their strength thus united, and were ready to call themselves the high allies; but, when the envoys were returning to their respective masters with the ratification of this treaty, Jeremiah gives each of them a yoke to carry to his master, to signify to him that he must either by consent or by compulsion become a servant to the king of Babylon, let him choose which he will. In the sermon upon this sign, 1. God asserts his own indisputable right to dispose of kingdoms as he pleases, *v.* 5. He is the Creator of all things; he *made the earth* at first, established it, and it abides: it is still the same, though *one generation passes away and another comes.* He still by a continued creation produces *man and beast upon the ground,* and it is by his *great power* and *outstretched arm.* His arm has infinite strength, though it be stretched out.

Upon this account he may give and convey a property and dominion to whomsoever he pleases. As he hath graciously *given the earth to the children of men* in general (Ps. 115:16), so he give to each his share of it, be it more or less. Note, Whatever any have of the good things of this world, it is what God sees fit to give them; we ourselves should therefore be content, though we have ever so little, and not envy any their share, though they have ever so much. 2. He publishes a grant of all these countries to Nebuchadnezzar. Know all men by these presents. *Sciant praesentes et futuri — Let those of the present and those of the future age know.* "This is to certify to all whom it may concern that I have *given all these lands,* with all the wealth of them, into *the hands of the king of Babylon;* even the beasts *of the field,* whether tame or wild, *have I given to him,* parks and pastures; they are all his own." Nebuchadnezzar was a proud wicked man, an idolater; and yet God, in his providence, gives him this large dominion, these vast possessions. Note, The things of this world are not the best things, for God often gives the largest share of them to bad men, that are rivals with him and rebels against him. He was a wicked man, and yet what he had he had by divine grant. Note, Dominion is not founded in grace. Those that have not any colourable title to eternal happiness may yet have a justifiable title to their temporal good things. Nebuchadnezzar is a very bad man, and yet God calls him his servant, because he employed him as an instrument of his providence for the chastising of the nations, and particularly his own people; and for his service therein he thus liberally repaid him. Those whom God makes use of shall not lose by him; much more will he be found the bountiful rewarder of all those that designedly and sincerely serve him. 3. He assures them that they should all be unavoidably brought under the dominion of the king of Babylon for a time (*v.* 7): *All nations,* all these nations and many others, shall serve *him, and his son, and his son's son.* His son was Evil-merodach, and his son's son Belshazzar, in whom his kingdom ceased: then the time of reckoning with his land came, when the tables were turned, and *many nations and great kings,* incorporated into the empire of the Medes and Persians, *served themselves of him,* as before, *ch.* 25:14. Thus Adonibezek was trampled upon himself, as he had trampled on other kings. 4. He threatens those with military execution that stood out and would not submit to the king of Babylon (*v.* 8): That nation that will not *put their neck under his yoke* I will *punish with sword and famine,* with one judgment after another, till it is *consumed by his hand.* Nebuchadnezzar was very unjust and barbarous in invading the rights and liberties of his neighbours thus, and forcing them into a subjection to him; yet God had just and holy ends in permitting him to do so, to punish these nations for their idolatry and gross immoralities. Those that would not serve the God that made them were justly made to serve their enemies that sought to ruin them. 5. He shows them the vanity of all the hopes they fed themselves with, that they should preserve their liberties, *v.* 9, 10. These nations had their prophets too, that pretended to foretell future events by the stars, or by dreams, or enchantments; and they, to please their patrons, and because they would themselves have it so, flattered them with assurances that they *should not serve the king of Babylon.* Thus they designed to animate them to a vigorous resistance; and, though they had no ground for it, they hoped hereby to do them service. But he tells them that it would prove to their destruction; for by resisting they would provoke the conqueror to deal severely with them, to *remove them,* and *drive them out* into a miserable captivity, in which they should all be lost and buried in oblivion. Particular prophecies against these nations that bordered on Israel severally, the ruin of which is here foretold in the general, we shall meet with, *ch.* 48 and 49, and Eze. 25, which had the same accomplishment with this here. Note, *When God judges he will overcome.* 6. He puts them in a fair way to prevent their destruction by a quiet and easy submission, *v.* 11. The nations that will be content to *serve the king of Babylon,* and pay him tribute for seventy years (ten apprenticeships), *those will I let remain still in their own land.* Those that will bend shall not break. Perhaps the dominion of the king of Babylon may bear no harder upon them than that of their own kings had done. It is often more a point of honour than true wisdom to prefer liberty before life. It is not mentioned to the disgrace of Issachar that because he saw *rest* was *good,* and the *land pleasant,* that he might peaceably enjoy it, he bowed *his shoulder to bear,* and *became a servant to tribute* (Gen. 49:14, 15), as these are here advised to do: *Serve the king of Babylon and you shall till the land* and *dwell therein.* Some would condemn this as the evidence of a mean spirit, but the prophet recommends it as that of a meek spirit, which yields to necessity, and by a quiet submission to the hardest turns of Providence makes the best of bad: it is better to do so than by struggling to make it worse.

> — Levius fit patientia
> Quicquid corrigere est nefas. — Hor.
> — When we needs must bear,
> Enduring patience makes the burden light. — Creech.

Many might have prevented destroying providences by humbling themselves under humbling providences. It is better to take up a lighter cross in our way than to pull a heavier on our own head.

Verses 12–22

What was said to all the nations is here with a particular tenderness applied to the nation of the Jews, for whom Jeremiah was sensibly concerned. The case at present stood thus: Judah and Jerusalem had often contested with the king of Babylon, and still were worsted; many both of their valuable persons and their valuable goods were carried to Babylon already, and some of the *vessels of the Lord's house* particularly. Now how this struggle would issue was the question. They had those among them at Jerusalem who pretended to be prophets, who bade them hold out and they should, in a little time, be too hard for the king of Babylon and recover all that they had lost. Now Jeremiah is sent to bid them yield and knock under, for that, instead of recovering what they had lost, they should otherwise lose all that remained; and to press them to this is the scope of these verses.

I. Jeremiah humbly addresses the king of Judah, to persuade him to surrender to the king of Babylon. His act would be the people's and would determine them, and therefore he speaks to him as to them all (*v.* 12): *Bring your necks under the yoke of the king of Babylon and live.* Is it their wisdom to submit to the heavy iron yoke of a cruel tyrant, that they may secure the lives of their bodies? And is it not much more our wisdom to submit to the sweet and easy yoke of our rightful Lord and Master Jesus Christ, that we may secure the lives of our souls? Bring down your spirits to repentance and faith, and that is the way to bring up your spirits to heaven and glory. And with much more cogency and compassion may we expostulate with perishing souls than Jeremiah here expostulates with a perishing people: *"Why will you die by the sword and the famine* — miserable deaths, which you inevitably run yourselves upon, under pretence of avoiding miserable lives?" What God had spoken, in general, of all those that would not submit to the king of Babylon, he would have them to apply to themselves and be afraid of. It were well if sinners would, in like manner, be afraid of the destruction threatened against all those that will not have *Christ to reign over them,* and reason thus with themselves, *"Why should we die* the second death, which is a thousand times worse than that by *sword and famine,* when we might submit and live?"

II. He addresses himself likewise to the priests and the people (*v.* 16), to persuade them to *serve the king of Babylon,* that they might *live,* and might prevent the desolation of the city (*v.* 17): *"Wherefore should it be laid waste,* as certainly it will be if you stand it out?" The priests had been Jeremiah's enemies, and had sought his life to destroy it, yet he approves himself their friend, and seeks their lives, to preserve and secure them, which is an example to us to render *good for evil.* When the *blood-thirsty hate the upright,* yet *the just seek his soul,* and the welfare of it, Prov. 29:10. The matter was far gone here; they were upon the brink of ruin, which they would not have been brought to if they would have taken Jeremiah's counsel; yet he continues his friendly admonitions to them, to save the last stake and manage that wisely, and now at length in this their day to understand the *things that belong to their peace,* when they had but one day to turn them in.

III. In both these addresses he warns them against giving credit to the false prophets that rocked them asleep in their security, because they saw that they loved to slumber: *"Hearken not to the words of the prophets* (*v.* 14), *your prophets, v.* 16. They are not God's prophets; he never sent them; they do not serve him, nor seek to please him; they are yours, for they say what you would have them say, and aim at nothing but to please you." Two things their prophets flattered them into the belief of: — 1. That the power which the king of Babylon had gained over them should now shortly be broken. They said (*v.* 14), *"You shall not serve the king of Babylon;* you need not submit voluntarily, for you shall not be compelled to submit." This they prophesied *in the name of the Lord* (*v.* 15), as if God had sent them to the people on this errand, in kindness to them, that they might not disparage themselves by an inglorious surrender. But it was a lie. They said that God sent them; but that was false; he disowns it: *I have not sent them, saith the Lord.* They said that they should never be brought into subjection to the king of Babylon; but that was false too, the event proved it so. They said that to hold out to the last would be the way to secure themselves and their city; but that was false, for it would certainly end in their being driven out and perishing. So that it was all a lie, from first to last; and the prophets that deceived the people with these lies did, in the issue, but deceive themselves; the blind leaders and the blind followers fell together into the ditch: That *you might perish, you, and the prophets that prophesy unto you,* who will be so far from warranting your security that they cannot secure themselves. Note, Those that encourage sinners to go on in their sinful ways will in the end perish with them. 2. They prophesied that the vessels of the temple, which the king of Babylon had already carried away, should now shortly be brought back (*v.* 16); this they fed the priests with the hopes of, knowing how acceptable it would be to them, who loved the *gold of the temple* better than the *temple that sanctified the gold.* These vessels were taken away when Jeconiah was carried captive into Babylon, *v.* 20. We have the story, and it is a melancholy one, 2 Ki. 24:13, 15; 2 Chr. 36:10. All the *goodly vessels* (that is, all the *vessels of gold* that were *in the house of the Lord*), with all the treasures, were taken as prey, and brought to Babylon. This was grievous to them above any thing; for the temple was their pride and confidence, and the stripping of that was too plain an indication of that which the true prophet told them, that their *God had departed from them.* Their false prophets therefore had no other way to make them easy than by telling them that the king of Babylon should be forced to restore them in a little while. Now here, (1.) Jeremiah bids them think of preserving the vessels that remained by their prayers, rather than of bringing back those that were gone by their prophecies (*v.* 18): *If they be prophets,* as they pretend, and if *the word of the Lord be with them* — if they have any intercourse with heaven and any interest there, let them improve it for the stopping of the progress of the judgment; let them step into the gap, and stand with their censer *between the living and the dead,* between that which is carried away and that which remains, that *the plague may be stayed; let them make intercession with the Lord of hosts,* that the vessels which are left go not after the rest. [1.] Instead of prophesying, let them pray. Note, Prophets must be praying men; by being much in prayer they must make it to appear that they keep up a correspondence with heaven. We cannot think that those do, as prophets, ever hear thence, who do not frequently by prayer send thither. By praying for the safety and prosperity of the sanctuary they must make it to appear that, as becomes prophets, they are of a public spirit; and by the success of their prayers it will appear that God favours them. [2.] Instead of being concerned for the retrieving of what they had lost, they must bestir themselves for the securing of what was left, and take it as a great favour if they can gain that point. When God's judgments are abroad we must not seek great things, but be thankful for a little. (2.) He assures them that even this point should not be gained, but the brazen vessels should go after the golden ones, *v.* 19, 22. Nebuchadnezzar had found so good a booty once that he would be sure to come again and take all he could find, not only in *the house of the Lord,* but in the *king's house.* They shall all be carried to Babylon in triumph, and *there shall they be.* But he concludes with a gracious promise that the time should come when they should all be returned: *Until the day that I visit them in mercy,* according to appointment, and *then I will bring* those vessels *up again, and restore them to this place,* to their place. Surely they were under the protection of a special Providence, else they would have been melted down and put to some other use; but there was to be a second temple, for which they were to be reserved. We read particularly of the return of them, Ezra 1:8. Note, Though the return of the church's prosperity do not come in our time, we must not therefore despair of it, for it will come in God's time. Though those who said, *The vessels of the Lord's house* shall *shortly* be brought again, prophesied a lie (*v.* 16), yet he that said, They shall *at length* be brought again, prophesied the truth. We are apt to set our clock before God's dial, and then to quarrel because they do not agree; but the Lord is a God of judgment, and it is fit that we should wait for him.

CHAPTER 28

In the foregoing chapter Jeremiah had charged those prophets with lies who foretold the speedy breaking of the yoke of the king of Babylon and the speedy return of the vessels of the sanctuary; how here we have his contest with a particular prophet upon those heads. I. Hananiah, a pretender to prophecy, in contradiction to Jeremiah, foretold the sinking of Nebuchadnezzar's power and the return both of the persons and of the vessels that were carried away (*v.* 1–4), and, as a sing of this, he broke the yoke from the neck of Jeremiah (*v.* 10, 11). II. Jeremiah wished his words might prove true, but appealed to the event whether they were so or no, not doubting but that would disprove them (*v.* 5–9). III. The doom both of the deceived and the deceiver is here read. The people that were deceived should have their yoke of wood turned into a yoke of iron (*v.* 12–14), and the prophet that was the deceiver should be shortly cut off by death, and he was so, accordingly, within two months (*v.* 15–17).

Verses 1–9

This struggle between a true prophet and a false one is said here to have happened *in the beginning of the reign of Zedekiah,* and yet *in the fourth year,* for the first four years of his reign might well be called *the beginning,* or former part, of it, because during those years he reigned under the dominion of the king of Babylon and as a tributary to him; whereas the rest of his reign, which might well be called the *latter part* of it, in distinction from that *former part,* he reigned in rebellion against the king of Babylon. In this fourth year of his reign he went in person to Babylon (as we find, *ch.* 51:59), and it is probable that this gave the people some hope that his negotiation in person would put a good end to the war, in which hope the false prophets encouraged them, this Hananiah particularly, who was of Gibeon, a priests' city, and therefore probably himself a priest, as well as Jeremiah. Now here we have,

I. The prediction which Hananiah delivered publicly, solemnly, *in the house of the Lord,* and in the name of the Lord, in an august assembly, *in the presence of the priests and of all the people,* who probably were expecting to have some message from heaven. In delivering this prophecy, he faced Jeremiah, he spoke it to him (*v.* 1), designing to confront and contradict him, as much as to say, "Jeremiah, thou liest." Now this prediction is that the king of Babylon's power, at least his power over Judah and Jerusalem, should be speedily broken, that *within two full years* the vessels of the temple should be brought back, and Jeremiah, and all the captives that were carried away with him, should return; whereas Jeremiah had foretold that the yoke of the king of Babylon should be bound on yet faster, and that the vessels and captives should not return for 70 years, *v.* 2–4. Now, upon the reading of this sham prophecy, and comparing it with the messages that God sent by the true prophets, we may observe what a vast difference there is between them. Here is nothing of the spirit and life, the majesty of style and sublimity of expression, that appear in the discourses of God's prophets, nothing of that divine flame and *flatus.* But that which is especially wanting here is an air of piety; he speaks with a great deal of confidence of the return of their prosperity, but here is not a word of good counsel given them to repent, and reform, and return to God, to pray, and seek his face, that they may be prepared for the favours God had in reserve for them. He promises them temporal mercies, in God's name, but makes no mention of those spiritual mercies which God always promised should go along with them, as *ch.* 24:7, *I will give them a heart to know me.* By all this it appears that, whatever he pretended, he had only the *spirit of the world,* not the *Spirit of God* (1 Co. 2:12), that he aimed to please, not to profit.

II. Jeremiah's reply to this pretended prophecy. 1. He heartily wishes it might prove true. Such an affection has he for his country, and so truly desirous is he of the welfare of it, that he would be content to lie under the imputation of a false prophet, so that their ruin might be prevented. He said, *Amen; the Lord do so; the Lord perform thy words, v.* 5, 6. This was not the first time that Jeremiah had prayed for his people, though he had prophesied against them, and deprecated the judgments which yet he certainly knew would come; as Christ prayed, *Father, if it be possible, let this cup pass from me,* when yet he knew it must not pass from him. Though, as a faithful prophet, he foresaw and foretold the destruction of Jerusalem, yet, as a faithful Israelite, he prayed earnestly for the preservation of it, in obedience to that command, *Pray for the peace of Jerusalem.* Though the will of God's purpose is the rule of prophecy and patience, the will of his precept is the rule of prayer and practice. God himself, though he has determined, does not desire, the death of sinners, but would *have all men to be saved.* Jeremiah often interceded for his people, *ch.* 18:20. The false prophets thought to ingratiate themselves with the people by promising them peace; now the prophet shows that he bore them as great a good-will as their prophets did, whom they were so fond of; and, though he had no warrant from God to promise them peace, yet he earnestly desired it and prayed for it. How strangely were those besotted who caressed those who did them the greatest wrong imaginable by flattering them and persecuted him who did them the greatest service imaginable by interceding for them! See *ch.* 27:18. 2. He appeals to the event, to prove it false, *v.* 7–9. The false prophets reflected upon Jeremiah, as Ahab upon Micaiah, because he never *prophesied good concerning them, but evil.* Now he pleads that this had been the purport of the prophecies that other prophets had delivered, so that it ought not to be looked upon as a strange thing, or as rendering his mission doubtful; for prophets of old prophesied against *many countries and great kingdoms,* so bold were they in delivering the messages which God sent by them, and so far from fearing men, or seeking to please them, as Hananiah did. They made no difficulty, any more than Jeremiah did, of threatening war, famine, and pestilence, and what they said was regarded as coming from God; why then should Jeremiah be run down as *a pestilent fellow, and a sower of sedition,* when he preached no otherwise than God's prophets had always done before him? Other prophets had foretold destruction did not come, which yet did not disprove their divine mission, as in the case of Jonah; for God is gracious, and ready to turn away his wrath from those that turn away from their sins. But the prophet that *prophesied of peace* and prosperity, especially as Hananiah did, absolutely and unconditionally, without adding that necessary proviso, that they do not by wilful sin put a bar in their own door and stop the current of God's favours, will be proved a true prophet only by the accomplishment of his prediction; if it come to pass, then it shall be known that *the Lord has sent him,* but, if not, he will appear to be a cheat and an impostor.

Verses 10–17

We have here an instance,

I. Of the insolence of the false prophet. To complete the affront he designed Jeremiah, *he took the yoke from off his neck* which he carried as a memorial of what he had prophesied concerning the enslaving of the nations to Nebuchadnezzar, and he broke it, that he might give a sign of the accomplishment of this prophecy, as Jeremiah had given of his, and might seem to have conquered him, and to have defeated the intention of his prophecy. See how the lying spirit, in the mouth of this false prophet, mimics the language of the Spirit of truth: *Thus saith the Lord, So will I break the yoke of the king of Babylon,* not only from the neck of this nation, but *from the neck of all nations, within two full years.* Whether by the force of a heated imagination Hananiah had persuaded himself to believe this, or whether he knew it to be false, and only persuaded them to believe it, does not appear; but it is plain that he speaks with abundance of assurance. It is no new thing for lies to be fathered upon the God of truth.

II. Of the patience of the true prophet. Jeremiah quietly *went his way,* and *when he was reviled he reviled not again,* and would not contend with one that was in the height of his fury and in the midst of the priests and people that were violently set against him. The reason why he went his way was not because he had nothing to answer, but because he was willing to stay till God was pleased to furnish him with a direct and immediate answer, which as yet he had not received. He expected that God would send a special message to Hananiah, and he would say nothing till he had received that. *I, as a deaf man, heard not, for thou wilt hear,* and *thou shalt answer, Lord, for me.* It may sometimes be our wisdom rather to retreat than to contend. *Currenti cede furori — Give place unto wrath.*

III. Of the justice of God in giving judgment between Jeremiah and his adversary. Jeremiah went his way, as a man *in whose mouth there was no rebuke,* but God soon put a word into his mouth; for he will appear for those who silently commit their cause to him. 1. The word of God, in the mouth of Jeremiah, is ratified and confirmed. Let not Jeremiah himself distrust the truth of what he had delivered in God's name because it met with such a daring opposition and contradiction. If what we have spoken be the truth of God, we must not unsay it because men gainsay it; for *great is the truth and will prevail.* It will stand, therefore let us stand to it, and not fear that men's unbelief or blasphemy will make it of no effect. Hananiah has broken the *yokes of wood,* but Jeremiah must make for them *yokes of iron,* which cannot be broken (*v.* 13), for (says God) *"I have put a yoke of iron upon the neck of all these nations,* which shall lie heavier, and bind harder, upon them (*v.* 14), *that they may serve the king of Babylon,* and not be able to shake off the yoke however they may struggle, for they shall serve him whether they will or no;" and who is he that can contend with God's counsel? What was said before is repeated again: *I have given him the beasts of the field also,* as if there were something significant in that. Men had by their wickedness made themselves *like the beasts that perish,* and therefore deserved to be ruled by an arbitrary power, as beasts are ruled, and such a power Nebuchadnezzar ruled with; for *whom he would he slew and whom he would he kept alive.* 2. Hananiah is sentenced to die for contradicting it, and Jeremiah, when he has received commission from God, boldly tells him so to his face, though before he received that commission he went away and said nothing. (1.) The crimes of which Hananiah stands convicted are cheating the people and affronting God: *Thou makest this people to trust in a lie,* encouraging them to hope that they shall have peace, which will make their destruction the more terrible to them when it comes; yet this was not the worst: *Thou hast taught rebellion against the Lord;* thou hast taught them to despise all the good counsel given them in God's name by the true prophets, and hast rendered it ineffectual. Those have a great deal to answer for who, by telling sinners that they shall have peace though they go on, harden their hearts in a contempt of the reproofs and admonitions of the word, and the means and methods God takes to bring them to repentance. (2.) The judgment given against him is, *"I will cast thee off from the face of the earth,* as unworthy to live upon it; thou shalt be buried in it. *This year thou shalt die,* and die as a rebel against the Lord, to whom death will come with a sting and a curse." This sentence was executed, *v.* 17. Hananiah died the same year, within two months; for his prophecy is dated the fifth month (*v.* 1) and his death the seventh. Good men may perhaps be suddenly taken off by death in the midst of their days, and in mercy to them, as Josiah was; but this being foretold as the punishment of his sin, and coming to pass accordingly, it may safely be construed as a testimony from Heaven against him and a confirmation of Jeremiah's mission. And, if the people's hearts had not been wretchedly hardened by the deceitfulness of sin, it would have prevented their being further hardened by the deceitfulness of their prophets.

CHAPTER 29

The contest between Jeremiah and the false prophets was carried on before by preaching, here by writing; there we had sermon against sermon, here we have letter against letter, for some of the false prophets are now carried away into captivity in Babylon, while Jeremiah remains in his own country. Now here is, I. A letter which Jeremiah wrote to the captives in Babylon, against their prophets that they had there (*v.* 1–3), in which letter, 1. He endeavours to reconcile them to their captivity, to be easy under it and to make the best of it (*v.* 4–7). 2. He cautions them not to give any credit to their false prophets, who fed them with hopes of a speedy release (*v.* 8, 9). 3. He assures them that God would restore them in mercy to their own land again, at the end of 70 years (*v.* 10–14). 4. He foretels the destruction of those who yet continued, and that they should be persecuted with one judgment after another, and sent at last into captivity (*v.* 15–19). 5. He prophesies the destruction of two of their false prophets that they had in Babylon, that both soothed them up in their sins and set them bad examples (*v.* 20–23), and this is the purport of Jeremiah's letter. II. Here is a letter which Shemaiah, a false prophet in Babylon, wrote to the priests at Jerusalem, to stir them up to persecute Jeremiah (*v.* 24–29), and a denunciation of God's wrath against him for writing such a letter (*v.* 30–32). Such struggles as these have there always been between the seed of the woman and the seed of the serpent.

Verses 1–7

We are here told,

I. That Jeremiah wrote to the captives in Babylon, in the name of the Lord. Jeconiah had surrendered himself a prisoner, with the queen his mother, the chamberlains of his household, called here the *eunuchs,* and many of *the princes of Judah and Jerusalem,* who were at that time the most active men; *the carpenters and smiths* likewise, being demanded, were yielded up, that those who remained might not have any proper hands to fortify their city or furnish themselves with weapons of war. By this tame submission it was hoped that Nebuchadnezzar would be pacified. *Satis est prostrasse leoni — It suffices the lion to have laid his antagonist prostrate;* but the imperious conqueror grows upon their concessions, like Benhadad upon Ahab's, 1 Ki. 20:5, 6. And, not content with this, when these had *departed from Jerusalem* he comes again, and fetches away many more of *the elders, the priests, the prophets, and the people* (*v.* 1), such as he thought fit, or such as his soldiers could lay hands on, and carries them to Babylon. The case of these captives was very melancholy, the rather because they, being thus distinguished from the rest of their brethren who continued in their own land, looked as if they were greater sinners than all men who dwelt at Jerusalem. Jeremiah therefore writes a letter to them, to comfort them, assuring them that they had no reason either to despair of succour themselves or to envy their brethren that were left behind. Note, 1. The word of God written is as truly given by *inspiration of God* as his word spoken was; and this was the proper way of spreading the knowledge of God's will among his *children scattered abroad.* 2. We may serve God and do good by writing to our friends at a distance pious letters of seasonable comforts and wholesome counsels. Those whom we cannot speak to we may write to; that which is written remains. This letter of Jeremiah's was sent to the captives in Babylon by the hands of the ambassadors whom king Zedekiah sent to Nebuchadnezzar, probably to pay him his tribute and renew his submission to him, or to treat of peace with him, in which treaty the captives might perhaps hope that they should be included, *v.* 3. By such messengers Jeremiah chose to send this message, to put an honour upon it, because it was a message from God, or perhaps because there was no settled way of sending letters to Babylon, but as such an occasion as this offered, and then it made the condition of the captives there the more melancholy, that they could rarely hear from their friends and relations they had left behind, which is some reviving and satisfaction to those that are separated from one another.

II. We are here told what he wrote. A copy of the letter at large follows here to *v.* 24. In these verses,

1. He assures them that he wrote in the name of the *Lord of hosts, the God of Israel,* who indited the letter; Jeremiah was but the scribe or amanuensis. It would be comfortable to them, in their captivity, to hear that God is *the Lord of hosts,* of all hosts, and is therefore able to help and deliver them; and that he is the *God of Israel* still, a God in covenant with his people, though he contend with them, and their enemies for the present are too hard for them. This would likewise be an admonition to them to stand upon their guard against all temptations to the idolatry of Babylon, because the *God of Israel,* the God whom they served, is *Lord of hosts.* God's sending to them in this letter might be an encouragement to them in their captivity, as it was an evidence that he had not cast them off, had not abandoned them and disinherited them, though he was displeased with them and corrected them; for, if the Lord had been pleased to kill them, he would not have written to them.

2. God by him owns the hand he had in their captivity: *I have caused you to be carried away, v.* 4 and again, *v.* 7. All the force of the king of Babylon could not have done it if God had not ordered it; nor could he have any power against them but what was given him from above. If God caused them to be carried captives, they might be sure that he neither did them any wrong nor meant them any hurt. Note, It will help very much to reconcile us to our troubles, and to make us patient under them, to consider that they are what God has appointed us to. *I opened not my mouth, because thou didst it.*

3. He bids them think of nothing but settling there; and therefore let them resolve to make the best of it (*v.* 5, 6): *Build yourselves houses and dwell in them,* etc. By all this it is intimated to them, (1.) That they must not feed themselves with hopes of a speedy return out of their captivity, for that would keep them still unsettled and consequently uneasy; they would apply themselves to no business, take no comfort, but be always tiring themselves and provoking their conquerors with the expectations of relief; and their disappointment at last would sink them into despair and make their condition much more miserable than otherwise it would be. Let them therefore reckon upon a continuance there, and accommodate themselves to it as well as they can. Let them *build,* and *plant,* and *marry,* and dispose of their children there as if they were at home in their own land. Let them take a pleasure in seeing their families built up and multiplied; for, though they must expect themselves to die in captivity, yet their children may live to see better days. If they live in the fear of God, what should hinder them but they may live comfortably in Babylon? They cannot but *weep* sometimes *when they remember Zion.* But let not weeping hinder sowing; let them not *sorrow as those that have no hope,* no joy; for they have both. Note, In all conditions of life it is our wisdom and duty to make the best of that which is, and not to throw away the comfort of what we may have because we have not all we would have. We have a natural affection for our native country; it strangely draws our minds; but it is with a *nescio qua dulcedine — we can give no good account of the sweet attraction;* and therefore, if providence remove us to some other country, we must resolve to live easy there, to bring our mind to our condition when our condition is not in every thing to our mind. If the *earth be the Lord's,* then, wherever a child of God goes, he does not go off his Father's ground. *Patria est ubicunque bene est — That place is our country in which we are well off.* If things be not as they have been, instead of fretting at that, we must live in hopes that they will be better than they are. *Non si male nunc, et olim sic erit — Though we suffer now we shall not always.* (2.) That they must not disquiet themselves with fears of intolerable hardships in their captivity. They might be ready to suggest (as persons in trouble are always apt to make the worst of things) that it would be in vain to build houses, for their lords and masters would not suffer them to dwell in them when they had built them, nor to eat the fruit of the vineyards they planted. "Never fear," says God; "if you live peaceably with them, you shall find them civil to you." Meek and quiet people, that work and mind their own business, have often found much better treatment, even with strangers and enemies, than they expected; and God has made his people to be *pitied of those that carry them captives* (Ps. 106:46), and a pity it is but that those who have built houses should dwell in them. Nay,

4. He directs them to seek the good of the country where they were captives (*v.* 7), to pray for it, to endeavour to promote it. This forbids them to attempt any thing against the public peace while they were subjects to the king of Babylon. Though he was a heathen, an idolater, an oppressor, and an enemy to God and his church, yet, while he gave them protection, they must pay him allegiance, and live *quiet and peaceable lives* under him, *in all godliness and honesty,* not plotting to shake off his yoke, but patiently leaving it to God in due time to work deliverance for them. Nay, they must pray to God for the peace of the places where they were, that they might oblige them to continue their kindness to them and disprove the character that had been given their nation, that they were *hurtful to kings and provinces,* and *moved sedition,* Ezra 4:15. Both the wisdom of the serpent and the innocency of the dove required them to be true to the government they lived under: *For in the peace thereof you shall have peace;* should the country be embroiled in war, they would have the greatest share in the calamitous effects of it. Thus the primitive Christians, according to the temper of their holy religion, prayed for the powers that were, though they were persecuting powers. And, if they were to pray for and seek the peace of the land of their captivity, much more reason have we to pray for the welfare of the land of our nativity, where we are a free people under a good government, *that in the peace thereof* we and ours *may have peace.* Every passenger is concerned in the safety of the ship.

Verses 8–14

To make the people quiet and easy in their captivity,

I. God takes them off from building upon the false foundation which their pretended prophets laid, *v.* 8, 9. They told them that their captivity should be short, and therefore that they must not think of taking root in Babylon, but be upon the wing to go back: "Now herein *they deceive you,*" says God; "they *prophesy a lie to you,* though they prophesy *in my name.* But *let them not deceive you,* suffer not yourselves to be deluded by them." As long as we have the word of truth to try the spirits by it is our own fault if we be deceived; for by it we may be undeceived. *Hearken not to your dreams, which you cause to be dreamed.* He means either the dreams or fancies which the people pleased themselves with, and with which they filled their own heads (by thinking and speaking of nothing else but a speedy enlargement when they were awake they caused themselves to dream of it when they were asleep, and then took that for a good omen, and with it strengthened themselves in their vain expectations), or the dreams which the prophets dreamed and grounded their prophecies upon. God tells the people, *They are your dreams,* because they pleased them, were the dreams that they desired and wished for. They *caused them to be dreamed;* for they hearkened to them, and encouraged the prophets to put such deceits upon them, desiring them to prophesy nothing but *smooth things,* Isa. 30:10. They were dreams of their own bespeaking. False prophets would not flatter people in their sins, but that they love to be flattered, and speak smoothly to their prophets that their prophets may speak smoothly to them.

II. He gives them a good foundation to build their hopes upon. We would not persuade people to pull down the house they have built upon the sand, but that there is a rock ready for them to rebuild upon. God here promises them that, though they should not return quickly, they should return at length, *after seventy years be accomplished.* By this it appears that the seventy years of the captivity are not to be reckoned from the last captivity, but the first. Note, Though the deliverance of the church do not come in our time, it is sufficient that it will come in God's time, and we are sure that that is the best time. The promise is that God will visit them in mercy; though he had long seemed to be strange to them, he will come among them, and appear for them, and put honour upon them, as great men do upon their inferiors by coming to visit them. He will put an end to *their captivity,* and *turn away* all the calamities of it. Though they are dispersed, some in one country and some in another, he will *gather them from all the places whither they are driven,* will set up a standard for them all to resort to, and incorporate them again in one body. And though they are at a great distance they shall be brought again to their own land, *to the place whence* they were *carried captive, v.* 14. Now, 1. This shall be the performance of God's promise to them (*v.* 10): *I will perform my good word towards you.* Let not the failing of those predictions which are delivered as from God lessen the reputation of those that really are from him. That which is indeed God's word is a *good word,* and therefore it will be made good, and not one iota or tittle of it shall fall to the ground. *Hath he said, and shall he not do it?* This will make their return out of captivity very comfortable, that it will be the performance of God's good word to them, the product of a gracious promise. 2. This shall be in pursuance of God's purposes concerning them (*v.* 11): *I know the thoughts that I think towards you.* Known unto God are all his works, for known unto him are all his thoughts (Acts 15:18) and his works agree exactly with his thoughts; he does all *according to the counsel of his will.* We often do not know our own thoughts, nor know our own mind, but God is never at any uncertainty within himself. We are sometimes ready to fear that God's designs concerning us are all against us; but he knows the contrary concerning his own people, that they are *thoughts of good and not of evil;* even that which seems evil is designed for good. His thoughts are all working towards the expected end, which he will give in due time. The end they expect will come, though perhaps not when they expect it. Let them have patience till the fruit is ripe, and then they shall have it. He will give them *an end, and expectation,* so it is in the original. (1.) He will give them to see *the end* (the comfortable termination) of their trouble; though it last long, it shall not last always. The *time to favour Zion,* yea, the *set time, will come.* When things are at the worst they will begin to mend; and he will give them to see the glorious perfection of their deliverance; for, as for God, his work is perfect. He that in the beginning finished the *heavens and the earth,* and all the *hosts* of both, will finish all the blessings of both to his people. When he begins in ways of mercy he will *make an end.* God does nothing by halves. (2.) He will give them to see the *expectation,* that *end* which they desire and hope for, and have been long waiting for. He will give them, not the expectations of their fears, nor the expectations of their fancies, but the expectations of their faith, the end which he has promised and which will turn for the best to them. 3. This shall be in answer to their prayers and supplications to God, *v.* 12–14. (1.) God will stir them up to pray: *Then shall you call upon me,* and *you shall go, and pray unto me.* Note, When God is about to give his people the expected good he pours out a spirit of prayer, and it is a good sign that he is coming towards them in mercy. Then, when you see the *expected end* approaching, *then you shall call upon me.* Note, Promises are given, not to supersede, but to quicken and encourage prayer: and when deliverance is coming we must by prayer go forth to meet it. When Daniel understood that the 70 years were near expiring, then he *set his face* with more fervency than ever *to seek the Lord,* Dan. 9:2, 3. (2.) He will then stir up himself to come and save them (Ps. 80:2): *I will hearken unto you,* and *I will be found of you.* God has said it, and we may depend upon it, *Seek and you shall find.* We have a general rule laid down (*v.* 13): *You shall find me when you shall search for me with all your heart.* In seeking God we must search for him, accomplish a diligent search, search for directions in seeking him and encouragements to our faith and hope. We must continue seeking, and take pains in seeking, as those that search; and this we must do with our heart (that is, in sincerity and uprightness), and with our whole heart (that is, with vigour and fervency, putting forth *all that is within us* in prayer), and those who thus *seek God* shall *find him,* and shall find him their bountiful rewarder, Heb. 11:6. He never said to such, *Seek you me in vain.*

Verses 15–23

Jeremiah, having given great encouragement to those among the captives whom he knew to be serious and well-affected, assuring them that God had very kind and favourable intentions concerning them, here turns to those among them who slighted the counsels and comforts that Jeremiah ministered to them and depended upon what the false prophets flattered them with. When this letter came from Jeremiah they would be ready to say, "Why should he make himself so busy, and take upon him to advise us? *The Lord has raised us up prophets in Babylon, v.* 15. We are satisfied with those prophets, and can depend upon them, and have no occasion to hear from any prophets in Jerusalem." See the impudent wickedness of this people; as the prophets, when they prophesied lies, said that they had them from God, so the people, when they invited those prophets thus to flatter them, fathered it upon God, and said that it was the Lord that raised them up those prophets. Whereas we may be sure that those who harden people in their sins, and deceive them with false and groundless hopes of God's mercy, are no prophets of God's raising up. These prophets of their own told them that no more should be carried captive, but that those who were in captivity should shortly return. Now, in answer to this, 1. The prophet here foretells the utter destruction of those who remained still at Jerusalem, notwithstanding what those false prophets said to the contrary: "As for the *king* and *people* that *dwell in the city,* who, you think, will be ready to bid you welcome when you return, you are deceived; they shall be followed with one judgment after another, *sword, famine,* and *pestilence,* which shall cut off multitudes; and the poor and miserable remains shall be *removed into all kingdoms of the earth,*" *v.* 16, 18. And thus God *will make them,* or rather deal with them accordingly, as the salt that has *lost its savour,* which, being good for nothing, is cast to the dunghill, and so are rotten figs. This refers to the vision and the prophecy upon it which we had *ch.* 24. And the reason given for these proceedings against them is the same that has often been given and will justify God in the eternal ruin of impenitent sinners (*v.* 19): *Because they have not hearkened to my words. I called, but they refused.* 2. He foretells the judgment of God upon the false prophets in Babylon, who deceived the people of God there. He calls upon all the children of the captivity, who boasted of them as prophets of God's raising up (*v.* 20): "Stand still, and hear the doom of the prophets you are so fond of." The two prophets are named here, *Ahab* and *Zedekiah, v.* 21. Observe, (1.) The crimes charged upon them — impiety and immorality: They *prophesied lies in God's name* (*v.* 21), and again (*v.* 23), They have *spoken lying words in my name.* Lying was bad, lying to the people of God to delude them into a false hope was worse, but fathering their lies upon the God of truth was worst of all. And no marvel if those that had the face to do that could allow themselves in the gratification of those vile affections to which God, in a way of righteous judgment, *gave them up.* They have done *villainy in Israel,* for *they have committed adultery with their neighbours' wives.* Adultery is villainy in Israel, and in such as pretend to be prophets, who by such wickednesses manifestly disprove their own pretensions. God never sent such profligate wretches on his errands. He is the *Lord God of the holy prophets,* not of such impure ones. Here it appears why they flattered others in their sins — because they could not reprove them without condemning themselves. These lewd practices of theirs they knew how to conceal from the eye of the world, that they might preserve their credit; but *I know* it *and am a witness, saith the Lord.* The most secret sins are known to God; he can see the villainy that is covered with the thickest cloak of hypocrisy, and there is a day coming when he will bring to light all these hidden works of darkness and every man will appear in his own colours. (2.) The judgments threatened against them: *The king of Babylon shall slay them before your eyes;* nay, he shall put them to a miserable death, *roast them in the fire, v.* 22. We may suppose that it was not for their impiety and immorality that Nebuchadnezzar punished them thus severely, but for sedition, and some attempts of their turbulent spirits upon the public peace, and stirring up the people to revolt and rebel. So much of their wickedness shall then be detected, and in such a wretched manner they shall end their days, that their names shall be a curse among the captives in Babylon, *v.* 22. When men would imprecate the greatest evil upon one they hated they would think they could not load them with a heavier curse, in fewer words, than to say, *The Lord make thee like Zedekiah and like Ahab.* Thus were they made ashamed of the prophets they had been proud of, and convinced at last of their folly in hearkening to them. God's faithful prophets were sometimes charged with being the troublers of the land, and as such were tortured and slain; but their names were a blessing when they were gone and their memory sweet, not as these false prophets. As malefactors are attended with infamy and disgrace, so martyrs with glory and honour.

Verses 24–32

We have perused the contents of Jeremiah's letter to the captives in Babylon, who had reason, with a great deal of thanks to God and him, to acknowledge the receipt of it, and lay it up among their treasures. But we cannot wonder if the false prophets they had among them were enraged at it; for it gave them their true character. Now here we are told concerning one of them,

I. How he manifested his malice against Jeremiah. this busy fellow is called *Shemaiah the Nehelamite,* the *dreamer* (so the margin reads it), because all his prophecies he pretended to have received from God in a dream. He had got a copy of Jeremiah's letter to the captives, or had heard it read, or information was given to him concerning it, and it nettled him exceedingly; and he will take pen in hand, and answer it, yea, that he will. But how? He does not write to Jeremiah in justification of his own mission, nor offer any rational arguments for the support of his prophecies concerning the speedy return of the captives; but he writes to the priests, those faithful patrons of the false prophets, and instigates them to persecute Jeremiah. He writes in his own name, not so much as pretending to have the people's consent to it; but, as if he must be dictator to all mankind, he sends a circular letter (as it should seem) among the priests at Jerusalem and the rest of the people, probably by the same messengers that brought the letter from Jeremiah. But it is chiefly directed to Zephaniah, who was either the immediate son of Maaseiah, or of the 24th course of the priests, of which Maaseiah was the father and head. He was not the high priest, but sagan or suffragan to the high priest, or in some other considerable post of command in the temple, as Pashur, *ch.* 20:1. Perhaps he was chairman of that committee of priests that was appointed in a particular manner to take cognizance of those that pretended to be prophets, of which there were very many at this time, and to give judgment concerning them. Now, 1. He puts him and the other priests in mind of the duty of their place (*v.* 26): *The Lord hath made thee priest instead of Jehoiada the priest.* Some think that he refers to the famous Jehoiada, that great reformer in the days of Joash; and (says Mr. Gataker) he would insinuate that this Zephaniah is for spirit and zeal such another as he, and raised up, as he was, for the glory of God and the good of the church; and therefore it was expected from him that he should proceed against Jeremiah. Thus (says he) there is no act so injurious or impious, but that wicked wretches and false prophets will not only attempt it, but colour it also with some specious pretence of piety and zeal for God's glory, Isa. 66:5; Jn. 16:2. Or, rather, it was some other Jehoiada, his immediate predecessor in this office, who perhaps was carried to Babylon among the priests, *v.* 1. Zephaniah is advanced, sooner than he expected, to this place of trust and power, and Shemaiah would have him think that Providence had preferred him that he might persecute God's prophets, that he had come to this government for such a time as this, and that he was unjust and ungrateful if he did not thus improve his power, or, rather, abuse it. Their hearts are wretchedly hardened who can justify the doing of mischief by their having a power to do it. These priests' business was to examine *every man that is mad and makes himself a prophet.* God's faithful prophets are here represented as prophets of their own making, usurpers of the office, and lay-intruders, as men that were mad, actuated by some demon, and not divinely inspired, or as distracted men and men in a frenzy. Thus the characters of the false prophets are thrown upon the true ones; and, if this had been indeed their character, they would have deserved to be bound as madmen and punished as pretenders, and therefore he concludes that Jeremiah must be so treated. He does not bid them examine whether Jeremiah could produce any proofs of his mission and could make it to appear that he was not mad. No; that is taken for granted, and, when once he has had a bad name given him, he must be run down of course. 2. He informs them of the letter which Jeremiah had written to the captives (*v.* 28): *He sent unto us in Babylon,* with the authority of a prophet, saying, *This captivity is long,* and therefore resolve to make the best of it. And what harm was there in this, that it should be objected to him as a crime? The false prophets had formerly said that the captivity would never come, *ch.* 14:13. Jeremiah had said that it would come, and the event had already proved him in the right, which obliged them to give credit to him who now said that it would be long, rather than to those who said that it would be short, but had once before been found liars. 3. He demands judgment against him, taking it for granted that he is *mad,* and *makes himself a prophet.* He expects that they will order him to be put *in prison* and *in the stocks* (*v.* 26), that they will thus punish him, and by putting him to disgrace possess the people with prejudices against him, ruin his reputation, and so prevent the giving of any credit to his prophecies at Jerusalem, hoping that, if they could gain that point, the captives in Babylon would not be influenced by him. Nay, he takes upon him to chide Zephaniah for his neglect (*v.* 27): *Why hast thou not rebuked and restrained Jeremiah of Anathoth?* See how insolent and imperious these false prophets had grown, that, though they were in captivity, they would give law to the priests who were not only at liberty, but in power. It is common for those that pretend to more knowledge than their neighbours to be thus assuming. Now here is a remarkable instance of the hardness of the hearts of sinners, and it is enough to make us all fear *lest our hearts be at any time hardened.* For here we find, (1.) That these sinners would not be convinced by the clearest evidence. God had confirmed his word in the mouth of Jeremiah; it had *taken hold* of them (Zec. 1:6); and yet, because he does not prophesy to them the smooth things they desired, they are resolved to look upon him as not duly called to the office of a prophet. None so blind as those that will not see. (2.) That they would not be reclaimed and reformed by the most severe chastisement. They were now sent into a miserable thraldom for *mocking the messengers of the Lord* and *misusing his prophets.* This was the sin for which God now contended with them; and yet in *their distress they trespass yet more against the Lord,* 2 Chr. 28:22. This very sin they are notoriously guilty of in their captivity, which shows that afflictions will not of themselves cure men of their sins, unless the grace of God work with them, but will rather exasperate the corruptions they are intended to mortify; so true is that of Solomon (Prov. 27:22), *Though thou shouldst bray a fool in a mortar, yet will not his foolishness depart from him.*

II. How Jeremiah came to the knowledge of this (*v.* 29): *Zephaniah read this letter in the ears of Jeremiah.* He did not design to do as Shemaiah would have him, but, as it should seem, had a respect for Jeremiah (for we find him employed in messages to him as a *prophet, ch.* 21:1, 37:3), and therefore protected him. He that continued in his dignity and power stood more in awe of God and his judgments than he that was now a captive. Nay, he made Jeremiah acquainted with the contents of the letter, that he might see what enemies he had even among the captives. Note, It is kindness to our friends to let them know their foes.

III. What was the sentence passed upon Shemaiah for writing this letter. God sent him an answer, for to him Jeremiah committed his cause: it was ordered to be sent not to him, but *to those of the captivity,* who encouraged and countenanced him as if he had been a prophet of God's raising up, *v.* 31, 32. Let them know, 1. That Shemaiah had made fools of them. He promised them peace in God's name, but God did not send him; he forged a commission, and counterfeited the broad seal of Heaven to it, and made the people *to trust in a lie,* and by preaching false comfort to them deprived them of true comfort. Nay, he had not only made fools of them, but, which was worse, he had made traitors of them; he had *taught rebellion against the Lord,* as Hananiah had done, *ch.* 28:16. And, if vengeance shall be taken on those that rebel, much more on those that teach rebellion by their doctrine and example. 2. That at his end *he shall also be a fool* (as the expression is, *ch.* 17:11); his name and family shall be extinct and shall be buried in oblivion; he shall leave no issue behind him to bear up his name; his pedigree shall end in him: *He shall not have a man to dwell among this people;* and neither he nor any that come from him shall *behold the good that I will do for my people.* Note, Those are unworthy to share in God's favours to his church that are not willing to stay his time for them. Shemaiah was angry at Jeremiah's advice to the captives to see to the building up of their families in Babylon, that they might be increased and not diminished, and therefore justly is he written childless there. Those that slight the blessings of God's word deserve to lose the benefit of them. See Amos 7:16, 17.

CHAPTER 30

The sermon which we have in this and the following chapter is of a very different complexion from all those before. The prophet does indeed, by direction from God, change his voice. Most of what he had said hitherto was by way of reproof and threatening; but these two chapters are wholly taken up with precious promises of a return out of captivity, and that typical of the glorious things reserved for the church in the days of the Messiah. The prophet is told not only to preach this, but to write it, because it is intended for the comfort of the generation to come (*v.* 1–3). It is here promised, I. That they should hereafter have a joyful restoration. 1. Though they were now in a great deal of pain and terror (*v.* 4–7). 2. Though their oppressors were very strong (*v.* 8–10). 3. Though a full end was made of other nations, and they were not restored (*v.* 11). 4. Though all means of their deliverance seemed to fail and be cut off (*v.* 12–14). 5. Though God himself had sent them into captivity, and justly, for their sins (*v.* 15, 16). 6. Though all about them looked upon their case as desperate (*v.* 17). II. That after their joyful restoration they should have a happy settlement, that their city should be rebuilt (*v.* 18), their numbers increased (*v.* 19, 20), their government established (*v.* 21), God's covenant with them renewed (*v.* 22), and their enemies destroyed and cut off (*v.* 23, 24).

Verses 1–9

Here, I. Jeremiah is directed to *write* what God had spoken to him, which perhaps refers to all the foregoing prophecies. He must write them and publish them, in hopes that those who had not profited by what he said upon once hearing it might take more notice of it when in reading it they had leisure for a more considerate review. Or, rather, it refers to the promises of their enlargement, which had been often mixed with his other discourses. He must collect them and put them together, and God will now add unto them many like words. He must write them for the generations to come, who should see them accomplished, and thereby have their faith in the prophecy confirmed. He must write them not *in a letter,* as that in the chapter before to the captives, but *in a book,* to be carefully preserved in the archives, or among the public rolls or registers of the state. Daniel understood by these books when the captivity was about coming to an end, Dan. 9:2. He must write them in a book, not in loose papers: *"For the days come,* and are yet at a great distance, when *I will bring again the captivity of Israel and Judah,* great numbers of the ten tribes, with those of the two," *v.* 3. And this prophecy must be written, that it may be read then also, that so it may appear how exactly the accomplishment answers the prediction, which is one end of the writing of prophecies. It is intimated that they shall be *beloved for their fathers' sake* (Rom. 11:28); for *therefore* God will bring them again to Canaan, because it was *the land that he gave to their fathers,* which therefore *they shall possess.*

II. He is directed what to write. The very words are such as the Holy Ghost teaches, *v.* 4. These are the words which God ordered to be written; and those promises which are written by his order are as truly his word as the ten commandments which were written with his finger. 1. He must write a description of the fright and consternation which the people were now in, and were likely to be still in upon every attack that the Chaldeans made upon them, which will much magnify both the wonder and the welcomeness of their deliverance (*v.* 5): *We have heard a voice of trembling* — the shrieks of terror echoing to the alarms of danger. The false prophets told them that they should have *peace,* but *there is fear and not peace,* so the margin reads it. No marvel that when *without are fightings within are fears.* The men, even the men of war, shall be quite overwhelmed with the calamities of their nation, shall sink under them, and yield to them, and shall look like *women in labour,* whose pains come upon them in great extremity and they know that they cannot escape them, *v.* 6. You never heard of a man travailing with child, and yet here you find not here and there a timorous man, but *every man with his hands on his loins,* in the utmost anguish and agony, *as women in travail,* when they see their cities burnt and their countries laid waste. But this pain is compared to that of a woman in travail, not to that of a death-bed, because it shall end in joy at last, and the pain, like that of a travailing woman, shall be forgotten. *All faces* shall be *turned into paleness.* The word signifies not only such paleness as arises from a sudden fright, but that which is the effect of a bad habit of body, the jaundice, or the green sickness. The prophet laments the calamity upon the foresight of it (*v.* 7): *Alas! for that day is great,* a day of judgment, which is called the *great day,* the *great and terrible day of the Lord* (Joel 2:31, Jude 6), great, so that *there has been none like it.* The last destruction of Jerusalem is thus spoken of by our Saviour as unparalleled, Mt. 24:21. *It is even the time of Jacob's trouble,* a sad time, when God's professing people shall be in distress above other people. The whole time of the captivity was a time of Jacob's trouble; and such times ought to be greatly lamented by all that are concerned for the welfare of Jacob and the honour of the God of Jacob. 2. He must write the assurances which God had given that a happy end should at length be put to these calamities. (1.) Jacob's troubles shall cease: *He shall be saved out of them.* Though the afflictions of the church may last long, they shall not last always. *Salvation belongs to the Lord,* and shall be wrought for his church. (2.) Jacob's troublers shall be disabled from doing him any further mischief, and shall be reckoned with for the mischief they have done him, *v.* 8. *The Lord of hosts,* who has all power in his hand, undertakes to do it: *"I will break his yoke from off thy neck,* which has long lain so heavy, and has so sorely galled thee. *I will burst thy bonds* and restore thee to liberty and ease, and thou shalt no more be at the beck and command of strangers, shalt no more serve them, nor shall they any more *serve themselves of thee;* they shall no more enrich themselves either by thy possessions or by thy labours." And, (3.) That which crowns and completes the mercy is that they shall be restored to the free exercise of their religion again, *v.* 9. They shall be delivered from serving their enemies, not that they may live at large and do what they please, but that they may *serve the Lord their God and David their king,* that they may come again into order, under the established government both in church and state. *Therefore* they were brought into trouble and made to *serve their enemies* because they had not *served the Lord their God* as they ought to have done, *with joyfulness and gladness of heart,* Deu. 28:47. But, when the time shall come that they should be *saved out of their trouble,* God will prepare and qualify them for it by giving them a *heart to serve him,* and will make it doubly comfortable by giving them opportunity to serve him. *Therefore* we are *delivered out of the hands of our enemies,* that we may *serve God,* Lu. 1:74, 75. And *then* deliverances out of temporal calamities are mercies indeed to us when by them we find ourselves engaged to and enlarged in the service of God. They shall serve their own God, and neither be inclined, as they had been of old in the day of their apostasy, nor compelled, as they had been of late in the day of their captivity, to serve other gods. They shall serve *David their king,* such governors as God should from time to time set over them, of the line of David (as Zerubbabel), or at least sitting on the *thrones of judgment, the thrones of the house of David,* as Nehemiah. But certainly this has a further meaning. The Chaldee paraphrase reads it, *They shall obey* (or *hearken to*) *the Messiah* (or *Christ*), the *Son of David, their king.* To him the Jewish interpreters apply it. That dispensation which commenced at their return out of captivity brought them to the Messiah. He is called *David their King* because he was the *Son of David* (Mt. 22:42) and he answered to the name, Mt. 20:31, 32. David was an illustrious type of him both in his humiliation and in his exaltation. The covenant of royalty made with David had principal reference to him, and in him the promises of that covenant had their full accomplishment. God gave him the *throne of his father David;* he *raised him up unto them, set him upon the holy hill of Zion.* God is often in the New Testament said to have *raised up Jesus,* raised him up as a King, Acts 3:26; 13:23, 33. Observe, [1.] Those that serve the Lord as their God must also serve *David their King,* must give up themselves to Jesus Christ, to be ruled by him. For all men must *honour the Son as they honour the Father,* and come into the service and worship of God by him as Mediator. [2.] Those that are delivered out of spiritual bondage must make it appear that they are so by giving up themselves to the service of Christ. Those to whom he gives rest must take his yoke upon them.

Verses 10–17

In these verses, as in those foregoing, the deplorable case of the Jews in captivity is set forth, but many precious promises are given them that in due time they should be relieved and a glorious salvation wrought for them.

I. God himself appeared against them: he *scattered* them (*v.* 11); he did *all these things unto them, v.* 15. All their calamities came from his hands; whoever were the instruments, he was the principal agent. And this made their case very sad that God, even their own God, spoke concerning them, to pull down and to destroy. Now, 1. This was intended by him as a fatherly chastisement, and no other (*v.* 11): *"I will correct thee in measure,* or *according to judgment,* with discretion, no more than thou deservest, nay, no more than thou canst well bear." What God does against his people is in a way of correction, and that correction is always moderated and always proceeds from love: *"I will not leave thee altogether unpunished,* as thou art ready to think I should, because of thy relation to me." Note, A profession of religion, though ever so plausible, will be far from securing to us impunity in sin. God is no respecter of persons, but will show his hatred of sin wherever he finds it, and that he hates it most in those that are nearest to him. God here corrects his people *for the multitude of their iniquity,* and *because their sins were increased, v.* 14, 15. Are our sorrows multiplied at any time and do they increase? We must acknowledge that it is because our sins have been multiplied and they have increased. Iniquities grow in us, and therefore troubles grow upon us. But, 2. What God intended as a fatherly chastisement they and others interpreted as an act of hostility; they looked upon him as having *wounded them with the wound of an enemy* and *with the chastisement of a cruel one* (*v.* 14), as if he had designed their ruin, and neither mitigated the correction nor had any mercy in reserve for them. It did indeed seem as if God had dealt thus severely with them, as if he had turned to be their enemy and had fought against them, Isa. 63:10. Job complains that God had become cruel to him and *multiplied his wounds.* When troubles are great and long we have need carefully to watch over our own hearts, that we entertain not such hard thoughts as these of God and his providence. His are the chastisements of a merciful one, not of a cruel one, whatever they may appear.

II. Their friends forsook them, and were shy of them. None of those who had courted them in their prosperity would take notice of them now in their distress, *v.* 13. It is commonly thus when families go to decay; those hang off from them that had been their hangers-on. In two cases we are glad of the assistance of our friends and need their service: — 1. If we be impeached, accused, or reproached, we expect that our friends should appear in vindication of us, should speak a good word for us when we cannot put on a face to speak for ourselves; but here *there is none to plead thy cause,* none to stand up in thy defence, none to intercede for thee with thy oppressors; therefore God will *plead their cause,* for he might well wonder there was none to uphold a people that had been so much the favourites of Heaven, Isa. 63:5. 2. If we be sick, or sore, or wounded, we expect our friends should attend us, advise us, sympathize with us, and, if occasion be, lend a hand for the applying of healing medicines; but here there is none to do that, none to bind up thy wounds, and by counsels and comforts to make proper applications to thy case; nay (*v.* 14), *All thy lovers have forgotten thee;* out of sight out of mind; instead of seeking thee, they forsake thee. Such as this has often been the case of religion and serious godliness in the world; those that from their education, profession, and hopeful beginnings, one might have expected to be its friends and lovers, its patrons and protectors, desert it, forget it, and have nothing to say in its defence, nor will do any thing towards the healing of its wounds. Observe, *Thy lovers have forgotten thee, for I have wounded thee.* When God is against a people who will be for them? Who can be for them so as to do them any kindness? See Job 30:11. Now, upon this account, their case seemed desperate and past relief (*v.* 12): *Thy bruise is incurable, thy wound grievous,* and (*v.* 15) *thy sorrow is incurable.* The condition of the Jews in captivity was such as no human power could redress the grievances of; there they were like a valley full of *dead and dry bones,* which nothing less than Omnipotence can put life into. Who could imagine that a people so diminished, so impoverished, should ever be restored to their own land and re-established there? So many were the aggravations of their calamity that their sorrow would not admit of any alleviation, but they seemed to be hardened in it, and their souls refused to be comforted, till divine consolations proved strong ones, too strong to be borne down even by the floods of grief that overwhelmed them. *Thy sorrow is incurable because thy sins,* instead of being repented of and forsaken, *were increased.* Note, Incurable griefs are owing to incurable lusts. Now in this deplorable condition they are looked upon with disdain (*v.* 17): *They called thee an outcast,* abandoned by all, abandoned to ruin; they said, *This is Zion, whom no man seeks after.* When they looked on the place where the city and temple had been built they called that an outcast; now all was in ruins, there was no resort to it, no residence in it, none asked the way to Zion, as formerly; *no man seeks after* it. When they looked on the people that formerly dwelt in Zion, but were now in captivity (and we read of *Zion dwelling with the daughter of Babylon,* Zec. 2:7), they called them outcasts; these are those who belong to Zion, and are wont to talk much of it and weep at the remembrance of it, but *no man seeks after* them, or enquires concerning them. Note, It is often the lot of Zion to be deserted and despised by those about her.

III. For all this God will work deliverance and salvation for them in due time. Though no other hand, nay, *because* no other hand, can cure their wound, his will, and shall. 1. Though he seemed to stand at a distance from them, yet he assures them of his presence with them, his powerful and gracious presence: *I will save thee, v.* 10. *I am with thee, to save thee, v.* 11. When they are in their troubles he is with them, to save them from sinking under them; when the time has come for their deliverance he is with them, to be ready upon the first opportunity, to save them out of their trouble. 2. Though they were at a distance, remote from their own land, *afar* off *in the land of their captivity,* yet there shall salvation find them out, thence shall it fetch them, them and their *seed,* for they also shall be known among the Gentiles, and distinguished from them, that they may *return, v.* 10. 3. Though they were now full of fears, and continually alarmed, yet the time shall come when they *shall be in rest and quiet,* safe and easy, *and none shall make them afraid, v.* 10. 4. Though the nations into which they were dispersed should be brought to ruin, yet they should be preserved from that ruin (*v.* 11): *Though I make a full end of the nations whither I have scattered thee,* and there might be danger of thy being lost among them, *yet I will not make a full end of thee.* It was promised that in the peace of these nations they should *have peace* (*ch.* 29:7), and yet in the destruction of these nations they should escape destruction. God's church may sometimes be brought very low, but he *will not make a full end of* it, *ch. v.* 10, 18. 5. Though God correct them, and justly, for their sins, their manifold transgressions and mighty sins, yet he will return in mercy to them, and even their sin shall not prevent their deliverance when God's time shall come. 6. Though their adversaries were mighty, God will bring them down, and break their power (*v.* 16): *All that devour thee shall be devoured,* and thus Zion's cause will be pleaded and will be made to appear to all the world a righteous cause. Thus Zion's deliverance will be brought about by the destruction of her oppressors; and thus her enemies will be recompensed for all the injury they have done her; for *there is a God that judges in the earth,* a God *to whom vengeance belongs.* "They *shall every one of them,* without exception, *go into captivity,* and the day will come when *those that* now *spoil thee shall be a spoil."* Those that *lead into captivity shall go into captivity,* Rev. 13:10. This might serve to oblige the present conquerors to use their captives well, because the wheel would turn round, and the day would come when they also should be captives, and let them do now as they would then be done by. 7. Though the wound seem incurable, God will make a cure of it (*v.* 17): *I will restore health unto thee.* Be the disease ever so dangerous, the patient is safe if God undertakes the cure.

IV. Upon the whole matter, they are cautioned against inordinate fear and grief, for in these precious promises there is enough to silence both. 1. They must not tremble as those that have no hope in the apprehension of future further trouble that might threaten them (*v.* 10): *Fear thou not, O my servant Jacob! neither be dismayed.* Note, Those that are God's servants must not give way to disquieting fears, whatever difficulties and dangers may be before them. 2. They must not sorrow as those that have no hope for the troubles which at present they lie under, *v.* 15. *"Why criest thou for thy affliction?* It is true thy carnal confidences fail thee, creatures are physicians of no value, but *I will heal thy wound,* and therefore, *Why criest thou?* Why dost thou fret and complain thus? It is *for thy sin* (*v.* 14, 15), and therefore, instead of repining, thou shouldest be repenting. *Wherefore should a man complain for the punishment of his sins?* The issue will be good at last, and therefore *rejoice in hope."*

Verses 18–24

We have here further intimations of the favour God had in reserve for them after the days of their calamity were over. It is promised,

I. That the city and temple should be rebuilt, *v.* 18. *Jacob's tents,* and *his dwelling places,* felt the effects of *the captivity,* for they lay in ruins when the inhabitants were carried away captives; but, when they have returned, the habitations shall be repaired, and raised up out of their ruins, and therein God will *have mercy upon their dwelling places,* that had been monuments of his justice. Then *the city* of Jerusalem *shall be built upon her own heap,* her own hill, though now it be no better than a ruinous heap. The situation was unexceptionable, and therefore it shall be rebuilt upon the same spot of ground. He that can *make of a city a heap* (Isa. 25:2) can when he pleases *make of a heap a city* again. *The palace* (the temple, God's palace) *shall remain after the manner thereof;* it shall be built after the old model; and the service of God shall be constantly kept up there and attended as formerly.

II. That the sacred feasts should again be solemnized (*v.* 19): *Out of* the city, and the temple, and all the dwelling-places of Jacob, *shall proceed thanksgiving and the voice of those that make merry.* They shall go with expressions of joy to the temple service, and with the like shall return from it. Observe, The voice of *thanksgiving* is the same with *the voice of those that make merry;* for whatever is the matter of our joy should be the matter of our praise. *Is any merry? Let him sing psalms.* What makes us cheerful should make us thankful. *Serve the Lord with gladness.*

III. That the people should be multiplied, and increased, and made considerable: *They shall not be few, they shall not be small,* but shall become numerous and illustrious, and make a figure among the nations; for *I will multiply them* and *I will glorify them.* It is for the honour of the church to have many added to it that shall be saved. This would make them be of some weight among their neighbours. Let a people be ever so much diminished and despised, God can multiply and glorify them. They shall be restored to their former honour: *Their children shall be as aforetime,* playing in the streets (Zec. 8:5); they shall inherit their parents' estates and honours as formerly; *and their congregation shall,* both in civil and sacred things, *be established before me.* There shall be a constant succession of faithful magistrates in the congregation of the elders, to establish that, and of faithful worshippers in the congregation of the saints. As one generation passes away another shall be raised up, and so the *congregation shall be established before* God.

IV. That they shall be blessed with a good government (*v.* 21): *Their nobles* and judges *shall be of themselves,* of their own nation, and they shall no longer be ruled by strangers and enemies; *their governor shall proceed from the midst of them,* shall be one that has been a sharer with them in the afflictions of their captive state; and this has reference to Christ our *governor, David our King* (*v.* 9); he is of ourselves, *in all things made like unto his brethren. And I will cause him to draw near;* this may be understood either, 1. Of the people, Jacob and Israel: *"I will cause* them *to draw near* to me in the temple service, as formerly, to come in to covenant with me, as *my people* (*v.* 22), to *approach to me* in communion; *for who* hath *engaged his heart,* made a covenant with it, and brought it into bonds, *to approach unto me?"* How few are there that do so! None can do it but by the special grace of God *causing them to draw near.* Note, Whenever we approach to God in any holy ordinance we must engage our hearts to do it; the heart must be prepared for the duty, employed in it, and kept closely to it. The heart is the main thing that God looks at and requires; but it is deceitful, and will start aside of a great deal of care and pains be not taken to engage it, to bind this *sacrifice with cords.* Or, 2. It may be understood of the governor; for it is a single person that is spoken of: *Their governor shall* be duly called to his office, shall *draw near* to God to consult him upon all occasions. God *will cause him to approach to* him, for, otherwise, who would engage to take care of so weak a people, and let this ruin come under their hand? But when God has work to do, though attended with many discouragements, he will raise up instruments to do it. But it looks further, to Christ, to him as Mediator. Note, (1.) The proper work and office of Christ, as Mediator, is *to draw near and approach unto* God, not for himself only, but for us, and in our name and stead, as the high priest of our profession. The priests are said to draw nigh to God, Lev. 10:3; 21:17. *Moses drew near,* Ex. 20:21. (2.) God the Father did *cause* Jesus Christ thus *to draw near and approach to* him as Mediator. He commanded and appointed him to do it; he sanctified and sealed him, anointed him for this purpose, accepted him, and declared himself well pleased in him. (3.) Jesus Christ, being caused by the Father to approach unto him as Mediator, did *engage his heart to* do it, that is, he bound and obliged himself to it, *undertook for his heart* (so some read it), for his soul, that, in the fullness of time, it should be *made an offering for sin.* His own voluntary undertaking, in compliance with his Father's will and in compassion to fallen man, engaged him, and then his own honour kept him to it. It also intimates that he was hearty and resolute, free and cheerful, in it, and made nothing of the difficulties that lay in his way, Isa. 63:3–5. (4.) Jesus Christ was, in all this, truly wonderful. We may well ask, with admiration, *Who is this that* thus *engages his heart* to such an undertaking?

V. That they shall be taken again into covenant with God, according to the covenant made with their fathers (*v.* 22): *You shall be my people;* and it is God's good work in us that makes us *to him a people, a people for his name,* Acts 15:14. *I will be your God.* It is his good-will to us that is the summary of that part of the covenant.

VI. That their enemies shall be reckoned with and brought down (*v.* 20): *I will punish all* those *that oppress them,* so that it shall appear to all a dangerous thing to *touch God's anointed,* Ps. 105:15. The last two verses come under this head: *The whirlwind of the Lord shall fall with pain upon the head of the wicked.* These two verses we had before (*ch.* 23:19, 20); *there* they were a denunciation of God's wrath against the wicked hypocrites in Israel; *here* against the wicked oppressors of Israel. The expressions, exactly agreeing, speak the same with that (Isa. 51:22, 23), *I will take the cup of trembling out of thy hand and put it into the hand of those that afflict thee.* The wrath of God against the wicked is here represented to be. 1. Very terrible, like a whirlwind, surprising and irresistible. 2. Very grievous. It *shall fall with pain upon their heads;* they shall be as much hurt as frightened. 3. It shall pursue them. Whirlwinds are usually short, but this shall be *a continuing whirlwind.* 4. It shall accomplish that for which it is sent: *The anger of the Lord shall not return till he have done it.* The purposes of his wrath, as well as the purposes of his love, will all be fulfilled; he will *perform the intents of his heart.* 5. Those that will not lay this to heart now will then be unable to put off the thoughts of it: *In the latter days you shall consider it,* when it will be too late to prevent it.

CHAPTER 31

This chapter goes on with the good words and comfortable words which we had in the chapter before, for the encouragement of the captives, assuring them that God would in due time restore them or their children to their own land, and make them a great and happy nation again, especially by sending them the Messiah, in whose kingdom and grace many of these promises were to have their full accomplishment. I. They shall be restored to peace and honour, and joy and great plenty (*v.* 1–14). II. Their sorrow for the loss of their children shall be at an end (*v.* 15–17). III. They shall repent of their sins, and God will graciously accept them in their repentance (*v.* 18–20). IV. They shall be multiplied and increased, both their children and their cattle, and not be cut off and diminished as they had been (*v.* 21–30). V. God will renew his covenant with them, and enrich it with spiritual blessings (*v.* 31–34). VI. These blessings shall be secured to theirs after them, even to the spiritual seed of Israel for ever (*v.* 35–37). VII. As an earnest of this the city of Jerusalem shall be rebuilt (*v.* 38–40). These exceedingly great and precious promises were firm foundations of hope and full fountains of joy to the poor captives; and we also may apply them to ourselves and mix faith with them.

Verses 1–9

God here assures his people,

I. That he will again take them into a covenant relation to himself, from which they seemed to be cut off. *At the same time,* when God's anger breaks out against the wicked (*ch.* 30:24), his own people shall be owned by him as the children of his love: *I will be the God* (that is, I will show myself to be the God) *of all the families of Israel* (*v.* 1), — not of the two tribes only, but of all the tribes, — not of the house of Aaron only, and the families of Levi, but of all their families; not only their state in general, but their particular families, and the interests of them, shall have the benefit of a special relation to God. Note, The families of good people, in their family capacity, may apply to God and stay themselves upon him as their God. If we and our houses serve the Lord, we and our houses shall be protected and blessed by him, Prov. 3:33.

II. That he will do for them, in bringing them out of Babylon, as he had done for their fathers when he delivered them out of Egypt, and as he had purposed to do when he first took them to be his people. 1. He puts them in mind of what he did for their fathers when he brought them out of Egypt, *v.* 2. They were then, as these were, a *people left of the sword,* that sword of Pharaoh with which he cut off all the male children as soon as they were born (a bloody sword indeed they had narrowly escaped) and that sword with which he threatened to cut them off when he pursued them to the Red Sea. They were then *in the wilderness,* where they seemed to be lost and forgotten, as these were now in a strange land, and yet they found grace in God's sight, were owned and highly honoured by him, and blessed with wonderful instances of his peculiar favour, and he was at this time going *to cause them to rest* in Canaan. Note, When we are brought very low, and insuperable difficulties appear in the way of our deliverance, it is good to remember that it has been so with the church formerly, and yet that it has been raised up from its low estate and has got to Canaan through all the hardships of a wilderness; and God is still the same. 2. They put him in mind of what God had done for their fathers, intimating that they now saw not such signs, and were ready to ask, as Gideon did, *Where are all the wonders that our fathers told us of?* It is true, *The Lord hath appeared of old unto me* (*v.* 3), in Egypt, in the wilderness, hath appeared with me and for me, hath been seen in his glory as my God. The years of ancient times were glorious years; but now it is otherwise; what good will it do us that he *appeared of old* to us when now he is *a God that hides himself* from us? Isa. 45:15. Note, It is hard to take comfort from former smiles under present frowns. 3. To this he answers with an assurance of the constancy of his love: *Yea, I have loved thee,* not only with an ancient love, but *with an everlasting love,* a love that shall never fail, however the comforts of it may for a time be suspended. It is *an everlasting love; therefore have I* extended or *drawn out lovingkindness unto thee* also, as well as to thy ancestors, or, *with lovingkindness have I drawn thee* to myself as thy God, from all the idols to which thou hadst turned aside. Note, It is the happiness of those who are through grace interested in the love of God that it is *an everlasting love* (from everlasting in the counsels of it, *to* everlasting in the continuance and consequences of it), and that nothing can separate them from that love. Those whom God loves with this love he will draw into covenant and communion with himself, by the influences of his Spirit upon their souls; he will *draw them with lovingkindness,* with the cords of a man and bands of love, than which no attractive can be more powerful.

III. That he will again form them into a people, and give them a very joyful settlement in their own land, *v.* 4, 5. Is the church of God his house, his temple? Is it now in ruins? It is so; but, *Again I will build thee, and thou shalt be built.* Are they parts of this building dispersed? They shall be collected and put together again, each in its place. If God undertake to build them, they shall be built, whatever opposition may be given to it? Is *Israel* a beautiful *virgin?* Is she now stripped of her ornaments and reduced to a melancholy state? She is so; but *thou shalt again be adorned* and made fine, adorned *with thy tabrets,* or timbrels, the ornaments of thy chamber, and made merry. They shall resume their harps which had been hung upon the willow-trees, shall tune them, and shall themselves be in tune to make use of them. They shall be adorned with their tabrets, for now their mirth and music shall be seasonable; it shall be a proper time for it, God in his providence shall call them to it, and then it shall be an ornament to them; whereas tabrets, at a time of common calamity, when God called to mourning, were a shame to them. Or it may refer to their use of tabrets in the solemnizing of their religious feasts and their *going forth in dances* then, as the *daughters of Shiloh,* Jdg. 21:19, 21. Our mirth is then indeed an ornament to us when we serve God and honour him with it. Is the joy of the city maintained by the products of the country? It is so; and therefore it is promised (*v.* 5), *Thou shalt yet plant vines upon the mountains of Samaria,* which had been the head city of the kingdom of Israel, in opposition to that of Judah; but they shall now be united (Eze. 37:22), and there shall be such perfect peace and security that men shall apply themselves wholly to the improvement of their ground: *The planters shall plant,* not fearing the soldiers' coming to eat the fruits of what they had planted, or to pluck it up; but they themselves *shall eat them* freely, *as common things,* not forbidden fruits, not forbidden by the law of God (as they were till the fifth year, Lev. 19:23–25), not forbidden by the owners, because there shall be such plenty as to yield enough for all, enough for each.

IV. That they shall have liberty and opportunity to worship God in the ordinances of his own appointment, and shall have both invitations and inclinations to do so (*v.* 6): *There shall be a day,* and a glorious day it will be, when *the watchmen upon Mount Ephraim,* that are set to stand sentinel there, to give notice of the approach of the enemy, finding that all is very quiet and that there is no appearance of danger, shall desire for a time to be discharged from their post, that they may *go up to Zion,* to praise God for the public peace. Or *the watchmen* that tend the vineyards (spoken of *v.* 5) shall stir up themselves, and one another, and all their neighbours, to go and keep the solemn feasts at Jerusalem. Now this implies that the service of God shall be again set up in Zion, that there shall be a general resort to it, with much affection and mutual excitement, as in David's time, Ps. 122:1. But that which is most observable here is *that the watchmen of Ephraim* are forward to promote the worship of God at Jerusalem, whereas formerly *the watchman of Ephraim was hatred against the house of his God* (Hos. 9:8), and, in stead of inviting people to Zion, laid snares for those that set their faces thitherward, Hos. 5:1. Note, God can make those who have been enemies to religion and the true worship of God to become encouragers of them and leaders in them. This promise was to have its full accomplishment in the days of the Messiah, when the gospel should be preached to all these countries, and a general invitation thereby given into the church of Christ, of which Zion was a type.

V. That God shall have the glory and the church both the honour and comfort of this blessed change (*v.* 7): *Sing with gladness for Jacob,* that is, let all her friends and well-wishers rejoice with her, Deu. 32:43. *Rejoice, you Gentiles with his people,* Rom. 15:10. The restoration of Jacob will be taken notice of by all the neighbours, it will be matter of joy to them all, and they shall all join with Jacob in his joys, and thereby pay him respect and put a reputation upon him. Even *the chief of the nations,* that make the greatest figure, shall think it an honour to them to congratulate the restoration of Jacob, and shall do themselves the honour to send their ambassadors on that errand. *Publish you, praise you.* In publishing these tidings, praise the God of Israel, praise the Israel of God, speak honourably of both. The publishers of the gospel must publish it with praise, and therefore it is often spoken of in the *Psalms* as mingled with *praises,* Ps. 67:2, 3; 96:2, 3. What we either bring to others or take to ourselves the comfort of we must be sure to give God the praise of. *Praise you, and say, O Lord! save thy people;* that is, perfect their salvation, go on to save *the remnant of Israel,* that are yet in bondage; as Ps. 126:3, 4. Note, When we are praising God for what he has done we must call upon him for the future favours which his church is in need and expectation of; and in praying to him we really praise him and give him glory; he takes it so.

VI. That, in order to a happy settlement in their own land, they shall have a joyful return out of the land of their captivity and a very comfortable passage homeward (*v.* 8, 9), and this beginning of mercy shall be to them a pledge of all the other blessings here promised. 1. Though they are scattered to places far remote, yet they shall be brought together *from the north country, and from the coasts of the earth;* wherever they are, God will find them out. 2. Though many of them are very unfit for travel, yet that shall be no hindrance to them: *The blind and the lame* shall come; such a good-will shall they have to their journey, and such a good heart upon it, that they shall not make their blindness and lameness an excuse for staying where they are. There companions will be ready to help them, will be *eyes to the blind and legs to the lame,* as good Christians ought to be to one another in their travels heavenward, Job 29:15. But, above all, their God will help them; and let none plead that he is blind who has God for his guide, or lame who has God for his strength. *The women with child* are heavy, and it is not fit that they should undertake such a journey, much less those *that travail with child;* and yet, when it is to return to Zion, neither the one nor the other shall make any difficulty of it. Note, When God calls we must not plead any inability to come; for he that calls us will help us, will strengthen us. 3. Though they seem to be diminished, and to have become few in numbers, yet, when they come all together, they shall be *a great company;* and so will God's spiritual Israel be when there shall be a general rendezvous of them, though now they are but a little flock. 4. Though their return will be matter of joy to them, yet prayers and tears will be both their stores and their artillery (*v.* 9): *They shall come with weeping and with supplications,* weeping for sin, supplication for pardon; for *the goodness of God* shall *lead them to repentance;* and they shall weep with more bitterness and more tenderness for sin, when they are delivered out of their captivity, than ever they did when they were groaning under it. Weeping and praying do well together; tears put life into prayers, and express the liveliness of the, and prayers help to wipe away tears. *With favours will I lead them* (so the margin reads it); in their journey they shall be compassed with God's favours, the fruits of his favour. 5. Though they have a perilous journey, yet they shall be safe under a divine convoy. Is the country they pass through dry and thirsty? *I will cause them to walk by the rivers of waters,* not the waters of a land-flood, which fail in summer. Is it a wilderness where there is no road, no track? *I will cause them t walk in a straight way,* which they shall not miss. Is it a rough and rocky country? Yet *they shall not stumble.* Note, Whithersoever God gives his people a clear call he will either find them or make them a ready way; and while we are following Providence we may be sure that Providence will not be wanting to us. And, *lastly,* here is a reason given why God will take all this care of his people: *For I am a Father to Israel,* a Father that begat him, and therefore will maintain him, that have the care and compassion of a father for him (Ps. 103:13); *and Ephraim is my first-born;* even *Ephraim,* who, having gone astray from God, was *no more worthy to be called a son,* shall yet be owned as a *first-born,* particularly dear, and heir of a double portion of blessings. The same reason that was given for their release out of Egypt is given for their release out of Babylon; they are freeborn and therefore must not be enslaved, are born to God and therefore must not be the servants of men. Ex. 4:22, 23, *Israel is my son, even my first-born; let my son go that he may serve me.* If we take God for our Father, and join ourselves to *the church of the first-born,* we may be assured that we shall want nothing that is good for us.

Verses 10–17

This paragraph is much to the same purport with the last, publishing to the world, as well as to the church, the purposes of God's love concerning his people. This is a *word of the Lord* which the *nations* must *hear,* for it is a prophecy of a work of the Lord which the nations cannot but take notice of. Let them hear the prophecy, that they may the better understand and improve the performance; and let those that hear it themselves declare it to others, *declare it in the isles afar off.* It will be a piece of news that will spread all the world over. it will look very great in history; let us see how it looks in prophecy.

It is foretold, 1. That those who are dispersed shall be brought together again from their dispersions: *He that scattereth Israel will gather him;* for he knows whither he scattered them and therefore where to find them, *v.* 10. *Una eademque manus vulnus opemque tulit — The hand that inflicted the wound shall heal it.* And when he has gathered him into one body, one fold, he will *keep him, as a shepherd does his flock,* from being scattered again. 2. That those who are sold and alienated shall be redeemed and brought back, *v.* 11. Though the enemy that had got possession of him was *stronger than he,* yet *the Lord,* who is stronger than all. *has redeemed and ransomed him,* not by price, but by power, as of old out of the Egyptians' hands. 3. That with their liberty they shall have plenty and joy, and God shall be honoured and served with it, *v.* 12, 13. When they shall have returned to their own land *they shall come and sing in the high place of Zion;* on the top of that holy mountain they shall sing to the praise and glory of God. We read that they did so when the foundation of the temple was laid there; they *sang together, praising and giving thanks to the Lord,* Ezra 3:11. They *shall flow together to the goodness of the Lord;* that is, they shall flock in great numbers and with great forwardness and cheerfulness, as streams of water, *to the goodness of the Lord,* to the temple where he causes his goodness to pass before his people. They shall come together in solemn assemblies, to *praise him for his goodness,* and to pray for the fruits of it and the continuance of it; they shall come to bless him for his goodness, in giving them *wheat, and wine, and oil, and the young of the flock and of the herd,* which, now that they have obtained their freedom, they have an uncontested property in and the quiet and peaceable enjoyment of, and which therefore they honour God with the first-fruits of and out of which they bring offerings to his altar. Note, It is comfortable to observe the goodness of the Lord in the gifts of common providence, and even in them to taste covenant-love. Having plenty (plenty out of want and scarcity) they shall greatly rejoice, *their soul shall be as a watered garden,* flourishing and fruitful (Isa. 58:11), pleasant and fragrant, and abounding in all good things. Note, Our souls are never valuable as gardens but when they are watered with the dews of God's Spirit and grace. It is a precious promise which follows, and which will not have its full accomplishment any where on this side the height of the heavenly Zion, that *they shall not sorrow any more at all;* for it is only in that new Jerusalem *that all tears shall be wiped away,* Rev. 21:4. However, so far it was fulfilled to the returned captives that they had not any more those causes for sorrow which they had formerly had; and therefore (*v.* 13) *young men and old shall rejoice together;* so grave shall the young men be in their joys as to keep company with the old men, and so transported shall the old men be as to associate with the young. *Salva res est, saltat senex — The state prospers, and the aged dance.* God *will turn their mourning into joy,* their fasts into solemn feasts, Zec. 8:19. It was in the return out of Babylon that those *who sowed in tears* were made to *reap in joy,* Ps. 126:5, 6. Those are comforted indeed whom God comforts, and may forget their troubles when he *makes them* to *rejoice from their sorrow,* not only rejoice after it, but rejoice from it their joy shall borrow lustre from their sorrow, which shall serve as a foil to it; and the more they think of their troubles the more they rejoice in their deliverance. 4. That both the ministers and those they minister to shall have abundant satisfaction in what God gives them (*v.* 14): *I will satiate the soul of the priests with fatness;* there shall be such a plenty of sacrifices brought to the altar that those who *live upon the altar* shall live very comfortably, they and their families shall be *satiated with fatness,* they shall have enough, and that of the best; *and my people shall be satisfied with my goodness,* and shall think there is enough in that to make them happy; and so there is. God's people have an abundant satisfaction in God's goodness, though they have but little of this world. Let them be satisfied of God's lovingkindness, and they will be satisfied with it and desire no more to make them happy. All this is applicable to the spiritual blessings which the redeemed of the Lord enjoy by Jesus Christ, infinitely more valuable than corn, and wine, and oil, and the satisfaction of soul which they have in the enjoyment of them. 5. That those particularly who had been in sorrow for the loss of their children who were carried into captivity should have that sorrow turned into joy upon their return, *v.* 15–17. Here we have, (1.) The sad lamentation which the mothers made for the loss of their children (*v.* 15): *In Ramah was there a voice heard,* at the time when the general captivity was, nothing but *lamentation, and bitter weeping,* more there than in other places, because there Nebuzaradan had the general rendezvous of his captives, as appears, *ch.* 40:1, where we find him sending Jeremiah back from Ramah. *Rachel* is here said to *weep for her children.* The sepulchre of Rachel was between Ramah and Bethlehem. Benjamin, one of the two tribes, and Ephraim, head of the ten tribes, were both descendants from Rachel. She had but two sons, the elder of whom was one for whom his father grieved and*refused to be comforted* (Gen. 37:35); the other she herself called *Benoni — the son of my sorrow.* Now the inhabitants of Ramah did in like manner *grieve for their sons and their daughters* that were carried away (as 1 Sa. 30:6), and such a voice of lamentation was there as, to speak poetically, might even have raised Rachel out of her grave to mourn with them. The tender parents even *refused to be comforted for their children, because they were not,* were not with them, but were in the hands of their enemies; they were never likely to see them any more. This is applied by the evangelists to the great mourning that was at Bethlehem for the murder of the infants there by Herod (Mt. 2:17–18), and this scripture is said to be then fulfilled. They wept for them, *and would not be comforted,* supposing the case would not admit any ground of comfort, *because they were not.* Note, Sorrow for the loss of children cannot but be great sorrow, especially if we so far mistake as to think *they are not.* (2.) Seasonable comfort administered to them in reference hereunto, *v.* 16, 17. They are advised to moderate that sorrow, and to set bounds to it: *Refrain thy voice from weeping and thy eyes from tears.* We are not forbidden to mourn in such a case; allowances are made for natural affection. But we must not suffer our sorrow to run into an extreme, to hinder our joy in God, or take us off from our duty to him. Though we mourn, we must not murmur, nor must we resolve, as Jacob did, to go to the grave mourning. In order to repress inordinate grief, we must consider that *there is hope in our end,* hope that there will be an end (the trouble will not last always), that it will be a happy and — the end will be peace. Note, It ought to support us under our troubles that we have reason to hope they will end well. *The righteous has hope in his death;* that will be the blessed period of his grief and the blessed passage to his joys. *"There is hope for thy posterity"* (so some read it); "though thou mayest not live to see these glorious days thyself, there is hope that thy posterity shall. Though one generation falls in the wilderness, the next shall enter Canaan. Two things thou mayest comfort thyself with the hope of:" — [1.] "The reward of thy work: — *Thy* suffering *work shall be rewarded.* The comforts of the deliverance shall be sufficient to balance all the grievances of thy captivity." God makes his people *glad according to the days wherein he has afflicted them,* and so there is a proportion between the joys and the sorrows, as between the reward and the work. The *glory to be revealed,* which the saints hope for in the end, will abundantly countervail *the sufferings of this present time,* Rom. 8:18. [2.] "The restoration of thy children: *They shall come again from the land of the enemy* (*v.* 16); they *shall come again to their own border,*" *v.* 17. *There is hope* that children at a distance may be brought home. Jacob had a comfortable meeting with Joseph after he had despaired of ever seeing him. There is hope concerning children removed by death that they shall *return to their own border,* to the happy lot assigned them in the resurrection, a lot in the heavenly Canaan, that border of his sanctuary. We shall see reason to repress our grief for the death of our children that are taken into covenant with God when we consider the hopes we have of their resurrection to eternal life. They are not lost, but gone before.

Verses 18–26

We have here,

I. Ephraim's repentance, and return to God. Not only Judah, but Ephraim the ten tribes, shall be restored, and therefore shall thus be prepared and qualified for it, Hos. 14:8. *Ephraim shall say, What have I do to any more with idols?* Ephraim the people, is here spoken of as a single person to denote their unanimity; they shall be as one man in their repentance and shall glorify God in it with one mind and one mouth, one and all. it is likewise thus expressed that it might be the better accommodated to particular penitents, for whose direction and encouragement this passage is intended. Ephraim is here brought in weeping for sin, perhaps because Ephraim, the person from whom that tribe had its denomination, was a man of a tender spirit, *mourned for his children many days* (1 Chr. 7:21, 22), and sorrow for sin is compared to that *for an only son.* This penitent is here brought in, 1. Bemoaning himself and the miseries of his present case. True penitents do thus bemoan themselves. 2. Accusing himself, laying a load upon himself as a sinner, a great sinner. He charges upon himself, in the first place, that sin which his conscience told him that he was more especially guilty of at this time, and that was impatience under correction: *"Thou has chastised me;* I have been under the rod, and I needed it, I deserved it; I was justly chastised, chastised *as a bullock,* who would never have felt the goad if he had not first rebelled against the yoke." True penitents look upon their afflictions as fatherly chastisements: *"Thou hast chastised me and I was chastised;* that is, it was well that I was chastised, otherwise I should have been undone; it did me good, or at least was intended to do me good; and yet I have been impatient under it." Or it may intimate his want of feeling under the affliction: *"Thou hast chastised me and I was chastised,* that was all; I was not awakened by it and quickened by it; I looked no further than the chastisement. *I have been* under the chastisement *as a bullock unaccustomed to the yoke,* unruly and unmanageable, kicking against the pricks, *like a wild bull in a net,"* Isa. 51:20. This is the sin he finds himself guilty of now; but (*v.* 19) he reflects upon his former sins and looks as far back as the days of his youth. The discovery of one sin should put us upon searching out more; now he remembers *the reproach of his youth.* Ephraim, as a people, reflect upon the misconduct of their ancestors when they were first formed in a people. It is applicable to particular persons. Note, The sin of our youth was the reproach of our youth, and we ought often to remember it against ourselves and to bear it in a penitential sorrow and shame. 3. He is here brought in angry at himself, having a holy indignation at himself for his sin and folly: He *smote upon his thigh,* as the publican upon his breast. He was even amazed at himself, and at his own stupidity and frowardness: He *was ashamed, yea even confounded,* could not with any confidence look up to God, nor with any comfort reflect upon himself. 4. He is here recommending himself to the mercy and grace of God. He finds he is bent to backslide from God, and cannot by any power of his own keep himself close with God, much less, when he has revolted, bring himself back to God, and therefore he prays, *Turn thou me and I shall be turned,* which implies that unless God do turn him by his grace he shall never be turned, but wander endlessly, that therefore he is very desirous of converting grace, has a dependence upon it, and doubts not but that that grace will be sufficient for him, to help him over all the difficulties that were in the way of his return to God. See *ch.* 17:14, *Heal me and I shall be healed.* God works with power, can make the unwilling willing; if he undertake the conversion of a soul, it will be converted. 5. He is here pleasing himself with the experience he had of the blessed effect of divine grace: *Surely after that I was turned I repented.* Note, All the pious workings of our heart towards God are the fruit and consequence of the powerful working of his grace in us. And observe, He was *turned,* he was *instructed,* his will was bowed to the will of God, by the right informing of his judgment concerning the truths of God. Note, The way God takes of converting souls to himself is by opening the eyes of their understandings, and all good follows thereupon: *After that I was instructed* I yielded, *I smote upon my thigh.* When sinners come to a right knowledge they will come to a right way. Ephraim was chastised, and that did not produce the desired effect, it went no further: *I was chastised,* and that was all. But, when the instructions of God's Spirit accompanied the corrections of his providence, then the work was done, then he *smote upon his thigh,* was so humbled for sin as to have no more to do with it.

II. God's compassion on Ephraim and the kind reception he finds with God, *v.* 20. 1. God owns him for a child and a prodigal: *Is Ephraim my dear son? Is he a pleasant child?* Thus when Ephraim bemoans himself God bemoans him, as *one whom his mother comforts,* though she had chidden him, Isa. 66:13. *Is this Ephraim my dear son? Is this that pleasant child?* Is it he that is thus sad in spirit and that complains so bitterly? So it is like that of Saul (1 Sa. 26:17), *Is this thy voice, my son David?* Or, as it is sometimes supplied, *Is not Ephraim my dear son? Is he not a pleasant child?* Yes, now he is, now he repents and returns. Note, Those that have been undutiful backsliding children, if they sincerely return and repent, however they have been under the chastisement of the rod, shall be accepted of God as dear and pleasant children. Ephraim had afflicted himself, but God thus heals him — had abased himself, but God thus honours him; as the returning prod-

igal who thought himself no more worthy to be *called a son,* yet, by his father, had the *best robe* put on him and *a ring on his hand.* 2. He relents towards him, and speaks of him with a great deal of tender compassion: *Since I spoke against him,* by the threatenings of the word and the rebukes of providence, *I do earnestly remember him still,* my thoughts towards him are thoughts of peace. Note, When God afflicts his people, yet he does not forget them; when he casts them out of their land, yet he does not cast them out of sight, nor out of mind. Even then when God is speaking against us, yet he is acting for us, and designing our good in all; and this is our comfort in our affliction, that *the Lord thinks upon us,* though we have forgotten him. *I remember him still,* and therefore *my bowels are troubled for him,* as Joseph's yearned towards his brethren, even when he *spoke roughly* to them. When Israel's afflictions extorted a penitent confession and submission it is said that his soul was grieved for the misery of Israel (Jdg. 10:16), for he always afflicts with the greatest tenderness. It was God's compassion that mitigated Ephraim's punishment: *My heart is turned within me* (Hos. 11:8, 9); and now the same compassion accepted Ephraim's repentance. Ephraim had pleaded (*v.* 18), *Thou art the Lord my God,* therefore to thee will I return, therefore on thy mercy and grace I will depend; and God shows that it was a valid plea and prevailing, for he makes it appear both that he is God and not man and that he is *his God.* 3. He resolves to do him good: *I will surely have mercy upon him, saith the Lord,* Note, God has mercy in store, rich mercy, sure mercy, suitable mercy, for all that in sincerity seek him and submit to him; and the more we are afflicted for sin the better prepared we are for the comforts of that mercy.

III. Gracious excitements and encouragements given to the people of God in Babylon to prepare for their return to their own land. Let them not tremble and lose their spirits; let them not trifle and lose their time; but with a firm resolution and a close application address themselves to their journey, *v.* 21, 22. 1. They must think of nothing but of coming back to their own country, out of which they had been driven: *"Turn again, O virgin of Israel!* a virgin to be again espoused to thy God; *turn again to these thy cities;* though they are laid waste and in ruins, they are *thy cities,* which thy God gave thee, and therefore *turn again* to them." They must be content in Babylon no longer than till they had liberty to return to Zion. 2. They must return the same way that they went, that the remembrance of the sorrows which attended them, or which their fathers had told them of, in such and such places upon the road, the sight of which would, by a local memory, put them in mind of them, might make them the more thankful for their deliverance. Those that have departed from God into the bondage of sin must return by the way in which they went astray, to the duties they neglected, must *do their first works.* 3. They must engage themselves and all that is within them in this affair: *Set thy heart towards the highway;* bring thy mind to it; consider thy duty, the interest, and go about it with a good-will. Note, The way from Babylon to Zion, from the bondage of sin to the glorious liberty of God's children, is a highway; it is right, it is plain, it is safe, it is well-tracked (Isa. 35:8); yet none are likely to walk in it, unless they *set their hearts towards it.* 4. They must furnish themselves with all needful accommodations for the journey: *Set thee up way-marks,* and *make thee high heaps* or *pillars;* send before to have such set up in all places where there is any danger of missing the road. Let those that go first, and are best acquainted with the way, set up such directions for those that follow. 5. They must compose themselves for their journey: *How long wilt thou go about, O backsliding daughter?* Let not their minds fluctuate, or be uncertain about it, but resolve upon it; let them not distract themselves with care and fear; let them not seek about to creatures for assistance, not hurry hither and thither in courting them, which had often been an instance of their backsliding from God; but let them cast themselves upon God, and then let their minds be fixed. 6. They are encouraged to do this by an assurance God gives them that he would *create a new thing* (strange and surprising) *in the earth* (in that land), *a woman shall compass a man.* The church of God, that is weak and feeble as a woman, altogether unapt for military employments and of a timorous spirit (Isa. 54:6), shall surround, besiege, and prevail

against a mighty man. The church is compared to a woman, Rev. 12:1. And, whereas we find *armies compassing the camp of the saints* (Rev. 20:9), now the camp of the saints shall compass them. Many good interpreters understand this *new thing* created in that land to be the incarnation of Christ, which God an eye to in bringing them back to that land, and which had sometimes been given them for a sign, Isa. 7:14; 9:6. *A woman,* the virgin Mary, enclosed in her womb *the Mighty One;* for so *Geber,* the word here used, signifies; and God is called *Gibbor, the Mighty God* (*ch.* 32:18), as also is Christ in Isa. 9:6, where his incarnation is spoken of, as it is supposed to be here. He is *El-Gibbor, the mighty God.* Let this assure them that God would not cast off this people, for that blessing was to be among them, Isa. 65:8.

IV. A comfortable prospect given them of a happy settlement in their own land again. 1. They shall have an interest in the esteem and good-will of all their neighbours, who will give them a good word and put up a good prayer for them (*v.* 23): *As yet* or rather *yet again* (though Judah and Jerusalem have long been an astonishment and a hissing), *this speech shall be used,* as it was formerly, *concerning the land of Judah and the cities thereof, The Lord bless you, O habitation of justice and mountain of holiness!* This intimates that they shall return much reformed and every way better; and this reformation shall be so conspicuous that all about them shall take notice of it. The *cities,* that used to be nests of pirates, shall be *habitations of justice;* the *mountain of Israel* (so the whole land is called, Ps. 78:54), and especially Mount Zion, shall be a *mountain of holiness.* Observe, Justice towards men, and holiness towards God, must go together. Godliness and honesty are what God has joined, and let no man think to put them asunder, not to make one to atone for the want of the other. It is well with a people when they come out of trouble thus refined, and it is a sure presage of further happiness. And we may with great comfort pray for the blessing of God upon those houses that are *habitations of justice,* those cities and countries that are *mountains of holiness.* There the Lord will undoubtedly *command the blessing.* 2. There shall be great plenty of all good things among them (*v.* 24, 25): *There shall dwell in Judah itself,* even in it, though it has now long lain waste, both husbandmen and shepherds, the two ancient and honourable employments of Cain and Abel, Gen. 4:2. It is comfortable dwelling in a *habitation of justice* and a *mountain of holiness.* "And the husbandmen and shepherds shall eat of the fruit of their labours; for I have *satiated the weary and sorrowful soul;"* that is, those that came weary from their journey, and have been long sorrowful in their captivity, shall now enjoy great plenty. This is applicable to the spiritual blessings God has in store for all true penitents, for all that are just and holy; they shall be abundantly satisfied with divine graces and comforts. In the love and favour of God the weary soul shall find rest and the sorrowful soul joy.

V. The prophet tells us what pleasure the discovery of this brought to his mind, *v.* 26. The foresights God had given him sometimes of the calamities of Judah and Jerusalem were exceedingly painful to him (as *ch.* 4:19), but these views were pleasant ones, though at a distance. *"Upon this I awaked,* overcome with joy, which burst the fetters of sleep; and I reflected upon my dream, and it was such as had made *my sleep sweet to me;* I was refreshed, as men are with quiet sleep." Those may sleep sweetly that lie down and rise up in the favour of God and in communion with him. Nor is any prospect in this world more pleasing to good men, and good ministers, than that of the flourishing state of the church of God. What can we see with more satisfaction than *the good of Jerusalem, all the days of our life, and peace upon Israel?*

Verses 27–34

The prophet, having found his sleep sweet, made so by the revelations of divine grace, sets himself to sleep again, in hopes of further discoveries, and is not disappointed; for it is here further promised,

I. That the people of God shall become both numerous and prosperous. Israel and Judah shall be replenished both with men and cattle, as if they were sown with the seed of both, *v.* 27. They shall increase and multiply like a field sown with corn; and this is the product of God's blessing (*v.* 23), for whom God blessed, to them he said, *Be fruit-*

ful. This should be a type of the wonderful increase of the gospel-church. God will build them, and plant them, *v.* 28. He *will watch over them* to do them good; no opportunity shall be lost that may further their prosperity. Every thing for a long time had turned so much against them, and all occurrences did so transpire to ruin them, that it seemed as if God had *watched over them to pluck up and to throw down;* but now every thing that falls out shall happily fall in to strengthen and advance their interests. God will be as ready to comfort those that repent of their sins, and are humbled for them, as he is to punish those that continue in love with their sins, and are hardened in them.

II. That they shall be reckoned with no further for the sins of their fathers (*v.* 29, 30),: *They shall say no more* (they shall have no more occasion to say) that *God visits the iniquity of the parents upon the children,* which God had done in the captivity, for the sins of their ancestors came into the account against them, particularly those of Manasseh: this they had complained of as a hardship. Other scriptures justify God in this method of proceeding, and our Saviour tells the wicked Jews in his days that they should smart for their fathers' sins, because they persisted in them, Mt. 23:35, 36. But it is here promised that this severe dispensation with them should now be brought to an end, that God would proceed no further in his controversy with them for their fathers' sins, but remember for them his covenant with their fathers and do them good according to that covenant: *They shall no more* complain, as they have done, that *the fathers have eaten sour grapes and the children's teeth are set on edge* (which speaks something of an absurdity, and is an invidious reflection upon God's proceedings), but *every one shall die for his own iniquity* still; though God will cease to punish them in their national capacity, yet he will still reckon with particular persons that provoke him. Note, Public salvations will give no impunity, no security, to private sinners: still every man that *eats the sour grapes* shall have his *teeth set on edge.* Note, Those that eat forbidden fruit, how tempting soever it looks, will find it a *sour grape,* and it will *set their teeth on edge;* sooner or later they will feel from it and reflect upon it with bitterness. There is as direct a tendency in sin to make a man uneasy as there is in sour grapes to set the teeth on edge.

III. That God will renew his covenant with them, so that all these blessings they shall have, not by providence only, but by promise, and thereby they shall be both sweetened and secured. But this covenant refers to gospel times, the latter days that *shall come;* for of gospel grace the apostle understands it (Heb. 8:8, 9, etc.), where this whole passage is quoted as a summary of the covenant of grace made with believers in Jesus Christ. Observe, 1. Who the persons are with whom this covenant is made — *with the house of Israel and Judah,* with the gospel church, *the Israel of God* on which *peace shall be* (Gal. 6:16), with the spiritual seed of believing Abraham and praying Jacob. Judah and Israel had been two separate kingdoms, but were united after their return, in the joint favours God bestowed upon them; so Jews and Gentiles were in the gospel church and covenant. 2. What is the nature of this covenant in general: it is a *new covenant* and *not according to the covenant made with them when they came out of Egypt;* not as if that made with them at Mount Sinai were a covenant of nature and innocency, such as was made with Adam in the day he was created; no, that was, for substance, a covenant of grace, but it was a dark dispensation of that covenant in comparison with this in gospel times. Sinners were saved by that covenant upon their repentance, and faith in a Messiah to come, whose blood, confirming that covenant, was typified by that of the legal sacrifices, Ex. 24:7, 8. Yet this may upon many accounts be called new, in comparison with that; the ordinances and promises are more spiritual and heavenly, and the discoveries much more clear. That covenant God made with them when he *took them by the hand,* as they had been blind, or lame, or weak, *to lead them out of the land of Egypt, which covenant they broke.* Observe, It was God that made this covenant, but it was the people that broke it; for our salvation is of God, but our sin and ruin are of ourselves. It was an aggravation of their breach of it that God *was a husband to them,* that he had espoused them to himself; it was a marriage-covenant that was between him and them, which they broke by idolatry, that spiritual adultery. It is a great aggravation of our treacherous departures from God that he has been a husband to us, a loving, tender, careful husband, faithful to us, and yet we false to him. 3. What are the particular articles of his covenant. They all contain spiritual blessings; not, "I will give them the land of Canaan and a numerous issue," but, "I will give them pardon, and peace, and grace, good heads and good hearts." He promises, (1.) That he will incline them to their duty; *I will put my law in their inward part and write it in their heart;* not, I will give them a new law (as Mr. Gataker well observes), for Christ *came not to destroy the law, but to fulfil it;* but the law shall be written in their hearts by the finger of the Spirit as formerly it was written in the tables of stone. God writes his law in the hearts of all believers, makes it ready and familiar to them, at hand when they have occasion to use it, as that which is *written in the heart,* Prov. 3:3. He makes them in care to observe it, for that which we are solicitous about is said to lie near our hearts. He works in them a disposition to obedience, a conformity of thought and affection to the rules of the divine law, as that of the copy to the original. This is here promised, and ought to be prayed for, that our duty may be done conscientiously and with delight. (2.) That he will take them into relation to himself: *I will be their God,* a God all-sufficient to them, *and they shall be my people,* a loyal obedient people to me. God's being to us a God is the summary of all happiness; heaven itself is no more, Heb. 11:16; Rev. 21:3. Our being to him a people may be taken either as the condition on our part (those and those only shall have God to be to them a God that are truly willing to engage themselves to be to him a people) or as a further branch of the promise that God will by his grace make us his people, a *willing people, in the day of his power;* and, whoever are his people, it is his grace that makes them so. (3.) That there shall be an abundance of the knowledge of God among all sorts of people, and this will have an influence upon all good: for those that rightly know God's name will seek him, and serve him, and put their trust in him (*v.* 34): *All shall know me;* all shall be welcome to the knowledge of God and shall have the means of that knowledge; *his ways shall be known upon earth,* whereas, for many ages, *in Judah only was God known.* Many more shall know God than did in the Old Testament times, which among the Gentiles were times of ignorance, the true God being to them an unknown God. The things of God shall in gospel times be made more plain and intelligible, and level to the capacities of the meanest, than they were while Moses had a *veil upon his face.* There shall be such a general knowledge of God that there shall not be so much need as had formerly been of teaching. Some take it as a hyperbolical expression (and the dulness of the Jews needed such expressions to awaken them), designed only to show that the knowledge of God in gospel times should vastly exceed that knowledge of him which they had under the law. Or perhaps it intimates that in gospel times there shall be such great plenty of public preaching, statedly and constantly, by men authorized and appointed to *preach the word in season and out of season,* much beyond what was under the law, that there shall be less need than there was then of fraternal teaching, by a neighbour and a brother. The priests preached but now and then, and in the temple, and to a few in comparison; but now all shall or may know God by frequenting the assemblies of Christians, wherein, through all parts of the church, the good knowledge of God shall be taught. Some give this sense of it (Mr. Gataker mentions it), That many shall have such clearness of understanding in the things of God that they may seem rather to have been taught by some immediate irradiation than by any means of instruction. In short, the things of God shall by the gospel of Christ be brought to a clearer light than ever (2 Tim. 1:10), and the people of God shall by the grace of Christ be brought to a clearer sight of those things than ever, Eph. 1:17, 18. (4.) That, in order to all these blessings, sin shall be pardoned. This is made the reason of all the rest: *For I will forgive their iniquity,* will not impute that to them, nor deal with them according to the desert of that, *will forgive* and forget: *I will remember their sin no more.* It is sin that keeps good things from us, that stops the current of God's favours; let sin betaken away by pardoning mercy, and the obstruction is removed, and divine grace runs down like a river, like a mighty stream.

Verses 35–40

Glorious things have been spoken in the foregoing verses concerning the gospel church, which that epocha of the Jewish church that was to commence at the return from captivity would at length terminate in, and which all those promises were to have their full accomplishment in. But may we depend upon these promises? Yes, we have here a ratification of them, and the utmost assurance imaginable given of the perpetuity of the blessings contained in them. The great thing here secured to us is that while the world stands God will have a church in it, which, though sometimes it may be brought very low, shall yet be raised again, and its interests re-established; it is *built upon a rock, and the gates of hell shall not prevail against it.* Now here are two things offered for the confirmation of our faith in this matter — the building of the world and the rebuilding of Jerusalem.

I. The building of the world, and the firmness and lastingness of that building, are evidences of the power and faithfulness of that God who has undertaken the establishment of his church. *He that built all things* at first *is God* (Heb. 3:4), and the same is he that makes all things now. The constancy of the glories of the kingdom of nature may encourage us to depend upon the divine promise for the continuance of the glories of the kingdom of grace, for *this is as the waters of Noah,* Isa. 54:9. Let us observe here,

1. The glories of the kingdom of nature, and infer thence how happy those are that have this God, the God of nature, to be their God for ever and ever. Take notice, (1.) Of the steady and regular motion of the heavenly bodies, which God is the first mover and supreme director of: *He gives the sun for a light by day* (*v.* 35), not only made it at first to be so, but still gives it to be so; for the light and heat, and all the influences of the sun, continually depend upon its great Creator. He gives *the ordinances of the moon and stars for a light by night;* their motions are called *ordinances* both because they are regular and by rule and because they are determined and under rule. See Job 38:31–33. (2.) Take notice of the government of the sea, and the check that is given to its proud billows: *The Lord of hosts divides the sea,* or (as some read it) *settles the sea, when the waves thereof roar (divide et impera — divide and rule);* when it is most tossed God keeps it within compass (Jer. 5:22), and soon quiets it and makes it calm again. The power of God is to be magnified by us, not only in maintaining the regular motions of the heavens, but in controlling the irregular motions of the seas. (3.) Take notice of the vastness of the heavens and the unmeasurable extent of the firmament; he must needs be a great God who manages such a great world as this is; the *heavens above cannot be measured* (*v.* 37), and yet God fills them. (4.) Take notice of the mysteriousness even of that part of the creation in which our lot is cast and which we are most conversant with. *The foundations of the earth cannot be searched out beneath,* for the Creator *hangs the earth upon nothing* (Job 26:7), and we *know not how the foundations thereof are fastened,* Job 38:6. (5.) Take notice of the immovable stedfastness of all these (*v.* 36): *These ordinances cannot depart from before God;* he has all the hosts of heaven and earth continually under his eye and all the motions of both; he has established them, and they abide, *abide according to his ordinance, for all are his servants,* Ps. 119:90, 91. The heavens are often clouded, and the sun and moon often eclipsed, the earth may quake and the sea be tossed, but they all keep their place, are moved, but not removed. Herein we must acknowledge the power, goodness, and faithfulness of the Creator.

2. The securities of the kingdom of grace inferred hence: we may be confident of this very thing that *the seed of Israel shall not cease from being a nation,* for the spiritual Israel, the gospel church, shall be *a holy nation, a peculiar people,* 1 Pt. 2:9. When Israel according to the flesh is no longer a nation the *children of the promise are counted for the seed* (Rom. 9:8) and God *will not cast off all the seed of Israel,* no, not *for all that they have done,* though they have done very wickedly, *v.* 37. He justly might cast them off, but he will not. Though he cast them out from their land, and cast them down for a time, yet he will not cast them off. Some of them he casts off, but not all; to this the apostle seems to refer (Rom. 11:1), *Hath God cast away his people? God forbid* that we should think so! For (*v.* 5) *at this time there is a remnant,* enough to save

the credit of the promise that God *will not cast off all the seed of Israel,* though many among them throw away themselves by unbelief. Now we may be assisted in the belief of this by considering, (1.) That the God that has undertaken the preservation of the church is a God of almighty power, who *upholds all things by his* almighty *word. Our help stands in his name who made heaven and earth,* and therefore can do any thing. (2.) That God would not take all this care of the world but that he designs to have some glory to himself out of it; and how shall he have it but by securing to himself a church in it, a people that *shall be to him for a name and a praise?* (3.) That if the order of the creation therefore continues firm because it was well-fixed at first, and is not altered because it needs no alteration, the method of grace shall for the same reason continue invariable, as it was a first well settled. (4.) That he who has promised to preserve a church for himself has approved himself faithful to the word which he has spoken concerning the stability of the world. He that is true to his covenant with Noah and his sons, because he established it for an *everlasting covenant* (Gen. 9:9, 16), will not, we may be sure, be false to his covenant with Abraham and his seed, his spiritual seed, for that also is an *everlasting covenant.* Even that which they have done amiss, though they have done much, shall not prevail to defeat the gracious intentions of the covenant. See Ps. 89:30, etc.

II. The rebuilding of Jerusalem which was now in ruins, and the enlargement and establishment of that, shall be an earnest of these great things that God will do for the gospel church, the *heavenly Jerusalem, v.* 38–40. *The days will come,* though they may be long in coming, when, 1. Jerusalem shall be entirely built again, as large as ever it was; the dimensions are here exactly described by the places through which the circumference passed, and no doubt the wall which Nehemiah built, and which, the more punctually to fulfil the prophecy, began about the *tower of Hananeel,* here mentioned (Neh. 3:1), enclosed as much ground as is here intended, though we cannot certainly determine the places here called *the gate of the corner, the hill Gareb,* etc. 2. When built it shall be consecrated to God and to his service. It *shall be built to the Lord* (v. 38), and even the suburbs and fields adjacent *shall be holy unto the Lord.* It shall not be polluted with idols as formerly, but God shall be praised and honoured there; the whole city shall be as it were one temple, one holy place, as the new Jerusalem is, which *therefore* has no temple, because it is all temple. 3. Being thus built by virtue of the promise of God, *it shall not be plucked up, nor thrown down, any more for ever;* that is, it shall continue very long, the time of the new city from the return to its last destruction being fully as long as that of the old from David to the captivity. But this promise was to have its full accomplishment in the gospel church, which, as it is the spiritual Israel, and therefore God will not cast it off, so it is the holy city, and therefore all the powers of men *shall not pluck it up, nor throw it down.* It may lie waste for a time, as Jerusalem did, but shall recover itself, shall weather the storm and gain its point, *and the gates of hell shall not prevail against it.*

CHAPTER 32

In this chapter we have, I. Jeremiah imprisoned for foretelling the destruction of Jerusalem and the captivity of king Zedekiah (v. 1–5). II. We have him buying land, by divine appointment, as an assurance that in due time a happy end should be put to the present troubles (v. 6–15). III. We have his prayer, which he offered up to God upon that occasion (v. 16–25). IV. We have a message which God thereupon entrusted him to deliver to the people. 1. He must foretel the utter destruction of Judah and Jerusalem for their sins (v. 26–35). But, 2. At the same time he must assure them that, though the destruction was total, it should not be final, but that at length their posterity should recover the peaceable possession of their own land (v. 36–44). The predictions of this chapter, both threatenings and promises, are much the same with what we have already met with again and again, but here are some circumstances that are very particular and remarkable.

Verses 1–15

It appears by the date of this chapter that we are now coming very nigh to that fatal year which completed the desolations of Judah and Jerusalem by the Chaldeans. God's judgments came gradually upon them, but, they not meeting him by repentance in the way of his judgments, he proceeded in his controversy till all was laid waste, which was in the eleventh year of Zedekiah; now what

is here recorded happened in the tenth. The king of Babylon's army had now invested Jerusalem and was carrying on the siege with vigour, not doubting but in a little time to make themselves masters of it, while the besieged had taken up a desperate resolution not to surrender, but to hold out to the last extremity. Now,

I. Jeremiah prophesies that both the city and the court shall fall into the hands of the king of Babylon. He tells them expressly that the besiegers shall take the city as a prize, for God, whose city it was in a peculiar manner, will give it into their hands and put it out of his protection (v. 3), — that, though Zedekiah attempt to make his escape, he shall be overtaken, and shall be delivered a prisoner into the hands of Nebuchadnezzar, shall be brought into his presence, to his great confusion and terror, he having made himself so obnoxious by breaking his faith with him, he shall hear the king of Babylon pronounce his doom, and see with what fury and indignation he will look upon him (*His eyes shall behold his eyes, v.* 4), — that Zedekiah shall be carried to Babylon, and continue a miserable captive there, *until God visit him,* that is, till God put an end to his life by a natural death, as Nebuchadnezzar had long before put an end to his days by putting out his eyes. Note, Those that live in misery may be truly said to be visited in mercy when God by death takes them home to himself. And, *lastly,* he foretels that all their attempts to force the besiegers from their trenches shall be ineffectual: *Though you fight with the Chaldeans, you shall not prosper;* how should they, when God did not fight for them? v. 5. See *ch.* 34:2, 3.

II. For prophesying thus he is imprisoned, not in the common gaol, but in the more creditable prison that was within the verge of the palace, *in the king of Judah's house,* and there not closely confined, but in *custodia libera* — *in the court of the prison,* where he might have good company, good air, and good intelligence brought him, and would be sheltered from the abuses of the mob; but, however, it was a prison, and Zedekiah shut him up in it for prophesying as he did, v. 2, 3. So far was he from *humbling himself before Jeremiah,* as he ought to have done (2 Chr. 36:12), that he *hardened himself* against him. Though he had formerly so far owned him to be a prophet as to desire him to *enquire of the Lord for them* (ch 21:2), yet now he chides him for prophesying (v. 3), and shuts him up in prison, perhaps not with design to punish him any further, but only to restrain him from prophesying any further, which was crime enough. Silencing God's prophets, though it is not so bad as mocking and killing them, is yet a great affront to the God of heaven. See how wretchedly the hearts of sinners are hardened by the deceitfulness of sin. Persecution was one of the sins for which God was now contending with them, and yet Zedekiah persists in it even now that he was in the depth of distress. No providences, no afflictions, will of themselves part between men and their sins, unless the grace of God work with them. Nay, some are made worse by those very judgments that should make them better.

III. Being in prison, he purchases from a near relation of his a piece of ground that lay in Anathoth, v. 6, 7, etc. 1. One would not have expected, (1.) That a prophet should concern himself so far in the business of this world; but why not? Though ministers must not entangle themselves, yet they may concern themselves in the affairs of this life. (2.) That one who had neither wife nor children should buy land. We find (ch. 16:2) that he had no family of his own; yet he may purchase for his own use while he lives, and leave it to the children of his relations when he dies. (3.) One would little have thought that a prisoner should be a purchaser; how should he get money beforehand to buy land with? It is probably that he lived frugally, and saved something out of what belonged to him as a priest, which is no blemish at all to his character; but we have no reason to think that the people were kind, or that his being beforehand was owing to their generosity. Nay, (4.) It was most strange of all that he should buy a *piece of land* when he himself knew that the whole land was now to be laid waste and fall into the hands of the Chaldeans, and then what good would this do him? But it was the will of God that he should buy it, and he submitted, though the money seemed to be thrown away. His kinsman came to offer it to him; it was not of his own seeking; he coveted not to lay house to house and field to field,

but Providence brought it to him, and it was probably a good bargain; besides, the *right of redemption* belonged to him (v. 8), and if he refused he would not do the kinsman's part. It is true he might lawfully refuse, but, being a prophet, in a thing of this nature he must do that which would be for the honour of his profession. *It became him to fulfil all righteousness.* It was land that lay within the suburbs of a priests' city, and, if he should refuse it, there was danger lest, in these times of disorder, it might be sold to one of another tribe, which was contrary to the law, to prevent which it was convenient for him to buy it. It would likewise be a kindness to his kinsman, who probably was at this time in great want of money. Jeremiah had but a little, but what he had he was willing to lay out in such a manner as might tend most to the honour of God and the good of his friends and country, which he preferred before his own private interests.

2. Two things may be observed concerning this purchase: —

(1.) How fairly the bargain was made. When Jeremiah knew by Hanameel's coming to him, as God had foretold he would, that *it was the word of the Lord,* that it was his mind that he should make this purchase, he made no more difficulty of it, but *bought the field.* And, [1.] He was very honest and exact in paying the money. He *weighted him the money,* did not press him to take it upon his report, though he was his near kinsman, but weighed it to him, current money. It was *seventeen shekels of silver,* amounting to about forty shillings of our money. The land was probably but a little field and of small yearly value, when the purchase was so low; besides, the *right of inheritance* was in Jeremiah, so that he had only to buy out his kinsman's life, the reversion being his already. Some think this was only the earnest of a greater sum; but we shall not wonder at the smallness of the price if we consider what scarcity there was of money at this time and how little lands were counted upon. [2.] He was very prudent and discreet in preserving the writings. They were subscribed *before witnesses.* One copy was *sealed up,* the other was *open.* One was the original, the other the counterpart; or perhaps that which was *sealed up* was for his own private use, the other that was *open* was to be laid up in the public register of conveyances, for any person concerned to consult. Due care and caution in things of this nature might prevent a great deal of injustice and contention. The deeds of purchase were lodged in the hands of Baruch, before witnesses, and he was ordered to lay them up in an *earthen vessel* (an emblem of the nature of all the securities this world can pretend to give us, brittle things and soon broken), that they might *continue many days,* for the use of Jeremiah's heirs, after the return out of captivity; for they might then have the benefit of this purchase. Purchasing reversions may be a kindness to those that come after us, and a good man thus *lays up an inheritance for his children's children.*

(2.) What was the design of having this bargain made. It was to signify that though Jerusalem was now besieged, and the whole country was likely to be laid waste, yet the time should come when *houses, and fields, and vineyards should be again possessed in this land, v.* 15. As God appointed Jeremiah to confirm his predictions of the approaching destruction of Jerusalem by his own practice in living unmarried, so he now appointed him to confirm his predictions of the future restoration of Jerusalem by his own practice in purchasing this field. Note, It concerns ministers to make it to appear in their whole conversation that they do themselves believe that which they preach to others; and that they may do so, and impress it the more deeply upon their hearers, they must many a time deny themselves, as Jeremiah did in both these instances. God having promised that this land should again come into the possession of his people, Jeremiah will, on behalf of his heirs, put in for a share. Note, It is good to manage even our worldly affairs in faith, and to do common business with an eye to the providence and promise of God. Lucius Florus relates it as a great instance of the bravery of the Roman citizens that in the time of the second Punic war, when Hannibal besieged Rome and was very near making himself master of it, a field on which part of his army lay, being offered to sale at that time, was immediately purchased, in a firm belief that the Roman valour would raise the siege, *lib. ii. cap.* 6. And have not we much more reason to venture our all upon the word of God, and to embark in Zion's interests, which will undoubtedly be the prevailing interests at last? *Non si male nunc et olim sic erit — Though now we suffer, we shall not suffer always.*

Verses 16–25

We have here Jeremiah's prayer to God upon occasion of the discoveries God had made to him of his purposes concerning this nation, to pull it down, and in process of time to build it up again, which puzzled the prophet himself, who, though he delivered his messages faithfully, yet, in reflecting upon them, was greatly at a loss within himself how to reconcile them; in that perplexity he poured out his soul before God in prayer, and so gave himself ease. That which disturbed him was not the bad bargain he seemed to have made for himself in purchasing a field that he was likely to have no good of, but the case of his people, for whom he was still a kind and faithful intercessor, and he was willing to hope that, if God had so much mercy in store for them hereafter as he had promised, he would not proceed with so much severity against them now as he had threatened. Before Jeremiah went to prayer he delivered the deeds that concerned his new purchase to Baruch, which may intimate to us that when we are going to worship God we should get our minds as clear as may be from the cares and incumbrances of this world. Jeremiah was in prison, in distress, in the dark about the meaning of God's providences, and then he prays. Note, Prayer is a salve for every sore. Whatever is a burden to us, we may by prayer cast it upon the Lord and then be easy.

In this prayer, or meditation,

I. Jeremiah adores God and his infinite perfections, and gives him the glory due to his name as the Creator, upholder, and benefactor, of the whole creation, thereby owning his irresistible power, that he can do what he will, and his incontestable sovereignty, that he may do what he will, *v.* 17–19. Note, When at any time we are perplexed about the particular methods and dispensations of Providence it is good for us to have recourse to our first principles, and to satisfy ourselves with the general doctrines of God's wisdom, power, and goodness. Let us consider, as Jeremiah does here, 1. That God is the fountain of all being, power, life, motion, and perfection: He *made the heaven and the earth with his outstretched arm;* and therefore who can control him? Who dares contend with him? 2. That with him nothing is impossible, no difficulty insuperable: *Nothing is too hard for thee.* When human skill and power are quite nonplussed, *with God are strength and wisdom* sufficient to master all the opposition. 3. That he is a God of boundless bottomless mercy; mercy is his darling attribute; it is his goodness that is his glory: "Thou not only art kind, but thou *showest lovingkindness,* not to a few, to here and there one, but *to thousands,* thousands of persons, thousands of generations." 4. That he is a God of impartial and inflexible justice. His reprieves are not pardons, but if in mercy he spares the parents, that they may be led to repentance, yet such a hatred has he to sin, and such a displeasure against sinners, that he *recompenses their iniquity into the bosom of their children,* and yet does them no wrong; so hateful is the unrighteousness of man, and so jealous of its own honour is the righteousness of God. 5. That he is a God of universal dominion and command: He is *the great* God, for he is *the mighty God,* and might among men makes them great. He is *the Lord of hosts,* of all hosts, that *is his name,* and he answers to his name, for all the hosts of heaven and earth, of men and angels, are at his beck. 6. That he contrives every thing for the best, and effects every thing as he contrived it: He is *great in counsel,* so vast are the reaches and so deep are the designs of his wisdom; and he is *mighty in doing,* according to the counsel of his will. Now such a God as this is not to be quarrelled with. His service is to be constantly adhered to and all his disposals cheerfully acquiesced in.

II. He acknowledges the universal cognizance God takes of all the actions of the children of men and the unerring judgment he passes upon them (*v.* 19): *Thy eyes are open upon all the sons of men,* wherever they are, beholding the evil and the good, and upon all *their ways,* both the course they take and every step they take, not as an unconcerned spectator, but as an observing judge, *to give every one according to his ways and according* to his deserts, which are *the fruit of his doings;* for men shall find God as they are found of him.

III. He recounts the great things God had done for his people Israel formerly. 1. He brought them out of Egypt, that house of bondage, with *signs and wonders,* which remain, if not in the marks of them, yet in the memorials of them, *even unto this day;* for it would never be forgotten, not only *in Israel,* who were reminded of it every year by the ordinance of the passover, but *among other men:* all the neighbouring nations spoke of it, as that which redounded exceedingly to the glory of the God of Israel, and made him *a name as at this day.* This is repeated (*v.* 21), that God *brought them forth,* not only with comforts and joys to them, but with glory to himself, *with signs and wonders* (witness the ten plagues), *with a strong hand,* too strong for the Egyptians themselves, *and with a stretched-out arm,* that reached Pharaoh, proud as he was, *and with great terror* to them and all about them. This seems to refer to Deu. 4:34. 2. He brought them into Canaan, that good land, that *land flowing with milk and honey.* He *swore to their fathers to give it them,* and, because he would perform his oath, he did give it to the children (*v.* 22) *and they came in and possessed it.* Jeremiah mentions this both as an aggravation of their sin and disobedience and also as a plea with God to work deliverance for them. Note, It is good for us often to reflect upon the great things that God did for his church formerly, especially in the first erecting of it, that work of wonder.

IV. He bewails the rebellions they had been guilty of against God, and the judgments God had brought upon them for these rebellions. It is a sad account he here gives of the ungrateful conduct of that people towards God. He had done every thing that he had promised to do (they had acknowledged it, 1 Ki. 8:56), but they had *done nothing of all that he commanded them to do* (*v.* 23); they made no conscience of any of *his laws;* they *walked not* in them, paid no respect to any of his calls by his prophets, for they *obeyed not his voice.* And therefore he owns that God was righteous in *causing all this evil to come upon them.* The city is besieged, is attacked *by the sword* without, is weakened and wasted by the *famine* and *pestilence* within, so that it is ready to fall *into the hands of the Chaldeans that fight against it* (*v.* 24); it is *given into their hands, v.* 25. Now, 1. He compares the present state of Jerusalem with the divine predictions, and finds that what God *has spoken* has *come to pass.* God had given them fair warning of it before; and, if they had regarded this, the ruin would have been prevented; but, if they will not do what God has commanded, they can expect no other than that he should do what he had threatened. 2. He commits the present state of Jerusalem to the divine consideration and compassion (*v.* 24): *Behold the mounts,* or *ramparts,* or the *engines* which they make use of to batter the city and beat down the wall of it. And again, *"Behold thou seest it,* and takest cognizance of it. Is this the city that thou has chosen to put thy name there? And shall it be thus abandoned?" He neither complains of God for what he had done nor prescribes to God what he should do, but desires he would behold their case, and is pleased to think that he does behold it. Whatever trouble we are in, upon a personal or public account, we may comfort ourselves with this, that God sees it and sees how to remedy it.

V. He seems desirous to be let further into the meaning of the order God had now given him to purchase his kinsman's field (*v.* 25): *"Though the city is given into the hand of the Chaldeans,* and no man is likely to enjoy what he has, yet *thou hast said unto me, Buy thou the field."* As soon as he understood that it was the mind of God he did it, and made no objections, was not disobedient to the heavenly vision; but, when he had done it, he desired better to understand why God had ordered him to do it, because the thing looked strange and unaccountable. Note, Though we are bound to follow God with an implicit obedience, yet we should endeavour that it may be more and more an intelligent obedience. We must never dispute God's statutes and judgments, but we may and must enquire, *What mean these statutes and judgments?* Deu. 6:20.

Verses 26–44

We have here God's answer to Jeremiah's prayer, designed to quiet his mind and make him easy; and it is a full discovery of the purposes of God's wrath against the present generation and the purposes of his grace concerning the future generations. Jeremiah knew not how to *sing both of mercy and judgment,* but God here teaches to sing unto him of both. When we know not how to reconcile one word of God with another we may yet be sure that both are true, both are pure, both shall be made good, and not one iota or tittle of either shall fall to the ground. When Jeremiah was ordered to buy the field in Anathoth he was willing to hope that God was about to revoke the sentence of his wrath and to order the Chaldeans to raise the siege. "No," says God, "the execution of the sentence shall go on; Jerusalem shall be laid in ruins." Note, Assurances of future mercy must not be interpreted as securities from present troubles. But, lest Jeremiah should think that his being ordered to buy this field intimated that all the mercy God had in store for his people, after their return, was only that they should have the possession of their own land again, he further informs him that that was but a type and figure of those spiritual blessings which should then be abundantly bestowed upon them, unspeakably more valuable than fields and vineyards; so that in this *word of the Lord,* which came to Jeremiah, we have first as dreadful threatenings and then as precious promises as perhaps any we have in the Old Testament; life and death, good and evil, are here set before us; let us consider and choose wisely.

I. The ruin of Judah and Jerusalem is here pronounced. The decree has gone forth, and shall not be recalled. 1. God here asserts his own sovereignty and power (*v.* 27): *Behold, I am Jehovah,* a self-existent self-sufficient being; *I am that I am; I am the God of all flesh,* that is, of all mankind, here called *flesh* because weak and unable to contend with God (Ps. 56:4), and because wicked and corrupt and unapt to comply with God. God is the Creator of all, and makes what use he pleases of all. He that is the God of Israel is the *God of all flesh* and of *the spirits of all flesh,* and, if Israel were cast off, could raise up a people to his name out of some other nation. If he be the *God of all flesh,* he may well ask, *Is any thing too hard for me?* What cannot he do from whom all the powers of men are derived, on whom they depend, and by whom all their actions are directed and governed? Whatever he designs to do, whether in wrath or in mercy, nothing can hinder him nor defeat his designs. 2. He abides by that he had often said of the destruction of Jerusalem by the king of Babylon (*v.* 28): *I will give this city into his hand,* now that he is grasping at it, *and he shall take it* and make a prey of it, *v.* 29. *The Chaldeans shall come and set fire to it,* shall burn it and all the *houses in it,* God's house not excepted, nor the king's neither. 3. He assigns the reason for these severe proceedings against the city that had been so much in his favour. It is sin, it is that and nothing else, that ruins it. (1.) They were impudent and daring in sin. They *offered incense to Baal,* not in corners, as men ashamed or afraid of being discovered, but upon the *tops of their houses* (*v.* 29), in defiance of God's justice. (2.) They designed an affront to God herein. They did it *to provoke me to anger, v.* 29. *They have only provoked me to anger with the works of their hands, v.* 30. They could not promise themselves any pleasure, profit, or honour out of it, but did it on purpose to offend God. And again (*v.* 32), *All the evil which they have done was to provoke me to anger.* They knew he was a jealous God in the matters of his worship, and there they resolved to try his jealousy and dare him to his face. "Jerusalem has been *to me a provocation of my anger and fury," v.* 31. Their conduct in every thing was provoking. (3.) They began betimes, and had continued all along provoking to God: "They have *done evil before me from their youth,* ever since they were first formed into a people (*v.* 30), witness their murmurings and rebellions in the wilderness." And as for Jerusalem, though it was the *holy city,* it has been *a provocation* to the holy God *from the day that they built it, even to this day, v.* 31. O what reason have we to lament the little honour God has from this world, and the great dishonour that is done him, when even in Judah, where *he is known* and *his name is great,* and in Salem where his *tabernacle is,* there was always that found that was a provocation to him! (4.) All orders and degrees of men contributed to the common guilt, and therefore were justly involved in the common ruin. Not only the *children of Israel,* that had revolted from the temple, but the *children of Judah* too, that still adhered to it — not only the common people, the *men of Judah* and *inhabitants of Jerusalem,* but those that should have reproved and restrained sin in others were themselves ringleaders in it, their *kings* and *princes,* their *priests* and *prophets.* (5.) God had again and again called them to repentance, but they turned a deaf ear to his calls, and rudely turned their back on him that called them, though he was their master, to whom they were bound in duty, and their benefactor, to whom they were bound in gratitude and interest, *v.* 33. "*I taught them* better manners, with as much care as ever any tender parent taught a child, *rising up early, in teaching them,* studying to adapt the teaching to their capacities, taking them betimes, when they might have been most pliable, but all in vain; they *turned not the face to me,* would not so much as look upon me, nay, they *turned the back upon me,*" an expression of the highest contempt. *As he called them,* like froward children, *so they went from him,* Hos. 11:2. *They have not hearkened to receive instruction;* they regarded not a word that was said to them, though it was designed for their own good. (6.) There was in their idolatries an impious contempt of God; for (*v.* 34) *they set their abominations* (their idols, which they knew to be in the highest degree abominable to God) *in the house which is called by my name, to defile it.* They had their idols not only in their high places and groves, but even in God's temple. (7.) They were guilty of the most unnatural cruelty to their own children; for they *sacrificed them to Moloch, v.* 35. Thus because they *liked not to retain God in their knowledge,* but *changed his glory* into shame, they were justly given up to vile affections and stripped of natural ones, and their glory was turned into shame. And, (8.) What was the consequence of all this? [1.] They *caused Judah to sin, v.* 35. The whole country was infected with the contagious idolatries and iniquities of Jerusalem. [2.] They brought ruin upon themselves. It was as if they had done it on purpose that God *should remove them from before his face* (*v.* 31); they would throw themselves out of his favour.

II. The restoration of Judah and Jerusalem is here promised, *v.* 36, etc. God will in judgment remember mercy, and there will a time come, a set time, to favour Zion. Observe, 1. The despair to which this people were now at length brought. When the judgment was threatened at a distance they had no fear; when it attacked them they had no hope. They said concerning the city (*v.* 36), *It shall be delivered into the hand of the king of Babylon,* not by any cowardice or ill conduct of ours, but by *the sword, famine, and pestilence.* Concerning the country they said, with vexation (*v.* 43), *It is desolate, without man or beast;* there is no relief, there is no remedy. *It is given into the hand of the Chaldeans.* Note, Deep security commonly ends in deep despair; whereas those that keep up a holy fear at all times have a good hope to support them in the worst of times. 2. The hope that God gives them of mercy which he had in store for them hereafter. Though their carcases must fall in captivity, yet their children after them shall again see this good land and the goodness of God in it. (1.) They shall be brought up from their captivity and shall come and settle again in this land, *v.* 37. They had been under God's *anger and fury, and great wrath;* but now they shall partake of his grace, and love, and great favour. He had dispersed them, and *driven them into all countries.* Those that fled dispersed themselves; those that fell into the enemies; hands were dispersed by them, in policy, to prevent combinations among them. God's hand was in both. But now God will find them out, and *gather them out of all the countries whither they were driven,* as he promised in the law (Deu. 30:3, 4) and the saints had prayed, Ps. 106:47; Neh. 1:9. He had banished them, but he will *bring them again to this place,* which they could not but have an affection for. For many years past, while they were in their own land, they were continually exposed, and terrified with the alarms of war; but now *I will cause them to dwell safely.* Being reformed, and having returned to God, neither their own consciences within nor their enemies without shall be a terror to them. He promises (*v.* 41): *I will plant them in this land assuredly;* not only I will certainly do it, but they shall here enjoy a holy a security and repose, and they shall take root here, shall be *planted in stability,* and not again be unfixed and shaken. (2.) God will renew his covenant with them, a covenant of grace, the blessings of which are spiritual, and such as will work good things in them, to qualify them for the great things God intended to do for them. It is called an *everlasting covenant* (*v.* 40), not only because God will be for ever faithful to it, but because the consequences of it will be everlasting. For, doubtless, here the promises look further than to Israel according to the flesh, and are sure to all believers, to every Israelite indeed. Good Christians may apply them to themselves and plead them with God, may claim the benefit of them and take the comfort of them. [1.] God will own them for his, and make over himself to them to be theirs (*v.* 38): *They shall be my people.* He will make them his by working in them all the characters and dispositions of his people, and then he will protect, and guide, and govern them as his people. "And, to make them truly, completely, and eternally happy, *I will be their God.*" They shall serve and worship God as theirs and cleave to him only, and he will approve himself theirs. All he is, all he has, shall be engaged and employed for their good. [2.] God will give them a heart to fear him, *v.* 39. That which he requires of those whom he takes into covenant with him as his people is that they fear him, that they reverence his majesty, dread his wrath, stand in awe of his authority, pay homage to him, and give him the glory due unto his name. Now what God requires of them he here promises to work in them, pursuant to his choice of them as his people. Note, As it is God's prerogative to fashion men's hearts, so it is his promise to his people to fashion theirs aright; and a heart to fear God is indeed a good heart, and well fashioned. It is repeated (*v.* 40): *I will put my fear in their hearts,* that is, work in them gracious principles and dispositions, that shall influence and govern their whole conversation. Teachers may put good things into our heads, but it is God only that can put them into our hearts, that can work in us *both to will and to do.* [3.] He will *give them one heart and one way.* In order to their walking in one way, he will give them one heart: as the heart is, so will the way be, and both shall be one; that is *First,* They shall be each of them one with themselves. *One heart* is the same with a *new heart,* Eze. 11:19. The heart is *then* one when it is fully determined for God and entirely devoted to God. When the eye is single and God's glory alone aimed at, when our hearts are fixed, trusting in God, and we are uniform and universal in our obedience to him, then the heart is one and way one; and, unless the heart be thus steady, the goings will not be stedfast. From this promise we may take direction and encouragement to pray, with David (Ps. 86:11), *Unite my heart to fear thy name;* for God says, *I will give them one heart, that they may fear me. Secondly,* They shall be all of them one with each other. All good Christians shall be incorporated into one body; Jews and Gentiles shall become *one sheep-fold;* and they shall all, as far as they are sanctified, have a disposition to love one another, the gospel they profess having in it the strongest inducements to mutual love, and the Spirit that dwells in them being the Spirit of love. Though they may have different apprehensions about minor things, they shall be all one in the great things of God, being renewed after the same image. Though they may have many paths, they have but *one way,* that of serious godliness. [4.] He will effectually provide for their perseverance in grace and the perpetuating of the covenant between himself and them. They would have been happy when there were first planted in Canaan, like Adam in paradise, if they had not departed from God. And therefore, now that they are restored to their happiness, they shall be confirmed in it by the preventing of their departures from God, and this will complete their bliss. *First,* God will never leave nor forsake them: *I will not turn away from them to do them good.* Earthly princes are fickle, and their greatest favourites have fallen under their frowns; but God's *mercy endures for ever. Whom he loves he loves to the end.* God may seem to turn from this people (Isa. 54:8), but even then he does not turn from doing and designing them good. *Secondly,* They shall never leave nor forsake him; that is the thing we are in danger of. We have no reason to distrust God's fidelity and constancy, but our own; and therefore it is here promised that God will *give them a heart to fear him for ever,* all days, to be in his fear every day and all the day long (Prov. 23:17), and to continue so to the end of their days. He will put such a principle into their hearts that they *shall not depart from him.* Even those who have given up their names to God, if they be left to themselves, will depart from him; but the fear of God ruling in the heart, will prevent their departure. That, and nothing else, will do it. If we continue close and faithful to God, it is owing purely to his almighty grace and not to any strength or resolution of our own. [5.] He will entail a blessing upon their seed, will give them grace to fear him, *for the good of them and of their children after them.* As their departures from God had been to the prejudice of their children, so their adherence to God should be to the advantage of their children. We cannot better consult the good of posterity than by setting up, and keeping up, the fear and worship of God in our families. [6.] He will take a pleasure in their prosperity and will do every thing to advance it (*v.* 41): *I will rejoice over them to do them good.* God will certainly do them good because he rejoices over them. They are dear to him; he makes his boast of them, and therefore will not only do them good, but will delight in doing them good. When he punishes them it is with reluctance. *How shall I give thee up, Ephraim?* But, when he restores them, it is with satisfaction; he rejoices in doing them good. We ought therefore to serve him with pleasure and to rejoice in all opportunities of serving him. He is himself a cheerful giver, and therefore loves a cheerful servant. *I will plant them* (says God) *with my whole heart and with my whole soul.* He will be intent upon it, and take delight in it; he will make it the business of his providence to settle them again in Canaan, and the various dispensations of providence shall concur to it. All things shall appear at last so to have been working for the good of the church that it will be said, The governor of the world is entirely taken up with the care of his church. [7.] These promises shall as surely be performed as the foregoing threatenings were; and the accomplishment of those, notwithstanding the security of the people, might confirm their expectation of the performance of these, notwithstanding their present despair (*v.* 42): *As I have brought all this great evil upon them,* pursuant to the threatenings, and for the glory of divine justice, *so I will bring upon them all this good,* pursuant to the promise, and for the glory of divine mercy. He that is faithful to his threatenings will much more be so to his promises; and he will comfort his people *according to the time that he has afflicted them.* The churches shall have rest after the days of adversity. [8.] As an earnest of all this, houses and lands shall again fetch a good price in Judah and Jerusalem, and, though now they are a drug, there shall again be a sufficient number of purchasers (*v.* 43, 44): *Fields shall be bought in this land,* and people will covet to have lands here rather than any where else. Lands, wherever they lie, will go off, not only in *the places about Jerusalem,* but *in the cities of Judah* and of Israel, too, whether they lie *on mountains,* or in valleys, or *in the south,* in all parts of the country, *men shall buy fields, and subscribe evidences.* Trade shall revive, for they shall have money enough to buy land with. Husbandry shall revive, for those that have money shall covet to lay it out upon lands. Laws shall again have their due course, for they shall *subscribe evidences and seal them.* This is mentioned to reconcile Jeremiah to his new purchase. Though he had bought a piece of ground and could not go to see it, yet he must believe that this was the pledge of many a purchase, and those but faint resemblances of the purchased possessions in the heavenly Canaan, reserved for all those who have God's fear in their hearts and do not depart from him.

CHAPTER 33

The scope of this chapter is much the same with that of the foregoing chapter — to confirm the promise of the restoration of the Jews, notwithstanding the present desolations of their country and dispersions of their people. And these promises have, both in type and tendency, a reference as far forward as to the gospel church, to which this second edition of the Jewish church was at length to resign its dignities and privileges. It is here promised, I. That the city shall be rebuilt and re-established "in statu quo — in its former state" (*v.* 1–6). II. That the captives, having their sins pardoned, shall be restored (*v.* 7, 8). III. That this shall redound very much to the glory of God (*v.* 9). IV. That the country shall have both joy and plenty (*v.* 10–14). V. That way shall be made for the coming of the Messiah (*v.* 15, 16). VI. That the house of David, the house of Levi, and the house of Israel, shall flourish again, and be established, and all three in the kingdom of Christ; a gospel ministry and the gospel church shall continue while the world stands (*v.* 17–26).

Verses 1–9

Observe here, I. The date of this comfortable prophecy which God entrusted Jeremiah with. It is not exact in the time, only that it was after that in the foregoing chapter, when things were still growing worse and worse; it was *the second time. God speaketh once, yea, twice,* for the encouragement of his people. We are not only so disobedient that we have need of *precept upon precept* to bring us to our duty, but so distrustful that we have need of promise upon promise to bring us to our comfort. This word, as the former, *came to Jeremiah* when *he was in prison.* Note, No confinement can deprive God's people of his presence; no locks nor bars can shut out his gracious visits; nay, oftentimes *as their afflictions abound their consolations much more abound,* and they have the most reviving communications of his favour when the world frowns upon them. Paul's sweetest epistles were those that bore date out of a prison.

II. The prophecy itself. A great deal of comfort is wrapped up in it for the relief of the captives, to keep them from sinking into despair. Observe,

1. Who it is that secures this comfort to them (*v.* 2): It is *the Lord, the maker thereof, the Lord that framed it,* He is the maker and former of heaven and earth, and therefore has all power in his hands; so it refers to Jeremiah's prayer, *ch.* 32:17. He is the maker and former of Jerusalem, of Zion, built them at first, and therefore can rebuild them — built them for his own praise, and therefore *will.* He *formed it, to establish it,* and therefore it shall be established till those things be introduced which cannot be shaken, but shall remain for ever. He is the maker and former of this promise; he has laid the scheme for Jerusalem's restoration, and he that has formed it will establish it, he that has made the promise will make it good; for Jehovah *is his name,* a God giving being to his promises by the performance of them, and when he does this he is known by that name (Ex. 6:3), a perfecting God. When the heavens and the earth were finished, then, and not till then, the creator is called *Jehovah,* Gen. 2:4.

2. How this comfort must be obtained and fetched in — by prayer (*v.* 3): *Call upon me, and I will answer them.* The prophet, having received some intimations of this kind, must be humbly earnest with God for further discoveries of his kind intentions. He had prayed (*ch.* 32:16), but he must pray again. Note, Those that expect to receive comforts from God must continue instant in prayer. We must call upon him, and then he will answer us. Christ himself must *ask, and it shall be given him,* Ps. 2:8. *I will show thee great and mighty things* (give thee a clear and full prospect of them), *hidden things, which,* though in part discovered already, yet *thou knowest not,* thou canst not understand or give credit to. Or this may refer not only to the prediction of these things which Jeremiah, if he desire it, shall be favoured with, but to the performance of the things themselves which the people of God, encouraged by this prediction, must pray for. Note, Promises are given, not to supersede, but to quicken and encourage prayer. See Eze. 36:37.

3. How deplorable the condition of Jerusalem was which made it necessary that such comforts as these should be provided for it, and notwithstanding which its restoration should be brought about in due time (*v.* 4, 5): *The houses of this city,* not excepting those *of the kings of Judah, are thrown down by the mounts,* or engines of battery, *and by the sword,* or axes, or hammers. It is the same word that is used Eze. 26:9, *With his axes he shall break down thy towers.* The strongest stateliest houses, and those that were best furnished, were levelled with the ground. The fifth verse comes in in a parenthesis, giving a further instance of the present calamitous state of Jerusalem. Those that *came to fight with the Chaldeans,* to beat them off from the siege, did more hurt than good, provoked the enemy to be more fierce and furious in their assaults, so that the houses in Jerusalem were filled *with the dead bodies of men,* who died of the wounds they received in sallying out upon the besiegers. God says that they were such as he had *slain in his anger,* for the enemies' sword was his sword and their anger his anger. But, it seems, the men that were slain were generally such as had distinguished themselves by their wickedness, for they were the very men *for whose wickedness* God did now *hide himself from this city,* so that he was just in all he brought upon them.

4. What the blessings are which God has in store for Judah and Jerusalem, such as will redress all their grievances.

(1.) Is their state diseased? Is it wounded? God will provide effectually for the healing of it, though the disease was thought mortal and incurable, *ch.* 7:22. *"The whole head is sick, and the whole heart faint* (Isa. 1:5); but (*v.* 6) *I will bring it health and cure;* I will prevent the death, remove the sickness, and set all to rights again," *ch.* 30:17. Note, Be the case ever so desperate, if God undertake the cure, he will effect it. The sin of Jerusalem was the sickness of it (Isa. 1:6); its reformation therefore will be its recovery. And the following words tell us how that is wrought: *"I will reveal unto them the abundance of peace and truth;* I will give it to them in due time, and give them an encouraging prospect of it in the mean time." *Peace* stands here for all good; *peace and truth* are peace according to the promise and in pursuance of that: or *peace and truth* are peace and the true religion, peace and the true worship of God, in opposition to the many falsehoods and deceits by which they had been led away from God. We may apply it more generally, and observe, [1.] That peace and truth are the great subject-matter of divine revelation. These promises here lead us to the gospel of Christ, and in that God has revealed to us *peace and truth,* the method of true peace — truth to direct us, peace to make us easy. *Grace and truth,* and abundance of both, *come by Jesus Christ.* Peace and truth are the life of the soul, and Christ *came that we might have* that *life, and might have it more abundantly.* Christ rules by the power of truth (Jn. 18:37) and by it he gives *abundance of peace,* Ps. 72:7; 85:10. [2.] That the divine revelation of peace and truth brings health and cure to all those that by faith receive it: it heals the soul of the diseases it has contracted, as it is a means of sanctification, Jn. 17:17. *He sent his word and healed them,* Ps. 107:20. And it puts the soul into good order, and keeps it in a good frame and fit for the employments and enjoyments of the spiritual and divine life.

(2.) Are they scattered and enslaved, and is their nation laid in ruins? *"I will cause their captivity to return* (*v.* 7), both that of Israel and that of Judah" (for though those who returned under Zerubbabel were chiefly of Judah, and Benjamin, and Levi, yet afterwards many of all the other tribes returned), *"and I will rebuild them, as* I built them *at first."* When they by repentance do their first works God will by their restoration do his first works.

(3.) Is sin the procuring cause of all their troubles? That shall be pardoned and subdued, and so the root of the judgments shall be killed, *v.* 8. [1.] By sin they have become filthy, and odious to God's holiness, but God will cleanse them, and purify *them from their iniquity.* As those that were ceremonially unclean, and were therefore shut out from the tabernacle, when they were sprinkled with the *water of purification* had liberty of access to it again, so had they to their own land, and the privileges of it, when God had *cleansed them from their iniquities.* In allusion to that sprinkling, David prays, *Purge me with hyssop.* [2.] By sin they have become guilty, and obnoxious to his justice; but he will *pardon all their iniquities,* will remove the punishment to which for sin they were bound over. All who by sanctifying grace are cleansed from the filth of sin, by pardoning mercy are freed from the guilt of it.

(4.) Have both their sins and their sufferings turned to the dishonour of God? Their reformation and restoration shall redound as much to his praise, *v.* 9. Jerusalem thus rebuilt, Judah thus repeopled, *shall be to me a name of joy,* as pleasing to God as ever they have been provoking, *and a praise and an honour before all the nations.* They, being thus restored, shall glorify God by their obedience to him, and he shall glorify himself by his favours to them. This renewed nation shall be as much a reputation to religion as formerly it has been a reproach to it. The nations *shall hear of all the good that* God has wrought in them by his grace and *of all the good* he has wrought for them by his providence. The wonders of their return out of Babylon shall make as great a noise in the world as ever the wonders of their deliverance out of Egypt did. and *they shall fear and tremble for all this goodness.* [1.] The people of God themselves shall fear and tremble; they shall be much surprised at it, shall be afraid of offending so good a God and of forfeiting his favour. Hos. 3:5, *They shall fear the Lord and his goodness.* [2.] The neighbouring nations shall fear because of the prosperity of Jerusalem, shall look upon the growing greatness of the Jewish nation as really formidable, and shall be afraid of making them their enemies. When the church is *fair as the moon,* and *clear as the sun,* she is *terrible as an army with banners.*

Verses 10–16

Here is a further prediction of the happy state of Judah and Jerusalem after their glorious return out of captivity, issuing gloriously at length in the kingdom of the Messiah.

I. It is promised that the people who were long in sorrow shall again be filled with joy. Every one concluded now that the country would lie for ever desolate, that *no beasts* would be found in the land of Judah, no inhabitant *in the streets of Jerusalem,* and consequently there would be nothing but universal and perpetual melancholy (*v.* 10); but, though weeping may endure for a time, joy will return. It was threatened (*ch.* 7:34 and 16:9) that *the voice of joy and gladness should cease* there; but here it is promised that they shall revive again, that *the voice of joy and gladness shall be heard* there, because *the captivity shall be returned;* for then was *their mouth filled with laughter,* Ps. 126:1, 2. 1. There shall be common joy there, *the voice of the bridegroom and the voice of the bride;* marriages shall again be celebrated, as formerly, with songs, which in Babylon they had laid aside, for their harps were hung on the willow-trees. 2. There shall be religious joy there; temple-songs shall be revived, *the Lord's songs,* which they could not *sing in a strange land.* There shall be heard in their private houses, and in the cities of Judah, as well as in the temple, *the voice of those that shall say, Praise the Lord of hosts.* Note, Nothing is more the praise and honour of a people than to have God the glory of it, the glory both of the power and of the goodness by which it is effected; they shall prise him both as *the Lord of hosts* and as the God who *is good* and whose *mercy endures for ever.* This, though a song of old, yet, being sung upon this fresh occasion, will be a new song. We find this literally fulfilled at their return out of Babylon, Ezra 3:11. They sang together in praising the Lord, *because he is good, for his mercy endures for ever.* The public worship of God shall be diligently and constantly attended upon: *They shall bring the sacrifice of praise to the house of the Lord.* All the sacrifices were intended for the praise of God, but this seems to be meant of the spiritual sacrifices of humble adorations and joyful thanksgivings, *the calves of our lips* (Hos. 14:2), which *shall please the Lord better than an ox of bullock.* The Jews say that in the days of the Messiah all sacrifices shall cease but *the sacrifice of praise,* and to those days this promise has a further reference.

II. It is promised that the country, which had lain long depopulated, shall be replenished and stocked again. It was now desolate, *without man and without beast;* but, after their return, the pastures shall again be *clothed with flocks,* Ps. 65:13. *In all the cities of Judah and Benjamin there shall be a habitation of shepherds, v.* 12, 13. This intimates, 1. The wealth of the country, after their return. It shall not be a habitation of beggars, who have nothing, but of shepherds and husbandmen, men of substance, with good stocks upon the ground they have returned to. 2. The peace of the country. It shall not be a habitation of soldiers, not shall there be tents and barracks set up to lodge them, but there shall be shepherds; tents; for they shall hear no more the alarms of war, nor shall there be any to make even the shepherds afraid. See Ps. 144:13, 14. 3. The industry of the country, and their return to their original plainness and simplicity, from which, in the corrupt ages, they had sadly degenerated. The seed of Jacob, in their beginning, gloried in this, that they were shepherds (Gen. 47:3), and so they shall now be again, giving themselves wholly to that innocent employment, *causing their flocks to lie down* (*v.* 12) and to *pass under the hands of him that telleth them* (*v.* 13); for, though their flocks are numerous, they are not numberless, nor shall they omit to number them, that they may know if any be missing and may seek after it. Note, It is the prudence of those who have ever so much of the world to keep an account of what they have. Some think that they *pass under the hand of him that telleth them* that they may be tithed, Lev. 27:32. *Then* we may take the comfort of what we have when God has had his dues out of it. Now because it seemed incredible that a people, reduced as now they were, should ever recover such a degree of peace and plenty as this, here is subjoined a general ratification of these promises (*v.* 14): *I will perform that good thing which I have promised.* Though the promise may sometimes work slowly towards an accomplishment, it works surely. *The days will come,* though they are long in coming.

III. To crown all these blessings which God has in store for them, here is a promise of the Messiah, and of that everlasting righteousness which he should bring in (*v.* 15, 16), and probably this is *that good thing,* that great good thing, which in the latter days, days that were yet to come, God would perform, as he had promised to Judah and Israel, and to which their return out of captivity and their settlement again in their own land was preparatory. *From the captivity to Christ* is one of the famous periods, Mt. 1:17. This promise of the Messiah we had before (*ch.* 23:5, 6), and there it came in as a confirmation of the promise of the shepherds whom God would set over them, which would make one think that the promise here concerning the shepherds and their flocks, which introduces it, is to be understood figuratively. Christ is here prophesied of, 1. As a rightful King. He is a *branch of righteousness,* not a usurper, for he *grows up unto David,* descends from his loins, with whom the covenant of royalty was made, and is that seed with whom that covenant should be established, so that his title is unexceptionable. 2. As a righteous king, righteous in enacting laws, waging wars, and giving judgment, righteous in vindicating those that suffer wrong and punishing those that do wrong: *He shall execute judgment and righteousness in the land.* This may point at Zerubbabel, in the type, who governed with equity, not as Jehoiakim had done (*ch.* 22:17); but it has a further reference to him to whom all judgment is committed and who shall *judge the world in righteousness.* 3. As a king that shall protect his subjects from all injury. By him *Judah shall be saved* from wrath and the curse, and, being so saved, *Jerusalem shall dwell safely,* quiet from the fear of evil, and enjoying a holy security and serenity of mind, in a dependence upon the conduct of this prince of peace, this prince of their peace. 4. As a king that shall be praised by his subjects: *"This is the name whereby they shall call him"* (so the Chaldee reads it, the Syriac, and vulgar Latin); "this name of his they shall celebrate and triumph in, and by this name they shall call upon him." It may be read, more agreeably to the original, *This is he who shall call her, The Lord our righteousness.* As Moses's altar is called *Jehovah-nissi* (Ex. 17:15), and Jerusalem *Jehovah-shammah* (Eze. 48:35), intimating that they glory in Jehovah as present with them and *their banner,* so here the city is called *The Lord our righteousness,* because they glory in Jehovah as their righteousness. That which was before said to be the name of Christ (says Mr. Gataker) is here made the name of Jerusalem, the city of the Messiah, the church of Christ. He it is that imparts righteousness to her, for he is *made of God to us righteousness,* and she, by bearing that name, professes to have her whole righteousness, not from herself, but from him. *In the Lord have I righteousness and strength,* Isa. 45:24. And *we are made the righteousness of God in him.* The inhabitants of Jerusalem shall have this name of the Messiah so much in their mouths that they shall themselves be called by it.

Verses 17–26

Three of God's covenants, that of royalty with David and his seed, that of the priesthood with Aaron and his seed, and that of Peculiarity with Abraham and his seed, seemed to be all broken and lost while the captivity lasted; but it is here promised that, notwithstanding that interruption and discontinuance for a time, they shall all three take place again, and the true intents and meaning of them all shall be abundantly answered in the New Testament blessings, typified by those conferred on the Jews after their return out of captivity.

I. The covenant of royalty shall be secured and the promises of it shall have their full accomplishment in the kingdom of Christ, the Son of David, *v.* 17. The throne of Israel was overturned in the captivity; the crown had fallen from their head; there was not *a man to sit on the throne of Israel;* Jeconiah was written childless. After their return the house of David made a figure again; but it in the Messiah that this promise is performed that *David shall never want a man to sit on the throne of Israel,* and that David shall have *always a son to reign upon his throne.* For as long as the man Christ Jesus sits on the right hand of the throne of God, rules the world, and rules it for the good of the church, to which he is a quickening head, and glorified head over all things, as long as he is *King upon the holy hill of Zion,* David does not want a successor, nor is the covenant with him broken. When the first-begotten was brought into the world it was declared concerning him, *The Lord God shall give him the throne of his father David and he shall reign over the house of Jacob for ever,* Lu. 1:32, 33. For the confirmation of this it is promised, 1. That the covenant with David shall be as firm as the ordinances of heaven, to the stability of which that of God's promise is compared, *ch.* 31:35, 36. There is a covenant of nature, by which the common course of providence is settled and on which it is founded, here called *a covenant of the day and the night* (*v.* 20, 25), because this is one of the articles of it, That there shall be *day and night in their season,* according to the distinction put between them in the creation, when God divided between the light and the darkness, and established their mutual succession, and a government to each, that *the sun* should *rule by day* and *the moon and stars by night* (Gen. 1:4, 5, 16), which establishment was renewed after the flood (Gen. 8:22), and has continued ever since, Ps. 19:2. The *morning* and *the evening* have both of them their regular *outgoings* (Ps. 65:8); the *day-spring knows its place, knows its time,* and keeps both, so do *the shadows of the evening;* and, while the world stands, this course shall not be altered, this covenant shall not be broken. *The ordinances of heaven and earth* (of this communication between heaven and earth, the dominion of these ordinances of heaven upon the earth), *which* God has *appointed* (*v.* 25; compare Job 38:33), shall never be disappointed. Thus firm shall the covenant of redemption be with the Redeemer — God's servant, but David our King, *v.* 21. This intimates that Christ shall have a church on earth to the world's end; he shall see a seed in which he shall prolong his days till time and day shall be no more. Christ's *kingdom is an everlasting kingdom;* and when *the end cometh,* and not till then, it *shall be delivered up to God,* even *the Father.* But it intimates that the condition of it in this world shall be intermixed and counterchanged, prosperity and adversity succeeding each other, as light and darkness, day and night. But this is plainly taught us, that, as sure as we may be that, though the sun will set tonight, it will rise again tomorrow morning, whether we live to see it or no, so sure we may be that, though the kingdom of the Redeemer in the world may for a time be clouded and eclipsed by corruptions and persecutions, yet it will shine forth again, and recover its lustre, in the time appointed. 2. That *the seed of David* shall be as numerous *as the host of heaven,* that is, the spiritual seed of the Messiah, that shall be born to him by the efficacy of his gospel and his Spirit working with it. *From the womb of the morning he shall have the dew of their youth,* to be his *willing people,* Ps. 110:3. Christ's seed are not, as David's were, his successors, but his subjects; yet the day is coming when they also shall reign with him (*v.* 22): *As the host of heaven cannot be numbered, so will I multiply the seed of David,* so that there shall be no danger of the kingdom's being extinct, or extirpated, for want of heirs. The children are numerous; *and, if children, then heirs.*

II. The covenant of priesthood shall be secured, and the promises of that also shall have their full accomplishment. This seemed likewise to be forgotten during the captivity, when there was no altar, no temple service, for the priests to attend upon; but this also shall revive. It did so; immediately upon their coming back to Jerusalem there were priests and Levites ready *to offer burnt-offerings* and to *do sacrifice continually* (Ezra 3:2, 3), as is here promised, *v.* 18. But that priesthood soon grew corrupt; *the covenant of Levi* was *profaned* (as appears Mal. 2:8), and in the destruction of Jerusalem by the Romans it came to a final period. We must therefore look elsewhere for the performance of this word, that the covenant with the Levites, the priests, God's ministers, shall be as firm, and last as long, as the covenant *with the day and the night.* And we find it abundantly performed, 1. In the priesthood of Christ, which supersedes that of Aaron, and is the substance of that shadow. While that great *high priest of our profession* is always appearing *in the presence of God for us,* presenting the virtue of his blood by which he made atonement in the incense of his intercession, it may truly be said that *the Levites do not want a man before God to offer continually,* Heb. 7:3, 17. He is a priest for ever. The covenant of the priesthood is called *a covenant of peace* (Num. 25:12), of *life and peace,* Mal. 2:5. Now we are sure that this covenant is not broken, nor in the least weakened, while Jesus Christ is himself our life and our peace. This covenant of priesthood is here again and again joined with that of royalty, for Christ is a *priest upon his throne,* as Melchizedek. 2. In a settled gospel ministry. While there are faithful ministers to preside in religious assemblies, and to offer up the spiritual sacrifices of prayer and praise, *the priests, the Levites,* do not want successors, and such as *have obtained a more excellent ministry.* The apostle makes those that preach the gospel to come in the room of those that served at the altar, 1 Co. 9:13, 14. 3. In all true believers, who are *a holy priesthood, a royal priesthood* (I Peter 2:5, 9), who are *made to our God kings and priests* (Rev. 1:6); they *offer up spiritual sacrifices, acceptable to God,* and themselves, in the first place, *living sacrifices.* Of these Levites this promise must be understood (*v.* 22), that they shall be as numerous *as the sand of the sea,* the same that is promised concerning Israel in general (Gen. 22:17); for all God's spiritual Israel are spiritual priests, Rev. 5:9, 10; 7:9, 15.

III. The covenant of peculiarity likewise shall be secured and the promises of that covenant shall have their full accomplishment in the gospel Israel. Observe, 1. How this covenant was looked upon as broken during the captivity, *v.* 24. God asks the prophet, "Hast though not heard, and dost *thou not consider, what this people have spoken?"* either the enemies of Israel, who triumphed in the extirpation of a people that had made such a noise in the world, or the unbelieving Israelites themselves, *"this people* among whom thou dwellest;" they have broken covenant with God, and then quarrel with him as if he had not dealt faithfully with them. *The two families which the Lord hath chosen,* Israel and Judah, whereas they were but one when he chose them, *he hath even cast them off. "Thus have they despised my people,* that is, despised the privilege of being my people as if it were a privilege of no value at all." The neighbouring nations despised them as now *no more a nation,* but the ruins of a nation, and looked upon all their honour as laid in the dust; but, 2. See how firm the covenant stands notwithstanding, as firm as that with day and night; sooner will God suffer day and night to cease then he will *cast away the seed of Jacob.* This cannot refer to the seed of Jacob according to the flesh, for they are cast away, but to the Christian church, in which all these promises were to be lodged, as appears by the apostle's discourse, Rom. 11:1, etc. Christ is that seed of David that is to be perpetual dictator to the seed of Abraham, Isaac, and Jacob; and, as this people shall never want such a king, so this king shall never want such a people. Christianity shall continue in the dominion of Christ, and the subjection of Christians to him, till day and night come to an end. And, as a pledge of this, that promise is again repeated, *I will cause their captivity to return;* and, having brought them back, *I will have mercy on them.* To whom this promise refers appears Gal. 6:16, where all that *walk according to the gospel rule* are made to be the *Israel of God,* on whom *peace and mercy* shall be.

CHAPTER 34

In this chapter we have two messages which God sent by Jeremiah. I. One to foretel the fate of Zedekiah king of Judah, that he should fall into the hands of the king of Babylon, that he should live a captive, but should at last die in peace in his captivity (*v.* 1–7). II. Another to read the doom both of prince and people for their treacherous dealings with God, in bringing back into bondage their servants whom they had released according to the law, and so playing fast and loose with God. They had walked at all adventures with God (*v.* 8–11), and therefore God would walk at all adventures with them, in bringing the Chaldean army upon them again when they began to hope that they had got clear of them (*v.* 12–22).

Verses 1–7

This prophecy concerning Zedekiah was delivered to Jeremiah, and by him to the parties concerned, before he was shut up in the prison, for we find this prediction here made the ground of his commitment, as appears by the recital of some passages out of it, *ch.* 32:4. Observe,

I. The time when this message was sent to Zedekiah; it was *when the king of Babylon,* with all his forces, some out of *all the kingdoms of the earth* that were within his jurisdiction, *fought against Jerusalem and the cities thereof* (*v.* 1), designing to destroy them, having often plundered them. The cities that now remained, and yet held out, are named (*v.* 7), *Lachish and Azekah.* This intimates that things were now brought to the last extremity, and yet Zedekiah obstinately stood it out, his heart being hardened to his destruction.

II. The message itself that was sent to him. 1. Here is a threatening of wrath. He is told that again which he had been often told before, that the city shall be taken by the Chaldeans *and burnt with fire* (*v.* 2), that he shall himself fall into the enemy's hands, shall be made a prisoner, shall be brought before that furious prince Nebuchadnezzar, and be carried away captive into Babylon (*v.* 3); yet Ezekiel prophesied that he *should not see Babylon;* nor did he, for his eyes were put out, Eze. 12:13. This Zedekiah brought upon himself from God by his other sins and from Nebuchadnezzar by breaking his faith with him. 2. Here is a mixture of mercy. He shall die a captive, but he *shall not die by the sword* he shall die a natural death (*v.* 4); he shall end his days with some comfort, *shall die in peace, v.* 5. He never had been one of the worst of the kings, but we are willing to hope that what evil he had *done in the sight of the Lord* he repented of in his captivity, as Manasseh had done, and it was forgiven to him; and, God being reconciled to him, he might truly be said to *die in peace,* Note, A man may die in a prison and yet *die in peace.* Nay, he shall end his days with some reputation, more than one would expect, all things considered. He shall be buried *with the burnings of his fathers,* that is, with the respect usually shown to their kings, especially those that had done good in Israel. It seems, in his captivity he had conducted himself so well towards his own people that they were willing to do him this honour, and towards Nebuchadnezzar that he suffered it to be done. If Zedekiah had continued in his prosperity, perhaps he would have grown worse and would have *departed* at last *without being desired;* but his afflictions wrought such a change in him that his death was looked upon as a great loss. It is better to live and die penitent in a prison than to live and die impenitent in a palace. *They will lament thee, saying, Ah lord!* an honour which his brother Jehoiakim had not, *ch.* 22:18. The Jews say that they lamented thus over him, *Alas! Zedekiah is dead, who drank the dregs of all the ages that went before him,* that is, who suffered for the sins of his ancestors, the measure of iniquity being filled up in his days. They shall thus lament him, *saith the Lord, for I have pronounced the word;* and what God hath spoken shall without fail be made good.

III. Jeremiah's faithfulness in delivering this message. Though he knew it would be ungrateful to the king, and might prove, as indeed it did, dangerous to himself (for he was imprisoned for it), yet he *spoke all these words to Zedekiah, v.* 6. It is a mercy to great men to have those about them that will deal faithfully with them, and tell them the evil consequences of their evil courses, that they may reform and live.

Verses 8–22

We have here another prophecy upon a particular occasion, the history of which we must take notice of, as necessary to give light to the prophecy.

I. When Jerusalem was closely besieged by the Chaldean army the princes and people agreed upon a reformation in one instance, and that was concerning their servants.

1. The law of God was very express, that those of their own nation should not be held in servitude above seven years, but, after they had served one apprenticeship, they should be discharged and have their liberty; yea, though they had sold themselves into servitude for the payment of their debts, or though they were *sold by the judges* for the punishment of their crimes. This difference was put between their brethren and strangers, that those of other nations taken in war, or bought with money, might be held in perpetual slavery, they and theirs; but their brethren must serve but for seven years at the longest. This God calls the covenant that he had made with them when he *brought them out of the land of Egypt, v.* 13, 14. This was the first of the judicial laws which God gave them (Ex. 21:2), and there was good reason for this law. (1.) God had put honour upon that nation, and he would have them thus to preserve the honour of it themselves and to put a difference between it and other nations. (2.) God had brought them out of slavery in Egypt, and he would have them thus to express their grateful sense of that favour, by letting those go to whom their houses were *houses of bondage,* as Egypt had been to their forefathers. That deliverance is therefore mentioned here (*v.* 13) as the ground of that law. Note, God's compassions towards us should engage our compassions towards our brethren; we must release as we are released, forgive as we are forgiven, and relieve as we are relieved. And this is called *a covenant;* for our performance of the duty required is the condition of the continuance of the favours God has bestowed.

2. This law they and their fathers had broken. Their worldly profit swayed more with them than God's command or covenant. When their servants had lived seven years with them they understood their business, and how to apply themselves to it, better than they did when they first came to them, and therefore they would then by no means part with them, though God himself by his law had made them free: *Your fathers hearkened not to me* in this matter (*v.* 14), so that from the days of their fathers they had been in this trespass; and they thought they might do it because their fathers did it, and their servants had by disuse lost the benefit of the provision God made for them; whereas against an express law, especially against an express law of God, no custom, usage, nor prescription, is to be admitted in plea. For this sin of theirs, and their fathers, God now brought them into servitude, and justly.

3. When they were besieged, and closely shut in, by the army of the Chaldeans, they, being told of their fault in this matter, immediately reformed, and let go all their servants that were entitled to their freedom by the law of God, as Pharaoh, who, when the plague was upon him, consented to *let the people go,* and bound themselves in a covenant to do so. (1.) The prophets faithfully admonished them concerning their sin. From them they heard that they should let their Hebrew servants *go free, v.* 10. They might have read it themselves in the book of the law, but did not, or did not heed it, therefore the prophets told them what the law was. See what need there is of the preaching of the word; people must hear the word preached because they will not make the use they ought to make of the word written. (2.) All orders and degrees of men concurred in this reformation. The *king,* and the *princes,* and *all the people,* agreed to *let go their servants,* whatever loss or damage they might sustain by so doing. When the king and princes led in this good work the people could not for shame but follow. The example and influence of great men would go very far towards extirpating the most inveterate corruptions. (3.) They bound themselves by a solemn oath and covenant that they would do this, whereby they engaged themselves to God and one another. Note, What God has bound us to by his precept, it is good for us to bind ourselves to by our promise. This covenant was very solemn: it was made in a sacred place, *made before me, in the house which is called by my name* (*v.* 15), in the special presence of God, the tokens of which, in the temple, ought to strike an awe upon them and make them very sincere in their appeals to him. It was ratified by a significant sign; they *cut a calf in two, and passed between the parts thereof* (*v.* 18, 19) with this dreadful imprecation, "Let us be in like manner cut asunder if we do not perform what we now promise." This calf was probably offered up in sacrifice to God, who was thereby made a party to the covenant. When God covenanted with Abraham, for the ratification of it, a *smoking furnace* and a *burning lamp passed between the pieces* of the sacrifice, in allusion to this federal rite, Gen. 15:17. Note, In order that we may effectually oblige ourselves to our duty, it is good to alarm ourselves with the apprehensions of the terror of the wrath and curse to which we expose ourselves if we live in the contempt of it, that wrath which will *cut sinners asunder* (Mt. 24:51), and sensible signs may be of use to make the impressions of it deep and durable, as here. (4.) They conformed themselves herein to the command of God and their covenant with him; they did *let their servants go,* though at this time, when the city was besieged, they could very ill spare them. Thus they did *right in God's sight, v.* 15. Though it was their trouble that drove them to it, yet he was well pleased with it; and if they had persevered in this act of *mercy to the poor,* to their poor servants, it might have been a lengthening of their tranquillity, Dan. 4:27.

II. When there was some hope that the siege was raised and the danger over they repented of their repentance, undid the good they had done, and forced the servants they had released into their respective services again. 1. The *king of Babylon's army* had now *gone up from them, v.* 21. Pharaoh was bringing an army of Egyptians to oppose the progress of the king of Babylon's victories, upon the tidings of which the Chaldeans raised the siege for a time, as we find, *ch.* 37:5. *They departed from Jerusalem.* See how ready God was to put a stop to his judgments, upon the first instance of reformation, so slow is he to anger and so swift to show mercy. As soon as ever they let their servants go free God let them go free. 2. When they began to think themselves safe from the besiegers they made their servants come back into subjection to them, *v.* 11, and again *v.* 16. This was a great abuse to their servants, to whom servitude would be more irksome, after they had had some taste of the pleasures of liberty. It was a great shame to themselves that they could not keep in a good mind when they were in it. But it was especially an affront to God; in doing this they *polluted his name, v.* 16. It was a contempt of the command he had given them, as if that were of no force at all, but they might either keep it or break it as they thought fit. It was a contempt of the covenant they had made with him, and of that wrath which they had imprecated upon themselves in case they should break that covenant. It was jesting with God almighty, as if he could be imposed upon by fallacious promises, which, when they had gained their point, they would look upon themselves no longer obliged by. it was *lying to God with their mouths* and *flattering him with their tongues.* It was likewise a contempt of the judgments of God and setting them at defiance; as if, when once the course of them was stopped a little and interrupted, they would never proceed again and the judgment would never be revived; whereas reprieves are so far from being pardons that if they be abused thus, and sinners take encouragement from them to return to sin, they are but preparatives for heavier strokes of divine vengeance.

III. For this treacherous dealing with God they are here severely threatened. *Be not deceived; God is not mocked.* Those that think to put a cheat upon God by a dissembled repentance, a fallacious covenant, and a partial temporary reformation, will prove in the end to have put the greatest cheat upon their own souls; for *the Lord, whose name is Jealous, is a jealous God.* it is here threatened, with an observable air of displeasure against them, 1. That, since they had not given liberty to their servants to go where they pleased, God would give all his judgments liberty to take their course against them without control (*v.* 17): *You have not proclaimed liberty to your servants.* Though they had done it (*v.* 10), yet they might truly be said not to have done it, because they did not stand to it, but undid it again; and *factum non dicitur quod non perseverat — that is not said to be done which does not last.* The righteousness that is forsaken and turned away from shall be forgotten, and *not mentioned* any more than if it had never been, Eze. 18:24. *"Therefore I will proclaim a liberty for you;* I will discharge you from my service, and put you out of my protection, which those forfeit that withdraw from their allegiance. You shall have liberty to choose which of these judgments you will be cut off by, *sword, famine, or pestilence;"* such a liberty as was offered to David, which put him into a *great strait,* 2 Sa. 24:14. Note, Those that will not be in subjection to the law of God put themselves into subjection to the wrath and curse of God. But this shows what liberty to *sin* really — it is but a liberty to the sorest judgments. 2. That, since they had brought their servants back into confinement in their houses, God would *make them to be removed into all the kingdoms of the earth,* where they should live in servitude, and, being strangers, could not expect the privileges of free-born subjects. 3. That, since they had broken the covenant which they ratified by a solemn imprecation, God would bring on them the evil which they imprecated upon themselves in case they should break it. out of their own mouth will he judge them, and so shall their doom be; the penalty of their bond shall be recovered, because they have not performed the condition; for so some read *v.* 18, *"I will make the men which have transgressed my covenant as the calf which they cut in twain;* I will divide them asunder as they divided it asunder." 4. That, since they would not let go their servants out of the hands, God would deliver them into the hands of those that hated them, even *the princes* and nobles both *of Judah and Jerusalem* (of the country and of the city), *the eunuchs* (chamberlains, or great officers of the court), *the priests, and all the people, v.* 19. They had all dealt treacherously with God, and therefore shall all be involved in the common ruin without exception. They shall all be *given unto the hand of their enemies, that seek,* not their wealth only, or their service, but *their life,* and they shall have what they seek; but neither shall that content them: when they have their lives they shall leave *their dead bodies* unburied, a loathsome spectacle to all mankind and an easy prey to *the fowls and beasts,* a lasting mark of ignominy being hereby fastened on them, *v.* 20. 5. That, since they had emboldened themselves in returning to their sin, contrary to their covenant, by the retreat of the Chaldean army from them, God would therefore bring it upon them again: "They have now *gone up from you,* and your fright is over for the present, but I *will command them* to face about as they were; they shall *return to this city, and take it and burn it," v.* 22. Note, (1.) As confidence in God is a hopeful presage of approaching deliverance, so security in sin is a sad omen of approaching destruction. (2.) When judgments are removed from a people before they have done their work, leave them, but leave them unhumbled and unreformed, it is *cum animo revertendi — with a design to return;* they do but retreat to come on again with so much the greater force; for when God judges he will overcome. (3.) It is just with God to disappoint those expectations of mercy which his providence had given cause for when we disappoint those expectations of duty which our professions, pretensions, and fair promises, had given cause for. If we repent of the good we had purposed, God will repent of the good he had purposed. *With the froward thou wilt show thyself froward.*

CHAPTER 35

A variety of methods is tried, and every stone turned, to awaken the Jews to a sense of their sin and to bring them to repentance and reformation. The scope and tendency of many of the prophet's sermons was to frighten them out of their disobedience, by setting before them what would be the end thereof if they persisted in it. The scope of this sermon, in this chapter, is to shame them out of their disobedience if they had any sense of honour left in them for a discourse of this nature to fasten upon. I. He sets before them the obedience of the family of the Rechabites to the commands which were left them by Jonadab their ancestor, and how they persevered in that obedience and would not be tempted from it (*v.* 1–11). II. With this he aggravates the disobedience of the Jews to God and their contempt of his precepts (*v.* 12–15). III. He foretels the judgments of God upon the Jews for their impious disobedience to God (*v.* 16, 17). IV. He assures the Rechabites of the blessing of God upon them for their pious obedience to their father (*v.* 18, 19).

Verses 1–11

This chapter is of an earlier date than many of those before; for what is contained in it was said and done *in the days of Jehoiakim* (*v.* 1); but then it must be in the latter part of his reign, for it was after the king of Babylon with his army *came up into the land* (*v.* 11), which seems to refer to the invasion mentioned 2 Ki. 24:2, which was upon occasion of Jehoiakim's rebelling against Nebuchadnezzar. After the judgments of God had broken in upon this rebellious people he continued to deal with them by his prophets to turn them from sin, that his wrath might turn away from the. For this purpose Jeremiah sets before them the example of the Rechabites, a family that kept distinct by themselves and were no more numbered with the families of Israel than they with the nations. They were originally Kenites, as appears 1 Chr. 2:55, *These are the Kenites that came out of Hemath, the father of the house of Rechab.* The Kenites, at least those of them that gained a settlement in the land of Israel, were of the posterity of Hobab, Moses's father-in-law, Jdg. 1:16. We find them separated from the Amalekites, 1 Sa. 15:6. See Jdg. 4:17. One family of these Kenites had their denomination from Rechab. His son, or a lineal descendant from him, was Jonadab, a man famous in his time for wisdom and piety. he flourished in the days of Jehu, king of Israel, nearly 300 years before this; for there we find him courted by that rising prince, when he affected to appear zealous for God (2 Ki. 10:15, 16), which he thought nothing more likely to confirm people in the opinion of than to have so good a man as Jonadab ride in the chariot with him. Now here we are told,

I. What the rules of living were which Jonadab, probably by his last will and testament, in writing, and duly executed, charged his children, and his posterity after him throughout all generations, religiously to observe; and we have reason to think that they were such as he himself had all his days observed.

1. They were comprised in two remarkable precepts: — (1.) He forbade them to *drink wine,* according to the law of the Nazarites. Wine is indeed given to *make glad the heart* of man and we are allowed the sober and moderate use of it; but we are so apt to abuse it and get hurt by it, and a good man, who has his heart made continually glad with the *light of God's countenance,* has so little need of it for that purpose (Ps. 4:6, 7), that it is a commendable piece of self-denial either not to use it at all or very sparingly and medicinally, as Timothy used it, 1 Tim. 5:23. (2.) He appointed them to *dwell in tents,* and not to build houses, nor purchase lands, nor rent or occupy either, *v.* 7. This was an instance of strictness and mortification beyond what the Nazarenes were obliged to. Tents were mean dwellings, so that this would teach them to be humble; they were cold dwellings, so that this would teach them to be hardy and not to indulge the body; they were movable dwellings, so that this would teach them not to think of settling or taking root any where in this world. They must dwell in tents *all their days.* They must from the beginning thus accustom themselves to endure hardness, and then it would be no difficulty to them, no, not under the decays of old age. Now,

2. Why did Jonadab prescribe these rules of living to his posterity? It was not merely to show his authority, and to exercise a dominion over them, by imposing upon them what he thought fit; but it was to show his wisdom, and the real concern he had for their welfare, by recommending to them what he knew would be beneficial to them, yet not tying them by any oath or vow, or under any penalty, to observe these rules, but only advising them to conform to this discipline as far as they found it for edification, yet to be dispensed with in any case of necessity, as here, *v.* 11. He prescribed these rules to them, (1.) That they might preserve the ancient character of their family, which, however looked upon by some with contempt, he thought its real reputation. His ancestors had addicted themselves to a pastoral life (Ex. 2:16), and he would have his posterity keep to it, and not degenerate from it, as Israel had done, who originally were shepherds and dwelt in tents, Gen. 46:34. Note, We ought not to be ashamed of the honest employments of our ancestors, though they were but mean. (2.) That they might comport with their lot and bring their mind to their condition. Moses had put them in hopes that they should be naturalized (Num. 10:32); but, it seems they were not; they were still *strangers in the land* (*v.* 7), had no inheritance in it, and therefore must live by their employments, which was a good reason why they should accustom themselves to hard fare and hard lodging; for strangers, such as they were, must not expect to live as the landed men, so plentifully and delicately. Note, It is our wisdom and duty to accommodate ourselves to our place and rank, and not aim to live above it. What has been the lot of our fathers why may we not be content that it should be our lot, and live according to it? *Mind not high things.* (3.) That they might not be envied and disturbed by their neighbours among whom they lived. If they that were strangers should live great, raise estates, and fare sumptuously, the natives would grudge them their abundance, and have a jealous eye upon them, as the Philistines had upon Isaac (Gen. 26:14), and would seek occasions to quarrel with them and do them a mischief; therefore he thought it would be their prudence to keep low, for that would be the way to continue long — to live meanly, that they might *live many days in the land where they were strangers.* Note, Humility and contentment in obscurity are often the best policy and men's surest protection. (4.) That they might be armed against temptations to luxury and sensuality, the prevailing sin of the age and place they lived in. Jonadab saw a general corruption of manners; the drunkards of Ephraim abounded, and he was afraid lest his children should be debauched and ruined by them; and therefore he obliged them to live by themselves, retired in the country; and, that they might not run into any unlawful pleasures, to deny themselves the use even of lawful delights. They must be very sober, and temperate, and abstemious, which would contribute to the health both of mind and body, and to their living many days, and easy ones, and such as they might reflect upon with comfort *in the land where they were strangers.* Note, The consideration of this, that we are strangers and pilgrims, should oblige us to abstain from all fleshly lusts, to live above the things of sense, and look upon them with a generous and gracious contempt. (5.) That they might be prepared for times of trouble and calamity. Jonadab might, without a spirit of prophecy, foresee the destruction of a people so wretchedly degenerated, and he would have his family provide, that, if they could not *in the peace thereof,* yet even in the midst of the troubles thereof, *they might have peace.* Let them therefore have little to lose, and then losing times would be the less dreadful to them: let them sit loose to what they had, and then they might with less pain be stripped of it. Note, Those are in the best frame to meet sufferings who are mortified to the world and life a life of self-denial. (6.) That in general they might learn to live by rule and under discipline. It is good for us all to do so, and to teach our children to do so. Those that have lived long, as Jonadab probably had done when he left this charge to his posterity, can speak by experience of the vanity of the world and the dangerous snares that are in the abundance of its wealth and pleasures, and therefore ought to be regarded when they warn those that come after them to stand upon their guard.

II. How strictly his posterity observed these rules, *v.* 8–10. They had in their respective generations all of them *obeyed the voice of Jonadab their father,* had *done according to all that he commanded them.* They *drank no wine,* though they dwelt in a country where was plenty of it; their wives and children drank no wine, for those that are temperate themselves should take care that all under their charge should be so too. They built no houses, tilled no ground, but lived upon the products of their cattle. This they did partly in obedience to their ancestor, and out of a veneration they had for his name and authority, and partly from the experience they themselves had of the benefit of living such a mortified life. See the force of tradition, and the influence that antiquity, example, and great names, have upon men, and how that which seems very difficult will by long usage and custom become easy and in a manner natural. Now, 1. As to one of the particulars he had given them in charge, we are here told how in a case of necessity they dispensed with the violation of it (*v.* 11): *When the king of Babylon came into the land* with his army, though they had hitherto dwelt in tents, they now quitted their tents, and came and dwelt in Jerusalem, and in such houses as they could furnish themselves with there. Note, The rules of a strict discipline must not be made too strict, but so as to admit of a dispensation when the necessity of a case calls for it, which therefore, in making vows of that nature, it is wisdom to provide expressly for, that the way may be made the more clear, and we may not afterwards be forced to say, *It was an error,* Eccles. 5:6. Commands of that nature are to be understood with such limitations. These Rechabites would have tempted God, and not trusted him, if they had not used proper means for their own safety in a time of common calamity, notwithstanding the law and custom of their family. 2. As to the other particular, we are here told how, notwithstanding the greatest urgency, they religiously adhered to it. Jeremiah took them into the temple (*v.* 2), into a *prophet's chamber,* there, rather than into the *chamber of the princes,* that joined to it, because he had a message from God, which would look more like itself when it was delivered in the *chambers of a man of God.* There he not only asked the Rechabites whether they would drink any wine, but he set *pots full of wine before them,* and cups to drink out of, made the temptation as strong as possible, and said, *"Drink you wine,* you shall have it on free cost. You have broken one of the rules of your order, in coming to live at Jerusalem; why may you not break this too, and when you are in the city do as they there do?" But they peremptorily refused. They all agreed in the refusal. "No, *we will drink no wine;* for with us it is against the law." The prophet knew very well they would deny it, and, when they did, urged it no further, for he saw they were stedfastly resolved. Note, Those temptations are of no force with men of confirmed sobriety which yet daily overcome such as, notwithstanding their convictions, are of no resolution in the paths of virtue.

Verses 12–19

The trial of the Rechabites' constancy was intended but for a sign; now here we have the application of it.

I. The Rechabites' observance of their father's charge to them is made use of as an aggravation of the disobedience of the Jews to God. Let them see it and be ashamed. The prophet asks them, in God's name, *"Will you not* at length *receive instruction? v.* 13. Will nothing affect you? Will nothing fasten upon you? Will nothing prevail to discover sin and duty to you? You see how obedient the Rechabites are to their father's commandment (*v.* 14); but *you have not inclined your ear to me"* (*v.* 15), though one might much more reasonably expect that the people of God should have obeyed him than that the sons of Jonadab should have obeyed him; and the aggravation is very high, for, 1. The Rechabites were obedient to one who was but a man like themselves, who had but the wisdom and power of a man, and was only the father of their flesh; but the Jews were disobedient to an infinite and eternal God, who had an absolute authority over them, as the Father of their spirits. 2. Jonadab was long since dead, and was ignorant of them, and could neither take cognizance of their disobedience to his orders nor give correction for it; but God lives for ever, to see how his laws are observed, and is in a readiness to revenge all disobedience. 3. The Rechabites were never put in mind of their obligations to their father; but God often sent his prophets to his people, to put them in mind of their duty to him, and yet they would not do it. This is insisted on here as a great aggravation of their disobedience: *"I have* myself *spoken to you, rising early and speaking* by the written word and the dictates and admonitions of conscience (*v.* 14); nay, *I have sent unto you all my servants the prophets,* men like yourselves, whose terrors shall not make you afraid, *rising up early and sending them* (*v.* 15), and yet all in vain." 4. Jonadab never did that for his seed which God had done for his people. He left them a charge, but left them no estate to bear the charge; but God had given his people a *good land,* and promised them that, if they would be obedient, they should still dwell in it, so that they were bound both in gratitude and interest to be obedient, and yet they *would not hear,* they would not *hearken.* 5. God did not tie up his people to so much hardship, and to such instances of mortification, as Jonadab obliged his seed to; and yet Jonadab's orders were obeyed and God's were not.

II. Judgments are threatened, as often before, against Judah and Jerusalem, for their disobedience thus aggravated. The Rechabites shall rise up in judgment against them, and shall condemn them; for they very punctually *performed the commandment of their father,* and continued and persevered in their obedience to it (*v.* 16); but *this people,* this rebellious and gainsaying people, *have not hearkened unto me;* and therefore (*v.* 17), because they have not obeyed the precepts of the word, God will perform the threatenings of it: *"I will bring upon them,* by the Chaldean army, *all the evil pronounced against them* both in the law and in the prophets, for *I have spoken to them, I have called to them* — spoken in a still small voice to those that were near and called aloud to those that were at a distance, tried all ways and means to convince and reduce them — spoken by my word, called by my providence, both to the same purport, and yet all to no purpose; they have not *heard* nor *answered."*

III. Mercy is here promised to the family of the Rechabites for their steady and unanimous adherence to the laws of their house. Though it was only for the shaming of Israel that their constancy was tried, yet, being unshaken, it was *found unto praise, and honour, and glory;* and God takes occasion from it to tell them that he had favours in reserve for them (*v.* 18, 19) and that they should have the comfort of them. 1. That the family shall continue as long as any of the families of Israel, among whom they were strangers and sojourners. it shall *never want a man* to inherit what they had, though they had no inheritance to leave. Note, Sometimes those that have the smallest estates have the most numerous progeny; but he that sends mouths will be sure to send meat. 2. That religion shall continue in the family: *"He shall not want a man to stand before me,* to serve me." Though they are neither priests nor levites, nor appear to have had any post in the temple service, yet in a constant course of regular devotion, they stand before God, to minister to him. Note, (1.) The greatest blessing that can be entailed upon a family is to have the worship of God kept up in it from generation to generation. (2.) Temperance, self-denial, and mortification to the world, do very much befriend the exercises of piety, and help to transmit the observance of them to posterity. The more dead we are to the delights of sense the better we are disposed for the service of God; but nothing is more fatal to the entail of religion in a family than pride and luxury.

CHAPTER 36

Here is another expedient tried to work upon this heedless and untoward people, but it is tried in vain. A roll of a book is provided, containing an abstract or abridgment of all the sermons that Jeremiah had preached to them, that they might be put in mind of what they had heard and might the better understand it, when they had it all before them at one view. Now here we have, I. The writing of this roll by Baruch, as Jeremiah dictated it (*v.* 1–4). II. The reading of the roll by Baruch to all the people publicly on a fast-day (*v.* 5–10), afterwards by Baruch to the princes privately (*v.* 11–19), and lastly by Jehudi to the king (*v.* 20, 21). III. The burning of the roll by the king, with orders to prosecute Jeremiah and Baruch (*v.* 22–26). IV. The writing of another roll, with large additions, particularly of Jehoiakim's doom for burning the former (*v.* 27–32).

Verses 1–8

In the beginning of Ezekiel's prophecy we meet with *a roll* written *in vision,* for discovery of the things therein contained to the prophet himself, who was to receive and digest them, Eze. 2:9, 10; 3:1. Here, in the latter end of Jeremiah's prophecy, we meet with *a roll* written *in fact,* for discovery of the things contained therein to the people, who were to hear and give heed to them; for the written word and other good books are of great use both to ministers and people. We have here,

I. The command which God gave to Jeremiah to write a summary of his sermons, of all the reproofs and all the warnings he had given in God's name to his people, ever since he first began to be a preacher, in the thirteenth year of Josiah, *to this day,* which was in the fourth year of Jehoiakim, *v.* 2, 3. What had been only spoken must now be written, that it might be reviewed, and that it might spread the further and last the longer. What had been spoken at large, with frequent repetitions of the same things, perhaps in the same words (which has its advantage one way), must now be contracted and put into less compass, that the several parts of it might be better compared together, which has its advantage another way. What they had heard once must be recapitulated, and rehearsed to them again, that what was forgotten might be called to mind again and what made no impression upon them at the first hearing might take hold of them when they heard it the second time. And what was perhaps already written, and published in single sermons, must be collected into one volume, that none might be lost. Note, The writing of the scripture is by divine appointment. And observe the reason here given for the writing of this roll (*v.* 3): *It may be the house of Judah will hear.* Not that the divine prescience was at any uncertainty concerning the event: with that there is no peradventure; God knew certainly *that they would deal very treacherously,* Isa. 48:8. But the divine wisdom directed to this as a proper means for attaining the desired end: and, if it failed, they would be the more inexcusable. And, though God foresaw that they would not hear, he did not tell the prophet so, but prescribed this method to him as a probably one to be used, in the hopes that they would *hear,* that is, heed and regard what they heard, take notice of it and mix faith with it: for otherwise our hearing the word, though an angel from heaven were to read or preach it to us, would stand us in no stead. Now observe here, 1. What it is hoped they will thus hear: *All that evil which I purpose to do unto them.* Note, The serious consideration of the certain fatal consequences of sin will be of great use to us to bring us to God. 2. What it is hoped will be produced thereby: *They will hear, that they may return every man from his evil way.* Note, The conversion of sinners from their evil courses is that which ministers should aim at in preaching; and people hear the word in vain if that point be not gained with them. To what purpose do we hear of the evil God will bring upon us for sin if we continue, notwithstanding, to do evil against him? 3. Of what vast advantage their consideration and conversion will be to them: *That I may forgive their iniquity.* This plainly implies the honour of God's justice, with which it is not consistent that he should forgive the sin unless the sinner repent of it and turn from it; but it plainly expresses the honour of his mercy, that he is very ready to forgive sin and only waits till the sinner be qualified to receive forgiveness, and therefore uses various means to bring us to repentance, *that he may forgive.*

II. The instructions which Jeremiah gave to Baruch his scribe, pursuant to the command he had received from God, and the writing of the roll accordingly, *v.* 4. God bade Jeremiah write, but, it should seem, he had not the *pen of a ready writer,* he could not write fast, or fair, so as Baruch could, and therefore he made use of him as his amanuensis. St. Paul wrote but few of his epistles with his own hand, Gal. 6:11; Rom. 16:22. God dispenses his gifts variously; some have a good faculty at speaking, others at writing, and neither can say to the other, We have *no need of you,* 1 Co. 12:21. The Spirit of God dictated to Jeremiah, and he to Baruch, who had been employed by Jeremiah as trustee for him in his purchase of the field (ch 32:12) and now was advanced to be his scribe and substitute in his prophetical office; and, if we may credit the apocryphal book that bears his name, he was afterwards himself a prophet to the captives in Babylon. Those that begin low are likely to rise high, and it is good for those that are designed for prophets to have their education under prophets and to be serviceable to them. Baruch wrote what Jeremiah dictated in a *roll of a book* on pieces of parchment, or vellum, which were joined together, the top of one to the bottom of the other, so making one long scroll, which was rolled perhaps upon a staff.

III. The orders which Jeremiah gave to Baruch to read what he had written to the people. Jeremiah, it seems was *shut up,* and *could not go to the house of the Lord* himself, *v.* 5. Though he was not a close prisoner, for then there would have been no occasion to send officers to seize him (*v.* 26), yet he was forbidden by the king to appear in the temple, was shut out thence where he might be serving God and doing good, which was as bad to him as if he had been shut up in a dungeon. Jehoiakim was ripening apace for ruin when he thus silenced God's faithful messengers. But, when Jeremiah could not go to the temple himself, he sent one that was deputed by him to read to the people what he would himself have said. Thus St. Paul wrote epistles to the churches which he could not visit in person. Nay, it was what he himself had often said to them. Note, The writing and repeating of the sermons that have been preached may contribute very much towards the answering of the great ends of preaching. what we have heard and known it is good for us to hear again, that we may know it better. To preach and write the same thing is safe and profitable, and many times very necessary (Phil. 3:1), and we must be glad to hear a good word from God, though we have it, as here, at second hand. Both ministers and people must do what they can when they cannot do what they would. Observe, When God ordered the reading of the roll he said, *It may be they will hear and return from their evil ways, v.* 3. When Jeremiah orders it, he says, *It may be they will pray* (they will *present their supplications before the Lord*) and will *return from their evil way.* Note, Prayer to God for grace to turn us is necessary in order to our turning; and those that are convinced by the word of God of the necessity of returning to him will present their supplications to him for that grace. And the consideration of this, that *great is the anger which God has pronounced against us* for sin, should quicken both our prayers and our endeavours. Now, according to these orders, Baruch did read *out of the book the words of the Lord,* whenever there was a *holy convocation, v.* 8.

Verses 9–19

It should seem that Baruch had been frequently reading out of the book, to all companies that would give him the hearing, before the most solemn reading of it altogether which is here spoken of; for the directions were given about it in the *fourth year of Jehoiakim,* whereas this was done *in the fifth year, v.* 9. But some think that the writing of the book fairly over took up so much time that it was another year ere it was perfected; and yet perhaps it might not be past a month or two; he might begin in the latter end of the fourth year and finish it in the beginning of the fifth, for *thee ninth month* refers to the computation of the year in general, not to the year of that reign. Now observe here, 1. The government appointed a public fast to be religiously observed (*v.* 9), on account either of the distress they were brought into by the army of the Chaldeans or of the want of rain (*ch.* 14:1): *They proclaimed a fast to the people;* whether the king and princes or the priests, ordered this fast, is not certain; but it was plain that God by his providence called them aloud to it. Note, Great shows of piety and devotion may be found even among those who, though they keep up these *forms of godliness,* are strangers and enemies to *the power* of it. But what will such hypocritical services avail? Fasting, without reforming and turning away from sin, will never turn away the judgments of God, Jon. 3:10. Notwithstanding this fast, God proceeded in his controversy with this people. 2. Baruch repeated Jeremiah's sermons publicly in the house of the Lord, on the fast-day. He stood in a chamber that belonged to Gemariah, and out of a window, or balcony, read to the people that were in the court, *v.* 10. Note, When we are speaking to God we must be willing to hear from him; and therefore, on days of fasting and prayer, it is requisite that the word be read and preached. *Hearken unto me, that God may hearken unto you.* Jdg. 9:7. For our help in suing out mercy and grace, it is proper that we should be told of sin and duty. 3. An account was brought of this to the princes that attended the court and were now together in the secretary's office, here called the *scribe's chamber, v.* 12. It should seem, though the princes had called the people to meet in the house of God, to fact, and pray, and hear the word, they did not think fit to attend there themselves, which was a sign that it was not from a principle of true devotion, but merely for fashion sake, that they proclaimed this fast. We are willing to hope that it was not with a bad design, to bring Jeremiah into trouble for his preaching, but with a good design, to bring the princes into trouble for their sins, that Michaiah informed the princes of what Baruch had read; for his father Gemariah so far countenanced Baruch as to lend him his chamber to read out of. Michaiah finds the princes sitting in *the scribe's chamber,* and tells them they had better have been where he had been, hearing a good sermon in the temple, which he gives them the heads of. Note, When we have heard some good word that has affected and edified us we should be ready to communicate it to others that did not hear it, for their edification. *Out of the abundance of the heart the mouth speaks.* 4. Baruch is sent for, and is ordered to sit down among them and read it all over again to them (*v.* 14, 15), which he readily did, not complaining that he was weary with his public work and therefore desiring to be excused, nor upbraiding the princes with their being absent from the temple, where they might have heard it when he read it there. Note, God's ministers must *become all things to all men, if by any means they may gain some,* must comply with them in circumstances, that they may secure the substance. St. Paul preached privately to those of reputation, Gal. 2:2. 5. The princes were for the present much affected with the word that was read to them, *v.* 16. Observe, *They heard all the words* they did not interrupt him, but very patiently attended to the reading of the whole book; for otherwise how could they form a competent judgment of it? And, *when they had heard all, they were afraid,* were all afraid, *one* as well as *another;* like Felix, who trembled at Paul's reasonings. The reproofs were just, the threatenings terrible, and the predictions now in a fair way to be fulfilled; so that, laying all together, they were in a great consternation. We are not told what impressions this reading of the roll made upon the people (*v.* 10), but the princes were put into a fright by it, and (as some read it) *looked one upon another,* not knowing what to say. They were all convinced that it was worthy to be regarded, but none of them had courage to second it, only they agreed to *tell the king of all these words;* and, if he think fit to give credit to them, they will, otherwise not, no, though it were to prevent the ruin of the nation. And yet at the same time they knew the king's mind so far that they advised Baruch and Jeremiah to hide themselves (*v.* 19) and to shift as they could for their own safety, expecting no other than that the king,

instead of being convinced, would be exasperated. Note, It is common for sinners, under convictions, to endeavour to shake them off, by shifting off the prosecution of them to other persons, as these princes here, or to another *more convenient season,* as Felix. 6. They asked Baruch a trifling question, *How he wrote all these words* (*v.* 17), as if they suspected there was something extraordinary in it; but Baruch gives them a plain answer, that there was nothing but what was common in the manner of the writing — Jeremiah dictated and he wrote, *v.* 18. But thus it is common for those who would avoid the convictions of the word of God to start needless questions about the way and manner of the inspiration of it.

Verses 20–32

We have traced the roll to the people, and to the princes, and here we are to follow it to the king; and we find, I. That, upon notice given him concerning it, he sent for it, and ordered it to be read to him, *v.* 20, 21. He did not desire that Baruch would come and read it himself, who could read it more intelligently and with more authority and affection than any one else; nor did he order one of his princes to do it (though it would have been no disparagement to the greatest of them), much less would he vouchsafe to read it himself; but Jehudi, one of his pages now in waiting, who was sent to fetch it, is bidden to read it, who perhaps scarcely knew how to make sense of it. But those who thus despise the word of God will soon make it to appear, as this king did, that they hate it too, and have not only low, but ill thoughts of it.

II. That he had not patience to hear it read through as the princes had, but, when he had heard *three or four leaves* read, in a rage he *cut it with his penknife,* and threw it piece by piece *into the fire,* that he might be sure to see it *all consumed, v.* 22, 23. This was a piece of as daring impiety as a man could lightly be guilty of, and a most impudent affront to the God of heaven, whose message this was. 1. Thus he showed his impatience of reproof; being resolved to persist in sin, he would by no means bear to be told of his faults. 2. Thus he showed his indignation at Baruch and Jeremiah; he would have cut them in pieces, and burnt them, if he had had them in his reach, when he was in this passion. 3. Thus he expressed an abstinent resolution never to comply with the designs and intentions of the warnings given him; he will do what he will, whatever God by his prophets says to the contrary. 4. Thus he foolishly hoped to defeat the threatenings denounced against him, as if God knew not how to execute the sentence when the roll was gone in which it was written. 5. Thus he thought he had effectually provided that the things contained in this roll should spread no further, which was the care of the chief priests concerning the gospel, Acts 4:17. They had told him how this roll had been read to the people and to the princes. "But," says he, "I will take a course that shall prevent its being read any more." See what an enmity there is against God in the carnal mind, and wonder at the patience of God, that he bears with such indignities done to him.

III. That neither the king himself nor any of his princes were at all affected with the word: *They were not afraid* (*v.* 24) no, not those princes that *trembled at the word* when they heard it the first time, *v.* 16. So soon, so easily, do good impressions wear off. They showed some concern till they saw how light the king made of it, and then they shook off all that concern. They *rent not their garments,* as Josiah, this Jehoiakim's own father, did when he had the *book of the law* read to him, though it was not so particular as the contents of this roll were, nor so immediately adapted to the present posture of affairs.

IV. That there were three of the princes who had so much sense and grace left as to interpose for the preventing of the burning of the roll, but in vain, *v.* 25. If they had from the first shown themselves, as they ought to have done, affected with the word, perhaps they might have brought the king to a better mind and have persuaded him to bear it patiently; but frequently those that will not do the good they should put it out of their own power to do the good they would.

V. That Jehoiakim, when he had thus in effect burnt God's warrant by which he was arrested, as it were in a way of revenge, now that he thought he had got the better, signed a warrant for the apprehending of Jeremiah and

Baruch, God's ministers (*v.* 26): *But the Lord hid them.* The princes bade them abscond (*v.* 19), but it was neither the princes' care for them nor theirs for themselves that secured them; it was under the divine protection that they were safe. Note, God will find out a shelter for his people, though their persecutors be ever so industrious to get them into their power, till their hour be come; nay, and then he will himself be their hiding place.

VI. That Jeremiah had orders and instructions to write in another roll the same words that were written in the roll which Jehoiakim had burnt, *v.* 27, 28. Note, Though the attempts of hell against the word of God are very daring, yet not one iota or tittle of it shall fall to the ground, nor shall the unbelief of man make the word of God of no effect. Enemies may prevail to burn many a Bible, but they cannot abolish the word of God, can neither extirpate it nor defeat the accomplishment of it. Though the tables of the law were broken, they were renewed again; and so out of the ashes of the roll that was burnt arose another Phoenix. *The word of the Lord endures for ever.*

VII. That the king of Judah, though a king, was severely reckoned with by the King of kings for this indignity done to the written word. God noticed what it was in the roll that Jehoiakim took so much offense at. Jehoiakim was angry because it was *written therein, saying,* Surely *the king of Babylon shall come and destroy this land, v.* 29. And did not *the king of Babylon* come two years before this, and go far towards *the destroying of this land?* He did so (2 Chr. 36:6, 7) in his third year, Dan. 1:1. So that God and his prophets had *therefore become his enemies because they told him the truth,* told him of the desolation that was coming, but at the same time putting him into a fair way to prevent it. But, if this be the thing he takes so much amiss, let him know, 1. That the wrath of God shall come upon him and his family, in the first place, by the hand of Nebuchadnezzar. He shall be cut off, and in a few weeks his son shall be dethroned, and exchange his royal robes for prison-garments, so that *he shall have none to sit upon the throne of David;* the glory of that illustrious house shall be eclipsed, and die in him; *his dead body* shall lie unburied, or, which comes all to one, *he shall be buried with the burial of an ass,* that is, thrown into the next ditch; it shall lie exposed to all weathers, *heat and frost,* which will occasion its putrefying and becoming loathsome the sooner. "Not that his body" (says Mr. Gataker) "could be sensible of such usage, or himself, being deceased, of aught that should befal his body; but that the king's body in such a condition should be a hideous spectacle, and a horrid monument of God's heavy wrath and indignation against him, unto all that should behold it." Even *his seed and his servants* shall fare the worse for their relation to him (*v.* 31), for they shall be punished, not for his iniquity, but so much the sooner for their own. 2. That all the evil pronounced against Judah and Jerusalem in that roll shall be brought upon them. Though the copy be burnt, the original remains in the divine counsel, which shall again be copied out after another manner in bloody characters. Note, There is no escaping God's judgments by struggling with them. *Who ever hardened his heart against God, and prospered?*

VIII. That, when the roll was written anew, *there were added* to the former *many like words* (*v.* 32), many more threatenings of wrath and vengeance; for, since they will yet *walk contrary to God,* he will *heat the furnace seven times hotter.* Note, As God is in one mind, and none can turn him, so he has still more arrows in his quiver; and those who contend with God's woes do but prepare for themselves heavier of the same kind.

CHAPTER 37

This chapter brings us very near the destruction of Jerusalem by the Chaldeans, for the story of it lies in the latter end of Zedekiah's reign; we have in it, I. A general idea of the bad character of that reign (*v.* 1, 2). II. The message which Zedekiah, notwithstanding, sent to Jeremiah to desire his prayers (*v.* 3). III. The flattering hopes which the people had conceived, that the Chaldeans would quit the siege of Jerusalem (*v.* 5). IV. The assurance God gave them by Jeremiah (who was now at liberty, *v.* 4) that the Chaldean army should renew the siege and take the city (*v.* 6–10). V. The imprisonment of Jeremiah, under pretence that he was a deserter (*v.* 11–15). VI. The kindness which Zedekiah showed him when he was a prisoner (*v.* 16–21).

Verses 1–10

Here is, 1. Jeremiah's preaching slighted, *v.* 1, 2. Zedekiah succeeded Coniah, or Jeconiah, and, though he saw in his predecessor the fatal consequences of contemning the word of God, yet he did not take warning, nor give any more regard to it than others had done before him. *Neither he, nor his* courtiers, *nor the people of the land, hearkened unto the words of the Lord,* though they already began to be fulfilled. Note, Those have hearts wretchedly hard indeed that see God's judgments on others, and feel them on themselves, and yet will not be humbled and brought to heed what he says. These had proof sufficient that it was the Lord who spoke by Jeremiah the prophet, and yet they would not hearken to him. 2. Jeremiah's prayers desired. Zedekiah sent messengers to him, saying, *Pray now unto the Lord our God for us.* He did so before (*ch.* 21:1, 2), and one of the messengers, Zephaniah, is the same there and here. Zedekiah is to be commended for his, and it shows that he had some good in him, some sense of his need of God's favour and of his own unworthiness to ask it for himself, and some value for good people and good ministers, who had an interest in Heaven. Note, When we are in distress we ought to desire the prayers of our ministers and Christian friends, for thereby we put an honour upon prayer, and an esteem upon our brethren. Kings themselves should look upon their praying people as the strength of the nation, Zec. 12:5, 10. And yet this does but help to condemn Zedekiah out of his own mouth. If indeed he looked upon Jeremiah as a prophet, whose prayers might avail much both for him and his people, why did he not then believe him, and *hearken to the words of the Lord* which he spoke by him? He desired his good prayers, but would not take his good counsel, nor be ruled by him, though he spoke in God's name, and it appears by this that Zedekiah knew he did. Note, It is common for those to desire to be prayed for who will not be advised; but herein they put a cheat upon themselves, for how can we expect that God should hear others speaking to him for us if we will not hear them speaking to us from him and for him? Many who despise prayer when they are in prosperity will be glad of it when they are in adversity. Now *give us of your oil.* When Zedekiah sent to the prophet to pray for him, he had better have sent for the prophet to pray with him; but he thought that below him: and how can those expect the comforts of religion who will not stoop to the services of it? 3. Jerusalem flattered by the retreat of the Chaldean army from it. Jeremiah was now at liberty (*v.* 4); he *went in and out among the people,* might freely speak to them and be spoken to by them. Jerusalem also, for the present, was at liberty, *v.* 5 Zedekiah, though a tributary to the king of Babylon, had entered into a private league with Pharaoh king of Egypt (Eze. 17:15), pursuant to which, when the king of Babylon came to chastise him for his treachery, the king of Egypt, though he came no more in person after that great defeat which Nebuchadnezzar gave him in the reign of Jehoiakim (2 Ki. 24:7), yet sent some forces to relieve Jerusalem when it was besieged, upon notice of the approach of which the Chaldeans raised the siege, probably not for fear of them but in policy, to fight them at a distance, before any of the Jewish forces could join them. From this they encouraged themselves to hope that Jerusalem was delivered for good and all out of the hands of its enemies and that the storm was quite blown over. Note, Sinners are commonly hardened in their security by the intermissions of judgments and the slow proceedings of them; and those who will not be awakened by the word of God may justly be lulled asleep by the providence of God. 4. Jerusalem threatened with the return of the Chaldean army and with ruin by it. Zedekiah sent to Jeremiah to desire him to pray for them, that the Chaldean army might not return; but Jeremiah sends him word back that the decree had gone forth, and that it was but a folly for them to expect peace, for God had begun a controversy with them, which he would make an end of: *Thus saith the Lord, Deceive not yourselves, v.* 9. Note, Satan himself, though he is the great deceiver, could not deceive us if we did not deceive ourselves; and thus sinners are their own destroyers by being their own deceivers, of which this is an aggravation that they are so frequently warned of it and cautioned not to deceive themselves, and they have the word of God, the great design of which is to undeceive them. Jeremiah uses no dark metaphors, but tells them plainly, (1.) That the Egyptians shall retreat, and either give back or be forced back, into *their own land* (Eze. 17:17), which was said of old (Isa. 30:7), and is here said again, *v.* 7. The Egyptians shall help in vain; they shall not dare to face the Chaldean army, but shall retire with precipitation. Note, If God help us not, no creature can. As no power can prevail against God, so none can avail without God nor countervail his departures from us. (2.) That the Chaldeans shall return, and shall renew the siege and prosecute it with more vigour than ever: *They shall not depart* for good and all (*v.* 9); *they shall come again* (*v.* 8); they shall *fight against the city.* Note, God has the sovereign command of all the hosts of men, even of those that know him not, that own him not, and they are all made to serve his purposes. He directs their marches, their counter-marches, their retreats, their returns, as it pleases him; and furious armies, like *stormy winds,* in all their motions are *fulfilling his word.* (3.) That Jerusalem shall certainly be delivered into the hand of the Chaldeans: *They shall take it, and burn it with fire, v.* 8. The sentence passed upon it shall be executed, and they shall be the executioners. "O but" (say they) "the Chaldeans have withdrawn; they have quitted the enterprise as impracticable." "And though they have," says the prophet, "nay, *though you had smitten* their army, so that many were slain and all the rest wounded, yet those *wounded men should rise up and burn this city," v.* 10. This is designed to denote that the doom passed upon Jerusalem is irrevocable, and its destruction inevitable; it must be laid in ruins, and these Chaldeans are the men that must destroy it, and it is now in vain to think of evading the stroke or contending with it. Note, Whatever instruments God has determined to make use of in any service for him, whether or mercy or judgment, they shall accomplish that for which they are designed, whatever incapacity or disability they may lie under or be reduced to. Those by whom God has resolved to save or to destroy, saviours they shall be and destroyers they shall be, yea, though there were all wounded; for as when God has work to do he will not want instruments to do it with, though they may seem far to seek, so when he has chosen his instruments they shall do the work, though they may seem very unlikely to accomplish it.

Verses 11–21

We have here a further account concerning Jeremiah, who relates more passages concerning himself than any other of the prophets; for the histories of the lives and sufferings of God's ministers have been very serviceable to the church, as well as their preaching and writing.

I. We are here told that Jeremiah, when he had an opportunity for it, attempted to retire out of Jerusalem into the country (*v.* 11, 12): *When the Chaldeans* had *broken up from Jerusalem* because *of Pharaoh's army,* upon the notice of their advancing towards them, Jeremiah determined *to go into the* country, and (as the margin reads it) *to slip away from Jerusalem in the midst of the people,* who, in that interval of the siege, went out into the country to look after their affairs there. He endeavoured to steal away in the crowd; for, though he was a man of great eminence, he could well reconcile himself to obscurity, though he was one of a thousand, he was content to be lost in the multitude and buried alive in a corner, in a cottage. Whether he designed for Anathoth or no does not appear; his concerns might call him thither, but his neighbours there were such as (unless they had mended since *ch.* 11:21) might discourage him from coming among them; or he might intend to hide himself somewhere where he was not known, and fulfil his own wish (*ch.* 9:2), *Oh that I had in the wilderness a lodging-place!* Jeremiah found he could do no good in Jerusalem; he laboured in vain among them, and therefore determined to leave them. Note, there are times when it is the wisdom of good men to retire into privacy, to *enter into the chamber and shut the doors about them,* Isa. 26:20.

II. That in this attempt he was seized as a deserter and committed to prison (*v.* 13–15): *He was in the gate of Benjamin,* so far he had gained his point, when *a captain of the ward,* who probably had the charge of that gate, discovered him and *took him* into custody. he was the grandson of Hananiah, who, the Jews say, was Hananiah the false prophet, who contested with Jeremiah (*ch.* 28:10), and they add that this young captain had a spite to Jeremiah upon that account. He could not arrest him without some pretence, and that which he charges upon his is, *Thou fallest away to the Chaldeans* — an unlikely story, for the Chaldeans had now gone off, Jeremiah could not reach them; or, if he could, who would go over to a baffled army? Jeremiah therefore with good reason, and with both the confidence and the mildness of an innocent man, denies the charge: *"It is false; I fall not away to the Chaldeans;* I am going upon my own lawful occasions." Note, it is no new thing for the church's best friends to be represented as in the interest of her worst enemies. Thus have the blackest characters been put upon the fairest purest minds, and, in such a malicious world as this is, innocency, nay, excellency itself, is no fence against the basest calumny. When at any time we are thus falsely accused we may do as Jeremiah did, boldly deny the charge and then commit our cause to him that judges righteously. Jeremiah's protestation of his integrity, though he is a prophet, a man of God, a man of honour and sincerity, though he is a priest, and is ready to say it *in verbo sacerdotis — on the word of a priest,* is not regarded; but he is brought before the privy-council, who without examining him and the proofs against him, but upon the base malicious insinuation of the captain, fell into a passion with him: they *were wroth;* and what justice could be expected from men who, being in anger, would hear no reason? They beat him, without any regard had to his coat and character, and then *put him in prison,* in the worst prison they had, that *in the house of Jonathan the scribe;* either it had been his house, and he had quitted it for the inconveniences of it, but it was thought good enough for a prison, or it was now his house, and perhaps he was a rigid severe man, that made it a house of cruel bondage to his prisoners. Into this prison Jeremiah was thrust, *into the dungeon,* which was dark and cold, damp and dirty, the most uncomfortable unhealthy place in it; in the cells, or *cabins,* there he must lodge, among which there is no choice, for they are all alike miserable lodging-places. *There Jeremiah remained many days, and* for aught that appears, nobody came near him or enquired after him. See what a world this is. The wicked princes, who are in rebellion against God, lie at ease, lie in state in their palaces, while godly Jeremiah, who is in the service of God, lies in pain, in a loathsome dungeon. It is well that there is a world to come.

III. That Zedekiah at length sent for him, and showed him some favour; but probably not till the Chaldean army had returned and had laid fresh siege to the city. When their vain hopes, with which they fed themselves (an in confidence of which they had re-enslaved their servants, *ch.* 34:11), had all vanished, then they were in a greater confusion and consternation then ever. "O then" (says Zedekiah) "send in all haste for the prophet; let me have some talk with him." When the Chaldeans had withdrawn, he only sent to the prophet to pray for him; but now that they had again invested the city, he sent for him to consult him. Thus gracious will men be when pangs come upon them. 1. The king sent for him to give him private audience as an ambassador from God. He *asked him secretly in his house,* being ashamed to be seen in his company, *"Is there any word from the Lord?* (*v.* 17) — any word of comfort? Canst thou give us any hopes that the Chaldeans shall again retire?" Note, Those that will not hearken to God's admonitions when they are in prosperity would be glad of his consolations when they are in adversity and expect that his ministers should then speak words of peace to them; but how can they expect it? What have they to do with peace? Jeremiah's life and comfort are in Zedekiah's hand, and he has now a petition to present to him for his favour, and yet, having this opportunity, he tells him plainly that *there is a word from the Lord,* but no word of comfort for him or his people: *Thou shalt be delivered into the hand of the king of Babylon.* If Jeremiah had consulted with flesh and blood, he would have given him a plausible answer, and, though he would not have told him a lie, yet he might have chosen whether he would tell him the worst at this time; what occasion was there for it, when he had so often told it him before? But Jeremiah was one that had *obtained mercy of the Lord to be faithful,* and would not, to obtain mercy of man, be unfaithful either to God or to his prince; he therefore tells him the truth, the whole truth. And, since there was no remedy, it would be a kindness to the king to know his doom, that, being no surprise to him, it might be the less a terror, and he might provide to make the best of bad. Jeremiah takes this occasion to upbraid him and his people with the credit they gave to the false prophets, who told them that *the king of Babylon* should *not come* at all, or, when he had withdrawn, should *not come* again *against* them, *v.* 19. *"Where are now your prophets,* who told you that you should have peace?" Note, Those who deceive themselves with groundless hopes of mercy will justly be upbraided with their folly when the event has undeceived them. 2. He improved this opportunity for the presenting of a private petition, as a poor prisoner, *v.* 18, 20. It was not in Jeremiah's power to reverse the sentence God had passed upon Zedekiah, but it was in Zedekiah's power to reverse the sentence which the princes had given against him; and therefore, since he thought him fit to be used as a prophet, he would not think him fit to be abused as the worst of malefactors. He humbly expostulates with the king: *"What have I offended against thee, or thy servants, or this people,* what law have I broken, what injury have I done to the common welfare, *that you have put me in prison?"* And many a one that has been very hardly dealt with has been able to make the same appeal and to make it good. He likewise earnestly begs, and very pathetically (*v.* 20), *Cause me to return* to yonder noisome gaol, *to the house of Jonathan the scribe, lest I die there.* This was the language of innocent nature, sensible of its own grievances and solicitous for its own preservation. Though he was not at all unwilling to die God's martyr, yet, having so fair an opportunity to get relief, he would not let it slip, lest he should die his own murderer. When Jeremiah delivered God's message he spoke as one having authority, with the greatest boldness; but, when he presented his own request, he spoke as one under authority, with the greatest submissiveness: *Near me, I pray thee, O my Lord the king! let my supplication, I pray thee, be accepted before thee.* Here is not a word of complaint of the princes that unjustly committed him, no offer to bring an action of false imprisonment against them, but all in a way of modest supplication to the king, to teach us that even when we act with the courage that becomes the faithful servants of God, yet we must conduct ourselves with the humility and modesty that become dutiful subjects to the government God hath set over us. A lion in God's cause must be a lamb in his own. And we find that God gave Jeremiah favour in the eyes of the king. (1.) He gave him his request, took care that he should not die in the dungeon, but ordered that he should have the liberty of the *court of the prison,* where he might have a pleasant walk and breathe a free air. (2.) He gave him more than his request, took care that he should not die for want, as many did that had their liberty, by reason of the straitness of the siege; he ordered him his *daily bread out of the* public stock (for the prison was within the verge of the court), *till all the bread was spent.* Zedekiah ought to have released him, to have made him a privy-counsellor, as Joseph was taken from prison to be the second man in the kingdom. But he had not courage to do that; it was well he did as he did, and it is an instance of the care God takes of his suffering servants that are faithful to him. He can make even their confinement turn to their advantage and the court of the of their prison to become as green pastures to them, and raise up such friends to provide for them that *in the days of famine they shall be satisfied. At destruction and famine thou shalt laugh.*

CHAPTER 38

In this chapter, just as in the former, we have Jeremiah greatly debased under the frowns of the princes, and yet greatly honoured by the favour of the king. They used him as a criminal; he used him as a privy-counsellor. Here, I. Jeremiah for his faithfulness is put into the dungeon by the princes (*v.* 1-6). II. At the intercession of Ebed-melech the Ethiopian, by special order from the king, he is taken up out of the dungeon and confined only to the court of the prison (*v.* 7-13). III. He has a private conference with the king upon the present conjuncture of affairs (*v.* 14-22). IV. Care is taken to keep that conference private (*v.* 24-28).

Verses 1-13

Here, 1. Jeremiah persists in his plain preaching; what he had many a time said, he still says (*v.* 3): *This city shall be given into the hand of the king of Babylon;* though it hold out long, it will taken at last. Nor would he have so often repeated this unwelcome message but that he could put them in a certain way, though not to save the city, yet to save themselves; so that every man might have his own life given him for a prey if he would be advised, *v.* 2. Let him not stay in the city, in hopes to defend that, for it will be to no purpose, but let him *go forth to the Chaldeans,* and throw himself upon their mercy, before things come to extremity, and then he *shall live;* they will not put him to the sword, but give him quarter *(satis est prostrasse leoni — it suffices the lion to lay his antagonist prostrate)* and he shall escape the *famine and pestilence,* which will be the death of multitudes within the city. Note, Those do better for themselves who patiently submit to the rebukes of Providence than those who contend with them. And, if we cannot have our liberty, we must reckon it a mercy to have our lives, and not foolishly throw them away upon a point of honour; they m ay be reserved for better times. 2. The princes persist in their malice against Jeremiah. He was faithful to his country and to his trust as a prophet, though he had suffered many a time for his faithfulness; and, though at this time he ate the king's bread, yet that did not stop his mouth. But his persecutors were still bitter against him, and complained that he abused the liberty he had of walking in the court of the prison; for, though he could not go to the temple to preach, yet he vented the same things in private conversation to those that came to visit him, and therefore (*v.* 4) they represented him to the king as a dangerous man, disaffected to his country and to the government he lived under: *He seeks not the welfare of this people, but the hurt* — an unjust insinuation, for no man had laid out himself more for the good of Jerusalem than he had done. They represent his preaching as having a bad tendency. The design of it was plainly to bring men to repent and turn to God, which would have been as much as any thing a strengthening to the hands both the soldiery and of the burghers, and yet they represented it *as weakening their hands* and discouraging them; and, if it did this, it was their own fault. Note, It is common for wicked people to look upon God's faithful ministers as their enemies, only because they show them what enemies they are to themselves while they continue impenitent. 3. Jeremiah hereupon, by the king's permission, is put into a dungeon, with a view to his destruction there. Zedekiah, though he felt a conviction that Jeremiah was a prophet, sent of God, had not courage to own it, but yielded to the violence of his persecutors (*v.* 5): *He is in your hand;* and a worse sentence he could not have passed upon him. We found in Jehoiakim's reign that the princes were better affected to the prophet than the king was (*ch.* 36:25); but now they were more violent against him, a sign that they were ripening apace for ruin. Had it been in a cause that concerned his own honour or profit, he would have let them know that the king is he who can do what he pleases, whether they will or no; but in the cause of God and his prophet, which he was very cool in, he basely sneaks, and truckles to them: *The king is not he that can do any thing against you.* Note, Those will have a great deal to answer for who, though they have a secret kindness for good people, dare not own it in a time of need, nor will do what they might do to prevent mischief designed them. The princes, having this general warrant from the king, immediately put poor *Jeremiah into the dungeon of Malchiah, that was in the court of the prison* (*v.* 6), a deep dungeon, for they *let* him *down* into it *with cords,* and a dirty one, for *there was no water* in it, *but mire;* and he *sunk in the mire, up to the neck,* says Josephus. Those that put him here doubtless designed that he should die here, die for hunger, die for cold, and so die miserably, die obscurely, fearing, if they should put him to death openly, the people might be affected with what he would say and be incensed against them. Many of God's faithful witnesses have thus been privately made away, and starved to death, in prisons, whose blood will be brought to account in the day of discovery. We are not here told what Jeremiah did in this distress, but he tells us himself (Lam. 3:55, 57), *I called upon thy name, O Lord! out of the low dungeon, and thou drewest near, saying, Fear not.* 4. Application is made to the king by an honest courtier, *Ebed-melech,* one of the gentlemen of the bed-chamber, in behalf of the poor sufferer. Though the princes carried on the matter as privately as they could, yet it came to the ear of this good man, who probably sought opportunities to do good. It may be he came to the knowledge of it by hearing Jeremiah's moans out of the dungeon, for it was in the king's house, *v.* 7. *Ebed-melech* was an Ethiopian, a *stranger to the commonwealth of Israel,* and yet had in him more humanity, and more divinity too, than native Israelites had. Christ found more faith among Gentiles than among Jews. Ebed-melech lived in a wicked court and in a very corrupt degenerate age, and yet had a great sense both of equity and piety. God has his remnant in all places, among all sorts. There were *saints* even *in Caesar's household.* The king was now *sitting in the gate of Benjamin,* to try causes and receive appeals and petitions, or perhaps holding a council of war there. Thither Ebed-melech went immediately to him, for the case would not admit delay; the prophet might have perished if he had trifled or put it off till he had an opportunity of speaking to the king in private. Not time must be lost when life is in danger, especially so valuable a life. He boldly asserts the Jeremiah had a great deal of wrong done him, and is not afraid to tell the king so, though they were princes that did it, though they were now present in court, and though they had the king's warrant for what they did. Whither should oppressed innocency flee for protection but to the throne, especially when great men are its oppressors? Ebed-melech appears truly brave in this matter. He does not mince the matter; though he had a place at court, which he would be in danger of losing for his plain dealing, yet he tells the king faithfully, let him take it as he will, *These men have done ill in all that they have done to Jeremiah.* They had dealt unjustly with him, for he had not deserved any punishment at all; and they had dealt barbarously with him, so as they used not to deal with the vilest malefactors. And they needed not to have put him to this miserable death; for, if they had let him alone where he was, he was *likely to die for hunger in the place where he was,* in the court of the prison to which he was confined, *for there was not more bread in the city:* the stores out of which he was to have his allowance (*ch.* 37:21) were in a manner spent. See how God can raise up friends for his people in distress where they little thought of them, and animate men for his service even beyond expectation. 5. Orders are immediately given for his release, and Ebed-melech takes care to see them executed. The king, who but now durst do nothing against the princes, had his heart wonderfully changed on a sudden, and will now have Jeremiah released in defiance of the princes, for therefore he orders no less than thirty men, and those of the lifeguard, to be employed in fetching him out of the dungeon, lest the princes should raise a party to oppose it, *v.* 10. Let this encourage us to appear boldly for God — we may succeed better that we could have thought, for *the hearts of kings are in the hand of God.* Ebed-melech gained his point, and soon brought Jeremiah the good news; and it is observable how particularly the manner of his drawing him out of the dungeon is related (for *God is not unrighteous to forget* any *work or labour of love* which is shown to his people or ministers, no, nor any circumstance of it, Heb. 6:10); special notice is taken of his great tenderness in providing old soft rags for Jeremiah to put under his arm-holes, to keep the cords wherewith he was to be drawn up from hurting him, his arm-holes being probably galled by the cords wherewith he was let down. Nor did he throw the rags down to him, lest they should be lost in the mire, but carefully let them down, *v.* 11, 12. Note, Those that are in distress should not only be relieved, but relieved with compassion and marks of respect, all which shall be placed to account and abound to a good account in the day of recompence. See what a good use even old rotten rags may be put to, which therefore should not be made waste of, any more than broken meat: even in the king's house, and *under the treasury* too, these were carefully preserved for the use of the poor or sick. Jeremiah is brought up out of the dungeon, and is now where he was, *in the court of the prison, v.* 13. Perhaps Ebed-melech could have made interest with the king to get him his discharge thence also, now that he had the king's ear; but he though him safer and better provided for there than he would be any where else. God can, when he pleases, make a prison to become a refuge and hiding-place to his people in distress and danger.

Verses 14-28

In the foregoing chapter we had the king in close conference with Jeremiah, and here again, though (*v.* 5) he had given him up into the hands of his enemies; such a struggle there was in the breast of this unhappy prince between his convictions and his corruptions. Observe,

I. The honour that Zedekiah did to the prophet. When he was newly fetched out of the dungeon he sent for him to advise with him privately. He met him in *the third entry,* or (as the margin reads it) *the principal entry,* that *is in,* or leads towards, or adjoins to, *the house of the Lord, v.* 14. In appointing this place of interview with the prophet perhaps he intended to show a respect and reverence for *the house of God,* which was proper enough now that he was desiring to hear *the word of God.* Zedekiah would ask *Jeremiah a thing;* it should rather be rendered, *a word.* "I am here asking thee for *a word of prediction,* of counsel, of comfort, *a word from the Lord, ch.* 37:17. Whatever word thou has for me *hide it not from me;* let me know the worst." He had been told plainly what things would come to in the foregoing chapter, but, like Balaam, he asks again, in hopes to get a more pleasing answer, as if God, who is *in one mind,* were altogether such a one as himself, who was in many minds.

II. The bargain that Jeremiah made with him before he would give him his advice, *v.* 15. He would stipulate, 1. For his own safety. Zedekiah would have him deal faithfully with him: "And if I do," says Jeremiah, *"wilt thou not put me to death?* I am afraid *thou wilt"* (so some take it); "what else can I expect when thou art led blindfold by the princes?" Not that Jeremiah was backward to seal the doctrine he preached with his blood, when he was called to do so; but, in doing our duty, we ought to use all lawful means for our own preservation; even the apostles of Christ did so. 2. He would answer for the success of his advice, being no less concerned for Zedekiah's welfare than for his own. He is willing to give him wholesome advice, and does not upbraid him with his unkindness in suffering him to be put into the dungeon, nor bid him go and consult with his princes, whose judgments he had such a value for. Ministers must with meekness instruct even those that oppose themselves, and render good for evil. He is desirous that he should *hear counsel and receive instruction: "Wilt thou not hearken unto me?* Surely thou wilt; I am in hopes to find thee pliable at last, and now *in this thy day* willing to know *the things that belong to thy peace."* Note, Then, and then only, there is hope of sinners, when they are willing to hearken to good counsel. Some read it as spoken despairingly: *"If I give thee counsel, thou wilt not hearken unto me;* I have reason to fear thou wilt not, and then I might as well keep my counsel to myself." Note, Ministers have little heart to speak to those who have long and often turned a deaf ear to them. Now, as to this latter concern of Jeremiah's, Zedekiah makes him no answer, will not promise to hearken to his advice: though he desires to know what is the mind of God, yet he will reserve himself a liberty, when he does know it, to do as he things fit; as if it were the prerogative of a prince not to have his ruin prevented by good counsel. But, as to the prophet's safety, he promises him, upon the word of a king, and confirms his promise with an oath, that, whatever he should say to him, no advantage should be taken against him for it: *I will neither put thee to death nor deliver thee into the hands of those that will, v.* 16. This, he thought, was a mighty favour, and yet Nebuchadnezzar and Belshazzar, when Daniel read their doom, not only protected him, but preferred and rewarded him, Dan. 2:48; *v.* 29. Zedekiah's oath on this occasion is solemn, and very observable: *"As the Lord liveth, who made us this soul,* who gave me my life and thee thine, I dare not take away thy life unjustly, knowing that then I should forfeit my own to him that is the Lord of life." Note, God is the Father of spirits; souls are his workmanship, and they are more *fearfully and wonderfully made* than bodies are. The soul both of the greatest prince and of the poorest prisoner is of God's making. *He fashioneth their hearts* alike easily. In all our appeals to God, and in all our dealings both with ourselves and others, we ought to consider this, that *the living God made us these souls.*

III. The good advice that Jeremiah gave him, with good reasons why he should take it, not from any prudence or politics of his own, but in the *name of the Lord, the God of hosts* and *God of Israel.* Not as a statesman, but as a prophet, he advises him by all means to surrender himself and his city *to the king of Babylon's princes: "Go forth to them,* and make the best terms thou canst with them," *v.* 17. This was the advice he had given to the people (*v.* 2, and before, *ch.* 21:9), to submit to divine judgments, and not think of contending with them. Note, In dealing with God, that which is good counsel to the meanest is so to the greatest, for *there is no respect of persons* with him. To persuade him to take this counsel, he sets before him good and evil, life and death. 1. If he will tamely yield, he shall save his children from the sword and Jerusalem from the flames. The white flag is yet hung out; if he will be acknowledge God's justice, he shall experience his mercy: *The city shall not be burnt,* and *thou shalt live and thy house.* But, 2. If he will obstinately stand it out, it will be the ruin both of his house and Jerusalem (*v.* 18); for when God judges he will overcome. This is the case of sinners with God; let them humbly submit to his grace and government and they shall live; let them *take hold on his strength, that they may make peace, and they shall make peace;* but, if they harden their hearts against his proposals, it will certainly be to their destruction: they must either bend or break.

IV. The objection which Zedekiah made against the prophet's advice, *v.* 19. Jeremiah spoke to him by prophecy, in the name of God, and therefore if he had had a due regard to the divine authority, wisdom, and goodness, as soon as he understood what the mind of God was he would immediately have acquiesced in it and resolved to observe it, without disputing; but, as if it had been the dictate only of Jeremiah's prudence, he advances against it some prudential considerations of his own: but human wisdom is folly when it contradicts the divine counsel. All he suggests is, *"I am afraid,* not of the Chaldeans; their princes are men of honour, but of the Jews, that have already gone over to the Chaldeans; when they see *me* follow them, and who had so much opposed their going, they will laugh at me, and say, *Hast thou also become weak as water?"* Isa. 14:10. Now, 1. It was not at all likely that he should be thus exposed and ridiculed, that the Chaldeans should so far gratify the Jews, or trample upon him, as to deliver him into their hands; nor that the Jews, who were themselves captives, should be in such a gay humour as to make a jest of the misery of their prince. Note, We often frighten ourselves from our duty by foolish, causeless, groundless, fears, that are merely the creatures of our own fancy and imagination. 2. If he should be taunted at a little by the Jews, could he not despise it and make light of it? What harm would it do him? Note, Those have very weak and fretful spirits indeed that cannot bear to be laughed at for that which is both their duty and their interest. 3. Though it had been really the greatest personal mischief that he could imagine it to be, yet he ought to have ventured it, in obedience to God, and for the preservation of his family and city. He thought it would be looked upon as a piece of cowardice to surrender; whereas it would be really an instance of true courage cheerfully to bear a less evil, the mocking of the Jews, for the avoiding of a greater, the ruin of his family and kingdom.

V. The pressing importunity with which Jeremiah followed the advice he had given the king. He assures him that, if he would comply with the will of God herein, the thing he feared should not come upon him (*v.* 20): *They shall not deliver thee up,* but treat thee as becomes thy character. He begs of him, after all the foolish games he had played, to manage wisely the last stake, and now at length to do well for himself: *Obey, I beseech thee, the voice of the Lord,* because it is his voice, so it *shall be well unto thee.* But he tells him what would be the consequence if he would not obey. 1. He himself would *fall into the hands of the Chaldeans,* as implacable enemies, whom he might now make his friends by throwing himself into their hands. if he must fall, he should contrive how to fall easily: *"Thou shalt not escape,* as thou hopest to do," *v.* 23. 2. He would himself be chargeable with the destruction of Jerusalem, which he pretended a concern for the preservation of: *"Thou shalt cause this city to be burnt with fire,* for by a little submission and self-denial thou mightest have prevented it." Thus subjects often suffer for the pride and wilfulness of their rulers, who should be their protectors, but prove their destroyers. 3. Whereas he causelessly feared an unjust reproach for surrendering, he should certainly fall under a just reproach for standing it out, and that from women too, *v.* 22. The court ladies who were left when Jehoiakim and Jeconiah were carried away will now at length fall into the hands of the enemy, and they shall say, *"The men of thy peace,* whom thou didst consult with and confide in, and who promised thee peace if thou wouldst be ruled by them, have *set thee on,* have encouraged thee to be bold and brace and hold out to the last extremity; and see what comes of it? They, by prevailing upon thee, have *prevailed against thee,* and thou findest those thy real enemies that would be thought thy only friends. *Now thy feet are sunk in the mire,* thou art embarrassed, and hast noway to help thyself; thy feet cannot get forward, but are *turned away back."* Thus will Zedekiah be bantered by the women, when all his wives and children shall be made a prey to the conquerors, *v.* 23. Note, What we seek to avoid by sin will be justly brought upon us by the righteousness of God. And those that decline the way of duty for fear of reproach will certainly meet with much greater reproach in the way of disobedience. *The fear of the wicked, it shall come upon him,* Prov. 10:24.

VI. The care which Zedekiah took to keep this conference private (*v.* 24): *Let no man know of these words.* he does not at all incline to take God's counsel, nor so much as promise to consider of it; for so obstinate has he been to the calls of God, and so wilful in the ways of sin, that though he has good counsel given him he seems to be given up to walk in his own counsels. He has nothing to object against Jeremiah's advice, and yet he will not follow it. Many hear God's words, but will not do them. 1. Jeremiah is charged to let no man know of what had passed between the king and him. Zedekiah is concerned to keep it private, not so much for Jeremiah's safety (for he knew the princes could do him no hurt without his permission), but for his own reputation. Note, Many have really a better affection to good men and good things than they are willing to own. God's prophets are manifest in their consciences (2 Co. 5:11), but they care not for manifesting that to the world; they would rather do them a kindness than have it known that they do: such, it is to be feared, *love the praise of men more than the praise of God.* 2. He is instructed what to say to the princes if they should examine him about it. He must tell them that he was petitioning the king not to remand him back to *the house of Jonathan the scribe* (*v.* 25, 26), and he did tell them so (*v.* 27), and no doubt it was true: he would not let slip so fair an opportunity of engaging the king's favour; so that this was no lie or equivocation, but a part of the truth, which it was lawful for him to put them off with when he was under no obligation at all to tell them the whole truth. Note, Though we must be harmless as doves, so as never to tell a wilful lie, yet we must be wise as serpents, so as not needlessly to expose ourselves to danger by telling all we know.

CHAPTER 39

As the prophet Isaiah, after he had largely foretold the deliverance of Jerusalem out of the hands of the king of Assyria, gave a particular narrative of the story, that it might appear how exactly the event answered to the prediction, so the prophet Jeremiah, after he had largely foretold the delivering of Jerusalem into the hands of the king of Babylon, gives a particular account of that sad event for the same reason. That melancholy story we have in this chapter, which serves to disprove the false flattering prophets and to confirm the word of God's messengers. We are here told, I. That Jerusalem, after eighteen months' siege, was taken by the Chaldean army (*v.* 1–3). II. That king Zedekiah, attempting to make his escape, was seized and made a miserable captive to the king of Babylon (*v.* 4–7). III. That Jerusalem was burnt to the ground, and the people were carried captive, except the poor (*v.* 8–10). IV. That the Chaldeans were very kind to Jeremiah, and took particular care of him (*v.* 11–14). V. That Ebed-melech too, for his kindness, had a protection from God himself in this day of desolation (*v.* 15–18).

Verses 1–10

We were told, in the close of the foregoing chapter, that *Jeremiah abode patiently in the court of the prison, until the day that Jerusalem was taken.* He gave the princes no further disturbance by his prophesying, nor they him by their persecutions; for he had no more to say than what he had said, and, the siege being carried on briskly, God found them other work to do. See here what it came to.

I. The city is at length taken by storm; for how could it hold out when God himself fought against it? Nebuchadnezzar's army sat down before it in the *ninth* year of Zedekiah, *in the tenth month* (*v.* 1), in the depth of winter. Nebuchadnezzar himself soon after retired to take his pleasure, and left his generals to carry on the siege: they intermitted it awhile, but soon renewed it with redoubled force and vigour. At length, *in the eleventh year, in the fourth month,* about midsummer, they entered the city, the soldiers being so weakened by famine, and all their provisions being now spent, that they were not able to make any resistance, *v.* 2. Jerusalem was so strong a place that nobody would have believed the enemy could ever enter its gates, Lam. 4:12. But sin had provoked God to withdraw his protection, and then, like Samson when his hair was cut, it was weak as other cities.

II. The princes of the king of Babylon take possession of the *middle gate, v.* 3. Some think that this was the same with that which is called the *second gate* (Zep. 1:10), which is supposed to be in the middle wall that divided between one part of the city and the other. Here they cautiously made a half, and durst not go forward into so large a city, among men that perhaps would sell their lives as dearly as they could, until they had given directions for the searching of all places, that they might not be surprised by any ambush. They sat in the *middle gate,* thence to take a view of the city and give orders. The princes are here named, rough and uncouth names they are, to intimate what a sad change sin had made; there, where *Eliakim* and *Hilkiah,* who bore the name of the God of Israel, used to sit, now sit *Nergal-sharezer,* and *Samgar-nebo,* etc., who bore the names of the heathen gods. *Rab-saris* and *Rab-mag* are supposed to be not the names of distinct persons, but the titles of those whose names go before. *Sarsechim* was *Rab-saris,* that is, *captain of the guard;* and *Nergal-sharezer,* to distinguish him from the other of the same name that is put first, is called *Ram-mag — camp-master,* either muster-master or quarter-master: these and the other great generals sat in the gate. And now was fulfilled what Jeremiah prophesied long since (*ch.* 1:15), that the families of the kingdoms of the north should set every one his throne at the entering of the gates of Jerusalem. Justly do the princes of the heathen set up themselves there, where the gods of the heathen had been so often set up.

III. Zedekiah, having in disguise perhaps seen the princes of the king of Babylon take possession of one of the gates of the city, thought it high time to shift for his own safety, and, loaded with guilt and fear, he *went out of the city,* under no other protection but that of *the night* (*v.* 4), which soon failed him, for he was discovered, pursued, and overtaken. Though he made the best of his way, he could make nothing of it, could not get forward, but *in the plains of Jericho* fell into the hands of the pursuers, *v.* 5. Thence he was brought prisoner to Riblah, where the king of Babylon passed sentence upon him as a rebel, not sentence of death, but, one many almost say, a worse thing. For, 1. He *slew his sons before his eyes,* and they must all be little, some of them infants, for Zedekiah himself was now but thirty-two years of age. The death of these sweet babes must needs be so many deaths to himself, especially when he considered that his own obstinacy was the cause of it, for he was particularly told of this thing: *They shall bring forth thy wives and children to the Chaldeans, ch.* 38:23. 2. He *slew all the nobles of Judah* (*v.* 6), probably not those princes of Jerusalem who had advised him to this desperate course (it would be a satisfaction to him to see them cut off), but the great men of the country, who were innocent of the matter. 3. He ordered *Zedekiah to have his eyes put out* (*v.* 7), so condemning *him* to darkness for life who had shut his eyes against the clear light of God's word, and was of those princes who *will not understand,* but *walk on in darkness,* Ps. 82:5. 4. He *bound him with two brazen chains or fetters* (so the margin reads it), to carry him away to Babylon, there to spend the rest of his days in misery. All this sad story we had before, 2 Ki. 25:4, etc.

IV. Some time afterwards the city was burnt, temple and palace and all, and the wall of it broken down, *v.* 8. *"O Jerusalem, Jerusalem!* this comes of *killing the prophets,* and *stoning those that were sent to thee. O Zedekiah, Zedekiah!* this thou mightest have prevented if thou wouldst but have taken God's counsel, and yielded in time."

V. The people that were left were all *carried away captives to Babylon, v.* 9. Now they must bid a final farewell to the land of their nativity, that pleasant land, and to all their possessions and enjoyments in it, must be driven some hundreds of miles, like beasts, before the conquerors, that were now their cruel masters, must lie at their mercy in a strange land, and be servants to those who would be sure to rule them with rigour. The word *tyrant* is originally a Chaldee word, and is often used for *lords* by the Chaldee paraphrast, as if the Chaldeans, when they were lords, tyrannized more than any other: we have reason to think that the poor Jews had reason to say so. Some few were left behind, but they were *the poor of the people,* that had nothing to lose, and therefore never made any resistance. And they not only had their liberty, and were left to tarry at home, but the *captain of the guard gave them vineyards and fields at the same time,* such as they were never masters of before, *v.* 10. Observe here, 1. The wonderful changes of Providence. Some are abased, others advanced, 1 Sa. 2:5. The *hungry are filled with good things, and the rich sent empty away.* The ruin of some proves the rise of others. Let us therefore in our abundance *rejoice as though we rejoiced not,* and in our distresses *weep as though we wept not.* 2. The just retributions or Providence. The rich had been proud oppressors, and now they were justly punished for their injustice; the poor had been patient sufferers, and now they were graciously rewarded for their patience and amends made them for all their losses; for *verily there is a God that judges in the earth,* even in this world, much more in the other.

Verses 11–18

Here we must sing of mercy, as in the former part of the chapter we sang of judgment, and must sing unto God of both. We may observe here,

I. A gracious providence concerning Jeremiah. When Jerusalem was laid in ruins, and all *men's hearts failed them for fear,* then might he *lift up his head* with comfort, *knowing that his redemption drew nigh,* as Christ's followers when the second destruction of Jerusalem was hastening on, Lu. 21:28. Nebuchadnezzar had given particular orders that care should be taken of him, and that he should be in all respects well used, *v.* 11, 12. Hebuzar-adan and the rest of the king of Babylon's princes observed these orders, discharged him out of prison, and did every thing to make him easy, *v.* 13, 14. Now we may look upon this, 1. As a very generous act of Nebuchadnezzar, who, though he was a haughty potentate, yet took cognizance of this poor prophet. Doubtless he had received information concerning him from the deserters, that he had foretold the king of Babylon's successes against Judah and other countries, that he had pressed his prince and people to submit to him, and that he had suffered very hard things for so doing; and in consideration of all this (though perhaps he might have heard also that he had foretold the destruction of Babylon at length) he gave him these extraordinary marks of his favour. Note, It is the character of a great soul to take notice of the services and sufferings of the meanest. It was honourably done of the king to give this charge even before the city was taken, and of the captains to observe it even in the heat of action, and it is recorded for imitation. 2. As a reproach to Zedekiah and the princes of Israel. They put him in prison, and the king of Babylon and his princes took him out. God's people and ministers have often found fairer and kinder usage among strangers and infidels than among those that call themselves of the holy city. Paul found more favour and justice with king Agrippa than with Ananias the high priest. 3. As the performance of God's promise to Jeremiah, in recompence for his services. *I will cause the enemy to treat thee well in the day of evil, ch.* 15:11. Jeremiah had been faithful to his trust as a prophet, and now God approves himself faithful to him and the promise he had made him. Now he is comforted according to the time wherein he had been afflicted, and sees thousands fall on each hand and himself safe. The false prophets fell by those judgments which they said should never come (*ch.* 14:15), which made their misery the more terrible to them. The true prophet escaped those judgments which he said would come, and that made his escape the more comfortable to him. The same that were the instruments of punishing the persecutors were the instruments of relieving the persecuted; and Jeremiah thought never the worse of his deliverance for its coming by the hand of the king of Babylon, but saw the more of the hand of God in it. A fuller account of this matter we shall meet with in the next chapter.

II. A gracious message to Ebed-melech, to assure him of a recompence for his kindness to Jeremiah. This message was sent to him by Jeremiah himself, who, when he returned him thanks for his kindness to him, thus turned him over to God to be his paymaster. He relieved *a prophet in the name of a prophet,* and thus he had *a prophet's reward.* This message was delivered to him immediately after he had done that kindness to Jeremiah, but it is mentioned here after the taking of the city, to show that, as God was kind to Jeremiah at that time, so he was to Ebed-melech for his sake; and it was a token of special favour to both, and they ought so to account it, that they were not involved in any of the common calamities. Jeremiah is directed to tell him, 1. That God would certainly bring upon Jerusalem the ruin that had been long and often threatened; and, for his further satisfaction in having been kind to Jeremiah, he should see him abundantly proved a true prophet, *v.* 16. 2. That God took notice of the fear he had of the judgments coming. Though he was bravely bold in the service of God, yet he was afraid of the rod of God. The enemies were *men of whom he was afraid,* Note, God knows how to adapt and accommodate his comforts to the fears and griefs of his people, for he *knows their souls in adversity.* 3. That he shall be delivered from having a share in the common calamity: *I will deliver thee; I will surely deliver thee.* He had been instrumental to deliver God's prophet out of the dungeon, and now God promises to deliver him; for he will be behind-hand with none for any service they do, directly or indirectly, for his name: "Thou has saved Jeremiah's life, that was precious to thee, and therefore *thy life shall be given thee for a prey.*" 4. The reason given for this distinguishing favour which God had in store for him is *because thou hast put thy trust in me, saith the Lord.* God, in recompensing men's services, has an eye to the principle they go upon in those services, and rewards according to those principles; and there is no principle of obedience that will be more acceptable to God, nor have a greater influence upon us, than a believing confidence in God. Ebed-melech trusted in God that he would own him, and stand by him, and then he was not afraid of the face of man. And those who trust God, as this good man did, in the way of duty, will find that their hope shall not make them ashamed in times of the greatest danger.

CHAPTER 40

We have attended Jerusalem's funeral pile, and have taken our leave of the captives that were carried to Babylon, not expecting to hear any more of them in this book: perhaps we may in Ezekiel; and we must in this and the four following chapters observe the story of those few Jews that were left to remain in the land after their brethren were carried away, and it is a very melancholy story; for, though at first there were some hopeful prospects of their well-doing, they soon appeared as obstinate in sin as ever, unhumbled and unreformed, till, all the rest of the judgments threatened in Deu. 28 being brought upon them, that which in the last verse of that dreadful chapter completes the threatenings was accomplished, "The Lord shall bring thee into Egypt again." In this chapter we have, I. A more particular account of Jeremiah's discharge and his settlement with Gedaliah (*v.* 1–6). II. The great resort of the Jews that remained scattered in the neighbouring countries to Gedaliah, who was made their governor under the king of Babylon; and the good posture they were in for a while under him (*v.* 7–12). III. A treacherous design formed against Gedaliah, by Ishmael, which we shall find executed in the next chapter (*v.* 13–16).

Verses 1–6

The title of this part of the book, which begins the chapter, seems misapplied *(The word which came to Jeremiah),* for here is nothing of prophecy in this chapter, but it is to be referred to *ch.* 42:7, where we have a message that God sent by Jeremiah to the captains and the people that remained. The story between is only to introduce that prophecy and show the occasion of it, that it may be the better understood, and Jeremiah, being himself concerned in the story, was the better able to give an account of it.

In these verses we have Jeremiah's adhering, by the advice of Nebuzar-adan, to Gedaliah. It should seem that Jeremiah was very honourably fetched out of the court of the prison by the king of Babylon's princes (*ch.* 39:13, 14), but afterwards, being found among the people in the city, when orders were given to the inferior officers to bind all they found that were of any fashion, in order to their being carried captives to Babylon, he, through ignorance and mistake, was bound among the rest and hurried away. Poor man! he seems to have been born to hardship and abuse — *man of sorrows* indeed! But when the captives were brought manacled to Ramah, not far off, where a council of war, or court-martial, was held for giving orders concerning them, Jeremiah was soon distinguished from the rest, and, by special order of the court, was discharged. 1. The captain of the guard solemnly owns him to be a true prophet (*v.* 2, 3): *"The Lord thy God,* whose messenger thou has been and in whose name thou hast spoken, *has* by thee *pronounced this evil upon this place;* they had fair warning given them of it, but they would not take the warning, and *now the Lord hath brought it,* and, as by thy mouth he said it, so by my hand *he hath done what he said."* He seems thus to justify what he had done, and to glory in it, that he had been God's instrument to fulfil that which Jeremiah had been his messenger to foretell; and upon that account it was indeed the most glorious action he had ever done. He tells all the people that were now in chains before him *It is because you have sinned against the Lord that this thing has come upon you.* The princes of Israel would never be brought to acknowledge this, though it was as evident as if it had been written with a sun-beam; but this heathen prince plainly sees it, that a people that had been so favoured as they had been by the divine goodness would never have been abandoned thus had they not been very provoking. The people of Israel had been often told this from the pulpit by their prophets, and they would not regard it; now they are told it from the bench by the conqueror, whom they dare not contradict and who will make them regard it. Note, Sooner or later men shall be made sensible that their sin is the cause of all their miseries. 2. He gives him free leave to dispose of himself as he thought fit. he *loosed him from his chains* a second time (*v.* 4), invited him to come along with him to Babylon, not as a captive, but as a friend, as a companion; and *I will set my eye upon thee* (so the word is), not only, *"I will look well to thee,"* but "I will show thee respect, will countenance thee, and will see that thou be safe and well provided for." If he was not disposed to go to Babylon, he might dwell where he pleased in his own country, for it was all now at the disposal of the conquerors. He may go to Anathoth if he please, and enjoy the field he has purchased there. A great change with this good man! He that but lately was tossed from one prison to another may now walk at liberty from one possession to another. 3. He advised him to go to Gedaliah and settle with him. This Gedaliah, *made governor of the* land under *the king of Babylon,* was an honest Jew, who (it is probably) betimes went over with his friends to the Chaldeans, and approved himself so well that he had this great trust put into his hands, *v.* 5. *While* Jeremiah had *not yet gone back,* but stood considering what he should do, Nebuzar-adan, perceiving him neither inclined to go to Babylon nor determined whither to go, turned the scale for him, and bade him by all means *go to Gedaliah.* Sudden thoughts sometimes prove wise ones. But when he gave this counsel he did not design to bind him by it, nor will he take ill if he do not follow it: *Go wheresoever it seemeth convenient unto thee.* It is friendly in such cases to give advice, but unfriendly to prescribe and to be angry if our advice be not take. Let Jeremiah steer what course he pleases, Nebuzar-adan will agree to it, and believe he does for the best. Nor does he only give him his liberty, and an approbation of the measures he shall take, but provides for his support: He *gave him victuals and a* present, either in clothes or money, *and so let him go.* See how considerate *the captain of the guard* was in his kindness to Jeremiah. He set him at liberty, but it was in a country that was laid waste, and in which, as the posture of it now was, he might have perished, though it was his own country, if he had not been thus kindly furnished with necessaries. Jeremiah not only accepted his kindness, but took his advice, and went to Gedaliah, to Mizpah, *and dwelt with him, v.* 6. Whether we may herein commend his prudence I know not; the event does not commend it, for it did not prove at all to his comfort. However, we may commend his pious affection to the land of Israel, that unless he were forced out of it, as Ezekiel, and Daniel, and other good men were, he would not forsake it, but chose rather to dwell with the poor in the holy land than with princes in an unholy one.

Verses 7–16

We have in these verses,

I. A bright sky opening upon the remnant of the Jews that were left in their own land, and a comfortable prospect given them of some peace and quietness after the many years of trouble and terror with which they had been afflicted. Jeremiah indeed had never in his prophecies spoken of any such good days reserved for the Jews immediately after the captivity; but Providence seemed to raise and encourage such an expectation, and it would be to that miserable people as life from the dead. Observe the particulars.

1. Gedaliah, one of themselves, is made *governor in the land,* by *the king of Babylon, v.* 7. To show that he designed to make and keep them easy he did not give this commission to one of the princes of Babylon, but to one of their brethren, who, they might be sure, would seek their peace. He was *the son of Ahikam, the son of Shaphan,* one of the princes. We read of his father (*ch.* 26:24) that he took Jeremiah's part against the people. He seems to have been a man of great wisdom and a mild temper, and under whose government the few that were left might have been very happy. The king of Babylon had a good opinion of him and reposed a confidence in him, for *to him he committed all that were* left behind.

2. There is great resort to him from all parts, and all those that were now the Jews of the dispersion came and put themselves under his government and protection. (1.) The great men that had escaped the Chaldeans by force came and quietly submitted to Gedaliah, for their own safety and common preservation. Several are here named, *v.* 8. *They came* with *their men,* their servants, their soldiers, and so strengthened one another; and the king of Babylon had such a good opinion of Gedaliah his delegate that he was not at all jealous of the increase of their numbers, but rather pleased with it. (2.) The poor men that had escaped by flight into the neighbouring countries of Moab, Ammon, and Edom, were induced by the love they bore to their own land to return to it again as soon as they heard that Gedaliah was in authority there, *v.* 11, 12. Canaan itself would be an unsafe unpleasant country if there were no government nor governors there, and those that loved it dearly would not come back to it till they heard there were. It would be a great reviving to those that were dispersed to come together again, to those that were dispersed into foreign countries to come together in their own country, to those that were under strange kings to be under a governor of their own nation. See here in wrath God remembered mercy, and yet admitted some of them upon a further trial of their obedience.

3. The model of this new government is drawn up and settled by an original contract, which Gedaliah confirmed with an oath, a solemn oath (*v.* 9): *He swore to them and to their men,* it is probably according to the warrant and instructions he had received from the king of Babylon, who empowered him to give them these assurances. (1.) They must own the property of their lands to be in the Chaldeans. "Come" (says Gedaliah), *"fear not to serve the Chaldeans.* Fear not the sin of it." Though the divine law had forbidden them to make leagues with the heathen, yet the divine sentence had obliged them to yield to the king of Babylon. "Fear not the reproach of it, and the disparagement it will be to your nation; it is what God has brought you to, has bound you to, and it is no disgrace to any to comply with him. Fear not the consequences of it, as if it would certainly make you and yours miserable; no, you will find the king of Babylon not so hard a landlord as you apprehend him to be; if you will but live peaceably, peaceably you shall live; disturb not the government, and it will not disturb you. *Serve the king of Babylon and it shall be well with you."* If they should make any difficulty of doing personal homage, or should be apprehensive of danger when the Chaldeans should come among them, Gedaliah, probably by instruction from the king of Babylon, undertakes upon all occasions to act for them, and make their application acceptable to the king (*v.* 10): *"As for me, behold, I will dwell at Mizpah, to serve the Chaldeans,* to do homage to them in the name of the whole body if there be occasion, to receive orders, and to pay them their tribute when the *come to us."* All that passes between them and the Chaldeans shall pass through his hand; and, if the Chaldeans put such a confidence in him, surely his own countrymen may venture to do it. Gedaliah is willing thus to give them the assurance of an oath that he will do his part in protecting them, but, being apt to err (as many good men are) on the charitable side, he did not require an oath from them that they would be faithful to him, else the following mischief might have been prevented. However, protection draws allegiance though it be not sworn, and by joining in with Gedaliah they did, in effect, consent to the terms of government, that they should *serve the king of Babylon.* But, (2.) Though they own the property of their lands to be in the Chaldeans, yet, upon that condition, they shall have the free enjoyment of them and all the profits of them (*v.* 10): *"Gather you wine and summer fruits,* and take them for your own use; *put them in your vessels,* to be laid up for winter-store, as those do that live in a land of peace and hope to *eat the labour of your hand,* nay, the labour of other people's hands, for you reap what they sowed." Or perhaps they were the spontaneous products of that fertile soil, for which none had laboured. And accordingly we find (*v.* 12) that they *gathered wine and summer fruits very much,* such as were at present upon the ground, for their corn-harvest was over some time before Jerusalem was taken. While Gedaliah was in care for the public safety he left them to enjoy the advantages of the public plenty, and, for aught that appears, demanded no tribute from them; for he sought not his own profit, but the profit of many.

II. Here is a dark cloud gathering over this infant state, and threatening a dreadful storm. How soon is this hopeful prospect blasted! For when God begins in judgment he will make an end. It is here intimated to us, 1. That *Baalis the king of the Ammonites* had a particular spite at Gedaliah, and was contriving to take him off, either out of malice to the nation of the Jews, whose welfare he hated the thought of, or a personal pique against Gedaliah, *v.* 14. Some make Baalis to signify the queen-mother of the king of the Ammonites, or queen-dowager, as if she were the first mover of the bloody and treacherous design. One would have thought this little remnant might be safe when the great king of Babylon protected it; and ye it is ruined by the artifices of this petty prince or princess. happy are those that have the King of kings of their side, who can take *the wise in their own craftiness;* for the greatest earthly king cannot with all his power secure us against fraud and treachery. 2. That he employed *Ishmael, the son of Nethaniah,* as the instrument of his malice, instigated him to murder Gedaliah, and, that he might have a fair opportunity to do it, directed him to go and enrol himself among his subjects and promise him fealty. Nothing could be more barbarous than the design itself, nor more base than the method of compassing it. How wretchedly is human nature corrupted and degenerated (even in those that pretend to the best blood) when it is capable of admitting the thought of such abominable wickedness! Ishmael was of the seed royal, and would therefore be easily tempted to envy and hate one that set up for a governor in Judah, who was not, as he was, of David's line, though he had ever so much of David's spirit. 3. That Johanan, a brisk and active man, having got scent of this plot, informed Gedaliah of it, yet taking it for granted he could not but know of it before, the proofs of the matter being so very plain: *Dost thou certainly know?* surely thou dost, *v.* 14. He gave him private intelligence of it (*v.* 15), hoping he would then take the more notice of it. He proffered his service to prevent it, by taking off Ishmael, whose very name was ominous to all the seed of Isaac: *I will slay* him. *Wherefore should he slay thee?* Herein he showed more courage and zeal than sense of justice; for, if it be lawful to kill for prevention, who then can be safe, since malice always suspects the worst? 4. That Gedaliah, being a man of sincerity himself, would by no means give credit to the information given him of Ishmael's treachery. He said, *Thou speakest falsely of Ishmael.* Herein he discovered more good humour than discretion, more of the innocency of the dove than the wisdom of the serpent. Princes become uneasy to themselves and all about them when they are jealous. Queen Elizabeth said that she would believe no more evil of her people than a mother would believe of her own children; yet many have been ruined by being over-confident of the fidelity of those about them.

CHAPTER 41

It is a very tragical story that is related in this chapter, and shows that evil pursues sinners. The black cloud that was gathering in the foregoing chapter here bursts in a dreadful storm. Those few Jews that escaped the captivity were proud to think that they were still in their own land, when their brethren had gone they knew not whither, were fond of the wine and summer-fruits they had gathered, and were very secure under Gedaliah's protectorship, when, on a sudden, even these remains prove ruins too. I. Gedaliah is barbarously slain by Ishmael (*v.* 1, 2). II. All the Jews that were with him were slain likewise (*v.* 3) and a pit filled with their dead bodies (*v.* 9). III. Some devout men, to the number of fourscore, that were going towards Jerusalem, were drawn in by Ishmael, and murdered likewise (*v.* 4–7). Only ten of them escaped (*v.* 8). IV. Those that escaped the sword were taken prisoners by Ishmael, and carried off towards the country of the Ammonites (*v.* 10). V. By the conduct and courage of Johanan, though the death of the slain is not revenged, yet the prisoners are recovered, and he now becomes their commander-in-chief (*v.* 11–16). VI. His project is to carry them into the land of Egypt (*v.* 17, 18), which we shall hear more of in the next chapter.

Verses 1–10

It is hard to say which is more astonishing, God's permitting or men's perpetrating such villanies as here we find committed. Such base, barbarous, bloody work is here done by men who by their birth should have been men of honour, by their religion just men, and this done upon those of their own nature, their own nation, their own religion, and now their brethren in affliction, when they were all brought under the power of the victorious Chaldeans, and smarting under the judgments of God, upon no provocation, nor with any prospect of advantage — all done, not only in cold blood, but with art and management. We have scarcely such an instance of perfidious cruelty in all the scripture; so that with John, when he saw the *woman drunk with the blood of the saints,* we may well *wonder with great admiration.* But God permitted it for the completing of the ruin of an unhumbled people, and the filling up of the measure of their judgments, who had filled up the measure of their iniquities. Let it inspire us with an indignation at the wickedness of men and an awe of God's righteousness.

I. Ishmael and his party treacherously killed Gedaliah himself in the first place. Though the king of Babylon had made him a great man, had given him a commission to be *governor of the land* which he had conquered, though God had made him a good man and a great blessing to his country, and his agency for its welfare was as life from the dead, yet neither could secure him. Ishmael was of *the seed royal* (*v.* 1) and therefore jealous of Gedaliah's growing greatness, and enraged that he should merit and accept a commission under the king of Babylon. He had *ten men* with him that were *princes of the king* too, guided by the same peevish resentments that he was; these had been with Gedaliah before, to put themselves under his protection (*ch.* 40:8), and now came again to make him a visit; *and they did eat bread together in Mizpah.* he entertained them generously, and entertained no jealousy of them, notwithstanding the information given him by Johanan. They pretended friendship to him, and gave him no warning to stand on his guard; he was in sincerity friendly to them, and did all he could to oblige them. But those that did *eat bread* with him *lifted up the heel* against him. They did not pick a quarrel with him, but watched an opportunity, when they had him alone, and assassinated him, *v.* 2.

II. They likewise put all to the sword that they found in arms there, both Jews and Chaldeans, all that were employed under Gedaliah or were in any capacity to revenge his death, *v.* 3. As if enough of the blood of Israelites had not been shed by the Chaldeans, their own princes here mingle it with the blood of the Chaldeans. The vine-dressers and the husbandmen were busy in the fields, and knew nothing of this bloody massacre; so artfully was it carried on and concealed.

III. Some good honest men, that were going all in tears to lament the desolations of Jerusalem, were drawn in by Ishmael, and murdered with the rest. Observe, 1. Whence they came (*v.* 5) — *from Shechem, Samaria,* and *Shiloh,* places that had been famous, but wee now reduced; they belonged to the ten tribes, but there were some in those countries that retained an affection for the worship of the God of Israel. 2. Whither they were going — *to the house of the Lord,* the temple at Jerusalem, which, no doubt, they had heard of the destruction of, and were going to pay their respects to its ashes, to see its ruins, that their eye might affect their heart with sorrow for them. They *favour the dust thereof,* Ps. 102:14. They took *offerings and incense in their hand,* that if they should find any altar there, though it were but an altar of earth, and any priest ready to officiate, they might not be without something to offer; if not, yet they showed their good-will, as Abraham, when he came to *the place of the altar,* though the altar was gone. The people of God used to go rejoicing to the *house of the Lord,* but these went in the habit of mourners, with *their clothes rent* and *their heads shaven;* for the providence of God loudly called to weeping and mourning, because it was not with the faithful worshippers of God as in months past. 3. How they were decoyed into a fatal snare by Ishmael's malice. Hearing of their approach, he resolved to be the death of them too, so bloodthirsty was he. He seemed as if he hated every one that had the name of an Israelite or the face of an honest man. These pilgrims towards Jerusalem he had a spite to, for the sake of their errand. Ishmael went out to meet them with crocodiles' tears, pretending to bewail the desolations of Jerusalem as much as they; and, to try how they stood affected to Gedaliah and his government, he courted them into the town and found them to have a respect for him, which confirmed him in his resolution to murder them. *He said, Come to Gedaliah,* pretending he would have them come and live with him, when really he intended that they should come and die with him, *v.* 6. They had heard such a character of Gedaliah that they were willing enough to be acquainted with him; but Ishmael, when he had them *in the midst of the* town, fell upon them and *slew them* (*v.* 7), and no doubt took the offerings they had and converted them to his own use; for he that would not stick at such a murder would not stick at sacrilege. Notice is taken of his disposing of the dead bodies of these and the rest that he had slain; he tumbled them all into a great *pit* (*v.* 7), the same pit that Asa king of Judah had digged long before, either in the city or adjoining to it, when he built or fortified Mizpah (1 Ki. 15:22), to be a frontier-garrison against *Baasha king of Israel* and *for fear of* him, *v.* 9. Note, Those that dig pits with a good intention know not what bad use they may be put to, one time or other. He slew so many that he could not afford them each a grave, or would not do them so much honour, but threw them all promiscuously into one pit. Among these last that were doomed to the slaughter there were ten that obtained a pardon, by working, not on the compassion, but the covetousness, of those that had them at their mercy, *v.* 8. They *said to Ishmael,* when he was about to suck their blood, like an insatiable horseleech, after that of the companions, *Slay us not, for we have treasurers in the field,* country treasures, large stocks upon the ground, abundance of such commodities as the country affords, *wheat and barley, and oil and honey,* intimating that they would discover it to him and put him in possession of it all, if he would spare them. *Skin for skin, and all that a man has, will he give for his life.* This bait prevailed. Ishmael saved them, not for the love of mercy, but for the love of money. Here were riches kept for the owners thereof, not *to their hurt* (Eccl. 5:13) and to cause them to *lose their lives* (Job 31:39), but to their good and the preserving of their lives. Solomon observes that sometimes *the ransom of a man's life is his riches.* But those who think thus to bribe death, when it comes with commission, and plead with it, saying, *Slay us not, for we have treasures in the field,* will find death inexorable and themselves wretchedly deceived.

IV. He carried off the people prisoners. *The king's daughters* (whom the Chaldeans cared not for troubling themselves with when they had the king's sons) and the poor of the land, the vine-dressers and husband-men, that were committed to Gedaliah's charge, were all led away prisoners towards the country of *the Ammonites* (*v.* 10), Ishmael probably intending to make a present of them, as the trophies of his barbarous victory, to the king of that country, that set him on. This melancholy story is a warning to us never to be secure in this world. Worse may be yet to come when we think the worst is over; and that end of one trouble, which we fancy to be the end of all trouble, may prove to be the beginning of another, of a greater. These prisoners thought, *Surely the bitterness of death,* and of captivity, *is past;* and yet some died by the sword and others went into captivity. When we think ourselves safe, and begin to be easy, destruction may come that way that we little expect it. There is many a ship wrecked in the harbour. We can never be sure of peace on this side heaven.

Verses 11–18

It would have been well if Johanan, when he gave information to Gedaliah of Ishmael's treasonable design, though he could not obtain leave to kill Ishmael and to prevent it that way, yet had staid with Gedaliah; for he, and his captains, and their forces, might have been a life-guard to Gedaliah and a terror to Ishmael, and so have prevented the mischief without the effusion of blood: but, it seems they were out upon some expedition, perhaps no good one, and so were out of the way when they should have been upon the best service. Those that affect to ramble are many times out of their place when they are most needed. However, at length they *hear of all the evil that Ishmael had done* (*v.* 11), and are resolved to try an after-game, which we have an account of in these verses. 1. We heartily wish Johanan could have taken revenge upon the murderers, but he prevailed only to rescue the captives. Those that had shed so much blood, it was a pity but their blood should have been shed; and it is strange that vengeance suffered them to live; yet it did. Johanan gathered what forces he could *and went to fight with Ishmael* (*v.* 12), upon notice of the murders he had committed (for though he concealed it for a time, *v.* 4, yet murder will out) and which way he was gone; he pursued him, and overtook him by the great *pool of Gibeon,* which we read of, 2 Sa. 2:13. And, upon his appearing with such a force, Ishmael's heart failed him, his guilty conscience flew in his face, and he durst not stand his ground against an enemy that was something like a match for him. The most cruel are often the most cowardly. The poor captives *were glad when they saw Johanan* and *the captains that were with him,* looking upon them as their deliverers (*v.* 13), and they immediately found a way to wheel about and come over to them (*v.* 14), Ishmael not offering to detain them when he saw Johanan. Note, Those that would be helped must help themselves. These captives staid not till their conquerors were beaten, but took the first opportunity to make their escape, as soon as they saw their friends appear and their enemies thereby disheartened. Ishmael quitted his pray to save his life, and *escaped with eight men, v.* 15. it seems, two of his ten men, that were his banditti or assassins (spoken of *v.* 1), either deserted him or were killed in the engagement; but he made the best of his way to the Ammonites, as a perfect renegado, that had quite abandoned all relation to the commonwealth of Israel, though he was of the seed royal, and we hear no more of him. 2. We heartily wish that Johanan, when he had rescued the captives, would have sat down quietly with them, and governed them peaceably, as Gedaliah did; but, instead of that, he is for leading them into the land of Egypt, as Ishmael would have led them into the land of the Ammonites; so that though he got the command over them in a better way than Ishmael did, and honestly enough, yet he did not use it much better. Gedaliah, who was of a meek and quiet spirit, was a great blessing to them; but Johanan, who was of a fierce and restless spirit, was set over them for their hurt, and to complete their ruin, even after they were, as they thought, redeemed. Thus did God still walk contrary to them. (1.) The resolution of Johanan and the captains was very rash; nothing would serve them but they would *go to enter into Egypt* (*v.* 17), and, in order to that, they encamped for a time *in the habitation of Chimham, by Bethlehem,* David's city. Probably it was some land which David gave to Chimham, the son of Barzillai, which, though it returned to David's family at the year of the Jubilee, yet still bore the name of *Chimham.* Here Johanan made his headquarters, steering his course towards Egypt, either from a personal affection to that country or an ancient national confidence in the Egyptians for help in distress. Some of the *mighty men of war,* it seems had escaped; those he took with him, *and the women and children, whom he had recovered from Ishmael,* who were thus emptied from vessel to vessel, because they were yet unchanged. (2.) The reason for this resolution was very frivolous. They pretended that *they were afraid of the Chaldeans,* that they would come and do I know not what with them, *because Ishmael had* killed *Gedaliah, v.* 18. I cannot think they really had any apprehensions of danger upon this account; for, though it is true that the Chaldeans had cause enough to resent the murder of their viceroy, yet they were not so unreasonable, or unjust, as to revenge it upon those who appeared so vigorously against the murderers. But they only make use of this as a sham to cover that corrupt inclination of their unbelieving ancestors, which was so strong in them, *to return into Egypt.* Those will justly lose their comfort in real fears that excuse themselves in sin with pretended fears.

CHAPTER 42

Johanan and the captains being strongly bent upon going into Egypt, either their affections or politics advising them to take that course, they had a great desire that God should direct them to do so too like Balaam, who, when he was determined to go and curse Israel, asked God leave. Here is, I. The fair bargain that was made between Jeremiah and them about consulting God in this matter (*v.* 1–6). II. The message at large which God sent them, in answer to their enquiry, in which, 1. They are commanded and encouraged to continue in the land of Judah, and assured that if they did so it should be well with them (*v.* 7–12). 2. They are forbidden to go to Egypt, and are plainly told that if they did it would be their ruin (*v.* 13–18). 3. They are charged with dissimulation in their asking what God's will was in this matter and disobedience when they were told what it was; and sentence is accordingly passed upon them (*v.* 19–22).

Verses 1–6

We have reason to wonder how Jeremiah the prophet escaped the sword of Ishmael; it seems he did escape, and it was not the first time that the Lord hid him. It is strange also that in these violent turns he was not consulted before now, and his advice asked and taken. But it should seem as if they knew not that a prophet was among them. Though this people were *as brands plucked out of the fire,* yet have they not *returned to the Lord.* This people has a *revolting and a rebellious heart;* and contempt of God and his providence, God and his prophets, is still *the sin that most easily besets* them. But now at length, to serve a turn, Jeremiah is sought out, and *all the captains, Johanan* himself not excepted, with *all the people from the least to the greatest,* make him a visit; they *came near* (*v.* 1), which intimates that hitherto they had kept at a distance from the prophet and had been shy of him. Now here,

I. They desire him by prayer to ask direction from God what they should do in the present critical juncture, *v.* 2, 3. They express themselves wonderfully well. 1. With great respect to the prophet. Though he was poor and low, and under their command, yet they apply to him with humility and submissiveness, as petitioners for his assistance, which yet they intimate their own unworthiness of: *Let, we beseech thee, our supplication be accepted before thee.* They compliment him thus in hopes to persuade him to say as they would have him say. 2. With a great opinion of his interest in heaven: *"Pray for us,* who know not how to pray for ourselves. *Pray to the Lord thy God,* for we are unworthy to call him ours, nor have we reason to expect any favour from him." 3. With a great sense of their need of divine direction. They speak of themselves as objects of compassion: *"We are but a remnant, but a few of many;* how easily will such a remnant be swallowed up, and yet it is a pity that it should. *Thy eyes* see what distress we are in, what a plunge we are at; if thou canst do any thing, help us." 4. With desire of divine direction: "Let *the Lord thy God* take this ruin into his thoughts and under his hand, and *show us the way wherein we may walk* and may expect to have his presence with us, *and the thing that we may do,* the course we may take for our own safety." Note, In every difficult doubtful case our eye must be up to God for direction. They then might expect to be directed by a *spirit of prophecy,* which has now ceased; but we may still in faith pray to be guided by a *spirit of wisdom* in our hearts and the hints of Providence.

II. Jeremiah faithfully promises them to pray for direction for them, and, whatever message God should send to them by him, he would deliver it to them just as he received it without adding, altering, or diminishing, *v.* 4. Ministers may hence learn, 1. Conscientiously to pray for those who desire their prayers: *I will pray for you according to your words.* Though they had slighted him, yet, like Samuel when he was slighted, he will not *sin against the Lord in ceasing to pray for* them, 1 Sa. 12:23. 2. Conscientiously to advise those who desire their advice as near as they can to the mind of God, not *keeping back any thing that is profitable for them,* whether it be pleasing or no, but to *declare to them the whole counsel of God,* that they may approve themselves true to their trust.

III. They fairly promise that they will be governed by the will of God, as soon as they know what it is (*v.* 5, 6), and they had the impudence to appeal to God concerning their sincerity herein, though at the same time they dissembled: *"The Lord be a true and faithful witness between us;* do thou in the fear of God tell us truly what his mind is and then we will in the fear of God comply with it, and for this the Lord the Judge be Judge between us." Note, Those that expect to have the benefit of good ministers' prayers must conscientiously hearken to their preaching and be governed by it, as far as it agrees with the mind of God. Nothing could be better than this was: *Whether it be good, or whether it be evil, we will obey the voice of the Lord our God, that it may be well with us.* 1. They now call God *their* God, for Jeremiah had encouraged them to call him so (*v.* 4): *I will pray to the Lord your God.* He is ours, and therefore *we will obey his voice.* Our relation to God strongly obliges us to obedience. 2. They promise to *obey his voice* because they sent the prophet to him to consult him. Note, We do not truly desire to know the mind of God if we do not fully resolve to comply with it when we do know it. 3. It is an implicit universal obedience that they here promise. They will do what God appoints them to do, *whether it be good or whether it be evil:* "Though it may seem evil to us, yet we will believe that if God command it it is certainly good, and we must not dispute it, but do it. Whatever God commands, whether it be easy or difficult, agreeable to our inclinations or contrary to them, whether it be cheap or costly, fashionable or unfashionable, whether we get or lose by it in our worldly interests, if it be our duty, we will do it." 4. It is upon a very good consideration that they promise this, a reasonable and powerful one, *that it may be well with us,* which intimates a conviction that they could not expect it should be well with them upon any other terms.

Verses 7–22

We have here the answer which Jeremiah was sent to deliver to those who employed him to ask counsel of God.

I. It did not come immediately, not till *ten days after, v.* 7. They were thus long held in suspense, perhaps, to punish them for their hypocrisy or to show that Jeremiah did not speak of himself, nor what he would, for he could not speak when he would, but must wait for instructions. However, it teaches us to continue waiting upon God for direction in our way. *The vision is for an appointed time, and at the end it shall speak.*

II. When it did come he delivered it publicly, both to the *captains* and to all the *people,* from the meanest to those in the highest station; he delivered it fully and faithfully as he received it, as he had promised that he would keep nothing back from them. If Jeremiah had been to direct them by his own prudence, perhaps he could not have told what to advise them to, the case was so difficult; but what he has to advise is what *the Lord the God of Israel saith,* to whom they had sent him, and therefore they were bound in honour and duty to observe it. And this he tells them,

1. That it is the will of God that they should stay where they are, and his promise that, if they do so, it shall undoubtedly be *well with them* he would have them still to *abide in this land, v.* 10. Their brethren were forced out of it into captivity, and this was their affliction; let those therefore count it a mercy that they may stay in it and a duty to stay in it. Let those whose lot is in Canaan never quit it while they can keep it. It would have been enough to oblige them if God had only said, "I charge you upon your allegiance to *abide still in the land;"* but he rather persuades them to it as a friend than commands it as a prince. (1.) He expresses a very tender concern for them in their present calamitous condition: *It repenteth me of the evil that I have done unto you.* Though they had shown small sign of their repenting of their sins, yet God, as one *grieved for the misery of Israel* (Jdg. 10:16), begins to repent of the judgments he had brought upon them for their sins. Not that he changed his mind, but he was very ready to change his way and to return in mercy to them. God's time to repent himself concerning his servants is when he sees that, as here, their strength is gone, and *there is none shut up or left,* Deu. 32:36. (2.) He answers the argument they had against abiding in this land. *They feared the king of Babylon* (*ch.* 41:18), lest he should come and avenge the death of Gedaliah upon them, though they were no way accessory to it, nay, had witnessed against it. The surmise was foreign and unreasonable; but, if there had been any ground for it, enough is here said to remove it (*v.* 11): *"Be not afraid of the king of Babylon,* though he is a man of great might and little mercy, and a very arbitrary prince, whose will is a law, and therefore you are afraid he will upon this pretence, though without colour of reason, take advantage against you; *be not afraid of him,* for that fear will bring a snare: fear not him, for *I am with you;* and, if God be for you to save you, who can be against you to hurt you?" Thus has God provided to obviate and silence even the causeless fears of his people, which discourage them in the way of their duty; there is enough in the promises to encourage them. (3.) He assures them that if they will still abide in this land they shall not only be safe from the king of Babylon, but be made happy by the King of kings: *"I will build you and plant you;* you shall take root again, and be the new foundation of another state, a phoenix-kingdom, rising out of the ashes of the last." It is added (*v.* 12), *I will show mercies unto you.* Note, In all our comforts we may read God's mercies. God will show them mercy in this, that not only the king of Babylon shall not destroy them, but he shall *have mercy upon them* and help to settle them. Note, Whatever kindness men do us we must attribute it to God's kindness. He makes those whom he pities to be pitied even by *those who carried them captives,* Ps. 16:46. "The king of Babylon, having now the disposal of the country, shall *cause you to return it to your own land,* shall settle you again in your own habitations and put you in possession of the lands that formerly belonged to you." Note, God has made that our duty which is really our privilege, and our obedience will be its own recompence. *"Abide in this land,* and it shall be your own land again and you shall continue in it. Do not quit it now that you stand so fair for the enjoyment of it again. Be no so unwise as to *forsake your own mercies* for *lying vanities."*

2. That as they tender the favour of God and their own happiness they must by no means think of going into Egypt, not thither of all places, not to that land out of which God had delivered their fathers and which he had so often warned them not to make alliance with nor to put confidence in. Observe here, (1.) The sin they are supposed to be guilty of (and to him that knew their hearts it was more than a supposition): "You begin to say, *We will not dwell in this land* (*v.* 13); we will never think that we can be safe in it, no, not though God himself undertake our protection. We will not continue in it, no, not *in obedience to the voice of the Lord our God.* He may say what he please, but we will do what we please. We will *go into the land of Egypt,* and *there will we dwell,* whether God give us leave and go along with us or no," *v.* 14. It is supposed that their hearts were upon it: *"If you wholly set your faces to enter into Egypt,* and are obstinately resolved that you will go and *sojourn there,* though God oppose you in it both by his word and by his providence, then take what follows." Now the reason they go upon in this resolution is that *"in Egypt we shall see no war, nor have hunger of bread,; as we have had for a long time in this land," v.* 14. Note, It is folly to quit our place, especially to quit the holy land, because we meet with trouble in it; but greater folly to think by changing our place to escape the judgments of God, and that evil which pursues sinners in every way of disobedience, and which there is no escaping but by returning to our allegiance. (2.) The sentence passed upon them for this sin, if they will persist in it. It is pronounced in God's name (*v.* 15): "Hear the word of the Lord, you remnant of Judah, who think that because you are a remnant you must be spared of course (*v.* 2) and indulged in your own humour." [1.] Did the sword and famine frighten them? Those very judgments shall pursue them into Egypt, shall overtake them, and overcome them there (*v.* 16, 17): "You think, because war and famine have long been raging in this land, that they are entailed upon it; whereas, if you trust in God, he can make even this land a land of peace to you; you think they are confined to it, and, if you can get clear of this land, you shall get out of the reach of them, but God will send them after you wherever you go." Note, the evils we think to escape by sin we certainly and inevitably run ourselves upon. The men that go to Egypt in contradiction to God's will, to escape *the sword and famine,* shall *die in Egypt by sword and famine.* We may apply it to the common calamities of human life; those that are impatient of them, and think to avoid them by changing their place, will find that they are deceived and that they do not at all better themselves. The

grievances common to men will meet them wherever they go. All our removes in this world are but from one wilderness to another; still we are where we were. [2.] Did the desolations of Jerusalem frighten them? Were they willing to get as far as they could from them? They shall meet with the second part of them too in Egypt (*v.* 18): *As my anger and fury have been poured out* here upon Jerusalem, so they shall be *poured out upon you in Egypt.* Note, Those that have by sin made God their enemy will find him a consuming fire wherever they go. And then you shall be *an execration and an astonishment.* The Hebrews were of old an abomination to the Egyptians (Gen. 43:32), and now they shall be made more so than ever. When God's professing people mingle with infidels, and make their court to them, they lose their dignity and make themselves a reproach.

3. That God knew their hypocrisy in their enquiries of him, and that when they asked what he would have them to do they were resolved to take their own way; and therefore the sentence which was before pronounced conditionally is made absolute. Having set before them good and evil, the blessing and the curse, in the close he makes application of what he had said. And here, (1.) He solemnly protests that he had faithfully delivered his message, *v.* 19. The conclusion of the whole matter is, *"Go not down into Egypt;* you disobey the command of God if you do, and what I have said to you will be a witness against you; for *know certainly* that, *whether you will hear or whether you will forbear,* I have plainly *admonished you;* you cannot now plead ignorance of the mind of God." (2.) He charges them with base dissimulation in the application they made to him for divine direction (*v.* 20): *"You dissembled in your hearts;* you professed one thing and intended another, promising what you never meant to perform." *You have used deceit against your soul* (so the margin reads it); for those that think to put a cheat upon God will prove in the end to have put a damning cheat upon themselves. (3.) He is already aware that they are determined to go contrary to the command of God; probably they discovered it in their countenance and secret mutterings already, before he had finished his discourse. However, he spoke from him who knew their hearts: *"You have not obeyed the voice of the Lord your God;* you have not a disposition to obey it." Thus Moses, in the close of his farewell sermon, had told them (Deu. 31:27, 29), *I know thy rebellion and thy stiff neck,* and *that you will corrupt yourselves.* Admire the patience of God, that he is pleased to speak to those who, he knows, will not regard him, and deal with those who, he knows, will *deal very treacherously,* Isa. 48:8. (4.) He therefore reads them their doom, ratifying what he had said before: *Know certainly that you shall die by the sword, v.* 22. God's threatenings may be vilified, but cannot be nullified, by the unbelief of man. *Famine and pestilence* shall pursue these sinners; for there is no place privileged from divine arrests, nor can any malefactors go out of God's jurisdiction. *You shall die in the place whither you desire to go.* Note, We know not what is good for ourselves; and that often proves afflictive, and sometimes fatal, which we are most fond of and have our hearts most set upon.

CHAPTER 43

Jeremiah had faithfully delivered his message from God in the foregoing chapter, and the case was made so very plain by it that one would have thought there needed no more words about it; but we find it quite otherwise. Here is, I. The people's contempt of this message; they denied it to be the word of God (*v.* 1–3) and then made no difficulty of going directly contrary to it. Into Egypt they went, and took Jeremiah himself along with them (*v.* 4–7). II. God's pursuit of them with another message, foretelling the king of Babylon's pursuit of them into Egypt (*v.* 8–13).

Verses 1–7

What God said to the builders of Babel may be truly said of this people that Jeremiah is now dealing with: *Now nothing will be restrained from them which they have imagined to do,* Gen. 11:6. They have a fancy for Egypt, and to Egypt they will go, whatever God himself says to the contrary. Jeremiah made them hear all he had to say, though he saw them uneasy at it; it was what the Lord their God had sent him to speak to them, and they shall have it all. And now let us see what they have to say to it.

I. They deny it to be a message from God: *Johanan, and all the proud men, said to Jeremiah, Thou speakest falsely, v.* 2. See here, 1. What was the cause of their disobedience — it was pride; only by that comes contention both with God and man. They were *proud men* that gave the lie to the prophet. They could not bear the contradiction of their sentiments and the control of their designs, no, not by the divine wisdom, by the divine will itself. Pharaoh said, *Who is the Lord, that I should obey him?* Ex. 5:2. The proud unhumbled heart of man is one of the most daring enemies God has on this side hell. 2. What was the colour for their disobedience. They would not acknowledge it to be the word of God: *The Lord hath not sent thee* on this errand to us. Either they were not convinced that what was said came from God or (which I rather think) though they were convinced of it they would not own it. The light shone strongly in their face, but they either shut their eyes against it or would not confess that they saw it. Note, The reason why men deny the scriptures to be the word of God is because they are resolved not to conform to scripture-rules, and so an obstinate infidelity is made the sorry subterfuge of a wilful disobedience. If God had spoken to them by an angel, or as he did from Mount Sinai, they would have said that it was a delusion. Had they not consulted Jeremiah as a prophet? Had he not waited to receive instructions from God what to say to them? Had not what he said all the usual marks of prophecy upon it? Was not the prophet himself embarked in the same bottom with them? What interests could he have separate from theirs? Had he not always approved himself an Israelite indeed? And had not God proved him a prophet indeed? Had any of his words ever fallen to the ground? Why, truly, they had some good thoughts of Jeremiah, but they suggest (*v.* 3), *Baruch sets thee on against us.* A likely thing, that Baruch should be in a plot to *deliver them into the hands of the Chaldeans;* and what would he get by that? If Jeremiah and he had been so well affected to the Chaldeans as they would represent them, they would have gone away at first with Nebuzaradan, when he courted them, to Babylon, and not have staid to take their lot with this despised ungrateful remnant. But the best services are no fences against malice and slander. Or, if Baruch had been so ill disposed, could they think Jeremiah would be so influenced by him as to make God's name an authority to patronise so villainous a purpose? Note, Those that are resolved to contradict the great ends of the ministry are industrious to bring a bad name upon it. When men will persist in sin they represent those that would turn them from it as designing men for themselves, nay, as ill-designing men against their neighbours. It is well for persons who are thus misrepresented that their witness is in heaven and their record on high.

II. They determine to go to Egypt notwithstanding. They resolve not to *dwell in the land of Judah,* as God had ordered them (*v.* 4), but to go themselves with one consent and to take all that they had under their power along with them to Egypt. Those that came *from all the nations whither they had been driven, to dwell in the land of Judah,* out of a sincere affection to that land, they would not leave to their liberty, but forced them to go with them into Egypt (*v.* 5), *men, women, and children* (*v.* 6), a long journey into a strange country, an idolatrous country, a country that had never been kind of faithful to Israel; yet thither they would go, though they deserted their own land and threw themselves out of God's protection. It is the folly of men that they know not when they are well off, and often ruin themselves by endeavouring to better themselves; and it is the pride of great men to force those they have under their power to follow them, though ever so much against their duty and interest. These proud men compelled even Jeremiah the prophet and Baruch his scribe to go along with them to Egypt; they carried them away as prisoners, partly to punish them (and a greater punishment they could not inflict upon them than to force them against their consciences; theirs is the worst of tyranny who say to men's souls, even to good men's souls, *Bow down, that we may go over*), partly to put some reputation upon themselves and their own way. Though the prophets were under a force, they would make the world believe that they were voluntary in going along with them; and who could have blamed them for acting contrary to the word of the Lord if the prophets themselves had acted so? They *came to Tahpanhes,* a famous city of Egypt (so called from a queen of that name, 1 Ki. 11:19), the same with *Hanes* (Isa. 30:4); it was now the metropolis, for Pharaoh's house was there, *v.* 9. No place could serve these proud men to settle in but the royal city and near the court, so little mindful were they of Joseph's wisdom, who would have his brethren settle in Goshen. If they had had the spirit of Israelites, they would have chosen rather to dwell in the wilderness of Judah than in the most pompous populous cities of Egypt.

Verses 8–13

We have here, as also in the next chapter, Jeremiah prophesying in Egypt. Jeremiah was now in Tahpanhes, for there his lords and masters were; he was there among idolatrous Egyptians and treacherous Israelites; but there, 1. He received *the word of the Lord;* it *came to him.* God can find his people, with the visits of his grace, wherever they are; and, when his ministers are bound, yet the word of the Lord is not bound. The spirit of prophecy was not confined to the land of Israel. When Jeremiah went into Egypt, not out of choice, but by constraint, God withdrew not his wonted favour from him. 2. What he received of the Lord he delivered to the people. Wherever we are we must endeavour to do good, for that is our business in this world. Now we find two messages which Jeremiah was appointed and entrusted to deliver when he was in Egypt. We may suppose that he rendered what services he could to his countrymen in Egypt, at least as far as they would be acceptable, in performing the ordinary duties of a prophet, praying for them and instructing and comforting them; but only two messages of his, which he had received immediately from God, are recorded, one in this chapter, relating to Egypt itself and foretelling its destruction, the other in the next chapter, relating to the Jews in Egypt. God had told them before that if they went into Egypt the sword they feared should follow them; here he tells them further that the sword of Nebuchadnezzar, which they were in a particular manner afraid of, should follow them.

I. This is foretold by a sign. Jeremiah must take *great stones,* such as are used for foundations, and *lay them in the clay of the* furnace, or *brick-kiln,* which is in *the open way,* or *beside the way* that leads *to Pharaoh's house* (*v.* 9), some remarkable place in view of the royal palace. Egypt was famous for brick-kilns, witness the slavery of the Israelites there, whom they forced to make bricks (Ex. 5:7), which perhaps was now remembered against them. The foundation of Egypt's desolation was laid in those brick-kilns, in *that clay.* This he must do, not in the sight of the Egyptians (they knew not Jeremiah's character), but *in the sight of the men of Judah* to whom he was sent, that, since he could not prevent their going into Egypt, he might bring them to repent of their going.

II. It is foretold in express words, as express as can be, 1. That the king, the present king of Babylon, Nebuchadnezzar, the very same that had been employed in the destruction of Jerusalem, should come in person against the land of Egypt, should make himself master even of this royal city, by the same token that he should *set his throne* in that very place where *these stones* were laid, *v.* 10. This minute circumstance is particularly foretold, that, when it was accomplished, they might be put in mind of the prophecy and confirmed in their belief of the extent and certainly of the divine prescience, to which the smallest and most contingent events are evident. God calls Nebuchadnezzar his servant, because herein he executed God's will, accomplished his purposes, and was instrumental to carry on his designs. Note, The world's princes are God's servants and he makes what use he pleases of them, and even those that know him not, nor aim at his honour, are the tools which his providence makes use of. 2. That he should destroy many of the Egyptians, and have them all at his mercy (*v.* 11): *He shall smite the land of Egypt;* and, though it has been always a warlike nation, yet none shall be able to make head against him, but whom he will he shall slay, and by what sort of death he will, whether pestilence (for that is here meant by *death,* as *ch.* 15:2) by shutting them up in places infected, or by the sword of war or justice, in cold blood or hot. And whom he will he shall save alive and carry into *captivity.* The Jews, by going into Egypt, brought the Chaldeans thither, and so did but ill repay those that entertained them. Those who promised to protect Israel from the king of Babylon exposed themselves to him. 3. That he shall destroy the idols of Egypt, both the temples and the images of their gods (*v.* 12): *He shall burn, the houses of the gods of Egypt,* but it shall be with a fire of God's kindling; the fire of God's wrath fastens upon them, and then he burns some of them and carries others captive, Isa. 46:1. *Beth-shemesh,* or *the house of the sun,* was so called from a temple there built to the sun, where at certain times there was a general meeting of the worshippers of the sun. The statues or standing images there he shall *break in pieces* (*v.* 13) and carry away the rich materials of them. It intimates that he should lay all waste when even the temple and the images should not escape the fury of the victorious army. The king of Babylon was himself a great idolater and a patron of idolatry; he had his temples and images in honour of the sun as well as the Egyptians; and yet he is employed to destroy the idols of Egypt. Thus God sometimes makes one wicked man, or wicked nation, a scourge and plague to another. 4. That he shall make himself master of the land of Egypt, and none shall be able to plead its cause or avenge its quarrel (*v.* 12): *He shall array himself with the rich spoils of the land of Egypt,* both beautify and fortify himself with them. He shall array himself with them as ornaments and as armour; and this, though it shall be a rich and heavy booty, being expert in war, and expeditious, he shall slip on with as much ease and in as little time, in comparison, *as a shepherd slips on his garment,* when he goes to turn out his sheep in a morning. And being loaded with the wealth of many other nations, the fruits of his conquests, he shall make no more of the spoils of the land of Egypt than of a shepherd's coat. And when he has taken what he pleases (as Benhadad threatened to do, 1 Ki. 20:6) he shall *go forth in peace,* without any molestation given him, or any precipitation for fear of it, so effectually reduced shall the land of Egypt be. This destruction of Egypt by the king of Babylon is foretold, Eze. 29:19 and 30:10. Babylon lay at a great distance from Egypt, and yet thence the destruction of Egypt comes; for God can make those judgments strike home which are far-fetched.

CHAPTER 44

In this chapter we have, I. An awakening sermon which Jeremiah preaches to the Jews in Egypt, to reprove them for their idolatry, notwithstanding the warnings given them both by the word and the rod of God and to threaten the judgments of God against them for it (*v.* 1–14). II. The impudent and impious contempt which the people put upon this admonition, and their declared resolution to persist in their idolatries notwithstanding, in despite of God and Jeremiah (*v.* 15–19). III. The sentence passed upon them for their obstinacy, that they should all be cut off and perish in Egypt except a very small number; and, as a sign or earnest of it, the king of Egypt should shortly fall into the hands of the king of Babylon and be unable any longer to protect them (*v.* 20–30).

Verses 1–14

The Jews in Egypt were now dispersed into various parts of the country, into *Migdol, and Noph,* and other places, and Jeremiah was sent on an errand from God to them, which he delivered either when he had the most of them together *in Pathros* (*v.* 15) or going about from place to place preaching to this purport. He delivered this message in the name of *the Lord of hosts, the God of Israel,* and in it,

I. God puts them in mind of the desolations of Judah and Jerusalem, which, though the captives *by the rivers of Babylon* were daily mindful of (Ps. 137:1), the fugitives in the cities of Egypt seem to have forgotten and needed to be put in mind of, though, one would have thought, they had not been so long out of sight as to become out of mind (*v.* 2): *You have seen* what a deplorable condition Judah and Jerusalem are brought into; now will you consider whence those desolations came? From the wrath of God; it was his fury and his anger that kindled the fire which made Jerusalem and *the cities of Judah waste and desolate* (*v.* 6); whoever were the instruments of the destruction, they were but instruments: it was a destruction from the Almighty.

II. He puts them in mind of the sins that brought those desolations upon Judah and Jerusalem. It was for *their wickedness.* It was this that *provoked God to anger,* and especially their idolatry, their *serving other gods* (*v.* 3) and giving that honour to counterfeit deities, the creatures of their own fancy and the work of their own hands, which should have been given to the true God only. They forsook the God who was known among them, and whose name was great, for gods that they knew not, upstart deities, whose original was obscure and not worth taking notice of: *"Neither they nor you, nor your fathers,* could give any rational account why *the God of Israel* was exchanged for such impostors." They knew not that they were gods; nay, they could not but know that they were no gods.

III. He puts them in mind of the frequent and fair warnings he had given them by his word not to serve other gods, the contempt of which warnings was a great aggravation of their idolatry, *v.* 4. *The prophets* were sent with a great deal of care to call to them, saying, *Oh! do not this abominable thing that I hate.* It becomes us to speak of sin with the utmost dread and detestation as an abominable thing; it is certainly so, for it is that which God hates, and we are sure that *hid judgment is according to truth.* Call it grievous, call it odious, that we may by all means possible put ourselves and others out of love with it. It becomes us to give warning of the danger of sin, and the fatal consequences of it, with all seriousness and earnestness: *"Oh! do not* do it. If you love God, do not, for it is provoking to him; if you love your own souls do not, for it is destructive to them." Let conscience do this for us in an hour of temptation, when we are ready to yield. O take heed! *do not this abominable thing* which the Lord hates; for, if God hates it, though shouldst hate it. But did they regard what God said to them? No: *"They hearkened not, nor inclined their ear* (*v.* 5); they still persisted in their idolatries; and you see what came of it, therefore God's *anger was poured* out upon them, *as at this day.* Now this was intended for warning to you, who have not only heard the judgments of God's mouth, as they did, but have likewise seen the judgments of his hand, by which you should be startled and awakened, for they were inflicted *in terrorem,* that others might hear and fear and do no more as they did, lest they should fare as they fared."

IV. He reproves them for, and upbraids them with, their continued idolatries, now that they had come into Egypt (*v.* 8): You *burn incense to other gods in the land of Egypt. Therefore* God forbade them to go into Egypt, because he knew it would be a snare to them. Those whom God sent into the land of the Chaldeans, though that was an idolatrous country, were there, by the power of God's grace, weaned from idolatry; but those who went against God's mind into the land of the Egyptians were there, by the power of their own corruptions, more wedded than ever to their idolatries; for, when we thrust ourselves without cause or call into places of temptation, it is just with God to leave us to ourselves. In doing this, 1. They did a great deal of injury to themselves and their families: *"You commit this great evil against your souls* (*v.* 7), you wrong them, you deceive them with that which is false, you destroy them, for it will be fatal to them." Note, In sinning against God we sin *against our own souls.* "It is the ready way to *cut yourselves off* from all comfort and hope (*v.* 8), to cut off your name and honour; so that you will, both by your sin and by your misery, become *a curse and a reproach among all nations.* It will become a proverb, As wretched as a Jew. It is the ready way *to cut off from you* all your relations, all that you shave have joy of and have your families built up in, *man and woman, child and suckling,* so that Judah shall be a land lost for want of heirs." 2. They filled up the measure of the iniquity of their fathers, and, as if that had been too little for them, added to it (*v.* 9): *"Have you forgotten the wickedness* of those who are gone before you, that you are not humbled for it as you ought to be, and afraid of the consequences of it?" *Have you forgotten the punishments of your fathers?* so some read it. "Do you not know how dear their idolatry cost them? And yet dare you continue in that vain conversation received by tradition from you fathers, though you received the curse with it?" He reminds them of the sins and punishments *of the kings of Judah,* who, great as they were, escaped not the judgments of God for their idolatry; yea, and they should have taken warning by *the wickedness of their wives,* who had seduced them to idolatry. In the original it is, *And of his wives,* which, Dr. Lightfoot thinks, tacitly reflects upon Solomon's wives, particularly his Egyptian wives, to whom the idolatry of the kings of Judah owed its original. "Have you forgotten this, and what came of it, that you dare venture upon the same wicked courses?" See Neh. 13:18, 26. "Nay, to come to your own times, *Have you forgotten your own wickedness and the wickedness of your wives,* when you lived in prosperity in Jerusalem, and what ruin it brought upon you? But, alas! to what purpose do I speak to them?" (says God to the prophet, *v.* 10) *"they are not humbled unto this day,* by all the humbling providences that they have been under. *They have not feared, nor walked in my law."* Note, Those that walk not in the law of God do thereby show that they are destitute of the fear of God.

V. He threatens their utter ruin for their persisting in their idolatry now that they were in Egypt. Judgment is given against them, as before (*ch.* 42:22), that they shall perish in Egypt; the decree has gone forth, and shall not be called back. They *set their faces to go into the land of Egypt* (*v.* 12), were resolute in their purpose against God, and now God is resolute in his purpose against them: *I will set my face to cut off all Judah, v.* 11. Those that think not only to affront, but to confront, God Almighty, will find themselves outfaced; for *the face of the Lord is against those that do evil,* Ps. 34:16. It is here threatened concerning these idolatrous Jews in Egypt, 1. That *they shall all be consumed,* without exception; no degree nor order among them shall escape: *They shall fall, from the least to the greatest* (*v.* 12), *high and low, rich and poor.* 2. That *they shall be consumed by* the very same judgments which God made use of for the punishment of Jerusalem, *the sword, famine, and pestilence, v.* 12, 13. They shall not be wasted by natural deaths, as Israel in the wilderness, but by these sore judgments, which, by flying into Egypt, they thought to get out of the reach of. 3. That none (except a very few that will narrowly escape) shall ever *return to the land of Judah* again, *v.* 14. They thought, being nearer, that they stood fairer for a return to their own land than those that were carried to Babylon; yet those shall return, and these shall not; for the way in which God has promised us any comfort is much surer than that in which we have projected it for ourselves. Observe, Those that are fretful and discontented will be uneasy and fond of change wherever they are. The Israelites, when they were in the land of Judah, desired to go into Egypt (*ch.* 42:22), but when they were in Egypt they desired to *return to the land of Judah* again; they *lifted up their soul* to it (so it is in the margin), which denotes an earnest desire. But, because they would not dwell there when God commanded it, they shall not dwell they were they desire it. If we walk contrary to God, he will walk contrary to us. How can those expect to be well off who would not know when they were so, though God himself told them?

Verses 15–19

We have here the people's obstinate refusal to submit to the power of the word of God in the mouth of Jeremiah. We have scarcely such an instance of downright daring contradiction to God himself as this, or such an avowed rebellion of the carnal mind. Observe,

I. The persons who thus set God and his judgments at defiance; it was not some one that was thus obstinate, but the generality of the Jews; and they were such as knew either themselves or their wives to be guilty of the idolatry Jeremiah had reproved, *v.* 15. We find, 1. That the women had been more guilty of idolatry and superstition than the men, not because the men stuck closer to the true God and the true religion than the women, but, I fear, because they were generally atheists, and were for no God and no religion at all, and therefore could easily allow their wives to be of a false religion, and to worship false gods. 2. That it was consciousness of guilt that made them impatient of reproof: *They knew that their wives had burnt incense to other gods,* and that they had countenanced them in it, *and the women that stood by* knew that they had joined with them in their idolatrous usages; so that what Jeremiah said touched them in a sore place, which made them *kick against the pricks,* as *children of Belial,* that will not *bear the yoke.*

II. The reply which these persons made to Jeremiah, and in him to God himself; it is in effect the same with theirs who had the impudence to say to the Almighty, *Depart from us; we desire not the knowledge of thy ways.*

1. They declare their resolution not to do as God commanded them, but what they themselves had a mind to do; that is, they would go on to worship the moon, here called *the queen of heaven;* yet some understand it of the sun, which was much worshipped in Egypt (*ch.* 43:13) and had been so at Jerusalem (2 Ki. 23:11), and they say that the Hebrew word for the sun being feminine it may not

unfitly be called *the queen of heaven.* And others understand it of all *the host of heaven,* or *the frame of heaven,* the whole machine, *ch.* 7:18. These daring sinners do not now go about to make excuses for their refusal to obey, nor suggest that Jeremiah spoke from himself and not from God (as before, *ch.* 43:2), but they own that he spoke to them *in the name of the Lord,* and yet tell him flatly, in so many words, "*We will not hearken unto thee;* we will do that which is forbidden and run the hazard of that which is threatened." Note, Those that live in disobedience to God commonly grow worse and worse, and the heart is more and more hardened by *the deceitfulness of sin.* Here is the genuine language of the rebellious heart: *We will certainly do whatsoever thing goes forth out of our own mouth,* let God and his prophets say what they please to the contrary. What they said many think who yet have not arrived at such a degree of impudence as to speak it out. It is that which the young man would be at *in the days of his youth;* he would *walk in the way of his heart and the sight of his eyes,* and would have and do every thing he has a mind to, Eccl. 11:9.

2. They give some sort of reasons for their resolution; for the most absurd and unreasonably wicked men will have something to say for themselves, till the day comes when *every mouth shall be stopped.*

(1.) They plead many of those things which the advocates for Rome make the marks of a true church, and not only justify but magnify themselves with; and these Jews have as much right to them as the Romanists have. [1.] They plead antiquity: We are resolved *to burn incense to the queen of heaven,* for *our fathers* did so; it is a practice that pleads prescription; and why should we pretend to be wiser than our fathers? [2.] They plead authority. Those that had power practised it themselves and prescribed it to others: *Our kings and our princes* did it, whom God set over us, and who were of the seed of David. [3.] They plead unity. It was not here and there one that did it, but *we,* we all with one consent, we that are *a great multitude* (*v.* 15), we did it. [4.] They plead universality. It was not done here and there, but *in the cities of Judah.* [5.] They plead visibility. It was not done in a corner, in dark and shady groves only, but *in the streets,* openly and publicly. [6.] They plead that it was the practice of the mother-church, the holy see; it was not now learned first in Egypt, but it had been done in *Jerusalem.* [7.] They plead prosperity: *They had we plenty of* bread, *and* of all good things; we *were well and saw no evil.* All the former pleas, I fear, were too true in fact; God's witnesses against their idolatry were few and hid; Elijah though that he was left alone: and this last might perhaps be true as to some particular persons, but, as to their nation, they were still under rebukes for their rebellions, and there was *no peace to those that went out or came in,* 2 Chr. 15:5. But, supposing all to be true, yet this does not at all excuse them from idolatry; it is the law of God that we must be ruled and judged by, hot the practice of men.

(2.) They suggest that the judgments they had of late been under were brought upon them for *leaving off to burn incense to the queen of heaven, v.* 18. So perversely did they misconstrue providence, though God, by his prophets, had so often explained it to them, and the thing itself spoke the direct contrary. *Since we* forsook our idolatries *we have wanted all things, and have been consumed by the sword,* the true reason of which was because they still retained their idols in their heart and an affection to their old sins; but they would have it thought that it was because they had forsaken the acts of sin. Thus the afflictions which should have been for their welfare, to separate between them and their sins, being misinterpreted did but confirm them in their sins. Thus, in the first ages of Christianity, when God chastised the nations by any public calamities for opposing the Christians and persecuting them, they put a contrary sense upon the calamities, as if they were sent to punish them for conniving at the Christians and tolerating them, and cried, *Christianos ad leones — Throw the Christians to the lions.* Yet, if it had been true, as they said here, that since they returned to the service of the true God, the God of Israel, they had been in want and trouble, was that a reason why they should revolt from him again? That was as much as to say that they served not him, but their own bellies. Those who know God, and put their trust in him, will serve him, though he starve them, though he slay them, though they never see a good day with him in this world, being well assured that they shall not lose by him in the end.

(3.) They plead that, though the women were most forward and active in their idolatries, yet they did it with the consent and approbation of their husbands; the women were busy to *make cakes* for meat-offerings *to the queen of heaven* and to prepare *and pour out the drink-offerings, v.* 19. We found, before, that this was their work, *ch.* 7:18. "But *did we* do it *without our husbands,* privately and unknown to them, so as to give them occasion to be jealous of us? No; the fathers kindled the fire while the women kneaded the dough; the men that were our heads, whom we were bound to learn of and to be obedient to, taught us to do it by their example." Note, It is sad when those who are in the nearest relation to each other, who should quicken each other to that which is good and so help one another to heaven, harden each other in sin and so ripen one another for hell. Some understand this as spoken by the husbands (*v.* 15), who plead that they did not do it *without their men,* that is, without their elders and rulers, their great men, and men in authority; but, because the making of the *cakes* and the pouring out of the *drink-offerings* are expressly spoken of as the women's work (*ch.* 7:18), it seems rather to be understood as their plea: but it was a frivolous plea. What would it avail them to be able to say that it was according to their husbands' mind, when they knew that it was contrary to their God's mind?

Verses 20–30

Daring sinners may speak many a bold word and many a big word, but, after all, God will have the last word; for he will be justified when he speaks, and all flesh, even the proudest, shall be silent before him. Prophets may be run down, but God cannot; nay, here the prophet would not.

I. Jeremiah has something to say to them from himself, which he could say without a spirit of prophecy, and that was to rectify their mistake (a wilful mistake it was) concerning the calamities they had been under and the true intent and meaning of them. They said that these miseries came upon them because they had now *left off burning incense to the queen of heaven.* "No," says he, "it was because you had formerly done it, not because you had now left it off." When they gave him that answer, he immediately replied (*v.* 20) that the incense which they and their fathers had burnt to other gods did indeed go unpunished a great while, for God was long-suffering towards them, and during the day of his patience it was perhaps, as they said, *well with them, and* they *saw no evil;* but at length they grew so provoking *that the Lord could no longer bear* (*v.* 22), but began a controversy with them, whereupon some of them did a little reform; their sins left them, for so it might be said, rather than that they left their sins. But their old guilt being still upon the score, and their corrupt inclinations still the same, God remembered against them the idolatries of *their fathers, their kings, and their princes, in the streets of Jerusalem,* which they, instead of being ashamed of, gloried in as a justification of them in their idolatries; they *all came into his mind* (*v.* 21), all the *abominations which they had committed* (*v.* 22) and all their disobedience to *the voice of the Lord* (*v.* 23), all were brought to account; and *therefore,* to punish them for these, *is their land a desolation and a curse, as at this day* (*v.* 22); *therefore,* not for their late reformation, but for their old transgressions, has all *this evil happened to them, as at this day, v.* 23. Note, The right understanding of the cause of our troubles, one would think, should go far towards the cure of our sins. Whatever *evil comes upon us,* it is *because we have sinned against the Lord,* and should therefore *stand in awe and sin not.*

II. Jeremiah has something to say to them, *to the women* particularly, from *the Lord of hosts, the God of Israel,* They have given their answer; now let them hear God's reply, *v.* 24. *Judah, that* dwells *in the land of Egypt,* has God speaking to them, even there; that is their privilege. Let them observe what he says; that is their duty, *v.* 26. Now God, in his reply, tells them plainly,

1. That, since they were fully determined to persist in their idolatry, he was fully determined to proceed in his controversy with them; if they would go on to provoke him, he would go on to punish them, and see which would get the better at last. God repeats what they had said (*v.* 25): "*You and your wives* are agreed in this obstinacy; *you have spoken with your mouths and fulfilled with your hands;* you have said it, and you stand to it, have said it and go on to do accordingly, *We will surely perform our vows that we have vowed, to burn incense to the queen of heaven,*" as if, though it were a sin, yet their having vowed to do it were sufficient to justify them in the doing of it; whereas no man can by his vow make that lawful to himself, much less duty, which God has already made sin. "Well" (says God), *"you will accomplish, you will perform, your* wicked *vows:* now hear what is my vow, what *I have sworn by my great name;"* and, if *the Lord hath sworn,* he *will not repent,* since they have sworn and will not repent. *With the froward he will show himself froward,* Ps. 18:26. (1.) He has sworn that what little remains of religion there were among them should be lost, *v.* 26. Though they joined with the Egyptians in their idolatries, yet they continued upon many occasions to make mention of the name of Jehovah, particularly in their solemn oaths; they said, *Jehovah liveth,* he is *the living God,* so they owned him to be, though they worshipped dead idols; they swear, *The Lord liveth* (*ch.* 5:2), but I fear they retained this form of swearing more in honour of their nation than of their God. But God declares that his *name shall no more be* thus *named* by *any man of Judah in all the land of Egypt;* that is, there shall be no Jews remaining to use this dialect of their country, or, if there be, they shall have forgotten it and shall learn to swear, as the Egyptians do, *by the life of Pharaoh,* not of Jehovah. Note, Those are very miserable whom God has so far left to themselves that they have quite forgotten their religion and lost all the remains of their good education. Or this may intimate that God would take it as an affront to him and would resent it accordingly, if they did make mention of his name and profess any relation to him. (2.) He hath sworn that what little remnant of people there was there should all be consumed (*v.* 27): *I will watch over them for evil;* no opportunity shall be let slip to bring some judgment upon them, *until there be an end of them* and they be rooted out. Note, To those whom God finds impenitent sinners he will be found an implacable Judge. And, when it comes to this, they *shall know* (*v.* 28) *whose word shall stand, mind or theirs.* They said that they should recover themselves when they returned to worship *the queen of heaven;* God said they should ruin themselves; and now the event will show which was in the right. The contest between God and sinners is whose word shall stand, whose will shall be done, and who shall get the better. Sinners say that they shall have peace though they go on; God says they shall have no peace. But *when God judges he will overcome;* God's word shall stand, and not the sinner's.

2. He tells them that a very few of them should *escape the sword,* and in process of time *return into the land of Judah, a small number* (*v.* 28), next to none, in comparison with the great numbers that should return out of the land of the Chaldeans. This seems designed to upbraid those who boasted of their numbers that concurred in sin; there were none to speak of that did not join in idolatry: "Well," says God, "and there shall be as few *that* shall *escape the sword and famine.*"

3. He gives them a sign that all these threatenings shall be accomplished in their season, that they shall be consumed here in Egypt and shall quite perish: *Pharaoh-hophra,* the present *king of Egypt,* shall be delivered *into the hand of his enemies that seek his life — of his own rebellious subjects* (so some) under Amasis, who usurped his throne — *of Nebuchadnezzar king of Babylon* (so others), who invaded his kingdom; the former is related by Herodotus, the latter by Josephus. It is likely that this Pharaoh had tempted the Jews to idolatry by promises of his favour; however, they depended upon him for his protection, and it would be more than a presage of their ruin, it would be a step towards it, if he were gone. They expected more from him than from Zedekiah king of Judah; he was a more potent and politic prince. "But," says God, *"I will give him into the hand of his enemies,* as I gave Zedekiah." Note, Those creature-comforts and confidences that we promise ourselves most from may fail us as soon as those that we promise ourselves least from, for they are all what God makes them, not what we fancy them.

The sacred history records not the accomplishment of this prophecy, but its silence is sufficient; we hear no more of these Jews in Egypt, and therefore conclude them, according to this prediction, lost there; for no word of God shall fall to the ground.

CHAPTER 45

The prophecy we have in this chapter concerns Baruch only, yet is intended for the support and encouragement of all the Lord's people that serve him faithfully and keep closely to him in difficult trying times. It is placed here after the story of the destruction of Jerusalem and the dispersion of the Jews, but was delivered long before, in the fourth year of Jehoiakim, as was the prophecy in the next chapter, and probably those that follow. We here find, I. How Baruch was terrified when he was brought into trouble for writing and reading Jeremiah's roll (*v.* 1–3). II. How his fears were checked with a reproof for his great expectations and silenced with a promise of special preservation (*v.* 4, 5). Though Baruch was only Jeremiah's scribe, yet this notice is taken of his frights, and this provision made for his comfort; for God despises not any of his servants, but graciously concerns himself for the meanest and weakest, for Baruch the scribe as well as for Jeremiah the prophet.

Verses 1–5

How Baruch was employed in writing Jeremiah's prophecies, and reading them, we had an account *ch.* 36, and how he was threatened for it by the king, warrants being out for him and he forced to abscond, and how narrowly he escaped under a divine protection, to which story this chapter should have been subjoined, but that, having reference to a private person, it is here thrown into the latter end of the book, as St. Paul's epistle to Philemon is put after his other epistles. Observe,

I. The consternation that poor Baruch was in when he was sought for by the king's messengers and obliged to hide his head, and the notice which God took of it. He cried out, *Woe is me now! v.* 3. he was a young man setting out in the world; he was well affected to the things of God, and was willing to serve God and his prophet; but, when it came to suffering, he was desirous to be excused. Being an ingenious man, and a scholar, he stood fair for preferment, and now to be driven into a corner, and in danger of a prison, or worse, was a great disappointment to him. When he read the roll publicly he hoped to gain reputation by it, that it would make him to be taken notice of and employed; but when he found that, instead of that, it exposed him to contempt, and brought him into disgrace, he cried out, "I am undone; I shall fall into the pursuers' hands, and be imprisoned, and put to death, or banished: *The Lord has added grief to my sorrow,* has loaded me with one trouble after another. After the grief of writing and reading the prophecies of my country's ruin, I have the sorrow of being treated as a criminal; for so doing; and, though another might make nothing of this, yet for my part I cannot bear it; it is a burden too heavy for me. *I fainted in my sighing* (or *I am faint with my sighing;* it just kills me) *and I find no rest,* no satisfaction in my own mind. I cannot compose myself as I should and would to bear it, not have I any prospect of relief or comfort." Baruch was a good man, but, we must say, this was his infirmity. Note, 1. Young beginners in religion, like freshwater soldiers, are apt to be discouraged with the little difficulties which they commonly meet with at first in the service of God. They do but *run with the footmen,* and it *wearies them;* they *faint* upon the very dawning of *the day of adversity,* and it is an evidence that *their strength is small* (Prov. 24:10), that their faith is weak, and that they are yet but babes, who cry for every hurt and every fright. 2. Some of the best and dearest of God's saints and servants, when they have seen storms rising, have been in frights, and apt to make the worst of things, and to disquiet themselves with melancholy apprehensions more than there was cause for. 3. God takes notice of the frets and discontents of his people and is displeased with them. Baruch should have rejoiced that he was counted worthy to suffer in such a good cause and with such good company, but, instead of that, he is vexed at it, and blames his lot, nay, and reflects upon his God, as if he had dealt hardly with him; what he said was spoken in a heat and passion, but God was offended, as he was with Moses, who paid dearly for it, when, his spirit being provoked, he *spoke unadvisedly with his lips. Thou didst say* so and so, and it was not well said. God keeps account what we say, even when we speak in haste.

II. The reproof that God gave him for talking at this rate. Jeremiah was troubled to see him in such an agitation, and knew not well what to say to him. He was loth to chide him, and yet thought he deserved it, was willing to comfort him, and yet knew not which way to go about it; but God tells him what he *shall say to him, v.* 4. Jeremiah could not be certain what was at the bottom of these complaints and fear, but God sees it. They came from his corruptions. That the hurt might therefore not be healed slightly, he searches the wound, and shows him that he had raised his expectations too high in this world and had promised himself too much from it, and that made the distress and trouble he was in so very grievous to him and so hard to be borne. Note, The frowns of the world would not disquiet us as they do if we did not foolishly flatter ourselves with the hopes of its smiles and court and covet them too much. It is our over-fondness for the good things of this present time that makes us impatient under its evil things. Now God shows him that it was his fault and folly, at this time of day especially, either to desire or to look for an abundance of the wealth and honour of this world. For, 1. The ship was sinking. Ruin was coming upon the Jewish nation, an utter and universal ruin: *"That which I have built,* to be a house for myself, *I am breaking down, and that which I have planted,* to be a vineyard for myself, *I am plucking up, even this whole land,* the Jewish church and state; and dost thou now *seek great things for thyself?* Dost thou expect to be rich and honourable and to make a figure now? No." 2. "It is absurd for thee to be now painting thy own cabin. Canst thou expect to be high when all are brought low, to be full when all about thee are empty?" To seek ourselves more than the public welfare, especially to seek great things to ourselves when the public is in danger, is very unbecoming Israelites. We may apply it to this world, and our state in it; God in his providence is breaking down and pulling up; every thing is uncertain and perishing; we cannot expect any continuing city here. What folly is it then to *seek great things for ourselves* here, where every thing is little and nothing certain!

III. The encouragement that God gave him to hope that though he should not be great, yet he should be safe: *"I will bring evil upon all flesh,* all nations of men, all orders and degrees of men, *but thy life will I give to thee for a prey" (thy soul,* so the word is) *"in all places whither thou goest.* Thou must expect to be hurried from place to place, and, wherever thou goest, to be in danger, but thou shalt escape, though often very narrowly, shalt have thy life, but it shall be as a prey, which is got with much difficulty and danger; thou shalt be saved as by fire." Note, The preservation and continuance of life are very great mercies, and we are bound to account them such, as they are the prolonging of our opportunity to glorify God in this world and to get ready for a better; and at some times, especially when the arrows of death fly thickly about us, life is a signal favour, and what we ought to be very thankful for, and while we have it must not complain though we be disappointed of the great things we expected. *Is not the life more than meat?*

CHAPTER 46

How judgment began at the house of God we have found in the foregoing prophecy and history; but now we shall find that it did not end there. In this and the following chapters we have predictions of the desolations of the neighbouring nations, and those brought upon them too mostly by the king of Babylon, till at length Babylon itself comes to be reckoned with. The prophecy against Egypt is here put first and takes up this whole chapter, in which we have, I. A prophecy of the defeat of Pharaoh-necho's army by the Chaldean forces at Carchemish, which was accomplished soon after, in the fourth year of Jehoiakim (*v.* 1–12) II. A prophecy of the descent which Nebuchadnezzar should make upon the land of Egypt, and his success in it, which was accomplished some years after the destruction of Jerusalem (*v.* 13–26). III. A word of comfort to the Israel of God in the midst of those calamities (*v.* 27, 28).

Verses 1–12

The first verse is the title of that part of this book, which relates to the neighbouring nations, and follows here. It is *the word of the Lord which came to Jeremiah against the Gentiles;* for God is King and Judge of nations, knows and will call to an account those who know him not nor take any notice of him. Both Isaiah and Ezekiel prophesied against these nations that Jeremiah here has a separate saying to, and with reference to the same events. In the Old Testament we have *the word of the Lord* against *the Gentiles;* in the New Testament we have *the word of the Lord* for *the Gentiles,* that those who were *afar off are made nigh.*

He begins with Egypt, because they were of old Israel's oppressors and of late their deceivers, when they put confidence in them. In these verses he foretells the overthrow of *the army of Pharaoh-necho,* by Nebuchadnezzar, *in the fourth year of Jehoiakim,* which was so complete a victory to the king of Babylon that thereby he recovered from the river of Egypt to *the river Euphrates, all that pertained to the king of Egypt,* and so weakened him that he *came not again any more out of his land* (as we find, 2 Ki. 24:7), and so made him pay dearly for his expedition against the king of Assyria four years before, in which he slew Josiah, 2 Ki. 23:29. This is the event that is here foretold in lofty expressions of triumph over Egypt thus foiled, which Jeremiah would speak of with a particular pleasure, because the death of Josiah, which he had lamented, was now avenged on Pharaoh-necho. Now here,

I. The Egyptians are upbraided with the mighty preparations they made for this expedition, in which the prophet calls to them to do their utmost, for so they would: "Come then, *order the buckler,* let the weapons of war be got ready," *v.* 3. Egypt was famous for *horses* — let them be *harnessed* and the cavalry well mounted: *Get up, you horsemen, and stand forth,* etc., *v.* 4. See what preparations the children of men make, with abundance of care and trouble and at a vast expense, to kill one another, as if they did not die fast enough of themselves. He compares their marching out upon this expedition to the rising of their river Nile (*v.* 7, 8): *Egypt* now *rises up like a flood,* scorning to keep within its own banks and threatening to overflow all the neighbouring lands. It is a very formidable army that the Egyptians bring into the field upon this occasion. The prophet summons them (*v.* 9): *Come up, you horses; rage, you chariots.* He challenges them to bring all their confederate troops together, *the Ethiopians,* that descended from the same stock with the Egyptians (Gen. 10:6), and were their neighbours and allies, *the Libyans and Lydians,* both seated in Africa, to the west of Egypt, and from them the Egyptians fetched their auxiliary forces. Let them strengthen themselves with all the art and interest they have, yet it shall be all in vain; they shall be shamefully defeated notwithstanding, for God will fight against them, and against him *there is no wisdom nor counsel,* Prov. 21:30, 31. It concerns those that go forth to war not only to *order the buckler,* and *harness the horses,* but to repent of their sins, and pray to God for his presence with them, and that they may have it to keep themselves from every wicked thing.

II. They are upbraided with the great expectations they had from this expedition, which were quite contrary to what God intended in bringing them together. They knew their own thoughts, and God knew them, and sat in heaven and laughed at them,; *but they knew not the thoughts of the Lord, for he gathers them as sheaves into the floor,* Mic. 4:11, 12. Egypt saith (*v.* 8): *I will go up; I will cover the earth,* and none shall hinder me; *I will destroy the city,* whatever city it is that stands in my way. Like Pharaoh of old, *I will pursue, I will overtake.* The Egyptians say that they shall have a day of it, but God saith that it shall be his day: *The is the day of the Lord God of hosts* (*v.* 10), the day in which he will be exalted in the overthrow of the Egyptians. They meant one thing, but God meant another; they designed it for the advancement of their dignity and the enlargement of their dominion, but God designed it for the great abasement and weakening of their kingdom. It is *a day of vengeance* for Josiah's death; it is a day of sacrifice to divine justice, to which multitudes of the sinners of Egypt shall fall as victims. Note, When men think to magnify themselves by pushing on unrighteous enterprises, let them expect that God will glorify himself by blasting them and cutting them off.

III. They are upbraided with their cowardice and inglorious flight when they come to an engagement (*v.* 5, 6): *"Wherefore have I seen them,* notwithstanding all these mighty and vast preparations and all these expressions of bravery and resolution, when the Chaldean army faces them, *dismayed, turned back,* quite disheartened, and no spirit left in them." 1. They make a shameful retreat. Even *their mighty ones,* who, one would think, should have stood their ground, *flee a flight,* flee by consent, make the best of their way, flee in confusion and with the utmost precipitation; they have neither time nor heart to *look back,* but *fear is round about* them, for they apprehend it so.

And yet, 2. They cannot make their escape. They have the shame of flying, and yet not the satisfaction of saving themselves by flight; they might as well have stood their ground and died upon the spot; for even *the swift shall not flee away.* The lightness of their heels shall fail them when it comes to the trial, as well as the stoutness of their hearts; the *mighty* shall not escape, nay, they *are beaten down* and broken to pieces. *They shall stumble* in their flight, *and fall towards the north,* towards their enemy's country; for such confusion were they in when they took to their feet that instead of making homeward, as men usually do in that case, they made forward. Note, *The race is not to the swift nor the battle to the strong.* Valiant men are not always victorious.

IV. They are upbraided with their utter inability ever to recover this blow, which should be fatal to their nation, *v.* 11, 12. The damsel, *the daughter of Egypt,* that lived in great pomp and state, is sorely wounded by this defeat. Let her now seek for *balm in Gilead* and physicians there; let her use all the medicines her wise men can prescribe for the healing of this hurt, and the repairing of the loss sustained by this defeat; but all in vain; *no cure shall be* to them; they shall never be able to bring such a powerful army as this into the field again. "*The nations that rang* of thy glory and strength *have* now *heard of thy shame,* how shamefully thou wast routed and how thou are weakened by it." It needs not be spread by the triumphs of the conquerors, the shrieks and outcries of the conquered will proclaim it: *Thy cry hath filled the* country about. For, when they fled several ways, one *mighty man stumbled* upon another and dashed against another, such confusion were they in, so that *both together* became a pray to the pursuers, an easy prey. A thousand such dreadful accidents there should be, which should fill the country with the cry of those that were overcome. *Let not the mighty man* therefore *glory in his might,* for the time may come when it will stand him in no stead.

Verses 13–28

In these verses we have,

I. Confusion and terror spoken to Egypt. The accomplishment of the prediction in the former part of the chapter disabled the Egyptians from making any attempts upon other nations; for what could they do when their army was routed? But still they remained strong at home, and none of their neighbours durst make any attempts upon them. Though the kings of Egypt came no more *out of their land* (2 Ki. 24:7), yet they kept safe and easy in their land; and what would they desire more than peaceably to enjoy their own? One would think all men should be content to do this, and not covet to invade their neighbours. But the measure of Egypt's iniquity is full, and now they shall not long enjoy their own; those that encroached on others shall not be themselves encroached on. The scope of the prophecy here is to show *how the king of Babylon should* shortly *come and smite the land of Egypt,* and bring the war into their own bosoms which they had formerly carried into his borders, *v.* 13. This was fulfilled by the same hand with the former, even Nebuchadnezzar's, but many years after, twenty at least, and probably the prediction of it was long after the former prediction, and perhaps much about the same time with that other prediction of the same event which we had *ch.* 43:10.

1. Here is the alarm of war sounded in Egypt, to their great amazement (*v.* 14), notice given to the country that the enemy is approaching, *the sword is devouring round about* in the neighbouring countries, and therefore it is time for the Egyptians to put themselves in a posture of defence, to prepare for war, that they may give the enemy a warm reception. This must be proclaimed in all parts of Egypt, particularly in Migdol, Noph, and Tahpanhes, because in these places especially the Jewish refugees, or fugitives rather, had planted themselves, in contempt of God's command (*ch.* 44:1), and let them hear what a sorry shelter Egypt is likely to be to them.

2. The retreat hereupon of the forces of other nations which the Egyptians had in their pay is here foretold. Some considerable number of those troops, it is probable, were posted upon the frontiers to guard them, where they were beaten off by the invaders and put to flights. Then were the *valiant men swept away* (*v.* 15) as with *a sweeping rain* (it is the word that is used Prov. 28:3); they can none of

them stand their ground, *because the Lord drives them* from their respective posts; he drives them by his terrors; he drives them by enabling the Chaldeans to drive them. It is not possible that those should fix whom the wrath of God chases. He it was (*v.* 16) that *made many to fall, yea,* when their day shall come to fall, the enemy needs not throw them down, they shall *fall one upon another,* every man shall be a stumbling-block to his fellow, to his follower; nay, if God please, they shall be made to *fall upon one another,* they shall be made to *fall upon one another, every man's sword* shall be *against his fellow. Her hired men,* the troops Egypt has in he service, are indeed *in the midst of her like fatted bullocks,* lusty men, able bodied and high spirited, who were likely for action and promised to make their part good against the enemy; but *they are turned back;* their hearts failed them, and, instead of fighting, they have *fled away together.* How could they withstand their fate when *the day of their calamity had come,* the day in which God will visit them in wrath? Some think they are compared to fatted bullocks for their luxury; they had wantoned in pleasures, so that they were very unfit for hardships, and therefore turned back and could not stand. In this consternation, (1.) They all made homeward towards their own country (*v.* 16): They said, "*Arise, and let us go again to our own people,* where we may be safe *from the oppressing sword* of the Chaldeans, that bears down all before it." In times of exigence little confidence is to be put in mercenary troops, that fight purely for pay, and have no interest in theirs whom they fight for. (2.) They exclaimed vehemently against Pharaoh, to whose cowardice or bad management, it is probably, their defeat was owing. When he posted them there upon the borders of his country it is probably that he told them he would within such a time come himself with a gallant army of his own subjects to support them; but he failed them, and, when the enemy advanced, they found they had none to back them, so that they were perfectly abandoned to the fury of the invaders. No marvel then that they quitted their post and deserted the service, crying out, *Pharaoh king of Egypt is but a noise* (*v.* 17); he can hector, and talk big of the mighty things he would do, but that is all; he brings nothing to pass. All his promises to those in alliance with him, or that are employed for him, vanish into smoke. He brings not the succours he engaged to bring, or not till it is too late: *He has passed the time appointed;* he did not keep his word, nor keep his day, and therefore they bid him farewell, they will never serve under him any more. Note, Those that make most noise in any business are frequently but a noise. Great talkers are little doers.

3. The formidable power of the Chaldean army is here described as bearing down all before it. *The King* of kings, *whose name is the Lord of hosts,* and before whom the mightiest kings on earth, though gods to us, are but as grasshoppers, he hath said it, he hath sworn it, *As I live, saith* this *king, as Tabor* overtops *the mountains and Carmel* overlooks *the sea, so shall* the king of Babylon overpower all the force of Egypt, such a command shall he have, such a sway shall he bear, *v.* 18. He and his *army shall come against* Egypt *with axes, as hewers of wood* (*v.* 22), and the Egyptians shall be no more able to resist them than the tree is to resist the man that comes with an axe to *cut it down;* so that Egypt shall be felled as a *forest is by the hewers of wood,* which (if there by many of them, and those well provided with instruments for the purpose) will be done in a little time. Egypt is very populous, full of towns and cities, like a forest, the trees of which *cannot be searched* or numbered, and very rich, full of hidden treasures, many of which will escape the searching eye of the Chaldean soldiers; but they shall make a great spoil in the country, for *they are more than the locusts,* that come in vast swarms and overrun a country, devouring every green thing (Joel 1:6, 7), so shall the Chaldeans do, for *they are innumerable.* Note, The Lord of hosts hath numberless hosts at his command.

4. The desolation of Egypt hereby is foretold, and the waste that should be made of that rich country. *Egypt is* now *like a very fair heifer,* or calf (*v.* 20), fat and shining, and not *accustomed to the yoke* of subjection, wanton as a heifer that is well fed, and very sportful. Some think here is an allusion to Apis, the bull or calf which the Egyptians worshipped, from whom the children of Israel learned to worship the golden calf. Egypt is as fair as a goddess, and

adores herself, *but destruction comes; cutting up comes* (so some read it); *it comes out of the north;* thence the Chaldean soldiers shall come, as so many butchers or sacrificers, to kill and cut up this *fair heifer.* (1.) The Egyptians shall be brought down, shall be tamed, and their tune changed: *The daughters of Egypt shall be confounded* (*v.* 24), shall be filled with astonishment. *Their voice shall go like a serpent,* that is, it shall be very low and submissive; they shall not low like a fair heifer, that makes a great noise, but hiss out of their holes like serpents. They shall not dare to make loud complaints of the cruelty of the conquerors, but vent their griefs in silent murmurs. They shall not now, as they used to do, answer roughly, but, with *the poor, use entreaties* and beg for their lives. (2.) They shall be carried away prisoners into their enemy's land (*v.* 19): "*O thou daughter! dwelling* securely and delicately *in Egypt,* that fruitful pleasant country, do not think this will last always, but *furnish thyself to go into captivity;* instead of rich clothes, which will but tempt the enemy to strip thee, get plain and warm clothes; instead of fine shoes, provide strong ones; and inure thyself to hardship, that thou mayest bear it the better." Note, It concerns us, among all our preparations, to prepare for trouble. We provide for the entertainment of our friends, let us not neglect to provide for the entertainment of our enemies, nor among all our furniture omit furniture for captivity. The Egyptians must prepare to flee; for their cities shall be evacuated. Noph particularly *shall be desolate, without an inhabitant,* so general shall the slaughter and the captivity be. There are some penalties which, we say, the king and the multitude are exempted from, but here even these are obnoxious: *The multitude of No shall be punished:* it is called *populous No,* Nah. 3:8. *Though hand join in hand,* yet they shall not escape; nor can any think to go off in the crowd. Be they ever so many, they shall find God will be too many for them. Their kings and all their petty princes shall fall; and their gods too (*ch.* 43:12, 13), their idols and their great men. Those which they call their tutelar deities shall be no protection to them. Pharaoh shall be brought down, and *all those that trust in him* (*v.* 25), particularly the Jews that came to sojourn in his country, trusting in him rather than in God. All these shall be *delivered into the hands of the northern nations* (*v.* 24), into the hand not only of Nebuchadnezzar that mighty potentate, but *into the hands of his servants,* according to the curse on Ham's posterity, of which the Egyptians were, that they should be the *servants of servants.* These seek their lives, and into their hands they shall be delivered.

5. An intimation is given that in process of time Egypt shall recover itself again (*v.* 26): *Afterwards it shall be inhabited,* shall be peopled again, whereas by this destruction it was almost dispeopled. Ezekiel foretels that this should be at the end of forty years, Eze. 29:13. See what changes the nations of the earth are subject to, how they are emptied and increased again; and let not nations that prosper be secure, nor those that for the present are in thraldom despair.

II. Comfort and peace are here spoken to the Israel of God, *v.* 27, 28. Some understand it of those whom the king of Egypt had carried into captivity with Jehoahaz, but we read not of any that were carried away captives with him; it may therefore rather refer to the captives in Babylon, whom God had mercy in store for, or, more generally, to all the people of God, designed for their encouragement in the most difficult times, when the judgments of God are abroad among the nations. We had these words of comfort before, *ch.* 30:10, 11. 1. Let the wicked of the earth tremble, they have cause for it; *but fear not thou, O my servant Jacob! and be not dismayed, O Israel!* and again, *Fear thou not, O Jacob!* God would not have his people to be a timorous people. 2. The wicked of the earth *shall be put away like dross,* not be looked after any more; but God's people, in order to their being saved, shall be found out and gathered though they be far off, shall be redeemed though they be held fast in captivity, and shall return. 3. The wicked *is like the troubled sea when it cannot rest;* they *flee when none pursues.* But Jacob, being at home in God, *shall be at rest and at ease, and none shall make him afraid;* for *what time he is afraid* he has a *God to trust to.* 4. The wicked God *beholds afar off;* but, wherever thou art, *O Jacob! I am with thee, a very present help.* 5. A *full end shall be made* of the nations that oppressed God's Israel, as Egypt and Babylon; but mercy shall be kept in store for the Israel of God: they shall be corrected, but not cast off; the correction shall be in measure, in respect of degree and continuance. Nations have their periods; the Jewish nation itself has come to an end as a nation; but the gospel church, God's spiritual Israel, still continues, and will to the end of time; in that this promise is to have its full accomplishment, that, though God correct it, he will never *make a full end of it.*

CHAPTER 47

This chapter reads the Philistines their doom, as the former read the Egyptians theirs and by the same hand, that of Nebuchadnezzar. It is short, but terrible; and Tyre and Zidon, though they lay at some distance from them, come in sharers with them in the destruction here threatened. I. It is foretold that the forces of the northern crowns should come upon them, to their great terror (*v.* 1–5). II. That the war should continue long, and their endeavours to put an end to it should be in vain (*v.* 6–7).

Verses 1–7

As the Egyptians had often proved false friends, so the Philistines had always been sworn enemies, to the Israel of God, and the more dangerous and vexatious for their being such near neighbours to them. They were considerably humbled in David's time, but, it seems they had got head again and were a considerable people till Nebuchadnezzar cut them off with their neighbours, which is the event here foretold. The date of this prophecy is observable; it was *before Pharaoh* smote Gaza. When this blow was given to Gaza by the king of Egypt is not certain, whether in his expedition against Carchemish or in his return thence, after he had slain Josiah, or when he afterwards came with design to relieve Jerusalem; but this is mentioned here to show that this word of the Lord came to Jeremiah against the Philistines when they were in their full strength and lustre, themselves and their cities in good condition, in no peril from any adversary or evil occurrent. When no disturbance of their repose was foreseen by any human probabilities, yet then Jeremiah foretold their ruin, which Pharaoh's smiting Gaza soon after would be but an earnest of, and, as it were, the beginning of sorrows to that country. It is here foretold, 1. That a foreign enemy and a very formidable one shall be brought upon them: *Waters rise up out of the north, v.* 2. Waters sometimes signify multitudes of people and nations (Rev. 17:15), sometimes great and threatening calamities (Ps. 69:1); here they signify both. They *rise out of the north,* whence fair weather and the wind that drives away rain are said to come; but now a terrible storm comes out of that cold climate. The Chaldean army shall overflow the land like a deluge. Probably this happened before the destruction of Jerusalem, for it should seem that in Gedaliah's time, which was just after, the army of the Chaldeans was quite withdrawn out of those parts. The country of the Philistines was but of small extent, so that it would soon be overwhelmed by so vast an army. 2. That they shall all be in a consternation upon it. The men shall have no heart to fight, but shall sit down and cry like children: *All the inhabitants of the land shall howl,* so that nothing but lamentation shall be heard in all places. The occasion of the fright is elegantly described, *v.* 3. Before it comes to killing and slaying, the very *stamping of the horses* and *rattling of the chariots,* when the enemy makes his approach, shall strike a terror upon the people, to such a degree that parents in their fright shall seem void of natural affection, *for they shall not look back to their children,* to provide for their safety, or so much as to see what becomes of them. Their *hands shall be so feeble* that they shall despair of carrying them off with them, and therefore they shall not care for seeing them, but leave them to take their lot; or they shall be in such a consternation that they shall quite forget even those pieces of themselves. Let none be overfond of their children, nor dote upon them, since such distress may come that they may either wish they had none or forget that they have, and have no heart to look upon them. 3. That the country of the Philistines shall be spoiled and laid waste, and the other countries adjoining to them and in alliance with them. It is a day *to spoil the Philistines, for the Lord will spoil them, v.* 4. Note, Those whom God will spoil must needs be spoiled; for, *if God be against them, who can be for them?* Tyre and Zidon were strong and wealthy cities, and they used to help the Philistines in a strait, but now they shall themselves be involved in the common ruin, and God will cut off from them every *helper that remains.* Note, Those that trust to help from creatures will find it cut off when they most need it and will thereby be put into the utmost confusion. Who the *remnant of the country of Caphtor* were is uncertain, but we find that the Caphtorim were near akin to the Philistines (Gen. 10:14), and probably when their own country was destroyed such as remained came and settled with their kinsmen the Philistines, and were now spoiled with them. Some particular places are here named, *Gaza, and Ashkelon, v.* 5. *Baldness has come upon them;* the invaders have stripped them of all their ornaments, or they have made themselves bald in token of extreme grief, and they are *cut off,* with the other cities that were in the plain or valley about them. The products of their fruitful valley shall be *spoiled,* and made a prey of, by the conquerors. 4. That these calamities should continue long. The prophet, in the foresight of this, with his usual tenderness, asks them first (*v.* 5), *How long will you cut yourselves,* as men in extreme sorrow and anguish do? O how tedious will the calamity be! not only cutting, but long cutting. But he turns from the effect to the cause: *They cut themselves,* for the sword of the Lord cuts them. And therefore, (1.) He bespeaks that to be still (*v.* 6): *O thou sword of the Lord! how long will it be ere thou be quiet?* He begs it would *put up itself into the scabbard,* would devour no more flesh, drink no more blood. This expresses the prophet's earnest desire to see an end of the war, looking with compassion, as became a man, even upon the Philistines themselves, when their country was made desolate by the sword. Note, War is the *sword of the Lord;* with it he punishes the crimes of his enemies and pleads the cause of his own people. When war is once begun it often lasts long; the sword, once drawn, does not quickly find the way into the scabbard again; nay, some when they draw the sword throw away the scabbard, for they *delight in war.* So deplorable are the desolations of war that the blessings of peace cannot but be very desirable. O that *swords might be beaten into ploughshares!* (2.) Yet he gives a satisfactory account of the continuance of the war and stops the mouth of his own complaint (*v.* 7): *How can it be quiet, seeing the Lord hath given it a charge* against such and such places, particularly specified in its commission? *There hath he appointed it.* Note, [1.] The sword of war hath its charge from the Lord of hosts. Every bullet has its charge; you call them blind bullets, but they are directed by an all-seeing God. The war itself has its charge; he saith to it, *Go, and it goes — Come, and it comes — Do this, and it does it;* for he is commander-in-chief. [2.] When the sword is drawn we cannot expect it should be sheathed till it has fulfilled its charge. As the word of God, so his rod and his sword, shall accomplish that for which he sends them.

CHAPTER 48

Moab is next set to the bar before Jeremiah the prophet, whom God has constituted judge over nations and kingdoms, from his mouth to receive its doom. Isaiah's predictions concerning Moab had had their accomplishment (we had the predictions Isa. 15 and 16 and the like Amos 2:1), and they were fulfilled when the Assyrians, under Salmanassar, invaded and distressed Moab. But this is a prophecy of the desolations of Moab by the Chaldeans, which were accomplished under Nebuzaradan, about five years after he had destroyed Jerusalem. Here is, I. The destruction foretold, that it should be great and general, should extend itself to all parts of the country (*v.* 1–6, 8, and again *v.* 21–25, 34), that spoilers should come upon them and force some to flee (*v.* 9), should carry many into captivity (*v.* 12, 46), that the enemy should come shortly (*v.* 16), come swiftly and surprise them (*v.* 40, 41), that he should make thorough work (*v.* 10) and lay the country quite waste, though it was very strong (*v.* 14, 15), that there should be no escaping (*v.* 42, 45), that this should force them to quit their idols (*v.* 13, 35) and put an end to all their joy (*v.* 33, 34), that their neighbours shall lament them (*v.* 17–19) and the prophet himself does (*v.* 31, 36, etc.). II. The causes of this destruction assigned; it was sin that brought this ruin upon them, their pride, and security, and carnal confidence (*v.* 7, 11, 14, 29), and their contempt of and enmity to God and his people (*v.* 26, 27, 30). III. A promise of the restoration of Moab (*v.* 47).

Verses 1–13

We may observe in these verses,

I. The author of Moab's destruction; it is *the Lord of hosts,* that has armies, all armies, at his command, and *the God of Israel* (*v.* 1), who will herein plead the cause of his Israel against a people that have always been vexatious to them, and will punish them now for the injuries done to Israel of old, though Israel was forbidden to meddle with them (Deu. 2:9), therefore the destruction of Moab is called *the work of the Lord* (*v.* 10), for it is he that pleads for Israel; and his work will exactly agree with his word, *v.* 8.

II. The instruments of it: *Spoilers shall come* (*v.* 8), shall come with a sword, a sword that shall *pursue them, v.* 2. *"I will send unto him wanderers,* such as come from afar, as if they were vagrants, or had missed their way, but they shall *cause him to wander;* they seem as wanderers themselves, but they shall make the Moabites to be really wanderers, some to flee and others to be carried into captivity." These destroyers stir up themselves to do execution; they *have devised evil against Heshbon,* one of the principal cities of Moab, and they aim at no less than the ruin of the kingdom: *Come, and let us cut it off from being a nation* (*v.* 2); nothing less will serve the turn of the invaders; they come, not to plunder it, but to ruin it. The prophet, in God's name, engages them to make thorough work of it (*v.* 10): *Cursed be he that does the work of the Lord deceitfully,* this bloody work, this destroying work; though it goes against the grain with men of compassion, yet it is *the work of the Lord,* and must not be done by the halves. The Chaldeans have it in charge, by a secret instinct (says Mr. Gataker), to destroy the Moabites, and therefore they must not spare, must not, out of foolish pity, *keep back their sword from blood;* they would thereby bring a sword, and a curse with it, upon themselves, as Saul did by sparing the Amalekites and Ahab by letting Benhadad go. *Thy life shall go for his life.* To this work is applied that general rule given to all that are employed in any service for God, *Cursed by he that does the work of the Lord deceitfully* or negligently, that pretends to do it, but does it not to purpose, makes a show of serving God's glory, but is really serving his own ends and carries on the work of the Lord no further than will suit his own purposes, or that is slothful in business for God and takes neither care nor pains to do it as it should be done, Mal. 1:14. Let not such deceive themselves, for God will not thus be mocked.

III. The woeful instances and effects of this destruction. The cities shall be laid in ruins; they shall be *spoiled* (*v.* 1) and cut down (*v.* 2); they shall be *desolate* (*v.* 9), *without any to dwell therein;* there shall be no houses to dwell in, or no people to dwell in them, or no safety and ease to those that would dwell in them. *Every city shall be spoiled and no city shall escape.* The strongest city shall not be able to secure itself against the enemies' power, nor shall the finest city be able to recommend itself to the enemies' pity and favour. The *country* also shall be wasted, the *valley shall perish,* and the *plain be destroyed, v.* 8. The corn and the flocks, which used to cover the plains and make the valleys rejoice, shall all be destroyed, eaten up, trodden down, or carried off. The most sacred persons shall not escape: The *priests and princes shall go together into captivity.* Nay, Chemosh, the god they worship, who, they hope, will protect them, shall share with them in the ruin; his temples shall be laid in ashes and his image carried away with the rest of the spoil. Now the consequence of all this will be, 1. Great shame and confusion: *Kirjathaim is confounded,* and Misgah is so. They shall be ashamed of the mighty boasts they have sometimes made of their cities: *There shall be no more vaunting in Moab concerning Heshbon* (so it might be read, *v.* 2); they shall no more boast of the strength of that city when the evil which is designed against it is brought upon it. Nor shall they any more boast of their gods (*v.* 13); they *shall be ashamed of Chemosh* (ashamed of all the prayers they have made to and all the confidence they put in that dunghill deity), *as Israel was ashamed of Beth-el,* of the golden calf they had at Beth-el, which they confided in as their protector, but were deceived in, for it was not able to save them from the Assyrians; nor shall Chemosh be able to save the Moabites from the Chaldeans. Note, Those that will not be convinced and made ashamed of the folly of their idolatry by the word of God shall be convinced and made ashamed of it by the judgments of God, when they shall find by woeful experience the utter inability of the gods they have served to do them any service. 2. There will be great sorrow; there is a *voice of crying* heard (*v.* 3) and the cry is nothing but *spoiling and great destruction.* Alas! alas! *Moab is destroyed, v.* 4. The great ones having quitted the cities to shift for their own safety, even the *little ones have caused a cry to be heard,* the meaner sort of people, or the little children, the innocent harmless ones, whose cries at such a time are the most piteous. Go up to the hills, go down to the valleys, and you meet with *continual weeping (weeping with weeping);* all are in tears; you meet none with dry eyes. Even the enemies have heard the cry, from whom it would have been policy to conceal it, for they will be animated and encouraged by it; but it is so great that it cannot be hid, 3. There will be great hurry; they will cry to one another, "Away, away! *flee; save your lives* (*v.* 6); shift for your own safety with all imaginable speed, though you escape as bare and naked as the *heath,* or grig, or dry shrub, *in the wilderness;* think not of carrying away any thing you have, for it may cost you your life to attempt it, Mt. 24:16–18. Take shelter, though it be in a barren wilderness, that you may have your lives for a prey. The danger will come suddenly and swiftly; and therefore *give wings unto Moab* (*v.* 9); that would be the greatest kindness you could do them; that is what they will call for, *O that we had wings like a dove!* for unless they have wings, and can fly, there will be no escaping."

IV. The sins for which God will now reckon with Moab, and which justify God in these severe proceedings against them. 1. It is because they have been secure, and have trusted in their wealth and strength, *in their works* and *in their treasures, v.* 7. They had taken a great deal of pains to fortify their cities and make large works about them, and to fill their exchequer and private coffers, so that they thought themselves in as good a posture for war as any people could be and that none durst invade them, and therefore set danger at defiance. They trusted *in the abundance of their riches and strengthened themselves in their wickedness,* Ps. 52:7. Now, for this reason, that they may have a sensible conviction of the vanity and folly of their carnal confidences, God will send an enemy that will master their works and rifle their treasures. Note, We forfeit the comfort of that creature which we repose that confidence in which should be reposed in God only. The reed will break that is leaned upon. 2. It is because they have not made a right improvement of the days of the peace and prosperity, *v.* 11. (1.) They had been long undisturbed: *Moab has been at ease from his youth.* It was an ancient kingdom before Israel was, and had enjoyed great tranquillity, though a small country and surrounded with potent neighbours. God's Israel were afflicted from their youth (Ps. 129:1, 2), but *Moab at ease from his youth.* He has *not been emptied from vessel to vessel,* has not known any troublesome weakening changes, but is as wine kept on the lees, and not racked or drawn off, by which it retains its strength and body. He has not been unsettled, nor any way made uneasy; he has not *gone into captivity,* as Israel have often done, and yet Moab is a wicked idolatrous nation, and one of the confederates against *God's hidden ones,* Ps. 83:3, 6. Note, There are many that persist in unrepented iniquity and yet enjoy uninterrupted prosperity. (2.) They had been as long corrupt and unreformed: He *has settled on his lees;* he has been secure and sensual in his prosperity, has rested in it, and fetched all the strength and life of the soul from it, as the wine from the lees. *His taste remained in him, and his scent is not changed;* he is still the same, as bad as ever he was. Note, While bad people are as happy as they used to be in the world it is no marvel if they are bad as they used to be. They have no changes of their peace and prosperity, *therefore fear not God,* their hearts and lives are unchanged, Ps. 55:19.

Verses 14–47

The destruction is here further prophesied of very largely and with a great copiousness and variety of expression, and very pathetically and in moving language, designed not only to awaken them by a national repentance and reformation to prevent the trouble, or by a personal repentance and reformation to prepare for it, but to affect us with the calamitous state of human life, which is liable to such lamentable occurrences, and with the power of God's anger and the terror of his judgments, when he comes forth to contend with a provoking people. In reading this long roll of threatenings, and meditating on the terror of them, it will be of more use to us to keep this in our eye, and to get our hearts thereby possessed with a holy awe of God and of his wrath, than to enquire critically into all the lively figures and metaphors here used.

I. It is a surprising destruction, and very sudden, that is here threatened. They were very secure, thought themselves *strong for war* and able to deal with the most powerful enemy (*v.* 14), and yet the calamity is near, and he is not able to keep it off, nor so much as to keep the enemy long in parley, for the *affliction hastens fast* (*v.* 16) and will soon come to a crisis. The enemy shall *fly as an eagle,* so swiftly, so strongly shall he come (*v.* 40), as an eagle flies upon his prey, and *he shall spread his wings,* the wings of his army, *over Moab;* he shall surround it, that none may escape. *The strong-holds* of Moab are taken by *surprise* (*v.* 41), so that all their strength stood them in no stead; and this made *the hearts* even of *their mighty men to fail,* for they had not time to recollect the considerations that might have animated them. It requires a more than ordinary degree of courage not to be *afraid of sudden fear.*

II. It is an utter destruction, and such as lays Moab all in ruins: *Moab is spoiled* (*v.* 15), quite spoiled, is *confounded and broken down* (*v.* 20); their cities are laid in ashes, or seized by the enemy so that they are forced to quit them, *v.* 15. Divers cities are here named, upon which judgment has come, and the list concludes with an *et cetera — and such like.* What occasion was there for him to mention more particulars when it comes *upon all the cities of Moab* in general, *far and near? v.* 21–24. Note, When iniquity is universal we have reason to expect that calamity should be so too. The kingdom is deprived of its dignity and authority: *The horn of Moab is cut off,* the horn of its strength and power, both offensive and defensive; *his arm is broken,* that he can neither give a blow nor prevent a blow, *v.* 25. Is the youth of the kingdom the strength and beauty of it? *His chosen young men have gone down to the slaughter, v.* 15. They went down to the battle promising themselves that they should return victorious; but God told them that they went *down to the slaughter;* so sure are those to fall against whom God fights. In a word, *Moab shall be destroyed from being a people, v.* 42. Those that are enemies to God's people will soon be made no people.

III. It is a lamentable destruction; it will be just matter of mourning and will turn joy into heaviness. 1. The prophet that foretels it does himself lament it, and mourns at the very foresight of it, from a principle of compassion to his fellow-creatures and concern for human nature. The prophet will himself *howl for Moab;* his very *heart shall mourn for* them (*v.* 31); he will *weep for the vine of Sibmah* (*v.* 32); his *heart shall sound like pipes for Moab, v.* 36. Though the destruction of Moab would prove him a true prophet, yet he could not think of it without trouble. The ruin of sinners is no pleasure to God, and therefore should be a pain to us; even those that give warning of it should lay it to heart. These passages, and many others in this chapter, are much the same with what Isaiah had used in his prophecies against Moab (Isa. 15:16); for, though there was a long distance of time between that prophecy and this, yet they were both dictated by one and the same Spirit, and it becomes God's prophets to speak the language of those that went before them. It is no plagiarism sometimes to make use of old expressions, provided it be with new affections and applications. 2. The Moabites themselves shall lament it; it will be the greatest mortification and grief imaginable to them. Those that sat in *glory,* in the midst of wealth, and mirth, and all manner of pleasure, shall *sit in thirst,* in a dry and thirsty land, where no water, no comfort is, *v.* 18. It is time for them to *sit in thirst,* and inure themselves to hardship, when *the spoiler has come,* who will strip them of all, and empty them. The Moabites in the remote corners of the country, that are furthest from the danger, will be inquisitive to know how the matter goes, what news from the army, will ask every one *that escapes, What is done? v.* 19. And when they are told that all is gone, that the invader is the conqueror, they will *howl and cry,* in bitterness and anguish of spirit (*v.* 20); they will abandon themselves to solitude, to lament the desolations of their country; they will *leave the cities* that used to be full of mirth, *and dwell in the rock* where they may have their full of melancholy; they shall no more be singing birds, but mourning birds, *like the dove* (*v.* 28); *the doves of the valley,* Eze. 7:16. Let those that give themselves up to mirth know that God can soon change their note. Their sorrow shall be so very extreme that they shall make themselves *bald and cut* themselves (*v.* 37), which were expressions of a desperate grief, such as tempted men to be even their own destroyers. *Job* indeed *rent his mantle and shaved his head,* but he did not cut himself. When the flood of passion rises ever so high wisdom and grace must set bounds to it, set banks to it, to restrain it from such barbarities. The sorrow shall be universal (*v.* 38): *There shall be a general lamentation upon all the house-tops of Moab,* where they worshipped their idols, to whom they shall in vain bemoan themselves, *and in* all *the streets,* where they conversed with one another, for they shall be free in communicating their grief and fears and in propagating them; for they see all lost: *"I have broken Moab like a vessel wherein is no pleasure,* which shall not be regarded and cannot be pieced again." That which Moab used to rejoice in was their pleasant fruits and the abundance of their rich wines. The delights of sense were all the matter of their joy. Take away these, destroy their gardens and vineyards, and you make *all their mirth to cease,* Hos. 2:11, 12. There is great weeping when their plants are transplanted, *have gone over the sea* (*v.* 32), are carried into other countries, to be planted there. *The spoiler has fallen upon thy summer-fruits and upon thy vintage,* and it is this that makes *the cry of Heshbon* to reach *even to Elealeh, v.* 34. *Take joy and gladness from the plentiful field,* and you take it *from the land of Moab, v.* 33. If *the wine fail from the wine-presses,* that used to be trodden with acclamations of joy, all their gladness is cut off. Take away that shouting, and there shall be no shouting. Note, Those who make the delights of sense their chief joy, their exceeding joy, since these are things they may easily be deprived of in a little time subject themselves to the tyranny of the greatest grief; whereas those who rejoice in God may do that even when *the fig-tree does not blossom and there is no fruit in the vine.* These Moabites lost not only their wine, but their water too: Even *the waters of Nimrim shall be desolate* (*v.* 34), and therefore their grief grew extravagantly loud and noisy, and their lamentations were heard in all placed like the lowing of *a heifer of three years old.* The expressions here are borrowed from Isa. 15:5, 6. 3. All their neighbours are called to mourn with them, and to condole with them on their ruin (*v.* 17): *All you that are about him bemoan him,* Let him have that allay to his grief, let him see himself pitied by the adjoining countries. Nay, let those at a distance, who do but *know his name* and have heard of his reputation, take notice of his fall, and say, *How is the strong staff broken,* whose strength was the terror of its enemies, *and the beautiful rod,* whose beauty was the pride of its friends! Let the nations take notice of this and receive instruction. Let none be puffed up with or put confidence in their strength or beauty, for neither will be a security against the judgments of God.

IV. It is a shameful destruction and such as shall expose them to contempt: *Moab is made drunk* (*v.* 26), and he that is made drunk is made vile; he *shall wallow in his vomit,* and become an odious spectacle, *and shall*justly *be in derision.* Let the Moabites be intoxicated with the cup of God's wrath till they stagger and fall, and be brought to *their wits' end,* and make themselves ridiculous by the wildness not only of their passions but of their counsels. And again (*v.* 39): *Moab shall be a derision and a dismaying to all about him;* they shall laugh at the fall of the pomp and power he was so proud of. Note, Those that are haughty are preparing reproach and ignominy for themselves.

V. It is the destruction of that which is dear to them, not only of their summer fruits and their vintage, but of their wealth (*v.* 36): *The riches that he has gotten have perished,* though he thought he had laid them up very safely, and promised himself a long enjoyment of them, yet they are gone. Note, The money that is hoarded in the chest is as liable to perishing as the summer-fruits that lie exposed in the open field. Riches are shedding things, and, like dust as they are, slip through our fingers even when we are in most care to hold them fast and gripe them hard. Yet this is not the worst; even those whose religion was false and foolish were fond of it above any thing, and, such as it was, would not part with it; and therefore, though it was really a promise, yet to them it was a threatening (*v.* 35), that God *will cause to cease him that offers in the high places,* for the high places shall be destroyed, and the fields of offerings shall be laid waste, and the priests themselves, *who burnt incense to their gods,* shall be slain or carried into captivity, *v.* 7. Note, It is only the true religion, and the worship and service of the true God, that will stand us in stead in a day of trouble.

VI. It is a just and righteous destruction, and that which they have deserved and brought upon themselves by sin.

1. The sin which they had been most notoriously guilty of, and for which God now reckoned with them, was pride. It is mentioned six times, *v.* 29. *We have* all *heard of the pride of Moab;* his neighbours took notice of it; it has testified to his face, as Israel's did; *he is exceedingly proud,* and grows worse and worse. Observe *his loftiness, his arrogancy, his pride, his haughtiness;* the multiplying of words to the same purport intimates in how many instances he discovered his pride, and how offensive it was both to God and man. It was charged upon them Isa, 16:6, but here it is expressed more largely that there. Since then they had been under humbling providences, and yet were unhumbled; nay, they grew more arrogant and haughty, which plainly marked them for that utter destruction of which pride is the forerunner. Two instances are here given of the pride of Moab: — (1.) He had conducted himself insolently towards God. He must be brought down with shame (*v.* 26), for *he* has *magnified himself against the Lord;* and again (*v.* 42), he *shall be destroyed from being a people,* for this very reason. The Moabites preferred Chemosh before Jehovah, and thought themselves a match for the God of Israel, whom they set at defiance. (2.) He had conducted himself scornfully towards Israel, particularly in their late troubles; therefore Moab shall fall into the same troubles; into the same hands, and be a derision, for Israel was *a derision to him, v.* 26, 27. The generality of the Moabites, when they heard of the calamities and desolations of their neighbours the Jews, instead of lamenting them, rejoiced in them, they *skipped for joy.* Many, in such a case, entertain in their minds a secret pleasure at the fall of those they had a dislike to, who yet have so much discretion as to conceal it; it is so invidious a thing. But the Moabites industriously proclaimed their joy, and avowed the enmity they had to Israel, triumphing over every Israelite they met with in distress and laughing at him, which was as inhuman as it was impious and an impudent affront both to man, whose nature they were of, and to God, whose name they were called by. Note, Those that deride others in distress will justly and certainly, sooner or later, come into distress themselves, and be had in derision. Those that are *glad at calamities,* especially the calamities of God's church, *shall not* long *go unpunished.*

2. Besides this they had been guilty of malice against God's people, and treachery in their dealings with them, *v.* 30. They made a jest of the desolations of Judah and Jerusalem, and pretended, when they laughed at them, that it was but in sport and to make themselves merry; but, says God, *"I know his wrath;* I know it comes from the old enmity he has to the seed of Abraham and the worshippers of the true God. *I know* he thinks these calamities of the Jewish nation will end in their utter extirpation. He now tells the Chaldeans what bad people the Jews are, and irritates them against them; *but it shall not be so* as he expects; *his lies shall not so effect it.* The nation, whose fall they triumph in, shall recover itself." Some read it, *I know his rage. Is it not so?* Is he not very furious against the people of God? And *his lies I know* also. *Do they not do so?* Do they not belie them? Note, All the fury and all the falsehood of the church's enemies are perfectly known to God, whatever the pretenses are with which they think to cover them, Isa. 37:28.

VII. It is a complicated destruction, and by one instance after another will at length be completed; for those that make their escape from one judgment shall perish by another: *Fear, and the pit, and the snare, shall be upon them, v.* 43. There shall be fear to drive them into the pit, and a snare to hold them fast in it when they are in it; so that they shall neither escape from the destruction nor escape out of it. What was said of sinners in general (Isa. 24:17, 18), that those who *flee from the fear shall fall into the pit* and those who come *up out of the pit shall be taken in the snare,* is here particularly foretold concerning the sinners of Moab (*v.* 44); for it is *the year of their visitation,* when God comes to reckon with them, and will be *known by the judgments which he executes,* for he is *the King whose name is the Lord of hosts* (*v.* 15); he is not only *the King* who has authority to give judgment, but he is *the Lord of hosts,* who is able to do what he has determined. The figurative expressions used *v.* 44 are explained in one instance (*v.* 45): *Those that fled* out of the villages for fear of the enemy's forces put themselves *under the shadow of Heshbon,* stood there, and supposed they stood safely, as now armies sometimes retire under the cannon of a fortified city, and it is their protection; but here they should be disappointed, for, when *they flee out of the pit, they fall into the snare;* Heshbon, which they thought would shelter them, devours them as Moses had foretold long since (Num. 21:28): *A fire has gone out of Heshbon,* and *a flame from the city of Sihon,* and devours those that come from all *the corners of Moab,* and fastens upon *the crown of the head of the tumultuous* noisy *ones,* or of the revellers, or children of noise, not meant of the rude clamorous multitude, but of the great men, who bluster, and hector, and make a noise; the judgments of God shall light on them. Shall we hear the conclusion of this whole matter? We have it (*v.* 46): *"Woe be to thee, O Moab!* thou art undone; *the people* that worship *Chemosh perish,* and are gone; farewell, Moab. *Thy sons* and *daughters,* the hopes of the next generation, have gone into captivity after the Jews, whose calamities they rejoiced in."

VIII. Yet it is not a perpetual destruction. The chapter concludes with a short promise of their return out of *captivity in the latter days.* God, who brings them into captivity, *will bring again* their *captivity, v.* 47. Thus tenderly does God deal with Moabites, much more with his own people! Even with Moabites he *will not contend for ever, nor be always wrath.* When Israel returned, Moab did; and perhaps the prophecy was intended chiefly for the encouragement of God's people to hope for that salvation which even Moabites shall share in. Yet it looks further, to gospel times; the Jews themselves refer it to the days of the Messiah; then the captivity of the Gentiles, under the yoke of sin and Satan, shall be brought back by divine grace, which shall *make them free, free indeed.* This prophecy concerning Moab is long, but here it ends; it ends comfortably: *Thus far is the judgment of Moab.*

CHAPTER 49

The cup of trembling still goes round, and the nations must all drink of it, according to the instructions given to Jeremiah, *ch.* 25:15. This chapter puts it into the hands, I. Of the Ammonites (*v.* 1–6). II. Of the Edomites (*v.* 7–22). III. Of the Syrians (*v.* 23–27). IV. Of the Kedarenes, and the kingdoms of Hazor (*v.* 28–33). V. Of the Elamites (*v.* 34–39). When Israel was scarcely saved where shall all these appear?

Verses 1–6

The Ammonites were next, both in kindred and neighbourhood, to the Moabites, and therefore are next set to the bar. Their country joined to that of the two tribes and a half, on the other side Jordan, and was but a bad neighbour; however, being a neighbour, they shall have a share in these circular predictions. 1. An action is here brought, in God's name, against the Ammonites, for an illegal encroachment upon the rightful possessions of the tribe of Gad, that lay next them, *v.* 1. A writ of enquiry is brought to discover what title they had to those territories, which, upon the carrying away of the Gileadites, by the king of Assyria (2 Ki. 15:29, 1 Chr. 5:26), were left almost dispeopled, at least unguarded, and an easy prey to the next invader. "What! Does it escheat *ob defectum sanguinis — for what of an heir? Hath Israel no sons? Hath he no heir?* Are there no Gadites left, to whom the right of inheritance belongs? Or, if there were not, are there no Israelites, none left of Judah, that are nearer akin to them than you are?" *Why then does their king,* as if he were entitled to the forfeited estates, or Milcom, their idol, as if he had the right to dispose of it to his worshippers, *inherit Gad, and his people dwell in the cities* which fell by lot to that tribe of God's people. Nay, there were sons and heirs of their own body, *en ventre de sa mere — in their mother's womb,* and the Ammonites, to prevent their claim, most barbarously murdered them (Amos 1:13): *They ripped up the women with child of Gilead, that they might enlarge their border,* that, having seized it, none might rise up hereafter to recover it from them. Thus *they magnified themselves against their border* and boasted it was their own, Zep. 2:8. Note, Though among men might often prevails against right, yet that might shall be controlled by the Almighty, who *sits in the throne, judging right;* and those will find themselves mistaken who think every thing their own which they can lay their hands on, or which none yet appears to lay claim to. As there is justice owing to owners, so also to their heirs, when they are dead, whom it is a great sin to defraud, though they either know not their right or know not how to come at it. This shall be reckoned for particularly, when injuries of this kind are done to God's people. 2. Judgment is here given against them for this violence. (1.) Terrors shall come upon them: God *will cause an alarm of war to be heard,* even *in Rabbah,* their capital city and a very strong one, *v.* 2. *The Lord God of hosts,* who has all armies at his command, *will bring a fear upon them from all that be about them, v.* 5. Note, God has many ways to terrify those who have been a terror to his people. (2.) Their cities shall be laid in ruins: *Rabbah,* the mother-city, *shall be a desolate heap, and her daughters,* the other cities that have a dependence upon her, and receive law from her as daughters, *shall be burnt with fire;* so that the inhabitants shall be forced to quit them, and they shall *cry,* and *gird themselves with sackcloth,* as having lost all they had, and not knowing whither to betake themselves. (3.) Their country, which they were so proud of, shall be wasted (*v.* 4): *Wherefore gloriest thou in the valleys,* and *trustest in thy treasures, O backsliding daughter?* They are charged with backsliding or turning away from God and from his worship, for they were the posterity of righteous Lot. It is true, they had never been so in covenant with God as Israel was; yet all idolaters may be called *backsliders,* for the worship of the true God was prior to that of false gods. *They were untoward and refractory* (so some read it); and, when they had forsaken their God, *they gloried in their valleys,* particularly one that was called *the flowing valley,* because it flowed with all good things. These they had violently taken away from Israel, and gloried in it when they had done so. They gloried in the strength of their valleys, so surrounded with mountains that they were inaccessible, gloried in the products of them, gloried *in the treasures* they got together out of them, *saying, Who shall come unto me?* While they bathed themselves in the pleasures of their country, they flattered themselves with a conceit that they should never be disturbed in the enjoyment of them: *To-morrow shall be as this day;* therefore they set God and his judgments at defiance; they are proud, voluptuous, and secure; but wherefore dost thou do so: Note, Those who backslide and turn away from God have little reason either to take complacency or to put confidence in any worldly enjoyments whatsoever, Hos. 9:1. (4.) Their people, from the least to the greatest, shall be forced out of the country. Some shall flee to seek for shelter, others shall be carried into captivity, so that their land shall be quite evacuated: *Their king and his princes,* nay, and Milcom, their god, *and his priests, shall go into captivity* (*v.* 3), *and every man shall be driven out right forth,* shall take the next way, and make the best of it in his flight (*v.* 5), forgetting the *valleys, the flowing valleys,* which now fail them. And, to complete their misery, *none shall gather up him that wanders,* none shall open their doors to them, as Jael to Sisera, to entertain them; and those that flee shall be so much in care to secure themselves that they shall not take notice of others, no, not of those that are nearest to them, that wander, and are at a loss which way to go, as *ch.* 47:3. (5.) Then the country of the Ammonites shall fall into the hands of the remaining Israelites (*v.* 2): *Then shall Israel be heir to those that were his heirs,* shall possess himself of their land who had possessed themselves of his, by way of reprisal. Note, The equity of divine Providence is to be acknowledged when the losses of the injured are recompensed out of the unjust gains of the injurious. Though the enemies of God's Israel may make a prey of them for a while, the tables will shortly be turned. 3. Yet there is a prospect given them of mercy hereafter (*v.* 6), as before to Moab. The day will come when *the captivity of the children of Ammon will* be *brought again;* for so it is in human affairs: the wheel goes round.

Verses 7–22

The Edomites come next to receive their doom from God, by the mouth of Jeremiah: they also were old enemies to the Israel of God; but their day will come to be reckoned with, and it is now at hand, and is foretold, not only for warning to them, but for comfort to the Israel of God, whose afflictions were very much aggravated by their triumphs over them and joy in their calamity, Ps. 137:7. Many of the expressions used in this prophecy *concerning Edom* are borrowed from the prophecy of Obadiah, which is *concerning Edom;* for, all the prophets being inspired by one and the same Spirit, there must needs be a wonderful harmony and agreement in their predictions. Now here it is foretold,

I. That the country of Edom should be all wasted and made desolate, that *the calamity of Esau* should be *brought upon him,* the calamity he has deserved, and God has long designed him, for his old sins, *v.* 8. The time is at hand when God *will visit him,* and call him to an account, and then they shall *flee* from the sword, *turn back* from the battle, and *dwell deep* in some close caverns, where they shall hide themselves. All they have shall be carried off by the conqueror; whereas *grape-gatherers* will *leave some gleanings,* and even *thieves* know when *they have enough* and *will destroy* no further, those that destroy them shall never be satiated, (*v.* 9, 10); they shall make *Esau* quite *bare,* shall strip the Edomites of all they have, shall find out ways and means to come at their most hidden treasure, shall discover even the *secret places* where they thought to secure their wealth, and rifle them, so that they shall none of them save their wealth, no, nor save themselves nor their children, that might be concealed in a little room: *He shall not be able to hide himself,* and *his seed* too *is spoiled. His brethren* the Moabites, *and his neighbours* the Philistines, whom he might have expected succours from, or at least shelter with, are spoiled as well as he and disabled to do him any service. *And he is not,* or *there is not he, there is none to him, none left him,* that may say what follows (*v.* 11), *Leave thy fatherless children, I will preserve them alive.* When they are flying, or dying, there shall be none left, no relation, no friend, no, not so much as any parish officers to take care of their wives and children that they leave behind. Edom is not, he is cut off and gone; nor is there any to say, *Leave me thy orphans.* If the master of a family be cut off, or forced away, it is some comfort if he have a friend to leave his family with, whom he can confide in; but they shall have none such, for they shall all be involved in the same calamity. The Chaldee makes these to be the words of God to his people, distinguishing them from the Edomites in this calamity; and they read it, *"But you, O house of Israel! you shall not leave your orphans; I will secure them, and let your widows rest on my word.* Whatever becomes of the widows and fatherless of the Edomites, I will take care of yours." Note, it is an unspeakable comfort to the people of God, when they are dying, that they may leave their surviving relations with God, may, in faith, commit them to him and encourage them to trust in him; and, though they cannot promise themselves great things in the world for them, yet they may hope that he will preserve them alive, always, provided that they trust in him. Let the Edomites, for their part, count upon no other than to be made *a desolation* and *a reproach;* for the decree has gone forth; God hath *sworn it by himself* (*v.* 13), that their *cities shall be wasted,* nay, they *shall be perpetual wastes,* they shall be made mean and despicable; they had made a mighty figure, but God will make *them small among the heathen;* and those that despised God's people shall themselves be *despised among men* (*v.* 15, Obad. 2), nay, they shall be made monstrous, and even a prodigy (*v.* 17): *Edom shall be* such a *desolation* that every one who goes by *shall be astonished;* nay, worse yet, they shall be made a terror; Edom shall be made like Sodom and Gomorrah, none shall care for coming near the ruins of it, *no man shall abide there* (*v.* 18), such a frightful place shall it be made.

II. That the instruments of this destruction should be very resolute and formidable. They have their commission from God; he summons them into this service (*v.* 14): *I have heard a rumour,* or report, *from the Lord,* heard it by the prophecy of Obadiah, heard it by a whisper to myself, that *an ambassador,* or herald, or messenger, *is sent to the* Gentiles, who are to lay Edom waste, *saying, Gather you together,* muster all the forces you can, *and come against her;* for (*v.* 20) this is *the counsel that he hath taken against Edom.* The matter is settled, the decree has gone forth, and there is no resisting it. God has determined that Edom shall be laid waste, and then he that is to be employed in wasting it shall come swiftly and strongly. Nebuchadnezzar is he or whom it is here foretold, 1. That he *shall come up like a lion,* with fierceness and fury, like a lion enraged by *the swelling of Jordan* overflowing his banks, which forces him out of his covert by the water-side into the higher grounds, *v.* 19. He shall come roaring, come to devour all that come in his way. He shall *come against the habitation of the strong,* the forts and castles; and I *will cause him to come suddenly into the land* (so the next words might well be read), so as to find them unprovided with necessaries for a defence; for I will look out *a chosen man to appoint over her,* to do this execution, a man fit for the purpose, one chosen out of the people; for when God has work to do he will find out the fittest instruments to be employed in doing it: *"Who is like me* for choosing the instruments, and spiriting them for the work? And *who will appoint me the time?* Who will challenge me, and fix a time and place to meet me? Who will join issue with me in battle? And, when I send a lion into the flock, *who is that shepherd* that can, or dare, stand before me, or against me, to oppose that lion, and think to rescue any of the flock?" Note, When God has work to do of any kind he will soon find those that are able to engage in it, and all the world cannot find those that are able to engage against it. Nay, if God will have Edom destroyed, and their peopled dislodged, there needs not a lion, a fierce lion to do it: *Even the least of the flock shall draw them out* (*v.* 20); the meanest servant in Nebuchadnezzar's retinue, the weakest of all that follow his camp, shall *draw them out* for the slaughter, shall force them to flee, or to surrender, and *make their habitations desolate with them.* God can bring to pass the greatest works by instruments least likely. When the Chaldean army comes against the Edomites all hands shall be employed and the poorest soldier in it shall have a pluck at them. 2. Nebuchadnezzar shall come, not only like a lion, the king of beasts, but like an eagle, the king of birds (*v.* 22): *He shall fly as the eagle* upon his prey, so swiftly, so strongly, shall clap his wings upon Bozrah, to secure it for himself (as before, ch 48:40), and immediately *the hearts of the mighty men* shall fail them, for they shall see he is an enemy that it is in vain to struggle with.

III. That the Edomites' confidences should all fail them in the day of their distress. 1. They trusted to their wisdom, but that shall stand them in no stead. This is the first thing fastened upon in this prophecy against Edom, *v.* 7. That nation used to be famous for wisdom, and their statesmen were thought to excel in politics; and yet now they shall take such wrong measures in all their counsels, and be so baffled in all their designs, that people shall ask, with wonder, What is the matter with the Edomites? *Is wisdom no more in Teman?* Have the wise men of the east country (1 Ki. 4:30) become fools? Are those at *their wits' end* that were thought to have the monopoly of prudence? *Has counsel perished from the understanding men?* It is so, when God is designing the ruin of a people; for whom he will destroy he infatuates. See Job 12:20. *Has their wisdom vanished? Is it tired?* (so some); *is it worn out?* (so others); *has it become useless?* so others. Yes, it will do them no service when God comes forth to contend with them. 2. They trusted to their strength, but neither shall that avail them, *v.* 16. They had been a terror to all their neighbours; every body feared them and truckled to them, and this made them proud and conceited of themselves and their own strength, and very secure; because no neighbouring nation durst meddle with them, they thought no nation in the world durst. Their country was much of it mountainous, having many passes which they thought themselves able to make good against any invader; but this terribleness of theirs deceived them, and so did their imaginary inaccessibleness; they did not prove so strong as they were formidable, nor so safe as they were secure. High as they are, God will bring them down; for, as *there is no wisdom,* so there is no might *against the Lord,* See these expressions, Obad. 3, 4, 8.

IV. That their destruction should be inevitable and very remarkable. 1. God hath determined it (*v.* 12); he hath said it; nay (*v.* 13), he hath *sworn it,* that *the Edomites shall not go unpunished,* but that they shall *drink the cup of trembling,* which is put into the hands of all their neighbours; even those *whose judgment,* or doom, *was not to drink of the cup,* who had not so well deserved it as they had done, nations that had not been such enemies to Israel as they had been, or Israel itself, that was God's peculiar people, and among whom there were many, very many, who kept his ordinances, upon which account they might have expected an exemption; and yet they had been made to drink of the bitter cup; and shall the Edomites think to pass it? No; they shall *surely drink of it.* Note, When God punishes the less guilty it is folly for the more guilty to promise themselves impunity; and when judgment begins at God's house it will reach the strangers. 2. All the world shall take notice of it (*v.* 21): *The earth is moved,* and all the nations are put into a concern, *at the noise of their fall;* the news of it shall make them tremble. *The noise of the outcry is heard to the Red Sea,* which flowed upon the coasts of Edom. So loud shall be the shouts of the conquerors and the shrieks of the conquered, and such a mighty noise shall the news of this destruction of Idumea make in the nations, that is shall be heard among the ships that lie in the Red Sea to take in lading (1 Ki. 9:26), and then they shall carry the news of it to the remotest shore. Note, The fall of those who have affected to make a noise with their pomp and power will make so much the greater noise.

Verses 23–27

The kingdom of Syria lay north of Canaan, as that of Edom lay south, and thither we must now remove and take a view of the approaching fate of that kingdom, which had been often vexatious to the Israel of God. Damascus was the metropolis of that kingdom, and the ruin of the whole is supposed in the ruin of that: yet Hamath and Arpad, two other considerable cities, are names (*v.* 23), and *the palaces of Ben-hadad,* which he built, are particularly marked for ruin, *v.* 27; see also Amos 1:4. Some think Ben-hadad (the son of Hadad, either their idol, or one of their ancient kings, whence the rest descended) was a common name of the kings of Syria, as Pharaoh of the kings of Egypt. Now observe concerning the judgment of Damascus, 1. It begins with a terrible fright and faint-heartedness. They *hear evil tidings,* that the king of Babylon, with all his force, is coming against them, and *they are confounded;* they know not what measures to take for their own safety, their souls are melted, *they are faint-hearted,* they have no spirit left them, they are like *the troubled sea, that cannot be quiet* (Isa. 57:20), or like men *in a storm* at sea (Ps. 17:26); or the sorrow that begins in the city shall go to the sea-coast, *v.* 23. See how easily God can dispirit those nations that have been most celebrated for valour. *Damascus* now *waxes feeble* (*v.* 24), a city that thought she could look the most formidable enemy in the face now *turns herself to flee,* and owns it is to no more purpose to think of contending with her fate than for *a woman in* labour to contend with her pains, which she cannot escape, but must yield to. It was a *city of praise* (*v.* 25), not praise to God, but to herself, a city much commended and admired by all strangers that visited it. It was a *city of joy,* where there was an affluence and confluence of all the delights of the sons of men, and abundance of mirth in the enjoyment of them. We read it (though there is no necessity for this) *the city of my joy,* which the prophet himself had sometimes visited with pleasure. Or it may be the speech of the king lamenting the ruin of *the city of* his *joy.* But now it is all overwhelmed with fear and grief. Note, Those deceive themselves who place their happiness in carnal joys; for God in his providence can soon cast a damp upon them and put an end to them. He can soon make a *city of praise* to be a reproach and a *city of joy* to be a terror to itself. 2. It ends with a terrible fall and fire. (1.) The inhabitants are slain (*v.* 26): The *young men,* who should fight the enemy and defend the city, *shall fall* by the sword *in her streets; and all the men of war,* mighty men, expert in war, and engaged in the service of their country, *shall be cut off.* (2.) The city is laid in ashes (*v.* 27): The *fire* is *kindled* by the besiegers *in the wall,* but it shall devour all before it, *the palaces of Ben-hadad* particularly, where so much mischief had formerly been hatched against God's Israel, for which it is now thus visited.

Verses 28–33

These verses foretell the desolation that Nebuchadnezzar and his forces should make among the people of Kedar (who descended from Kedar the son of Ishmael, and inhabited a part of Arabia the Stony), and of the kingdoms, the petty principalities, of Hazor, that joined to them, who perhaps were originally Canaanites, of the kingdom of Hazor, in the north of Canaan, which had Jabin for its king, but, being driven thence, settled in the deserts of Arabia and associated themselves with the Kedarenes. Concerning this people we may here observe,

I. What was their present state and posture? They dwelt in *tents* and had no walls, but *curtains* (*v.* 20), no fortified cities; they had *neither gates nor bars, v.* 31. They were shepherds, and had no treasures, but stock upon land, no money, but flocks and camels. They had no soldiers among them, for they were in no fear of invaders, no merchants, for they *dwelt alone, v.* 31. Those of other nations neither came among them nor traded with them; but they lived within themselves, content with the products and pleasures of their own country. This was their manner of living, very different from that of the nations that were round about them. And, 1. They were very rich; though they had not trade, no treasures, yet they are here said to be a *wealthy nation* (*v.* 31), because they had a sufficiency to answer all the occasions of human life and they were content with it. Note, Those are truly rich who have enough to supply their necessities, and know when they have enough. We need not go to the treasures of kings and provinces, or to the cash of merchants, to look for wealthy people; they may be found among shepherds *that dwell in tents.* 2. They were very easy: *They dwelt without care.* Their wealth was such as nobody envied them, or, if any did, they might come peaceably and enjoy the like; and therefore they feared nobody. Note, Those that live innocently and honestly may live very securely, though they have *neither gates nor bars.*

II. The design of the king of Babylon against them and the descent he make upon them: *He has taken counsel against you and has conceived a purpose against you, v.* 30. That proud man resolves it shall never be said that he, who had conquered so many strong cities, will leave those unconquered *that dwell in tents.* It was strange that that eagle should stoop to catch these flies, that so great a prince should play at such small game; but all is fish that comes to the ambitious covetous man's net. Note, It will not always secure men from suffering wrong to be able to say that they have done no wrong; not to have given offence will not be a defence against such men as Nebuchadnezzar. Yet, how unrighteous soever he was in doing it, God was righteous in directing it. These people had lived inoffensively among their neighbours, as many do, who yet, like them, are guilty before God; and it was to punish them for their offences against him that God said (*v.* 28): *Arise, go up to Kedar, and spoil the men of the east.* They will do it to gratify their own covetousness and ambition, but God orders it for the correcting of an unthankful people, and for warning to a careless world to expect trouble when they seem to be most safe. God says to the Chaldeans (*v.* 31): *"Arise, get up to the wealthy nation that dwells without care;* go and give them an alarm, that none may imagine *their mountain stands so strong that it cannot be moved."*

III. The great amazement that this put them into, and the great desolation hereby made among them: *They shall cry unto them;* those on the borders shall send the alarm into all parts of the country, which shall be put into the utmost confusion by it; they shall cry, *"Fear is on every side* — We are surrounded by the enemy." the very terror of which shall drive them all to their feet and they shall none of them have any heart to make resistance. The enemy shall *proclaim fear upon them,* or *against them, on every side.* They need not strike a stroke; they shall shout them out of their tents, *v.* 29. Upon the first alarm, they shall *flee, get far off,* and *dwell deep* (*v.* 30), as the Edomites, *v.* 8. And it will be found that this *fear on every side* is not groundless, for *their calamity* shall be *brought from all sides thereof, v.* 32. No marvel there are *fears on every side* when there are foes on every side. The issue will be, 1. What they have will be a prey to the Chaldeans; they shall *take to themselves their curtains and vessels;* though they are but plain and coarse, and they have better of their own, yet they shall take them for spite, and spoil for spoiling sake. *They shall carry away their tents and their flocks, v.* 29. *Their camels* shall be a booty to those that came for nothing else, *v.* 32. 2. It is not said that any of them shall be slain, for they attempt not to make any resistance and their tents and flocks are accepted as a ransom for their lives; but they shall be dislodged and dispersed; though now they dwell *in the utmost corners,* out of the way, and therefore they think out of the reach, of danger (by this character those people were distinguished, *ch.* 9:26, 25, 23), yet they shall be *scattered* thence *into all winds,* into all parts of the world. Note, Privacy and obscurity are not always a protection and security. Many that affect to be strangers to the world may yet by unthought-of providences be forced into it; and those that live most retired may have the same lot with those that thrust themselves forth and lie most exposed. 3. Their country shall lie uninhabited; for, lying remote and out of all high roads, and having neither cities nor lands inviting to strangers, none shall care to succeed them, so that *Hazor shall be a desolation for ever, v.* 33. If busy men be displaced, many strive to get into their placed, because they lived great; but here are easy quiet men displaced, and *no man* cared to *abide* where they did, because they lived meanly.

Verses 34–39

This prophecy is dated in the beginning of Zedekiah's reign; it is probable that the other prophecies against the Gentiles, going before, were at the same time. The Elamites were the Persians, descended from Elam the son of Shem (Gen. 10:22); yet some think it was only that part of Persia which lay nearest to the Jews which was called *Elymais,* and adjoined to Media-Elam, which, say they, had acted against God's Israel, *bore the quiver* in an expedition against them (Isa. 22:6), and therefore must be reckoned with among the rest. It is here foretold, in general, that God will *bring evil upon them, even* his *fierce anger,* and that is evil enough, it has *all evil in it, v.* 37. In particular, 1. Their forces shall be disabled, and rendered incapable of doing them any service. The Elamites were famous archers, but, *Behold, I will break the bow of Elam* (*v.* 35), will ruin their artillery, and then *the chief of their might* is gone. God often orders it so that that which we most trust to first fails us, and that which was *the chief of our might* proves the least of our help. 2. Their people shall be dispersed. There shall come enemies against them from all parts of the world, and they shall all carry some of them away captive into their respective countries; while others shall flee, some one way and some another, to shift for themselves, so that *there shall be no nation whither the outcasts of Elam shall not come, v.* 36. *The four winds* shall be brought upon them; the storm shall come sometimes from one point and sometimes from another, to toss and hurry them several ways. We know not from what point the wind of trouble may blow; but, if God encompass us with his favour, we are safe, and may be easy, which way soever the storm comes. Fear shall drive them into other countries; they shall *be dismayed before their enemies;* but, as if that were not enough, *I will send the sword after them, v.* 37. Note, God can make his judgments follow those that think by flight to escape them and to get out of the reach of them. *Evil pursues sinners.* 3. Their princes shall be destroyed and the government quite changed (*v.* 38): *I will set my throne in Elam.* The throne of Nebuchadnezzar shall be set there, or the throne of Cyrus, who began his conquests with Elymais. Or it may be meant of the throne on which God sits for judgment; he will make them know that he reigns, that he *judges in the earth,* that *kings and princes* are accountable to him, and that high as they are he is above them. The king of Elam was famous of old, Gen. 14:1. Chedorlaomer was king of Elam, and a mighty man he was in his day; the nations about him served him; his successors, we may suppose, made a great figure; but the king of Elam is no more to God than another man. When God *sets his throne in Elam* he *will destroy thence the king and the princes* that are, and set up whom he pleases. 4. Yet the destruction of Elam shall not be perpetual (*v.* 39): *In the latter days I will bring again the captivity of Elam.* When Cyrus had destroyed Babylon, brought the empire into the hands of the Persians, the Elamites no doubt returned in triumph out of all the countries whither they were scattered, and settled again in their own country. But this promise was to have its full and principal accomplishment in the days of the Messiah, when we find Elamites particularly among those who, when the Holy Ghost was given, heard spoken *in their own tongues the wonderful works of God* (Acts 2:9, 11), and that is the most desirable return of the captivity. *If the Son make you free, then you shall be free indeed.*

CHAPTER 50

In this chapter, and that which follows, we have the judgment of Babylon, which is put last of Jeremiah's prophecies against the Gentiles because it was last accomplished; and when the cup of God's fury went round (25:17) the king of Sheshach, Babylon, drank last. Babylon was employed as the rod in God's hand for the chastising of all the other nations, and now at length that rod shall be thrown into the fire. The destruction of Babylon by Cyrus was foretold, long before it came to its height, by Isaiah, and now again, when it has come to its height, by Jeremiah; for, though at this time he saw that kingdom flourishing "like a green bay-tree," yet at the same time he foresaw it withered and cut down. And as Isaiah's prophecies of the destruction of Babylon and the deliverance of Israel out of it seem designed to typify the evangelical triumphs of all believers over the powers of darkness, and the great salvation wrought out by our Lord Jesus Christ, so Jeremiah's prophecies of the same events seem designed to point at the apocalyptic triumphs of the gospel church in the latter days over the New-Testament Babylon, many passages in the Revelation being borrowed hence. The kingdom of Babylon being much larger and stronger than any of the kingdoms here prophesied against, its fall was the more considerable in itself; and, it having been more oppressive to the people of God than any of the other, the prophet is very copious upon this subject, for the comfort of the captives; and what was foretold in general often before (25:12 and 27:7) is here more particularly described, and with a great deal of prophetic heat as well as light. The terrible judgments God had in store for Babylon, and the glorious blessings he had in store for his people that were captives there, are intermixed and counterchanged in the prophecy of this chapter; for Babylon was destroyed to make way for the turning again of the captivity of God's people. Here is, I. The ruin of Babylon (*v.* 1–3, 9–16, 21–32, and 35–46). II. The redemption of God's people (*v.* 4–8, 17–20, and 33, 34). And these being set the one against the other, it is easy to say which one would choose to take one's lot with, the persecuting Babylonians, who, though now in pomp, are reserved for so great a ruin, or the persecuted Israelites, who, though now in thraldom, are reserved for so great a glory.

Verses 1–8

I. Here is a word spoken against Babylon by him whose works all agree with his word and none of whose words fall to the ground. The king of Babylon had been very kind of Jeremiah, and yet he must foretel the ruin of that kingdom; for God's prophets must not be governed by favour or affection. Whoever are our friends, if, notwithstanding, they are God's enemies, we dare not speak peace to them. 1. The destruction of Babylon is here spoken of as a thing done, *v.* 2. let it be published to the nations as a piece of news, true news, and great news, and news they are all concerned in; let them hang out the flag, as is usual on days of triumph, to give notice of it; let all the world take notice of it: *Babylon is taken.* Let God have the honour of it, let his people have the comfort of it, and therefore do not conceal it. Take care that it be known, that *the Lord may be known by those judgments which he executes,* Ps. 9:16. 2. It is spoken of as a thing done thoroughly. For, (1.) The very idols of Babylon, which the people would protect with all possible care, and from which they expected protection, shall be destroyed. Bel and Merodach were their two principal deities; they shall be *confounded,* and the images of them *broken to pieces.* (2.) The country shall be laid waste (*v.* 3) out *of the north,* from Media, which lay north of Babylon, and from Assyria, through which Cyrus made his descent upon Babylon; thence the nation shall come that shall make *her land desolate.* Their land was north of the countries that they destroyed, who were therefore threatened with evil from the north *(Omne malum ab aquilone — Every evil comes from the north);* but God will find out nations yet further north to come upon them. The pomp and power of old Rome were brought down by northern nations, the Goths and Vandals.

II. Here is a word spoken for the people of God, and for their comfort, both *the children of Israel* and *of Judah;* for many there were of the ten tribes that associated with those of the two tribes in their return out of Babylon. Now here,

1. It is promised that they shall return to their God first and then to their own land; and the promise of their conversion and reformation is that which makes way for all the other promises, *v.* 4, 5. (1.) They shall *lament after the Lord* (as the whole house of Israel did in Samuel's time, 1 Sa. 7:2); they shall *go weeping.* These tears flow not from the sorrow of the world as those when they went into captivity, but from godly sorrow; they are tears of repentance for sin, tears of joy for the goodness of God, in the dawning of the day of their deliverance, which, for aught that appears, does more towards the bringing of them to mourn for sin than all the calamities of their captivity; that prevails to *lead them to repentance* when the other did not prevail to drive them to it. Note, It is a good sign that God

is coming towards a people in ways of mercy when they begin to be tenderly affected under his hand. (2.) They shall *enquire after the Lord;* they shall not sink under their sorrows, but bestir themselves to find out comfort where it is to be had: *They shall go weeping to seek the Lord their God.* Those that seek the Lord must *seek him sorrowing,* as Christ's parents sought him, Lu. 2:48. And those that sorrow must seek the Lord, and then their sorrow shall soon be turned into joy, for he will be found of those that so seek him. They shall *seek the Lord as their God,* and shall now have no more to do with idols. When they shall hear that the idols of Babylon are *confounded and broken* it will be seasonable for them to enquire after their own God and to return to him who lives for ever. *Therefore* men are deceived in false gods, that they may depend on the true God only. (3.) They shall think of returning to their own country again; they shall think of it not only as a mercy, but as a duty, because there only is the *holy hill of Zion,* on which once stood *the house of the Lord their God* (*v.* 5): *They shall ask the way to Zion with their faces thitherward.* Zion was the city of their solemnities; they often thought of it in the depth of their captivity (Ps. 137:1); but, now that the ruin of Babylon gave them some hopes of a release, they talk of nothing else but of going back to Zion. Their hearts were upon it before, and now they *set their faces thitherward.* They long to be there; they set out for Zion, and resolve not to take up short of it. The journey is long and they know not the road, but they will *ask the way,* for they will press forward till they come to Zion; and, as they are determined not to turn back, so they are in care not to miss the way. This represents the return of poor souls to God. Heaven is the Zion they aim at as their end; on this they have set their hearts; towards this they have *set their faces,* and therefore they *ask the way* thither. They do not ask the way to heaven and set their faces towards the world; nor set their faces towards heaven and go on at a venture without asking the way. But in all true converts there are both a sincere desire to attain the end and a constant care to keep in the way; and a blessed sight it is to see people thus asking the way to heaven with their faces thitherward. (4.) They shall renew their covenant to walk with God more closely for the future: *Come, and let us join ourselves to the Lord in a perpetual covenant.* They had broken covenant with God, had in effect separated themselves from him, but now they resolve to *join themselves* to him again, by engaging themselves afresh to be his. Thus, when backsliders return, they must *do their first works,* must renew the covenant they first made; and it must be a *perpetual covenant,* that must never be broken; and, in order to that, must never be forgotten; for a due remembrance of it will be the means of a due observance of it.

2. Their present case is lamented as very sad, and as having been long so: *"My people"* (for he owns them as his now that they are returning to him) *"have been lost sheep* (*v.* 6); they have *gone from mountain to hill,* have been hurried from place to place, and could find no pasture; *they have forgotten their resting-place* in their own country and cannot find their way to it." And that which aggravated their misery was, (1.) That they were *led astray by their own shepherds,* their own princes and priests; they turned them from their duty, and so provoked God to turn them out of their own land. It is bad with a people when their leaders cause them to err, when those that should direct them, and when those that should secure and advance their interests are the betrayers of them. (2.) That in their wanderings they lay exposed to the beasts of prey, who thought they were entitled to them, as waifs and strays that had no owner (*v.* 7); it is with them as with wandering sheep, *all that found them have devoured them* and made a prey of them; and when they did them the greatest injuries they laughed at them, telling them it was what their own prophets had many a time told them they deserved; that was far from justifying those who did them wrong, yet they bantered them with this excuse, *We offend not, because they have sinned against the Lord;* but they could not pretend that they had sinned against them. And see what notion they had of the Lord they had sinned against, not as the only true and living God, but only as *the habitation of justice and the hope of their fathers;* they had put a contempt upon the temple and upon the tradition of their ancestors, and therefore deserved to suffer these hard things. And yet it was indeed an aggravation of their sin, and justified God, though it did not justify their adversaries in what was done to them, that they had *forsaken the habitation of justice* and him that was *the hope of their fathers.*

3. They are called upon to hasten away, as soon as ever the door of liberty was opened to them (*v.* 8): *"Remove,* not only out of the borders, but *out of the midst of Babylon;* though you be ever so well seated there, think not to settle there, but hasten to Zion, and *be as the he-goats before the flocks;* strive which shall be foremost, which shall lead in so good a work:" a he-goat is *comely in going* (Prov. 30:31) because he goes first. It is a graceful thing to be forward in a good work and to set others a good example.

Verses 9–20

God is here by his prophet, as afterwards in his providence, proceeding in his controversy with Babylon. Observe,

I. The commission and charge given to the instruments that were to be employed in destroying Babylon. The army that is to do it is called *an assembly of great nations* (*v.* 9), the Medes and Persians, and all their allies and auxiliaries; it is called *an assembly,* because regularly formed by the divine will and counsel to do this execution. God will *raise them up* to do it, will incline them to and fir them for this service, and then he will *cause them to come up,* for all their motions are under his conduct and direction: he shall give the word of command, shall order them to *put themselves in array against Babylon* (*v.* 14), and then *they shall put themselves in array* (*v.* 9), for what God appoints to be done shall be done; and *thence she shall be* quickly *taken;* from their first sitting down before it they shall be still gaining ground against it till it be taken. God shall bid them *shoot at her and spare no arrows* (*v.* 14), and then *their arrows shall be as of a mighty expert man,* that has both skill and strength, a good eye and a good hand (*v.* 9); *none shall return in vain.* When God gives commission he will give success. Nay, they are bidden not only to *shoot at her* (*v.* 14), but to *shout against her* (*v.* 15) with a triumphant shout, as those that are already sure of victory. Those whom God directs to shoot may do so with shouting, for they are sure not to miss the mark.

II. The desolation and destruction itself that shall be brought upon Babylon. This is here set forth in a great variety of expressions. 1. The wealth of Babylon shall be a rich and easy prey to the conquerors (*v.* 10): *Chaldea shall be a spoil* to all her destroyers, who shall enrich themselves by plundering her, and, which is strange, *all that spoil her shall be satisfied;* they shall have so much that even they themselves shall say that they have enough. 2. The country of Babylon shall be depopulated and lie uninhabited: *It shall be wholly desolate* (*v.* 13) to such a degree that *every one who goes by* shall triumph in her fall, and, instead of condoling with them, shall *hiss at all her plagues, v.* 13. 3. Their ancestors shall be ashamed of their cowardice, in fleeing from the first onset (*v.* 12), or, *Your mother,* Babylon itself, the mother-city, *shall be confounded,* when she sees herself deserted by those that should have been her guards. Thus the former ages of Christians may justly be confounded and ashamed to see how unlike them the latter ages are, and how wretchedly they have degenerated; and no sin brings a surer and sorer ruin upon persons, or people, than apostasy. 4. The great admirers of Babylon shall see it rendered very despicable: the last of kingdoms, the very tail of the nations, *shall it be, a wilderness, a dry land, a desert, v.* 12. The country that was populous shall be dispeopled, that was enriched with a fertile soil shall become barren. 5. The great city, the head of it, shall be quite ruined. *Her foundations have fallen,* and therefore *her walls are thrown down;* for how can the walls stand when divine vengeance is at the door and shakes the very foundations? It is the vengeance of the Lord, which nothing can contend with either in law or battle. 6. There shall not be left in Babylon so much as *the poor of the land, for vine-dressers and husbandmen,* as there was in Israel (*v.* 16): *The sower shall be cut off from Babylon, and he that handles the sickle;* the country shall be so emptied of people that there shall be none to till the ground and gather in the fruits of it. Harvest shall come, and there shall be no reapers; seed-time shall come, but there shall be no sower; God will do his part, but there shall be no men to do theirs. 7. All their auxiliary forces, which they have hired into their service, shall ??desert them, as mercenary men often do upon the approach of danger (*v.* 16): *For fear of the oppressing sword they shall turn every one to his people.* This was threatened before concerning Egypt, *ch.* 46:16.

III. The procuring provoking cause of this destruction. It comes from God's displeasure; it is *because of the wrath of the Lord* that Babylon *shall be wholly desolate* (*v.* 13), and his wrath is righteous, for (*v.* 14) *she hath sinned against the Lord,* therefore *spare no arrows.* Note, It is sin that makes men a mark for the arrows of God's judgments. An abundance of idolatry and immorality was to be found in Babylon, yet those are not mentioned as the reason of God's displeasure against them, but the injuries they had done to the people of God, from a principle of enmity to them as his people. They have been *the destroyers of God's heritage* (*v.* 11); herein indeed God made use of them for the necessary correction of his people, and yet it is laid to their charge as a heinous crime, because they designed nothing but their utter destruction. 1. What they did against Jerusalem they did with pleasure (*v.* 11): *You were glad, you rejoice.* God does not afflict his people willingly, and therefore takes it very ill if the instruments he employs afflict them willingly. When Titus Vespasian destroyed Jerusalem he wept over it, but these Chaldeans triumphed over it. 2. The spoils of Jerusalem they made use of to feed their own luxury: *"You have grown fat as the heifer at grass, and bellow as bulls;* your having conquered Jerusalem has made you very wanton and proud, easy to yourselves and formidable to all about you, and therefore you must *be a spoil."* Those that have thus swallowed down riches must vomit them up again. Therefore they have *given their hand* (*v.* 15); they have surrendered themselves to the conqueror, have tamely yielded so that now you may *take vengeance on her,* now you may make reprisals and *do unto her as she hath done.* 3. They aimed at nothing less than the utter ruin of God's Israel: *Israel is a scattered sheep,* as before (*v.* 6), that is not only barked at and worried by dogs, but even lions, the most potent adversaries, have roared upon him and *driven him away, v.* 17. One king of Assyria carried the ten tribes quite away and devoured them; another invaded Judah, and plundered and impoverished it, tore the fleece and flesh of this poor sheep; and now at last this Nebuchadnezzar, that is the terror and plague of all his neighbours, has taken advantage of the low condition to which he is reduced, and he has fallen upon him and *broken his bones,* has quite ruined him, and therefore the king of Babylon must be punished as the king of Assyria was, *v.* 18. Note, Those who pursue and prosecute the sins of their predecessors must expect to be pursued and prosecuted by their plagues; if they do as they did, let them fare as they fared.

IV. The mercy promised to the Israel of God, which shall not only accompany, but accrue from, the destruction of Babylon. 1. God will return their captivity; they shall be released out of their bondage, and *brought again to their own habitation* as sheep that were scattered to their own fold *v.* 19. They still retained a title to the land of Canaan; it is their habitation still. The discontinuance of their possession was not the destruction of their right. But now they shall recover the enjoyment of it again. 2. He will restore their prosperity; they shall not only live, but live comfortably, in their own land again; they shall *feed upon Carmel and Bashan,* the richest and most fruitful parts of the country. These sheep shall be gathered from the deserts to which they were dispersed, and put again into good pasture, which their soul shall be satisfied with though they shall come hungry to it, having been so long stinted, and straitened, and kept short, yet they shall find enough to satiate them and shall have hearts to be satiated with it. They *enquired the way to Zion* (*v.* 5), where God was to be served and worshipped. This was what they chiefly aimed at in their return; but God will not only bring them thither, but bring them also to Carmel and Bashan, where they shall abundantly feed themselves. Note, Those that return to God and their duty shall find true satisfaction of soul in so doing; and those that *seek first the kingdom of God and the righteousness thereof,* that aim to make their habitation in Zion, the holy hill, shall have *other things added to them,* even all the comforts of *Ephraim and Gilead,* the fruitful hills. 3. God will pardon their iniquity; this is the root of all the rest (*v.* 20): *In those days the iniquity of Israel shall be sought for, and there shall be none.* Not only the punishments of their iniquity shall be taken off, but the offence which it gave to God shall be forgotten, and he will be reconciled to them. Their sin shall be before him as if it had never been; it shall be blotted out as a cloud, crossed out as a debt, shall be cast behind his back; nay, it shall be cast into the depth of the sea, shall be no longer sealed up among God's treasures, nor in any danger of appearing again or rising up against them. This denotes how fully God forgives sin; he *remembers it no more.* Note, Deliverances out of trouble are then comforts indeed when they are the fruits of the forgiveness of sin, Isa. 38:17. Judah and Israel were so fully forgiven when they were brought back out of Babylon that they are said to have *received of the Lord's hand double for all their sins,* Isa. 40:2. This may include also a thorough reformation of their hearts and lives, as well as a full remission of their sins. If any seek for idols or any idolatrous customs among them, after their return, *there shall be none,* they *shall not find them;* their dross shall be purely purged away, and by that it shall appear that their guilt is so; *for I will pardon those whom I reserve; I will be propitious to them* (so the word is) and that must be through him who is the great propitiation. Note, Those whose sins God pardons he reserves for something very great; for *whom he justifies them he* glorifies.

Verses 21–32

Here, 1. The forces are mustered and commissioned to destroy Babylon, and every thing is got ready for a descent upon that potent kingdom: *Go up against* that *land* by *Merathaim,* the country of the Mardi, that lay part in Assyria and part in Armenia; and go among *the inhabitants of Pekod,* another country (mentioned Eze. 23:23) which Cyrus took in his way to Babylon. The forces of Cyrus are called to go up against Babylon (*v.* 21), to *come against her from the utmost border.* Let all come together, for there will be both work and pay enough for them all, *v.* 26. Distance of place must not be their hindrance from engaging in this work. *The archers* particularly must be *called together against Babylon, v.* 29. Thus *the Lord hath opened his armoury* (*v.* 25), *his treasury* (so the word is), *and hath brought forth the weapons of his indignation,* as great princes fetch out of their magazines and stores all necessary provisions for their armies when they undertake any great expedition. Media and Persia are now God's armoury; thence he fetches the weapons of his wrath, Cyrus and his great officers and armies, whom he will make use of for the destruction of Babylon. Note, Great men are but instruments which the great God makes use of to serve his own purposes. He has variety of instruments, has them at command, has armouries ready to be opened according as the occasion is. *This is the work of the Lord God of hosts.* Note, When God has work to do he will make it appear that he is *God of hosts,* and will not want instruments to do it with. 2. Instructions are given them what to do. In general, *Do according to all that I have commanded thee, v.* 21. It was said of Cyrus (Isa. 44:28), *He shall perform all my pleasure,* in his expedition against Babylon. They must *waste and utterly destroy after them;* when they have destroyed once they must go over them again, or destroy their posterity that should come after them. They must *open her store-houses* (*v.* 26), rifle her treasures, and turn her artillery against herself. They must *cast her up as heaps;* let all the wealth and pomp of Babylon be shovelled up in a heap of ruins and rubbish. *Tread her down as heaps* (so the margin reads it) *and destroy her utterly.* See how little account the great God makes of those things which men so much value and value themselves so much upon. Their princes and great men, who are fat and bulky, shall fall by the sword, not as men of war in the field of battle, which we call a bed of honour, but as beasts by the butcher's hand (*v.* 27): *Slay all her bullocks,* all her mighty men; *let them go down* sottishly and insensibly, as an ox *to the slaughter. Woe unto them!* their case is the more sad for the little sense they have of it. *Their day has come* to fall, *the time* when they must be reckoned with, and they are not aware of it. 3. Assurances are given them of success. Let them do what God commands, and they shall accomplish what he threatens. A *great destruction* shall be made, *v.* 22. *Babylon* shall *become a desolation* (*v.* 23); *her young men and all her men of war shall be cut off in that day* which should have been her defence, *v.* 30. God is *against* her (*v.* 31); he has *laid a snare for* her (*v.* 24); he has formed this enterprise against her, that she should be surprised as a bird taken in a snare. Cyrus shall no doubt prevail, for he fights under God. God *will kindle a fire* in the cities of Babylon (*v.* 32); and who can stand before him when he is angry, or quench the fire that he has kindled? 4. Reasons are given for these severe dealings with Babylon. Those that are employed in this war may, if they please, know the grounds of it, and be satisfied in the justice of it, which it is fit all should be that are called to such work. (1.) Babylon has been very troublesome, vexatious, and injurious, to all its neighbours; it has been *the hammer of the whole earth* (*v.* 23), beating, beating down, and beating to pieces, all the nations far and near. It has done so long enough; it is time now that it be *cut asunder and broken.* Note, He that is the god of nations will sooner or later assert the injured rights of nations against those that unjustly and violently invade them. The God of the whole earth will break *the hammer of the whole earth.* (2.) Babylon has bidden defiance to God himself: *Thou has striven against the Lord* (*v.* 24), *hast joined issue with him* (so the word signifies) as in law or battle, hast openly opposed him, set up rivals with him, raised rebellion against him; therefore *thou art* now *found, and caught,* as in a snare. Note, Those that strive against the Lord will soon find themselves over-matched. (3.) Babylon ruined Jerusalem, the holy city, and the holy house there, and must now be called to an account for that. This is the manifesto published in Zion, in the day of Babylon's visitation; it is *the vengeance of the Lord our God, the vengeance of his temple, v.* 28. The burning of the temple, and the carrying away of its vessels, were articles in the charge against Babylon on which greater stress was laid than upon its being *the hammer of the whole earth;* for Zion was *the joy* and glory *of the whole earth.* Note, Whatever wrong is done to God's church (his temple in the world) it will certainly be reckoned for; and no vengeance will be sorer nor heavier than *the vengeance of the temple.* (4.) Babylon has been very haughty and insolent, and therefore must have a fall; for it is the glory of God to *look upon those that are proud and to abase them,* Job 40:12. *I am against thee, O thou most proud! v.* 31 and again *v.* 32. *Thou pride* (so the word is), as proud as pride itself. Note, the pride of men's hearts sets God against them and ripens them apace for ruin; for God *resists the proud* and will bring them down. *The most proud shall stumble and fall;* they shall fall not so much by others' thrusting them down as by their own stumbling; for they hold their heads so high that they never look under their feet, to choose their way and avoid stumbling-blocks, but walk at all adventures. Babylon's pride must unavoidably be her ruin; for *she has been proud against the Lord, against the Holy One of Israel* (*v.* 29), has insulted him in insulting over his people; she has made him her enemy, and therefore, when she has *fallen, none shall raise her up, v.* 32. Who can help those up whom God will throw down?

Verses 33–46

We have in these verses,

I. Israel's sufferings, and their deliverance out of those sufferings. God takes notice of the bondage of his people in Babylon, as he did of their bondage in Egypt; he has *surely seen* it, and has *heard their cry. Israel and Judah were oppressed together, v.* 33. Those that remained of the captives of the ten tribes, upon the uniting of the kingdoms of Assyria and Chaldea, seem to have come and mingled with t hose of the two tribes, and to have mingled tears with them, so that they were *oppressed together.* They were humble suppliants for their liberty, and that was all; they could not attempt any thing towards it, for *all that took them captives held them fast,* and were much too hard for them. But this is their comfort in distress, that, though they are weak, *their Redeemer is strong* (*v.* 34), *their Avenger* (so the word signifies), he that has a right to them, and will claim his right and make good his claim. He is stronger than their enemies that hold them fast; he can overpower all the force that is against them, and put strength into his own people though they are very weak. *The Lord of hosts is his name,* and he will answer to his name, and make it to appear that he is what his people call him, and will be that to them for which they depend upon him. Note, It is the unspeakable comfort of the people of God that, though they have hosts against them, they have *the Lord of hosts* for them and *he shall thoroughly plead their cause,* pleading he shall plead it, plead it with jealousy, plead it effectually, plead it and carry it, *that he may give rest to the land,* and to his people's land, rest from all their enemies round about. This is applicable to all believers, who complain of the dominion of sin and corruption, and of their own weakness and manifold infirmities. Let them know that *their Redeemer is strong;* he is able to keep what they commit to him, and he will plead their cause. Sin shall not have dominion over them; he will *make them free,* and they shall be *free indeed;* he will give them *rest,* that *rest which remains for the people of God.*

II. Babylon's sin, and their punishment for that sin.

1. The sins they are here charged with are idolatry and persecution. (1.) They oppressed the people of God; they *held them fast,* and would not *let them go.* They *opened not the house of his prisoners,* Isa. 14:17. This was God's quarrel with them, as of old with Pharaoh; it cost him dear, and yet they would not take warning. *The inhabitants of Babylon* must be *disquieted* (*v.* 34) because they have disquieted God's people, whose honour and comfort he is jealous for, and therefore will *recompense tribulation to those that trouble them,* as well as *rest to those that are troubled,* 2 Th. 1:6, 7. (2.) They wronged God himself, and robbed him, giving that glory to others which is due to him alone; for (*v.* 38) *it is the land of graven images.* All parts of the country abounded with idols, and they were mad upon them, were in love with them and doted on them, cared not what cost and pains they were at in the worship of them, were unwearied in paying their respects to them; and in all this they were wretchedly infatuated and acted like men out of their wits; they were carried on in their idolatry without reason or discretion, like men in a perfect fury. The word here used for idols properly signifies *terrors — Enim,* the name given to giants that were formidable, because they made the images of their gods to look frightful, to strike a terror upon fools and children. Their idols were scarecrows, yet they doted on them. Babylon was *the mother of harlots* (Rev. 17:5), the source of idolatry. Note, It is the maddest thing in the world to make a god of any creature; and those who are proud against the Lord, the true God, are justly given up to strong delusions, to be mad upon idols that cannot profit. But this madness is wickedness, for which sinners will be certainly and severely reckoned with.

2. The judgments of God upon them for these sins are such as will quite lay them waste and ruin them.

(1.) All that should be their defence and support shall be cut off by the sword. The Chaldeans had long been God's sword, wherewith he had done execution upon the sinful nations round about: but now, they being as bad as any of them, or worse, *a sword* is brought upon them, even *upon the inhabitants of Babylon* (*v.* 35), a sword of war; and, as it is in God's hand, sent and directed by him, it is a sword of justice. It shall be, [1.] *Upon their princes;* they shall fall by it, and their dignity, wealth, and power, shall not secure them. [2.] *Upon their wise men,* their philosophers, their statesmen, and privy-counsellors; their learning and policy shall neither secure them nor stand the public in any stead. [3.] *Upon* their soothsayers and astrologers, here called *the liars* (*v.* 36), for they cheated with their prognostications of peace and prosperity; the sword upon them shall make them dote, so that they shall talk like fools, and be as men that have lost all their wits. Note, God has a sword that can reach the soul and affect the mind, and bring men under spiritual plagues. [4.] *Upon their mighty men.* A sword shall be upon their spirits; if they are not slain, yet *they shall be dismayed,* and shall be no longer *mighty men;* for what stead will their hands stand them in when their hearts fail them? [5.] Upon their militia (*v.* 37): *The sword shall be upon their horses and chariots;* the invaders shall make themselves masters of all their warlike stores, shall seize their horses and chariots for themselves, or destroy them. The troops of other nations that were in their service shall be quite disheartened: *The mingled people shall become as* weak and timorous as *women.* [6.] Upon their exchequer: The *sword* shall be *upon her treasures,* which are the sinews of war, *and they shall be robbed,* and made use of by the enemy against them. See what universal destruction the sword makes when it comes with commission.

(2.) The country shall be made desolate (*v.* 38): *The waters shall be dried up,* the water that secures the city. Cyrus drew the river Euphrates into so many channels as made it passable for his army, so that they got with ease to the walls of Babylon, which, if was thought, that river had rendered inaccessible. "The water likewise that made the country fruitful shall *be dried up,* so that it shall be turned into barrenness, and shall be no more inhabited by the children of men, but by *the wild beasts of the desert," v.* 39. This was foretold concerning Babylon, Isa. 13:19–22. It shall become like *Sodom and Gomorrah, v.* 40. The same was foretold concerning Edom, *ch.* 49:18. As the Chaldeans had laid Edom waste, so they shall themselves be laid waste.

(3.) The king and kingdom shall be put into the utmost confusion and consternation by the enemies' invading them, *v.* 41–43. All the expressions here used to denote the formidable power of the invaders, the terrors wherewith they should array themselves, and the great fright which both court and country should be put into thereby, we met with before (*ch.* 6:22–24) concerning the Chaldeans' invading the land of Judah. The battle which is there said to be *against thee, O daughter of Zion!* is here said to be *against thee, O daughter of Babylon!* to intimate that they should be paid in their own coin. God can find out such as shall be for terror and destruction to those that are for terror and destruction to others; and those who have dealt cruelly, and have shown no mercy, may expect to be cruelly dealt with, and to find no mercy. Only there is one difference between these passages; there it is said, *We have heard the fame thereof and our hands wax feeble;* here it is said, *The king of Babylon has heard the report and his hands waxed feeble,* which intimates that that proud and daring prince shall, in the day of his distress, be as weak and dispirited as the meanest Israelites were in the day of their distress.

(4.) That they shall be as much hurt as frightened, for the invader shall *come up like a lion* to tear and destroy (*v.* 44) and shall make them and their *habitation desolate* (*v.* 45), and the desolation shall be so astonishing that all the nations about shall be terrified by it, *v.* 46. These three verses we had before (*ch.* 49:19–21) in the prophecy of the destruction of Edom, which was accomplished by the Chaldeans, and they are here repeated, *mutatis mutandis — with a few necessary alterations,* in the prophecy of the destruction of Babylon, which was to be accomplished upon the Chaldeans, to show that though the distributions of Providence may appear unequal for a time its retributions will be equal at last; when thou shalt make *an end to spoil thou shalt be spoiled,* Isa. 33:1; Rev. 13:10.

CHAPTER 51

The prophet, in this chapter, goes on with the prediction of Babylon's fall, to which other prophets also bore witness. He is very copious and lively in describing the foresight God had given him of it, for the encouragement of the pious captives, whose deliverance depended upon it and was to be the result of it. Here is, I. The record of Babylon's doom, with the particulars of it, intermixed with the grounds of God's controversy with her, many aggravations of her fall, and great encouragements given thence to the Israel of God, that suffered such hard things by her (*v.* 1–58). II. The representation and ratification of this by the throwing of a copy of this prophecy into the river Euphrates (*v.* 59–64).

Verses 1–58

The particulars of this copious prophecy are dispersed and interwoven, and the same things left and returned to so often that it could not well be divided into parts, but we must endeavor to collect them under their proper heads. Let us then observe here,

I. An acknowledgment of the great pomp and power that Babylon had been in and the use that God in his providence had made of it (*v.* 7): *Babylon hath been a golden cup,* a rich and glorious empire, *a golden city* (Isa. 14:4), *a head of gold* (Dan. 2:38), filled with all good things, as a cup with wine. Nay, she had been *a golden cup in the Lord's hand;* he had in a particular manner filled and favoured her with blessings; he had made the earth *drunk with this cup;* some were intoxicated with her pleasures and debauched by her, others intoxicated with her terrors and destroyed by her. In both senses the New-Testament Babylon is said to have made the kings of the earth drunk, Rev. 17:2; 18:3. Babylon had also been God's *battle-axe;* it was so at this time, when Jeremiah prophesied, and was likely to be yet more so, *v.* 20. The forces of Babylon were God's *weapons of war,* tools in his hand, with which he broke in pieces, and knocked down, *nations and kingdoms, — horses* and *chariots,* which are so much the strength of kingdoms (*v.* 21), *— man and woman, young and old,* with which kingdoms are replenished (*v.* 22), *— the shepherd and his flock, the husbandman and his oxen,* with which kingdoms are maintained and supplied, *v.* 23. Such havoc as this the Chaldeans had made when God employed them as instruments of his wrath for the chastising of the nations; and yet now Babylon itself must fall. Note, Those that have carried all before them a great while will yet at length meet with their match, and their day also will come to fall; the rod will itself be thrown into the fire at last. Nor can any think it will exempt them from God's judgments that they have been instrumental in executing his judgments on others.

II. A just complaint made of Babylon, and a charge drawn up against her by the Israel of God. 1. She is complained of for her incorrigible wickedness (*v.* 9): *We would have healed Babylon, but she is not healed.* The people of God that were captives among the Babylonians endeavoured, according to the instructions given them (Jer. 10:11), to convince them of the folly of their idolatry, but they could not do it; still they doted as much as ever upon their graven images, and therefore the Israelites resolved to quit them and go to their own country. Yet some understand this as spoken by the forces they had hired for their assistance, declaring that they had done their best to save her from ruin, but that it was all to no purpose, and therefore they might as well go home to their respective countries; "for *her judgment reaches unto heaven,* and it is in vain to withstand it or think to avert it." 2. She is complained of for her inveterate malice against Israel. Other nations had been hardly used by the Chaldeans, but Israel only complains to God of it, and with confidence appeals to him (*v.* 34, 35): *"The king of Babylon has devoured me, and crushed me,* and never thought he could do enough ruin to me; *he has emptied me* of all that was valuable, has *swallowed me up as a dragon,* or whale, swallows up the little fish by shoals; *he has filled his belly,* filled his treasures, *with my delicates,* with all my pleasant things, *and has cast me out,* cast me away as a *vessel in which there is no pleasure;* and now let them be accountable for all this." *Zion and Jerusalem shall say,* "Let *the violence done to me and* my children, that are *my* own *flesh,* and pieces of myself, and all the blood of my people, which they have shed like water, *be upon* them; let the guilt of it lie upon them, and let it be required at their hands." Note, Ruin is not far off from those that lie under the guilt of wrong done to God's people.

III. Judgment given upon this appeal by the righteous Judge of heaven and earth, on behalf of Israel against Babylon. he *sits in the throne judging right,* is ready to receive complaints, and answers (*v.* 36): *"I will plead thy cause.* Leave it with me; I will in due time plead it effectually *and take vengeance for thee,* and every drop of Jerusalem's blood shall be accounted for with interest." Israel and Judah seemed to have been neglected and forgotten, but God had an eye to them, *v.* 5. It is true *their land was filled with sin against the Holy One of Israel.* They were a provoking people and their sings were a great offence to God, as a holy God, and as their God, their Holy One; and therefore he justly delivered them up into the hands of their enemies, and might justly have abandoned them and left them to perish in their hands; but God deals better with them than they deserve, and, notwithstanding their iniquities and his severities, *Israel is not forsaken,* is not cast off, though he be cast out, but is owned and looked after by his God, by the Lord of hosts. God is his God still, and will act for him as the Lord of hosts, a God of power. Note, Though God's people may have broken his laws and fallen under his rebukes, yet it does not therefore follow that they are thrown out of covenant; but God's care of them and love to them will *flourish again,* Ps. 89:30–33. The Chaldeans thought they should never be called to an account for what they had done against God's Israel; but there is *a time* fixed *for vengeance, v.* 6. We cannot expect it should come sooner than the time fixed, but then it will come; he *will render unto Babylon a recompence,* for the avenging of Israel is *the vengeance of the Lord,* who espouses their cause; it is *the vengeance of his temple, v.* 11, as before, *ch.* 50:28. *The Lord God of recompences,* the *God to whom vengeance belongs, will surely requite* (*v.* 56), will pay them home; he will *render unto Babylon all the evil they have done in Zion* (*v.* 24); he will return it *in the sight* of his people. They shall have the satisfaction to see their cause pleaded with jealousy. They shall not only live to see those judgments brought upon Babylon, but they shall plainly see them to be the punishment of the wrong they have done to Zion; any man may see it, and say, *Verily there is a God that judges in the earth;* for just as *Babylon has caused the slain of Israel to fall,* has not only slain those that were found in arms, but all without distinction, even *all the land* (almost all were put to the sword), so *at Babylon shall fall* the slain not only of the city, but of *all the country, v.* 49. Cyrus shall measure to the Chaldeans the same that they measured to the Jews, so that every observer may discern that God is recompensing them for what they did against his people; but Zion's children shall in a particular manner triumph in it (*v.* 10): *The Lord has brought forth our righteousness;* he has appeared in our behalf against those that dealt unjustly with us, and has given us redress; he has also made it to appear that he is reconciled to us and that we are yet in his eyes a *righteous nation.* Let it therefore be spoken of to his praise: *Come and let us declare in Zion the work of the Lord our God,* that others may be invited to join with us in praising him.

IV. A declaration of the greatness and sovereignty of that God who espouses Zion's cause and undertakes to reckon with this proud and potent enemy, *v.* 14. It is *the Lord of hosts* that has said it, that has *sworn it,* has *sworn it by himself* (for he could swear by no greater), that he will fill Babylon with vast and incredible numbers of the enemy's forces, will *fill it with men as with caterpillars,* that shall overpower it will multitudes, and need only to *lift up a shout* against it, for that shall be so terrible as to dispirit all the inhabitants and make them an easy prey to this numerous army. But who, and where, is he that can break so powerful a kingdom as Babylon? The prophet gives an account of him from the description he had formerly given of him, and of his sovereignty and victory over all pretenders (Jer. 10:12–16), which was there intended for the conviction of the Babylonian idolaters and the confirmation of God's Israel in the faith and worship of the God of Israel; and it is here repeated to show that God will convince those by his judgments who would not be convinced by his word that he is *God over all.* Let not any doubt but that he who has determined to destroy Babylon is able to make his words good, for, 1. he is the God that made the world (*v.* 15), and therefore nothing is too hard for him to do; it is in his name that our help stands, and on him our hope is built. 2. He has the command of all the creatures that he has made (*v.* 16); his providence is a continued creation. He has *wind and rain* at his disposal. if he speak the word, there is a *multitude of waters in the heavens* (and it is a wonder how they hang there), fed by *vapours out of the earth,* and it is a wonder how they ascend thence. *Lightnings and rain* seem contraries, as fire and water, and yet they are produced together; and the wind, which seems arbitrary in its motions, and we *know not whence it comes,* is yet, we are sure, brought *out of his treasures.* 3. The idols that oppose the accomplishment of his word are a mere sham and their worshippers brutish people, *v.* 17, 18. The idols are falsehood, they are vanity, they are *the work of errors;* when they come to be visited (to be examined and enquired into) *they perish,* that is, their reputation sinks and they appear to be nothing; and those *that make them are like unto them.* But between the God of Israel and these gods of the heathen there is no comparison (*v.* 19): *The portion of Jacob is not like them;* the God who speaks this and will do it is the *former of all things* and *the Lord of all hosts,* and therefore can do what he will; and there is a near relation between him and his people, for he is *their portion* and they are his; they put a confidence in him as their portion and he is pleased to take a complacency in them and a particular care of them as the *lot of his inheritance;* and therefore he will do what is best for them. The repetition of these things here, which were said before, intimates both the certainty and the importance of them, and obliges us to take special notice of them; *God hath spoken once; yea, twice have we heard this, that power belongs to God,* power to destroy the most formidable enemies of his church; and if God thus *speak once, yea, twice,* we are inexcusable if we do not perceive it and attend to it.

V. A description of the instruments that are to be employed in this service. God has *raised up the spirit of the kings of the Medes* (*v.* 11), Darius and Cyrus, who come against Babylon by a divine instinct; for *God's device is against Babylon to destroy it.* They do it, but God devised it, he designed it; they are but accomplishing his purpose, and acting as he directed. Note, God's counsel shall stand, and according to it all hearts shall move. Those whom God employs against Babylon are compared (*v.* 1) to a *destroying wind,* which either by its coldness blasts the fruits of the earth or by its fierceness blows down all before it. This wind is *brought out of God's treasuries* (*v.* 16), and it is here said to be *raised up against those that dwell in the midst of the Chaldeans,* those of other nations that inhabit among them and are incorporated with them. The Chaldeans rise up against God by falling down before idols, and against them God will raise up destroyers, for he will be too hard for those that contend with him. These enemies are compared to fanners (*v.* 2), who shall *drive them away as chaff* is driven away by the fan. The Chaldeans had been fanners to winnow God's people (*ch.* 15:7) and to empty them, and now they shall themselves be in like manner despoiled and dispersed.

VI. An ample commission given them to destroy and lay all waste. Let them *bend their bow* against the archers of the Chaldeans (*v.* 3) and *not spare her young men,* but *utterly destroy them,* for the Lord has *both devised and done what he spoke against Babylon, v.* 12. This may animate the instruments he employs, but assuring them of success. The methods they take are such as God has devised and therefore they shall surely prosper; what he has spoken shall be done, for he himself will do it; and therefore let all necessary preparations be made. This they are called to, *v.* 27, 28. Let *a standard be set up,* under which to enlist soldiers for this expedition; *let a trumpet be blown* to call men together to it and animate them in it; let the nations, out of which Cyrus's army is to be raised, prepare their recruits; let the kingdoms of *Ararat,* and *Minni, and Ashkenaz,* of Armenia, both the higher and the lower, and of Ascania, about Phrygia and Bithynia, send in their quota of men for his service; let general officers be appointed and the cavalry advance; let the horses come up in *great numbers,* as the *caterpillars,* and come, like them, leaping and pawing in the valley; let them lay the country waste, as *caterpillars* do (Joel 1:4), especially rough caterpillars; let the kings and captains prepare nations against Babylon, for the service is great and there is occasion for many hands to be employed it.

VII. The weakness of the Chaldeans, and their inability to make head against this threatening destroying force. When God employed them against other nations they had spirit and strength to act offensively, and went on with admirable resolution, conquering and to conquer; but now that it comes to their turn to be reckoned with all their might and courage are gone, their hearts fail them, and none of all their men of might and mettle have found their hands to act so much as defensively. They are called upon here to prepare for action, but it is ironically and in an upbraiding way (*v.* 11): *Make bright the arrows,* which have grown rusty through disuse; *gather the shields,* which in a long time of peace and security have been scattered and thrown out of the way (*v.* 12); *set up the standard upon the walls of Babylon,* upon the towers on those walls, to summon all that owed suit and service to that mother-city, now to come in to her assistance; let them make the watch as strong as they can, and appoint the sentinels to their respective posts, and prepare ambushes for the reception of the enemy. This intimates that they would be found very secure and remiss, and would need to be thus quickened (and they were so to such a degree that they were in the midst of their revels when the city was taken), but that all their preparations should come to no purpose. Whoever will may call them to it, but they shall have no heart to come at the call, *v.* 29. *The* whole *land shall tremble, and sorrow* (a universal consternation) shall seize upon them; for they shall see both the irresistible arm and the irreversible counsel and decree of God against them. They shall see that God is making *Babylon a desolation,* and therein is performing what he has purposed; and then *the mighty men of Babylon have forborne to fight, v.* 30. God having taken away their strength and spirit, so that they have *remained in their holds,* not daring so much as to peep forth, the might both of their hearts and of their hands fails; they *become* as timorous *as women,* so that the enemy has, without any resistance, *burnt her dwelling-places* and *broken her bars.* It is to the same purport with *v.* 56–58. When the spoiler comes upon Babylon her mighty men, who should make head against him, are immediately taken, their weapons of war fail them, *every one of their bows is broken* and stands them in no stead. Their politics fail them; they call councils of war, but their princes and captains, who sit in council to concert measures for the common safety, are made drunk; they are as men intoxicated through stupidity or despair; they can form no right notions of things; they stagger and are unsteady in their counsels and resolves, and dash one against another, and, like drunken men, fall out among themselves. At length they *sleep a perpetual sleep,* and never *awake* from their wine, the wine of God's wrath, for it is to them an opiate that lays them into a fatal lethargy. The *walls of their city* fail them, *v.* 58. When the enemy had found ways to ford Euphrates, which was thought impassable, yet surely, think they, the walls are impregnable, they are *the broad walls of Babylon* or (as the margin reads it), *the walls of broad Babylon.* The compass of the city, within the walls, was 385 furlongs, some say 480, that is, about sixty miles; the walls were 200 cubits high, and fifty cubits broad, so that two chariots might easily pass by one another upon them. Some say that there was a threefold wall about the inner city and the like about the outer, and that the stones of the wall, being laid in pitch instead of mortar (Gen. 11:3), were scarcely separable; and yet these shall be *utterly broken,* and *the high gates and towers shall be burnt,* and the people that are employed in the defence of the city shall *labour in vain in the fire;* they shall quite tire themselves, but shall do no good.

VIII. The destruction that shall be made of Babylon by these invaders. 1. It is a certain destruction; the doom has passed and it cannot be reversed; a divine power is engaged against it, which cannot be resisted (*v.* 8): *Babylon is fallen and destroyed,* is as sure to fall, to fall into destruction, as if it were fallen and destroyed already; though when Jeremiah prophesied this, and many a year after, it was in the height of its power and greatness. God declares, God appears against Babylon (*v.* 25): *Behold, I am against thee;* and those cannot stand long whom God is against. He will *stretch out his hand upon it,* a hand which no creature can bear the weight of nor withstand the force of. It is his purpose, which shall be performed, that *Babylon* must be a *desolation, v.* 29. 2. It is a righteous destruction. Babylon has made herself meet for it, and therefore cannot fail to meet with it. For (*v.* 25) *Babylon* has been *a destroying mountain,* very lofty and bulky as a mountain, and *destroying all the earth,* as the stones that are tumbled from high mountains spoil the grounds about them; but now it shall itself be *rolled down from its rocks,* which were as the foundations on which it stood. It shall be levelled, its pomp and power broken. It is now a burning mountain, like Aetna and the other volcanoes, that throw out fire, to the terror of all about them. But it shall be a burnt mountain; it shall at length have consumed itself, and shall remain a heap of ashes. So will this world be at the end of time. Again (*v.* 33), *"Babylon is like a threshing-floor,* in which the people of God have been long threshed, as sheaves in the floor; but now the time has come that she shall herself be threshed and her sheaves in her; her princes and great men, and all her inhabitants, shall be beaten in their own land, as in the threshing-floor. The threshing-floor is prepared. Babylon is by sin made meet to be a seat of war, and her people, like corn in harvest, are ripe for destruction," Rev. 14:15; Mic. 4:12. 3. It is an unavoidable destruction. Babylon seems to be well-fenced and fortified against it: *She dwells upon many waters* (*v.* 13); the situation of her country is such that it seems inaccessible, it is so surrounded, and the march of an enemy into it so embarrassed, by rivers. In allusion to this, the New-Testament Babylon is said to *sit upon many waters,* that is, to rule over many nations, as the other Babylon did, Rev. 17:15. *Babylon is abundant in treasures;* and yet *"thy end has come,* and neither they waters nor thy wealth shall secure thee." This end that comes shall be *the measure of thy covetousness;* it shall be the stint of thy gettings, it shall set bounds to thy ambition and avarice, which otherwise would have ben boundless. God, by the destruction of Babylon, said to its proud waves, *Hitherto shall you come, and no further.* Note, if men will not set a measure to their covetousness by wisdom and grace, God will set a measure to it by his judgments. Babylon, thinking herself very safe and very great, was very proud; but she will be deceived (*v.* 53): *Though Babylon should mount* her walls and palaces *up to heaven,* and though (because what is high is apt to totter) she should take care to *fortify the height of her strength,* yet all will not do; God will send spoilers against her, that shall break through her strength and bring down her height. 4. It is a gradual destruction, which, if they had pleased, they might have foreseen and had warning of; for (*v.* 46) *"A rumor will come one year* that Cyrus is making vast preparations for war, *and after that, in another year, shall come a rumour* that his design is upon Babylon, and he is steering his course that way;" so that when he was a great way off they might have sent and desired conditions of peace; but they were too proud, too secure, to do that, and their hearts were hardened to their destruction. 5. Yet, when it comes, it is a surprising destruction: *Babylon has suddenly fallen* (*v.* 8); the destruction came upon them when they did not think of it and was perfected in a little time, as that of the New-Testament *Babylon — in one hour,* Rev. 18:17. The king of Babylon, who should have been observing the approaches of the enemy, was himself at such a distance from the place where the attack was made that it was a great while ere he had notice that the city was taken; so that those who were posted near the place sent one messenger, one courier, after another, with advice of it, *v.* 31. The foot-posts shall meet at the court from several quarters with this intelligence to the king of Babylon that his *city is taken at one end,* and there is nothing to obstruct the progress of the conquerors, but they will be at the other end quickly. They are to tell him that the enemy has *seized the passes* (*v.* 32), the forts or blockades upon the river, and that, having got over the river, he has set fire to the reeds on the river side, to alarm and terrify the city, so that all the men of war are affrighted and have thrown down their arms and surrendered at discretion. The messengers come, like Job's, one upon the heels of another, with these tidings, which are immediately confirmed with a witness by the enemies' being in the palace and slaying the king himself, Dan. 5:30. That profane feast which they were celebrating at the very time when the city was taken, which was both an evidence of their strange security and a great advantage to the enemy, seems here to be referred to (*v.* 38, 39): *They shall roar together like lions,* as men in their revels do, when the wine has got into their heads. They call it *singing;* but in scripture-language, and in the language of sober men, it is called *yelling like lions' whelps.* It is probable that they were drinking confusion to Cyrus and his army with loud huzzas. Well, says God, in their heat, when they are inflamed (Isa. 5:11) and their heads are hot with hard drinking, I will *make their feasts,* I will *give them their portion.* They have passed their cup round; now *the cup of the Lord's right hand shall be turned unto them* (Hab. 2:15, 16), a cup of fury, which shall *make them drunk that they may rejoice* (or rather *that they may revel it)* and *sleep a perpetual sleep;* let them be as merry as they can with that bitter cup, but it shall lay them to sleep never to wake more (as *v.* 57); for *on that night,* in the midst of the jollity, was *Belshazzar slain.* 6. It is to be a universal destruction. God will make thorough work of it; for, as he will perform what he has purposed, so he will perfect what he has begun. *The slain shall fall* in great abundance throughout *the land of the Chaldeans;* multitudes shall be *thrust through in her streets, v.* 4. They are *brought down like lambs to the slaughter* (*v.* 40), in such great numbers, so easily, and the enemies make no more of killing them than the butcher does of killing lambs. The strength of the enemy, and their invading them, are here compared to an irruption and inundation of waters (*v.* 42): *The sea has come up upon Babylon,* which, when it has once broken through its bounds, there is no fence against, so that she is *covered with the multitude of its waves,* overpowered by a numerous army; *her cities* then become *a desolation,* an uninhabited uncultivated desert, *v.* 43. 7. It is a destruction that shall reach the gods of Babylon, the idols and images, and fall with a particular weight upon them. "In token that *the whole land shall be confounded* and all *her slain shall fall* and that throughout all the country *the wounded shall groan, I will do judgment upon her graven images," v.* 47 and again *v.* 52. All must needs perish if their gods perish, from whom they expect protection. Though the invaders are themselves idolaters, yet they shall destroy the images and temples of the gods of Babylon, as an earnest of the abolishing of all counterfeit deities. Bel was the principal idol that the Babylonians worshipped, and therefore that is by name here marked for destruction (*v.* 44): *I will punish Bel,* that great devourer, that image to which such abundance of sacrifices are offered and such rich spoils dedicated, and to whose temple there is such a vast resort. He shall disgorge what he has so greedily regaled himself with. God will bring forth out of his temple all the wealth laid up there, Job 20:15. His altars shall be forsaken, none shall regard him any more, and so that idol which was thought to be a wall to Babylon shall fall and fail them. 8. It shall be a final destruction. You may *take balm for her pain,* but in vain; she that *would not be healed* by the word of God *shall not be healed* by his providence, *v.* 8, 9. *Babylon* shall *become heaps* (*v.* 37), and, to complete its infamy, no use shall be made even of the ruins of Babylon, so execrable shall they be, and attended with such ill omens (*v.* 26): *They shall not take of thee a stone for a corner, nor a stone for foundations.* People shall not care for having any thing to do with Babylon, or whatever belonged to it. Or it denotes that there shall be nothing left in Babylon on which to ground any hopes or attempts of raising it into a kingdom again; for, as it follows here, *it shall be desolate for ever.* St. Jerome says that in his time, though the ruins of Babylon's walls were to be seen, yet the ground enclosed by them was a forest of wild beasts.

IX. Here is a call to God's people to go out of Babylon. It is their wisdom, when the ruin is approaching, to quit the city and retire into the country (*v.* 6): *"Flee out of the midst of Babylon,* and get into some remote corner, that you may save your lives, and may not be cut off in her iniquity." When God's judgments are abroad it is good to get as far as we can from those against whom they are levelled, as Israel from the tents of Korah. This agrees with the advice Christ gave his disciples, with reference to the destruction of Jerusalem. *Let those who shall be in Judea flee to the mountains,* Mt. 24:16. It is their wisdom to *get out of the midst of Babylon,* lest they be involved, if not in her ruins, yet in her fears (*v.* 45, 46): *Lest your heart faint, and you fear for the rumour that shall be heard in the land.* Though God had told them that Cyrus should be their deliverer, and Babylon's destruction their deliverance, yet they had been told also that *in the peace thereof they should have peace,* and therefore the alarms given to Babylon would put them into a fright, and perhaps they might not have faith and consideration enough to suppress those fears, for which reason they are here advised to get out of the hearing of the alarms. Note, Those who have not grace enough to keep their temper in temptation should have wisdom enough to keep out of the way of temptation. But this is not all; it is not only their wisdom to quit the city when the ruin is approaching, but it is their duty to quit the country too when the ruin is accomplished, and they are set at liberty by the pulling down of the prison over their heads. This they are told, *v.* 50, 51: *"You* Israelites, *who have escaped the sword of the Chaldeans* your oppressors, and of the Persians their destroyers, now that the year of release has come, *go away, stand not still;* hasten to your own country again, however you may be comfortably seated in Babylon, for this is not your rest, but Canaan is." 1. He puts them in mind of the inducements they had to return: *"Remember the Lord afar off,* his presence with you now, though you are here afar off from your native soil; his presence with your fathers formerly in the temple, though you are now afar off from the ruins of it." Note, Wherever we are, in the greatest depths, at the greatest distances, we may and must remember the Lord our God; and in the time of the greatest fears and hopes it is seasonable to *remember the Lord.* "And let Jerusalem come into your mind. Though it be now in ruins, yet *favour its dust* (Ps. 102:14); though few of you ever saw it, yet believe the report you have had concerning it from those that *wept when they remembered Zion;* and think of Jerusalem until you come up to a resolution to make the best of your way thither." Note, When the city of our solemnities is out of sight, yet it must not be out of mind; and it will be of great use to us, in our journey through this world, to let the heavenly Jerusalem come often into our mind. 2. He takes notice of the discouragement which the returning captives labour under (*v.* 51); being reminded of Jerusalem, they cry out, *"We are confounded;* we cannot bear the thought of it; *shame covers our faces* at the mention of it, for *we have heard of the reproach of the sanctuary,* that is profaned and ruined by strangers; how can we think of it with any pleasure?" To this he answers (*v.* 52) that the God of Israel will now triumph over the gods of Babylon, and so that reproach will be for ever rolled away. Note, The believing prospect of Jerusalem's recovery will keep us from being ashamed of Jerusalem's ruins.

X. Here is the diversified feeling excited by Babylon's fall, and it is the same that we have with respect to the *New-Testament Babylon,* Rev. 18:9, 19. 1. Some shall lament the destruction of Babylon. There is *the sound of a cry,* a great outcry coming from Babylon (*v.* 54), lamenting this great destruction, the voice of mourning, because the Lord has *destroyed the voice* of the multitude, that great voice of mirth which used to be heard in Babylon, *v.* 55. We are told what they shall say in their lamentations (*v.* 41): *"How is Sheshach taken,* and how are we mistaken concerning her! How is that city surprised and become an *astonishment among the nations* that was the praise, and glory, and admiration of the whole earth!" See how that may fall into a general contempt which has been universally cried up. 2. Yet some shall rejoice in Babylon's fall, not as it is the misery of their fellow-creatures, but as it is the manifestation of the righteous judgment of God and as it opens the way for the release of God's captives; upon these accounts *the heaven and the earth, and all that is in both, shall sing for Babylon* (*v.* 48); the church in heaven and the church on earth shall give to God the glory of his righteousness, and take notice of it with thankfulness to his praise. Babylon's ruin is Zion's praise.

Verses 59–64

We have been long attending the judgment of Babylon in this and the foregoing chapter; now here we have the conclusion of that whole matter. 1. A copy is taken of this prophecy, it should seem by Jeremiah himself, for Baruch his scribe is not mentioned here (*v.* 60): *Jeremiah wrote in a book all these words that are here written against Babylon.* He received this notice that he might give it to all whom it might concern. It is of great advantage both to the propagating and to the perpetuating of the word of God to have it written, and to have copies taken of the law, prophets, and epistles. 2. It is sent to Babylon, to the captives there, by the hand of Seraiah, who went there attendant on or ambassador for king Zedekiah, *in the fourth year of his reign, v.* 59. He *went with Zedekiah,* or (as the margin reads it) *on the behalf of Zedekiah, into Babylon.* The character given of him is observable, that this *Seraiah was a quiet prince,* a prince of rest. He was in honour and power, but not, as most f the princes then were, hot and heady, making parties, and heading factions, and driving things furiously. He was of a calm temper, studied the things that made for peace, endeavoured to preserve a good understanding between the king his master and the king of Babylon, and to keep his master from rebelling. He was no persecutor of God's prophets, but a moderate man. Zedekiah was happy in the choice of such a man to be his envoy to the king of Babylon, and Jeremiah might safely entrust such a man with his errand too. Note, it is the real honour of great men to be quiet men, and it is the wisdom of princes to put such into places of trust. 3. Seraiah is desired to read it to his countrymen that had already gone into captivity: *"When thou shalt come to Babylon, and shalt see* what a magnificent place it is, how large a city, how strong, how rich, and how well fortified, and shalt therefore be tempted to think, Surely, it will stand forever" (as the disciples, when they observed the buildings of the temple, concluded that nothing would *throw them down* but the end of the world, Mt. 24:3), *"then thou shalt read all these words* to thyself and thy particular friends, for their encouragement in their captivity: let them with an eye of faith see to the end of these threatening powers, and comfort themselves and one another herewith." 4. He is directed to make a solemn protestation of the divine authority and unquestionable certainty of that which he had read (*v.* 62): *Then thou shalt* look up to God, and say, *O Lord! it is thou that hast spoken against this place, to cut it off.* This is like the angel's protestation concerning the destruction of the New-Testament Babylon. *These are the true sayings of God,* Rev. 19:9. *These words are true and faithful,* Rev. 21:5. Though Seraiah sees Babylon flourishing, having read this prophecy he must foresee Babylon falling, and by virtue of it must curse its habitation, though it be *taking root* (Job *v.* 3): *"O Lord! thou hast spoken against this place,* and I believe what thou hast spoken, that, as thou knowest every thing, so thou canst do every thing. Thou hast passed sentence upon Babylon, and it shall be executed. *Thou hast spoken against this place, to cut it off,* and therefore we will neither envy its pomp nor fear its power." When we see what this world is, how glittering its shows are and how flattering its proposals, let us read in the book of the Lord that its *fashion passes away,* and it shall shortly be *cut off* and be *desolate for ever,* and we shall learn to look upon it with a holy contempt. Observe here, When we have been reading the word of God it becomes us to direct to him whose word it is a humble believing acknowledgment of the truth, equity, and goodness, of what we have read. 5. He must then tie a stone to the book and throw it into the midst of the river Euphrates, as a confirming sign of the things contained in it, saying, *"Thus shall Babylon sink, and not rise;* for they *shall be weary,* they shall perfectly succumb, as men tired with a burden, under the load of *the evil that I will bring upon them,* which they shall never shake off, nor get from under," *v.* 53, 64. In the sign it was the stone that sunk the book, which otherwise would have swum. But in *the thing signified* it was rather the book that sunk the stone; it was the divine sentence passed upon Babylon in this prophecy that sunk that city, which seemed *as firm as a stone.* The fall of the New-Testament Babylon was represented by something like this, but much more magnificent, Rev. 18:21. *A mighty angel cast a great millstone into the sea, saying, Thus shall Babylon fall.* Those that sink under the weight of God's wrath and curse sink irrecoverably. The last words of the chapter seal up the vision and prophecy of this book: *Thus far are the words of Jeremiah.* Not that this prophecy against Babylon was the last of his prophecies; for it was dated in the *fourth* year of Zedekiah (*v.* 59), long before he finished his testimony; but this is recorded last of his prophecies because it was to be last accomplished of all his prophecies against the Gentiles, *ch.* 46:1. And the chapter which remains is purely historical, and, as some think, was added by some other hand.

CHAPTER 52

History is the best expositor of prophecy; and therefore, for the better understanding of the prophecies of this book which relate to the destruction of Jerusalem and the kingdom of Judah, we are here furnished with an account of that sad event. It is much he same with the history we had 2 Ki. 24 and 25, and many of the particulars we had before in that book, but the matter is here repeated and put together, to give light to the book of the Lamentations, which follows next, and to serve as a key to it. That article in the close concerning the advancement of Jehoiachin in his captivity, which happened after Jeremiah's time, gives colour to the conjecture of those who suppose that this chapter was not written by Jeremiah himself, but by some man divinely inspired among those in captivity, for a constant memorandum to those who in Babylon preferred Jerusalem above their chief joy. In this chapter we have, I. The bad reign of Zedekiah, very bad in regard both of sin and of punishment (*v.* 1–3). II. The besieging and taking of Jerusalem by the Chaldeans (*v.* 4–7). III. The severe usage which Zedekiah and the princes met with (*v.* 8–11). IV. The destruction of the temple and the city (*v.* 12–14). V. The captivity of the people (*v.* 15, 16) and the numbers of those that were carried away into captivity (*v.* 28–30). VI. The carrying off of the plunder of the temple (*v.* 17–23). VII. The slaughter of the priests, and some other great men, in cold blood (*v.* 24–27). VIII. The better days which king Jehoiachin lived to see in the latter end of his time, after the death of Nebuchadnezzar (*v.* 31–34).

Verses 1–11

This narrative begins no higher than the beginning of the reign of Zedekiah, though there were two captivities before, one in the fourth year of Jehoiakim, the other in the first of Jeconiah; but probably it was drawn up by some of those that were carried away with Zedekiah, as a reproach to themselves for imagining that they should not go into captivity after their brethren, with which hopes they had long flattered themselves. We have here, 1. God's just displeasure against Judah and Jerusalem for their sin, *v.* 3. His anger was against them to such a degree that he determined to *cast them out from his presence,* his favourable gracious presence, as a father, when he is extremely angry with an undutiful son, bids him get out of his presence, he expelled them from that good land that had such tokens of his presence in providential bounty and that holy city and temple that had such tokens of his presence in covenant-grace and love. Note, Those that are banished from God's ordinances have reason to complain that they are in some degree *cast out of his presence;* yet none are cast out from God's gracious presence but those that by sin have first thrown themselves out of it. This fruit of sin we should therefore deprecate above any thing, as David (Ps. 51:11), *Cast me not away from thy presence.* 2. Zedekiah's bad conduct and management, to which God left him, in displeasure against the people, and for which God punished him, in displeasure against him. Zedekiah had arrived at years of discretion when he came to the throne; he *was twenty-one years old* (*v.* 1); he was none of the worst of the kings (we never read of his idolatries), yet his character is that he *did evil in the eyes of the Lord,* for he did not do the good he should have done. But that evil deed of his which did in a special manner hasten this destruction was his *rebelling against the king of Babylon,* which was both his sin and his folly, and brought ruin upon his people, not only meritoriously, but efficiently. God was greatly displeased with him for his perfidious dealing with the king of Babylon (as we find, Eze. 17:15, etc.); and, because he was angry at Judah and Jerusalem, he put him into the hand of his own counsels, to do that foolish thing which proved fatal to him and his kingdom. 3. The possession which the Chaldeans at length gained of Jerusalem, after eighteen months' siege. They sat down before it, and blocked it up, in the ninth year of Zedekiah's reign, in the tenth month (*v.* 4), and made themselves masters of it in the *eleventh year in the fourth month, v.* 6. In remembrance of these two steps towards their ruin, while they were in captivity, they kept *a fast in the fourth month, and a fast in the tenth* (Zec. 8:19): that in the *fifth month* was in remembrance of the burning of the temple, and that in the *seventh* of the murder of Gedaliah. We may easily imagine, or rather cannot imagine, what a sad time it was with Jerusalem, during this year and half that it was besieged, when all provisions were cut off from coming to them and they were ever and anon alarmed by the attacks of the enemy, and, being obstinately resolved to hold out to the last extremity, nothing remained but a *certain fearful looking for of judgment.* That which disabled them to hold out, and yet could not prevail with them to capitulate, was the *famine in the city* (*v.* 6); there was *no bread for the people of the land,* so that the soldiers could not make good their posts, but were rendered wholly unserviceable; and then no wonder that *the city was broken up, v.* 7. Walls, in such a case, will not hold out long without men, any more than men without walls; nor will both together stand people in any stead without God and his protection. 4. The inglorious retreat of the king and his mighty men. They got out of the city *by night* (*v.* 7) and made the best of their way, I know not whither, nor perhaps they themselves; but the king was overtaken by the pursuers *in the plains of Jericho,* his guards were dispersed, and all his army was *scattered from him, v.* 8. His fright was not causeless, for there is no escaping the judgments of God; they will *come upon the sinner,* and will *overtake him,* let him flee where he will (Deu. 28:15), and these judgments particularly that are here executed were there threatened, *v.* 52, 53, etc. 5. The sad doom passed upon Zedekiah by the king of Babylon, and immediately put in execution. he treated him as a rebel, *gave judgment upon him, v.* 9. One cannot think of it without the utmost vexation and regret that a king, a king of Judah, a king of the house of David, should be arraigned as a criminal at the bar of this heathen king. But he *humbled not himself before Jeremiah* the prophet; therefore God thus humbled him. Pursuant to the sentence passed upon him by the haughty conqueror, *his sons were slain before his eyes,* and all *the princes of Judah* (*v.* 10); then *his eyes were put out,* and he was *bound in chains,* carried in triumph to Babylon; perhaps they made sport with him, as they did with Samson when his eyes were put out; however, he was condemned to perpetual imprisonment, wearing out the remainder of his life (I cannot say his days, for he saw day no more) in darkness and misery. He was kept in prison till *the day of his death,* but had some honour done him at his funeral, *ch.* 34:5. Jeremiah had often told him what it would come to, but he would not take warning when he might have prevented it.

Verses 12–23

We have here an account of the woeful havoc that was made by the Chaldean army, a month after the city was taken, under the command of Nebuzaradan, who was *captain of the guard,* or general of the army, in this action. In the margin he is called the *chief of the slaughter-men,* or *executioners;* for soldiers are but slaughter-men, and God employs them as executioners of his sentence against a sinful people. Nebuzaradan was chief of those soldiers, but, in the execution he did, we have reason to fear he had no eye to God, but he served the king of Babylon and his own designs, now that he came into Jerusalem, into the very bowels of it, as captain of the slaughter-men there. And, 1. He laid the temple in ashes, having first plundered it of every thing that was valuable: He *burnt the house of the Lord,* that holy and beautiful house, where their *fathers praised him,* Isa. 64:11. 2. He burnt the royal palace, probably that which Solomon built after he had built the temple, which was, ever since, *the king's house.* 3. He burnt *all the houses of Jerusalem,* that is, all the houses of the great men, or those particularly; if any escaped, it was only some sorry cottages for the poor of the land. 4. He *broke down all the walls of Jerusalem,* to be revenged upon them for standing in the way of his army so long. Thus, of a defenced city, it was made a ruin, Isa. 25:2. 5. He *carried away many into captivity* (*v.* 15); he took away *certain of the poor of the people,* that is, of the people in the city, for *the poor of the land* (the poor of the country) he left for *vine-dressers and husbandmen.* He also carried off *the residue of the people that remained in the city,* that had escaped the sword and famine, and the deserters, such as he thought fit, or rather such as God thought fit; for he had already determined some for the *pestilence,* some for the *sword,* some for *famine,* and some for *captivity, ch.* 15:2. But, 6. Nothing is more particularly and largely related here than the carrying away of the appurtenances of the temple. All that were of great value were carried away before, *the vessels of silver and gold,* yet some of that sort remained, which were now carried away, *v.* 19. But most of the temple-prey that was now seized was of brass, which, being of less value, was carried off last. When the gold was gone, the brass soon went after it, because the people repented not, according to Jeremiah's prediction, *ch.* 27:19, etc. When the walls of the city were demolished, the pillars of the temple were pulled down too, and both in token that God, who was the strength and stay both of their civil and their ecclesiastical government, had departed from them. No walls can protect those, nor pillars sustain those, from whom God withdraws. These pillars of the temple were not for support (for there was nothing built upon them), but for ornament and significancy. They were called *Jachin — He will establish;* and *Boaz — In him is strength;* so that the breaking of these signified that God would no longer establish his house nor be the strength of it. These pillars are here very particularly described (*v.* 21–23, from 1 Ki. 7:15), that the extraordinary beauty and stateliness of them may affect us the more with the demolishing of them. All the vessels that belonged to the brazen altar were carried away; for the iniquity of Jerusalem, like that of Eli's house, was not to be purged by sacrifice or offering, 1 Sa. 3:14. It is said (*v.* 20), *The brass of all these vessels was without weight;* so it was in the making of them (1 Ki. 7:47), *the weight of the brass was not* then *found out* (2 Chr. 4:18), and so it was in the destroying of them. Those that made great spoil of them did not stand to weigh them, as purchasers do, for, whatever they weighted, it was all their own.

Verses 24–30

We have here a very melancholy account, 1. Of the slaughter of some great men, in cold blood, at Riblah, seventy-two in number (according to the number of the elders of Israel, Num. 11:24, 25), so they are computed, 2 Ki. 25:18, 19. We read there of five out of the temple, two out of the city, five out of the court, and sixty out of the country. The account here agrees with that, except in one article; there it is said that there were five, here there were seven, of those that were *near the king,* which Dr. Lightfoot reconciles thus, that he took away seven of those that were near the king, but two of them were Jeremiah himself and Ebed-melech, who were both discharged, as we have read before, so that there were only five of them put to death, and so the number was reduced to seventy-two, some of all ranks, for they had all corrupted their way; and it is probable that such were made examples of as had been most forward to excite and promote the rebellion against the king of Babylon. *Seraiah the chief priest* is put first, whose sacred character could not exempt him from this stroke; how should it, when he himself had profaned it by sin? Seraiah the prince was *a quiet prince* (*ch.* 51:59), but perhaps Seraiah the priest was not so, but unquiet and turbulent, by which he had made himself obnoxious to the king of Babylon. The leaders of this people had caused them to err, and now they are in a particular manner made monuments of divine justice. 2. Of the captivity of the rest. Come and see how *Judah was carried away captive out of his own land* (*v.* 27), and how it spued them out as it spued out the Canaanites that went before them, which God had told them it would certainly do if they trod in their steps and copied out their abominations, Lev. 18:28. Now here is an account, (1.) Of two captivities which we had an account of before, one in the seventh year of Nebuchadnezzar (the same with that which is said to be in his eighth year, 2 Ki. 24:12), another in his eighteenth year, the same with that which is said (*v.* 12) to be in his nineteenth year. But the sums here are very small, in comparison with what we find expressed concerning the former (2 Ki. 24:14, 16), when there were 18,000 carried captive, whereas here they are said to be 3023; they are also small in comparison with what we may reasonably suppose concerning the latter; for, when all the residue of the people were carried away (*v.* 15), one would think there should be more than 832 souls; therefore Dr. Lightfoot conjectures that, these accounts being joined to the story of the putting to death of the great men at Riblah, all that are here said to be carried away were *put to death* as rebels. (2.) Of a third captivity, not mentioned before, which was in the twenty-third year of Nebuchadnezzar, four years after the destruction of Jerusalem (*v.* 30): Then *Nebuzaradan* came, and *carried away* 745 Jews; it is probable that this was done in revenge of the murder of Gedaliah, which was another rebellion against the king of Babylon, and that those who were now taken were aiders and abetters of Ishmael in that murder, and were not only carried away, but put to death for it; yet this is uncertain. If this be the sum total of the captives (*all the persons were* 4600, *v.* 30), we may see how strangely they were reduced from what they had been, and may wonder as much how they came to be so numerous again as afterwards we find them; for it should seem that, as at first in Egypt, so again in Babylon, the Lord made them fruitful in the land of their affliction, and the more they were oppressed the more they multiplied. And the truth is, this people were often miracles both of judgment and mercy.

Verses 31–34

This passage of story concerning the reviving which king Jehoiachin had in his bondage we had likewise before (2 Ki. 25:27–30), only there it is said to be done on *the twenty-seventh day of the twelfth month,* here *on the twenty-fifth;* but in a thing of this nature two days make a very slight difference in the account. It is probable that the orders were given for his release on the twenty-fifth day, but that he was not presented to the king till the twenty-seventh. We may observe in this story, 1. That new lords make new laws. Nebuchadnezzar had long kept this unhappy prince in prison; and his son, though well-affected to the prisoner, could not procure him any favour, not one smile, from his father, any more than Jonathan could for David from his father; but, when the old peevish man was dead, his son countenanced Jehoiachin and made him a favourite. It is common for children to undo what their fathers have done; it were well if it were always as much for the better as this was. 2. That the world we live in is a changing world. Jehoiachin, in his beginning, fell from a throne into a prison, but here he is advanced again to a throne of state (*v.* 32), though not to a throne of power. As, before, the robes were changed into prison-garments, so now they were converted into robes again. Such chequer-work is this world; prosperity and adversity are set the one over-against the other, that we may learn to *rejoice as though we rejoiced not and weep as though we wept not.* 3. That, though the night of affliction be very long, yet we must not despair but that the day may dawn at last. Jehoiachin was thirty-seven years a prisoner, in confinement, in contempt, ever since he was eighteen years old, in which time we may suppose him so inured to captivity that he had forgotten the sweets of liberty; or, rather, that after so long an imprisonment it would be doubly welcome to him. Let those whose afflictions have been lengthened out encourage themselves with this instance; the vision will at the end speak comfortably, and therefore wait for it. *Dum spiro spero — While there is life there is hope. Non si male nunc, et olim sic erit — Though now we suffer, we shall not always suffer.* 4. That god can make his people to find favour in the eyes of those that are their oppressors, and unaccountably turn their hearts to pity them, according to that word (Ps. 106:46), *He made them to be pitied of all those that carried them captives.* He can bring those that have spoken roughly to speak kindly, and those to feed his people that have fed upon them. Those therefore that are under oppression will find that it is not in vain to hope and quietly to *wait for the salvation of the Lord. Therefore* our times are in God's hand, because the hearts of all we deal with are so. 5. And now, upon the whole matter, comparing the prophecy and the history of this book together, we may learn, in general, (1.) That it is no new thing for churches and persons highly dignified to degenerate, and become very corrupt. (2.) That iniquity tends to the ruin of those that harbour it; and, if it be not repented of and forsaken, will certainly end in their ruin: (3.) That external professions and privileges will not only not amount to an excuse for sin and an exemption from ruin, but will be a very great aggravation of both. (4.) That no word of God shall fall to the ground, but the event will fully answer the prediction; and the unbelief of man shall not make God's threatenings, any more than his promises, of no effect. The justice and truth of God are here written in bloody characters, for the conviction or the confusion of all those that make a jest of his threatenings. Let them *not be deceived, God is not mocked.*

AN EXPOSITION, WITH PRACTICAL OBSERVATIONS, OF

THE LAMENTATIONS OF JEREMIAH

Since what Solomon says, though contrary to the common opinion of the world, is certainly true, that *sorrow is better than laughter,* and *it is better to go to the house of mourning than to the house of feasting,* we should come to the reading and consideration of the melancholy chapters of this book, not only willingly, but with an expectation to edify ourselves by them; and, that we may do this, we must compose ourselves to a holy sadness and resolve to weep with the weeping prophet. Let us consider, I. The title of this book; in the Hebrew it has one, but is called (as the books of Moses are) from the first word *Ecah — How;* but the Jewish commentators call it, as the Greeks do, and we from them, *Kinoth — Lamentations.* As we have sacred odes or songs of joy, so have we sacred elegies or songs of lamentation; such variety of methods has Infinite Wisdom taken to work upon us and move our affections, and so soften our hearts and make them susceptible of the impressions of divine truths, as the wax of the seal. We have not only *piped unto you,* but have *mourned* likewise, Mt. 11:17. II. The penman of this book; it was Jeremiah the prophet, who is here Jeremiah the poet, and *vates* signifies both; therefore this book is fitly adjoined to the book of his prophecy, and is as an appendix to it. We had there at large the predictions of the desolations of Judah and Jerusalem, and then the history of them, to show how punctually the predictions were accomplished, for the confirming of our faith: now here we have the expressions of his sorrow upon occasion of them, to show that he was very sincere in the protestations he had often made that he did not desire the woeful day, but that, on the contrary, the prospect of it filled him with bitterness. When he saw these calamities at a distance, he wished that his *head were waters and his eyes fountains of tears;* and, when they came, he made it to appear that he did not dissemble in that wish, and that he was far from being disaffected to his country, which was the crime his enemies charged him with. Though his country had been very unkind to him, and though the ruin of it was both a proof that he was a true prophet and a punishment of them for prosecuting him as a false prophet, which might have tempted him to rejoice in it, yet he sadly lamented it, and herein showed a better temper than that which Jonah was of with respect to Nineveh. III. The occasion of these Lamentations was the destruction of Judah and Jerusalem by the Chaldean army and the dissolution of the Jewish state both civil and ecclesiastical thereby. Some of the rabbies will have these to be the Lamentations which Jeremiah penned upon occasion of the death of Josiah, which are mentioned 2 Chr. 35:25. But, though it is true that that opened the door to all the following calamities, yet these Lamentations seem to be penned in the sight, not in the foresight, of those calamities — when they had already come, not when they were at a distance; and these is nothing of Josiah in them, and his praise, as was no question, in the lamentations for him. No, it is Jerusalem's funeral that this is an elegy upon. Others of them will have these Lamentations to be contained in the roll which Baruch wrote from Jeremiah's mouth, and which Jehoiakim burnt, and they suggest that at first there were in it only the 1st, 2nd, and 4th chatpers, but that the 3rd and 5th were the *many like words* that were afterwards added; but this is a groundless fancy; that roll is expressly said to be a repetition and summary of the prophet's sermons, Jer. 36:2. IV. The composition of it; it is not only poetical, but alphabetical, all except the 5th chatper, as some of David's psalms are; each verse begins with a several letter in the order of the Hebrew alphabet, the first *aleph,* the second *beth,* etc., but the 3rd chapter is a triple alphabet, the first three beginning with *aleph,* the next three with *beth,* etc., which was a help to memory (it being designed that these mournful ditties should be got by heart) and was an elegance in writing then valued and therefore not now to be despised. They observe that in the 2nd, 3rd, and 4th chapters, the letter *pe* is put before *ain,* which in all the Hebrew alphabets follows it, for a reason of which Dr. Lightfoot offers this conjecture, That the letter *ajin,* which is the numeral letter for Septuagint, was thus, by being displaced, made remarkable, to put them in mind of the seventy years at the end of which God would turn again their captivity. V. The use of it: of great use, no doubt, it was to the pious Jews in their sufferings, furnishing them with spiritual language to express their natural grief by, helping to preserve the lively remembrance of Zion among them, and their children that never saw it, when they were in Babylon, directing their tears into the right channel (for they are here taught to mourn for sin and mourn to God), and withal encouraging their hopes that God would yet return and have mercy upon them; and it is of use to us, to affect us with godly sorrow for the calamities of the church of God, as becomes those that are living members of it and are resolved to take our lot with it.

CHAPTER 1

We have here the first alphabet of this lamentation, twenty-two stanzas, in which the miseries of Jerusalem are bitterly bewailed and her present deplorable condition is aggravated by comparing it with her former prosperous state; all along, sin is acknowledged and complained of as the procuring cause of all these miseries; and God is appealed to for justice against their enemies and applied to for compassion towards them. The chapter is all of a piece, and the several remonstrances are interwoven; but here is, I. A complaint made to God of their calamities, and his compassionate consideration desired (*v.* 1–11). II. The same complaint made to their friends, and their compassionate consideration desired (*v.* 12–17). III. An appeal to God and his righteousness concerning it (*v.* 18–22), in which he is justified in their affliction and is humbly solicited to justify himself in their deliverance.

Verses 1–11

Those that have any disposition to *weep with those that weep,* one would think, should scarcely be able to refrain from tears at the reading of these verses, so very pathetic are the lamentations here.

I. The miseries of Jerusalem are here complained of as very pressing and by many circumstances very much aggravated. Let us take a view of these miseries.

1. As to their civil state. (1.) A city that was populous is now depopulated, *v.* 1. It is spoken of by way of wonder — Who would have thought that ever it should come to this! Or by way of enquiry — What is it that has brought it to this? Or by way of lamentation — Alas! alas! (as Rev. 18:10, 16, 19) *how doth the city sit solitary that was full of people!* She was full of her own people that replenished her, and full of the people of other nations that resorted to her, with whom she had both profitable commerce and pleasant converse; but now her own people are carried into captivity, and strangers make no court to her: she *sits solitary.* The *chief places of the city* are not now, as they used to be, *place of concourse,* where *wisdom cried* (Prov. 1:20, 21); and justly are they left unfrequented, because wisdom's cry there was not heard. Note, Those that are ever so much increased God can soon diminish. *How has she become as a widow!* Her king that was, or should have been, as a husband to her, is cut off, and gone; her God has departed from her, and has given her a bill of divorce; she is emptied of her children, is solitary and sorrowful as a widow. Let no family, no state, not Jerusalem, no, nor Babylon herself, be secure, and say, *I sit as a queen,* and shall never *sit as a widow,* Isa. 47:8; Rev. 18:7. (2.) A city that had dominion is now in subjection. She had been *great among the nations,* greatly loved by some and greatly feared by others, and greatly observed and obeyed by both; some made her presents, and others padi her taxes; so that she was really *princess among the provinces,* and every sheaf bowed to hers; even the princes of the people entreated her favour. But now the tables are turned; she has not only lost her friends and *sits solitary,* but has lost her freedom too and sits *tributary;* she paid tribute to Egypt first and then to Babylon. Note, Sin brings a people not only into solitude, but into slavery. (3.) A city that used to be full of mirth has now become melancholy and upon all accounts full of grief. Jerusalem had been a joyous city, whither the tribes went up on purpose to rejoice before the Lord; she was *the joy of the whole earth,* but now *she weeps sorely,* her laughter if turned into mourning, her solemn feasts are all gone; she weeps *in the night,* as true mourners do who weep in secret, in silence and solitude; *in the night,* when others compose themselves to rest, her thoughts are most intent upon her troubles, and grief then plays the tyrant. What the prophet's head was for her, when she regarded it not, now her head is — *as waters, and* her *eyes fountains of tears,* so that she *weeps day and night* (Jer. 9:1); *her tears are* continually *on her cheeks.* Though nothing dries away sooner than a tear, yet fresh griefs extort fresh tears, so that her cheeks are never free from them. Note, There is nothing more commonly seen *under the sun* than *the tears of the oppressed,* with whom *the clouds return after the rain,* Eccl. 4:1. (4.) Those that were separated from the heathen now *dwell among the heathen;* those that were a peculiar people are now a mingled people (*v.* 3): *Judah has gone into captivity,* out of her own land into the land of her enemies, and there she abides, and is likely to abide, among those that are aliens to God and the covenants of promise, with whom *she finds no rest,* no satisfaction of mind, nor any settlement of abode, but is continually hurried from place to place at the will of the victorious imperious tyrants. And again (*v.* 5): *"Her children have gone into captivity before the enemy;* those that were to have been the seed of the next generation are carried off; so that the land that is now desolate is likely to be still desolate and lost for want of heirs." Those that dwell among their own people, and that a free people, and

in their own land, would be more thankful for the mercies they thereby enjoy if they would but consider the miseries of those that are forced into strange countries. (5.) Those that used in their wars to conquer are now conquered and triumphed over: *All her persecutors overlook her between the straits* (*v.* 3); they gained all possible advantages against her, sot hat her people unavoidably *fell into the hand of the enemy,* for there was no way to escape (*v.* 7); they were hemmed in on every side, and, which way soever they attempted to flee, they found themselves embarrassed. When they made the best of their way they could make nothing of it, but were overtaken and overcome; so that every where *her adversaries are the chief and her enemies prosper* (*v.* 5); which way soever their sword turns they get the better. Such straits do men bring themselves into by sin. If we allow that which is our greatest adversary and enemy to have dominion over us, and to be chief in us, justly will our other enemies be suffered to have dominion over us. (6.) Those that had been not only a distinguished by a dignified people, on whom God had put honour, and to whom all their neighbours had paid respect, are now brought into contempt (*v.* 8): *All that honoured her* before *despise her;* those that courted an alliance with her now value it not; those that caressed her when she was in pomp and prosperity slight her now that she is in distress, *because they have seen her nakedness.* By the prevalency of the enemies against her they perceive her weakness, and that she is not so strong a people as they thought she had been; and by the prevalency of God's judgments against her they perceive her wickedness, which now comes to light and is every where talked of. Now it appears how they have vilified themselves by their sins: *The enemies magnify themselves* against them (*v.* 9); they trample upon them, and insult over them, and in their eyes they have *become vile,* the tail of the nations, though once they were the head. Note, *Sin is the reproach of any people.* (7.) Those that lived in a fruitful land were ready to perish, and many of them did perish, for want of necessary food (*v.* 11): *All her people sigh* in despondency and despair; they are ready to faint away; their spirits fail, and therefore they sigh, *for they seek bread* and seek it in vain. They were brought at last to that extremity that there was *no bread for the people of the land* (Jer. 52:6), and in their captivity they had much ado to get break, *ch.* 5:6. *They have given their pleasant things,* their jewels and pictures, and all the furniture of their closets and cabinets, which they used to please themselves with looking upon, they have sold these to buy bread for themselves and their families, have parted with them *for meat to relieve the soul,* or (as the margin is) *to make the soul come again,* when they were ready to faint away. They desired no other cordial than meat. *All that a man has will he give for life,* and for break, which is the staff of life. Let those that abound in pleasant things not be proud of them, nor fond of them; for the time may come when they may be glad to let them go for necessary things. And let those that have competent food to relieve their soul be content with it, and thankful for it, though they have not pleasant things.

2. We have here an account of their miseries in their ecclesiastical state, the ruin of their sacred interest, which was much more to be lamented than that of their secular concerns. (1.) Their religious feasts were no more observed, no more frequented (*v.* 4): *The ways of Zion do mourn;* they look melancholy, overgrown with grass and weeds. It used to be a pleasant diversion to see people continually passing and repassing in the highway that led to the temple, but now you may stand there long enough, and see nobody stir; for *none come to the solemn feasts;* a full end is put to them by the destruction of that which was the *city of our solemnities,* Isa. 33:20. *The solemn feasts* had been neglected and profaned (Isa. 1:11, 12), and therefore justly is an end now put to them. But, when thus *the ways of Zion* are made to *mourn,* all the sons of Zion cannot but mourn with them. It is very grievous to good men to see religious assemblies broken up and scattered, and those restrained from them that would gladly attend them. And, as *the ways of Zion mourned,* so *the gates of Zion,* in which the faithful worshippers used to meet, *are desolate;* for there is none to meet in them. Time was when *the Lord loved the gates of Zion more than all the dwellings of Jacob,* but now he has forsaken them, and is provoked to withdraw from them, and therefore it cannot but fare with them as it did with the temple when Christ quitted it. *Behold, you house is left unto you desolate,* Mt. 23:38. (2.) Their religious persons were quite disabled from performing their wonted services, were quite dispirited: *Her priests sigh* for the desolations of the temple; their songs are turned into sighs; they sigh, for they have nothing to do, and therefore there is nothing to be had; they sigh, as the people (*v.* 11), *for want of bread,* because the offerings of the Lord, which were their livelihood, failed. It is time to sigh when the priests, the Lord's ministers, sigh. *Her virgins* also, that used, with their music and dancing, to grace the solemnities of their feasts, *are afflicted* and *in heaviness.* Notice is taken of their service in the day of Zion's prosperity (Ps. 68:25, *Among them were the damsels playing with timbrels),* and therefore notice is taken of the failing of it now. *Her virgins are afflicted,* and therefore *she is in bitterness;* that is, all the inhabitants of Zion are so, whose character it is that they are *sorrowful for the solemn assembly,* and that to them *the reproach of it is a burden,* Zep. 3:18. (3.) Their religious places were profaned (*v.* 10): *The heathen entered into her sanctuary,* into the temple itself, into which no Israelite was permitted to enter, though ever so reverently and devoutly, but the priests only. *The stranger that comes nigh,* even to worship there, *shall be put to death.* Thither the heathen now crows rudely in, not to worship, but to plunder. God had commanded that *the heathen should not* so much as *enter into the congregation,* nor be incorporated with the people of the Jews (Deu. 23:3); yet now they *enter into the sanctuary* without control. Note, Nothing is more grievous to those who have a true concern for the glory of God, nor is more lamented, than the violation of God's laws, and the contempt they see put upon sacred things. What *the enemy did wickedly in the sanctuary* was complained of, Ps. 74:3, 4. (4.) Their religious utensils, and all the rich things with which the temple was adorned and beautified, and which were made use of in the worship of God, were made a prey to the enemy (*v.* 10): *The adversary has spread out his hand upon all her pleasant things,* has grasped them all, seized them all, for himself. What these pleasant things are we may learn from Isa. 64:11, where, to the complaint of the burning of the temple, it is added, *All our pleasant things are laid waste;* the ark and the altar, and all the other tokens of God's presence with them, these were their pleasant things above any other things, and these were now broken to pieces and carried away. Thus from *the daughter of Zion all her beauty has departed, v.* 6. *The beauty of holiness* was the *beauty of the daughter of Zion;* when the temple, that holy and beautiful house, was destroyed, her beauty was gone; that was the breaking of *the staff of beauty,* the taking away of the pledges and seals of the covenant, Zec. 11:10. (5.) Their religious days were made a jest of (*v.* 7): *The adversaries saw her, and did mock at her sabbaths.* They laughed at them for observing one day in seven as a day of rest from worldly business. Juvenal, a heathen poet, ridicules the Jews in his time for losing a seventh part of their time: —

— cui septima quaeque fuit lux
Ignava et vitae partem non attigit ullam —
They keep their sabbaths to their cost,
For thus one day in sev'n is lost;

whereas sabbaths, if they be sanctified as they ought to be, will turn to a better account than all the days of the week besides. And whereas the Jews professed that they did it in obedience to their God, and to his honour, their adversaries asked them, "What do you get by it now? What profit have you in keeping the ordinances of your God, who now deserts you in your distress?" Note, it is a very great trouble to all that love God to hear his ordinances mocked at, and particularly his sabbaths. Zion calls them *her sabbaths,* for the sabbath was made for men; they are his institutions, but they are her privileges; and the contempt put upon sabbaths all the sons of Zion take to themselves and lay to heart accordingly; nor will they look upon sabbaths, or any other divine ordinances, as less honourable, nor value them less, for their being mocked at. (6.) That which greatly aggravated all these grievances was that her state at present was just the revers of what it had been formerly, *v.* 7. Now, *in the days of affliction and misery,* when every thing was black and dismal, *she remembers all her pleasant things that she had in the days of old,* and now knows how to value them better than formerly, when she had the full enjoyment of them. God often makes us know the worth of mercies by the want of them; and adversity is borne with the greatest difficulty by those that have fallen into it from the height of prosperity. This cut David to the heart, when he was banished from God's ordinances, that he could remember when he *went with the multitude to the house of God,* Ps. 42:4.

II. The sins of Jerusalem are here complained of as the procuring provoking cause of all these calamities. Whoever are the instruments, God is the author of all these troubles; it is *the Lord* that *has afflicted her* (*v.* 5) and he has done it as a righteous Judge, for *she has sinned.* 1. Her sins are for number numberless. Are her troubles many? Her sins are many more. it is *for the multitude of her transgressions* that *the Lord has afflicted her.* See Jer. 30:14. When the transgressions of a people are multiplied we cannot say, as Job does in his own case, that *wounds are multiplied without cause,* Job 9:17. 2. They are for nature exceedingly heinous (*v.* 8): *Jerusalem has grievously sinned,* has *sinned sin* (so the word is), sinned wilfully, deliberately, has sinned that sin which of all others is the abominable things that the Lord hates, the sin of idolatry. The sins of Jerusalem, that makes such a profession and enjoys such privileges, are of all others the most grievous sins. She has *sinned grievously* (*v.* 8), and therefore (*v.* 9) she *came down wonderfully.* note, Grievous sins bring wondrous ruin; there are some workers of iniquity to whom there is a strange punishment, Job 31:3. They are such sins as may plainly be read in the punishment. (1.) They have been very oppressive and therefore are justly oppressed (*v.* 3): *Judah has gone into captivity,* and it is *because of affliction and great servitude,* because the rich among them afflicted the poor and made them serve with rigour, and particularly (as the Chaldee paraphrases it) because they had oppressed their Hebrew servants, which is charged upon them, Jer. 34:11. Oppression was one of their crying sins (Jer. 6:6, 7) and it is a sin that cries aloud. (2.) They have made themselves vile, and therefore are justly vilified. They all *despise her* (*v.* 8), for *her filthiness is in her skirts;* it appears upon her garments that she has rolled them in the mire of sin. None could stain our glory if we did not stain it ourselves. (3.) They have been very secure and therefore are justly surprised with this ruin (*v.* 9): *She remembers not her last end;* she did not take the warning that was given her to *consider her latter end,* to consider what would be the end of such wicked courses as she took, and therefore she *came down wonderfully,* in an astonishing manner, that she might be made to feel what she would not fear; therefore God shall *make their plagues wonderful.*

III. Jerusalem's friends are here complained of as false and faint-hearted, and very unkind: They *have all dealt treacherously with her* (*v.* 2), so that, in effect, *they have become here enemies.* Her deceivers have created her as much vexation as her destroyers. The staff that breaks under us may do us as great a mischief as the *staff that beats us,* Eze. 29:6, 7. *Her princes,* that should have protected her, have not courage enough to make head against the enemy for their own preservation; they *are like harts,* that, upon the first alarm, betake themselves to flight and make no resistance; nay, they *are like harts* that are famished for want of *pasture,* and therefore *are gone without strength before the pursuer,* and, having no strength for flight, are soon run down and made a prey of. her neighbours are unneighbourly, for, 1. There is none *to help her* (*v.* 7); either they could not or they would not; nay, 2. *She has not comforter,* none to sympathize with her, or suggest any thing to alleviate her griefs, *v.* 7, 9. Like Job's friends, they saw it was to no purpose, her *grief was so great;* and *miserable comforters were they all* in such a case.

IV. Jerusalem's God is here complained to concerning all these things, and all is referred to his compassionate consideration (*v.* 9): *"O Lord! behold my affliction,* and take cognizance of it;" and (*v.* 11), *"See, O Lord! and consider,* take order about it." Note, The only way to make ourselves easy under our burdens is to cast them upon God first, and leave it to him to do with us as seemeth him good.

Verses 12–22

The complaints here are, for substance, the same with those in the foregoing part of the chapter; but in these verses the prophet, in the name of the lamenting church, does more particularly acknowledge the hand of god in these calamities, and the righteousness of his hand.

I. The church in distress here magnifies her affliction, and yet no more than there was cause for; her groaning was not heavier than her strokes. She appeals to all spectators: *See if there be any sorrow like unto my sorrow, v.* 12. This might perhaps be truly said of Jerusalem's griefs; but we are apt to apply it too sensibly to ourselves when we are in trouble and more than there is cause for. Because we feel most from our own burden, and cannot be persuaded to reconcile ourselves to it, we are ready to cry out, Surely never was *sorrow like unto our sorrow;* whereas, if our troubles were to be thrown into a common stock with those of others, and then an equal dividend made, share and share alike, rather than stand to that we should each of us say, "Pray, give me my own again."

II. She here looks beyond the instruments to the author of her troubles, and owns them all to be directed, determined, and disposed of by him: "It is *the Lord* that *has afflicted me,* and he has *afflicted me* because he is angry with me; the greatness of his displeasure may be measured by the greatness of my distress; it is *in the day of his fierce anger," v.* 12. Afflictions cannot but be very much our griefs when we see them arising from God's wrath; so the church does here. 1. She is as one in a fever, and the fever is of God's sending: *"He has sent fire into my bones* (*v.* 13), a preternatural heat, which *prevails against them,* so that they are *burnt like a hearth* (Ps. 102:3), pained and wasted, and dried away." 2. She is as one in a net, which the more he struggles to get out of the more he is entangled in, and this net is of God's spreading. "The enemies could not have succeeded in their stratagems had not God *spread a net for my feet."* 3. She is as one in a wilderness, whose way is embarrassed, solitary, and tiresome: *"He has turned me back,* that I cannot go on, *has made me desolate,* that I have nothing to support me with, but am *faint all the day."* 4. She is as one in a yoke, not yoked for service, but for penance, tied neck and heels together (*v.* 14): *The yoke of my transgressions is bound by his hand.* Observe, We never are entangled in any yoke but what is framed out of our own transgressions. The sinner is *holden with the cords of his own sins,* Prov. *v.* 22. The yoke of Christ's commands is an *easy yoke* (Mt. 11:30), but that of our own transgressions is a heavy one. God is said to bind this yoke when he charges guilt upon us, and brings us into those inward and outward troubles which our sins have deserved; when conscience, as his deputy, binds us over to his judgment, then *the yoke is bound* and *wreathed by the hand* of his justice, and nothing but the hand of his pardoning mercy will unbind it. 5. She is as one in the dirt, and he it is that has *trodden under foot all her mighty men,* that has disabled them to stand, and overthrown them by one judgment after another, and so left them to be trampled upon by their proud conquerors, *v.* 15. Nay, she is as one in a wine-press, not only trodden down, but trodden to pieces, crushed as grapes in the wine-press of God's wrath, and her blood pressed out as wine, and it is God that has thus *trodden the virgin, the daughter of Judah.* 6. She is in the hand of her enemies, and it is the Lord that has delivered her *into their hands* (*v.* 14): *He has made my strength to fall,* so that *I am not able to* make head against them; nay, not only not able to rise up against them, but *not able to rise up* from them, and then *he has delivered me into their hands;* nay (*v.* 15), *he has called an assembly against me, to crush my young men,* and such an assembly as it is in vain to think of opposing; and again (*v.* 17), *The Lord has commanded concerning Jacob that his adversaries should be round about him.* He that has many a time *commanded deliverances for Jacob* (Ps. 44:4) now commands an invasion against Jacob, because Jacob has disobeyed the commands of his law.

III. She justly demands a share in the pity and compassion of those that were the spectators of her misery (*v.* 12): *"Is it nothing to you, all you that pass by?* Can you look upon me without concern? What! are your hearts as adamants and your eyes as marbles, that you cannot bestow upon me one compassionate thought, or look, or tear? Are not you also in the body? Is it nothing to you that your neighbor's house is on fire?" There are those to whom Zion's sorrows and ruins are nothing; they are not *grieved for the affliction of Joseph.* How pathetically does she beg their compassion! (*v.* 18): *"Hear, I pray you, all people, and behold my sorrow:* hear my complaints, and see what cause I have for them." This is a request like that of Job (*ch.* 19:21), *Have pity upon me, have pity upon me, O you my friends!* It helps to make a burden sit lighter if our friends sympathize with us, and mingle their tears with ours, for this is an evidence that, though we are in affliction, we are not in contempt, which is commonly as much dreaded in an affliction as any thing.

IV. She justifies her own grief, though it was very extreme, for these calamities (*v.* 16): *"For these things I weep,* I weep in the night (*v.* 2), when none sees; *my eye, my eye, runs down with water."* Note, This world is a vale of tears to the people of God. Zion's sons are often Zion's mourners. *Zion spreads forth her hands* (*v.* 17), which is here an expression rather of despair than of desire; she flings out her hands as giving up all for gone. Let us see how she accounts for this passionate grief. 1. Her God has withdrawn from her; and Micah, that had but gods of gold, when they were stolen from him cried out, *What have I more? And what is it that you say unto me? What aileth thee?* The church here grieves excessively; for, says she, *the comforter that should relieve my soul is far from me.* God is the comforter; he used to be so to her; he only can administer effectual comforts; it is his word that speaks them; it is his Spirit that speaks them to us. His are strong consolations, able to *relieve the soul,* to *bring it back* when it is gone, and we cannot of ourselves *fetch it again;* but now he has departed in displeasure, he is *far from me,* and beholds me *afar off.* Note, It is no marvel that the souls of the saints faint away, when God, who is the only Comforter that can relieve them, keeps at a distance. 2. Her children are removed from her, and are in no capacity to help her: it is for them that she weeps, as Rachel for hers, *because they were not,* and therefore she *refuses to be comforted. Her children were desolate, because the enemy prevailed* against them; there is *none of all her sons to take her by the hand* (Isa. 51:18); they cannot help themselves, and how should they help her? Both the damsels and the youths, that were her joy and hope, *have gone into captivity, v.* 18. It is said of the Chaldeans that they had *no compassion upon young men nor maidens,* not on the fair sex, not on the blooming age, 2 Chr. 36:17. 3. Her friends failed her; some would not and others could not give her any relief. She *spread forth her hands,* as begging relief, but *there is none to comfort her* (*v.* 17), none that can do it, none that cares to do it; she *called* for her *lovers,* and, to engage them to help her, *called* them her *lovers,* but they *deceived* her (*v.* 19), they proved like the brooks in summer to the thirsty traveller, Job 6:15. Note, Those creatures that we set our hearts upon and raise our expectations from we are commonly deceived and disappointed in. Her idols were her lovers. Egypt and Assyria were her confidants. But they deceived her. Those that made court to her in her prosperity were shy of her, and strange to her, in her adversity. Happy are those that have made God their friend and keep themselves in his love, for he will not deceive them! 4. Those whose office it was to guide her were disabled from doing her any service. The *priests* and the *elders,* that should have appeared at the head of affairs, died for hunger (*v.* 19); they *gave up the ghost,* or were ready to expire, *while they sought their meat;* they went a begging for bread to keep them alive. *The famine* is *sore* indeed *in the land* when there is no bread to the wise, when priests and elders are starved. The priests and elders should have been her comforters; but how should they comfort others when they themselves were comfortless? *"They have heard that I sigh,* which should have summoned them to my assistance; but *there is none to comfort me. Lover and friend hast thou put far from me."* 5. Her enemies were too hard for her, and they insulted over her; they have *prevailed, v.* 16. *Abroad the sword bereaves* and slays all that comes in its way, and *at home* all provisions are cut off by the besiegers, so that *there is as death,* that is, famine, which is as bad as the pestilence, or worse — *the sword without and terror within,* Deu. 32:25. And as the enemies, that were the instruments of the calamity, were very barbarous, so were those that were the standers by, the Edomites and Ammonites, that bore ill will to Israel: They have *heard of my trouble, and are glad that thou hast done it* (*v.* 21); they rejoice in the trouble itself; they rejoice that it is God's doing; it pleases them to find that God and his Israel have fallen out, and they act accordingly with a great deal of strangeness towards them. *Jerusalem is as a menstruous woman among them,* that they are afraid of touching and are shy of, *v.* 17. Upon all these accounts it cannot be wondered at, nor can she be blamed, that *her sighs are many,* in grieving for what is, and that *her heart is faint* (*v.* 22) in fear of what is yet further likely to be.

V. She justifies God in all that is brought upon her, acknowledging that her sins had deserved these severe chastenings. The yoke that lies so heavily, and binds so hard, is *the yoke of her transgressions, v.* 14. The fetters we are held in are of our own making, and it is with our own rod that we are beaten. When the church had spoken here as if she thought the Lord severe she does well to correct herself, at least to explain herself, but acknowledging (*v.* 18), *The Lord is righteous.* He does us no wrong in dealing thus with us, nor can we charge him with any injustice in it; how unrighteous soever men are, we are sure that the *Lord is righteous,* and manifests his justice, though they contradict all the laws of theirs. Note, Whatever our troubles are, which God is pleased to inflict upon us, we must own that therein he *is righteous;* we understand neither him nor ourselves if we do not own it, 2 Chr. 12:6. she owns the equity of God's actions, but owning the iniquity of her own: *I have rebelled against his commandments* (*v.* 18); and again (*v.* 20), *I have grievously rebelled.* We cannot speak ill enough of sin, and we must always speak worst of our own sin, must call it *rebellion, grievous rebellion;* and very grievous sins is to all true penitents. It is this that lies more heavily upon her than the afflictions she was under: *"My bowels are troubled;* they work within me as the troubled sea; *my heart is turned within me,* is restless, is turned upside down; *for I have grievously rebelled."* Note, Sorrow for our sin must be great sorrow and must affect the soul.

VI. She appeals both to the mercy and to the justice of God in her present case. 1. She appeals to the mercy of God concerning her own sorrows, which had made her the proper object of his compassion (*v.* 20): *"Behold, O Lord! for I am in distress;* take cognizance of my case, and take such order for my relief as thou pleasest." Note, It is matter of comfort to us that the troubles which oppress our spirits are open before God's eye. 2. She appeals to the justice of God concerning the injuries that her enemies did her (*v.* 21, 22): *"Thou wilt bring the day that thou hast called,* the day that is fixed in the counsels of God and published in the prophecies, when my enemies, that now prosecute me, *shall be made like unto me,* when the cup of trembling, now put into my hands, shall be put into theirs." It may be read as a prayer, "Let the day appointed come," and so it goes on, *"Let their wickedness come before thee,* let it come to be remembered, let it come to be reckoned for; take vengeance on them for all the wrongs they have done to me (Ps. 109:14, 15); hasten the time when thou wilt *do to them* for their transgressions *as thou hast done to me* for mine." This prayer amounts to a protestation against all thoughts of a coalition with them, and to a prediction of their ruin, subscribing to that which God had in his word spoken of it. Note, Our prayers may and must agree with God's word; and what day God has here called we are to call for, and no other. And though we are bound in charity to forgive our enemies, and to pray for them, yet we may in faith pray for the accomplishment of that which God has spoken against his and his church's enemies, that will not repent to give him glory.

CHAPTER 2

The second alphabetical elegy is set to the same mournful tune with the former, and the substance of it is much the same; it begins with Ecah, as that did, "How sad is our case! Alas for us!" I. Here is the anger of Zion's God taken notice of as the cause of her calamities (*v.* 1–9). II. Here is the sorrow of Zion's children taken notice of as the effect of her calamities (*v.* 10–19). III. The complaint is made to God, and the matter referred to his compassionate consideration (*v.* 20–22). The hand that wounded must make whole.

Verses 1–9

It is a very sad representation which is here made of the state of God's church, of Jacob and Israel, of Zion and Jerusalem; but the emphasis in these verses seems to be laid all along upon the hand of God in the calamities which they were groaning under. The grief is not so much that such and such things are done as that God has done them, that he appears angry with them; it is he that chastens them, and chastens them *in wrath* and *in his hot displeasure;* he has become their enemy, and fights against them; and this, this is the wormwood and the gall in the affliction and the misery.

I. Time was when God's delight was in his church, and he appeared to her, and appeared for her, as a friend. But now his displeasure is against her; he is angry with her, and appears and acts against her as an enemy. This is frequently repeated here, and sadly lamented. What he has done he has done *in his anger;* this makes the present day a melancholy day indeed with us, that it is *the day of his anger* (*v.* 1), and again (*v.* 2) it is *in his wrath,* and (*v.* 3) it is *in his fierce anger,* that he has *thrown down* and *cut off,* and (*v.* 6) *in the indignation of his anger.* Note, To those who know how to value God's favour nothing appears more dreadful than his anger; corrections in love are easily borne, but rebukes in love wound deeply. It is God's wrath that *burns against Jacob like a flaming fire* (*v.* 3), and it is a consuming fire; it *devours round about,* devours all her honours, all her comforts. This is the *fury that is poured out like fire* (*v.* 4), like the fire and brimstone which were rained upon Sodom and Gomorrah; but it was their sin that kindled this fire. God is such a tender Father to his children that we may be sure he is never angry with them but when they provoke him, and give him cause to be angry; nor is he ever angry more than there is cause for. God's covenant with them was that if they would *obey his voice* he would be *an enemy to their enemies* (Ex. 23:22), and he had been so as long as they kept close to him; but now he is an enemy to them; at least he is *as an enemy, v.* 5. He has *bent his bow like an enemy, v.* 4. He stood *with his right hand* stretched out against them, and a sword drawn in it *as an adversary.* God is not really an enemy to his people, no, not when he is angry with them and corrects them in anger. We may be sorely displeased against our dearest friends and relations, whom yet we are far from having an enmity to. But sometimes he is *as an enemy* to them, when all his providences concerning them seem in outward appearance to have a tendency to their ruin, when every thing made against them and nothing for them. But, blessed be God, Christ is *our peace,* our peacemaker, who has slain the enmity, and in him we may *agree with our adversary,* which it is our wisdom to do, since it is in vain to contend with him, and he offers us advantageous conditions of peace.

II. Time was when God's church appeared very bright, and illustrations, and considerable among the nations; but now *the Lord has covered the daughter of Zion with a cloud* (*v.* 1), a dark cloud, which is very terrible to himself, and through which she cannot see his face; *a thick cloud* (so that word signifies), a *black cloud,* which eclipses all her glory and conceals her excellency; not such a cloud as that under which God conducted them through the wilderness, or that in which God took possession of the temple and filled it with his glory: no, that side of the cloud is now turned towards them which was turned towards the Egyptians in the Red Sea. The *beauty of Israel is now cast down from heaven to the earth;* their princes (2 Sa. 1:19), their religious worship, their beauty of holiness, all that which recommended them to the affection and esteem of their neighbours and rendered them amiable, which had *lifted them up to heaven,* was now withered and gone, because God had covered it with a cloud. He has *cut off all the horn of Israel* (*v.* 3), all her beauty and majesty (Ps. 132:17), all her plenty and fulness, and all her power and authority. They had, in their pride, lifted up their horn against God, and therefore justly will God *cut off their horn.* He disabled them to resist and oppose their enemies; he *turned back their right hand,* so that they were not able to follow the blow which they gave nor to ward off the blow which was given them. What can their right hand do against the enemy when God draws it back, and withers it, as he did Jeroboam's? Thus was the *beauty of Israel cast down,* when a people famed for courage were not able to stand their ground nor make good their post.

III. Time was when Jerusalem and the cities of Judah were strong and well fortified, were trusted to by the inhabitants and let alone by the enemy as impregnable. But now the lord has in anger *swallowed them up;* they are quite gone; the forts and barriers are taken away, and the invaders meet with no opposition: the stately structures, which were their strength and beauty, are pulled down and laid waste. 1. The Lord has in anger *swallowed up all the habitations of Jacob* (*v.* 2), both the cities and the country houses; they are burnt, or otherwise destroyed, so totally ruined that they seem to have been *swallowed up,* and no remains left of them. He has *swallowed up, and has not pitied.* One would have thought it a pity that such sumptuous houses, so well built, so well furnished, should be quite destroyed, ad that some pity should have been had for the poor inhabitants that were thus dislodged and driven to wander; but God's wonted compassion seemed to fail: *He has swallowed up Israel,* as a lion swallows up his prey, *v.* 5. 2. He has *swallowed up* not only her common habitations, but her palaces, *all her palaces,* the habitations of their princes and great men (*v.* 5), though those were most stately, and strong, and rich, and well guarded. God's judgments, when they come with commission, level palaces with cottages, and as easily swallow them up. If palaces be polluted with sin, as theirs were, let them expect to be visited with a curse, which shall *consume them, with the timber thereof and the stones thereof,* Zec. *v.* 4. 3. He had destroyed not only their dwelling-places, but their *strong-holds,* their castles, citadels, and places of defence. These he has *thrown down in his wrath,* and *brought them to the ground;* for shall they stand in the way of his judgments, and give check to the progress of them? No; let them drop like leaves in autumn; let them be rased to the foundations, and made to touch the *ground, v.* 2. And again (*v.* 5), *He has destroyed his strong-holds;* for what strength could they have against God? And thus he *increased in the daughter of Judah mourning and lamentation,* for they could not but be in a dreadful consternation when they saw all their defence departed from them. This is again insisted on, *v.* 7–9. In order to the *swallowing up of her palaces,* he has *given up into the hand of the enemy the walls of her palaces,* which were their security, and, when they are *broken down,* the palaces themselves are soon broken into. The walls of palaces cannot protect them, unless God himself be a wall of fire round about them. This God did *in his anger,* and yet he has done it deliberately. It is the result of a previous purpose, and is done by a wise and steady providence; for the Lord has *purposed to destroy the wall of the daughter of Zion;* he brought the Chaldean army in on purpose to do this execution. Note, Whatever desolations God makes in his church, they are all according to his counsels; he *performs the thing that is appointed for us,* even that which makes most against us. But, when it is done, he has *stretched out a line,* a measuring line, to do it exactly and by measure: hitherto the destruction shall go, and no further; no more shall be cut off than what is marked to be so. Or it is meant of *the line of confusion* (Isa. 34:11), a levelling line; for he will go on with his work; he *has not withdrawn his hand from destroying,* that right hand which he stretched out against his people as *an adversary, v.* 4. As far as the purpose went the performance shall go, and his hand shall accomplish his counsel to the utmost, and not be withdrawn. Therefore he made the *rampart and the wall,* which the people had rejoiced in and upon which perhaps they had *made merry,* to *lament,* and they *languished together;* the *walls and the ramparts,* or bulwarks, upon them, fell together, and were left to condole with one another on their fall. *Her gates* are gone in an instant, so that one would think they were sunk into the ground with their own weight, and *he has destroyed and broken her bars,* those bars of Jerusalem's gates which formerly *he had strengthened,* Ps. 147:13. Gates and bars will stand us in no stead when God has withdrawn his protection.

IV. Time was when their government flourished, their princes made a figure, their kingdom was great among the nations, and the balance of power was on their side; but now it is quite otherwise: *He has polluted the kingdom and the princes thereof, v.* 2. They had first polluted themselves with their idolatries, and then God dealt with them as with polluted things; he threw them to the dunghill, the fittest place for them. he has given up their glory, which was looked upon as sacred (that is a character we give to majesty), to be trampled upon and profaned; and no marvel that the king and the priest, whose characters were always deemed venerable and inviolable, are despised by every body, when God has, *in the indignation of his anger, despised the king and the priest, v.* 6. He has abandoned them; he looks upon them as no longer worthy of the honours conveyed to them by the covenants of royalty and priesthood, but as having forfeited both; and then Zedekiah the king was used despitefully, and Seraiah the chief priest put to death as a malefactor. The crown has fallen from their heads, for *her king and her princes are among the Gentiles,* prisoners among them, insulted over by them (*v.* 9), and treated not only as common persons, but as the basest, without any regard to their character. Note, It is just with God to debase those by his judgments who have by sin debased themselves.

V. Time was when the ordinances of God were administered among them in their power and purity, and they had those tokens of God's presence with them; but now those were taken from them, that part of the *beauty of Israel* was gone which was indeed their greatest beauty. 1. The ark was God's footstool, under the mercy-seat, between the cherubim; this was of all others the most sacred symbol of God's presence (it is called his *footstool,* 1 Chr. 28:2; Ps. 99:5; 132:7); there the Shechinah rested, and with an eye to this Israel was often protected and saved; but now he *remembered not his footstool.* The ark itself was suffered, as it should seem, to fall into the hands of the Chaldeans. God, being angry, threw that away; for it shall be no longer his footstool; the earth shall be so, as it had been before the ark was, Isa. 66:1. Of what little value are the tokens of his presence when his presence is gone! Nor was this the first time that God agave his ark into captivity, Ps. 78:61. God and his kingdom can stand without that footstool. 2. Those that ministered in holy things had been *pleasant to the eye in the tabernacle of the daughter of Zion* (*v.* 4); they had been *purer than snow, whiter than mile* (*ch.* 4:7); none more pleasant in the eyes of all good people than those that did the service of the tabernacle. But now these are slain, and their *blood is mingled with their sacrifices.* Thus is the priest despised as well as the king. Note, When those that were pleasant to the eye in Zion's tabernacle are slain God must be acknowledged in it; he has done it, and the *burning which the Lord has kindled must be bewailed* but the whole house of Israel, as in the case of Nadab and Abihu, Lev. 10:6. 3. The temple was God's tabernacle (as the tabernacle, while that was in being, was called *his temple,* Ps. 27:4) and this *he has violently taken away* (*v.* 6); he has plucked up the stakes of it and cut the cords; it shall be no more a tabernacle, much less his; he has *taken it away,* as the keeper *of a garden* takes away his hovel or shade, when he has done with it and has no more occasion for it; he takes it down as easily, as speedily, and with a little regret and reluctance as if it were but a *cottage in a vineyard or a lodge in a garden of cucumbers* (Isa. 1:8), but a *booth which the keeper makes,* Job 27:18. When men profane God's tabernacle it is just with him to take it from them. God has justly refused to *smell their solemn assemblies* (Amos *v.* 21); they had provoked him to withdraw from them, and then no marvel that he has *destroyed his places of the assembly;* what should they do with the places when the services had become an abomination? He has now *abhorred his sanctuary* (*v.* 7); it has been defiled with sin, that only thing which he hates, and for the sake of that he abhors even his sanctuary, which he had delighted in and called *his rest for ever,* Ps. 132:14. Thus he had *done to Shiloh.* Now the enemies have made as great *a noise* of revelling and blaspheming *in the house of the Lord* as ever had been made with the temple-songs and music *in the day of a solemn feast,* Ps. 74:4. Some, by the *places of the assembly* (*v.* 6), understand not only the temple, but the synagogues, and the schools of the prophets, which the enemy had *burnt up,* Ps. 74:8. 4. The solemn feasts and the sabbaths had been carefully remembered, and the people constantly put in mind of them; but now the Lord has *caused those to be forgotten,* not only in the country, among those that lived at a distance, but even in Zion itself; for there were none left to remember them, nor were there the places left where they used to be observed. Now that Zion was in ruins no difference was made between sabbath time and other times; every day was a day of mourning, so that all the *solemn feasts were forgotten.* Note, It is just with God to deprive those of the benefit and comfort of sabbaths and solemn feasts who have not duly valued them, nor conscientiously observed them, but have profaned them, which was one of the sins that the Jews were often charged with. Those that have *seen the days of the Son of man,* and slighted them, may *desire to see one of those days* and not be permitted, Lu. 17:22. 5. The altar that had sanctified their gifts is now cast off, for God will no more accept their gifts, nor be honoured by their sacrifices, *v.* 7. The altar was *the table of the Lord,* but God will no longer keep house among them; he will neither feast them nor feast with them. 6. They had been blest with prophets and teachers of the law; but now *the law is no more (v.* 9); it is no more read by the people, no more expounded by the scribes; the tables of the law are gone with the ark; the book of the law is taken from them, and the people are forbidden to have it. What should those do with Bibles who had made no better improvement of them when they had them? *Her prophets also find no vision from the Lord;* God *answers them no more by prophets and dreams,* which was the melancholy case of Saul, 1 Sa. 28:15. They had persecuted God's prophets, and despised the visions they had from the Lord, and therefore it is just with God to say that they shall have no more prophets, no more visions. Let them go to the prophets that had flattered and deceived them with visions of their own hearts, for they shall have none from God to comfort them, or tell them *how long.* Those that misuse God's prophets justly lose them.

Verses 10–22

Justly are these called *Lamentations,* and they are very pathetic ones, the expressions of grief in perfection, mourning and woe, and nothing else, like the contents of Ezekiel's roll, Eze. 2:10.

I. Copies of lamentations are here presented and they are painted to the life. 1. The judges and magistrates, who used to appear in robes of state, have laid them aside, or rather are stripped of them, and put on the habit of mourners *(v.* 10); the elders now sit no longer in the judgmentseats, the *thrones of the house of David,* but they *sit upon the ground,* having no seat to repose themselves in, or in token of great grief, as Job's friends *sat with him upon the ground,* Job 2:13. They open not their mouth in the gate, as usual, to give their opinion, but they *keep silence,* overwhelmed with grief, and not knowing what to say. They have *cast dust upon their heads, and girded themselves with sackcloth,* as deep mourners used to do; they had lost their power and wealth, and that made the grieve thus. *Ploratur lachrymis amissa pecunia veris — Genuine are the tears which we shed over lost property.* 2. The young ladies, who used to dress themselves so richly, and *walk with stretched-forth necks* (Isa. 3:16), now are humbled; *The virgins of Jerusalem hang down their heads to the ground;* those are made to know sorrow who seemed to bid defiance to it and were always disposed to be merry. 3. The prophet himself is a pattern to the mourners, *v.* 11. His *eyes do fail with tears;* he has wept till he can weep no more, has almost wept his eyes out, wept himself blind. Nor are the inward impressions of grief short of the outward expressions. *His bowels are troubled,* as they were when he saw these calamities coming (Jer. 4:19, 20), which, one would think, might have excused him now; but even he, to whom they were no surprise, felt them an insupportable grief, to such a degree that his *liver is poured out on the earth;* he felt himself a perfect colliquation; all his entrails were melted and dissolved, as Ps. 22:14. Jeremiah himself had better treatment than his neighbours, better than he had had before from his own countrymen, nay, their destruction was his deliverance, their captivity his enlargement; the same that made them prisoners made him a favourite; and yet his private interests are swallowed up in a concern for the public, and he bewails the *destruction of the daughter of his people* as sensibly as if he himself had been the greatest sufferer in that common calamity. Note, The judgments of God upon the land and nation are to be lamented by us, though we, for our parts, may escape pretty well.

II. Calls to lamentation are here given: *The heart of the people cried unto the Lord, v.* 18. Some fear it was a cry, not of true repentance, but of bitter complaint; their heart was as full of grief as it could hold, and they gave vent to it in doleful shrieks and outcries, in which they made use of God's name; yet we will charitably suppose that many of them did in sincerity cry unto God for mercy in their distress; and the prophet bids them go on to do so: *"O wall of the daughter of Zion!* either you that stand upon

the wall, you *watchmen on the walls* (Isa. 62:6), when you see the enemies encamped about the walls and making their approaches towards them, or *because of the wall* (that is the subject of the lamentation), because of the *breaking down of the wall* (which was not done till about a month after the city was taken), because of this further calamity, let *the daughter of Zion lament* still." This was a thing which Nehemiah lamented long after, Neh. 1:3, 4. *"Let tears run down like a river day and night,* weep without intermission, give thyself no rest from weeping, *let not the apple of thy eye cease."* This intimates, 1. That the calamities would be continuing, and the causes of grief would frequently recur, and fresh occasion would be given them every day and every night to bemoan themselves. 2. That they would be apt, by degrees, to grow insensible and stupid under the hand of God, and would need to be still called upon to afflict their souls yet more and more, till their proud and hard hearts were thoroughly humbled and softened.

III. Causes for lamentation are here assigned, and the calamities that are to be bewailed are very particularly and pathetically described.

1. Multitudes perish by famine, a very sore judgment, and piteous is the case of those that fall under it. God had corrected them by scarcity of provisions through want of rain some time before (Jer. 14:1), and they were not brought to repentance by that lower degree of this judgment, and therefore now by the straitness of the siege God brought it upon them in extremity; for, (1.) The children died for hunger in their mothers' arms: *The children and sucklings,* whose innocent and helpless state entitles them to relief as soon as any, *swoon in the streets* (*v.* 11) *as the wounded (v.* 12), there being no food to be had for them; those that are starved die as surely as those that are stabbed. They lie a great while crying to their poor mothers for corn to feed them and wine to refresh them, for they are such as had been bred up to the use of wine and wanted it now; but there is none for them, so that at length *their soul is poured into their mothers' bosom,* and there they breathe their last. This is mentioned again (*v.* 19): *They faint for hunger in the top of every street.* Yet this is not the worst, (2.) There were some little children that were slain by their mothers' hands and eaten, *v.* 20. Such was the scarcity of provision that the *women ate the fruit* of their own bodies, even their children when they were but of *a span long,* according to the threatening, Deu. 28:53. The like was done in the siege of Samaria, 2 Ki. 6:29. Such extremities, nay, such barbarities, were they brought to by the famine. Let us, in our abundance, thank God that we have food convenient, not only for ourselves, but for our children.

2. Multitudes fall by the sword, which devours one as well as another, especially when it is in the hand of such cruel enemies as the Chaldeans were. (1.) They spared no character, no, not the most distinguished; even the *priest and the prophet,* who of all men, one would think, might expect protection from heaven and veneration on earth, *are slain,* not abroad in the field of battle, where they are out of their place, as Hophni and Phinehas, but in *the sanctuary of the Lord,* the place of their business and which they hoped would be a refuge to them. (2.) They spared no age, no, not those who, by reason of their tender or their decrepit age, were exempted from taking up the sword; for even they *perished by the sword.* "The young, who have not yet come to bear arms, and the old, who have had their *discharge, lie on the ground, slain in the streets,* till some kind hand is found that will bury them." (3.) They spared no sex: *My virgins and my young men have fallen by the sword.* In the most barbarous military executions that ever we read of the virgins were spared, and made part of the spoil (Num. 31:18, Judges 5:30), but here the virgins were put to the sword, as well as the young men. (4.) This was the *Lord's doing;* he suffered the sword of the Chaldeans to devour thus without distinction: *Thou has slain them in the day of thy anger,* for it is God that *kills and makes alive,* and saves alive, as he pleases. But that which follows is very harsh: *Thou has killed, and not pitied;* for his soul is *grieved for the misery of Israel.* The enemies that used them thus cruelly were such as he had both mustered and summoned (*v.* 22): *"Thou hast called in, as in a solemn day, my terrors round about,* that is, the Chaldeans, who are such a terror to me;" enemies crowd-

ed into Jerusalem now as thickly as ever worshippers used to do on a solemn festival, so that they were quite overpowered with numbers, and none escaped nor remained; Jerusalem was made a perfect slaughter-house. Mothers are cut to the heart to see those whom they have taken such care of, and pains with, and whom they have been so tender of, thus inhumanly used, suddenly cut off, though not soon reared: *Those that I have swaddled, and brought up, has my enemy consumed,* as if they were brought forth for the murderer, like lambs for the butcher, Hosea 9:13. Zion, who was a mother to them all, lamented to see those who were brought up in her courts, and under the tuition of her oracles, thus made a prey.

3. Their false prophets cheated them, *v.* 14. This was a thing which Jeremiah had lamented long before, and had observed with a great concern (Jer. 14:13): *Ah! Lord God, the prophets say unto them, You shall not see the sword;* and here he inserts it among his lamentations: *Thy prophets have seen vain and foolish things for thee;* they pretended to discover for thee, and then to discover to thee, the mind and will of God, to see *the visions of the Almighty* and then to speak his words; but they were all vain and foolish things; their visions were all their own fancies, and, if they thought they had any, it was only the product of a crazed head or a heated imagination, as appeared by what they delivered, which was all idle and impertinent: nay, it is most likely that they themselves knew that the visions they pretended were counterfeit, and all a sham, and made use of only to colour that which they designedly imposed upon the people with, that they might make an interest in them for themselves. They are thy prophets, not God's prophets; he never sent them, nor were they pastors after his heart, but the people set them up, told them what they should say, so that they were *prophets after their hearts.* (1.) Prophets should tell people of their faults, should show them their sins, that they may bring them to repentance, and so prevent their ruin; but these prophets knew that would lose them the people's affections and contributions, and knew they could not reprove their hearers without reproaching themselves at the same time, and therefore *they have not discovered thy iniquity;* they saw it not themselves, or, if they did, saw so little evil in it, or danger from it, that they would not tell them of it, though that might have been a means, by taking away their iniquity, to turn away their captivity. (2.) Prophets should warn people of the judgments of God coming upon them, but these *saw for them false burdens;* the messages they pretended to deliver to them from God they knew to be false, and falsely ascribed to God; so that, by soothing them up in carnal security, they caused that banishment which, by plain dealing, they might have prevented.

4. Their neighbours laughed at them (*v.* 15): *All that pass by thee clap their hands at thee.* Jerusalem had made a great figure, got a great name, and borne a great sway, among the nations; it was the envy and terror of all about; and, when the city was thus reduced; they all (as men are apt to do in such a case) triumphed in its fall; *they hissed, and wagged the head,* pleasing themselves to see how much it had fallen from its former pretensions. *Is this the city* (said they) *that men called the perfection of beauty?* Ps. 50:2. How is it now the perfection of deformity! Where is all its beauty now? *Is this the city which was called the joy of the whole earth* (Ps. 48:2), which rejoiced in the gifts of God's bounty and grace more than any other place, and which all the earth rejoiced in? Where is all its joy now and all its glorying? It is a great sin thus to make a jest of others' miseries, and adds very much affliction to the afflicted.

5. Their enemies triumphed over them, *v.* 16. Those that wished ill to Jerusalem and her peace now vent their spite and malice, which before they concealed; they now *open their mouths,* nay, they widen them; they *hiss and gnash their teeth* in scorn and indignation; they triumph in their own success against her, and the rich prey they have got in making themselves masters of Jerusalem: *"We have swallowed her up;* it is our doing, and it is our gain; it is all our own now. Jerusalem shall never be either courted or feared as she has been. *Certainly this is the day that we have long looked for; we have found it; we have seen it; aha! so would we have it."* Note, The enemies of the church are apt to take its shocks for its ruins, and to triumph in them accordingly; but they will find themselves

deceived; *for the gates of hell shall not prevail against the church.*

6. Their God, in all this, appeared against them (*v.* 17): *The Lord has done that which he had devised.* The destroyers of Jerusalem could have *no power against her unless it were given them from above.* They are but the sword in God's hand; it is he that has *thrown down, and has not pitied.* "In this controversy of his with us we have not had the usual instances of his compassion towards us." *He has caused they enemy to rejoice over thee* (see Job 30:11); *he has set up the horn of thy adversaries,* has given them power and matter for pride. This is indeed the highest aggravation of the trouble, that God has become their enemy, and yet it is the strongest argument for patience under it; we are bound to submit to what God does, for, (1.) It is the performance of his purpose: *The Lord has done that which he had devised;* it is done with counsel and deliberation, not rashly, or upon a sudden resolve; it is the *evil that he has framed* (Jer. 18:11), and we may be sure it is framed so as exactly to answer the intention. What God devises against his people is designed for them, and so it will be found in the issue. (2.) It is the accomplishment of his predictions; it is the fulfilling of the scripture; he has now *put in execution his word that he had commanded in the days of old.* When he gave them his law by Moses he told them what judgments he would certainly inflict upon them if they transgressed that law; and now that they have been guilty of the transgression of this law he had executed the sentence of it, according to Lev. 26:16, etc., Deu. 28:15. Note, In all the providences of God concerning his church it is good to take notice of the fulfilling of his word; for there is an exact agreement between the judgments of God's hand and the judgments of his mouth, and when they are compared they will mutually explain and illustrate each other.

IV. Comforts for the cure of these lamentations are here sought for and prescribed.

1. They are sought for and enquired after, *v.* 13. The prophet seeks to find out some suitable acceptable words to say to her in this case: *Wherewith shall I comfort thee, O virgin! daughter of Zion?* Note, We should endeavour to comfort those whose calamities we lament, and, when our passions have made the worst of them, our wisdom should correct them and labour to make the best of them; we should study to make our sympathies with or afflicted friends turn to their consolation. Now the two most common topics of comfort, in case of affliction, are here tried, but are laid by because they would not hold. We commonly endeavour to comfort our friends by telling them, (1.) That their case is not singular, nor without precedent; there are many whose trouble is greater, and lies heavier upon them, than theirs does; but Jerusalem's case will not admit this argument: *"What thing shall I liken to thee,* or *what shall I equal to thee, that I may comfort thee?* What city, what country, is there, whose case is parallel to thine? What witness shall I produce to prove an example that will reach thy present calamitous state? Alas! there is none, no sorrow like thine, because there is none whose honour was like thine." (2.) We tell them that their case is not desperate, but that it may easily be remedied; but neither will that be admitted here, upon a view of human probabilities; for *thy breach is great, like the sea,* like the breach which the sea sometimes makes upon the land, which cannot be repaired, but still grows wider and wider. Thou art wounded, and *who shall heal thee?* No wisdom nor power of man can repair the desolations of such a broken shattered state. It is to no purpose therefore to administer any of these common cordials; therefore,

2. The method of cure prescribed is to address themselves to God, and by a penitent prayer to commit their case to him, and to be instant and constant in such prayers (*v.* 19): *"Arise* out of thy dust, out of thy despondency, *cry out in the night,* watch unto prayer; when others are asleep, be thou upon thy knees, importunate with God for mercy; *in the beginning of the watches,* of each of the four watches, of the night (let thy *eyes prevent* them, Ps. 119:148), then *pour out thy heart like water before the Lord,* be free and full in prayer, be sincere and serious in prayer, open thy mind, spread thy case before the Lord; *lift up thy hands towards him* in holy desire and expectation; beg for the *life of thy young children.* These poor lambs, what have they done? 2 Sa. 24:17. Take with you words, take with you these words (*v.* 20), *Behold, O Lord! and consider to whom thou hast done this,* with whom thou hast dealt thus. Are they not thy own, the seed of Abraham thy friend and of Jacob thy chosen? Lord, take their case into thy compassionate consideration!" Note, Prayer is a salve for every sore, even the sorest, a remedy for every malady, even the most grievous. And our business in prayer is not to prescribe, but to subscribe to the wisdom and will of God; to refer our case to him, and then to leave it with him. *Lord, behold and consider,* and *thy will be done.*

CHAPTER 3

The scope of this chapter is the same with that of the two foregoing chapters, but the composition is somewhat different; that was in long verse, this is in short, another kind of metre; that was in single alphabets, this is in a treble one. Here is, I. A sad complaint of God's displeasure and the fruits of it (*v.* 1–20). II. Words of comfort to God's people when they are in trouble and distress (*v.* 21–36). III. Duty prescribed in this afflicted state (*v.* 37–41). IV. The complaint renewed (*v.* 42–54). V. Encouragement taken to hope in God, and continue waiting for his salvation, with an appeal to his justice against the persecutors of the church (*v.* 55–66). Some make all this to be spoken by the prophet himself when he was imprisoned and persecuted; but it seems rather to be spoken in the person of the church now in captivity and in a manner desolate, and in the desolations of which the prophet did in a particular manner interest himself. But the complaints here are somewhat more general than those in the foregoing chapter, being accommodated to the case as well of particular persons as of the public, and intended for the use of the closet rather than of the solemn assembly. Some think Jeremiah makes these complaints, not only as an intercessor for Israel, but as a type of Christ, who was thought by some to be Jeremiah the weeping prophet, because he was much in tears (Mt. 16:14) and to him many of the passages here may be applied.

Verses 1–20

The title of the 102nd Psalm might very fitly be prefixed to this chapter — *The prayer of the afflicted, when he is overwhelmed, and pours out his complaint before the Lord;* for it is very feelingly and fluently that the complaint is here poured out. Let us observe the particulars of it. The prophet complains, 1. That God is angry. This gives both birth and bitterness to the affliction (*v.* 1): *I am the man,* the remarkable man, *that has seen affliction,* and has felt it sensibly, *by the rod of his wrath.* Note, God is sometimes angry with his own people; yet it is to be complained of, not as a sword to cut off, by only as a rod to correct; it is to them *the rod of his wrath,* a chastening which, though grievous for the present, will in the issue be advantageous. By this rod we must expect to *see affliction,* and, if we be made to see more than ordinary affliction by that rod, we must not quarrel, for we are sure that the anger is just and affliction mild and mixed with mercy. 2. That he is at a loss and altogether in the dark. Darkness is put for great trouble and perplexity, the want both of comfort and of direction; this was the case of the complainant (*v.* 2): *"He has led me* by his providence, and an unaccountable chain of events, *into darkness and not into light,* the darkness I feared and not into the light I hoped for." And (*v.* 6), *He has set me in dark places,* dark as the grave, *like those that are dead of old,* that are quite forgotten, nobody knows who or what they were. Note, The Israel of God, though children of light, sometimes *walk in darkness.* 3. That God appears against him as an enemy, as a professed enemy. God had been for him, but no *"Surely against me is he turned* (*v.* 3), as far as I can discern; for *his hand is turned against me all the day. I am chastened every morning,"* Ps. 73:14. And, when God's hand is continually turned against us, we are tempted to think that his heart is turned against us too. God had said once (Hos. *v.* 14), *I will be as a lion to the house of Judah,* and now he has made his word good (*v.* 10): *"He was unto me as a bear lying in wait,* surprising me with his judgments, *and as a lion in secret places;* so that which way soever I went I was in continual fear of being set upon and could never think myself safe." Do men shoot at those thy are enemies to? *He has bent his bow,* the bow that was ordained against the church's prosecutors, that is bent against her sons, *v.* 12. *He has set me as a mark for his arrow,* which he aims at, and will be sure to hit, and then *the arrows of his quiver enter into my reins,* give me a mortal wound, an inward wound, *v.* 13. Note, God has many arrows in his quiver, and they fly swiftly and pierce deeply. 4. That he is as one sorely afflicted both in body and mind. The Jewish state may now be fitly compared to a man wrinkled with age, for which there is no remedy (*v.* 4): *"My flesh and my skin has he made old;* they are wasted and withered, and I look like one that is ready to drop into the grave; nay, *he has broken my bones,* and so disabled me to help myself, *v.* 15. *He has filled me with bitterness,* a bitter sense of his calamities." God has access to the spirit, and can so embitter that as thereby to embitter all the enjoyments; as, when the stomach is foul, whatever is eaten sours in it: *"He has made me drunk with wormwood,* so intoxicated me with the sense of my afflictions that I know not what to say or do. *He has* mingled *gravel* with my bread, so that *my teeth* are *broken* with it (*v.* 16) and what I eat is neither pleasant nor nourishing. *He has covered me with ashes,* as mourners used to be, or (as some read it) *he has fed me with ashes. I have eaten ashes like bread,"* Ps. 102:9. 5. That he is not able to discern any way of escape or deliverance (*v.* 5): *"He has built against me,* as forts and batteries are built against a besieged city. Where there was a way open it is now quite made up: *He has compassed me* on ever side *with gall and travel;* I vex, and fret, and tire myself, to find a way of escape, but can find none, *v.* 7. *He has hedged me about, that I cannot get out."* When Jerusalem was besieged it was said to be *compassed in on every side,* Lu. 19:43. "I am chained; and as some notorious malefactors are double-fettered, and loaded with irons, so he *has made my chain heavy. He has* also (*v.* 9) *enclosed my ways with hewn stone,* not only hedged up my way *with thorns* (Hos. 2:6), but stopped it up with a stone wall, which cannot be broken through, so that *my paths are made crooked;* I traverse to and fro, to the right hand, to the left, to try to get forward, but am still turned back." It is just with God to make those who walk in the crooked paths of sin, crossing God's laws, walk in the crooked paths of affliction, crossing their designs and breaking their measures. So (*v.* 11), *"He has turned aside my ways;* he has blasted all my counsels, ruined my projects, so that I am necessitated to yield to my own ruin. He has *pulled me in pieces;* he has torn and is gone away (Hos. *v.* 14), and has *made me desolate,* has deprived me of all society and all comfort in my own soul." 6. That God turns a deaf ear to his prayers (*v.* 8): *"When I cry and shout,* as one in earnest, as one that would make him hear, yet he *shuts out my prayer* and will not suffer it to have access to him." God's ear is wont to be open to the prayers of his people, and his door of mercy to those that knock at it; but now both are shut, even to one that *cries and shouts.* Thus sometimes God seems to be angry even against *the prayers of his people* (Ps. 80:4), and their case is deplorable indeed when they are denied not only the benefit of an answer, but the comfort of acceptance. 7. That his neighbours make a laughing matter of his troubles (*v.* 14): *I was a derision to all my people,* to all the wicked among them, who made themselves an one another merry with the public judgments, and particularly the prophet Jeremiah's griefs. I am their song, their *neginath,* or hand-instrument of music, their *tabret* (Job 17:6), that they play upon, as Nero on his harp when Rome was on fire. 8. That he was ready to despair of relief and deliverance: "Thou hast not only taken peace from me, but hast *removed my soul far off from peace* (*v.* 17), so that it is not only not within reach, but no within view. *I forget prosperity;* it is so long since I had it, and so unlikely that I should ever recover it, that I have lost the idea of it. I have been so inured to sorrow and servitude that I know not what joy and liberty mean. I have even given up all for gone, concluding, *My strength and my hope have perished from the Lord* (*v.* 18); I can no longer stay myself upon God as my support, for I do not find that he gives me encouragement to do so; nor can I look for his appearing in my behalf, so as to put an end to my troubles, for the case seems remediless, and even my God inexorable." Without doubt it was his infirmity to say this (Ps. 77:10), for with God there is *everlasting strength,* and he is his people's never-failing hope, whatever they may think. 9. That grief returned upon every remembrance of his troubles, and his reflections were as melancholy as his prospects, *v.* 19, 20. Did he endeavour as Job did (Job 9:27), to *forget his complaint?* Alas! it was to no purpose; he remembers, upon all occasions, *the affliction and the misery, the wormwood and the gall.* Thus emphatically does he speak of his affliction, for thus did he think of it, thus heavily did it lie when he reviewed it! It was an affliction that was misery itself. *My affliction and my transgression* (so some read it), my trouble and my sin that brought it upon me; this was *the wormwood and the gall* in *the affliction and the misery.* It is sin that makes the cup of affliction a bitter cup. *My soul has them still in remembrance.* The captives in Babylon had all the miseries of the siege in their mind continually and the flames and ruins of Jerusalem still before their eyes, and *wept when* they *remembered Zion;* nay, they could *never forget Jerusalem,* Ps. 137:1, 5. *My soul,* having *them in remembrance, is humbled in me,* not only oppressed with a sense of the trouble, but in bitterness for sin. Note, It becomes us to have humble hearts under humbling providences, and to renew our penitent humiliations for sin upon every remembrance of our afflictions and miseries. Thus we may get good by former corrections and prevent further.

Verses 21–36

Here the clouds begin to disperse and the sky to clear up; the complaint was very melancholy in the former part of the chapter, and yet here the tune is altered and the mourners in Zion begin to look a little pleasant. But for hope, the heart would break. To save the heart from being quite broken, here is something *called to mind,* which gives ground for *hope* (*v.* 21), which refers to what comes after, not to what goes before. *I make to return to my heart* (so the margin words it); what we have had in our hearts, and have laid to our hearts, is sometimes as if it were quite lost and forgotten, till God by his grace make it return to our hearts, that it may be ready to us when we have occasion to use it. *"I recall* it *to mind; therefore have I hope,* and am kept from downright despair." Let us see what these things are which he calls to mind.

I. That, bad as things are, it is owing to the mercy of God that they are not worse. We are *afflicted by the rod of his wrath,* but *it is of the lord's mercies that we are not consumed, v.* 22. When we are in distress we should, for the encouragement of our faith and hope, observe what makes for us as well as what makes against us. Things are bad but they might have been worse, and therefore there is hope that they may be better. Observe here, 1. The streams of mercy acknowledged: *We are not consumed.* Note, The church of God is like Moses's bush, burning, yet *not consumed;* whatever hardships it has met with, or may meet with, it shall have a being in the world to the end of time. It is *persecuted* of men, *but not forsaken* of God, and therefore, though it is *cast down,* it is *not destroyed* (2 Co. 4:9), corrected, yet *not consumed,* refined in the furnace as silver, but *not consumed* as dross. 2. These streams followed up to the fountain: *It is of the Lord's mercies.* here are mercies in the plural number, denoting the abundance and variety of those mercies. God is an inexhaustible *fountain of mercy, the Father of mercies.* Note, We all owe it to the sparing mercy of God *that we are not consumed.* Others have been consumed round about us, and we ourselves have been in the consuming, and yet *we are not consumed;* we are out of the grave; we are out of hell. Had we been dealt with *according to our sins,* we should have been consumed long ago; but we have been dealt with *according to God's mercies,* and we are bound to acknowledge it to his praise.

II. That even in the depth of their affliction they still have experience of the tenderness of the divine pity and the truth of the divine promise. They had several times complained that God had not pitied (*ch.* 2:17, 21), but here they correct themselves, and own, 1. That *God's compassions fail not;* they do not really fail, no, not even when in anger he seems to have *shut up his tender mercies.* These rivers of mercy run fully and constantly, but never run dry. No; *they are new every morning;* every morning we have fresh instances of God's compassion towards us; he visits us with them *every morning* (Job 7:18); *every morning does he bring his judgment to light,* Zep. 3:5. When our comforts fail, yet God's compassions do not. 2. That *great is his faithfulness.* Though the covenant seemed to be broken, they owned that it still continued in full force; and, though Jerusalem be in ruins, *the truth of the Lord endures for ever.* Note, Whatever hard things we suffer, we must never entertain any hard thoughts of God, but must still be ready to own that he is both kind and faithful.

III. That God is, and ever will be, the all-sufficient happiness of his people, and they have chosen him and depend upon him to be such (*v.* 24): *The Lord is my portion, saith my soul;* that is, 1. "When I have lost all I have in the world, liberty, and livelihood, and almost life itself, yet I have not lost my interest in God." Portions on earth are perishing things, but God is *portion for ever.* 2. "While I have an interest in God, therein I have enough; I have that which is sufficient to counterbalance all my troubles and make up all my losses." Whatever we are robbed of our portion is safe. 3. "This is that which I depend upon and rest satisfied with: *Therefore will I hope in him.* I will stay myself upon him, and encourage myself in him, when all other supports and encouragements fail me." Note, It is our duty to make God the portion of our souls, and then to make use of him as our portion and to take the comfort of it in the midst of our lamentations.

IV. That those who deal with God will find it is not in vain to trust in him; for, 1. He is good to those who do so, *v.* 25. He is good to all; *his tender mercies are over all his works;* all his creatures taste of his goodness. But he is in a particular manner *good to those that wait for him, to the soul that seeks him.* Note, While trouble is prolonged, and deliverance is deferred, we must patiently wait for God and his gracious returns to us. While we *wait for him* by faith, we must *seek him* by prayer: our *souls* must *seek him,* else we do not seek so as to find. Our seeking will help to keep up our waiting. And to those who thus wait and seek God will be gracious; he will show them his *marvellous lovingkindness.* 2. Those that do so will find it good for them (*v.* 26): *It is good* (it is our duty, and will be our unspeakable comfort and satisfaction) *to hope and quietly to wait for the salvation of the Lord,* to hope that it will come, thought eh difficulties that lie in the way of it seem insupportable, to wait till it does come, though it be long delayed, and while we wait to be quiet and silent, not quarrelling with God nor making ourselves uneasy, but acquiescing in the divine disposals. *Father, thy will be done.* If we call this to mind, we may have hope that all will end well at last.

V. That afflictions are really good for us, and, if we bear them aright, will work very much for our good. it is not only good to hope and wait for the salvation, but it is good to be under the trouble in the mean time (*v.* 27): *It is good for a man that he bear the yoke in his youth.* Many of the young men were carried into captivity. To make them easy in it, he tells them that it was good for them to *bear the yoke* of that captivity, and they would find it so if they would but accommodate themselves to their condition, and labour to answer God's ends in laying that heavy yoke upon them. It is very applicable to the yoke of God's commands. it is good for young people to take that yoke upon them in their youth; we cannot begin too soon to be religious. it will make our duty the more acceptable to God, and easy to ourselves, if we engage in it when we are young. But here it seems to be meant of the yoke of affliction. Many have found it good to bear this in youth; it has made those humble and serious, and has weaned them from the world, who otherwise would have been proud and unruly, and *as a bullock unaccustomed to the yoke.* But when do we *bear the yoke* so that it is really *good for us to bear it in our youth?* He answers in the following verses, 1. When we are sedate and quiet under our afflictions, when we *sit alone and keep silence,* do not run to and fro into all companies with our complaints, aggravating our calamities, and quarrelling with the disposals of Providence concerning us, but retire into privacy, that we may *in a day of adversity consider, sit alone,* that we may converse with God and *commune with our own hearts,* silencing all discontented distrustful thoughts, and laying our hand upon our mouth, as Aaron, who, under a very severe trial, held his peace. We must keep silence under the yoke as those that have borne it upon us, not wilfully pulled it upon our own necks, but patiently submitted to it when God laid it upon us. When those who are afflicted in their youth accommodate themselves to their afflictions, fit their necks to the yoke and study to answer God's end in afflicting them, then they will find it good for them to bear it, for it yields *the peaceable fruit of righteousness to those who are* thus *exercised thereby.* 2. When we are humble and patient under our affliction. *He* gets good by the yoke who *puts his mouth in the dust,* not only *lays his hand upon his mouth,* in token of submission to the will of God in the affliction, but *puts it in the dust,* in token of sorrow, and shame, and self-loathing, at the remembrance of sin, and as one perfectly reduced and reclaimed, and brought as those that are vanquished to *lick the dust,* Ps. 72:9. And we must thus humble ourselves, *if so be there may be hope,* or (as it is in the original) *peradventure there is hope.* If there be any way to acquire and secure a good hope under our afflictions, it is this way, and yet we must be very modest in our expectations of it, must look for it with an *it may be,* as those who own ourselves utterly unworthy of it. Note, Those who are truly humbled for sin will be glad to obtain a good hope, through grace, upon any terms, though they *put their mouth in the dust* for it; and those who would have hope must do so, and ascribe it to free grace if they have any encouragements, which may keep their hearts from sinking into the dust when they put their mouth there. 3. When we are meek and mild towards those who are the instruments of our trouble, and are of a forgiving spirit, *v.* 30. *He* gets good by the yoke who *gives his cheek to him that smites him,* and rather *turns the other cheek* (Mt. *v.* 39) than returns the second blow. Our Lord Jesus has left us an example of this, for he *gave his back to the smiter,* Isa. 50:6. he who can bear contempt and reproach, and not *render railing for railing,* and bitterness for bitterness, who, when he is *filled full with reproach,* keeps it to himself, and does not retort it and empty it again upon those who filled him with it, but *pours it out before the Lord* (as those did, Ps. 123:4, whose *souls were exceedingly filled with the contempt of the proud),* he shall find that *it is good to bear the yoke,* that it shall turn to his spiritual advantage. The sum is, *If tribulation work patience,* that *patience* will work *experience,* and that *experience a hope that makes not ashamed.*

VI. That God will graciously return to his people with seasonable comforts *according to the time that he has afflicted them, v.* 31, 32. *Therefore* the sufferer is thus penitent, thus patient, because he believes that God is gracious and merciful, which is the great inducement both to evangelical repentance and to Christian patience. We may bear ourselves up with this, 1. That, when we are cast down, yet we are not cast off; the father's correcting his son is not a disinheriting of him. 2. That though we may seem to be cast off for a time, while sensible comforts are suspended and desired salvations deferred, yet we are not really cast off, because not *cast off for ever;* the controversy with us shall not be perpetual. 3. That, whatever sorrow we are in, it is what God has allotted us, and his hand is in it. It is he that causes grief, and therefore we may be assured it is ordered wisely and graciously; and it is but *for a season,* and when need is, that we *are in heaviness,* 1 Pt. 1:6. 4. That God has compassions and comforts in store even for those whom he has himself grieved. We must be far from thinking that, though God cause grief, the world will relieve and help us. No; the very same that caused the grief must bring in the favour, or we are undone. *Una eademque manus vulnus opemque tulit — The same hand inflicted the wound and healed it.* he has torn, and he will heal us, Hos. 6:1. 5. That, when God returns to deal graciously with us, it will not be according to our merits, but according to his mercies, *according to the multitude,* the abundance, *of his mercies.* So unworthy we are that nothing but an abundant mercy will relieve us; and from that what may we not expect? And God's causing our grief ought to be no discouragement at all to those expectations.

VII. That, when God does cause grief, it is for wise and holy ends, and he takes not delight in our calamities, *v.* 33. he does indeed *afflict, and grieve the children of men;* all their grievances and afflictions are from him. But he does not do it *willingly,* not *from the heart;* so the word is. 1. He never afflicts us but when we give him cause to do it. He does not dispense his frowns as he does his favours, *ex mero motu — from his mere good pleasure.* If he show us kindness, it is because *so it seems good* unto him; but, if he write bitter things against us, it is because we both deserve them and need them. 2. He does not afflict with pleasure. he delights not in the death of sinners, or the disquiet of saints, but punishes with a kind of reluctance. He comes out of his place to punish, for his place is the mercy-seat. He delights not in the misery of any of his creatures, but, as it respects his own people, he is so far from it that in all their afflictions he is afflicted and his soul is grieved for the misery of Israel. 3. He retains his kindness for his people even when he afflicts them. If he does not *willingly grieve the children of men,* much less his own children. However it be, yet *God is good* to them (Ps. 73:1), and they may by faith see love in his heart even when they see frowns in his face and a rod in his hand.

VIII. That though he makes use of men as his hand, or rather instruments in his hand, for the correcting of his people, yet he is far from being pleased with the injustice of their proceedings and the wrong they do them, *v.* 34–36. Though God serves his own purposes by the violence of wicked and unreasonable men, yet it does no therefore follow that he countenances that violence, as his oppressed people are sometimes tempted to think. Hab. 1:13, *Wherefore lookest thou upon those that deal treacherously?* Two ways the people of God are injured and oppressed by their enemies, and the prophet here assures us that God does not approve of either of them: — 1. If men injure them by force of arms, God does not approve of that. he does not himself *crush under his feet the prisoners of the earth,* but he regards the cry of the prisoners; nor does he approve of men's doing it; nay, he is much displeased with it. It is barbarous to trample on those that are down, and to crush those that are bound and cannot help themselves. 2. If men injure them under colour of law, and in the pretended administration of justice, — if they *turn aside the right of a man,* so that he cannot discover what his rights are or cannot come at them, they are out of his reach, — if they *subvert a man in his cause,* and bring in a wrong verdict, or give a false judgment, let them know, (1.) That God sees them. It is *before the face of the Most High* (*v.* 35); it is in his sight, under his eye, and is very displeasing to him. They cannot but know it is so, and therefore it is in defiance of him that they do it. he is *the Most High,* whose authority over them they contemn by abusing their authority over their subjects, not considering that *he that is higher than the highest regardeth,* Eccl. 5:8. (2.) That God does not approve of them. More is implied than is expressed. The perverting of justice, and the subverting of the just, are a great affront to God; and, though he may make use of them for the correction of his people, yet he will sooner or later severely reckon with those that do thus. Note, However God may for a time suffer evil-doers to prosper, and serve his own purposes by them, yet he does not therefore approve of their evil doings. *Far be it from God that he should do iniquity,* or countenance those that do it.

Verses 37–41

That we may be entitled to the comforts administered to the afflicted in the foregoing verses, and may taste the sweetness of them, we have here the duties of an afflicted state prescribed to us, in the performance of which we may expect those comforts.

I. We must see and acknowledge the hand of God in all the calamities that befal us at any time, whether personal or public, *v.* 37, 38. This is here laid down as a great truth, which will help to quiet our spirits under our afflictions and to sanctify them to us. 1. That, whatever men's actions are, it is God that overrules them: *Who is he that saith, and it cometh to pass* (that designs a thing and bring his designs to effect), if *the Lord commandeth it not?* Men can do nothing but according to the counsel of God, nor have any power or success but what is given them from above. *A man's heart devises his way;* he projects and purposes; he says that he will do so and so (Jam. 4:13); *but the Lord directs his steps* far otherwise than he designed them, and what he contrived and expected does not *come to pass,* unless it be what God's hand and his counsel had determined before to be done, Prov. 16:9; Jer. 10:23. The Chaldeans said that they would destroy Jerusalem, and it came to pass, not because they said it, but because God commanded it and commissioned them to do it. Note, Men are but tools which the great God makes use of, and manages as he pleases, in the government of this lower world; and they cannot accomplish any of their designs without him. 2. That, whatever men's lot is, it is God that orders it: *Out of the mouth of the Most High do not evil and good proceed?* Yes, certainly they do; and it is more emphatically expressed in the original: *Do not* this *evil, and* this *good, proceed out of the mouth of the Most High?* Is it not what he has ordained and appointed for us? Yes, certainly it is; and for the reconciling of us to our own afflictions, whatever they be, this general truth must thus be particularly applied. This comfort I receive *from the hand of God, and shall I not receive* that *evil* also? so Job argues, *ch.* 2:10. Are we healthful or sickly, rich or poor? Do we succeed in our designs, or are we crossed in them? It is all what God orders; *every man's judgment proceeds from him. The Lord gave, and the Lord has taken away;* he forms the light and creates the darkness, as he did at first. Note, All the events of divine Providence are the products of a divine counsel; whatever is done God has the directing of it, and the works of his hands agree with the words of his mouth; *he speaks, and it is done,* so easily, so effectually are all his purposes fulfilled.

II. We must not quarrel with God for any affliction that he lays upon us at any time (*v.* 39): *Wherefore does a living man complain?* The prophet here seems to check himself for the complaint he had made in the former part of the chapter, wherein he seemed to reflect upon God as unkind and severe. "Do I well to be angry? Why do I fret thus?" Those who in their haste have chidden with God must, in the reflection, chide themselves for it. From the doctrine of God's sovereign and universal providence, which he had asserted in the verses before, he draws this inference, *Wherefore does a living man complain?* What God does we must not open our mouths against, Ps. 39:9. Those that blame their lot reproach him that allotted it to them. The sufferers in the captivity must submit to the will of God in all their sufferings. Note, Though we may pour out our complaints before God, we must never exhibit any complaints against God. What! Shall *a living man complain, a man for the punishment of his sins?* The reasons here urged are very cogent. 1. We are men; let us herein show ourselves men. Shall *a man complain?* And again, *a man!* We are men, and not brutes, reasonable creatures, who should act with reason, who should look upward and look forward, and both ways may fetch considerations enough to silence our complaints. We are men, and not children that cry for every thing that hurts them. We are men, and not gods, subjects, not lords; we are not our own masters, not our own carvers; we are bound and must obey, must submit. We are men, and not angels, and therefore cannot expect to be free from troubles as they are; we are not inhabitants of that world where there is no sorrow, but this where there is nothing but sorrow. We are men, and not devils, are not in that deplorable, helpless, hopeless, state that they are in, but have something to comfort ourselves with which they have not. 2. We are living men. Through the good hand of our God upon us we are alive yet, though dying daily; and shall *a living man complain?* No; he has more reason to be thankful for life than to complain of any of the burdens and calamities of life. Our lives are frail and forfeited, and yet we are alive; now *the living, the living, they* should *praise,* and not complain (Isa. 38:19); while there is life there is hope, and therefore, instead of complaining that things are bad, we should encourage ourselves with the hope that they will be better. 3. We are sinful men, and that which we complain of is the just *punishment of our sins;* nay, it is far less than our iniquities have deserved. WE have little reason to complain of our trouble, for it is our own doing; we may thank ourselves. Our own wickedness corrects us, Prov. 19:3. We have no reason to quarrel with God, for he is righteous in it; he is the governor of the world, and it is necessary that he should maintain the honour of his government by chastising the disobedient. Are we suffering for our sins? Then let us not complain; for we have other work to do; instead of repining, we must be repenting; and, as an evidence that God is reconciled to us, we must be endeavouring to reconcile ourselves to his holy will. Are we *punished for our sins?* It is our wisdom then to submit, and to kiss the rod; for, if we still walk contrary to God, he will punish us yet seven times more; for *when he judges he will overcome.* But, if we accommodate ourselves to him, though we be *chastened of the Lord* we shall not be *condemned with the world.*

III. We must set ourselves to answer God's intention in afflicting us, which is to bring sin to our remembrance, and to bring us home to himself, *v.* 40. These are the two things which our afflictions should put us upon. 1. A serious consideration of ourselves and a reflection upon our past lives. *Let us search and try our ways,* search what they have been, and then try whether they have been right and good or no; search as for a malefactor in disguise, that flees and hides himself, and then try whether guilty or not guilty. Let conscience be employed both to search and to try, and let it have leave to deal faithfully, to accomplish a diligent search and to make an impartial trial. *Let us try our ways,* that by them we may try ourselves, for we are to judge of our state not by our faint wishes, but by our steps, not by one particular step, but by our ways, the ends we aim at, the rules we go by, and the agreeableness of the temper of our minds and the tenour of our lives to those ends and those rules. When we are in affliction it is seasonable to *consider our ways* (Hag. 1:5), that what is amiss may be repented of and amended for the future, and so we may answer the intention of the affliction. We are apt, in times of public calamity, to reflect upon other people's ways, and lay blame upon them; whereas our business is to *search and try our* own *ways.* We have work enough to do at home; we must each of us say, "What have I done? What have I contributed to the public flames?" that we may each of us mend one, and then we should all be mended. 2. A sincere conversion to God: "Let us *turn again to the Lord,* to him who is turned against us and whom we have turned from; to him let us turn by repentance and reformation, as to our owner and ruler. We have been with him, and it has never been well with us since we forsook him; let us therefore now turn again to him." This must accompany the former and be the fruit of it; *therefore* we must *search and try our ways,* that we may turn from the evil of them to God. This was the method David took. Ps. 119:59, *I thought on my ways, and turned my feet unto thy testimonies.*

IV. We must offer up ourselves to God, and our best affections and services, in the flames of devotion, *v.* 41. When we are in affliction, 1. We must look up to God as a *God in the heavens,* infinitely above us, and who has an incontestable dominion over us; for *the heavens do rule,* and are therefore not to be quarrelled with, but submitted to. 2. We must pray to him, with a believing expectation to receive mercy from him; for that is implied in our *lifting up our hands* to him (a gesture commonly used in prayer and sometimes put for it, as Ps. 141:2, *Let the lifting up of my hands be as the evening sacrifice);* it signifies our requesting mercy from him and our readiness to receive that mercy. (3.) Our hearts must go along with our prayers. We must *lift up our hearts with our hands,* as we must pour out our souls with our words. it is the heart that God looks at in that and every other service; for what will a sacrifice without a heart avail? If inward impressions be not in some measure answerable to outward expressions, we do but mock God and deceive ourselves. Praying is lifting up the soul to God (Ps. 25:1) as to *our Father in heaven;* and the soul that hopes to be with God in heaven for ever will thus, by frequent acts of devotion, be still learning the way thither and pressing forward in that way.

Verses 42–54

It is easier to chide ourselves for complaining than to chide ourselves out of it. The prophet had owned that a living man should not complain, as if he checked himself for his complaints in the former part of the chapter; and yet here the clouds return after the rain and the wound bleeds afresh; for great pains must be taken with a troubled spirit to bring it into temper.

I. They confess the righteousness of God in afflicting them (*v.* 42): *We have transgressed and have rebelled.* Note, It becomes us, when we are in trouble, to justify God, by owning our sins, and laying the load upon ourselves for them. Call sin a transgression, call it a rebellion, and you do not miscall it. This is the result of their searching and trying their ways; the more they enquired into them the worse they found them. Yet,

II. They complain of the afflictions they are under, not without some reflections upon God, which we are not to imitate, but, under the sharpest trials, must always think and speak highly and kindly of him.

1. They complain of his frowns and the tokens of his displeasure against them. Their sins were repented of, and yet (*v.* 42), *Thou hast not pardoned.* They had not the assurance and comfort of the pardon; the judgments brought upon them for their sins were not removed, and therefore they thought they could not say the sin was pardoned, which was a mistake, but a common mistake with the people of God when their souls are cast down and disquieted within them. Their case was really pitiable, yet they complain, *Thou hast not pitied, v.* 43. Their enemies persecuted and slew them, but that was not the worst of it; they

were but the instruments in God's hand: *"Thou hast persecuted us, and thou hast slain us,* though we expected thou wouldst protect and deliver us." They complain that there was a wall of partition between them and God, and, (1.) This hindered God's favours from coming down upon them. The reflected beams of God's kindness to them used to be the beauty of Israel; but now *"thou hast covered* us *with anger,* so that our glory is concealed and gone; now God is angry with us, and we do not appear that illustrious people that we have formerly been thought to be." Or, *"Thou hast covered us* up as men that are buried are covered up and forgotten." (2.) It hindered their prayers from coming up unto God (*v.* 44): *"Thou hast covered thyself with a cloud,"* not like that bright cloud in which he took possession of the temple, which enabled the worshippers to draw near to him, but like that in which he came down upon Mount Sinai, which obliged the people to stand at a distance. "This cloud is so thick *that our prayers* seem as if they were lost in it; they cannot *pass through;* we cannot obtain an audience." Note, The prolonging of troubles is sometimes a temptation, even to praying people, to question whether God be what they have always believed him to be, a prayer-hearing God.

2. They complain of the contempt of their neighbours and the reproach and ignominy they were under (*v.* 45): *"Thou hast made us as the off-scouring,* or scrapings, of the first floor, which are thrown to the dunghill." This St. Paul refers to in his account of the sufferings of the apostles. 1 Co. 4:13, *We are made as the filth of the world and are the off-scouring of all things.* "We are the *refuse,* or dross, *in the midst of the people,* trodden upon by every body, and looked upon as the vilest of the nations, and good for nothing but to be cast out as *salt* which *has lost its savour. Our enemies have opened their mouths against us* (*v.* 46), have *gaped upon us as roaring lions,* to swallow us up, or made mouths at us, or have taken liberty to say what they please of us." These complaints we had before, *ch.* 2:15, 16. Note, It is common for base and ill-natured men to run upon, and run down, those that have fallen into the depths of distress from the height of honour. But this they brought upon themselves by sin. If they had not made themselves vile, their enemies could not have made them so: but *therefore men call them reprobate silver, because the Lord has rejected them* for rejecting him.

3. They complain of the lamentable destruction that their enemies made of them (*v.* 47): *Fear and a snare have come upon us;* the enemies have not only terrified us with those alarms, but prevailed against us by their stratagems, and surprised us with the ambushes they laid for us; and then follows nothing but *desolation and destruction,* the *destruction of the daughter of my people* (*v.* 48), *of all the daughters of my city, v.* 51. The enemies, having taken some of them *like a bird* in a snare, *chased* others as a harmless bird is chased by a bird of prey (*v.* 52): *My enemies chased me sorely like a bird* which is beaten from bush to bush, as Saul hunted David *like a partridge.* Thus restless was the enmity of their persecutors, and yet causeless. They have done it *without cause,* without any provocation given them. Though God was righteous, they were unrighteous. David often complains of those that *hated him without cause;* and such are the enemies of Christ and his church, Jn. 15:25. Their enemies chased them till they had quite prevailed over them (*v.* 53): *They have cut off my life in the dungeon.* They have shut up their captives in close and dark prisons, where they are as it were cut off *from the land of the living* (as *v.* 6), or the state and kingdom are sunk and ruined, the life and being of them are gone, and they are as it were thrown into the dungeon or grave and a *stone cast upon them,* such as used to be *rolled to the door of the sepulchres.* They look upon the Jewish nation as dead and buried, and imagine that there is not possibility of its resurrection. Thus Ezekiel saw it, in vision, *a valley full of dead and dry bones.* Their destruction is compared not only to the burying of a dead man, but to the sinking of a living man into the water, who cannot long be a living man there, *v.* 54. *Waters* of affliction *flowed over my head.* The deluge prevailed and quite overwhelmed them. The Chaldean forces broke in upon them *as the breaking forth of waters,* which rose so high as to *flow over their heads;* they could not wade, they could not swim, and therefore must unavoidably sink. Note, The distresses of God's people sometimes prevail to such a degree that they cannot find any footing for their faith, nor keep their head above water, with any comfortable expectation.

4. They complain of their own excessive grief and fear upon this account. (1.) The afflicted church is drowned in tears, and the prophet for her (*v.* 48, 49): *My eye runs down with rivers of water,* so abundant was their weeping; *it trickles down and ceases not,* so constant was their weeping, *without* any *intermission,* there being no relaxation of their miseries. The distemper was in continual extremity, and they had no better day. It is added (*v.* 51), *"My eye affects my heart.* My seeing eye affects my heart. The more I look upon the desolation of the city and country the more I am grieved. Which way soever I cast my eye, I see that which renews my sorrow, even *because of all the daughters of my city,"* all the neighbouring towns, which were as daughters to Jerusalem the mother-city. Or, *My weeping eye affects my heart;* the venting of the grief, instead of easing it, did but increase and exasperate it. Or, *My eye melts my soul;* I have quite wept away my spirits; not only *my eye is consumed with grief, but my soul and my life are spent with it,* Ps. 31:9, 10. Great and long grief exhausts the spirits, and brings not only many a *gray head,* but many a green head too, *to the grave.* I weep, ways the prophet, *more than all the daughters of my city* (so the margin reads it); he outdid even those of the tender sex in the expressions of grief. And it is no diminution to any to be much in tears for the sins of sinners and the sufferings of saints; our Lord Jesus was so; for, *when he came near, he beheld* this same *city and wept over it,* which the daughters of Jerusalem did not. (2.) She is overwhelmed with fears, not only grieves for what is, but fears worse, and gives up all for gone (*v.* 54): *"Then I said, I am cut off,* ruined, and see no hope of recovery; I am as one dead." Note, Those that are cast down are commonly tempted to think themselves cast off, Ps. 31:22; Jon. 2:4.

5. In the midst of these sad complaints here is one word of comfort, by which it appears that their case was not altogether so bas as they made it, *v.* 50. We continue thus weeping *till the Lord look down and behold from heaven.* This intimates, (1.) That they were satisfied that God's gracious regard to them in their miseries would be an effectual redress of all their grievances. "If God, who now *covers himself with a cloud,* as if he took no notice of our troubles (Job 22:13), would but shine forth, all would be well; if he look upon us, *we shall be saved,"* Ps. 80:19; Dan. 9:17. Bad as the case is, one favourable look from heaven will set all to rights. (2.) That they had hopes that he would at length look graciously upon them and relieve them; nay, they take it for granted that he will: "Though he contend long, he will not contend for ever, thou we deserve that he should." (3.) That while they continued weeping they continued waiting, and neither did nor would expect relief and succour from any hand but his; nothing shall comfort them but his gracious returns, nor shall any thing wipe tears from their eyes *till he look down.* Their eyes, which now *run down with water,* shall still *wait upon the Lord their God until he have mercy upon them,* Ps. 123:2.

Verses 55–66

We may observe throughout this chapter a struggle in the prophet's breast between sense and faith, fear and hope; he complains and then comforts himself, yet drops his comforts and returns again to his complaints, as Ps. 42. But, as there, so here, faith gets the last word and comes off a conqueror; for in these verses he concludes with some comfort. And here are two things with which he comforts himself: —

I. His experience of God's goodness even in his affliction. This may refer to the prophet's personal experience, with which he encourages himself in reference to the public troubles. He that has seasonably succoured particular saints will not fail the church in general. Or it may include the remnant of good people that were among the Jews, who had found that it was not in vain to wait upon God. In three things the prophet and his pious friends had found God good to them: — 1. He had *heard their prayers;* though they had been ready to fear that the cloud of wrath was such as their *prayers could not pass through* (*v.* 44), yet upon second thoughts, or at least upon further trial, they find it otherwise, and that God had not said unto them, *Seek you me in vain.* When they were *in the low dungeon,* as *free among the dead,* they *called upon God's name* (*v.* 55); their weeping did not hinder praying. Note, Though we are cast into ever so low a dungeon, we may thence find a way of access to God in the highest heavens. *Out of the depths have I cried unto thee* (Ps. 130:1), as Jonah out of the whale's belly. And could God hear them out of the low dungeon, and would he? Yes, he did: *Thou hast heard my voice;* and some read the following words as carrying on the same thankful acknowledgment: *Thou didst not hide thy ear at my breathing, at my cry;* and the original will bear that reading. We read it as a petition for further audience: *Hide not thy ear.* God's having heard our voice when we *cried to him,* even out of *the low dungeon,* is an encouragement for us to hope that he will not at any time *hide his ear.* Observe how he calls prayer *his breathing;* for in prayer we breathe towards God, we breathe after him. Though we be but weak in prayer, cannot cry aloud, but only *breathe* in *groanings that cannot be uttered,* yet we shall not be neglected if we be sincere. Prayer is the breath of the new man, sucking in the air of mercy in petitions and returning it in praises; it is both the evidence and the maintenance of the spiritual life. Some read it, *at my gasping.* "When I lay gasping for life, and ready to expire, and thought i was breathing my last, then thou tookest cognizance of my distressed case." 2. He had silenced their fears and quieted their spirits (*v.* 57): *"Thou drewest near in the day that I called upon thee;* thou didst graciously assure me of thy presence with me, and give me to see thee nigh unto me, whereas I had thought thee to be at a distance from me." Note, When we draw nigh to God in a way of duty we may by faith see him drawing nigh to us in a way of mercy. But this was not all: *Thou saidst, Fear not.* This was the language of God's prophets preaching to them not to fear (Isa. 41:10, 13, 14), of his providence preventing those things which they were afraid of, and of his grace quieting their minds, and making them easy, by the witness of his Spirit with their spirits that they were his people still, though in distress, and therefore ought not to fear. 3. He had already begun to appear for them (*v.* 58): *"O Lord! thou hast pleaded the causes of my soul"* (that is, as it follows), *"thou hast redeemed my life,* hast rescued that out of the hands of those who would have taken it away, hast saved that when it was ready to be swallowed up, hast given me that for a prey." And this is an encouragement to them to hope that he would yet further appear for them: *"Thou hast delivered my soul from death,* and therefore wilt deliver *my feet from falling;* thou hast *pleaded the causes of my life,* and therefore wilt plead my other causes."

II. He comforts himself with an appeal to God's justice, and (in order to the sentence of that) to his omniscience.

1. He appeals to God's knowledge of the matter of fact, how very spiteful and malicious his enemies were (*v.* 59): *"O Lord! thou hast seen my wrong,* that I have done no wrong at all, but suffer a great deal." He that knows all things knew, (1.) The malice they had against him: *"Thou hast seen all their vengeance,* how they desire to do me a mischief, as if it were by way of reprisal for some great injury I had done them." Note, We should consider, to our terror and caution, that God knows all the revengeful thoughts we have in our minds against others, and therefore we should not allow of those thoughts nor harbour them, and that he knows all the revengeful thoughts others have causelessly in their minds against us, and therefore we should not be afraid of them, but leave it to him to protect us from them. (2.) The designs and projects they had laid to do him a mischief: *Thou hast seen all their imaginations against me* (*v.* 60), and again, *"Thou hast heard all their imaginations against me* (*v.* 61), both the desire and the device they have to ruin me; whether it show itself in word or deed, it is known to thee; nay, though the products of it are not to be seen nor heard, yet their device against me all the day is perceived and understood by him to whom all things are naked and open." Note, The most secret contrivances of the church's enemies are perfectly known to the church's God, from whom they can hide nothing. (3.) The contempt and calumny wherewith they loaded him, all that they spoke slightly of him, and all that they spoke reproachfully: *"Thou hast heard their reproach* (*v.* 61), all the bad characters they give me, laying to my charge things that I know not, all the methods they use to make me odious and contemptible, even the *lips of those that rose up against me* (*v.* 62), the contu-

melious language they use whenever they speak of me, and that at their sitting down and rising up, when they lie down at night and get up in the morning, when they sit down to their meat and with their company, and when they rise from both, still I am their music; they make themselves and one another merry with my miseries, as the Philistines made sport with Samson." Jerusalem was the tabret they played upon. Perhaps they had some tune or play, some opera or interlude, that was called *the destruction of Jerusalem,* which, though in the nature of a tragedy, was very entertaining to those who wished ill to the holy city. Note, God will one day call sinners to account for all the hard speeches which they have spoken against him and his people, Jude 15.

2. He appeals to God's judgment upon this fact: *"Lord, thou hast seen my wrong;* there is no need of any evidence to prove it, nor any prosecutor to enforce and aggravate it; thou seest it in its true colours; and now I leave it with thee. *Judge thou my cause, v.* 59. Let them be dealt with," (1.) "As they deserve (*v.* 64): *Render to them a recompence according to the work of their hands.* Let them be dealt with as they have dealt with us; let thy hand be against them as their hand has been against us. They have created us a great deal of vexation; now, Lord, *give them sorrow of heart* (*v.* 65), *perplexity of heart"* (so some read it); "let them be surrounded with threatening mischiefs on all sides, and not be able to see their way out. Give them *despondence of heart"* (so others read it); "let them be driven to despair, and give themselves up for gone." God can entangle the head that thinks itself clearest, and sink the heart that thinks itself stoutest. (2.) "Let them be dealt with according to the threatenings: *Thy curse unto them;* that is, let thy curse come upon them, all the evils that are pronounced in thy word against the enemies of thy people, *v.* 65. They have loaded us with curses; as they loved cursing, so let it come unto them, thy curse which will make them truly miserable. Theirs is causeless, and therefore fruitless, it shall not come; but thine is just, and shall take effect. Those whom thou cursest are cursed indeed. Let the curse be executed, *v.* 66. *Persecute and destroy them in anger,* as they persecute and destroy us in their anger. *Destroy them from under the heavens of the Lord;* let them have no benefit of the light and influence of the heavens. Destroy them in such a manner that all who see it may say, It is a destruction from the Almighty, who *sits in the heavens and laughs at them* (Ps. 2:4), and may own *that the heavens do rule,"* Dan. 4:26. What is said of the idols is here said of their worshippers (who in this also shall be like unto them), *They shall perish from under these heavens,* Jer. 10:11. They shall be not only excluded from the happiness of the invisible heavens, but cut off from the comfort even of these visible ones, which are the *heavens of the Lord* (Ps. 115:16) and which those therefore are unworthy to be taken under the protection of who rebel against him.

CHAPTER 4

This chapter is another single alphabet of Lamentations for the destruction of Jerusalem, like those in the first two chapters. I. The prophet here laments the injuries and indignities done to those to whom respect used to be shown (*v.* 1, 2). II. He laments the direful effects of the famine to which they were reduced by the siege (*v.* 3–10). III. He laments the taking and sacking of Jerusalem and its amazing desolations (*v.* 11, 12). IV. He acknowledges that the sins of their leaders were the cause of all these calamities (*v.* 13–16). V. He gives up all as doomed to utter ruin, for their enemies were every way too hard for them (*v.* 17–20). VI. He foretels the destruction of the Edomites who triumphed in Jerusalem's fall (*v.* 21). VII. He foretels the return of the captivity of Zion at last (*v.* 22).

Verses 1–12

The elegy in this chapter begins with a lamentation of the very sad and doleful change which the judgments of God had made in Jerusalem. The city that was formerly *as gold,* as *the most fine gold,* so rich and splendid, *the perfection of beauty and the joy of the whole earth,* has become dim, and is changed, has lost its lustre, lost its value, is not what it was; it has become dross. Alas! what an alteration is here!

I. The temple was laid waste, which was the glory of Jerusalem and its protection. it is given up into the hands of the enemy. And some understand the gold spoken of (*v.* 1) to be the *gold of the temple,* the fine gold with which it was overlaid (1 Ki. 6:22); when the temple was burned the gold of it was smoked and sullied, as if it had been of little value. it was thrown among the rubbish; it *was changed,* converted to common uses and made nothing of. *The stones of the sanctuary,* which were curiously wrought, were thrown down by the Chaldeans, when they demolished it, or were brought down by the force of the fire, and were *poured out,* and thrown about *in the top of every street;* they lay mingled without distinction among the common ruins. When the God of the sanctuary was by sin provoked to withdraw no wonder that the stones of the sanctuary were thus profaned.

II. The princes and priests, who were in a special manner the *sons of Zion,* were trampled upon and abused, *v.* 2. Both the house of God and the house of David were in Zion. The sons of both those houses were upon this account precious, that they were heirs to the privileges of those two covenants of priesthood and royalty. They were *comparable to fine gold.* Israel was more rich in them than in treasures of gold and silver. But now they are *esteemed as earthen pitchers;* they are broken as *earthen pitchers,* thrown by as vessels in which there is no pleasure. They have grown poor, and are brought into captivity, and thereby are rendered mean and despicable, and every one treads upon them and insults over them. Note, The contempt put upon God's people ought to be matter of lamentation to us.

III. Little children were starved for want of bread and water, *v.* 3, 4. The nursing-mothers, having no meat for themselves, had no milk for the babes at their breast, so that, though in disposition they were really compassionate, yet in fact they seemed to be cruel, *like the ostriches in the wilderness, that leave their eggs in the dust* (Job 39:14, 15); having no food for their children, they were forced to neglect them and do what they could to forget them, because it was a pain to them to think of them when they had nothing for them; in this they were worse than the seals, or *sea-monsters,* or *whales* (as some render it), for they *drew out the breast, and gave suck to their young,* which *the daughter of my people* will not do. Children cannot shift for themselves as grown people can; and therefore it was the more painful to see *the tongue of the sucking-child cleave to the roof of his mouth for thirst,* because there was not a drop of water to moisten it; and to hear the young children, that could but just speak, *ask bread* of their parents, who had none to give them, no, nor any friend that could supply them. As doleful as our thoughts are of this case, so thankful should our thoughts be of the great plenty we enjoy, and the food convenient we have for ourselves and for our children, and for *those of our own house.*

IV. Persons of good rank were reduced to extreme poverty, *v.* 5. Those who were well-born and well bred, and had been accustomed to the best, both for food and clothing, who had *fed delicately,* had every thing that was curious and nice (they call it *eating well,* whereas those only eat well who eat to the glory of God), and *fared sumptuously every day;* they had not only been *advanced to the scarlet,* but from their beginning were *brought up in scarlet,* and were never acquainted with any thing mean or ordinary. They were *brought up upon scarlet* (so the word is); their foot-cloths, and the carpets they walked on, were scarlet, yet these, being stripped of all by the war, are *desolate in the streets,* have not a house to put their head in, nor a bed to lie on, nor clothes to cover them, nor fire to warm them. They *embrace dunghills;* on them they were glad to lie to get a little rest, and perhaps raked in the dunghills for something to eat, as the prodigal son who *would fain have filled his belly with the husks.* Note, Those who live in the greatest pomp and plenty know not what straits they may be reduced to before they die; as sometimes the *needy* are *raised out of the dunghill. Those who were full have hired out themselves for bread,* 1 Sa. 2:5. It is therefore the wisdom of those who have abundance not to use themselves too nicely, for then hardships, when they come, will be doubly hard, Deu. 28:56.

V. Persons who were eminent for dignity, nay, perhaps for sanctity, shared with others in the common calamity, *v.* 7, 8. *Her Nazarites* are extremely charged. Some understand it only of her honourable ones, the young gentlemen, who were very clean, and neat, and well-dressed, washed and perfumed; but I see not why we may not understand it of those devout people among them who *separated themselves to the Lord* by the *Nazarites'* vow, Num. 6. 2. That there were such among them in the most degenerate times appears from Amos 2:11, *I raised up of your young men for Nazarites.* These *Nazarites,* though they were not to cut their hair, yet by reason of their temperate diet, their frequent washings, and especially the pleasure they had in devoting themselves to God and conversing with him, which made their faces to shine as *Moses's,* were *purer than snow* and *whiter than milk;* drinking no wine nor strong drink, they had a more healthful complexion and cheerful countenance than those who regaled themselves daily with the blood of the grape, as *Daniel* and his fellows with *pulse and water.* Or it may denote the great respect and veneration which all good people had for them; though perhaps to the eye they had *no form nor comeliness,* yet, being separated to the Lord, they were valued as if they had been *more ruddy than rubies and their polishing had been of sapphire.* But now *their visage is marred* (as is said of Christ, Isa. 52:14); it is *blacker than a coal;* they look miserably, partly through hunger and partly through grief and perplexity. *They are not known in the streets;* those who respected them now take no notice of them, and those who had been intimately acquainted with them now scarcely knew them, their countenance was so altered by the miseries that attended the long siege. *Their skin cleaves to their bones,* their flesh being quite consumed and wasted away; it is *withered;* it has *become like a stick,* as dry and hard as a piece of wood. Note, It is a thing to be much lamented that even those who are separated to God are yet, when desolating judgments are abroad, often involved with others in the common calamity.

VI. Jerusalem came down slowly, and died a lingering death; for the famine contributed more to her destruction than any other judgment whatsoever. Upon this account the destruction of *Jerusalem was greater than that of Sodom* (*v.* 6), for that was *overthrown in a moment;* one shower of fire and brimstone dispatched it; *no hand staid on her;* she did not endure any long siege, as Jerusalem has done; she fell immediately into the *hands of the Lord,* who strikes home at a blow, and did not *fall into the hands of man,* who, being weak, is long in doing execution, Jdg. 8:21. Jerusalem is kept many months upon the rack, in pain and misery, and dies by inches, dies so as to feel herself die. And, when the iniquity of Jerusalem is more aggravated than that of Sodom, no wonder that the punishment of it is so. Sodom never had the means of grace the Jerusalem had, the oracles of God and his prophets, and therefore the condemnation of Jerusalem will be *more intolerable* than that of Sodom, Mt. 11:23, 24. The extremity of the famine is here set forth by two frightful instances of it: — 1. The tedious deaths that it was the cause of (*v.* 9); many were slain with hunger, were famished to death, their stores being spent, and the public stores so nearly spent that they could not have any relief out of them. They were *stricken through, for want of the fruits of the field;* those who were starved were as sure to die as if they had been stabbed and stricken through; only their case was much more miserable. *Those who are slain with the sword* are soon put out of their pain; *in a moment they go down to the grave,* Job 21:13. They have not the terror of seeing death make its advances towards them, and scarcely feel it when the blow is given; it is but one sharp struggle, and the work is done. And, if we be ready for another world, we need not be afraid of a short passage to it; the quicker the better. But those who die by famine pine away; hunger preys upon their spirits and wastes them gradually; nay, and it frets their spirits, and fills them with vexation, and is as great a torture to the mind as to the body. There are *bands in their death,* Ps. 73:4. 2. The barbarous murders that it was the occasion of (*v.* 10): *The hands of the pitiful women have* first slain and then *sodden their own children.* This was lamented before (*ch.* 2:20); and it was a thing to be greatly lamented that any should be so wicked as to do it and that they should be brought to such extremities as to be tempted to it. But this horrid effect of long sieges had been threatened in general (Lev. 26:29, Deu. 28:53), and particularly against Jerusalem in the siege of the Chaldeans, Jer. 19:9; Eze. *v.* 10. The case was sad enough that they had not wherewithal to feed their children and make meat for them (*v.* 4), but much worse that they could find in their hearts to feed upon their children and make meat of them. I know not whether to make it an instance of the power of necessity or of the power of iniquity; but, as the Gentile idolaters were justly *given up to vile affections* (Rom. 1:26), so these Jewish idolaters, and the women particularly, who had *made cakes to the queen of heaven* and taught their children to do so too, were *stripped of natural affection* and that to their own children. Being thus left to *dishonour their own nature* was a righteous judgment upon them for the dishonour they had done to God.

VII. Jerusalem comes down utterly and wonderfully. 1. The destruction of Jerusalem is a complete destruction (*v.* 11): *The Lord has accomplished his fury;* he has made thorough work of it, has executed all that he purposed in wrath against Jerusalem, and has remitted no part of the sentence. He has poured out the full vials of his fierce anger, poured them out to the bottom, even the dregs of them. He has *kindled a fire in Zion,* which has not only consumed the houses, and levelled them with the ground, but, beyond what other fires do, has *devoured the foundations thereof,* as if they were to be no more built upon. 2. It is an amazing destruction, *v.* 12. It was a surprise to the kings of the earth, who are acquainted with, and inquisitive about, the state of their neighbours; nay, it was so to *all the inhabitants of the world* who knew Jerusalem, or had ever heard or read of it; they *could not have believed that the adversary and enemy would ever enter into the gates of Jerusalem;* for, (1.) They knew that Jerusalem was strongly fortified, not only by walls and bulwarks, but by the numbers and strength of its inhabitants; the strong hold of Zion was thought to be impregnable. (2.) They knew that it was the *city of the great King,* where the Lord of the whole earth had in a more peculiar manner his residence; it was the holy city, and therefore they thought that it was so much under the divine protection that it would be in vain for any of its enemies to make an attack upon it. (3.) They knew that many an attempt made upon it had been baffled, witness that of Sennacherib. They were therefore amazed when they heard of the Chaldeans making themselves masters of it, and concluded that it was certainly by an immediate hand of God that Jerusalem was given up to them; it was by a commission from him that the enemy broke through and entered the gates of Jerusalem.

Verses 13–20

We have here,

I. The sins they were charged with, for which God brought this destruction upon them, and which served to justify God in it (*v.* 13, 14): It is *for the sins of her prophets,* and the *iniquities of her priests.* Not that the people were innocent; no, they *loved to have it so* (Jer. *v.* 31), and it was to please them that the prophets and priests did as they did; but the fault is chiefly laid upon them, who should have taught them better, should have reproved and admonished them, and told them what would be in the end hereof; of the hands of those watchmen who did not give them warning will their blood be required. Note, Nothing ripens a people more for ruin, nor fills the measure faster, than the sins of their priests and prophets. The particular sin charged upon them is persecution; the false prophets and corrupt priests joined their power and interest to *shed the blood of the just in the midst of her,* the blood of God's prophets and of those that adhered to them. They not only shed the blood of their innocent children, whom they sacrificed to Moloch, but the blood of the righteous men that were among them, whom they sacrificed to that more cruel idol of enmity to the truth and true religion. This was that sin which the Lord would not pardon (2 Ki. 24:4) and which brought the last destruction upon Jerusalem (Jam. *v.* 6): *You have condemned and killed the just.* And the priests and prophets were the ringleaders in persecution, as in Christ's time the chief priests and scribes were the men that incensed the people against him, who otherwise would have persisted in their hosannas. Now these are those that *wandered as blind men in the streets, v.* 14. They strayed from the paths of justice, were blind to every thing that is good, but to do evil they were quick-sighted. God says of corrupt judges, *They know not, neither do they understand; they walk in darkness* (Ps. 82:5); and Christ says of the corrupt teachers, *They are blind leaders of the blind,* Mt. 15:14. They have so *polluted themselves with* innocent *blood,* the blood of the saints, that *men could not touch their garments;* they made themselves odious to all about them, so that good men were as shy of touching them as of touching a dead body, which contracted a ceremonial pollution, or of touching the bloody clothes of one slain, which tender spirits care not to do. There is nothing that will make prophets and priests to be abhorred so much as a spirit of persecution.

II. The testimony of their neighbours produced in evidence against them, both to convict them of sin and to show the equity of God's proceedings against them. Some that have grown very impudent in sin boast that they *care not what people say of them;* but God, by the prophet, would have the Jews to take notice of what people said of them and what was the opinion of the standers by concerning them (*v.* 15, 16), what they said, nay, what *they cried unto them,* especially to the corrupt priests and prophets, *among the heathen.* 1. They upbraided them with their pretended purity, while they lived in all manner of real iniquity. They cried to them, *"Depart you; it is unclean.* You were so precise that you would not touch a Gentile, by cried, *Depart, depart; stand by thyself; I am holier than thou,"* Isa. 65:5. Thus the prosecutors of Christ would not go *into the judgment-hall, lest they should be defiled.* "But can you now keep the Gentiles from touching you, when God has delivered you into their hands? When you flee away and wander you will bid them stand off and not touch you, because they are unclean. But in vain; these serpents will not be charmed or enchanted thus; no, they will no *respect the persons of the priests,* nor *favour the elders;* the most venerable persons will to them be despicable." 2. They upbraided them with their sins, and the anger of God against them for their sins, and the direful effects of that anger. *They cried to them, Depart you; it is unclean.* They all cried out shame on them, and could easily foresee that God would not long suffer so provoking a people to continue in so good a land. They knew their *statutes and judgments were righteous,* and expected they should be *a wise and understanding people,* Deu. 4:6. But, when they saw them quite otherwise, they cried, *Depart, depart;* they soon read their doom, that the land would spue them out, as it had done their predecessors, and, when they saw the dispersed of *Jacob fleeing and wandering,* they told them of it. They said, Now *the anger of the Lord has divided them,* has dispersed them into all countries, because *they respected not the persons of the priests,* the pious priests that were among them, such as Zechariah the son of Jehoiada, Jeremiah, and others; neither did they *favour the elders,* but despised them and their authority when they went about to check them for their vicious courses. The very heathen foresaw that this would ruin them. 3. They triumphed in their ruin as irrecoverable. They said, when they saw them expelled out of their own land, "Now *they shall no more sojourn there;* they have bidden it a final farewell, never more to return to it, for *God will no more regard them,* and how then can they help themselves?" Herein they were mistaken. God had not cast them off, for all this. yet thus much is intimated, that all about them observed them to be so very provoking to their God that there was not reason to expect any other than that they should be quite abandoned.

III. The despair which they themselves were almost brought to under their calamities. Having heard what they said concerning them *among the heathen,* let us now hear what they say concerning themselves (*v.* 17): *"As for us,* we look upon our case to be in a manner helpless. *Our end is near* (*v.* 18), the end both of our church and of our state; we are just at the brink of the ruin of both; nay, *our end has come;* we are utterly undone; a fatal final period is put to all our comforts; the days of our prosperity are fulfilled; they are numbered and finished." Thus their fears concurred with the hopes of their enemies that the *Lord would no more regard them.* For, 1. The refuges they fled to disappointed them. They looked for help from this and the other powerful ally, but to no purpose; it proved vain help. The succours they expected did not come in, or at least they had not the success they expected, and their eyes failed with looking for that which never came (*v.* 17); they *watched in watching;* they watched long, and with a great deal of earnestness and impatience, *for a nation* that promised them assistance, but failed the, and frustrated their expectation. They *could not save them;* they were too weak to contend with the Chaldean army and therefore retired. Help from creatures is vain help (Ps. 60:11), and we may look for it till our eyes fail, till our hearts fail, and come short of it at last. 2. The persecutors they fled from overtook them and overcame them (*v.* 18): *They hunt our steps, that we cannot go in our streets.* When the Chaldeans besieged the city they raised their batteries so high above the walls that they could command the town, and shoot at people as they went along the streets. They *hunted them* with their arrows from place to place. When the city was broken up, and all the men of war fled, their *persecutors were swifter than the eagles of heaven* when they fly upon their prey, *v.* 19. There was no escaping them; they *pursued them upon the mountains,* and, when they thought they had got clear of them, they fell into the hands of those that *laid wait for them in the wilderness,* to cut off their retreat, and to pick up stragglers. nay, the king himself, though he may be supposed to have had all the advantages the exigence of the case would admit to favour his flight, yet could not escape, for divine vengeance pursued him with them, and then (*v.* 20), *The breath of our nostrils, the anointed of the Lord, was taken in their pits.* Some apply it to Josiah, who was killed in battle by the king of Egypt; but it is rather to be understood of Zedekiah, who was the last king of the house of David, and who was pursued by the Chaldeans and seized in the plains of Jericho, Jer. 39:5. He was *the anointed of the Lord,* heir of that family which God had appointed to the government. he was very much confided in by the Jewish state: *They said, Under his shadow we shall live among the heathen.* They promised themselves that the remnant which were left after Jeconiah's captivity should, under the protection of his government, yet again *take root downward and bear fruit upward.* They thought, though they were so reduced that they could not think of reigning over the heathen, as they had done, yet they might make a shift to live among them and not be insulted and pulled to pieces by them. Thus apt are sinking interests not only to catch at every twig, but to think it will recover them. Jerusalem died of a consumption, a flattering distemper. Even when she was ready to expire she formed some hopeful symptoms to herself, and on them grounded a hope that she should recover; but what came of it? The shadow under which they thought they should live proved like that of Jonah's gourd, which *withered in a night.* He that was *the anointed of the Lord was taken in their pits,* as if he had been but a beast of prey; so little account did they make of a person deemed sacred and not to be violated. Note, When we make any creature *the breath of our nostrils,* and promise ourselves that we shall live by it, it is just with God to stop that breath, and deprive us of the life we expected by it; for God will have the honour of being himself along *our life and the length of our days.*

Verses 21–22

David's psalms of lamentation commonly conclude with some word of comfort, which is as life from the dead and light shining out of darkness; so does this lamentation here in this chapter. The people of God are now in great distress, their aspects all doleful, their prospects all frightful, and their ill-natured neighbours the Edomites insult over them and do all they can to exasperate their destroyers against them. Such was their violence against their brother Jacob (Obad. 10), such their spleen at Jerusalem, of which they cried, *Rase it, rase it,* Ps. 137:7. Now it is here foretold, for the encouragement of God's people,

I. That an end shall be put to Zion's troubles (*v.* 22): *The punishment of they iniquity is accomplished, O daughter of Zion!* not the fulness of that punishment which it deserves, but of that which God has designed and determined to inflict, and which was necessary to answer the end, the glorifying of God's justice and the taking away of their sin. The captivity, which is *the punishment of thy iniquity, is accomplished* (Isa. 40:2), and *he will no longer keep thee in captivity;* so it may be read, as well as, *he will no more carry thee into captivity;* he will turn again thy captivity and work a glorious release for thee. Note, The troubles of God's people shall be continued no longer than till they have done their work for which they were sent.

II. That an end shall be put to Edom's triumphs. It is spoken ironically (*v.* 21): *"Rejoice and be glad, O daughter of Edom!* go on to insult over Zion in distress, till thou hast filled up the measure of thy iniquity. Do so; rejoice in thy own present exemption from the common fate of thy neighbours." This is like Solomon's upbraiding the young man with his ungoverned mirth (Eccl. 11:9): *"Rejoice, O young man! in thy youth;* rejoice, if thou canst, when God comes to reckon with thee, and that he will do ere long. *The cup* of trembling, which it is now Jerusalem's turn to drink deeply of, *shall pass through unto thee;* it shall go round till it comes to be thy lot to pledge it." Note, This is a good reason why we should not insult over any who are in misery, because we ourselves also are in the body, and we know not how soon their case may be ours. But those who please themselves in the calamities of God's church must expect to have their doom, as aiders and abettors, with those that are instrumental in those calamities. The destruction of the Edomites was foretold by this prophet (Jer. 49:7. etc.), and the people of God must encourage themselves against their present rudeness and insolence with the prospect of it. 1. It will be a shameful destruction: *"The cup* that *shall pass unto thee* shall intoxicate thee" (and that is shame enough to any man); *"thou shalt be drunken,* quite infatuated, and at thy wits' end, shalt stagger in all thy counsels and stumble in all thy enterprises, and then, as Noah when he was drunk, *thou shalt make thyself naked* and expose thyself to contempt." Note, Those who ridicule God's people will justly be left to themselves to do that, some time or other, by which they will be made ridiculous. 2. It will be a righteous destruction. God will herein *visit thy iniquity* and *discover thy sins;* he will punish them, and, to justify himself therein, he will discover them, and make it to appear that he has just cause thus to proceed against them. Nay, the punishment of the sin shall so exactly answer the sin that it shall itself plainly discover it. Sometimes God does so visit the iniquity that he that runs may read the sin in the punishment. But, sooner or later, sin will be visited and discovered, and all the hidden works of darkness brought to light.

CHAPTER 5

This chapter, though it has the same number of verses with the 1st, 2nd, and 4th, is not alphabetical, as they were, but the scope of it is the same with that of all the foregoing elegies. We have in it, I. A representation of the present calamitous state of God's people in their captivity (*v.* 1–16). II. A protestation of their concern for God's sanctuary, as that which lay nearer their heart than any secular interest of their own (*v.* 17, 18). III. A humble supplication to God and expostulation with him, for the returns of mercy (*v.* 19–22); for those that lament and do not pray sin in their lamentations. Some ancient versions call this chapter, "The Prayer of Jeremiah."

Verses 1–16

Is any afflicted? let him pray; and let him in prayer pour out his complaint to God, and make known before him his trouble. The people of God do so here; being overwhelmed with grief, they give vent to their sorrows at the footstool of the throne of grace, and so give themselves ease. They complain not of evils feared, but of evils felt: *"Remember what has come upon us, v.* 1. What was of old threatened against us, and was long in the coming, has now at length *come upon us,* and we are ready to sink under it. *Remember what is* past, *consider and behold* what is present, and *let not all the trouble* we are in *seem little to thee,* and not worth taking notice of," Neh. 9:32. Note, As it is a great comfort to us, so it ought to be a sufficient one, in our troubles, that God sees, and considers, and remembers, all that *has come upon us;* and in our prayers we need only to recommend our case to his gracious and compassionate consideration. The one word in which all their grievances are summer up is *reproach: Consider, and behold our reproach.* The troubles they were in compared with their former dignity and plenty, were a greater reproach to them than they would have been to any other people, especially considering their relation to God and dependence upon him, and his former appearances for them; and therefore this they complain of very sensibly, because, as it was a reproach, it reflected upon the name and honour of that God who had owned them for his people. *And what wilt thou do unto thy great name?*

I. They acknowledge the reproach of sin which they bear, *the reproach of their youth* (which Ephraim bemoans himself for, Jer. 31:19), of the early days of their nation. This comes in in the midst of their complaints (*v.* 7), but may well be put in the front of them: *Our fathers have sinned and are not;* they are dead and gone, but *we have borne their iniquities.* This is not here a peevish complaint, nor an imputation of unrighteousness to God, like that which we have, Jer. 31:29, Eze. 18:2. *The fathers did eat sour grapes, and the children's teeth are set on edge,* and therefore *the ways of the Lord are not equal.* But it is a penitent confession of the sins of their ancestors, which they themselves also had persisted in, for which they now justly suffered; the judgments God brought upon them were so very great that it appeared that God had in them an eye to the sins of their ancestors (because they had not been remarkably punished in this world) as well as to their own sins; and thus God was justified both in his connivance at their ancestors (he *laid up their iniquity for their children*) and in his severity with them, on whom he visited that iniquity, Mt. 23:35, 36. Thus they do here, 1. Submit themselves to the divine justice: "Lord, thou art just in all that is brought upon us, for we are a seed of evil doers, children of wrath, and heirs of the curse; we are sinful, and we have it by kind." Note, The sins which God looks back upon in punishing we must look back upon in repenting, and must take notice of all that which will help to justify God in correcting us. 2. They refer themselves to the divine pity: "Lord, *our fathers have sinned,* and we justly smart for their sins; but *they are not;* they were taken away from the evil to come; they lived not to see and share in these miseries that have *come upon us,* and we are left to *bear their iniquities.* Now, though herein God is righteous, yet it must be owned that our case is pitiable, and worthy of compassion." Note, If we be penitent and patient under what we suffer for the sins of our fathers, we may expect that he who punishes will pity, and will soon return in mercy to us.

II. They represent the reproach of trouble which they bear, in divers particulars, which tend much to their disgrace.

1. They are disseised of that good land which God gave them, and their enemies have got possession of it, *v.* 2. Canaan was their inheritance; it was theirs by promise. God gave it to them and their seed, and they held it by grant from his crown, (Ps. 136:21, 22); but now, "It is turned to strangers; those possess it who have no right to it, who are *strangers to the commonwealth of Israel and aliens from the covenants of promise;* they dwell in the houses that we built, and this is our reproach." It is the happiness of all God's spiritual Israel that the heavenly Canaan is an inheritance that they cannot be disseised of, that shall never be turned to strangers.

2. Their state and nation are brought into a condition like that of widows and orphans (*v.* 3): *"We are fatherless* (that is, helpless); we have none to protect us, to provide for us, to take any care of us. Our king, who is the father of the country, is cut off; nay, God our Father seems to have forsaken us and cast us off; *our mothers,* our cities, that were as fruitful mothers in Israel, *are* now *as widows,* are as wives whose husbands are dead, destitute of comfort, and exposed to wrong and injury, and this is our reproach; for we who made a figure are now looked on with contempt."

3. They are put hard to it to provide necessaries for themselves and their families, whereas once they lived in abundance and had plenty of every thing. Water used to be free and easily come by, but now (*v.* 4), *We have drunk our water for money,* and the saying is no longer true, *Usus communis aquarum — Water is free to all.* So hardly did their oppressors use them that they could not have a draught of fair water but they must purchase it either with money or with work. Formerly they had fuel too for the fetching; but now, *"Our wood is sold to us,* and we pay dearly for every faggot." Now were they punished for employing their children to gather wood for fire with which to *bake cakes for the queen of heaven,* Jer. 7:18. They were perfectly proscribed by their oppressors, were forbidden the use both of fire and water, according to the ancient form, *Interdico tibi aqua et igni — I forbid thee the use of water and fire.* But what must they do for bread? Truly that was as hard to come at as any thing, for (1.) Some of them sold their liberty for it (*v.* 6): *"We have given the hand to the Egyptians and to the Assyrians,* have made the best bargain we could with them, to serve them, that we might *be satisfied with bread.* We were glad to submit to the meanest employment, upon the hardest terms, to get a sorry livelihood; we have yielded ourselves to be their vassals, have parted with all to them, as the Egyptians did to Pharaoh in the years of famine, that we might have something for ourselves and families to subsist on." The neighbouring nations used to trade with Judah for wheat (Eze. 27:17), for it was a fruitful land; but now it *eats up the inhabitants,* and they are glad to make court to the Egyptians and Assyrians. (2.) Others of them ventured their lives for it (*v.* 9): *We got our bread with the peril of our lives;* when, being straitened by the siege and all provisions cut off, they either sallied or stole out of the city, to fetch in some supply, they were in danger of falling into the hands of the besiegers and being put to the sword, *the sword of the wilderness* it is called, or *of the plain* (for so the word signifies), the besiegers lying dispersed every where in the plains that were about the city. Let us take occasion hence to bless God for the plenty that we enjoy, that we get our bread so easily, scarcely with the sweat of our face, much less *with the peril of our lives;* and for the peace we enjoy, that we can go out, and enjoy not only the necessary productions, but the pleasures of the country, without any fear of *the sword of the wilderness.*

4. Those are brought into slavery who were a free people, and not only their own masters, but masters of all about them, and this is as much as any thing their reproach (*v.* 5): *Our necks are under* the grievous and intolerable yoke of *persecution* (the iron yoke which Jeremiah foretold should be laid upon them, Jer. 28:14); we are used like beasts in the yoke, that wholly serve their owners, and are at the command of their drivers. That which aggravated the servitude was, (1.) That their labours were incessant, like those of Israel in Egypt, who were daily tasked, nay, overtasked: *We labour and have no rest,* neither leave nor leisure to rest. The oxen in the yoke are unyoked at night and have rest; so they have, by a particular provision of the law, on the sabbath day; but the poor captives in Babylon, who were compelled to work for their living, *laboured and had no rest,* no night's rest, no sabbath-rest; they were quite tired out with continual toil. (2.) That their masters were insufferable (*v.* 8): *Servants have ruled over us;* and nothing is more vexatious than *a servant when he reigns,* Prov. 30:22. They were not only the great men of the Chaldeans that commanded them, but even the meanest of their servants abused them at pleasure, and insulted over them; and they must be at their beck too. The curse of Canaan had now become the doom of Judah: *A servant of servants shall he be.* They would not be ruled by their God, and by his servants the prophets, whose rule was gentle and gracious, and therefore justly are they ruled with rigour by their enemies and their servants. (3.) That they saw no probable way for the redress of their grievances: *"There is none that doth deliver us out of their hand;* not only none to rescue us out of our captivity, but none to check and restrain the insolence of the servants that abuse us and trample upon us," which one would think their masters should have done, because it was a usurpation of their authority; but, it should seem, they connived at it and encouraged it, and, as if they were not worthy of the correction of gentlemen, they are turned over to the footmen to be spurned by them. Well might they pray, *Lord, consider and behold our reproach.*

5. Those who used to be feasted are now famished (*v.* 10): *Our skin was black like an oven,* dried and parched too, *because of the terrible famine,* the *storms of famine* (so the word is); for, though famine comes gradually upon a people, yet it comes violently, and bears down all before it, and there is no resisting it; and this also is their disgrace; hence we read of *the reproach of famine,* which in captivity their received among the heathen, Eze. 36:30.

6. All sorts of people, even those whose persons and characters were most inviolable, were abused and dishonoured. (1.) The *women* were *ravished,* even *the women in Zion,* that holy mountain, *v.* 11. The committing of such abominable wickednesses there is very justly and sadly complained of. (2.) The great men were not only put to death, but put to ignominious deaths. *Princes were hanged,* as if they had been slaves, *by the hands* of the Chaldeans (*v.* 12), who took a pride in doing this barbarous execution with *their own hands.* Some think that the dead bodies of the princes, after they were slain with the sword, were hung up, as the bodies of Saul's sons, in disgrace to them, and as it were to expiate the nation's guilt. (3.) No respect was shown to magistrates and those in authority: *The faces of elders,* elders in age, elders in office, *were not*

honoured. This will be particularly remembered against the Chaldeans another day. Isa. 47:6, *Upon the ancient hast thou very heavily laid thy yoke.* (4.) The tenderness of youth was no more considered than the gravity of old age (*v.* 13): *They took the young men to grind* at the hand-mills, nay, perhaps at the horse-mills. *The young men have carried the grist* (so some), *have carried the mill,* or *mill-stones,* so others. They loaded them as if they had been beasts of burden, and so broke their backs while they were young, and made the rest of their lives the more miserable. Nay, they made *the* little *children* carry their wood home for fuel, and laid such burdens upon them that they *fell* down *under* them, so very inhuman were these cruel taskmasters!

7. An end was put to all their gladness, and their joy was quite extinguished (*v.* 14): *The young men,* who used to be disposed to mirth, have ceased *from their music,* have hung their harps upon the willow-trees. It does indeed well become old men to cease from their music; it is time to lay it by with a gracious contempt when *all the daughters of music are brought low;* but it speaks some great calamity upon a people when their young men are made to cease from it. It was so with the body of the people (*v.* 15): *The joy of their heart ceased;* they never knew what joy was since the enemy came in upon them like a flood, for ever since *deep called unto deep,* and one wave flowed in upon the neck of another, so that they were quite overwhelmed: *Our dance is turned into mourning,* instead of leaping for joy, as formerly, we sink and lie down in sorrow. This may refer especially to the joy of their solemn feasts, and the dancing used in them (Jdg. 21:21), which was not only modest, but sacred, dancing; this was *turned into mourning,* which was doubled on their festival days, in remembrance of their former pleasant things.

8. An end was put to all their glory. (1.) The public administration of justice was their glory, but that was gone: *The elders have ceased from the gate* (*v.* 14); the course of justice, which used to run down like a river, is now stopped; the courts of justice, which used to be kept with so much solemnity, are put down; for the judges are slain, or carried captive. (2.) The royal dignity was their glory, but that also was gone: *The crown has fallen from our head,* not only the *king* himself fallen into disgrace, but *the crown;* he has no successor; the regalia are all lost. Note, Earthly crowns are fading falling things; but, blessed be God, there is *a crown of glory that fades not away,* that never falls, *a kingdom that cannot be moved.* Upon this complaint, but with reference to all the foregoing complaints, they make that penitent acknowledgment, *"Woe unto us that we have sinned!* Alas for us! Our case is very deplorable, and it is all owing to ourselves; we are undone, and, which aggravates the matter, we are undone by our own hands. God is righteous, for *we have sinned."* Note, All our woes are owing to our own sin and folly. If *the crown of our head be fallen* (for so the words run), if we lose our excellency and become mean, we may thank ourselves, we have by our own iniquity profaned our crown and *laid our honour in the dust.*

Verses 17–22

Here, I. The people of God express the deep concern they had for the ruins of the temple, more than for any other of their calamities; the interests of God's house lay nearer their hearts than those of their own (*v.* 17, 18): *For this our heart is faint,* and sinks under the load of its own heaviness; *for these things our eyes are dim,* and our sight is gone, as is usual in a deliquium, or fainting fit. "It is *because of the mountain of Zion, which is desolate,* the holy mountain, and the temple built upon that mountain. For other desolations our hearts grieve and our eyes weep; but for this our hearts faint and our eyes are dim." Note, Nothing lies so heavily upon the spirits of good people as that which threatens the ruin of religion or weakens its interests; and it is a comfort if we can appeal to God that that afflicts us more than any temporal affliction to ourselves. "The people have polluted the *mountain of Zion* with their sins, and therefore God has justly made it *desolate,* to such a degree that *the foxes walk upon it* as freely and commonly as they do in the woods." It is sad indeed when the *mountain of Zion* has become *a portion for foxes* (Ps. 63:10); but sin had first made it so, Eze. 13:4.

II. They comfort themselves with the doctrine of God's eternity, and the perpetuity of his government (*v.* 19): But *thou, O Lord! remainest for ever.* This they are taught to do by that psalm which is entitled, *A prayer of the afflicted,* Ps. 102:27, 28. When all our creature-comforts are removed from us, and our hearts fail us, we may then encourage ourselves with the belief, 1. Of God's eternity: *Thou remainest for ever.* What shakes the world gives no disturbance to him who made it; whatever revolutions there are on earth there is no change in the Eternal Mind; God is still the same, and *remains for ever* infinitely wise and holy, just and good; with him there is *no variableness nor shadow of turning.* 2. Of the never-failing continuance of his dominion: *Thy throne is from generation to generation;* the throne of glory, the throne of grace, and the throne of government, are all unchangeable, immovable; and this is matter of comfort to us when *the crown has fallen from our head.* When the thrones of princes, that should be our protectors, are brought to the dust, and buried in it, God's throne continues still; he still rules the world, and rules it for the good of the church. The Lord reigns, reigns for ever, even *thy God, O Zion!*

III. They humbly expostulate with God concerning the low condition they were now in, and the frowns of heaven they were now under (*v.* 20): *"Wherefore dost thou forsake us so long time,* as if we were quite deprived of the tokens of thy presence? Wherefore dost thou defer our deliverance, as if thou hadst utterly abandoned us? Thou art the same, and, though the throne of thy sanctuary is demolished, thy throne in heaven is unshaken. But wilt thou not be the same to us?" Not as if they thought God had forgotten and forsaken them, much less feared his forgetting and forsaking them for ever; but thus they express the value they had for his favour and presence, which they thought it long that they were deprived of the evidence and comfort of. The last verse may be read as such an expostulation, and so the margin reads it: *"For wilt thou utterly reject us? Wilt thou be perpetually wroth with us,* not only not smile upon us and remember us in mercy, but frown upon us and lay us under the tokens of thy wrath, not only not draw nigh to us, but cast us out of thy presence and forbid us to draw nigh unto thee? How ill this be reconciled with thy goodness and faithfulness, and the stability of thy covenant?" We read it, *"But thou hast rejected us;* thou hast given us cause to fear that thou hast. Lord, how long shall we be in this temptation?" Note, Thou we may not quarrel with God, yet we may plead with him; and, though we may not conclude that he has cast off, yet we may (with the prophet, Jer. 12:1) humbly reason with him concerning his judgments, especially the continuance of the desolations of his sanctuary.

IV. They earnestly pray to God for mercy and grace: "Lord, do not reject *us for ever,* but *turn thou us unto thee; renew our days," v.* 21. Though these words are not put last, yet the Rabbin, because they would not have the book to conclude with those melancholy words (*v.* 22), repeat this prayer again, that the sun may not set under a cloud, and so make these the last words both in writing and reading this chapter. They here pray, 1. For converting grace to prepare and qualify them for mercy: *Turn us to thee, O Lord!* They had complained that God had forsaken and forgotten them, and then their prayer is not, *Turn thou to us,* but, *Turn us to thee,* which implies an acknowledgment that the cause of the distance was in themselves. God never leaves any till they first leave him, nor stands afar off from any longer than while they stand afar off from him; if therefore he turn them to him in a way of duty, no doubt but he will quickly return to them in a way of mercy. This agrees with that repeated prayer (Ps. 80:3, 7, 19), *Turn us again, and then cause thy face to shine. Turn us* from our idols to thyself, by a sincere repentance and reformation, *and* then *we shall be turned.* This implies a further acknowledgment of their own weakness and inability to turn themselves. There is in our nature a proneness to backslide from God, but no disposition to return to him till his grace works in us both *to will and to do.* So necessary is that grace that we may truly say, *Turn us or we shall not be turned,* but shall wander endlessly; and so powerful and effectual is that grace that we may as truly say, *Turn us, and we shall be turned;* for it is a day of power, almighty power, in which God's people are made a *willing people,* Ps. 110:3. 2. For restoring mercy: *Turn us to thee,* and then *renew our days as of old,* put us into the same happy state that our ancestors were in long ago and that they continued long in; let it be with us as it was *at the first,* and *at the beginning,* Isa. 1:26. Note, If God by his grace renew our hearts, he will be his favour *renew our days,* so that we shall *renew our youth as the eagle,* Ps. 103:5. Those that *repent, and do their first works,* shall rejoice, and recover their first comforts. God's mercies to his people have been *ever of old* (Ps. 25:6); and therefore they may hope, even then when he seems to have forsaken and forgotten them, that the mercy which was *from everlasting* will be *to everlasting.*

AN EXPOSITION, WITH PRACTICAL OBSERVATIONS, OF

THE BOOK OF THE PROPHET EZEKIEL

When we entered upon the writings of the prophets, which speak of the *things that should be hereafter,* we seemed to have the same call that St. John had (Rev. 4:1), *Come up hither;* but, when we enter upon the prophecy of this book, it is as if the voice said, *Come up higher;* as we go forward in time (for Ezekiel prophesied in the captivity, as Jeremiah prophesied just before it), so we soar upward in discoveries yet more sublime of the divine glory. These waters of the sanctuary still grow deeper; so far are they from being fordable that in some places they are scarcely fathomable; yet, deep as they are, out of them flow streams which *make glad the city of our God, the holy place of the tabernacles of the Most High.* As to this prophecy now before us, we may enquire, I. Concerning the penman of it — it was Ezekiel; his name signifies, *The strength of God,* or one *girt* or *strengthened of God.* He girded up the loins of his mind to the service, and God put strength into him. Whom God calls to any service he will himself enable for it; if he give commission, he will give power to execute it. Ezekiel's name was answered when God said (and no doubt did as he said), *I have made thy face strong against their faces.* The learned Selden, in his book *De Diis Syris,* says that it was the opinion of some of the ancients that the prophet Ezekiel was the same with that Nazaratus Assyrius whom Pythagoras (as himself relates) had for his tutor for some time, and whose lectures he attended. It is agreed that they lived much about the same time; and we have reason to think that many of the Greek philosophers were acquainted with the sacred writings and borrowed some of the best of their notions from them. If we may give credit to the tradition of the Jews, he was put to death by the captives in Babylon, for his faithfulness and boldness in reproving them; it is stated that they dragged him upon the stones till his brains were dashed out. An Arabic historian says that he was put to death and was buried in the sepulchre of Shem the son of Noah. So Hottinger relates, *Thesaur. Philol. lib. 2 cap. 1.* II. Concerning the date of it — the place whence it is dated and the time when. The scene is laid in Babylon, when it was a *house of bondage* to the *Israel of God;* there the prophecies of this book were preached, there they were written, when the prophet himself, and the people to whom he prophesied, were captives there. Ezekiel and Daniel are the only writing prophets of the Old Testament who lived and prophesied any where but in the land of Israel, except we add Jonah, who was sent to Nineveh to prophesy. Ezekiel prophesied in the beginning of the captivity, Daniel in the latter end of it. It was an indication of God's good-will to them, and his gracious designs concerning them in their affliction, that he raised up prophets among them, both to convince them when, in the beginning of their troubles, they were secure and unhumbled, which was Ezekiel's business, and to comfort them when, in the latter end of their troubles, they were dejected and discouraged. If the Lord had been pleased to kill them, he would not have used such apt and proper means to cure them. III. Concerning the matter and scope of it. 1. There is much in it that is very mysterious, dark, and hard to be understood, especially in the beginning and the latter end of it, which therefore the Jewish rabbin forbade the reading of to their young men, till they came to be thirty years of age, lest by the difficulties they met with there they should be prejudiced against the scriptures; but if we read these difficult parts of scripture with humility and reverence, and search them diligently, though we may not be able to untie all the knots we meet with, any more than we can solve all the phenomena in the book of nature, yet we may from them, as from the book of nature, gather a great deal for the confirming of our faith and the encouraging of our hope in the God we worship. 2. Though the visions here be intricate, such as an elephant may swim in, yet the sermons are mostly plain, such as a lamb may wade in; and the chief design of them is to *show God's people their transgressions,* that in their captivity they might be repenting and not repining. It should seem the prophet was constantly attended (for we read of their *sitting before him as God's people sat to hear his words,* 33:31), and that he was occasionally consulted, for we read of the elders of Israel who came to *enquire of the Lord* by him, 14:1, 3. And as it was of great use to the oppressed captives themselves to have a prophet with them, so it was a testimony to their holy religion against their oppressors who ridiculed it and them. 3. Though the reproofs and the threatenings here are very sharp and bold, yet towards the close of the book very comfortable assurances are given of great mercy God had in store for them; and there, at length, we shall meet with something that has reference to gospel times, and which was to have its accomplishment in the kingdom of the Messiah, of whom indeed this prophet speaks less than almost any of the prophets. But by opening the *terrors of the Lord* he prepares Christ's way. By the law is the knowledge of sin, and so it becomes our *school-master to bring us to Christ.* The visions which were the prophet's credentials we have *ch.* 1–3, the reproofs and threatenings *ch.* 4–24 betwixt which and the comforts which we have in the latter part of the book we have messages sent to the nations that bordered upon the land of Israel, whose destruction is foretold (*ch.* 25–35), to make way for the restoration of God's Israel and the re-establishment of their city and temple, which are foretold *ch.* 36 to the end. Those who would apply the comforts to themselves must apply the convictions to themselves.

CHAPTER 1

In this chapter we have, I. The common circumstances of the prophecy now to be delivered, the time when it was delivered (*v.* 1), the place where (*v.* 2), and the person by whom (*v.* 3). II. The uncommon introduction to it by a vision of the glory of God, 1. In his attendance and retinue in the upper world, where his throne is surrounded with angels, here called "living creatures," (*v.* 4–14). 2. In his providences concerning the lower world, represented by the wheels and their motions (*v.* 15–25). 3. In the face of Jesus Christ sitting upon the throne (*v.* 26–28). And the more we are acquainted, and the more intimately we converse, with the glory of God in these three branches of it, the more commanding influence will divine revelation have upon us and the more ready shall we be to submit to it, which is the thing aimed at in prefacing the prophecies of this book with these visions. When such a God of glory speaks, it concerns us to hear with attention and reverence; it is at our peril if we do not.

Verses 1–3

The circumstances of the vision which Ezekiel saw, and in which he received his commission and instructions, are here very particularly set down, that the narrative may appear to be authentic and not romantic. It may be of use to keep an account when and where God has been pleased to manifest himself to our souls in a peculiar manner, that the *return of the day,* and our return to *the place of the altar* (Gen. 13:4), may revive the pleasing grateful remembrance of God's favour to us. "Remember, O my soul! and never forget what communications of divine love thou didst receive at such a time, at such a place; tell others what God did for thee."

I. The time when Ezekiel had this vision is here recorded. It was *in the thirtieth year, v.* 1. Some make it the thirtieth year of the prophet's age; being a priest, he was at that age to enter upon the full execution of the priestly office, but being debarred from that by the iniquity and calamity of the times, now that they had neither temple nor altar, God at that age called him to the dignity of a prophet. Others make it to be the thirtieth year from the beginning of the reign of Nabopolassar, the father of Nebuchadnezzar, from which the Chaldeans began a new computation of time, as they had done from Nabonassar 123 years before. Nabopolassar reigned nineteen years, and this was the eleventh of his son, which makes the thirty. And it was proper enough for Ezekiel, when he was in Babylon, to use the computation they there used, as we in foreign countries date by the new style; and he afterwards uses the melancholy computation of his own country, observing (*v.* 2) that it was the fifth year of Jehoiachin's captivity. But the Chaldee paraphrase fixes upon another era, and says that this was the thirtieth year after *Hilkiah the priest found the book of the law in the house of the sanctuary, at midnight, after the setting of the moon, in the days of Josiah the king.* And it is true that this was just thirty years from that time; and that was an event so remarkable (as it put the Jewish state upon a new trial) that it was proper enough to date form it; and perhaps therefore the prophet speaks indefinitely of thirty years, as having an eye both to that event and to the Chaldean computation, which were coincident. It was in the *fourth month,* answering to our June, and in the *fifth day of the month,* that Ezekiel had this vision, *v.* 2. It is probably that it was on the sabbath day, because we read (*ch.* 3:16) that *at the end of seven days,* which we may well suppose to be the next sabbath, the word of the Lord came to him again. Thus *John was in the Spirit on the Lord's day,* when he *saw the visions of the Almighty,* Rev. 1:10. God would hereby put an honour upon his sabbaths, when *the enemies mocked at them,* Lam. 1:7. And he would thus encourage his people to keep up their attendance on the ministry of his prophets every sabbath day, by the extraordinary manifestations of himself on some sabbath days.

II. The melancholy circumstances he was in when God honoured him, and thereby favoured his people, with this vision. he was *in the land of the Chaldeans, among the captives, by the river of Chebar, and it was in the fifth year of king Jehoiachin's captivity.* Observe,

1. The people of God were now, some of them, *captives in the land of the Chaldeans.* The body of the Jewish nation yet remained in their own land, but these were the first-fruits of the captivity, and they were some of the best; for in Jeremiah's vision these were the *good figs,* whom God had *sent into the land of the Chaldeans for their good* (Jer. 24:5); and, that it might be for their good, God raised up a prophet among them, to *teach them out of the law,* then when he chastened them, Ps. 94:12. Note, It is a great mercy to have the word of God brought to us, and a great duty to attend to it diligently, when we are in affliction. The word of instruction and the rod of correction may be of great service to us, in concert and concurrence with each other, the word to explain the rod and the rod to enforce the word: both together give wisdom. It is happy for a man, when he is sick and in pain, to have a messenger with him, an interpreter, *one among a thousand,* if he have but his *ear open to discipline,* Job 23:23. One of the quarrels God had with the Jews, when he sent them into captivity, we for *mocking his messengers* and *misusing his prophets;* and yet, when they were suffering for this sin, he favoured them with this forfeited mercy. It were ill with us if God did not sometimes graciously thrust upon us those means of grace and salvation which we have foolishly thrust from us. In their captivity they were destitute of ordinary helps for their souls, and therefore God raised them up these extraordinary ones; for God's children, if they be hindered in their education one way, shall have it made up another way. But observe, *It was in the fifth year of the captivity* that Ezekiel was raised up amongst them, and not before. So long God left them without any prophet, till they began to *lament after the Lord* and to complain that they *saw not their signs* and there was none to *tell them how long* (Ps. 74:9), and then they would know how to value a prophet, and God's discoveries of himself to them by him would be the more acceptable and comfortable. The Jews that remained in their own land had Jeremiah with them, those that had gone into captivity had Ezekiel with them; for wherever the children of God are scattered abroad he will find out tutors for them.

2. The prophet was himself among the captives, those of them that were posted by *the river Chebar;* for it was *by the rivers of Babylon* that they *sat down,* and on the willow-trees by the river's side that they *hanged their harps,* Ps. 137:1, 2. The planters in America keep along by the sides of the rivers, and perhaps those captives were employed by their masters in improving some parts of the country by the rivers' sides that were uncultivated, the natives being generally employed in war; or they employed them in manufactures, and therefore chose to fix them by the sides of rivers, that the good they made might the more easily be conveyed by water-carriage. Interpreters agree not what river this of Chebar was, but *among the captives* by that river Ezekiel was, and himself a captive. Observe here, (1.) The best men, and those that are dearest to God, often share, not only in the common calamities of this life, but in the public and national judgments that are inflicted for sin; those feel the smart who contributed nothing to the guilt, by which it appears that the difference between good and bad arises not from the events that befal them, but from the temper and disposition of their spirits under them. And since not only righteous men, but prophets, share with the worst in present punishments, we may infer thence, with the greatest assurance, that there are rewards reserved for them in the future state. (2.) Words of conviction, counsel, and comfort, come best to those who are in affliction from their fellow sufferers. The captives will be best instructed by one who is a captive among them and experimentally knows their sorrows. (3.) The spirit of prophecy was not confined to the land of Israel, but some of the brightest of divine revelations were revealed *in the land of the Chaldeans,* which was a happy presage of the carrying of the church, with that divine revelation upon which it is built, into the Gentile world; and, as now, so afterwards, when the gospel kingdom was to be set up, the dispersion of the Jews contributed to the spreading of the knowledge of God. (4.) Wherever we are we may keep up our communion with God. *Undique ad coelos tantundem est viae — From the remotest corners of the earth we may find a way open heavenward.* (5.) When God's ministers are bound *the word of the Lord is not bound,* 2 Tim. 2:9. When St. Paul was a prisoner the gospel had a free course. When St. John was banished into the Isle of Patmos Christ visited him there. Nay, God's suffering servants have generally been treated as favourites, and their consolations have much more abounded when affliction has abounded, 2 Co. 1:5.

III. The discovery which God was pleased to make of himself to the prophet when he was in these circumstances, to be by him communicated to his people. He here tells us what he saw, what he heard, and what he felt. 1. He *saw visions of God, v.* 1. No man can *see God and live;* but many have seen visions of God, such displays of the divine glory as have both instructed and affected them; and commonly, when God first revealed himself to any prophet, he did it by an extraordinary vision, as to Isaiah (*ch.* 6), to Jeremiah (*ch.* 1), to Abraham (Acts 7:2), to settle a correspondence and a satisfactory way of intercourse, so that there needed not afterwards a vision upon ever revelation. Ezekiel was employed in turning the hearts of the people to the Lord their God, and therefore he must himself see the visions of God. Note, It concerns those to be well acquainted with God themselves, and much affected with what they know of him, whose business it is to bring others to the knowledge and love of him. That he might see the *visions of God the heavens were opened;* the darkness and distance which hindered his visions were conquered, and he was let into the light of the glories of the upper world, as near and clear as if heaven had been opened to him. 2. He heard the voice of God (*v.* 3): *The word of the Lord came expressly* to him, and what he saw was designed to prepare him for what he was to hear. The expression is emphatic. *Essendo fuit verbum Dei — The word of the Lord was a really it was to him.* There was no mistake in it; it came to him in the fulness of its light and power, in the evidence and demonstration of the Spirit; it came close to him, nay, it came into him, took possession of him and dwelt in him richly. It *came expressly,* or accurately, to him; he did himself clearly understand what he said and was abundantly satisfied f the truth of it. *The essential Word* (so we may take it), *the Word who is, who is what he is, came to Ezekiel,* to send him on his errand. 3. He felt the power of God opening his eyes to see the visions, opening his ear to hear the voice, and opening his heart to receive both: *The hand of the Lord was there upon him.* Note, *The hand of the Lord* goes along with *the word f the Lord,* and so it becomes effectual; those only understand and *believe the report to whom the arm of the Lord is revealed. The hand of God was upon him,* as upon Moses, to cover him, that he should not be overcome by the dazzling light and lustre of the visions he saw, Ex. 33:22. It *was upon him* (as upon St. John, Rev. 1:17), to revive and support him, that he might bear up, and not faint, under these discoveries, that he might neither be lifted up nor cast down with the abundance of the revelations. God's *grace is sufficient for him,* and, in token of that, his *hand is upon him.*

Verses 4–14

The visions of God which Ezekiel here saw were very glorious, and had more particulars than those which other prophets saw. It is the scope and intention of these vision, 1. To possess the prophet's mind with very great, and high, and honourable thoughts of that God by whom he was commissioned and for whom he was employed. It is *the likeness of the glory of the Lord* that he sees (*v.* 28), and hence he may infer that it is his honour to serve him, for he is one whom angels serve. He may serve him with safety, for he has power sufficient to bear him out in his work. It is at his peril to draw back from his service, for he has power to pursue him, as he did Jonah. So great a God as this must be served *with reverence and godly fear;* and with assurance may Ezekiel foretel what this God will do, for he is able to make his words good. 2. To strike a terror upon the sinners who remained in Zion, and those who had already come to Babylon, who were secure, and bade defiance to the threatenings of Jerusalem's ruin, as we have found in Jeremiah's prophecy, and shall find in this, many did. "Let those who said, *We shall have peace though we go on,* know that *our God is a consuming fire,* whom they cannot stand before." That this vision had a reference to the destruction of Jerusalem seems plain from *ch.* 43:3, where he says that it was *the vision which he saw when he came to destroy the city,* that is, to prophesy the destruction of it. 3. To speak comfort to those that feared God, and trembled at his word, and humbled themselves under his mighty hand. "Let them know that, though they are captives in Babylon, yet they have God nigh unto them; though they have not *the place of the sanctuary* to be their glorious high throne, they have the God of the sanctuary." Dr. Lightfoot observes, "Now that the church is to be planted for a long time in another country, the Lord shows a glory in the midst of them, as he had done at their first constituting into a church in the wilderness; and out of *a cloud and fire,* as he had done there, he showed himself; and from between *living creatures,* as from between the cherubim, he gives his oracles." This put an honour upon them, by which they might value themselves when the Chaldeans insulted over them, and this might encourage their hopes of deliverance in due time.

Now, to answer these ends, we have in these verses the first part of the vision, which represents God as attended and served by an innumerable company of angels, who are all his messengers, his ministers, *doing his commandments* and *hearkening to the voice of his word.* This denotes his grandeur, as it magnifies an earthly prince to have a splendid retinue and numerous armies at his command, which engages his allies to trust him and his enemies to fear him.

I. The introduction to this vision of the angels is very magnificent and awakening, *v.* 4. The prophet, observing the heavens to open, *looked,* looked up (as it was time), to see what discoveries God would make to him. Note, When the heavens are opened it concerns us to have our eyes open. To clear the way, *behold, a whirlwind came out*

of the north, which would drive away the interposing mists of this lower region. Fair weather *comes out of the north,* and thence *the wind* comes that *drives away rain.* God can by a whirlwind clear the sky and air, and produce that serenity of mind which is necessary to our communion with Heaven. Yet this whirlwind was attended with *a great cloud.* When we think that the clouds which arise from this earth are dispelled and we can see beyond them, yet still there is a cloud which heavenly things are wrapped in, a cloud from above, so that *we cannot order our speech* concerning them *by reason of darkness.* Christ here descended, as he ascended, *in a cloud.* Some by this *whirlwind and cloud* understand the Chaldean army coming *out of the north* against the land of Judah, bearing down all before them as a tempest; and so it agrees with that which was signified by one of the first of Jeremiah's visions (Jer. 1:14, *Out of the north an evil shall break forth*); but I take it here as an introduction rather to the vision than to the sermons. This whirlwind came to Ezekiel (as that to Elijah, 1 Ki. 19:11), to *prepare the way of the Lord,* and to demand attention. *He* that has eyes, *that has ears,* let him see, *let him hear.*

II. The vision itself. *A great cloud* was the vehicle of this vision, in which it was conveyed to the prophet; for God's pavilion in which he rests, his chariot in which he rides, is *darkness and thick clouds,* Ps. 18:11; 104:3. Thus he *holds back the face of his throne,* lest its dazzling light and lustre should overpower us, by *spreading a cloud upon it.* Now,

1. The cloud is accompanied with *a fire,* as upon Mount Sinai, where God resided in a *thick cloud;* but *the sight of his glory was like a devouring fire* (Ex. 24:16, 17), and his first appearance to Moses was *in a flame of fire in the bush;* for *our God is a consuming fire.* This was *a fire enfolding itself,* a globe, or orb, or wheel of fire. God being his own cause, his own rule, and his own end, if he be as *a fire,* he is as *a fire enfolding itself,* or (as some read it) *kindled by itself.* The fire of God's glory shines forth, but it quickly enfolds itself; for he lets us know but part of his ways; the fire of God's wrath breaks forth, but it also quickly enfolds itself, for the divine patience suffers not all his wrath to be stirred up. If it were not a fire thus enfolding itself, *O Lord! who shall stand?*

2. The fire is surrounded with a glory: *A brightness was about it,* in which it enfolded itself, yet it made some discovery of itself. Though we cannot see into the fire, cannot by searching find out God to perfection, yet we see the brightness that is round about it, the reflection of this fire from the thick cloud. Moses might see God's back parts, but not his face. We have some light concerning the nature of God, from the brightness which encompasses it, though we have not an insight into it, by reason of the cloud spread upon it. Nothing is more easy than to determine that God is, nothing more difficult than to describe what he is. When God displays his wrath as fire, yet there is a brightness about it; for his holiness and justice appear very illustrious in the punishment of sin and sinners: even about the devouring fire there is a brightness, which glorified saints will for ever admire.

3. Out of this fire there shines *the colour of amber.* We are not told who or what it was that had this colour of amber, and therefore I take it to be the whole frame of the following vision, which came into Ezekiel's view *out of the midst of the fire and brightness;* and the first thing he took notice of before he viewed the particulars was that it was *of the colour of amber,* or *the eye of amber;* that is, it looked as amber does to the eye, of a bright flaming fiery colour, the colour of *a burning coal;* so some think it should be read. The *living creatures* which he saw coming *out of the midst of the fire* were *seraphim — burners;* for *he maketh his angels spirits, his ministers a flaming fire.*

4. That which comes out of the fire, of a fiery amber colour, when it comes to be distinctly viewed, is *the likeness of four living creatures;* not the *living creatures* themselves (angels are spirits, and cannot be seen), but *the likeness* of them, such a hieroglyphic, or representation, as God saw fit to make use of for the leading of the prophet, and us with him, into some acquaintance with the world of angels (a matter purely of divine revelation), so far as is requisite to possess us with an awful sense of the greatness of that God who has angels for his attendants, and the goodness of that God who has appointed them to be

attendants on his people. *The likeness of these living creatures came out of the midst of the fire;* for angels derive their being and power from God; they are in themselves, and to us, what he is pleased to make them; their glory is a ray of his. The prophet himself explains this vision (*ch.* 10:20): *I knew that the living creatures were the cherubim,* which is one of the names by which the angels are known in scripture. To Daniel was made known their number, *ten thousand times ten thousand,* Dan. 7:10. But, though they are many, yet they are one, and that is made known to Ezekiel here; they are one in nature and operation, as an army, consisting of thousands, is yet called a body of men. We have here an account of,

(1.) Their nature. They are living creatures; they are the creatures of God, the work of his hands; their being is derived; they have not life in and of themselves, but receive it from him who is *the fountain of life.* As much as the living creatures of this lower world excel the vegetables that are the ornaments of earth, so much do the angels, the living creatures of the upper world, excel the sun, moon, and stars, the ornaments of the heavens. The sun (say some) is a flame of *fire enfolding itself,* but it is not a living creature, as angels, those flames of fire, are. Angels are living creatures, living beings, emphatically so. Men on earth are dying creatures, dying daily *(in the midst of life we are in death),* but angels in heaven are living creatures; they live indeed, live to good purpose; and, when saints come to be *equal unto the angels,* they shall not *die any more,* Lu. 20:36.

(2.) Their number. They are four; so they appear here, though they are innumerable; not as if these were four particular angels set up above the rest, as some have fondly imagined, Michael and Gabriel, Raphael and Uriel, but for the sake of the four faces they put on, and to intimate their being sent forth towards *the four winds of heaven,* Mt. 24:31. Zechariah saw them as four chariots going forth east, west, north, and south, Zec. 6:1. God has messengers to send every way; for his kingdom is universal, and reaches to all parts of the world.

(3.) Their qualifications, by which they are fitted for the service of their Maker and Master. These are set forth figuratively and by similitude, as is proper in visions, which are parables to the eye. Their description here is such, and so expressed, that I think it is not possible by it to form an exact idea of them in our fancies, or with the pencil, for that would be a temptation to worship them; but the several instances of their fitness for the work they are employed in are intended in the several parts of this description. Note, It is the greatest honour of God's creatures to be in a capacity of answering the end of their creation; and the more ready we are to every good work the nearer we approach to the dignity of angels. These living creatures are described here, [1.] By their general appearance: *They had the likeness of a man;* they appeared, for the main, in a human shape, *First,* To signify that these living creatures are reasonable creatures, intelligent beings, who have the *spirit of a man* which is the *candle of the Lord. Secondly,* To put an honour upon the nature of man, who is made lower, yet but *a little lower, than the angels,* in the very next rank of beings below them. When the invisible intelligences of the upper world would make themselves visible, it is in *the likeness of man. Thirdly,* To intimate that their *delights are with the sons of men,* as their Master's are (Prov. 8:31), that they do service to men, and men may have spiritual communion with them by faith, hope, and holy love. *Fourthly,* The angels of God appear in *the likeness of man* because in the *fulness of time* the Son of God was not only to appear in that likeness, but to assume that nature; they therefore show this love to it. [2.] By their faces: *Every one had four faces,* looking four several ways. In St. John's vision, which has a near affinity with this, each of the four living creatures has one of these faces here mentioned (Rev. 4:7); here each of them has all four, to intimate that they have all the same qualifications for service; though, perhaps, among the angels of heaven, as among the angels of the churches, some excel in one gift and others in another, but all for the common service. Let us contemplate their faces till we be in some measure changed into the same image, that we may do the will of God as the angels do it in heaven. They *all four had the face of a man* (for in that likeness they appeared, *v.* 5), but, besides that, they had *the face of a lion, an ox, and an eagle,* each masterly in its kind, *the lion* among *wild* beasts, *the ox* among *tame* ones, and *the eagle* among fowls, *v.* 10. Does God make use of them for the executing of judgments upon his enemies? They are fierce and strong as the lion and the eagle in tearing their prey. Does he make use of them for the good of his people? They are as *oxen strong for labour* and inclined to serve. And in both they have *the understanding of a man.* The scattered perfections of the living creatures on earth meet in the angels of heaven. They have *the likeness of man;* but, because there are some things in which man is excelled even by the inferior creatures, they are therefore compared to some of them. They have *the understanding of a man,* and such as far exceeds it; they also resemble man in tenderness and humanity. But, *First, A lion* excels man in strength and boldness, and is much more formidable; therefore the angels, who in this resemble them, put on the *face of a lion. Secondly, An ox* excels man in diligence, and patience, and painstaking, and an unwearied discharge of the work he has to do; therefore the angels, who are constantly employed in the service of God and the church, put on *the face of an ox. Thirdly, An eagle* excels man in quickness and piercingness of sight, and in soaring high; and therefore the angels, who seek things above, and see far into divine mysteries, put on *the face of a flying eagle.* [3.] By their wings: *Every one had four wings, v.* 6. In the vision Isaiah had of them they appeared with six, now with four; for they appeared above the throne, and had occasion for two to cover their faces with. The angels are fitted with wings to fly swiftly on God's errands; whatever business God sends them upon they lose no time. Faith and hope are the soul's wings, upon which it soars upward; pious and devout affections are its wings on which it is carried forward with vigour and alacrity. The prophet observes here, concerning their wings, *First,* That they were *joined one to another, v.* 9 and again *v.* 11. They did not make use of their wings for fighting, as some birds do; there is no contest among the angels. God makes *peace,* perfect peace, *in his high places.* But their wings were joined, in token of their perfect unity and unanimity and the universal agreement there is among them. *Secondly,* That *they were stretched upward,* extended, and ready for use, not folded up, or flagging. Let an angel receive the least intimation of the divine will, and he has nothing to seek, but is upon the wings immediately; while our poor dull souls are like the ostrich, that with much difficulty lifts up herself on high. *Thirdly,* That two of their wings were made use of in covering their bodies, the spiritual bodies they assumed. The clothes that cover us are our hindrance in work; angels need no other covering than their own wings, which are their furtherance. They cover their bodies from us, so forbidding us needless enquiries concerning them. Ask not after them, for they are wonderful, Jdg. 13:18. They cover them before God, so directing us, when we approach to God, to see to it that we be so clothed with Christ's righteousness *that the shame of our nakedness may not appear.* [4.] By their feet, including their legs and thighs: They were *straight feet* (*v.* 7); they stood straight, and firm, and steady; no burden of service could make their legs to bend under them. The spouse makes this part of the description of her beloved, that *his legs* were *as pillars of marble set upon sockets of fine gold* (Cant. 5:15); such are the angels' legs. *The sole of their feet was like* that *of a calf's foot,* which divides the hoof and is therefore clean: *as it were the sole of a round foot* (as the Chaldee words it); they were ready for motion any way. *Their feet were winged* (so the Septuagint); they went so swiftly that it was as if they flew. And their very feet *sparkled like the colour of burnished brass;* not only the faces, but the very feet, of those are beautiful whom God sends on his errands (Isa. 52:7); every step the angels take is glorious. In the vision John had of Christ it is said, *His feet were like unto fine brass, as if they burned in a furnace,* Rev. 1:15. [5.] By their hands (*v.* 8): *They had the hands of a man under their wings on their four sides,* an arm and a hand under every wing. They had not only wings for motion, but hands for action. Many are quick who are not active; they hurry about a great deal, but do nothing to purpose, bring nothing to pass; they have wings, but no hands: whereas God's servants, the angels, not only go when he sends them and come when he calls them, but do what he bids them. They are *the hands of a man,* which are wonderfully made and fitted for service, which are guided by reason and understanding; for what angels do they do intelligently and with judgment. They have calves' feet; this denotes the swiftness of their motion (the cedars of Lebanon are said to *skip like a calf,* Ps. 29:6); but they have a man's hand, which denotes the niceness and exactness of their performances, as the heavens are said to be the work of God's fingers. Their hands were *under their wings,* which concealed them, as they did the rest of their bodies. Note, The agency of angels is a secret thing and their work is carried on in an invisible way. In working for God, though we must not, with *the sluggard, hide our hand in our bosom,* yet we must, with the humble, *not let our left hand know what our right hand doeth.* We may observe that where these wings were their hands were *under their wings;* wherever their wings carried them they carried hands along with them, to be still doing something suitable something that the duty of the place requires.

(4.) Their motions. The living creatures are moving. Angels are active beings; it is not their happiness to sit still and do nothing, but to be always well employed; and we must reckon ourselves then best when we are doing good, doing it as the angels do it, or whom it is here observed, [1.] That whatever service they went about *they went every one straight forward* (*v.* 9, 12), which intimates, *First,* That they sincerely aimed at the glory of God, and had a single eye to that, in all they did. Their going *straight forward* supposes that they looked straight forward, and never had any sinister intentions in what they did. And, if thus *our eye be single,* our *whole body will be full of light.* The singleness of the eye is the sincerity of the heart. *Secondly,* That they were intent upon the service they were employed in, and did it with a close application of mind. They went forward with their work; for what their hand found to do they did *with all their might* and did not loiter in it. *Thirdly,* That they were unanimous in it: *They went straight forward,* every one about his own work; they did not thwart or jostle one another, did not stand in one another's light, in one another's way. *Fourthly,* That they perfectly understood their business, and were thoroughly apprised of it, so that they needed not to stand still, to pause of hesitate, but pursue their work with readiness, as those that knew what they had to do and how to do it. *Fifthly,* They were steady and constant in their work. They did not fluctuate, did not tire, did not vary, but were of a piece with themselves. They moved in a direct line, and so went the nearest way to work in all they did and lost no time. When we go straight we go forward; when we serve God with one heart we rid ground, we rid work. [2.] *They turned not when they went, v.* 9, 12. *First,* They made no blunders or mistakes, which would give them occasion to turn back to rectify them; their work needed no correction, and therefore needed not to be gone over again. *Secondly,* They minded no diversions; as they turned not back, so they turned not aside, to trifle with any thing that was foreign to their business. [3.] *They went whither the Spirit was to go* (*v.* 12), either, *First, Whither* their own *spirit was* disposed *to go;* thither *they went,* having no bodies, as we have, to clog or hinder them. It is our infelicity and daily burden that, when *the spirit if willing,* yet *the flesh is weak* and cannot keep pace with it, so that *the good which we would do we do it not;* but angels and glorified saints labour under no such impotency; whatever they incline or intend to do they do it, and never come short of it. Or, rather, *Secondly,* Whithersoever *the Spirit* of God would have them *go,* thither *they went.* Though they had so much wisdom of their own, yet in all their motions and actions they subjected themselves to the guidance and government of the divine will. Whithersoever the divine Providence *was to go they went,* to serve its purposes and to execute its orders. The Spirit of God (says Mr. Greenhill) is the great agent that sets angels to work, and it is their honour that they are led, they are easily *led, by the Spirit.* See how tractable and obsequious these noble creatures are. Whithersoever *the Spirit* is *to go* they go immediately, with all possible alacrity. Note, Those that *walk after the Spirit* do the will of God as the angels do it. [4.] They *ran and returned like a flash of lightning, v.* 14. This intimates, *First,* That they made haste; they were quick in their motions, as quick as lightning. Whatever business they went about they despatched it immediately, in a moment, in the twinkling of an eye. Happy they that have no bodies to retard their motion in holy exercises. And happy shall we be when we come to have spiritual bodies for spiritual work. Satan *falls like lightning* into his own ruin, Lu. 10:18. Angels fly *like lightning* in their Master's work. The angel Gabriel flew swiftly. *Secondly,* That they made haste back: They *ran and returned;* ran to do their work and execute their orders, and then returned to give an account of what they had done and receive new instructions, that they might be always doing. They *ran* into the lower world, to do what was to be done there; but, when they had done it, they *returned like flash of lightning* to the upper world again, to the beatific vision of their God, which they could not with any patience be longer from than their service did require. Thus we should be in the affairs of this world as out of our element. Though we run into them, we must not repose in them, but our souls must quickly return like lightning to God their rest and centre.

5. We have an account of the light by which the prophet saw these living creatures, or the looking-glass in which he saw them, *v.* 13. (1.) He saw them by their own light, for *their appearance was like burning coals of fire;* they are *seraphim — burners,* denoting the ardour of their love to God, their fervent zeal in his service, their splendour and brightness, and their terror against God's enemies. When God employs them to fight his battles they are as *coals of fire* (Ps. 18:12) to *devour the adversaries,* as lightnings shot out to discomfit them. (2.) He saw them by the light of some *lamps,* which *went up and down among* them, the shining whereof *was* very *bright.* Satan's works are works of darkness; he is *the ruler of the darkness of this world.* But the angels of light are in the light, and, though they conceal their working, they show their work, for it will bear the light. But we see them and their works only by candle-light, but the dim light *of lamps* that go *up and down among* them; when *the day breaks, and the shadows flee away,* we shall see them clearly. Some make the *appearance* of these *burning coals,* and of the *lightning* that issues *out of the fire,* to signify the wrath of God, and his judgments, that were now to be executed upon Judah and Jerusalem for their sins, in which angels were to be employed; and accordingly we find afterwards *coals of fire scattered upon the city* to consume it, which were *fetched from between the cherubim, ch.* 10:2. But by *the appearance of the lamps* then we may understand the light of comfort which shone forth to the people of God in the darkness of this present trouble. If the ministry of the angels is as a consuming fire to God's enemies, it is as a rejoicing light to his own children. To the one this *fire* is *bright,* it is very reviving and refreshing; to the other, *out of the fire* comes fresh *lightning* to destroy them. Note, Good angels are our friends, or enemies, according as God is.

Verses 15–25

The prophet is very exact in making and recording his observations concerning this vision. And here we have,

I. The notice he took of the *wheels, v.* 15–21. The glory of God appears not only in the splendour of his retinue in the upper world, but in the steadiness of his government here in this lower world. Having seen how God does according to his will in the armies of heaven, let us now see how he does according to it among the inhabitants of the earth; for there, *on the earth,* the prophet saw the *wheels, v.* 15. *As he beheld the living creatures,* and was contemplating the glory of that vision and receiving instruction from it, this other vision presented itself to his view. Note, Those who make a good use of the discoveries God has favoured them with may expect further discoveries; for *to him that hath shall be given.* We are sometimes tempted to think there is nothing glorious but what is in the upper world, whereas, could we with an eye of faith discern the beauty of Providence and the wisdom, power, and goodness, which shine in the administration of that kingdom, we should see, and say, *Verily he is a God that judgeth in the earth* and acts like himself. There are many things in this vision which give us some light concerning the divine Providence. 1. The dispensations of Providence are compared to *wheels,* either the wheels of a chariot, in which the conqueror rides in triumph, or rather the wheels of a clock or watch, which all contribute to the regular motion of the machine. We read of *the course* or *wheel of nature* (James 3:6), which is here set before us as under the direction of the God of nature. *Wheels,* though they move not of themselves, as *the living creatures* do, are yet made movable and are almost continually kept in action. Providence, represented by these *wheels,* produces changes; sometimes one spoke of the wheel is uppermost and sometimes another; but the motion of the wheel on its own axletree, like that of the orbs above, is very regular and steady. The motion of the wheels is circular; by the revolutions of Providence things are brought to the same posture and pass which they were in formerly; for *the thing that is is that which has been, and there is no new thing under the sun,* Eccl. 1:9, 10. 2. The wheel is said to be *by the living creatures,* who attended it to direct its motion; for the angels are employed as the ministers of God's providence, and have a greater hand in directing the motions of second causes to serve the divine purpose than we think they have. Such a close connexion is there between *the living creatures* and the *wheels* that they moved and rested together. Were angels busily employed? Men were busily employed as instruments in their hand, whether of mercy or judgment, though they themselves were not aware of it. Or, Are men active to compass their designs? Angels at the same time are acting to control and overrule them. This is much insisted on here (*v.* 19): *When the living creatures went,* to bring about any business, *the wheels went by them;* when God has work to do by the ministry of angels second causes are all found, or made, ready to concur in it; and (*v.* 21) *when those stood these stood;* when the angels had done their work the second causes had done theirs. If *the living creatures were lifted up from the earth,* were elevated to any service above the common course of nature and out of the ordinary road (as suppose in the working of miracles, the dividing of the water, the standing still of the sun), *the wheels,* contrary to their own natural tendency, which is towards the earth, move in concert with them, and *are lifted up over against them;* this is thrice mentioned, *v.* 19–21. Note, All inferior creatures are, and move, and act, as the Creator, by the ministration of angels, directs and influences them. Visible effects are managed and governed by invisible causes. The reason given of this is because *the spirit of the living creatures was in the wheels;* the same wisdom, power, and holiness of God, the same will and counsel of his, that guides and governs the angels and all their performances, does, by them, order and dispose of all the motions of the creatures in this lower world and the events and issues of them. God is the soul of the world, and animates the whole, both that above and that beneath, so that they move in perfect harmony, as the upper and lower parts of the natural body do, so that *whithersoever the Spirit is to go* (whatever God wills and purposes to be done and brought to pass) *thither their spirit is to go;* that is, the angels, knowingly and designedly, set themselves to bring it about. And *their spirit is in the wheels,* which are therefore *lifted up over against them;* that is, both the powers of nature and the wills of men are all made to serve the intention, which they infallibly and irresistibly effect, though perhaps *they mean not so, neither doth their heart think so,* Isa. 10:7; Mic. 4:11, 12. Thus, though the will of God's precept be not *done on earth as it is done in heaven,* yet the will of his purpose and counsel is, and shall be. 3. The wheel is said to have four *faces,* looking four several ways (*v.* 15), denoting that the providence of God exerts itself in all parts of the world, east, west, north, and south, and extends itself to the remotest corners of it. Look which way you will upon the wheel of Providence, and it has a face towards you, a beautiful one, which you may admire the features and complexion of; it looks upon you as ready to speak to you, if you be but ready to hear the voice of it; like a well-drawn picture, it has an eye upon all that have an eye upon it. The wheel had so four *faces* that it had in it four *wheels,* which *went upon their four sides, v.* 17. At first Ezekiel saw it as *one wheel* (*v.* 15), one sphere; but afterwards he saw it was four, but *they* four *had one likeness* (*v.* 16); not only they were like one another, but they were as if they had been one. This intimates, (1.) That one event of providence is like another; what happens to us is *that which is common to men* and what we are not to think strange. (2.) That various events have a tendency to the same issue and concur to answer the same intention. 4. *Their appearance and their work* are said to be *like the colour of a beryl* (*v.* 16), *the colour of Tarshish* (so the word is), that is, of the sea; the beryl is of that colour, sea-green; *blue Neptune* we call it. The nature of things in this world is like that of the sea, which is in a continual flux and yet there is a constant coherence and succession of its parts. There is a chain of events which is always drawing one way or other. The sea ebbs and flows, so does Providence in its disposals, but always in the stated appointed times and measures. The sea looks blue, as the air does, because of the shortness and feebleness of our sight, which can see but a little way of either; to that colour therefore are *the appearance and work* of Providence fitly compared, because we cannot find out that which God does *from the beginning to the end,* Eccl. 3:11. We see but *parts of his ways* (Job 26:14), and all beyond looks blue, which gives us to understand no more concerning it but that in truth we know it not; it is *far above out of our sight.* 5. *Their appearance and their work* are likewise said to be *as it were a wheel in the middle of a wheel.* Observe here again, Their *appearance* to the prophet is designed to set forth what *their work* really is. Men's appearance and their work often differ, but the appearance of God's providence and its work agree; if they seem to differ, it is through our ignorance and mistake. Now both *were as a wheel in a wheel,* a less wheel moved by a greater. We pretend not to give a mathematical description of it. The meaning is that the disposals of Providence seem to us intricate, perplexed, and unaccountable, and yet that they will appear in the issue to have been all wisely ordered for the best; so that though *what God does we know not now,* yet *we shall know hereafter,* Jn. 13:7. 6. The motion of these wheels, like that of the living creatures, was steady, regular, and constant: *They returned not when they went* (*v.* 17), because they never went amiss, nor otherwise than they should do. God, in his providence, takes his work before him, and he will have it forward; and it is going on even when it seems to us to be going backward. *They went* as the Spirit directed them, and therefore *returned not.* We should not have occasion to return back as we have, and to undo that by repentance which we have done amiss, and to do it over again, if we were but *led by the Spirit* and followed his direction. *The Spirit of life* (so some read it) *was in the wheels,* which carried them on with ease and evenness, and then *they returned not when they went.* 7. The *rings,* or rims, *of the wheels were so high that they were dreadful, v.* 18. They were of a vast circumference, so that when they were reared, and put in motion, the prophet was even afraid to look upon them. Note, The vast compass of God's thought, and the vast reach of his design, are really astonishing; when we go about to describe the circle of Providence we are struck with amazement and are even swallowed up. O the height and depth of God's councils! The consideration of them should strike an awe upon us. 8. They were *full of eyes round about.* This circumstance of the vision is most surprising of all, and yet most significant, plainly denoting that the motions of Providence are all directed by infinite wisdom. The issues of things are not determined by a blind fortune, but by those *eyes of the Lord* which *run to and fro through the earth,* and *are in every place, beholding the evil and the good.* Note, It is a great satisfaction to us, and ought to be so, that, though we cannot account for the springs and tendencies of events, yet they are all under the cognizance and direction of an all-wise all-seeing God.

II. The notice he took of *the firmament* above *over the heads of the living creatures.* When he saw *the living creatures* moving, and *the wheels by* them, he looked up, as it is proper for us to do when we observe the various motions of providence in this lower world; looking up, he saw *the firmament stretched forth over the heads of the living creatures, v.* 22. What is done on earth is done under the heaven (as the scripture often speaks), under its inspection and influence. Observe, 1. What he saw: *The firmament was as the colour of the terrible crystal,* truly glorious, but terribly so; the vastness and brightness of it put the prophet into an amazement and struck him with an awful reverence. *The terrible ice,* or *frost* (so it may be read), the colour of snow congealed, or as mountains of ice in the northern seas, which are very frightful. Daring sinners ask, *Can God judge through the dark cloud?* Job 22:13. But that which we take to be a dark cloud is to him transparent as crystal, through which, *from the place of his habitation, he looks upon all the inhabitants of the earth,* Ps. 33:14. *Under the firmament* he saw *the wings of the living creatures* erect, *v.* 23. When they pleased they used them either for flight or for covering. God is on high, *above the firmament;* the angels are *under the firmament,* which denotes their subjection to God's dominion and their readiness to fly on his errands *in the open firmament of heaven,* and to serve him unanimously. 2. What he heard. (1.) He heard the *noise of the angels' wings, v.* 24. Bees and other insects make a great noise with the vibration of their wings; here the angels do so, to awaken the attention of the prophet to that which God was about to say to him from *the firmament, v.* 25. Angels, by the providences they are employed in, sound God's alarms to the children of men and stir them up to *hear his voice;* for that is it that *cries in the city* and is heard and understood by *the men of wisdom. The noise of their wings* was loud and terrible, *as the noise of great waters* (like the rout or roaring of the sea), and *as the noise of a host,* the noise of war; but it was articulate and intelligible, and did not *give an uncertain sound;* for it was *the voice of speech;* nay, it was *as the voice of the Almighty,* for *God,* by his providences, *speaks once, yea, twice,* if we could by *perceive it,* Job 33:14. The *Lord's voice cries,* Mic. 6:9. (2.) He heard a *voice from the firmament,* from him that sits upon the throne there, *v.* 25. When the angels moved they *made a noise with their wings;* but, when with that they had roused a careless world, they stood still, and *let down their wings,* that there might be a profound silence, and so God's voice might be the better heard. The voice of Providence is designed to open men's ears to the voice of the word, to do the office of the crier, who with a loud voice charges silence while the judge passes sentence. *He that has ears to hear, let him hear.* Note, Noises on earth should awaken our attention to the *voice from the firmament;* for *how shall we escape if we turn away from him that speaks from heaven!*

Verses 26–28

All the other parts of this vision were but a preface and introduction to this. God in them had made himself known as Lord of angels and supreme director of all the affairs of this lower world, whence it is easy to infer that whatever God by his prophets either promises or threatens to do he is able to effect it. Angels are his servants; men are his tools. But now that a divine revelation is to be given to a prophet, and by him to the church, we must look higher than the living creatures or the wheels, and must expect that from the eternal Word, of whom we have an account in these verses. Ezekiel, hearing a voice from the firmament, looked up, as John did, to *see the voice that spoke with him,* and he *saw one like unto the Son of man,* Rev. 1:12, 13. The second person sometimes tried the *fashion of a man* occasionally before he clothed himself with it for good and all; and the Spirit of prophecy is called the *Spirit of Christ* (1 Pt. 1:11) and the *testimony of Jesus,* Rev. 19:10. 1. This glory of Christ that the prophet saw *was above the firmament* that was *over the heads* of the living creatures, *v.* 26. Note, The heads of angels themselves are under the feet of the Lord Jesus; for the firmament that is over their heads is under his feet. *Angels, principalities, and powers are made subject to him,* 1 Pt. 3:22. This dignity and dominion of the Redeemer before his incarnation magnify his condescension in his incarnation, when he was *made a little lower than the angels,* Heb. 2:9. 2. The first thing he observed was a *throne;* for divine revelation comes backed and supported with a royal authority. We must have an eye of faith to God and Christ as upon a throne. The first thing that John discovered in his visions was *a throne set in heaven* (Rev. 4:2), which commands reverence and subjection. It is a throne of glory, a throne of grace, a throne of triumph, a throne of government, a throne of judgment. *The Lord has prepared his throne in the heavens,* has prepared it for his Son, whom he has set *King on his holy hill of Zion.* 3. On the throne he saw *the appearance of a man.* This is good new to the children of men, that the throne above the firmament is filled with one that is not ashamed to appear, even there, in the likeness of man. Daniel, in vision, saw the kingdom and dominion given to one *like the Son of man,* who *therefore* has *authority given him to execute judgment because he is the Son of man* (John *v.* 27), so appearing in these visions. 4. He saw him as a prince and judge upon this throne. Though he appeared *in fashion as a man,* yet he appeared in more than human glory, *v.* 27. (1.) Is God a *shining light?* So is he: when the prophet saw him he saw *as the colour of amber,* that is, a *brightness round about;* for God dwells in light, and *covers himself with light as with a garment.* How low did the Redeemer stoop for us when, to bring about our salvation, he suffered his glory to be eclipsed by the veil of his humanity! (2.) Is God a *consuming fire?* So is he: from his loins, both upward and downward, there was the *appearance of fire.* The fire above the loins was *round about within the amber;* it was inward and involved. That below the loins was more outward and open, and yet that also had *brightness round about.* Some make the former to signify Christ's divine nature, the glory and virtue of which are hidden within the *colour of amber;* it is what no man has seen nor can see. The latter they suppose to be his human nature, the glory of which there were those who saw; the glory as of *the only begotten of the Father, full of grace and truth,* Jn. 1:14. He had *rays coming out of his hand, and yet there was the hiding of his power,* Hab. 3:4. The fire in which the Son of man appeared here might be intended to signify the judgments that were ready to be executed upon Judah and Jerusalem, coming form that *fiery indignation* of the Almighty which *devours the adversaries.* Nothing is more dreadful to the most daring sinners than *the wrath of him that sits upon the throne, and of the Lamb,* Rev. 6:16. The day is coming when *the Lord Jesus shall be revealed in flaming fire,* 2 Th. 1:7, 8. It concerns us therefore *to kiss the Son lest he be angry.* 5. The throne is surrounded with a rainbow, *v.* 28. It is so in St. John's vision, Rev. 4:3. The brightness about it was of divers colours, *as the bow that is in the cloud in the day of rain,* which, as it is a display of majesty, and looks very great, so it is a pledge of mercy, and looks very kind; for it is a confirmation of that gracious promise God has made that he will not drown the world again, and he has said, *I will look upon the bow and remember the covenant,* Gen. 9:16. This intimates that he who *sits upon the throne* is the *Mediator of the covenant,* that his dominion is for our protection, not our destruction, that he interposes between us and the judgments our sins have deserved, and that *all the promises of God are in him yea and amen.* Now that the fire of God's wrath was breaking out against Jerusalem bounds should be set to it, and he would not make an utter destruction of it, for he would *look upon the bow and remember the covenant,* as he promised in such a case, Lev. 26:42.

Lastly, We have the conclusion of this vision. Observe, 1. What notion the prophet himself had of it: *This was the appearance of the likeness of the glory of the Lord.* Here, as all along, he is careful to guard against all gross corporeal thoughts of God, which might derogate from the transcendent purity of his nature. he does not say, *This was the Lord* (for he is invisible), but, *This was the glory of the Lord,* in which he was pleased to manifest himself a glorious being; yet it is not *the glory of the Lord,* but *the likeness of that glory,* some faint resemblance of it; nor is it any adequate likeness of that glory, but only *the appearance of that likeness,* a shadow of it, and not the very *image of the thing,* Heb. 10:1. 2. What impressions it made upon him: *When I saw it, I fell upon my face.* (1.) He was overpowered by it; the dazzling lustre of it conquered him and threw him upon his face; for *who is able to stand before this holy Lord God?* Or, rather, (2.) He prostrated himself in a humble sense of his own unworthiness of the honour now done him, and of the infinite distance which he now, more than ever, perceived to be between him and God; he fell upon his face in token of that holy awe and reverence of God with which his mind was possessed and filled. Note, The more God is pleased to make known of himself to us the more low we should be before him. He *fell upon his face* to adore the majesty of God, to implore his mercy and to deprecate the wrath he saw ready to break out against the children of his people. 3. What instructions he had from it. All he saw was only to prepare him for that which he was to hear; for *faith comes by hearing.* He therefore *heard a voice of one that spoke;* for we are taught by words, not merely by hieroglyphics. When *he fell on his face,* ready to received the word, then he *heard the voice of one that spoke;* for God delights to teach the humble.

CHAPTER 2

What our Lord Jesus said to St. Paul (Acts 26:16) may fitly be applied to the prophet Ezekiel, to whom the same Jesus is here speaking, "Rise and stand upon thy feet, for I have appeared unto thee for this purpose, to make thee a minister." We have here Ezekiel's ordination to his office, which the vision was designed to fit him for, not to entertain his curiosity with uncommon speculations, but to put him into business. Now here, I. He is commissioned to go as a prophet to the house of Israel, now captives in Babylon, and to deliver God's messages to them from time to time (*v.* 1–5). II. He is cautioned not to be afraid of them (*v.* 6). III. He is instructed what to say to them, and has words put into his mouth, signified by the vision of a roll, which he was ordered to eat (*v.* 7–10), and which, in the next chapter, we find he did eat.

Verses 1–5

The title here given to Ezekiel, as often afterwards, is very observable. God, when he speaks to him, calls him, *Son of man* (*v.* 1, 3), *Son of Adam, Son of the earth.* Daniel is once called so (Dan. 8:17) and but once; the compellation is used to no other of the prophets but to Ezekiel all along. We may take it, 1. As a humble diminishing title. Lest Ezekiel should be lifted up with the abundance of the revelations, he is put in mind of this, that sill he is a *son of man,* a mean, weak, mortal creature. Among other things made known to him, it was necessary he should be made to know this, that he was a *son of man,* and therefore that it was wonderful condescension in God that he was pleased thus to manifest himself to him. Now he is among the living creatures, the angels; yet he must remember that he is himself a man, a dying creature. *What is man, or the son of man,* that he should be thus visited, thus dignified? Though God had here a splendid retinue of holy angles about his throne, who were ready to go on his errands, yet he passes them all by, and pitches on Ezekiel, a *son of man,* to be his messenger to the *house of Israel;* for we *have this treasure in earthen vessels,* and God's messages sent us by men like ourselves, whose terror shall not *make us afraid* nor *their hand be heavy upon us.* Ezekiel was a priest, but the priesthood was brought low and the honour of it laid in the dust. It therefore became him, and all of his order, to humble themselves, and to lie low, as sons of men, common men. he was now to be employed as a prophet, God's ambassador, and a ruler over the kingdoms (Jer. 1:10), a post of great honour, but he must remember that he is a *son of man,* and, whatever good he did, it was not by any might of his own, for he was a *son of man,* but in the strength of divine grace, which must therefore have all the glory. Or, 2. We may take it as an honourable dignifying title; for it is one of the titles of the Messiah in the Old Testament (Dan. 7:13, *I saw one like the Son of man come with the clouds of heaven),* whence Christ borrows the title he often calls himself by, *The Son of man.* The prophets were types of him, as they had near access to God and great authority among men; and therefore as David the king is called the *Lord's anointed,* or *Christ,* so Ezekiel the prophet is called *son of man.*

I. Ezekiel is here set up, and made to stand, that he might receive his commission, *v.* 1, 2. He is set up,

1. By a divine command: *Son of man, stand upon thy feet.* His lying prostrate was a posture of greater reverence, but his standing up would be a posture of greater readiness and fitness for business. Our adorings of God must not hinder, but rather quicken and excite, our actings for God. He *fell on his face* in a holy fear and awe of God, but he was quickly raised up again; for those that *humble themselves shall be exalted.* God delights no in the dejections of his servants, but the same that brings them low will raise them up; the same that is a Spirit of bondage will be a Spirit of adoption. *Stand, and I will speak to thee.* Note, We may expect that God will speak to us when we stand ready to do what he commands us.

2. By a divine power going along with that command, *v.* 2. God bade him *stand up;* but, because he had not strength of his own to recover his feet nor courage to face the vision, *the Spirit entered into him* and *set him upon his feet.* Note, God is graciously pleased to work that in us which he requires of us and raises those whom he bids rise. We must stir up ourselves, and then God will put strength into us; we must *work out our salvation,* and then God will *work in us.* He observed that the Spirit entered into him when Christ spoke to him; for Christ conveys his Spirit by his word as the ordinary means and makes the word effectual by the Spirit. *The Spirit set* the prophet *upon his feet,* to raise him up from his dejections, for *he is the Comforter.* Thus, in a similar case, Daniel was strengthened by a divine touch (Dan. 10:18) and John was raised by the right hand of Christ laid upon him, Rev. 1:17. The *Spirit set him upon his feet,* made him willing and forward to do as he was bidden, and then he *heard him that spoke* to him. He heard the voice before (*ch.* 1:28), but now he heard it more distinctly and clearly, heard it and submitted to it. The Spirit sets us upon our feet by inclining our will to our duty, and thereby disposes the understanding to receive the knowledge of it.

II. Ezekiel is here sent, and made to go, with a message to the children of Israel (*v.* 3): *I send thee to the children of Israel.* God had for many ages been sending to them his servants the prophets, rising up betimes and sending them, but to little purpose; they were now sent into captivity for abusing God's messengers, and yet even there God sends this prophet among them, to try if their ears were open to discipline, now that they were holden in the cords of affliction. As the supports of life, so the means of grace, are continued to us after they have been a thousand times forfeited. Now observe,

1. The rebellion of the people to whom this ambassador is sent; he is sent to reduce them to their allegiance, to bring back the children of Israel to the Lord their God. let the prophet know that there is occasion for his going on this errand, for they are a *rebellious nation* (*v.* 3), *a rebellious house, v.* 5. They are called *children of Israel;* they retain the name of their pious ancestors, but they have wretchedly degenerated, they have become *Goim — nations,* the word commonly used for the Gentiles. The *children of Israel* have become as the *children of the Ethiopian* (Amos 9:7), for they are *rebellious;* and rebels at home are much more provoking to a prince than enemies abroad. Their idolatries and false worships were the sins which, more than any thing, denominated them a *rebellious nation;* for thereby they set up another prince in opposition to their rightful Sovereign, and did homage and paid tribute to the usurper, which is the highest degree of rebellion that can be. (1.) They had been all along a rebellious generation and had persisted in their rebellion: *They and their fathers have transgressed against me.* Note, Those are not always in the right that have antiquity and the fathers on their side; for there are errors and corruptions of long standing: and it is so far from being an excuse for walking in a bad way that our fathers walked in it that it is really an aggravation, for it is justifying the sin of those that have gone before us. They have continued in their rebellion *even unto this very day;* notwithstanding the various means and methods that have been made use of to reclaim them, *to this day,* when they are under divine rebukes for their rebellion, they continue *rebellious;* many among them, like Ahaz, even *in their distress, trespass yet more;* they are not the better for all the changes that have befallen them, but still remain unchanged. (2.) They were now hardened in their rebellion. They are *impudent children,* brazen-faced, and cannot blush; they are still-hearted, self-willed, and cannot bend, cannot stoop, neither ashamed nor afraid to sin; they will not be wrought upon by the sense either of honour or duty. We are willing to hope this was not the character of all, but of many, and those perhaps the leading men. Observe, [1.] God knew this concerning them, how inflexible, how incorrigible, they were. Note, God is perfectly acquainted with every man's true character, whatever his pretensions and professions may be. [2.] He told the prophet this, that he might know the better how to deal with them and what handle to take them by. He must rebuke such men as those sharply, cuttingly, must deal plainly with them, though they call it *dealing roughly.* God tells him this, that it might be no surprise or stumbling-block to him if he found that his preaching should not make that impression upon them, which he had reason to think it would.

2. The dominion of the prince by whom this ambassador is sent. (1.) He has authority to command him whom he sends: *"I do send thee unto them,* and therefore *thou shalt say* thus and thus unto them," *v.* 4. Note, it is the prerogative of Christ to send prophets and ministers and to enjoin them their work. St. Paul thanked Christ Jesus who put him into the ministry (1 Tim. 1:12); for, as he was sent of the Father, ministers are sent by him; and as he received the Spirit without measure he gives the Spirit by measure,

saying, *Receive you the Holy Ghost.* They are *impudent* and *rebellious*, and yet *I send thee unto them.* Note, Christ gives the means of grace to many who he knows will not make a good use of those means, puts many a price into the hand of fools to get wisdom, who not only have no heart to it, but have their hearts turned against it. Thus he will magnify his own grace, justify his own judgment, leave them inexcusable, and make their condemnation more intolerable. (2.) He has authority by him to command those to whom he sends him: *Thou shalt say unto them, Thus saith the Lord God.* All he said to them must be spoken in God's name, enforced by his authority, and delivered as from him. Christ delivered his doctrines as a Son — *Verily, verily, I say unto you;* the prophets as *servants — Thus saith the Lord God,* our Master and yours. Note, The writings of the prophets are the word of God, and so are to be regarded by every one of us. (3.) He has authority to call those to an account to whom he sends his ambassadors. *Whether they will hear or whether they will forbear,* whether they will attend to the word or turn their backs upon it, *they shall know that there has been a prophet among them,* shall know by experience. [1.] If they hear and obey, they will know by comfortable experience that the word which did them good was brought to them by one that had a commission from God and a divine power going along with him in the execution of it. Thus those who were converted by St. Paul's preaching are said to be *the seals of his apostleship,* 1 Co. 9:2. When men's hearts are made to burn under the word, and their wills to bow to it, then they know and bear the witness in themselves that it is not the *word of men, but of God.* [2.] If they forbear, if they turn a deaf ear to the word (as it is to be feared they will, *for they are a rebellious house),* yet they shall be made to know that he whom they slighted was indeed a prophet, by the reproaches of their own consciences and the just judgments of God upon them for refusing him; they shall know it to their cost, know it to their confusion, know it by sad experience, what a pernicious dangerous thing it is to despise God's messengers. They shall know by the accomplishment of the threatenings that the prophet who denounced them was sent of God; thus the word will *take hold of men,* Zec. 1:6. Note, *First,* Those to whom the word of God is sent are upon their trial *whether they will hear* or *whether they will forbear,* and accordingly will their doom be. *Secondly,* Whether we be edified by the word or no, it is certain that God will be glorified and his word magnified and made honourable. Whether it be a *savour of life unto life* or *of death unto death,* either way it will appear to be of divine original.

Verses 6–10

The prophet, having received his commission, here receives a charge with it. It is a post of honour to which he is advanced, but withal it is a post of service and work, and it is here required of him,

I. That he be bold. He must act in the discharge of this trust with an undaunted courage and resolution, and not be either driven off from his work or made to drive on heavily, by the difficulties and oppositions that he would be likely to meet with in it: *Son of man, be not afraid of them, v.* 6. Note, Those that will do any thing to purpose in the service of God must not be afraid of the face of man; for the fear of men will bring a snare, which will be very entangling to us in the work of God. 1. God tells the prophet what was the character of those to whom he sent him, as before, *v.* 3, 4. They are *briers and thorns,* scratching, and tearing, and vexing a man, which way soever he turns. They are continually teazing God's prophets and entangling them in their *talk* (Mt. 22:15); they are *pricking briers* and *grieving thorns.* The best of them is as a brier, and *the most upright sharper than a thorn-hedge,* Mic. 7:4. Thorns and briers are the fruit of sin and the curse, and of equal date with the enmity between the seed of the woman and the seed of the serpent. Note, Wicked men, especially the persecutors of God's prophets and people, are as briers and thorns, which are hurtful to the ground, choke the good seed, hinder God's husbandry, are vexatious to his husbandmen; but they are *nigh unto cursing* and *their end is to be burned.* Yet God makes use of them sometimes for the correction and instruction of his people, as *Gideon taught the men of Succoth with thorns and briers,* Jdg. 8:16. Yet this is not the worst of their character: they are *scorpions,* venomous and malignant. The sting of a scorpion is a thousand times more hurtful than the scratch of a brier. persecutors are a *generation of vipers,* are of the serpent's seed, and the *poison of asps is under their tongue;* and they are *more subtle than any beast of the field.* And, which makes the prophet's case the more grievous, he dwells among these scorpions; they are continually about him, so that he cannot be safe nor quiet in his own house; these bad men are his bad neighbours, who thereby have many opportunities, and will let slip none, to do him a mischief. God takes notice of this to the prophet, as Christ to the angel of one of the churches, Rev. 2:13. *I know thy works, and where thou dwellest, even where Satan's seat is.* Ezekiel had been, in vision, conversing with angels, but when he comes down from this mount he finds he *dwells with scorpions.* 2. He tells him what would be their conduct towards him, that they would do what they could to frighten him with *their looks* and *their words;* they would hector him and threaten him, would look scornfully and spitefully at him, and do their utmost to face him down and put him our of countenance, that they might drive him off from being a prophet, or at least from telling them of their faults and threatening them with the judgments of God; or, if they could not prevail in this, that they might vex and perplex him, and disturb the repose of his mind. They were now themselves in subjection, divested of all power, so that they had no other way of persecuting the prophet than with *their looks and their words;* and so they did persecute him. *Behold, thou hast spoken and done evil things as thou couldest,* Jer. 3:5. If they had had more power, they would have done more mischief. They were now in captivity, smarting for their rebellion, and particularly their misusing God's prophets; and yet they are as bad as ever. *Though thou brag a fool in a mortar, yet will not his foolishness depart from him;* no providences will of themselves humble and reform men, unless the grace of God work with them. But, how malicious soever they were, Ezekiel must not be *afraid of them* nor *dismayed,* he must not be deterred from his work, or any part of it, nor be disheartened or dispirited in it by all their menaces, but go on in it with resolution and cheerfulness, assuring himself of safety under the divine protection.

II. It is required that he be faithful, *v.* 7. 1. he must be faithful to Christ who sent him: *Thou shalt speak my words unto them.* Note, As it is the honour of prophets that they are entrusted to speak God's words, so it is their duty to cleave closely to them and to speak nothing but what is agreeable to the words of God. Ministers must always speak according to that rule. 2. He must be faithful to the souls of those to whom he was sent: *Whether they will hear of whether they will forbear,* he must deliver his message to them as he received it. He must bring them to comply with the word, and not study to accommodate the word to their humours. "It is true they are *most rebellious,* they are rebellion itself; but, however, *speak my words* to them, whether they are pleasing or unpleasing." Note, The untractableness and unprofitableness of people under the word are no good reason why ministers should leave off preaching to them; nor must we decline an opportunity by which good may be done, though we have a great deal of reason to think no good will be done.

III. It is required that he be observant of his instructions.

1. Here is a general intimation what the instructions were that were given him, in the contents of the book which was *spread before him, v.* 10. (1.) His instructions were large; for the roll was *written within and without,* on the inside and on the outside of the roll. It was as a sheet of paper written on all the four sides. One side contained their sins; the other side contained the judgments of God coming upon them for those sins. Note, God has a great deal to say to his people when they have degenerated and become rebellious. (2.) His instructions were melancholy. He was sent on a sad errand; the matter contained in the book was, *lamentations, and mourning, and woe.* The idea of his message is taken from the impression it would make upon the minds of those that carefully attended to it; it would set them a weeping and crying out, *Woe! and, Alas!* Both the discoveries of sin and the denunciations of wrath would be matter of lamentation. What could be more lamentable, more mournful, more woeful, than to see a holy happy people sunk into such a state of sin and misery as it appears by the prophecy of this book the Jews were at this time? Ezekiel echoes to Jeremiah's lamentations. Note, Though God is rich in mercy, yet impenitent sinners will find there are even among his words *lamentations and woe.*

2. Here is an express charge given to the prophet to observe his instructions, both in receiving his message and delivering it. he is now to receive it and is here commanded, (1.) To attend diligently to it: *son of man, hear what I say unto thee, v.* 8. Note, Those that speak from God to others must be sure to hear from God themselves and be obedient to his voice: *"Be not thou rebellious;* do not refuse to go on this errand, or to deliver it; do not fly off, as Jonah did, for fear of disobliging thy countrymen. They are a *rebellious house,* among whom thou livest; but be not thou like them, do not comply with them in any thing that is evil." If ministers, who are reprovers by office, connive at sin and indulge sinners, either show them not their wickedness or show them not the fatal consequences of it, for fear of displeasing them and getting their ill-will, they hereby make themselves partakers of their guilt and are rebellious like them. If people will not do their duty in reforming, yet let ministers do theirs in reproving, and they will have the comfort of it in the reflection, whatever the success be, as that prophet had, Isa. 50:5. *The Lord God has opened my ear, and I was not rebellious.* Even the best of men, when their lot is cast in bad times and places, have need to be cautioned against the worst of crimes. (2.) To digest it in his own mind by an experience of the favour and power of it: "Do not only *hear what I say unto thee,* but *open thy mouth, and eat that which I give thee.* Prepare to eat it and eat it willingly and with an appetite." All God's children are content to be at their heavenly father's finding, and to eat whatever he gives them. That which God's hand reached out to Ezekiel was *a roll of a book,* or *the volume of a book,* a book or scroll of paper or parchment fully written and rolled up. Divine revelation comes to us from the hand of Christ; he gave it to the prophets, Rev. 1:1. When we look at *the roll of thy book* we must have an eye to the hand by which it is sent to us. He that brought it to the prophet *spread it before him,* that he might now swallow it with an implicit faith, but might fully understand the contents of it, and then receive it and make it his own. *Be not rebellious,* says Christ, but *eat what I give thee.* If we receive not what Christ in his ordinances and providences allots for us, if we submit not to his word and rod, and reconcile not ourselves to both, we shall be accounted rebellious.

CHAPTER 3

In this chapter we have the further preparation of the prophet for the work to which God called him. I. His eating the roll that was presented to him in the close of the foregoing chapter (*v.* 1–3). II. Further instructions and encouragements given him to the same purport with those in the foregoing chapter (*v.* 4–11). III. The mighty impulse he was under, with which he was carried to those that were to be his hearers (*v.* 12–15). IV. A further explication of his office and business as a prophet, under the similitude of a watchman (*v.* 16–21). V. The restraining and restoring of the prophet's liberty of speech, as God pleased (*v.* 22–27).

Verses 1–15

These verses are fitly joined by some translators to the foregoing chapter, as being of a piece with it and a continuation of the same vision. The prophets received the word from God that they might deliver it to the people of God, furnished themselves that they might furnish them with the knowledge of the mind and will of God. Now here the prophet is taught,

I. How he must receive divine revelation himself, *v.* 1. Christ (whom he saw *upon the throne, ch.* 1:26) said to him, *"Son of man, eat this roll,* admit this revelation into thy understanding, take it, take the meaning of it, understand it aright, admit it into thy heart, apply it, and be affected with it; imprint it in thy mind, ruminate and chew the cud upon it; take it as it is entire, and make no difficulty of it, nay, take a pleasure in it as thou dost in thy meat, and let thy soul be nourished and strengthened by it; let it be meat and drink to thee, and as thy necessary food; be full of it, as thou art of the meat thou hast eaten." Thus ministers should in their studies and meditations take in that word of God which they are to preach to others. *Thy words were found, and I did eat them,* Jer. 15:16. They must be both well acquainted and much affected with the things of God, that they may speak of them both clearly and warmly, with a great deal of divine light and heat. Now observe, 1. How this command is inculcated upon the prophet. In the foregoing chapter, *Eat what I give thee;* and here (v. 1), "*Eat that thou findest,* that which is presented to thee by the hand of Christ." Note, Whatever we find to be the word of God, whatever is brought to us by him who is the Word of God, we must receive it without disputing. What we find set before us in the scripture, that we must eat. And again (v. 3), "*Cause thy belly to eat, and fill thy bowels with this roll;* do not eat it and bring it up again, as that which is nauseous, but eat it and retain it, as that which is nourishing and grateful to the stomach. Feast upon this vision till thou be *full of matter,* as Elihu was, Job 32:18. Let the word have a place in thee, the innermost place." We must take pains with our own hearts, that we may cause them duly to receive and entertain the word of God, that every faculty may do its office, in order to the due digesting of the word of God, that it may be turned *in succum et sanguinem* — *into blood and spirits.* We must empty ourselves of worldly things, that we may *fill our bowels with this roll.* 2. How this command is explained (v. 10): "*All my words that I shall speak unto thee,* to be spoken unto the people, *thou must receive in thy heart,* as well as *hear with thy ears,* receive them in the love of them." *Let these sayings sink down into your ears,* Lu. 9:44. Christ demands the prophet's attention not only to what he now says, but to all that he shall at any time hereafter speak: *Receive* it all *in thy heart; meditate on these things and give thyself wholly to them,* 1 Tim. 4:15. 3. How this command was obeyed in vision. He *opened his mouth* and Christ *caused him to eat the roll, v.* 2. If we be truly willing to receive the word into our hearts, Christ will by his Spirit bring it into them and cause it to *dwell in us richly.* If he that *opens the roll,* and by his Spirit, as a *Spirit of revelation,* spreads it before us, did not also *open our understanding,* and by his Spirit, as a *Spirit of wisdom,* give us the knowledge of it and *cause us to eat* it, we should be for ever strangers to it. The prophet had reason to fear that the roll would be an unpleasant morsel and a sorry dish to make a meal of, but it proved to be in his *mouth as honey for sweetness.* Note, if we readily obey even the most difficult commands, we shall find that comfort in the reflection which will make us abundant amends for all the hardships we meet with in the way of our duty. Though *the roll was filled with lamentations, and mourning, and woe,* yet it was to the prophet *as honey for sweetness.* Note, Gracious souls can receive those truths of God with great delight which speak most terror to wicked people. We find St. John let into some part of the revelation by such a sign as this, Rev. 10:9, 10. He *took the book out of the angel's hand, and ate it up, and it was,* as this, *in his mouth sweet as honey;* but it was *bitter in the belly;* and we shall find that this was so too, for (v. 14) the prophet *went in bitterness.*

II. How he must deliver that divine revelation to others which he himself had received (v. 1): *Eat this roll,* and then go, *speak to the house of Israel.* He must not undertake to preach the things of God to others till he did himself fully understand them; let him not go without his errand, nor take it by the halves. But when he does himself fully understand them he must be both busy and bold to preach them for the good of others. We must not *conceal the words of the Holy One* (Job 6:10), for that is burying a talent which was given us to trade with. He must *go and speak to the house of Israel;* for it is their privilege to have God's statutes and judgments made known to them; as *the giving of the law* (the lively oracles), so prophecy (the living oracles) *pertains to them.* He is not sent to the Chaldeans to reprove them for their sins, but *to the house of Israel* to reprove them for theirs; for the father corrects his own child if he do amiss, not the child of a stranger.

1. The instructions given him in speaking to them are much the same with those in the foregoing chapter.

(1.) He must speak to them all that, and that only, which God spoke to him. he had said before (*ch.* 2:7): *Thou shalt speak my words to them;* here he says (v. 4), *Thou shalt speak with my words unto them,* or *in my words.* He must not only say that which for substance is the same that God had said to him, but as near as may be in the same language and expressions. Blessed Paul, though a man of a very happy invention, yet speaks of the things of God in

the words which the Holy Ghost teaches, 1 Co. 2:13. Scripture truths look best in scripture language, their native dress; and how can we better speak God's mind than with his words?

(2.) He must remember that they are *the house of Israel* whom he is sent to speak to, God's house and his own; and therefore such as he ought to have a particular concern for and to deal faithfully and tenderly with. They were such as he had an intimate acquaintance with, being not only their countryman, but their *companion in tribulation;* they and he were fellow-sufferers, and had lately been fellow-travellers, in very melancholy circumstances, from Judea to Babylon, and had often mingled their tears, which could not but knit their affections to each other. It was well for the people that they had a prophet who knew experimentally how to sympathize with them, and could not but be touched with the feeling of their infirmities. It was well for the prophet that he had to do with those of his own nation, not *with a people of strange speech and a hard language,* deep of lip, so that thou canst not fathom their meaning, and heavy of tongue, whom it is intolerable and impossible to converse with. Every strange language seems to us to be deep and heavy. "Thou art not sent to *many such people,* whom thou couldst neither speak to nor hear from, neither understand nor be understood among but by an interpreter." The apostles indeed were sent to *many people of a strange speech,* but they could not have done any good among them if they had not had *the gift of tongues;* but Ezekiel was sent only to one people, those but a few, and his own, whom having acquaintance with he might hope to find acceptance with.

(3.) He must remember what God had already told him of the bad character of those to whom he was sent, that, if he met with discouragement and disappointment in them, he might not be offended. They *are impudent and hard-hearted* (v. 7), no convictions of sin would make them blush, no denunciations of wrath would make them tremble. Two things aggravated their obstinacy: — [1.] That they were more obstinate than their neighbours would have been if the prophet had been sent to them. had God sent him to any other people, though of a *strange speech, surely they would have hearkened* to him; they would at least have given him a patient hearing and shown him that respect which he could not obtain of his own countrymen. The Ninevites were wrought upon by Jonah's preaching when the house of Israel, that was compassed about with so great a cloud of prophets, was unhumbled and unreformed. But what shall we say to these things? The means of grace are given to those that will not improve them and withheld from those that would have improved them. We must resolve this into the divine sovereignty, and say, Lord, *thy judgments are a great deep.* [2.] That they were obstinate against God himself: "They *will not hearken unto thee,* and no marvel, *for they will not hearken unto me;*" they will not regard the word of the prophet, for they will not regard the rod of God, by which the *Lord's voice cries in the city.* If they believe not God speaking to them by a minister, neither would they believe though he should speak to them by *a voice from heaven;* nay, *therefore* they reject what the prophet says, because it comes from God, whom *the carnal mind is enmity* to. They are prejudiced against the law of God, and for that reason turn a deaf ear to his prophets, whose business it is to enforce his law.

(4.) He must resolve to put on courage, and Christ promises to steel him with it, *v.* 8, 9. He is sent to such as are *impudent and hard-hearted,* who will receive no impressions nor be wrought upon either by fair means or foul, who will take a pride in affronting God's messenger and confronting the message. It will be a hard task to know how to deal with them; but, [1.] God will enable him to put a good face on it: "*I have made thy face strong against their faces,* endued thee with all the firmness and boldness that the case calls for." Perhaps Ezekiel was naturally bashful and timorous, but, if God did not find him fit, yet by his grace he made him fit, to encounter the greatest difficulties. Note, The more impudent wicked people are in their opposition to religion the more openly and resolutely should God's people appear in the practice and defence of it. let the *innocent stir up himself against the hypocrite,* Job 17:8. When vice is daring let not virtue be sneaking. And, when God has work to do, he will animate men for it and give them strength according to the day. If there

be occasion, God can and will by his grace make the *foreheads* of faithful ministers *as an adamant,* so that the most threatening powers shall not dash them out of countenance. *The Lord God will help men, therefore have I set my face like a flint,* Isa. 50:7. [2.] He is therefore commanded to have a good heart on it, and to go on in his work with a holy security, not valuing either the censures or the threats of his enemies: "*Fear not, neither be dismayed at their looks;* let not the menaces of their impotent malice cast either a damp upon thee or a stumblingblock before thee." Bold sinners must have bold reprovers; *evil beasts* must be *rebuked* cuttingly (Tit. 1:12, 13), must be *saved with fear,* Jude 23. Those that keep closely to the service of God may be sure of the favour of God, and then they need not be dismayed at the proud looks of men. Let not the angry countenance that drives away a backbiting tongue give any check to a reproving tongue.

(5.) He must continue instant with them in his preaching, whatever the success was, *v.* 11. he must *go to those of the captivity,* who, being in affliction, it was to be hoped would receive instruction; he must look upon them as *the children of his people,* to whom he was nearly allied, and for whom he therefore ought to have a very tender concern, as Paul for his kinsmen, Rom. 9:3. And he must *tell them* not only what the Lord said, but that the Lord said it; let him speak in God's name, and back what he said with his authority: *Thus saith the Lord God; tell them* so, *whether they will hear or whether they will forbear.* Not that it may be indifferent to us what success our ministry has, but, whatever it be, we must go on with our work and leave the issue to God. We must not say "Here are some so good that we do not need to speak to them," or, "Here are others so bad that it is to no purpose to speak to them;" but, however it be, deliver thy message faithfully, *tell them, The Lord God saith* so and so, let them reject it at their peril.

2. Full instructions being thus given to the prophet, pursuant to his commission, we are here told,

(1.) With what satisfaction this mission of his was applauded by the holy angels, who were very well pleased to see one of a nature inferior to their own thus honourable employed and entrusted. He *heard a voice of a great rushing* (v. 12), as if the angels thronged and crowded to see the inauguration of a prophet; for to them *is known by the church* (that is, by reflection from the church) *the manifold wisdom of God,* Eph. 3:10. They seemed to strive who should get nearest to this great sight. he *heard the noise of their wings that touched,* or (as the word is) *kissed one another,* denoting the mutual affections and assistances of the angels. He heard also *the noise of the wheels* of Providence moving *over-against* the angels and in concert with them. All this was to engage his attention and to convince him that the God who sent him, having such a glorious train of attendants, no doubt had power sufficient to bear him out in his work. But all this noise ended in the voice of praise. He heard them saying, *Blessed be the glory of the Lord from his place.* [1.] From heaven, his place above, whence his glory was now in vision descending, or whither perhaps it was now returning. Let the innumerable company of angels above join with those employed in this vision in saying, *Blessed be the glory of the Lord. Praise you the Lord from the heavens. Praise him, all his angels,* Ps. 148:1, 2. [2.] From the temple, his place on earth, whence his glory was now departing. They lament the departure of the glory, but adore the righteousness of God in it: however it be, yet God is blessed and glorious, and ever will be so. The prophet Isaiah heard God thus praised when he received his commission (Isa. 6:3); and a comfort it is to all the faithful servants of God, when they see how much God is dishonoured in this lower world, to think how much he is admired and glorified in the upper world. *The glory of the Lord* has many slights from our place, but many *praises from his place.*

(2.) With what reluctance of his own spirit, and yet with what a mighty efficacy of *the Spirit of God,* the prophet was himself brought to the execution of his office. *The grace given to him was not in vain;* for, [1.] The Spirit led him with a strong hand. God bade him go, but he stirred not till *the Spirit took him up. The Spirit of the living creatures* that was *in the wheels* now was in the prophet too, and *took him up,* first to hear more distinctly the acclamations of the angels (v. 12), but afterwards (v. 14) *lifted him up, and took him away* to his work, which he was backward to, being very loth either to bring trouble upon himself or foretel it to his people. he would gladly have been excused, but must own, as another prophet does (Jer. 20:7), *Thou was stronger than I, and hast prevailed.* Ezekiel would willingly have kept all he heard and saw to himself, that it might go no further, *but the hand of the Lord was strong upon him* and overpowered him; he was carried on contrary to his own inclinations by the prophetical impulse, so that he could not *but speak the things which he had heard and seen,* as the apostles, Acts 4:20. Note, Those whom God calls to the ministry, as he furnishes their heads for it, so he bows their hearts to it. [2.] He followed with a sad heart: *The Spirit took me away,* says he, *and* then *I went,* but it was *in bitterness, in the heat of my spirit.* He had perhaps seen what a hard task Jeremiah had at Jerusalem when he appeared as a prophet, what pains he took, what opposition he met with, how he was abused by hand and tongue, and what ill treatment he met with, and all to no purpose. "And" (thinks Ezekiel) "must I be set up for a mark like him?" The life of a captive was bad enough; but what would the life of a prophet in captivity be? Therefore he went in this fret and under this discomposure. Note, There may in some cases be a great reluctance of corruption even where there is a manifest predominance of grace. *"I went,* not *disobedient to the heavenly vision,* or shrinking from the work, as Jonah, but *I went in bitterness,* not at all pleased with it." When he received the divine revelation himself, it was to him *sweet as honey* (*v.* 3); he could with abundance of pleasure have spent all his days in meditating upon it; but when he is to preach it to others, who, he foresees, will be hardened and exasperated by it, and have their condemnation aggravated, then he goes *in bitterness.* Note, It is a great grief to faithful ministers, and makes them go on in their work with a heavy heart, when they find people untractable and hating to be reformed. he *went in the heat of his spirit,* because of the discouragements he foresaw he should meet with; *but the hand of the Lord was strong upon* him, not only to compel him to his work, but to fit him for it, to carry him through it, and animate him against the difficulties he would meet with (so we may understand it); and, when he found it so, he was better reconciled to his business and applied himself to it: *Then he came to those of the captivity* (*v.* 15), to some place where there were many of them together, *and sat where they sat,* working, or reading, or talking, and continued *among them seven days* to hear what they said and observe what they did; and all that time he was waiting for *the word of the Lord* to come to him. Note, Those that would speak suitably and profitably to people about their souls must acquaint themselves with them and with their case, must do as Ezekiel did here, must *sit where they sit,* and speak familiarly to them of the things of God, and put themselves into their condition, yea, though they *sit by the rivers of Babylon.* But observe, He was *there astonished,* overwhelmed with grief for the sins and miseries of his people and overpowered by the pomp of the vision he had seen. he was *there desolate* (so some read it); God showed him no visions, men made him no visit. Thus was he left to digest his grief, and come to a better temper, before *the word of the Lord* should come to him. Note, Those whom god designs to exalt and enlarge he first humbles and straitens for a time.

Verses 16–21

These further instructions God gave to the prophet *at the end of seven days,* that is, on the seventh day after the vision he had; and it is very probably that both that and this were on the sabbath day, which *the house of Israel,* even in their captivity, observed as well as they could in those circumstances. We do not find that their conquerors and oppressors tied them to any constant service, as their Egyptian task-masters had formerly done, but that they might observe the sabbath-rest for a sign to distinguish between them and their neighbours; but for the sabbath-work they had not the convenience of temple or synagogue, only it should seem they had a *place by the river side where prayer was wont to be made* (as Acts 16:13); there they met on the sabbath day; there their enemies upbraided them with *the songs of Zion* (Ps. 137:1, 3); there Ezekiel met them, and *the word of the Lord* then and there *came to* him. He that had been musing and meditating on the things of God all the week was fit to speak to the people in God's name on the sabbath day, and disposed to hear God speak to him. This sabbath day Ezekiel was not so honoured with visions of the glory of God as he had been the sabbath before; but he is plainly, and by a very common similitude, told his duty, which he is to communicate to the people. Note, Raptures and transports of joy are not the daily bread of God's children, however they may upon special occasions be feasted with them. We must not deny but that we have truly communion with God (1 Jn. 1:3) though we have it not always so sensibly as at some times. And, though the mysteries of the kingdom of heaven may sometimes be looked into, yet ordinarily it is plain preaching that is most for edification. God here tells the prophet what his office was, and what the duty of that office; and this (we may suppose) he was to tell the people, that they might attend to what he said and improve it accordingly. Note, It is good for people to know and consider what a charge their ministers have of them and what an account they must shortly give of that charge. Observe,

I. What the office is to which the prophet is called: *Son of man, I have made thee a watchman to the house of Israel, v.* 17. The vision he saw astonished him: he knew not what to make of that, and therefore God used this plain comparison, which served better to lead him to the understanding of his work and so to reconcile him to it. he sat among the captives, and said little, but God comes to him, and tells him that will not do; he is *a watchman,* and has something to say to them; he is appointed to be as *a watchman* in the city, to guard against fire, robbers, and disturbers of the peace, as *a watchman* over the flock, to guard against thieves and beasts of prey, but especially as *a watchman* in the camp, in an invaded country or a besieged town, that is to watch the motions of the enemy, and to sound an alarm upon the approach, nay, upon the first appearance, of danger. This supposes *the house of Israel* to be in a military state, and exposed to enemies, who are subtle and restless in their attempts upon it; yea, and each of the particular members of that house to be in danger and concerned to stand upon their guard. Note, Ministers are *watchmen on the church's walls* (Isa. 62:6), *watchmen that go about the city,* Cant. 3:3. It is a toilsome office. Watchmen must keep awake, be they ever so sleepy, and keep abroad, be it ever so cold; they must stand all weathers *upon the watch-tower,* Isa. 21:8; Gen. 31:40. It is a dangerous office. Sometimes they cannot keep their post, but are in peril of death from the enemy, who gain their point if they kill the sentinel; and yet they dare not quit their post upon pain of death from their general. Such a dilemma are the church's watchmen in; men will curse them if they be faithful, and God will curse them if they be false. But it is a needful office; *the house of Israel* cannot be safe without watchmen, and yet, *except the Lord keep* it, *the watchman waketh but in vain,* Ps. 127:1, 2.

II. What is the duty of this office. The work of a watchman is to take notice and to give notice.

1. The prophet, as a watchman, must take notice of what God said concerning this people, not only concerning the body of the people, to which the prophecies of Jeremiah and other prophets had most commonly reference, but concerning particular persons, according as their character was. He must not, as other watchmen, look round to spy danger and gain intelligence, but he must look up to God, and further he need not look: *Hear the word at my mouth, v.* 17. Note, Those that are to preach must first hear; for how can those teach others who have not first learned themselves?

2. He must give notice of what he heard. As a watchman must have eyes in his head, so he must have a tongue in his head; if he be dumb, it is as bad as if he were blind, Isa. 56:10. Thou shalt *give them warning from me,* sound an alarm in the *holy mountain;* not in his own name, or as from himself, but in God's name, and from him. Ministers are God's mouth to the children of men. The scriptures are written for our admonition. *By them is thy servant warned,* Ps. 19:11. But, because that which is delivered *vivâ voce — by the living voice,* commonly makes the deepest impression, God is pleased, by men like ourselves, who are equally concerned, to enforce upon us the warnings of the written word. Now the prophet, in his preaching, must distinguish between the wicked and the righteous, the precious and the vile, and in his applications must suit his alarms to each, giving every one his portion; and, if he did this, he should have the comfort of it, whatever the success was, but, if not, he was accountable.

(1.) Some of those he had to do with were wicked, and he must warn them not to go on in their wickedness, but to turn from it, *v.* 18, 19. We may observe here, [1.] That the God of heaven has said, and does say, to every wicked man, that if he go on still in his trespasses he *shall surely die. His iniquity* shall undoubtedly be his ruin; it tends to ruin and will end in ruin. Dying *thou shalt die, thou shalt die* so great a death, *shalt die* eternally, be ever dying, but never dead. *The wicked man shall die in his iniquity, shall fie* under the guilt of it, *die* under the dominion of it. [2.] That if a *wicked man turn from his wickedness,* and *from his wicked way, he shall live,* and the ruin he is threatened with shall be prevented; and, that he may do so, he is warned of the danger he is in. *The wicked man shall die* if he go on, but *shall live* if he repent. Observe, he is to turn *from his wickedness* and *from his wicked way.* It is not enough for a man to turn *from his wicked way* by an outward reformation, which may be the effect of his sins leaving him rather than of his leaving his sins, but he must *turn from his wickedness,* from the love of it and the inclination to it, by an inward regeneration; if he do not so much as turn *from his wicked way,* there is little hope that he will turn *from his wickedness.* [3.] That it is the duty of ministers both to warn sinners of the danger of sin and to assure them of the benefit of repentance, to set before them how miserable they are if they go on in sin, and how happy they may be if they will but repent and reform. Note, The ministry of the word is concerning matters of *life and death,* for those are the things it sets before us, *the blessing and the curse,* that we may escape the curse and inherit the blessing. [4.] That, though ministers do not warn wicked people as they ought of their misery and danger, yet that shall not be admitted as an excuse for those that go on still in their trespasses; for, though the watchman did not *give them warning,* yet they *shall die in their iniquity,* for they had sufficient warning given them by the providence of God and their own consciences; and, if they would have taken it, they might have *saved* their *lives.* [5.] That if ministers be not faithful to their trust, if they do not warn sinners of the fatal consequences of sin, but suffer them to go on unreproved, the *blood* of those that perish through their carelessness *will be required at their hand.* It shall be charged upon them in the day of account that it was owing to their unfaithfulness that such and such precious souls perished in sin; for who knows but if they had had fair warning given them they might have fled in time *from the wrath to come?* And, if it contract so heinous a guilt as it does to be accessory to the murder of a dying body, what is it to be accessory to the ruin of an immortal soul? [6.] That if ministers do their duty in giving warning to sinners, though the warning be not taken, yet they may have this satisfaction, that they are j*clear from* their *blood,* and have *delivered their own souls,* though they cannot prevail to deliver theirs. Those that are faithful shall have their reward, though they be not successful.

(2.) Some of those he had to deal with were *righteous,* at least he had reason to think, in a judgment of charity, that they were so; and he must warn them not to apostatize and *turn away from their righteousness, v.* 20, 21. We may observe here, [1.] That the best men in the world have need to be warned against apostasy, and to be told of the danger they are in of it and the danger they are in by it. God's servants must be warned (Ps. 19:11) that they do not neglect his work and quit his service. One good means to keep us from falling is to keep up a holy fear of falling, Heb. 4:1. *Let us therefore fear;* and (Rom. 11:20) even those that *stand by faith* must *not be high-minded, but fear,* and must therefore be warned. [2.] There is a *righteousness* which a man may *turn from,* a seeming *righteousness,* and, if men turn from this, it thereby appears that it was never sincere, how passable, nay, how plausible soever it was; for, *if they had been of us, they would no doubt have continued with us,* 1 Jn. 2:19. There are many that *begin in the spirit,* but *end in the flesh,* that set their faces heavenward, but look back; that had a first love, but have lost it, and *turned from the holy commandment.*

[3.] When men *turn from their righteousness* they soon learn to commit iniquity. When they grow careless and remiss in the duties of God's worship, neglect them, or a re negligent in them, they become an easy prey to the tempter. Omissions make way for commissions. [4.] *When men turn from their righteousness, and commit iniquity,* it is just with God to lay *stumbling-blocks before them,* that they may grow worse and worse, till they are ripened for destruction. When Pharaoh hardened his heart God hardened it. When sinners turn their back upon God, desert his service, and so cast a reproach upon it, he does, in a way of righteous judgment, not only withdraw his restraining grace and give them up to their own hearts' lusts, but order them by his providence into such circumstances as occasion their sin and hasten their ruin. There are those to whom Christ himself is *a stone of stumbling and a rock of offence,* 1 Pt. 2:8. [5.] The righteousness which men relinquish shall never be remembered to their honour or comfort; it will stand them in no stead in this world or the other. Apostates lose all that they have wrought; their services and sufferings are all in vain, and shall never be brought to an account, because not continued in. It is a rule in the law, *Factum non dicitur, quod non perseverat — We are said to do only that which we do perseveringly,* Gal. 3:3, 4. [6.] If ministers do no give fair warning, as they ought, of the weakness of the best, their aptness to stumble and fall, the particular temptations they are in and the fatal consequences of apostasy, the ruin of those that do apostatize will be laid at their door, and they shall answer for it. Not but that there are those who are warned against it, and yet *turn from their righteousness;* but that case is not put here, as was concerning the wicked man, but, on the contrary, that a *righteous man,* being warned, takes the warning and *does not sin* (*v.* 21); for, if you *give instruction to a wise man, he will be yet wiser.* We must not only not flatter the wicked, but not flatter even the righteous as if they were perfectly safe any where on this side heaven. [7.] If ministers give warning, and people take it, it is well for both. Nothing is more beautiful than *a wise reprover upon an obedient ear;* the one *shall live because he is warned* and the other *has delivered his soul.* What can a good minister desire more than to *save himself and those that hear him?* 1 Tim. 4:16.

Verses 22–27

After all this large and magnificent discovery which God had made of himself to the prophet, and the full instructions he had given him how to deal with those to whom he sent him with an ample commission, we should have expected presently to see him preaching the word of God to a great congregation of Israel; but here we find it quite otherwise. his work here, at first, seems not at all proportionable to the pomp of his call.

I. We have him here retired for further learning. By his unwillingness to go it should seem as if he were not so thoroughly convinced as he might have been of the ability of him that sent him to bear him out; and therefore, to encourage him against the difficulties he foresaw, God will favour him with another vision of his glory, which (if any thing) would put life into him and animate him for his work. In order for this, God calls him out *to the plain* (*v.* 22) and there he will have some *talk with him.* See and admire the condescension of God in conversing thus familiarly with a man, a *son of man,* a poor captive, nay, with a sinful man, who, when God sent him *went in bitterness of spirit,* and was at this time out of humour with his work. And let us own ourselves for ever indebted to the mediation of Christ for this blessed intercourse and communion between God and man, between heaven and earth. See here the benefit of solitude, and how much it befriends contemplation. It is very comfortable to be alone with God, withdrawn from the word for converse with him, to hear from him, to speak to him; and a good man will say that he is never less along than when thus alone. Ezekiel *went forth into the plain* more willingly than he went *among those of the captivity* (*v.* 15); for those that know what it is to have communion with God cannot but prefer that before any converse with this world, especially such as is commonly met with. He *went out into the plain,* and there he saw the same vision that he had seen *by the river of Chebar;* for God is not tied to places. Note, Those who follow God shall meet with his consolations, wherever they go. God called him out to *talk with him,* but did more than that: he showed him his *glory, v.* 23. We are not now to expect such visions, but we must own that we have a favour done us no way inferior if we so by faith *behold the glory of the Lord* as to be *changed into the same image, by the Spirit of the Lord;* and this *honour have all his saints. Praise you the Lord,* 2 Co. 3:18.

II. We have him here restrained from further teaching for the present. When he saw *the glory of the Lord* he *fell on his face,* being struck with an awe of God's majesty and a dread of his displeasure; but *the Spirit entered into* him to raise him up, and then he recovered himself and got *upon his feet* and heard what the Spirit whispered to him, which is very surprising. One would have expected now that God would send him directly to the chief place of concourse, would give him favour in the eyes of his brethren, and make him and his message acceptable to them, that he would have a wider door of opportunity opened to him and that God would give him a door of utterance to open his mouth boldly; but what is here said to him is the reverse of all this.

1. Instead of sending him to a public assembly, he orders him to confine himself to his own lodgings: *Go, shut thyself within thy house, v.* 24. He was not willing to appear in public, and, when he did, the people did not regard him, nor show him the respect he deserved, and as a just rebuke both to him and them, to him for his shyness of them and to them for their coldness towards him, God forbids him to appear in public. Note, Our choice is often made our punishment; and it is a righteous thing with God to remove teachers into corners when they, or their people, or both, grow indifferent to solemn assemblies. Ezekiel must shut up himself, some think, to give a sign of the besieging of Jerusalem, in which the people should be closely shut up as he was in his house, and which he speaks of in the next chapter. He must *shut himself within his house,* that he might receive further discoveries of the mind of God and might abundantly furnish himself with something to say to the people when he went abroad. We find that *the elders of Judah* visited him and *sat before* him sometimes *in his house* (*ch.* 8:1), to be witnesses of his ecstasies; but it was not till *ch.* 11:25 that he *spoke to those of the captivity all the things that the Lord had shown him.* Note, Those that are called to preach must find time to study, and a great deal of time too, must often shut themselves up in their houses, that they may give attendance to reading and meditation, and so their profiting may appear to all.

2. Instead of securing him an interest in the esteem and affections of those to whom he sent him he tells him that *they shall put bands upon him and bind him* (*v.* 25), either (1.) As a criminal. *They shall bind him* in order to the further punishing of him as a disturber of the peace; though they were themselves sent into bondage in Babylon for persecuting the prophets, yet there they continue to persecute them. Or, rather, (2.) As a distracted man. *They* would go about to *bind him* as one beside himself; for to that they imputed his violent motions in his raptures. The captains asked Jehu, *Wherefore came this mad fellow unto thee?* Festus said to Paul, *Thou art beside thyself;* and so the Jews said of our Lord Jesus, mark 3:21. Perhaps this was the reason why he must keep within doors, because otherwise they would bind him, under pretence of his being mad, and therefore he must not *go out among them.* Justly are prophets forbidden to go to those that will abuse them.

3. Instead of opening his lips that his mouth might show forth God's praise, God silence him, made his *tongue cleave to the roof of his mouth,* so that he was dumb for a considerable time, *v.* 26. The pious captives in Babylon used this imprecation upon themselves, that, *if* they should *forget Jerusalem,* there *tongue* might *cleave to the roof of their mouth,* Ps. 137:6. Ezekiel remembers Jerusalem more than any of them, and yet his *tongue cleaves to the roof of his mouth,* and he that can speak best is forbidden to speak at all; and the reason given is because *they are a rebellious house* to whom he is sent, and they are not worthy to have him for *a reprover.* He shall not give them instructions and admonitions, for they are lost and thrown away upon them. he is before commanded to speak boldly to them because *they are most rebellious* (*ch.* 2:7); but, since that proves to no purpose, he is now for that reason enjoined silence and shall not speak at all to them. Note, Those whose hearts are hardened against conviction are justly deprived of the mans of conviction. Why should not the reprovers be dumb, if, after long trials, it be found that the reproved resolve to be deaf? If Ephraim be *joined to idols, let him alone. Thou shalt be dumb, and not be a reprover,* implying that unless he were dumb he would be reproving; if he could speak at all, he would witness against the wickedness of the wicked. *But when* God *speaks with* him, and designs to speak by him, he *will open* his *mouth, v.* 27. Note, Though God's prophets may be silenced awhile, there will come a time when God will give them the opening of the mouth again. And, when God speaks to his ministers, he not only opens their ears to hear what he says, but opens their mouth to return an answer. Moses, who had a veil on his face when he went down to the people, took it off when he went up again to God, Ex. 34:34.

4. Instead of giving him assurance of success when he should at any time speak to the people, he here leaves the matter very doubtful, and Ezekiel must not perplex and disquiet himself about it, but let it be as it will. *He that hears, let him hear,* and he is welcome to the comfort of it; *let him hear, and his soul shall live;* but *he that forbears, let him forbear* at his peril, and take what comes. If *thou scornest, thou alone shalt bear it;* neither God nor his prophet shall be any losers by it; but the prophet shall be rewarded for his faithfulness in reproving the sinner, and God will have the glory of his justice in condemning him for not taking the reproof.

CHAPTER 4

Ezekiel was now among the captives in Babylon, but they there had Jerusalem still upon their hearts; the pious captives looked towards it with an eye of faith (as Daniel 6:10), the presumptuous ones looked towards it with an eye of pride, and flattered themselves with a conceit that they should shortly return thither again; those that remained corresponded with the captives, and, it is likely, bouyed them up with hopes that all would be well yet, as long as Jerusalem was standing in its strength, and perhaps upbraided those with their folly who had surrendered at first; therefore, to take down this presumption, God gives the prophet, in this chapter, a very clear and affecting foresight of the besieging of Jerusalem by the Chaldean army and the calamities which would attend that siege. Two things are here represented to him in vision: — I. The fortifications that should be raised against the city; this is signified by the prophet's laying siege to the portraiture of Jerusalem (*v.* 1–3) and laying first on one side and then on the other side before it (*v.* 4–8). II. The famine that should rage within the city; this is signified by his eating very coarse fare, and confining himself to a little of it, so long as this typical representation lasted (*v.* 9–17).

Verses 1–8

The prophet is here ordered to represent to himself and others by signs which would be proper and powerful to strike the fancy and to affect the mind, *the siege of Jerusalem;* and this amounted to a prediction.

I. He was ordered to engrave a draught of Jerusalem upon a tile, *v.* 1. It was Jerusalem's honour that while she kept her integrity God had *graven her upon the palms of his hands* (Isa. 49:16), and the names of the tribes were engraven in precious stones on the breast-plate of the high priest; but, now that *the faithful city has become a harlot,* a worthless brittle tile or brick is thought good enough to *portray it upon.* This the prophet must lay before him, that the eye may affect the heart.

II. He was ordered to build little forts against this portraiture of the city, resembling the batteries raised by the besiegers, *v.* 2. Between the city that was besieged and himself that was the besieger he was to set up an *iron pan,* as an *iron wall, v.* 3. This represented the inflexible resolution of both sides; the Chaldeans resolved, whatever it cost them, that they would make themselves masters of the city and would never quit it till they had conquered it; on the other side, the Jews resolved never to capitulate, but to hold out to the last extremity.

III. He was ordered to lie upon his side before it, as it were to surround it, representing the Chaldean army lying before it to block it up, to keep the meat from going in and the mouths from going out. He was to lie on his left side 390 *days* (*v.* 5), about thirteen months; the siege of Jerusalem is computed to last eighteen months (Jer. 52:4–6), but if we deduct from that five months' interval, when the besiegers withdrew upon the approach of Pharaoh's army (Jer. 37:5–8), the number of the days of the close siege will be 390. Yet that also had another signification. The 390 days, according to the prophetic dialect, signified 390 years; and, when the prophet lies so many days on his side, he bears the guilt of that iniquity which *the house of Israel,* the ten tribes, had borne 390 years, reckoning from their first apostasy under Jeroboam to the destruction of Jerusalem, which completed the ruin of those small remains of them that had incorporated with Judah. He is then to lie forty days *upon his right side,* and so long to bear *the iniquity of the house of Judah,* the kingdom of the two tribes, because the measure-filling sins of that people were those which they were guilty of during the last forty years before their captivity, since the thirteenth year of Josiah, when Jeremiah began to prophesy (Jer. 1:1, 2), or, as some reckon it, since the eighteenth, when the book of the law was found and the people renewed their covenant with God. When they persisted in their impieties and idolatries, notwithstanding they had such a prophet and such a prince, and were brought into the bond of such a covenant, what could be expected but ruin without remedy? Judah, that had such helps and advantages for reformation, fills the measure of its iniquity in less time than Israel does. Now we are not to think that the prophet lay constantly night and day upon his side, but every day, for so many days together, at a certain time of the day, when he received visits, and company came in, he was found lying 390 *days on his left side* and *forty days on his right side* before his portraiture of Jerusalem, which all that saw might easily understand to mean the close besieging of that city, and people would be flocking in daily, some for curiosity and some for conscience, at the hour appointed, to see it and to take their different remarks upon it. His being found constantly on the same side, as if *bands were laid upon him* (as indeed they were by the divine command), so that he could not *turn himself from one side to another till he had ended the days of the siege,* did plainly represent the close and constant continuance of the besiegers about the city during that number of days, till they had gained their point.

IV. He was ordered to prosecute the siege with vigour (*v.* 7): *Thou shalt set thy face towards the siege of Jerusalem,* as wholly intent upon it and resolved to carry it; so the Chaldeans would be, and neither bribed nor forced to withdraw from it. Nebuchadnezzar's indignation at Zedekiah's treachery in breaking his league with him made him very furious in pushing on this siege, that he might chastise the insolence of that faithless prince and people; and his army promised themselves a rich booty of that pompous city; so that both set their faces against it, for they were very resolute. Nor were they less active and industrious, exerting themselves to the utmost in all the operations of the siege, which the prophet was to represent by the *uncovering of his arm,* or, as some read it, the *stretching out* of his arm, as it were to deal blows about without mercy. When God is about to do some great work he is said to *make bare his arm,* Isa. 52:10. In short, The Chaldeans will go about their business, and go on in it, as men in earnest, who resolve to go through with it. Now, 1. This is intended to be a *sign to the house of Israel* (*v.* 3), both to those in Babylon, who were eye-witnesses of what the prophet did, and to those also who remained in their own land, who would hear the report of it. The prophet was *dumb* and *could not speak* (*ch.* 3:26); but as his silence had a voice, and upbraided the people with their deafness, so even then God *left not himself without witness,* but ordered him to make signs, as dumb men are accustomed to do, and as Zacharias did when he was dumb, and by them to *make known his mind* (that is, the mind of God) to the people. And thus likewise the people were upbraided with their stupidity and dulness, that they were not capable of being taught as men of sense are, by words, but must be taught as children are, by pictures, or as deaf men are, by signs. Or, perhaps, they are hereby upbraided with their malice against the prophet. Had he spoken in words at length what was signified by these figures, they would have entangled him in his talk, would have indicted him for treasonable expressions, for they knew how to *make a man an offender for a word* (Isa. 29:21), to avoid which he is ordered to make use of signs. Or the prophet made use of signs for the same reason that Christ made use of parables, that *hearing they might hear and not understand,* and *seeing they might see and not perceive,* Mt. 13:14, 15. They would not understand what was plain, and therefore shall be taught by that which is difficult; and herein the Lord was righteous. 2. Thus the prophet *prophesies against Jerusalem* (*v.* 7); and there were those who not only understood it so, but were the more affected with it by its being so represented, for images to the eye commonly make deeper impressions upon the mind than words can, and for this reason sacraments are instituted to represent divine things, that we might see and believe, might see and be affected with those things; and we may expect this benefit by them, and a blessing to go along with them, while (as the prophet here) we make use only of such signs as God himself has expressly appointed, which, we must conclude, are the fittest. Note, The power of imagination, if it be rightly used, and kept under the direction and correction of reason and faith, may be of good use to kindle and excite pious and devout affections, as it was here to Ezekiel and his attendants. *"Methinks I see* so and so, myself dying, time expiring, the world on fire, the dead rising, the great tribunal set, and the like, may have an exceedingly good influence upon us: for fancy is like fire, a *good servant, but a bad master."* 3. This whole transaction has that in it which the prophet might, with a good colour of reason, have hesitated at and excepted against, and yet, in obedience to God's command, and in execution of his office, he did it according to order. (1.) It seemed childish and ludicrous, and beneath his gravity, and there were those that would ridicule him for it; but he knew the divine appointment put honour enough upon that which otherwise seemed mean to save his reputation in the doing of it. (2.) It was toilsome and tiresome to do as he did; but our ease as well as our credit must be sacrificed to our duty, and we must never call God's service in any instance of it a hard service. (3.) It could not but be very much against the grain with him to appear thus against Jerusalem, the city of God, the holy city, to act as an enemy against a place to which he was so good a friend; but he is a prophet, and must follow his instructions, not his affections, and must plainly preach the ruin of a sinful place, though its welfare is what he passionately desires and earnestly prays for. 4. All this that the prophet sets before the children of his people concerning the destruction of Jerusalem is designed to bring them to repentance, by showing them sin, the provoking cause of this destruction, sin the ruin of that once flourishing city, than which surely nothing could be more effectual to make them hate sin and turn from it; while he thus in lively colours describes the calamity with a great deal of pain and uneasiness to himself, he is *bearing the iniquity of Israel and Judah.* "Look here" (says he) "and see what work sin makes, what an *evil and bitter thing it is to depart form God;* this comes of sin, your sins and the sin of your fathers; let that therefore be the daily matter of your sorrow and shame now in your captivity, that you may make your peace with God and he may return in mercy to you." But observe, It is a day of punishment for a year of sin: *I have appointed thee each day for a year.* The siege is a calamity of 390 days, in which God reckons for the iniquity of 390 years; justly therefore d they acknowledge that God had *punished them less than their iniquity deserved,* Ezra 9:13. But let impenitent sinners know that, though now God is long-suffering towards them, in the other world there is an everlasting punishment. When God *laid bands* upon the prophet, it was to show them how they were *bound with the cords of their own transgression* (Lam. 1:14), and therefore they were now *holden in the cords of affliction.* But we may well think of the prophet's case with compassion, when God laid upon him the bands of duty, as he does on all his ministers (1 Co. 9:16, *Necessity is laid upon me, and woe unto me if I preach not the gospel*); and yet men laid upon him bonds of restraint (*ch.* 3:25); but under both it is satisfaction enough that they are serving the interests of God's kingdom among men.

Verses 9–17

The best exposition of this part of Ezekiel's prediction of Jerusalem's desolation is Jeremiah's lamentation of it, Lam. 4:3, 4, etc., and *v.* 10, where he pathetically describes the terrible famine that was in Jerusalem during the siege and the sad effects of it.

I. The prophet here, to affect the people with the foresight of it, must confine himself for 390 days to coarse fare and short commons, and that ill-dressed, for they should want both food and fuel.

1. His meat, for the quality of it, was to be of the worst bread, made of but little wheat and barley, and the rest of beans, and lentiles, and millet, and fitches, such as we feed horses or fatted hogs with, and this mixed, as mill corn, or as that in the beggar's bag, that has a dish full of one sort of corn at one house and of another at another house; of such corn as this must the prophet's bread be made while he underwent the fatigue of lying on his side, and needed something better to support him, *v.* 9. Note, It is our wisdom not to be too fond of dainties and pleasant bread, because we know not what hard meat we may be tied to, nay, and may be glad of, before we die. The meanest sort of food is better than we deserve, and therefore must not be despised nor wasted, nor must those that use it be looked upon with disdain, because we know not what may be our own lot.

2. For the quantity of it, it was to be of the least that a man could be kept alive with, to signify that the besieged should be reduced to short allowance and should hold out till all *the bread in the city was spent,* Jer. 37:21. The prophet must eat but twenty *shekels'* weight of bread a day (*v.* 10), that was about ten ounces; and he must drink but the *sixth part of a hin of water,* that was half a pint, about eight ounces, *v.* 11. The stint of the Lessian diet is fourteen ounces of meat and sixteen of drink. The prophet in Babylon had bread enough and to spare, and was by the river side, where there was plenty of water; and yet, that he might confirm his own prediction and be a sign to the children of Israel, God obliges him to live thus sparingly, and he submits to it. Note, God's servants must learn to endure hardness, and to deny themselves the use of lawful delights, when they may thereby serve the glory of God, evidence the sincerity of their faith, and express their sympathy with their brethren in affliction. The body must be *kept under and brought into subjection.* Nature is content with a little, grace with less, but lust with nothing. It is good to stint ourselves of choice, that we may the better bear it if ever we should come to be stinted by necessity. And in times of public distress and calamity it ill becomes us to make much of ourselves, as those that *drank wine in bowls* and *were not grieved for the affliction of Joseph,* Amos 6:4–6.

3. For the dressing of it, he must *bake it with a man's dung* (*v.* 12); that must be dried, and serve for fuel to heat his oven with. The thought of it would almost turn one's stomach; yet the coarse bread, thus baked, he must *eat as barley-cakes,* as freely as if it were the same bread he had been used to. This nauseous piece of cookery he must exercise publicly *in their sight,* that they might be the more affected with the calamity approaching, which was signified by it, that in the extremity of the famine they should not only have nothing that was dainty, but nothing that was cleanly, about them; they must take up with what they could get. *To the hungry soul every bitter thing is sweet.* This circumstance of the sign, the baking of his bread with man's dung, the prophet with submission humbly desired might be dispensed with (*v.* 14); it seemed to have in it something of a ceremonial pollution, for there was a law that man's dung should *be covered with earth,* that God might *see no unclean thing in their camp,* Deu. 23:13, 14. And must he go and gather a thing so offensive, and use it in the dressing of his meat in the sight of the people? *"Ah! Lord God,"* says he, *"behold, my soul has not been polluted,* and I am afraid lest by this it be polluted." Note, The pollution of the soul by sin is what good people dread more than any thing; and yet sometimes tender consciences fear it without cause, and perplex themselves with scruples about lawful things, as the prophet here, who had not yet learned that it is not that which *goes into the mouth that defiles the man,* Mt. 15:11. But observe he does not plead, "Lord, from my youth I have been brought up delicately and have never been used to any thing but what was clean and nice" (and there were those who were so brought up, who in the siege of Jerusalem did *embrace dunghills,* Lam. 4:5), but that he had been brought up conscientiously, and had never eaten any thing that was forbidden by the law, that *died of itself* or was *torn in pieces;* and therefore, "Lord, do not put this upon me now." Thus Peter pleaded (Acts 10:14), *Lord, I have never eaten any thing that is common or unclean.* Note, it will be comfortable to us, when we are reduced to hardships, if our hearts can witness for us that we have always been careful to abstain from sin, even from little sins, and the *appearances of evil.* Whatever God commands us, we may be sure, is

good; but, if we be put upon any thing that we apprehend to be evil, we should argue against it, from this consideration, that hitherto we have preserved our purity — and shall we lose it now? Now, because Ezekiel with a manifest tenderness of conscience made this scruple, God dispensed with him in this matter. Note, Those who have power in their hands should not be rigorous in pressing their commands upon those that are dissatisfied concerning them, yea, though their dissatisfactions be groundless or arising from education and long usage, but should recede from them rather than grieve or offend the weak, or put a stumbling-block before them, in conformity to the example of God's condescension to Ezekiel, though we are sure his authority is incontestable and all his commands are wise and good. God allowed Ezekiel to use *cow's dung* instead of *man's dung, v.* 15. This is a tacit reflection upon man, as intimating that he being polluted with sin his filthiness is more nauseous and odious than that of any other creature. *How much more abominable and filthy is man!* Job 15:16.

II. Now this sign is particularly explained here; it signified,

1. That those who remained in Jerusalem should be brought to extreme misery for want of necessary food. All supplies being cut off by the besiegers, the city would soon find the want of the country, for *the king himself is served of the field;* and thus *the staff of bread* would be *broken in Jerusalem, v.* 16. God would not only take away from the bread its power to nourish, so that *they should eat and not be satisfied* (Lev. 26:26), but would take away the bread itself (Isa. 3:1), so that what little remained should be *eaten by weight,* so much a day, so much a head, that they might have an equal share and might make it last as long as possible. But to what purpose, when they could not make it last always, and the besieged must be tired out before the besiegers? They should eat and drink *with care,* to make it go as far as might be, and with *astonishment,* when they saw it almost spent and knew not which way to look for a recruit. They should *be astonished one with another;* whereas it is ordinarily some alleviation of a calamity to have others share with us in it *(Solamen miseris socios habuisse doloris),* and some ease to the spirit to complain of the burden, it should be an aggravation of the misery that it was universal, and their complaining to one another should but make them all the more uneasy and increase the *astonishment.* And the event shall be as bad as their fears; they cannot make it worse than it is, for *they shall consume away for their iniquity;* multitudes of them shall die of famine, a lingering death, worse than that by *the sword* (Lam. 4:9); they shall dies so as to *feel themselves die.* And it is sin that brings all this misery upon them: *They shall consume away in their iniquity* (so it may be read); they shall continue hardened and impenitent, and shall die in their sins, which is more miserable than to die on a dunghill. Now, (1.) Let us see here what woeful work sin makes with a people, and acknowledge the righteousness of God herein. Time was when *Jerusalem was filled with the finest of the wheat* (Ps. 147:14); but now it would be glad of the coarsest, and cannot have it. *Fulness of bread,* as it was one of Jerusalem's mercies, so it had become one of her sins, Eze. 16:49. The plenty was abused to luxury and excess, which were therefore thus justly punished with famine. It is a righteous thing with God to deprive us of those enjoyments which we have made the food and fuel of our lusts. (2.) Let us see what reason we have to bless God for plenty, not only for the fruits of the earth, but for the freedom of commerce, that the husbandman can have money for his bread and the tradesman bread for his money, that there is abundance not only in the field, but in the market, that those who live in cities and great towns, though they *sow not,* neither do they *reap,* are yet fed from day to day with food convenient.

2. It signified that those who were carried into captivity should be forced to *eat their defiled bread among the Gentiles* (*v.* 13), to eat meat made up by Gentile hands otherwise than according to the law of the Jewish church, which they were always taught to call *defiled,* and which they would have as great an aversion to as a man would have to bread prepared with dung, that is (as perhaps it may be understood) kneaded and moulded with dung. Daniel and his fellows confined themselves to *pulse and water,* rather than they would *eat the portion of the king's meat* assigned them, because they apprehended it would defile them, Dan. 1:8. Or they should be forced to eat putrid meat, such as their oppressors would allow them in their slavery, and such as formerly they would have scorned to touch. Because they *served not God* with cheerfulness in the abundance of all things, God will make them serve their enemies in the want of all things.

CHAPTER 5

In this chapter we have a further, and no less terrible, denunciation of the judgments of God, which were coming with all speed and force upon the Jewish nation, which would utterly ruin it; for when God judges he will overcome. This destruction of Judah and Jerusalem is here, I. Represented by a sign, the cutting, and burning, and scattering of hair (*v.* 1–4). II. That sign is expounded, and applied to Jerusalem. 1. Sin is charged upon Jerusalem as the cause of this desolation — contempt of God's law (*v.* 5–7) and profanation of his sanctuary (*v.* 11). 2 Wrath is threatened, great wrath (*v.* 8–10), a variety of miseries (*v.* 12, 16, 17), such as should be their reproach and ruin (*v.* 13–15).

Verses 1–4

We have here the sign by which the utter destruction of Jerusalem is set forth; and here, as before, the prophet is himself the sign, that the people might see how much he affected himself with, and interested himself in, the case of Jerusalem, and how it lay to his heart, even when he foretold the desolations of it. he was so much concerned about it as to take what was done to it as done to himself, so far was he from desiring the woeful day.

I. He must *shave off the hair of his head and beard* (*v.* 1), which signified God's utter rejecting and abandoning that people, as a useless worthless generation, such as could well be spared, nay, such as it would be his honour to part with; his judgments, and all the instruments he made use of in cutting them off, were this *sharp knife* and this *razor,* that were proper to be made use of, and would do execution. Jerusalem had been the head, but, having degenerated, had become as the *hair,* which, when it grows thick and long, is but a burden which a man wishes to get clear of, as God of the sinners in Zion. *Ah! I will ease me of my adversaries,* Isa. 1:24. Ezekiel must not cut off that hair only which was superfluous, but *cut it all off,* denoting the full end that God would make of Jerusalem. The hair that would not be trimmed and kept neat and clean by the admonitions of the prophets must be all shaved off by utter destruction. Those will be ruined that will not be reformed.

II. He must *weigh the hair* and *divide it into three parts.* This intimates the very exact directing of God's judgments according to equity (by him men and their actions are *weighed* in the unerring balance of truth and righteousness) and the proportion which divine justice observes in punishing some by one judgment and others by another; one way or other, they shall all be met with. Some make the shaving of the hair to denote the loss of their liberty and of their honour: it was looked upon as a mark of ignominy, as in the disgrace Hanun put on David's ambassadors. It denotes also the loss of their joy, for they shaved their heads upon occasion of great mourning; I may add the loss of their Nazariteship, for the shaving of the head was a period to that vow (Num. 6:18), and Jerusalem was now no longer looked upon as a *holy city.*

III. He must dispose of the hair so that it might all be destroyed or dispersed, *v.* 2. 1. One *third part* must *be burnt in the midst of the city,* denoting the multitudes that should perish by famine and pestilence, and perhaps many in the conflagration of the city, *when the days of the siege were fulfilled.* Or the laying of that glorious city in ashes might well be looked upon as a third part of the destruction threatened. 2. Another third part was to be *cut in pieces with a knife,* representing the many who, during the siege, were slain by the sword, in their sallies out upon the besiegers, and especially when the city was taken by storm, the Chaldeans being then most furious and the Jews most feeble. 3. Another third part was to be *scattered in the wind,* denoting the carrying away of some into the land of the conqueror and the flight of others into the neighbouring countries for shelter; so that they were hurried, some one way and some another, like loose hairs in the wind. But, lest they should think that this dispersion would be their escape, God adds, *I will draw out a sword after them,* so that wherever they go evil shall pursue them. Note, God has variety of judgments wherewith to accomplish the destruction of a sinful people and to make an end when he begins.

IV. He must preserve a small quantity of the third sort that were to be *scattered in the wind,* and *bind them in his skirts,* as one would bind that which he is very mindful and careful of, *v.* 3. This signified perhaps that little handful of people which were left under the government of Gedaliah, who, it was hoped, would keep possession of the land when the body of the people was carried into captivity. Thus God would have done well for them if they would have done well for themselves. But these few that were reserved must be taken and *cast into the fire, v.* 4. When Gedaliah and his friends were slain the people that put themselves under his protection were scattered, some gone into Egypt, others carried off by the Chaldeans, and in short the land totally cleared of them; then this was fulfilled, for out of those combustions *a fire came forth into all the house of Israel,* who, as fuel upon the fire, kindled and consumed one another. Note, It is ill with a people when those are taken away in wrath that seemed to be marked for monuments of mercy; for then there is no remnant or escaping, none shut up or left.

Verses 5–17

We have here the explanation of the foregoing similitude: *This is Jerusalem.* Thus it is usual in scripture language to give the name of the thing signified to the sign; as when Christ said, *This is my body.* The prophet's head, which was to be shaved, signified Jerusalem, which by the judgments of God was now to be stripped of all its ornaments, to be emptied of all its inhabitants, and to be set *naked and bare,* to be *shaved with a razor that is hired,* Isa. 7:20. The head of one that was a priest, a prophet, a holy person, was fittest to represent Jerusalem the holy city. Now the contents of these verses are much the same with what we have often met with, and still shall, in the writings of the prophets. Here we have,

I. The privileges Jerusalem was honoured with (*v.* 5): *I have set it in the midst of the nations and countries that are round about her,* and those famous nations and very considerable. Jerusalem was not situated in a remote obscure corner of the world, far from neighbours, but in the midst of kingdoms that were populous, polite, and civilized, famed for learning, arts, and sciences, and which then made the greatest figure in the world. But there seems to be more in it than this. 1. Jerusalem was dignified and preferred above the neighbouring nations and their cities. it was *set in the midst* of them as excelling them all. This *holy mountain was exalted above all the hills,* Isa. 2:2. *Why leap you, you high hills? This is the hill which God desires to dwell in,* Ps. 68:16. Jerusalem was a city upon a hill, conspicuous and illustrious, and which all the neighbouring nations had an eye upon, some for good-will, some for ill-will. 2. Jerusalem was designed to have a good influence upon *the nations and countries round about,* was set in the midst of them as a candle upon a candlestick, to spread the light of divine revelation, which she was blessed with, to all the dark corners of the neighbouring nations, that from them it might diffuse itself further, even to the ends of the earth. Jerusalem was set *in the midst* of the nations, to be as the heart in the body, to invigorate this dead world with a divine life as well as to enlighten this dark world with a divine light, to be an example of every thing that was good. The nations that observed what excellent *statutes and judgments* they had concluded them to be *a wise and understanding people* (Deu. 4:6), fit to be consulted as an oracle, as they were in Solomon's time, 1 Ki. 4:34. And, had they preserved this reputation and made a right use of it, what a blessing would Jerusalem have been to all the nations about! But, failing to be so, the accomplishment of this intention was reserved for its latter days, *when out of Zion went forth the* gospel *law and the word of the Lord* Jesus *from Jerusalem,* and there *repentance and remission* began to be preached, and thence the preachers of them *went forth into all nations.* And, when that was done, Jerusalem was levelled with the ground. Note, When places and persons are made great, it is with design that they may do good and that those about them may be the better for them, that their *light may shine before men.*

II. The provocations Jerusalem was guilty of. A very high charge is here drawn up against that city, and proved beyond contradiction sufficient to justify God in seizing its privileges and putting it under military execution. 1. She has *not walked in God's statutes,* nor *kept his judgments* (*v.* 7); nay, the inhabitants of Jerusalem had *refused his judgments and his statutes* (*v.* 6); they did not do their duty, nay, they *would not,* they said that they would not. Those *statutes and judgments* which their neighbours admired they despised, which they should have set before their face they cast behind their back. Note, A contempt of the word and law of God opens a door to all manner of iniquity. God's statutes are the terms on which he deals with men; those that refuse his terms cannot expect his favours. 2. She had *changed God's judgments into wickedness* (*v.* 6), a very high expression of profaneness, that the people had not only broken God's laws, but had so perverted and abused them that they had made them the excuse and colour of their wickedness. They introduced the abominable customs and usages of the heathen, instead of God's institutions; this was changing *the truth of God into a lie* (Rom. 1:25) and the *glory of God into shame,* Ps. 4:2. Note, Those that have been well educated, if they live ill, put the highest affront imaginable upon God, as if he were the patron of sin and *his judgments* were *turned into wickedness.* 3. She had been worse than the neighbouring nations, to whom she should have set a good example: *She has changed my judgments,* by idolatries and false worship, *more than the nations* (*v.* 6), and she has *multiplied* (that is, multiplied idols and altars, gods and temples, multiplied those things the unity of which was their praise) *more than the nations that were round about.* Israel's God is one, and his name one, his altar one; but they, not content with this one God, multiplied their gods to such a degree that *according to the number of their cities so were their gods,* and their altars were *as heaps in the furrows of the field;* so that they exceeded all their neighbours in having *gods many and lords many.* They corrupted revealed religion more than the Gentiles had corrupted natural religion. Note, If those who have made a profession of religion, and have had a pious education, apostatize from it, they are commonly more profane and vicious than those who never made any profession; they have *seven other spirits more wicked.* 4. She had *not done according to the judgments of the nations, v.* 7. Israel had not acted towards their God, as the nations had acted towards their gods, though they were false gods; they had not been so observant of him nor so constant to him. Has a nation *changed its gods,* or slighted them, so as they have? Jer. 2:11. or it may refer to their morals; instead of reforming their neighbors, they came short of them; and many who were of the *uncircumcision kept the righteousness of the law* better than those who were *of the circumcision,* Rom. 2:26, 27. Those who had the light of scripture did not *according to the judgments* of many who had only the light of nature. Note, There are those who are called *Christians* who will in the great day be condemned by the better tempers and better lives of sober heathens. 5. The particular crime charged upon Jerusalem is profaning the holy things, which she had been both entrusted and honoured with (*v.* 11): *Thou hast defiled my sanctuary with all thy detestable things,* with thy idols and idolatries. The images of their pretended deities, and the groves erected in honour of them, were brought into the temple; and the ceremonies used by idolaters were brought into the worship of God. Thus every thing that is sacred was polluted. Note, Idols are detestable things any where, but more especially so in the sanctuary.

III. The punishments that Jerusalem should fall under for these provocations: *Shall not God visit for these things?* No doubt he shall. The matter of the sentence here passed upon Jerusalem is very dreadful, and the manner of expression makes it yet more so; the judgments are various, and the threatenings of them varied, reiterated, inculcated, that one may well say, *Who is able to stand in God's sight when once he is angry?*

1. God will take this work of punishing Jerusalem into his own hands; and *who knows the power of his anger* and what *a fearful thing it is to fall into his hands?* Observe what a strong emphasis is laid upon it (*v.* 8): *I, even I, am against thee.* God had been for Jerusalem, to defend and save it; but miserable is its case when he has turned to be its enemy and fights against it. If God be against us, the whole creation is at war with us, and nothing can be for us so as to stand us in any stead: "You think it is only the Chaldean army that is against you, but they are God's hand, or rather the staff in his hand; it is *I, even I,* that *am against thee,* not only to speak against thee by prophets, but to act against thee by providence. *I will execute judgments in thee* (*v.* 10), *in the midst of thee* (*v.* 8), not only in the suburbs, but in the heart of the city, not only in the borders, but in the bowels of the country." Note, Those who will not observe the judgments of God's mouth shall not escape the judgments of his hand; and God's judgments, when they come with commission, will penetrate into the midst of a people, will enter into the soul, *into the bowels like water* and *like oil into the bones. I will execute judgments.* Note, God himself undertakes to execute his own judgments, according to the true and full intent of them; whatever are the instruments, he is the principal agent.

2. These punishments shall come from his displeasure. As to the body of the people, it shall not be a correction in love, but he will *execute judgments in anger, and in fury, and in furious rebukes* (*v.* 15), strange expressions to come from a God who has said, *Fury is not in me,* and who has declared himself *gracious, and merciful,* and *slow to anger.* But they are designed to show the malignity of sin, and the offence it gives to the just and holy God. That must needs be a very evil thing which provokes him to such resentments, and against his own people too, that had been so high in his favour, and expressed with so much satisfaction (*v.* 13): *"My anger,* which has long been withheld, *shall* now *be accomplished, and I will cause my fury to rest upon them;* it shall not only light upon them, but lie upon them, and fill them as vessels of wrath fitted by their own wickedness to destruction; *and,* justice being hereby glorified, *I will be comforted,* I will be entirely satisfied in what I have done." As, when God is dishonoured by the sins of men, he is said to be *grieved* (Ps. 95:10), so when he is honoured by their destruction he is said to *be comforted.* The struggle between mercy and judgment is over, and in this case judgment triumphs, triumphs indeed; for mercy that has been so long abused is now silent and gives up the cause, has not a word more to say on the behalf of such an ungrateful incorrigible people: *My eye shall not spare, neither will I have any pity, v.* 11. Divine compassion defers the punishment, or mitigates it, or supports under it, or shortens it; but here is *judgment without mercy,* wrath without any mixture or allay of pity. These expressions are thus sharpened and heightened perhaps with design to look further, to the vengeance of eternal fire, which some of the destructions we read of in the Old Testament were typical of, and particularly that of Jerusalem; for surely it is nowhere on this side hell that this word has its full accomplishment, *My eye shall not spare,* but *I will cause my fury to rest.* Note, Those who live and die impenitent will perish for ever unpitied; there is a day coming when *the Lord will not spare.*

3. Punishments shall be public and open: *I will execute* these *judgments in the sight of the nations* (*v.* 8); the judgments themselves shall be so remarkable that all the nations far and near shall take notice of them; they shall be all the talk of that part of the world, and the more for the conspicuousness of the place and people on which they are inflicted. Note, Public sins, as they call for public reproofs *(those that sin rebuke before all),* so, if those prevail not, they call for public judgments. *He strikes them as wicked men in the open sight of others* (Job 34:26), that he may maintain and vindicate the honour of his government, for (as Grotius descants upon it here) *why should he suffer it to be said, See what wicked lives those lead who profess to be the worshippers of the only true God!* And, as the publicity of the judgments will redound to the honour of God, so it will serve, (1.) To aggravate the punishment, and to make it lie the more heavily. Jerusalem, being made *waste,* becomes *a reproach among the nations in the sight of all that pass by, v.* 14. The more conspicuous and the more peculiar any have been in the day of their prosperity the greater disgrace attends their fall; and that was Jerusalem's case. The more Jerusalem had been *a praise in the earth* the more it is now *a reproach and a taunt, v.* 15. This she was warned of as much as any thing when her glory commenced (1 Ki. 9:8), and this was lamented as much as any thing when it was laid in the dust, Lam. 2:15. (2.) To teach the nations to fear before the God of Israel, when they see what a jealous God he is, and how severely he punishes sin even in those that are nearest to him: *It shall be an instruction to the nations, v.* 15. Jerusalem should have taught her neighbours the fear of God by her piety and virtue, but, she not doing that, God will teach it to them by her ruin; for they have reason to say, *If this be done in the green tree, what shall be done in the dry?* If *judgment begin at the house of God,* where will it end? If those be thus punished who only had some idolaters among them, what will become of us who are all idolaters? Note, The destruction of some is designed for the instruction of others. Malefactors are publicly punished *in terrorem — that others may take warning.*

4. These punishments, in the kind of them, shall be very severe and grievous. (1.) They shall be such as have no precedent or parallel. Their sins being more provoking than those of others, the judgments executed upon them should be uncommon (*v.* 9): *"I will do in thee that which I have not done* in thee before, though thou hast long since deserved it; nay, that which I have not done in any other city." This punishment of Jerusalem is said to be *greater than that of Sodom* (Lam. 4:6), which was more grievous than all that went before it; nay, it is such as *"I will not do any more the like,* all the circumstances taken in, to any other city, till the like come to be done again to this city, in the final overthrow by the Romans." This is a rhetorical expression of the most grievous judgments, like that character of Hezekiah, that there was *none like him, before or after him.* (2.) They shall be such as will force them to break the strongest bonds of natural affection to one another, which will be a just punishment of them for their wilfully breaking the bonds of their duty to God (*v.* 10): *The fathers shall eat the sons, and the sons shall eat the fathers,* through the extremity of the famine, or shall be compelled to do it by their barbarous conquerors. (3.) There shall be a complication of judgments, any one of them terrible enough, and desolating; but what then would they be when they came all together and in perfection? Some shall be taken away by the plague (*v.* 12); the *pestilence shall pass through thee* (*v.* 17), sweeping all before it, as the destroying angel; others *shall be consumed with famine,* shall gradually waste away as men in a consumption (*v.* 12); this is again insisted on (*v.* 16): *I will send upon them the evil arrows of famine;* hunger shall make them pine, and shall pierce them to the heart, as if arrows, *evil arrows,* poisoned darts, were shot into them. God has many arrows, *evil arrows,* in his quiver; when some are discharged, he has still more in reserve. *I will increase the famine upon you.* A famine in a bereaved country may *decrease* as fruits spring forth; but a famine in a besieged city will *increase* of course; yet god speaks of it as his act: *"I will increase it, and will break your staff of bread,* will take away the necessary supports of life, will disappoint you of all that which you depend upon, so that there is no remedy, but you must fall to the ground." Life is frail, is weak, is burdened, so that, if it have not daily bread for its staff to lean upon, it cannot but sink, and is soon gone if that staff be broken. Others *shall fall by the sword round about* Jerusalem, when they sally out upon the besiegers; it is a *sword* which God *will bring, v.* 17. The sword of the Lord, that used to be drawn for Jerusalem's defence, is now drawn for its destruction. Others are devoured by *evil beasts,* which will make a prey of those that fly for shelter to the deserts and mountains. They shall meet their ruin where they expected refuge, for there is no escaping the judgments of God, *v.* 17. And, *lastly,* those who escape shall be *scattered into* all parts of the world, *into all the winds* (so it is expressed, *v.* 10, 12), intimating that they should not only be dispersed, but hurried, and tossed, and driven to and fro, as *chaff before the wind.* Nay, and Cain's curse (to be fugitives and vagabonds) is not the worst of it neither; their restless life shall be cut off by a bloody death: *"I will draw out a sword after them,* which shall follow them wherever they go." *Evil pursues sinners;* and the curse shall come upon them and overtake them.

5. These punishments will prove their ruin by degrees. They shall be *diminished* (*v.* 11); their strength and glory shall grow less and less. They shall be *bereaved* (*v.* 17), emptied of all that which was their joy and confidence. God sends these judgments on purpose to destroy them, *v.* 16. The arrows are not sent (as those which Jonathan shot) for their direction, but *for their destruction;* for god will *accomplish his fury upon them* (*v.* 13); the day of God's pa-

tience is over, and the ruin is remediless. Though this prophecy was to have its accomplishment now quickly, in the destruction of Jerusalem by the Chaldeans, yet the executioners not being named here, but the criminal only (this is Jerusalem), we may well suppose that it looks further, to the final destruction of that great city by the Romans when God made a full end of the Jewish nation, and caused his fury to rest upon them.

6. All this is ratified by the divine authority and veracity: I the Lord have spoken it, v. 15 and again v. 17. The sentence is passed by him that is Judge of heaven and earth, whose judgment is according to truth, and the judgments of whose hand are according to the judgments of his mouth. he has spoken it who can do it, for with him nothing is impossible. He has spoken it who will do it, for he is not a man that he should lie. He has spoken it whom we are bound to hear and heed, whose ipse dixit — word commands the most serious attention and submissive assent: And they shall know that I the Lord have spoken it, v. 13. There were those who thought it was only the prophet that spoke it in his delirium; but God will make them know, by the accomplishment of it, that he has spoken it in his zeal. Note, Sooner or later, God's word will prove itself.

CHAPTER 6

In this chapter we have, I. A threatening of the destruction of Israel for their idolatry, and the destruction of their idols with them (v. 1–7). II. A promise of the gracious return of a remnant of them to God, by true repentance and reformation (v. 8–10). III. Directions given to the prophet and others, the Lord's servants, to lament both the iniquities and the calamities of Israel (v. 11–14).

Verses 1–7

Here, I. The prophecy is directed to the mountains of Israel (v. 1, 2); the prophet must set his face towards them. If he could see so far off as the land of Israel, the mountains of that land would be first and furthest seen; towards them therefore he must look, and look boldly and stedfastly, as the judge looks at the prisoner, and directs his speech to him, when he passes sentence upon him. Though the mountains of Israel be ever so high and ever so strong, he must set his face against them, as having judgments to denounce that should shake their foundation. The mountains of Israel had been holy mountains, but now that they had polluted them with their high places God set his face against them and therefore the prophet must. Israel is here put, not, as sometimes, for the ten tribes, but for the whole land. The mountains are called upon to hear the word of the Lord, to shame the inhabitants that would not hear. The prophets might as soon gain attention from the mountains as from that rebellious and gainsaying people, to whom they all day long stretched out their hands in vain. Hear, O mountains! the Lord's controversy (Mic. 6:1, 2), for God's cause will have a hearing, whether we hear it or no. But from the mountains the word of the Lord echoes to the hills, to the rivers, and to the valleys; for to them also the Lord God speaks, intimating that the whole land is concerned in what is now to be delivered and shall be witnesses against this people that they had fair warning given them of the judgments coming, but they would not take it; nay, they contradicted the message and persecuted the messengers, so that God's prophets might more safely and comfortably speak to the hills and mountains than to them.

II. That which is threatened in this prophecy is the utter destruction of the idols and the idolaters, and both by the sword of war. God himself is commander-in-chief of this expedition against the mountains of Israel. It is he that says, Behold, I, even I, will bring a sword upon you (v. 3); the sword of the Chaldeans is at God's command, goes where he sends it, comes where he brings it, and lights as he directs it. In the desolations of that war,

1. The idols and all their appurtenances should be destroyed. The high places, which were on the tops of mountains (v. 3), shall be levelled and made desolate (v. 6); they shall not be beautified, shall not be frequented as they had been. The altars, on which they offered sacrifice and burnt incense to strange gods, shall be broken to pieces and laid waste; the images and idols shall be defaced, shall be broken and cease, and be cut down, and all the fine costly works about them shall be abolished, v. 4, 6. Observe here, (1.) That war makes woeful desolations, which those persons, places, and things that were esteemed most sacred

cannot escape; for the sword devours one as well as another. (2.) That God sometimes ruins idolatries even by the hands of idolaters, for such the Chaldeans themselves were; but, as if the deity were a local thing, the greatest admirers of the gods of their own country were the greatest despisers of the gods of other countries. (3.) It is just with God to make that a desolation which we make an idol of; for he is a jealous God and will not bear a rival. (4.) If men do not, as they ought, destroy idolatry, God will, first or last, find out a way to do it. When Josiah had destroyed the high places, altars, and images, with the sword of justice, they set them up again; but God will now destroy them with the sword of war, and let us see who dares re-establish them.

2. The worshippers of idols and all their adherents should be destroyed likewise. As all their high places shall be laid waste, so shall all their dwelling-places too, even all their cities, v. 6. Those that profane God's dwelling-place as they had done can expect no other than that he should abandon theirs, ch. v. 11. If any man defile the temple of God, him will God destroy, 1 Co. 3:17. It is here threatened that their slain shall fall in the midst of them (v. 7); there shall be abundance slain, even in those places which were thought most safe; but it is added as a remarkable circumstance that they shall fall before their idols (v. 4), that their dead carcases should be laid, and their bones scattered, about their altars, v. 5. (1.) Thus their idols should be polluted, and those places profaned by the dead bodies which they had had in veneration. If they will not defile the covering of their graven images, God will, Isa. 30:22. The throwing of the carcases among them, as upon the dunghill, intimates that they were but dunghill-deities. (2.) Thus it was intimated that they were but dead things, unfit to be rivals with the living God; for the carcases of dead men, that, like them, have eyes and see not, ears and hear not, were the fittest company for them. (3.) Thus the idols were upbraided with their inability to help their worshippers, and idolaters were upbraided with the folly of trusting in them; for, it should seem, they fell by the sword of the enemy when they were actually before their idols imploring their aid and putting themselves under their protection. Sennacherib was slain by his sons when he was worshipping in the house of his god. (4.) The sin might be read in this circumstance of the punishment; the slain men are cast before the idols, to show that therefore they are slain, because they worshipped those idols; see Jer. 8:1, 2. let the survivors observe it, and take warning not to worship images; let them see it, and know that God is the Lord, that the Lord he is God and he alone.

Verses 8–10

Judgment had hitherto triumphed, but in these verses mercy rejoices against judgment. A sad end is made of this provoking people, but not a full end. The ruin seems to be universal, and yet will I leave a remnant, a little remnant, distinguished from the body of the people, a few of many, such as are left when the rest perish; and it is God that leaves them. This intimates that they deserved to be cut off with the rest, and would have been cut off if God had not left them. See Isa. 1:9. And it is God who by his grace works that in them which he has an eye to in sparing them. Now,

I. It is a preserved remnant, saved from the ruin which the body of the nation is involved in (v. 8): That you may have some who shall escape the sword. God said (ch. v. 12) that he would draw a sword after those who were scattered, that destruction should pursue them in their dispersion; but here is mercy remembered in the midst of that wrath, and a promise that some of the Jews of the dispersion, as they were afterwards called, should escape the sword. None of those who were to fall by the sword about Jerusalem shall escape; for they trust to Jerusalem's walls for security, and shall be made ashamed of that vain confidence. but some of them shall escape the sword among the nations, where, being deprived of all other stays, they stay themselves upon God only. They are said to have those who shall escape; for they shall be the seed of another generation, out of which Jerusalem shall flourish again.

II. It is a penitent remnant (v. 9): Those who escape of you shall remember me. Note, To those whom God designs for life he will give repentance unto life. They are reprieved, and escape the sword, that they may have time to return

to God. Note, God's patience both leaves room for repentance and is an encouragement to sinners to repent. Where God designs grace to repent he allows space to repent; yet many who have the space want the grace, many who escape the sword do not forsake the sin, as it is promised that these shall do. This remnant, here marked for salvation, is a type of the remnant reserved out of the body of mankind to be monuments of mercy, who are made safe in the same way that these were, by being brought to repentance. Now observe here,

1. The occasion of their repentance, and that is a mixture of judgment and mercy — judgment, that they were carried captives, but mercy, that they escaped the sword in the land of their captivity. They were driven out of their own land, but not out of the land of the living, not chased out of the world, as other were and they deserved to be. Note, The consideration of the just rebukes of Providence we are under, and yet of the mercy mixed with them, should engage us to repent, that we may answer God's end in both. And true repentance shall be accepted of God, though we are brought to it by our troubles; nay, sanctified afflictions often prove means of conversion, as to Manasseh.

2. The root and principle of their repentance: They shall remember me among the nations. Those who forgot God in the land of their peace and prosperity, who waxed fat and kicked, were brought to remember him in the land of their captivity. The prodigal son never bethought himself of his father's house till he was ready to perish for hunger in the far country. Their remembering God was the first step they took in returning to him. Note, Then there begins to be some hopes of sinners when they have sinned against, and to enquire, Where is God my Maker? Sin takes rise in forgetting God, Jer. 3:21. Repentance takes rise from the remembrance of him and of our obligations to him. God says, They shall remember me, that is, "I will give them grace to do so;" for otherwise they would for ever forget him. That grace shall find them out wherever they are, and by bringing God to their mind shall bring them to their right mind. The prodigal, when he remembered his father, remembered how he has sinned against Heaven and before him; so do these penitents. (1.) They remember the base affront they had put upon God by their idolatries, and this is that which an ingenuous repentance fastens upon and most sadly laments. They had departed from God to idols, and given that honour to pretended deities, the creatures of men's fancies and the work of men's hands, which they should have given to the God of Israel. They departed from God, from his word, which they should have made their rule, from his work, which they should have made their business. Their hearts departed from him. The heart, which he requires and insists upon, and without which bodily exercise profits nothing, the heart, which should be set upon him, and carried out towards him, when that departs from him, is as the treacherous elopement of a wife from her husband or the rebellious revolt of a subject from his sovereign. Their eyes also go after their idols; they doted on them, and had great expectations from them. Their hearts followed their eyes in the choice of their gods (they must have gods that they could see), and then their eyes followed their hearts in the adoration of them. Now the malignity of this sin is that it is spiritual whoredom; it is a whorish heart that departs from God; and they are eyes that go a whoring after their idols. Note, Idolatry is spiritual whoredom; it is the breach of a marriage-covenant with God; it is the setting of the affections upon that which is a rival with him, and the indulgence of a base lust, which deceives and defiles the soul, and is a great wrong to God in his honour. (2.) They remember what a grief this was to him and how he resented it. They shall remember that I am broken with their whorish heart and their eyes that are full of this spiritual adultery, not only angry at it, but grieved, as a husband is at the lewdness of a wife whom he dearly loved, grieved to such a degree that he is broken with it; it breaks his heart to think that he should be so disingenuously dealt with; he is broken as an aged father is with the undutiful behaviour of a rebellious and disobedient son, which sinks his spirits and makes him to stoop. Forty years long was I grieved with this generation, Ps. 95:10. God's measures were broken (so some); a stop was put to the current of his favours towards them, and he was even compelled to punish them. This they shall

remember in the day of their repentance, and it shall affect and humble them more than any thing, not so much that their peace was broken, and their country broken, as *that God was broken* by their sin. Thus *they shall look on him whom they have pierced and shall mourn,* Zec. 12:10. Note, Nothing grieves a true penitent so much as to think that his sin has been a grief to God and to the Spirit of his grace.

3. The product and evidence of their repentance: *They shall loathe themselves for the evils which they have committed in all their abominations.* Thus God will give them grace to qualify them for pardon and deliverance. Though he had been *broken by their whorish heart,* yet he would not quite cast them off. See Isa. 57:17, 18; Hos. 2:13, 14. His goodness takes occasion from their badness to appear the more illustrious. note, (1.) True penitents see sin to be an abominable thing, that *abominable thing which the Lord hates* and which makes sinners, and even their services, odious to him, Jer. 44:4; Isa. 1:11. It defiles the sinner's own conscience, and makes him, unless he be past feeling, an abomination to himself. An idol is particularly called *an abomination,* Isa. 44:19. Those gratifications which the hearts of sinners were set upon as delectable things the hearts of penitents are turned against as detestable things. (2.) There are many *evils committed in these abominations,* many included in them, attendant on them, and flowing from them, many transgressions in one sin, Lev. 16:21. In their idolatries they were sometimes guilty of whoredom (as in the worship of Peor), sometimes of murder (as in the worship of Moloch); these were *evils committed in their abominations.* Or it denotes the great malignity there is in sin; it is an abomination that has abundance of evil in it. (3.) Those that truly loathe sin cannot but loathe themselves because of sin; self-loathing is evermore the companion of true repentance. Penitents quarrel with themselves, and can never be reconciled to themselves till they have some ground to hope that God is reconciled to them; nay, *then* they shall lie down in their shame, when he is pacified towards them, *ch.* 16:63.

4. The glory that will redound to God by their repentance (*v.* 10): *"They shall know that I am the Lord;* they shall be convinced of it by experience, and shall be ready to own it, *and that I have not said in vain that I would do this evil unto them,* finding that what I have said is made good, and made to work for good, and to answer a good intention, and that it was not without just provocation that they were thus threatened and thus punished." Note, (1.) One way or other God will make sinners to know and own that he is the lord, either by their repentance or by their ruin. (2.) All true penitents are brought to acknowledge both the equity and the efficacy of the word of God, particularly the threatenings of the word, and to justify God in them and in the accomplishment of them.

Verses 11–14

The same threatenings which we had before in the foregoing chapter, and in the former part of this, are here repeated, with a direction to the prophet to lament them, that those he prophesied to might be the more affected with the foresight of them.

I. He must by his gestures in preaching express the dep sense he had both of the iniquities and of the calamities of the house of Israel (*v.* 11): *Smite with thy hand and stamp with thy foot.* Thus he must make it to appear that he was in earnest in what he said to them, that he firmly believed it and laid it to heart. Thus he must signify the just displeasure he had conceived at their sins, and the just dread he was under of the judgments coming upon them. Some would reject this use of these gestures, and call them antic and ridiculous; but God bids him use them because they might help to enforce the word upon some and give it the setting on; and those that know the worth of souls will be content to be laughed at by the wits, so they may but edify the weak. Two things the prophet must thus lament: — 1. National sins. *Alas! for all the evil abominations of the house of Israel.* Note, The sins of sinners are the sorrows of God's faithful servants, especially the *evil abominations of the house of Israel,* whose sins are more abominable and have more evil in them than the sins of others. Alas! *What will be in the end hereof?* 2. National judgments. To punish them for these abominations *they shall fall by the sword, by the famine, and by the pestilence.* Note, It is our duty to be affected not only with our own sins and sufferings, but with the sins and sufferings of others; and to look with compassion upon the miseries that wicked people bring upon themselves; as Christ *beheld Jerusalem and wept over it.*

II. He must inculcate what he had said before concerning the destruction that was coming upon them. 1. They shall be run down and ruined by a variety of judgments which shall find them out and follow them wherever they are (*v.* 12): *He that is far off,* and thinks himself out of danger, because out of the reach of the Chaldeans' arrows, shall find himself not out of the reach of God's arrows, which fly day and night (Ps. 91:5): *He shall die of the pestilence. He that is near* a place of strength, which he hopes will be to him a place of safety, *shall fall by the sword,* before he can retreat. *He that* is so cautious as not to venture out, but *remains* in the city, *shall* there *die by the famine,* the saddest death of all. *Thus will* God *accomplish his fury,* that is, do all that against them which he had purposed to do. 2. They shall read their sin in their punishment; for *their slain men shall be among their idols, round about their altars,* as was threatened before, *v.* 5–7. There, where they had prostrated themselves in honour of their idols, God will lay them dead, to their own reproach and the reproach of their idols. They lived among them and shall die among them. They had offered sweet odours to their idols, but there shall their dead carcases send forth an offensive smell, as it were to atone for that misplaced incense. 3. The country shall be all laid waste, as, before, *the cities* (*v.* 6): *I will make the land desolate.* That fruitful, pleasant, populous country, that has been as the garden of the Lord, the glory of all lands, shall be *desolate, more desolate than the wilderness towards Diblath, v.* 14. It is called Diblathaim (Num. 33:46; Jer. 48:22), that *great and terrible wilderness* which is described, Deu. 8:15, wherein were *fiery serpents and scorpions.* The land of Canaan is at this day one of the most barren desolate countries in the world. City and country are thus depopulated, *that the altars may be laid waste and made desolate, v.* 6. Rather than their idolatrous altars shall be left standing, both town and country shall be laid in ruins. Sin is a desolating thing; therefore *stand in awe and sin not.*

CHAPTER 7

In this chapter the approaching ruin of the land of Israel is most particularly foretold in affecting expressions often repeated, that if possible they might be awakened by repentance to prevent it. The prophet must tell them, I. That it will be a final ruin, a complete utter destruction, which would make an end of them, a miserable end (*v.* 1–6). II. That it is an approaching ruin, just at the door (*v.* 7–10). III. That it is an unavoidable ruin, because they had by sin brought it upon themselves (*v.* 10–15). IV. That their strength and wealth should be no fence against it (*v.* 16–19). V. That the temple, which they trusted in, should itself be ruined (*v.* 20–22). VI. That it should be a universal ruin, the sin that brought it having been universal (*v.* 23–27).

Verses 1–15

We have here fair warning given of the destruction of the land of Israel, which was now hastening on apace. God, by the prophet, not only sends notice of it, but will have it inculcated in the same expressions, to show that the thing is certain, that it is near, that the prophet is himself affected with it and desires they should be so too, but finds them deaf, and stupid, and unaffected. When the town is on fire men do no seek for fine words and quaint expressions in which to give an account of it, but cry about the streets, with a loud and lamentable voice, "Fire! fire!" So the prophet here proclaims, *An end! an end! it has come, it has come; behold, it has come. He that hath ears to hear let him hear.*

I. *An end has come, the end has come* (*v.* 2), and again (*v.* 3, 6), *Now has the end come upon thee* — the end which all their wickedness had a tendency to, and which God had often told them it would come to at last, when by his prophets he had asked them, *What will you do in the end hereof?* — the end which all the foregoing judgments had been working towards, as means to bring it about (their ruin shall now be completed) — or *the end,* that is, the period of their state, the final destruction of their nation, as the deluge was *the end of all flesh,* Gen. 6:13. They had flattered themselves with hopes that they should shortly *see an end* of their troubles. "Yea," says God, *"An end has come,* but a miserable one, not *the expected end"* (which is promised to the pious remnant among them, Jer. 29:11); *"it is the end, that end* which you have been so often warned of, *that last end* which Moses wished you to *consider* (Deu. 32:29), and which, because *Jerusalem remembered not, therefore she came down wonderfully,"* Lam. 1:9. This end was long in coming, but *now it has come.* Though the ruin of sinners comes slowly, it comes surely. *"It has come;* it watches for thee, ready to receive thee." This perhaps looks further, to the last destruction of that nation by the Romans, which that by the Chaldeans was an earnest of; and still further to the final destruction of the world of the ungodly. *The end of all things is at hand;* and Jerusalem's last end was a type of *the end of the world,* Mt. 24:3. Oh that we could all see that end of time and days very near, and the end of our own time and days much nearer, that we may secure a happy lot *at the end of the days!* Dan. 12:13. This *end comes upon the four corners of the land.* The ruin, as it shall be final, so it shall be total; no part of the land shall escape; no, not that which lies most remote. Such will the destruction of the world be; all these things shall be dissolved. Such will the destruction of sinners be; none can avoid it. *Oh that the wickedness of the wicked* might *come to an end,* before it bring them to *an end!*

II. *An evil, an only evil, behold, has come, v.* 5. Sin is *an evil, an only evil, an evil* that has no good in it; it is the worst of evils. But this is spoken of the evil of trouble; it is *an evil,* one *evil,* and that one shall suffice to affect and complete the ruin of the nation; there needs no more to do its business; this one shall *make an utter end,* affliction needs not *rise up a second time,* Nah. 1:9. It is *an evil* without precedent or parallel, *an evil* that stands alone; you cannot produce such another instance. It is to the impenitent *an evil, an only evil;* it hardens their hearts and irritates their corruptions, whereas there were those to whom it was sanctified by the grace of God and made a means of much good; they were *sent into Babylon for their good,* Jer. 24:5. The wicked have *the dregs of that cup* to drink which to the righteous is full of *mixtures of mercy,* Ps. 75:8. The same affliction is to us either a half *evil* or *an only evil* according as we conduct ourselves under it and make use of it. But when *an end, the end, has come* upon the wicked world, then *an evil, an only evil,* comes upon it, and not till then. The sorest of temporal judgments have their allays, but the torments of the damned are *an evil, an only evil.*

III. *The time has come,* the set time, for the inflicting of this *only evil* and the making of this *full end;* for to all God's purposes *there is a time,* a proper time, and that prefixed, in which the purpose shall have its accomplishment; particularly the time of reckoning with wicked people, and rendering to them according to their desserts, is fixed, *the day of the revelation of the righteous judgment of god;* and *he sees,* whether we see it or no, that *his day is coming.* This they are here told of again and again (*v.* 10): *Behold, the day* that has lingered so long *has come* at last, *behold, it has come. The time has come, the day draws near, the day of trouble is near, v.* 7, 12. Though threatened judgments may be long deferred, yet they shall not be dropped; the time for executing them will come. Though God's patience may put them off, nothing but man's sincere repentance and reformation will put them by. *The morning has come unto thee* (*v.* 7), and again (*v.* 10), *The morning has gone forth;* the day of trouble dawns, the day of destruction is already begun. *The morning* discovers that which was hidden; they thought their secret sins would never come to light, but now they will be brought to light. They used to try and execute malefactors in the morning, and such a morning of judgment and execution is now coming upon them, *a day of trouble* to sinners, *the year of their visitation.* See how stupid these people were, that, though the day of their destruction was already begun, yet they were not aware of it, but must be thus told of it again and again. *The day of trouble,* real trouble, *is near, and not the sounding again of the mountains,* that is, not a mere echo or report of troubles, as they were willing to think it was, nothing but a groundless surmise; as if the *men that came against them* were but *the shadow of the mountains* (as Zebul suggested to Gaal, Jdg. 9:36) and the intelligence they received were but *an empty sound,* reverberated from the mountains. No; the trouble is not a fancy, and so you will soon find.

IV. All this comes from God's wrath, not allayed, as sometimes it has been, with mixtures of mercy. This is the fountain from which all these calamities flow; and this is *the wormwood and the gall* in *the affliction and the misery,* which make it bitter indeed (*v.* 3): *I will send my anger upon thee.* Observe, God is Lord of his anger; it does not break out but when he pleases, nor fasten upon any but as he directs it and gives it commission. The expression rises higher (*v.* 8): *Now will I shortly pour out my fury upon thee* in full vials, *and accomplish my anger,* all the purposes and all the products of it, *upon thee.* This wrath does not single out here and there one to be made examples, but it *is upon all the multitude thereof* (*v.* 12, 14); the whole body of the nation has become a *vessel of wrath, fitted for destruction.* God does sometimes *in wrath remember mercy,* but now he says, *My eye shall not spare thee, neither will I have pity, v.* 4 and again *v.* 9. Those shall *have judgment without mercy* who made light of mercy when it was offered them.

V. All this is the just punishment of their sins, and it is what they have by their own folly brought upon themselves. This is much insisted on here, that they might be brought to justify God in all he had brought upon them. God never sends his anger but in wisdom and justice; and therefore it follows, *"I will judge thee according to thy ways, v.* 3. I will examine what thy ways have been, compare them with the law, and then deal with thee according to the merit of them, and *recompense* them to *thee," v.* 4. Note, In the heaviest judgments God inflicts upon sinners he does but *recompense their own ways upon them;* they are beaten with their own rod. And, when God comes to reckon with a sinful people, he will bring every provocation to account: *"will recompense upon thee all thy abominations* (*v.* 3); and now *thy iniquity shall be found to be hateful* (Ps. 36:2) *and thy abominations shall be in the midst of thee"* (*v.* 4); that is, the secret wickedness shall now be brought to light, and that shall appear to have been in the midst of thee which before was not suspected; and thy sin shall now become an *abomination* to thyself. So the abomination of iniquity will be when it comes to be an *abomination of desolation,* Mt. 24:15. Or, *Thy abominations* (that is, the punishments of them) *shall be in the midst of thee;* they shall *reach to thy heart.* See Jer. 4:18. Or therefore *God will not spare, nor have pity,* because, even when he is *recompensing their ways* upon them, yet *in their distress they trespass yet more;* their *abominations* are still *in the midst of them,* indulged and harboured in their hearts. It is repeated again (*v.* 8, 9), *I will judge thee, I will recompense thee.* Two sins are particularly specified as provoking God to bring these judgments upon them — pride and oppression. 1. God will humble them by his judgments, for they have magnified themselves. *The rod* of affliction *has blossomed,* but it was *pride* that *budded, v.* 10. What buds in sin will blossom in some judgment or other. The pride of Judah and Jerusalem appeared among all orders and degrees of men, as buds upon the tree in spring. 2. Their enemies shall deal hardly with them, for they have dealt hardly with one another (*v.* 11): *Violence has risen up into a rod of wickedness;* that is, their injuriousness to one another is protected and patronised by the power of the magistrate. The rod of government had become a *rod of wickedness,* to such a degree of impudence was *violence risen up. I saw the place of judgment, that wickedness was there,* Eccl. 3:16; Isa. 5:7. Whatever are the fruits of God's judgments, it is certain that our sin is the root of them.

VI. There is no escape from these judgments nor fence against them, for they shall be universal and shall bear down all before them, without remedy. 1. Death in its various shapes shall ride triumphantly, both in town and in country, both within the city and without it, *v.* 15. Men shall be safe nowhere; for *he that is in the field shall die by the sword* (every field shall be to them a field of battle) *and he that is in the city,* though it be a holy city, yet it shall not be his protection, but *famine and pestilence shall devour him.* Sin had abounded both in city and country, *Iliacos intra muros peccator et extra — Trojans and Greeks offend alike;* and therefore among both desolations are made. 2. None of those that are marked for death shall escape: There *shall none of them remain.* None of those proud oppressors that did violence to their poor neighbours with *the rod of wickedness,* none of them shall be left, but they shall be all swept away by the desolation that is coming (*v.* 11): *None of their multitude,* that is, of the rabble, whom they set on to do mischief, and to countenance them in doing it, to cry, "Crucify, crucify," when they were resolved on the destruction of any, *none of them shall remain, nor any of theirs;* their families shall all be destroyed, and neither root nor branch left them. This multitude, this mob, divine vengeance will in a particular manner fasten upon; *for wrath is upon all the multitude thereof* (*v.* 12, 14) and *the vision was touching the whole multitude thereof* (*v.* 13), the bulk of the common people. The judgments coming shall carry them away by wholesale, and they shall neither secure themselves nor their masters whose creatures and tools they were. God's judgments, when they come with commission, cannot be overpowered by multitudes. *Though hand join in hand, yet shall not the wicked go unpunished.* 3. Those that fall shall not be lamented (*v.* 11): *There shall be no wailing for them,* for there shall be none left to bewail them, but such as are hastening apace after them. And the times shall be so bad that men shall rather congratulate than lament the death of their friends, as reckoning those happy that are taken away from seeing these desolations and sharing in them, Jer. 16:4, 5. 4. They shall not be able to make any resistance. The decree has gone forth, and *the vision* concerning them *shall not return, v.* 13. God will not reveal it, and they cannot defeat it; and therefore it *shall not return re infecta — without having accomplished any thing,* but shall *accomplish that for which he sends it.* God's word will take place, and then, (1.) Particular persons cannot make their part good against God: No man *shall strengthen himself in the iniquity of his life;* it will be to no purpose for sinners to set God and his judgments at defiance as they used to do. *None ever hardened his heart against God and prospered.* Those that strengthen themselves in their wickedness will be found not only to weaken, but to ruin, themselves, Ps. 52:7. (2.) *The multitude* cannot resist the torrent of these judgments, nor make head against them (*v.* 14): *They have blown the trumpet,* to call their soldiers together, and to animate and encourage those whom they have got together, and thus they think *to make all ready;* but all in vain; none enlist themselves, or those that do have not courage to face the enemy. Note, If God be against us, none can be for us to do us any service. 5. They shall have no hope of the return of their prosperity, with which to support themselves in their adversity; they shall have given up all for gone; and therefore, *"Let not the buyer rejoice* that he is increasing his estate and has become a purchaser; nor let *the seller mourn* that he is lessening his estate and has become a bankrupt," *v.* 12. See the vanity of the things of this world, and how worthless they are — that in a time of trouble, when we have most need of them, we may perhaps make least account of them. Those that have sold are the more easy, having the less to lose, and those that have bought have but increased their own cares and fears. Because *the fashion of this world passes away,* let *those that buy be as though they possessed not,* because they know not how soon they may be dispossessed, 1 Co. 7:29–31. It is added (*v.* 13), *"The seller shall not return,* at the year of jubilee, *to that which is sold,* according to the law, though he should escape the sword and pestilence, and live till that year comes; for no inheritances shall be enjoyed here till the seventy years be accomplished, and then men shall return to their possessions, shall claim and have their own again." In the belief of this, Jeremiah, about this time, *bought his uncle's field,* yet, according to the charge, the buyer did not rejoice, but complain, Jer. 32:25. 6. God will be glorified in all: *"You shall know that I am the Lord* (*v.* 4), *that I am the Lord that smiteth, v.* 9. You look at second causes, and think it is Nebuchadnezzar that smites you, but you shall be made to know he is but the staff: it is the hand of the Lord that smiteth you, and who knows the weight of his hand?" Those who would not know it was the *Lord that did them goo* shall be made to know it is *the Lord that smiteth* them; for, one way or other, he will be owned.

Verses 16–22

We have attended the fate of those that are cut off, and are now to attend the flight of those that have an opportunity of escaping the danger; some of them *shall escape* (*v.* 16), but what the better? As good die once as, in a miserable life, die a thousand deaths, and escape only like Cain to be *fugitives and vagabonds,* and afraid of being slain by every one they meet; so shall these be.

I. They shall have no comfort or satisfaction in their own minds, but be in continual anguish and terror; for, wherever they go, they carry about with them guilty consciences, which make them a burden to themselves. 1. They shall be always solitary and under prevailing melancholy; they shall not be in the cities, or places of concourse, but all alone *upon the mountains,* not caring for society, but shy of it, as being ashamed of the low circumstances to which they are reduced. 2. They shall be always sorrowful. Those have reason to be so that are under the tokens of God's displeasure; and God can make those so that have been most jovial and have set sorrow at defiance. Those that once thought themselves as the lions of the mountains, so daring were they, now become as the *doves of the valleys,* so timid are they, and so dispirited, ready to *flee when none pursues* and to tremble at the shaking of a leaf. They are all of them mourning (not with a *godly sorrow,* but with the *sorrow of the world,* which *works death), every one for his iniquity,* that is, for those calamities which they now see their iniquity has brought upon them, not only the iniquity of the land, but their own: they shall then be brought to acknowledge what they have each of them contributed to the national guilt. Note, Sooner or later sin will have sorrow of one kind or other; and those that will not repent of their iniquity may justly be left to pine away in it; those that will not mourn for it as it is an offence to God shall be made to mourn for it as it is a shame and ruin to themselves, to *mourn at the last, when the flesh and the body are consumed, and to say, How have I hated instruction!* Prov. 5:11, 12. 3. They shall be deprived of all their strength of body and mind (*v.* 17): *All hands shall be feeble,* so that they shall not be able to fight, or defend themselves, and *all knees shall be weak as water,* so that they shall neither be able to flee nor to stand their ground; they shall feel a universal colliquation: their knees *shall flow as water,* so that they must fall of course. Note, It is folly for the *strong man to glory in his strength,* for God can soon weaken it. 4. They shall be deprived of all their hopes and shall abandon themselves to despair (*v.* 18); they shall have nothing to hold up their spirits with; their aspects shall show what are their prospects, all dreadful, for they shall *gird themselves with sackcloth,* as having no expectation ever to wear better clothing. *Horror shall cover them,* and *shame,* and *baldness,* all the expressions of a desperate sorrow, Isa. 17:11. Note, Those that will not be kept from sin by fear and shame shall by fear and shame be punished for it; such is the confusion that sin will end in.

II. They shall have no benefit from their wealth and riches, but shall be perfectly sick of them, *v.* 19. Those that were reduced to this distress were such as had had abundance of *silver and gold,* money, and plate, and jewels, and other valuable goods, from which they promised themselves a great deal of advantage in times of public trouble. They thought their wealth would be *their strong city,* that with it they could bribe enemies and buy friends, that it would be the ransom of their lives, that they could never want bread as long as they had money, and that *money would answer all things;* but see how it proved. 1. Their wealth had been a great temptation to them in the *day of their prosperity;* they set their affections upon it, and put their confidence in it. By their eager pursuit of it they were drawn into sin, and by their plentiful enjoyment of it they were hardened in sin; and thus it was the stumbling-block of their iniquity; it occasioned their falling into sin and obstructed their return to God. Note, There are many whose wealth is their snare and ruin. The gaining of the world is the losing of their souls; it makes them proud, secure, covetous, oppressive, voluptuous; and that which, it well used, might have been the servant of their piety, being abused, becomes *the stumbling-block of their iniquity.* 2. It was no relief to them now in the day of their adversity; for, (1.) Their *gold and silver* could not protect them from the judgments of God. They *shall not be able to deliver them in the day of the wrath of the Lord;* they shall not serve to atone his justice, or turn away his wrath, nor to screen them from the judgments he is bringing upon them. Note, *Riches profit not in the day of wrath,* Prov. 11:4. They neither set them so high that god's judgments cannot reach them nor make them so strong that they cannot conquer them. There is a day of wrath coming, when it will appear that men's wealth is utterly unable to deliver them or do them any service. What the better was the rich man for his full barns when his soul was required of him, or that other rich man for his *purple, and scarlet, and sumptuous fare,* when in hell he could not procure a drop of water to *cool his tongue?* Money is no defence against the arrests of death, nor any alleviation to the miseries of the damned. (2.) Their *gold and silver* could not give them any content under their calamities. [1.] They could not fill their bowels; when there was no bread left in the city, none to be had for love or money, their silver and gold could not satisfy their hunger, nor serve to make one meal's meat for them. Note, We could better be without mines of gold than fields of corn; the products of the earth, which may easily be gathered from the surface of it, are much greater blessings to mankind than its treasures, which are with so much difficulty and hazard dug out of its bowels. If God give us daily bread, we have reason to be thankful, and no reason to complain, though silver and gold we have none. [2.] Much less could they satisfy their souls, or yield them any inward comfort. Note, The wealth of this world has not that in it which will answer the desires of the soul, or be any satisfaction to it in a day of distress. *He that loves silver shall not be satisfied with silver,* much less he that loses it. (3.) Their *gold and silver shall be thrown into the streets,* either by the hands of the enemy, who shall have more spoil than they care for or can carry away (silver shall be nothing accounted of; they shall *cast that in the streets;* but the *gold,* which is more valuable, shall be removed and brought to Babylon); or they themselves shall *throw away their silver and gold,* because it would be an incumbrance to them and retard their flight, or because it would expose them and be a temptation to the enemy to cut their throats for their money, or in indignation at it, because, after all the care and pains they had taken to scrape it together and hoard it up, they found that it would stand them in no stead, but do them a mischief rather. Note, *The world passes away, and the lusts thereof,* 1 Jn. 2:17. The time may come when worldly men will be as weary of their wealth as now they are wedded to it, when those will fare best that have least.

III. God's temple shall stand them in no stead, *v.* 20–22. This they had prided themselves in, and promised themselves security from (Jer. 7:4; Mic. 3:11); but this confidence of theirs shall fail them. Observe, 1. The great honour God had done to that people in setting up his sanctuary among them (*v.* 20): *As for the beauty of his ornament,* that *holy and beautiful house,* where *they and their fathers praised God* (Isa. 64:11), which was therefore beautiful because holy (it was called the *beauty of holiness,* and holiness is the beauty of its ornament; it was also adorned with gold and gifts) — as for this, *he set it in majesty;* every thing was contrived to make it magnificent, that it might help to make the people of Israel the more illustrious among their neighbours. *He built his sanctuary like high palaces,* Ps. 78:69. It was a *glorious high throne from the beginning,* Jer. 17:12. But, 2. Here is the great dishonour they had done to God in profaning his sanctuary; they *made the images of their* counterfeit deities, which they set up in rivalship with God, and which are here called *their abominations* and *their detestable things* (for so they were to God, and so they should have been to them), and these they set up in God's temple, than which a greater affront could not be put upon him. And therefore, 3. It is here threatened that they shall be deprived of the temple, and it shall be no succour to them: *Therefore have I set it far from them,* that is, sent them far from it, so that it is out of the reach of their services and they are out of the reach of its influences. Note, God's ordinances, and the privileges of a profession of religion, will justly be taken away from those that despise and profane them. Nay, they shall not only be kept at a distance from the temple, but the temple itself shall be involved in the common desolation (*v.* 21); the Chaldeans, who are *strangers,* and therefore have no veneration for it, who are *the wicked of the earth,* and therefore have an antipathy to it, shall *have it for a prey* and for *a spoil;* all the ornaments and treasures of it shall fall into their hands, who will make no difference between that and other plunder. This was a grief to the saints in Zion, who complained of nothing so much as of that which *the enemy did wickedly in the sanctuary* (Ps. 74:3); but it was the punishment of the sinners in Zion, who, by profaning the temple with *strange gods,* provoked God to suffer it to be profaned by *strange nations,* and to *turn his face from those that did it* as if he had not seen them and their crimes and from those that deprecated it as not regarding them and their prayers. Let the soldiers do as they will; let them *enter into the secret place,* into the holy of holies, as robbers; let them strip it, let them pollute it; its defence has departed, and then farewell all its glory. Note, Those are unworthy to be honoured with the form of godliness who will not be governed by the power of godliness.

Verses 23–27

Here is, I. The prisoner arraigned: *Make a chain,* in which to drag the criminal to the bar, and set him before the tribunal of divine justice; let him stand in fetters (as a notorious malefactor), stand pinioned to receive his doom. Note, Those that break the bands of God's law *asunder,* and *cast away those cords from them,* will find themselves bound and held by the chains of his judgments, which they cannot break nor cast from them. The chain signified the siege of Jerusalem, or the slavery of those that were carried into captivity, or that they were all bound over to the righteous judgment of God, *reserved in chains.*

II. The indictment drawn up against the prisoner: *The land is full of bloody crimes,* full of *the judgments of blood* (so the word is), that is, of the guilt of blood which they had shed under colour of justice and by forms of law, with the solemnity of a judgment. The innocent blood which Manasseh shed, probably thus shed, by the *judgment of the blood,* was the measure-filling sin of Jerusalem, 2 Ki. 24:4. Or, It is full of such crimes as by the law were to be punished with death, *the judgment of blood.* Idolatry, blasphemy, witchcraft, Sodomy, and the like, were *bloody crimes,* for which particular sinners were to die; and therefore, when they had become national, there was no remedy but the nation must be cut off. Note, Bloody crimes will be punished with bloody judgments. *The city,* the city of David, the holy city, that should have been the pattern of righteousness, the protector of it, and the punisher of wrong, *is now full of violence;* the rulers of that city, having greater power and reputation, are greater oppressors than any others. This was sadly to be lamented. *How has the faithful city become a harlot!*

III. Judgment given upon this indictment. God will reckon with them not only for the profaning of his sanctuary, but for the perverting of justice between man and man; for, as *holiness becomes his house,* so the *righteous Lord loves righteousness* and is the avenger of unrighteousness. Now the judgment given is, 1. That since they had walked in the way of the heathen, and done worse than they, God would *bring the worst of the heathen upon them* to destroy them and lay them waste, the most barbarous and outrageous, that have the least compassion to mankind and the greatest antipathy to the Jews. Note, Of the heathen some are worse than others, and God sometimes picks out the worst to be a scourge to his own people, because he intends them for the fire when the work is done. 2. That since they had filled their houses with goods unjustly gotten, and used their pomp and power for the crushing and oppressing of the weak, God would give their houses to be possessed and all the furniture of them to be enjoyed by strangers, and *make the pomp of the strong to cease,* so that their great men should not dazzle the eyes of the weak-sighted with their pomp, nor with their might at any time prevail against right, as they had done. 3. That, since they had *defiled the holy places* with their idolatries, God would defile them with his judgments, since they had set up the images of other gods in the temple, God would remove thence the tokens of the presence of their own God. When the holy places are deserted by their God they will soon be defiled by their enemies. 4. Since they had followed one sin with another, God would pursue them with one judgment upon another: *"Destruction comes, utter destruction* (*v.* 25); for there shall come *mischief upon mischief* to ruin you, and *rumour upon rumour* to frighten you, like the waves in a storm, one upon the neck of another." Note, Sinners that are marked for ruin shall be prosecuted to it; for God will overcome when he judges. 5. Since they had disappointed God's expectations from them, he would disappoint their expectations from him; for, (1.) They shall not have the *deliverance out of their troubles* that they expect. They shall *seek peace;* they shall desire it and pray for it; they shall aim at and expect it: but *there shall be none;* their attempts both to court their enemies and to conquer them shall be in vain, and their troubles shall grow worse and worse. (2.) They shall not have the direction in the trouble that they expect (*v.* 26): *They shall seek a vision of the prophet,* shall desire, for their support under their troubles, to be assured of a happy issue out of them. They did not desire a vision to reprove them for sin, nor to warn them of danger, but to promise them deliverance. Such messages they longed to hear. But *the law shall perish from the priest;* he shall have no words either of counsel or comfort to say to them. They would not hear what God had to say to them by ways of conviction, and therefore he has nothing to say to them by way of encouragement. *Counsel shall perish from the ancients;* the elders of the people, that should advise them what to do in this difficult juncture, shall be infatuated and at their wits' end. It is bad with a people when those that should be their counsellors know not how to consider within themselves, consult with one another, or counsel them. 6. Since they had animated and encouraged one another to sin, God would dispirit and dishearten them all, so that they should not be able to make head against the judgments of God that were breaking in upon them. All orders and degrees of men shall lie down by consent under the load (*v.* 27): *The king,* that should inspire life into them, and *the prince,* that should lead them onto attack the enemy, *shall mourn* and be *clothed with desolation;* their heads and hearts shall fail, their politics and their courage; and then no wonder if *the hands of the people of the land,* that should fight for them, be *troubled.* None of the men of might shall *find their hands.* What can men contrive or do for themselves when God has departed from them and appears against them? All must needs be in *tears,* all in *trouble,* when God comes to *judge them according to their deserts,* and so make then know, to their cost, that he is the Lord, the *God to whom vengeance belongs.*

CHAPTER 8

God, having given the prophet a clear foresight of the people's miseries that were hastening on, here gives him a clear insight into the people's wickedness, by which God was provoked to bring these miseries upon them, that he might justify God in all his judgments, might the more particularly reprove the sins of the people, and with the more satisfaction foretel their ruin. Here God, in vision, brings him to Jerusalem, to show him the sins that were committed there, though God had begun to contend with them (*v.* 1–4), and there he sees, I. The image of jealousy set up at the gate of the altar (*v.* 5, 6). II. The elders of Israel worshipping all manner of images in a secret chamber (*v.* 7–12). III. The women weeping for Tammuz (*v.* 13, 14). IV. The men worshipping the sun (*v.* 15, 16). And then appeals to him whether such a provoking people should have any pity shown them (*v.* 17, 18).

Verses 1–6

Ezekiel was now in Babylon; but the messages of wrath he had delivered in the foregoing chapters related to Jerusalem, for in the peace or trouble thereof the captives looked upon themselves to have peace or trouble, and therefore here he has a vision of what was done at Jerusalem, and this vision is continued to the close of the 11th chapter.

I. Here is the date of this vision. The first vision he had was in *the fifth year of the captivity, in the fourth month* and *the fifth day of the month, ch.* 1:1, 2. This was just fourteen months after. Perhaps it was after he had lain 390 days on his left side, to bear the iniquity of Israel, and before he began the forty days on his right side, to bear the iniquity of Judah; for now he was sitting in the house, not lying. Note, God keeps a particular account of the messages he sends to us, because he will shortly call us to account about them.

II. The opportunity is taken notice of, as well as the time. 1. The prophet was himself *sitting in his house,* in a sedate composed frame, deep perhaps in contemplation. Note, The more we retreat from the world, and retire into our own hearts, the better frame we are in for communion with God: those that sit down to consider what they have learned shall be taught more. Or, he *sat in his house,* ready to preach to the company that resorted to him, but waiting for instructions what to say. God will communicate more knowledge to those who are communicative of what they do know. 2. *The elders of Judah,* that were now in captivity with him, *sat before him.* It is probable that it was on the sabbath day, and that it was usual for them to attend on the prophet every sabbath day, both to hear the word from him and to join with him and prayer and praise: and how could they spend the sabbath better, now that they had neither temple nor synagogue, neither priest nor altar? It was a great mercy that they had opportunity to spend it so well, as the good people in Elisha's time, 2 Ki. 4:23. But some think it was on some extraordinary occasion that they attended him, to enquire of the Lord, and *sat down* at his feet to *hear his word.* Observe here, (1.) When the *law had perished from the priests* at Jerusalem, whose *lips should keep knowledge* (*ch.* 7:26), those in Babylon had a prophet to consult. God is not tied to places or persons. (2.) Now that the elders of Judah were in captivity they paid more respect to God's prophets, and his word in their mouth, than they did when they lived in peace in their own land. When God brings men into the *cords of affliction,* then he *opens their ears to discipline,* Job 36:8, 10; Ps. 141:6. Those that despised vision in the *valley of vision* prized it now that the word of the Lord precious and there was *no open vision.* (3.) When our teachers are driven into corners, and are forced to preach in private houses, we must diligently attend them there. A minister's house should be a church for all his neighbours. Paul preached in his own hired house at Rome, and God owned him there, and *no man forbad him.*

III. The divine influence and impression that the prophet was now under: *The hand of the Lord fell there upon me.* God's hand took hold of him, and arrested him, as it were, to employ him in this vision, but at the same time supported him to bear it.

IV. The vision that the prophet saw, *v.* 2. He *beheld a likeness,* of a man we may suppose, for that was the likeness he saw before, but it was all *brightness* above the girdle and all *fire* below, fire and flame. This agrees with the description we had before of the apparition he saw, *ch.* 1:27. It is probably that it was the same person, the man Christ Jesus. It is probable that the elders that *sat with him* (as the men that journeyed with Paul) saw a light and were afraid, and this happy sight they gained by attending the prophet in a private meeting, but they had no distinct view of him that spoke to him, Acts 22:9.

V. The prophet's remove, in vision, to Jerusalem. The apparition he saw *put forth the form of a hand,* which *took him by a lock of his head,* and the Spirit was that hand which was put forth, for the Spirit of God is called *the finger of God.* Or, The spirit within him *lifted him up,* so that he was borne up and carried on by an internal principle, not an external violence. A faithful ready servant of God will be drawn by a hair, by the least intimation of the divine will, to his duty; for he has that within him which inclines him to a compliance with it, Ps. 27:8. He was miraculously *lifted up between heaven and earth,* as if he were to fly away upon eagles' wings. This, it is probable (so Grotius thinks), the elders that sat with him saw; they were witnesses of *the hand taking him by the lock* of hair, and *lifting him up,* and then perhaps laying him down again in a trance of ecstasy, while he had the following visions, *whether in the body or out of the body,* we may suppose, he *could not tell,* any more than Paul in a like case, much less can we. Note, Those are best prepared for communion with God and the communications of divine light that by divine grace are raised up above the earth and the things of it, to be out of their attractive force. But, being lifted up towards heaven, he was carried in vision to Jerusalem, and to God's sanctuary there; for those that would go to heaven must take that in their way. The Spirit represented to his mind the city and temple as plainly as if he had been there in person. O that by faith we could thus enter into the Jerusalem, the holy city, above, and see the things that are invisible!

VI. The discoveries that were made to him there.

1. There he saw the glory of God (*v.* 4): *Behold, the glory of the god of Israel was there,* the same appearance of the living creatures, and the wheels, and the throne, that he had seen, *ch.* 1. Note, God's servants, wherever they are and whithersoever they go, ought to carry about with them a believing regard to the glory of God and to set that always before them; and those that have seen God's power and glory in the sanctuary should desire to see them again, so as they have seen them, Ps. 63:2. Ezekiel has this repeated vision of the glory of God both to give credit to and to put honour upon the following discoveries. But it seems to have a further intention here; it was to aggravate this sin of Israel, in changing their own God, the God of Israel (who is a God of so much glory as here he appears to be), for dunghill gods, scandalous gods, false gods, and indeed no gods. Note, The more glorious we see God to be the more odious we shall see sin to be, especially idolatry, which turns his truth into a lie, his glory into shame. It was also to aggravate their approaching misery, when this glory of the Lord should remove from them (*ch.* 11:23) and leave the house and city desolate.

2. There he saw the reproach of Israel — and that was *the image of jealousy,* set *northward, at the gate of the altar, v.* 3, 5. What image this was is uncertain, probably an image of Baal, or of the grove, which Manasseh made and set in the temple (2 Ki. 21:7, 2 Chr. 33:3), which Josiah removed, but his successors, it seems, replace there, as probably they did the *chariots of the sun* which he found *at the entering in of the house of the Lord* (2 Ki. 23:11), and this is here said to be *in the entry.* But the prophet, instead of telling us what image it was, which might gratify our curiosity, tells us that it was *the image of jealousy,* to convince our consciences that, whatever image it was, it was in the highest degree offensive to God and *provoked him to jealousy.* he resented it as a husband would resent the whoredoms of his wife, and would certainly revenge it; for *God is jealous, and the Lord revenges,* Nah. 1:2.

(1.) The very setting up of this image *in the house of the Lord* was enough to *provoke him to jealousy;* for it is in the matters of his worship that we are particularly told, *I the Lord thy God am a jealous God.* Those that placed this image at *the door of the inner gate,* where the people assembled, called *the gate of the altar* (*v.* 5), thereby plainly intended, [1.] To affront God, to provoke him to his face, by advancing an idol to be a rival with him for the adoration of his people, in contempt of his law and in defiance of his justice. [2.] To debauch the people, and pick them up as they were entering into the courts of the Lord's house to bring their offerings to him, and to tempt them to offer them to this image; like the adulteress Solomon describes, that *sits at the door of her house, to call passengers who go right on their ways, Whoso is simple, let him turn in hither,* Prov. 9:14–16. With good reason therefore is this called *the image of jealousy.*

(2.) We may well imagine what a surprise and what a grief it was to Ezekiel to see this image in the house of God, when he was in hopes that the judgments they were under had, by this time, wrought some reformation among them; but there is more wickedness in the world, in the church, than good men think there is. And now, [1.] God appeals to him whether this was not bad enough, and a sufficient ground for God to go upon in casting off this people and abandoning them to ruin. Could he, or any one else, expect any other than *that God should go far from his sanctuary,* when there were such abominations committed there, in that very place; nay, was he not perfectly driven thence? They did these things designedly, and on purpose that he should leave his sanctuary, and so shall their doom be; they have hereby, in effect, like the Gadarenes, desired him *to depart out of their coasts,* and therefore he will depart; he will no more dignify and protect his sanctuary, as he has done, but will give it up to reproach and ruin. But, [2.] Though this is bad enough, and serves abundantly to justify God in all that he brings upon them, yet the matter will appear to be much worse: *But turn thyself yet again,* and thou wilt be amazed to *see greater abominations than these.* Where there is one abomination it will be found that there are many more. Sins do not go alone.

Verses 7–12

We have here a further discovery of the abominations that were committed at Jerusalem, and within the confines of the temple, too. Now observe,

I. How this discovery is made. God, in vision, brought Ezekiel to the *door of the court,* the outer court, along the sides of which the priests' lodgings were. God could have introduced him at first into *the chambers of imagery,* but he brings him to them by degrees, partly to employ his own industry in searching out these mysteries of iniquity, and partly to make him sensible with what care and caution those idolaters concealed their idolatries. Before the priests' apartments they had run up a wall, to make them the more private, that they might not lie open to the observation of those who passed by — a shrews sign that they did something which they had reason to be ashamed of. *He that doth evil hates the light.* They were not willing that those who saw them in God's house should see them in their own, lest they should see them contradict themselves and undo in private what they did in public. But, *behold, a hole in the wall,* (*v.* 7), a spy-hole, by which you might see that which would give cause to suspect them. When hypocrites screen themselves behind the wall of an external profession, and with it think to conceal their wickedness from the eye of the world and carry on their designs the more successfully, it is hard for them to manage it with so much art by that there is some hole or other left in the wall, something that betrays them, to those who look diligently, not to be what they pretend to be. The ass's ears in the fable appeared from under the lion's skin. This *hole in the wall* Ezekiel made wider, and *behold a door, v.* 8. This door he goes in by into *the treasury,* or some of the apartments of the priests, and sees *the wicked abominations that they do there, v.* 9. Note, Those that would discover the mystery of iniquity in others, or in themselves, must accomplish a diligent search; for Satan has his wiles, and depths, and devices, which we should not be ignorant of, and *the heart is deceitful above all things;* in the examining of it therefore we are concerned to be very strict.

II. What the discovery is. It is a very melancholy one. 1. He sees a chamber set round with idolatrous pictures (*v.* 10): *All the idols of the house of Israel,* which they had borrowed from the neighbouring nations, were *portrayed upon the wall round about,* even the vilest of them, *the forms of creeping things,* which they worshipped, and *beasts,* even *abominable ones,* which are poisonous and venomous; at least they were abominable when they were worshipped. This was a sort of panthenon, a collection of all the idols together which they paid their devotions to. Though the second commandment, in the letter of it, forbids only graven images, yet painted ones are as bad and as dangerous. 2. He sees this chamber filled with idolatrous worshippers (*v.* 11): There were *seventy men of the elders of Israel* offering incense to these painted idols. here was a great number of idolaters strengthening one another's hands in this wickedness; though it was in a private chamber, and the meeting industriously concealed, yet here were seventy men engaged in it. I doubt these elders were many more than those in Babylon that sat before the prophet in his house, *v.* 1. They were *seventy men,* the number of the great Sanhedrim, or chief council of the nation, and, we have reason to fear, the same men; for they were *the ancients of the house of Israel,* not only in age, but in office, who were bound, by the duty of their place, to restrain and punish idolatry and to destroy and abolish all superstitious images wherever they found them; yet these were those that did themselves worship them in private, so undermining that religion which in public they professed to own and promote only because by it they held their preferments. They had *every man his censer in his hand;* so fond were they of the idolatrous service that they would all be their own priests, and very prodigal they were of their perfumes in honour of these images, for *a thick cloud of incense went up,* that filled the room. O that the zeal of these idolaters might shame the worshippers of the true God out of their indifference to his service! The prophet took particular notice of one whom he knew, who *stood in the midst of* these idolaters, as chief among them, being perhaps president of the great council at this time or most forward in this wickedness. No wonder the people were corrupt when the elders were so. The sins of leaders are leading sins.

III. What the remark is that made upon it (*v.* 12): *"Son of man, hast thou seen this?* Couldst thou have imagined that there was such wickedness committed?" It is here observed concerning it, 1. That it was done *in the dark;* for sinful works are *works of darkness.* They concealed it, lest they should lose their places, or at least their credit. There is a great deal of secret wickedness in the world, which the day will declare, *the day of the revelation of the righteous judgment of God.* 2. That this one idolatrous chapel was but a specimen of many the like. Here they met together, to worship their images in concert, but, it should seem, they had *every man the chamber of his imagery* besides, a room in his own house for this purpose, in which every man gratified his own fancy with such pictures as he liked best. Idolaters had their household gods, and their family worship of them in private, which is a shame to those who call themselves Christians and yet have no church in their house, no worship of God in their family. Had they *chambers of imagery,* and shall not we have chambers of devotion? 3. That atheism was at the bottom of their idolatry. They worship images *in the dark,* the images of the gods of other nations, and *they say,* "Jehovah, the God of Israel, whom we should serve, *seeth us not.* Jehovah *hath forsaken the earth,* and we may worship what God we will; he regards us not." (1.) They think themselves out of God's sight: *They say, The Lord seeth us not.* They imagined, because the matter was carried on so closely that men could not discover it, nor did any of their neighbours suspect them to be idolaters, that therefore it was hidden from the eye of God; as if there were any *darkness, or shadow of death, where the workers of iniquity may hide themselves.* Note, A practical disbelief of God's omniscience is at the bottom of our treacherous departures from him; but the church argues justly, as to this very sin of idolatry (Ps. 44:20, 21), *If we have forgotten the name of our God, and stretched forth our hand to a strange god, will not God search this out?* No doubt he will. (2.) They think themselves out of God's care: "*The Lord has forsaken the earth,* and looks not after the affairs of it; and then we may as well worship any other god as him." Or, "He has forsaken our land, and left it to be a prey to its enemies; and therefore it is time for us to look out for some other god, to whom to commit the protection of it. Our one God cannot, or will not, deliver us; and therefore let us have many." This was a blasphemous reflection upon God, as if he had forsaken them first, else they would not have forsaken him. Note, Those are ripe indeed for ruin who have arrived at such a pitch of impudence as to lay the blame of their sins upon God himself.

Verses 13–18

Here we have,

I. More and greater abominations discovered to the prophet. He thought that what he had seen was bad enough and yet (*v.* 13): *Turn thyself again, and thou shalt see yet greater abominations,* and greater still, *v.* 15, as before, *v.* 6. There are those who live in retirement who do no think what wickedness there is in this world; and the more we converse with it, and the further we go abroad into it, the more corrupt we see it. When we have seen that which is bad we may have our wonder at it made to cease by the discovery of that which, upon some account or other, is a great deal worse. We shall find it so in examining our own hearts and searching into them; there is a world of iniquity in them, a great abundance and variety of abominations, and, when we have found out much amiss, still we shall find more; for *the heart is desperately wicked, who can know it* perfectly? Now the abominations here discovered were, 1. *Women weeping for Tammuz, v.* 14. An abominable thing indeed, that any should choose rather to serve an idol in tears than to serve the true God *with joyfulness and gladness of heart!* Yet such absurdities as these are those guilty of who *follow after lying vanities* and *forsake their own mercies.* Some think it was for Adonis, an idol among the Greeks, other for Osiris, an idol of the Egyptians, that they shed these tears. The image, they say, was made to weep, and then the worshippers wept with it. They bewailed the death of this Tammuz, and anon rejoiced in its returning to life again. These mourning women *sat at the door of the gate of the Lord's house,* and there shed their idolatrous tears, as it were in defiance of God and the sacred rites of his worship, and some think, with their idolatry, prostrating themselves also to corporeal whoredom; for these two commonly went together, and those that dishonoured the divine nature by the one were justly *given up to vile affections* and a reprobate sense to dishonour the human nature, which nowhere ever sunk so far below itself as in these idolatrous rites. 2. *Men worshipping the sun, v.* 16. And this was so much the greater an abomination that it was practised *in the inner court of the Lord's house at the door of the temple of the lord, between the porch and the altar.* There, where the most sacred rites of their holy religion used to be performed, was this abominable wickedness committed. Justly might God in jealousy say to those who thus

affronted him at his own door, as the king to Haman, *Will he force the queen also before me in the house?* Here *were about twenty-five men* giving that honour to the sun which is due to God only. Some think they were the king and his princes; it should rather seem that they were priests, for this was the court of the priests, and the proper place to find them in. Those that were entrusted with the true religion, had it committed to their care and were charged with the custody of it, they were the men that betrayed it. (1.) They turned *their backs towards the temple of the Lord,* resolvedly forgetting it and designedly slighting it and putting contempt upon it. Note, When men turn their backs upon God's institutions, and despise them, it is no marvel if they wander endlessly after their own inventions. Impiety is the beginning of idolatry and all iniquity. (2.) They turned *their faces towards the east, and worshipped the sun,* the rising sun. This was an ancient instance of idolatry; it is mentioned in Job's time (Job 31:26), and had been generally practised among the nations, some worshipping the sun under one name, others under another. These priests, finding it had antiquity and general consent and usage on its side (the two pleas which the papists use at this day in defence of their superstitious rites, and particularly this of worshipping towards the east), practised it in the court of the temple, thinking it an omission that it was not inserted in their ritual. See the folly of idolaters in worshipping that as a god, and calling it *Baal — a lord,* which God made to be a servant to the universe (for such the sun is, and so his name *Shemesh* signified, Deu. 4:19), and in adoring the borrowed light and despising the *Father of lights.*

II. The inference drawn from these discoveries (*v.* 17): "*Hast thou seen this, O son of man!* and couldst thou have thought ever to see such things done in the temple of the Lord?" Now, 1. he appeals to the prophet himself concerning the heinousness of the crime. Can he think it *is a light thing to the house of Judah,* who know and profess better things, and are dignified with so many privileges above other nations? Is it an excusable thing in those that have God's oracles and ordinances *that they commit the abominations which they commit here?* Do not those deserve to suffer that thus sin? Should not such abominations as these *make desolate?* Dan. 9:27. 2. He aggravates it from the fraud and oppression that were to be found in all parts of the nations: *They have filled the land with violence.* It is not strange if those that wrong God thus make no conscience of wronging one another, and with all that is sacred trample likewise upon all that is just. And their wickedness in their conversations made even the worship they paid to their own God an abomination (Isa. 1:11, etc.): "*They fill the land with violence,* and then they return to the temple *to provoke me to anger* there; for even their sacrifices, instead of making an atonement, do but add to their guilt. They *return to provoke me* (they repeat the provocation, do it, and do it again), *and, lo, they put the branch to their nose*" — a proverbial expression denoting perhaps their scoffing at God and having him in derision; they snuffed at his service, as men do when they *put a branch to their nose.* Or it was some custom used by idolaters in honour of the idols they served. We read of garlands used in their idolatrous worships (Acts 14:13), out of which every zealot took a branch which they smelled to as a nosegay. Dr. Lightfoot (*Hor. Heb. in John* 15.6) gives another sense of this place: *They put the branch to their wrath,* or *to his wrath,* as the Masorites read it; that is, they are still bringing more fuel (such as the withered branches of the vine) to the fire of divine wrath, which they have already kindled, as if that wrath did not burn hot enough already. Or putting the branch to the nose may signify the giving of a very great affront and provocation either to God or man; they are an abusive generation of men. 3. he passes sentence upon them that they shall be utterly cut off: *Therefore, because they are thus furiously bent upon sin, I will also deal in fury with them, v.* 18. They filled the land with *their violence,* and God will fill it with the violence of their enemies; and he will not lend a favourable ear to the suggestions either, (1.) Of his own pity: *My eye shall not spare, neither will I have pity;* repentance shall be hidden from his eyes; or, (2.) Of their prayers: *Though they cry in my ears with a loud voice, yet will I not hear them;* for still their sins cry more loudly for vengeance than their prayers cry for mercy. God will now be as deaf to their prayers

as their own idols were, on whom they cried aloud, but in vain, 1 Ki. 18:26. Time was when God was ready to hear even *before they cried* and to *answer while they were yet speaking;* but now *they shall seek me early and not find me,* Prov. 1:28. It is not the loud voice, but the upright heart, that God will regard.

CHAPTER 9

The prophet had, in vision, seen the wickedness that was committed at Jerusalem, in the foregoing chapter, and we may be sure that it was not represented to him worse than really it was; now here follows, of course, a representation of their ruin approaching; for when sin goes before judgments come next. Here is, I. Preparation made of instruments that were to be employed in the destruction of the city (*v.* 1, 2). II. The removal of the Shechinah from the cherubim to the threshold of the temple (*v.* 3). III. Orders given to one of the persons employed, who is distinguished from the rest, for the marking of a remnant to be preserved from the common destruction (*v.* 3, 4). IV. The warrant signed for the execution of those that were not marked, and the execution begun accordingly (*v.* 5–7). V. The prophet's intercession for the mitigation of the sentence, and a denial of any mitigation, the decree having now gone forth (*v.* 8–10). VI. The report made by him that was to mark the pious remnant of what he had done in that matter (*v.* 11). And this shows a usual method of Providence in the government of the world.

Verses 1–4

In these verses we have,

I. The summons given to Jerusalem's destroyers to come forth and give their attendance. He that appeared to the prophet (*ch.* 8:2), that had brought him to Jerusalem and had shown the wickedness that was done there, *he cried, Cause those that have charge over the city to draw near* (*v.* 1), or, as it might better be read, and nearer the original, *Those that have charge over the city are drawing near.* He had said (*ch.* 8:18), *I will deal in fury;* now, says he to the prophet, thou shalt see who are to be employed as the instruments of my wrath. *Appropinquaverunt visitationes civitatis — The visitations* (or visitors) *of the city are at hand.* They would not *know the day of their visitations* in mercy, and now they are to be visited in wrath. Observe, 1. how the notice of this is given to the prophet: *He cried it in my ears with a loud voice,* which intimates the vehemency of him that spoke; when men are highly provoked, and threaten in anger, they speak aloud. Those that regard not the counsels God gives them in a still small voice shall be made to hear the threatenings, to hear and tremble. It denotes also the prophet's unwillingness to be told this: he was deaf on that ear, but there is no remedy, their sin will not admit an excuse and therefore their judgment will not admit a delay: "*He cried it in my ears with a loud voice; he made me hear it, and I heard it with a sad heart.*" 2. What this notice is. There are those *that have charge over the city* to destroy it, not the Chaldean armies, they are to be indeed employed in this work, but they are not the visitors, they are only the servants, or tools rather. God's angels have received a charge now to lay that city waste, which they had long had a charge to protect and watch over. They are at hand, as destroying angels, as ministers of wrath, for *every man has his destroying weapon in his hand,* as the angel that kept the way of the tree of life with a flaming sword. Note, Those that have by sin made God their enemy have made the good angels their enemies too. These visitors are called and *caused to draw near.* Note, God has ministers of wrath always within call, always at command, invisible powers, by whom he accomplishes is purposes. The prophet is made to see this in vision, that he might with the greater assurance in his preaching denounce these judgments. God told it him with a loud voice, *taught it him with a strong hand* (Isa. 8:11), that it might make the deeper impression upon him and that he might thus proclaim it in the people's ears.

II. Their appearance, upon this summons, is recorded. Immediately *six men came* (*v.* 2), one for each of the principal gates of Jerusalem. Two destroying angels were sent against Sodom, but six against Jerusalem; for Jerusalem's doom in the judgment will be thrice as heavy as that of Sodom. There is an angel watching at every gate to destroy, to bring in judgments from every quarter, and to take heed that none escape. One angel served to destroy the first-born of Egypt, and the camp of the Assyrians, but here are six. In the Revelation we find seven that were to *pour out the vials of God's wrath,* Rev. 16:1. They came with every one *a slaughter-weapon in his hand,* prepared for the work to which they were called. The nations of which the king of Babylon's army was composed, which some reckon to be six, and the commanders of his army (of whom *six* are named as principal, Jer. 39:3), may be called *the slaughter-weapons* in the hands of the angels. The angels are thoroughly furnished for every service. 1. Observe whence they came — *from the way of the higher gate, which lies towards the north* (*v.* 2), either because the Chaldeans came from the north (Jer. 1:14, *Out of the north an evil shall break forth)* or because the image of jealousy was set up *at the door of the inner gate that looks towards the north, ch.* 8:3, 5. At that gate of the temple the destroying angels entered, to show what it was that opened the door to them. Note, That way that sin lies judgments may be expected to come. 2. Observe where they placed themselves: *They went in and stood beside the brazen altar,* on which sacrifices were wont to be offered and atonement made. When they acted as destroyers they acted as sacrificers, not from any personal revenge or ill-will, but with a pure and sincere regard to the glory of God; for to his justice all they slew were offered up as victims. *They stood by the altar,* as it were to protect and vindicate that, and plead its righteous cause, and avenge the horrid profanation of it. At the altar they were to receive their commission to destroy, to intimate that the iniquity of Jerusalem, like that of Eli's house, was *not to be purged by sacrifice.*

III. The notice taken of one among the destroying angels distinguished in his habit from the rest, from whom some favour might be expected; it should seem he was not one of the six, but *among them,* to see that mercy was mixed with judgment, *v.* 2. This *man was clothed with linen,* as the priests were, and he had a *writer's inkhorn* hanging at *his side,* as anciently attorneys and lawyers' clerks had, which he was to make use of, as the other six were to make use of their *destroying weapons.* Here the honours of the pen exceeded those of the sword, but he was the Lord of angels that made use of the *writer's inkhorn;* for it is generally agreed, among the best interpreters, that this man represented Christ as Mediator saving those that are his from the flaming sword of divine justice. He is our *high priest,* clothed with holiness, for that was signified by the *fine linen,* Rev. 19:8. As prophet he wears the *writer's inkhorn.* The book of life is the Lamb's book. The great things of the law and gospel which God has written to us are of his writing; for it is the Spirit of Christ, in the writers of the scripture, that testifies to us, and the Bible is *the revelation of Jesus Christ.* Note, It is a matter of great comfort to all good Christians that, in the midst of the destroyers and the destructions that are abroad, there is a Mediator, a great high priest, who has an interest in heaven, and whom saints on earth have an interest in.

IV. The removal of the appearance of the divine glory from over the cherubim. Some think this was that usual display of the divine glory which was between the cherubim over the mercy seat, in the most holy place, that took leave of them now, and never returned; for it is supposed that it was not in the second temple. Others think it was that display of the divine glory which the prophet now saw over the cherubim in vision; and this is more probable, because this is called *the glory of the God of Israel* (*ch.* 8:4), and this is it which he had now his eye upon; this was gone *to the threshold of the house,* as it were to call to the servants that attended without the door, to send them on their errand and give them their instructions. And the removal of this, as well as the former, might be significant of God's departure from them, and leaving them their house desolate; and when God goes all good goes, but he goes from none till they first drive him from them. He went at first no further than *the threshold,* that he might show how loth he was to depart, and might give them both time and encouragement to invite his return to them and his stay with them. Note, God's departures from a people are gradual, but gracious souls are soon award of the first step he takes towards a remove. Ezekiel immediately observed that *the glory of the god of Israel had gone up from the cherub:* and what is a vision of angels if God be gone?

V. The charge given *to the man clothed in linen* to secure the pious remnant from the general desolation. We do not read that this Saviour was summoned and sent for, as the destroyers were; for he is always ready, *appearing in the presence of God for us;* and to him, as the most proper person, the care of those that are marked for salvation is committed, *v.* 4. Now observe, 1. The distinguishing character of this remnant that is to be saved. They are such as *sigh and cry,* sigh in themselves, as men in pain and distress, cry to God in prayer, as men in earnest, because of *all the abominations that* are committed in Jerusalem. It was not only the idolatries they were guilty of, but all their other enormities, that were abominations to God. These pious few had witnessed against those abominations and had done what they could in their places to suppress them; but, finding all their attempts for the reformation of manners fruitless, they sat down, and *sighted, and cried,* wept in secret, and complained to God, because of the dishonour done to his name by their wickedness and the ruin it was bringing upon their church and nation. Note, It is not enough that we do not delight in the sins of others, and that we have not fellowship with them, but we must mourn for them, and lay them to heart; we must grieve for that which we cannot help, as those that hate sin for its own sake, and have a tender concern for the souls of others, as David (Ps. 119:136), and Lot, who *vexed his righteous soul* with the wicked conversation of his neighbours. The abominations committed in Jerusalem are to be in a special manner lamented, because they are in a particular manner offensive to God. 2. The distinguishing care taken of them. Orders are given to find those all out that are of such a pious public spirit: *"Go through the midst of the city* in quest of them, and though they are ever so much dispersed, and ever so closely hid from the fury of their persecutors, yet see that you discover them, *and set a mark upon* their *foreheads,"* (1.) To signify that God owns them for his, and he will confess them another day. A work of grace in the soul is to God *a mark upon the forehead,* which he will acknowledge as his mark, and by which *he knows those that are his.* (2.) To give to them who are thus marked an assurance of God's favour, that they may know it themselves; and the comfort of knowing it will be the most powerful support and cordial in calamitous times. Why should we perplex ourselves about this temporal life if we know by the mark that we have eternal life? (3.) To be a direction to the destroyers whom to pass by, as the blood upon the door-posts was an indication that that was an Israelite's house, and the first-born there must not be slain. Note, Those who keep themselves pure in times of common iniquity God will keep safe in times of common calamity. Those that distinguish themselves shall be distinguished; those that cry for other men's sins shall not need to cry for their own afflictions, for they shall be either delivered from them or comforted under them. God will set a mark upon his mourners, will book their sighs and bottle their tears. The *sealing of the servants of God in their foreheads* mentioned in Rev. 7:3 was the same token of the care God has of his own people with this related here; only this was to secure them from being destroyed, that from being seduced, which is equivalent.

Verses 5–11

In these verses we have,

I. A command given to the destroyers to do execution according to their commission. *They stood by the brazen altar,* waiting for orders; and orders are here given them to cut off and destroy all that were either guilty of, or accessory to, the abominations of Jerusalem, and that did not *sigh and cry* for them. Note, When God has *gathered his wheat into his garner* nothing remains but to *burn up the chaff,* Mt. 3:12.

1. They are ordered to destroy all, (1.) Without exception. They must *go through the city, and smite;* they must *slay utterly,* slay to destruction, give them their death's wound. They must make no distinction of age or sex, but cut off *old and young;* neither the beauty of the virgins, nor the innocency of the babes, shall secure them. This was fulfilled in the death of multitudes by famine and pestilence, especially by the sword of the Chaldeans, as far as the military execution went. Sometimes even such bloody work as this has been God's work. But what an evil thing is sin, then, which provokes the God of infinite mercy to such severity! (2.) Without compassion: *"Let not your eye spare, neither have you pity* (*v.* 5); you must not save any whom God has doomed to destruction, as Saul did Agag and the Amalekites, for that is *doing the work of God deceitfully,* Jer. 48:10. None need to be more merciful than God is; and he had said (*ch.* 8:18), *My eye shall not spare, neither will I have pity."* Note, Those that live in sin, and hate to be reformed, will perish in sin, and deserve not to be pitied; for they might easily have prevented the ruin, and would not.

2. They are warned not to do the least hurt to those that were marked for salvation: *"Come not near any man upon whom is the mark;* do not so much as threaten or frighten any of them; it is promised them that there shall no evil come nigh them, and therefore you must keep at a distance from them." The king of Babylon gave particular orders that Jeremiah should be protected. Baruch and Ebed-melech were secured, and, it is likely, others of Jeremiah's friends, for his sake. God had promised that *it should go well with his remnant* and they *should be well treated* (Jer. 15:11); and we have reason to think that none of the mourning praying remnant fell by the sword of the Chaldeans, but that God found out some way or other to secure them all, as, in the last destruction of Jerusalem by the Romans, the Christians were all secured in a city called *Pella,* and none of them perished with the unbelieving Jews. Note, None of those shall be lost whom God has marked for life and salvation; for the foundation of God stands sure.

3. They are directed to *begin at the sanctuary* (*v.* 6), that sanctuary which, in the chapter before, he had seen the horrid profanation of; they must begin there because there the wickedness began which provoked God to send these judgments. The debaucheries of the priests were the poisoning of the springs, to which all the corruption of the streams was owing. The wickedness of the sanctuary was of all wickedness the most offensive to God, and therefore there the slaughter must begin: *"Begin* there, to try if the people will take warning by the judgments of God upon their priests, and will repent and reform; *begin* there, that all the world may see and know that the Lord, whose name is *Jealous,* is *a jealous God,* and hates sin most in those that are nearest to him." Note, When judgements are abroad they commonly *begin at the house of God,* 1 Pt. 4:17. *You only have I known, and therefore I will punish you,* Amos 3:2. God's temple is a sanctuary, a refuge and protection for penitent sinners, but not for any that *go on still in their trespasses;* neither the sacredness of the place nor the eminency of their place in it will be their security. It should seem the destroyers made some difficulty of putting men to death in the temple, but God bids them not to hesitate at that, but (*v.* 7), *Defile the house, and fill the courts with slain.* They will not be *taken from the altar* (as was appointed by the law, Ex. 21:14), but think to secure themselves by *keeping hold of the horns of* it, like Joab, and therefore, like him, let them *die there,* 1 Ki. 2:30, 31. There the blood of one of God's prophets had been shed (Mt. 23:35) and therefore let their blood be shed. Note, If the servants of God's house defile it with their idolatries, God will justly suffer the enemies of it to defile it with their violences, Ps. 79:1. But these acts of necessary justice were really, whatever they were ceremonially, rather a purification than a pollution of the sanctuary; it was *putting away evil from among them.* 4. They are appointed to *go forth into the city, v.* 6, 7. Note, Wherever sin has gone before judgement will follow after; and, though *judgement begins at the house of God,* yet it shall not end there. The holy city shall be no more a protection to the wicked people then the holy house was to the wicked priests.

II. Here is execution done accordingly. They observed their orders, and, 1. *They began at the* elders, *the ancient men that were before the house,* and slew them first, either those seventy ancients who worshipped idols in their chambers (*ch.* 8:12) or those twenty-five who *worshipped the sun between the porch and the altar,* who might more properly be said to be *before the house.* Note, Ringleaders in sin may expect to be first met with by the judgements of God; and the sins of those who are in the most eminent and public stations call for the most exemplary punishments. 2. They proceeded to the common people: *They went forth and slew in the city;* for, when the decree has gone forth, there shall be no delay; if God begin, he will make an end.

III. Here is the prophet's intercession for a mitigation of the judgement, and a reprieve for some (*v.* 8): *While they were slaying them, and I was left, I fell upon my face.* Observe here, 1. How sensible the prophet was of God's mercy to him, in that he was spared when so many round about him were cut off. *Thousands fell on his right hand, and on his left,* and yet *the destruction* did *not come nigh him; only with his eyes did he behold the just reward of the wicked,* Ps. 91:7, 8. He speaks as one that narrowly escaped the destruction, attributing it to God's goodness, not his own deserts. Note, The best saints must acknowledge themselves indebted to sparing mercy that they are not consumed. And when desolating judgements are abroad, and multitudes fall by them, it ought to be accounted a great favor if we have our *lives given us for a prey;* for we might justly have perished with those that perished. 2. Observe how he improved this mercy; he looked upon it that *therefore* he was left that he might stand in the gap to turn away the wrath of God. Note, We must look upon it that for this reason we are spared, that we may do good in our places, may do good by our prayers. Ezekiel did not triumph in the slaughter he made, but his *flesh trembled for the fear of God,* (as David's, Ps. 119:120); he *fell on his face, and cried,* not in fear for himself (he was one of those that were marked), but in compassion to his fellow-creatures. Those that sigh and cry for the sins of sinners cannot but sigh and cry for their miseries too; yet the day is coming when all this concern will be entirely swallowed up in a full satisfaction in this, that God is glorified; and those that now *fall on their faces, and cry, Ah! Lord God,* will lift up their heads, and sing, *Hallelujah,* Rev. 19:1, 3. The prophet humbly expostulates with God: *"Wilt thou destroy all the residue of Israel,* and shall there be none left but the few that are marked? Shall the Israel of God be destroyed, utterly destroyed? When there are but a few left shall those be cut off, who might have been the seed of another generation? And will the God of Israel be himself their destroyer? Wilt thou now destroy Israel, who wast wont to protect and deliver Israel? Wilt thou so *pour out thy fury upon Jerusalem* as by the total destruction of the city to ruin the whole country too? Surely thou wilt not!" Note, Though we acknowledge that *God is righteous,* yet we have leave to *plead with him concerning his judgements,* Jer. 12:1.

IV. Here is God's denial of the prophet's request for a mitigation of the judgement and his justification of himself in that denial, *v.* 9, 10. 1. Nothing could be said in extenuation of this sin. God was willing to show mercy as the prophet could desire; he always is so. But here the case will not admit of it; it is such that mercy cannot be granted without wrong to justice; and it is not fit that one attribute of God should be glorified at the expense of another. Is it any pleasure to the Almighty that he should destroy, especially that he should destroy Israel? By no means. But the truth is their crimes are so flagrant that the reprieve of the sinners would be a connivance at the sin: *"The iniquity of the house of Judah and Israel is exceedingly great;* there is no suffering them to go on at this rate. *The land is filled with the innocent blood,* and, when the city courts are appealed to for the defence of injured innocency, the remedy is as bad as the disease, for *the city is full of perverseness,* or *wrestling of judgement;* and that which they support themselves with in this iniquity is the same atheistical profane principle with which they flattered themselves in their idolatry, *ch.* 8:12. *The Lord has forsaken the earth,* and left it to us to do what we will in it; he will not intermeddle in the affairs of it; and, whatever wrong we do, he *sees not;* he either knows it not, or will not take cognizance of it." Now how can those expect benefit by the mercy of God who thus bid defiance to his justice? No; nothing can be offered by an advocate in excuse of the crimes while the criminal puts in such a plea as this in his own vindication; and therefore. 2. Nothing can be done to mitigate the sentence (*v.* 10): "Whatever thou thinkest of it, *as for me, my eye shall not spare, neither will I have pity;* I have borne with them as long as it was fit that such impudent sinners should be borne with; and therefore now *I will recompense their way on their head."* Note, Sinners sink and perish under the weight of their own sins; it is their own way, which they deliberately chose rather than the way of God, and which they obstinately persisted in, in contempt of the word of God, that is *recompensed on* them. Great iniquities justify God in great severities; nay, he is ready to justify himself, as he does here to the prophet, for he will be *clear when he judges.*

V. Here is a return made of the writ of protection which was issued out for the securing of those that mourned in Zion (*v.* 11): *The man clothed with linen reported the matter,* gave an account of what he had done in pursuance of his commission; he had found out all that mourned in secret for the sins of the land, and cried out against them by a public testimony, and had marked them all in the forehead. Lord, *I have done as thou hast commanded me.* We do not find that those who were commissioned to destroy reported what destruction they had made, but he who was appointed to protect reported his matter; for it would be more pleasing both to God and to the prophet to hear of those that were saved than of those that perished. Or this report was made now because the thing was finished, whereas the destroying work would be a work of time, and when it was brought to an end then the report should be made. See how faithful Christ is to the trust reposed in him. Is he commanded to secure eternal life to the chosen remnant? He has done as was commanded him. *Of all that thou hast given me I have lost none.*

CHAPTER 10

The prophet had observed to us (8:4) that when he was in vision at Jerusalem he saw the same appearance of the glory of God there that he had seen by the river Chebar; now, in this chapter, he gives us some account of the appearance there, as far as was requisite for the clearing up of two further indications of the approaching destruction of Jerusalem, which God here gave the prophet: — I. The scattering of the coals of fire upon the city, which were taken from between the cherubim (*v.* 1-7). II. The removal of the glory of God from the temple, and its being upon the wing to be gone (*v.* 8-22). When God goes out from a people all judgments break in upon them.

Verses 1-7

To inspire us with a holy awe and dread of God, and to fill us with his fear, we may observe, in this part of the vision which the prophet had,

I. The glorious appearance of his majesty. Something of the invisible world is here in the visible, some faint representations of its brightness and beauty, some shadows, but such as are no more to be compared with the truth and substance than a picture with the life; yet here is enough to oblige us all to the utmost reverence in our thoughts of God and approaches to him, if we will but admit the impressions this discovery of him will make. 1. He is here *in the firmament above the head of the cherubim, v.* 1. He manifests his glory in the upper world, where purity and brightness are both in perfection; and the vast expanse of the firmament aims to speak the God that dwells there infinite. It is *the firmament of his power* and of his prospect too; for thence *he beholds* all *the children of men.* The divine nature infinitely transcends the angelic nature, and God is *above the head of the cherubim,* in respect not only of his dignity above them, but of his dominion over them. Cherubim have great power, and wisdom, and influence, but they are all subject to God and Christ. 2. He is here upon the throne, or that which had *the appearance of the likeness of a throne* (for God's glory and government infinitely transcend all the brightest ideas our minds can either form or receive concerning them); and it was *as it were a sapphire-stone,* pure and sparkling; such a throne has God *prepared in the heavens,* far exceeding the thrones of any earthly potentates. 3. He is here attended with a glorious train of holy angels. When God came into his temple *the cherubim stood on the right side of the house* (*v.* 3), as the prince's life-guard, attending the gate of his palace. Christ has angels at command. The orders given to all the angels of God are, to *worship him.* Some observe that they *stood on the right side of the house,* that is, the south side, because on the north side the image of jealousy was, and other instances of idolatry, from which they would place themselves at as great a distance as might be. 4. The appearance of his glory is veiled with a cloud, and yet out of that cloud darts forth a dazzling lustre; in *the house* and *inner court* there was *a cloud* and darkness, which filled them, and yet either the outer court, or the same court after some time, *was full of the brightness of the Lord's glory, v.* 3, 4. There was a darting forth of light and brightness; but if any over curious eye pried into it, it would find itself lost in a cloud. His righteousness is conspicuous *as the great mountains,* and the brightness of it *fills the court;* but *his judgements are a great deep,* which we cannot fathom, *a cloud* which we cannot see through. *The brightness* discovers enough to awe and direct our consciences, but the *cloud* forbids us to expect the gratifying of our curiosity; for *we cannot order our speech by rea-*

sons of darkness. Thus (Hab. 3:4) he had rays coming out of his hand, and yet there was the hiding of his power. Nothing is more clear than that God *is,* nothing more dark than *what* he is. God *covers himself with light,* and yet, as to us, *makes darkness his pavilion.* God took possession of the tabernacle and the temple in a cloud, which was always the symbol of his presence. In the temple above there will be no cloud, but we shall see *face to face.* 5. The cherubim, made a dreadful sound with their wings, *v.* 5. The vibration of them, as of the strings of musical instruments, made a curious melody; bees, and other winged insects, make a noise with their wings. Probably this intimated their preparing to remove, by stretching forth and lifting up their wings, which made this noise as it were to give warning of it. This noise is said to be *as the voice of the almighty God when he speaks,* as the thunder, which is called *the voice of the Lord* (Ps. 29:3), or *as the voice of the Lord* when he spoke to Israel on Mount Sinai; and *therefore* he then gave the law with abundance of terror, to signify with what terror he would reckon for the violation of it, which he was now about to do. This noise of their wings *was heard even to the outer court,* the court of the people; for the Lord's voice, in his judgements, *cries in the city,* which those may hear that do not, as Ezekiel, see the visions of them.

II. The terrible directions of his wrath. This vision has a further tendency than merely to set forth the divine grandeur; further orders are to be given for the destruction of Jerusalem. The greatest devastations are made by fire and sword. For a general slaughter of the inhabitants of Jerusalem orders were given in the foregoing chapter; now here we have a command to lay the city in ashes, by *scattering coals of fire* upon it, which in the vision were fetched *from between the cherubim.*

1. For the issuing out of orders to do this *the glory of the Lord* was lifted *up from the cherub* (as in the chapter before for the giving of orders there, *v.* 3) *and stood* upon *the threshold of the house,* in imitation of the courts of judgement, which they kept in the gates of their cities. The people would not hear the oracles which God had delivered to them from his holy temple, and therefore they shall thence be made to hear their doom.

2. *The man clothed in linen* who had marked those that were to be preserved is to be employed in this service; for *the same Jesus* that is the protector and Saviour of those that believe, having *all judgement committed to him,* that of condemnation as well as that of absolution, will *come in a flaming fire to take vengeance on those that obey not his gospel.* He that sits on the throne calls *to the man clothed in linen* to go in between the wheels, and fill his hand with coals of fire from between the cherubim, and scatter them over the city. This intimates, (1.) That the burning of the city and temple by the Chaldeans was a consumption determined, and that therein they executed God's counsel, did what he designed before should be done. (2.) That the fire of divine wrath, which kindles judgement upon a people, is just and holy, for it is fire fetched *from between the cherubim.* The fire on God's altar, where atonement was made, had been slighted, to avenge which fire is here fetched from heaven, like that by which Nadab and Abihu were killed for offering strange fire. If a city, or town, or house, be burnt, whether by design or accident, if we trace it in its original, we shall find that the *coals* which kindled the *fire* came from *between the wheels;* for there is not any evil of that kind in the city, but the Lord has done it. (3.) That Jesus Christ acts by commission from the Father, for from him he *receives authority to execute judgement, because he is the Son of man.* Christ came to *send fire on the earth* (Lu. 12:49) and in the great day will speak this world into ashes. By fire from his hand, the earth, and all the works that are therein, will be burnt up.

3. This *man clothed with linen* readily attended to this service; though, being *clothed with linen,* he was very unfit to go among the burning *coals,* yet, being called, he said, *Lo, I come;* this commandment he had received of his Father, and he complied with it; the prophet saw him go in, *v.* 2. *He went in, and stood beside the wheels,* expecting to be furnished there with the coals he was to scatter; for what Christ was to give he first received, whether for mercy or judgement. He was directed to take fire, but he staid till he had it given him, to show how slow he is to execute judgement, and how long-suffering to us-ward.

4. One of the cherubim reached him a handful of fire from the midst of the living creatures. The prophet, when he first saw this vision, observed that there were *burning coals of fire,* and *lamps,* that *went up and down among the living creatures* (*ch.* 1:13); thence this fire was taken, *v.* 7. The *spirit of burning, the refiner's fire,* by which Christ purifies his church, is of a divine original. It is by a celestial fire, *fire* from *between the cherubim,* that wonders are wrought. *The cherubim put it into* his *hand;* for the angels are ready to be employed by the Lord Jesus and to serve all his purposes.

5. When he had taken the fire he *went out,* no doubt to *scatter* it up and down upon *the city,* as he was directed. And *who can abide the day of his coming?* Who can stand before him when he goes out in his anger?

Verses 8–22

We have here a further account of the vision of God's glory which Ezekiel saw, here intended to introduce that direful omen of the departure of that glory from them, which would open the door for ruin to break in.

I. Ezekiel sees the glory of God shining in the sanctuary, as he had seen it *by the river of Chebar,* and gives an account of it, that those who had by their wickedness provoked God to depart from them might know what they had lost and might lament after the Lord, groaning out their Ichabod, *Where is the glory?* Ezekiel here sees the operations of divine Providence in the government of the lower world, and the affairs of it, represented by the *four wheels;* and the perfections of the holy angels, the inhabitants of the upper world, and their ministrations, represented by the *four living creatures,* every one of which had *four faces.* The agency of the angels in directing the affairs of this world is represented by the close communication that was between the *living creatures* and the *wheels,* the wheels being guided by them in all their motions, as the chariot is by him that drives it. But the same Spirit being both in the *living creatures* and in the *wheels* denoted the infinite wisdom which serves its own purposes by the ministration of angels and all the occurrences of this lower world. So that this vision gives out faith a view of that throne which the Lord has *prepared in the heavens,* and that kingdom of which *rules over all,* Ps. 103:19. The prophet observes that this was *the same vision* with that he saw by the river of Chebar (*v.* 15, 22), and yet in one thing there seems to be a material difference, that that which was there *was the face of an ox,* and was *on the left side* (*ch.* 1:10), is here the *face of a cherub,* and is the *first face* (*v.* 14), whence some have concluded that the peculiar face of a cherub was that of an ox, which the Israelites had an eye to when they made the golden calf. I rather think that in this latter vision the first face was the proper appearance or figure of a cherub, which Ezekiel knew very well, being a priest, by what he had seen in the temple of the Lord (1 Ki. 6:29), but which we now have no certainty of at all; and by this Ezekiel knew assuredly, whereas before he only conjectured it, that they were all cherubim, though putting on different faces, *v.* 20. And this first appearing in the proper figure of a cherub, and yet it being proper to retain the number of four, that of the ox is left out and dropped, because the face of the cherub had been most abused by the worship of an ox. As sometimes when God appeared to deliver his people, so now when he appeared to depart from them, *he rode on a cherub, and did fly.* Now observe here, 1. That this world is subject to turns, and changes, and various revolutions. The course of affairs in it is represented by *wheels* (*v.* 9); sometimes one spoke is uppermost and sometimes another; they are still ebbing and flowing like the sea, waxing and waning like the moon, 1 Sa. 2:4, etc. Nay, their appearance is as if there were a *wheel in the midst of a wheel* (*v.* 10), which intimates the mutual references of providence to each other, their dependences on each other, and the joint tendency of all to one common end, while their motions as to us are intricate, and perplexed, and seemingly contrary. 2. That there is an admirable harmony and uniformity in the various occurrences of providence (*v.* 13): *As for the wheels,* though they moved several ways, yet *it was cried to them, O wheel!* they were all as one, being guided by one Spirit to one end; for God works all according to the counsel of his own will, which is one, for his own glory, which is one. And this makes the disposal of Providence truly admirable, and to be looked upon with wonder. As the works of his creation, considered separately, were *good,* but all together *very good,* so the wheels of Providence, considered by themselves, are wonderful, but put them together and they are very wonderful. *O wheel!* 3. That the motions of Providence are steady and regular, and whatever the Lord pleases that he does and is never put upon new counsels. *The wheels turned not as they went* (*v.* 11), and the *living creatures went every one straight forward, v.* 22. Whatever difficulties lay in their way, they were sure to get over them, and were never obliged to stand still, turn aside, or go back. So perfectly known to God are all his works that he never put upon to new counsels. 4. That God make more use of the ministration of angels in the government of this lower world than we are aware of: *The four wheels were by the cherubim, one wheel by one cherub and another wheel by another cherub, v.* 9. What has been imagined by some concerning the spheres above, that every orb has its intelligence to guide it, is here intimated concerning the wheels below, that every wheel has its cherub to guide it. We think it a satisfaction to us if under the wise God there are wise men employed in managing the affairs of the kingdoms and churches; whether there be so or no, it appears by this that there are wise angels employed, *a cherub to every wheel.* 5. That all the motions of Providence and all the ministrations of angels are under the government of the great God. They are all *full of eyes,* those eyes of the Lord which run to and fro through the earth and which the angels have always an eye to, *v.* 12. The *living creatures* and *the wheels* concur in their motions and rests (*v.* 17); for *the Spirit of life,* as it may be read, or *the Spirit of the living creatures, is in the wheels.* The Spirit of God directs all the creatures, both upper and lower, so as to make them serve the divine purpose. Events are not determined by the *wheel of fortune,* which is blind, but by the *wheels of Providence,* which are full of eyes.

II. Ezekiel sees the glory of God removing out of the sanctuary, the place where God's honour had long dwelt, and this sight is as sad as the other was grateful. It was pleasant to see that God had not *forsaken the earth* (as the idolaters suggested, *ch.* 9:9), but sad to see that he was forsaking his sanctuary. The *glory of the Lord stood over the threshold,* having thence given the necessary orders for the destruction of the city, and it *stood over the cherubim,* not those in the most holy place, but those that Ezekiel now saw in vision, *v.* 18. It ascended that stately chariot, as the judge, when he comes off the bench, goes into his coach and is gone. And immediately *the cherubim lifted up their wings* (*v.* 19), as they were directed, and they *mounted up from the earth,* as birds upon the wing; and, *when they went out,* the wheels of this chariot were not drawn, but went by instinct, *beside them,* by which it appeared that *the Spirit of the living creatures was in the wheels.* Thus, when God is leaving a people in displeasure, angels above, and all events here below, shall concur to further his departure. But observe here, In the courts of the temple where the people of Israel had dishonoured their God, had cast off his yoke and withdrawn the shoulder from it, blessed angels appear very ready to serve him, to draw in his chariot, and to *mount upwards* with it. God has shown the prophet how the will of God was disobeyed by men on earth (*ch.* 8); here he shows him how readily it is obeyed by angels and inferior creatures; and it is a comfort to us, when we grieve for the wickedness of the wicked, to think how his angels do his commandments, *hearkening to the voice of his word,* Ps. 103:20. Let us now, 1. Take a view of this chariot in which *the glory of the God of Israel rides triumphantly.* He that is the God of Israel is the God of heaven and earth, and has the command of all the powers of both. Let the faithful Israelites comfort themselves with this, that he who is their God is above the cherubim; their Redeemer is so (1 Pt. 3:22) and has the sole and sovereign disposal of all events; *the living creatures* and *the wheels* agree to serve him, so that he is *head over all things to the church.* The rabbin call this vision that Ezekiel had *Mercabah — the vision of the chariot;* and thence they call the more abstruse part of divinity, which treats concerning God and spirits, *Opus currus — The work of the chariot,* as they do the other part, that is more plain and familiar, *Opus bereshith — The work of the creation.* — 2. Let us attend the motions of this chariot: The *cherubim, and the glory of God above them, stood at the door of the east gate of the Lord's house, v.* 19. But observe with how many stops and pauses God departs, as loth to go, as if to see if there be any that will intercede with him to return. None of the priests in the inner court, between the temple and the altar, would court his stay; therefore he leaves their court, and stands at the *east gate,* which led into the *court of the people,* to see if any of them would yet at length stand in the gap. Note, God removes by degrees from a provoking people; and, when he is ready to depart in displeasure, would return to them in mercy if they were but a repenting praying people.

CHAPTER 11

This chapter concludes the vision which Ezekiel saw, and this part of it furnished him with two messages: — I. A message of wrath against those who continued still at Jerusalem, and were there in the height of presumption, thinking they should never fall (*v.* 1–13). II. A message of comfort to those who were carried captives into Babylon and were there in the depth of despondency, thinking they should never rise. And, as the former are assured that God has judgments in store for them notwithstanding their present security, so the later are assured that God has mercy in store for them notwithstanding their present distress (*v.* 14–21). And so the glory of God removes further (*v.* 22, 23). The vision disappears (*v.* 24), and Ezekiel faithfully gives his hearers an account of it (*v.* 25).

Verses 1–13

We have here,

I. The great security of the prince's of Jerusalem, notwithstanding the judgements of God that were upon them, The prophet was brought, in vision, to the gate of the temple where these princes sat in council upon the present arduous affairs of the city: *The Spirit lifted me up, and brought me to the east gate of the Lord's house, and behold twenty-five men were there.* See how obsequious the prophet was to the Spirit's orders and how observant of all the discoveries that were made to him. It should seem, these twenty-five men were not the same with those twenty-five whom we saw at the door of the temple, *worshipping towards the east* (*ch.* 8:16); those seen to have been priests or Levites, for they were between the porch and the altar, but these were princes sitting *in the gate of the Lord's house,* to try causes (Jer. 26:10), and they are here charged, not with corruptions in worship, but with mal-administration in the government; two of them are named, because they were the most active leading men, and perhaps because the prophet knew them, though he had been some years absent — *Pelatiah* and *Jaazaniah,* not that mentioned *ch.* 8:11, for he was the son of *Shaphan,* this is the *son of Azur.* Some tell us that Jerusalem was divided into twenty-four wards, and that these were the governors or aldermen of those wards, with their mayor or president. Now observe, 1. The general character which God gives of these men to the prophet (*v.* 2): *"These are the men that devise mischief;* under pretence of concerting measures for the public safety they harden people in their sins, and take off their fear of God's judgements which they are threatened with by the prophets; they *gave wicked counsel in this city,* counselling them to restrain and silence the prophets, to rebel against the king of Babylon, and to resolve upon holding *the city* out to the last extremity." Note, It is bad with a people when the things that belong to their peace are hidden from the eyes of those who are entrusted with their counsels. And, when mischief is done, God knows at whose door to lay it, and, in the day of discovery and recompence, will be sure to lay it at the right door, and will say, *These are the men that devised it,* though they are great men, and pass for wise men, and must not now be contradicted or controlled. 2. The particular charge exhibited against them in proof of this character. They are indicted for words spoken at their council-board, which he that *stands in the congregation of the mighty* would take cognizance of (*v.* 3); they said to this effect, *"It is not near;* the destruction of our city, that has been so often threatened by the prophets, *is not near,* not so near as they talk of." They are conscious to themselves of such an enmity to reformation that they cannot but conclude it will come at last; but they have such an opinion of God's patience (though they have long abused it) that they are willing to hope it will not come this great while. Note, Where Satan cannot persuade men to look upon the judgement to come as a thing doubtful and uncertain, yet he gains his point by persuading them to look upon it as a thing at a distance, so that it loses its force: if it be sure, yet *it is not near;* whereas, in truth, *the Judge stands before the door.* Now, if the destruction is not near, they conclude, *Let us build houses;* let us count upon a continuance, for *this city is the caldron and we are the flesh.* This seems to be a proverbial expression, signifying no more than this, "We are as safe in this city as flesh in a boiling pot; the walls of the city shall be to us as *walls of brass,* and shall receive no more damage from the besiegers about it than the *cauldron* does from *the fire under it.* Those that think to force us out of our city into captivity shall find it to be as much at their peril as it would be to take the flesh out of a boiling pot with their hands." This appears to be the meaning of it, by the answer God gives to it (*v.* 9): *"I will bring you out of the midst of the city,* where you think yourselves safe, and then it will appear (*v.* 11) that *this is not your caldron, neither are you the flesh."* Perhaps it has a particular reference to *the flesh of the peace-offerings,* which it was so great an offence for the priests themselves to take out of the *caldron* while it was in seething (as we find 1 Sa. 2:13, 14), and then it intimates that they were the more secure because Jerusalem was the holy city, and they thought themselves a holy people in it, not to be meddled with. Some think this was a banter upon Jeremiah, who in one of his first visions saw Jerusalem represented by a *seething pot,* Jer. 1:13. "Now," say they, in a way of jest and ridicule, "if it be a seething pot, we are as the flesh in it, and who dares meddle with us?" Thus they continued mocking the messengers of the Lord, even while they suffered for so doing; but *be you not mockers, lest your bands be made strong.* Those hearts are indeed which are made more secure by those words of God which were designed for warning to them.

II. The method taken to awaken them out of their security. One would think that the providences of God which related to them were enough to startle them; but, to help them to understand and improve those, the word of God is sent to them to give them warning (*v.* 4): *Therefore prophesy against them,* and try to undeceive them; *prophesy, O son of man!* upon these dead and dry bones. Note, The greatest kindness ministers can do to secure sinners is to preach against them, and to show them their misery and danger, though they are ever so unwilling to see them. We then act most for them when we appear most against them. But the prophet, being at a loss what to say to men that were hardened in sin, and that bade defiance to the judgments of God, *the Spirit of the Lord fell upon him,* to make him full of power and courage, and *said unto him, Speak.* Note, When sinners are flattering themselves into their own ruin it is time to speak, and to tell them that they shall have no peace if they go on. Ministers are sometimes so bashful and timorous, and so much at a loss, that they must be put on to speak, and to speak boldly. But he that commands the prophet to speak gives him instructions what to say; and he must address himself to them as *the house of Israel* (*v.* 5), for not the princes only, but all the people, were concerned to know the truth of their cause, to know the worst of it. They are the *house of Israel,* and therefore the *God of Israel* is concerned, in kindness to them, to give them warning; and they are concerned in duty to him to take the warning. And what is it that the must say to them in God's name? 1. Let them know that the God of heaven takes notice of the vain confidences with which they support themselves (*v.* 5): *"I know the things which come into your minds every one of them,* what secret reasons you have for these resolutions, and what you aim at in putting so good a face upon a matter you know to be bad." Note, God perfectly knows not only the things that come out of our mouths, but the things that come into our minds, not only all we say, but all we think; even those thoughts that are most suddenly darted into our minds, and that as suddenly slip out of them again, so that we ourselves are scarcely aware of them, yet God knows them. He knows us better than we know ourselves; *he understands our thoughts afar off.* The consideration of this should oblige us to keep our hearts with all diligence, that no vain thoughts come into them or lodge within them. 2. Let them know that those who advised the people to stand it out should be accounted before God the murderers of all who had fallen, or should yet fall, in Jerusalem, by the sword of the Chaldeans; and those slain were the only ones that should *remain in the city,* as the *flesh in the caldron. "You have multiplied your slain in the city,* not only those whom you have by the sword of justice unjustly put to death under colour of law, but those whom you have by your wilfulness and pride unwisely exposed to the sword of war, though you were told by the prophets that you should certainly go by the worst. Thus you, with your stubborn humour, have *filled the streets of Jerusalem with the slain," v.* 6. Note, Those who are either unrighteous or imprudent in beginning or carrying on a war bring upon themselves a great deal of the guilt of blood; and those who are slain in the battles or sieges which they, by such a reasonable peace as the war aimed at, might have prevented, will be called *their slain.* Now these slain are the only flesh that shall be left in this *caldron, v.* 7. There shall none remain to keep possession of the city but those that are buried in it. There shall be no inhabitants of Jerusalem but the inhabitants of the graves there, no freemen of the city but the free among the dead. 3. Let them know that, how impregnable soever they thought their city to be, they should be forced out of it, either driven to flight or dragged into captivity: *I will bring you forth out of the midst of it,* whether you will or no, *v.* 7, 9. They had provoked God to forsake the city, and thought they should do well enough by their own policy and strength when he was gone; but God will make them know that there is no peace to those that have left their God. If they have by their sins driven God from his house, he will soon by his judgments drive them from theirs; and it will be found that those are least safe that are most secure: "This city shall not be your *caldron, neither shall you be the flesh;* you shall not soak away in it as you promise yourselves, and die in your nest; you think yourself safe *in the midst thereof,* but you shall not be long there." 4. Let them know that when God has got them out of the midst of Jerusalem he will pursue them with his judgments wherever he finds them, the judgments which they thought to shelter themselves from by keeping close in Jerusalem. They feared the sword if they should go out to the Chaldeans, and therefore would abide in their *caldron,* but, says God, I will *bring a sword upon you* (*v.* 8) and *you shall fall by the sword, v.* 10. Note, The fear of the wicked shall come upon him. And there is no fence against the judgments of God when they come with commission, no, not in walls of brass. They were afraid of trusting to the mercy of strangers. "But," says God, *"I will deliver you into the hands of strangers,* whose resentments you shall feel, since you were not willing to lie at their mercy." See Jer. 38:17, 18. They thought to escape the judgments of God, but God says that he will *execute judgments upon them;* and whereas they resolved, if they must be judged, that it should be in Jerusalem, God tells them (*v.* 10 and again *v.* 11) that he will judge them *in the borders of Israel,* which was fulfilled when Nebuchadnezzar slew all the nobles of Judah at Riblah in the land of Hamath, on the utmost border of the land of Canaan. Note, Those who have taken ever so deep root in the place where they live cannot be sure that in that place they shall die. 5. Let them know that all this is the due punishment of their sin, and *the revelation of the righteous judgment of God* against them: *You shall know that I am the Lord, v.* 10 and again *v.* 12. Those shall be made to know by the sword of the Lord who would not be taught by his word what a hatred he has to sin, and what a fearful thing it is for impenitent sinners to fall into his hands. *I will execute judgments,* and then you shall *know that I am the Lord,* for the Lord is known by the judgments which he executes upon those *that have not walked in his statutes.* Hereby it is known that he made the law, because he punishes the breach of it. *I will execute judgments among you* (says God) because *you have not executed my judgments, v.* 12. Note, The executing of the judgments of God's mouth by us, in a uniform steady course of obedience to his law, is the only way to prevent the executing of the judgments of his hand upon us in our ruin and confusion. One way or other. God's judgments will be executed; the law will take place either in its precept or in its penalty. If we do not give honour to God by executing his judgments as he has commanded, he will *get him honour* upon us by executing his judgments as he has threatened; and thus we shall know that he is the Lord, the sovereign Lord of all, that will not be mocked. And observe, When they cast off God's statutes, and walked not in them, they did *after the manners of the heathen that were round about them,* and introduced into their worship all their impure, ridiculous, and barbarous usages. When men leave the settled rule of divine institutions, they wander endlessly. Justly therefore was this made the reason why they should *keep God's ordinances,* that they might not *commit the abominable customs of the heathen,* Lev. 18:30.

III. This awakening word is here immediately followed by an awakening providence, *v.* 13. Here we may observe, 1. With what power Ezekiel prophesied, or, rather, what a divine power went along with it: *It came to pass, when I prophesied, that Pelatiah the son of Benaiah died;* he was mentioned (*v.* 1) as a principal man among the twenty-five princes that made all the mischief in Jerusalem. It should seem, this was done in vision now, as the slaying of the ancient men (*ch.* 9:6) upon occasion of which Ezekiel prayed (*v.* 8) as he did here; but it was an assurance that when this prophecy should be published it should be done in fact. The death of Pelatiah was an earnest of the complete accomplishment of this prophecy. Note, God is pleased often-times to single out some sinners, and to make them monuments of his justice, for warning to others of what is coming; and some that thought themselves very safe and snatched away suddenly, and drop down dead in an instant, as Ananias and Sapphira at Peter's feet when he prophesied. 2. With what pity Ezekiel prayed. Thought the sudden death of Pelatiah was a confirmation of Ezekiel's prophecy, and really an honour to him, yet he was in deep concern about it, and laid it to heart as if he had been his relation or friend: *He fell on his face and cried with a loud voice,* as one in earnest, *"Ah! Lord God, wilt thou make a full end of the remnant of Israel?* Many are swept away by the judgments we have been under; and shall the remnant which have escaped the sword die thus by the immediate hand of heaven? Then thou wilt indeed make a full end." Perhaps it was Ezekiel's infirmity to bewail the death of this wicked prince thus, as it was Samuel's to mourn so long for Saul; but thus he showed how far he was from desiring the woeful day he foretold. David lamented the sickness of those that hated and persecuted him. And we ought to be much affected with the sudden death of others, yea, though they are wicked.

Verses 14–21

Prophecy was designed to exalt *every valley* as well as to bring low *every mountain and hill* (Isa. 40:4), and prophets were to speak not only conviction to the presumptuous and secure, but comfort to the despised and desponding that trembled at God's word. The prophet Ezekiel, having in the former part of this chapter received instructions for the awakening of those that were *at ease in Zion,* is in these verses furnished with comfortable words for those that mourned in Babylon and *by the rivers* there sat *weeping* when they *remembered Zion.* Observe,

I. How the pious captives were trampled upon and insulted over by those who continued in Jerusalem, *v.* 15. God tells the prophet what the inhabitants of Jerusalem said of him and the rest of them that were already carried away to Babylon. God had owned them as *good figs,* and declared it was for their good that he had sent them into Babylon; but the inhabitants of Jerusalem abandoned them, supposing those that were really the best saints to be the greatest sinners of all men that dwelt in Jerusalem. Observe, 1. How they are described: They are *thy brethren* (says God to the prophet), whom thou hast a concern and affection for; they are *the men of thy kindred (the men of thy redemption,* so the word is), thy next of kin, to whom the right of redeeming the alienated possession belongs, but who are so far from being able to do it that they have themselves gone into captivity. They are *the whole house of Israel;* God so accounts of them because they only have retained their integrity, and are bettered by their captivity. They were not only of the same family and nation with Ezekiel, but of the same spirit; they were his hearers, and he had communion with them in holy ordinances; and perhaps upon that account they are called *his brethren and the men of his kindred.* 2. How they were disowned by *the inhabitants of Jerusalem;* they said of them, *Get you far from the Lord.* Those that were at ease and proud themselves scorned their brethren that were humbled and under humbling providences. (1.) They cut them off from being members of their church. Because they had separated themselves from their rulers and in compliance with the will of God had surrendered themselves to the king of Babylon, they excommunicated them, and said, *"Get you far from the Lord;* we will have nothing to do with you." Those that were superstitious were very willing to shake off those that were conscientious, and were severe in their censures of them and sentences against them, as if they were forsaken and forgotten of the Lord and were cut off from the communion of the faithful. (2.) They cut them off from being members of the commonwealth too, as if they had no longer any part or lot in the matter: *"Unto us is this land given in possession,* and you have forfeited your estates by surrendering to the king of Babylon, and we have thereby become entitled to them." God takes notice of, and is much displeased with, the contempt which those that are in prosperity put upon their brethren that are in affliction.

II. The gracious promises which God made to them in consideration of the insolent conduct of their brethren towards them. Those that hated them and cast them out said, *Let the Lord be glorified;* but *he shall appear to their joy,* Isa. 66:5. God owns that his hand had gone out against them, which had given occasion to their brethren to triumph over them (*v.* 16): "It is true *I have cast them far off among the heathen* and *scattered them among the countries;* they look as if they were an abandoned people, and so mingled with the nations that they will be lost among them; but I have mercy in store for them." Note, God takes occasion from the contempts which are put upon his people to speak comfort to them, as David hoped God would reward him good for Shimei's cursing. His time to support his people's hopes is when their enemies are endeavouring to drive them to despair. Now God promises,

1. That he will make up to them the want of the temple and the privileges of it (*v.* 16): *I will be to them as a little sanctuary, in the countries where they shall come.* Those at Jerusalem have the temple, but without God; those in Babylon have God, though without the temple. (1.) God *will be a sanctuary to them;* that is, a place of refuge; to him they shall flee, and in him they shall be safe, as he was that took hold on *the horns of the altar.* Or, rather, they shall have such communion with God in the land of their captivity as it was thought could be had nowhere but in the temple. They shall there *see God's power and his glory,* as they used *to see them in the sanctuary;* they shall have the tokens of God's presence with them, and his grace in their hearts shall sanctify their prayers and praises, as well as ever the altar sanctified the gift, so that they shall *please the Lord better than an ox or bullock.* (2.) He *will be a little sanctuary,* not seen or observed by their enemies, who looked with an evil and an envious eye upon *that house* at Jerusalem which was high and great, 1 Ki. 9:8. They were but few and mean, and a little sanctuary was fittest for them. God regards the low estate of his people, and suits his favours to their circumstances. Observe the condescensions of divine grace. The great God will be to his people a little sanctuary. Note, Those that are deprived of the benefit of public ordinances, if it be not their own fault, may have the want of them abundantly made up in the immediate communications of divine grace and comforts.

2. That God would in due time put an end to their afflictions, bring them out of the land of their captivity, and settle them again, them or their children, in their own land (*v.* 17): *"I will gather* even *you* that are thus dispersed, thus despised, and given over for lost by your own countrymen; *I will gather you from the people,* distinguish you from those with whom you are mingled, deliver you from those by whom you are held captives, *and assemble you* in a body out of the countries *where you have been scattered;* you shall not come back one by one, but all together, which will make your return more honourable, safe, and comfortable; and then *I will give you the land of Israel,* which now your brethren look upon you as for ever shut out from." Note, It is well for us that men's severe censures cannot cut us off from God's gracious promises. There are many that will be found to have a place in the holy land whom uncharitable men, by their monopolies of it to themselves, had secluded from it. *I will give you the land of Israel,* give it to you again by a new grant, *and they shall come thither.* If there be any thing in the change of the person from *you* to *them,* it may signify the posterity of those to whom the promise is made. *"You* shall have the title as the patriarchs had, and *those* that come after shall have the possession."

3. That God by his grace would part between them and their sins, *v.* 18. Their captivity shall effectually cure them of their idolatry: *When they come thither* to their own land again *they shall take away all the detestable things thereof.* Their idols, that had been their delectable things, should now be looked upon with detestation, not only the idols of Babylon, where they were captives, but the idols of Canaan, where they were natives; they should not only not worship them as they had done, but they should not suffer any monuments of them to remain: *They shall take all the abominations thereof thence.* Note, *Then* it is in mercy that we return to a prosperous estate, when we return not to the sins and follies of that state. *What have I to do any more with idols?*

4. That God would powerfully dispose them to their duty; they shall not only *cease to do evil,* but they shall *learn to do well,* because there shall be not only an end of their troubles, but a return to their peace.

(1.) God will plant good principles in them; he will make the tree good, *v.* 19. This is a gospel promise, and is made good to all those whom God designs for the heavenly Canaan; for God prepares all for heaven whom he has prepared heaven for. It is promised, [1.] That God *will give them one heart,* a heart entire for the true God and not divided as it had been among many gods, a heart firmly fixed and resolved for God and not wavering, steady and uniform, and not inconstant with itself. *One heart* is a sincere and upright heart, its intentions of a piece with its professions. [2.] That he *will put a new spirit within them,* a temper of mind agreeable to the new circumstances into which God in his providence would bring them. All that are sanctified have *a new spirit,* quite different from what it was; they act from new principles, walk by new rules, and aim at new ends. A new name, or a new face, will not serve without a new spirit. *If any man be in Christ, he is a new creature.* [3.] That he *will take* away *the stony heart out of their flesh,* out of their corrupt nature. Their hearts shall no longer be, as they have been, dead and dry, and hard and heavy, as a stone, no longer incapable of bearing good fruit, so that the good seed is lost upon it, as it was on the *stony ground.* [4.] That he *will give them a heart of flesh,* not dead or proud flesh, but living flesh; he will make their hearts sensible of spiritual pains and spiritual pleasures, will make them tender, and apt to receive impressions. This is God's work, it is his gift, his gift by promise; and a wonderful and happy change it is that is wrought by it, from death to life. This is promised to those whom God would bring back to their own land; for *then* such a change of the condition is for the better indeed when it is accompanied with such a change of the heart; and such a change must be wrought in all those that shall be brought to the *better country,* that is, the heavenly.

(2.) Their practices shall be consonant to those principles: *I will give them a new spirit,* not that they may be able to discourse well of religion and to dispute for it, but *that they may walk in my statues* in their whole conversation *and keep my ordinances* in all acts of religious worship, *v.* 20. These two must go together; and those to whom God has given *a new heart and a new spirit* will make conscience of both; and then *they shall be my people and I will be their God.* The ancient covenant, which seemed to be broken and forgotten, shall be renewed. By their idolatry, it should seem, they had cast God off; by their captivity, it should seem, God had cast them off. But when they were cured of their idolatry, and delivered out of their captivity, God and his Israel own one another again. God, by his good work in them, will make them his *people;* and then, by the tokens of his good-will towards them, he will show that he is *their God.*

III. Here is a threatening of wrath against those who hated to be reformed. As, when judgments are threatened, the righteous are distinguished so as not to share in the evil of those judgments, so, when favours are promised, the wicked are distinguished so as not to share in the comfort of those favours; they have no part nor lot in the matter, *v.* 21. *But, as for those* that have no grace, what have they *to do with peace?* Observe, 1. Their description. Their *heart walks after the heart of their detestable things;* they have as great a minds to worship devils as devils have to be worshipped. Or, in opposition to the *new heart* which God gives his people, which is a heart after his own heart, they have a *heart after the heart of their idols;* in their temper and practice they conformed to the characters and accounts given them of their idols, and the ideas they had of them, and of them they learned lewdness and cruelty. Here lies the root of all their wickedness, the corruption of the heart; as the root of their reformation is laid in the renovation of the heart. The heart has its walks, and according as those are the man is. 2. Their doom. It carries both justice and terror in it: *I will recompense their way upon their own heads;* I will deal with them as they deserve. There needs no more than this to speak God righteous, that he does but render to men according to their deserts: and yet such are the deserts of sin that there needs no more than this to speak the sinner miserable.

Verses 22–25

Here is, 1. The departure of God's presence from the city and temple. When the message was committed to the prophet, and he was fully apprized of it, fully instructed how to separate between *the precious and the vile, then the cherubim lifted up their wings and the wheels beside them* (*v.* 22) as before, *ch.* 10:19. Angels, when they have done their errands in this lower world, are upon the wing to be gone, for they lose no time. We left *the glory of the Lord* last at *the east gate of the temple* (*ch.* 10:19), which is here said to be in the *midst of the city.* Now here we are told that, finding and wondering that there was none to intercede, none to uphold, none to invite its return, it removed next to *the mountain which is on the east side of the city* (*v.* 23); that was the *mount of Olives.* On this mountain they had set up their idols, to confront God in his temple, when he dwelt there (1 Ki. 11:7), and thence it was called *the mount of corruption* (2 Ki. 23:13); therefore there God does as it were set up his standard, his tribunal, as it were to confront those who thought to keep possession of the temple for themselves now that God had left it. From that mountain there was a full prospect of the city; thither God removed, to make good what he had said (Deu. 32:20), *I will hide my face from them, I will see what their end shall be.* It was from this mountain that Christ *beheld the city and wept over it,* in the foresight of its last destruction by the Romans. *The glory of the Lord* removed thither, to be as it were yet within call, and ready to return if now at length, *in this their day,* they would have *understood the things that belonged to their peace.* Loth to depart bids oft farewell. God, by going away thus slowly, thus gradually, intimated that he left them with reluctance, and would not have gone if they had not perfectly forced him from them. He did now, in effect, say, *How shall I give thee up, Ephraim? How shall I deliver thee, Israel?* But, though he bear long, he will not bear always, but will at length forsake those, and cast them off for ever, who have forsaken him and cast him off. 2. The departure of this vision from the prophet. At length it *went up from him* (*v.* 24); he saw it mount upwards, till it went out of sight, which would be a confirmation to his faith that it was a heavenly vision, that it descended from above, for thitherward it returned. Note, The visions which the saints have of the glory of God will not be constant will they come to heaven. They have glimpses of that glory, which they soon lose again, visions which go up from them, tastes of divine pleasures, but not a continual feast. It was from the mount of Olives that the vision went up, typifying the ascension of Christ to heaven from that very mountain, when those that had seen him *manifested in the flesh* saw him no more. It was foretold (Zec. 14:4) that *his feet should stand upon the mount of Olives,* stand last there. 3. The prophet's return to those of the captivity. The same spirit that had carried him in a trance or ecstasy to Jerusalem brought him back to Chaldea; for there the bounds of his habitation are at present appointed, and that is the place of his service. The Spirit came to him, not to deliver him out of captivity, but (which was equivalent) to support and comfort him in his captivity. 4. The account which he gave to his hearers of all he had seen and heard, *v.* 25. He received that he might give, and he was *faithful to him that appointed him;* he delivered his message very honestly: he *spoke all that,* and that only, which God *had shown* him. He told them of the great wickedness he had seen at Jerusalem, and the ruin that was hastening towards that city, that they might not repent of their surrendering themselves to the king of Babylon as Jeremiah advised them, and blame themselves for it, nor envy those that staid behind, and laughed at them for going when they did, nor wish themselves there again, but be content in their captivity. Who would covet to be in a city so full of sin and so near to ruin? It is better to be in Babylon under the favour of God than in Jerusalem under his wrath and curse. But, though this was delivered immediately to those of the captivity, yet we may suppose that they sent the contents of it to those at Jerusalem, with whom they kept up a correspondence; and well would it have been for Jerusalem if she had taken the warning hereby given.

CHAPTER 12

Though the vision of God's glory had gone up from the prophet, yet his word comes to him still, and is by him sent to the people, and to the same purport with that which was discovered to him in the vision, namely, to set forth the terrible judgments that were coming upon Jerusalem, by which the city and temple should be entirely laid waste. In this chapter, I. The prophet, by removing his stuff, and quitting his lodgings, must be a sign to set forth Zedekiah's flight out of Jerusalem in the utmost confusion when the Chaldeans took the city (*v.* 1–16). II. The prophet, by eating his meat with trembling, must be a sign to set forth the famine in the city during the siege, and the consternation that the inhabitants should be in (*v.* 17–20). III. A message is sent from God to the people, to assure them that all these predictions should have their accomplishment very shortly, and not be deferred, as they flattered themselves they would be (*v.* 21–28).

Verses 1–16

Perhaps Ezekiel reflected with so much pleasure upon the vision he had had of the glory of God that often, since it went up from him, he was wishing it might come down to him again, and, having seen it once and a second time, he was willing to hope he might be a third time so favoured; but we do not find that he ever saw it any more, and yet *the word of the Lord comes to* him; for God did *in divers manners speak to the fathers* (Heb. 1:1) and they often *heard the words of God* when they did not *see the visions of the Almighty.* Faith comes by hearing that word of prophecy which is more sure than vision. We may keep up our communion with God without raptures and ecstasies. In these verses the prophet is directed,

I. By what signs and actions to express the approaching captivity of Zedekiah king of Judah; that was the thing to be foretold, and it is foretold to those that are already in captivity, because as long as Zedekiah was upon the throne they flattered themselves with hopes that he would make his part good with the king of Babylon, whose yoke he was now projecting to shake off, from which, it is probable, these poor captives promised themselves great things; and it may be, when he was forming that design, he privately sent encouragement to them to hope that he would rescue them shortly, or procure their liberty by exchange of prisoners. While they were fed with these vain hopes they could not set themselves either to submit to their affliction or to get good by their affliction. It was therefore necessary, but very difficult, to convince them that Zedekiah, instead of being their deliverer, should very shortly be their fellow-suffered. Now, one would think it might have been sufficient if the prophet had only told them this in God's name, as he does afterwards (*v.* 10); but, to prepare them for the prophecy of it, he must first give them a sign of it, must speak it to their eyes first and then to their ears: and here we have, 1. The reason why he must take this method (*v.* 2): It is because they are a stupid, dull, unthinking people, that will not heed or will soon forget what they only hear of, or at least will not be at all affected with it; it will make no impression at all upon them: *Thou dwellest in the midst of a rebellious house,* whom it is next to impossible to work any good upon. *They have eyes and ears,* they have intellectual powers and faculties, but they *see not,* they *hear not.* They were idolaters, whose character it was that they were like the idols they worshipped, which *have eyes and see not, ears and hear not,* Ps. 115:5, 6, 8. Note, Those are to be reckoned rebellious that shut their eyes against the divine light and stop their ears to the divine law. The ignorance of those that are wilfully ignorant, that have faculties and means and will not use them, is so far from being their excuse that it adds rebellion to their sin. None so blind, so deaf, as those that will not see, that will not hear. They *see not,* they *hear not; for they are a rebellious house.* The cause is all from themselves: the darkness of the understanding is owing to the stubbornness of the will. Now this is the reason why he must speak to them by signs, as deaf people are taught, that they might be either instructed or ashamed. Note, Ministers must accommodate themselves not only to the weakness, but to the wilfulness of those they deal with, and deal with them accordingly: if they dwell among those that are rebellious they must speak to them the more plainly and pressingly, and take that course that is most likely to work upon them, that they may be left inexcusable. 2. The method he just take to awaken and affect them; he must furnish himself with all necessaries *for removing* (*v.* 3), provide for a journey clothes and money; he must *remove from one place to another,* as one unsettled and forced to shift; this he must do *by day, in the sight* of the people; he must bring out all his household goods, to be packed up and sent away (*v.* 4); and, because all the doors and gates were either locked up that they could not pass through them or so guarded by the enemy that they durst not, he must therefore *dig through the wall,* and convey his goods away clandestinely through that breach in the wall, *v.* 5. He must carry his goods away himself upon his own shoulders, for want of a servant to attend him; he must do this *in the twilight,* that he might not be discovered; and, when he has made what shift he can to secure some of the best of his effects, he must himself steal away *at evening in their sight,* with fear and trembling, and must go *as those that go forth into captivity* (*v.* 4); that is, he must *cover* his *face* (*v.* 6) as being ashamed to be seen and afraid to be known, or in token of very great sorrow and concern; he must go away as a poor broken tradesman, who, when he is forced to shut up shop, hides his head, or quits his country. Thus Ezekiel must be himself a sign to them; and when perhaps he seemed somewhat backward to put himself to all this trouble, and to expose himself to be bantered and ridiculed for it, to reconcile him to it God says (*v.* 3) *"It may be they will consider,* and will by it be taken off from their vain confidence, *though they be a rebellious house."* Note, We must not despair even of the worst, but that yet they may be brought to bethink themselves and repent; and therefore we must continue the use of proper means for their conviction and conversion, because, while there is life, there is hope. And ministers must be willing to go through the most difficult and inconvenient offices (for such was this of Ezekiel's removing), though there be but the *it may be* of success. If but one soul be awakened to consider, our care and pains will be well bestowed. 3. Ezekiel's ready and punctual obedience to the orders God gave him (*v.* 7): *I did so as I was commanded.* Hereby he teaches us all, and ministers especially, (1.) To obey with cheerfulness every command of God, even the most difficult. Christ himself *learned obedience,* and so we must all. (2.) To do all we can for the good of the souls of others, to put ourselves to any trouble or pains for the conviction of those that are unconvinced. *We do all things* (that is, we are willing to do any thing), *dearly beloved, for your edifying.* (3.) To be ourselves affected with those things wherewith we desire to affect others. When Ezekiel would give his hearers a melancholy prospect he does himself put on a melancholy aspect. (4.) To sit loose to this world, and prepare to leave it, to carry out our *stuff for removing,* because *we have here no continuing city. Arise, depart, this it not your rest, for it is polluted.* Thou dwellest *in a rebellious house,* therefore prepare for removing; for who would not be willing to leave such a house, such a wicked world as this is?

II. He is directed by what words to explain those signs and actions, as Agabus, when he bound his own hands and feet, told whose binding was thereby signified. But observe, It was not till morning that God gave him an exposition of the sign, till the next morning, to keep up in him a continual dependence upon God for instruction. As what God does, so what he directs us to do, perhaps we know not now, but shall know hereafter.

1. It was supposed that the people would ask the meaning of this sing, or at least they should (*v.* 9): *"Hath not the house of Israel said unto thee, What doest thou?* Yes, I know they have. *Though they* are *a rebellious house,* yet they are inquisitive concerning the mind of God," as those (Isa. 58:2) who *sought God daily. Therefore* the prophet must do such a strange uncouth thing, that they might enquire what it meant; and then, it may be hoped, people will take notice of what is told them, and profit by it, when it comes to them in answer to their enquiries. But some understand it as an intimation that they had not made any such enquiries: *"Hath not this rebellious house* so much as asked thee, *What dost thou?* No; they take no notice of it; but tell them the meaning of it, though they do not ask." Note, When God sends to us by his ministers he observes what entertainment we give to the messages he sends us; he hearkens and hears what we say to them, and what enquiries we make upon them, and is much displeased if we pass them by without taking any notice of them. When we have heard the word we should apply to our ministers for further instruction; and then we shall know if we thus follow on to know.

2. The prophet is to tell them the meaning of it. In general (*v.* 10), *This burden concerns the prince in Jerusalem;* they knew who that was, and gloried in it now that they were in captivity that they had a prince of their own in Jerusalem, and that *the house of Israel* was yet entire there, and therefore doubted not but in time to do well enough. "But tell them," says God, "that in what thou hast done they may read the doom of their friends at Jerusalem. *Say, I am your sign,*" *v.* 11. As the conversation of ministers should teach the people what they should do, so the providences of God concerning them are sometimes intended to tell them what they must expect. The unsettled state and removals of ministers give warning to people what they must expect in this world, no continuance, but constant changes. When times of trouble are coming on Christ tells his disciples, *They shall first lay their hands on you,* Lu. 21:12. (1.) The people shall be led away into captivity (*v.* 11): *As I have done, so shall it be done unto them;* they shall be forced away from their own houses, no more to return to them, neither shall *their place know them any more.* We cannot say concerning our dwelling-place that it is our resting-place; for how far we may be tossed from it before we die we cannot foresee. (2.) The prince shall in vain attempt to make his escape; for he also shall go into captivity. Jeremiah had told Zedekiah the same to his face (Jer. 34:3): *Thou shalt not escape, but shalt surely be taken.* Ezekiel here foretels it to those who made him their confidence and promised themselves relief from him. [1.] That he shall himself carry away his own goods: *He shall bear upon his shoulder* some of his most valuable effects. Note, The judgments of God can turn a prince into a porter. He that was wont to have the regalia carried before him, and to march through the city at noon-day, shall now himself carry his goods on his back and steal away out of the city in the twilight. See what a change sin makes with men! All the avenues to the palace being carefully watched by the enemy, *they shall dig through the wall to carry out thereby.* Men shall be their own house-breakers, and steal away their own goods; so it is when the sword of war has cancelled all right and property. [2.] That he shall attempt to escape in a disguise, with a mask or a visor on, which *shall cover his face,* so that he shall be able only to look before him, and shall *not see the ground with his eyes.* He who, when he was in pomp, affected to be seen, now that he is in his flight is afraid to be seen; let none therefore either be proud of being looked at or over-much pleased with looking about them, when they see a king with *his face covered, that he cannot see the ground.* [3.] That he shall be made a prisoner and carried captive into Babylon (*v.* 13): *My net will I spread upon him and he shall be taken in my snare.* It seemed to be the Chaldeans' net and their snare, but God owns them for his. Those that think to escape the sword of the Lord will find themselves taken in his net. Jeremiah had said that king Zedekiah should *see the king of Babylon* and that he should *go to Babylon;* Ezekiel says, He shall be *brought to Babylon,* yet he *shall not see it,* though *he shall die there.* Those that were disposed to cavil would perhaps object that these two prophets contradicted one another; for one said, He shall *see the king of Babylon,* the other said, He shall *not see Babylon;* and yet both proved true: he did *see the king of Babylon* at Riblah, where he passed sentence upon him for his rebellion, but there he had his eyes put out, so that he did *not see Babylon* when he was brought thither. These captives expected to see their prince come to Babylon as a conqueror, to bring them out of their trouble; but he shall come thither a prisoner, and his disgrace will be a great addition to their troubles. Little joy could they have in seeing him when he could not see them. [4.] That all his guards should be dispersed and utterly disabled for doing

him any service (*v.* 14): *I will scatter all that are about him to help him,* so that he shall be left helpless; *I will scatter them among the nations and disperse them in the countries* (*v.* 15), to be monuments of divine justice wherever they go. But are there not hopes that they may rally again? (he that flies one time may fight another time); no: *I will draw out the sword after them,* which shall cut them off wherever if finds them; for the sword that God draws out will be sure to do the execution designed. Yet of Zedekiah's scattered troops some shall escape (*v.* 16): *I will leave a few men of them.* Though they shall all be scattered, yet they shall not all be cut off; some shall have their *lives given them for a prey.* And the end for which they are thus remarkably spared is very observable: *That they may declare all their abominations among the heathen whither they come;* the troubles they are brought into will bring them to themselves and to their right mind, and then they will acknowledge the justice of God in all that is brought upon them and will make an ingenuous confession of their sins, which provoked God thus to contend with them; and, as by this it shall appear that they were spared in mercy, so hereby they will make a suitable grateful return to God for his favours to them in sparing them. Note, When God has remarkably delivered us from the deaths wherewith we were surrounded we must look upon it that for this end, among others, we were spared, that we might glorify God and edify others by making a penitent acknowledgment of our sins. Those that by their afflictions are brought to this are then made to know *that God is the Lord* and may help to bring others to the knowledge of him. See how God brings good out of evil. The dispersion of sinners, who had done God much dishonour and disservice in their own country, proves the dispersion of penitents, who shall do him much honour and service in others countries. The Levites are by a curse *divided in Jacob* and *scattered in Israel,* yet it is turned into a blessing, for thereby they have the fairest opportunity to *teach Jacob God's laws.*

Verses 17–20

Here again the prophet is made a sign to them of the desolations that were coming on Judah and Jerusalem. 1. He must himself eat and drink in care and fear, especially when he was in company, *v.* 17, 18. Though he was under no apprehension of danger to himself, but lived in safety and plenty, yet he must *eat his bread with quaking* (the bread of sorrows, Ps. 127:2) *and drink his water with trembling and with carefulness,* that he might express the calamitous condition of those that should be in Jerusalem during the siege; not that he must dissemble and pretend to be in fear and care when really he was not; but having to foretel this judgment, to show that he firmly believed it himself, and yet was far from desiring it, in the prospect of it he was himself affected with grief and fear. Note, When ministers speak of the ruin coming upon impenitent sinners they must endeavour to speak feelingly, as those that *know the terrors of the Lord;* and they must be content to endure hardness, so that they may but do good. 2. He must tell them that *the inhabitants of Jerusalem* should in like manner eat and drink with care and fear, *v.* 19, 20. Both those that have their home in Jerusalem and those *of the land of Israel* that come to shelter themselves there, *shall eat their bread with carefulness and drink their water with astonishment,* either because they are afraid it will not hold out, but they shall want shortly, or because they are continually expecting the alarms of the enemy, *their life hanging in doubt before them* (Deu. 28:66), so that what they have they shall have no enjoyment of nor will it do them any good. Note, Care and fear, if they prevail, are enough to embitter all our comforts and are themselves very sore judgments. They shall be reduced to these straits that thus by degrees, and by the hand of those that thus straiten them, both city and country may be laid in ruins; for it is no less than an utter destruction of both that is aimed at in these judgments — *that her land may be desolate from all* the fulness thereof, may be stripped of all its ornaments and robbed of all its fruits, and then of course *the cities that are inhabited shall be laid waste,* for they are *served by the field.* This universal desolation was coming upon them, and then no wonder that they eat their bread with care and fear. Now we are here told, (1.) How bad the cause of this judgment was; it is *because of the violence of all those that dwell therein,* their injustice and oppression, and the mischief they did one another, for which God would reckon with them, as well as for the affronts put upon him in his worship. Note, The decay of virtue in a nation brings on a decay of every thing else; and when neighbours devour one another it is just with God to bring enemies upon them to devour them all. (2.) How good the effect of this judgment should be: *You shall know that I am the Lord;* and if, by these judgments, they learn to know him aright, that will make up the loss of all they are deprived of by these desolations. Those are happy afflictions, how grievous soever to flesh and blood, that help to introduce us into and improve us in an acquaintance with God.

Verses 21–28

Various methods had been used to awaken this secure and careless people to an expectation of the judgments coming, that they might be stirred up, by repentance and reformation, to prevent them. The prophecies of their ruin were confirmed by visions, and illustrated by signs, and all with such evidence and power that one would think they must needs be wrought upon; but here we are told how they evaded the conviction, and guarded against it, namely, by telling themselves, and one another, that though these judgments threatened should come at last yet they would not come of a long time. This suggestion, with which they bolstered themselves up in their security, is here answered, and shown to be vain and groundless, in two separate messages which God sent to them by the prophet at different times, both to the same purport; such care, such pains, must the prophet take to undeceive them, *v.* 21, 26. Observe,

I. How they flattered themselves with hopes that the judgments should be delayed. One saying they had, which had become proverbial *in the land of Israel, v.* 22. They said, *"The days are prolonged;* the judgments have not come when they were expected to come, but seem to be still put off *de die in diem — from day to day,* and therefore we may conclude that *every vision fails,* because it should seem that some do, that because the destruction has not come yet it will never come; we will never trust a prophet again, for we have been more frightened than hurt." And another saying they had which, if it would not conquer their convictions, yet would cool their affections and abate their concern, and that was, *"The vision* is *for* a great while *to come;* it refers to events at a vast distance, *and he prophesies of* things which, though they may be true, are yet very *far off,* so that we need not trouble our heads about them (*v.* 27); we may die in honour and peace before these troubles come." And, if indeed the troubles had been thus adjourned, they might have made themselves easy, as Hezekiah did. *Is it not well if peace and truth shall be in my days?* But it was a great mistake, and they did but deceive themselves into their own ruin; and God is here much displeased at it; for, 1. It was a wretched abuse of the patience of God, who, because for a time he kept silence, was thought to be *altogether such a one as themselves,* Ps. 50:21. That forbearance of God which should have led them to repentance hardened them in sin. They were willing to think their works were not *evil because sentence against* them was *not executed speedily;* and therefore concluded the *vision* itself *failed,* because *the days were prolonged.* 2. It received countenance form the false prophets that were among them, as should seem from the notice God takes (*v.* 24) of the *vain visions,* and *flattering divinations,* even *within the house of Israel,* to whom *were committed the oracles of God.* No marvel if those that deceived themselves by worshipping pretended deities deceived themselves also by crediting pretended prophecies, to which *strong delusions* God justly *gave them up* for their idolatries. 3. These sayings had become proverbial; they were industriously spread among the people, so that they had got into very one's mouth, and not only so, but were generally assented to, as proverbs usually are, not only the proverbs of the ancients, but those of the moderns too. Note, It is a token of universal degeneracy in a nation when corrupt and wicked sayings have grown proverbial; and it is an artifice of Satan by them to confirm men in their prejudices against the word and ways of God, and a great offence to the God of heaven. It will not serve for an excuse, in saying ill, to plead that it is a common saying.

II. How they are assured that they do but deceive themselves, for the judgments shall be hastened, these profane proverbs shall be confronted: *Tell them, therefore, The days are at hand* (*v.* 23), and again, *There shall none of my words be prolonged any more, v.* 28. Their putting the evil day far from them does but provoke God to bring it the sooner upon them; and it will be so much the sorer, so much the heavier, so much the more a surprise and terror to them when it does come. He must tell them,

1. That God will certainly silence the lying proverbs, and the lying prophecies, with which they buoyed up their vain hopes, and will make them ashamed of both: (1.) *I will make this proverb to cease;* for when they find the days of vengeance have come, and not one iota or tittle of the prediction falls to the ground, they will be ashamed to *use it as a proverb in Israel, The days are prolonged, and the vision fails.* Note, Those that will not have their eyes opened and their mistakes rectified, by the word of God, shall be undeceived by his judgments: for *every mouth* that speaks perverse things *shall be stopped.* (2.) *There shall be no more any vain vision, v.* 24. The false prophets, who told the people they should have peace and should soon see an end of their troubles, shall be disproved by the event, and then shall be ashamed of their pretensions, and shall hide their heads and impose silence upon themselves. Note, As truth was older than error, so it will survive it; it got the start, and it will get the race. The true prophets' visions and predictions stand, and are in full force, power, and virtue; they give law, and receive credit, when the *vain visions,* and the *flattering divinations,* are lost and forgotten, and *shall be no more in the house of Israel;* for *great is the truth, and will prevail.*

2. That God will certainly, and very shortly, accomplish every word that he has spoken. With what majesty does he say it (*v.* 25): I *am the* LORD! *I am Jehovah!* That glorious name of his speaks him a God giving being to his word by the performance of it, and therefore to the patriarchs, who lived by faith in a promise not yet performed, he was not known by his name *Jehovah,* Ex. 6:3. But, as he is Jehovah in making good his promise, so he is in making good his threatenings. Let them know then that God, *with whom they have to do,* is the great Jehovah, and therefore, (1.) He will speak, *whether they will hear or whether they will forbear: I am the Lord, I will speak.* God will have his saying, whoever gainsays it. God's oracles are called *lively* ones, for they still speak when the pagan oracles are long ago struck dumb. There has been, and shall be, a succession of God's ministers to the end of the world, by whom he will speak; and, though contempt may be put upon them, that shall not put a period to their ministration: *In your days, O rebellious house! will I say the word.* Even in the worst ages of the church God *left not himself without witness,* but raised up men that spoke for him, that spoke from him. *I will say the word,* the word that shall stand. (2.) The word that he speaks shall come to pass; it shall infallibly be accomplished according to the true intent and meaning of it, and according to the full extent and compass of it: *I will say the word and will perform it* (*v.* 25), for his mind is never changed, nor his arm shortened, nor is Infinite Wisdom ever nonplussed. With men saying and doing are two things, but they are not so with God; with him it is *dictum, factum — said, and done.* In the works of providence, as in those of creation, *he speaks and it is done;* for he said, *Let there be light, and there was light — Let there be a firmament, and there was a firmament,* Num. 23:19; 1 Sa. 15:29. Whereas they had said, *Every vision fails* (*v.* 22), God says, "No, there shall be *the effect of every vision* (*v.* 23); it shall not return void, but every sign shall be answered by the thing signified." Those that *see the visions of the Almighty* do not see *vain visions;* God *confirms the word of his servants* by performing it. (3.) It shall be accomplished very shortly: *"The days are at hand* when you shall see *the effect of every vision, v.* 23. It is said, it is sworn, that delay *shall be no longer* (Rev. 10:6); the year of God's patience has now just expired, and he will no longer defer the execution of the sentence. *It shall be no more prolonged* (*v.* 25); he has borne with you a great while, but he will not bear always. *In your days, O rebellious house!* shall the word that is said be *performed,* and you shall see the threatened judgments and share in them. *Behold, the Judge stands at the door.* The *righteous are taken away from the evil to come,* but this

rebellious house shall not be so quietly taken away; no, they shall live to be hurried away, to *be chased out of the world.*" This is repeated (*v.* 28): "*There shall none of my words be prolonged any more,* but judgment shall now hasten on apace; and the longer the bow has been in the drawing the deeper shall the arrow pierce." When we tell sinners of death and judgment, heaven and hell, and think by them to persuade them to a holy life, though we do not find them downright infidels (they will own that they do believe there is a state of rewards and punishments in the other world), yet they put by the force of those great truths, and void the impressions of them, by looking upon the things of the other world as very remote; they tell us, "*The vision* you *see is for many days to come, and* you *prophesy of the times that are* very *far off;* it will be time enough to think of them when they come nearer," whereas really there is but a step between us and death, between us and an awful eternity; *yet a little while and the vision shall speak and not lie,* and therefore it concerns us to redeem time, and get ready with all speed for a future state; for, though it is future, it is very near, and while impenitent sinners slumber their *damnation slumbers not.*

CHAPTER 13

Mention had been made, in the chapter before, of the vain visions and flattering divinations with which the people of Israel suffered themselves to be imposed upon (*v.* 24); now this whole chapter is levelled against them. God's faithful prophets are nowhere so sharp upon any sort of sinners as upon the false prophets, not because they were the most spiteful enemies to them, but because the put the highest affront upon God and did the greatest mischief to his people. The prophet here shows the sin and punishment, I. Of the false prophets (*v.* 1–16). II. Of the false prophetesses (*v.* 17–23). Both agreed to sooth men up in their sins, and, under pretence of comforting God's people, to flatter them with hopes that they should yet have peace; but the prophets shall be proved liars, their prophecies mere shams, and the expectations of the people illusions; for God will let them know that "the deceived and the deceiver are his," are both accountable to him, Job 12:16.

Verses 1–9

The false prophets, who are here prophesied against, were some of them at Jerusalem (Jer. 23:14): *I have seen in the prophets at Jerusalem a horrible thing;* some of them among the captives in Babylon, for to them Jeremiah writes (Jer. 29:8), *Let not your diviners, that be in the midst of you, deceive you.* And as God's prophets, though at a distance from each other in place or time, yet preached the same truths, which was an evidence that they were guided by one and the same good Spirit, so the false prophets prophesied the same lies, being actuated by one and the same spirit of error. There were little hopes of bringing them to repentance, they were so hardened in their sin; yet Ezekiel must prophesy against them, in hopes that the people might be cautioned not to hearken to them; and thus a testimony will be left upon record against them, and they will thereby be left inexcusable.

Ezekiel had express orders to *prophesy against the prophets of Israel;* so they called themselves, as if none but they had been worthy of the name of Israel's prophets, who were indeed Israel's deceivers. But it is observable that Israel was never imposed upon by pretenders to prophecy till after they had rejected and abused the true prophets; as, afterwards, they were never deluded by counterfeit messiahs till after they had refused the true Messiah and rejected him. These false prophets must be required to *hear the word of the Lord.* They took upon them to speak what concerned others as from God; let them now hear what concerned themselves as from him. And two things the prophet is directed to do: —

I. To discover their sin to them, and to convince them of that if possible, or thereby to prevent their proceeding any further, by making *manifest their folly unto all men,* 2 Tim. 3:9. They are here called *foolish prophets* (*v.* 3), men that did not at all understand the business they pretended to; to make fools of the people they made fools of themselves, and put the greatest cheat upon their own souls. Let us see what is here laid to their charge. 1. They pretend to have a commission from God, whereas he never sent them. They thrust themselves into the prophetic office, without warrant from him who is *the Lord God* of the holy prophets, which was a foolish thing; for how could they expect that God should own them in a work to which he never called them? They are *prophets out of their own hearts* (so the margin reads it, *v.* 2), prophets of their own making, *v.* 6. *They say, The Lord saith;* they pretend to be his messengers, but *the Lord has not sent them,* has not given them any orders. They counterfeit the broad seal of heaven, than which they cannot do a greater indignity to mankind, for hereby they put a reproach upon divine revelation, lessen its credit, and weaken its credibility. When these pretenders are found to be deceivers atheists and infidels will thence infer, They are all so. *The Lord has not sent them;* for though crafty enough in other things *like the foxes,* and very wise for the world, yet they are *foolish prophets* and have no experimental acquaintance with the things of God. Note, Foolish prophets are not of God's sending, for whom he sends he either finds fit or makes fit. Where he gives warrant he gives wisdom. 2. They pretend to have instructions from God, whereas he never made himself and his mind known to them: *They followed their own spirit* (*v.* 3); they delivered that as a message from God which was the product either of their subtle invention, to serve a turn for themselves, or of their own crazed and heated imagination, to give vent to a fancy. For *they have seen nothing,* they have not really had any heavenly vision; they pretend that what they say *the Lord saith it,* but God disowns it: "*I have not spoken it,* I never said it, never meant any such thing." What they delivered was not what they had seen or heard, as that is which the ministers of Christ deliver (1 Jn. 1:1), but either what they had dreamed or what they thought would please those they coveted to make an interest in; this is called their *seeing vanity and lying divination* (*v.* 6); they pretended to have seen that which they did not see, and produced that as a divine truth which they knew to be false. To the same purport (*v.* 7): *You have see a vain vision and spoken a lying divination,* which had no divine original and would have no effect, but would certainly be disproved by the event; the words are changed (*v.* 8): *You have spoken vanity and seen lies;* what they saw and what they said was all alike, a mere sham; they saw nothing, they said nothing, to the purpose, nothing that could be relied on or that deserved regard. Again (*v.* 9), They *see vanity and divine lies;* they pretended to have had visions, as the true prophets had, whereas really they had none, but either it was the creature of their own fancy (they thought they had a vision, as men in a delirium do, that was *seeing vanity)* or it was a fiction of their own politics, and they knew they had none, and then they *saw lies, and divined lies.* See Jer. 23:16, etc. Note, Since the devil is universally know to be the father of lies, those put the highest affront imaginable upon God who tell lies, and then father them upon him. But those that had put God's character upon Satan, in worshipping devils, arrived at length at such a pitch of impiety as to put Satan's character upon God. 3. They took no care to prevent the judgments of God that were breaking in upon the kingdom. They are like *the foxes in the deserts,* running to and fro, and seeming to be in a great hurry, but it was to get away and shift for their own safety, not to do any good: *The hireling flees, and leaves the sheep.* They are like foxes that are greedy of prey for themselves, crafty and cruel to feed themselves. But (*v.* 5), "You *have not gone up into the gaps, nor made up the hedge of the house of Israel.* A breach is made in their fences, at which judgments are ready to pour in upon them, and then, if ever, is the time to do them service; but you have done nothing to help them." They should have made intercession for them, to turn away the wrath of God; but they were not praying prophets, had no interest in heaven nor intercourse with heaven (as prophets used to have, Gen. 20:7) and so could do them no service that way. They should have made it their business by preaching and advice to bring people to repentance and reformation, and so have *made up the hedge,* and put a stop to the judgments of God; but this was none of their care: they contrived how to pleased people, not how to profit them. They saw a deluge of profaneness and impiety breaking in upon the land, waging war with virtue and holiness, and threatening to crush them and bear them down, and then they should have come in *to the help of the Lord, to the help of the Lord against the mighty,* by witnessing against the wickedness of the time and place they lived in; but they thought that would be as dangerous a piece of service as standing in a breach to make it good against the besiegers, and therefore they declined it, did nothing to stem the tide, stood not in the battle against vice and immorality, but basely deserted the cause of religion and reformation, *in the day of the Lord,* when it was proclaimed, *Who is on the Lord's side? Who will rise up for me against the evildoers?* Ps. 94:16. Those were unworthy the name of prophets that could think so favourably of sin, and had so little zeal for God and the public welfare. 4. They flattered people into a vain hope that the judgments God had threatened would never come, whereby they hardened those in sin whom they should have endeavoured to turn from sin (*v.* 6): *They have made others to hope* that all should be well, and they should have peace, though they went on still in their trespasses, and that the event would confirm the word. They were still ready to say, "We will warrant you that these troubles will be at an end quickly, and we shall be in prosperity again." as if their warrants would confirm false prophecies, in defiance of God himself.

II. He is directed to denounce the judgments of God against them for these sins, from which their pretending to the character of prophets would not exempt them. 1. In general, here is a *woe* against them (*v.* 3), and what that woe is we are told (*v.* 8). *Behold, I am against you, saith the Lord God.* Note, Those are in a woeful condition that have God against them. Woe, and a thousand woes, to those that have made him their enemy. 2. In particular, they are sentenced to be excluded from all the privileges of the commonwealth of Israel, for they are adjudged to have forfeited them all (*v.* 9): God's *hand shall be upon them,* to seize them and bring them to his bar, to shut them out from his presence, and they will find it a *fearful thing to fall into his hands.* They pretend to be prophets, particular favourites of heaven, and authorized to preside in the congregation of his church on earth; but, by pretending to the honours they were not entitled to, they lost those that otherwise they might have enjoyed, Mt. 5:19. Their doom is, (1.) To be expelled from the communion of saints, and not to be looked upon as belonging to it: *They shall not be in the secret of my people;* their folly shall be so clearly manifested that they shall never be consulted, nor their advice asked; they shall not be present at any debates about public affairs. Or, rather, they shall not be in the assembly of God's people for religious worship, for they shall be ashamed to show their heads there, when they are proved by the events to be false prophets, and, like Cain, shall *go out from the presence of the Lord.* The people that are deceived by them shall abandon them, and resolve to have no more to do with them. Those that usurped Moses's chair shall not be allowed so much as a door-keeper's place. In the great day they shall *not stand in the congregation of the righteous* (Ps. 1:5), when God *gathers his saints together to him* (Ps. 50:5, 16), *to be for ever with him.* (2.) To be expunged out of the book of the living. They shall die in their captivity, and shall die childless, shall leave no posterity to take their denomination from them, and so their names shall not be found among those who either themselves or their posterity returned out of Babylon, of whom a particular account was kept in a public register, which was called *the writing of the house of Israel,* such as we have Ezra 2. They shall not be found among the living in Jerusalem, Isa. 4:3. Or they shall not be found written among those whom God has from eternity chosen to be vessels of his mercy to eternity. We read of those who *prophesied in Christ's name,* and yet he will tell them that he *never knew them* (Mt. 7:22, 23), because they were not among those that were *given to him.* The Chaldee paraphrase reads it, *They shall not be written in the writing of eternal life, which is written for the righteous of the house of Israel.* See Ps. 69:28. (3.) To be for ever excluded from the land of Israel. God has *sworn in his wrath* concerning them that *they shall never enter* with the returning captives into the land of Canaan, which a second time remains a rest for them. Note, Those who oppose the design of God's threatenings, and will not be awed and influenced by them, forfeit the benefit of his promises, and cannot expect to be comforted and encouraged by them.

Verses 10–16

We have here more plain dealing with the false prophets, and some further articles of their doom. We have seen the people made ashamed of the false prophets (though sometimes they had been fond of them) and casting them away, as they shall do their false gods, with indignation;

now here we find them as much ashamed of their false prophecies, which they had sometimes depended upon with much assurance. Observe,

I. How the people are deceived by the false prophets. Those flatterers seduce them, saying, *Peace, and there was no peace, v.* 10. They pretended to have *seen visions of peace, v.* 16. But that could not be, for *there was no peace, saith the Lord God.* There was no prosperity designed for them, and therefore there could be no ground for their security; yet they told them that God was at peace with them, and had mercy in reserve for them, and that the war they were engaged in with the Chaldeans should soon end in an honourable peace, and their land should enjoy a happy repose and tranquillity. They told the idolaters and other sinners that there was neither harm nor danger in the way they were in. Thus they *seduced God's people;* they put a cheat upon them, led them into mistakes, and drew them aside out of that way of repentance and reformation which the other prophets were endeavouring to bring them into. Note, Those are the most dangerous seducers who suggest to sinners that which tends to lessen their dread of sin and their fear of God. Now this is compared to the building of a slight rotten wall, or, according to our Saviour's similitude, which is to the same purport with this (Mt. 7:26), the *building of a house upon the sand,* which seems to be a shelter and protection for a while, but will fall when a storm comes. One false prophet built the wall, set up the notion that God was not at all displeased with Jerusalem, but that the city should be confirmed in its flourishing state, and be victorious over the powers that now threatened it. This notion was very pleasing, and he that started it made himself very acceptable by it and was caressed by every body, which invited others to say the same. They made the matter look yet more plausible and promising; they *daubed the wall,* which the first had built, but it was with *untempered mortar,* sorry stuff, that will not bind nor hold the bricks together; they had no ground for what they said, nor had it any consistency with itself, but was like ropes of sand. They did not strengthen the wall, were in no care to make it firm, to see that they went upon sure grounds; they only daubed it to hide the cracks and make it look well to the eye. And the wall thus built, when it comes to any stress, much more to any distress, will bulge and totter, and come down by degrees. Note, Doctrines that are groundless, though ever so grateful, that are not built upon a scripture foundation nor fastened with a scripture cement, though ever so plausible, ever so pleasing, are not of any worth, nor will stand men in any stead; and those hopes of peace and happiness which are not warranted by the word of God will but cheat men, like a wall that is well daubed indeed, but ill-built.

II. How they will be soon undeceived by the judgment of God, which, we are sure, is according to truth. 1. God will in anger bring a terrible storm that shall beat fiercely and furiously upon the wall. The descent which the Chaldean army shall make upon Judah, and the siege which they shall lay to Jerusalem, will be as *an overflowing shower,* or inundation (such as Solomon calls a *sweeping rain that leaves no food,* Prov. 28:3), will bear down all before it, as the deluge did in Noah's time: *You, O great hailstones! shall fall,* the artillery of heaven, every hailstone like a cannon-ball, battering this wall, and with these a *stormy wind,* which is sometimes so strong as to *rend the rocks* (1 Ki. 19:11), much more an ill-built wall, *v.* 11. But that which makes this *rain,* and *hail,* and *wind,* most terrible is that they arise from the wrath of God, and are enforced by that; it is that which sends them; it is that which gives them the setting on (*v.* 13); it is *a stormy wind in my fury,* and *an overflowing shower in my anger,* and *great hailstones in my fury.* The fury of Nebuchadnezzar and his princes, who highly resented Zedekiah's treachery, made the invasion very formidable, but that was nothing in comparison with God's displeasure. *The staff in their hand is my indignation,* Isa. 10:5. Note, An angry God has winds and storms at command wherewith to alarm secure sinners; and his wrath makes them frightful and forcible indeed; for *who can stand before him when he is angry?* 2. This storm shall overturn the wall: *it shall fall,* and the wind shall *rend it* (*v.* 11), the *hailstones shall consume it* (*v.* 13); I will *break it down* (*v.* 14) and *bring it to the ground,* so that the *foundation thereof shall be discovered;* it will appear how false, how rotten it was, to the prophetical reproach of the builders. When the Chaldean army has made Judah and Jerusalem desolate then this credit of the prophets, and the hopes of the people, will both sink together; the former will be found false in flattering the people and the latter foolish in suffering themselves to be imposed upon by them, and so exposed to so much the greater confusion, when the judgment shall surprise them in their security. Note, Whatever men think to shelter themselves with against the judgments of God, while they continue unreformed, will prove but a *refuge of lies* and will not profit them *in the day of wrath.* See Isa. 28:17. Men's anger cannot shake that which God has built (for *the blast of the terrible ones is but as a storm against the wall,* which makes a great noise, but never stirs the wall; see Isa. 25:4), but God's anger will overthrow that which men have built in opposition to him. They and all their attempts, they and all the securities wherein they intrench themselves, shall be *as a bowing wall and as a tottering fence* (Ps. 62:3, 10); and when their vain predictions are disproved, and their vain expectations disappointed, then it will be discovered that there was no ground for either, Hab. 3:13. The *day will declare* what every man's work is, and *the fire will try* it, 1 Co. 3:13. 3. The builders of the wall, and those that daubed it, will themselves be buried in the ruins of it: *It shall fall, and you shall* be *consumed in the midst thereof, v.* 14. And thus the threatenings of God's wrath, and all the just intentions of it, shall be accomplished to the uttermost, both upon *the wall* and upon those *that have daubed it, v.* 15. The same judgments that will prove the false prophets to be false will punish them for their falsehood; and they themselves shall be involved in the calamity which they made the people believe there was no danger of, and become monuments of that justice which they bade defiance to. Thus, if *the blind lead the blind,* both the blind leaders and the blind followers will *fall together into the ditch.* Note, Those that deceive others will in the end prove to have deceived themselves; and no doom will be more fearful than that of unfaithful ministers, that flattered sinners in their sins. 4. Both the deceivers and the deceived, when they thus perish together, will justly be ridiculed and triumphed over (*v.* 12): *When the wall has fallen shall it not be said unto you,* by those that gave credit to the true prophets, and feared the word of the Lord, "Now *where is the daubing wherewith you have daubed the wall?* What has become of all the fine soft words and fair promises wherewith you flattered your wicked neighbours, and all the assurances you gave them that the troubles of the nation should soon be at an end?" The *righteous shall laugh at them,* the righteous God shall, righteous men shall, saying, *Lo, this is the man that made not God his strength,* Ps. 52:6, 7. *I also will laugh at your calamity,* Prov. 1:26. They will say unto you (*v.* 15), *"The wall is no more, neither he that daubed it;* your hopes have vanished, and those that supported them, even *the prophets of Israel," v.* 16. Note, Those that usurp the honours that do not belong to them will shortly be filled with the shame that does.

Verses 17–23

As God has promised that when he pours out his Spirit upon his people both *their sons and their daughters shall prophesy,* so the devil, when he acts as a spirit of lies and falsehood, is so in the mouth not only of false prophets, but of false prophetesses too, and those are the deceivers whom the prophet is here directed to prophesy against; for they are not such despicable enemies to God's truths as deserve not to be taken notice of, nor yet will either the weakness of their sex excuse their sin or the tenderness and respect that are owing to it exempt them from the reproaches and threatenings of the word of God. No: *Son of man, set thy face against the daughters of thy people, v.* 17. God takes no pleasure in owning them for his people. They are *thy people,* as Ex. 32:7. The women pretend to a spirit of prophecy, and are in the same song with the men, as Ahab's prophets were: *Go on, and prosper.* They *prophesy out of their own heart* too; they say what comes uppermost and what they know nothing of. Therefore *prophesy against them* from God's own mouth. The prophet must *set his face against them,* and try if they can look him in the face and stand to what they say. Note, When sinners grow very impudent it is time for reprovers to be very bold. Now observe,

I. How the sin of these false prophetesses is described, and what are the particulars of it. 1. They told deliberate lies to those who consulted them, and came to them to be advised, and to be told their fortune: "You do mischief *by your lying to my people that hear your lies* (*v.* 19); they come to be told the truth, but you tell them lies; and, because you humour them in their sins, they are willing to hear you." Note, It is ill with those people who can better hear pleasing lies than unpleasing truths; and it is a temptation to those who lie in wait to deceive to tell lies when they find people willing to hear them and to excuse themselves with this, *Si populus vult decipi, decipiatur — If the people will be deceived, let them.* 2. They profaned the name of God by pretending to have received those lies from him (*v.* 19): *"You pollute my name among my people,* and make use of that for the patronising of your lies and the gaining of credit to them." Note, Those greatly pollute God's holy name that make use of it to give countenance to falsehood and wickedness. Yet this they did *for handfuls of barley and pieces of bread.* They did it for gain; they cared not what dishonour they did to God's name by their lying, so they could but make a hand of it for themselves. There is nothing so sacred which men of mercenary spirits, in whom the love of this world reigns, will not profane and prostitute, if they can but get money by the bargain. But they did it for poor gain; if they could get no more for it, rather than break they would sell you a false prophecy that should please you to a nicety for the beggar's dole, a *piece of bread* or *a handful of barley;* and yet that was more than it was worth. Had they asked it as an alms, for God's sake, surely they might have had it, and God would have been honoured; but, taking it as a fee for a false prophecy, God's name if polluted, and the smallness of the reward heightens the offence. *For a piece of bread that man will transgress,* Prov. 28:21. Had their poverty been their temptation to *steal, and so to take the name of the Lord in vain,* it would not have been nearly so bad as when it tempted them to *prophesy lies in his name* and so to profane it. 3. They kept people in awe, and terrified them with their pretensions: *"You hunt the souls of my people* (*v.* 18), *hunt them to make them flee* (*v.* 20), *hunt them into gardens* (so the margin reads it); you use all the arts you have to court or compel them into those places where you deliver your pretended predictions, or you have got such an influence upon them that you make them do just as you would have them to do, and tyrannise over them." It was indeed the people's fault that they did regard them, but it was their fault by lies and falsehoods to command that regard; they pretended to *save the souls alive that came to them, v.* 18. If they would but be hearers of them, and contributors to them, they might be sure of salvation; thus they beguiled unstable souls that had a concern about salvation as their end but did not rightly understand the way, and therefore hearkened to those who were most confident in promising it to them. "But will you pretend to save souls, or secure salvation to your party?" Those are justly suspected that make such pretensions. 4. They discouraged those that were honest and good, and encouraged those that were wicked and profane: *You slay the souls that should not die, and save those alive that should not live, v.* 19. This is explained (*v.* 22): *You have made the heart of the righteous sad, whom I have not made sad;* because they would not, they durst not, countenance your pretensions, you thundered out the judgments of God against them, to their great grief and trouble; you put them under invidious characters, to make them either despicable or odious to the people, and pretended to do it in God's name, which made them go many a time with a sad heart; whereas it was the will of God that they should be comforted, and by having respect put upon them should have encouragement given them. But on the other side, and which is still worse, you have *strengthened the hands of the wicked* and emboldened them to go on in their *wicked ways* and not to return from them, which was the thing the true prophets with earnestness called them to. "You have promised sinners life in their sinful ways, have told them that they shall have peace though they go on, by which their *hands have been strengthened* and their hearts hardened." Some think this refers to the severe censures they passed upon those who had already gone into captivity (who were humbled under their affliction, by *which their hearts were made sad),* and the commendations they gave to those who rebelled against the king of Babylon, who were hardened in their impieties, by which their *hands were strengthened;* or by their polluting the name of God they saddened the hearts of good people who have a value and veneration for the word of God, and confirmed atheists and infidels in their contempt of divine revelation and furnished them with arguments against it. Note, Those have a great deal to answer for who grieve the spirits, and weaken the hands, of good people, and who gratify the lusts of sinners, and animate them in their opposition to God and religion. Nor can any thing strengthen the hands of sinners more than to tell them that they may be saved in their sins without repentance, or that there may be repentance though they do not return from their wicked ways. 5. They mimicked the true prophets, by giving signs for the illustrating of their false predictions (as Hananiah did, Jer. 28:10), and they were signs agreeable to their sex; they *sewed little pillows to the people's arm-holes,* to signify that they might be easy and repose themselves, and needed not be disquieted with the apprehensions of trouble approaching. And they *made kerchiefs upon the head of every stature,* of persons of every age, young and old, distinguishable by their stature, *v.* 18. These kerchiefs were badges of liberty or triumph, intimating that they should not only be delivered from the Chaldeans, but be victorious over them. Some think these were some superstitious rites which they used with those to whom they delivered their divinations, preparing them for the reception of them by putting enchanted pillows under their arms and handkerchiefs on their heads, to raise their fancies and their expectations of something great. Or perhaps the expressions are figurative: they did all they could to make people secure, which is signified by laying them easy, and to make people proud, which is signified by dressing them fine with handkerchiefs, perhaps laid or embroidered on their heads.

II. How the wrath of God against them is expressed. Here is a woe to them (*v.* 18), and God declares himself against the methods they took to delude and deceive, *v.* 20. But what course will God take with them? 1. They shall be confounded in their attempts, and shall proceed no further; for (*v.* 23) you shall *see no more vanity nor divine revelations;* not that they shall themselves lay down their pretensions in a way of repentance, but when the event gives them the lie they shall be silent for shame; or their fancies and imaginations shall not be disposed to receive impressions which assist them in their divinations as they have been; or they themselves shall be cut off. 2. God's people shall be delivered out of their hands. When they see themselves deluded by them into a false peace and a fool's paradise, and that though they would not leave their sin their sin has left them, and they *see no more vanity nor divine divinations,* they shall turn their back upon them, shall slight their predictions. The righteous shall be no more saddened by them, no, nor the wicked strengthened: The *pillows shall be torn from their arms,* and the *kerchiefs from their heads;* the fallacies shall be discovered, their frauds detected, and the people of God shall no more be in their hand, to be hunted as they had been. Note, It is a great mercy to be delivered from a servile regard to, and fear of, those who, under colour of a divine authority, impose upon and tyrannise over the consciences of men, and say to their souls, *Bow down, that we may go over.* But it is a sore grief to those who delight in such usurpations to have their power broken and the prey delivered; such was the reformation to the church of Rome. And, when God does this, he makes it to appear that he is the Lord, that it is his prerogative to give law to souls.

CHAPTER 14

Hearing the word, and prayer, are two great ordinances of God, in which we are to give honour to him and may hope to find favour and acceptance with him; and yet in this chapter, to our great surprise, we find some waiting upon God in the one and some in the other and yet not meeting with success as they expected. I. The elders of Israel come to hear the word, and enquire of the prophet, but, because they are not duly qualified, they meet with a rebuke instead of acceptance (*v.* 1–5) and are called upon to repent of their sins and reform their lives, else it is at their peril to enquire of God (*v.* 6–11). II. Noah, Daniel, and Job, are supposed to pray for this people, and yet, because the decree has gone forth, and the destruction of them is determined by a variety of judgments, their prayers shall not be answered (*v.* 12–21). And yet it is promised, in the close, that a remnant shall escape (*v.* 22, 23).

Verses 1–11

Here is, I. The address which some of the elders of Israel made to the prophet, as an oracle, to enquire of the Lord by him. They *came, and sat before him, v.* 1. It is probable that they were not of those who were now his fellow-captives, and constantly attended his ministry (such as those we read of *ch.* 8:1), but some occasional hearers, some of the grandees of Jerusalem who had come upon business to Babylon, perhaps public business, on an embassy from the king, and in their way called on the prophet, having heard much of him and being desirous to know if he had any message from God, which might be some guide to them in their negotiation. By the severe answer given them one would suspect they had a design to ensnare the prophet, or to try if they could catch hold of any thing that might look like a contradiction to Jeremiah's prophecies, and so they might have occasion to reproach them both. However, they feigned themselves just men, complimented the prophet, and sat before him gravely enough, as God's people used to sit. Note, It is no new thing for bad men to be found employed in the external performances of religion.

II. The account which God gave the prophet privately concerning them. They were strangers to him; he only knew that they were *elders of Israel;* that was the character they wore, and as such he received them with respect, and, it is likely, was glad to see them so well disposed. But God gives him their real character (*v.* 3); they were idolaters, and did only consult Ezekiel as they would any oracle of a pretended deity, to gratify their curiosity, and therefore he appeals to the prophet himself whether they deserved to have any countenance or encouragement given them: "*Should I be enquired of at all by them?* Should I accept their enquiries as an honour to myself, or answer them for satisfaction to them? No; they have no reason to expect it;" for, 1. They *have set up their idols in their heart;* they not only have idols, but they are in love with them, they dote upon them, are wedded to them, and have laid them so near their hearts, and have given them so great a room in their affections, that there is no parting with them. The idols they have set up in their houses, though they are now at a distance from *the chambers of their imagery,* yet they have them in their hearts, and they are ever and anon worshipping them in their fancies and imaginations. *They have made their idols to ascend upon their hearts* (so the word is); they have subjected their hearts to their idols, they are upon the throne there. Or when they came to enquire of the prophet they pretended to put away their idols, but it was in pretence only; they still had a secret reserve for them. They kept them *up in their hearts;* and, if they left them for a while, it was *cum animo revertendi — with an intention to return to them,* not a final farewell. Or it may be understood of spiritual idolatry; those whose affections are placed upon the wealth of the world and the pleasures of sense, whose god is their money, *whose god is their belly,* they *set up their idols in their heart.* Many who have no idols in their sanctuary have idols in their hearts, which is no less a usurpation of God's throne and a profanation of his name. *Little children, keep yourselves from* those *idols.* 2. They *put the stumbling-block of their iniquity before their face.* Their *silver and gold* were called *the stumbling-block of their iniquity* (*ch.* 7:19), their *idols of silver and gold,* by the beauty of which they were allured to idolatry, and so it was the block at which they stumbled, and fell into that sin; or *their iniquity* is their *stumbling-block,* which throws them down, so that they fall into ruin. Note, Sinners are their own tempters *(every man is tempted when he is drawn aside of his own lust),* and so they are their own destroyers. *If thou scornest, thou alone shalt bear it;* and thus *they put the stumbling-block of their iniquity before their* own *faces,* and stumble upon it though they see it before their eyes. It intimates that they are resolved to go on in sin, whatever comes of it. *I have loved strangers, and after them I will go;* that is the language of their hearts. And *should* God *be enquired of* by such wretches? Do they not hereby rather put an affront upon him than do him any honour, as those did who *bowed the knee* to Christ in mockery? Can those expect an answer of peace from God who thus continue their acts of hostility against him? "Ezekiel, what thinkest thou of it?"

III. The answer which God, in just displeasure, orders Ezekiel to give them, *v.* 4. Let them know that it is not out of any disrespect to their persons that God refuses to give them an answer, but it is laid down as a rule for *every man of the house of Israel,* whoever he be, that if he continue in love and league with his idols, and come to enquire of God, God will resent it as an indignity done to him, and will answer him according to his real iniquity, not according to his pretended piety. He *comes to the prophet,* who, he expects, will be civil to him, but God will give him his answer, by punishing him for his impudence: *I the Lord,* who *speak and it is done, I will answer him that cometh, according to the multitude of his idols.* Observe, Those who *set up idols in their hearts,* and set their hearts upon their idols, commonly have a multitude of them. Humble worshippers God answers *according to the multitude of his mercies,* but bold intruders he answers *according to the multitude of their idols,* that is, 1. According to the desire of their idols; he will give them up *to their own hearts' lust,* and leave them to themselves to be as bad as they have a mind to be, till they *have filled up the measure of their iniquity.* Men's corruptions are *idols in their hearts,* and they are of their own setting up; their temptations are *the stumbling-block of their iniquity,* and they are of their own putting, and God will answer them accordingly; let them take their course. 2. According to the desert of their idols; they shall have such an answer as it is just that such idolaters should have. God will punish them as he usually punishes idolaters, that is, when they stand in need of his help he will *send them to the gods whom they have chosen,* Jdg. 10:13, 14. Note, The judgment of God will dwell with men according to what they are really (that is, according to what their hearts are), not according to what they are in show and profession. And what will be the end of this? What will this threatened answer amount to? He tells them (*v.* 5): *That I may take the house of Israel in their own heart,* may lay them open to the world, that they may be ashamed; nay, lay them open to the curse, that they may be ruined. Note, The sin and shame, and pain and ruin, of sinners, are all from themselves, and their own hearts are the snares in which they are taken; they seduce them, they betray them; their own consciences witness against them, condemn them, and are a terror to them. If God take them, if he discover them, if he convict them, if he bind them over to his judgment, it is all by *their own hearts. O Israel! thou hast destroyed thyself. The house of Israel* is ruined by its own hands, *because they are all estranged from me through their idols.* Note, (1.) The ruin of sinners is owing to their estrangement from God. (2.) It is through some idol or other that the hearts of men are estranged from God; some creature has gained that place and dominion in the heart that God should have.

IV. The extent of this answer which God had given them — to all *the house of Israel, v.* 7, 8. The same thing is repeated, which intimates God's just displeasure against hypocrites, who mock him with the shows and forms of devotion, while their hearts are estranged from him and at war with him. Observe, 1. To whom this declaration belongs. It concerns not only every one of the house of Israel (as before, *v.* 4), but *the stranger that sojourns in Israel;* let him not think it will be an excuse for him in his idolatries that he is but a stranger and a sojourner in Israel, and does but worship the gods that his father served and that he himself was bred up in the service of; no, let him not expect any benefit from Israel's oracles or prophets unless he thoroughly renounce his idolatry. Note, Even proselytes shall not be countenanced if they be not sincere: a dissembled conversion is no conversion. 2. The description here given of hypocrites: They *separate themselves from* God by their fellowship with idols; they cut themselves off from their relation to God and their interest in him; they break off their acquaintance and intercourse with him, and set themselves at a distance from him. Note, Those that join themselves to idols separate themselves from God; nor shall any be for ever separated from the vision and fruition of God, but such as now separate themselves from his service and wilfully withdraw their allegiance from him. But there are those who thus separate themselves from God, and yet come to the prophets with a seeming respect and deference to their office, *to enquire of them concerning* God, in order to satisfy a vain curiosity, to stop the mouth of a clamorous conscience, or to get or save a reputation among men, but without any desire to be acquainted with God or any design to be ruled by him. 3. The doom of those who thus trifle with God and think to impose upon him: *"I the Lord will answer him by myself;* let me alone to deal with him; I will give him an answer that shall fill him with confusion, that shall make him repent of his daring impiety." He shall have his answer, not by the words of the prophet, but by the judgments of God. *And I will set my face against that man,* which denotes great displeasure against him and a fixed resolution to ruin him. God can outface the most impenitent sinner. The hypocrite thought to save his credit, nay, and to gain applause, but, on the contrary, God *will make him a sign and a proverb,* will inflict such judgments upon him as shall make him remarkable and contemptible in the eyes of all about him; his misery shall be made use of to express the greatest misery, as when the worst of sinners are said to have *their portion appointed them with hypocrites,* Mt. 24:51. God will make him an example; his judgments upon him shall be for warning to others to take heed of mocking God: for *thus shall it be done to the man that separates himself from* God, and yet pretends to *enquire concerning him.* The hypocrite thought to pass for one of God's people, and to crowd into heaven among them; but God *will cut him off from the midst of his people,* will discover him, and pluck him out from the thickest of them; and by this, says God, *you shall know that I am the Lord.* By the discovery of hypocrites it appears that God is omniscient: ministers know not how people stand affected when they come to hear the word, by God does. And by the punishment of hypocrites it appears that he is a jealous God, and one that cannot and will not be imposed upon.

V. The doom of those pretenders to prophecy who give countenance to these pretenders to piety, *v.* 9, 10. These hypocritical enquirers, though Ezekiel will not give them a comfortable answer, yet hope to meet with some other prophets that will; and if they do, as perhaps they may, let them know that God permits those lying prophets to deceive them in part of punishment: *"If the prophet that flatters them be deceived,* and gives them hopes which there is no ground for, *I the Lord have deceived that prophet,* have suffered the temptation to be laid before him, and suffered him to yield to it, and overruled it for the hardening of those in their wicked courses who were resolved to go on in them." We are sure that God is not the author of sin, but we are sure that he is the Lord of all and the Judge of sinners, and that he often makes use of one wicked man to destroy another, and so of one wicked man to deceive another. Both are sins in him who does them, and so they are *not* from God; both are punishments to him to whom they are done, and so they *are* from God. We have a full instance of this in the story of Ahab's prophets, who were deceived by a lying spirit, which God put into their mouths (1 Ki. 22:23), and another in those whom God *gives up to strong delusions, to believe a lie, because they received not the love of the truth,* 2 Th. 2:10, 11. But read the fearful doom of the lying prophet: *I will stretch out my hand upon him and will destroy him.* When God has served his own righteous purposes by him he shall be reckoned with for his unrighteous purposes. As, when God had made use of the Chaldeans for the wasting of a sinful people, he justly punished them for their rage, so when he had made use of *false prophets,* and afterwards of *false Christs,* for the deceiving of a sinful people, he justly punished them for their falsehood. But herein we must acknowledge (as Calvin upon this place reminds us) that God's *judgments are a great deep,* that we are incompetent judges of them, and that, though we cannot account for the equity of God's proceedings to the satisfying and silencing of every caviller, yet there is a day coming when he will be justified before all the world, and particularly in this instance, when *the punishment of the prophet that flattereth the hypocrite in his evil way shall be as the punishment of the hypocrite that seeketh to him and bespeaks smooth things* only, Isa. 30:10. The ditch shall be the same to the blind leader and the blind followers.

VI. The good counsel that is given them for the preventing of this fearful doom (*v.* 6): *"Therefore repent, and turn yourselves from your idols.* Let this separate between you and them, that they separate between you and God; because they set God's face against you, do you *turn away*

your faces from them," which denotes, not only forsaking them, but forsaking them with loathing and detestation: "Turn from them as from abominations that you are sick of; and then you will be welcome to enquire of the Lord. *Come now, and let us reason together."*

VII. The good issue of all this as to the house of Israel; *therefore* the pretending prophets, and the pretending saints, shall perish together by the judgments of God, that, some being made examples, the body of the people may be reformed, *that the house of Israel may go no more astray from me, v.* 11. Note, The punishments of some are designed for the prevention of sin, that others may hear, and fear, and take warning. When we see what becomes of those that go astray from God we should thereby be engaged to keep close to him. And, if *the house of Israel go not astray, they will not be polluted any more.* Note, Sin is a polluting thing; it renders the sinner odious in the eyes of the pure and holy God, and in his own eyes too whenever conscience is awakened; and therefore they shall *no more be polluted, that they may be my people and I may be their God.* Note, Those whom God takes into covenant with himself must first be cleansed from the pollutions of sin; and those who are so cleansed shall not only be saved from ruin, but be entitled to all the privileges of God's people.

Verses 12–23

The scope of these verses is to show,

I. That national sins bring national judgments. When virtue is ruined and laid waste every thing else will soon be ruined and laid waste too (*v.* 13): *When the land sins against me,* when vice and wickedness become epidemical, *when the land sins by trespassing grievously,* when the sinners have become very numerous and their sins very heinous, when gross impieties and immoralities universally prevail, *then will I stretch forth my hand upon it,* for the punishment of it. The divine power shall be vigorously and openly exerted; the judgments shall be extended and stretched forth to all the corners of the land, to all the concerns and interests of the nation. Grievous sins bring grievous plagues.

II. That God has a variety of sore judgments wherewith to punish sinful nations, and he has them all at command and inflicts which he pleases. He did indeed give David his choice what judgment he would be punished with for his sin in numbering the people; for any of them would serve to answer the end, which was to lessen the numbers he was proud of; but David, in effect, referred it to God again: *"Let us fall into the hands of the Lord;* let him choose with what rod we shall be beaten." But he uses a variety of judgments that it may appear he has a universal dominion, and that in all our concerns we may see our dependence on him. *Four sore judgments* are here specified: — 1. *Famine, v.* 13. The denying and withholding of common mercies is itself judgment enough, there needs no more to make a people miserable. God needs not bring the staff of oppression, it is but *breaking the staff of bread* and the work is soon done; he *cuts off man and beast* by cutting off the provisions which nature makes for both in the annual products of the earth. God *breaks the staff of bread* when, though we have bread, yet we are not nourished and strengthened by it. Hag. 1:6, *You eat, but you have not enough.* 2. Hurtful *beasts, noisome* and noxious, either as poisonous or as ravenous. God can make these *to pass through the land* (*v.* 15), to increase in all parts of it, and to bereave it, not only of the tame cattle, preying upon their flocks and herds, but of their people, devouring men, women, and children, so *that no man may pass through because of the beasts;* none dare travel even in the high roads for fear of being pulled in pieces by lions, or other beasts of prey, as the children of Beth-el by two bears. Note, When men revolt from their allegiance to God, and rebel against him, it is just with God that the inferior creatures should rise up in arms against men, Lev. 26:22. 3. War. God often chastises sinful nations by bringing a sword upon them, the sword of a foreign enemy, and he gives it its commission and orders what execution it shall do (*v.* 17): he says, *Sword, go through the land.* It is bad enough if the sword do but enter into the borders of a land, but much worse when it goes through the bowels of a land. By it God *cuts off man and beast,* horse and foot. What execution the sword does God does by it; for it is his sword,

and it acts as he directs. 4. *Pestilence* (*v.* 19), a dreadful disease, which has sometimes depopulated cities; by it God *pours out his fury in blood* (that is, in death); the pestilence kills as effectually as if the blood were shed by the sword, for it is poisoned by the disease, *the sickness* we call it. See how miserable the case of mankind is that lies thus exposed to deaths in various shapes. See how dangerous the case of sinners is against whom God has so many ways of fighting, so that, though they escape one judgment, God has another waiting for them.

III. That when God's professing people revolt from him, and rebel against him, they may justly expect a complication of judgments to fall upon them. God has various ways of contending with a sinful nation; but if Jerusalem, the holy city, *become a harlot,* God will send upon her all his *four sore judgments* (*v.* 21); for the nearer any are to God in name and profession the more severely will he reckon with them if they reproach that worthy name by which they are called and give the lie to that profession. They shall be punished *seven times more.*

IV. That there may be, and, commonly are, some few very good men, even in those places that by sin are ripened for ruin. It is no foreign supposition that, even in a land that has *trespassed grievously,* there may be *three* such *men* as *Noah, Daniel, and Job.* Daniel was now living, and at this time had scarcely arrived at the prime of his eminency, but he was already famous (at least this word of God concerning him would without fail make him so); yet he was carried away into captivity with the first of all, Dan. 1:6. Some of the better sort of people in Jerusalem might perhaps think that, if Daniel (of whose fame in the king of Babylon's court they had heard much) had but continued in Jerusalem, it would have been spared for his sake, as the magicians in Babylon were. "No," says God, "though you had him, who was as eminently good in bad times and places as Noah in the old world and Job in the land of Uz, yet a reprieve should not be obtained." In the places that are most corrupt, and in the ages that are most degenerate, *there is a remnant* which God reserves to himself, and which *still hold fast their integrity* and stand fair for the honour of *delivering the land,* as *the innocent* are said to do, Job 22:30.

V. That God often spares very wicked places for the sake of a few godly people in them. This is implied here as the expectation of Jerusalem's friends in the day of its distress: "Surely God will stay his controversy with us; for are there not some among us that are emptying the measure of national guilt by their prayers, as others are filling it by their sins? And, rather than God will *destroy the righteous with the wicked,* he will preserve *the wicked with the righteous.* If Sodom might have been spared for the sake of ten good men, surely Jerusalem may."

VI. That such men as Noah, Daniel, and Job, will prevail, if any can, to turn away the wrath of God from a sinful people. Noah was a perfect man, and kept his integrity when all flesh had corrupted their way; and, for his sake, his family, though one of them was wicked (Ham), was saved in the ark. Job was a great example of piety, and mighty in prayer for his children, for his friends; and God turned his captivity when he prayed. Those were very ancient examples, before Moses, that great intercessor; and therefore God mentions them, to intimate that he had some very peculiar favourites long before the Jewish nation was formed or founded, and would have such when it was ruined, for which reason, it should seem, those names were made use of, rather than Moses, Aaron, or Samuel; and yet, lest any should think that God was partial in his respects to the ancient days, here is a modern instance, a living one, placed between those two that were the glories of antiquity, and he now a captive, and that is Daniel, to teach us not to lessen the useful good men of our own day by over-magnifying the ancients. Let the children of the captivity know that Daniel, their neighbour, and *companion in tribulation,* being a man of great humility, piety, and zeal for God, and instant and constant in prayer, had as good an interest in heaven as Noah or Job had. Why may not God raise up as great and good men now as he did formerly, and do as much for them?

VII. That when the sin of a people has come to its height, and the decree has gone forth for their ruin, the piety and prayers of the best men shall not prevail to finish the controversy. This is here asserted again and again, that, *though these three men were in* Jerusalem at this time, yet they should *deliver neither son nor daughter;* not so much as the little ones should be spared for their sakes, as the little ones of Israel were upon the prayer of Moses, Num. 14:31. No; *the land shall be desolate,* and God would not hear their prayers for it, though *Moses and Samuel stood before him,* Jer. 15:1. Note, Abused patience will turn at last into inexorable wrath; and it should seem as if God would be more inexorable in Jerusalem's case than in another (*v.* 6), because, besides the divine patience, they had enjoyed greater privileges than any other people, which were the aggravations of their sin.

VIII. That, though pious praying men may not prevail to deliver others, yet *they shall deliver their own souls by their righteousness,* so that, though they may suffer in the common calamity, yet to them the property of it is altered; it is not to them what it is to the wicked; it is unstrung, and does them no hurt; it is sanctified, and does them good. Sometimes *their souls* (their lives) are remarkably *delivered,* and *given them for a prey;* at least *their souls* (their spiritual interests) are secured. If their bodies be not *delivered,* yet *their souls* are. *Riches* indeed *profit not in the day of wrath,* but *righteousness delivers from death,* from so great a death, so many deaths as are here threatened. This should encourage us to keep our integrity in times of common apostasy, that, if we do so, we shall be *hidden in the day of the Lord's anger.*

IX. That, even when God makes the greatest desolations by his judgments, he reserves some to be the monuments of his mercy, *v.* 22, 23. In Jerusalem itself, though marked for utter ruin, yet *there shall be left a remnant,* who shall not be cut off by any of those *sore judgments* before mentioned, but shall be carried into captivity, both *sons and daughters,* who shall be the seed of a new generation. The young ones, who had not grown up to such an obstinacy in sin as their fathers had who were therefore cut off as incurable, these *shall be brought forth* out of the ruins of Jerusalem by the victorious enemy, and *behold they shall come forth to you* that are in captivity, they shall make a virtue of a necessity, and shall come the more willingly to Babylon because so many of their friends have gone thither before them and are there ready to receive them; and, when they come, *you shall see their ways and their doing;* you shall hear them make a free and ingenuous confession of the sins they had formerly been guilty of, and a humble profession of repentance for them, with promises of reformation; and you shall see instances of their reformation, shall see what good their affliction has done them, and how prudently and patiently they conduct themselves under it. Their narrow escape shall have a good effect upon them; it shall change their temper and conversation, and make them new men. And this will redound, 1. To the satisfaction of their brethren: *They shall comfort you when you see their ways.* Note, It is a very comfortable sight to see people, when they are under the rod, repenting and humbling themselves, justifying God and accepting the punishment of their iniquity. When we sorrow (as we ought to do) for the afflictions of others, it is a great comfort to us in our sorrow to see them improving their afflictions and making a good use of them. When those captives told their friends how bad they had been, and how righteous God was in bringing these judgments upon them, it made them very easy, and helped to reconcile them to the calamities of Jerusalem, to the justice of God in punishing his own people so, and to the goodness of God, which now appeared to have had kind intentions in all; and thus *"You shall be comforted concerning all the evil that I have brought upon Jerusalem,* and, when you better understand the thing, shall not have such direful apprehensions concerning it as you have had." Note, It is a debt we owe to our brethren, if we have got good by our afflictions, to comfort them by letting them know it. 2. It will redound to the honour of God: *"You shall know that I have not done without cause,* not without a just provocation, and yet not without a gracious design, *all that I have done in it."* Note, When afflictions have done their work, and have accomplished that for which they were sent, then will appear the wisdom and goodness of God in sending them, and God will be not only justified, but glorified in them.

CHAPTER 15

Ezekiel has again and again, in God's name, foretold the utter ruin of Jerusalem; but, it should seem, he finds it hard to reconcile himself to it, and to acquiesce in the will of God in this severe dispensation; and therefore God takes various methods to satisfy him not only that it shall be so, but that there is no remedy: it must be so; it is fit that it should be so. Here, in this short chapter, he shows him (probably with design that he should tell the people) that it was as requisite Jerusalem should be destroyed as that the dead and withered branches of a vine should be cut off and thrown into the fire. I. The similitude is very elegant (*v.* 1–5), but, II. The explanation of the similitude is very dreadful (*v.* 6–8).

Verses 1–8

The prophet, we may suppose, was thinking what a glorious city Jerusalem was, above any city in the world; it was the crown and *joy of the whole earth;* and therefore what a pity it was that it should be destroyed; it was a noble structure, the city of God, and the city of Israel's solemnities. But, if these were the thoughts of his heart, God here returns an answer to them by comparing Jerusalem to a vine. 1. It is true, if a vine be fruitful, it is a most valuable tree, none more so; it was one of those that were courted to have dominion over the trees, and the fruit of it is such as *cheers God and man* (Jdg. 9:12, 13); it *makes glad the heart,* Ps. 104:15. So Jerusalem was *planted a choice and noble vine, wholly a right seed* (Jer. 2:21); and, if it had brought forth fruit suitable to its character as a holy city, it would have been the glory both of God and Israel. It was a vine which *God's right hand had planted,* a *branch out of a dry ground,* which, though its original was mean and despicable, God had *made strong for himself* (Ps. 80:15), to be *to him for a name and for a praise.* 2. But, if it be not fruitful, it is good for nothing, it is as worthless and useless a production of the earth as even thorns and briers are: *What is the vine-tree,* if you take the tree by itself, without consideration of the fruit? *What is it more than any tree,* that it should have so much care taken of it and so much cost laid out upon it? What is a branch of the vine, though it spread *more than a branch which is among the trees of the forest,* where it grows neglected and exposed? Or, as some read it, *What is the vine more than any tree if the branch of it be as the trees of the forest;* that is, if it bear no fruit, as forest-trees seldom do, being designed for timber-trees, not fruit-trees? Now there are some fruit-trees which, if they do not bear, are nevertheless of good use, as the wood of them may be made to turn to a good account; but the vine is not of this sort: if that do not answer its end as a fruit-tree, it is worth nothing as a timber-tree. Observe,

I. How this similitude is expressed here. The wild vine, that *is among the trees of the forest,* or the empty vine (which Israel is compared to, Hos. 10:1), that bears no more fruit than a forest-tree, is good for nothing; it is as useless as a brier, and more so, for that will add some sharpness to the thorny hedge, which the vine-branch will not do. He shows, 1. That it is fit for no use. The *wood* of it is not *taken to do any work;* one cannot so much as make *a pin of it to hand a vessel upon, v.* 3. See how variously the gifts of nature are dispensed for the service of man. Among the plants, the roots of some, the seeds or fruits of others, the leaves of others, and of some the stalks, are most serviceable to us; so, among trees, some are strong and not fruitful, as the oaks and cedars; others are weak but very fruitful, as the vine, which is unsightly, low, and depending, yet of great use. Rachel is comely but barren, Leah homely but fruitful. 2. That therefore it is made use of *for fuel;* it will serve to heat the oven with. Because *it is* not *meet for any work, it is cast into the fire, v.* 4. When it is good for nothing else it is useful this way, and answers a very needful intention, *for fuel* is a thing we must have, and to burn any thing for fuel which is good for other work is bad husbandry. *To what purpose is this waste?* The unfruitful vine is disposed of in the same way with the briers and thorns, which are rejected, and *whose end is to be burnt,* Heb. 6:8. And what care is taken of it then? If a piece of solid timber be kindled, somebody perhaps may snatch it *as a brand out of the burning,* and say, "It is a pity to burn it, for it may be put to some better use;" but if the branch of a vine be on fire, and, as usual, both the ends of it and the middle be kindled together, nobody goes about to save it. *When it was whole it was meet for no work, much less when the fire has devoured it* (*v.* 5); even the ashes of it are not worth saving.

II. How this similitude is applied to Jerusalem. 1. That holy city had become unprofitable and good for nothing. It had been as *the vine-tree among the trees of the* vineyard, abounding in the fruits of righteousness to the glory of God. When religion flourished there, and the pure worship of God was kept up, many a joyful vintage was then gathered in from it; and, while it continued so, God made a hedge about it; it was his *pleasant plant* (Isa. 5:7); he *watered it every moment* and *kept it night and day* (Isa. 27:3); but it had now become *the degenerate plant of a strange vine,* of a wild vine (such as we read of 2 Ki. 4:39), *a vine-tree among the trees of the wild grapes* (Isa. 5:4), which are not only of no use, but are nauseous and noxious (Deu. 32:32), *their grapes are grapes of gall, and their clusters are bitter.* It is explained (*v.* 8): *"They have trespassed a trespass,* that is, they have treacherously prevaricated with God and perfidiously apostatized from him;" for so the word signifies. Note, Professors of religion, if they do not live up to their profession, but contradict it, if they degenerate and depart from it, are the most unprofitable creatures in the world, like the *salt* that has *lost its savour* and is thenceforth *good for nothing,* Mk. 9:50. Other nations were famed for valour or politics, some for war, others for trade, and retained their credit; but the Jewish nation, being famous as a holy people, when they lost their holiness, and became wicked, were thenceforth *good for nothing;* with that they lost all their credit and usefulness, and became the most base and despicable people under the sun, *trodden under foot of the Gentiles.* Daniel, and other pious Jews, were of great use in their generation; but the idolatrous Jews then, and the unbelieving Jews now since the preaching of the gospel, have been, and are, of no common service, not fit *for any work.* 2. Being so, it is *given to the fire for fuel, v.* 6. Note, Those who are not fruitful to the glory of God's grace will be fuel to the fire of his wrath; and thus, if they give not honour to him, he will *get himself honour upon them,* honour that will shine brightly in that flaming fire by which impenitent sinners will be for ever consumed. He will not be a loser at last by any of his creatures. *The Lord has made all things for himself,* yea, *even the wicked,* that would not otherwise be for him, *for the day of evil* (Prov. 16:4); and in those who would not glorify him as *the God to whom* duty *belongs* he will be glorified as *the God to whom vengeance belongs.* The fire of God's wrath had before *devoured both the ends of* the Jewish nation (*v.* 4), Samaria and the cities of Judah; and now Jerusalem, that was *the midst of it,* was thrown *into the fire,* to be *burnt* too, for *it is meet for no work;* it will not be wrought upon, by any of the methods God has taken, to be serviceable to him. *The inhabitants of Jerusalem* were like a vine-branch, rotten and awkward; and therefore (*v.* 7), *"I will set my face against them,* to thwart all their counsels," as they set their faces against God, to contradict his word and defeat all his designs. It is decreed; the consumption is determined: *I will make the land* quite *desolate,* and therefore, when they *go out from one fire, another fire shall devour them* (*v.* 7); the end of one judgment shall be the beginning of another, and their escape from one only a reprieve till another comes; they shall go from misery in their own country to misery in Babylon. Those who kept out of the way of the sword perished by famine or pestilence. When one descent of the Chaldean forces upon them was over, and they thought, *Surely the bitterness of death is past,* yet soon after they returned again with double violence, till they had made a full end. Thus *they shall know that I am the Lord,* a God of almighty power, *when I set my face against them.* Note, God shows himself to be *the Lord,* by perfecting the destruction of his implacable enemies as well as the deliverances of his obedient people. Those whom God *sets his face,* though they may come out of one trouble little hurt, will fall into another; though they *come out of the pit,* they will be *taken in the snare* (Isa. 24:18); though they escape *the sword of Hazael,* they will fall by that of Jehu (1 Ki. 19:17); for *evil pursues sinners.* Nay, though *they go out from the fire* of temporal judgments, and seem to die in peace, yet there is an everlasting fire that will *devour them;* for, *when God judges,* first or last *he will overcome,* and he will be *known by the judgments which he executes.* See Mt. 3:10; Jn. 15:6.

CHAPTER 16

Still God is justifying himself in the desolations he is about to bring upon Jerusalem; and very largely, in this chapter, he shows the prophet, and orders him to show the people, that he did but punish them as their sins deserved. In the foregoing chapter he had compared Jerusalem to an unfruitful vine, that was fit for nothing but the fire; in this chapter he compares it to an adulteress, that, in justice, ought to be abandoned and exposed, and he must therefore show the people their abominations, that they might see how little reason they had to complain of the judgments they were under. In this long discourse are set forth, I. The despicable and deplorable beginnings of that church and nation (*v.* 3–5). II. The many honours and favours God had bestowed upon them (*v.* 6–14). III. Their treacherous and ungrateful departures from him to the services and worship of idols, here represented by the most impudent whoredom (*v.* 15–34). IV. A threatening of terrible destroying judgments, which God would bring upon them for this sin (*v.* 35–43). V. An aggravation both of their sin and of their punishment, by comparison with Sodom and Samaria (*v.* 44–59). VI. A promise of mercy in the close, which God would show to a penitent remnant (*v.* 60–63). And this is designed for admonition to us.

Verses 1–5

Ezekiel is now among the captives in Babylon; but, as Jeremiah at Jerusalem wrote for the use of the captives though they had Ezekiel upon the spot with them (*ch.* 29), so Ezekiel wrote for the use of Jerusalem, though Jeremiah himself was resident there; and yet they were far from looking upon it as an affront to one another's help both by preaching and writing. Jeremiah wrote to the captives for their consolation, which was the thing they needed; Ezekiel here is directed to write to the inhabitants of Jerusalem for their conviction and humiliation, which was the thing they needed.

I. This is his commission (*v.* 2): *"Cause Jerusalem to know her abominations* (that is, her sins); set them in order before her." Note, 1. Sins are not only *provocations* which God is angry at, but *abominations* which he hates, as contrary to his nature, and which we ought to hate, Jer. 44:4. 2. The sins of Jerusalem are in a special manner so. The practice of profaneness appears most odious in those that make a profession of religion. 3. Though Jerusalem is a place of great knowledge, yet she is loth *to know her abominations;* so partial are men in their own favour that they are hardly made to see and own their own badness, but deny it, palliate or extenuate it. 4. It is requisite that we should know our sins, that we may confess them, and may justify God in what he brings upon us for them. 5. It is the work of ministers to cause sinners, sinners in Jerusalem, *to know their abominations,* to set before them the glass of the law, that in it they may see their own deformities and defilements, to tell them plainly of their faults. *Thou art the man.*

II. That Jerusalem may be made *to know her abominations,* and particularly the abominable ingratitude she had been guilty of, it was requisite that she should be put in mind of the great things God had done for her, as the aggravations of her bad conduct towards him; and, to magnify those favours, she is in these verses made to know the meanness and baseness of her original, from what poor beginnings God raised her, and how unworthy she was of his favour and of the honour he had put upon her. Jerusalem is here put for the Jewish church and nation, which is here compared to an outcast child, base-born and abandoned, which the mother herself has no affection nor concern for. 1. The extraction of the Jewish nation was mean: *"Thy birth is of the land of Canaan* (*v.* 3); thou hadst from the very first the spirit and disposition of a Canaanite." The patriarchs dwelt in Canaan, and they were there but *strangers and sojourners,* had no possession, no power, not one foot of ground of their own but a burying-place. Abraham and Sarah were indeed their *father and mother,* but they were only inmates with the Amorites and Hittites, who, having the dominion, seemed to be as parents to the seed of Abraham, witness the court Abraham made to the *children of Seth* (Gen. 23:4, 8), the dependence they had upon their neighbours the Canaanites, and the fear they were in of them, Gen. 13:7; 34:30. If the patriarchs, at their first coming to Canaan, had conquered it, and made themselves masters of it, this would have put an honour upon their family and would have looked great in history; but, instead of that, they *went from one nation to another* (Ps. 105:13), as tenants from one farm to another, almost as beggars from one door to another, when they *were but few in number,* yea, very few. And yet this was not the worst; their fathers had *served other gods in Ur of the Chaldees* (Jos. 24:2); even in Jacob's family there were *strange gods,* Gen. 35:2. Thus early had they a genius leading them to idolatry; and upon this account their ancestors were Amorites and Hittites. 2. When they first began to multiply their condition was really very deplorable, like that of a new-born child, which must of necessity die from the womb if the knees prevent it not, Job 3:11, 12. The children of Israel, when they began to increase into a people and became considerable, were thrown out from the country that was intended for them; a famine drove them thence. Egypt was *the open field* into which they were cast; there they had no protection or countenance from the government they were under, but, on the contrary, were ruled with rigour, and their lives embittered; they had no encouragement given them to build up their families, no help to build up their estates, no friends or allies to strengthen their interests. Joseph, who had been the *shepherd and stone of Israel,* was dead; the king of Egypt, who should have been kind to them for Joseph's sake, set himself to *destroy this man-child as soon as it was born* (Rev. 12:4), ordered all the males to be slain, which, it is likely, occasioned the exposing of many as well as Moses, to which perhaps the similitude here has reference. The founders of nations and cities had occasion for all the arts and arms they were masters of, set their heads on work, by policies and stratagems, to preserve and nurse up their infant states. *Tantae molis erat Romanam condere gentem — So vast were the efforts requisite to the establishment of the Roman name.* Virgil. But the nation of Israel had no such care taken of it, no such pains taken with it, as Athens, Sparta, Rome, and other commonwealths had when they were first founded, but, on the contrary, was doomed to destruction, like an infant new-born, exposed to wind and weather, *the navel-string not cut,* the poor babe *not washed,* not clothed, *no swaddled,* because not *pitied, v.* 4, 5. Note, We owe the preservation of our infant lives to the natural pity and compassion which the God of nature has put into the hearts of parents and nurses towards new-born children. This infant is said to be *cast out, to the loathing of her person;* it was a sign that she was loathed by those that bore her, and she appeared loathsome to all that looked upon her. *The Israelites were an abomination to the Egyptians,* as we find Gen. 43:32; 46:34. Some think that this refers to the corrupt and vicious disposition of that people from their beginning: they were not only the weakest and *fewest of all people* (Deu. 7:7), but the worst and most ill-humoured of all people. *God giveth thee this good land, not for thy righteousness, for thou art a stiff-necked people,* Deu. 9:6. And Moses tells them there (*v.* 24), *You have been rebellious against the Lord from the day that I knew you.* They were not *suppled,* nor *washed,* nor *swaddled;* they were not at all tractable or manageable, nor cast into any good shape. God took them to be his people, not because he saw any thing in them inviting or promising, but *so it seemed good in his sight.* And it is a very apt illustration of the miserable condition of all the children of men by nature. *As for our nativity, in the day that we were born* we were shapen in iniquity and conceived in sin, our understandings darkened, our minds alienated from the life of God, polluted with sin, which rendered us loathsome in the eyes of God. *Marvel not* then that we are told, *You must be born again.*

Verses 6–14

In there verses we have an account of the great things which God did for the Jewish nation in raising them up by degrees to be very considerable. 1. God saved them from the ruin they were upon the brink of in Egypt (*v.* 6): *"When I passed by thee, and saw thee polluted in thy own blood,* loathed and abandoned, and appointed to die, *as sheep for the slaughter,* then *I said unto thee, Live.* I designed thee for life when thou wast doomed to destruction, and resolved to save thee from death." Those shall live to whom God commands life. God looked upon the world of mankind as thus cast off, thus cast out, thus polluted, thus weltering in blood, and his thoughts towards it were thoughts of good, designing it *life, and that more abundantly.* By converting grace, he says to the soul, *Live.* 2. He looked upon them with kindness and a tender affection, not only pitied them, but *set his love upon them,* which was unaccountable, for there was nothing lovely in them; but *I looked upon thee,* and, *behold, thy time was the time of love, v.* 8. It was *the kindness and love of God our Saviour* that sent Christ to redeem us, that sends the Spirit to sanctify us, that brought us out of a state of nature into a state of grace. That *was a time of love* indeed, distinguishing love, when God manifested his love to us, and courted our love to him. *Then was I in his eyes as one that found favour,* Cant. 8:10. 3. He took them under his protection: *"I spread my skirt over thee,* to shelter thee from wind and weather, and to *cover thy nakedness,* that the shame of it might not appear." Boaz *spread his skirt over* Ruth, in token of the special favour he designed her, Ruth 3:9. God took them into his care, as an *eagle bears her young ones upon her wings,* Deu. 32:11, 12. When God owned them for his people, and sent Moses to Egypt to deliver them, which was an expression of the good-will of him *that dwelt in the bush,* then he *spread his skirt over them.* 4. He cleared them from the reproachful character which their bondage in Egypt laid them under (*v.* 9): *"Then washed I thee with water,* to make thee clean, *and anointed thee with oil,* to make thee sweet and supple thee." All the disgrace of their slavery was rolled away when they were brought, *with a high hand and a stretched-out arm, into the glorious liberty of the children of God.* When God said, *Israel is my son, my first-born — Let my people go, that they may serve me,* that word, backed as it was with so many works of wonder, *thoroughly washed away their blood;* and when God led them under the convoy of *the pillar of cloud and fire* he *spread his skirt over them.* 5. He multiplied them and built them up into a people. This is here mentioned (*v.* 7) before his *spreading his skirt over them,* because *their numbers increased exceedingly* while they were yet bond-slaves in Egypt. They *multiplied as the bud of the field* in spring time; they *waxed great, exceedingly mighty,* Ex. 1:7. 20. Their *breasts were fashioned* when they were formed into distinct tribes and had officers of their own (Ex. 5:19); their *hair grew* when they grew numerous, whereas they had been *naked and bare,* very few and therefore contemptible. 6. He admitted them into covenant with himself. See what glorious nuptials this poor forlorn infant is preferred to at last. How she is dignified who at first had scarcely her life *given her for a prey: I swore unto thee and entered into covenant with thee.* This was done at Mount Sinai: "when the covenant between God and Israel was sealed and ratified then *thou becamest mine."* God called them his people, and himself the God of Israel. Note, Those to whom God gives spiritual life he takes into covenant with himself; by that covenant they become his subjects and servants, which intimates their duty — his portion, his treasure, which intimates their privilege; and it is *confirmed with an oath, that we might have strong consolation.* 7. He beautified and adorned them. This maid cannot forget her ornaments, and she is gratified with abundance of them, *v.* 10–13. We need not be particular in the application of these. Her wardrobe was well furnished with rich apparel; they had *embroidered work* to wear, shoes of fine *badgers' skins, linen* girdles, and *silk* veils, *bracelets* and *necklaces, jewels* and *ear-rings,* and even *a beautiful crown,* or coronet. Perhaps this may refer to the jewels and other rich goods which they took from the Egyptians, which might well be spoken of thus long after as a merciful circumstance of their deliverance, when it was spoken of long before, Gen. 15:14. *They shall come out with great substance.* Or it may be taken figuratively for all those blessings of heaven which adorned both their church and state. In a little time they came to *excellent ornaments, v.* 7. The laws and ordinances which God gave them were to them as *ornaments of grace to the head and chains about the neck,* Prov. 1:9. God's sanctuary, which he set up among them, was *a beautiful crown upon their head;* it was the *beauty of holiness.* 8. He fed them with abundance, with plenty, with dainty: *Thou didst eat fine flour, and honey, and oil —* manna, angels' food *— honey out of the rock, oil out of the flinty rock.* In Canaan they did eat bread to the full, the finest of the wheat, Deu. 32:13, 14. Those whom God takes into covenant with himself are fed with the bread of life, clothed with the robe of righteousness, adorned with the graces and comforts of the spirit. The *hidden man of the heart is that which is incorruptible.* 9. He gave them great reputation among their neighbours, and made them considerable, acceptable to their friends and allies and formidable to their adversaries: *Thou didst prosper into a kingdom* (*v.* 13), which speaks both dignity and dominion; and, *They renown went forth among the heathen for thy beauty, v.* 14. The nations about had their eye upon them, and admired them for the excellent laws by which they were governed, the privilege they had of access to God, Deu. 4:7, 8. Solomon's wisdom, and Solomon's temple, were very much *the renown* of that nation; and, if we put all the privileges of the Jewish church and kingdom together, we must own that it was the most accomplished beauty of all the nations of the earth. The beauty of it was perfect; you could not name the thing that would be the honour of a people but it was to be found in Israel, in David's and Solomon's time, when that kingdom was in its zenith — piety, learning, wisdom, justice, victory, peace, wealth, and all sure to continue if they had kept close to God. *It was perfect, saith God, through my comeliness which I had put upon thee,* through the beauty of their holiness, as they were a people set apart for God, and devoted to him, to be to him *for a name, and for a praise, and for a glory.* It was this that put a lustre upon all their other honours and was indeed the perfection of their beauty. We may apply this spiritually. Sanctified souls are truly beautiful; they are so in God's sight, and they themselves may take the comfort of it. But God must have all the glory, for they were by nature deformed and polluted, and, whatever comeliness they have, it is that which God has put upon them and beautified them with, and he will be well pleased with the work of his own hands.

Verses 15-34

In these verses we have an account of the great wickedness of the people of Israel, especially in worshipping idols, notwithstanding the great favours that God had conferred upon them, by which, one would think, they should have been for ever engaged to him. This wickedness of theirs is here represented by the lewd and scandalous conversation of that beautiful maid which was rescued from ruin, brought up and well provided for by a kind friend and benefactor, that had been in all respects as a father and a husband to her. Their idolatry was the great provoking sin that they were guilty of; it began in the latter end of Solomon's time (for from Samuel's till then I do not remember that we read any thing of it), and thenceforward continued more or less the crying sin of that nation till the captivity; and, though it now and then met with some check from the reforming kings, yet it was never to tally suppressed, and for the most part appeared to a high degree impudent and barefaced. They not only worshipped the true God by images, as the ten tribes by the calves at Dan and Bethel, but they worshipped false gods, Baal and Moloch, and all the senseless rabble of the pagan deities.

This is that which is here all along represented (as often elsewhere) under the similitude of whoredom and adultery, 1. Because it is the violation of a marriage-covenant with God, forsaking him and embracing the bosom of a stranger; it is giving that affection and that service to his rivals which are due to him alone. 2. Because it is the corrupting and defiling of the mind, and the enslaving of the spiritual part of the man, and subjecting it to the power and dominion of sense, as whoredom is. 3. Because it debauches the conscience, sears and hardens it; and those who by their idolatries dishonour the divine nature, and change the truth of God into a lie and his glory into shame, God justly punishes by giving them over to a reprobate mind, to dishonour the human nature with vile affections, Rom. 1:23, etc. It is a besotting bewitching sin; and, when men are given up to it, they seldom recover themselves out of the snare. 4. Because it is a shameful scandalous sin for those that have joined themselves to the Lord to join themselves to an idol. Now observe here,

I. What were the causes of this sin. How came the people of God to be drawn away to the service of idols? How came a virgin so well taught, so well educated, to be debauched? Who would have thought it? But, 1. They grew proud (*v.* 15): "*Thou trustedst to thy beauty,* and didst expect that that should make thee an interest, and didst *play the harlot because of thy renown.*" They thought, because they were so complimented and admired by their neighbours, that, further to ingratiate themselves with them and return their compliments, they must join with them in their worship and conform to their usages. Solomon admitted idolatry, to gratify his wives and their relations. Note, Abun-

dance of young people are ruined by pride and particularly pride in their beauty. *Rara est concordia formae atque pudicitiae — Beauty and chastity are seldom associated* 2. They forgot their beginning (*v.* 22) "*Thou hast not remembered the days of thy youth,* how poor, and mean, and despicable thou wast, and what great things God did for thee and what lasting obligations he laid upon thee thereby." Note, It should be an effectual check to our pride and sensuality to consider what we are and how much we are beholden to the free grace of God. 3. They were weak in understanding and in resolution (*v.* 30): *How weak is thy heart, seeing thou dost all these things.* Note, The strength of men's lusts is an evidence of the weakness of their hearts; they have no acquaintance with themselves, nor government of themselves. She is weak, and yet an imperious whorish woman. Note, Those that are most foolish are commonly most imperious, and think themselves fit to manage others when they are far from being able to manage themselves.

II. What were the particulars of it. 1. They worshipped all the idols that came in their way, all that they were ever courted to the worship of; they were at the beck of all their neighbours (*v.* 15): *Thou pouredst out thy fornications on every one that passed by; his it was.* They were ready to close with every temptation of this kind, though ever so absurd. No foreign idol could be imported, no new god invented, but they were ready to catch at it, as a common trumpet that prostitutes herself to all comers and *multiplies her whoredoms, v.* 25. Thus some common drunkards will be company for every one that puts up the finger to them; how weak are the hearts of such! 2. They adorned their idol-temples, and groves, and high places, with the fine rich clothing that God had given them (*v.* 16, 18): *Thou deckedst thy high places with divers colours,* with the coats of divers colours, like Joseph's, which God had given them as particular marks of his favour, *and hast played the harlot* (that is, worshipped idols) *thereupon.* Of this he saith, "*The like things shall not come, neither shall it be so;* that is, this is a thing by no means to be suffered; I will never endure such practices as these without showing my resentments." 3. They made images for worship of the jewels which God had given them (*v.* 17): *The jewels of my gold and my silver which I had given thee.* Note, It is God that gives us our gold and silver; the products of trade, of art and industry, are the gifts of God's providence to us, as well as the fruits of the earth. And what God gives us the use of he still retains a property in. "It is *my silver* and *my gold,* though I have *given it to thee.*" It is his still, so that we ought to serve and honour him with it, and are accountable to him for the disposal of it. Every penny has God's image upon it as well as Caesar's. Should we make our silver and gold, our plate, money, and jewels, the matter of our pride and contention, our covetousness and prodigality, if we duly considered that they were God's silver and his gold? The Israelites began betimes to turn their jewels into idols, when Aaron made the golden calf of their earrings. 4. They served their idols with the good things which God gave them for their own use and to serve him with (*v.* 18): "*Thou hast set my oil and my incense before the,* upon their altars, as perfumes to these dunghill-deities; *my meat, and fine flour, and oil,* and that honey which Canaan flowed with, and *wherewith I fed thee,* thou hast regaled them and their hungry priests with, hast made an offering of it to them for *a sweet savour,* to purify them, and procure acceptance with them: and *thus it was, saith the Lord God.* It is too plain to be denied, too bad to be excused. *These things thou hast done.* He that knows all things knows it." See how fond they were of their idols, that they would part with that which was given them for the necessary subsistence of themselves and their families to honour them with, which may shame our niggardliness and strait-handedness in the service of the true and living God. 5. They had sacrificed their children to their idols. This is insisted upon here, and often elsewhere, as one of the worst instances of their idolatry, as indeed there was none in which the devil triumphed so much over the children of men, both their natural reason and their natural affection, as in this (see Jer. 7:31; 19:5; 32:35): *Thou hast taken thy sons and thy daughters,* and not only made them to pass through the fire, or between two fires, in token of their being dedicated to Moloch, but thou hast *sacrificed them to be devoured, v.* 20. Never was

there such an instance of the degenerating of the paternal authority into the most barbarous tyranny as this was. Yet that was not the worst of it: it was an irreparable wrong to God himself, who challenged a special property in their children more than in their gold and silver and their meat: They are *my children* (*v.* 21), the *sons and daughters which thou hast borne unto me, v.* 20. He is the *Father of spirits,* and rational souls are in a particular manner his; and therefore the taking away of life, human life, unjustly, is a high affront to the *God of life.* But the children of Israelites were his by a further right; they were the *children of the covenant,* born in God's house. He had said to Abraham, *I will be a God to thee and to thy seed;* they had the seal of the covenant in their flesh from eight days old; they were to bear God's name, and keep up his church; to murder them was in the highest degree inhuman, but to murder them in honour of an idol was in the highest degree impious. One cannot think of it without the utmost indignation: to see the pitiless hands of the parents shedding the guiltless blood of their own children, and by offering those pieces of themselves to the devil for buying sacrifices openly avowing the offering up of themselves to him for living sacrifices! How absurd was this, that the children which were born to God should be *sacrificed to devils!* Note, The children of parents that are members of the visible church are to be looked upon as born unto God, and his children,; as such, and under that character, we are to love them, and pray for them, bring them up for him, and, if he calls for them, cheerfully part with them to him; for *may he not do what he will with his own?* Upon this instance of their idolatry, which indeed ought not to pass without a particular brand, this remark is made (*v.* 20), *Is this of thy whoredoms a small matter?* which intimates that there were those who made a small matter of it, and turned it into a jest. Note, There is no sin so heinous, so apparently heinous, which men of profligate consciences will not make a mock at. But is whoredom, is spiritual whoredom, a small matter? Is it a small matter for men to make their children brutes and the devil their god? It will be a great matter shortly. 6. They built temples in honour of their idols, that others might be invited to resort thither and join with them in the worship of their idols: "*After all thy wickedness* of this kind committed in private, for which, *woe, woe, unto thee*" (that comes in in a sad parenthesis, denoting those to be in a woeful condition who are going on in sin, and giving them warning in time, if they would but take it), "thou hast at length arrived at such a pitch of impudence as to proclaim it; thou hast long had a whore's heart, but now thou hast come to have a whore's forehead, and canst not blush," *v.* 23-35. *Thou hast built there an eminent place,* a *brothel-house* (so the margin reads it), and such their idol temples were. *Thou hast made for thyself a high place,* for one idol or other, *in every street,* and *at every head of the way;* and again *v.* 31. They did all they could to seduce and debauch others, and to spread the contagion, by making the temptations to idolatry as strong as possibly they could; and hereby the ringleaders in idolatry did but *make themselves vile,* and even those that had courted them to it, finding themselves outdone by them, began to be surfeited with the abundance and violence of their idolatries: *Thou hast made thy beauty to be abhorred,* even by those that had admired it. The Jewish nation, by leaving their own God, and doting on the gods of the nations round about them, had made themselves mean and despicable in the eyes even of their heathen neighbours; much more was their *beauty abhorred* by all that were wise and good, and had any concern for the honour of God and religion. Note, Those shame themselves that bring a reproach on their profession. And justly will that beauty, that excellency, at length be made the object of the loathing of others which men have made the matter of their own pride.

III. What were the aggravations of this sin.

1. They were fond of the idols of those nations which had been their oppressors and persecutors. As, (1.) The Egyptians. They were a people notorious for idolatry, and for the most sottish senseless idolatries; they had of old abused Israel by their barbarous dealings, and of late by their treacherous dealings — were always either cruel or false to them; and yet so infatuated were they that *they committed fornication with the Egyptians their neighbours,* not only by joining with them in their idolatries, but by

entering into leagues and alliances with them, and depending upon them for help in their straits, which was an adulterous departure from God. (2.) The Assyrians. They had also been vexatious to Israel: "And *yet thou hast played the whore with them* (*v.* 28); though they lived at a greater distance, yet thou hast entertained their idols and their superstitious usages, and so *hast multiplied thy fornications unto Chaldea,* hast borrowed images of gods, patterns of altars, rites of sacrificing, and one foolery or other of that kind, from that remote country, that enemy's country, and hast imported them *into the land of Canaan,* enfranchised and established them there." Thus Mr. George Herbert long since foretold, or feared at least,

That Seine shall swallow Tiber, and the Thames
By letting in them both pollute her streams.

2. They had been under the rebukes of Providence for their sins, and yet they persisted in them (*v.* 27): *I have stretched out my hand over thee,* to threaten and frighten thee. So God did before he *laid his hand upon them* to ruin and destroy them; and that is his usual method, to try to bring men to repentance first by less judgments. He did so here. Before he brought such a famine upon them as broke the staff of bread he *diminished their ordinary food,* but them short before he cut them off. When the overplus is abused, it is just with God to diminish that which is for necessity. Before he delivered them to the Chaldeans to be destroyed he delivered them *to the daughters of the Philistines* to be ridiculed for their idolatries; for they hated them, and, though they were idolaters themselves, yet were ashamed of the lewd way of the Israelites, who had grown more profane in their idolatries than any of their neighbours, who changed their gods, whereas other nations did not change theirs, Jer. 2:10, 11. For this they were justly chastised by the Philistines. Or it may refer to the inroads which the Philistines made upon the south of Judah in the reign of Ahaz, by which it was weakened and impoverished, and which was the beginning of sorrows to them (2 Chr. 28:18); but they did not take warning by those judgments, and therefore were justly abandoned to ruin at last. Note, In the account which impenitent sinners shall be called to they will be told not only of the mercies for which they have been ungrateful, but of the afflictions under which they have been incorrigible, Amos 4:11.

3. They were insatiable in their spiritual whoredom: Thou *couldst not be satisfied, v.* 28 and again *v.* 29. When they had multiplied their idols and superstitious usages beyond measure, yet still they were enquiring after new gods and new fashions in worship. Those that in sincerity join themselves to the true God find enough in him for their satisfaction; and, though they still desire more of God, yet they never desire more than God. But those that forsake this living fountain for broken cisterns will find themselves soon surfeited, but never satisfied; they have soon enough of the gods they have, and are still enquiring after more.

4. They were at great expense with their idolatry, and laid out a great deal of wealth in purchasing patterns of images and altars, and hiring priests to attend upon them from other countries. Harlots generally had their hire; but this impudent adulteress, instead of being hired to serve idols, hired idols to protect her and accept her homage. This is much insisted on, *v.* 31–34. "In this respect *the contrary is in thee from other women in thy whoredoms:* others are courted, but thou makest court to those that do not follow thee, art fond of making leagues and alliances with those heathen nations that despise thee; others have gifts given them, but thou givest thy gifts, the gifts which God had graciously given thee, to thy idols; herein thou art like a wife that commits adultery, not for gain, as harlots do, but entirely for the sin's sake." Note, Spiritual lusts, those of the mind, such as theirs after idols were, are often as strong and impetuous as any carnal lusts are. And it is a great aggravation of sin when men are their own tempters, and, instead of proposing to themselves any worldly advantage by their sin, are at great expense with it; such are *transgressors without cause* (Ps. 25:3), wicked transgressors indeed.

And now is not Jerusalem in all this made to know her abominations? For what greater abominations could she be guilty of than these? Here we may see with wonder and horror what the corrupt nature of men is when God leaves them to themselves, yea, though they have the greatest advantages to be better and do better. And the way of sin is down-hill. *Nitimur in vetitum — We incline to what is forbidden.*

Verses 35–43

Adultery was by the law of Moses made a capital crime. This notorious adulteress, the criminal at the bar, being in the foregoing verses found guilty, here has sentence passed upon her. It is ushered in with solemnity, *v.* 35. The prophet, as the judge, in God's name calls to her, *O harlot! hear the word of the Lord.* Our Saviour preached to harlots, for their conversion, to bring them into the kingdom of God, not as the prophet here, to expel them out of it. Note, An apostate church is a harlot. Jerusalem is so if she become idolatrous. *How has the faithful city become a harlot!* Rome is so represented in the Revelation, when it is marked for ruin, as Jerusalem here. Rev. 17:1, *Come, and I will show thee the judgments of the great whore.* Those who will not hear the commanding word of the Lord and obey it shall be made to hear the condemning word of the Lord and shall tremble at it. Let us attend while judgment is given.

I. The crime is stated and the articles of the charge are summed up (*v.* 36) and (as is usual) with the attendant aggravations (*v.* 43); for when God speaks in wrath he will be justified, and clear when he judges, clear when he is judged; and sinners, when they are condemned, shall have their sins so set in order before them that their mouth shall be stopped and they shall not have a word to object against the equity of the sentence. The crimes which this harlot stands convicted of, and is now to be condemned for, are, 1. The violation of the first two commandments of the first table by idolatry, which is here called her *whoredoms with her lovers* (so she called them, Hos. 2:12, because she loved them as if they had been indeed her benefactors), that is, with *all the idols of her abominations,* the abominable idols which she served and worshipped. This was the sin which provoked God to jealousy. 2. The violation of the first two commandments of the second table by the murder of their own innocent infants: *The blood of thy children which thou didst give unto them.* It is not strange if those that have cast off God and his fear break through the strongest and most sacred bonds of natural affection. Their sins are aggravated from the consideration, (1.) Of the dishonour they had thereby done to themselves: "Hereby *thy filthiness was poured out;* the uncleanness that was in thy heart was hereby discovered and brought to light, and thy nakedness was exposed to view, and thou wast thereby exposed to contempt." God is displeased with his professing people for shaming themselves by their sins. (2.) Their base ingratitude is another aggravation of their sins: *"Thou hast not remembered the days of thy youth,* and the kindness that was done thee then, when otherwise thou wouldst have perished," *v.* 43. And, (3.) The vexation which their sins gave to God, whom they ought to have pleased: *"Thou hast fretted me in all these things,* not only angered me, but grieved me." It is a strange expression, and, one would think, enough to melt a heart of stone, that the great God, who cannot admit any uneasiness, is pleased to speak of the sins and follies of his professing people as *fretting* to him. *Forty years long was I grieved with this generation.*

II. The sentence is passed in general: *I will judge thee as women that break wedlock and shed blood are judged* (*v.* 38), and those two crimes were punished with death, with an ignominious death. "Thou hast *shed blood,* and therefore I will *give thee blood;* thou hast *broken wedlock,* and therefore I will give it thee, not only in justice, but in jealousy, not only as a righteous Judge, but as an injured and incensed husband, who *will not spare in the day of vengeance,"* Prov. 6:34, 35. He will *recompense their way upon their head, v.* 43. In all the judgments God executes upon sinners we must see *their own way recompensed upon their head;* they are dealt with not only as they deserved, but as they procured. It is the end which their sin, as a way, had a direct tendency to. More particularly, 1. This criminal must be (as is usually done with criminals) exposed to public shame, *v.* 37. Malefactors are not executed privately, but are made a spectacle to the world. Care is here taken to bring spectators together: *"All those whom thou hast loved, with whom thou hast taken pleasure,* shall come to be witnesses of the execution, that they may take warning and prevent their own like ruin; and those also *whom thou hast hated,* who will insult over thee and triumph in thy fall." Both ways the calamities of Jerusalem will be aggravated, that they will be the grief of her friends and the joy of her foes. These shall not only be gathered *around her,* but *gathered against her;* even those with whom she took unlawful pleasure, with whom she contracted unlawful leagues, the Egyptians and Assyrians, shall now contribute to her ruin. As, *when a man's ways please the Lord, he makes even his enemies to be at peace with him,* so when a man's ways displease the Lord he makes even his friends to be at war with him; and justly makes those a scourge and a plague to sinners, and instruments of their destruction, who were their tempters, and with whom they were partakers in wickedness. Those whom they have suffered to strip them of their virtue shall see them stripped, and perhaps help to strip them, of all their other ornaments; to *see the nakedness of the land* will they come. It is added, to the same purport (*v.* 41), *I will execute judgments upon thee in the sight of many women;* thou shalt be made an example of *in terrorem — that others may see and fear* and do no more presumptuously. 2. The criminal is *condemned to die,* for her sins are such as death is the wages of (*v.* 40): *They shall bring up a company* (that is, a company shall be brought up) *against thee,* and *they shall stone thee with stones,* and *thrust thee through with their swords;* so great a death, so many deaths in one, is this adulteress adjudged to. When the walls of Jerusalem were battered down with stones shot against them, and the inhabitants of Jerusalem were put to the sword, then this sentence was executed in the letter of it. 3. The estate of the criminal is confiscated, and all that belonged to her destroyed with her (*v.* 39): *They shall throw down thy eminent place,* and (*v.* 41) they *shall burn thy houses,* as the habitations of bad women are destroyed, in detestation of their lewdness. Their high places, erected in honour of their idols, by which they thought to ingratiate themselves with their neighbours, shall be an offence to them, and even *they* shall *break them down.* It was long the complaint, even in some of the best reigns of the kings of Judah, that *the high places were not taken away;* but now the army of the Chaldeans, when they lay all waste, shall break them down. If iniquity be not taken away by the justice of the nation, it shall be taken away by the judgments of God upon the nation. 4. Thus both the sin and the sinners shall be abolished together, and an end put to both: *Thou shalt cease from playing the harlot;* there shall be no remainders of idolatry in the land, because the inhabitants shall be wholly extirpated, and they shall *give no more hire* because they shall have no more to give. Some that will not leave their sins live till their sins leave them. When all that with which they honoured their idols is taken from them they shall not *give hire any more* (*v.* 41): "Then *thou shalt not commit this lewdness* of sacrificing thy children, which was a crime provoking *above all thy abominations,* for thy children shall all be cut off by the sword or carried into captivity, so that thou shalt have none to sacrifice," *v.* 43. Or it may be meant of the reformation of those of them that escape and survive the punishment; they shall take warning, and shall *do no more presumptuously.* The captivity in Babylon made the people of Israel to cease for ever *from playing the harlot;* it effectually cured them of their inclination to idolatry. And then all shall be well, when this is the fruit, even the *taking away of sin;* then (*v.* 42) *my jealousy shall depart. I will be quiet, and no more angry.* When we begin to be at war with sin God will be at peace with us; for he continues the affliction no longer than till it has done its work. When sin departs God's jealousy will soon depart, for he is never jealous but when we give him just cause to be so. Yet some understand this as a threatening of utter ruin, that God will *make a full end* and the fire of his anger shall burn as long as there is any fuel for it. *His fury shall rest upon them,* and not remove. Compare this with that doom of unbelievers, Jn. 3:36. *The wrath of God abideth on them.* They shall drink the dregs of the cup, and then God will be *no more angry,* for he is *eased of his adversaries* (Isa. 1:24), is satisfied in the abandoning of them, and therefore will be *no more angry,* because there are no more for his anger to fasten upon. They had fretted him, when judgment and mercy were contesting; but now *he is quiet,* as he will be in the eternal damnation of sinners, wherein he will be glorified, and therefore he will be satisfied.

Verses 44–59

The prophet here further shows Jerusalem her abominations, by comparing her with those places that had gone before her, and showing that she was worse than any of them, and therefore should, like them, be utterly and irreparably ruined. We are all apt to judge of ourselves by comparison, and to imagine that we are sufficiently good if we are but as good as such and such, who are thought passable; or that we are not dangerously bad if we are no worse than such and such, who, though bad, are not of the worst. Now God by the prophet shows Jerusalem,

I. That she was as bad as *her mother,* that is, as the accursed devoted Canaanites that were the possessors of this land before her. Those that use proverbs, as most people do, shall apply that proverb to Jerusalem, *As is the mother, so is her daughter, v.* 44. She is her *mother's own child.* The Jews are as like the Canaanites in temper and inclination as if they had been their own children. The character of the mother was that she *loathed her husband and her children,* she had all the marks of an adulteress; and that is the character of the daughter: she *forsakes the guide of her youth,* and is barbarous to the children of her own bowels. When God brought Israel into Canaan he particularly warned them not to do according to the abominations of *the men of that land, who went before them* (for which *it had spued them out,* Lev. 18:27, 28), the monuments of whose idolatry, with the remains of the idolaters themselves, would be a continual temptation to them; but they learned their way, and trod in their steps, and were as well affected to the *idols of Canaan* as ever they were (Ps. 106:38), and thus, in respect of imitation, it might truly be said that *their mother* was a *Hittite* and their *father* an *Amorite* (*v.* 45), for they resembled them more than Abraham and Sarah.

II. That she was worse than her sisters Sodom and Samaria, that were adulteresses too, that *loathed their husbands and their children,* that were weary of the gods of their fathers, and were for introducing new gods, *a-la-mode — quite in style,* that came newly up, and new fashions in religion, and were given to change. On this comparison between Jerusalem and *her sisters* the prophet here enlarges, that he might either shame them into repentance or justify God in their ruin. Observe,

1. Who Jerusalem's sisters were, *v.* 45. Samaria and Sodom. Samaria is called the *elder* sister, or rather the *greater,* because it was a much larger city and kingdom, richer and more considerable, and more nearly allied to Israel. If Jerusalem look northward, this is partly *on her left hand.* This city of Samaria, and the towns and villages, that were as *daughters* to that *mother-city,* these had been *lately* destroyed for their *spiritual whoredom.* Sodom, and the adjacent towns and villages that were her daughters, dwelt at Jerusalem's *right hand,* and was her *less sister,* less than Jerusalem, less than Samaria, and these were of old destroyed for their corporeal whoredom, Jude 7.

2. Wherein Jerusalem's sins resembled her sisters', particularly Sodom's (*v.* 49): *This was the iniquity of Sodom* (it is implied, and this is *thy* iniquity too), *pride, fulness of bread, and abundance of idleness.* Their *going after strange flesh,* which was Sodom's most flagrant wickedness, is not mentioned, because notoriously known, but those sins which did not look so black, but opened the door and led the way to these more enormous crimes, and began to fill that measure of her sins, which was filled up at length by their unnatural filthiness. Now these initiating sins were, (1.) Pride, in which the heart lifts up itself above and against both God and man. Pride was the first sin that turned angels into devils, and the *garden of the Lord* into a *hell upon earth.* It was the pride of the Sodomites that they despised *righteous Lot,* and would not bear to be reproved by him; and this ripened them for ruin. (2.) Gluttony, here called *fulness of bread.* It was God's great mercy that they had plenty, but their great sin that they abused it, glutted themselves with it, ate to excess and drank to excess, and made that the gratification of their lusts which was given them to be the support of their lives. (3.) Idleness, *abundance of idleness,* a dread of labour and a love of ease. Their country was fruitful, and the abundance they had they came easily by, which was a temptation to them to indulge themselves in sloth, which disposed them to all that abominable filthiness which kindled their flames. Note, Idleness is an inlet to much sin. The men of Sodom, who were idle, were *wicked,* and *sinners before the Lord exceedingly,* Gen. 13:13. The standing waters gather filth and the sitting bird is the fowler's mark. When David *arose from off his bed at evening* he saw Bathsheba. *Quaeritur, Aegisthus quare sit factus adulter? In promptu causa est; desidiosus erat — What made Aegisthus an adulterer? Indolence.* (4.) Oppression: Neither did she *strengthen the hands of the poor and needy;* probably it is implied that she weakened their hands and *broke* their arms; however, it was bad enough that, when she had so much wealth, and consequently power and interest and leisure, she did nothing for the relief of the poor, in providing for whose wants those that themselves are *full of bread* may employ their time well; they need not be so abundantly idle as too often they are. These were the sins of the Sodomites, and these were Jerusalem's sins. Their pride, the cause of their sins, is mentioned again (*v.* 50): *They were haughty,* with the horrid effects of their sins, their *abominations* which they *committed before God.* Men arrive gradually at the height of impiety and wickedness. *Nemo repente fit turpissimus — No man reaches the height of vice at once.* But, where pride has got the ascendant in a man, he is in the high road to all abominations.

3. How much the sins of Jerusalem exceeded those of Sodom and Samaria; they were more heinous in the sight of God, either in themselves or by reason of several aggravations: *"Thou hast not only walked after their ways,* and trod in their steps, but hast quite outdone them in wickedness, *v.* 47. Thou thoughtest it *a very little thing* to do as they did; didst laugh at them as sneaking sinners and silly ones; thou wouldst be more cunning, more daring, in wickedness, wouldst triumph more boldly over thy convictions, and bid more open defiance to God and religion: 'if a man will break, let him break for *something.*' Thus *thou wast corrupted more than they in all thy ways."* Jerusalem was more polite, and therefore sinned with more wit, more art and ingenuity, than Sodom and Samaria could. Jerusalem had more wealth and power, and its government was more absolute and arbitrary, and therefore had the more opportunity of oppressing the poor, and shedding malignant influences around her, than Sodom and Samaria had. Jerusalem had the temple, and the ark, and the priesthood, and kings of the house of David; and therefore the wickedness of that holy city, that was so dignified, so near, so dear to God, was more provoking to him than the wickedness of Sodom and Samaria, that had not Jerusalem's privileges and means of grace. Sodom has *not done as thou hast done, v.* 48. This agrees with what Christ says. Mt. 11:24, *It shall be more tolerable for the land of Sodom in the day of judgment than for thee.* The kingdom of the ten tribes had been very wicked; and yet *Samaria has not committed half thy sins* (*v.* 51), has not worshipped half so many idols, nor slain half so many prophets. It was bad enough that those of Jerusalem were guilty of Sodom's sins, Sodomy itself not excepted, 1 Ki. 14:24; 2 Ki. 23:7. And though the Dead Sea, the standing monument of Sodom's sin and ruin, bordered upon their country (Num. 34:12), and that sulphureous lake was always under their nose (God having *taken away Sodom and her daughters* in such way and manner as he *saw good,* as he says here, *v.* 50, so as that one thing should effectually make their *overthrow* an *example to those that afterwards should live ungodly,* 2 Pt. 2:6), yet they did not take warning, but *multiplied their abominations more than they;* and, (1.) By this they *justified Sodom and Samaria, v.* 51. They pretended, in their haughtiness and superciliousness, to *judge them,* and in the days of old, when they retained their integrity, they did judge them, *v.* 52. But now they justify them comparatively: *Sodom and Samaria* are *more righteous than thou,* that is, less wicked. It will look like some extenuation of their sins that, bad as they were, Jerusalem was worse, though it was God's own city. Not that it will serve for a plea to justify Sodom, but it condemns Jerusalem, against which Sodom and Samaria will *rise up in judgment.* (2.) For this they ought themselves to be greatly ashamed: "Thou who hast *judged thy sisters,* and cried out shame on them, now *bear thy own shame, for thy sins which thou hast committed,* which, though of the same kind with theirs, yet, being committed *by thee,* are *more abominable than theirs," v.* 52. This may be taken either as foretelling their ruin *(Thou shalt bear thy shame)* or as inviting them to repentance: *"Be thou confounded and bear thy shame;* take the shame to thyself that is due to thee." It may be hoped that sinners will forsake their sins when they begin to be heartily ashamed of them. And therefore they shall go into captivity, and there they shall lie, that they may be *confounded in all that they have done,* because they had been a comfort and encouragement to Sodom and Samaria, *v.* 54. Note, There is nothing in sin which we have more reason to be ashamed of than this, that by our sin we have encouraged others in sin, and comforted them in that for which they must be grieved or they are undone. Another reason why they must now be ashamed is because in the day of their prosperity they had looked with so much disdain upon their neighbours: *Thy sister Sodom was not mentioned by thee in the day of they pride, v.* 56. They thought Sodom not worthy to be named the same day with Jerusalem, little dreaming that Jerusalem would at length lie under a worse and more scandalous character than Sodom herself. Those that are high may perhaps come to stand upon a level with those they contemn. Or "Sodom was *not mentioned,* that is, the warning designed to be given to thee by Sodom's ruin was not regarded." If the Jews had but talked more frequently and seriously to one another, and to their children, concerning *the wrath of God revealed from heaven* against *Sodom's ungodliness and unrighteousness,* it might have kept them in awe, and prevented their treading in their steps; but they kept the thought of it at a distance, would not bear the mention of it, and (as the ancients say) put Isaiah to death for putting them in mind of it, when he called them *rulers of Sodom* and *people of Gomorrah,* Isa. 1:10. Note, Those are but preparing judgments for themselves that will not take notice of God's judgments upon others.

4. What desolations God had brought and was bringing upon Jerusalem for these wickednesses, wherein they had exceeded Sodom and Samaria. (1.) She has already long ago been disgraced, and has fallen into contempt, among her neighbours (*v.* 57): *Before her wickedness was discovered,* before she came to be so grossly and openly flagitious, she bore the just punishment of her secret and more concealed lewdness, when she fell under *the reproach of the daughters of Syria, of the Philistines,* who were said to *despise her* and *be ashamed of her* (*v.* 27), and under the reproach of *all that were round about her,* which seems to refer to the descent made upon Judah by the Syrians in the days of Ahaz, and soon after another by the Philistines, 2 Chr. 28:5, 18. Note, Those that disgrace themselves by yielding to their lusts will justly be brought into disgrace by being made to yield to their enemies; and it is observable that before God brought potent enemies upon them, for *their destruction,* he brought enemies upon them that were less formidable, *for their reproach.* If less judgments would do the work, God would not send greater. In this *thou hast borne thy lewdness, v.* 58. Those that will not cast off their sins by repentance and reformation shall be made to bear their sins to their confusion. (2.) She is now *in captivity,* or hastening into captivity, and therein is reckoned with, not only for her lewdness (*v.* 58), but for her perfidiousness and covenant-breaking (*v.* 59): *"I will deal with thee as thou hast done;* I will forsake thee as thou hast forsaken me, and cast thee off as thou hast cast me off, for thou hast *despised the oath, in breaking the covenant."* This seems to be meant of the covenant God made with their fathers at Mount Sinai, whereby he took them and theirs to be a peculiar people to himself. They flattered themselves with a conceit that because God had hitherto continued his favour to them, notwithstanding their provocations, he would do so still. "No," says God, "you have *broken covenant with me,* have despised both the promises of the covenant and the obligations of it, and therefore I will *deal with thee as thou hast done."* Note, Those that will not adhere to God as their God have no reason to expect that he should continue to own them as his people. (3.) The captivity of the wicked Jews, and their ruin, shall be as irrevocable as that of Sodom and Samaria. In this sense, as a threatening, most interpreters take *v.* 53, 55. *"When I shall bring again the captivity of Sodom and Samaria, and when they shall return to their former estate, then I will bring again the captivity of thy captives in the midst of them,* and as it were for their sakes, and under their shadow and protection, because they are *more righteous than thou,* and *then thou shalt return to thy former estate,"* But Sodom and Samaria were never brought

back, nor ever returned to their former estate, and therefore let not Jerusalem expect it, that is, those who now remained there, whom God would *deliver to be removed into all the kingdoms of the earth for their hurt,* Jer. 24:9, 10. Sooner shall the Sodomites arise out of the salt sea, and the Samaritans return out of the land of Assyria, than they enjoy their peace and prosperity again; for, to their shame be it spoken, it is *a comfort* to those of the ten tribes, who are dispersed and in captivity, to see those of the two tribes who had been as bad as they, or worse, in like manner dispersed and in captivity; and therefore they shall live and die, shall stand and fall, together. The bad ones of both shall perish together; the good ones of both shall return together. Note, Those who do as the worst of sinners do must expect to fare as they fare. *Let my enemy be as the wicked.*

Verses 60–63

Here, in the close of the chapter, after a most shameful conviction of sin and a most dreadful denunciation of judgments, mercy is remembered, mercy is reserved, for those who shall come after. As was when God swore in his wrath concerning those who came out of Egypt that they should not enter Canaan, "Yet" (says God) "your little ones shall;" so here. And some think that what is said of the return of Sodom and Samaria (*v.* 53, 55), and of Jerusalem with them, is a promise; it may be understood so, if by Sodom we understand (as Grotius and some of the Jewish writers do) the Moabites and Ammonites, the posterity of Lot, who once dwelt in Sodom; their captivity was returned (Jer. 48:47; 49:6), as was that of many of the ten tribes, and Judah's with them. But these closing verses are, without doubt, a *previous* promise, which was in part fulfilled at the return of the penitent and reformed Jews out of Babylon, but was to have its full accomplishment in gospel-times, and in that *repentance and* that *remission of sins* which should then be *preached* with success *to all nations, beginning at Jerusalem.* Now observe here,

I. Whence this mercy should take rise — from *God himself,* and his *remembering his covenant* with them (*v.* 60): *Nevertheless,* though they had been so provoking, and God had been provoked to such a degree that one would think they could never be reconciled again, yet "*I will remember my covenant with thee,* that covenant which I made with thee *in the days of thy youth,* and will revive it again. Though thou hast *broken the covenant* (*v.* 59), I will remember it, and it shall flourish again." See how much it is our comfort and advantage that God is pleased to deal with us in a covenant-way, for thus the mercies of it come to be *sure mercies* and *everlasting* (Isa. 55:3); and, while this root stands firmly in the ground, there is *hope of the tree,* though it be *cut down,* that *through the scent of water it will bud again.* We do not find that they put him in mind of the covenant, but *ex mero motu* — *from his own mere good pleasure,* he *remembers* it as he had promised. Lev. 26:42, *Then will I remember my covenant, and will remember the land.* He that bids us to be ever mindful of the covenant no doubt will himself be ever mindful of it, the word *which he commanded* (and what he commands stands fast for ever) to *a thousand generations.*

II. How they should be prepared and qualified for this mercy (*v.* 61): "*Thou shalt remember thy ways,* thy evil ways; God will put thee in mind of them, will set them in order before thee, that thou mayest be *ashamed of them.*" Note, God's good work in us commences and keeps pace with his good-will towards us. When he remembers his covenant for us, that he may not remember our sins against us, he puts us upon remembering our sins against ourselves. And if we will but be brought to remember our ways, how crooked and perverse they have been and how we have walked contrary to God in them, we cannot but be ashamed; and, when we are so, we are best prepared to receive the honour and comfort of a sealed pardon and a settled peace.

III. What the mercy is that God has in reserve for them. 1. He will take them into covenant with himself (*v.* 60): *I will establish unto thee an everlasting covenant;* and again (*v.* 62), *I will establish,* re-establish, and establish more firmly than ever, *my covenant with thee.* Note, It is an unspeakable comfort to all true penitents that the covenant of grace is so well ordered in all things that every transgression in the covenant does not throw us out of the covenant, for

that is inviolable. 2. He will bring the Gentiles into church-communion with them (*v.* 61): "*Thou shalt receive thy sisters,* the Gentile nations that are found about thee, *thy elder and thy younger,* greater than thou art and less, ancient nations and modern, and *I will give them unto thee for daughters;* they shall be founded, nursed, taught, and educated, by that gospel, that *word of the Lord,* which shall *go forth from* Zion and from *Jerusalem;* so that all the neighbours shall call Jerusalem *mother,* while the church continues there, and shall acknowledge the Jerusalem which is from above, and *which is free,* to be *the mother of us all,* Gal. 4:26. They shall be thy *daughters,* but *not by thy covenant,* not by the covenant of peculiarity, not as being proselytes to the Jewish religion and subject to the yoke of the ceremonial law, but as being converts with thee to the Christian religion." Or *not by thy covenant* may mean, "not upon such terms as thou shalt think fit to impose upon them as conquered nations, as captives and homagers to whom thou mayest give law at pleasure" (such a dominion as that the carnal Jews hope to have over the nations); "no, they shall be thy daughters *by my covenant,* the covenant of grace made with thee and them in concert, as in *indenture tripartite.* I will be a Father, a common Father, both to Jews and Gentiles, and so they shall become sisters to one another. And, when thou *shalt receive them,* thou shalt be *ashamed of thy own evil ways* wherein thou wast conformed to them. Thou shalt blush to look a Gentile in the face, remembering how much worse than the Gentiles thou wast in the day of thy apostasy."

IV. What the fruit and effect of this will be. 1. God will hereby be glorified (*v.* 62): "*Thou shalt know that I am the Lord.* It shall hereby be known that the God of Israel is Jehovah, a God of power, and faithful to his covenant; and thou shalt know it who hast hitherto lived as if thou didst not know or believe it." It had often been said in wrath, *You shall know that I am the Lord,* shall know it to your cost; here it is said in mercy, You shall know it to your comfort; and it is one of the most precious promises of the new covenant which God has made with us that *all shall know him from the least to the greatest.* 2. They shall hereby be more humbled and abased for sin (*v.* 63): "*That thou mayest be* the more *confounded* at the *remembrance of all that thou hast done* amiss, mayest reproach thyself for it and call thyself a thousand times unwise, undutiful, ungrateful, and unlike what thou wast, and mayest never *open thy mouth any more* in contradiction to God, reflection on him, or complaints of him, but mayest be for ever silent and submissive *because of thy shame.*" Note, Those that rightly remember their sins will be truly ashamed of them; and those that are truly ashamed of their sins will see great reason to be patient under their afflictions, to be dumb, and not open their mouths against what God does. But that which is most observable is, that all this shall be *when I am pacified towards thee, saith the Lord God.* Note, It is the gracious ingenuousness of true penitents that the clearer evidences and the fuller instances they have of God's being reconciled to them the more grieved and ashamed they are that ever they have offended God. God is in Jesus Christ *pacified towards us;* he is our peace, and it is by his cross that we are reconciled, and in his gospel that God is reconciling the world to himself. Now the consideration of this should be powerful to melt our hearts into a godly sorrow for sin. This is repenting because the *kingdom of heaven is at hand.* The prodigal, after he had received the kiss which assured him that his father was *pacified towards him,* was ashamed and confounded, and said, *Father, I have sinned against heaven and before thee.* And the more our shame for sin is increased by the sense of pardoning mercy the more will our comfort in God be increased.

CHAPTER 17

God was, in the foregoing chapter, reckoning with the people of Judah, and bringing ruin upon them for their treachery in breaking covenant with him; in this chapter he is reckoning with the king of Judah for his treachery in breaking covenant with the king of Babylon; for when God came to contend with them he found many grounds of his controversy. The thing was now in doing: Zedekiah was practising with the king of Egypt underhand for assistance in a treacherous project he had formed to shake off the yoke of the king of Babylon, and violate the homage and fealty he had sworn to him. For this God by the prophet here, I. Threatens the ruin of him and his kingdom, by a parable of two eagles and a vine (*v.* 1–10),

and the explanation of that parable (*v.* 11–21). But, in the close, II. He promises hereafter to raise the royal family of Judah again, the house of David, in the Messiah and his kingdom (*v.* 22–24).

Verses 1–21

We must take all these verses together, that we may have the parable and the explanation of it at one view before us, because they will illustrate one another. 1. The prophet is appointed to *put forth a riddle* to the *house of Israel* (*v.* 2), not to puzzle them, as Samson's riddle was put forth to the Philistines, not to hide the mind of God from them in obscurity, or to leave them in uncertainty about it, one advancing one conjecture and another another, as is usual in expounding riddles; no, he is immediately to tell them the meaning of it. *Let him that speaks in an unknown tongue pray that he may interpret,* 1 Co. 14:13. But he must deliver this message in a riddle or parable that they might take the more notice of it, might be the more affected with it themselves, and might the better remember it and tell it to others. For these reasons God often used similitudes by his servants the prophets, and Christ himself *opened his mouth in parables.* Riddles and parables are used for an amusement to ourselves and an entertainment to our friends. The prophet must make use of these to see if in this dress the things of God might find acceptance, and insinuate themselves into the minds of a careless people. Note, Ministers should study to find out acceptable words, and try various methods to do good; and, as far as they have reason to think will be for edification, should both bring that which is familiar into their preaching and their preaching too into their familiar discourse, that there may not be so vast a dissimilitude as with some there is between what they say in the pulpit and what they say out. 2. He is appointed to expound this riddle to *the rebellious house, v.* 12. Though being *rebellious* they might justly have been left in ignorance, to see and hear and not perceive, yet the thing shall be explained to them: *Know you not what these things mean?* Those that knew the story, and what was now in agitation, might make a shrewd guess at the meaning of this riddle, but, that they might be left without excuse, he is to give it to them in plain terms, stripped of the metaphor. But the enigma was first propounded for them to study on awhile, and to send to their friends at Jerusalem, that they might enquire after and expect the solution of it some time after.

Let us now see what the matter of this message is.

I. Nebuchadnezzar had some time ago carried off Jehoiachin, the same that was called *Jeconiah,* when he was but eighteen years of age and had reigned in Jerusalem but *three months,* him and his princes and great men, and had brought them captives to Babylon, 2 Ki. 24:12. This in the parable is represented by an eagle's cropping the top and tender branch of *a cedar,* and carrying it into a *land of traffic,* a *city of merchants* (*v.* 3, 4), which is explained *v.* 12. The *king of Babylon* took the *king of Jerusalem,* who was no more able to resist him than a young twig of a tree is to contend with the strongest bird of prey, that easily crops it off, perhaps towards the making of *her nest.* Nebuchadnezzar, in Daniel's vision, is *a lion,* the king of beasts (Dan. 7:4); there he has *eagle's wings,* so swift were his motions, so speedy were his conquests. Here, in this parable, he is *an eagle,* the king of birds, a *great eagle,* that lives upon spoil and rapine, whose young ones *suck up blood,* Job 39:30. His dominion extends itself far and wide, like the great and long wings of an eagle; the people are numerous, for it is *full of feathers;* the court is splendid, for it has *divers colours,* which look like *embroidering,* as the word is. Jerusalem is Lebanon, a forest of houses, and very pleasant. The royal family is *the cedar;* Jehoiachin is the *top branch,* the *top of the young twigs,* which he crops off. Babylon is the *land of traffic and city of merchants* where it is set. And the king of Judah, being of the house of David, will think himself much degraded and disgraced to be lodged among tradesmen; but he must make the best of it.

II. When he carried him to Babylon he made his uncle Zedekiah king in his room, *v.* 5, 6. His name was *Mattaniah* — *the gift of the Lord,* which Nebuchadnezzar changed into *Zedekiah* — *the justice of the Lord,* to remind him to be just like the God he called his, for fear of his justice. This was *one of the seed of the land,* a native, not a foreigner, not one of his Babylonian princes;

he was *planted in a fruitful field,* for so Jerusalem as yet was; he *placed it by great waters,* where it would be likely to grow, like *a willow-tree,* which grows quickly, and grows best in moist ground, but is never designed nor expected to be a stately tree. He *set it with* care and *circumspection* (so some read it); he wisely provided that it might grow, but that it might not grow too big. *He took of the king's seed* (so it is explained, *v.* 13) and *made a covenant with him* that he should have the kingdom, and enjoy the regal power and dignity, provided he held it as his vassal, dependent on him and accountable to him. He *took an oath of him,* made him swear allegiance to him, swear by his own God, the God of Israel, that he would be a faithful tributary to him, 2 Chr. 36:13. He also *took away the mighty of the land,* the chief of the men of war, partly as hostages for the performance of the covenant, and partly that, the land being thereby weakened, the king might be the less able, and therefore the less in temptation, to break his league. What he designed we are told (*v.* 14): *That the kingdom might be base,* in respect both of honour and strength, might neither be a rival with its powerful neighbours, nor a terror to its feeble ones, as it had been, that *it might not left up itself* to vie with the kingdom of Babylon, or to bear down any of the petty states that were in subjection to it. But yet he designed that by *the keeping of this covenant it might stand,* and continue a kingdom. Hereby the pride and ambition of that haughty potentate would be gratified, who aimed to be *like the Most High* (Isa. 14:14), to have all about him subject to him. Now see here, 1. How sad a change sin made with the royal family of Judah. Time was when all the nations about were tributaries to that; now that has not only lost its dominion over other nations, but has itself become a tributary. *How has the gold become dim!* Nations by sin sell their liberty, and princes their dignity, and *profane their crowns by casting them to the ground.* 2. How wisely Zedekiah did for himself in accepting these terms, though they were dishonourable, when necessity brought him to it. A man may live very comfortably and contentedly, though he cannot bear a part, and make a figure, as formerly. A kingdom may stand firmly and safely, though it do not stand so high as it has sometimes done; and so may a family.

III. Zedekiah, while he continued faithful to the king of Babylon, did very well, and, if he would but have reformed his kingdom, and returned to God and his duty, he would have done better, and by that means might soon have recovered his former dignity, *v.* 6. This plant grew, and though it was *set as a willow-tree,* and little account was made of it, yet it became *a spreading vine of low stature,* a great blessing to his own country, and his fruits *made glad their hearts;* and it is better to be a spreading vine of low stature than a lofty cedar of no use. Nebuchadnezzar was pleased, for *the branches turned towards him,* and rested on him as the vine on the wall, and he had his share of the fruits of this vine; *the roots thereof* too were *under him,* and at his disposal. The Jews had reason to be pleased, for they sat under their own vine, which *brought forth branches, and shot forth sprigs,* and looked pleasant and promising. See how gradually the judgments of God came upon this provoking people, how God gave them respite and so gave them space to repent. He made *their kingdom base,* to try if that would humble them, before he made it no kingdom; yet left it easy for them, to try if that would win upon them to return to him, that the troubles threatened might be prevented.

IV. Zedekiah knew not when he was well off, but grew impatient of the disgrace of being a tributary to the king of Babylon, and, to get clear of it, entered into a private league with the king of Egypt. He had no reason to complain that the king of Babylon put any new hardships upon him or improved his advantages against him, that he oppressed or impoverished his country, for, as the prophet had said before (*v.* 6) to aggravate his treachery, he shows again (*v.* 8) what a fair way he was in to be considerable: *He was planted in a good soil by great waters;* his family was likely enough to be built up, and his exchequer to be filled, in a little time, so that, if he had dealt faithfully, he might have been *a goodly vine.* But there was *another great eagle* that he had an affection for, and put a confidence in, and that was the *king of Egypt, v.* 7. Those two great potentates, the kings of Babylon and Egypt, were but two great eagles, *birds of prey.* This great eagle of Egypt is said to have *great wings,* but not to be *long-winged* as the king of Babylon, because, though the kingdom of Egypt was strong, yet it was not of such a vast extent as that of Babylon was. The great eagle is said to have *many feathers,* much wealth and many soldiers, which he depended upon as a substantial defence, but which really were no more than so *may feathers.* Zedekiah, promising himself liberty, made himself a vassal to the king of Egypt, foolishly expecting ease by changing his master. Now *this vine* did secretly and under-hand *bend her roots towards* the king of Egypt, that great eagle, and after awhile did openly *shoot forth her branches towards him,* give him an intimation how much she coveted an alliance with him, *that he might water it by the furrows of her plantation,* whereas it was *planted by great waters,* and did not need any assistance from him. This is expounded, *v.* 15. Zedekiah rebelled against the king of Babylon in *sending his ambassadors into Egypt,* that they might *give him horses and much people,* to enable him to contend with the king of Babylon. See what a change sin had made with the people of God! God promised that they should be a numerous people, as the sand of the sea; yet now, if their king had occasion for *much people,* he must send to Egypt for them, they being for sin *diminished and brought low,* Ps. 107:39. See also the folly of fretful discontented spirits, that ruin themselves by striving to better themselves, whereas they might be easy and happy enough if they would but *make the best of that which is.*

V. God here threatens Zedekiah with the utter destruction of him and his kingdom, and, in displeasure against him, passes that doom upon him for his treacherous revolt from the king of Babylon. This is represented in the parable (*v.* 9, 19) by the *plucking up of this vine by the roots, the cutting off of the fruit,* and *the withering of the leaves,* the leaves *of her spring,* when they are in their greenness (Job 8:12), before they begin in autumn to wither of themselves. The project shall be blasted; it shall *utterly wither.* The affairs of this perfidious prince shall be ruined past retrieve; as a vine when the east wind blasts it, so that it shall be fit for nothing but the fire (as we had it in that parable, *ch.* 15:4), it shall wither even *in the furrows where it grew,* though they were ever so well watered. It shall be destroyed *without great power or many people to pluck it up;* for what need is there of raising the militia to pluck up a vine? Note, God can bring great things to pass without much ado. He needs not great power and many people to effect his purposes; a handful will serve if he pleases. He can without any difficulty ruin a sinful king and kingdom, and make no more of it than we do of rooting up a tree that cumbers the ground. In the explanation of the parable the sentence is very largely recorded: *Shall be prosper? v.* 15. Can he expect to do ill and fare well? Nay, shall he that does such wicked things *escape?* Shall he *break the covenant, and be delivered* from that vengeance which is the just punishment of his treachery? No; can he expect to do ill and not suffer ill? Let him hear his doom.

1. It is ratified by the oath of God (*v.* 16): *As I live, saith the Lord God, he shall die* for it. This intimates how highly God resented the crime, and how sure and severe the punishment of it would be. God *swears in his wrath,* as he did Ps. 95:11. Note, As God's promises are confirmed with an oath, for comfort to the saints, so are his threatenings, for terror to the wicked. As sure as God lives and is happy (I may add, and as long), so sure, so long, shall impenitent sinners die and be miserable.

2. It is justified by the heinousness of the crime he had been guilty of. (1.) He had been very ungrateful to his benefactor, who had *made him king,* and undertook to protect him, had made him a prince when he might as easily have made him a prisoner. Note, It is a sin against God to be unkind to our friends and to lift up the heel against those that have helped to raise us. (2.) He had been very false to him whom he had covenanted with. This is mostly insisted on: He *despised the oath.* When his conscience or friends reminded him of it he made a jest of it, put on a daring resolution, and *broke it, v.* 15, 16, 18, 19. He broke through it, and took a pride in making nothing of it, as a great tyrant in our own day, whose maxim (they say) it is, *That princes ought not to be slaves to their word any further than it is for their interest.* That which aggravated Zedekiah's perfidiousness was that the oath by which he had bound himself to the king of Babylon was, [1.] A solemn oath. An emphasis is laid upon this (*v.* 18): *When, lo, he had given his hand,* as a confederate with the king of Babylon, not only as his subject, but as his friend, the joining of hands being a token of the joining of hearts. [2.] As sacred oath. God says (*v.* 19): It is *my oath* that he has despised and *my covenant that he has broken.* In every solemn oath God is appealed to as a witness of the sincerity of him that swears, and invocated as a judge and revenger of his treachery if he now swear falsely or at any time hereafter break his oath. But the oath of allegiance to a prince is particularly called *the oath of God* (Eccl. 8:2), as if that had something in it more sacred than another oath; for princes are *ministers of God to us for good,* Rom. 13:4. Now Zedekiah's breaking this oath and covenant is the sin which God will *recompense upon his own head* (*v.* 19), the *trespass which he has trespassed against God,* for which God will *plead with him, v.* 20. Note, Perjury is a heinous sin and highly provoking to the God of heaven. It would not serve for an excuse, *First,* That he who took this oath was a king, a king of the house of David, whose liberty and dignity might surely set him above the obligation of oaths. No; though kings are gods to us, they are men to God, and not exempt from his law and judgment. The prince is doubtless as firmly bound before God to the people by his coronation-oath as the people are to the princes by the oath of allegiance. *Secondly,* Nor that this oath was sworn to the king of Babylon, a heathen prince, worse than a heretic, with whom the church of Rome says, *No faith is to be kept.* No; though Nebuchadnezzar was a worshipper of false gods, yet the true God will avenge this quarrel when one of his worshippers breaks his league with him; for truth is a debt due to all men; and, if the professors of the true religion deal perfidiously with those of a false religion, their profession will be so far from excusing, much less justifying them, that it aggravates their sin, and God will the more surely and severely punish it, because by it they give occasion to the enemies of the Lord to blaspheme; as that Mahometan prince, who, when the Christians broke their league with him, cried out, *O Jesus! are these thy Christians? Thirdly,* Nor would it justify him that the oath was extorted from him by a conqueror, for the covenant was made upon a valuable consideration. He held his life and crown upon this condition, that he should be faithful and bear true allegiance to the king of Babylon; and, if he enjoy the benefit of his bargain, it is very unjust if he do not observe the terms. Let him know then that, having *despised the oath,* and *broken the covenant,* he *shall not escape.* And if the contempt and violation of such an oath, such a covenant as this, would be so punished, of how much sorer punishment shall those be thought worthy who break covenant with God (when, *lo, they had given their hand* upon it that they would be faithful), who *tread under foot the blood* of that *covenant* as an unholy thing? Between the covenants there is no comparison.

3. It is particularized in divers instances, wherein the punishment is made to answer the sin. (1.) He had rebelled against the king of Babylon, and the king of Babylon should be his effectual conqueror. In the place where that king *dwells* whose *covenant he broke,* even *with him in the midst of Babylon he shall die, v.* 16. He thinks to get out of his hands, but he shall fall, more than before, into his hands. God himself will now take part with the king of Babylon against him: *I will spread my net upon him, v.* 20. God has a net for those who deal perfidiously and think to escape his righteous judgments, in which those shall be taken and held who would not be held by the bond of an oath and covenant. Zedekiah dreaded Babylon: "Thither I will bring him," says God, "and *plead with him there."* Men will justly be forced upon that calamity which they endeavour by sin to flee from. (2.) He had *relied upon the king of Egypt,* and the king of Egypt should be his ineffectual helper: *Pharaoh with his mighty army shall not make for him in the war* (*v.* 17), shall to him no service, nor give any check to the progress of the Chaldean forces; he shall not assist him in the *siege* by *casting up mounts and building forts,* nor in battle by *cutting off many person.* Note, Every creature is that to us which God makes it to be; and he commonly weakens and withers that *arm of flesh* which we trust in and stay ourselves upon. Now was again fulfilled what was spoken on a former similar occasion (Isa. 30:7), *The Egyptians shall help in vain.* They

did so; for though, upon the approach of the Egyptian army, the Chaldeans withdrew from the siege of Jerusalem, upon their retreat they returned to it again and took it. It should seem, the Egyptians were not hearty, had strength enough, but no good-will, to help Zedekiah. Note, Those who deal treacherously with those who put a confidence in them will justly be dealt treacherously with by those they put a confidence in. Yet the Egyptians were not the only states Zedekiah stayed himself upon; he had bands of his own to stand by him, but those bands, though we may suppose they were veteran troops and the best soldiers his kingdom afforded, shall become *fugitives,* shall quit their posts, and make the best of their way, and shall *fall by the sword* of the enemy, and the *remains of them shall be scattered, v.* 21. This was fulfilled *when the city was broken up and all the men of war fled,* Jer. 52:7. This *you shall now that I the Lord have spoken it.* Note, Sooner or later God's word will prove itself; and those who will not believe shall find by experience the reality and weight of it.

Verses 22–24

When the royal family of Judah was brought to desolation by the captivity of Jehoiachin and Zedekiah it might be asked, "What has now become of the covenant of royalty made with David, that *his children should sit upon his throne for evermore?* Do the *sure mercies of David* prove thus unsure?" To this it is sufficient for the silencing of the objectors to answer that the promise was conditional. If *they will keep my covenant,* then they shall continue, Ps. 132:12. But David's posterity broke the condition, and so forfeited the promise. But the unbelief of man shall not invalidate the promise of God. He will find out another *seed of David* in which it shall be accomplished; and that is promised in these verses.

I. The house of David shall again be magnified, and out of its ashes another phoenix shall arise. The metaphor of a tree, which was made us of in the threatening, is here presented in the promise, *v.* 22, 23. This promise had its accomplishment in part when Zerubbabel, a branch of the house of David, was raised up to head the Jews in their return out of captivity, and to rebuild the city and temple and re-establish their church and state; but it was to have its full accomplishment in the kingdom of the Messiah, who was a root out of a dry ground, and to whom God, according to promise, gave *the throne of his father David,* Lu. 1:32. 1. God himself undertakes the reviving and restoring of the house of David. Nebuchadnezzar was the *great eagle* that had attempted the re-establishing of the house of David in a dependence upon him, *v.* 5. But the attempt miscarried; his plantation withered and was plucked up. "Well," says God, "the next shall be of my planting: *I will also take of the highest branch of the high cedar and I will set it.*" Note, As men have their designs, God also has his designs; but his will prosper when theirs are blasted. Nebuchadnezzar prided himself in setting up kingdoms at his pleasure, Dan. 5:19. But those kingdoms soon had an end, whereas the *God of heaven sets up a kingdom that shall never be destroyed,* Dan. 2:44. 2. The house of David is revived in a *tender one cropped from the top of his young twigs.* Zerubbabel was so; that which was hopeful in him was but the *day of small things* (Zec. 4:10), yet before him *great mountains* were *made plain.* Our Lord Jesus was *the highest branch of the high cedar,* the furthest of all from *the root* (for soon after he appeared the *house of David* was all cut off and extinguished), but the nearest of all to heaven, for his kingdom was not of this world. He was *taken from the top of the young twigs,* for he is *the man, the branch, a tender* plant, and a *root out of a dry ground* (Isa. 53:2), but a *branch of righteousness, the planting of the Lord, that he may be glorified.* 3. This branch is planted *in a high mountain* (*v.* 22), in the *mountain of the height of Israel, v.* 23. Thither he brought Zerubbabel in triumph; there he raised up his son Jesus, sent him to gather the *lost sheep of the house of Israel* that were *scattered upon the mountains,* set him *his king* upon *his holy hill of Zion,* sent forth the gospel from *Mount Zion, the word of the Lord from Jerusalem;* there, in the *height of Israel,* a nation which all its neighbours had an eye upon as conspicuous and illustrious, was the Christian church first planted. The churches of Judea were the most primitive churches. The unbelieving Jews did what they could to prevent its being planted there; but who can pluck up what God will plant? 4. Thence it spreads far and wide. The Jewish state, though it began very low in Zerubbabel's time, was set as a tender branch, which might easily be plucked up, yet took root, spread strangely, and after some time became very considerable; those of other nations, *fowl of every wing,* put themselves under the protection of it. The Christian church was at first like a grain of mustard-seed, but became, like this tender branch, a great tree, its beginning small, but its latter end increasing to admiration. When the Gentiles flocked into the church then did the *fowl of every wing* (even the birds of prey, which those preyed upon, as the *wolf and the lamb* feeding together, Isa. 11:6) come and *dwell under the shadow of this goodly cedar.* See Dan. 4:21.

II. God himself will herein be glorified, *v.* 24. The setting up of the Messiah's kingdom in the world shall discover more clearly than ever to the children of men that *God is the King of all the earth,* Ps. 47:7. Never was there a more full conviction given of this truth, that all things are governed by an infinitely wise and mighty Providence, than that which was given by the exaltation of Christ and the establishment of his kingdom among men; for by that it appeared that God has all hearts in his hand, and the sovereign disposal of all affairs. *All the trees of the field shall know,* 1. That the tree which God will have to be *brought down,* and *dried up,* shall be so, though it be ever so high and stately, ever so green and flourishing. Neither honour nor wealth, neither external advancements nor internal endowments, will secure men from humbling withering providence. 2. That the tree which God will have to be exalted, and to flourish, shall so be, shall so do, though ever so low, and ever so dry. The house of Nebuchadnezzar, that now makes so great a figure, shall be extirpated, and the house of David, that now makes so mean a figure, shall become famous again; and the Jewish nation, that is now despicable, shall be considerable. The kingdom of Satan, that has borne so long, so large, a sway, shall be broken, and the kingdom of Christ, that was looked upon with contempt. shall be established. The Jews, who, in respect of church-privileges, had been high and green, shall be thrown out, and the Gentiles, who had been low and dry trees, shall be taken in their room, Isa. 54:1. All the enemies of Christ shall be abased and made his footstool, and his interests shall be confirmed and advanced: *I the Lord have spoken* (it is the decree, the declared decree, that Christ must be exalted, must be the headstone of the corner), and *I have done it,* that is, I will do it in due time, but it is as sure to be done as if it were done already. With men *saying and doing are two things,* but they are not so with God. What he has spoken we may be sure that he will do, nor shall one iota or tittle of his word fall to the ground, for *he is not a man, that he should lie, or the son of man, that he should repent* either of his threatenings or of his promises.

CHAPTER 18

Perhaps, in reading some of the foregoing chapters, we may have been tempted to think ourselves not much concerned in them (though they also were written for our learning); but this chapter, at first view, appears highly and nearly to concern us all, very highly, very nearly; for, without particular reference to Judah and Jerusalem, it lays down the rule of judgment according to which God will deal with the children of men in determining them to their everlasting state, and it agrees with that very ancient rule laid down, Gen. 4:7, "If though doest well, shalt thou not be accepted?" But, "if not, sin," the punishment of sin,"lies at the door." Here is, I. The corrupt proverb used by the profane Jews, which gave occasion to the message here sent them, and made it necessary for the justifying of God in his dealings with them (*v.* 1–3). II. The reply given to this proverb, in which God asserts in general his own sovereignty and justice (*v.* 4). Woe to the wicked; it shall be ill with them (*v.* 4, 20). But say to the righteous, It shall be ill with them (*v.* 4, 20). But say to the righteous, It shall be well with them (*v.* 5–9). In particular, as to the case complained of, he assures us, 1. That it shall be ill with a wicked man, though he had a good father (*v.* 10–13). 2. That it shall be well with a good man, though he had a wicked father (*v.* 14–18). And therefore in this God is righteous (*v.* 19, 20). 3. That it shall be well with penitents, though they began ever so ill (*v.* 21–23 and 27, 28). 4. That it shall be ill with apostates, though they began ever so well (*v.* 24, 26). And the use of all this is, (1.) To justify God and clear the equity of all his proceedings (*v.* 25, 29). (2.) To engage and encourage us to repent of our sins and turn to God (*v.* 30–32). And these are things which belong to our everlasting peace. O that we may understand and regard them before they be hidden from our eyes!

Verses 1–9

Evil manners, we say, beget good laws; and in like manner sometimes unjust reflections occasion just vindications; evil proverbs beget good prophecies. Here is,

I. An evil proverb commonly used by the Jews in their captivity. We had one before (*ch.* 12:22) and a reply to it; here we have another. *That* sets God's justice at defiance: "*The days are prolonged and every vision fails;* the threatenings are a jest." *This* charges him with injustice, as if the judgments executed were a wrong: "You use this proverb *concerning the land of Israel,* now that it is laid waste by the judgments of God, saying, *The fathers have eaten sour grapes and the children's teeth are set on edge;* we are punished for the sins of our ancestors, which is as great an absurdity in the divine regimen as if the children should have their teeth set on edge, or stupefied, by the fathers' eating sour grapes, whereas, in the order of natural causes, if men eat or drink any thing amiss, they only themselves shall suffer by it." Now, 1. It must be owned that there was some occasion given for this proverb. God had often said that he would *visit the iniquity of the fathers upon the children,* especially the sin of idolatry, intending thereby to express the evil of sin, of that sin, his detestation of it, and just indignation against it, and the heavy punishments he would bring upon idolaters, that parents might be restrained from sin by their affection to their children and that children might not be drawn to sin by their reverence for their parents. He had likewise often declared by his prophets that in bringing the present ruin upon Judah and Jerusalem he had an eye to the sins of Manasseh and other preceding kings; for, looking upon the nation as a body politic, and punishing them with national judgments for national sins, and admitting the maxim in our law that *a corporation never dies,* reckoning with them now for the iniquities of former ages was but like making a man, *when he is old,* to *possess the iniquities of his youth,* Job 13:26. And there is no unrighteousness with God in doing so. But, 2. They intended it as a reflection upon God, and an impeachment of his equity in his proceedings against them. Thus far that is right which is implied in this proverbial saying, That those who are guilty of wilful sin *eat sour grapes;* they do that which they will feel from, sooner or later. The grapes may look well enough in the temptation, but they will be bitter as bitterness itself in the reflection. They will set the sinner's teeth on edge. When conscience is awake, and sets the sin in order before them, it will spoil the relish of their comforts as when the teeth are set on edge. But they suggest it as unreasonable that the children should smart for the fathers' folly and feel the pain of that which they never tasted the pleasure of, and that God was unrighteous in thus taking vengeance and could not justify it. See how wicked the reflection is, how daring the impudence; yet see how witty it is, and how sly the comparison. Many that are impious in their jeers are ingenious in their jests; and thus the malice of hell against God and religion is insinuated and propagated. It is here put into a proverb, and that proverb used, commonly used; they had it up ever and anon. And, though it had plainly a blasphemous meaning, yet they sheltered themselves under the similitude from the imputation of downright blasphemy. Now by this it appears that they were unhumbled under the rod, for, instead of condemning themselves and justifying God, they condemned him and justified themselves; but *woe to him that* thus *strives with his Maker.*

II. A just reproof of, and reply to, this proverb: *What mean you* by using it? That is the reproof. "Do you intend hereby to try it out with God? Or can you think any other than that you will hereby provoke him to be *angry with you will he has consumed you?* Is this the way to reconcile yourselves to him and make your peace with him?" The reply follows, in which God tells them,

1. That the use of the proverb should be taken away. This is said, it is sworn (*v.* 3): *You shall not have occasion any more to use this proverb;* or (as it may be read), *You shall not have the use of this parable.* The taking away of this parable is made the matter of a promise, Jer. 31:29. Here it is made the matter of a threatening. There it intimates that God will return to them in ways of mercy; here it intimates that God would proceed against them in ways of judgment. He will so punish them for this impudent saying that they shall not dare to use it any more; as in another case, Jer. 23:34, 36. God will find out effectual ways to silence those cavillers. Or God will so manifest both to themselves and others that they have wickedness of their own enough to bring all these desolating judgments upon them that they shall no longer for shame lay it upon the

sins of their fathers that they were thus dealt with: "Your own consciences shall tell you, and all your neighbours shall confirm it, that you yourselves have eaten the same sour grapes that your fathers ate before you, or else your teeth would not have been set on edge."

2. That really the saying itself was unjust and a causeless reflection upon God's government. For,

(1.) God does not punish the children for the fathers' sins unless they tread in their fathers' steps and *fill up the measure of their iniquity* (Mt. 23:32), and then they have no reason to complain, for, whatever they suffer, it is less than their own sin has deserved. And, when God speaks of *visiting the iniquity of the fathers upon the children,* that is so far from putting any hardship upon the children, to whom he only renders *according to their works,* that it accounts for God's patience with the parents, whom he therefore does not punish immediately, because he *lays up their iniquity for their children,* Job 21:19.

(2.) It is only in temporal calamities that children (and sometimes innocent ones) fare the worse for their parents' wickedness, and God can alter the property of those calamities, and make them work for good to those that are visited with them; but as to spiritual and eternal misery (and that is the death here spoken of) the children shall by no means smart for the parents' sins. This is here shown at large; and it is a wonderful piece of condescension that the great God is pleased to reason the case with such wicked and unreasonable men, that he did not immediately strike them dumb or dead, but vouchsafed to state the matter before them, that he may be clear when he is judged. Now, in his reply,

[1.] He asserts and maintains his own absolute and incontestable sovereignty: *Behold, all souls are mine, v.* 4. God here claims a property in all the souls of the children of men, one as well as another. *First,* Souls are his. He that is the Maker of *all things* is in a particular manner the *Father of spirits,* for his image is stamped on the souls of men; it was so in their creation; it is so in their renovation. He *forms the spirit of man within him,* and is therefore called the *God of the spirits of all flesh,* of embodied spirits. *Secondly,* All souls are his, all created by him and for him, and accountable to him. *As the soul of the father, so the soul of the son, is mine.* Our earthly parents are only the *fathers of our flesh;* our souls are not theirs; God challenges them. Now hence it follows, for the clearing of this matter, 1. That God may certainly do what he pleases both with fathers and children, and none may say unto him, *What doest thou?* He that gave us our being does us no wrong if he takes it away again, much less when he only takes away some of the supports and comforts of it; it is as absurd to quarrel with him as for *the thing formed to say to him that formed it, Why hast thou made me thus?* 2. That God as certainly bears a good-will both to father and son, and will put no hardship upon either. We are sure that God hates nothing that he has made, and therefore (speaking of the adult, who are capable of acting for themselves) he has such a kindness for all souls that none die but through their own default. *All souls are his,* and therefore he is not partial in his judgment of them. Let us subscribe to his interest in us and dominion over us. He says, *All souls are mine;* let us answer, "Lord, my soul is thine; I devote it to thee to be employed for thee and made happy in thee." It is with good reason that God says, *"My son, give me thy heart,* for it is my own," to which we must yield, *"Father, take my heart,* it is thy own."

[2.] Though God might justify himself by insisting upon his sovereignty, yet he waives that, and lays down the equitable and unexceptionable rule of judgment by which he will proceed as to particular persons; and it is this: — *First,* The sinner that persists in sin shall certainly die, his iniquity shall be his ruin: *The soul that sins shall die,* shall die as a soul can die, shall be excluded from the favour of God, which is the life and bliss of the soul, and shall lie for ever under his wrath, which is its death and misery. Sin is the act of the *soul,* the body being only the *instrument of unrighteousness;* it is called the *sin of the soul,* Mic. 6:7. And therefore the punishment of sin is the *tribulation and the anguish of the soul,* Rom. 2:9. *Secondly,* The righteous man that perseveres in his righteousness shall certainly live. *If a man be just,* have a good principle, a good spirit and disposition, and, as an evidence of that, *do judgment and justice (v.* 5), *he shall surely live,*

saith the Lord God, v. 9. He that makes conscience of conforming in every thing to the will of God, that makes it his business to serve God and his aim to glorify God, shall without fail be happy here and for ever in the love and favour of God; and, wherein he comes short of his duty, it shall be forgiven him, through a Mediator. Now here is part of the character of this just man. 1. He is careful to keep himself clean from the pollutions of sin, and at a distance from all the appearances of evil. (1.) From sins against the second commandment. In the matters of God's worship he is jealous, for he knows God is so. He has not only not sacrificed in the high places to the images there set up, but he has not so much as *eaten upon the mountains,* that is, not had any communion with idolaters by *eating things sacrificed to idols,* 1 Co. 10:20. He would not only not kneel with them at their altars, but not sit with them at their tables in their high places. He detests not only the idols of the heathen but *the idols of the house of Israel,* which were not only allowed of, but generally applauded and adored, by those that were accounted the professing people of God. He has not only not worshipped those idols, but he has not so much as *lifted up his eyes* to them; he has not given them a favourable look, has had no regard at all to them, neither desired their favour nor dreaded their frowns. He has observed so many bewitched by them that he has not dared so much as to look at them, lest he should be taken in the snare. The eyes of idolaters are said to *go a whoring,* Eze. 6:9. See Deu. 4:19. (2.) From sins against the seventh commandment. He is careful to possess his vessel in *sanctification and honour,* and not *in the lusts of uncleanness;* and therefore he has not dared to *defile his neighbour's wife,* nor said or done any thing which had the least tendency to corrupt or debauch her, no, nor will he make any undue approaches to his own wife when she is *put apart for her uncleanness,* for it was forbidden by the law, Lev. 18:19; 20:18. Note, It is an essential branch of wisdom and justice to keep the appetites of the body always in subjection to reason and virtue. (3.) From sins against the eighth commandment. He is a *just man,* who has not, by fraud and under colour of law and right, *oppressed any,* and who has not with force and arms *spoiled any by violence,* not spoiled them of their goods or estates, much less of their liberties and lives, *v.* 7. Oppression and violence were the sins of the old world, that brought the deluge, and are sins of which still God is and will be the avenger. Nay, he is one that has not lent his money *upon usury,* nor *taken increase (v.* 8), though, being done by contract, it may seem free from injustice *(Volenti non fit injuria — What is done to a person with his own consent is no injury to him),* yet, as far as it is forbidden by the law, he dares not do it. A moderate usury they were allowed to receive from strangers, but not from their brethren. A just man will not take advantage of his neighbour's necessity to make a prey of him, nor indulge himself in ease and idleness to live upon the sweat and toil of others, and therefore will not take increase from those who cannot make increase of what he lends them, nor be rigorous in exacting what was agreed for from those who by the act of God are disabled to pay it; but he is willing to share in loss as well as profit. *Qui sentit commodum, sentire debet et onus — He who enjoys the benefit should bear the burden.* 2. He makes conscience of doing the duties of his place. He has *restored the pledge* to the poor debtor, according to the law. Ex. 22:26. *"If thou take thy neighbour's raiment* for a pledge, the raiment that is for necessary use, thou shalt *deliver it* to him again, that he may sleep in his own bedclothes." Nay, he has not only restored to the poor that which was their own, but has *given his bread to the hungry.* Observe, It is called *his bread,* because it is honestly come by; that which is given to some is not unjustly taken from others; for God has said, *I hate robbery for burnt-offerings.* Worldly men insist upon it that their bread is *their own,* as Nabal, who therefore would not give of it to David (1 Sa. 25:11); yet let them know that it is not so their own but that they are bound to do good to others with it. Clothes are necessary as well as food, and therefore this just man is so charitable as *to cover the naked* also *with a garment, v.* 7. The coats which Dorcas had made for the poor were produced as witnesses of her charity, Acts 9:39. This just man has *withdrawn his hands from iniquity, v.* 8. If at any time he has been drawn in through inadvertency to that which afterwards has ap-

peared to him to be a wrong thing, he does not persist in it because he has begun it, but *withdraws his hand* from that which he now perceives to be *iniquity;* for he *executes true judgment between man and man,* according as his opportunity is of doing it (as a judge, as a witness, as a juryman, as a referee), and in all commerce is concerned that justice be done, that no man be wronged, that he who is wronged be righted, and that every man have his own, and is ready to interpose himself, and do any good office, in order hereunto. This is his character towards his neighbours; yet it will not suffice that he be just and true to his brother, to complete his character he must be so to his God likewise (v. 9): *He has walked in my statutes,* those which relate to the duties of his immediate worship; *he has kept* those and all his other *judgments,* has had respect to them all, has made it his constant care and endeavour to conform and come up to them all, to deal truly, that so he may approve himself faithful to his covenant with God, and, having joined himself to God, he does not treacherously *depart from him,* nor *dissemble with him.* This is a just man, and *living he shall live;* he shall certainly live, shall have life and shall have it more abundantly, shall live truly, live comfortably, live eternally. *Keep the commandments,* and thou shalt *enter into life,* Mt. 19:17.

Verses 10-20

God, by the prophet, having laid down the general rule of judgment, that he will render eternal life to those that *patiently continue in well-doing,* but indignation and wrath to those that do not *obey the truth,* but *obey unrighteousness* (Rom. 2:7, 8), comes, in these verses, to show that men's parentage and relation shall not alter the case either one way or other.

I. He applied it largely and particularly both ways. As it was in the royal line of the kings of Judah, so it often happens in private families, that godly parents have wicked children and wicked parents have godly children. Now here he shows,

1. That a wicked man shall certainly perish in his iniquity, though he be the son of a pious father. If that righteous man before described *beget a son* whose character is the reverse of his father's, his condition will certainly be so too. (1.) It is supposed as no uncommon case, but a very melancholy one, that the child of a very godly father, notwithstanding all the instructions given him, the good education he has had and the needful rebukes that have been given him, and the restraints he has been laid under, after all the pains taken with him and prayers put up for him, may yet prove notoriously wicked and vile, the grief of his father, the shame of his family, and the curse and plague of his generation. He is here supposed to allow himself in all those enormities which his good father dreaded and carefully avoided, and to shake off all those good duties which his father made conscience of and took satisfaction in; he undoes all that his father did, and goes counter to his example in every thing. He is here described to be a highwayman — *a robber and a shedder of blood.* He is an idolater: *He has eaten upon the mountains (v.* 11) and has *lifted up his eyes to the idols,* which his good father never did, and has come at length not only to feast with the idolaters, but to sacrifice with them, which is here called *committing abomination,* for the way of sin is downhill. He is an adulterer, has *defiled his neighbour's wife.* He is an oppressor even of *the poor and needy;* he robs the spital, and squeezes those who, he knows, cannot defend themselves, and takes a pride and pleasure in trampling upon the weak and impoverishing those that are poor already. He *takes away* from those to whom he should *give.* He has *spoiled by violence* and open force; he has *given forth upon usury,* and so spoiled by contract; and he *has not restored the pledge,* but unjustly detained it even when the debt was paid. Let those good parents that have wicked children not look upon their case as singular; it is a case put here; and by it we see that grace does not run in the blood, nor always attend the means of grace. The race is not always to the swift, nor the battle to the strong, for then the children that are well taught would do well, but God will let us know that his grace is his own and his Spirit a free-agent, and that though we are tied to give our children a good education he is not tied to bless it. In this, as much as any thing, appears the power of original sin and the necessity of special grace. (2.) We are here assured

that this wicked man shall perish for ever in his iniquity, notwithstanding his being the son of a good father. He may perhaps prosper awhile in the world, for the sake of the piety of his ancestors, but, having *committed all these abominations,* and never repented of them, *he shall not live,* he shall not be happy in the favour of God; though he may escape the sword of men, he shall not escape the curse of God. *He shall surely die;* he shall be for ever miserable; *his blood shall be upon him.* He may thank himself; he is his own destroyed. And his relation to a good father will be so far from standing him in stead that it will aggravate his sin and his condemnation. It made his sin the more heinous, nay, it made him really the more vile and profligate, and, consequently, will make his misery hereafter the more intolerable.

2. That a righteous man shall be certainly happy, though he be the son of a wicked father. Though the father did eat the sour grapes, if the children do not meddle with them, they shall fare never the worse for that. Here, (1.) It is supposed (and, blessed be God, it is sometimes a case in fact) that the son of an ungodly father may be godly, that, observing how fatal his father's errors were, he may be so wise as to *take warning,* and not tread in his father's tests, *v.* 14. Ordinarily, children partake of the parents' temper and are drawn in to imitate their example; but here the son, instead of *seeing his father's sins,* and, as is usual, doing the like, sees them and dreads doing the like. *Men* indeed do not *gather grapes of thorns,* but God sometimes does, takes a branch from a wild olive and grafts it into a good one. Wicked Ahaz begets a good Hezekiah, who *sees all his father's sins which he has done,* and though he will not, like Ham, proclaim his father's shame, or make the worst of it, yet he loathes it, and blushes at it, and thinks the worse of sin because it was the reproach and ruin of his own father. *He considers and does not such like;* he considers how ill it became his father to do such things, what an offence it was to God and all good men, what a wound and dishonour he got by it, and what calamities he brought into his family, and therefore he *does not such like.* Note, If we did but duly *consider the ways* of wicked men, we should all dread being associates with them and followers of them. The particulars are here again enumerated almost in the same words with that character given of the just man (*v.* 6, etc.), to show how good men *walk in the same spirit and in the same steps.* This just man here, when he took care to avoid his father's sins, took care to imitate his grandfather's virtues; and, if we look back, we shall find some examples for our imitation, as well as others for our admonition. This just man can not only say, as the Pharisee, *I am no adulterer, no extortioner,* no oppressor, no usurer, no idolater; but he has *given his bread to the hungry* and *covered the naked.* He has *taken off his hand from the poor;* where he found his father had put hardships upon poor servants, tenants, neighbours, he eased their burden. He did not say, "What my father has done I will abide by, and if it was a fault it was his and not mine;" as Rehoboam, who contemned the taxes his father had imposed. No; he *takes his hand off from the poor,* and restores them to their rights and liberties again, *v.* 15–17. Thus he has *executed God's judgments* and *walked in his statutes,* not only done his duty for once, but one on in a course and way of obedience. (2.) We are assured that the graceless father alone shall die in his iniquity, but his gracious son shall fare never the worse for it. As for his father (*v.* 18), because he was a cruel oppressor, and *did hurt,* nay, because, though he had wealth and power, he did not with them do good among his people, lo, *even he,* great as he is, *shall die in his iniquity,* and be undone for ever; but he that kept his integrity *shall surely live,* shall be easy and happy, and he shall *not die for the iniquity of his father.* Perhaps his father's wickedness has lessened his estate and weakened his interest, but it shall be no prejudice at all to his acceptance with God and his eternal welfare.

II. He appeals to themselves then whether they did not wrong God with their proverb. "Thus plain the case is, and *yet you say, Does not the son bear the iniquity of the father?* No, he does not; he shall not if he will himself *do that which is lawful and right,"* *v.* 19. But this people that bore the iniquity of their fathers had not done that which is lawful and right, and therefore justly suffered for their own sin and had no reason to complain of God's proceedings against them as at all unjust, though they had reason to complain of the bad example their fathers had left them as very unkind. *Our fathers have sinned and are not, and we have borne their iniquity,* Lam. 5:7. It is true that there is a curse entailed upon wicked families, but it is as true that the entail may be cut off by repentance and reformation; let the impenitent and unreformed therefore thank themselves if they fall under it. The settled rule of judgment is therefore repeated (*v.* 20): *The soul that sins shall die,* and not another for it. What direction God has given to earthly judges (Deu. 24:16) he will himself pursue: *The son shall not die,* not die eternally, *for the iniquity of the father,* if he do not tread in the steps of it, nor the father *for the iniquity of the son,* if he endeavour to do his duty for the preventing of it. In *the day of the revelation of the righteous judgment of God,* which is now clouded and eclipsed, *the righteousness of the righteous shall* appear before all the world to be *upon him,* to his everlasting comfort and honour, upon him as a robe, upon his as a crown; and *the wickedness of the wicked* shall be *upon him,* to his everlasting confusion, upon him as a chain, upon him as a load, as a mountain of lead to sink him to the bottomless pit.

Verses 21–29

We have here another rule of judgment which God will go by in dealing with us, by which is further demonstrated the equity of his government. The former showed that God will reward or punish according to the change made in the family or succession, for the better or for the worse; here he shows that he will reward or punish according to the change made in the person himself, whether for the better or the worse. While we are in this world we are in a state of probation; the time of trial lasts as long as the time of life, and according as we are found at last it will be with us to eternity. Now see here,

I. The case fairly stated, much as it had been before (*ch.* 3:18, etc.), and here it is laid down once (*v.* 21–24) and again (*v.* 26–28), because it is a matter of vast importance, a matter of life and death, of life and death eternal. Here we have,

1. A fair invitation given to wicked people, to turn from their wickedness. Assurance is here given us that, *if the wicked will turn,* he shall *surely live, v.* 21, 27. Observe,

(1.) What is required to denominate a man a true convert, how he must be qualified that he may be entitled to this act of indemnity. [1.] The first step towards conversion is consideration (*v.* 28): *Because he considers and turns.* The reason why sinners go on in their evil ways is because they do not consider what will be *in the end thereof;* but if the prodigal once *come to himself,* if he sit down and consider a little how bad his state is and how easily it may be bettered, he will soon *return to his father* (Lu. 15:17), and the adulteress *to her first husband* when she considers that *then it was better with her than now,* Hos. 2:7. [2.] This consideration must produce an aversion to sin. When he considers he must turn *away from his wickedness,* which denotes a change in the disposition of the heart; he must turn from *his sins and his transgression,* which denotes a change in the life; he must break off from all his evil courses, and, wherein he has done iniquity, must resolve to do so no more, and this from a principle of hatred to sin. *What have I to do any more with idols?* [3.] This aversion to sin must be universal; he must turn from *all* his sins and *all* his transgressions, without a reserve for any Delilah, any house of Rimmon. We do not rightly turn from sin unless we truly hate it, and we do not truly hate sin, as sin, if we do not hate all sin. [4.] This must be accompanied with a conversion to God and duty; he must *keep all God's statutes* (for the obedience, if it be sincere, will be universal) and must *do that which is lawful and right,* that which agrees with the word and will of God, which he must take for his rule, and not the will of the flesh and the way of the world.

(2.) What is promised to those that do thus turn from sin to God. [1.] They shall *save their souls alive, v.* 27. They shall *surely live, they shall not die, v.* 21. and again *v.* 28. Whereas it was said, *The soul that sins it shall die,* yet let not those that have sinned despair but that the threatened death may be prevented if they will but turn and repent in time. When David penitently acknowledges, *I have sinned,* he is immediately assured of his pardon: *"The Lord has taken away thy sin, thou shalt not die* (2 Sa. 12:13), thou shalt not die eternally." He shall *surely live;* he shall be restored to the favour of God, which is the life of the soul, and shall not lie under *his wrath,* which is as *messengers of death* to the soul. [2.] The sins they have repented of and forsaken shall not rise up in judgment against them, nor shall they be so much as upbraided with them: *All his transgressions that he has committed,* though numerous, though heinous, though very provoking to God, and redounding very much to his dishonour, yet *they shall not be mentioned unto him* (*v.* 22), not mentioned against them; not only they shall not be imputed to him to ruin him, but in the great day they shall not be remembered against him to grieve or shame him; they shall be covered, shall be sought for and not found. This intimates the fulness of pardoning mercy; when sin is forgiven it is *blotted out,* it is *remembered no more.* [3.] In *their righteousness they shall live;* not for their righteousness, as if that were the purchase of their pardon and bliss and an atonement for their sins, but in their righteousness, which qualifies them for all the blessings purchased by the Mediator, and is itself one of those blessings.

(3.) What encouragement a repenting returning sinner has to hope for pardon and life according to this promise. He is conscious to himself that his obedience for the future can never be a valuable compensation for his former disobedience; but he has this to support himself with, that God's nature, property, and delight, is to have mercy and to forgive, for he has said (*v.* 23): *"Have I any pleasure at all that the wicked should die?* No, by no means; you never had any cause given you to think so." It is true God has determined to punish sinners; his justice calls for their punishment, and, pursuant to that, impenitent sinners will lie for ever under his wrath and curse; that is the will of his decree, his consequent will, but it is not his antecedent will, the will of his delight. Though the righteousness of his government requires that sinners die, yet the goodness of his nature objects against it. *How shall I give thee up, Ephraim?* It is spoken here comparatively; he has not pleasure in the ruin of sinners, for he would rather they should *turn from their ways and live;* he is better pleased when his mercy is glorified in their salvation than when his justice is glorified in their damnation.

2. A fair warning given to righteous people not to turn from their righteousness, *v.* 24–26. Here is, (1.) The character of an apostate, that *turns away from his righteousness.* He never was in sincerity a righteous man (as appears by that of the apostle, 1 Jn. 2:19, *If they had been of us, they would, no doubt, have continued with us),* but he passed for a righteous man. He had the denomination and all the external marks of a righteous man; he thought himself one, and others thought him one. But he throws of his profession, leaves his first love, disowns and forsakes the truth and ways of God, and so *turns away from his righteousness* as one sick of it, and now shows, what he always had, a secret aversion to it; and, having *turned away from his righteousness,* he *commits iniquity,* grows loose, and profane, and sensual, intemperate, unjust, and, in short, *does according to all the abominations that the wicked man does;* for, when the unclean spirit recovers his possession of the heart, he *brings with him seven other spirits more wicked than himself and they enter in and dwell there,* Lu. 11:26. (2.) The doom of an apostate: *Shall he live* because he was once a *righteous man?* No; *factum non dicitur quod non perseverat — that which does not abide is not said to be done. In his trespass* (*v.* 24) and for his iniquity (that is the meritorious cause of his ruin), *for the iniquity that he has done, he shall die,* shall die eternally, *v.* 26. *The backslider in heart shall be filled with his own ways.* But will not his former professions and performances stand him in some stead — will they not avail at least to mitigate his punishment? No: *All his righteousness that he has done,* though ever so much applauded by men, *shall not be mentioned* so as to be either a credit or a comfort to him; the righteousness of an apostate is forgotten, as the wickedness of a penitent is. Under the law, if a Nazarite was polluted he lost all the foregoing days of his separation (Num. 6:12), so those that have *begun in the spirit and end in the flesh* may reckon all their past services and sufferings *in vain* (Gal. 3:3, 4); unless we persevere we *lose what we have gained,* 2 Jn. 8.

II. An appeal to the consciences even of the house of

Israel, though very corrupt, concerning God's equity in all these proceedings; for he will be justified, as well as sinners judged, out of their own mouths. 1. The charge they drew up against God is blasphemous, *v.* 25, 29. The *house of Israel* has the impudence to say, *The way of the Lord is not equal,* than which nothing could be more absurd as well as impious. *He that formed the eye, shall he not see?* Can his ways be unequal whose will is the eternal rule of good and evil, right and wrong? *Shall not the Judge of all the earth do right?* No doubt he shall; he cannot do otherwise. 2. God's reasonings with them are very gracious and condescending, for even these blasphemers God would rather have convinced and saved than condemned. One would have expected that God would immediately vindicate the honour of his justice by making those that impeached it eternal monuments of it. Must those be suffered to draw another breath that have once breathed out such wickedness as this? Shall that tongue ever speak again any where but in hell that has once said, *The ways of the Lord are not equal?* Yes, because this is the day of God's patience, he vouchsafes to argue with them; and he requires them to own, for it is so plain that they cannot deny, (1.) The equity of his ways: *Are not my ways equal?* No doubt they are. He never lays upon man more than is right. In the present punishments of sinners and the afflictions of his own people, yea, and in the eternal damnation of the impenitent, *the ways of the Lord are equal.* (2.) The iniquity of their ways: *"Are not your ways unequal?* It is plain that they are, and the troubles you are in you have brought upon your own heads. God does you no wrong, but you have wronged yourselves." *The foolishness of man perverts his way,* makes that unequal, and then *his heart frets against the Lord,* as if his ways were unequal, Prov. 19:3. In all our disputes with God, and in all his controversies with us, it will be found that his ways are equal, but ours are unequal, that he is in the right and we are in the wrong.

Verses 30–32

We have here the conclusion and application of this whole matter. After a fair trial at the bar of right reason the verdict is brought in on God's side; it appears that *his ways are equal.* Judgment therefore is next to be given; and one would think it should be a judgment of condemnation, nothing short of *Go, you cursed, into everlasting fire.* But, behold, a miracle of mercy; the day of grace and divine patience is yet lengthened out; and therefore, though God will at last judge *every one according to his ways,* yet he waits to be gracious, and closes all with a call to repentance and a promise of pardon upon repentance.

I. Here are four necessary duties that we are called to, all amounting to the same: — 1. We must repent; we must change our mind and change our ways; we must be sorry for what we have done amiss and ashamed of it, and go as far as we can towards the undoing of it again. 2. We must *turn ourselves from all our transgressions, v.* 30 and again *v.* 32. *Turn yourselves,* face about; turn from sin, nay, turn against it as the enemy you loathe, turn to God as the friend you love. 3. We must *cast away from us all our transgressions;* we must abandon and forsake them with a resolution never to return to them again, give sin a bill of divorce, break all the leagues we have made with it, throw it overboard, as the mariners did Jonah (for it has raised the storm), cast it out of the soul, and crucify it as a malefactor. 4. We must *make us a new heart and a new spirit.* This was the matter of a promise, *ch.* 11:19. Here it is the matter of a precept. We must do our endeavour, and then God will not be wanting to us to give us his grace. St. Austin well explains this precept. *Deus non jubet impossibilia, sed jubendo monet et facere quod possis et petere quod non possis — God does not enjoin impossibilities, but by his commands admonishes us to do what is in our power and to pray for what is not.*

II. Here are four good arguments used to enforce these calls to repentance: — 1. It is the only way, and it is a sure way, to prevent the ruin which our sins have a direct tendency to: *So iniquity shall not be your ruin,* which implies that, if we do not repent, iniquity will be our ruin, here and for ever, but that, if we do, we are safe, we are snatched as brands out of the burning. 2. If we repent not, we certainly perish, and our blood will be upon our own heads. *Why will you die, O house of Israel?* What an absurd thing it is for you to choose death and damnation rather than life and salvation. Note, The reason why sinners die is because they *will die;* they will go down the way that leads to death, and not come up to the terms on which life is offered. Herein sinners, especially sinners of the house of Israel, are most unreasonable and act most unaccountably. 3. The God of heaven has no delight in our ruin, but desires our welfare (*v.* 32): *I have no pleasure in the death of him that dies,* which implies that he has pleasure in the recovery of those that repent; and this is both an engagement and an encouragement to us to repent. 4. We are made for ever if we repent: *Turn yourselves, and live.* He that says to us, *Repent,* thereby says to us, *Live,* yea, he says to us, *Live;* so that life and death are here set before us.

CHAPTER 19

The scope of this chapter is much the same with that of the 17th, to foretel and lament the ruin of the house of David, the royal family of Judah, in the calamitous exit of the four sons and grandsons of Josiah — Jehoahaz, Jehoiakim, Jeconiah, and Zedekiah, in whom that illustrious line of kings was cut off, which the prophet is here ordered to lament (*v.* 1). And he does it by similitudes. I. The kingdom of Judah and house of David are here compared to a lioness, and those princes to lions, that were fierce and ravenous, but were hunted down and taken in nets (*v.* 2–9). II. That kingdom and that house are here compared to a vine, and these princes to branches, which had been strong and flourishing, but were now broken off and burnt (*v.* 10–14). This ruin of that monarchy was now in the doing, and this lamentation of it was intended to affect the people with it, that they might not flatter themselves with vain hopes of the lengthening out of their tranquility.

Verses 1–9

Here are, I. Orders given to the prophet to bewail the fall of the royal family, which had long made so great a figure by virtue of a covenant of royalty made with David and his seed, so that the eclipsing and extinguishing of it are justly lamented by all who know what value to put upon the *covenant of our God,* as we find, after a very large account of that covenant with David (Ps. 89:3, 20, etc.), a sad lamentation for the decays and desolations of his family (*v.* 38, 39): *But thou hast cast off and abhorred, hast made void the covenant of thy servant and profaned his crown,* etc. The kings of Judah are here called *princes of Israel;* for their glory was diminished and they had become but as princes, and their purity was lost; they had become corrupt and idolatrous as the *kings of Israel,* whose ways they had learned. The prophet must *take up a lamentation* for them; that is, he must describe their lamentable fall as one that did himself lay it to heart, and desired that those he preached and wrote to might do so to. And how can we expect that others should be affected with that which we ourselves are not affected with? Ministers, when they boldly foretel, must yet bitterly lament the destruction of sinners, as those that have not *desired the woeful day.* He is not directed to give advice to the princes of Israel (that had been long and often done in vain), but, the decree having gone forth, he must *take up a lamentation* for them.

II. Instructions given him what to say. 1. He must compare the kingdom of Judah to a *lioness,* so wretchedly degenerated was it from what it had been formerly, when it sat as a queen among the nations, *v.* 2. *What is thy mother?* thine, O king? (we read of Solomon's crown wherewith his mother crowned him, that is, his people, Cant. 3:11), thine, O Judah? The royal family is as a mother to the kingdom, a nursing mother. She is a *lioness,* fierce, and cruel, and ravenous. When they had left their divinity they soon lost their humanity too; and, when they *feared not God,* neither did they *regard man.* She *lay down among lions.* God had said, *The people* shall dwell alone, but they *mingled with the nations* and *learned their works.* She *nourished her whelps among young lions,* taught the young princes the way of tyrants, which was then used by the arbitrary kings of the east, filled their heads betimes with notions of their absolute despotic power, and possessed them with a belief that they had a right to enslave their subjects, that their liberty and property lay at their mercy: thus *she nourished her whelps among young lions.* 2. He must compare the kings of Judah to *lions' whelps, v.* 3. Jacob had compared Judah, and especially the house of David, to a *lion's whelp,* for its being strong and formidable to its enemies abroad (Gen. 49:9, *He is an old lion; who shall stir him up?)* and, if they had adhered to the divine law and promise, God would have preserved to them the might, and majesty, and dominion of a lion, and does it in Christ, the *Lion of the tribe of Judah.* But these *lions' whelps* were so to their own subjects, were cruel and oppressive to them, preyed upon their estates and liberties; and, when they thus by their tyranny made themselves a terror to those whom they ought to have protected, it was just with God to make those a terror to them whom otherwise they might have subdued. Here is lamented, (1.) The sin and fall of Jehoahaz, one of the whelps of this lioness. He *became a young lion* (*v.* 3); he was made king, and thought he was made so that he might do what he pleased, and gratify his own ambition, covetousness, and revenge, as he had a mind; and so he was soon master of all the arts of tyranny; he *learned to catch the prey and devoured men.* When he got power into his hand, all that had before in any thing disobliged him were made to feel his resentments and become a sacrifice to his rage. But what came of it? He did not prosper long in his tyranny: *The nations heard of him* (*v.* 4), heard how furiously he drove at his first coming to the crown, how he trampled upon all that is just and sacred, and violated all his engagements, so that they looked upon him as a dangerous neighbour, and prosecuted him accordingly, *as a multitude of shepherds is called forth against a lion roaring on his prey,* Isa. 31:4. And *he was taken,* as a beast of prey, *in their pit.* His own subjects durst not stand up in defence of their liberties, but God raised up a foreign power that soon put an end to his tyranny, and *brought him in chains to the land of Egypt.* Thither Jehoahaz was carried captive, and never heard of more. (2.) The like sin and fall of his successor Jehoiakim. The *kingdom of Judah* for some time expected the return of Jehoahaz out of Egypt, but at length despaired of it, and then *took another* of the *lion's* whelps, and *made him a young lion, v.* 5. And he, instead of taking warning by his brother's fate to use his power with equity and moderation, and to seek the good of his people, trod in his brother's steps: *He went up and down among the lions, v.* 6. He consulted and conversed with those that were fierce and furious like himself, and took his measures from them, as Rehoboam took the advice of the rash and not-headed young men. And he soon learned to *catch the prey,* and he *devoured men* (*v.* 6); he seized his subjects' estates, fined and imprisoned them, filled his treasury by rapine and injustice, sequestrations and confiscations, fines and forfeitures, and swallowed up all that stood in his way. He had got the art of discovering what effects men had that lay concealed, and where the treasures were which they had hoarded up; he *knew their desolate places* (*v.* 7), where they his *their money* and sometimes hid *themselves;* he knew where to find both out; and by his oppression he *laid waste their cities,* depopulated them by forcing the inhabitants to remove their families to some place of safety. *The land was desolate,* and the country villages were deserted; and though there was great plenty, and a fulness of all good things, yet people quitted it all for fear of *the noise of his roaring.* He took a pride in making all his subjects afraid of him, as the lion makes all the beasts of the forest to tremble (Amos 3:8), and by his terrible roaring so astonished them that they fell down for fear, and, having not spirit to make their escape, became an easy prey to him, as they say the lions do. He hectored, and threatened, and talked big, and bullied people out of what they had. Thus he thought to establish his own power, but it had a contrary effect, it did but hasten his own ruin (*v.* 8): *The nations set against him on every side,* to restrain and reduce his exorbitant power, which they joined in confederacy to do for their common safety; and *they spread their net over him,* formed designs against him. God brought against Jehoiakim bands of the Syrians, Moabites, and Ammonites, with the Chaldees (2 Ki. 24:2), and he was *taken in their pit. Nebuchadnezzar bound him in fetters to carry him to Babylon,* 2 Chr. 36:6. They put this lion within grates, bound him *in chains,* and *brought him to the king of Babylon, v.* 9. What became of him we know not; but *his voice was nowhere heard* roaring *upon the mountains of Israel.* There was an end of his tyranny: he was *buried with the burial of an ass* (Jer. 22:19), though he had been as a lion, *the terror of the mighty in the land of the living.* Note, The righteousness of God is to be acknowledged when those who have terrified and enslaved others are themselves terrified and enslaved, when those who by the abuse of their power to destruction which was given them for edification make themselves as wild beasts, as *roaring lions and ranging bears* (for such, Solomon says, *wicked rulers* are *over the poor people*, Prov. 28:15), are treated as such — when those who, like Ishmael, have their *hand against every man*, come at last to have *every man's hand against them.* It was long since observed that bloody tyrants seldom die in peace, but have blood given them to drink, for they are worthy.

> Ad generum Cereris sine caede et sanguine pauci
> Descendunt reges et sicca morte tyranni —
> How few of all the boastful men that reign
> Descend in peace to Pluto's dark domain!
>   — Juvenal

Verses 10–14

Jerusalem, the mother-city, is here represented by another similitude; she is a vine, and the princes are her branches. This comparison we had before, *ch.* 15:1. Jerusalem is as *a vine;* the Jewish nation is so: *Like a vine in they blood* (*v.* 10), the blood-royal, like a vine set in blood and watered with blood, which contributes very much to the flourishing and fruitfulness of vines, as if the blood which had been shed had been designed for the fattening and improving of the soil, in such plenty was it shed; and for a time it seemed to have that effect, for she was *fruitful and full of branches* by reason of the waters, the *many waters* near which she was *planted.* Places of great wickedness may prosper for a while; and a vine set in blood may be full of branches. Jerusalem was full of able magistrates, men of sense, men of learning and experience, that were *strong rods,* branches of this vine of uncommon bulk and strength, or poles for the support of this vine, for such magistrates are. The boughs of this vine had grown to such maturity that they were fit to make white staves of for the *sceptres of those that bore rule, v.* 11. And those are *strong rods* that are fit for *sceptres,* men of strong judgments and strong resolutions that are fit for magistrates. When the royal family of Judah was numerous, and the courts of justice were filled with men of sense and probity, then *Jerusalem's stature was exalted among thick branches;* when the government is in good able hands a nation is thereby made considerable Then she was not taken for a weak and lowly vine, but *she appeared in her height,* a distinguished city, *with the multitude of her branches. Tanquam lenta solent inter viburna cupressi — Midst humble withies thus the cypress soars. "In thy quietness"* (so some read that, *v.* 10, which we translate *in thy blood)* "thou wast such a vine as this." When Zedekiah was quiet and easy under the king of Babylon's yoke his kingdom flourished thus. See how slow God is to anger, how he defers his judgments, and waits to be gracious. 2. This vine is now quite destroyed. Nebuchadnezzar, being highly provoked by Zedekiah's treachery, *plucked it up in fury* (*v.* 12), ruined the city and kingdom, and cut off all the branches of the royal family that fell in his way. The vine was *cut off close to the ground,* though not plucked up by the roots. The *east wind dried up the fruit* that was blasted. The young people fell by the sword, or were carried into captivity. The aspect of it had nothing that was pleasing, the prospect nothing that was promising. Her *strong rods were broken and withered;* her great men were cut off, judges and magistrates deposed. *The vine itself is planted in the wilderness, v.* 13. Babylon was as a wilderness to those of the people that were carried captives thither; the land of Judah was as a wilderness to Jerusalem, now that the whole country was ravaged and laid waste by the Chaldean army — a *fruitful land turned into barrenness.* "It is *burnt with fire* (Ps. 80:16) and that fire has *gone out of a rod of her branches* (*v.* 14); the king himself, by rebelling against the king of Babylon, has given occasion to all this mischief. She may thank herself for the fire that consumes her; she has by her wickedness made herself like tinder to the sparks of God's wrath, so that her own branches serve as fuel for her own consumption; in them the fire is kindled which *devoured the fruit,* the sins of the elder being the judgments which destroy the younger; her *fruit* is burned with her own branches, so that she *has no strong rod to be a sceptre to rule,* none to be found now that are fit for the government or dare take *this ruin under their hand,* as the complaint is (Isa. 3:6, 7), none of the house of David left that have a right to rule, no wise men, or men of sense, that are able to rule." It goes ill with any state, and is like-

ly to go worse, when it is thus deprived of the blessings of government and has *no strong rods for sceptres. Woe unto thee, O land! when thy king is a child,* for it is as well to have no rod as not a strong rod. Those strong rods, we have reason to fear, had been instruments of oppression, assistant to the king in *catching the prey and devouring men,* and now they are destroyed with him. Tyranny is the inlet to anarchy; and, when the rod of government is turned into the serpent of oppression, it is just with God to say, "There shall be no strong rod to be a sceptre to rule; but let men be as *are the fishes of the sea,* where the greater devour the less." Note, *This is a lamentation and shall be for a lamentation.* The prophet was bidden (*v.* 1) *to take up a lamentation;* and, having done so, he leaves it to be made use of by others. *"It is a lamentation* to us of this age, and, the desolations continuing long, it *shall be for a lamentation* to those that shall come after us; the child unborn will rue the destruction made of Judah and Jerusalem by the present judgments. They were a great while in coming; the bow was long in the drawing; but now that they have come they will continue, and the sad effects of them will be entailed upon posterity." Note, Those who fill up the measure of their fathers' sins are laying up in store for their children's sorrows and furnishing them with matter for lamentation; and nothing is more so than the overthrow of government.

CHAPTER 20

In this chapter, I. The prophet is consulted by some of the elders of Israel (*v.* 1). II. He is instructed by his God what answer to give them. He must, 1. Signify God's displeasure against them (*v.* 2, 3). And, 2. He must show them what just cause he had for that displeasure, by giving them a history of God's grateful dealings with their fathers and their treacherous dealings with God. (1.) In Egypt (*v.* 5–9). (2.) In the wilderness (*v.* 10–26). (3.) In Canaan (*v.* 27–32). 3. He must denounce the judgments of God against them (*v.* 33–36). 4. He must tell them likewise what mercy God had in store for them, when he would bring a remnant of them to repentance, re-establish them in their own land, and set up his sanctuary among them again (*v.* 37–44). 5. Here is another word dropped towards Jerusalem, which is explained and enlarged upon in the next chapter (*v.* 45–49).

Verses 1–4

Here is, 1. The occasion of the message which we have in this chapter. That sermon which we had *ch.* 18 was occasioned by their presumptuous reflections upon God; this was occasioned by their hypocritical enquiries after him. Each shall have his own. This prophecy is exactly dated, in the *seventh year of the* captivity, about two years after Ezekiel began to prophesy. God would have them to keep account how long their captivity lasted, that they might see how the years went on towards their deliverance, though very slowly. *Certain of the elders of Israel came to enquire of the Lord,* not statedly (as those *ch.* 8:1), but, as it should seem, occasionally, and upon a particular emergency. Whether they were of those that were now in captivity, or elders lately come from Jerusalem upon business to Babylon, is not certain; but, by what the prophet says to them (*v.* 32), it should seem, their enquiry was whether now that they were captives in Babylon, at a distance from their own country, where they had not only no temple, but no synagogue, for the worship of God, it was not lawful for them, that they might ingratiate themselves with their lords and masters, to join with them in their worship and do *as the families of these countries* do, that *serve wood and stone.* This matter was palliated as well as it would bear, like Naaman's pleading with Elisha for leave to bow in the house of Rimmon, in compliment to the king; but we have reason to suspect that their enquiry drove at this. Note, Those hearts are wretchedly hardened which ask God leave to go on in sin, and that when they are suffering for it. They came and *sat* very demurely and with a show of devotion *before the prophet, ch.* 33:31. 2. The purport of this message. (1.) They must be made to know that *God is angry with them;* he takes it as an affront that they come to enquire of him when they are resolved to go on still in their trespasses: *As I live, saith the Lord God, I will not be enquired of by you, v.* 3. Their shows of devotion shall be neither acceptable to God nor advantageous to themselves. God will not take notice of their enquiries, nor give them any satisfactory answers. Note, A hypocritical attendance on God and his ordinances is so far from being pleasing to him that it is provoking. (2.) They must be made to know that God is justly angry with them (*v.* 4): "*Wilt thou judge them, son of man, wilt*

thou judge them? Thou art a prophet, surely thou wilt not *plead for them,* as an intercessor with God; but surely thou wilt *pass sentence* on them as a judge for God. *See, I have set thee over the nation;* wilt thou not declare to them the judgments of the Lord? Cause them therefore *to know the abominations of their fathers.*" So the orders run now, as before (*ch.* 16:2) he must cause them to *know their own abominations.* Though their own abominations were sufficient to justify God in the severest of his proceedings against them, yet it would be of use for them to know the *abominations of their fathers,* that they might see what a righteous thing it was with God now at last to cut them off from being a people, who from the first were such a provoking people.

Verses 5–9

The history of the ingratitude and rebellion of the people of Israel here begins as early as their beginning; so does the history of man's apostasy from his Maker. No sooner have we read the story of our first parents' creation than we immediately meet with that of their rebellion; so we see here it was with Israel, a people designed to represent the body of mankind both in their dealings with God and in his with them. Here is,

I. The gracious purposes of God's law concerning Israel in Egypt, where they were bond-slaves to Pharaoh. Be it spoken, be it written, to the immortal honour of free grace, that then and there, 1. He chose Israel to be a peculiar people to himself, though their condition was bad and their character worse, that he might have the honour of mending both. He *therefore* chose them, because they were *the seed of the house of Jacob,* the posterity of that prince with God, *that he might keep the oath which he had sworn unto their fathers,* Deu. 7:7, 8. 2. He *made himself known to them* by his name Jehovah (a new name, Ex. 6:3), when by reason of their servitude they had almost lost the knowledge of that name by which he was known to their fathers, *God Almighty.* Note, As the foundation of our blessedness is laid in God's choosing us, so the first step towards it is God's making himself known to us. And whatever distance we are at, whatever distress we are in, he that made himself known to Israel even in the land of Egypt can find us out, and follow us with the gracious discoveries and manifestations of his favour. 3. He made over himself to them as their God in covenant: *I lifted up my hand unto them,* saying it, and confirming it with an oath. *"I am the Lord your God,* to whom you are to pay your homage, and from whom and in whom you are to expect your bliss." 4. He promised to bring them out of Egypt; and made good what he promised. He *lifted up his hand,* that is, he swore unto them, that he would deliver them; and, they being very unworthy, and their deliverance very unlikely, it was requisite that the promise of it should be *confirmed by an oath.* Or, He *lifted up his hand,* that is, he put forth his almighty power to do it; he did it with an *outstretched arm,* Ps. 136:12. 5. He assured them that he would put them in possession of the land of Canaan. He *therefore* brought them out of Egypt, that *he might bring them into a land that he had spied* out *for them,* a second garden of Eden, which was *the glory of all lands.* So he found it, the climate being temperate, the soil fruitful, the situation pleasant, and every thing agreeable (Deu. 8:7; 11:12); or, however this might be, so he made it, by setting up his sanctuary in it.

II. The reasonable commands he gave them, and the easy conditions of his covenant with them at that time. Having told them what they might expect from him, he next tells them what was all he expected from them; it was no more than this (*v.* 7): *"Cast you away every man* his images that he uses for worship, that are the adorations, but should be the *abominations, of his eyes.* Let him abominate them, and put them out of his sight, and *defile not yourselves with the idols of Egypt.*" Of these, it seems, many of them were fond; the golden calf was one of them. It was just, and what might reasonably be expected, that, being delivered from the Egyptian slavery, they should quit the Egyptian idolatry, especially when God, at bringing them out, *executed judgment upon the gods of Egypt* (Num. 33:4) and thereby showed himself above them. And, whatever other idols they might have an inclination to, one would think they should have had a rooted aversion to the gods of Egypt for Egypt's sake, which had been to them a house of bondage. Yet, it seems, they needed this caution, and it is backed with a good reason: *I am the Lord your God,* who neither need an assistant nor will admit a rival.

III. Their unreasonable disobedience to these commands, for which God might justly have cut them off as soon as ever they were formed into a people (*v.* 8): *They rebelled against God,* not only refused to comply with his particular precepts, but shook off their allegiance, and in effect told him that they should be at liberty to worship what God they pleased. And even then when God came down to deliver them, and sent Moses for that purpose, yet they would not *forsake the idols of Egypt,* which perhaps made them speak so affectionately of the *onions of Egypt* (Num. 11:5), for among other things the Egyptians worshipped an onion. It was strange that all the plagues of Egypt would not prevail to cure them of their affection to the *idols of Egypt.* For this God said he would *pour out his fury upon them,* even while they were yet *in the midst of the land of Egypt.* Justly might he have said, "Let them die with the Egyptians." This magnifies the riches of God's goodness, that he was pleased to work so great a salvation for them even when he saw them ripe for ruin. Well might Moses tell them, It is *not for your righteousness,* Duet. 9:4, 5.

IV. The wonderful deliverance which God wrought for them, notwithstanding. Though they forfeited the favour while it was in the bestowing, and when God *would have healed them* then their *iniquity was discovered* (Hos. 7:1), yet *mercy rejoiced against judgment,* and God did what he designed purely *for his own name's sake, v.* 9. When nothing in us will furnish him with a reason for his favours he furnishes himself with one. God *made himself known* to them *in the sight of the heathen* when he ordered Moses publicly to say to Pharaoh, Israel is *my son, my first-born,* let them go, *that they may serve me.* Now, if he had left them to perish for their wickedness as they deserved, the Egyptians would have reflected upon him for it, and his name would have been polluted, which ought to be sanctified and shall be so. Note, The church is secured, even when it is corrupt, because God will secure his own honour.

Verses 10–26

The history of the struggle between the sins of Israel, by which they endeavoured to ruin themselves, and the mercies of God, by which he endeavoured to save them and make them happy, is here continued: and the instances of that struggle in these verses have reference to what passed between God and them in the wilderness, in which God honoured himself and they shamed themselves. The story of Israel in the wilderness is referred to in the New Testament (1 Co. 10 and Heb. 3), as well as often in the Old, for warning to us Christians; and therefore we are particularly concerned in these verses. Observe,

I. The great things God did for them, which he puts them in mind of, not as grudging them his favours, but to show how ungrateful they had been. And we say, If you call a man ungrateful, you can call him no worse. It was a great favour, 1. That God *brought them forth out of Egypt* (*v.* 10), though, as it follows, he *brought them into the wilderness* and not into Canaan immediately. It is better to be at liberty in a wilderness than bond-slaves in a land of plenty, to enjoy God and ourselves in solitude than to lose both in a crowd; yet there were many of them who had such base servile spirits as not to understand this, but, when they met with the difficulties of a desert, wished themselves in Egypt again. 2. That he gave them the law upon Mount Sinai (*v.* 11), not only instructed them concerning good and evil, but by his authority bound them from the evil and to the good. He *gave them his statutes,* and a valuable gift it was. *Moses commanded them a law that was the inheritance of the congregation of Israel,* Deu. 33:4. God *made them to know his judgments,* not only enacted laws for them, but showed them the reasonableness and equity of those laws, with what judgment they were formed. The laws he gave them they were encouraged to observe and obey; for, *if a man do them, he shall even live in them;* in keeping God's commandments there is abundance of comfort and a great reward. Christ says, *If thou wilt into enter life,* and enjoy it, *keep the commandments.* Though those who are the most strict in their obedience are thus far unprofitable servants that they do no more than is their duty to do, yet it is thus richly recompensed: *This do, and thou shalt live.* The Chaldee says, *He shall live an eternal life in them.* St. Paul quotes this (Gal. 3:12) to show that *the law is not of faith,* but proposes life upon condition of perfect obedience, which we are not capable of rendering, and therefore must have recourse to the grace of the gospel, without which we are all undone. 3. That he revived the ancient institution of the sabbath day, which was lost and forgotten while they were bond-slaves in Egypt; for their task-masters there would by no means allow them to rest one day in seven. In the wilderness indeed every day was a day of rest; for what need had those to labour who lived upon manna, and whose raiment waxed not old? But one day in seven must be a holy rest (*v.* 12): *I gave them my sabbaths to be a sign between me and them* (the institution of the sabbath was a sign of God's good-will to them, and their observance of it a sign of their regard to him), *that they might know that I am the Lord that sanctify them.* By this God made it to appear that he had distinguished them from the rest of the world, and designed to model them for a peculiar people to himself; and by their attendance on God in solemn assemblies on sabbath days they were made to increase in the knowledge of God, in an experimental knowledge of the powers and pleasures of his sanctifying grace. Note, (1.) Sabbaths are privileges, and are so to be accounted; the church acknowledges as a great favour, in that chapter which is parallel to this and seems to have a reference to this (Neh. 9:14), *Thou madest known unto them thy holy sabbaths.* (2.) Sabbaths are signs; it is a sign that men have a sense of religion, and that there is some good correspondence between them and God, when they make conscience of keeping holy and sabbath day. (3.) Sabbaths, if duly sanctified, are the means of our sanctification; if we do the duty of the day, we shall find, to our comfort, *it is the Lord that sanctifies us,* makes us holy (that is, truly happy) here, and prepares us to be happy (that is, perfectly holy) hereafter.

II. Their disobedient undutiful conduct towards God, for which he might justly have thrown them out of covenant as soon as he had taken them into covenant (*v.* 13): *They rebelled in the wilderness.* There where they received so much mercy from God, and had such a dependence upon him, and were in their way to Canaan, yet there they broke out in many open rebellions against the God that led them and fed them. They did not only not *walk in God's statutes,* but they *despised his judgments* as not worth observing; instead of sanctifying the sabbaths, they polluted them, greatly polluted them; one gathered sticks, many went out to gather manna on this day. Hereupon God was ready sometimes to cut them off; he said, more than once, that he would *consume them in the wilderness.* But Moses interceded, so did God's own mercy more powerfully, and most of all a concern for his own glory, that *his name might not be polluted and profaned among the heathen* (*v.* 14), that the Egyptians might not say that for mischief he brought them thus far, or that he was not able to bring them any further, or that he had no such good land as was talked of to bring them to, Ex. 32:12; Num. 14:13, etc. Note, God's strongest reasons for his sparing mercy are those which are fetched from his own glory.

III. God's determination to cut off that generation of them in the wilderness. He who *lifted up his hand* for them (*v.* 6) now *lifted up his hand against them;* he who by an oath confirmed his promise to bring them out of Egypt now by an oath confirmed his threatenings that he would not bring them into Canaan (*v.* 15, 16): *I lifted up my hand unto them,* saying, *As truly as I live, these men who have tempted me these ten times shall never see the land which I swore unto their fathers,* Num. 14:22, 23; Ps. 95:11. By their contempt of God's laws, and particularly of his sabbaths, they put a bar in their own door; and that which was at the bottom of their disobedience to God, and their neglect of his institutions, was a secret affection to the gods of Egypt: *Their heart went after their idols.* Note, The bias of the mind towards the world and the flesh, the money and the belly (those two great objects of spiritual idolatry), is the root of bitterness from which springs all disobedience to the divine law. The heart that goes after those idols despises God's judgments.

IV. The reservation of a seed that should be admitted upon a new trial, and the instructions given to that seed, *v.* 17. Though they thus deserved ruin, and were doomed to it, yet *my eye spared them.* When he looked upon them he had compassion on them, and did not *make an end of them,* but reprieved them till a new generation was reared. Note, It is owing purely to the mercy of God that he has not long ago *made an end of us.* This new generation is well educated. Moses in Deuteronomy reported and enforce the laws which had been given to those that came out of Egypt, that their children might have them as it were sounding in their ears afresh when they entered Canaan (*v.* 18): *"I said unto their children in the wilderness,* in the plains of Moab, Walk in the statutes of your God and *walk not in the statutes of your fathers;* do not imitate their superstitious usages nor retain their foolish wicked customs; away with their vain conversation, which has nothing else to say for itself but that it was *received by the tradition of your fathers,* 1 Pt. 1:18. *Defile not yourselves with their idols,* for you see how odious they rendered themselves to God by them. But *keep my judgments* and *hallow my sabbaths," v.* 19, 20. Note, If parents be careless, and do not give their children good instructions as they ought, the children ought to make up the want by studying the word of God so much the more carefully and diligently themselves when they grow up; and the bad examples of parents must be made use of by their children for admonition, and not for imitation.

V. The revolt of the next generation from God, by which they also made themselves obnoxious to the wrath of God (*v.* 21): *The children rebelled against me* too. And the same that was said of the fathers' rebellion is here said *of the children's,* for they were a seed of evil-doers. Moses told them that he *knew their rebellion and their stiff neck,* Deu. 31:27. And Deu. 9:24, *You have been rebellious against the Lord from the day that I knew you. They walked not in my statutes* (*v.* 21); nay, *they despised my statutes, v.* 24. Those who disobey God's statutes despise them, they show that they have a mean opinion of them and of him whose statutes they are. They *polluted God's sabbaths,* as their fathers. Note, The profanation of the sabbath day is an inlet to all impiety; those who pollute holy time will keep nothing pure. It was said of the fathers (*v.* 16) that *their heart went after their idols;* they worshipped idols because they had an affection for them. It is said of the children (*v.* 24) that *their eyes went after their fathers' idols;* they had grown atheistical, and had no affection for any gods at all, but they worshipped *their fathers' idols* because they were their fathers' and they had them before their eyes. They were used to them; and, if they must have gods, they would have such as they could see, such as they could manage. And that which aggravated their disobedience to God's statutes was that, *if they had done them, they might have lived in them* (*v.* 21), might have been a happy thriving people. Note, Those that go contrary to their duty go contrary to their interest; they will not obey, will not come to Christ, that they may have life, Jn. 5:40. And it is therefore just that those who will not live and flourish as they might in their obedience should die and perish in their disobedience. Now the great instance of that generation's rebellion and inclination to idolatry was the *iniquity of Peor,* as that of their fathers was the *golden calf.* Then *the anger of the Lord was kindled against Israel,* Num. 25:3. Then there was a plague in the congregation of the Lord, which, if it had not been seasonably stayed by Phinehas's zeal, had cut them all off; and yet they owned, in Joshua's time, We ware not *cleansed from that iniquity unto this day,* Jos. 22:17; Ps. 106:29. Then it was that God said he would *pour out his fury upon them* (*v.* 21), that he *lifted up his hand unto them in the wilderness,* when they were a second time just ready to enter Canaan, *that he would scatter them among the heathen.* This very thing he said to them by Moses in his parting song, Deu. 32:20. Because they *provoked him to jealousy with strange gods,* he said, *I will hide my face form them;* and (*v.* 26, 27) he said, *I would scatter them into corners, were it not that I feared the wrath of the enemy,* which explains this (*v.* 21, 22), *I said I would pour out my fury upon them,* but *I withdrew* my hand *for my name's sake.* Note, When the corruptions of the visible church are such, and so provoking, that we have reason to fear its total extirpation, yet then we may be confident of this, to our comfort, that God will secure his own honour, by making good his purpose, that while the world stands he will have a church in it.

VI. The judgments of God upon them for their rebellion. They would not regard the statutes and judgments by which God prescribed them their duty, but despised them, and therefore God *gave them statutes and judgments* which *were not good,* and *by which they should not live, v.* 25. By this we may understand the several ways by which God punished them while they were in the wilderness — the plague that broke in upon them, the fiery serpent, and the like — which, in allusion to the law they had broken, are called *judgments,* because inflicted by the justice of God, and *statutes,* because he gave orders concerning them and commanded desolations as sometimes he had commanded deliverances, and appointed Israel's plagues as he had done the plagues of Egypt. When God said, *I will consume them in a moment* (Num. 16:21), when he said, *Take the heads of the people and hang them up* (Num. 25:4), when he threatened them with the curse and obliged them to say *Amen* to every curse (Deu. 27:28), then he gave them judgments by *which they should not live.* More is implied than is expressed; they are judgments by which they should die. Those that will not be bound by the precepts of the law shall be bound by the sentence of it; for one way or other the word of God will *take hold* of men, Zec. 1:6. Spiritual judgments are the most dreadful; and these God punished them with. The statutes and judgments which the heathen observed in the worship of their idols were not good, and in practising them they could not live; and God gave them up to those. He made their sin to be their punishment, gave them up to a *reprobate mind,* as he did the Gentile idolaters (Rom. 1:24, 26), gave them up to their own heart's lusts (Ps. 81:12), punished them for those superstitious customs which were against the written law by giving them up to those which were against the very light and law of nature; he left them to themselves to be guilty of the most impure idolatries, as in the worship of Baal-peor (he *polluted them,* that is, her permitted them to pollute themselves, *in their own gifts, v.* 26), and of the most barbarous idolatries, as in the worship of Moloch, when they *caused their children,* especially their first-born, which God challenged a particular property in *(the first-born of thy sons shalt thou give unto me),* to pass *through the fire,* to be sacrificed to their idols; that thus he might *make them desolate,* not only that he might justly do it, but that he might do it by their own hands; for this must needs be a great weakening to their families and a diminution of the honour and strength of their country. Note, God sometimes makes sin to be its own punishment, and yet is not the author of sin; and there needs no more to make men miserable than to give them up to their own vile appetites and passions. Let them be put into the hand of their own counsels, and they will ruin themselves and make themselves desolate. And thus God makes them know that he is the Lord, and that he is a righteous God, which they themselves will be compelled to own when they see how much their wilful transgressions contribute to their own desolations. Note, Those who will not acknowledge God as the Lord their ruler shall be made to acknowledge him as the Lord their judge when it is too late.

Verses 27–32

Here the prophet goes on with the story of their rebellions, for their further humiliation, and shows,

I. That they had persisted in them after they were settled in the land of Canaan. Though God had so many times testified his displeasure against their wicked courses, "yet *in this* (that is, in the very same thing) *your fathers have blasphemed me,* continued to affront me, that they *also have trespassed a trespass against me," v.* 27. Note, It is a great aggravation of sin when men will not take warning by the mischievous consequences of sin in those that have gone before them: this is *blaspheming God;* it is speaking reproachfully of his judgments, as if they were of no significancy and were not worth regarding. 1. God had made good his promise: *I brought them into the land* that I had sworn to give them. Though their unbelief and disobedience had made the performance slow, and much retarded it, yet it did not *make the promise of no effect.* They were often very near being cut off in the wilderness, but a step between them and ruin, and yet they came to Canaan at last. Note, Even God's Israel get to heaven by hell-gates; so many are their transgressions, and so strong their corruptions, that it is a miracle of mercy they are happy at last; as hypocrites go to hell by heaven-gates. *The righteous scarcely are saved. Per tot discrimina rerum tendimus ad coelum — Ten thousand dangers fill the road to haven.* 2. They had broken his precept by their abominable idolatries. God had appointed them to destroy all the monuments of idolatry, that they might not be tempted to desert his sanctuary; but, instead of defacing them, they fell in love with them, and when they *saw every high hill* whence they had the most delightful prospects, and all the *thick trees* where they had the most delightful shades (the former to show forth their pompous idolatries, the latter to conceal their shameful ones), *there they offered their sacrifices* and *made their sweet savour,* which should have been presented upon God's altar only. *There they presented the provocation of their offering* (*v.* 28), that is, their offerings, which, instead of pacifying God, or pleasing him, were highly provoking — sacrifices which, though costly, yet being misplaced, were an abomination to the Lord. 3. They obstinately persisted herein notwithstanding all the admonitions that were given them (*v.* 29): *"Then I told them,* by my servants the prophets, told them *where the high place was, to which they went;* nay, I put them upon considering it, and asking their own consciences concerning it, by putting this question to them, *Which is the high place whereunto you go?* What do you find there so inviting that you will leave God's altars, where he requires your attendance, to frequent such places as he has forbidden you to worship in? Do you not know that those high places are of a heathenish extraction, and that the things which the Gentiles sacrificed they sacrificed to devils and not to God? Did not Moses tell you so? Deu. 32:17. *And will you have fellowship with devils? What is that high place to which you go* when you turn your back on God's altars? *O foolish* Israelites, *who* or what *has bewitched you,* that you will forsake the fountain of life for broken cisterns, that worship which God appoints, and will accept, for that which he forbids, which he abhors, and which he will punish?" And yet *the name is called Bamah unto this day;* they will have their way, let God and his prophets say what they please to the contrary. They are wedded to their *high places;* even in the best reigns those were not taken away; you could not prevail to take away the name of *Bamah — the high place,* out of their mouths, but still they would have that in the place of their worship. The sin and the sinner are with difficulty parted.

II. That this generation, after they were unsettled, continued under the dominion of the same corrupt inclinations to idolatry, *v.* 30. He must *say to* the present *house of Israel,* some of whose elders were now sitting before him, *"Are you polluted after the manner of your fathers?* After all that God has said against you by a succession of prophets, and done against you by a series of judgments, yet will you take no warning? Will you still be as bad as your fathers were, and commit the same abominations that they committed? I see you will; you are bent upon returning to the old abominations; you *offer your gifts* in the high places, and you *make your sons to pass through the fire;* either you actually do it or you do it in purpose and imagination, and so you continue idolaters *to this day."* These elders seem now to have been projecting a coalition with the heathen; their hearts they will reserve for the God of Israel, but their knees they will be at liberty to bow to the gods of the nations among whom they live, that they may have the more respect and the fairer quarter among them. Now the prophet is here ordered to tell those who were forming this scheme, and were for compounding the matter between God and Baal, that they should have no comfort or benefit from either. 1. They should have no benefit by their consulting in private with the prophets of the Lord; for, because they were hearkening after idols, God would have nothing to do with them (*v.* 31): *As I live, saith the Lord God, I will not be enquired of by you.* What he had said before (*v.* 3), having largely shown how just it was, he here repeats, as that which he would abide by. Let them not think that they honoured him by their enquiries, nor expect an answer of peace from him, as long as they continued in love and league with their idols. Note, Those reap no benefit by their religion that are not entire and sincere in it; nor can we have any comfortable communion with God in ordinances of worship unless we be inward and upright with him therein. We make nothing of our profession if it be but a profession. Nay, 2. They should have no benefit from their conforming in public to the practice of their neighbours (*v.* 32): *"That which comes into your mind* as a piece of refined politics in the present difficult juncture, and which you would be advised to for your own preservation, and that you may not by being singular expose yourselves to abuses, it *shall not be at all,* it shall turn to no account to you. You say, *'We will be as the heathen,* we will join with them in worshipping their gods, though at the same time we do not believe them to be gods, but *wood and stone,* and then we should be taken *as the families of the countries;* they will not know, or in a little while will have forgotten, that we are Jews, and will allow us the same privileges with their own countrymen.' Tell them," says God, "that this project shall *never prosper.* Either their neighbours will not admit them to join with them in their worship, or, if they do, will think never the better, but the worse, of them for it, and will look upon them as dissemblers, and not fit to be trusted, who are thus false to their God, and put a cheat upon their neighbours." Note, There is nothing got by sinful compliances; and the carnal projects of hypocrites will stand them in no stead. It is only integrity and uprightness that will preserve men, and recommend them to God and man.

Verses 33–44

The design which was now on foot among the elders of Israel was that the people of Israel, being scattered among the nations, should lay aside all their peculiarities and conform to those among whom they lived; but God had told them that the design should not take effect, *v.* 32. Now, in these verses, he shows particularly how it should be frustrated. They aimed at the *mingling* of the families of *Israel with the families of the countries;* but it will prove in the issue that the wicked Israelites, notwithstanding their compliances, shall not mingle with them in their prosperity, but shall be distinguished from them for destruction; for idolatrous Israelites, that are apostates from God, shall be sooner and more sorely punished than idolatrous Babylonians that never knew the way of righteousness. Read and tremble at the doom here passed upon them; it is backed with an oath not to be reversed: *As I live, saith the Lord God,* thus and thus will I deal with you. They think to make both Jerusalem and Babylon their friends by halting between two; but God threatens that neither of them shall serve for a rest or refuge for them.

I. Babylon shall not protect them, nor any of the countries of the heathen; for God will cast them out of his protection and then what prince, what people, what place, can serve to be a sanctuary to them? God was Israel's King of old, and had they continued his loyal subjects he would have *ruled over them* with care and tenderness for their good, but now *with a stretched-out arm, and with fury poured out, will I rule over them, v.* 33. That power which should have been exerted fore their protection shall be exerted for their destruction. Note, There is no shaking off God's dominion; rule he will, either with the golden sceptre or with the iron rod; and those that will not yield to the power of his grace shall be made to sink under the power of his wrath. Now when God is angry with them, though they may think that they shall be lost in the crowd of the heathen among whom they are scattered, they will be disappointed; for (*v.* 34) *I will gather you out of the countries wherein you are scattered,* as, when the rebels are dispersed in battle, those that have escaped the sword of war are pursued and brought together out of all the places whither they were scattered, to be punished by the sword of justice. They shall be brought *into the wilderness of the people* (*v.* 35), either into Babylon, which is called a *wilderness* (*ch.* 19:13), and the *desert of the sea* (Isa. 21:1), or into some place which, though full of people, shall be to them as the wilderness was to Israel after they came out of Egypt, a place where God will *plead with them face to face,* as he *pleaded with their fathers in the wilderness of Egypt* (*v.* 36), — where their carcases shall fall and where he will swear concerning them that they shall never return to Canaan, as he did swear concerning their fathers that they should never come into Canaan, — where he will avenge the breach of his law with as much terror as that with which he gave it in the wilderness of Sinai. Note, God has a good action against apostates, and will find not only time, but a proper place, to plead with them in upon that action, a wilderness even in the midst of the people for that purpose.

II. Israel shall be no more able to protect them than Babylon could; nor shall their relation to God's people stand them in any more stead for the other world than their compliance with idolaters shall for this world; nor shall they stand *in the congregation of the righteous* any more than in the congregation of evil-doers; for there will come a distinguishing day, when God will separate between the precious and the vile; he will *cause them,* as the shepherd causes his sheep, to *pass under the rod,* when he tithes them (Lev. 27:32), that he may mark which is for God. God will take particular notice of each of them, one by one, as sheep are counted, and *he will bring them into the bond of the covenant* (*v.* 37); he will try them and judge of them according to the tenour of the covenant, and the difference made between some and others by the blessings and curses of the covenant. Or it may refer to those among them that repented and reformed; he will cause them to pass under the rod of affliction, and, having done them good by it, he will bring them again *into the bond of the covenant,* will be to them a God in covenant, and use them again as *heirs of promise.*

1. He will separate the wicked from among them (*v.* 38): "*I will purge out from among you the rebels,* who have been a grief and scandal to you, and who have by their rebellions brought all these calamities upon you." The judgments of God shall find them out, and their naming the name of Israel shall be no shelter to them. They shall be *brought out of the countries where they sojourn,* and shall not have that rest in them which they promised themselves. But they *shall not enter into the land of Israel,* nor enjoy the benefit of that rest which God has promised to his people. Note, Though godly people may share with the wicked in the calamities of the world, yet wicked people shall have no share with the godly in the heavenly Canaan; but it shall be part of the blessedness of that world that they shall be *purged out from among them,* the tares from the wheat, the chaff from the corn, *ch.* 13:9. But wherever these idolaters of *the house of Israel* were contriving to worship both God and their idols, thinking to please both, God here protests against it (*v.* 39), as Elijah had done in his name: "*If the Lord be God, then follow him, but, if Baal, then follow him;* if you will serve your idols, do, and take what comes of it; but then do not pretend relation to God and a religious regard to him, nor *pollute his holy name with your gifts* at his altar." Spiritual judgments are the sorest judgments. Two of that kind of judgments are threatened in this verse against those that were for dividing between the God of Israel and the gods of the nations: — (1.) That they should be given up to the service of their idols. To them he said ironically, "*Since you will not hearken unto me, go you, serve every one his idols,* now that you think it will be for your interest, *and hereafter also.* You shall go on in it. *Ephraim is joined to idols, let him alone;* let him take his course, and see what he will get by it at last." Note, Those who think to serve themselves by sin will find in the end that they have but enslaved themselves to sin. (2.) That they should be cut off from the service of God and communion with God: "You *shall not pollute my holy name* with your *vain oblations,* Isa. 1:11. You bring your gifts in your hands, wherewith you pretend to honour me, but at the same time you bring your idols in your hearts, and therefore you do but pollute me, which I will not suffer any more," Amos 5:21, 22. Note, Those are justly forbidden God's house that profane his house.

2. He will separate them to himself again. (1.) He will *gather them* in mercy *out of the countries whither they were scattered,* to be monuments of mercy, as the incorrigible were gathered to be vessels of wrath, *v.* 41. Not one of God's jewels shall be lost in the lumber of this world. (2.) He will *bring them to the land of Israel,* which he had promised to *give to their fathers;* and the discontinuance of their possession shall be no defeasance of their right; it is the *land of Israel* still, and thither God will bring them safely again, *v.* 42. (3.) He will re-establish his ordinances among them, will set up his sanctuary in his holy mountain, which is here called *the mountain of the height of Israel;* for, though the Mount Zion was none of the highest mountains, yet the temple there was one of the highest honours of Israel. It is promised that those who preserved their integrity, and would not serve idols, in other lands, shall return to their prosperity and shall serve the true God in their own land: *All of them in the land shall serve me.* Note, It is the true happiness of a people, and a sure token for good to them, when there is a prevailing disposition in them to serve God. Whereas God had forbidden the idolaters to bring their gifts to his altar, of these he will *require offerings and first-fruits,* and will accept them, *v.* 40. What he does not require he will not accept, but what is done with a regard to his precepts he will be well pleased with. He will *accept them with their sweet savour,* or *savour of rest* (*v.* 41), as being very grateful to him and what he takes a complacency in; whereas, to hypocritical worshippers, he says, *I will not smell in your solemn assemblies.* (4.) He will give them true repentance for their sins, *v.* 43. When they find how gracious God is to them they will be overcome with his kindness, and blush to think of their bad behaviour towards so *good a God:* "There, in *my holy mountain,* when you come to enjoy the privileges of that again, *there* shall you *remember your doings,* wherein you have been defiled." Note, The more conversant we are with God's holiness the more we shall see of the odious nature of sin. There *you shall loathe yourselves in your own sight.* Note, Ingenuous evangelical repentance makes people loathe themselves for their sins, as Job 42:5, 6. (5.) He will give them the knowledge of himself: *They shall know* by experience that *he is the Lord,* that he is a God of almighty power and inexhaustible goodness, kind to his people and faithful to his covenant with them. Note, All the favours we receive from God should lead us into a more intimate acquaintance with him. (6.) He will do all this for his own name's sake, notwithstanding their undeservings and ill-deservings (*v.* 44); he has *wrought with them,* that is, wrought for them, wrought in favour of them, wrought in concurrence with them, they doing their endeavour; he has wrought with them purely *for his name's sake.* His reasons were all fetched from himself. Had he dealt with them *according to their wicked ways and their corrupt doings,* though they were the better and sounder part of the house of Israel, he would have left them to be scattered and lost with the rest; but he recovered and restored them for the sake of his own name, not only that it might not be *polluted* (*v.* 14), but that he might be *sanctified in them before the heathen* (*v.* 41), that he might *sanctify himself* (so the word is); for it is God's work to glorify his own name. He will do well for his people that he may have the glory of it, that he may manifest himself to be a God pardoning sin and so keeping promise, that his people may praise him, and that their neighbours may likewise take notice of him, as they did when God *burned again their captivity,* Ps. 126:3. *Then said they among the heathen, The Lord has done great things for them.*

Verses 45–49

We have here a prophecy of wrath against Judah and Jerusalem, which would more fitly have begun the next chapter than conclude this; for it has no dependence on what goes before, but that which follows in the beginning of the next chapter is the explication of it, when the people complained that this was a parable which they understood not. In this parable, 1. It is a forest that is prophesied against, *the forest of the south field,* Judah and Jerusalem. These lay south from Babylon, where Ezekiel now was, and therefore he is directed to *set his face towards the south* (*v.* 46), to intimate to them that God had set his face against them, was displeased with them, and determined to destroy them. But, though it be a message of wrath which he has to deliver, he must deliver it with mildness and tenderness; he must *drop his word towards the south;* his doctrine must *distil as the rain* (Deu. 32:2), that people's hearts might be softened by it, as the earth by the *river of God,* which *drops upon the pastures of the wilderness* (Ps. 65:12) and which a south land more especially calls for, Jos. 15:19. Judah and Jerusalem are called *forests,* not only because they had been full of people, as a wood of trees, but because they had been empty of fruit, for fruit-trees grow not in a forest; and a forest is put in opposition to a fruitful field, Isa. 32:15. Those that should have been as the garden of the Lord, and his vineyard, had become like a forest, all overgrown with *briers and thorns;* and those that are so, that bring not forth the fruits of righteousness, God's word prophesies against. 2. It is a fire kindled in his forest that is prophesied of, *v.* 47. All those judgments which wasted and consumed both the city and the country — sword, famine, pestilence, and captivity, are signified by this fire. (1.) It is a fire of God's own kindling: *I will kindle a fire in thee;* the *breath of the Lord* is not as a drop, but *as a stream, of brimstone* to set it on fire, Isa. 30:33. He that had been himself a protecting fire about Jerusalem is now a consuming fire in it. *All flesh shall see* by the fury of this fire, and the desolations it shall make, especially when they compare it with the sins which had made them fuel for this fire, that it is *the Lord* that *has kindled it* (*v.* 48), as a just avenger of his own injured honour. (2.) This conflagration shall be general: all orders and degrees of men shall be devoured by it — young and old, rich and poor, high and low. Even *green trees,* which the fire does not easily fasten upon, shall be devoured by this fire; even good people shall some of them be involved in these calamities; and *if this be done in the green trees, what shall be done in the dry?* The dry trees shall be as tinder and touch-wood to this fire. *All faces* (that is, all that covers the face of the earth) *from the south* of Canaan to the north, from Beer-sheba to Dan, shall be *burnt therein.* (3.) The fire *shall not be quenched;* no attempts to give check to the dissolution shall prevail. When God will ruin a nation, who or what can save it?

Now observe, 1. The people's reflection upon the prophet on occasion of this discourse. They said, *Does he not speak parables?* This was the language either of their ignorance or infidelity (the plainest truths were as parables to them), or of their malice and ill-will to the prophet. Note. It is common for those who will not be wrought upon by the word to pick quarrels with it; it is either too plain or too obscure, too fine or too homely, too common or too singular; something or other is amiss in it. 2. The prophet's complaint to God: *Ah, Lord God! they say* so and so of me. Note, It is a comfort to us, when people speak ill of us unjustly, that we have a God to complain to.

CHAPTER 21

In this chapter we have, I. An explication of the prophecy in the close of the foregoing chapter concerning the fire in the forest, which the people complained they could not understand (*v.* 1–5), with directions to the prophet to show himself deeply affected with it (*v.* 6, 7). II. A further prediction of the sword that was coming upon the land, by which all should be laid waste; and this expressed very emphatically (*v.* 8–17). III. A prospect given of the king of Babylon's approach to Jerusalem, to which he was determined by divination (*v.* 18–24). IV. Sentence passed upon Zedekiah king of Judah (*v.* 25–27). V. The destruction of the Ammonites by the sword foretold (*v.* 28–32). Thus is this chapter all threatenings.

Verses 1–7

The prophet had faithfully delivered the message he was entrusted with, in the close of the foregoing chapter, in the terms wherein he received it, not daring to add his own comment upon it; but, when he complained that the people found fault with him for speaking parables, the word of the Lord came to him again, and gave him a key to that figurative discourse, that with it he might let the people into the meaning of it and so silence that objection. For all men shall be rendered inexcusable at God's bar and every mouth shall be stopped. Note, He that *speaks with tongues* should *pray that he may interpret,* 1 Co. 14:13. When we speak to people about their souls we should study plainness, and express ourselves as we may be the best understood. Christ *expounded his parables to his disciples,* Mk. 4:34. 1. The prophet is here more plainly directed against whom to level the arrow of this prophecy. He must *drop his word towards the holy places* (*v.* 2), towards Canaan the holy land, Jerusalem the holy city, the temple the holy house. These were highly dignified above other places; but, when they polluted them, that word which used to drop in the holy places shall now drop against them: *Prophesy against the land of Israel.* It was the honour of Israel that it had prophets and prophecy; but these, being despised by them, are turned against them. And justly is Zion battered with her own artillery, which used to be employed against her adversaries, seeing she knew not how to value it. 2. He is instructed, and is to instruct the people, in the meaning of the fire that was threatened to consume the forest of the south: it signified a sword drawn, the sword of war which should make the land desolate (*v.* 3): *Behold, I am against thee, O land of Israel!* There needs no more to make a people miserable than to have God against them; for as, if he be for us, we need not fear, whoever are against us, so, if he be against us, we cannot hope, whoever are for us. And God's professing people, when they revolt from him, set him against them, who used to be for them. Was the fire there of God's kindling? The sword here is his sword, which he has prepared, and which he will give commission to; it is he that will *draw it out of its sheath,* where it had laid quiet and threatened no harm. Note, When the sword is unsheathed among the nations God's hand must be eyed and owned in it. Did the fire devour *every green tree* and *every dry tree?* The sword in like manner shall *cut off the righteous and the wicked.* Good and bad were involved in the common calamities of the nation; the righteous were *cut off from the land of Israel* when they were sent captives in Babylon, though perhaps few or none of them were cut off from the land of the living; and it was a threatening omen to the land of Israel that in the beginning of its troubles such excellent men as Daniel and his fellows, and Ezekiel, were cut off from it and conveyed to Babylon. But though the sword *cut off the righteous and the wicked* (for it *devours one as well as another,* 2 Sa. 11:25), yet far be it from us to think that *the righteous are as the wicked,* Gen. 18:25. No; God's graces and comforts make a great difference when his providence seems to make none. The *good figs* are sent into Babylon *for their good,* Jer. 24:5, 6. It is only in outward appearance that there is *one event to the righteous and to the wicked,* Eccl. 9:2. But it speaks the greatness of God's displeasure against the land of Israel. Well might it be said, *His eye shall not spare,* when it shall not spare, no, not the *righteous* in it. Since there are not righteous men sufficient to save the land, to make the justice of God the more illustrious the few that there are shall suffer with it, and God's mercy shall make it up to them some other way. Did the fire *burn up all faces from the south to the north?* The sword shall go *forth against all flesh from the south to the north,* shall go forth, as God's sword, with a commission that cannot be contested, with a force that cannot be resisted. Were all flesh made to know that God kindled the fire? They shall be made to know that he has *drawn forth the sword, v.* 5. And, *lastly,* Shall the fire that is *kindled never be quenched?* So when this sword of the Lord is drawn against Judah and Jerusalem the scabbard is thrown away, and it shall never be sheathed: It *shall not return any more,* till it has made a full end. 3. The prophet is ordered, by expressions of his own grief and concern for these calamities that were coming on, to try to make impressions of the like upon the people. When he has delivered his message he must *sigh* (*v.* 6), must fetch many deep sighs, *with the breaking of his loins;* he must sign as if his heart would burst, *sigh with bitterness,* with other expressions of bitter sorrow, and this publicly, *in the sight* of those to whom he delivered the foregoing message, that this might be a sermon to their eyes as that was to their ears; and it was well if both would work upon them. The prophet must sign, though it was painful to himself and made his breast sore, and though it is probable that the profane among the people would ridicule him for it and call him a whining canting preacher. But, *if we be beside ourselves it is to God;* and, if *this be to be vile, we will be yet more so.* Note, Ministers, if they would affect others with the things they speak of, must show that they are themselves in the greatest sincerity affected with them, and must submit to that which may create uneasiness to themselves, so that it will promote the ends of their ministry. The people, observing the prophet to sigh so much and seeing no visible occasion for it, would ask, *"Wherefore sighest thou?* These sighs have some mystical meaning; let us know what it is." And he must answer them (*v.* 7): "It is *for the tidings,* the heavy tidings, that we shall hear shortly; the *tidings come* (the judgments come which we hear the tidings of), they come apace, and then you will all sigh; nay, that will not serve. *every heart shall melt* and *every spirit fail;* your courage will all be gone and you will have no animating considerations to support yourselves with. And, when *heart* and *spirit* fail, it will follow of course that *all hands will be feeble* and unable to fight, and all *knees will* be *weak as water* and unable to flee or to stand their ground." Those who have God for them when flesh and heart fail have him to be *the strength of their heart;* but those who have God against them have no cordial for a fainting spirit, but are as Belshazzar when *his thoughts troubled him,* Dan. 5:6. But some people are worse frightened than hurt; may not the case be so here and the event prove better than likely? No: *Behold it cometh,* and *shall be brought to pass.* It is not a bugbear that they are frightened with, but *according to the fear so is the wrath,* and more grievous than is feared.

Verses 8–17

Here is another prophecy of the sword, which is delivered in a very affecting manner; the expressions here used are somewhat intricate, and perplex interpreters. The sword was unsheathed in the foregoing verses; here it is fitted up to do execution, which the prophet is commanded to lament. Observe,

I. How the sword is here described. 1. It is *sharpened,* that it may cut and wound, and make *a sore slaughter.* The wrath of God will put an edge upon it; and, whatever instruments God shall please to make use of in executing his judgments, he will fill them with strength, courage, and fury, according to the service they are employed in. Out of the mouth of Christ goes a *sharp sword,* Rev. 19:15. 2. It is *furbished,* that *it may glitter,* to the terror of those against whom it is drawn. It shall be a kind of *flaming sword.* If it have rusted in the scabbard for want of use, it shall be rubbed and brightened; for though the glory of God's justice may seem to have been eclipsed for a while, during the day of his patience and the delay of his judgments, yet it will shine out again and be made to glitter. 3. It is a victorious sword, nothing shall stand before it (*v.* 10): *It contemneth the rod of my son as every tree. Israel,* said God once, *is my son, my first-born.* The government of that people was called a *rod,* a *strong rod;* we read (*ch.* 19:11) of the *strong rods* they had *for sceptres.* But when the sword of God's justice is drawn it *contemns this rod,* makes nothing of it; though it be a *strong rod,* and the *rod of his son,* it is no more than *any other tree.* When God's professing people have revolted from him, and are in rebellion against him, his sword *despises* them. What are they to him more than another people? The marginal reading gives another notion of this sword: *It is the rod of my son;* and we know of whom God has said (Ps. 2:7), *Thou art my Son, this day have I begotten thee,* and (*v.* 9) *Thou shalt break them with a rod of iron.* This sword is *that rod of iron* which *contemns every tree* and will bear it down. Or, This sword is *the rod of my son,* a correcting rod, for the chastening of the transgression of God's people (2 Sa. 7:14), not to cut them off from being a people. It is a sword to others, a rod to my son.

II. How the sword is here put into the hand of the executioners: "It is *the rod of my Son,* and he has *given it that it may be handled* (*v.* 11), that it may be made use of for the end for which it was drawn. *It is given into the hand,* not of the fencer to be played with, but *of the slayer* to do execution with. The sword of war my Son makes use of as a sword of justice, and to him *all judgment is committed.* It is *made bright* (*v.* 15), *it is wrapped up,* that it may be kept safe, and clean, and sharp *for the slaughter,* not as Goliath's sword was wrapped *up in a cloth* only for a memorial," 1 Sa. 21:9.

III. How the sword is directed, and against whom it is sent (*v.* 12): *It shall be upon my people;* they shall fall by this sword. It is repeated again, as that which is scarcely credible, that *the sword* of the heathen shall be upon God's own people; nay, it shall be *upon all the princes of Israel;* their dignity and power as princes shall be no more their security than their profession of religion as princes of Israel. But, if the sword be at any time upon God's people, have they not comfort within sufficient to arm them against every thing in it that is frightful? Yes, they have, while they conduct themselves as becomes his people; but these had not done so, and therefore *terrors, by reason of the sword,* shall be upon those that call themselves *my people.* Note, While good men are quiet, not only from evil, but from the fear of it, wicked men are disturbed not only with the sword, but with the terrors of it, arising from a consciousness of their own guilt. This sword is directed particularly *against the great men,* for they had been the greatest sinners among them; they had *altogether broken the yoke and burst the bonds* (Jer. 5:5), and therefore with them in a special manner God's controversy is, who had been the ringleaders in sin. The *sword of the slain* is *the sword of the great men that are slain, v.* 14. Though they have furnished themselves with places of retirement, places of concealment, where they flatter themselves with hopes that they shall be safe, they will find that the sword will *enter into their privy chambers,* and find them out there, as the *frogs,* when they were one of Egypt's plagues, found admission into the *chambers of their kings.* The sword, the *point of this sword,* is directed *against their gates,* against *all their gates* (*v.* 15), against all those things with which they thought to keep it out and fortify themselves against it. Note, The strongest gates, though they be *gates of brass,* ever so well barred, ever so well guarded, are no fence against the point of the sword of God's judgments. But when that is pointed against sinners, 1. They are ready to fear the worst; *their hearts faint,* so that they are not able to make any resistance. 2. The worst comes; whatever resistance they make, it is to no purpose, but they are ruined, and *their ruins are multiplied.* But what need have we to observe the particular directions of this sword when it has a general commission, is sent with a running warrant? (*v.* 16): *"Go thee, one way or other,* which way thou wilt, turn *to the right hand or to the left,* thou wilt find those that are obnoxious, for there are none free from guilt; and thou hast authority against them, for there are none exempt from punishment; and therefore, *whithersoever thy face is set,* that way do thou proceed, and, like Jonathan's sword, *from the blood of the slain, from the fat of the mighty, thou shalt never return empty,"* 2 Sa. 1:22. Note, So full is the world of wicked people that, which way soever God's judgments go forth, they will find work, will find matter to work upon. That fire will never go out on this earth for want of fuel. And such various methods God has of meeting with sinners that the sword of his justice is still as it was at first when it flamed in the hand of the cherubim: it *turns every way,* Gen. 3:24.

IV. What is the nature of this sword, and what are the intentions and limitations of it as to the people of God, *v.* 13. It is a correction; it is designed to be so; the sword to others is a rod to them. This is a comfortable word which comes in in the midst of these terrible ones, though it be expressed somewhat obscurely. 1. The people of God begin to be afraid that *the sword will contemn even the rod,* that the sword will go on with such fury that it will despise its commission to be a rod only, will forget its bounds and become a sword indeed, even to God's own people. They fear lest the Chaldeans' sword, which is the rod of God's anger, contemn its being called a rod, and become as the *axe* that *boasts itself against him that heweth therewith* or *the staff that lifts up itself as if it were no wood,* Isa. 10:15. Or, *"What if the sword contemn even the rod?* that is, what if this sword make the former rods, as that or Sennacherib, to be contemned as nothing to this? What if this should prove not a correcting rod, but a destroying sword, to make a full end of our church and nation?" This is that which the thinking, but timorous, few are apprehensive of. Note, When threatening judgments are abroad it is good to suppose the worst that may be the consequences of them, that we may provide accordingly. *What if the sword contemn the tribe or sceptre?* namely, that of Judah and the house of David (so some think *Shebet* here signifies); what if it should aim at the ruin of our government? If it do, *the Lord is righteous* and *will be gracious* notwithstanding. But, 2. These fears are silenced with an assurance that it is not so; the sword shall not forget itself, nor the errand on which it is sent: *It is a trial,* and it is *no more than a trial.* He that sends it makes what use of it, and sets what bounds to it, he pleases. Here shall its proud waves be stayed. Note, It is matter of comfort to the people of God, when his judgments are abroad, and they are ready to tremble for fear of them, that, whatever they are to others, to them they are but trials; and, *when they are tried, they shall come forth as gold,* and the proving of their faith shall be the improving of it.

V. Here the prophet and the people must show themselves affected with these judgments threatened. 1. The prophet must be very serious in denouncing these judgments. He must say, *A sword! a sword! v.* 9. Let him not study for fine words, and a variety of quaint expressions; when the town is on fire people do not so give notice of it, but cry, with a frightful doleful voice, *Fire! fire!* So must the prophet cry, *A sword! a sword!* and (*v.* 14), *Let the sword be doubled the third time* in thy preaching. God speaks once, yea, twice, yea, thrice; it were well if men, after all, would perceive and regard it. It shall be *doubled the third time* in God's providence; for it was Nebuchadnezzar's third descent upon Jerusalem that *made a full end* of it. Ruin comes gradually, but at last comes effectually, upon a provoking people. Yet this is not all: the prophet is not only as a herald at arms to proclaim war, and to cry, *A sword! a sword!* once and again, and a third time, but, as a person nearly concerned, he must *cry and howl* (*v.* 12), must sadly lament the desolations that the sword would make, as one that did himself not only sympathize with the sufferers, but feel from the sufferings. Again (*v.* 14), *Prophesy, and smite thy hands together,* wring *thy hands,* as lamenting the desolation, or clap thy hands, as by thy prophecy instigating and encouraging those that were to be the instruments of it, or as one standing amazed at the suddenness and severity of the judgment. The prophet must *smite his hands together;* for (says God) *I will also smite my hands together, v.* 17. God is in earnest in pronouncing this sentence upon them, and therefore the prophet must show himself in earnest in publishing it. God's *smiting his hands together,* as well as the prophet's smiting, is in token of a holy indignation at their wickedness, which was really very astonishing. When Balak's anger was kindled against Balaam he *smote his hands together,* Num. 24:10. Note, God and his ministers are justly angry at those who might be saved and yet will be ruined. Some make it an expression of triumph and exultation, agreeing with that (Isa. 1:24), *Ah! I will ease me of my adversaries;* and that (Prov. 1:26), *I also will laugh at their calamity.* And so it follows here, *I will cause my fury to rest,* not only it shall be perfected, but it shall be pleased. And observe with what solemnity, with what authority, this sentence is ratified: *"I the Lord have said it,* who can and will make good what I have said. I have said it, and will never unsay it. I have said it, and who can gainsay it?" 2. The people must be very serious in the prospect of these judgments. An intimation of this comes in in a parenthesis (*v.* 10): *Should we then make mirth?* Seeing God has drawn the sword, and the prophet sighs and cries, *Should we then make mirth?* The prophet seems to give this as a reason why he sighs; as Neh. 2:3, *Why should not my countenance be sad,* when Jerusalem lies waste? Note, Before we allow ourselves to be merry, we ought to consider whether we should be merry or no. Should we make mirth, we who are sentenced to the sword, who lie under the wrath and curse of God? Shall we *make mirth as other people,* who have *gone a whoring from our God?* Hos. 9:1. Should we now make mirth, when the hand of God has gone out against us, when God's judgments are abroad in the land and he by them *calls to weeping and mourning?* Isa. 22:11, 13. Shall we now make mirth as the king and Haman, when the church is in perplexity (Esther 3:15), when we should be *grieving for the affliction of Joseph?* Amos 6:6.

Verses 18–27

The prophet, in the verses before, had shown them the sword coming; he here shows them that sword coming against them, that they might not flatter themselves that by some means or other it should be diverted a contrary way.

I. He must see and show the Chaldean army coming against Jerusalem and determined by a supreme power so to do. The prophet must *appoint him two ways,* that is, he must upon a paper draw out two roads (*v.* 19), as sometimes is done in maps; and he must bring the king of Babylon's army to the place where the roads part, for there they will make a stand. They both *come out of the same land;* but when they come to the place where one road leads to Rabbath, the head city of the Ammonites, and the other to Jerusalem, he makes a pause; for, though he is resolved to be the ruin of both, yet he is not determined which to attack first; here his politics and his politicians leave him at a loss. The sword must go either to Rabbath or *to Judah in Jerusalem.* Many of the inhabitants of Judah had now taken shelter in Jerusalem, and all the interests of the country were bound up in the safety of the city, and therefore it is called *Judah in Jerusalem the defenced;* so strongly fortified was it, both by nature and art, that it was thought impregnable, Lam. 4:12. The prophet must describe this dilemma that the king of Babylon is at (*v.* 21); for *the king of Babylon stood* (that is, he shall stand considering what course to take) *at the head of the two ways.* Though he was a prince of great foresight and great resolution, yet, it seems, he knew neither his own interest nor his own mind. Let not the wise man then glory in his wisdom nor the mighty man in his arbitrary power, for even those that may do what they will seldom know what to do for the best. Now observe, 1. The method he took to come to a resolution; he *used divination,* applied to a higher and invisible power, perhaps to the determination of Providence by a lot, in order to which he *made his arrows bright,* that were to be drawn for the lots, in honour of the solemnity. Perhaps *Jerusalem* was written on one arrow and *Rabbath* on the other, and that which was first drawn out of the quiver he determined to attack first. Or he applied to the direction of some pretended oracle: he *consulted with images* or *teraphim,* expecting to receive audible answers from them. Or to the observations which the augurs made upon the entrails of the sacrifices: *he looked in the liver,* whether the position of that portended good or ill luck. Note, It is a mortification to the pride of the wise men of the earth that in difficult cases they have been glad to make their court to heaven for direction; as it is an instance of their folly that they have taken such ridiculous ways of doing it, when in cases proper for an appeal to Providence it is sufficient that *the lot be cast into the lap,* with that prayer, *Give a perfect lot,* and a firm belief that the *disposal thereof* is not fortuitous, but *of the Lord,* Prov. 16:33. 2. The resolution he was hereby brought to. Even by these sinful practices God served his own purposes and directed him to go to Jerusalem, *v.* 22. *The divination for Jerusalem* happened to be *at his right hand,* which, according to the rules of divination, determined him *that way.* Note, What services God designs men for he will be sure in his providence to lead them to, though perhaps they themselves are not aware what guidance they are under. Well, Jerusalem being the mark set up, the campaign is presently opened with the siege of that important place. *Captains* are appointed for the command of the forces to be employed in the siege, who must *open the mouth in the slaughter,* must give directions to the soldiers what to do and make speeches to animate them. Orders are given to provide every thing necessary for carrying on the siege with vigour; *battering rams* must be prepared and *forts built.* O what pains, what cost, are men at to destroy one another!

II. He must show both the people and the prince that they bring this destruction upon themselves by their own sin.

1. The people do so, *v.* 23, 24. They slight the notices that are given them of the judgment coming. Ezekiel's prophecy is to them a *false divination;* they are not moved or awakened to repentance by it. When they hear that Nebuchadnezzar by his divination is directed to Jerusalem, and assured of success in that enterprise, they laugh at it and continue *secure,* calling it a *false divination;* because *they have sworn oaths,* that is, they have joined in a solemn league with the Egyptians, and they depend upon the promise they have made them to *raise the siege,* or upon the assurances which the false prophets have given them that it shall be raised. Or it may refer to the oaths of allegiance they had sworn to the king of Babylon, but had violated, for which treachery of theirs God had given them up to a judicial blindness, so that the fairest warnings given them were slighted by them as false divinations. Note, It is not strange if those who make a jest of the most sacred oaths can make a jest likewise of the most sacred oracles; for where will a profane mind stop? But shall their unbelief invalidate the counsel of God? Are they safe because they are secure? By no means; nay, the contempt they put upon divine warnings is a sin that brings to remembrance their other sins, and they may thank themselves if they be now remembered against them. (1.) Their present wickedness is discovered. Now that God is contending with them so perverse and obstinate are they that whatever they offer in their own defence does but add to their offence; they never conducted themselves so ill as they did now that they had the loudest call given them to repent and reform: *"So that in all your doings your sins do appear.* Turn yourselves which way you will, you show a black side." This is too true of every one of us; for not only there is *none that lives and sins not,* but *there is not a must man upon earth that does good and sins not.* Our best services have such allays of weakness, and folly, and imperfection, and so much *evil* is *present with us* even when we *would do good,* that we may say, with sorrow and shame, *In all our doings,* and in all our sayings too, *our sins do appear,* and witness against us, so that if we were under the law we were undone. (2.) This brings to mind their former wickedness: *"You have made your iniquity to be remembered,* not by yourselves that it might be repented of, but by the justice of God that it might be reckoned for. Your own sins make the sins of your fathers to be remembered against you, which otherwise you should never have smarted for." Note, God remembers former iniquities against those only who by the present discoveries of their wickedness show that they do not repent of them. (3.) That they may suffer for all together, they are turned over to the destroyed, that they may be taken (*v.* 23): *"You shall be taken with the hand* that God had appointed to seize you and to hold you and out of which you cannot escape." Men are said to be *God's hand* when they are made use of as the ministers of his justice, Ps. 17:14. Note, Those who will not be taken with the word of God's grace shall at last be taken by the hand of his wrath.

2. The prince likewise brings his ruin upon himself. Zedekiah is the *prince of Israel,* to whom the prophet here, in God's name, addresses himself; and, if he had not spoken in God's name, he would not have spoken so boldly, so bluntly; for *is it fit to say to a king, Thou art wicked?* (1.) He gives him his character, *v.* 25. Thou profane and *wicked prince of Israel!* He was not so bad as some of his predecessors, and yet bad enough to merit his character. He was himself profane, lost to every thing that is virtuous and sacred. And he was wicked, as he promoted sin among his people; he sinned, and *made Israel to sin.* Note, Profaneness and wickedness are bad in any, but worst of all in a prince, a prince of Israel, who as an Israelite should know better himself, and as a prince should set a better example and have a better influence on those about him. (2.) He reads him his doom. His iniquity *has an end;* the measure of it is full, and therefore *his day has come,* the day of his punishment, the day of divine vengeance. Note, Though those who are wicked and profane may flourish awhile, yet *their day will come* to fall. The sentence here passed is, [1.] That Zedekiah shall be deposed. He has forfeited his crown, and he shall no longer wear it; he has by his profaneness profaned his crown, and it shall be *cast to the ground* (*v.* 26): *Remove the diadem.* Crowns and diadems are losable things; it is only in the other world that there is a crown of glory that fades not away, a *kingdom that cannot be moved.* The Chaldee paraphrase expounds it thus: *Take away the diadem from Seraiah the chief priest, and I will take away the crown from Zedekiah the king; neither this nor that shall abide in his place, but shall be removed. This shall not be the same,* not the same that he has been; *this not this* (so the word is); profane and wicked perhaps he is as he has been. Note, Men lose their dignity by their iniquity. Their profaneness and wickedness remove their diadem, and take off their crown, and make them the reverse of what they were. [2.] That great confusion and disorder in the state shall follow hereupon. Every thing shall be turned upside down. The conqueror shall take a pride in *exalting him that is low* and *abasing him that is high,* preferring some and degrading others, at his pleasure, without any regard either to right or merit. [3.] Attempts to re-establish the government shall be blasted and come to nothing, Gedaliah's particularly, and Ishmael's who was *of the seed-royal* (to which the Chaldee paraphrase refers this); neither of them shall be able to make any thing of it. *I will overturn, overturn, overturn,* first one project and then another; for who can build up what God will throw down? [4.] This monarchy shall never be restored till it is fixed for perpetuity in the hands of the Messiah. There *shall be no more* kings of the house of David after Zedekiah, till Christ comes, *whose right the kingdom is,* who is that seed of David in whom the promise was to have its full accomplishment, and *I will give it to him.* He shall have *the throne of his father David,* Lu. 1:32. Immediately before the coming of Christ there was a long eclipse of the royal dignity, as there was also a failing of the spirit of prophecy, that his shining forth in the fulness of time both as king and prophet might appear the more illustrious. Note, Christ has an incontestable title to the dominion and sovereignty both in the church and in the world; the kingdom is his right. And, having the right, he shall in due time have the possession: *I will give it to him;* and there shall be a general overturning of all rather

than he shall come short of his right, and a certain overturning of all the opposition that stands in his way to make room for him, Dan. 2:45; 1 Co. 15:25. This is mentioned here for the comfort of those who feared that the promise made in David would fail for evermore. "No," says God, "that promise is sure, for the Messiah's kingdom shall last for ever."

Verses 28–32

The prediction of the destruction of the Ammonites, which was effected by Nebuchadnezzar about five years after the destruction of Jerusalem, seems to come in here upon occasion of the king of Babylon's diverting his design against Rabbath, when he turned it upon Jerusalem. Upon this the Ammonites grew very insolent, and triumphed over Jerusalem; but the prophet must let them know that forbearance is no acquittance; the reprieve is not a pardon; their day also is at hand; their turn comes next, and it will be but a poor satisfaction to them that they are to be devoured last, to be last executed.

I. The sin of the Ammonites is here intimated; it is *their reproach, v.* 28. 1. The reproach they put upon themselves when they hearkened to their false prophets (for such it seems there were among them as well as among the Jews), who pretended to foretel their perpetual safety in the midst of the desolations that were made of the countries round about them: "They *see vanity unto thee and divine a lie, v.* 29. They flatter thee with promises of peace, and thou art such a fool as to suffer thyself to be imposed upon by them and to encourage them therein by giving credit to them." Note, Those that feed themselves with a self-conceit in the day of their prosperity prepare matter for a self-reproach in the day of their calamity. 2. The reproach they put upon the Israel of God, when they triumphed in their afflictions, and thereby added affliction to them, which was very barbarous and inhuman. Their divines, by puffing them up with a conceit that they were a better people than Israel, being spared when they were cut off, and with a confidence that their prosperity should always continue, made them so very haughty and insolent that they did even *tread on the necks of the Israelites that were slain, slain by the wicked Chaldeans,* who had commission to execute God's judgments upon them when their *iniquity had an end,* that is, when the measure of it was full. We shall meet with this again, *ch.* 25:3, etc. Note, Those are ripening apace for misery who trample upon the people of God in their distress, whereas they ought to tremble when *judgment begins at the house of God.*

II. The utter destruction of the Ammonites is threatened. For the reproach cast on the church by her neighbours will be returned into their own bosom, Ps. 79:12. Let us see how terrible the threatening is and the destruction will be. 1. It shall come *from the wrath of God,* who resents the indignities and injuries done to his people as done to himself (*v.* 31): *I will pour out my indignation* as a shower of fire and brimstone *upon thee.* The least drop of divine *indignation and wrath* will create *tribulation and anguish* enough to the *soul of man that does evil;* what then would a full stream of that indignation and wrath do? *"I will blow against thee in the fire of my wrath;* that is, I will blow up the fire of my wrath against thee; it shall burn with the utmost vehemence." *Thou shalt be for fuel to this fire, v.* 32. Note, Wicked men make themselves fuel to the fire of God's wrath; they are consumed by it, and it is inflamed by them. 2. It shall be effected by the sword of war; to them he must cry, as before to Israel, because they had triumphed in Israel's overthrow: *The sword, the sword is drawn* (*v.* 28, compare *v.* 9, 10); it is drawn *to consume because of the glittering,* because it is brandished and glitters, and is fit to be made use of. God's executions will answer his preparations. This sword, when it is drawn, *shall not return into its sheath* (*v.* 30) till it has done the work for which it was drawn. When the sword is drawn it does not return till *God causes it to return,* and *he is in one mind and who can turn him?* Who can change his purpose? 3. The persons employed in it are *brutish men, and skilful to destroy.* Men of such a bad character as this, who have the wit of men to do the work of wild beasts — human reason, which makes them skilful, but no human compassion, which makes them skilful only to destroy — though they are the scandal of mankind, yet sometimes are made use of to serve God's purposes. God *delivers the Ammonites into the hands of such,* and justly, for they themselves were brutish, and delighted in the destruction of God's Israel. We have reason to pray, as Paul desired to be prayed for, that we may be *delivered from wicked and unreasonable men* (2 Th. 3:2), men that seem made for doing mischief. 4. The place where they should thus be reckoned with: *"I will judge thee where thou wast created,* where thou wast first formed into a people, and where thou hast been settled ever since, and therefore where thou seemest to have taken root; *the land of thy nativity* shall be the land of thy destruction." Note, God can bring ruin upon us even where we are most secure, and turn us out of that land which we thought we had a title to not to be disputed and a possession of not to be disturbed. *Thy blood shall be shed* not only in thy borders, but *in the midst of thy land. Lastly,* I shall be an irreparable ruin: "Though thou mayest think to recover thyself, it is in vain to think of it; thou *shalt be no more remembered* with any respect," Ps. 9:6. Justly is their name blotted out who would have Israel's name for ever lost.

CHAPTER 22

Here are three separate messages which God entrusts the prophet to deliver concerning Judah and Jerusalem, and all to the same purport, to show them their sins and the judgments that were coming upon them for those sins. I. Here is a catalogue of their sins, by which they had exposed themselves to shame and for which God would bring them to ruin (*v.* 1–16). II. They are here compared to dross, and are condemned as dross to the fire (*v.* 17–22). III. All orders and degrees of men among them are here found guilty of the neglect of the duty of their place and of having contributed to the national guilt, which therefore, since none appeared as intercessors, they must all expect to share in the punishment of (*v.* 23–31).

Verses 1–16

In these verses the prophet by a commission from Heaven sits as a judge upon the bench, and Jerusalem is made to hold up her hand as a prisoner at the bar; and, if prophets were set over other nations, much more over God's nation, Jer. 1:10. This prophet is authorized to *judge the bloody city,* the *city of bloods.* Jerusalem is so called, not only because she had been guilty of the particular sin of blood-shed, but because her crimes in general were bloody crimes (*ch.* 7:23), such as polluted her in her blood, and for which she deserved to have blood given her to drink. Now the business of a judge with a malefactor is to convict him of his crimes, and then to pass sentence upon him for them. These two things Ezekiel is to do here.

I. He is to find Jerusalem guilty of many heinous crimes here enumerated in a long bill of indictment, and it is *billa vera — a true bill;* so he writes upon it whose judgment we are sure is according to truth. He must *show her all her abominations* (*v.* 2), that God may be justified in all the desolations brought upon her. Let us take a view of all the particular sins which Jerusalem here stands charged with; and they are all exceedingly sinful.

1. Murder: *The city sheds blood,* not only in the suburbs, where the strangers dwell, but *in the midst of it,* where, one would think, the magistrates would, if any where, be vigilant. Even there people were murdered either in duels or by secret assassinations and poisonings, or in the courts of justice under colour of law, and there was no care taken to discover and punish the murderers according to the law (Gen. 9:6), no, nor so much as the ceremony used to expiate an uncertain murder (Deu. 21:1), and so the guilt and pollution remains upon the city. Thus *thou hast become guilty in thy blood that thou hast shed, v.* 4. This crime is insisted most upon, for it was Jerusalem's measure-filling sin more than any; it is said to be that *which the Lord would not pardon,* 2 Ki. 24:4. (1.) The *princes of Israel,* who should have been the protectors of injured innocence, *every one were to their power to shed blood, v.* 6. They thirsted for it, and delighted in it, and whoever came within their power were sure to feel it; whoever lay at their mercy were sure to find none. (2.) There were those who *carried tales to shed blood, v.* 9. They told lies of men to the princes, to whom they knew it would be pleasing, to incense them against them; or they betrayed what passed in private conversation, to make mischief among neighbours, and set them together by the ears, to bite, and devour, and worry one another, even to death. Note, Those who, by giving invidious characters and telling ill-natured stories of their neighbours, sow discord among brethren, will be accountable for all the mischief that follows upon it; as he that kindles a fire will be accountable for all the hurt it does. (3.) There were those who *took gifts to shed blood* (*v.* 12), who would be hired with money to swear a man out of his life, or, if they were upon a jury, would be bribed to find an innocent man guilty. When so much barbarous bloody work of this kind was done in Jerusalem we may well conclude, [1.] That men's consciences had become wretchedly profligate and seared and their hearts hardened; for those would stick at no wickedness who would not stick at this. [2.] That abundance of quiet, harmless, good people were made away with, whereby, as the guilt of the city was increased, so the number of those that should have stood in the gap to turn away the wrath of God was diminished.

2. Idolatry: *She makes idols against herself to destroy herself, v.* 3. And again (*v.* 4), *Thou hast defiled thyself in thy idols which thou hast made.* Note, Those who make idols for themselves will be found to have made them against themselves, for idolaters put a cheat upon themselves and prepare destruction for themselves; besides that thereby they pollute themselves, they render themselves odious in the eyes of the just and jealous God, and even *their mind and conscience are defiled,* so that to them *nothing is pure.* Those who did not make idols themselves were yet found guilty of *eating upon the mountains,* or high places (*v.* 9), in honour of the idols and in communion with idolaters.

3. Disobedience to parents (*v.* 7): *In thee have* the children *set light by their father and mother,* mocked them, cursed them, and despised to obey them, which was a sign of a more than ordinary corruption of nature as well as manners, and a disposition to all manner of disorder, Isa. 3:5. Those that set light by their parents are in the highway to all wickedness. God had made many wholesome laws for the support of the paternal authority, but no care was taken to put them in execution; nay, the Pharisees in their day taught children, under pretence of respect to the Corban, to set light by their parents and refuse to maintain them, Mt. 15:5.

4. Oppression and extortion. To enrich themselves they wronged the poor (*v.* 7): *They dealt by oppression* and *deceit with the stranger,* taking advantage of his necessities, and his ignorance of the laws and customs of the country. In Jerusalem, that should have been a sanctuary to the oppressed, *they vexed the fatherless and widows* by unreasonable demands and inquisitions, or troublesome lawsuits, in which might prevails against right. *"Thou hast taken usury and increase* (*v.* 12); not only there are those in thee that do it, but thou hast done it." It was an act of the city or community; the public money, which should have been employed in public charity, was put out to usury, with extortion. *Thou hast greedily gained of thy neighbours* by *violence* and *wrong.* For neighbours to gain by one another in a way of fair trading is well, but those who are *greedy of gain* will not be held within the rules of equity.

5. Profanation of the sabbath and other holy things. This commonly goes along with the other sins for which they here stand indicted (*v.* 8): *Thou hast despised my holy things,* holy oracles, holy ordinances. The rites which God appointed were thought too plain, too ordinary; they despised them, and therefore were fond of the customs of the heathen. Note, Immorality and dishonesty are commonly attended with a contempt of religion and the worship of God. *Thou hast profaned my sabbaths.* There was not in Jerusalem that face of sabbath-sanctification that one would have expected in the *holy city.* Sabbath-breaking is an iniquity that is an inlet to all iniquity. Many have owned it to contribute as much to their ruin as any thing.

6. Uncleanness and all manner of seventh-commandment sins, fruits of those vile affections to which God in a way of righteous judgment gives men up, to punish them for their idolatry and profanation of holy things. Jerusalem had been famous for its purity, but now *in the midst of thee they commit lewdness* (*v.* 9); lewdness goes bare-faced, though in the most scandalous instances, as that of a man's having his father's wife, which is the *discovery of the father's nakedness* (*v.* 10) and is a sin not *to be named among Christians* without the utmost detestation (1 Co. 5:1), and was made a capital crime by the law of Moses, Lev. 20:11. The time *to refrain from embracing* has not been observed (Eccles. 3:6), for *they have humbled her that was set apart for her pollution.* They made nothing of committing lewdness with a *neighbour's wife,* with a *daughter-*

in-law, or a sister, *v.* 11. And *shall not God visit for these things?*

7. Unmindfulness of God was at the bottom of all this wickedness (*v.* 12): *"Thou hast forgotten me*, else thou wouldst not have done thus." Note, Sinners do that which provokes God because they forget him; they forget their descent from him, dependence on him, and obligations to him; they forget how valuable his favour is, which they make themselves unfit for, and how formidable his wrath, which they make themselves obnoxious to. Those that *pervert their ways forget the Lord their God,* Jer. 3:21.

II. He is to pass sentence upon Jerusalem for these crimes.

1. Let her know that she has filled up the measure of her iniquity, and that her sins are such as forbid delays and call for speedy vengeance. She has made *her time to come* (*v.* 3), *her days to draw near;* and she *has come to her years* of maturity for punishment (*v.* 4), as an heir that has *come to age* and is ready for his inheritance. God would have borne longer with them, but they had arrived at such a pitch of impudence in sin that God could not in honour give them a further day. Note, Abused patience will at last be weary of forbearing. And, when sinners (as Solomon speaks) grow *overmuch wicked*, they *die before their time* (Eccl. 7:17) and shorten their reprieves.

2. Let her know that she has exposed herself, and therefore God has justly exposed her, to the contempt and scorn of all her neighbours (*v.* 4): *I have made thee a reproach to the heathen,* both *those who are near,* who are eyewitnesses of Jerusalem's apostasy and degeneracy, and *those afar off,* who, though at a distance, will think it worth taking notice of (*v.* 5); they shall all *mock thee.* While they were reproached by their neighbours for their adherence to God it was their honour, and they might be sure that God would roll away their reproach. But, now that they are laughed at for their revolt from God, they must lie down in their shame, and must say, The Lord is righteous. They make a mock at Jerusalem, both because her sins had been very *scandalous* (she is *infamous, polluted in name,* and has quite lost her credit), and because her punishment is very *grievous* — she is *much vexed* and frets without measure at her troubles. Note, Those who fret most at their troubles have commonly those about them who will be so much the more apt to make a jest of them.

3. Let her know that God is displeased, highly displeased, at her wickedness, and does and will witness against it (*v.* 13): *I have smitten my hand at thy dishonest gain.* God, both by his prophets and by his providence, revealed his wrath from heaven against their *ungodliness* and *unrighteousness*, the oppressions they were guilty of, though they got by them, and *their murders* (the *blood which has been in the midst of thee)*, and all their other sins. Note, God has sufficiently discovered how angry he is at the wicked courses of his people; and, that they may not say that they have not had fair warning, he *smites his hand* against the sin before he *lays his hand* upon the sinner. And this is a good reason why we should despise dishonest gain, even the *gain of oppressions*, and *shake our hands from holding bribes,* because these are sins against which God *shakes his hands,* Isa. 33:15.

4. Let her know that, proud and secure as she is, she is no match for God's judgments, *v.* 14. (1.) She is assured that the destruction she has deserved will come: *I the Lord have spoken it, and will do it.* He that is true to his promises will be true to his threatenings too, for he is not a man that he should repent. (2.) It is supposed that she thinks herself able to contend with God, and so stand a siege against his judgments. She bade defiance to the day of the Lord, Isa. 5:19. But, (3.) She is convinced of her utter inability to make her part good with him: *"Can thy heart endure, or can thy hand be strong, in the days that I shall deal with thee?* Thou thinkest thou hast to do only with men like thyself, but shalt be made to know that thou fallest into the hands of a living God." Observe here, [1.] There is a day coming when God will *deal with sinners,* a day of visitation. He deals with some to bring them to repentance, and there is no resisting the force of convictions when he sets them on; he deals with others to bring them to ruin. He deals with sinners in this life, when he brings upon them his sore judgments; but the days of eternity are especially the days in which God will deal with them, when the full vials of God's wrath will be poured out without

mixture. [2.] The wrath of God against sinners, when he comes to deal with them, will be found both intolerable and irresistible. There is no heart stout enough to endure it; it is none of the infirmities which *the spirit of a man will sustain.* Damned sinners can neither forget nor despise their torments, nor have they any thing wherewith to support themselves under their torments. There are no hands strong enough either to ward off the strokes of God's wrath or to break the chains with which sinners are bound over to the day of wrath. *Who knows the power of God's anger?*

5. Let her know that, since she has walked in the way of the heathen, and learned their works, she shall have enough of them (*v.* 15): *"I will* not only send thee *among the heathen,* out of thy own land, but *I will scatter thee* among them and *disperse thee in the countries,* to be abused and insulted over by strangers." And since her *filthiness* and *filthy ones* continued in her, notwithstanding all the methods God had taken to *refine* her (she *would not be made clean,* Jer. 13:27), he will be his judgments *consume her filthiness out of her;* he will destroy those that are incurably bad and reform those that are inclined to be good.

6. Let her know that God has disowned her and cast her off. He had been her heritage and portion; but now (*v.* 16), *"Thou shalt take thy inheritance in thyself,* shift for thyself, make the best hand thou canst for thyself, for God will no longer undertake for thee." Note, Those that give up themselves to be ruled by their lusts will justly be given up to be portioned by them. Those that resolve to be their own masters, let them expect no other comfort and happiness than what their own hands can furnish them with, and a miserable portion it will prove. *Verily, I say unto you, They have their reward. Thou in thy life-time receivedst thy good things.* These are the same with this, *"Thou shalt take thy inheritance in thyself,* and then, when it is too late, shalt own *in the sight of the heathen that I am the Lord,* who alone am a portion sufficient for my people." Note, Those that have lost their interest in God will know how to value it.

Verses 17–22

The same melancholy string is still harped upon, and various turns are given it, to make it affecting, that it may be influencing. The prophet must here show, or at least it is here shown him, that the whole house of Israel has become as dross and that as dross they shall be consumed. What David has said concerning the wicked ones of the world is here said concerning the wicked ones of the church, now that it is corrupt and degenerate (Ps. 119:119): *Thou puttest away all the wicked of the earth like dross.*

I. See here how the wretched degeneracy of the house of Israel is described. That state, in David's and Solomon's time, had been *a head of gold;* when the kingdoms were divided it was as the *arms of silver.* But now, 1. It has degenerated into baser metal, of no value in comparison with what it formerly was: *They are all brass, and tin, and iron, and lead,* which some make to signify divers sorts of sinners among them. Their being brass denotes the impudence of some in their wickedness; they are *brazen-faced,* and cannot blush; their *shoes* had been *iron and brass* (Deu. 33:25), but now their brow is so, Isa. 48:4. Their being tin denotes the hypocritical profession of piety with which many of them cover their iniquity; they have a specious show, but no intrinsic worth. Their being iron denotes the cruel disposition of some, and their delight in war, according to the character of the *iron age.* Their being lead denotes their dulness, sottishness, and stupidity: though soft and pliable to evil, yet heavy and not movable to good. *How has the gold become dross! How has the most fine gold changed!* So is Jerusalem's degeneracy bewailed, Lam. 4:1. Yet this is not the worst; these metals, though of less value, are yet of good use. But, 2. The *house of Israel has become dross to me.* So she is in God's account, whatever she is in her own and her neighbours' account. They were silver, but now they are *even the dross of silver;* the word signifies all the dirt, and rubbish, and worthless stuff, that are separated from the silver in the washing, melting, and refining of it. Note, Sinners, and especially degenerate professors, are in God's account as dross, vile, and contemptible, and of no account, as the *evil figs* which *could not be eaten, they were so evil.* They are useless and fit

for nothing; of no consistency with themselves and no service to man.

II. How the woeful destruction of this degenerate house of Israel is foretold. They are all gathered together in Jerusalem; thither people fled from all parts of the country as to a city of refuge, not only because it was a strong city, but because it was the holy city. Now God tells them that their flocking into Jerusalem, which they intended for their security, should be as the gathering of various sorts of metal into the furnace or crucible, to be melted down, and to have the dross separated from them. They are *in the midst of Jerusalem,* surrounded by the forces of the enemy; and, being thus enclosed, 1. The *fire of God's wrath* shall be kindled upon this furnace, and it shall be *blown,* to make it burn fiercely and strongly, *v.* 20, 21. God will *gather them in his anger and fury.* The blowing of the fire makes a great noise, so will the judgments of God upon Jerusalem. When God stirs up himself to execute judgments upon a provoking people, from the consideration of his own glory and the necessity of making some examples, then he may be said to *blow the fire of his wrath* against sin and sinners, to *heat the furnace seven times hotter.* 2. The several sorts of metal gathered in it shall be melted; by a complication of judgments, as by a raging fire, their constitution shall be dissolved, they shall lose all their former shape and strength, and shall be utterly unable to stand before the wrath of God. The various sorts of sinners shall be melted down together, and united in a common overthrow, as *brass* and *lead* in the same furnace, as trees are *bound in bundles for the fire.* They came together into Jerusalem as a place of defence, but God brought them together there as unto a place of execution. 3. God will leave them in the furnace (*v.* 20): I will *gather you into the furnace* and will *leave you there.* When God brings his own people into the furnace he sits by them, as the refiner by his gold, to see that they be not continued there any longer than is fitting and needful; but he will bring these people into the furnace, as men throw dross into it, which they design shall be consumed, and therefore are in no care about it, but *leave it there.* Compare with this Hos. 5:14, *I will tear and go away.* 4. Hereby the dross shall be wholly separated and the good metal purified, the impenitent shall be destroyed and the penitent reformed and fitted for deliverance. *Take away the dross from the silver, and there shall come forth a vessel for the finer,* Prov. 25:4. This judgment shall do that in the house of Israel for the doing of which other methods had been tried in vain, and *reprobate silver shall they no more be called,* Jer. 6:30.

Verses 23–31

Here is, I. A general idea given of the land of Israel, how well it deserved the judgments coming to destroy it and how much it needed these judgments to refine it. Let the prophet tell her plainly, *"Thou art the land that is not cleansed,* not refined as metal is, and therefore needest to be again put into the furnace. Means and methods of reformation have been ineffectual; thou art *not rained upon in the day of indignation."* This was one of the judgments which God brought upon them in the day of his wrath, he *withheld the rain* from them, Jer. 14:4. Or, "When thou art under the tokens of God's displeasure, even in the day of indignation thou art *not rained upon;* thou hast not received instruction by the prophets, whose doctrine is said to *descend as the rain."* Or, "When thou art corrected thou art not cleansed; thy filth is not carried away as that in the streets is by a sweeping rain. Nay, though it be a *day of indignation* with thee, yet thy filthiness, which should be done away, has become more *offensive,* as that of a city is in dry weather, when it is not rained upon." Or, "Thou hast nothing to refresh and comfort thyself with *in the day of indignation;* thou art not rained upon by divine consolations." So the rich man in torment had not a *drop of water,* or rain, *to cool his tongue.*

II. A particular charge drawn up against the several orders and degrees of men among them, which shows that they had all helped to fill the measure of the nation's guilt, but none had done any thing towards the emptying of it; they are therefore all alike.

1. They have every one *corrupted his way,* and those who should have been the brightest examples of virtue were ringleaders in iniquity and patterns of vice.

(1.) The *prophets*, who pretended to make known the

mind of God to them, were not only *deceivers,* but *devourers* (*v.* 25), and hardened them in their wickedness both by their preaching, wherein they promised them impunity and prosperity, and by their conversation, in which they were as profligate as any. *There is a conspiracy of her prophets* against God and religion, against the true prophets and all good men; they conspired together to be all in one song, as Ahab's prophets were, to assure them of peace in their sinful ways. Note, The unity which is found among pretenders to infallibility, and which they so much boast of, is only the result of a secret *conspiracy* against the truth. Satan is not *divided against himself.* The prophets are *in conspiracy* with the murderers and oppressors, to patronise and protect them in their wickedness, and justify what they did with their false prophecies, provided they may come in sharers with them in the profits of it. They are like *a roaring lion ravening the prey;* they thunder out threats against those whose ruin is aimed at, terrify them, or make them odious to the people, and so make themselves masters, [1.] Of their lives: They *have devoured souls,* have been accessory to the shedding of the blood of many an innocent person, and so have made many to become sorrowful widows who were comfortable wives. They have persecuted those to death who witnessed against their pretensions to prophecy and would not be imposed upon by their counterfeit commission. Or, They devoured souls by flattering sinners into a false peace and a vain hope, and seducing them into the paths of sin, which would be their eternal ruin. Note, Those who draw men to wickedness, and encourage them in it, are the devourers and murderers of their souls. [2.] Of their estates. When Naboth is slain they take possession of his vineyard; *They have seized the treasure and precious things,* as forfeited; some way or other they had of *devouring the widows' houses,* as the Pharisees, Mt. 23:14. Or, They got this *treasure,* and all these *precious things,* as fees for false and flattering prophecies; for *he that puts not into their mouths, they even prepare war against him,* Mic. 3:5. It was said with Jerusalem when such men as these passed for prophets.

(2.) The priests, who were teachers by office, and had the custody of the sacred things, and should have called the false prophets to account, were as bad as they, *v.* 26. [1.] They violated the law of God, which they should have observed and taught others to observe. They made no conscience of the law of the priesthood, but openly broke it, and with contempt, as Hophni and Phinehas. They did what they had a mind, with an express *non obstante — notwithstanding* to the word of God. And how should those teach the people their duty who lived in contradiction to their own? [2.] They *profaned God's holy things,* about which they were to minister, and which they ought to have restrained others from the profanation of. They suffered those to eat of the holy things who were unqualified by the law. The table of the Lord was contemptible with them. By dealing in holy things with such unhallowed hands they did themselves profane them. [3.] They did not themselves put a difference, nor did they show the people how to *put a difference, between the holy and profane, the clean and the unclean,* according to the directions and distinctions of the law. They did not exclude those from God's courts who were excluded by the law, nor teach the people to observe the difference the law had made between food clean and unclean, between times and places holy and common; but they lived at large themselves and encouraged the people to do so too. [4.] They *hid their eyes from God's sabbaths;* they took no care about them; it was all one to them whether God's sabbaths were kept holy or no; they neither gave countenance to those who observed them nor check to those who profaned them, nor did they themselves show any regard to them or veneration for them. They winked at those who did servile works on that day, and looked another way when they should have inspected the behaviour of the people on sabbath days. God's sabbaths have such a beauty and glory put upon them by the divine institution as may command respect; but they *hid their eyes* from them and would not see that excellency in them. [5.] By all this God himself was *profaned among them;* his authority was slighted, his goodness made light of, and the highest affront and contempt imaginable were put upon his holiness. Note, The profanation of the honour of the scriptures, of sabbaths and sacred things, is a profanation of the honour of God himself, who is interested in them.

(3.) The princes, who should have interposed with their authority to redress these grievances, were as daring transgressors of the law as any (*v.* 27): *They are like wolves ravening the prey;* for such is power without justice and goodness to direct it. All their business was to gratify, [1.] Their own pride and ambition, by making themselves arbitrary and formidable. [2.] Their own malice and revenge, by *shedding blood* and *destroying souls,* sacrificing to their cruelty all those that stood in their way or had in any thing disobliged them. [3.] Their own avarice; all they aim at is to *get dishonest gain,* by crushing and oppressing their subject. *Lucri bonus est odor ex re qualibet. Rem, rem, quocunque modo rem — Sweet is the odour of gain, from whatever substance it ascends. Money, money, by fairness or by fraud, get money.* But, though they had power sufficient to carry them on in their oppressive courses, yet how could they answer it both to their credit and to their consciences? We are told how (*v.* 28): The prophets *daubed them with untempered mortar,* told them in God's name (horrid wickedness!) that there was no harm in what they did, that they might dispose of the lives and estates of their subjects as they pleased, and could do no wrong, nay, that in prosecuting such and such whom they had marked out they did God service; and thus they stopped the mouth of their consciences. They also justified what they did, to the people, nay, and *magnified* it as if it were all for the public good, and so saved their reputation, and kept their oppressed subjects from murmuring. Note, Daubing prophets are the great supporters of ravening princes, but will prove at last their great deceivers, for they daub with untempered mortar which will not hold, nor will the wall stand long that is built up with it. They pretend to be seers, but they *see vanity;* they pretend to be diviners, but they *divine lies;* they pretend a warrant from Heaven for what they say, and that it is all as true as gospel; they say, *Thus saith the Lord God,* but it is all a sham, for *the Lord has not spoken any such thing.*

(4.) The people that had any power in their hands learned of their princes to abuse it, *v.* 29. Those that should have complained of the oppression of the subject, and have put in a *claim of rights* on behalf of the injured, that should have stood up for liberty and property, were themselves invaders of them: *The people of the land have used oppression and exercised robbery.* The rich oppress the poor, masters their servants, landlords their tenants, and even parents their own children; nay, the buyers and sellers will find some way to oppress one another. This is such a sin as, when it is national, is indeed a national judgment, and is threatened as such. Isa. 3:5, *The people shall be oppressed every one by his neighbour.* It is an aggravation of the sin that they have *vexed the poor and needy,* whom they should have relieved, and have *oppressed the stranger* and deprived him of *his right,* to whom they ought to have been not only just, but kind. Thus was the apostasy universal and the disease epidemical.

2. There is none that appears as an intercessor for them (*v.* 30): *I sought for a man among them that should stand in the gap, but I found none.* Note, (1.) Sin makes a gap in the hedge of protection that is about a people at which good things run out from them and evil things pour in upon them, a gap by which God enters to destroy them. (2.) There is a way of standing in the gap, and making up the breach against the judgments of God, by repentance, and prayer, and reformation. Moses stood in the gap when he made intercession for Israel to *turn away the wrath of God,* Ps. 106:23. (3.) When God is coming forth against a sinful people to destroy them he expects some to intercede for them, and enquires if there be but one that does; so much is it his desire and delight to show mercy. If there be but a man that stands in the gap, as Abraham for Sodom, he will discover him and be well pleased with him. (4.) It bodes ill to a people when judgments are breaking in upon them, and the spirit of prayer is restrained, so that *not one is found* that will either give them a good word or speak a good word for them. (5.) When it is so, what can be expected but utter ruin? *Therefore have I poured out my indignation upon them* (*v.* 31), have given it full scope, that it may come upon them in a full stream; yet, whatever God's wrath inflicts upon a people, it is *their own way* that is therein *recompensed upon their heads,* and God deals with them no worse, but even much better, than their iniquity deserves.

CHAPTER 23

This long chapter (as before *ch.* 16 and 20) is a history of the apostasies of God's people from him and the aggravations of those apostasies under the similitude of corporal whoredom and adultery. Here the kingdoms of Israel and Judah, the ten tribes and the two, with their capital cities, Samaria and Jerusalem, are considered distinctly. Here is, I. The apostasy of Israel and Samaria from God (*v.* 1–8) and their ruin for it (*v.* 9, 10). II. The apostasy of Judah and Jerusalem from God (*v.* 11–21) and sentence passed upon them, that they shall in like manner be destroyed for it (*v.* 22–35). III. The joint wickedness of them both together (*v.* 36–44) and the joint ruin of them both (*v.* 45–49). And all that is written for warning against the sins of idolatry, and confidence in an arm of flesh, and sinful leagues and confederacies with wicked people (which are the sins here meant by committing whoredom), is that others may hear and fear, and not sin after the similitude of the transgressions of Israel and Judah.

Verses 1–10

God had often spoken to Ezekiel, and by him to the people, to this effect, but now his word *comes again;* for *God speaks* the same thing *once, yea, twice,* yea, many a time, and all little enough, and too little, for *man perceives it not.* Note, To convince sinners of the evil of sin, and of their misery and danger by reason of it, there is need of *line upon line,* so loth we are to know the worst of ourselves. The sinners that are here to be exposed are *two women,* two kingdoms, sister-kingdoms, Israel and Judah, *daughters of one mother,* having been for a long time but *one people.* Solomon's kingdom was so large, so populous, that immediately after his death it divided into two. Observe, 1. Their character when they were one (*v.* 3): *They committed whoredoms in Egypt,* for there they were guilty of idolatry, as we read before, *ch.* 20:8. The representing of those sins which are most provoking to God and most ruining to a people by the sin of whoredom plainly intimates what an exceedingly sinful sin uncleanness is, how offensive, how destructive. Doubtless it is itself one of the worst of sins, for the worst of other sins are compared to it here and often elsewhere, which should increase our detestation and dread of all manner of *fleshly lusts,* all appearances of them and approaches to them, as *warring against the soul,* infatuating sinners, bewitching them, alienating their minds from God and all that is good, debauching conscience, rendering them odious in the eyes of the pure and holy God, and drowning them at last in destruction and perdition. 2. Their names when they became two, *v.* 4. The kingdom of Israel is called the *elder sister,* because that first made the breach, and separated from the family both of kings and priests that God had appointed — the *greater sister* (so the word is), for ten tribes belonged to that kingdom and only two to the other. God says of them both, *They were mine,* for they were the seed of Abraham *his friend* and of Jacob *his chosen;* they were in covenant with God, and carried about with them the sign of *their circumcision,* the seal of the covenant. *They were mine;* and therefore their apostasy was the highest injustice. It was alienating God's property, it was the basest ingratitude to the best of benefactors, and a perfidious treacherous violation of the most sacred engagements. Note, Those who have been in profession the people of God, but have revolted from him, have a great deal to answer for more than those who never made any such profession. *"They were mine;* they were espoused tome, and to me *they bore sons and daughters;"* there were many among them that were devoted to God's honour, and employed in his service, and were the strength and beauty of these kingdoms, as children are of the families they are born in. In this parable Samaria and the kingdom of Israel shall bear the name of *Aholah — her own tabernacle,* because the places of worship which that kingdom had were of their own devising, their own choosing, and the worship itself was their own invention; God never owned it. *Her tabernacle to herself* (so some render it); "let her take it to herself, and make her best of it." Jerusalem and the kingdom of Judah bear the name of *Aholibah — my tabernacle is in her,* because *their* temple was the place which God himself had *chosen* to *put his name there.* He acknowledged it to be his, and honoured them with the tokens of his presence in it. Note, Of those that stand in relation to God, and make profession of his name, some have greater privileges and advantages than others; and, as those who have greater are thereby rendered the more inexcusable if they revolt from God, so those who have less will not thereby be rendered inexcusable. 3. The treacherous departure of the kingdom of Israel from God (*v.* 5): *Aholah played the harlot when she was mine.* Though the ten tribes had deserted the house of David, yet God owned them for *his* still; though Jeroboam, in setting up the golden calves, *sinned, and made Israel to sin,* yet, as long as they worshipped the God of Israel only, though by images, he did not quite cast them off. But they way of sin is downhill. Aholah played the harlot, brought in the worship of Baal (1 Ki. 16:31), set up that other god, that dunghill-god, in competition with Jehovah (1 Ki. 18:21), as a vile adulteress *dotes on her lovers,* because they are well dressed and make a figure, because they are young and handsome (*v.* 6), *clothed with blue, captains and rulers, desirable young* men, genteel, and that pass for men of honour, so she doted upon her neighbours, particularly the Assyrians, who had extended their conquests near them; she admired their idols and worshipped them, admired the pomp of their courts and their military strength and courted alliances with them upon any terms, as if her own God were not sufficient to be depended upon. We find one of the kings of Israel giving a *thousand talents* to the *king of Assyria,* to engage him in his interests, 2 Ki. 15:19. She doted on the *chosen men of Assyria,* as worthy to be trusted and employed in the service of the state (*v.* 7), and *on all their idols with which she defiled herself.* Note, Whatever creature we dote upon, pay homage to, and put a confidence in, we make an idol of that creature; and whatever we make an idol of we defile ourselves with. And now again the conviction looks back as far as the original of their nation: *Neither left she her whoredoms which she brought from Egypt, v.* 8. Their being idolaters in Egypt was a thing never to be forgotten — that they should be in love with Egypt's idols even when they were continually in fear of Egypt's tyrants and task-masters! But (as some have observed) therefore, at that time, when Satan boasted of his having *walked through the earth* as all his own, to disprove his pretensions God did not say, Hast thou considered *my people Israel in Egypt?* (for they had become idolaters, and were not to be boasted of), but, *Hast thou considered my servant Job in the land of Uz?* And this corrupt disposition in them, when they were first formed into a people, is an emblem of that original corruption which is born with us and is woven into our constitution, a strong bias towards the world and the flesh, like that in the Israelites towards idolatry; it was *bred in the bone* with them, and was charged upon them long after, that they *left not their whoredoms brought from Egypt.* It would never *out of the flesh,* though Egypt had been a house of bondage to them. Thus the corrupt affections and inclinations which we brought into the world with us we have not lost, nor got clear of, but still retain them, though the iniquity we were born in was the source of all the calamities which human life is liable to. 4. The destruction of the kingdom of Israel for their apostasy from God (*v.* 9, 10): *I have delivered her into the hand of her lovers.* God first justly gave her up to her lust *(Ephraim is joined to idols, let him alone),* and then gave her up *to her lovers.* The neighbouring nations, whose idolatries she had conformed to and whose friendship she had confided in, and in both had affronted God, are now made use of as the instruments of her destruction. The *Assyrians, on whom she doted,* soon spied out the *nakedness of the land,* discovered her blind side, on which to attack her, stripped her of all her ornaments and all her defences, and so *uncovered* her, and *made her naked and bare,* carried her *sons and daughters* into captivity, *slew her with the sword,* and quite destroyed that kingdom and put an end to it. We have the story at large 2 Ki. 17:6, etc., where the cause of the ruin of that once flourishing kingdom by the Assyrians is shown to be their forsaking the God of Israel, *fearing other gods,* and *walking in the statutes of the heathen;* it was for this that God was very *angry with them and removed them out of his sight, v.* 18. And that the Assyrians, whom they had been so fond of, should be employed in *executing judgments* upon them was very remarkable, and shows how God, in a way of righteous judgment, often makes that a scourge to sinners which they have inordinately set their hearts upon. The devil will for ever be a tormentor to those impenitent sinners who now hearken to him and comply with him as a tempter. Thus Samaria became *famous among women,* or *infamous* rather; she *became a name* (so the word is); not only she came to be the subject of discourse, and much talked of, as the desolations of cities and kingdoms fill the newspapers, but she was thus ruined for her idolatries *in terrorem — for warning* to all people to take heed of doing likewise; as the public execution of notorious malefactors makes them such *a name,* such an ill name, as may serve to frighten others from those wicked courses which have brought them to a miserable and shameful end. Deu. 21:21, *All Israel shall hear and fear.*

Verses 11–21

The prophet Hosea, in his time, observed that the two tribes retained their integrity, in a great measure, when the ten tribes had apostatized (Hos. 11:12, *Ephraim indeed compasses me about with lies, but Judah yet rules with God and is faithful with the saints;* and this was justly expected from them: Hos. 4:15, *Though thou Israel play the harlot, yet let not Judah offend);* but this lasted not long. By some unhappy matches made between the house of David and the house of Ahab the worship of Baal had been brought into the kingdom of Judah, but had been by the reforming kings worked out again; and at the time of the captivity of the ten tribes, which was in the reign of Hezekiah, things were in a good posture: but it lasted not long. In the reign of Manasseh, soon after the kingdom of Judah had seen the destruction of the kingdom of Israel, they became more corrupt than Israel had been in their inordinate love of idols, *v.* 11. Instead of being made better by the warning which that destruction gave them, they were made worse by it, as if they were *displeased because the Lord had made that breach upon Israel,* and for that reason became disaffected to him and to his service. Instead of being made to stand in awe of him as a *jealous God,* they therefore grew strange to him, and liked those gods better that would admit of partners with them. Note, Those may justly expect God's judgments upon themselves who do not take warning by his judgments upon others, who see in others what is the end of sin and yet continue to make a light matter of it. But it is bad indeed with those who are made worse by that which should make them better, and have their lusts irritated and exasperated by that which was designed to suppress and subdue them. Jerusalem grew worse *in her whoredoms* than her sister Samaria had been *in her whoredoms.* This was observed before (*ch.* 16:51), *Neither has Samaria committed half of thy sins.*

I. Jerusalem, that had been a *faithful city, became a harlot,* Isa. 1:21. She also *doted upon the Assyrians* (*v.* 12), joined in league with them, joined in worship with them, grew to be in love with their *captains and rulers,* and cried them up as finer and more accomplished gentlemen than any that ever the land of Israel produced. "See how richly, how neatly, they are dressed, *clothed most gorgeously;* how well they sit a horse; they are *horsemen riding on horses;* how charmingly they look, *all of them desirable young men.*" And thus they grew to affect every thing that was foreign and to despise their own nation; and even the religion of it was mean and homely, and not to be compared with the curiosity and gaiety of the heathen temples. Thus she *increased her whoredoms;* she fell in love, fell in league, with the Chaldeans. Hezekiah himself was faulty this way when he was proud of the court which the king of Babylon made to him and complimented his ambassadors with the sight of all his treasures, Isa. 39:2. And the humour increased (*v.* 14); she doted upon the pictures of the Babylonian captains (*v.* 15, 16), joined in alliance with that kingdom, invited them to come and settle in Jerusalem, that they might refine the genius of the Jewish nation and make it more polite; nay, they sent for patterns of their images, altars, and temples, and made use of them in their worship. Thus was she *polluted with her whoredoms* (*v.* 17), and thereby she *discovered her own whoredom* (*v.* 18), her own strong inclination to idolatry. And when she had had enough of the Chaldeans, and grew tired of them and disposed to break her league with them, as Jehoiakim and Zedekiah did, *her mind being alienated from them,* she courted the *Egyptians, doted upon their paramours* (*v.* 20), would come into an alliance with them, and, to strengthen the alliance, would join with them in their idolatries and then depend upon them to be their protectors from all other nations; for so wise, so rich, so strong, was the Egyptian nation, and came to such perfection in idolatry, that there was no nation now which they could take such satisfaction in as in Egypt. Thus they *called to remembrance the days of their youth* (*v.* 19), the *lewdness of their youth, v.* 21. 1. They pleased themselves with the remembrance of it. When they began to set their affections upon Egypt, they encouraged themselves to put a confidence in that kingdom, because of the old acquaintance they had with it, as if they still retained the gust and relish of the *leeks and onions* they ate there, or rather of the idolatrous worship they learned there, and brought up with them thence. When they began an acquaintance with Egypt they remembered how merrily their fathers worshipped the golden calf, what music and dancing they had at that sport, which they learned in Egypt; and they hoped they should now have a fair pretence to come to that again. Thus *she multiplied her whoredoms,* repeated her former whoredoms, and encouraged herself to close with present temptations, by calling *to remembrance the days of her youth.* Note, Those who, instead of reflecting upon their former sins with sorrow and shame, reflect upon them with pleasure and pride, contract new guilt thereby, strengthen their own corruptions, and in effect bid defiance to repentance. This is returning *with the dog to his vomit.* 2. They called it *God's remembrance,* and provoked him to remember it against them. God had said indeed that he would reckon with them for *the golden calf,* that *idol of Egypt* (Ex. 32:34); but such was his patience that he seemed to have forgotten it till they, by their league now with the Egyptians against the Chaldeans, did, as it were, put him in mind of it; and in the day *when he visits he will now,* as he has said, *visit for that.* It is very observable how this adulteress changes her lovers: she dotes first on the Assyrians; then she thought the Chaldeans finer and courted them; after a while her mind was alienated from them, and she thought the Egyptians more powerful (*v.* 20) and she must contract an intimacy with them. This shows the folly, (1.) Of fleshly lusts; when they are indulged they grow humoursome and fickle, are soon surfeited but never satisfied; they must have variety, and what is loved one day is loathed the next. *Unius adulterium matrimonium vocant — One adultery is called marriage,* as Seneca observes. (2.) Of idolatry. Those who think one God too little will not think a hundred sufficient, but will still be for trying more, as finding all insufficient. (3.) Of seeking to creatures for help; we go from one to another, but are disappointed in them all, and can never rest till we have made the God of Israel our help.

II. The faithful God justly gives a bill of divorce to this now faithless city, that has *become a harlot.* His jealousy soon discovered her lewdness (*v.* 13): *I saw that she was defiled,* that she was debauched, and saw which way her inclination was, that the *two sisters both took one way,* and that Jerusalem grew worse than Samaria. For, *if we stretch out our hand to a strange god, will not God search this out?* No doubt he will; and when he has found it can he be pleased with it? No (*v.* 18): *Then my mind was alienated from her, as it was from her sister.* How could the pure and holy God any longer take delight in such a lewd generation? Note, Sin alienates God's mind from the sinner, and justly, for it is the alienation of the sinner's mind from God; but woe, and a thousand woes, to those from whom God's mind is alienated; for whom he turns from he will turn against.

Verses 22–35

Jerusalem stands indicted by the name of *Aholibah,* for that she, as a false traitor to her sovereign Lord the God of heaven, not having his fear before her eyes, but moved by the instigation of the devil, had revolted from her allegiance to him, had compassed and imagined to shake off his government, had kept up a correspondence had joined in confederacy with his enemies, and the pretenders to a deity, in contempt of his crown and dignity. To this indictment she has pleaded, Not guilty: *I am not polluted; I have not gone after Baalim.* But it is found against her by the notorious evidence of the fact, and she stands convicted of it, nor has any thing material to offer why judgment should not be given and execution awarded according to law. In these verses, therefore, we have the sentence.

I. Her old confederates must be her executioners; and

those whom she had courted to be her leaders in sin are now to be employed as instruments of her punishment (*v.* 22): *"I will raise up thy lovers against thee,* the Chaldeans, whom formerly thou didst so much admire and covet an acquaintance with, but from whom thy mind is since alienated and with whom thou hast perfidiously broken covenant." They are called *thy lovers* (*v.* 22) and yet (*v.* 28) *those whom thou hatest.* Note, It is common for sinful love soon to turn into hatred; as Amnon's to Tamar. Those of headstrong and unreasonable passions are often very hot against those persons and things that a little before they were as hot for. Fools run into extremes; nay, and wise men may see cause to change their sentiments. And therefore, as we should rejoice and weep as if we rejoiced not and wept not, so we should love and hate as if we loved not and hated not. *Ita ama tanquam osurus — Love as one who may have cause to feel aversion.*

II. The execution to be done upon her is very terrible. 1. Her enemies shall come against her *on every side* (*v.* 22), those of the several nations that constituted the Chaldean army (*v.* 23), all of them *great lords and renowned,* whose pomp, and grandeur, and splendid appearance made them look the more amiable when they came as friends to protect and patronise Jerusalem, but the more formidable when they came to chastise its treachery and aimed at no less than its ruin. (1.) They shall come with a great deal of military force (*v.* 24), with *chariots and wagons* furnished with all necessary provisions for a camp, with arms and ammunition, bag and baggage, with a vast army, and well armed. (2.) They shall have justice on their side: *"I will set judgment before them"* (they shall have right with them as well as might; for the king of Babylon had just cause to make war upon the king of Judah, because he had broken his league with him), "and therefore they *shall judge thee,* not only according to God's judgments, as the instruments of his justice, to punish thee for the indignities done to him, but *according to their judgments,* according to the law of nations, to punish thee for thy perfidious dealings with them." (3.) They shall prosecute the war with a great deal of fury and resentment. It being a war of revenge, *they shall deal with thee hatefully, v.* 29. This will make the execution the more severe that their swords will be dipped in poison. Thou hatest them, and they shall deal hatefully with thee; those that hate will be hated and will be hatefully dealt with. (4.) God himself will lead them on, and his anger shall be mingled with theirs (*v.* 25): *I will set my jealousy against thee;* that shall kindle this fire, and then *they shall deal furiously with thee.* If men deal ever so hatefully, ever so furiously, with us, yet, if we have God on our side, we need not fear them; they can do us no real hurt. But if men deal furiously with us, and God set his jealousy against us too, what will become of us?

2. The particulars of the sentence here passed upon this notorious adulteress are, (1.) That all she has shall be seized on. The *clothes* and the *fair jewels,* with which she had endeavoured to recommend herself to her lovers, these she shall be stripped of, *v.* 26. All those things that were the ornaments of their state shall be taken away: *"They shall take away all thy labour,* all that thou hast gotten by thy labour, and shall *leave thee naked and bare," v.* 29. Both city and country shall be impoverished and all the wealth of both swept away. (2.) That her children shall go into captivity. "They shall *take thy sons and thy daughters,* and make slaves of them (*v.* 25); for they are *children of whoredoms,* unworthy the dignities and privileges of Israelites," Hos. 2:4. (3.) That she shall be stigmatized and deformed: "They shall *take away thy nose and thy ears,* shall mark thee for a harlot, and render thee for ever odious," *v.* 25. This intimates the many cruelties of the Chaldean soldiers towards the Jews that fell into their hands, whom, it is probable, they used barbarously. Some will have this to be understood figuratively; and by the nose they think is meant the kingly dignity, and by the ears that of the priesthood. (4.) That she shall be exposed to shame: *Thy lewdness and thy whoredoms shall be discovered* (*v.* 29), as, when a malefactor is punished, all his crimes are ripped up, and repeated to his disgrace; what was secret then comes to light, and what was done long since is then called to mind. (5.) That she shall be quite cut off and ruined: "The *remnant* of thy people that have escaped the famine and pestilence shall fall *by the sword;* and the residue of thy houses that have not been battered down about thy ears shall be *devoured by the fire," v.* 25. And this shall be the end of Jerusalem.

III. Because she has trod in the steps of Samaria's sins, she must expect no other than Samaria's fate. It is common, in giving judgment, to have an eye to precedents; so has God in passing this sentence on Jerusalem (*v.* 31, etc.): *"Thou hast walked in the way of thy sister,* notwithstanding the warning thou hast had given thee, by the fatal consequences of her wickedness; and therefore I *will give her cup,* her portion of miseries, *into thy hand,* the cup of the Lord's fury, which will be to thee a *cup of trembling."* Now, 1. This cup is said to be *deep and large,* and to *contain much* (*v.* 32), abundance of God's wrath and abundance of miseries, the fruits of that wrath. It is such a cup as that which we read of, Jer. 25:15, 16. The cup of divine vengeance holds a great deal, and so those will find into whose hand it shall be put. 2. They shall be made to drink the very dregs of this cup, as the *wicked* are said to do (Ps. 75:8): *"Thou shalt drink it and suck it out,* not because it is pleasant, but because it is forced upon thee (*v.* 34); *thou shalt break the shreds thereof,* and *pluck off thy own breasts,* for indignation at the extreme bitterness of this cup, being *full of the fury of the Lord* (Isa. 51:20), as men in great anguish tear their hair, and throw every thing from them. Finding there is no remedy, but it must be drank (for *I have spoken it, saith the Lord God*), thou shalt have no manner of patience in the drinking of it." 3. They shall be intoxicated by it, made sick, and be at their wits' end, as men in drink are, staggering, and stumbling, and ready to fall (*v.* 33): *Thou shalt be filled with drunkenness and sorrow.* Note, Drunkenness has sorrow attending it, to such a degree that the utmost confusion and astonishment are here represented by it. Who would think that that which is such a force upon nature, such a scandal to it, which deprives men of their reason, disorders them to the last degree, and is therefore expressive of the greatest misery, should yet be with many a beloved sin, that they should damn their own souls to distemper their own bodies? *Who has woe* and *sorrow* like them? Prov. 23:29. 4. Being so intoxicated, they shall become, as drunkards deserve to be, a laughing-stock to all about them (*v.* 32): *Thou shalt be laughed to scorn and had in derision,* as acting ridiculously in every thing thou goest about. When God is about to ruin a people he *makes their judges fools* and *pours contempt on their princes,* Job 12:17, 21.

IV. In all this God will be justified, and by all this they will be reformed; and so the issue even of this will be God's glory and their good. 1. They have been bad, very bad, and that justifies God in all that is brought upon them (*v.* 30): *I will do these things unto thee because thou hast gone a whoring after the heathen,* and (*v.* 35) *because thou hast forgotten me and cast me behind thy back.* Note, Forgetfulness of God, and a contempt of him, of his eye upon us and authority over us, are at the bottom of all our treacherous adulterous departures from him. *Therefore* men wander after idols, because they forget *God,* and their obligations to him; nor could they look with so much desire and delight upon the baits of sin if they did not first cast God *behind their back,* as not worthy to be regarded. And those who put such an affront upon God, how can they think but that it should turn upon themselves at last? *Therefore bear thou also thy lewdness and thy whoredoms;* that is, thou shalt *suffer the punishment* of them, and thou alone must *bear the blame.* Men need no more to sink them than the weight of their own sins; and those who will not part with their lewdness and their whoredoms must bear them. 2. They shall be better, much better, and this fire, though consuming to many, shall be refining to a remnant (*v.* 27): *Thus will I make thy lewdness to cease from thee.* The judgments which were brought upon them by their sins parted between them and their sins, and taught them at length to say, *What have we to do any more with idols?* Observe, (1.) How inveterate the disease was: *Thy whoredoms were brought from the land of Egypt.* Their disposition to idolatry was early and innate, their practice of it was ancient, and had gained a sort of prescription by long usage. (2.) How complete the cure was notwithstanding: "Though it has taken root, yet it shall be made to cease, so that thou shalt not so much as *lift up thy eyes* to the idols again, nor *remember Egypt* with pleasure *any more."* They shall avoid the occasions of this sin, for they shall not so much as look upon an idol, lest their hearts should unawares *walk after their eyes.* And they shall abandon all inclinations to it: "They shall *not remember Egypt;* they shall not retain any of that affection for idols which they had from the very infancy of their nation." They got it, through the corruption of nature, in their bondage in Egypt, and lost it, through the grace of God, in their captivity in Babylon, which this was the blessed fruit of, even *the taking away of sin,* of *that* sin; so that whereas, before the captivity, no nation (all things considered) was more impetuously bent upon idols and idolatry than they were, after that captivity no nation was more vehemently set against idols and idolatry than they were, insomuch that at this day the image-worship which is practised in the church of Rome confirms the Jews as much as any thing in their prejudices against the Christian religion.

Verses 36–49

After the ten tribes were carried into captivity, and that kingdom was made quite desolate, the remains of it by degrees incorporated with the kingdom of Judah, and gained a settlement (many of them) in Jerusalem; so that the *two sisters* had in effect become *one* again; and therefore, in these verses, the prophet takes those to task jointly who were thus conjoined: *"Wilt thou judge Aholah and Aholibah* together? *v.* 36. Wilt thou go about to frame an excuse for them? Thou seest the matter is so bad as not to bear an excuse." Or, rather, "Thou shalt now be employed, in God's name, to *judge them, ch.* 20:4. The matter is rather worse than better since the union."

I. Let them be made to see the sins they are guilty of: *Declare unto them* openly and boldly *their abominations.* 1. They have been guilty of gross idolatry, here called *adultery. With their idols they have committed adultery* (*v.* 37), have broken their marriage-covenant with God, have lusted after the gratifications of a carnal sensual mind in the worship of God. This is the first and worst of the abominations he is to charge them with. 2. They have committed the most barbarous murders, in sacrificing their children to Moloch, a sin so unnatural that they deserve to hear of it upon all occasions: *Blood is in their hands,* innocent blood, the blood of their own children, which they have *caused to pass through the fire* (*v.* 37), not that they might be dedicated to the idols, but that they might be devoured, a sign that they loved their idols better than that which was dearest to them in the world. 3. They have profaned the sacred things with which God had dignified and distinguished them: This *they have done unto me,* this indignity, this injury, *v.* 38. Every contempt put upon that which is holy reflects upon him who is the fountain of holiness, and from a relation to whom whatever is called holy has its denomination. God had set up his sanctuary among them, but they defiled it, by making it a house of merchandise, a den of thieves; nay, and much worse; there they set up their idols and worshipped them, and there they shed the blood of God's prophets. God had revealed to them his holy sabbaths, but they profaned them, by doing all manner of servile work therein, or perhaps by sports and recreations on that day, not only practised, but allowed and encouraged by authority. They *defiled the sanctuary* on *the same day* that they *profaned the sabbath.* To defile the sanctuary was bad enough on any day, but to do it on the sabbath day was an aggravation. We commonly say, *The better day the better deed;* but here, the better day the worse deed. God takes notice of the circumstances of sin which add to the guilt. He shows (*v.* 39) what was their profanation both of the sanctuary and of the sabbath. *They slew their children,* and sacrificed them *to their idols,* to the great dishonour both of God and of human nature; and then came, on *the same day,* their hands imbrued with the blood of their children and their clothes stained with it, to attend in *God's sanctuary,* not to ask pardon for what they had done, but to present themselves before him, as other Israelites did, expecting acceptance with him, notwithstanding these villanies which they were guilty of; as if God either did not know their wickedness or did not hate it. Thus they *profaned the sanctuary,* as if that were a protection to the worst of malefactors; for thus they did *in the midst of his house.* Note, It is a profanation of God's solemn ordinances when those that are grossly and openly profane and vicious impudently and impenitently so intrude upon the services and privileges of them. *Give not that which is holy unto dogs. Friend, how camest thou in hither?* 4. They have courted foreign alliances, been proud of them, and reposed a confidence in them. This also is represented by the sin of adultery, for it was a departure from God, not only *to whom* alone they ought to pay their homage and not to idols, but *in* whom alone they ought to put their trust, and not in creatures. Israel was a peculiar people, must *dwell alone* and not be *reckoned among the nations;* and they profane their crown, and lay their honour in the dust, when they covet to be like them or in *league* with them. But this they have now done; they have entered into strict alliances with the Assyrians, Chaldeans, and Egyptians, the most renowned and potent kingdoms at that time; but they scorned alliances with the petty kingdoms and states that lay near them, which yet might have been of more real service to them. Note, Affecting an acquaintance and correspondence with great people has often been a snare to good people. Let us see how Jerusalem courts her high allies, thinking thereby to make herself considerable. (1.) She privately requested that a public embassy might be sent to her (*v.* 40): You *sent a messenger for men to come from far.* It seems, then, that the neighbours had no desire to come into a confederacy with Jerusalem, but she thrust herself upon them, and sent under-hand to desire them to court her: and, *lo, they came.* The wisest and best may be drawn unavoidably into company and conversation with profane and wicked people: but it is no sign either of wisdom or goodness to covet an intimacy with such and to court it. (2.) Great preparation was made for the reception of these foreign ministers, for their public entry and public audience, which is compared to the pains that an adulteress takes to make herself look handsome. Jezebel-like, thou *paintedst thy face* and *deckedst thyself with ornaments, v.* 40. The king and princes made themselves new clothes, fitted up the rooms of state, beautified the furniture, and made it look fresh. Thou *sattest upon a stately bed* (*v.* 41), a stately throne; *a table was prepared, whereon thou has set my oil and my incense.* This was either, [1.] A feast for the ambassadors, a noble treat, agreeable to the other preparations. There was incense to perfume the room and oil to anoint their heads. Or, [2.] An altar already furnished for the ambassadors' use in the worship of their idols, to let them know that the Israelites were not so strait-laced but that they could allow foreigners the free exercise of their religion among them, and furnish them with chapels, yea, and complimented them so far as to join with them in their devotions; though the law of their God was against it, yet they could easily dispense with themselves to oblige a friend. The oil and incense God calls *his,* not only because they were the gift of his providence, but because they should have been offered at his altar, which was an aggravation of their sin in serving idols and idolaters with them. See Hos. 2:8. (3.) There was great joy at their coming, as if it were such a blessing as never happened to Jerusalem before (*v.* 42): *A voice of a multitude being at east was with her.* The people were very easy, for they thought themselves very safe and happy now that they had such powerful allies; and therefore attended the ambassadors with loud huzzas and acclamations of joy. A great confluence of people there was to the court upon this occasion. The *men of the common sort* were there to grace the solemnity, and to increase the crowd; and *with them were brought Sabeans from the wilderness.* The margin reads it *drunkards from the wilderness,* that would drink healths to the prosperity of this grand alliance, and force them upon others, and be most noisy in shouting upon this occasion. Whoever they were, in honour of the ambassadors they put *bracelets upon their hands and beautiful crowns upon their heads,* which made the cavalcade appear very splendid. (4.) God by his prophets warned them against making these dangerous leagues with foreigners (*v.* 43): *"Then said I unto her that was old in adulteries,* that from the first was fond of leagues with the heathen, of matching with their families (Jdg. 3:6), and afterwards of making alliances with their kingdoms, and, though often disappointed therein, would never be dissuaded from it (this was the adultery she was old in), I said, *Will they now commit whoredoms with her and she with them?* Surely experience and observation will by this time have convinced both them and her that an alliance between the nation of the Jews and a heathen nation can never be for the advantage of either." They are *iron and clay,* that will not mix, nor will God bless such an alliance, or smile upon it. But, it seems, her being old in these adulteries, instead of weaning her from them, as one would expect, does but make her the more impudent and insatiable in them; for, though she was thus admonished of the folly of it, *yet they went in unto her, v.* 44. A bargain was soon clapped up, and a league made, first with this, and then with the other, foreign state. Samaria did so, Jerusalem did so, like lewd women. They could not rest satisfied in the embraces of God's laws and care, and the assurances of protection he gave them; they could not think his covenant with them security enough. But they must by treaties and leagues, politic ones (they thought) and well-concerted, throw themselves into the arms of foreign princes, and put their interests under their protection. Note, Those hearts go a whoring from God that take a complacency in the pomp of the world and put a confidence in its wealth, and in an *arm of flesh,* Jer. 17:5.

II. Let them be made to foresee the judgments that are coming upon them for these sins (*v.* 45): *The righteous men, they shall judge them.* Some make the instruments of their destruction to be the righteous men that shall judge them. The Assyrians that destroyed Samaria, the Chaldeans that destroyed Jerusalem, those were comparatively righteous, had a sense of justice between man and man and justly resented the treachery of the Jewish nation; however, they executed God's judgments, which, we are sure, are all righteous. Others understand it of the prophets, whose office it was, in God's name, to judge them and pass sentence upon them. Or we may take it as an appeal to all righteous men, to all that have a sense of equity; they shall all judge concerning these cities, and agree in their verdict, that forasmuch as they have been notoriously guilty of adultery and murder, and the guilt is national, therefore they ought to suffer the pains and penalties which by law are inflicted upon women in their personal capacity that shed blood and are adulteresses. Righteous men will say, "Why should bloody filthy cities escape any better than bloody filthy persons? *Judge, I pray thee,*" Isa. 5:3. This judgment being given by the righteous men, the righteous God will award execution. See here, 1. What the execution will be. *v.* 46, 47. The same as before, *v.* 23, etc. God will *bring a company* of enemies *upon them,* who shall be made to serve his holy purposes even when they are serving their own sinful appetites and passions. These enemies shall easily prevail, for God will *give them* into their hands *to be removed and spoiled;* this company shall *stone them with stones* as malefactors, shall *single them out* and *dispatch them with their swords;* and, as was sometimes done in severe executions (witness that of Achan), they shall *slay their children and burn their houses.* 2. What will be the effects of it. (1.) Thus they shall suffer for their sins: Their *lewdness shall be recompensed upon them* (*v.* 49); and they shall *bear the sins of their idols, v.* 35, 49. Thus God will assert the honour of his broken law and injured government, and let the world know what a just and jealous God he is. (2.) Thus they shall be broken off from their sins: *I will cause lewdness to cease out of the land, v.* 27, 48. The destruction of God's city, like the death of God's saints, shall do that for them which ordinances and providences before could not do; it shall quite take away their sin, so that Jerusalem shall rise out of its ashes a new lump, as gold comes out of the furnace purified from its dross. (3.) Thus other cities and nations will have fair warning given them to keep themselves from idols. That *all women may be taught not to do after your lewdness.* This is the end of the punishment of malefactors, that they may be made examples to others, who will *see and fear. Smite the scorner and the simple will beware.* The judgments of God upon some are designed to teach others, and happy are those who receive instruction from them not to tread in the steps of sinners, lest they be taken in their snares; those who would be taught this must *know God is the Lord* (*v.* 49), that he is the governor of the world, a God that judges in the earth, and with whom there is *no respect of persons.*

CHAPTER 24

Here are two sermons in this chapter, preached on a particular occasion, and they are both from Mount Sinai, the mount of terror, both from Mount Ebal, the mount of curses; both speak the approaching fate of Jerusalem. The occasion of them was the king of Babylon's laying siege to Jerusalem, and the design of them is to show that in the issue of that siege he should be not only master of the place, but destroyer of it. I. By the sign of flesh boiling in a pot over the fire are shown the miseries that Jerusalem should suffer during the siege, and justly, for her filthiness (*v.* 1–14). II. By the sign of Ezekiel's not mourning for the death of his wife is shown that the calamities coming upon Jerusalem were too great to be lamented, so great that they should sink down under them into a silent despair (*v.* 15–27).

Verses 1–14

We have here,

I. The notice God gives to Ezekiel in Babylon of Nebuchadnezzar's laying siege to Jerusalem, just at the time when he was doing it (*v.* 2): *"Son of man,* take notice, *the king of Babylon,* who is now abroad with his army, thou knowest not where, *set himself against Jerusalem this same day."* It was many miles, it was many days' journey, from Jerusalem to Babylon. Perhaps the last intelligence they had from the army was that the design was upon Rabbath of the children of Ammon and that the campaign was to be opened with the siege of that city. But God knew, and could tell the prophet, *"This day,* at this time, Jerusalem is invested, and the Chaldean army has sat down before it." Note, As all times, so all places, even the most remote, are present with God and under his view. He tells the prophet, that the prophet might tell the people, that so when it proved to be punctually true, as they would find by the public intelligence in a little time, it might be a confirmation of the prophet's mission, and they might infer that, since he was right in his news, he was so in his predictions, for he owed both to the same correspondence he had with Heaven.

II. The notice which he orders him to take of it. He must enter it in his book, *memorandum,* that *in the ninth year* of Jehoiachin's captivity (for thence Ezekiel dated, *ch.* 1:2, which was also the ninth year of Zedekiah's reign, for he began to reign when Jehoiachin was carried off), in the tenth month, on the tenth day of the month, the king of Babylon laid siege to Jerusalem; and the date here agrees exactly with the date in the history, 2 Ki. 25:1. See how God reveals things to his servants the prophets, especially those things which serve to confirm their word, and so to confirm their own faith. Note, It is good to keep an exact account of the date of remarkable occurrences, which may sometimes contribute to the manifesting of God's glory so much the more in them, and the explaining and confirming of scripture prophecies. *Known unto God are all his works.*

III. The notice which he orders him to give to the people thereupon, the purport of which is that this siege of Jerusalem, now begun, will infallibly end in the ruin of it. This he must say *to the rebellious house,* to those of them that were in Babylon, to be by them communicated to those that were yet in their own land. A rebellious house will soon be a ruinous house.

1. He must show them this by a sign; for that stupid people needed to be taught as children are. The comparison made use of is that of a *boiling pot.* This agrees with Jeremiah's vision many years before, when he first began to be a prophet, and probably was designed to put them in mind of that (Jer. 1:13, *I see a seething pot, with the face towards the north;* and the explanation of it, *v.* 15, makes it to signify the besieging of Jerusalem by the *northern* nations); and, as this comparison is intended to confirm Jeremiah's vision, so also to confront the vain confidence of the princes of Jerusalem, who had said (*ch.* 11:3), *This city is the caldron and we are the flesh,* meaning, "We are as safe here as if we were surrounded with walls of brass." "Well," says God, "it shall be so; you shall be boiled in Jerusalem, as the *flesh in the caldron,* boiled to pieces; let the pot be set on with water in it (*v.* 4); let it be filled with the flesh of the *choice of the flock* (*v.* 5), with the choice pieces (*v.* 4), and the marrow-bones, and let the other bones serve for fuel, that, one way or other, either in the pot or under it, the whole beast may be made use of." A fire of bones, though it be a slow fire (for the siege was to be long), is yet a sure and lasting fire; such was God's wrath against them, and not like the *crackling of thorns under a pot,* which has noise and blaze, but no intense heat. Those that from all parts of the country fled into Jerusalem for safety would be sadly disappointed when the siege laid to it would soon make the place too hot for them; and yet there was not getting out of it, but they must be forced to abide by it, as the flesh in a boiling pot.

2. He must give them a comment upon this sign. It is to be construed as a *woe to the bloody city, v.* 6. And again (*v.* 9), being *bloody,* let it *go to pot,* to be boiled; that is the fittest place for it. Let us here see,

(1.) What is the course God takes with it. Jerusalem, during the siege, is like a pot boiling over the fire, all in a heat, all in a hurry. [1.] Care is taken to keep a good fire under the pot, which signifies the closeness of the siege, and the many vigorous attacks made upon the city by the besiegers, and especially the continued wrath of God burning against them (*v.* 9): *I will make the pile for fire great.* Commission is given to the Chaldeans (*v.* 10) to *heap on wood, and kindle the fire,* to make Jerusalem more and more hot to the inhabitants. Note, The fire which God kindles for the consuming of impenitent sinners shall never abate, much less go out, for want of fuel. *Tophet has fire and much wood,* Isa. 30:33. [2.] The meat, as it is boiled, is taken out, and given to the Chaldeans for them to feast upon. *"Consume the flesh;* let it be thoroughly boiled, boiled to rags. *Spice it well,* and make it savoury, for those that will fees sweetly upon it. *Let the bones be burnt."* either the bones *under* the pot ("let them be consumed with the other fuel") or, as some think, the bones *in* the pot — "let it boil so furiously that not only the flesh may be sodden, but even the bones softened; let all the inhabitants of Jerusalem be by sickness, sword, and famine, reduced to the extremity of misery." And then (*v.* 6), *"Bring it out piece by piece;* let every man be delivered into the enemy's hand, to be either put to the sword or made a prisoner. Let them be an easy prey to them, and let the Chaldeans fall upon them as eagerly as a hungry man does upon a good dish of meat when it is set before him. *Let no lot fall upon it;* every piece in the pot shall be fetched out and devoured, first or last, and therefore it is no matter for casting lots which shall be fetched out first." It was a very severe military execution when David measured Joab with *two lines to put to death and one full line to keep alive,* 2 Sa. 8:2. But here is no line, no lot of mercy, made use of; all goes one way, and that is to destruction. [3.] When all the broth is boiled away the pot is set empty upon the coals, that it may burn too, which signifies the setting of the city on fire, *v.* 11. The scum of the meat, or (as some translate it) *the rust of the meat,* has so got into the pot that there is no making it clean by washing or scouring it, and therefore it must be done by fire; so let the filthiness be burnt out of it, or, rather, *melted in it* and burnt with it. Let the vipers and their nest be consumed together.

(2.) What is the quarrel God has with it. He would not take these severe methods with Jerusalem but that he is provoked to it; she deserves to be thus dealt with, for, [1.] It is a bloody city (*v.* 7, 8): *Her blood is in the midst of her.* Many a barbarous murder has been committed in the very heart of the city; nay, and they have a disposition to cruelty in their hearts; they inwardly delight in blood-shed, and so it is *in the midst of them.* Nay, they commit their murders in the face of the sun, and openly and impudently avow them, in defiance of the justice both of God and man. She did not *pour out* the blood she shed *upon the ground, to cover it with dust,* as being ashamed of the sin or afraid of the punishment. She did not look upon it as a filthy thing, proper to be concealed (Deu. 23:13), much less dangerous. Nay, she poured out the innocent blood she shed upon a rock, where it would not soak in, upon *the top of a rock,* in despite of divine views and vengeance. They shed innocent blood under colour of justice; so that they gloried in it, as if they had done God and the country good service, so put it, as it were, *on the top of a rock.* Or it may refer to the sacrificing of their children on their high places, perhaps on the top of rocks. Now thus they *caused fury to come up and take vengeance, v.* 8. It could not be avoided but that God *must* in anger *visit for these things; his soul must be avenged on such a nation as this.* It is absolutely necessary that such a bloody city as this should have blood given her to drink, for she is worthy, for the vindicating of the honour of divine justice. And, the crime having been public and notorious, it is fit that the punishment should be so too: *I have set her blood on the top of a rock.* Jerusalem was to be made an example, and therefore was made a spectacle, to the world; God dealt with her according to the law of retaliation. It is fit that those who *sin before all* should be *rebuked before all;* and that the reputation of those should not be consulted by the concealment of their punishment who were so impudent as not to desire the concealment of their sin. [2.] It is a filthy city. Great notice is taken, in this explanation of the comparison, of the *scum of this pot,* which signifies the sin of Jerusalem, working up and appearing when the judgments of God were upon her. It is the pot *whose scum is therein* and has *not gone out of it, v.* 6. The *great scum* that *went not forth out of her* (*v.* 12), that stuck to the pot when all was boiled away, and was *molten in it* (*v.* 11), some of this runs over *into the fire* (*v.* 12), inflames that, and makes it burn the more furiously, but *it shall all be consumed* at last, *v.* 11. When the hand of God had gone out against them, instead of humbling themselves under it, repenting and reforming, and accepting the punishment of their iniquity, they grew more impudent and outrageous in sin, quarrelled with God, persecuted his prophets, were fierce to one another, enraged to the last degree against the Chaldeans, snarled at the stone, gnawed their chain, and were like a wild bull in a net. This as *their scum;* in their distress they *trespassed yet more against the Lord,* like *that king Ahaz,* 2 Chr. 28:22. There is little hope of those who are made worse by that which should make them better, whose corruptions are excited an exasperated by those rebukes both of the word and of the providence of God which were designed for the suppressing and subduing of them, or of those whose scum boiled up once in convictions, and confessions of sin, as if it would be taken off by reformation, but afterwards returned again, in a revolt from their good overtures; and the heart that seemed softened is hardened again. This was Jerusalem's case: *She has wearied with lies,* wearied her God with purposes and promises of amendment, which she never stood to, wearied herself with her carnal confidences, which have all deceived her, *v.* 12. Note, Those that follow after lying vanities weary themselves with the pursuit. Now see her doom, *v.* 13, 14. Because she is incurably wicked she is abandoned to ruin, without remedy. *First,* Methods and means of reformation had been tried in vain (*v.* 13): *"In thy filthiness is lewdness;* thou hast become obstinate and impudent in it; thou hast got a habit of it, which is confirmed by frequent acts. *In thy filthiness* thee is a rooted lewdness; as appears by this, *I have purged thee and thou wast not purged.* I have given thee medicine, but it has done thee no good. I have used the means of cleansing thee, but they have been ineffectual; the intention of them has not been answered." Note, It is sad to think how many there are on whom ordinances and providences are all lost. *Secondly,* It is therefore resolved that no more such methods shall be sued: *Thou shalt not be purged from thy filthiness any more.* The fire shall no longer be a refining fire, but a consuming fire, and therefore shall not be mitigated and shortened, as it has been, but shall be continued in extremity, till it has done its destroying work. Note, Those that will not be healed are justly given up and their case adjudged desperate. There is a day coming when it will be said, *He that is filthy, let him be filthy still. Thirdly,* Nothing remains then but to bring them to utter ruin: *I will cause my fury to rest upon thee.* This is the same with what is said of the later Jews, that *wrath has come upon them to the uttermost,* 1 Th. 2:16. They deserve it: *According to thy doings they shall judge thee, v.* 14. And God will do it. The sentence is bound on with repeated ratifications, that they might be awakened to see how certain their ruin was: *"I the Lord have spoken it,* who am able to make good what I have spoken; *it shall come to pass,* nothing shall prevent it, for *I will do it* myself, *I will not go back* upon any entreaties; the decree has gone forth, and *I will not spare* in compassion to them, *neither will I repent."* He will neither change his mind nor his way. Hereby the prophet was forbidden to interceded for them, and they were forbidden to flatter themselves with hopes of an escape. God hath said it, and he will do it. Note, The declarations of God's wrath against sinners are as inviolable as the assurances he has given of favour to his people; and the case of such is sad indeed, who have brought it to this issue, that either God must be false or they must be damned.

Verses 15–27

These verses conclude what we have been upon all along from the beginning of this book, to wit, Ezekiel's prophecies of the destruction of Jerusalem; for after this, though he prophesied much concerning other nations, he said no more concerning Jerusalem, till he heard of the destruction of it, almost three years after, *ch.* 33:21. He had assured them, in the former part of this chapter, that there was no hope at all of the preventing of the trouble; here he assures them that they should not have the ease of weeping for it. Observe here,

I. The sign by which this was represented to them, and it was a sign that cost the prophet very dear; the more shame for them that when he, by a divine appointment, was at such an expense to affect them with what he had to deliver, yet they were not affected by it

1. He must lose a good wife, that should suddenly be taken from him by death. God gave him notice of it before, that it might be the less surprise to him (*v.* 16): *Behold, I take away from thee the desire of thy eyes with a stroke.* Note, (1.) A married state may very well agree with the prophetical office; it is *honourable in all,* and therefore not sinful in ministers. (2.) Much of the comfort of human life lies in agreeable relations. No doubt Ezekiel found a prudent tender yoke-fellow, that shared with him in his griefs and cares, to be a happy companion in his captivity. (3.) Those in the conjugal relation must be to each other not only a *covering of the eyes* (Gen. 20:16), to restrain wandering looks after others; but a *desire of the eyes,* to engage pleasing looks on one another. A beloved wife is the *desire of the eyes,* which find not any object more grateful. (4.) That is least safe which is most dear; we know not how soon the desire of our eyes may be removed from us and may become the sorrow of our hearts, which is a good reason why those that *have wives* should be *as though they had none,* and those *who rejoice* in them *as though they rejoiced not,* 1 Co. 7:29, 30. Death is a stroke which the most pious, the most useful, the most amiable, are not exempted from. (5.) When the desire of our eyes is taken away with a stroke we must see and own the hand of God in it: *I take away the desire of thy eyes.* He takes our creature-comforts from us when and how he pleases; he gave them to us, but reserved to himself a property in them; and *may he not do what he will with his own?* (6.) Under afflictions of this kind it is good for us to remember that we are *sons of men;* for so God calls the prophet here. If thou art a *son of Adam,* thy wife is a daughter of *Eve,* and therefore a dying creature. It is an affliction which the children of men are liable to; and *shall the earth be forsaken for us?* According to this prediction, he tells us (*v.* 18), *I spoke unto the people in the morning;* for God sent his prophets, *rising up early* and sending them; then he thought, if ever, they would be disposed to hearken to him. Observe, [1.] Though God had given Ezekiel a certain prospect of this affliction coming upon him, yet it did not take him off from his work, but he resolved to go on in that. [2.] We may the more easily bear an affliction if it find us in the way of our duty; for nothing can hurt us, nothing come amiss to us, while we keep ourselves in the love of God.

2. He must deny himself the satisfaction of mourning for his wife, which would have been both an honour to her and an ease to the oppression of his own spirit. He must not use the natural expressions of sorrow, *v.* 16. He must not give vent to his passion by *weeping,* or letting *his tears run down,* though tears are a tribute due to the dead, and, when the body is sown, it is fit that it should thus be watered. But Ezekiel is not allowed to do this, though he thought he had as much reason to do it as any man and would perhaps be ill thought of by the people if he did it not. Much less might he use the customary formalities of mourners. He must dress himself in his usual attire, must bind his turban on him, here called the *tire of his head,* must *put on his shoes,* and not go barefoot, as was usual in such cases; he must not *cover his lips,* not throw a veil over his face (as mourners were wont to do, Lev. 13:45), must not be of a *sorrowful countenance, appearing unto men to fast,* Mt. 6:18. He must not *eat the bread of men,* nor expect that his neighbours and friends should send him in provisions, as usually they did in such cases, presuming the mourners had no heart to provide meat for themselves; but, if it were sent, he must not eat of it, but go on in his business as at other times. It could not but be greatly against the grain to flesh and blood not to lament the death of one he loved so dearly, but so God commands; and *I did in the morning as I was command-*

ed. He appeared in public, in his usual habit, and looked as he used to do, without any signs of mourning. (1.) Here there was something peculiar, and Ezekiel, to make himself a sign to the people, must put a force upon himself and exercise an extraordinary piece of self-denial. Note, Our dispositions must always submit to God's directions, and his command must be obeyed even in that which is most difficult and displeasing to us. (2.) Though mourning for the dead be a duty, yet it must always be kept under the government of religion and right reason, and we must not *sorrow as those that have no hope,* nor lament the loss of any creature, even the most valuable, and that which we could worst spare, as if we had lost our God, or as if all our happiness were gone with it; and, of this moderation in mourning, ministers, when it is their case, ought to be examples. We must at such a time study to improve the affliction, to accommodate ourselves to it, and to get our acquaintance with the other world increased, by the removal of our dear relations, and learn with holy Job *to bless the name of the Lord* even when he takes as well as when he gives.

II. The explication and application of this sign. The people enquired the meaning of it (*v.* 19): *Wilt thou not tell us what these things are to us that thou doest so?* They knew that Ezekiel was an affectionate husband, that the death of his wife was a great affliction to him, and that he would not appear so unconcerned at it but for some good reason and for instruction to them; and perhaps they were in hopes that it had a favourable signification, and gave them an intimation that God would now comfort them again according to the time he had afflicted them, and make them look pleasant again. Note, When we are enquiring concerning the things of God our enquiry must be, "What are those thing *to us?* What are we concerned in them? What conviction, what counsel, what comfort, do they speak to us? Wherein do they reach our case?" Ezekiel gives them an answer *verbatim* — *word for word* as he had received it from the Lord, who had told him what he must *speak to the house of Israel.*

1. Let them know that as Ezekiel's wife was taken from him by a stroke so would God take from them all that which was dearest to them, *v.* 21. If this was *done to the green tree, what shall be done to the dry?* If a faithful servant of God was thus afflicted only for his trial, shall such a generation of rebels against God go unpunished? By this awakening providence God showed that he was in earnest in his threatenings, and inexorable. We may suppose that Ezekiel prayed that, if it were the will of God, his wife might be spared to him, but God would not hear him; and should he be heard then in his intercessions for this provoking people? No, it is determined: *God will take away the desire of your eyes.* Note, The removal of the comforts of others should awaken us to think of parting with ours too; for *are we better than they?* We know not how soon the same cup, or a more bitter one, may be put into our hands, and should therefore weep with those that weep, as being ourselves also in the body. God will *take away that which their soul pities,* that is, of which they say, What a pity is it that it should be cut off and destroyed! That *for which your souls are afraid* (so some read it); you shall lose that which you most dread the loss of. And what is that? (1.) That which was their public pride, the temple: *"I will profane my sanctuary,* by giving that into the enemy's hand, to be plundered and burnt." This was signified by the death of a wife, a dear wife, to teach us that God's sanctuary should be dearer to us, and more *the desire of our eyes,* than any creature-comfort whatsoever. Christ's church, that is his spouse, should be ours too. Though this people were very corrupt, and had themselves profaned the sanctuary, yet it is called *the desire of their eyes.* Note, Many that are destitute of *the power of godliness* are yet very fond of *the form* of it; and it is just with God to punish them for their hypocrisy by depriving them of that too. The sanctuary is here called the *excellency of their strength;* they had many strong-holds and places of defence, but the temple excelled them all. It was the *pride of their strength;* they prided in it as their strength that they were *the temple of the Lord,* Jer. 7:4. Note, The church-privileges that men are proud of are profaned by their sins, and it is just with God to profane them by his judgments. And with these God will take away, (2.) That which was their family-pleasure, which they looked upon with delight: *"Your sons and your daughters* (which are the dearer to you because they are but few left of many, the rest having perished by famine and pestilence) shall *fall by the sword* of the Chaldeans." What a dreadful spectacle would it be to see their own children, pieces, pictures, of themselves, whom they had taken such care and pains to bring up, and whom they loved as their own souls, sacrificed to the rage of the merciless conquerors! This, this, was the punishment of sin.

2. Let them know that as Ezekiel wept not for his affliction so neither should they weep for theirs. He must say, *You shall do as I have done, v.* 22. *You shall not mourn nor weep, v.* 23. Jeremiah had told them the same, that men *shall not lament for the dead nor cut themselves* (Jer. 16:6); not that there shall be any such merciful circumstance without, or any such degrees of wisdom and grace within, as shall mitigate and moderate the sorrow; but they *shall not mourn,* for, (1.) Their grief shall be so great that they shall be quite overwhelmed with it; their passions shall stifle them, and they shall have no power to ease themselves by giving vent to it. (2.) Their calamities shall come so fast upon them, one upon the neck of another, that by long custom they shall be *hardened in their sorrows* (Job 6:10) and perfectly stupefied, and moped (as we say), with them. (3.) They shall not dare to express their grief, for fear of being deemed disaffected to the conquerors, who would take their lamentations as an affront and disturbance to their triumphs. (4.) They shall not have hearts, nor time, nor money, wherewith to put themselves in mourning, and accommodate themselves with the ceremonies of grief: "You will be so entirely taken up with solid substantial grief that you will have no room for the shadow of it." (5.) Particular mourners shall not need to distinguish themselves by *covering their lips,* and laying aside their ornaments, and *going barefoot;* for it is well known that every body is a mourner. (6.) There shall be none of that sense of their affliction and sorrow for it which would help to bring them to repentance, but that only which shall drive them to despair; so it follows: *"You shall pine away for your iniquities,* with seared consciences and reprobate minds, and *you shall mourn,* not to God in prayer and confession of sin, but *one towards another,"* murmuring, and fretting, and complaining of God, thus making their burden heavier and their wound more grievous, as impatient people do under their afflictions by mingling their own passions with them.

III. An appeal to the event, for the confirmation of all this (*v.* 24): *"When this comes,* as it is foretold, when Jerusalem, which is this day besieged, is quite destroyed and laid waste, which now you cannot believe will ever be, *then you shall know that I am the Lord God,* who have given you this fair warning of it. Then you will remember that Ezekiel was to you a sign." Note, Those who regard not the threatenings of the word when they are preached will be made to remember them when they are executed. Observe,

1. The great desolation which the siege of Jerusalem should end in (*v.* 25): *In that day,* that terrible day, when the city shall be broken up, *I will take from them,* (1.) That which they depended on — *their strength,* their walls, their treasures, their fortifications, their men of war; none shall stand them in stead. (2.) That which they boasted of — the *joy of their glory,* that which they looked upon as most their glory, and which they most rejoiced in, the temple of their God and the palaces of their princes. (3.) That which they delighted in, which was the *desire of their eyes,* and on which they *set their minds.* Note, Carnal people set their minds upon that on which they can set their eyes; they look at, and dote upon, *the things that are seen;* and it is their folly to *set their minds* upon that which they have no assurance of and which may be taken from them in a moment, Prov. 23:5. *Their sons and their daughters* were all this — *their strength, and joy, and glory;* and these shall go into captivity.

2. The notice that should be brought to the prophet, not be revelation, as the notice of the siege was brought to him (*v.* 2), but in an ordinary way (*v.* 26): *"He that escapes in that day* shall, by a special direction of Providence, *come to thee,* to bring thee intelligence of it," which we find was done, *ch.* 33:21. The ill-news came slowly, and yet to Ezekiel and his fellow-captives it came too soon.

3. The divine impression which he should be under upon receiving that notice, *v.* 27. Whereas, from this time to that, Ezekiel was thus far dumb that he prophesied no more against the land of Israel, but against the neighbouring nations, as we shall find in the following chapters, then he shall have orders given him to *speak again to the children of his people* (*ch.* 33:2, 22); then *his mouth shall be opened.* He was suspended from prophesying against them in the mean time, because, Jerusalem being besieged, his prophecies could not be sent into the city, — because, when God was speaking so loudly by the rod, there was the less need of speaking by the word, — and because then the accomplishment of his prophecies would be the full confirmation of his mission, and would the more effectually clear the way for him to begin again. It being referred to that issue, that issue must be waited for. Thus Christ forbade his disciples to preach openly that he was Christ till after his resurrection, because that was to be the full proof of it. "But then *thou shalt speak* with the greater assurance, and the more effectually, either to their conviction or to their confusion." Note, God's prophets are never silenced but for wise and holy ends. And when God gives them the opening of the mouth again (as he will in due time, for even the witnesses that are *slain* shall *arise*) it shall appear to have been for his glory that they were for a while silent, that people may the more certainly and fully *know* that *God is the Lord.*

CHAPTER 25

Judgment began at the house of God, and therefore with them the prophets began, who were the judges; but it must not end there, and therefore they must not. Ezekiel had finished his testimony which related to the destruction of Jerusalem. As to that he was ordered to say no more, but stand upon his watch-tower and wait the issue; and yet he must not be silent; there are divers nations bordering upon the land of Israel, which he must prophesy against, as Isaiah and Jeremiah had done before; and must proclaim God's controversy with them, chiefly for the injuries and indignities which they had done to the people of God in the day of their calamity. In this chapter we have his prophecy, I. Against the Ammonites (*v.* 1–7). II. Against the Moabites (*v.* 8–11). III. Against the Edomites (*v.* 11–14). IV. Against the Philistines (*v.* 15–17). That which is laid to the charge of each of them is their barbarous and insolent conduct towards God's Israel, for which God threatens to put the same cup of trembling into their hand. God's resenting it thus would be an encouragement to Israel to believe that though he had dealt thus severely with them yet he had not cast them off, but would still own them and plead their cause.

Verses 1–7

Here, I. The prophet is ordered to address himself to the Ammonites, in the name of *the Lord Jehovah* the *God of Israel,* who is also the God of the whole earth. But what can Chemosh, the god of the children of Ammon, say, in answer to it? He is bidden to *set his face against the Ammonites,* for he is God's representative as a prophet, and thus he must signify that God *set his face against them,* for *the face of the Lord is against those that do evil,* Ps. 34:16. He must speak with boldness and assurance, as one that knew whose errand he went upon, and that he should be borne out in delivering it. He must therefore *set his face as a flint,* Isa. 1:7. He must show his displeasure against these proud enemies of Israel, and face them down, though they were very impudent, and thus must show that, though he had prophesied so much and so long *against Israel,* yet still he was for Israel, and, while he witnessed against their corruptions, he adhered to and gloried in God's covenant with them. Note, Those are miserable that have the preaching and praying of God's prophets against them, against whom their faces are set.

II. He is directed what to say to them. Ezekiel is now a captive in Babylon, and has been so many years, and knows little of the state of his own nation, much less of the nations that were about it; but God tells him both what they were doing and what he was about to do with them. And thus by the spirit of prophecy he is enabled to speak as pertinently to their case as if he had been among them.

1. He must upbraid the Ammonites with their insolent and barbarous triumphs over the people of Israel in their calamities, *v.* 3. The Ammonites said, when all went against the Jews, *Aha! so would we have it.* They were glad to see, (1.) The temple burned, *the sanctuary profaned* by the victorious Chaldeans. This is put first, to intimate what was the cause of the controversy; they had an enmity to the Jews for the sake of their religion, though it was only some poor remains of the profession of it that were to be found among them. (2.) The nation ruined. They rejoiced when *the land of Israel was made desolate,* the cities burnt, the

country wasted, and both depopulated, and when the house of *Judah went into captivity.* When they had not power to oppress God's Israel themselves they were pleased to see the Chaldeans oppress them, partly because they envied their wealth and the good land they enjoyed, partly because they feared their growing power, and partly because they hated their religion and the divine oracles they were favoured with. It is repeated again (*v.* 6): *They clapped with their hands,* to irritate the rage of the Chaldeans, and to set them on as dogs upon the game; or they clapped their hands in triumph, attended this tragedy with their *Plaudite — Give us your applause,* thinking it well acted; never was there any thing more diverting or entertaining to them. They *stamped with their feet,* ready to leap and dance for joy upon this occasion; they not only *rejoiced in heart,* but they could not forbear showing it, though every one that had any sense of honour and humanity would cry shame upon them for it, especially considering that they rejoiced thus, not for any thing they got by Israel's fall (if so, they would have been the more excusable: most people are for themselves); but this as purely from a principle of malice and enmity: *Thou hast rejoiced in heart with all thy despite* (which signifies both scorn and hatred) *against the land of Israel.* Note, The people of God have always had a great deal of ill-will borne them by this wicked world; and their calamities have been their neighbours' entertainments. See to what unnatural instances of malice the enmity that is in the seed of the serpent against the seed of the woman will carry them. The Ammonites, of all people, should not have rejoiced in Jerusalem's ruin, but should rather have trembled, because they themselves had such a narrow escape at the same time; it was but "cross or pile" [the toss of a halfpenny] which should be besieged first, Rabbath or Jerusalem, *ch.* 21:20. And they had reason to think that the king of Babylon would set upon them next. But thus were their hearts hardened to their ruin, and their insolence against Jerusalem was to them an *evident token of perdition,* Phil. 1:28. It is a very wicked thing to be glad at the calamities of any, especially of God's people, and a sin that God will surely reckon for; such delight has God in showing mercy, and so backward is he to punish, that nothing is more pleasing to him than to be stopped in the ways of his judgments by intercessions, not any thing more provoking than to *help forward the affliction* when he is but *a little displeased,* Zec. 1:15.

2. He must threaten the Ammonites with utter ruin for this insolence which they were guilty of. God turns away his wrath from Israel against them, as is said, Prov. 24:17, 18. God is jealous for his people's honour, because his own is so nearly interested in it. And therefore those that touch that shall be made to know that they touch the apple of his eye. He had before predicted the destruction of the Ammonites, *ch.* 21:28. Had they repented, that would have been revoked; but now it is ratified. (1.) A destroying enemy is brought against them: *I will deliver thee to the men of the east,* first to the Chaldeans, who came from the north-east, and whose army, under the command of Nebuchadnezzar, destroyed the country of the Ammonites, about five years after the destruction of Jerusalem (as Josephus relates, *Antiq.* 10.181), and then to the Arabians, who were properly the *children of the east,* who, when the Chaldeans had made the country desolate, and quitted it, came and took possession of it for themselves, probably with the consent of the conquerors. Shepherds' tents were their palaces; these they set up in the country of the Ammonites; there they *made their dwellings, v.* 4. They enjoyed the products of the country: *They shall eat thy fruit and drink thy milk;* and the milk from the cattle is the fruit of the ground at second-hand. They made use even of the royal city for their cattle (*v.* 5): *I will make Rabbath,* that was a nice and splendid city, to be *a stable for camels;* for its new masters, whose wealth lies all in cattle, will not think they can put the palaces of Rabbath to a better use. Rabbath had been a habitation of brutish men; justly therefore is it now made a *stable for camels* and the country a *couching-lace for flocks,* more innocent beasts than those with which it had been before replenished. (2.) God himself acts as an enemy to them (*v.* 7): *I will stretch out my hand upon thee,* a hand that will reach far and strike home, which there is no resisting the blow of, for it is a mighty hand, nor bearing the weight of, for it is a heavy hand. God's hand stretched out against the Ammonites will not only deliver them *for a spoil to the heathen,* so that all their neighbours shall prey upon them, but will *cut them off from the people* and *made them perish out of the countries,* so that there shall be no remains of them in that place. Compare with this, Jer. 49:1, etc. What can sound more terrible than that resolution (*v.* 7), *I will destroy thee?* For the almighty God is able both *to save and to destroy,* and it is *a fearful thing to fall into his hands.* Both the threatenings here (*v.* 5 and *v.* 7) conclude with this, *You shall know that I am the Lord.* For, [1.] Thus God will maintain his own honour, and will make it appear that he is the God of Israel, though he suffers them for a time to be captives in Babylon. [2.] Thus he will bring those that were strangers to him into an acquaintance with him, and it will be a blessed effect of their calamities. Better know God and be poor than be rich and ignorant of him.

Verses 8–17

Three more of Israel's ill-natured neighbours are here arraigned, convicted, and condemned to destruction, for contributing to and triumphing in Jerusalem's fall.

I. The Moabites. Seir, which was the seat of the Edomites, is joined with them (*v.* 8), because they said the same as the Moabites; but they were afterwards reckoned with by themselves, *v.* 12. Now observe,

1. What was the sin of the Moabites; they said, *Behold, the house of Judah is like unto all the heathen.* They triumphed, (1.) In the apostasies of Israel, were please to see them forsake their God and worship idols, and hoped that in a while their religion would be quite lost and forgotten and the *house of Judah* would be *like all the heathen,* perfect idolaters. When those that profess religion walk unworthy of their profession they encourage the enemies of religion to hope that it will in time sink, and be run down, and quite abandoned; but let the Moabites know that, though there are those of the house of Judah who have made themselves *like the heathen,* yet there is a remnant that retain their integrity, the religion of the house of Judah shall recover itself, its peculiarities shall be preserved, it shall not lose itself *among the heathen,* but distinguish itself from them, till it deliver itself honourably into a better institution. (2.) In the calamities of Israel. They said, *"The house of Judah is like all the heathen,* in as bad a state as they; their God is no more able to deliver them from this *overflowing scourge* of these parts of the world than the gods of the heathen are to deliver them. Where are the promises they gloried in and all the wonders which they and their fathers told us of? What the better are they for the covenant of peculiarity, upon which they so much valued themselves? Those that looked with so much scorn upon *all the heathen* are now set upon a level with them, or rather sunk below them." Note, Those who judge only by outward appearance are ready to conclude that the people of God have lost all their privileges when they have lost their worldly prosperity, which does not follow, for good men, even in affliction, in captivity among the heathen, have graces and comforts within sufficient to distinguish them from all the heathen. Though the event seem one to the *righteous and wicked,* yet indeed it is vastly different.

2. What should be the punishment of Moab for this sin; because they triumphed in the overthrow of Judah, their country shall be in like manner overthrown with that of the Ammonites, who were guilty of the same sin (*v.* 9, 10): *"I will open the side of Moab,* will uncover its shoulder, will take away all its defences, that it may become an easy prey to any that will make a prey of it." (1.) See here how it shall be exposed; the frontier-towns, that were its strength and guard, shall be demolished by the Chaldean forces, and laid open. Some of the cities are here named, which are said to be *the glory of the country,* which they trusted in, and boasted of as impregnable; these shall decay, be deserted, or betrayed, or fall into the enemies' hands, so that Moab shall lie exposed, and whoever will may penetrate into the heart of the country. Note, Those who glory in any other defence and protection than that of the divine power, providence, and promise, will sooner or later see cause to be ashamed of their glorying. (2.) See here to whom it shall be exposed: *The men of the east,* when they come to take possession of the country of the Ammonites, shall seize that of the Moabites too. God, the Lord of all lands, will give them that land; for the kingdoms of men he gives to whomsoever he will. The Arabians, who are shepherds, and live quietly, plain men dwelling in tents, shall by an overruling Providence be put in possession of the land of the Moabites, who are soldiers, men of war, and cunning hunters, that live turbulently. The Chaldeans shall get it by war, and the Arabians shall enjoy it in peace. Concerning the Ammonites it is said, They shall no *more be remembered among the nations* (*v.* 10), for they had been accessory to the murder of Gedaliah, Jer. 40:14. But of the Moabites it is said, *I will execute judgments upon Moab;* they shall feel the weight of God's displeasure, but perhaps not to that degree that the Ammonites shall; however, so far as that *they shall know that I am the Lord,* that the God of Israel is a God of power, and that his covenant with his people is not broken.

II. The Edomites, the posterity of Esau, between whom and Jacob there had been an old enmity. And here is,

1. The sin of the Edomites, *v.* 12. They not only triumphed in the ruin of Judah and Jerusalem, as the Moabites and Ammonites had done, but they took advantage from the present distressed state to which the Jews were reduced to do them some real mischiefs, probably made inroads upon their frontiers and plundered their country: *Edom has dealt against the house of Judah by taking vengeance.* The Edomites had of old been tributaries to the Jews, according to the sentence that the elder should serve the younger. In Jehoram's time they revolted. Amaziah severely chastised them (2 Ki. 14:7), and for this they *took vengeance.* Now they would pay off all the old scores, and not only incensed the Babylonians against Jerusalem, crying, *Rase it, rase it* (Ps. 137:7), but cut *off those that escaped,* as we find in the prophecy of Obadiah, which is wholly directed against Edom, *v.* 11, 12, etc. It is called here *revenging a revenge,* which intimates that they were not only eager upon it, but very cruel in it, and recompensed to the Jews more than double. "Herein he *has greatly offended."* Note, It is a great offence to God for us to revenge ourselves upon our brother; for God has said, *Vengeance is mine.* We are forbidden to *revenge* or to *bear a grudge.* Suppose Judah had been hard upon Edom formerly, it was a base thing for the Edomites now, in revenge for it, *to smite them secretly.* But the Jews had a divine warrant to reign over the Edomites, for that therefore they ought not to have made reprisals; and it was the more disingenuous for them to retain the old enmity when God had particularly commanded his people to forget it. Deu. 23:7, *Thou shalt not abhor an Edomite.*

2. The judgments threatened against them for this sin. God will take them to task for it (*v.* 13): *I will stretch out my hand upon Edom* Their country shall be desolate *from Teman,* which lay in the south part of it; and *they shall fall by the sword unto Dedan,* which lay north; the desolations of war should go through the nation. (1.) They had taken vengeance, and therefore God will *lay his vengeance* upon them (*v.* 14): *They shall know my vengeance.* Those that will not leave it to God to take vengeance for them may expect that he will take vengeance on them; and those that will not believe and fear his vengeance shall be made to know and feel his vengeance; they shall be dealt with *according to God's anger* and *according to his fury,* not according to the weakness of the instruments that are employed in it, but according to the strength of the arm that employs them. (2.) They had taken vengeance on Israel, and God will lay his vengeance on them *by the hand of his people Israel.* They suffered much by the Chaldeans, which seems to be referred to, Jer. 49:8. But besides that there were *saviours* to come *upon Mount Zion,* who should judge the mount of Esau (Obad. 21), and Israel's Redeemer comes *with dyed garments from Bozrah* (Isa. 63:1), this implies a promise that Israel should recover itself again to such a degree as to be in a capacity of curbing the insolence of its neighbours. And we find (1 Mac. 5:3) that *Judas Maccabeus fought against the children of Esau in Idumea, gave them a great overthrow, abated their courage, and took their spoil;* and Josephus says (*Antiq.* 13.257), that Hircanus made the Edomites tributaries to Israel. Note, The equity of God's judgments is to be observed when he not only avenges injuries upon those that did them, but by those against whom they were done.

III. The Philistines. And, 1. Their sin is much the same with that of the Edomites: They have *dealt by revenge* with the people of Israel, and have *taken vengeance with a despiteful heart,* not to disturb them only, but to *destroy them,* for *the old hatred* (v. 15), the old grudge they bore them, or (as the margin reads it) *with perpetual hatred,* a hatred that began long since and which they resolved to continue. The anger was implacable: they *dealt by revenge,* traded in the acts of malice; it was their constant practice, and their heart, their spiteful heart, was upon it. 2. Their punishment likewise is much the same, v. 16. Those that were for destroying God's people shall themselves be cut off and destroyed; and (v. 17) those that were for avenging themselves shall find that God will *execute great vengeance upon them.* This was fulfilled when that country was wasted by the Chaldean army, not long after the destruction of Jerusalem, which is foretold, Jer. 47. It was strange that these nations, which bordered upon the land of Israel, were not alarmed by the success of the Chaldean army, and made to tremble in the apprehension of their own danger; when their neighbour's house was on fire it was time to look to their own; but their impiety and malice made them forget their politics, till God by his judgments convinced them that the cup was going round, and they were the less safe for being secure.

CHAPTER 26

The prophet had soon done with those four nations that he set his face against in the foregoing chapters; for they were not at that time very considerable in the world, nor would their fall make any great noise among the nations nor any figure in history. But the city of Tyre is next set to the bar; this, being a place of vast trade, was known all the world over; and therefore here are three whole chapters, this and the two that follow, spent in the prediction of the destruction of Tyre. We have "the burden of Tyre," Isa. 23. It is but just mentioned in Jeremiah, as sharing with the natives in the common calamity, 25:22; 27:3; 47:4. But Ezekiel is ordered to be copious upon that head. In this chapter we have, I. The sin charged upon Tyre, which was triumphing in the destruction of Jerusalem (v. 2). II. The destruction of Tyrus itself foretold. 1. The extremity of this destruction: it shall be utterly ruined (v. 4–6, 12–14). 2. The instruments of this destruction, many nations (v. 3), and the king of Babylon by name with his vast victorious army (v. 7–11). 3. The great surprise that this should give to the neighbouring nations, who would all wonder at the fall of so great a city and be alarmed at it (v. 15–21).

Verses 1–14

This prophecy is dated in the eleventh year, which was the year that Jerusalem was taken, and *in the first day of the month,* but it is not said what month, some think the month in which Jerusalem was taken, which was the fourth month, others the month after; or perhaps it was the first month, and so it was the first day of the year. Observe here,

I. The pleasure with which the Tyrians looked upon the ruins of Jerusalem. Ezekiel was a great way off, in Babylon, but God told him what Tyrus said against Jerusalem (v. 2): *"Aha! she is broken,* broken to pieces, that was *the gates of the people,* to whom there was a great resort and where there was a general rendezvous of all nations, some upon one account and some upon another, and I shall get by it; all the wealth, power, and interest, which Jerusalem had, it is hoped, shall be turned to Tyre, and so *now* that *she is laid waste I shall be replenished."* We do not find that the Tyrians had such a hatred and enmity to Jerusalem and the sanctuary as the Ammonites and Edomites had, or were so spiteful and mischievous to the Jews. They were men of business, and of large acquaintance and free conversation, and therefore were not so bigoted, and of such a persecuting spirit, as the narrow souls that lived retired and knew not the world. All their care was to get estates, and enlarge their trade, and they looked upon Jerusalem not as an enemy, but as a rival. Hiram, king of Tyre, was a good friend to David and Solomon, and we do not read of any quarrels the Jews had with the Tyrians; but Tyre promised herself that the fall of Jerusalem would be an advantage to her in respect of trade a commerce, that now she shall have Jerusalem's customers, and the great men from all parts that used to come to Jerusalem for the accomplishing of themselves, and to spend their estates there, will now come to Tyre and spend them there; and whereas many, since the Chaldean army became so formidable in those parts, had retired into Jerusalem, and brought their estates thither for safety, as the Rechabites did, now they will come to Tyre, which, being in a manner surrounded with the sea, will be thought a place of greater strength than Jerusalem, and thus the prosperity of Tyre will rise out of the ruins of Jerusalem. Note, To

be secretly pleased with the death or decay of others, when we are likely to get by it, with their fall when we may thrive upon it, is a sin that does most easily beset us, but is not thought to be such a bad thing, and so provoking to God, as really it is. We are apt to say, when those who stand in our light, in our way, are removed, when they break of fall into disgrace, "We shall be *replenished* now that they are *laid waste."* But this comes from a selfish covetous principle, and a desire to be *placed alone in the midst of the earth,* as if we grudged that any should live by us. This comes from a want of that love to our neighbour as to ourselves which the law of God so expressly requires, and from that inordinate love of the world as our happiness which the love of God so expressly forbids. And it is just with God to blast the designs and projects of those who thus contrive to raise themselves upon the ruins of others; and we see they are often disappointed.

II. The displeasure of God against them for it. The providence of God had done well for Tyrus. Tyrus was a pleasant and wealthy city, and might have continued so if she had, as she ought to have done, sympathized with Jerusalem in her calamities and sent her an address of condolence; but when, instead of that, she showed herself pleased with her neighbour's fall, and perhaps sent an address of congratulation to the conquerors, then God says, *Behold, I am against thee, O Tyrus!* v. 3. And let her not expect to prosper long if God be against her.

1. God will bring formidable enemies upon her: *Many nations shall come against thee,* an army made up of many nations, or one nation that shall be as strong as many. Those that have God against them may expect all the creatures against them; for what peace can those have with whom God is at war? They shall come pouring in as *the waves of the sea,* one upon the neck of another, with an irresistible force. The person is named that shall bring this army upon them — *Nebuchadnezzar king of Babylon, a king of kings,* that had many kings tributaries to him and dependents on him, besides those that were his captives, Can 2:37, 38. He is that *head of gold.* He shall come with a vast army, *horses and chariots,* etc., all land-forces. We do not find that he had any naval force, or any thing wherewith he might attack it by sea, which made the attempt the more difficult, as we find *ch.* 29:18, where it is called a *great service which he served against Tyrus.* He shall besiege it in form (v. 8), *make a fort, and cast a mount,* and (v. 9) shall *set engines of war against the walls.* His troops shall be so numerous as to raise a dust that shall cover the city, v. 10. They shall make a noise that shall even *shake the walls;* and they shall shout at every attack, as soldiers do when they *enter a city* that is *broken up;* the horses shall prance with so much fury and violence that they shall even *tread down the streets* though so ever well paved.

2. They shall do terrible execution. (1.) The enemy shall make themselves masters of all their fortifications, shall *destroy the walls* and *break down the towers,* v. 4. For what walls are so strongly built as to be a fence against the judgments of God? Her *strong garrisons shall go down to the ground,* v. 11. And the walls shall be broken down, v. 12. The city held out a long siege, but it was taken at last. (2.) A great deal of blood shall be shed: *Her daughters who are in the field,* the cities upon the continent, which were subject to Tyre as the mother-city, the inhabitants of them *shall be slain by the sword,* v. 6. The invaders begin with those that come first in their way. And (v. 11) *he shall slay thy people with the sword;* not only the soldiers that are found in arms, but the burghers, shall be *put to the sword,* the king of Babylon being highly incensed against them for holding out so long. (3.) The wealth of the city shall all become a spoil to the conqueror (v. 12): They *shall make a prey of the merchandise.* It was in hope of the plunder that the city was set upon with so much vigour. See the vanity of riches, that they are *kept for the owners to their hurt;* they entice and recompense thieves, and not only cease to benefit those who took pains for them and were duly entitled to them, but are made to serve their enemies, who are thereby put into a capacity of doing them so much the more mischief. (4.) The city itself shall be laid in ruins. All the *pleasant houses* shall be *destroyed* (v. 12), such as were pleasantly situated, beautified, and furnished, shall become a heap of rubbish. Let none please themselves too much in their pleasant houses, for they know not how soon they may see the desolation of them. Tyre

shall be utterly ruined; the enemy shall not only pull down the houses, but shall carry away *the stones and the timber,* and shall *lay them in the midst of the water,* not to be recovered, or ever made use of again. Nay (v. 4), *I will scrape her dust from her;* not only shall the loose dust be blown away, but the very ground it stands upon shall be torn up by the enraged enemy, carried off, and laid *in the midst of the water,* v. 12. The *foundation is in the dust;* that dust shall be all taken away, and then the city must fall of course. When Jerusalem was destroyed it was *ploughed like a field,* Mic. 3:12. But the destruction of Tyre is carried further than that; the very soil of it shall be scraped away, and it shall be made *like the top of a rock* (v. 4. 14), pure rock that has no earth to cover it; it shall only be a place *for the spreading of nets* (v. 5. 14); it shall serve fishermen to dry their nets upon and mend them. (5.) There shall be a full period to all its mirth and joy (v. 13): *I will cause the noise of thy songs to cease.* Tyre had been a joyous city (Isa. 23:7).; with her songs she had courted customers to deal with her in a way of trade. But now farewell all her profitable commerce and pleasant conversation; Tyre is no more a place either of business or of sport. *Lastly,* It shall be *built no more* (v. 14), not built any more as it had been, with such state and magnificence, nor built any more in the same place, within the sea, nor built any where for a long time; the present inhabitants shall be destroyed or dispersed, so that this Tyre shall be *no more.* For *God has spoken it* (v. 5, 14); and when what he has said is accomplished *they shall know* thereby that *he is the Lord,* and *not a man that he should lie nor the son of man that he should repent.*

Verses 15–21

The utter ruin of Tyre is here represented in very strong and lively figures, which are exceedingly affecting.

1. See how high, how great, Tyre had been, how little likely ever to come to this. The remembrance of men's former grandeur and plenty is a great aggravation of their present disgrace and poverty. Tyre was *a renowned city* (v. 17), famous among the nations, the *crowning* city (so she is called Isa. 23:8), a city that had crowns in her gift, honoured all she smiled upon, crowned herself and all about her. She was *inhabited of seas,* that is, of those that trade at sea, of those who from all parts came thither by sea, bringing with them the *abundance of the seas* and *the treasures hidden in the sand.* She was *strong in the sea,* easy of access to her friends, but to her enemies inaccessible, fortified by a *wall of water,* which made her impregnable. So that *she* with her pomp, *and her inhabitants* with their pride, *caused their terror to be on all that haunted* that city, and upon any account frequented it. It was well fortified, and formidable in the eyes of all that acquainted themselves with it. Every body stood in awe of the Tyrians and was afraid of disobliging them. Note, Those who know their strength are too apt to cause terror, to pride themselves in frightening those they are an over-match for.

2. See how low, how little, Tyre is made, v. 19, 20. This *renowned city* is made a *desolate city,* is no more frequented as it has been; there is no more resort of merchants to it; it is *like the cities not inhabited,* which are no cities, and having none to keep them in repair, will go to decay of themselves. Tyre shall be like a city overflowed by an inundation of waters, which *cover* it, and upon which the *deep* is *brought up.* As the waves had formerly been its defence, so now they shall be its destruction. She shall be *brought down with those that descend into the pit,* with the cities of the old world that were under water, and with *Sodom and Gomorrah,* that lie in the bottom of the Dead Sea. Or, she shall be in the condition of those who have been long buried, of the *people of old time,* who are old inhabitants of the silent grace, who are quite rotted away under ground and quite forgotten above ground; such shall Tyre be, *free among the dead, set in the lower parts of the earth,* humbled, mortified, reduced. It shall be *like the places desolate of old,* as well as like persons dead of old; it shall be like other cities that have formerly been in like manner deserted and destroyed. It shall *not be inhabited* again; none shall have the courage to attempt the rebuilding of it upon that spot, so that *it shall be no more;* The Tyrians shall be lost among the nations, so that people will look in vain for Tyre in Tyre: *Thou shalt be sought for, and never found again.* New persons may build a new city upon

a new spot of ground hard by, which they may call *Tyre,* but Tyre, as it is, shall never be any more. Note, The strongest cities in this world, the best-fortified and best-furnished, are subject to decay, and may in a little time be brought to nothing. In the history of our own island many cities are spoken of as in being when the Romans were here which now our antiquaries scarcely know where to look for, and of which there remains no more evidence than Roman urns and coins digged up there sometimes accidentally. But in the other world we look for a city that shall stand for ever and flourish in perfection through all the ages of eternity.

3. See what a distress the inhabitants of Tyre are in (*v.* 15): *There is a great slaughter made in the midst of thee,* many slain, and great men. It is probable that, when the city was taken, the generality of the inhabitants were put to the sword. Then did *the wounded cry,* and they cried in vain, to the pitiless conquerors; they cried *quarter,* but it would not be given them; the wounded are *slain* without mercy, or, rather, that is the only mercy that is shown them, that the second blow shall rid them out of their pain.

4. See what a consternation all the neighbours are in upon the fall of Tyre. This is elegantly expressed here, to show how astonishing it should be. (1.) the *islands* shall *shake at the sound of thy fall* (*v.* 15), as, when a great merchant breaks, all that he deals with are shocked by it, and begin to look about them; perhaps they had effects in his hands, which they are afraid they shall lose. Or, when they see one fail and become bankrupt of a sudden, in debt a great deal more than he is worth, it makes them afraid for themselves, lest they should do so too. Thus *the isles,* which thought themselves safe in the embraces of the sea, when they see Tyrus fall, shall *tremble* and *be troubled,* saying, "What will become of us?" And it is well if they make this good use of it, to take warning by it not to be secure, but to stand in awe of God and his judgments. The sudden fall of a great tower shakes the ground round about it; thus all the islands in the Mediterranean Sea shall feel themselves sensibly touched by the destruction of Tyre, it being a place they had so much knowledge of, such interests in, and such a constant correspondence with. (2.) The *princes of the sea* shall be affected with it, who ruled in those islands. Or the rich merchants, who live like princes (Isa. 23:8), and the masters of ships, who command like princes, these shall condole the fall of Tyre in a most compassionate and pathetic manner (*v.* 16): *They shall come down from their thrones,* as neglecting the business of their thrones and despising the pomp of them. They shall *lay away their robes* of state, *their broidered garments,* and shall *clothe themselves* all over with *tremblings,* with sackcloth that will make them shiver. Or they shall by their own act and deed make themselves to tremble upon this occasion; they shall *sit upon the ground* in shame and sorrow; they shall *tremble every moment* at the thought of what has happened to Tyre, and for fear of what may happen to themselves; for what island is safe if Tyre be not? They shall *take up a lamentation for thee,* shall have elegies and mournful poems penned upon the fall of Tyre, *v.* 17. *How art thou destroyed!* [1.] It shall be a great surprise to them, and they shall be affected with wonder, that a place so well fortified by nature and art, so famed for politics and so full of money, which is the sinews of war, that held out so long and with so much bravery, should be taken at last (*v.* 21): *I make thee a terror.* Note, It is just with God to make those a terror to their neighbours, by the suddenness and strangeness of their punishment, who make themselves a terror to their neighbours by the abuse of their power. Tyre had *caused her terror* (*v.* 17) and now is made a terrible example. [2.] It shall be a great affliction to them, and they shall be affected with sorrow (*v.* 17); they shall *take up a lamentation for Tyre,* as thinking it a thousand pities that such a rich and splendid city should be thus laid in ruins. When Jerusalem, the holy city, was destroyed, there were no such lamentations for it; it was *nothing* to *those that passed by* (Lam. 1:12); but when Tyre, the trading city, fell, it was universally bemoaned. Note, Those who have the world in their hearts lament the loss of great men more than the loss of good men. [3.] It shall be a loud alarm to them: *They shall tremble in the day of thy fall,* because they shall have reason to think that their own turn will be next. If Tyre fall, who can stand? *Howl, fir-trees, if such a cedar be shaken.* Note, The fall of others should awaken us out of our security. The death or decay of others in the world is a check to us, when we dream that our mountain *stands strongly and shall not be moved.*

5. See how the irreparable ruin of Tyre is aggravated by the prospect of the restoration of Israel. Thus shall Tyre sink *when I shall set glory in the land of the living, v.* 20. Note, (1.) The holy land is the *land of the living;* for none but holy souls are properly living souls. Where living sacrifices are offered to the living God, and where the lively oracles are, there *the land of the living* is; there David hoped to *see the goodness of the Lord,* Ps. 27:13. That was a type of heaven, which is indeed the *land of the living.* (2.) Though this land of the living may for a time lie under disgrace, yet God will again *set glory* in it; the glory that had departed shall return, and the restoration of what they had been deprived of shall be so much more their glory. God will himself be the glory of the lands that are the lands of the living. (3.) It will aggravate the misery of those that have their portion in the land of the dying, of those that are for ever dying, to behold the happiness of those, at the same time, that shall have their everlasting portion in the land of the living. When the rich man was himself in torment he saw Lazarus in the bosom of Abraham, and glory set for him in the land of the living.

CHAPTER 27

Still we are attending the funeral of Tyre and the lamentations made for the fall of that renowned city. In this chapter we have, I. A large account of the dignity, wealth, and splendour of Tyre, while it was in its strength, the vast trade it drove, and the interest it had among the nations (*v.* 1–25), which is designed to make its ruin the more lamentable. II. A prediction of its fall and ruin, and the confusion and consternation which all its neighbours shall thereby be put into (*v.* 26–36). And this is intended to stain the pride of all worldly glory, and, by setting the one over-against the other, to let us see the vanity and uncertainty of the riches, honours, and pleasures of the world, and what little reason we have to place our happiness in them or to be confident of the continuance of them; so that all this is written for our learning.

Verses 1–25

Here, I. The prophet is ordered to take up a lamentation for Tyrus, *v.* 2. It was yet in the height of its prosperity, and there appeared not the least symptom of its decay; yet the prophet must lament it, because its prosperity is its snare, is the cause of its pride and security, which will make its fall the more grievous. Even those that live at ease are to be lamented if they be not preparing for trouble. He must lament it because its ruin is hastening on apace; it is sure, it is near; and though the prophet foretel it, and justify God in it, yet he must lament it. Note, We ought to mourn for the miseries of other nations, as well as for our own, out of an affection for mankind in general; it is a part of the honour we owe to all men to bewail their calamities, even those which they have brought upon themselves by their own folly.

II. He is directed what to say, and to say it in the name of *the Lord Jehovah,* a name not unknown in Tyre, and which shall be better known, *ch.* 26:6.

1. He must upbraid Tyre with her pride: *O Tyrus! thou hast said, I am of perfect beauty* (*v.* 3), of *universal beauty* (so the word is), every way accomplished, and therefore every where admired. Zion, that had the *beauty of holiness,* is called indeed the *perfection of beauty* (Ps. 1. 2); that is the *beauty of the Lord.* But Tyre, because well-built and well-filled with money and trade, will set up for a perfect beauty. Note, It is the folly of the children of this world to value themselves on the pomp and pleasure they live in, to call themselves beauties for the sake of them, and, if in these they excel others, to think themselves perfect. But God takes notice of the vain conceits men have of themselves in their prosperity when the mind is lifted up with the condition, and often, for the humbling of the spirit, finds a way to bring down the estate. Let none reckon themselves beautified any further than they are sanctified, nor say that they are of perfect beauty till they come to heaven.

2. He must upbraid Tyre with her prosperity, which was the matter of her pride. In elegies it is usual to insert encomiums of those whose fall we lament; the prophet, accordingly, praises Tyre for all that she had that was praiseworthy. He has nothing to say of her religion, her piety, her charity, her being a refuge to the distressed or using her interest to do good offices among her neighbours; but she lived great, and had a great trade, and all the trading part of mankind made court to her. The prophet must describe her height and magnificence, that God may be the more glorified in her fall, as the God who *looks upon every one that is proud and abases him, hides the proud in the dust together, and binds their faces in secret,* Job 40:12.

(1.) The city of Tyre was advantageously situated, *at the entry of the sea* (*v.* 3), having many commodious harbours each way, not as cities seated on rivers, which the shipping can come but one way to. It stood at the east end of the Mediterranean, very convenient for trade by land into all the Levant parts; so that she became a *merchant of the people for many isles.* Lying between Greece and Asia, it became the great emporium, or mart-town, the rendezvous of merchants from all parts: *They borders are in the heart of the seas, v.* 4. It was surrounded with water, which was a great advantage to its trade; it was the darling of the sea, laid in its bosom, in its heart. Note, It is a great convenience, upon many accounts, to live in an island: seas are the most *ancient land-mark,* not *which our fathers have set,* but the God of our fathers, and which cannot be removed as other land-marks may, nor so easily got over. The people so situated may the more easily *dwell alone,* if they please, as *not reckoned among the nations,* and yet, if they please, may the more easily traffic abroad and keep a correspondence with the nations. We therefore of this island must own that he who determines the bounds of men's habitations has determined well for us.

(2.) It was curiously built, according as the fashion then was; and, being a city on a hill, it made a glorious show and tempted the ships that sailed by into her ports (*v.* 4): *They builders have perfected thy beauty;* they have so improved in architecture that nothing appears in the buildings of Tyre that can be found fault with; and yet it wants that perfection of beauty into which the Lord does and will build up his Jerusalem.

(3.) It had its haven replenished with abundance of *gallant ships,* Isa. 33:21. The ship-carpenters did their part, as well as the house-carpenters theirs. The Tyrians are thought to be the first that invented the art of navigation; at least they improved it, and brought it to as great a perfection perhaps as it could be without the loadstone. [1.] They made the *boards,* or planks, for the hulk of the ship, of *fir-trees* fetched from *Senir,* a mount in the land of Israel, joined with Hermon, Cant. 4:8. Planks of fir were smooth and light, but not so lasting as our English oak. [2.] They had cedars from Lebanon, another mountain of Israel, for their masts, *v.* 5. [3.] They had oaks from Bashan (Isa. 2:13), to make oars of; for it is probable that their ships were mostly galleys, that go with oars. The people of Israel built few ships for themselves, but they furnished the Tyrians with timber for shipping. Thus one country uses what another produced, and so they are serviceable one to another, and cannot say to each other, *I have no need of thee.* [4.] Such magnificence did they affect in building their ships that they made the very *benches of ivory,* which they fetched from *the isles of Chittim,* from Italy or Greece, and had workmen from the Ashurites or Assyrians to make them, so rich would they have their staterooms in their ships to be. [5.] So very prodigal were they that they made their *sails* of *fine linen* fetched from Egypt, and that *embroidered* too, *v.* 7. Or it may be meant of their *flags* (which they hoisted to notify what city they belonged to), which were very costly. The word signifies a *banner* as well as a *sail.* [6.] They hung those rooms on ship-board with *blue and purple,* the richest cloths and richest colours they could get from the isles they traded with. For though Tyre was itself famous for purple, which is therefore called the *Tyrian dye,* yet they must have that which was far-fetched.

(4.) These gallant ships were well-manned, by men of great ingenuity and industry. The pilots and masters of the ships, that had command in their fleets, were of their own city, such as they could put a confidence in (*v.* 8): *Thy wise men, O Tyrus! that were in thee, were thy pilots.* But, for common sailors, they had men from other countries; *The inhabitants of Arvad and Zidon were thy mariners.* These came from cities hear them; Zidon was sister to Tyre, not two leagues off, to the northward; there they bred able seamen, which it is the interest of the maritime powers to support and give all the countenance they can to. They sent to Gebal in Syria for *calkers,* or *strengtheners of the clefts* or *chinks,* to stop them when the ships come home, after long voyages, to be repaired. To do this they had the *ancients* and *wise men* (*v.* 9); for there is more need of wisdom and prudence to repair what has gone to decay than to build anew. In public matters there is occasion for the *ancients* and *wise men* to be the *repairers of the breaches and the restorers of paths to dwell in.* Nay, all the countries they traded with were at their service, and were willing to send men into their pay, to put their youths apprentice in Tyre, or to put them on board their fleets; so that *all the ships in the sea with their mariners were* ready *to occupy thy merchandise.* Those that give good wages shall have hands at command.

(5.) Their city was guarded by a military force that was very considerable, *v.* 10, 11. The Tyrians were themselves wholly given to trade; but it was necessary that they should have a good army on foot, and therefore they took those of other states into their pay, such as were fittest for service, though they had them from afar (which perhaps was their policy), from Persia, Lud, and Phut. These bore their arms when there was occasion, and in time of peace *hung up the shield and buckler* in the armoury, as it were to proclaim peace, and let the world know that they had at present no need of them, but they were ready to be taken down whenever there was occasion for them. Their *walls* were *guarded* by the *man of Arvad;* their *towers* were garrisoned by *the Gammadim,* robust men, that had a great deal of strength in *their arms;* yet the vulgar Latin renders it *pygmies,* men no longer than one's arm. They *hung their shields upon the walls* in their magazines or places of arms; or hung them out upon the walls of the city, that none might dare to approach them, seeing how well provided they were with all things necessary for their own defence. "Thus *they set forth thy comeliness* (*v.* 10), and *made they beauty perfect,*" *v.* 11. It contributed as much as any thing to the glory of Tyre that it had those of all the surrounding nations in its service, except the land of Israel (though it lay next them), which furnished them with timber, but we do not find that it furnished them with men; that would have trenched upon the liberty and dignity of the Jewish nation, 2 Chr. 2:17, 18. It was also the glory of Tyre that it had such a militia, so fit for service, and in constant pay, and such an armoury, like that in the tower of David, where hung the *shields of mighty men,* Cant. 4:4. It is observable that there and here the armouries are said to be furnished with *shields* and *helmets,* defensive arms, not with swords and spears, offensive, though it is probable that there were such, to intimate that the military force of a people must be intended only for their own protection and not to invade and annoy their neighbours, to secure their own right, not to encroach upon the rights of others.

(6.) They had a vast trade and a correspondence with all parts of the known world. Some nations they dealt with in one commodity and some in another, according as either its products or its manufactures were, and the fruits of nature or art were, with which it was blessed. This is very much enlarged upon here, as that which was the principal glory of Tyre, and which supported all the rest. We do not find any where in scripture so many nations named together as are here; so that this chapter, some think, gives much light to the first account we have of the settlement of the nations after the flood, Gen. 10. The critics have abundance of work here to find out the several places and nations spoken of. Concerning many of them their conjectures are different and they leave us in the dark and at much uncertainty; it is well that it is not material. Modern surveys come short of explaining the ancient geography. And therefore we will not amuse ourselves here with a particular enquiry either concerning the traders or the goods they traded in. We leave it to the critical expositors, and observe that only which is improvable. [1.] We have reason to think that Ezekiel knew little, of his own knowledge, concerning the trade of Tyre. He was a priest, carried away captive far enough from the neighbourhood of Tyre, we may suppose when he was young, and there he had been eleven years. And yet he speaks of the particular merchandises of Tyre as nicely as if he had been comptroller of the custom-house there, by which it appears that he was divinely inspired in what he spoke and wrote. It is God that *saith this, v.* 3. [2.] This account of the trade of Tyre intimates to us that God's eye is upon men, and that he takes cognizance of what they do when they are employed in their worldly business, not only when they are at church, praying and hearing, but when they are in their markets and fairs, and upon the exchange, buying and selling, which is a good reason why we should in all our dealings *keep a conscience void of offence,* and have our eye always upon him whose eye is always upon us. [3.] We may here observe the wisdom of God, and his goodness, as the common Father of mankind, in making one country to abound in one commodity and another in another, and all more or less serviceable either to the necessity or to the comfort or ornament of human life. *Non omis fert omnia tellus — One land does not supply all the varieties of produce.* Providence dispenses its gifts variously, some to each, and all to none, that there may be a mutual commerce among those whom God has *made of one blood,* though they are made *to dwell on all the face of the earth,* Acts 17:26. Let every nations therefore thank God for the productions of its country; though they be not so rich as those of others, yet there is use for them in the public service of the world. [4.] See what a blessing trade and merchandise are to mankind, especially when followed in the fear of God, and with a regard not only to private advantage, but to a common benefit. *The earth is full of God's riches,* Ps. 104:24. There is a *multitude of all kinds of riches* in it (as it is here, *v.* 12), gathered off its surface and dug out of its bowels. The earth is also full of the fruits of men's ingenuity and industry, according as their genius leads them. Now by exchange and barter these are made more extensively useful; thus what can be spared is helped off, and what is wanted is fetched in, in lieu of it, from the most distant countries. Those that are not tradesmen themselves have reason to thank God for tradesmen and merchants, by whom the productions of other countries are brought to our hands, as those of our own are by our husbandmen. [5.] Besides the necessaries that are here traded in, see what abundance of things are here mentioned that only serve to please fancy, and are made valuable only by men's humour and custom; and yet God allows us to use them, and trade in them, and part with those things for them which we can spare that are of an intrinsic worth much beyond them. Here are *horns of ivory and ebony* (*v.* 15), that are *brought for a present,* exposed to sale, and offered in exchange, or (as some think) presented to the city, or the great men of it, to obtain their favour. Here are *emeralds, coral,* and *agate* (*v.* 16), all *precious stones, and gold* (*v.* 22), which the world could better be without than iron and common stones. Here are, to please the taste and smell, the *chief of all spices* (*v.* 22), *cassia and calamus* (*v.* 19), and, for ornament, *purple, broidered work, and fine linen* (*v.* 16), *precious clothes for chariots* (*v.* 20), *blue clothes* (which Tyre was famous for), *broidered work,* and *chests of rich apparel, bound with* rich *cords,* and *made of cedar,* a sweet wood to perfume the garments kept in them, *v.* 24. Upon the review of this invoice, or bill of parcels, we may justly say, What a great many things are here that we have no need of, and can live very comfortably without! [6.] It is observable that Judah and the *land of Israel* were merchants in Tyre too; in a way of trade they were allowed to converse with the heathen. But they traded mostly *in wheat,* a substantial commodity, and necessary, *wheat of Minnith and Pannag,* two countries in Canaan famous for the best wheat, as some think. The whole land indeed was a *land of wheat* (Deu. 8:8); it had *the fat of kidneys of wheat,* Deu. 32:14. Tyre was maintained by corn fetched from the land of Israel. They traded likewise in *honey, and oil,* and *balm,* or *rosin;* all useful things, and not serving to pride or luxury. And the land which these were the staple commodities of was that which was the *glory of all lands,* which God reserved for his peculiar people, not those that traded in spices and *precious stones;* and the Israel of God must reckon themselves well provided for if they have *food convenient;* for those that are acquainted with the delights of the children of God will not set their hearts on the *delights of the sons and daughters of men,* or the *treasures of kings and provinces.* We find indeed that the New-Testament Babylon trades in such things as Tyre traded in, Rev. 18:12, 13. For, notwithstanding its pretensions to sanctity, it is a mere worldly interest. [7.] Though Tyre was a city of great merchandise, and they got abundance by buying and selling, importing commodities from one place and exporting them to another, yet manufacture-trades were not neglected. The *wares of their own making,* and a *multitude of such wares,* are here spoken of, *v.* 16, 18. It is the wisdom of a nation to encourage art and industry, and not to bear hard upon the handicraft-tradesmen; for it contributes much to the wealth and honour of a nation to send abroad *wares of their own making,* which may bring them in the *multitude of all riches.* [8.] All this made Tyrus very great and very proud: *The ships of Tarshish did sing of thee in they market* (*v.* 25); thou wast admired and cried up by all the nations that had dealings with thee; for *thou wast replenished* in wealth and number of people, wast beautified, and *made very glorious, in the midst of the seas.* Those that grow very rich are cried up as very glorious; for riches are glorious things in the eyes of carnal people, Gen. 31:1.

Verses 26–36

We have seen Tyre flourishing; here we have Tyre falling, and great is the fall of it, so much the greater for its having made such a figure in the world. Note, The most mighty and magnificent kingdoms and states, sooner or later, have their day to come down. They have their period; and, when they are in their zenith, they will begin to decline. But the destruction of Tyre was sudden. Her *sun went down at noon.* And all her wealth and grandeur, pomp and power, did but aggravate her ruin, and make it the more grievous to herself and astonishing to all about her. Now observe here, 1. How the ruin of Tyrus will be brought about, *v.* 26. She is as a great ship richly laden, that is split or sunk by the indiscretion of her steersmen: *Thy rowers have* themselves *brought thee into great* and dangerous *waters;* the governors of the city, and those that had the management of their public affairs, by some mismanagement or other involved them in that war with the Chaldeans which was the ruin of their state. By their insolence, by some affront given to the Chaldeans or some attempt made upon them, in confidence of their own ability to contend with them, they provoked Nebuchadnezzar to make a descent upon them, and, by their obstinacy in standing it out to the last, enraged him to such a degree that he determined on the ruin of their state, and, *like an east wind, broke them in the midst of the seas.* Note, It is ill with a people when those that sit at the stern, instead of putting them into the harbour, run them aground. 2. How great and general the ruin will be. All her wealth shall be buried with her, *her riches, her fairs, and her merchandise* (*v.* 27); all that had any dependence upon her, and dealings with her, in trade, in war, in conversation, shall *ball with her into the midst of the seas, in the day of her ruin.* Note, Those who make creatures their confidence, place their happiness in their interest in them and rest their hopes upon them, will of course fall with them; *happy* therefore *are those that have the God of Jacob for their help,* and *whose hope is in the Lord their God,* who lives for ever. 3. What sad lamentation would be made for the destruction of Tyre. The pilots, her princes and governors, when they see how wretchedly they have mismanaged and how much they have contributed to their own ruin, shall *cry out* so loud as to make even the *suburbs shake* (*v.* 28), such a vexation shall it be to them to reflect upon their own bad conduct. The inferior officers, that were as the mariners of the state, shall be forced to come down from their respective posts (*v.* 29), and they shall *cry out against thee,* as having deceived them, in not proving so well able to hold out as they thought thou hadst been; they shall *cry bitterly* for the common ruin, and their own share in it. They shall use all the most solemn expressions of grief; they shall *cast dust on their heads,* in indignation against themselves, shall *wallow themselves in ashes,* as having bid a final farewell to all ease and pleasure; they shall *make themselves bald* (*v.* 31), with *tearing their hair;* and, according to the custom of great mourners, those shall *gird themselves with sackcloth* who used to wear find linen, and, instead of merry songs, they shall *weep with bitterness of heart.* Note, Losses and crosses are very grievous, and hard to be borne, to those that have long been wallowing in pleasure and sleeping in carnal security. 4. How Tyre should be upbraided with her former honour and prosperity (*v.* 32, 33); she that was Tyrus the *renowned* shall now be called *Tyrus the destroyed* in the *midst of the sea.* *"What city is like Tyre?* Did ever any city come down from such a height of prosperity to such a depth of adversity? Time was when *thy wares,* those of thy own making and those that passed through thy hands, *went forth out of the seas,* and were exported to all parts of the world; then *thou filledst many people,* and didst *enrich the kings of the earth* and their kingdoms." The Tyrians, though they bore such a sway in trade, were yet, it seems, fair merchants, and let their neighbours not only live, but thrive by them. All that dealt with them were gainers; they did not cheat or oppress the people, but did enrich them with *the multitude of their merchandise.* "But now those that used to be enriched by thee shall be ruined with thee" (as is usual in trade); *"when thou shalt be broken,* and all thou hast is seized on, *all thy company shall fall too," v.* 34. There is an end of Tyre, that made such a noise and bustle in the world. This great blaze goes out in a snuff. 5. How the fall of Tyre should be matter of terror to some and laughter to others, according as they were differently interested and affected. Some shall be *sorely afraid,* and shall *be troubled* (*v.* 35), concluding it will be their own turn to fall next. Others shall *hiss at her* (*v.* 36), shall ridicule her pride, and vanity, and bad management, and think her ruin just. She triumphed in Jerusalem's fall, and there are those that will triumph in hers. When God casts his judgments on the sinner *men* also *shall clap their hands at him* and *shall hiss him out of his place,* Job 27:22, 23. *Is this the city which men called the perfection of beauty?*

CHAPTER 28

In this chapter we have, I. A prediction of the fall and ruin of the king of Tyre, who, in the destruction of that city, is particularly set up as a mark for God's arrows (*v.* 1–10). II. A lamentation for the king of Tyre, when he has thus fallen, though he falls by his own iniquity (*v.* 11–19). III. A prophecy of the destruction of Zidon, which as in the neighbourhood of Tyre and had a dependence upon it (*v.* 20–23). IV. A promise of the restoration of the Israel of God, though in the day of their calamity they were insulted over by their neighbours (*v.* 24–26).

Verses 1–10

We had done with Tyrus in the foregoing chapter, but now the prince of Tyrus is to be singled out from the rest. Here is something to be said to him by himself, a *message to him from God,* which the prophet must send him, whether he will hear or whether he will forbear.

I. He must tell him of his pride. His people are proud (*ch.* 27:3) and so is he; and they shall both be made to know that *God resists the proud.* Let us see, 1. What were the expressions of his pride: *His heart was lifted up, v.* 2. He had a great conceit of himself, was puffed up with an opinion of his own sufficiency, and looked with disdain upon all about him. Out of the abundance of the pride of his heart he said, *I am a god;* he did not only say it in his heart, but had the impudence to speak it out. God has said of princes, *They are gods* (Ps. 82:6); but it does not become them to say so of themselves; it is a high affront to him who is *God alone,* and will not give his glory to another. He thought that the city of Tyre had as necessary a dependence upon him as the world has upon the God that made it, and that he was himself independent as God and unaccountable to any. He thought himself to have as much wisdom and strength as God himself, and as incontestable an authority, and that his prerogatives were as absolute and his word as much a law as the word of God. He challenged divine honours, and expected to be praised and admired as a god, and doubted not to be deified, among other heroes, after his death as a great benefactor to the world. Thus the king of Babylon said, *I will be like the Most High* (Isa. 14:14), not like the *Most Holy. "I am the strong God,* and therefore will not be contradicted, because I cannot be controlled. *I sit in the seat of God;* I sit *as high* as God, my throne equal with his. *Divisum imperium cum Jove Caesar habet — Caesar divides dominion with Jove.* I sit as safely as God, as safely *in the heart of the seas,* and as far out of the reach of danger, as he in the *height of heaven."* He thinks his guards of men of war about his throne as pompous and potent as the hosts of angels that are about the throne of God. He is put in mind of his meanness and mortality, and, since he needs to be told, he shall be told, that self-evident truth, *Thou art a man, and not God,* a depending creature; thou art *flesh, and not spirit,* Isa. 31:3. Note, Men must be made to know that they are *but men,* Ps. 9:20. The greatest wits, the greatest potentates, the greatest saints, are *men, and not gods.* Jesus Christ was both God and man. The king of Tyre, though he has such a mighty influence upon all about him, and with the help of his riches bears a mighty sway, though he has tribute and presents brought to his court with as much devotion as if they were sacrifices to his altar, though he is flattered by his courtiers and made a god of by his poets, yet, after all, he is *but a man;* he knows it; he fears it. But *he sets his heart as the heart of God;* "Thou hast conceited thyself to be a god, hast compared thyself with God, thinking thyself as wise and strong, and as fit to govern the world, as he." It was the ruin of our first parents, and ours in them, that they would be *as gods,* Gen. 3:5. And still that corrupt nature which inclines men to set up themselves as their own masters, to do what they will, and their own carvers, to have what they will, their own end, to live to themselves, and their own felicity, to enjoy themselves, *sets their hearts as the heart of God,* invades his prerogatives, and catches at the flowers of his crown — a presumption that cannot go unpunished.

2. We are here told what it was that he was proud of. (1.) His wisdom. It is probable that this prince of Tyre was a man of very good natural parts, a philosopher, and well read in all the parts of learning that were then in vogue, at least a politician, and one that had great dexterity in managing the affairs of state. And then he thought himself *wiser than Daniel, v.* 3. We found, before, that Daniel, though now but a young man, was celebrated for his prevalency in prayer, *ch.* 14:14. Here we find he was famous for his prudence in the management of the affairs of this world, a great scholar and statesman, and withal a great saint, and yet not a prince, but a poor captive. It was strange that under such external disadvantages his lustre should shine forth, so that he had become *wise to a proverb.* When the king of Tyre dreams himself to be a god he says, I am *wiser than Daniel. There is no secret that they can hide from thee.* Probably he challenged all about him to *prove him with questions,* as Solomon was proved, and he had unriddled all their enigmas, had solved all their problems, and none of them all could puzzle him. He had perhaps been successful in discovering plots, and diving into the counsels of the neighbouring princes, and therefore thought himself omniscient, and that no thought could be withholden from him; therefore he said, *I am a god.* Note, *Knowledge puffeth up;* it is hard to know much and not to know it too well and to be elevated with it. He that was *wiser than Daniel* was prouder than Lucifer. Those therefore that are knowing must study to be humble and to evidence that they are so. (2.) His wealth. That way his wisdom led him; it is not said that by his wisdom he searched into the arcana either of nature or government, modelled the state better than it was, or made better laws, or advanced the interests of the commonwealth of learning; but his *wisdom and understanding* were of use to him in *traffic.* As some of the kings of Judah *loved husbandry* (2 Chr. 26:10), so the king of Tyre loved merchandise, and by it he *got riches, increased his riches, and filled his treasures with gold and silver, v.* 4, 5. See what the wisdom of this world is; those are cried up as the wisest men that know how to get money and by right or wrong to raise estates; and yet really *this their way is their folly,* Ps. 49:13. It was the folly of the king of Tyre, [1.] That he attributed the increase of his wealth to himself and not to the providence of God, forgetting him who *gave him power to get wealth,* Deu. 8:17, 18. [2.] That he thought himself a wise man because he was a rich man; whereas a fool may have an estate (Eccl. 2:19), yea, and a fool may get an estate, for the world has been often observed to favour such, *when bread is not to the wise,* Eccl. 9:11. [3.] That *his heart was lifted up because of his riches,* because of the increase of his wealth, which made him so haughty and secure, so insolent and imperious, and which *set his heart as the heart of God.* The *man of sin,* when he had a great deal of worldly pomp and power, *showed himself as a god,* 2 Th. 2:4. Those who are rich in this world have therefore need to charge that upon themselves which the word of God charges upon them, *that they be not highminded,* 1 Tim. 6:17.

II. Since *pride goes before destruction, and a haughty spirit before a fall,* he must bell him of that destruction, of that fall, which was now hastening on as the just punishment of his presumption in setting up himself a rival with God. "Because thou hast pretended to be a god (*v.* 6), therefore thou shalt not be long a man," *v.* 7. Observe here,

1. The instruments of his destruction: *I will bring strangers upon thee* — the Chaldeans, whom we do not find mentioned among the many nations and countries that traded with Tyre, *ch.* 27. If any of those nations had been brought against it, they would have had some compassion upon it, for old acquaintance-sake; but these strangers will have none. They are people of a *strange language,* which the king of Tyre himself, wise as he is, perhaps understands not. They are the *terrible of the nations;* it was an army made up of many nations, and it was at this time the most formidable both for strength and fury. These God has at command, and these he will bring upon the king of Tyre.

2. The extremity of the destruction: *They shall draw their swords against the beauty of thy wisdom* (*v.* 7), against all those things which thou gloriest in as thy beauty and the production of thy wisdom. Note, It is just with God that our enemies should make that their prey which we have made our pride. The king of Tyre's palace, his treasury, his city, his navy, his army, these he glories in as his brightness, these, he thinks, made him illustrious and glorious as a god on earth. But all these the victorious enemy shall defile, shall deface, shall deform. He thought them sacred, things that none durst touch; but the conquerors shall seize them as common things, and spoil the brightness of them. But, whatever becomes of what he has, surely his person is sacred. No (*v.* 8): *They shall bring thee down to the pit,* to the grave; thou shalt *die the death.* And, (1.) It shall not be an honourable death, but an ignominious one. He shall be so vilified in his death that he may despair of being deified after his death. He shall die *the deaths of those that are slain in the midst of the seas,* that have no honour done them at their death, but their dead bodies are immediately thrown overboard, without any ceremony or mark of distinction, to be a feast for the fish. Tyre is *likely to be destroyed in the midst of the sea* (*ch.* 27:32) and the prince of Tyre shall fare no better than the people. (2.) It shall not be a happy death, but a miserable one. He shall *die the deaths of the uncircumcised* (*v.* 10), of those that are strangers to God and not in covenant with him, and therefore die under his wrath and curse. It is *deaths,* a double death, temporal and eternal, the death both of body and soul. He shall die the *second death;* that is dying miserably indeed. The sentence of death here passed upon the king of Tyre is ratified by a divine authority: *I have spoken it, saith the Lord God.* And what he has said he will do. None can gainsay it, nor will he unsay it.

3. The effectual disproof that this will be of all his pretensions to deity (*v.* 9): "When the conqueror sets his sword to thy breast, and thou seest no way of escape, *wilt thou then say, I am God?* Wilt thou then have such a conceit of thyself as thou now hast? No; thy being overpowered by death, and by the fear of it, will force thee to own that thou art not a god, but a weak, timorous, trembling, dying man. *In the hand of him that slays thee* (in the hand of God, and of the instruments that he employed) *thou shalt be a man, and not God,* utterly unable to resist, and help thyself." *I have said, You are gods; but you shall die like men,* Ps. 82:6, 7. Note, Those who pretend to be rivals with God shall be forced one way or other to let fall their claims. Death at furthest, when we come into his hand, will make us know that we are men.

Verses 11–19

As after the prediction of the ruin of Tyre (*ch.* 26) followed a pathetic lamentation for it (*ch.* 27), so after the ruin of the king of Tyre is foretold it is bewailed.

I. This is commonly understood of the prince who then reigned over Tyre, spoken to, *v.* 2. His name was *Ethbaal,* or *Ithobalus,* as Diodorus Siculus calls him that was king of Tyre when Nebuchadnezzar destroyed it. He was, it seems, upon all external accounts an accomplished man, very great and famous; but his iniquity was his ruin. Many expositors have suggested that besides the literal sense of this lamentation there is an allegory in it, and that it is an allusion to the fall of the angels that sinned, who undid themselves by their pride. And (as is usual in texts that have a mystical meaning) some passages here refer primarily to the king of Tyre, as that of his merchandises, others to the angels, as that of being *in the holy mountain of God.* But, if there be any thing mystical in it (as perhaps there may), I shall rather refer it to the fall of Adam, which seems to be glanced at, *v.* 13. *Thou hast been in Eden the garden of God, and that in the day thou wast created.*

II. Some think that by *the king of Tyre* is meant the whole royal family, this including also the foregoing kings, and looking as far back as Hiram, king of Tyre. The then governor is called *prince* (*v.* 2); but he that is here lamented is called *king.* The court of Tyre with its kings had for many ages been famous; but sin ruins it. Now we may observe two things here: —

1. What was the renown of the king of Tyre. He is here spoken of as having lived in great splendour, *v.* 12–15. He as a man, but it is here owned that he was a very considerable man and one that made a mighty figure in his day. (1.) He far exceeded other men. Hiram and other kings of Tyre had done so in their time; and the reigning king perhaps had not come short of any of them: *Thou sealest up the sum full of wisdom and perfect in beauty.* But the powers of human nature and the prosperity of human life seemed in him to be at the highest pitch. He was looked upon to be as wise as the reason of men could make him, and as happy as the wealth of this world and the enjoyment of it could make him; in him you might see the utmost that both could do; and therefore *seal up the sum,* for nothing can be added; he is a complete man, perfect *in suo genere — in his kind.* (2.) He seemed to be as wise and happy as Adam in innocency (*v.* 13): *"Thou hast been in Eden,* even *in the garden of God;* thou hast lived as it were in paradise all thy days, hast had a full enjoyment of every thing that is *good for food* or *pleasant to the eyes,* and an uncontroverted dominion over all about thee, as Adam had." One instance of the magnificence of the king of Tyre is, that he outdid all others princes in jewels, which those have the greatest plenty of that trade most abroad, as he did: *Every precious stone* was *his covering.* There is a great variety of precious stones; but he had of every sort and in such plenty that besides what were treasured up in his cabinet, and were the ornaments of his crown, he had his clothes trimmed with them; they were his *covering.* Nay (*v.* 14), he *walked up and down in the midst of the stones of fire,* that is, these precious stones, which glittered and sparkled like fire. His rooms were in a manner set round with jewels, so that he walked in the midst of them, and then fancied himself as glorious as if, like God, he had been surrounded by so many angels, who are compared to a *flame of fire.* And, if he be such an admirer of precious stones as to think them as bright as angels, no wonder that he is such an admirer of himself as to think himself as great as God. Nine several sorts of previous stones are here named, which were all in the high priest's ephod. Perhaps they are particularly named because he, in his pride, used to speak particularly of them, and tell those about him, with a great deal of foolish pleasure, "This is such a precious stone, of such a value, and so and so are its virtues." Thus is he upbraided with his vanity. *Gold* is mentioned last, as far inferior in value to those precious stones; and he used to speak of it accordingly. Another thing that made him think his palace a paradise was the curious music he had, the *tabrets and pipes,* hand-instruments and wind-instruments. The *workmanship* of these was extraordinary, and they were prepared for him on purpose; prepared *in thee,* the pronoun is feminine — *in thee,* O Tyre! or it denotes that the king was effeminate in doting on such things. They were prepared *in the day he was created,* that is, either born, or created king; they were made on purpose to celebrate the joys either of his birth-day or of his coronation-day. These he prided himself much in, and would have all that came to see his palace take notice of them. (3.) He looked like an incarnate angel (*v.* 14): *Thou art the anointed cherub that covers* or *protects;* that is, he looked upon himself as a guardian angel to his people, so bright, so strong, so faithful, appointed to this office and qualified for it. Anointed kings should be to their subjects as anointed cherubim, that cover them with the wings of their power; and, when they are such, God will own them. Their advancement was from him: *I have set thee so.* Some think, because mention was made of Eden, that it refers to the cherub set on the east of Eden to cover it, Gen. 3:24. He thought himself as able to guard his city from all invaders as that angel was for his charge. Or it may refer to the cherubim in the most holy place, whose wings covered the ark; he thought himself as bright as one of them. (4.) He appeared in as much splendour as the high priest when he was clothed with his garments for glory and beauty: *"Thou wast upon the holy mountain of God,* as president of the temple built on that holy mountain; thou didst look as great, and with as much majesty and authority, as ever the high priest did when he walked in the temple, which was *garnished with precious stones* (2 Chr. 3:6), and had his habit on, which had precious stones both in the breast and on the shoulders; in that he seemed to *walk in the midst of the stones of fire."* Thus glorious is the king of Tyre; at least he thinks himself so.

2. Let us now see what was the ruin of the king of Tyre, what it was that stained his glory and laid all this honour in the dust (*v.* 15): *"Thou wast perfect in thy ways;* thou didst prosper in all thy affairs and every thing went well with thee; thou hadst not only a clear, but a bright reputation, *from the day thou wast created,* the day of thy accession to the throne, *till iniquity was found in thee;* and that spoiled all." This may perhaps allude to the deplorable case of the angels that fell, and of our first parents, both of whom *were perfect in their ways till iniquity was found in them.* And when iniquity was once *found in him* it increased; he grew worse and worse, as appears (*v.* 18): *"Thou hast defiled thy sanctuaries;* thou hast lost the benefit of all that which thou thoughtest sacred, and in which, as in a sanctuary, thou thoughtest to take refuge; these thou hast *defiled,* and so exposed thyself *by the multitude of thy iniquities."* Now observe,

(1.) What the iniquity was that was the ruin of the king of Tyre. [1.] The *iniquity of his traffic* (so it is called, *v.* 18), both his and his people's, for their sin is charged upon him, because he connived at it and set them a bad example (*v.* 16):*By the multitude of thy merchandise they have filled the midst of thee with violence,* and thus *thou hast sinned.* The king had so much to do with his merchandise, and was so wholly intent upon the gains of that, that he took no care to do justice, to give redress to those that suffered wrong and to protect them from violence; nay, in the multiplicity of business, wrong was done to many by oversight; and in his dealings he made use of his power to invade the rights of those he dealt with. Note, Those that have much to do in the world are in great danger of doing much amiss; and it is hard to deal with many without violence to some. Trades are called mysteries; but too many make them mysteries of iniquity. [2.] His pride and vain-glory (*v.* 17): *"Thy heart was lifted up because of thy beauty;* thou wast in love with thyself, and thy own shadow. And thus *thou hast corrupted thy wisdom by reason of the brightness,* the pomp and splendour, wherein thou livedst." He gazed so much upon this that it dazzled his eyes and prevented him from seeing his way. He appeared so puffed up with his greatness that it bereaved him both of his wisdom and of the reputation of it. He really became a *fool in glorying.* Those make a bad bargain for themselves that part with their wisdom for the gratifying of their gaiety, and, to please a vain humour, lose a real excellency.

(2.) What the ruin was that this iniquity brought him to. [1.] He was thrown out of his dignity and dislodged from his palace, which he took to be his paradise and temple (*v.* 16): *I will cast thee as profane out of the mountain of God.* His kingly power was high as a *mountain,* setting him above others; it was a *mountain of God,* for the powers that be are ordained of God, and have something in them that is sacred; but, having abused his power, he is reckoned profane, and is therefore deposed and expelled. He disgraces the crown he wears, and so has forfeited it, and shall be destroyed *from the midst of the stones of fire,* the precious stones with which his palace was garnished, as the temple was; and they shall be no protection to him. [2.] He was exposed to contempt and disgrace, and trampled upon by his neighbours: *"I will cast thee to the ground* (*v.* 17), will cast thee among the *pavement-stones,* from the midst of the *precious stones,* and will *lay thee* a rueful spectacle *before kings, that they may behold thee* and take warning by thee not to be proud and oppressive." [3.] He was quite consumed, his city and he in it: *I will bring forth a fire from the midst of thee.* The conquerors, when they have plundered the city, will kindle a fire in the heart of it, which shall lay it, and the palace particularly, in ashes. Or it may be taken more generally for the fire of God's judgments, which shall devour both prince and people, and bring all the glory of both *to ashes upon the earth;* and this fire shall be *brought forth from the midst of thee.* All God's judgments upon sinners take rise from themselves; they are devoured by a fire of their own kindling. [4.] He was hereby made a terrible example of divine vengeance. Thus he is reduced *in the sight of all those that behold him* (*v.* 18): *Those that know him shall be astonished at him,* and shall wonder how one that stood so high could be brought so low. The king of Tyre's palace, like the temple at Jerusalem, when it is destroyed shall be *an astonishment and a hissing,* 2 Chr. 7:20, 21. So fell the king of Tyre.

Verses 20–26

God's glory is his great end, both in all the good and in all the evil which *proceed out of the mouth of the Most High;* so we find in these verses. 1. God will be glorified in the destruction of Zidon, a city that lay near to Tyre, was more ancient, but not so considerable, had a dependence upon it and stood and fell with it. God says here, *I am against thee, O Zidon! and I will be glorified in the midst of thee, v.* 22. And again, "Those that would not know be gentler methods shall be made to *know that I am the Lord,* and I alone, and that I am a just and jealous God, *when I shall have executed judgments in her,* destroying judgments, when I shall have done execution according to justice and according to the sentence passed, and so shall be *sanctified in her."* The Zidonians, it should seem, were more addicted to idolatry than the Tyrians were, who, being men of business and large conversation, were less under the power of bigotry and superstition. The Zidonians were noted for the worship of Ashtaroth; Solomon introduced it, 1 Ki. 11:5. Jezebel was daughter to the king of Zidon, who brought the worship of Baal into Israel (1 Ki. 16:31); so that God had been much dishonoured by the Zidonians. Now, says he, *I will be glorified, I will be sanctified.* The Zidonians were borderers upon the land of Israel, where God was known, and where they might have got the knowledge of him and have learned to glorify him; but, instead of that, they seduced Israel to the worship of their idols. Note, When God is sanctified he is glorified, for his holiness is his glory; and those whom he is not sanctified and glorified by he will be sanctified and glorified upon, by executing judgments upon them, which declare him a just avenger of his own and his people's injured honour. The judgments that shall be executed upon Zidon are war and pestilence, two wasting depopulating judgments, *v.* 23. They are God's messengers, which he sends on his errands, and they shall accomplish that for which he sends them. *Pestilence* and *blood* shall be sent *into her streets;* there the dead bodies of those shall lie who perished, some by the plague, occasioned perhaps through ill diet when the city was besieged, and some by the sword of the enemy, most likely the Chaldean armies, when the city was taken, and all were put to the sword. Thus the wounded shall be judged; when they are dying of their wounds they shall judge themselves, and others shall say, They justly fall. Or, as some read it, *They shall be punished by the sword,* that sword which has commission to destroy *on every side.* It is God that judges, and he will overcome. Nor is it Tyre and Zidon only on which God would execute judgments, but on all those that despised his people Israel, and triumphed in their calamities; for this was now God's controversy with the nations that were *round about them, v.* 26. Note, When God's people are under his correcting hand for their faults he takes care, as he did concerning malefactors that were scourged, *that they shall not seem vile* to those that are about them, and therefore takes it ill of those who despise them and so *help forward the affliction* when he is but *a little displeased,* Zec. 1:15. God regards them even in their low estate; and therefore let not men despise them. 2. God will be glorified in the restoration of his people to their former safety and prosperity. God had been dishonoured by the sins of his people, and their sufferings too had given occasion to the enemy to blaspheme (Isa. 52:5); but God will now both cure them of their sins and ease them of their troubles, and so *will be sanctified in them in the sight of the heathen,* will recover the honour of his holiness, to the satisfaction of all the world, *v.* 25. For, (1.) They shall return to the possession of their own land again: *I will gather the house of Israel* out of their dispersions, in answer to that prayer (Ps.

106:27), *Save us, O Lord our God! and gather us from among the heathen;* and in pursuance of that promise (Deu. 30:4), Thence will *the Lord thy God gather thee.* Being gathered, they shall be brought in a body, to *dwell in the land that I have given to my servant Jacob.* God had an eye to the ancient grant, in bringing them back, for that remained in force, and the discontinuance of the possession was not a defeasance of the right. He that gave it will again give it. (2.) They shall enjoy great tranquillity there. When those that have been vexatious to them are taken off they shall live in quietness; there shall be no more *a pricking brier nor a grieving thorn, v.* 24. They shall have a happy settlement, for they shall *build houses,* and *plant vineyards;* and they shall enjoy a happy security and serenity there; they shall *dwell safely,* shall *dwell with confidence,* and there shall be none to disquiet them or make them afraid, *v.* 26. This never had full accomplishment in the body of that people, for after their return out of captivity they were ever and anon molested by some bad neighbour or other. Nor has the gospel-church been ever quite free from pricking briers and grieving thorns; yet sometimes *the church has rest,* and believers always dwell safely under the divine protection and may be *quiet from the fear of evil.* But the full accomplishment of this promise is reserved for the heavenly Canaan, when all the saints shall be gathered together, and every thing that offends shall be removed, and all griefs and fears for ever banished.

CHAPTER 29

Three chapters we had concerning Tyre and its king; next follow four chapters concerning Egypt and its king. This is the first of them. Egypt had formerly been a house of bondage to God's people; of late they had had but too friendly a correspondence with it, and had depended too much upon it; and therefore, whether the prediction reached Egypt or no, it would be of use to Israel, to take them off from their confidence in their alliance with it. The prophecies against Egypt, which are all laid together in these four chapters, were of five several dates; the first in the 10th year of the captivity (*v.* 1), the second in the 27th (*v.* 17), the third in the 11th year and the first month (30:20), the fourth in the 11th year and the third month (31:1), the fifth in the 12th year (32:1), and another in the same year (*v.* 17). In this chapter we have, I. The destruction of Pharaoh foretold, for his dealing deceitfully with Israel (*v.* 1–7). II. The desolation of the land of Egypt foretold (*v.* 8–12). III. A promise of the restoration thereof, in part, after forty years (*v.* 13–16). IV. The possession that should be given to Nebuchadnezzar of the land of Egypt (*v.* 17–20). V. A promise of mercy to Israel (*v.* 21).

Verses 1–7

Here is, I. The date of this prophecy against Egypt. It was in the *tenth year of the captivity,* and yet it is placed after the prophecy against Tyre, which was delivered in the eleventh year, because, in the accomplishment of the prophecies, the destruction of Tyre happened before the destruction of Egypt, and Nebuchadnezzar's gaining Egypt was the reward of his service against Tyre; and *therefore* the prophecy against Tyre is put first, that we may the better observe that. But particular notice must be taken of this, that the first prophecy against Egypt was just at the time when the king of Egypt was coming to relieve Jerusalem and raise the siege (Jer. 37:5), but did not answer the expectations of the Jews from them. Note, It is good to foresee the failing of all our creature-confidences, then when we are most in temptation to depend upon them, that we may *cease from man.*

II. The scope of this prophecy. It is directed against *Pharaoh king of Egypt, and against all Egypt, v.* 2. The prophecy against Tyre began with the people, and then proceeded against the prince. But this begins with the prince, because it began to have its accomplishment in the insurrections and rebellions of the people against the prince, not long after this.

III. The prophecy itself. Pharaoh Hophrah (for so was the reigning Pharaoh surnamed) is here represented by a *great dragon,* or crocodile, that *lies in the midst of his rivers,* as Leviathan in the waters, to *play therein, v.* 3. Nilus, the river of Egypt, was famed for crocodiles. And what is the king of Egypt, in God's account, but a *great dragon,* venomous and mischievous? Therefore says God, *I am against thee. I am above thee;* so it may be read. How high soever the princes and potentates of the earth are, there is a *higher than they* (Eccl. 5:8), a God above them, that can control them, and, if they be tyrannical and oppressive, a God against them, that will be free to reckon with them. Observe here,

1. The pride and security of Pharaoh. He *lies in the midst of his rivers,* rolls himself with a great deal of satisfaction in his wealth and pleasures; and he says, *My river is my own.* He boasts that he is an absolute prince (his subjects are his vassals; Joseph bought them long ago, Gen. 47:23), — that he is a sole prince, and has neither partner in the government nor competitor for it, — that he is out of debt (what he has is his *own,* and none of his neighbours have any demands upon him), — that he is independent, neither tributary nor accountable to any. Note, Worldly carnal minds please themselves with, and pride themselves in, their property, forgetting that whatever we have we have only the use of it, the property is in God. We ourselves are not our own, but his. Our *tongues are not our own,* Ps. 12:4. Our river is not *our own,* for its springs are in God. The most potent prince cannot call what he has his own, for, though it be so against all the world, it is not so against God. But Pharaoh's reason for his pretensions is yet more absurd: *My river is my own,* for *I have made it for myself.* Here he usurps two of the divine prerogatives, to be the author and the end of his own being and felicity. He only that is the great Creator can say of this world, and of every thing in it, *I have made it for myself.* He calls his river his own because he *looks not unto the Maker thereof, nor has respect unto him that fashioned it long ago,* Isa. 22:11. What we have we have received from God and must use for God, so that we cannot say, We made it, much less, We made it for ourselves; and why then do we boast? Note, Self is the great idol that all the world worships, in contempt of God and his sovereignty.

2. The course God will take with this proud man, to humble him. He is a great dragon in the waters, and God will accordingly deal with him, *v.* 4, 5. (1.) He will draw him out of his rivers, for he has *a hook and a cord* for this *leviathan,* with which he can manage him, though none on earth can (Job 41:1): *"I will bring thee up out of the midst of thy rivers,* will cast thee out of thy palace, out of thy kingdom, out of all those things in which thou takest such a complacency and placest such a confidence." Herodotus related of this Pharaoh, who was now king of Egypt, that he had reigned in great prosperity for twenty-five years, and was so elevated with his successes that he said that *God himself would not cast him out of his kingdom;* but he shall soon be convinced of his mistake, and what he depended on shall be no defence. God can force men out of that in which they are most secure and easy. (2.) *All his fish* shall be drawn out with him, his servants, his soldiers, and all that had a dependence on him, as he thought, but really such as he had dependence upon. These shall *stick to his scales,* adhere to their king, resolving to live and die with him. But, (3.) The king and his army, the dragon and all the fish that stick to his scales, shall perish together, as fish cast upon dry ground, and shall be *meat to the beasts and fowls, v.* 5. Now this is supposed to have had its accomplishment soon after, when this Pharaoh, in defence of Aricius king of Libya, who had been expelled his kingdom by the Cyrenians, levied a great army, and went out against the Cyrenians, to re-establish his friend, but was defeated in battle, and all his forces were put to flight, which gave such disgust to his kingdom that they rose in rebellion against him. Thus was he left *thrown into the wilderness, he and all the fish of the river* with him. Thus issue men's pride, and presumption, and carnal security. Thus men justly lose what they might call their own, under God, when they call it their own against him.

3. The ground of the controversy God has with the Egyptians; it is because they have cheated his people. They encouraged them to expect relief and assistance from them when they were in distress, but failed them (*v.* 6, 7): *Because they have been a staff of reed to the house of* Israel. They pretended to be a staff for them to lean upon, but, when any stress was laid upon them, they were either weak and could not or treacherous and would not do that for them which was expected. They *broke under them,* to their great disappointment and amazement, so that they *rent their shoulder* and *made all their loins to be at a stand.* The king of Egypt, it is probable, had encouraged Zedekiah to break his league with the king of Babylon, with a promise that he would stand by him, which, when he failed to do, to any purpose, it could not but put them into a great consternation. God had told them, long since, that the Egyptians were broken reeds, Isa. 30:6, 7. Rabshakeh had told them so, Isa. 36:6. And now they found it so. It was indeed the folly of Israel to trust them, and they were well enough served when they were deceived in them. God was righteous in suffering them to be so. But that is no excuse at all for the Egyptians' falsehood and treachery, nor shall it secure them from the judgments of that God who is and will be the avenger of all such wrongs. It is a great sin, and very provoking to God, as well as unjust, ungrateful, and very dishonourable and unkind, to put a cheat upon those that put a confidence in us.

Verses 8–16

This explains the foregoing prediction, which was figurative, and looks something further. Here is a prophecy,

I. Of the ruin of Egypt. The threatening of this is very full and particular; and the sin for which this ruin shall be brought upon them is their pride, *v.* 9. They said, *The river is mine and I have made it;* therefore their land shall spue them out. 1. God is against them, both against the king and against the people, *against thee and against thy rivers.* Waters signify *people and multitudes,* Rev. 17:15. 2. Multitudes of them shall be cut off by the sword of war, a sword which God will bring upon them to destroy *both man and beast,* the sword of civil war. 3. The country shall be depopulated. The *land of Egypt shall be desolate and waste* (*v.* 9), the country not cultivated, the cities not inhabited. The wealth of both was their pride, and that God will take away. It *shall be utterly waste (wastes of waste,* so the margin reads it), *and desolate* (*v.* 10); *neither men nor beasts shall pass through it, nor shall it be inhabited* (*v.* 11); it shall be *desolate in the midst of the countries that are so, v.* 12. This was the effect not so much of those wars spoken of before, which were made by them, but of the war which the king of Babylon made upon them. It shall be desolate from one end of the land to the other, *from the tower of Syene even unto the border of Ethiopia.* The sin of pride is enough to ruin a whole nation. 4. The people shall be dispersed and scattered among the nations (*v.* 12), so that those who thought the balance of power was in their hand should now become a contemptible people. Such a fall does a haughty spirit go before.

II. Of the restoration of Egypt after awhile, *v.* 13. Egypt shall lie *desolate forty years* (*v.* 12) and then *I will bring again the captivity of Egypt, v.* 14. Some date the forty years from Nebuchadnezzar's destroying Egypt, others from the desolation of Egypt some time before; however, they end about the first year of Cyrus, when the seventy years' captivity of Judah ended, or soon after. Then this prediction was accomplished, 1. That God will gather the Egyptians out of all the countries into which they were dispersed, and make them to *return to the land of their habitation,* and give them a settlement there again, *v.* 14. Note, Though God will find out a way to humble the proud, yet he will not contend for ever, no, not with them in this world. 2. That yet they shall not make a figure again as they have done. Egypt shall be *a kingdom* again, but it shall be the *basest of the kingdoms* (*v.* 15); it shall have but little wealth and power, and shall not extend its conquests as formerly; it shall be the tail of the nations, and not the head. It is a mercy that it shall become a kingdom again, but, to humble it, it shall be a despicable kingdom; it shall be a long time before it recover any thing like its ancient lustre. For two reasons it shall be thus mortified: — (1.) That it may not domineer over its neighbours, that it may not *exalt itself above the nations,* nor *rule over the nations,* as it has done, but that it may know what it is to be low and despised. Note, Those who abuse their power will justly be stripped of it; and God, as King of nations, will find out a way to maintain the injured rights and liberties, not only of his own, but of other nations. (2.) That it may not deceive the people of God (*v.* 16): *It shall no more be the confidence of the house of Israel;* they shall no more be in temptation to trust in it as they have done, which is a sin that *brings their iniquity to remembrance,* that is, provokes God to punish them not for that only, but for all their other sins. Or it *puts them in mind* of their idolatries to return to them, *when they look* to the idolaters, to repose a confidence in them. Note, The creatures we confide in are often *therefore* ruined, because there is no other way effectually to cure us of our confidence in them. Rather than Israel shall be ensnared again, the whole land of Egypt shall be laid waste. He that once *gave Egypt for their ransom* (Isa. 43:3) will now give Egypt for their cure; and it shall be destroyed rather than Israel shall not in this particular be reformed. God, not only in justice, but in wisdom and goodness to us, breaks those creature-stays which we lean too much upon, and makes them to be no more, that they may be no more our confidence.

Verses 17–21

The date of this prophecy is observable; it was in the twenty-seventh year of Ezekiel's captivity, sixteen years after the prophecy in the former part of the chapter, and almost as long after those which follow in the next chapters; but it comes in here for the explication of all that was said against Egypt. After the destruction of Jerusalem Nebuchadnezzar spent two or three campaigns in the conquest of the Ammonites and Moabites and making himself master of their countries. Then he spent thirteen years in the siege of Tyre. During all that time the Egyptians were embroiled in war with the Cyrenians and one with another, by which they were very much weakened and impoverished; and just at the end of the siege of Tyre God delivers this prophecy to Ezekiel, to signify to him that that utter destruction of Egypt which he had foretold fifteen or sixteen years before, which had been but in part accomplished hitherto, should now be completed by Nebuchadnezzar. The prophecy which begins here, it should seem, is continued to the twentieth verse of the next chapter. And Dr. Lightfoot observes that it is the last prophecy we have of this prophet, and should have been last in the book, but is laid here, that all the prophecies against Egypt might come together. The particular destruction of Pharaoh-Hophrah, foretold in the former part of this chapter, was likewise foretold Jer. 44:30. This general devastation of Egypt by Nebuchadnezzar was foretold Jer. 43:10. Observe,

I. What success God would give to Nebuchadnezzar and his forces against Egypt. God gave him *that land,* that he might *take the spoil* and *prey* of it, *v.* 19, 20. It was a cheap and easy prey. He subdued it with very little difficulty; the blood and treasure expended upon the conquest of it were inconsiderable. But it was a rich prey, and he carried off a great deal from it that was of value. Their having been divided among themselves, no doubt, gave a common enemy great advantage against them, who, when they had been so long preying upon one another, soon made a prey of them all. *En! quo discordia cives perduxit miseros — What wretchedness does civil discord bring!* Jeremiah foretold that Nebuchadnezzar should *array himself with the land of Egypt as a shepherd puts on his coat,* which intimates what a rich and cheap prey it should be.

II. Upon what considerations God would give Nebuchadnezzar this success against Egypt; it was to be a recompence to him for the hard service with which he had caused his army to serve against Tyre, *v.* 18, 20. 1. The taking of Tyre was a tedious piece of work; it cost Nebuchadnezzar abundance of blood and treasure. It held out thirteen years; all that time the Chaldean army was hard at it, to make themselves masters of it. A large current of the sea, between Tyre and the continent, was filled up with earth, and many other difficulties which were thought insuperable they had to struggle with; but so great a prince, having begun such an undertaking, thought himself bound in honour to push it on, whatever it cost him. How many thousand lives have been sacrificed to such points of honour as this as! In prosecuting this siege *every head was made bald, and every shoulder peeled,* with carrying burdens and labouring in the water when they had a strong tide and a strong town to contend with. Egypt, a large kingdom, being divided within itself, is easily conquered; Tyre, a single city, being unanimous, is with difficulty subdued. Those that have much to do in the world find some affairs go on a great deal more readily and easily than others. But, 2. In this service God own that they *wrought for him, v.* 20. He set them at work, for the humbling of a proud city and its king, though *they meant not so, neither did their heart think so,* who were employed in it. Note, Even great men and bad men are tools that God makes use of, and are *working for him* even when they are pursuing their own covetous and ambitious designs; so wonderfully does God overrule all to his own glory. Yet, 3. For this service he had *no wages* nor *his army.* He was at a vast expense to take Tyre; and when he had it, though it was a very rich city, and he promised himself good plunder for his army from it, he was disappointed; the Tyrians sent away by ship their best effects, and threw the rest into the sea, so that they had nothing but bare walls. Thus are the children of this world ordinarily frustrated in their highest expectations from it. Therefore, 4. He shall have the spoil of Egypt to recompense him for his service against Tyre. Note, God will be behind-hand with none for any service they do for him, but, one way or other, will recompense them for it; none shall kindle a fire on his altar for nought. The service done for him by worldly men, with worldly designs, shall be recompensed with a mere worldly reward, which his faithful servants, that have a sincere regard to his will and glory, would not be put off with. This accounts for the prosperity of wicked men in this world; God is in it paying them for some service or other, in which he has made use of them. *Verily they have their reward.* Let none envy it them. The conquest of Egypt is spoken of as Nebuchadnezzar's *full reward,* for that completed his dominion over the then known world in a manner; that was the last of the kingdoms he subdued; when he was master of that he became the *head of gold.*

III. The mercy God had in store for the house of Israel soon after. When the tide is at the highest it will turn, and so it will when it is at the lowest. Nebuchadnezzar was in the zenith of his glory when he had conquered Egypt, but within a year after he ran mad (Can. 4), was so seven years, and within a year or two after he had recovered his senses he resigned his life. When he was at the highest Israel was at the lowest; then were they in the depth of their captivity, their bones dead and dry; but *in that day the horn of the house of Israel shall bud forth, v.* 21. The day of their deliverance shall begin to dawn, and they shall have some little reviving in their bondage, in the honour that shall be done, 1. To their princes; they are the *horns of the house of Israel,* the seat of their glory and power. These began to bud forth when Daniel and his fellows were highly preferred in Babylon; Daniel *sat in the gate of the city; Shadrach, Meshach, and Abednego, were set over the affairs of the province* (Dan. 2:49); these were all *of the king's seed, and of the princes,* Dan. 1:3. And it was within a year after the conquest of Egypt that they were thus preferred; and, soon after, three of them were made famous by the honour God put upon them in bringing them alive out of the burning fiery furnace. This might very well be called the *budding forth of the horn of the house of Israel.* And, some years after, this promise had a further accomplishment in the enlargement and elevation of Jehoiachin king of Judah, Jer. 52:31, 32. They were both tokens of God's favour to Israel, and happy omens. 2. To their prophets. And *I will give thee the opening of the mouth.* Though none of Ezekiel's prophecies, after this, are recorded, yet we have reason to think he went on prophesying, and with more liberty and boldness, when Daniel and his fellows were in power, and would be ready to protect him not only from the Babylonians, but from the wicked ones of his own people. Note, It bodes well to a people when God enlarges the liberties of his ministers and they are countenanced and encouraged in their work.

CHAPTER 30

In this chapter we have, I. A continuation of the prophecy against Egypt, which we had in the latter part of the foregoing chapter, just before the desolation of that once flourishing kingdom was completed by Nebuchadnezzar, in which is foretold the destruction of all her allies and confederates, all her interests and concerns, and the several steps which the king of Babylon should take in pushing on this destruction (*v.* 1–19). II. A repetition of a former prophecy against Egypt, just before the desolation of it begun by their own bad conduct, which gradually weakened them and prepared the way for the king of Babylon (*v.* 20–26). It is all much to the same purport with what we had before.

Verses 1–19

The prophecy of the destruction of Egypt is here very full and particular, as well as, in the general, very frightful. What can protect a provoking people when the righteous God comes forth to contend with them?

I. It shall be a very lamentable destruction, and such as shall occasion great sorrow (*v.* 2, 3): *"Howl you;* you may justly shriek now that it is coming, for you will be made to shriek and make hideous outcries when it comes. Cry out, *Woe worth the day!* or, *Ah the day! alas because of the day!* the terrible day! *Woe and alas!* For *the day is near;* the day we have so long dreaded, so long deserved. It is the *day of the Lord,* the day in which he will manifest himself as a God of vengeance. You have your day now, when you carry all before you, and trample on all about you, but God will have his day shortly, the day of the revelation of his righteous judgment," Ps. 37:13. It will be *a cloudy day,* that is, dark and dismal, without the shining forth of any comfort; and it shall threaten a storm — *fire, and brimstone, and a horrible tempest. It shall be the time of the heathen,* of reckoning with the heathen for all their heathenish practices, that time which David spoke of when God would *pour out his fury upon the heathen* (Ps. 79:6), when *they should sink,* Ps. 9:15.

II. It shall be the destruction of Egypt, and of all the states and countries in confederacy with her and in her neighbourhood. 1. Egypt herself shall fall (*v.* 4): The *sword shall come upon Egypt,* the sword of the Chaldeans, and it shall be a victorious sword, for the *slain shall fall in Egypt,* fall by it, fall before it. Is the country populous? They shall *take away her multitude.* Is it strong, and well-fixed? *Her foundations shall be broken down,* and then the fabric, though built ever so fine, ever so high, will fall of course. 2. Her neighbours and inmates shall fall with her. When the slain fall so thickly in Egypt *great pain shall be in Ethiopia,* both that in Africa, which is in the neighbourhood of Egypt on one side, and that in Asia, which is near to it on the other side. When their neighbour's house was on fire they could not but apprehend their own in danger; nor were their fears groundless, for they shall all *fall with them by the sword, v.* 5. *Ethiopia and Libya* (Cush and Phut, so the Hebrew names are, two of the sons of Ham who are mentioned, and Mizraim, that is, Egypt, between them, Gen. 10:6), *and the Lydians* (who were famous archers, and are spoken of as confederates with Egypt, Jer. 46:9), these shall fall with Egypt and *Chub* (the Chaldeans, the inhabitants of the inner Libya); these and others were the *mingled people;* there were those of all these and other countries who upon some account or other resided in Egypt, as did also *the men of the land that is in league,* some of the remains of the people of Israel and Judah, the *children of the covenant,* or league, as they are called (Acts 3:25), the *children of the promise,* Gal. 4:28. These sojourned in Egypt contrary to God's command, and these shall *fall with them.* Note, Those that will take their lot with God's enemies shall have their lot with them, yea, though they be in profession the men of the land that is in league with God.

III. All that pretend to support the sinking interests of Egypt shall come down under her, shall come down with her (*v.* 6): *Those that uphold Egypt shall fall,* and then Egypt must fall of course. See the justice of God; Egypt pretended to uphold Jerusalem when that was tottering, but proved a deceitful reed; and now those that pretended to uphold Egypt shall prove no better. Those that deceive others are commonly paid in their own coin; they are themselves deceived. 1. Does Egypt think herself upheld by the absolute authority and dominion of her king? The *pride of her power* shall *come down, v.* 6. The power of the king of Egypt was his pride; but that shall be broken, and humbled. 2. Is the multitude of her people her support? These shall *fall by the sword,* even *from the tower of Syene,* which is in the utmost corner of the land, from that side of it by which the enemy shall enter. Both the *countries* and the *cities,* the husbandmen and the merchants, shall be desolate, *v.* 7, as before, *ch.* 29:12. Even *the multitude of Egypt shall be made to cease, v.* 10. That populous country shall be depopulated. The land shall be even *filled with the slain, v.* 11. 3. Is the river Nile her support, and are the several channels of it a defence to her? *"I will make the rivers dry* (*v.* 12), so that those natural fortifications which were thought impregnable, because impassable, shall stand them in no stead." 4. Are her idols a support to her? They shall be destroyed; those imaginary upholders shall appear more than ever to be imaginary, for so images are when they pretend to be deliverers and strongholds (*v.* 13): *I will cause their images to cease out of Noph.* 5. Is her royal family her support? *There shall be no more a prince in the land of Egypt;* the royal family shall be extirpated and extinguished, which had continued so long. 6. Is her courage her support, and does she think to uphold herself by the bravery of her men of war, who have now of late been inured to service? That shall fail: *I will put a fear in the land of Egypt.* 7. Is the rising generation her support? is she upheld by her children, and does she think herself happy because she has her quiver full of them? Alas! *the young men shall fall by the sword* (v. 17) and *the daughters shall go into captivity* (v. 18), and so she shall be robbed of all her hopes.

IV. God shall inflict these desolating judgments on Egypt (v. 8): *They shall know that I am the Lord,* and greater than all gods, than all *their* gods, when I have *set a fire in Egypt.* The fire that consumes nations is of God's kindling; and, when he sets fire to a people, *all their helpers shall be destroyed.* Those that go about to quench the fire shall themselves be devoured by it; for who can stand before him when he is angry? When he *pours out his fury* upon a place, when he sets fire to it (v. 15, 16), neither its strength nor its multitude can stand it in any stead.

V. The king of Babylon and his army shall be employed as instruments of this destruction: *The multitude of Egypt shall be made to cease* and be quite cut off *by the hand of the king of Babylon, v.* 10. Those that undertook to protect Israel from the king of Babylon shall not be able to protect themselves. It is said of the Chaldeans, who should destroy Egypt, 1. That they are *strangers* (v. 12), who therefore shall show no compassion for old acquaintance-sake, but shall behave strangely towards them. 2. That they are *the terrible of the nations* (v. 11), both in respect of force and in respect of fierceness; and, being terrible, they shall make terrible work. (3.) That they are *the wicked,* who will not be restrained by reason and conscience, the laws of nature or the laws of nations, for they are without law: *I will sell the land into the hand of the wicked.* They do violence *unjustly,* as they are wicked; yet, so far as they are instruments in God's hand of executing his judgments, it is on his part justly done. Note, God often makes one wicked man a scourge to another; and even wicked men acquire a title to prey, *jure belli — by the laws of war,* for God *sells it into their hands.*

VI. No place in the land of Egypt shall be exempted from the fury of the Chaldean army, not the strongest, not the remotest: *The sword shall go through the land.* Various places are here named: *Pathros, Zoan,* and *No* (v. 14), *Sin* and *Noph* (v. 15, 16), *Aven* and *Pi-beseth* (v. 17), and *Tehaphnehes, v.* 18. These shall be made desolate, shall be fired, and God's judgments shall be executed upon them, and his fury poured out upon them. Their strength and multitude shall be *cut off;* they shall have *great pain,* shall be *rent asunder* with fear, and shall *have distresses daily.* Their *day shall be darkened;* their honours, comforts, and hopes, shall be extinguished. Their *yokes shall be broken,* so that they shall no more oppress and tyrannize as they have done. The *pomp of their strength shall cease,* and *a cloud shall cover them,* a cloud so thick that through it they shall not see any hopes, nor shall their glory *be seen,* or *shine further.* And, *lastly,* the Ethiopians, who are at a distance from them, as well as those who are mingled with them, shall share in their pain and terror. God will by his providence spread the rumour, and the *careless Ethiopians* shall be *made afraid, v.* 9. Note, God can strike a terror upon those that are most secure; fearfulness shall, when he pleases, surprise the most presumptuous hypocrites.

The close of this prediction leaves, 1. The land of Egypt mortified: *Thus will I execute judgments on Egypt, v.* 19. The destruction of Egypt is the *executing of judgments,* which intimates not only that it is done justly, for its sins, but that it is done regularly and legally, by a judicial sentence. All the executions God does are according to his judgments. 2. The God of Israel herein glorified: *They shall know that I am the Lord.* The Egyptians shall be made to know it and the people of God shall be made to know it better. *The Lord is known by the judgments which he executes.*

Verses 20–26

This short prophecy of the weakening of the power of Egypt was delivered about the time that the army of the Egyptians, which attempted to raise the siege of Jerusalem, was frustrated in its enterprises, and returned *re infectâ — without accomplishing their purpose;* whereupon the king of Babylon renewed the siege and carried his point. The kingdom of Egypt was very ancient, and had been for many ages considerable. That of Babylon had but lately arrived at its great pomp and power, being built upon the ruins of the kingdom of Assyria. Now it is with them

as it is with families and states, some are growing up, others are declining and going back; one must increase and the others must of course decrease.

I. It is here foretold that the king of Egypt shall grow weaker and weaker. The extent of his territories shall be abridged, his wealth and power shall be diminished, and he shall become less able than ever to help either himself or his friend. 1. This was in part done already (v. 21): *I have broken the arm of Pharaoh,* some time ago. One arm of that kingdom might well be reckoned broken when the king of Babylon routed the forces of Pharaoh-Necho at Carchemish (Jer. 46:2), and made himself master of *all that pertained to Egypt from the river of Egypt to Euphrates,* 2 Ki. 24:7. Egypt had been long in gathering strength and extending its dominions, and therefore, that there may be a proportion observed in providence, it loses its strength slowly and by degrees. It was soon after the king of Egypt slew good king Josiah, and in the same reign, that its arm was thus broken, and it received that fatal blow which it never recovered. Before Egypt's heart and neck were broken its arm was. God's judgments come upon a people by steps, that they may meet him repenting. When the arm of Egypt is broken *it shall not be bound up to be healed,* for none can heal the wounds that God gives but he himself. Those whom he disarms, whom he disables, cannot again hold the sword. 2. This was to be done again. One arm was broken before, and something was done towards the setting of it, towards the healing of the deadly wound that was given to the beast. But now (v. 22), *I am against Pharaoh, and will break both his arms,* both *the strong* and that *which was broken* and set again. Note, If less judgments do not prevail to humble and reform sinners, God will send greater. Now God will *cause the sword to fall out of his hand,* which he caught hold of as thinking himself strong enough to hold it. It is repeated (v. 24), *I will break Pharaoh's arms.* He had been a cruel oppressor to the people of God formerly, and of late the *staff of a broken rod* to them; and now God by breaking his arms reckons with him for both. God justly breaks that power which is abused either to put wrongs upon people or to put cheats upon them. But this is not all; (1.) The king of Egypt shall be dispirited when he finds himself in danger of the king of Babylon's forces: he *shall groan before him with the groaning of a deadly wounded man.* Note, It is common for those that are most elated in their prosperity to be most dejected and disheartened in their adversity. Pharaoh, even before the sword touches him, shall groan as if he had received his death's wound. (2.) The people of Egypt shall be dispersed (v. 23) and again v. 26): *I will scatter them among the nations.* Other nations had mingled with them (v. 5); now they shall be mingled with other nations, and seek shelter in them, and so be made to know that the Lord is righteous.

II. It is here foretold that the king of Babylon shall grow stronger and stronger, v. 24, 25. *Put strength* into the king of Babylon's arms, that he may be able to go through the service he is designed for. 2. That he will *put a sword,* his sword, into the king of Babylon's hand, which signified his giving him a commission and furnishing him with arms for carrying on a war, particularly against Egypt. Note, As judges on the bench, like Pilate (Jn. 19:11), so generals in the field, like Nebuchadnezzar, have no power but what is given them from above.

CHAPTER 31

The prophecy of this chapter, as the two chapters before, is against Egypt, and designed for the humbling and mortifying of Pharaoh. In passing sentence upon great criminals it is usual to consult precedents, and to see what has been done to others in the like case, which serves both to direct and to justify the proceedings. Pharaoh stands indicted at the bar of divine justice for his pride and haughtiness, and the injuries he had done to God's people; but he thinks himself so high, so great, as not to be accountable to any authority, so strong, and so well guarded, as not to be conquerable by any force. The prophet is therefore directed to make a report to him of the case of the king of Assyria, whose head city was Nineveh. I. He must show him how great a monarch the king of Assyria had been, what a vast empire he had, what a mighty sway he bore; the king of Egypt, great as he was could not go beyond him (v. 3–9). II. He must then show him how like he was to the king of Assyria in pride and carnal security (v. 10). III. He must next read him the history of the fall and ruin of the king of Assyria, what a noise it made among the nations and what a warning it gave to all potent princes to take heed of pride (v. 11–17). IV. He must leave the king of Egypt to apply all this to himself, to see his own face in the looking-glass of the king of Assyria's sin, and to foresee his own fall through the perspective glass of his ruin (v. 18).

Verses 1–9

This prophecy bears date the month before Jerusalem was taken, as that in the close of the foregoing chapter about four months before. When God's people were in the depth of their distress, it would be some comfort to them, as it would serve likewise for a check to the pride and malice of their neighbours, that insulted over them, to be told from heaven that the cup was going round, even the cup of trembling, that it would shortly be taken out of the hands of God's people and put into the hands of those that hated them, Isa. 51:22, 23. In this prophecy,

I. The prophet is directed to put Pharaoh upon searching the records for a case parallel to his own (v. 2): *Speak to Pharaoh and to his multitude,* to the multitude of his attendants, that contributed so much to his magnificence, and the multitude of his armies, that contributed so much to his strength. These he was proud of, these he put a confidence in; and they were as proud of him and trusted as much in him. Now ask him, *Whom art thou like in thy greatness?* We are apt to judge of ourselves by comparison. Those that think highly of themselves fancy themselves as great and as good as such and such, that have been mightily celebrated. The flatterers of princes tell them whom they equal in pomp and grandeur. "Well," says God, "let him pitch upon the most famous potentate that ever was, and it shall be allowed that he is *like him in greatness* and no way inferior to him; but, let him pitch upon whom he will, he will find that *his day came to fall;* he will see there was *an end* of all *his perfection,* and must therefore expect the end of his own in like manner." Note, The falls of others, both into sin and ruin, are intended as admonitions to us not to be secure or *high-minded,* nor to think we stand out of danger.

II. He is directed to show him an instance of one whom he resembles in greatness, and that was the Assyrian (v. 3), whose monarchy had continued from Nimrod. Sennacherib was one of the mighty princes of that monarchy; but it sunk down soon after him, and the monarchy of Nebuchadnezzar was built upon its ruins, or rather grafted upon its stock. Let us now see what a flourishing prince the king of Assyria was. He is here compared to a stately cedar, v. 3. The glory of the house of David is illustrated by the same similitude, *ch.* 17:3. The olive-tree, the fig-tree, and the vine, which were all fruit-trees, had refused to be *promoted over the trees* because they would not leave their fruitfulness (Jdg. 9:8, etc.), and therefore the choice falls upon the cedar, that is stately and strong, and casts a great shadow, but bears no fruit. 1. The Assyrian monarch was a tall cedar, such as the cedars in Lebanon generally were, of a *high stature,* and *his top among the thick boughs;* he was attended by other princes that were tributaries to him, and was surrounded by a life-guard of brave men. He surpassed all the princes in his neighbourhood; they were all shrubs to him (v. 5): *His height was exalted above all the trees of the field;* they were many of them very high, but he overtopped them all, *v.* 8. The cedars, even those in the garden of Eden, which we may suppose were the best of the kind, *would not hide him,* but his top branches outshot theirs. 2. He was a spreading cedar; his branches did not only run up in height, but run out in breadth, denoting that this mighty prince was not only exalted to great dignity and honour, and had a name above the names of the great men of the earth, but that he obtained great dominion and power; his territories were large, and he extended his conquests far and his influences much further. This cedar, like *a vine,* sent forth *his branches to the sea, to the river,* Ps. 80:11. *His boughs were multiplied; his branches became long* (v. 5); so that *he had a shadowing shroud, v.* 3. This contributed very much to his beauty, that he grew proportionably large as well as high. He was *fair in his greatness, in the length of his branches* (v. 7), very comely as well as very stately, *fair by the multitude of his branches, v.* 9. His large dominions were well managed, like a spreading tree that is kept in shape and good order by the skill of the gardener, so as to be very beautiful to the eye. His government was as amiable in the eyes of wise men as it was admirable in the eyes of all men. The *fir-trees* were not *like his boughs,* so straight, so green, so regular; nor were the branches of *the chestnut-trees like his branches,* so thick, so spreading. In short, *no tree in the garden of God,* in Eden, in Babylon (for that stood where paradise was planted), where there was every tree that was *pleasant to the sight* (Gen. 2:9), was like *to this cedar in beauty;* that is, in all the surrounding nations there was no prince so much admired, so much courted, and whom every body was so much in love with, as the king of Assyria. Many of them *did virtuously,* but he *excelled them all,* outshone them all. *All the trees of Eden envied him,* v. 9. When they found they could not compare with him they were angry and grieved that he so far outdid them, and secretly grudged him the praise due to him. Note, It is the unhappiness of those who in any thing excel others that thereby they make themselves the objects of envy; and *who can stand before envy?* 3. He was serviceable, as far as a standing growing cedar could be, and that was only by his shadow (v. 6): *All the fowls of heaven,* some of all sorts, *made their nests in his boughs,* where they were sheltered from the injuries of the weather. The *beasts of the field* put themselves under the protection of *his branches.* There they were *levant — rising up,* and *couchant — lying down;* there they *brought forth their young;* for they had there a natural covert from the heat and from the storm. The meaning of all is, *Under his shadow dwelt all great nations;* they all fled to him for safety, and were willing to swear allegiance to him if he would undertake to protect them, as travellers in a shower come under thick trees for shelter. Note, Those who have power ought to use it for the protection and comfort of those whom they have power over; for to that end they are entrusted with power. Even the bramble, if he be anointed king, invites the trees to come and *trust in his shadow,* Jdg. 9:15. But the utmost security that any creature, even the king of Assyria himself, can give, is but like the shadow of a tree, which is but a scanty and slender protection, and leaves a man many ways exposed. Let us therefore flee to God for protection, and he will take us *under the shadow of his wings,* where we shall be warmer and safer than under the shadow of the strongest and stateliest cedar, Ps. 17:8; 91:4. 4. He seemed to be settled and established in his greatness and power. For, (1.) It was God that *made him fair,* v. 9. For by him kings reign. He was comely with the comeliness that God put upon him. Note, God's hand must be eyed and owned in the advancement of the great men of the earth, and therefore we must not envy them; yet that will not secure the continuance of their prosperity, for he that gave them their beauty, if they be deprived of it, knows how to turn it into deformity. (2.) He seemed to have a good bottom. This cedar was not like the *heath in the desert, made to inhabit the parched places* (Jer. 17:6); it was not a *root in a dry ground,* Isa. 53:2. No; he had abundance of wealth to support his power and grandeur (v. 4): *The waters made him great;* he had vast treasures, large stores and magazines, which were as *the deep that set him up on high,* constant revenues coming in by taxes, customs, and crown-rents, which were *as rivers running round about his plants;* these enabled him to strengthen and secure his interests every where, for he *sent out his little rivers,* or conduits, *to all the trees of the field,* to water them; and when they had *maintenance from the king's palace* (Ezra 4:14), and *their country was nourished by the king's country* (Acts 12:20), they would be serviceable and faithful to him. Those that have wealth flowing upon them in great rivers find themselves obliged to send it out again in little rivers; for, *as goods are increased, those are increased that eat them,* and the more men have the more occasion they have for it; yea, and still the more they have occasion for. The *branches* of this cedar *became long,* because of the *multitude of waters* which fed them (v. 5 and 7); *his root was by great waters,* which seemed to secure it that *its leaf should never wither* (Ps. 1:3), that it should not *see when heat came,* Jer. 17:8. Note, Worldly people may seem to have an established prosperity, yet it only seems so, Job 5:3; Ps. 37:35.

Verses 10–18

We have seen the king of Egypt resembling the king of Assyria in pomp, and power, and prosperity, how like he was to him in his greatness; now here we see,

I. How he does likewise resemble him in his pride, v. 10. For, as face answers to face in a glass, so does one corrupt carnal heart to another; and the same temptations of a prosperous state by which some are overcome are fatal to many others too. *"Thou,* O king of Egypt! *hast lifted up thyself in height,* hast been proud of thy wealth and power,

ch. 29:3. And just so *he* (that is, the king of Assyria); when he had *shot up his top among the thick boughs his heart* was immediately *lifted up in his height,* and he grew insolent and imperious, set God himself at defiance, and trampled upon his people;" witness the messages and letter which *the great king, the king of Assyria,* sent to Hezekiah, Isa. 36:4. How haughtily does he speak of himself and his own achievements! how scornfully of that great and good man! There were other sins in which the Egyptians and the Assyrians did concur, particularly that of oppressing God's people, which is charged upon them both together (Isa. 52:4); but here that sin is traced up to its cause, and that was pride; for it is the *contempt of the proud* that they are *filled with.* Note, When men's outward condition rises their minds commonly rise with it; and it is very rare to find a humble spirit in the midst of great advancements.

II. How he shall therefore resemble him in his fall; and for the opening of this part of the comparison,

1. Here is a history of the fall of the king of Assyria. For his part, says God (v. 11), *I have therefore,* because he was thus lifted up, *delivered him into the hand of the mighty one of the heathen.* Cyaxares, king of the Medes, in the twenty-sixth year of his reign, in conjunction with Nebuchadnezzar king of Babylon in the first year of his reign, destroyed Nineveh, and with it the Assyrian empire. Nebuchadnezzar, though he was not then, yet afterwards became, very emphatically, the *mighty one of the heathen,* most mighty among them and most mighty over them, to prevail against them.

(1.) Respecting the fall of the Assyrian three things are affirmed: — [1.] It is God himself that orders his ruin: *I have delivered him into the hand* of the executioner; *I have driven him out.* Note, God is the Judge, who puts down one and sets up another (Ps. 75:7); and when he pleases he can extirpate and expel those who think themselves, and seem to others, to have taken deepest root. And the mightiest ones of the heathens could not gain their point against those they contended with if the Almighty did not himself deliver them into their hands. [2.] It is his own sin that procures his ruin: *I have driven him out for his wickedness.* None are driven out from their honour, power, and possessions, but it is *for their wickedness.* None of our comforts are ever lost but what have been a thousand times forfeited. If the wicked are *driven away,* it is *in their wickedness.* [3.] It is a *mighty one of the heathen* that shall be the instrument of his ruin; for God often employs one wicked man in punishing another. *He shall surely deal with him,* shall know how to manage him, great as he is. Note, Proud imperious men will, sooner or later, meet with their match.

(2.) In this history of the fall of the Assyrian observe, [1.] A continuation of the similitude of the cedar. He grew very high, and extended his boughs very far; but his day comes to fall. *First,* This stately cedar was cropped: *The terrible of the nations cut him off.* Soldiers, who being both armed and commissioned to kill, and slay, and destroy, may well be reckoned among *the terrible of the nations.* They have lopped off his branches first, have seized upon some parts of his dominion and forced them out of his hands; so that in all *mountains* and *valleys* of the nations about, in the high-lands and low-lands, and *by all the rivers,* there were cities or countries that were broken off from the Assyrian monarchy, that had been subject to it, but had either revolted or were recovered from it. Its feathers were borrowed; and, when every bird had fetched back its own, it was naked like the stump of a tree. *Secondly,* It was deserted: *All the people of the earth,* that had fled to him for shelter, have *gone down from his shadow and have left him.* When he was disabled to give them protection they thought they no longer owed him allegiance. Let not great men be proud of the number of those that attend them and have a dependence upon them; it is only for what they can get. When Providence frowns upon them their retinue is soon dispersed and scattered from them. *Thirdly,* It was insulted over, and its fall triumphed in (v. 13): *Upon his ruin shall all the fowls of the heaven remain,* to tread upon the broken branches of this cedar. Its fall is triumphed in by the other trees, who were angry to see themselves overtopped so much: *All the trees of Eden, that were cut down and had fallen before him, all that drank water of the rain of heaven, as the stump of the tree that is left*

in the *south* is said to be *wet with the dew of heaven* (Dan. 4:23) and to bud *through the scent of water* (Job 14:9), *shall be comforted in the nether parts of the earth* when they see this proud cedar brought as low as themselves. *Solamen miseris socios habuisse doloris — To have companions in woe is a solace to those who suffer.* But, on the contrary, the trees of Lebanon, that are yet standing in their height and strength, *mourned for him,* and *the trees of the field fainted for him,* because they could not but read their own destiny in his fall. *Howl, fir-trees, if the cedar be shaken,* for they cannot expect to stand long, Zec. 11:2. [2.] An explanation of the similitude of the cedar. By the cutting down of this cedar is signified the slaughter of this mighty monarch and all his adherents and supporters; they are all *delivered to death,* to fall by the sword, as the cedar by the axe. He and his princes, who, he said, were *altogether kings,* go down to the grace, *to the nether parts of the earth, in the midst of the children of men,* as common persons of no quality or distinction. *They died like men* (Ps. 82:7); they were carried away with *those that go down to the pit,* and their pomp did neither protect them nor *descend after them.* Again (v. 16), He was *cast down to hell with those that descend into the pit;* he went into the state of the dead, and was buried as others are, in obscurity and oblivion. Again (v. 17), *They all that were his arm,* on whom he stayed, by whom he acted and exerted his power, all *that dwelt under his shadow,* his subjects and allies, and all that had any dependence on him, they all *went down* into ruin, down into the grace *with him, unto those that were slain with the sword,* to those that were cut off by untimely deaths before them, under the load of guilt and shame. When great men fall a great many fall with them, as a great many in like manner have fallen before them. [3.] What God designed, and aimed at, in bringing down this mighty monarch and his monarchy. He designed thereby, *First, To give an alarm* to the nations about, to put them all to a stand, to put them all to a gaze (v. 16): *I made the nations to shake at the sound of his fall.* They were all struck with astonishment to see so mighty a prince brought down thus. It give a shock to all their confidences, every one thinking his turn would be next. *When he went down to the grace* (v. 15) *I caused a mourning,* a general lamentation, as the whole kingdom goes into mourning at the death of the king. In token of this general grief, *I covered the deep for him,* put that into black, gave a stop to business, in complaisance to this universal mourning. *I restrained the floods, and the great waters were stayed,* that they might run into another channel, that of lamentation. Lebanon particularly, the kingdom of Syria, that was sometimes in confederacy with the Assyrian, mourned for him; as the allies of Babylon, Rev. 18:9. *Secondly,* To give an admonition to the nations about, and to their kings (v. 14): *To the end that none of all the trees by the waters,* though ever so advantageously situated, *may exalt themselves for their height,* may be proud and conceited of themselves and *shoot up their top among the thick boughs,* looking disdainfully upon others, nor *stand upon themselves for their height,* confiding in their own politics and powers, as if they could never be brought down. Let them all take warning by the Assyrian, for he once held up his head as high, and thought he kept his footing as firm, as any of them; but his pride went before his destruction, and his confidence failed him. Note, The fall of proud presumptuous men is intended for warning to others to keep humble. It would have been well for Nebuchadnezzar, who was himself active in bringing down the Assyrian, if he had taken the admonition.

2. Here is a prophecy of the fall of the king of Egypt in like manner, v. 18. He thought himself like the Assyrian *in glory and greatness,* over-topping *all the trees of Eden,* as the cypress does the shrubs. "But *thou also shalt be brought down,* with the other trees that are pleasant to the sight, as those in Eden. Thou shalt be *brought to the grave,* to the nether or lower *parts of the earth;* thou shalt *lie in the midst of the uncircumcised,* that die in their uncleanness, die ingloriously, die under a curse and at a distance from God; then shall those whom thou hast trampled upon triumph over thee, saying, *This is Pharaoh and all his multitude.* See how mean he looks, how low he lies; see what all his pomp and pride have come to; here is all that is left of him." Note, Great men and great multitudes, with the great figure and great noise they make in the

world, when God comes to contend with them, will soon become little, less than nothing, such as Pharaoh and all his multitude.

CHAPTER 32

Still we are upon the destruction of Pharaoh and Egypt, which is wonderfully enlarged upon, and with a great deal of emphasis. When we read so very much of Egypt's ruin, no less than six several prophecies at divers times delivered concerning it, we are ready to think, Surely there is some special reason for it. And, I. Perhaps it may look as far back as the book of Genesis, where we find (15:14) that God determined to judge Egypt for oppressing his people; and, though that was in part fulfilled in the plagues of Egypt and the drowning of Pharaoh, yet, in this destruction, here foretold, those old scores were reckoned for, and that was to have its full accomplishment. II. Perhaps it may look as far forward as the book of the Revelation, where we find that the great enemy of the gospel-church, that makes war with the Lamb, is spiritually called Egypt, Rev. 11:8. And, if so, the destruction of Egypt and its Pharaoh was a type of the destruction of that proud enemy; and between this prophecy of the ruin of Egypt and the prophecy of the destruction of the antichristian generation there is some analogy. We have two distinct prophecies in this chapter relating to Egypt, both in the same month, one on the 1st day, the other that day fortnight, probably both on the sabbath day. They are both lamentations, not only to signify how lamentable the fall of Egypt should be, but to intimate how much the prophet himself should lament it, from a generous principle of love to mankind. The destruction of Egypt is here represented under two similitudes: — 1. The killing of a lion, or a whale, or some such devouring creature (*v.* 1–16). 2. The funeral of a great commander or captain-general (*v.* 17–32). The two prophecies of this chapter are much of the same length.

Verses 1–16

Here, I. The prophet is ordered to *take up a lamentation for Pharaoh king of Egypt, v.* 2. It concerns ministers to be much of a serious spirit, and, in order thereunto, to be frequent in taking up lamentations for the fall and ruin of sinners, as those that have not desired, but dreaded, the woeful day. Note, Ministers that would affect others with the things of God must make it appear that they are themselves affected with the miseries which sinners bring upon themselves by their sins. It becomes us to weep and tremble for those that will not weep and tremble for themselves, to try if thereby we may set them a weeping, set them a trembling.

II. He is ordered to show cause for that lamentation.

1. Pharaoh has been a troubler of the nations, even of his own nation, which he should have procured the repose of: He is *like a young lion of the nations* (*v.* 2), loud and noisy, hectoring and threatening as a lion when he roars. Great potentates, if they by tyrannical and oppressive, are in God's account no better than beasts of prey. He is like *a whale,* or dragon, like a crocodile (so some) *in the seas,* very turbulent and vexatious, as the *leviathan* that *makes the deep to boil like a pot,* Job 41:31. When Pharaoh engaged in an unnecessary war with the Cyrenians he *came forth with his rivers,* with his armies, *troubled the waters,* disturbed his own kingdom and the neighbouring nations, *fouled the rivers,* and made them muddy. Note, A great deal of disquiet is often given to the world by the restless ambition and implacable resentments of proud princes. Ahab is he that troubles Israel, and not Elijah.

2. He that has troubled others must expect to be himself troubled; for the Lord is righteous, Jos. 7:25.

(1.) This is set forth here by a comparison. Is Pharaoh like a *great whale,* which, when it comes up the river, gives great disturbance, a leviathan which Job cannot *draw out with a hook?* (Job 41:1), yet God has a net for him which is large enough to enclose him and strong enough to secure him (*v.* 3): *I will spread my net over thee,* even the army of the Chaldeans, a *company of many people;* they shall force him out of his fastnesses, dislodge him out of his possessions, throw him like a great fish upon dry ground, *upon the open field* (*v.* 4), where being out of his element, he must die of course, and be a prey to the birds and beasts, as was foretold, *ch.* 29:5. What can the strongest fish do to help itself when it is out of the water and lies gasping? *The flesh* of this great whale shall be *laid upon the mountains* (*v.* 5) and the *valleys* shall be *filled with his height.* Such numbers of Pharaoh's soldiers shall be slain that the dead bodies shall be scattered upon the hills and there shall be heaps of them piled up in the valleys. Blood shall be shed in such abundance as to swell the rivers in the valleys. Or, Such shall be the bulk, such the height, of this leviathan, that, when he is laid upon the ground, he shall fill a valley. Such vast quantities of blood shall issue from this *leviathan* as shall *water the land of Egypt,* the land wherein *now he swims,* now he sports himself, *v.* 6. It shall reach *to the mountains,* and the waters of Egypt shall again be *turned into blood* by this means: *The rivers shall be full of thee.* The judgments executed upon Pharaoh of old are expressed by the *breaking* of *the heads of leviathan in the waters,* Ps. 74:13, 14. But now they go further; this old serpent not only has now his head bruised, but is all crushed to pieces.

(2.) It is set forth by a prophecy of the deep impression which the destruction of Egypt should make upon the neighbouring nations; it would put them all into a consternation, as the fall of the Assyrian monarchy did, *ch.* 31:15, 16. When Pharaoh, who had been like a blazing burning torch, is *put out* and *extinguished* it shall make all about him look black, *v.* 7. The heavens shall be hung with black, the *stars darkened,* the sun eclipsed, and the moon be deprived of her borrowed light. It is from the upper world that this lower receives its light; and therefore (*v.* 8), when the *bright lights of heaven* are *made dark* above, darkness by consequence is *set upon the land,* upon the earth; so it shall be on the land of Egypt. Here the plague of darkness, which was upon Egypt of old for three days, seems to be alluded to, as, before, the turning of the waters into blood. For, when former judgments are forgotten, it is just that they should be repeated. When their privy-counsellors, and statesmen, and those that have the direction of the public affairs, are deprived of wisdom and made fools, and the things that belong to their peace are hidden from their eyes, then their lights are darkened and the land is in a mist. This is foretold, Isa. 19:13. *The princes of Zoan have become fools.* Now upon the spreading of the report of the fall of Egypt, and the bringing of the news to remote countries, *countries which they had not known* (*v.* 9), people shall be much affected, and shall feel themselves sensibly touched by it. [1.] It shall fill them with vexation to see such an ancient, wealthy, potent kingdom thus humbled and brought down, and the pride of worldly glory, which they have such a value for, stained. The *hearts of many people* will be *vexed* to see the word of the God of Israel fulfilled in the destruction of Egypt, and that all the *gods of Egypt* were not able to relieve it. Note, The destruction of some wicked people is a vexation to others. [2.] It shall fill them with admiration (*v.* 10): They shall be *amazed at thee,* shall wonder to see such *great riches* and power *come to nothing,* Rev. 18:17. Note, Those that admire with complacency the pomp of this world will admire with consternation the ruin of that pomp, which to those that know the vanity of all things here below is no surprise at all. [3.] It shall fill them with fear: even *their kings* (that think it their prerogative to be secure) shall be *horribly afraid for thee,* concluding their own house to be in danger when their neighbour's is on fire. *When I shall brandish my sword before them they shall tremble every man for his own life.* Note, When the sword of God's justice is drawn against some, to cut them off, it is thereby brandished before others, to give them warning. And those that will not be admonished by it, and made to reform, shall yet be frightened by it, and made to tremble. They shall *tremble at every moment, because of thy fall.* When others are ruined by sin we have reason to quake for fear, as knowing ourselves guilty and obnoxious. *Who is able to stand before this holy Lord God?*

(3.) It is set forth by a plain and express prediction of the desolation itself that should come upon Egypt. [1.] The instruments of the desolation appear here very formidable. It is the *sword of the king of Babylon,* that warlike, that victorious prince, that shall *come upon thee* (*v.* 11), the *swords of the mighty,* even the *terrible of the nations, all of them* (*v.* 12), an army that there is no standing before. Note, Those that delight in war, and are upon all occasions entering into contention, may expect, some time or other, to be engaged with those that will prove too hard for them. Pharaoh had been forward to quarrel with his neighbour and to come forth *with his rivers,* with his armies, *v.* 2. But God will now give him enough of it. [2.] The instances of the desolation appear here very frightful, much the same with what we had before, *ch.* 29:10–12; 30:7. *First,* The multitude of Egypt shall be destroyed, not decimated, some picked out to be made examples, but all cut off. Note, The numbers of sinners, though they be a multitude, will neither secure them against God's power nor entitle them to his pity. *Secondly,* The pomp of Egypt shall be spoiled, the pomp of their court, what they have been proud of. Note, in renouncing the pomps of this world we did ourselves a great kindness, for they are things that are soon spoiled and that cheat their admirers. *Thirdly,* The cattle of Egypt, that used to feed by the rivers, shall be destroyed (*v.* 13), either cut off by the sword or carried off for a prey. Egypt was famous for horses, which would be an acceptable booty to the Chaldeans. The rivers shall be no more frequented as they have been by man and beast, that came thither to drink. *Fourthly,* The *waters of Egypt,* that used to flow briskly, shall now grow deep, and slow, and heavy, and shall *run like oil* (*v.* 14), a figurative expression signifying that there should be such universal sadness and heaviness upon the whole nation that even the rivers should go softly and silently like mourners, and quite forget their rapid motion. *Fifthly,* The whole country of Egypt shall be stripped of its wealth; it shall be *destitute of what whereof it was full* (*v.* 15), corn, and cattle, and all the pleasant fruits of the earth; when those are *smitten that dwell therein* the ground is untilled, and that which is gathered becomes an easy prey to the invader. Note, God can soon empty those of this world's goods that have the greatest fulness of those things and are full of them, that enjoy most and have their hearts set upon those enjoyments. The Egyptians were full of their pleasant and plentiful country, and its rich productions. Every one that talked with them might perceive how much it filled them. But God can soon make their *country destitute of that whereof it is full;* it is therefore our wisdom to be full of treasures in heaven. When the country is made destitute, 1. It shall be an instruction to them: *Then shall they know that I am the Lord.* A sensible conviction of the vanity of the world, and the fading perishing nature of all things in it, will contribute much to our right knowledge of God as our portion and happiness. 2. It shall be a lamentation to all about them: *The daughters of the nations shall lament her* (*v.* 16), either because, being in alliance with her, they share in her grievances and suffer with her, or, being admirers of her, they at least share in her grief and sympathize with her. They shall lament *for Egypt and all her multitude;* it shall excite their pity to see so great a devastation made. By enlarging the matters of our joy we increase the occasions of our sorrow.

Verses 17–32

This prophecy concludes and completes the burden of Egypt, and leaves it and all its multitude in the pit of destruction.

I. We are here invited to attend the funeral of that once flourishing kingdom, to lament its fall, and to take a view of those who attend it to the grave and accompany it in the grave.

1. This dead corpse of a kingdom is here brought to the grave. The prophet is ordered to *cast them down* to the pit (*v.* 18), to foretel their destruction as one that had authority, as Jeremiah was set over the kingdoms, Jer. 1:10. He must speak in God's name, and as from him who will cast them down. Yet he must foretel it as one that had an affectionate concern for them; he must *wail for the multitude of Egypt,* even when he *casts them down.* When Egypt is slain, let her have an honourable funeral, befitting her quality; let her be buried *with the daughters of the famous nations,* in their burying-places and with the same ceremony. It is but a poor allay to the reproach and terror of death to be buried with those that were famous; yet this is all that is allowed to Egypt. Shall Egypt think to exempt herself from the common fate of proud and imperious nations? No; she must take her lot with them (*v.* 19): *"Whom dost thou surpass in beauty?* Art thou so much fairer than any other nation that thou shouldst expect therefore to be excused? No; others as fair as thou have sunk into the pit; *go down* therefore, and *be thou laid with the uncircumcised.* Thou art like them and art likely to lie among them. The multitude of Egypt shall all *fall in the midst of those that are slain with the sword,* now that there is a general slaughter made among the nations." Egypt with the rest must drink of the bloody cup, and therefore she is *delivered to the sword,* to the sword of war (but, in God's hand, the sword of justice), is delivered to be publicly executed. *Draw her and all her multitude;* draw them either as the dead bodies of great men are drawn in honour to the grave, in a hearse, or as malefactors are drawn in dis-

grace to the place of execution, on a sledge; draw them to the pit, and let them be made a spectacle to the world.

2. This corpse of a kingdom is bid welcome to the grave, and Pharaoh is made free of the congregation of the dead, and admitted into their regions, not without some pomp and ceremony. As the surprising fall of the king of Babylon is thus illustrated, *Hell from beneath is moved for thee to meet thee at thy coming,* and to introduce thee into those mansions of darkness (Isa. 14:9, etc.), so here (*v.* 21), *They shall speak to him out of the midst of hell,* as it were congratulating his arrival and calling him to join with them in acknowledging that which neither he nor they would be brought to own when they were in their pomp and pride, that it is in vain to think of contesting with God, and none ever hardened their hearts against him and prospered. They shall say to him, and to those that pretended to help him, Where are you now? What have you brought your attempts to at last? Divers nations are here mentioned as gone down to the grave before Egypt that are ready to give her a scornful reception and upbraid her with coming to them at last. These nations here spoken of were probably such as had been of late years ruined and wasted by the king of Babylon, and their princes cut off; let Egypt know that she has *neighbour's fare.* When she goes to the grave she does but *migrare ad plures — migrate to the majority;* there are *innumerable before her.* But it is observable that though Judah and Jerusalem were just about this time, or a little before, utterly ruined and laid waste, yet they are not mentioned here among the nations that welcome Egypt to the pit; for though they suffered the same things that these nations suffered, and by the same hand, yet the kind intentions of their affliction, and its happy issue at last, and the mercy God had yet in reserve for them, altered the property of it; it was not to them a *going down to the pit,* as it was to the heathen; they were not *smitten as others were,* nor *slain according to the slaughter of other nations,* Isa. 27:7. But let us see who those are that have *gone to the grave* before Egypt, that *lie uncircumcised, slain by the sword,* with whom she must now take up her lodging. (1.) There lie the Assyrian empire, and all the princes and mighty men of that monarchy (*v.* 22): *Asshur is there and all her company,* all the countries that were tributaries to and had dependence upon that crown. That mighty potentate who used to lie in state, with his guards and grandees about him, now lies in obscurity, with his *graves about him* and his soldiers in them, unable any longer to do him service or honour; they are *all of them slain, fallen by the sword.* The number of their months was *cut off in the midst,* and, being *bloody* and *deceitful men,* they were not suffered to *live out half their days.* Their *braves were set in the sides of the pit,* all in a row, like beds in a common chamber, *v.* 23. All their company is such as were *slain, fallen by the sword;* a vast congregation there is of such, who had *caused terror in the land of the living.* But as the death of those to whom they were a terror put an end to their fears (in the grave *the prisoners rest together* and *hear not the voice of the oppressor,* Job 3:18), so the death of these mighty men puts an end to their terrors. Who is afraid of *a dead lion?* Note, Death will be a king of terrors to those who, instead of making themselves blessings, make themselves terrors, in their generation. (2.) There lies the kingdom of Persia, which perhaps within the memory of man at that time had been wasted and brought down: *There is Elam and all her multitude,* the king of Elam and his numerous armies, *v.* 24, 25. They also had *caused their terror in the land of the living,* had made a fearful noise and bluster among the nations in their day. But Elam has now a grave by herself, and the graves of the common people *round about her, fallen by the sword;* she has *her bed in the midst of the slain* that went down *uncircumcised, unsanctified,* unholy, and not in covenant with God. They have *borne their shame with those that go down to the pit;* they have fallen under the common disgrace and mortification of mankind, that they die and are buried; nay, they die under particular marks of ignominy, which God and man put upon them. Note, Those who cause their terror shall, sooner or later, bear their *shame,* and be made a terror to themselves. The king of Elam is *put in the midst of those that are slain.* All the honour he can now pretend to is to be buried in the chief sepulchre. (3.) There lies the Scythian power, which, about this time, was busy in the world. *Me-*

shech and *Tubal,* those barbarous northern nations, had lately made a descent upon the Medes, and *caused their terror* among them, lived among them upon free quarter for some years, making every thing their own that they could lay their hands on; but at length Cyaxares, king of the Medes, drew them by a wile into his power, but off abundance of them, and obliged them to quit his country, *v.* 26. There lie Meshech and Tubal, and all their multitude; there is a burying place for them, with their chief commander in the midst of them, *all of them uncircumcised, slain by the sword.* These Scythians, dying ingloriously as they lived, are not laid, as the other nations spoken of before, in the bed of honour (*v.* 27): *They shall not lie with the mighty,* shall not be buried in state, as those are, even by consent of the enemy, that are slain in the field of battle, that *go down to their graves with their weapons of war* carried before the hearse, or trailed after it, that have particularly *their swords laid under their heads,* as if they could sleep the sweeter in the grave when they laid their heads on such a pillow. These Scythians are not buried with these marks of honour, but *their iniquities shall be upon their sons;* they shall, for their iniquity, be left unburied, though they were the *terror even of the mighty in the land of the living.* (4.) There lies the kingdom of Edom, which had flourished long, but about this time, at least before the destruction of Egypt, was made quite desolate, as was foretold, *ch.* 25:13. Among the sepulchres of the nations *there is Edom, v.* 29. There lie, not dignified with monuments or inscriptions, but mingled with common dust, *her kings and all her princes,* her wise statesmen (which Edom was famous for), and her brave soldiers. These *with their might are laid by those that were slain by the sword;* their might could not prevent it, nay, their might helped to procure it, for that both encouraged them to engage in war and incensed their neighbours against them, who thought it necessary to curb their growing greatness. A great deal of pains they took to ruin themselves, as many do, who *with their might,* with all their might, are *laid by those that were slain with the sword.* The Edomites retained circumcision, being of the seed of Abraham. But that shall stand them in no stead; they shall *lie with the uncircumcised.* (5.) There lie the *princes of the north, and all the Zidonians.* These were as well acquainted with maritime affairs as the Egyptians were, who relied much upon that part of their strength, but they have *gone down with the slain* (*v.* 30), down to the pit. Now they are *ashamed of their might,* ashamed to think how much they boasted of it and trusted to it; and, as the *Edomites with their might,* so these *with their terror,* are laid with those that are *slain by the sword* and are forced to take their lot with them. They *bear their shame with those that go down to the pit,* die in as much disgrace as those that are cut off by the hand of public justice. (6.) All this is applied to Pharaoh and the Egyptians, who have no reason to flatter themselves with hopes of tranquillity when they see how the wisest, and wealthiest, and strongest, of their neighbours have been laid waste (*v.* 28): "*Yea, thou shalt be broken in the midst of the uncircumcised;* when God is pulling down the unhumbled and unreformed nations thou must expect to come down with them." [1.] It will be some extenuation of the miseries of Egypt to observe that it has been the case of so many great and mighty nations before (*v.* 31): *Pharaoh shall see them and be comforted;* it will be some ease to his mind that he is not the first king that has been slain in battle — his not the first army that has been routed, his not the first kingdom that has been made desolate. Mr. Greenhill observes here, "The comfort which wicked ones have after death is poor comfort, not real, but imaginary." They will find little satisfaction in having so many fellow-sufferers; the rich man in hell dreaded it. It is only in point of honour that Pharaoh can *see and be comforted.* [2.] But nothing will be an exemption from these miseries; for (*v.* 32) *I have caused my terror in the land of the living.* Great men have caused their terror, have studied how to make every body *fear them. Oderint dum metuant — Let them hate, so that they do but fear.* But now the great God has *caused his terror in the land of the living;* and therefore he laughs at theirs, because he sees that *his day is coming,* Ps. 37:13. In this day of terror Pharaoh *and all his multitude* shall be *laid with those that are slain by the sword.*

II. The view which this prophecy gives us of ruined states may show us something, 1. Of this present world,

and the empire of death in it. Come, and see the calamitous state of human life; see what a dying world this is. The strong die, the mighty die, Pharaoh and all his multitude. See what a killing world this is. They are all *slain with the sword.* As if men did not die fast enough of themselves, men are ingenious at finding out ways to destroy one another. It is not only a great pit, but a great cock-pit. 2. Of the other world. Though it is the destruction of nations as such that perhaps is principally intended here, yet here is a plain allusion to the final and everlasting ruin of impenitent sinners, of those that are uncircumcised in heart; they are *slain by the sword* of divine justice; their *iniquity is upon them,* and with it they *bear their shame.* Those, Christ's enemies, that would not have him to reign over them, *shall be brought forth* and *slain before him,* though they be as pompous, though they be as numerous, as Pharaoh and *all his multitude.*

CHAPTER 33

The prophet has now come off his circuit, which he went as judge, in God's name, to try and pass sentence upon the neighbouring nations, and, having finished with them, and read them all their doom, in the eight chapters foregoing, he now returns to the children of his people, and receives further instructions what to say to them. I. He must let them know what office he was in among them as a prophet, that he was a watchman, and had received a charge concerning them, for which he was accountable (*v.* 1–9). The substance of this we had before, 3:17, etc. II. He must let them know upon what terms they stand with God, that they are upon their trial, upon their good behaviour, that if a wicked man repent he shall not perish, but that if a righteous man apostatize he shall perish (*v.* 10–20). III. Here is a particular message sent to those who yet remained in the land of Israel, and (which is very strange) grew secure there, and confident that they should take root there again, to tell them that their hopes would fail them because they persisted in their sins (*v.* 21–29). IV. Here is a rebuke to those who personally attended Ezekiel's ministry, but were not sincere in their professions of devotion (*v.* 30–33).

Verses 1–9

The prophet had been, by express order from God, taken off from prophesying to the Jews, just then when the news came that Jerusalem was invested, and close siege laid to it, *ch.* 24:27. But now that Jerusalem is taken, two years after, he is appointed again to direct his speech to them; and there his commission is renewed. If God had abandoned them quite, he would not have sent prophets to them; nor, if he had not had mercy in store for them, would he have *shown them such things as these.* In these verses we have,

I. The office of a watchman laid down, the trust reposed in him, the charge given him, and the conditions adjusted between him and those that employ him, *v.* 2, 6. 1. It is supposed to be a public danger that gives occasion for the appointing of a watchman — when *God brings the sword upon a land, v.* 2. The sword of war, whenever it comes upon a land, is of God's bringing; it is the *sword of the Lord,* of his justice, how unjustly soever men draw it. At such a time, when a country is in fear of a foreign invasion, that they may be informed of all the motions of the enemy, may not be surprised with an attack, but may have early notice of it, in order to their being at their arms and in readiness to give the invader a warm reception, they *set a man of their coast,* some likely person, that lives upon the borders of their country, where the threatened danger is expected, and is therefore well acquainted with all the avenues of it, and make him *their watchman.* Thus *wise* are the *children of this world in their generation.* Note, One man may be of public service to a whole country. Princes and statesmen are the watchmen of a kingdom; they are continually to employ themselves, and, if occasion be, as watchmen, to expose themselves for the public safety. 2. It is supposed to be a public trust that is lodged in the watchman and that he is accountable to the public for the discharge of it. His business is, (1.) To discover the approaches and advances of the enemy; and therefore he must not be blind nor asleep, for then he cannot *see the sword coming.* (2.) To give notice of them immediately by sound of trumpet, or, as sentinels among us, by the discharge of a gun, as a signal of danger. A special trust and confidence is reposed in him by those that set him to be their watchman that he will faithfully do these two things; and they venture their lives upon his fidelity. Now, [1.] If he do his part, if he be betimes aware of all the dangers that fall within his cognizance, and give warning of them, he has discharged his trust, and has not only *delivered his soul,* but earned his wages. If the people do not take warning, if they either will not believe the notice he gives them, will not believe the danger to be so great or so near as really it is, or will not regard it, and so are surprised by the enemy in their security, it is their own fault; the blame is not to be laid upon the watchman, but their blood is upon their own head. If any person goes presumptuously into the mouth of danger, though he heard the sound of the trumpet, and was told by it where the danger was, and *so the sword comes* and *takes him away* in his folly, he is *felo de se — a suicide;* foolish man, he has *destroyed himself.* But, [2.] If the watchman do not do his duty, if he might have seen the danger, and did not, but was asleep, or heedless, or looking another way, or if he did *see the danger* (for so the case is put here) and shifted only for his own safety, and *blew not the trumpet* to *warn the people,* so that some are surprised and cut off *in their iniquity* (*v.* 6), cut off suddenly, without having time to cry, *Lord, have mercy upon me,* time to repent and make their peace with God (which makes the matter much the worse, that the poor creature is *taken away in his iniquity),* his blood shall be required *at the watchman's hand;* he shall be found guilty of his death, because he did not *give him warning* of his danger. But if the watchman do his part, and the people do theirs, all is well; both he that gives warning and he that takes warning have delivered their souls.

II. The application of this to the prophet, *v.* 7, 9.

1. He is a *watchman to the house of Israel.* He had occasionally given warning to the nations about, but to the house of Israel he was a watchman by office, for they were the *children of the prophets and the covenant* They did not *set him for a watchman,* as the people of the land, *v.* 2 (for they were not so wise for their souls as to secure the welfare of them, as they would have been for the protection of their temporal interests); but God did it for them; he appointed them a watchman.

2. His business as a watchman is to give warning to sinners of their misery and danger by reason of sin. This is the word he must *hear from God's mouth* and *speak to them.* (1.) God has said, *The wicked man shall surely die;* he shall be miserable. Unless he repent, he shall be cut off from God and all comfort and hope in him, shall be cut off from all good. He shall fall and lie for ever under the wrath of God, which is the death of the soul, as his favour is its life. The righteous God has said it, and will never unsay it, nor can all the world gainsay it, that the *wages of sin is death. Sin, when it is finished, brings froth death.* The wrath of God is revealed from heaven, not only against wicked nations, speaking ruin to them as nations, but against wicked persons, speaking ruin to them in their personal capacity, their personal interests, which pass into the other world and last to eternity, as national interests do not. (2.) It is the will of God that the wicked man should be warned of this: *Warn them from me.* This intimates that there is a possibility of preventing it, else it were a jest to give warning of it; nay, and that God is desirous it should be prevented. Sinners are *therefore* warned of the wrath to come, that they may *flee from it,* Mt. 3:7. (3.) It is the work of ministers to give him warning, to say to the wicked, *It shall be ill with thee,* Isa. 3:11. God ways in general, *The soul that sinneth it shall die.* The minister's business is to apply this to particular persons, and to say, *"O wicked man! thou shalt surely die,* whoever thou art; if thou go on still in thy trespasses, they will inevitably be thy ruin. O adulterer! O robber! O drunkard! O swearer! O sabbath-breaker! *thou shalt surely die."* And he must say this, not in passion, to provoke the sinner, but in compassion, to *warn the wicked from hi way,* warn him to *turn from it,* that he may live. This is to be done by the faithful preaching of the word in public, and by personal application to those whose sins are open.

3. If souls perish through his neglect of his duty, he brings guilt upon himself. "If the prophet do not warn the wicked of the ruin that is at the end of his wicked way, that *wicked man shall die in his iniquity;* for, though the watchman did not do his part, yet the sinner might have taken warning from the written word, from his own conscience, and from God's judgments upon others, by which his mouth shall be stopped, and God will be justified in his destruction." Note, It will not serve impenitent sinners to plead in the great day that their watchmen did not give them warning, that they were careless and unfaithful; for, though they were so, it will be made to appear that *God left not himself without witness.* "But he shall not perish alone in his iniquity; the watchman also shall be called to an account: *His blood will I require at thy hand.* The blind leader shall fall with the blind follower into the ditch." See what a desire God has of the salvation of sinners, in that he resents it so ill if those concerned do not what they can to prevent their destruction. And see what a great deal those ministers have to answer for another day who palliate sin, and flatter sinners in their evil way, and by their wicked lives countenance and harden them in their wickedness, and encourage them to believe that they shall have peace though they go on.

4. If he do his duty, he may take the comfort of it, though he do not see the success of it (*v.* 9): *"If thou warn the wicked of his way,* if thou tell him faithfully what will be the end thereof, and call him earnestly to turn from it, and he do not turn, but persist in it, *he shall die in his iniquity,* and the fair warning given him will be an aggravation of his sin and ruin; but *thou hast delivered thy soul."* Note, It is a comfort to ministers that they may through grace save themselves, though they cannot be instrumental to save so many as they wish of those that hear them.

Verses 10–20

These verses are the substance of what we had before (*ch.* 18:20, etc.) and they are so full and express a declaration of the terms on which people stand with God (as the former were of the terms on which ministers stand) that it is no wonder that they are here repeated, as those were, though we had the substance of them before. Observe here,

I. The cavils of the people against God's proceedings with them. God was now in his providence contending with them, but their uncircumcised hearts were not as yet humbled, for they were industrious to justify themselves, though thereby they reflected on God. Two things they insisted upon, in their reproaches of God, and in both they added iniquity to their sin and misery to their punishment: — 1. They quarrelled with his promises and favours, as having no kindness nor sincerity in them, *v.* 10. God had *set life before them,* but they plead that he had set it out of their reach, and therefore did but mock them with the mention of it. The prophet had said, some time ago (*ch.* 24:23), *You shall pine away for your iniquities;* with that word he had concluded his threatenings against Judah and Jerusalem; and this they now upbraided him with, as if it had been spoken absolutely, to drive them to despair; whereas it was spoken conditionally, to bring them to repentance. Thus are the sayings of God's ministers perverted by men of corrupt minds, who are inclined to pick quarrels. He puts them in hopes of life and happiness; and herein they would make him contradict himself; "for" (say they) *"if our transgressions and our sins be upon us,* as thou hast often told us they are, and if we must, as thou sayest, *pine away in them,* and wear out a miserable captivity in a fruitless repentance, *how shall we then live?* If this be our doom, there is no remedy. *We die, we perish, we all perish."* Note, It is very common for those that have been hardened with presumption when they were warned against sin to sink into despair when they are called to repent, and to conclude there is no hope of life for them. 2. They quarrelled with his threatenings and judgments, as having no justice or equity in them. They said, *The way of the Lord is not equal* (*v.* 17:20), suggesting that God was partial in his proceedings, that with him there was respect of persons and that he was more severe against sin and sinners than there was cause.

II. Here is a satisfactory answer given to both these cavils.

1. Those that despaired of finding mercy with God are here answered with a solemn declaration of God's readiness to show mercy, *v.* 11. When they spoke of *pining away in their iniquity* God sent the prophet to them, with all speed, to tell them that though their case was sad it was not desperate, but there was yet *hope in Israel.* (1.) It is certain that God has no delight in the ruin of sinners, nor does he desire it. If they will destroy themselves, he will glorify himself in it, but he has no pleasure in it, but would rather they should *turn and live,* for his goodness is that attribute of his which is most his glory, which is most his delight. He would rather sinners should turn and live than go on and die. He has said it, he has sworn it, that by these two immutable things, in both which it is impossible for God to lie, we might have strong consolation. We have his word and his oath; and, since he could *swear by no greater, he swears by himself: As I live.* They questioned whether they should *live,* though they did repent and reform; yea, says God, as sure *as I live,* true penitents shall live also; for *their life is hid with Christ in God.* (2.) It is certain that God is sincere and in earnest in the calls he gives sinners to repent: *Turn you, turn you, from your evil way.* To repent is to turn from our evil way; this God requires sinners to do; this he urges them to do by repeated pressing instances: *Turn you, turn you.* O that they would be prevailed with to turn, to turn quickly, without delay! This he will enable them to do if they will but *frame their doings to turn to the Lord,* Hos. 5:4. For he has said, *I will pour out my Spirit unto you,* Prov. 1:23. And in this he will accept of them; for it is not only what he commands, but what he courts them to. (3.) It is certain that, if sinners perish in their impenitency, it is owing to themselves; they die because they will die; and herein they act most absurdly and unreasonably: *Why will you die, O house of Israel?* God would have heard them, and they would not be heard.

2. Those that despaired of finding justice with God are here answered with a solemn declaration of the rule of judgment which God would go by in dealing with the children of men, which carries along with it the evidence of its own equity; he that runs may read the justice of it. The Jewish nation, as a nation, was now *dead;* it was ruined to all intents and purposes. The prophet must therefore deal with particular persons, and the rule of judgment concerning them is much like that concerning a nation, Jer. 18:8–10. If God speak concerning it to build and to plant, and it do wickedly, he will recall his favours and leave it to ruin. But if he speak concerning it to pluck up and destroy, and it repent, he will revoke the sentence and deliver it. So it is here. In short, The most plausible professors, if they apostatize, shall certainly perish for ever in their apostasy from God; and the most notorious sinners, if they repent, shall certainly be happy for ever in their return to God. This is here repeated again and again, because it ought to be again and again considered, and preached over to our own hearts. This was necessary to be inculcated upon this stupid senseless people, that said, *The way of the Lord is not equal;* for these rules of judgment are so plainly just that they need no other confirmation of them than the repetition of them.

(1.) If those that have made a great profession of religion throw off their profession, quit the good ways of God and grow loose and carnal, sensual and worldly, the profession they made and all the religious performances with which they had for a great while kept up the credit of their profession shall stand them in no stead, but they shall certainly perish in their iniquity, *v.* 12, 13, 18. [1.] God says to the *righteous man* that *he shall surely live, v.* 13. He says it by his word, by his ministers. He that lives regularly, his own heart tells him, his neighbours tell him, He shall live. Surely such a man as this cannot but be happy. And it is certain, if he proceed and persevere in his righteousness, and if, in order to that, he be upright and sincere in it, if he be really as good as he seems to be, he shall live; he shall continue in the love of God and be for ever happy in that love. [2.] Righteous men, who have very good hopes of themselves and whom others have a very good opinion of, are yet in danger of turning to iniquity by trusting to their righteousness. So the case is put here: *If he trust to his own righteousness, and commit iniquity,* and come to make a trade of sin — if he not only take a false step, but turn aside into a false way and persist in it. This may possibly be the case of a righteous man, and it is the effect of his trusting to his own righteousness. Note, Many eminent professors have been ruined by a proud conceitedness of themselves and confidence in themselves. He trust to the merit of his own righteousness, and thinks he has already made God so much his debtor that now he may venture to commit iniquity, for he has righteousness enough in stock to make amends for it; he fancies that whatever evil deeds he may do hereafter he can be in no danger from them, having so many good deeds beforehand to counterbalance them. Or, He trust to the strength of his own righteousness, thinks himself now so well established in a course of virtue that he may thrust himself into any temptation and it cannot overcome him, and so by presuming on his own sufficiency he is brought to commit iniquity. By making bold on the confines of sin he is drawn at length into the depths of hell. This ruined the Pharisees; they *trusted to themselves that they were righteous,* and that their long prayers, and fasting twice in the week, would atone for their devouring widows' houses. [3.] If righteous men *turn to iniquity,* and return not to their righteousness, they shall certainly perish in their iniquity, and all the righteousness they have formerly done, all their prayers, and all their alms, shall be forgotten. No mention shall be made, no remembrance had, of their good deeds; they shall be overlooked, as if they had never been. The *righteousness of the righteous shall not deliver him* from the wrath of God, and the curse of the law, *in the day of his transgression.* When he becomes a traitor and a rebel, and takes up arms against his rightful Sovereign, it will not serve for him to plead in his own defence that formerly he was a loyal subject, and did many good services to the government. No; *he shall not be able to live.* The remembrance of his former righteousness shall be no satisfaction either to God's justice or his own conscience *in the day that he sins,* but rather shall, in the estimate of both, highly aggravate the sin and folly of his apostasy. And therefore *for his iniquity that he committed he shall die, v.* 13. And again (*v.* 18), *He shall even die thereby;* and it is owing to himself.

(2.) If those that have lived a wicked life repent and reform, forsake their wicked ways and become religious, their sins shall be pardoned, and they shall be justified and saved, if they persevere in their reformation. [1.] God says *to the wicked, "Thou shalt surely die.* The way that thou art in leads to destruction. The wages of thy sin is death, and thy iniquity will shortly be thy ruin." It was said to the righteous man, *Thou shalt surely live,* for his encouragement to proceed and persevere in the way of righteousness; but he made an ill use of it, and was emboldened by it to commit iniquity. It was said to the wicked man, *Thou shalt surely die,* for warning to him not to persist in his wicked ways; and he makes a good use of it, and is quickened thereby to return to God and duty. Thus even the threatenings of the word are to some, by the grace of God, a savour of life unto life, while even the promises of the word become to others, by their own corruption, a savour of death unto death. When God says to the wicked man, *Thou shalt surely die,* die eternally, it is to frighten him, not out of his wits, but out of his sins. [2.] There is many a wicked man who was hastening apace to his own destruction who yet is wrought upon by the grace of God to return and repent, and live a holy life. He *turns from his sin* (*v.* 14), and is resolved that he will have no more to do with it; and, as an evidence of his repentance for wrong done, he *restores the pledge* (*v.* 15) which he had taken uncharitably from the poor, *he gives again that which he had robbed* and taken unjustly from the rich. Nor does he only *cease to do evil,* but he *learns to do well;* he *does that which is lawful and right,* and makes conscience of his duty both to God and man — a great change, since, awhile ago, he neither feared God nor regarded man. But many such amazing changes, and blessed ones, have been wrought by the power of divine grace. He that was going on in the paths of death and the destroyer now walks in *the statues of life,* in the way of God's commandments, which has both life in it (Prov. 12:28) and life at the end of it, Mt. 19:17. And in this good way he perseveres *without committing iniquity,* though not free from remaining infirmity, yet under the dominion of no iniquity. He repents not of his repentance, nor returns to the commission of those gross sins which he before allowed himself in. [3.] He that does thus repent and return shall escape the ruin he was running into, and his former sins shall be no prejudice to his acceptance with God. Let him not pine away in his iniquity, for, if he confess and forsake it, he shall find mercy. He *shall surely live; he shall not die, v.* 15. Again (*v.* 16), *He shall surely live.* Again (*v.* 19), *He has done that which is lawful and right,* and *he shall live thereby.* But will not his wickednesses be remembered against him? No; he shall not be punished for them (*v.* 12): *As for the wickedness of the wicked,* though it was very heinous, *yet he shall not fall thereby in the day that he turns from his wickedness.* Now that it has become his grief it shall not be his ruin. Now that there is a settled separation between him and sin there shall be no longer a separation between him and God. Nay, he shall not be so much as upbraided with them (*v.* 16): *None of his sins that he has committed shall be mentioned unto him,* either as a clog to his pardon or an allay to the comfort of it, or as any blemish and diminution to the glory that is prepared for him.

Now lay all this together, and then judge whether the *way of the Lord be not equal,* whether this will not justify God in the destruction of sinners and glorify him in the salvation of penitents. The conclusion of the whole matter is (*v.* 20): *"O you house of Israel,* though you are all involved now in the common calamity, yet there shall be a distinction of persons made in the spiritual and eternal state, and *I will judge you every one after his ways."* Though they were sent into captivity by the lump, good fish and bad enclosed in the same net, yet there he will separate between the precious and the vile and will *render to every man according to his works.* Therefore God's way is equal and unexceptionable; but, as for the *children of thy people,* God turns them over to the prophet, as he did to Moses (Ex. 32:7): "They are thy people; I can scarcely own them for mine." As for them, *their way is unequal;* this way which they have got of quarrelling with God and his prophets is absurd and unreasonable. In all disputes between God and his creatures it will certainly be found that he is in the right and they are in the wrong.

Verses 21–29

Here we have,

I. The tidings brought to Ezekiel of the burning of Jerusalem by the Chaldeans. The city was burnt in the eleventh year of the captivity and the fifth month, Jer. 52:12, 13. Tidings hereof were brought to the prophet by one that was an eye-witness of the destruction, in the twelfth year, and the tenth month (*v.* 21), which was a year and almost five months after the thing was done; we may well suppose that, there being a constant correspondence at this time more than ever kept up between Jerusalem and Babylon, he had heard the news long before. But this was the first time he had an account of it from a refugee, from one who escaped, who could be particular, and would be pathetic, in the narrative of it. And the sign given him was the coming of such a one to him as had himself narrowly escaped the flames (*ch.* 24:26): *He that escapes in that day shall come unto thee,* to *cause thee to hear it with thy ears,* to hear it more distinctly than ever, from one that could say, *Quaeque ipse miserrima vidi — These miserable scenes I saw.*

II. The divine impressions and influences he was under, to prepare him for those heavy tidings (*v.* 22): *The hand of the Lord was upon me before he came, and had opened my mouth* to speak to the house of Israel what we had in the former part of this chapter. And now *he was no more dumb;* he prophesied now with more freedom and boldness, being by those the event proved a true prophet, to the confusion of those that contradicted him. All the prophecies from *ch.* 24 to this chapter have relation purely to the nations about, it is probable that the prophet, when he received them from the Lord, did not deliver them by word of mouth, but in writing; for he could not *Say to the Ammonites, Say unto Tyrus, Say unto Pharaoh,* etc., so and so, but by letters directed to the persons concerned, as Zacharias, when he could not speak, wrote; and herein he was as truly executing his prophetic office as ever. Note, Even silenced ministers may be doing a great deal of good by writing letters and making visits. But now the prophet's *mouth is opened,* that he may *speak to the children of his people.* It is probable that he had, during these three years, been continually speaking to them as a friend, putting them in mind of what he had formerly delivered to them, but that he never spoke to them as a prophet, by inspiration, till now, when *the hand of the Lord came upon him,* renewed his commission, gave him fresh instructions, and *opened his mouth,* furnished him with power to speak to the people *as he ought to speak.*

III. The particular message he was entrusted with, relating to these Jews that yet remained in the *land of Israel,* and *inhabited the wastes* of that land, *v.* 24. See what work sin had made. *The cities of* Israel had now become the wastes of Israel, for they lay all in ruins; some few that had escaped the sword and captivity still continued there and began to think of re-settling. This was so long after the destruction of Jerusalem that it was some time before this that Gedaliah (a modest humble man) and his friends were slain; but probably at this time Johanan, and the *proud men* that joined with him, were at the height (Jer. 43:2); and before they came to a resolution to go into Egypt, wherein Jeremiah opposed them, it is probable that the project was to establish themselves in the wastes of the land of Israel, in which Ezekiel here opposed them, and probably despatched the message away by the person that brought him the news of Jerusalem's destruction. Or, perhaps, those here prophesied against might be some other party of Jews, that remained in the land, hoping to take root there and to be sole masters of it, after Johanan and his forces had gone into Egypt. Now here we have,

1. An account of the pride of these remaining Jews, who dwelt in the *wastes of the land of* Israel. Though the providence of God concerning them had been very humbling, and still was very threatening, yet they were intolerably haughty and secure, and promised themselves peace. He that brought the news to the prophet that Jerusalem was smitten could not tell him (it is likely) what these people said, but God tells him, *They say, "The land is given us for inheritance, v.* 24. Our partners being gone, it is now all our own by survivorship, or, for want of heirs, it comes to us as occupants; we shall now be placed alone in the midst of the earth and have it all to ourselves." This argues great stupidity under the weighty hand of God, and a reigning selfishness and narrow-spiritedness; they pleased themselves in the ruin of their country as long as they hoped to find their own account in it, cared not though it were *all waste,* so that they might have the sole property — a poor inheritance to be proud of! They have the impudence to compare their case with Abraham's, glorying in this, *We have Abraham to our father.* "Abraham," say they, *"was one,* one family, and *he inherited the land,* and lived many years in the peaceable enjoyment of it; *but we are many,* many families, more numerous than he; *the land is given us for inheritance."* (1.) They think they can make out as good a title from God to this land as Abraham could: "If God *gave this land* to him, who was but one worshipper of him, as a reward of his service, much more will he give it to us, who are many worshippers of him, as the reward of our service." This shows the great conceit they had of the own merits, as if they were greater than those of Abraham their father, who yet was not justified by works. (2.) They think they can make good the possession of this land against the Chaldeans and all others invaders, as well as Abraham could against those that were competitors with him for it: "If he, who was but one, could hold it, much more shall we, who are many, and have many more at command than his 300 *trained servants."* This shows the confidence they had in their own might; they had got possession, and were resolved to keep it.

2. A check to this pride. Since God's providences did neither humble them nor terrify them, he sends them a message sufficient to do both.

(1.) To humble them, he tells them of the wickedness they still persisted in, which rendered them utterly unworthy to possess this land, so that they could not expect God should give it to them. They had been followed with one judgment after another, but they had not profited by those means of grace as might be expected; they were still unreformed, and how could they expect *that they should possess the land? "Shall you possess the land?* What! such wicked people as you are? *How shall I put thee among the children, and give thee a pleasant land?* Jer. 3:19. Surely you never reflect upon yourselves, else you would rather wonder that you are in the land of the living than expect to possess this land. For do you now know how bad you are?" [1.] "You make no conscience of forbidden fruit, forbidden food: *You eat with the blood,"* directly contrary to one of the precepts given to Noah and his sons when God gave them possession of the earth, Gen. 9:4. [2.] "Idolatry, that covenant-breaking sin, that sin which the jealous God has been in a particular manner provoked by to lay your country waste, is still the sin that most easily besets you and which you have a strong inclination to: *You lift up your eyes towards your idols,* which is a sign that though perhaps you do not bow your knee to them so much as you have done, yet you set your hearts upon them and hanker after them." [3.] "You are as fierce, and cruel, and barbarous as ever: *You shed blood,* innocent blood."

[4.] "You confide in your own strength, your own arm, your own bow, and have no dependence on, or regard to, God and his providence: *You stand upon your sword* (*v.* 26); you think to carry all before you, and make all your own, by force of arms." How can those expect the inheritance of Isaac (as these did) who are of Ishmael's disposition, that had *his hand against every man* (Gen. 16:12), and Esau's resolution to *live by his sword?* Gen. 27:40. We met with those (*ch.* 32:27) who, when they died, thought they could not lie easy underground unless they had their swords under their heads. Here we meet with those who, while they live, think they cannot stand firmly above ground unless they have their swords under their feet, as if swords were both the softest pillows and the strongest pillars; though it was sin, it was sin, that first drew the sword. But, blessed be God, there are those who know better, who stand upon the support of the divine power and promise and lay their heads in the bosom of divine love, *not trusting in their own sword,* Ps. 44:3. [5.] "You are guilty of all manner of abominations, and, particularly, *you defile every one his neighbour's wife,* which is an abomination of the first magnitude, *and shall you possess the land?* What! such vile miscreants as you?" Note, Those cannot expect to *possess the land,* nor to enjoy any true comfort or happiness here or hereafter, who live in rebellion against the Lord.

(2.) To terrify them, he tells them of the further judgments God had in store for them, which should make them utterly unable to possess this land, so that they could not stand it out against the enemy. Do they say that they shall possess the land? God has said they shall not, he has sworn it, *As I live, saith the Lord.* Though he has sworn that he delights not *in the death of sinners,* yet he has sworn also that those who persist in impenitency and unbelief *shall not enter into his rest.* [1.] Those that are in the cities, here called the *wastes,* shall *fall by the sword,* either by the sword of the Chaldeans, who come to avenge the murder of Gedaliah, or by one another's swords, in their intestine broils. [2.] Those that are in the open field shall be *devoured by* wild *beasts,* which swarmed, of course, in the country when it was dispeopled, and there were none to master them and keep them under, Ex. 23:29. When the army of the enemy had quitted the country still there was no safety in it. *Noisome beasts* constituted one of the four *sore judgments, ch.* 14:15. [3.] Those that are *in the forts and in the caves,* that think themselves safe in artificial or natural fastnesses, because men's eyes cannot discover them nor men's darts reach them, there the arrows of the Almighty shall find them out; they shall *die of the pestilence.* [4.] The whole land, even the land of Israel, that had been the glory of all lands, shall be *most desolate, v.* 28. *It shall be desolation, desolation,* all over as desolate as desolation itself can make it. The *mountain of Israel,* the fruitful mountains, Zion itself the holy mountain not excepted, *shall be desolate,* the roads unfrequented, the houses uninhabited, that *none shall pass through;* as it was threatened (Deu. 28:62), *You shall be left few in number.* [5.] The *pomp of her strength,* whatever she glories in as her pomp and trusts to as her strength, shall be made to cease. [6.] The cause of all this was very bad; it is for *all their abominations which they have committed.* It is sin that does all this mischief, that makes nations desolate; and therefore we ought to call it an abomination. [7.] Yet the effect of all this will be very good: *Then shall they know that I am the Lord,* am their Lord, and shall return to their allegiance, *when I have made the land most desolate.* Those are untractable unteachable indeed that are not made to know their dependence upon God when all their creature-comforts fail them and are made desolate.

Verses 30–33

The foregoing verses spoke conviction to the Jews who remained in the land of Israel, who were monuments of sparing mercy and yet returned not to the Lord; in these verses those are reproved who were now in captivity in Babylon, under divine rebukes, and yet were not reformed by them. They are not indeed charged with the same gross enormities that the others are charged with. They made some show of religion and devotion; but their hearts were not right with God. The thing they are here accused of is *mocking the messengers of the lord,* one of their measure-filling sins, which brought this ruin upon them, and yet they were not cured of it. Two ways they mocked the prophet Ezekiel: —

I. By invidious ill natured reflections upon him, privately among themselves, endeavouring by all means possible to render him despicable. The prophet did not know it, but charitably thought that those who spoke so well to him to his face, with so much seeming respect and deference, would surely not speak ill of him behind his back. But God comes and tells him, *The children of thy people are still talking against thee* (*v.* 30), or *talking of thee,* no good, I doubt. Note, Public persons are a common theme or subject of discourse; every one takes a liberty to censure them at pleasure. Faithful ministers know not how much ill is said of them every day; it is well that they do not; for, if they did, it might prove a discouragement to them in their work not to be easily got over. God takes notice of all that is said against his ministers, not only what is decreed against them, or sworn against them, not only what is written against them, or spoken with solemnity and deliberation, but of what is said against them in common talk, among neighbours when they meet in an evening, *by the walls and in the doors of their houses,* where whatever freedom of speech they use, if they reproach and slander any of God's ministers, God will reckon with them for it; his prophets shall not be made the song of the drunkards always. They had no crime to lay to the prophet's charge, but they loved to talk of him in a careless, scornful, bantering way; they said, jokingly, *"Come, and let us hear what is the word that comes forth from the Lord;* perhaps it will be something new, and will entertain us, and furnish us with matter for discourse." Note, Those have arrived as a great pitch of profaneness who can make so great a privilege, and so great a duty, as the preaching and hearing of the word of God, a matter of sport and ridicule, yea though it be not done publicly, but in private conversation among themselves. Serious things should be spoken of seriously.

II. By dissembling with him in their attendance upon his ministry. Hypocrites mock God and mock his prophets. But their hypocrisy is open before God, and the day is coming when, as here, it will be laid open. Observe here,

1. The plausible profession which these people made and the speciousness of their pretensions. They are like those (Mt. 15:8) who *draw nigh to God with their mouths and honour him with their lips, but their hearts are far from him.* (1.) They were diligent and constant in their attendance upon the means of grace: *They come unto thee as the people come.* In Babylon they had no temple or synagogue, but they went to the prophet's house (*ch.* 8:1), and there, it is probable, they spent their *new moons and their sabbaths* in religious exercises, 2 Ki. 4:23. When the prophet was bound the word of the Lord was not bound; and the people, when they had not the help for their souls that they wished for, were thankful for what they had; it was a reviving in their bondage. Now these hypocrites came, *according to the coming of the people,* as duly and as early as any of the prophet's hearers. Their being said to come *as the people came* seems to intimate that the reason why they came was because other people came; they did not come out of conscience towards God, but only for company, for fashion-sake, and because it was now the custom of their countrymen. Note, Those that have no inward principle of love to God's ordinances may yet be found much in the external observance of them. Cain brought his sacrifice as well as Abel; and the Pharisee went up to the temple to pray as well as the publican. (2.) They behaved themselves very decently and reverently in the public assembly; there were none of them whispering, or laughing, or gazing about them, or sleeping. But *they sit before thee as my people,* with all the shows of gravity, and sereneness, and composure of mind. They sit out the time, without weariness, or wishing the sermon done. (3.) They were very attentive to the word preached: "They are not thinking of something else, but they *hear thy words,* and take notice of what thou sayest." (4.) They pretended to have a great kindness and respect for the prophet. Though, behind his back, they could not give him a good word, yet, to his face, *they showed much love* to him and his doctrine; they pretended to have a great concern lest he should spend himself too much in preaching or expose himself to the Chaldeans, for they would be thought to be some of his best friends and well-wishers. (5.) They took a great deal of pleasure in the word; they *delighted to know God's word,* Isa. 58:2. *Herod heard John Baptist gladly,* Mk. 6:20. *Thou art unto them as a very lovely song.* Ezekiel's matter was surprising, his language fine, his expressions elegant, his similitudes apt, his voice melodious, and his delivery graceful; so that they could sit with as much pleasure to hear him preach as (if I may speak in the language of our times) to see a play or an opera, or to hear a concert of music. Ezekiel was to them as one *that had a pleasant voice* and could sing well, *or play well on an instrument.* Note, Men may have their fancies pleased by the word, and yet not have their consciences touched nor their hearts changed, the itching ear gratified and yet not the corrupt nature sanctified.

2. The hypocrisy of these professions and pretensions; it is all a sham, it is all a jest. (1.) They have no cordial affection for the word of God. While they *show much love* it is only *with the mouth,* from the teeth outward, but *their heart goes after their covetousness;* they are as much set upon the world as ever, as much in love and league with it as ever. Hearing the word is only their diversion and recreation, a pretty amusement now and then for an hour or two. But still their main business is with their farm and merchandise; the bent and bias of their souls are towards them, and their *inward thoughts* are employed in projects about them. Note, Covetousness is the ruining sin of multitudes that make a great profession of religion; it is the love of the world that secretly eats the love of God out of their hearts. *The cares of* this world and the deceitfulness of riches are the *thorns* that *choke the seed,* and choke the soul too. And those neither please God nor profit themselves who, when they are hearing the word of God, are musing upon their worldly affairs. God has his eye on the hearts that do so. (2.) They yield no subjection to it. They *hear thy words,* but it is only a hearing that they *give thee,* for they *will not do them, v.* 31. And again (*v.* 32), they *do them not.* They will not be persuaded by all the prophet can say, either by authority or argument, to cross themselves in any instance, to part with any one beloved sin, or apply themselves to any one duty that is against the grain to flesh and blood. Note, There are many who take pleasure in hearing the word, but make no conscience of doing it; and so they build upon the sand, and deceive themselves.

3. Let us see what will be in the end hereof: *Shall their unbelief* and carelessness *make the word of God of no effect?* By no means. (1.) God will confirm the prophet's word, though they contemn it, and make light of it, *v.* 33. What he says will come to pass, and not one jot or one tittle shall fall to the ground. Note, The curses of the law, though they may be bantered by profane wits, cannot be baffled. (2.) They themselves shall rue their folly when it is too late. When it comes to pass *they shall know,* shall know to their cost, know to their confusion, that *a prophet has been among them,* though they made no more of him than as one that *had a pleasant voice.* Note, Those who will not consider that a prophet is among them, and who improve not the day of their visitation while it is continued, will be made to remember that a prophet has been among them when the things that belong to their peace are *hidden from their eyes.* The day is coming when vain and worldly men will have other thoughts of things than now they have, and will feel a weight in that which they made light of. They shall know that *a prophet has been among them* when they see the event exactly answer the prediction, and the prophet himself shall be a witness against them that they had fair warning given them, but would not take it. When Ezekiel is gone, whom now they speak against, and *there is no more any prophet,* nor any *to show them how long,* then they will remember that once they had a prophet, but knew not how to use him well. Note, Those who will not know the worth of mercies by the improvement of them will justly be made to know the worth of them by the want of them, as those who should desire to see one of the days of the Son of man, which now they slighted, and might not see it.

CHAPTER 34

The iniquities and calamities of God's Israel had been largely and pathetically lamented before, in this book. Now in this chapter the shepherds of Israel, their rulers both in church and state, are called to an account, as having been very much accessory to the sin and ruin of Israel, by their neglecting to do the duty of their place. Here is, I. A high charge exhibited against them for their negligence, their unskillfulness, and unfaithfulness in the management of public affairs (*v.* 1–6 and *v.* 8). II. Their discharge from their trust, for their insufficiency and treachery (*v.* 7–10). III. A gracious promise that God would take care of his flock, though they did not, and that it should not always suffer as it had done by their maladministrations (*v.* 11–16). IV. Another charge exhibited against those of the flock that were fat and strong, for the injuries they did to those that were weak and feeble (*v.* 17–22). V. Another promise that God would in the fulness of time send the Messiah, to be the great and good Shepherd of the sheep, who should redress all grievances and set every thing to rights with the flock (*v.* 23–31).

Verses 1–6

The prophecy of this chapter is not dated, nor any of those that follow it, till *ch.* 40. It is most probable that it was delivered after the completing of Jerusalem's destruction, when it would be very seasonable to enquire into the causes of it.

I. The prophet is ordered to *prophesy against the shepherds of Israel* — the princes and magistrates, the priests and Levites, the great Sanhedrim or council of state, or whoever they were that had the direction of public affairs in a higher or lower sphere, the kings especially, for there were two of them now captives in Babylon, who, as well as the people, must have their transgressions shown them, that they might repent, as Manasseh in his captivity. God has something to *say to the shepherds,* for they are but under-shepherds, accountable to him who is the great *Shepherd of Israel,* Ps. 80:1. And that which he says is, *Woe to the shepherds of Israel!* Though they are shepherds, and shepherds of Israel, yet he must not spare them, must not flatter them. Note, If men's dignity and power do not, as they ought, keep them from sin, they will not serve to exempt them from reproof, to excuse their repentance, or to secure them from the judgments of God if they do not repent. We had a *woe to the pastors,* Jer. 23:1. God will in a particular manner reckon with them if they be false to their trust.

II. He is here directed what to charge the shepherds with, in God's name, as the ground of God's controversy with them; for it is not a causeless quarrel. Two things they are charged with: — 1. That all their care was to advance and enrich themselves and to make themselves great. Their business was to take care of those that were committed to their charge: *Should not the shepherds feed the flocks?* No doubt they should; they betray their trust if they do not. Not that they are to put the meat into their mouths, but to provide it for them and bring them to it. But *these* shepherds made this the least of their care; they *fed themselves,* contrived every thing to gratify and indulge their own appetite, and to make themselves rich and great, fat and easy. They made sure of the profits of their places; they did *eat the fat,* the *cream* (so some), for he *that feeds a flock eats of the milk of it* (1 Co. 9:7), and they made sure of the best of the milk. They made sure of the fleece, and *clothed themselves with the wool,* getting into their hands as much as they could of the estates of their subjects, yea, and *killed those that were* well *fed,* that what they had might be fed upon, as Naboth was put to death for his vineyard. Note, There is a woe to those who are in public trusts, but consult only their own private interest, and are more inquisitive about the benefice than about the office, what money is to be got than what good to be done. It is an old complaint, *All seek their own,* and too many *more than their own.* 2. That they took no care for the benefit and welfare of those that were committed to their charge: *You feed not the flock.* They neither knew how to do it, so ignorant were they, nor would they take any pains to do it, so lazy and slothful were they; nay, they never desired nor designed it, so treacherous and unfaithful were they. (1.) They did not do their duty to those of the flock that were distempered, did not strengthen them, nor heal them, nor bind them up, *v.* 4. When any of the flock were sick or hurt, worried or wounded, it was all one to them whether they lived or died; they never looked after them. The princes and judges took no care to right those that suffered wrong or to shelter injured innocency. They took no care of the poor to see them provided for; they might starve, for them. The priests took no care to instruct the ignorant, to rectify the mistakes of those that were in error, to warn the unruly, or to comfort the feeble-minded. The ministers of state took no care to check the growing distempers of the kingdom, which threatened the vitals of it. Things were amiss, and out of course, every where, and nothing was done to rectify them. (2.) They did not do their duty to those of the flock that were dispersed, that were driven away by the enemies that invaded the country, and were forced to seek for shelter where they could find a place, or that *wandered* of choice upon *the mountains and hills* (*v.* 6), where they were exposed to the beasts of prey and became *meat to them, v.* 5. Every one is ready to seize a waif and stray. Some went abroad and begged, some went abroad and traded, and thus the country became thin of inhabitants, and was weakened and impoverished, and wanted hands both in the fields of corn and in the fields of battle, both in harvest and in war: *My flock was scattered upon all the face of the earth, v.* 6. And they were never enquired after, were never encouraged to return to their own country: *None did search or seek after them.* Nay, *with force and cruelty they ruled them,* which drove more away, and discouraged those that were driven away from all thoughts of returning. *Their* case is bad who have reason to expect better treatment among strangers than in their own country. It may be meant of those of the flock that went astray from God and their duty; and the priests, that should have taught the good knowledge of the Lord, used no means to convince and reclaim them, so that they became an easy prey to seducers. Thus were *they scattered because there was no shepherd, v.* 5. There were those that called themselves shepherds, but really they were not. Note, Those that do not do the work of shepherds are unworthy of the name. And if those that undertake to be shepherds are *foolish shepherds* (Zec. 11:15), if they are proud and above their business, idle and do not love their business, or faithless and unconcerned about it, the case of the flock is as bad as if it were without a shepherd. Better no shepherd than such shepherds. Christ complains that his flock were *as sheep having no shepherd,* when yet the scribes and Pharisees *sat in Moses' seat,* Mt. 9:36. It is ill with the patient when his physician is his worst disease, ill with the flock when the shepherds drive them away and disperse them, *by ruling them with force.*

Verses 7–16

Upon reading the foregoing articles of impeachment drawn up, in God's name, against the shepherds of Israel, we cannot but look upon the shepherds with a just indignation, and upon the flock with a tender compassion. God, by the prophet, here expresses both in a high degree; and the shepherds are called upon (*v.* 7, 9) to *hear the word of the Lord,* to hear this word. Let them hear how little he regards them, who made much of themselves, and how much he regards the flock, which they made nothing of; both will be humbling to them. Those that will not *hear the word of the Lord* giving them their direction shall be made to hear the word of the Lord reading them their doom. Now see here,

I. How much displeased God is at the shepherds. Their crimes are repeated, *v.* 8. God's flock became a prey to the deceivers first that drew them to idolatry, and then to the destroyers that carried them into captivity; and these shepherds took no care to prevent either the one or the other, but were as if there had been *no shepherds;* and therefore God says (*v.* 10), and confirms it with an oath (*v.* 8), *I am against the shepherds.* They had a commission from God to feed the flock, and made use of this name in what they did, expecting he would stand by them. "No," says God, "so far from that, *I am against them.*" Note, It is not our having the name and authority of shepherds that will engage God for us, if we do not the work enjoined us, and be not faithful to the trust reposed in us. God is *against them,* and they shall know it; for, 1. They shall be made to account for the manner in which they have discharged their trust: *"I will require my flock at their hands,* and charge it upon them that so many of them are missing." Note, Those will have a great deal to answer for in the judgment-day who take upon them the care of souls and yet take no care of them. Ministers must *watch* and work as those that *must give account,* Heb. 13:17. 2. They shall be deprived *officio et beneficio — both of the work and of the wages. They shall cease from feeding the flock,* that is, from pretending to feed it. Note, It is just with God to take out of men's hands that power which they have abused and that trust which they have betrayed. But, if this were all their punishment, they could bear it well enough; therefore it is added, *"Neither shall the shepherds feed themselves any more,* for *I will deliver my flock from their mouth,* which, instead of protecting, they had made a prey of." Note, Those that are enriching themselves with the spoils of the public cannot expect that they shall always be suffered to do so. Nor will God always permit his people to be trampled upon by those that should support them, but will find a time to deliver them from the shepherds their false friends, as well as from the lions their open enemies.

II. How much concerned God is for the flock; he speaks as if he were the more concerned for them because he saw them thus neglected, for *with him the fatherless finds mercy.* Precious promises are made here upon the occasion, which were to have their accomplishment in the return of the Jews out of their captivity and their re-establishment in their own land. Let the shepherds *hear this word of the Lord,* and know that they have no part nor lot in the matter. But let the poor sheep hear it and take the comfort of it. Note, Though magistrates and ministers fail in doing their part, for the good of the church, yet God will not fail in doing his; he will take the flock into his own hand rather than the church shall come short of any kindness he has designed for it. The under-shepherds may prove careless, but the chief Shepherd *neither slumbers nor sleeps.* They may be false, but God *abides faithful.*

1. God will gather his sheep together that were scattered, and bring those back to the fold that had wandered from it: *"I, even I,* who alone can do it, will do it, and will have all the glory of it. *I will both search my sheep and find them out* (*v.* 11) as a *shepherd* does (*v.* 12), and bring them back as he does the stray-sheep, upon his shoulders, *from all the places where they have been scattered in the cloudy and dark day."* There are cloudy and dark days, windy and stormy ones, which scatter God's sheep, which send them hither and thither, to divers and distant places, in quest of secresy and safety. But, (1.) Wherever they are the eye of God will *find them out;* for his eyes run to and fro through the earth, in favour of them. *I will seek out my sheep;* and not one that belongs to the fold, though driven ever so far off, shall be lost. *The Lord knows those that are his;* he *knows their work* and *where they dwell* (Rev. 2:13), and where they are hidden. (2.) When his time shall come his arms will *fetch them home* (*v.* 13): *I will bring them out from the people.* God will both incline their hearts to come by his grace and will by his providence open a door for them and remove every difficulty that lies in the way. They shall not return one by one, clandestinely stealing away, but they shall return in a body: *"I will gather them from the countries* into which they are dispersed, not only the most considerable families of them, but every particular person. *I will seek that which was lost and bring again that which was driven away," v.* 16. This was done when so many thousand Jews returned triumphantly out of Babylon, under the conduct of Zerubbabel, Ezra, and others. When those that have gone astray from God into the paths of sin are brought back by repentance, when those that erred come to the acknowledgment of the truth, when God's outcasts are gathered and restored, and religious assemblies, that were dispersed, rally again, upon the ceasing of persecution, and when the churches have rest and liberty, then this promise has a further accomplishment.

2. God will feed his people as the *sheep of his pasture,* that had been famished. God will bring the returning captives safely to their own land (*v.* 13), *will feed them upon the mountains of Israel,* and that is a *good pasture,* and a *fat pasture* (*v.* 14); there shall their *feeding* be, and there shall be *their fold;* and it is a *good fold.* There God will not only *feed them,* but *cause them to lie down* (*v.* 15), which denotes a comfortable rest after they had tired themselves with their wanderings, and a constant continuing residence; they shall not be driven out again from these green pastures, as they have been, nor shall they be disturbed, but shall lie down in a sweet repose and there shall be *none to make them afraid.* Ps. 23:2, *He makes me to lie down in green pastures.* Compare this with the like promise (Jer. 23:3, 4), when God restored them not only to the milk and honey of their own land, to the enjoyment of its fruits, but to the privileges of his sanctuary on Mount Zion, the chief of the mountains of Israel. When

they had an altar and a temple again, and the benefit of a settled priesthood, then they were fed in a good pasture.

3. He will succour those that are hurt, will *bind up that which was broken and strengthen that which was sick,* will comfort those that *mourn in Zion* and with Zion. If ministers, who should speak peace to those who are of a sorrowful spirit, neglect their duty, yet the Holy Ghost the Comforter will be faithful to his office. But, as it follows, the *fat and the strong shall be destroyed.* He that has rest for disquieted saints has terror to speak to presumptuous sinners. As *every valley* shall be *filled,* so *every mountain and hill shall be brought low,* Lu. 3:5.

Verses 17–31

The prophet has no more to say to the shepherds, but he has now a message to deliver to the flock. God had ordered him to speak tenderly to them, and to assure them of the mercy he had in store for them. But here he is ordered to make a difference between some and others of them, to separate between the precious and the vile and then to give them a promise of the Messiah, by whom this distinction should be effectually made, partly at his first coming (for *for judgment he came into this world,* Jn. 9:39, to *fill the hungry with good things and to send the rich empty away,* Lu. 1:53), but completely at his second coming, when he shall, as it is here said, *judge between cattle and cattle, as a shepherd divides between the sheep and the goats, and shall set the sheep on his right hand and the goats on his left* (Mt. 25:32, 33), which seems to have reference to this. We have here,

I. Conviction spoken to those of the flock that were fat and strong, the *rams and the he-goats* (v. 17), those that, though they had not power, as shepherds and rulers, to oppress with, yet, being rich and wealthy, made use of the opportunity which this gave them to bear hard upon their poor neighbours. Those that have much would have more, and, if they set to it, will have more, so many ways have they of encroaching upon their poor neighbours, and forcing from them the one ewe-lamb, 2 Sa. 12:4. Do not the rich oppress the poor merely with the help of their riches, and *draw them before the judgment-seats?* Jam. 2:6. Poor servants and tenants are hardly used by their rich lords and masters. The *rams* and the *he-goats* not only kept all the good pasture to themselves, ate the fat and drank the sweet, but they would not let the poor of the flock have any comfortable enjoyment of the little that was left them; they *trod down the residue of the pastures and fouled the residue of the waters,* so that the flock was obliged to eat that which they had trodden into the dirt, and drink that which they had muddied, v. 18, 19. This intimates that the great men not only by extortion and oppression made and kept their neighbours poor, and scarcely left them enough to subsist on, but were so vexatious to them that what little coarse fare they had was embittered to them. And this *seemed a small thing* to them; they thought there was no harm in it, as if it were the privilege of their quality to be injurious to all their neighbours. Note, Many that live in pomp and at ease themselves care not what straits those about them are reduced to, so they may but have every thing to their mind. Those that *are at ease,* and *the proud,* grudge that any body should live by them with any comfort. But this as not all; they not only robbed the poor, to make them poorer, but were troublesome to the sick and weak of the flock (v. 21): They *thrust with side and shoulder* those that were feeble (for the weakest goes to the wall) and *pushed the diseased with their horns,* because they knew they could be too hard for them, when they durst not meddle with their match. It has been observed concerning sheep that if one of the flock be sick and faint the rest will secure it as well as they can, and shelter it from the scorching heat of the sun; but these, on the contrary, were most injurious to the diseased. Those that they could not serve themselves of they did what they could to rid the country of, and so *scattered them abroad,* as if the poor, whom, Christ says, we must have always with us, were public nuisances, not to be relieved, but sent far away from us. Note, It is a barbarous thing to *add affliction to the afflicted.* Perhaps these *rams* and *he-goats* are designed to represent the scribes and Pharisees, for they are such troublers of the church as Christ himself must come to deliver it from. v. 23. They devoured widows' houses, took away the key of knowledge, corrupted the pure water of divine truths, and oppressed the consciences of men with the traditions of the elders, besides that they were continually vexatious and injurious to *the poor of the flock* that *waited on the Lord,* Zec. 11:11. Note, It is no new thing for the flock of God to receive a great deal of damage and mischief from those that are themselves of the flock, and in eminent stations in it, Acts 20:30.

II. Comfort spoken to those of the flock that are poor and feeble, and that wait for the consolation of Israel (v. 22): "*I will save my flock,* and they shall no more be spoiled as they have been by the beasts of prey, by their own shepherds or by the rams and he-goats among themselves." Upon this occasion, as is usual in the prophets, comes in a prediction of the coming of the Messiah, and the setting up of his kingdom, and the exceedingly great and precious benefits which the church should enjoy under the protection and influence of that kingdom. Observe what is here foretold,

1. Concerning the Messiah himself. (1.) He shall have his commission from God himself: I will *set him up* (v. 23); *I will raise him up,* v. 29. He sanctified and sealed him, appointed and anointed him. (2.) He shall be the great *Shepherd* of the sheep, who shall do that for his flock which no one else could do. He is the *one Shepherd,* under whom Jews and Gentiles should be *one fold.* (3.) He is *God's servant,* employed by him and for him, and doing all in obedience to his will, with an eye to his glory — his servant, to re-establish his kingdom among men and advance the interests of that kingdom. (4.) He is David, one after God's own heart, set as his King upon the holy hill of Zion, made the head of the corner, with whom the covenant of royalty is made, and to whom God would *give the throne of his father David.* He is both the *root and offspring of David.* (5.) He is the *plant of renown,* because a *righteous branch* (Jer. 23:5), a branch of the Lord, that is *beautiful and glorious,* Isa. 4:2. He has a name above every name, a throne above every throne, and may therefore well be called a *branch of renown.* Some understand it of the church, the *planting of the Lord,* Isa. 61:3. *Its name shall be remembered* (Ps. 45:17) and Christ's in it.

2. Concerning the great charter by which the kingdom of the Messiah should be incorporated, and upon which it should be founded (v. 25): *I will make with them a covenant of peace.* The covenant of grace is a covenant of peace. In it God is at peace with us, speaks peace to us, and assures us of peace, of all good, all the good we need to make us happy. The tenour of this covenant is: "*I the Lord will be their God,* a God all-sufficient to them (v. 24), will own them and will be owned by them; in order to this *my servant David shall be a prince among them,* to reduce them to their allegiance, to receive their homage, and to reign over them, in them, and for them." Note, Those, and those only, that have the Lord Jesus for *their prince* have the Lord Jehovah for *their God.* And then *they, even the house of Israel, shall be my people.* If we take God to be *our God,* he will take us to be *his people.* From this covenant between God and Israel there results communion: "*I the Lord their God am with them,* to converse with them; and *they shall know it,* and have the comfort of it."

3. Concerning the privileges of those that are the faithful subjects of this kingdom of the Messiah and interested in the covenant of peace. These are here set forth figuratively, as the blessings of the flock. But we have a key to it, v. 31. Those that belong to this flock, though they are spoken of as *sheep,* are really men, men that have *the Lord for their God,* and are in covenant with him. Now to them it is promised,

(1.) That they shall enjoy a holy security under the divine protection. Christ, our good Shepherd, has *caused the evil beasts to cease out of the land* (v. 25), having vanquished all our spiritual enemies, broken their power, and triumphed over them; the roaring lion is not a roaring devouring lion to them; *they shall no more be a prey to the heathen* nor the heathen a terror to them, *neither shall the beasts of the land devour them.* Sin and Satan, death and hell, are conquered. And then *they shall dwell safely,* not only in the folds, but in the fields, *in the wilderness, in the woods,* where the beasts of prey are; they shall not only dwell there, but they shall sleep there, which denotes not only that the beasts being *made to cease* there shall be no danger, but, their consciences being purified and pacified, they shall be in no apprehension of danger; not only safe from evil, but quiet from the fear of evil. Note, Those may lay down and sleep securely, sleep at ease, that have Christ for their prince; for he will be their protector, and make them to dwell in safety. None shall hurt them, nay, *none shall make them afraid.* If God be for us, who can be against us? *Therefore will not we fear, though the earth be removed.* Through Christ, God delivers his people not only from the things they have reason to fear, but from their fear even of death itself, from all that fear that has torment. This safety from evil is promised (v. 27): *They shall be safe in their land,* in no danger of being invaded and enslaved, though their great plenty be a temptation to their neighbours to *desire their land;* and that which shall make them think themselves safe is their confidence in the wisdom, power, and goodness of God: *They shall know that I am the Lord.* All our disquieting fears arise from our ignorance of God and mistakes concerning him. Their experience of his particular care concerning them encourages their confidence in him: "*I have broken the bands of their yoke,* with which they have been brought and held down under oppression, and have *delivered them out of the hand of those that served themselves of them,* whence they shall argue, He that has delivered does and will, therefore will we dwell safely." This is explained, and applied to our gospel-state, Lu. 1:74. *That we, being delivered out of the hand of our enemies, might serve him without fear,* as those may do that serve him in faith.

(2.) That they shall enjoy a spiritual plenty of all good things, the best things, for their comfort and happiness: *They shall no more be consumed with hunger in the land,* v. 29. Famine and scarcity, when Israel was punished with that judgment, turned as much to their reproach among the heathen as any other, because the fruitfulness of Canaan was so much talked of. But now *they shall not bear that shame of the heathen any more.* For the *showers shall come down in their season,* even *showers of blessing,* v. 26. Christ is a Shepherd that will feed his people, and they shall *go in and out, and find pasture.* [1.] They shall not be consumed with hunger; for they shall not be put off with the world for a portion, which is not bread, which satisfies not, and which leaves those that are put off with it to be *consumed with hunger.* The ordinances of the ceremonial law are called *beggarly elements,* for there was little in them, compared with the Christian institutes, *wherewith the mower fills his hand and he that binds sheaves his bosom.* Those that *hunger and thirst after righteousness* shall not be consumed with that hunger, for *they shall be filled.* And he that drinks of the water that Christ gives him, the still waters by which he leads his sheep, shall *never thirst.* [2.] *Showers of blessings* shall come upon them, v. 26, 27. The heavens shall yield their dews; the *trees of the field* also shall *yield their fruit.* The seat of this plenty is *God's hill,* his holy hill of Zion, for on that mountain, in the gospel-church, it is, that God has *made to all nations a feast;* to that those must join themselves who would partake of gospel benefits. The cause of this plenty is the *showers that come down in their season,* that descend upon the mountains of Zion, the graces of Christ, his doctrine that drops as the dew, the graces of Christ, and the fruits and comforts of his Spirit, by which we are made fruitful in the fruits of righteousness. The instances of this plenty are the blessings of heaven poured down upon us and the productions of grace brought forth by us, our comfort in God's favour and God's glory in our fruit-bearing. The extent of this plenty is very large, to all the *places round about my hill;* for *out of Zion shall go forth the law,* shall go forth light to a dark world, and the river that shall water a dry and desert world; all that are in the neighbourhood of Zion shall fare the better for it; and the nearer the church the nearer its God. And, *lastly,* The *effect of this plenty* is, *I will make them a blessing,* eminently and exemplarily blessed, patterns of happiness, Isa. 19:24. Or, They shall be blessings to all about them, diffusively useful. Note, Those that are the *blessed of the Lord* must study to make themselves blessings to the world. He that is good, let him do good; he that has received the gift, the grace, let him minister the same.

Now this promise of the Messiah and his kingdom spoke much comfort to those to whom it was then made, for they might be sure that God would not utterly *destroy* their nation, how low soever it might be brought, as long as that *blessing* was *in* the womb of *it,* Isa. 65:8. But it speaks much more comfort to us, to whom it is fulfilled, who are the sheep of this good Shepherd, are fed in his pastures, and *blessed with all spiritual blessings in heavenly things* by him.

CHAPTER 35

It was promised, in the foregoing chapter, that when the time to favour Zion, yea, the set time, should come, especially the time for sending the Messiah and setting up his kingdom in the world, God would cause the enemies of his church to cease and the blessings and comforts of the church to abound. This chapter enlarges upon the former promise, concerning the destruction of the enemies of the church; the next chapter upon the latter promise, the replenishing of the church with blessings. Mount Seir (that is, Edom) is the enemy prophesied against in this chapter, but fitly put here, as in the prophecy of Obadiah, for all the enemies of the church; for, as those all walked in the way of Cain that hated Abel, so those all walked in the way of Esau who hated Jacob, but over whom Jacob, by virtue of a particular blessing, was to have dominion. Now here we have, I. The sin charged upon the Edomites, and that was their spite and malice to Israel (*v.* 5, 10–13). II. The ruin threatened, that should come upon them for this sin. God will be against them (*v.* 3) and then their country shall be laid waste (*v.* 4), depopulated, and made quite desolate (*v.* 6–9), and left so when other nations that had been wasted should recover themselves (*v.* 14, 15).

Verses 1–9

Mount Seir was mentioned as partner with Moab in one of the threatenings we had before (*ch.* 25:8); but here it is convicted and condemned by itself, and has woes of its own. The prophet must boldly *set his face against Edom,* and *prophesy* particularly *against it;* for the God of Israel has said, *O Mount Seir! I am against thee.* Note, Those that have God against them have the word of God against them, and the face of his ministers, nor dare they prophesy any good to them, but evil. The prophet must tell the Edomites that God has a controversy with them, and let them know,

I. What is the cause and ground of that controversy, *v.* 5. God espouses his people's cause, and will plead it, takes what is done against them as done against himself, and will reckon for it; and it is upon their account that God now contends with the Edomites. 1. Because of the enmity they had against the people of God, that was rooted in the heart. "Thou hast had a *perpetual hatred* to them, to the very name of an Israelite." The Edomites kept up an *hereditary* malice against Israel, the same that Esau bore to Jacob, because he got the birth-right and the blessing. Esau had been reconciled to Jacob, had embraced and kissed him (Gen. 33), and we do not find that ever he quarrelled with him again. But the posterity of Esau would never be reconciled to the seed of Jacob, but hated them with a perpetual hatred. Note, Children will be more apt to imitate the vices than the virtues of their parents, and to tread in the steps of their sin than in the steps of their repentance. Parents should therefore be careful not to set their children any bad example, for though, through the grace of God, they may return, and prevent the mischief of what they have done amiss to themselves, they may not be able to obviate the bad influence of it upon their children. It is strange how deeply rooted national antipathies sometimes are, and how long they last; but it is not to be wondered at that profane Edomites hate pious Israelites, since the old *enmity* that was put between the *seed of the woman* and the seed of the serpent (Gen. 3:15) will continue to the end. *Marvel not if the world hate you.* 2. Because of the injuries they had done to the people of God. They *shed their blood by the force of the sword, in the time of their calamity;* they did not attack them as fair and open enemies, but laid wait for them, to *cut off* those of them that had escaped (Obad. 14), or they drove them back upon the sword of the pursuers, by which they fell. It was cowardly, as well as barbarous, to take advantage of their distress; and for neighbours, with whom they had lived peaceably, to *smite them secretly* when strangers openly invaded them. It was in the time *that their iniquity had an end,* when the measure of it was full and destruction came. Note, Even those that suffer justly, and for their sins, are yet to be pitied and not trampled upon. If the father corrects one child, he expects the rest should tremble at it, not triumph in it.

II. What should be the effect and issue of that controversy. If God stretch out his hand against the country of Edom, he will *make it most desolate, v.* 3. *Desolation and desolation.* 1. The inhabitants shall be slain with the sword

(*v.* 6): *I will prepare thee unto blood.* Edom shall be gradually weakened, and so be the more easily conquered, and the enemy shall gather strength the more effectually to subdue it. Thus preparation is in the making a great while before for this destruction. *Thou hast not hated blood;* it implies, "Thou hast delighted in it and thirsted after it." Those that do not keep up a rooted hatred of sin, when a temptation to it is very strong, will be in danger of yielding to it. Some read it, *"Unless thou hatest blood"* (that is, "unless thou dost repent, and put off this bloody disposition) *blood shall pursue thee."* And then it is an intimation that the judgment may yet be prevented by a thorough reformation. *If he turn not, he will whet his sword,* Ps. 7:12. But, if he turn, he will lay it by. *Blood shall pursue thee,* the *guilt* of the blood which thou hast shed or the *judgment* of blood; thy blood-thirsty enemies shall pursue thee, which way soever thou seekest to make thy escape. A great and general slaughter shall be made of the Idumeans, such as had been foretold (Is. 34:6): The *mountains and hills, the valleys and rivers,* shall be *filled with the slain, v.* 8. The pursuers shall overtake those that flee and shall give no quarter, but put them all to the sword. Note, When God comes to make inquisition for blood those that have shed the blood of his Israel shall have blood given them to drink, for they are worthy. *Satia te sanguine quem sitisti — Glut thyself with blood, after which thou hast thirsted.* 2. The country shall be laid waste. The cities shall be destroyed (*v.* 4), the *country made most desolate* (*v.* 7; for God will *cut off* from both him that *passes out* and *him that returns;* and when the inhabitants are cut off that should keep the cities in repair they will decay and go into ruins, and when those are cut off that should till the land that will soon be over-run with briers and thorns and become a wilderness. Note, Those that help forward the desolations of Israel may expect to be themselves made desolate. And that which completes the judgment is that Edom shall be made *perpetual desolations* (*v.* 9) and the cities shall never return to their former state, nor the inhabitants of them come back from their captivity and dispersion. Note, Those that have a perpetual enmity to God and his people, as the carnal mind has, can expect no other than to be made a perpetual desolation. Implacable malice will justly be punished with irreparable ruin.

Verses 10–15

Here is, I. A further account of the sin of the Edomites, and their bad conduct towards the people of God. We find the church complaining of them for setting on the Babylonians, and irritating them against Jerusalem, saying, *Rase it, rase it,* down with it, down with it (Ps. 137:7), inflaming a rage that needed no spur; here it is further charged upon them that they triumphed in Jerusalem's ruin and in the desolations of the country. Many *blasphemies* they spoke against the *mountains of Israel,* saying, with pride and pleasure, *They are laid desolate, v.* 12. Note, The troubles of God's church, as they give proofs of the constancy and fidelity of its friends, so they discover and draw out the corruptions of its enemies, in whom there then appears more brutish malice than one would have thought of. Now their triumphing in Jerusalem's ruin is here said to proceed, 1. From a sinful passion against the people of Israel; from *anger* and *envy,* and *hatred against them* (*v.* 11), that *perpetual hatred* spoken of *v.* 5. Though they were not a match for them, and therefore could not do them a mischief themselves, yet they were glad when the Chaldeans did them a mischief. 2. From a sinful appetite to the land of Israel. They pleased themselves with hopes that when the people of Israel were destroyed they should be let into the possession of their country, which they had so often grudged and envied them. They thought they could make out something of a title to it, *ob defectum sanguinis — for want of other heirs.* If Jacob's issue fail, they think that they are next in the entail, and that the remainder will be to his brother's issue: *"These two nations of Judah and Israel shall be mine.* Now is the time for me to put in for them." At least they hope to come in as first occupants, being near neighbours: *We will possess it* when it is deserted. *Ceditur occupanti — Let us get possession and that will be title enough.* Note, Those have the spirit of Edomites who desire the death of others because they hope to get by it, or are pleased with their failing because they expect to come into their business. When we see the

vanity of the world in the disappointments, losses, and crosses, that others meet with in it, instead of showing ourselves, upon such an occasion, greedy of it, we should rather be made thereby to sit more loose to it, and both take our affections off it and lower our expectations from it. But in this case of the Edomites' coveting the land of Israel, and gaping for it, there was a particular affront to God, when they said, *"These lands are given us to devour,"* and we shall have our bellies full of their riches." God says, *You have boasted against me and have multiplied your words against me;* for they expected possession upon a vacancy, because Israel was driven out, *whereas the Lord was still there, v.* 10. His temple indeed was burnt, and the other tokens of his presence were gone; but his promise to give that land to the seed of Jacob for an inheritance was not made void, but remained in full force and virtue; and by that promise he did in effect still keep possession for Israel, till they should in due time be restored to it. That was Immanuel's land (Isa. 8:8); in that land he was to be born, and therefore that people shall continue in it of whom he is to be born, till he has passed his time in it, and then let who will take it. *The Lord is there,* the Lord Jesus is to be there; and therefore Israel's discontinuance of possession is no defeasance of their right, but it shall be kept for them, and they shall have, hold, and enjoy it by virtue of the divine grant, till the promise of this Canaan shall by the Messiah be changed into the promise of a far better. Note, It is a piece of presumption highly offensive to God for Edomites to lay claim to those privileges and comforts that are peculiar to God's chosen Israel and are reserved for them. It is *blasphemy against the mountains of Israel,* the holy mountains, to say, because they are for the present made a prey of and *trodden under foot of the Gentiles* (Rev. 11:2), even the *holy city* itself, that therefore the *Lord has forsaken them,* their *God has forgotten them.* The apostle will by no means admit such a thought as this, that *God hath cast away his people,* Rom. 11:1. No; though they are cast down for a time, they are not cast off for ever. Those *reproach the Lord* who say they are.

II. The notice God took of the barbarous insolence of the Edomites, and the doom passed upon them for it: *I have heard all thy blasphemies, v.* 12. And again (*v.* 13), *You have multiplied your words against me,* and *I have heard them,* I have observed them, I have kept an account of them. Note, In the multitude of words, not one escapes God's cognizance; let men speak ever so much, ever so fast, though they multiply words, which they themselves regard not, but forget immediately, yet none of them are lost in the crowd, not the most idle words; but God hears them, and will be able to charge the sinner with them. All the haughty and hard speeches, particularly, which are spoken against the Israel of God, the words which are *magnified* (as it is in the margin, *v.* 13) as well as the words which are multiplied, God takes notice of. For, as the most trifling words are not below his cognizance, so the most daring are not above his rebuke. *I have heard all thy blasphemies.* This is a good reason why we should bear reproach as if we heard it not, because *God will hear,* Ps. 38:13, 15. God has heard the Edomites' blasphemy; let them therefore hear their doom, *v.* 14, 15. It was a national sin (the blasphemies charged upon them were the sense and language of all the Edomites), and therefore shall be punished with a national desolation. And, 1. It shall be a distinguishing punishment. As God has peculiar favours for Israelites, so he has peculiar plagues for Edomites: so that *"When the whole earth rejoices I will make thee desolate;* when other nations have their desolations repaired, to their joy, thine shall be *perpetual," v.* 9. 2. The punishment shall answer to the sin: *"As thou didst rejoice in the desolation of the house of Israel,* God will give thee enough of desolation; since thou art so fond of it, *thou shalt be desolate; I will make thee so."* Note, Those who, instead of weeping with the mourners, make a jest of their grievances, may justly be made to weep like the mourners, and themselves to feel the weight, to feel the smart, of those grievances which they set so light by. Some read *v.* 14 so as to complete the resemblance between the sin and the punishment: *The whole earth shall rejoice when I make thee desolate, as thou didst rejoice when Israel* was made desolate. Those that are glad at the death and fall of others may expect that others will be glad of their death, of their fall. 3. In the destruction of the enemies of the church God designs his own glory, and we may be sure that he will not come short of his design. (1.) That which he intends is to manifest himself, as a just and jealous God, firm to his covenant and faithful to his people and their injured cause (*v.* 11): *I will make myself known among them when I have judged thee.* The Lord is and will be known by the judgments which he executes. (2.) His intention shall be fully answered; not only his own people shall be made to know it to their comfort, but even the Edomites themselves, and all the other enemies of his name and people, *shall know that he is the Lord, v.* 4, 9, 15. As the works of creation and common providence demonstrate that there is a God, so the care taken of Israel shows that Jehovah, the God of Israel, is that God alone, the true and living God.

CHAPTER 36

We have done with Mount Seir, and left it desolate, and likely to continue so, and must now turn ourselves, with the prophet, to the mountains of Israel, which we find desolate too, but hope before we have done with the chapter to leave in better plight. Here are two distinct prophecies in this chapter: — I. Here is one that seems chiefly to relate to the temporal estate of the Jews, wherein their present deplorable condition is described and the triumphs of their neighbours in it; but it is promised that their grievances shall be all redressed and that in due time they shall be settled again in their own land, in the midst of peace and plenty (*v.* 1–15). II. Here is another that seems chiefly to concern their spiritual estate, wherein they are reminded of their former sins and God's judgments upon them, to humble them for their sins and under God's mighty hand (*v.* 16–20). But it is promised, 1. That God would glorify himself in showing mercy to them (*v.* 21–24). 2. That he would sanctify them, by giving them his grace and fitting them for his service; and this for his own name's sake and in answer to their prayers (*v.* 25–38).

Verses 1–15

The prophet had been ordered to set his face *towards the mountains of Israel* and *prophesy against them, ch.* 6:2. Then God was coming forth to contend with his people; but now that God is returning in mercy to them he must speak good words and comfortable words to these mountains, *v.* 1 and again *v.* 4. *You mountains of Israel, hear the word of the Lord;* and what he says to them he says *to the hills, to the rivers, to the valleys, to the desolate wastes* in the country, and to the cities *that are forsaken, v.* 4. and again *v.* 6. The people were gone, some one way and some another; nothing remained there to be spoken to but the places, the mountains and valleys; these the Chaldeans could not carry away with them. *The earth abides for ever.* Now, to show the mercy God had in reserve for the people, he is to speak of him as having a dormant kindness for the place, which, if the Lord had been pleased for ever to abandon, he would not have called upon to *hear the word of the Lord,* nor *would he as at this time have shown it such things as these.* Here is,

I. The compassionate notice God takes of the present deplorable condition of the land of Israel. It has become both a *prey* and a *derision to the heathen that are round about, v.* 4. 1. It has become a prey to them; and they are all enriched with the plunder of it. When the Chaldeans had conquered them all their neighbours flew to the spoil as to a shipwreck, every one thinking all his own that he could lay his hands on (*v.* 3): *They have made you desolate, and swallowed you up on every side, that you might be a possession to the heathen,* to the *residue* of them, even such as had themselves narrowly escaped the like desolation. No one thought it any crime to strip an Israelite. *Turba Romae sequitur fortunam ut semper — The mob of Rome still praise the elevated and despise the fallen.* It is the common dry, when a man is down, *Down with him.* 2. It has become a derision to them. They took all they had and laughed at them when they had done. *The enemy said, "Aha! even the ancient high places are ours in possession, v.* 2. Neither the antiquity, nor the dignity, neither the sanctity nor the fortifications, of the land of Israel, are its security, but we have become masters of it all." The more honours that land had been adorned with, and the greater figure it had made among the nations, the more pride and pleasure did they take in making a spoil of it, which is an instance of a base and sordid spirit; for the more glorious and prosperity was the more piteous is the adversity. God takes notice of it here as an aggravation of the present calamity of Israel: *You are taken up in the lips of talkers and are an infamy of the people, v.* 3. All the talk of the country about was concerning the overthrow of the Jewish nation; and every one that spoke of it had some peevish ill-natured reflection or other upon them. They were the *scorning of those that were at ease and the contempt of the proud,* Ps. 123:4. There are some that are noted for talkers, that have something to say of every body, but cannot find in their hearts to speak well of any body; God's people, among such people, were sure to be a reproach when the crown had fallen from their head. Thus it was the lot of Christianity, in its suffering days, to be *every where spoken against.*

II. The expressions of God's just displeasure against those who triumphed in the desolations of the land of Israel, as many of its neighbours did, even the residue of the brethren, and Idumea particularly. Let us see, 1. How they dealt with the Israel of God. They carved out large possessions to themselves out of their land, out of God's land; for so indeed it was: *"They have appointed my land into their possession* (*v.* 5), and so not only invaded their neighbour's property, but intrenched upon God's prerogative." It was the holy land which they laid their sacrilegious hands upon. They did not own any dependence upon God, as the God of that land, nor acknowledge any remaining interest that Israel had in it, but *cast it out for a prey,* as if they had won it in a lawful war. And this they did without any dread of God and his judgments and without any compassion for Israel and their calamities, but with the *joy of all their hearts,* because they got by it, and *with despiteful minds* to Israel that lost by it. Increasing wealth, by right or wrong, is all the joy of a worldly heart; and the calamities of God's people are all the joy of a despiteful mind. And those that had not an opportunity of making a prey of God's people made a reproach of them; so that they were *the shame of the heathen, v.* 6. Every body ridiculed them and made a jest of them; and the truth is they had by their own sin made themselves vile; so that God was righteous herein, but men were unrighteous and very barbarous. 2. How God would deal with those who were thus in word and deed abusive to his people. He has *spoken against the heathen;* he has passed sentence upon them; he has determined to reckon with them for it, and this *in the fire of his jealousy,* both for his own honour and for the honour of his people, *v.* 5. Having a *love* for both as *strong as death,* he has a *jealousy* for both as *cruel as the grave.* They spoke in their malice against God's people, and he will speak in his jealousy against them; and it is easy to say which will speak most powerfully. God will speak *in his jealousy and in his fury, v.* 6. Fury is not in God; but he will exert his power against them and handle them as severely as men do when they are in a fury. He will so *speak to them in his wrath as to vex them in his sore displeasure.* What he says he will stand to, for it is backed with an oath. He has *lifted up his hand* and sworn by himself, has sworn and will not repent. And what is it that is said with so much heat, and yet with so much deliberation? It is this (*v.* 7), *Surely the heathen that are about you, they shall bear their shame.* Note, The righteous God, to whom vengeance belongs, will render shame for shame. Those that put contempt and reproach upon God's people will, sooner or later, have it *burned upon themselves,* perhaps in this world (either their follies or their calamities, their miscarriages or their mischances, shall be their reproach), at furthest in that day when all the impenitent shall *rise to shame and everlasting contempt.*

III. The promises of God's favour to his Israel and assurances given of great mercy God had in store for them. God takes occasion from the outrage and insolence of their enemies to show himself so much the more concerned for them and ready to do them good, as David hoped that God would recompense him good for Shimei's cursing him. *Let them curse, but bless thou.* In this way, as well as others, the enemies of God's people do them real service, even by the injuries they do them, against their will and beyond their intention. We shall have no reason to complain if, the more unkind men are, the more kind God is — if, the more kindly he speaks to us by his word and Spirit, the more kindly he acts for us in his providence. The prophet must say so to the *mountains of Israel,* which were now *desolate and despised,* that God is *for them* and will *burn to them, v.* 9. As the curse of God reaches the ground for man's sake, so does the blessing. Now that which is promised is, 1. That their rightful owners should return to the possession of them: *My people Israel are at hand to come, v.* 8. Though they are at a great distance from their own country, though they are dispersed in many countries, and though they are detained by the power of their enemies, yet they shall *come again to their own border,* Jer. 31:17. The time is at hand for their return. Though there were above forty years of the seventy (perhaps fifty) yet remaining, it is spoken of as near, because it is sure, and there were some among them that should live to see it. A *thousand years are* with God but *as one day.* The mountains of Israel are now desolate; but God will *cause men to walk upon them* again, *even his people Israel,* not as travellers passing over them, but as inhabitants — not tenants, but freeholders: *They shall possess thee,* not for term of life, but for themselves and their heirs; *thou shalt be their inheritance.* It was a type of the heavenly Canaan, to which all God's children are heirs, every Israelite indeed, and into which they shall shortly be all brought together, out of the countries where they are now scattered. 2. That they should afford a plentiful comfortable maintenance for their owners at their return. When the land had *enjoyed her sabbaths* for so many years, it should be so much the more fruitful afterwards, as we should be after rest, especially a sabbath rest: *You shall be tilled and sown* (*v.* 9) and shall *yield your fruit to my people Israel, v.* 8. Note, It is a blessing to the earth to be made serviceable to men, especially to good men, that will serve God with cheerfulness in the use of those good things which the earth serves up to them. 3. That the people of Israel should have not only a comfortable sustenance, but a comfortable settlement, in their own land: The *cities shall be inhabited; the wastes shall be builded, v.* 10 And *I will settle you after your old estates, v.* 11. Their own sin had unsettled them, but now God's favour shall resettle them. When the prodigal son has become a penitent he is settled again in his father's house, according to his former estate. Bring hither the *first robe,* and put it on him. Nay, *I will do better unto you* now *than at your beginnings.* There is more joy for the sheep that is brought back than there would have been if it had never gone astray. And God sometimes multiplies his people's comforts in proportion to the *time that he has afflicted them.* Thus God blessed the latter end of Job more than his beginning, and doubled to him all he had. 4. That the people, after their return, should be *fruitful, and multiply, and replenish the land,* so that it should not only be inhabited again, but as thickly inhabited, and as well peopled, as ever. God will bring back to it *all the house of Israel, even all of it* (observe what an emphasis is laid upon that, *v.* 10), all *whose spirits God stirred up* to return; and those only were reckoned of *the house of Israel,* the rest had cut themselves off from it; or, though but few, in comparison, returned at first, yet afterwards, at divers times, they *all* returned; and then (says God) *I will multiply these men* (*v.* 10), *multiply man and beast; and they shall increase, v.* 11. Note, God's kingdom in the world is a growing kingdom; and his church, though for a time it may be diminished, shall recover itself and be again replenished. 5. That the reproach long since cast upon the land of Israel by the evil spies, and of late revived, that *it was a land that ate up the inhabitants* of it by famine, sickness, and the sword, should be quite rolled away, and there should never be any more occasion for it. Canaan had got into a bad name. It had of old *spued out the inhabitants* (Lev. 18:28), the natives, the aborigines, which was turned to its reproach by those that should have put another construction upon it, Num. 13:32. It had of late devoured the Israelites, and spued them out too; so that it was commonly said of it, It is a land which, instead of supporting its nations or tribes that inhabit it, *bereaves* them, *overthrows* them, and *causes them to fall;* it is a tenement which breaks all the tenants that come upon it. This character it had got among the neighbours; but God now promises that it shall be so no more: *Thou shalt no more bereave them of men* (*v.* 12), shalt *devour men no more, v.* 14. But the inhabitants shall live to a good old age, and not have the number of their months cut off in the midst. Compare this with that promise, Zec. 8:4. Note, God will take away the reproach of his people by taking away that which was the occasion of it. When the nation is made to flourish in peace, plenty, and power, then they *hear no more the shame of the heathen* (*v.* 15), especially when it is reformed; when sin, which is the reproach of any people, particularly of God's professing people, is taken away, then they *hear no more the reproach of the people.* Note, When

God returns in mercy to a people that return to him in duty, all their grievances will be soon redressed and their honour retrieved.

Verses 16–24

When God promised the poor captives a glorious return, in due time, to their own land, it was a great discouragement to their hopes that they were unworthy, utterly unworthy, of such a favour; therefore, to remove that discouragement, God here shows them that he would do it for them purely *for his own name's sake,* that he might be glorified in them and by them, that he might manifest and magnify his mercy and goodness, that attribute which of all others is most his glory. And, the restoration of that people being typical of our redemption by Christ, this is intended further to show that the ultimate end aimed at in our salvation, to which all the steps of it were made subservient, was the glory of God. To this end Christ directed all he did in that short prayer, *Father, glorify thy name;* and God declared it was his end in all he did in the immediate answer given to that prayer, by a voice from heaven: *I have glorified it, and I will glorify it yet again,* Jn. 12:28. Now observe here,

I. How God's name had suffered both by the sins and by the miseries of Israel; and this was more to be regretted than all their sorrow, which they had brought upon themselves; for the honour of God lies nearer the hearts of good men than any interests of their own. 1. God's glory had been injured by the sin of Israel when they were in their own land, *v.* 17. It was a good land, a holy land, a land that had the eye of God upon it. *But they defiled it by their own way,* their wicked way; that is *our own* way, the way of our own choice; and we ourselves must bear the blame and shame of it. The sin of a people defiles their land, renders it abominable to God and uncomfortable to themselves; so that they cannot have any holy communion with him nor with one another. What was unclean might not be made use of. By the abuse of the gifts of God's bounty to us we forfeit the use of them; and, the mind and conscience being defiled with guilt, no comfort is allowed us, *nothing is pure* to us. Their way in the eye of God was like the pollution of a woman during the days of her separation, which shut her out from the sanctuary and made very things she touched ceremonially unclean, Lev. 15:19. Sin is that *abominable thing which the Lord hates,* and which he cannot endure to look upon. They *shed blood* and *worshipped idols* (*v.* 18) and with those sins *defiled the land.* For this God *poured out his fury* upon them, *scattered them among the heathen.* Their own land was sick of them, and they were sent into other lands. Herein God was righteous, and was justified in what he did; none could say that he did them any wrong, nay, he did justice to his own honour, for he *judged them according to their way and according to their doings, v.* 19. And yet, the matter being not rightly understood, he was not glorified in it; for the enemies did say, as Moses pleaded the Egyptians would say if he had destroyed them in the wilderness, that *for mischief he brought them forth.* Their neighbours considered them rather as a holy people than as a sinful people, and therefore took occasion from the calamities they were in, instead of glorifying God, as they might justly have done, to reproach him and put contempt upon him; and God's name was *continually every day blasphemed* by their oppressors, Isa. 52:5. 2. When they *entered into the land of the heathen* God had no glory by them there; but, on the contrary, his holy name was profaned, *v.* 20. (1.) It was profaned by the sins of Israel; they were no credit to their profession wherever they went, but, on the contrary, a reproach to it. The *name of God* and his holy religion was *blasphemed through them,* Rom. 2:24. When those that pretended to be in relation to God, in covenant and communion with him, were found corrupt in their morals, slaves to their appetites and passions, dishonest in their dealings, and false to their words and the trust reposed in them, the enemies of the Lord had thereby great occasion given them to blaspheme, especially when they quarrelled with their God for correcting them, than which nothing could be more scandalous. (2.) It was profaned by the sufferings of Israel; for from them the enemies of God took occasion to reproach God, as unable to protect his own worshippers and to make good his own grants. They said, in scorn, *"These are the people of the*

land, these wicked people (you see he could not keep them in their obedience to his precepts), these *miserable people* — you see he could not keep them in the enjoyment of his favours. These are *the people that came out of Jehovah's land,* they are the very scum of the nations. Are these those that had statues so righteous whose lives are so unrighteous? Is this the nation that is so much celebrated for a *wise and understanding people,* and that is said to have *God so nigh unto them?* Do these belong to that brave, that holy nation, who appear here so vile, so abject?" Thus God sold his people and did not *increase his wealth by their price,* Ps. 44:12. The reproach they were under reflected upon him.

II. Let us now see how God would retrieve his honour, secure it, and advance it, by working a great reformation upon them and then working a great salvation for them. He would have *scattered them among the heathen, were it not that he feared the wrath of the enemy,* Deu. 32:26, 27. But, though they were unworthy of his compassion, yet *he had pity for his own holy name,* and a thousand pities it was that that should be trampled upon and abused. He looked with compassion on his own honour, which lay bleeding among the heathen, on that jewel which was trodden into the dirt, which *the house of Israel,* even in the land of their captivity, *had profaned, v.* 21. In pity to that God brought them out from the heathen, because their sins were more scandalous there than they had been in their own land. "Therefore I *will gather you out of all countries and bring you into your own land, v.* 24. *Not for your sake,* because you are worthy of such a favour, for you are most unworthy, but *for my holy name's sake* (*v.* 22), that *I may sanctify my great name," v.* 23. Observe, by the way, God's holy name is his great name. His holiness is his greatness; so he reckons it himself. Nor does any thing make a man truly great but being truly good, and partaking of God's holiness. God will magnify his name as a holy name, for he will sanctify it: *I will sanctify my name which you have profaned.* When God performs that which he has sworn by his holiness, then he sanctifies his name. The effect of this shall be very happy: *The heathen shall know that I am the Lord when I shall be sanctified in you before their eyes* and yours. When God proves his own holy name, and his saints praise it, then he is sanctified in them, and this contributes to the propagating of the knowledge of him. Observe, 1. God's reasons of mercy are all fetched from within himself; he will bring his people out of Babylon, not for their sakes, but *for his own name's sake,* because he will be glorified. 2. God's goodness takes occasion from man's badness to appear so much the more illustrious; *therefore* he will sanctify his name by the pardon of sin, because it has been profaned by the commission of sin.

Verses 25–38

The people of God might be discouraged in their hopes of a restoration by the sense not only of their unworthiness of such a favour (which was answered, in the foregoing verses, with this, that God, in doing it, would have an eye to his own glory, not to their worthiness), but of their unfitness for such a favour, being still corrupt and sinful; and that is answered in these verses, with a promise that God would by his grace prepare and qualify them for the mercy and then bestow it on them. And this was in part fulfilled in that wonderful effect which the captivity in Babylon had upon the Jews there, that it effectually cured them of their inclination to idolatry. But it is further intended as a draught of the covenant of grace, and a specimen of those spiritual blessings with which we are blessed in heavenly things by that covenant. As (ch. 34) after a promise of their return the prophecy insensibly slid into a promise of the coming of Christ, the great Shepherd, so here it insensibly slides into a promise of the Spirit, and his gracious influences and operations, which we have as much need of for our sanctification as we have of Christ's merit for our justification.

I. God here promises that he will work a good work in them, to qualify them for the good work he intended to bring about for them, *v.* 25–27. We had promises to the same purport, ch. 11:18–20. 1. That God would cleanse them from the pollutions of sin (*v.* 25): *I will sprinkle clean water upon you,* which signifies both the book of Christ sprinkled upon the conscience to purify that and to take

away the sense of guilt (as those that were sprinkled with the water of purification were thereby discharged from their ceremonial uncleanness) and the grace of the Spirit sprinkled on the whole soul to purify it from all corrupt inclinations and dispositions, as Naaman was cleansed from his leprosy by dipping in Jordan. Christ was himself clean, else his blood could not have been cleansing to us; and it is a Holy Spirit that makes us holy: *From all your filthiness and from all your idols will I cleanse you.* And (*v.* 29) *I will save you from all your uncleannesses.* Sin is defiling, idolatry particularly is so; it renders sinners odious to God and burdensome to themselves. When guilt is pardoned, and the corrupt nature sanctified, then we are cleansed from our filthiness, and there is no other way of being saved from it. This God promises his people here, in order to his being sanctified in them, *v.* 23. We cannot sanctify God's name unless he sanctify our hearts, nor live to his glory, but by his grace. 2. That God would give them a *new heart,* a disposition of mind excellent in itself and vastly different from what it was before. God will work an inward change in order to a universal change. Note, All that have an interest in the new covenant, and a title to the new Jerusalem, have a new heart and a new spirit, and these are necessary in order to their walking in *newness of life.* This is that *divine nature* which believers are by the promises made partakers of. 3. That, instead of a *heart of stone,* insensible and inflexible, unapt to receive any divine impressions and to return any devout affections, God would give a *heart of flesh,* a soft and tender heart, that has spiritual senses exercised, conscious to itself of spiritual pains and pleasures, and complying in every thing with the will of God. Note, Renewing grace works as great a change in the soul as the turning of a dead stone into living flesh. 4. That since, besides our inclination to sin, we complain of an inability to do our duty, God will *cause them to walk in his statutes,* will not only show them the way of his statutes before them, but incline them to walk in it, and thoroughly furnish them with wisdom and will, and active powers, for every good work. In order to this he will *put his Spirit within them,* as a teacher, guide, and sanctifier. Note, God does not force men to walk in his statutes by external violence, but causes them to walk in his statutes by an internal principle. And observe what use we ought to make of this gracious power and principle promised us, and put within us: *You shall keep my judgments.* If God will do his part according to the promise, we must do ours according to the precept. Note, The promise of God's grace to enable us for our duty should engage and quicken our constant care and endeavour to do our duty. God's promises must drive us to his precepts as our rule, and then his precepts must send us back to his promises for strength, for without his grace we can do nothing.

II. God here promises that he will take them into covenant with himself. The sum of the covenant of grace we have, *v.* 28. *You shall be my people, and I will be your God.* It is not, "If you will be my people, I will be your God" (though it is very true that we cannot expect to have God to be to us a God unless we be to him a people), but he has chosen us, and loved us, first, not we him; therefore the condition is of grace, is by promise, as well as the reward; not of merit, not of works: *"You shall be my people;* I will make you so; I will give you the nature and spirit of my people, and then *I will be your God."* And this is the foundation and top-stone of a believer's happiness; it is heaven itself, Rev. 21:3, 7.

III. He promises that he will bring about all that good for them which the exigence of their case calls for. When they are thus prepared for mercy, 1. Then they shall return to their possessions and be settled again in them (*v.* 28): *You shall dwell in the land that I gave to your fathers.* God will, in bringing them back to it, have an eye not to any merit of theirs, but to the promise made to the fathers; for therefore he gave it to them at first, Deu. 7:7, 8. *Therefore* he is gracious, because he has said that he will be so. This shall follow upon the blessed reformation God would work among them (*v.* 33): *"In the day that I shall have cleansed you from all your iniquities,* and so shall have made you meet for the inheritance, *I will cause you to dwell in the cities,* and so put you in possession of the inheritance." This is God's method of mercy indeed, first to part men from their sins, and then to restore them to their comforts. 2. Then they shall enjoy a plenty of all good things. When they are saved *from their uncleanness,* from their sins which kept good things from them, then *I will call for the corn and will increase it, v.* 29. Plenty comes at God's call, and the plenty he calls for shall be still growing; and when he speaks the word the fruit both of the tree and of the field shall multiply. As the inhabitants multiply the productions shall multiply for their maintenance; for he that sends mouths will send meat. Famine was one of the judgments which they had laboured under, and it had been as much as any a reproach to them, that they should be starved in a land so famed for fruitfulness. But now *I will lay no famine upon you;* and none are under that rod without having it laid on by him. Then they *shall receive no more reproach of famine,* shall never be again upbraided with that, nor shall it ever be said that God is a Master that keeps his servants to short allowance. Nay, they shall not only be cleared from the reproach of famine, but they shall have the credit of abundance. The land that had long *lain desolate in the sight of all that passed by,* that looked upon it, some with contempt and some with compassion, shall again *be tilled* (*v.* 34), and, having long lain fallow, it will now be the more fruitful. Observe, God will *call for the corn* and yet they must *till the ground* for it. Note, Even promised mercies must be laboured for; for the promise is not to supersede, but to quicken and encourage our industry and endeavour. And such a blessing will God command on the *hand of the diligent* that all who pass by shall take notice of it, with wonder, *v.* 35. They shall say, "See what a blessed change here is, how *this land that was desolate* has *become like the garden of Eden,* the desert turned again into a paradise." Note, God has honours in reserve for his people to be crowned with sufficient to counterbalance the contempt they are now loaded with, and in them he will be honoured. This wonderful increase both of the people of the land and of its products is compared (*v.* 38) to the large flocks of cattle that are brought to Jerusalem, to be sacrificed at one of the solemn feasts. Even the cities that now lie waste shall be filled with *flocks of men,* not like the flocks with which the pastures are *covered over* (Ps. 65:13), but like the holy flock which is brought to the courts of the Lord's house. Note, *Then* the increase of the numbers of a people is honourable and comfortable indeed when they are all dedicated to God as a holy flock, to be presented to him for *living sacrifices.* Crowds are a lovely sight in God's temple.

IV. He shows what shall be *the happy effects of this blessed change.* 1. It shall have a happy effect upon the people of God themselves, for it shall bring them to an ingenuous repentance for their sins (*v.* 31): *Then shall you remember your own evil ways and shall loathe yourselves.* See here what sin is; it is an *abomination,* a loathsome thing, that abominable thing which the Lord hates. See what is the first step towards repentance; it is *remembering our own evil ways,* reflecting seriously upon the sins we have committed and being particular in recapitulating them. We must remember against ourselves not only our gross enormities, *our own evil ways,* but our defects and infirmities, *our doings that were not good,* not so good as they should have been; not only our direct violations of the law, but our coming short of it. See what is evermore a companion of true repentance, and that is self-loathing, a holy shame and confusion of face: "You shall *loathe yourselves in your own sight,* seeing how loathsome you have made yourselves in the sight of God." Self-love is at the bottom of sin, which we cannot but blush to see the absurdity of; but our quarrelling with ourselves is in order to our being, upon good grounds, reconciled to ourselves. And, *lastly,* see what is the most powerful inducement to an evangelical repentance, and that is a sense of the mercy of God; when God settles them in the midst of plenty, *then they shall loathe themselves for their iniquities.* Note, The goodness of God should overcome our badness and *lead us to repentance.* The more we see of God's readiness to receive us into favour upon our repentance the more reason we shall see to be ashamed of ourselves that we could ever sin against so much love. That heart is hard indeed that will not be thus melted. 2. It shall have a happy effect upon their neighbours, for it shall bring them to a more clear knowledge of God (*v.* 36): *"Then the heathen that are left round about you,* that spoke ignorantly of God (for so all those do that speak *ill* of him) when they saw the land of Israel desolate, shall begin to know better, and to speak more intelligently of God, being convinced that he is able to rebuild the most desolate cities and to replant the most desolate countries, and that, though the course of his favours to his people may be obstructed for a time, they shall not be cut off for ever." They shall be made to know the truth of divine revelation by the exact agreement which they shall discern between God's word which he has spoken to Israel and his works which he has done for them: *I the Lord have spoken it, and I will do it.* With us saying and doing are two things, but they are not so with God.

V. He proposes these things to them, not as the *recompence* of their merits, but as the return of their prayers.

1. Let them not think that they have deserved it: *Not for your sakes do I this, be it known to you* (*v.* 22, 32); no, *be you ashamed and confounded for your own ways.* God is *doing* this, all this which he has promised; it is as sure to be done as if it were done already, and present events have a tendency towards it. But then, (1.) They must renounce the merit of their own good works, and be brought to acknowledge that it is not for their sakes that it is done; so, when God brought Israel into Canaan the first time, an express *caveat* was entered against this thought. Deu. 9:4–6, *It is not for thy righteousness.* It is not for the sake of any of their good qualities or good deeds, not because God had any need of them, or expected any benefit by them. No, in showing mercy he acts by prerogative, not for our deserts, but for his own honour. See how emphatically this is expressed: *Be it known to you,* it is *not for your sakes,* which intimates that we are apt to entertain a high conceit of our own merits and are with difficulty persuaded to disclaim a confidence in them. But, one way or other, God will make all his favourites to know and own that it is his grace, and not their goodness, his mercy, and not their merit, that made them so; and that therefore not unto them, not unto them, but unto him, is all the glory due. (2.) They must repent of the sin of their own evil ways. They must own that the mercies they receive from God are not only not merited, but that they are a thousand times forfeited; and therefore they must be so far from boasting of their good works that they must be ashamed and confounded for their evil ways, and then they are best prepared for mercy.

2. Yet let them know that they must desire and expect it (*v.* 37): *I will yet for this be enquired of by the house of Israel.* God has spoken, and he will do it, and he will be sought unto for it. He requires that his people should *seek unto him,* and he will incline their hearts to do it, when he is coming towards them in ways of mercy. (1.) They must pray for it, for by prayer God is sought unto, and enquired after. What is the matter of God's promises must be the matter of our prayers. By asking for the mercy promised we must give glory to the donor, express a value for the gift, own our dependence, and put honour upon prayer which God has put honour upon. Christ himself must ask, and then God will *give him the heathen for his inheritance,* must *pray the Father,* and then he will *send the Comforter;* much more must we ask that we may receive. (2.) They must consult the oracles of God, and thus also God is sought unto and enquired after. The mercy must be, not an act of providence only, but a child of promise; and therefore the promise must be looked at, and prayer made for it with an eye of faith fastened upon the promise, which must be both the guide and the ground of our expectations. Both these ways we find God enquired of by Daniel, in the name of the house of Israel, when he was about to do those great things for them; he consulted the oracles of God, for he *understood by books,* the book of the prophet Jeremiah, both what was to be expected and when; and then he *set his face* to seek God by prayer, Dan. 9:2, 3. Note, Our communion with God must be kept up by the word and prayer in all the operations of his providence concerning us and in both he must be enquired of.

CHAPTER 37

The threatenings of the destruction of Judah and Jerusalem for their sins, which we had in the former part of this book, were not so terrible, but the promises of their restoration and deliverance for the glory of God, which we have here in the latter part of the book, are as comfortable; and as those were illustrated with many visions and similitudes, for the awakening of a holy fear, so are these, for the encouraging of a humble faith. God had assured them, in the foregoing chapter, that he would gather the house of Israel, even all of it, and would bring them out of their captivity, and return them to their own land; but there were two things that rendered this very unlikely: — I. That they were so dispersed among their enemies, so destitute of all helps and advantages which might favour or further their return, and so dispirited likewise in their own minds; upon all these accounts they are here, in vision, compared to a valley full of the dry bones of dead men, which should be brought together and raised to life. The vision of this we have (*v.* 1–10) and the explication of it, with its application to the present case (*v.* 11–14). II. That they were so divided among themselves, too much of the old enmity between Judah and Ephraim remaining even in their captivity. But, as to this, by a sign of two sticks made one in the hand of the prophet is foreshown the happy coalition that should be, at their return, between the two nations of Israel and Judah (*v.* 15–22). In this there was a type of the uniting of Jews and Gentiles, Jews and Samaritans, in Christ and his church. And so the prophet slides into a prediction of the kingdom of Christ, which should be set up in the world with God's tabernacle in it, and of the glories and graces of that kingdom (*v.* 23–28).

Verses 1–14

Here is, I. The vision of a resurrection from death to life, and it is a glorious resurrection. This is a thing so utterly unknown to nature, and so contrary to its principles *(a privatione ad habitum non datur regressus — from privation to possession there is no return),* that we could have no thought of it but *by the word of the Lord;* and that it is certain by that word that there shall be a general resurrection of the dead some have urged from this vision, "For" (say they) "otherwise it would not properly be made a sign for the confirming of their faith in the promise of their deliverance out of Babylon, as the coming of the Messiah is mentioned for the confirming of their faith touching a former deliverance," Isa. 7:14. But,

1. Whether it be a confirmation or no, it is without doubt a most lively representation of a threefold resurrection, besides that which it is primarily intended to be the sign of. (1.) The resurrection of souls from the death of sin to the life or righteousness, to a holy, heavenly, spiritual, and divine life, by the power of divine grace going along with the word of Christ, Jn. 5:24, 25. (2.) The resurrection of the gospel church, or any part of it, from an afflicted persecuted state, especially under the yoke of the New-Testament Babylon, to liberty and peace. (3.) The resurrection of the body at the great day, especially the bodies of believers that shall rise to life eternal.

2. Let us observe the particulars of this vision.

(1.) The deplorable condition of these dead bones. The prophet was made, [1.] to take an exact view of them. By a prophetic impulse and a divine power he was, in vision, carried out and set *in the midst of a valley,* probably that plain spoken of *ch.* 3:22, where God then *talked with him;* and it was *full of bones,* of dead men's bones, not piled up on a heap, as in a charnel-house, but scattered upon the face of the ground, as if some bloody battle had been fought here, and the slain left unburied till all the flesh was devoured or putrefied, and nothing left but the bones, and those disjointed from one another and dispersed. He *passed by them round about,* and he observed not only that they were very many (for there are multitudes gone to the congregation of the dead), but that, *lo, they were very dry,* having been long exposed to the sun and wind. The bones that have been *moistened with marrow* (Job 21:24), when they have been any while dead, lose all their moisture, and are dry as dust. The body is now fenced with bones (Job 10:11), but then they will themselves be defenceless. The Jews in Babylon were like those dead and dry bones, unlikely ever to come together, to be so much as a skeleton, less likely to be formed into a body, and least of all to be a living body. However, they lay *unburied* in the *open valley,* which encouraged the hopes of their resurrection, as of the two witnesses, Rev. 11:8, 9. The bones of Gog and Magog shall be buried (*ch.* 39:12, 15), for their destruction is final; but the bones of Israel are in the *open valley,* under the eye of Heaven, for there is *hope in their end.* [2.] He was made to own their case deplorable, and not to be helped by any power less than that of God himself (*v.* 3): "Son of man, *can these bones live?* Is it a thing likely? Cast thou devise how it should be done? Can thy philosophy reach to put life into dry bones, or thy politics to restore a captive nation?" "No," says the prophet, "I know not how it should be done, but *thou knowest.*" He does not say, "They cannot live," lest he should seem to limit the Holy One of Israel; but, "Lord, thou knowest whether they can and whether they shall; if thou dost not put life into them, it is certain that they cannot life." Note, God is perfectly acquainted with his own power and his own purposes, and will have us to refer all to them, and to see and own that his wondrous works are such as could not be effected by any counsel or power but his own.

(2.) The means used for the bringing of these dispersed bones together and these dead and dry bones to life. It must be done by prophecy. Ezekiel is ordered to *prophesy upon these bones* (*v.* 4 and again *v.* 9), to *prophesy to the wind.* So he *prophesied as he was commanded, v.* 7, 10. [1.] He must preach, and he did so; and the dead bones lived by a power that went along with the word of God which he preached. [2.] He must pray, and he did so; and the dead bones were made to live in answer to prayer; for *a spirit of life* entered into them. See the efficacy of the word and prayer, and the necessity of both, for the raising of dead souls. God bids his ministers *prophesy upon the dry bones.* Say unto them, *Live;* yea, say unto them, *Live;* and they do as they are commanded, calling to them again and again, *O you dry bones! hear the word of the Lord.* But we call in vain, still they are dead, still they are very dry; we must therefore be earnest with God in prayer for the working of the Spirit with the word: *Come, O breath!* and breathe upon them. God's grace can save souls without our preaching, but our preaching cannot save them without God's grace, and that grace must be sought by prayer. Note, Ministers must faithfully and diligently use the means of grace, even with those that there seems little probability of gaining upon. To prophesy upon dry bones seems as great a penance as to water a dry stick; and yet, whether they will hear or forbear, we must discharge our trust, must *prophesy as we are commanded,* in the name of him who raises the dead and is the fountain of life.

(3.) The wonderful effect of these means. Those that do as they are commanded, as they are commissioned, in the face of the greatest discouragements, need not doubt of success, for God will own and enrich his own appointments. [1.] Ezekiel looked down and prophesied upon the bones in the valley, and they became human bodies. *First,* That which he had to *say to them* was that God would infallibly raise them to life: *Thus saith the Lord God unto these bones, You shall live, v.* 5 and again *v.* 6. And he that speaks the word will thereby do the work; he that says, They *shall live,* will make them alive: He will *clothe them with skin and flesh* (*v.* 6), as he did at first, Job 10:11. He that made us so fearfully and wonderfully, and curiously wrought us, can in like manner new-make us, for *his arm is not shortened. Secondly,* That which was immediately done for them was that they were moulded anew into shape. We may well suppose it was with great liveliness and vigour that the prophet prophesied, especially when he found what he said begin to take effect. Note, The opening, sealing, and applying of the promises, are the ordinary means of our participation of a new and divine nature. As Ezekiel prophesied in this vision *there was a noise,* a word of command, from heaven, seconding what he said; or it signified the motion of the angels that were to be employed as the ministers of the divine Providence in the deliverance of the Jews, and we read of the *noise of their wings* (Eze. 1:24) and the *sound of their going,* 2 Sa. 5:24. *And, behold, a shaking,* or commotion, among the bones. Even dead and dry bones begin to move when they are called to hear the word of the Lord. This was fulfilled when, upon Cyrus's proclamation of liberty, those whose spirits God had stirred up began to think of making use of that liberty, and getting ready to be gone. When *there was a noise, behold, a shaking;* when David heard *the sound of the going on the tops of the mulberry-trees* then he *bestirred himself;* then there was *a shaking.* When Paul heard the voice saying, *Why persecutest thou me?* behold, a shaking of the dry bones; he *trembled* and was *astonished.* But this was not all: *The bones came together bone to his bone,* under a divine direction; and, though there is in man a multitude of bones, yet of all the bones of those numerous slain not one was missing, not one missed its way, not one missed its place, but, as it were by instinct, each knew and found its fellow. The dispersed bones came together and the displaced bones were knit together, the divine power supplying that to these dry bones which in a living body *every joint supplies.* Thus shall it be in the resurrection of the dead; the scattered atoms shall be ranged and marshalled in their proper place and order, and *every bone come to his bone,* by the same wisdom and power by which the bones were first *formed in the womb of her that is with child.* Thus it was in the return of the Jews; those that were scattered in several parts of the province of Babylon came to their respective families, and all as it were by consent to the general rendezvous, in order to their return. By degrees *sinews* and *flesh* came upon these bones, and the *skin covered them, v.* 8. This was fulfilled when the captives got their effects about them, and the *men of their place helped them* with *silver,* and *gold,* and whatever they needed for their remove, Ezra 1:4. But still there was *no breath in them;* they wanted spirit and courage for such a difficult and hazardous enterprise as this was of returning to their own land. [2.] Ezekiel then looked up and prophesied to the *wind,* or *breath,* or *spirit,* and said, *Come, O breath! and breathe upon these slain.* As good have been still dry bones as dead bodies: but as for God *his work is perfect;* he is not the God of the dead, but of the living; therefore *breathe upon them that they may live.* In answer to this request, *the breath* immediately came *into them, v.* 10. Note, the spirit of life is from God; he at first in the creation breathed into man the breath of life, and so he will at last in the resurrection. The dispirited despairing captives were wonderfully animated with resolution to break through all the discouragements that lay in the way of their return and applied themselves to it with all imaginable vigour. And then they *stood upon their feet, an exceedingly great army;* not only living men, but effective men, fit for service in the wars and formidable to all that gave them any opposition. Note, With God nothing is impossible. He can *out of stones raise up children unto Abraham* and out of dead and dry bones levy an exceedingly great army to fight his battles and plead his cause.

II. The application of this vision to the present calamitous condition of the Jews in captivity: *These bones are the whole house of Israel,* both the ten tribes and the two. See in this what they are and what they shall be.

1. The depth of despair to which they are now reduced, *v.* 11. They all give up themselves for lost and gone; they say, *"Our bones are dried,* our strength is exhausted, our spirits are gone, *our hope is* all *lost;* every thing we looked for succour and relief from fails us, and *we are cut off for our parts.* Let who will cherish some hope, we see no ground for any." Note, When troubles continue long, hopes have been often frustrated, and all creature-confidences fail, it is not strange if the spirits sink; and nothing but an active faith in the power, promise, and providence of God will keep them from quite dying away. 2. The height of prosperity to which, notwithstanding this, they shall be advanced: *"therefore,* because things have come thus to the last extremity, *prophesy to them,* and tell them, now is God's time to appear for them. *Jehovah-jireh — in the mount of the Lord it shall be seen, v.* 12–14. Tell them," (1.) "That they shall be brought out of the land of their enemies, where they are as it were buried alive: *I will open your graves."* Those shall be restored, not only whose *bones* are *scattered at the grave's mouth* (Ps. 141:7), but who are buried in the grave; though the power of the enemy is like the *bars of the pit,* which one would think it impossible to break through, strong as death and cruel as the grave, yet it shall be conquered. God can *bring* his people *up from the depths of the earth,* Ps. 71:20. (2.) "That they shall be brought into their own land, where they shall live in prosperity: *I will bring you into the land of Israel* (*v.* 12) and *place you there* (*v.* 14), and will *put my spirit in you* and then *you shall live."* Note, *Then* God puts spirit in us to good purpose, and so that we shall indeed live, when he puts his Spirit in us. And *(lastly)* in all this God will be glorified: *You shall know that I am the Lord* (*v.* 13), and that I have *spoken it and performed it, v.* 14. Note, God's quickening the dead redounds more than any thing to his honour, and to the honour of his word, which he has magnified above all his name, and will magnify more and more by the punctual accomplishment of every tittle of it.

Verses 15–28

Here are more exceedingly great and precious promises made of the happy state of the Jews after their return to their own land; but they have a further reference to the kingdom of the Messiah and the glories of gospel-times.

I. It is here promised that Ephraim and Judah shall be happily united in brotherly love and mutual serviceableness; so that whereas, ever since the desertion of the ten tribes from the house of David under Jeroboam, there had been continual feuds and animosities between the two kingdoms of Israel and Judah, and it is to be feared there had been some clashings between them even in the land of their captivity (Ephraim upon all occasions envying Judah and Judah vexing Ephraim), now it should be no longer, but there should be a coalition between them, and, notwithstanding the old differences that had been between them, they should agree to love one another and to do one another all good offices. This is here illustrated by a sign. The prophet was to take *two sticks,* and write upon one, *For Judah* (including Benjamin, those of the *children of Israel* that were *his companions),* upon the other, *For Joseph,* including the rest of the tribes, *v.* 16. These two sticks must be so framed as to fall into *one in his hand, v.* 17. The people took notice of this, and desired him to *tell them the meaning of it,* for they knew he did not play with sticks for his diversion, as children do. Those that would know the meaning should ask the meaning of the word of God which they read and hear, and of the instituted signs by which spiritual and divine things are represented to us; the ministers' *lips* should *keep the knowledge* hereof and the people should *ask it at their mouth,* Mal. 2:7. It is a necessary question for grown people, as well as children, to ask, *What mean you by this service,* by this sign? Ex. 12:26. The meaning was that Judah and Israel should become *one in the hand of God, v.* 19. 1. They shall be one, one nation, *v.* 22. They shall have no separate interests, and, consequently, no divided affections. There shall be no mutual jealousies and animosities, no remembrance, no remains, of their former discord. But there shall be a perfect harmony between them, a good understanding one of another, a good disposition one to another, and a readiness to all good offices and services for one another's credit and comfort. They had been two sticks crossing and thwarting one another, nay, beating and bruising one another; but now they shall become one, supporting and strengthening one another. *Vix unita fortior — Force added to force is proportionally more efficient. Behold, how good and how pleasant a thing it is* to see Judah and Israel, that had long been at variance, now *dwelling together in unity.* Then they shall become acceptable to their God, amiable to their friends, and formidable to their enemies, Isa. 11:13, 14. 2. They shall be one in *God's hand;* by his power they shall be united, and, being by his hand brought together, his hand shall keep them together, so that they shall not fly off, to be separated again. They shall be one in his hand, for his glory shall be the centre of their unity and his grace the cement of it. In him, in a regard to him and in his service and worship, they shall unite, and so shall become one. Both sides shall agree to put themselves into his hand, and so they shall be one. *Qui conveniunt in aliquo tertio inter se conveniunt — Those who agree in a third agree with each other.* Note, Those are best united that are one in God's hand, whose union with each other results from their union with Christ and their communion with God through him, Eph. 1:10. *One in us,* Jn. 17:21. 3. They shall be one in their return out of captivity (*v.* 21): *I will take them from among the heathen,* and *gather them on every side,* and *bring them* together incorporated into one body *to their own land.* They shall be one in their separation from the heathen with whom they had mingled themselves: they shall both agree to part from them, and take their affections off from them, and no longer to comply with their usages, and then they will soon agree to join together in walking according to the rule of God's word. Their having been joint-sufferers will contribute to this blessed comprehension, when they begin to come to themselves and to consider things. Put many pieces of metal together into the furnace, and, when they are melted, they will run all together. It was time for them to strengthen one another when their oppressors were so busy to weaken and ruin them all. Likewise their being joint-sharers in the favour of God, and the great and common deliverance wrought out for them all, should help to unite them. God's loving them all was a good reason why they should love one another. Times of common joy, as well as times of common suffering, should be healing loving times. 4. They shall all be the subjects of one king, and so they shall become one. The Jews, after their return, were under one government, and not divided as formerly. But this certainly looks further, to the kingdom of Christ; he is that one King in allegiance to whom all God's spiritual Israel shall cheerfully unite, and under whose protection they shall all be gathered. All believers unite in *one Lord, one faith,* and *one baptism.* And the uniting of Jews and Gentiles in the gospel church, their becoming one fold under Christ the one great Shepherd, is doubtless the union that is chiefly looked at in this prophecy. By Christ and partition-wall between them was taken down, and the enmity slain, and of them *twain* was made *one new man,* Eph. 2:14, 15.

II. It is here promised that the Jews shall by their captivity be cured of their inclination to idolatry; this shall be the happy fruit of that affliction, even the taking away of their sin (*v.* 23): *Neither shall they defile themselves any more with their idols,* those detestable defiling things, no, nor *with any of their* former *transgressions.* Note, When one sin is sincerely parted with all sin is abandoned too, for he that hates sin, as sin, will hate all sin. And those that are cured of their spiritual idolatry, their inordinate affection to the world and the flesh, that no longer make a god of their money or their belly, have a happy blow given to the root of all their transgressions. Two ways God will take to cure them of their idolatry: — 1. By bringing them out of the way of temptation to it: *"I will save them out of all their dwelling-places wherein they have sinned,* because there they met with the occasion of sin and allurements to it." Note, It is our wisdom to avoid the places where we have been overcome by temptations to sin, not to remain in them, or return to them, but to *save ourselves* out of them, as we would out of infected places; see Zec. 2:7; Rev. 18:4. And it is a great mercy when God, in his providence, *saves us out of the dwelling-places where we have sinned,* and keeps us from harm by keeping us out of harm's way, in answer to our prayer, *Lead us not into temptation, but deliver us from evil.* 2. By changing the disposition of their mind: *"I will cleanse them* (*v.* 28); that is, I will sanctify them, will work in them an aversion to the pollutions of sin and a complacency in the pleasures of holiness, and then you may be sure they will not defile themselves any more with their idols." Those whom God has cleansed he will keep clean.

III. It is here promised that they shall be the people of God, as *their God,* and the subjects and sheep of Christ their King and Shepherd. These promises we had before, and they are here repeated (*v.* 23, 24) for the encouragement of the faith of Israel: *They shall be my people,* to serve me, and *I will be their God,* to save them and to make them happy. *David, my servant, shall be king over them,* to fight their battles, to protect them from injury, and to rule them, and overrule all things that concern them for their good. He shall be *their shepherd,* to guide them and provide for them. Christ is this David, Israel's King of old; and those whom he subdues to himself, and makes willing in the day of his power, he makes to *walk in his judgments and to keep his statutes.*

IV. It is here promised that they shall dwell comfortably, *v.* 25, 26. They shall dwell in the land of Israel; for where else should Israelites dwell? And many things will concur to make their dwelling agreeable. 1. They shall have it by covenant; they shall come in again upon their old title, by virtue of the grant made unto *Jacob,* God's *servant.* As Christ was David, God's servant, so the church is Jacob, his servant too; and the members of the church shall come in for a share, as born in God's house. He will make a *covenant of peace* with them (*v.* 26), and in pursuance of that covenant he will *place them, and multiply them.* Note, Temporal mercies are doubly sweet when they come from the promise of the covenant, and not merely from common providence. 2. They shall come to it by prescription: "It is *the land wherein your fathers have dwelt,* and for that reason you cannot but have a special kindness for it, which God will graciously gratify." It was the inheritance of their ancestors, and therefore shall be theirs. They are *beloved for their fathers' sakes.* 3. They shall have it entailed upon them and the heirs of their body, and shall have their families built up, so that it shall not be lost for want of heirs. *They shall dwell therein* all their time, and never be turned out of possession, and they shall leave it for an inheritance *to their children and their children's children for ever,* who shall enjoy it when they are gone, the prospect of which will be a satisfaction to them. 4. They shall live under a good government, which will contribute very much to the comfort of their lives: *My servant David shall be their prince for ever.* This can be no other than Christ, of whom it was said, when he was brought into the world, *He shall reign over the house of Jacob for ever,* Lu. 1:33. Note, It is the unspeakable comfort of all Christ's faithful subjects that, as his *kingdom* is *everlasting,* so he is an *everlasting King,* he lives to reign for ever; and, as sure and as long as he lives and reigns, they shall live and reign also. 5. The charter by which they hold all their privileges is indefeasible. God's covenant with them shall be an *everlasting covenant;* so the covenant of grace is, for it secures to us an everlasting happiness.

V. It is here promised that God will dwell among them; and this will make them dwell comfortably indeed: *I will set my sanctuary in the midst of them for evermore; my tabernacle also shall be with them, v.* 26, 27. 1. They shall have the tokens of God's special presence with them and his gracious residence among them. God will *in very deed dwell with them upon the earth,* for where his sanctuary is he is; when they profaned his sanctuary he took it from them (Isa. 64:11), but now that they are purified God will dwell with them again. 2. They shall have opportunity of conversing with God, of hearing from him, speaking to him, and so keeping up communion with him, which will be the comfort of their lives. 3. They shall have the means of grace. By the oracles of God in his tabernacle they shall be made wiser and better, and all their children shall be taught of the Lord. 4. Thus their covenant relation to God shall be improved and the bond of it strengthened: *"I will be their God and they shall be my people,* and they shall know it by having my sanctuary among them, and shall have the comfort of it."

VI. Both God and Israel shall have the honour of this among the heathen, *v.* 26. "Now the heathen observe how Israel have profaned their own crown by their sins, and God has profaned it by his judgments; but then, when Israel is reformed and God has returned in mercy to them, the very heathen shall be made to know that *the Lord sanctifies* Israel, has a title to them and an interest in them more than other people, because his sanctuary is, and shall be, in the midst of them." Note, God designs the sanctification of those among whom he sets up his sanctuary. And blessed and holy are those who, enjoying the privileges of the sanctuary, give such proofs and evidences of their sanctification that the heathen may know it is no less than the almighty grace of God that sanctifies them. Such have God's sanctuary in the midst of them, the kingdom of God within them, in the principles of the spiritual life, and shall have it so for evermore in the enjoyments of an eternal life.

CHAPTER 38

This chapter, and that which follows it, are concerning Gog and Magog, a powerful enemy to the people of Israel, that should make a formidable descent upon them, and put them into a consternation, but their army should be routed and their design defeated; and this prophecy, it is most probable, had its accomplishment some time after the return of the people of Israel out of their captivity, whether in the struggles they had with the kings of Syria, especially Antiochus Epiphanes, or perhaps in some other way not recorded, we cannot tell. If the sacred history of the Old Testament had reached as far as the prophecy, we should have been better able to understand these chapters, but, for want of that key, we are locked out of the meaning of them. God had by the prophet assured his people of happy times after their return to their own land; but lest they should mistake the promises which related to the kingdom of the Messiah and the spiritual privileges of that the kingdom of the Messiah and the spiritual privileges of that kingdom, as if from them they might promise themselves an uninterrupted temporal prosperity, he here tells them, as Christ told his disciples to prevent the like mistake, that in the world they shall have tribulation, but they may be of good cheer, for they shall be victorious at last. This prophecy here of Gog and Magog is without doubt alluded to in that prophecy which relates to the latter days, and which seems to be yet unfulfilled (Rev. 20:8), that Gog and Magog shall be gathered to battle against the camp of the saints, as the Old-Testament prophecies of the destruction of Babylon are alluded to, Rev. 18. But, in both, the Old-Testament prophecies had their accomplishment in the Jewish church as the New-Testament prophecies shall have when the time comes in the Christian church. In this chapter we have intermixed, I. The attempt that Gog and Magog should make upon the land of Israel, the vast army they should bring into the field, and their vast preparations (*v.* 4–7), their project and design in it (*v.* 8–13), God's hand in it (*v.* 4). II. The great terror that this should strike upon the land of Israel (*v.* 15, 16, 18–20). III. The divine restraint that these enemies should be under, and the divine protection that Israel should be under (*v.* 2–4 and *v.* 14). IV. The defeat that should be given to those enemies by the immediate hand of God (*v.* 21–23), which we shall hear more of in the next chapter.

Verses 1–13

The critical expositors have enough to do here to enquire out Gog and Magog. We cannot pretend either to add to their observations or to determine their controversies. Gog seems to be the king and Magog the kingdom; so that Gog and Magog are like Pharaoh and the Egyptians. Some think they find them afar off, in Scythia, Tartary, and Russia. Others think they find them nearer the land of Israel, in Syria, and Asia the Less. Ezekiel is appointed to prophesy against Gog, and to tell him that *God is against him, v.* 2, 3. Note, God does not only see those that are now the enemies of his church and set himself against them, but he foresees those that will be so and lets them know by his word that he is against them too, and yet is pleased to make use of them to serve his own purposes, for the glory of his own name; surely *their wrath* shall *praise him,* and the *remainder thereof he will restrain,* Ps. 76:10. Let us observe here,

I. The confusion which God designed to put this enemy to. It is remarkable that this is put first in the prophecy; before it is foretold that God will *bring him forth* against Israel it is foretold that God will *put hooks into his jaws* and *turn him back* (*v.* 4), that they might have assurance of their deliverance before they had the prospect given them of their danger. Thus tender is God of the comfort of his people, thus careful that they may not be frightened; even before the trouble begins he tells them it will end well.

II. The undertaking which he designed to engage him in, in order to this defeat and disappointment. 1. The nations that shall be confederate in this enterprise against Israel are many, and great, and mighty (*v.* 5, 6), *Persia, Ethiopia,* etc. Antiochus had an army made up of all the nations here named, and many others. These people had been at variance with one another, and yet in combination against Israel. How are those increased that trouble God's people! 2. They are well furnished with arms and ammunition, and bring a good train of artillery into the field — *horses and horsemen* (*v.* 4) bravely equipped *with all sorts of armour, bucklers and shields* for defence, *and all handling swords* for offence. Orders are given to make all imaginable preparation for this expedition (*v.* 7): *"Be thou prepared, and do thou prepare.* See what warlike preparations thou hast already in store, and, lest that should not suffice, make further preparation, *thou and all thy company,"* Let Gog himself be a guard to the rest of the confederates. As commander-in-chief, let him engage to take care of them and their safety; let him pass his word for their security, and take them under his particular protection. The leaders of an army, instead of exposing their soldiers needlessly and presumptuously, and throwing away their lives upon desperate undertakings, should study to be a guard to them, and, whenever they send them forth in danger, should contrive to support and cover them. This call to prepare seems to be ironical — *Do thy worst,* but I will *turn thee back;* like that Isa. 8:9. *Gird yourselves, and you shall be broken in pieces.* 3. Their design is against *the mountains of Israel* (*v.* 8), against *the land that is brought back from the sword.* It is not long since it was harassed with the sword of war, and it has been always wasted, more or less, with one judgment or other; it is but newly *gathered out of many people,* and *brought forth out of the nations;* it has enjoyed comparatively but a short breathing-time, has scarcely recovered any strength since it was brought down by war and captivity; and therefore its neighbours need not fear its being too great, nay, and therefore it is very barbarous to pick a quarrel with it so soon. It is a people that *dwell safely, all of them, in unwalled villages,* very secure, and *having neither bars nor gates, v.* 11. It is a certain sign that they intend no mischief to their neighbours, for they fear no mischief from them. It cannot be thought that those will offend others who do not take care to defend themselves; and this aggravates the sin of these invaders. It is base and barbarous to *devise evil against thy neighbour while he dwells securely by thee,* and has no distrust of thee, Prov. 3:29. But see here how *the clouds return after the rain* in this world, and what little reason we have ever to be secure till we come to heaven. It is not long since Israel was brought back from the sword of one enemy, and behold the sword of another is drawn against it. Former troubles will not excuse us from further troubles; but when we think we have *put off the harness,* at least for some time, by a fresh and sudden alarm we may be called to *gird it on again;* and therefore we must never boast nor be off our guard. 4. That which the enemy has in view, in forming this project, is to enrich himself and to make himself master, not of the country, but of the wealth of it, to spoil and plunder it, and make a prey of it: *At the same* time that God intends to bring this matter about *things shall come into the mind* of this enemy, and *he shall think an evil thought, v.* 10. Note, All the mischief men do, and particularly the mischief they do to the church of God, arises from evil thoughts that come into their mind, ambitious thoughts, covetous thoughts, spiteful thoughts against those that are good, for the sake of their goodness. It came into Antiochus's mind what a singular people these religious Jews were, and how their worship witnessed against and condemned the idolatries of their neighbours, and therefore, in enmity to their religion, he would plague them. It came into his mind what a wealthy people they were, that they had *gotten cattle and goods in the midst of the land* (v. 12), and withal how weak they were, how unable to make any resistance, how easy it would be to carry off what they had, and how much glory this rapine would add to his victorious sword; these things coming into his mind, and one evil thought drawing on another, he came at last to this resolve (v. 11, 12): *"I will go up to the land of unwalled villages;* yea, that I will; it will cost me nothing to make them all my own. I will go and disturb *those that are at rest,* without giving them any notice, not to crush their growing greatness, or chastise their insolence, or make reprisals upon them for any wrong they have done us (they had none of these pretences to make war upon them), but purely *to take a spoil and to take a prey"* (v. 12), in open defiance to all the laws of justice and equity, as much as the highwayman's killing the traveller that he may take his money. These were the thoughts that came into the mind of this wicked prince, and God knew them; nay, he knew them before they came into his mind, for he *understands our thoughts afar off,* Ps. 139:2. 5. According to the project thus formed he pours in all his forces upon the land of Israel, and finds those that are ready to come in to his assistance with the same prospects (v. 9): *"Thou shalt ascent and come like a storm,* with all the force, and fury, and fierceness imaginable, and *thou shalt be like a cloud to cover the land,* to darken it, and to threaten it, *thou and* not only *all thy bands,* all the force thou canst bring into the field, but *many people with thee"* (such as are spoken of v. 13), *"Sheba and Dedan,* the Arabians and the Edomites, *and the merchants of Tarshish,* of Tyre and Sidon and other maritime cities, they and their *young lions* that are greedy of spoil and live upon it, *shall say, Hast thou come to take the spoil* of this land?" Yes he has; and therefore they wish him success. Or perhaps they envy him, or grudge it to him. "Hast thou come for riches who art thyself so rich already?" Or, knowing that God was on Israel's side, they thus ridicule his attempts, foreseeing that they would be baffled and that he would be disappointed of the prey he promised himself. Or, if he come to *take the prey,* they will come and join with him, and add to his forces. When Lysias, who was general of Antiochus's army, came against the Jews, the neighbouring nations joined with him (1 Mac. 3:41), to share in the guilt, in hopes to share in the prey. *When thou sawest a thief then thou consentedst with him.*

Verses 14–23

This latter part of the chapter is a repetition of the former; the dream is doubled, for the thing is certain and to be very carefully regarded.

I. It is here again foretold that this spiteful enemy should make a formidable descent upon the land of Israel (v. 15): *"Thou shalt come out of the north parts* (Syria lay on the north of Canaan) with *a mighty army,* shalt come like a *cloud,* and *cover the land of my people Israel,"* v. 16. These words (v. 14), *When my people Israel dwell safely, shalt thou not know it?* may be taken two ways: — 1. As intimating his inducements to this attempt. "Thou shalt have intelligence brought thee how securely, and therefore how carelessly, the people of Israel dwell, which shall give rise to thy project against them; for when thou knowest not only what a rich, but what an easy prey they are likely to be, thou wilt soon determine to fall upon them" Note, God's providence is to be acknowledged in the occasion, the small occasion perhaps, that is given, and that not designedly neither, to those first thoughts from which great enterprises take their original. God, to bring about his own purposes, lets men know that which yet he knows they

will make a bad use of, as here. Or, 2. As intimating his disappointment in this attempt, which here, as before, the prophecy begins with: *"When my people Israel dwell safely,* not in their own apprehension only, but in reality, forasmuch as they dwell safely under the divine protection, shalt not thou be made to know it by the fruitlessness of thy endeavours to destroy them?" Thou shalt soon find that there is *no enchantment against Jacob,* that *no weapon formed against them shall prosper;* thou shalt know to thy cost, shalt know to thy shame, that though they have no walls, nor bars, nor gates, they have God himself, a *wall of fire,* round about them, and that he who *touches them touches the apple of his eye;* whosoever meddles with them meddles to his own hurt. And it is for the demonstrating of this to all the world that God will bring this mighty enemy against his people. Those that *gathered themselves against Israel* said, *Let us take the spoil and take they prey,* but they *knew not the thoughts of the Lord,* Mic. 4:11, 12. *I will bring thee against my land.* This is strange news, that God will not only permit his enemies to come against his own children, but will himself bring them; but, if we understand what he aims at, we shall be well reconciled even to this: it is *"that the heathen may know me* to be the only living and true God *when I shall be sanctified in thee,* O Gog! that is, in thy defeat and destruction *before their eyes,* that all the nations may see, and say, *There is none like unto the God of Jeshurun, that rides on the heavens for the help of his people."* Note, God brings his people into danger and distress that he may have the honour of bringing about their deliverance, and suffers the enemies of his church to prevail awhile, though they profane his name by their sin, that he may have the honour of prevailing at last and sanctifying his own name in their ruin. Now it is said, This shall be *in the latter days,* namely, in the latter days of the Old-Testament church; so the mischief that Antiochus did to Israel was; but in the latter days of the New-Testament church another like enemy should arise, that should in like manner be defeated. Note, Effectual securities are treasured up in the word of God against the troubles and dangers the church may be brought into a great while hence, even in the latter days.

II. Reference is herein had to the predictions of the former prophets (v. 17): *Art thou he of whom I have spoken in old time,* of whom Moses spoke in his prophecy of the latter days (Deu. 32:43, *He will render vengeance to his adversaries),* and David, Ps. 9:15 *(The heathen are sunk down into the pit that they made)* and often elsewhere in the Psalms? This is the leviathan of whom Isaiah spoke (Isa. 27:1), that congress of the nations of which Joel spoke, Joel 3:1. Many of the prophets had perhaps spoken particularly of this event, though it be not written, as they all had spoken and written too that which is applicable to it. Note, There is an amiable admirable harmony and agreement between the Lord's prophets, though they lived in several ages, for they were all guided by one and the same Spirit.

III. It is here foretold that this furious formidable enemy should be utterly cut off in this attempt upon Israel, and that it should issue in his own ruin. This is supposed by many to have its accomplishment in the many defeats given by the Maccabees to the forces of Antiochus and the remarkable judgments of God executed upon his own person, for he died of sore diseases. But these things are here foretold, as usual, in figurative expressions, which we are not to look for the literal accomplishment of, and yet they might be fulfilled nearer the letter than we know of. 1. God will be highly displeased with this bold invader: *When he comes up* in pride and anger *against the land of Israel,* and thinks to carry all before him with a high hand, then *God's fury shall come up in his face,* which is an allusion to the manner of men, whose colour rises in their faces when some high affront is offered them and they are resolved to show their resentment of it, v. 18. God will speak against them in his *jealousy* for his people and in *the fire of his wrath* against his and their enemies, v. 19. See how God's permitting sin, his laying occasions of sin before men, and his making use of it to serve his own purposes, consist with his hatred of sin and his displeasure against it. God *brings this enemy against his land,* letting him know what an easy prey it might be and determining thereby to glorify himself; and yet, *when he comes against the land,* God's *fury comes up,* and *he speaks to him in the fire of his wrath.* If any ask, Why does he thus find fault? for who

has resisted his will? It is easy to answer, *Nay, but, O man! who art thou that repliest against God?* 2. His forces shall be put into the greatest confusion and consternation imaginable (v. 19): *There shall be a great shaking of* them *in the land of Israel,* a universal concussion (v. 20), such as shall affect the *fishes* and *fowls,* the *beasts* and *creeping things,* and much more *the men that are upon the face of the earth,* who sooner receive impressions of fear. There shall be such an earthquake as shall *throw down the mountains,* those natural heights, and the *steep places,* towers and *walls,* those artificial heights; they shall all *fall to the ground.* Some understand this of the fright which the land of Israel should be put into by the fury of the enemy. But it is rather to be understood of the fright which the enemy should be put into by the wrath of God; all those things which they both raise themselves and stay themselves upon shall be shaken down, and their hearts shall fail them. 3. He shall be routed and utterly ruined; both earth and heaven shall be armed against him (1.) The earth shall muster up its forces to destroy him. If the people of Israel have not strength and courage to resist him, God will *call for a sword against him, v.* 21. And he has swords always at command, that are *bathed in heaven,* Isa. 35:5. Throughout all the mountains of Israel, where he hoped to meet with spoil to enrich him, he shall meet with swords to destroy him, and, rather than fail, *every man's sword shall be against his brother,* as in *the day of Midian,* Ps. 83:9. The great men of Syria shall undermine and overthrow one another, shall accuse one another, shall fight duels with one another. Note, God can, and often does, make the destroyers of his people to be their own destroyers and the destroyers of one another. However, he will himself be their destroyer, will take the work into his own hand, that it may be done thoroughly (v. 22): *I will plead against him with pestilence and blood.* Note, Whom God acts against he pleads against; he shows them the ground of his controversy with them, that their mouths may be stopped, and he may be clear when he judges. (2.) The artillery of heaven shall also be drawn out against them: *I will rain upon him an overflowing rain, v.* 22. He comes like a storm upon Israel, v. 9. But God will come like a storm upon him, will rain upon him *great hailstones* as upon the Canaanites (Jos. 10:11), fire and brimstone as upon Sodom, and a *horrible tempest,* Ps. 11:6. Thus the Gog and Magog in the New Testament shall be devoured with *fire from heaven,* and cast into the *lake of brimstone,* Rev. 20:9, 10. That will be the everlasting portion of all the impenitent implacable enemies of God's church and people. 4. God, in all this, will be glorified. The end he aimed at (v. 16) shall be accomplished (v. 23): *Thus will I magnify myself and sanctify myself.* Note, In the destruction of sinners God makes it to appear that he is a great and holy God, and he will do so to eternity. And, if men do not magnify and sanctify him as they ought, he will magnify himself, and sanctify himself; and this we should desire and pray for daily, *Father, glorify thy own name.*

CHAPTER 39

This chapter continues and concludes the prophecy against Gog and Magog, in whose destruction God crowns his favour to his people Israel, which shines very brightly after the scattering of that black cloud in the close of this chapter. Here is, I. An express prediction of the utter destruction of Gog and Magog, agreeing with what we had before (v. 1-7). II. An illustration of the vastness of that destruction, in three consequences of it: the burning of their weapons (v. 8-10), the burning of their slain (v. 11-16), and the feasting of the fowls with the dead bodies of those that were unburied (v. 17-22). III. A declaration of God's gracious purposes concerning his people Israel, in this and his other providences concerning them, and a promise of further mercy that he had yet in store for them (v. 23-29).

Verses 1–7

This prophecy begins as that before (ch. 38:3, 4, *I am against thee, and I will turn thee back);* for there is need of line upon line, both for the conviction of Israel's enemies and the comfort of Israel's friends. Here, as there, it is foretold that God will bring this enemy *from the north parts,* as formerly the Chaldeans were fetched from the north, Jer. 1:14 *(Omne malum ab aquilone — Every evil comes from the north),* and, long after, the Roman empire was overrun by the northern nations, that he will bring him *upon the mountains of Israel* (v. 2), first as a place of temptation, where the measures of his iniquity shall be filled up, and then as a place of execution, where his ruin shall be completed. And that is it which is here enlarged upon. 1. His soldiers shall be disarmed and so disabled to carry on their enterprise. Though the men of might may *find their hands,* yet to what purpose, when they find it is put out of their power to do mischief, when God shall smite their *bow out of their left hand* and their *arrow out of their right? v.* 3. Note, The weapons formed against Zion shall not prosper. 2. He and the greatest part of his army shall be slain in the field of battle (*v.* 4): *Thou shalt fall upon the mountains of Israel;* there they sinned, and there they shall perish, even upon the holy *mountains of Israel,* for *there broke he the arrows of the bow,* Ps. 76:3. The mountains of Israel shall be moistened, and fattened, and made fruitful, with the blood of the enemies. "Thou shalt *fall upon the open field* (*v.* 5) and shalt not be able even there to make thy escape." Even upon the mountains he shall not find a pass that he shall be able to maintain, and upon the open field he shall not find a road that he shall be able to make his escape by. He and *his bands;* his regular troops, and the people that are *with him* that follow the camp to share in the plunder, shall all *fall with him.* Note, Those that *cast in their lot* among wicked people (Prov. 1:14), that they *may have one purse* with them, must expect to *take their lot with them,* and fare as they fare, taking the worse with the better. There shall be such a general slaughter made that but *a sixth part shall be left* (*v.* 2), the other five shall all be cut off. Never was army so totally routed as this. And, for its greater infamy and reproach, their bodies shall be a feast to the birds of prey, *v.* 4. Compare *v.* 17, *Thou shalt fall,* for *I have spoken it.* Note, Rather shall the most illustrious princes (Antiochus was called *Epiphanes — the illustrious*) and the most numerous armies *fall to the ground* than any word of God; for he that has spoken will *make it good.* 3. His country also shall be made desolate: *I will send a fire on Magog* (*v.* 6) and *among those that dwell carelessly,* or confidently, *in the isles,* that is, the nations of the Gentiles. He designed to destroy the land of Israel, but shall not only be defeated in that design, but shall have his own destroyed by some fire, some consuming judgment or other. Note, Those who invade other people's rights justly lose their own. 4. God will by all this advance the honour of his own name, (1.) Among his people Israel; they shall hereby know more of God's name, of his power and goodness, his care of them, his faithfulness to them. His providence concerning them shall lead them into a better acquaintance with him; every providence should do so, as well as every ordinance: *I will make my holy name known in the midst of my people.* In Judah is God known; but those that know much of God should know more of him; we should especially increase in the knowledge of his name as a holy name. They shall know him as a God of perfect purity and rectitude and that hates all sin, and then it follows, *I will not let them pollute my holy name any more.* Note, Those that rightly know God's holy name will not dare to profane it; for it is through ignorance of it that men make light of it and make bold with it. And this is God's method of dealing with men, first to enlighten their understandings, and by that means to influence the whole man; he first makes us to know his holy name, and so keeps us from polluting it and engages us to honour it. And this is here the blessed effect of God's glorious appearances on the behalf of his people. Thus he completes his favours, thus he sanctifies them, thus he makes them blessings indeed; by them he instructs his people and reforms them. *When the Almighty scattered kings for her she was white as snow in Salmon,* Ps. 68:14. (2.) Among the heathen; those that never knew it, or would not own it, shall *know that I am the Lord, the Holy One in Israel.* They shall be made to know by dearbought experience that he is a God of power, and his people's God and Saviour; and it is in vain for the greatest potentates to contend with him; none ever hardened their heart against him and prospered.

Verses 8–22

Though this prophecy was to have its accomplishment in the latter days, yet it is here spoken of as if it were already accomplished, because it is certain (*v.* 8): *"Behold it has come, and it is done;* it is as sure to be done when the time shall come as if it were done already; *this is the day whereof I have* long and often *spoken,* and, though it has been long in coming, yet at length *it has come."* Thus it was said unto John (Rev. 21:6), *It is done.* To represent the routing of the army of Gog as very great, here are three things specified as the consequences of it. It was God himself that gave the defeat; we do not find that the people of Israel drew a sword or struck a stroke: but,

I. They shall *burn their weapons,* their *bows and arrows,* which *fell out of their hands* (*v.* 3), *their shields and bucklers,* their *javelins, spears, leading staves, truncheons,* and *half-pikes,* every thing that is combustible. They shall not lay them up in their armouries, nor reserve them for their own use, lest they should be tempted to put a confidence in them, but they shall burn them; not all at once, for a bonfire (to what purpose would be that waste?) but as they had occasion to use them for fuel in their houses, instead of other fire-wood, so that they should have no occasion to *take wood out of the field or forests* for *seven years* together (*v.* 10), such vast quantities of weapons shall there be left upon the open field where the enemy fell, and in the roads which they passed in their flight. The weapons were dry and fitter for fuel than green wood; and, by saving the wood in their coppices and forests, they gave it time to grow. Though the mountains of Israel produce plenty of all good things, yet it becomes the people of Israel to be good husbands of their plenty and to save what they can for the benefit of those that come after them, as Providence shall give them opportunity to do so. We may suppose that when those who dwelt in the cities of Israel came forth to *spoil those who spoiled them,* and make reprisals upon them, they found upon them silver, and gold, and ornaments; yet no mention is made of any thing particularly that they converted to their own use but the wood of the weapons for fuel, which is one of the necessaries of human life, to teach us to think it enough if we be well supplied with those, though we have but little of the delights and gaieties of it and of those things which we may very well live without. And every time they put fuel to the fire, and warmed themselves at it, they would be put in mind of the number and strength of their enemies, and the imminent peril they were in of falling into their hands, which would help to enlarge their hearts in thankfulness to that God who had so wonderfully, so seasonably, delivered them. As they sat by *the fire* with their children about them (their fire-side), they might from it take occasion to tell them what great things God had done for them.

II. They shall bury their dead. Usually, after a battle, when many are slain, the enemy desire time to bury their own dead. But here the slaughter shall be so general that there shall not be a sufficient number of the enemies left alive to bury the dead. And, besides, the slain lie so dispersed on the mountains of Israel that it would be a work of time to find them out; and therefore it is left to the house of Israel to bury them as a piece of triumph in their overthrow. 1. A place shall be appointed on purpose for the burying of them, *the valley of the passengers, on the east of the sea,* either the salt sea or the sea of Tiberias, a valley through which there was great passing and repassing of travellers between Egypt and Chaldea. There shall be such a multitude of dead bodies, putrefying above ground, with such a loathsome stench, that the travellers who go that way shall be forced to *stop their noses.* See what vile bodies ours are; when the soul has been a little while from them the smell of them becomes offensive, no smell more nauseous or more noxious. There therefore where the greatest number lay slain shall the burying-place be appointed. In the place where the tree falls there let it lie. And it shall be called, *The valley of Hamon-gog,* that is, *of the multitude of Gog;* for that was the thing which was in a particular manner to be had in remembrance. How numerous the forces of the enemy were which God defeated and destroyed for the defence of his people Israel! 2. A considerable time shall be spent in burying them, no less than *seven months* (*v.* 12), which is a further intimation that the *slain of the Lord* in this action should be many and that great care should be taken by the house of Israel to leave none unburied, that so *they might cleanse the land* from the ceremonial pollution it contracted by the lying of so many dead corpses unburied in it, for the prevention of which it was appointed that those who were *hanged on a tree* should be speedily *taken down and buried,* Deut, 21:23. This is an intimation that times of eminent deliverances should be times of reformation. The more God has done for the saving of a land from ruin the more the inhabitants should do for the cleansing of the land from sin. 3. Great numbers shall be employed in this work: *All the people of the land* shall be ready to lend a helping hand to it, *v.* 13. Note, Every one should contribute the utmost he can in his place towards the cleansing of the land from the pollutions of it, and from every thing that is a reproach to it. Sin is a common enemy, which every man should take up arms against. *In publico discrimine unusquisque homo miles est — In the season of public danger every man becomes a soldier.* And whoever shall assist in this work *it shall be to them a renown;* though the office of grave-makers, or common scavengers of the country, seem but mean, yet, when it is for the cleansing and purifying of the land from dead works, it shall be mentioned to their honour. Note, Acts of humanity add much to the renown of God's Israel; it is a credit to religion when those that profess it are ready to every good work; and a good work it is to bury the dead, yea, though they be strangers and enemies to the commonwealth of Israel, for even they shall rise again. *It shall be a renown* to them in *the day when God will be glorified.* Note, It is for the glory of God when his Israel do that which adorns their profession; others *will see their good works and glorify their Father,* Mt. 5:16. And when God is honoured he will put honour upon his people. His glory is their renown. 4. Some particular persons shall make it their business to search out the dead bodies, or any part of them that should remain unburied. The *people of the land* will soon grow weary of burying the pollutions of the country, and therefore they shall appoint *men of continual employment,* that shall apply themselves to it and do nothing else till the land be thoroughly cleansed; for, otherwise, that which is every one's work would soon become nobody's work. Note, Those that are engaged in public work, especially for the cleansing and reforming of a land, ought to be *men of continual employments,* men that will stick to what they undertake and go through with it, men that will apply themselves to it; and those that will do good according to their opportunities will find themselves *continually employed.* 5. Even the passengers shall be ready to give information to those whose business it is to cleanse the land of what public nuisances they meet with, which call for their assistance. Those that *pass through the land,* though they will not stay to bury the dead themselves, lest they should contract a ceremonial pollution, will yet give notice of those that they find unburied. If they but discover a bone, they will *set up a sign,* that *the buriers may come and bury it,* and that, till it is buried, others may take need of touching it, for which reason their sepulchres among the Jews were whitened, that people might keep at a distance from them. Note, When good work is to be done every one should lend a hand to further it, even the passengers themselves, who must not think themselves unconcerned, in a common calamity, or a common iniquity, to put a stop to it. Those whose work it is to cleanse the land must not countenance any thing in it that is defiling; though it were not the body, but only *the bone, of a man,* that was found unburied, they must encourage those who will give information of it (private information, by a sign, concealing the informer), that they may take it away, and bury it out of sight. Nay, *after the end of seven months,* which was allowed them for this work, when all is taken away that appeared at first view, *they shall search* for more, that what is hidden may be brought to light; they shall *search out iniquity till they find none.* In memory of this they shall give a new name to their city. It shall be called *Hamonah — The multitude.* O what a multitude of our enemies have we of this city buried! *Thus shall they cleanse the land,* with all this care, with all this pains, *v.* 16. Note, After conquering there must be cleansing. Moses appointed those Israelites that had been employed in the war with the Midianites to *purify themselves,* Num. 31:24. Having received special favours from God, *let us cleanse ourselves from all filthiness.*

III. The birds and beasts of prey shall rest upon the carcases of the slain while they remain unburied and it shall be impossible to prevent them, *v.* 17, etc. We find a great slaughter represented by this figure, Rev. 19:17, etc., which is borrowed from this.

1. There is a general invitation given, *v.* 17. It is *to the fowl of every wing* and to *every beast of the field,* from the greatest to the least, that preys upon carcases, from the eagle to the raven, from the lion to the dog; let them

all gather themselves on every side; here is meat enough for them, and they are all welcome. Let them come to God's *sacrifice,* to his *feast;* so the margin reads it. Note, The judgments of God, executed upon sin and sinners, are both a sacrifice and a feast, a sacrifice to the justice of God and a feast to the faith and hope of God's people. When God *broke the head of leviathan,* he gave him to be *meat to Israel,* Ps. 74:14. *The righteous shall rejoice* as at a feast *when he sees the vengeance,* and shall *wash his foot,* as at a feast, *in the blood of the wicked.* This sacrifice is *upon the mountains of Israel;* these are the high places, the altars, where God has been dishonoured by the idolatries of the people, but where he will now glorify himself in the destruction of his enemies.

2. There is great preparation made: They shall *eat the flesh of the mighty* and *drink the blood of the princes of the earth, v.* 18, 18. (1.) It is the flesh and blood of men that they shall be treated with. This has sometimes been an instance of the rebellion of the inferior creatures against man their master, which is an effect of his rebellion against God his Maker. (2.) It is the flesh and blood of great men, here called *rams,* and *bullocks,* and *great goats, all of them fatlings of Bashan.* It is the blood of *the princes of the earth* that they shall regale themselves with. What a mortification is this to the princes of the blood, as they call themselves, that God can make that blood, that royal blood, which swells their veins, a feast for the birds and beasts of prey! (3.) It is the flesh and blood of wicked men, the enemies of God's church and people, that they are invited to. They had accounted the Israel of God as *sheep for the slaughter,* and now they shall themselves be so accounted; they had thus used the *dead bodies of Gods' servants* (Ps. 79:2), or would have done, and now it shall come upon themselves.

3. They shall all be fed, they shall all be feasted to the full (*v.* 19, 20): "*You shall eat fat, and drink blood,* which are satiating surfeiting things. The sacrifice is great and the feast upon the sacrifice is accordingly: *You shall be filled at my table.*" Note, God keeps a table for the inferior creatures; he *provides food for all flesh.* The *eyes of all wait upon him,* and he *satisfies their desires,* for he keeps a plentiful table. And if the birds and beasts shall be filled at God's table, which he has prepared for them, much more shall his children be abundantly satisfied with the goodness of his house, even of his holy temple. They shall be filled *with horses and chariots;* that is, those who ride in the chariots, *mighty men and men of war,* who triumphed over nations, are now themselves triumphed over by the *ravens of the valley* and the *young eagles,* Prov. 30:17. They thought to make an easy prey of God's Israel, and now they are themselves an easy prey to the birds and beasts. See how *evil pursues sinners* even after death. This exposing of their bodies to be a prey is but a type and sign of those terrors which, after death, shall prey upon their consciences (which the poetical fictions represented by a vulture continually pecking at the heart), and this shame is but an earnest of the everlasting shame and contempt they shall rise to.

IV. This shall redound very much both to the glory of God and to the comfort and satisfaction of his people. 1. It shall be much for the honour of God, for the heathen shall hereby be made to know that he is the Lord (*v.* 21): *All the heathen shall see* and observe *my judgments that I have executed,* and thereby my *glory shall be set among them.* This principle shall be admitted and established among them more than ever, that the God of Israel is a great and glorious God. He is known to be so even among the heathen, that have not, or read not, his written word, by *the judgments which he executes.* 2. It shall be much for the satisfaction of his people; for they shall hereby be made to know that he is their God (*v.* 22): *The house of Israel shall know,* abundantly to their comfort, that *I am the Lord their God from that day and forward.* (1.) He will be so from that day and forward. God's present mercies are pledges and assurances of further mercies. If God evidence to us that he is our God he assures us that he will never leave us. *This God is our God for ever and ever.* (2.) They shall know it with more satisfaction from that day and forward. They had sometimes been ready to question whether the Lord was with them or no; but the events of this day shall silence their doubts, and, the matter being thus settled and made clear, it shall not be doubted of for the future. As boasting in themselves is hereby for ever excluded, so boasting in God is hereby for ever secured.

Verses 23–29

This is the conclusion of the whole matter going before, and has reference not only to the predictions concerning Gog and Magog, but to all the prophecies of this book concerning the captivity of the house of Israel, and then concerning their restoration and return out of their captivity.

I. God will let the heathen know the meaning of his people's troubles, and rectify the mistake of those concerning them who took occasion from the troubles of Israel to reproach the God of Israel, as unable to protect them and untrue to his covenant with them. When God, upon their reformation and return to him, turned again their captivity, and brought them back to their own land, and, upon their perseverance in their reformation, wrought such great salvations for them as that from the attempts of Gog upon them, then it would be made to appear, even to the heathen that would but consider and compare things, that there was no ground at all for their reflection, that Israel went into captivity, not because God could not protect them, but because they had by sin forfeited his favour and thrown themselves out of his protection (*v.* 23, 24): *The heathen shall know that the house of Israel went into captivity for their iniquity,* that iniquity which they learned from the heathen their neighbours, *because they trespassed against God.* That was the true reason why God *hid his face from them* and *gave them into the hand of their enemies.* It was *according to their uncleanness* and *according to their transgressions.* Now the evincing of this will not only silence their reflections on God, but will redound greatly to his honour; when the troubles of God's people are over, and we see the end of them, we shall better understand them than we did at first. And it will appear much for the glory of God when the world is made to know, 1. That God punishes sin even in his own people, because he hates it most in those that are nearest and dearest to him, Amos 3:2. It is the praise of justice to be impartial. 2. That, when God gives up his people for a prey, it is to correct them and reform them, not to gratify their enemies, Isa. 10:7; 42:24. Let not them therefore exalt themselves. 3. That no sooner do God's people humble themselves under the rod than he returns in mercy to them.

II. God will give his own people to know what great favour he has in store for them notwithstanding the troubles he had brought them into (*v.* 25, 26): *Now will I bring again the captivity of Jacob.*

1. Why now? Now God will *have mercy upon the whole house of Israel,* (1.) Because it is time for him to stand up for his own glory, which suffers in their sufferings: *Now will I be jealous for my holy name,* that that may no longer be reproached. (2.) Because now they repent of their sins: They *have borne their shame, and all their trespasses.* When sinners repent, and take shame to themselves, God will be reconciled and put honour upon them. It is particularly pleasing to God that these penitents look a great way back in their penitential reflections, and are ashamed of all their trespasses which they were guilty of *when they dwelt safely in their land and none made them afraid.* The remembrance of the mercies they enjoyed in their own land, and the divine protection they were under there, shall be improved as an aggravation of the sins they committed in that land; they dwelt safely, and might have continued to dwell so, and none should have given them any disquiet or disturbance if they had continued in the way of their duty. Nay, *therefore* they trespassed because *they dwelt safely.* Outward safety is often a cause of inward security, and that is an inlet to all sin, Ps. 73. Now this they are willing to bear the shame of, and acknowledge that God has justly brought them into a land of trouble, where every one makes them afraid, because they had trespassed against him in a land of peace, where none made them afraid. And, when they thus humble themselves under humbling providences, God will bring again their captivity: and,

2. What then? When God has gathered them out of their enemies' hands, and brought them home again, (1.) Then God will have the praise of it: I will be *sanctified in them in the sight of many nations, v.* 27. As God was reproached in the reproach they were under during their captivity, so he will be sanctified in their reformation and the making of them a holy people again, and will be glorified in their restoration and the making of them a happy glorious people again. (2.) Then they shall have the benefit of it (*v.* 28): *They shall know that I am the Lord their God.* Note, The providences of God concerning his people, that are designed for their good, have the grace of God going along with them to teach them to eye God as the Lord, and their God, in all; and then they do them good. They shall eye him as the Lord and their God, [1.] In their calamities, that it was he who *caused them to be led into captivity;* and therefore they must not only submit to his will, but endeavour to answer his end in it. [2.] In their comfort, that it is he who has *gathered them to their own land,* and left none of them among the heathen. Note, By the variety of events that befal us, if we look up to God in all, we may come to acquaint ourselves better with his various attributes and designs. (3.) Then God and they will never part, *v.* 29. [1.] God will *pour out his Spirit* upon them, to prevent their departures from him and returns to folly again, and to keep them close to their duty. And then, [2.] He will *never hide his face any more from them,* will never suspend his favour as he had done; he will never turn from doing them good, and, in order to that, he will effectually provide that they shall never turn from doing him service. Note, The indwelling of the Spirit is an infallible pledge of the continuance of God's favour. He will hide his face no more from those on whom he has *poured out his Spirit.* When therefore we pray that God would never *cast us away from his presence* we must as earnestly pray that, in order to that, he would *never take his Holy Spirit away from us,* Ps. 51:11.

CHAPTER 40

The waters of the sanctuary which this prophet saw in vision (47:1) are a proper representation of this prophecy. Hitherto the waters have been sometimes but to the ankles, in other places to the knees, or to the loins, but now the waters have risen, and have become "a river which cannot be passed over." Here is one continued vision, beginning at this chapter, to the end of the book, which is justly looked upon to be one of the most difficult portions of scripture in all the book of God. The Jews will not allow any to read it till they are thirty years old, and tell those who do read it that, though they cannot understand every thing in it, "when Elias comes he will explain it." Many commentators, both ancient and modern, have owned themselves at a loss what to make of it and what use to make of it. But because it is hard to be understood we must not therefore throw it by, but humbly search concerning it, get as far as we can into it and as much as we can out of it, and, when we despair of satisfaction in every difficulty we meet with, bless God that our salvation does not depend upon it, but that things necessary are plain enough, and wait till God shall reveal even this unto us. These chapters are the more to be regarded because the last two chapters of the Revelation seem to have a plain allusion to them, as Rev. 20 has to the foregoing prophecy of Gog and Magog. Here is the vision of a glorious temple (in this chapter and *ch.* 41 and 42), of God's taking possession of it (*ch.* 43), orders concerning the priests that are to minister in this temple (*ch.* 44), the division of the land, what portion should be allotted for the sanctuary, what for the city, and what for the prince, both in his government of the people and his worship of God (*ch.* 45), and further instructions for him and the people, *ch.* 46. After the vision of the holy waters we have the borders of the holy land, and the portions assigned to the tribes, and the dimensions and gates of the holy city, *ch.* 47, 48. Some make this to represent what had been during the flourishing state of the Jewish church, how glorious Solomon's temple was in its best days, that the captives might see what they had lost by sin and might be the more humbled. But that seems not probable. The general scope of it I take to be, 1. To assure the captives that they should not only return to their own land, and be settled there, which had been often promised in the foregoing chapters, but that they should have, and therefore should be encouraged to build, another temple, which God would own, and where he would meet them and bless them, that the ordinances of worship should be revived, and the sacred priesthood should there attend; and, though they should not have a king to live in such splendour as formerly, yet they should have a prince or ruler (who is often spoken of in this vision), who should countenance the worship of God among them and should himself be an example of diligent attendance upon it, and that prince, priests, and people, should have a very comfortable settlement and subsistence in their own land. 2. To direct them to look further than all this, and to expect the coming of the Messiah, who had before been prophesied of under the name of David because he was the man that projected the building of the temple and that should set up a spiritual temple, even the gospel-church, the glory of which should far exceed that of Solomon's temple, and which should continue to the end of time. The dimensions of these visionary buildings being so large (the new temple more spacious than all the old Jerusalem and the new Jerusalem of greater extent than all the land of Canaan) plainly intimates, as Dr. Lightfoot observes, that these things cannot be literally, but must spiritually, understood. At the gospel-temple, erected by Christ and his apostles, was so closely connected with the second material temple, was erected so carefully just at the time when that fell into decay, that it might be ready to receive its glories when it resigned them, that it was proper enough that they should both be referred to in one and the same vision. Under the type and figure of a temple and altar, priests and sacrifices, is foreshown the spiritual worship that should be performed in gospel times, more agreeable to the nature both of God and man, and that perfected at last in the kingdom of glory, in which perhaps these visions will have their full accomplishment, and some think in some happy and glorious state of the gospel-church on this side heaven, in the latter days.

In this chapter we have, I. A general account of this vision of the temple and city (*v.* 1–4). II. A particular account of it entered upon; and a description given, 1. Of the outside wall (*v.* 5). 2. Of the east gate (*v.* 6–19). 3. Of the north gate (*v.* 20–23). 4. Of the south gate (*v.* 24–31) and the chambers and other appurtenances belonging to these gates. 5. Of the inner court, both towards the east and towards the south (*v.* 32–38). 6. Of the tables (*v.* 39–43). 7. Of the lodgings for the singers and the priests (*v.* 44–47). 8. Of the porch of the house (*v.* 48, 49).

Verses 1–4

Here is, 1. The date of this vision. It was in the twenty-fifth year of Ezekiel's captivity (*v.* 1), which some compute to be the thirty-third year of the first captivity, and is here said to be the *fourteenth year after the city was smitten.* See how seasonably the clearest and fullest prospects of their deliverance were given, when they were in the depth of their distress, and an assurance of the return of the morning when they were in the midnight of their captivity: "Then *the hand of the Lord was upon me* and *brought me thither* to Jerusalem, now that it was in ruins, desolate and deserted" — a pitiable sight to the prophet. 2. The scene where it was laid. The prophet was brought, *in the visions of God, to the land of Israel, v.* 2. And it was not the first time that he had been brought thither in vision. We had him carried to Jerusalem to see it in its iniquity and shame (*ch.* 8:3); here he is carried thither to have a pleasing prospect of it in its glory, though its present aspect, now that it was quite depopulated, was dismal. He was set *upon a very high mountain,* as Moses upon the top of Pisgah, to view this land, which was now a second time a *land of promise,* not yet in possession. From the top of this mountain he saw *as the frame of a city,* the plan and model of it; but this city was a temple as large as a city. The *New Jerusalem* (Rev. 21:22) had *no temple therein;* this which we have here is *all temple,* which comes much to one. It is a city for men to dwell in; it is a temple for God to dwell in; for in the church on earth God dwells with men, in that in heaven men dwell with God. Both these are framed in the counsel of God, framed by infinite wisdom, and all very good. 3. The particular discoveries of this city (which he had at first a general view of) were made to him by *a man whose appearance was like the appearance of brass* (*v.* 3), not a created angel, but Jesus Christ, who should be found in fashion as a man, that he might both discover and build the gospel-temple. He brought him to this city, for it is through Christ that we have both acquaintance with and access to the benefits and privileges of God's house. He it is that *shall build the temple of the Lord,* Zec. 6:13. His appearing like brass intimates both his brightness and his strength. John, in vision, saw *his feet like unto fine brass,* Rev. 1:15. 4. The dimensions of this city or temple, and the several parts of it, were taken with a *line of flax* and a *measuring reed,* or *rod* (*v.* 3), as carpenters have both their line and a wooden measure. The temple of God is built by line and rule; and those that would let others into the knowledge of it must do it by that line and rule. The church is formed according to the scripture, *the pattern in the mount.* That is the line and the measuring reed that is in the hand of Christ. With that doctrine and laws ought to be measured, and examined by that; for then peace is upon the Israel of God when they *walk according to that rule.* 5. Directions are here given to the prophet to receive this revelation from the Lord and transmit it pure and entire to the church, *v.* 4. (1.) He must carefully observe every thing that was said and done in this vision. His attention is raised and engaged (*v.* 4): "*Behold with thy eyes* all that is *shown thee* (do not only see it, but look intently upon it), and *hear with thy ears* all that is *said to thee;* diligently hearken to it, and be sure *to set thy heart upon it;* attend with a fixedness of thought and a close application of mind." What we see of the works of God, and what we hear of the word of God, will do us no good unless we set out hearts upon it, as those that reckon ourselves nearly concerned in it, and expect advantage to our souls by it. (2.) He must faithfully *declare it to the house of Israel,* that they may have the comfort of it. Therefore he receives, that he may give. Thus the *Revelation of Jesus Christ* was lodged in the hands of John, that he might signify it to the churches, Rev. 1:1. And, because he is to declare it as a message from God, he must therefore be fully apprised of it himself and much affected with it. Note, Those who are to preach God's word to others ought to study it well themselves and set their hearts upon it. Now the reason given why he must both observe it himself and declare it to the house of Israel is because to this intent he is brought hither, and has it shown to him. Note, When the things of God are shown to us it concerns us to consider to what intent they are shown to us, and, when we are sitting under the ministry of the word, to consider to what intent we are brought thither, that we may answer the end of our coming, and may not receive the grace of God, in showing us such things, in vain.

Verses 5–26

The measuring-reed which was in the hand of the surveyor-general was mentioned before, *v.* 3. Here we are told (*v.* 5) what was the exact length of it, which must be observed, because the house was measured by it. It was *six cubits long,* reckoning, not by the common cubit, but the *cubit of the sanctuary,* the sacred cubit, by which it was fit that this holy house should be measured, and that was a hand-breadth (that it, four inches) longer than the common cubit: the common cubit was eighteen inches, this twenty-two, see *ch.* 43:13. Yet some of the critics contend that this *measuring-reed* was but six common cubits in length, and one handbreadth added to the whole. The former seems more probable. Here is an account,

I. Of the outer wall of the house, which encompassed it round, which was three yards thick and three yards high, which denotes the separation between the church and the world on every side and the divine protection which the church is under. If a wall of this vast thickness will not secure it, God himself will be *a wall of fire round about it;* whoever attack it will do so at their peril.

II. Of the several gates with the chambers adjoining to them. Here is no mention of the outer court of all, which was called the *court of the Gentiles,* some think because in gospel-times there should be such a vast confluence of Gentiles to the church that their court should be left unmeasured, to signify that the worshippers in that court should be unnumbered, Rev. 7:9, 11, 12.

1. He begins with the *east gate,* because that was the usual way of entering into the lower end of the temple, the holy of holies being at the west end, in opposition to the idolatrous heathen that worshipped towards the east. Now, in the account of this gate, observe, (1.) That he went up to it by *stairs* (*v.* 6), for the gospel-church was exalted above that of the Old Testament, and when we go to worship God we must ascend; so is the call, Rev. 4:1. Come up hither. *Sursum corda — Up with your hearts.* (2.) That the chambers adjoining to the gates were but *little chambers,* about ten feet square, *v.* 7. These were for those to lodge in who attended the service of the house. And it becomes such as are made spiritual priests to God to content themselves with little chambers and not to seek great things to themselves; so that we may but have a place within the verge of God's court we have reason to be thankful though it be in a little chamber, a mean apartment, though we be but door-keepers there. (3.) The chambers, as they were each of them four-square, denoting their stability and due proportion and their exact agreement with the rule (for they were each of them one reed long and one reed broad), so they were all of *one measure,* that there might be an equality among the attendants on the service of the house. (4.) The chambers were very many; for in our Father's house there are *many mansions* (Jn. 14:2), in his house above, and in that here on earth. In the secret of his tabernacle shall those be hid, and in a safe pavilion, whose desire is to dwell in the house of the Lord all the days of their life, Ps. 27:4, 5. Some make these chambers to represent the particular congregations of believers, which are parts of the great temple, the universal church, which are, and must be, framed by the scripture-line and rule, and which Jesus Christ takes the measure of, that is, takes cognizance of, for he walks in the midst of the seven golden candle-sticks. (5.) It is said (*v.* 14), *He made also the posts.* He that now measured them was the same that made them; for Christ is the builder of his church and therefore is best able to give us the knowledge of it. And his reducing them to the rule and standard is called his making them, for no account is made of them further than they agree with that. *To the law and to the testimony.* (6.) Here are posts of sixty cubits, which, some think, was literally fulfilled when Cyrus, in his edict for rebuilding the temple at Jerusalem, ordered that the height thereof should be sixty cubits, that is, thirty yards and more, Ezra 6:3. (7.) Here were windows to the little chambers, and windows to *the posts and arches* (that is, to the cloisters below), and *windows round about* (*v.* 16), to signify the light from heaven with which the church is illuminated; divine revelation is let into it for instruction, direction, and comfort, to those that dwell in God's house, light to work by, light to walk by, light to see themselves and one another by. There were lights to the little chambers; even the least, and least considerable, parts and members of the church, shall have light afforded them. *All thy children shall be taught of the Lord.* But they are *narrow windows,* as those in the temple, 1 Ki. 6:4. The discoveries made to the church on earth are but narrow and scanty compared with what shall be in the future state, when we shall no longer *see through a glass darkly.* (8.) Divers courts are here spoken of, an outermost of all, then an outer court, then an inner, and then the innermost of all, into which the priests only entered, which (some think) may put us in mind "of the diversities of gifts, and graces, and offices, in the several members of Christ's mystical body here, as also of the several degrees of glory in the courts and mansions of heaven, as there are stars in several spheres and stars of several magnitudes in the fixed firmament." *English Annotations.* Some draw nearer to God than others and have a more intimate acquaintance with divine things; but to a child of God a day in any of his courts is *better than a thousand* elsewhere. These courts had porches, or piazzas, round them, for the shelter of those that attended in them from wind and weather; for when we are in the way of our duty to God we may believe ourselves to be under his special protection, that he will graciously provide for us, nay, that he will himself be to us *a covert from the storm and tempest,* Isa. 4:5, 6. (9.) On the posts were palm-trees engraven (*v.* 16), to signify that *the righteous shall flourish like the palm-tree* in the courts of God's house, Ps. 92:12. The more they are depressed with the burden of affliction the more strongly do they grow, as they say of the palm-trees. It likewise intimates the saints' victory and triumph over their spiritual enemies; they have *palms in their hands* (Rev. 7:9); but lest they should drop these, or have them snatched out of their hands, they are here engraven upon the posts of the temple as perpetual monuments of their honour. *Thanks be to God, who always causes us to triumph.* Nay, believers shall themselves be made pillars in the temple of our God, and shall *go no more out,* and shall have his name engraven on them, which will be their brightest ornament and honour, Rev. 3:12. (10.) Notice is here taken of the pavement of the court, *v.* 17, 18. The word intimates that the pavement was made of *porphyry-stone,* which was of the colour of *burning coals;* for the brightest and most sparkling glories of this world should be put and kept under our feet when we draw near to God and are attending upon him. The stars are, as it were, the *burning coals,* or stones of a *fiery colour,* with which the pavement of God's celestial temple is laid; and, if the pavement of the court be so bright and glittering, how glorious must we conclude the mansions of that house to be!

2. The gates that looked towards the north (*v.* 20) and towards the south (*v.* 24), with their appurtenances, are much the same with that towards the east, *after the measure of the first gate, v.* 21. But the description is repeated very particularly. And thus largely was the structure of the tabernacle related in Exodus, and of the temple in the books of Kings and Chronicles, to signify the special notice God does take, and his ministers should take, of all that belong to his church. His delight is in them; his eye is upon them. He knows all that are his, all his living temples and all that belongs to them. Observe, (1.) This temple had not only a gate towards the east, to let into it the *children of the east,* that were famous for their wealth and wisdom, but it had a gate to the north, and another to the south, for the admission of the poorer and less civilized nations. The new Jerusalem has *twelve gates,* three towards each quarter of the world (Rev. 21:13); for many shall come from all parts to sit down there, Mt. 8:11. (2.) To those gates they went up by steps, *seven steps* (*v.* 22–26), which,

as some observe, may remind us of the necessity of advancing in grace and holiness, adding one grace to another, going from step to step, *from strength to strength,* still pressing forward towards perfection — upward, upward, towards heaven, the temple above.

Verses 27–38

In these verses we have a delineation of the inner court. The survey of the outer court ended with the south side of it. This of the inner court begins with the south side (*v.* 27), proceeds to the east (*v.* 32), and so to the north (*v.* 35); for here is no gate either of the outer or inner court towards the *west.* It should seem that in Solomon's temple there were gates westward, for we find porters towards the west, 1 Chr. 9:24; 26:8. But Josephus says that in the second temple there was no gate on the west side. Observe, 1. These gates into the inner court were exactly uniform with those into the outer court, the dimensions the same, the chambers adjoining the same, the galleries or rows round the court the same, and the very engravings on the posts the same. The work of grace, and its workings, are the same, for substance, in grown Christians that they are in young beginners, only that the former have got so much nearer their perfection. The faith of all the saints is alike precious, though it be not alike strong. There is a great resemblance between one child of God and another; for *all they are brethren* and bear the same image. 2. The ascent into the outer court at each gate was by *seven steps,* but the ascent into the inner court at each gate was by *eight steps.* This is expressly taken notice of (*v.* 31, 34, 37), to signify that the nearer we approach to God the more we should rise above this world and the things of it. The people, who worshipped in the outer court, must rise seven steps above other people, but the priests, who attended in the inner court, must rise eight steps above them, must exceed them at least one step more than they exceed other people.

Verses 39–49

In these verses we have an account,

I. Of the tables that were in the porch of the gates of the inner court. We find no description of the altars of burnt-offerings in the midst of that court till *ch.* 43:13. But, because the one altar under the law was to be exchanged for a multitude of tables under the gospel, here is *early notice* taken of the tables, at our entrance into the inner court; for till we come to partake of the *table of the Lord* we are but professors at large; our admission to that is our entrance into the inner court. But in this gospel-temple we meet with no altar till after the glory of the Lord has taken possession of it, for Christ is our altar, that sanctifies every gift. Here were eight tables provided, whereon to *slay the sacrifices, v.* 41. We read not of any tables for this purpose either in the tabernacle or in Solomon's temple. But here they are provided, to intimate the multitude of spiritual sacrifices that should be brought to God's house in gospel-times, and the multitude of hands that should be employed in offering up those sacrifices. Here were the shambles for the altar; here were the dressers on which they laid the flesh of the sacrifice, the knives with which they cut it up, and the hooks on which they hung it up, that it might be ready to be offered on the altar (*v.* 43), and there also they washed the burnt-offerings (*v.* 38), to intimate that before we draw near to God's altar we must have every thing in readiness, must wash our hands, our hearts, those spiritual sacrifices, and so *compass God's altar.*

II. The use that some of the chambers mentioned before were put to. 1. Some were for the *singers, v.* 44. It should seem they were first provided for before any other that attended this temple-service, to intimate, not only that the singing of psalms should still continue a gospel-ordinance, but that the gospel should furnish all that embrace it with abundant matter for joy and praise, and give them occasion to *break forth into singing,* which is often foretold concerning gospel times, Ps. 96:1; 98:1. Christians should be singers. *Blessed are those that dwell in God's house,* they will be *still praising him.* 2. Others of them were for *the priests,* both those that kept *the charge of the house,* to cleanse it, and to see that none came into it to pollute it, and to keep it in good repair (*v.* 45), and those that *kept the charge of the altar* (*v.* 46), that *came near to the Lord to minister to him.* God will find convenient lodging for all his servants. Those that do the work of his house shall enjoy the comforts of it.

III. Of the inner court, the court of the priests, which was fifty yards square, *v.* 47. The altar that *was before the house* was placed in the midst of this court, over-against the three gates, and, standing in a direct line with the three gates of the outer court, when the gates were set open all the people in the outer court might through them be spectators of the service done at the altar. Christ is both our altar and our sacrifice, to whom we must look with an eye of faith in all our approaches to God, and he is salvation in the midst of the earth (Ps. 74:12), to be looked unto from all quarters.

IV. Of the porch of the house. The temple is called the house, emphatically, as if no other house were worthy to be called so. Before this house there was a porch, to teach us not to rush hastily and inconsiderately into the presence of God, but gradually, that is, gravely, and with solemnity, passing first through the outer court, then the inner, then the porch, ere we enter into the house. Between this porch and the altar was a place where the priests used to pray, Joel 2:17. In the porch, besides the posts on which the doors were hung, there were pillars, probably for state and ornament, like *Jachin* and *Boaz — He will establish; in him is strength, v.* 49. In the gospel church every thing is strong and firm, and every thing ought to be kept in its place and to be done decently and in order.

CHAPTER 41

An account was given of the porch of the house in the close of the foregoing chapter; this brings us to the temple itself, the description of which here given creates much difficulty to the critical expositors and occasions differences among them. Those must consult them who are nice in their enquiries into the meaning of the particulars of this delineation; it shall suffice us to observe, I. The dimensions of the house, the posts of it (*v.* 1), the door (*v.* 2), the wall and the side-chambers (*v.* 5, 6), the foundations and wall of the chambers, their doors (*v.* 8–11), and the house itself (*v.* 13). II. The dimensions of the oracle, or most holy place (*v.* 3, 4). III. An account of another building over against the separate place (*v.* 12–15). IV. The manner of the building of the house (*v.* 7, 16, 17). V. The ornaments of the house (*v.* 18–20). VI. The altar of incense and the table (*v.* 22). VII. The doors between the temple and the oracle (*v.* 23–26). There is so much difference both in the terms and in the rules of architecture between one age and another, one place and another, that it ought not to be any stumbling-block to us that there is so much in these descriptions dark and hard to be understood, about the meaning of which the learned are not agreed. To one not skilled in mathematics the mathematical description of a modern structure would be scarcely intelligible; and yet to a common carpenter or mason among the Jews at that time we may suppose that all this, in the literal sense of it, was easy enough.

Verses 1–11

We are still attending a prophet that is under the guidance of an angel, and therefore attend with reverence, though we are often at a loss to know both what this is and what it is to us. Observe here, 1. After the prophet had observed the courts he was at length *brought to the temple, v.* 1. If we diligently attend to the instructions given us in the plainer parts of religion, and profit by them, we shall be led further into an acquaintance with the mysteries of the kingdom of heaven. Those that are willing to dwell in God's courts shall at length be brought into his temple. Ezekiel was himself a priest, but by the iniquity and calamity of the times was cut short of his birthright privilege of ministering in the temple; but God makes up the loss to him by introducing him into this prophetical, evangelical, celestial temple, and employing him to transmit a description of it to the church, in which he was dignified above all the rest of his order. 2. When our Lord Jesus spoke of the destroying of *this temple,* which his hearers understood of this second temple of Jerusalem, he spoke of the temple of his body (Jn. 2:19, 21); and with good reason might he speak so ambiguously when Ezekiel's vision had a joint respect to them both together, including also his mystical body the church, which is called the *house of God* (1 Tim. 3:15), and all the members of that body, which are *living temples,* in which the Spirit dwells. 3. The very posts of this temple, the door-posts, were as far one from the other, and consequently the door was as wide, as *the* whole *breadth of the tabernacle* of Moses (*v.* 1), namely, twelve cubits, Ex. 26:16, 22, 25. In comparison with what had been under the law we may say, *Wide is the gate* which leads into the church, the ceremonial law, that wall of partition which had so much straitened the gate, being taken down. 4. The most holy place was an exact square, twenty cubits each way, *v.* 4. For the new Jerusalem is exactly square (Rev. 21:16), denoting its stability; for we look for a city that cannot be moved. 5. The upper stories were larger than the lower, *v.* 7. The walls of the temple were six cubits thick at the bottom, five in the middle story, and four in the highest, which gave room to enlarge the chambers the higher they went; but care was taken that the timber might have *fast hold* (though God builds high, he builds firmly), yet so as not to weaken one part for the strengthening of another; they had hold, but not *in the wall of the house.* By this spreading gradually, the *side-chambers* that were on *the height of the house* (in the uppermost story of all) were six cubits, whereas the lowest were but four; they gained a cubit every story. The higher we build up ourselves in our most holy faith the more should our hearts, those living temples, be enlarged.

Verses 12–26

Here is, 1. An account of a building that was *before the separate place* (that is, before the temple), *at the end towards the west* (*v.* 12), which is here measured, and compared (*v.* 13) with the measure of the house, and appears to be of equal dimensions with it. This stood in a court by itself, which is measured (*v.* 15) and its galleries, or chambers belonging to it, its posts and windows, and the ornaments of them, *v.* 15–17. But what use was to be made of this other building we are not told; perhaps, in this vision, it signified the setting up of a church among the Gentiles not inferior to the Jewish temple, but of quite another nature, and which should soon supersede it. 2. A description of the ornaments of the temple, and the other building. The walls on the inside from top to bottom were adorned with *cherubim and palm-trees,* placed alternately, as in Solomon's temple, 1 Ki. 6:29. Each cherub is here said to have two *faces,* the *face of a man* towards the palm tree on one side and the *face of a young lion towards the palm-tree* on the other side, *v.* 19. These seem to represent the angels, who have more than the wisdom of a man and the courage of a lion; and in both they have an eye to the palms of victory and triumph which are set before them, and which they are sure of in all their conflicts with the powers of darkness. And in the assemblies of the saints angels are in a special manner present, 1 Co. 11:10. 3. A description of the posts of the doors both of the temple and of the sanctuary; they were *squared* (*v.* 21), not round like pillars; and *the appearance of the one was as the appearance of the other.* In the tabernacle, and in Solomon's temple, the door of the sanctuary, or most holy, was narrower than that of the temple, but here it was fully as broad; for in gospel-times *the way into the holiest of all is made* more *manifest* than it was under the Old Testament (Heb. 9:8) and therefore the door is wider. These doors are described, *v.* 23, 24. The temple and the sanctuary had each of them its door, and they were *two-leaved,* folding doors. 4. We have here the description of the altar of incense, here said to be an *altar of wood, v.* 22. No mention is made of its being *over-laid with gold;* but surely it was intended to be so, else it would not bear the fire with which the incense was to be burned, unless we will suppose that it served only to put the censers upon. Or else it intimates that the incense to be offered in the gospel-temple shall be purely spiritual, and the fire spiritual, which will not consume an altar of wood. Therefore this altar is called a table. *This is the table that is before the Lord.* Here, as before, we find the altar turned into a table; for, the great sacrifice being now offered, that which we have to do is to feast upon the sacrifice at the Lord's table. 5. Here is the adorning of the doors and windows with palm-trees, that they might be of a piece with the walls of the house, *v.* 25, 26. Thus the living temples are adorned, not with gold, or silver, or costly array, but with *the hidden man of the heart, in that which is not corruptible.*

CHAPTER 42

This chapter continues and concludes the describing and measuring of this mystical temple, which it is very hard to understand the particular architecture of, and yet more hard to comprehend the mystical meaning of. Here is, I. A description of the chambers that were about the courts, their situation and structure (*v.* 1–13), and the uses for which they were designed (*v.* 13, 14). II. A survey of the whole compass of ground which was taken up with the house, and the courts belonging to it (*v.* 15–20).

Verses 1–14

The prophet has taken a very exact view of the temple and the buildings belonging to it, and is now brought again into the outer court, to observe the chambers that were in that square.

I. Here is a description of these chambers, which (as that which went before) seems to us very perplexed and intricate, through our unacquaintedness with the Hebrew language and the rules of architecture at that time. We shall only observe, in general, 1. That about the temple, which was the place of public worship, there were private chambers, to teach us that our attendance upon God in solemn ordinances will not excuse us from the duties of the closet. We must not only worship in the courts of God's house, but must, both before and after our attendance there, enter into our chambers, enter into our closets, and read and meditate, and *pray to our Father in secret;* and a great deal of comfort the people of God have found in their communion with God in solitude. 2. That these chambers were many; there were *three stories* of them, and, though the higher stories were not so large as the lower, yet they served as well for retirement, *v.* 5, 6. There were many, that there might be conveniences for all such devout people as Anna the prophetess, who *departed not from the temple night or day,* Lu. 2:37. *In my Father's house are many mansions.* In his house on earth there are so; multitudes by faith have taken lodgings in his sanctuary, and *yet there is room.* 3. That these chambers, though they were private, yet were near the temple, within view of it, within reach of it, to teach us to prefer public worship before private *(the Lord loves the gates of Zion more than all the dwellings of Jacob,* and so must we), and to refer our private worship to the public. Our religious performances in our chambers must be to prepare us for the exercises of devotion in public, and to further us in our improvement of them, as our opportunities are. 4. That before these chambers there were *walks of five yards broad* (*v.* 4), in which those that had lodgings in these chambers might meet for conversation, might walk and talk together for their mutual edification, might communicate their knowledge and experiences. For we are not to spend all our time between the church and the chamber, though a great deal of time may be spent to very good purpose in both. But man is made for society, and Christians for the communion of saints; and the duties of that communion we must make conscience of, and the privileges and pleasures of that communion we must take the comfort of. It is promised to Joshua, who was high priest in the second temple, that God will *give him places to walk in among those that stand by,* Zec. 3:7.

II. Here is the use of these chambers appointed, *v.* 13, 14. 1. They were *for the priests* that approach unto the Lord, that they may be always near their business and may not be non-residents. *Therefore* they are called *holy chambers,* because they were for use of those that ministered in holy things during their ministration. Those that have public work to do for God and the souls of men have need to be much in private, to fit themselves for it. Ministers should spend much time in their chambers, in reading, meditation, and prayer, that their *profiting may appear;* and they ought to be provided with conveniences for this purpose. 2. There the priests were to deposit *the most holy things,* those parts of the offerings which fell to their share; and there they were to *eat them,* they and their families, in a religious manner, for *the place is holy;* and thus they must make a difference between those feasts upon the sacrifice and other meals. 3. There (among other uses) they were to lay their vestments, which God had appointed them to wear when they ministered at the altar, their linen ephods, coats, girdles, and bonnets. We read of the providing of priests garments after their return out of captivity, Neh. 7:70, 72. When they had ended their service at the altar they must lay by those garments, to signify that the use of them should continue only during that dispensation; but they must *put on other garments,* such as other people wear, when they *approached to those things which were for the people,* that is, to do that part of their service which related to the people, to teach them the law and to answer their enquiries. Their holy garments must be *laid up,* that they may be kept clean and decent for the credit of their service.

Verses 15–20

We have attended the measuring of this mystical temple and are now to see how far the holy ground on which we tread extends; and that also is here measured, and found to take in a great compass. Observe, 1. What the dimensions of it were. It extended each way 500 reeds (*v.* 16–19), each reed above three yards and a half, so that it reached every way about an English measured mile, which, the ground lying square, was above four miles round. Thus large were the suburbs (as I may call them) of this mystical temple, signifying the great extent of the church in gospel-times, when all nations should be discipled and the kingdoms of the world made Christ's kingdoms. Room should be made in God's courts for the numerous forces of the Gentiles that shall flow into them, as was foretold, Isa. 49:18; 60:4. It is in part fulfilled already in the accession of the Gentiles to the church; and we trust it shall have a more full accomplishment when the *fulness of the Gentiles shall come in* and *all Israel shall be saved.* 2. Why the dimensions of it were made thus large. It was to *make a separation,* by putting a very large distance *between the sanctuary* and *the profane place;* and *therefore* there was a wall surrounding it, to keep off those that were unclean and to separate between the *previous and the vile.* Note, A difference is to be put between common and sacred things, between God's name and other names, between his day and other days, his book and other books, his institutions and other observances; and a distance is to be put between our worldly and religious actions, so as still to go about the worship of God with a solemn pause.

CHAPTER 43

The prophet, having given us a view of the mystical temple, the gospel-church, as he received it from the Lord, that it might appear not to be erected in vain, comes to describe, in this and the next chapter, the worship that should be performed in it, but under the type of the Old-Testament services. In this chapter we have, I. Possession taken of this temple, by the glory of God filling it (*v.* 1–6). II. A promise given of the continuance of God's presence with his people upon condition of their return to, and continuance in, the instituted way of worship, and their abandoning idols and idolatry (*v.* 7–12). III. A description of the altar of burnt-offerings (*v.* 13–17). IV. Directions given for the consecration of that altar (*v.* 18–27). Ezekiel seems here to stand between God and Israel, as Moses the servant of the Lord did when the sanctuary was first set up.

Verses 1–6

After Ezekiel has patiently surveyed the temple of God, the greatest glory of this earth, he is admitted to a higher form, and honoured with a sight of the glories of the upper world; it is said to him, *Come up hither.* He has seen the temple, and sees it to be very spacious and splendid; but, till the glory of God comes into it, it is but like the dead bodies he had seen in vision (*ch.* 37), that had *no breath* till the Spirit of life entered into them. Here therefore he sees the house filled with God's glory.

I. He has a vision of *the glory of God* (*v.* 2), *the glory of the God of Israel,* that God who is in covenant with Israel, and whom they serve and worship. The idols of the heathen have no glory but what they owe to the goldsmith or the painter; but this is the glory of the God of Israel. This glory *came from the way of the east,* and therefore he was brought to the *gate that leads towards the east,* to expect the appearance and approach of it. Christ's *star was seen in the east,* and he is that *other angel that ascends out of the east,* Rev. 7:2. For he is the morning star, he is the sun of righteousness. Two things he observed in this appearance of the glory of God: — 1. The power of his word which he heard: *His voice was like a noise of many waters,* which is heard very far, and makes impressions; the noise of purling streams is grateful, of a roaring sea dreadful, Rev. 1:15; 14:2. Christ's gospel, in the glory of which he shines, was to be proclaimed aloud, the report of it to be heard far; to some it is a savour of life, to others of death, according as they are. 2. The brightness of his appearance which he saw: *The earth shone with his glory;* for God is light, and none can bear the lustre of his light, none *has seen* nor *can see it.* Note, That glory of God which shines in the church shines on the world. When God appeared for David *the brightness that was before him* dispersed the clouds, Ps. 18:12. This appearance of the glory of God to Ezekiel he observed to be the same with the vision he saw when he first received his commission (*ch.* 1:4), *according to that by the river Chebar* (*v.* 3); because God is the same, he was pleased to manifest himself in the same manner, for with him is *no variableness.* "It was the same" (says he) "as that which I saw *when I came to destroy the city,* that is, to foretel the city's destruction," which he did with such authority and efficacy, and the event did so certainly answer the prediction, that he might be said to destroy it. As a judge, in God's name, he passed a sentence upon it, which was soon executed. God appeared in the same manner when he sent him to speak words of terror and when he sent him to speak words of comfort; for in both God is and will be glorified. *He kills and he makes alive;* he *wounds and he heals,* Deu. 32:39. To the same hand that destroyed we must look for deliverance. *He has smitten, and he will bind up. Una eademque manus vulnus opemque tulit — The same hand inflicted the wound and healed it.*

II. He has a vision of the entrance of this glory into the temple. When he saw this glory he *fell upon his face* (*v.* 3), as not *able* to bear the lustre of God's glory, or rather as one willing to give him the glory of it by a humble and reverent adoration. But the Spirit *took him up* (*v.* 5) when the *glory of the Lord* had *come into the house* (*v.* 4), that he might see how the house was filled with it. He saw how the glory of the Lord in this same appearance departed from the temple, because it was profaned, to his great grief; now he shall see it return to the temple to his great satisfaction. See *ch.* 10:18, 19; 11:23. Note, Though God may forsake his people for a small moment, he will return with everlasting loving-kindness. God's glory *filled the house* as it had filled the tabernacle which Moses set up and the temple of Solomon, Ex. 40:34; 1 Ki. 8:10. Now we do not find that ever the Shechinah did in that manner take possession of the second temple, and therefore this was to have its accomplishment in that glory of the divine grace which shines so brightly in the gospel church, and fills it. Here is no mention of a cloud filling the house as formerly, for we now *with open face behold the glory of the Lord,* in the face of Christ, and not as of old through the cloud of types.

III. He receives instructions more immediately from the glory of the Lord, as Moses did when God had taken possession of the tabernacle (Lev. 1:1): *I heard him speaking to me out of the house, v.* 6. God's glory shining in the church, we must thence expect to receive divine oracles. *The man stood by me;* we could not bear to hear the voice of God any more than to see the face of God if Jesus Christ did not stand by us as Mediator. Or, if this was a created angel, it is observable that when God began to speak to Ezekiel he stood by and gave way, having no more to say. Nay, he stood by the prophet, as a learner with him; for *to the principalities and powers,* to the angels themselves, who *desire to look into* these things, *is known by the church the manifold wisdom of God,* Eph. 3:10. The man stood by him to conduct him thither where he might receive further discoveries, *ch.* 44:1.

Verses 7–12

God does here, in effect, renew his covenant with his people Israel, upon his retaking possession of the house, and Ezekiel negotiates the matter, as Moses formerly. This would be of great use to the captives at their return both for direction and encouragement; but it looks further, to those that are blessed with the privileges of the gospel-temple, that they may understand how they are before him on their good behaviour.

I. God, by the prophet, puts them in mind of their former provocations, for which they had long lain under the tokens of his displeasure. This conviction is spoken to them to make way for the comforts designed them. Though God *gives and upbraids not,* it becomes us, when he forgives, to upbraid ourselves with our unworthy conduct towards him. Let them now remember therefore, 1. That they had formerly *defiled God's holy name,* had profaned and abused all those sacred things by which he had made himself known among them, *v.* 7. *They and their kings* had brought contempt on the religion they professed, and their relation to God, by their spiritual whoredom, their idolatry, and by worshipping images, which they called *their kings* (for so *Moloch* signifies) or lords (for so *Baal* signifies), but which were really the *carcases of kings,* not only lifeless and useless, but loathsome and abominable as dead carcases, *in their high places,* set up in honour of them. They had defiled God's name by their abominations. And what were they? It was *in setting their threshold by my thresholds, and their post by my posts,* that is, adding their own inventions to God's institutions, and urging all to a compliance with them, as if they had been of equal authority and efficacy, *teaching for doctrines the commandments of men* (Isa. 29:13); or, rather, setting up altars to their idols even in the courts of the temple, than which a more impudent affront could not be put upon the divine Majesty. Thus they set up a separation *wall between him and them,* which stopped the current of his favours to them and spoiled the acceptableness of their services to him. See what an indignity sinners do to God, setting up their walls in opposition to his, and thrusting him out from what is his right; and see what injury they do to themselves, for the nearer any come to God with their sins the further they set him at a distance from them. Some give this sense of it: Though their houses joined close to God's house, their posts and thresholds to hi, so that they were in a manner his next neighbours, *there was but a wall between me and them* (so it is in the margin), so that it might have been expected they would acquaint themselves with him and be in care to please him, yet they were not so much as neighbourly. Note, It often proves too true, *The nearer the church the further from God.* They were, by profession, in covenant with God, and yet they had *defiled the place of his throne* and of *the soles of his feet,* his temple, where he did both reside and reign. Jerusalem is called the *city of the great king* (Ps. 48:2) and his *footstool,* Ps. 99:5; 132:7. Note, When God's ordinances are profaned his holy name is polluted. 2. That for this God had had a controversy with them in their late troubles. They could not condemn him, for he had but brought upon them the desert of their sins: *Wherefore I have consumed them in my anger.* Note, Those that pollute God's holy name fall under his just displeasure.

II. He calls upon them to repent and reform, and, in order to that, to be ashamed of their iniquities (*v.* 9): "*Now let them put away their whoredom;* now that they have smarted so severely for it, and now that God is returning in mercy to them and setting up his sanctuary again in the midst of them, now let them cast away their idols and have no more to do with them, that they may not again forfeit the privileges which they have been taught to know the worth of by the want of them. Let them put away their idols, those loathsome *carcases of their kings, far from me,* from being a provocation to me." This was seasonable counsel now that the prophet had the model or pattern of the temple to set before them; for, 1. If *they see that pattern,* they will surely be ashamed of their sins (*v.* 10): when they see what mercy God has in store for them, notwithstanding their utter unworthiness of it, they will be ashamed to think of their disingenuous conduct towards him. Note, The goodness of God to us should lead us to repentance, especially to a penitential shame. Let *them measure the pattern* themselves, and see how much it exceeds the former pattern, and guess by that what great things God has in store for them; and surely it will put them out of countenance to think what the desert of their sins was. And then, 2. If *they be ashamed* of their sins, they shall surely see more of the pattern, *v.* 11. If they *be ashamed of all that they have done,* upon a general view of the goodness of God, let them have a more distinct particular account of the temple. Note, Those that improve what they see and know of the goodness of God shall see and know more of it. And then, and not till then, we are qualified for God's favours, when we are truly humbled for our own follies. "*Show them the form of the house;* let them see what a stately structure it will be; and withal show them the ordinances and laws of it." Note, With the foresights of our comforts it is fit that we should get the knowledge of our duty; with the privileges of God's house we must acquaint ourselves with the rules of it. *Show them* these ordinances, that they may *keep them* and *do them.* Note, *Therefore* we are made to know our duty, that we may do it, and be blessed in our deed.

III. He promises that they shall be such as they should be, and then he will be to them such as they would have him to be, *v.* 7. 1. The house of *Israel shall no more defile my holy name.* This is pure gospel. The precept of the law says, You must not defile my name: the grace of the gospel says, You shall not. Thus what is required in the covenant is promised in the covenant, Jer. 32:40. 2. Then *I will dwell in the midst of them for ever;* and the same again *v.* 9. God secures to us his good-will be confirming in us his good work. If we do not defile his name, we may be sure that he will not depart from us.

IV. The general law of God's house is laid down (*v.* 12), That, whereas formerly only the chancel, or sanctuary, was *most holy,* now the whole *mountain of the house* shall be so; the *whole limit thereof,* including all the courts and all the chambers, shall be as the most holy place, signifying that in gospel-times, 1. The whole church shall have the privilege of the *holy of holies,* that of a near access to God. All believers have now, under the gospel, *boldness to enter into the holiest* (Heb. 10:19), with this advantage, that whereas the high priest entered in the virtue of the blood of bulls and goats, we enter in the virtue of the blood of Jesus, and, wherever we are, we have through him *access to the Father.* 2. The whole church shall be under a mighty obligation to press towards the perfection of holiness, *as he who has called us is holy.* All must now be most holy. *Holiness becomes God's house* for ever, and in gospel-times more than ever. Behold this is the *law of the house;* let none expect the protection of it that will not submit to this law.

Verses 13–27

This relates to the altar in this mystical temple, and that is mystical too; for Christ is our altar. The Jews, after their return out of captivity, had an altar long before they had a temple, Ezra 3:3. But this was an altar in the temple. Now here we have,

I. The measures of the altar, *v.* 13. It was six yards square at the top and seven yards square at the bottom; it was four yards and a half high; it had a lower bench or shelf, here called a *settle,* a yard from the ground, on which some of the priests stood to minister, and another two yards above that, on which others of them stood, and these were each of them half a yard broad, and had ledges on either side, that they might stand firmly upon them. The sacrifices were killed at the table spoken of before, *ch.* 40:39. What was to be burnt on the altar was given up to those on the lower bench, and handed by them to those on the higher, and they laid it on the altar. Thus in the service of God we must be assistant to one another.

II. The ordinances of the altar. Directions are here given, 1. Concerning the dedication of the altar at first. *Seven days* were to be spent in the dedication of it, and every day sacrifices were to be offered upon it, and particularly a goat for a *sin-offering* (*v.* 25), besides a young bullock for a *sin-offering* on the first day (*v.* 19), which teaches us in all our religious services to have an eye to Christ the great sin-offering. Neither our persons nor our performances can be acceptable to God unless sin be taken away, and that cannot be taken away but by the blood of Christ, which both sanctifies the altar (for Christ entered by his own blood, Heb. 9:12) and the gift upon the altar. There were also to be a *bullock* and a ram offered for a *burnt-offering* (*v.* 24), which was intended purely for the glory of God, to teach us to have an eye to that in all our services; we present ourselves as living sacrifices, and our devotions as spiritual sacrifices, that we and they may be to him for a name, and for a praise, and for a glory. The dedication of the altar is here called the *cleansing* and *purging* of it, *v.* 20, 26. Christ, our altar, though he had no pollution to be cleansed from, yet sanctified himself (Jn. 17:19); and when we consecrate the altars of our hearts to God, to have the fire of holy love always burning upon them, we must see that they be purified and cleansed from the love of the world and the lusts of the flesh. It is observable that there are several differences between the rites of dedication here and those which were appointed Ex. 29, to intimate that the ceremonial institutions were mutable things, and the changes in them were earnests of their period in Christ. Only here, according to the general law, that all the sacrifices must be seasoned with salt (Lev. 2:13), particular orders are given (*v.* 24) that the priests shall *cast salt upon the sacrifices. Grace* is the *salt* with which all our religious performances must be seasoned, Col. 4:6. An everlasting covenant is called a *covenant of salt,* because it is incorruptible. The *glory* reserved for us is incorruptible and undefiled; and the *grace* wrought in us is the hidden man of the heart in that *which is not corruptible.* 2. Concerning the constant use that should be made of it, when it was dedicated: *Henceforward* the priests shall *make their burnt-offerings and peace-offerings upon this altar* (*v.* 27), for *therefore* it was *sanctified,* that it might *sanctify the gift* that was offered upon it. Observe further, (1.) Who were to serve at the altar: The *priests of the seed of Zadok, v.* 19. That family was substituted in the room of Abiathar by Solomon, and God confirms it. His name signifies *righteous,* for they are the righteous seed that are priests to God, through Christ *the Lord our righteousness.* (2.) How they should prepare for this service (*v.* 26): *They shall consecrate themselves,* shall *fill their hand* with the offerings, in token of the giving up of themselves with their offerings to God and to his service. Note, Before we minister to the Lord in holy things we must consecrate ourselves by getting our hands and hearts filled with those things. (3.) How they should speed in it (*v.* 27): *I will accept you.* And if God now accept our works, if our services be pleasing to him, it is enough, we need no more. Those that give themselves to God shall be accepted of God, their persons first and then their performances, through the Mediator.

CHAPTER 44

In this chapter we have, I. The appropriating of the east gate of the temple to the prince (*v.* 1–3). II. A reproof sent to the house of Israel for their former profanations of God's sanctuary, with a charge to them to be more strict for the future (*v.* 4–9). III. The degrading of those Levites that had formerly been guilty of idolatry and the establishing of the priesthood in the family of Zadok, which had kept their integrity (*v.* 10–16). IV. Divers laws and ordinances concerning the priests (*v.* 17–31).

Verses 1–3

The prophet is here brought to review what he had before once surveyed; for, though we have often looked into the things of God, they will yet bear to be looked over again, such a copiousness there is in them. The lessons we have learned we should still repeat to ourselves. Every time we review the sacred fabric of holy things, which we have in the scriptures, we shall still find something new which we did not before take notice of. The prophet is brought a third time to the east gate, and finds it shut, which intimates that the rest of the gates were open at all times to the worshippers. But such an account is given of this gate's being shut as puts honour, 1. Upon the God of Israel. It is for the honour of him that the gate of the inner court, at which his glory entered when he took possession of the house, was ever after kept shut, and no man was allowed to enter in by it, *v.* 2. The difference ever after made between this and the other gates, that this was shut when the others were open, was intended both to perpetuate the remembrance of the solemn entrance of the glory of the Lord into the house (which it would remain a traditional evidence of the truth of) and also to possess the minds of people with a reverence for the Divine Majesty, and with very awful thoughts of his transcendent glory, which was designed in God's charge to Moses at the bush, *Put off thy shoe from off thy foot.* God will have a way by himself. 2. Upon the prince of Israel, *v.* 3. It is an honour to him that though he may not enter in by this gate, for no man may, yet, (1.) He shall *sit in this gate* to *eat* his share of the peace-offerings, that sacred food, *before the Lord.* (2.) He shall *enter by the way of the porch of that gate,* by some little door or wicket, either in the gate or adjoining to it, which is called the *say of the porch.* This as to signify that God puts some of his glory upon magistrates, upon the princes of his people, for he has said, *You are gods.* Some by the prince here understand the high priests, or the sagan or second priest; and that he only was allowed to enter by this gate, for he was God's representative. Christ is the high priest of our profession, who entered himself into the holy place, and *opened the kingdom of heaven to all believers.*

Verses 4–9

This is much to the same purport with what we had in the beginning of *ch.* 43. As the prophet must look again upon what he had before seen, so he must be told again what he had before heard. Here, as before, he sees the house *filled with the glory of the Lord,* which strikes an awe upon him, so that he falls prostrate at the sight, the humblest posture of adoration and the expression of a holy awe: *I fell upon my face, v.* 4. Note, The more we see of the glory of God the more low we shall lie in our own eyes. Now here,

I. God charges the prophet to take a very particular notice of all he saw, and all that was said to him (v. 5): "*Behold with thy eyes* what is *shown* thee, particularly the *entering in of the house* and *every going forth* of it, all the inlets and all the outlets of the sanctuary;" those he must take special notice of. Note, In acquainting ourselves with divine things we must not aim so much at an abstract speculation of the things themselves as at finding the plain appointed way of converse and communion with those things, that we may *go in and out and find pasture.* 2. *Hear with thy ears all that I say unto thee* about *the laws* and *ordinances* of *the house*, which he was to instruct the people in. Note, Those who are appointed to be teachers have need to be very diligent careful learners, that they may neither forget any of the things they are entrusted with nor mistake concerning them.

II. He sends him upon an errand to the people, *to the rebellious, even to the house of Israel, v.* 6. It is sad to think that the house of Israel should deserve this character from him who perfectly knew them, that a people in covenant with God should be rebellious against him. Who are his subjects if the house of Israel be rebels? But it is an instance of God's rich mercy that, though they had been *rebellious*, yet, being the *house of Israel*, he does not cast them off, but sends an ambassador to them, to invite and encourage them to return to their allegiance, which he would not have done if he had been pleased to kill them. The whole race of mankind has fallen under the character here given of the house of Israel; but our Lord Jesus, when he ascended on high, received gifts for men, *yea, even for the rebellious also, that*, as here, *the Lord God might dwell among them,* Ps. 68:18.

1. He must tell them of their faults, must show them their rebellions, must show the house of Jacob their sins. Note, Those that are sent to comfort God's people must first convince them, and so prepare them for comfort. *Let it suffice you of all your abominations, v.* 6. Note, It is time for those that have continued long in sin to reckon it long enough, and too long, and to begin to think of taking up in time, and leaving off their evil courses. "*Let the time past of your lives suffice*, for by this time, surely, you have surfeited upon your abominations and have become sick of them," 1 Pt. 4:3. That which is here charged upon them is, (1.) That they had admitted those to the privileges of the sanctuary that were not entitled to them; whereas God had said, *The stranger that comes nigh shall be put to death*, they had not only connived at the intrusion of strangers into the sanctuary, but had themselves introduced them (v. 7): *You brought in strangers uncircumcised in flesh*, and therefore under a legal incapacity to enter into the sanctuary, which was a *breaking of the covenant* of circumcision, throwing down the hedge of their peculiarity, and laying themselves in common with the rest of the world. Yet if these strangers had been devout and good, though they were not circumcised, the crime would not have been so great; but they were *uncircumcised in heart* too, unhumbled, unreformed, and strangers indeed to God and all goodness. When they came to offer sacrifice they brought these with them to feast with them upon the sacrifice, because they were fond of their company, and this was one of their abominations, wherewith they *polluted God's sanctuary;* it was *giving that which was holy unto dogs*, Mt. 7:6. Note, The admission of those who are openly wicked and profane to special ordinances is a polluting of God's sanctuary and a great provocation to him. (2.) That they had employed those in the service of the sanctuary who were not fit for it. Though none but priests and Levites were to minister in the sanctuary, yet we may suppose that all who were priests and Levites did not immediately attend there, but chosen men of them, who were best qualified, who were most wise, serious, and conscientious, and most likely to keep the charge of the holy things carefully; but, in making this choice, they had not regard to merit and qualification for the work: "*You have set keepers of my charge in my sanctuary for yourselves*, such as you had some favour or affection for, such as you either had got, or hoped to get, money by, or such as would comply with your humours and would dispense with the laws of the sanctuary to please you; *thus you have not kept the charge of my holy things.*" Note, Those who have the choice of the keepers of the holy things, if, to serve some secular selfish purpose, they choose such as are unfit and unfaithful, will justly have it laid at their

door, that they have betrayed the holy things by lodging them in bad hands.

2. He must tell them their duty (v. 9): "*No stranger shall enter into my sanctuary* till he has first submitted to the laws of it." But, lest any should think that this excluded the penitent believing Gentiles from the church, the stranger here is described to be one that is *uncircumcised in heart*, not in sincerity consenting to the covenant, nor putting away the filth of the flesh; whereas the believing Gentiles were *circumcised with the circumcision made without hands*, Col. 2:11. This circumcision of the heart, in the *spirit, not in the letter*, was what the unbelieving Jews were strangers to and unconcerned about, while yet they were zealous to keep out of the sanctuary uncircumcised Gentiles, witness their rage against Paul when they did but suspect him to have brought *Greeks into the temple*, Acts 21:28.

Verses 10–16

The Master of the house, being about to set up house again, takes account of his servants the priests, and sees who are fit to be turned out of their places and who to be kept in, and takes a course with them accordingly.

I. Those who have been treacherous are degraded and put lower those Levites — or priests who were carried down the stream of the apostasy of Israel formerly, who *went astray from God after their idols* (v. 10), who had complied with the idolatrous kings of Israel or Judah, who *ministered to them before their idols* (v. 12), bowed with them in the house of Rimmon, or set up altars for them, as Urijah did for Ahaz, and so *caused the house of Israel to fall into iniquity*, led them to sin and hardened them in sin; for, if the priests go astray, many will follow *their pernicious ways.* Perhaps in Babylon some of the Jewish priests had complied with the idolaters of the place, to the great scandal of their religion. Now these priests who had thus prevaricated were justly put under the mark of God's displeasure; or, if they were dead (as it is probable that they were, if the crime were committed before the captivity), the iniquity was visited upon their children. Or perhaps it was the whole family of Abiathar that had been guilty of this trespass, which was now called to account for it. And, 1. They are sentenced to be deprived, in part, of their office, and from the dignity of priests are put down into the condition or ordinary Levites. God has *lifted up his hand against them*, has said it, and sworn it, that *they shall bear their iniquity* (v. 12); assuredly they shall suffer for it, shall suffer disgrace for it; *they shall bear their shame* (v. 13), for though they have (we charitably hope) repented of it, *yet they shall not come near to do the office of a priest*, that is, those parts of the office that were peculiar to them, they shall not come near to *any of the holy things* within the sanctuary, v. 13. Note, those who have robbed God of his honour will justly be deprived of their honour. And it is really a great punishment to be forbidden to come near to God; and justly might those who have once gone away from him be rejected as unworthy ever to come near to him and put at an everlasting distance. 2. Yet there is a mixture of mercy in this sentence. God deals not in severity, as he might have done, with those who had dealt treacherously with him, but mitigates the sentence, v. 11, 14. They are deprived but in part, *ab officio* — of their office, and, it should seem, not at all *à beneficio* — of their emoluments. They shall help to *slay the sacrifice*, which the Levites were permitted to do, and which in this temple was done, not at the altar, but *at the tables*, ch. 40:29. They shall be porters *at the gates of the house*, and they shall be *keepers of the charge of the house, for all the service thereof.* Note, Those who may not be fit to be employed in one kind of service may yet be fit to be employed in another; and even those who have offended may yet be made use of, and not quite thrown aside, much less thrown away.

II. Those who have been faithful are honoured and established, v. 15, 16. These are remarkably distinguished from the other: "*But the sons of Zadok*, who kept their integrity in a time of general apostasy, who *went not astray* when others did, *they shall come near to me, shall come near to my table.*" Note, God will put marks of honour upon those who give proofs of their fidelity and constancy to him in shaking trying times, and will employ those in his service who have kept close to his service when others

deserted it and drew back. And it ought to be reckoned a true and great reward of stability in duty to be established in it. If we keep close to God, God will keep us close to him.

Verses 17–31

God's priests must be *regulars*, not *seculars;* and therefore here are rules laid down for them to govern themselves by and due encouragement given them to live up to those rules. Directions are here given,

I. Concerning their clothes; they must wear *linen garments* when they *went in to minister* or do any service in the inner court, or in the sanctuary, and nothing that was *woollen*, because it would *cause sweat, v.* 17, 18. They must dress themselves cool, that they might go the more readily about their work; and they had the more need to do so because they were to attend the altars, which had constant fires upon them. And they must dress themselves clean and sweet, and avoid every thing that was sweaty and filthy, to signify the purity of mind with which the service of God is to be attended to. Sweat came in with sin and was part of the curse. *In the sweat of thy face shalt thou eat bread.* Clothes came in with sin, coats of skins did; and therefore the priests must use as little and as light clothing as possible, and not such as caused sweat. When they had finished their service they must change their clothes again, and lay up their linen garments in the chambers appointed for that purpose, v. 19, as before, *ch.* 42:14. They must not go among the people with their holy garments on, lest they should imagine themselves sanctified by the touch of them; or, *They shall sanctify the people*, that is (as it is explained, *ch.* 42:14), they shall *approach to those things which are for the people*, in their ordinary *garments.*

II. Concerning their hair; in that they must avoid extremes on both hands (v. 20): *They must not shave their heads*, in imitation of the Gentile priests, and as the priests of the Romish church do; nor, on the other hand, must they *suffer their locks to grow long*, as the *beaux*, or that they might be thought Nazarites, when really they were not; but they must be grave and modest, must *poll their heads* and keep their hair short. If a *man*, especially a minister, wear *long hair*, it is not becoming (1 Co. 11:14); it is effeminate.

III. Concerning their diet; they must be sure to *drink no wine* when they went in to minister, lest they should rink to excess, should drink and forget the law, v. 21. *It is not for kings to drink wine*, more than will do them good, much less for priests. See Lev. 10:9; Prov. 31:4, 5.

IV. Concerning their marriages, v. 22. Here they must consult the credit of their office, and not marry one that had been *divorced*, that was at least under the suspicion of immodesty, nor a *widow*, unless she were a priest's widow, that had been accustomed to the usages of the priests' families. Others may do that which ministers may not do, but must deny themselves in, in honour of their character. Their wives as well as themselves must be of good report.

V. Concerning their preaching and church-government. 1. It was part of their business to teach the people; and herein they must approve themselves both skilful and faithful (v. 23): *They shall teach my people the difference between the holy and the profane*, between good and evil, lawful and unlawful, that they may neither scruple what is lawful nor venture upon what is unlawful, that they may not pollute what is holy nor pollute themselves with what is profane. Ministers must take pains to cause *people to discern between the clean and the unclean*, that they may not confound the distinctions between right and wrong, nor mistake concerning them, so as to *put darkness for light and light for darkness*, but may have a good judgment of discretion concerning their own actions. 2. It was part of their business to judge upon appeals made to them (Deu. 17:8, 9); and *in controversy they shall stand in judgment, v.* 24. They shall have the honesty to stand up for what is right, and, when they have passed a right judgment, shall have the courage to stand to it and stand by it. They must judge, not according to their own fancies, or inclinations, or secular interests, but *according to my judgments;* that must be their rule and standard. Note, Ministers must decide controversies according to the word of God, *to the law and to the testimony. Sit liber judex — Let the judge be unbiased.* Their business is to keep courts in God's name, to preside in the congregations of his people. And herein they must go to the statute-book: They shall *keep my statutes in all my assemblies.* God calls the assemblies of his people *his* assemblies, because they are held in his name, to his glory. Ministers are the masters of those assemblies, are to preside in them, and in all their acts must keep close to God's laws. Another part of their work, as church governors, is to *hallow God's sabbaths,* to do the public work of that day with a becoming care and reverence, as the work of a holy day should be done, and to see that God's people also sanctify that day and do nothing to pollute it.

VI. Concerning their mourning for dead relations; the rule here agrees with the law of Moses, Lev. 21:1, 11. A priest shall not come near any *dead body* (for they must be purified *from dead works)* except of his next relations, *v.* 25. Decent expressions of a pious sorrow for dear relations, when they are removed by death, are not disagreeable to the character of a minister. Yet by this approach to the dead body of a relation they contracted a ceremonial pollution, from which they must be cleansed by a *sin-offering* before they went in again to minister, *v.* 26, 27. Note, Though sorrow for the dead is very allowable and commendable, yet there is danger of sinning in it, either by excess or dissimulation; and those tears have too often need to be *wept over again.*

VII. Concerning their maintenance; they must live upon the altar at which they served, and live comfortably (*v.* 28): *"You shall give them no possession in Israel,* no lands or tenements, lest they should be entangled with the affairs of this life;" for God has said, *I am their inheritance,* and they need no other in reserve; *I am their possession,* and they need no other in hand. Some land was allowed them (*ch.* 48:10), but their principal subsistence was by their office. What God appropriated to himself they were the receivers of, for their own proper use and behoof; they lived upon the holy things, and so God himself was the portion both of their inheritance and of their cup. Note, Those who have God for their inheritance and their possession may be content with a little, and ought not to covet a great deal of the possessions and inheritances of this earth. If we have God, we have *all;* and therefore may well reckon that we have enough. Observe,

1. What the priests were to have from the people, for their maintenance and encouragement. (1.) They must have the flesh of many of the offerings, the *sin-offering and trespass-offering,* which would supply them and their families with flesh-meat, and the *meat-offerings,* which would supply them with bread. What we offer to God will redound to our own advantage. (2.) They must have every dedicated devoted thing in Israel, which was in many cases to be turned into money and given to the priest. This is explained, *v.* 20. *Every oblation* or free-will offering (which in times of reformation and devotion would be many and considerable) *of all, of every sort of your oblations, shall be the priest's.* We have the law concerning them Lev. 27. (3.) They were to have *the first of the dough* when it was going to the oven, as well as the first of their fruits when they were going to the barn. God, who is the first, must have the first; and, if it belong to him, his priests must have it. We may *then* comfortably enjoy what we have, when a share of it has been first set apart for works of piety and charity. To this the apostle's rule bears some analogy, to *begin the week* with laying by for pious uses, 1 Co. 16:2. The priests being so well provided for, it would be inexcusable in them if they (contrary to the law which every Israelite is bound by) should *eat that which is torn or which died of itself, v.* 31. Those that were in want of necessary food might perhaps expect to be dispensed with in such a case. Poverty has its temptations, but the priests were so well provided for that they could have no pretence for it.

2. What the people might expect from the priest for their recompence. Those that are kind to a prophet, to a priest, shall have a prophet's, a priest's reward: *That he may cause the blessing to rest in thy house* (*v.* 30), that God may cause it by commanding it, that the priest may cause it by praying for it; and it was part of the priest's work to *bless the people in the name of the Lord,* not only their congregations, but their families. Note, It is all in all to the comfort of any house to have the blessing of God upon it and to have the blessing to rest in it, to dwell where we dwell and to attend the entail of it upon those that shall come after us. And the way to have the blessing of God abide upon our estates is to honour God with them, and to give him and his ministers, him and his poor, their share out of them. God blesses, he surely blesses, the habitation of those who are thus just, Prov. 3:33. And ministers, by instructing and praying for the families that are kind to them, should do their part towards causing the blessing to rest there. *Peace be to this house.*

CHAPTER 45

In this chapter is further represented to the prophet, in vision, I. The division of the holy land, so much for the temple, and the priests that attended the service of it (*v.* 1–4), so much for the Levites (*v.* 5), so much for the city (*v.* 6), so much for the prince, and the residue to the people (*v.* 7, 8). II. The ordinances of justice that were given both to prince and people (*v.* 9–12). III. The oblations they were to offer, and the prince's part in those oblations (*v.* 13–17). Particularly in the beginning of the year (*v.* 18–20) and in the passover, and the feast of tabernacles (*v.* 21–25). And all this seems to point at the new church-state that should be set up under the gospel, which, both for extent and for purity, should far exceed that of the Old Testament.

Verses 1–8

Directions are here given for the dividing of the land after their return to it; and, God having warranted them to do it, would be an act of faith, and not of folly, thus to divide it before they had it. And it would be welcome news to the captives to hear that they should not only return to their own land, but that, whereas they were now but few in number, they should *increase and multiply,* so as to *replenish* it. But this never had its accomplishment in the Jewish state after the return out of captivity, but was to be fulfilled in the model of the Christian church, which was perfectly new (as this division of the land was quite different from that in Joshua's time) and much enlarged by the accession of the Gentiles to it; and it will be perfected in the heavenly kingdom, of which the land of Canaan had always been a type. Now, 1. Here is the portion of land assigned to *the sanctuary,* in the midst of which the temple was to be built, with all its courts and purlieus; the rest round about it was for the priests. This is called (*v.* 1) *an oblation to the Lord;* for what is given in works of piety, for the maintenance and support of the worship of God and the advancement of religion, God accepts as given to him, if it be done with a single eye. It is a *holy portion of the land,* which is to be set out first, as the *first-fruits* that sanctify the lump. The appropriating of lands for the support of religion and the ministry is an act of piety that bids as fair for perpetuity, and the benefit of posterity, as any. This *holy portion of the land* was to be measured, and the borders of it fixed, that the sanctuary itself might not have more than its share and in time engross the whole land. So far the lands of the church shall extend and no further; as in our own kingdom donations to the church were of old limited by the *statute of mortmain.* The lands here allotted to the sanctuary were 25,000 *reeds* (so our translation makes it, though some make them only *cubits*) in length, and 10,000 in breadth — about eighty miles one way and thirty miles another way (say some); twenty-five miles one way and ten miles the other way, so others. The priests and Levites that were to come near to minister were to have their dwellings in this *portion of the land* that was round about the sanctuary, that they might be near their work; whereas by the distribution of land in Joshua's time the cities of the priests and Levites were dispersed all the nation over. This intimates that gospel ministers should reside upon their charge; where their service lies there must they live. 2. Next to the lands of the sanctuary the city-lands are assigned, in which the holy city was to be built, and with the issues and profits of which the citizens were to be maintained (*v.* 6): *It shall be for the whole house of Israel,* not appropriated, as before, to one tribe or two, but some of all the tribes shall dwell in the city, as we find they did, Neh. 11:1, 2. The portion for the city was fully as long, but only half as broad, as that for the sanctuary; for the city was enriched by trade and therefore had the less need of lands. 3. The next allotment after the church-lands and the city-lands is of the crown-lands, *v.* 7, 8. Here is no admeasurement of these, but they are said to lie *on the one side and on the other side* of the church-lands and city-lands, to intimate that the prince with his wealth and power was to be a protection to both. Some make the prince's share equal to the church's and city's share both together; others make it to be a thirteenth part of the rest of the land, the other twelve parts being for the twelve tribes. The prince that attends continually to the administration of public affairs must have wherewithal to support his dignity, and have abundance, that he may not be in temptation to oppress the people, which yet with many does not prevent that; but the grace of God shall prevent it, for it is promised here, *My princes shall no more oppress my people;* for God will make the *officers peace* and the *exactors righteousness.* Notwithstanding this, we find that after the return of the Jews to their own land the princes were complained of for their exactions. But Nehemiah was one that did not do as the *former governors,* and yet kept a handsome court, Neh. *v.* 15, 18. But so much is said of the prince in this mystical holy state, to intimate that in the gospel-church magistrates should be as *nursing fathers* to it and Christian princes its patrons and protectors; and the holy religion they profess, as far as they are subject to the power of it, will restrain them from oppressing God's people, because they are more his people than theirs. 4. The rest of the lands were to be distributed to the people *according to their tribes,* who had reason to think themselves well settled, when they had both the *testimony of Israel* and the *throne of judgment* so near them.

Verses 9–12

We have here some general rules of justice laid down both for prince and people, the rules of distributive and commutative justice; for godliness without honesty is but a form of godliness, will neither please God nor avail to the benefit of any people. Be it therefore enacted, by the authority of the church's King and God, 1. That *princes do not oppress their subjects,* but duly and faithfully administer justice among them (*v.* 9): *"Let it suffice you, O princes of Israel!* that you have been oppressive to the people and have enriched yourselves by spoil and violence, that you have so long fleeced the flock instead of feeding them, and henceforward do so no more." Note, Even princes and great men that have long done amiss must at length think it time, high time, to reform and amend; for no prescription will justify a wrong. Instead of saying that they have been long accustomed to oppress, and therefore may persist in it, for the custom will bear them out, they should say that they have been long accustomed to it and therefore, as here, *Let the time pass suffice,* and let them now remove *violence and spoil;* let them drop wrongful demands, cancel wrongful usages, and turn out those from employments under them that do violence. Let them *take away their exactions,* ease their subjects of those taxes which they find lie heavily upon them, and let them *execute judgment and justice* according to the law, as the duty of their place requires. Note, All princes, but especially the princes of Israel, are concerned to do justice; for of their people God says, They are my people, and they in a special manner *rule for God.* 2. That one neighbour do not cheat another in commerce (*v.* 10): *You shall have just balances,* in which to weigh both money and goods, a *just ephah* for dry measure of corn and flour, a *just bath* for the measure of liquids, wine, and oil; and the *ephah* and *bath* shall be *one measure,* the tenth part of a *chomer,* or *cor, v.* 11. So that the ephah and bath contained (as the learned Dr. Cumberland has computed) seven wine gallons and four pints, and something more. An omer was but the tenth part of an ephah (Ex. 16:36) and the one hundredth part of a *chomer,* or *homer,* and contained about six pints. The *shekel* is here settled (*v.* 13); it is twenty *gerahs,* just half a *Roman* ounce, in our money 2*s.* 4¼*d.* and almost the eighth part of a farthing, as the aforesaid learned man exactly computes it. By the shekels the *maneh,* or pound, was reckoned, which, when it was set for a mere weight (says bishop Cumberland), without respect to coinage, contained just 100 shekels, as appears by comparing 1 Ki. 10:17, where it is said three *manehs,* or *pounds, of gold, went to one shield,* with the parallel place, 2 Chr. 9:16, where it is said 300 *shekels of gold went to one shield.* But when the *maneh* is set for a sum of money or coin it contains but sixty shekels, as appears here, where twenty shekels, twenty-five shekels, and fifteen shekels, which in all make sixty, shall be the *maneh.* But it is thus reckoned because they had one piece of money that weighed twenty shekels, another twenty-five, another fifteen, all of which made up one pound, as a learned writer here observes. Note, It concerns God's Israel to be very honest and just in all their dealings, very punctual and exact in rendering to all their due, and very cautious to do wrong to none, because otherwise they spoil the acceptableness of their profession with God and the reputation of it before men.

Verses 13–25

Having laid down the rules of the righteousness toward men, which is really a branch off true religion, he comes next to give some directions for their religion towards God, which is a branch of universal righteousness.

I. It is required that they offer an oblation to the Lord out of what they have (*v.* 13): *All the people of the land* must give an oblation, *v.* 16. As God's tenants, they must pay a quitrent to their great landlord. They had offered an oblation out of their real estates (*v.* 1), a *holy portion of their land;* now they are directed to offer an oblation out of their personal estates, their goods and chattels, as an acknowledgement of their receivings from him, their dependence on him, and their obligations to him. Note, Whatever our substance is we must honour God with it, by giving him his dues out of it. Not that God has need of or may be benefited by any thing that we can give him, Ps. 50:9. No; it is but an *oblation;* we only *offer it* to him; the benefit of it returns back to ourselves, to his poor, who, as our neighbours, are ourselves, or to his ministers who serve continually for our good.

II. The proportion of this oblation is here determined, which was not done by the law of Moses. No mention is made of the title, but only of this oblation. And the *quantum* of this is thus settled: — 1. Out of their corn they were to offer a sixtieth part; out of every *homer of wheat and barley,* which contained ten ephahs, they were to offer the sixth part of one ephah, which was a sixtieth part of the whole, *v.* 13. 2. Out of their oil (and probably their wine too) they were to offer a hundredth part, for this oblation; out of every cor, or homer, which contained ten baths they were to offer the tenth part of one bath, *v.* 14. This was given to the altar; for in eery meat-offering there was *flour mingled with oil.* 3. Out of their flocks they were to give *one lamb* out of 200; that was the smallest proportion of all, *v.* 15. But it must be *out of the fat pastures of Israel.* They must not offer to God that which was taken up from the common, but the fattest and best they had, for *burnt-offerings* and *peace-offerings:* the former were offered for the giving of glory to God, the latter for the fetching in of mercy, grace, and peace, from God, and in our spiritual sacrifices these are our two great errands at the throne of grace; but, in order to the acceptance of both, these sacrifices were to *make reconciliation* for them. Christ is our sacrifice of atonement, by whom reconciliation is made, and to him we must have an eye in our sacrifices of acknowledgment.

III. This oblation must be given *for the prince in Israel, v.* 16. Some read it *to* the prince, and understand it of Christ, who is indeed the prince in Israel, to whom we must offer our oblations, and into whose hands we must put them, to be presented to the Father. Or, They shall give it *with* the prince; every private person shall bring his oblation, to be offered with that of the prince; for it follows (*v.* 17). It *shall be the prince's part to provide* all the offerings, *to make reconciliation for the house of Israel.* The people were to bring their oblations to him according to the foregoing rules, and he was to bring them to the sanctuary, and to make up what fell short out of his own. Note, It is the duty of rulers to take care of religion, and to see that the duties of it be regularly and carefully performed by those under their charge, and that nothing be wanting that is requisite thereto: the magistrate is the keeper of both tables; and it is a happy thing when those that are above others in power and dignity go before them in the service of God.

IV. Some particular solemnities are here appointed.

1. Here is one in the beginning of the year, which seems to be altogether new, and not instituted by the law of Moses; it is the annual solemnity of cleansing the sanctuary. (1.) *On the first day of the first month* (upon new-year's day) they were to offer a sacrifice for the *cleansing of the sanctuary* (*v.* 18), that is, to make atonement for the iniquity of the holy things the year past, that they might bring none of the guilt of them into the services of the new year, and to implore grace for the preventing of that iniquity, and for the better performance of the service of the sanctuary the ensuing year. And, in token of this, the blood of this *sin-offering* was to be put upon the *posts of the gate of the inner court* (*v.* 19), to signify that by it atonement was intended to be made for the sins of all the servants that attended that house, priests, Levites, and people, even the sins that were found in all their services. Note, Even sanctuaries on earth need cleansing, frequent cleansing; that above needs none. Those what worship God together should often join in renewing their repentance for their manifold defects, and applying the blood of Christ for the pardon of them, and in renewing their covenants to be more careful for the future; and it is very seasonable to begin the year with this work, as Hezekiah did when it had been long neglected, 2 Chr. 29:17. They were here appointed to *cleanse the sanctuary* upon the first day of the month, because on the fourteenth day of the month they were to eat the *passover,* an ordinance which, of all Old-Testament institutions, had most in it of Christ and gospel grace, and therefore it was very fit that they should begin to prepare for it a fortnight before by cleansing the sanctuary. (2.) This sacrifice was to be repeated *on the seventh day of the first month, v.* 20. And then it was intended to make atonement *for every one that errs, and for him that is simple.* Note, He that sins *errs and is simple;* he mistakes, he goes out of the way, and shows himself to be foolish and unwise. But here it is spoken of those sins which are committed through ignorance, mistake, or inadvertency, whether by any of the priests, or of the Levites, or of the people. Sacrifices were appointed to atone for such sins as men were surprised into, or did before they were aware, which they would not have done if they had known and remembered aright, which they were overtaken in, and for which, afterwards, they condemn themselves. But for presumptuous sins, committed with a high hand, there was no sacrifice appointed, Num. 15:30. By these repeated sacrifices you shall *reconcile the house,* that is, God will be reconciled to it, and continue the tokens of his presence in it, and will *let it alone this year also.*

2. The passover was to be religiously observed at the time appointed, *v.* 21. Christ is *our passover,* that is *sacrificed for us.* We celebrate the memorial of that sacrifice and feast upon it, triumphing in our deliverance out of the Egyptian slavery of sin and our preservation from the sword of the destroying angel, the sword of divine justice, in the Lord's supper, which is our passover-feast, as the whole Christian life is, and must be, the feast of unleavened bread. It is here appointed that the prince shall prepare a *sin-offering,* to be offered *for himself and the people,* a bullock on the *first* day (*v.* 22) and a *kid of the goats* every other day (*v.* 23), to teach us, in all our attendance upon God for communion with him, to have an eye to the great sin-offering, by which *transgression* was *finished* and an *everlasting righteousness brought in.* On every day of the feast there was to be a *burnt-offering,* purely for the honour of God, of no less than seven bullocks and seven rams, with their meat-offering, which were wholly consumed upon the altar, and yet *no waste, v.* 23, 24.

3. The feast of tabernacles; that is spoken of next (*v.* 25), and there is no mention of the feast of pentecost, which came between that of the passover and that of tabernacles. Orders are here given (above what were given by the law of Moses) for the same sacrifices to be offered during the seven days of the passover. See the deficiency of the legal sacrifices for sin; they were therefore often repeated, not only every year, but every feast, every day of the feast, because *they could not make the comers thereunto perfect,* Heb. 10:1, 3. See the necessity of our frequently repeating the same religious exercises. Though the sacrifice of atonement is offered *once for all,* yet the sacrifices of acknowledgement, that of a broken heart, that of a thankful heart, those spiritual sacrifices which are acceptable to God through Christ Jesus, must be every day offered. We should, as here, fall into a method of holy duties, and keep to it.

CHAPTER 46

In this chapter we have, I. Some further rules given both to the priests and to the people, relating to their worship (*v.* 1–15). II. A law concerning the prince's disposal of his inheritance (*v.* 16–18). III. A description of the places provided for the boiling of the sacrifices and the baking of the meat-offerings (*v.* 19–24).

Verses 1–15

Whether the rules for public worship here laid down were designed to be observed, even in those things wherein they differed from the law of Moses, and were so observed under the second temple, is not certain; we find not in the history of that latter part of the Jewish church that they governed themselves in their worship by these ordinances, as one would think they should have done, but only by law of Moses, looking upon this *then* in the next age after as mystical, and not literal. We may observe, in these verses,

I. That the place of worship was fixed, and rules were given concerning that, both to prince and people.

1. The east gate, which was kept shut at other times, was to be opened on the sabbath days, on the moons (*v.* 1), and whenever the prince offered a voluntary offering, *v.* 12. Of the keeping of this gate ordinarily shut we read before (*ch.* 44:2); whereas the other gates of the court were opened every day, this was opened only on high days and on special occasions, when it was opened for the prince, who was to *go in by the way of the porch of that gate, v.* 2, 8. Some think he went in with the priests and Levites into the *inner court* (for into that court this gate was the entrance), and they observe that magistrates and ministers should join forces, and go the same way, hand in hand, in promoting the service of God. But it should rather seem that he did not go *through* the gate (as the glory of the Lord had done), though it was open, but he went *by the way of the porch of the gate,* stood *at the post of the gate,* and *worshipped at the threshold of the gate* (*v.* 2), where he had a full view of the priests' performances at the altar, and signified his concurrence in them, for himself and for the people of the land, that stood behind him *at the door of that gate, v.* 3. Thus must every prince show himself to be of David's mind, who would very willingly be a *doorkeeper in the house of his God,* and, as the word there is, *lie at the threshold,* Ps. 84:10. Note, The greatest of men are less than the least of the ordinances of God. Even princes themselves, when they draw near to God, must worship *with reverence and godly fear,* owning that even they are unworthy to approach to him. But Christ is *our prince,* whom God causes to *draw near* and *approach to him,* Jer. 30:21.

2. As to the north gate and south gate, by which they entered into the *court of the people* (not into the inner court), there was this rule given, that whoever came in at the *north gate* should go out at the *south gate,* and whoever came in at the *south gate* should go out at the *north gate, v.* 9. Some think this was to prevent thrusting and jostling one another; for God is *the God of order, and not of confusion.* We may suppose that they came in at the gate that was next their own houses, but, when they went away, God would have them go out at that gate which would lead them *the furthest way about,* that they might have time for meditation; being thereby obliged to go a great way round the sanctuary, they might have an opportunity *to consider the palaces* of it, and, if they improved their time well in fetching this circuit, they would call it the nearest way home. Some observe that this may remind us, in the service of God, to be still pressing forward (Phil. 3:13) and not to *look back,* and, in our attendance upon ordinances, not to go back as we came, but more holy, and heavenly, and spiritual.

3. It is appointed that *the people shall worship at the door of the east gate,* where the prince does, he at the head and they attending him, both *on the sabbath and on the new moons* (*v.* 3), and that, when they come in and go out, the prince shall be *in the midst of them, v.* 10. Note, Great men should, by their constant and reverent attendance on God in public worship, give a good example to their inferiors, both engaging them and encouraging them to do likewise. It is a very graceful becoming thing for persons of quality to go to church with their servants, and tenants, and poor neighbours about them, and to behave themselves there with an air of seriousness and devotion; and those who thus honour God with their honour he will delight to honour.

II. That the ordinances of worship were fixed. Though

the prince is supposed himself to be a very hearty zealous friend to the sanctuary, yet it is not left to him, no, not in concert with the priests, to appoint what sacrifices shall be offered, but God himself appoints them; for it is his prerogative to institute the rites and ceremonies of religious worship. 1. Every morning, as duly as the morning came, they must offer *a lamb* for a *burnt-offering, v.* 13. It is strange that no mention is made of the evening sacrifice; but Christ having come, and having offered himself now *in the end of the world* (Heb. 9:26), we are to look upon him as the evening sacrifice, about the time of the offering up of which he died. 2. On the sabbath days, whereas by the law of Moses four lambs were to be offered (Num. 28:9), it is here appointed that (at the prince's charge) there shall be *six lambs* offered, *and a ram* besides (*v.* 4), to intimate how much we should abound in sabbath work, now in gospel-time, and what plenty of the spiritual sacrifices of prayer and praise we should offer up to God on that day; and, if *with such sacrifice God is well-pleased,* surely we have a great deal of reason to be so. 3. On the new moons, in the beginning of their months, there was over and above the usual sabbath-sacrifices the additional offering of a young bullock, *v.* 6. Those who do much for God and their souls, statedly and constantly, must yet, upon some occasions, do still more. 4. All the sacrifices were to be *without blemish;* so Christ, the great sacrifice, was (1 Pt. 1:19), and so Christians, who are to present themselves to God as living sacrifices, should aim and endeavour to be — *blameless, and harmless, and without rebuke.* 5. All the sacrifices were to have their meat-offerings annexed to them, for so the law of Moses had appointed, to show what a good table God keeps in his house and that we ought to honour him with the fruit of our ground as well as with the fruit of our cattle, because in both he has blessed us, Duet. 28:4. In the beginning, Cain offered the one and Abel the other. Some observe that the meat-offerings here are much larger in proportion than they were by the law of Moses. Then the proportion was *three tenth-deals to a bullock,* and *two to a ram* (so many tenth parts of an ephah) and half a hin of oil at the most (Num. 15:6–9); but here, for every bullock and every ram, a whole ephah and a whole hin of oil (p. 7), which intimates that under the gospel, the great atoning sacrifice having been offered, these unbloody sacrifices shall be more abounded in; or, in general, it intimates that as now, under the gospel, God abounds in the gifts of his grace to us, more than under the law, so we should abound in the returns of praise and duty to him. But it is observable that in the meat-offering *for the lambs* the prince is allowed to offer *as he shall be able to give* (*v.* 5, 7, 11), *as his hand shall attain unto.* Note, Princess themselves must spend as they can afford; and even in that which is laid out in works of piety God expects and requires but that we should do according to our ability, every man *as God has prepared him,* 1 Co. 16:2. God has not *made us to serve with an offering* (Isa. 43:23), but considers our frame and state. Yet this will not countenance those who pretend a disability that is not real, or those who by their extravagances in other things disable themselves to do the good they should. And we find those praised who, in an extraordinary case of charity, went not *only to their power,* but *beyond their power.*

Verses 16–18

We have here a law for the limiting of the power of the prince in the disposing of the crown-lands. 1. If he have a *son* that is a favourite, or has merited well, he may, if he please, as a token of his favour and in recompence for his services, settle some parts of his lands upon him and his heirs for ever (*v.* 16), provided it do not go out of the family. There may be a cause for parents, when their children have grown up, to be more kind to one than to another, as Jacob gave to Joseph one portion *above his brethren,* Gen. 48:22. 2. Yet, if he have a servant that is a favourite, he may not in like manner settle lands upon him, *v.* 17. The servant might have the rents, issues, and profits, for such a term, but the inheritance, the *jus proprietarium — the right of proprietorship,* shall remain in the prince and his heirs. It was fit that a difference should be put between a child and a servant, like that Jn. 8:35. *The servant abides not in the house for ever,* as the son does. 3. What estates he gives his children must be of his own (*v.* 18): He *shall not take of the people's inheritance,* under pretence of having many children to provide for; he shall not find ways to make them forfeit their estates, or to force them to sell them and so *thrust his subjects out of their possession;* but let him and his sons be content with their own. It is far from being a prince's honour to increase the wealth of his family and crown by encroaching upon the rights and properties of his subjects; nor will he himself be a gainer by it at last, for he will be but a poor prince when the people are *scattered every man from his possession,* when they quit their native country, being forced out of it by oppression, choosing rather to live among strangers that are free people, and where what they have they can call their own, be it ever so little. It is the interest of princes to rule in the hearts of their subjects, and then all they have is, in the best manner, at their service. It is better for themselves to gain their affections by protecting their rights than to gain their estates by invading them.

Verses 19–24

We have here a further discovery of buildings about the temple, which we did not observe before, and those were places to boil the flesh of the offerings in, *v.* 20. He that kept such a plentiful table at his altar needed large kitchens; and a wise builder will provide conveniences of that kind. Observe, 1. Where those boiling-places were situated. There were some at the entry into the inner court (*v.* 19) and others under the rows, in the four corners of the outer court, *v.* 21–23. These were the places where, it is likely, there was most room to spare for this purpose; and this purpose was found for the spare room, that none might be lost. It is a pity that holy ground should be waste ground. 2. What use they were put to. In those places they were to *boil the trespass-offering and the sin-offering,* those parts of them which were allotted to the priests and which were more sacred than the flesh of the peace-offerings, of which the offerer also had a share. There also they were to *bake the meat-offering,* their share of it, which they had from the altar for their own tables, *v.* 20. Care was taken that they should not *bear them out into the outer court, to sanctify the people.* Let them not pretend to sanctify the people with this holy flesh, and so impose upon them; or let not the people imagine that by touching those sacred things they were sanctified, and made any the better or more acceptable to God. It should seem (from Hag. 2:12) that there were those who had such a conceit; and therefore the priests must not carry any of the holy flesh away with them, lest they should encourage that conceit. Ministers must take heed of doing any thing to bolster up ignorant people in their superstitious vanities.

CHAPTER 47

In this chapter we have, I. The vision of the holy waters, their rise, extent, depth, and healing virtue, the plenty of fish in them, and an account of the trees growing on the banks of them (*v.* 1–12). II. An appointment of the borders of the land of Canaan, which was to be divided by lot to the tribes of Israel and the strangers that sojourned among them (*v.* 13–23).

Verses 1–12

This part of Ezekiel's vision must so necessarily have a mystical and spiritual meaning that thence we conclude the other parts of his vision have a mystical and spiritual meaning also; for it cannot be applied to the waters brought by pipes into the temple for the washing of the sacrifices, the keeping of the temple clean, and the carrying off of those waters, for that would be to turn this pleasant river into a sink or common sewer. That prophecy, Zec. 14:8, may explain it, of *living waters* that shall *go out* from Jerusalem, *half of them towards the former sea and half of them towards the hinder sea.* And there is plainly a reference to this in St. John's vision of a *pure river of water of life,* Rev. 22:1. That seems to represent the glory and joy which are grace perfected. This seems to represent the grace and joy which are glory begun. Most interpreters agree that these waters signify the gospel of Christ, which went forth from Jerusalem, and spread itself into the countries about, and the gifts and powers of the Holy Ghost which accompanied it, and by virtue of which it spread far and produced strange and blessed effects. Ezekiel had walked round the house again and again, and yet did not till now take notice of those waters; for God makes known his mind and will to his people, not all at once, but by degrees. Now observe,

I. The rise of these waters. He is not put to trace the streams to the fountain, but has the fountain-head first discovered to him (*v.* 1): *Waters issued out from the threshold of the house eastward,* and from *under the right side of the house,* that is, the south side of *the alter.* And again (*v.* 2), *There ran out waters on the right side,* signifying that *from Zion should go forth the law and the word of the Lord from Jerusalem,* Isa. 2:3. There it was that the Spirit was poured out upon the apostles, and endued them with the gift of tongues, that they might carry these waters to all nations. In the temple first they were to stand and *preach the words of this life,* Acts 5:20. They must preach the gospel to all nations, but must *begin at Jerusalem,* Lu. 24:47. But that is not all: Christ is the temple; he is the door; from him those living waters flow, out of his pierced side. It is the water that he gives us that is *the well of water which springs up,* Jn. 4:14. And it is by believing in him that we receive from him *rivers of living water;* and *this spoke he of the Spirit,* Jn. 7:38, 39. The original of these waters was not above-ground, but they sprang up from under the threshold; for the fountain of a believer's life is a mystery; it is *hid with Christ in God,* Col. 3:3. Some observe that they came forth *on the right side of the house* to intimate that gospel-blessings are right-hand blessings. It is also an encouragement to those who attend at Wisdom's gates, at the posts of her doors, who are willing to lie at the threshold of God's house, as David was, that they lie at the fountainhead of comfort and grace; the very entrance into God's word gives light and life, Ps. 119:130. David speaks it to the praise of Zion, *All my springs are in thee,* Ps. 87:7. They came *from the side of the altar,* for it is in and by Jesus Christ, the great altar (who *sanctifies our gifts* to God), that God has *blessed us with spiritual blessings in holy heavenly places.* From God as the fountain, in him as the channel, flows the river which *makes glad the city of our God, the holy place of the tabernacles of the Most High,* Ps. 46:4. But observe how much the blessedness and joy of glorified saints in heaven exceed those of the best and happiest saints on earth; here the streams of our comfort arise *from under the threshold;* there they proceed *from the throne* the throne *of God and of the Lamb,* Rev. 22:1.

II. The progress and increase of these waters: They *went forth eastward* (*v.* 3), *towards the east country* (*v.* 8), for so they were directed. The prophet and his guide followed the stream as it ran down from the holy mountains, and when they had followed it about *a thousand cubits* they went over across it, to try the depth of it, and it was *to the ankles, v.* 3. Then they walked along on the bank of the river on the other side, a thousand cubits more, and then, to try the depth of it, they waded through it the second time, and it was up to *their knees, v.* 4. They walked along by it a thousand cubits more, and then forded it the third time, and then it was up to their middle — *the waters were to the loins.* They then walked a thousand cubits further, and attempted to repass it the fourth time, but found it impracticable: *The waters had risen,* by the addition either of brooks that fell into it above ground or by springs under ground, so that they were *waters to swim in, a river that could not be passed over, v.* 5. Note, 1. The waters of the sanctuary are running waters, as those of a river, not standing waters, as those of a pond. The gospel, when it was first preached, was still spreading further. Grace in the soul is still pressing forward; it is an active principle, *plus ultra — onward still,* till it comes to perfection. 2. They are increasing waters. This river, as it runs constantly, so the further it goes the fuller it grows. The gospel-church was very small in its beginnings, like a little purling brook; but by degrees it came to be *to the ankles, to the knees:* many were added to it daily, and the *grain of mustard seed* grew up to be a *great tree.* The gifts of the Spirit increase by being exercised, and grace, where it is true, is growing, like the light of the morning, which *shines more and more to the perfect day.* 3. It is good for us to follow these waters, and go along with them. Observe the progress of the gospel in the world; observe the process of the work of grace in the heart; attend the motions of the blessed Spirit, and walk after them, under a divine guidance, as Ezekiel here did. 4. It is good to be often searching into the things of God, and trying the depth of them, not only to look on the surface of those waters, but to go to the bottom of them as far as we can, to be often digging, often diving, into the mysteries of the kingdom of heaven, as those who covet to be intimately acquainted with those things. 5. If we search into the things of God, we shall find some things very plain and easy to be understood, as the waters that were but to the ankles, others more difficult, and which require a deeper search, as the water to the knees or the loins, and some quite beyond our reach, which we cannot penetrate into, or account for, but, despairing to find the bottom, must, as St. Paul, sit down at the brink, and adore the *depth,* Rom. 11:33. It has been often said that in the scripture, like these waters of the sanctuary, there are some places so shallow that a lamb may wade through them, and others so deep that an elephant may swim in them. And it is our wisdom, as the prophet here, to begin with that which is most easy, and get our hearts washed with those things before we proceed to that which is *dark and hard to be understood;* it is good to take our work before us.

III. The extent of this river: *It issues towards the east country,* but thence it either divide itself into several streams or fetches a compass, so that it *goes down into the desert,* and so *goes into the sea,* either into the *dead sea,* which lay *south-east,* or the sea of Tiberias, which lay *north-east,* or the great sea, which lay *west, v.* 8. This was accomplished when the gospel was preached with success throughout all the regions of Judea and Samaria (Acts 8:1), and afterwards the nations about, nay, and those that lay most emote, even in the isles of the sea, were enlightened and leavened by it. The sound of it went forth *to the end of the world;* and the enemies of it could no more prevail to stop the progress of it than that of a mighty river.

IV. The healing virtue of this river. The waters of the sanctuary, wherever they come and have a free course, will be found a wonderful restorative. Being *brought forth into the sea,* the sulphureous lake of Sodom, that standing monument of divine vengeance, even those *waters shall be healed* (*v.* 8), shall become sweet, and pleasant, and healthful. This intimates the wonderful and blessed change that the gospel would make, wheresoever it came in its power, a a great change, in respect both of character and condition, as the turning of the dead sea into a fountain of gardens. When children of wrath became children of love, and those that were dead in trespasses an sins were made alive, then this was fulfilled. The gospel was as that salt which Elisha cast into the spring of the waters of Jericho, with which he *healed them,* 2 Ki. 2:20, 21. Christ, coming into the world to be its physician, sent his gospel as the great medicine, the *panpharmacon;* there is in it a remedy for every malady. Nay, wherever these rivers come, they *make things to live* (*v.* 9), both plants and animals; they are the *water of life,* Rev. 22:1, 17. Christ came, *that we might have life* and for that end he sends his gospel. *Every thing shall live whither the river comes.* The grace of God makes dead sinners alive and living saints lively; everything is made fruitful and flourishing by it. But its effect is according as it is received, and as the mind is prepared and disposed to receive it; for (*v.* 11) with respect to the marshes and *miry places thereof,* that are settled in the mire of their own sinfulness, and will not be healed, or settled in the moisture of their own righteousness, and think they need no healing, their doom is, *They shall not be healed;* the same gospel which to others is a savour of life unto life shall to them be a savour of death unto death; *they shall be given to salt,* to perpetual barrenness, Deu. 29:23. Those that will not be watered with the grace of God, and made fruitful, shall be abandoned to their own hearts' lusts, and left for ever unfruitful. *He that is filthy, let him be filthy still. Never fruit grow on thee more for ever.* They shall be given to *salt,* that is, to be monuments of divine justice, as Lot's wife that was turned into a *pillar of salt,* to season others.

V. The great plenty of fish that should be in this river. Everything living moving thing shall be found here, shall *live here* (*v.* 9), shall come on and prosper, shall be the best of the kind, and shall increase greatly; so that there shall be a *very great multitude of fish, according to their kinds, as the fish of the great sea, exceedingly many.* There shall be as great plenty of the river fish, and as vast shoals of them, as there is of salt-water fish, *v.* 10. There shall be no great numbers of Christians in the church, and those multiplying like fishes in the rising generations and *the dew of their youth.* In the creation the *waters brought forth* the fish *abundantly* (Gen. 1:20, 21), and they still live in and by the waters that produced them; so believers are *begotten by the word of truth* (James 1:18), and *born by it* (1 Pt. 1:23), that river of God; by it they live, from it they have their maintenance and subsistence; in the waters of the sanctuary they are as in their element, out of them they are as fish *upon dry ground;* so David was when he thirsted and panted for God, for the living God. Where the fish are known to be in abundance, thither will the fishers flock, and there they will *cast their nets;* and therefore, to intimate the replenishing of these waters and their being made every way useful, it is here foretold that the fishers shall stand upon the banks of this river, from *En-gedi,* which lies on the border of the dead sea, to *En-eglaim,* another city, which joins to that sea, and all along shall *spread their nets.* The dead sea, which before was shunned as noisome and noxious, shall be frequented. Gospel-grace makes those persons and places which were unprofitable and good for nothing to become serviceable to God and man.

VI. The trees that were on the banks of this river — *many trees on the one side and on the other* (*v.* 7), which made the prospect very pleasant and agreeable to the eye; the shelter of these trees also would be a convenience to the fishery. But that is not all (*v.* 12); they *are trees for meat,* and the *fruit of them shall not be consumed,* for it shall produce fresh fruit *every month.* The *leaf* shall be *for medicine,* and it *shall not fade,* This part of the vision is copied out into St. John's vision very exactly (Rev. 22:2), where, on either side of the river, is said to grow the *tree of life,* which *yielded her fruit every month,* and *the leaves were for the healing of the nations.* Christians are supposed to be these trees, ministers especially, *trees of righteousness, the planting of the Lord* (Isa. 61:3), set by *the rivers of water,* the waters of the sanctuary (Ps. 1:3), grafted into Christ the tree of life, and by virtue of their union with him made trees of life too, *rooted* in him, Col. 2:7. There is a great variety of these trees, through the diversity of gifts with which they are endued by that *one Spirit who works all in all.* They grow *on the bank of the river,* or they keep close to holy ordinances, and through them derive from Christ sap and virtue. They are *fruit-trees,* designed, as the fig tree and the olive, with their fruits to *honour God and man,* Jdg. 9:9. *The fruit thereof shall be for meat,* for the *lips of the righteous feed many.* The fruits of their righteousness are one way or other beneficial. The very leaves of these trees *are for medicine,* for *bruises* and sores, *margin.* Good Christians with their good discourses, which are as their leaves, as well as with their charitable actions, which are as their fruits, do good to those about them; they *strengthen the weak,* and bind up the broken-hearted. Their cheerfulness *does good like a medicine,* not only to themselves, but to others also. They shall be enabled by the grace of God to persevere in their goodness and usefulness; their *leaf shall not fade,* or lose its medicinal virtue, having not only life in their root, but sap in all their branches; their profession *shall not wither* (Ps. 1:3), *neither shall the fruit thereof be consumed;* that is, they shall not lose the principle of their fruitfulness, but *shall still bring forth fruit in old age,* to *show that the Lord is upright* (Ps. 92:14, 15), or the reward of their fruitfulness shall abide for ever; they bring forth fruit that shall abound to their account in the great day, *fruit to life eternal;* that is indeed *fruit which shall not be consumed.* They bring *new fruit according to their months,* some in one month and others in another: so that still there shall be one or other found to serve the glory of God for the purpose he designs. Or each one of them shall bring forth fruit monthly, which denotes an abundant disposition to fruit-bearing (they shall never be weary of well-doing), and a very happy climate, such that there shall be a perpetual spring and summer. And the reason of this extraordinary fruitfulness is *because their waters issued out of the sanctuary;* it is not to be ascribed to any thing in themselves, but to the continual supplies of divine grace, with which they are *watered every moment* (Isa. 27:3); for, whoever planted them, it was that which *gave the increase.*

Verses 13–23

We are now to pass from the affairs of the sanctuary to those of the state, from the city to the country. 1. The Land of Canaan is here secured to them for an inheritance (*v.* 14): *I lifted up my hand to give it unto your fathers,* that is, promised it upon oath to them and their posterity. Though the possession had been a great while discontinued, yet God had not forgotten his oath which he swore to their fathers. Though God's providences may for a time seem to contradict his promises, yet the promise will certainly take place at last, for God will be *ever mindful of his covenant. I lifted up my hand to give it,* and therefore it shall without fail *fall to you for an inheritance.* Thus the heavenly Canaan is sure to all the seed, because it is what *God, who cannot lie, has promised.* 2. It is here circumscribed, and the bounds and limits of it are fixed, which they must not pass over to encroach upon their neighbours and which their neighbours shall not break through to encroach upon them. We had such a draught of the borders of Canaan when Joshua was to put the people in possession of it, Num. 34:1, etc. That begins with the salt sea in the south, goes round and ends there. This begins with Hamath about Damascus in the north, and so goes round and ends there, *v.* 20. Note, It is God that *appoints the bounds of our habitation;* and his Israel shall always have cause to say that *the lines have fallen to them in pleasant places.* The lake of Sodom is here called *the east sea,* for it, being healed by the waters of the sanctuary, it is no more to be called a *salt sea,* as it was in Numbers. 3. It is here ordered to be divided among the tribes of Israel, reckoning Joseph for two tribes, to make up the number of twelve, when Levi was taken out to attend the sanctuary, and had his lot adjoining to that (*v.* 13, 21): *You shall inherit it, one as well as another, v.* 14. The tribes shall have an equal share, one as much as another. As the tribes returned out of Babylon, this seems unequal, because some tribes were much more numerous than the other, and indeed the most were of Judah and Benjamin and very few of the other ten tribes; but as the twelve tribes stand, in type and vision, for the gospel-church, the Israel of God, it was very equal, because we find in another vision an equal number of each of the twelve tribes *sealed* for the *living God,* just 12,000 of each, Rev. 7:5, etc. And to those sealed ones these allotments did belong. It intimates likewise that all the subjects of Christ's kingdom have *obtained like precious faith.* Male and female, Jew and Gentile, bond and free, are all alike welcome to Christ and made partakers of him. 4. The strangers who sojourn among them, *who shall beget children* and be built up into families, and so help to people their country, *shall have inheritance among* the tribes, as if they had been native Israelites (*v.* 22, 23), which was by no means allowed in Joshua's division of the land. This is an act for a general naturalization, which would teach the Jews who was their neighbour, not those only of their own nation and religion, but those, whoever they were, that they had an opportunity of showing kindness to, because from them they would be willing to receive kindness. It would likewise invite strangers to come and settle among them, and put themselves under the wings of the divine Majesty. But it certainly looks at gospel-times, when the partition-wall between Jew and Gentile was taken down, and both one in Christ, in whom *there is no difference,* Rom. 10:12. This land was a type of the heavenly Canaan, that *better country* (Heb. 11:16), in which believing Gentiles shall have a blessed lot, as well as believing Jews, Isa. 56:3.

CHAPTER 48

In this chapter we have particular directions given for the distribution of the land, of which we had the metes and bounds assigned in the foregoing chapter. I. The portions of the twelve tribes, seven to the north of the sanctuary (*v.* 1–7) and five to the south (*v.* 23–29). II. The allotment of land for the sanctuary, and the priests (*v.* 8–11), for the Levites (*v.* 12–14), for the city (*v.* 15–20), and for the prince (*v.* 21, 22). Much of this we had before, *ch.* 45. III. A plan of the city, its gates, and the new name given to it (*v.* 30–35), which seals up, and concludes, the vision and prophecy of this book.

Verses 1–30

We have here a very short and ready way taken for the dividing of the land among the twelve tribes, not so tedious and so far about as the way that was taken in Joshua's time; for in the distribution of spiritual and heavenly blessings there is not that danger of murmuring and quarrelling that there is in the participation of the temporal blessings. When God gave to the labourers every one his penny those that were uneasy at it were soon put to silence with, *May I not do what I will with my own?* And such is the equal distribution here among the tribes. In this distribution of the land we may observe, 1. That it differs very much from the division of it in Joshua's time, and agrees not with the order of their birth, nor with that of their blessing by Jacob or Moses. Simeon here is not *divided* in Jacob, nor is Zebulun a *haven of ships,* a plain intimation that it is not so much to be understood literally as spiritually, though the mystery of it is very much hidden from us. In gospel times old things have passed away; *behold, all things have become new.* The Israel of God is cast into a new method. 2. That the tribe of Dan, which was last provided for in the first division of Canaan (Jos. 19:40), is first provided for here, *v.* 1. Thus in the gospel the last shall be first, Mt. 19:30. God, in the dispensation of his grace, does not follow the same method that he does in the disposals of his providence. But Dan had now his portion thereabouts where he had only one city before, northward, on the border of Damascus, and furthest of all from the sanctuary, because that tribe had revolted to idolatry. 3. That all the ten tribes that were carried away by the king of Assyria, as well as the two tribes that were long afterwards carried to Babylon, have their allotment in this visionary land, which some think had its accomplishment in the particular persons and families of those tribes who returned with Judah and Benjamin, of which we find many instances in Ezra and Nehemiah; and it is probable that there were returns of many more afterwards at several times, which are not recorded; and the Jews having Galilee, and other parts, that had been the possessions of the ten tribes, put into their hands, in common with them, they enjoyed them. Grotius says, If the ten tribes had repented and returned to God, as the *chief fathers of Judah and Benjamin did, and the priests and Levites* (Ezra 1:5), they would have fared as those two tribes did, but they forfeited the benefit of this glorious prophecy by sin. However, we believe it has its designed accomplishment in the establishment and enlargement of the gospel church, and the happy settlement of all those who are Israelites indeed in the sure and sweet enjoyment of the privileges of the new covenant, in which there is enough for all and enough for each. 4. That every tribe in this visionary distribution had its particular lot assigned it by a divine appointment; for it was never the intention of the gospel to pluck up the hedge of property and lay all in common; it was in a way of charity, not of legal right, that the first Christians had all things common (Acts 2:44), and many precepts of the gospel suppose that every man should know his own. We must not only acknowledge, but acquiesce in, the hand of God appointing us our lot, and be well pleased with it, believing it fittest for us. *He shall choose our inheritance for us,* Ps. 47:4. 5. That the tribes lay contiguous. By *the border* of one tribe was *the portion* of another, all in a row, in exact order, so that, like stones in an arch, they fixed, and strengthened, and wedged in one another. *Behold how good and how pleasant a thing it is for brethren* thus *to dwell together!* It was a figure of the communion of churches and saints under the gospel-government; thus, though they are many, yet they are one, and should hold together in holy love and mutual assistance. 6. That the lot of Reuben, which before lay at a distance beyond Jordan, now lies next to Judah, and next but one to the sanctuary; for the scandal he lay under, for which he was told *he should not excel,* began by this time to wear off. What has turned to the reproach of any person or people ought not to be remembered for ever, but should at length be kindly forgotten. 7. That the sanctuary was *in the midst* of them. There were seven tribes to the north of it and the Levites, the prince's, and the city's portion, with that of five tribes more, to the south of it; so that it was, as it ought to be, *in the heart of the kingdom,* that it might diffuse its benign influences to the whole, and might be the centre of their unity. The tribes that lay most remote from each other would meet there in a mutual acquaintance and fellowship. Those of the same parish or congregation, though dispersed, and having no occasion otherwise to know each other, yet by meeting statedly to worship God together should have their hearts knit to each other in holy love. 8. That where the sanctuary was the priests were: *For them, even for the priests, shall this holy oblation be, v.* 10. As, on the one hand, this denotes honour and comfort to ministers, that what is given for their support and maintenance is reckoned *a holy oblation to the Lord,* so it intimates their duty, which is that, since they are appointed and maintained for the service of the sanctuary, they ought to *attend continually to this very thing,* to reside on their cures. Those that live upon the altar must serve at the altar, not take the wages to themselves and devolve the work upon others; but how can they serve the altar, his altar they live upon, if they do not live near it? 9. Those priests had the priests' share of these lands that had approved themselves faithful to God in times of trial (*v.* 11): *It shall be for the sons of Zadok,* who, it seems, had signalized themselves in some critical juncture, and *went not astray* when the *children of Israel,* and the other Levites, went astray. God will put honour upon those who keep their integrity in times of general apostasy, and he has special favours in reserve for them. Those are swimming upwards, and so they will find at last, that are swimming against the stream. 10. The land which was appropriated to the ministers of the sanctuary might by no means be alienated. It was in the nature of the *first-fruits of the land,* and was therefore *holy to the Lord;* and, though the priests and Levites had both the use of it and the inheritance of it to them and their heirs, yet they might not *sell it nor exchange it, v.* 14. It is sacrilege to convert that to other uses which is dedicated to God. 11. The land allotted for the city and its suburbs is called a *profane place* (*v.* 15), or *common;* not but that the city was a holy city above other cities, for the Lord was there, but, in comparison with the sanctuary, it was a profane place. Yet it is too often true in the worst sense that great cities, even those which, like this, have the sanctuary near them, are profane places, and it ought to be deeply lamented. It was the complaint of old, *From Jerusalem has profaneness gone forth into all the land,* Jer. 23:15. 12. The city is made to be exactly square, and the suburbs extending themselves equally on all sides, as the Levites' cities did in the first division of the land (*v.* 16, 17), which, never being literally fulfilled in any city, intimates that it is to be understood spiritually of the beauty and stability of the gospel church, that *city of the living God,* which is formed according to the wisdom and counsel of God, and is made firm and immovable by his promise. 13. Whereas, before, the inhabitants of Jerusalem were principally of Judah and Benjamin, in whose tribe it lay, now the head city lies not in the particular lot of any of the tribes, but *those that serve the city,* and bear office in it, *shall serve it out of all the tribes of Israel, v.* 19. The most eminent men must be picked out of all the tribes of Israel for the service of the city, because many eyes were upon it, and there was great resort to it from all parts of the nation and from other nations. Those that live in the city are said to serve the city, for, wherever we are, we must study to be serviceable to the place, some way or other, according as our capacity is. They must not come out of the tribes of Israel to the city to take their ease, and enjoy their pleasures, but to serve the city, to do all the good they can there, and in so doing they would have a good influence upon the country too. 14. Care was taken that those who applied themselves to public business in the city, as well as in the sanctuary, should have an honourable comfortable maintenance; lands are appointed, *the increase* whereof *shall be food unto those that serve the city, v.* 18. Who goes a warfare at his own charges? Magistrates, that attend the service of the state, as well as ministers, that attend the service of the church, should have all due encouragement and support in so doing; and *for this cause pay we tribute also.* 15. The prince had a lot for himself, suited to the dignity of his high station (*v.* 21); we took an account of it before, *ch.* 45. He was seated near the sanctuary, where the testimony of Israel was, and near the city, where the *thrones of judgment* were, that he might be a protection to both and might see the that duty of both was carefully and faithfully done; and herein he was a minister of God for good to the whole community. Christ is the church's prince, that defends it on every side, and creates a defense; nay, he is himself a defence upon all its glory and encompasses it with his favour. 16. As Judah had his lot next the sanctuary on one side, so Benjamin had, of all the tribes, his lot nearest to it on the other side, which honour was reserved for those who adhered to the house of David and the temple at Jerusalem when the other ten tribes went astray from both. It is enough if treachery and apostasy, upon repentance, he pardoned, but constancy and fidelity shall be rewarded and preferred.

Verses 31–35

We have here a further account of the city that should be built for the metropolis of this glorious land, and to be the receptacle of those who would come from all parts to worship in the sanctuary adjoining. It is nowhere called Jerusalem, nor is the land which we have had such a particular account of the dividing of any where called the land of Canaan; for the old names are forgotten, to intimate that the *old things are done away, behold all things have become new.* Now, concerning this city, observe here, 1. The measures of its out-lets, and the grounds belonging to it, for its several conveniences; each way its appurtenances extended 4500 *measures* 18,000 in all, *v.* 35. But what these measures were is uncertain. It is never said, in all this chapter, whether so many *reeds* (as our translation determines by inserting that word, *v.* 8, each reed containing six cubits and span, *ch.* 40:5, and why should the measurer appear with the measuring reed in his hand of that length if he did not measure with *that,* except where it is expressly said he measured by cubits?) or whether, as others think, it is so many cubits, because those are mentioned *ch.* 45:2 and *ch.* 47:3. Yet that makes me incline rather to think that where cubits are not mentioned must be intended so many lengths of the measuring reed. But those who understand it of so many cubits are not agreed whether it be meant of the common cubit, which was half a yard, or the geometrical cubit, which, for better expedition, is supposed to be mostly used in surveying lands, which, some say, contained six cubits, others about three cubits and a half, so making 1000 cubits the same with 1000 paces, that is, an English mile. But our being left at this uncertainty is an intimation that these things are to be understood spiritually, and that what is principally meant is that there is an exact and just proportion observed by Infinite Wisdom in modelling the gospel church, which though now we cannot discern we shall when we come to heaven. 2. The number of its gates. It had twelve gates in all, three on each side, which was very agreeable when it lay four square; and these twelve gates were inscribed to the twelve tribes. Because the city was to be served *out of all the tribes of Israel* (*v.* 19) it was fit that each tribe should have its gate; and, Levi being here taken in, to keep to the number twelve Ephraim and Manasseh are made one in Joseph, *v.* 32. On the north side were the gates of Reuben, Judah, and Levi (*v.* 31), on the east the gates of Joseph, Benjamin, and Dan (*v.* 32), on the south the gates of Simeon, Issachar, and Zebulun (*v.* 33), and on the west the gates of Gad, Asher, and Naphtali, *v.* 34. Conformable to this, in St. John's vision, the new Jerusalem (for so the holy city is called there, though not here) has *twelve gates,* three on a side, and on them are written *the names of the twelve tribes of the children of Israel,* Rev. 21:12, 13. Note, Into the church of Christ, both militant and triumphant, there is a free access by faith for all that come of every tribe, from every quarter. Christ has *opened the kingdom of heaven for all believers.* Whoever will may come and *take of the water of life,* of the tree of life, *freely.* 3. The name given to this city: *From that day,* when it shall be newly-erected according to this model, the name of it shall be, not, as before, *Jerusalem — The vision of peace,* but which is the original of that, and more than equivalent to it, *Jehovah Shammah — The Lord is there, v.* 35. This intimated, (1.) That the captives, after their return, should have manifest tokens of God's presence with them and his residence among them, both in his ordinances and his providences. They shall have no occasion to ask, as their fathers did, *Is the Lord among us, or is he not?* for they shall see and say that he is with them of a truth. And then, though their troubles were many and threatening, they were like the bush which burned but was not consumed, because *the Lord was there.* But when God departed from their temple, when he said, *Migremus hinc — Let us go hence,* their house was soon *left unto them desolate.* Being no longer his, it was not much longer theirs. (2.) That the gospel-church should likewise have the presence of God in it, though not in the *Shechinah,* as of old, yet in a token of it no less sure, that of his Spirit. Where the gospel is faithfully preached, gospel ordinances are duly administered, and God is worshipped in the name of Jesus Christ only, it may truly be said, *The Lord is there;* for faithful is he that has said, and he will be as good as his word, *Lo, I am with you always even unto the end of the world.*

The Lord is there in his church, to rule and govern it, to protect and defend it, and graciously to accept and own his sincere worshippers, and to be *nigh unto them in all that they call upon him for.* This should engage us to keep close to the communion of saints, for *the Lord is there;* and then whither shall we go to better ourselves? Nay, it is true of every good Christian; he dwells in God, and God in him; whatever soul has in it a living principle of grace, it may be truly said, *The Lord is There.* (3.) That the glory and happiness of heaven should consist chiefly in this, that *the Lord is there.* St. John's representation of that blessed state does indeed far exceed this in many respects. That is all gold, and pearls, and precious stones; it is much larger than this, and much brighter, for it *needs not the light of the sun.* But, in making the presence of God the principal matter of its bliss, they both agree. There the happiness of the glorified saints is made to be that *God himself shall be with them* (Rev. 21:3), that *he who sits on the throne shall dwell among them,* Rev. 7:15. And here it is made to crown the bliss of this holy city that *the Lord is there.* Let us therefore give all diligence to make sure to ourselves a place in that city, that we may be *for ever with the Lord.*

AN EXPOSITION, WITH PRACTICAL OBSERVATIONS, OF

THE BOOK OF THE PROPHET DANIEL

The book of Ezekiel left the affairs of Jerusalem under a doleful aspect, all in ruins, but with a joyful prospect of all in glory again. This of Daniel fitly follows. Ezekiel told us what was seen, and what was foreseen, by him in the former years of the captivity: Daniel tells us what was seen, and foreseen, in the latter years of the captivity. When God employs different hands, yet it is about the same work. And it was a comfort to the poor captives that they had first one prophet among them and then another, to show them *how long,* and a sign that God had not quite cast them off. Let us enquire, I. Concerning this prophet His Hebrew name was *Daniel,* which signifies the *judgment of God;* his Chaldean name was *Belteshazzar.* He was of the tribe of Judah, and, as it should seem, of the royal family. He was betimes eminent for wisdom and piety. Ezekiel, his contemporary, but much his senior, speaks of him as an oracle when thus he upbraids the king of Tyre with his conceitedness of himself: *Thou art wiser then Daniel,* Eze. 38:3. He is likewise there celebrated for success in prayer, when Noah, Daniel, and Job are reckoned as three men that had the greatest interest in heaven of any, Eze. 14:14. He began betimes to be famous, and continued long so. Some of the Jewish rabbin are loth to acknowledge him to be a prophet of the higher form, and therefore rank his book among the *Hagiographa,* not among the prophecies, and would not have their disciples pay much regard to it. One reason they pretend is because he did not live such a mean mortified life as Jeremiah and some other of the prophets did, but lived like a prince, and was a prime-minister of state; whereas we find him persecuted as other prophets were (*ch.* 6), and mortifying himself as other prophets did, when he *ate no pleasant bread* (10:3), and fainting sick when he was under the power of the Spirit of prophecy, 8:27. Another reason they pretend is because he wrote his book in a heathen country, and *there* had his visions, and not in the land of Israel; but, for the same reason, Ezekiel also must be expunged out of the roll of prophets. But the true reason is that he speaks so plainly of the time of the Messiah's coming that the Jews cannot avoid the conviction of it and therefore do not care to hear of it. But Josephus calls him one of the *greatest* of *the prophets,* nay, the angel Gabriel calls him a *man greatly beloved.* He lived long an active life in the courts and councils of some of the greatest monarchs the world ever had, Nebuchadnezzar, Cyrus, Darius; for we mistake of we confine the privilege of an intercourse with heaven to speculative men, or those that spend their time in contemplation; no, who was more intimately acquainted with the mind of God than Daniel, a courtier, a statesman, and a man of business? The Spirit, as the wind, blows where it lists. And, if those that have much to do in the world plead that as an excuse for the infrequency and slightness of their converse with God, Daniel will condemn them. Some have thought that he returned to Jerusalem, and was one of the masters of the Greek synagogue; but nothing of that appears in scripture; it is therefore generally concluded that he died in Persia at Susan, where he lived to be very old. II. Concerning this book. The first six chapters of it are historical, and are plain and easy; the last six are prophetical, and in them are many things dark, and hard to be understood, which yet would be more intelligible if we had a more complete history of the nations, and especially the Jewish nation, from Daniel's time to the coming of the Messiah. Our Saviour intimates the difficulty of apprehending the sense of Daniel's prophecies when, speaking of them, he says, *Let him that readeth understand,* Mt. 24:15. The first chapter, and the first three verses of the second chapter, are in Hebrew; thence to the eighth chapter is in the Chaldee dialect; and thence to the end is in Hebrew. Mr. Broughton observes that, as the Chaldeans were kind to Daniel, and gave cups of cold water to him when he requested it, rather than the king's wine, God would not have them lose their reward, but made that language which they taught him to have honour in his writings through all the world, unto this day. Daniel, according to his computation, continues the holy story from the first surprising of Jerusalem by the Chaldean Babel, when he himself was carried away captive, until the last destruction of it by Rome, the mystical Babel, for so far forward his predictions look, 9:27. The fables of Susannah, and of Bel and the Dragon, in both which Daniel is made a party, are apocryphal stories, which we think we have no reason to give any credit to, they being never found in the Hebrew or Chaldee, but only in the Greek, nor ever admitted by the Jewish church. There are some both of the histories and of the prophecies of this book that bear date in the latter end of the Chaldean monarchy, and others of both that are dated in the beginning of the Persian monarchy. But both Nebuchadnezzar's dream, which Daniel interpreted, and his own visions, point at the Grecian and Roman monarchies, and very particularly at the Jews' troubles under Antiochus, which it would be of great use to them to prepare for; as his fixing the very time for the coming of the Messiah was of use to all those that waited for the consolation of Israel, and is to us, for the confirming of our belief, That this is he who should come, and we are to look for no other.

CHAPTER 1

This chapter gives us a more particular account of the beginning of Daniel's life, his original and education, than we have of any other of the prophets. Isaiah, Jeremiah, and Ezekiel, began immediately with divine visions; but Daniel began with the study of human learning, and was afterwards honoured with divine visions; such variety of methods has God taken in training up men for the service of his church. We have here, I. Jehoiakim's first captivity (*v.* 1, 2), in which Daniel, with others of the seed-royal, was carried to Babylon. II. The choice made of Daniel, and some other young men, to be brought up in the Chaldean literature, that they might be fitted to serve the government, and the provision made for them (*v.* 3–7). III. Their pious refusal to eat the portion of the king's meat, and their determining to live upon pulse and water, which, having tried it, the master of the eunuchs allowed them to do, finding that it agreed very well with them (*v.* 8–16). IV. Their wonderful improvement, above all their fellows, in wisdom and knowledge (*v.* 17–21).

Verses 1–7

We have in these verses an account,

I. Of the first descent which Nebuchadnezzar, king of Babylon, in the first year of his reign, made upon Judah and Jerusalem, in the third year of the reign of Jehoiakim, and his success in that expedition (*v.* 1, 2.): He *besieged Jerusalem,* soon made himself master of it, seized the king, took whom he pleased and what he pleased away with him, and then left Jehoiakim to reign as tributary to him, which he did about eight years longer, but then rebelled, and it was his ruin. Now from this *first* captivity most interpreters think the seventy years are to be dated, though Jerusalem was not destroyed, nor the captivity completed, till about nineteen years after, In that first year Daniel was carried to Babylon, and there continued the whole seventy years (see *v.* 21), during which time all nations shall serve Nebuchadnezzar, and his son, and his son's son, Jer. 25:11. This one prophet therefore saw within the compass of his own time the rise, reign, and ruin of that monarchy; so that it was *res unius aetatis — the affair of a single age,* such short-lived things are the kingdoms of the earth; but the kingdom of heaven is everlasting. The righteous, that see them taking root, shall *see their fall,* Job 5:3; Prov. 29:16. Mr. Broughton observes the proportion of times in God's government since the coming out of Egypt: thence to their entering Canaan forty years, thence seven years to the dividing of the land, thence seven Jubilees to the first year of Samuel, in whom prophecy began, thence to this first year of the captivity seven seventies of years, 490 (ten Jubilees), thence to the return one seventy, thence to the death of Christ seven seventies more, thence to the destruction of Jerusalem forty years.

II. The improvement he made of this success. He did not destroy the city or kingdom, but did that which just accomplished the first threatening of mischief by Babylon. It was denounced against Hezekiah, for showing his treasures to the king of Babylon's ambassadors (Isa. 39:6, 7), that the treasures and the children should be carried away, and, if they had been humbled and reformed by this, hitherto the king of Babylon's power and success should have gone, but *no further.* If less judgments do the work, God will not send greater; but, if not, he will heat the furnace seven times hotter. Let us see what was now done. 1. The vessels of the sanctuary were carried away, *part* of them, *v.* 2. They fondly trusted to the temple to defend them, though they went on in their iniquity. And now, to show them the vanity of that confidence, the temple is first plundered. Many of the holy vessels which used to be employed in the service of God were taken away by the king of Babylon, those of them, it is likely, which were most valuable, and he brought them as trophies of victory to the *house of his god,* to whom, with a blind devotion, he gave praise of his success; and having appropriated these vessels, in token of gratitude, to his god, he *put them in the treasury* of his temple. See the righteousness of God; his people had brought the images of other gods into his temple, and now he suffers the vessels of the temple to be carried into the treasuries of those other gods. Note, When men profane the vessels of the sanctuary with their sins it is just with God to profane them by his judgments. It is probable that the treasures of the king's house were rifled, as was foretold, but particular mention is made of the taking away of the *vessels of the sanctuary* because we shall find afterwards that the profanation of them was that which filled up the measure of the Chaldeans' iniquity, *ch.* 5:3. But observe, It was only *part of them* that went now; some were left them yet upon trial, to see if they would take the right course to prevent the carrying away of the remainder. See Jer. 27:18. 2. The children and young men, especially such as were of noble or royal extraction, that were sightly and promising, and of good natural parts, were carried away. Thus was the iniquity of the fathers visited upon the children. These were taken away by Nebuchadnezzar, (1.) As trophies, to be made a show of for the evidencing and magnifying of his success. (2.) As hostages for the fidelity of their parents in their own land, who would be concerned to conduct themselves well that their children might have the better treatment. (3.) As a seed to serve him. He took them away to train them up for employments and preferments under him, either out of an unaccountable affectation, which great men often have, to be attended by foreigners, though they be blacks, rather than by those of their own nation, or because he knew that there were no such witty, sprightly, ingenious young men to be found among his Chaldeans as abounded among the youth of Israel; and, if that were so, it was much for the honour of the Jewish nation, as of an uncommon genius above other people, and a fruit of the blessing. But it was a shame that a people who had so much wit should have so little wisdom and grace. Now observe, [1.] The directions which the king of Babylon gave for the choice of these youths, *v.* 4. They must not choose such as were deformed in body, but comely and well-favoured, whose countenances were indexes of ingenuity and good humour. But that is not enough; they must be *skilful in all wisdom,* and *cunning,* or *well-seen in knowledge,* and *understanding science,* such as were quick and sharp, and could give a ready and intelligent account of their own country and of the learning they had hitherto been brought up in. He chose such as were young, because they would be pliable and tractable, would forget their own people and incorporate with the Chaldeans. He had an eye to what he designed them for; they must be such as had ability in them to *stand in the king's palace,* not only to attend his royal person, but to preside in his affairs. This is an instance of the policy of this rising monarch, now in the beginning of his reign, and was a good omen of his prosperity, that he was in care to raise up a succession of persons fit for public business. He did not, like Ahasuerus, appoint them to choose him out young women for the service of his government. It is the interest of princes to have wise men employed under them; it is therefore their wisdom to take care for the finding out and training up of such. It is the misery of this world that so many who are fit for public stations are buried in obscurity, and so many who are unfit for them are preferred to them. [2.] The care which he took concerning them. *First,* For their education. He ordered that they should be taught *the learning and tongue of the Chaldeans.* They are supposed to be wise and knowing young men, and yet they must be further taught. *Give instructions to a wise man and he will increase in learning.* Note, Those that would do good in the world when they grow up must learn when they are young. That is the learning age; if that time be lost, it will hardly be redeemed. It does not appear that Nebuchadnezzar designed they should learn the unlawful arts that were used among the Chaldeans, magic and divination; if he did, Daniel and his fellows would not defile themselves with them. Nay, we do not find that he ordered them to be taught the religion of the Chaldeans, by which it appears That he was at this time no bigot; if men were skilful and faithful, and fit for his business, it was not material to him what religion they were of, provided they had but some religion. They must be trained up in the language and laws of the country, in history, philosophy, and mathematics, in the arts of husbandry, war, and navigation, in such learning as might qualify them to serve their generation. Note, It is real service to the public to provide for the good education of the youth. *Secondly,* For their maintenance. He provided for them *three years,* not only necessaries, but dainties for their encouragement in their studies. They had *daily provision of the king's meat, and of the wine which he drank, v.* 5. This was an instance of his generosity and humanity; though they were captives, he considered their birth and quality, their spirit and genius, and treated them honourably, and studied to make their captivity easy to them. There is a respect due to those who are well-born and bred when they have fallen into distress. With a liberal education there should be a liberal maintenance.

III. A particular account of Daniel and his fellows. They were of the *children of Judah,* the royal tribe, and probably of the house of David, which had grown a numerous family; and God told Hezekiah that of the children that should *issue from him* some should be taken and made eunuchs, or chamberlains, *in the palace of the king of Babylon.* The *prince of the eunuchs* changed the names of Daniel and his fellows, partly to show his authority over them and their subjection to him, and partly in token of their being naturalized and made Chaldeans. Their Hebrew names, which they received at their circumcision, had something of God, or Jah, in them: *Daniel — God is my Judge; Hananiah — The grace of the Lord; Mishael — He that is the strong God; Azariah — The Lord is a help.* To make them forget the God of their fathers, the guide of their youth, they give them names that savour of the Chaldean idolatry. *Belteshazzar* signifies the *keeper of the hidden treasures of Bel; Shadrach — The inspiration of the*

sun, which the Chaldeans worshipped; *Meshach — Of the goddess Shach,* under which name Venus was worshipped; *Abed-nego,* The *servant of the shining fire,* which they worshipped also. Thus, though they would not force them from the religion of their fathers to that of their conquerors, yet they did what they could by fair means insensibly to wean them from the former and instil the latter into them. Yet see how comfortably they were provided for; though they suffered for their fathers' sins they were preferred for their own merits, and the land of their captivity was made more comfortable to them than the land of their nativity at this time would have been.

Verses 8–16

We observe here, very much to our satisfaction,

I. That Daniel was a favourite with the *prince of the eunuchs* (*v.* 9), as Joseph was with the keeper of the prison; he had a *tender love* for him. No doubt Daniel deserved it, and recommended himself by his ingenuity and sweetness of temper (he was *greatly beloved, ch.* 9:23); and yet it is said here that it was God that *brought him into favour with the prince of the eunuchs,* for every one does not meet with acceptance according to his merits. Note, The interest which we think we make for ourselves we must acknowledge to be God's gift, and must ascribe to him the glory of it. Whoever are in favour, it is God that has brought them into favour; and it is by him that they *find good understanding.* Herein was again verified That work (Ps. 106:46), *He made them to be pitied of all those that carried them captives.* Let young ones know that the way to be acceptable is to be tractable and dutiful.

II. That Daniel was still firm to his religion. They had changed his name, but they could not change his nature. Whatever they pleased to call him, he still retained the spirit of an Israelite indeed. He would apply his mind as closely as any of them to his books, and took pains to make himself master of the *learning and tongue of the Chaldeans,* but he was resolved that *he would not defile himself with the portion of the king's meat,* he would not meddle with it, nor *with the wine which he drank, v.* 8. And having communicated his purpose, with the reasons of it, to his fellows, they concurred in the same resolution, as appears, *v.* 11. This was not out of sullenness, or peevishness, or a spirit of contradiction, but from a principle of conscience. Perhaps it was not in itself unlawful for them to *eat of the king's meat* or to *drink of his wine.* But, 1. They were scrupulous concerning the meat, lest it should be sinful. Sometimes such meat would be set before them as was expressly forbidden by their law, as swine's flesh; or they were afraid lest it should have been offered in sacrifice to an idol, or blessed in the name of an idol. The Jews were distinguished from other nations very much by their meats (Lev. 11:45, 46), and these pious young men, being in a strange country, thought themselves obliged to keep up the honour of their being a peculiar people. Though they could not keep up their dignity as princes, they would not lose it as Israelites; for on that they most valued themselves. Note, When God's people are in Babylon they have need to take special care that they *partake not in her sins.* Providence seemed to lay this meat before them; being captives they must eat what they could get and must not disoblige their masters; yet, if the command be against it, they must abide by that. Though Providence says, *Kill and eat,* conscience says, *Not so, Lord, for nothing common or unclean has come into my mouth.* 2. They were jealous over themselves, lest, though it should not be sinful in itself, it should be an *occasion of sin* to them, lest, by indulging their appetites with these dainties, they should grow sinful, voluptuous, and in love with the pleasures of Babylon. They had learned David's prayer, *Let me not eat of their dainties* (Ps. 141:4), and Solomon's precept, *Be not desirous of dainties, for they are deceitful meat* (Prov. 23:3), and accordingly they form their resolution. Note, It is very much the praise of all, and especially of young people, to be dead to the delights of sense, not to covet them, not to relish them, but to look upon them with indifference. Those that would excel in wisdom and piety must learn betimes to *keep under the body and bring it into subjection.* 3. However, they thought it unseasonable now, when Jerusalem was in distress, and they themselves were in captivity. They had no heart to *drink wine in bowls,* so much were they *grieved for the affliction of Joseph.* Though

they had royal blood in their veins, yet they did not think it proper to have royal dainties in their mouths when they were thus brought low. Note, It becomes us to be humble under humbling providences. *Call me not Naomi; call me Marah.* See the benefit of affliction; by the account Jeremiah gives of the princes and great men now at Jerusalem it appears that they were very corrupt and wicked, and defiled themselves with things offered to idols, while these young gentlemen that were in captivity would not defile themselves, no, not with their *portion of the king's meat.* How much better is it with those that retain their integrity in the depths of affliction than with those that retain their iniquity in the heights of prosperity! Observe, The great thing that Daniel avoided was defiling himself with the pollutions of sin; that is the thing we should be more afraid of than of any outward trouble. Daniel, having taken up this resolution, *requested of the prince of the eunuchs that he might not defile himself,* not only that he might not be compelled to do it, but that he might not be tempted to do it, that the bait might not be laid before him, that he might not see the portion appointed him of the king's meat, nor look upon the wine when it was red. It will be easier to keep the temptation at a distance than to suffer it to come near and then be forced to *put a knife to our throat.* Note, We cannot better improve our interest in any with whom we have found favour than by making use of them to keep us from sin.

III. That God wonderfully owned him herein. When Daniel requested that he might have none of the king's meat or wine set before him the prince of the eunuchs objected that, if he and his fellows were not found in as good case as any of their companions, he should be in danger of having anger and of losing his head, *v.* 10. Daniel, to satisfy him that there would be no danger of any bad consequence, desires the matter might be put to a trial. He applies himself further to the under-officer, Melzar, or the steward: "*Prove us for ten days;* during that time let us have nothing but *pulse to eat,* nothing but herbs and fruits, or parched peas or lentils, and nothing but *water to drink,* and see how we can live upon that, and proceed accordingly," *v.* 13. People will not believe the benefit of abstemiousness and a spare diet, nor how much it contributes to the health of the body, unless they try it. Trial was accordingly made. Daniel and his fellows lived for ten days upon *pulse and water,* hard fare for young men of genteel extraction and education, and which one would rather expect they should have indented against than petitioned for; but *at the end of the ten days* they were compared with the other children, and were found *fairer and fatter in flesh,* of a more healthful look and better complexion, than *all those who did eat the portion of the king's meat, v.* 15. This was in part a natural effect of their temperance, but it must be ascribed to the special blessing of God, which will make a little to go a great way, a *dinner of herbs* better than a *stalled ox.* By this it appears that *man lives not by bread alone;* pulse and water shall be the most nourishing food if God speak the word. See what it is to keep ourselves pure from the pollutions of sin; it is the way to have that comfort and satisfaction which will be *health to the navel and marrow to the bones,* while the pleasures of sin are *rottenness to the bones.*

IV. That his master countenanced him. The steward did not force them to eat against their consciences, but, as they desired, *gave them pulse and water* (*v.* 16), the pleasures of which they enjoyed, and we have reason to think were not envied the enjoyment. Here is a great example of temperance and contentment with mean things; and (as Epicurus said) "he that lives according to nature will never be poor, but he that lives according to opinion will never be rich." This wonderful abstemiousness of these young men in the days of their youth contributed to the fitting of them, 1. For their eminent services. Hereby they kept their minds clear and unclouded, and fit for contemplation, and saved for the best employments a great deal both of time and thought; and thus they prevented those diseases which indispose men for the business of age that owe their rise to the intemperances of youth. 2. For their eminent sufferings. Those that had thus inured themselves to hardship, and lived a life of self-denial and mortification, could the more easily venture upon the fiery furnace and the den of lions, rather than sin against God.

Verses 17–21

Concerning Daniel and his fellows we have here,

I. Their great attainments in learning, *v.* 17. They were very sober and diligent, and studied hard; and we may suppose their tutors, finding them of an uncommon capacity, took a great deal of pains with them, but, after all, their achievements are ascribed to God only. It was he that *gave them knowledge and skill in all learning and wisdom;* for *every good and perfect gift is from above, from the Father of the lights.* It is the Lord our God that *gives men power to get* this wealth; the mind is furnished only by him that formed it. The great learning which God gave these four children was, 1. A balance for their losses. They had, for the iniquity of their fathers, been deprived of the honours and pleasures that would have attended their noble extraction; but, to make them amends for that, God, in giving them learning, gave them better honours and pleasures than those they had been deprived of. 2. A recompence for their integrity. They kept to their religion, even in the minutest instances of it, and would not so much as defile themselves with the king's meat or wine, but became, in effect, Nazarites; and now God rewarded them for it with eminency in learning; for God *gives to a man that is good in his sight, wisdom, and knowledge, and joy* with them, Eccl. 2:26. To Daniel he gave a double portion; he had *understanding in visions and dreams;* he knew how to interpret dreams, as Joseph, not by rules of art, such as are pretended to be given by the oneirocritics, but by a divine sagacity and wisdom which God gave him. Nay, he was endued with a prophetic spirit, by which he was enabled to converse with God, and to receive the notices of divine things in dreams and visions, Num. 12:6. According to this gift given to Daniel, we find him, in this book, all along employed about dreams and visions, interpreting or entertaining them; for, *as every one has received the gift,* so shall he have an opportunity, and so should he have a heart, to *minister the same,* 1 Pt. 4:10.

II. Their great acceptance with the king. After *three years* spent in their education (they being of some maturity, it is likely, when they came, perhaps about twenty years old) they were presented to the king with the rest that were of their standing, *v.* 18. And the king examined them and *communed with them* himself, *v.* 19. He could do it, being a man of parts and learning himself, else he would not have come to be so great; and he would do it, for it is the wisdom of princes, in the choice of the persons they employ, to see with their own eyes, to exercise their own judgment, and not trust too much to the representation of others. The king examined them not so much in the languages, in the rules of oratory or poetry, as *in all matters of wisdom and understanding,* the rules of prudence and true politics; he enquired into their judgment about the due conduct of human life and public affairs; not "Were they wits?" but, "Were they wise?" And he not only found them to excel the young candidates for preferment that were of their own standing, but found that they had *more understanding than the ancients, than all their teachers,* Ps. 119:99, 100. So far was the king from being partial to his own countrymen, to seniors, to those of his own religion and of an established reputation, that he freely owned that, upon trial, he found those poor young captive Jews ten times wiser and *better than all the magicians that were in all his realm, v.* 20. He was soon aware of something extraordinary in these young men, and, which gave him a surprising satisfaction, was soon aware that a little of their true divinity was preferable to a great deal of the divination he had been used to. *What is the chaff to the wheat?* what are the magicians' rods to Aaron's? There was no comparison between them. These four young students were better, were *ten times* better, than all the old practitioners, put them all together, that were *in all his realm,* and we may be sure that they were not a few. This contempt did God pour upon the pride of the Chaldeans, and this honour did he put upon the low estate of his own people; and thus did he make not only these persons, but the rest of their nation for their sakes, the more respected in the land of their captivity. *Lastly,* This judgment being given concerning them, they *stood before the king (v.* 19); they attended in the presence-chamber, nay, and in the council-chamber, for to *see the king's face* is the periphrasis of a privy-counsellor, Esth. 1:14. This confirms Solomon's observation, *Seest thou a man dil-igent in his business,* sober and humble? *he shall stand before kings; he shall not stand before mean men.* Industry is the way to preferment. How long the other three were about the court we are not told; but Daniel, for his part, *continued to the first year of Cyrus (v.* 21), though not always alike in favour and reputation. He lived and prophesied after the first year of Cyrus; but that is mentioned to intimate that he lived to see the deliverance of his people out of their captivity and their return to their own land. Note, Sometimes God favours his servants that mourn with Zion in her sorrows to let them live to see better times with the church than they saw in the beginning of their days and to share with her in her joys.

CHAPTER 2

It was said (1:17) that Daniel had understanding in dreams; and here we have an early and eminent instance of it, which soon made him famous in the court of Babylon, as Joseph by the same means came to be so in the court of Egypt. This chapter is a history, but it is the history of a prophecy, by a dream and the interpretation of it. Pharaoh's dream, and Joseph's interpretation of it, related only to the years of plenty and famine and the interest of God's Israel in them; but Nebuchadnezzar's dream here, and Daniel's interpretation of that, look much higher, to the four monarchies, and the concerns of Israel in them, and the kingdom of the Messiah, which should be set up in the world upon the ruins of them. In this chapter we have, I. The great perplexity that Nebuchadnezzar was put into by a dream which he had forgotten, and his command to the magicians to tell him what it was, which they could not pretend to do (*v.* 1–11). II. Orders given for the destroying of all the wise men of Babylon, and of Daniel among the rest, with his fellows (*v.* 12–15). III. The discovery of this secret to him, in answer to prayer, and the thanksgiving he offered up to God thereupon (*v.* 16–23). IV. His admission to the king, and the discovery he made to him both of his dream and of the interpretation of it (*v.* 24–45). V. The great honour which Nebuchadnezzar put upon Daniel, in recompence for this service, and the preferment of his companions with him (*v.* 46–49).

Verses 1–13

We meet with a great difficulty in the date of this story; it is said to be in the second year of the reign of Nebuchadnezzar, *v.* 1. Now Daniel was carried to Babylon in his first year, and, it should seem, he was three years under tutors and governors before he was presented to the king, *ch.* 1:5. How then could this happen in *the second year?* Perhaps, though three years were appointed for the education of other children, yet Daniel was so forward that he was taken into business when he had been but one year at school, and so in the second year he became thus considerable. Some make it to be the second year after he began to reign alone, but the fifth or sixth year since he began to reign in partnership with his *father.* Some read it, *and in the second year,* (the second after Daniel and his fellows stood before the king), *in the kingdom of Nebuchadnezzar,* or *in his reign,* this happened; as Joseph, in the second year after his skill in dreams, showed and expounded Pharaoh's, so Daniel, in the second year after he commenced master in that art, did this service. I would much rather take it some of these ways than suppose, as some do, that it was in the second year after he had conquered Egypt, which was the thirty-sixth year of his reign, because it appears by what we meet with in Ezekiel, that Daniel was famous both for wisdom and prevalence in prayer long before that; and therefore this passage, or story, which shows how he came to be so eminent for both these must be laid early in Nebuchadnezzar's reign. Now here we may observe,

I. The perplexity that Nebuchadnezzar was in by reason of a dream which he had dreamed but had forgotten (*v.* 1): *He dreamed dreams,* that is, a dream consisting of divers distinct parts, or which filled his head as much as if it had been many dreams. Solomon speaks of a *multitude of dreams,* strangely incoherent, in which *there are divers vanities,* Eccl. 5:7. This dream of Nebuchadnezzar's had nothing in the thing itself but what might be paralleled in many a common dream, in which are often represented to men things as foreign as are here mentioned; but there was something in the impression it made upon him which carried with it an incontestable evidence of its divine original and its prophetic significancy. Note, The greatest of men are not exempt from, nay, they lie most open to, those cares and troubles of mind which disturb their repose in the night, while *the sleep of the labouring man is sweet* and sound, and the sleep of the sober temperate man free from confused dreams. The abundance of the rich will not suffer them to sleep at all for care, and the excesses of gluttons and drunkards will not suffer them to sleep quietly for dreaming. But this recorded here was not from natural causes. Nebuchadnezzar was a troubler of God's Israel, but God here troubled him; for he that made the soul can *make his sword to approach to it.* He had his guards about him, but they could not keep trouble from his spirit. We know not the uneasiness of many that live in great pomp, and, one would think, in pleasure, too. We look into their houses, and are tempted to envy them; but, could we look into their hearts, we should pity them rather. All the treasures and all the delights of the children of men, which this mighty monarch had command of, could not procure him a little repose, when by reason of the trouble of his mind his *sleep broke from him.* But God *gives his beloved sleep,* who return to him as their rest.

II. The trial that he made of his magicians and astrologers whether they could tell him what his dream was, which he had forgotten. They were immediately sent for, to *show the king his dreams, v.* 2. There are many things which we retain the impressions of, and yet have lost the images of the things; though we cannot tell what the matter was, we know how we were affected with it; so it was with this king. His dream had slipped out of his mind, and he could not possibly recollect it, but he was confident he should know it if he heard it again. God ordered it so that Daniel might have the more honour, and, in him, the God of Daniel. Note, God sometimes serves his own purposes by putting things out of men's minds as well as by putting things into their minds. The magicians, it is likely, were proud of their being sent for into the king's bed-chamber, to give him a taste of their office, not doubting but it would be for their honour. He tells them that he had *dreamed a dream, v.* 3. They speak to him in the Syriac tongue, which was then the same with the Chaldee, but now they differ much. And henceforward Daniel uses that language, or dialect of the Hebrew, for the same reason that those words, Jer. 10:11, are in that language because designed to convince the Chaldeans of the folly of their idolatry and to bring them to the knowledge and worship of the true and living God, which the stories of these chapters have a direct tendency to. But *ch.* 8 and forward, being intended for the comfort of the Jews, is written in their peculiar language. They, in their answer, complimented the king with their good wishes, desired him to tell his dream, and undertook with all possible assurance to interpret it, *v.* 4. But the king insisted upon it that they must tell him the dream itself, because he had forgotten it and could not tell it to them. And, if they could not do this, they should all be put to death as deceivers (*v.* 5), themselves *cut to pieces* and *their houses made a dunghill.* If they could, they should be rewarded and preferred, *v.* 6. And they knew, as Balaam did concerning Balak, that he was able to *promote them to great honour,* and give them that *wages of unrighteousness* which, like him, *they loved* so dearly. No question therefore that they will do their utmost to gratify the king; if they do not, it is not for want of good-will, but for want of power, Providence so ordering it that the magicians of Babylon might now be as much confounded and put to shame as of old the magicians of Egypt had been, that, how much soever his people were both in Egypt and Babylon vilified and made contemptible, his oracles might in both be magnified and made honourable, by the silencing of those that set up in competition with them. The magicians, having reason on their side, insist upon it that the king must tell them the dream, and then, if they do not tell him the interpretation of it, it is their fault, *v.* 7. But arbitrary power is deaf to reason. The king falls into a passion, gives them hard words, and, without any colour of reason, suspects that they could tell him but would not; and instead of upbraiding them with impotency, and the deficiency of their art, as he might justly have done, he charges them with a combination to affront him: *You have prepared lying and corrupt words to speak before me.* How unreasonable and absurd is this imputation! If they had undertaken to tell him what his dream was, and had imposed upon him with a sham, he might have charged them with lying and corrupt words; but to say this of them when they honestly confessed their own weakness only shows what senseless things indulged passions are, and how apt great men are to think it is their prerogative to pursue their humour in defiance of reason and equity, and all the dictates of both. When the magicians begged of him to tell them the dream, though the request was highly rational and just, he tells them that they did but dally with him, to gain time (*v.* 8), *till the time be changed* (*v.* 9), either till the king's desire to know his dream be over, and he grown indifferent whether he be told it or no, though now he is so hot upon it, or till they may hope he has so perfectly forgotten his dream (the remaining shades of which are slipping from him apace as he catches at them) that they may tell him what they please and make him believe it was his dream, and, when the thing which is going, is quite *gone from him,* as it will be in a little time, he will not be able to disprove them. And therefore, without delay, they must tell him the dream. In vain do they plead, 1. That there is *no man on earth* that can retrieve the king's dream, *v.* 10. There are settled rules by which to discover what the meaning of the dream was; whether they will hold or no is the question. But never were any rules offered to be given by which to discover what the dream was; they cannot work unless they have something to work upon. They acknowledge that the gods may indeed *declare unto man what is his thought* (Amos 4:13), for God *understands our thoughts afar off* (Ps. 139:2), what they will be before we think them, what they are when we do not regard them, what they have been when we have forgotten them. But those who can do this are gods, that *have not their dwelling with flesh* (*v.* 11), and it is they alone that can do this. As for men, their *dwelling is with flesh;* the wisest and greatest of men are clouded with a veil of flesh, which quite obstructs and confounds all their acquaintance with spirit, and their powers and operations; but the gods, that are themselves pure spirit, know what is in man. See here an instance of the ignorance of these magicians, that they speak of many gods, whereas there is but one and can be but one infinite; yet see their knowledge of that which even the light of nature teaches and the works of nature prove, that there is a God, who is a Spirit, and perfectly knows the spirits of men and all their thoughts, so as it is not possible that any man should. This confession of the divine omniscience is here extorted from these idolaters, to the honour of God and their own condemnation, who though they knew there is a God in heaven, *to whom all hearts are open, all desires known, and from whom no secret is hid,* yet offered up their prayers and praises to dumb idols, that have *eyes and see not, ears and hear not.* 2. That there is no king on earth that would expect or require such a thing, *v.* 10. This intimates that they were *kings, lords,* and *potentates,* not ordinary people, that the magicians had most dealings with, and at whose devotion they were, while the oracles of God and the gospel of Christ are dispensed *to the poor.* Kings and potentates have often required unreasonable things of their subjects, but they think that never any required so unreasonable a thing as this, and therefore hope his imperial majesty will not insist upon it. But it is all in vain; when passion is in the throne reason is under foot: He was *angry and very furious, v.* 12. Note, It is very common for those that will not be convinced by reason to be provoked and exasperated by it, and to push on with fury what they cannot support with equity.

III. The doom passed upon all the magicians of Babylon. There is but *one decree for them all* (*v.* 9); they all stand condemned without exception or distinction. The decree has gone forth, they must every man of them be slain (*v.* 13), Daniel and his fellows (though they knew nothing of the matter) not excepted. See here, 1. What are commonly the unjust proceedings of arbitrary power. Nebuchadnezzar is here a tyrant in true colours, speaking death when he cannot speak sense, and treating those as traitors whose only fault is that they would serve him, but cannot. 2. What is commonly the just punishment of pretenders. How unrighteous soever Nebuchadnezzar was in this sentence, as to the ringleaders in the imposture, God was righteous. Those that imposed upon men, in pretending to do what they could not do, are now sentenced to death for not being able to do what they did not pretend to.

Verses 14–23

When the king sent for his wise men to tell them his dream, and the interpretation of it (*v.* 2), Daniel, it seems, was not summoned to appear among them; the king, though he was highly pleased with him when he examined him, and thought him *ten times* wiser than the rest of his wise men, yet forgot him when he had most occasion for him; and no wonder, when all was done in a

heat, and nothing with a cool and deliberate thought. But Providence so ordered it; that the magicians being nonplussed might be the more taken notice of, and so the more glory might redound to the God of Daniel. But, though Daniel had not the honour to be consulted with the rest of the wise men, contrary to all law and justice, by an undistinguishing sentence, he stands condemned with them, and till he has notice brought him to prepare for execution he knows nothing of the matter. How miserable is the case of those who live under arbitrary government, as this of Nebuchadnezzar's! How happy are we, whose lives are under the protection of the law and methods of justice, and lie not thus at the mercy of a peevish and capricious prince!

We have found already, in Ezekiel, that Daniel was famous both for prudence and prayer; as a prince he had power with God and by man; by prayer he had power with God, by prudence he had power with man, and in both he prevailed. Thus did he *find favour and good understanding* in the sight of both, and in these verses we have a remarkable instance of both.

I. Daniel by prudence knew how to deal with men, and he prevailed with them. When *Arioch, the captain of the guard,* that was appointed to slay all the wise men of Babylon, the whole college of them, seized Daniel (for the sword of tyranny, like the sword of war, *devours one as well as another*), he *answered with counsel and wisdom* (*v.* 14); he did not fall into a passion, and reproach the king as unjust and barbarous, much less did he contrive how to make resistance, but mildly asked, *Why is the decree so hasty? v.* 15. And whereas the rest of the wise men had insisted upon it that it was utterly impossible for him ever to have his demand gratified, which did but make him more outrageous, Daniel undertakes, if he may but have a little time allowed him, to give the king all the satisfaction he desired, *v.* 16. The king, being now sensible of his error in not sending for Daniel sooner, whose character he began to recollect, was soon prevailed upon to respite the judgment, and make trial of Daniel. Note, The likeliest method to turn away wrath, even the wrath of a king, which is as the messenger of death, is by a *soft answer,* by that yielding which *pacifies great offences;* thus, though *where the word of a king is there is power,* yet even that word may be repelled, and that so as to be repealed; and so some read it here (*v.* 14): *Then Daniel returned,* and stayed *the counsel and edict, through Arioch, the king's provost-marshal.*

II. Daniel knew how by prayer to converse with God, and he found favour with him, both in petition and in thanksgiving, which are the two principal parts of prayer. Observe,

1. His humble petition for this mercy, that God would discover to him what was the king's dream, and the interpretation of it. When he had gained time he did not go to consult with the rest of the wise men whether there was anything in their art, in their books, that might be of use in this matter, but *went to his house,* there to be alone with God, for from him alone, who is the Father of lights, he expected this great gift. Observe, (1.) He did not only pray for this discovery himself, but he engaged his companions to pray for it too. He *made the thing known* to those who had been all along his bosom-friends and associates, requesting *that they would desire mercy of God concerning this secret, v.* 17, 18. Though Daniel was probably their senior, and every way excelled them, yet he engaged them as partners with him in this matter, *Vis unita fortior — The union of forces produces greater force.* See Esth. 4:16. Note, Praying friends are valuable friends; it is good to have an intimacy with and an interest in those that have fellowship with God and an interest at the throne of grace; and it well becomes the greatest and best of men to desire the assistance of the prayers of others for them. St. Paul often entreats his friends to pray for him. Thus we must show that we put a value upon our friends, upon prayer, upon their prayers. (2.) He was particular in this prayer, but had an eye to, and a dependence upon, the general mercy of God: *That they would desire the mercies of the God of heaven concerning this secret, v.* 18. We ought in prayer to look up to God as the *God of heaven,* a God above us, and who has dominion over us, to whom we owe adoration and allegiance, a God of power, who can do everything. Our savior has taught us to pray to God

as *our Father in heaven.* And, whatever good we pray for, our dependence must be upon the *mercies of God* for it, and an interest in those mercies we must desire; we can expect nothing by way of recompence for our merits, but all as the gift of God's mercies. They desired mercy *concerning this secret.* Note, Whatever is the matter of our care must be the matter of our prayer; we must desire mercy of God concerning this thing and the other thing that occasions us trouble and fear. God gives us leave to be humbly free with him, and in prayer to enter into the detail of our wants and burdens. *Secret things belong to the Lord our God,* and therefore, if there be any mercy we stand in need of that concerns a secret, to him we must apply; and, though we cannot in faith pray for miracles, yet we may in faith pray to him who has all hearts in his hand, and who in his providence does wonders without miracles, for the discovery of that which is out of our view and the obtaining of that which is out of our reach, as far as is for his glory and our good, believing that to him nothing is hidden, nothing is hard. (3.) Their plea with God was the imminent peril they were in; they desired mercy of God in this matter, that so Daniel and his *fellows might not perish with the rest of the wise men of Babylon,* that the righteous might not be destroyed with the wicked. Note, When the lives of good and useful men are in danger it is time to be earnest with God for mercy for them, as for Peter in prison, Acts 12:5. (4.) The mercy which Daniel and his fellows prayed for was bestowed. The *secret was revealed unto Daniel* in a *night-vision, v.* 19. Some think he dreamed the same dream, when he was asleep, that Nebuchadnezzar had dreamed; it should rather seem that when he was awake, and continuing *instant in prayer,* and *watching in the same,* the dream itself, and the interpretation of it, were communicated to him by the ministry of an angel, abundantly to his satisfaction. Note, The *effectual fervent prayer of righteous men avails much.* There are mysteries and secrets which by prayer we are let into; with that key the cabinets of heaven are unlocked, for Christ has said, Thus *knock, and it shall be opened unto you.*

2. His grateful thanksgiving for this mercy when he had received it: *Then Daniel blessed the God of heaven, v.* 19. He did not stay till he had told it to the king, and seen whether he would own it to be his dream or no, but was confident that it was so, and that he had gained his point, and therefore he immediately turned his prayers into praises. As he had prayed in a full assurance that God would do this for him, so he gave thanks in a full assurance that he had done it; and in both he had an eye to God as the *God of heaven.* His prayer was not recorded, but his thanksgiving is. Observe,

(1.) The honour he gives to God in this thanksgiving, which he studies to do in a great variety and copiousness of expression: *Blessed be the name of God for ever and ever.* There is that *for ever* in God which is to be blessed and praised; it is unchangeably and eternally in him. And it is to be blessed *for ever and ever;* as the matter of praise is God's eternal perfection, so the work of praise shall be everlastingly in the doing. [1.] He gives to God the glory of what he is in himself: *Wisdom and might are his, wisdom and courage* (so some); whatever is fit to be done he will do; whatever he will do he can do, he dares do, and he will be sure to do it in the best manner, for he has infinite wisdom to design and contrive and infinite power to execute and accomplish. *With him are strength and wisdom,* which in men are often parted. [2.] He gives him the glory of what he is to the world of mankind. He has a universal influence and agency upon all the children of men, and all their actions and affairs. Are the times changed? Is the posture of affairs altered? Does every thing lie open to mutability? It is God that *changes the times and the seasons,* and the face of them. No change comes to pass by chance, but according to the will and counsel of God. Are those that were kings removed and deposed? Do they abdicate? Are they laid aside? It is God that *removes kings.* Are the *poor raised out of the dust,* to be *set among princes?* It is God that *sets up kings;* and the making and unmaking of kings is a flower of his crown who is the fountain of all power, *King of kings and Lord of lords.* Are there men that excel others in wisdom, philosophers and statesmen, that think above the common rate, contemplative penetrating men? It is *God that gives wisdom to the wise,* whether they be so wise as to acknowledge it or no; they have it not of themselves, but it is he that *gives knowledge to those that know understanding,* which is a good reason why we should not be proud of our knowledge, and why we should serve and honour God with it and make it our business to know him. [3.] He gives him the glory of this particular discovery. He praises him, *First,* For that he could make such a discovery (v. 22): *He reveals the deep and secret things* which are hidden from the eyes of all living. It was he that revealed to man what is true wisdom when none else could (Job 27:27, 28); it is he that reveals things to come to his servants and prophets. He does himself perfectly discern and distinguish that which is most closely and most industriously concealed, for he will *bring into judgment every secret thing;* the truth will be evident in the great day. He *knows what is in the darkness,* and what is done in the darkness, for that *hides not from him,* Ps. 139:11, 12. *The light dwells with him,* and he *dwells in the light* (1 Tim. 6:16), and yet, as to us, he *makes darkness his pavilion.* Some understand it of the light of prophecy and divine revelation, which dwells with God and is derived from him; for he is the *Father of lights,* of all lights; they are all at home in him. *Secondly,* For that he had made this discovery to him. Here he has an eye to God as the *God of his fathers;* for, though the Jews were now captives in Babylon, yet they were *beloved for their father's sake.* He praises God, who is the fountain of wisdom and might, for the wisdom and might he had given him, wisdom to know this great secret and might to bear the discovery. Note, What wisdom and might we have we must acknowledge to be God's gift. *Thou hast made this known to me,* v. 23. What was hidden from the celebrated Chaldeans, who made the interpreting of dreams their profession, is revealed to Daniel, a captive-Jew, a babe, much their junior. God would hereby put honour upon the *Spirit of prophecy* just when he was putting contempt upon the *spirit of divination.* Was Daniel thus thankful to God for making known that to him which was the saving of the lives of him and his fellows? Much more reason have we to be thankful to him for making known to us the great salvation of the soul, to us and *not to the world,* to us and *not to the wise and prudent.*

(2.) The respect he puts upon his companions in this thanksgiving. Though it was by his prayers principally that this discovery was obtained, and to him that it was made, yet he owns their partnership with him, both in praying for it (it is what *we desired of thee*) and in enjoying it — Thou hast *made known unto us the king's matter.* Either they were present with Daniel when the discovery was made to him, or as soon as he knew it he told it them (*heurēka, heurēka — I have found it, I have found it*), that those who had assisted him with their prayers might assist him in their praises; his joining them with him is an instance of his humility and modesty, which well become those that are taken into communion with God. Thus St. Paul sometimes joins Sylvanus, Timotheus, or some other minister, with himself in the inscriptions to many of his epistles. Note, What honour God puts upon us we should be willing that our brethren may share with us in.

Verses 24–30

We have here the introduction to Daniel's declaring the dream, and the interpretation of it.

I. He immediately bespoke the reversing of the sentence against the wise men of Babylon, v. 24. He went with all speed to Arioch, to tell him that his commission was now superseded: *Destroy not the wise men of Babylon.* Though there were those of them perhaps that deserved to die, as magicians, by the law of God, yet here that which they stood condemned for was not a crime worth of death or of bonds, and therefore let them not die, and be *unjustly destroyed,* but let them live, and be justly shamed, as having been nonplussed and unable to do that which a prophet of the Lord could do. Note, Since God shows common kindness to the evil and good, we should do so too, and be ready to save the lives of even bad men, Mt. 5:45. A good man is a common good. To Paul in the ship God gave the souls of all that sailed with him; they were saved for his sake. To Daniel was owing the preservation of all the wise men, who yet rendered not according to the benefit done to them, ch. 3:8.

II. He offered his service, with great assurance, to go to the king, and tell him his dream and the interpretation

of it, and was admitted accordingly, v. 24, 25. Arioch brought him in haste to the king, hoping to ingratiate himself by introducing Daniel; he pretends he had sought him to interpret the king's dream, whereas really it was to execute upon him the king's sentence that he sought him. But courtiers' business is every way to humour the prince and make their own services acceptable.

III. He contrived as much as might be to reflect shame upon the magicians, and to give honour to God, upon this occasion. The king owned that it was a bold undertaking, and questioned whether he could make it good (v. 26): *Art thou able to make known unto me the dream?* What! Such a babe in this knowledge, such a stripling as thou are, wilt thou undertake that which thy seniors despair of doing? The less likely it appeared to the king that Daniel should do this the more God was glorified in enabling him to do it. Note, In transmitting divine revelation to the children of men it has been God's usual way to make use of the *weak and foolish things* and persons *of the world,* and such as were *despised* and despaired of, *to confound the wise and mighty,* that the excellency of the power might be of him, 1 Co. 1:27, 28. Daniel from this takes occasion, 1. To put the king out of conceit with his magicians and soothsayers, whom he had such great expectations from (v. 27): *"This secret they cannot show to the king;* it is out of their power; the rules of their art will not reach to it. Therefore let not the king be angry with them for not doing that which they cannot do; but rather despise them, and cast them off, because they cannot do it." Broughton reads it generally: "This secret *no sages, astrologers, enchanters, or entrail-cookers, can show unto the king;* let not the king therefore consult them any more." Note, The experience we have of the inability of all creatures to give us satisfaction should lessen our esteem of them, and lower our expectations from them. They are baffled in their pretensions; we are baffled in our hopes from them. Hitherto they come, and no further; let us therefore say to them, as Job to his friends, *Now you are nothing; miserable comforters are you all.* 2. To bring him to the knowledge of the one only living and true God, the God whom Daniel worshipped: "Though they cannot find out the secret, let not the king despair of having it found out, for *there is a God in heaven that reveals secrets,"* v. 28. Note, The insufficiency of creatures should drive us to the all-sufficiency of the Creator. *There is a God in heaven* (and it is well for us there is) who can do that for us, and make known that to us, which none on earth can, particularly the secret history of the work of redemption and the secret designs of God's love to us therein, the mystery which was *hidden from ages and generations;* divine revelation helps us out where human reason leaves us quite at a loss, and makes known that, not only to kings, but to the poor of this world, which none of the philosophers or politicians of the heathens, with all their oracles and arts of divination to help them, could ever pretend to give us any light into, Rom. 16:25, 26.

IV. He confirmed the king in his opinion that the dream he was thus solicitous to recover the idea of was really well worth enquiring after, that it was of great value and of vast consequence, not a common dream, the idle disport of a ludicrous and luxuriant fancy, which was not worth remembering or telling again, but that it was a divine discovery, a ray of light darted into his mind from the upper world, relating to the great affairs and revolutions of this lower world. God in it *made known to the king what should be in the latter days* (v. 28), that is, in the times that were to come, reaching as far as the setting up of Christ's kingdom in the world, which was to be *in the latter days,* Heb. 1:1. And again (v. 29): *"The thoughts which came into thy mind* were not the repetitions of what had been before, as our dreams usually are" —

Omnia quae sensu volvuntur vota diurno
Tempore sopito reddit amica quies —

The sentiments which we indulge throughout the day
often mingle with the grateful slumbers of the night.
— Claudian

"But they were predictions of *what should come to pass hereafter,* which he that *reveals secrets makes known unto thee;* and therefore thou art in the right in taking the hint and pursuing it thus." Note, Things that are to come to pass hereafter are secret things, which God only can reveal; and what he has revealed of those things, especially with reference to the last days of all, to the end of time, ought

to be very seriously and diligently enquired into and considered by every one of us. Some think that the *thoughts* which are said to have come into the king's mind upon his bed, what should come to pass hereafter, were his own thoughts when he was awake. Just before he fell asleep, and dreamed this dream, he was musing in his own mind what would be the issue of his growing greatness, what his kingdom would hereafter come to; and so the dream was an answer to those thoughts. What discoveries God intends to make he thus prepares men for.

V. He solemnly professes that he could not pretend to have merited from God the favour of this discovery, or to have obtained it by any sagacity of his own (v. 30): *"But, as for me,* this secret is not found out by me, but is *revealed to me,* and that *not for any wisdom that I have more than any living,* to qualify me for the receiving of such a discovery." Note, It well becomes those whom God has highly favoured and honoured to be very humble and low in their own eyes, to lay aside all opinion of their own wisdom and worthiness, that God alone may have all the praise of the good they are, and have, and do, and that all may be attributed to the freeness of his good-will towards them and the fulness of his good work in them. The secret was made known to him not for his own sake, but, 1. For the sake of his people, for *their sakes that shall make known the interpretation to the king,* that is, for the sake of his brethren and companions in tribulation, who had by their prayers helped him to obtain this discovery, and so might be said to make known the interpretation — that their lives might be spared, that they might come into favour and be preferred, and all the people of the Jews might fare the better, in their captivity, for their sakes. Note, Humble men will be always ready to think that what God does for them and by them is more for the sake of others than for their own. 2. For the sake of *his prince;* and some read the former clause in this sense, "Not for any wisdom of mine, *but that the king may know the interpretation, and that thou mightest know the thoughts of thy heart,* that thou mightest have satisfaction given thee as to what thou wast before considering, and thereby instruction given thee how to behave towards the church of God." God revealed this thing to Daniel that he might make it known to the king. Prophets receive that they may give, that the discoveries made to them may not be lodged with themselves, but communicated to the persons that are concerned.

Verses 31–45

Daniel here gives full satisfaction to Nebuchadnezzar concerning his dream and the interpretation of it. That great prince had been kind to this poor prophet in his maintenance and education; he had been brought up at the king's cost, preferred at court, and the land of his captivity had hereby been made much easier to him than to others of his brethren. And now the king is abundantly repaid for all the expense he had been at upon him; and for receiving this prophet, though not in the name of a prophet, he had a prophet's reward, such a reward as a prophet only could give, and for which that wealthy mighty prince was now glad to be beholden to him. Here is,

I. The dream itself, v. 31, 45. Nebuchadnezzar perhaps was an admirer of statues, and had his palace and gardens adorned with them; however, he was a worshipper of images, and now behold a *great image* is set before him in a dream, which might intimate to him what the images were which he bestowed so much cost upon, and paid such respect to; they were mere dreams. The creatures of fancy might do as well to please the fancy. By the power of imagination he might shut his eyes, and represent to himself what forms he thought fit, and beautify them at his pleasure, without the expense and trouble of sculpture. This was the image of a man erect: *It stood before him,* as a living man; and, because those monarchies which were designed to be represented by it were admirable in the eyes of their friends, the *brightness* of this image *was excellent;* and because they were formidable to their enemies, and dreaded by all about them, the *form* of this image is said to be *terrible;* both the features of the face and the postures of the body made it so. But that which was most remarkable in this image was the different metals of which it was composed — the *head of gold* (the richest and most durable metal), the *breast and arms of silver* (the next to it in worth), the *belly and sides (or thighs) of brass,* the *legs of iron* (still baser metals), and lastly the feet *part of iron and part of clay.* See what the things of this world are; the further we go in them the less valuable they appear. In the life of a man youth is a head of gold, but it grows less and less worthy of our esteem; and old age is half clay; a man is then *as good as dead.* It is so with the world; later ages degenerate. The first age of the Christian church, of the reformation, was a head of gold; but we live in an age that is iron and clay. Some allude to this in the description of a hypocrite, whose practice is not agreeable to his knowledge. He has a head of gold, but feet of iron and clay: he knows his duty, but does it not. Some observe that in Daniel's visions the monarchies were represented by four beasts (*ch.* 7), for he looked upon that wisdom from beneath, by which they were turned to be earthly and sensual, and a tyrannical power, to have more in it of the beast than of the man, and so the vision agreed with his notions of the thing. But to Nebuchadnezzar, a heathen prince, they were represented by a gay and pompous image of a man, for he was an admirer of the *kingdoms of this world and the glory of them.* To him the sight was so charming that he was impatient to see it again. But what became of this image? The next part of the dream shows it to us calcined, and brought to nothing. He saw a stone cut out of the quarry by an unseen power, without hands, and this stone fell upon the *feet of the image,* that were of *iron and clay,* and *broke them to pieces;* and then the image must fall of course, and so the gold, and silver, and brass, and iron, were all broken to pieces together, and beaten so small that they became like the *chaff of the summer threshing-floors,* and there were not to be found any the least remains of them; but the stone *cut out of the mountain* became itself a *great mountain, and filled the earth.* See how God can bring about great effects by weak and unlikely causes; when he pleases a *little one shall become a thousand.* Perhaps the destruction of this image of gold, and silver, and brass, and iron, might be intended to signify the abolishing of idolatry out of the world in due time. The *idols of the heathen are silver and gold,* as this image was, and *they shall perish from off the earth and from under these heavens,* Jer. 10:11.; Isa. 2:18. And whatever power destroys idolatry is in the ready way to magnify and exalt itself, as this stone, when it had broken the image to pieces, became a great mountain.

II. The interpretation of this dream. Let us now see what is the meaning of this. It was from God, and therefore from him it is fit that we take the explication of it. It should seem, Daniel had his fellows with him, and speaks for them as well as for himself, when he says, *We will tell the interpretation, v.* 36. Now,

1. This image represented the kingdoms of the earth that should successively bear rule among the nations and have influence on the affairs of the Jewish church. The four monarchies were not represented by four distinct statues, but by one image, because they were all of one and the same spirit and genius, and all more or less against the church. It was the same power, only lodged in four different nations, the two former lying eastward of Judea, the two latter westward. (1.) The *head of gold* signified the Chaldean monarchy, which was now in being (*v.* 37, 38): *Thou, O king! art* (or rather, *shalt be*) *a king of kings,* a universal monarch, to whom many kings and kingdoms shall be tributaries; or, Thou art the *highest of kings* on earth at this time (as a *servant of servants* is the meanest servant); thou dost outshine all other kings. But let him not attribute his elevation to his own politics or fortitude. No; it is *the God of heaven* that has *given thee a kingdom, power, and strength, and glory,* a kingdom that exercises great authority, stands firmly, and shines brightly, acts by a puissant army with an arbitrary power. Note, The greatest of princes have no power but what is given them from above. The extent of his dominion is set forth (*v.* 38), that *wheresoever the children of men dwell,* in all the nations of that part of the world, he was *ruler over them all,* over them and all that belonged to them, all their cattle, not only those which they had a property in, but those that were *ferae naturae — wild,* the *beasts of the field* and *the fowls of the heaven.* He was lord of all the woods, forests, and chases, and none were allowed to hunt or fowl without his leave. Thus *"thou art the head of gold;* thou, and thy son, and thy son's son, for seventy years." Compare this with Jer. 25:9, 11, especially Jer. 27:5–7. There were other powerful kingdoms in the world at this time, as that of the Scythians; but it was the kingdom of Babylon that reigned over the Jews, and that began the government which continued in the succession here described till Christ's time. It is called a *head,* for its wisdom, eminency, and absolute power, a head of *gold* for its wealth (Isa. 14:4); it was a golden city. Some make this monarchy to begin in Nimrod, and so bring into it all the Assyrian kings, about fifty monarchs in all, and compute that it lasted above 1600 years. But it had not been so long a monarchy of such vast extent and power as is here described, nor any thing like it; therefore others make only Nebuchadnezzar, Evil-merodach, and Belshazzar, to belong to this *head of gold;* and a glorious high throne they had, and perhaps exercised a more despotic power than any of the kings that went before them. Nebuchadnezzar reigned forty-five years current, Evil-merodach twenty-three years current, and Belshazzar three. Babylon was their metropolis, and Daniel was with them upon the spot during the seventy years. (2.) The *breast and arms of silver* signified the monarchy of the Medes and Persians, of which the king is told no more than this, *There shall arise another kingdom inferior to thee* (*v.* 39), not so rich, powerful, or victorious. This kingdom was founded by Darius the Mede and Cyrus the Persian, in alliance with each other, and therefore represented by two arms, meeting in the breast. Cyrus was himself a Persian by his father, a Mede by his mother. Some reckon that this second monarchy lasted 130 years, others 204 years. The former computation agrees best with the scripture chronology. (3.) The *belly and thighs of brass* signified the monarchy of the Grecians, founded by Alexander, who conquered Darius Codomannus, the last of the Persian emperors. This is the *third kingdom, of brass,* inferior in wealth and extent of dominion to the Persian monarchy, but in Alexander himself it shall by the power of the sword *bear rule over all the earth;* for Alexander boasted that he had conquered the world, and then sat down and wept because he had not another world to conquer. (4.) The *legs and feet of iron* signified the Roman monarchy. Some make this to signify the latter part of the Grecian monarchy, the two empires of Syria and Egypt, the former governed by the family of the Seleucidae, from Seleucus, the latter by that of the Lagidae, from Ptolemaeus Lagus; these they make the two legs and feet of this image: Grotius, and Junius, and Broughton, go this way. But it has been the more received opinion that it is the Roman monarchy that is here intended, because it was in the time of that monarchy, and when it was at its height, that the kingdom of Christ was set up in the world by the preaching of the everlasting gospel. The Roman kingdom was strong as iron (*v.* 40), witness the prevalency of that kingdom against all that contended with it for many ages. That kingdom *broke in pieces* the Grecian empire and afterwards quite destroyed the nation of the Jews. Towards the latter end of the Roman monarchy it grew very weak, and branched into ten kingdoms, which were as the toes of these feet. Some of these were weak as clay, others strong as iron, *v.* 42. Endeavours were used to unite and cement them for the strengthening of the empire, but in vain: *They shall not cleave one to another, v.* 43. This empire divided the government for a long time between the senate and the people, the nobles and the commons, but they did not entirely coalesce. There were civil wars between Marius and Sylla, Caesar and Pompey, whose parties were as iron and clay. Some refer this to the declining times of that empire, when, for the strengthening of the empire against the irruptions of the barbarous nations, the branches of the royal family intermarried; but the politics had not the desired effect, when the day of the fall of that empire came.

2. The stone *cut out without hands* represented the kingdom of Jesus Christ, which should be set up in the world in the time of the Roman empire, and upon the ruins of Satan's kingdom in the *kingdoms of the world.* This is *the stone cut out of the mountain without hands,* for it should be neither raised nor supported by human power or policy; no visible hand should act in the setting of it up, but it should be done invisibly the *Spirit of the Lord of hosts.* This was *the stone which the builders refused,* because it was not cut out by their hands, but it has now become the *head-stone of the corner.* (1.) The gospel-church is a kingdom, which Christ is the sole and sovereign monarch of, in which he rules by his word and Spirit, to which he gives protection and law, and from which he receives homage and tribute. It is a kingdom *not of this world,* and yet set up in it; it is the kingdom of God among men. (2.) The *God of heaven* was to set up this kingdom, to give authority to Christ to execute judgment, to set him as *King upon his holy hill of Zion,* and to bring into obedience to him a willing people. Being set up by the God of heaven, it is often in the *New Testament* called the *kingdom of heaven,* for its original is from above and its tendency is upwards. (3.) It was to be set up *in the days of these kings,* the kings of the fourth monarchy, of which particular notice is taken (Lu. 2:1), That Christ was born when, by the decree of the emperor of Rome, *all the world was taxed,* which was a plain indication that that empire had become as universal as any earthly empire ever was. When these kings are contesting with each other, and in all the struggles each of the contending parties hopes to find its own account, God will do his own work and fulfil his own counsels. *These kings* are all enemies to Christ's kingdom, and yet it shall be set up in defiance of them. (4.) It is a kingdom that knows no decay, is in no danger of destruction, and will not admit any succession or revolution. It shall *never be destroyed* by any foreign force invading it, as many other kingdoms are; fire and sword cannot waste it; the combined powers of earth and hell cannot deprive either the subjects of their prince or the prince of his subjects; nor shall this *kingdom be left to other people,* as the kingdoms of the earth are. As Christ is a monarch that has no successor (for he himself shall reign for ever), so his kingdom is a monarchy that has no revolution. The kingdom of God was indeed taken from the Jews and given to the Gentiles (Mt. 21:43), but still it was Christianity that ruled, the kingdom of the Messiah. The Christian church is still the same; it is fixed on a rock, much fought against, but never to be prevailed against, by the gates of hell. (5.) It is a kingdom that shall be victorious over all opposition. It shall *break in pieces and consume all those kingdoms,* as the *stone cut out of the mountain without hands* broke in pieces the image, *v.* 44, 45. The kingdom of Christ shall *wear out* all other kingdoms, shall outlive them, and flourish when they are sunk with their own weight, and so wasted that their place *knows them no more.* All the kingdoms that appear against the kingdom of Christ shall be broken with a *rod of iron,* as a *potter's vessel,* Ps. 2:9. And in the kingdoms that submit to the kingdom of Christ tyranny, and idolatry, and every thing that is their reproach, shall, as far as the gospel of Christ gets ground, be broken. The day is coming when Jesus Christ shall have *put down all rule, principality, and power,* and have made *all his enemies his footstool;* and then this prophecy will have its full accomplishment, and not till then, 1 Co. 15:24, 25. Our savior seems to refer to this (Mt. 21:44), when, speaking of himself as the stone set at nought by the Jewish builders, he says, *On whomsoever* this stone *shall fall, it will grind him to powder.* (6.) It shall be an everlasting kingdom. Those kingdoms of the earth that had *broken in pieces* all about them at length came, in their turn, to be in like manner broken; but the kingdom of Christ shall break other kingdoms in pieces and shall itself *stand for ever.* His throne shall be as the days of heaven, his seed, his subjects, as the stars of heaven, not only so innumerable, but so immutable. Of the *increase* of Christ's *government and peace* there shall be *no end. The Lord shall reign for ever,* not only to the end of time, but when time and days shall be no more, and God *shall be all in all* to eternity.

III. Daniel having thus interpreted the dream, to the satisfaction of Nebuchadnezzar, who gave him no interruption, so full was the interpretation that he had no question to ask, and so plain that he had no objection to make, he closes all with a solemn assertion, 1. Of the divine original of this dream: *The great God* (so he calls him, to express his own high thoughts of him, and to beget the like in the mind of this great king) has *made known to the king what shall come to pass hereafter,* which the gods of the magicians could not do. And thus a full confirmation was given to that great argument which Isaiah had long before urged against idolaters, and particularly the idolaters of Babylon, when he challenged the gods they worshipped to *show things that are to come hereafter, that we may know that you are gods* (Isa. 41:23), and by *this* proved the God of Israel to be the true God, that he *declares the end from the beginning,* Isa. 46:10. 2. Of the undoubted certainty of the things foretold by this dream. He who makes known these things is the same that has himself designed and determined them, and will by his providence effect them; and we are sure that *his counsel shall stand,* and cannot be altered, and therefore *the dream is certain and the interpretation thereof sure.* Note, Whatever God has made known we may depend upon.

Verses 46–49

One might have expected that when Nebuchadnezzar was contriving to make his own kingdom everlasting he would be enraged at Daniel, who foretold the fall of it and that another kingdom of another nature should be the everlasting kingdom; but, instead of resenting it as an affront, he received it as an oracle, and here we are told what the expressions were of the impressions it made upon him. 1. He was ready to look upon Daniel as a little god. Though he saw him to be a man, yet from this wonderful discovery which he had made both of his secret thoughts, in telling him the dream, and of things to come, in telling him the interpretation of it, he concluded that he had certainly a divinity lodged in him, worthy his adoration; and therefore he *fell upon his face and worshipped Daniel, v.* 46. It was the custom of the country by prostration to give honour to kings, because they have something of a divine power in them *(I have said, You are gods);* and therefore this king, who had often received such veneration from others, now paid the like to Daniel, whom he supposed to have in him a divine knowledge, which he was so struck with an admiration of that he could not contain himself, but forgot both that Daniel was a man and that himself was a king. Thus did God magnify divine revelation *and make it honourable,* extorting from a proud potentate such a veneration but for one glimpse of it. He *worshipped Daniel,* and *commanded that they should offer an oblation to him,* and burn incense. Herein he cannot be justified, but may in some measure be excused, when Cornelius was thus ready to worship Peter, and John the angel, who both knew better. But, though it is not here mentioned, yet we have reason to think that Daniel refused these honours that he paid him, and said, as Peter to Cornelius, *Stand up, I myself also am a man,* or, as the angel to St. John, *See thou do it not;* for it is not said that the oblation was offered unto him, though the king commanded it, or rather *said it,* for so the word is. He said, in his haste, *Let an oblation be offered to him.* And that Daniel did say something to him which turned his eyes and thoughts another way is intimated in what follows (*v.* 47), *The king answered Daniel.* Note, It is possible for those to express a great honour for the ministers of God's word who yet have no true love for the word. *Herod feared John,* and *heard him gladly,* and yet went on in his sins, Mk. 6:20. 2. He readily acknowledged the God of Daniel to be the great God, the true God, the only living and true God. If Daniel will not suffer himself to be worshipped, he will (as Daniel, it is likely, directed him) *worship God,* by confessing (*v.* 47), *Of a truth your God is a God of gods,* such a God as there is no other, above all gods in dignity, over all gods in dominion. He is a Lord *of kings,* from whom they derive their power and to whom they are accountable; and he is both a discoverer and a *revealer of secrets;* what is most secret he sees and can reveal, and what he has revealed is what was secret and which none but himself could reveal, 1 Co. 2:10. 3. He preferred Daniel, made him a great man, *v.* 48. God made him a great man indeed when he took him into communion with himself, a greater man than Nebuchadnezzar could make him; but, because God had magnified him, therefore the king magnified him. Does wealth make men great? The king *gave him many great gifts;* and he had no reason to refuse them, when they all put him into so much the greater capacity of doing good to his brethren in captivity. These gifts were grateful returns for the good services he had done, and not aimed at, nor bargained for, by him, as the rewards of divination were by Balaam. Does power make a man great? He made him *ruler over the whole province of Babylon,* which no doubt had great influence upon the other provinces; he made him likewise chancellor of the university, *chief of the governors over all the wise men of Babylon,* to instruct those whom he had thus outdone; and, since they could not do what the king would have them do, they shall be obliged to do what Daniel would have them do. Thus it is fit that

the *fool should be servant to the wise in heart.* Seeing Daniel *could reveal this secret* (*v.* 47), the king thus advanced him. Note, It is the wisdom of princes to advance and employ those who receive divine revelation, and are much conversant with it, who, as Daniel here, show themselves to be well acquainted with the kingdom of heaven. Joseph, like Daniel here, was advanced in the court of the king of Egypt for his interpreting his dreams; and he called him *Zaphnath-paaneah — a revealer of secrets,* as the king of Babylon here calls Daniel; so that the preambles to their patents of honour are the same — for, and in consideration of, their good services done to the crown in *revealing secrets.* 4. He preferred his companions for his sake, and upon his special instance and request, *v.* 49. Daniel himself *sat in the gate of the king,* as president of the council, chief-justice, or prime-minister of state, or perhaps chamberlain of the household; but he used his interest for his friends as became a good man, and procured places in the government for Shadrach, Meshach, and Abednego. Those that helped him with their prayers shall share with him in his honours, such a grateful sense had he even of that service. The preferring of them would be a great stay and help to Daniel in his place and business. And these pious Jews, being thus preferred in Babylon, had great opportunity of serving their brethren in captivity, and of doing them many good offices, which no doubt they were ready to do. Thus, sometimes, before God brings his people into trouble, he prepares it, that it may be easy to them.

CHAPTER 3

In the close of the foregoing chapter we left Daniel's companions, Shadrach, Meshach, and Abednego, in honour and power, princes of the provinces, and preferred for their relation to the God of Israel and the interest they had in him. I know not whether I should say. It were well if this honour had all the saints. No, there are many whom it would not be good for; the saints' honour is reserved for another world. But here we have those same three men as much under the king's displeasure as when they were in his favour, and yet more truly, more highly, honoured by their God than there they were honoured by their prince, both by the grace wherewith he enabled them rather to suffer than to sin and by the miraculous and glorious deliverance which he wrought for them out of their sufferings. It is a very memorable story, a glorious instance of the power and goodness of God, and a great encouragement to the constancy of his people in trying times. The apostle refers to it when he mentions, among the believing heroes, those who by faith "quenched the violence of fire," Heb. 11:34. We have here, I. Nebuchadnezzar's erecting and dedicating a golden image, and his requiring all his subjects, of what rank or degree soever, to fall down and worship it, and the general compliance of his people with that command (*v.* 1–7). II. Information given against the Jewish princes for refusing to worship this golden image (*v.* 8–12). III. Their constant persisting in that refusal, notwithstanding his rage and menaces (*v.* 13–18). IV. The casting of them into the fiery furnace for their refusal (*v.* 19–23). V. Their miraculous preservation in the fire by the power of God, and their invitation out of the fire by the favour of the king, who was by this miracle convinced of his error in casting them in (*v.* 24–27). VI. The honour which the king gave to God hereupon, and the favour he showed to those faithful worthies (*v.* 28–30).

Verses 1–7

We have no certainty concerning the date of this story, only that if this image, which Nebuchadnezzar dedicated, had any relation to that which he dreamed of, it is probable that it happened not long after that; some reckon it to be about the seventh year of Nebuchadnezzar, a year before Jehoiachin's captivity, in which Ezekiel was carried away. Observe,

I. A *golden image set up* to be worshipped. Babylon was full of idols already, yet nothing will serve this imperious prince but they must have one more; for those who have forsaken the one only living God, and begin to set up many gods, will find the gods they set up so unsatisfying, and their desire after them so insatiable, that they will multiply them without measure, wander after them endlessly, and never know when they have sufficient. Idolaters are fond of novelty and variety. *They choose new gods.* Those that have many will wish to have more. Nebuchadnezzar the king, that he might exert the prerogative of his crown, to make what god he thought fit, *set up* this image, *v.* 1. Observe, 1. The *valuableness* of it; it was *an image of gold,* not all gold surely; rich as he was, it is probable that he could not afford that, but overlaid with gold. Note, The worshippers of false gods are not wont to mind charges in setting up images and worshipping them; they *lavish gold out of the bag* for that purpose (Isa. 46:6), which shames our niggardliness in the worship of the true God. 2. The vastness of it; it was *threescore cubits high and six cubits broad.* It exceeded the ordinary stature of a man

fifteen times (for that is reckoned but four cubits, or six feet), as if its being monstrous would make amends for its being lifeless. But why did Nebuchadnezzar set up this image? Some suggest that it was to clear himself from the imputation of having turned a Jew, because he had lately spoken with great honour of the God of Israel and had preferred some of his worshippers. Or perhaps he set it up as an image of himself, and designed to be himself worshipped in it. Proud princes affected to have divine honours paid them; Alexander did so, pretending himself to be the son of Jupiter Olympius. He was told that in the image he had seen in his dream he was represented by the *head of gold,* which was to be succeeded by kingdoms of baser metal; but here he sets up to be himself the whole image, for he makes it all of gold. See here, (1.) How the good impressions that were then made upon him were quite lost, and quickly. He then acknowledged that the God of Israel is of a truth a *God of gods* and a *Lord of kings;* and yet now, in defiance of the express law of that God, he sets up an image to be worshipped, not only continues in his former idolatries, but contrives new ones. Note, Strong convictions often come short of a sound conversion. Many a pang have owned the absurdity and dangerousness of sin, and yet have gone on in it. (2.) How that very dream and the interpretation of it, which then made such good impressions upon him, now had a quite contrary effect. Then it made him fall down as a humble worshipper of God; now it made him set up for a bold competitor with God. Then he thought it a great thing to be the golden head of the image, and owned himself obliged to God for it; but, his mind rising with his condition, now he thinks that too little, and, in contradiction to God himself and his oracle, he will be *all in all.*

II. A general convention of the states summoned to attend the solemnity of the dedication of this image, *v.* 2, 3. Messengers are despatched to all parts of the kingdom to *gather together the princes,* dukes, and lords, all the peers of the realm, with all officers civil and military, *the captains* and commanders of the forces, *the judges, the treasurers or general receivers, the counsellors,* and *the sheriffs, and all the rulers of the provinces;* they must all *come to the dedication of this image* upon pain and peril of what shall fall thereon. He summons the great men, for the great honour of his idol; it is therefore mentioned to the glory of Christ that *kings shall bring presents unto him.* If he can bring them to pay homage to his golden image, he doubts not but the inferior people will follow of course. In obedience to the king's summons all the magistrates and officers of that vast kingdom leave the services of their particular countries, and come to Babylon, to the dedication of this golden image; long journeys many of them took, and expensive ones, upon a very foolish errand; but, as the idols are senseless things, such are the worshippers.

III. A proclamation made, commanding all manner of persons present before the image, upon the signal given, to fall down prostrate, and worship the image, under the style and title of *The golden image which Nebuchadnezzar the king has set up.* A herald proclaims this aloud throughout this vast assembly of grandees, with their numerous train of servants and attendants, and a great crowd of people, no doubt, that were not sent for; let them all take notice, 1. That the king does strictly charge and command all manner of persons to fall down and *worship the golden image;* whatever other gods they worship at other times, now they must worship this. 2. That they must all do this just at the same time, in token of their communion with each other in this idolatrous service, and that, in order hereunto, notice shall be given by a concert of music, which would likewise serve to adorn the solemnity and to sweeten and soften the minds of those that were loth to yield and bring them to comply with the king's command. This mirth and gaiety in the worship would be very agreeable to carnal sensual minds, that are strangers to that spiritual worship which is due to God who is a spirit.

IV. The general compliance of the assembly with this command, *v.* 7. They heard the sound of the musical instruments, both wind-instruments and hand-instruments, *the cornet and flute,* with the *harp, sackbut, psaltery,* and *dulcimer,* the melody of which they thought was ravishing (and fit enough it was to excite such a devotion as they were then to pay), and immediately they all, as one man, as soldiers that are wont to be exercised by beat of drum, *all the people, nations, and languages, fell down and worshipped the golden image.* And no marvel when it was proclaimed, That whosoever would not *worship this golden image* should be immediately thrown *into the midst of a burning fiery furnace,* ready prepared for that purpose, *v.* 6. Here were the charms of music to allure them into a compliance and the terrors of the fiery furnace to frighten them into a compliance. Thus beset with temptation, they all yielded. Note, That way that sense directs the most will go; there is nothing so bad which the careless world will not be drawn to by a concert of music, or driven to by a fiery furnace. And by such methods as these false worship has been set up and maintained.

Verses 8-18

It was strange that Shadrach, Meshach, and Abednego, would be present at this assembly, when, it is likely, they knew for what intent it was called together. Daniel, we may suppose, was absent, either his business calling him away or having leave from the king to withdraw, unless we suppose that he stood so high in the king's favour that none durst complain of him for his noncompliance. But why did not his companions keep out of the way? Surely because they would obey the king's orders as far as they could, and would be ready to bear a public testimony against this gross idolatry. They did not think it enough not to bow down to the image, but, being in office, thought themselves obliged to stand up against it, though it was the image which the king their master set up, and would be a golden image to those that worshipped it. Now,

I. Information is brought to the king by *certain Chaldeans* against these three gentlemen that they did not obey the king's edict, *v.* 8. Perhaps these Chaldeans that accused them were some of those *magicians or astrologers* that were particularly called *Chaldeans* (*ch.* 2:2, 4) who bore a grudge to Daniel's companions for his sake, because he had eclipsed them, and so had these companions. They by their prayers had obtained the mercy which saved the lives of these Chaldeans, and, behold, how they requite them evil for good! for their love they are their adversaries. Thus Jeremiah *stood before God, to speak good for those* who afterwards *dug a pit for his life,* Jer. 18:20. We must not think it strange if we meet with such ungrateful men. Or perhaps they were such of the Chaldeans as expected the places to which they were advanced, and envied them their preferments; *and who can stand before envy?* They appeal to the king himself concerning the edict, with all due respect to his majesty, and the usual compliment, *O king! live forever* (as if they aimed at nothing but his honour, and to serve his interest, when really they were putting him upon that which would endanger the ruin of him and his kingdom); they beg leave, 1. To put him in mind of the law he had lately made, That all manner of persons, without exception of nation or language, should *fall down and worship this golden image;* they put him in mind also of the penalty which by the law was to be inflicted upon recusants, that they were to be *cast into the midst of the burning fiery furnace, v.* 10, 11. It cannot be denied but that this was the law; whether a righteous law or no ought to be considered. 2. To inform him that these three men, Shadrach, Meshach, and Abednego, had not conformed to this edict, *v.* 12. It is probable that Nebuchadnezzar had no particular design to ensnare them in making the law, for then he would himself have had his eye upon them, and would not have needed this information; but their enemies, that sought an occasion against them, laid hold on this, and were forward to accuse them. To aggravate the matter, and incense the king the more against them, (1.) They put him in mind of the dignity to which the criminals had been preferred. Though they were Jews, foreigners, captives, men of a despised nation and religion, yet the king had *set them over the affairs of the province of Babylon.* It was therefore very ungrateful, and an insufferable piece of insolence, for them to disobey the king's command, when they had shared so much of the king's favour. And, besides, the high station they were in would make their refusal the more scandalous; it would be a bad example, and have a bad influence upon others; and therefore it was necessary that it should be severely animadverted upon. Thus princes that are incensed enough against innocent people commonly have but too many about them who do all they can to make

them worse. (2.) They suggest that it was done maliciously, contumaciously, and in contempt of him and his authority: "They have *set no regard upon thee;* for they *serve not the gods* which thou servest, and which thou requirest them to serve, nor *worship the golden image which thou hast set up."*

II. These three pious Jews are immediately brought before the king, and arraigned and examined upon this information. Nebuchadnezzar fell into a great passion, and *in his rage and fury commanded* them to be seized, *v.* 13. How little was it the honour of this mighty prince that he had rule over so many nations when at the same time he had no *rule over his own spirit,* that there were so many who were subjects and captives to him when he was himself a perfect slave to his own brutish passions and led captive by them! How unfit was he to rule reasonable men who could not himself be ruled by reason! It needed not be a surprise to him to hear that these three men did not now serve his gods, for he knew very well they never had served them, and that their religion, which they had always adhered to, forbade them to do it. Nor had he any reason to think that they designed any contempt of his authority, for they had in all instances shown themselves respectful and dutiful to him as their prince. But it was especially unseasonable at this time, when he was in the midst of his devotions, dedicating his golden image, to be in such a rage and fury, and so much to discompose himself. The *discretion of a man,* one would think, should at least have *deferred this anger.* True devotion calms the spirit, quiets and meekens it; but superstition, and a devotion to false gods, inflame men's passions, inspire them with rage, and fury, and turn them into brutes. *The wrath of a king is as the roaring of a lion;* so was the wrath of this king; and yet, when he was in such a heat, these three men were *brought before him,* and appeared with an undaunted courage, and unshaken constancy.

III. The case is laid before them in short, and it is put to them whether they will comply or no. 1. The king asked them whether it was true that they had not worshipped the golden image when others did, *v.* 14. *"Is it of purpose?"* so some read it. "Was it designedly and deliberately done, or was it only through inadvertency, that you have not *served my gods?* What! you that I have nourished and brought up, that have been educated and maintained at my charge, that I have been so kind to and done so much for, you that have been in such reputation for wisdom, and therefore should better have known your duty to your prince; what! do not you *serve my gods nor worship the golden image which I have set up?"* Note, The faithfulness of God's servants to him has often been the wonder of their enemies and persecutors, who *think it strange* that they *run not with them to the same excess of riot.* 2. He was willing to admit them to a new trial; if they did on purpose not do it before, yet, it may be, upon second thoughts, they will change their minds; it is therefore repeated to them upon what terms they now stand, *v.* 15. (1.) The king is willing that music shall play again, only for their sakes, to soften them into a compliance; and if they will not, like the deaf adder, stop their ears, but will hearken to the voice of the charmers and will *worship the golden image,* well and good; their former omission shall be pardoned. But, (2.) The king is resolved, if they persist in their refusal, that they shall immediately be *cast into the fiery furnace,* and shall not have so much as an hour's reprieve. Thus does the matter lie in a little compass — *Turn, or burn;* and, because he knew they buoyed themselves up in their refusal with a confidence in their God, he insolently set him a defiance: *"And who is that God that shall deliver you out of my hands?* Let him, if he can." Now he forgot what he himself once owned, that their God was a *God of gods* and a *Lord of kings, ch.* 2:47. Proud men are still ready to say, as Pharaoh, *Who is the Lord that I should obey his voice?* or, as Nebuchadnezzar, Who is the Lord, that I should *fear his power?*

IV. They give in their answer, which they all agree in, that they still adhere to their resolution not to worship the golden image, *v.* 16-18. We have here such an instance of fortitude and magnanimity as is scarcely to be paralleled. We call these the *three children* (and they were indeed *young men),* but we should rather call them the three champions, the *first three* of the *worthies* of God's *kingdom among men.* They did not break out into any intemperate

heat or passion against those that did worship the golden image, did not insult or affront them; nor did they rashly thrust themselves upon the trial, or go out of their way to court martyrdom; but, when they were duly called to the fiery trial, they acquitted themselves bravely, with a conduct and courage that became sufferers for so good a cause. The king was not so daringly bad in making this idol, but they were as daringly good in witnessing against it. They keep their temper admirably well, do not call the king a tyrant or an idolater (the cause of God needs not the wrath of man), but, with an exemplary calmness and sedateness of mind, they deliberately give in their answer, which they resolve to abide by. Observe,

1. Their gracious and generous contempt of death, and the noble negligence with which they look upon the dilemma that they are put to: *O Nebuchadnezzar! we are not careful to answer thee in this matter.* They do not in sullenness deny him an answer, nor stand mute; but they tell him that they are in no care about it. *There needs not an answer* (so some read it); they are resolved not to comply, and the king is resolved they shall die if they do not; the matter therefore is determined, and why should it be disputed? But it is better read, *"We want not an answer for thee,* nor have it to seek, but come prepared." (1.) They needed no time to deliberate concerning the matter of their answer; for they did not in the least hesitate whether they should comply or no. It was a matter of life and death, and one would think they might have considered awhile before they had resolved; life is desirable, and death is dreadful. But when the sin and duty that were in the case were immediately determined by the letter of the second commandment, and no room was left to question what was right, the life and death that were in the case were not to be considered. Note, Those that would avoid sin must not parley with temptation. When that which we are allured or affrighted to is manifestly evil the motion is rather to be rejected with indignation and abhorrence than reasoned with; stand not to pause about it, but say, as Christ has taught us, *Get thee behind me, Satan.* (2.) They needed no time to contrive how they should *word* it. While they were advocates for God, and were called out to witness in his cause, they doubted not but it should be *given them in that same hour what they should speak,* Mt. 10:19. They were not contriving an evasive answer, when a direct answer was expected from them; no, nor would they seem to court the king not to insist upon it. Here is nothing in their answer that looks like compliment; they begin not, as their accusers did, with, *O king! live for ever,* no artful insinuation, *ad captandam benevolentiam* — to put him *into a good humour,* but every thing that is plain and downright: O Nebuchadnezzar! *we are not careful to answer thee.* Note, Those that make their duty their main care need not be careful concerning the event.

2. Their believing confidence in God and their dependence upon him, *v.* 17. It was this that enabled them to look with so much contempt upon death, death in pomp, death in all its terrors: they trusted in the living God, and by that faith chose rather to suffer than to sin; they therefore *feared not the wrath of the king,* but endured, because by faith they had an eye to *him that is invisible* (Heb. 11:25, 27): *"If it be so,* if we are brought to this strait, if we must be thrown into the fiery furnace unless we serve thy gods, know then," (1.) "That though we worship not *thy gods* yet we are not atheists; there is a God whom we can call ours, to whom we faithfully adhere." (2.) "That we serve this God; we have devoted ourselves to his honour; we employ ourselves in his work, and depend upon him to protect us, provide for us, and reward us." (3.) "That we are well assured that this God is *able to deliver us from the burning fiery furnace;* whether he will or no, we are sure that he can either prevent our being cast into the furnace or rescue us out of it." Note, The faithful servants of God will find him a Master able to bear them out in his service, and to control and overrule all the powers that are armed against them. *Lord, if thou wilt, thou canst.* (4.) "That we have reason to hope *he will deliver us,"* partly because, in such a vast appearance of idolaters, it would be very much for the honour of his great name to deliver them, and partly because Nebuchadnezzar had defied him to do it — *Who is that God that shall deliver you?* God sometimes appears wonderfully for the silencing of the blasphemies of the enemy, as well as for the answering of the

prayers of his people, Ps. 74:18–22; Deu. 32:27. "But, if he do not deliver us from the fiery furnace, he will *deliver us out of thy hand.*" Nebuchadnezzar can but torment and kill the body, and after that, there is no more that he can do; then they are got out of his reach, delivered out of his hand. Note, Good thoughts of God, and a full assurance that he is with us while we are with him, will help very much to carry us through sufferings; and, if he be for us, we need not fear what man can do unto us; let him do his worst. God will deliver us either from death or in death.

3. Their firm resolution to adhere to their principles, whatever might be the consequence (*v.* 18): *"But, if not,* though God should not think fit to deliver us from the fiery furnace (which yet we know he can do), if he should suffer us to *fall into thy hand,* and fall by thy hand, yet *be it known unto thee, O king! we will not serve* these gods, though they are *thy gods, nor worship this golden image,* though thou thyself hast *set it up."* They are neither ashamed nor afraid to own their religion, and tell the king to his face that they do not fear him, they will not yield to him; had they consulted with flesh and blood, much might have been said to bring them to a compliance, especially when there was no other way of avoiding death, *so great a death.* (1.) They were not required to abjure their own God, or to renounce his worship, no, nor by any verbal profession or declaration to own this golden image to be a god, but only to bow down before it, which they might do with a secret reserve of their hearts for the God of Israel, inwardly detesting this idolatry, as Naaman bowed in the house of Rimmon. (2.) They were not to fall into a course of idolatry; it was but one single act that was required of them, which would be done in a minute, and the danger was over, and they might afterwards declare their sorrow for it. (3.) The king that commanded it had an absolute power; they were under it, not only as subjects, but as captives; and, if they did it, it was purely by coercion and duress, which would serve to excuse them. (4.) He had been their benefactor, had educated and preferred them, and in gratitude to him they ought to go as far as they could, though it were to strain a point, a point of conscience. (5.) They were now driven into a strange country, and to those that were so driven out it was, in effect, said, *Go, and serve other gods,* 1 Sa. 26:19. It was taken for granted that in their disposition they would *serve other gods,* and it was made a part of the judgment, Deu. 4:28. They might be excused if they should go down the stream, when it is so strong. (6.) Did not their kings, and their princes, and their fathers, yea, and their priests too, set up idols even in God's temple, and worship them there, and not only bow down to them, but erect altars, burn incense, and offer sacrifices, even their own children, to them? Did not all the ten tribes, for many ages, worship gods of gold at Dan and Bethel? And shall they be more precise than their fathers? *Communis error facit jus — What all do must be right.* (7.) If they should comply, they would save their lives and keep their places, and so be in a capacity to do a great deal of service to their brethren in Babylon, and to do it long; for they were young men, and rising men. But there is enough in that one word of God wherewith to answer and silence these and many more such like carnal reasonings: *Thou shalt not bow down thyself to any images, nor worship them.* They know they must obey God rather than man; they must rather suffer than sin, and must not do evil that good may come. And therefore none of these things move them; they are resolved rather to die in their integrity than live in their iniquity. While their brethren, who yet remained in their own land, were worshipping images by choice, they in Babylon would not be brought to it by constraint, but, as if they were good by *antiperistasis,* were most zealous against idolatry in an idolatrous country. And truly, all things considered, the saving of them from this sinful compliance was as great a miracle in the kingdom of grace as the saving of them out of the fiery furnace was in the kingdom of nature. These were those who formerly resolved not to defile themselves with the *king's meat,* and now they as bravely resolve not to defile themselves with his gods. Note, A stedfast self-denying adherence to God and duty in less instances will qualify and prepare us for the like in greater. And in this we must be resolute, never, under any pretence whatsoever, to worship images, or to say "A confederacy" with those that do so.

Verses 19–27

In these verses we have,

I. The casting of these three faithful servants of God into the fiery furnace. Nebuchadnezzar had himself known and owned so much of the true God that, one would have thought, though his pride and vanity induced him to make this golden image, and set it up to be worshipped, yet what these young men now said (whom he had formerly found to be wiser than all his wise men) would revive his convictions, and at least engage him to excuse them; but it proved quite otherwise. 1. Instead of being convinced by what they said, he was exasperated, and made more outrageous, *v.* 19. It made him *full of fury,* and the *form of his visage was changed* against these men. Note, Brutish passions the more they are indulged the more violent they grow, and even change the countenance, to the great reproach of the wisdom and reason of a man. Nebuchadnezzar, in this heat, exchanged the awful majesty of a prince upon his throne, or a judge upon the bench, for the frightful fury of a *wild bull in a net.* Would men in a passion but view their faces in a glass, they would blush at their own folly and turn all their displeasure against themselves. 2. Instead of mitigating their punishment, in consideration of their quality and the posts of honour they were in, he ordered it to be heightened, that they should *heat the furnace seven times more than it was wont to be heated* for other malefactors, that is, that they should put seven times more fuel to it, which, though it would not make their death more grievous, but rather dispatch them sooner, was designed to signify that the king looked upon their crime as seven times more heinous than the crimes of others, and so made their death more ignominious. But God brought glory to himself out of this foolish instance of the tyrant's rage; for, though it would not have made their death the more grievous, yet it did make their deliverance much the more illustrious. 3. He ordered them to be bound in their clothes, and cast into the midst of the burning fiery furnace, which was done accordingly, *v.* 20, 21. They were bound, that they might not struggle, or make any resistance, were bound in their clothes, for haste, or that they might be consumed the more slowly and gradually. But God's providence ordered it for the increase of the miracle, in that their clothes were not so much as singed. They were bound in their *coats* or mantles, their *hosen* or breeches, and their *hats* or turbans, as if, in detestation of their crime, they would have their clothes to be burnt with them. What a terrible death was this — to be *cast bound into the midst of a burning fiery furnace! v.* 23. It makes one's flesh tremble to think of it, and horror to take hold on one. It is amazing that the tyrant was so hard-hearted as to inflict such a punishment, and that the confessors were so stout-hearted as to submit to it rather than sin against God. But what is this to the *second death,* to that furnace into which the tares shall be cast in bundles, to that lake which burns eternally with fire and brimstone? Let Nebuchadnezzar heat his furnace as hot as he can, a few minutes will finish the torment of those who are cast into it; but hell-fire tortures and does not kill. The pain of damned sinners is more exquisite, and the *smoke of their torment ascends for ever and ever,* and *those have no rest,* no intermission, no cessation of their pains, *who have worshipped the beast and his image* (Rev. 14:10, 11), whereas their pain would be soon over that were cast into this furnace for not worshipping this Babylonian beast and his image. 4. It was a remarkable providence that the men, the *mighty men,* that bound them, and threw them into the furnace, were themselves consumed or suffocated by the flame, *v.* 22. The *king's commandment was urgent,* that they should dispatch them quickly, and be sure to do it effectually; and therefore they resolved to go to the very mouth of the furnace, that they might throw them *into the midst* of it, but they were in such haste that they would not take time to arm themselves accordingly. The apocryphal additions to Daniel say that the flame ascended forty-nine cubits above the mouth of the furnace. Probably God ordered it so that the wind blew it directly upon them with such violence that it smothered them. God did thus immediately plead the cause of his injured servants, and take vengeance for them on their persecutors, whom he punished, not only in the very act of their sin, but by it. But these men were only the instruments of cruelty; he that bade them do it had the greater sin; yet they suffered justly for executing an unjust decree, and it is very probable that they did it with pleasure and were glad to be so employed. Nebuchadnezzar himself was reserved for a further reckoning. There is a day coming when proud tyrants will be punished, not only for the cruelties they have been guilty of, but for employing those about them in their cruelties, and so exposing them to the judgments of God.

II. The deliverance of these three faithful servants of God out of the furnace. When they were cast bound into the midst of that devouring fire we might well conclude that we should hear no more of them, that their very bones would be calcined; but, to our amazement, we here find that Shadrach, Meshach, and Abednego, are yet alive.

1. Nebuchadnezzar finds them walking in the fire. *He was astonished, and rose up in haste, v.* 24. Perhaps the slaying of the men that executed his sentence was that which astonished him, as well it might, for he had reason to think his own turn would be next; or it was some unaccountable impression upon his own mind that astonished him, and made him rise up in haste, and go to the furnace, to see what had become of those he had cast into it. Note, God can strike those with astonishment whose hearts are most hardened both against him and against his people. He that made the soul can make his sword to approach to it, even to that of the greatest tyrant. In his astonishment he calls his counsellors about him, and appeals to them. *Did we not cast three men bound into the fire?* It seems, it was done by order, not only of the king, but of the council. They durst not but concur with him, which he forced them to do, that they might share with him in the guilt and odium? *"True, O king!"* say they; "we did order such an execution to be done and it was done." "But now," says the king, "I have been looking into the furnace, and I *see four men, loose, walking in the midst of the fire," v.* 25. (1.) They were loosed from their bonds. The fire that did not so much as singe their clothes burnt the cords wherewith they were bound, and set them at liberty; thus God's people have their hearts enlarged, through the grace of God, by those very troubles with which their enemies designed to straiten and hamper them. (2.) They had no hurt, made no complaint, felt no pain or uneasiness in the least; the flame did not scorch them; the smoke did not stifle them; they were alive and as well as ever in the midst of the flames. See how God of nature can, when he pleases, control the powers of nature, to make them serve his purposes. Now was fulfilled in the letter gracious promise (Isa. 43:2), *When thou walkest through the fire thou shalt not be burnt, neither shall the flame kindle upon thee.* By faith they *quench the violence of the fire, quench the fiery darts of the wicked.* (3.) They *walked in the midst of the fire.* The furnace was large, so that they had room to walk; they were unhurt, so that they were able to walk; their minds were easy, so that they were disposed to walk, as in a paradise or garden of pleasure. *Can a man walk upon hot coals and his feet not be burnt?* Prov. 6:28. Yes, they did it with as much pleasure as the king of Tyrus *walked up and down in the midst of his stones of fire,* his precious stones that sparkled as fire, Eze. 28:14. They were not striving to get out, finding themselves unhurt; but, leaving it to that God who preserved them in the fire to bring them out of it, they walked up and down *in the midst of it* unconcerned. One of the apocryphal writings relates at large the prayer which Azariah, one of the three, prayed in the fire (wherein he laments the calamities and iniquities of Israel, and entreats God's favour to his people), and the song of praise which they all three sang in the midst of the flames, in both which there are remarkable strains of devotion; but we have reason to think, with Grotius, that they were composed by some Jew of a later age, not as what were used, but only as what might have been used, on this occasion, and therefore we justly reject them as no part of holy writ. (4.) There was a fourth seen with them in the fire, whose form, in Nebuchadnezzar's judgment, was *like the Son of God;* he appeared as a divine person, a messenger from heaven, not as a servant, but as a son. *Like an angel* (so some); and angels are called *sons of God,* Job 38:7. In the apocryphal narrative of this story it is said, *The angel of the Lord came down into the furnace;* and Nebuchadnezzar here says (*v.* 28), God *sent his angel and delivered them;* and it was an angel that shut the lions' mouths when Dan-

iel was in the den, *ch.* 6:22. But some think it was the eternal Son of God, the angel of the covenant, and not a created angel. He appeared often in our nature before he assumed it in his incarnation, and never more seasonable, nor to give a more proper indication and presage of his great errand into the world in the fulness of time, than now, when, to deliver his chosen out of the fire, he came and walked with them in the fire. Note, Those that suffer for Christ have his gracious presence with them in their sufferings, even in the fiery furnace, even in the valley of the shadow of death, and therefore even there they need *fear no evil.* Hereby Christ showed that what is done against his people he takes as done against himself; whoever throws them into the furnace does, in effect, throw him in. *I an Jesus, whom thou persecutest,* Isa. 63:9.

2. Nebuchadnezzar calls them out of the furnace (*v.* 26): He *comes near to the mouth of the burning fiery furnace,* and bids them *come forth and come hither. Come forth, come* (so some read it); he speaks with a great deal of tenderness and concern, and stands ready to lend them his hand and help them out. He is convinced by their miraculous preservation that he did evil in casting them into the furnace; and therefore he does not *thrust them out privily; no verily, but he will come himself and fetch them out,* Acts 16:37. Observe the respectful title that he gives them. When he was in the heat of his fury and rage against them it is probable that he called them rebels, and traitors, and all the ill names he could invent; but now he owns them *for the servants of the most high God,* a God who now appears *able to deliver them out of his hand.* Note, Sooner or later, God will convince the proudest of men that he is the most high God, and above them, and too hard for them, even in those things wherein they deal proudly and presumptuously, Ex. 18:11. He will likewise let them know are who his servants, and that he owns them and will stand by them. Elijah prayed (1 Ki. 18:36), *Let it be known that thou art God and that I am thy servant.* Nebuchadnezzar now embraces those whom he had abandoned, and is very officious about them, now that he perceives them to be the favourites of Heaven. Note, What persecutors have done against God's servants, when God opens their eyes, they must as far as they can undo again. How the *fourth,* whose *form was like the Son of God,* withdrew, and whether he vanished away or visibly ascended, we are not told, but of the other three we are informed, (1.) That they *came forth out of the midst of the fire,* as Abraham their father out of Ur (that is, *the fire) of the Chaldees,* into which, says this tradition of the Jews, he was cast, for refusing to worship idols, and out of which he was delivered, as those his *three children* were. When they had their discharge they did not tempt God by staying in any longer, but came forth as brands out of the burning. (2.) That it was made to appear, to the full satisfaction of all the amazed spectators, that they had not received the least damage by the fire, *v.* 27. All the great men came together to view them, and found that there was not so much as *a hair of their head singed.* Here that was true in the letter which our Saviour spoke figuratively, for an assurance to his suffering servants that they should sustain no real damage (Lu. 21:18), *There shall not a hair of your head perish.* Their clothes did not so much as change colour, nor smell of fire, much less were their bodies in the least scorched or blistered; no, *the fire had no power on them.* The Chaldeans worshipped the fire, as a sort of image of the sun, so that, in restraining the fire now, God put contempt, not only upon their king, but upon their god too, and showed that *his voice divides the flames of fire* as well as the floods of water (Ps. 29:7), when he pleases to make a way for his people through the midst of it. It is our God only that is *the consuming fire* (Heb. 12:29); other fire, if he but speak the word, shall not consume.

Verses 28–30

The strict observations that were made, *super visum corporis — on inspecting their bodies,* by the princes and governors, and all the great men who were present upon this public occasion, and who could not be supposed partial in favour of the confessors, contributed much to the clearing of this miracle and the magnifying of the power and grace of God in it. *That indeed a notable miracle has been done is manifest, and we cannot deny it,* Acts 4:16. Let us now see what effect it had upon Nebuchadnezzar.

I. He gives glory to the God of Israel as a God able and ready to protect his worshippers (*v.* 28): *"Blessed be the God of Shadrach, Meshach, and Abednego.* Let him have the honour both of the faithful allegiance which his subjects bear to him and the powerful protection he grants to them, neither of which can be paralleled by any other nation and their gods." The king does himself acknowledge and adore him, and thinks it is fit that he should be acknowledged and adored by all. *Blessed be thee God of Shadrach.* Note, God can extort confessions of his blessedness even from those that have been ready to curse him to his face. 1. He gives him the glory of his power, that he was able to protect his worshippers against the most mighty and malignant enemies: *There is no other God that can deliver after this sort* (*v.* 29), no, not this golden image which he had set up. For this reason there was no other god that obliged his worshippers to cleave to him only, and to suffer death rather than worship any other, as the God of Israel did, for they could not engage to bear them out in so doing, as he could. If God can work such deliverance as no other can, he may demand such obedience as no other may. 2. He gives him the glory of his goodness, that he was ready to do it (*v.* 28): *He has sent his angel and delivered his servants.* Bel could not save his worshippers from being burnt at the mouth of the furnace, but the God of Israel saved his from being burnt when they were cast into the midst of the furnace because they refused to *worship any other god.* By this Nebuchadnezzar was plainly given to understand that all the great success which he had had, and should yet have, against the people of Israel, which he gloried in, as he had therein overpowered the God of Israel, was owing purely *to their sin:* if the body of that nation had faithfully adhered to their own God and the worship of him only, as these three men did, they would all have been delivered out of his hand as these three men were. And this was a necessary instruction for him at this time.

II. He applauds the constancy of these three men in their religion, and describes it to their honour, *v.* 28. Though he is not himself persuaded to own their God for his and to worship him, because, if he do so, he knows he must worship him only and renounce all others, and he calls him *the God of Shadrach,* not *my* God, yet he commends them for cleaving to him, and *not serving nor worshipping any other God but their own.* Note, There are many who are not religious themselves, and yet will own that those are clearly in the right that are religious and are stedfast in their religion. Though they are not themselves persuaded to close with it, they will commend those who, having closed with it, cleave to it. If men have given up their names to that God who will alone be served, let them keep to their principles, and serve him only, whatever it cost them. Such a constancy in the true religion will turn to men's praise, even among those that are without, when unsteadiness, treachery, and double dealing, are what all men will cry shame on. He commends them that they did this, 1. With a generous contempt of their lives, which they valued not, in comparison with the favour of God and the testimony of a good conscience. The *yielded their* own *bodies* to be cast into the fiery furnace rather than they would not only not forsake their God, but not affront him, by once paying that homage to any other which is due to him alone. Note, Those shall have their praise, if not of men, yet of God, who prefer their souls before their bodies, and will rather lose their lives than forsake their God. Those know not the worth and value of religion who do not think it worth suffering for. 2. They did it with a glorious contradiction to their prince: They *changed the king's word,* that is, they were contrary to it, and thereby put contempt upon both his precepts and threatenings, and made him repent and revoke both. Note, Even kings themselves must own that, when their commands are contrary to the commands of God, he is to be obeyed and not they. (3.) They did it with a gracious confidence in their God. They *trusted in him* that he would stand by them in what they did, that he would either bring them out of the fiery furnace back to their place on earth or lead them through the fiery furnace forward to their place in heaven; and in this confidence they became fearless of the king's wrath and regardless of their own lives. Note, A stedfast faith in God will produce a stedfast faithfulness to God. Now this honourable testimony, thus publicly borne by the king himself to these servants of God, we may well think, would have a good influence upon the rest of the Jews that were, or should be, captives in Babylon. Their neighbours could not with any confidence urge them to do that, nor could they for shame do that, which their brethren were so highly applauded by the king himself for not doing. Nay, and what God did for these his servants would help not only to keep the Jews close to their religion while they were in captivity, but to cure them of their inclination to idolatry, for which end they were sent into captivity; and, when it had had that blessed effect upon them, they might be assured that God would deliver them out of that furnace, as now he delivered their brethren out of this.

III. He issues a royal edict, strictly forbidding any to speak evil of the God of Israel, *v.* 29. We have reason to think that both the sins and the troubles of Israel had given great occasion, though no just occasion, to the Chaldeans to blaspheme the God of Israel, and, it is likely, Nebuchadnezzar himself had encouraged it; but now, though he is no true convert, nor is wrought upon to worship him, yet he resolves never to speak ill of him again, nor to suffer others to do so: *"Whoever shall speak any thing amiss,* any *error* (so some), or rather any reproach or blasphemy, whoever shall speak with contempt of *the God of Shadrach, Meshach, and Abednego,* they shall be counted the worst of malefactors, and dealt with accordingly, they shall be *cut in pieces,* as Agag was by the sword of Samuel, and their houses shall be demolished and made a *dunghill."* The miracle now wrought by the power of this God in defence of his worshippers, publicly in the sight of the thousands of Babylon, was a sufficient justification of this edict. And it would contribute much to the ease of the Jews in their captivity to be by this law screened from the fiery darts of reproach and blasphemy, with which otherwise they would have been continually annoyed. Note, It is a great mercy to the church, and a good point gained, when its enemies though they have not their hearts turned, yet have their mouths stopped and their tongues tied. If a heathen prince laid such a restraint upon the proud lips of blasphemers, much more should Christian princes do it; nay, in this thing, one would think that men should be a law to themselves, and that those who have so little love to God that they care not to speak well of him, yet could never find in their hearts, for we are sure they could never find cause, to *speak any thing amiss* of him.

IV. He not only reverses the attainder of these three men, but restores them to their places in the government *(makes them to prosper,* so the word is), and prefers them to greater and more advantageous trusts than they had been in before: He *promoted them in the province of* Babylon, which was much to their honour and the comfort of their brethren in captivity there. Note, It is the wisdom of princes to prefer and employ men of stedfastness in religion; for those are most likely to be faithful to them who are faithful to God, and it is likely to be well with them when God's favourites are made theirs.

CHAPTER 4

The penman of this chapter is Nebuchadnezzar himself: the story here recorded concerning him is given us in his own words, as he himself drew it up and published it; but Daniel, a prophet, by inspiration, inserts it in his history, and so it has become a part of sacred writ and a very memorable part. Nebuchadnezzar was as daring a rival with God Almighty for the sovereignty as perhaps any mortal man ever was; but here he fairly owns himself conquered, and gives it under his hand that the God of Israel is above him. Here is, I. The preface to his narrative, wherein he acknowledges God's dominion over him (*v.* 1–3). II. The narrative itself, wherein he relates, 1. His dream, which puzzled the magicians (*v.* 1–18). 2. The interpretation of his dream by Daniel, who showed him that it was a prognostication of his own fall, advising him therefore to repent and reform (*v.* 19–27). 3. The accomplishment of it in his running stark mad for seven years, and then recovering the use of his reason again (*v.* 28–36). 4. The conclusion of the narrative, with a humble acknowledgment and adoration of God as Lord of all (*v.* 37). This was extorted from him by the overruling power of that God who has all men's hearts in his hand, and stands upon record a lasting proof of God's supremacy, a monument of his glory, a trophy of his victory, and a warning to all not to think of prospering while they lift up or harden their hearts against God.

Verses 1–3

Here is, I. Something of form, which was usual in writs, proclamations, or circular letters, issued by the king, *v.* 1. The royal style which Nebuchadnezzar makes use of has nothing in it of pomp or fancy, but is plain, short, and unaffected — *Nebuchadnezzar the king.* If at other times he made use of great swelling words of vanity in his title, how he laid them all aside; for he was old, he had lately recovered from a distraction which had humbled and mortified him, and was now in the actual contemplation of God's greatness and sovereignty. The declaration is directed not only to his own subjects, but to all to whom this present writing shall come — *to all people, nations, and languages, that dwell in all the earth.* He is not only willing that they should all hear of it, though it carry the account if his own infamy (which perhaps none durst have published if he had not done it himself, and therefore Daniel published the original paper), but he strictly charges and commands all manner of persons to take notice of it; for all are concerned, and it may be profitable to all. He salutes those to whom he writes, in the usual form, *Peace be multiplied unto you.* Note, It becomes kings with their commands to disperse their good wishes, and, as fathers of their country, to bless their subjects. So the common form with us. We send greeting, *Omnibus quibus hae praesentes literae pervenerint, salutem — To all to whom these presents shall come, health;* and sometimes *Salutem sempiternam — Health and salvation everlasting.*

II. Something of substance and matter. He writes this, 1. To acquaint others with the providences of God that had related to him (*v.* 2): *I thought it good to show the signs and wonders that the high God* (so he calls the true God) *has wrought towards me.* He thought it *seemly* (so the word is), that it was his duty, and did well become him, that it was a debt he owed to God and the world, now that he had recovered from his distraction, to relate to distant places, and record for future ages, how justly God had humbled him and how graciously he had at length restored him. All the nations, no doubt, had heard what befell Nebuchadnezzar, and rang of it; but he thought it fit that they should have a distinct account of it from himself, that they might know the hand of God in it, and what impressions were made upon his own spirit by it, and might speak of it not as a matter of news, but as a matter of religion. The events concerning him were not only wonders to be admired, but signs to be instructed by, signifying to the world that Jehovah is greater than all gods. Note, We ought to show to others God's dealings with us, both the rebukes we have been under and the favours we have received; and though the account hereof may reflect disgrace upon ourselves, as this did upon Nebuchadnezzar, yet we must not conceal it, as long as it may redound to the glory of God. Many will be forward to tell what God has done *for their souls,* because that turns to their own praise, who care not for telling what God has done against them, and how they deserved it; whereas we ought to give glory to God, not only by praising him for his mercies, but by confessing our sins, accepting the punishment of our iniquity, and in both taking shame to ourselves, as this mighty monarch here does. 2. To show how much he was himself affected with them and convinced by them, *v.* 3. We should always speak of the word and works of God with concern and seriousness and show ourselves affected with those great things of God which we desire others should take notice of. (1.) He admires God's doings. He speaks of them as one amazed: *How great are his signs, and how mighty are his wonders!* Nebuchadnezzar was now old, had reigned above forty years, and had seen as much of the world and the revolutions of it as most men ever did; and yet never till now, when himself was nearly touched, was he brought to admire surprising events as God's signs and his wonders. Now, *How great, how mighty,* are they! Note, The more we see events to be *the Lord's doing,* and see in them the product of a divine power and the conduct of a divine wisdom, the more marvellous they will appear in our eyes, Ps. 118:23; 66:2. (2.) He thence infers God's dominion. This is that which he is at length brought to subscribe to: *His kingdom is an everlasting kingdom;* and not like his own kingdom, which he saw, and long since foresaw, in a dream, hastening towards a period. He now owns that there is a God that governs the world and has a universal, incontestable, absolute dominion in and over all the affairs of the children of men. And it is the glory of this kingdom that it is everlasting. Other reigns are confined to one generation, and other dynasties to a few generations, but God's *dominion is from generation to generation.* It should seem, Nebuchadnezzar here refers to what Daniel had foretold of a kingdom which the God of heaven would set up, that should *never be destroyed* (*ch.* 2:44), which, though meant of the kingdom of the Messiah, he understood of the providential kingdom. Thus we may make a profitable practical use and application of those prophetical scriptures which yet we do not fully, and perhaps not rightly, comprehend the meaning of.

Verses 4–18

Nebuchadnezzar, before he relates the judgments of God that had been wrought upon him for his pride, gives an account of the fair warning he had of them before they came, a due regard to which might have prevented them. But he was *told of them,* and of the issue of them, *before they came to pass, that, when they did come to pass,* by comparing them with the prediction of them, he might see, and say, that they were the Lord's doing, and might be brought to believe that there is a divine revelation in the world, as well as a divine Providence, and that the works of God agree with his word.

Now, in the account he here gives of his dream, by which he had notice of what was coming, we may observe,

I. The time when this alarm was given to him (*v.* 4); it was when he was *at rest in his house, and flourishing in his palace.* He had lately conquered Egypt, and with it completed his victories, and ended his wars, and made himself monarch of all those parts of the world, which was about the thirty-fourth or thirty-fifth year of his reign, Eze. 29:17. Then he had this dream, which was accomplished about a year after. Seven years his distraction continued, upon his recovery from which he penned this declaration, lived about two years after, and died in his forty-fifth year. He had undergone a long fatigue in his wars, had made many a tedious and dangerous campaign in the field; but now at length he is *at rest in his house,* and there is *no adversary, nor any evil occurrent.* Note, God can reach the greatest of men with his terrors even when they are most secure, and think themselves at rest and flourishing.

II. The impression it made upon him (*v.* 5): *I saw a dream which made me afraid.* One would think no little thing would frighten him that had been a man of war from his youth, and used to look the perils of war in the face without change of countenance; yet, when God pleases, a dream strikes a terror upon him. His bed, no doubt, was soft, and easy, and well-guarded, and yet his own *thoughts upon his bed* made him uneasy, and the *visions of his head,* the creatures of his own imagination, *troubled him.* Note, God can make the greatest of men uneasy even when they say to their souls, *Take your ease, eat, drink, and be merry;* he can make those that have been the troublers of the world, and have tormented thousands, to be their own troublers, their own tormentors, and those that have been *the terror of the mighty* a terror to themselves. By the consternation which this dream put him into, and the impression it made upon him, he perceived it to be, not an ordinary dream, but sent of God on a special errand.

III. His consulting, in vain, with the magicians and astrologers concerning the meaning of it. He had not now forgotten the dream, as before, *ch.* 2. He had it ready enough, but he wanted to know the interpretation of it and what was prefigured by it, *v.* 6. Orders are immediately given to summon *all the wise men of Babylon* that were such fools as to pretend by magic, divination, inspecting the entrails of beasts, or observations of the stars, to predict things to come: they must all come together, to see if any, or all of them in consultation, could interpret the king's dream. It is probable that these people had sometimes, in a like case, given the king some sort of satisfaction, and by the rules of their art had answered the king's queries so as to please him, whether it were right or wrong, hit or missed; but now his expectation from them was disappointed: He *told them the dream* (*v.* 7), but they *could not tell him the interpretation of it,* though they had boasted, with great assurance (*ch.* 2:4, 7), that, if they had but the dream told them, they would without fail interpret it. But the key of this dream was in a sacred prophecy (Eze. 31:3, etc.), where the Assyrian is compared, as Nebuchadnezzar here, to a *tree cut down,* for his pride; and that was a book they had not studied, nor acquainted themselves with, else they might have been let into the mystery of this dream. Providence ordered it so that they should be first puzzled with it, that Daniel's interpreting it afterwards might redound to the glory of the God of Daniel. Now was fulfilled what Isaiah foretold (*ch.* 47:12, 13), that when the ruin of Babylon was drawing on her *enchantments and sorceries,* her *astrologers* and *star-gazers,* should not be able to do her any service.

IV. The court he made to Daniel, to engage him to expound his dream to him: *At the last Daniel came in. v.* 8. Either he declined associating with the rest because of their badness, or they declined his company because of his goodness; or perhaps the king would rather that his own magicians should have the honour of doing it if they could than that Daniel should have it; or Daniel, being *governor* of the wise men (*ch.* 2:48), was, as is usual, last consulted. Many make God's word their last refuge, and never have recourse to it till they are driven off from all other succours. He compliments Daniel very highly, takes notice of the name which he had himself given him, in the choice of which he thinks he was very happy and that it was a good omen: "His *name was Belteshazzar,* from *Bel, the name of my god.*" He applauds his rare endowments: He has *the spirit of the holy gods,* so he tells him to his face (*v.* 9), with which we may suppose that Daniel was so far from being puffed up that he was rather very much grieved to hear that which he had by gift from the God of Israel, the true and living God, ascribed to Nebuchadnezzar's god, a dunghill deity. Here is a strange medley in Nebuchadnezzar, but such as is commonly found in those that side with their corruptions against their convictions. 1. He retains the language and dialect of his idolatry, and therefore, it is to be feared, is no convert to the faith and worship of the living God. He is an idolater, and his speech betrayeth him. For he speaks of many gods, and is brought to acquiesce in one as sufficient, no, not in him who is all-sufficient. And some think, when he speaks of *the spirit of the holy gods,* that he supposes there are some evil malignant deities, whom men are concerned to worship, only to prevent their doing them a mischief, and some who are good beneficent deities, and that by the spirit of the latter Daniel was animated. He also owns that Bel was his god still, though he had once and again acknowledged the *God of Israel* to be Lord of all, *ch.* 2:47; 3:29. He also applauds Daniel, not as *a servant of God,* but as *master of the magicians* (*v.* 9), supposing his knowledge to differ from theirs, not in kind, but only in degree; and he consulted him not as a prophet, but as a celebrated magician, so endeavouring to save the credit of the art when those blundered and were nonplussed who were masters of the art. See how close his idolatry sat to him. He has got a notion of many gods, and has chosen Bel for his god, and he cannot persuade himself to quit either his notion or his choice, though the absurdity of both had been evidenced to him, more than once, beyond contradiction. He, like other heathens, would not change his gods, though they were no gods, Jer. 2:11. Many persist in a false way only because they think they cannot in honour leave it. See how loose his convictions sat, and how easily he had dropped them. He once called the God of Israel a *God of gods, ch.* 2:47. Now he sets him upon a level with the rest of those whom he calls the *holy gods.* Note, If convictions be not speedily prosecuted, it is a thousand to one but in a little time they will be quite lost and forgotten. Nebuchadnezzar, not going forward with the acknowledgements he had been brought to make of the sovereignty of the true God, soon *went backwards,* and relapsed to the same veneration he had always had for his false gods. And yet, 2. He professes a great opinion of Daniel, whom he knows to be a servant of the true God, and of him only. He looked upon him as one that had such an insight, such a foresight, as none of his magicians had: *I know that no secret troubles thee.* Note, The spirit of prophecy quite outdoes the spirit of divination, even the enemies themselves being judges; for so it was adjudged here, upon a fair trial of skill.

V. The particular account he gives him of his dream.

1. He saw a stately flourishing tree, remarkable above all the trees of the wood. This tree was *planted in the midst of the earth* (*v.* 10), fitly representing him who reigned in Babylon, which was about the midst of the then known world. His dignity and eminency above all his neighbours were signified by the height of this tree, which was *exceedingly great;* it *reached unto heaven.* He over-topped those about him, and aimed to have divine honours given him; nay, he over-powered those about him, and the potent armies he had the command of, with which he car-

ried all before him, are signified by the strength of this tree: it *grew and was strong.* And so much were Nebuchadnezzar and his growing greatness the talk of the nations, so much had they their eye upon him (some a jealous eye, all a wondering eye), that the sight of this tree is said to be *to the end of all the earth.* This tree had every thing in it that was pleasant to the eye and good for food (*v.* 12); *The leaves thereof were fair,* denoting the pomp and splendour of Nebuchadnezzar's court, which was the wonder of strangers and the glory of his own subjects. Nor was this tree for sight and state only, but for use. (1.) For protection; the boughs of it were for shelter both to the beasts and to the fowls. Princes should be a screen to their subjects *from the heat* and *from the storm,* should expose themselves to secure them, and study how to make them safe and easy. If the bramble be *promoted over the trees,* he invites them to come and *trust in his shadow,* such as it is, Jdg. 9:15. It is protection that draws allegiance. The kings of the earth are to their subjects but as the shadow of a great tree; but Christ is to his subjects as the *shadow of a great rock,* Isa. 32:2. Nay, because that, though strong, may be cold, they are said to be hidden under the *shadow of his wings* (Ps. 17:8), where they are not only safe, but warm. (2.) For provision, The Assyrian was compared to a *cedar* (Eze. 31:6), which affords shadow only; but this tree here had much fruit — in it was *meat for all* and *all flesh was fed of it.* This mighty monarch, it should seem by this, not only was great, but did good; he did not impoverish, but enrich his country, and by his power and interest abroad brought wealth and trade to it. Those that *exercise authority* would be called *benefactors* (Lu. 22:25), and the most effectual course they can take to support their authority is to be really benefactors. And see what is the best that great men, with their wealth and power can attain to, and that is to have the honour of having many to live upon them and to be maintained by them; for, *as goods are increased, those are increased that eat them.*

2. He heard the doom of this tree read, which he perfectly remembered, and related here, perhaps word for word as he heard it. The sentence was passed upon it by an angel, whom he saw *come down from heaven,* and heard proclaim this sentence aloud. This angel is here called a *watcher,* or *watchman,* not only because angels by their nature are spirits, and therefore neither slumber nor sleep, but because by their office they are *ministering spirits,* and attend continually to their ministrations, watching all opportunities of serving their great Master. They, as watchers, encamp round those that fear God, to deliver them, and *bear them up in their hands.* This angel was a *messenger,* or *ambassador* (so some read it), and a *holy one. Holiness becomes God's house;* therefore angels that attend and are employed by him are *holy ones;* they preserve the purity and rectitude of their nature, and are in every thing conformable to the divine will. Let us review the doom passed upon the tree.

(1.) Orders are given that it be cut down (*v.* 14); now also *the axe is laid to the root* of this tree. Though it is ever so high, ever so strong, that cannot secure it when its day comes to fall; the beasts and fowls, that are sheltered in and under the boughs of it, are driven away and dispersed; the branches are cropped, the leaves shaken off, and the fruit scattered. Note, Worldly prosperity in its highest degree is a very uncertain thing; and it is no uncommon thing for those that have lived in the greatest pomp and power to be stripped of all that which they trusted to and gloried in. By the turns of providence, those who made a figure become captives, those who lived in plenty, and above what they had, are reduced to straits, and live far below what they had, and those perhaps are brought to be beholden to others who once had many depending upon them and making suit to them. But the *trees of righteousness,* that are *planted in the house of the Lord* and bring forth fruit to him, shall not be cut down, nor shall their leaf wither.

(2.) Care is taken that the root be preserved (*v.* 15); *"Leave the stump of it in the earth,* exposed to all weathers. There let it lie neglected and buried in the grass. Let the beasts that formerly sheltered themselves under the boughs now repose themselves upon the stump; but that it may not be raked to pieces, nor trodden to dirt, and to show that it is yet reserved for better days, let it be hooped round with *a band of iron and brass,* to keep it firm." Note, God in judgment remembers mercy; and may yet have good things in store for those whose condition seems most forlorn. There is *hope of a tree, if it be cut down, that it will sprout again, that through the scent of water it will bud,* Job 14:7–9.

(3.) The meaning of this is explained by the angel himself to Nebuchadnezzar, *v.* 16. Whoever is the person signified by this tree he is sentenced to be deposed from the honour, state, and dignity of a man, to be deprived of the use of his reason, and to be and live like a brute, till *seven times pass over him. Let a beast's heart be given unto him.* This is surely the saddest and sorest of all temporal judgments, worse a thousand times than death, and though, like it, least felt by those that lie under it, yet to be dreaded and deprecated more than any other. Nay, whatever outward affliction God is pleased to lay upon us, we have reason to bear it patiently, and to be thankful that he continues to us the use of our reason and the peace of our consciences. But those proud tyrants who *set their heart as the heart of God* (Eze. 27:2) may justly be deprived of the heart of man, and have a beast's heart given them.

(4.) The truth of it is confirmed (*v.* 17); *This matter is by the decree of the watchers and the demand by the word of the holy ones.* God has determined it, as a righteous Judge; he has signed this edict; pursuant to his eternal counsel, the decree has gone forth, And, [1.] The angels of heaven have subscribed to it, as attesting it, approving it, and applauding it. It is by *the decree of the watchers;* not that the great God needs the counsel or concurrence of the angels in any thing he determines or does, but, as he uses their ministration in executing his counsels, so he is sometimes represented, after the manner of men, as if he consulted them. *Whom shall I send?* Isa. 6:8. *Who shall persuade Ahab?* I kings 22:20. So it denotes the solemnity of this sentence. The king's breves, or short writs, pass, *Teste me ipso — in my presence;* but charters used to be signed, *His testibus — In the presence of us whose names are underwritten;* such was Nebuchadnezzar's doom; it was by the *decree of the watchers.* [2.] The saints on earth petitioned for it, as well as the angels in heaven: *The demand is by the word of the holy ones.* God's suffering people, that had long groaned under the heavy yoke of Nebuchadnezzar's tyranny, cried to him for vengeance; they made the demand, and God gave this answer to it; for, when the *oppressed cry to God, he will hear,* Ex. 22:27. Sentence was passed, in Ahab's time, that there should be no more rain, at Elijah's word, when he *made intercession against Israel,* 1 Ki. 17:1.

(5.) The design of it is declared. Orders are given for the cutting down of this tree, *to the intent that the living may know that the Most High rules.* This judgment must be executed, to convince the unthinking, unbelieving, world, that *verily there is a God that judges in the earth,* a God that governs the world, that not only has a kingdom of his own in it, and administers the affairs of that kingdom, but rules also *in the kingdom of men,* in the dominion that one man has over another, and *gives* that *to whomsoever he will;* from him promotion comes, Ps. 75:6, 7. He advances men to power and dominion that little expected it, and crosses the projects of the ambitious and aspiring. Sometimes he *sets up the basest of men,* and serves his own purposes by them. He sets up mean men, as David from the sheepfold; *he raises the poor out of the dust,* to *set them among princes,* Ps. 113:7, 8. Nay, sometimes he sets up bad men, to be a scourge to a provoking people. Thus he can do, thus he may do, thus he often does, and *gives not account of any of his matters.* By humbling Nebuchadnezzar it was designed that the living should be made to know this. The dead know it, that have gone to the world of spirits, the world of retribution; they know that *the Most High rules;* but the living must be made to know it and lay it to heart, that they may make their peace with God before it be too late.

Thus has Nebuchadnezzar fully and faithfully related his dream, what he saw and what he heard, and then demands of Daniel the interpretation of it (*v.* 18), for he found that no one else was able to interpret it, but was confident that he was: *For the spirit of the holy gods is in thee,* or of the *Holy God,* the proper title of the God of Israel. Much may be expected from those that have in them the *Spirit of the Holy God.* Whether Nebuchadnezzar had any jealousy that it was his own doom that was read by this dream does not appear; perhaps he was so vain and secure as to imagine that it was some other prince that was a rival with him, whose fall he had the pleasing prospect of given him in this dream; but, be it for him or against him, he is very solicitous to know the true meaning of it and depends upon Daniel to give it to him. Now, When God gives us general warnings of his judgments we should be desirous to understand his mind in them, to hear *the Lord's voice crying in the city.*

Verses 19–27

We have here the interpretation of Nebuchadnezzar's dream; and when once it is applied to himself, and it is declared that he is the tree in the dream *(Mutato nomine de te fabula narratur — Change but the name, the fable speaks of thee),* when once it is said, *Thou art the man,* there needs little more to be said for the explication of the dream. *Out of his own mouth he is judged; so shall his doom be, he himself has decided it.* The thing was so plain that Daniel, upon hearing the dream, was *astonished for one hour, v.* 19. He was struck with amazement and terror at so great a judgment coming upon so great a prince. *His flesh trembled for fear of God.* He was likewise struck with confusion when he found himself under a necessity of being the man that must bring to the king *these heavy tidings,* which, having received so many favours from the king, he had rather he should have heard from any one else; so far is he from desiring the woeful day that he dreads it, and the thoughts of it trouble him. Those that come after the ruined sinner are said to be *astonished at his day,* as *those that went before,* and saw it coming (as Daniel here), *were affrighted,* Job 18:20.

I. The preface to the interpretation is a civil compliment which, as a courtier, he passes upon the king. The king observed him to stand as one astonished, and, thinking he was loth to speak out for fear of offending him, he encouraged him to deal plainly and faithfully with him; *Let not the dream, nor the interpretation thereof, trouble thee.* This he speaks either, 1. As one that sincerely desired to know this truth. Note, Those that consult the oracles of God must be ready to receive them as they are, whether they be for them or against them, and must accordingly give their ministers leave to be free with them. Or, 2. As one that despised the truth, and set it at defiance. When we see how regardless he was of this warning afterwards we are tempted to think that this was his meaning; *"Let it not trouble thee,* for I am resolved it shall not trouble me; nor will I lay it to heart." But, whether he have any concern for himself or no, Daniel is concerned for him, and therefore wishes, *"The dream be to those that hate thee.* Let the ill it bodes light on the head of thy enemies, not on thy head." Though Nebuchadnezzar was an idolater, a persecutor, and an oppressor of the people of God, yet he was, at present, Daniel's prince; and therefore, though Daniel foresees, and is now going to foretell, ill concerning him, he dares not wish ill to him.

II. The interpretation itself is only a repetition of the dream, with application to the king. "As for *the tree* which thou sawest *flourishing* (*v.* 20, 21), *it is thou, O king!" v.* 22. And willing enough would the king be to hear this (as, before, to hear, *Thou art the head of gold),* but for that which follows. He shows the king his present prosperous state in the glass of his own dream; *"Thy greatness has grown and reaches* as near *to heaven* as human greatness can do, and *thy dominion is to the end of the earth," ch.* 2:37, 38. "As for the doom passed upon the tree (*v.* 23), it is *the decree of the Most High, which comes upon my lord the king," v.* 24. He must not only be deposed from his throne, *but driven from men,* and being deprived of his reason, and having a beast's heart given him, his dwelling shall be *with the beasts of the field,* and with them he shall be a fellow-commoner: he shall *eat grass as oxen,* and, like them, lie out all weathers, and be *wet with the dew of heaven,* and this till *seven times* pass over him, that is, *seven years;* and then he shall know that the *Most High rules,* and when he is brought to know and own this he shall be restored to his dominion again (*v.* 26): *"Thy kingdom shall be sure unto thee,* shall remain as firm as the *stump of the tree* in the ground, and thou shalt have it, *after thou shalt have known* that *the heavens do rule."* God is here called *the heavens,* because it is in heaven that he has *prepared his throne* (Ps. 103:19), thence he *beholds all the sons of men,* Ps. 33:13. The *heavens, even the heavens, are the Lord's;* and the influence which the visible heavens have upon this earth is intended as a faint representation of the dominion the God of heaven has over this lower world; we are said to *sin against heaven,* Lu. 15:18. Note, Then only we may expect comfortably to enjoy our right in, and government of, both ourselves and others, when we dutifully acknowledge God's title to, and dominion over, us and all we have.

III. The close of the interpretation is the pious counsel which Daniel, as a prophet, gave the king, *v.* 27. Whether he appeared concerned or not at the interpretation of the dream, a word of advice would be very seasonable — if careless, to awaken him, if troubled, to comfort him; and it is not inconsistent with the dream and the interpretation of it, for Daniel knew not but it might be conditional, like the prediction of Nineveh's destruction. Observe, 1. How humbly he gives his advice, and with what tenderness and respect: *"O king! let my counsel be acceptable unto thee;* take it in good part, as coming from love, and well-meant, and let it not be misinterpreted." Note, Sinners need to be courted to their own good, and respectfully entreated to do well for themselves. The apostle beseeches men to *suffer the word of exhortation,* Heb. 13:22. We think it a good point gained if people will be persuaded to take good counsel kindly; nay, if they will take it patiently. 2. What his advice is. He does not counsel him to enter into a course of physic, for the preventing of the distemper in his head, but to break off a course of sin that he was in, to reform his life. He wronged his own subjects, and dealt unfairly with his allies; and he must *break off* this *by righteousness,* by rendering to all their due, making amends for wrong done, and not triumphing over right with might. He had been cruel to the poor, to God's poor, to the poor Jews; and he must *break off* this *iniquity* by *showing mercy* to those poor, pitying those oppressed ones, setting them at liberty or making their captivity easy to them. Note, It is necessary, in repentance, that we not only *cease to do evil, but learn to do well,* not only do no wrong to any, but do good to all. 3. What the motive is with which he backs this advice: *If it may be a lengthening of thy tranquility.* Though it should not wholly prevent the judgment, yet by this means a reprieve may be obtained, as by *Ahab's humbling himself,* 1 Ki. 21:29. Either the trouble may be the longer before it comes or the shorter when it does come; yet he cannot assure him of this, but *it may be,* it may prove so. Note, The mere probability of preventing a temporal judgment is inducement enough to a work so good in itself as the leaving off of our sins and reforming of our lives, much more the certainty of preventing our eternal ruin. *"That will be a healing of thy error"* (so some read it); "thus the quarrel will be taken up, and all will be well again."

Verses 28–33

We have here Nebuchadnezzar's dream accomplished, and Daniel's application of it to him justified and confirmed. How he took it we are not told, whether he was pleased with Daniel or displeased; but here we have,

I. God's patience with him: *All this came upon him,* but not till *twelve months after* (*v.* 29), so long there was a *lengthening of his tranquility,* though it does not appear that he *broke off his sins,* or showed any *mercy to the poor* captives, for this was still God's quarrel with him, that he *opened not the house of his prisoners,* Isa. 14:17. Daniel having counselled him to repent, God so far confirmed his word that he gave him space to repent; he *let him alone this year also,* this *one* year more, before he brought this judgment upon him. Note, God is long-suffering with provoking sinners, because he is not willing that *any should perish, but that all should come to repentance,* 2 Pt. 3:9.

II. His pride, and haughtiness, and abuse of that patience. He walked *in the palace of the kingdom of Babylon,* in pomp and pride, pleasing himself with the view of that vast city, which, with all the territories thereunto belonging, was under his command, and *he said,* either to himself or to those about him, perhaps some foreigners to whom he was showing his kingdom and the glory of it, *Is not this great Babylon?* Yes, it is great, of vast extent, no less that forty-five miles compass within the walls. It is full of inhabitants, and they are full of wealth. It is a *golden city,* and that is enough to proclaim it great, Isa. 14:4. See the grandeur of the houses, walls, towers, and public edifices. Every thing in Babylon he thinks looks great; "and this *great Babylon I have built."* Babylon was built many ages before he was born, but because he fortified and beautified it, and we may suppose much of it was rebuilt during his long and prosperous reign, he boasts that he has built it, as Augustus Caesar boasted concerning Rome, *Lateritiam inveni, marmoream reliqui — I found it brick, but I left it marble.* He boasts that he built it *for the house of the kingdom,* that is, the metropolis of his empire. This vast city, compared with the countries that belonged to his dominions, was but as one house. He built it with the assistance of his subjects, yet boasts that he did it *by the might of his power;* he built it for his security and convenience, yet, as if he had no occasion for it, boasts that he built it purely *for the honour of his majesty.* Note, Pride and self-conceitedness are sins that most easily beset great men, who have great things in the world. They are apt to take the glory to themselves which is due to God only.

III. His punishment for his pride. When he was thus strutting, and vaunting himself, and adoring his own shadow, *while the* proud *word was in the king's mouth* the powerful word came from heaven, by which he was immediately deprived, 1. Of his honour as a king: *The kingdom has departed from thee.* When he thought he had erected impregnable bulwarks for the preserving of his kingdom, now, in an instant, it *has departed from him;* when he thought it so well guarded that none could take it from him, behold, it departs of itself. As soon as he becomes utterly incapable to manage it, it is of course taken out of his hands. 2. He is deprived of his honour as a man. He loses his reason, and by that means loses his dominion: *They shall drive thee from men, v.* 32. And it was fulfilled (*v.* 33): he was *driven from men the same hour.* On a sudden he fell stark mad, distracted in the highest degree that ever any man was. His understanding and memory were gone, and all the faculties of a rational soul broken, so that he became a perfect brute in the shape of a man. He went naked, and on all four, like a brute, did himself shun the society of reasonable creatures and run wild into the fields and woods, and was driven out by his own servants, who, after some time of trial, despairing of his return to his right mind, abandoned him, and looked after him no more. He had not the spirit of a beast of prey (that of the royal lion), but of the abject and less honourable species, for he was made to *eat grass as oxen;* and, probably, he did not speak with human voice, but lowed like an ox. Some think that his body was all covered with hair; however, *the hair* of his head and beard, being never cut nor combed, grew like *eagles feathers,* and *his nails like birds' claws.* Let us pause a little, and view this miserable spectacle; and let us receive instruction from it. (1.) Let us see here what a mercy it is to have the use of our reason, how thankful we ought to be for it, and how careful we ought to be not to do any thing which may either provoke God or may have a natural tendency to put us out of the possession of our own souls. Let us learn how to value our own reason, and to pity the case of those that are under the prevailing power of melancholy or distraction, or are delirious, and to be very tender in our censures of them and conduct towards them, for it is a trial common to men, and a case which, some time or other, may be our own. (2.) Let us see here the vanity of human glory and greatness. Is this Nebuchadnezzar the Great? What this despicable animal that is meaner than the poorest beggar? Is this he that looked so glorious on the throne, so formidable in the camp, that had politics enough to subdue and govern kingdoms, and now has not so much sense as to keep his own clothes on his back? *Is this the man that made the earth to tremble, that did shake kingdoms?* Isa. 14:16. Never let the *wise man* then *glory in his wisdom,* nor *the mighty man in his strength.* (3.) Let us see here how God resists the proud, and delights to abase them and put contempt upon them. Nebuchadnezzar would be more than a man, and therefore God justly makes him less than a man, and puts him upon a level with the beasts who set up for a rival with his Maker. See Job 40:11–13.

Verses 34–37

We have here Nebuchadnezzar's recovery from his distraction, and his return to his right mind, *at the end of the days* prefixed, that is, of the seven years. So long he continued a monument of God's justice and a trophy of his victory over the children of pride, and he was made more so by being struck mad than if he had been in an instant struck dead with a thunderbolt; yet it was a mercy to him that he was kept alive, for while there is life there is hope that we may yet praise God, as he did here: *At the end of the days* (says he), *I lifted up my eyes unto heaven* (*v.* 34), looked no longer down towards the earth as a beast, but begun to look up as a man. *Os homini sublime dedit — Heaven gave to man an erect countenance.* But there was more in it than this; he looked up as a devout man, as a penitent, as a humble petitioner for mercy, being perhaps never till now made sensible of his own misery. And now,

I. He has the use of his reason so far restored to him that with it he glorifies God, and humbles himself under his mighty hand. He was told that he should continue in that forlorn case till he should know that the Most High rules, and here we have him brought to the knowledge of this: *My understanding returned to me, and I blessed the Most High.* Note, Those may justly be reckoned void of understanding that do not bless and praise God; nor do men ever rightly use their reason till they begin to be religious, nor live as men till they live to the glory of God. As reason is the substratum or subject of religion (so that creatures which have no reason are not capable of religion), so religion is the crown and glory of reason, and we have our reason in vain, and shall one day wish we had never had it, if we do not glorify God with it. This was the first act of Nebuchadnezzar's returning reason; and, when this became the employment of it, he was then, and not till then, qualified for all the other enjoyments of it. And till he was for a great while disabled to exercise it in other things he never was brought to apply it to this, which is the great end for which our reason is given us. His folly was the means whereby he became wise; he was not recovered by his dream of this judgment (that was soon forgotten like a dream), but he is made to feel it, and then his *ear is opened to discipline.* To bring him to himself, he must first be *beside himself.* And by this it appears that what good thoughts there were in his mind, and what good work was wrought there, were not of himself (for he was not his own man), but it was the gift of God. Let us see what Nebuchadnezzar is now at length effectually brought to the acknowledgment of; and we may learn from it what to believe concerning God. 1. That the *most high* God *lives for ever,* and his being knows neither change nor period, for he has it of himself. His flatterers often complimented him with, *O king! live for ever.* But he is now convinced that no king lives for ever, but the God of Israel only, who is still the same. 2. That his kingdom is like himself, *everlasting,* and his *dominion from generation to generation;* there is no succession, no revolution, in his kingdom. As he lives, so he reigns, for ever, and of his government there is no end. 3. That *all nations* before him are *as nothing.* He has no need of them; he makes no account of them. The greatest of men, in comparison with him, are less than nothing. Those that think highly of God think meanly of themselves. 4. That his kingdom is universal, and both *the armies of heaven* and *the inhabitants of the earth* are his subjects, and under his check and control. Both angels and men are employed by him, and are accountable to him; the highest angel is not above his command, nor the meanest of the children of men beneath his cognizance. The angels of heaven are his armies, the inhabitants of the earth his tenants. 5. That his power is irresistible, and his sovereignty uncontrollable, for he *does according to his will,* according to his design and purpose, according to his decree and counsel; whatever he pleases that he does; whatever he appoints that he performs; and none can resist his will, change his counsel, nor *stay his hand, nor say unto him, What doest thou?* None can arraign his proceedings, enquire into the meaning of them, nor demand a reason for them. Woe to him that strives with his Maker, that says to him, *What doest thou?* Or, *Why doest thou so?* 6. That every thing which God does is well done: His *works are truth,* for they all agree with his word. *His ways are judgment,* both wise and righteous, exactly consonant to the rules both of prudence and equity, and no fault is to be found with them. 7. That he has power to humble the haughtiest of his enemies that act in contradiction to him or competition with him: *Those that walk in pride he is able to abuse* (*v.* 37); he is able to deal with those that are most confident of their own sufficiency to contend with him.

II. He has the use of his reason so far restored to him as with it to re-enjoy himself, and the pleasures of his re-established prosperity (*v.* 36): *At the same time my reason returned to me;* he had said before (*v.* 34) that his *understanding returned* to him, and here he mentions it again, for the use of our reason is a mercy we can never be sufficiently thankful for. Now his *lords sought to him;* he did not need to seek to them, and they soon perceived, not only that he had recovered his reason and was fit to rule, but that he had recovered it with advantage, and was more fit to rule than ever. It is probable that the dream and the interpretation of it were well known, and much talked of, at court; and the former part of the prediction being fulfilled, that he should go distracted, they doubted not but that, according to the prediction, he should come to himself again at seven years' end, and, in confidence of that, when the time had expired they were ready to receive him; and then *his honour and brightness returned to him,* the same that he had before his madness seized him. He is now established in his kingdom as firmly as if there had been no interruption given him. *He becomes a fool, that he may be wise,* wiser than ever; and he that but the other day was in the depth of disgrace and ignominy has now *excellent majesty added to him,* beyond what he had when he went from kingdom to kingdom conquering and to conquer. Note, 1. When men are brought to honour God, particularly by a penitent confession of sin and a believing acknowledgment of his sovereignty, then, and not till then, they may expect that God will put honour upon them, will not only restore them to the dignity they lost by the sin of the first Adam, but *add excellent majesty to them* from the righteousness and grace of the second Adam. 2. Afflictions shall last no longer than till they have done the work for which they were sent. When this prince is brought to own God's dominion over himself. 3. All the accounts we take and give of God's dealing with us ought to conclude with praises to him. When Nebuchadnezzar is restored to his kingdom he *praises, and extols, and honours the King of heaven* (*v.* 37), before he applies himself to his secular business. Therefore we have our reason, that we may be in a capacity of praising him, and therefore our prosperity, that we may have cause to praise him.

It was not long after this that Nebuchadnezzar ended his life and reign. Abydenus, quoted by Eusebius (Prap. Evang. 1.9), reports, from the tradition of the Chaldeans, that upon his death-bed he foretold the taking of Babylon by Cyrus. Whether he continued in the same good mind that here he seems to have been in we are not told, nor does any thing appear to the contrary but that he did: and, if so great a *blasphemer and persecutor* did find mercy, he was not the last. And, if our charity may reach so far as to hope he did, we must admire free grace, by which he lost his wits for a while that he might save his soul for ever.

CHAPTER 5

The destruction of the kingdom of Babylon had been long and often foretold when it was at a distance; in this chapter we have it accomplished, and a prediction of it the very same night that it was accomplished. Belshazzar now reigned in Babylon; some compute he had reigned seventeen years, others but three; we have here the story of his exit and the period of his kingdom. We must know that about two years before this Cyrus king of Persia, a growing monarch, came against Babylon with a great army; Belshazzar met him, fought him, and was routed by him in a pitched battle. He and his scattered forces retired into the city, where Cyrus besieged them. They were very secure, because the river Euphrates was their bulwark, and they had twenty years; provision in the city; but in the second year of the siege he took it, as is here related. We have in this chapter, I. The riotous, idolatrous, sacrilegious feast which Belshazzar made, in which he filled up the measure of his iniquity (*v.* 1–4). II. The alarm given him in the midst of his jollity by a hand-writing on the wall, which none of his wise men could read or tell him the meaning of (*v.* 5–9). III. The interpretation of the mystical characters by Daniel, who was at length brought in to him, and dealt plainly with him, and showed him his doom written (*v.* 10–28). IV. The immediate accomplishment of the interpretation in the slaying of the king and seizing of the kingdom (*v.* 30, 31).

Verses 1–9

We have here Belshazzar the king very gay, but all of a sudden very gloomy, and in straits in the fulness of his sufficiency. See how he affronts God, and God affrights him; and wait what will be the issue of this contest; and whether he that hardened his heart against God prospered.

I. See how the king affronted God, and put contempt upon him. He *made a great feast,* or *banquet of wine;* probably it was some anniversary solemnity, in honour off his birth-day or coronation-day, or in honour of some of their idols. Historians say that Cyrus, who was now with his army besieging Babylon, knew of this feast, and presuming that they then would be off their guard, *somno vinoque sepulti — buried in sleep and wine,* took that opportunity to attack the city, and so with the more ease made himself master of it. Belshazzar upon this occasion invited *a thousand of his lords* to come and drink with him. Perhaps they were such as had signalized themselves in defense of the city against the besiegers; or these were his great council of war, with whom, when they had well drunk, he would advise what was further to be done. And they were to look upon it as a great favour that he *drank wine before* them, for it was the pride of those eastern kings to be seldom seen. He drank wine before them, for he made this feast, as Ahasuerus did, to show the *honour of his majesty.* Now in this sumptuous feast, 1. He put an affront upon the providence of God and bade defiance to his judgments. His city was now besieged; a powerful enemy was at his gates; his life and kingdom lay at stake. In all this the hand of the Lord had gone out against him, and by it he called him to *weeping, and mourning, and girding with sackcloth.* God's voice cried in the city, as Jonah to Nineveh, *Yet forty days,* or fewer, *and Babylon shall be destroyed.* He should therefore, like the king of Nineveh, have proclaimed a fast; but, as one resolved to walk contrary to God, he proclaims a feast, and behold *joy and gladness, slaying oxen, killing sheep, eating flesh, and drinking wine,* as if he dared the Almighty to do his worst, Isa. 22:12, 13. To show how little fear he had of being forced to surrender, for want of provisions, he spent thus extravagantly. Note, Security and sensuality are sad presages of approaching ruin. Those that will not be warned by judgments of God may expect to be wounded by them. 2. He put an affront upon the temple of God, and bade defiance to his sanctuary, *v.* 2. *While he tasted the wine, he commanded to bring the vessels of* the temple, that they might drink in them. When he tasted how rich and fine the wine was, "O," said he, "it is a pity but we should have holy vessels to drink such delicious wine as this in," which was looked upon as a piece of wit, and, to carry on the humour, the vessels of the temple were immediately sent for. Nay, there seems to have been something more in it than a frolic, and that it was done in a malicious despite to the God of Israel. The heart of his people was very much upon these sacred vessels, as appears from Jer. 27:16, 18. Their principal care, at their return, was about these, Ezra 1:7. Now, we may suppose, they had an expectation of their deliverance approaching, reckoning the seventy years of their captivity near a period; and some of them might perhaps have given out some words to that purport, that shortly they should have the vessels of the sanctuary restored to them, in defiance of which Belshazzar here proclaims them to be his own, will keep them in store no longer, but will make use of them among his own plate. Note, That mirth is sinful indeed, and fills the measure of men's iniquity apace, which profanes sacred things and jests with them. This ripened Babylon for ruin — that no songs would serve them but the *songs of Zion* (Ps. 137:3), no vessels but the vessels of the sanctuary. Let those who thus sacrilegiously alienate what is dedicated to God and his honour know that he *will not be mocked.* 3. He put an affront upon God himself, and bade defiance to his deity; for *they drank wine, and praised the gods of gold and silver, v.* 4. They gave that glory to images, the work of their own hands and creatures of their own fancy, which is due to the true and living God only. They praised them either with sacrifices offered to them or with songs sung in honour of them. When their heads were giddy, and their hearts merry, with wine, they were in the fittest frame to *praise the gods of gold and silver, wood and stone;* for one would think that men in their senses, who had the command of a clear and sober thought, could not be guilty of so gross an absurdity; they must be intoxicated ere they could be so infatuated. Drunken worshippers, who are not men, but beasts, are the most proper for the service of dunghill deities, that are not gods, but devils. *They have erred through wine,* Isa. 27:7. They drank wine, and praised their idol-gods, as if they had been the founders of their feast and the givers of all good things to them. Or, when they were drinking wine, they praised their gods by drinking healths to them; and the king *drank wine before* them (*v.* 1), that is, he began the health, first to this god, and then to the other, till they went through the *bead-roll* or *farrago* of them, those of *wood and stone* not excepted. Note, Immorality and impiety, vice and profaneness, strengthen the hands and advance the interests one of another. Drunken frolics were an introduction to idolatry, and then idolatrous healths were a shoeing-horn to further drunkenness.

II. See how God affrighted the king, and struck a terror upon him. Belshazzar and his lords are in the midst of their revels, the cups going round apace, and all upon the merry pin, drinking confusion, it may be, to Cyrus and his army, and roaring out huzzas, in confidence of the speedy raising of the siege; but the hour had come when that must be fulfilled which had been long ago said of the king of Babylon, when his city should be besieged by the Persians and Medes, Isa. 21:2–4. *The night of my pleasures has he turned into fear to me.* The mirth of this ball at court must be spoiled, and a damp cast upon their jollity, though the king himself be master of the revels; immediately, when God speaks the word, we have him and all his guests in the utmost confusion, and the end of their mirth is heaviness. 1. There appear the *fingers of a man's hand writing on the plaster of the wall,* before the king's face (*v.* 5), "the angel Gabriel," say the rabbin, "directing these fingers and writing by them." "That divine hand" (says a rabbi of our own, Dr. Lightfoot) "that had written the two tables for a law to his people now writes the doom of Babel and Belshazzar upon the wall." Here was nothing sent to frighten them which made a noise, or threatened their lives, no claps of thunder nor flashes of lightning, no destroying angel with his sword drawn in his hand, only a pen in the hand, writing upon the wall, *over-against the candlestick,* where they might all see it by the light of their own candle. Note, God's written word is sufficient to put the proudest boldest sinners into a fright, when he is pleased to give it the setting on. The king saw *the part of the hand that wrote,* but saw not the person whose hand it was, which made the thing more frightful. Note, What we see of God, the part of the hand that writes in the book of the creatures and the book of the scriptures *(Lo, these are parts of his ways,* Job 26:14), may serve to possess us with awful thoughts concerning that of God which we do not see. If this be *the finger of God,* what is his arm made bare? And what is he? 2. The king is immediately seized with a panic fear (*v.* 6): *His countenance was changed* (his colour went and came); *the joints of his loins were loosed,* so that he had no strength in them, but was struck with a pain in his back, as is usual in a great fright; *his knees smote one against another,* so violently did he tremble like an aspen leaf. But what was the matter? Why is he in such a fright? He perceives not what is written, and how does he know but it may be some happy presage of deliverance to him and to his kingdom? But the business was *his thoughts troubled him;* his own guilty conscience flew in his face, and told him that he had no reason to expect any good news from Heaven, and that the hand of an angel could write nothing but terror to him. He that knew himself liable to the justice of God immediately concluded this to be an arrest in his name, a summons to appear before him. Note, God can soon awaken the most secure and make the heart of the stoutest sinner to tremble; and there needs no more to do it than to let loose his own thoughts upon him; they will soon play the tyrant, and give him trouble enough. 3. The wise men of Babylon are immediately called in, to see what they can make of this writing upon the wall, *v.* 7. The king *cried aloud,* as one in haste, as one in earnest, to bring the whole college of magicians, to try if they can *read this writing,* and *show the interpretation of it;* for the king and all his lords cannot pretend to it, it is out of their sphere. The study of divine revelation (such as they had, or thought they had) and converse with the world of spirits were by the heathen confined to one profession, and no other meddled with it; but what is written to us by the finger of God is legible to all; whoever will may read the mind of God in the scriptures. To engage these wise men to exert the utmost of their skill in this matter, and provoke them to an emulation in the attempt, he promised that whoever would give him a satisfactory account of this writing should be dignified with the highest honours of the court. He knew what these pretenders to wisdom aimed at, and what would please them, and therefore promised them a *scarlet robe* and a *gold chain*, glorious things in the eyes of those that know no better. Nay, he should be *primus par regni — chief minister of state, the third ruler* in the kingdom, next to the king and his heir apparent. 4. The king is disappointed in his expectations from them; they can none of them *read the writing*, much less interpret it (*v.* 8), which increases the king's confusion, *v.* 9. He likes the thing yet worse and worse, and fears that mischief is towards him. *His lords* also, that had been partners with him in his jollity, are now sharers with him in his terrors; they also were *astonished* at their wits' end; and neither their numbers nor their refreshment by wine would serve to keep up their spirits. The reason why the wise men could not read the writing was not because it was written in any language or characters unknown to them, but God either cast a mist before their eyes or put such confusion upon their spirits that they could not read it, that the honour of expounding this mystical writing might be reserved for Daniel. Note, The terror of an awakened convinced conscience may justly be increased by the utter insufficiency of all creatures to give it ease or satisfaction.

Verses 10–29

Here is, I. The information given to the king, by the queen-mother, concerning Daniel, how fit he was to be consulted in this difficult case. It is supposed that this queen was the widow of Evil-Merodach, and was that famous Nitocris whom Herodotus mentions as a woman of extraordinary prudence. She was not present at the feast, as the king's *wives and concubines were* (*v.* 2); it was not agreeable to her age and gravity to keep a merry night. But, tidings of the fright which the king and his lords were put into being brought to her apartment, she came herself to the banqueting-house, to recommend to the king a physician for his melancholy. She entreated him not to be discouraged by the insufficiency of his wise men to solve this riddle, for that there was *a man in his kingdom* that had more than once helped his grandfather at such a dead lift, and, no doubt, could help him, *v.* 11, 12. She could not undertake to read the writing herself, but directed him to one that could; let *Daniel be called* now, who should have been called first. Now observe, 1. The high character she gives of Daniel: He is a *man in whom is the spirit of the holy gods*, who has something in him more than human, not only the *spirit of a man*, which, in all, is the *candle of the Lord*, but a divine spirit. According to the language of her country and religion, she could not give a higher encomium of any man; she speaks honourably of him as a man that had, (1.) An admirably good head: *Light, and understanding, and wisdom, like the wisdom of the gods, were found in him.* Such an insight had he into things secret, and such a foresight of things to come, that it was evident he was divinely inspired; he had *knowledge* and *understanding* beyond all the other wise men for *interpreting dreams*, explaining enigmas or hard sentences, untying knots, and resolving doubts. Solomon had a wonderful sagacity of this kind; but it should seem that in these things Daniel had more of an immediate divine direction. *Behold, a greater than Solomon* himself *is here.* Yet what was the wisdom of them both compared with the treasures of wisdom hidden in Christ? (2.) He had an admirably good heart: *An excellent spirit was found in him*, which was a great ornament to his wisdom and knowledge, and qualified him to receive that gift; for God *gives to a man that is good in his sight wisdom, and knowledge, and joy.* He was of a humble, holy, heavenly spirit, had a devout and gracious spirit, a spirit of zeal for the glory of God and the good of men. This was indeed an excellent spirit. 2. The account she gives of the respect that Nebuchadnezzar had for him; he was much in his favour, and was preferred by him: "*The king thy father*" (that is, thy grandfather, but even to many generations Nebuchadnezzar might well be called the father of that royal family, for he it was that raised it to such a pitch of grandeur), "*the king, I say, thy father, made him master of the magicians.*" Perhaps Belshazzar had sometimes, in his pride, spoken slightly of Nebuchadnezzar, and his politics, and the methods of his government, and the ministers he employed, and thought himself wiser than he; and therefore his mother

harps upon that. "*The king,* I say, *thy father*, to whose good management all thou hast owing, he pronounced him chief of, and gave him dominion over, all the wise men of Babylon, and *named him Belteshazzar*, according to the name of his god, thinking thereby to put honour upon him;" but Daniel, by constantly making use of his Jewish name himself (which he resolved to keep, in token of his faithful adherence to his religion), had worn out that name; only the queen-dowager remembered it, otherwise he was generally called *Daniel.* Note, It is a very good office to revive the remembrance of the good services of worthy men, who are themselves modest, and willing that they should be forgotten. 3. The motion she makes concerning him: *Let Daniel be called, and he will show the interpretation.* By this it appears that Daniel was now forgotten at court. Belshazzar was a stranger to him, knew not that he had such a jewel in his kingdom. With the new king there came in a new ministry, and the old one was laid aside. Note, There are a great many valuable men, and such as might be made very useful, that lie long buried in obscurity, and some that have done eminent services that live to be overlooked and taken no notice of; but, whatever men are, God is not unrighteous to forget the services done to his kingdom. Daniel, being turned out of his place, lived privately, and sought not any opportunity to come into notice again; yet he lived near the court and within call, though Babylon was now besieged, that he might be ready, if there were occasion, to do any good office, by what interest he had among the great ones, for the children of his people. But Providence so ordered it that now, just at the fall of that monarchy, he should by the queen's means be brought to court again, that he might lie there ready for preferment in the ensuing government. Thus do *the righteous shine forth out of obscurity*, and *before honour is humility.*

II. The introducing of Daniel to the king, and his request to him to read and expound the writing. Daniel was *brought in before the king, v.* 13. He was now nearly ninety years of age, so that his years, and honours, and former preferments, might have entitled him to a free admission into the king's presence; yet he was willing to be conducted in, as a stranger, by the master of the ceremonies. Note, 1. The king asks, with an air of haughtiness: *Art thou that Daniel who art of the children of the captivity?* Being a Jew, and a captive, he was loth to be beholden to him if he could help it. 2. He tells him what an encomium he had heard of him (*v.* 14), *that the spirit of the gods was in him;* and he had sent for him to try whether he deserved so high a character or no. 3. He acknowledges that all the wise men of Babylon were baffled; they could not *read this writing*, nor *show the interpretation, v.* 16. But, 4. He promises him the same rewards that he had promised them if he would do it, *v.* 16. It was strange that the magicians, when now, and in Nebuchadnezzar's time, once and again, they were nonplussed, did not attempt something to save their credit; if they had with a good assurance said, "This is the meaning of such a dream, such a writing," who could disprove them? But God so ordered it that they had nothing at all to say, as, when Christ was born, the heathen oracles were struck dumb.

III. The interpretation which Daniel gave of these mystic characters, which was so far from easing the king of his fears that we may suppose it increased them rather. Daniel was now in years, and Belshazzar was young; and therefore he seems to take a greater liberty of dealing plainly and roundly with him than he had done upon the like occasions with Nebuchadnezzar. In reproving any man, especially great men, there is need of wisdom to consider all circumstances; for they are *the reproofs of instruction* that are *the way of life.* In Daniel's discourse here,

1. He undertakes to read the writing which gave them this alarm, and to show them the interpretation of it, *v.* 17. He slights the offer he made him of rewards, is not pleased that it was mentioned, for he is not one of those that *divine for money;* what gratuities Nebuchadnezzar gave him afterwards he gladly accepted, but he scorned to bargain for them, or to read the *writing to the king* for and in consideration of such and such honours promised him. No: "*Let thy gifts be to thyself,* for they will not be long thine, and *give thy fee to another,* to any of the wise men whom thou wouldst have most wished to earn it; I value it not." Daniel sees his kingdom now at its last gasp, and therefore looks with contempt upon his gifts and rewards. And

thus should we despise all the gifts and rewards that this world can give did we see, as we may by faith, its final period hastening on. Let it give its perishing gifts to another; there are better gifts which we have our eyes and hearts upon; but let us do our duty in the world, do it all the real service we can, read God's writing to it in a profession of religion, and by an agreeable conversation make known the interpretation of it, and then trust God for his gifts, his rewards, in comparison with which all the world can give is mere trash and trifles.

2. He largely recounts to the king God's dealings with his father Nebuchadnezzar, which were intended for instruction and warning to him, *v.* 18, 21. This is not intended for a flourish or an amusement, but is a necessary preliminary to the interpretation of the writing. Note, That we may understand aright what God is doing with us, it is of use to us to review what he has done with others.

(1.) He describes the great dignity and power to which the divine Providence had advanced Nebuchadnezzar, *v.* 18, 19. He had *a kingdom, and majesty, and glory, and honour*, for aught we know, above what any heathen prince ever had before him; he thought that he got his glory by his own extraordinary conduct and courage, and ascribed his successes to a projecting active genius of his own; but Daniel tells him who now enjoyed what he had laboured for that it was the *most high God, the God of gods and Lord of kings* (as Nebuchadnezzar himself had called him), that gave him *that kingdom*, that vast dominion, that majesty wherewith he presided in the affairs of it, and that *glory and honour* which by his prosperous management he acquired. Note, Whatever degree of outward prosperity any arrive at, they must own that it is of God's giving, not their own getting. Let it never be said, *My might*, and *the power of my hand, have gotten me this wealth*, this preferment; but let it always be remembered that it is *God that gives men power to get wealth*, and gives success to their endeavours. Now the power which God gave to Nebuchadnezzar is here described to be very great in respect both of ability and of authority. [1.] His ability was so strong that it was irresistible; such was the majesty that God gave him, so numerous were the forces he had at command, and such an admirable dexterity he had at commanding them, that, which way soever his sword turned, it prospered. He could captivate and subdue nations by threatening them, without striking a stroke, for *all people trembled and feared before him*, and would compound with him for their lives upon any terms. See what force is, and what the fear of it does. It is that by which the brutal part of the world, even of the world of mankind, both governs and is governed. [2.] His authority was so absolute that it was uncontrollable. The power which was allowed him, which descended upon him, or which, at least, he assumed, was without contradiction, was absolute and despotic, none shared with him either in the legislative or in the executive part of it. In dispensing punishments he condemned or acquitted at pleasure: *Whom he would he slew, and whom he would he saved alive*, though both were equally innocent or equally guilty. The *jus vitae et necis — the power of life and death* was entirely in his hand. In dispensing rewards he granted or denied preferment at pleasure: *Whom he would he set up, and whom he would he put down*, merely for a humour, and without giving a reason so much as to himself; but it is all *ex mero motu — of his own good pleasure*, and *stat pro ratione voluntas — his will stands for a reason.* Such was the constitution of the eastern monarchies, such the manner of their kings.

(2.) He sets before him the sins which Nebuchadnezzar had been guilty of, whereby he had provoked God against him. [1.] He behaved insultingly towards those that were under him, and grew tyrannical and oppressive. The description given of his power intimates his abuse of his power, and that he was directed in what he did by humour and passion, not by reason and equity; so that he often condemned the innocent and acquitted the guilty, both which are an *abomination to the Lord.* He deposed men of merit and preferred unworthy men, to the great detriment of the public, and for this he was accountable to the most high God, that gave him his power. Note, It is a very hard and rare thing for men to have an absolute arbitrary power, and not to make an ill use of it. Camden has a distich of Giraldus, wherein he speaks of it as a rare instance, concerning our king Henry II of England, that never any man had so much power and did so little hurt with it.

> Glorior hoc uno, quod nunquam vidimus unum,
> Nec potuisse magis, nec nocuisse minus —
> Of him I can say, exulting, that with the same power
> to do harm no one was ever more inoffensive.

But that was not all. [2.] He behaved insolently towards the God above him, and grew proud and haughty (*v.* 20): *His heart was lifted up,* and there his sin and ruin began; his *mind was hardened* in pride, hardened against the commands of God and his judgments; he was willful and obstinate, and neither the word of God nor his rod made any lasting impression upon him. Note, Pride is a sin that hardens the heart in all other sin and renders the means of repentance and reformation ineffectual.

(3.) He reminds him of the judgments of God that were brought upon him for his pride and obstinacy, how he was deprived of his reason, and so *deposed from his kingly throne* (*v.* 20), *driven from among men,* to *dwell with the wild asses, v.* 21. He that would not govern his subjects by rules of reason had not reason sufficient for the government himself. Note, Justly does God deprive men of their reason when they become unreasonable and will not use it, and of their power when they become oppressive and use it ill. He continued like a brute till *he knew* and embraced that first principle of religion, *That the most high God rules.* And it is rather by religion than reason that man is distinguished from, and dignified above, the beasts; and it is more his honour to be a subject to the supreme Creator than to be lord of the inferior creatures. Note, Kings must know, or shall be made to know, that the most high God rules in their kingdoms (that is an *imperium in imperio — an empire within an empire,* not to be excepted against), and that he appoints over them whomsoever he will. As he makes heirs, so he makes princes.

3. In God's name, he exhibits articles of impeachment against Belshazzar. Before he reads him his doom, from the hand-writing on the wall, he shows him his crime, that God may be *justified when he speaks, and clear when he judges.* Now that which he lays to his charge is, (1.) That he had not taken warning by the judgments of God upon his father (*v.* 22): *Thou his son, O Belshazzar! hast not humbled thy heart, though thou knewest all this.* Note, It is a great offence to God if our hearts be not humbled before him to comply both with his precepts and with his providences, humbled by repentance, obedience, and patience; nay, he expects from the greatest of men that their hearts should be humbled before him, by an acknowledgment that, great as they are, to him they are accountable. And it is a great aggravation of the unhumbledness of our hearts when we know enough to humble them but do not consider and improve it, particularly when we know how others have been broken that would not bend, how others have fallen that would not stoop, and yet we continue stiff and inflexible. It makes the sin of children the more heinous if they tread in the steps of their parents' wickedness, though they have seen how dearly it has cost them, and how pernicious the consequences of it have been. Do we know this, do we know all this, and yet are we not humbled? (2.) That he had affronted God more impudently than Nebuchadnezzar himself had done, witness the revels of this very night, in the midst of which he was seized with this horror (*v.* 23): *"Thou hast lifted up thyself against the Lord of heaven,* hast swelled with rage against him, and taken up arms against his crown and dignity, in this particular instance, that thou hast profaned the *vessels of his house,* and made the utensils of his sanctuary instruments of thy iniquity, and, in an actual designed contempt of him, hast *praised the gods of silver and gold, which see not, nor hear, nor know* anything, as if they were to be preferred before the God that sees, and hears, and knows every thing." Sinners that are resolved to go on in sin are well enough pleased with gods that *neither see, nor hear, nor know,* for then they may sin securely; but they will find, to their confusion, that though those are the gods they choose those are not the gods they must be judged by, but one to whom *all things are naked and open.* (3.) That he had not answered the end of his creation and maintenance: *The God in whose hand thy breath is, and whose are all thy ways, hast thou not glorified.* This is a general charge, which stands good against us all; let us consider how we shall answer it. Observe, [1.] Our dependence upon God as our creator, preserver, benefactor, owner, and ruler; not only from his hand our breath was at first, but *in his hand our breath is* still; it is he that *holds our souls in life,* and, if he *take away our breath, we die.* Our times being *in his hand,* so is our breath, by which our times are measured. *In him we live, and move, and have our being;* we live by him, live upon him, and cannot live without him. *The way of man is not in himself,* not at his own command, at his own disposal, *but his are all our ways;* for our hearts are in his hand, and so are the hearts of all men, even of kings, who seem to act most as free-agents. [2.] Our duty to God, in consideration of this dependence; we ought to glorify him, to devote ourselves to his honour and employ ourselves in his service, to make it our care to please him and our business to praise him. [3.] Our default in this duty, notwithstanding that dependence; we have not done it; for we have *all sinned, and come short of the glory of God.* This is the indictment against Belshazzar; there needs no proof, it is made good by the notorious evidence of the fact, and his own conscience cannot but plead guilty to it. And therefore,

4. He now proceeds to read the sentence, as he found it *written upon the wall: "Then"* (says Daniel) "when thou hast come to such a height of impiety as thus to trample upon the most sacred things, *then* when thou wast in the midst of thy sacrilegious idolatrous feast, then was *the part of the hand,* the writing fingers, sent *from him,* from that God whom thou didst so daringly affront, and who had borne so long with thee, but would bear no longer; he *sent them,* and *this writing,* thou now seest, *was written, v.* 24. It is he that now *writes bitter things against thee,* and *makes thee to possess thy iniquities,"* Job 13:26. Note, As the sin of sinners is written in the book of God's omniscience, so the doom of sinners is written in the book of God's law; and the day is coming when those *books shall be opened,* and they shall be judged by them. Now the writing was, *Mene, Mene, Tekel, Upharsin, v.* 25. It is well that we have an authentic exposition of these words annexed, else we could make little of them, so concise are they; the signification of them is, *He has numbered, he has weighed, and they divide.* The Chaldean wise men, because they knew not that there is but one God only, could not understand who this *He* should be, and for that reason (some think) the writing puzzled them. (1.) *Mene;* that is repeated, for the thing is certain — *Mene, mene;* that signifies, both in Hebrew and Chaldee, *He has numbered and finished,* which Daniel explains thus (*v.* 26): *"God has numbered thy kingdom,* the years and days of the continuance of it; these were numbered in the counsel of God, and now they are finished; the term has expired for and during which thou wast to hold it, and now it must be surrendered. Here is an end of thy kingdom." (2.) *Tekel;* that signifies, in Chaldee, *Thou art weighed,* and, in Hebrew, *Thou art too light.* So Dr. Lightfoot. For this king and his actions are weighed in the just and unerring balances of divine equity. God does as perfectly know his true character as the goldsmith knows the weight of that which he has weighed in the nicest scales. God does not give judgment against him till he has first pondered his actions, and considered the merits of his case. "But thou art *found wanting,* unworthy to have such a trust lodged in thee, a vain, light, empty man, a man of no weight or consideration." (3.) *Upharsin,* which should be rendered, *and Pharsin,* or *Peres. Parsin,* in Hebrew, signifies the *Persians; Paresin,* in Chaldee, signifies *dividing;* Daniel puts both together (*v.* 28): *"Thy kingdom is divided,* is rent from thee, and *given to the Medes and Persians,* as a prey to be divided among them." Now this may, without any force, be applied to the doom of sinners. *Mene, Tekel, Peres,* may easily be made to signify *death, judgment,* and *hell.* At death, the sinner's days are *numbered* and *finished;* after death the judgment, when he will be *weighed in the balance and found wanting;* and after judgment the sinner will be *cut asunder,* and given as a prey to the devil and his angels. Daniel does not here give Belshazzar such advice and encouragement to repent as he had given Nebuchadnezzar, because he saw the decree had gone forth and he would not be allowed any space to repent.

One would have thought that Belshazzar would be exasperated against Daniel, and, seeing his own case desperate, would be in a rage against him. But he was so far convicted by his own conscience of the reasonableness of all he said that he objected nothing against it; but, on the contrary, gave Daniel the reward he promised him, put on him the *scarlet gown* and the *gold chain,* and proclaimed him the *third ruler in the kingdom* (*v.* 29), because he would be as good as his word, and because it was not Daniel's fault if the exposition of the hand-writing was not such as he desired. Note, Many show great respect to God's prophets who yet have no regard to his word. Daniel did not value these titles and ensigns of honour, yet would not refuse them, because they were tokens of his prince's goodwill: but we have reason to think that he received them with a smile, foreseeing how soon they would all wither with him that bestowed them. They were like Jonah's gourd, which came up in a night and perished in a night, and therefore it was folly for him to be *exceedingly glad* of them.

Verses 30–31

Here is, 1. The death of the king. Reason enough he had to tremble, for he was just falling into the hands of the *king of terrors, v.* 30. *In that night,* when his heart was merry with wine, the besiegers broke into the city, aimed at the palace; there they found the king, and gave him his death's wound. He could not find any place so secret as to conceal him, or so strong as to protect him. Heathen writers speak of Cyrus's taking Babylon by surprise, with the assistance of two deserters that showed him the best way into the city. And it was foretold what a consternation it would be to the court, Jer. 51:11, 39. Note, Death comes as a snare upon those whose hearts are overcharged with surfeiting and drunkenness. 2. The transferring of the kingdom into other hands. From the head of gold we now descend to the breast and arms of silver. *Darius the Mede took the kingdom* in partnership with, and by the consent of, Cyrus, who had conquered it, *v.* 31. They were partners in war and conquest, and so they were in dominion, *ch.* 6:28. Notice is taken of his age, that he was now sixty-two years old, for which reason Cyrus, who was his nephew, gave him the precedency. Some observe that being now sixty-two years old, in the last year of the captivity, he was born in the eighth year of it, and that was the year when Jeconiah was carried captive and all the nobles, etc. See 2 Ki. 24:13–15. Just at that time when the most fatal stroke was given was a prince born that in process of time should avenge Jerusalem upon Babylon, and heal the wound that was now given. Thus deep are the counsels of God concerning his people, thus kind are his designs towards them.

CHAPTER 6

Daniel does not give a continued history of the reigns in which he lived, nor of the state-affairs of the kingdoms of Chaldea and Persia, though he was himself a great man in those affairs; for what are those to us? But he selects such particular passages of story as serve for the confirming of our faith in God and the encouraging of our obedience to him, for the things written aforetime were written for our learning. It is a very observable improvable story that we have in this chapter, how Daniel by faith "stopped the mouths of lions," and so "obtained a good report," Heb. 11:33. The three children were cast into the fiery furnace for not committing a known sin, Daniel was cast into the lions' den for not omitting a known duty, and God's miraculously delivering both them and him is left upon record for the encouragement of his servants in all ages to be resolute and constant both in their abhorrence of that which is evil and in their adherence to that which is good, whatever it cost them. In this chapter we have, I. Daniel's preferment in the court of Darius (*v.* 1–3). II. The envy and malice of his enemies against him (*v.* 4, 5). III. The decree they obtained against prayer for thirty days (*v.* 6–9). IV. Daniel's continuance and constancy in prayer, notwithstanding that decree (*v.* 10). V. Information given against him for it, and the casting of him into the den of lions (*v.* 11–17). VI. His miraculous preservation in the lions' den, and deliverance out of it (*v.* 18–23). VII. The casting of his accusers into the den, and their destruction there (*v.* 24). VIII. The decree which Darius made upon this occasion, in honour of the God of Daniel, and the prosperity of Daniel afterwards (*v.* 25–28). And this God is our God for ever and ever.

Verses 1–5

We are told concerning Daniel,

I. What a *great man* he was. When Darius, upon his accession to the crown of Babylon by conquest, new-modelled the government, he made Daniel prime-minister of state, set him at the helm, and made him first commissioner both of the treasury and of the great seal. Darius's dominion was very large; all he got by his conquests and acquests was that he had so many more countries to take care of; no more can be expected from himself than what one man can do, and therefore others must be employed under him. He *set over the kingdom 120 princes* (*v.* 1), and appointed them their districts, in which they were to administer justice, preserve the public peace, and levy the king's revenue. Note, Inferior magistrates are ministers of God to us for good as well as the sovereign; and therefore we must submit ourselves both to the king as supreme and to the governors that are constituted and commissioned by him, 1 Pt. 2:13, 14. Over these princes there was a *triumvirate,* or *three presidents,* who were to take and state the public accounts, to receive appeals from the princes, or complaints against them in case of maladministration, *that the king should have no damage* (*v.* 2), that he should not sustain loss in his revenue and that the power he delegated to the princes might not be abused to the oppression of the subject, for by that the king (whether he thinks so or no) receives real damage, both as it alienates the affections of his people from him and as it provokes the displeasure of his God against him. Of these three Daniel was chief, because he was found to go beyond them all in all manner of princely qualifications. He was *preferred above the presidents and princes* (*v.* 3), and so wonderfully well pleased the king was with his management that *he thought to set him over the whole realm,* and let him place and displace at his pleasure. Now, 1. We must take notice of it to the praise of Darius that he would prefer a man thus purely for his personal merit, and his fitness for business; and those sovereigns that would be well served must go by that rule. Daniel had been a great man in the kingdom that was conquered, and for that reason, one would think, should have been looked upon as an enemy, and as such imprisoned or banished. He was a native of a foreign kingdom, and a ruined one, and upon that account might have been despised as a stranger and captive. But, Darius, it seems, was very quick-sighted in judging of men's capacities, and was soon aware that this Daniel had something extraordinary in him, and therefore, though no doubt he had creatures of his own, not a few, that expected preferment in this newly-conquered kingdom, and were gaping for it, and those that had been long his confidants would depend upon it that they should be now his presidents, yet so well did he consult the public welfare that, finding Daniel to excel them all in prudence and virtue, and probably having heard of his being divinely inspired, he made him his right hand. 2. We must take notice of it, to the glory of God, that, though Daniel was now very old (it was above seventy years since he was brought a captive to Babylon), yet he was as able as ever for business both in body and mind, and that he who had continued faithful to his religion through all the temptations of the foregoing reigns in a new government was as much respected as ever. He kept in by being an oak, not by being a willow, by a constancy in virtue, not by a pliableness to vice. Such honesty is the best policy, for it secures a reputation; and those who thus honour God he will honour.

II. What a good man he was: *An excellent spirit was in him, v.* 3. And he was faithful to every trust, dealt fairly between the sovereign and the subject, and took care that neither should be wronged, so that there was *no error,* or *fault, to be found in him, v.* 4. He was not only not chargeable with any treachery or dishonesty, but not even with any mistake or indiscretion. He never made any blunder, nor had any occasion to plead inadvertency or forgetfulness for his excuse. This is recorded for an example to all that are in places of public trust to approve themselves both careful and conscientious, that they may be free, not only from fault, but from error, not only from crime, but from mistake.

III. What ill-will was borne him, both for his greatness and for his goodness. The presidents and princes envied him because he was advanced above them, and probably hated him because he had a watchful eye upon them and took care they should not wrong the government to enrich themselves. See here, 1. The cause of envy, and that is every thing that is good. Solomon complains of it as a vexation that *for every right work a man is envied of his neighbour* (Eccl. 4:4), that the better a man is the worse he is thought of by his rivals. Daniel is envied because he has a more excellent spirit than his neighbours. 2. The effect of envy, and that is every thing that is bad. Those that envied Daniel sought no less than his ruin. His disgrace would not serve them; it was his death that they desired. *Wrath is cruel, and anger is outrageous, but who can stand before envy?* Prov. 27:4. Daniel's enemies set spies upon him, to observe him in the management of his place; they *sought to find occasion against him,* something on which to ground an accusation *concerning the kingdom,* some instance of neglect or partiality, some hasty word spoken, some person borne hard upon, or some necessary business overlooked. And if they could but have found the mote, the mole-hill, of a mistake, it would have been soon improved to the beam, to the mountain, of an unpardonable misdemeanour. But *they could find no occasion against* him; they owned that they could not. Daniel always acted honestly, and now the more warily, and stood the more upon his guard, *because of his observers,* Ps. 27:11. Note, We have all need to walk circumspectly, because we have many eyes upon us, and some that watch for our halting. Those especially have need to carry their cup even that have it full. They concluded, at length, that they should not find any occasion against him except *concerning the law of his God v.* 5. It seems then that Daniel kept up the profession of his religion, and held it fast without wavering or shrinking, and yet that was no bar to his preferment; there was no law that required him to be of the king's religion, or incapacitated him to bear office in the state unless he were. It was all one to the king what God he prayed to, so long as he did the business of his place faithfully and well. He was at the king's service *usque ad aras — as far as the altars;* but there he left him. In this matter therefore his enemies hoped to ensnare him. *Quaerendum est crimen laesae religionis ubi majestatis deficit — When treason could not be charged upon him he was accused of impiety.* Grotius. Note, It is an excellent thing, and much for the glory of God, when those who profess religion conduct themselves so inoffensively in their whole conversation that their most watchful spiteful enemies may find no occasion of blaming them, save only in the matters of their God, in which they walk according to their consciences. It is observable that, when Daniel's enemies could find no occasion against him concerning the kingdom, they had so much sense of justice left that they did not suborn witnesses against him to accuse him of crimes he was innocent of, and to swear treason upon him, wherein they shame many that were called Jews and are called Christians.

Verses 6–10

Daniel's adversaries could have no advantage against him from any law now in being; they therefore contrive a new law, by which they hope to ensnare him, and in a matter in which they knew they should be sure of him; and such was his fidelity to his God that they gained their point. Here is,

I. Darius's impious law. I call it *Darius's,* because he gave the royal assent to it, and otherwise it would not have been of force; but it was not properly his: he contrived it not, and was perfectly wheedled to consent to it. The presidents and princes framed the edict, brought in the bill, and by their management it was agreed to by the convention of the states, who perhaps were met at this time upon some public occasion. It is pretended that this bill which they would have to pass into a law was the result of mature deliberation, that *all the presidents of the kingdom, the governors, princes, counsellors, and captains, had consulted together* about it, and that they not only agreed to it, but *advised it,* for *divers good causes and considerations,* that they had done what they could to *establish it for a firm decree;* nay, they intimate to the king that it was carried *nemine contradicente — unanimously: "All the presidents* are of this mind;" and yet we are sure that Daniel, the chief of the three presidents, did not agree to it, and have reason to think that many more of the princes excepted against it as absurd and unreasonable. Note, It is no new thing for that to be represented, and with great assurance too, as the sense of the nation, which is far from being so; and that which few approve of is sometimes confidently said to be that which all agree to. But, O the infelicity of kings, who, being under a necessity of seeing and hearing with other people's eyes and ears, are often wretchedly imposed upon! These designing men, under colour of doing honour to the king, but really intending the ruin of his favourite, press him to pass this into a law, and make it a royal statute, that *whosoever shall ask a petition of any god or man for thirty days, save of the king, shall be* put to death after the most barbarous manner, shall be *cast into the den of lions, v.* 7. This is the bill they have been hatching, and they lay it before the king to be signed and passed into a law. Now, 1. There is nothing in it that has the least appearance of good, but that it magnifies the king, and makes him seem both very great and very kind to his subjects, which, they suggest, will be of good service to him now that he has newly come to his throne, and will confirm his interests. All men must be made to believe that the king is so rich, and withal so ready to all petitioners, that none in any want or distress need to apply either to God or man for relief, but to him only. And for thirty days together he will be ready to give audience to all that have any petition to present to him. It is indeed much for the honour of kings to be benefactors to their subjects and to have their ears open to their complaints and requests; but if they pretend to be their sole benefactors, and undertake to be to them instead of God, and challenge that respect from them which is due to God only, it is their disgrace, and not their honour. But, 2. There is a great deal in it that is apparently evil. It is bad enough to forbid asking a petition of any man. Must not a beggar ask an alms, or one neighbour beg a kindness of another? If the child want bread, must he not ask it of his parents, or be cast into the den of lions if he do? Nay, those that have business with the king, may they not petition those about him to introduce them? But it was much worse, and an impudent affront to all religion, to forbid asking a petition *of any god.* It is by prayer that we give glory to God, fetch in mercy from God; and so keep up our communion with God; and to interdict prayer for thirty days is for so long to rob God of all the tribute he has from man and to rob man of all the comfort he has in God. When the light of nature teaches us that the providence of God has the ordering and disposing of all our affairs does not the law of nature oblige us by prayer to acknowledge God and seek to him? Does not every man's heart direct him, when he is in want or distress, to call upon God, and must this be made high treason? We could not live a day without God; and can men live thirty days without prayer? Will the king himself be tied up for so long from praying to God; or, if it be allowed him, will he undertake to do it for all his subjects? Did ever any nation thus slight their gods? But see what absurdities malice will drive men to. Rather than not bring Daniel into trouble for praying to his God, they will deny themselves and all their friends the satisfaction of praying to theirs. Had they proposed only to prohibit the Jews from praying to their God, Daniel would have been as effectually ensnared; but they knew the king would not pass such a law, and therefore made it thus general. And the king, puffed up with a fancy that this would set him up as a little god, was fond of the *feather in his cap* (for so it was, and not a *flower in his crown)* and *signed the writing and the decree* (*v.* 9), which, being once done, according to the constitution of the united kingdom of the Medes and Persians, was not upon any pretence whatsoever to be altered or dispensed with, or the breach of it pardoned.

II. Daniel's pious disobedience to this law, *v.* 10. He did not retire into the country, nor abscond for some time, though he knew the law was levelled against him; but, because he knew it was so, therefore he stood his ground, knowing that he had now a fair opportunity of honouring God before men, and showing that he preferred his favour, and his duty to him, before life itself. *When Daniel knew that the writing was signed* he might have gone to the king, and expostulated with him about it; nay, he might have remonstrated against it, as grounded upon a misinformation that *all the presidents* had consented to it, whereas he that was chief of them had never been consulted about it; but *he went to his house,* and applied himself to his duty, cheerfully trusting God with the event. Now observe,

1. Daniel's constant practice, which we were not informed of before this occasion, but which we have reason to think was the general practice of the pious Jews. (1.) He *prayed in his house,* sometimes alone and sometimes with his family about him, and made a solemn business of it. Cornelius was a man that *prayed in his house,* Acts 10:30. Note, Every house not only may be, but ought to be, a house of prayer; where we have a tent God must have

an alter, and on it we must offer spiritual sacrifices. (2.) In every prayer he gave thanks. When we pray to God for the mercies we want we must praise him for those we have received. Thanksgiving must be a part of every prayer. (3.) In his prayer and thanksgiving he had an eye to God as his God, his in covenant, and set himself as in his presence. He did this *before his God,* and with a regard to him. (4.) When he prayed and gave thanks he *kneeled upon his knees,* which is the most proper gesture in prayer, and most expressive of humility, and reverence, and submission to God. Kneeling is a begging posture, and we come to God as beggars, beggars for our lives, whom it concerns to be importunate. (5.) He *opened the windows of his chamber,* that the sight of the visible heavens might affect his heart with an awe of that God who dwells above the heavens; but that was not all: he *opened them towards Jerusalem,* the holy city, though now in ruins, to signify the affection he had for its very stones and dust (Ps. 102:14) and the remembrance he had of its concerns daily in his prayers. Thus, though he himself lived great in Babylon, yet he testified his concurrence with the meanest of his brethren the captives, in remembering Jerusalem and preferring it before his *chief joy,* Ps. 137:5, 6. Jerusalem was the place which God had chosen to put his name there; and, when the temple was dedicated, Solomon's prayer to God was that if his people should *in the land of their enemies* pray unto him with their eye towards the land which he gave them, and the city he had chosen, and the house which was built to his name, then he would *hear* and *maintain their cause* (1 Ki. 8:48, 49), to which prayer Daniel had reference in this circumstance of his devotions. (6.) He did this *three times a day,* three times every day according to the example of David (Ps. 55:17), *Morning, evening, and at noon, I will pray.* It is good to have our hours of prayer, not to bind, but to remind conscience; and, if we think our bodies require refreshment by food thrice a day, can we think seldomer will serve our souls? This is surely as little as may be to answer the command of *praying always.* (7.) He did this so openly and avowedly that all who knew him knew it to be his practice; and he thus showed it, not because he was proud of it (in the place where he was there was no room for that temptation, for it was not reputation, but reproach, that attended it), but because he was not ashamed of it. Though Daniel was a great man, he did not think it below him to be thrice a day upon his knees before his Maker and to be his own chaplain; though he was an old man, he did not think himself past it; nor, though it had been his practice from his youth up, was he weary of this well doing. Though he was a man of business, vast business, for the service of the public, he did not think that would excuse him from the daily exercises of devotion. How inexcusable then are those who have but little to do in the world, and yet will not do thus much for God and their souls! Daniel was a man famous for prayer, and for success in it (Eze. 14:14), and he came to be so by thus making a conscience of prayer and making a business of it daily; and in thus doing God blessed him wonderfully.

2. Daniel's constant adherence to this practice, even when it was made by the law a capital crime. When he knew that *the writing was signed* he continued to do *as he did aforetime,* and altered not one circumstance of the performance. Many a man, yea, and many a good man, would have thought it prudence to omit it for these thirty days, when he could not do it without hazard of his life; he might have prayed so much oftener when those days had expired and the danger was over, or he might have performed the duty at another time, and in another place, so secretly that it should not be possible for his enemies to discover it; and so he might both satisfy his conscience and keep up his communion with God, and yet avoid the law, and continue in his usefulness. But, if he had done so, it would have been thought, both by his friends and by his enemies, that he had thrown up the duty for this time, through cowardice and base fear, which would have tended very much to the dishonour of God and the discouragement of his friends. Others who moved in a lower sphere might well enough act with caution; but Daniel, who had so many eyes upon him, must act with courage; and the rather because he knew that the law, when it was made, was particularly levelled against him. Note, We must not omit duty for fear of suffering, so, nor so much as *seems to come short* of it. In trying times great stress is laid upon our *confessing Christ before men* (Mt. 10:32), and we must take heed lest, under pretence of discretion, we be found guilty of cowardice in the cause of God. If we do not think that this example of Daniel obliges us to do likewise, yet I am sure it forbids us to censure those that do, for God owned him in it. By his constancy to his duty it now appears that he had never been used to admit any excuse for the omission of it; for, if ever any excuse would serve to put it by, this would have served now, (1.) That it was forbidden by the king his master, and in honour of the king too; but it is an undoubted maxim, in answer to that, We are to obey God rather than men. (2.) That it would be the loss of his life, but it is an undoubted maxim, in answer to that, Those who throw away their souls (as those certainly do that live without prayer) to save their lives make but a bad bargain for themselves; and though herein they make themselves, like the king of Tyre, *wiser than Daniel,* at their end they will be fools.

Verses 11–17

Here is 1. Proof made of Daniel's praying to his God, notwithstanding the late edict to the contrary (*v.* 11): *These men assembled;* the *came tumultuously together,* so the word is, the same that was used *v.* 6, borrowed from Ps. 2:1, *Why do the heathen rage?* They came together to visit Daniel, perhaps under pretence of business, at that time which they knew to be his usual hour of devotion; and, if they had not found him so engaged, they would have upbraided him with his faint-heartedness and distrust of his God, but (which they rather wished to do) they *found him on his knees praying* and *making supplication before his God. For his love they are his adversaries;* but, like his father David, he *gives himself unto prayer,* Ps. 109:4. 2. Complaint made of it to the king. When they had found occasion against Daniel concerning *the law of his God* they lost no time, but applied to the king (*v.* 12), and having appealed to his whether there was not such a law made, and gained from him a recognition of it, and that it was so ratified that it might not be altered, they proceeded to accuse Daniel, *v.* 13. They so describe him, in the information they give, as to exasperate the king and incense him the more against him: "He is *of the children of the captivity of Judah;* he is of Judah, that despicable people, and now a captive in a despicable state, that can call nothing his own but what he has by the king's favour, and yet *he regards not thee, O king! nor the decree that thou hast signed.*" Note, It is no new thing for that which is done faithfully, in the conscience towards God, to be misrepresented as done obstinately and in contempt of the civil powers, that is, for the best saints to be reproached as the worst men. Daniel regarded God, and therefore prayed, and we have reason to think prayed for the king and his government, yet this is construed as not regarding the king. That excellent spirit which Daniel was endued with, and that established reputation which he had gained, could not protect him from these poisonous darts. They do not say, He makes his petition to his God, lest Darius should take notice of that to his praise, but only, *He makes his petition,* which is the thing the law forbids. 3. The great concern the king was in hereupon. He now perceived that, whatever they pretended, it was not to honour him, but in spite to Daniel, that they had proposed that law, and now he is *sorely displeased with himself* for gratifying them in it, *v.* 14. Note, When men indulge a proud vain-glorious humour, and please themselves with that which feeds it, they know not what vexations they are preparing for themselves; their flatterers may prove their tormentors, and are but *spreading a net for their feet.* Now, the king *sets his heart to deliver Daniel;* both by argument and by authority he labours *till the going down of the sun* to *deliver him,* that is, to persuade his accusers not to insist upon his prosecution. Note, We often do that, through inconsideration, which afterwards we see cause a thousand times to wish undone again, which is a good reason why we should *ponder the path of our feet,* for then *all our ways will be established.* 4. The violence with which the prosecutors demanded judgment, *v.* 15. We are not told what Daniel said; the king himself is his advocate, he needs not plead his own cause, but silently commits himself and it to him that judges righteously. But the prosecutors insist upon it that the law must have its course; it is a fundamental maxim in the constitution of the government of the Medes and Persians, which had now become the universal monarchy, that *no decree or statute which the king establishes may be changed.* The same we find Esth. 1:19; 8:8. The Chaldeans magnified the will of their king, by giving him a power to make and unmake laws at his pleasure, to slay and keep alive whom he would. The Persians magnified the wisdom of their king, by supposing that whatever law he solemnly ratified it was so well made that there could be no occasion to alter it, or dispense with it, as if any human foresight could, in framing a law, guard against all inconveniences. But, if this maxim be duly applied to Daniel's case (as I am apt to think it is not, but perverted), while it honours the king's legislative power it hampers his executive power, and incapacitates him to show that mercy which upholds the throne, and to pass acts of indemnity, which are the glories of a reign. Those who allow not the sovereign's power to dispense with a disabling statute, yet never question his power to pardon an offence against a penal statute. But Darius is denied this power. See what need we have to pray for princes that God would give them wisdom, for they are often embarrassed with great difficulties, even the wisest and best are. 5. The executing of the law upon Daniel. The king himself, with the utmost reluctance, and against his conscience, signs the warrant for his execution; and Daniel, that venerable grave man, who carried such a mixture of majesty and sweetness in his countenance, who had so often looked great upon the bench, and at the council-board, and greater upon his knees, who had power with God and man, and had prevailed, is brought, purely for worshipping his God, as if he had been one of the vilest of malefactors, and *thrown into the den of lions,* to be devoured by them, *v.* 16. One cannot think of it without the utmost compassion to the gracious sufferer and the utmost indignation at the malicious prosecutors. To make sure work, the stone *laid upon the mouth of the den* is *sealed,* and the king (an over-easy man) is persuaded to seal it *with his own signet* (*v.* 17), that unhappy signet with which he had confirmed the law that Daniel falls by. But his lords cannot trust him, unless they add their signets too. Thus, when Christ was buried, his adversaries *sealed the stone* that was rolled to the door of his sepulchre. 6. The encouragement which Darius gave to Daniel to trust in God: *Thy God whom thou servest continually, he will deliver thee, v.* 16. Here (1.) He justifies Daniel from guilt, owning all his crime to be serving his God continually, and continuing to do so even when it was made a crime. (2.) He leaves it to God to free him from punishment, since he could not prevail to do it: *He will deliver thee.* He is sure that his God can deliver him, for he believes him to be an almighty God, and he has reason to think he will do it, having heard of his delivering Daniel's companions in a like case from the fiery furnace, and concluding him to be always faithful to those who approve themselves faithful to him. Note, Those who serve God continually he will continually preserve, and will bear them out in his service.

Verses 18–24

Here is, I. The melancholy night which the king had, upon Daniel's account, *v.* 18. He had said, indeed, that God would deliver him out of the danger, but at the same time he could not forgive himself for throwing him into the danger; and justly might God deprive him of a friend whom he had himself used so barbarously. He *went to his palace,* vexed at himself for what he had done, and calling himself unwise and unjust for not adhering to the law of God and nature with a *non obstante — a negative* to the law of the Medes and Persians. He ate no supper, but *passed the night fasting;* his heart was already full of grief and fear. He forbade the music; nothing is more unpleasing that songs sung to a heavy heart. He went to bed, but got no sleep, was full of *tossings to and fro* till the dawning of the day. Note, the best way to have a good night is to keep a good conscience, then we may lie down in peace.

II. The solicitous enquiry he made concerning Daniel the next morning, *v.* 19, 20. He was up early, *very early;* for how could he lie in bed when he could not sleep for dreaming of Daniel, nor lie awake quietly for thinking of him? And he was no sooner up than he *went in haste to the den of lions,* for he could not satisfy himself to send a servant (that would not sufficiently testify his affection for Daniel), nor had he patience to stay so long as till a servant would return. When he comes to the den, not without some hopes that God had graciously undone what he had wickedly done, he cries, *with a lamentable voice,* as one full of concern and trouble, *O Daniel!* art thou alive? He longs to know, yet trembles to ask the question, fearing to be answered with the roaring of the lions after more prey: *O Daniel! servant of the living God,* has *thy God whom thou servest* made it to appear that he is *able to deliver thee from the lions?* If he rightly understood himself when he called him *the living God,* he could not doubt of his ability to keep Daniel alive, for he that has life in himself quickens whom he will; but has he thought fit in this case to exert his power? What he doubted of we are sure of, that the *servants of the living God* have a Master who is well able to protect them and bear them out in his service.

III. The joyful news he meets with — that Daniel is alive, is safe, and well, and unhurt in the lions' den, *v.* 21, 22. Daniel knew the king's voice, though it was now a lamentable voice, and spoke to him with all the deference and respect that were due to him: *O king! live for ever.* He does not reproach him for his unkindness to him, and his easiness in yielding to the malice of his persecutors; but, to show that he has heartily forgiven him, he meets him with his good wishes. Note, We should not upbraid those with the diskindnesses they have done us who, we know, did them with reluctance, and are very ready to upbraid themselves with them. The account Daniel gives the king is very pleasant; it is triumphant. 1. God has preserved his life by a miracle. Darius had called him Daniel's god *(thy God whom thou servest),* to which Daniel does as it were echo back, Yea, he is *my God,* whom I own, and who owns me, for *he has sent his angel.* The same bright and glorious being that was seen in *the form of the Son of God* with the three children in the fiery furnace had visited Daniel, and, it is likely, in a visible appearance had enlightened the dark den, and kept Daniel company all night, and had *shut the lions' mouths, that they* had not in the least *hurt him.* The angel's presence made even the lions' den his strong-hold, his palace, his paradise; he had never had a better night in his life. See the power of God over the fiercest creatures, and believe his power to restrain the roaring lion that *goes about continually seeking to devour* from hurting those that are his. See the care God takes of his faithful worshippers, especially when he calls them out to suffer for him. If he keeps their souls from sin, comforts their souls with his peace, and receives their souls to himself, he does in effect *stop the lions' mouths,* that they cannot hurt them. See how ready the angels are to minister for the good of God's people, for they own themselves their *fellow servants.* 2. God has therein pleaded his cause. He was represented to the king as disaffected to him and his government. We do not find that he said any thing in his own vindication, but left it to God to clear up his integrity as the light; and he did it effectually, by working a miracle for his preservation. Daniel, in what he had done, had not offended either God or the king: *Before him* whom I prayed to *innocency was found in me.* He pretends not to a meritorious excellence, but the testimony of his conscience concerning his sincerity is his comfort — *As also that before thee, O king! I have done no hurt,* nor designed thee any affront.

IV. The discharge of Daniel from his confinement. His prosecutors cannot but own that the law is satisfied, though they are not, or, if it be altered, it is by a power superior to that of the Medes and Persians; and therefore no cause can be shown why Daniel should not be fetched out of the den (*v.* 23): *The king was exceedingly glad* to find him alive, and gave orders immediately that they should *take him out of the den,* as Jeremiah out of the dungeon; and, when they searched, *no manner of hurt was found upon him;* he was nowhere crushed nor scarred, but was kept perfectly well, *because he believed in his God.* Note, Those who boldly and cheerfully trust in God to protect them in the way of their duty shall never be made ashamed of their confidence in him, but shall always find him a present help.

V. The committing of his prosecutors to the same prison, or place of execution rather, *v.* 24. Darius is animated by this miracle wrought for Daniel, and now begins to take courage and act like himself. Those that would not suffer him to show mercy to Daniel shall, now that God has done it for him, be made to feel his resentments; and he will do justice for God who had shown mercy for him. Daniel's accusers, now that his innocency is cleared, and Heaven itself has become his compurgator, have the same punishment inflicted upon them which they designed against him, according to the law of retaliation made against false accusers, Deu. 19:18, 19. Such they were to be reckoned now that Daniel was proved innocent; for, though the fact was true, yet it was not a fault. They were *cast into the den of lions,* which perhaps was a punishment newly invented by themselves; however, it was what they maliciously designed for Daniel. *Nec lex est justior ulla quàm necis artifices arte perire suâ — No law can be more just than that which adjudges the devisers of barbarity to perish by it,* Ps. 7:15, 16; 9:15, 16. And now Solomon's observation is verified (Prov. 11:8), *The righteous is delivered out of trouble,* and *the wicked cometh in his stead.* In this execution we may observe, 1. The king's severity, in ordering their wives and children to be thrown to the lions with them. How righteous are God's statutes above those of the nations! for God commanded that the children should not die for the fathers' crimes, Deu. 24:16. Yet they were put to death in extraordinary cases, as those of Achan, and Saul, and Haman. 2. The lion's fierceness. They had the *mastery of them* immediately, and tore them to pieces *before they came to the bottom of the den.* This verified and magnified the miracle of their sparing Daniel; for hereby it appeared that it was not because they had not appetite, but because they had not leave. Mastiffs that are kept muzzled are the more fierce when the muzzle is taken off; so were these lions. And the Lord is known by those judgments which he executes.

Verses 25–28

Darius here studies to make some amends for the dishonour he had done both to God and Daniel, in casting Daniel into the lions' den, by doing honour to both.

I. He gives honour to God by a decree published to all nations, by which they are required to fear before him. And this is a decree which is indeed fit to be made unalterable, according to the laws of the Medes and Persians, for it is the *everlasting gospel,* preached to those that *dwell on the earth,* Rev. 14:7. *Fear God, and give glory to him.* Observe, 1. To whom he sends this decree — *to all people, nations and languages, that dwell in all the earth, v.* 25. These are great words, and it is true that all the inhabitants of the earth are obliged to that which is here decreed; but here they mean no more than *every dominion of his kingdom,* which, though it contained many nations, did not contain all nations; but so it is, those that have much are ready to think they have all. 2. What the matter of the decree is — that *men tremble and fear before the God of Daniel.* This goes further than Nebuchadnezzar's decree upon a similar occasion, for that only restrained people from *speaking amiss* of this God, but this requires them to *fear before him,* to keep up and express awful reverent thoughts of him. And well might this decree he prefaced, as it is, with *Peace be multiplied unto you,* for the only foundation of true and abundant peace is laid in the fear of God, for that is true wisdom. If we live in the fear of God, and walk according to that rule, peace shall be upon us, peace shall be multiplied to us. But, though this decree goes far, it does not go far enough; had he done right, and come up to his present convictions, he would have commanded all men not only to tremble and fear before this God, but to love him and trust in him, to forsake the service of their idols, and to worship him only, and call upon him as Daniel did. But idolatry had been so long and so deeply rooted that it was not to be extirpated by the edicts of princes, nor by any power less than that which went along with the glorious gospel of Christ. 3. What are the causes and considerations moving him to make this decree. They are sufficient to have justified a decree for the total suppression of idolatry, much more will they serve to support this. There is good reason why all men should fear before this God, for, (1.) His being is transcendent. "He is the *living God,* lives as a God, whereas the gods we worship are dead things, have not so much as an animal life." (2.) His government is incontestable. He has a *kingdom,* and a *dominion;* he not only lives, but reigns as an absolute sovereign. (3.) Both his being and his government are unchangeable. He is himself *stedfast for ever,* and with him is no shadow of turning. And his *kingdom* too is *that which shall not be destroyed* by any external force, nor has his *dominion* any thing in itself that threatens a decay or tends towards it, and therefore it shall be *even to the end.* (4.) He has an ability sufficient to support such an authority, *v.* 27. He delivers his faithful servants from trouble and rescues them out of trouble; he *works signs and wonders,* quite above the utmost power of nature to effect, both *in heaven and on earth,* by which it appears that he is sovereign Lord of both. (5.) He has given a fresh proof of all this in *delivering* his servant *Daniel from the power of the lions.* This miracle, and that of the delivering of the three children, were wrought in the eyes of the world, were seen, published, and attested by two of the greatest monarchs that ever were, and were illustrious confirmations of the first principles of religion, abstracted from the narrow scheme of Judaism, effectual confutations of all the errors of heathenism, and very proper preparations for pure catholic Christianity.

II. He puts honour upon Daniel (*v.* 28): *So this Daniel prospered.* See how God brought to him good out of evil. This bold stroke which his enemies made at his life was a happy occasion of taking them off, and their children too, who otherwise would still have stood in the way of his preferment, and have been upon all occasions vexatious to him; and now he *prospered more than ever,* was more in favour with his prince and in reputation with the people, which gave him a great opportunity of doing good to his brethren. Thus *out of the eater* (and that was a lion too) *comes forth meat, and out of the strong sweetness.*

CHAPTER 7

The six former chapters of this book were historical; we now enter with fear and trembling upon the six latter, which are prophetical, wherein are many things dark and hard to be understood, which we dare not positively determine the sense of, and yet many things plain and profitable which I trust God will enable us to make a good use of. In this chapter we have, I. Daniel's vision of the four beasts (*v.* 1–8). II. His vision of God's throne of government and judgment (*v.* 9–14). III. The interpretation of these visions, given him by an angel that stood by (*v.* 15–28). Whether those visions look as far forward as the end of time, or whether they were to have a speedy accomplishment, is hard to say, nor are the most judicious interpreters agreed concerning it.

Verses 1–8

The date of this chapter places it before *ch.* 5, which was in the last year of Belshazzar, and *ch.* 6, which was in the first of Darius; for Daniel had those visions in the first year of Belshazzar, when the captivity of the Jews in Babylon was drawing near a period. Belshazzar's name here is, in the original, spelt differently from what it used to be; before it was *Bel-she-azar — Bel is he that treasures up riches.* But this is *Bel-eshe-zar — Bel is on fire by the enemy.* Bel was the god of the Chaldeans; he had prospered, but is now to be consumed.

We have, in these verses, Daniel's vision of the four monarchies that were oppressive to the Jews. Observe,

I. The circumstances of this vision. Daniel had interpreted Nebuchadnezzar's dream, and now he is himself honoured with similar divine discoveries (*v.* 1): He *had visions of his head upon his bed,* when he was asleep; so God sometimes revealed himself and his mind to the children of men, when deep sleep fell upon them (Job 33:15); for when we are most retired from the world, and taken off from the things of sense, we are most fit for communion with God. But when he was awake he *wrote the dream* for his own use, lest he should forget it as a dream which passes away; and he *told the sum of the matters* to his brethren the Jews for their use, and gave it to them in writing, that it might be communicated to those at a distance and preserved for their children after them, who shall see these things accomplished. The Jews, misunderstanding some of the prophecies of Jeremiah and Ezekiel, flattered themselves with hopes that, after their return to their own land, they should enjoy a complete and uninterrupted tranquility; but that they might not so deceive themselves, and their calamities be made doubly grievous by the disappointment, God by this prophet lets them know that they shall have tribulation: those promises of their prosperity were to be accomplished in the spiritual blessings of the kingdom of grace; as Christ has told his disciples they must expect persecution, and the promises they depend upon will be accomplished in the eternal blessings of the kingdom of glory. Daniel both wrote these things and spoke them, to intimate that the church should be taught both by the scriptures and by ministers' preaching, both by the written word and by word of mouth; and ministers in their preaching are to *tell the sum of the matters* that are written.

II. The vision itself, which foretels the revolutions of government in those nations which the church of the Jews, for the following ages, was to be under the influence of. 1. He observed the *four winds to strive upon the great sea, v.* 2. They strove which should blow strongest, and, at length, blow alone. This represents the contests among princes for empire, and the shakings of the nations by these contests, to which those mighty monarchies, which he was now to have a prospect of, owed their rise. One wind from any point of the compass, if it blow hard, will cause a great commotion in the sea; but what a tumult must needs be raised when the four winds strive for mastery! This is it which the kings of the nations are contending for in their wars, which are as noisy and violent as the battle of the winds; but how is the poor sea tossed and torn, how terrible are its concussions, and how violent its convulsions, while the winds are at strife which shall have the sole power of troubling it! Note, This world is like a stormy tempestuous sea; thanks to the proud ambitious winds that vex it. 2. He saw *four great beasts come up from the sea,* from the *troubled waters,* in which aspiring minds love to fish. The monarchs and monarchies are represented by *beasts,* because too often it is by brutish rage and tyranny that they are raised and supported. These beasts were *diverse one from another* (*v.* 3), of different shapes, to denote the different genius and complexion of the nations in whose hands they were lodged. (1.) *The first* beast *was like a lion, v.* 4. This was the Chaldean monarchy, that was fierce and strong, and made the kings absolute. This lion had *eagle's wings,* with which to fly upon the prey, denoting the wonderful speed that Nebuchadnezzar made in his conquest of kingdoms. But Daniel soon sees the *wings plucked,* a full stop put to the career of their victorious arms. Divers countries that had been tributaries to them revolt from them, and make head against them; so that this monstrous animal, this winged lion, is made to *stand upon the feet as a man, and a man's heart is given to it.* It has lost the heart of a lion, which it had been famous for (one of our English kings was called *Caeur de Lion — Lion-heart*), has lost its courage and become feeble and faint, dreading every thing and daring nothing; they are put in fear, and made to know themselves to be but men. Sometimes the valour of a nation strangely sinks, and it becomes cowardly and effeminate, so that what was the head of the nations in an age or two becomes the tail. (2.) The *second* beast was *like a bear, v.* 5. This was the Persian monarchy, less strong and generous than the former, but no less ravenous. This bear *raised up itself on one side* against the lion, and soon mastered it. It *raised up one dominion;* so some read it. Persia and Media, which in Nebuchadnezzar's image were the *two arms* in one breast, now set up a joint government. This bear had *three ribs in the mouth of it between the teeth,* the remains of those nations it had devoured, which were the marks of its voraciousness, and yet an indication that though it had devoured much it could not devour all; some ribs still stuck in the teeth of it, which it could not conquer. Whereupon it was said to it, *"Arise, devour much flesh;* let alone the bones, the ribs, that cannot be conquered, and set upon that which will be an easier prey." The princes will stir up both the kings and the people to push on their conquests, and let nothing stand before them. Note, Conquests, unjustly made, are but like those of the beasts of prey, and in *this* much worse, that the beasts prey not upon those of their own kind, as wicked and unreasonable men do. (3.) The third beast was *like a leopard, v.* 6. This was the Grecian monarchy, founded by *Alexander the Great,* active, crafty, and cruel, like a *leopard.* He had *four wings of a fowl;* the lion seems to have had but two wings; but the leopard had four, for though Nebuchadnezzar made great despatch in his conquests Alexander made much greater. In six years' time he gained the whole empire of Persia, a great part besides of Asia, made himself master of Syria, Egypt, India, and other nations. This beast had *four heads;* upon Alexander's death his conquests were divided among his four chief captains; Seleucus Nicanor had Asia the Great; Perdiccas, and after him Antigonus, had Asia the Less; Cassander had Macedonia; and Ptolemeus had Egypt. *Dominion* was *given* to this *beast;* it was given of God, from whom alone promotion comes. (4.) The fourth beast was more fierce, and formidable, and mischievous, than any of them, unlike any of the other, nor is there any among the beasts of prey to which it might be compared, *v.* 7. The learned are not agreed concerning this anonymous beast; some make it to be the Roman empire, which, when it was in its glory, comprehended ten kingdoms, Italy, France, Spain, Germany, Britain, Sarmatia, Pannonia, Asia, Greece, and Egypt; and then the little horn which rose by the fall of three of the other horns (*v.* 8) they make to be the Turkish empire, which rose in the room of Asia, Greece, and Egypt. Others make this fourth beast to be the kingdom of Syria, the family of the Seleucidae, which was very cruel and oppressive to the people of the Jews, as we find in Josephus and the history of the Maccabees. And herein that empire was diverse from those which went before, that none of the preceding powers compelled the Jews to renounce their religion, but the kings of Syria did, and used them barbarously. Their armies and commanders were the *great iron teeth* with which they *devoured and broke in pieces* the people of God, and they *trampled upon the residue* of them. The *ten horns* are then supposed to be ten kings that reigned successively in Syria; and then the *little horn* is Antiochus Epiphanes, the last of the ten, who by one means or other undermined three of the kings, and got the government. He was a man of great ingenuity, and therefore is said to have eyes *like the eyes of a man;* and he was very bold and daring, had a *mouth speaking great things.* We shall meet with him again in these prophecies.

Verses 9–14

Whether we understand the fourth beast to signify the Syrian empire, or the Roman, or the former as the figure of the latter, it is plain that these verses are intended for the comfort and support of the people of God in reference to the persecutions they were likely to sustain both from the one and from the other, and from all their proud enemies in every age; for it is written for their learning on whom the ends of the world have come, that they also, through patience and comfort of this scripture, might have hope. Three things are here discovered that are very encouraging: —

I. That there is a judgment to come, and God is the Judge. Now men have their day, and every pretender thinks he should have his day, and struggles for it. But *he that sits in heaven laughs at them,* for he sees that *his day is coming,* Ps. 37:13. *I beheld* (*v.* 9) *till the thrones were cast down,* not only the thrones of these beasts, but *all rule, authority, power,* that are set up in opposition to the kingdom of God among men (1 Co. 15:24): such are the thrones of the kingdoms of the world, in comparison with God's kingdom; those that see them set up need but wait awhile, and they will see them cast down. *I beheld till thrones were set up* (so it may as well be read), Christ's throne and the throne of his Father. One of the rabbin confesses that these thrones are *set up,* one for *God,* another for the *Son of David.* It is the *judgment* that is here *set, v.* 10. Now, 1. This is intended to proclaim God's wise and righteous government of the world by his providence; and an unspeakable satisfaction it gives to all good men, in the midst of the convulsions and revolutions of states and kingdoms, that *the Lord has prepared his throne in the heavens and his kingdom rules over all* (Ps. 103:19), *that verily there is a God that judges in the earth,* Ps. 58:11. 2. Perhaps it points at the destruction brought by the providence of God upon the empire of Syria, or that of Rome, for their tyrannizing over the people of God. But, 3. It seems principally designed to describe the last judgment, for though it follow not immediately upon the dominion of the fourth beast, nay, though it be yet to come, perhaps many ages to come, yet it was intended that in every age the people of God should encourage themselves, under their troubles, with the belief and prospect of it. Enoch, the seventh from Adam, prophesied of it, Jude 14. Does the mouth of the enemy *speak great things, v.* 8. Here are far greater things which the mouth of the Lord has spoken. Many of the New-Testament predictions of the judgment to come have a plain allusion to this vision, especially St John's vision of it, Rev. 20:11, 12. (1.) The Judge is *the Ancient of days* himself, *God the Father,* the glory of whose presence is here described. He is called *the Ancient of days,* because he is God *from everlasting to everlasting.* Among men we reckon that *with the ancient is wisdom,* and *days shall speak;* shall not all flesh then be silent before him who is *the Ancient of days?* The glory of the Judge is here set forth by his garment, which was *white as snow,* denoting his splendour and purity in all the administrations of his justice; and the *hair of his head* clean and white, *as the pure wool,* that, as the white and hoary head, he may appear venerable. (2.) The throne is very formidable. It is *like the fiery flame,* dreadful to the wicked that shall be summoned before it. And the throne being movable upon wheels, or at least the chariot in which he rode the circuit, the *wheels* thereof are *as burning fire,* to devour the adversaries; for *our God is a consuming fire,* and with him are *everlasting burnings,* Isa. 33:14. This is enlarged upon, *v.* 10. As to all his faithful friends there *proceeds out of the throne of God and the Lamb a pure river of water of life* (Rev. 22:1), so to all his implacable enemies there *issues and comes forth from* his throne a *fiery stream, a stream of brimstone* (Isa. 30:33), a *fire* that shall *devour before him.* He is a swift witness, and his word a word upon the wheels. (3.) The attendants are numerous and very splendid. The Shechinah is always attended with angels; it is so here (*v.* 10): *Thousand thousands minister to him,* and *ten thousand times ten thousand stand before him.* It is his glory that he has such attendants, but much more his glory that he neither needs them nor can be benefited by them. See how numerous the heavenly hosts are (there are *thousands of angels),* and how obsequious they are — they *stand before God,* ready to go on his errands and to take the first intimation of his will and pleasure. They will particularly be employed as ministers of his justice in the last judgment day, when the *Son of man shall come, and all the holy angels with him.* Enoch prophesied that the Lord should come *with his holy myriads.* (4.) The process is fair and unexceptionable: *The judgment is set,* publicly and openly, that all may have recourse to it; and *the books are opened.* As in courts of judgment among men the proceedings are in writing and upon record, which is laid open when the cause comes to a hearing, the examination of witnesses is produced, and affidavits are read, to clear the matter of fact, and the statute and common-law books are consulted to find out what is the law, so, in the judgment of the great day, the equity of the sentence will be as incontestably evident as if there were books opened to justify it.

II. That the proud and cruel enemies of the church of God will certainly be reckoned with and brought down in due time, *v.* 11, 12. This is here represented to us, 1. In the destroying of the fourth beast. God's quarrel with this beast is *because of the voice of the great words which the horn spoke,* bidding defiance to Heaven, and triumphing over all that is sacred; this provokes God more than any thing, for the *enemy to behave himself proudly,* Deu. 32:27. *Therefore* Pharaoh must be humbled, because he has said, *Who is the Lord?* and has said, *I will pursue, I will overtake.* Enoch foretold that *therefore* the Lord would come to *judge the world,* that he might *convince all that are ungodly of their hard speeches,* Jude 15. Note, Great words are but idle words, for which men must give account in the great day. And see what becomes of this beast that talks so big: He *is slain,* and *his body destroyed and given to the burning flame.* The Syrian empire, after Antiochus, was destroyed. He himself died of a miserable disease, his family was rooted out, the kingdom wasted by the Parthians and Armenians, and at length made a province of the Roman empire by Pompey. And the Roman empire itself (if we take that for the fourth beast), after it began to persecute Christianity, declined and wasted away, and the body of it was destroyed. *So shall all thy enemies perish, O Lord!* and be *slain before thee.* 2. In the diminishing and weakening of the other three beasts (*v.* 12): They had *their dominion taken away,* and so were disabled from doing the mischiefs they had done to the church and people of God; but *a prolonging in life was given them, for a time and a season,* a set time, the bounds of which they could not pass. The power of the foregoing kingdoms was quite broken, but the people of them still remained in a mean, weak, and low condition. We may allude to this in describing the remainders of sin in the hearts of good people; they have corruptions in them, the lives of which are prolonged, so that they are not perfectly free from sin, but the dominion of them is taken away, so that sin does not *reign in their mortal bodies.* And thus God deals with his church's enemies; sometimes he breaks the teeth of them (Ps. 3:7), when he does not break the neck of them, crushes the persecution, but reprieves the persecutors, that they may have space to repent. And it is fit that God, in doing his own work, should take his own time and way.

III. That the kingdom of the Messiah shall be set up, and kept up, in the world, in spite of all the opposition of the powers of darkness. Let the heathen rage and fret as long as they please, God will *set his King upon his holy hill of Zion.* Daniel sees this in vision, and comforts himself and his friends with the prospect of it. This is the same with Nebuchadnezzar's foresight of the *stone cut out of the mountain without hands,* which broke in pieces the image; but in this vision there is much more of pure gospel than in that. 1. The Messiah is here called the Son of man — *one like unto the Son of man;* for he was *made in the likeness of sinful flesh,* was *found in fashion as a man. I saw one like unto the Son of man,* one exactly agreeing with the idea formed in the divine counsels of him that in the fulness of time was to be the Mediator between God and man. He is *like unto the son of man,* but is indeed the Son of God. Our Savior seems plainly to refer to this vision when he says (Jn. 5:27) that the *Father* has therefore *given him authority to execute judgment* because he is *the Son of man,* and because he is the person whom Daniel saw in vision, to whom a kingdom and dominion were to be given. 2. He is said to *come with the clouds of heaven.* Some refer this to his incarnation; he descended *in the clouds of heaven,* came into the world unseen, as the glory of the Lord took possession of the temple in a cloud. The empires of the world were beasts that *rose out of the sea;* but Christ's kingdom is from above: he is the *Lord from heaven.* I think it is rather to be referred to his ascension; when he returned to the Father the eye of his disciples followed him, till *a cloud received him out of their sight,* Acts 1:9. He made that cloud his chariot, wherein he rode triumphantly to the upper world. He comes swiftly, irresistibly, and comes in state, for he *comes with the clouds of heaven.* 3. He is here represented as having a mighty interest in Heaven. When the cloud received him out of the sight of his disciples, it is worth while to enquire (as the sons of the prophets concerning Elijah in a like case) whither it carried him, where it lodged him; and here we are told, abundantly to our satisfaction, that *he came to the Ancient of days;* for he ascended to *his Father and our Father,* to *his God and our God* (Jn. 20:17); from him he came forth, and to him he returns, to be glorified with him, and to sit down at his right hand. It was with a great deal of pleasure that he said, *Now I go to him that sent me.* But was he welcome? Yes, not doubt, he was, for *they brought him near before him;* he was introduced into his Father's presence, with the attendance and adorations of *all the angels of God,* Heb. 1:6. God *caused him to draw near and approach to him,* as an advocate and undertaker for us (Jer. 30:21), that we through him might be *made nigh.* By this solemn near approach which he made to the Ancient of days it appears that the Father accepted the sacrifice he offered, and the satisfaction he made, and was entirely well pleased with all he had done. He was *brought near,* as our high priest, who for us enters within the veil, and as our forerunner, 4. He is here represented as having a mighty influence upon this earth, *v.* 14. When he went to be glorified with his Father he had a *power given him over all flesh,* Jn. 17:2, 5. With the prospect of this Daniel and his friends are here comforted, that not only the dominion of the church's enemies shall be taken away (*v.* 12), but the church's head and best friend shall have *the dominion given him;* to him *every knee shall bow* and *every tongue confess.* Phil. 2:9, 10. To him are given *glory and a kingdom,* and they are given by him who has an unquestionable right to give them, which, some think with an eye to these words, our Savior teaches us to acknowledge in the close of the Lord's prayer, *For thine is the kingdom, the power, and the glory.* It is here foretold that the kingdom of the exalted Redeemer shall be, (1.) A universal kingdom, the only universal monarchy, whatever others have pretended to, or aimed at: *All people, nations, and languages,* shall *fear him,* and be under his jurisdiction, either as his willing subjects or as his conquered captives, to be either ruled or overruled by him. One way or other, the kingdoms of the world shall all become his kingdoms. (2.) An everlasting kingdom. His *dominion* shall not *pass away* to any successor, much less to any invader, and his kingdom is *that* which *shall bot be destroyed.* Even the gates of hell, or the infernal powers and policies, shall not prevail against it. The church shall continue militant to the end of time, and triumphant to the endless ages of eternity.

Verses 15–28

Here we have, I. The deep impressions which these visions made upon the prophet. God in them put honour upon him, and gave him satisfaction, yet not without a great allay of pain and perplexity (*v.* 15): *I Daniel was grieved in my spirit, in the midst of my body.* The word here used for the *body* properly signifies a *sheath* or *scabbard,* for the body is no more to the soul; that is the weapon; it is that which we are principally to take care of. The *visions of my head troubled me,* an again (*v.* 28), *my cogitations much troubled me.* The manner in which these things were discovered to him quite overwhelmed him, and put his thoughts so much to the stretch that his spirits failed him, and the trance he was in tired him and made him faint. The things themselves that were discovered amazed and astonished him, and put him into a confusion, till by degrees he recollected and conquered himself, and set the comforts of the vision over against the terrors of it.

II. His earnest desire to understand the meaning of them (*v.* 16): *I came near to one of those that stood by, to* one of the angels that appeared attending the *Son of man* in his glory, and *asked him the truth* (the true intent and meaning) *of all this.* Note, It is a very desirable thing to take the right and full sense of what we see and hear from God; and those that would know must ask by faithful and fervent prayer and by *accomplishing a diligent search.*

III. The key that was given him, to let him into the understanding of this vision. The angel *told him,* and told him so plainly that he made him *know the interpretation of the thing,* and so made him somewhat more easy.

1. *The great beasts* are great *kings* and their kingdoms, great monarchs and their monarchies, *which shall arise out of the earth,* as those beasts did *out of the sea, v.* 17. They are but *terraefilii — from beneath;* they savour of the earth, and their foundation is *in the dust;* they are of the earth earthy, and they are written in the dust, and to the dust they shall return.

2. Daniel pretty well understands the first three beasts, but concerning the fourth he desires to be better informed, because it differed so much from the rest, and was *exceedingly dreadful,* and not only so, but very mischievous, or it *devoured and broke in pieces, v.* 19. Perhaps it was this that put Daniel into such a fright, and this part of the visions of his head troubled him more than any of the rest. But especially he desired to know what the *little horn* was, that *had eyes,* and a *mouth that spoke very great things,* and whose countenance was more fearless and formidable than that of *any of his fellows, v.* 20. And this he was most inquisitive about because it was this horn that *made war with the saints, and prevailed against them, v.* 21. While no more is intimated than that the children of men make war with one another, and prevail against one another, the prophet does not show himself so much concerned (*let the potsherds strive with the potsherds of the earth,* and be dashed in pieces one against another); but when they *make war with the saints,* when the *precious sons of Zion, comparable to fine gold,* are broken as *earthen pitchers,* it is time to ask, "What is the meaning of this? Will the Lord cast off his people? Will he suffer their enemies to trample upon them and triumph over them? What is this same horn that shall prevail so far against the saints?" To this his interpreter answers (*v.* 23–25) that this *fourth beast* is a *fourth kingdom,* that *shall devour the whole earth,* or (as it may be read) *the whole land.* That the *ten horns are ten kings,* and the *little horn* is another king that shall subdue three kings, and shall be very abusive to God and his people, shall act, (1.) Very impiously towards God. He shall *speak great words against the Most High,* setting him, and his authority and justice, at defiance. (2.) Very imperiously towards the people of God. He shall *wear out the saints of the Most High;* he will not cut them off at once, but wear them out by long oppressions and a constant course of hardships put upon them, ruining their estates and weakening their families. The design of Satan has been to *wear out the saints of the Most High,* that they may be no more in remembrance; but the attempt is vain, for while the world stands God will have a church in it. He shall *think to change times and laws,* to abolish all the ordinances and institutions of religion, and to bring every body to say and do just as he would have them. He shall trample upon laws and customs, human and divine. *Diruit, aedificut, mutat quadrata rotundis — He pulls down, he builds, he changes square into round,* as if he meant to alter even the ordinances of heaven themselves. And in these daring attempts he shall for a time prosper and have success; they shall be given into his hand *until time, times, and half a time* (that is, for three years and a half), that famous prophetical measure of time which we meet with in the Revelation, which is sometimes called forty-two months, sometimes 1260 days, which come all to one. But at the end of that time the *judgment shall sit and take away his dominion* (*v.* 26), which he expounds (*v.* 11) of the beast being *slain and his body destroyed.* And (as Mr. Mede reads *v.* 12) *as to the rest of the beast,* the ten horns, especially the little *ruffling* horn (as he calls it), they had their dominion taken away. Now the question is, Who is this enemy, whose rise, reign, and ruin, are foretold? Interpreters are not agreed. Some will have the fourth kingdom to be that of the Seleucidae, and the little horn to be Antiochus, and show the accomplishment of all this in the history of the Maccabees; so Junius, Piscator, Polanus, Broughton, and many others: but others will have the fourth kingdom to be that of the Romans, and the *little horn* to be Julius Caesar, and the succeeding emperors (says Calvin), the antichrist, the papal kingdom (says Mr. Joseph Mede), that *wicked one,* which, as this *little horn,* is to be consumed by the *brightness of Christ's second coming.* The pope assumes a power to *change times and laws, potestas autokratorikē — an absolute and despotic power,* as he calls it. Others make the *little horn* to be the *Turkish empire;* so Luther, Vatablus, and others. Now I cannot prove either side to be wrong; and therefore, since prophecies sometimes have many fulfillings, and we ought to give scripture its full latitude (in this as in many other controversies), I am willing to allow that they are both in the right, and that this prophecy has primary reference to the Syrian empire, and was intended for the encouragement of the Jews who suffered under Antiochus, that they might see even these melancholy times foretold, but might foresee a glorious issue of them at last, and the final overthrow of their proud oppressors; and, which is best of all, might foresee, not long after, the setting up of the kingdom of the Messiah in the world, with the hopes of which it was usual with the former prophets to comfort the people of God in their distresses. But yet it has a further reference, and foretels the like persecuting power and rage in Rome heathen, and no less in Rome papal, against the Christian religion, that was in Antiochus against the pious Jews and their religion. And St. John, in his visions and prophecies, which point primarily at Rome, has plain reference, in many particulars, to these visions of Daniel.

3. He has a joyful prospect given him of the prevalency of God's kingdom among men, and its victory over all opposition at last. And it is very observable that in the midst of the predictions of the force and fury of the enemies this is brought in abruptly (*v.* 18 and again *v.* 22), before it comes, in the course of the vision, to be interpreted, *v.* 26, 27. And this also refers, (1.) To the prosperous days of the Jewish church, after it had weathered the storm under Antiochus, and the power which the Maccabees obtained over their enemies. (2.) To the setting up of the kingdom of the Messiah in the world by the preaching of his gospel. *For judgment Christ comes into this world,* to rule by his Spirit, and to make all his saints *kings and priests to their God.* (3.) To the second coming of Jesus Christ, when the saints shall judge the world, shall sit down with him on his throne and triumph in the complete downfall of the devil's kingdom. Let us see what is here foretold. [1.] *The Ancient of days shall come, v.* 22. God shall judge the world by his Son, to whom he has *committed all judgment,* and, as an earnest of that, he *comes* for the deliverance of his oppressed people, comes for the setting up of his kingdom in the world. [2.] *The judgment shall sit, v.* 26. God will make it appear that he *judges in the earth,* and will, both

in wisdom and in equity, plead his people's righteous cause. At the great day he will *judge the world in righteousness by that man whom he has ordained.* [3.] The *dominion* of the enemy shall be *taken away, v.* 26. All Christ's enemies shall be made his footstool, and shall be *consumed and destroyed* to the end: these were the apostle uses concerning the man of sin, 2 Th. 2:8. He shall be *consumed* with the *spirit of Christ's mouth* and *destroyed with the brightness of his coming.* [4.] *Judgment is given to the saints of the Most High.* The apostles are entrusted with the preaching of a gospel by which the *world shall be judged.* All the saints by their faith and obedience condemn an unbelieving disobedient world; in Christ their head they shall judge the world, shall *judge the twelve tribes of Israel,* Mt. 19:28. See what reason we have to honour those that fear the Lord; how mean and despicable soever the saints now appear in the eye of the world, and how much contempt soever is poured upon them; they are the *saints of the Most High;* they are near and dear to God, and he owns them for his, and *judgment is given to them.* [5.] That which is most insisted upon is that *the saints of the Most High shall take the kingdom, and possess the kingdom for ever, v.* 18. And again (*v.* 22), The *time came that the saints possessed the kingdom.* And again (*v.* 27), The *kingdom and dominion, and the greatness of the kingdom under the whole heavens, shall be given to the people of the saints of the Most High.* Far be it from us to infer hence that dominion is founded on grace, or that this will warrant any, under pretence of saintship, to usurp kingship. No; *Christ's kingdom is not of this world;* but this intimates the spiritual dominion of the saints over their own lusts and corruptions, their victories over Satan and his temptations, and the triumphs of the martyrs over death and its terrors. It likewise promises that the gospel kingdom shall be set up, a kingdom of grace, the privileges and comforts of which now, *under the heavens,* shall be the earnest and first-fruits of the kingdom of *glory in the heavens.* When the empire became Christian, and princes used their power for the defence and advancement of Christianity, then the *saints possessed the kingdom.* The saints rule by the Spirit's ruling in them (and *this is the victory overcoming the world, even their faith)* and by making the kingdoms of this world to become Christ's kingdom. But the full accomplishment of this will be in the everlasting happiness of the saints, the kingdom that cannot be moved, which we, according to his promise, look for (that is the *greatness of the kingdom),* the crown of glory that fades not away — that is the *everlasting kingdom.* See what an emphasis is laid upon this (*v.* 18): The saints shall possess the kingdom *for ever, even for ever and ever;* and the reason is because he whose saints they are is the *Most High* and *his kingdom is an everlasting kingdom, v.* 27. He is so, and therefore theirs shall be so. *Because I live, you shall live also,* Jn. 14:19. His kingdom is theirs; they reckon themselves exalted in his exaltation, and desire no greater honour and satisfaction to themselves than that *all dominions* should *serve and obey him,* as they shall do, *v.* 27. They shall either be brought into subjection to his golden sceptre or brought to destruction by his iron rod.

Daniel, in the close, when he ends that matter, tells us what impressions this vision made upon him; it overwhelmed his spirits to such a degree that his *countenance* was *changed,* and it made him look pale; but he *kept the matter in his heart.* Note, The heart must be the treasury and store-house of divine things; there we must hide God's word, as the Virgin Mary kept the sayings of Christ, Lu. 2:51. Daniel kept *the matter in his heart,* with a design, not to keep it from the church, but to keep it for the church, that what he had received from the Lord he might fully and faithfully deliver to the people. Note, It concerns God's prophets and ministers to treasure up the things of God in their minds, and there to digest them well. If we would have God's word ready in our mouths when we have occasion for it, we must keep it in our hearts at all times.

CHAPTER 8

The visions and prophecies of this chapter look only and entirely at the events that were then shortly to come to pass in the monarchies of Persia and Greece, and seem not to have any further reference at all. Nothing is here said of the Chaldean monarchy, for that was now just at its period; and therefore this chapter is written not in Chaldee, as the six foregoing chapters were, for the benefit of the Chaldeans, but in Hebrew, and so are

the rest of the chapters to the end of the book, for the service of the Jews, that they might know what troubles were before them and what the issue of them would be, and might provide accordingly. In this chapter we have, I. The vision itself of the ram, and the he-goat, and the little horn that should fight and prevail against the people of God, for a certain limited time (*v.* 1-14). II. The interpretation of this vision by an angel, showing that the ram signified the Persian empire, the he-goat the Grecian, and the little horn a king of the Grecian monarchy, that should set himself against the Jews and religion, which was Antiochus Epiphanes (*v.* 15-27). The Jewish church, from its beginning, had been all along, more or less, blessed with prophets, men divinely inspired to explain God's mind to them in his providences and give them some prospect of what was coming upon them; but, soon after Ezra's time, divine inspiration ceased, and there was no more any prophet till the gospel day dawned. And therefore the events of that time were here foretold by Daniel, and left upon record, that even then God might not leave himself without witness, nor them without a guide.

Verses 1-14

Here is, I. The date of this vision, *v.* 1. It was *in the third year of the reign of Belshazzar,* which proved to be his last year, as many reckon; so that this chapter also should be, in order of time, before the fifth. That Daniel might not be surprised at the destruction of Babylon, now at hand, God gives him a foresight of the destruction of other kingdoms hereafter, which in their day had been as potent as that of Babylon. Could we foresee the changes that shall be hereafter, when we are gone, we should the less admire, and be less affected with, the changes in our own day; for *that which is done is that which shall be done,* Eccl. 1:9. Then it was that a *vision appeared to me, even to me, Daniel.* Here he solemnly attests the truth of it: it was to him, even to him, that the vision was shown; he was the eye-witness of it. And this vision puts him in mind of a former vision which *appeared to him at the first,* in the first year of this reign, which he makes mention of because this vision was an explication and confirmation of that, and points at many of the same events. That seems to have been a dream, a vision in his sleep; this seems to have been when he was awake.

II. The scene of this vision. The place where that was laid was in *Shushan the palace,* one of the royal seats of the kings of Persia, situated on the banks of the river Ulai, which surrounded the city; it was in the province of Elam, that part of Persia which lay next to Babylon. Daniel was not there in person, for he was now in Babylon, a captive, in some employment under Belshazzar, and might not go to such a distant country, especially being now an enemy's country. But he was there in vision; as Ezekiel, when a captive in Babylon, was often brought, in the spirit, to the land of Israel. Note, The soul may be a liberty when the body is in captivity; for, when we are bound, the Spirit of the Lord is not bound. The vision related to that country, and therefore there he was made to fancy himself to be as strongly as if he had really been there.

III. The vision itself and the process of it.

1. He saw a *ram* with *two horns, v.* 3. This was the second monarchy, of which the kingdoms of Media and Persia were the two horns. The horns were *very high;* but that which came up last was the higher, and got the start of the former. So the last shall be first, and the first last. The kingdom of Persia, which rose last, in Cyrus, became more eminent than that of the Medes.

2. He saw this *ram pushing* all about him with his horns (*v.* 4), *westward* (towards Babylon, Syria, Greece, and Asia the less), *northward* (towards the Lydians, Armenians, and Scythians), and *southward* (towards Arabia, Ethiopia, and Egypt), for all these nations did the Persian empire, one time or other, make attempts upon for the enlarging of their dominion. And at last he became so powerful that *no beasts might stand before him.* This *ram,* though of a species of animal often preyed upon, became formidable even to the beasts of prey themselves, so that there was *no standing* before him, no escaping him, none that *could deliver out of his hand,* but all must yield to him: the kings of Persia did according *to their will,* prospered in all their ways abroad, had an uncontrollable power at home, and *became great.* He thought himself great because he did what he would; but to do good is that which makes men truly great.

3. He saw this ram overcome by a he-goat. He was considering the *ram* (wondering that so weak an animal should come to be so prevalent) and thinking what would be the issue; and, *behold, a he-goat came, v.* 5. This was Alexander the Great, the son of Philip king of Macedonia. He *came from the west,* from Greece, which lay west from Per-

sia. He fetched a great compass with his army: he came *upon the face of the whole earth;* he did in effect conquer the world, and then sat down and wept because there was not another world to be conquered. *Unus Pellaeo juveni non sufficit orbis — One world was too little for the youth of Pellae.* This he-goat (a creature famed for comeliness in going, Prov. 30:31) went on with incredible swiftness, so that he *touched not the ground,* so lightly did he move; he rather seemed to fly above the ground than to go upon the ground; or *none touched him in the earth,* that is, he met with little or no opposition. This he-goat, or buck, had a *notable horn between his eyes,* like a unicorn. He had strength, and knew his own strength; he saw himself a match for all his neighbours. Alexander pushed his conquests on so fast, and with so much fury, that none of the kingdoms he attacked had courage to make a stand, or give check to the progress of his victorious arms. In six years he made himself master of the greatest part of the then known world. Well might he be called a *notable horn,* for his name still lives in history as the name of one of the most celebrated commanders in war that ever the world knew. Alexander's victories and achievements are still the entertainment of the ingenious. This *he-goat* came to the *ram that had two horns, v.* 6. Alexander with his victorious army attacked the kingdom of Persia, an army consisting of no more than 30,000 foot and 5000 horse. He *ran unto him,* to surprise him ere he could get intelligence of his motions, *in the fury of his power.* He came *close to the ram.* Alexander with his army came up with Darius Codomannus, then emperor of Persia, being *moved with choler against him, v.* 7. It was with the greatest violence that Alexander pushed on his war against Darius, who, though he brought vast numbers into the field, yet, for want of skill, was an unequal match for him, so that Alexander was too hard for him whenever he engaged him, *smote him, cast him down to the ground,* and *stamped upon him,* which three expressions, some think, refer to the three famous victories that Alexander obtained over Darius, at Granicus, at Issus, and at Arbela, by which he was at length totally routed, having, in the last battle, had 600,000 men killed, so that Alexander became absolute master of all the Persian empire, *broke his two horns,* the kingdoms of Media and Persia. The ram that had destroyed *all before him* (*v.* 4) now is himself destroyed; Darius has *no power to stand* before Alexander, not has he any friends or allies to help to *deliver him out of his hand.* Note, Those kingdoms which, when they had power, abused it, and, because none could oppose them, withheld not themselves from the doing of any wrong, may expect to have their power at length taken from them, and to be served in their own kind, Isa. 33:1.

4. He saw the he-goat made hereby very considerable; but the *great horn,* that had done all this execution, *was broken, v.* 8. Alexander was about twenty years old when he began his wars. When he was about twenty-six he conquered Darius, and became master of the whole Persian empire; but when he was about thirty-two or thirty-three *years of age,* when he was *strong,* in his full strength, he was *broken.* He was not killed in war, in the bed of honour, but died of a drunken surfeit, or, as some suspect, by poison and left no child living behind him to enjoy that which he had endlessly laboured for, but left a lasting monument of the vanity of worldly pomp and power, and their insufficiency to make a man happy.

5. He saw this kingdom divided into four parts, and that instead of that one great horn there came up *four notable ones.* Alexander's four captains, to whom he bequeathed his conquests; and he had so much that, when it was divided among four, they had each of them enough for any one man. These *four notable horns* were towards the *four winds of heaven,* the same with the *four heads* of the leopard (ch. 7:6), the kingdoms of Syria and Egypt, Asia and Greece — Syria lying to the *east,* Greece to the *west,* Asia Minor to the *north,* and Egypt to the *south.* Note, Those that heap up riches know not who shall gather them, nor whose all those things shall be which they have provided.

6. He saw a *little horn* which became a great persecutor of the church and people of God; and this was the principal thing that was intended to be shown to him in this vision, as afterwards, *ch.* 11:30, etc. All agree that this was *Antiochus Epiphanes* (so he called himself) — *the illustrious,* but others called him *Antiochus Epimanes —*

Antiochus the furious. He is called here (as before, *ch.* 7:8), a *little horn,* because he was in his original contemptible; there were others between him and the kingdom, and he was of a base servile disposition, had nothing in him of princely qualities, and had been for some time a hostage and prisoner at Rome, whence he made his escape, and, though, the youngest brother, and his elder living, got the kingdom. He waxed exceedingly great *towards the south,* for he seized upon Egypt, and towards *the east,* for he invaded Persia and Armenia. But that which is here especially taken notice of is the mischief that he did to the people of the Jews. They are not expressly named, or prophecies must not be too plain; but they are here so described that it would be easy for those who understood scripture-language to know who were meant; and the Jews, having notice of this before, might be awakened to prepare themselves and their children beforehand for these suffering trying times. (1.) He set himself against *the pleasant land,* the land of Israel, so called because it was the *glory of all lands,* for fruitfulness and all the delights of human life, but especially for the tokens of God's presence in it, and its being blessed with divine revelations and institutions; it was Mount Zion that was *beautiful for situation, the joy of the whole earth,* Ps. 48:2. The pleasantness of that land was that there the Messiah was to be born, who would be both the consolation and *the glory of his people Israel.* Note, We have reason to reckon that a pleasant place which is a holy place, in which God dwells, and where we may have opportunity of communing with him. Surely, *It is good to be here.* (2.) He fought against the *host of heaven,* that is, the people of God, the church, which is the kingdom of heaven, the church-militant here on earth. The saints, being born from above, and citizens of heaven, and doing the will of God, by his grace, in some measure, as the angels of heaven do it, may be well called a *heavenly host.* Or the priests and Levites, who were employed in the service of the tabernacle, and there *warred a good warfare,* were this *host of heaven.* These Antiochus set himself against; he *waxed great to the host of heaven,* in opposition to them and in defiance of them. (3.) He *cast down some of the host* (that is, *of the stars,* for they are called the host of heaven) *to the ground, and stamped upon them.* Some of those that were most eminent both in church and state, that were burning and shining lights in their generation, he either forced to comply with his idolatries or put them to death; he got them into his hands, and then trampled upon them and triumphed over them; as good old Eleazar, and the *seven brethren,* whom he put to death with cruel tortures, because they would not eat swine's flesh, 2 Mac. 6:7. He gloried in it that herein he insulted Heaven itself and *exalted his throne above the stars of God,* Isa. 14:13. (4.) He *magnified himself even to the prince of the host.* He set himself against the high priest, Onias, whom he deprived of his dignity, or rather against God himself, who was Israel's *King of old,* who *reigns for ever* Zion's King, who himself heads his own host that fight his battles. Against him Antiochus magnified himself; as Pharaoh, when he said, *Who is the Lord?* Note, Those who persecute the people of God persecute God himself. (5.) He *took away the daily sacrifice.* The morning and evening lamb, which God appointed to be offered every day upon his altar to his honour, Antiochus forbade and restrained the offering of. No doubt he took away all other sacrifices, but only the *daily sacrifice* is mentioned, because that was the greatest loss of all, for in that they kept up their constant communion with God, which they preferred before that which is only occasional. God's people reckon their daily sacrifices, their morning and evening exercises of devotion, the most needful of their daily business and the most delightful of their daily comforts, and would not for all the world part with them. (6.) He *cast down the place of his sanctuary.* He did not burn and demolish the temple, but he cast it down, when he profaned it, made it the temple of Jupiter Olympius, and set up his image in it. He also *cast down the truth to the ground,* trampled upon the book of the law, that word of truth, tore it, and burnt it, and did what he could to destroy it quite, that it might be lost and forgotten for ever. These were the projects of that wicked prince. In these he practised. And (would you think it?) in these he prospered. He carried the matter very far, seemed to have gained his point, and went near to extirpate that holy religion which God's right hand had plant-

ed. But lest he or any other should triumph, as if herein he had prevailed against God himself and been too hard for him, the matter is here explained and set in a true light. [1.] He could not have done this if God had not permitted him to do it, could have had no power against Israel unless it had been given him from above. God put this power into his hand, and *gave him a host against the daily sacrifice.* God's providence put that sword into his hand by which he was enabled thus to bear down all before him. Note, We ought to eye and own the hand of God in all the enterprises and all the successes of the church's enemies against the church. They are but the rod in God's hand. [2.] God would not have permitted it if his people had not provoked him to do so. It is *by reason of transgression,* the transgression of Israel, to correct them for that, that Antiochus is employed to give them all this trouble. Note, When the pleasant land and all its pleasant things are laid waste, it must be acknowledged that sin is the procuring cause of all the desolation. *Who gave Jacob to the spoil? Did not the Lord, he against whom we have sinned?* Isa. 42:24. The great transgression of the Jews after the captivity (when they were cured of idolatry) was a contempt and profanation of the holy things, *snuffing* at the service of God, *bringing the torn and the lame for sacrifice,* as if the *table of the Lord* were a *contemptible* thing (so we find Mal. 1:7, 8, etc., and that the priests were guilty of this Mal. 2:1, 8), and therefore God sent Antiochus to *take away the daily sacrifice* and *cast down the place of his sanctuary.* Note, It is just with God to deprive those of the privileges of his house who despise and profane them, and to make those know the worth of ordinances by the want of them who would not know it by the enjoyment of them.

7. He heard the time of this calamity limited and determined, not the time *when it should come* (that is not here fixed, because God would have his people always prepared for it), but *how long it should last,* that, when they had no more any *prophets to tell them how long* (Ps. 74:9, which psalm seems to have been calculated for this dark and doleful day), they might have this prophecy to give them a prospect of deliverance in due time. Now concerning this we have here,

(1.) The question asked concerning it, *v.* 13. Observe [1.] By whom the question was put: *I heard one saint speaking* to this purport, and then *another saint* seconded him. "O that we knew how long this trouble will last!" The angels here are called *saints,* for they are *holy ones* (*ch.* 4:13), the *holy myriads,* Jude 14. The angels concern themselves in the affairs of the church, and enquire concerning them, if, as here, concerning its temporal salvations, much more do they desire to *look into the great salvation,* 1 Pt. 1:12. One saint *spoke* of the thing, and another *enquired* concerning it. Thus John, who lay in Christ's bosom, was beckoned to by Peter to ask Christ a question, Jn. 13:23, 24. [2.] To whom the question was put. He said *unto Palmoni that spoke.* Some make this *certain saint* to be a superior angel who understood more than the rest, to whom therefore they came with their enquiries. Others make it to be the *eternal Word,* the *Son of God.* He is the *unknown One. Palmoni* seems to be compounded of *Peloni Almoni,* which is used (Ruth 4:1) for *Ho, such a one,* and (2 Ki. 6:8) for *such a place.* Christ was yet the nameless One. Wherefore *asked thou after my name, seeing it is secret?* Jdg. 13:18. He is the *numberer of secrets* (as some translate it), for from him there is nothing hidden — the *wonderful numberer,* so others; his name is called *Wonderful.* Note, If we would know the mind of God, we must apply to Jesus Christ, who lay in the bosom of the Father, and *in whom are hidden all the treasures of wisdom and knowledge,* not hidden from us, but hidden for us. [3.] The question itself that was asked: "*How long shall be the vision concerning the daily sacrifice?* How long shall the prohibition of it continue? How long shall the pleasant land be made unpleasant by that severe interdict? How long shall *the transgression of desolation* (the image of Jupiter), that great transgression which makes all our sacred things desolate, how long shall that stand in the temple? How long shall *the sanctuary and the host,* the holy place and the holy persons that minister in it, be *trodden under foot by the oppressor?*" Note, Angels are concerned for the prosperity of the church on earth and desirous to see an end of its desolations. The angels asked, for the satisfaction of Daniel, not doubting

but he was desirous to know, how long these calamities should last? The question takes it for granted that they should not last always. *The rod of the wicked shall not rest upon the lot of the righteous,* though it may come upon their lot. Christ comforted himself in his sufferings with this, *The things concerning me have an end* (Lu. 22:37), and so may the church in hers. But it is desirable to know how long they shall last, that we may provide accordingly.

(2.) The answer given to this question, *v.* 14. Christ gives instruction to the holy angels, for they are our fellow-servants; but here the answer was given to Daniel, because for his sake the question was asked: *He said unto me.* God sometimes gives in great favours to his people, in answer to the enquiries and requests of their friends for them. Now, [1.] Christ assures him that the trouble shall end; it shall continue *2300 days and no longer,* so many *evenings and mornings* (so the word is), so many *nychthēmerai,* so many *natural days,* reckoned, as in the beginning of Genesis, by the evenings and mornings, because it was the evening and the morning sacrifice that they most lamented the loss of, and thought the time passed very slowly while they were deprived of them. Some make the morning and the evening, in this number, to stand for two, and then 2300 evenings and as many mornings will make but 1150 days; and about so many days it was that the daily sacrifice was interrupted: and this comes nearer to the computation (*ch.* 7:25) of a *time, times,* and the *dividing of a time.* But it is less forced to understand them of so many natural days; 2300 days make *six years* and *three months,* and about eighteen days; and just so long they reckon from the defection of the people, procured by Menelaus the high priest in the 142nd year of the kingdom of the Seleucidae, the sixth month of that year, and the 6th day of the month (so Josephus dates it), to the cleansing of the sanctuary, and the reestablishment of religion among them, which was in the 148th year, the 9th month, and the 25th *day of the month,* 1 Mac. 4:52. God reckons the time of his people's afflictions he is afflicted. Rev. 2:10, Thou shalt have *tribulation ten days.* [2.] He assures him that they shall see better days afterwards: *Then shall the sanctuary be cleansed.* Note, The cleansing of the sanctuary is a happy token for good to any people; when they begin to be reformed they will soon be relieved. Though the righteous God may, for the correction of his people, suffer his sanctuary to be profaned for a while, yet the jealous God will, for his own glory, see to the cleansing of it in due time. Christ died to cleanse his church, and he will so cleanse it as at length to present it blameless to himself.

Verses 15–27

Here we have,

I. Daniel's earnest desire to have this vision explained to him (*v.* 15): *I sought the meaning.* Note, Those that rightly know the things of God cannot but desire to know more and more of them, and to be led further into the mystery of them; and those that would find the meaning of what they have seen or heard from God must seek it, and seek it diligently. *Seek and you shall find.* Daniel considered the thing, compared it with the former discoveries, to try if he could understand it; but especially he sought by prayer (as he had done *ch.* 2:18), and he did not seek in vain.

II. Orders given to the angel Gabriel to inform him concerning this vision. One *in the appearance of a man* (who, some think, was Christ himself, for who besides could command angels?) orders Gabriel to *make Daniel understand this vision.* Sometimes God is pleased to make use of the ministration of angels, not only to protect his children, but to instruct them, to serve the kind intentions, not only of his providence, but of his grace.

III. The consternation that Daniel was in upon the approach of his instructor (*v.* 17): *When he came near I was afraid.* Though Daniel was a man of great prudence and courage, and had been conversant with the visions of the Almighty, yet the approach of an extraordinary messenger from heaven put him into this fright. He *fell upon his face,* not to worship the angel, but because he could no longer bear the dazzling lustre of his glory. Nay, being prostrate upon the ground, he *fell into a deep sleep,* (*v.* 18), which came not from any neglect of the vision, or indifference towards it, but was an effect of his faintness and the oppression of spirit he was under, through the abundance of revelations. The disciples in the garden slept for sorrow; and, as there, so here, *the spirit was willing, but the flesh was weak.* Daniel would have kept awake, and could not.

IV. The relief which the angel gave to Daniel, with great encouragement to him to expect a satisfactory discovery of the meaning of this vision. 1. He *touched him*, and *set him upon his feet*, v. 18. Thus when John, in a similar case, was in similar consternation, Christ *laid his right hand upon him*, Rev. 1:17. It was a gentle touch that the angel here gave to Daniel, to show that he came not to hurt him, not to *plead against him with his great power,* or with a hand *heavy upon him*, but to help him, to *put strength into him* (Job 23:6), which God can do with a touch. When we are slumbering and grovelling on this earth we are very unfit to hear from God, and to converse with him. But, if God design instruction for us, he will be his grace awaken us out of our slumber, raise us from things below, and *set us upright.* 2. He promised to inform him: *"Understand, O son of man! v.* 17. Thou shalt understand, if thou wilt but apply thy mind to understand." He calls him *son of man* to intimate that he would consider his frame, and would deal tenderly with him, accommodating himself to his capacity as a man. Or thus he preaches humility to him; though he be admitted to converse with angels, he must not be puffed up with it, but must remember that he is a son of man. Or perhaps this title puts honour upon him: the Messiah was lately called the *Son of man (ch.* 7:13), and Daniel is akin to him, and is a figure of him as a prophet and one *greatly beloved.* He assures him that he shall be made to know *what shall be in the last end of the indignation, v.* 19. Let it be laid up for a comfort to those who shall live to see these calamitous times that there shall be an end of them; *the indignation shall cease* (Isa. 10:25); it *shall be overpast,* Isa. 26:20. It may intermit and return again, but the *last end* shall be glorious; good will follow it, nay, and good will be brought out of it. He tells him (v. 17), *"At the time of the end shall be the vision;* when the last end of the indignation comes, when the course of this providence is completed, then the vision shall be made plain and intelligible by the event, as the event shall be made plain and intelligible by the vision." Or, *"At the time of the end* of the Jewish church, in the latter days of it, *shall this vision* be accomplished, 300 or 400 years hence; understand it therefore, that thou mayest leave it on record for the generations to come." But is he ask more particularly, "When is the time of the end? And how long will it be before it arrive?" let this answer suffice (v. 19): *At the time appointed the end shall be;* it is fixed in the divine counsel, which cannot be altered and which must not be pried into.

V. The exposition which he gave him of the vision. 1. Concerning the two monarchies of Persia and Greece, v. 20–22. The *ram* signified the succession of the kings of Media and Persia; the *rough goat* signified the kings of Greece; the *great horn* was Alexander; the *four horns* that rose in his room were the four kingdoms into which his conquests were cantoned, of which before, v. 8. They are said to *stand up out of the nations,* but *not in his power;* none of them ever made the figure that Alexander did. Josephus relates that when Alexander had taken Tyre, and subdued Palestine, and was upon his march to Jerusalem, Jaddas, who was them high priest (Nehemiah mentions one of his name, *ch.* 12:11), fearing his rage, had recourse to God by prayer and sacrifice for the common safety, and was by him warned in a dream that upon Alexander's approach he should throw open the gates of the city, and that he and the rest of the priests should go forth to meet him in their habits, and all the people in white. Alexander, seeing this company at a distance, went himself alone to the high priest, and, having prostrated himself before that God whose name was engraven in the golden plate of his mitre, he first saluted him; and, being asked by one of his own captains why he did so, he said that while he was yet in Macedon, musing on the conquest of Asia, there appeared to him a man like unto this, and thus attired, who invited him into Asia, and assured him of success in the conquest of it. The priests led him to the temple, where he offered sacrifice to the God of Israel as they directed him; and there they showed him this book of the prophet Daniel, that it was there foretold that a Grecian should come and destroy the Persians, which animated him very much in the expedition he was now meditating against Dar-

ius. Hereupon he took the Jews and their religion under his protection, promised to be kind to those of their religion in Babylon and Media, whither he was now marching, and in honour of him all the priests that had sons born that year called them *Alexander. Joseph. lib.* 11.

2. Concerning Antiochus, and his oppression of the Jews. This is said to be in the *latter time of the* kingdom of the Greeks, *when the transgressors are come to the full* (v. 23); that is, when the degenerate Jews have filled up the measure of their iniquity, and are ripe for this destruction, so that God cannot in honour bear with them any longer then shall *stand up* this king, to be *flagellum Dei* — the *rod in God's hand* for the chastising of the Jews. Now observe here, (1.) His character: He shall be a *king of fierce countenance,* insolent and furious, neither fearing God nor regarding man, *understanding dark sentences,* or (rather) *versed in dark practices,* the *hidden things of dishonesty;* he was master of all the arts of dissimulation and deceit, and knew the *depths of Satan* as well as any man. He was *wise to do evil.* (2.) His success. He shall make dreadful havoc of the nations about him: *His power shall be mighty,* bear down all before it, but not *by his own power* (v. 24), but partly by the assistance of his allies, Eumenes and Attalus, partly by the baseness and treachery of many of the Jews, even of the priests that came into his interests, and especially by the divine permission. it was not by his own power, but by a power given him from above, that he *destroyed wonderfully,* and thought he made himself a great man by being a great destroyer. He destroys wonderfully indeed, for he destroys, [1.] The *mighty people,* and they cannot resist him by their power. The princes of Egypt cannot stand before him with all their forces, but he practises against them and prospers. Note, The mighty ones of the earth commonly meet with those at length that are too hard for them, that are more mighty than they. Let not the strong man then glory in his strength, be it ever so great, unless he could be sure that there were none stronger than he. [2.] He destroys the *holy people,* or *the people of the holy ones;* and their sacred character does neither deter him from destroying them nor defend them from being destroyed. *All things come alike to all,* and there is one event to the mighty and to the holy in this world. [3.] The methods by which he will gain this success, not by true courage, wisdom, or justice, but by his *policy* and *craft* (v. 25), by fraud and deceit, and serpentine subtlety: He shall *cause craft to prosper;* so cunningly shall he carry on his projects that he shall gain his point by the art of wheedling. *By peace he shall destroy many,* as others do by war; under the pretence of treaties, leagues, and alliances, with them, he shall encroach on their rights, and trick them into a subjection to him. Thus sometimes what a nation truly brave has gained in a righteous war a nation truly base has regained in a treacherous peace, and craft has been caused to prosper. [4.] The mischief that he shall do to religion: *He shall magnify himself in his heart,* and think himself fit to prescribe and give law to every body, so that he shall *stand up against the Prince of princes,* that is, against God himself. He will profane his temple and altar, prohibit his worship, and persecute his worshippers. See what a height of impudence some men's impiety brings them to; they openly bid defiance to God himself though he is the Kings of kings. [5.] The ruin that he shall be brought to at last: *He shall be broken without hand,* that is, without the hand of man. He shall not be slain in war, nor shall he be assassinated, as tyrants commonly were, but he shall fall into the hand of the living God and die by an immediate stroke of his vengeance. He, hearing that the Jews had cast the image of Jupiter Olympius out of the temple, where he had placed it, was so enraged at the Jews that he vowed he would make Jerusalem *a common burial-place,* and determined to march thither immediately; but no sooner had he spoken these proud words than he was struck with an incurable plague in his bowels; worms bred so fast in his body that whole flakes of flesh sometimes dropped from him; his torments were violent, and the stench of his disease such that none could endure to come near him. He continued in this misery very long. At first he persisted in his menaces against the Jews; but at length, despairing of his recovery, he called his friends together, and acknowledged all those miseries to have fallen upon him for the injuries he had done to the Jews and his profaning the temple at Jerusalem. Then

he wrote courteous letters to the Jews, and vowed that if he recovered he would let them have the free exercise of their religion. But, finding his disease grow upon him, when he could no longer endure his own smell, he said, *It is meet to submit to God, and for man who is mortal not to set himself in competition with God,* and so died miserably in a strange land, on the mountains of Pacata near Babylon: so Ussher's Annals, *A.M.* 3840, about 160 years before the birth of Christ.

3. As to the time fixed for the continuance of the cessation of the daily sacrifice, it is not explained here, but only confirmed (v. 26). That *vision of the evening and morning is true,* in the proper sense of the words, and needs no explication. How unlikely soever it might be that God should suffer his own sanctuary to be thus profaned, yet it is true, it is too true, so it shall be.

VI. Here is the conclusion of this vision, and here, 1. The charge given to Daniel to keep it private for the present: *Shut thou up the vision;* let it not be publicly know among the Chaldeans, lest the Persians, who were now shortly to possess the kingdom, should be incensed against the Jews by it, because the downfall of their kingdom was foretold by it, which would be unseasonable now that the edict for their release was expected from the king of Persia. *Shut it up, for it shall be for many days.* It was about 300 years from the time of this vision to the time of the accomplishment of it; therefore he must *shut it up* for the present, even from the people of the Jews, lest it should amaze and perplex them, but let it be kept safely for the generations to come, that should live about the time of the accomplishment of it, for to them it would be both most intelligible and most serviceable. Note, What we know of the things of God should be carefully laid up, that hereafter, when there is occasion, it may be faithfully laid out; and what we have not now any use for, yet we may have another time. Divine truths should be sealed up among our treasures, that we may find them again after many days. 2. The care he took to keep it private, having received such a charge, v. 27. He *fainted, and was sick,* with the multitude of his thoughts within him occasioned by this vision, which oppressed and overwhelmed him the more because he was forbidden to publish what he had seen, so that *his belly was as wine which has no vent,* he was *ready to burst like new bottles,* Job 32:19. However, he kept it to himself, stifled and smothered the concern he was in; so that those he conversed with could not perceive it, but he *did the king's business* according to the duty of his place, whatever it was. Note, As long as we live in this world we must have something to do in it; and even those whom God has most dignified with his favours must not think themselves above their business; nor must the pleasure of communion with God take us off from the duties of our particular callings, but still we must in them *abide with God.* Those especially that are entrusted with public business must see to it that they conscientiously discharge their trust.

CHAPTER 9

In this chapter we have, I. Daniel's prayer for the restoration of the Jews who were in captivity, in which he confesses sin, and acknowledges the justice of God in their calamities, but pleads God's promises of mercy which he had yet in store for them (v. 1–19). II. An immediate answer sent him by an angel to his prayer, in which, 1. He is assured of the speedy release of the Jews out of their captivity (v. 20–23). And, 2. He is informed concerning the redemption of the world by Jesus Christ (of which that was a type), what should be the nature of it and when it should be accomplished (v. 24–27). And it is the clearest, brightest, prophecy of the Messiah, in all the Old Testament.

Verses 1–3

We left Daniel, in the close of the foregoing chapter, employed in the *king's business;* but here we have him employed in better business than any king had for him, speaking to God and hearing from him, not for himself only, but for the church, whose mouth he was to God, and for whose use the *oracles* of God were *committed to him,* relating to the days of the Messiah. Observe, 1. When it was that Daniel had this communion with God (v. 1), *in the first year of Darius the Mede,* who was newly made king of the Chaldeans, Babylon being conquered by him and his nephew, or grandson, Cyrus. In this year the seventy years of the Jews' captivity ended, but the decree for their release was not yet issued out; so that this address of Daniel's to God seems to have been ready in that year, and, probably, before he was cast into the lions' den. And one powerful inducement, perhaps, it was to him then to keep so close to the duty of prayer, though it cost him his life, that he had so lately experienced the benefit and comfort of it. 2. What occasioned his address to God by prayer (*v.* 2): He *understood by books* that seventy years was the time fixed for the continuance of *the desolations of Jerusalem. v.* 2. The *book* by which he understood this was the book of the prophecies of Jeremiah, in which he found it expressly foretold (Jer. 29:10), *After seventy years be accomplished in Babylon* (and therefore they must be reckoned from the first captivity, in the *third year* of Jehoiakim, which Daniel had reason to remember by a good token, for it was in that captivity that he was carried away himself, *ch.* 1:1), *I will visit you, and perform my good word towards you.* It was likewise said (Jer. 25:11), *This whole land shall be seventy years a desolation (chorbath),* the same word that Daniel here uses for the *desolations of Jerusalem,* which shows that he had that prophecy before him when he wrote this. Though Daniel was himself a great prophet, and one that was well acquainted with the visions of God, yet he was a diligent student in the scripture, and thought it no disparagement to him to consult Jeremiah's prophecies. He was a great politician, and prime-minister of state to one of the greatest monarchs upon earth, and yet could find both heart and time to converse with the word of God. The greatest and best men in the world must not think themselves above their Bibles. 3. How serious and solemn his address to God was when he understood that the seventy years were just upon expiring (for it appears, by Ezekiel's dating of his prophecies, that they exactly computed the years of their captivity), then he *set his face to seek God by prayer.* Note, God's promises are intended, not to supersede, but to excite and encourage, our prayers; and, when we see the day of the performance of them approaching, we should the more earnestly plead them with God and put them in suit. So Daniel did here; he prayed three times a day, and, no doubt, in every prayer made mention of the desolations of Jerusalem; yet he did not think that enough, but even in the midst of his business set time apart for an extraordinary application to Heaven on Jerusalem's behalf. God had said to Ezekiel that though Daniel, among others, stood before him, his intercession should not prevail to prevent the judgment (Eze. 14:14), yet he hopes, now that *the warfare is accomplished* (Isa. 40:2), his prayer may be heard for the removing of the judgment. When the day of deliverance dawns it is time for God's praying people to bestir themselves; something extraordinary is then expected and required from them, besides their daily sacrifice. Now *Daniel sought by prayer and supplications,* for fear lest the sins of the people should provoke him to defer their deliverance longer than was intended, or rather that the people might be prepared by the grace of God for the deliverance now that the providence of God was about to work it out for them. Now observe, (1.) The intenseness of his mind in this prayer; *I set my face unto the Lord God to seek him,* which denotes the fixedness of his thoughts, the firmness of his faith, and the fervour of his devout affections, in the duty. We must, in prayer, set God before us, an set ourselves as in his presence; to him we must *direct our prayer* and must *look up.* Probably, in token of his setting his face towards God, he did, as usual, set his face towards Jerusalem, to affect his own heart the more with the desolations of it. (2.) The mortification of his body in this prayer. In token of his deep humiliation before God for his own sins, and the sins of his people, and the sense he had of his unworthiness, when he prayed he *fasted,* put on *sackcloth,* and lay in *ashes,* the more to affect himself with the desolations of Jerusalem, which he was praying for the repair of, and to make himself sensible that he was now about an extraordinary work.

Verses 4–19

We have here Daniel's prayer to God as his God, and the confession which he joined with that prayer: I *prayed, and made my confession.* Note, In every prayer we must make confession, not only of the sins we have been guilty of (which we commonly call *confession),* but of our faith in God and dependence upon him, our sorrow for sin and our resolutions against it. It must be our confession, must be the language of our own convictions and that which we ourselves do heartily subscribe to.

Let us go over the several parts of this prayer, which we have reason to think that he offered up much more largely than is here recorded, these being only the heads of it.

I. Here is his humble, serious, reverent address to God, 1. As a God to be feared, and whom it is our duty always to stand in awe of: *"O Lord! the great and dreadful God,* that art able to deal with the greatest and most terrible of the church's enemies." 2. As a God to be trusted, and whom it is our duty to depend upon and put a confidence in: *Keeping the covenant and mercy to those that love him,* and, as a proof of their love to him, *keep his commandments.* If we fulfil our part of the bargain, he will not fail to fulfil his. He will be to his people as good as his word, for he keeps covenant with them, and not one iota of his promise shall fall to the ground; nay, he will be better than his word, for he keeps mercy to them, something more than was in the covenant. It was proper for Daniel to have his eye upon God's mercy now that he was to lay before him the miseries of his people, and upon God's covenant now that he was to sue for the performance of a promise. Note, We should, in prayer, look both at God's greatness and his goodness, his majesty and mercy in conjunction.

II. Here is a penitent confession of sin, the procuring cause of all the calamities which his people had for so many years been groaning under, *v.* 5, 6. When we seek to God for national mercies we ought to humble ourselves before him for national sins. These are the sins Daniel here laments; and we may here observe the variety of words he makes use of to set forth the greatness of their provocations (for it becomes penitents to lay load upon themselves): *We have sinned* in many particular instances, nay, *we have committed iniquity,* we have driven a trade of sin, *we have done wickedly* with a hard heart and a stiff neck, and herein we have *rebelled,* have taken up arms against the King of kings, his crown and dignity. Two things aggravated their sins: — 1. That they had violated the express laws God had given them by Moses: "We have *departed from they precepts and from thy judgments,* and have not conformed to them. And (*v.* 10) *we have not obeyed the voice of the Lord our God."* That which speaks the nature of sin, that it is *the transgression of the law,* does sufficiently speak the malignity of it; if sin be made to *appear sin,* it cannot be made to appear worse; its *sinfulness* is its greatest hatefulness, Rom. 7:13. God has *set his laws before us* plainly and fully, as the copy we should write after, yet *we have not walked in* them, but turned aside, or turned back. 2. That they had slighted the fair warnings God had given them by the prophets, which in every age he had sent to them, *rising up betimes and sending them* (*v.* 6): *"We have not hearkened to thy servants the prophets,* who have put us in mind of thy laws, and of the sanctions of them; though they *spoke in thy name,* we have not regarded them; though they delivered their message faithfully, with a universal respect to all orders and degrees of men, to *our kings and princes,* whom they had the courage and confidence to speak to, *to our fathers,* and to all the *people of the land,* whom they had the condescension and compassion to speak to, yet *we have not hearkened to them,* nor heard them, or not heeded them, or not complied with them." Mocking God's messengers, and despising his words, were Jerusalem's measure-filling sins, 2 Chr. 36:16. This confession of sin is repeated here, and much insisted on; penitents should again and again accuse and reproach themselves till they find their hearts thoroughly broken. *All Israel have transgressed thy law, v.* 11. It is *Israel,* God's professing people, who have known better, and from whom better is expected — Israel, God's peculiar people, whom he has surrounded with his favours; not here and there one, but it is *all* Israel, the generality of them, the body of the people, that *have transgressed by departing* and getting out of the way, *that they might not* hear, and so might not *obey, thy voice.* This disobedience is that which all true penitents do most sensibly charge upon themselves (*v.* 14): *We obeyed not his voice, and* (*v.* 15) *we have sinned, we have done wickedly.* Those that would find mercy must thus confess their sins.

III. Here is a self-abasing acknowledgment of the righteousness of God in all the judgments that were brought upon them; and it is evermore the way of true penitents thus to justify God, that he may be clear when he judges, and the sinner may bear all the blame. 1. He acknowledges that it was sin that plunged them in all these troubles. Israel is *dispersed* through *all the countries* about, and so weakened, impoverished, and exposed. God's hand has *driven them* hither and thither, some *near,* where they are known and therefore the more ashamed, others *afar off,* where they are not known and therefore the more abandoned, and it is *because of their trespass that they have trespassed* (*v.* 7); they mingled themselves with the nations that they might be debauched by them, and now God mingles them with the nations that they might be stripped by them. 2. He owns the righteousness of God in it, that he had done them no wrong in all he had brought upon them, but had dealt with them as they deserved (*v.* 7): *"O Lord! righteousness belongs to thee;* we have no fault to find with thy providence, no exceptions to make against thy judgments, for (*v.* 14) *the Lord our God is righteous in all his works which he does,* even in the sore calamities we are now under, for *we obeyed not the words* of his mouth, and therefore justly feel the weight of his hand." This seems to be borrowed from Lam. 1:18. 3. He takes notice of the fulfilling of the scripture in what was brought upon them. *In very faithfulness he afflicted them;* for it was according to the word which he had spoken. *The curse is poured upon us and the oath,* that is, the curse that was ratified by an oath in the law of Moses, *v.* 11. This further justifies God in their troubles, that he did but inflict the penalty of the law, which he had given them fair notice of. It was necessary for the preserving of the honour of God's veracity, and saving his government from contempt, that the threatenings of his word should be accomplished, otherwise they look but as bugbears, nay, they seem not at all frightful. Therefore *he has confirmed his words which spoke against us* because we broke his laws, *and against our judges that judged us* because they did not according to the duty of their place punish the breach of God's laws. He told them many a time that if they did not execute justice, as terrors to evil-workers, he must and would take the work into his own hands; and now he has *confirmed* what he said *by bringing upon us a great evil,* in which the princes and judges themselves deeply shared. Note, It contributes very much to our profiting by the *judgments of God's hand* to observe how exactly they agree with the *judgments of his mouth.* 4. He aggravates the calamities they were in, lest they should seem, having been long used to them, to make light of them, and so to lose the benefit of the chastening of the Lord by despising it. "It is not some of the common troubles of life that we are complaining of, but that which has in it some special marks of divine displeasure; for *under the whole heaven has not been done as has been done upon Jerusalem," v.* 12. It is Jeremiah's lamentation in the name of the church, *Was ever sorrow like unto my sorrow?* which must suppose another similar question, *Was ever sin like unto my sin?* 5. He puts shame upon the whole nation, from the highest to the lowest; and if they will say *Amen* to his prayer, as it was fit they should if they would come in for a share in the benefit of it, they must all put their hand upon their mouth, and their mouth in the dust: *"To us belongs confusion of faces as at this day* (*v.* 7); we lie under the shame of the punishment of our iniquity, for shame is our due." If Israel had retained their character, and had continued a holy people, they would have been *high above all nations in praise, and mane, and honour* (Duet. 26:19); but now that they have *sinned and done wickedly* confusion and disgrace belong to them, to *the men of Judah and the inhabitants of Jerusalem,* the inhabitants both of the country and of the city, for they have been all alike guilty before God; it belongs to *all Israel,* both to the two tribes, *that are near,* by the rivers of Babylon, and to the ten tribes, *that are afar off,* in the land of Assyria. "Confusion belongs not only to the common people of our land, but to *our kings, our princes,* and *our fathers* (*v.* 8), who should have set a better example, and have used their authority and influence for the checking of the threatening torrent of vice profaneness." 6. He imputes the continuance of the judgment to their incorrigibleness under it (*v.* 13, 14): *"All this evil has come upon us,* and has lain long upon us, *yet made we not our prayer before the Lord our God,* not in a right manner, as we should have made it, *with a humble, lowly, penitent, and obedient heart.* We have been smitten, but have not returned to him that smote us. *We have not entreated the face of the Lord our God"* (so the word is); "we have taken no care to make our peace with God and reconcile ourselves to him." Daniel set his brethren a good example of praying continually, but he was sorry to see how few there were that followed his example; in their *affliction* it was expected that they would *seek God early,* but they sought him not, that they might *turn from their iniquities* and *understand his truth.* The errand upon which afflictions are sent is to bring men to *turn from their iniquities* and to *understand God's truth;* so Elihu had explained them, Job 36:10. God by them *opens men's ears to discipline* and *commands that they return from iniquity.* And if men were brought rightly to *understand God's truth,* and to submit to the power and authority of it, they would turn from the error of their ways. Now the first step towards this is to *make our prayer before the Lord our God,* that the affliction may be sanctified before it is removed, and that the grace of God may go along with the providence of God, to make it answer the end. Those who in their affliction *make not their prayer to God,* who *cry not when he binds them,* are not likely to *turn from iniquity* or to *understand his truth. "Therefore,* because we have not improved the affliction, *the Lord has watched upon the evil,* as the judge takes care that execution be done according to the sentence. Because we have not been melted, he has kept us still in the furnace, and *watched over it,* to make the heat yet more intense;" for when God judges he will overcome, and will be justified in all his proceedings.

IV. Here is a believing appeal to the mercy of God, and to the ancient tokens of his favour to Israel, and the concern of his own glory in their interests. 1. It is some comfort to them (and not a little) that God has been always ready to pardon sin (*v.* 9): *To the Lord our God belong mercies and forgiveness;* this refers to that proclamation of his name, Ex. 34:6, 7, *The Lord God, gracious and merciful, forgiving iniquity.* Note, It is very encouraging to poor sinners to recollect that *mercies belong to God,* as it is convincing and humbling to them to recollect that righteousness belongs to him; and those who give him the glory of his righteousness may take to themselves the comfort of his mercies, Ps. 62:12. There are abundant mercies in God, and not only forgiveness but *forgivenesses;* he is a *God of pardons* (Neh. 9:17, marg.); he *multiplies to pardon,* Isa. 55:7. *Though we have rebelled against him,* yet with him there is mercy, pardoning mercy, even *for the rebellious.* 2. It is likewise a support to them to think that God had formerly glorified himself by delivering them out of Egypt; so far he looks back for the encouragement of his faith (*v.* 15): *"Thou hast* formerly *brought thy people out of Egypt with a mighty hand,* and wilt thou not now with the same mighty hand bring them out of Babylon? Were they then formed into a people, and shall they not now be reformed and new-formed? Are they now sinful and unworthy, and were they not so then? Are their oppressors now mighty and haughty, and were they not so then? And has not God said the their deliverance out of Babylon shall outshine even that out of Egypt?" Jer. 16:14, 15. The force of this plea lies in that, *"Thou hast gotten thyself renown,* hast *made thyself a name"* (so the word is) *"as at this day,* even to this day, by bringing us out of Egypt; and wilt thou lose the credit of that by letting us perish in Babylon? Didst thou get a renown by that deliverance which we have so often commemorated, and wilt thou not now get thyself a renown by this which we have so often prayed for, and so long waited for?"

V. Here is a pathetic complaint of the reproach that God's people lay under, and the ruins that God's sanctuary lay in, both which redounded very much to the dishonour of God and the diminution of that name and renown which God had gained by bringing them out of Egypt. 1. God's holy people were despised. By *their sins and the iniquities of their fathers* they had profaned their crown and made themselves despicable, and then though they are, in name and profession, God's people, and upon that account truly great and honourable, yet they become *a reproach to all that are round about them.* Their neighbours laugh them to scorn, and triumph in their disgrace. Note, *Sin is a reproach to any people,* but especially to God's people, that have more eyes upon them and have more honour to lose than other people. 2. God's holy place was desolate. Jerusalem, the holy city, was a reproach (*v.* 16) when it lay in ruins; it was an *astonishment* and a hissing to all that passed by. The sanctuary, the holy house, was desolate (*v.* 17), the altars were demolished, and all the buildings laid in ashes. Note, The desolations of the sanctuary are the grief of all the saints, who reckon all their comforts in this world buried in the ruins of the sanctuary.

VI. Here is an importunate request to God for the restoring of the poor captive Jews to their former enjoyments again. The petition is very pressing, for God gives us leave in prayer to wrestle with him: *"O Lord! I beseech thee, v.* 16. If ever thou wilt do any thing for me, do this; it is my heart's desire and prayer. *Now therefore, O our God! hear the prayer of thy servant and his supplication* (*v.* 17), and grant an answer of peace." Now what are his petitions? What are his requests? 1. That God would turn away his wrath from them; that is it which all the saints dread and deprecate more than any thing: O let *thy anger be turned away from thy Jerusalem, thy holy mountain! v.* 16. He does not pray for the turning again of their captivity (let the Lord do with them as seems good in his eyes), but he prays first for the *turning away of God's wrath.* Take away the cause, and the effect will cease. 2. That he would lift up the light of his countenance upon them (*v.* 17): *"Cause thy face to shine upon thy sanctuary that is desolate;* return in thy mercy to us, and show that thou art reconciled to us, and then all shall be well." Note, The shining of God's face upon the desolations of the sanctuary is all in all towards the repair of it; and upon that foundation it must be rebuilt. If therefore its friends would begin their work at the right end, they must first be earnest with God in prayer for his favour, and recommend his desolate sanctuary to his smiles. *Cause thy face to shine* and then *we shall be saved,* Ps. 80:3. 3. That he would forgive their sins, and then hasten their deliverance (*v.* 19): *O Lord! hear; O Lord! forgive.* "That the mercy prayed for may be granted in mercy, let the sin that threatens to come between us and it be removed: *O Lord! hearken and do,* not hearken and speak only, but hearken and do; do that for us which none else can, and that speedily — *defer not, O my God!"* Now that he saw the appointed day approaching he could in faith pray that God would make haste to them and not defer. David often prays, *Make haste, O God! to help me.*

VII. Here are several pleas and arguments to enforce the petitions. God gives us leave not only to pray, but to plead with him, which is not to move him (he himself knows what he will do), but to move ourselves, to excite our fervency and encourage our faith. 1. They disdain a dependence upon any righteousness of their own; they pretend not to merit any thing at God's hand but wrath and the curse (*v.* 18): *"We do not present our supplications before thee* with hope to speed *for our righteousness,* as if we were worthy to receive thy favour for any good in us, or done by us, or could demand any thing as a debt; we cannot insist upon our own justification, no, though we were more righteous than we are; nay, though we knew nothing amiss of ourselves, yet are we not thereby justified, nor *would we answer,* but we would *make supplication to our Judge."* Moses had told Israel long before that, whatever God did for them, it was *not for their righteousness,* Deu. 9:4, 5. And Ezekiel had of late told them that their return out of Babylon would be *not for their sakes,* Eze. 36:22, 32. Note, Whenever we come to God for mercy we must lay aside all conceit of, and confidence in, our own righteousness. 2. They take their encouragement in prayer from God only, as knowing that his reasons of mercy are fetched from within himself, and therefore from him we must borrow all our pleas for mercy, and so give honour to him when we are suing for grace and mercy from him. (1.) "Do it *for thy own sake* (*v.* 19), for the accomplishment of thy own counsel, the performance of thy own promise, and the manifestation of thy own glory." Note, God will do his own work, not only in his own way and time, but for his own sake, and so we must take it. (2.) "Do it *for the Lord's sake,* that is, for the Lord Christ's sake," for the sake of the Messiah promised, who is the Lord (so the most and best of our Christian interpreters understand it), *for the sake of Adonai,* so David called the Messiah (Ps. 110:1), and mercy is prayed for for the church for the sake of the *Son of man* (Ps. 80:17), and *for thy Word's sake,* he is Lord of all. It is for his sake that God causes his face to shine upon sinners when they repent and turn to him, because of the satisfaction he has made. In all our prayers that therefore must be our plea; we must *make mention of his righteousness, even of his only,* Ps. 71:16. *Look upon the face of the anointed.* He has himself directed us to *ask in his name.* (3.) "Do it *according to all thy righteousness* (*v.* 16), that is, plead for us against our persecutors and oppressors *according to thy righteousness.* Though we are ourselves unrighteous before God, yet with reference to them we have a righteous cause, which we leave it with the righteous God to appear in the defence of." Or, rather, by the *righteousness of God* here is meant his faithfulness to his promise. God had, *according to his righteousness,* executed the threatening, *v.* 11. "Now, Lord, wilt thou not do according to *all* thy righteousness? Wilt thou not be as true to thy promises as thou hast been to thy threatenings and accomplish them also?" (4.) "Do it *for thy great mercies* (*v.* 18), to make it to appear that thou art a merciful God." The good things we ask of God we call *mercies,* because we expect them purely from God's mercy. And, because misery is the proper object of mercy, the prophet here spreads the deplorable condition of the church before God, as it were to move his compassion: *"Open thy eyes and behold our desolations,* especially the desolations of the sanctuary. O look with pity upon a pitiable case!" Note, The desolations of the church must in prayer be laid before God and then left with him. (5.) "Do it for the sake of the relation we stand in to thee. The sanctuary that is desolate is thy sanctuary (*v.* 17), dedicated to thy honour, employed in thy service, and the place of thy residence. Jerusalem is *thy* city and *thy holy mountain* (*v.* 16); it is *the city which is called by thy name," v.* 18. It was the city which God had *chosen out of all the tribes of Israel, to put his name there.* "The people that have *become a reproach* are *thy people,* and thy name suffers in the reproach cast upon them (*v.* 16); they are *called by thy name, v.* 19. Lord, thou hast a property in them, and therefore art interested in their interests; wilt thou not provide for thy own, for those of thy own house? They are *thine, save them,"* Ps. 119:94.

Verses 20–27

We have here the answer that was immediately sent to Daniel's prayer, and it is a very memorable one, as it contains the most illustrious prediction of Christ and gospel-grace that is extant in all the *Old Testament.* If John Baptist was the morning-star, this was the day-break to the Sun of righteousness, the *day-spring from on high.* Here is,

I. The time when this answer was given.

1. It was while Daniel was at prayer. This he observed and laid a strong emphasis upon: *While I was speaking* (*v.* 20), yea, *while I was speaking in prayer* (*v.* 21), before he rose from his knees, and while there was yet more which he intended to say.

(1.) He mentions the two heads he chiefly insisted upon in prayer, and which perhaps he designed yet further to enlarge upon. [1.] He was confessing sin and lamenting that — "both *my sin and the sin of my people Israel."* Daniel was a very great and good man, and yet he finds sin of his own to confess before God and is ready to confess it; for there is not a *just man upon earth that does good and sins not,* nor that sins and repents not. St. John puts himself into the number of those who deceive themselves if they say that they *have no sin,* and who therefore *confess their sins,* 1 Jn. 1:8. Good men find it an ease to their consciences to pour out their complaints before the Lord against themselves; and that is *confessing sin.* He also confessed the *sin of his people,* and bewailed that. Those who are heartily concerned for the glory of God, the welfare of the church, and the souls of men, will mourn for the sins of others as well as for their own. [2.] He was *making supplication before the Lord his God,* and presenting it to him as an intercessor for Israel; and in this prayer his concern was for *the holy mountain of his God,* Mount Zion. The desolations of the sanctuary lay nearer his heart than those of the city and the land; and the repair of that, and the setting up of the public worship of God of Israel again, were the things he had in view, in the deliverance he was preparing for, more than re-establishment of their civil interests. Now,

(2.) While Daniel was thus employed, [1.] He had a grant made him of the mercy he prayed for. Note, God is very ready to hear prayer and to give an answer of peace. Now was fulfilled what God had spoken Isa. 65:24, *While they are yet speaking, I will hear.* Daniel grew very fervent in prayer, and his affections were very strong, v. 18, 19. And, *while he was speaking* with such fervour and ardency, the angel came to him with a gracious answer. God is well pleased with lively devotions. We cannot now expect that God should send us answers to our prayer by angels, but, if we pray with fervency for that which God has promised, we may by faith take the promise as an immediate answer to the prayer; for *he is faithful that has promised.* [2.] He had a discovery made to him of a far greater and more glorious redemption which God would work out for his church in the latter days. Note, Those that would be brought acquainted with Christ and his grace must be *much in prayer.*

2. It was *about the time of the evening oblation, v.* 21. The altar was in ruins, and there was no oblation offered upon it, but, it should seem, the pious Jews in their captivity were daily thoughtful of the time when it should have been offered, and at that hour were ready to weep at the remembrance of it, and desired and hoped that their prayer should be *set forth before God as incense,* and the *lifting up of their hands,* and their hearts with their hands, should be acceptable in his sight *as the evening-sacrifice,* Ps. 141:2. The evening oblation was a type of the great sacrifice which Christ was to offer in the evening of the world, and it was in the virtue of that sacrifice that Daniel's prayer was accepted when he prayed *for the Lord's sake;* and for the sake of that this glorious discovery of redeeming love was made to him. The Lamb *opened the seals* in the virtue of his own blood.

II. The messenger by whom this answer was sent. It was not given him in a dream, nor by a voice from heaven, but, for the greater certainty and solemnity of it, an angel was sent on purpose, appearing in a human shape, to give this answer to Daniel. Observe,

1. Who this angel, or messenger, was; it was *the man Gabriel.* If Michael the archangel be, as many suppose, no other than Jesus Christ, this Gabriel is the only created angel that is named in scripture. Gabriel signifies the *mighty one of God;* for the angels are *great in power and might,* 2 Pt. 2:11. It was he *whom I had seen in the vision at the beginning.* Daniel heard him called by his name, and thence learned it (Dan. 8:16); and, though then he trembled at his approach, yet he observed him so carefully that now he knew him again, knew him to be the same that he had seen at the beginning, and, being somewhat better acquainted with him, was not now so terrified at the sight of him as he had been at first. When this angel said to *Zacharias, I am Gabriel* (Lu. 1:19), he intended thereby to put him in mind of this notice which he had given to Daniel of the Messiah's coming when it was at a distance, for the confirming of his faith in the notice he was then about to give of it as at the door.

2. The instructions which this messenger received from the Father of lights to whom Daniel prayed (v. 23): *At the beginning of thy supplications* the word, *the commandment, came forth* from God. Notice was given to the angels in heaven of this counsel of God, which they were desirous to look into; and orders were given to Gabriel to go immediately and bring the notice of it to Daniel. By this it appears that it was not any thing which Daniel said that moved God, for the answer was given as he began to pray; but God was well pleased with his serious solemn address to the duty, and, in token of that, sent him this gracious message. Or perhaps it was *at the beginning of Daniel's supplications* that *Cyrus's word,* or *commandment, went forth to restore and to build Jerusalem,* that going forth spoken of v. 25. "The thing was done *this very day;* the proclamation of liberty to the Jews was signed this morning, just when thou wast praying for it;" and now, at the close of this fast-day, Daniel had notice of it, as, at the close of the *day of atonement,* the jubilee-trumpet sounded to proclaim liberty.

3. The haste he made to deliver his message: He was *caused to fly swiftly, v.* 21. Angels are winged messengers, quick in their motions, and delay not to execute the orders they receive; they run and *return like a flash of lightning,* Eze. 1:14. But, it should seem, sometimes they are more expeditious than at other times, and make a quicker despatch, as here the angel was *caused to fly swiftly;* that is, he was ordered and he was enabled to fly swiftly. Angels do their work in obedience to divine command and

in dependence upon divine strength. Though they excel in wisdom, they fly swifter or slower as God directs; and, though they excel in power, they fly but as God causes them to fly. Angels themselves are to us what he makes them to be; they are *his ministers,* and *do his pleasure,* Ps. 103:21.

4. The prefaces or introductions to his message. (1.) He *touched him* (v. 21), as before (ch. 8:18), not to awaken him out of sleep as then, but to give him a hint to break off his prayer and to attend to that which he has to say in answer to it. Note, In order to the keeping up of our communion with God we must not only be forward to speak to God, but as forward to hear what he has to say to us; when we have prayed we must look up, must look after our prayers, must set ourselves upon our watch-tower. (2.) He *talked with him* (v. 22), talked familiarly with him, as one friend talks with another, that *his terror might not make him afraid.* He informed him on what errand he came, that he was sent from heaven on purpose with a kind message to him: "*I have come to show thee* (v. 23), to tell thee that which thou didst not know before." He had shown him the troubles of the church under Antiochus, and the period of those troubles (ch. 8:19); but now he has greater things to show him, for he that is faithful in a little shall be entrusted with more. "Nay, *I have now come forth to give thee skill and understanding* (v. 22), not only to show thee these things, but to *make thee understand them."* (3.) He assured him that he was a favourite of Heaven, else he would not have had this intelligence sent him, and he must take it for a favour: "*I have come to show thee, for thou art greatly beloved.* Thou art *a man of desires,* acceptable to God, and whom he has a favour for." Note, Though God loves all his children, yet there are some that are more than the rest *greatly beloved.* Christ had one disciple that lay in his bosom; and that *beloved disciple* was he that was entrusted with the prophetical visions of the New Testament, as Daniel was with those of the Old. For what greater token can there be of God's favour to any man than for the secrets of the Lord to be with him? Abraham is the *friend of God;* and therefore *Shall I hide from Abraham that thing which I do?* Gen. 18:17. Note, Those may reckon themselves greatly beloved of God to whom, and in whom, he *reveals his Son.* Some observe that the title which this angel Gabriel gives to the Virgin Mary is much the same with this which he here gives to Daniel, as if he designed to put her in mind of it — *Thou that art highly favoured;* as Daniel, *greatly beloved.* (4.) He demands his serious attention to the discovery he was now about to make to him: *Therefore understand the matter, and consider the vision, v.* 23. This intimates that it was a thing well worthy of his regard, above any of the visions he had been before favoured with. Note, Those who would understand the things of God must consider them, must apply their minds to them, ponder upon them, and compare spiritual things with spiritual. The reason why we are so much in the dark concerning the revealed will of God, and mistake concerning it, is want of consideration. This vision both requires and deserves consideration.

III. The message itself. It was delivered with great solemnity, received no doubt with great attention, and recorded with great exactness; but in it, as is usual in prophecies, there are things dark and hard to be understood. Daniel, who understood by the book of the prophet Jeremiah the expiration of the seventy years of the captivity, is now honourably employed to make known to the church another more glorious release, which that was but a shadow of, at the end of another seventy, not years, but weeks of years. He prayed over that prophecy, and received this in answer to that prayer. He had prayed for *his people* and the *holy city* — that *they* might be released, that *it* might be rebuilt; but God answers him *above what he was able to ask or think.* God not only grants, but outdoes, the desires of those that fear him, Ps. 21:4.

1. The times here determined are somewhat hard to be understood. In general, it is *seventy weeks,* that is, *seventy times seven years,* which makes just 490 years. The great affairs that are yet to come concerning the people of Israel, and the city of Jerusalem, will lie within the compass of these years.

(1.) These years are thus described by weeks, [1.] In conformity to the prophetic style, which is, for the most part, abstruse, and out of the common road of speaking, that

the things foretold might not lie too obvious. [2.] To put an honour upon the division of time into weeks, which is made purely by the sabbath day, and to signify that that should be perpetual. [3.] With reference to the seventy years of the captivity; as they had been so long kept out of the possession of their own land, so, being now restored to it they should seven times as long be kept in the possession of it. So much more does God delight in showing mercy than in punishing. The land had *enjoyed its sabbaths,* in a melancholy sense, seventy years, Lev. 26:34. But now the people of the Lord shall, in a comfortable sense, enjoy their sabbaths seven times seventy years, and in them seventy sabbatical years, which makes ten jubilees. Such proportions are there in the disposals of Providence, that we might see and admire the wisdom of him who has *determined the times before appointed.*

(2.) The difficulties that arise about these seventy weeks are, [1.] Concerning the time when they commence and whence they are to be reckoned. They are here dated *from the going forth of the commandments to restore and to build Jerusalem, v.* 25. I should most incline to understand this of the edict of Cyrus mentioned Ezra 1:1, for by it the people were *restored;* and, though express mention be not made there of the building of Jerusalem, yet that is supposed in the building of the temple, and was foretold to be done by Cyrus, Isa. 44:28. He shall *say to Jerusalem, Thou shalt be built.* That was, both in prophecy and in history, the most famous decree for the building of Jerusalem; nay, it should seem, this *going forth of the commandment* (which may as well be meant of God's command concerning it as of Cyrus's) is the same with that going forth of the commandment mentioned v. 23, which was *at the beginning of Daniel's supplications.* And it looks very graceful that the seventy weeks should begin immediately upon the expiration of the seventy years. And there is nothing to be objected against this but that by this reckoning the *Persian monarchy,* from the taking of Babylon by Cyrus to Alexander's conquest of Darius, lasted but 130 years; whereas, by the particular account given of the reigns of the Persian emperors, it is computed that it continued 230 years. So Thucydides, Xenophon, and others reckon. those who fix it to that first edict set aside these computations of the heathen historians as uncertain and not to be relied upon. But others, willing to reconcile them, begin the 490 years, not at the edict of Cyrus (Ezra 1:1), but at the second edict for the building of Jerusalem, issued out by Darius Nothus above 100 years after, mentioned Ezra vi. Others fix on the seventh year of Artaxerxes Mnemon, who sent Ezra with a commission, Ezra 7:8–12. The learned Mr. Poole, in his Latin Synopsis, has a vast and most elaborate collection of what has been said, *pro* and *con,* concerning the different beginnings of these weeks, with which the learned may entertain themselves. [2.] Concerning the termination of them; and here likewise interpreters are not agreed. Some make them to end at the death of Christ, and think the express words of this famous prophecy will warrant us to conclude that from this very hour when Gabriel spoke to Daniel, at the time of the evening oblation, to the hour when Christ died, which was towards evening too, it was exactly 490 years; and I am willing enough to be of that opinion. But others think, because it is said that *in the midst of the weeks* (that is, the last of the seventy weeks) he *shall cause the sacrifice and the oblation to cease,* they end *three years and a half* after the death of Christ, when the Jews having rejected the gospel, the apostles turned to the Gentiles. But those who make them to end precisely at the death of Christ read it thus, "He shall *make strong the testament to the many;* the last seven, or the last week, yea, *half that seven,* or *half that week* (namely, the latter half, the three years and a half which Christ spent in his public ministry), shall bring to an end sacrifice and oblation." Others make these 490 years to end with the destruction of Jerusalem, about thirty-seven years after the death of Christ, because these seventy weeks are said to be *determined upon the people* of the Jews *and the holy city;* and much is said here concerning the destruction of the city and the sanctuary. [3.] Concerning the division of them into seven weeks, and sixty-two weeks, and one week; and the reason of this is as hard to account for as any thing else. In the first seven weeks, or forty-nine years, the temple and city were built; and in the last single week Christ preached his gospel, by which the Jewish economy was taken down, and the foundations were laid of the gospel city and temple, which were to be built upon the ruins of the former.

(3.) But, whatever uncertainty we may labour under concerning the exact fixing of these times, there is enough clear and certain to answer the two great ends of determining them. [1.] It did serve them to raise and support the expectations of believers. There were general promises of the coming of the Messiah made to the patriarchs; the preceding prophets had often spoken of him as *one that should come,* but never was the time fixed for his coming until now. And, though there might be so much doubt concerning the date of this reckoning that they could not ascertain the time just to a year, yet by the light of this prophecy they were directed about what time to expect him. And we find, accordingly, that when Christ came he was generally *looked for* as the *consolation of Israel,* and *redemption in Jerusalem* by him, Lu. 2:25, 38. There were those that for this reason thought the *kingdom of God should immediately appear* (Lu. 19:11), and some think it was this that brought a more than ordinary concourse of people to Jerusalem, Acts 2:5. [2.] It does serve still to refute and silence the expectations of unbelievers, who will not own that Jesus is he who *should come,* but still *look for another.* This prediction should silence them, and will condemn them; for, reckon these seventy weeks from which of the commandments to build Jerusalem we please, it is certain that they have expired above 1500 years ago; so that the Jews are for ever *without excuse,* who will not own that the Messiah has come when they have gone so far beyond their utmost reckoning for his coming. But by this we are confirmed in our belief of the Messiah's being come, and that our Jesus is he, that he came just at the time prefixed, a time worthy to be had in everlasting remembrance.

2. The events here foretold are more plain and easy to be understood, at least to us now. Observe what is here foretold,

(1.) Concerning the return of the Jews now speedily to their own land, and their settlement again there, which was the thing that Daniel now principally prayed for; and yet it is but briefly touched upon here in the answer to his prayer. Let this be a comfort to the pious Jews, that a *commandment* shall *go forth to restore and to build Jerusalem, v.* 25. And the commandment shall not be in vain; for though the times will be very troublous, and this good work will meet with great opposition, yet it shall be carried on, and brought to perfection at last. The *street* shall be *built again,* as spacious and splendid as ever it was, and *the walls, even in troublous times.* Note, as long as we are here in this world we must expect *troublous times,* upon some account or other. Even when we have *joyous times* we must rejoice with trembling; it is but a gleam, it is but a lucid interval of peace and prosperity; the clouds will *return after the rain.* When the Jews are restored in triumph to their own land, yet there they must expect troublous times, and prepare for them. But this is our comfort, that God will carry on his own work, will build up his Jerusalem, will beautify it, will fortify it, *even in troublous times;* nay, the troublousness of the times may by the grace of God contribute to the advancement of the church. The more it is afflicted the more it multiplies.

(2.) Concerning the Messiah and his undertaking. The carnal Jews looked for a Messiah that could deliver them from the Roman yoke and give them temporal power and wealth, whereas they were here told that the Messiah should come upon another errand, purely spiritual, and upon the account of which he should be the more welcome. [1.] Christ came to *take away sin,* and to abolish that. Sin had made a quarrel between God and man, had alienated men from God and provoked God against man; it was this that put dishonour upon God and brought misery upon mankind; this was the great mischief-maker. He that would do God a real service, and man a real kindness, must be the destruction of this. Christ undertakes to be so, and *for this purpose* he is *manifested, to destroy the works of the devil.* He does not say to *finish your* transgressions and your sins, but *transgression* and *sin* in general, for he is the propitiation not only for *our sins,* that are Jews, but *for the sins of the whole world.* He came, *First,* To *finish transgression,* to *restrain* it (so some), to break the power of it, to *bruise the head* of that serpent that had done so much mischief, to take away the usurped dominion of that tyrant, and to set up a kingdom of holiness and love in the hearts of men, upon the ruins of Satan's kingdom there, that, where *sin and death* had *reigned, righteousness* and *life* through grace might *reign.* When he died he said, *It is finished;* sin has now had its death-wound given it, like Samson's, *Let me die with the Philistines. Animamque in vulnere ponit — He inflicts the wound and dies. Secondly,* To *make an end of sin,* to abolish it, that it may not rise up in judgment against us, to obtain the pardon of it, that it may not be our ruin, to *seal up sins* (so the margin reads it), that they may not appear or break out against us, to accuse and condemn us, as, when Christ cast the devil into the bottomless pit, he *set a seal upon him,* Rev. 20:3. When sin is pardoned it is *sought for and not found,* as that which is *sealed up. Thirdly,* To *make reconciliation for iniquity,* as by a sacrifice, to satisfy the justice of God and so to *make peace* and bring God and man together, not only as an arbitrator, or referee, who only brings the contending parties to a good understanding one of another, but as a surety, or undertaker, for us. He is not only the *peace-maker,* but the *peace.* He is the *atonement.* [2.] He came to *bring in an everlasting righteousness.* God might justly have made an end of the sin by making an end of the sinner; but Christ found out another way, and so made an end of sin as to save the sinner from it, by providing a righteousness for him. We are all guilty before God, and shall be condemned as guilty, if we have not a righteousness wherein to appear before him. Had we stood, our innocency would have been our righteousness, but, having fallen, we must have something else to plead; and Christ has provided us a plea. The merit of his sacrifice is *our righteousness;* with this we answer all the demands of the law; *Christ has died, yea, rather, has risen again.* Thus Christ is *the Lord our righteousness,* for he is *made of God to us righteousness,* that we might be *made the righteousness of God in him.* By faith we apply this to ourselves and plead it with God, and our *faith is imputed to us for righteousness,* Rom. 4:3, 5. This is an *everlasting* righteousness, for Christ, who is *our righteousness,* and the *prince* of our *peace,* is the *everlasting Father.* It was from everlasting in the counsels of it and will be to everlasting in the consequences of it. The application of it was from the beginning, for Christ was *the Lamb slain from the foundation of the world;* and it will be to the end, for he is *able to save to the uttermost.* It is of everlasting virtue (Heb. 10:12); it is the *rock that follows us* to Canaan. [3.] He came to *seal up the vision and prophecy,* all the prophetical visions of the Old Testament, which had reference to the Messiah. He *sealed them up,* that is, he accomplished them, answered to them to a tittle; all things that were written in the law, the prophets, and the psalms, concerning the Messiah, were fulfilled in him. Thus he confirmed the truth of them as well as his own mission. He *sealed them up,* that is, he put an end to that method of God's discovering his mind and will, and took another course by completing the scripture-canon in the New Testament, which is the more sure word of prophecy than that *by vision,* 2 Pt. 1:19; Heb. 1:1. [4.] He came to *anoint the most holy,* that is, himself, the Holy One, who was *anointed* (that is, appointed to his work and qualified for it) by the Holy Ghost, that oil of gladness which he received *without measure,* above his fellows; or to *anoint* the gospel-church, his spiritual temple, or holy place, to sanctify and cleanse it, and appropriate it to himself (Eph. 5:26), or to consecrate for us *a new and living way into the holiest,* by his own blood (Heb. 10:20), as the sanctuary was *anointed,* Ex. 30:25, etc. He is called *Messiah* (*v.* 25, 26), which signifies *Christ — Anointed* (Jn. 1:41), because he received the unction both for himself and for all that are his. [5.] In order to all this the Messiah must be *cut off,* must die a violent death, and so be *cut off from the land of the living,* as was foretold, Isa. 53:8. Hence, when Paul preaches the death of Christ, he says that he preached nothing but *what the prophet said should come,* Acts 26:22, 23. And *thus it behoved Christ to suffer.* He must be *cut off, but not for himself* — not for any sin of his own, but, as Caiaphas prophesied, he must *die for the people,* in our stead and for our good, — not for any *advantage of his own* (the glory he purchased for himself was no more than the glory he had before, Jn. 17:4, 5); no; it was to atone for our sins, and to purchase life for us, that he was *cut off.* [6.] He must *confirm the covenant with many.* He shall introduce a new covenant between God and man, a covenant of grace, since it had become impossible for us to be saved by a covenant of innocence. This covenant he shall confirm by his doctrine and miracles, by his death and resurrection, by the ordinances of baptism and the Lord's supper, which are the *seals* of the New Testament, assuring us that God is willing to accept us upon gospel-terms. His death made *his testament* of force, and enabled us to claim what is bequeathed by it. He confirmed it to *the many,* to the common people; the poor were *evangelized,* when the *rulers* and *Pharisees believed not on him.* Or, he confirmed it *with many,* with the Gentile world. The New Testament was not (like the Old) confined to the Jewish church, but was committed to all nations. Christ gave his life a *ransom for many.* [7.] He must *cause the sacrifice and oblation to cease.* By offering himself a sacrifice once for all he shall put an end to all the Levitical sacrifices, shall supercede them and set them aside; when the substance comes the shadows shall be done away. He causes all the peace-offerings to cease when he has made peace by the blood of his cross, and by it confirmed the covenant of peace and reconciliation. By the preaching of his gospel to the world, with which the apostles were entrusted, he took men off from expecting remission by the blood of bulls and goats, and so *caused the sacrifice and oblation to cease.* The apostle in his epistle to the Hebrews shows what a better priesthood, altar, and sacrifice, we have now than they had under the law, as a reason why we should *hold fast our profession.*

(3.) Concerning the final destruction of Jerusalem, and of the Jewish church and nation; and this follows immediately upon the cutting off of the Messiah, not only because it was the *just punishment* of those that put him to death, which was the sin that filled up the measure of their iniquity and brought ruin upon them, but because, as things were, it was necessary to the perfecting of one of the great intentions of his death. He died to take away the ceremonial law, quite to abolish *that law of commandments,* and to vacate the obligation of it. But the Jews would not be persuaded to quit it; still they kept it up with more zeal than ever; they would hear no talk of parting with it; they stoned Stephen (the first Christian martyr) for saying that Jesus should *change the customs which Moses delivered them* (Acts 6:14); so that there was no way to abolish the Mosaic economy but by destroying the temple, and the holy city, and the Levitical priesthood, and that whole nation which so incurably doted on them. This was effectually done in less than forty years after the death of Christ, and it was a desolation that could *never be repaired* to this day. And this is it which is here largely foretold, that the Jews who returned out of captivity might not be overmuch lifted up with the rebuilding of their city and temple, because in process of time they would be finally destroyed, and not as now for seventy years only, but might rather rejoice in hope of the coming of the Messiah, and the setting up of his spiritual kingdom in the world, which should *never be destroyed.* Now, [1.] It is here foretold that *the people of the prince that shall come* shall be the instruments of this destruction, that is, the Roman armies, belonging to a monarchy yet to come (Christ is *the prince that shall come,* and they are employed by him in this service; they are *his armies,* Mt. 22:7), or the Gentiles (who, though now strangers, shall become the people of the Messiah) shall destroy the Jews. [2.] That the destruction shall be *by war,* and the *end* of that *war* shall be this *desolation determined.* The *wars of the Jews* with the Romans were by their own obstinacy made very long and very bloody, and they issued at length in the utter extirpation of that people. [3.] That the *city* and *sanctuary* shall in a particular manner be *destroyed* and laid quite waste. Titus the Roman general would fain have saved the temple, but his soldiers were so enraged against the Jews that he could not restrain them from burning it to the ground, that this prophecy might be fulfilled. [4.] That all the resistance that shall be made to this destruction shall be in vain: *The end of it shall be with a flood.* It shall be a deluge of destruction, like that which swept away the old world, and which there will be no making head against. [5.] That hereby the *sacrifice and oblation* shall be *made to cease.* And it must needs cease when the family of the priests was so extirpated, and the genealogies of it were so confounded, that (they say) there is no man in the world that can prove himself of the seed of Aaron. [6.] that there shall be *an overspreading of abominations,* a general corruption of the Jewish nation and an abounding of iniquity among them, for which it shall be *made desolate,* 1 Th. 2:16. Or it is rather to be understood of the armies of the Romans, which were abominable to the Jews (they could not endure them), which *overspread the nation,* and by which it was *made desolate;* for these are the words which Christ refers to, Mt. 24:15, *When you shall see the abomination of desolation, spoken of by Daniel, stand in the holy place, then let those who shall be in Judea flee,* which is explained Lu. 21:20, *When you shall see Jerusalem encompassed with armies then flee.* [7.] That the desolation shall be total and final: *He shall make it desolate, even until the consummation,* that is, he shall make it completely desolate. It is a *desolation determined,* and it will be accomplished to the utmost. And when it is made desolate, it should seem, there is something more determined that is to be *poured upon the desolate* (*v.* 27), and what should that be but the *spirit of slumber* (Rom. 11:8, 25), that blindness which has happened to Israel until the fulness of the Gentiles shall come in? And *then all Israel shall be saved.*

CHAPTER 10

This chapter and the two next (which conclude this book) make up one entire vision and prophecy, which was communicated to Daniel for the use of the church, not by signs and figures, as before (*ch.* 7 and 8), but by express words; and this was about two years after the vision in the foregoing chapter. Daniel prayed daily, but had a vision only now and then. In this chapter we have some things introductory to the prophecy, in the eleventh chapter the particular predictions, and *ch.* 12 the conclusion of it. This chapter shows us, I. Daniel's solemn fasting and humiliation, before he had this vision (*v.* 1–3). II. A glorious appearance of the Son of God to him, and the deep impression it made upon him (*v.* 4–9). III. The encouragement that was given him to expect such a discovery of future events as should be satisfactory and useful both to others and to himself, and that he should be enabled both to understand the meaning of this discovery, though difficult, and to bear up under the lustre of it, though dazzling and dreadful (*v.* 10–21).

Verses 1–9

This vision is dated in the *third year of Cyrus,* that is, of his reign after the conquest of Babylon, his third year since Daniel became acquainted with him and a subject to him. Here is,

I. A general idea of this prophecy (*v.* 1): *The thing was true;* every word of God is so; it was true that Daniel had such a vision, and that such and such things were said. This he solemnly attests upon the word of a prophet. *Et hoc paratus est verificare — He was prepared to verify it;* and, if it was a word *spoken from heaven,* no doubt it is stedfast and may be depended upon. *But the time appointed was long,* as long as to the end of the reign of Antiochus, which was 300 years, a long time indeed when it is looked upon as to come. Nay, and because it is usual with the prophets to glance at things spiritual and eternal, there is that in this prophecy which looks in type as far forward as to the end of the world and the resurrection of the dead; and then he might well say, *The time appointed was long.* It was, however, made as plain to him as if it had been a history rather than a prophecy; he *understood the thing;* so distinctly was it delivered to him, and received by him, that he could say he *had understanding of the vision.* It did not so much operate upon his fancy as upon his understanding.

II. An account of Daniel's mortification of himself before he had this vision, not in expectation of it, nor, when he prayed that solemn prayer *ch.* 9, does it appear that he had any expectation of the vision in answer to it, but purely from a principle of devotion and pious sympathy with the afflicted people of God. He *was mourning full three weeks* (*v.* 2), for his own sins and the sins of his people, and their sorrows. Some think that the particular occasion of his mourning was slothfulness and indifference of many of the Jews, who, though they had liberty to return to their own land, continued still in the land of their captivity, not knowing how to value the privileges offered them; and perhaps it troubled him the more because those that did so justified themselves by the example of Daniel, though they had not that reason to stay behind which he had. Others think that it was because he heard of the obstruction given to the building of the temple by the enemies of the Jews, who *hired counsellors against them, to frustrate their purpose* (Ezra 4:4, 5), *all the days of Cyrus,* and gained their point from his son Cambyses, or Artaxerxes, who governed while Cyrus was absent in the Scythian war. Note, Good men cannot but mourn to see how slowly the work of God goes on in the world and what opposition it meets with, how weak its friends are and how active its enemies. During the days of Daniel's mourning he *ate no pleasant bread;* he could not live without meat, but he ate little, and very sparingly, and mortified himself in the quality as well as the quantity of what he ate, which may truly be reckoned fasting, and a token of humiliation and sorrow. He did not eat the pleasant bread he used to eat, but that which was course and unpalatable, which he would not be tempted to eat any more of than was just necessary to support nature. As ornaments, so delicacies, are very disagreeable to a day of humiliation. *Daniel ate no flesh, drank no wine, nor anointed himself,* for those three week's time, *v.* 3. Though he was now a very old man, and might plead that the decay of his nature required what was nourishing, though he was a very great man, and might plead that, being used to dainty meats, he could not do without them, it would prejudice his health if he were, yet, when it was both to testify and to assist his devotion, he could thus deny himself; let this be noted to the shame of many young people in the common ranks of life who cannot persuade themselves thus to deny themselves.

III. A description of that glorious person whom Daniel saw in vision, which, it is generally agreed, could be no other that Christ himself, the eternal Word. He was by the side of the river Hiddekel (*v.* 4), probably walking there, not for diversion, but devotion and contemplation, as Isaac walked in the field, to meditate; and, being a person of distinction, he had his servants attending him at some distance. There he *looked up,* and saw *one man Christ Jesus.* It must be he, for he appears in the same resemblance wherein he appeared to St. John in the isle of Patmos, Rev. 1:13–15. His dress was priestly, for he is the high priest of our profession, *clothed in linen,* as the high priest himself was on the day of atonement, that great day; *his loins were girded* (in St. John's vision his *paps* were *girded) with a golden girdle* of the finest gold, that of Uphaz, for every thing about Christ is the best in its kind. The *girding of the loins* denotes his ready and diligent application to his work, as his Father's servant, in the business of our redemption. His shape was amiable, *his body like the beryl,* a precious stone of a sky-colour. His countenance was awful, and enough to strike a terror on the beholders, for his face was *as the appearance of lightning,* which dazzles the eyes, both brightens and threatens. His *eyes* were bright and sparkling, *as lamps of fire.* His *arms and feet* shone *like polished brass, v.* 6. His *voice* was loud, and strong, and very piercing, *like the voice of a multitude.* The *vox Dei — voice of God* can overpower the *vox populi — voice of the people.* Thus glorious did Christ appear, and it should engage us, 1. To think highly and honourably of him. *Now consider how great this man is,* and in all things let him have the pre-eminence. 2. To admire his condescension for us and our salvation. Over all this splendour he drew a veil when he took upon him the form of a servant, and *emptied himself.*

IV. The wonderful influence that this appearance had upon Daniel and his attendants, and the terror that it struck upon him and them.

1. His attendants *saw not the vision;* it was not fit that they should be honoured with the sight of it. There is a divine revelation vouchsafed to all, from converse with which none are excluded who do not exclude themselves; but such a vision must be peculiar to Daniel, who was a favourite. Paul's companions were aware of the *light,* but *saw no man,* Acts 9:7; 22:9. Note, It is the honour of those who are beloved of God that, what is hidden from others, is known to them. Christ *manifests himself to them, but not to the world,* Jn. 14:22. But, though they saw not the vision, they were seized with an unaccountable trembling; either from the voice they heard, or from some strange concussion or vibration of the air they felt, so it was that a *great quaking fell upon them, so that they fled to hide themselves,* probably among the willows that grew by the river's side. Note, Many have a *spirit of bondage to fear* who never receive *a spirit of adoption,* to whom Christ has been, and will be, never otherwise than a terror. Now the fright that Daniel's attendants were in is a confirmation of the truth of the vision; it could not be Daniel's fancy, or the product of a heated imagination of his own, or it had a real, powerful, and strange effect upon those about him.

2. He himself saw it, and saw it alone, but he was not able to bear the sight of it. It not only dazzled his eyes, but overwhelmed his spirit, so that *there remained no strength in him, v.* 8. He said, as Moses himself, *I exceedingly fear and quake.* His spirits were all so employed, either in an intense speculation of the glory of this vision or in the fortifying of his heart against the terror of it, that his body was left in a manner lifeless and spiritless. He had no vigour in him, and was but one remove from a dead carcase; he looked as pale as death, his colour was gone, his *comeliness* in him was *turned into corruption,* and he *retained no strength.* Note, the greatest and best of men cannot bear the immediate discoveries of the divine glory; no man can see it and live; it is next to death to see a glimpse of it, as Daniel here; but glorified saints see Christ as he is and can bear the sight. But, though Daniel was thus dispirited with the vision of Christ, yet he *heard the voice of his words* and knew what he said. Note, We must take heed lest our reverence of God's glory, by which we should be awakened to hear his voice both in his word and in his providence, should degenerate into such a dread of him as will disable or indispose us to hear it. It should seem that when the vision of Christ terrified Daniel the voice of his words soon pacified and composed him, silenced his fear, and laid him to sleep in a holy security and serenity of mind: *When I heard the voice of his words I fell into a slumber,* a sweet slumber, *on my face,* and *my face towards the ground.* When he saw the vision he threw himself prostrate, into a posture of the most humble adoration, and dropped asleep, not as careless of what he heard and saw, but charmed with it. Note, How dreadful soever Christ may appear to those who are under convictions of sin, and in terror by reason of it, there is enough in his word to quiet their spirits and make them easy, if they will but attend to it and apply it.

Verses 10–21

Much ado here is to bring Daniel to be able to bear what Christ has to say to him. Still we have him in a fright, hardly and very slowly recovering himself; but he is still answered and *supported* with *good words* and *comfortable words.* Let us see how Daniel is by degrees brought to himself, and gather up the several passages that are to the same purport.

I. Daniel is in a great consternation and finds it very difficult to get clear of it. The hand that *touched him* set him at first *upon his knees and the palms of his hands, v.* 10. Note, Strength and comfort commonly come by degrees to those that have been long cast down and disquieted; they are first helped up a little, and then more. *After two days he will revive us, and* then *the third day he will raise us up.* And we must not *despise the day of small things,* but be thankful for the beginnings of mercy. Afterwards he is helped up, but he *stands trembling* (*v.* 11), for fear lest he fall again. Note, Before God *gives strength and power unto his people* he makes them sensible of their own weakness. *I trembled in myself, that I might rest in the day of trouble,* Hab. 3:16. But when, afterwards, Daniel recovered so much strength in his limbs that he could stand steadily, yet he tells us (*v.* 15) that he *set his face towards the ground and became dumb;* he was as a man astonished, who knew not what to say, struck dumb with admiration and fear, and was loth to enter into discourse with one so far *above him;* he *kept silence,* yea, *even from good,* till he had recollected himself a little. Well, at length he recovered, not only the use of his feet, but the use of his tongue; and, when he *opened his mouth* (*v.* 16), that which he had to say was to excuse his having been so long silent, for really he durst not speak, he could not speak: *"O my lord"* (so, in great humility, this prophet calls the angel, though the angels, in great humility, called themselves *fellow-servants to the prophets,* Rev. 22:9), *"by the vision my sorrows are turned upon me;* they break in upon me with violence; the sense of my sinful sorrowful state *turns upon me* when I see thy purity and brightness." Note, Man, who has lost his integrity, has reason to blush, and be ashamed of himself, when he sees or considers the glory of the blessed angels that keep their integrity. *"My sorrows are turned upon me, and I have retained no strength* to resist them or bear up a head against them." And again (*v.* 17), like one half dead with the fright, he complains, "As for me, *straightway there remained no strength in me* to receive these displays of the divine glory and these discoveries of the divine will; nay, *there is no breath left in me.*" Such a *deliquium* did he suffer that he could not draw one breath after another, but panted and languished, and was in a manner breathless. See how well it is for us that the treasure of divine revelation is put into *earthen vessels,* that God speaks to us *by men like ourselves* and not by angels. Whatever we may wish, in a peevish dislike of the method God takes in dealing with us, it is certain that if we were tried we should all be of Israel's mind at Mt. Sinai, when they said to Moses, *Speak thou to us, and we will hear, but let not God speak to us lest we die,* Ex. 20:19. If Daniel could not bear it, how could we? Now this he insists upon as an excuse for his irreverent silence, which otherwise would have been blame-worthy: *How can the servant of this my lord talk with this my lord? v.* 17. Note, Whenever we enter into communion with God it becomes us to have a due sense of the vast distance and disproportion that there are between us and the holy angels, and of the infinite distance, and no proportion at all, between us and the holy God, and to acknowledge that we cannot *order our speech by reason of darkness.* How shall we that are dust and ashes speak to the Lord of glory?

II. The blessed angel that was employed by Christ to converse with him gave him all the encouragement and comfort that could be. It should seem, it was not he whose glory he saw in vision (*v.* 5, 6) that here *touched him,* and *talked with him;* that was Christ, but this seems to have been the angel Gabriel, whom Christ had once before ordered to instruct Daniel, *ch.* 8:16. That glorious appearance (as that of the *God of glory* to Abraham, Acts 7:2) was to give authority and to gain attention to what the angel should say. Christ himself comforted John when he in a like case *fell at his feet as dead* (Rev. 1:17); but here he did it by *the angel,* whom Daniel saw in a glory much inferior to that of the vision in the verses before; for he was *like the similitude of the sons of men* (*v.* 16), one like the appearance *of a man, v.* 18. When *he* only *appeared,* as he had done before (*ch.* 9:21), we do not find that Daniel was put into any disorder by it, as he was by this vision; and therefore he is here employed a third time with Daniel.

1. He lent him his hand to help him, *touched him, and set him upon his hands and knees* (*v.* 10), else he would still have lain grovelling, *touched his lips* (*v.* 16), else he would have been still dumb; again he *touched him* (*v.* 18), and put strength into him, else he would still have been staggering and trembling. Note, The hand of God's power going along with the word of his grace is alone effectual to redress all our grievances, and to rectify whatever is amiss in us. One touch from heaven brings us to our knees, sets us on our feet, opens our lips, and strengthens us; for it is God that works on us, and *works in us, both to will and to do* that which is good.

2. He assured him of the great favour that God had for him: Thou art *a man greatly beloved* (*v.* 11); and again (*v.* 19), *O man greatly beloved!* Note, Nothing is more likely, nothing more effectual, to revive the drooping spirits of the saints than to be assured of God's love to them. Those are greatly beloved indeed whom God loves; and it is comfort enough to know it.

3. He silenced his fears, and encouraged his hopes, with good words and comfortable words. He said unto him, *Fear not, Daniel* (*v.* 12); and again (*v.* 19), *O man greatly beloved! fear not; peace be unto thee; be strong, yea, be strong.* Never did any tender mother quiet her child, when any thing had grieved or frightened it, with more compassion and affection than the angel here quieted Daniel. Those that are beloved of God have no reason to be afraid of any evil; peace is to them; God himself speaks peace to them; and they ought, upon the warrant of that, to speak peace to themselves; and that peace, that *joy of the Lord,* will be *their strength.* Will God *plead against us with his great power?* will he take advantage against us of our being overcome by his terror? *No, but he will put strength into us,* Job 23:6. So he did into Daniel here, when, by reason of the lustre of the vision, *no strength* of his own *remained in him;* and he acknowledges it (*v.* 19): *When he had spoken to me I was strengthened.* Note, God by his word puts life, and strength, and spirit into his people; for if he says, *Be strong,* power goes along with the word. And, now that Daniel has experienced the efficacy of God's strengthening word and grace, he is ready for any thing: *"Now, Let my lord speak,* and I can hear it, I can bear it, and am ready to do according to it, *for thou hast strengthened me."* Note, To those that (like Daniel here) have no might God *increases strength,* Isa. 40:29. And we cannot keep up our communion with God but by strength derived from him; but, when he is pleased to put strength into us, we must make a good use of it, and say, *Speak, Lord, for thy servant hears.* Let God enable us to comply with his will, and them, whatever it is, we will stand complete in it. *Da quod jubes, et jube quod vis — Give what thou commandest, and then command what thou wilt.*

4. He assured him that his fastings and prayers had come up for a memorial before God, as the angel told Cornelius (Acts 10:4): *Fear not, Daniel, v.* 12. It is natural to fallen man to be afraid of an extraordinary messenger from heaven, as dreading to hear evil tidings thence; but Daniel need not fear, for he has by his three weeks' humiliation and supplication sent *extraordinary* messengers to heaven, which he may expect to return with an olive-branch of peace: *"From the first day that thou didst set thy heart to understand* the word of God, which is to be the rule of thy prayers, and to *chasten thyself before thy God,* that thou mightest put an edge upon thy prayers, *thy words were heard,"* as, before, *at the beginning of thy supplication, ch.* 9:23. Note, As the *entrance of God's word is enlightening* to the upright, so the entrance of their prayers is pleasing to God, Ps. 119:130. From the first day that we begin to look towards God in a way of duty he is ready to meet us in a way of mercy. Thus ready is God to hear prayer. *I said, I will confess, and thou forgavest.* 5. He informed him that he was sent to him on purpose to bring him a prediction of the future state of the church, as a token of God's accepting his prayers for the church: *"Knowest thou wherefore I come unto thee?* If thou knewest on what errand I come, thou wouldst not be put into such a consternation by it." Note, If we rightly understood the meaning of God's dealings with us, and the methods of his providence and grace concerning us, we should be better reconciled to them. *"I have come for thy words* (*v.* 12), to bring thee a gracious answer to thy prayers." Thus, when God's praying people call to him, he says, *Here I am* (Isa. 58:9); *what would you* have with me? See the power of prayer, what glorious things it has, in its time, fetched from heaven, what strange discoveries! On what errand did this angel come to Daniel? He tells him (*v.* 14): *I have come to make thee understand what shall befal thy people in the latter days.* Daniel was a curious inquisitive man, that had all his days been searching into secret things, and it would be a great gratification to him to be let into the knowledge of things to come. Daniel had always been concerned for the church; its interests lay much upon his heart, and it would be a particular satisfaction to him to know what its state should be, and he would know the better what to pray for as long as he lived. He was now lamenting the difficulties which his people met with in the present day; but, that he might not be offended in those, the angel must tell him what greater difficulties are yet before them; and, if they be *wearied* now that they only *run with the footmen, how will they contend with horses?* Note, It would abate our resentment of present troubles to consider that we know not but much greater are before us, which we are concerned to provide for. Daniel must be made to know what shall befal his people *in the latter days* of the church, after the cessation of prophecy, and when the time drew nigh for the Messiah to appear, *for yet the vision is for many days;* the principal things that this vision was intended to give the church the foresight of would come to pass in the days of Antiochus, nearly 300 years after this. Now that which the angel is entrusted to communicate to Daniel, and which Daniel is encouraged to expect from him, is not any curious speculations, moral prognostications, nor rational prospects of his own, though he is an angel, but what he has *received from the Lord.* It was the *revelation of Jesus Christ* that the angel gave to St. John to be *delivered to the churches,* Rev. 1:1. So here (*v.* 21): *I will show thee what is written in the scriptures of truth,* that is, what is fixed in the determinate counsel and foreknowledge of God. The *decree of God* is a thing written, it is a *scripture* which remains and cannot be altered. *What I have written.* As there are scriptures for the revealed will of God, the letters-patent, which are published to the world, so there are scriptures for the secret will of God, the close rolls, which are *sealed among his treasures,* the book of his decrees. Both are *scriptures of truth;* nothing shall be added to nor taken from either of them. The *secret things belong not to us,* only now and then some few paragraphs have been copied out from the book of God's counsels, and delivered to the prophets for the use of the church, as here to Daniel; but they are the *things revealed,* even the *words of this law,* which belong *to us and to our children;* and we are concerned to study what is written in these *scriptures of truth,* for they are things which *belong to our everlasting peace.*

6. He gave him a general account of the adversaries of the church's cause, from whom it might be expected that troubles would arise, and of its patrons, under whose protection it might be assured of safety and victory at last. (1.) The *kings of the earth* are and will be its adversaries; for they set themselves against the Lord, and against his Anointed, Ps. 2:2. The angel told Daniel that he was to have come to him with a gracious answer to his prayers, but that the *prince of the kingdom of Persia withstood him one and twenty days,* just the three weeks that Daniel had been fasting and praying. Cambyses king of Persia had been very busy to embarrass the affairs of the Jews, and to do them all the mischief he could, and the angel had been all that time employed to counter-work him; so that he had been constrained to defer his visit to Daniel till now, for angels can be but in one place at a time. Or, as Dr. Lightfoot says, This new king of Persia, by hindering the temple, had hindered those good tidings which otherwise he should have brought him. The kings and kingdoms of the world were indeed sometimes helpful to the church, but more often they were injurious to it. "When *I have gone forth* from the kings of Persia, when their monarchy is brought down for their unkindness to the Jews, then *the prince of Grecia shall come," v.* 20. The Grecian monarchy, though favourable to the Jews at first, as the Persian was, will yet come to be vexatious to them. Such is the state of the church-militant; when it has got clear of one enemy it has another to encounter: and such a hydra's head is that of the old serpent; when one storm has *blown over* it is not long before another rises. (2.) The *God of heaven* is, and will be, its protector, and, under him, the angels of heaven are its patrons and guardians. [1.] Here is the angel Gabriel busy in the service of the church, making his part good in defence of it twenty-one days, *against the prince of Persia,* and *remaining there with the kings of Persia,* as consul, or liege-ambassador, to take care of the affairs of the Jews in that court, and to do them service, *v.* 13. And, though much was done against them by the kings of Persia (God permitting it), it is probably that much more mischief would have been done them, and they would have been quite ruined (witness Haman's plot) if God had not prevented it by the ministration of angels. Gabriel resolves, when he has despatched this errand to Daniel, that he will return *to fight with the prince of Persia,* will continue to oppose him, and will at length humble and bring down that proud monarchy (*v.* 20), though he knows that another as mischievous, even that of Grecia, will rise instead of it. [2.] Here is Michael our prince, the great protector of the church, and the patron of its just but injured cause: *The first of the chief princes, v.* 13. Some understand it of a created angel, but an archangel of the highest order, 1 Th. 4:16; Jude 9. Others think that *Michael the archangel* is no other than Christ himself, the *angel of the covenant,* and the Lord of the angels, he whom Daniel saw in vision, *v.* 5. He *came to help me* (*v.* 13); and there is *none but he that holds with me in these things, v.* 21. Christ is the church's prince; angels are not, Heb. 2:5. He presides in the affairs of the church and effectually provides for its good. He is said to *hold with the angels,* for it is he that makes them serviceable to the *heirs of salvation;* and, if he were not on the church's side, its case were bad. But, says David, and so says the church, *The Lord takes my part with those that help me,* Ps. 118:7. *The Lord is with those that uphold my soul,* Ps. 54:4.

CHAPTER 11

The angel Gabriel, in this chapter, performs his promise made to Daniel in the foregoing chapter, that he would "show him what should befal his people in the latter days," according to that which was "written in the scriptures of truth:" very particularly does he here foretel the succession of the kings of Persia and Grecia, and the affairs of their kingdoms, especially the mischief which Antiochus Epiphanes did in his time to the church, which was foretold before (*ch.* 8:11–12). Here is, I. A brief prediction of the setting up of the Grecian monarchy upon the ruins of the Persian monarchy, which was now newly begun (*v.* 1–4). II. A prediction of the affairs of the two kingdoms of Egypt and Syria, with reference to each other (*v.* 5–20). III. Of the rise of Antiochus Epiphanes, and his actions and successes (*v.* 21–29). IV. Of the great mischief that he should do to the Jewish nation and religion, and his contempt of all religion (*v.* 30–39). V. Of his fall and ruin at last, when he is in the heat of his pursuit (*v.* 40–45).

Verses 1–4

Here, 1. The angel Gabriel lets Daniel know the good service he has done to the Jewish nation (*v.* 1): *"In the first year of Darius the Mede,* who destroyed Babylon and released the Jews out of that house of bondage, *I stood a strength and fortress to him,* that is, I was instrumental to protect him, and give him success in his ward, and, after he had conquered Babylon, to confirm him in his resolution to release the Jews," which, it is likely, met with much opposition. Thus by the angel, and at the request of *the watcher,* the golden head was broken, and the axe laid to the root of the tree. Note, We must acknowledge the hand of God in the strengthening of those that are friends to the church for the service they are to do it, and confirming them in their good resolutions; herein he uses the ministry of angels more than we are aware of. And the many instances we have known of God's care of his church formerly encourage us to depend upon him in further straits and difficulties. 2. He foretels the reign of four Persian kings (*v.* 2): *Now I will tell thee the truth,* that is, the true meaning of the visions of the great image, and of the four beasts, and expound in plain terms what was before represented by dark types. (1.) There shall stand up *three kings in Persia,* besides Darius, in whose reign this prophecy is dated, *ch.* 9:1. Mr. Broughton makes these three to be Cyrus, Artaxasta or Artaxerxes, called by the Greeks *Cambyses,* and Ahasuerus that married Esther, called *Darius son of Hystaspes.* To these three the Persians gave these attributes — Cyrus was a father, Cambyses a master, and Darius a hoarder up. So Herodotus. (2.) There shall be a fourth, *far richer than they all,* that is, Xerxes, of whose wealth the Greek authors take notice. By *his strength* (his vast army, consisting of 800,000 men at least) and *his riches,* with which he maintained and paid that vast army, he *stirred up all* against *the realm of Greece.* Xerxes's expedition against Greece is famous in history, and the shameful defeat that he met with. He who when he went out was the terror of Greece in his return was the scorn of Greece. Daniel needed not to be told what disappointment he would meet with, for he was a hinderer of the building of the temple; but soon after, about thirty years after the first return from captivity, Darius, a young king, revived the building of the temple, owning the hand of God against his predecessors for hindering it, Ezra 6:7. 3. He foretels Alexander's conquests and the partition of his kingdom, *v.* 3. He is that *mighty king* that shall *stand up* against the kings of Persia, and he shall *rule with great dominion,* over many kingdoms, and with a despotic power, for he shall *do according to his will,* and undo likewise, which, by the law of the Medes and Persians, their kings could not. When Alexander, after he had conquered Asia, would be worshipped as a god, then this was fulfilled, that he shall *do according to his will.* That is God's prerogative, but was his pretension. But (*v.* 4) his *kingdom* shall soon be *broken,* and *divided* into four parts, *but not to his posterity,* nor shall any of his successors reign *according to his dominion;* none of them shall have such large territories nor such an absolute power. His *kingdom was plucked up for others besides those* of his own family. Arideus, his brother, was made king in Macedonia; Olympias, Alexander's mother, killed him, and poisoned Alexander's two sons, Hercules and Alexander. Thus was his family rooted out by its own hands. See what decaying perishing things worldly pomp and possessions are, and the powers by which they are got. Never was the vanity of the world and its greatest things shown more evidently than in the story of Alexander. *All is vanity and vexation of spirit.*

Verses 5–20

Here are foretold,

I. The rise and power of two great kingdoms out of the remains of Alexander's conquests, *v.* 5. 1. The kingdom of Egypt, which was made considerable by Ptolemaeus Lagus, one of Alexander's captains, whose successors were, from him, called the *Lagidae.* He is called the king of the *south,* that is, Egypt, named here, *v.* 8, 42, 43. The countries that at first belonged to Ptolemy are reckoned to be Egypt, Phoenicia, Arabia, Libya, Ethiopia, etc. Theocr. Idyl. 17. 2. The kingdom of Syria, which was set up by Seleucus Nicanor, or the *conqueror;* he was one of Alexander's princes, and became stronger than the other, and *had the greatest dominion of all,* was the most powerful of all Alexander's successors. It was said that he had no fewer than seven-two kingdoms under him. Both these were strong against Judah (the affairs of which are particularly eyed in this prediction); Ptolemy, soon after he gained Egypt, invaded Judea, and took Jerusalem *on a sabbath,* pretending a friendly visit. Seleucus also gave disturbance to Judea.

II. The fruitless attempt to unite these two kingdoms as iron and clay in Nebuchadnezzar's image (*v.* 6): *"At the end of certain years,* about seventy after Alexander's death, the Lagidae and the Seleucidae shall associate, but not in sincerity. Ptolemy Philadelphus, king of Egypt, shall marry his daughter Berenice to Antiochus Theos, king of Syria," who had already a wife called *Laodice.* "Berenice shall come to the *king of the north,* to make an agreement, but it shall not hold: *She shall not retain the power of the arm;* neither she nor her posterity shall establish themselves in the kingdom of the north, neither shall Ptolemy her father, nor Antiochus her husband (between whom there was to be a great alliance), *stand,* nor their arm, but *she shall be given up and those that brought her,"* all that projected that unhappy marriage between her and Antiochus, which occasioned so much mischief, instead of producing a coalition between the northern and southern crowns, as was hoped. Antiochus divorced Berenice, took his former wife Laodice again, who soon after poisoned him, procured Berenice and her son to be murdered, and set up her own son by Antiochus to be king, who was called *Seleucus Callinicus.*

III. A war between the two kingdoms, *v.* 7, 8. A branch from the same root with Berenice *shall stand up in his estate.* Ptolemaeus Euergetes, the son and successor of Ptolemaeus Philadelphus, shall come with an army against Seleucus Callinicus, king of Syria, to avenge his sister's quarrel, and shall prevail; and he shall carry away a rich booty both of persons and goods into Egypt, and shall *continue more years than the king of the north.* This Ptolemy reigned forty-six years; and Justin says that if his own affairs had not called him home he would, in this war, have made himself master of the whole kingdom of Syria. But (*v.* 9) he shall be forced to *come into his kingdom* and *return into his own land,* to keep peace there, so that he can no longer carry on the war abroad. Note, It is very common for a treacherous peace to end in a bloody war.

IV. The long and busy reign of *Antiochus the Great,* king of Syria. Seleucus Callinicus, that king of the north that was overcome (*v.* 7) and died miserably, left two sons, Seleucus and Antiochus; these are his sons, the sons of the *king of the north,* that shall be *stirred up, and shall assemble a multitude of great forces,* to recover what their father had lost, *v.* 10. But Seleucus the elder, being weak, and unable to rule his army, was poisoned by his friends, and reigned only two years; and his brother Antiochus succeeded him, who reigned thirty-seven years, and was called *the Great.* And therefore the angel, though he speaks of *sons* at first, goes on with the account of *one only,* who was but fifteen years old when he began to reign, and he shall *certainly come, and overflow,* and *over-run,* and shall *be restored* at length to what his father lost. 1. The *king of the south,* in this war, shall at first have very great success. Ptolemaeus Philopater, moved with indignation at the indignities done by *Antiochus the Great,* shall (though otherwise a slothful prince) *come forth, and fight with him,* and shall bring a vast army into the field of 70,000 foot, and 5000 horse, and seventy-three elephants. And the *other multitude* (the army of Antiochus, consisting of 62,000 foot, and 6000 horse, and 102 elephants) shall *be given into his hand.* Polybius, who lived with Scipio, has given a particular account of this battle of Raphia. Ptolemaeus Philopater, having gained this victory, grew very insolent; *his heart was lifted up;* then he went into the temple of God at Jerusalem, and, in defiance of the law, entered the most holy place, for which God has a controversy with him, so that, though he shall *cast down many myriads,* yet he shall *not be strengthened by it,* so as to secure his interest. For, 2. The *king of the north, Antiochus the Great,* shall *return* with a *greater army* than *the former;* and, at the *end of times (that is, years)* he shall *come with a mighty army, and great riches,* against the *king of the south,* that is, Ptolemaeus Epiphanes, who succeeded Ptolemaeus Philopater his father, when he was a child, which gave advantage to Antiochus the Great. In this expedition he had some powerful allies (*v.* 14): *Many shall stand up against the king of the south.* Philip of Macedon was confederate with Antiochus against the king of Egypt, and Scopas his general, whom he sent into Syria; Antiochus routed him, destroyed a great part of his army; whereupon the Jews willingly yielded to Antiochus, joined with him, helped him to besiege Ptolemaeus's garrisons. They *the robbers of thy people shall exalt themselves to establish the vision,* to help forward the accomplishment of this prophecy; but *they shall fall, and shall come to nothing, v.* 14. Hereupon (*v.* 15) the *king of the north,* this same Antiochus Magnus, shall carry on his design against the king of the south another way. (1.) He shall surprise his strong-holds; all that he has got in Syria and Samaria, and the arms of the south, all the power of the king of Egypt, shall not be able to withstand him. See how dubious and variable the turns of the scale of war are; like buying and selling, it is winning and losing; sometimes one side gets the better and sometimes the other; yet neither by chance; it is not, as they call it, the *fortune of war,* but according to the will and counsel of God, who brings some low and raises others up. (2.) He shall make himself master of the land of Judea (*v.* 16): *He that comes against him* (that is, the king of the north) shall carry all before him and do what he pleases, and *he shall stand* and get footing *in the glorious land;* so the land of Israel was, and *by his hand* it was wasted and consumed, for with the spoil of that good land he victualled his vast army. The land of Judea lay between these two potent kingdoms of Egypt and Syria, so that in all the struggles between them that was sure to suffer, for to it they both bore *ill will.* Yet some read this, *By his hand it shall be perfected;* as if it intimated that the land of Judea, being taken under the protection of this Antiochus, shall flourish, and be in better condition than it had been. (3.) He shall still push on his war against the king of Egypt, and *set his face* to *enter with the strength of his whole kingdom,* taking advantage of the infancy of Ptolemy Epiphanes, and the *upright ones,* many of the pious Israelites, siding with him, *v.* 17. In prosecution of his design, he shall give him his daughter Cleopatra to wife, designing, as Saul in giving his daughter Cleopatra to David, that she should be a *snare to him,* and do him a mischief; but she *shall not stand on her father's* side, nor be *for him,* but for her husband, and so that plot failed him. (4.) His war with the Romans is here foretold (*v.* 18): He shall *turn his face to the isles* (*v.* 18), the isles of the Gentiles (Gen. 10:5), Greece and Italy. He took many of the isles about the Hellespont — Rhodes, Samos, Delos, etc., which by war or treaty he made himself master of; but a *prince,* or *state* (so some), even the Roman senate, or a *leader,* even the Roman general, shall *return his reproach* with which he abused the Romans *upon himself,* or shall *make his shame rest on himself,* and *without his own shame,* or any disgrace to himself, shall *pay him again.* This was fulfilled when the two Scipios were sent with an army against Antiochus. Hannibal was then with him, and advised him to invade Italy and waste it as he had done; but he did not take hid advice; and Scipio joined battle with him, and gave him a total defeat, though Antiochus had 70,000 men and the Romans but 30,000. Thus he caused the *reproach offered by him to cease.* (5.) His fall. When he was totally routed by the Romans, and was forced to abandon to them all he had in Europe, and had a very heavy tribute exacted from him, he *turned to his own land,* and, not knowing which way to raise money to pay his tribute, he plundered a temple of Jupiter, which so incensed his own subjects against him that they set upon him, and killed him; so he was overthrown, and *fell,* and *was no more found, v.* 19. (6.) His next successor, *v.* 20. There rose up one in his place, a *raiser of taxes,* a *sender forth of the extortioner,* or extorter. This character was remarkably answered in Seleucus Philopater, the elder son of Antiochus the Great, who was a great oppressor of his own subjects, and exacted abundance of money from them; and, when he was told he would thereby lose his friends, he said he knew no better friend he had then *money.* He likewise attempted to rob the temple at Jerusalem, which this seems especially to refer to. But *within a few days he shall be destroyed, neither in anger nor in battle,* but poisoned by Heliodorus, one of his own servants, when he had reigned but twelve years, and done nothing remarkable.

V. From all this let us learn, 1. That God in his providence sets up one, and pulls down another, as he pleases, advances some from low beginnings and depresses others that were very high. Some have called great men the *footballs of fortune;* or, rather, they are the *tools of Providence.* 2. This world is full of *wars and fightings,* which come *from men's lusts,* and make it a theatre of sin and misery. 3. All the changes and revolutions of states and kingdoms, and every event, even the most minute and contingent, were plainly and perfectly foreseen by the God of heaven, and to him nothing is *new.* 4. No word of God shall fall to the ground; but what he has designed, what he has declared, shall infallibly come to pass; and even the sins of men shall be made to serve his purpose, and contribute to the b ringing of his counsels to birth in their season; and yet *God is not the author of sin.* 5. That, for the right understanding of some parts of scripture, it is necessary that heathen authors be consulted, which give light to the scripture, and show the accomplishment of what is there foretold; we have therefore reason to bless God for the human learning with which many have done great service to divine truths.

Verses 21-45

All this is a prophecy of the reign of Antiochus Epiphanes, the *little horn* spoken of before (ch. 8:9) a sworn enemy to the Jewish religion, and a bitter persecutor of those that adhered to it. What troubles the Jews met with in the reigns of the Persian kings were not so particularly foretold to Daniel as these, because then they had living prophets with them, Haggai and Zechariah, to encourage them; but these troubles in the days of Antiochus were foretold, because, before that time, prophecy would cease, and they would find it necessary to have recourse to the written word. Some things in this prediction concerning Antiochus are alluded to in the New-Testament predictions of the antichrist, especially *v.* 36, 37. And as it is usual with the prophets, when they foretel the prosperity of the Jewish church, to make use of such expressions as were applicable to the *kingdom of Christ,* and insensibly to slide into a prophecy of that, so, when they foretel the troubles of the church, they make use of such expressions as have a further reference to the kingdom of the antichrist, the rise and ruin of that. Now concerning Antiochus, the angel foretels here,

I. His character: He shall be a *vile person.* He called himself *Epiphanes — the illustrious,* but his character was the reverse of his surname. The heathen writers describe him to be an *odd-humoured* man, rude and boisterous, base and sordid. He would sometimes steal out of the court into the city, and herd with any infamous company *incognito — in disguise* he made himself a companion of the common sort, and of the basest strangers that came to town. He had the most unaccountable whims, so that some took him to be silly, others to be mad. Hence he was called *Epimanes — the madman.* He is called a *vile person,* for he had been a long time a hostage at Rome for the fidelity of his father when the Romans had subdued him; and it was agreed that, when the other hostages were exchanged, he should continue a prisoner at large.

II. His accession to the crown. By a trick he got his elder brother's son, Demetrius, to be sent a hostage to Rome, in exchange for him, contrary to the cartel; and, his elder brother being made away with by Heliodorus (*v.* 20), he took the kingdom. The states of Syria did not *give it to him* (*v.* 21), because they knew it belonged to his elder brother's son, nor did he get it by the sword, but *came in peaceably,* pretending to reign for his brother's son, Demetrius, then a hostage at Rome. But with the help of Eumenes and Attalus, neighbouring princes, he gained an interest in the people, and by *flatteries obtained the kingdom,* established himself in it, and crushed Heliodorus, who made head against him *with the arms of a flood;* those

that opposed him were *overflown* and *broken before him,* even *the prince of the covenant,* his nephew, the rightful heir, whom he pretended to covenant with that he would resign to him whenever he should return, *v.* 22. But (*v.* 23) *after the league made with him he shall work deceitfully,* as one whose avowed maxim it is that princes ought not to be bound by their word any longer than it is for their interest. And *with a small people,* that at first cleave to him, he shall *become strong,* and (*v.* 24) *he shall enter peaceably upon the fattest places* of the kingdom of Syria, and, very unlike his predecessors, shall *scatter* among the people the *prey, and the spoil, and riches,* to insinuate himself into their affections; but, at the same time, he shall *forecast his devices against the strong-holds,* to make himself master of them, so that his generosity shall last but for a time; when he has got the garrisons into his hands he will scatter his spoil no more, but rule by force, as those commonly do that come in by fraud. He that comes in like a fox reigns like a lion. Some understand these verses of his first expedition into Egypt, when he came not as an enemy, but as a friend and guardian to the young king Ptolemaeus Philometer, and therefore brought with him but few followers, yet those stout men, and faithful to his interest, whom he placed in divers of the strong-holds in Egypt, thereby making himself master of them.

III. His war with Egypt, which was his second expedition thither. This is described, *v.* 25, 27. Antiochus shall *stir up his power and courage* against Ptolemaeus Philometer king of Egypt. Ptolemy, thereupon, shall *be stirred up to battle* against him, shall come against him *with a very great and mighty army;* but Ptolemy, though he has such a vast army, shall not be able to stand before him; for Antiochus's army shall *overthrow* his, and overpower it, and great multitudes of the Egyptian army shall *fall down slain.* And no marvel, for the king of Egypt shall be betrayed by his own counsellors; those that *feed of the portion of his meat,* that eat of his bread and live upon him, being bribed by Antiochus, shall *forecast devices against him,* and even *they shall destroy him;* and what fence is there against such treachery? After the battle, a treaty of peace shall be set on foot, and these two kings shall meet *at one council-board,* to adjust the articles of peace between them; but they shall neither of them be sincere in it, for they shall, in their pretences and promises of amity and friendship, *lie to one another,* for their hearts shall be at the same time to do one another all the mischief they can. And then no marvel that *it shall not prosper.* The peace shall not last; but *the end* of it shall be *at the time appointed* in the divine Providence, and then the war shall break out again, as a sore that is only skinned over.

IV. Another expedition against Egypt. From the former he *returned with great riches* (*v.* 28), and therefore took the first occasion to invade Egypt again, *at the time appointed* by the divine Providence, two years after, in the eighth year of his reign, *v.* 29. He shall come *towards the south.* But this attempt shall not succeed, as the two former did, nor shall he gain his point, as he had done before once and again; for (*v.* 30) *the ships of Chittim shall come against him,* that is, the navy of the Romans, or only ambassadors from the Roman senate, who came in ships. Ptolemaeus Philometer, king of Egypt, being now in a strict alliance with the Romans, craved their aid against Antiochus, who had besieged him and his mother Cleopatra in the city of Alexandria. The Roman senate thereupon sent an embassy to Antiochus, to command him to raise the siege, and, when he desired some time to consider of it and consult with his friends about it, Popilius, one of the ambassadors, with his staff drew a circle about him, and told him, as one having authority, he should give a positive answer before he came out of that circle; whereupon, fearing the Roman power, he was forced immediately to give orders for the raising of the siege and the retreat of his army out of Egypt. So Livy and others relate the story which this prophecy refers to. *He shall be grieved, and return;* for it was a great vexation to him to be forced to yield thus.

V. His rage and cruel practices against the Jews. This is that part of his government, or mis-government rather, which is most enlarged upon in this prediction. In his return from his expedition into Egypt (which is prophesied of, *v.* 28) he *did exploits* against the Jews, in the sixth year

of his reign; then he spoiled the city and temple. But the most terrible storm was in his return from Egypt, two years after, prophesied of *v.* 30. Then he took Judea in his way home; and, because he could not gain his point in Egypt by reason of the Romans interposing, he wreaked his revenge upon the poor Jews, who gave him no provocation, but had greatly provoked God to permit him to do it, Dan. 8:23.

1. He had a rooted antipathy to the Jews' religion: *His heart* was *against the holy covenant, v.* 28. And (*v.* 30) *he had indignation against the holy covenant,* that covenant of peculiarity by which the Jews were incorporated a people distinct from all other nations, and dignified above them. He hated the law of Moses and the worship of the true God, and was vexed at the privileges of the Jewish nation and the promises made to them. Note, That which is the hope and joy of the people of God is the envy of their neighbours, and that is *the holy covenant.* Esau hated Jacob because he had got the blessing. Those that are strangers to the covenant are often enemies to it.

2. He carried on his malicious designs against the Jews by the assistance of some perfidious apostate Jews. He kept up *intelligence with those that forsook the holy covenant* (*v.* 30), some of the Jews that were false to their religion, and introduced the customs of the heathen, with whom they made a covenant. See the fulfilling of this, 1 Mac. 1:11-15, where it is expressly said, concerning those renegado Jews, that they *made themselves uncircumcised and forsook the holy covenant.* We read (2 Mac. 4:9) of Jason, the brother of Onias the high priest, who by the appointment of Antiochus set up a school at Jerusalem, *for the training up of youth in the fashions of the heathen;* and (2 Mac. 4:23, etc.) of Menelaus, who fell in with the interests of Antiochus, and was the man that helped him into Jerusalem, now in his last return from Egypt. We read much in the book of the Maccabees of the mischief done to the Jews by these treacherous men of their own nation, Jason and Menelaus, and their party. These upon all occasions he made use of. "*Such as do wickedly against the covenant,* such as throw up their religion, and comply with the heathen, he shall *corrupt with flatteries,* to harden them in their apostasy, and to make use of them as decoys to draw in others," *v.* 32. Note, It is not strange if those who do not live up to their religion, but in their conversations *do wickedly against the covenant,* are easily *corrupted by flatteries* to quit their religion. Those that make shipwreck of a good conscience will soon *make shipwreck of the faith.*

3. He profaned the temple. *Arms stand on his part* (*v.* 31), not only his own army which he now brought from Egypt, but a great party of deserters from the Jewish religion that joined with them; and they *polluted the sanctuary of strength,* not only the holy city, but the temple. The story of this we have, 1 Mac. 1:21, etc. He *entered proudly into the sanctuary,* took *away the golden altar, and the candlestick,* etc. And therefore (*v.* 25) *there was a great mourning in Israel; the princes and elders mourned,* etc. And (2 Mac. 5:15, etc.) *Antiochus went into the most holy temple, Menelaus, that traitor to the laws and to his own country, being his guide.* Antiochus, having resolved to bring all about him to be of his religion, *took away the daily sacrifice, v.* 31. Some observe that the word *Tammidh,* which signifies no more than *daily,* is only here, and in the parallel place, used for the *daily sacrifice,* as if there were a designed liberty left to supply it either with *sacrifice,* which was suppressed by Antiochus, or with *gospelworship,* which was suppressed by the Antichrist. Then he *set up the abomination of desolation upon the altar* (1 Mac. 1:54), even an *idol altar* (*v.* 59), and called the temple the temple of *Jupiter Olympius,* 2 Mac. 6:2.

4. He persecuted those who retained their integrity. Though there are many who *forsake the covenant and do wickedly* against it, yet there is a people who do *know their God* and retain the knowledge of him, and *they shall be strong and do exploits, v.* 32. When others yield to the tyrant's demands, and surrender their consciences to his impositions, they bravely keep their ground, resist the temptation, and make the tyrant himself ashamed of his attempt upon them. Good old Eleazar, one of the *principal scribes,* when he had swine's flesh thrust into his mouth, did bravely spit it out again, though he knew he must be tormented to death for so doing, and was so, 2 Mac. 6:19. The mother and her seven sons were put to

death for adhering to their religion, 2 Mac. 7. This might well be called *doing exploits;* for to choose suffering rather than sin is a great exploit. And it was *by faith,* by being *strong in faith,* that they did those exploits, that *they were tortured, not accepting deliverance,* as the apostle speaks, probably with reference to that story, Heb. 11:35. Or it may refer to the military courage and achievements of Judas Maccabaeus and others in opposition to Antiochus. Note, The right knowledge of God is, and will be, the strength of the soul, and, in the strength of that, gracious souls do exploits. *Those that know his name will put their trust in him,* and by that trust will do great things. Now, concerning this people that knew their God, we are here told, (1.) That *they shall instruct many, v.* 33. They shall make it their business to show others what they have learned themselves of the difference between truth and falsehood, good and evil. Note, Those that have the knowledge of God themselves should communicate their knowledge to those about them, and this spiritual charity must be extensive: they must *instruct many.* Some understand this of a society newly erected for the propagating of divine knowledge, called *Assideans,* godly men, *pietists* (so the name signifies), that were both knowing and zealous in the law; these instructed many. Note, In times of persecution and apostasy, which are trying times, those that have knowledge ought to make use of it for the strengthening and establishing of others. Those that understand aright themselves ought to do what they can to bring others to understand; for knowledge is a talent that must be traded with. Or, They shall instruct many by their perseverance in their duty and their patient suffering for it. Good examples instruct many, and with many are the most powerful instructions. (2.) *They shall fall* by the cruelty of Antiochus, shall be put to the torture, and put to death, by his rage. Though they are so excellent and intelligent themselves, and so useful and serviceable to others, yet Antiochus shall show them no mercy, but *they shall fall for some days;* so it may be read, Rev. 2:10, *Thou shalt have tribulation ten days.* We read much, in the books of the Maccabees, of Antiochus's barbarous usage of the pious Jews, how many he slew in wars and how many he murdered in cold blood. Women were *put to death* for having their children *circumcised,* and their *infants were hanged about their necks,* 1 Mac. 1:60, 61. But why did God suffer this? How can this be reconciled with the justice and goodness of God? I answer, Very well, if we consider what it was that God aimed at in this (*v.* 35): *Some of those of understanding shall fall,* but it shall be for the good of the church and for their own spiritual benefit. *It shall* be to *try them, and to purge, and to make them white.* They *needed* these afflictions themselves. The best have their spots, which must be washed off, their dross, which must be purged out; and their troubles, particularly their *share in the public troubles,* help to do this; being sanctified to them by the grace of God, they are means of mortifying their corruptions, weaning them from the world, and awakening them to greater seriousness and diligence in religion. They try them, as silver in the furnace is refined from its dross; they purge them, as wheat in the barn is winnowed from the chaff; and they *make them white,* as cloth by the fuller is cleared from its spots. See 1 Pt. 1:7. Their sufferings *for righteousness' sake* would try and purge the nation of the Jews, would convince them of the truth, excellency, and power of that holy religion which these *understanding* men died for their adherence to. The blood of the martyrs is the seed of the church; it is precious blood, and not a drop of it should be shed but upon such a valuable consideration. (3.) The cause of religion, though it be thus run upon, shall not be run down. *When they shall fall* they shall not be utterly cast down, but *they shall be holpen with a little help, v.* 34. Judas Maccabaeus, and his brethren, and a few with them, shall *make head* against the tyrant, and assert the injured cause of their religion; they *pulled down the* idolatrous *altars, circumcised the children that they found uncircumcised, recovered the law out of the hand of the Gentiles, and the work prospered in their hands,* 1 Mac. 2:45, etc. Note, Those that stand by the cause of religion when it is threatened and struck at, though they may not immediately be delivered and made victorious, shall yet have *present help.* And a *little help* must not be despised; but, when times are very bad, we must be thankful for *some reviving.* It is likewise foretold that *many shall cleave to them with flatteries;* when they see the Maccabees prosper some Jews shall join with them that are no true friends to religion, but will only pretend friendship either with design to *betray them* or in hope to *rise with them;* but the *fiery trial* (*v.* 35) will separate between the *precious and the vile,* and by it *those that are perfect will be made manifest* and those that are not. (4.) Though these troubles may continue long, yet they will have *an end.* They are *for a time appointed,* a limited time, fixed in the divine counsels. This warfare shall be accomplished. *Hitherto* the power of the enemy shall come, and *no further;* here shall its *proud waves* be *stayed.*

5. He grew very proud, insolent, and profane, and, being puffed up with his conquests, bade defiance to Heaven, and trampled upon every thing that was sacred, *v.* 36, etc. And here some think begins a prophecy of the antichrist, the papal kingdom. It is plain that St. Paul, in his prophecy of the rise and reign of the man of sin, alludes to this (2 Th. 2:4), which shows that Antiochus was a type and figure of that enemy, as Babylon also was; but, this being joined in a continued discourse with the foregoing prophecies concerning Antiochus, to me it seems probably that it principally refers to him, and in him had its primary accomplishment, and has reference to the other only by way of accommodation. (1.) He shall impiously dishonour the God of Israel, the only living and true God, called here the *God of gods.* He shall, in defiance of him and his authority, *do according to his will* against his people and his holy religion; he shall *exalt himself* above him, as Sennacherib did, and shall *speak marvellous things against him* and against his laws and institutions. This was fulfilled when Antiochus forbade *sacrifices* to be *offered* in God's temple, and ordered the *sabbaths* to be *profaned,* the *sanctuary* and the *holy people* to be *polluted,* etc., to *the end that they might forget the law and change all the ordinances,* and this upon pain of death, 1 Mac. 1:45. (2.) He shall proudly put contempt upon *all other gods,* shall *magnify himself above every god,* even the gods of the nations. Antiochus wrote to his own kingdom that every one should leave the gods he had worshipped, and worship such as he ordered, contrary to the practice of all the conquerors that went before him, 1 Mac. 1:41, 42. And *all the heathen agreed according to the commandment of the king;* fond as they were of their gods, they did not think them worth suffering for, but, their gods being idols, it was all alike to them what gods they worshipped. Antiochus did not *regard any god,* but *magnified himself above all, v.* 37. He was so proud that he thought himself above the condition of a mortal man, that he could *command the waves of the sea, and reach to the stars of heaven,* as his insolence and haughtiness are expressed, 2 Mac. 9:8, 10. Thus he carried all before him, *till the indignation was accomplished* (*v.* 36), till he had run his length, and filled up the measure of his iniquity; for *that which is determined shall be done,* and nothing more, nothing short. (3.) He shall, contrary to the way of the heathen, disregard the god of his fathers, *v.* 37. Though an affection to the religion of their ancestors was, among the heathen, almost as natural to them as *the desire of women* (for, if you search through *the isles of Chittim,* you will not find an instance of a nation that has *changed its gods,* Jer. 2:10, 11), yet Antiochus shall not *regard the god of his fathers;* he made laws to abolish the religion of his country, and to bring in the idols of the Greeks. And though his predecessors had honoured the God of Israel, and given great gifts to the temple at Jerusalem (2 Mac. 3:2, 3), he offered the greatest indignities to God and his temple. His not regarding the *desire of women* may denote his barbarous cruelty (he shall spare no age or sex, no, not the tender ones) or his unnatural lusts, or, in general, his contempt of every thing which men of honour have a concern for, or it might be accomplished in something we meet not with in history. Its being joined to his not *regarding the god of his fathers* intimates that the idolatries of his country had in them more of the gratifications of the flesh than those of other countries (Lucian has written of the Syrian goddesses), and yet that would not prevail to keep him to them. (4.) He shall set up an unknown god, a new god, *v.* 38. *In his estate,* in the room of the god of his fathers (Apollo and Diana, deities of pleasure), he shall *honour the god of forces,* a supposed deity of power, a *god whom his fathers knew not,* nor worshipped; because he will be thought in wisdom and strength to excel his fathers, he shall *honour this god with gold, and silver, and precious stones,* thinking nothing too good for the god he has taken a fancy to. This seems to be Jupiter Olympius, known among the Phoenicians by the name of *Baal-Semen, the lord of heaven,* but never introduced among the Syrians till Antiochus introduced it. Thus shall he do *in the most strong holds,* in the temple of Jerusalem, which is called *the sanctuary of strength* (*v.* 31), and here the *fortresses of munitions; there* he shall set up the image of this *strange god.* Some read it, *He shall commit the munitions of strength,* or of the most strong God (that is, the city Jerusalem), to *a strange god;* he put it under the protection and government of Jupiter Olympius. This god he shall not only acknowledge, but shall *increase with glory,* by setting his image even upon God's altar. And he shall *cause those* that minister to this idol *to rule over many,* shall put them into places of power and trust, and they shall *divide the land for gain,* shall be maintained richly out of the profits of the country. Some by the *Mahuzzim,* or *god of forces,* that Antiochus shall worship, understand *money,* which is said to *answer all things,* and which is the great idol of worldly people.

Now here is very much that is applicable to the *man of sin;* he *exalts himself above all that is called god or that is worshipped; magnifies himself above all;* his flatterers call him *our lord god the pope.* By forbidding marriage, and magnifying the single life, he pretends not to regard the desire of women; and honours the *god of forces,* the god *Mahuzzim,* or *strong holds,* saints and angels, whom his followers take for their protectors, as the heathen did of old their demons; these they make presidents of several countries, etc. These they honour with vast treasures dedicated to them, and therein the learned Mr. Mede thinks that this prophecy was fulfilled, and that it is referred to 1 Tim. 4:1, 2.

VI. Here seems to be another expedition into Egypt, or, at least, a struggle with Egypt. The Romans had tied him up from invading Ptolemy, but now that *king of the south pushes at him* (*v.* 40), makes an attempt upon some of his territories, whereupon Antiochus, the *king of the north, comes against him like a whirlwind,* with incredible swiftness and fury, *with chariots, and horses, and many ships,* a great force. He shall *come trough countries, and shall overflow and pass over.* In this flying march *many countries shall be overthrown by him;* and he shall enter into *the glorious land,* the land of Israel; it is the same word that is translated *the pleasant land, ch.* 8:9. He shall make dreadful work among the nations thereabout; yet some shall escape his fury, particularly Edom and Moab, and *the chief of the children of Ammon, v.* 41. He did not put these countries under contribution, because they had joined with him against the Jews. But especially the land of Egypt *shall not escape,* but he will quite beggar that, so bare will he strip it. This some reckon his fourth and last expedition against Egypt, in the tenth or eleventh year of his reign, under pretence of assisting the younger brother of Ptolemaeus Philometer against him. We read not of any great slaughter made in this expedition, but great plunder; for, it should seem, that was what he came for: *He shall have power over the treasures of gold and silver, and all the precious things of Egypt, v.* 43. Polybius, in Athenaeus, relates that Antiochus, having got together abundance of wealth, by spoiling young Philometer, and breaking league with him, and by the contributions of his friends, bestowed a vast deal upon a triumph, in imitation of Paulus Aemilius, and describes the extravagance of it; here we are told how he got that money which he spent so profusely. Notice is here taken likewise of the use he made of the Lybians and Ethiopians, who bordered upon Egypt; they *were at his steps;* he had them at his foot, had them at his beck, and they made inroads upon Egypt to serve him.

VII. Here is a prediction of the fall and ruin of Antiochus, as before (*ch.* 8:25), when he is in the height of his honour, flushed with victory, and laden with spoils, tidings *out of the east* and *out of the north* (out of the north-east) shall trouble him, *v.* 44. Or, He shall have intelligence, both from the eastern and northern parts, that the king of Parthia is invading his kingdom. This obliged him to drop the enterprises he had in hand, and to go against the Persians and Parthians that were revolting from him; and this *vexed* him, for now he thought utterly to ruin and extirpate the Jewish nation, when that expedition called him off, in which he perished. This is explained by a passage in Tacitus (though an impious one) where he commends Antiochus for his attempt to *take away the superstition of the Jews*, and *bring in the manners of the Greeks*, among them *(ut teterrimam gentem in melius mutaret — to meliorate an odious nation)*, and laments that he was hindered from accomplishing it by the Parthian war. Now here is, 1. The last effort of his rage against the Jews. When he finds himself perplexed and embarrassed in his affairs he shall *go forth with great fury to destroy and utterly to make away many*, *v.* 44. The story of this we have 1 Mac. 3:27, etc., what a rage Antiochus was in when he heard of the successes of Judas Maccabaeus, and the orders he gave to Lysias to destroy Jerusalem. Then *he planted the tabernacles of his palace*, or *tents of his court, between the seas*, between the Great Sea and the Dead Sea. He set up his royal pavilion at Emmaus near Jerusalem, in token that, though he could not be present himself, yet he gave full power to his captains to prosecute the war against the Jews with the utmost rigour. He placed his tent there, as if he had taken possession *of the glorious holy mountain* and called it *his own*. Note, When impiety grows very impudent we may see its ruin near. 2. His exit: *He shall come to his end and none shall help him;* God shall cut him off in the midst of his days and none shall be able to prevent his fall. This is the same with that which was foretold *ch.* 8:25 *(He shall be broken without hand)*, where we took a view of his miserable end. Note, When God's time shall come to bring proud oppressors to their end none shall be able to help them, nor perhaps inclined to help them; for those that covet to be feared by all when they are in their grandeur, when they come to be in distress will find themselves loved by none; none will lend them so much as a hand or a prayer to help them; and, if the Lord do not help, who shall?

Of the kings that came after Antiochus nothing is here prophesied, for that was the most malicious mischievous enemy to the church, that was a type of the son of perdition, whom the Lord shall consume with the breath of his mouth and destroy with the brightness of his coming, and none shall help him.

CHAPTER 12

After the prediction of the troubles of the Jews under Antiochus, prefiguring the troubles of the Christian church under the anti-christian power, we have here, I. Comforts, and very precious ones, prescribed as cordials for the support of God's people in those times of trouble; and they are such as may indifferently serve both for those former times of trouble under Antiochus and those latter which were prefigured by them (*v.* 1–4). II. A conference between Christ and an angel concerning the time of the continuance of these events, designed for Daniel's satisfaction (*v.* 5–7). III. Daniel's enquiry for his own satisfaction (*v.* 8). And the answer he received to that enquiry (*v.* 9–12).

Verses 1–4

It is usual with the prophets, when they foretel the grievances of the church, to furnish it at the same time with proper antidotes, a remedy for every malady. And no relief is so sovereign, of such general application, so easily accommodated to every case, and of such powerful efficacy, as those that are fetched from Christ and the future state; thence the comforts here are fetched.

I. Jesus Christ shall appear his church's patron and protector: *At that time*, when the persecution is at the hottest, *Michael shall stand up*, *v.* 1. The angel had told Daniel what a firm friend Michael was to the church, *ch.* 10:21. He all along showed this friendship in the upper world; the angels knew it; but now *Michael shall stand* up in his providence, and work deliverance for the Jews, *when he sees that their power is gone*, Deu. 32:3. 6. Christ is *that great prince*, for he is the *prince of the kings of the earth*, Rev. 1:5. And, if he stand up for his church, who can be against it? But this is not all: *At that time* (that is, soon after) Michael shall stand up for the working out of our eternal salvation; the Son of God shall be incarnate, shall be *manifested to destroy the works of the devil*. Christ *stood for the children of our people* when he was made sin and a curse for them, stood in their stead as a sacrifice, bore the cure for them, to bear it from them. He stands for them in the intercession he ever lives to make within the veil, stands up for them, and stands their friend. And after the destruction of antichrist, of whom Antiochus was a type, Christ shall *stand at the latter day upon the earth*, shall appear for the complete redemption of all his.

II. When Christ appears he will recompense tribulation to those that trouble his people. There shall *be a time of trouble*, threatening to all, but ruining to all the implacable enemies of God's kingdom among men, such *trouble as never was since there was a nation*. This is applicable. 1. To the destruction of Jerusalem, which Christ calls (perhaps with an eye to this prediction) such a *great tribulation as was not since the beginning of the world to this time*, Mt. 24:21. This the angel had spoken much of (*ch.* 9:26, 27); and it happened about the same time that Christ set up the gospel-kingdom in the world, that Michael our prince *stands up*. Or, 2. To the judgment of the great day, that day that shall *burn as an oven*, and consume the proud and all that do wickedly; that will be such a *day of trouble* as never was to all those whom Michael our prince stands against.

III. He will work salvation for his people: *"At that time thy people shall be delivered*, delivered from the mischief and ruin designed them by Antiochus, even all those that were marked for preservation, that were *written among the living,"* Isa. 4:3. When Christ comes into the world he will save his spiritual Israel from sin and hell, and will, at his second coming, complete their salvation, even the salvation of as many as were given him, as many as have *their names in the book of life*, Rev. 20:15. They were written there before the world, and will be *found written* there at the end of the world, when the books shall be opened.

IV. There shall be a distinguishing resurrection of those that *sleep in the dust, v.* 2. 1. When God works deliverance for his people from persecution it is a kind of resurrection; so the Jews' release out of Babylon was represented in vision (Eze. 37) and so the deliverance of the Jews from Antiochus, and other restorations of the church to outward prosperity; they were as *life from the dead. Many of those* who had long slept in the dust of obscurity and calamity shall then awake, some to that life, and honour, and comfort which will be lasting, everlasting; but to others, who, when they return to their prosperity, will return to their iniquity, it will be a resurrection to shame and contempt, for the *prosperity of fools* will but expose them and destroy them. 2. When, upon the appearing of Michael our prince, his gospel is preached, many of those who *sleep in the dust*, both Jews and Gentiles, shall be awakened by it to take upon them a profession of religion, and shall rise out of their heathenism or Judaism; but, since there will be always a mixture of hypocrites with true saints, it is but some of those who are *raised to life* to whom the gospel is a *savour of life unto life*, but others will be raised by it *to shame and contempt*, to whom the gospel of Christ will be a *savour of death unto death*, and Christ himself set for their fall. The net of the gospel encloses both good and bad. But, 3. It must be meant of the general resurrection at the last day: *The multitude of those that sleep in the dust shall awake*, that is, all, which shall be a great many. Or, *Of those that sleep in the dust* many shall arise to life and many to shame. The Jews themselves understand this of the resurrection of the dead at the end of time; and Christ seems to have an eye to it when he speaks of the *resurrection of life* and the *resurrection of damnation* (Jn. 5:29); and upon this the Jews are said by St. Paul to expect a *resurrection of the dead both of the just and of the unjust*, Acts 24:15. And nothing could come in more seasonably here, for, under Antiochus's persecution, some basely betrayed their religion, others bravely adhered to it. Now it would be a trouble to them that, when the storm was over, they could neither reward the one nor punish the other; this therefore would be a satisfaction to them, that they would both be recompensed according to their works in the resurrection. And the apostle, speaking of the pious Jews that suffered martyrdom under Antiochus, tells us that though they were tortured yet they *accepted not deliverance*, because they *hoped to obtain this better resurrection*, Heb. 11:35.

V. There shall be a glorious reward conferred on those who, in the day of trouble and distress, being themselves *wise*, did *instruct many*. Such were taken particular notice of in the prophecy of the persecution (*ch.* 11:33), that they should do eminent service, and yet should *fall by the sword and by flame;* now, if there were not another life after this, they would be *of all men most miserable*, and therefore we are here assured that they shall be recompensed *in the resurrection of the just* (*v.* 3): *Those that are wise* (that are *teachers*, so some read it, for teachers have need of wisdom, and those that have wisdom themselves should communicate it to others) *shall shine as the brightness of the firmament*, shall shine in glory, heavenly glory, the glory of the upper world; and those that by the wisdom they have, and the instructions they give, are instrumental *to turn* any, especially to *turn many to righteousness*, shall shine *as the stars for ever and ever*. Note, 1. There is a glory reserved for all the saints in the future state, for all that are wise, wise for their souls and eternity. A man's wisdom now *makes his face to shine* (Eccles. 8:1), but much more will it do so in that state where its power shall be perfected and its services rewarded. 2. The more good any do in this world, especially to the souls of men, the greater will be their glory and reward in the other world. Those that turn *men to righteousness*, that *turn sinners from the errors of their ways* and help to *save their souls from death* (Jam. 5:20), will share in the glory of those they have helped to heaven, which will be a great addition to their own glory. 3. Ministers of Christ, who have obtained mercy of him to be faithful and successful, and so are made *burning and shining lights* in this world, shall shine very brightly in the other world, shall shine *as the stars*. Christ is *the sun*, the fountain, of the lights both of grace and glory; ministers, as stars, shine in both, with a light derived from him, and a diminutive light in comparison of him; yet to those that are *earthen vessels* it will be a glory infinitely transcending their deserts. They shall *shine as the stars* of different magnitudes, some in less, others in greater lustre; but, whereas the day is coming when the stars shall fall from heaven as leaves in autumn, these stars shall *shine for ever and ever*, shall never set, never be eclipsed.

VI. That this prophecy of those times, though sealed up now, would be of great use to those that should live then, *v.* 4. Daniel must now *shut up the words and seal the book* because the *time would be long* ere these things would be accomplished: and it was some comfort that the Jewish nation, though, in the infancy of their return from Babylon, while they were few and weak, they met with obstructions in their work, were not persecuted for their religion till a long time after, when they had grown to some strength and maturity. He must *seal the book* because it would not be *understood*, and therefore would not be regarded, till the things contained in it were accomplished; but he must keep it safely, as a treasure of great value, laid up for the ages to come, to whom it would be of great service; for *many shall then run to and fro, and knowledge shall be increased*. Then this hidden treasure shall be opened, and many shall search into it, and dig for the knowledge of it, as for silver. They shall *run to and fro*, to enquire out copies of it, shall collate them, and see that they be true and authentic. They shall read it over and over, shall meditate upon it, and run it over in their minds; *discurrent — they shall discourse* of it, and talk it over among themselves, and compare notes about it, if by any means they may *sift out* the meaning of it; and thus *knowledge shall be increased*. By consulting this prophecy on this occasion they shall be led to *search* other *scriptures*, which shall contribute much to their advancement in useful knowledge; for *then shall we know if we follow on to know the Lord*, Hos. 6:3. Those that would have their knowledge increased must take pains, must not sit still in slothfulness and bare wishes but *run to and fro*, must make use of all the means of knowledge and improve all opportunities of getting their mistakes rectified, their doubts resolved, and their acquaintance with the things of God improved, to know more and to know better what they do know. And let us here see reason to hope that, 1. Those things of God which are now dark and obscure will hereafter be made clear, and easy to be understood. *Truth is the daughter of time*. Scripture prophecies will be expounded by the accomplishment of them; *therefore* they are given, and for that explication they are reserved. *Therefore* they are *told us before*, that, *when they do come to pass*, we may believe. 2. Those things of God which are despised and neglected, and thrown by as useless, shall be brought into reputation, shall be found to be of great service, and be brought into request; for divine revelation, however slighted for a time, shall be *magnified and made honourable*, and, above all, in the *judgment of the great day*, when the books shall be opened, and that book among the rest.

Verses 5–13

Daniel had been made to foresee the amazing revolutions of states and kingdoms, as far as the Israel of God was concerned in them; in them he foresaw troublous times to the church, suffering trying times, the prospect of which much affected him and filled him with concern. Now there were two questions proper to be asked upon this head: — *When* shall the *end be?* And, *What* shall the *end be?* These two questions are asked and answered here, in the close of the book; and though the comforts prescribed in the foregoing verses, one would think, were satisfactory enough, yet, for more abundant satisfaction, this is added.

I. The question, *When shall the end be?* is asked by an angel, *v.* 5, 6. Concerning this we may observe,

1. Who it was that asked the question. Daniel had had a vision of Christ in his glory, the *man clothed in linen, ch.* 10:5. But his discourse had been with the angel Gabriel, and now he *looks,* and *behold other two* (*v.* 5), two angels that he had not seen before, *one upon the bank of the river on one side and the other on the other side,* that, the river being between them, they might not whisper to one another, but what they said might be heard. Christ stood *on the waters of the river,* (*v.* 6), *between the banks of Ulai;* it was therefore proper that the angels his attendants should stand on either bank, that they might be ready to go, one one way and the other the other way, as he should order them. These angels appeared, (1.) To adorn the vision, and make it the more illustrious; and to add to the glory of the Son of man, Heb. 1:6. Daniel had not seen them before, though it is probable that they were there; but now, when they began to speak, he looked up, and saw them. Note, The further we look into the things of God, and the more we converse with them, the more we shall see of those things, and still new discoveries will be made to us; those that know much, if they improve it, shall know more. (2.) To confirm the discovery, that *out of the mouth of two or three witnesses the word might be established.* Three angels appeared to Abraham. (3.) To inform themselves, to hear and ask questions; for the mysteries of God's kingdom are things which the *angels desire to look into* (1 Pt. 1:12) and they are *known to the church,* Eph. 3:10. Now one of these two angels said, *When shall the end be?* Perhaps they both asked, first one and then the other, but Daniel heard only one.

2. To whom this question was put, to the *man clothed in linen,* of whom we read before (*ch.* 10:5), to Christ our great high priest, *who was upon the waters of the river,* and whose spokesman, or interpreter, the angel Gabriel had all this while been. This river was Hiddekel (*ch.* 10:4), the same with Tigris, the place whereabout many of the events prophesied of would happen; there therefore is the scene laid. Hiddekel was mentioned as one of the rivers that watered the garden of Eden (Gen. 2:14); fitly therefore does Christ stand upon that river, for by him the trees in the paradise of God are watered. *Waters* signify *people,* and so his standing upon the waters denotes his dominion over all; he *sits upon the flood* (Ps. 29:10); *he treads upon the waters of the sea,* Job 9:8. And Christ, to show that this was he, in the days of his flesh *walked upon the waters,* Mt. 14:25. He was *above the waters of the river* (so some read it); he appeared in the air over the river.

3. What the question was: *How long shall it be to the end of these wonders?* Daniel would not ask the question, because he would not pry into what was hidden, nor seem inquisitive concerning the times and the seasons, which the Father has *put in his own power,* Acts 1:7. But, that he might have the satisfaction of the answer, the angel put the question in his hearing. Our Lord Jesus sometimes answered the questions which his disciples were afraid or ashamed to ask, Jn. 16:19. The angel asked as one concerned, *How long shall it be?* What is the time prefixed in the divine counsels for the *end of these wonders,* these suffering trying times, that are to pass over the people of God? Note, (1.) The troubles of the church are the *wonder* of angels. They are astonished that God will suffer his church to be thus afflicted, and are anxious to know what good he will do his church by its afflictions. (2.) Good angels know no more of things to come than God is pleased to discover to them, much less do evil angels. (3.) The holy angels in heaven are concerned for the church on earth, and lay to heart its afflictions; how much more then should we, who are more immediately related to it, and have so much of our peace in its peace?

4. What answer was returned to it by him who is indeed the *numberer of secrets,* and knows things to come.

(1.) Here is a more general account given of the continuance of these troubles to the angel that made the enquiry (*v.* 7), that they shall continue *for a time, times, and a half,* that is, a year, two years, and half a year, as was before intimated (*ch.* 7:25), but the one half of a prophetical week. Some understand it indefinitely, a certain time for an uncertain; it shall be *for a time* (a considerable time), for *times* (a longer time yet, double what it was thought at first that it would be), and yet indeed it shall be but *half a time,* or a part of a time; when it is over it shall seem not half so much as was feared. But it is rather to be taken for a certain time; we meet with it in the Revelation, under the title sometimes of three days and a half, put for three years and a half, sometimes forty-two months, sometimes 1260 days. Now this determination of the time is here [1.] Confirmed by an oath. The man *clothed in linen* lifted up both his hands *to heaven, and swore by him that lives for ever and ever* that it should be so. Thus the *mighty angel* whom St. John saw is brought in, with a plain reference to this vision, standing with his *right foot on the sea* and *his left foot on the earth,* and with his hand lifted up to heaven, swearing *that there shall be no longer delay,* Rev. 10:5, 6. This Mighty One that Daniel saw stood with *both feet* on the water, and swore with *both hands* lifted up. Note, An oath is of use for confirmation; God only is to be sworn by, for he is the proper Judge to whom we are to appeal; and lifting up the hand is a very proper and significant sign to be used in a solemn oath. [2.] It is illustrated with a reason. God will suffer him to prevail *till he shall have accomplished to scatter the power of the holy people.* God will suffer him to do his worst, and run his utmost length, and then *all these things shall be finished.* Note, God's time to succour and relieve his people is when their affairs are brought to the last extremity; *in the mount of the Lord it shall be seen* that Isaac is saved just when he lies ready to be sacrificed. Now the event answered the prediction; Josephus says expressly, in his book of the *Wars of the Jews,* that Antiochus, surnamed Epiphanes, surprised Jerusalem by force, *and held it three years and six months,* and was then *cast out of the country* by the Asmoneans or Maccabees. Christ's public ministry continued *three years and a half,* during which time he endured the contradiction of sinners against himself, and lived in poverty and disgrace; and then when his power seemed to be quite scattered at his death, and his enemies triumphed over him, he obtained the most glorious victory and said, *It is finished.*

(2.) Here is something added more particularly concerning the time of the continuance of those troubles, in what is said to Daniel, *v.* 11, 12, where we have, [1.] The event fixed from which the time of the trouble is to be dated, from the *taking away of the daily sacrifice* by Antiochus, and the *setting up* of the image of Jupiter upon the altar, which was the *abomination of desolation.* They must reckon their troubles to begin indeed when they were deprived of the benefit of public ordinances; that was to them the *beginning of sorrows;* that was what they laid most to heart. [2.] The continuance of their trouble; it shall last 1290 days, *three years* and *seven months,* or (as some reckon) *three years, six months,* and *fifteen days;* and then, it is probable, the daily sacrifice was restored, and the abomination of desolation taken away, in remembrance of which the *feast of dedication* was observed even to our Saviour's time, Jn. 10:22. Though it does not appear by the history that it was exactly so long to a day, yet it appears that the beginning of the trouble was in the 145th year of the Seleucidae, and the end of it in the 148th year; and either the restoring of the sacrifice, and the taking away of the image, were just so many days after, or some other previous event that was remarkable, which is not recorded. There are many particular times fixed in the scripture-prophecies, which it does not appear by any history, sacred or profane, that the event answered, and yet no doubt it did punctually; as Isa. 16:14. [3.] The completing of their deliverance, or at least a further advance towards it, which is here set forty-five days after the former, and, some think, points at the death of Antiochus, 1335 days after his profaning the temple. *Blessed is he that waits and comes* to that time. It is said (1 Mac. 9:28; 10:1) that the Maccabees, under a divine conduct, *recovered the temple and the city.* Many good interpreters make these to be prophetical days (that is, so many years), and date them from the destruction of Jerusalem by the Romans; but what events they then fall upon they are not agreed. Others date them from the corruption of the gospel-worship by the antichrist, whose reign is confined in the Apocalypse to 1260 days (that is, years), at the end of which he shall begin to fall; but thirty years after he shall be quite fallen, at the end of 1290 days; and whoever lives forty years longer, to 1335 days, will see glorious times indeed. Whether it looks so far forward or no I cannot tell; but this, however, we may learn, *First,* That there is a time fixed for the termination of the church's troubles, and the bringing about of her deliverance, and that this time will be punctually observed to a day. *Secondly,* That this time must be waited for with faith and patience. *Thirdly,* That, when it comes, it will abundantly recompense us for our long expectations of it. *Blessed is he* who, having waited long, comes to it at last, for he will then have reason to say, *Lo, this is our God, and we have waited for him.*

II. The question, *What shall the end be?* is asked by Daniel, and an answer given to it. Observe,

1. Why Daniel asked this question; it was because, though he *heard what was said* to the angel, yet he did not *understand* it, *v.* 8. Daniel was a very intelligent man, and had been conversant in visions and prophecies, and yet here he was puzzled; he did not understand the meaning of the *time, times, and the part of a time,* at least not so clearly and with so much certainty as he wished. Note, The best men are often much at a loss in their enquiries concerning divine things, and meet with that which they do not *understand.* But the better they are the more sensible they are of their own weaknesses and ignorance, and the more ready to acknowledge them.

2. What the question was: *O my Lord! What shall be the end of these things?* He directs his enquiry not to the angel that talked with him, but immediately to Christ, for to whom else should we go with our enquiries? "What shall be the final issue of these events? What do they tend to? What will then end in?" Note, When we take a view of the affairs of this world, and of the church of God in it, we cannot but think, What will be the end of these things? We see things move as if they would end in the utter ruin of God's kingdom among men. When we observe the prevalence of vice and impiety, the decay of religion, the sufferings of the righteous, and the triumphs of the ungodly over them, we may well ask, *O my Lord! what will be the end of these things?* But this may satisfy us in general, that all will end well at last. Great is the truth, and will prevail at long-run. All opposing rule, principality, and power, will be put down, and holiness and love will triumph, and be in honour, to eternity. The end, this end, will come.

3. What answer is returned to this question. Besides what refers to the time (*v.* 11, 12), of which before, here are some general instructions given to Daniel, with which he is dismissed from further attendance.

(1.) He must content himself with the discoveries that had been made to him, and not enquire any further: *"Go thy way, Daniel;* let it suffice thee that thou has been admitted thus far to the foresight of things to come, but stop here. *Go thy way* about the king's business again, *ch.* 8:27. *Go thy way,* and record what thou hast seen and heard, for the benefit of posterity, and covet not to see and hear more at present." Note, Communion with God is not our continual feast in this world; we sometimes are taken to be witnesses of Christ's glory, and we say, *It is good to be here;* but we must go down from the mount, and have there no continuing city. Those that know much *know but in part,* and still see there is a great deal that they are kept in the dark about, and are likely to be so till the veil is rent; hitherto their knowledge shall go, but no further. *"Go thy way, Daniel,* satisfied with what thou hast."

(2.) He must not expect that what had been said to him would be fully understood till it was accomplished: *The words are closed up and sealed,* are involved in perplexities, and are likely to be so, *till the time of the end,* till the end of these things; nay, till the end of all things. Daniel was ordered to *seal the book to the time of the end, v.* 4. The Jews used to say, *When Elias comes he will tell us all things.* "They are *closed up and sealed,* that is, the discovery designed to be made by them is now fully settled and completed; nothing is to be added to it nor taken from it, for it is *closed up* and *sealed;* ask not therefore after more." *Nescire velle quae magister maximus docere non vult erudita inscitia est — He has learned much who is willing to be ignorant of those things which the great teacher does not choose to impart.*

(3.) He must count upon no other than that, as long as the world stands, there will still be in it such a mixture as now we see there is of good and bad, *v.* 10. We long to see all wheat and no tares in God's field, all corn and no chaff in God's floor; but it will not be till the time of ingathering, till the winnowing day, comes; both must *grow together until the harvest.* As it has been, so it is, and will be, *The wicked shall do wickedly,* but *the wise shall understand.* In this, as in other things, St. John's Revelation closes as Daniel did. Rev. 22:11, *He that is filthy, let him be filthy still; and he that is holy, let him be holy still.* [1.] There is no remedy but that wicked people *will do wickedly;* and such people there are and will be in the world to the end of time. *So said the proverb of the ancients, Wickedness proceeds from the wicked* (1 Sa. 24:13); and the observation of the moderns says the same. Bad men will do bad things; and a *corrupt tree* will *never bring forth good fruit.* Do men *gather grapes of thorns,* or bring forth good things from an evil treasure in the heart? No; wicked practices are the natural products of wicked principles and dispositions. *Marvel not at the matter* then, Eccl. 5:8. We are told, before, that the *wicked will do wickedly;* we can expect no better from them: but, which is worse, *none of the wicked shall understand.* This is either, *First,* A part of their sin. They *will not understand;* they shut their eyes against the light, and none so blind as those that will not see. *Therefore* they are *wicked* because they *will not understand.* If they did but rightly know the truths of God, they would readily obey the laws of God, Ps. 82:5. Wilful sin is the effect of wilful ignorance; they *will not understand* because *they are wicked;* they *hate the light,* and come not to the light, *because their deeds are evil,* Jn. 3:19. Or, *Secondly,* It is a part of their punishment; they will do wickedly, and therefore God has given them up to *blindness of mind,* and has said concerning them, *They shall not understand,* nor be *converted and healed,* Mt. 13:14, 15. God will not *give them eyes to see,* because they will do wickedly, Deu. 29:4. [2.] Yet, bad as the world is, God will secure to himself a remnant of good people in it; still there shall be some, there shall be many, to whom the providences and ordinances of God shall be *a savour of life unto life,* while to others they are *a savour of death unto death. First,* the providences of God shall do them good: *Many shall be purified, and made white, and tried,* by their troubles (compare *ch.* 11:35), by the same troubles which will but stir up the corruptions of the wicked and make them do more wickedly. Note, The afflictions of good people are designed for their trial; but by these trials they are *purified* and *made white,* their corruptions are purged out, their graces are brightened, and made both more vigorous and more conspicuous, and are *found to praise, and honour, and glory,* 1 Pt. 1:7. To those who are themselves sanctified and good every event is sanctified, and works for good, and helps to make them better. *Secondly,* The word of God shall do them good. When the *wicked understand not,* but stumble at the word, the *wise shall understand.* Those who are wise in practice shall understand doctrine; those who are influenced and governed by the divine law and love shall be illuminated with a divine light. For if any man will *do his will* he shall *know the truth,* Jn. 7:17. *Give instruction to a wise man, and he will be yet wiser.*

(4.) He must comfort himself with the pleasing prospect of his own happiness in death, in judgment, and to eternity, *v.* 13. Daniel was now very old, and had been long engaged both in an intimate acquaintance with heaven and in a great deal of public business on this earth. And now he must think of bidding farewell to this present state: *Go thou thy way till the end be.* [1.] It is good for us all to think much of going away from this world; we are still going, and must be gone shortly, gone the way of all the earth. That must be our way; but this is our comfort, We shall not go till God calls for us to another world, and till he has done with us in this world, till he says, *"Go thou thy way;* thou hast finished thy testimony, done thy work, and accomplished as a hireling thy day, therefore now, *Go thy way,* and leave it to others to take thy room." [2.] When a good man goes his way from this world he enters into rest: *"Thou shalt rest* from all thy present toils and agitations, and shalt not see the evils that are coming on the next generation." Never can a child of God say more pertinently than in his dying moments, *Return unto thy rest, O my soul!* [3.] Time and days will have an end; not only our time and days will end very shortly, but all times and days will have an end at length; yet a little while, and time shall be no more, but all its revolutions will be numbered and finished. [4.] Our rest in the grave will be but *till the end of the days;* and then the peaceful rest will be happily disturbed by a joyful resurrection. Job foresaw this when he said of the dead, *Till the heavens be no more,* they *shall not awake, nor be raised out of their sleep,* implying that then they shall, Job 14:12. [5.] We must every one of us *stand in our lot at the end of the days.* In the judgment of the great day we must have our allotment according to what we were, and what we did, in the body, either, *Come, you blessed* or, *Go, you cursed;* and we must *stand for ever in that lot.* It was a comfort to Daniel, it is a comfort to all the saints, that, whatever their lot is in the days of time, they shall have a happy lot in *the end of the days,* shall have their *lot among the chosen.* And it ought to be the great care and concern of every one of us to secure a happy lot at last in the *end of the days,* and they we may well be content with our present lot, welcome the will of God. [6.] A believing hope and prospect of a blessed lot in the heavenly Canaan, at the end of the days, will be an effectual support to us when we are going our way out of this world, and will furnish us with living comforts in dying moments.

AN EXPOSITION, WITH PRACTICAL OBSERVATIONS, OF

THE BOOK OF THE PROPHET HOSEA

I. We have now before us the twelve minor prophets, which some of the ancients, in reckoning up the books of the Old Testament, put all together, and reckon but as *one book.* They are called the minor prophets, not because their writings are of any less authority or usefulness than those of the greater prophets, or as if these prophets were less in God's account or might be so in ours than the other, but only because they are shorter, and less in bulk, than the other. We have reason to think that these prophets preached as much as the others, but that they did not write so much, nor is so much of their preaching kept upon record. Many excellent prophets wrote nothing, and others but little, who yet were very useful in their day. And so in the Christian church there have been many burning and shining lights, who are not known to posterity by their writings, and yet were no way inferior in gifts, and graces, and serviceableness to their own generation, than those who are; and some who have left but little behind them, and make no great figure among authors, were yet as valuable men as the more voluminous writers. These twelve small prophets, Josephus says, were put into one volume by the *men of the great synagogue* in Ezra's time, of which learned and pious body of men the last three of these twelve prophets are supposed to have been themselves members. These are what remained of the scattered pieces of inspired writing. Antiquaries value the *fragmenta veterum — the fragments of antiquity;* these are the fragments of prophecy, which are carefully gathered up by the divine Providence and the care of the church, that nothing might be lost, as St. Paul's short epistles after his long ones. The son of Sirach speaks of these twelve prophets with honour, as men that *strengthened Jacob, Ecclus.* 49:10. Nine of these prophets prophesied before the captivity, and the last three after the return of the Jews to their own land. Some difference there is in the order of these books. We place them as the ancient Hebrew did; and all agree to put Hosea first; but the ancient thing is not material. And, if we covet to place them according to their seniority, as to some of them we shall find no certainty.

II. We have before us the prophecy of Hosea, who was the first of all the writing prophets, being raised up somewhat before the time of Isaiah. The ancients say, He was of Bethshemesh, and of the tribe of Issachar. He continued very long a prophet; the Jews reckoned that he prophesied nearly fourscore and ten years; so that, as Jerome observes, he prophesied of the destruction of the kingdom of the ten tribes when it was at a great distance, and lived himself to see and lament it, and to improve it when it was over, for warning to its sister kingdom. The scope of his prophecy is to discover sin, and to denounce the judgments of God against a people that would not be reformed. The style is very concise and sententious, above any of the prophets; and in some places it seems to be like the book of Proverbs, without connexion, and rather to be called Hosea's *sayings* than Hosea's *sermons.* And a weighty adage may sometimes do more service than a laboured discourse. Huetius observes that many passages in the prophecies of Jeremiah and Ezekiel seem to refer to, and to be borrowed from, the prophet Hosea, who wrote a good while before them. As Jer. 7:34; 16:9; 25:10; and Eze. 26:13, speak the same with Hos. 2:11; so Eze. 16:16, etc., is taken from Hos. 2:8. And that promise of *serving the Lord their God,* and *David their king,* Jer. 30:8, 9. Eze. 34:23, *Hosea* had before, 3:5. And Eze. 19:12 is taken from Hos. 13:15. Thus one prophet confirms and corroborates another; and all these worketh that one and the self-same Spirit.

CHAPTER 1

The mind of God is revealed to this prophet, and by him to the people, in the first three chapters, by signs and types, but afterwards only by discourse. In this chapter we have, I. The general title of the whole book (*v.* 1). II. Some particular instructions which he was ordered to give to the people of God. 1. He must convince them of their sin in going a whoring from God, by marrying a wife of whoredoms (*v.* 2, 3). 2. He must foretel the ruin coming upon them for their sin, in the names of his sons, which signified God's disowning and abandoning them (*v.* 4–6, 8, 9). 3. He must speak comfortable to the kingdom of Judah, which still retained the pure worship of God, and assure them of the salvation of the Lord (*v.* 7). 4. He must give an intimation of the great mercy God had in store both for Israel and Judah, in the latter days (*v.* 10, 11), for in this prophecy many precious promises of mercy are mixed with the threatenings of wrath.

Verse 1

1. Here is the prophet's name and surname; which he himself, as other prophets, prefixes to his prophecy, for the satisfaction of all that he is ready to attest what he writes to be of God; he sets his hand to it, as that which he will stand by. His name, *Hosea,* or *Hosea* (for it is the very same with Joshua's original name), signifies a *saviour;* for prophets were instruments of salvation to the people of God, so are faithful ministers; they help to save many a soul from death, by saving it from sin. his surname was *Ben-Beeri,* or *the son of Beeri.* As with us now, so with them then, some had their surname from their place, as Micah the Morashite, Nahum the Elkoshite; others from their parents, as Joel the son of Bethuel, and here Hosea the son of Beeri. And perhaps they made use of that distinction when the eminence of their parents was such as would bring honour upon them; but it is a groundless conceit of the Jews that where a prophet's father is names he also was a proph-

et. *Beeri* signifies a *well,* which may put us in mind of the fountain of life and living waters from which prophets are drawn and must be continually drawing. 2. Here are his authority and commission: *The word of the Lord came to him. It was to him;* it came with power and efficacy to him; it was revealed to him as a real thing, and not a fancy or imagination of his own, in some such way as God then discovered himself to his servants the prophets. What he said and wrote was by divine inspiration; it was *by the word of the Lord,* as St. Paul speaks concerning that which he had purely by revelation, 1 Th. 4:15. Therefore this book was always received among the canonical books of the Old Testament, which is confirmed by what is quoted out of it in the New Testament, Mt. 2:15; 9:13; 12:7; Rom. 9:25, 26; 1 Pt. 2:10. For the word of the Lord endures for ever. 3. Here is a particular account of the times in which he prophesied — *in the days of Uzziah, Jotham, Ahaz, and Hezekiah, kings of Judah, and in the days of Jeroboam the son of Joash, king of Israel.* We have only this general date of his prophecy; and not the date of any particular part of it, as, before, in Isaiah, Jeremiah, Ezekiel, and Daniel, and, afterwards, in Haggai and Zechariah. Here is only one king of Israel named, though there were many more within this time, because, having mentioned the kings of Judah, there was no necessity of naming the other; and, they being all wicked, he took no pleasure in naming them, nor would do them the honour. Now by this account here given of the several reigns in which Hosea prophesied (and it should seem the word of the Lord still came to him, more or less, at times, throughout all these reigns) it appears, (1.) That he prophesied a long time, that he began when he was very young, which gave him the advantage of strength and sprightliness, and that he continued at his work till he was very old, which gave him the advantage of experience and authority. It was a great honour to him to be thus long employed in such good work, and a great mercy to the people to have a minister so long among them that so well knew their state, and naturally cared for it, one they had been long used to and who therefore was the more likely to be useful to them. And yet, for aught that appears, he did but little good among them; the longer they enjoyed him the less they regarded him; they despised his youth first, and afterwards his age. (2.) That he passed through a variety of conditions. Some of these kings were very good, and, it is likely, countenanced and encouraged him; others were very bad, who (we may suppose) frowned upon him and discouraged him; and yet he was still the same. God's ministers must expect to pass through *honour and dishonour, evil report and good report,* and must resolve in both to hold fast their integrity and keep close to their work. (3.) That he began to prophesy at a time when the judgments of God were abroad, when God was himself contending in a more immediate way with that sinful people, who *fell into the hands of the Lord,* before they were turned over *into the hands of man;* for in the days of Uzziah, and of Jeroboam his contemporary, the dreadful earthquake was, mentioned Zec. 14:5 and Amos 1:1. And then was the plague of locusts, Joel 1:2–4; Amos 7:1; Hos. 4:3. The rod of God is sent to enforce the word and the word of God is sent to explain the rod, yet neither prevails till God by his Spirit opens the ear to instruction and discipline. (4.) That he began to prophesy in Israel at a time when their kingdom was in a flourishing prosperous condition, for so it was in the reign of Jeroboam the second, as we find 2 Ki. 14:25, *He restored the coast of Israel,* and God *saved them by his hand;* yet then Hosea boldly tells them of their sins and foretels their destruction. Men are not to be flattered in their sinful ways because they prosper in the world, but even then must be faithfully reproved, and plainly told that their prosperity will not be their security, nor will it last long if they *go on still in their trespasses.*

Verses 2–7

These words, *The beginning of the word of the Lord by Hosea,* may refer either, 1. To that glorious set of prophets which was raised up about this time. About this time there lived and prophesied Joel, Amos, Micah, Jonah, Obadiah, and Isaiah; but Hosea was the first of them that foretold the destruction of Israel; the *beginning of this word of the Lord was by him.* We read in the history of this Jeroboam here named (2 Ki. 14:27) that *the Lord* had *not* yet *said* he would *blot out the name of Israel,* but soon after he said he would, and Hosea was the man that began to say it, which made it so much the harder task to him, to be the first that should carry an unpleasing message and some time before any were raised up to second him. Or, rather, 2. To Hosea's own prophecies. This was the first message God sent him upon to this people, to tell them that they were *an evil and an adulterous generation.* He might have desired to be excused from dealing so roughly with them till he had gained authority and reputation, and some interest in their affections. No; he must *begin with this,* that they might know what to expect from a prophet of the Lord. Nay, he must not only preach this to them, but he must write it, and publish it, and leave it upon record as a witness against them. Now here,

I. The prophet must, as it were in a looking-glass, show them *their sin,* and show it to be exceedingly sinful, exceedingly hateful. The prophet is ordered to *take unto him a wife of whoredoms and children of whoredoms, v.* 2. And he did so, *v.* 3. He married a woman of ill fame, *Gomer the daughter of Diblaim,* not one that had been married and had committed adultery, for then she must have been put to death, but one that had lived scandalously in the single state. To marry such a one was not *malum in se — evil in itself,* but only *malum per accidens — incidentally an evil,* not prudent, decent, or expedient, and therefore forbidden to the priests, and which, if it were really done, would be an affliction to the prophet (it is threatened as a curse on Amaziah that his wife should be a harlot, Amos 7:17), but not a sin when God commanded it for a holy end; nay, if commanded, it was his duty, and he must trust God with his reputation. But most commentators think that it was done *in vision,* or that it is no more than a parable; and that was a way of teaching commonly used among the ancients, particularly prophets; what they meant of others they *transferred to themselves in a figure,* as St. Paul speaks, 1 Co. 4:6. He must take *a wife of whoredoms,* and have such children by her as every one would suspect, though born in wedlock, to be *children of whoredoms,* begotten in adultery, because it is too common for those who have lived lewdly in the single state to live no better in the married state. "Now" (saith God) "Hosea, this people is to me such a dishonour, and such a grief and vexation, as a *wife of whoredoms* and *children of whoredoms* would be to thee. *For the land has committed great whoredoms.*" In all instances of wickedness they had departed from the Lord; but their idolatry especially is the whoredom they are here charged with. Giving that glory to any creature which is due to God alone is such an injury and affront to God as for a wife to embrace the bosom of a stranger is to her husband. It is especially so in those that have made a profession of religion, and have been taken into covenant with God; it is breaking the marriage-bond; it is a heinous odious sin, and, as much as any thing, besots the mind and takes away the heart. *Idolatry* is *great whoredom,* worse than any other; it is departing from *the Lord,* to whom we lie under greater obligations than any wife does or can do to her husband. *The land has committed whoredom;* it is not here and there a particular person that is guilty of idolatry, but the whole land is polluted with it; the sin has become national, the disease epidemical. What an odious thing would it be for the prophet, a *holy man,* to have a whorish wife, and children whorish like her! What an exercise would it be of his patience, and, if she persisted in it, what could be expected but that he should give her a bill of divorce! And is it not then much more offensive to the *holy God* to have such a people as this to be called by his name and have a place in his house? How great is his patience with them! And how justly may he cast them off! It was as if he should have married Gomer the daughter of Diblaim, who probably was at that time a noted harlot. The land of Israel was like Gomer the daughter of Diblaim. *Gomer* signifies *corruption; Diblaim* signifies *two cakes,* or *lumps of figs;* this denotes that Israel was near to ruin, and that their luxury and sensuality were the cause of it. They were as the *evil figs* that could not be eaten, they were so evil. It intimates sin to be the daughter of plenty and destruction the daughter of the abuse of plenty. Some give this sense of the command here given to the prophet: "Go, take thee a wife of *whoredoms,* for, if thou shouldst go to seek for an honest modest woman, thou wouldst not find any such, for the whole land, and all the people of it, are given to whoredom, the usual concomitant of idolatry."

II. The prophet must, as it were through a perspective glass, show them their ruin; and this he does in the names given to the children born of this adulteress; for as *lust,* when it has *conceived, brings forth sin,* so *sin, when it is finished, brings forth death.*

1. He foretels the fall of the royal family in the name he is appointed to give to his first child, which was a son: *Call his name Jezreel, v.* 4. We find that the prophet Isaiah gave prophetical names to his children (Isa. 7:3; 7:3), so this prophet here. Jezreel signifies *the seed of God* (so they should have been); but it signifies also the *scattered of God;* they shall be as sheep on the mountains that have no shepherds. *Call them not Israel,* which signifies *dominion,* they have lost all the honour of that name; but call them Jezreel, which signifies *dispersion,* for those that have departed from the Lord will wander endlessly. Hitherto they have been scattered as seek; let them now be scattered as chaff. Jezreel was the name of one of the royal seats of the kings of Israel; it was a beautiful city, seated in a pleasant valley, and it is with allusion to that city that this child is called *Jezreel,* for *yet a little while and I will avenge the blood of Jezreel upon the house of Jehu,* from whom the present king, Jeroboam, was lineally descended. The house of Jehu smarted for the sins of Jehu, for God often lays up men's iniquity for their children and visits it upon them. It is *the kingdom of the house of Israel,* which may be meant either of the present royal family, that of Jehu, which God did quickly *cause to cease* (for the son of this Jeroboam, Zechariah, reigned but *six months,* and he was the last of Jehu's race), or of the whole kingdom in general, which continued corrupt and wicked, and which was *made to cease* in the reign of Hoshea, about seventy years after; and with God that is but a *little while.* Note, Note, Neither the pomp of kings nor the power of kingdoms can secure them from God's destroying judgments, if they continue to rebel against him. (2.) What is the ground of this controversy: *I will revenge the blood of Jezreel upon the house of Jehu,* the blood which Jehu shed at Jezreel, when by commission from God and in obedience to his command, he utterly destroyed the house of Ahab, and all that were in alliance with it, with all the worshippers of Baal. God approved of what he did (2 Ki. 10:30): *Thou has done well in executing that which is right in my eyes;* and yet here God will avenge that *blood upon the house of Jehu,* when the time has expired during which it was promised that his family should reign, even to the fourth generation. But how comes the same action to be both rewarded and punished? Very justly; the matter of it was good; it was the execution of a righteous sentence passed upon the house of Ahab, and, as such, it was rewarded; but Jehu did it not in a right manner; he aimed at his own advancement, not at the glory of God, and mingled his own resentments with the execution of God's justice. He did it with a malice against the sinners, but not with any antipathy to the sin; for he kept up the worship of the golden calves, and *took no heed to walk in the law of God,* 2 Ki. 10:31. And therefore when the measure of the iniquity of his house was full, and God came to reckon with them, the first article in the account is (and, being first, it is put for all the rest) for the blood of the house of Ahab, here called the *blood of Jezreel.* Thus when the house of Baasha was rooted out it was because he did *like the house of Jeroboam, and because he killed him,* 1 Ki. 16:7. Note, Those that are entrusted with the administration of justice are concerned to see to it that they do it from a right principle and with a right intention, and that they do not themselves live in those sins which they punish in others, lest even their just executions should be reckoned for, another day, as little less than murders. (3.) How far the controversy shall proceed; it shall be not a correction, but a destruction. Some make those words, *I will visit, or appoint, the blood of Jezreel upon the house of Jehu,* to signify, not as we read it the revenging of that bloodshed, but the repeating of that bloodshed: "I will punish the house of Jehu, as I punished the house of Ahab, because Jehu did not take warning by the punishment of his predecessors, but trod in the steps of their idolatry. And after the house of Jehu is destroyed *I will cause to cease the kingdom of the house of Israel;* I will begin to bring it down, though now it flourish." After the death of Zech-

ariah, the last of the house of Jehu, the kingdom of the ten tribes went to decay, and dwindled sensibly. And, in order to the ruin of it, it is threatened (v. 5), *I will break the bow of Israel in the valley of Jezreel;* the *strength of the warriors of Israel,* so the Chaldee. God will disable them either to defend themselves or to resist their enemies. And the *bow abiding in strength,* and being *renewed in the hand,* intimates a growing power, so the *breaking of the bow* intimates a sinking ruined power. The bow shall be broken *in the valley of Jezreel,* where, probably, the armoury was; or, it may be, in that valley some battle was fought, wherein the kingdom of Israel was very much weakened. Note, There is no fence against God's controversy; when he comes forth against a people their strong bows are soon broken and their strong-holds broken down. In the valley of Jezreel they shed that blood which the righteous God would in that very place avenge upon them; as some notorious malefactors are hanged in chains just where the villainy they suffer for was perpetrated, that the punishment may answer the sin.

2. He foretels God's abandoning the whole nation in the name he gives to the second child. This was a daughter, as the former was a son, to intimate that both sons and daughters had corrupted their way. Some make to signify that Israel grew effeminate, and was thereby enfeebled and made weak. Call the name of this daughter *Loruhamah — not beloved* (so it is translated Rom. 9:25), or *not having obtained mercy,* so it is translated 1 Pt. 2:10. It comes all to one. This reads the doom of the *house of Israel: I will no more have mercy* upon them. It intimates that God had shown them great mercy, but they had abused his favours, and forfeited them, and now he would show them favour no more. Note, Those that forsake their own mercies for lying vanities have reason to expect that their own mercies should forsake them, and that they should be left to their *lying vanities,* Jonah 2:8. Sin turns away the mercy of God even from *the house of Israel,* his own professing people, whose case is sad indeed when God says that he will no more have mercy upon them. And then it follows, *I will utterly take them away,* will utterly *remove them* (so some), will utterly *pluck them up,* so others. Note, When the streams of mercy are stopped we can expect no other than that the vials of wrath should be opened. Those whom God will no more have mercy upon shall be utterly taken away, as dross and dung. The word for *taking away* sometimes signifies to *forgive* sin; and some take it in that sense here: *I will no more have mercy upon them, though in pardoning I have pardoned them* heretofore. Though God has borne long, he will not bear always, with a people that hate to be reformed. Or, *I will no more have mercy upon them, that I should in any wise pardon them,* or (as our margin reads it) *that I should altogether pardon them.* If pardoning mercy is denied, no other mercy can be expected, for that opens the door to all the rest. Some make this to speak comfort: *I will no more have mercy upon them till in pardoning I shall pardon them,* that is, till the Redeemer comes to Zion to turn away ungodliness from Jacob. The Chaldee reads it, *But, if they repent, in pardoning I will pardon them.* Even the greatest sinners, if in time they bethink themselves and return, will find that *there is forgiveness with God.*

III. He must show them what mercy God had in store for the house of Judah, at the same time that he was thus contending with the house of Israel (v. 7): *But I will have mercy upon the house of Judah.* Note, Though some are justly cast off for their disobedience, yet God will always secure to himself a remnant that shall be the vessels and monuments of mercy. When divine justice is glorified in some, yet there are others in whom free grace is glorified. And, though some through unbelief are broken off, yet God will have a church in this world till the end of time. It aggravates the rejection of Israel that God will have mercy on Judah, and not on them, and magnifies God's mercy to Judah that, though they also have done wickedly, yet God did not reject them, as he rejected Israel: *I will have mercy upon them and will save them.* Note, Our salvation is owing purely to God's mercy, and not to any merit of our own. Now,

1. This, without doubt, refers to the temporal salvations which God wrought for Judah in a distinguishing way, the favours shown to them and not to Israel. When the Assyrian armies had destroyed Samaria, and carried the ten

tribes away into captivity, they proceeded to besiege Jerusalem; but God had mercy on the house of Judah, and saved them by the vast slaughter which an angel made, in one night, in the camp of the Assyrians; then they were *saved by the Lord their God* immediately, and not by sword or bow. When the ten tribes were continued in their captivity, and their land was possessed by others, they being *utterly taken away,* God *had mercy on the house of Judah* and *saved them,* and, after seventy years, brought them back, *not by might or power, but by the Spirit of the Lord of hosts,* Zec. 4:6. *I will save them by the Lord their God,* that is, by myself. God will be exalted *in his own strength,* will take the work into his own hands. That salvation is sure which he undertakes to be the author of; for, if he will work, none shall hinder. And that salvation is most acceptable which he does *by himself. So the Lord alone did lead him.* The less there is of man in any salvation, and the more of God, the brighter it shines and the sweeter it tastes. I will save them *in the word of the Lord* (so the Chaldee), for the sake of Christ, the eternal word, and by his power. *I will save them not by bow nor by sword,* that is, (1.) They shall be saved when they are reduced to so low an ebb that they have neither bow nor sword to defend themselves with, Jdg. 5:8; 1 Sa. 13:22. (2.) They shall be saved by the Lord when they are brought off from trusting to their own strength and their weapons of war, Ps. 44:6. (3.) They shall be saved easily, without the trouble of sword and bow, v. 7. Isa. 9:5, *I will save them by the Lord their God.* In the calling him *their God,* he upbraids the ten tribes who had *cast him off* from being *theirs,* for which reason he had *cast them off,* and intimates what was the true reason why he had mercy, distinguishing mercy, for the house of Judah, and saved them: it was in pursuance of his covenant with them as the Lord their God, and in recompence for their faithful adherence to him and to his word and worship. But,

2. This may refer also to the salvation of Judah from idolatry, which qualified and prepared them for their other salvations. And this is indeed a salvation *by the Lord their God;* it is wrought only by the power of his grace, and can never be wrought by *sword or bow.* Just at the time that the kingdom of Israel was *utterly taken away,* under Hoshea, the kingdom of Judah was gloriously reformed, under Hezekiah, and was therefore preserved; and in Babylon God saved them from their idolatry first, and then from their captivity.

3. Some make this promise to look forward to the great salvation which, in the fulness of time, was to be wrought out *by the Lord our God,* Jesus Christ, who came into the world to *save his people from their sins.*

Verses 8-11

We have here a prediction,

I. Of the rejection of Israel for a time, which is signified by the name of another child that Hosea had by his adulterous spouse, v. 8, 9. And still we must observe that those children whose names carried these direful omens in them to Israel were all *children of whoredoms* (v. 2), all born of the harlot that Hosea married, to intimate that the ruin of Israel was the natural product of the sin of Israel. If they had not first revolted from God, they would never have been rejected by him; God never leaves any till they first leave him. Here is, 1. The birth of this child: *When she had weaned her daughter, she conceived and bore a son.* Notice is taken of the delay of the birth of this child, which was to carry in its name a certain presage of their utter rejection, to intimate God's patience with them, and his unwillingness to proceed to extremity. Some think that her bearing another son signifies that people's persisting in their wickedness; lust still *conceived* and *brought forth sin.* They *added to do evil* (so the Chaldee paraphrase expounds it); they were old in adulteries, and obstinate. 2. The name given him: *Call him Lo-ammi — Not my people.* When they were told that God would *no more have mercy on them* they regarded it not, but buoyed up themselves with this conceit, that they were God's people, whom he could not but have mercy on. And therefore he plucks that staff from under them, and disowns all relation to them: *You are not my people, and I will not be your God.* "I will not be yours (so the word it); I will be in no relation to you, will have nothing to do with you; I will not be *your King, your Father, your* patron and protector." We supply it very well

with that which includes all, *"I will not be your God; I will not be to you* what I have been, nor what you vainly expect I should be, nor what I would have been if you had kept close to me." Observe, *"You are not my people;* you do not act as becomes my people; you are not observant of me and obedient to me, as my people should be; you are not my people, but the people of this and the other dunghill-deity; and therefore I will not own you for my people, will not protect you, will not put in any claim to you, not demand you, not deliver you out of the hands of those that have seized you; let them take you; you are none of mine. You will not have me to be your God, but pay your homage to the pretenders, and therefore *I will not be your God;* you shall have no interest in me, shall expect no benefit from me." Note, Our being taken into covenant with God is owing purely to him and to his grace, for then it begins on his side: *I will be to them a God,* and then they shall be *to me a people; we love him because he first loved us.* But our being cast out of covenant is owing purely to ourselves and our own folly. The breach is on man's side: *You are not my people,* and therefore *I will not be your God;* if God *hate any,* it is because they *first hated him.* This was fulfilled in Israel when they were *utterly taken away* into the *land of Assyria,* and their place knew them no more. They were no longer *God's people,* for they lost the knowledge and worship of him; no prophets were sent to them, no promises made to them, as were to the two tribes in their captivity; nay, they were no longer *a people,* but, for aught that appears, were mingled with the nations into which they were carried, and lost among them.

II. Of the reduction and restoration of Israel in the fulness of time. Here, as before, mercy is remembered in the midst of wrath; the rejection, as it shall not be total, so it shall not be final (v. 10, 11): *Yet the number of the children of Israel shall be as the sand of the sea.* See how the same hand that wounded is stretched forth to heal, and how tenderly he that has *torn binds up;* though God *cause grief* by his threatenings, yet *he will have compassion,* and will gather with everlasting kindness. They are very precious promises which are here made concerning the Israel of God, and which may be of use to us now.

1. Some think that these promises had their accomplishment in the return of the Jews out of their captivity in Babylon, when many of the ten tribes joined themselves to Judah, and took the benefit of the liberty which Cyrus proclaimed, came up in great numbers out of the several countries into which they were dispersed, to their own land, appointed Zerubbabel their head, and coalesced into one people, whereas before they had been two distinct nations. And in their own land, where God had by his prophets disowned and rejected them as none of his, he would by his prophets own them and appear for them as his children; and from all parts of the country they should come up to the temple to worship. And we have reason to think that, though this promise has a further reference, yet it was graciously intended and piously used for the support and comfort of the captives in Babylon, as giving them a general assurance of mercy which God had in store for them and their land; their nation could not be destroyed so long as this blessing was in it, was in reserve for it.

2. Some think that these promises will not have their accomplishment, at least not in full, till the general conversion of the Jews in the latter days, which is expected yet to come, when the vast incredible numbers of Jews, that are now dispersed as the sand of the sea, shall be brought to embrace the faith of Christ and be incorporated in the gospel-church. Then, and not till then, God will own them as his people, his children, even there where they had lain under the dismal tokens of their rejection. The Jewish doctors look upon this promise as not having had its accomplishment yet. But,

3. It is certain that this promise had its accomplishment in the setting up of the kingdom of Christ, by the preaching of the gospel, and the bringing in both of Jews and Gentiles to it, for to this these words are applied by St. Paul (Rom. 9:25, 26), and by St. Peter when he writes to the Jews of the dispersion, 1 Pt. 2:10. Israel here is the gospel-church, the spiritual Israel (Gal. 6:16), all believers who follow the steps, and inherit the blessing of faithful Abraham, who is the father of all that believe, whether Jews or Gentiles, Rom. 4:11, 12. Now let us see what is promised concerning this Israel.

(1.) That it shall greatly multiply, and the numbers of it be increased; it shall be *as the sand of the sea, which cannot be measured nor numbered.* Though Israel according to the flesh be diminished and made few, the spiritual Israel shall be numerous, shall be innumerable. In the vast multitudes that by the preaching of the gospel have been brought to Christ, both in the first ages of Christianity and ever since, this promise is fulfilled, thousands out of every tribe in Israel, and out of other nations, *a multitude which no man can number,* Rev. 7:4, 9; Gal. 4:27. In this the promise made to Abraham, when God called him Abraham the *high father of a multitude,* had its full accomplishment (Gen. 17:5), and that Gen. 22:17. Some observe that they are here compared to the *sand of the sea,* not only for their numbers, but as the sand of the sea serves for a boundary to the waters, that they shall not overflow the earth, so the Israelites indeed are a wall of defence to the places where they live, to keep off judgments. God can do nothing against Sodom while Lot is there.

(2.) That God will renew his covenant with the gospel-Israel, and will incorporate it a church to himself, by as full and ample a charter as that whereby the Old-Testament church was incorporated; nay, and its privileges shall be much greater: *"In the place where it was said unto them, You are not my people,* there shall you be again admitted into covenant, and owned as my people." The *abandoned Gentiles* in their respective places, and the *rejected Jews* in theirs, shall be favoured and blessed. There, where the fathers were cast off for their unbelief, the children, upon their believing, shall be taken in. This is a blessed resurrection, the making of those the people of God that were *not a people.* Nay, but the privilege is enlarged; now it is not only, *You are my people,* as formerly, but *You are the sons of the living God,* whether by birth you were Jews or Gentiles. Israel under the law was *God's son, his first-born,* but then they were as children *under age;* now, under the gospel, they have grown up both to greater understanding and greater liberty, Gal. 4:1, 2. Note, [1.] It is the unspeakable privilege of all believers that they have the living God for their Father, the ever-living God, and may look upon themselves as his children by grace and adoption. [2.] The sonship of believers shall be owned and acknowledged; it shall be *said to them,* for their comfort and satisfaction, nay, and it shall be said for their honour in the hearing of the world, *You are the sons of the living God.* Let not the saints disquiet themselves; let not others despise them; for, sooner or later, there shall be a manifestation of the children of God, and all the world shall be made to know their excellency and the value God has for them. [3.] It will add much to their comfort, very much to their honour, when they are dignified with the tokens of God's favour in that very place where they had long lain under the tokens of his displeasure. This speaks comfort to the believing Gentiles, that they need not go up to Jerusalem, to be received and owned as God's children; no, they may stay where they are, and *in that place,* though it be in the remotest corner of the earth, *in that place* where they were at a distance, where it was said to them, *"You are not God's people,"* but are separated from them (Isa. 56:3, 6), even there, without leaving their country and kindred, they may by faith receive the *Spirit of adoption,* witnessing with their spirits that *"they are the children of God."*

(3.) That those who had been at variance should be happily brought together (*v.* 11): *Then shall the children of Judah and the children of Israel be gathered together.* This uniting of Judah and Israel, those two kingdoms that were now so much at variance, biting and devouring one another, is mentioned only as a specimen, or one instance, of the happy effect of the setting up of Christ's kingdom in the world, the bringing of those that had been at the greatest enmity one against another to a good understanding one of another and a good affection one to another. This was literally fulfilled when the Galileans, who inhabited that part of the country which belonged to the ten tribes, and probably for the most part descended from them, so heartily joined with those that were probably called *Jews* (that were of Judea) in following Christ and embracing his gospel; and his first disciples were partly Jews and partly Galileans. The first that were blessed with the light of the gospel were of the *land of Zebulun and Naphtali* (Mt. 4:15); and, though there was no good-will at all between the Jews and the Galileans, yet, upon their believing in Christ, they were happily consolidated, and there were no remains of the former disaffection they had to one another; nay, when the Samaritans believed, though between them and the Jews there was a much greater enmity, yet in Christ there was a perfect unanimity, Acts 8:14. Thus Judah and Israel were *gathered together;* yet this was but a type of the much more celebrated coalition between Jews and Gentiles, when, by the death of Christ, the partition-wall of the ceremonial law was taken down. See Eph. 2:14–16. Christ died, to *gather together in one all the children of God that were scattered abroad,* Jn. 11:51; Eph. 1:10.

(4.) That Jesus Christ should be the centre of unity to all God's spiritual Israel. They shall all agree to *appoint to themselves one head,* which can be no other than he whom God has appointed, even Christ. Note, Jesus Christ is the head of the church, the one only head of it, not only a head of government, as of the body politic, but a head of vital influence, as of the natural body. To believe in Christ is to appoint him to ourselves for our head, that is, to consent to God's appointment, and willingly commit ourselves to his guidance and government; and this in concurrence and communion with all good Christians that make him their head; so that, though they are many, yet in him they are one, and so become one with each other. *Qui conveniunt in aliquo tertio inter se conveniunt — Those who agree with a third agree with each other.*

(5.) That, having appointed Christ for their head, *they shall come up out of the land;* they shall come, some of all sorts, from all parts, to join themselves to the church, as, under the Jewish economy, they came up from all corners of the land of Israel to Jerusalem, to worship (Ps. 122:4), *Thither the tribes go up,* to which there is a plain allusion in that prophecy of the accession of the Gentiles to the church (Isa. 2:3), *Come, and let us go up to the mountain of the Lord.* It denotes not a local remove (for they are said to be in the same place, *v.* 10), but a change of their mind, a spiritual ascent to Christ. They shall *come up from the earth* (so it may be read); for those who have given up themselves to Christ as their head take their affections off from *this earth,* and the things of it, to set them upon *things above* (Col. 3:1, 2); for they are not of the world (Jn. 15:19), but have their conversation in heaven. They shall *come up out of the land,* though it be the land of their nativity; they shall, in affection, come out from it, that they may *follow the Lamb withersoever he goes.* Thus the learned Dr. Pocock takes it.

(6.) That, when all this comes to pass, *great shall be the day of Jezreel.* Though *great* is *the day of Jezreel's* affliction (so some understand it), yet *great shall be the day* of Jezreel's glory. This shall be Israel's day; the day shall be *their own,* after their enemies have long had their day. Israel is here called *Jezreel,* the *seed of God,* the *holy seed* (Isa. 6:13), the *substance* of the land. This seed is now sown in the earth, and buried under the clods; but great shall be its day when the harvest comes. Great was the church's day when there were *added to it daily such as should be saved;* then did the Almighty *do great things* for it.

CHAPTER 2

The scope of this chapter seems to be much the same with that of the foregoing chapter, and to point at the same events, and the causes of them. As there, so here, I. God, by the prophet, discovers sin to them, and charges it home upon them, the sin of their idolatry, their spiritual whoredom, their serving idols and forgetting God and their obligations to him (*v.* 1, 2, 5, 8). II. He threatens to take away from them that plenty of all good things with which they had served their idols, and to abandon them to ruin without remedy (*v.* 3, 4, 6, 7, 9–13). III. Yet he promises at last to return in ways of mercy to them for his own sake (*v.* 14), to restore them to their former plenty (*v.* 15), to cure them of their inclination to idolatry (*v.* 16, 17), to renew his covenant with them (*v.* 18–20), and to bless them with all good things (*v.* 21–23).

Verses 1–5

The first words of this chapter some make the close of the foregoing chapter, and add them to the promises which we have here of the great things God would do for them. When they shall have appointed Christ their head, and centered in him, then let them say to one another, with triumph and exultation (*let the prophets say it* to them, so the Chaldee — *Comfort you, comfort you, my people,* is now their commission), "say to them, *Ammi,* and *Ruhamah;* call them so again, for they shall no longer lie under the reproach and doom of *Lo-ammi* and *Lo-ruhamah;* they shall now be *my people* again, and shall *obtain mercy.*" God's spiritual Israel, made up of Jews and Gentiles without distinction, shall call one another brethren and sisters, shall own one another for the people of God and beloved of him, and, for that reason, shall embrace one another, and stir up one another both to give thanks for and to walk worthy of this *common salvation* which they partake of. Or rather, because the following words seem to have a coherence with these, these also are designed for conviction and humiliation. The *mother* (*v.* 2) seems to be the same with the *brethren* and *sisters* (*v.* 1), the church of the ten tribes, the body of the people, who were brethren, and in a special manner with the heads and leaders, who were as the mother by whom the rest were brought up and nursed. But who are the children that must *plead with their mother* thus? Either, 1. The godly that were among them, that witnessed against the iniquities of the times, let them boldly go on to bear their testimony against the idolatries and gross corruptions that prevail among them. Let those that had not bowed the knee to Baal reason the case with those that had, and endeavour to convince them with such arguments as are here put into their mouths. Note, Private persons may, and ought in their places, to appear and plead against the public profanations of God's name and worship. Children may humbly and modestly argue with their parents when they do amiss: *Plead with your mother, plead,* as Jonathan with Saul concerning David. Or, 2. The sufferers among them, that shared in the calamities of the times, let them not complain of God, let them not quarrel with him, nor lay the blame on him, as if he had dealt hardly with them, and not like a tender father. No; let them *plead with their mother,* and lay the fault on her, where it ought to be laid; compare Isa. 50:1. *"For her transgressions is your mother put away;* she may thank herself, and you may thank her for all your miseries." Let us see now how they must plead with her.

I. They must put here in mind of the relation wherein she had stood to God, the kindness he had had for her, the many favours he had bestowed upon her, and the further favours he had designed her. Let them tell their *brethren* and *sisters* that they had been *Ammi* and *Ruhamah,* that they had been God's people and vessels of his mercy, and might have been so still if it had not been their own fault, *v.* 1. Note, Our relation to God and dependence on him are a great aggravation of our revolts from him and rebellions against him.

II. They must, in God's name, charge her with the violation of the marriage-covenant between her and God. Let them tell her that God does not look upon her as his wife, nor upon himself as her husband any longer. Tell her (*v.* 2) that *she is not my wife, neither am I her husband,* that by her spiritual whoredom she has forfeited all the honour and comfort of her relation to God, and provoked him to give her a bill of divorce. Note, No consideration can be more powerful to awaken us to repentance than the provocation we have by sin given to God to disown and cast us off. It is time to look about us, and to think what course we must take, when God threatens to reject us; for woe unto us if he be not *our husband.* They must charge this home upon her (*v.* 5): *Their mother has played the harlot; their congregation has run a whoring after false prophets* (so the Chaldee), or, rather, *after idols,* wherein they were encouraged by their false prophets; *she that conceived them has done shamefully,* in making and worshipping idols. An idol is called a *shame* (*ch.* 9:10) and idolatry is a *shameful thing.* It is not only an affront to God, but a reproach to men, to *fall down to the stock of a tree,* as the prophet speaks. Or it denotes that the sinner was shameless, impudent in sin, and could not blush; Jer. 6:15. Or, *She has made ashamed,* has made all that see her ashamed of her; her own children are ashamed of their relation to her.

III. They must upbraid her with her horrid ingratitude to God her benefactor, in ascribing to her idols the glory of the gifts he had given her, and then giving that for a reason why she paid them the homage due to him only, *v.* 5. In this she *did shamefully* indeed, that *she said, I will go after my lovers that give me my bread and my water.* Observe here, 1. Her wicked resolution to persist in idolatry, notwithstanding all that God said, both by his prophets and by his providences, to draw her from it. *She said,*

Whatever is offered to the contrary, *I will go after my lovers,* or *those that cause me to love them,* whom I cannot but be in love with. The Chaldee understands it of the nations whose alliance Israel courted and depended upon, who supplied them with what they needed. But it is rather to be understood of the idols they worshipped, to justify their love of which they called them their lovers. See who do shamefully; those that are wilful and resolute in sin, and those that openly profess and own their resolution to go on in it. See the folly of idolaters, to call those their lovers that had not so much as life; yet let us learn to call our God our lover; let us keep up good thoughts of him, and put a high value upon our interest in him and in his love. 2. The gross mistake upon which this resolution was grounded: "I will go after my lovers, because they give me my *bread and my water,* which are necessary to sustain the body, *my wool and my flax,* which are necessary to clothe the body, and pleasant things, *my oil,* and *my drink,* my liquors" (so the word is), "wine and strong drink." Note, (1.) The things of sense are the best things with carnal hearts, and the most powerful attractives, in pursuit of which they care not what they follow after. The God of Israel set before them his *statutes* and *judgments* (Deu. 4:8), *more to be desired than gold, and sweeter than honey* (Ps. 119:10), promised them his favour, which would *put gladness in their hearts more than corn, wine, and oil* (Ps. 4:7); but they had no relish at all for these things. Whence they thought their oil and their drink came, thither they would return their best affections. *O curvae in terram animae et coelestium inanes! — O degenerate minds, bending towards the earth, and devoid of every thing heavenly!* (2.) It is a great abuse and injury to God, in pursuance of the pleasures and delights of sense to forsake him, who not only gives us better things, but gives us even those things too. The idolaters made Ceres the goddess of their corn, Bacchus the god of their wine, etc., and then foolishly fancied they had their corn and wine from these, forgetting the Lord their God, who both gave them that good land and *gave them power to get wealth* out of it. (3.) Many are hardened in sin by their worldly prosperity. They had an abundance of those things when they served their idols, and then imagined them to be given them by their idols, which kept them to their service; thus they argued (Jer. 44:17, 18), *While we burnt incense to the queen of heaven we had plenty of victuals.*

IV. They must persuade her to repent and reform. God will disown her if she persist in her whoredoms; *let her therefore put away her whoredoms, v.* 2. Let her be convinced that it is possible for her to reform; the idols, dear as they are, may yet be parted with; and it will certainly be well with her if she do reform. Note, Our pleading with sinners must be to drive them to repentance, not to drive them to despair. Let her *put away her whoredoms and her adulteries;* the doubling of words to the same purport, and both plural, denotes the abundance of idolatries they were guilty of, all which must be abandoned ere God would be reconciled to them. Let her put them *out of her sight,* as detestable things which she cannot endure to look upon; let her say unto them, *Get you hence,* Isa. 30:22. Let her put them *from her face* and from *between her breasts,* that is, let her not do as harlots use to do, that both discover their own wicked disposition, and allure others to wickedness, by painting their faces, and exposing their naked breasts, and adorning them; let her not thus, by annexing all possible gaieties and pleasures to the worship of idols, engage herself and allure others to it. let her put away all these. Every sinful course, persisted in, is an adulterous departure from God. And here we may see what it is truly to repent of it and turn from it. 1. True penitents will forsake both open sins, will put away not only the whoredoms that lie in sight, but those that lie in secret *between their breasts,* the sin that is *rolled under the tongue as a sweet morsel.* 2. They will both avoid the outward occasions of sin and mortify the inward disposition to it. Idolaters walked after their own eyes, which *went a whoring* after their idols (Eze. 6:9, Deu. 4:19), and *therefore* they must put them away *out of their sight,* lest they should be tempted to worship them. *Look not upon the wine when it is red.* But that is not enough: the axe must be *laid to the root;* the corrupt bent and inclination of the heart must be changed, and it must be put away *from between the breasts,* that Christ alone may have the innermost and uppermost place there. Cant. 1:13.

V. They must show her the utter ruin that will certainly be the fatal consequence of her sin if she do not repent and reform (*v.* 3): *Lest I strip her naked.* This comes in here not by way of sentence passed upon her, but by way of warning given to her, that she may prevent it: *Let her put away her whoredoms, that I may not strip her naked* (so it may be read), intimating that God waits to show mercy to sinners, if they would but qualify themselves for that mercy. It is here threatened that God will deal with her as the just and jealous husband at length does with an adulterous wife, that has filled his house with a spurious brood, and will not be reclaimed; he turns her and her children out of doors and sends them a begging; *I will not have mercy upon her children* (*v.* 4); the particular persons that share in the calamity of the nation, and the rising generation, shall be ruined by it, for they are *children of whoredoms,* and keep up the *vain conversation received by tradition from their fathers.* Now it is here threatened that they shall be both stripped and starved. They thought their idols gave them *their bread and their water, their wool and their flax;* but God, by taking them away, will let them know that it was he that gave them. 1. She shall be stripped: *Lest I strip her* of all her ornaments which she is proud of, and with which she courts her lovers, *strip her* and set her *as in the day that she was born,* send her as naked out of the world as she came into it; this death does, Job 1:21. *I will strip her,* and so expose her to cold, and expose her to shame; and justly is she exposed to shame that *did shamefully, v.* 5. The day when God brought them out of Egypt, where they were no better than slaves and beggars, was *the day in which they were born;* and God threatens to bring them back to as low and miserable a condition as he then found them in. Whatever they had that either gained them respect or screened them from contempt, among their neighbours, should be taken from them. See Eze. 16:4, 39. 2. She shall be starved, shall be deprived not only of her honours, but of her comforts and necessary supports. She shall be famished, shall be made *as a wilderness* and *a dry land,* and *slain with thirst.* She that boasted so much of her bread and water, her oil and her drinks, which her lovers had *given her,* shall not have so much as necessary food. The land shall not afford subsistence for the inhabitants, for want of the rain of heaven; or, if it do, it shall be taken from them by the enemy, so that the rightful owners shall perish for want of it. Some understand it thus: *I will make her as* she was in the *wilderness,* and set her as she was *in the desert land,* where she was sometimes ready to perish *for thirst.* So it explains the former part of the verse: I will set her *as in the day that she was born;* for it was in the vast howling wilderness that Israel was first formed into a people. They shall be in as deplorable a condition as their fathers were, whose carcases fell in the wilderness, and in this respect, worse, that then the children were reserved to be heirs of the land of promise, but now *I will not have mercy upon her children,* for *their mother has played the harlot.*

Verses 6–13

God here goes on to threaten what he would do with this treacherous idolatrous people; and he warns that he may not wound, he threatens that he may not strike. *If he turn not, he will whet his sword* (Ps. 7:12); but, if he turn, he will sheathe it. They did not turn, and therefore all this came upon them: and its being threatened before shows that it was the execution of a divine sentence upon them for their wickedness; and it is written for admonition to us.

I. They shall be perplexed and embarrassed in all their counsels, and disappointed in all their expectations. This is threatened *v.* 6, 7. But to the threatening is annexed a promise that this shall be a means to convince them of their folly, and bring them home to their duty; and so good shall be brought out of evil, in token of the mercy God has yet in reserve for them. And, this being the happy fruit and effect of the distress, it is hard to say whether the prediction, or the distress itself, should be called a threatening or a promise.

1. God will raise up difficulties and troubles in their way, so that their public counsels and affairs shall have no success, nor shall they be able to get forward in them: *I will hedge up thy way with thorns,* with such crosses as, like thorns and briers, are the product of sin and the curse, and are scratching, and tearing, and vexing, and, when the way we are in is hedged up with them, stop our progress, and force us to turn back. She said, *"I will go after my lovers;* I will pursue my leagues and alliances with foreign powers, and depend upon them." But God says, "She shall be frustrated in these projects, and not be able to proceed in them. *I will hedge up thy way with thorns,* and, if that do not serve, *I will make a wall."* If some smaller difficulties be got over, and prevail not to break her measures, God will raise greater, for he will overcome when he judges. It shall be such a hedge, and such a wall, that *she shall not find her paths.* The change of the person here, I will hedge up *thy way,* and then, *She* shall not find *it,* is usual in scripture, especially in an earnest way of speaking. "Sinner, do thou take notice, *I will hedge up thy way,* and all you that are bystanders take notice what will be the effect of this, you may observe that *she* cannot find her paths." She shall be as a traveller that not only knows not which way to go, of many that are before him, but that finds no way at all to go forward. And then *she shall follow after her lovers, but she shall not overtake them;* she shall endeavour to make an interest in the Assyrians and Egyptians, and to have them for her protectors, but she shall not gain her point; they shall either not come into confederacy with her or not do her any service, shall *help in vain* and be as the *staff of a broken reed. She shall seek them, but shall not find them,* shall seek to her idols, but shall not find that satisfaction in them which she promised herself; the gods whom she trusted and courted not only can do nothing for her, but have nothing to say to her to encourage her. Now, (1.) This is such a just judgment as the Sodomites met with, that were *struck with blindness,* and *wearied themselves to find the door* (Gen. 19:11), and the Syrians, 2 Ki. 6:18. Note, Those that are most resolute in their sinful pursuits are commonly most crossed in them. *Thorns and snares are in the way of the froward* (Prov. 22:5); and thus with them God *shows himself froward* (Ps. 18:26), and *walks contrary to those that walk contrary to him,* Lev. 26:23, 24. The lamenting prophet complains, *He has enclosed my ways,* Lam. 3:7, 9. The way of God and duty is often hedged about with thorns, but we have reason to think it is a sinful way that is hedged up with thorns. (2.) This is such a kind rebuke, and indeed such a mercy, as Balaam met with, when the angel stood in his way, to hinder his going forward to *curse Israel,* Num. 22:22. Note, Crosses and obstacles in an evil course are great blessings, and are so to be accounted. They are God's hedges, to keep us from transgressing, to restrain us from wandering out of the green pastures, to *withdraw man from his purpose* (Job 33:17), to make the way of sin difficult, that we may not go on in it, and to keep us from it whether we will or not. We have reason to bless God both for restraining grace and for restraining providences.

2. These difficulties that God raises up in their way shall raise up in their minds thoughts of turning back: *"Then shall she say,* Since I cannot overtake my lovers, I will even *go and return to my first husband,* that is, will return to God, and humble myself to him, and desire him to take me in again; for, when I kept close to him, it was every way *better with me than now."* Two things are here extorted from this degenerate apostate people: — (1.) A just acknowledgement of the folly of their apostasy. They are now brought to own that it was better with them while they kept close to their God than ever it was since they forsook him. Note, Whoever have exchanged the service of God for the services of the world and the flesh have, sooner or later, been made to own that they *changed for the worse,* and that while they continued in good company, and went on in the way of good duties, and made conscience how they spent their time and what they said or did, it was better with them; they had more true comfort and enjoyment of themselves than ever they had since they went astray. (2.) A good purpose, to come back again to their duty: *I will go, and return to my first husband;* and she knows so much of his goodness and readiness to forgive that she speaks without any doubt of his receiving her again into favour and making her condition as good as ever. Note, The disappointments we meet with in our pursuits of satisfaction in the creature should, if nothing else will do it, drive us at length to the Creator, in whom alone

it is to be had. When Moab is *weary of the high place* he shall *go to the sanctuary,* Isa. 16:12. And when the prodigal son is reduced to husks, short allowance indeed, and remembers that *in his father's house there is bread enough,* then he says, *I will arise and go to my father's house,* Lu. 15:17, 18.

II. The necessary supports and comforts of life shall be taken from them, because they had dishonoured God with them, *v.* 8, 9. Their land was plenteous. Now see here, 1. How graciously their plenty was given to them. God gave them not only corn for necessity, but wine for delight, and oil for ornament. Nay, he *multiplied their silver and gold,* wherewith to traffic with other nations and bring home their products, and which they might hoard up for posterity. *Silver and gold* will keep longer than *corn, and wine, and oil.* He gave them *wool and flax* too, to *cover their nakedness,* and to serve for ornament enough to them, Eze. 16:10. Note, God is a bountiful benefactor even to those who, he foresees, will be ungrateful and unthankful to him.

2. How basely their plenty was abused by them. (1.) They robbed God of the honour of his gifts: *She did not know that I gave her corn and wine;* she did not remember it. The law and the prophets had told them, again and again, that all their comforts they received from God's bountiful providence; but they were so often told by their false prophets and idolatrous priests that they had their corn from such an idol, and their wine from such an idol, etc., that they had quite forgotten their relation to their great benefactor and their obligations to him. She did not consider it; she would not acknowledge it. This they were *willingly ignorant of,* and more brutish than the ox, that *knows his owner,* and the *ass, that knows his master's crib. She did not know it,* for she did not return thanks to him for his gifts, nor study what she should render; nor did she give him his dues out of them, but acted as if she were ignorant who was the donor. (2.) They served and honoured his enemies with them: *They prepared them for Baal;* they adorned their images with *gold and silver* (Jer. 10:4), and adorned themselves for the worship of their images, *v.* 13. See Eze. 16:17–19. *Wherewith they made Baal* (so the margin reads it), that is, the image of Baal. Note, It is a very great dishonour to the God of heaven to make those gifts of his providence the food and fuel of our lusts which he gave us for our support in his service, and to be oil to the wheels of our obedience.

3. How justly their plenty should be taken from them: *"Therefore will I return;* I will alter my dealings with them, will take another course, *and will take away my corn* and other good things that I gave her." I will *recover* them, a law term, as a man by due course of law recovers what is unjustly detained from him, or as, when the tenant has committed waste, the landlord recovers *locum vastatum* — *dilapidations.* Observe, God calls their abundance *my corn* and *my wine, my wool* and *my flax.* They called it theirs (*my bread* and *my water, v.* 5), but God lets them know that it is not theirs; he only allowed them the use of it as tenants, entrusted them with the management of it as stewards, but still reserved the property in himself. "It is *my* corn and *my* wine." God will have us to know, not only that we have all our creature-comforts and enjoyments from him, but that he has still an incontestable right and title to them, that they are more his than ours, and therefore are to be used for him, and accounted for to him. He will therefore take their plenty away from them, because they have forfeited it by disowning his right, as a tenant by copy of court-roll, who holds at the will of his lord, forfeits his estate if he makes a feoffment of it as though he were a freeholder. He will *recover* it, will *free* or *deliver* it, that it may be no longer abused, as the creature is said to be *delivered from the bondage of corruption* under which *it groans,* Rom. 8:21. He will take it away *in the time thereof,* and *in the season thereof,* just when they expected it, and thought that they were sure of it. It shall suffer shipwreck in the harbour; and *the harvest shall be a heap.* He will take it away by unseasonable weather or by unreasonable men. Note, Those that abuse the mercies God gives them, to his dishonour, cannot expect to enjoy them long.

III. They shall lose *all their honour,* and be exposed to contempt (*v.* 10): *"I will discover her lewdness,* will bring to light all her secret wickedness, and make it public, to her shame; I will show by the punishment of it how hei-

nous, how odious, how offensive it is. The fact has been denied, but now it shall appear; the fault has been diminished, but now it shall appear exceedingly sinful. And this *in the sight of her lovers,* in the sight of the neighbouring nations, with whom she courted an alliance, and on whom she had a dependence; they shall despise her and be ashamed of her because of her weakness, and poverty, and ill conduct; they shall not think her any longer worthy of their friendship." See this fulfilled, Lam. 1:8, *All that honoured her despise her, because they have seen her nakedness.* Or in the sight of *the sun and moon,* which she worshipped as *her lovers;* before them shall *her lewdness be discovered.* Compare this with Jer. 7:1, 2, *They shall bring out the bones of their kings and princes, and spread them before the sun and moon, whom they have loved and served.* Note, Sin will have shame; let those expect it that have done shamefully. What other lot can this impudent adulteress expect but that of a common harlot, to be carted through the town? And, when God comes to deal thus with her, *none shall deliver her out of his hands,* neither the gods nor the men they confide in. Note, Those who will not deliver themselves into the hand of God's mercy cannot be delivered out of the hand of his justice.

IV. They shall lose all their pleasure, and shall be left melancholy (*v.* 11): *I will cause her mirth to cease.* It seems, then, though they had *gone a whoring from their God,* yet they could find in their hearts to *rejoice as other people,* which is forbidden, *ch.* 9:1. Note, Many who lie under guilt and wrath are yet very jocund and merry, and live jovially; but, whether in their laughter their hearts be sad or no, it is certain that the *end of their mirth* will be *heaviness;* for God *will cause all their mirth to cease.* It is as Mr. Burroughs observes here, *Sin and mirth can never hold long together;* but, *if men will not take away sin from their mirth, God will take away mirth from their sin.*

1. God will take away the occasions of their sacred mirth — *their feast-days, their new moons, their sabbaths, and all their solemn feasts.* These God instituted to be observed in a religious manner, and they were to be observed with rejoicing; and, it seems, though they had departed from the pure worship of God, yet they kept up the observance of these, not at God's temple at Jerusalem, for they had long since forsaken that, but probably at Dan and Bethel, where the calves were, or in some other places of meeting that they had. They observed them, not for the honour of God, nor with any true devotion towards him, but only because they were times of mirth and feasting, music and dancing, and meeting of friends, received by tradition from their fathers. Thus, when they had lost the power of godliness, and denied that, yet, for the pleasing of a vain and carnal mind, they kept up the form of it; and by this means their new-moons and their sabbaths became an iniquity which God *could not away with,* Isa. 1:13. Now observe, (1.) God calls them their new-moons and their sabbaths, not his (he disowns them), but theirs. (2.) He will *cause them to cease.* Note, When men by their sins have caused the life and substance of ordinances to cease it is just with God by his judgments to cause the remaining show and shadow of them to cease.

2. He will take away the supports of their carnal mind. They loved the new-moons and the sabbaths only for the sake of the good cheer that was stirring then, not for the sake of any religious exercises then performed; these they had dropped long ago; and now God will take away their provisions for these solemnities (*v.* 12): *I will destroy her vines and her fig-trees.* Note, If men destroy God's words and ordinances, by which he should be honoured on their feast-days, it is just with him to destroy their vines and fig-trees, with which they regale themselves. While they took the pleasure of these, they gave their lovers the praise of them: *"These are my rewards which my lovers have given me;* I may thank my stars for these, and my worship of them; I may thank my neighbours for these, and my alliance with them." And therefore God will destroy them, will wither them with a blast, or bring in a foreign enemy that shall lay the country waste, so that their vineyards shall become *a forest;* the enclosures shall be thrown down, as is usual in war; all shall be laid in common, so that the *beasts of the field* shall eat their grapes and their figs. Or they shall be so blasted with the east wind that fruit-trees shall be of no more use than forest-trees; but, being withered and good for nothing, what fruit there is shall be left

to the *beasts of the field.* Or it shall be devoured by their enemies, by men as barbarous as wild beasts. Now, (1.) This shall be the ruin of their mirth: God will *cause all her mirth to cease.* How will he do it? Taking away the new-moons and the sabbaths will not do it; they can very easily part with them, and find no loss; but "I will *destroy her vines and her fig-trees,* will take away her sensual pleasures, and then she will think herself undone indeed." Note, The destruction of the vines and the fig-trees causes all the mirth of a carnal heart to cease; it will say, as Micah, You have *taken away my gods, and what have I more?* (2.) This shall be the punishment of her idolatry (*v.* 13): *"I will visit upon her the days of Baalim;* I will reckon with her for all the worship of all the Baals they have made gods of, from the days of their fathers unto this day." We read of their worshipping Baal as long ago as the time of the Judges, and, for aught I know, this may look as far back as those times, those *days of Baalim;* for it is in the second commandment, which forbids idolatry, that God threatens to *visit the iniquities of the fathers upon the children;* and justly is that sin so visited, more than any other, because it commonly supports itself by prescription and long usage. Now that the measure of the iniquity of Israel was full all their former sins came into the account, and shall be *required of this generation.* Or the *days of Baalim* are the solemn festival days which they kept in honour of their idols. Days of sinful mirth must be visited in days of mourning. These were the days wherein she *burnt incense* to idols, and, to grace the solemnity, *decked herself with her ear-rings and her jewels,* that, appearing honourable, the honour she did to Baal might be thought the greater. Or she was as a wife that decks herself with the ear-rings and jewels that her husband gave her, to make herself amiable to her lovers, whom she follows after, and is ever mindful of. But *she forgot me, saith the Lord.* Note, Our treacherous departures from God are owing to our forgetfulness of him, of his nature and attributes, his relation to us and our obligations to him. Many who plead that they have weak memories, and forget the things of God, can remember other things well enough; nay, it is because they are so mindful of lying vanities that they are so forgetful of their own mercies.

Verses 14–23

The state of Israel ruined by their own sin did not look so black and dismal in the former part of the chapter, but that the state of Israel, restrained by the divine grace, looks as bright and pleasant here in the latter part of the chapter, and the more surprisingly so as the promises follow thus close upon the threatenings; nay, which is very strange, they are by a note of connexion joined to, and inferred from, that declaration of their sinfulness upon which the threatenings of their ruin are grounded: *She went after her lovers, and forgot me, saith the Lord; therefore I will allure her.* Fitly therefore is that *therefore* which is the note of connexion immediately followed with a note of admiration: *Behold I will allure her!* When it was said, *She forgot me,* one would think it should have followed, "Therefore I will abandon her, I will forget her, I will never look after her more." No, *Therefore I will allure her.* Note, God's thoughts and ways of mercy are infinitely above ours; his reasons are all fetched from within himself, and not from any thing in us; nay, his goodness takes occasion from man's badness to appear so much the more illustrious, Isa. 57:17, 18. *Therefore,* because she will not be restrained by the denunciations of wrath, God will try whether she will be wrought upon by the offers of mercy. Some think it may be translated, *Afterwards,* or *nevertheless,* I will allure her. It comes all to one; the design is plainly to magnify free grace to those on whom God will have mercy purely for mercy's sake. Now that which is here promised to Israel is,

I. That though now they were disconsolate, and ready to despair, they should again be revived with comforts and hopes, *v.* 14, 15. This is expressed here with an allusion to God's dealings with that people when he brought them out of Egypt, through the wilderness to Canaan, as their forlorn and deplorable condition in their captivity was compared to their state in *Egypt in the day that they were born, v.* 3. They shall be new-formed by such miracles of love and mercy as they were first-formed by, and such a transport of joy shall they be in as they were in then. It is hard to say when this had its accomplishment in the kingdom of the ten tribes; but it principally aims, no doubt, at the bringing in both of Jews and Gentiles into the church by the gospel of Christ; and it is applicable, nay, we have reason to think it was designed that it should be applied, to the conversion of particular souls to God. Now observe,

1. The gracious methods God will take with them. (1.) He will *bring them into the wilderness,* as he did at first when he brought them out of Egypt, where he instructed them, and took them into covenant with himself. The land of their captivity shall be to them now, as that wilderness was then, the *furnace of affliction,* in which God will *choose them.* See Eze. 20:35, 36, *I will bring you into the wilderness of the people, and there will I plead with you.* God had said that he would *make them as a wilderness* (*v.* 3), which was a threatening; now, when it is here made part of a promise that he would bring them into the wilderness, the meaning may be that he would by his grace bring their minds to their condition: "They shall have humble hearts under humbling providences; being poor, they shall be poor in spirit, shall *accept of the punishment of their iniquity,* and then they are prepared to have comfort spoken to them." When God delivered Israel out of Egypt he led them into the wilderness, to *humble them and prove them, that he might do them good* (Deu. 8:2, 3, 15, 16), and so he will do again. Note, Those whom God has mercy in store for he first *brings into a wilderness* — into solitude and retirement, that they may the more freely converse with him out of the noise of this world, — into distress of mind, through sense of guilt and dread of wrath, which brings a soul to be quite at a loss in itself and bewildered, and by those convictions he prepares for consolations, — and sometimes into outward distress and trouble, thereby to open the ear to discipline. (2.) He will then *allure them and speak comfortably to them,* will *persuade them* and *speak to their hearts,* that is, he will by his word and Spirit incline their hearts to return to him, and encourage them to do so. He will allure them with the promises of his favour, as before he had terrified them with the threatenings of his wrath, will speak friendly to them, both by his prophets and by his providences, as before he had spoken roughly, Isa. 40:1, 2. *By the hand of my servants the prophets I will speak comfort to her heart;* so the Chaldee. This refers to the gospel of Christ, and the offers of divine grace in the gospel, by which we are allured to forsake our sins and to turn to God, and which speaks to the heart of a convinced sinner that which is every way suited to his case, speaks abundant consolation to those that sorrow for sin and lament after the Lord. And when by the Spirit it is indeed spoken to the heart effectually, and so as to reach the conscience (which it is God's prerogative to do), O what a blessed change is wrought by it! Note, The best way of reducing wandering souls to God is by fair means. By the promise of rest in Christ we are invited to take his yoke upon us; and the work of conversion may be forwarded by comforts as well as by convictions. (3.) *He will give her her vineyards thence.* From that time and from that place where he has afflicted her, and brought her to see her folly and to humble herself, thenceforward he will *do her good;* not only speak comfortably to her, but do well for her, and undo what he had done against her. He had *destroyed her vines* (*v.* 12), but now he will give her whole *vineyards,* as if for every vine destroyed she should have a vineyard restored, and so be repaid with interest; she shall not only have corn for necessity, but vineyards for delight. These denote the privileges and comforts of the gospel, which are prepared for those that *come up out of the wilderness leaning upon* Christ as *their beloved,* Cant. 8:5. Note, God has vineyards of consolation ready to bestow on those who repent and return to him; and he can give vineyards *out of a wilderness,* which are of all others the most welcome, as rest to the weary. (4.) He will give her *the valley of Achor for a door of hope. The valley of Achor* was that in which Achan was stoned; it signifies *the valley of trouble,* because he troubled Israel, and there God troubled him. This was the beginning of the wars of Canaan; and their putting away the accursed thing in that place gave them ground to hope that God would continue his presence with them and complete their victories. So when God returns to his people in mercy, and they to him in duty, it will be to them as happy an omen as any thing. If they put away the accursed thing from among them, if by mortifying sin they stone the Achan that has troubled their camp, their subduing that enemy within themselves is an earnest to them of victory over all the kings of Canaan. Or, if the allusion be to the name, it intimates that trouble for sin, if it be sincere, opens a door of hope; for that sin which truly troubles us shall not ruin us. The valley of Achor was a very fruitful pleasant valley, some think the same with the valley of Engedi, famous for vineyards, Cant. 1:14. This God gave to Israel as a pattern and pledge of the whole land of Canaan; so "God will by his gospel give to all believers such gifts, graces, and comforts in this life, as shall be a taste of those more perfect good things of the kingdom of heaven, and shall give them as assured hope of a full possession of them in due time." So the learned Dr. Pocock expounds it; and, to the same purport, this whole context.

2. The great rejoicing with which they shall receive God's gracious returns towards them: *She shall sing there as in the days of her youth.* This plainly refers to that triumphant and prophetic song which Moses and the children of Israel sang at the *Red Sea,* Ex. 15:1. When they are delivered out of captivity they shall repeat that song, and to them it shall be a new song, because sung upon a new occasion, not inferior to the former. God had said (*v.* 11) that he would *cause all her mirth to cease,* but now he would cause it to revive: She shall sing *as in the day that she came out of Egypt.* Note, When God repeats former mercies we must repeat former praises; we find the song of Moses sung in the New Testament, Rev. 15:3. This promise of Israel's singing has its accomplishment in the gospel of Christ, which furnishes us with abundant matter for joy and praise, and wherever it is received in its power enlarges the heart in joy and praise; and this is that land flowing with milk and honey which *the valley of Achor* opens *a door of hope to.* We *rejoice in tribulation.*

II. That, though they had been much addicted to the worship of Baal, they should now be perfectly weaned from it, should relinquish and abandon all appearances of idolatry and approaches towards it, and cleave to God only, and worship him as he appoints, *v.* 16, 17. Note, The surest pledge and token of God's favour to any people is his effectual parting between them and their beloved sins. The worship of Baal was the sin that did most easily beset the people of Israel; it was their own iniquity, the sin that had dominion over them; but now that idolatry shall be quite abolished, and there shall not be the least remains of it among them. 1. The idols of Baal shall not be mentioned, not any of the Baals that *in the days of Baalim* had made so great a noise with, *O Baal! hear us; O Baal! hear us.* The very *names of Baalim* shall be *taken out of their mouths;* they shall be so disused that they shall be quite forgotten, as if their names had never been known in Israel; they shall be so detested that people will not bear to mention them themselves, nor to hear others mention them, so that posterity shall scarcely know that ever there were such things. They shall be so ashamed of their former love to Baal that they shall do all they can to blot out the remembrance of it. They shall tie themselves up to the strictest literal meaning of that law against idolatry (Ex. 23:13), *Make no mention of the names of other gods, neither let it be heard out of thy mouth,* as David, Ps. 16:4. Thus the apostle expresses the abhorrence we ought to have of all fleshly lusts: *Let them not be once named among you,* Eph. 5:3. But how can such a change of the Ethiopian's skin be wrought? It is answered, The power of God can do it, and will. *I will take away the names of Baalim;* as Zec. 13:2, *I will cut off the names of the idols.* Note, God's grace in the heart will change the language by making that iniquity to be loathed which was beloved. Zep. 3:9, *I will turn to the people a pure language.* One of the rabbin says, This promise relates to the Gentiles, by the gospel of Christ, from the idolatries which they had been wedded to, 1 Th. 1:9. 2. The very word Baal shall be laid aside, even in its innocent signification. God says, *Thou shalt call me Ishi, and call me no more Baali;* both signify *my husband,* and both had been made use of concerning God. Isa. 54:5, *Thy Maker is thy husband,* thy *Baal* (so the word is), thy owner, patron, and protector. It is probable that many good people had, accordingly, made use of the word *Baali* in worshipping the God of Israel; when their wicked neighbours bowed the knee to Baal they gloried in this, that God was their Baal. "But," says God, "you shall call me so no more, because I will have the very names of Baalim taken away." Note, That which is very innocent in itself should, when it has been abused to idolatry, be abolished, and the very use of it taken away, that nothing may be done to keep idols in remembrance, much less to keep them in reputation. When calling God *Ishi* will do as well, and signify as much, as *Baali,* let that word be chosen rather, lest, by calling him Baali, others should be put in mind of their *quondam* Baals. Some think that there is another reason intimated why God would be called *Ishi* and not *Baali;* they both signify *my husband,* but *Ishi* is a compellation of love, and sweetness, and familiarity, *Baali* of reverence and subjection. Ishi is *vir meus — my man;* Baali is *dominus meus — my lord.* In gospel-times God has so revealed himself to us as to encourage us to come boldly to the throne of his grace, and to use a holy humble freedom there; we ought to call God our Master, for so he is, but we are more taught to call him our Father. *Ishi* is *a man the Lord* (Gen. 4:1), and intimates that in gospel-times the church's husband shall be *the man Christ Jesus,* made like unto his brethren, and therefore they shall call him *Ishi,* not *Baali.*

III. That though they had been in continual troubles, as if the whole creation had been at war with them, now they shall enjoy perfect peace and tranquillity, as if they were in a league of friendship with the whole creation (*v.* 18): *In that day,* when they have forsaken their idols, and put themselves under the divine protection, *I will make a covenant for them.* 1. They shall be protected from evil; nothing shall hurt them, nor do them any mischief. *Tranquillus Deus tranquillat amnia — When God is at peace with us he makes every creature to be so too.* The inferior creatures shall do them no harm, as they had done when the *beasts of the field* ate up their vineyards (*v.* 12) and when *noisome beasts* were one of God's *sore judgments,* Eze. 14:15. The *fowl* and the *creeping things* are taken into this covenant; for they also, when God makes use of them as the instruments of his justice, may be come very hurtful, but they shall be no more so; nay, by virtue of this covenant, they shall be made serviceable to them and brought into their interests. Note, God has the command of the inferior creatures, and brings them into what covenant he pleases; he can make *the beasts of the field* to *honour* him (so he has promised, Isa. 43:20) and to contribute to his people's comfort. And, if the inferior creatures are thus laid under an engagement to serve us, it is our part of the covenant not to abuse them, but to serve God with them. Some think that this had its accomplishment in the miraculous power Christ gave his disciples to *take up serpents,* Mk. 16:17, 18. It agrees with the promises made particularly to Israel, in their return out of captivity (Eze. 34:25, *I will cause the evil beasts to cease out of the land*), and the more general ones to all the saints. Job 5:22, 23, *The beasts of the field shall be at peace with thee;* and Ps. 91:13, *Thou shalt tread upon the lion and the adder.* But this is not all; men are more in danger from one another than from the brute beast, and therefore it is further promised that God will *make wars to cease,* will disarm the enemy: *I will break the bow, and sword, and battle.* He can do it when he pleases (Ps. 44:9), and will do it for those whose *ways please him,* for he *makes even their enemies to be at peace with them,* Prov. 16:7. This agrees with the promise that in gospel-times *swords shall be beaten into ploughshares,* Isa. 2:4. 2. They shall be quiet from the fear of evil. God will not only keep them safe, but *make them to lie down safely,* as those that know themselves to be under the protection of Heaven, and therefore are not afraid of the powers of hell.

IV. That, though God had given them a bill of divorce for their whoredoms, yet, upon their repentance, he would again take them into covenant with himself, into a marriage-covenant, *v.* 19, 20. God's making a covenant for them with the inferior creatures was a great favour; but it was nothing to this, that he took them into covenant with himself and engaged himself to do them good. Observe,

1. The nature of this covenant; it is a *marriage-covenant,* founded in choice and love, and founding the nearest relation: *I will betroth thee unto me;* and again, and a third time, *I will betroth thee.* Note, All that are sincerely devoted to God are betrothed to him; God gives them the most sacred and inviolable security imaginable that he will love them, protect them, and provide for them, that he will do the part of a husband to them, and that he will

incline their hearts to join themselves to him and will graciously accept of them in so doing. Believing souls are espoused to Christ, 2 Co. 11:2. The gospel-church is *the bride, the Lamb's wife;* and they would never come into that relation to him if he did not by the power of his grace betroth them to himself. The separation begins on our side; we alienate ourselves from God. The coalition begins on his side; he betroths us to himself.

2. The duration of this covenant: *"I will betroth thee for ever.* The covenant itself shall be inviolable; God will not break it on his part, and you shall not on yours; and the blessings of it shall be everlasting." One of the Jewish rabbin says, This is a promise that *she shall attain to the life of the world to come, which is absolute eternity or perpetuity.*

3. The manner in which this covenant shall be made. (1.) In *righteousness and judgment,* that is, God will deal sincerely and uprightly in covenant with them; they have broken covenant, and God is righteous. "But," says God, "I will renew the covenant *in righteousness."* The matter shall be so ordered that God may receive even these backsliding children into his family again, without any reflection upon his justice, nay, his justice being satisfied by the Mediator of this covenant very much to the honour of it. But what reason can there be why God should take a people into covenant with him that had so often dealt treacherously? Will it not reflect upon his wisdom? "No," says God; "I will do it *in judgment,* not rashly, but upon due consideration; let me alone to give a reason for it and to justify my own conduct." (2.) *In lovingkindness and in mercies.* God will deal tenderly and graciously in covenanting with them; and will be not only as good as his word, but better; and, as he will be just in keeping covenant with them, so he will be merciful in keeping them in the covenant. They are subject to many infirmities, and, if he be extreme to mark what they do amiss, they will soon lose the benefit of the covenant. He therefore promises that it shall be a covenant of grace, made in a compassionate consideration of their infirmities, so that every transgression in the covenant shall not throw them out of covenant; he will *gather with everlasting lovingkindness.* (3.) *In faithfulness.* Every article of the covenant shall be punctually performed. *Faithful is he that has called them, who also will do it;* he cannot *deny himself.*

4. The means by which they shall be kept tight and faithful to the covenant on their part: *Thou shalt know the Lord.* This is not only a promise that God will reveal himself to them more fully and clearly than ever, but that he will give them *a heart to know him;* they shall know more of him, and shall know him in another manner than ever yet. The ground of their apostasy was their not knowing God to be their benefactor (*v.* 8); therefore, to prevent the like, they shall all be *taught of God* to know him. Note, God keeps up his interest in men's souls by giving them a good understanding and a right knowledge of things, Heb. 8:11.

V. That, though the heavens had been to them as brass, and the earth as iron, now the heavens shall yield their dews, and by that means the earth its fruits, *v.* 21, 22. God having betrothed the gospel-church and in it all believers to himself, how shall he not with himself and with his Son freely *give them all things,* all things pertaining both to life and godliness, all things they need or can desire? *All is theirs,* for they are *Christ's,* betrothed to him; and with the righteousness of the kingdom of God, which they *seek first,* all *other things* shall be *added unto them.* And yet this promise of *corn and wine* is to be taken also in a spiritual sense (so the learned Dr. Pocock thinks): it is an effusion of those blessings and graces which relate to the soul that is here promised under the metaphor of temporal blessings, the dew of heaven, as well as the fatness of the earth, and that put first, as in the blessing of Jacob, Gen. 27:28. God had threatened (*v.* 9) that he would *take away the corn and the wine;* but now he promises to restore them, and that in the common course and order of nature. While they lay under the judgment of famine they called to the earth for *corn and wine* for the support of themselves and their families. Very gladly would the earth have supplied them, but she cannot give unless she receive, cannot produce *corn and wine* unless she be *enriched with the river of God* (Ps. 65:9); and therefore she calls to the heavens for rain, the former and latter rain in their season, grapes for it, and by her melancholy aspect when rain is denied pleads for it. "But," say the heavens, "we have no rain to give unless he who has the key of the clouds unlock them, and open these bottles; so that, *if the Lord do not help you,* we cannot." But, when God takes them into covenant with himself, then the wheel of nature shall be set a-going again in favour of them, and the streams of mercy shall flow in the usual channel: Then *I will hear, saith the Lord; I will receive your prayers* (so the Chaldee interprets the first *hearing*); God will graciously take notice of their addresses to him. And then *I will hear the heavens;* I will *answer* them (so it may be read); and then they shall *hear and answer the earth,* and pour down seasonable rain upon it; and then the *earth* shall *hear the corn and vines,* and supply them with moisture, and *they shall hear Jezreel,* and be nourishment and refreshment for those that inhabit Jezreel. See here the coherence of second causes with one another, as links in a chain, and the necessary dependence they all have upon God, the first Cause. Note, We must expect all our comforts from God in the usual method and by the appointed means; and, when we are at any time disappointed in them, we must look up to God, *above the hills and the mountains,* Ps. 121:1, 2. See how ready the creatures are to serve the people of God, how desirous of the honour: the corn cries to the earth, the earth to the heavens, the heavens to God, and all that they may supply them. And see how ready God is to give relief: *I will hear,* saith the Lord, *yea, I will hear.* And, if God will hear the cry of the heavens for his people, much more will he hear the intercession of his Son for them, who is made *higher than the heavens.* See what a peculiar delight those that are in covenant with God may take in their creature-comforts, as seeing them all come to them from the hand of God; they can trace up all the streams to the fountain, and taste covenant-love in common mercies, which makes them doubly sweet.

VI. That whereas they were now dispersed, not only, as Simeon and Levi, divided in Jacob and scattered in Israel, but divided and scattered all the world over, God will turn this curse, as he did that, into a blessing: "I will not only water the earth for her, but will *sow her unto me in the earth;* her dispersion shall be not like that of the chaff in the floor, which *the wind drives away,* but like that of the seed in the field, in order to its greater increase; wherever they are scattered they shall *take root downward and bear fruit upward. The good seed are the children of the kingdom. I will sow her unto me."* This alludes to the name of Jezreel, which signifies *sown of God,* or *for God;* as she was scattered of him (which is one signification of the words) so she shall be sown of him; and to what he sows he will give the increase. When in all parts of the world Christianity got footing, and every where there were professors of it, then this promise was fulfilled, *I will sow her unto me in the earth.* Note, The greatest blessing of this earth is that God has a church in it, and from that arises all the tribute of glory which he has out of it; it is what he has sown to himself, and what he will therefore secure to himself.

VII. That, whereas they had been *Lo-ammi — not a people,* and *Lo-ruhamah — not finding mercy* with God, now they shall be restored to his favour and taken again into covenant with him (*v.* 23): They *had not obtained mercy,* but seemed to be abandoned; they were *not my people,* not distinguished, not dealt with, as my people, but left to lie in common with the nations. This was the case with the rejected Jews; and the same, or more deplorable, was that of the Gentile world (to whom the apostle applies this, Rom. 9:24, 25), that had *no hope,* and was *without God in the world;* but when great multitudes both of Jews and Gentiles were, upon their believing in Christ, incorporated into a Christian church, then, 1. God had mercy on those who *had not obtained mercy.* Those found favour with God, and became the children of his love, who had been long out of favour and the children of his wrath, and, if infinite mercy had not interposed, would have been for ever so. Note, God's mercy must not be despaired of any where on this side hell. 2. He took those into a covenant-relation to himself who had been strangers and foreigners. He says to them, *"Thou art my people,* whom I will own and bless, protect and provide for;" and they shall say, *"Thou art my God,* whom I will serve and worship, and to whose honour I will be entirely and for ever devoted." Note, (1.) The sum total of the happiness of believers is the mutual relation that is between them and God, that he is theirs and they are his; this is the crown of all the promises. (2.) This relation is founded in free grace. We have not chosen him, but he has chosen us. He first says, They are my people, and makes them willing to be so in the day of his power, and then they avouch him to be theirs. (3.) As we need desire no more to make us happy than to be the people of God, so we need desire no more to make us easy and cheerful than to have him to assure us that we are so, to say unto us, by his Spirit witnessing with ours, *Thou art my people.* (4.) Those that have accepted the Lord for their God must avouch him to be so, must go to him in prayer and tell him so, *Thou art my God,* and must be ready to make profession before men. (5.) It adds to the comfort of our covenant with God that in it there is a communion of saints, who, though they *are many,* yet here are one. It is not, I will *say to them, You are my people,* but, *Thou* art; for he looks upon them as all *one in Christ,* and, as such in him, he speaks to them and covenants with them; and they also do not say, Thou art *our God,* for they look upon themselves as one body, and desire with one mind and one mouth to glorify him, and therefore say, *Thou art my God.* Or it intimates that such a covenant as God made of old with his people Israel, in general, now under the gospel he makes with particular believers, and says to *each of them,* even the meanest, with as much pleasure as he did of old to the *thousands of Israel, Thou art my people,* and invites and encourages each of them to say, *Thou art my God,* and to triumph therein, as Moses and all Israel did. Ex. 15:2, He is *my God,* and my *father's God.*

CHAPTER 3

God is still by the prophet inculcating the same thing upon this careless people, and much in the same manner as before, by a type or sign, that of the dealings of a husband with an adulterous wife. In this chapter we have, I. The bad character which the people of Israel now had; they were, as is said of the Athenians (Acts 17:16), "wholly given to idolatry," (*v.* 1). II. The low condition which they should be reduced to by their captivity, and the other instances of God's controversy with them (*v.* 2–4). III. The blessed reformation that should at length be wrought upon them in the latter days (*v.* 5).

Verses 1–5

Some think that this chapter refers to Judah, the two tribes, as the adulteress the prophet married (*ch.* 1:3) represented the *ten tribes;* for this was not to be divorced, as the ten tribes were, but to be left desolate for a long time, and then to return, as the two tribes did. But these are called the *children of Israel,* which was the ten tribes, and therefore it is more probable that of them this parable, as well as that before, is to be understood. *Go,* and repeat it, says God to the prophet; *Go yet again.* Note, For the conviction and reduction of sinners it is necessary that precept be upon precept, and line upon line. If they will not believe one sign, try another, Ex. 4:8, 9. Now,

I. In this parable we may observe,

1. God's goodness and Israel's badness strangely serving for a foil to each other, *v.* 1. Israel is as a woman *beloved of her friend,* either of him that has married her or of him that only courts her, and *yet an adulteress;* such is the case between God and Israel. We say of those whose affection is mutual that there is *no love lost* between them; but here we find a great deal of the love even of God himself lost and thrown away upon an unworthy ungrateful people. The God of Israel retains a very great love for the *children of Israel,* and yet they are an evil and adulterous generation. *Be astonished, O heavens! at this, and wonder, O earth!* (1.) That God's goodness has not put an end to their badness; the Lord loves them, has a kindness for them, and is continually showing kindness to them; they know it, they cannot but own it, that he has been as a friend and Father to them; and yet they *look to other gods,* gods that they can see, and to the love of which they are drawn by the eye; they look to them with an eye of adoration (they offer up all their services to them) and with an eye of dependence (they expect all their comforts from them); if they were restrained from bowing the knee to idols, yet they gave them an amorous glance, and had *eyes full of that* spiritual *adultery.* And they loved *flagons of wine;* they joined with idolaters because they lived merrily and drank hard; they had a kindness for *other gods* for the sake of the plenty of good wine with which they

had been sometimes treated in their temples. Idolatry and sensuality commonly go together; those that make a god of their belly, as drunkards do, will easily be brought to make a god of any thing else. God's priests were to *drink no wine* when they went in to minister, and his Nazarites none at all. But the worshippers of other gods *drank wine in bowls;* nay, no less than *flagons of wine* would content them. (2.) That their badness had not stopped the current of his favours to them. This is a wonder of mercy indeed, that she is thus *beloved of her friend, though an adulteress;* such is the *love of the Lord towards the children of Israel.* "Go," says God, *"love* such a woman; see if thou canst find in thy heart to do it. No, thou canst not, the breast of no man would admit such a love; yet such is my *love to the children of Israel;* it is love to the loveless, to the unlovely, to those that have a thousand times forfeited it." Note, In God's goodwill to poor sinners his thoughts and ways are infinitely above ours, and his love is more condescending and compassionate than ours is, or can be; in this, as much as any thing, he is *God, and not man,* Hos. 11:9.

2. The method found for the bringing of a God so very good and a people so very bad together again; this is the thing aimed at, and what God aims at he will accomplish. To our great surprise, we find a breach thus wide as the sea effectually healed; miracles cease not so long as divine mercy does not cease. Observe here, (1.) The course God takes to humble them and make them know themselves (*v.* 2): *I bought her to me for fifteen pieces of silver, and a homer and a half of barley,* that is, I courted her to be reconciled, to leave her ill courses, and return to her first husband, as *ch.* 2:14. I *allured* her, and *spoke comfortably* to her; as the *Levite who went after* his concubine that had *played the harlot* from him, and had run away with another man, *spoke friendly to her,* Jdg. 19:3. But here the present which the prophet brought her for the purchasing of her favour is observed to be a very small one; but it was all that was intended for her separate maintenance, and in it she is reduced to a short allowance, and, to punish her for her pride, is made to look very mean. When Samson went to be reconciled to his wife that had disobliged him he *visited her with a kid* (Jdg. 15:1), which was a genteel entertainment. But the prophet here visited his wife with *fifteen pieces of silver,* a small sum, which yet she must be content to live upon a great while, so long as till her husband thought fit to restore her to her first estate. She shall also have *a homer and a half of barley,* for bread-corn, and that is all she must expect till she be sufficiently humbled, and, by a competent time of trial, satisfactory proof given that she is indeed reformed. Let her be made sensible that it is not for her own merit that her husband makes court to her; it is but a lame price that he values her at. The price of a servant was thirty shekels, Ex. 21:32. This was but half so much; yet let her know that it is more than she is worth. God had given Egypt for Israel's ransom once, so precious were they then in his sight, and so honourable, Isa. 43:3, 4. But now that they have gone a whoring from him he will give but fifteen pieces of silver for them, so much have they lost in their value by their iniquity. Note, Those whom God designs honour and comfort for he first makes sensible of their own worthlessness, and brings them to acknowledge, with the prodigal, *I am no more worthy to be called thy son.* Time was when Israel was *fed with the finest of the wheat,* but they grew wanton, *and loved flagons of wine,* and therefore, in order to the humbling and reducing of them, they must be brought in the land of their captivity to eat barley-bread, and be thankful they can get it, and to eat that too by weight and measure, whereas they did not use to be stinted. Note, Poverty and disgrace sometimes prove a happy means of making great sinners true penitents. (2.) The new terms upon which God is willing to come with them (*v.* 3): *Thou shalt abide for me many days, and shalt not be for another, so will I be for thee.* He might justly have given them a bill of divorce, and have resolved to have no more to do with them; but he is willing to show them kindness, and that the matter should be compromised; he deals not with them in strict justice, according to the rigour of the law, but according to the multitude of his mercies; and it represents God's gracious dealings with the apostate race of mankind, that had gone a whoring from him; he bought them indeed with an inestimable price, not for their honour, but for the honour of his own justice; and now this is the proposal he makes to them, the covenant of grace he is willing to enter into with them — they must be to him a people, and he will be to them a God, the same with the proposal here made to Israel. [1.] They must take to themselves the shame of their apostasy from him, must submit to, and accept of, the punishment of their iniquity: *Thou shalt abide for me many days* in *solitude* and *silence,* as a widow that is *desolate* and in sorrow; they must *lay aside their ornaments,* and wait with patience and submission to know what God will do with them, and whether he will please to admit such unworthy wretches into his favour again, as they did Ex. 33:4, 5. *Their father,* their husband, has *spit in their face* (as God said concerning Miriam), has put them under the marks of his displeasure, and therefore, like her, they must be *ashamed seven days,* and be *shut out of the camp* (Num. 12:14), till *their uncircumcised hearts be humbled,* Lev. 26:41. Let them *sit alone* and *keep silence, waiting for the salvation of the Lord,* and in the mean time let them *bear the yoke,* Lam. 3:26–28. Let them not expect that God should speedily return in mercy to them,; no, let them want it, let them wait for it *many days,* during all the days of their captivity, and reckon it a miracle of mercy, and well worth waiting for, it if come at last. Note, Those whom God designs mercy for he will first bring to abase themselves and to put a high value upon his favours. [2.] They must never return to folly again; that is the condition upon which God will *speak peace to his people and to his saints* (Ps. 85:8), and no other. *"Thou shalt not play the harlot,* shalt not worship idols in the land of thy captivity, while thou art there set apart for the uncleanness." Note, It is not enough to take shame to ourselves for the sins we have committed, and to justify God in correcting us for them, but we must resolve, in the strength of God's grace, that we will not offend any more, that we will not again go a whoring from God, after the world and the flesh. Blessed be God, though it is the law of the covenant, it is not the condition of it that we shall never in any thing do amiss: "But thou shalt not *play the harlot;* thou shalt not serve other gods, *shalt not be for another man."* In the land of their captivity they would be courted to worship the idols of the country; that would be a trial for them, a *long* trial, many days: "But if thou keep thy ground, and hold fast thy integrity, if, when *all this comes upon thee,* thou dost not *stretch out thy hand to a strange god,* thou wilt be qualified for the returns of God's favour." Note, It is a certain sign that our afflictions are means of much good to us, and earnests of more, when we are kept by the grace of God from being overcome by the temptations of an afflicted state. [3.] Upon these terms their Maker will again be their husband: *So will I also be for thee.* This is the covenant between God and returning sinners, that, if they will be for him to serve him, he will be for them to save them. Let them renounce and abjure all rivals with God for the throne in the heart, and devote themselves entirely to him and him only, and he will be to them a God all-sufficient. If we be faithful and constant to God in a way of duty, and will never leave nor forsake him, he will be so to us in a way of mercy, and will never leave nor forsake us. And a fairer proposal could not be made.

II. In the last two verses we have the interpretation of the parable and the application of it to Israel.

1. They must long *sit like a widow,* stripped of all their joys and honours, Lam. 4:1, 2. *They shall abide many days without a king, and without a prince;* and a nation in this condition may well be called *a widow.* They want the blessing, (1.) Of civil government: They shall abide *without a king,* and *without a prince,* of their own. There were kings and princes over them to oppress them and rule them with rigour, but they had no king nor prince to protect them, to fight their battles for them, to administer justice to them, and to take care of their common safety and welfare. Note, Magistracy is a very great blessing to a people, and it is a sad and sore judgment to want it. (2.) Of public worship: *They shall* abide *without a sacrifice,* and *without an image* (or a *statue,* or *pillar;* the word is used concerning the pillars Jacob erected, Gen. 28:18; 31:45; 35:20), and *without an ephod and teraphim.* The *teraphim* being here closely joined to the *ephod,* some thing the *urim* and *thummim* were meant by it in the breast-plate of the high priest. The meaning is that in their captivity they should not only have no face of a nation upon them, but no face of a church; they should not have (as a learned expositor speaks) liberty of any public profession or exercise of religion, either true or false, according to their choice. They shall have *no sacrifice or altar* (so the Septuagint), and therefore no sacrifice because no altar. They shall have *no ephod,* nor *teraphim,* no legal priesthood, no means of knowing God's mind, no oracle to consult in doubtful cases, but shall be all in the dark. Note, The case of those is very melancholy that are deprived of all opportunities to worship God in public. This was the case of the Jews in their captivity; and it is so far the case of the scattered Jews at this day that, though they have their synagogues, they have no temple-service. Desolate indeed is their condition that are shut out from communion with God, that have no opportunity of directing their addresses to God by sacrifice and altar, and of receiving instruction from him by ephod and teraphim.

2. They shall at length be received again as a wife (*v.* 5): *Afterwards,* in process of time, when they have gone through this discipline, *they shall return,* that is, they shall repent of their idolatries and forsake them, they shall apply themselves to God and adhere to him, and herein they shall be accepted of him. Two things are here promised as instances of their return, and steps towards their acceptance with God in their return: — (1.) The enquiries they shall make after God: *They shall seek the Lord their God, and David their king.* Note, Those that would find God, and find favour with him, must seek him, must ask after him, covet acquaintance with him, desire to be reconciled to him, set their love on him, and labour in this that they may be accepted of him. Their seeking him implies that they had lost him, that they were lamenting their loss, and that they were solicitous to retrieve what they had lost. They shall seek him as *their God;* for *should not a people seek unto their God?* And they shall seek *David their King,* who can be no other than the Messiah, our Lord Jesus Christ, the Son of David, the *root and offspring of David,* whom David himself called *Lord* (Ps. 110:1), and to whom God gave the *throne of his father David,* Lu. 1:32. The Chaldee reads it, They shall *seek the service of the Lord their God,* and *shall obey Messiah, the Son of David their king.* Compare this with Jer. 30:9; Eze. 34:23; 37:25. Note, Those that would seek the Lord so as to find him must apply to Jesus Christ, and must seek to him as their King, and become his willing people, and take an oath of fealty and allegiance to him. (2.) The reverence they shall have of God: *They shall fear the Lord and his goodness.* Some by his *goodness* here understand the temple, towards which they shall look, in worshipping God. The Jews say, There were three things which Israel cast off in the days of Rehoboam — the *kingdom of heaven,* the *family of David,* and the *house of the sanctuary;* and it will never be well with them till they return, and seek them all three, which is here promised. They shall seek the kingdom of heaven in *the Lord their God,* the royal family in *David their King,* and the temple in *the goodness of the Lord.* Others by *his goodness* understand Christ, the same *with David their King.* But it is rather to be taken for that attribute of God which he showed as his glory, and by which he proclaimed his name. Note, It is not only the Lord and his greatness that we are to fear, but the Lord and his goodness, not only his majesty, but his mercy. They shall *flee for fear to the Lord and his goodness* (so some take it), shall flee to it as their city of refuge. We must *fear God's goodness,* that is, we must admire it, and stand amazed at it, must adore it, and *worship* as Moses did at the proclaiming of this name, Ex. 34:6. We must be afraid of offending his goodness, of making any ungrateful returns for it, and so forfeiting it. *There is forgiveness with God, that he may be feared,* Ps. 130:4. We must *rejoice with trembling* in the goodness of God, must not be *high-minded, but fear.* Now this promise had its accomplishment when by the gospel of Christ great multitudes both of Jews and Gentiles were brought home to God, and incorporated in the New-Testament church, served God in Christ, with a filial fear of divine grace, and were accepted of God as his Israel. And some think it is to be yet further accomplished in the conversion of those Jews to the faith of Christ who shall remain in unbelief, when they shall seek their Messiah as *David their King,* and by him *all Israel shall be saved,* when the *fulness of the Gentiles is brought in.* Time was when

they sought him to put him to death, saying, *We have no king but Caesar;* but the day is coming when they shall seek him to *appoint him their head,* and to lay their necks under his yoke. He that has here promised that they shall do it will enable them to do it, and bring about this great work in his own way and time, *in the latter days* of the *last times,* the times of the Messiah: but, alas! who shall live when God does this? How far we are to expect a general conversion of that nation I cannot say; but I am sure we ought to pray that the Jews may be converted.

CHAPTER 4

Prophets were sent to be reprovers, to tell people of their faults, and to warn them of the judgments of God, to which by sin they exposed themselves; so the prophet is employed in this and the following chapters. He is here, as counsel for the King of kings, opening an indictment against the people of Israel, and labouring to convince them of sin, and of their misery and danger because of sin, that he might prevail with them to repent and reform. I. He shows them what were the grounds of God's controversy with them, a general prevalency of vice and profaneness (*v.* 1, 2), ignorance and forgetfulness of God (*v.* 6, 7), the worldly-mindedness of the priests (*v.* 8), drunkenness and uncleanness (*v.* 11), using divination and witchcraft (*v.* 12), offering sacrifice in the high places (*v.* 13), whoredoms (*v.* 14, 18), and bribery among magistrates (*v.* 18). II. He shows them what would be the consequences of God's controversy. God would punish them for these things (*v.* 9). The whole land should be laid waste (*v.* 3), all sorts of people cut off (*v.* 5), their honour lost (*v.* 7), their creature-comforts unsatisfying (*v.* 10), and themselves made ashamed (*v.* 19). And, which is several times mentioned here as the sorest judgment of all, they should be let alone in their sins (*v.* 17), they shall not reprove one another (*v.* 4), God will not punish them (*v.* 14), nay, he will let them prosper (*v.* 16). III. He gives warning to Judah not to tread in the steps of Israel, because they saw their steps went down to hell (*v.* 15).

Verses 1–5

Here is, I. The court set, and both attendance and attention demanded: *"Hear the word of the Lord, you children of Israel,* for to you is the word of this conviction sent, whether you will hear or whether you will forbear." Whom may God expect to give him a fair hearing, and take from him a fair warning, but the children of Israel, his own professing people? Yea, they will be ready enough to hear when God speaks comfortably to them; but are they willing to hear when he has a controversy with them? Yes, they must hear him when he pleads against them, when he has something to lay to their charge: *The Lord has a controversy with the inhabitants of the land,* of this land, of this holy land. Note, Sin is the great mischief-maker; it sows discord between God and Israel. God sees sin in his own people, and a good action he has against them for it. Some more particular actions lie against his own people, which do not lie against other sinners. He has a controversy with them for breaking covenant with him, for bringing a reproach upon him, and for an ungrateful return to him for his favours. God's controversy will be pleaded, pleaded by the judgments of his mouth before they are pleaded by the judgments of his hand, that he may be justified in all he does and may make it appear that he desires not the death of sinners; and God's pleadings ought to be attended to, for, sooner or later, they shall have a hearing.

II. The indictment read, by which the whole nation stands charged with crimes of a heinous nature, by which God is highly provoked. 1. They are charged with national omissions of the most important duties: *There is no truth nor mercy,* neither justice nor charity, these most *weighty matters of the law,* as our Saviour accounts them (Mt. 23:23), *judgment, mercy, and faith.* The generality of the people seemed to have no sense at all of the thing called honesty; they made no conscience of what they said and did, though ever so contrary to the truth and injurious to their neighbour. Much less had they any sense of mercy, or any obligation they were under to pity and help the poor. And it is not strange that there is no truth and mercy when there is *no knowledge of God in the land.* What good can be expected where there is no knowledge of God? It was the privilege of that land that *in Israel God was* made *known,* and his *name* was *great,* which was an aggravation of their sin, that they did not *know him,* Ps. 76:1. 2. Hence follows national commissions of the most enormous sins against both the first and second table, for they had no regard at all to either. *Swearing,* and *lying,* and *killing,* and *stealing,* and *committing adultery,* against the third, ninth, sixth, eighth, and seventh commandments, were to be found in all corners of the land, and among all orders and degrees of men among them, *v.* 2. The corruption was universal; what good people there were among them were either lost or hid, or they hid themselves. By these they *break out,* that is, they transgress all bounds of reason and conscience, and the divine law; *they have exceeded* (Job 36:9); they have been *overmuch wicked* (Eccl. 7:17); they suffer their corruptions to break out; they themselves break over, and break through, all that stands in their way and would stop them in their sinful career, as water overflows the banks. Note, Sin is a violent thing and its power exorbitant; when men's hearts are *fully set in them to do evil* (Eccl. 8:11) *what will be restrained from them?* Gen. 11:6. When they break out thus *blood touches blood,* that is, abundance of murders are committed in all parts of the country, and, as it were, in a constant series and succession. *Caedes aliae aliis sunt contiguae — Murders touch murders;* a stream of blood runs down among them, even royal blood. It was about this time that there was so much blood shed in grasping at the crown; Shallum slew Zechariah, and Menahem slew Shallum, Pekah slew Pekahiah, and Hoshea slew Pekah; and the like bloody work, it is likely, there was among other contenders, so that the land was *polluted with blood* (Ps. 106:38); *it was filled with blood from one end to the other,* 2 Ki. 21:16.

III. Sentence passed upon this guilty and polluted land, *v.* 3. It shall be utterly destroyed and laid waste. The whole land is infected with sin, and therefore *the whole land shall mourn* under God's sore judgments, shall sit in mourning, being stripped of all its wealth and beauty. As the valleys are said to *shout for joy, and sing,* when there are plenty and peace, so here they are said to *mourn* when by war and famine they are made desolate. The *whole land shall be brimstone, and salt, and burning,* was as threatened in the law, Deu. 29:33. They had broken all God's commandments, and now God threatens to take away all their comforts. The *land mourns* when there is neither *grass for the cattle nor herbs for the service of man;* and then *every one that dwells therein shall languish* for want of nice food to support a wasting life, and fret for want of the usual dainties for delight. The *beasts of the field* will languish, Jer. 14:5, 6. Nay, the destruction of the fruits of the earth shall be so great that there shall not be picking for the *fowls of the air,* to keep them alive; they shall suffer with man, and their dying, or growing lean, will be a punishment to those who used to have their tables replenished with wild-fowl. Nay, *the fishes of the sea shall be taken away,* or *gathered together,* that they may go away in shoals to some other coast, and then the fishing trade will be worth nothing. This desolation shall be in that respect more general than that by Noah's flood, for that did not affect the fishes of the sea, but this shall. It was part of one of the plagues of Egypt that he *slew their fish* (Ps. 105:29); when the waters are dried the *fish die,* Isa. 50:2; Zep. 1:2, 3. Note, When man becomes disobedient to God, it is just that the inferior creatures should be made unserviceable to man. Oh what reason have we to admire God's patience and mercy to our land, that though there is in it so much swearing, and lying, and killing, and stealing, and adultery, yet there is plenty of flesh, and fish, and fowl, on our tables!

IV. An order of court that no pains should be taken with the condemned criminal to bring him to repentance, with the reason for that order. Observe, 1. The order itself (*v.* 4): *Yet let no man strive nor reprove another;* let no means be used to reduce and reclaim them; let their physicians give them up as desperate and past cure. It intimates that as long as there is any hope we ought to reprove sinners for their sins; it is a duty we owe to one another to give and to take reproofs; it was one of the laws of Moses (Lev. 19:17), *Thou shalt in any wise rebuke thy neighbour;* it is an instance of brotherly love. Sometimes there is need to rebuke sharply, not only to reprove, but to strive, so loth are men to part with their sins. But it is a sign that persons and people are abandoned to ruin when God says, *Let them not be reproved.* Yet this is to be understood as God's commands sometimes to the prophets not to *pray for them,* notwithstanding which they did pray for them; but the meaning is, They are so hardened in sin, and so ripened for ruin, that it will be to little purpose either to deal with them or to deal with God for them. Note, It bodes ill to a people when reprovers are silenced, and when those who should witness against the sins of the times, retire into a corner, and give up the cause. See 2 Chr. 25:16. 2. The reasons of this order. Let them not reprove one another; for, (1.) They are determined to *go on in sin,* and no reproofs will cure them of that: *Thy people are as those that strive with the priests;* they have grown so very impudent in sin, so very insolent, and impatient of reproof, that they will fly in the face even of a priest himself if he should but give them the least check, without any regard to his character and office; and how then can it be thought that they should take a reproof from a private person? Note, Those sinners have their hearts wickedly hardened who quarrel with their ministers for dealing faithfully with them; and those who rebel against ministerial reproof, which is an ordinance of God for their reformation, have forfeited the benefit of brotherly reproof too. Perhaps this may refer to the late wickedness of Joash king of Judah, and his people, who stoned Zechariah, the son of Jehoiada, for delivering them a message from God, 2 Chr. 24:21. He was a *priest;* with him they *strove* when he was officiating *between the temple and the altar;* and Dr. Lightfoot thinks the prophet had an eye to his case when he spoke (*v.* 2) of *blood touching blood;* the blood of the *sacrificer was mingled with the blood of the sacrifice,* That, says he, was the *apex* of *their wickedness* — thence their ruin was to be dated (Mt. 23:35), as this is of *their incorrigibleness,* that they are as those who *strive with the priest,* therefore let no man reprove them; for, (2.) God also is determined to *proceed in their ruin* (*v.* 5): *"Therefore,* because thou wilt take no reproof, no advice, *thou shalt fall,* and it is in vain for any to think of preventing it, for the *decree* has *gone forth.* Thou shalt stumble and *fall in the day,* and *the prophet,* the false prophet that flattered and seduced thee, shall *fall with thee in the night;* both thou and thy prophet shall fall *night and day,* shall be continually falling into one calamity or other; the darkness of the night shall not help to cover thee from trouble nor the light of the day help thee to flee from it." The prophets are blind leaders and the people blind followers; and to the blind day and night are alike, so that whether it be day or night both shall *fall together into the ditch.* "Thou shalt fall *in the day,* when thy fall is least feared by thyself and thou art very *secure;* and *in the day,* when it will be seen and observed by others, and turn most to thy shame; and the prophet shall *fall in the night,* when to himself it will be most terrible." Note, The ruin of those who have helped to ruin others will, in a special manner, be intolerable. And did the children think that when they were in danger of falling their mother would help them? It shall be in vain to expect it, for *I will destroy thy mother,* Samaria, the mother-city, the whole *state,* or *kingdom,* which is as a mother to every part. It shall all be *made silent.* Note, When all are involved in guilt nothing less can be expected than that all should be involved in ruin.

Verses 6–11

God is here proceeding in his controversy both with the priests and with the people. *The people* were as those *that strove with the priests* (*v.* 4) when they had priests that did their duty; but the generality of them lived in the neglect of their duty, and here is a word for those priests, and for the people that love to have it so, Jer. 5:31. And it is observable here how the punishment answers to the sin, and how, for the justifying of his own proceedings, God sets the one over-against the other.

I. The people *strove with the priests* that should have taught them the knowledge of God; justly therefore were they *destroyed for lack of knowledge, v.* 6. Note, Those that rebel against the light can expect no other than to perish in the dark. Or it is a charge upon the priests, who should have been still *teaching the people knowledge* (Eccl. 12:9), but they did not, or did it in such a manner that it was as if they had not done it at all, so there was *no knowledge of God in the land;* and because there was no vision, or none to any purpose, the people *perished,* Prov. 29:18. Note, Ignorance is so far from being the mother of devotion that it is the mother of destruction; lack of knowledge is ruining to any person or people. They are *my people* that are thus *destroyed;* their relation to God as his people aggravates both their sin in not taking pains to get the knowledge of that God whose command they were under and with whom they were taken into covenant, and likewise the sin of those who should have taught them; God set his children to school to them, and they never minded them nor took any pains with them.

II. Both priests and people rejected knowledge; and justly therefore will God *reject them.* The reason why the people did not learn, and the priests did not teach, was not because they had not the light, but because they hated it — not because they had not ways of coming to the knowledge of God and of communicating it, but because they had no heart to it; they *rejected* it. They *desired not the knowledge of God's ways,* but put it from them, and shut their eyes against the light; and therefore *"I will also reject thee;* I will refuse to take cognizance of thee and to own thee; you will not know me, but bid me *depart;* I will therefore say, *Depart from me, I know you not. Thou* shalt be *no priest to me."* 1. The priests shall be no longer admitted to the privileges, or employed in the services, of the priesthood, nor shall they ever be received again, as we find, Eze. 44:13. Note, Ministers that reject knowledge, that are grossly ignorant and scandalous, ought not to be owned as ministers; but that which they *seem to have* should be *taken away,* Lu. 8:18. 2. The people shall be no longer as they have been, a *kingdom of priests,* a royal priesthood, Ex. 19:6. God's people, by rejecting knowledge, forfeit their honour and profane their own crown.

III. They *forgot the law of God,* neither desired nor endeavoured to retain it in mind, nor to transmit the remembrance of it to their posterity, and therefore justly will God *forget* them and *their children,* the people's children; they did not educate them, as they ought to have done, in the knowledge of God and their duty to him, and therefore God will disown them, as not in covenant with him. Note, If parents do not teach their children, when they are young, to *remember their Creator,* they cannot expect that their Creator should remember them. Or it may be meant of the priests' children; they shall not succeed them in the priests' office, but shall be reduced to poverty, as is threatened against Eli's house, 1 Sa. 2:20.

IV. They dishonoured God with that which was their honour, and justly therefore will God strip them of it, *v.* 7. It was their honour that they were increased in number, wealth, power, and dignity. The beginning of their nation was small, but in process of time it *greatly increased,* and grew very considerable; the family of the priests increased wonderfully. But, *as they were increased, so they sinned* against God. The more populous the nation grew, the more sin was committed and the more profane they were; their wealth, honour, and power, did but make them the more daring in sin. Therefore, says God, *will I change their glory into shame.* Are their numbers their glory? God will diminish them and make them few. Is their wealth their glory? God will impoverish them and bring them low; so that they shall themselves be ashamed of that which they gloried in. Their priests shall be made *contemptible and base,* Mal. 2:9. Note, That which is our honour, if we dishonour God with it, will sooner or later be turned into shame to us: for *those that despise God shall be lightly esteemed,* 1 Sa. 2:30.

V. The priests ate up the sin of God's people, and therefore *they shall eat and not have enough.* 1. They abused the maintenance that was allowed to the priests, to the priests of the house of Aaron, by the law of God, and to the mock-priests of the calves by their constitution (*v.* 8): *They eat up the sin of my people,* that is, their sin-offerings. If it be meant of the priests of the calves, it intimates their seizing that which they had no right to; they usurped the revenues of the priests, though they were no priests. If it be meant of those who were legal priests, it intimates their greediness of the profits and perquisites of their office, when they took no care at all to do the duty of it. They feasted upon their part of the offerings of the Lord, but forgot the work for which they were so well paid. They *set their heart* upon the people's *iniquities;* they *lifted up their soul* to them, that is, they were glad then people did commit iniquity, that they might be obliged to bring an offering to make atonement for it, which they should have their share of; the more sins the more sacrifices, and therefore they cared not how much sin people were guilty of. Instead of warning the people against sin, from the consideration of the sacrifices, which showed them what an offence sin was to God, since it needed such an expiation, they emboldened and encouraged the people to sin, since an atonement might be made at so small an expense. Thus they glutted themselves upon the sins of the people, and helped to keep up that which they should have beaten down. Note, It is a very wicked thing to be well pleased with the sins of others because, in some way or other, they may turn to our advantage. 2. God will therefore deny them his blessing upon their maintenance (*v.* 10): *They shall eat and not have enough.* Though they have great plenty by the abundance of offerings that are brought in, yet they shall have no satisfaction in it. Either their food shall yield no good nourishment or their greedy appetites shall not be satisfied with it. Note, What is unlawfully gained cannot be comfortably used; no, nor that which is inordinately coveted; it is just that the desires which are insatiable should always be unsatisfied, and that those should never have enough who never know when they have enough. See Mic. 6:14; Hag. 1:6.

VI. The more they increased the more they sinned (*v.* 7), and therefore though they *commit whoredom,* though they take the most wicked methods to multiply their people, yet *they shall not increase.* Though they have many wives and concubines, as Solomon had, yet they shall not have their families built up thereby in a numerous progeny, any more than he had. Note, Those that hope any way to increase by unlawful means will be disappointed. And therefore God will thus blast all their projects *because they have left off to take heed to the Lord;* time was when they had some regard to God, and to his authority over them and interest in them, but they have *left it off;* they take no heed to his word nor to his providences; they do not eye him in either. They *forsake him, so as not to take heed to him;* they have apostatized to such a degree that they have no manner of regard to God, but are perfectly *without God in the world.* Note, Those that leave off to take heed to the Lord leave off all good, and can expect no other than that all good should leave them.

VII. The people and the priests did harden one another in sin; and therefore justly shall they be sharers in the punishment (*v.* 9): *There shall be, like people, like priest.* So they were in character; people and priest were both alike ignorant and profane, regardless of God and their duty, and addicted to idolatry: and so they shall be in condition; God will bring judgments upon them, that shall be the destruction both of priest and people; the famine that deprives the people of their meat shall deprive the priests of their *meat-offerings,* Joel 1:9. It is part of the description of a universal desolation that it shall be *as with the people, so with the priest,* Isa. 24:2. God's judgments, when they come with commission, will make no difference. Note, Sharers in sin must expect to be sharers in ruin. Thus God will *punish them* both *for their ways,* and *reward them for their doings.* God will *cause their doings to return upon them* (so the word is); when a sin is committed the sinner thinks *it is gone* and he shall hear no more of it, but he shall find it *called over again,* and made to *return,* either to his humiliation or to his condemnation.

VIII. They indulged themselves in the delights of sense, to hold up their hearts; but they shall find that they *take away their hearts* (*v.* 11): *Whoredom, and wine, and new wine take away the heart.* Some join this with the foregoing words. *They have forsaken the Lord, to take heed to whoredom, and wine, and new wine.* Or, *Because* these *have taken away their heart.* Their sensual pleasures have taken them off from their devotions and drowned all that is good in them. Or we may take it as a distinct sentence, containing a great truth which we see confirmed by every day's experience, that drunkenness and uncleanness are sins which besot and infatuate men, weaken and enfeeble them. They take away both the understanding and the courage.

Verses 12–19

In these verses we have, as before,

I. The sins charged upon the people of Israel, for which God had a controversy with them, and they are,

1. Spiritual whoredom, or idolatry. They have in them a *spirit of whoredoms,* a strong inclination to that sin; the bent and bias of their hearts are that way; it is *their own iniquity;* they are carried out towards it with an unaccountable violence, and this *causes them to err.* Note, The errors and mistakes of the judgment are commonly owing to the corrupt affections; men *therefore* have a good opinion of sin, because they have a disposition towards it. And having such erroneous notions of idols, and such passionate motions towards them, no marvel that with such a head and such a heart they have *gone a whoring from under their God, v.* 12. They ought to have been in subjection to him as their head and husband, to have been under his guidance and command, but they revolted from their allegiance, and put themselves under the guidance and protection of false gods. So (*v.* 15) Israel has *played the harlot;* their conduct in the worship of their idols was like that of a harlot, wanton and impudent. And (*v.* 16), *Israel slideth back as a backsliding heifer,* as an *untamed* heifer (so some), or as a *perverse* or *refractory* one (so others), as a heifer that is turned loose runs madly about the pasture, or, if put under the yoke (which seems rather to be alluded to here), will draw back instead of going forward, will struggle to get her neck out of the yoke and her feet out of the furrow. Thus unruly, ungovernable, untractable, were the people of Israel. They had begun to draw in the yoke of God's ordinances, but they drew back, as *children of Belial,* that will not endure the yoke; and when the prophets were sent with the goads of reproof, to put them forward, they *kicked against the pricks,* and ran backwards. The sum of all is (*v.* 17), *Ephraim is joined to idols,* is perfectly wedded to them; his affections are glued to them, and his heart is upon them. There are two instances given of their spiritual whoredom, in both which they gave that honour to their idols which is due to God only: — (1.) They consulted them as oracles, and used those arts of divination which they had learned from their idolatrous priests (*v.* 12): *My people ask counsel at their stocks,* their wooden gods; they apply to them for advice and direction in what they should do and for information concerning the event. They *say to a stock, Thou art my father* (Jer. 2:27); and, if it were indeed a father, it were worthy of this honour; but it was a great affront to God, who was indeed their Father, and whose lively oracles they had among them, with which they had liberty to consult at any time, thus to *ask counsel at their stocks.* And they expect that their *staff* should *declare to them* what course they should take and what the event should be. It is probable that this refers to some wicked methods of divination used among the Gentiles, and which the Jews learned from them, by a *piece of wood,* or by *a staff,* like Nebuchadnezzar's divining by *his arrows,* Eze. 21:21. Note, Those who forsake the oracles of God, to take their measures from the world and the flesh, do in effect but consult with their stocks and their staves. (2.) They offered sacrifice to them as gods, whose favour they wanted and whose wrath they dreaded and deprecated (*v.* 13): *They sacrifice to them,* to atone and pacify them, and *burn incense* to them, to please and gratify them, and hope by both to recommend themselves to them. God had pitched upon the place where he would record his name; but they, having forsaken that, chose places for their irreligious rites which pleased their own fancies; they chose, [1.] High places, *upon the tops of the mountains* and *upon the hills,* foolishly imagining that the height of the ground gave them some advantage in their approaches towards heaven. [2.] Shady places, *under oaks, and poplars, and elms, because the shadow thereof* is pleasant to them, especially in those hot countries, and therefore they thought it was pleasing to their gods; or they fancied that a thick shade befriends contemplation, possesses the mind with something of awe, and therefore is proper for devotion.

2. Corporal whoredom is another crime here charged upon them: *They have committed whoredom continually, v.* 18. They drove a trade of uncleanness; it was not a single act now and then, but their constant practice, as it is of many that have *eyes full of adultery* and *which cannot cease from* that *sin,* 2 Pt. 2:14. Now the abominable filthiness and lewdness that was found in Israel is here spoken of, (1.) As a concomitant of their idolatry; their false gods drew them to it; for the devil whom they worshipped, though a spirit, is an unclean spirit. Those that worshipped idols were *separated with harlots,* and they *sacrificed with harlots;* for because they *liked not to retain God in their knowledge,* but dishonoured him, therefore God *gave them up to vile affections,* by the indulging of which they *dishonoured themselves,* Rom. 1:24, 28. (2.) As a punishment of it. The *men* that worshipped idols were *separated with harlots* that attended the idolatrous rites, as in the worship of *Baal-peor,* Num. 25:1, 2. To punish them for that God gave up their wives and daughters to the like vile affections: They *committed whoredom and adultery* (*v.* 13), which could not but be a great grief and reproach to their

husbands and parents; for those that are not chaste themselves desire to have their wives and daughters so. But thus they might read their sin in their punishment, as David's adultery was punished in the debauching of his concubines by his own son, 2 Sa. 12:11. Note, When the same sin in others is made men's grief and affliction which they have themselves been guilty of they must own that the Lord is righteous.

3. The perverting of justice, *v.* 18. *Their rulers* (be it spoken to their shame) *do love, Give ye,* that is, they love bribes, and have it continually in their mouths, *Give, give.* They are given to *filthy lucre;* every one that has any business with them must expect to be asked, What will you give? Though, as rulers, they are bound by office to do justice, yet none can have justice done them without a fee; and you may be sure that for a fee they will do injustice. Note, The love of money is the ruin of equity and the root of all iniquity. But of all men it is a shame for rulers (who should be men *fearing God* and *hating covetousness*) to love *Give ye.* Perhaps this is intended in that part of the charge here, *Their drink is sour;* it is *dead;* it is *gone.* Justice, duly administered, is refreshing, like drink to the thirsty, but when it is perverted, and rulers take rewards either to acquit the guilty or to condemn the innocent, the *drink is sour;* they *turn judgment into wormwood,* Amos 5:7. Or it may refer in general to the depraved morals of the whole nation; they had lost all their life and spirit, and were as offensive to God as dead and sour drink is to us. See Deu. 31:32, 33.

II. The tokens of God's wrath against them for their sins. 1. Their wives and daughters should not be punished for the injury and disgrace they did to their families (*v.* 14): *I will not punish your daughters;* and, not being punished for their sin, they would go on in it. Note, The impunity of one sinner is sometimes made the punishment of another. Or, *"I will not punish* them as I will punish you; for you must own, as Judah did concerning his daughter-in-law, that *they are more righteous than you,"* Gen. 38:26. 2. They themselves should prosper for a while, but their prosperity should help to destroy them. It comes in as a token of God's wrath (*v.* 16): *The Lord will feed them as a lamb in a large place;* they shall have a fat pasture, and a large one, in which they shall be fed to the full, and fed of the best, but it shall be only to prepare them for the slaughter, as a lamb is that is so fed. If they *wax fat and kick,* they do but wax fat for the butcher. But others make them feed as *a lamb on the common,* a large place indeed, but where it has short grass and lies exposed. The Shepherd of Israel will turn them both out of his pastures and out of his protection. 3. No means should be used to bring them to repentance (*v.* 17): *"Ephraim is joined to idols,* is in love with them and addicted to them, and therefore *let him alone,* as *v.* 4, *Let no man reprove* him. Let him be given up to *his own heart's lusts,* and walk *in his own counsel;* we *would have healed* him, and he *would not be healed,* therefore *forsake* him," See *what their end will be,* Deu. 32:20. Note, It is a sad and sore judgment for any man to be let alone in sin, for God to say concerning a sinner, "He is joined to his idols, the world and the flesh; he is incurably proud, covetous, or profane, an incurable drunkard or adulterer; *let him alone;* conscience, let him alone; minister, let him alone; providences, let him alone. Let nothing awaken him till the flames of hell do it." The father corrects not the rebellious son any more when he determines to disinherit him. "Those that are not disturbed in their sin will be destroyed for their sin." 4. They should be hurried away with a swift and shameful destruction (*v.* 19): *The wind has bound her up in her wings,* to carry her away into captivity, suddenly, violently, and irresistibly; he shall take *them away as with a whirlwind,* Ps. 58:9. And then *they shall be ashamed because of their sacrifices,* ashamed of their sin in offering sacrifice to idols, ashamed of their folly in putting themselves to such an expense upon gods that have no power to help them, and thereby making that God their enemy who has almighty power to destroy them. Note, There are sacrifices that men will one day be ashamed of. Those that have sacrificed their time, strength, honour, and all their comforts, to the world and the flesh, will shortly be ashamed of it. Yea, and those that bring to God blind, and lame, and heartless sacrifices, will be ashamed of them too.

III. The warning given to Judah not to sin after the similitude of Israel's transgression. It is said in the close of *v.* 14, *Those that do not understand shall fall;* those must needs fall that do not understand how to avoid, or get over, the stumbling-blocks they meet with (and therefore *let him that thinks he stands take heed lest he fall*), particularly the two tribes (*v.* 15): *Though thou, Israel, play the harlot, yet let not Judah offend.* Though Israel be given to idolatry, yet let not Judah take the infection. Now, 1. This was a very needful caution. The men of Israel were brethren, and near neighbours, to the men of Judah; Israel was more numerous, and at this time in a prosperous condition, and therefore there was danger lest the men of Judah should learn their way and get a snare to their souls. Note, The nearer we are to the infection of sin the more need we have to stand upon our guard. 2. It was a very rational caution: *"Let Israel play the harlot,* yet let not Judah do so; for Judah has greater means of knowledge than Israel, has the temple and priesthood, and a king of the house of David; from Judah Shiloh is to come; and for Judah God has reserved great blessings in store; therefore *let not Judah offend,* for more is expected from them than from Israel, they will have more to answer for if they do offend, and from them God will take it more unkindly. If *Israel play the harlot,* let not Judah do so too, for then God will have no professing people in the world." God bespeaks Judah here, as Christ does the twelve, when many turned their backs upon him, *Will you also go away?* Jn. 6:67. Note, Those that have hitherto kept their integrity should, for that reason, still hold it fast, even in times of general apostasy. Now, to preserve Judah from offending as Israel had done, two rules are here given: — (1.) That they might not be guilty of idolatry they must keep at a distance from the places of idolatry: *Come not you unto Gilgal,* where *all their wickedness was* (*ch.* 9:15; 12:11); there they *multiplied transgression* (Amos 4:4); and perhaps they contracted a veneration for that place because there it was said to Joshua, The place *where thou standest is holy ground* (Jos. 5:15); therefore they are forbidden to *enter into Gilgal,* Amos 5:5. And for the same reason they must *not go up to Bethel,* here called the *house of vanity,* for so *Bethaven* signifies, not the *house of God,* as *Bethel* signifies. Note, Those that would be kept from sin, and not fall into the devil's hands, must studiously avoid the occasions of sin and not come upon the devil's ground. (2.) That they might not be guilty of idolatry they must take heed of profaneness, and *not swear, The Lord liveth.* They are commanded to swear, *The Lord liveth in truth and righteousness* (Jer. 4:2); and therefore that which is here forbidden is swearing so in untruth and unrighteousness, swearing rashly and lightly, or falsely and with deceit, or swearing by the Lord and the idol, Zep. 1:5. Note, Those that would be steady in their adherence to God must possess themselves with an awe and reverence of God, and always speak of him with solemnity and seriousness; for those that can make a jest of the true God will make a god of any thing.

CHAPTER 5

The scope of this chapter is the same with that of the foregoing chapter, to discover the sin both of Israel and Judah, and to denounce the judgments of God against them. I. They are called to hearken to the charge (*v.* 1, 8). II. They are accused of many sins, which are here aggravated. 1. Persecution (*v.* 1, 2). 2. Spiritual whoredom (*v.* 3, 4). 3. Pride (*v.* 5). 4. Apostasy from God (*v.* 7). 5. The tyranny of the princes, and the tameness of the people in submitting to it (*v.* 10, 11). III. They are threatened with God's displeasure for their sins; he knows all their wickedness (*v.* 3) and makes known his wrath against them for it (*v.* 9). 1. They shall fall in their iniquity (*v.* 5). 2. God will forsake them (*v.* 6). 3. Their portions shall be devoured (*v.* 7). 4. God will rebuke them, and pour out his wrath upon them (*v.* 9, 10). 5. They shall be oppressed (*v.* 11). 6. God will be as a moth to them in secret judgments (*v.* 12) and as a lion in public judgments (*v.* 14). IV. They are blamed for the wrong course they took under their afflictions (*v.* 13). V. It is intimated that they shall at length take a right course (*v.* 15). The more generally these things are expressed of so much the more general use they are for our learning, and particularly for our admonition.

Verses 1–7

Here, I. All orders and degrees of men are cited to appear and answer to such things as shall be laid to their charge (*v.* 1): *Hear you this, O priests!* whether *in holy orders* (as those in Judah, and perhaps many in Israel too, for in the ten tribes there were divers cities of priests and Levites, who, it is probable, staid in their own lot after the revolt of the ten tribes and did so much of their office as might be done at a distance from the temple) or *pretending holy orders,* as the priests of the calves, who, some think, are included here. "Hearken, *you house of Israel,* the common people, and *give ear, O house of the king!"* let them all take notice, for they have all contributed to the national guilt, and they shall all share in the national judgments. Note, If neither the sanctity of the priesthood nor the dignity of the royal family will prevail to keep out sin, it cannot be expected that they should avail to keep out wrath. If the priests, and the house of the king, though they bear such noble characters, sin like others, their noble characters will not excuse them, but they must smart like others. Nor shall it be any plea for *the house of Israel* that they were misled by their priests and princes, but they shall receive their doom with them, and neither their meanness nor their multitude shall be their exemption.

II. Witness is produced against them, one instead of a thousand; it is God's omniscience (*v.* 3): *I know Ephraim, and Israel is not hidden from me.* They have *not known the Lord* (*v.* 4), but the Lord has known them, knows their true character however disguised, knows their secret wickedness however concealed. Note, Men's rejecting the knowledge of God will not secure them from his knowledge of them; and when he contends with them he will prove their sins upon them by his own knowledge, so that is will be in vain to plead *Not guilty.*

III. Very bad things are laid to their charge. 1. They had been very ingenious and very industrious to draw people either into sin or into trouble: You have been *a snare on Mizpah, and a net spread upon Tabor* (*v.* 1), that is, such snares and nets as the huntsmen used to lay upon those mountains in pursuit of their game. When the worship of the calves was set up in Israel the patrons of that idolatry, and sticklers for it, contrived by all possible arts and wiles to draw men into it and reconcile those to it that at first had a dread of it. Note, Those that allure and entice men to sin, however they may pretend friendship and goodwill, are to be looked upon as *snares and nets* to them, and *their hands as bands,* Eccl. 7:26. But to those whom they could not seduce into sin they were as a net and a snare to bring them into trouble. Some think it was their practice to set spies in the road, and particularly upon the mountains of Mizpah and Tabor, at the times of the solemn feasts at Jerusalem, to watch if any of their people who were piously affected went thither, and to inform against them, that they might be prosecuted for it, thus doing the devil's work, who disquiets those whom he cannot debauch. 2. They had been both very crafty and very cruel in carrying on their designs (*v.* 2): *The revolters are profound to make slaughter.* Note, Those who have themselves apostatized from the truths of God are often the most subtle and barbarous persecutors of those who still adhere to them. Nothing will serve them but to *make slaughter* (it is the blood of the saints that they thirst after): and with the serpent's sting they have his head; they are *profound* to do it. O the depth of *the depths of Satan,* of the wickedness of his agents, of those that have *deeply revolted!* Isa. 31:6. Now that which aggravated this was the many reproofs and warnings that had been given them: *Though I have been a rebuker of them all.* The prophet had been so, a reprover by office. He had many a time told them of the evil of their ways and doings, had dealt plainly *with them all,* and had not spared either the priests or the house of the king. God himself had been *a rebuker of them all* by their own consciences and by his providences. Note, Sins against reproof are doubly sinful, Prov. 29:1. 3. They had *committed whoredom,* had defiled their own bodies with fleshly lusts, had defiled their own souls with the worship of idols, *v.* 3. This God was a witness to, though secretly committed and artfully palliated. Nay, the piercing eye of God saw *the spirit of whoredom* that was *in the midst of them,* their secret inclination and disposition to those sins, the love they had to their sins, and the dominion their sins had over them, how much they were under the power of a *spirit of whoredom,* that *root of bitterness* which bore all this gall and wormwood, that corrupt and poisoned fountain. 4. They had no disposition at all to come into acquaintance and communion with God. The *spirit of whoredoms,* having *caused them to err* from him, keeps them wandering endlessly, *v.* 4. (1.) They *have not known the Lord,* nor desire to know him, but have rather declined, nay dreaded, the knowledge of him, for that would disturb them in their sinful ways. (2.) Therefore *they will not frame their doings to turn to their God,* by which it appeared that they did not know him aright. This intimates their obstinate persistence in their apostasy from God; they would not *turn to God,* though he was *their God,* theirs in covenant, by whose name they had been called, and whom they were bound to *serve.* They would not return to the worship of him, from which they had turned aside. Nay, *they would not frame their doings to turn to God.* They would not *consider their ways,* nor dispose themselves into a serious temper, nor apply their minds to think of those things that would bring them to God. It is true we cannot by our own power, without the special grace of God, turn to him; but we may by the due improvement of our faculties, and the common aids of his Spirit, *frame our doings* to turn to him. Those that will not do this, that *prepare not their hearts to seek the Lord* (2 Chr. 12:14), owe it to themselves that they are not turned; they die because they will die; and to those that will do this further grace shall not be wanting. (5.) They were guilty of notorious arrogancy, and insolence in sin (*v.* 5): *The pride of Israel doth testify to his face,* doth witness against him that he is a rebel to God and his government. The *spirit of whoredoms* which was *in the midst of them* showed itself in the gaiety and gaudiness of their worship, as a harlot is known by her attire, Prov. 7:10. The wantonness of her dress testifies to her face that she is not a modest woman. Or their pride in confronting the prophets God sent them and the message they brought (Jer. 43:2), or a haughty scornful conduct towards their brethren and those that were under them, *witnessed against* them that they were not God's people and justified God in all the humbling judgments he brought upon them. His pride testifies *in his face;* so some read it, agreeing with Isa. 3:9, *The show of their countenance doth witness against them.* They have that *proud look* which *the Lord hates.* (6.) They departed from God to idols, and bred up their children in idolatry (*v.* 7): *They have dealt treacherously against the Lord,* as a wife, who, in contempt of the marriage covenant, forsakes her husband, and lives in adultery with another. Thus those who are guilty of spiritual idolatry, whose god is their money, whose god is their belly, *deal treacherously against the Lord;* they violate their engagements to him and frustrate his expectations from them. Note, Wilful sinners are treacherous dealers. *They have begotten strange children,* that is, their children which they have begotten are estranged from God, and trained up in a false way of worship; they are a spurious brood, as *children of fornication* (Jn. 8:41), whom God will disown. Note, Those deal treacherously with God indeed who not only turn from following him themselves but train up their children in wicked ways.

IV. Very sad things are made to be their doom. In general (*v.* 1), *"Judgment is towards you.* God is coming forth to contend with you, and to testify his displeasure against you for your sins." It is time to hearken when judgment is towards us. In particular,

1. They shall *fall in their iniquity.* This follows upon their *pride testifying to their face* (*v.* 5) *Therefore shall Israel and Ephraim fall in their iniquity.* Note, Pride will have a fall; it is the certain presage and forerunner of it. Those that exalt themselves shall be abased. The face in which pride testifies shall be filled with confusion. They shall not only fall, but fall in their iniquity, the saddest fall of any. Their pride kept them from repenting of their iniquity, and therefore they shall fall in it. Note, Those that are not humbled for their sins are likely to perish for ever in their sins. it is added, *Judah also shall fall with them* in her iniquity. As the ten tribes were carried captive into Assyria, for their idolatry, so the two tribes, in process of time, were carried into Babylon for following their bad example; but the former fell and were utterly cast down, the latter fell and were raised up again. Judah had the temple and priesthood, and yet these shall not secure them, but, if they sin with Israel and Ephraim, with them they shall fall.

2. They shall fall short of God's favour when they profess to seek it (*v.* 6): *They shall go with their flocks and with their herds to seek the Lord,* but in vain; *they shall not find him.* This seems to be spoken principally of Judah, when they fell into their iniquity, and when they fell in their iniquity. (1.) When they fell into their iniquity they *sought the Lord;* but they did not *seek him only,* and therefore he was not *found of them.* When they worshipped strange gods, yet they kept up the show and shadow of the worship of the true God; they went as usual, at the solemn feasts, *with their flocks and herds to seek the Lord;* but their hearts were not *upright with him,* because they were not *entire for him,* and therefore he would not accept them; for *then* only shall we find him when we *seek him with our whole heart,* not divided between God and Baal, Eze. 14:3. (2.) When they fell in their iniquity, or found themselves falling by it, they *sought the Lord;* but they did not seek him *early,* and therefore he will not be found of them. They shall see ruin coming upon them, and shall then, in their distress, flee to God, and think to make him their friend with burnt-offerings and sacrifices; but it will be too late then to turn away his wrath when *the decree has gone forth.* Even Josiah's reformation did not prevail to *turn away the wrath of God,* 2 Ki. 23:25, 26. Those that go *with their flocks and their herds* only to seek the Lord, and not with their hearts and souls, cannot expect to find him, for his favour is not to be purchased with *thousands of rams.* Nor shall those speed who do not seek the Lord *while he may be found,* for there is a time when he will not be found. They shall not find him, for he has withdrawn himself; he will not be enquired of by them, but will turn a deaf ear to their sacrifices. See how much it is our concern to seek God early, now while the accepted time is, and the day of salvation.

3. They and their portions shall all be swallowed up. They have *dealt treacherously against the Lord,* and have thought to strengthen themselves in it by their alliances with strange children; but *now shall a month devour them with their portions,* that is, their estates and inheritances, all those things which they have taken, and taken up with, as their portion; or by their *portions* is meant their idols, whom they chose for their portion instead of God. Note, Those that make an idol of the world, by taking it for their portion, will themselves perish with it. A *month* shall *devour* them, or eat them up — a certain time prefixed, and a short time. When God's judgments begin with them they shall soon make an end; one month will do their business. How much may a body be weakened by one month's sickness, or a kingdom wasted by one month's war! *Three shepherds* (says God) *I cut off in one month,* Zec. 11:8. Note, The judgments of God sometimes make quick work with a sinful people. A month devours more, and more portions, than many years can repair.

Verses 8–15

Here is, I. A loud alarm sounded, giving notice of judgments coming (*v.* 8): *Blow you the cornet in Gibeah* and *in Ramah,* two cities near together in the confines of the two kingdoms of Judah and Israel, Gibeah a frontier-town of the kingdom of Judah, Ramah of Israel; so that the warning is hereby sent into both kingdoms. *"Cry aloud at Beth-aven,* or Bethel, which place seems to be already seized upon by the enemy, and therefore the trumpet is not sounded there, but you hear the outcries of those that shout for mastery, mixed with theirs that are overcome." Let them *cry aloud, "After thee, O Benjamin!* comes the enemy. The tribe of Ephraim is already vanquished, and the enemy will be upon thy back, O Benjamin! in a little time; thy turn comes next. The cup of trembling shall go round." The prophet had described God's controversy with them as a trial at law (*ch.* 4:1); here he describes it as a trial by battle; and here also *when he judges he will overcome.* Let all therefore prepare to meet their God. He had before spoken of the judgments as certain; here he speaks of them as near; and, when they are apprehended as just at the door, they are very startling and awakening. The blowing of this cornet is explained, *v.* 9. *Among the tribes of Israel have I made known that which shall surely be,* that which is *true* or *certain,* so the word is. Note, The destruction of impenitent sinners is a thing which shall surely be; it is not mere talk, to frighten them, but it is an irrevocable sentence. And it is a mercy to us that it is *made known* to us, that we have timely warning given us of it, that we may *flee from the wrath to come.* It is the privilege of the tribes of Israel that, as they are told their duty, so they are told their danger, by the oracles of God committed to them.

II. The ground of God's controversy with them. 1. He has a quarrel with *the princes of Judah,* because they were daring leaders in sin, *v.* 10. They are *like those that remove the bound,* or the ancient land-marks. God has given them his law, to be a fence about his own property; but they have sacrilegiously broken through it, and set it aside; they have encroached even upon God's rights, have trampled upon the distinctions between good and evil, and the most sacred obligations of reason and equity, thinking, because they were princes, that they might do any thing, Quicquid libet, licet — Their will was a law. Or it may be understood of their invading the liberty and property of the subject for the advancing of the prerogative, which was like removing the ancient land-marks. Some have observed that the princes of Judah were more absolute, and assumed a more arbitrary power, than the princes of Israel did; now, for this, God has a controversy with them: *I will pour out my wrath upon them like water,* in great abundance, like the waters of the flood, which were poured upon the *giants* of the *old world,* for the violence which the earth was filled with through them, Gen. 6:13. Note, There are *bounds* which even princes themselves must not remove, bounds both of religion and justice, which they are limited by, and, if they break through them, they must know that there is a God above them that will call them to account for it. 2. He has a quarrel with the *people of Ephraim,* because they were sneaking followers in sin (*v.* 11): *He willingly walked after the commandment,* that is, the commandment of Jeroboam and the succeeding kings of Israel, who obliged all their subjects by a law to worship the calves at Dan and Bethel, and never to go up to Jerusalem to worship. This was *the commandment;* it was the law of the land, and backed with reasons of state; and the people not only walked after it in a blind implicit obedience to authority, but they willingly walked after it, from a secret antipathy they had to the worship of idols. Note, An easy compliance with the commandments of men that thwart the commandments of God ripens a people for ruin as much as any thing. And the punishment of the sequacious disobedience (if I may so call it) answers to the sin; for it is for this that *Ephraim is oppressed and broken in judgment,* has all his civil rights and liberties broken in upon and trodden down; and, (1.) It is just with God that it should be so, that those who betray God's property should lose their own, that those who subject their consciences to an infallible judge, and an arbitrary power, should have enough of both. (2.) There is a natural tendency in the thing itself towards it. *Those* that *willingly walk after the commandment,* even when it walks contrary to the command of God, will find the commandment an encroaching thing, and that the more power is given it the more it will claim. Note, Nothing gives greater advantage to a mastiff-like tyranny, that is fierce and furious, than a spaniel-like submission, that is fawning and flattering. Thus is *Ephraim oppressed and broken in judgment,* that is, he is wronged under a face and colour of right. Note, It is a sad and sore judgment upon any people to be oppressed under pretence of having justice done them. This explains the threatening *v.* 9, *Ephraim shall be desolate in the day of rebuke.* Note, Daring sinners must expect that a day of rebuke will come, and such a day of rebuke as will make them desolate, will deprive them of the comfort of all they have and all they hope for.

III. The different methods that God would take both with Judah and Ephraim, sometimes one method and sometimes the other, and sometimes both together, or rather by which, first the one and then the other, he would advance towards their complete ruin.

1. He would begin with less judgments, which should sometimes work silently and insensibly (*v.* 12): *I will be* (that is, my providences shall be) *unto Ephraim as a moth;* nay (as it might better be supplied), they *are unto Ephraim as a moth,* for it is such *a sickness* as Ephraim now sees, *v.* 13. Note, The judgments of God are sometimes to a sinful people *as a moth,* and *as rottenness,* or as *a worm.* The former signifies the little animals that breed in clothes, the latter those that breed in wood; as these consume the clothes and the wood, so shall the judgments of God consume them. (1.) Silently, so as not to make any noise in the world, nay, so as they themselves shall not be sensible of it; they shall think themselves safe and thriving, but, when they come to look more narrowly into their state, shall find themselves wasting and decaying. (2.) Slowly, and with long delays and intervals, that he may give them *space to repent.* Many a nation, as well as many a person, in the prime of its time, dies of a consumption. (3.) Gradually. God comes upon sinners with less judgments, so to prevent greater,

if they will be wise and take warning; he comes upon them step by step, to show he is not willing that they should perish. (4.) The moth breeds in the clothes, and the worm or rottenness in the wood; thus sinners are consumed by a fire of their own kindling.

2. When it appeared that those had not done their work he would come upon them with greater (*v.* 14): *I will be unto Ephraim as a lion, and to the house of Judah as a young lion,* though Judah is himself, in Jacob's blessing, a *lion's whelp.* Lest any should think his power weakened, because he was said to be *as a moth* to them, he says that he will now be as *a lion* to them, not only to frighten them with his roaring, but to pull them to pieces. Note, If less judgments prevail not to do their work, it may be expected that God will send greater. *Christ* is sometimes a lion of the tribe of Judah, here he is a lion against that tribe. See what God will do to a people that are secure in sin: *Even I will tear.* He seems to glory in it, as his prerogative, to be able to *destroy,* as the *alone lawgiver,* Jam. 4:12. *"I, even I,* will take the work into my own hands; I *say it* that will *do it."* There is a more immediate work of God in some judgments than in others. *I will tear, and go away.* He will go away, (1.) As not fearing them; he will go away in state, and with a majestic face, as the lion from his prey. (2.) As not helping them. If God tear by afflicting providences, and yet by his graces and comforts stays with us, it is well enough; but our condition is sad indeed if he *tear* and *go away,* if, when he deprives us of our creature comforts, he does himself depart from us. When he goes away he will take away all that is valuable and dear, for, when God goes, all good goes along with him. He will take away, *and none shall rescue him,* as the prey cannot be rescued from the lion, Mic. 5:8. Note, None can be delivered out of the hands of God's justice but those that are delivered into the hands of his grace. It is in vain for a man to strive with his Maker.

IV. The different effects of those different methods. 1. When God contended with them by less judgments they neglected him, and sought to creatures for relief, but sought in vain, *v.* 13. When God was to them *as a moth,* and *as rottenness,* they perceived *their sickness* and *their wound;* after a while they found themselves going down the hill, and that they were behind-hand in their affairs, their estate was sensibly decaying, and then they sent *to the Assyrian,* to come in to their assistance, made their court to king Jareb, which some think, was one of the names of Pul, or Tiglathpileser, kings of Assyria, to whom both Israel and Judah applied for relief in their distress, hoping by an alliance with them to repair and re-establish their declining interests. Note, Carnal hearts, in time of trouble, see their sickness and see their wound, but do not see the sin that is the cause of it, nor will be brought to acknowledge that, no, nor to acknowledge the hand of God, his *mighty hand,* much less his righteous hand, in their trouble; and therefore, instead of going the next way to the Creator, who could relieve them, they take a great deal of pains to go about to creatures, who can do them no service. Those who repent not that they have offended God by their sins are loth to be beholden to him in their afflictions, but would rather seek relief any where than with him. And what is the consequence? *Yet could he not heal you, nor cure you of your wound.* Note, Those who neglect God, and seek to creatures for help, will certainly be disappointed; those who depend upon them for support will find them, not *foundations,* but *broken reeds;* those who depend upon them for supply will find them, not *fountains,* but *broken cisterns;* those who depend upon them for comfort and a cure will find them *miserable comforters,* and *physicians of no value.* The kings of Assyria, whom Judah and Israel sought unto, *distressed them* and *helped them not,* 2 Chr. 28:16, 28. Some make king *Jareb* to signify the *great, potent,* or *magnificent king,* for they built much upon his power; others *the king that will plead,* or *should plead,* for they built much upon his wisdom and eloquence, and in his interesting himself in their affairs. They had sent him *a present* (*ch.* 10:6), a good fee, and, having so retained him of counsel for them, they doubted not of his fidelity to them; but he deceived them, as an arm of flesh does those that trust in it, Jer. 17:5, 6. 2. When, to convince them of their folly, God brought greater judgments upon them, then they would at length be forced to apply to him, *v.* 15. When he has *torn* as a *lion,* (1.) He will leave them: *I will go and return to my place,* to heaven, or to the mercy-seat, the throne of grace, which is his glory. When God punishes sinners he *comes out of his place* (Isa. 26:21); but, when he designs them favour, he *returns to his place,* where he *waits to be gracious,* upon their submission. Or he will *return to his place* when he has corrected them, as not regarding them, hiding his face from them, and not taking notice of their troubles or prayers; and this for their further humiliation, till they are qualified in some measure for the returns of his favour. (2.) He will at length work upon them, and bring them home to himself, by their afflictions, which is the thing he waits for; and then he will no longer withdraw from them. Two things are here mentioned as instances of their return: — [1.] Their penitent confession of sin: *Till they acknowledge their offence;* marg. *Till they be guilty,* that is, till they be sensible of their guilt, and be brought to own it, and humble themselves before God for it. Note, When men begin to complain more of their sins than of their afflictions then there begins to be some hope of them; and this is that which God requires of us, when we are under his correcting hand, that we own ourselves in a fault and justly corrected. [2.] Their humble petition for the favour of God: Till they *seek my face,* which, it may be expected, they will do when they are brought to the last extremity, and they have tried other helpers in vain. *In their affliction they will seek me early,* that is, diligently and earnestly, and with great importunity; and if they seek him thus, and be sincere in it, though it might be called seeking him late, because it was long ere they were brought to it, yet it is not too late, nay, he is pleased to call it seeking him early, so willing is he to make the best of true penitents in their return to him. Note, When we are under the convictions of sin, and the corrections of the rod, our business is to seek God's face; we must desire the knowledge of him, and an acquaintance with him, that he may manifest himself to us, and for us, in token of his being at peace with us. And it may reasonably be expected that affliction will bring those to God that had long gone astray from him, and kept at a distance. *Therefore* God for a time turns away from us, that he may turn us to himself, and then return to us. *Is any among you afflicted? Let him pray.*

CHAPTER 6

The closing words of the foregoing chapter gave us some hopes that God and his Israel, notwithstanding their sins and his wrath, might yet be happily brought together again, that they would seek him and he would be found of them; now this chapter carries that matter further, and some join the beginning of this chapter with the end of that, "They will seek me early," saying, "Come and let us return." But God doth again complain of the wickedness of this people; for, though some did repent and reform, the greater part continued obstinate. Observe, I. Their resolution to return to God, and the comforts wherewith they encourage themselves in their return (*v.* 1–3). II. The instability of many of them in their professions and promises of repentance, and the severe course which God therefore took with them (*v.* 4, 5). III. The covenant God made with them, and his expectations from them (*v.* 6); their violation of that covenant and frustrating those expectations (*v.* 7–11).

Verses 1–3

These may be taken either as the words of the prophet to the people, calling them to repentance, or as the words of the people to one another, exciting and encouraging one another to *seek the Lord,* and to humble themselves before him, in hopes of finding mercy with him. God had said, *In their affliction they will seek me;* now the prophet, and the good people his friends, would strike while the iron was hot, and set in with the convictions their neighbours seemed to be under. Note, Those who are disposed to turn to God themselves should do all they can to excite, and engage, and encourage others to return to him. Observe,

I. What it is they engage to do: *"Come, and let us return to the Lord, v.* 1. Let us go no more to the Assyrian, nor send to king Jareb; we have had enough of that. But let us *return to the Lord,* return to the worship of him from our idolatries, and to our hope in him from all our confidences in the creature." Note, It is the great concern of those who have revolted from God to return to him. And those who have gone from him by consent, and in a body, drawing one another to sin, should by consent, and in a body, return to him, which will be for his glory and their mutual edification.

II. What inducements and encouragements to do this they fasten upon, to stir up one another with.

1. The experience they had had of his displeasure: "Let us return to him, for *he has torn, he has smitten.* We have been torn, and it was he that tore us; we have been smitten, and it was he that smote us. *Therefore* let us return to him, because it is for our revolts from him that he has torn and smitten us in anger, and we cannot expect that he should be reconciled to us till we return to him; and for this end he has afflicted us thus, that we might be wrought upon to return to him. His hand will be stretched out still against us if the people *turn not to him that smites them,"* Isa. 9:12, 13. Note, The consideration of the judgments of God upon us and our land, especially when they are tearing judgments, should awaken us to return to God by repentance, and prayer, and reformation.

2. The expectation they had of his favour: "He that has torn will *heal us,* he that has smitten will *bind us up,"* as the skilful surgeon with a tender hand binds up the broken bone or bleeding wound. Note, The same providence of God that afflicts his people relieves them, and the same Spirit of God that convinces the saints comforts them; that which is first *a Spirit of bondage* is afterwards *a Spirit of adoption.* This is an acknowledgement of the power of God (he can heal though we be ever so ill torn), and of his mercy (he will do it); nay, *therefore* he has torn that he may heal. Some think this points particularly to the return of the Jews out of Babylon, when they sought the Lord, and joined themselves to him, in the prospect of his gracious return to them in a way of mercy. Note, It will be of great use to us, both for our support under our afflictions and for our encouragement in our repentance, to keep up good thoughts of God and of his purposes and designs concerning us. Now this favour of God which they are here in expectation of is described in several instances: —

(1.) They promise themselves that their deliverance out of their troubles should be to them as *life from the dead* (*v.* 2): *"After two days he will revive us* (that is, in a short time, in a day or two), *and the third day,* when it is expected that the dead body should putrefy and corrupt, and be buried *out of our sight,* then will he *raise us up,* and *we shall live in his sight,* we shall see his face with comfort and it shall be reviving to us. Though he *forsake* for *a small moment,* he will *gather* with *everlasting kindness."* Note, The people of God may not only be torn and smitten, but left for dead, and may lie so a great while; but they shall not always lie so, nor shall they long lie so; God will in a little time revive them; and the assurance given them of this should engage them to return and adhere to him. But this seems to have a further reference to the resurrection of Jesus Christ; and the time limited is expressed by *two days* and the *third day,* that it may be a type and figure of Christ's rising the *third day,* which he is said to do *according to the scriptures,* according to this scripture; for all the prophets testified of *the sufferings of Christ and the glory that should follow.* Let us see and admire the wisdom and goodness of God, in ordering the prophet's words so that when he foretold the deliverance of the church out of her troubles he should at the same time point out our salvation by Christ, which other salvations were both figures and fruits of; and, though they might not be aware of this mystery in the words, yet now that they are fulfilled in the letter of them in the resurrection of Christ it is a confirmation to our faith that *this is he that should come,* and we are to *look for no other.* And it is every way suitable that a prophecy of Christ's rising should be thus expressed, "He will raise *us up,* and *we* shall live," for Christ rose as the first-fruits, and we revive with him, we live through him; he rose for our justification, and all believers are said to be *risen with Christ.* See Isa. 26:19. And it would serve for a comfort to the church then, and an assurance that God would raise them out of their low estate, for in his fulness of time he would raise his Son from the grave, who would be the life and glory of his people Israel. Note, A regard by faith to a rising Christ is a great support to a suffering Christian, and gives abundant encouragement to a repenting returning sinner; for he has said, *Because I live, you shall live also.*

(2.) That then they shall improve in the knowledge of God (*v.* 3): *Then shall we know, if we follow on to know, the Lord. Then,* when God returns in mercy to his people and designs favour for them, he will, as a pledge and fruit of his favour, give them more of the knowledge of himself; the earth shall be *full of that knowledge*, Isa. 11:9. *Knowledge shall be increased*, Dan. 12:4. *All shall know God*, Jer. 31:34. *We shall know, we shall follow to know, the Lord*, (so the words are); and it may be taken as the fruit of Christ's resurrection, and the life we live in God's sight by him, that we shall have not only greater means of knowledge, but grace to improve in knowledge by those means. Note, When God designs mercy for a people he gives them *a heart to know him*, Jer. 24:7. Those that have *risen with Christ* have the spirit of wisdom and revelation given them. And if we understand our living in his sight, as the Chaldee paraphrast does, of the day of the resurrection of the dead, it fitly follows, *We shall know, we shall follow to know, the Lord;* for in that day we shall see him be perfected, and yet be eternally increasing. Or, taking it as we read it, *If we follow on to know,* we have here, [1.] A precious blessing promised: *Then shall we know,* shall *know the Lord*, then when *we return to God;* those that come to God shall be brought into an acquaintance with him. When we are designed to *live in his sight*, then he gives us to know him; for this is *life eternal to know God*, Jn. 17:3. [2.] The way and means of obtaining this blessing. We must *follow on to know* him. We must value and esteem the knowledge of God as the best knowledge, we must *cry after it*, and *dig for it* (Prov. 2:3, 4), must *seek and intermeddle with all wisdom* (Prov. 18:1), and must proceed in our enquiries after this knowledge and our endeavours to improve in it. And, if we do the prescribed duty, we have reason to expect the promised mercy, that we shall know more and more of God, and be at last perfect in this knowledge.

(3.) That then they shall abound in divine consolations: *His going forth is prepared as the morning,* that is, the returns of his favour, which he had withdrawn from us when he went and *returned to his place*. His out-goings again are prepared and secured to us as firmly as the return of the morning after a dark night, and we expect it, as those do that *wait for the morning* after a long night, and are sure that it will come at the time appointed and will not fail; and the light of his countenance will be both welcome to us and growing upon us, unto the perfect day, as the light of the morning is. *He shall come to us*, and be welcome to us, *as the rain, as the latter and former rain unto the earth,* which refreshes it and makes it fruitful. Now this looks further than their deliverance out of captivity, and, no doubt, was to have its full accomplishment in Christ, and the grace of the gospel. The Old-Testament saints *followed on to know him,* earnestly looked for redemption in Jerusalem; and at length the out-goings of divine grace in him, in his going forth to visit this world, were [1.] As the morning to this earth when it is dark for he went forth as the *sun of righteousness*, and in him *the day-spring from on high visited us. His going forth was prepared as the morning,* for he came in the fulness of time; John Baptist was his fore-runner, nay, he was himself the *bright and morning star.* [2.] As the rain to this earth when it is *dry. He shall come down as the rain upon the mown grass,* Ps. 72:6. In him showers of blessings descend upon this world, which *give seed to the sower and bread to the eater,* Isa. 55:10. And the favour of God in Christ is what is said of the king's favour, *like the cloud of the latter rain,* Prov. 16:15. The grace of God in Christ is both the *latter and the former rain,* for by it the good work of our fruit-bearing is both begun and carried on.

Verses 4–11

Two things, two evil things, both Judah and Ephraim are here charged with, and justly accused of: —

I. That they were not firm to their own convictions, but were unsteady, *unstable as water, v.* 4, 5. *O Ephraim! what shall I do unto thee? O Judah! what shall I do unto thee?* This is a strange expression. Can Infinite Wisdom be at a loss what to do? Can it be nonplussed, or put upon taking new measures? By no means; but God speaks after the manner of men, to show how absurd and unreasonable they were, and how just his proceedings against them were. Let them not complain of him as harsh and severe in tearing them, and smiting them, as he has done; for what else should he do? What other course could he take with them? God had tried various methods with them (*What could*

have been done more to his vineyard than he had done? Isa. 5:4), and very loth he was to let things go to extremity; he reasons with himself (as *ch.* 11:9), *How shall I give thee up, Ephraim?* God would have done them good, but they were not qualified for it: *"What shall I do unto thee? What else can I do but cast thee off, when I cannot in honour save thee?"* Note, God never destroys sinners till he sees there is no other way with them. See here, 1. What their conduct was towards God: *Their goodness,* or *kindness,* was *as the morning cloud.* Some understand it of their kindness to themselves and their own souls, in their repentance; it is indeed mercy to ourselves to repent of our sins, but they soon retracted that kindness to themselves, undid it again, and wronged their own souls as much as ever. But it is rather to be taken for their piety and religion; what good appeared in them sometimes, it soon vanished and disappeared again, *as the morning cloud and the early dew.* Such was the goodness of Israel in Jehu's time, and of Judah in Hezekiah's and Josiah's time; it was soon gone. In time of drought the *morning-cloud* promises rain, and the *early dew* is some present refreshment to the earth; but the cloud is dispersed (and hypocrites are compared to *clouds without water,* Jude 12) and the dew does not soak into the ground, but is drawn back again into the air, and the earth is parched still. What shall he do with them? Shall he accept their goodness? No, for it *passes away;* and *factum non dicitur quod non perseverat — that which does not continue can scarcely be said to be done.* Note, That goodness will never be either pleasing to God or profitable to ourselves which is as the morning cloud and the early dew. When men promise fair and do not perform, when they begin well in religion and do not hold on, when they leave their first love and their first works, or, though they do not quite cast off religion, are yet unsteady, uneven, and inconstant in it, then is their *goodness as the morning cloud and the early dew.* 2. What course God had taken with them (*v.* 5): *"Therefore,* because they were so rough and ill-shapen, *I have hewn them by the prophets,* as timber or stone is hewn for use; *I have slain them by the words of my mouth."* What the prophets did was done by the word of God in their mouths, which never returned void. By it they thought themselves slain, were ready to say that the prophets killed them, or cut them to the heart when they dealt faithfully with them. (1.) The prophets hewed them by convictions of sin, endeavouring to cut off their transgressions from them. They were uneven in religion (*v.* 4), therefore God hewed them. The hearts of sinners are not only as stone, but as rough stone, which requires a great deal of pains to bring it into shape, or as knotty timber, that is not squared without a great deal of difficulty; ministers' work is to hew them, and God by the minister hews them, *for with the froward will he show himself froward.* And there are those whom ministers must rebuke sharply; every word should cut, and though the chips fly in the face of the workman, though the reproved fly in the face of the reprover and reckon him an enemy because he tells the truth, yet he goes on with his work. (2.) They slew them by the denunciations of wrath, foretelling that they should be slain, as Ezekiel is said to destroy the city when he prophesied of the destruction of it, Eze. 43:3. And God accomplished that which was foretold: *"I have slain them* by my judgments, according to the words of my mouth."* Note, The word of God will be the death either of the sin or of the sinner, a savour either of life unto life or of death unto death. Some read it, *"I have hewn the prophets, and slain them by the words of my mouth,* that is, I have employed them in laborious service for the people's good, which has wasted their strength; they have spent themselves, and hews away all their spirits, in their work, and in hazardous service, which has cost many of them their lives."* Note, Ministers are the tools which God makes use of in working upon people; and, though with many they labour in vain, yet God will reckon for the wearing out of his tools. (3.) God was hereby justified in the severest proceedings against them afterwards. His prophets had taken a great deal of pains with them, had admonished them of their sin and warned them of their danger, but the means used had not the desired effect; some good impressions perhaps were made for the present, but they wore off, and passed away as the morning cloud, and now they cannot charge God with severity if he bring upon them the miseries threat-

ened. The prophet turns to him and acknowledges, *Thy judgments are as the light that goes forth,* evidently just and righteous. Note, Though sinners be not reclaimed by the pains that ministers take with them, yet thereby God will be *justified when he speaks and clear when he judges.* See Mt. 11:17–19.

II. That they were not faithful to God's covenant with them, *v.* 6, 7. Here observe,

1. What the covenant was that God made with them, and upon what terms they should obtain his favour and be accepted of him (*v.* 6): *I desired mercy and not sacrifice* (that is, rather than sacrifice), and insisted upon *the knowledge of God more than* upon *burnt-offerings. Mercy* here is the same word which in *v.* 4 is rendered *goodness —* cheses — *piety, sanctity;* it is put for all practical religion; it is the same with *charity* in the New Testament, the reigning love of God and our neighbour, and this accompanied with and flowing from the *knowledge of God,* as he has revealed himself in his word, a firm belief that he is, and is the *rewarder of those that diligently seek him,* a good affection to divine things guided by a good judgment, which cannot but produce a very good conversation; this is that which God by his covenant requires, and not *sacrifice and offering.* This is fully explained, Jer. 7:22, 23. *I spoke not to your fathers concerning burnt-offerings* (that was the smallest of the matters I spoke to them of, and on which the least stress was laid), but *this I said, Obey my voice,* Mic. 6:6–8. To love God and our neighbour is *better than all burnt offering and sacrifice,* Mk. 12:33; Ps. 51:16, 17. Not but that sacrifice and offering were required, and to be paid, and had their use, and, when they were accompanied with mercy and the knowledge of God, were acceptable to him, but, without them, God regarded them not, he despised them, Isa. 1:10, 11. Perhaps this is mentioned here to show a difference between the God whom they deserted and the gods whom they went over to. The true God aimed at nothing but that they should be good men, and live good lives for their own good, and the ceremony of honouring him with sacrifices was one of the smallest matters of his law; whereas the false gods required that only; let their priests and altars be regaled with sacrifices and offerings, and the people might live as they listed. What fools were those then that left a God who aimed at giving his worshippers a new nature, for gods who aimed at nothing but making themselves a new name! It is mentioned likewise to show that God's controversy with them was not for the omission of sacrifices (*I will not reprove thee for them,* Ps. 50:8), but because there was no *justice, nor mercy,* nor *knowledge of God,* among them (*ch.* 4:1), and to teach us all that the *power of godliness* is the main thing God looks at and requires, and without it the *form of godliness* is of no avail. Serious piety in the heart and life is the *one thing needful,* and, separate from that, the performances of devotion, though ever so plausible, ever so costly, are of no account. Our Saviour quotes this to show that moral duties are to be preferred before rituals whenever they come in competition, and to justify himself in *eating with publicans and sinners,* because it was in mercy to the souls of men, and in healing on the sabbath day, because it was in mercy to the bodies of men, to which the ceremony of singularity in eating and the sabbath-rest must give way, Mt. 9:13; 12:7.

2. How little they had regarded this covenant, though it was so well ordered in all things, though they, and not God, would be the gainers by it. See here what came of it.

(1.) In general, they broke with God, and proved unfaithful; there were *good things committed* to them to keep, the jewels of mercy and piety, and the knowledge of God, in the cabinet of sacrifice and burnt-offering, but they betrayed their trust, kept the cabinet, but pawned the jewels for the gratification of a base lust, and this is that for which God has justly a quarrel with them (*v.* 7): *They, like men, have transgressed the covenant,* that covenant which God made with them; they have broken the conditions of it, and so forfeited the benefit of it. By casting off mercy and the knowledge of God, and other instances of disobedience, [1.] They had contracted the guilt of perjury and covenant-breaking; they were like men that *transgress a covenant* by which they had solemnly bound themselves, which is a thing that all the world cries out shame on; men that have done so deserve not again to be valued, or trusted, or dealt with. *"There,* in that thing, *they have dealt treacherously against me;* they have been perfidious, base, and false children, in whom is no faith, though I depended upon their being *children that would not lie.*" [2.] In this they had but acted like themselves, *like men,* who are generally false and fickle, and in whose nature (their corrupt nature) it is to deal treacherously; *all men are liars,* and they are like the rest of that degenerate race, *all gone aside,* Ps. 14:2, 3. They have *transgressed the covenant* like *men* (like the Gentiles that transgressed the covenant of nature), like *mean men* (the word here used is sometimes put for *men of low degree*); they have dealt deceitfully, like base men that have no sense of honour. [3.] Herein they trod in the steps of our first parents: *They, like Adam, have transgressed the covenant* (so it might very well be read); as he transgressed the covenant of innocency, so they transgressed the covenant of grace, so treacherously, so foolishly; *there* in paradise he violated his engagements to God, and there in Canaan, another paradise, they violated their engagements. And by their treacherous dealing they, like Adam, have ruined themselves and theirs. Note, Sin is so much the worse the more there is in it of the *similitude of Adam's transgression,* Rom. 5:14. [4.] Low thoughts of God and of his authority and favour were at the bottom of all this; for so some read it: *They have transgressed the covenant, as of a man,* as if it had been but the covenant of a man, that stood upon even ground with them, as if the commands of the covenant were but like those of a man like themselves, and the kindness conveyed by it no more valuable than that of a man. There is something sacred and binding in *a man's covenant* (as the apostle shows, Gal. 3:15), but much more in the covenant of God, which yet they made small account of; and *there* in that covenant they *dealt treacherously,* promised fair, but performed nothing. Dealing treacherously with God is here called dealing treacherously against him, for it is both an affront and an opposition. Deserters are traitors, and will be so treated; the revolting heart is a rebellious heart.

(2.) Some particular instances of their treachery are here given: *There they dealt treacherously,* that is, in the places hereafter named [1.] Look on the other side Jordan, to the country which lay most exposed to the insults of the neighbouring nations, and where therefore the people were concerned to keep themselves under the divine protection, and yet there you will find the most daring provocations of the divine Majesty, *v.* 8. Gilead, which lay in the lot of Gad and the half tribe of Manasseh, was *a city of the workers of iniquity.* Wickedness was the trade that was driven there; the country was called *Gilead,* but it was all called a *city,* because they were all as it were incorporated in one society of rebels against God. Or (as most think) Ramoth Gilead is the city here meant, one of the three cities of refuge on the other side Jordan, and a Levites' city; the inhabitants of it, though of the sacred tribe, were *workers of iniquity,* contrived it, and practised it. Note, It is bad indeed when a Levites' city is *a city of those that work iniquity,* when those that are to preach good doctrine live bad lives. Particularly it is *polluted with blood,* as if that were a sin which the wicked Levites were in a special manner guilty of. In popish countries the clergy are observed to be the most bloody persecutors. Or, as it was a *city of refuge,* by abusing the power it had to judge of murders it became *polluted with blood.* They would, for a bribe, protect those that were guilty of wilful murder, whom they ought to have put to death, and would deliver those to the avenger of blood who were guilty but of chance-medley, if they were poor and had nothing to give them; and both these ways they were *polluted with blood.* Note, Blood defiles the land where it is shed, and where no inquisition is made or no vengeance taken for it. See how the best institutions, that are ever so well designed to keep the balance even between justice and mercy, are capable of being abused and perverted to the manifest prejudice and violation of both. [2.] Look among those whose business it was to minister in holy things, and they were as bad as the worst and as vile as the vilest (*v.* 9): *The company of priests* are so, not here and there one that is the scandal of his order, but the whole order and body of them, the *priests* go all one way *by consent, with one shoulder* (as the word is), one and all; and they make one another worse, more daring, and fierce, and impudent, in sin, more crafty and more cruel. A *company of priests* will say and do that in conspiracy which none of them would dare to say or do singly. The *companies of priests* were as *troops of robbers,* as *banditti,* or gangs of highwaymen, that cut men's throats to get their money. *First,* They were cruel and blood-thirsty. They *murder* those that they have a pique against, or that stand in their way; nothing less will satisfy them. *Secondly,* They were cunning. They *laid wait* for men, that they might have a fair opportunity to compass their mischievous malicious designs; thus the company of priests laid wait for Christ to take him, saying, *Not on the feast-day. Thirdly,* They were concurring as one man: *They murder in the way;* in the highway, where travellers should be safe, there *they murder by consent,* aiding and abetting one another in it. See how unanimous wicked people are in doing mischief; and should not good people be so then in doing good? *They murder in the way to Shechem* (so the margin reads it, as a proper name) such as were going to Jerusalem (for that way Shechem lay) to worship. Or *in the way to Shechem* (some think) means in the same manner that their father Levi, with Simeon his brother, murdered the Shechemites (Gen. 34), by fraud and deceit; and some understand it of their destroying the souls of men by drawing them to sin. *Fourthly,* They did it with contrivance: *They commit lewdness;* the word signifies such wickedness as is committed with deliberation, and of malice prepense, as we say. The more there is of device and design in sin the worse it is. [3.] Look into the body of the people, take a view of the whole house of Israel, and they are all alike (*v.* 10): *I have seen a horrible thing in the house of Israel,* and, though it be ever so artfully managed, God discovers it, and will discover it to them; and who can deny that which God himself says that he has seen? *There is the whoredom of Ephraim,* both corporal and spiritual whoredom; there it is too plain to be denied. Note, The sin of sinners, especially sinners of the house of Israel, has enough in it to make them tremble, for it is a horrible thing, it is amazing, and it is threatening, enough to make them blush, for Israel is thereby defiled and rendered odious in the sight of God. [4.] Look into Judah, and you find them sharing with Israel (*v.* 11): *Also, O Judah! he has set a harvest for thee;* thou must be reckoned with as well as Ephraim; thou art ripe for destruction too, and the time, even the set time, of thy destruction is hastening on, when thou that hast *ploughed iniquity,* and *sown wickedness,* shalt *reap the same.* The general judgment is compared to *a harvest* (Mt. 13:39), so are particular judgments, Joel 3:13; Rev. 14:15. I have appointed a time to call thee to account, even *when I returned the captivity of my people,* that is, when those captives of Judah which were taken by the men of Israel were restored, in obedience to the command of God sent them by Oded the prophet, 2 Chr. 28:8–15. When God spared them that time he *set them a harvest,* that is, he designed to reckon with them another time for all together. Note, Preservations from present judgments, if a good use be not made of them, are but reservations for greater judgments.

CHAPTER 7

In this chapter we have, I. A general charge drawn up against Israel for those high crimes and misdemeanors by which they had obstructed the course of God's favours to them (*v.* 1, 2). II. A particular accusation, 1. Of the court — the king, princes, and judges (*v.* 3–7). 2. Of the country. Ephraim is here charged with conforming to the nations (*v.* 8), senselessness and stupidity under the judgments of God (*v.* 9–11), ingratitude to God for his mercies (*v.* 13), incorrigibleness under his judgments (*v.* 14), contempt of God (*v.* 15), and hypocrisy in their pretences to return to him (*v.* 16). They are also threatened with a severe chastisement, which shall humble them (*v.* 12), and, if that prevail not, then with an utter destruction (*v.* 13), particularly their princes (*v.* 16).

Verses 1–7

Some take away the last words of the foregoing chapter, and make them the beginning of this: *"When I returned,* or *would have returned, the captivity of my people,* when I was about to come towards them in ways of mercy, even *when I would have healed Israel, then the iniquity of Ephraim* (the country and common people) *was discovered, and the wickedness of Samaria,* the court and the chief city." Now, in these verses, we may observe,

I. A general idea given of the present state of Israel, *v.* 1, 2. See how the case now stood with them.

1. God graciously designed to do well for them: *I would have healed Israel.* Israel were sick and wounded; their disease was dangerous and malignant, and likely to be fatal, Isa. 1:6. But God offered to be their physician, to undertake the cure, and there was balm in Gilead sufficient to recover the health of the daughter of his people; their case was bad, but it was not desperate, nay, it was hopeful, when God *would have healed Israel.* (1.) He would have reformed them, would have separated between them and their sins, would have purged out the corruptions that were among them, by his laws and prophets. (2.) He would have delivered them out of their troubles, and restored to them their peace and prosperity. Several healing attempts were made, and their declining state seemed sometimes to be in a hopeful way of recovery; but their own folly put them back again. Note, If sinful miserable souls be not healed and helped, but perish in their sin and misery, they cannot lay the blame on God, for he both could and *would have healed them;* he offered to take the ruin under his hand. And there are some special seasons when God manifests his readiness to heal a distempered church and nation, now and then a hopeful crisis, which, if carefully watched and improved, might, even when the case is very bad, turn the scale for life and health.

2. They stood in their own light and put a bar in their own door. When God *would have healed them,* when they bade fair for reformation and peace, then their *iniquity* was *discovered* and their *wickedness,* which stopped that current of God's favours, and undid all again. (1.) *Then,* when their case came to be examined and enquired into, in order to their cure, that wickedness which had been concealed and palliated was *found out;* not that it was ever hid from God, but he speaks after the manner of men; as a surgeon, when he probes a wound in order to the cure of it and finds that it touches the vitals and is incurable, goes no further in his endeavour to cure it, so, when God *came down to see* the case of Israel (as the expression is, Gen. 18:21), with kind intentions towards them, he found their wickedness so very flagrant, and them so hardened in it, so impudent and impenitent, that he could not in honour show them the favour he designed them. Note, Sinners are not healed because they would not be healed. Christ *would have gathered* them, and they *would not.* (2.) *Then,* when some endeavours were used to reform and reclaim them, that wickedness which had been restrained and kept under *broke out;* and from God's steps towards the healing of them they took occasion to be so much the more provoking. When endeavours were used to reform them vice grew more impetuous, more outrageous, and swelled so much the higher, as a stream when it is damned up. When they began to prosper they grew more proud, wanton, and secure, and so stopped the progress of their cure. Note, It is sin that turns away good things from us when they are coming towards us; and it is the folly and ruin of multitudes that, when God would do well for them, they do ill for themselves. And what was it that did them this mischief? In one word, *they commit falsehood;* they worship idols (so some), defraud one another (so others), or, rather, they dissemble with God in their professions of repentance and regard to him. They say that they are desirous to be healed by him, and, in order to that, willing to be ruled by him; but they *lie unto him with their mouth and flatter him with their tongue.*

3. A practical disbelief of God's omniscience and government was at the bottom of all their wickedness (*v.* 2): *"They consider not in their hearts,* they never say it to their own hearts, never think of this, *that I remember all their wickedness."* As if God could not see it, though he is all eye, or did not heed it, though his name is Jealous, or had forgotten it, though he is an eternal mind that can never be unmindful, or would not reckon for it, though he is the *Judge of heaven and earth.* This is the sinner's atheism; as good say that there is *no God* as say that he is either ignorant or forgetful, that there is *none that judges in the earth* as that he remembers not the things he is to give judgment upon. It is a high affront they put upon God; it is a damning cheat they put upon themselves; they say, *The Lord shall not see,* Ps. 94:7. They cannot but know that *God remembers all their works;* they have been told it many a time; nay, if you ask them, they cannot but own it, and yet they do not *consider it;* they do not think of it when they should, and with application to themselves and their own works, else they would not, they durst not, do as they do. But the time will come when those who thus deceive themselves shall be undeceived: *"Now their own doings have beset them about,* that is, they have come

at length to such a pitch of wickedness that their sins appear on every side of them; all their neighbours see how bad they are, and can they think that God does not see it?" Or, rather, "The punishment of their doings besets them about; they are surrounded and embarrassed with troubles, so that they cannot get out, by which it appears that the sins they smart for are *before my face,* not only that I have seen them, but that I am displeased at them;" for, till God by pardoning our sins has cast them behind his back, they are still before his face. Note, Sooner or later, God will convince those who do not now consider it that he *remembers all their works.*

4. God had begun to contend with them by his judgments, in earnest of what was further coming: *The thief comes in, and the troop of robbers spoils without.* Some take this as an instance of their wickedness, that they robbed and spoiled one another. *Nec hospes ab hospite tutus — The host and the guest stand in fear of each other.* It seems rather to be a punishment of their sin; they were infested with secret thieves among themselves, that robbed their houses and shops and picked their pockets, and *troops of robbers,* foreign invaders, that with open violence *spoiled abroad;* so far was Israel from being healed that they had fresh wounds given them daily by robbers and spoilers; and all this the effect of sin, all to punish them for robbing God, Isa. 42:24; Mal. 3:8, 11.

II. A particular account of the sins of the court, of the king and princes, and those about them, and the tokens of God's displeasure that they were under for them.

1. Their king and princes were pleased with the wickedness and profaneness of their subjects, who were emboldened thereby to be so much them ore wicked (*v.* 3): *They make the king and princes glad with their wickedness.* It pleased them to see the people conform to their wicked laws and examples, in the worship of their idols, and other instances of impiety and immorality, and to hear them flatter and applaud them in their wicked ways. When Herod saw that his wickedness pleased the people he proceeded further in it, much more will the people do so when they see that it pleases the prince, Acts 12:3. Particularly, they made them glad *with their lies,* with the lying praises with which they crowned the favourites of the prince and the lying calumnies and censures with which they blackened those whom they knew the princes had a dislike to. Those who show themselves pleased with slanders and ill-natured stories shall never want those about them who will fill their ears with such stories. Prov. 29:12, *If a ruler hearken to lies, all his servants are wicked,* and will make him glad with their lies.

2. Drunkenness and revelling abound much at the court, *v.* 5. The *day of our king* was a merry day with them, either his birth-day or his inauguration-day, of which it is probable that they had an anniversary observation, or perhaps it was some holiday of his appointing, which was therefore called *his day;* on that day the princes met to drink the king's health, and got him among them, to be merry, and *made him sick with bottles of wine.* It should seem the king did not ordinarily drink to excess, but he was not upon a high day brought to it by the artifices of the princes, tempted by the goodness of the wine, the gaiety of the company, or the healths they urged; and so little was he used to it that it *made him sick;* and it is justly charged as a crime, as *crimen laesae majestatis — treason,* upon those who thus imposed upon him and *made him sick;* nor would it serve for an excuse that it was *the day of their king,* but was rather an aggravation of the crime, that, whey they pretended to do him honour, they dishonoured him to the highest degree. If it is a great affront and injury to a common person to make him drunk, and there is a woe to those that do it (Hab. 2:15), much more to a crowned head; for the greater any man's dignity is the greater disgrace it is to him to be drunk. *It is not for kings, O Lemuel! it is not for kings, to drink wine,* Prov. 31:4, 5. See what a prejudice the sin of drunkenness is to a man, to a king. (1.) In his health; it *made him sick.* It is a force upon nature; and strange it is by what charms men, otherwise rational enough, can be drawn to that which besides the offence it gives to God, and the damage it does to their spiritual and eternal welfare, is a present disorder and distemper to their own bodies. (2.) In his honour; for, when he was thus intoxicated, he *stretched out his hand with scorners;* then he that was entrusted with the government of a kingdom lost the government of himself, and so far forgot, [1.] The dignity of a king that he made himself familiar with players and buffoons, and those whose company was a scandal. [2.] The duty of a king that he joined in confederacy with atheists, and the profane scoffers at religion, whom he ought to have silenced and put to shame; he *sat in the seat of the scornful,* of those that had arrived at the highest pitch of impiety; he struck in with them, said as they said, did as they did, and exerted his power, and *stretched forth the hand* of his government, in concurrence with them. Goodness and good men are often made *the song of the drunkards* (Ps. 69:12; 35:16); but *woe unto thee, O land!* when *thy king is such a child* as to *stretch forth his hand* with those that make them so, Eccl. 10:16.

3. Adultery and uncleanness prevailed much among the courtiers. This is spoken of *v.* 4, 6, 7, and the charge of drunkenness comes in in the midst of this article; for wine is oil to the fire of lust, Prov. 23:33. Those that are inflamed with fleshly lusts, that are *adulterers* (*v.* 4), are here again and again compared to an oven heated by the baker (*v.* 4): *They have made ready their heart like an oven* (*v.* 6); *they are all hot as an oven, v.* 7. Note, [1.] An unclean heart is like an oven heated; and the unclean lusts and affections of it are as the fuel that makes it hot. It is an inward fire, it keeps the heat within itself; so adulterers and fornicators secretly *burn in lust,* as the expression is, Rom. 1:27. The heat of the oven is an intense heat, especially as it is here described; he that heats it *stirs up* the fire, and *ceases not from raising* it up, till the bread is ready to be put in, being *kneaded* and *leavened,* all which only signifies that they are like an oven when it is at the hottest; nay, when it is *too hot for the baker* (so the learned Dr. Pocock), when it is *hotter than he would have it,* so that the raiser up of the fire ceases as long as while the dough that is kneaded is in the fermenting, that the heat may abate a little. Thus fiery hot are the lusts of an unclean heart. (2.) The unclean wait for an opportunity to compass their wicked desires; having made ready their heart like an oven, they lie in wait to catch their prey. *The eye of the adulterer waits for the twilight,* Job 24:15. *Their baker sleeps all the night, but in the morning it burns as a flaming fire.* As the baker, having kindled a fire in his oven and laid sufficient fuel to it, goes to bed, and sleeps all night, and in the morning finds his oven well heated, and ready for his purpose, so these wicked people, when they have laid some wicked plot, and formed a design for the gratifying of some covetous, ambitious, revengeful, or unclean lusts, have their hearts so fully set in them to do evil that, though they may stifle them for a while, yet the fire of corrupt affections is still glowing within, and, as soon as ever there is an opportunity for it, their purposes which they have compassed and imagined break out into overt acts, as a fire flames out when it has vent given it. Thus *they are all hot as an oven.* Note, Lust in the heart is like fire in an oven, puts it into a heat; but the day is coming when those who thus make themselves like a fiery oven with their own vile affections, if that fire be not extinguished by divine grace, shall be made as a fiery oven by divine wrath (Ps. 21:9), when *the day comes* that shall *burn as an oven,* Mal. 4:1.

4. They resist the proper methods of reformation and redress: *They have devoured their judges,* those few good judges that were among them, that would have put out these fires with which they were heated; they fell foul upon them, and would not suffer them to do justice, but were ready to stone them, and perhaps did so; or, as some think, they provoked God to deprive them of the blessing of magistracy and to leave all in confusion: *All their kings* have *fallen* one after another, and their families with them, which could not but put the kingdom into confusion, crumble it into contending parties, and occasion a great deal of bloodshed. There are heart-burnings among them; they are *hot as an oven* with rage and malice at one another, and this occasions the *devouring of their judges,* the *falling* of their *kings. For the transgressions of a land many are the princes thereof,* Prov. 28:2. But in the midst of all this trouble and disorder *there is none among them that calls unto God,* that sees his hand stretched out against them in these judgments, and deprecates the strokes of it, none, or next to none, that stir up themselves to take hold on God, Isa. 64:7. Note, Those are not only heated with sin, but hardened in sin, that continue to live without prayer even when they are in trouble and distress.

Verses 8–16

Having seen how vicious and corrupt the court was, we now come to enquire how it is with the country, and we find that to be no better; and no marvel if the distemper that has so seized the head affect the whole body, so that there is *no soundness* in it; the *iniquity of Ephraim is discovered,* as well as *the sin of Samaria,* of the people as well as the princes, of which here are divers instances.

I. They were not peculiar and entire for God, as they should have been, *v.* 8. 1. They did not distinguish themselves from the heathen, as God had distinguished them: *Ephraim, he has mingled himself among the people,* has associated with them, and conformed himself to them, and has in a manner confounded himself with them and lost his character among them. God had said, *The people shall dwell alone;* but they *mingled themselves with the heathen and learned their works,* Ps. 16:35. They went up and down among the heathen, to beg help of one of them against another (so some); whereas, if they had kept close to God, they would not have needed the help of any of them. 2. They were not entirely devoted to God: *Ephraim is a cake not turned,* and so is burnt on one side and dough on the other side, but good for nothing on either side. As in Ahab's time, so now, they *halted between God and Baal;* sometimes they seemed zealous for God, but at other times as hot for Baal. Note, It is sad to think how many, who, after a sort, profess religion, are made up of contraries and inconsistencies, *as a cake not turned,* a constant self-contradiction, and always in one extreme or the other.

II. They were strangely insensible of the judgments of God, which they were under, and which threatened their ruin, *v.* 9. Observe, 1. The condition they were in. God was not to them, in his judgments, as *a moth* and as *rottenness;* they were silently and slowly drawing towards the ruin of their state partly by the encroachments of foreigners upon them: *Strangers have devoured his strength,* and eaten him up; they have wasted his wealth and treasure, lessened his numbers, and consumed the fruits of the earth. Some devoured them by open wars (as 2 Ki. 13:7, when the king of Syria made them *like the dust by threshing*), others by pretending treaties of peace and amity, in which they extorted abundance of wealth from them, and made them pay dearly for that which did them no good, but which afterwards they paid more dearly for, as 2 Ki. 16:9. This Ephraim got by mingling with the heathen, and suffering them to mingle with him; they devoured that which he rested upon and supported himself with. Note, Those that make not God their strength (Ps. 52:7) make that their strength which will soon be devoured by strangers. They were thus reduced partly by their own mal-administrations among themselves: *Yea, gray hairs are here and there upon him* (are *sprinkled* upon him, so the word is), that is, the sad symptoms of a decaying declining state, which is *waxing old* and *ready to vanish away,* and the effects of trouble and vexation. *Cura facit canos — Care turns gray.* The *almond-tree* does not as yet *flourish,* but it begins to turn colour, which speaks aloud to him that the *evil days* are coming, and the *years of which he shall say, I have no pleasure in them,* Eccl. 12:1, 5. 2. Their regardlessness of these warnings: *He knows it not;* he is not aware of the hand of God gone out against him; it is lifted up, but he *will not see,* Isa. 26:11. He does not know how near his ruin is, and takes no care to prevent it. Note, Stupidity under less judgments is a presage of greater coming.

III. They went on frowardly in their wicked ways, and were not reclaimed by the rebukes they were under (*v.* 10): *The pride of Israel* still *testifies to his face,* as it had done before (*ch.* 5:5); under humbling providences their hearts were still unhumbled, their lusts unmortified; and it is *through the pride of their countenance* that they *will not seek after God* (Ps. 10:4); they *do not return to the Lord their God* by repentance and reformation, *nor do they seek him* by faith and prayer *for all this;* though they suffer for going astray from him, though it can never be well with them till they come back to him, and though they have in vain sought to others for relief, yet they think not of applying to God.

IV. They were infatuated in their counsels, and took very wrong methods when they were in distress (*v.* 11, 12):

Ephraim is like a silly dove without heart. To be harmless as a dove, without gall, and not to hurt or injure others, is commendable; but to be sottish as a dove, without heart, that knows not how to defend herself and provide for her own safety, is a shame.

1. The silliness of this dove is, (1.) That she laments not the loss of her young that are taken from her, but will make her nest again in the same place; so they have their people carried away by the enemy, and are not affected with it, but continue their dealings with those that deal barbarously with them. (2.) That she is easily enticed by the bait into the net, and has *no heart,* no understanding, to discern her danger, as many other fowls do, Prov. 1:17. She *hastes to the snare, and knows not that it is for her life* (Prov. 7:23); so they were drawn into leagues with neighbouring nations that were their ruin. (3.) That, when she is frightened, she has not courage to stay in the dove-house, where she is safe, and under the careful protection of her owner, but flutters and hovers, seeking shelter first in one place, then in another, and thereby exposes herself so much the more; so this people, when they were in distress, sought not to God, did not fly *like the doves to their windows* where they might have been secured from all the birds of prey that struck at them, but threw themselves out of God's protection, and then *called to Egypt* to help them, and went in all haste *to Assyria,* to seek for that aid in vain which they might, by repentance and prayer, have found nearer home, in their God. Note, It is a silly senseless thing for those who have a God in heaven to trust to creatures for the refuge and relief which are to be had in him only; and those that do so are a *people of no understanding,* they are *without heart.* Now,

2. See what becomes of this *silly dove* (*v.* 12): *When they shall go* to Egypt and Assyria, *I will spread my net upon them.* Note, Those that will not abide by the mercy of God must expect to be pursued by the justice of God. Here, (1.) They are ensnared: *"I will spread my net upon them,* bring them into straits, that they may see their folly and think of returning." Note, It is common for those that go away from God to find snares where they expected shelters. (2.) They are humbled; they soar upward, proud of their foreign alliances and confiding in them; but *I will bring them down,* let them fly ever so high, *as the fowls of heaven,* that are shot flying. Note, God can and will *bring those down* that *exalt themselves as the eagle,* Obad. 3, 4. (3.) They are made to smart for their folly: *I will chastise them.* Note, The disappointments we meet with in the creature, when we put a confidence in it, are a necessary chastisement, or discipline, that we may learn to be wiser another time. (4.) In all this the scripture is fulfilled. It is *as their congregation has heard;* they have been many a time told by the word of God, read, and preached, and sung, in their religious assemblies, that *"vain is the help of man,* that *in the son of man there is no help;* they have heard both from the law and from the prophets what judgments God would bring upon them for their wickedness; and *as they have heard* now *they shall see,* they shall feel." Note, It concerns us to take notice of the word of God which we hear from time to time *in the congregation,* and to be governed by it, for we must shortly be judged by it; and it will justify God in the condemnation of sinners, and aggravate it to them, that they have had plain public warning given them of it; it is what their congregation has heard many a time, but they would not take warning. *"Son, remember* thou wast told what would come of it; and now thou seest they were not vain words." See Zec. 1:6.

V. They revolted from God and rebelled against him, notwithstanding the various methods he took to retain them in their allegiance, *v.* 13–15. Here observe,

1. How kindly and tenderly God had dealt with them, as a gracious sovereign towards a people dear unto him, and whose prosperity he had much at heart. He had *redeemed them* (*v.* 13), brought them, at first, out of the land of Egypt, and, since, delivered them out of many a distress. He had *bound and strengthened their arms, v.* 15. When their power was weakened, like an arm broken or out of joint, God set it again, and bound it, as a surgeon does a broken bone, to make it knit. God had given Israel victories over the Syrians (2 Ki. 13:16, 17), had *restored their coast* (2 Ki. 14:25, 26), had *girded them with strength for battle.* "Though *I have chastened* them" (so the margin reads it), "sometimes corrected them for their faults and thereby taught them, at other times *strengthened their arms* and relieved them, though I have used both fair means and foul to work upon them, it was all to no purpose; they were mercy-proof and judgment-proof."

2. How impudent their conduct had been towards him notwithstanding, which is described here for the conviction and humiliation of all those who have gone on in any way of wickedness, that they may see how exceedingly sinful their sin is, how heinous, how the God of heaven interprets it, how he resents it. (1.) He had courted them to him, and taken them into covenant with himself; but *they fled from him,* as if he had been their dangerous enemy who had always approved himself their faithful friend. They wandered from him, as the silly dove from her nest, for those who forsake God will find no rest nor settlement in the creature, but wander endlessly. They fled from God when they forsook the worship of him, and ran away from his service, and withdrew themselves from their allegiance to him. (2.) He had given them his laws, which were all holy, just, and good, by which he designed to keep them in the right way; but they *transgressed against him;* they sinned with a high hand and a stiff neck, wilfully and presumptuously (so the words signifies); they broke through the fence of the divine law, and therein thwarted the design of the divine love. (3.) He had made known his truths to them, and given them all possible proofs of the sincerity of his good-will to them; and yet they *spoke lies against him.* They set up false gods in competition with him; they denied his providence and power; thus they *belied the Lord,* Jer. *v.* 12. They rejected his messages sent them by his prophets, and said that they should have peace, though they went on in sin, directly against what he said. In their hypocritical professions of religion, shows of devotion, and promises of amendment, they lied to the Lord, which he took as lying against him. (4.) He was their rightful Lord and King, and had always ruled in Jacob with equity, and for the public good; and yet they *rebelled against him, v.* 14. They not only went off from him, but took up arms against him, would have deposed him if they could and set up another. (5.) He designed well for them, but they *imagined mischief against him, v.* 15. Sin is a mischievous thin; it is mischief against God, for it is treason against his crown and dignity; not that the sinners can do any thing to hurt their Creator (as one of the ancients observes on these words), but *what they can they do;* and it is so much the worse when it is not done by surprise, or through inadvertency, but designedly and with contrivance. The Jews have a saying, which Dr. Pocock quotes here, *The thoughts of transgression are worse than the transgression.* The designing of mischief is doing it, in God's account. *Compassing and imagining* the death of the king is treason by our law. Those that imagine an evil thing, though it prove a vain thing (Ps. 2:1), will be reckoned with for the imagination.

3. How they shall be punished for this (*v.* 13): *Woe unto them! for they have fled from me.* Note, Those who flee from God have woes sent after them, and are, without doubt, in a woeful case. The wrath of God is revealed from heaven against them; the word of God says, *Woe to them!* And observe what follows immediately, *Destruction unto them!* Note, The woes of God's word have real effects; destruction makes them good. The judgments of his hand shall verify the judgments of his mouth. Those whom he curses, and pronounces woeful, they are cursed, they are woeful indeed.

VI. Their shows of devotion and reformation were but shows, and in them they did but mock God.

1. They pretended devotion, but it was not sincere, *v.* 14. When the hand of God had gone forth against them they made some sort of application to him. *When he slew them, then they sought him. Lord, in trouble have they visited thee.* But it was all in hypocrisy. (1.) When they were under personal troubles, and called upon God in secret, they were not sincere in that: *They have not cried unto me with their heart, when they howled upon their beds.* When they were *chastened with pain upon their beds,* and the *multitude of their bones with strong pains,* perhaps ill of the wounds they received in war, they cried, and groaned, and complained in the forms of devotion, and, it may be, they used many good words, proper enough for the circumstances they were in; they cried, *God help us,* and, *Lord, look upon us.* But they did not *cry with their heart,* and therefore God reckons it as no crying to him. Moses is said to *cry unto God* when he spoke not a word, only his heart prayed with faith and fervency, Ex. 14:15. These made a great noise, and said a great deal, and yet did not *cry to God,* because their hearts were not *right with him,* not subjected to his will, devoted to his honour, nor employed in his service. To pray is to *lift up the soul* to God, this is the essence of prayer. If this be not done, *words,* though ever so well chosen, *are but wind;* but, if it be, it is an acceptable prayer, though the *groanings cannot be uttered.* Note, Those do not pray to God at all that do not pray *in the spirit.* Nay, God is so far from approving their prayer and accepting it that he calls it *howling.* Some think it intimates the *noisiness* of their prayers (they cried to God as they used to cry to Baal, when they thought he must be awakened), or the brutish violent passions which they vented in their prayers; they snarled at the stone, and howled under the whip, but regarded not the hand. Or it denotes that their hypocritical prayers were so far from being pleasing to God that they were offensive to him; he *was angry at their prayers.* The *songs of the temple shall be howlings,* Amos 8:3. God will be so far from pitying them that he will justly *laugh at their calamity,* who have so often laughed at his authority. (2.) When they were under public troubles, and met together to implore God's favour, in that also they were hypocritical; they *assembled themselves,* for fashion-sake, because it was usual to *call a solemn assembly* in times of general mourning, Zep. 2:1. But it was only to pray *for corn and wine* that they came together, which were the things they wanted, and feared being deprived of by the want of rain, the judgment they now laboured under. They did not pray for the favour or grace of God, that God would give them repentance, pardon their sins, and turn away his wrath, but only that he would not take away from them *their corn and wine.* Note, Carnal hearts, in their prayers to God, covet temporal mercies only, and dread and deprecate no other but temporal judgments, for they have no sense of any other.

2. They pretended reformation, but neither was that sincere, *v.* 16. Here is, (1.) The sin of Israel: *They return,* that is, they make as if they would return; they pretend to repent and amend their doings, but they make nothing of it; they do not come home to God nor return to their allegiance, whereas God says (Jer. 4:1), *If thou wilt return, O Israel! return to me;* do not only *turn towards me,* but *return to me.* This dissimulation of theirs makes them like a *deceitful bow,* which looks as if it were fit for business, and is bent and drawn accordingly, but, when strength comes to be laid to it, either the bow or the string breaks, and the arrow, instead of flying to the mark, drops at the archer's foot. Such were their essays towards repentance and reformation. (2.) The sin of the princes of Israel. That which is charged upon them is *the rage of their tongue,* quarrelling with God and his providence and with all about them when they are crossed. Princes think they may say what they will, and that it is their prerogative to huff and bluster, to curse and rail, and to call names at their pleasure, but let them know there is a God above them that will call them to an account for the *rage of their tongues* and make *their own tongues to fall upon them.* (3.) The punishment of Israel and their princes for their sin. As for the princes, they shall *fall by the sword* either of their enemies or of their own people, some by one and some by the other; and *this shall be their derision,* this is that for which they shall be derided *in the land of Egypt,* when they flee to the Egyptians for succour, *v.* 11. Their sin and punishment shall make them a laughing-stock to all about them. Note, Those that are treacherous and deceitful in their dealings with God, and passionate and outrageous in their conduct towards men, will justly be made a derision to their neighbours, for they make themselves ridiculous.

CHAPTER 8

This chapter, as that before, divides itself into the sins and punishments of Israel; every verse almost declares both, and all to bring them to repentance. When they saw the malignant nature of their sin, in the descriptions of that, they could not but be convinced now much it was their duty to repent of what was so bad in itself; and when they saw the mischievous consequences of their sin, in the predictions of them, they could not but see how much it was their interest to repent for the preventing of them. I. The sin of Israel is here set forth, 1. In many general expressions (*v.* 1, 3, 12, 14). 2. In many particular instances; setting up kings without God (*v.* 4), setting up idols against God (*v.* 4–6, 11), and courting alliances with the neighbouring nations, (*v.* 8–10). 3. In this aggravation of it, that they still kept up a profession of religion and relation to God (*v.* 2, 13, 14). II. The punishment of Israel is here set forth as answering to the sin. God would bring an enemy upon them (*v.* 1, 3). All their projects should be blasted (*v.* 7). Their confidence both in their idols and in their foreign alliances should disappoint them (*v.* 6, 8, 10). Their strength at home should fail them (*v.* 14). Their sacrifices should have no reckoning made of them, and their sins should have a reckoning made for them (*v.* 13).

Verses 1–7

The reproofs and threatenings here are introduced with an order to the prophet to *set the trumpet to his mouth* (*v.* 1), thus to call a solemn assembly, that all might take notice of what he had to deliver and take warning by it. He must sound an alarm, must, in God's name, proclaim war with this rebellious nation. An enemy is coming with speed and fury to seize their land, and he must awaken them to expect it. Thus the prophet must do the part of a watchman, that was by sound of trumpet to call the besieged to stand to their arms, when he saw the besiegers making their attack, Eze. 33:3. The prophet must *lift up his voice like a trumpet* (Isa. 58:1), and the people must hearken to the sound of the trumpet, Jer. 6:17. Now,

I. Here is a general charge drawn up against them as sinners, as rebels and traitors against their sovereign Lord. 1. They have *transgressed my covenant, v.* 1. They have not only transgressed the command (every sin does that), but they have *transgressed the covenant;* they have been guilty of such sins as break the original contract; they have revolted from their allegiance, and violated the marriage-covenant by their spiritual whoredom; they have, in effect, declared that they will be no longer God's people, nor take him for their God; that is *transgressing the covenant.* They have not only done foolishly, but have dealt deceitfully. 2. They have *trespassed against my law* in many particular instances. God's law is the rule by which we are to walk; and this is the malignity of sin, that it trespasses upon the bounds set us by that law. 3. They have *cast off the thing that is good.* They have *put away* and *rejected good,* that is, God himself; so some understand it, and very fitly. He is good, and does good, and is our goodness. *There is none good but one, that is God,* the fountain of all good. They have *cast him off,* as not desiring to have any thing more to do with him. God was abandoning them to ruin, and here gives the reason for it. Note, God never casts off any till they first cast him off. Or, as we read it, They have cast off *the thing that is good;* they have cast off the service and worship of God, which is, in effect, *casting God off.* They have cast off that which denominates men good; they have cast off the fear of God, and the regard of man, and all sense of virtue and honesty. Observe, *They have transgressed my covenant;* it has come to this at last; for *they trespassed against my law.* Breaking the command made way for breaking the covenant; and they did that, for they *cast off that which was good;* there it began first. They *left off to be wise and to do good,* and then they went all to naught, Ps. 36:3. See the method of apostasy; men first cast off that which is good; then those omissions make way for commissions; and frequent actual transgressions of God's law bring men at length to an habitual renunciation of his covenant. When men cast off praying, and hearing, and sabbath-sanctification, and other things that are good, they are in the high road to a total forsaking of God.

II. Here are general threatenings of wrath and ruin for their sin: *The enemy shall come as an eagle against the house of the Lord,* and (*v.* 3) *shall pursue him.* If by *the house of the Lord* we understand the temple at Jerusalem, by the eagle that comes against it we must suppose to be meant either Sennacherib, who had taken all the fenced cities of Judah, laid siege to Jerusalem (and, no doubt, aimed at the house of the Lord, to lay that waste, as he had done the temples of the gods of other nations), or Nebuchadnezzar, who burnt the temple and made a prey of the vessels of the temple. But, if we make it to point at the destruction of the kingdom of the ten tribes by the king of Assyria, we must reckon it is the body of that people which as Israelites, to whom *pertained the adoption, the glory, and the covenants,* is here called the *house of the Lord.* They thought their being so would be their protection; but the prophet is directed to tell them that now they had lost the life and spirit of their religion, though they still retained the name and form of it, they were but as a carcase to which the eagles and other birds of prey should be gathered together. The enemy shall pursue them *as an eagle,* so swiftly, so strongly, so furiously. Note, Those who break their covenant of friendship with God expose themselves to the enmity of all about them, to whom they make themselves a cheap and easy prey; and their having been *the house of the Lord,* and his living temples, will be no excuse nor refuge to them. See Amos 3:2.

III. Here is the people's hypocritical claim of relation to God, when they were in trouble and distress (*v.* 2): *Israel shall cry unto me;* when either they are threatened with these judgments, and would plead an exemption, or when the judgments are inflicted on them and they apply to God for relief, *pouring out a prayer when God's chastening is upon them,* they will plead that among them *God is known* and his *name is great* (Ps. 76:1) and in their distress will pretend to that knowledge of God's ways which in their prosperity they *desired not,* but *despised.* They will then cry unto God, will call him their God, and (as impudent beggars) will tell him they are well acquainted with him, and have known him long. Note, There are many who in works deny God, and disown him, yet, to serve a turn, will profess that they *know him,* that they know more of him than some of their neighbours do. But what stead will it stand a man in to be able to say, *My God, I know thee,* when he cannot say, "My God, I love thee," and "My God, I serve thee, and cleave to thee only?"

IV. Here is the prophet's expostulation with them, in God's name (*v.* 5): *How long will it be ere they attain to innocency?* It is not meant of absolute innocency (that is what the guilty can never attain to); but how long will it be ere they repent and reform, ere they become innocent in this matter, and free from the sin of idolatry? They are wedded to their idols; how long will it be ere they are weaned from them, ere *they are able to get clear of them?* so it might be rendered. This intimates that custom in sin makes it very difficult for men to part with it. It is hard to cleanse from that filthiness, either of flesh or spirit, which has been long wallowed in. But God speaks as if he thought the time long till sinners cast away their iniquities and come to live a new life. He complains of their obstinacy; it is that which keeps his anger against them burning, which would soon be turned away if they did but *attain to innocency* from those sins that kindled it. They in trouble cry, *How long* will it be ere God return to us in a way of mercy? but they do not hear him ask, *How long* will it be ere they return to God in a way of duty?

V. Here are some particular sins which they are charged with, are convicted of the folly of, and warned of the fatal consequences of, and for which God's *anger is kindled against them.*

1. In their civil affairs. They set *up kings without God,* and in contempt of him, *v.* 4. So they did when they rejected Samuel, in whom the Lord was their king, and chose Saul, that they might be *like the nations.* So they did when they revolted from their allegiance to the house of David, and set up Jeroboam, wherein, though they fulfilled God's secret counsel, yet they aimed not at his glory, nor consulted his oracle, nor applied to him by prayer for direction, nor had any regard to his providence, but were led by their own humour and hurried on by the impetus of their own passions. So they did now about the time when Hosea prophesied, when it seems to have grown fashionable to *set up kings,* and depose them again, according as the contenders for the crown could make an interest, 2 Ki. 15:8, etc. Note, We cannot expect comfort and success in our affairs when we go about them, and go on in them, without consulting God and acknowledge not him in all our ways: "They *set up kings,* and *I knew it not,* that is, I did not know it from them, they did not ask *counsel at my mouth,* whether they might lawfully do it or whether it would be best for them to do it, though they had prophets and oracles with whom they might have advised." They *looked not to the Holy One of Israel,* Isa. 31:1. Nor did the princes do as Jephthah, who, before he took upon him the government, *uttered all his words before the Lord in Mizpeh,* Jdg. 11:11. Note, Those that are entrusted with public concerns, and particularly with the election and nomination of magistrates, ought to take God along with them therein, by desiring his direction and designing his honour.

2. In their religious matters they did much worse; for they *set up calves against God,* in competition with him and contradiction to him. "Of *their silver and their gold* which God *gave them,* and *multiplied* to them, that they might serve and honour him with them, they have *made them idols.*" They called them *gods* (1 Ki. 12:28, *Behold thy gods, O Israel!*) but God calls them *idols;* the word signifies *griefs,* or *troubles,* because they are offensive to God and will be ruining to those that worship them. *Their silver and their gold they have made to them idols;* so the words are, referring primarily to the images of their gods, which they made of gold and silver, especially the golden calves at Dan and Bethel. Idolaters spare no cost in worshipping their idols. But they are very applicable to the spiritual idolatry of the covetous: *Their silver and their gold* are the gods they place their happiness in, set their hearts upon, to which they pay their homage, and in which they put their confidence. Now, to show them the folly of their idolatry, he tells them,

(1.) Whence their gods came. Trace them to their original, and they will be found the creatures of their own fancies and the work of their own hands, *v.* 6. The calf they worshipped is here called *the calf of Samaria,* because it is probable that when Samaria, in Ahab's time, became the metropolis of the kingdom, a calf was set up there to be near the court, besides those at Dan and Bethel, or perhaps one of those was removed thither; for those that are for new gods will still be for newer. Now let them consider what this god of theirs owed its rise and being to. [1.] To their own invention and institution: *From Israel was it also,* not from the God of Israel (he expressly forbade it), but from Israel; it was a device of their own (some think), not borrowed from any of their neighbours, no, not from the Egyptians, for, though they worshipped Apis in a living cow, they never worshipped a *golden calf;* that was from Israel; it was *their own iniquity.* Now could that be worthy of their worship which was a contrivance of their own? It was *from Israel,* that is, the gold and silver of which it was made were collected from the people of Israel by a brief: it was a poor god that was framed by contribution. [2.] It was owing to the skill and labour of the craftsman, Deu. 27:15. *The workmen made it, therefore it is not God, v.* 6. This is a very cogent conclusive argument, and the inference so very plain that one would think their own thoughts should have suggested it to them, so as to make them ashamed of their idolatry. What can be more absurd than for men to worship that as a god, giving being and good to them, which they themselves gave being to (both matter and form), but could not give life to? A made god is no God. This is a self-evident truth; and yet St. Paul was accused as a criminal for preaching that *those are no gods which are made with hands,* Acts 19:26. And, here, this which should have turned them from their idols comes in as a reason why they were inseparably wedded to them; therefore they could not attain to innocency because it was *from themselves;* they were willing to have gods of their own to do what they pleased with, that they themselves might do what they pleased.

(2.) What their gods would come to. If they are not gods, they will not last; nay, if they pretend to be gods, they will be reckoned with: *The calf of Samaria shall be broken to pieces,* and those that would not yield to the force of the former argument shall be convinced by this that it is not God, but an *unprofitable idol,* as the Chaldee calls it. It shall be *broken to shivers,* like a potter's vessel, though it be a golden calf. It shall be *chips* or *saw-dust;* it shall be a *spider's web;* so St. Jerome. It seems to allude to Moses's grinding to powder the golden calf that was in his time. This shall be served as that was. Sennacherib boasted what he had done to *Samaria and her idols,* Isa. 10:11. Note, Deifying any creature makes way for the destruction of it. If they had made vessels and ornaments for themselves of their silver and gold, they might have remained; but, if they make gods of them, they shall be *broken to pieces.*

(3.) What their gods would bring them to. The breaking of them to pieces would be a disappointment to those who trusted in them. But that was not all: *They have* made to themselves idols, *that they may be cut off* (*v.* 4), that their gold and silver, which they so abused, may be cut off (so some take it), nay, that they may themselves be cut off from God, from their own land, from the land of the living. Their idolatry will as certainly end in their extirpation as if they had purposely designed it. And, when this proves to be the effect of their sin, what relief will they have from the gods wherein they trusted? None at all: *"Thy calf, O Samaria! has cast thee off;* it cannot give thee any help in thy distress, and the pleasure thou now takest in it will vanish, and be no pleasure to thee." Those that were justly sent to the gods whom they had chosen found them *miserable comforters,* Jdg. 10:14. If men will not quit the love and service of sin, yet they shall certainly lose all the delights and profits of it. If Samaria had continued firm and faithful to the God of Israel, he would have been a present powerful help to her; but the calf she preferred before him was a broken reed. The case will be the same with those that make their silver and their gold their god. It will *cast them off,* and not *profit them in the day of wrath,* Eze. 7:12. Note, Those that suffer themselves to be deceived into any idolatries will certainly find themselves deceived in them. Cardinal Wolsey owned that if he had served his God as faithfully as he had served his prince he would not have *cast him off,* as his prince did, in his old age. Their disappointment in their idols is illustrated (*v.* 7) by a similitude which intimates both that and the destruction which God brought upon them for their idolatry. [1.] They got no good to themselves by worshipping idols: *They have sown the wind.* They have put themselves to a great deal of trouble and expense to make and worship their idols, have made a business of it as much as the husbandman does of sowing his corn, in expectation of reaping some mighty advantage from it, and that they should be as prosperous and victorious as the neighbouring nations were, that worshipped idols. But it is all a cheat; it is like *sowing the wind,* which can yield no increase; they *labour in vain, labour for the wind,* Eccl. 5:16. They take great pains to no purpose, and *weary themselves for very vanity,* Hab. 2:13. Those that make an idol of this world do so; they *set their eyes on that which is not,* which, like the wind, makes a great noise, but has nothing substantial in it. [2.] They brought ruin upon themselves by it: They shall *reap the whirlwind,* a *great whirlwind* (so the word signifies), which shall hurry them away and dash them to pieces. They not only have not their false gods for them but they set the true God against them; their favour will stand them in no more stead than the wind, but his wrath will do them more mischief than a whirlwind. As a man sows, so shall he reap. "If it may be supposed that a man should sow the wind, and cover it with earth, or keep it there for a while penned up, what could he expect but that it should be forced by its being shut up, and the accession of what might increase its strength, to break forth again in greater quantities with greater violence?" So Dr. Pocock. They promise themselves plenty, peace, and victory, by worshipping idols, but their expectations come to nothing. What they sow never comes up; it has *no stalk,* no blade, or, if it have, *the bud shall yield no meal;* it shall be as the thin ears in Pharaoh's dream, that were blasted with the *east wind,* and there was nothing in them. Or *if it yield,* if they do prosper for a while in their idolatrous courses, *the strangers shall swallow it up;* it shall be so far from doing them any service that it shall be but as a bait to invite strangers to invade them, and as a spoil to enrich those strangers and enable them to do so much the more mischief. Note, The service of idols is an unprofitable service, and the works of darkness are unfruitful; nay, in the end they will be pernicious. Rom. 6:21, *The end of those things is death.* Those that *sow iniquity* reap *vanity:* nay, those that *sow to the flesh, reap corruption.* The hopes of sinners will be cheats, and their gains will be snares.

Verses 8–14

It was the honour and happiness of Israel that they had but one God to trust to and he all-sufficient in every strait, and but one God to serve, and he well worthy of all their devotions. But it was their sin, and folly, and shame, that they knew not when they were well off, that they forsook their own mercies for lying vanities; for,

I. They multiplied their alliances (*v.* 9): *They have hired lovers,* or (as the margin reads it) *they have hired loves.* They were at great expense to purchase the friendship of the nations about them, that otherwise had no value nor affection at all for them, nor cared for having any thing to do with them but only upon the Shechemites' principles — *Shall not their cattle and their substance be ours?* Gen. 34:23. Had Israel maintained the honour of their peculiarity, the surrounding nations would have continued to admire them *as a wise and understanding people;* but, when they profaned their own crown, their neighbours despised them, and they had no interest in them further than they paid dearly for it. But those surely have behaved ill among their neighbours who have no loves, no lovers, but what they hire. See here, 1. The contempt that Israel lay under among the nations (*v.* 8): *Israel is swallowed up,* devoured by strangers, their land eaten up (*v.* 7), and themselves too, and, being impoverished, they have quite lost their credit and reputation, like a merchant that has become a bankrupt, so that they are *among the Gentiles as a vessel wherein is no pleasure,* a vessel of *dishonour* (2 Tim. 2:20), a *despised broken vessel,* Jer. 22:28. None of their neighbours have any value for them, nor care to have any thing to do with them. Note, Those that have professed religion, if they degenerate and grow profane, are of all men the most contemptible. *If the salt have lost its savour,* it is fit for nothing but to be *trodden under foot of men.* Or it denotes their dispersion and captivity *among the Gentiles;* they shall be among them poor and prisoners; and who has pleasure in such? 2. The court that Israel made to the nations notwithstanding (*v.* 9): They have *gone to Assyria,* to engage the king of Assyria to help them; and herein they are as a *wild ass alone by himself,* foolish, headstrong, and unruly; they will have their way, and nothing shall *hold them in,* no, not the bridle of God's laws, nothing shall *turn them back,* no, not the sword of God's wrath. They take a course by themselves, and the effect will be that, like a *wild ass by himself,* they will be the easier and surer prey to the lion. See Job 11:12; Jer. 2:24. Note, Man is in nothing more like the wild ass's colt than in seeking for that succour and that satisfaction in the creature which are to be had in God only. 3. The crosses that they were likely to meet with in their alliances with the neighbouring nations (*v.* 10): *Though they have hired among the nations,* and hoped thereby to prevent their own ruin, yet *now will I gather them,* as *the sheaves in the floor* (Mic. 4:12); so that what they provided for their own safety shall but make them the easier prey to their enemies. Note, There is no fence against the judgments of God, when they come with commission; nay, that which men hire for their own preservation often contributes to their own destruction. See Isa. 7:20. The king of Assyria, whose friendship they courted, called himself a *king of princes,* Isa. 10:8. *Are not my princes altogether kings?* He laid *burdens* upon Israel, levied taxes upon them, 2 Ki. 15:19, 20. And for these *they shall sorrow a little;* this shall be but a little burden to them in comparison of what they may further expect; or they will be but little sensible of this grievance, will not lay it to heart, and therefore may expect heavier judgments. *They have begun to be diminished* (so some read it), *by the burden of the king of princes;* but this is only the *beginning of sorrows* (Mt. 24:8), *the beginning of revenges,* Deu. 32:42. Note, God often comes gradually with his judgments upon a provoking people, that he may show how slow he is to wrath, and may awaken them to repentance; but those that are made to *sorrow a little,* if they are not thereby brought to sorrow after a godly sort, will, another day, be made to sorrow a great deal, to sorrow everlastingly.

II. They multiplied their altars and temples. Observe,

1. How they denied *the power of godliness,* and wholly cast that off (*v.* 12): *I have written to him the great things of my law;* this intimates the privilege they enjoyed, as having God's statutes and judgments made known to them, and being entrusted with the lively oracles. Note, (1.) The things of God's law are *magnalia Dei — the great things of God.* They are things that proclaim the greatness of the Law-maker, and things of great use and great importance to us; they are our life, and our eternal welfare depends upon our observance of them and obedience to them; they will make us great if we make a right use of them; and they are things which God will magnify and make honourable. (2.) It is a great privilege to have the things of God's law written; thus they are reduced to a greater certainty, spread the further, and last the longer, with much less danger of being embezzled and corrupted than if they were transmitted by word of mouth only. (3.) The things of God's law are of his own writing; for Moses and the prophets were his amanuenses, and holy men wrote as they were moved by the Holy Ghost. (4.) It is the advantage of those that are members of the visible church that these great things are written *to them,* are intended for their direction, and so they must receive them; what things were written in former ages *were written for our learning,* and are profitable for us. And, if those were happy who had the *great things of God's law* written to them, how much happier are we who have the gospel written to us! But see how this privilege was slighted; these great things of the law were *counted as a strange thing,* as unintelligible and unreasonable (which might *therefore* be slighted, because not to be fathomed, not to be accounted for), or as foreign, and things of no concernment to them, things that they had nothing to do with nor were to be governed by; they used those things as strangers, which they were shy of, and knew not how to bid welcome. *We desire not the knowledge of thy ways.* Note, [1.] God having written to us the great things of his law, we ought to make them familiar to us, as our nearest relations (Prov. 7:3, 4); for *therefore* we have them written, that they may *talk with us,* Prov. 6:22. [2.] We make nothing of the things of God's law if we make strange of them, as if they did not affect us and therefore we need not be affected with them.

2. How they kept up the form of godliness notwithstanding, and to what little purpose they did so.

(1.) They multiplied their altars (*v.* 11): *Ephraim made many altars to sin.* God appointed that there should be but one altar for sacrifice (Deu. 12:3, 5); but the ten tribes, having forsaken that, would still be thought very devout, and zealous for the honour of God, and, as if they would make amends for the affront they put on God's altar, they made *many altars,* dedicated to the God of Israel, whom hereby they intended, or at least pretended, to give glory to; but that would not justify their violation of God's express command, nor would the example of the patriarchs, who before the law of Moses had many altars. No, they *made many altars to sin* (that is, they did that which turned into sin to them), and therefore these *altars shall be unto* them *to sin,* that is, God will charge it upon them as a heinous sin, and put that upon the score of their crimes which they designed to be for the expiation of their crimes. Or they shall be to them an occasion of further sin. Their multiplying of altars dedicated to the God of Israel would introduce altars dedicated to other gods. Note, It is a great sin to corrupt the worship of God, and it will be charged as sin upon those that do it, how plausible soever their pretensions may be. And the way of this, as other sins, is down-hill; those that once deviate from the fixed rule of God's commands will wander endlessly.

(2.) They multiplied their sacrifices, *v.* 13. Their altars were smoking altars: They *sacrificed flesh for the sacrifices of God's offerings,* and they celebrated their feasts upon their sacrifices; they were at a great expense upon their devotions, and (as those commonly are who set up their own inventions in the room of divine institutions) were very zealous in their way; as if they hoped by their impositions on themselves to atone for the contempt of the great atonement, and by their observing a ceremonial law of their own to excuse themselves from the obligation of all God's moral precepts. But how did they speed? [1.] God makes no reckoning of their services: *The Lord accepts them not.* How should he, when they did not offer their sacrifice upon that altar which alone *sanctified the gift,* and when they only sacrificed flesh, but not the spiritual sacrifice of a penitent believing heart? Note, Those services only are acceptable to God which are performed according to the rule of his word, and *through Jesus Christ,* 1 Pt. 2:5. [2.] He takes that occasion to reckon with them for their sins; now will he, instead of pardoning their iniquity and blotting out their sins, as they expected, *remember their iniquity* and *visit their sins.* Such an *abomination to the Lord* are the *sacrifices of the wicked* that they provoke him to call them to an account for all their other abominations. When they think by their sacrifices to bribe the Judge of heaven and earth into a connivance at their wickedness he will resent that as the highest affront they can put upon him, and it shall be the measure-filling sin. Note, A petition for leave to sin amounts to an imprecation of the curse for sin, and so it shall be answered, *according to the multitude of the idols.* "I will punish their sins, *for they shall return to Egypt;*" they shall be carried captive into Assyria, which shall be to them a house of bondage, as Egypt was to their fathers. Or it refers to Deu. 28:68, where returning to Egypt is made to close and complete the miseries of that sinful nation.

(3.) They multiplied their temples, and these also in honour of the true God, as they pretended, but really in contempt of the choice he had made of Jerusalem to *put his name there. Israel has forgotten his Maker, v.* 14. They pretended to know him, and yet forgot him, for they *liked not to retain God in their knowledge,* when the remembrance of him would give check to their lusts. It was an aggravation of their sin in forgetting God that he was *their Maker* (Deu. 32:15, 18; Job 35:10), as nothing obliges us more to remember him than that he is *our Creator,* Eccl. 12:1. "He has *forgotten his Maker, and builds temples;* he seems by the temples he builds to me mindful of his Maker, and to be desirous still to keep him in mind, and yet really he has forgotten him, because he has cast off the fear of him." Some by temples here understand *palaces,* for so the word sometimes signifies. *"He has forgotten his Maker,* and yet is so secure and haughty that he sets his judgments at defiance, as Nebuchadnezzar did when he said, *Is not this great Babylon that I have built?"* Judah is likewise charged with *multiplying fenced cities,* and trusting in them for safety, when the judgments of God were abroad. To fortify their cities in subjection and subordination to God was well enough; but to fortify them in opposition to God, and without any regard to him or his providence (Isa. 22:11), shows their hearts to be desperately *hardened through the deceitfulness of sin.* But *none ever hardened his heart against God and prospered,* nor shall they. *God will send a fire upon his cities,* upon the cities both of Judah and Israel, not only the head-cities of Jerusalem and Samaria, but all the other cities of those two kingdoms, and it shall devour not only the cottages, but *the palaces thereof;* though ever so strong, the fire shall master them; though ever so stately and sumptuous, the fire shall not spare them. This was fulfilled when all the cities of Israel were laid in ashes by the king of Assyria, and all the cities of Judah by the king of Babylon. The fires they both kindled were of his sending; and when he judges he will overcome.

CHAPTER 9

In this chapter, I. God threatens to deprive this degenerate seed of Israel of all their worldly enjoyments, because by sin they had forfeited their title to them; so that they should have no comfort either in receiving them themselves or in offering them to God (v. 1–5). II. He dooms them to utter ruin, for their own sins and the sins of their prophets (v. 6–8). III. He upbraids them with the wickedness of their fathers before them, whose steps they trod in (v. 9, 10). IV. He threatens them with the destruction of their children and the rooting out of their posterity (v. 11–17).

Verses 1–6

Here, I. The people of Israel are charged with spiritual adultery: *O Israel! thou hast gone a whoring from thy God, v.* 1. Their covenant with God was a marriage-covenant, by which they were joined to him as their God, renouncing all others. But when they set up idols and worshipped them, when they fled to creatures for succour and put a confidence in them, they *went a whoring from God* as their God, and honoured the pretenders and rivals with the affection, adoration, and confidence, which were due to God only. Other people were idolaters, but that sin was not, in them, going a whoring from God, as it was in Israel that had been married to him. Note, The sins of those who have made a profession of religion and relation to God are more provoking to him than the sins of others. As a proof of their going a whoring from God, it is charged upon them that *they loved a reward upon every corn-floor.* 1. They loved to give rewards to their idols, in the offerings and first-fruits they presented to them out of every corn-floor. They took a strange pleasure in serving their idols with that which they would have grudged to consecrate to God and employ in his service. Note, It is common for those that are niggardly in the expenses of their religion to be very prodigal in spending upon their lusts. Or, 2. They loved to receive rewards from their idols; and such they reckoned the fruits of the earth to be: *These are my rewards, which my lovers have given me,* ch. 2:12. Note, Those are directly disposed to spiritual idolatry that love a reward in the corn-floor better than a reward in the favour of God and eternal life.

II. They are forbidden to rejoice as other people do:

"Rejoice not, O Israel! for joy. Do not expect to rejoice. *What peace,* what joy, what hast thou to do with either, while thy whoredoms and witchcrafts are so many?" 2 Ki. 9:19–22. Be not disposed to rejoice, for it does not become thee, but rather to *be afflicted, and mourn, and weep,* Jam. 4:9. Judah, that keeps close to the true God, nay, and other people that never knew him nor could ever be charged with revolting from him, may be allowed to rejoice, as not having so much cause to be ashamed as Israel has, that has gone a whoring from him. Some think that they had at this time particular occasions for joy, probably upon the account of some losses recovered, or some advantages gained, or some league made with a potent ally, for which they had public rejoicings, as other people used to have upon such occasions; but God sends to them not to rejoice. Note, Joy is forbidden fruit to wicked people. They must not rejoice, because they have gone a whoring from their God; and therefore, 1. Whatever it was that they rejoiced in, it would be no security nor advantage to them, so long as they were at a distance from God and at war with him. Note, We are likely to have small joy of any of our creature-comforts if we make not God our chief joy. 2. The sense of sin and dread of wrath ought to be a damp upon their joy and a strong alloy to all their comforts. Note, Those who by departing from God have made work for repentance have thereby marred their own mirth, till they return and make their peace with God.

III. They are threatened with destroying judgments for their spiritual whoredoms, according to what was said long before. Ps. 72:27, *Thou hast destroyed all those that go a whoring from thee.* It is here threatened,

1. That their land shall not yield its wonted increase. Canaan, that *fruitful land,* shall be *turned into barrenness for the wickedness of those that dwell therein.* They *love the reward in the corn-floor,* and are so full of the *joy of harvest* that they have no disposition at all to mourn for their sins; and therefore God will, for their effectual humiliation, take away from them, not only their delights and dainties, but even their necessary food (v. 2): *The floor and the wine-press shall not feed them,* much less feast them; they shall either be blasted by the hand of God or plundered by the hand of man. The *new wine* with which they used to make merry shall *fail in her.* Note, When we make the world, and the things of it, our idol and portion, above what they were designed for, it is just with God to deny us even support and nourishment from them, according to that which they were designed for, to show us our folly and correct us for it. Let those miss of their food in the corn-floor that look for their reward in the corn-floor. We forfeit the good things of this world if we love them as the best things.

2. That their land shall not only cease to feed them, but cease to lodge them and to be a habitation for them; it shall *spue them out,* as it had done the Canaanites before them (v. 3): *They shall not dwell any longer in the Lord's land.* The land of Canaan was in a peculiar manner the *Lord's land, the land of the Shechinah* (so the Chaldee), *the land of the Lord of the world* (so the Arabic); he whose all the earth is (Ps. 24:1) took that for his demesne. *The land is mine,* says God, Lev. 25:23. They had used it, or abused it rather, as if it had been their own, had not paid the rent, nor done the services, due to God as their landlord, and therefore God justly *enters,* and takes possession of it, they having forfeited their lease. "It is *my land"* (says God) "and I will make it appear, for they shall be turned off, as bad tenants, and be made to know that, though they thought themselves freeholders, they were but tenants at will." Note, It is for the honour of God's justice and holiness that those who go a whoring from God should not be suffered to dwell upon his land; and therefore, sooner or later, the wicked shall be *chased out of the world.* Or it is called the Lord's land because it was the holy land, *Immanuel's land,* the land that had peculiar tokens of God's favour to it, and presence in it, where God was known and his name was great, where God's prophets and oracles were; it was a kind of copy of the earthly paradise, and a type of the heavenly one. It was a great privilege to have a lot in such a land as this. It was a great sin and folly to rebel against God, and go a whoring from him, in such a land as this, to *deal unjustly in a land of uprightness,* Isa. 26:10. And it was a sad and sore judgment to be driven out from such a land as this; it was like driving our first parents out of the garden of Eden, and almost amounted to an exclusion out of the heavenly Canaan. Note, Those cannot expect to dwell in the Lord's land that will not be subject to the Lord's laws, nor be influenced by his love. Those have forfeited the privileges of the church that conform not to the rules of it.

3. That, when they are turned out from the Lord's land, they shall have no rest nor satisfaction in any other land. When Cain was *driven out from the presence of the Lord* he was *a fugitive and a vagabond* ever after, and dwelt in the land of *trembling.* So Israel here. Some shall *return into Egypt,* the old house of bondage; thither they shall flee from the Assyrian (*ch.* 8:13) and they shall lose and ruin themselves where they thought to hide and help themselves. Others shall be carried captives to Assyria and there shall be forced to *eat unclean things,* either (1.) Such things as were not fit for men to eat, that which is rotten and putrefied, intimating that they shall be reduced to the utmost poverty, as the prodigal that would fain have filled his belly *with the husks.* Or, (2.) Such things as were not fit for Jews to eat, being prohibited by their law. It is probable that while they were in their own land, however disobedient in other things, they kept up the distinction of meats, and prided themselves in that; but, since they would not keep the law of God in other things, they should not be suffered to keep it in that, and it was a just punishment of their sin in eating things offered to idols. Note, When at any time we suffer in our food, and either through want or for our health are forced to eat or drink that which is unpleasing, we must acknowledge that God is righteous, because we have sinned about our food, and have indulged ourselves too much in that which is pleasing.

4. That in the land of their enemies, to which they shall be driven, they shall have no opportunity either of giving honour to God or obtaining favour with God, by offering any acceptable sacrifice to him; they should not be in a capacity of keeping up any face or show of religion among them; "and so" (as Dr. Pocock expresses it) "should be as it were quite cut off from any expression of relation to him, from all signs of grace, and means of reconciliation with him, which would be to them a token of their being rejected of God, estranged from him, and no more owned by him as his people." (1.) They shall have no sacrifices to offer, nor any altar to offer them on, nor priests to offer them; they shall not so much as *offer drink-offerings* to the Lord, much less any other sacrifices. (2.) If they should offer them, neither they nor their sacrifices shall be pleasing to him, for they cannot have any legal offerings, nor are their hearts humbled. (3.) Instead of their sacrifices of joy and praise, they shall *eat the bread of mourners;* they shall live desolate and disconsolate, mourning for the death of their relations and their own miseries, so that if they had opportunity of sacrificing they should never be themselves in a frame fit for it; for they were forbidden to eat of the holy things in *their mourning,* Deu. 26:14. *All that eat* of the bread of mourners *are polluted,* and incapacitated to *partake of the altar.* (4.) Their *bread for their soul,* the bread which they must either eat or starve, the bread which they shall have for the support of their lives, *shall not come into the house of the Lord;* they shall have no house of the Lord to bring it to, or, if they had, it is such as is not fit to be brought, nor are they rightly disposed to bring it. (5.) The return of the days of their sacred and solemn feasts would therefore be very melancholy and uncomfortable to them (v. 5): *What will you do in the solemn day,* in the sabbath, *the solemn day* of every week, in the *new moons,* the solemn days of every month, at the return of the times for keeping the passover, pentecost, and feast of the tabernacles, the solemn days of every year, the *days of the feasts of the Lord?* Note, The feasts of the Lord are solemn days; and, when we are invited to those feasts, we ought to consider seriously what we shall do. But the question is here put to those who were to be deprived of the benefit and comfort of those solemn feasts, *"What will you do then?* You will then spend those days in sorrow and lamentation which, if it had not been your own fault, you might have been spending in joy and praise. You will then be made to know the worth of mercies by the want of them and to prize spiritual bread by being made to feel a famine of it." Note, When we enjoy the means of grace we ought to consider what we shall do if ever we should know the want

of them, if either they should be taken from us or we be disabled to attend upon them.

5. That they should perish in the land of their dispersion (*v.* 6): *For, lo, they have gone* out of the Lord's land, where they might have spent both their sabbath days and other days with comfort, *gone because of destruction,* gone to Egypt because of the destruction of their own country by the Assyrians, flattering themselves with hopes that they shall return when the storm is over; but those hopes also shall fail them; they shall find there are *graves in Egypt,* as their murmuring ancestors said (Ex. 14:11), graves for them; for *Egypt shall gather them up,* as dead men are gathered up and carried forth to the grave, and Memphis (one of the chief cities of Egypt) *shall bury them. Gathering* and *burying* are put together, Jer. 8:2; Job 27:19. Note, Those that think presumptuously to flee from the judgments of God are likely enough tp meet their death where they hoped to save their lives.

6. That their land, which they left behind and to which they hoped to return, should become a desolation: As for *their tabernacles,* where they formerly dwelt and where they kept their stores, *the pleasant places for their silver,* they shall be demolished and laid in ruins, to such a degree that they shall be overgrown with *nettles;* so that if they should survive the trouble, and return to their own land again, they would find it neither fruitful nor habitable; it would afford them neither food nor lodging. Note, Those that make their money their god reckon the *places of their silver* their *pleasant places,* as those that make the Lord their God reckon his tabernacles amiable and his ordinances their pleasant things, Isa. 64:11. But, while the pleasures of communion with God are out of the reach of chance and change, the *pleasant places of men's silver,* which were purchased with silver, or in which they deposited their silver, or which were beautified and adorned with silver, are liable to be laid in ruins, in nettles, and therewith all the pleasure men took in them.

Verses 7–10

For their further awakening, it is here threatened,

I. That the destruction spoken of shall come speedily. They shall have no reason to hope for a long reprieve, for the judgment slumbers not; it is at the door (*v.* 7): *The days of visitation have come,* and there shall be no more delay; *the days of recompence have come,* which they have been so often warned to expect; their prophets have told them that destruction *would come,* and now *it has come,* and the time of the divine patience has expired. Note, 1. The day of God's judgments is both a *day of visitation,* in which men's sins are enquired into and brought to light, and a *day of recompence,* in which men's doom will be passed, and a reward given to every man according to his work; the strict visitation is in order to a just retribution. 2. This day of visitation and recompence is hastening on apace. It is sure; it is near; as if it had already come.

II. That hereby they shall be made ashamed of their sentiments concerning their prophets. When the day of visitation comes *Israel shall know it,* shall be made to know that by sad experience which they would not know by instruction. *Israel shall know* then what an *evil and bitter thing it* is to *depart from God,* and what a *fearful thing* it is to *fall into his hands. When thy hand is lifted up they will not see, but they shall see.* Israel shall know the difference between true prophets and false. 1. They shall know then that the pretenders to prophecy, who flattered them in their sins, and rocked them asleep in their security, and told them that they should have peace though they went on, however they pretended to be *spiritual men* (as Ahab's prophets did, 1 Ki. 22:24) were *fools* and *madmen,* and not true prophets; they deceived themselves and those to whom they prophesied. But why would God suffer his people Israel to be imposed upon by those false prophets? He answers, *"It is for the multitude of thy iniquity* which, in contempt of the divine law, thou hast persisted in, *and, for the great hatred of* the true prophets, that reproved thee, in God's name, for it." Note, Because men receive not the love of the truth, but conceive a hatred of it, and by the multitude of their iniquities bid defiance to it, therefore God shall *send them strong delusions, to believe a lie,* so strong that they shall not be undeceived till the day of visitation and recompence comes, which will convince them of the folly and madness of those that seduced them and of their own folly and madness in suffering themselves to be seduced by them. 2. They shall know then whether the *true prophets,* that were really *spiritual men,* guided by the Spirit of God, were such as they called and counted them, *fools and madmen;* and they shall be convinced that they were so far from being so that they were the wise men of their times, and God's faithful ambassadors to them. When Israel saw that none of Samuel's words *fell to the ground* they knew he was *established to be a prophet* (1 Sa. 3:20); and so here, when God fulfils the word of his messengers, by bringing the days of recompence they foretold, then those that despised and ridiculed them, and thought Bedlam the fittest place for them, will be ashamed of *the multitude of their iniquities* of that kind, and of *their great hatred,* for which God brings upon them this swift destruction. Mocking the messengers of the Lord was the sin they were punished for, and so made ashamed of.

III. That hereby the wickedness of the false prophets themselves shall be manifested to their shame (*v.* 8): *"The watchman of Ephraim was with my God;* he had been formerly. They had a set of worthy good ministers, that kept close to God and maintained communion with him; but now they have a race of corrupt, malignant, persecuting prophets, that are the ring-leaders of all mischief." Or, "The *watchman of Ephraim* now pretends to have been *with my God,* and prefaces his lies with, *Thus saith the Lord;* but he is *a snare of a fowler in all his ways,* and is cunning to draw the simple into sin and the upright into trouble; and he is so full of hatred and enmity to goodness and good men that he has become *hatred* itself *in the house of his God,* or *against the house of his God."* Note, Wicked prophets are the worst of men; their sins against God are most heinous, and their plots against religion most dangerous. They may boast that they are *watchmen, speculators,* and, as far as speculation goes, they may be right, and *with my God,* may have their heads full of good notions; but look into their lives, and they are the *snare of a fowler in all their ways,* catching for themselves and making a prey of others; look into *their hearts,* and they are *hatred in the house of my God,* very malicious and spiteful against good ministers and good people. Woe unto thee, O land! unto thee, O church! that hast such watchmen, such prophets, that are seers, but not doers! *Corruptio optimi est pessima — The best things, when corrupted, become the worst.*

IV. That God will now reckon with them for the sins of their fathers, which they have trod in the steps of, *v.* 9, 10. 1. They were as bad as their fathers: *They have deeply corrupted themselves;* they are rooted and riveted in sin; they are far gone in the *depths of Satan* (Isa. 31:6), so that it is next to impossible that they should be recovered; the stain of their corruption is deep, not to be got out; it is as scarlet and crimson, or as the spots of the leopard: and it is their own fault; they have *corrupted themselves,* have polluted and hardened their own hearts, as *in the days of Gibeah,* when the Levite's concubine was abused to death by the men of Gibeah and the whole tribe of Benjamin patronised the villany; that was a time of deep corruption indeed, and such were the present days. Lewdness and wickedness were as impudent and daring now as in the days of Gibeah; and therefore what can be expected but such a vengeance as was then taken on Gibeah? Every tribe is now as bad as the tribe of Benjamin then was, and therefore may expect to be brought as low as that tribe then was. 2. They shall therefore be reckoned with for their fathers' sins: *He will remember their iniquity and visit their sins,* the iniquity they have by kind and by entail, the sin that runs in the blood; the *sin of the father* shall now be *visited upon the children.* Hence God takes occasion to upbraid them with the degeneracy and apostasy of their ancestors, their perfidiousness and base ingratitude, *v.* 10. Here observe, (1.) The great honour God put upon Israel when he first formed them into a people: *I found Israel like grapes in the wilderness.* He took as much delight and pleasure in them as a poor traveller would do if he found grapes in a wilderness, where he most needed them and least expected them. Or when they were *in the wilderness* he *found them as grapes,* not precious in themselves, but precious to him, and pleasant as the first-ripe grapes to the lord of the vineyard. They were *precious in his sight, and honourable* (Isa. 43:4); he planted them a *choice vine,* a *right seed* (Jer. 2:21), and found them no better than he himself made them, good grapes at first. *I saw them* with pleasure, *as the first-ripe in the fig-tree at the first time.* Good people are compared to the *good things that are first ripe,* Jer. 24:2. One then is worth more than many afterwards. This intimates the delight God took in them and in doing them good, not for their sakes, but because he loved their fathers. He preserved them carefully, as a man does the first and choicest fruits of his vineyard. Now when he put all this honour upon them, and they stood so fair for preferment, one would think they should have maintained their excellency; but, (2.) See the great disgrace they put upon themselves. God set them apart for himself as a peculiar people, but they went to Baal-peor, joined with the Moabites in sacrificing to that dirty dunghill deity (Num. 25:2, 3), and they *separated themselves unto that shame,* that shameful idol, so Baal-peor was in a particular manner, if (as should seem) the *whoredom* which the people *committed with the daughters of Moab* was a part of the service done to Baal-peor. Note, Whatever those separate themselves to that forsake God it will certainly be a shame to them, first or last. *Their abominations* are here said to be *as they loved;* their practices which were an abomination to God were as the best-beloved of their souls. Or when they had once forsaken God they multiplied *their abominations,* their idols and abominable idolatries, at their pleasure. This was the way of their fathers; God had done well for them, but they had acted ungratefully towards him, and in the same manner had the present generation *deeply corrupted themselves.*

Verses 11–17

In the foregoing verses we saw the sin of Israel derived from their fathers; here we see the punishment of Israel derived to their children; for, as death entered by sin at first, so it is still entailed with it. We may observe, in these verses,

I. The sin of Ephraim. Some expressions are here which describe that. 1. *They did not hearken to God* (*v.* 17); they did not give attention to the voice either of his word or of his rod; they did not believe what he said, nor would they be ruled by him. He told them their duty, their interest, their danger, but they regarded him not; all he said to them by his words and by his prophets was to them as a tale that is told; and then no wonder that we hear, 2. Of the *wickedness of their doings* (*v.* 15), the downright malice that was in their sins; they were not infirmities, but daring presumptions. How can those but do wickedly who will not hearken to the word of God, that would teach and persuade them to do well? And no wonder that there were wicked doings among them when, 3. Their worship was corrupt (*v.* 15): *All their wickedness is in Gilgal,* which was a place infamous for idolatry, as appears, *ch.* 4:15; 12:11; Amos 4:4; 5:5. It is probable that the idolaters chose that place for their head-quarters because it had been famous in other ages for solemn transactions between God and Israel, as Jos. 5:2, 10; 1 Sa. 10:8; 11:15. There, where the source of idolatry was, whence it spread through the kingdom, there it might be said that *all their wickedness* was, for all other wickedness owed its origin to that. Corruptions in worship make way for corruptions in morals. The *mother of harlots* is the *mother of* all other *abominations,* Rev. 17:5. The learned Grotius conjectures that there is a mystical sense here. Golgotha in Syriac is the same with Gilgal in Hebrew, and therefore he thinks this may have reference to the putting of Christ to death at Golgotha, which was the greatest sin of the Jewish nation, and of which it might truly be said, *All their wickedness* was summed up in that. And no wonder that the people did wickedly, both in worship and conversation, when 4. *All their princes were revolters;* the whole succession of the kings of the ten tribes did evil in the sight of the Lord, or all the set of judges and magistrates at this time were wicked; they turned aside to sinful ways and persisted in those ways.

II. The displeasure of God against Ephraim for sin. This is variously expressed here, to show what a provocation sin is to the pure eyes of his glory, and how odious it makes the sinner to him. 1. He *departs from them, v.* 12. When they revolt from him, and withdraw from their allegiance to him, how can they expect but that he should depart from them and withdraw both his protection and his bounty? And well may his threatening be enforced as it is, and made terrible: *Woe also unto them when I depart from them!* Note, Those are in a woeful condition indeed whom God has forsaken. Our weal or woe depends upon the gracious presence of God with us; and, if he goes, all weal goes with him and all woes come upon us. *God has forsaken him; persecute and take him.* Saul knew this when he laid such an emphasis upon this part of his complaint, *The Philistines make war against me, and God has departed from me.* Nay, he does not only depart from them, but, 2. He hates them. *In Gilgal, where all their wickedness is, there I hated them.* There, where the abominations of sin are committed, there God abominates the sinners. In Gilgal he had bestowed many tokens of his favour upon their ancestors, but now that is the place where he hates them for their base ingratitude. Nay, he not only hates them, but, 3. He *will love them no more,* will never take them into his favour again; the breach between God and Israel is wide as the sea, which cannot be healed. This agrees with what he had said, (*ch.* 1:6, 7), *I will no more have mercy upon the house of Israel,* the ten tribes. 4. He will discard them, and have no more to do with them: *For the wickedness of their doings, I will drive them out of my house.* He will no longer own them as his, or as belonging to his family in the world; he will turn them out of doors as unfaithful tenants that pay him no rent, as unprofitable servants that do him neither credit nor work. Note, Those that profane God's house can expect no other than to be expelled his house, and no longer suffered to be either lodgers in it or retainers to it. Nay, he will not only drive them out of his house, but, 5. He will drive them far enough (*v.* 17): *My God will cast them away,* not only out of his house, but out of his sight; he will quite abandon and reject them; they shall be *cast-aways.* God said that he would *drive them out of his house,* and here the prophet seconds it, as one that knew his Master's mind very well: *My God will cast them away.* See with what comfort and pleasure he calls God his God. Note, When others disown God, and are disowned by him, it is a very great satisfaction to good people that they can call God their God, can cheerfully own him and see themselves owned by him — all revolters, all ruined, yet God is *my God.*

III. The fruit of this displeasure, in the cutting off and abandoning of their posterity, which is the judgment here threatened again and again. Observe here,

1. How numerous Ephraim seemed likely to be. The name *Ephraim* is derived from *fruitfulness,* Gen. 41:51. Joseph is a *fruitful bough,* Gen. 49:22. And Moses's blessing foretold the *ten thousands of Ephraim,* Deu. 33:17. This was his glory, *v.* 11. For this he seemed designed by him that appoints the bounds of men's habitation; for *Ephraim, as I saw Tyrus, is planted in a pleasant place,* to encourage his increase, which one may expect as from a tree planted by the river's side. Ephraim is as strong and rich as ever Tyre was, and as proud and secure. The Chaldee paraphrase gives this sense of it, *The congregation of Israel, while they observed the law, was like to Tyrus in prosperity and security.*

2. How few Ephraim should be (*v.* 11): *Their glory shall fly away like a bird;* their children shall be taken away and the hopes of their families cut off. All their glory shall fly *as an eagle towards heaven,* swiftly and irrecoverably. Note, Worldly glory is glory that will *fly away;* but those that have their God their glory have in him an unfading everlasting glory. Ephraim has been as a fruitful tree. But now *Ephraim is smitten,* is blasted; *their root is dried up; they shall bear no fruit, v.* 16. If the root be dried, the branch must wither of course. Observe,

(1.) God's threatening this judgment of the destroying of their children. [1.] They shall perish of themselves by the immediate hand of God (*v.* 11): They shall *fly away from the birth, and from the womb, and from the conception.* Some of their children shall die as soon as they are born; the cradle shall be presently turned into a coffin. Others of them shall be *still-born,* or the womb shall be their grave, and their death there their mothers' death too. Of others their mothers shall miscarry almost as soon as they have conceived, and they shall be as untimely fruit. See how easily God can, and how justly we are sure he might, root out the whole race of mankind, that degenerate, guilty, obnoxious race, and blot out the name of it from under heaven; it is but doing as he does by Ephraim here, writ-

ing them all childless, making all their glory to *fly away from the birth, the womb, and the conception,* drying up their root, that they bear no fruit, and their business is done in a few years. [2.] They shall perish by the hand of their enemies; they shall die violent deaths (*v.* 12): "*Though they bring up their children* to some maturity, though they escape the diseases and deaths which the infant age is liable to, and are thought to be reared past danger, *yet will I bereave them* (*v.* 12), by one judgment or other, so that *there shall not be a man left* to build up their families and bear up their name." Again (*v.* 13), *Ephraim shall bring forth his children to the murderer.* The mothers shall travail with pain to bear their children, and a great deal of care, and pains, and cost shall be bestowed upon the nursing of them, and when a cruel enemy comes and puts all to the word, young and old, without mercy, then they seem but as lambs that were all this while fed for the slaughter. Note, It is a great alloy to the comfort parents have in their children that they know not what they have brought them forth and brought them up for, perhaps *for the murderer,* or, which is worse, to be themselves the plagues of their generation. It is threatened again (*v.* 16), *Though they bring forth, yet will I slay even the beloved fruit of their womb,* those children that they are most fond of. Note, The parents' love is no security to the children's lives; nay, sometimes death is commissioned to take the darlings of the family and leave the burdens of it. When sentence was passed upon Israel in the wilderness, that they should all perish there, this mercy was mixed with the wrath, that their children should nevertheless enter into that rest which they through unbelief could not enter into. But this is a total and final rejection; even their children shall be cut off, and the land shall escheat to the crown, *ob defectum sanguinis* — *shall be lost for want of heirs.* The Chaldee-paraphrase, and many of the rabbin, by the *murderers* to whom the children were brought forth, understand those that sacrificed their children to Moloch, a sin which was its own punishment, which showed the parents void of bowels and justly left them void of blessings. [3.] Those few that escape and remain shall be dispersed (*v.* 17): They shall be *wanderers among the nations;* so the remains of the Jews are at this day, and there is no place in the world where they are a distinct nation.

(2.) The prophet's prayer relating to it (*v.* 14): *Give them, O Lord! what wilt thou give?* What shall I ask for a people thus doomed to destruction? It is this; since the decree has gone forth, that they must either die from the womb or be brought forth for the murderer, of the two let them rather *die from the womb.* Rather let them have no children than have them to be made miserable; for the same reason, when a total ruin was coming on the Jewish nation, Christ said, *Blessed is the womb that never bore and the paps that never gave suck,* Lu. 23:29. "Give therefore *a miscarrying womb and dry breasts;* for it is better to fall into the hands of the Lord, whose mercies are great, than into the hands of man." Note, Those that are childless may with this reconcile themselves to the will of God herein, that the time may come when, if they were not so, they would wish they had been so.

CHAPTER 10

In this chapter, I. The people of Israel are charged with gross corruptions in the worship of God and are threatened with the destruction of their images and altars (*v.* 1, 2, 5, 6, 8). II. They are charged with corruptions in the administration of the civil government and are threatened with the ruin of that (*v.* 3, 4, 7). III. They are charged with imitating the sins of their fathers, and with security in their own sins, and are threatened with smarting humbling judgments (*v.* 9–11). IV. They are earnestly invited to repent and reform, and are threatened with ruin if they did not (*v.* 12–15).

Verses 1–8

Observe, I. What the sins are which are here laid to Israel's charge, the national sins which bring down national judgment. The prophet deals plainly with them; for what good would it do them to be flattered?

1. They were not fruitful in the fruits of righteousness to the glory of God. Here all their other wickedness began (*v.* 1): *Israel is an empty vine.* The church of God is fitly compared to a *vine,* weak, and of an unpromising outside, yet spreading and fruitful; believers are branches of that vine, and partake of its root and fatness. But this was the character of Israel, they were as *an empty vine,* a vine that had no sap or virtue in it, and therefore none of those good

fruits produced by it that were expected from it, with which God and man should be honoured. Note, There are many who, though they have not become *degenerate* vines, are yet *empty vines,* have no good in them. A vine is of all trees least serviceable if it do not bear fruit. It is thenceforth good for nothing, Eze. 15:3, 5. And those that bring forth no grapes will soon come to bring forth wild grapes; those that do no good will do hurt. He is an *empty vine,* for *he brings forth fruit to himself.* What good there is in him is not directed to the glory of God, but he takes the praise of it to himself, and prides himself in it. Christians live not to themselves (Rom. 14:6), but hypocrites make self their centre; they *eat and drink to themselves,* Zec. 7:5, 6. Or Israel is by the judgments of God *emptied* and *spoiled* of all his wealth, because he made use of it in the service of his lusts, and not to the honour of God who gave it to him. Note, What we do not rightly employ we may justly expect to be emptied of.

2. They multiplied their altars and images, and the more bountiful God's providence was to them the more prodigal they were in serving their idols: *According to the multitude of his fruit* which his land brought forth *he has increased the altars,* and *according to the goodness of his land they have made goodly images.* Note, It is a great affront to God, and an abuse of his goodness, when the more mercies we receive from him the more sins we commit against him, and when the more wealth men have the more mischief they do. Should not we be thus abundant in the service of our God, as they were in the service of their idols? As we find our estates increasing, we should proportionably abound the more in works of piety and charity.

3. Their hearts were divided, *v.* 2. (1.) They were divided among themselves. They were at variance about their idols, some for one, some for another, at variance about their kings, whose separate interests made parties in the kingdom, and in them their very hearts were divided, and alienated one from another, and there was no such thing as cordial friendship to be found among them; it follows therefore, *Now shall they be found faulty.* Note, The divisions and animosities of a people are the causes of much sin and the presages of ruin. (2.) They were divided between God and their idols. They had a remaining affection in their hearts for God, but a reigning affection for their idols. They *halted between God and Baal,* that was the dividing of their heart. But God is the sovereign of the heart and he will by no means endure a rival; he will either have all or none. Satan, like the pretended mother, says, *Let it be neither mine nor thine, but divide it;* but, if this be yielded to, God says, Nay, *let him take it all.* A heart thus divided will be *found faulty,* and be rejected as treacherous in covenanting with God. Note, A heart divided between God and mammon, though it may trim the matter so as to appear plausible, will, in the day of discovery, be *found faulty.*

4. They made no conscience of what they said and what they did in the most solemn manner, *v.* 4. (1.) Not of what they said in swearing, which is the most solemn speaking: *They have spoken words,* and words only, for they meant not as they said; they did *verba dare* — *give words.* They *swore falsely in making a covenant;* they were deceitful in their covenanting with God, the covenant of circumcision, the fair promises they made of reformation when they were in distress; and no marvel if those that were false to their God were false to all mankind. They contracted such a habit of treachery that they broke through the most sacred bonds, and made nothing of them; subjects violated their oaths of allegiance and their kings their coronation-oaths; they broke their leagues with the nations they were in alliance with, nor was any conscience made of contracts between private persons. (2.) Nor of what they did in judgment, which is the most solemn acting. Justice could not take place when men made nothing of forswearing themselves; for thus *judgment,* which should have been a healing medicinal plant and of a sweet smell, *sprang up as hemlock,* which is both nauseous and noxious, *in the furrows of the field,* in the field that was ploughed and furrowed for good corn. Note, God is greatly offended with corruptions, not only in his own worship, but in the administration of justice between man and man, and the dishonesty of a people shall be the ground of his controversy with them as well as their idolatry and impiety; for God's

laws are intended for man's benefit and the good of the community, as well as for God's honour, and the profanation of courts of justice shall be avenged as surely as the profanation of temples.

II. What the judgments are with which Israel should be punished for these sins; they sinned both in civil and religious matters, and in both they shall be punished. 1. They shall have no joy of their kings and of their government. Because justice is turned into oppression, therefore those who are entrusted with the administration of it, and should be blessings to the state, shall be complained of as the burdens of it (v. 3), and those that would not rule their people well shall not be able to protect them: *Now they shall say, "We have no king,* that is, we are as if we had none, we have none to do us any good nor stand us in any stead, none to keep us from destroying ourselves or being destroyed by our enemies, none to preserve the public peace nor to fight our battles; and justly has this come to us. *Because we feared not the Lord,* when we were safe under the protection of our kings, therefore we are rejected by him, and then *what shall a king do for us?* What good can we expect from a king when we have forfeited the favour of our God?" Note, Those that cast off the fear of God are not likely to have joy of any of their creature-comforts; nor will men's loyalty to their prince befriend them without religion, for, though that may engage him to be for them, what good will that do them if God be against them? Those that keep themselves in the fear and favour of God may say, with triumph, "What can the greatest of men do against us?" But those that throw themselves out of his protection must say, with despair, "What can the greatest of men do for us?" He was a king that said, *If the Lord do not help thee, whence should I help thee?* Yet he is a fool that says, If a king cannot help us, we must perish (as these intimate here), for God can do that for us which kings cannot. Time was when they doted upon having a king; but now what can a king (who, they thought, could do any thing) do for them? God can make people sick of those creature-confidences which they were most fond of. This is their complaint when their king is disabled to help them, yet this is not the worst; their civil government shall not only be weakened, but quite destroyed (v. 7): *As for Samaria,* the royal city, which is now almost all that is left, *her king is cut off as the foam from the water.* The foam swims uppermost, and makes a great show upon the face of the water, yet it is but a heap of bubbles raised by the troubling of the water. Such were the kings of Israel, after their revolt from the house of David, a mere scum; their government had no foundation. No better are the greatest of kings when they set up in opposition to God; when God comes to contend with them by his judgments he can as easily disperse and dissolve them, and bring them to nothing, as the froth upon the water. 2. They shall have no joy of their idols and of their worship of them. And miserable is the case of that people whose gods fail them when their kings do. (1.) The idols they had made, and the altars they had set up in honour of them, should be broken down, and spoiled, and carried away, as common plunder, by the victorious enemy: He *shall break down their altars.* God shall do it by the hand of the Assyrians: the Assyrians shall do it by order from God. *He shall spoil their images, v.* 2. Note, What men make idols of it is just with God to *break down* and *spoil.* But the calf at Bethel was the sovereign idol; it was this that the inhabitants of Samaria doted most upon; now it is here foretold that this should be destroyed: *The glory of it has departed from it (v.* 5) when it is thrown down and defaced, no more to be worshipped; but this is not all: *It shall also be carried to Assyria* (as some think that the calf at Dan was some time before) *for a present to king Jareb.* It was carried to him as a rich booty (for it was a golden calf, and probably adorned with the gifts and offerings of its worshippers) and as a trophy of victory over their enemies: and what more glorious trophy could they bring than this, or more incontestable proof of an absolute conquest? Thus it is said, *The sin of Israel shall be destroyed* (v. 8), that is, the idols which they made the matter of their sin; it is said of them, *They became a sin to all Israel,* 1 Ki. 12:30. Note, If the grace of God prevail not to destroy the love of sin in us, it is just that the providence of God should destroy the food and fuel of sin about us. With the idols, *the high places* shall be destroyed, the *high places of Aven,* that is, of Bethaven (v. 5) or Bethel;

it was called *the house of God* (so Bethel signifies), but now it is called *the house of iniquity,* nay, *iniquity* itself. The kings did not, as they ought to have done, *take away the high places* by the sword of justice, and therefore God will take them away by the sword of war; so that *the thorn and the thistle* shall *come up on their altars,* that is, they shall lie in ruins. Their altars, while they stood, were as thorns and thistles, offensive to God and good men, and fruits of sin and the curse; justly therefore are they buried in thorns and thistles. (2.) The destruction of their idols, their altars, and their high places, shall be the occasion of sorrow, and shame, and terror to them. [1.] It shall be an occasion of sorrow to them. When the calf at Bethel is broken *the people thereof shall mourn over it.* They looked upon the calf to be the protector of their nation, and, when that was gone, thought they must all be undone, which made the poor ignorant people that were deluded into the love of it lament bitterly, as Micah did (Jdg. 18:24), *You have taken away my gods, and what have I more?* The priests that had rejoiced in it shall now mourn for it with the people. Note, Whatever men make a god of they will mourn for the loss of; and an inordinate sorrow for the loss of any worldly good is a sign we made an idol of it. They used to be very merry in the worship of their idols, but now they shall mourn over them; for sinful mirth shall, sooner or later, be turned into mourning. [2.] It shall be an occasion of shame to them (v. 6): *Ephraim shall receive shame* when he sees the gods he trusted to carried into captivity, and *Israel shall be ashamed of his own counsel,* in putting such confidence in them and paying such adoration to them. God's ark and altars were never thrown down till the people rejected them; but the idolatrous altars were thrown down when the people were doting on them, which shows that the contempt of the former, and the veneration for the latter, were the sins for which God visited them. [3.] It shall be an occasion of fear to them (v. 5): *The inhabitants of Samaria shall fear;* they shall be in pain for their gods and afraid of losing them; or, rather, they shall be in pain for themselves and their children and families, when they see the judgments of God breaking in upon them and beginning with their idols, as he *executed judgment against the gods of Egypt,* Ex. 12:12. Thus idolaters are brought in trembling when God arises to *shake terribly the earth,* Isa. 2:21. And here (v. 8), *They shall say to the mountains, Cover us; and to the hills, Fall on us.* The supporters of idolatry (Rev. 6:15, 16) are brought in calling thus in vain to rocks and mountains to shelter them from God's wrath.

Verses 9–15

Here, I. They are put in mind of the sins of their fathers and predecessors, for which God would now reckon with them. It was told them (ch. 9:9) that they had *corrupted themselves, as in the days of Gibeah,* and here (v. 9), *O Israel! thou hast sinned from the days of Gibeah.* Not only the wickedness that was committed in that age is revived in this, and reacted, a copy from that original, but the wickedness that was committed in that age has been continued in a constant series and succession through all the intervening ages down to this; so that the measure of iniquity had been long in filling; and still there had been made additions to it. Or, "*Thou has sinned more than in the days of Gibeah*" (so it may be read); "the sins of this age exceed those of the worst of former ages. The case was bad then, for *there they stood;* the criminals stood in their own defence, and the tribes of Israel, who undertook to chastise them for their wickedness, were *at a stand,* when both in the first and in the second battle the malefactors were the victors; and *the battle in Gibeah against the children of iniquity did not overtake them* till the third engagement, and then did not overtake them all, for 600 made their escape. But thy sin is worse than theirs, and therefore thou canst not expect but that the battle against the children of iniquity should overtake thee, and overcome thee."

II. They have warning given them, fair warning, of the judgments of God that were coming upon them, v. 10. God had hitherto pitied and spared them. Though they had been very provoking, he had a mind to try whether they would be wrought upon by patience and forbearance; but now, "*It is in my desire that I should chastise them;* it is what I have a purpose of and will take pleasure in." He

will *rejoice over them to do them hurt,* Deu. 28:63. Note, Because God does not desire the death and ruin of sinners, therefore he does desire their chastisement. And see what the chastisement it: *The people shall be gathered against them,* as all the other tribes were against Benjamin in the battle of Gibeah. One of the rabbin thus descants upon it: "Because they receive not chastisement from me by my prophets, who in my name rebuke them, I will chastise them by the hands of the people who shall be *gathered against them, when they shall bind themselves in their two furrows,*" that is, when they shall think to fortify themselves, as it were, within a double entrenchment. or, *When I shall bind them for their two transgressions* (so the margin reads it), meaning their corporal and spiritual whoredom, which they are so often charged with, or the *two calves* at Dan and Bethel, or those two great evils mentioned Jer. 2:13. Or, *When I shall bind them to their two furrows,* that is, bring them into servitude to the Assyrians, who shall keep them under the yoke as oxen in the plough, who are bound to the two furrows up the field and down it, and dare not, for fear of the goad, stir a step out of them. The Chaldee says, Those that are *gathered against them shall exercise dominion over them,* in like manner *as a pair of heifers are tied to their two furrows.* Thus those that would not be God's freemen shall be their enemies' slaves, and shall be made to know the difference between *God's service* and *the service of the kingdoms of the countries,* 2 Chr. 12:8.

III. They are made to know that their unacquaintedness with sufferings and hardships should not excuse them from a very miserable captivity, v. 11. See how nice, and tender, and delicate, Ephraim is; he is *as a heifer that is taught to tread out the corn, and loves* that work, because, being not allowed to be muzzled, she has liberty to eat at pleasure, and the work itself was dry and easy, and both its own diversion and its own wages. "But," says God, "I have a yoke to put upon *her fair neck,* fair as it is. *I will make Ephraim to ride,* that is, I will tame them, or cause them to be ridden by the Assyrians and other conquerors that shall rule them with rigour, as men do the beasts they ride upon (Ps. 66:12); and *Judah* too shall be made to *plough,* and *Jacob to break the clods,*" that is, they shall be used hardly, but not so hardly as Ephraim. Note, It is just with God to make those know what hardships mean that indulge themselves too much in their own ease and pleasure. The learned Dr. Pocock inclines to another sense of these words, as intimating the tender gentle methods God took with this people, to bring them into obedience to his law, as a reason why they should return to that obedience; he had managed them as the husbandman does his cattle that he trains up for service. Ephraim being as a docile heifer, fit to be employed, God took hold of *her fair neck,* to accustom her to the hand, *harnessed her,* or put the yoke of his commandments upon her, gave his people Israel a law, that, being trained up in his institutions, they might not be tempted by the usages of the heathen; he had used all fair and likely means with them to keep them in their obedience, had set *Judah to plough* and *Jacob to break the clods,* had employed them in the observance of precepts proper for them; and yet they would not be retained in their obedience, but started aside.

IV. They are invited and encouraged to return to God by prayer, repentance, and reformation, v. 12, 13. See here,

1. The duties they are called to. They are *God's husbandry* (1 Co. 3:9), and the duties are expressed in language borrowed from the husbandman's calling. If they would not be brought into bondage by their oppressors, let them return to God's service. (1.) Let them *break up the fallow ground;* let them cleanse their hearts from all corrupt affections and lusts, which are as weeds and thorns, and let them be humbled for their sins, and be of a broken and contrite spirit in the sense of them; let them be full of sorrow and shame at the remembrance of them, and prepare to receive the divine precepts, as the ground that is ploughed is to receive the seed, that it may take root. See Jer. 4:3. (2.) Let them *sow to themselves in righteousness;* let them return to the practice of good works, according to the law of God, which is the rule of righteousness; let them abound in works of piety towards God, and of justice and charity towards one another, and herein let them *sow to the Spirit,* as the apostle speaks, Gal. 6:7, 8. Every action is seed sown. Let them *sow in right-*

eousness; let them sow what they should sow, do what they should do, and they themselves shall have the benefit of it. (3.) Let them *seek the Lord;* let them look up to him for his grace, and beg of him to bless the *seed sown.* The husbandman must plough and sow with an eye to God, asking of him rain in the season thereof.

2. The arguments used for the pressing of these duties. Consider, (1.) It is time to do it; it is *high time.* The husbandman sows in seed-time, and, if that time be far spent, he applies to the work with the more diligence. Note, Seeking the Lord is to be every day's work, but there are some special occasions given by the providence and grace of God when it is, in a particular manner, time to seek him. (2.) If we do our part, God will do his. If we *sow to ourselves in righteousness* — if we be careful and diligent to do our duty, in a dependence upon his grace — he will shower down his grace upon us, will *rain righteousness,* the very thing that those need most who are to sow *in righteousness;* for *by the grace of God we are what we are.* Some apply it to Christ, who should come in the fulness of time, and for whose coming they must prepare themselves; he shall come as *the Lord our righteousness,* and shall *rain righteousness upon us,* that everlasting righteousness which he has brought in; he will grant us of it abundantly. It is foretold (Ps. 72:6) that *he shall come down like rain.* (3.) If we *sow in righteousness,* we shall *reap in mercy,* which agrees with that promise, If we *sow to the Spirit,* we shall *of the Spirit reap life everlasting.* We shall reap *according to the measure of mercy* (so the word is); it shall be a great reward, according to the *riches of mercy,* such a reward, not as becomes such mean creatures as we are to receive, but as becomes a God of infinite mercy to give, a reward, *not of debt,* but *of grace.* We reap not in merit, but in mercy. It is what is sown; God gives a body as it has pleased him. (4.) We have *ploughed wickedness and reaped iniquity;* and the time *past of our life may suffice* that we have done so, *v.* 13. "You have taken a great deal of pains in the service of sin, have laboured at it in the very fire; and will you grudge to bear the burden and heat of the day in God's service and in doing that which will be for your own advantage? You have done much to damn your souls; will you not undo it again, and do something to save them?" (5.) We never got any thing in the service of sin. They have *ploughed wickedness* (that is, they have done the drudgery of sin), and they have *reaped iniquity,* that is, they have got all that is to be got by it; they have carried it on to the *harvest,* and what the better? It is all a cheat. *They have eaten the fruit of lies,* fruit that is but a lie, which looks fair, but is rotten within; the *works of darkness* are *unfruitful works,* Eph. 5:11; Rom. 6:21. Even the gains of sin yield the sinner no satisfaction. (6.) As our comforts, so our confidences, in the service of sin will certainly fail us: *"Thou didst trust in thy ways, in the multitude of thy mighty men;* thou has stayed thyself upon creatures, thy own power and policy, and therefore hast ventured to plough wickedness, and thy hopes have deceived thee; come therefore, and seek the Lord, and thy hope in him shall not deceive thee."

V. They are threatened with utter destruction, both for their carnal practices and for their carnal confidences, *v.* 14, 15. *Therefore,* because thou has sown wickedness, and trusted in thy own way, *a tumult shall arise among thy people,* either by insurrections at home or invasions from abroad, either of which will put a kingdom into confusion and make a noise, much more both together. 1. Their cities and strongholds shall be a prey to the enemy: The *fortresses* which they confided in, and in which they had laid up their effects, shall be seized and rifled, as *Shalman spoiled Beth-arbel in the day of battle.* This refers to some event that had lately happened, not elsewhere recorded; and probably Shalman is the same with Shalmaneser king of Assyria, who had lately put some town, or castle, or house *(Beth-arbel is the house of Arbel),* under *military execution,* which perhaps he used with severity in the beginning of his conquests, to terrify other garrisons into a speedy surrender at the first summons. God tells them that thus Samaria should be *spoiled.* 2. The inhabitants shall be put to the *sword,* as it was at *Beth-arbel;* when it was taken *the mother was dashed in pieces upon her children,* that is, they were both dashed in pieces together by the fury of the soldiers. See what cruel work war makes. *Jusque datum sceleri — Wickedness has free course.* It is

strange that any of the human race could be so inhuman; but see what comes of sin. *Homo homini lupus — Man is a wolf to man,* and then, *Homo homini agnus — Man is a lamb to man.* 3. Even royal blood shall be mingled with common gore: *In a morning shall the king of Israel utterly be cut off, v.* 15. Hoshea was the last king of Israel; in him the whole kingdom was *cut off* and came to a period; it may refer either to him or to some of his predecessors that were cut off by treachery. It shall be done *in a morning,* in a very little time, as suddenly as the dawning of the morning, or at the time appointed, for so the morning comes, punctually at its time. Or *in the morning,* when they think the night of calamity is over, and expect a returning day, then shall all their hopes be dashed by the sudden cutting off of their king, *v.* 7. Kings, though gods to us, are men to God, and shall die like men. And *(lastly)* what does all this desolation owe its rise to? What is the spring of this bloodshed? He tells us *(v.* 15): *So shall Bethel do unto you.* Bethel was the place where one of the calves was; Gilgal, where *all their wickedness* is said to have been, was hard by; there was their *great wickedness,* the *evil of their evil* (so the word is), the sum and quintessence of their sin; and that was it that *did this to them,* that made all this havoc, for that was it that provoked God to bring it upon them. He does not say, "So shall the *king of Assyria* do to you;" but, "So shall *Bethel* do to you." Note, Whatever mischief is done to us it is sin that does it. Are the fortresses spoiled? Are the women and children murdered? Is the king cut off? It is sin that does all this. It is sin that ruins soul, body, estate, all. *So shall Bethel do unto you.* It is *thy own wickedness* that *corrects thee* and *thy backslidings* that *reprove thee.*

CHAPTER 11

In this chapter we have, I. The great goodness of God towards his people Israel, and the great things he had done for them (*v.* 1, 3, 4). II. Their ungrateful conduct towards him, notwithstanding his favours towards them (*v.* 2–4, 7, 12). III. Threatenings of wrath against them for their ingratitude and treachery (*v.* 5, 6). IV. Mercy remembered in the midst of wrath (*v.* 8, 9). V. Promises of what God would yet do for them (*v.* 10, 11). VI. An honourable character given of Judah (*v.* 12).

Verses 1–7

Here we find,

I. God very gracious to Israel. They were a people for whom he had done more than for any people under heaven, and to whom he had given more, which they are here, I will not say upbraided with (for God gives, and upbraids not), but put in mind of, as an aggravation of their sin and an encouragement to repentance. 1. He had a kindness for them when they were young (*v.* 1): *When Israel was a child then I loved him;* when they first began to multiply into a nation in Egypt God then *set his love upon them,* and *chose them because he loved them,* because he would love them, Deu. 7:7, 8. When they were weak and helpless as children, foolish and froward as children, when they were outcasts, and children exposed, then God *loved them;* he pitied them, and testified his goodwill to them; he bore them as the nurse does the sucking child, nourished them, and suffered their manners. Note, Those that have grown up, nay, those that have grown old, ought often to reflect upon the goodness of God to them in their childhood. 2. He delivered them out of the house of bondage: *I called my son out of Egypt,* because a son, because a beloved son. When God demanded Israel's discharge from Pharaoh he called them *his son,* his *first-born.* Note, Those whom God loves he calls out of the bondage of sin and Satan into the glorious liberty of his children. These words are said to have been fulfilled in Christ, when, upon the death of Herod, he and his parents were *called out of Egypt* (Mt. 2:15), so that the words have a double aspect, speaking historically of the calling of Israel out of Egypt and prophetically of the bringing of Christ thence; and the former was a type of the latter, and a pledge and earnest of the many and great favours God had in reserve for that people, especially the sending of his Son into the world, and the bringing him again into the land of Israel when they had unkindly driven him out, and he might justly never have returned. The calling of Christ out of Egypt was a figure of the calling of all that are his, through him, out of spiritual slavery. 3. He gave them a good education, took care of them, took pains with them, not only as a father or tutor, but, such is the condescension of di-

vine grace, as a mother or nurse (*v.* 3): *I taught Ephraim also to go,* as a child in leading-strings is taught. When they were in the wilderness God led them by the pillar of cloud and fire, showed them the way in which they should go, and bore them up, *taking them by the arms.* He taught *them to go* in the way of his commandments, by the institutions of the ceremonial law, which were as tutors and governors to that people under age. He took them by the arms, to guide them, that they might not stray, and to hold them up, that they might not stumble and fall. God's spiritual Israel are thus supported. *Thou has holden me by my right hand,* Ps. 73:23. 4. When any thing was amiss with them, or they were ever so little out of order, he was their physician: *"I healed them;* I not only took a tender care of them (a friend may do that), but wrought an effectual cure: it is a God only that can do that. *I am the Lord that healeth thee* (Ex. 15:26), that redresseth all thy grievances." 5. He brought them into his service by mild and gentle methods (*v.* 4): *I drew them with cords of a man, with bands of love.* Note, It is God's work to draw poor souls to himself; and none can come to him except he draw them, Jn. 6:44. He draws, (1.) *With the cords of a man,* with such cords as men draw with that have a principle of humanity, or such cords as men are drawn with; he dealt with them *as men,* in an equitable rational way, in an easy gentle way, *with the cords of Adam.* He dealt with them as with Adam in innocency, bringing them at once into a paradise, and into covenant with himself. (2.) *With bands of love,* or *cartropes* of love. This word signifies stronger cords than the former. He did not drive them by force into his service, whether they would or no, nor rule them with rigour, nor detain them by violence, but his attractives were all loving and endearing, all sweet and gentle, that he might overcome them with kindness. Moses, whom he made their guide, was the meekest man in the world. *Kindnesses* among men we commonly call *obligations,* or *bonds,* bonds of love. Thus *God draws with the savour of his good ointments* (Cant. 1:4), draws *with lovingkindness,* Jer. 31:3. Thus God deals with us, and we must deal in like manner with those that are under our instruction and government, deal rationally and mildly with them. 6. He eased them of the burdens they had been long groaning under: *I was to them as those that take off the yoke on their jaws,* alluding to the care of the good husbandman, who is merciful to his beast, and will not tire him with hard and constant labour. Probably, in those times, the yoke on the neck of the oxen was fastened with some bridle, or headstall, over the jaws, which *muzzled the mouth of the ox.* Israel in Egypt were thus restrained from the enjoyments of their comforts and constrained to hard labour; but God eased them, *removed their shoulder from the burden,* Ps. 81:6. Note, Liberty is a great mercy, especially out of bondage. 7. He supplied them with food convenient. In Egypt they fared hard, but, when God brought them out, he *laid meat unto them,* as the husbandman, when he has unyoked his cattle, fodders them. God rained manna about their camp, bread from heaven, angels' food; other creatures *seek their meat,* but God laid meat to his own people, as we do to our children, was himself their caterer and carver, anticipated *them with the blessings of goodness.*

II. Here is Israel very ungrateful to God.

1. They were deaf and disobedient to his voice. He spoke to them by his messengers, Moses and his other prophets, called them from their sins, called them to himself, to their work and duty; but *as they called them so they went from them;* they rebelled in those particular instances wherein they were admonished; the more pressing and importunate the prophets were with them, to persuade them to that which was good, the more refractory they were, and the more resolute in their evil ways, disobeying for disobedience-sake. This foolishness is bound in the hearts of children, who, as soon as they are taught to go, will go from those that call them.

2. They were fond of idols, and worshipped them: They *sacrificed to Baalim,* first one Baal and then another, and *burnt incense to graven images,* though they were called to by the prophets of the Lord again and again not to do this abominable thing which he hated. Idolatry was the sin which from the beginning, and all along, had most easily beset them.

3. They were regardless of God, and of his favours to them: *They knew not that I healed them.* They looked only

at Moses and Aaron, the instruments of their relief, and, when any thing was amiss, quarrelled with them, but looked not through them to God who employed them. Or, When God corrected them, and kept them under a severe discipline, they understood not that it was for their good, and that God thereby *healed them,* and it was necessary for the perfecting of their cure, else they would have been better reconciled to the methods God took. Note, Ignorance is at the bottom of ingratitude, *ch.* 2:8.

4. They were strongly inclined to apostasy. This is the blackest article in the charge (*v.* 7): *My people are bent to backsliding from me.* Every word here is aggravating. (1.) They *backslide.* There is no hold of them, no stedfastness in them; they seem to come forward, towards God, but they quickly slide back again, and are as a deceitful bow. (2.) They backslide *from me,* from God, the chief good, the fountain of life and living waters, from their God who never turned from them, nor war as a wilderness to them. (3.) They are *bent to backslide;* they are ready to sin; there is in their natures a propensity to that which is evil; at the best they hang in suspense between God and the world, so that a little thing serves to draw them the wrong way; they are forward to close with every temptation. It also intimates that they are resolute in sin; their hearts are *fully set in them to do evil* the bias is strong that way; and they persist in their backslidings, whatever is said or done to stop them; and yet, (4.) "They are, in profession, *my people.* They are *called by my name,* and profess relation to me; they are mine, whom I have done much for and expect much from, whom I have *nourished* and *brought up, as children,* and yet they backslide *from me.*" Note, In our repentance we ought to lament not only our backslidings, but our *bent to backslide,* not only our actual transgressions, but our original corruption, the sin that dwells in us, the carnal mind.

5. They were strangely averse to repentance and reformation. Here are two expressions of their obstinacy: — (1.) *They refused to return, v.* 5. So much were they bent to backslide that, though they could not but find, upon trial, the folly of their backslidings, and that when they forsook God they changed for the worse, yet they went on frowardly. *I have loved strangers, and after them I will go.* They were commanded to return, were courted and entreated to return, were promised that if they would they should be kindly received, but they refused. (2.) Though *they called them to the Most High.* God's prophets and ministers called them to return to the God from whom they had revolted, to the most high God, from whom they had sunk into this wretched degeneracy; they called them from the worship of the idols, which were so much below them, and the worship of which was therefore their disparagement, to the true God, who was so much above them, and the worship of whom was therefore their preferment; they called them from this earth to high and heavenly things; but they called in vain. *None at all would exalt him.* Though he is the most high God they would not acknowledge him to be so, would do nothing to honour him nor give him the glory due to his name. Or, They would not *exalt themselves,* would not rise out of that state of apostasy and misery into which they had precipitated themselves; but there they contentedly lay still, would not lift up their heads nor lift up their souls. Note, God's faithful ministers have taken a great deal of pains, to no purpose, with backsliding children, have called them to the Most High; but none would stir, *none at all would exalt him.*

III. Here is God very angry, and justly so, with Israel; see what are the tokens of God's displeasure with which they are here threatened. 1. God, who brought them out of Egypt, to take them for a people to himself, since they would not be faithful to him, shall bring them into a worse condition than he at first found them in (*v.* 5): *"He shall not return into the land of Egypt,* though that was a house of bondage grievous enough; but he shall go into a harder service, for *the Assyrian shall be his king,* who will use him worse than ever Pharaoh did." They shall not return into Egypt, which lies near, where they may hear often from their own country, and whence they may hope shortly to return to it again; but they shall be carried into Assyria, which lies much more remote, and where they shall be cut off from all correspondence with their own land and from all hopes of returning to it, and justly, because *they refused to return.* Note, Those that will not return to the duties they have left cannot expect to return to the comforts they have lost. 2. God, who gave them Canaan, that good land, and a very safe and comfortable settlement in it, shall bring his judgments upon them there, which shall make their habitation unsafe and uncomfortable (*v.* 6): *The sword* shall come upon them, the sword of war, the sword of a foreign enemy, prevailing against them and triumphing over them. (1.) This judgment shall spread far. The sword shall fasten upon their *cities,* those nests of people and store-houses of wealth; it shall likewise reach to their *branches,* the country villages (so some), the citizens themselves (so others), or the *bars* (so the word signifies) and gates of their city, or all the branches of their revenue and wealth, or their children, the branches of their families. (2.) It shall last long: It shall *abide on their cities.* David thought *three months* flying before his enemies was the only judgment of the three that was to be excepted against; but this *sword* shall abide much longer than three months on the cities of Israel. They continued their rebellions against God, and therefore God continued his judgments on them. (3.) It shall *make a full end:* It shall *consume their branches, and devour them,* and lay all waste, and this *because of their own counsels,* that is, because they would have their own projects, which God therefore, in a way of righteous judgment, gave them up to. Note, The confusion of sinners is owing to their contrivance. God's counsels would have saved them, but their own counsels ruined them.

Verses 8–12

In these verses we have,

I. God's wonderful backwardness to destroy Israel (*v.* 8, 9): *How shall I give thee up?* Here observe,

1. God's gracious debate within himself concerning Israel's case, a debate between justice and mercy, in which victory plainly inclines to mercy's side. Be astonished, O heavens! at this, and wonder, O earth! at the glory of God's goodness. Not that there are any such struggles in God as there are in us, or that he is ever fluctuating or unresolved; no, he is in one mind, and knows it; but they are expressions after the manner of men, designed to show what severity the sin of Israel had deserved, and yet how divine grace would be glorified in sparing them notwithstanding. The connexion of this with what goes before is very surprising; it was said of Israel (*v.* 7) that they were *bent to backslide from God,* that though they were called to him they *would not exalt him,* upon which, one would think, it should have followed, "Now I am determined to destroy them, and never show them mercy any more." No, such is the sovereignty of mercy, such the freeness, the fulness, of divine grace, that it follows immediately, *How shall I give thee up?* See here, (1.) The proposals that justice makes concerning Israel, the suggestion of which is here implied. Let Ephraim be given up, as an incorrigible son is given up to be disinherited, as an incurable patient is given over by his physician. Let him be given up to ruin. Let Israel be delivered into the enemy's hand, as a lamb to the lion to be torn in pieces; let them be made as Admah and set as Zeboim, the two cities that with Sodom and Gomorrah were destroyed by fire and brimstone rained from heaven upon them; let them be utterly and irreparably ruined, and be made as like these cities in desolation as they have been in sin. Let that curse which is written in the law be executed upon them, that the *whole land* shall be *brimstone and salt, like the overthrow of Sodom and Gomorrah, Admah and Zeboim,* Deu. 29:23. Ephraim and Israel deserve to be thus abandoned, and God will do them no wrong if he deal thus with them. (2.) The opposition that mercy makes to these proposals: *How shall I do it?* As the tender father reasons with himself, "How can I cast off my untoward son? for he is my son, though he be untoward; how can I find in my heart to do it?" Thus, "Ephraim has been a dear son, a pleasant child: *How can I do it?* He is ripe for ruin; judgments stand ready to seize him; there wants nothing but *giving him up,* but I cannot do it. They have been a people near unto me; there are yet some good among them; theirs are the children of the covenant; if they be ruined, the enemy will triumph; it may be they will yet repent and reform; and therefore how can I do it?" Note, The God of heaven is slow to anger, and is especially loth to abandon a people to utter ruin that have been in special relation to him. See how mercy works upon the mention of those severe proceedings: *My heart is turned within me,* as we say, Our heart fails us, when we come to do a thing that is against the grain with us. God speaks as if he were conscious to himself of a strange striving of affections in compassion to Israel: as Lam. 1:20, *My bowels are troubled; my heart is turned within me.* As it follows here, *My repentings are kindled together.* His bowels yearned towards them, and *his soul was grieved* for their sin and *misery,* Jdg. 10:16. Compare Jer. 31:20. *Since I spoke against him my bowels are troubled for him.* When God was to give up his Son to be a sacrifice for sin, and a Saviour for sinners, he did not say, How shall I give him up? No, he *spared not his own Son;* it *pleased the Lord to bruise him;* and *therefore* God spared not him, that he might spare us. But this is only the language of the day of his patience; when men have sinned that away, and the great day of his wrath comes, then no difficulty is made of it; nay, *I will laugh at their calamity.*

2. His gracious determination of this debate. After a long contest mercy in the issue rejoices against judgment, has the last word, and carries the day, *v.* 9. It is decreed that the reprieve shall be lengthened out yet longer, and *I will not* now *execute the fierceness of my anger,* though I am angry; though they shall not go altogether unpunished, yet he will mitigate the sentence and abate the rigour of it. He will show himself to be justly angry, but not implacably so; they shall be corrected, but not consumed. *I will not return to destroy Ephraim;* the judgments that have been inflicted shall not be repeated, shall not go so deep as they have deserved. He will not *return to destroy,* as soldiers, when they have pillaged a town once, return a second time, to take more, as when *what the palmerworm has left the locust has eaten.* It is added, in the close of the verse, *"I will not enter into the city,* into Samaria, or any other of their cities; I will not enter into them as an enemy, utterly to destroy them, and lay them waste, as I did the cities of Admah and Zeboim."

3. The ground and reason of this determination: *For I am God and not man, the Holy One of Israel.* To encourage them, to hope that they shall find mercy, consider, (1.) What he is in himself: *He is God, and not man,* as in other things, so in pardoning sin and sparing sinners. If they had offended a man like themselves, he would not, he could not have borne it; his passion would have overpowered his compassion, and he would have executed the fierceness of his anger; but *I am God, and not man.* He is *Lord of his anger,* whereas men's anger commonly lords it over them. If an earthly prince were in such a strait between justice and mercy, he would be at a loss how to compromise the matter between them; but he who is God, and not man, knows how to find out an expedient to secure the honour of his justice and yet advance the honour of his mercy. Man's compassions are nothing in comparison with the tender mercies of our God, whose thoughts and ways, in receiving returning sinners, are as much above ours as heaven is above the earth, Isa. 55:9. Note, It is a great encouragement to our hope in God's mercies to remember that he is *God, and not man.* He is *the Holy One.* One would think this were a reason why he should reject such a provoking people. No; God knows how to spare and pardon poor sinners, not only without any reproach to his holiness, but very much to the honour of it, as he is *faithful and just to forgive us our sins,* and therein *declares his righteousness,* now Christ has purchased the pardon and he has promised it. (2.) What he is to them; he is the *Holy One in the midst of thee;* his holiness is engaged for the good of his church, and even in this corrupt and degenerate land and age there were some that gave thanks at the remembrance of his holiness, and he required of them all to be *holy as he is,* Lev. 19:2. As long as we have the *Holy One in the midst of us* we are safe and well; but woe to us when he leaves us! Note, Those who submit to the influence may take the comfort of God's holiness.

II. Here is his wonderful forwardness to do good for Israel, which appears in this, that he will qualify them to receive the good he designs for them (*v.* 10, 11): *They shall walk after the Lord.* This respects the same favour with that (*ch.* 3:5), *They shall return, and seek the Lord their God;* it is spoken of the ten tribes, and had its accomplishment, in part, in the return of some of them with those of the two tribes in Ezra's time; but it had its more full accomplishment in God's spiritual Israel, the gospel-church, brought together and incorporated by the gospel of Christ. The ancient Jews referred it to the time of the Messiah; the learned Dr. Pocock looks upon it as a prophecy of Christ's coming to preach the gospel to the dispersed children of Israel, the children of God that were scattered abroad. And then observe, 1. How they were to be called and brought together: *The Lord shall roar like a lion.* The *word of the Lord* (so says the Chaldee) *shall be as a lion that roars.* Christ is called *the lion of the tribe of Judah,* and his gospel, in the beginning of it, was *the voice of one crying in the wilderness.* When Christ cried with a loud voice it was as *when a lion roared,* Rev. 10:3. The voice of the gospel was heard afar, as the *roaring of a lion,* and it was a *mighty voice.* See Joel 3:16. 2. What impression this call should make upon them, such an impression as the roaring of a lion makes upon all the beasts of the forest: *When he shall roar then the children shall tremble.* See Amos 3:8, *The lion has roared; the Lord* God *has spoken;* and then *who will not fear?* When those whose hearts the gospel reached trembled, and were astonished, and cried out, *What shall we do?* — when they were by it put upon working out their salvation, and worshipping God with fear and trembling, then this promise was fulfilled. *The children shall tremble from the west.* The dispersed Jews were carried eastward, to Assyria and Babylon, and those that returned came from the east; therefore this seems to have reference to the calling of the Gentiles that lay westward from Canaan, for that way especially the gospel spread. They shall *tremble;* they shall move and come with trembling, with care and haste, *from the west,* from the nations that lay that way, to the mountain of the Lord (Isa. 2:3), to the gospel-Jerusalem, upon hearing the alarm of the gospel. The apostle speaks of *mighty signs and wonders* that were wrought by the preaching of the gospel from *Jerusalem round about to Illyricum,* Rom. 15:19. Then the children trembled from the west. And, whereas Israel after the flesh was dispersed in Egypt and Assyria, it is promised that they shall be effectually summoned thence (*v.* 11): *They shall tremble;* they shall come trembling, and with all haste, *as a bird* upon the wing, *out of Egypt,* and *as a dove out of the land of Assyria;* a dove is noted for swift and constant flight, especially when she flies *to her windows,* which the flocking of Jews and Gentiles to the church is here compared to, as it is Isa. 60:8. Wherever those are that belong to the election of grace — east, west, north, or south — they shall *hear the joyful sound,* and be wrought upon by it; those of Egypt and Assyria shall come together; those that lay most remote from each other shall meet in Christ, and be incorporated in the church. Of the uniting of Egypt and Assyria, it was prophesied, Isa. 19:23. 3. What effect these impressions should have upon them. Being *moved with fear,* they shall flee to the ark: *They shall walk after the Lord,* after *the service of the Lord* (so the Chaldee); they shall take the Lord Christ for their *leader and commander;* they shall enlist themselves under him as the captain of their salvation, and give up themselves to the direction of the Spirit as their guide by the word; they shall *leave all* to *follow Christ,* as becomes *disciples.* Note, Our holy trembling at the word of Christ will draw us to him, not drive us from him. When he *roars like a lion* the slaves tremble and flee from him, the children tremble and flee to him. 4. What entertainment they shall meet with at their return (*v.* 11): *I will place them in their houses* (all those that come at the gospel-call shall have a place and a name in the gospel-church, in the particular churches which are their houses, to which they pertain; they shall dwell in God, and be at home in him, both easy and safe, as a man in his own house; they shall have mansions, for there are many in *our Father's house*), in his tabernacle on earth and his temple in heaven, in *everlasting habitations,* which may be called *their houses,* for they are *the lot* they shall stand in *at the end of the days.*

III. Here is a sad complaint of the treachery of Ephraim and Israel, which may be an intimation that it is not Israel after the flesh, but the spiritual Israel, to whom the foregoing promises belong, for as for this Ephraim, this Israel, they *compass God about with lies and deceit;* all their services of him, when they pretended to compass his altar, were feigned and hypocritical; when they surrounded him with their prayers and praises, every one having a petition to present to him, they *lied to him with their mouth and flattered him with their tongue;* their pretensions were so fair, and yet their intentions so foul, that they would, if possible, have imposed upon God himself. Their professions and promises were all a cheat, and yet with these they thought to compass God about, to enclose him as it were, to keep him among them, and prevent his leaving them.

IV. Here is a pleasant commendation of the integrity of the two tribes, which they held fast, and this comes in as an aggravation of the perfidiousness of the ten tribes, and a reason why God had that mercy in store for Judah which he had not for Israel (*ch.* 1:6, 7), for *Judah yet rules with God and is faithful with the saints,* or *with the Most Holy.* 1. *Judah rules with God,* that is, he serves God, and the service of God is not only true liberty and freedom, but it is dignity and dominion. *Judah rules,* that is, the princes and governors of Judah *rule with God;* they use their power for him, for his honour, and the support of his interest. Those *rule with God* that *rule in the fear of God* (2 Sa. 23:3), and it is their honour to do so, and their praise shall be *of God,* as Judah's here is. Judah is *Israel — a prince with God.* 2. He is *faithful with the holy God,* keeps close to his worship and *to his saints,* with Abraham, Isaac, and Jacob, whose steps they faithfully tread in. They *walk in the way of good men;* and those that do so *rule with God,* they have a mighty interest in Heaven. Judah *yet* does thus, which intimates that the time would come when Judah also would revolt and degenerate. Note, When we see how many there are that compass God about *with lies and deceit* it may be a comfort to us to think that God has his remnant that cleave to him with purpose of heart, and are faithful to his saints; and for those who are thus faithful unto death is reserved a crown of life, when hypocrites and all liars shall have their portion without.

CHAPTER 12

In this chapter we have, I. A high charge drawn up against both Israel and Judah for their sins, which were the ground of God's controversy with them (*v.* 1, 2). Particularly the sin of fraud and injustice, which Ephraim is charged with (*v.* 7), and justifies himself in (*v.* 8). And the sin of idolatry (*v.* 11), by which God is provoked to contend with them (*v.* 14). II. The aggravations of the sins they are charged with, taken from the honour God put upon their father Jacob (*v.* 3–5), the advancement of them into a people from low and mean beginnings (*v.* 12, 13), and the provision he had made them of helps for their souls by the prophets he sent them (*v.* 10). III. A call to the unconverted to turn to God (*v.* 6). IV. An intimation of mercy that God had in store for them (*v.* 9).

Verses 1–6

In these verses,

I. Ephraim is convicted of folly, in staying himself upon Egypt and Assyria, when he was in straits (*v.* 1): *Ephraim feeds on wind,* that is, feeds himself with vain hopes of assistance from man, when he is at variance with God; and, when he meets with disappointments, he still pursues the same game, and greedily pants and *follows after the east wind,* which he cannot catch holy of, nor, if he could, would it be nourishing, nay, would be noxious. We say of the *wind in the east,* It is *good neither for man nor beast.* It was said (*ch.* 8:7), He *sows the wind;* and as he sows so he reaps (He *reaps the whirlwind*); and as he reaps so he feeds — He feeds on the wind, the *east wind.* Note, Those that make creatures their confidence make fools of themselves, and take a great deal of pains to put a cheat upon their own souls and to prepare vexation for themselves: *He daily increaseth lies,* that is, multiplies his correspondences and leagues with his neighbours, which will all prove deceitful to him; nay, they will prove desolation to him. Those very nations that he makes his refuge will prove his ruin. Those that stay themselves upon lies will be still coveting to increase them, that they may build their hopes firmly upon them; as if many lies twisted together would make one truth, or many broken reeds and rotten supports one sound one, which is a great delusion and will prove to them a great desolation; for those that *observe lying vanities* the more they increase them the more disappointments they prepare for themselves and the further they run from *their own mercies.* The men of Ephraim did so when they thought to secure the Assyrians in their interests by a *solemn league,* signed, sealed, and sworn to: *They make a covenant with the Assyrians,* but they will find there is no hold of them; that potent prince will be a slave to his word no longer than he pleases. They thought to secure the Egyptians for their confederates by a rich present of the commodities of their country, not only to purchase their favour, but to show that their friendship was worth having: *Oil is carried into Egypt.* But the Egyptians, when they had got the bribe, dropped the cause, and Ephraim was never the better for them. *Oleum perdidit et operam — The oil and the labour are both lost.* This was *feeding on wind;* this was *increasing lies and desolation.*

II. Judah is contended with too, and Jacob, which includes both Ephraim and Judah (*v.* 2): *The Lord has also a controversy with Judah;* for though he had a while ago *ruled with God,* and been *faithful with the saints,* yet now he begins to degenerate. Or though, in keeping close to the house of David and the house of Aaron, and in them to the covenants of royalty and priesthood, they were so far *in the right,* in the former they *ruled with God* and in the latter were *faithful to the saints,* yet upon other accounts God *had a controversy* with them, and would punish them. Note, Mens *being in the right in some things, in the main things, will not exempt them from correction, and therefore should not exempt them from reproof, for those things wherein they are in the wrong. There were those of the seven churches of Asia whom Christ approved and commended, and yet he adds, Nevertheless I have something against thee.* So here; though the seed of Jacob are a people near to God, yet God will punish them according to the evil ways they are found in and the evil doings they are found guilty of; for God sees sin even in his own people, and will reckon with them for it.

III. Both Ephraim and Judah are put in mind of their father Jacob, whose seed they were and whose name they bore (and it was their honour), of the extraordinary things which he did and which God did for him, that they might be the more ashamed of themselves for degenerating from so illustrious a progenitor and staining the lustre of so great a name, and yet that they might be engaged and encouraged to return to God, the God of their father Jacob, in hopes for his sake to find favour with him. He had called this people Jacob (*v.* 2), threatening to punish them; but *how shall I give them up?* How shall that dear name be forgotten?

1. Three glorious things concerning Jacob the person Jacob the people are here put in mind of; but by brief hints only, for it is presumed that they knew the story: — (1.) His struggling with Esau in the womb: There *he took his brother by the heel, v.* 3. We have the story Gen. 25:26. It was an early act of bravery, and an effort for the best precedency, a pious ambition for that birthright in the covenant which Esau is justly branded as profane for despising. But his degenerate seed, by mingling with the nations, and making leagues with them, profaned that crown, and laid that honour in the dust, which he so gloriously put in for. Then it was that the dominion was given to him: *The elder shall serve the younger.* Then he was owned of God as his beloved: *Jacob have I loved, but Esau have I hated.* But they had by their sin forfeited both the love of God and dominion over their neighbours. (2.) His wrestling with the angel. "Remember how your father Jacob had *power with God by his* own *strength,* the strength he had by the gift of God, who *pleaded* not *against him by his great power,* but *put strength into him,*" Job 22:6. The angel he wrestled with is called *God,* and therefore is supposed to be the *Son of God,* the angel of the covenant. "God was both a combatant with Jacob and an assistant of him, showing, in the latter respect, greater strength than in the former, fighting as it were against him with his left hand and for him with his right, and to that putting greater force." So, Dr. Pocock. The providence of God fought against him when he met with one danger after another, in his return homewards; but the grace of God enabled him to go on cheerfully in his way, and, when his faith acted upon the divine promise that was for him prevailed above his fears that arose from the divine providences that were against him, then *by his strength he had power with God.* But it refers especially to his prayer for deliverance from Esau, and for a blessing: *He had power over the angel and prevailed,* for he *wept and made supplication.* Here was a mixture of the greatest courage and the greatest tenderness, Jacob wrestling like a champion and yet weeping like a child. Note, Prayers and tears are the weapons with which the saints have obtained the most glorious victories. Thus Jacob commenced *Israel — a prince with God;*

his posterity was called *Israel,* but they were unworthy the name, for they had forfeited and lost their communion with God, and their interest in him, by revolting from their duty to him. (3.) His meeting with God at Bethel: God *found him* in Bethel, *and there he spoke with us.* God found him the first time in Bethel, as he went to Padanaram (Gen. 28:10), and a second time after his return, Gen. 35:9, etc. It is probable that this refers to both; for in both God spoke to Jacob, and renewed the covenant with him, and the prophet might very well say, *There he spoke with us* who are the seed of Jacob, for both times that God spoke with Jacob at Bethel he spoke with him concerning his seed. Gen. 28:14, *Thy seed shall be as the dust of the earth;* and Gen. 35:12, *This land I will give unto thy seed.* Thus God then covenanted with him and his seed after him. Now justly are they upbraided with this; for in that very place which their father Jacob called *Bethel — the house of God,* in remembrance of the communion he there had with God, did they set up one of the calves, and worship it; thus they turned that Bethel into a *Beth-aven* — a *house of iniquity.* There God *spoke with them* exceedingly great and precious promises, which they had despised and lost the benefit of.

2. Two inferences are here drawn from these stories concerning Jacob, for instruction to his seed: —

(1.) Here is a use of information. From what passed between God and Jacob we may learn that *Jehovah, the Lord God of hosts,* is *the God of Israel;* he was the God of Jacob, and this is *his memorial* throughout all the generations of the seed of Jacob (*v.* 5) — the more shame for those who forgot the memorial of their church, deserted the God of their fathers, and exchanged a *Lord of hosts* for Baalim. Note, Those only are accounted the people of God that keep up a memorial of God, such a memorial of him as he himself has instituted, by which he makes himself known and will have us to remember him. Here are two memorials of his, by which he is distinguished from all others, and is to be acknowledged and adored by us. [1.] The former denotes his *existence of himself.* He is Jehovah, much the same with *I AM,* the same that *was, and is, and is to come,* infinite, eternal, and unchangeable. Jehovah is *his memorial,* his peculiar name. [2.] The latter denotes his dominion over all: He is the *God of hosts,* that has all the hosts of heaven and earth at his beck and command, and makes what use he pleases of them. Jacob saw *Mahanaim* — God's *two hosts,* about the time that he *wrestled with the angel* (Gen. 32:1, 2), and so learned to call God the *God of hosts,* and transmitted it to us as his memorial. God's names, titles, and attributes, are the memorials of him; there is no need for images to be such. And that which was a revelation of God to one is his memorial to many, to all generations.

(2.) Here is a use of exhortation, *v.* 6. "Is this so, that Jacob thy father had this communion with the Lord God of hosts, and is this still his memorial?" Then, [1.] Let those that have gone astray from God be converted to him: *Therefore turn thou to thy God.* He that was the God of Jacob is the God of Israel, is *thy God;* from him thou hast unjustly and unkindly revolted; therefore turn thou to him by repentance and faith, turn to him as thine, to love him, obey him, and depend upon him. [2.] Let those that are converted to him walk with him in all holy conversation and godliness: *"Keep mercy and judgment,* mercy in relieving and succouring the poor and distressed, judgment in rendering to all their due; be kind to all; do wrong to none. *Keep piety and judgment"* (so it may be read); "live *righteously and godly in this present world;* be devout and be honest. Do not only practise these occasionally, but be careful, and constant, and conscientious in the practice of them." [3.] Let those that walk with God be encouraged to live a life of dependence upon him: *"Wait on thy God continually,* with a believing expectation to receive from him all the succours and supplies thou standest in need of." Those that live a life of conformity to God may live a life of confidence and comfort in him, if it be not their own fault. Let our *eyes* be *ever towards the Lord,* and let us preserve a holy security and serenity of mind under the protection of the divine power and the influence of the divine favour, looking, without anxiety, for a dubious event, and by faith keeping our spirits sedate and even; this is waiting on God as our God in covenant, and this we must do continually.

Verses 7–14

Here are intermixed, in these verses,

I. Reproofs for sin. When God is coming forth to contend with a people, that he may demonstrate his own righteousness, he will demonstrate their unrighteousness. Ephraim was called to turn to his God and *keep judgment* (*v.* 6); now, to show that he had need of that call, he is charged with turning from his God by idolatry, and breaking the laws of justice and judgment.

1. He is here charged with injustice against the precepts of the second table, *v.* 7, 8. Here observe,

(1.) What the sin is wherewith he is charged: *He is a merchant.* The margin reads it as a proper name, *He is Canaan,* or a Canaanite, unworthy to be denominated from Jacob and Israel, and worthy to be cast out with a curse from this good land, as the Canaanites were. See Amos 9:7. But Canaan sometimes signifies *a merchant,* and therefore is most likely to do so here, where Ephraim is charged with deceit in trade. Though God had given his people a land flowing with milk and honey, yet he did not forbid them to enrich themselves by merchandise, and they succeeded the Canaanites in that as well as in their husbandry; they sucked *the abundance of the seas and the treasures hidden in the sand,* Deu. 33:19. And, if they had been fair merchants, it would have been no reproach at all to them, but an honour and a blessing. But he is such a merchant as the Canaanites were, who were honest only with good looking to, and, if they could, cheated all they dealt with. Ephraim does so; he deceives and thereby oppresses. Note, There is oppression by fraud as well as oppression by force. It is not only princes, lords, and masters, that oppress their subjects, tenants, and servants, but merchants and traders are often guilty of oppressing those they deal with, when they impose upon their ignorance, or take advantage of their necessity, to make hard bargains with them, or are rigorous and severe in exacting their debts. Ephraim cheated, [1.] With a great deal of art and cunning: *The balances of deceit are in his hand.* He uses balances, and delivers his goods by weight and measure, as if he would be very exact, but they are balances of deceit, false weights and false measures, and thus, under colour of doing right, he does the greatest wrong. Note, God has his eye upon merchants and traders, when they are weighing their goods and paying their money, whether they do honestly or deceitfully. He observes what balances they have in their hand, and how they hold them; and, though those they deal with may not be aware of that sleight of hand with which they make them balances of deceit, God sees it, and knows it. Trades by the wit of man are made *mysteries,* but it is a pity that by the sin of man they should ever be made *mysteries of iniquity.* [2.] With a great deal of pleasure and pride: *He loves to oppress.* To oppress is bad enough, but to love to do so is much worse. His conscience does not check and reprove him for it, as it ought to do; if it did, though he committed the sin, he could not delight in it; but his corruptions are so strong, and have so triumphed over his convictions, that he not only loves the gain of oppression, but he loves to oppress, sins for sinning-sake, and takes a pleasure in out-witting and over-reaching those that suspect him not.

(2.) How he justifies himself in this sin, *v.* 8. Wicked men will have something to say for themselves now when they are told of their faults, some frivolous turn-off or other wherewith to evade the convictions of the word. Ephraim stands indicted for a common cheat. Now see what he pleads to the indictment. He does not deny the charge, nor plead, Not guilty, yet does not make a penitent confession of it and ask pardon, but insists upon his own justification. Suppose it were so that he did use balances of deceit, yet, [1.] He pleads that he had got a good estate. Let the prophet say what he pleased of his deceit, of the sin of it and the curse of God that attended it, he could not be convinced there was any harm or danger in it, for this he was sure of that he had thriven in it: *"Yet I have become rich, I have found me out substance.* Whatever you make of it, I have made a good hand of it." Note, Carnal hearts are often confirmed in a good opinion of their evil ways by their worldly prosperity and success in those ways. But it is a great mistake. Every word in what Ephraim says here proclaims his folly. *First,* It is folly to call the riches of this world substance, for they are things that are not, Prov. 23:5. *Secondly,* It is folly to think that we have them of ourselves, to say (as some read it), *I have made myself rich;* what *substance* I have is owing purely to my ingenuity and industry — *I have found it; my might and the power of my hand have gotten me this wealth. Thirdly,* It is folly to think that what we have is for ourselves. *I have found me out substance,* as if we had it for our own proper use and behoof, whereas we hold it in trust, only as stewards. *Fourthly,* It is folly to think that riches are things to be gloried in, and to say with exultation, *I have become rich.* Riches are not the honours of the soul, are not peculiar to the best men, nor sure to us; and therefore *let not the rich man glory in his riches,* Jam. 1:9, 10. *Fifthly,* It is folly to think that growing rich in a sinful way makes us innocent, or will make us safe, or may make us easy, in that way; for the prosperity of fools deceives and destroys them. See Isa. 47:10; Prov. 1:32. [2.] He pleads that he had kept a good reputation. It is common for sinners, when they are justly reproved by their ministers, to appeal to their neighbours, and because they know no ill of them, or will say none, or think well of what the prophets charge them with as bad, fly in the face of their reprovers: *In all my labours* (says Ephraim) *they shall find no iniquity in me that were sin.* Note, Carnal hearts are apt to build a good opinion of themselves upon the fair character they have among their neighbours. Ephraim was very secure; for, *First,* All his neighbours knew him to be diligent in his business; they had an eye upon *all his labours,* and commended him for them. *Men will praise thee when thou doest well for thyself. Secondly,* None of them knew him to be deceitful in his business. He acted with so much policy that nobody could say to the contrary but that he acted with integrity. For either, 1. He concealed the fraud, so that none discovered it: "Whatever iniquity there is, *they shall find* none;" as if no iniquity were displeasing to God, and damning to the soul, but that which is open and scandalous before men. What will it avail us that men shall find no iniquity in us, when God finds a great deal, and will bring every secret work, even secret frauds, into judgment? Or, 2. He excused the fraud, so that none condemned it: *"They shall find no iniquity in me that were sin,* nothing very bad, nothing but what is very excusable, only some venial sins, sins not worth speaking of," which they think God will make nothing of because they do not. It is a fashionable iniquity; it is customary; it is what every body does; it is pleasant; it is gainful; and this, they think, is no iniquity that is sin; nobody will think the worse of them for it. But God sees not as man sees; he judges not as man judges.

2. He is here charged with idolatry, against the precepts of the first table, with that iniquity which is in a special manner vanity, the making and worshipping of images, which are vanities (*v.* 11): *Surely they are vanity;* they do not profit, but deceive. Now the prophet mentions two places notorious for idolatry: — (1.) Gilead on the other side Jordan, which had been branded for it before (*ch.* 6:8): *Is there iniquity in Gilead?* It is a thing to be wondered at; it is a thing to be sadly lamented. What! iniquity in Gilead? idolatry there? Gilead was a fruitful pleasant country (pleasant to a proverb, Jer. 22:6), and does it so ill requite the Lord? It was a frontier-country, and lay much exposed to the insults of enemies, and therefore stood in special need of the divine protection; what! and yet by iniquity throw itself out of that protection? *Is there iniquity in Gilead?* Yea, (2.) And in Gilgal too; there they *sacrifice bullocks* (*ch.* 9:15), and there *their altars* which they have set up, either to strange gods in opposition to his own appointed altar, are as thick *as heaps* of manure *in the furrows of the field* that is to be sown, *ch.* 8:11. *Is there iniquity in Gilead* only? so some. Is it only in those remote parts of the nation that people are so superstitious, where they border upon other nations? No; they are as bad at Gilgal. In Gilead God protected Jacob their father (of whom he had been speaking) from the rage of Laban; and will you there commit iniquity?

II. Here are threatenings of wrath for sin. Some make that to be so (*v.* 9), *I will make thee to dwell in tabernacles as in the days of the appointed time,* that is, I will bring thee into such a condition as the Israelites were in when they dwelt in tents and wandered for forty years; that was the *time appointed in the wilderness.* Ephraim forgot that God brought him out of Egypt and brought him up to be what he was, and was proud of his wealth, and took sinful courses to increase it; and therefore God threatens to bring him to a tabernacle-state again, to a poor, mean, desolate, unsettled condition. Note, It is just with God, when men have by their sins turned their tents into houses, by his judgments to turn their houses into tents again. However, that is certainly a threatening (*v.* 14), *Ephraim provoked him to anger most bitterly.* See how men are deceived in their opinion of themselves, and how they will one day be undeceived. Ephraim thought that there was no iniquity in him that deserved to be called sin (*v.* 8); but God told him that there was that in him which was sin, and would be found so if he did not repent and reform; for, 1. It was extremely offensive to his God: *Ephraim provoked him to anger most bitterly* with his iniquities, which were so distasteful to God, and to him too would be *bitterness in the latter end.* He was so wilful in sinning against his knowledge and convictions that any one might see, and say, that he designed no other than to provoke God in the highest degree. 2. It would certainly be destructive to himself; that cannot be otherwise which provokes God against him, and kindles the fire of his wrath. Therefore, (1.) He shall take away his forfeited life: *He shall leave his blood upon him,* that is, he shall not hold him guiltless, but bring upon him that death which is the wages of sin. *His blood shall be upon his own head* (2 Sa. 1:16), for his own iniquity has testified against him and he alone shall bear it. Note, When sinners perish their blood is left upon them. (2.) He shall take away his forfeited honour: *His reproach shall his Lord return upon him.* God is *his Lord;* he had by idolatry and other sins reproached the Lord, and done dishonour to him, and to his name and family, and had given occasion to others to reproach him; and now God will return the reproach upon him, according to the word he has spoken, that *those who despise him shall be lightly esteemed.* Note, Shameful sins shall have shameful punishments. If Ephraim put contempt on his God, he shall be so reduced that all his neighbours shall look with contempt upon him.

III. Here are memorials of former mercy, which come in to convict them of base ingratitude in revolting from God. Let them blush to remember,

1. That God had raised them from meanness. When Ephraim had become rich, and was proud of that, he forgot that which God (that he might not forget it) obliged them every year to acknowledge (Deu. 26:5), *A Syrian ready to perish was my father.* But God here puts them in mind of it, *v.* 12. Let them remember, not only the honours of their father Jacob, what a *mighty prince* he was with God, *v.* 3 (an honour which they had no share in while they were in rebellion against God), but what a poor servant he was to Laban, which was sufficient to mortify those that were puffed up with the estates they had raised. *Jacob fled into Syria* from a malicious brother, and there served a covetous uncle *for a wife,* and *for a wife he kept sheep,* because he had not estate to endow a wife with. Jacob was poor, and low, and a fugitive; therefore his posterity ought not to be proud. He was a plain man, dwelling in tents, and keeping sheep; therefore *balances of deceit* ill became them. He *served for a wife* that was not a Canaanitess, as Esau's wives were; therefore it was a shame for them to degenerate into Canaanites, and mingle with the nations. God wonderfully preserved him in his flight and preserved him in his service, so that he multiplied exceedingly, and from that *root* in a dry ground sprang an illustrious nation, that bore his name, which magnifies the goodness of God both to him and them and leaves them under the stain of base ingratitude to that God who was their founder and benefactor.

2. That God had rescued them from misery, had raised them to what they were, not only out of poverty, but out of slavery (*v.* 13), which laid them under much stronger obligations to serve him and under a yet deeper guilt in serving other gods. (1.) God *brought Israel out of Egypt* on purpose that they might serve him, and by redeeming them out of bondage acquired a special title to them and to their service. (2.) He preserved them, as sheep are kept by the shepherd's care. He preserved them from Pharaoh's rage at the sea, even at the Red Sea, protected them from all the perils of the wilderness, and provided for them. (3.) He did this *by a prophet,* Moses, who, though he is called *king in Jeshurun* (Deu. 33:5), yet did what he did for Israel *as a prophet,* by direction from God and by the power of his word. The ensign of his authority was not a royal sceptre, but the *rod of God;* with that he summoned both Egypt's plagues and Israel's blessings. Moses, as a prophet, was a type of Christ (Acts 3:22), and it is by Christ as a prophet that we are brought out of the Egypt of sin and Satan by the power of his truth. Now this shows how very unworthy and ungrateful this people were, [1.] In rejecting their God, who had brought them out of Egypt, which, in the preface to the commandments, is particularly mentioned as a reason for the first, why they should have no other gods before him. [2.] In despising and persecuting his prophets, whom they should have loved and valued, and have studied to answer God's end in sending them, for the sake of that prophet by whom God had brought them out of Egypt and preserved them in the wilderness. Note, The benefit we have had by the word of God greatly aggravates our sin and folly if we put any slight upon the word of God.

3. That God had taken care of their education as they grew up. This instance of God's goodness we have, *v.* 10. As by a prophet he delivered them, so *by prophets* he still continued to speak to them. Man, who is formed out of the earth, is fed out of the earth; so that nation, that was formed by prophecy, by prophecy was fed and taught; *beginning at Moses,* and so going on *to all the prophets* through the several ages of that church, we find that divine revelation was all along their tuition. (1.) They had prophets raised up among themselves (Amos 2:11), a succession of them, were scarcely ever without a Spirit of prophecy among them more or less, from Moses to Malachi. (2.) These prophets were *seers;* they had *visions,* and *dreams,* in which God discovered his mind to them immediately, with a full assurance that it was his mind, Num. 12:6. (3.) These visions were multiplied; God spoke not only *once, yea, twice,* but many a time; if one vision was not regarded, he sent another. The prophets had variety of visions, and frequent repetitions of the same. (4.) God *spoke* to them *by the prophets.* What the prophets *received from the Lord* they plainly and faithfully delivered to them. The people at Mount Sinai begged that God would speak to them by men like themselves, and he did so. (5.) In speaking to them by the prophets he *used similitudes,* to make the messages he sent by them intelligible, more affecting, and more likely to be remembered. The visions they saw were often similitudes, and their discourses were embellished with very apt comparisons. And, as God by his prophets, so by his Son, he *used similitudes,* for *he opened his mouth in parables.* Note, God keeps an account, whether we do or no, of the sermons we hear; and those that have long enjoyed the means of grace in purity, plenty, and power, that have been frequently, faithfully, and familiarly, told the mind of God, will have a great deal to answer for another day if they persist in a course of iniquity.

IV. Here are intimations of further mercy, and this remembered too in the midst of sin and wrath (as some understand *v.* 9): *"I that am the Lord thy God from the land of Egypt,* who then and there took thee to be my people, and have approved myself thy God ever since, in a constant series of merciful providences, have yet a kindness for thee, bad as thou art; and I will *make thee to dwell in tabernacles,* not as in the wilderness, but *as in the days of the solemn feast,"* the feast of tabernacles, which was celebrated with great joy, Lev. 23:40. 1. They shall be made to see, by the grace of God, that though they are rich, and have found out substance, yet they are but in a tabernacle-state, and have in their worldly wealth *no continuing city.* 2. They shall yet have cause to rejoice in God, and have opportunity to do it in public ordinances. The feast of tabernacles was the first solemn feast the Jews kept after their return out of Babylon, Ezra 3:4. 3. This, as other promises, was to have its full accomplishment in the grace of the gospel, which provides tabernacles for believers in their way to heaven, and furnishes them with matter of joy, holy joy, joy in God, such as was in the feast of tabernacles, Zec. 14:18, 19.

CHAPTER 13

The same strings, though generally unpleasing ones, are harped upon in this chapter that were in those before. People care not to be told either of their sin or of their danger by sin; and yet it is necessary, and for their good, that they should be told of both, nor can they better hear of either than from the word of God and from their faithful ministers, while the sin may be repented of and the danger prevented. Here, I. The people of Israel are reproved and threatened for their idolatry (*v.* 1–4). II. They are reproved and threatened for their wantonness, pride, and luxury, and other abuses of their wealth and prosperity (*v.* 5–8). III. The ruin that is coming upon them for these and all their other sins is foretold as very terrible (*v.* 12, 13, 15, 16). IV. Those among them that yet retain a respect for their God are here encouraged to hope that he will yet appear for their relief, though their kings and princes, and all their other supports and succours, fail them (*v.* 9–11, 14).

Verses 1–4

Idolatry was the sin that did most easily beset the Jewish nation till after the captivity; the ten tribes from the first were guilty of it, but especially after the days of Ahab; and this is the sin which, in these verses, they are charged with. Observe,

I. The provision that God made to prevent their falling into idolatry. This we have, *v.* 4. God did what was fit to be done to keep them close to himself; what could have been done more? 1. He made known himself to them as *the Lord their God,* and took them to be his people in a peculiar manner. Both by his word and by his works all along *from the land of Egypt* he declared, *I am the Lord thy God;* he told them so from heaven at Mount Sinai, that he was *the Lord* and *their God,* who *brought them out of the land of Egypt.* This he continued both to declare and to prove to them by his prophets and by his providences. 2. He gave them a law forbidding them to worship any other: *"Thou shalt know no God but me;* not only shalt not own and worship any other, but shalt not acquaint thyself with any other, nor make the rites and usages of the Gentiles familiar to thee." Note, It is a happy ignorance not to know that which we ought not to meddle with. We find those commended who *have not known the depths of Satan.* 3. He gave them a good reason for it: *There is no saviour besides me.* Whatever we take for our God we expect to have for our saviour, to make us happy here and hereafter; as, where we have protection, we owe allegiance, so where we have salvation, and hope for it, we owe adoration.

II. The honour that Ephraim had, while he kept himself clear from idolatry (*v.* 1): *While Ephraim spoke trembling,* or *with trembling* (that is, as Dr. Pocock understands it, while he behaved himself towards God as his father Jacob did, with *weeping and supplications,* and spoke not proudly and insolently against God and his prophets, while he kept up a holy fear of God, and worshipped him in that fear) so long *he exalted himself in Israel,* that is, he was very considerable among the tribes and made a figure. Jeroboam, who was of that tribe, exalted himself and his family. *When he spoke there was trembling,* that is, all about him stood in awe of him; so some understand it. Note, *Those that humble themselves,* especially that humble themselves before God, *shall be exalted.* When people speak with modesty and jealousy of themselves, with a diffidence of their own judgment and a deference to others, they exalt themselves, they gain a reputation. But as for Ephraim he soon lost himself: *When he offended in Baal he died,* that is, he lost his reputation, his honour soon dwindled and sunk, and was laid in the dust. Baal is here put for all idolatry; when Ephraim forsook God, and took to worship images, the state received its death's wound and was never good for any thing afterwards. Note, Deserting God is the death of any person or persons.

III. The lamentable growth of idolatry among them (*v.* 2): *Now they sin more and more.* When once he began to *offend in Baal* the ice was broken, and he grew worse and worse, coveted more idols, doted more upon those he had, and grew more ridiculous in the worship of them. Note, The way of idolatry, as of other sins, is down-hill, and men cannot easily stop themselves. It is the sad case of all those who have forsaken God that they sin yet more and more. Let us trace them in their apostasy. 1. They made themselves *molten images,* proud to have gods that they could cast into what mould they pleased; probably these were the calves in miniature like the silver shrines for Diana; the zealots for the calf-worship carried about with them, it may be, images of the gods they worshipped, made on purpose *for themselves.* 2. They made them of *their silver,* and then doubted not of their property in them, when they purchased them with their own money or made them of their own plate melted down for that purpose. See what cost they put themselves to in the service of their idols, which they honoured with the best they had, and therefore made their molten images of silver. 3. They made them *according to their own understanding,* according to their own fancy. They consulted with themselves what shape they should make their idol in, and made it accordingly, *a god* according to the *best of their judgment.* Or *according to their own likeness,* in the form of a man. And, when they made their idols men like themselves in shape, they made themselves stocks and stones like them in reality; for *those that make them are like unto them, and so is every one that trusts in them.* 4. It was *all the work of the craftsmen.* Their images did not pretend, like that of Diana, to have come down from Jupiter (Acts 19:35); no, perhaps the workmen stamped their names upon them, such an idol was such a man's work. See *ch.* 8:6; Isa. 44:9, etc. 5. Though they were thus the work of their hands, yet they were the beloved of their souls; for they say of them, *Let the men that sacrifice kiss the calves.* Either the priests called upon the people thus to pay their homage, or the people, who were not allowed to come so near themselves, called upon the *men that sacrificed,* the priests that attended for them, to *kiss the calves* in their name and stead, because they could not reach to do it, so very fond were they of paying their utmost respects to such an idol as they were taught to have a veneration for. Though they were calves, yet, if they were gods, the worshippers, by themselves or their proxies, thus made their honours to them. They *kissed the calves,* in token of the adoration of them, affection for them, and allegiance to them, as theirs. Thus we are directed to *kiss the Son,* to take him for our Lord and our God.

IV. Threatenings of wrath for their idolatry. The Lord, whose name is *Jealous,* is a jealous God, and will not give his glory to another; and therefore all those that *worship images* shall be *confounded,* especially if Ephraim do it, Ps. 97:7. Because they are so fond of kissing their calves, therefore God will give them sensible convictions of their folly, *v.* 3. They promise themselves a great del of safety and satisfaction in the worship of their idols, and that their prosperity will thereby be established; but God tells them that they shall be disappointed, and *driven away in their wickedness.* This is illustrated by four similitudes: — They shall be, 1. As the *morning cloud,* which promises showers of rain to the parched ground. 2. As the *early dew,* which seems to be an earnest of such showers. But both *pass away,* and the day proves as dry and hot as ever; so fleet and transitory their profession of piety was (*ch.* 6:4), and so had they disappointed God's expectation from them, and therefore it is just that so their prosperity should be, and so their expectations from their idols should be disappointed, and so will all theirs be that make an idol of this world. 3. They are *as the chaff,* light and worthless; and they shall be driven *as the chaff is driven with the whirlwind out of the floor,* Ps. 1:4; 25:5; Job 21:18. Nay, 4. They are *as the smoke,* noisome and offensive (see Isa. 65:5), and they shall be driven away *as the smoke out of the chimneys,* that is soon dissipated and disappears, Ps. 68:2. Note, No solid lasting comfort is to be expected any where but in God.

Verses 5-8

We may observe here, 1. The plentiful provision God had made for Israel and the seasonable supplies he had blessed them with (*v.* 5): "*I did know thee in the wilderness,* took cognizance of thy case and made provision for thee, even in *a land of great drought,* when thou wast in extreme distress, and when no relief was to be had in an ordinary way." See a description of this wilderness, Deu. 8:15, Jer. 2:6, and say, The God that knew them, and owned them, and fed them there, was a *friend indeed,* for he was a *friend at need* and an all-sufficient friend, that could victual so vast an army when all ordinary ways of provision were cut off, and where, if miracles had not been their daily bread, they must all have perished. Note, Help at an exigency lays under peculiar obligations and must never be forgotten. 2. Their unworthy ungrateful abuse of God's favour to them. God not only took care of them in the wilderness, but put them in possession of Canaan, a good land, a large and fat pasture. And (*v.* 6) *according to their pasture so were they filled.* God gave them both plenty and dainties, and they did not spare it, but, having been long confined to manna, when they came into Canaan they fed

themselves *to the full.* And this was no hopeful presage; it would have looked better, and promised better, if they had been more modest and moderate in the use of their plenty, and had learned to deny themselves; but what was the effect of it? *They were filled, and their heart was exalted.* Their luxury and sensuality made them proud, insolent, and secure. The best comment upon this is that of Moses, Deu. 32:13-15. But *Jeshurun waxed fat and kicked.* When the body was stuffed up with plenty the soul was puffed up with pride. Then they began to think their religion a thing below them, and they could not persuade themselves to stoop to the services of it. *The wicked, through the pride of his countenance, will not seek after God.* When they were poor and lame in the wilderness they thought it was necessary for them to keep in with God; but when they were replenished and established in Canaan they began to think they had no further need of him: *Their heart was exalted, therefore have they forgotten me.* Note, Worldly prosperity, when it feeds men's pride, makes them forgetful of God; for they remember him only when they want him. When Israel was filled, what more could the Almighty do for them? And therefore they said to him, *Depart from us,* Job 22:17. It is sad that those favours which ought to make us mindful of God, and studious what we shall render to him, should make us unmindful of him, and regardless what we do against him. We ought to know that we live upon God when we live upon common providence, though we do not, as Israel in the wilderness, live upon miracles. 3. God's just resentment of their base ingratitude, *v.* 7, 8. The judgments threatened (*v.* 3) intimated the departure of all good from them. The threatenings here go further, and intimate the breaking in of all evils upon them; for God, who had so much befriended them, now *turns to be their enemy and fights against them,* which is expressed here very terribly: *I will be unto them as a lion* and *as a leopard.* The lion is strong, and there is no resisting him. The leopard is here taken notice of to be crafty and vigilant: *As a leopard by the way will I observe them.* As that beast of prey lies in wait by the road-side to catch travellers, and devour them, so will God by his judgments *watch over them* to do them hurt, as he had watched over them to do them good, Jer. 44:27. No opportunity shall be let slip that may accelerate or aggravate their ruin (Jer. 5:6): *A leopard shall watch over their cities.* A lynx, or spotted beast (and such the leopard is), is noted for quicksightedness above any creature *(lynx visu* — the eyes of a lynx*),* and so it intimates that not only the power, but the wisdom of God is engaged against those whom he has a controversy with. Some read it (and the original will bear it), *I will be as a leopard in the way of Assyria.* The judgments of God shall surprise them just when they are going to the Assyrians to seek for protection and help from them. It is added, *I will meet them as a bear that is bereaved,* and thereby exasperated and made more cruel (2 Sa. 17:8, Prov. 28:15), which intimates how highly God was provoked, and he would make them feel it: He will *rend the caul of their heart.* The lion is observed to aim at the heart of the beasts he preys upon, and thus will God *devour them like a lion.* He will send such judgments upon them as shall prey upon their spirits and consume their vitals. Their heart was exalted (*v.* 6), but God will take an effectual course to bring it down: *The wild beast shall tear them;* not only God will be as a lion and leopard to them, but the metaphor shall be fulfilled in the letter, for *noisome beasts* are one of the *four sore judgments* with which God will destroy a provoking people, Eze. 14:15.

Now all this teaches us, 1. That abused goodness turns into the greater severity. Those who despise God and affront him, when he is to them as a careful tender shepherd, shall find he will be even to his own flock as the beasts of prey are. Those whom God has in vain *endured with much long-suffering,* and invited with much affection, in them he will *show his wrath* and make them *vessels* of it, Rom. 9:22. *Patientia laesa fit furor — Despised patience will turn into fury.* 2. That the judgments of God, when they come with commission against impenitent sinners, will be irresistible and very terrible. They will *rend the caul of the heart,* will fill the soul with confusion, and tear that in pieces; and we are as unable to grapple with them as a lamb is to make his part good against a roaring lion, for *who knows the power of God's anger?* Knowing

therefore the terror of the Lord, let us be persuaded to make peace with him; for are we stronger then he?

Verses 9-16

The first of these verses is the summary, or contents, of all the rest (*v.* 9), where we have, 1. All the blame of Israel's ruin laid upon themselves: *O Israel! thy perdition is thence;* it is of and from thyself; or, "*It has destroyed thee, O Israel!* that is, all that sin and folly of thine which thou art before charged with. As *thy own wickedness* has many a time *corrected thee,* so that has now at length destroyed thee." Note, Wilful sinners are self-destroyers. Obstinate impenitence is the grossest self-murder. Those that are *destroyed of the destroyer* have their blood upon their own head; they have *destroyed themselves.* 2. All the glory of Israel's relief ascribed to God: *But in me is thy help.* That is, (1.) It might have been: "I would have helped thee and healed thee, but thou wouldst not be healed and helped, but wast resolutely set upon thy own destruction." This will aggravate the condemnation of sinners, not only that they did that which tended to their own ruin, but that they opposed the offers God made them and the methods he took with them to prevent it: *I would have gathered them,* and they *would not.* They might have been easily and effectually helped, but they put the help away from them. Nay, (2.) It may be: "Thy case is bad, but it is not desperate. *Thou hast destroyed thyself;* but come to me, and I will help thee." This is a plank thrown out after shipwreck, and greatly magnifies not only the power of God, that he can help when things are at the worst, can help those that cannot help themselves, but the riches of his grace, that he will help those that have destroyed themselves and therefore might justly be left to perish, that he will help those that have long refused his help. Dr. Pocock gives a different reading and sense of this verse: "*O Israel! this has destroyed thee, that in me is thy help.* Presuming upon God and his favour has emboldened thee in those wicked ways which have been thy ruin."

Now, in the rest of these verses, we may see,

I. How Israel destroyed themselves. It is said (*v.* 16), They *rebelled against God,* revolted from their allegiance to him, entered into a confederacy with his enemies, and took up arms against him; and this was the thing that ruined them, for never any hardened themselves against God and prospered. Note, Those that rebel against their God destroy themselves, for they make him their enemy for whom they are an unequal match.

1. They treasure up wrath against the day of wrath, and so they destroy themselves. They are doing that, every day, which will be remembered against them another day (*v.* 12): *The iniquity of Ephraim is bound up, and his sin is hid;* God took notice of it, kept it upon record, and will produce it against him and reckon with him for it afterwards. Their former sins contributed to their present destruction; for they were *laid up in store with God,* Deu. 32:34, 35; Job 14:17. It is laid up in safety, and will not be forgotten, nor the evidence against him lost; but it is laid up in secret; it is hid; the sinner himself is not aware of it. It is bound up in God's omniscience, in the sinner's own conscience. Note, The sin of sinners is not forgotten till it is pardoned, but an exact account is kept of it, which will be opened in proper time.

2. They make no haste to repent and help themselves when they are under divine rebukes; they are their own ruin because they will not do what they should do towards their own salvation, *v.* 13. (1.) They are brought into trouble and distress by sin: *The sorrows of a travailing woman shall come upon him.* They shall smart for sin, and so be made sensible of it; they shall be thrown into pangs and agonies by it, very sharp and severe, and yet, like the pains of a woman in labour, hopeful and promising, and in order to deliverance; and by these, though God corrects them, yet he designs their good. They are chastened, that they may not be destroyed. But, (2.) They are not by these forwarded as they ought to be towards repentance and reformation, which would cause their sorrows to issue in true joy: *He is an unwise son, for he should not stay long,* as he does, *in the place of the breaking forth of children,* but, being *brought to the birth,* should struggle to *get forth,* lest he be stifled and *still-born at last.* Were the child which the mother is in travail of capable of understanding its own case, we should reckon it an unwise child that would

choose to stay long in the birth; for the *captive exile hasteth to be loosed, lest he die in the pit,* Isa. 51:14. Note, Those may justly be reckoned their own destroyers who defer and put off their repentance, by which alone they might help themselves. Those are in danger of miscarrying in conversion who delay it, and will not put forth themselves to speed the work and bring it to an issue.

3. *Therefore* they are destroyed because they have done that which will be their certain ruin and neglected that which would have been their only relief. Here is a sad description of the desolation they are doomed to, *v.* 15, 16. It is here taken for granted that *Ephraim* is *fruitful among his children;* his name signifies *fruitfulness.* He is fruitful in respect of the plentiful products of his country and the great numbers of its inhabitants; it was both a rich and a populous tribe, as was foretold concerning it; but sin turns this fruitful tribe into barrenness. *Joseph* was a *fruitful bough,* but for sin it was blasted. The instrument is an *east wind,* representing a foreign enemy that should invade it. It is called the *wind of the Lord,* not only because it shall be a very great and strong wind, but because it shall be sent by divine direction; it shall come *from the Lord,* and do whatever he appoints; and see what effect it shall have upon that flourishing tribe, what desolations war shall make. (1.) Was it a rich tribe? The foreign enemy shall make it poor enough. This *wind of the Lord* shall come up *from the wilderness,* a freezing blasting wind, and shall *dry up* the *springs* and *fountains* with which this tree is watered, shall exhaust the sources of its wealth. The invader shall waste the country and so impoverish the husbandman, shall intercept trade and commerce and so impoverish the merchant; and let not the great men, whose wealth lies in their rich furniture, think that they shall be exempted from the judgment, for he shall *spoil the treasure of all pleasant vessels.* See the folly of those that lay up their treasure on earth, that lay it up in *pleasant vessels (vessels of desire,* so the word is), on which they set their affections, and in which they place their comfort and satisfaction. This is treasure that may be spoiled and that they may be spoiled of; it is what either moth or rust may corrupt, or what thieves and soldiers may steal and carry away. But wise and happy are those who have laid up their treasures in heaven, and in the pleasant things of that world, which cannot be spoiled, which they cannot be stripped of; ever happy are they, and therefore truly wise. (2.) Was it a populous tribe, and numerous? The enemy shall depopulate it and make its men few: *Samaria shall become desolate,* without inhabitants. [1.] Those shall be cut off who are the guard and joy of the present generation; the men who bear arms shall bear them to no purpose, for *they shall fall by the sword,* so that there shall be none to make head against the fury of the conqueror nor to take care of the concerns either of the public or of private families. [2.] Those shall be cut off who are the seed and hope of the next generation, who should rise up in the places of those who fell by the sword; the whole nation must be rooted out, and therefore *the infants shall be dashed to pieces,* in the most cruel and barbarous manner, and, which is if possible yet more inhuman, *the women with child shall be ripped up.* Thus shall the glory of *Samaria flee away from the birth, and from the womb, ch.* 9:11; 10:14. See instances of this cruelty, 2 Ki. 8:12; 15:16; Amos 1:13.

II. Let us now see how God was the help of this self-destroying people, how he was their only help (*v.* 10): *I will be thy King,* to rule and save thee. Though they had refused to be his subjects and had rebelled against him, yet he would still be their King and would not abandon them. The business and care of a good king is to keep his people, not only from ruined by foreign enemies, but from ruining themselves and one another. Thus will God yet be Israel's King, as he was *their King of old.* Note, Our case would be sad indeed if God were not better to us than we are to ourselves.

1. God will be their King when they have no other king; he will protect and save them when those are cut off and gone who should have been their protectors and saviours: *I will be he* (so *v.* 10 may be read), he that shall help thee. *"Where is the king that may save thee in all thy cities,* that may go in and out before thee, and fight thy battles, when thy cities are invaded by a foreign power, and suppress the more dangerous quarrels of thy citizens among themselves? *Where are thy judges,* who by administering public justice should preserve the public peace? For it is *righteousness* and *peace* that *kiss each other. Where are thy judges* that thou hadst such a desire of and such a dependence upon, of whom thou saidst, *Give me a king and princes?* This refers, (1.) To the foolish wicked desire which the whole nation had of a kingly government, being weary of the theocracy, or divine government, which they had been under during the time of the *Judges,* because it looked too mean for them. They rejected Samuel, and in him *the Lord,* when they said, *Give us a king* like the nations, whereas the *Lord was their King.* (2.) To the desire which the ten tribes had of a kingly government different from that of the house of David, because they thought that was too absolute and bore too hard upon them, and they hoped to better themselves by setting up Jeroboam. Both these are instances, [1.] Of men's improvidence for themselves. When they are uneasy with their present lot they are fond of novelty, and think to better themselves by a change; but they are commonly disappointed, and do not find that advantage in the alteration which they promised themselves. [2.] Of men's impiety towards God, in thinking to refine upon his appointments and amend them. God gave Israel judges and prophets for their guidance; but they were weary of them, and cried, *Give us a king and princes.* God gave them the house of David, established it by a covenant of royalty; but they were soon weary of that too, and cried, *We have no part in David.* Those destroy themselves who are not pleased with what God does for them, but think they can do better for themselves. Well, in both these requests, Providence humoured them, gave them Saul first, and afterwards Jeroboam. And what the better were they for them? Saul was *given in anger* (given in *thunder,* 1 Sa. 12:18, 19) and soon after was *taken away in wrath,* upon Mount Gilboa. The kingly government of the ten tribes was given in anger, not only against Solomon for his defection, but against the ten tribes that desired it, for their discontent and disaffection to the house of David; and God was now about to take that away in wrath by the power of the king of Assyria. And then, *where is thy King?* He is gone, and thou shalt abide many days *without a king, and without a prince* (*ch.* 3:4), shalt have none to save thee, none to rule thee. Note, *First,* God often gives in anger what we sinfully and inordinately desire, gives it with a curse, and with it gives us up to our own hearts' lusts. Thus he gave Israel quails. *Secondly,* What we inordinately desire we are commonly disappointed in, and it cannot save us, as we expected it should. *Thirdly,* What God gives in anger he takes away in wrath; what he gives because we did not desire it well he takes away because we did not use it well. It is the happiness of the saints that, whether God gives or takes, it is all in love, and furnishes them with matter for praise. *To the pure all things are pure.* It is the misery of the wicked that, whether God gives or takes, it is all in wrath; to them nothing is pure, nothing is comfortable.

2. God will do that for them which no other king could do if they had one (*v.* 14): *I will ransom them from the power of the grave.* Though Israel, according to the flesh, be abandoned to destruction, God has mercy in store for his spiritual Israel, in whom all the promises were to have their accomplishment, and this among the rest, for to them the apostle applies it (1 Co. 15:55), and particularly to the blessed resurrection of believers at the great day, yet not excluding their spiritual resurrection from the death of sin to a holy, heavenly, spiritual, and divine life. It is promised, (1.) That the captives shall be delivered, *shall be ransomed, from the power of the grave.* Their deliverance shall be by ransom; and we know who it was that paid their ransom, and what the ransom was, for it was the Son of man that *gave his life a ransom for many,* Mt. 20:28. It is he that thus redeemed them. Those who, upon their repenting and believing, are, for the sake of Christ's righteousness, acquitted from the guilt of sin and saved from death and hell, which are the *wages of sin,* are those *ransomed of the Lord* that shall, in the great day, be brought out of the grave in triumph, and it shall be as impossible for the banks of death to hold them as it was to hold their Master. (2.) That the conqueror shall be destroyed: *O death! I will be thy plagues.* Jesus Christ was the plague and destruction of death and the grave when by death he *destroyed him that had the power of death,* and when in his own resurrection he triumphed over the grave. But the complete destruction of them will be in the resurrection of believers at the great day, when death shall for ever be swallowed up in victory, and it is the last enemy that shall be destroyed. But the word which we translate *I will* may as well be rendered *Ubi nunc — Where now* are thy plagues? And so the apostle took it: *'O death! where is thy plague,* or *sting,* with which thou hast so long pestered the world? *O grave! where is thy victory,* or thy *destruction,* wherewith thou has destroyed mankind?" Christ has abolished death, has broken the power of it and altered the property of it, and so enabled us to triumph over it. This promise he has made, and it shall be made good to all that are his; for *repentance shall be hidden from his eyes;* he will never recall this sentence passed on death and the grave, for he is not a man that he should repent. Thanks be to God therefore who gives us the victory.

CHAPTER 14

The strain of this chapter differs from that of the foregoing chapters. Those were generally made up of reproofs for sin and threatenings of wrath; but this is made up of exhortations to repentance and promises of mercy, and with these the prophet closes; for all the foregoing convictions and terrors he had spoken were designed to prepare and make way for these. He wounds that he may heal. The Spirit convinces that he may comfort. This chapter is a lesson for penitents; and some such there were in Israel at this day, bad as things were. We have here, I. Directions in repenting, what to do and what to say (*v.* 1–3). II. Encouragements to repent taken from God's readiness to receive returning sinners (*v.* 4, 8) and the comforts he has treasured up for them (*v.* 5–7). III. A solemn recommendation of these things to our serious thoughts (*v.* 9).

Verses 1–3

Here we have,

I. A kind invitation given to sinners to repent, *v.* 1. It is directed to Israel, God's professing people. They are called to *return.* Note, Conversion must be preached even to those that are within the pale of the church as well as to heathen. "Thou are Israel, and therefore art bound to thy God in duty, gratitude, and interest; thy revolt from him is so much the more heinous, and thy return to him so much the more necessary." Let Israel see, 1. What work he has made for repentance: *"Thou has fallen by thy iniquity." Thou has stumbled;* so some read it. Their idols were their *stumbling-blocks.* "Thou has fallen from God into sin, fallen off from all good, fallen down under the load of guilt and the curse." Note, Sin is a fall; and it concerns those that have fallen by sin to get up again by repentance. 2. What work he has to do in his repentance: *"Return to the Lord thy God;* return to him as *the Lord* whom thou has a dependence upon, as *thy God,* thine in covenant, whom thou has an interest in." Note, It is the great concern of those that have revolted from God to *return to God,* and so to do their *first works.* "Return to him from whom thou has fallen, and who alone is able to raise thee up. Return *even to the Lord,* or *quite home* to the Lord; do not only look to him, or take some steps towards him, but make thorough work of it." The ancient Jews had a saying grounded on this, *Repentance is a great thing, for it brings men quite up to the throne of glory.*

II. Necessary instructions given them how to repent. 1. They must bethink themselves what to say to God when they come to him: *Take with you words.* They are required to bring, not sacrifices and offerings, but penitential prayers and supplications, the *fruit of thy lips,* yet not of the lips only, but of the heart, else words are but wind. One of the rabbin says, They must be such words as proceed *from what is spoken first in the inner man;* the heart must dictate to the tongue. We must take good words with us, by taking good thoughts and good affections with us. *Verbaque praevisam rem non invita sequentur — Those who master a subject are seldom at a loss for language.* Note, When we come to God we should consider what we have to say to him; for, if we come without an errand, we are likely to go without an answer. Ezra 9:10, *What shall we say?* We must take with us words from the scripture, take them from the Spirit of grace and supplication, who teaches us to cry, Abba, Father, and makes intercession in us. 2. They must bethink themselves what to do. They must not only take with them words, but must *turn to the Lord;* inwardly in their hearts, outwardly in their lives.

III. For their assistance herein, and encouragement, God is pleased to put words into their mouths, to teach them what they shall say. Surely we may hope to speed with

God, when he himself has ordered our address to be drawn up ready to our hands, and his own Spirit has indited it for us; and no doubt we shall speed if the workings of our souls agree with the words here recommended to us. They are,

1. Petitioning words. Two things we are here directed to petition for: — (1.) To be acquitted from guilt. When we return to the Lord we must say to him, Lord, *take away all iniquity.* They were now smarting for sin, under the load of affliction, but are taught to pray, not as Pharaoh, Take away *this death,* but, *Take away this* sin. Note, When we are in affliction we should be more concerned for the forgiveness of our sins than for the removal of our trouble. "*Take away iniquity,* lift it off as a *burden* we are ready to sink under or as the stumbling-block which we have often fallen over. Lord, take it away, that it may not appear against us, to our confusion and condemnation. Take it all away by a free and full remission, for we cannot pretend to strike any of it off by a satisfaction of our own." When God pardons sin he pardons *all,* that *great debt;* and when we pray against sin we must pray against it all and not except any. (2.) To be accepted as righteous in God's sight: "*Receive us graciously.* Let us have thy favour and love, and have thou respect to us and to our performances. Receive our prayer graciously; be well pleased with that good which by thy grace we are enabled to do." *Take good* (so the word is); take it to bestow upon us, so the margin reads it — *Give good.* This follows upon the petition for the taking away of iniquity; for, till iniquity is taken away, we have no reason to expect any good from God, but the taking away of iniquity makes way for the conferring of good *removendo prohibens — by taking that out of the way which hindered. Give good;* they do not say what good, but refer themselves to God; it is not good of the world's showing (Ps. 4:6), but good of God's giving. "*Give good,* that good which we have forfeited, and which thou has promised, and which the necessity of our case calls for." Note, God's gracious acceptance, and the blessed fruits and tokens of that acceptance, are to be earnestly desired and prayed for by us in our returning to God. "*Give good,* that good which will make us good and keep us from returning to iniquity again."

2. Promising words. These also are put into their mouths, not to move God, or to oblige him to show them mercy, but to move themselves, and oblige themselves to returns of duty. Note, Our prayers for pardon and acceptance with God should be always accompanied with sincere purposes and vows of new obedience. Two things they are to promise and vow: — (1.) Thanksgiving. "Pardon our sins, and accept of us, so *will we render the calves of our lips.*" The *fruit of our lips* (so the Septuagint), a word they used for *burnt-offerings,* and so it agrees with the Hebrew. The apostle quotes this phrase (Heb. 13:15), and by the *fruit of our lips* understands the *sacrifice of praise to God, giving thanks to his name.* Note, Praise and thanksgiving are our spiritual sacrifice, and, if they come from an upright heart, shall please the Lord *better than an ox or bullock,* Ps. 69:30, 32. And the sense of our pardon and acceptance with God will enlarge our hearts in praise and thankfulness. Those that are *received graciously* may, and must, *render the calves of their lips* — poor returns for rich receivings, yet, if sincere, more acceptable than the calves of the stall. (2.) Amendment of life. They are taught to promise, not only verbal acknowledgements, but a real reformation. And we are taught here, [1.] In our returns to God to covenant against sin. We cannot expect that God should take it away by forgiving it if we do not put it away by forsaking it. [2.] To be particular in our covenants and resolutions against sin, as we ought to be in our confession, because deceit lies in generals. [3.] To covenant especially and expressly against those sins which we have been most subject to, which have most easily beset us, and which we have been most frequently overcome by. We must keep ourselves from, and therefore must thus fortify ourselves against, *our own iniquity,* Ps. 18:23. The sin they here covenant against, owning thereby that they had been guilty of it, is giving that glory to another which is due to God only; this they promise they will never do, *First,* By putting that confidence in creatures which should be put in God only. They will not trust to their alliances abroad: *Asshur* (that is, Assyria) *shall not save us.* "We will not court the help of the Assyrians when we are in distress, as we have done (*ch.* 5:13; 7:11; 8:9); we will not contract for it, nor will we confide in it, or depend upon it. Having a God to go to, a God all-sufficient to trust to, we scorn to be beholden to the Assyrians for help." They will not trust to their warlike preparations at home, especially not those which they were forbidden to multiply: "*We will not ride upon horses,* that is, we will not make court to Egypt," for thence they fetched their horses, Deu. 17:16; Isa. 30:16; 31:1, 3. "When our enemies invade us we will depend upon our God to succour our infantry, and will be in no care to remount our cavalry." Or, "We will not *post on horseback,* for haste, from one creature to another, to seek relief, but will take the nearest way, and the only sure way, by addressing ourselves to God," Isa. 20:5. Note, True repentance takes us off from trusting to an arm of flesh, and brings us to rely on God only for all the good we stand in need of. *Secondly,* Nor will they do it by paying that homage to creatures which is due to God only. We *will not say any more to the works of our hands, You are our gods.* They must promise never to worship idols again, and for a good reason, because it is the most absurd and senseless thing in the world to pray to that as a god which is the work of our hands. We must promise that we will not set our hearts upon the gains of this world, nor pride ourselves in our external performances in religion, for that is, in effect, to say to the work of our hands, *You are our gods.*

3. Pleading words are here put into their mouths: For *in thee the fatherless find mercy.* We must take our encouragement in prayer, not from any merit God finds in us, but purely from the mercy we hope to find in God. This contains in itself a great truth, that God takes special care of fatherless children, Ps. 68:4, 5. So he did in his law, Ex. 22:22. So he does in his providence, Ps. 27:10. It is God's prerogative to help the helpless. In him there is mercy for such, for they are proper objects of mercy. In him they find it; there it is laid up for them, and there they must seek it; *seek and you shall find.* It comes in here as a good plea for mercy and grace and an encouraging one to their faith. (1.) They plead the distress of their state and condition: "We are fatherless orphans, destitute of help." Those may expect to find help in God that are truly sensible of their helplessness in themselves and are willing to acknowledge it. This is a good step towards comfort. "If we have not yet boldness to call God *Father,* yet we look upon ourselves as fatherless without him, and therefore lay ourselves at his feet, to be looked upon by him with compassion." (2.) They plead God's wonted lovingkindness to such as were in that condition: *With thee the fatherless* not only may find, but *does find,* and shall find, *mercy.* It is a great encouragement to our faith and hope, in returning to God, that it is his glory to father the fatherless and help the helpless.

Verses 4–7

We have here an answer of peace to the prayers of returning Israel. They seek God's face, and they shall not *seek in vain.* God will be sure to meet those in a way of mercy who return to him in a way of duty. If we speak to God in good prayers, God will speak to us in good promises, as he *answered the angel with good words and comfortable words,* Zec. 1:13. If we take with us the foregoing words in our coming to God, we may take home with us these following words for our faith to feast upon; and see how these answer those.

I. Do they dread and deprecate God's displeasure, and therefore return to him? He assures them that, upon their submission, his *anger is turned away from them.* This is laid as the ground of all the other favours here promised. I will do so and so, for my *anger is turned away,* and thereby a door is opened for all good to flow to them, Isa. 12:1. Note, Though God is justly and greatly angry with sinners, yet he is not implacable in his anger; it may be turned away; it shall be turned away, from those that turn away from their iniquity. God will be reconciled to those that are reconciled to him and to his whole will.

II. Do they pray for the *taking away of iniquity?* He assures them that he will *heal their backslidings;* so he promised, Jer. 3:22. Note, Though backslidings from God are the dangerous diseases and wounds of the soul, yet they are not incurable, for God has graciously promised that if backsliding sinners will apply to him as their physician, and comply with his methods, he will heal their backslidings. He will heal the guilt of their backslidings by pardoning mercy and their *bent to backslide* by renewing grace. Their *iniquity* shall *not be their ruin.*

III. Do they pray that God will receive them graciously? In answer to that, behold, it is promised, *I will love them freely.* God had hated them while they went on sin (*ch.* 9:15); but now that they return and repent he loves them, not only ceases to be *angry* with them, but takes complacency in them and designs their good. He *loves them freely,* with an *absolute entire* love (so some), so that there are no remains of his former displeasure, with a *liberal bountiful* love (so others); he will be open-handed in his love to them, and will think nothing too much to bestow upon them or to do for them. Or with a *cheerful willing* love; he will love them without reluctancy or renitency. He will not say in the day of thy repentance, *How shall I receive thee again?* as he said in the day of thy apostasy, *How shall I give thee up?* Or with an *unmerited preventing* love. Whom God loves he loves *freely,* not because they deserve it, but of his own good pleasure. He loves because he *will* love, Deut, 7:7, 8.

IV. Do they pray that God will *give good,* will make them good? In answer to that, behold, it is promised, *I will be as the dew unto Israel, v.* 5. Observe,

1. What shall be the favour God will bestow upon them. It is the blessing of their father Jacob, *God give thee the dew of heaven,* Gen. 27:28. Nay, what they need God will not only give them, but he will himself be *that* to them, all that which they need: I *will be as the dew unto Israel.* This ensures *spiritual blessings in heavenly things;* and it follows upon the healing of their backslidings, for pardoning mercy is always accompanied with renewing grace. Note, To Israelites indeed God himself will be *as the dew.* He will instruct them; his doctrine shall drop upon them as the dew, Deu. 32:2. They shall know more and more of him, for he will come to them *as the rain,* Hos. 6:3. He will refresh them with his comforts, so that their souls shall be as a *watered garden,* Isa. 58:11. He will be to true penitents *as the dew to Israel* when they were in the wilderness, dew that had manna in it, Ex. 16:14; Num. 11:9. The graces of the Spirit are the hidden manna, hidden in the dew; God will give them bread from heaven, as he did to Israel in the dew in abundance, Jn. 1:16.

2. What shall be the fruit of that favour which shall be produced in them. The grace thus freely bestowed on them *shall not be in vain.* Those souls, those Israelites, to whom God is as the dew, on whom his grace distils,

(1.) Shall be growing. The bad being by the grace of God made good, they shall by the same grace be made better; for grace, wherever it is true, is growing. [1.] They shall grow upwards, and be more flourishing, *shall grow as the lily,* or (as some read it) shall *blossom as the rose.* The growth of the lily, as that of all bulbous roots, is very quick and speedy. The root of the lily seems lost in the ground all winter, but, when it is refreshed with the dews of the spring, it starts up in a little time; so the grace of God improves young converts sometimes very fast. The lily, when it has come to its height, is a lovely flower (Mt. 6:29), so grace is the comeliness of the soul, Eze. 16:14. it is the *beauty of holiness* that is produced by the *dew of the morning,* Ps. 110:3. [2.] They shall grow downwards, and be more firm. The lily indeed grows fast, and grows fine, but it soon fades and is easily plucked up; and therefore it is here promised to Israel that with the flower of the lily he shall have the root of the cedar: He shall *cast forth his roots as Lebanon,* as the *trees of Lebanon,* which, having taken deep root, cannot be plucked up, Amos 9:15. Note, Spiritual growth consists most in the growth of the root, which is out of sight. The more we depend upon Christ and draw sap and virtue from him, the more we act in religion from a principle and the more steadfast and resolved we are in it, the more we *cast forth our roots.* [3.] They shall grow round about (*v.* 6): *His branches shall spread* on all sides. And (*v.* 7) he shall *grow as the vine,* whose branches extend furthest of any tree. Joseph was to be *a fruitful bough,* Gen. 49:22. When many are added to the church from without, when a hopeful generation rises up, then Israel's branches spread. When particular believers abound in good works, and increase in the knowledge of God and in every good gift, then their branches may be said to spread. The *inward man is renewed day by day.*

(2.) They shall be graceful and acceptable both to God and man. Grace is the amiable thing, and makes those that have it truly amiable. They are here compared to such trees as are pleasant, [1.] To the sight: *His beauty shall be as the olive-tree,* which is always green. *The Lord called thy name a green olive-tree,* Jer. 11:16. Ordinances are the beauty of the church, and in them it is, and shall be, ever green. Holiness is the beauty of a soul; when those that believe with the heart make profession with the mouth, and justify and adorn that profession with an agreeable conversation, then their beauty is as the olive-tree, Ps. 52:8. It is a promise to the trees of righteousness that their leaf shall not wither. [2.] To the smell: *His smell shall be as Lebanon* (v. 6) and his *scent as the wine of Lebanon,* v. 7. This was the praise of their father Jacob, *The smell of my son is as the smell of a field which the Lord has blessed,* Gen. 27:27. The church is compared to a *garden of spices* (Cant. 4:12, 14), which *all her garments smell of.* True believers are *acceptable to God* and *approved of men.* God *smells a sweet savour* from their *spiritual sacrifices* (Gen. 8:21), and they are *accepted of the multitude of the brethren.* Grace is the perfume of the soul, the perfume of the name, makes it like a precious ointment, Eccl. 7:1. *The memorial thereof shall be as the wine of Lebanon* (so the margin reads it), not only their reviving comforts now, but their surviving honours when they are gone, shall be as *the wine of Lebanon,* that has a delicate flavour. Flourishing churches have *their faith spoken of throughout the world* (Rom. 1:8) and *leave their name to be remembered* (Ps. 45:17); and *the memory of flourishing saints is blessed,* and shall be so, as theirs who *by faith obtained a good report.*

(3.) They shall be fruitful and useful. The church is compared here to the vine and the olive, which brings forth useful fruits, to the honour of God and man. Nay, the very shadow of the church shall be agreeable (v. 7): *Those that dwell under his shadow shall return* — under God's *shadow* (so some), under the shadow of the Messias, so the Chaldee. Believers *dwell under God's shadow* (Ps. 91:1), and there they are and may be safe and easy. But it is rather *under the shadow of Israel,* under the shadow of the church. Note, God's promises pertain to those, and those only, that dwell under the church's shadow, that attend on God's ordinances and adhere to his people, not those that flee to that shadow only for shelter in a hot gleam, but those that *dwell under it.* Ps. 27:4. We may apply it to particular believers; when a man is effectually brought home to God all that *dwell under his shadow* — children, servants, subjects, friends. *This day has salvation come to this house.* Those that dwell under the shadow of the church shall return; their drooping spirits shall return, and they shall be refreshed and comforted. He *restores my soul,* Ps. 23:3. *They shall revive as the corn,* which, when it is sown, dies first, and then revives, and *brings forth much fruit,* Jn. 12:24. It is promised that God's people shall be blessings to the world, as corn and wine are. And a very great and valuable mercy it is to be serviceable to our generation. Comfort and honour attend it.

Verses 8–9

Let us now hear the conclusion of the whole matter.

I. Concerning Ephraim; he is spoken of and spoken to, *v.* 8. Here we have,

1. His repentance and reformation: *Ephraim shall say, What have I to do any more with idols?* As some read it, God here reasons and argues with him, why he should renounce idolatry: "O Ephraim! what to me and idols? What

concord or agreement can there be *between me and idols? What communion between light and darkness, between Christ and Belial?* 2 Co. 6:14, 15. Therefore thou must break off thy league with them if thou wilt come into covenant with me." As we read it, God promises to bring Ephraim and keep him to this: *Ephraim shall say,* God will put it into his heart to say it, *What have I to do any more with idols?* He has promised (v. 3) not to *say any more to the works of his hands, You are my gods.* But God's promises to us are much more our security and our strength for the mortifying of sin than our promises to God; and therefore God himself is here *surety for his servant to good,* will put in into his heart and into his mouth. And, whatever good we say or do at any time, it is he that works it in us. Ephraim had solemnly engaged not to call his idols *his gods;* but God here engages further for him that he shall resolve to have *no more to do with them.* He shall abolish them, he shall abandon them, and that with the utmost detestation; for it is necessary not only that in our lives we be turned from sin, but that in our hearts we be turned against sin. See here, (1.) The power of divine grace. Ephraim had been *joined to his idols* (ch. 4:17), was so fond of them that one would have thought he could never fall out with them; and yet God will work such a change in him that he shall loathe them as much as ever he loved them. (2.) See the benefit of sanctified afflictions. Ephraim had smarted for his idolatry; it had brought one judgment after another upon him, and this at length is the fruit, even the *taking away of his sin,* Isa. 27:9. (3.) See the nature of repentance; it is a firm and fixed resolution to have no more to do with sin. This is the language of the penitent: "I am ashamed that ever I had to do with sin; but I have had enough of it; I hate it, and by the grace of God I will never have any thing to do with it again, no, not with the occasions of it." Thou shalt say to thy idol, *Get thee hence* (Isa. 30:22), shalt say to the tempter, *Get thee behind me, Satan.*

2. The gracious notice God is pleased to take of it: *I have heard him, and observed him. I have heard, and will look upon him;* so some read it. Note, The God of heaven takes cognizance of the penitent reflections and resolutions of returning sinners. He expects and desires the repentance of sinners, because he has no pleasure in their ruin. *He looks upon men* (Job 33:27), *hearkens and hears,* Jer. 8:6. And, if there be any disposition to repent, he is well pleased with it. When *Ephraim bemoans himself* before God, he is a *dear son,* he is a *pleasant child,* Jer. 31:20. He meets penitents with mercy, as the father of the prodigal met his returning son. God *observed* Ephraim, to see whether he would bring forth fruits meet for this profession of repentance that he made, and whether he would continue in this good mind. He observed him to do him good, and comfort him, according to the exigencies of his case.

3. The mercy of God designed for him, in order to his comfort and perseverance in his resolutions; still God will be all in all to him. Before, Israel was compared to a tree, now God compares himself to one. He will be to his people, (1.) As the branches of a tree: "*I am like a green fir-tree,* and will be so to thee." The fir-trees, in those countries, were exceedingly large and thick, and a shelter against sun and rain. God will be to all true converts both a delight and a defence; under his protection and influence they shall both dwell in safety and dwell in ease. He with be either *a sun and a shield* or a *shade and a shield,* according as their case requires. They shall sit down *under his shadow with delight,* Cant. 2:3. He will be so all weathers, Isa. 4:6. (2.) As the root of a tree: *From me is thy fruit found,* which may be understood either of the fruit brought

forth to us (to him we owe all our comforts) or of the fruit brought forth by us — from him we receive grace and strength to enable us to do our duty. Whatever fruits of righteousness we brought forth, all the praise of them is due to God; for he works in us both to will and to do that which is good.

II. Concerning every one that hears and reads the words of the prophecy of this book (v. 9): *Who is wise? and he shall understand these things.* Perhaps the prophet was wont to conclude that sermons he preached with these words, and now he closes with them the whole book, in which he has committed to writing some fragments of the many sermons he had preached. Observe, 1. The character of those that do profit by the truths he delivered: *Who is wise and prudent? He shall understand these things, he shall know them.* Those that set themselves to understand and know these things thereby make it to appear that they are truly wise and prudent, and will thereby be made more so; and, if any do not understand and know them, it is because they are foolish and unwise. Those that are wise in the doing of their duty, that are prudent in practical religion, are most likely to know and understand both the truths and providences of God, which are a mystery to others, Jn. 7:17. *The secret of the Lord is with those that fear him,* Ps. 25:14. *Who is wise?* This intimates a desire that those who read and hear these things would understand them *(O that they were wise!)* and a complaint that few were so — *Who has believed our report?* 2. The excellency of these things concerning which we are here instructed: *The ways of the Lord are right;* and therefore it is our wisdom and duty to know and understand them. The way of God's precepts, in which he requires us to walk, is right, agreeing with the rules of eternal reason and equity and having a direct tendency to our eternal felicity. The ways of God's providence, in which he walks toward us, are all right; no fault is to be found with any thing that God does, for it is all well done. His judgments upon the impenitent, his favours to the penitent, are all right; however they may be perverted and misinterpreted, God will at last be justified and glorified in them all. His *ways are equal.* 3. The different use which men make of them. (1.) The right ways of God to those that are good are, and will be, a savour of life unto life: *The just shall walk in them;* they shall conform to the will of God both in his precepts and in his providences, and shall have the comfort of so doing. They shall well understand the mind of God both in his word and in his works; they shall be well reconciled to both, and shall accommodate themselves to God's intention in both. *The just shall walk* in *those ways* towards their great end, and shall not come short of it. (2.) The right ways of God will be to those that are wicked a savour of death unto death: *The transgressors shall fall* not only in their own wrong ways, but even *in the right ways of the Lord.* Christ, who is a foundation stone to some, is to others a *stone of stumbling* and a *rock of offence.* That which was *ordained to life* becomes through their abuse of it, death to them. God's providences, being not duly improved by them, harden them in sin and contribute to their ruin. God's discovery of himself both in the judgments of his mouth and in the judgments of his hand is to us according as we are affected under it. *Recipitur ad modum recipientis — What is received influences according to the qualities of the receiver.* The same sun softens wax and hardens clay. But of all transgressors those certainly have the most dangerous fatal falls that fall *in the ways of God,* that split on the rock of ages, and suck poison out of the balm of Gilead. *Let the sinners in Zion be afraid* of this.

AN EXPOSITION, WITH PRACTICAL OBSERVATIONS, OF
THE BOOK OF THE PROPHET JOEL

We are altogether uncertain concerning the time when this prophet prophesied; it is probable that it was about the same time Amos prophesied, not for the reason that the rabbin give, "Because Amos begins his prophecy with that wherewith Joel concludes his, *The Lord shall roar out of Zion,*" but for the reason Dr. Lightfoot gives, "Because he speaks of the same judgments of locusts, and drought, and fire, that Amos laments, which is an in-timation that they appeared about the same time, Amos in Israel and Joel in Judah. Hosea and Obadiah prophesied about the same time; and it appears that Amos prophesied in the says of Jeroboam, the second king of Israel, Amos 7:10. God sent a variety of prophets, that they might strengthen the hands one of another, and that out of the mouth of two or three witnesses every word might be established. In this prophecy, I. The desolations made by hosts of noxious insects is described, *ch.* 1 and part of *ch.* 2. II. The people are hereupon called to repentance, *ch.* 2. III. Promises are made of the return of mercy upon their repentance (*ch.* 2), and promises of the pouring out of the Spirit in the latter days. IV. The cause of God's people is pleaded against their enemies, whom God would in due time reckon with (*ch.* 3); and glorious things are spoken of the gospel-Jerusalem and of the prosperity and perpetuity of it.

CHAPTER 1

This chapter is the description of a lamentable devastation made of the country of Judah by locusts and caterpillars. Some think that the prophet speaks of it as a thing to come and gives warning of it beforehand, as usually the prophets did of judgments coming. Others think that it was now present, and that his business was to affect the people with it and awaken them by it to repentance. I. It is spoken of as a judgment which there was no precedent of in former ages (*v.* 1–7). II. All sorts of people sharing in the calamity are called upon to lament it (*v.* 8–13). III. They are directed to look up to God in their lamentations, and to humble themselves before him (*v.* 14–20).

Verses 1–7

It is a foolish fancy which some of the Jews have, that this Joel the prophet was the same with that Joel who was the son of Samuel (1 Sa. 8:2); yet one of their rabbin very gravely undertakes to show why Samuel is here called *Pethuel.* This Joel was long after that. He here speaks of a sad and sore judgment which was now brought, or to be brought, upon Judah, for their sins. Observe,

I. The greatness of the judgment, expressed here in two things: — 1. It was such as could not be paralleled in the ages that were past, in history, or in the memory of any living, *v.* 2. The *old men* are appealed to, who could remember what had happened long ago; nay, and *all the inhabitants of the land* are called on to testify, if they could any of them remember the like. Let them go further than any man's memory, and *prepare themselves for the search of their fathers* (Job 8:8), and they would not find an account of the like in any record. Note, Those that outdo their predecessors in sin may justly expect to fall under greater and sorer judgments than any of their predecessors knew. 2. It was such as would not be forgotten in the ages to come (*v.* 3): "*Tell you your children of it;* let them know what dismal tokens of the wrath of God you have been under, that they make take warning, and may learn obedience by the things which you have suffered, for it is designed for warning to them also. Yea, let *your children tell their children, and their children another generation;* let them tell it not only as a strange thing, which may serve for matter of talk" (as such uncommon accidents are records in our almanacs — It is so long since the plague, and fire — so long since the great frost, and the great wind), "but let them tell it to *teach their children* to stand in awe of God and of his judgments, and to tremble before him." Note, We ought to transmit to posterity the memorial of God's judgments as well as of his mercies.

II. The judgment itself; it is an invasion of the country of Judea by a great army. Many interpreters both ancient and modern understand it of armies of men, the forces of the Assyrians, which, under Sennacherib, *took all the defenced cities of Judah,* and then, no doubt, made havoc of the country and destroyed the products of it: nay, some make the four sorts of animals here names (*v.* 4) to signify the four monarchies which, in their turns, were oppressive to the people of the Jews, one destroying what had escaped the fury of the other. Many of the Jewish expositors think it is a parabolic expression of the coming of enemies, and their multitude, to lay all waste. So the Chaldee paraphrast mentions these animals (*v.* 4); but afterwards (*ch.* 2:25) puts instead of them, *Nations, peoples, tongues, languages, potentates,* and *revenging kingdoms.* But it seems much rather to be understood literally of armies of insects coming upon the land and eating up the fruits of it. Locusts were one of the plagues of Egypt. Of them it is said, There never were any like them, nor should be (Ex. 10:14), none such as those in Egypt, none such as these in Judah — none like those locusts for bigness, none like these for multitude and the mischief they did. The plague of locusts in Egypt lasted but for a few days; this seems to have continued for four years successively (as some think), because here are four sorts of insects mentioned (*v.* 4), one destroying what the other left; but others think they came all in one year. We are not told, in the history of the Old Testament, when this happened, but we are sure that no word of God fell to the ground; and, though a devastation by these insects is primarily intended here, yet it is expressed in such a language as is very applicable to the destruction of the country by a foreign enemy invading it, because, if the people were not humbled and reformed by that less judgment which devoured the land, God would send this greater upon them, which would devour the inhabitants; and by the description of that they are bidden to take it for a warning. If this nation of worms do not subdue them, another nation shall come to ruin them. Observe, 1. What these animals are that are sent against them — *locusts* and *caterpillars, palmer-worms* and *canker-worms, v.* 4. We cannot now describe how these differed one from another; they were all little insects, any one of them despicable, and which a man might easily crush with his foot or with his finger; but when they came in vast swarms, or shoals, they were very formidable and ate up all before them. Note, God is Lord of hosts, has all creatures at his command, and, when he pleases, can humble and mortify a proud and rebellious people by the weakest and most contemptible creatures. Man is said to be a worm; and by this it appears that he is *less than a worm,* for, when God pleases, worms are too hard for him, plunder his country, eat up that for which he laboured, destroy the forage, and cut off the subsistence of a potent nation. The weaker the instrument is that God employs the more is his power magnified. 2. What fury and force they came with. They are here called a *nation* (*v.* 6), because they are embodied, and act by consent, and as it were with a common design; for, though *the locusts have no king, yet they go forth all of them by bands* (Prov. 30:27), and it is there mentioned as an instance of their *wisdom.* It is prudence for those that are weak severally to unite and act jointly. They are *strong,* for they are *without number.* The *small dust of the balance* is light, and easily blown away, but a heap of dust is weighty; so a worm can do little (yet one worm served to destroy Jonah's gourd), but numbers of them can do wonders. They are said to have *teeth of a lion,* of a *great lion,* because of the great and terrible execution they do. Note, Locusts become as lions when they come armed with a divine commission. We read of the locusts out of the bottomless pit, that *their teeth were as the teeth of lions,* Rev. 9:8. 3. What mischief they do. They *eat up* all before them (*v.* 4); what one leaves the other devours; they destroy not only the grass and corn, but the trees (*v.* 7): The *vine is laid waste.* There vermin eat the leaves which should be a shelter to the fruit while it ripens, and so that also perishes and comes to nothing. They eat the very bark of the fig-tree, and so kill it. Thus the *fig-tree does not blossom,* nor is there *fruit in the vine.*

III. A call to the drunkards to lament this judgment (*v.* 5): *Awake and weep, all you drinkers of wine.* This intimates, 1. That they should suffer very sensibly by this calamity. It should touch them in a tender part; the *new wine* which they loved so well should be *cut off from their mouth.* Note, It is just with God to take away those comforts which are abused to luxury and excess, to *recover* the *corn and wine* which are *prepared* for Baal, which are made the food and fuel of a base lust. And to them judgments of that kind are most grievous. The more men place their happiness in the gratification of sense the more pressing temporal afflictions are upon them. The drinkers of water need not to care when the vine was laid waste; they could live as well without it as they had done; it was no trouble to the Nazarites. But the *drinkers of wine* will *weep and howl.* The more delights we make necessary to our satisfaction the more we expose ourselves to trouble and disappointment. 2. It intimates that they had been very senseless and stupid under the former tokens of God's displeasure; and therefore they are here called to *awake and weep.* Those that will not be roused out of their security by the word of God shall be roused by his rod; those that will not be startled by judgments at a distance shall be themselves arrested by them; and when they are going to partake of the forbidden fruit a prohibition of another nature shall come *between the cup and the lip,* and *cut off the wine from their mouth.*

Verses 8–13

The judgment is here described as very lamentable, and such as all sorts of people should share in; it shall not only rob the drunkards of their pleasure (if that were the worst of it, it might be the better borne), but it shall deprive others of their necessary subsistence, who are therefore called to lament (*v.* 8), as a virgin laments the death of her lover to whom she was espoused, but not completely married, yet so that he was in effect her husband, or as a young woman lately married, from whom the *husband of her youth,* her young husband, or the husband to whom she was married when she was young, is suddenly taken away by death. Between a new-married couple that are young, that married for love, and that are every way amiable and agreeable to each other, there is great fondness, and consequently great grief if either be taken away. Such lamentation shall there be for the loss of their corn and wine. Note, The more we are wedded to our creature-comforts that harder it is to part with them. See that parallel place, Isa. 32:10–12. Two sorts of people are here brought in, as concerned to lament this devastation, countrymen and clergymen.

I. Let the husbandmen and vine-dressers lament, *v.* 11. Let them be ashamed of the care and pains they have taken about their vineyards, for it will be all labour lost, and they shall gain no advantage by it; they shall see the fruit of their labour eaten up before their eyes, and shall not be able to save any of it. Note, Those who labour only *for the meat that perishes* will, sooner or later, be ashamed of their labour. The *vine-dressers* will then express their extreme grief by *howling,* when they see their vineyards stripped of leaves and fruit, and the vines withered, so that nothing is to be had or hoped for from them, wherewith they might pay their rent and maintain their families. The destruction is particularly described here: *The field is laid waste* (*v.* 10); all is consumed that is produced; *the land mourns;* the ground has a melancholy aspect, and looks ruefully; all the inhabitants of the land are in tears for what they have lost, are in fear of perishing for want, Isa. 24:4; Jer. 4:28. "The *corn,* the bread-corn, which is the staff of life, is *wasted;* the *new wine,* which should be brought into the cellars for a supply when the old is drunk, is *dried up,* is *ashamed* of having promised so fair what it is not now able to perform; the oil *languishes,* or is *diminished,* because (as the Chaldee renders it) *the olives have fallen off.*" The people were not thankful to God as they should have been for the *bread that strengthens man's heart,* the *wine* that *makes glad the heart,* and the *oil that makes the face to shine* (Ps. 104:14, 15); and therefore they are justly brought to lament the loss and want of them, of all the products of the earth, which God had given either for necessity or for delight (this is repeated, *v.* 11, 12) — the *wheat and barley,* the two principal grains bread was then made of, wheat for the rich and barley for the poor, so that the rich and poor meet together in the calamity. The trees are destroyed, not only the *vine and the fig-tree* (as before, *v.* 7), which were more useful and necessary, but other trees also that were for delight — the *pomegranate, palm-tree,* and *apple-tree,* yea, all the *trees of the field,* as well as those of the orchard, timber-trees as well as fruit-trees. In short, all *the harvest of the field has perished, v.* 11. And by this means *joy has withered away from the children of men* (*v.* 11); the *joy of harvest,* which is used to express great and general joy, has come to nothing, is turned into shame, is turned into lamentation. Note, The perishing of the harvest is the withering of the joy of the children of men. Those that place their happiness in the delights of the sense, when they are deprived of them, or in any way disturbed in the enjoyment of them, lose all their joy; whereas the children of God, who look upon the pleasures of sense with holy indifference and contempt, and know what it is to make God their hearts' delight, can rejoice in him as the *God of their salvation* even when the *fig-tree does not blossom;* spiritual joy is so far from withering then, that it flourishes more than ever, Hab. 3:17, 18. Let us see here, 1. What perishing uncertain things all our creature-comforts are. We can never be sure of the continuance of them. Here the heavens had given their rains in due season, the earth had yielded her strength, and, when the appointed weeks of harvest were at hand, they saw no reason to doubt but that they should have a very plentiful crop; yet then they are invaded by these unthought-of enemies, that lay all waste, and not by fire and sword. It is our wisdom not to lay up our treasure in those things which are liable to so many untoward accidents. 2. See what need we have to live in continual dependence upon God and his providence, for our own hands are not sufficient for us. When we see the *full corn in the ear,* and think we are sure of it — nay, when we have *brought it home,* if *he blow upon it,* nay, if he do not bless it, we are not likely to have any good of it. 3. See what ruinous work sin makes. A paradise is turned into a wilderness, a fruitful land, the most fruitful land upon earth, *into barrenness,* for the *iniquity of those that dwelt therein.*

II. Let the priests, the Lord's ministers, lament, for they share deeply in the calamity: *Gird yourselves* with sackcloth (*v.* 13); nay, they *do mourn, v.* 9. Observe, The priests are called the *ministers of the altar,* for on that they attended, and the *ministers of the Lord* (of *my God,* says the prophet), for in attending on the altar they served him, did is work, and did him honour. Note, Those that are employed in holy things are therein God's ministers, and on him they attend. The ministers of the altar used to rejoice before the Lord, and to spend their time very much in singing; but now they must *lament and howl,* for the *meat-offering* and *drink-offering* were *cut off from the house of the Lord* (*v.* 9), and the same again (*v.* 13), *from the house of your God.* "He is your God in a particular manner; you are in a nearer relation to him than other Israelites are; and therefore it is expected that you should be more concerned than others for that which is a hindrance to the service of his sanctuary." It is intimated, 1. That the people, as long as they had the fruits of the earth brought in in their season, presented to the Lord his dues out of them, and brought the offerings to the altar and tithes to those that served at the altar. Note, A people may be filling up the measure of their iniquity apace, and yet may keep up a course of external performances in religion. 2. That, when the meat and drink failed, the meat-offering and drink-offering failed of course; and this was the sorest instance of the calamity. Note, As far as any public trouble is an obstruction to the course of religion it is to be upon that account, more than any other, sadly lamented, especially by the priests, the Lord's ministers. As far as poverty occasions the decay of piety and the neglect of divine offices, and starves the cause of religion among a people, it is indeed a sore judgment. When the famine prevailed God could not have his sacrifices, nor could the priests have their maintenance; and therefore let *the Lord's ministers mourn.*

Verses 14–20

We have observed abundance of tears shed for the destruction of the fruits of the earth by the locusts; now here we have those tears turned into the right channel, that of repentance and humiliation before God. The judgment was very heavy, and here they are directed to own the hand of God in it, his *mighty hand,* and to *humble themselves* under it. Here is,

I. A proclamation issued out for a general fast. The priests are ordered to appoint one; they must not only mourn themselves, but they must call upon others to mourn too: *"Sanctify a fast;* let some time be set apart from all worldly business to be spent in the exercises of religion, in the expressions of repentance and other extraordinary instances of devotion." Note, Under public judgments there ought to be public humiliations; for by them the *Lord God calls to weeping and mourning.* With all the marks of sorrow and shame sin must be confessed and bewailed, the righteous of God must be acknowledged, and his favour implored. Observe what is to be done by a nation at such a time. 1. A day is to be appointed for this purpose, a *day of restraint* (so the margin reads it), a day in which people must be restrained from their other ordinary business (that they may more closely attend God's service), and from all bodily refreshments; for, 2. It must be a *fast,* a religious abstaining from meat and drink, further than is of absolute necessity. The king of Nineveh appointed a fast, in which they were to *taste nothing,* Jonah 3:7. Hereby we own ourselves unworthy of our necessary food, and that we have forfeited it and deserve to be wholly deprived of it, we punish ourselves and mortify the body, which has been the occasion of sin, we keep it in a frame fit to serve the soul in serving God, and, by the appetite's craving food, the desires of the soul towards that which is better than life, and all the supports of it, are excited. This was in a special manner seasonable now that God was depriving them of their *meat and drink;* for hereby they accommodated themselves to the affliction they were under. When God says, *You shall fast,* it is time to say, *We will fast.* 3. There must be a solemn assembly. The *elders* and the *people,* magistrates and subjects, must be *gathered together,* even *all the inhabitants of the land,* that God might be honoured by their public humiliations, that they might thereby take the more shame to themselves, and that they might excite and stir up one another to the religious duties of the day. All had contributed to the national guilt, all shared in the national calamity, and therefore they must all join in the professions of repentance. 4. They must come together in the temple, *the house of the Lord* their *God,* because that was the house of prayer, and there they might be hope to meet with God because it was the place which he had *chosen to put his name there,* there they might hope to speed because it was a type of Christ and his mediation. Thus they interested themselves in Solomon's prayer for the acceptance of all the requests that should be put up in or towards this house, in which their present case was particularly mentioned. 1 Ki. 7:37, *If there be locust, if there be caterpillar.* 5. They must *sanctify* this fast, must observe it in a religious manner, with sincere devotion. What is a fast worth if it be not sanctified? 6. They must *cry unto the Lord.* To him they must make their complaint and offer up their supplication. When we cry in our affliction we must *cry to the Lord;* this is *fasting to him,* Zec. 7:5.

II. Some considerations suggested to induce them to proclaim this fast and to observe it strictly.

1. God was beginning a controversy with them. It is time to *cry unto the Lord,* for *the day of the Lord is at hand, v.* 15. Either they mean the continuance and consequences of this present judgment which they now saw but breaking in upon them, or some greater judgments which this was but a preface to. However it be, this they are taught to make the matter of their lamentation: *Alas, for the day! for the day of the Lord is at hand.* Therefore *cry to God.* For, (1.) "The day of his judgment is very near, it is *at hand;* it *will not slumber,* and therefore you should not. It is time to fast and pray, for you have but a little time to turn yourselves in." (2.) It will be very terrible; there is no escaping it, no resisting it: *As a destruction from the Almighty shall it come.* See Isa. 13:6. It is not a correction, but a destruction; and it comes from the hand, not of a weak creature, but *of the Almighty;* and *who knows* (nay, who does not know) *the power of his anger?* Whither should we go with our cries but to him from whom the judgment we dread comes? There is no fleeing from him but by fleeing to him, no escaping destruction from the Almighty but by making our submission and supplication to the Almighty; this is *taking hold on his strength, that we may make peace,* Isa. 27:5.

2. They saw themselves already under the tokens of his displeasure. It is time to fast and pray, for their distress is very great, *v.* 16. (1.) Let them look into their own houses, and was no plenty there, as used to be. Those who kept a good table were now obliged to retrench: *Is not the meat cut off before our eyes?* If, when God's hand is lifted up, men *will not see,* when his hand is laid on *they shall see.* Is not the meat many a time cut off before our eyes? Let us then labour for that spiritual meat which is not before our eyes, and which cannot be cut off. (2.) Let them look into God's house, and see the effects of the judgment there; joy and gladness were *cut off from the house of God.* Note, The house of our God is the proper place of joy and gladness; when David goes to the *altar of God,* it is to God *my exceeding joy;* but when *joy and gladness* are *cut off from God's house,* either by corruption of holy things or the persecution of holy persons, when serious godly decays and love waxes cold, then it time to cry to the Lord, time to cry, *Alas!*

3. The prophet returns to describe the grievousness of the calamity, in some particulars of it. Corn and cattle are the husbandman's staple commodities; now here he is deprived of both. (1.) The caterpillars have devoured the corn, *v.* 17. The *garners,* which they used to fill with corn, *are laid desolate,* and *the barns broken down,* because *the corn has withered,* and the owners think it not worth while to be at the charge of repairing them when they have nothing to put in them, nor are likely to have any thing; for *the seed it rotten under the clods,* either through too much rain or (which was the more common case in Canaan) for want of rain, or perhaps some insects under ground ate it up. When one crop fails the husbandman hopes the next may make it up; but here they despair of that, the seedness being as bad as the harvest. (2.) The cattle perish too for want of grass (*v.* 18): *How do the beasts groan!* This the prophet takes notice of, that the people might be affected with it and lay to heart the judgment. The groans of the cattle should soften their hard and impenitent hearts. *The herds of cattle,* the large cattle (black cattle we call them), *are perplexed;* nay, even *the flocks of sheep,* which will live upon a common and be content with very short grass, *are made desolate.* See here the inferior creatures suffering for our transgression, and groaning under the double burden of being serviceable to the sin of man and subject to the curse of God for it. *Cursed is the ground for thy sake.*

III. The prophet stirs them up to cry to God, with the consideration of the examples given them for it.

1. His own example (*v.* 19): *O Lord! to thee will I cry.* He would not put them upon doing that which he would not resolve to do himself; nay, whether they would do it or no, he would. Note, If God's ministers cannot prevail to affect others with the discoveries of divine wrath, yet they ought to be themselves affected with them; if they cannot bring others to cry to God, yet they themselves be much in prayer. In time of trouble we must not only pray, but cry, must be fervent and importunate in prayer; and to God, from whom both the destruction is and the salvation must be, ought our cry to be always directed. That which engaged him *to cry to God* was, not so much any personal affliction, as the national calamity: The *fire has devoured the pastures of the wilderness,* which seems to be meant of some parching scorching heat of the sun, which was as fire to the fruits of the earth; it consumed them all. Note, When God *calls to contend by fire* it concerns those that have any interest in heaven to cry mightily to him for relief. See Num. 11:2; Amos 7:4, 5.

2. The example of the inferior creatures: *"The beasts of the field* do not only *groan,* but *cry unto thee, v.* 20. They appeal to thy pity, according to their capacity, and as if, though they are not capable of a rational and revealed religion, yet they had something of dependence upon God by natural instinct." At least, when they groan by reason of their calamity, he is pleased to interpret it as if they cried to him; much more will he put a favourable construction upon the groanings of his own children, though sometimes so feeble that they *cannot be uttered,* Rom. 8:26. The beasts are here said to *cry unto God,* as from him the *lions seek their meat* (Ps. 104:21) and the young *ravens,* Job 38:41. The complaints of the brute-creatures here are for want of water (*The rivers are dried up,* through the excessive heat), and for want of grass, for the *fire has devoured the pastures of the wilderness.* And what better are those than beasts who never cry to God but for corn and wine, and complain of nothing but the want of delight of sense? Yet their crying to God in those cases shames the stupidity of those who cry not to God in any case.

CHAPTER 2

In this chapter we have, I. A further description of that terrible desolation which should be made in the land of Judah by the locusts and caterpillars (*v.* 1–11). II. A serious call to the people, when they are under this sore judgment, to return and repent, to fast and pray, and to seek unto God for mercy, with directions how to do this aright (*v.* 12–17). III. A promise that, upon their repentance, God would remove the judgment, would repair the breaches made upon them by it, and restore unto them plenty of all good things (*v.* 18–27). IV. A prediction of the setting up of the kingdom of the Messiah in the world, by the pouring out of the Spirit in the latter days (*v.* 28–32). Thus the beginning of this chapter is made terrible with the tokens of God's wrath, but the latter end of it made comfortable with the assurances of his favour, and it is in the way of repentance that this blessed change is made; so that, though it is only the last paragraph of the chapter that points directly at gospel-times, yet the whole may be improved as a type and figure, representing the curses of the law invading men for their sins, and the comforts of the gospel flowing in to them upon their repentance.

Verses 1–11

Here we have God contending with his own professing people for their sins and executing upon them the judgment written in the law (Deu. 28:42), *The fruit of thy land shall the locust consume,* which was one of those diseases of Egypt that God would bring upon them, *v.* 60.

I. Here is the war proclaimed (*v.* 1): *Blow the trumpet in Zion,* either to call the invading army together, and then the trumpet sounds a charge, or rather to give notice to Judah and Jerusalem of the approach of the judgment, that they might *prepare to meet their God* in the way of his judgments and might endeavor by prayers and tears, the church's best artillery, to put by the stroke. It was the priests' business to sound the trumpet (Num. 10:8), both as an appeal to God in the day of their distress and a summons to the people to come together to seek his face. Note, It is the work of ministers to give warning from the word of God of the fatal consequences of sin, and to reveal his wrath from heaven against the ungodliness and unrighteousness of men. And though it is not the privilege of Zion and Jerusalem to be exempted from the judgments of God, if they provoke him, yet it is their privilege to be warned of them, that they might make their peace with him. Even in *the holy mountain* the *alarm* must be *sounded,* and then it sounds most dreadful, Amos 3:2. Now, *shall a trumpet be blown in the city,* in the holy city, *and the people not be afraid?* Surely they will. Amos 3:6. *Let all the inhabitants of the land tremble;* they shall be made to tremble by the judgment itself; let them therefore tremble at the alarm of it.

II. Here is a general idea given of the day of battle, which *cometh,* which is *nigh at hand,* and there is no avoiding it. It is the *day of the Lord,* the day of his judgment, in which he will both manifest and magnify himself. It is *a day of darkness and gloominess* (*v.* 2), literally so, the swarms of locusts and caterpillars being so large and so thick as to darken the sky (Ex. 10:15), or rather figuratively; it will be a melancholy time, a time of grievous affliction. And it will come *as the morning spread upon the mountains;* the darkness of this day will come as suddenly as the morning light, as irresistibly, will spread as far, and grow upon them as the morning light.

III. Here is the army drawn up in array (*v.* 2): They are a *great people, and a strong.* Any one sees the vast numbers that there shall be of locusts and caterpillars, destroying the land, will say (as we are all apt to be most affected with what is present), "Surely, never was the like before, nor ever will be the like again." Note, Extraordinary judgments are rare things, and seldom happen, which is an instance of God's patience. When God had drowned the world once he promised never to do it again. The army is here describe to be, 1. Very bold and daring: *They are as horses,* as war-horses, that rush into the battle and *are not affrighted* (Job 39:22); and *as horsemen,* carried on with martial fire and fury, *so they shall run, v.* 4. Some of the ancients have observed that the head of a locust is very like, in shape, to the head of a horse. 2. Very loud and noisy — *like the noise of chariots,* of many chariots, when driven furiously over rough ground, *on the tops of the mountains, v.* 5. Hence is borrowed part of the description of the locusts which St. John saw rise out of the bottomless pit. Rev. 9:7, 9, *The shapes of the locusts were like unto horses prepared to the battle; and the sound of their wings was as the sound of chariots, of many horses running to the battle.* Historians tell us that the noise made by swarms of locusts in those countries that are infested with them has sometimes been heard six miles off. The noise is likewise compared to that of a *roaring fire;* it is like the *noise of a flame* that *devours the stubble,* which noise is the more terrible because that which it is the indication of is devouring. Note, When God's judgments are abroad they make a great noise; and it is necessary for the awakening of a secure and stupid world that they should do so. (3.) They are very regular, and keep ranks in their march; though numerous and greedy of spoil, yet they are *as a strong people set in battle array* (*v.* 5.): *They shall march every one on his ways,* straight forward, as if they had been trained up by the discipline of war to keep their post and observe their right-hand man. *They shall not break their ranks, nor one thrust another, v.* 7, 8. Their number and swiftness shall breed no confusion. See how God can make creatures to act by rule that have no reason to act by, when he designs to serve his own purposes by them. And see how necessary it is that those who are employed in any service for God should observe order, and keep ranks, should diligently go on in their own work and stand in one another's way. 4. They are very *swift;* they *run like horsemen* (*v.* 4), run *like mighty men* (*v.* 7); they *run to and fro in the city,* and *run upon the wall, v.* 9. When God *sends forth his command on earth* his word *runs very swiftly,* Ps. 147:15. Angels have wings, and so have locusts, when God makes use of them.

IV. Here is the terrible execution done by this formidable army, 1. In the country, *v.* 3. View the army in the front, and you will see a *fire devouring before them;* they consume all as if they breathed fire. View it in the rear, and you will see those that come behind as furious as the foremost: *Behind them a flame burns.* When they are gone, then it will appear what destruction they have made. Look upon the fields that they have not yet invaded, and they are *as the garden of Eden,* pleasant to the eye, and full of good fruits; they are the pride and glory of the country. But look upon the fields that they have eaten up and they are *as a desolate wilderness;* one would not think that these had ever been like the former, and yet so they were perhaps but the day before, or that those should ever be made like these, and yet so they shall be perhaps by to-morrow night; yea, and *nothing shall escape them* than can possibly be made food for them. Let none be proud of the beauty of their grounds any more than of their bodies, for God can soon change the face of both. 2. In the city. They shall *climb the wall* (*v.* 7), they shall *run upon the houses,* and *enter in at the windows like a thief* (*v.* 9); when Egypt was plagued with *locusts,* they filled *Pharaoh's houses* and the *houses of his servants,* Ex. 10:5, 6. The locusts out of the bottomless pit, Satan's emissaries, and missionaries of the man of sin, do as these locusts. God's judgments too, when they come with commission, cannot be kept out with bars and bolts; they will find or force their way.

V. The impressions that should hereby be made upon the people. They shall find it to no purpose to make opposition. These enemies are invulnerable and therefore irresistible: *When they fall upon the sword they shall not be wounded, v.* 8. And those that cannot be hurt cannot be stopped; and therefore *before their faces the people shall be much pained* (*v.* 6), as the merchants are in pain for their trading ships when they hear they are just in the mouth of a squadron of the enemies. "One is in pain for his field, another for his vineyard, *and all faces gather blackness,*" which denotes the utmost consternation imaginable. Men in fear look pale, but men in despair look black; the whiteness of a sudden fright, when it is settled, turns into blackness. What is the matter of our pride and pleasure God can soon make the matter of our pain. The terror that the country should be in is described (*v.* 10) by figurative expressions: *The earth shall quake and the heavens tremble;* even the hearts that seemed undaunted, so firm that nothing would frighten them, as immovable as heaven or earth, shall be seized with astonishment. Or when the inhabitants of the land are made to quake it seems to them as if all about them trembled too. Through the prevalency of their fear, or for want of the supports of life which they used to have, their eye shall wax dim and their sight fail them, so that to them *the sun and moon shall seem* to be *dark,* and the stars to *withdraw their shining.* Note, When God frowns upon men the lights of heaven will be small joy to them; for man, by rebelling against his Creator, has forfeited the benefit of all the creatures. But, though this is to be understood figuratively, there is a day coming when it will be accomplished in the letter, when the *heavens* shall be *rolled together like a scroll,* and *the earth, and all the works that are therein,* shall be *burnt up.* Particular judgments should awaken us to think of the general judgment.

VI. We are here directed to look up both him who is the commander-in-chief of this formidable army, and that is God himself, *v.* 11. It is *his army;* it is *his camp.* He raised it; he gives it commission; he *utters his voice before it,* as the general gives orders to his army what to do and makes a speech to animate the soldiers; it is the Lord that gives the word of command to all these animals, which they exactly observe. Some think that with this cloud of locusts God sent terrible thunder, for that is called, *The voice of the Lord,* and was another of the plagues of Egypt, and this made the heavens and the earth tremble. It is the *day of the Lord* (as it was called, *v.* 1), for in this war we are sure he carries the day; it must needs be his, for *his camp is great* and numerous. Those whom he makes war upon he can, as here, overpower with numbers; and whoever he employs to *execute his word,* as the minister of his justice, is sure to be made *strong* and *par negotio — equal to what he undertakes;* whom God gives commission to he girds with strength for the executing of that commission. And this makes the *great day* of the Lord *very terrible* to all those who in that day are to be made the monuments of his justice; for *who can abide it?* None can escape the arrests of God's wrath, can make head against the force of it, or bear up under the weight of it, 1 Sa. 6:20; Ps. 76:7.

Verses 12–17

We have here an earnest exhortation to repentance, inferred from that desolating judgment described and threatened in the foregoing verses: *Therefore now turn you to the Lord.* 1. "Thus you must answer the end and intention of the judgment; for it was sent for this end, to convince you of your sins, to humble you for them, to reduce you to your right minds and to your allegiance." God brings us into straits, that he may bring us to repentance and so bring us to himself. 2. "Thus you may stay the progress of the judgment. Things are bad with you, but thus you may prevent their growing worse; nay, if you take this course, they will soon grow better." Here is a gracious invitation,

I. To a personal repentance, exercised in the soul, *every family apart, and their wives apart,* Zec. 12:12. When the judgments of God are abroad, each person is concerned to contribute his *quota* to the common supplications, having contributed to the common guilt. Every one must mend one and mourn for one, and then we should all be mended and all found among God's mourners. Observe,

1. What we are here called to, which will teach us what it is to repent, for it is the same that the Lord our God still requires of us, we having all made work for repentance. (1.) We must be truly humbled for our sins, must be sorry we have by sin offended God, and ashamed we have by sin wronged ourselves, both wronged our judgments and wronged our interests. There must be outward expressions of sorrow and shame, *fasting,* and *weeping,* and *mourning;* tears for the sin that procured it. But what will the outward expressions of sorrow avail if the inward impressions be not agreeable, and not only accompany them, but be the root and spring of them, and give rise to them? And therefore it follows, *Rend your heart, and not your garments;* not but that, according to the custom of that age, it was proper for them to rend their garments, in token of great grief for their sins and a holy indignation against themselves for their folly; but, "Rest not in the doing of that, as if that were sufficient, but be more in care to accommodate your spirits than to accommodate your dress to a day of fasting and humiliation; nay, rend not your garments at all, unless withal you rend your hearts, for the sign without the thing signified is but a jest and a mockery, and an affront to God." Rending the heart is that which God looks for and requires; that is the *broken and contrite heart* which he *will not despise,* Ps. 51:17. When we are greatly grieved in soul for sin, so that it even *cuts us to the heart* to think how we have dishonoured God and disparaged ourselves by it, when we conceive an aversion to sin, and earnestly desire and endeavor to get clear of the principles of it and never to return to the practice of it, then we rend our hearts for it, and then will God *rend the heavens* and come down to us with mercy. (2.) We must be thoroughly converted to our God, and come home to him when we fall out with sin. *Turn you even to me, said the Lord* (*v.* 12), and again (*v.* 13), *Turn unto the Lord your God.* Our fasting and weeping are worth nothing if we do not with them turn to God as our God. When we are fully convinced that it is our duty and interest to keep in with him, and are heartily sorry we have ever turned the back upon him, and thereupon, by a firm and fixed resolution,

make his glory our end, his will our rule, and his favour our felicity, then we *return to the Lord our God,* and this we are all commanded and invited to do, and to do it quickly.

2. What arguments are here used to persuade this people thus to turn to the Lord, and to turn to him *with all their hearts.* When the heart is rent for sin, and rent from it, then it is prepared to turn entirely to God, and to be devoted entirely to him, and he will have it all or none. Now, to bring ourselves to this, let us consider, (1.) We are sure that he is, in general, a good God. We must *turn to the Lord our God,* not only because he has been just and righteous in punishing us for our sins, the fear of which should drive us to him, but because he is *gracious and merciful,* in receiving upon us our repentance, the hope of which should draw us to him. He is gracious and merciful, delights not in the death of sinners, but desires that they may turn and live. *He is slow to anger* against those that offend him, but of *great kindness* towards those that desire to please him. These very expressions are used in God's proclamation of his name when he caused *his goodness,* and with it all his glory, to *pass before Moses,* Ex. 34:6, 7. *He repents him of the evil,* not that he changes his mind, but, when the sinner's mind is changed, God's way towards him is changed; the sentence is reversed, and the curse of the law is taken off. Note, That is genuine, ingenuous, and evangelical repentance, which arises from a firm belief of the mercy of God, which we have sinned against, and yet are not in despair. *Repent, for the kingdom of heaven is at hand.* The goodness of God, if it be rightly understood, instead of emboldening us to go on in sin, will be the most powerful inducement to repentance, Ps. 130:4. The act of indemnity brings those to God whom the act of attainder frightened from him. (2.) We have reason to hope that he will, upon our repentance, give us that good which by sin we have forfeited and deprived ourselves of (*v.* 14), that he will *return and repent,* that he will not proceed against us as he has done, but will act in favour of us. *Therefore* let us repent of our sins against him, and return to him in a way of duty, because then we may hope that he will repent of his judgments against us and return to us in a way of mercy. Now observe, [1.] The manner of expectation is very humble and modest: *Who knows if he will?* Some think it is expressed thus doubtfully to check the presumption and security of the people, and to quicken them to a holy carefulness and liveliness in their repentance, as Jos. 24:19. Or, rather, it is expressed doubtfully because it is the removal of a temporal judgment that they here promise themselves, of which we cannot be so confident as we can that, in general, God is gracious and merciful. There is no question at all to be made but that if we truly repent of our sins God will forgive them, and be reconciled to us; but whether he will remove this or the other affliction which we are under may well be questioned, and yet the probability of it should encourage us to repent. Promises of temporal good things are often made with a peradventure. *It may be, you shall be hid,* Zep. 2:3. David's sin is pardoned, and yet the child shall die, and, when David prayed for its life, he said, as here, *Who can tell whether God will begracious to me* in this matter likewise? 2 Sa. 12:22. The Ninevites repented and reformed upon such a consideration as this, Jonah 3:9. [2.] The matter of expectation is very pious. They hope God will return and repent, and *leave a blessing behind him,* not as if he were about to go from them, and they could be content with any blessing in lieu of his presence, but *behind him,* that is, "After he has ceased his controversy with us, he will bestow a blessing upon us;" and what is it? It is a *meat-offering and a drink-offering to the Lord our God.* The fruits of the earth are called *a blessing* (Isa. 45:8) because they depend upon God's blessing and are necessary blessings to us. They had been deprived of these, and that which grieved them most while they were so was that God's altar was deprived of its offerings and God's priests of their maintenance; that therefore which they comfort themselves with the prospect of in their return of plenty is that then there shall be meat-offerings and drink-offerings in abundance brought to God's altar, which they more desired than to see the wonted abundance of meat and drink brought to their own tables. Thus when Hezekiah was in hopes that he should recover of his sickness he asked, *What is the sign that I shall go up,* not to the thrones of judgment, or to the councilboard, but *to the house of the Lord?* Isa. 38:22. Note, The plentiful enjoyment of God's ordinances in their power and purity is the most valuable instance of a nation's prosperity and the greatest blessing that can be desired. If God give the blessing of meat-offering and the drink-offering, that will bring along with it other blessings, will sanctify them, sweeten them, and secure them.

II. They are here called to a public national repentance, to be exercised in the solemn assembly, as a national act, for the glory of God and the excitement of one another, and that the neighbouring nations might know and observe what it was that qualified them for God's gracious returns in mercy to them, which they would be the admiring witnesses of. Let us see here, 1. How the congregation must be called together, *v.* 15, 16. The trumpet was blown (*v.* 1), to sound an *alarm of war;* but now it must be blown in order to a treaty of peace. God is willing to show mercy to his people if he do but find them in a frame fit for it; and therefore, Call them together; *sanctify a fast.* By the law many annual feasts were appointed, but only one day in the year was to be observed as a fast, the *day of atonement,* a day to *afflict the soul;* and, if they had kept close to God and their duty, there would have been no occasion to observe any more; but now that they had by sin brought the judgments of God upon them they are often called to fasting. What was said *ch.* 1:14 is here repeated: *"Call a solemn assembly; gather the people* (press them to come together upon this errand); *sanctify the congregation;* appoint a time for solemn preparation beforehand and put them in mind to prepare themselves. Let not the greatest be excused, but *assemble the elders,* the judges and magistrates. Let not the meanest be passed by, but *gather the children, and those that suck the breasts."* It is good to bring little children, as soon as they are capable of understanding any thing, to religious assemblies, that they may be trained up betimes in the way wherein they should go; but these were brought even when they were at the breast and were kept fasting, that by their cries for the breast the hearts of the parents might be moved to repent of sin, which God might justly so visit upon their children that the *tongue of the sucking child* might *cleave to the roof of his mouth* (Lam. 4:4), and that on them God might have compassion, as he had on the infants of Nineveh, Jonah 4:11. New-married people must not be exempted: *Let the bridegroom go forth of his chamber and the bride out of her closet;* let them not take state upon them as usual, not put on their ornaments, nor indulge themselves in mirth, but address themselves to the duties of the public fast with as much gravity and sadness as any of their neighbours. Note, Private joys must always give way to public sorrows, both those for affliction and those for sin. 2. How the work of the day must be carried on, *v.* 17. (1.) The priests, *the Lord's ministers,* must preside in the congregation, and be God's mouth to the people, and theirs to God; who should stand in the gap to turn away the wrath of God but those whose business it was to make intercession upon ordinary occasions? (2.) They must officiate *between the porch and the altar.* There they used to attend about the sacrifices, and therefore now that they have no sacrifices to offer, or next to none, there they must offer up spiritual sacrifices. There the people must see them weeping and wrestling, like their father Jacob, and be helped into the same devout frame. Ministers must themselves be affected with those things wherewith they desire to affect others. It was *between the porch and the altar* that Zechariah the son of Jehoiada was put to death for his faithfulness; that precious blood God would require at their hands, and therefore, to turn away the judgment threatened for it, there they must *weep.* (3.) They must pray. Words here are put into their mouths, which they might in their prayers enlarge upon. Their petition must be, *Spare thy people, O Lord!* God's people, when they are in distress, can expect no relief against God's justice but what comes from his mercy. They cannot say, Lord, *right us,* but, Lord, *spare us.* We deserve the correction; we need it; but, Lord, mitigate it. The sinner's supplication is, *Spare us, good Lord.* Their plea must be taken from the relation wherein they stand to God ("They are *thy people,* and *thy heritage,* therefore have compassion on them"), but especially from the concern of God's glory in their trouble — "Lord, *give not thy heritage to reproach,* to the reproach of famine; let not the land of Canaan, that has so long been celebrated as the glory of all lands, now be made the scorn of all lands; let not *the heathen rule over them,* as they will easily do when thy heritage is thus impoverished and disabled to subsist. Let not the heathen make them *a proverb,* or a *by-word"* (so some read it); "let it never be said, *As poor and beggarly as an Israelite."* Note, The maintaining of the credit of the nation among its neighbours is a blessing to be desired and prayed for by all that wish well to it. But that reproach of the church is especially to be dreaded and deprecated which reflects upon God: "Let them not *say among the people, Where is their God* — that God who has promised to help them, whom they have boasted so much of and put such a confidence in?" If God's heritage be destroyed, the neighbours will say, "God was either weak and could not relieve them or unkind and would not." Deu. 32:37, *Where are now their gods in whom they trusted?* And Sennacherib thus triumphs over them. *Where are they gods of Hamath and Arpad?* But it must by no means be suffered that they should say of Israel, *Where is their God?* For we are sure that our God is in the heavens (Ps. 115:2, 3), is in his temple, Ps. 11:4.

Verses 18–27

See how ready God is to succour and relieve his people, how he *waits to be gracious;* as soon as ever they humble themselves under this hand, and pray, and seek his face, he immediately meets them with his favours. They prayed that God would *spare them,* and see here with what *good words and comfortable words* he answered them; for God's promises are real answers to the prayers of faith, because with him saying and doing are not two things. Now observe,

I. Whence this mercy promised shall take rise (*v.* 18): God will be *jealous for his land* and *pity his people.* He will have an eye, 1. To his own honour, and the reputation of his covenant with Israel, by which he had conveyed to them that good land and had given in the value of it very high; now he will not suffer it to be despised nor disparaged, but will be jealous for the credit of his land, and the inhabitants of it, who had been praised as a happy people and therefore must not lie open to reproach as a miserable people. 2. To their distress: He will *pity his people,* and, in pity to them, he will restore them their forfeited comforts. God's compassion is a great encouragement to those that come humbly to him as penitents and as petitioners.

II. What his mercy shall be, in several instances: — 1. The destroying army shall be dispersed and defeated (*v.* 20): *"I will remove far off from you the northern army,* that army of locusts and caterpillars that invaded you from the north, brought in upon the wings of a north wind, an army which you could put no stop to the progress of; but, when you have made your peace with God, he will ease you of these soldiers that are quartered upon you and will *drive them into a land barren and desolate,* into that vast howling wilderness that Israel wandered in, where, after having surfeited upon the plenty of Canaan, they shall perish for want of sustenance. Those that have their *face to the east sea* (the Dead Sea, which lay east of Judea) shall perish in that, and the rear of the army shall be lost in the Great Sea," called here the *utmost sea.* They had made the land barren and desolate, and now God will cast them into a land barren and desolate. Thus those whom God employs for the correction of his people come afterwards to be themselves reckoned with; and the rod is thrown into the fire. Nothing shall remain of these swarms of insects but the ill savour of them. When Egypt was eased of the plague of locusts they were carried away to the Red Sea, Ex. 10:19. Note, When an affliction has done its work it shall be removed in mercy, as the locusts of Canaan were from a penitent people, not as the locusts of Egypt were removed, in wrath, from an impenitent prince, only to make room for another plague. Many interpreters, by this northern army, understand that of Sennacherib, which was dispersed when God by it had *accomplished his whole work upon Mount Zion and upon Jerusalem,* Isa. 10:12. This enemy shall be driven away, because *he has done great things,* has done a great deal of mischief, and has *magnified* to do it, has done it in the pride of his heart; therefore it follows (*v.* 21), *The Lord will do great things for* his people, as the enemy has done great things against them, to convince them that wherein they deal proudly he is, and will be, above them, that, what great things soever they did, they did no more than God commissioned them to do; and as, when he said to them, Go, they went, so, when he said to them, Come, they came, to show that they were *soldiers under him.* 2. The destroyed land shall be watered and made fruitful. When the army is scattered, yet what shall we do if the desolation they have made continue? It is therefore promised (*v.* 22) that *the pastures of the wilderness,* the pastures which the locusts had left as bare as the wilderness, shall again *spring* and the *trees shall again bear their fruit,* particularly the *fig-tree and the vine.* But, when we see how the country is wasted, we are tempted to say, *Can these dry bones live? If the Lord should make windows in heaven,* it cannot be; but it shall be, for (*v.* 23) *the Lord has given* and will give you *the former rain and the latter rain,* and, if he give them in mercy, he will give them moderately, so that the rain shall not turn into a judgment, and he will give them in due season, the *latter rain in the first month,* when it was wanted and expected. It would make it comfortable to them to see it coming from the hand of God, and ordered by his wisdom, for then we are sure it is well ordered. *He has given you a teacher of righteousness,* (so the margin reads it, for the same word that signifies the *rain* signifies a *teacher.* and that which we translate *moderately is according to righteousness*), and this *teacher of righteousness,* says one of the rabbin, is the King Messias, and of him many others understand this; for he is a *teacher come from God,* and he shows us the way of *righteousness.* But others understand it of any prophet that *instructs unto righteousness,* and some of Hezekiah particularly, others of Isaiah. Note, It is a good sign that God has mercy in store for a people when he sends them teachers of righteousness, pastors after his own heart. 3. All their losses shall be repaired (*v.* 25): *"I will restore to you the years that the locust has eaten;* you shall be comforted according to the time that you have been afflicted, and shall have years of plenty to balance the years of famine." Thus does it *repent the Lord concerning his servants,* when they repent, and, to show how perfectly he is reconciled to them, he makes good the damage they have sustained by his judgments, and, like the jailer, *washes their stripes.* Though, in justice, he distrained upon them, and did them no wrong, yet, in compassion, he makes restitution; as the father of the prodigal, upon his return, made up all he had lost by his sin and folly, and took him into his family, as in his former estate. The locusts and caterpillars are here called *God's great army which he sent among them,* and he will repair what they had devoured because they were his army. 4. They shall have great abundance of all good things. The earth shall yield her increase, and they shall enjoy it. Look into the stores where they lay up, and you shall find *the floors full of wheat, and the fats overflowing with wine and oil* (*v.* 24), whereas, in the day of their distress, the *wine and oil languished* and *the barns were broken down, ch.* 1:10, 17. Look upon their tables, where they lay out what they have laid up, and you shall find that they *eat in plenty and are satisfied, v.* 26. They do not eat to excess, nor are surfeited; we hope the *drunkards* are cured by the late affliction of their inordinate love of wine and strong drink, for, though they were brought in howling for their scarcity (*ch.* 1:5), they are now brought in again here singing for the plenty of it; but now all shall have enough, and shall known when they have enough, for God will make their food nourishing and give them to be content with it.

These are the mercies promised, and in these *God does great things* (*v.* 21), *He deals wondrously with his people, v.* 26. Herein he glorifies his power, and shows that he can relieve his people though their distress be ever so great, and glorifies his goodness, that he will do it upon their repentance though their provocations were ever so great. Note, When God deals graciously with poor sinners that return to him it must be acknowledged that he deals wondrously and does great things. Some expositors understand these promises figuratively, as pointing at gospel-grace, and having their accomplishment in the abundant comforts that are treasured up for believers in the covenant of grace and the satisfaction of soul they have therein. When God sends us his promises to be the matter of our comfort, his graces to be the grounds of it, and his Spirit to be the author of it, we may well own that he has sent us (according to his promise here, *v.* 19) *corn, and wine, and oil,* or that which is unspeakably better, and we have reason to be satisfied therewith.

III. What use shall be made of these returns of God's mercy to them and the good account they shall turn to.

1. God shall have the glory thereof, for they shall *rejoice in the Lord their God* (*v.* 23), and what is the matter of their rejoicing shall be the matter of their thanksgiving; they shall *praise the name of the Lord their God* (*v.* 26) and not praise their idols, nor call their corn and wine the *rewards that their lovers had given them.* Note, The plenty of our creature-comforts is a mercy indeed to us when by them our hearts are enlarged in love and thankfulness to God, who gives us all things richly to enjoy, though we serve him but poorly. When God restores to us plenty after we have known scarcity, as it is doubly pleasant to us, so it should make us the more thankful to God. When Israel comes out of a wilderness into a Canaan, and there eats and is full, surely he will then *bless the Lord,* with a very sensible pleasure, for *that good land* which *he has given him,* Deu. 8:10.

2. They shall have the credit, and comfort, and spiritual benefit, thereof. When God gives them plenty again, and gives them to be satisfied with it, (1.) Their reputation shall be retrieved; they and their God shall be no more reflected upon as unfaithful to one another when they have returned to him in a way of duty and he to them in a way of mercy (*v.* 19): *"I will no more make you a reproach among the heathen,* that triumphed in your calamities and insulted over you;" and *v.* 26, 27, *"My people shall never be ashamed,* as they have been, of their good land which they used to boast of, but shall again and ever have the same occasion to boast of it." Note, It redounds much to the honour of God when he does that which saves the honour of his people; and those that are his people indeed, though they may be for a time, shall not be always, a *reproach among the heathens;* if we be rightly ashamed of our sins against God, we shall never be ashamed of our glorying in God. (2.) Their joys shall be revived (*v.* 23): *Be glad and rejoice, O land!* and all the inhabitants of it. Times of plenty are commonly times of joy; yet the favour of God *puts gladness into the heart* more than those who have *corn, and wine, and oil increase.* But especially *be glad them, you children of Zion, and rejoice in the Lord your God, v.* 23. They *mourned in Zion* (*v.* 15), and therefore there in a particular manner they shall rejoice; for those that sow in penitential tears shall certainly reap in thankful joys. The children of Zion, who led the rest in fasting, must lead the rest in rejoicing. But observe, They shall *rejoice in the Lord their God,* not so much in the good themselves that are given them as in the good hand that gives them and in the return of his favour to them, as theirs in covenant, which these good things are the tokens and pledges of. The *joy of harvest* and the joy of a feast must both terminate in God, whose love we should taste in all the gifts of his bounty, that we may make him our chief joy, as he is our chief good, and the fountain of all good to us. (3.) Their faith in God shall be confirmed and increased. When temporal mercies are made by the grace of God to be of spiritual advantage to us, and plenty for the body is so far from being an enemy (as with many it proves) that it becomes a friend to the prosperity of the soul, then they are mercies indeed to us. This is promised here (*v.* 27): *You shall know that I am in the midst of Israel,* the *Holy One in the midst of thee* (Hos. 11:9), *and that I am the Lord your God, and none else.* As it proves that the Lord is God, and there is none other, because he *wounds* and he *heals,* he *forms light and darkness,* he does *good and evil* (Isa. 45:7; Deu. 32:39), so it proves him to be *God of Israel,* a God in covenant with his people and a father to them, that as a father he both corrects them when they offend and comforts them when they repent. It was the burden of the threatenings in Ezekiel's prophecy, Such and such evils I will bring upon you, *and you shall know that I am the Lord;* and the same is here made the crown of the promises: You shall *eat, and be satisfied,* and rejoice, and thus *you shall know that I am the Lord.* Note, We should labour to grow in our acquaintance with God by all providences, both merciful and afflictive. When God gives to his people plenty, and peace, and joy, upon their return to him, he thereby gives them to understand that he is pleased with their repentance, that he has pardoned their sins, and that he is theirs as much as ever — that they are taken into the same covenant with him, for he is the Lord their God, and into the same communion, for he is in the midst of them, *nigh unto them in all that they call upon him for,* and, as the sun in the centre of the worlds, so in the midst of them as to diffuse his benign influences to all the parts of his land.

3. Even the inferior creatures shall share therein and be made easy thereby: *Fear not, O land! v.* 21. *Be not afraid, you beasts of the field, v.* 22. They had suffered for the sin of man, and for God's quarrel with him; and now they shall fare the better for man's repentance and God's reconciliation to him. Nay, the beasts were said to *cry unto God* (*ch.* 1:20); and now that cry is answered, and they are directed not to *be afraid,* for they shall have plenty of all that which their nature craves. God, in sparing Nineveh, had an eye to the cattle (Jonah 4:11), for the cattle had fasted, *ch.* 3:8. This may lead us to think of the restitution of all things, when the *creature,* that is now *made subject to vanity* and *groans* under it, *shall be brought,* though not into the glorious joy, yet *into the glorious liberty, of the children of God,* Rom. 8:21.

Verses 28–32

The promises of corn, and wine, and oil, in the foregoing verses, would be very acceptable to a wasted country; but here we are taught that we must not rest in those things. God has reserved some better things for us, and these verses have reference to those better things, both the kingdom of grace and the kingdom of glory, with the happiness of true believers in both. We are here told,

I. How the kingdom of grace shall be introduced by a plentiful *effusion of the Spirit,* (*v.* 28, 29). We are not at a loss about the meaning of this promise, nor in doubt what it refers to and wherein it had its accomplishment, for the apostle Peter has given us an infallible explication and application of it, assuring us that when the Spirit was poured out upon the apostles, on the day of Pentecost (Acts 2:1, etc.), that was the very thing *which was spoken of here by the prophet Joel, v.* 16, 17. That was the gift of the Spirit, which, according to this prediction, was *to come,* and we are not to *look for any other,* any more than for another accomplishment of the promise of the Messiah. Now, 1. The blessing itself here promised is the *pouring out of the Spirit of God,* his gifts, graces, and comforts, which the blessed Spirit is the author of. We often read in the Old Testament of the Spirit of the Lord coming by drops, as it were, upon the judges and prophets whom God raised up for extraordinary services; but now the Spirit shall be poured out plentifully in a full stream, as was promised with an eye to gospel-times, Isa. 44:3. *I will pour my Spirit upon thy seed.* 2. The time fixed for this is *afterwards;* after the fulfilling of the foregoing promises this shall be fulfilled. St. Peter expounds this of *the last days,* the days of the Messiah, by whom the world was to have its last revelation of the divine will and grace in the last days of the Jewish church, a little before its dissolution. 3. The extent of this blessing, in respect of the persons on whom it shall be bestowed. The Spirit shall be *poured out upon all flesh,* not as hitherto upon Jews only, but upon Gentiles also; for in Christ there is no distinction between Jew and Greek, Rom. 10:11, 12. Hitherto divine revelation was confined to the seed of Abraham, none but those of the land of Israel had the Spirit of prophecy; but, in the last days, *all flesh shall see the glory of God* (Isa. 40:5) and shall come to *worship before him,* Isa. 66:23. The Jews understand it of all flesh in the land of Israel, and Peter himself did not fully understand it as speaking of the Gentiles till he saw it accomplished in the descent of the Holy Ghost upon Cornelius and his friends, who were Gentiles (Acts 10:44, 45), which was but a continuation of the same gift which was bestowed on the day of Pentecost. The Spirit shall be poured out *upon all flesh,* that is, upon all those whose hearts are made hearts of flesh, soft and tender, and so prepared to receive the impressions and influences of the Holy Ghost. *Upon all flesh,* that is, upon some of all sorts of men; the gifts of the Spirit shall not be so sparing, or so much confined, as they have been, but shall be more general and diffusive of themselves. (1.) The Spirit shall be poured out upon some of each sex. Not *your sons* only, but *your daughters,* shall prophesy; we read of four sisters in one family that were prophetesses, Acts 21:9. Not the parents only, but the children, shall be filled with the Spirit, which intimates the continuance of this gift for some ages successively in the church. (2.) Upon some of each age: "*Your old men,* who are past their vigour and whose spirits begin to decay, *your young men,* who have yet but little acquaintance with and experience of divine things, shall yet *dream dreams* and *see visions;*" God will reveal himself by dreams and visions both to the young and old. (3.) Upon those of the meanest rank and condition, even *upon the servants and the handmaids.* The Jewish doctors say, *Prophecy does not reside on any* but such as are *wise, valiant, and rich,* not upon the soul of a *poor man,* or a man *in sorrow.* But in Christ Jesus there is *neither bond nor free,* Gal. 3:28. There were many that *were called being servants* (1 Co. 7:21), but that was no obstruction to their receiving the Holy Ghost. (4.) The effect of this blessing: *They shall prophesy;* they shall receive new discoveries of divine things, and that not for their own use only, but for the benefit of the church. They shall interpret scripture, and speak of things secret, distant, and future, which by the utmost sagacities of reason, and their natural powers, they could not have any insight into nor foresight of. By these extraordinary gifts the Christian church was first founded and set up, and the scriptures were written, and the ministry settled, by which, with the ordinary operations and influences of the Spirit, it was to be afterwards maintained and kept up.

II. How the kingdom of glory shall be introduced by the universal change of nature, *v.* 30, 31. The pouring out of the Spirit will be very comfortable to the righteous; but let the unrighteous hear this, and tremble. There is a *great and terrible day of the Lord* coming, which shall be ushered in with *wonders* in *heaven and earth, blood, and fire, and pillars of smoke,* the turning of *the sun into darkness and the moon into blood.* This is to have its full accomplishment (as the learned Dr. Pocock thinks) in the day of judgment, at the end of time, before which these signs will be performed in the letter of them, yet so that it was accomplished in part in the death of Christ (which is called the *judgment of this world,* when the earth quaked and the sun was darkened, and a *great and terrible day* it was), and more fully in the destruction of Jerusalem, which was a type and figure of the general judgment, and before which there were many amazing prodigies, besides the convulsions of states and kingdoms prophesied of under the figurative expressions of turning the *sun into darkness and the moon into blood,* and the *wars and rumours of wars,* and *distress of nations,* which our Saviour spoke of as the *beginning of* these *sorrows,* Mt. 24:6, 7. But before the last judgment there will be *wonders* indeed *in heaven and earth,* the dissolution of both, without a metaphor. The judgments of God upon a sinful world, and the frequent destruction of wicked kingdoms by fire and sword, are prefaces to and presages of the judgment of the world in the last day. Those on whom the Spirit is poured out shall foresee and foretel that *great and terrible day of the Lord,* and expound the *wonders in heaven and earth* that go before it; for, as to his first coming, so to his second, all the prophets did and do bear witness, Rev. 10:7.

III. The safety and happiness of all true believers both in the first and second coming of Jesus Christ, *v.* 32. This speaks of particular persons, for to them the New Testament has more respect, and less to kingdoms and nations, than the Old. Now observe here, 1. That there is a salvation wrought out. Though the day of the Lord will be great and terrible, yet *in Mount Zion and in Jerusalem there shall be deliverance* from the terror of it. It is the day of the Lord, the day of his judgment, who knows how to separate between the precious and the vile. In the everlasting gospel, which *went from Zion,* in the church of the first-born typified by Mount Zion, and which is the Jerusalem that is from above, there is *deliverance;* a way of escaping the *wrath to come* is found out and laid open. Christ is himself not only the *Saviour,* but *the salvation;* he is so *to the ends of the earth.* This deliverance, laid up for us in the covenant of grace, is in performance of the promises made to the fathers. *There shall be deliverance, as the Lord has said.* See Lu. 1:72. Note, This is ground of comfort and hope to sinners, that, whatever danger there is in their case, there is also deliverance, deliverance for them, if it be not their own fault. And, if we would share in this deliverance, we must ourselves apply to the gospel-Zion, to God's Jerusalem. 2. That there is a remnant interested in this salvation, and for whom the deliverance is wrought. It is *in that remnant* (that is, among them) that the deliverance is, or in their souls and spirits; there are the earnests and evidences of it. *Christ in you, the hope of glory.* They are called a *remnant,* because they are but a few in comparison with the multitudes that are left to perish; a little remnant but a chosen one, a *remnant according to the election of grace.* And here we are told who they are that shall be delivered in the great day. (1.) Those that sincerely call upon God: *Whosoever shall call upon the name of the Lord,* whether Jew or Gentile (for the apostle so expounds it, Rom. 10:13, where he lays this down as the great rule of the gospel by which we must all be judged), *shall be delivered.* This calling on God supposes knowledge of him, faith in him, desire towards him, dependence on him, and, as an evidence of the sincerity of all this, a conscientious obedience to him; for, without that, crying *Lord, Lord,* will not stand us in any stead. Note, It is the praying remnant that shall be the saved remnant. And it will aggravate the ruin of those who perish that they might have been saved on such easy terms. (2.) Those that are effectually called to God. The deliverance is sure to the *remnant whom the Lord shall call,* not only with the common call of the gospel, with which many are called that are not chosen, but with a special call into the fellowship of Jesus Christ, whom *the Lord predestinates,* or *prepares,* so the Chaldee. St. Peter borrows this phrase, Acts 2:39. Note, Those only shall be delivered in the great day that are now effectually called from sin to God, from self to Christ, from things below to things above.

CHAPTER 3

In the close of the foregoing chapter we had a gracious promise of deliverance in Mount Zion and Jerusalem; now this whole chapter is a comment upon that promise, showing what that deliverance shall be, how it shall be wrought by the destruction of the church's enemies, and how it shall be perfected in the everlasting rest and joy of the church. This was in part accomplished in the deliverance of Jerusalem from the attempt that Sennacherib made upon it in Hezekiah's time, and afterwards in the return of the Jews out of their captivity in Babylon, and other deliverances wrought for the Jewish church between that and Christ's coming. But it has a further reference, to the great redemption wrought out for us by Jesus Christ, and the destruction of our spiritual enemies and all their agents, and will have its full accomplishment in the judgment of the great day. Here is a prediction, I. Of God's reckoning with the enemies of his people for all the injuries and indignities that they had done them, and returning them upon their own head (*v.* 1–8). II. Of God's judging all nations when the measure of their iniquity is full, and appearing publicly, to the everlasting confusion of all impenitent sinners and the everlasting comfort of all his faithful servants (*v.* 9–17). III. Of the provision God has made for the refreshment of his people, for their safety and purity, when their enemies shall be made desolate (*v.* 18–21). These promises were not of private interpretation only, but were written for our learning, "that we, through patience and comfort of this scripture, might have hope."

Verses 1–8

We have often heard of the *year of the redeemed,* and the *year of recompences for the controversy of Zion;* now here we have a description of the transactions of that year, and a prophecy of what shall be done when it comes, whenever it comes, for it comes often, and at the end of time it will come once for all.

I. It shall be the *year of the redeemed,* for God will *bring again the captivity of Judah and Jerusalem, v.* 1. Though the bondage of God's people may be grievous and very long, yet it shall not be everlasting. That in Egypt ended at length in their deliverance into the glorious liberty of the children of God. *Let my son go, the he may serve me.* That in Babylon shall likewise end well. And the Lord Jesus will provide for the effectual redemption of poor enslaved souls from under the dominion of sin and Satan, and will proclaim that *acceptable year,* the year of jubilee, the release of debts and servants, and the *opening of the prison to those that were bound.* There is a day, there is a time, fixed for the *bringing again of the captivity* of God's children, for the redeeming of them *from the power of the grave;* and it shall be the *last day* and the end of all time.

II. It shall be the *year of recompences for the controversy of Zion.* Though God may suffer the enemies of his people to prevail against them very far and for a long time, yet he will call them to an account for it, and will lead captivity captive (Ps. 68:18), will lead those captive that led his people captive, Rev. 13:10. Observe,

1. Who those are that shall be reckoned with — *all nations, v.* 2. This intimates, (1.) That all the nations had made themselves liable to the judgment of God for wrong done to his people. Persecution is the reigning crying sin of the world; that *lying in wickedness* itself is set against godliness. The enmity that is in the old serpent, *the god of this world,* against the seed of the woman, appears more or less in the *children of this world. Marvel not if the world hate you.* (2.) That, whatsoever nation injured God's nation, they should not go unpunished; for he that touches the Israel of God shall be made to know that he touches the apple of his eye. Jerusalem will be a *burdensome stone to all people,* Zec. 12:3. But the neighboring nations shall be particularly reckoned with — *Tyre, and Sidon, and all the coasts of Palestine,* or the Philistines, who have been troublesome neighbours to the Israel of God, *v.* 4. When the more remote and potent nations that laid Israel wastes are reckoned with the impotent malice of those that lay near them, and *helped forward the affliction,* (Zec. 1:15), and made a hand of it (Eze. 26:2), shall not be passed by. Note, Little persecutors shall be called to an account as well as great ones; and, though they could not do much mischief, shall be reckoned with according to the *wickedness of their endeavors* and the mischief they would have done.

2. The sitting of this court for judgment. They shall all be *gathered* (*v.* 2), that those who have combined together against God's people, *with one consent* (Ps. 83:5), may together receive their doom. They shall be *brought down into the valley of Jehoshaphat,* which lay near Jerusalem, and there *God will plead with them,* (1.) Because it is fit that criminals should be tried in the same country where they did the fact. (2.) For their greater confusion, when they shall see that Jerusalem which they have so long endeavored and hoped for the ruin of, in spite of all their rage, made a *praise in the earth.* (3.) For the greater comfort and honor of God's Jerusalem, which shall see God pleading their cause. (4.) Then shall be re-acted what God did for Jehoshaphat when he gave him victory over those that invaded him, and furnished him and his people with matter of joy and praise, in the *valley of Berachah.* See 2 Chr. 20:26. (5.) It was in this valley of Jehoshaphat (as Dr. Lightfoot suggests) that Sennacherib's army, or part of it, lay, when it was destroyed by an angel. They came together to ruin Jerusalem, but God brought them together for their own ruin, *as sheaves into the floor,* Mic. 4:12.

3. The plaintiff called, on whose behalf this prosecution is set on foot; it is for *my people,* and *for my heritage Israel.* It is their cause that God will now plead with jealousy. Note, God's people are *his heritage,* his *peculiar,* his *portion,* his *treasure,* above all people, Ex. 19:5; Deu. 32:9. They are his demesne, and therefore he has a good action against those that trespass upon them.

4. The charge exhibited against them, which is very particular. Many affronts they had put upon God by their idolatries, but that for which God has a quarrel with them is the affront they have put upon his people and upon the vessels of his sanctuary.

(1.) They had been very abusive to the people of Israel, had *scattered them among the nations* and forced them to seek for shelter where they could find a place, or carried them captive into their respective countries and there industriously dispersed them, for fear of their incorporating for their common safety. They *parted their land,* and took every one his share of it as their own; nay, they have *cast lots for my people,* and *sold them.* When they had taken them prisoners, [1.] They made a jest of them, made a scorn of them as of no value. They would not release them and yet thought them not worth the keeping; they made nothing of playing them away at dice. Or they made a dividend of the prisoners *by lot,* as the soldiers did of Christ's garments. [2.] They made a gain of them. When they had them they *sold* them, yet with so much contempt that they did *not increase their wealth by their price,* but sold them for their pleasure rather than their profit; they *gave a boy* taken in war for the *hire of a harlot,* and *a girl* for so many bottles of wine as would serve them for one sitting, a *goodly price* at which they valued them, and goodly preferment for a son and daughter of Israel to be a slave and a drudge in a tavern or a brothel. Observe, here, how that which is got by sin is commonly spent upon another. The spoil which these enemies of the Jews gathered by injustice and violence they scattered and threw away in drinking and whoring; such is frequently the character, and such the conversation, of the enemies and persecutors of the people of God. The Tyrians and Philistines, when they seized any of the children of Judah and Jerusalem, either took them prisoners in war or kidnapped them, they sold them to the Grecians (with whom the men of Tyre traded in the *persons of men,* Eze. 27:13), that they *might remove them far from their* own *border, v.* 6. It was a great reproach to Israel, God's first-born, his free-born, to be thus bought and sold among the heathen.

(2.) They had unjustly seized *God's silver and gold* (*v.* 5), by which some understand the wealth of Israel. The silver and gold which God's people had he calls his, because they had received it from him and devoted it to him; and whosoever robbed them God took it as if they had robbed him and would make reprisals accordingly. Those who take away the estates of good men for well-doing will be found guilty of sacrilege; they take God's *silver and gold.* But it seems rather to be meant of the *vessels* and *treasures of the temple,* which God here calls his *goodly pleasant things,* precious and desirable to him and all that are his. These they *carried into their temples* as trophies of their victory over God's Israel, thinking that therein they triumphed over Israel's God, nay, and that their idols triumphed over him. Thus the ark was put in Dagon's temple. Thus they did unjustly. *"What have you to do with me* (*v.* 4), with my people; what wrong have they done you? What provocation have they given you? You had nothing to do with them, and yet you do all this against them. Devices are devised against the *quiet in the land,* and those offended and harmed that are harmless and inoffensive: *Will you render me a recompence?"* Can they pretend that either God or his people have done them any injury, for which they may justify themselves by the law of retaliation in doing them these mischiefs? No; they have no colour for it. Note, It is no new thing for those who have been very civil and obliging to their neighbours to find them very unkind and unneighbourly and for those who do no injuries to suffer many.

5. The sentence passed upon them. In general (*v.* 4), "If *you recompense me,* if you pretend a quarrel with me, if you provoke me thus to jealousy, if you touch the apple of my eye, *I will swiftly and speedily return your recompence upon your own head."* Those that contend with God will find themselves unable to make their part good with him. He will recompense them *suddenly,* when they little think of it, and have not time to prevent it; if he take them to task, he will soon effect their ruin. Particularly, it is threatened, (1.) That they should not gain their end in the mischief they designed against God's people. They thought to *remove them so far from their border* that they should never return to it again, *v.* 6. But (says God) *"I will raise them out of the place whither you have sold them,* and they shall not, as you intended, be buried alive there." Men's selling the people of God will not deprive him of his property in them. (2.) That they shall be paid in their own coin, as Adonibezek was (*v.* 8): *"I will sell your sons and your daughters into the hands of the children of Judah;* you shall lie as much at their mercy as they have been at yours," Isa. 60:14. Thus the Jews *had rule over those that hated them,* Esther 9:1. And then they shall justly be *sold to the Sabeans,* to a *people far off.* This (some think) had its accomplishment in the victories obtained by the Maccabees over the enemies of the Jews; others think it looks as far forward as the last day, when the *upright shall have dominion* (Ps. 49:14) and *the saints shall judge the world.* It is certain that none ever hardened his heart against God, or his church, and prospered long; no, not Pharaoh himself, for *the Lord has spoken it,* for the comfort of all his suffering servants, that *vengeance is his and he will repay.*

Verses 9–17

What the psalmist had long before ordered to be *said among the heathen* (Ps. 96:10) the prophet here will have in like manner to be published to all nations, That *the Lord reigns,* and that *he comes, he comes to judge the earth,* as he had long been judging in the earth. The notice here given of God's judging the nations may have reference to the destruction of Sennacherib, Nebuchadnezzar, Antiochus, and to the Antichrist especially, and all the proud enemies of the Christian church; but some of the best interpreters, ancient and modern (particularly the learned Dr. Polock), think the scope of these verses is to set forth the day of the last judgment under the similitude of God's making war upon the enemies of his kingdom, and his gathering in the harvest of the earth, both which similitudes we find used in the Revelation, *ch.* 19:11; 14:18. Here we have,

I. A challenge given to all the enemies of God's kingdom to do their worst. To signify to them that God is preparing war against them, they are called upon to prepare war against him, *v.* 9–11. When the hour of God's judgment shall come effectual methods shall be taken to gather all nations *to the battle of that great day of God Almighty,* Rev. 16:14; 20:8. It seems to be here spoken ironically: *"Proclaim you this among the Gentiles;* let all the forces of the nations be summoned to join in confederacy against God and his people." It is like that, Isa. 7:9, *"Associate yourselves, O you people!* and *gird yourselves,* but you shall be *broken to pieces. Prepare war;* muster up all your strength; *wake up the mighty men;* call them into your service; excite them to vigilance and resolution; *let all the men of war draw near. Let them come* and enter the lists with Omnipotence if they dare; let them not complain for want of weapons, but let them *beat their ploughshares into swords* and their *pruning-hooks into spears.* Let them resolve, if they will, never to return to their husbandry again, but either to conquer or die; let none plead unfitness to bear arms, but *let the weak say, I am strong* and will venture into the field of battle." Thus does a God of almighty power bid defiance to all the opposition of the powers of darkness; let the *heathen rage,* and the *kings of the earth take counsel together, against the Lord and his Christ;* let them *assemble, and come,* and *gather themselves together;* but he that sits in heaven shall laugh at them, and, while he thus calls them, he has them in derision, Ps. 2:1, 4. The heathen must be wakened, must be raised from the dead, that they may *come up to the valley of Jehoshaphat,* to receive their doom (*v.* 12), may come up out of their graves, come up *into the air,* to meet the Lord there. Jehoshaphat signifies *the judgment of the Lord.* Let them come to the place of God's judgment, which perhaps is the chief reason for the using of this name here, but it is put together as a proper name for the sake of allusions to the place so called, which we observed before; let them come thither where God will *sit to judge the heathen,* to that *throne of glory* before which shall be *gathered all nations* (Mt. 25:32), for before the judgment-seat of Christ *we must all appear.* The challenge (*v.* 9) is turned into a summons, *v.* 12. It is not only, *Come if you dare,* but *You shall come* whether you will or no, for there is no escaping the judgments of God.

II. A charge given to the ministers of God's justice to appear and act against these daring enemies of his kingdom among men: And therefore *cause thy mighty ones to come down, O Lord! v.* 11. When they bring their forces into the field, let God bring his, let the archangel's trumpet sound a charge, to call together his *mighty ones,* that is, his angels. Perhaps it is with reference to this that Christ's coming from heaven at the last day is said to be *with his mighty angels,* 2 Th. 1:7. These are the *hosts of the Lord,* that shall fight his battles when he shall put down all opposing rule, principality, and power when he shall *judge among the heathen,* Ps. 110:6. Some think these words (*v.* 9, 10), *Prepare war, wake up the mighty men,* are not a challenge to the enemies' hosts, but a charge to God's hosts; let them *draw near, and come up.* When God's cause is to be pleaded, either by the law or by the sword, he has those ready that shall please it effectually, witnesses ready to appear for him in the court of judgment, soldiers ready to appear for him in the field of battle. They shall *beat ploughshares into swords,* if need be. However, it is plain that to them the charge in given (*v.* 13), *Put you in the sickle, for the harvest is ripe;* that is, *their wickedness is great,* the measure of it is full, and they are ripe for ruin. Our Saviour has expounded this, Mt. 13:39. *The harvest is the end of the world, and the reapers are the angels.* And they are commanded to *thrust* in their *sickle. their sharp sickle,* and gather in both the *harvest* and the *vintage,* Rev. 14:15, 18. Note, The greatness of men's wickedness makes them ripe for God's judgment.

III. The vast appearance that shall be in that great and solemn day (*v.* 14): *Multitudes, multitudes, in the valley of decision,* the same which before was called the *valley of Jehoshaphat,* or *of the judgment of the Lord,* for the *day of the Lord is near* in that valley. Note, 1. The judgment-day, that day of the Lord, has all along been looked upon, and spoken of, as *nigh at hand.* Enoch said, *Behold, the Lord comes,* as if the Judge were then standing before the door, because it is certain that that day will come and will come according to the appointment, and a *thousand years with God are but as one day;* things are ripening apace for it; we ought always to be ready for it, because our judgment is at hand. 2. The day of judgment will be the *day of decision,* when every man's eternal state will be determined, and the controversy that has been long depending between the kingdom of Christ and that of Satan shall be finally decided, and an end put to the struggle. *The valley of the distribution of judgment* (so the Chaldee), when *every man shall receive according to the things done in the body. The valley of threshing* (so the margin), carrying on the metaphor of the *harvest, v.* 13. The proud enemies of God's people will then be crushed and broken to pieces, and made as the *dust of the summer threshing-floors.* 3. Innumerable multitudes will be gathered together to receive their final doom in that day, as in the destruction of Gog we read of the valley of *Hamon-Gog,* and the city of *Hamonah* (Eze. 39:15, 16), both signifying the *multitude* of the vanquished enemies; it is the word here used, *Hamonim, Hamonim,* expressed by the way of admiration — O what vast multitudes of sinners will divine justice be glorified in the ruin of at that day! *A multitude of living* (says one of the rabbin) *and a multitude of dead,* for Christ shall come *to judge both the quick and the dead.*

IV. The amazing change that shall then be made in the kingdom of nature (*v.* 15): *The sun and moon shall be darkened,* as before, *ch.* 2:31. Their glory and lustre shall be eclipsed by the far greater brightness of that glory in which the Judge shall then appear. Nay, they shall themselves be set aside in the dissolution of all things; for the damned sinners in hell shall not be allowed their light, for God himself will be *their everlasting light,* Isa. 60:19. Those that fall under the wrath of God in that day of wrath shall be cut off from all comfort and joy, signified by the darkening not only of sun and moon, but of the stars also.

V. The different impressions which that day will make upon the children of this world and the children of God, according as it will be to them. 1. To the wicked it will be a terrible day. *The Lord* shall then speak *from Zion and Jerusalem,* from the throne of his glory, from heaven, where he manifests himself in a peculiar manner, as sometimes he has done in the *glorious high throne of his sanctuary,* which yet was but a faint resemblance of the glory of that day. He shall speak *from heaven,* from *the midst* of his saints and angels (so some understand it), the holy society of which may be called *Zion* and *Jerusalem;* for, when we come to the *heavenly Jerusalem,* we come to the *innumerable company of angels;* see Heb. 12:22, 25. Now is speaking in that day will be to the wicked as *roaring,* terrible as the roaring of a lion (for so the word signifies); he long kept silence, but now *our God shall come, and shall not keep silence,* Ps. 50:3, 21. Note, The judgment of the great day will make the ears of those to tingle that continue the implacable enemies of God's kingdom. God's voice will then *shake terribly* both *heaven and earth* (Isa. 2:21), yet *once more,* Hag. 2:6; Heb. 12:26. This denotes that the voice of God will in the great day speak such terror to the wicked as were enough to put even heaven and earth into a consternation. When God comes to pull down and destroy his enemies, and make them all his footstool, though heaven and earth should stand up in defence of them and undertake their protection, it shall be all in vain. Even they shall shake before him and be an insufficient shelter to those whom he comforts forth to contend with. Note, As blessings out of Zion are the sweetest blessings, and enough to make heaven and earth sing, so terrors out of Zion are the sorest terrors, and enough to make heaven and earth shake. 2. To the righteous it will be a joyful day. When the heaven and earth shall tremble, and be dissolved and burnt up, then will the Lord be the *hope of his people* and the *strength of the children of Israel* (*v.* 16), and *then shall Jerusalem be holy, v.* 17. The saints are the Israel of God; they are *his people;* the church is his Jerusalem. They are in covenant and communion with him; now in the great day, (1.) Their longings shall be satisfied: *The Lord will be the hope of his people.* As he always was the founder and foundation of their hopes, so he then will be the crown of their hopes. He will be the *harbour* of his people (so the word is), their receptacle, refuge, and home. The saints in the great day shall arrive at the desired haven, shall put to shore after a stormy voyage; they shall go to be for ever at home with God, to their Father's house, the house *not made with hands.* (2.) Their happiness shall be confirmed. God will be in that day the *strength of the children of Israel,* enabling them to bid that day welcome and to bear up under the weight of its glories and joys. In this world, when the judgments of God are abroad, and sinners are falling under them, God is and will be the hope and strength of his people, the strength of their heart, and their portion, when other men's hearts fail them for fear. (3.) Their holiness shall be completed (*v.* 17): *Then shall Jerusalem be holy,* the *holy city* indeed; such shall the heavenly Jerusalem be, such the glorious church, *without spot, or wrinkle, or any such thing. Jerusalem shall be holiness* (so the word is); it shall be perfectly holy; there shall be no remainder of sin in it. The gospel-church is a holy society, even in its militant state, but will never be holiness itself till it comes to be triumphant. Then *no stranger shall pass through her any more;* there shall not enter into the New Jerusalem any thing that defiles or works iniquity; none shall be there but those who have a right to be there, none but its own citizens; for it shall be an unmixed society. (4.) God shall in all this be manifested and magnified: *So shall you know that I am the Lord your God.* By the sanctifying and glorifying of the church God will be known in his holiness and glory, as the God that dwells in his holy mountain and makes it holy by dwelling in it; and those that are sanctified and glorified are so *through the knowledge of him* that called them. The knowledge which true believers have of God is, [1.] An appropriating knowledge. They know that he is *the Lord their God,* yet not theirs only, but theirs in common with the whole church, that he is their God, but *dwelling in Zion his holy mountain;* for, though faith appropriates, it does not engross or monopolize the privileges of the covenant. [2.] It is an experimental knowledge. They shall find him their *hope and strength* in the worst of times, and so they shall *know that he is the Lord their God.* Those know best the goodness of God who have tasted and seen it, and have found him good to them.

Verses 18–21

These promises with which this prophecy concludes have their accomplishments in part in the kingdom of grace, and the comforts and graces of all the faithful subjects of that kingdom, but will have their full accomplishment in the kingdom of glory; for, as to the Jewish church, we know not of any event concerning that which answers to the extent of these promises, and what instances of peace and prosperity they were blessed with, which they may be supposed to be a hyperbolical description of, they were but figures of *better things* reserved *for us, that they* in their best estate *without us might not be made perfect.*

I. It is promised that the enemies of the church shall be vanquished and brought down, *v.* 19. Egypt, that old enemy of Israel, and Edom, which had an inveterate enmity to Israel, derived from Esau, these *shall be a desolation,* a *desolate wilderness,* no more to be inhabited; they have become the *people of God's curse;* so the Idumeans were, Isa. 34:5. No strength nor wealth of a nation is a defence against the judgment of God. But what is the quarrel God has with these potent kingdoms? It is for their *violence against the children of Judah,* and the injuries they had done them; see Eze. 25:3, 8, 12, 15; 26:2. They had *shed* the *innocent blood* of the Jews that fled to them for shelter or were making their escape through their country. Note, The innocent blood of God's people is very precious to him, and not a drop of it shall be shed but it shall be reckoned for. In the last day this earth, which has been filled with violence against the people of God, shall be made a desolation, when it and all the works that are therein shall be burnt up. And, sooner or later, the oppressors and persecutors of God's Israel shall be brought down and laid in the dust, nay, they will at length be brought down and laid in the flames.

II. It is promised that the church shall be very happy; and truly happy it is in spiritual privileges, even during its militant state, but much more when it comes to be triumphant. Three things are here promised it: —

1. Purity. This is put last here, as a reason for the rest (*v.* 21); but we may consider it first, as the ground and foundation of the rest: *I will cleanse their blood that I have not cleansed,* that is, their bloody heinous sins, especially shedding innocent blood; that filth and guilt they had contracted by sin, which rendered them unfit for communion with God, and made them odious to his holiness and obnoxious to his justice; this they shall be washed from in the *fountain opened,* Zec. 13:1. That shall be cleansed by the blood of Christ which could not be cleansed by the sacrifices and purifications of the ceremonial law. Or, if we apply it to the happiness of a future state, it intimates the cleansing of the saints from all these corruptions from which they were not cleansed either by ordinances or providences in the world; there shall not be the least remains of sin in them there. Here, though they are washing daily, there is still something that is not cleansed; but in heaven, even that also shall be done away. Ands the reason is because *the Lord dwells in Zion,* dwells with his church, and much more gloriously with that in heaven, and *holiness becomes his house for ever,* for which reason, where he dwells there must be, there shall be, a perfection of holiness. Note, Though the refining and reforming of the church is work that goes on slowly, and still there is something we complain of that is *not cleansed,* yet there is a day coming when every thing that is amiss shall be amended, and the church shall be all fair, and no spot, no stain in her; and we must wait for that day.

2. Plenty, *v.* 18. This is put first, because it is the reverse of the judgment threatened in the foregoing chapters. (1.) The streams of this plenty overflow the land and enrich it: *The mountains shall drop new wine* and *the hills shall flow with milk,* such great abundance shall they have of suitable provision, both for *babes* and for *strong men.* It intimates the abundance of vineyards, and all fruitful; and the abundance of cattle in the pastures that fill them with milk. And, to make the corn-land fruitful, the *rivers of Judah shall flow with water,* so that the country shall be like the garden of Eden, well-watered every where and greatly enriched, Ps. 65:9. But this seems to be meant spiritually; the graces and comforts of the new covenant are compared to *wine and milk* (Isa. 55:1), and the Spirit to *rivers of living water,* Jn. 7:38. And these gifts abound much more under the New Testament than they did under the Old; when believers receive *grace for grace* from Christ's fulness, when they are enriched with *everlasting consolations,* and *filled with joy and peace in believing,* then *the mountains drop new wine,* and *the hills flow with milk. Drink you,* drink abundantly, *O beloved!* When there is plentiful effusion of the Spirit of grace, then the *rivers of Judah flow with water,* and make glad, not only *the city of our God* (Ps. 46:4), but the whole land. (2.) The fountain of this plenty is in the *house of God,* whence the streams take their rise, as those *waters of the sanctuary* (Eze. 47:1) from *under the threshold of the house,* and the river of life *out of the throne of God and the Lamb,* Rev. 22:1. The psalmist, speaking of Zion, says, *All my springs are in thee,* Ps. 87:7. Those that take temporal blessings to be meant in the former part of the verse, yet by this *fountain* out of *the house of the Lord* understand the grace of God, which, if we abound in temporal blessings, we have so much more need of, that we may not abuse them. Christ himself is the fountain; his merit and grace cleanse us, refresh us, and make us fruitful. This is said to water *the valley of Shittim,* which lay a great way off from the temple at Jerusalem, on the other side of Jordan, and was a dry and barren valley, which intimates that gospel-grace, flowing from Christ, shall reach far, even to the Gentile world, to the most remote regions of it, and shall make those to abound in the fruits of righteousness who had long lain as the barren wilderness. This grace is a fountain overflowing, ever-flowing, from which we may be continually drawing, and yet need not fear its being drawn dry. This fountain comes *out of the house of the Lord* above, from his temple in heaven, flows all that good which here we are daily tasting the streams of, but hope to be shortly, hope to be eternally, drinking at the fountain-head of.

3. Perpetuity. This crowns all the rest (*v.* 20): *Judah shall dwell for ever* (when Egypt and Edom are made *a desolation*), and Jerusalem shall continue *from generation to generation.* This is a promise, and a precious promise it is, (1.) That the church of Christ shall continue in the world to the end of time. As one generation of professing Christians passes away, another shall come, in whom the *throne* of Christ *shall endure for ever,* and *the gates of hell shall not prevail* against it. (2.) That all the living members of that church (Judah and Jerusalem are put for the *inhabitants* of that city and country, Mt. 3:5) shall be established in their happiness to the utmost ages of eternity. This new Jerusalem shall be *from generation to generation,* for it is a city that has foundations, not made with hands, but eternal in the heavens.

AN EXPOSITION, WITH PRACTICAL OBSERVATIONS, OF

THE PROPHECY OF AMOS

Though this prophet appeared a little before Isaiah, yet he was not, as some have mistaken, that Amos who was the father of Isaiah (Isa. 1:1), for in the Hebrew their names are very different; their families too were of a different character, for Isaiah was a courtier, Amos a country-farmer. Amos signifies a *burden,* whence the Jews have a tradition that he was of a slow tongue and spoke with stammering lips; we may rather, in allusion to his name, say that his speech was *weighty* and his word the *burden of the Lord.* He was (as most think) of Judah, yet prophesied chiefly against Israel, and at Bethel, 7:13. Some think his style savours of his extraction, and is more plain and rustic than that of some other of the prophets; I do not see it so; but it is plain that his matter agreed with that of his contemporary Hosea, that *out of the mouth of these two witnesses the word might be established.* It appears by his contest with Amaziah the priest of Bethel that he met with opposition in his work, but was a man of undaunted resolution in it, faithful and bold in reproving sin and denouncing the judgments of God for it, and pressing in his exhortations to repentance and reformation. He begins with threatenings against the neighbouring nations that were enemies to Israel, *ch.* 1 and 2. He then calls Israel to account, and judges them for their idolatry, their unworthy walking under the favours God had bestowed upon them, and their incorrigibleness under his judgments, *ch.* 3 and 4. He calls them to repentance (*ch.* 5), rejecting their hypocritical sacrifices unless they did repent. He foretels the desolations that were coming upon them notwithstanding their security (*ch.* 6), some particular judgments (*ch.* 7), particularly on Amaziah; and, after other reproofs and threatenings (*ch.* 8 and 9), concludes with a promise of the setting up of the Messiah's kingdom and the happiness of God's spiritual Israel therein, just as the prophecy of Joel concluded. These prophets, having opened the wound in their reproofs and threatenings, which show all wrong, in the promises of gospel-grace open the remedy, which alone will set all to rights.

CHAPTER 1

In this chapter we have, I. The general title of this prophecy (*v.* 1), with the general scope of it (*v.* 2). II. God's particular controversy with Syria (*v.* 3–5), with Palestine (*v.* 6–8), with Tyre (*v.* 9, 10), with Edom (*v.* 11, 12), and with Ammon (*v.* 13–15), for their cruelty to his people and the many injuries they had done them. This explains God's pleading with the nations, Joel 3:2.

Verses 1–2

Here is, I. The general character of this prophecy. It consists of *the words which the prophet saw.* Are words to be seen? Yes, God's words are; the apostles speak of the *word of life,* which they had not only *heard,* but *which they had seen with their eyes, which they had looked upon, and which their hands had handled* (1 Jn. 1:1), such a real substantial thing is the word of God. The prophet saw these words, that is, 1. They were revealed to him in a *vision,* as John is said to see *the voice* that spoke to him, Rev. 1:12. 2. That which was foretold by them was to him as certain as if he had seen it with his bodily eyes. It intimates how strong he was in that faith which is *the evidence of things not seen.*

II. The person by whom this prophecy was sent — *Amos, who was among the herdmen of Tekoa,* and was one of them. Some think he was a rich dealer in cattle; the word is used concerning the king of Moab (2 Ki. 3:4, *He was a sheep-master*); it is probable that he got money by that business, and yet he must quit it, to follow God as a prophet. Others think he was a poor keeper of cattle, for we find (*ch.* 7:14, 15) that he was withal a *gatherer of wild figs,* a poor employment by which we may suppose he could but just get his bread, and that God took him, as he did David, from following the flock, and Elisha from following the plough. Many were trained up for great employments, in the quiet, innocent, contemplative business of shepherds. When God would send a prophet to reprove and warn his people, he employed a shepherd, a herdsman, to do it; for they had made themselves *as the horse and mule that have no understanding,* nay, worse than the *ox that knows his owner.* God sometimes *chooses the foolish things of the world to confound the wise,* 1 Co. 1:27. Note, Those whom God has endued with abilities for his service ought not to be despised nor laid aside for the meanness either of their origin or of their beginnings. Though Amos himself is not ashamed to own that he was a herdsman, yet others ought not to upbraid him with it nor think the worse of him for it.

III. The persons concerned in the prophecy of this book; it is *concerning Israel,* the *ten tribes,* who were now ripened in sin and ripening apace for ruin. God has raised them up prophets among themselves (*ch.* 2:11), but they regarded them not; therefore God sends them one from Tekoa, in the land of Judah, that, coming from another country, he might be the more valued, and perhaps he was the rather sent out of his own country because there he was despised for his having been a herdsman. See Mt. 13:55–57.

IV. The time when these prophecies were delivered. 1. The book is dated, as laws used to be, by the reigns of the kings under whom the prophet prophesied. It was in the days of *Uzziah king of Judah,* when the affairs of that kingdom went very well, and of Jeroboam the second kind of Israel, when the affairs of that kingdom went pretty well; yet then they must both be told both of the sins they were guilty of and of the judgments that were coming upon them for those sins, that they might not with the present gleam of prosperity flatter themselves either into an opinion of their innocence or a confidence of their perpetual security. 2. It is dated by a particular event to which is prophecy had a reference; it was *two years before the earthquake,* that earthquake which is mentioned to have been *in the days of Uzziah* (Zec. 14:5), which put the nation into a dreadful fright, for it is there said, They *fled before it.* But how could they flee from it? Some conjecture that this earthquake was at the time of Isaiah's vision, when the *posts of the door were moved,* Isa. 6:4. The tradition of the Jews is that it happened just at the time when Uzziah presumptuously invaded the priest's office and went in to burn incense, 2 Chr. 26:16. Josephus mentions this earthquake, *Antiq.* 9.225, and says, "By it half of a mountain was removed and carried to a plain four furlongs off; and it spoiled the king's gardens." God by this prophet gave warning of it *two years* before, that God by it would shake down their houses, *ch.* 3:15.

V. The introduction to these prophecies, containing the general scope of them (*v.* 2): *The Lord will roar from Zion.* His threatenings by his prophets, and the executions of those threatenings in his providence, will be as terrible as the roaring of a lion is to the shepherds and their flocks. Amos here speaks the same language with his contemporaries, Hosea (*ch.* 11:10) and Joel, *ch.* 3:16. The lion roars before he tears; God gives warning before he strikes. Observe, 1. Whence this warning comes — *from Zion* and Jerusalem, from the oracles of God there delivered; for *by them is they servant warned,* Ps. 19:11. Our God, whose special residence is there, will issue out warrants, *given at that court,* as it were, for the executing of judgments on the land. See Jer. 25:30. In Zion was the mercy-seat; thence the Lord roars, intimating that God's acts of justice are consistent with mercy, allayed and mitigated by mercy, nay, as they are warnings, they are really acts of mercy. We are chastened, that we may be not be condemned. 2. What effect the warning has: *The habitations of the shepherds mourn,* either because they fear the roaring lion or because they feel what is signified by that comparison, the consequences of a *great drought* (*ch.* 4:7), which made *the top of Carmel* (of the most fruitful fields) to *wither* and become a desert, Joel 1:12–17.

Verses 3–15

What the Lord says here may be explained by what he says Jer. 12:14, *Thus said the Lord, against all my evil neighbours that touch the inheritance of my people Israel, Behold, I will pluck them out.* Damascus was a near neighbour to Israel on the north, Tyre and Gaza on the west, Edom on the south, Ammon and (in the next chapter) Moab on the east; and all of them had been, one time, one way, or other, *pricking briers and grieving thorns* to Israel, evil neighbours to them; and, because God espouses his people's cause, he there calls them *his evil neighbours,* and here comes forth to reckon with them. The method is taken in dealing with each of them is, in part, the same, and therefore we put them together, and yet in each there is something peculiar.

I. Let us see what is repeated, both by way of charge and by way of sentence, concerning them all. The controversy God has with each of them is prefaced with, *Thus said the Lord,* Jehovah the God of Israel. Though those nations will not worship him as their God, yet they shall be made to know that they are accountable to him as their Judge. The God of Israel is *the God of the whole earth,* and has something to say to them that shall make them tremble. Against them the Lord *roars out of Zion.* And before God, by the prophet, threatens Israel and Judah, he denounces judgments against those nations whom he made use of as scourges to them for their being so, which might serve for a check to their pride and insolence and a relief to his people under their dejections; for hereby they might see that God had not quitted his interest in them, and therefore might hope they had not lost their interest in him. Now as to all these nations here arraigned,

1. The indictment drawn up against them all is thus far the same, (1.) That they are charged in general with *three transgressions, and with four,* that is, with many transgressions (as by one or two we mean *a few,* so by three or four we mean many, as in Latin a man that is very happy is said to be *terque quarterque beatus — three and four times happy*); or *with three and four,* that is, with seven transgressions, a number of perfection, intimating that they have *filled up the measure of their iniquities,* and are ripe for ruin; or *with three* (that is, a variety of sins) *and with a fourth* especially, which is specified concerning each of them, though the other three are not, as Prov. 30:15, 18, 21, 29, where we read of *three things, yea, four,* generally one seems to be more especially intended. (2.) That the particular sin which is fastened upon as the fourth, and which alone is specified, is the sin of persecution: it is some mischief or other done to the people of God that is particularly charged upon every one of them, for persecution is the measure-filling sin of any people, and it is this sin that will be particularly reckoned for — *I was hungry, and you gave me no meat;* much more if it may be said, *I was hungry, and you took my meat from me.*

2. The judgment given against them all is thus far the same, (1.) That, their sin having risen to such a height, *God will not turn away the punishment thereof.* Though he has granted them a long reprieve, and has often *turned away their punishment,* yet now he will turn it away no longer, but justice shall take its course. *"I will not revoke it* (so some read it); I will not recall *the voice* which has *gone forth* from Zion to Jerusalem (*v.* 2), speaking death and terror to the sinful nations." It is an irrevocable sentence. God has spoken it, and he will not *call it back.* Note, Though God bear long, he will not bear always, with those that provoke him; and, when the decree brings forth, it will bring up. (2.) That God will *kindle a fire* among them; this is said concerning all these *evil neighbours, v.* 4, 7, 10, 12, 14. God will *send a fire* into their cities. When fires are kindled that lay cities, towns, and houses in ashes, whether designedly or casually, God must be acknowledged in it; they are of his sending. Sin stirs up the fire of his jealousy, and that kindles other fires.

II. Let us see what is mentioned, both by way of charge and by way of sentence, that is peculiar to each of them, that every one may take his portion.

1. Concerning Damascus, the head-city of Syria, a kingdom that was often vexatious to Israel. (1.) The peculiar sin of Damascus was using the Gileadites barbarously: *They threshed Gilead with threshing-instruments of iron* (*v.* 3), which may be understood literally of their putting to the torture, or to cruel deaths, the inhabitants of Gilead whom they got into their hands, as David put the Ammonites under *saws and harrows* 2 Sa. 12:31. We read with what inhumanity Hazael king of Syria prosecuted his wars with Israel (2 Ki. 8:12); he *dashed their children,* and *ripped up their women with child;* and see what desolations he made in their land, 2 Ki. 10:32, 33. Or it may be taken figuratively, for his laying the country waste, and this very similitude is used in the history of it. 2 Ki. 13:7, He *destroyed them, and made them like the dust by threshing.* Note, Men often do that unjustly and wickedly, and shall be severely reckoned with for it, which yet God just permits them to do. The church is called *God's threshing, and the corn of his floor* (Isa. 21:10); but if men make it their threshing, and the chaff of their floor, they shall be sure to hear of it. (2.) The peculiar punishment of Damascus is [1.] That the fire which shall be sent shall fasten upon the court in the first place, not on the chief city, nor the country towns, but on *the house of Hazael,* which he built; and *it shall devour the palaces of Ben-hadad,* the royal palaces inhabited by the kings of Syria, many of whom were of that name. Note, Even royal palaces are no defence against the judgments of God, though ever so richly furnished, though ever so strongly fortified. [2.] That the enemy shall force his way into the city (*v.* 5): *I will break the bar of Damascus,* and then the gate flies open. Or it may be understood figuratively: all that which is depended upon as the strength and safety of that great city shall fail, and prove insufficient. When God's judgments come with commission it is in vain to think of *turning them out.* [3.] That the people shall be destroyed with the sword: *I will cut off the inhabitant from the plain of Aven,* the *valley of idolatry,* for the gods of the Syrians were *gods of the valleys* (1 Ki. 20:23), were worshipped in valleys; as the idols of Israel were worshipped on *the hills; him also that holdeth the sceptre* of power, some petty king or other that used to boast of the sceptre he held from Beth-Eden, the *house of pleasure.* Both those that were given to idolatry and those that were given to sensuality should be cut off together. [4.] That the body of the nation shall be carried off. The *people shall go into captivity unto Kir,* which was in the country of the Medes. We find this fulfilled (2 Ki. 16:9) about fifty years after this, when *the king of Assyria went up against Damascus,* and *took it, and carried the people of it captive to Kir, and slew Rezin,* at the instigation of Ahaz king of Judah.

2. Concerning Gaza, a city of the Philistines, and now the metropolis of that country. (1.) The peculiar sin of the Philistines was *carrying away captive the whole captivity,* either of Israel or Judah, which some think refers to that inroad made upon Jehoram when they took away *all the king's sons* and *all his substance* (2 Chr. 21:17), or, perhaps, it refers to their seizing those that fled to them for shelter when Sennacherib invaded Judah, and *selling them to the Grecians* (Joel 3:4–6), or (as here) to the Edomites, who were always sworn enemies to the people of God. They

spared none, but carried off all they could lay their hands on, designing, if possible, to *cut off the name of Israel,* Ps. 83:4–7. (2.) The peculiar punishment of the Philistines is that the fire which God will send shall devour the palaces of Gaza, and that the *inhabitants* of the other cities of the Philistines, Ashdod (or Azotus), Ashkelon, and Ekron, shall all be *cut off,* and God will make as thorough work with them in their ruin as they would have made with God's people when they carried away the whole captivity; for even the *remnant* of them *shall perish, v.* 8. Note, God will make a full end of those that think to make a full end of his church and people.

3. Concerning Tyre, that famous city of wealth and strength, that was itself a kingdom, *v.* 9. (1.) The peculiar sin of Tyre is *delivering up the whole captivity to Edom,* that is, selling to the Edomites those of Israel that fled to them for shelter, or in any way fell into their hands; not caring what hardships they put upon them, so that they could but make gain of them to themselves. Herein they forgot the *brotherly covenant,* the league that was between Solomon and Hiram king of Tyre (1 Ki. 5:12), which was intimate that Hiram called Solomon his *brother,* 1 Ki. 9:13. Note, It is a great aggravation of enmity and malice when it is the violation of friendship and of a *brotherly covenant.* (2.) Here is nothing peculiar in the punishment of Tyrus but that *the palaces thereof* shall be *devoured,* which was done when Nebuchadnezzar took it after thirteen years' siege. Their merchants were all princes, and their private houses were as palaces; but the fire shall make no more of them than of cottages.

4. Concerning Edom, the posterity of Esau. (1.) Their peculiar sin was an unmerciful, unwearied, pursuit of the people of God, and their taking all advantages against them to do them a mischief, *v.* 11. He did *pursue his brother with the sword,* not only of old, when the king of Edom took up arms to oppose the children of Israel's passage *through his border* (Num. 20:18), but ever since upon all occasions; they had not strength and courage enough to face them in the field of battle, but, whenever any other enemy had put Judah or Israel to flight, then the Edomites set in with the pursuers, fell upon the rear, slew those that were half dead already, and (as is usual with cowards when they have an enemy at an advantage) they did *cast off all pity.* Those that are least courageous are commonly most cruel. Edom was so; his malice *destroyed his compassion* (so the word is); he stripped himself of the tenderness of a man, and put on the fierceness of a beast of prey; and, as such a one, he did tear, his *anger did tear perpetually.* His cruelty was insatiable, and he never knew when he had sucked enough of the blood of Israel, but, like the horse-leech, still cried, *Give, give.* Nay, he *kept his wrath for ever;* when he wanted objects of his wrath, and opportunity to show it, yet he kept it in reserve (it *rested in his bosom*), he rolled it under his tongue as a sweet morsel, and had it ready to spit in the face of Israel upon the next occasion. Cursed be such cruel wrath, and anger so fierce, so outrageous, which makes men like the devil, who *continually seeks to devour,* and unlike to God, who *keeps not his anger for ever.* Edom's malice was unnatural, for thus he pursued his brother, whom he ought to have protected: it was hereditary, as if it had been entailed upon the family ever since Esau hated Jacob, and time itself could not wear it out, no, nor the brotherly conduct of Israel towards them (Deu. 2:4), and the express law given to Israel (Deu. 23:7), *Thou shalt not abhor an Edomite, for he is thy brother.* (2.) Here is nothing peculiar in their punishment; but (*v.* 12) a *fire* shall be *sent to devour their palaces.* Note, The fire of our anger against our brethren kindles the fire of God's anger against us.

5. Concerning the Ammonites, *v.* 13–15. (1.) See how violently the fire of their anger turned against the people of God; they not only triumphed in their calamities (as we find, Eze. 25:2, 6), but they did themselves use them barbarously; they *ripped up the women with child of Gilead,* a piece of cruelty the very mention of which strikes a horror upon one's mind; one would think it is not possible that any of the human race should be so inhuman. Hazael was guilty of it, 2 Ki. 8:12. It was done not only in a brutish rage, which falls without consideration upon all that comes before it, but with a devilish design to extirpate the race of Israel by killing not only all that were born, but all that were to be born, worse than Egyptian cruelty. It was *that they might enlarge their border,* that they might make the land of Gilead their own, and there might be none to lay claim to it or given them any disturbance in the possession of it. We find (Jer. 49:1) that the Ammonites inherited *Gad* (that is, Gilead) under pretence that Israel had no sons, no heirs. We know how heavy the doom of those was, and how heinous their crime, who said, *This is the heir; come, let us kill him, and the inheritance shall be ours* by occupancy. See what cruelty covetousness is the cause of, and what horrid practices those are often put upon that are greedy to *enlarge their own border.* (2.) See how violently the fire of God's anger burned against them; shall not God *visit for these things* done to any of mankind, especially when they are done to his own people? *Shall not his soul be avenged on such a nation as this?* No doubt, it shall. The fire shall be kindled *with shouting in the day of battle,* that is, war shall kindle the fire; it shall be a fire accompanied with the sword, or a roaring fire, which shall make a noise like that of soldiers ready to engage, and it shall be as a *tempest* in the *day of the whirlwind,* which comes swiftly, furiously, and bears down all before it. Or this tempest and whirlwind shall be as bellows to the fire, to make it burn the stronger, and spread the further. It is particularly threatened that *their king and his princes shall go together into captivity,* carried away by the king of Babylon, not long after Judah was. See what changes God's providence often makes with men, or rather their own sin; kings become captives, and princes prisoners. *Milchom shall go into captivity;* some understand it of the god of the Ammonites, whom they called *Moloch — a king. He, and his princes,* and his priests that attended him, shall to *into captivity;* their idol shall be so far from protecting them that it shall itself go into captivity with them. Note, Those who by violence and fraud seek to enlarge their own border will justly be expelled and excluded their own border; nor is it strange if those who make no conscience of invading the rights of others be able to make no resistance against those who invade theirs.

CHAPTER 2

In this chapter, I. God, by the prophet, proceeds in a like controversy with Moab as before with other nations (*v.* 1–3). II. He shows what quarrel he had with Judah (*v.* 4, 5). III. He at length begins his charge against Israel, to which all that goes before is but an introduction. Observe, 1. The sins they are charged with — injustice, oppression, whoredom (*v.* 6–8). 2. The aggravations of those sins — the temporal and spiritual mercies God had bestowed upon them, for which they had made him such ungrateful returns (*v.* 9–12). 3. God's complaint of them for their sins (*v.* 13) and his threatenings of their ruin, and their utter inability to prevent it (*v.* 14–16).

Verses 1–8

Here is, I. The judgment of Moab, another of the nations that bordered upon Israel. They are reckoned with and shall be punished *for three transgressions and for four,* as those before. Now, 1. Moab's fourth transgression, as theirs who were before set to the bar, was cruelty. The instance given refers not to the people of God, but to a heathen like themselves: The king of Moab *burnt the bones of the king of Edom into lime.* We find there was war between the Edomites and the Moabites, in which the king of Moab, in distress and rage, offered his own son for a burnt-offering, to appease his deity, 2 Ki. 3:26, 27. And it should seem that afterwards he, or some of his successors, in revenge upon the Edomites for bringing him to that extremity, having an advantage against the *king of Edom,* seized him alive and burnt him to ashes, or slew him and burnt his body, or dug up the bones of their dead king, of that particularly who had so straitened him, and, in token of his rage and fury, *burnt them to lime.* and perhaps made use of the powder of his bones for the white-washing of the walls and ceilings of his palace, that he might please himself with the sight of that monument of his revenge. *Est vindicta bonum vita jucundius ipsa — Revenge is sweeter than life itself.* It is barbarous to abuse human bodies, for we ourselves also are *in the body;* it is senseless to abuse dead bodies, nay, it is impious, for we believe and look for their resurrection; and to abuse the dead bodies of kings (whose persons and names ought to be in a particular manner respected and had in veneration) is an affront to majesty; it is an argument of a base spirit for those to trample upon a dead lion who, were he alive, would tremble before him. 2. Moab's doom for this transgression is, (1.) A judgment of death. Those that deal cruelly shall be cruelly dealt with (*v.* 2): *Moab shall die;* the Moabites shall be cut off with the sword of war, which kills *with tumult, with shouting, and with sound of trumpet,* circumstances that make it so much the more terrible, as the lion's roaring aggravates his tearing. *Every battle of the warrior is with confused noise,* Isa. 9:5. (2.) It is a judgment upon their judge, who had passed the sentence upon the bones of the king of Edom that they should be burnt to lime: *I will cut him off,* says God (*v.* 3); he shall know there is a judge that is higher than he. The king, the chief judge, and all the inferior judges and princes, shall be cut off together. If the people sometimes suffer for the sin of their princes, yet the princes themselves shall not escape, Jer. 48:47. *Thus far is the judgment of Moab.*

II. Judah also is a near neighbour to Israel, and therefore, now that justice is riding the circuit, that shall not be passed by; that nation has made itself like the heathen and mingled with them, and therefore the indictment here runs against them in the same form in which it had run against all the rest: *For these transgressions of Judah, and for four, I will not turn away the punishment thereof;* their sins are as many as the sins of other nations, and we find them huddled up with them in the same character, Jer. 9:26, "As for *Egypt, and Judah, and Edom,* jumble them together; they are all alike;" the sentence here also is the same (*v.* 5): *"I will send a fire upon Judah,* though it is the land where God is known, and it shall *devour the palaces of Jerusalem,* though it is the holy city, and God has formerly been *known in its palaces for a refuge,"* Ps. 48:3. But the sin here charged upon Judah is different from all the rest. The other nations were reckoned with for injuries done to men, but Judah is reckoned with for indignities done to God, *v.* 4. 1. They put contempt upon his statutes and persisted in disobedience to them: *They have despised the law of the Lord,* as if it were not worth taking notice of, nor had any thing in it valuable; and herein they despised the wisdom, justice, and goodness, as well as the authority and sovereignty, of the Lawmaker; this they did, in effect, when they *kept not his commandments,* made no conscience of them, took no care about them. 2. They put honour upon his rivals, their idols, here called *their lies* which caused *them to err;* for *an image is a teacher of lies,* Hab. 2:18. And those that are led away into the error of idolatry are by that led into a multitude of other errors, *Uno dato absurdo mille sequuntur — One absurdity draws after it a thousand.* God is an infinite eternal Spirit; but, when the *truth of God* is by idolatry *changed into a lie,* all his other truths are in danger of being so changed likewise; thus their idols caused them to err, and God justly gave them up to strong delusions; nor was it any excuse for their sin that they were lies *after which their father walked,* for they should rather have taken warning than taken pattern by those that perished with these *lies in their right hand.*

III. We now at length come to *the words* which *Amos saw concerning Israel.* The reproofs and threatenings having walked the round, here they centre, here they settle. He begins with them as with the rest: *For three transgressions of Israel, and for four, I will not turn away the punishment thereof;* it all these nations must be punished for their iniquities, shall Israel go unpunished? Observe here what their sins were, for which God would reckon with them. 1. Perverting justice. This was the sin of those who were entrusted with the administration of justice, the judges and magistrates, and all parties concerned. They made nothing of selling a righteous man, and his righteous cause when it came to be tried before them, for a piece of silver; sentence was passed, not according to the merits of the cause, but the bribe always turned the scale, and judgment was set to sale by auction to the highest bidder. They would sell the life and livelihood of a *poor* man *for a pair of shoes,* for the least advantage to themselves that could be proposed to them; give them but a *pair of shoes,* and the cause of a poor man, who could not give them as much as that, should be betrayed, and left at the mercy of those that will have no mercy. They will rather play at small game that sit out. *For a piece of bread such a man will transgress.* Note, Those who will wrong their consciences for any thing will come at length to do it for next to nothing; those who begin to sell justice for silver will in time be so sordid as to see it *for a pair of shoes,* for a pair of old shoes. 2. Oppressing the poor, and seeking to benefit themselves by doing them a mischief: *They pant after the dust of the earth on the head of the poor;* they swallow up the poor with the utmost greediness, and make a prey of those that are in sorrow with dust on their heads, poor orphans that are in mourning for their parents; they catch at them to get their estates into their hands; they never rest till they have got the heads of the poor in the dust, to be trodden on. Or, *They pant after the dust of the earth,* that is, silver and gold, white and yellow dust; they covet it earnestly, and levy it *upon the head of the poor* by their unjust exactions. Note, Men's seeking to enrich themselves by the impoverishing of others is a transgression which God will not long *turn away the punishment of.* This is *turning aside the way of the meek,* contriving to do injury to those who, they know, are mild and patient and will bear injury. They invade their rights, break their measures, and obstruct the course of justice in favour of them, not suffering them to go on with their righteous cause; this is *turning aside their way.* Note, The more patiently men bear injuries that are done them the greater is the sin of those that injure them, and the more occasion they have to expect that God will give them redress, and take vengeance for them. I, *as a deaf man, heard not,* and then *thou wilt hear.* 3. Abominable uncleanness, even incest itself, such as it not named among the Gentiles, that *a man should have his father's wife* (1 Co. 5:1), his father's concubine: *A man and his father will go in unto the same young woman,* as black an instance as any other of an unbounded promiscuous lust; and yet where the former iniquities of oppression and extortion are this also is found; for laws of modesty seldom hold those that have broken the bands of justice and *cast away its cords* from them. This wickedness is such a scandal to religion, and the profession of it, that those who are guilty of it are looked upon as designing thereby to *profane God's holy name,* and to render it odious among the heathen, as if he countenanced the villainies which those who pretend relation to him allow themselves in, and were altogether such a one as they. 4. Regaling themselves and yet pretending to honour their God with that which they had got by oppression and extortion, *v.* 8. They add idolatry to their injustice, and then think to atone for their injustice with their idolatry. (1.) They make merry with that which they have unjustly squeezed from the poor. They *lay themselves down* at ease, and in state, and stretch themselves upon *clothes laid to pledge,* which they ought to have restored the same night, according to the law, Deu. 24:12, 13. And they *drink the wine of the condemned,* of such as they have fined and laid heavy mulcts upon, spending that in sensuality which they have got by injustice. (2.) They think to make atonement for this by feasting on the gains of oppression *before their altars,* and *drinking this wine in the house of their God,* in the temples where they worshipped their calves, as if they would make God a *partner in their crimes* by making him a *partner of the profits* of them — service good enough for false gods; but the true God will not thus be mocked; he has declared that he *hates robbery for burnt-offerings,* and cannot be served acceptably but with that which is got honestly.

Verses 9–16

Here, I. God puts his people Israel in mind of the great things he has done for them, in putting them into possession of the land of Canaan, the greatest part of which these ten tribes now enjoyed, *v.* 9, 10. Note, We need often to be reminded of the mercies we have received, which are the heaviest aggravations of the sins we have committed. God gives liberally, and upbraids us not with our meanness and unworthiness, and the disproportion between his gifts and our merits; but he justly upbraids us with our ingratitude, and ill requital of his favours, and tells us what he has done for us, to shame us for not rendering again according to the benefit done to us. *"Son, remember;* Israel, remember, 1. That God brought thee out of a house of bondage, rescued thee out of the *land of Egypt,* where thou wouldst otherwise have perished in slavery." 2. That he *led thee forty years* through a desert land, and fed thee in a *wilderness,* where thou wouldst otherwise have perished with hunger. Mercies to our ancestors were mercies to us, for, if they had been cut off, we should not have been. 3. That he made room for them in Canaan, by extirpating the natives by a series of wonders little inferior to those by which they were redeemed out of Egypt: *I destroyed the Amorite before them,* here put for all the devoted nations. Observe the magnificence of the enemies that stood in their way, which is taken notice of, that God may be the more magnified in the subduing of them. They were of great stature *(whose height was like the height of the cedars)* and the people of Israel were as shrubs to them; and they were also of great strength, not only tall, but well-set: *He was strong as the oaks.* Their kingdom was eminent among the nations, and over-topped all its neighbours. The supports and defences of it seemed impregnable; it was as fine as the stately cedar; it was as firm as the sturdy oak; yet, when God had a vine to plant there (Ps. 80:8, 9), this Amorite was not only cut down, but plucked up: *I destroyed his fruit from above and his roots from beneath,* so that the Amorites were no more a nation, nor ever read of any more. Thus highly did God value Israel. He gave men *for them and people for their life,* Is. 43:4. How ungrateful then were those who put such contempt upon him! 4. That he made them *possess the land of the Amorite,* not only put it into their hands, so that they became masters of it *jure belli — by right of conquest,* but gave them a better title to it, so that it became theirs by promise.

II. He likewise upbraids them with the spiritual privileges and advantages they enjoyed as a holy nation, *v.* 11. They had helps for their souls, which taught them how to make good use of their temporal enjoyments and were therefore more valuable. It is true the *ten tribes* had not God's temple, altar, and priesthood, and it was their own fault that they deserted them, and for that they might justly have been left in utter darkness; but God *left not himself without witness,* nor them without guides to show them the way. 1. They had prophets that were powerful instructors in piety, divinely inspired, and commissioned to make known the mind of God to them, to show them what is pleasing to God and what displeasing, to reprove them for their faults and warn them of their dangers, to direct them in their difficulties and comfort them in their troubles. God raised them up prophets, animated them for that work and employed them in it. He *raised* them *up of their sons,* from among themselves, as Moses and Christ were raised up *from among their brethren,* Deu. 18:15. It was an honour put upon their nation, and upon their families, that they had children of their own to be God's messengers to them, of their own language, not strangers sent from another country, whom they might suspect to be prejudiced against them and their land, but those who, they knew, wished well to them. Note, Faithful ministers are great blessings to any people, and it is God that raises them up to be so, that they may justly be reckoned an honour to the families they are of. 2. They had Nazarites that were bright examples of piety: *I raised up of your young men for Nazarites,* men that bound themselves by a vow to God and his service, and, in pursuance of that, denied themselves many of the lawful delights of sense, as drinking wine and eating grapes. There were some of their young men that were in their prime for the enjoyment of the pleasures of this life and yet voluntarily abridged themselves of them; these God raised up by the power of his grace, to be *monuments of his grace,* to his glory, and to be his witnesses against the impieties of that degenerate age. Note, It is as great a blessing to any place to have eminent good Christians in it as to have eminent good ministers in it; for so they have examples to their rules. We must acknowledge that it bodes well to any people when God raises up numbers of hopeful young people among them, when he makes their young men Nazarites, devout, and conscientious, and mortified to the pleasures of sense; and those that are such Nazarites are *purer than snow, whiter than milk;* they are indeed the polite young men, for their *polishing is of sapphires,* Lam. 4:7. Those that have such men, such young men, among them, have therein such an advantage, both for direction and encouragement, to be religious, as they will be called to an account for another day if they do not improve. Israel is here reckoned with, not only for the prophets, but for the Nazarites, raised up among them. Concerning the truth of this, he appeals to themselves: *"Is it not even thus, O you children of Israel?* Can you deny it? Have not you yourselves been sensible of the advantage you had by the prophets and Nazarites raised up among you?" Note, Sinners' own consciences will be witnesses for God that he has not been wanting to them in the means of grace, so that, if they perish, it is because they have been wanting to themselves in not improving those means. The men of Judah shall themselves *judge between God and his vineyard,* whether he could have done more for it, Isa. 5:3, 4.

III. He charges them with the abuse of the means of grace they enjoyed, and the opposition they gave to God's designs in affording them those means, *v.* 12. They were so far from walking in the light that they rebelled against it, and did what they could to extinguish it, that it might not shine in their faces, to their conviction. 1. They did what they could to debauch good people, to draw them off from their seriousness in devotion and their strictness in conversation: *You gave the Nazarites wine to drink,* contrary to their vow, that, having broken it in that instance, they might not pretend to keep it in any other. Some they surprised, or allured into it, and *with their much fair speech caused them to yield;* others they forced and frightened into it, reproached and threatened them if they were more precise than their neighbours; and, by drawing them in to drink wine, they spoiled them for Nazarites. Note, Satan and his agents are very busy to corrupt the minds of young people that look heavenward; and many that we thought would have been Nazarites they have overcome by giving them wine to drink, by drawing them in to the love of mirth and pleasure, and drinking company. Multitudes of young men that bade fair for eminent professors of religion have *erred through wine,* and been undone for ever. And how do the factors for hell triumph in the debauching of a Nazarite! 2. They did what they could to silence good ministers, and to stop their mouths: *"You commanded the prophets, saying, Prophesy not,* and threatened them if they did prophesy (*ch.* 7:12), as if God's messengers were bound to observe your orders, and might not deliver their errand unless you gave them leave, and so you not only *received the grace of God,* in raising up those prophets, *in vain,* but put the highest affront imaginable upon that God in whose name the prophets spoke." Note, Those have a great deal to answer for that cannot bear faithful preaching, and those much more that suppress it.

IV. He complains of the wrong they did him by their sins (*v.* 13): *"I am pressed under you,* I am *straitened* by you, and can no longer bear it, and therefore *I will ease myself of my adversaries,* Isa. 1:24. *I am pressed under you* and the load of your sins *as a cart is pressed that is full of sheaves,* is loaded with corn, in the midst of the *joy of harvest,* as long as any will lie on." Note, The great God complains of sin, especially the sins of his professing people, as a burden to him. He is *grieved with this generation* (Ps. 95:10), *is broken with their whorish heart* (Eze. 6:9), a consideration which, if it make not the sinner's repentance very deep, will make his ruin very great. The great God that upholds the world, and never complains that his is pressed under the weight of it (he *fainteth not, neither is weary*), yet complains of the sins of Israel, yea, and of their hypocritical services too, that he is *weary of bearing them,* Isa. 1:14. No wonder the *creature groans being burdened* (Rom. 8:22), when the Creator says, *I am pressed under them.*

V. He threatens them with unavoidable ruin. And so some read, *v.* 13, *"Behold I will press,* or straiten, *your place, as a cart full of sheaves presses;* they shall be loaded with judgments till they shall sink under them, and shall make a noise, as a cart overloaded does." Those that will not submit to the convictions of the word, that will neither be won by that nor by the conversation of those about them, shall be made to sink under the weight of God's judgments. If God load us daily with his benefits, and we, notwithstanding that, load him with our sins, how can we expect any other than that he should load us with his judgments? And it is here threatened in the last three verses that, when God comes forth to contend with this provoking people, they shall not be able to stand before him, to flee from him, nor to make their part good with him; for when God judges he will overcome. Though his patience be tired out, his power is not, and so the sinner shall find, to his cost. When the Assyrian army comes to lay the country waste by sword and captivity none shall escape, but every one shall have his share in the common desolation. 1. It will be in vain to think of fleeing from the enemy that comes armed with a commission to make all desolate: *The flight shall perish from the swift;* those that have been famed for happy escapes and happy retreats shall now find their arts fail them; they shall have no time to flee, or shall find no way to take, or they shall have no strength or spirit to attempt it; they shall be at their wits' end, and then they are soon at their flight's end. Are they, as Asahel, as *swift of foot as a wild roe?* (2 Sa. 2:18), yet, like him, they shall run the faster upon their own destruction: *He that is swift of foot shall not deliver himself, v.* 15. Or do they say (as those, Isa. 30:16), *We will flee upon horses,* and *we will ride upon the swift?* Yet they shall be overtaken: *Neither shall he that rides the horse deliver himself* from his pursuers. *A horse is a vain thing for safety.* 2. It will be in vain to think of fighting it out. God is at war with them; and *are they stronger than he?* Is there any military force that can pretend to be a match for Omnipotence? No: *The strong shall not strengthen his force.* He that has a habit of strength shall not be able to exert it when he has occasion for it. And *the mighty,* whose should protect and deliver others, shall not be able to *deliver himself,* to deliver *his soul* (so the word is), shall not save his life. Let not the *strong man* then *glory in his strength,* nor trust in it, but *strengthen himself in the Lord his God,* for in him is *everlasting strength.* And, as the bodily strength shall fail, so shall the weapons of war. The armour as well as the arm shall become insufficient: *Neither shall he stand that handles the bow,* though he stand at a distance, but shall betake himself to flight, and not trust to his own bow to save him. Though the arm be ever so strong, and the armour ever so well fixed, neither will avail when the spirit fails (*v.* 16): *He that is courageous among the mighty,* that used to look danger in the face, and not be dismayed at it, shall *flee away naked in that day,* not only disarmed, having thrown away his weapons both offensive and defensive, but plundered of his treasure, which he thought to carry away with him, and he shall think it as much as he could expect that he has *his life for a prey.* Thus when God pleases *he takes away the heart of the chief of the people of the earth,* and causes those who used to boast of their courage, and their daring enterprises in the field, to *wander* and sneak *in a wilderness where there is no way,* Job 12:24.

CHAPTER 3

A stupid, senseless, heedless people, are, in this chapter, called upon to take notice, I. Of the judgments of God denounced against them and the warnings he gave them of those judgments, and to be hereby awakened out of their security (*v.* 1–8). II. Of the sins that were found among them, by which God was provoked thus to threaten, thus to punish, that they might justify God in his controversy with them, and, unless they repented and reformed, might expect no other than that God should proceed in his controversy (*v.* 9–15).

Verses 1–8

The scope of these verses is to convince the people of Israel that God had a controversy with them. That which the prophet has to say to them is to let them know that the Lord has something to say against them, *v.* 1. They were his peculiar people above others, knew his name, and were called by it; *nevertheless he had something against them,* and they were called to hear what it was, that they might consider what answer they should make, as the prisoner at the bar is told to hearken to his indictment. The *children of Israel* would not regard the words of counsel and comfort that God had many a time spoken to them, and now they shall be made to hear the word of reproof and threatening that the Lord has spoken against them; for he will act as he has spoken.

I. Let them know that the gracious cognizance God has taken of them, and the favours he has bestowed upon them, should not exempt them from the punishment due to them for their sins. Israel is a *family* that *God brought up out of the land of Egypt,* (*v.* 1), and it was no more than a family when it went down thither; thence God delivered it; thence he fetched it to be a family to himself. It is not only the ten tribes, the kingdom of Israel, that must take notice of this, but that of Judah also, for it is spoken against the whole *family* that God *brought up out of Egypt.* It is a family that God has bestowed distinguishing favours upon, has owned in a peculiar manner. *You only have I known of all the families of the earth.* Note, God's church in the world is a family dignified above all the families of the earth. Those that know God are known of him. *In Judah is God known,* and therefore Judah is more than any people known of God. God has *known* them, that is, he has chosen them, covenanted with them, and conversed with them as his acquaintance. Now, one would think, it should follow, "Therefore I will spare you, will connive at your faults, and excuse you." No: *Therefore I will punish you for all your iniquities.* Note, The distinguishing favours of God to us, if they do not serve to restrain us from sin, shall not serve to exempt us from punishment; nay, the nearer any are to God in profession, and the kinder notice he has taken of them, the more surely, the more quickly, and the more severely will he reckon with them, if they by a course of wilful sin profane their character, disgrace their relation to him, violate their engagements, and put a slight upon the favours and honours with which they have been distinguished. *Therefore* they shall be punished, because their sins dishonour him, affront him, and grieve him, more than the sins of others, and because it is necessary that God should vindicate his own honour by making it appear that he hates sin and hates it most in those that are nearest to him; if they be but as bad as others, they shall be punished worse than others, because it is justly expected that they should be so much better than others. *Judgment begins at the house of God,* begins at the sanctuary; for God will be sanctified either by or upon those that *come nigh unto him,* Lev. 10:3.

II. Let them know that they could not expect any comfortable communion with God unless they first made their peace with him (*v.* 3): *Can two walk together except they be agreed?* No; how should they? Where there is not friendship there can be no fellowship; if two persons be at variance, they must first accommodate the matters in difference between them before there can be any interchanging of good offices. Israel has affronted God, had broken their covenant with him, and ill-requited his favours to them; and yet they expected that he should continue to walk with them, should take their part, act for them, and give them assurances of his presence with them, though they took no care by repentance and reformation to *agree with their adversary* and to turn away his wrath. "But how can that be?" says God. "While you continue to *walk contrary to God* you can look for no other than that he should *walk contrary to you,*" Lev. 26:23, 24. Note, We cannot expect that God should be present with us, or act for us, unless we be reconciled to him. God and man cannot *walk together except they be agreed.* Unless we agree with God in our end, which is his glory, we cannot walk with him by the way.

III. Let them know that the warnings God gave them of judgments approaching were not causeless and groundless, merely to amuse them, but certain declarations of the wrath of God against them, which (if they did not speedily repent) they would infallibly feel the effects of (*v.* 4): *"Will a lion roar in the forest when he has no prey* in view? No: he roars upon his prey. Nor will a *young lion cry out of his den* if the old lion *have taken nothing* to bring home to him; nor would God thus give you warning both by the threatenings of his word, and by less judgments, if you had not by your sins made yourselves a prey to his wrath, nor if he were not really about to fall upon you with desolating destroying judgments." Note, The threatenings of the word and providence of God are not bugbears, to frighten children and fools, but are certain inferences from the sin of man and certain presages of the judgments of God.

IV. Let them know that, as their own wickedness was the procuring cause of these judgments, so they shall not be removed till they have done their work, *v.* 5. When God has come forth to contend with a sinful people it is necessary that they should understand, 1. That it is their own sin that has entangled them; for *can a bird fall in a snare upon the earth where no gin is for him?* No, nature does not lay snares for the creatures, but the art of men; a bird is not taken in a snare by chance, but with the fowler's design; so the providence of God prepares trouble for sinners, and it is *in the work of their own hands* that they *are snared.* Affliction does not *spring out of the dust,* but it is God's justice, and *our own wickedness,* that *correct us.* 2. It is nothing but their own repentance that can disentangle them; for *shall one take up a snare from the earth,* which he laid with design, except he have *taken something* as he designed? So neither will God remove the affliction he has sent till it have done its work and accomplished that for which he sent it. If our hearts be duly humbled, and we are brought by our afflictions to confess and forsake our sins, then the snare has taken something, then the point is gained, the end is answered, and then, and not till then, the *snare is broken,* is taken up from the earth, and *we are delivered* in love and mercy.

V. Let them know that all their troubles came from the hand of God's providence and from the counsel of his will (*v.* 6): *Shall there be evil in a city,* in a family, in a nation, *and the Lord has not done it,* appointed it, and performed what he appointed? The evil of sin is from ourselves; it is our own doing. But the evil of trouble, personal or public, is from God, and is his doing; whoever are the instruments, God is the principal agent. *Out of his mouth both evil and good proceed.* This consideration, that, whatever evil is in the city, the Lord has done it, should engage us patiently to bear our share in public calamities and to study to answer God's intention in them.

VI. Let them know that their prophets, who give them warning of judgments approaching, deliver nothing to them but what they have *received from the Lord* to be delivered to his people. 1. God makes it known beforehand to the prophets (*v.* 7): *Surely the Lord Jehovah will do nothing,* none of that evil in the city spoken of (*v.* 6), *but he reveals it to his servants the prophets,* though to others it is a secret. Therefore those know not what they do who make light of the warnings which the prophets give them, in God's name. Observe, God's prophets are *his servants,* whom he employs to go on his errands to the children of men. The *secret* of God is with them; it is in some sense with all *the righteous* (Prov. 3:32), with *all that fear God* (Ps. 25:14), but in a peculiar manner with the prophets, to whom the Spirit of prophecy is a Spirit of revelation. It would have put honour enough upon prophets if it had been only said that sometimes God is pleased to reveal to his prophets what he designs to do, but it speaks something very great to say that he *does nothing* but what he *reveals to them,* as if they were *the men of his counsel. Shall I hide from Abraham,* who is a prophet, *the thing which I do?* Gen. 18:17. God will therefore be sure to reckon with those that put contempt on the prophets, whom he puts this honour upon. 2. The prophets cannot but make that known to the people which God has made known to them (*v.* 8): *The Lord God has spoken; who can but prophesy?* His prophets, to whom he has spoken in secret by dreams and visions, cannot but speak in public to the people what they have heard from God. They are so full of those things themselves, so well assured concerning them, and so much affected with them, that they cannot but speak of them; for *out of the abundance of the heart* the mouth will speak. *I believed; therefore have I spoken,* Acts 4:20. Nay, and besides the prophetic impulse which went along with the inspiration, and made the word *like a fire in their bones* (Jer. 20:9), they received a command from God to deliver what they had been charged with; and they would have been false to their trust if they had not done it. *Necessity was laid upon them,* as upon the preachers of the gospel, 1 Co. 9:16.

VII. Let them know that they ought to tremble before God upon the fair warning he had given them, as they would, 1. Upon the sounding of a trumpet, to give notice of the approach of the enemy, that all may stand upon their guard and stand to their arms: *Shall a trumpet be blown in the city, and the people be not afraid,* or *run together?* so some read it, *v.* 6. Will they not immediately come together in a fright, to consider what is best to be done for the common safety? Yet when God by his prophets gives them notice of their danger, and summons them to come and enlist themselves under his banner, it makes no impression; they will sooner give credit to a watchman on their walls than to a prophet sent of God, will sooner obey the summons of the governor of their city than the orders given them by the Governor of the world. God says, *Hearken to the voice of the trumpet;* but *they will not hearken,* nay, and they tell him plainly that they will not, Jer. 6:17. 2. Upon the roaring of a lion. God is sometimes *as a lion, and a young lion, to the house of Judah,* Hos. 5:14. The lion roars before he tears; thus God warns before he wounds. If therefore the lion roars upon a poor traveller (as he did against Samson, Jdg. 14:5), he cannot but be put into great consternation; yet the *Lord roars out of Zion* (*ch.* 1:2), and none are afraid, but they go on securely as if they were in no danger. Note, The fair warning given to a careless world, if it be not taken, will aggravate its condemnation another day. The lion roared, and they were not moved with fear to prepare an ark. O the amazing stupidity of an unbelieving world, that will not be wrought upon, no, not by the *terrors of the Lord!*

Verses 9–15

The Israelites are here again convicted and condemned, and particular notice given of the crimes they are convicted of and the punishment they are condemned to.

1. Notice is given of it to their neighbours. The prophet is ordered to *publish it in the palaces of Ashdod,* one of the chief cities of the Philistines; nay, the summons must go further, even to *the palaces in the land of Egypt.* "The great men of both those nations, that dwell in the palaces, that are inquisitive concerning the affairs of the neighboring nations, and are conversant with the public intelligence, let them *assemble themselves upon the mountains of Samaria,*" *v.* 9. There, upon *a throne high and lifted up,* the judgment is set. Samaria is the criminal that is to be tried; let them be present at the trial, for it shall be (as other trials are) public, in the face of the country; let them make an appointment to meet there from all parts, to judge between God and his vineyard. God appeals to all impartial righteous men, Eze. 23:45. They will all subscribe to the equity of his proceedings when they see how the case stands. Note, God's controversies with sinners do not fear a scrutiny; even Philistines and Egyptians will be made to see, and say, that *the ways of the Lord are equal,* but *our ways are unequal.* They are likewise summoned to attend, not only that they may justify God and be witness for him that he deals fairly, but that they may themselves take warning; for, if *judgment begin at the house of God,* as they see it does, what shall be the end of those that are strangers to him? 1 Pt. 4:17. *If this be done in a green tree, what shall be done in a dry?* Or this intimates that the sin of Israel had been so notorious that the neighboring nations could come in witnesses against them, and therefore it was fit that their punishment should be so. "If it could have been concealed, we would have said, *Tell it not in Gath; publish it not in the streets of Ashkelon;*" but why should their friends consult their reputation, when they themselves do not consult it? If they have grown impudent in sin, let them bear the shame: *"Publish* it in *Ashdod,* in *Egypt."*

1. Let them see how black the charge is, and how well proved. Let them observe the behaviour of the inhabitants of Samaria; let them look off from the adjacent hills, and they may see how rude and boisterous they are, and hear how loud they cry of their sin is, as was that of Sodom. (1.) Look into their streets and you will see nothing but riot and disorder, *great tumults in the midst thereof;* reason and justice are upon all occasions run down by the noise and fury of an outrageous mob, the dominion of which is the sin and shame of any people, and is likely to be their ruin. (2.) Look into their prisons, and you will see them filled with injured innocents: *The oppressed are in the midst thereof,* thrown down and crushed by their oppressors, overpowered and overwhelmed, and *they had no comforter,* Eccl. 4:1. (3.) Look into their courts of justice, and you will see that those who preside in those courts *know not to do right,* because they have always been accustomed to do wrong; they act as if they had no notion at all of the thing called justice, are in no care to do justice themselves nor to see that others do justice. (4.) Look into their treasures and stores, and you will see them replenished with *violence and robbery,* with that which was unjustly got and is still unjustly kept. Thus *they have heaped treasures together for the last days,* but it will prove a *treasure of wrath against the day of wrath.* It may well be said, Those *know not to do right* who think to enrich themselves by doing wrong.

2. Let them see how heavy the doom is, and how well executed, *v.* 11, 12.

(1.) Their country shall be invaded and ruined; and observe how the punishment answers to the sin. [1.] *Great tumults* are *in the midst of the land,* and therefore *an adversary shall be even round about the land;* the Assyrian forces shall surround it and break in upon it on every side. Note, When sin is harboured and indulged in the midst of a people they can expect no other than that adversaries should be round about them, so that, go which way they will, they go into the mouth of danger, Lu. 19:43. [2.] They strengthened themselves in their wickedness, but the enemy shall *bring down their strength* from them, that strength which they abused in oppressing the poor, and doing violence to all about them. Note, That power which is made an instrument of unrighteousness will justly be brought down and broken. [3.] They *stored up robbery in their palaces,* and therefore their *palaces shall be spoiled;* for what is got and kept wrongfully will not be kept long. Even palaces will be no protection to fraud and oppression; but the greatest of men, if they have spoiled others, shall themselves be spoiled, for *the Lord is the avenger of all such.*

(2.) Their countrymen shall not escape, *v.* 12. They shall be in the hands of the enemy, as a lamb in the mouth of a lion, all devoured and eaten up, and they shall be utterly unable to make an resistance; and if any do make their escape, so as neither to fall by the sword or go into captivity, yet they shall be very few, and those of the meanest and least considerable, like *two legs,* or *shanks,* of a lamb, *or,* it may be, *a piece of an ear,* which the lion drops, or *the shepherd* takes from him, when he has eaten the whole body; so, perhaps, here and there one may escape from Samaria and from Damascus, when the king of Assyria shall fall upon them both, but none to make any account of; and those that do escape shall do so with the utmost difficult and hazard, by hiding themselves in the *corner of a bed* or under the *bed's feet,* which intimates that their spirits shall sneak shamefully in the time of danger. They shall not hide themselves in dens and caves, but in the *corner of a bed,* or the *piece of a bed,* such as poor people must be content with. They shall very narrowly escape, as it is foretold concerning the last destruction of Jerusalem that there shall be *two in a bed together, one taken and the other left.* Note, When God's judgments come forth against a people with commission it will be in vain to think of escaping them. Some make their *dwelling in the corner of a bed,* and *in a couch,* to denote their present security and sensuality; they are at ease, as *in a bed,* or *on a couch,* but, when God comes to contend with them, he shall make them uneasy, shall take them away out of the bed of their sloth and slumber. Those that stretch themselves lazily upon their couches when God's judgments are abroad shall *go captive with the first that go captive.*

II. Notice is given of it to themselves, *v.* 13. Let this be *testified,* and *heard, in the house of Jacob,* among all the seed of Israel, for it is spoken by *the Lord God, the God of hosts,* who has authority to pass this sentence and ability to execute it; let them know from him that the day is at hand when God will *visit the transgressions of Israel upon him,* when he will enquire into them and reckon for them: there will come *a day of visitation,* a day of punishment, and in that day all those things they are proud of, and put confidence in, shall fail them, and so they shall smart for the sins they have been guilty of about them. 1. Woe to *their altars,* for God will *visit* them. He will enquire into the sins they have been guilty of at their altars, and bring into the account all their superstition and idolatry, all their expenses on their false gods, and all their expectations from them; and he will lay the altars themselves under the marks of his displeasure, for *the horns of the altar shall be cut off,* and *fall to the ground,* and with them the altar itself demolished and broken to pieces. We find the altar at Bethel prophesied against (1 Ki. 13:2), and immediately *rent* (*v.* 3), and that prophecy fulfilled with *Josiah burnt men's bones upon it,* 2 Ki. 23:15, 16. This seconds that prophecy, and seems to point at the same event. Note, If men will not destroy idolatrous altars, God will, and those with them that had them in veneration. Some make *the horns of the altar* to signify all those things which they flee to for refuge, and trust in, and which they make their sanctuary: they shall all be cut off, so that they shall have nothing to take hold of. 2. Woe to their houses, for God will visit them too. He will enquire into the sins they have been guilty of in their houses, the robbery that have stored up in their houses, and the luxury in which they lived: *and I will smite the winter-house with the summer-house, v.* 15. Their nobility, and gentry, and rich merchants, had their winter-houses in the city and their summer-houses in the country, so nice were they in guarding against the inconveniences of the winter when the country was thought too cold, and of the summer when the city was thought too hot, though the climate of that good land was so temperate, like that of ours, that neither the cold nor heat was ever in extremity. They indulged a foolish affectation of change and variety; but God will, either by war or by the earthquake, smite both the winter-house and the summer-house; neither shall serve to shelter them from his judgments. *The houses of ivory* (so called because the ceiling, or wainscot, or some of the ornaments of them, were edged or inlaid with ivory) *shall perish,* shall be burnt or pulled down; *and the great houses shall have an end;* the most splendid and spacious houses, the houses of their great men, shall no longer be, or at least be no longer theirs. Note, The pomp or pleasantness of men's houses will be so far from fortifying them against God's judgments that it will make them the more grievous and vexatious, as their extravagance about them will be put to the score of their sins and follies.

CHAPTER 4

In this chapter, I. The oppressors in Israel are threatened for their oppression of the poor (*v.* 1–3). II. The idolaters in Israel, being joined to idols, are given up to their own heart's lusts (*v.* 4, 5). III. All the sins of Israel are aggravated from their incorrigibleness in them, and their refusal to return and reform, notwithstanding the various rebukes of Providence which they had been under (*v.* 6–11). IV. They are invited yet at length to humble themselves before God, since it is impossible for them to make their part good against him (*v.* 12, 13).

Verses 1–5

It is here foretold, in the name of God, that oppressors shall be humbled and idolaters shall be hardened.

I. That proud oppressors shall be humbled for their oppressions: for *he that does wrong shall receive according to the wrong that he has done.* Now observe,

1. How their sin is described, *v.* 1. They are compared to the *kine of Bashan,* which were a breed of cattle very large and strong, especially if, though bred there, they were fed upon *the mountain of Samaria,* where the pastures were extraordinarily fat. Amos had been a herdsman, and he speaks in a dialect of his calling, comparing the rich and great men, that lived in luxury and wantonness, to the *kine of Bashan,* which were wanton and unruly, would not be kept within the bounds of their own pasture, But broke through the hedges, broke down all the fences, and trespassed upon the neighboring grounds; and not only so, but pushed and gored the smaller cattle that were not a match for them. Those that had their summer-houses upon the mountains of Samaria when they went thither for fresh air were as mischievous as the kine upon the mountains of Bashan and as injurious to those about them. (1.) They oppress the poor and needy themselves; they *crush* them, to squeeze something to themselves out of them. They took advantage of their poverty, and necessity, and inability to help themselves, to make them poorer and more necessitous than they were. They made use of their power as judges and magistrates for the invading of men's rights and properties, the poor not excepted; for they made no conscience of robbing even the hospital. (2.) They are in confederacy with those that do so. They *say to their masters* (to the masters of the poor, that abuse them and violently take from them what they have, when they ought to relieve them), *"Bring, and let us drink;* let us feast with you upon the gains of our oppression, and then we will protect you, and stand by you in it, and reject the appeals of the poor against you." Note, What is got by extortion is commonly made use of as *provisions for the flesh, to fulfil the lusts thereof;* and *therefore* men are tyrants to the poor because they are slaves to their appetites. *Bring, and let us drink,* is the language of those that *crush the needy,* as if the *tears of the oppressed,* mingled with their wine, made it drink the better. And by their associations for drinking and reveling, and an excess of riot, they strengthen their combinations for persecution and oppression, and harden the hearts of one another in it.

2. How their punishment is described, *v.* 2, 3. God will *take them away with hooks, and their posterity with fish-hooks;* he will send the Assyrian army upon them, that shall make a prey of them, shall not only enclose the body of the nation in their net, but shall angle for particular persons, and take them prisoners and captives as with hooks and fish-hooks, shall draw them out of their own land as fish are drawn out of the water, which is their element, them and their children with them, or, They in their day

shall be drawn out by one victorious enemy, and their posterity in their day by another, so that by a succession of destroying judgments they shall at length be wholly extirpated. These *kine of Bashan* thought they could no more be drawn out with a hook and a cord than the Leviathan can, Job 41:1, 2. But God will make them know that he has a *hook for their nose* and a *bridle for their jaws,* Isa. 37:29. The enemy shall take them away as easily as the fisherman takes away the little fish, and shall make it their sport and recreation. When the enemy has made himself master of Samaria, then, (1.) Some shall attempt to escape by flight: *You shall go out at the breaches* made in the wall of the city, *every cow at that which is before her,* to shift for her own safety, and make the best of her way; and now the unruly kine of Bashan are tamed, and are themselves crushed, as they crushed the poor and needy. Note, Those to whom God has given a good pasture, if they are wanton in it, will justly be turned out of it; and those who will not be kept within the hedge of God's precept forfeit the benefit of the hedge of God's protection, and will be forced in vain to flee through the breaches they have themselves fearfully made in that hedge. (2.) Others shall think to shelter themselves, or at least their best effects, in the palace, because it is a castle well fortified and a garrison well manned: *You shall throw yourselves* (so some read it), or *throw them* (that is, your posterity, your children, or whatever is dear to you), *into the palace,* where the enemy will find it ready to be seized. Note, What is got by oppression cannot long be enjoyed with satisfaction.

3. How their sentence to this punishment is ratified: *The Lord God has sworn it by his holiness.* He had often said it, and they regarded it not; they thought God and his prophets did but jest with them; therefore he *swears* it *in his wrath,* and what he has sworn he will not revoke. He swears by *his holiness,* that attribute of his which is so much his glory, and which is so much glorified in the punishment of wicked people; for, as sure as God is a holy God, those that *plough iniquity and sow wickedness shall reap the same.*

II. That obstinate idolaters shall be hardened in their idolatries (*v.* 4, 5): *Come to Bethel, and transgress.* It is spoken ironically: "Do so; take your course; *multiply* your *transgressions* by multiplying your sacrifices, *for this liketh you;* but what will you do in the end hereof?" Here we see, 1. How intent they were upon the service of their idols, and how willing they were to be at cost upon them; they *brought their sacrifices,* and their *tithes,* and their *freewill offerings,* hoping that therein they should be accepted of God, but it was all an abomination to him. The profuseness of idolaters in the service of their false gods may shame our strait-handedness in the service of the true and living God. 2. How they mimicked God's institutions. They had their *daily sacrifice* at the altar of Bethel, as God had at his altar; they had their *thank-offerings* as God had, only they allowed *leaven* in them, which God had forbidden, because their priests did not like to have the bread to heavy and tasteless as it would be if it had not leaven in it, for something to ferment it. Holy bread would not serve them, unless it were pleasant bread. 3. How well pleased they were with these services themselves: *This liketh you, O you children of Israel! So you love.* What was their own invention they were fond of and wedded to, and thought it must be pleasing to God because it was agreeable to their own fancy. 4. How they upbraided with it: "*Come to Bethel, to Gilgal; bring the sacrifices* and *tithes* yourselves; *proclaim* and *publish* to the nation the *free-offerings,* pressing them to bring in abundance of such; *go on* in this way;" that is, (1.) "It is plain that you are resolved to do it, whatever God and conscience say to the contrary." (2.) "Your prophets shall let you alone in it, and not admonish you as they have done, for it is to no purpose. *Let no man strive nor rebuke his neighbour.*" (3.) "Your foolish hearts shall be more and more darkened and besotted, and you shall be quite *given up* to these *strong delusions, to believe a lie.*" (4.) "What will you get by it? *Come to Bethel* and *multiply your sacrifices,* and see what the better you will be, what returns you will have to your sacrifices, what stead they will stand you in in the day of distress. *You shall be ashamed of Bethel your confidence,*" Jer. 48:13. (5.) "*Come, and transgress,* come, and *multiply your transgression,* that you may *fill up the measure* of your iniquity and be ripened for ruin." Thus Christ said to Judas, *What thou doest*

do quickly; and to the Jews, *Fill you up the measure of your fathers,* Mt. 23:32.

Verses 6–13

Here, I. God complains of his people's incorrigibleness under the judgments which he had brought upon them in order to their humiliation and reformation. He had by several tokens intimated to them his displeasure, with this design, that they might by repentance make their peace with him; but it had not that effect.

1. It is five times repeated in these verses, as the burden of the charge, *"Yet have you not returned unto me, saith the Lord;* you have been several times corrected, but in vain; you are not reclaimed, there is no sign of amendment. You have been sent for by one messenger after another, but you have not come back, you have not come home." (1.) This intimates that that which God designed in all his providential rebukes was to reduce them to their allegiance, to influence them to return to him. (2.) That, if they had returned to their God, they would have been accepted, he would have bidden them welcome, and the troubles they were in would have been removed. (3.) That the reason why God sent further troubles was because former troubles had not done the work, otherwise it is *no pleasure to the Almighty that he should afflict.* (4.) That God was grieved at their obstinacy, and took it unkindly that they should force him to do that which he did so unwillingly: "*You have not returned to me* from whom you have revolted, *to me* with whom you are in covenant, *to me* who stands ready to receive you, *to me* who have so often called you." Now,

2. To aggravate their incorrigibleness, and to justify himself in inflicting greater judgments, he recounts the less judgments with which he had tried to bring them to repentance.

(1.) There had sometimes been a scarcity of provisions, though there was no visible cause of it (*v.* 6): "*I have given you cleanness of teeth in all your cities,* for you had no meat to chew, whereby your teeth might be fouled," especially no flesh, which dirties the teeth. Or, *I have given you emptiness of teeth,* nothing to fill your mouths with. "*Bread,* the staff of life, has been wanting, for you have *sown much* and *brought in little,*" as Hag. 1:9. Some think this refers to that *seven years' famine* that was in Elisha's time, which we read of 2 Ki. 8:1. Now when God thus *took away their corn in the season thereof,* because they had prepared it for Baal, they should have said, We will *go and return to our first husband,* having paid dearly for leaving him; but it had not that effect. *They have not returned to me,* saith the Lord.

(2.) Sometimes they had wanted rain, and then of course they wanted the fruits of the earth. This evil was of the Lord: *I have withholden the rain from you.* God has the key of the clouds, and, if he shut up, who can open? *v.* 7. The rain was withheld *when there were yet three months to the harvest,* at the time when they used to have it, and therefore the withholding of it was an extraordinary thing, and, if the course of nature was altered, they must therein own the hand of the God of nature; and it was at a time when they most needed it, and therefore the want of it was a very sore judgment, and blasted their expectations of a crop at harvest. And one circumstance which made this very remarkable was that when there were some places that wanted rain, and withered for want of it, there were other places near adjoining that had it in abundance. God *caused it to rain upon one city, and not upon another,* in the same country; nay, he caused it to rain *upon one field,* one *piece* of a field, and it was thereby made fruitful and flourishing, but on the next field, on the other side of the hedge, nay, on another part of the same field, *it rained not* at all, and it was so long without rain that all the products of it *withered.* No doubt this was literally true, and there were many instances of it which were generally taken notice of. Now, [1.] By this it appeared that the withholding of the rain was not casual, but by a divine direction and disposal, and that the cloud which waters the earth is *turned round about by the counsels of God, to do whatsoever he commands it, whether for correction, or for his land, or for his mercy,* Job 37:12–18. Rain does not go by planets (as common people speak), but as God sends it by his winds. [2.] We have reason to think that those cities on which it rained not were the most infamous for

wickedness, such as Bethel and Gilgal (*v.* 4), and that those on which it rained were such as retained something of religion and virtue among them. And so in the town-fields it rained or rained not, upon the piece, according as the owner was; for we are sure *the curse of the Lord is in the house,* and upon the ground, *of the wicked, but he blesses the habitation of the just,* and his field is a *field that the Lord has blessed.* [3.] It would be the greater grief and vexation to those whose fields withered for want of rain to see their neighbours' fields well watered and flourishing. *My servants shall eat, but you shall be hungry,* Isa. 65:13. The *wicked shall see it, and be grieved.* Probably those that were oppressed were rained upon, and so they recovered their losses, while the oppressors withered, and so lost their gains. [4.] Yet, as to the nation in general, it was a mixture of mercy with the judgment, and, consequently, strengthened the call to repentance and reformation, and encouraged them to hope for all mercy, in their returns to God, since there was so much mercy even in God's rebukes of them. But, because they did not make good use of this gracious allay to the extremity of the judgment, they had not the benefit of it, which otherwise they might have had, for (*v.* 8) *two or three cities wandered* at uncertainty, as beggars, *unto one city, to drink water,* and, if possible, to have some to carry home with them, but *they were not satisfied;* it was but here and there one city that had water, while many wanted, and then it was not, as usual, *Usus communis aquarum — Water is free to all.* Those that had it had occasion for it, or knew not how soon they might, and therefore could afford but little to those that wanted, saying, *Lest there be not enough for us and you.* Those that came *drank water,* but *they were not satisfied,* because they drank it *by measure, and with astonishment;* and those that *drink of this water shall thirst again,* Jn. 4:13. They were not satisfied, because their desires were greedy, and what they had God did not bless to them, Hag. 1:6. And now, one would think, when they met with all this disappointment, they should have considered their ways and repented; but it had not that effect: "*Yet have you not returned to me,* no, not so much as to pray in a right manner for the former and latter rain," Zec. 10:1. See the folly of carnal hearts; they will wander from city to city, from one creature to another, in pursuit of satisfaction, and still they miss of it; they *labour for that which satisfies not* (Isa. 55:2), and yet, after all, they *will not return to God,* will not incline their ear to him in whom they might have satisfaction. The preaching of the gospel is as rain; God sometimes blesses one place with it more than another; some countries, some cities, are, like Gideon's fleece, wet with this dew, while the ground about is dry; all withers where this rain is wanting. But it were well if people were but as wise for their souls as they are for their bodies, and, when they have not this rain near them, would go and seek it where it is to be had; and, if they seek aright, they shall not seek in vain.

(3.) Sometimes the fruits of their ground were eaten up by caterpillars, or blasted with mildew, *v.* 9. Heaven and earth are armed against those who have made God their enemy. When God pleased, that is, when he was displeased, [1.] They suffered by a malignant air, the influence of which, either too hot or too cold, blasted their fruits, with a force that could be neither discerned nor resisted, and against which there was no defence. [2.] They suffered by malignant animals. Their *vineyards* and *gardens* yielded their increase in great abundance, so did their *fig-trees* and *olive-trees;* but the *palmer-worm devoured them* before the fruits were ripe, and fit to be gathered in. This was either the same judgment with that which we read of Joel 1:4–6, or a less judgment of the same nature, sent before to give warning of that. But they did not take warning: *Yet have you not returned unto me.*

(4.) Sometimes the plague had raged among them, and the sword of war had cut off multitudes, *v.* 10. The *pestilence* is God's messenger; this he *sent among* them, with directions whom to strike dead, and it was done. It was a *pestilence after the manner of Egypt;* deaths were scattered among them by the hand of a *destroying angel at midnight.* And perhaps this pestilence, as that of Egypt, fastened upon the first-born. *In the way of Egypt* (so the margin); when they were making their escape to Egypt, or going thither to seek for aid, the pestilence seized them by the way and stopped their journey. The sword of war is likewise *the sword of the Lord;* this was drawn among them with commission; and then it *slew their young men,* the strength of the present generation and the seed of the next. God says, *I have slain them;* he avows the execution. *The slain of the Lord are many.* The enemy *took away their horses,* and converted them to their own use; and the dead carcases of those that were slain either with sword or pestilence were so many, and for want of surviving friends were left so long unburied, that the *stench of their camps came up into their nostrils,* and was both noisome and dangerous, and might put them in mind of the offensiveness of their sin to God. And yet this did not prevail to humble and reclaim them: *You have not returned to* him that smites you. Such a rueful woeful sight as this prevailed not to make them religious.

(5.) In these and other judgments some were remarkably cut off, and made monuments of justice, others were remarkably spared, and made monuments of mercy, the setting of which the one over against the other one would have thought likely to work upon them, but it had not its effect, *v.* 11. [1.] Some were quite ruined, their families destroyed, and themselves in them: *I have overthrown some of you, as God overthrew Sodom and Gomorrah.* Perhaps they were consumed with lightning, as Sodom was, or the houses were, in some other way, burnt to the ground, and the inhabitants in them. Sodom and Gomorrah are said to be *condemned with an overthrow, and so made an example,* 2 Pt. 2:6. God had threatened to destroy the whole land with such an overthrow as that of Sodom, Deu. 29:23. But he began with some particular places first, to give them warning, or perhaps with some particular persons, whose *sins went beforehand to judgment.* [2.] Others very narrowly escaped: "You *were* many of you as a *firebrand plucked out of the burning,* like Lot out of Sodom, when the fire had already kindled upon you; and yet you hate sin never the more for the danger it has brought you to, nor love God ever the more for the deliverance he wrought for you. You that have been so signally delivered, and in such a distinguishing way, *have not returned unto me.*"

II. God, in the close, calls upon his people, now at length, in this their day, to understand the things that belong to their peace, before they were hidden from their eyes, *v.* 12, 13. Observe here,

1. How God threatens them with sorer judgments than any they had yet been under: "Therefore, seeing you have not been wrought upon by correction hitherto, *thus will I do unto thee, O Israel!*" He does not say how he will do, but it shall be something worse than had come yet, Jn. 5:14. Or, *"Thus I will* go on to *do unto thee,* following one judgment with another, like the plagues of Egypt, till I have made a full end." Nothing but reformation will prevent the ruin of a sinful people. If they turn not to him, his anger is not *turned away,* but *his hand is stretched out still. I will punish you yet seven times more, if you will not be reformed;* so it was written in the law, Lev. 26:23, 24.

2. How he awakens them therefore to think of making their peace with God: *"Seeing I will do this unto thee,* and there is no remedy, *prepare to meet they God, O Israel!"* that is, (1.) "Consider how unable thou art to meet him as a combatant." Some make it to be spoken by way of irony or challenge: "Prepare to meet God, who is coming forth to contend with thee. What armour of proof canst thou put on? What courage canst thou steel thyself with? Alas! it is but putting *briers and thorns* before a consuming fire, Isa. 27:4, 5. Art thou able with less than 10,000 to meet him that comes forth against thee with more than 20,000?" Lu. 14:31. (2.) "Resolve therefore to meet him as a penitent, as a humble suppliant, to meet him as *thy God,* in covenant with thee, to submit, and stand it out no longer." We must prepare to *meet God in the way of his judgments* (Isa. 26:8), to *take hold on his strength, that we may make peace.* Note, Since we cannot flee from God we are concerned to prepare to meet him; and therefore he gives us warning, that we may prepare. When we are to meet him in his ordinances we must prepare to meet him, prepare to seek him.

3. How he sets forth the greatness and power of God as a reason why we should prepare to meet him, *v.* 13. If he be such a God as he is here described to be, it is folly to contend with him, and our duty and interest to make our peace with him; it is good having him our friend and bad having him our enemy. (1.) He *formed the mountains,* made the earth, the strongest stateliest parts of it, and by the word of his power still upholds it and them. Whatever are the products of the everlasting mountains, he formed them; whatever *salvation is hoped for from hills and mountains,* he is the founder of it, Ps. 89:11, 12. He that formed the *great mountains* can *make them plain,* when they stand in the way of his people's salvation. (2.) He *creates the wind.* The power of the air is derived from him, and directed by him; he brings the wind out of his treasures, and orders from what point of the compass it shall blow; and he that made it rules it; even *the winds and the seas obey him.* (3.) He *declares unto man what is his thought.* He makes known his counsel by his servants the prophets to the children of men, the thought of his justice against impenitent sinners, and the thought of good he thinks towards those that repent. He can also make known, for he perfectly knows, the thought that is in man's heart; he *understands it afar off,* and in the day of conviction will set the evil thoughts among the other sins of sinners *in order before them.* (4.) He often *makes the morning darkness,* by thick clouds overspreading the sky immediately after the sun rose bright and glorious; so when we look for prosperity and joy he can dash our expectations with some unlooked-for calamity. (5.) He *treads upon the high places of the earth,* is not only higher than the highest, but has dominion over all, tramples upon proud men, and upon the idols that were worshipped in the highest places. (6.) *Jehovah the God of hosts is his name,* for he has his being of himself, and is the fountain of all being, and all the hosts of heaven and earth are at his command. Let us humble ourselves before this God, prepare to meet him, and give all diligence to make him our God, for happy are the people whose God he is, who have all this power engaged for them.

CHAPTER 5

The scope of this chapter is to prosecute the exhortation given to Israel in the close of the foregoing chapter to prepare to meet their God; the prophet here tells them, I. What preparation they must make; they must "seek the Lord," and not seek any more to idols (*v.* 4–8); they must seek good, and love it (*v.* 14, 15). II. Why they must make this preparation to meet their God, 1. Because of the present deplorable condition they were in (*v.* 1–3). 2. Because it was by sin that they were brought into such a condition (*v.* 7, 10–12). 3. Because it would be their happiness to seek God, and he was ready to be found of them (*v.* 8, 9, 14). 4. Because he would proceed, in his wrath, to their utter ruin, if they did not seek him (*v.* 5, 6, 13, 16, 17). 5. Because all their confidences would fail them if they did not seek unto God, and make him their friend. (1.) Their profane contempt of God's judgments, and setting them at defiance, would not secure them (*v.* 18–20). (2.) Their external services in religion, and the shows of devotion, would not avail to turn away the wrath of God (*v.* 21–24). (3.) Their having been long in possession of church-privileges, and in a course of holy duties, would not be their protection, while all along they had kept up their idolatrous customs (*v.* 25–27). They have therefore no way left them to save themselves, but by repentance and reformation.

Verses 1–3

This chapter begins, as those two next foregoing began, with, *Hear this word.* Where God has a mouth to speak we must have an ear to hear; it is our duty, it is our interest, yet so stupid are most men that they need to be again and again called upon to *hear the word of the Lord,* to give audience, to give attention. *Hear this word.* this convincing awakening word must be heard and heeded, as well as words of comfort and peace; the word that is taken up against us, as well as that which makes for us; for, whether we hear or forbear, the word of God shall take effect, and not a tittle of it shall fall to the ground. It is the *word which I take up* — not the prophet only, but the God that sent him. It is *the word that the Lord has spoken, ch.* 3:1. The word to be heard is *a lamentation,* a lamentable account of the present calamitous state of the kingdom of Israel, and a lamentable prediction of its utter destruction. Their condition is sad: *The virgin of Israel has fallen* (*v.* 2), has come down from what she was; that state, though not pure and chaste as a virgin, yet was beautiful and gay, and had its charms; she looked high herself, and was courted by many as a virgin; but *she has fallen* into contempt and poverty, and is universally slighted. Nay, and their condition is helpless: *She shall no more rise,* shall never recover her former dignity again. God had lately begun to *cut Israel short* (2 Ki. 10:32), and, because they repented not, it was not long before he *cut Israel down.* 1. Their princes, that should have helped them up, were disabled: *She is forsaken upon her land.* Not only those she was in alliance with abroad failed her, but her friends at home deserted her; she would not have been carried captive into a strange land if she had not first been *forsaken upon her own land* and *thrown to the ground* there, and all her true interests abandoned by those that should have had them at heart. *There is none to raise her up,* none that can do it, not that cares to lend her a hand. 2. Their people, that should have helped them up, were diminished, *v.* 3. "The city that had a militia, 1000 strong, and, in the beginning of the war, had furnished out 1000 effective men, able-bodied and well-armed, when they come to review their troops after the battle, shall find but 100 *left;* and, in proportion, the city that sent out 100 shall have but *ten* come back, so great a slaughter shall be made, and so few left to the house of Israel for the public service and safety." Scarcely one in ten shall escape of the hands that should relieve this abject, this dejected, nation. Note, The lessening of the numbers of God's spiritual Israel, by death or desertion, is just a matter for lamentation; for *by whom shall Jacob arise,* by whom shall the decays of piety be repaired, when he is thus *made small?*

Verses 4–15

This is a message from God to the house of Israel, in which,

I. They are told of their faults, that they might see what occasion there was for them to repent and reform, and that, when they were called to return, they might not need to ask, *Wherein shall we return?*

1. God tells them, in general (*v.* 12), *"I know your manifold transgressions, and your mighty sins;* and you shall be made to know them too." In our penitent reflections upon our sins we must consider, as God does in his judicial remarks upon them, and will do in the great day, (1.) That they are very numerous; they are our *manifold transgressions,* sins of various kinds and often repeated. Oh what a multitude of vain and vile thoughts lodge within us! What a multitude of idle, foolish, wicked words have been spoken by us! In what a multitude of instances have we gratified and indulged our corrupt appetites and passions! And how many our own omissions of duty and in duty! Who can understand his errors? Who can tell how often he offends? God knows how many, just how many, our transgressions are; none of them pass him unobserved; we know that they are to us innumerable; *more than the hairs of our head;* and we have reason to see what danger we have brought ourselves into, and what abundance of work we have made for repentance, by our *manifold transgressions,* by the numberless number of our sins of daily incursion. (2.) That some of them are very heinous; they are *our mighty* sins; sins that are more exceedingly sinful in their own nature and by being committed presumptuously and with a high hand, sins against the light of nature, flagrant crimes, that are mighty to overpower your convictions and to pull down judgments upon you.

2. He specifies some of these mighty sins. (1.) They corrupted the worship of God, and turned to idols; this is implied *v.* 5. They had *sought to Bethel,* where one of the golden calves was; they had frequented Gilgal, a place which they chose to set up idols in, because it had been made famous in the days of Joshua by God's wonderful appearances to and for his people. Beer-sheba likewise, a place that had been famous in the days of the patriarchs, was now another rendezvous of idols; as we find also, *ch.* 8:14. And thither *they passed,* though it lay at a distance, in the land of Judah. Now, having thus shamefully gone a whoring from God, no doubt they should have felt themselves concerned to return to him. (2.) They perverted justice among themselves (*v.* 7): *"You turn judgment to wormwood,* that is, you make your administrations of justice bitter and nauseous, and highly displeasing both to God and man." That fruit has become a *weed,* a weed in the garden; as nothing is more venerable, nothing more valuable, than justice duly administered, so nothing is more hurtful, nothing more abominable, than designedly doing wrong under colour and pretence of doing right. *Corruptio optimi est pessima — The best, when corrupted, becomes the worst. "You leave off righteousness in the earth,* as if those that do wrong were accountable to the God of heaven only, and not to the princes and *judges of the earth."* Thus it was as before the flood, when the *earth was filled with violence.* (3.) They were very oppressive to the poor, and

made them poorer; they trod upon the poor (*v.* 11), trampled upon them, hectored over them, made them their footstool, and were most imperious and barbarous to those that were most obsequious and submissive; they care not what shame and slavery they put those to who were poor and such as they could get nothing by. The judges aimed at nothing but to enrich themselves; and therefore they *took from* the poor *burdens of wheat,* took it by extortion, either by way of bribe or by usury. The poor had no other way to save themselves from being trodden upon, and trodden to dirt, by them, than by presenting to them horse-loads of that corn which they and their families should have had to subsist upon, and they forced them to do it. They took from the poor *debts of wheat,* so some read it. It was legally due either for rent or for corn lent, but they exacted it with rigour from those who were disabled by the providence of God to pay it, as Neh. 5:2, 5. In demanding and recovering even a just debt we must take heed left we act either unjustly or uncharitably. This sin of oppression by are again charged with (*v.* 12): *They afflict the just,* by turning the edge of the law and of the sword of justice against those that are the innocent and *quiet in the land;* they hated men because they were more righteous than themselves, and he that *departed from evil* thereby *made himself a prey* to them. They take a bribe from the rich to patronize and protect them in oppressing the poor, so that he who has money in his hand is sure to have the judgment on his side, be his cause ever so bad. Thus they *turn aside the poor in the gate,* in the courts of justice, *from their right.* If the poor sue for their right, who cannot bribe them, or are so honest that they will not, though they have it ever so clear in view and ever so *near,* yet they are turned away from it by their unrighteous sentence and cannot come at it. And *therefore the prudent will keep silence, v.* 13. Men will reckon it their prudence, when they are wronged and injured, to be silent, and make no complaints to the magistrates, for it will be to no purpose; they shall not have justice done them. (4.) They were malicious persecutors of God's faithful ministers and people, *v.* 10. Their hearts were so fully set in them to do evil that they could not bear to be reproved, [1.] By the ministry of the word, by the reading and expounding of the law, and the messages which prophets delivered to them in the name of the Lord. *They hate him that rebukes in the gate,* in the gate of the Lord's house, or in their courts of justice, or in the places of concourse, where Wisdom is lifting up her voice, Prov. 1:21. Reprovers in the gate are reprovers by office; these they hated, counting them their *enemies because they told them the truth,* as Ahab hated Micaiah. They not only despised them, but had an enmity to them, and sought to do them mischief. Those that hate reproof love ruin. [2.] By the conversation of their honest neighbours. Though things were generally very bad, yet there were some among them that *spoke uprightly* that made conscience of what they said, and, as it was their praise, so it was the shame of those that spoke deceitfully, and condemned them, as Noah's faith condemned the unbelief of the old world, and for that reason *they abhorred them;* they were such inveterate enemies to the thing called honesty that they could not endure the sight of an honest man. All that have any sense of the common interest of mankind will love and value such as speak uprightly, for veracity is the bond of human society; to what a pitch of folly and madness then have those arrived who, having banished all notions of justice out of their own hearts, would have them banished out of the world too, and so put mankind into a state of war, for the *abhor him that speaks uprightly!* And for this reason *the prudent shall keep silence in that time, v.* 13. Prophets cannot, dare not, keep silence; the impulse they are under will not allow them to act on prudential considerations; they must *cry aloud, and not spare.* But as for other wise and good men they shall keep silence, and shall reckon it is their prudence to do so, because it is an evil time. *First,* They shall think it dangerous to complain, and therefore shall keep silence; this was one way in which they afflicted the just, that by false suggestions and strained innuendos they made men *offenders for a word* (Isa. 19:21); and therefore the *prudent,* who were *wise as serpents,* because they knew not how what they said might be misinterpreted and misrepresented, were so cautious as to say nothing, lest they should run themselves into a premunire, because it was an evil time. Note, Through the iniquity of the times, as good men are hidden, so good men are silent, and it is their wisdom to be so; *little said soon amended.* But it is their comfort that they may speak freely to God when they know not to whom else they can speak freely. *Secondly,* They shall think if fruitless to reprove. They see what wickedness is committed, and their spirits are stirred up, as Paul's at Athens; but they shall think it prudent not to bear an open testimony against it, because it is to no purpose. They are *joined to their idols; let them alone. Let no man strive or rebuke another;* for it is but *casting pearls before swine.* The cautious men will say to a bold reprover, as Erasmus to Luther, *"Abi in cellam, et dic, Miserere mei, Domine — Away to they cell, and cry, Have mercy on me, O Lord!"* Let grave lessons and counsels be kept for better men and better times. And there is *a time to keep silence* as well as *a time to speak,* Eccl. 3:7. *Evil times* will not bear plain dealing, that is *evil men* will not; and the men the prophet here speaks of had reason to think themselves evil men indeed, when wise and good them thought it in vain to speak to them and were afraid of having any thing to do with them.

II. They are told of their danger and what judgments they lay exposed to for their sins. 1. The places of their idolatry are in danger of being ruined in the first place, *v.* 5. *Gilgal,* the head-quarters of idolatry, *shall go into captivity,* not only its inhabitants, but its images, *and Bethel,* with its golden calf *shall come to nought.* The victorious enemy shall make nothing of it, so easily shall it be spoiled, and shall bring it to nothing, so effectually shall it be spoiled. Idols were always vanity, and *things of nought,* and so they shall prove when God appears to abolish them. 2. The body of the kingdom is in danger of being ruined with them, *v.* 6. There is danger lest, if you seek him not in time, he *break out like a fire in the house of Joseph and devour it;* for our God is a righteous Judge, is a *consuming fire,* and the men of Israel, as criminals, are stubble before him; woe to those that make themselves fuel to the fire of God's wrath. It follows, *And there shall be none to quench it in Bethel.* There their idols were, and their idolatrous priests; thither they brought their sacrifices, and there they offered up their prayers. But God tells them that when the fire of his judgments should kindle upon them all the gods they served at Bethel should not be able to quench it, should not turn away the judgment, nor be any relief to them under it. Thus those that make an idol of the world will find it insufficient to protect them when God comes to reckon with them for their spiritual idolatry. 3. What they have got by oppression and extortion shall be taken from them (*v.* 11): *"You have built houses of hewn stone,* which you thought would be lasting; *but you shall not dwell in them,* for your enemies shall burn them down, or possess them for themselves, or take you into captivity. *You have planted pleasant vineyards,* have contrived how to make them every way agreeable, and have promised yourselves many a pleasant walk in them; but you shall be forced to walk off, and shall never *drink wine of them."* The law had tenderly provided that if a man had *built a house,* or *planted a vineyard,* he should be at his liberty to return from the wars, Deu. 20:5, 6. But now the necessity would be so urgent that it would not be allowed; all must go to the battle, and many of those who had lately been building and planting should fall in battle, and never enjoy what they had been labouring for. What is not honestly got is not likely to be long enjoyed.

III. They are told their duty, and have great encouragement to set about it in good earnest, and good reason. The duties here prescribed to them are godliness and honesty, seriousness in their applications to God and justice in their dealings with men; and each of these is here pressed upon them with proper arguments to enforce the exhortation.

1. They are here exhorted to be sincere and devout in their addresses to God, *v.* 4. God says to the *house of Israel, Seek you me,* and with good reason, for *should not a people seek unto their God?* Isa. 8:19. Whither else should they go but to their protector? Israel was a *prince with God;* let his descendants *seek the Lord,* as he did, and they shall be so too. Now, in order to their doing this, they must abandon their idolatries. God is not sought truly if he be not sought exclusively, for he will endure no rivals: *"Seek you the Lord, and seek not Bethel* (*v.* 5), consult not your idol-oracles, nor ask at the mouth of the priests of Bethel; seek not to the golden calf there for protection, nor bring your prayers and sacrifices any longer thither, or to Gilgal, for you *forsake your own mercies* if you observe those *lying vanities.* But *seek the Lord* (*v.* 6, 8); enquire after him; enquire of him; seek to know his mind as your rule, to secure his favour as your felicity." To press this exhortation we are told to consider, (1.) What we shall get by seeking God; it will be *our life;* we shall find him, and shall be happy in him. So he tells them himself (*v.* 4): *Seek you me, and you shall live.* Those that seek perishing gods shall perish with them (*v.* 5), but those that seek the living God shall live with him: "You shall be delivered from the killing judgments which you are threatened with; your nation shall live, shall recover from its present languishings; your souls shall live; you shall be sanctified and comforted, and made for ever blessed. *You shall live."* (2.) What a God he is whom we are to *seek, v.* 8, 9. [1.] He is a God of almighty power himself. The idols were impotent things, could do neither good nor evil, and therefore it was folly either to fear or trust them; but the God of Israel does every thing, and can do any thing, and therefore we ought to seek him; he challenges our homage who has all power in his hand, and it is our interest to have him on our side. Divers proofs and instances are here given of God's power, as Creator, in the kingdom of nature, as both founding and governing that kingdom. Compare *ch.* 4:13. *First,* The stars are the work of his hands; those stars which the heathens worshipped (*v.* 26), the *stars of your god,* those stars are God's creatures and servants. He *makes the seven stars and Orion,* two very remarkable constellations, which Amos, a herdsman, while he kept his cattle by night, had particularly observed the motions of. He made them at the first, he still makes them to be what they are to this earth and either *binds* or *looses* the *sweet influences of Peliades* and *Orion,* the two constellations here mentioned. See Job 38:31; 9:9, to which passages Amos seems here to refer, putting them in mind of those ancient discoveries of the glory of God before he was called the *God of Israel. Secondly,* The constant succession of day and night is under his direction, and is kept up by his power and providence. It is he that *turns* the night (which is dark as *the shadow of death*) *into the morning* by the rising of the sun, and by the setting of the sun *makes the day dark with night;* and the same power can, for humble penitents, easily turn affliction and sorrow into prosperity and joy, but can as easily turn the prosperity of presumptuous sinners into darkness, into utter darkness. *Thirdly,* The rain rises and falls as he appoints. He *calls for the waters of the sea;* out of them vapours are drawn up by the heat of the sun, which gather into clouds, and are *poured out upon the face of the earth,* to water it and make it fruitful. This was the mercy that had been *withholden from them* of late (*ch.* 4:7); and therefore to whom should they apply but to him who had power to give it? For all the *vanities of the heathen* could not *give rain,* nor could the *heavens* themselves *give showers* Jer. 14:22. It is God that has *made these things; Jehovah is his name,* the name by which the God of nature, the God of the whole earth, has made himself known to his people Israel and covenanted with them. [2.] As he is God of almighty power himself, so he *gives strength and power unto his people* that seek him, and *renews strength* to those that had lost it, if they *wait upon him* for it; for (*v.* 9) he *strengthens the spoiled against the strong* to such a degree that the spoiled come *against the fortress* and make bold and brave attacks upon those that had spoiled them. This is an encouragement to the people to *seek the Lord,* that, if they do so, they shall find him above to retrieve their affairs, when they are brought to the lowest ebb; though they are the spoiled, and their enemies are the strong, if they can but engage God for them, they shall soon recruit so as the next time to be not only the aggressors, but the conquerors; they *come against the fortress,* to make reprisals and become masters of it.

2. They are here exhorted to be honest and just in their dealings with men, *v.* 14, 15, where observe, (1.) The duty required: *Seek good, and not evil. Hate the evil, and love the good, and establish judgment in the gate;* re-establish it there, whence it has been banished, *v.* 7. Note, Things are not so bad but that they may be amended if the right course be taken; we must not despair but that grievances may be redressed and abuses rectified; justice may yet

triumph where injustice tyrannizes. In order to this, good must be loved and sought, evil must be hated and no longer sought. We must love good principles and adhere to them, love to do good and abound in doing it, love good people, and good converse, and good duties; and, whatever good we do, we must do it from a principle of love, do it of choice and with delight. Those who thus *love good* will *seek it,* will contrive to do all the good they can, enquire for opportunities of doing it, and endeavor to do it to the utmost of their power. They will also *hate evil,* will abhor the thought of doing an unjust thing, and abstain from all appearance of it. In vain do we pretend to seek God in our devotions if we do not seek good in our whole conversations. (2.) The reasons annexed. [1.] This is the sure way to be happy ourselves and to have the continual presence of God with us: *"Seek good, and not evil, that you may live,* may escape the punishment of the evil you have sought and loved *(righteousness delivereth from death),* that you may have the favour of God, which is your life, which is better than life itself, that you may have comfort in yourselves and may live to some good purpose. You shall live, for *so the Lord God of hosts shall be with you* and be your life." Note, Those that keep in the way of duty have the presence of God with them, as the *God of hosts,* a God of almighty power. "He will be with you *as you have spoken,* that is, as you have *gloried;* you shall have that really which, while you went on in unrighteous ways, you only seemed to have and boasted of as if you had." Those that truly repent and reform enter into the enjoyment of that comfort which before they had only flattered themselves with the imagination of. Or, "As you have prayed when *you sought the Lord.* Live up to your prayers, and you shall have what you pray for." [2.] This is the likeliest way to make the nation happy: "If you seek and love that which is good, you may contribute to the saving of the land from ruin." *It may be, the Lord God of hosts will be gracious to the remnant of Joseph;* though there is but a remnant left, yet, if God be gracious to that remnant, it will rise to a great nation again; and if some among them turn from sin, especially if *judgment* be *established in the gate,* though we cannot be certain, yet there is a great probability that public affairs will take a new and happy turn, and every thing will mend if men mend their lives. Temporary promises are made with an *It may be;* and our prayers must be made accordingly.

Verses 16–20

Here is, I. A very terrible threatening of destruction approaching, *v.* 16, 17. Since they would not take the right course to obtain the favour of God, God would take an effectual course to make them feel the weight of his displeasure. The threatening is introduced with more than ordinary solemnity, to strike an awe upon them; it is not the word of the prophet only (if so, it might be made light of) but it is the *Lord Jehovah,* who has an infinite eternal being; it is the *God of hosts,* who has a boundless irresistible power, and it is *Adonai — the Lord,* who has an absolute incontestable sovereignty, and a universal dominion; it is he who says it, who can and will make his words good, and he has said, 1. That the land of Israel shall be put in mourning, true mourning, that all places shall be filled with lamentation for the calamities coming upon them. Look into the cities, and *wailing shall be in all streets,* in the great streets, in the by-streets. Look into the country, and *they shall say in all the highways, Alas! alas!* we are all undone! The lamentation shall be so great as not to be confined within doors, nor kept within the bounds of decency, but it shall be proclaimed in the streets and highways, and shall run wild. The husbandman shall be called from the plough by the calamities of his country to the natural expressions of mourning; and, because those who will come short of the merits of the cause, such as are skilful of lamentation shall be called to artificial mourning, to put accents upon the lamentations of the real mourners with their *Ahone, ahone.* Even in all vineyards, where there used to be nothing but mirth and pleasure, there shall be general wailing, when a foreign force invades the country, lays all waste, and there is no making any head against it, no weapons left but prayers and tears. 2. That the land of Israel shall be brought to ruin, and the advances of that ruin are the occasion of all this wailing: *I will pass through thee,* as the destroying angel passed through the land of Egypt to destroy the first-born, but then passed over the houses of the Israelites. God's judgments had often passed by them, but now they shall pass through them, shall run them through.

II. A just and severe reproof to those who made light of these threatenings, and impudently bade defiance to the justice of God and his judgments, *v.* 18. Woe unto you that *desire the day of the Lord,* that really wish for times of war and confusion, as some do who have restless spirits, and long for changes, or who choose to *fish in troubled waters,* hoping to raise their families, as some had done, upon the ruins of their country; but the prophet tells them that this should be so great a desolation that nobody could get by it. Or it is spoken to those who, in their wailings and lamentations for the calamities they were in, wished they might die, and be delivered out of their misery, as Job did, with passion. The prophet shows them the folly of this. Do they know what death is to those who are unprepared for it, and how much more terrible it will be than any thing that can befal them in this life? Or, rather, it is spoken to those who speak jestingly of that day of the Lord which the prophet spoke so seriously of; they desired it, that is, they challenged it; they said, Let him do his worst; *let him make speed,* and *hasten his work,* Isa. 5:19. *Where is the promise of his coming?* 2 Pt. 3:4. It intimates, 1. That they do not believe it. They say that they wish it would come because they do not believe it will ever come; nor will they believe it unless they see it. 2. That they do not fear it; though they may have some belief of it, yet they had so little consideration of it, and their mind is so intent upon other things, that they are under no apprehension at all of peril from it; instead of having the conscience to dread it, they have the curiosity to desire it. In answer to this, (1.) He shows the folly of those who impudently wished for any of God's judgments, and made a jest of any of the terrors of the Lord: *"To what end is it for you* that the day of the Lord should come? You will find it both certain and sad; not a thing to be bantered, for it is neither a thing to be questioned whether it will come or no nor a thing to be turned off with a slight when it does come. *The day of the Lord is darkness, and not light, v.* 18. *Shall it not be so? v.* 20. Do not your own consciences tell you that it will be so, that it will be *very dark,* and *no brightness in it?"* Note, The *day of the Lord* will be a dark, dismal, gloomy day to all impenitent sinners; the *day of judgment* will be so; and sometimes the day of their present trouble. And, when God makes a day dark, all the world cannot make it light. (2.) He shows the folly of those who impatiently wished for a change of God's judgment, in hopes that the next would be better and more tolerable. They desire *the day of the Lord,* in hopes to better themselves (though their hearts and lives be not amended), or, at least, to know the worst. But the prophet tells them that they know not what they ask. *v.* 19. It is *as if a man did flee from a lion and a bear met him,* a beast of prey more cruel and ravenous than a lion, or as if a man, to escape all dangers abroad, *went into the house for security,* and *leaned his hand on the wall* to rest himself, and there a *serpent bit him.* Note, Those who are not reformed by the judgments of God will be pursued by them; and, if they escape one, another stands ready to seize them; *fear and the pit and snare* surround them, Isa. 24:17, 18. It is madness therefore to *defy the day of the Lord.*

Verses 21–27

The scope of these verses is to show how little God valued their shows of devotion, nay, how much he detested them, while they went on in their sins. Observe,

I. How unpleasing, nay, how displeasing, their hypocritical services were to God. They had their *feast-days* at Bethel, in imitation of those at Jerusalem, in which they pretended to rejoice before God. They had their *solemn assemblies* for religious worship, in which they put on the gravity of those who *come before God as his people come, and sit before him as his people sit.* They offered to God *burnt-offerings,* to the honour of God, together with the *meat-offerings* which by the law were to be offered with them; they offered the *peace-offerings,* to implore the favour of God, and they offered them of the *fat beasts* that they had, *v.* 21, 22. In imitation likewise of the temple-music, they had the *noise of their songs* and the *melody of their viols* (*v.* 23), vocal and instrumental music, with which they praised God. With these services they hoped to make God amends for the sins they had committed, and to obtain leave to go on in sin; and therefore they were so far from being acceptable to God that they were abominable. He *hated,* he *despised,* their *feast-days,* not only despised them as no valuable services done to him, but hated them as an affront and provocation to him, as we hate to see men dissemble with us, pretend a respect for us when really they have none. Nothing more hateful, more despicable, than hypocrisy. *He that blesseth his friend with a loud voice, it shall be counted a curse,* when it appears that his heart is not with him. God will not *smell* in *their solemn assemblies,* for there is nothing in them that is grateful to him, but a great deal that is offensive. Their sacrifices are not to him *of a sweet smelling savour,* as Noah's was, Gen. 8:21. He will not accept them; he will not regard them, will not take any notice of them; he will not hear the melody of their viols; for, when sin is a jar in the harmony, it grates in his ears: *"Take it away,"* says God, "I cannot bear it." Now this intimates, 1. That sacrifice itself is of small account with God in comparison with moral duties; to love God and our neighbour is *better than all burnt offering and sacrifice.* 2. That the sacrifice of the wicked is really an abomination to him, Prov. 15:8. Dissembled piety is double iniquity, and so it will be found when, if any place in hell be hotter than another, that will be the hypocrite's portion.

II. What it was that he required in order to the acceptableness of their sacrifices and without which no sacrifice would be acceptable (*v.* 24): *Let judgment run down as waters,* among you, *and righteousness as a mighty stream,* that is 1. "Let there be a general reformation of manners among you; let religion (God's *judgment*) and *righteousness* have their due influence upon you; let your land be watered with it, and let it bear down all the opposition of vice and profaneness; let it run wide as overflowing waters, and yet run strong as might stream." (2.) "In particular, let justice be duly administered by magistrates and rulers; let not the current of it be stopped by partiality and bribery, but let it come freely as waters do, in the natural course; let it be pure as running waters, not muddied with corruption or whatever may pervert justice; let it run *like a might stream,* and not suffer itself to be obstructed, or its course retarded, by the fear of man; let all have free access to it as a common stream, and have benefit by it as *trees planted by the rivers of waters."* The great thing laid to Israel's charge was *turning judgment into wormwood* (*v.* 7); in that matter therefore they must reform, Zec. 7:9. This was what God desired *more than sacrifices,* Hos. 6:6; 1 Sa. 15:22.

III. What little stress God had laid upon the law of sacrifices, though it was his own law, in comparison with the moral precepts (*v.* 25): *"Did you offer unto me sacrifices in the wilderness forty years?* No, you did not." For the greatest part of that time sacrifice was very much neglected, because of the unsettledness of their state; after the second year, the passover was not kept till they came into Canaan, and other institutions were in like manner intermitted; and yet, because God will have mercy and not sacrifice, he never imputed the omission to them as their fault, but continued his care of them and kindness to them: it was not that, but their murmuring and unbelief, for which God was displeased with them. He that so owned his people, though they did not sacrifice, when in other things they kept close to him, will certainly disown them, though they do sacrifice, if in other things they depart from him. But, though ritual sacrifices may thus be dispensed with, spiritual sacrifices will not; even justice and honesty will not excuse for the want of prayer and praise, a broken heart and the love of God. Stephen quotes this passage (Acts 7:42), to show the Jews that they ought not to think it strange that ceremonial law was repealed when from the beginning it was comparatively made light of. Compare Jer. 7:22, 23.

II. What little reason they had to expect that their sacrifices should be acceptable to God, when they and their fathers had been all along addicted to the worship of other gods. So some take *v.* 25, *"Did you offer to me sacrifices,* that is, to me only? No, and therefore not at all to me acceptably;" for the law of worshipping the Lord our God is, *Him only we must serve. "But you have borne the tabernacle of your Moloch* (*v.* 26), little shrines that you made to carry about with you, pocket-idols for your private superstition, when you durst not be seen to do it publicly. You have had the images of your *Moloch — your king*" (probably representing *the sun,* that sits king among the heavenly bodies), "and *Chiun,* or *Remphan*" (as Stephen calls it, Acts 7:43, after the Septuagint), which it is supposed, represented Saturn, the highest of the seven planets. The worship of the sun, moon, and stars, was the most ancient, most general, and most plausible idolatry. They *made to themselves* the *star of their God,* some particular star which they took to be their god, or the name of which they gave to their god. This idolatry Israel was from the beginning prone to (Deu. 4:19); and those that retain an affection for false gods cannot expect the favour of the true God.

V. What punishment God would inflict upon them for their persisting in idolatry (*v.* 27): *I will cause you to go into captivity beyond Damascus.* They were led captive by Satan into idolatry, and therefore God caused them to go into captivity among idolaters, and hurried them into a strange land, since they were so fond of strange gods. They were carried *beyond Damascus.* Their captivity by the Assyrians was far beyond that by the Syrians; for, if less judgments do not work that for which they were sent, God will send greater. Or the captivity of Israel under Shalmaneser was far beyond that of Damascus under Tiglath-pileser, and much more grievous and destructive, which was foretold *ch.* 1:5. For, as the sins of God's professing people are greater than the sins of others, so it may be expected that their punishments will be proportionable. We find the spoil of Damascus and that of Samaria carried off together by the king of Assyria, Isa. 8:4. Stephen reads it, *I will carry you away beyond Babylon* (Acts 7:43), further than Judah shall be carried, so far further as not to return. And, to make this sentence appear both the more certain and the more dreadful, he that passes it calls himself *the Lord, whose name is, The God of hosts,* and who is therefore able to execute the sentence, having hosts at command.

CHAPTER 6

In this chapter we have, I. A sinful people studying to put a slight upon God's threatenings and to make them appear trivial, confiding in their privileges and pre-eminences above other nations (*v.* 2, 3), and their power (*v.* 13), and wholly addicted to their pleasures (*v.* 4–6). II. A serious prophet studying to put a weight upon God's threatenings and to make them appear terrible, by setting forth the severity of those judgments that were coming upon these sensualists (*v.* 7), God's abhorring them, and abandoning them and theirs to death (*v.* 8–11), and bringing utter desolation upon them, since they would not be wrought upon by the methods he had taken for their conviction (*v.* 12–14).

Verses 1–7

The first words of the chapter are the contents of these verses; but they sound very strangely, and contrary to the sentiments of a vain world: *Woe to those that are at ease!* We are ready to say, *Happy are those that are at ease,* that neither feel any trouble nor fear any, that lie soft and warm, and lay nothing to heart; and wise we think are those that do so, that bathe themselves in the delights of sense and care not how the world goes. Those are looked upon as doing well for themselves that do well for their bodies and make much of them; but against them this woe is denounced, and we are here told what their ease is, and what the woe is.

I. Here is a description of their pride, security, and sensuality, for which God would reckon with them.

1. They were vainly conceited of their own dignities, and thought those would secure them from the judgments threatened and be their defence against the wrath both of God and man. (1.) Those that dwelt in Zion thought that was honour and protection enough for them, and they might there be quiet from all fear of evil, because it was a strong city, well fortified both by nature and art (we read of Zion's *strong-holds* and her *bulwarks*), and because it was a royal city, where were set the thrones of the house of David (it was the head-city of Judah, and therefore truly great), and especially because it was the holy city, where the temple was, and the testimony of Israel; those that dwelt there doubted not but that God's sanctuary would be a sanctuary to them and would shelter them from his judgments. The *temple of the Lord are these,* Jer. 7:4. They are *haughty because of the holy mountain,* Zep. 3:11. Note, Many are puffed up with pride, and rocked asleep in carnal security, by their church-privileges, and the place they have in Zion. (2.) Those that dwelt *in the mountain of Samaria,* though it was not a holy hill, like that of Zion, yet they trusted in it, because it was the metropolis of a potent kingdom, and perhaps, in imitation of Jerusalem, was the head-quarters of its religion; and by lapse of time the hill of Shemer became with them in as good repute as the hill of Zion ever was. They hoped for salvation from these hills and mountains. (3.) Both these two kingdoms valued themselves upon their relation to Israel, that prince with God, which they looked upon as masking them the *chief of the nations,* more ancient and honourable than any of them; the *first-fruits of the nations* (so the word is), dedicated to God and sanctifying the whole harvest. The *house of Israel* came to them, that is, was divided into those kingdoms, of which Zion and Samaria were the mother cities. Those that were at ease were the princes and rulers, the great men, that were *chief of the nations,* chief of those two kingdoms, and to whom, having their residence in Zion and Samaria, the whole house of Israel applied for judgment. Note, It is hard to be great and not to be proud. Great nations and great men are apt to overvalue themselves, and to overlook their neighbours, because they think they a little overtop them. But, for a check to their pride and security, the prophet bids them take notice of those cities that were within the compass of their knowledge, that had been as illustrious in their time as ever Zion or Samaria was, and yet were destroyed, *v.* 2. "Go *to Calneh* (which was an ancient city built by Nimrod, Gen. 10:10), and see what has become of that, it is now in ruins; so is *Hamath the great,* one of the chief cities of Syria. Sennacherib boasts of *destroying the gods of Hamath.* Gath was likewise made desolate by Hazael, and not long ago, 2 Ki. 12:17. Now *were they better than these kingdoms* of Judah and Israel? Yes, they were, and *their border greater than your border,* so that they had more reason than you to be confident of their own safety; yet you see what has become of them, and dare you be secure? *Art thou better than populous No?*" Nah. 3:8. Note, The examples of others' ruin forbid us to be secure.

2. They persisted in their wicked courses upon a presumption that they should never be called to an account for them (*v.* 3): "*You put far away the evil day,* the day of reckoning, as a thing that shall never come, or you look upon it as at such a distance that it makes no impression at all upon you; you *put it far away,* and think you can still put it yet further, and adjourn it *de die in diem — from day to day,* and therefore you *cause the seat of violence to draw near;* you venture upon all acts of injustice and oppression, and have *fellowship with the throne of iniquity, which frames mischief by a law,* Ps. 94:20. You cause that to come near, as if that would be your protection from these judgments which really ripens you for them." Note, *Therefore* men take sin to be near them, because they take judgment to be far off from them; but those deceive themselves who thus mock God.

3. They indulged themselves in all manner of sensual pleasures and delights, *v.* 4–6. These Israelites were perfect epicures and slaves to their appetites. Their dignities (in consideration of which they ought to have been examples of self-denial and mortification), they thought, would justify them in their sensuality; the gains of their oppression and violence, they thought, would bear the charge of it; and they put the evil day at a distance, that they might give them no disturbance in it. That which they are here charged with is not in itself sinful (these things might be soberly and moderately used), but they placed their happiness in the gratification of their carnal appetites; and though they were men in office, that had business to mind, they gave themselves up to their pleasures, spent their time in them, and threw away their thoughts, and cares, and estates upon them. They were in these enjoyments as in their element. Their hearts were upon them; they exceeded all bounds in them, and this at a time when God in his providence was calling them to *weeping and mourning,* Isa. 22:12, 13. When they were under guilt and wrath, and the judgments of God were ready to break in upon them, they called for *wine and strong drink,* presuming that *to-morrow shall be as this day, and much more abundant* (Isa. 56:12), thus walking contrary to God and setting his justice at defiance. (1.) They were extravagant in their furniture. Nothing would serve them but *beds of ivory* to sleep upon, or to sit on at their meat, when sackcloth and ashes would have become them better. (2.) They were lazy, and humoured themselves in the love of ease. They did not only lie down, but *stretched themselves* upon their couches, when they should have stirred up themselves to their business; they were willingly slothful, and took a pride in doing nothing; they *abound in superfluities* (so the margin reads it), when many of their poor brethren wanted necessaries. (3.) They were nice and curious in their diet, must have every thing of the best and abundance of it: They ate *the lambs out of the flock* (lambs by wholesale) and the *calves out of the midst of the stall,* the fattest they could lay their hand on; and these perhaps not out of their own flock and their own stall, but taken by oppression from the poor. (4.) They were merry and jovial, and diverted themselves at their feasts with music and singing: They *chant to the sound of the viol,* sing and play in concert, and they invent new-fashioned *instruments of music,* striving herein, more than in any thing else, to excel their ancestors; they set their wits on work to contrive how to please their fancy. Some men never show their ingenuity but in their luxury; on that they bestow all their faculty of invention and contrivance. They invent *instruments of music, like David,* entertain themselves with that which formerly used to be the entertainment of kings only. Or it intimates their profaneness in their mirth; they mimicked the temple-music, and made a jest of that, because, it may be, it was old-fashioned, and they took a pride in bantering it as the Babylonians did when they urged the captives to sing to them the *songs of Zion;* such was Belshazzar's profaneness when he drank wine in temple-bowls, and such is theirs that sing vain and loose songs in psalm-tunes, on purpose to ridicule a divine institution. (5.) They drank to excess, and never thought they could pour down enough: They *drank wink in bowls,* not in glasses, or cups (as Jer. 35:5); they hate to be stinted, and must have large draughts, and therefore make use of vessels that they can steal a draught out of. (6.) They affected the strongest perfumes: They *anoint themselves with the chief ointments,* to please the smell, and to make them more in love with their own bodies, and to guard against those presages of putrefaction which they carry about with them while they live. No ordinary ointments would serve their turn; they must have the chief, such as were far-fetched and dear-bought, when cheaper would have served as well.

4. They had no concern at all for the interests of the church of God, and of the nation, that were sinking and going to decay: *They are not grieved for the affliction of Joseph;* the church of God, including both the kingdoms of Judah and Israel (which are called *Joseph,* Ps. 80:1), was in distress, invaded, insulted, and broken in upon. As to their own kingdom which they were entrusted with the government of, the affairs of which they were directors of, the peace of which they were the conservators of, great breaches were made upon it, upon its peace and welfare; and they were so besotted that they were not aware of them, so indulgent of their pleasures that they never laid them to heart, and had such an aversion to the thing called business that they were in no care or concern to get them repaired. It is all one to them whether the nation sink or swim, so that they can but lie at ease and live in pleasure. Particular persons that belonged to Joseph were in affliction, and they took no cognizance of their case of the wrongs and hardships they sustained and the troubles they were in, nor took any care to relieve them, and right them, contrary to the temper of holy Job, who, when he was in prosperity, *wept with him* that *was in misery* and his *soul was grieved for the poor,* Job 30:25. Some think that, in calling the afflicted church *Joseph,* there is an allusion to the story of Pharaoh's butler, who, when he preferred to give the cup again into his master's hand, *remembered not Joseph, but forgot him,* Gen. 40:21, 23. Thus they *drank wine in bowls,* but *were not grieved for the affliction of Joseph.* Note, Those are commonly careless of the troubles of others who are set upon their own pleasures; and it is a great offence to God when his church is in affliction and we are not grieved for it, nor lay it to heart.

II. Here is the doom passed upon them (*v.* 7): *Therefore now shall they go captive with the first that go captive,* and shall fall into all the miseries that attend captives; and the *banquet of those* that *stretched themselves* upon their couches *shall be removed.* Their plenty shall be taken from them, and they from it, because they made it the food and fuel of their lusts. 1. Those who lived in luxury shall lose even their liberty; and by being brought into servitude shall be justly punished for the abuse of their dignity and dominion. 2. Those who trusted in the delights and pleasures of their own land shall be carried away into a strange land, and so made ashamed of their pride and confidence; they shall *go captive*. 3. Those who placed their happiness in the pleasures of sense, and set their hearts upon them, shall be deprived of those pleasures; their banquet shall be removed, and they shall know what it is to fare hard. 4. Those who *stretched themselves* shall be made to contract themselves, and to come into a less compass. 5. Those who *put the evil day far from them* shall find it nearer to them than it is to others; *those shall go captive with the first* who flattered themselves with hopes that if trouble did come they should be the last who should be seized by it. Those are ripening apace for trouble themselves who lay not to heart the trouble of others and of the church of God. Those who give themselves to mirth, when God calls them to mourning, will find it a sin that shall not go unpunished, Isa. 22:14.

Verses 8–14

In the former part of the chapter we had these secure Israelites loading themselves with pleasures, as if they could never be made merry enough; here we have God loading them with punishments, as if they could never be made miserable enough. And observe,

I. How strongly this burden is bound on, not to be shaken off by their presumption and security; for it is bound by *the Lord the God of hosts*, by his mighty, his almighty, hand, which none can resist; it is bound with an oath, which puts the sentence past revocation: *The Lord God has sworn, and he will not repent*, and, since he could swear by no greater, he has sworn by himself. How dreadful, how miserable, is the case of those whose ruin, whose eternal ruin, God himself has sworn, who can execute his purpose and cannot alter it!

II. How heavily this burden lies! Let us see the particulars. 1. God will abhor and abandon them, and that implies misery enough, all misery: *I abhor the excellency of Jacob*, all that which they are proud of, and value themselves upon, and for which they call and count themselves the *chief of nations*. Their visible church-membership, and the privileges of that, their temple, altar, and priesthood, these were, more than any thing, the excellencies of Jacob; but, when these were profaned and polluted by sin, God abhorred them; he hated and despised them, *ch.* 5:21. Note, God abhors that form of godliness which hypocrites keep up, while they abhor the power of it. And if he abhors their temple, for the iniquity of that, no marvel that he hates their palaces, for the injustices and oppression he finds there. Note, that creature which we take such a complacency and put such a confidence in as to make it a rival with God is thereby made abominable to him. He *hates the palaces* of sinners, for the sake of wickedness of those that dwell therein. Prov. 3:33, *The curse of the Lord is in the house of the wicked*. And, if God abhor them, immediately it follows, He will *deliver up the city with all that is therein*, deliver it up into the hands of the enemy, that will lay it waste, and make a prey of all its wealth. Note, Those that are abhorred and abandoned of God are undone to all intents and purposes. 2. There shall be a great and general mortality among them (*v.* 9): *If there remain ten men in one house*, that have escaped the sword of the enemy, yet they shall be met with another way; *they shall all die* by famine or pestilence. In the most sickly times, if there be ten in a house, one may hope that at least the one-half of them will escape, according to the proportion of two in a bed, *one taken and the other left*; but here not one of ten shall live to bury the rest. Another instance of the greatness of the mortality is (*v.* 10) that the nearest relations of the dead shall be forced with their own hands to wind up their bodies, and bury them, for want of other hands to be employed in it; that is all that the *next of kin*, to whom the right of redemption belongs, can do for them, and with great reluctance will they do that. It intimates that the young people shall be cut off soonest; for the uncle that survives is, ordinarily, the senior relation. "When the uncle comes with the sexton (or *him that burns*), *to bring out the bones out of the house*, he *shall say* to him that

he sees next about the house, '*Is there any yet with thee? Are there any left alive?*' And he shall say, 'No, this is the last; now the whole family is cut off by death, and neither root nor branch remains.'" But that which makes the judgment the more grievous is that their hearts seem to be hardened under it. "When he that is found by the sides of the house begin to enter into discourse with those that are carrying off the dead, they shall say, '*Hold thy tongue; do not stand preaching to us about the hand of Providence* in this calamity, for *we may not make mention of the name of the Lord;* God is so angry with us that there is no speaking to him; he is so extreme to mark what we do amiss that we dare not so much as make mention of his name.'" Thus *the foolishness of men perverts their way*, and brings them into distress, and then *their heart frets against the Lord*. Even then they will not take notice of his hand, nor suffer those about them to do it. Perhaps it was forbidden by some of the idolatrous kings to make mention of the name of *Jehovah*, as by the law of Moses it was forbidden to make mention of the names of the heathen-gods: "We may not do it without incurring the penalty." Note, Those hearts are wretchedly hardened indeed that will not be brought to make mention of God's name, and to worship him, when the hand of God has gone out against them, and when, as here, sickness and death are in their families. Thus those *heap up wrath* who *cry not when God binds them*. 3. Their houses shall be destroyed, *v.* 11. God *will smite the great house with breaches, and the little house with clefts;* they shall both be cracked so as to lose their beauty and strength, and to be hastening towards a fall. The princes' palaces are not above the rebuke of divine justice, nor the poor men's cottages beneath it; neither shall escape. When sin has marked them for ruin God will find ways to bring it about. It is by order from him that breaches are made.

III. How justly they are thus burdened. If we understand the matter aright, we shall say, The *Lord is righteous*. 1. The methods used for their reformation had been all fruitless and ineffectual (*v.* 12): *Shall horses run upon the rock*, to hurl or harrow the ground there? Or will *one plough there with oxen?* No, for there will be no profit to countervail the pains. God has sent them his prophets, to *break up their fallow-ground;* but they found them as hard and inflexible as the rock, rough and rugged, and they could do no good with them, nor work upon them, and therefore they shall not attempt it any more. They will not be reclaimed, and therefore shall not be reproved, but quite abandoned. Note, Those who will not be cultivated as fields and vineyards shall be rejected as barren rocks and deserts, Heb. 6:7, 8. 2. They had abused their power to the wrong and oppression of many, whose injured cause the sovereign Judge would not only right, but revenge: *You have turned judgment into gall*, which is nauseous, and *the fruit of righteousness into hemlock*, which is noxious; it would make one sick to see how those that were entrusted with the administration of public justice bore down equity with that power which they out to have defended and supported it, and so turned its own artillery against itself. Note, When our services of God are soured with sin his providences will justly be embittered to us. 3. They had set the judgments of God at defiance, and, confiding in their own strength, thought themselves a match for Omnipotence, *v.* 13. They *rejoiced in a thing of nought*, pleased themselves with a fancy that no evil should befal them, though they had no ground at all for that confidence, nothing to trust to that would bear any weight. They said, "*Have we not taken to us horns;* have we not arrived to great dignity and dominion, have we not pushed down our enemies and pushed on our victories, and this *by our own strength*, our own skill and courage, our own wealth and military force? Who then need we be afraid of? Who then need we make court to? Not God himself." Note, Prosperity and success commonly make men secure and haughty; and those that have done much think they can do any thing, any thing without God, nay, any thing against him. But those who trust in their own strength rejoice in a *thing of nought*, and so they will find. Probably they did not say this with their lips, *totidem verbis* — *in so many words*, but it was the language of their hearts and of their actions, both which God understands.

IV. How easily and effectually this burden shall be brought upon them, *v.* 14. He that brings it upon them is

the Lord the God of hosts, who both may do and can do what he pleases, who has all creatures at his command, and who, when he has work to do, will not be at a loss for instruments to do it with; though they are the house of Israel, yet he will *raise up against them a nation* which they feared not, but had many a time hoped in, even the Assyrians, and this nation shall *afflict them*, bring them into straits, and put them to pain, from the *entering in of Hamath*, in the north, to *the river of the wilderness*, the river of Egypt, Sihor or Nile, in the south. The whole nation has shared in the iniquity, and therefore must expect to share in the calamity. Note, When men are in any way instruments of affliction to us we must see God raising them up against us, for they are in his hand — the rod, the sword, in his hand. The Lord has bidden Shimei curse David.

CHAPTER 7

In this chapter we have, I. God contending with Israel, by the judgments, but are reprieved, and the judgments turned away at the prayer of Amos (*v.* 1–6). 2. God's patience is at length worn out by their obstinacy, and they are rejected, and sentenced to utter ruin (*v.* 7–9). II. Israel contending with God, by the opposition given to his prophet. 1. Amaziah informs against Amos (*v.* 10, 11) and does what he can to rid the country of him as a public nuisance (*v.* 12, 13). 2. Amos justifies himself in what he did as a prophet (*v.* 14, 15) and denounces the judgments of God against Amaziah his prosecutor (*v.* 16, 17); for, when the contest is between God and man, it is easy to foresee, it is very easy to foretel, who will come off with the worst of it.

Verses 1–9

We here see that God bears long, but that he will not bear always, with a provoking people, both these God here showed the prophet: *Thus hath the Lord God showed me, v.* 1, 4, 7. He showed him what was present, foreshowed him what was to come, gave him the knowledge both of what he did and of what he designed; for the *Lord God reveals his secret unto his servants the prophets, ch.* 3:7.

I. We have here two instances of God's sparing mercy, remembered in the midst of judgment, the narratives of which are so much like one another that they will be best considered together, and very considerable they are.

1. God is here coming forth against this sinful nation, first by one judgment and then by another. (1.) He begins with the judgment of famine. The prophet saw this in vision. He saw God *forming grasshoppers*, or *locusts*, and bringing them up upon the land, to eat up the fruits of it, and so to strip it of its beauty and starve its inhabitants, *v.* 1. God formed these grasshoppers, not only as they were his creatures (and much of the wisdom and power of God appears in the formation of minute animals, as much in the structure of an ant as of an elephant), but as they were instruments of his wrath. God is said to *frame evil* against a sinful people, Jer. 18:11. These grasshoppers were framed on purpose to *eat up the grass of the land;* and vast numbers of them were prepared accordingly. They were sent *in the beginning of the shooting up of the latter growth, after the king's mowings*. See here how the judgment was mitigated by the mercy that went before it. God could have sent these insects to eat up the grass at the beginning of the first growth, in the spring, when the grass was most needed, was most plentiful, and was the best in its kind; but God suffered that to grow, and suffered them to gather it in; the king's mowings were safely housed, for the *king himself is served from the field* (Eccl. 5:9), and could as ill be without his mowings as without any other branch of his revenues. Uzziah, who was now king of Judah, *loved husbandry*, 2 Chr. 26:10. But the grasshoppers were commissioned to eat up only the *latter growth* (the edgrew we call it in the country), the after-grass, which is of little value in comparison with the former. The mercies which God give us, and continues to us, are more numerous and more valuable than those he removes from us, which is a good reason why we should be thankful and not complain. The remembrance of the mercies of the former growth should make us submissive to the will of God when we meet with disappointments in the latter growth. The prophet, in vision, saw this judgment prevailing far. These grasshoppers *ate up the grass of the land*, which should have been for the cattle, which the owners must of course suffer by. Some understand this figuratively of a wasting destroying army brought upon them. In the days of Jeroboam the kingdom of Israel began to recover itself from the desolations it had been under in the former reigns (2 Ki. 14:25); the latter growth shot up, after the mowings of the kings of

Syria, which we read of 2 Ki. 13:3. And then God commissioned the king of Assyria with an army of caterpillars to come upon them and lay them waste, that nation spoken of *ch.* 6:14, which afflicted them *from the entering of Hamath to the river of the wilderness,* which seems to refer to 2 Ki. 14:25, where Jeroboam is said to have restored their coast *from the entering of Hamath to the sea of the plain.* God can bring all to ruin when we think all is in some good measure repaired. (2.) He proceeds to the judgment of fire, to show that he has many arrows in his quiver, many ways of humbling a sinful nation (*v.* 4): *The Lord God called to contend by fire.* He contended, for God's judgment upon a people are his controversies with them; in them he prosecutes his action against them; and his controversies are neither causeless nor groundless. He *called to contend;* he did by his prophets give them notice of his controversy, and drew up a declaration, setting forth the meaning of it. Or he called for his angels, or other ministers of his justice, that were to be employed in it. A fire was kindled among them, by which perhaps is meant a great drought (the heat of the sun, which should have warmed the earth, scorched it, and burnt up the roots of the grass which the locusts had eaten the spires of), or a raging fever, which was as a fire in their bones, which devoured and ate up multitudes, or lightning, fire from heaven, which consumed their houses, as Sodom and Gomorrah were consumed (*ch.* 4:11), or it was the burning of their cities, either by accident or by the hand of the enemy, for fire and sword used to go together; thus were the towns wasted, as the country was by the grasshoppers. This fire, which God called for, did terrible execution; it *devoured the great deep,* as the fire that fell from heaven on Elijah's altar licked up the water that was in the trench. Though the water designed for the stopping and quenching of this fire was as the water of the great deep, yet it devoured it; for who, or what, can stand before a fire kindled by the wrath of God! It did *eat up a part,* a great part, of the cities where it was sent; or it was as the fire at Taberah, which *consumed the outermost parts of the camp* (Num. 11:1); when some were overthrown others were *as brands plucked out of the fire.* All deserved to be devoured, but it ate up only a part, for God does not stir up all his wrath.

2. The prophet goes forth to meet him in the way of his judgments, and by prayer seeks to turn away his wrath, *v.* 2. When he saw, in vision, what dreadful work these caterpillars made, that they had eaten up in a manner *all the grass of the land* (he foresaw they would do so, if suffered to go on), then he said, *O Lord God! forgive, I beseech thee* (*v.* 2); *cease, I beseech thee, v.* 5. He that foretold the judgment in his preaching to the people, yet deprecated it in his intercessions for them. *He is a prophet, and he shall pray for thee.* It was the business of prophets to pray for those to whom they prophesied, and so to make it appear that though they denounced they did not *desire the woeful day. Therefore,* God showed his prophets the evils coming, that they might befriend the people, not only by warning them, but by praying for them, and *standing in the gap,* to turn away God's wrath, as Moses, that great prophet, often did. Now observe here,

(1.) The prophet's prayer: *O Lord God!* [1.] *Forgive, I beseech thee,* and take away the sin, *v.* 2. He sees sin at the bottom of the trouble, and therefore concludes that the pardon of sin must be at the bottom of deliverance, and prays for that in the first place. Note, Whatever calamity we are under, personal or public, the forgiveness of sin is that which we should be most earnest with God for. [2.] *Cease, I beseech thee,* and take away the judgment; cease the fire, cease the controversy; *cause they anger towards us to cease.* This follows upon the forgiveness of sin. Take away the cause and effect will cease. Note, Those whom God contends with will soon find what need they have to cry for a cessation of arms; and there are hopes that though God has begun, and proceeded far, in his controversy, yet it may be obtained.

(2.) The prophet's plea to enforce this prayer: *By whom shall Jacob arise, for he is small? v.* 2. And it is repeated (*v.* 5) and yet no vain repetition. Christ, *in his agony,* prayed earnestly, *saying the same words,* again and again. [1.] It is Jacob that he is interceding for, the professing people of God, called by his name, calling on his name, the seed of Jacob, his chosen, and in covenant with him. It it Jacob's case that is in this prayer spread before the God of Jacob. [2.] *Jacob is small,* very small already, weakened and brought low by former judgments; and therefore, it these come, he will be quite ruined and brought to nothing. The people are few; *the dust of Jacob,* which was once innumerable, is now soon counted. Those few are feeble (it is *the worm Jacob,* Isa. 41:14); they are unable to help themselves or one another. Sin will soon make a great people small, will diminish the numerous, impoverish the plenteous, and weaken the courageous. [3.] *By whom shall he arise?* He has fallen, and cannot help himself up, and he has no friend to help him, none to raise him, unless the hand of God do it; what will become of him, then, if the hand that should raise him to stretched out against him? Note, When the state of God's church is very low and very helpless it is proper to be recommended by our prayers to God's pity.

3. God graciously lets fall his controversy, in answer to the prophet's prayer, once and again (*v.* 3): *The Lord repented for this.* He did not change his mind, for he is one mind and who can turn him? But he changed is way, took another course, and determined to deal in mercy and not in wrath. He said, *It shall not be.* And again (*v.* 6), *This also shall not be.* The caterpillars were countermanded, were remanded; a stop was put to the progress of the fire, and thus a reprieve was granted. See the power of prayer, of *effectual fervent* prayer, and how much it *avails,* what great things it prevails for. A stop has many a time been put to a judgment by making *supplication to the Judge.* This was not the first time that Israel's life was begged, and so saved. See what a blessing praying people, praying prophets, are to a land, and therefore how highly they ought to be valued. Ruin would many a time have broken in if they had not stood in the breach, and made good the pass. See how ready, how swift, God is to show mercy, how he *waits to be gracious.* Amos moves for a reprieve, and obtains it, because God inclines to grant it and looks about to see if there be any that will intercede for it, Isa. 59:16. Nor are former reprieves objected against further instances of mercy, but are rather encouragements to pray and hope for them. This also shall not be, any more than that. It is the glory of God that he *multiplies to pardon,* that he spares, and forgives, to more than seventy times seven times.

II. We have here the rejection of those at last who had been often reprieved and yet never reclaimed, reduced to straits and yet never reduced to their God and their duty. This is represented to the prophet by a vision (*v.* 7, 8) and an express prediction of utter ruin, *v.* 9.

1. The vision is of a *plumb-line,* a line with a plummet at the end of it, such as masons and bricklayers use to run up a wall by, that they may work it straight and true, and by rule. (1.) Israel was a wall, a strong wall, which God himself had reared, as a bulwark, or wall of defence, to his sanctuary, which he set up among them. The Jewish church says of herself (Cant. 8:10), *I am a wall, and my breasts are like towers.* This wall was *made by a plumb-line,* very exact and firm. So happy was its constitution, so well compacted, and every thing so well ordered according to the model; it had long stood fast as a wall of brass. But, (2.) God now *stands upon* this wall, not to hold it up, but to tread it down, or, rather, to consider what he should do with it. He *stands upon it with a plumb-line in his hand,* to take measure of it, that it may appear to be a bowing, bulging wall. *Recti est index sui et oblique — This plumb-line would discover where it was crooked.* Thus God would bring the people of Israel to the trial, would discover their wickedness, and show wherein they erred; and he would likewise bring his judgments upon them according to equity, would set a *plumb-line in the midst of them,* to mark how far their wall must be pulled down, as David measured the *Moabites with a line* (2 Sa. 8:2) to *put them to death.* And, when God is coming to the ruin of a people, he is said to *lay judgment to the line and righteousness to the plummet;* for when he punishes it is with exactness. It is now determined: *"I will not again pass by them any more;* they shall not be spared and reprieved as they have been; their punishment shall not be *turned away," ch.* 1:3. Note, God's patience, which has long been sinned against, will at length be sinned away; and the time will come when those that have been spared often shall be no longer spared. *My spirit shall not always strive.* After frequent reprieves, yet a day of execution will come.

2. The prediction is of utter ruin, *v.* 9. (1.) The body of the people shall be destroyed, with all those things that were their ornament and defence. They are here called *Isaac* as well as *Israel, the house of Isaac* (*v.* 16), some think in allusion to the signification of Isaac's name; it is *laughter;* they shall become a jest among all their neighbours; their neighbours shall *laugh at them.* The desolation shall fasten upon their high places and their *sanctuaries,* either their *castles* or their *temples,* both built on high places. Their castles they thought safe, and their temples sacred as sanctuaries. These shall be *laid waste,* to punish them for their idolatry and to make them ashamed of their carnal confidences, which were the two things for which God had a controversy with them. When these were made desolate they might read their sin and folly in their punishment. (2.) The royal family shall sink first, as an earnest of the ruin of the whole kingdom: *I will rise against the house of Jeroboam,* Jeroboam the second, who was now king of the ten tribes; his family was extirpated in his son Zecharias, who was *slain with the sword before the people,* by Shallum who *conspired against him,* 2 Ki. 15:10. How unrighteous soever the instruments were, God was righteous, and in them God rose up against that idolatrous family. Even king's houses will be no shelter against the sword of God's wrath.

Verses 10–17

One would have expected, 1. That what we met with in the former part of the chapter would awaken the people to repentance, when they saw that they were reprieved in order that they might have *space to repent* and that they could not obtain a pardon unless the did repent. 2. That it would endear the prophet Amos to them, who had not only shown his good-will to them in praying against the judgments that invaded them, but had prevailed to turn away those judgments, which, if they had had any sense of gratitude, would have gained him an interest in their affections. But it fell out quite contrary; they continue impenitent, and the next news we hear of Amos is that he is persecuted. Note, As it is the praise of great saints that they pray for those that are enemies to them, so it is the shame of many great sinners that they are enemies to those who pray for them, Ps. 35:13, 15; 109:4. We have here,

I. The malicious information brought to the king against the prophet Amos, *v.* 10, 11. The informer was *Amaziah the priest of Bethel,* the chief of the priests that ministered to the golden calf there, the *president of Bethel* (so some read it), that had the principal hand in civil affairs there. He complained against Amos, not only because he prophesied without license from him, but because he prophesied against his altars, which would soon be deserted and demolished if Amos's preaching could but gain credit. Thus the shrine-makers at Ephesus hated Paul, because his preaching tended to spoil their trade. Note, Great pretenders to sanctity are commonly the worst enemies to those who are really sanctified. Priests have been the most bitter persecutors. Amaziah brings an information to Jeroboam against Amos. Observe, 1. The crime he is charged with is no less than treason: *"Amos has conspired against thee,* to depose and murder thee; he aims at succeeding thee, and therefore is taking the most effectual way to weaken thee. He sows the seeds of sedition in the hearts of the good subjects of the king, and makes them disaffected to him and his government, that he may draw them by degrees from their allegiance; upon this account *the land is not able to bear his words."* It is slyly insinuated to the king that the country was exasperated against him, and it is given in as their sense that his preaching was intolerable, and such as nobody could be reconciled to, such as the times would by no means bear, that is, the men of the times would not. Both the impudence of his supposed treason, and the bad influence it would have upon the country, are intimated in that part of the charge, that he conspired against the king in the midst of the house of Israel. Note, It is no new thing for the accusers of the brethren to misrepresent them as enemies to the king and kingdom, as traitors to their prince and troublers of the land, when really they are the best friends to both. And it is common for designing men to assert that as the sense of the country which is far from being so. And yet here, I doubt, it was too true, that the people could not bear plain dealing any more than the priests. 2. The words laid in the indictment for the support of this charge (v. 11): *Amos says* (and they have witnesses ready to prove it) *Jeroboam shall die by the sword, and Israel shall be led away captive;* and hence they infer that he is an enemy to his king and country, and not to be tolerated. See the malice of Amaziah; he does not tell the king how Amos had interceded for Israel, and by his intercession had turned away first one judgment and then another, and did not let fall his intercession till he saw the decree had gone forth; he does not tell him that these threatenings were conditional, and that he had often assured them that if they would repent and reform the ruin should be prevented. Nay, it was not true that he said, *Jeroboam shall die by the sword,* nor did he so die (2 Ki. 14:28), but that God would *rise against the house of Jeroboam with the sword, v. 9.* God's prophets and ministers have often had occasion to make David's complaint (Ps. 56:5), *Every day they wrest my words.* But shall it be made the watchman's crime, when he sees the sword coming, to give warning to the people, that they may get themselves secured? or the physician's crime to tell his patient of the danger of his disease, that he may use means for the cure of it? What enemies are foolish men to themselves, to their own peace, to their best friends! It does not appear that Jeroboam took any notice of this information; perhaps he reverenced a prophet, and stood more in awe of the divine authority than Amaziah his priest did.

II. The method he used to persuade Amos to withdraw and quit the country (v. 12, 13); when he could not gain his point with the king to have Amos imprisoned, banished, or put to death, or at least to have him frightened into silence or flight, he tried what he could do by fair means to get rid of him; he insinuated himself into his acquaintance, and with all the arts of wheedling endeavored to persuade him to go and prophesy in the *land of Judah,* and not at Bethel. He owns him to be a seer, and does not pretend to enjoin him silence, but suggests to him,

1. That Bethel was not a proper place for him to exercise his ministry in, for it was *the king's chapel,* or *sanctuary,* where he had his idols and their altars and priests; and it was *the king's court,* or *the house of the kingdom,* where the royal family resided and where were set the thrones of judgment; and therefore *prophesy not any more* here. And why not? (1.) Because Amos is too plain and blunt a preacher for the court and the king's chapel. Those that *wear silk and fine clothing,* and speak silken soft words, are fit for king's palaces. (2.) Because the worship that is in the king's chapel will be a continual vexation and trouble to Amos; let him therefore get far enough from it, and what the eye sees not the heart grieves not for. (3.) Because it was not fit that the king and his house should be affronted in their own court and chapel by the reproofs and threatenings which Amos was continually teazing them with in the name of the Lord; as if it were the prerogative of the prince, and the privilege of the peers, when they are running headlong upon a precipice, not to be told of their danger. (4.) Because he could not expect any countenance or encouragement there, but, on the contrary, to be bantered and ridiculed by some and to be threatened and brow-beaten by others; however, he could not think to make any converts there, or to persuade any from that idolatry which was supported by the authority and example of the king. To preach his doctrine there was but (as we say) to run his head against a post; and therefore *prophesy no more* there. But,

2. He persuades him that the land of Judah was the fittest place for him to set up in: *Flee thee away* thither with all speed, and *there eat bread,* and *prophesy there.* There thou wilt be safe; there thou wilt be welcome; the king's court and chapel there are on thy side; the prophets there will second thee; the priests and princes there will take notice of thee, and allow thee an honourable maintenance. See here, (1.) How willing wicked men are to get clear of their faithful reprovers, and how ready to *say to the seers, See not,* or See not for us; the two witnesses were a torment to those that dwelt on the earth (Rev. 11:10), and it were indeed a pity that men should be *tormented before the time,* but that it is in order to the preventing of eternal torment. (2.) How apt worldly men are to measure others by themselves. Amaziah, as a priest, aimed at nothing but the profits of his place, and he thought Amos, as a prophet, had the same views, and

therefore advised him to prophesy were he might *eat bread,* where he might be sure to have as much as he chose; whereas Amos was to prophesy where God appointed him, and where there was most need of him, not where he would get most money. Note, Those that make gain their godliness, and are governed by the hopes of wealth and preferment themselves, are ready to think these the most powerful inducements with others also.

III. The reply which Amos made to these suggestions of Amaziah's. He did not *consult with flesh and blood,* nor was it his care to enrich himself, but to *make full proof of his ministry,* and to be found faithful in the discharge of it, not to sleep in a whole skin, but to keep a good conscience; and therefore he resolved to abide by his post, and, in answer to Amaziah,

1. He justified himself in his constant adherence to his work and to his place (v. 14, 15); and that which he was sure would not only bear him out, but bind him to it, was that he had a divine warrant and commission for it: *"I was no prophet, nor prophet's son,* neither born nor bred to the office, not originally designed for a prophet, as Samuel and Jeremiah, not educated in the schools of the prophets, as many others were; but *I was a herdsman,* a keeper of cattle, and *a gatherer of sycamore-fruit."* Our sycamores bear no fruit, but, it seems, theirs did, which Amos gathered either for his cattle or for himself and his family, or to sell. He was a plain country-man, bred up and employed in country work and used to country fare. He *followed the flocks* as well as the herds, and thence God *took him,* and bade him *go* and *prophesy to his people Israel,* deliver to them such messages as he should from time to time *receive from the Lord.* God made him a prophet, and a prophet to them, appointed him his work and appointed him his post. Therefore he ought not to be silenced, for, (1.) He could produce a divine commission for what he did. He did not run before he was sent, but pleads, as Paul, that he was *called to be an apostle;* and men will find it is at their peril if they contradict and oppose any that come in God's name, if they say to his *seers, See not,* or silence those whom he has bidden to speak; such *fight against God.* An affront done to an ambassador is an affront to the prince that sends him. Those that have a warrant from God ought not to *fear the face of man.* (2.) The mean character he wore before he received that commission strengthened his warrant, so far was it from weakening it. [1.] He had no thoughts at all of ever being a prophet, and therefore his prophesying could not be imputed to a raised expectation or a heated imagination, but purely to a divine impulse. [2.] He was not educated nor instructed in the art or mystery of prophesying, and therefore he must have his abilities for it immediately from God, which is an undeniable proof that he had his mission from him. The apostles, being originally unlearned and ignorant men, evidenced that they owed their knowledge to their having *been with Jesus,* Acts 4:13. When the treasure is put into such earthen vessels, it is thereby made to appear that the *excellency of the power is of God, and not of man,* 2 Co. 4:7. [3.] He had an honest calling, by which he could comfortably maintain himself and his family; and therefore did not need to prophesy for bread, as Amaziah suggested (v. 12), did not take it up as a trade to live by, but as a trust to honour God and do good with. [4.] He had all his days been accustomed to a plain homely way of living among poor husbandmen, and never affected either gaieties or dainties, and therefore would not have thrust himself so near the king's court and chapel if the business God had called him to had not called him thither. [5.] Having been so meanly bred, he could not have the courage to speak to kings and great men, especially to speak such bold and provoking things to them, if he had not been animated by a greater spirit than his own. If God, that sent him, had not strengthened him, he could not thus have *set his face as a flint,* Isa. 50:7. Note, God often chooses the *weak and foolish things of the world* to confound the wise and mighty; and a herdman of Tekoa puts to shame a priest of Bethel, when he receives from God authority and ability to act for him.

2. He condemns Amaziah for the opposition he gave them, and denounces the judgments of God against him, not from any private resentment or revenge, but in the name of the Lord and by authority from him, v. 16, 17. Amaziah would not suffer Amos to preach at all, and there-

fore he is particularly ordered to preach against him: *Now therefore hear thou the word of the Lord,* hear it and tremble. Those that cannot bear general woes may expect woes of their own. The sin he is charged with is forbidding Amos to prophesy; we do not find that he beat him, or put him in the stocks, only he enjoined him silence: *Prophesy not against Israel, and drop not thy word against the house of Isaac;* he must not only thunder against them, but he must not so much as drop a word against them; he cannot bear, no, not the most gentle distilling of that rain, that small rain. Let him therefore hear his doom.

(1.) For the opposition he gave to Amos God will bring ruin upon himself and his family. This was the sin that filled the measure of his iniquity. [1.] He shall have no comfort in any of his relations, but be afflicted in those that were nearest to him: *His wife shall be a harlot;* either she shall be forcibly abused by the soldiers, as the Levite's concubine by the men of Gibeah (they *ravish the women of Zion,* Lam. 5:11), or she shall herself wickedly play the harlot, which, though her sin, her great sin, would be his affliction, his great affliction and reproach, and a just punishment upon him for promoting spiritual whoredom. Sometimes the sins of our relations are to be looked upon as judgments of God upon us. His children, though they keep honest, yet shall not keep alive: *His sons and his daughters shall fall by the sword* of war, and he himself shall live to see it. He has trained them up in iniquity, and therefore God will cut them off in it. [2.] He shall be stripped of all his estate; it shall fall into the hand of the enemy, and be *divided by line,* by lot, among the soldiers. What is ill begotten will not be long kept. [3.] He shall himself perish in a strange country, not in the *land of Israel,* which had been holiness to the Lord, but in a *polluted land,* in a heathen country, the fittest place for such a heathen to end his days in, that hated and silenced God's prophets and contributed so much to the polluting of his own land with idolatry.

(2.) Notwithstanding the opposition he gave to Amos, God will bring ruin upon the land and nation. He was accused for saying, *Israel shall be led away captive* (v. 11), but he stands to it, and repeats it; for the unbelief of man shall not make the word of God of no effect. The *burden of the word of the Lord* may be striven with, but it cannot be shaken off. Let Amaziah rage, and fret, and say what he will to the contrary, *Israel shall surely go into captivity forth of his land.* Note, it is to no purpose to contend with the judgments of God; for when God judges he will overcome. Stopping the mouths of God's ministers will not stop the progress of God's word, for it shall not return void.

CHAPTER 8

Sinful times are here attended with sorrowful times, so necessary is the connexion between them; it is threatened here again and again that the laughter shall be turned into mourning. I. By the vision of "basket of summer-fruit" is signified the hastening on of the ruin threatened (v. 1–3) and that shall change their note. II. Oppressors are here called to an account for their abusing the poor; and their destruction is foretold, which will set them a mourning (v. 4–10). III. A famine of the word of God is here made the punishment of a people that go a whoring after other gods (v. 11–14); yet for this, which is the most mournful judgment of all, they are not here brought in mourning.

Verses 1–3

The great reason why sinners defer their repentance *de die in diem — from day to day,* is because they think God thus defers his judgments, and there is no song wherewith they so effectually sing themselves asleep as that, *My Lord delays his coming;* and therefore God, by his prophets, frequently represents to Israel the day of his wrath not only as just and certain, but as very near and hastening on apace; so he does in these verses.

I. The approach of the threatened ruin is represented by *a basket of summer-fruit* which Amos saw in vision; for the Lord *showed it* to him (v. 1) and obliged him to take notice of it (v. 2): *Amos, what seest thou?* Note, It concerns us to enquire whether we do indeed see that which God has been pleased to show us, and hear what he has been pleased to say to us; for many a thing God speaks, God shows *once, yea twice,* and men *perceive it not.* Are we in the midst of the visions of the Almighty? Let us consider what we see. He saw *a basket of summer-fruit* gathered and ready to be eaten, which signified, 1. That they were ripe for destruction, rotten ripe, and it was time for God to put in the sickle of his judgments and to cut them off; nay, the thing was in effect done already, and they lay ready to be eaten up. 2. That the year of God's patience was drawing towards a conclusion; it was autumn with them, and their year would quickly have its period in a dismal winter. 3. Those we call *summer-fruits* that will not keep till winter, but must be used immediately, an emblem of this people, that had nothing solid or consistent in them.

II. The intent and meaning of this vision is no more than this: It signifies that *the end has come upon my people Israel.* The word that signifies *the end* is *ketz,* which is of near affinity with *kitz,* the word used for *summer-fruit.* God has long spared them, and borne with them, but now his patience is tired out; they are indeed *his people Israel,* but their end, that *latter end* they have been so often reminded of, but have so long forgotten, has now come. Note, If sinners do not make an end of sin, God will make an end of them, yea though they be *his people Israel.* What was said *ch.* 7:8 is here repeated as God's determined resolution, *I will not again pass by them any more;* they shall not be connived at as they have been, nor the judgment coming turned away.

III. The consequence of this shall be a universal desolation (*v.* 3): When *the end* shall come sorrow and death shall ride in triumph; they are accustomed to go together, and shall at length go away together, when in heaven *there shall be no more death, nor sorrow,* Rev. 21:4. But here in a sinful world, in a sinful nation, 1. Sorrow reigns, reigns to such a degree that *the songs of the temple shall be howlings* — the songs of God's temple at Jerusalem, or rather of their idol-temples, where they used, when, in honour of the golden calves, they had *eaten and drunk,* to *rise up to play.* They were perhaps wanton profane songs; and it is certain that sooner or later those will be turned into howlings. Or, if they had a sound and show of piety and religion, yet, not coming from the heart, nor being sung to the glory of God, he valued them not, but would justly turn them into howlings. Note, Mourning will follow sinful mirth, yea, and sacred mirth too, if it be not sincere. And, when God's judgments are abroad, they will soon turn the greatest joy into the greatest heaviness, the temple-songs, which used to sound so pleasantly, not only into sighs and groans, but into loud howlings, which sound dismally. They shall come to the temple, and, finding that in ruins, there they shall howl most bitterly. 2. Death reigns, reigns to such a degree that there shall be *dead bodies, many* dead bodies *in every place* (Ps. 110:6), slain by sword or pestilence, so many that the survivors shall not bury them with the usual pomp and solemnity of funerals; they shall not so much as have the bell tolled, but they shall *cast them forth with silence,* shall bury them in the dead of the night, and charge all about them to be silent and to take notice of it, either because they have not wherewithal to bear the charges of a funeral, or because, the killing disease being infectious, none will come near them, or for fear the enemy should be provoked, if they should be known to lament their slain. Or they shall charge themselves and one another silently to submit to the hand of God in these desolating judgments, and not to repine and quarrel with him. Or it may be taken not for a patient, but a sullen silence; their hearts shall be hardened, and all these judgments shall not extort from them one word of acknowledgment either of God's righteousness or their own unrighteousness.

Verses 4–10

God is here contending with proud oppressors, and showing them,

I. The heinousness of the sin they were guilty of; in short, they had the character of the unjust judge (Lu. 18:2) that neither *feared God* nor *regarded man.*

1. Observe them in their devotions, and you will say, "They had no reverence for God." Bad as they are, they do indeed keep up a show and form of godliness; they observe the *sabbath* and the *new moon;* they put some difference between those days and other days, but they were soon weary of them, and had no affection at all to them, for their hearts were wholly set upon the world and the things of it. It is a sad character which this gives of them, that they said, *When will the sabbath be gone, that we may sell corn?* Yet is still the character of many that are called Christians. (1.) They were weary of sabbath days. "When will they be *gone?"* They were weary of the restraints of the sabbaths and the new-moons, and wished them over because they might *do no servile work therein.* They were weary of the work or business of the sabbaths and new-moons, snuffed at it (Mal. 1:13), and were, as *Doeg, detained before the Lord* (1 Sa. 21:7); they would rather have been any where else than about God's altars. Note, Sabbath days and sabbath work are a burden to carnal hearts, that are always afraid of doing too much for God and eternity. Can we spend our time better than in communication with God? And how much time do we spend pleasantly with the world? Will not the sabbath be gone before we have done the work of it and reaped the gains of it? Why then should we be in such haste to part with it? (2.) They were fond of market-days: they longed to be *selling corn* and *setting forth wheat.* When they were employed in religious services they were thinking of their marketings; their hearts *went after their covetousness* (Eze. 33:31), and thus made my Father's house a house of merchandise, nay, a den of thieves. They were weary of holy duties because their worldly business stood still the while; in this they were as in their element, but in God's sanctuary as a fish upon dry ground. Note, Those are strangers to God, and enemies to themselves, that love market days better than sabbath days, that would rather be selling corn than worshipping God.

2. Observe them in their conversations, and you will see they have no regard to man; and this commonly follows upon the former; those that have lost the savour of piety will not long retain the sense of common honesty. They neither *do justly* nor *love mercy.* (1.) They cheat those they deal with. When they *sell their corn* they impose upon the buyer, both in giving out the goods and in receiving the money for them. They measure him the corn by their own measure, and pretend to give him what he agreed for, but they *make the ephah small.* The measure is scanty, and not statute-measure, and so they wrong him that way. When they receive his money they must weigh fit in their own scales, by their own weights, and the *shekel* they weigh by is above standard: *They make the shekel great,* so that the money, being found too light, must have more added to it; and so they cheat that way too, and this under colour and pretence of exactness in doing justice. By such wicked practices as these men show such a greediness of the world, such a love of themselves, such a contempt of mankind in general, of the particular persons they deal with, and of the sacred laws of justice, as prove them to have in their hearts neither the fear nor the love of that God who has so plainly said that *false weights and balances are an abomination to him.* Another instance of their fraudulent dealing is that they *sell the refuse of the wheat,* and, taking advantage of their neighbour's ignorance or necessity, make them take it at the same price at which they sell the *finest of the wheat.* (2.) The are barbarous and unmerciful to the poor: *They swallow up the needy,* and *make the poor of the land to fail.* [1.] They valued themselves so much on their wealth that they looked upon all that were poor with the highest contempt imaginable; they hated them, could not endure them, but abandoned them, and therefore did what they could to make them cease, not by relieving them to make them cease to be poor, but by banishing and destroying them to make them cease to be, or at least to be in their land. But he who thus *reproaches the poor despises his Maker,* in whose hands *rich and poor meet together.* [2.] They were so eager to increase their wealth, and make it more, that they robbed the poor to enrich themselves; and they fastened upon the poor, to *make a prey* of them, because they were not able to obtain any redress nor to resist or revenge the violence of their oppressors. Those riches that are got by the ruin of the poor will bring ruin on those that get them. They swallowed up the poor by making them hard bargains, and cheating them in those bargains; for *therefore* they *falsify the balances by deceit,* not only that they *may enrich themselves,* may have money at command, and so may have every thing else (as they think) at command too, but that they may impoverish those about them, and bring them so low that they may force them to become slaves to them, and so, having drained them of every thing else, they may have their labour for nothing, or next to nothing. Thus *they buy the poor for silver;* they bring them and their *children into bondage,* because they have not wherewithal to pay for the corn they have bought; see Neh. 5:2–5. And there were so many that they were reduced to this extremity that the price was very low; and the oppressors had beaten it down so that you might buy a poor man to be your slave *for a pair of shoes.* Property was first invaded and then liberty; it is the method of oppressors first to make men beggars and then to make them their vassals. Thus is the dignity of the human nature lost in the misery of those that are trampled on and the tenderness of it in the sin of those that trample on them.

II. The grievousness of the punishment that shall be inflicted on them for this sin. When the poor are injured they will *cry unto God,* and he will hear their cry, and reckon with those that are injurious to them, for, they being his receivers, he takes the wrongs done to them as done to himself, Ex. 22:23, 24.

1. God will remember their sin against them: *He has sworn by the excellency of Jacob* (*v.* 7), by himself, for he can swear by no greater; and who but he is the glory and magnificence of Jacob? He has sworn by those tokens of his presence with them, and his favour to them, which they had profaned and abused, and had done what they could to make them detestable to him; for he is said (ch 6:8) to *abhor the excellency of Jacob.* He swears *in his wrath,* swears by his own name, that name which was so well known and was so great in Israel. He swears, *Surely I will never forget any of their works,* but upon all occasions they shall be remembered against them, for more is implied than is expressed. *I will never forget them* is as much as to say, *I will never forgive them;* and then it proclaims the case of these unjust unmerciful men to be miserable indeed, eternally miserable; woe, and a thousand woes, to that man that is cut off by an oath of God from all benefit by pardoning mercy; and those have reason to fear judgment without mercy that have *shown no mercy.*

2. He will bring utter ruin and confusion upon them. It is here described largely, and in a great variety of emphatic expressions, that, if possible, they might be frightened into a sincere repentance and reformation. (1.) There shall be a universal terror and consternation: *Shall not the land tremble for this* (*v.* 8), *this land,* out of which you thought to drive the poor? *Shall not every one mourn that dwells therein?* Certainly he shall. Note, Those that will not tremble and mourn as they ought for national sins shall be made to tremble and mourn for national judgments; those that look without concern upon the sins of the oppressors, which should make them tremble, and upon the miseries of the oppressed, which should them mourn, God will find out a way to make them tremble at the fury of those that oppress them and mourn for their own losses and sufferings by it. (2.) There shall be a universal deluge and desolation. When God comes forth against them the waters of trouble and calamity shall *rise up wholly as a flood,* that swells, when it is dammed up, and soon overflows its banks. Every thing shall make against them. That with which they thought to check the progress of God's judgments shall but make them rise the higher. Judgments shall force their way as the *breaking forth of waters.* The whole land *shall be cast out, and drowned,* and laid under water, as the land of Egypt is every year by the overflowing of its river Nile. Or the expressions may allude to some former judgments of God. Their ruin *shall rise up wholly as a flood,* as Noah's flood, which overwhelmed the whole world, so shall this the whole land; and the land shall be *cast out, and drowned, as by the flood of Egypt,* as Pharaoh and his Egyptians were buried in the Red Sea, which was to them the *flood of Egypt,* both which judgments, as this which is here threatened, were the punishment of violence and oppression, which the Lord is the avenger of.

3. It shall surprise them, and come upon them when they little think of it (*v.* 9): *"I will cause the sun to go down at noon,* when it is in its full strength and lustre, at their noon, when they promise themselves a long afternoon, and think they have at least half a day good before them. The *earth* shall be *darkened in the clear day,* when every thing looks pleasant and hopeful." Thus uncertain are all our creature-comforts and enjoyments, even life itself; the highest degree of health and prosperity often proves the next degree to sickness and adversity; Job's sun *went down at noon;* many are taken away in the midst of their days, and their sun goes down at noon. In the midst of life we are in death. Thus *terrible* are the judgments of God to those that sleep in security; they are to them as the sun's *going*

down at noon; the less they are expected the more confounding they are. When they *cry Peace and safety* then *sudden destruction* comes, comes *as a snare,* Lu. 21:35.

4. It shall change their note, and mar all their mirth (*v.* 10): *I will turn your feasts into mourning,* as (*v.* 3) the *songs of the temple into howlings.* Note, The end of the sinner's mirth and jollity is heaviness. As *to the upright there arises light in the darkness,* which gives them *the oil of joy for mourning,* so on the wicked their falls darkness in the midst of light, which turns their *laughter into mourning,* their *joy into heaviness.* So great, so general, shall the desolation be, that *sackcloth shall be brought upon all loins, and baldness upon every head,* instead of the *well-set hair* and the rich garments they used to wear. The mourning at that day shall be as *mourning for an only son,* which denotes the most bitter and lasting lamentation. But are there are no hopes that when things are at the worst they will mend, and that at evening time it will yet be light? No, even *the end thereof shall be as a bitter day,* a day of bitter mourning; that state of impenitent sinners grows worse and worse, and the last of all will be the worst of all. *This shall you have at my hand, you shall lie down in sorrow.*

Verses 11–14

In these verses is threatened,

I. A general judgment of spiritual famine coming upon the whole land, a *famine of the word of God,* the failing of oracles and the scarcity of good preaching. This is spoken of as a thing at some distance: *The days come,* they will come hereafter, when another kind of darkness shall come upon that land of light. When Amos prophesied, and for a considerable time after, they had great plenty of prophets, abundant opportunities of *hearing the word of God,* in season and out of season; they had precept upon precept and line upon line; prophecy was their daily bread; and it is probable that they surfeited upon it, as Israel on the manna, and therefore God threatens that hereafter he will deprive them of this privilege. Probably in the land of Israel there were not so many prophets, about the time that their destruction came upon them, as there were in the land of Judah; and when the ten tribes went into captivity they *saw not their signs,* there were *no more any prophets,* none to *show them how long,* Ps. 74:9. The Jewish church, after Malachi, had no prophets for many ages; and some think this threatening looks further yet, to the blindness which has in part happened to Israel in the days of the Messiah, and the veil that is on the heart of the unbelieving Jews. They reject the gospel, and the ministers of it that God sends to them, and covet to have prophets of their own, as their fathers had, but they shall have none, *the kingdom of God* being *taken from them* and *given to another people.* Observe here,

1. What the judgment itself is that is threatened. It is a famine, a scarcity, not of bread and water (which are the necessary support of the body, and the want of which is very grievous), but a much sorer judgment than that, even a *famine of hearing the words of the Lord.* There shall be no congregations for ministers to preach to, nor any ministers to preach, nor any instructions and abilities given to those that do set up for preachers, to fit them for their work. The *word of the Lord* shall be *precious* and scarce; there shall be no *vision,* 1 Sa. 3:1. They shall have the written word, Bibles to read, but no ministers to explain and apply it to them, the water in the well, but nothing to draw with. It is a gracious promise (Isa. 30:20) that though they have a scarcity of bread they shall have plenty of the means of grace. God will *give them the bread of adversity and the water of affliction,* but their eyes shall see their teachers; and it was a common saying among the Puritans that brown bread and the gospel are good fare. But it is here a threatening that on the contrary they should have plenty enough of bread and water, and yet their teachers should be removed. Now, (1.) This was the departure of a great part of their glory from their land. This made their nation great and high, that *to them were committed the oracles of God;* but, when these were taken from them, their beauty was stained and their honour laid in the dust. (2.) This was a token of God's highest displeasure against them. Surely he was angry indeed with them when he would no more speak to them as he had done, and had abandoned them to ruin when he would no more afford them the means of bringing them to repentance. (3.) This made all the other calamities that were upon them truly melancholy, that they had no prophets to instruct and comfort them from the word of God, nor to give them any hopeful prospect. We should say at any time, and shall say in a time of trouble, that a famine of the word of God is the sorest famine, the heaviest judgment.

2. What will be the effect of this (*v.* 12): *They shall wander from sea to sea,* from the sea of Tiberias to the Great Sea, from one border of the country to another, to see if God will send them prophets, either by sea or land, from other countries; since they have none among themselves, they shall go from the *north to the east;* when they are disappointed in one place they shall try another, and shall *run to and fro,* as men at a loss, and in a hot pursuit to *seek the word of the Lord,* to enquire if there be any prophets, any prophecy, any message from God, but they *shall not find it.* (1.) Though to many this is no affliction at all, yet some will be very sensible of it as a great grievance, and will gladly travel far to hear a good sermon; but they shall sensibly feel the loss of those mercies which others have foolishly sinned away. (2.) Even those that slighted prophets when they had them shall wish for them as Saul did for Samuel, when they are deprived of them. Many never know the worth of mercies till they feel the want of them. Or it may be meant thus, Though they should thus wander from sea to sea, in quest of the word of God, yet shall they not find it. Note, The means of grace are moveable things; and the candlestick, when we think it stands most firmly, may be removed out of its place (Rev. 2:5); and those that now slight the *days of the son of man* may wish in vain to see them. And *in the day* of this famine *the fair virgins and the young men shall faint for thirst* (*v.* 13); those who, one would think, could well enough have borne the toil, shall sink under it. The *Jewish churches,* and the *masters of their synagogues,* some take to be meant by the *virgins* and the *young men;* these shall lose the word of the Lord, and the benefit of divine revelation, and shall faint away for want of it, shall lose all their strength and beauty. Those that trust in their own merit and righteousness, and think they have no need of Christ, others take to be meant by the *fair virgins* and the *choice young men;* they shall *faint for thirst,* when those that *hunger and thirst after the righteousness* of Christ shall be abundantly satisfied and filled.

II. The particular destruction of those that were ringleaders in idolatry, *v.* 14. Observe, 1. The sin they are charged with: They *swear by the sin of Samaria,* that is, by the god of Samaria, the idol that was worshipped at Bethel, not far off from Samaria. Thus did they glory in their shame, and swear by them as their god which was their iniquity, thinking that could help them which would certainly ruin them, and giving the highest honour to that which they should have looked upon with the utmost abhorrence and detestation. They say, *Thy god, O Dan! liveth;* that was the other golden calf, a dumb deal idol, and yet caressed and complimented as if it had been the living and true God. They say, *The manner,* or way, of *Beer-sheba liveth;* they swore by the *religion* of Beer-sheba, the way and manner of worship used there, which they looked upon as sacred, and therefore swore by and appealed to as a judge of controversy. Thus the papists swear by the mass, as the *manner of Beer-sheba.* 2. The destruction they are threatened with. Those who thus give that honour to idols which is due to God alone will find that the God they affront is thereby made their enemy, so that *they shall fall,* and the gods they serve cannot stand their friends, so that they shall *never rise again.* They will find that God is jealous and will resent the indignity done him, and that he will be victorious and it is to no purpose to contend with him.

CHAPTER 9

In this chapter we have, I. Judgment threatened, which the sinners shall not escape (*v.* 1–4), which an almighty power shall inflict (*v.* 5, 6), which the people of Israel have deserved as a sinful people (*v.* 7, 8); and yet it shall not be the utter ruin of their nation (*v.* 8), for a remnant of good people shall escape (*v.* 9). But the wicked ones shall perish (*v.* 10). II. Mercy promised, which was to be bestowed in the latter days (*v.* 11–15), as appears by the application of it to the days of the Messiah, Acts 15:16. And with those comfortable promises, after all the foregoing rebukes and threatenings, the book concludes.

Verses 1–10

We have here the justice of God passing sentence upon a provoking people; and observe,

I. With what solemnity the sentence is passed. The prophet saw in vision *the Lord standing upon the altar* (*v.* 1), the altar of burnt-offerings; for the *Lord has a sacrifice,* and multitudes must fall as victims to his justice. He is removed from the *mercy-seat* between the *cherubim,* and stands upon *the altar,* the *judgment-seat,* on which the fire of God used to fall, to devour the sacrifices. He stands upon *the altar,* to show that the ground of his controversy with this people was their profanation of his holy things; here he stands to avenge the quarrel of his altar, as also to signify that the sin of the house of Israel, like that of the house of Eli, shall *not be purged with sacrifice nor offering for ever,* 1 Sa. 3:14. He stands on the altar, to prohibit sacrifice. Now the order given is, *Smite the lintel of the door* of the temple, the chapiter, smite it with such a blow *that the posts may shake,* and *cut them,* wound them *in the head, all of them;* break down the doors of God's house, or of the courts of his house, in token of this, that he is going out from it, and forsaking it, and then all judgments are breaking in upon it. Or it signifies the destruction of those in the first place that should be as the door-posts to the nation for its defence, so that, they being broken down, it becomes as a *city without gates and bars.* "Smite the king, who is as the lintel of the door, that the princes, who are as *the posts,* may *shake; cut them in the head,* cleave them down, *all of them,* as wood for the fire; and *I will slay the last of them,* the posterity of them, them and their families, or the *least* of them, them and all that are employed under them; or, I will *slay them all,* them and all that remain of them, till it comes to the last man; the slaughter shall be general." There is no living for those on whom God has said, *I will slay* them, no standing before his sword.

II. What effectual care is taken that none shall escape the execution of this sentence. This is enlarged upon here, and is intended for warning to all that *provoke the Lord to jealousy.* Let sinners read it, and tremble; as there is no fighting it out with God, so there is no fleeing from him. His judgments, when they come with commission, as they will overpower the strongest that think to outface them, so they will overtake the swiftest that think to out-run them, *v.* 2. Those of them that flee, and take to their heels, shall soon be out of breath, and shall not flee away out of the reach of danger; for, as sometimes *the wicked flee when none pursues,* so he cannot flee away when God pursues, though *he would fain flee out of his hand.* Nay, *he that escapes of them,* that thinks he has gained his point, *shall not be delivered. Evil pursues sinners,* and will arrest them. This is here enlarged upon by showing that wherever sinners flee for shelter from God's justice, it will overtake them, and the shelter will prove but a *refuge of lies.* What David says of the ubiquity of God's presence (Ps. 139:7–10) is here said of the extent of God's power and justice. (1.) Hell itself, though it has its name in English from its being *hilled,* or *covered over,* or *hidden,* cannot hide them (*v.* 2): "Though *they dig into hell,* into the centre of the earth, or the darkest recesses of it, yet *thence shall my hand take them,* and bring them forth to be made public monuments of divine justice." The grave is a hiding-place to the righteous from the malice of the world (Job 3:17), but it shall be no hiding-place to the righteous from the justice of God; thence God's hands shall take them, when they shall rise in the great day to *everlasting shame and contempt.* (2.) Heaven, though it has its name from being *heaved,* or lifted up, shall not put them out of reach of God's judgments; as hell cannot hide them, so heaven will not. Though they *climb up to heaven* in their conceit, yet *thence will I bring them down.* Those whom God brings to heaven by his grace shall never be brought down; but those who climb thither themselves, by their own presumption, and confidence in themselves, will be brought down and filled with shame. (3.) *The top of Carmel,* one of the highest parts of the dust of the world in that country, shall not protect them: *"Though they hide themselves there,* where they imagine nobody will look for them, *I will search, and take them out thence;* neither the thickest bushes, nor the darkest caves, in the *top of Carmel,* will serve to hide them." (4.) The *bottom of the sea* shall not serve to conceal them; though they think to hide themselves there, even there the judgments of God shall find them out, and lay hold on them: *Thence will I command the serpent, and he shall bite them,* the *crooked serpent,* even *the dragon that is in the sea,* Isa. 27:1. They shall find their plague and death where they hope to find shelter and protection; diving will stand them in no more stead than climbing. (5.) Remote countries will not befriend them, nor shall less judgments excuse them from greater (*v.* 4): *Thought they go into captivity before their enemies,* who carry them to places at a great distance, and mingle them with their own people, among whom they seem to be lost, yet that shall not serve their turn: *Thence will I command the sword, and it shall slay them,* the sword of the enemy, or one another's sword. When God judges he will overcome. That which binds on all this, makes their escape impossible and their ruin inevitable, is that God will *set his eyes upon them for evil, and not for good.* His eyes are in every place, are upon all men and upon all the ways of men, upon some for good, to *show himself strong* on their behalf, but upon others for evil, to take notice of their sins (Job 13:27) and take all opportunities of punishing them for their sins. *Their* case is truly miserable who have the providence of God: and all the dispensations of it, against them, working for their hurt.

3. What a great and mighty God he is that passes this sentence upon them, and will take the executing of it into his own hands. Threatenings are more or less formidable according to the power of him that threatens. We laugh at impotent wrath; but the wrath of God is not so; it is omnipotent wrath. *Who knows the power* of it? What he had before said he would do (*ch.* 8:8) is here repeated, that he would *make the land melt* and tremble, and *all that dwell therein mourn,* that the judgment should *rise up wholly like a flood,* and the country should be *drowned,* and laid under water, *as by the flood of Egypt, v.* 5. But is he able to make his words good? Yes, certainly he is; he does but *touch the land* and *it melts, touch the mountains* and they smoke; he can do it with the greatest ease, for, (1.) He is *the Lord God of hosts,* who undertakes to do it, the God who has all the power in his hand, and all creatures at his beck and call, who having made them all, and given them their several capacities, makes what use he pleases of them and all their powers. Very miserable is the case of those who have the Lord of hosts against them, for they have hosts against them, the whole creation at war with them. (2.) He is the Creator and governor of the upper world: *It is he that builds his stories in the heavens,* the celestial orbs, or spheres, one over another, as so many stories in a high and stately palace. They are his, for he built them at first, when he said, *Let there be a firmament, and he made the firmament;* and he builds them still, is continually building them, not that they need repair, but by his providence he still upholds them; his power is the pillars of heaven, by which it is borne up. Now he that has the command of those stories is certainly to be feared, for thence, as from a castle, he can fire upon his enemies, or cast upon them great hailstones, as on the Canaanites, or make the stars in their courses, the furniture of those stories, to fight against them, as against Sisera. (3.) He has the management and command of this lower world too, in which we dwell, the terraqueous globe, both *earth* and *sea,* so that, which way soever his enemies think to make their escape, he will meet them, or to make opposition, he will match them. Do they think to make a land-fight of it? He *has founded his troop in the earth,* his troop of guards, which he has at command, and makes use of for the protection of his subjects and the punishment of his enemies. All the creatures on earth make one bundle (as the margin reads it), one bundle of arrows, out of which he takes what he pleases to discharge against the persecutors, Ps. 7:13. They are all one *army,* one *body,* so closely are they connected, and so harmoniously and so much in concert do they act for the accomplishing of their Creator's purposes. Do they think to make a sea-fight of it? He will be too hard for them there, for he has the waters of the sea at command; even its waves, the most tumultuous rebellious waters, do obey him. He *calls for the waters of the sea* in the course of his common providence, *causes vapours to ascend* out of it, and *pours them out* in showers, the small rain and the great rain of his strength, *upon the face of the earth;* this was mentioned before as a reason why we should *seek the Lord* (*ch.* 5:8) and make him our friend, as it is here made a reason why we should fear him and dread having him for our enemy.

4. How justly God passes this sentence upon the people of Israel. He does not destroy them by an act of sovereignty, but by an act of righteousness; for (*v.* 8), it is a *sinful kingdom,* and the *eyes of the Lord* are upon it, discovering it to be so; he sees the great sinfulness of it, and therefore he will *destroy it from off the face of the earth.* Note, When those kingdoms that in name and profession were holy kingdoms, and kingdoms of priests, as Israel was, become sinful kingdoms, no other can be expected than that they should be cut off and abandoned. Let sinful kingdoms, and sinful families, and sinful persons too, see the eyes of the Lord upon them, observing all their wickedness, and reserving the notice of it for the day of reckoning and recompence. This being a sinful kingdom, see how light God makes of it, *v.* 7.

(1.) Of the relation wherein he stood to it: *Are you not as children of Ethiopians unto me, O children of Israel?* A sad change! Children of Israel become as children of the Ethiopians! [1.] They were so in themselves; that was their sin. It is a thing to be greatly lamented that the children of Israel often become as children of the Ethiopians; this children of godly parents degenerate, and become the reverse of those that went before them. Those that were well-educated, and trained up in the knowledge and fear of God, and set out well, and promised fair, throw off their profession and become as bad as the worst. *How has the gold become dim!* [2.] The were so in God's account, and that was their punishment. He valued them no more, though they were children of Israel, than if they had been *children of the Ethiopians.* We read of one in the title of Ps. 7 that was *Cush* (an *Ethiopian,* as some understand it) and yet a Benjamite. Those that by birth and profession are children of Israel, if they degenerate, and become wicked and vile, are to God no more than children of the Ethiopians. This is an intimation of the rejection of the unbelieving Jews in the days of the Messiah; because they embraced not the doctrine of Christ, the kingdom of God was taken from them, they were unchurched, and cast out of covenant, became as children of the Ethiopians, and are so to this day. And it is true of those that are called Christians, but do no live up to their name and profession, that rest in the form of piety, but live under the power of reigning iniquity, that they are to God as children of the Ethiopians; he rejects them, and their services.

(2.) See how light he makes of the favours he had conferred upon them; they thought he would not, he could not, cast them off, and put them upon a level with other nations, because he had done that for them which he had not done for other nations, whereby they thought he was bound to them, so as never to leave them. "No," says he, "The favours shown to you are not so distinguishing as you think they are: *Have I not brought up Israel out of the land of Egypt?"* It is true I have; but I have also brought the *Philistines from Caphtor,* or *Cappadocia,* where they were natives, or captives, or both; they are called the *remnant of the country of Caphtor* (Jer. 47:4), and the Philistim are joined with the Caphtorim, Gen. 10:14. In like manner the Syrians were brought up from Kir when they had been carried away thither, 2 Ki. 16:9. Note, If God's Israel lose the peculiarity of their holiness, they lose the peculiarity of their privileges; and what was designed as a favour of special grace shall be set in another light, shall have its property altered, and shall become an act of *common providence;* if professors liken themselves to the world, God will level them with the world. And, if we live not up to the obligation of God's mercies, we forfeit the honour and comfort of them.

5. How graciously God will separate between the precious and the vile in the day of retribution. Though the wicked Israelites shall be as the wicked Ethiopians, and their being called Israelites shall stand them in no stead, yet the pious Israelites shall not be as the *wicked* ones; no, the *Judge of all the earth will do right,* more right than to *slay the righteous with the wicked,* Gen. 18:25. His *eyes are upon the sinful kingdom,* to spy out those in it who preserve their integrity and swim against the stream, who sigh and cry for the abominations of their land, and they shall be marked for preservation, so that the destruction shall not be total: *I will not utterly destroy the house of Jacob,* not ruin them by wholesale and in the gross, good and bad together, but I will distinguish, as becomes a righteous judge. The house of Israel shall be *sifted as corn is sifted;* they shall be greatly hurried, and shaken, and tossed, but still in the hands of God, in both his hands, as the sieve in the hands of him that sifts (*v.* 9): *I will sift the house of Israel among all nations.* Wherever they are shaken and scattered, God will have his eye upon them, and will take care to separate between the corn and chaff, which was the thing he designed in sifting them. (1.) The righteous ones among them, that are as the solid wheat, shall none of them perish; they shall be delivered either from or through the common calamities of the kingdom; *not the least grain shall fall on the earth,* so as to be lost and forgotten — not the least *stone* (so the word is), for the good corn is weighty as a stone in comparison with that which we call *light corn.* Note, Whatever shakings there may be in the world, God does and will effectually provide that none who are truly his shall be truly miserable. (2.) The wicked ones among them who are hardened in their sins shall all of them perish, *v.* 10. See what a height of impiety they have come to: *They say, The evil shall not overtake nor prevent us.* They think they are innocent, and do not deserve punishment, or that the profession they make of relation to God will be their exemption and security from punishment, or that they shall be able to make their part good against the judgments of God, that they shall flee so swiftly from them that they shall not overtake them, or guard so carefully against them that they shall not prevent or surprise them. Note, Hope of impunity is the deceitful refuge of the impenitent. But see what it will come to at last: *All the sinners* that thus flatter themselves, and affront God, shall *die by the sword,* the sword of war, which to them shall be the sword of divine vengeance; yea, though they be the *sinners of my people,* for their profession shall not be their protection. Note, Evil is often nearest those that put it at the greatest distance from them.

Verses 11–15

To him to whom all the prophets bear witness this prophet, here in the close, bears his testimony, and speaks of *that day,* those days that shall come, in which God will do great things for his church, by the setting up of the kingdom of the Messiah, for the rejecting of which the rejection of the Jews was foretold in the foregoing verses. The promise here is said to agree to the planting of the Christian church, and in that to be fulfilled, Acts 15:15–17. It is promised,

I. That in the Messiah the kingdom of David shall be restored (*v.* 11); the *tabernacle of David* it is called, that is, his house and family, which, though great and fixed, yet, in comparison with the kingdom of heaven, was mean and movable as a tabernacle. The church militant, in its present state, dwelling as in shepherds' tents to feed, as in soldiers' tents to fight, is the *tabernacle of David.* God's tabernacle is called the tabernacle of David because David desired and chose to *dwell in God's tabernacle for ever,* Ps. 61:4. Now, 1. These tabernacles had fallen an gone to decay, the royal family was so impoverished, its power abridged, its honour stained, and laid in the dust; for many of that race degenerated, and in the captivity it lost the imperial dignity. Sore breaches were made upon it, and at length it was laid in ruins. So it was with the church of the Jews; in the latter days of it its glory departed; it was like a tabernacle broken down and brought to ruin, in respect both of purity and of prosperity. 2. By Jesus Christ these tabernacles were raised and rebuilt. In him God's covenant with David had its accomplishment; and the glory of that house, which was not only sullied, but quite sunk, revived again; the *breaches* of it were *closed* and its *ruins raised up, as in the days of old;* nay, the spiritual glory of the family of Christ far exceeded the temporal glory of the family of David when it was at its height. In him also God's covenant with Israel had its accomplishment, and in the gospel-church the tabernacle of God was set up among men again, and raised up out of the ruins of the Jewish state. This is quoted in the first council at Jerusalem as referring to the calling in of the Gentiles and God's *taking out of them a people for his name.* Note, While the world stands God will have a church in it, and, if it be fallen down in one place and among one people, it shall be raised up elsewhere.

II. That that kingdom shall be enlarged, and the territories of it shall extend far, by the accession of many countries to it (*v.* 12), that the house of David may possess the *remnant of Edom, and of all the heathen,* that is, that Christ may have them given him for his *inheritance,* even the *uttermost parts of the earth for his possession,* Ps. ii. 8. Those that had been strangers and enemies shall become willing faithful subjects to the Son of David, shall be *added to the church,* or those of them that are *called by my name, saith the Lord,* that is, that belong to the election of grace and are ordained to eternal life (Acts 13:48), for it is true of the Gentiles as well as of the Jews that *the election hath obtained* and *the rest were blinded,* Rom. 11:7. Christ died *to gather together in one the children of God that were scattered abroad,* here said to be those that were *called by his name.* The promise is to all that are *afar off,* even as *many* of them *as the Lord our God shall call,* Acts 2:39. St. James expounds this as a promise *that the residue of men should seek after the Lord, even all the Gentiles upon whom my name is called.* But may the promise be depended upon? Yes, the Lord says this, who does this, who can do it, who has determined to do it, the power of whose grace is engaged for the doing of it, and with whom saying and doing are not two things, as they are with us.

III. That in the kingdom of the Messiah there shall be great plenty, an abundance of all good things that the country produces (*v.* 13): *The ploughman shall overtake the reaper,* that is, there shall be such a plentiful harvest every year, and so much corn to be gathered in, that it shall last all summer, even till autumn, when it is time to begin to plough again; and in like manner the vintage shall continue till seed-time, and there shall be such abundance of grapes that even the *mountains shall drop new wine* into the vessels of the grape-gatherers, and the hills that were dry and barren shall be moistened and shall melt with the *fatness* or *mellowness* (as we call it) *of the soil.* Compare this with Joel 2:24, and 3:18. This must certainly be understood of the abundance of spiritual blessings in heavenly things, which all those are, and shall be, blessed with, who are in sincerity added to Christ and his church; they shall be abundantly replenished with the goodness of God's house, with the graces and comforts of his Spirit; they shall have bread, the bread of life, to *strengthen their hearts,* and the wine of divine consolations to *make them glad — meat indeed* and *drink indeed* — all the benefit that comes to the souls of men from the word and Spirit of God. These had been long confined to the vineyard of the Jewish church; divine revelation, and the power that attended it, were to be found only within that enclosure; but in gospel-times the mountains and hills of the Gentile world shall be enriched with these privileges by the gospel of Christ preached, and professed, and received in the power of it. When great multitudes were converted to the faith of Christ, and nations were born at once, when the preachers of the gospel were *always caused to triumph in* the success of their preaching, then the *ploughman overtook the reaper;* and when, the Gentile churches were *enriched in all utterance, and in all knowledge,* and all manner of *spiritual gifts* (1 Co. 1:5), then the *mountains dropped sweet wine.*

IV. That the kingdom of the Messiah shall be well peopled; as the country shall be replenished, so shall the cities be; there shall be mouths for this meat, *v.* 14. Those that were carried captives shall be brought back out of their captivity; their enemies shall not be able to detain them in the land of their captivity, nor shall they themselves incline to settle in it, but the remnant shall return, and shall *build the waste cities and inhabit them,* shall form themselves into Christian churches and set up pure doctrine, worship, and discipline among them, according to the gospel charter, by which Christ's cities are incorporated; and they shall enjoy the benefit and comfort thereof; they shall *plant vineyards,* and *make gardens.* Though the mountains and hills drop wine, and the privileges of the gospel-church are laid in common, yet they shall enclose for themselves, not to monopolize these privileges, to the exclusion of others, but to appropriate and improve these privileges, in communion with others, and they shall *drink the wine,* and *eat the fruit,* of their own *vineyards and gardens;* for those that take pains in religion, as men must do about their vineyards and gardens, shall have both the pleasure and profit of it. The *bringing again* of the *captivity* of God's Israel, which is here promised, may refer to the cancelling of the ceremonial law, which had been long to God's Israel as a *yoke of bondage,* and the investing of them in the liberty wherewith Christ came to make his church free, Gal. 5:1.

V. That the kingdom of the Messiah shall take such deep rooting in the world as never to be rooted out of it (*v.* 15): *I will plant them upon their land.* God's spiritual Israel shall be planted by the right hand of God himself upon the land assigned them, and *they shall no more be pulled up out of it,* as the old Jewish church was. God will preserve them from throwing themselves out of it by a total apostasy, and will preserve them from being thrown out of it by malice of their enemies; the church may be corrupted, but shall not quite forsake God, may be persecuted, but shall not quite be forsaken of God, so that the gates of hell, neither with their temptations nor with their terrors, shall prevail against it. Two things secure the perpetuity of the church: — 1. God's grants to it: It *is the land which I have given them;* and God will confirm and maintain his own grants. The part he has given to his people is that good part which shall never be taken from them; he will not revoke his grant, and all the powers of earth and hell shall not invalidate it. 2. Its interest in him: He is *the Lord thy God,* who has said it, and will make it good, *thine, O Israel!* who shall *reign for ever* as thine *unto all generations.* And because he lives the church shall live also.

AN EXPOSITION, WITH PRACTICAL OBSERVATIONS, OF

THE PROPHECY OF OBADIAH

This is the shortest of all the books of the Old Testament, the least of those tribes, and yet is not to be passed by, or thought meanly of, for this penny has Caesar's image and superscription upon it; it is stamped with a divine authority. There may appear much of God in a short sermon, in a little book; and much good may be done by it, *multum in parvo — much in a little.* Mr. Norris says, "If angels were to write books, we should have few folios." That may be very precious which is not voluminous. This book is entitled, *The Vision of Obadiah.* Who this Obadiah was does not appear from any other scripture. Some of the ancients imagined him to be the same with that Obadiah that was steward to Ahab's household (1 Ki. 18:3); and, if so, he that hid and fed the prophets had indeed a prophet's reward, when he was himself made a prophet. But that is a conjecture which has no ground. This Obadiah, it is probable, was of a later date, some think contemporary with Hosea, Joel, and Amos; others think he lived about the time of the destruction of Jerusalem, when the children of Edom so barbarously triumphed in that destruction. However, what he wrote was what he saw; it is his *vision.* Probably there was much more which he was divinely inspired to speak, but this is all he was inspired to write; and all he writes is concerning Edom. It is a foolish fancy of some of the Jews that because he prophesies only concerning Edom he was himself an Edomite by birth, but a proselyte to the Jewish religion. Other prophets prophesied against Edom, and some of them seem to have borrowed from him in their predictions against Edom, as Jer. 49:7, etc.; Eze. 25:12, etc. Out of the mouth of these two or three witnesses every word will be established.

This book is wholly concerning Edom, a nation nearly allied and near adjoining to Israel, and yet an enemy to the seed of Jacob, inheriting the enmity of their father Esau to Jacob. Now here we have, after the preface (*v.* 1). I. Threatenings against Edom, 1. That their pride should be humbled (*v.* 2–4). 2. That their wealth should be plundered (*v.* 5–7). 3. That their wisdom should be infatuated (*v.* 8, 9). 4. That their spiteful behaviour towards God's Israel should be avenged (*v.* 10–16). II. Gracious promises to Israel; that they shall be restored and reformed, and shall be victorious over the Edomites, and become masters of their land and the lands of others of their neighbours (*v.* 17–20), and that the kingdom of the Messiah shall be set up by the bringing in of the great salvation (*v.* 21).

Verses 1–9

Edom is the nation against which this prophecy is levelled, and which, some think, is put for all the enemies of Israel, that shall be brought down first or last. The rabbin by Edom understand Rome. Rome Christians they understand it of, and have an implacable enmity to it a such; but, if we understand it of Rome antichristian, we shall find the passages of it applicable enough. And though Edom was mortified in the times of the Maccabees, as it had been before by Jehoshaphat, yet its destruction seems to have been typical, as their father Esau's rejection, and to have had further reference to the destruction of the enemies of the gospel-church; for so shall all God's enemies perish; and we find (Isa. 34:5) the *sword of the Lord* coming down *upon Idumea,* to signify the general day of God's recompences for the controversy of Zion, *v.* 8. Some have well observed that it could not but be a great temptation to the people of Israel, when they saw themselves, who were the children of beloved Jacob, in trouble, and the Edomites, not only prospering, but triumphing over them in their troubles; and therefore God gives them a prospect of the destruction of Edom, which should be total and final, and of a happy issue of their own correction. Now we may observe here,

I. A declaration of war against Edom, (*v.* 1): *"We have heard a rumour,* or rather *an order, from the Lord,* the God of hosts; he has given the word of command; it is his counsel and decree, which can neither be reversed nor resisted, that all who do mischief to his people shall certainly bring mischief upon themselves. We have heard a report that God is raised up out of his holy habitation, and is preparing his throne for judgment; and *an ambassador is sent among the heathen,"* a *herald* rather, some minister or messenger of Providence, to alarm the nations, or the Lord's prophets, who gave each nation its burden. Those whom God employs cry to each other, *Arise ye,* stir up yourselves and one another, and let *us rise up against Edom in battle.* The confederate forces under Nebuchadnezzar thus animate themselves and one another to make a descent upon that country: *Gather yourselves together, and come against her;* so it is in the parallel place, Jer. 49:14. Note, When God has bloody work to do among the enemies of his church he will find out and fit up both hands and hearts to do it.

II. A prediction of the success of that war. Edom shall certainly be subdued, and spoiled, and brought down; for all her confidences shall fail her and stand her in no stead, and in like manner shall all the enemies of God's church be disappointed in those things which they stayed themselves upon.

1. Do they depend upon their grandeur, the figure they make among the nations, their influence upon them, and interest in them? That shall dwindle (*v.* 2): *"Behold, I have made thee small among the heathen,* so that none of thy neighbours will court thy friendship, or court an alliance with thee; *thou art greatly despised* among them, and looked upon with contempt, as an infatuated and unfaithful nation." And thus (*v.* 3) *the pride of thy heart has deceived thee.* Note, (1.) Those that think well of themselves are apt to fancy that others think well of them too; but, when they come to make trial of them, they will find themselves mistaken, and thus their pride deceives them and by it slays them. (2.) God can easily lay those low that have magnified and exalted themselves, and will find out a way

to do it, for he *resists the proud;* and we often see those small and greatly despised who once looked very big and were greatly caressed and admired.

2. Do they depend upon the fortifications of their country, both by nature and art, and glory in the advantages they have thereby? Those also shall deceive them. They *dwelt in the clefts of the rock,* as an eagle in her nest, and their *habitation* was *high,* not only exalted above their neighbours, which was the matter of their pride, but fortified against their enemies, which was the matter of their security, so high as to be out of the reach of danger. Now observe, (1.) What Edom says in the pride of his heart: *Who shall bring me down to the ground?* He speaks with a confidence of his own strength, and a contempt of God's judgments, as if almighty power itself could not overpower him. As for *all his enemies,* even God himself, he *puffs at them* (Ps. 10:5), sets them all at defiance. Their father Esau had *sold his birthright,* and yet they lifted up themselves, as if to them had still pertained the *excellency of dignity and power.* Many forfeit their privileges, and yet boast of them. Because Edom is high and lifted up, he imagines none can bring him down. Note, Carnal security is a sin that most easily besets men in the day of their pomp, power, and prosperity, and does, as much as any thing, both ripen men for ruin and aggravate it when it comes. (2.) What God says to this, *v.* 4. If men will dare to challenge Omnipotence, their challenge shall be taken up: *Who shall bring me down?* says Edom. *"I will,"* says God. *"Though thou exalt thyself as the eagle* that soars high and builds high, nay, *though thou set thy nest among stars,* higher than ever any eagle flew, it is but in thy own imagination, and *thence will I bring thee down."* This we had Jer. 49:15, 16. Note, Sinners will certainly be made ashamed of their pride and security of their pride when it has a fall and of their security when their confidences fail their expectation.

3. Do they depend upon their wealth and treasure, the abundance of which is looked upon as the sinews of war? Is their money their defence? Is that their strong city? It is so only in their own conceit, for it shall rather expose them than protect them; it shall be made a prey to the enemy, and they for the sake of it, *v.* 5. 6. Much to this purport we had Jer. 49:9, 10. Only here comes in, in a parenthesis, *How art thou cut off!* thou and all thy stores. The prophet foretels it, but laments it, that the thread of their prosperity was cut off. How art thou fallen, and how great is thy fall! *How art thou stupefied!* so the Chaldee words it. How senseless art thou under these desolating judgments, as if they were but common strokes! But he shows that it should be an utter ruin, not a usual calamity; for, (1.) It is indeed a usual calamity for those that have wealth to have it stolen, and to lose a little out of their great deal. *Thieves come to them* (for where the carcase is, there will the birds of prey be gathered together), *robbers come by night,* and they *steal till they have enough,* what they have occasion for, what they have a mind for; they steal no more than they think they can carry away, and out of a great stock it is scarcely missed. Those that rob orchards, or vineyards, carry off what they think fit; but they *leave some grapes,* some fruit for the owner, who easily bears his loss perhaps and soon recruits it. But, (2.) It shall not be so with Edom; his wealth shall all be taken away, and nothing shall escape the hands of the destroying army, not that which is most precious and valuable, *v.* 6. *How are the things of Esau,* the things he sets his heart upon and places his happiness in, his good things, his best things, how are these things, which were so carefully treasured up and concealed, now *searched out* by the enemy and seized! *How are the hidden things,* his hidden treasures, plundered, rifled, and *sought up!* His hoards, that had not see the light for many years, are now a spoil to the enemy. Note, Treasures on earth, though ever so fast locked up and ever so artfully hidden, cannot be so safely laid up but that thieves may break through and steal; it is therefore our wisdom to *lay up for ourselves treasures in heaven.*

4. Do they depend upon their alliances with neighbouring states and potentates? Those also shall fail them (*v.* 7): "The *men of thy confederacy,* all of them, the Ammonites and Moabites, and other thy high allies that were at *peace with thee,* that entered into a league offensive and defensive with thee, that solemnly engaged not only to do thee no hurt, but to do thee all the service the could, *did eat thy bread,* were magnificently treated and entertained by thee, lived upon thee; their soldiers had free quarter in thy country, and took pay as thy auxiliaries; they *brought thee even to the border* of thy land, were very respectful to thy ambassadors, and brought them on their way home, even to the utmost limits of their country; they seemed forward to serve thee with their forces when thou hadst occasion for them, and came along with thee *to the border,* till thou wast just ready to engage the invading enemy; but then," (1.) "They had *deceived thee;* they flew back and retreated when thou wast in extremity, and proved as a broken reed to the traveller that is weary, and as the brooks in summer to the traveller that is thirsty; they bear no weight, yield no relief." Nay, (2.) "They have *prevailed against thee;* they were too hard for thee in the treaty imposed upon thee, and by cheating thee ruined thee, brought thee into danger, and there left thee an easy prey to thy enemy." Note, Those that make flesh their arm arm it against them. Yet this was not the worst. (3.) "They have *laid a wound under thee;* that is, they have laid that under thee for a stay and support, for a foundation to rely on, for a pillow to repose on, which will prove a wound to thee; not as thorns only, but as swords." If God lay under us the arms of his power and love, these will be firm and easy under us; the God of our covenant will never deceive us. But if we trust to *the men of our confederacy,* and what they will lay under us, it may prove to us a *wound* and *dishonour.* And observe the just censure here passed upon Edom for trusting to those who thus played tricks with him: *"There is no understanding in him,* or else he would never have put it into their power to betray him by putting such a confidence in them." Note, Those show they have no understanding in them who, when they are encouraged to trust in the Creator, put a cheat upon themselves by reposing a confidence in the creature.

5. Do they depend upon the politics of their counsellors? These shall fail them, *v.* 8. Edom had been famous for great statesmen, men of learning and experience, that sat at the help of government, and were masters of all the arts of management, that in all treaties used to outwit their neighbours; but now the *counsellors* have become *fools,* and the wise God makes them so: *Shall I not in that day destroy the wise men out of Edom?* As men they shall fall by the sword in common with others (Ps. 49:10), and their wisdom shall not secure them; as wise men they shall be infatuated in all their counsels; their best-laid designs shall be baffled, their measures broken, and those very projects by which they thought to establish themselves and the public interests shall be the ruin of both. Thus *wisdom perishes from Teman,* as it is in the parallel place, Jer. 49:7. This was, (1.) The just punishment of their folly in trusting to an arm of flesh: *There is no understanding in them, v.* 7. They have not sense to trust in a living God, and a God of truth, but put confidence in men that are frail, fickle, and false; and therefore God will *destroy their understanding.* Note, God will justly deny those understanding to keep out of the way of danger that will not use their understanding to keep out of the way of sin. He that will be foolish, let him be foolish still. (2.) It was the forerunner of their destruction. A nation is certainly marked for ruin when God hides the things that belong to its peace from the eyes of those that are entrusted with its counsels. *Quos Deus vult perdere, eos dementat — God infatuates those whom he designs to destroy.* Job 12:17.

6. Do they depend upon the strength and courage of their soldiers? They are not only able-bodied, but men of spirit and courage, that can face an enemy and stand their ground; but now (*v.* 9), *Thy mighty men, O Teman! shall be dismayed;* their courage shall fail them, *to the end that every one of the mount of Esau may be cut off by slaughter,* and none escape. The weak, and feeble, and unarmed must fall of course into the hand of the destroyer when the *mighty men are dismayed,* and not only lose the day, but lose their lives, because they have lost their spirit. *Howl, fir-trees, if the cedars be shaken.* Note, The death or disuniting of the mighty often proves the death and destruction of the many; and it is in vain to depend upon mighty men for our protection if we have not an almighty God for us, much less if we have an almighty God against us.

Verses 10–16

When we have read Edom's doom, no less than utter ruin, it is natural to ask, *Why, what evil has he done?* What is the ground of God's controversy with him? Many things, no doubt, were amiss in Edom; they were a sinful people, and *a people laden with iniquity.* But that one single crime which is laid to their charge, as filling their measure and bringing this ruin upon them, that for which they here stand indicted, of which they are convicted, and for which they are condemned, is the injury they had done to the people of God (*v.* 10): "It is *for thy violence against thy brother Jacob,* that ancient and hereditary grudge which thou hast borne to the people of Israel, that all this *shame shall cover thee* and *thou shalt be cut off for ever."* Note, Injuries to men are affronts to God, the righteous God, that loveth righteousness and hateth wickedness; and, as the Judge of all the earth, he will give redress to those that suffer wrong and take vengeance on those that do wrong. All violence, all *unrighteousness, is sin;* but it is a great aggravation of the violence if it be done either, 1. Against any of our own people; it is violence *against thy brother,* thy near relation, to whom thou shouldst be a *goël — a redeemer,* whom it is thy duty to right if others wronged him; how wicked is it then for thee thyself to wrong him! Thou *slanderest* and abusest *thy own mother's son;* this makes the sin *exceedingly sinful,* Ps. 50:20. Or, 2. Much more if it be done against any of God's people; "it is thy brother Jacob that is in covenant with God, and dear to him. Thou hatest him whom God has loved, and because God espouses and will plead with jealousy, and in whose interests God is pleased so far to interest himself that he takes the violence done to him as done to himself. *Whoso touches Jacob touches the apple of the eye of Jacob's God."* So that it is *crimen laesae majestatis — high treason,* for which, as for high treason, let Edom expect an ignominious punishment: *Shame shall cover thee,* and a ruining one; *thou shalt be cut off for ever.*

In the following verses we are told more particularly, I. What the violence was which Edom did against his brother Jacob, and what are the proofs of this charge. It does not appear that the Edomites did themselves invade Israel, but that was more for want of power than will; they had malice enough to do it, but were not a match for them. But that which is laid to their charge is their barbarous conduct towards Judah and Jerusalem when they were in distress, and ready to be destroyed, probably by the Chaldeans, or upon occasion of some other of the calamities of the Jews; for this seems to have been always their temper towards them. See this charged upon the Edomites (Ps. 137:7), that *in the day of Jerusalem they said, Rase it, rase it,* and Eze. 25:12. They are here told particularly what they did, by being told what they should not have done (*v.* 12–14): "Thou *shouldst not have looked,* thou *shouldst not have entered;* but thou didst so." Note, In reflecting upon ourselves it is good to compare what we have done with what we should have done, our practice with the rule, that we may discover wherein we have done amiss, have *done those things which we ought not to have done.* We should not have been where we were at such a time, should not have been in such and such company, should not have said what we said, nor have taken the liberty that we took. Sin thus looked upon, in the glass of the commandment, will appear exceedingly sinful. Let us see,

1. What was the case of Judah and Jerusalem when the Edomites behaved themselves thus basely and insulted over them. (1.) It was a day of distress with them (*v.* 12): It was the *day of their calamity,* so it is called three times, *v.* 13. With the Edomites it was a day of prosperity and peace when with the Israelites it was a day of distress and calamity, for judgment commonly *begins at the house of God.* Children are corrected when strangers are let alone. (2.) It was the day of *their destruction* (*v.* 12), when both city and country were laid waste, were laid *in ruins.* (3.) It was a day when *foreigners entered into the gates of Jerusalem,* when the city, after a long siege, was broken up, and the great officers of the king of Babylon's army came, and sat in the gates, as judges of the land; when they cast lots upon the spoils of Jerusalem, as the soldiers on Christ's garments, what shares each of the conquerors shall have, what shares of the lands, what shares of the goods; or they cast lots to determine when and where they should attack it. (4.) It was a day when the *strangers carried away captive his forces* (*v.* 11), took the men of war prisoners of war, and carried them off, in poverty and shame, to their own

country, or such a multitude of captives that they were as an army. (5.) "It was a day when thy brother himself, that had long been at home, at rest in his own land, *became a stranger,* an exile in a strange land." Now, when this was the woeful case of the Jews, the Edomites, their neighbours and brethren, should have pitied them and helped them, condoled with them and comforted them, and should have trembled to think that their own turn would come next; for, *if this was done in the green tree, what shall be done in the dry?* But,

2. See what was the conduct of the Edomites towards them when they were in this distress, for which they are here condemned. (1.) They looked with pleasure upon the affliction of God's people; they *stood on the other side* (*v.* 11), afar off, when they should have come in to the relief of their distressed neighbours, and *looked upon them,* and *their day, looked on their affliction* (*v.* 12, 13), with a careless unconcerned eye, as the priest and Levite looked upon the wounded man, and *passed by on the other side.* Those have a great deal to answer for that are idle spectators of the troubles and afflictions of their neighbours, when they are capable of being their active helpers. But this was not all; they looked upon it with a scornful eye, with an eye of complacency and satisfaction; they looked and laughed to see Israel in distress, saying, *Aha! so we would have it.* They fed their eyes with the rueful spectacle of Jerusalem's ruin, and looked at it as those that had long looked for it and often wished to see it. Note, We must take heed with what eye we look upon the afflictions of our brethren; and, if we cannot look upon them with a gracious eye of sympathy and tenderness, it is better not to look upon them at all: *Thou shouldst not have looked* as thou didst *upon the day of thy brother.* (2.) They triumphed and insulted over them, upbraided their brethren with their sorrows, and made themselves and their companions merry with them. They *rejoiced over the children of Judah in the day of their destruction.* They had not the good manners to conceal the pleasure they took in Judah's destruction and to dissemble it, but openly declared it, and rudely and insolently declared it *to them; they rejoiced over them,* crowed, and hectored, and trampled upon them. Those have the spirit of Edomites that can rejoice over any, especially over Israelites, in the day of their calamity. (3.) They *spoke proudly — magnified the mouth* (so the word is), against Israel, talked with a great disdain of the suffering Israelites, and with an air of haughtiness of the present safety and prosperity of Edom, as it if might be inferred from their present different state that the tables were turned, and now Esau was beloved, and the favourite of heaven, and Jacob hated and rejected. Note, Those must expect to be in some way or other effectually humbled and mortified themselves that are puffed up and made proud by the humiliations and mortifications of others. (4.) They went further yet, for they *entered into the gate* of God's people in the day of their calamity, and *laid hands on their substance.* Though they did not help to conquer them, they helped to plunder them, and put in for a share in the prey, *v.* 13. Jerusalem was thrown open, and then they entered in; its wealth was thrown about, and they seized it for themselves, excusing it with this, that they might as well take it as let it be lost; whereas it was taking what was not their own. Babylon lays Jerusalem waste, but Edom, by meddling with the spoil, becomes *particeps criminis — partaker of the crime,* and shall be reckoned with as an accessary *ex post facto — after the fact.* Note, Those do but impoverish themselves that think to enrich themselves by the ruins of the people of God; and those deceive themselves who think they may call all that substance their own which they can lay their hands on in a day of calamity. (5.) They did yet worse things; they not only robbed their brethren, but murdered them, in the day of their calamity; laid hands not only on their substance, but on their persons, *v.* 14. When the victorious sword of the Chaldeans was making bloody work among the Jews many made their escape, and were in a fair way to save themselves by flight; but the Edomites basely intercepted them, *stood in the cross-way* where several roads met, by each of which the trembling Israelites were making the best of their way from the fury of the pursuers, and there they stopped them: some they barbarously and cowardlike cut off themselves; others they took prisoners, and delivered up to the pursuers, only to ingratiate themselves with them, because they were now the conquerors. They *should not have been* thus *cruel* to those that lay at their mercy, and never had done, nor were every likely to do, them any hurt; they should not have betrayed those whom they had such a fair opportunity to protect; but such are the *tender mercies of the wicked.* One cannot read this without a high degree of compassion towards those who were thus basely abused, who when they fled from the sword of an open enemy, and thought they had got out of the reach of it, fell upon and fell by the sword of a treacherous neighbour, whom they were not apprehensive of any danger from. Nor can one read this without a high degree of indignation towards those who were so perfectly lost to all humanity as to exercise such cruelty upon such proper objects of compassion. (6.) In all this they joined with the open enemies and persecutors of Israel: *Even thou wast as one of them,* an accessary equally guilty with the principals. He that joins in with the evil doers, and is aiding and abetting in their evil deeds, shall be reckoned, and shall be reckoned with, as one of them.

II. What the shame is that shall cover them for this violence of theirs. 1. They shall soon find that the cup is going round, even the cup of trembling; and, when they come to be in the same calamitous condition that the Israel of God is now in, they will be ashamed to remember how they triumphed over them (*v.* 15): *The day of the Lord is near upon all the heathen,* when God will recompense tribulation to the troublers of his church. Though judgment begin at the house of God, it shall not end there. This should effectually restrain us from triumphing over others in their misery, that we know not how soon it may be our own case. 2. Their enmity to the people of God, and the injuries they had done them, shall be recompensed into their own bosoms: *As thou hast done, it shall be done unto thee.* The righteous God will render both to nations and to particular persons *according to their works;* and the punishment is often made exactly to answer to the sin, and those that have abused others come to be themselves abused in like manner. The just and jealous God will find out a time and way to avenge the wrongs done to his people on those that have been injurious to them. *As you have drunk upon my holy mountain* (*v.* 16), that is, as God's professing people, who inhabit his holy mountain, have drunk deeply of the cup of affliction (and their being of the holy mountain would not excuse them), *so shall all the heathen drink,* in their turn, of the same bitter cup; for, if God *bring evil on the city that is called by his name, shall those be unpunished* that never knew his name? See Jer. 25:29. And it is part of the burden of Edom (Jer. 49:12), *Those whose judgment was not to drink of the cup* (who had reason to promise themselves an exemption from it) have assuredly drunken, and *shall Edom* that is the generation of God's wrath *go unpunished?* No, *thou shalt surely drink of it;* the *cup of trembling shall be taken out of the hand* of God's people, and put *into the hand of those that afflict them,* Isa. 51:22, 23. Nay, they may expect their case to be worse in the day of their distress than that of Israel was in their day; for, (1.) The afflictions of God's people were but for a moment, and soon had an end, but their enemies shall *drink continually* the *wine of God's wrath,* Rev. 14:10. (2.) The dregs of the cup are reserved for the *wicked of the earth* (Ps. 75:8); they shall *drink and swallow down,* or *sup up* (as the margin reads it), shall drink it to the bottom. (3.) The people of God, though they may be made to drink of the wine of astonishment for a while (Ps. 60:3), shall yet recover, and come to themselves again; but the heathen shall drink and be *as though they had not been;* there shall be neither any remains nor any remembrance of them, but they shall be wholly extirpated and rooted out. *So let all thy enemies perish, O Lord!* so they shall perish, if the turn not.

Verses 17–21

After the destruction of the church's enemies is threatened, which will be completely accomplished in the great day of recompence, and that judgment for which Christ came once, and will come again, into this world, here follow precious promises of the salvation of the church, with which this prophecy concludes, and those of Joel and Amos did, which, however they might be in part fulfilled in the return of the Jews out of Babylon notwithstanding the triumphs of Edom in their captivity, as if it were perpetual, are yet, doubtless, to have their full accomplishment in that great salvation wrought out by Jesus Christ, to which all the prophets bore witness. It is promised here,

I. That there shall be salvation upon Mount Zion, that holy hill where God sets his anointed King (Ps. 2:6): *Upon Mount Zion shall be deliverance, v.* 17. There shall be *those that escape;* so the margin. A remnant of Israel, *upon the holy mountain* shall be saved, *v.* 16. Christ said, *Salvation is of the Jews,* Jn. 4:22. God wrought deliverances for the Jews, typical of our redemption by Christ. But Mount Zion is the gospel-church, from which the New-Testament law *went forth,* Isa. 2:3. There salvation shall be preached and prayed for; to the gospel-church those are added who *shall be saved;* and for those who come in faith and hope to this Mount Zion deliverance shall be wrought from wrath and the curse, from sin, and death, and hell, while those who continue afar off shall be left to perish.

II. That, where there is salvation, there shall be sanctification in order to it: *And there shall be holiness,* to prepare and qualify the children of Zion for this deliverance; for wherever God designs glory he gives grace. Temporal deliverances are indeed wrought for us in mercy when with them there is holiness, when there is wrought in us a disposition to receive them with love and gratitude to God; when we are sanctified, they are sanctified to us. Holiness is itself a great deliverance, and an earnest of that eternal salvation which we look for. *There,* upon Mount Zion, in the gospel-church, *shall be holiness;* for that is it which *becomes God's house for ever,* and the great design of the gospel, and its grace, is to plant and promote holiness. There shall be the Holy Spirit, the holy ordinances, the holy Jesus, and a select remnant of holy souls, in whom, and among whom, the holy God will delight to dwell. Note, Where there is holiness there shall be deliverance.

III. That this salvation and sanctification shall spread, and prevail, and get ground in the world: The *house of Jacob,* even this *Mount Zion,* with the deliverance and their holiness there wrought, shall *possess their possessions;* that is, the gospel-church shall be set up among the heathen, and shall replenish the earth; the apostles of Christ by their preaching shall gain possession of the hearts of men for him whose messengers and ministers they are, and when they possess their hearts they shall *possess their possessions,* for those who have given up themselves to the Lord give up all they have to him. When Lydia's heart was opened to Christ her house was opened to his ministers. When the Gentile nations became *nations of those that were saved,* were disciplined, *walked in the light* of the Lord, and *brought their glory and honour into the new Jerusalem* (Rev. 21:24), then the *house of Jacob possessed their possessions.* This is the part fulfilled by the planting of the Christian religion in the world, and shall be fulfilled yet more and more by the setting up of Christ's throne where Satan's seat is, and the erecting of trophies of his victory upon the ruins of the devil's kingdom. Now here is foretold,

1. How this possession shall be *gained,* and the opposition given to it got over (*v.* 18): *The house of Jacob shall be a fire, and the house of Joseph a flame,* for their God is, and will be, a *consuming fire;* and the house of Esau shall be for *stubble,* easily devoured and consumed by this fire. This is fulfilled, (1.) In the conversion of multitudes by the grace of Christ; the gospel, preached in the house of Jacob and Joseph, and there owned and professed, shall be as a fire and a flame to melt and to soften hard hearts, to burn up the dross of sin and corruption, that they may be purified and refined with the *spirit of judgment and* the *spirit of burning.* Christ, when he comes, shall be *as a refiner's fire,* Mal. 3:1, 2. (2.) In the confusion of all the impenitent implacable enemies of the gospel of Christ, that oppose it and do all they can to hinder the setting up of the kingdom of the Messiah by it. The gospel day is a day that *burns like an oven,* in which *all the proud, and all that do wickedly, shall be a stubble,* Mal. 4:1. Jacob and Joseph shall be as a fire and a flame; for those that meddle with them, to do them hurt, will find that they do so at their peril; they shall be to them as *a torch of fire in a sheaf,* Zec. 12:6. The word of God in the mouth of his ministers is said to be like fire, and the people as wood to be devoured by it, Jer. 5:14. And the *man of sin* is to be *consumed by the breath of Christ's mouth,* 2 Th. 2:8.

Those that are not refined as gold by fire of the gospel shall be consumed as dross by it; for it will be a savour either of life or of death. When idols and idolatry were abolished, and the wealth and power of nations were brought into the service of Christ and his gospel, and the spoils of the *strong man armed* were divided by him that was *stronger than he,* then the house of Jacob and Joseph devoured *the house of Esau,* so that there was none of them left remaining. This the Lord *spoke* by his prophets, and this he did by his apostles.

2. How far this possession shall extend, *v.* 19, 20. This is described in Jewish language, which speaks the accession made to the land of Israel, after the return out of captivity into Babylon. The *captivity of this host of Israel,* that is, this host of Israel that have been so long in captivity and now they have come back are still called the *children of the captivity,* these shall not only recover their own land, but shall gain ground upon their neighbours adjoining to them, some of whom shall become proselytes and shall incorporate with the Jews, who, by possessing them in a holy communion, possess their land. We must reckon ourselves truly enriched by the conversion of our neighbours to the fear of God and the faith of Christ, and their coming to join with us in the worship of God. Such an accession to our Christian communion we must reckon to be more our wealth and strength than an accession to our estates. Or, The ancient inhabitants of those lands that were carried away into captivity being lost, and never returning to their estates, the children of Israel shall take possession of that which lies next them; for their numbers shall so increase that their own land shall be too strait for them, and their neighbours' estates shall escheat to them *ob defectum sanguinis — through default of heirs.* They shall enter upon that which is adjoining to them. The country of Esau shall be possessed by those *of the south* parts of Canaan, for to them it lies contiguous. Those *of the plain,* on the *west* of Canaan, which was a champaign country, shall enter upon *the land of the Philistines,* their neighbours. Those of Judah, which was the chief of the two returning tribes, shall possess *the field of Ephraim and Samaria,* which before belonged to the ten tribes; and Benjamin, the other tribe, shall possess Gilead on the other side of Jordan, which had belonged to the two tribes and a half. The kingdom of Israel shall join with that of Judah both in civil and sacred interests, and, as friends and brethren, shall mutually possess and enjoy one another; and both together shall *possess the Canaanites,* even to Zarephath, which *belongeth to Zidon;* and Jerusalem shall possess the *cities of the south,* even to Sepharad. Thus did the Jews enlarge their borders on all sides. The modern rabbin teach their scholars by Zarephath and Sepharad to understand France and Spain, grounding upon this a foolish groundless expectation that some time or other the Jews shall be masters of those countries; and they call and count the Christians *Edomites,* over whom they are to have dominion. But the promise here, no doubt, has a spiritual signification, and had its accomplishment in the setting up of the Christian church, the gospel-Israel, in the world, and shall have its accomplishment more and more in the enlargement of it and the additions made to it, till the mystical body is completed. When ministers and Christians prevail with their neighbours to come to Christ, to yield themselves to the Lord, they possess them. The converts that Abraham had are said to be the *souls that he had gotten,* Gen. 12:5. The possession is gained, not *vi et armis — by force and arms;* for the *weapons of our warfare are not carnal,* but *spiritual;* it is by the preaching of the gospel, and the power of divine grace going along with it, that this possession is got and kept.

IV. That the kingdom of the Redeemer shall be erected and maintained, to the comfort of his loyal subjects and the terror and shame of all his enemies (*v.* 21): *The kingdom shall be the Lord's,* the Lord Christ's. God shall give it to him, by putting all things into his hand, all power both in heaven and in earth; men shall give it to him, by resigning themselves to him as his willing people, and appointing him their head. Now the work of kings is to protect their subjects and suppress their enemies; and this Christ will do; he will both reward and punish. 1. The mountain of Zion shall be saved; on it *saviours* shall *come,* the preachers of the gospel, who are called saviours, because their business is to save themselves and those that hear them; and in this they are *workers together with Christ,* but to little purpose if he by his grace did not *work together with them.* 2. The mountain of Esau shall be judged; and the same that come as saviours on Mount Zion shall *judge* the *mountain of Esau;* for the word of the gospel in their mouth, that saves believers, judges unbelievers, convinces and condemns them. Christ's ministers are *saviours on Mount Zion* when they preach that he *that believes shall be saved;* but they judge the mount of Esau when they preach *that he that believeth not shall be damned,* which they are not only commissioned, but commanded to do, Mk. 16:16. And in the course of God's providence his scripture is fulfilled; when God raises up friends to the church in her distress (as he *raised up judges* to deliver Israel of old, Jdg. 2:16), then *saviours come on Mount Zion,* to save it from being sunk and ruined; and when the enemies of the church are brought down, and their power broken, then is the *mount of Esau judged;* and this shall be done in every age in such a way as God thinks best; we may depend upon it that the gates of hell shall not prevail against the church, but the church shall prevail against them; *for the kingdom shall be the Lord's;* the kingdoms of the world shall become his, and he has taken, and will take, to himself his great power and reign.

AN EXPOSITION, WITH PRACTICAL OBSERVATIONS, OF

THE BOOK OF JONAH

This book of Jonah, though it be placed here in the midst of the prophetical books of scripture, is yet rather a history than a prophecy; one line of prediction there is in it, *Yet forty days, and Nineveh shall be overthrown;* the rest of the book is a narrative of the preface to and the consequences of that prediction. In the midst of the obscure prophecies before and after this book, wherein are many things dark and hard to be understood, which are puzzling to the learned, and are *strong meat for strong men,* comes in this plain and pleasant story, which is entertaining to the weakest, and *milk for babes.* Probably Jonah was himself the penman of this book, and he, as Moses and other inspired penmen, records his own faults, which is an evidence that in these writings they designed God's glory and not their own. We read of this same Jonah 2 Ki. 14:25, where we find that he was of Gath-hepher in Galilee, a city that belonged to the tribe of Zebulun, in a remote corner of the land of Israel; for the Spirit, which like the wind, *blows where it listeth,* will as easily find out Jonah in Galilee as Isaiah at Jerusalem. We find also that he was a messenger of mercy to Israel in the reign of Jeroboam the second; for the success of his arms, in the *restoring of the coast of Israel,* is said to be *according to the word of the Lord which he spoke by the hand of his servant Jonah the prophet.* Those prophecies were not committed to writing, but this against Nineveh was, chiefly for the sake of the story that depends upon it, and that is recorded chiefly for the sake of Christ, of whom Jonah was a type; it contains also very remarkable instances of human infirmity in Jonah, and of God's mercy both in pardoning repenting sinners, witness Nineveh, and in bearing with repining saints, witness Jonah.

CHAPTER 1

In this chapter we have, I. A command given to Jonah to preach at Nineveh (*v.* 1, 2). II. Jonah's disobedience to that command (*v.* 3). III. The pursuit and arrest of him for that disobedience by a storm, in which he was asleep (*v.* 4–6). IV. The discovery of him, and his disobedience, to be the cause of the storm (*v.* 7–10). V. The casting of him into the sea, for the stilling of the storm (*v.* 11–16). VI. The miraculous preservation of his life there in the belly of a fish (*v.* 17), which was his reservation for further services.

Verses 1–3

Observe, 1. The honour God put upon Jonah, in giving him a commission to go and prophesy against Nineveh. *Jonah* signifies *a dove,* a proper name for all God's prophets, all his people, who ought to be *harmless as doves,* and to *mourn as doves* for the sins and calamities of the land. His father's name was *Amittai — My truth;* for God's prophets should be sons of truth. To him *the word of the Lord came — to him it was* (so the word signifies), for God's word is a real thing; men's words are but wind, but God's words are substance. He has been before acquainted with the *word of the Lord,* and knew his voice from that of a stranger; the orders now given him were, *Arise, go to Nineveh, that great city, v.* 2. Nineveh was at this time the metropolis of the Assyrian monarchy, an eminent city (Gen. 10:11), *a great city, that great city,* forty-eight miles in compass (some make it much more), great in the number of the inhabitants, as appears by the multitude of infants in it (*ch.* 4:11), great in wealth (there was no end of its store, Nah. 2:9), great in power and dominion; it was the city that for some time *ruled over the kings of the earth.* But great cities, as well as great men, are under God's government and judgment. Nineveh was a great city, and yet a heathen city, without the knowledge and worship of the true God. How many great cities and great nations are there that *sit in darkness* and *in the valley of the shadow of death!* This great city was a wicked city: *Their wickedness has come up before me* (their *malice,* so some read it); *their wickedness was presumptuous,* and they sinned with *a high hand.* It is sad to think what a great deal of sin is committed in great cities, where there are many sinners, who are not only all sinners, but making one another sin. *Their wickedness has come up,* that is, it has come to a high degree, to the highest pitch; the *measure of it* is *full* to the brim; *their wickedness has come up,* as that of Sodom, Gen. 18:20, 21. It has come up *before me — to my face* (so the word is); it is a bold and open affront to God; it is sinning against him, *in his sight;* therefore Jonah must *cry against it;* he must witness against their great wickedness, and must warn them of the destruction that was coming upon them for it. God is coming forth against it, and he sends Jonah before, to proclaim war, and to sound an alarm. *Cry aloud, spare not.* He must not whisper his message in a corner, but publish it in the streets of Nineveh; *he that hath ears let him hear* what God has to say by his prophet against that wicked city. When the cry of sin comes up to God the cry of vengeance comes out against the sinner. He must *go to Nineveh,* and cry there upon the spot against the wickedness of it. Other prophets were ordered to send messages to the neighbouring nations, and the prophecy of Nahum is particularly *the burden of Nineveh;* but Jonah must go and carry the message himself: *"Arise* quickly; apply thyself to the business with speed and courage, and the resolution that becomes a prophet; *arise, and go to Nineveh."* Those that go on God's errands must rise and go, must stir themselves to the work cut out for them. The prophets were sent first to the *lost sheep of the house of Israel,* yet not to them only; they had the children's bread, but Nineveh eats of the crumbs. 2. The dishonour Jonah did to God in refusing to obey his orders, and to go on the errand on which he was sent (*v.* 3): *But Jonah,* instead of rising to go to Nineveh, *rose up to flee to Tarshish,* to *the sea,* not bound for any port, but desirous to get away *from the presence of the Lord;* and, if he might but do that, he card not whither he went, not as if he thought he could go any where from under the eye of God's inspection, but from his special presence, from the spirit of prophecy, which, when it put him upon this work, he thought himself haunted with, and coveted to get out of the hearing of. Some think Jonah went upon the opinion of some of the Jews that the spirit of prophecy was confined to the land of Israel (which in Ezekiel and Daniel was effectually proved to be a mistake), and therefore he hoped he should get clear of it if he could but get out of the borders of that land. (1.) Jonah would not go to Nineveh to cry against it either because it was a long and dangerous journey thither, and in a road he knew not, or because he was afraid it would be as much as his life was worth to deliver such an ungrateful message to that great and potent city. He *consulted with flesh and blood*, and declined the embassy because he could not go with safety, or because he was jealous for the prerogatives of his country, and not willing that any other nation should share in the honour of divine revelation; he feared it would be the beginning of the removal of the kingdom of God from the Jews to another nation, that would bring forth more of the fruits of it. He owns himself (*ch.* 4:2) that the reason of his aversion to this journey was because he foresaw that the Ninevites would repent, and God would forgive them and take them into favour, which would be a slur upon the people of Israel, who had been so long a peculiar people to God. (2.) He therefore went to Tarshish, to Tarsus in Cilicia (so some), probably because he had friends and relations there, with whom he hoped for some time to sojourn. He went to Joppa, a famous seaport in the land of Israel, in quest of a ship bound for Tarshish, and there he found one. Providence seemed to favour his design, and give him an opportunity to escape. We may be out of the way of duty and yet may meet with a favourable gale. The ready way is not always the right way. He found the ship just ready to weigh anchor perhaps, and to set sail for Tarshish, and so he lost no time. Or, perhaps, he went to Tarshish because he found the ship going thither; otherwise all places were alike to him. He did not think himself out of his way, the way he would go, provided he was not in his way, the way he should go. So he *paid the fare thereof;* for he did not regard the charge, so he could but gain his point, and get to a distance *from the presence of the Lord.* He went *with them*, with the mariners, with the passengers, with the merchants, whoever they were that were going to Tarshish. Jonah, forgetting his dignity as well as his duty, herded with them, and *went down* into the ship to go *with them to Tarshish.* See what the best of men are when God leaves them to themselves, and what need we have, when the *word of the Lord* comes to us, to have the *Spirit of the Lord* come along with the word, to bring every thought within us into obedience to it. The prophet Isaiah owns that *therefore* he was not *rebellious*, neither *turned away back*, because God not only spoke to him, but *opened his ear*, Isa. 50:5. Let us learn hence to *cease from man*, and not to be too confident either of ourselves or others in a time of trial; but *let him that thinks he stands take heed lest he fall.*

Verses 4–10

When Jonah was set on ship-board, and under sail for Tarshish, he thought himself safe enough; but here we find him pursued and overtaken, discovered and convicted as a deserter from God, as one that had *run his colours.*

I. God sends a pursuer after him, *a mighty tempest in the sea, v.* 4. God has the *winds in his treasure* (Ps. 135:7), and out of these treasures God *sent forth*, he *cast forth* (so the word is), with force and violence, *a great wind into the sea;* even *stormy winds fulfil his word*, and are often the messengers of his wrath; he *gathers the winds in his fist* (Prov. 30:4), where he holds them, and whence he squeezes them when he pleases; for though, as to us, the *wind blows where it listeth*, yet not as to God, but where he directs. The effect of this wind as *a mighty tempest;* for when the winds rise the waves rise. Note, Sin brings storms and tempests into the soul, into the family, into churches and nations; it is a disquieting disturbing thing. The tempest prevailed to such a degree that *the ship was likely to be broken;* the mariners expected no other; *that ship* (so some read it), that and no other. Other ships were upon the same sea at the same time, yet, it should seem, that ship in which Jonah was was tossed more than any other and was more in danger. This wind was sent after Jonah, to fetch him back again to God and to his duty; and it is

a great mercy to be reclaimed and called home when we go astray, though it be by a tempest.

II. The ship's crew were alarmed by this mighty tempest, but Jonah only, the person concerned, was unconcerned, *v.* 5. The mariners were affected with their danger, though it was not with them that God has this controversy. 1. They were *afraid;* though, their business leading them to be very much conversant with dangers of this kind, they used to make light of them, yet now the oldest and stoutest of them began to tremble, being apprehensive that there was something more than ordinary in this tempest, so suddenly did it rise, so strongly did it rage. Note, God can strike a terror upon the most daring, and make even *great men and chief captains* call for shelter from rocks and mountains. 2. They *cried every man unto his god;* this was the effect of their fear. Many will not be brought to prayer till they are frightened to it; he that would learn to pray, let him go to sea. *Lord, in trouble they have visited thee. Every man* of them prayed; they were not some praying and others reviling, but every man engaged; as the danger was general, so was the address to heaven; there was not one praying for them all, but every one for himself. They cried *every man to his god*, the god of his country or city, or his own tutelar deity; it is a testimony against atheism that every man had a god, and had the belief of a God; but it is an instance of the folly of paganism that they had gods many, every man the god he had a fancy for, whereas there can be but one God, there needs to be no more. But, though they had lost that dictate of the light of nature that there is but *one God*, they still were governed by that direction of the law of nature that God is to be prayed to (*Should not a people seek under their God?* Isa. 8:19), and that he is especially to be prayed to when we are in distress and danger. *Call upon me in the time of trouble. Is any afflicted?* Is any frightened? *Let him pray.* 3. Their prayers for deliverance were seconded with endeavours, and, having called upon their gods to help them, they did what they could to help themselves; for that is the rule, *Help thyself and God will help thee.* They *cast forth the wares that were in the ship into the sea, to lighten it of them*, as Paul's mariners in a like case cast forth even the *tackling of the ship*, and the *wheat*, Acts 27:18, 19, 38. They were making a trading voyage, as it should seem, and were laden with many goods and much merchandise, by which they hoped to get gain; but now they are content to suffer loss by throwing them overboard, to save their lives. See how powerful the natural love of life is. *Skin for skin*, and *all that a man has, will he give for it.* And shall we not put a like value upon the spiritual life, the life of the soul, reckoning that the gain of all the world cannot countervail the loss of the soul? See the vanity of worldly wealth, and the uncertainty of its continuance with us. Riches make themselves wings and fly away; nay, and the case may be such that we may be under a necessity of making wings for them, and driving them away, as here, when they could not be *kept for the owners thereof* but to their hurt, so that they themselves are glad to be rid of them, and sink that which otherwise would sink them, though they have no prospect of ever recovering it. Oh that men would be thus wise for their souls, and would be willing to part with that wealth, pleasure, and honour which they cannot keep without *making shipwreck of faith and a good conscience* and ruining their souls for ever! Those that thus quit their temporal interests for the securing of their spiritual welfare will be unspeakable gainers at last; for what they lose upon those terms they shall find again to life eternal. But where is Jonah all this while? One would have expected gone down into his cabin, nay, into the *hold, between the sides of the ship*, and there he lies, and is *fast asleep;* neither the noise without, for the sense of guilt within, awoke him. Perhaps for some time before he had avoiding sleeping, for fear of God's speaking to him again in a dream; and now that he imagined himself out of the reach of that danger, he slept so much the more soundly. Note, Sin is of a stupifying nature, and we are concerned to *take heed lest at any time our hearts be hardened by the deceitfulness of it.* It is the policy of Satan, when by his temptations he has drawn men from God and their duty, to rock them asleep in carnal security, that they may not be sensible of their misery and danger. It concerns us all to *watch therefore.*

III. The master of the ship called Jonah up to his prayers,

v. 6. The *ship-master came to him*, and bade him for shame get up, both to *pray for life* and to *prepare for death;* he gave him, 1. A just and necessary chiding: *What meanest thou, O sleeper?* Here we commend the ship-master, who gave him this reproof; for, though he was a stranger to him, he was, for the present, as one of his family; and whoever has a precious soul we must help, as we can, to *save it from death.* We pity Jonah, who needed this reproof; as a prophet of the Lord, if he had been in his place, he might have been reproving the king of Nineveh, but, being out of the way of his duty, he does himself lie open to the reproofs of a sorry ship-master. See how men by their sin and folly diminish themselves and make themselves mean. Yet we must admire God's goodness in sending him this seasonable reproof, for it was the first step towards his recovery, as the crowing of the cock was to Peter. Note, Those that sleep in a storm may well be asked what they mean. 2. A pertinent word of advice: *"Arise, call upon thy God;* we are here crying every man to his god, why dost not thou get up and cry to thine? Art not thou equally concerned with the rest both in the danger dreaded and in the deliverance desired?"* Note, The devotions of others should quicken ours; and those who hope to share in a common mercy ought in all reason to contribute their quota towards the prayers and supplications that are made for it. In times of public distress, if we have any interest at the throne of grace, we ought to improve it for the public good. And the servants of God themselves have sometimes need to be called and stirred up to this part of their duty. 3. A good reason for this advice: *If so be that God will think upon us, that we perish not.* It should seem, the many gods they called upon were considered by them only as mediators between them and the supreme God, and intercessors for them with him; for the ship-master speaks of one God still, from whom he expected relief. To engage prayer, he suggested that the danger was very great and imminent: "We are all likely to *perish;* there is but a step between us and death, and that just ready to be stepped." Yet he suggested that there was some hope remaining that their destruction might be prevented and they might *not perish.* While there is still life there is hope, and while there is hope there is room for prayer. He suggested also that it was God only that could effect their deliverance, and it must come from his power and his pity. "If he *think upon us*, and act for us, we may yet be saved." And therefore to him we must look, and in him we must put our trust, when the danger is ever so imminent.

IV. Jonah is found out to be the cause of the storm.

1. The mariners observed so much peculiar and uncommon either in the storm itself or in their own distress by it that they concluded it was a messenger of divine justice sent to arrest some one of those that were in that ship, as having been guilty of some enormous crime, judging as the barbarous people (Acts 28:4), *"no doubt one of us is a murderer*, or guilty of sacrilege, or perjury, or the like, who is thus *pursued* by the *vengeance of the sea*, and it is for his sake that we all suffer."* Even the light of nature teaches that in extraordinary judgments the wrath of God is revealed from heaven against some extraordinary sins and sinners. Whatever evil is upon us at any time we must conclude *there is a cause* for it; there is evil done by us, or else this evil would not be upon us; there is a ground for God's controversy.

2. They determined to refer it to the lot which of them was the criminal that had occasioned this storm: *Let us cast lots, that we may know for whose cause the evil is upon us.* None of them suspected himself, or said, *Is it I, Lord; is it I?* But they suspected one another, and would find out the man. Note, It is a desirable thing, when any evil is upon us, to know for what cause it is upon us, that what is amiss may be amended, and, the grievance being redressed, the grief may be removed. In order to this we must look up to heaven, and pray, Lord, *show me wherefore thou contendest with me; that which I see not teach thou me.* These mariners desired to know the person that was the dead weight in their ship, the accursed thing, that that one man might *die for the people* and that the whole ship *might not be lost;* this was not only expedient, but highly just. In order to this they cast lots, by which they appealed to the judgment of God, to whom *all hearts are open, and from whom no secret is hid*, agreeing to acquiesce in his discovery and determination, and to take

that for true which the lot spoke; for they knew by the light of nature, what the scripture tells us, that *the lot is cast into the lap, but the whole disposal thereof is of the Lord.* Even the heathen looked upon the casting of lots to be a sacred thing, to be done with seriousness and solemnity, and not to be made a sport of. It is a shame for Christians if they have not a like reverence for an appeal to Providence.

3. The *lot fell upon Jonah,* who could have saved them this trouble if he would but have told them what his own conscience told him, *Thou are the man;* but as is usual with criminals, he never confesses till he finds he cannot help it, till *the lot falls upon him.* We may suppose there were those in the ship who, upon other accounts, were greater sinners than Jonah, and yet he is the man that the tempest pursues and that the lot pitches upon; for it is his own child, his own servant, that the parent, that the master, corrects, if they do amiss; others that offend he leaves to the law. The storm is sent after Jonah, because God has work for him to do, and it is sent to fetch him back to it. Note, God has many ways of bringing to light concealed sins and sinners, and making manifest that folly which was thought to be hidden from the eyes of all living. God's right hand will find out all his servants that desert him, as well as all his enemies that have designs against him; yea, though they flee to the uttermost parts of the sea, or go down to the sides of the ship.

4. Jonah is hereupon brought under examination before the master and mariners. He was a stranger; none of them could say that they knew the prisoner, or had any thing to lay to his charge, and therefore they must extort a confession from him and judge him *out of his own mouth;* and for this there needed no rack, the shipwreck they were in danger of was sufficient to frighten him, so as to make him tell the truth. Though it was discovered by the lot that he was the person for whose sake they were thus damaged and exposed, yet they did not fly outrageously upon him, as one would fear they might have done, but calmly and mildly enquired into his case. There is a compassion due to offenders when they are discovered and convicted. They give him no hard words, but, *"Tell us, we pray thee,* what is the matter?" Two things they enquire of him: — (1.) Whether he would himself own that he was the person for whose sake the storm was sent, as the lot had intimated: *"Tell us for whose cause this evil is upon us;* is it indeed for thy cause, and, if so, *for what cause?* What is this offence for which thou art thus prosecuted?" Perhaps the gravity and decency of Jonah's aspect and behaviour made them suspect that the lot had missed its man, had missed its mark, and therefore they would not trust it, unless he would himself own his guilt; they therefore begged of him that he would satisfy them in this matter. Note, Those that would find out the cause of their troubles must not only begin, but pursue the enquiry, must descend to particulars and *accomplish a diligent search.* (2.) What his character was, both as to his calling and as to his country. [1.] They enquire concerning his calling: *What is thy occupation?* This was a proper question to be put to a vagrant. Perhaps they suspected his calling to be such as might bring this trouble upon them: "Art thou a diviner, a sorcerer, a student in the black art? Hast thou been conjuring for this wind? Or what business are thou now going on? It is like Balaam's, to curse any of God's people, and is this wind send to stop thee?" [2.] They enquire concerning his country. One asked, *Whence comest thou?* Another, not having patience to stay for an answer to that, asked, *What is thy country?* A third to the same purport, *"Of what people art thou?* Art thou of the Chaldeans," that were noted for divination, "or of the Arabians," that were noted for stealing? They wished to know of what country he was, that, knowing who was the god of his country, they might guess whether he was one that could do them any kindness in this storm.

5. In answer to these interrogatories Jonah makes a full discovery. (1.) Did they enquire concerning his country? He tells them he is *a Hebrew* (*v.* 9), not only of the nation of Israel, but of their religion, which they received from their fathers. He is a Hebrew, and therefore is the more ashamed to own that he is a criminal; for the sins of Hebrews, that make such a profession of religion and enjoy such privileges, are greater than the sins of others, and more exceedingly sinful. (2.) Did they enquire concerning his calling — *What is thy occupation?* In answer to that he gives an account of his religion, for that was his calling, that was his occupation, that was it that he made a business of: *"I fear the Lord Jehovah;* that is the God I worship, the God I pray to, even *the God of heaven,* the sovereign Lord of all, that has *made the sea and the dry land* and has command of both." Not the god of one particular country, which they enquired after, and such as the gods were that they had been every man calling upon, but *the God of the whole earth,* who, having made both the sea and the dry land, makes what work he pleases in both and makes what use he pleases of both. This he mentions, not only as condemning himself for his folly, in fleeing from the presence of this God, but as designing to bring these mariners from the worship and service of their many gods to the knowledge and obedience of the one only living and true God. When we are among those that are strangers to us we should do what we can to bring them acquainted with God, by being ready upon all occasions to own our relation to him and our reverence for him. (3.) Did they enquire concerning his crime, for which he is now persecuted? He owns that he *fled from the presence of the Lord,* that he was here running away from his duty, and the storm was sent to fetch him back. We have reason to think that he told them this with sorrow and shame, justifying God and condemning himself and intimating to the mariners what a great God Jehovah is, who could send such a messenger as this tempest was after a runagate servant.

6. We are told what impression this made upon the mariners: *The men were exceedingly afraid,* and justly, for they perceived, (1.) That God was angry, even that God that made *the sea and the dry land.* This tempest comes from the hand of an offended justice, and therefore they have reason to fear it will go hard with them. Judgments inflicted for some particular sin have a peculiar weight and terror in them. (2.) That God was angry with one that feared and worshipped him, only for once running from his work in particular instance; this made them afraid for themselves. "If a prophet of the Lord be thus severely punished for one offence, what will become of us that have been guilty of so many, and great, and heinous offences?" If *the righteous be* thus *scarcely saved,* and for a single act of disobedience thus closely pursued, *where shall the ungodly and the sinner appear?* 1 Pt. 4:17, 18. They said to him, *"Why hast thou done this?* If thou fearest the God that *made the sea and the dry land,* why wast thou such a fool as to think thou couldst flee from his presence? What an absurd unaccountable thing is it!" *Thus he was reproved,* as Abraham by Abimelech (Gen. 20:16); for if the professors of religion do a wrong thing they must expect to hear of it from those that make no such profession. *"Why hast thou done this to us?"* (so it may be taken) "Why has thou involved us in the prosecution?" Note, Those that commit a willful sin know not how far the mischievous consequences of it may reach, nor what mischief may be done by it.

Verses 11–17

It is plain that Jonah is the man for whose sake this evil is upon them, but the discovery of him to be so was not sufficient to answer the demands of this tempest; they had found him out, but something more was to be done, for still *the sea wrought and was tempestuous* (*v.* 11), and again (*v.* 13), it *grew more and more tempestuous* (so the margin reads it); for if we discover sin to be the cause of our troubles, and do not forsake it, we do but make bad worse. Therefore they went on with the prosecution.

I. They enquired of Jonah himself what he thought they must do with him (*v.* 11): *What shall we do unto thee, that the sea may be calm to us?* They perceived that Jonah is a prophet of the Lord, and therefore will not do any thing, no, not in his own case, without consulting him. He appears to be a delinquent, but he appears also to be a penitent, and therefore they will not insult over him, nor offer him any rudeness. Note, We ought to act with great tenderness towards those that are overtaken in a fault and are brought into distress by it. They would not *cast him into the sea* if he could think of any other expedient by which to *save the ship.* Or, perhaps, thus they would show how plain the case was, that there was no remedy but he must be thrown overboard; let him be his own judge as he had been his own accuser, and he himself will say so. Note, When sin has raised a storm, and laid us under the tokens of God's displeasure, we are concerned to enquire what we shall do that the sea may be calm; and what shall we do? We must pray and believe, when we are in a storm, and study to answer the end for which it was sent, and then the storm shall become a calm. But especially we must consider what is to be done to the sin that raised the storm; that must be discovered, and penitently confessed; that must be detested, disclaimed, and utterly forsaken. What have I to do any more with it? Crucify it, crucify it, for this evil it has done.

II. Jonah reads his own doom (*v.* 12): *Take me up, and cast me forth into the sea.* He would not himself leap into the sea, but he put himself into their hands, to cast him into the sea, and assured them that then the *sea would be calm,* and not otherwise. He proposed this, in tenderness to the mariners, that the might no suffer for his sake. *"Let thy hand be upon me"* (says David, 1 Chr. 21:17), "who am guilty; let me die for me own sin, but let not the innocent suffer for it." This is the language of true penitents, who earnestly desire that none but themselves may ever smart, or fare the worse, for their sins and follies. He proposed it likewise in submission to the will of God, who sent this tempest in pursuit of him; and *therefore* judged himself to be cast into the sea, because to that he plainly saw God judging him, that he might not be *judged of the Lord* to eternal misery. Note, Those who are truly humbled for sin will cheerfully submit to the will of God, even in a sentence of death itself. If Jonah sees this to be the punishment of his iniquity, he accepts it, he subjects himself to it, and justifies God in it. No matter though the *flesh* be *destroyed,* no matter how it is destroyed, so that the *spirit may* be *but saved in the day of the Lord Jesus,* 1 Co. 5:5. The reason he gives is, *For I know that for my sake this great tempest is upon you.* See how ready Jonah is to take all the guilt upon himself, and to look upon all the trouble as theirs: "It is purely for my sake, who have sinned, that this tempest is upon you; therefore cast me forth into the sea; for," 1. "I deserve it. I have wickedly departed from my God, and it is upon my account that he is angry with you. Surely I am unworthy to breathe in that air which for my sake has been hurried with winds, to live in that ship which for my sake has been thus tossed. Cast me into the sea after the wares which for my sake you have thrown into it. Drowning is too good for me; a single death is punishment too little for such a complicated offence." 2. "Therefore there is no way of having the sea calm. If it is I that have raised the storm, it is not casting the wares into the sea that will lay it again; no, you must cast me thither." When conscience is awakened, and a storm raised there, nothing will turn it into a calm but parting with the sin that occasioned the disturbance, and abandoning that. It is not parting with our money that will pacify conscience; no, it is the Jonah that be thrown overboard. Jonah is herein a type of Christ, that he *gives his life a ransom for many;* but with this material difference, that the storm Jonah gave himself up to still was of his own raising, but that storm which Christ gave himself up to still was of our raising. Yet, as Jonah delivered himself up to be cast into a raging sea that it might be calm, so did our Lord Jesus, when he died that we might live.

III. The poor mariners did what they could to save themselves from the necessity of throwing Jonah into the sea, but all in vain (*v.* 13): *They rowed hard to bring the ship to the land,* that, if they must part with Jonah, they might set him safely on shore; *but they could not.* All their pains were to no purpose; *for the sea wrought* harder than they could, and *was tempestuous against them,* so that they could by no means *make the land.* If they thought sometimes that they had gained their point, they were quickly thrown off to sea again. Still their ship was overladen; their lightening it of the wares made it never the lighter as long as Jonah was in it. And, besides, they rowed against wind and tide, the wind of God's vengeance, the tide of his counsels; and it is in vain to contend with God, in vain to think of saving ourselves any other way than by destroying our sins. By this it appears that these mariners were very loth to execute Jonah's sentence upon himself, though they knew it was for his sake that this tempest was upon them. They were thus very backward to it partly from a dread of bringing upon themselves the guilt of blood, and partly from a compassion they could not but have for poor Jonah, as a good man, as a man in distress, and as a man of sincerity. Note, The more sinners humble and abase themselves, judge and condemn themselves, the more likely they are to find pity both with God and man. The more forward Jonah was to say, *Cast me into the sea,* the more backward they were to do it.

IV. When they found it necessary to cast Jonah into the sea they first prayed to God that the guilt of his blood might not lie upon them, nor be laid to their charge, *v.* 14. When they found it in vain to row hard they quitted their oars and went to their prayers: *Wherefore they cried unto the Lord,* unto *Jehovah,* the true and living God, and no more to the *gods many.* and *lords many,* that the had *cried to, v.* 5. They prayed to the *God of Israel,* being now convinced, by the providences of God concerning Jonah and the information he had given them, that he is God *alone.* Having determined to cast Jonah into the sea, they first enter a protestation in the court of heaven that they do not do it willingly, much less maliciously, or with any design to be revenged upon him because it was for his sake that this tempest was upon them. No; *his god forgive him,* as *they do!* But they are forced to do it *se defendendo — in self-defence,* having no other way to save their own lives; and they do it as ministers of justice, both God and himself having sentenced him to *so great a death.* They *therefore* present a humble petition to the God whom Jonah feared, that they might not *perish for his life.* See, 1. What a fear they had of contracting the guilt of blood, especially the blood of one that feared God, and worshipped him, and had fellowship with him, as they perceived Jonah had, though in a single instance he had been faulty. Natural conscience cannot but have a dread of blood-guiltiness, and make men very earnest in prayer, as David was, to be delivered from it, Ps. 51:14. So they were here: *We beseech thee, O Lord! we beseech thee, lay not upon us innocent blood.* They are now as earnest in praying to be saved from the peril of sin as they were before in praying to be saved from the peril of the sea, especially because Jonah appeared to them to be no ordinary person, but a very good man, a man of God, a worshipper of the great Creator of heaven and earth, upon which account even these rude mariners conceived a veneration for him, and trembled at the thought of taking away his life. Innocent blood is precious, but saints' blood, prophets' blood, is much more precious, and so those will find to their cost that any way bring themselves under the guilt of it. The mariners saw Jonah pursued by divine vengeance, and yet could not without horror think of being his executioners. Though his God has a controversy with him, yet, think they, *Let not our hand be upon him.* The Israelites were at this time killing the prophets for doing their duty (witness Jezebel's late persecution), and were prodigal of their lives, which is aggravated by the tenderness these heathens had for one whom they perceived to be a prophet, though he was now out of the way of his duty. 2. What a fear they had of incurring the wrath of God; they were jealous lest he should be angry if they should be the death of Jonah, for he had said, *Touch not my anointed, and do my prophets no harm;* it is at your peril if you do. "Lord," say they, *"let us not perish for this man's life.* Let it not be such a fatal dilemma to us. We see we must perish if we spare his life; Oh let us not perish for taking away his life." And their plea is good: *"For thou, O Lord! hast done as it pleased thee;* thou had laid us under a necessity of doing it; the wind that pursued him, the lot that discovered him, were both under thy direction, which we are herein governed by; we are but the instruments of Providence, and it is sorely against our will that we do it; but we must say, *The will of the Lord be done."* Note, When we are manifestly led by Providence to do things contrary to our own inclinations, and quite beyond our own intentions, it will be some satisfaction to us to be able to say, *Thou, O Lord! has done as it pleased thee.* And, if God please himself, we ought to be satisfied though he do not please us.

V. Having deprecated the guilt they dreaded, they proceeded to execution (*v.* 15): *They took up Jonah,* and *cast him forth into the sea.* They cast him out of their ship, out of their company, and cast him into the sea, a raging stormy sea, that cried, "Give, give; surrender the traitor, or expect no peace." We may well think what confusion and amazement poor Jonah was in when he saw himself ready to be hurried into the presence of that God as a Judge whose presence as a Master he was now fleeing from. Note, Those know not what ruin they run upon that run away from God. *Woe unto them! for they have fled from me.* When sin is the Jonah that raises the storm, that must thus be cast forth into the sea; we must abandon it, and be the death of it, must drown that which otherwise will *drown us in destruction and perdition.* And if we thus by a thorough repentance and reformation cast our sins forth into the sea, never to recall them or return to them again, God will by pardoning mercy subdue our iniquities, and *cast them into the depths of the sea* too, Mic. 7:19.

VI. The throwing of Jonah into the sea immediately put an end to the storm. The sea has what she came for, and therefore rests contended; she *ceases from her raging.* It is an instance of the sovereign power of God that he can soon turn the storm into a calm, and of the equity of his government that when the end of an affliction is answered and attained the affliction shall immediately be removed. He will not contend for ever, will not contend any longer till we submit ourselves and give up the cause. If we turn from our sins, he will soon turn from his anger.

VII. The mariners were hereby more confirmed in their belief that Jonah's God was the only true God (*v.* 16): *Then the men feared the Lord with a great fear,* were possessed with a deep veneration for the God of Israel, and came to a resolution that they would worship him only for the future; for *there is no other God that can* destroy, that *can deliver, after this sort.* When they saw the power of God in raising and laying the tempest, when they saw his justice upon Jonah his own servant, and when they saw his goodness to them in saving them from the brink of ruin, *then they feared the Lord,* Jer. 5:22. As an evidence of their fear of him, they *offered sacrifice* to him when they came ashore again in the land of Israel, and for the present made vows that they would do so, in thankfulness for their deliverance, and to make atonement for their souls. Or, perhaps, they had something yet on board which might be for a sacrifice to God immediately. Or it may be meant of the spiritual sacrifices of prayer and praise, with which God is better pleased than with that of an ox or bullock that has horns and hoofs. See Ps. 107:2, etc. We must make vows, not only when we are in the pursuit of mercy, but, which is much more generous, when we have received mercy, as those that are still studying what we shall render.

VIII. Jonah's life, after all, is saved by a miracle, and we shall hear of him again for all this. In the midst of judgment God *remembers mercy.* Jonah shall be more frightened than hurt, not so much punished for his sin as reduced to his duty. Though he flees from the presence of the Lord, and seems to fall into his avenging hands, yet God has more work for him to do, and therefore has *prepared a great fish to swallow up Jonah* (*v.* 17), *a whale* our Saviour calls it (Mt. 12:40), one of the largest sorts of whales, that have wider throats than others, in the belly of which has sometimes been found the dead body of a man in armour. Particular notice is taken, in the history of creation, of God's *creating great whales* (Gen. 1:21) and the *leviathan* in the waters *made to play therein,* Ps. 104:26. But God finds work for this leviathan, has *prepared* him, has *numbered* him (so the word is), has appointed him to be Jonah's receiver and deliverer. Note, God has command of all the creatures, and can make any of them serve his designs of mercy to his people, even the fishes of the sea, that are most from under man's cognizance, even the great whales, that are altogether from under man's government. This fish was prepared, lay ready under water close by the ship, that he might keep Jonah from sinking to the bottom, and save him alive, though he deserved to die. Let us *stand still and see this salvation of the Lord,* and admire his power, that he could thus save a drowning man, and his pity, that he would thus save one that was running from him and had offended him. It was of the Lord's mercies that Jonah was not now consumed. The fish swallowed up Jonah, not to devour him, but to protect him. *Out of the eater comes forth meat;* for Jonah was alive and well *in the belly of the fish three days and three nights,* not consumed by the heat of the animal, nor suffocated for want of air. It is granted that to nature this was impossible, but not to the God of nature, with whom all things are possible. Jonah by this miraculous preservation was designed to be made, 1. A monument of divine mercy, for the encouragement of those that have sinned, and gone away from God, to return and repent. 2. A successful preacher to Nineveh; and this miracle wrought for his deliverance, if the tidings of it reached Nineveh, would contribute to his success. 3. An illustrious type of Christ, who was buried and rose again according to the scriptures (1 Co. 15:4), according to this scripture, for, *as Jonah was three days and three nights in the whale's belly, so was the Son of man three days and three nights in the heart of the earth,* Mt. 12:40. Jonah's burial was a figure of Christ's. God prepared Jonah's grave, so he did Christ's, when it was long before ordained that he should *make his grave with the rich,* Isa. 53:9. Was Jonah's grave a strange one, a new one? So was Christ's, one in which never man before was laid. Was Jonah there the best part of three days and three nights? So was Christ; but both in order to their rising again for the bringing of the doctrine of repentance to the Gentile world. *Come, see the place where the Lord lay.*

CHAPTER 2

We left Jonah in the belly of the fish, and had reason to think we should hear no more of him, that if he were not destroyed by the waters of the sea he would be consumed in the bowels of that leviathan, "out of whose mouth go burning lamps, and sparks of fire, and whose breath kindles coals," Job 41:19, 21. But God brings his people through fire, and through water (Ps. 66:12); and by his power, behold, Jonah the prophet is yet alive, and is heard of again. In this chapter God hears from him, for we find him praying; in the next Nineveh hears from him, for we find him preaching. In his prayer we have, I. The great distress and danger he was in (*v.* 2, 3, 5, 6). II. The despair he was thereby almost reduced to (*v.* 4). III. The encouragement he took to himself, in this deplorable condition (*v.* 4, 7). IV. The assurance he had of God's favour to him (*v.* 6, 7). V. The warning and instruction he gives to others (*v.* 8). VI. The praise and glory of all given to God (*v.* 9). In the last verse we have Jonah's deliverance out of the belly of the fish, and his coming safe and sound upon dry land again.

Verses 1–9

God and his servant Jonah had parted in anger, and the quarrel began on Jonah's side; he fled from his country that he might outrun his work; but we hope to see them both together again, and the reconciliation begins on God's side. In the close of the foregoing chapter we found God returning to Jonah in a way of mercy, *delivering him from going down to the pit,* having *found a ransom;* in this chapter we find Jonah returning to God in a way of duty; he was called up in the former chapter to pray to his God, but we are not told that he did so; however, now at length he is brought to it. Now observe here,

I. When he prayed (*v.* 1): *Then Jonah prayed;* then when he was in trouble, under the sense of sin and the tokens of God's displeasure against him for sin, then he prayed. Note, When we are in affliction we must pray; then we have occasion to pray, then we have errands at the throne of grace and business there; then, if ever, we shall have a disposition to pray, when the heart is humbled, and softened, and made serious; then God expects it (*in their affliction they will seek me early,* seek me earnestly); and, though we bring our afflictions upon ourselves by our sins, yet, if we pray in humility and godly sincerity, we shall be welcome to the throne of grace, as Jonah was. Then when he was in a hopeful way of deliverance, being preserved alive by miracle, a plain indication that he was reserved for further mercy, then he prayed. An apprehension of God's good-will to us, notwithstanding our offences, gives us boldness of access to him, and opens the lips in prayer which were closed with the sense of guilt and dread of wrath.

II. Where he prayed — in *the fish's belly.* No place is amiss for prayer. *I will that men pray every where.* Wherever God casts us we may find a way open to heavenward, if it be not our own fault. *Undique ad coelos tantundem est viae — The heavens are equally accessible from every part of the earth.* He that has Christ dwelling in his heart by faith, wherever he goes carries the altar along with him, that *sanctifies the gift,* and is himself a *living temple.* Jonah was here in confinement; the belly of the fish was his prison, was a close and dark dungeon to him; yet there he had freedom of access to God, and walked at liberty in communion with him. Men may shut us out from communion with one another, but not from communion with God. Jonah was now in the bottom of the sea, yet *out of the depths he cries to God;* as Paul and Silas prayed in the prison, in the stocks.

III. To whom he prayed — *to the Lord his God.* He had been fleeing from God, but now he sees the folly of it, and returns to him; by prayer he draws near to that God whom he had gone aside from, and *engages his heart to approach him.* In prayer he has an eye to him, not only as *the Lord,* but as *his God,* a God in covenant with him; for, thanks be to God, every transgression in the covenant does not throw us out of covenant. This encourages even backsliding children to return. Jer. 3:22, *Behold, we come unto thee, for thou art the Lord our God.*

IV. What his prayer was. He afterwards recollected the substance of it, and left it upon record. He reflects upon the workings of his heart towards God when he was in his distress and danger, and the conflict that was then in his breast between faith and sense, between hope and fear.

1. He reflects upon the earnestness of his prayer, and God's readiness to hear and answer (*v.* 2): He said, *I cried, by reason of my affliction, unto the Lord.* Note, Many that prayed not at all, or did but whisper prayer, when they were in prosperity, are brought to pray, nay, are brought to cry, *by reason of their affliction;* and it is for this end that afflictions are sent, and they are in vain if this end be not answered. Those *heap up wrath* who *cry not when God binds them,* Job 36:13. *"Out of the belly of hell* and the grave *cried I."* The fish might well be called a grave, and, as it was a prison to which Jonah was condemned for his disobedience and in which he lay under the wrath of God, it might well be called the belly of hell. Thither this good man was cast, and yet thence he cried to God, and it was not in vain; God *heard him, heard the voice* of his affliction, the voice of his supplication. There is a hell in the other world, out of which there is no crying to God with any hope of being heard; but, whatever hell we may be *in the belly of* in this world, we may thence *cry to God.* When Christ lay, as Jonah, three days and three nights in the grave, though he prayed not, as Jonah did, yet his very lying there cried to God for poor sinners, and the cry was heard.

2. He reflects upon the very deplorable condition that he was in when he was in the belly of hell, which, when he lay there, he was very sensible of and made particular remarks upon. Note, If we would get good by our troubles, we must take notice of our troubles, and of the hand of God in them. Jonah observes here, (1.) How low he was thrown (*v.* 3): *Thou hadst cast me into the deep.* The mariners cast him there; but he looked above them, and saw the hand of God casting him there. Whatever deeps we are cast into, it is God that casts us into them, and he it is who, *after he has killed, has power to cast into hell.* He was *cast into the midst of the seas — the heart of the seas* (so the word is), and thence Christ borrows that Hebrew phrase, when he applies it to his own lying so long in the *heart of the earth.* For he that is laid dead in the grave, though it be ever so shallow, is cut off as effectually from the land of the living as if he were laid in the *heart of the earth.* (2.) How terribly he was beset: *The floods compassed me about.* The channels and springs of the waters of the sea surrounded him on every side; it was always high-water with him. God's dear saints and servants are sometimes encompassed with the floods of affliction, with troubles that are very forcible and violent, that bear down on all before them, and that run constantly upon them, as the waters of a river in a continual succession, one trouble upon the neck of another, as Job's messengers of evil tidings; they are enclosed by them on all sides, as the church complains, Lam. 3:7. *He has hedged me about, that I cannot get out,* nor see which way I may flee for safety. *All thy billows and they waves passed over me.* Observe, He calls them God's billows and his waves, not only because he made them *(the sea is his, and he made it),* and because he *rules* them (for *even the winds and the seas obey him*), but because he had now commissioned them against Jonah, and limited them, and ordered them to afflict and terrify him, but not to destroy him. These words are plainly quoted by Jonah from Ps. 42:7, where, though the translations differ a little, in the original David's complaint is the same *verbatim — word for word,* with this of Jonah's: *All thy billows and thy waves passed over me.* What David spoke figuratively and metaphorically Jonah applied to himself as literally fulfilled. For the reconciling of ourselves to our afflictions, it is good to search precedents, that we may find *there has no temptation taken us but such as is common to men.* If ever any man's case was singular, and not to be paralleled, surely Jonah's was, and yet, to his great satisfaction, he finds even the man after God's own heart making the same complaint of God's *waves and billows going over him* that he has now occasion to make. When God *performs the thing that is appointed for us* we shall find that *many such things are with him,* that even our path of trouble is no untrodden path, and that God deals with us no otherwise than as he *uses to deal with those that love his name.* And therefore for our assistance in our addresses to God, when we are in trouble, it is good to make use of the complaints and prayers which the saints that have been before us made use of in the like case. See how good it is to be ready in the scriptures; Jonah, when he could make no use of his Bible, by the help of his memory furnished himself from the scripture with a very proper representation of his case: *All thy billows and thy waves passed over me.* To the same purport, *v.* 5, *The waters compassed me about even to the soul;* they threatened his life, which was hereby brought into imminent danger; or they made an impression upon his spirit; he saw them to be tokens of God's displeasure, and in them the *terrors of the Almighty set themselves in array against him;* this reached to his soul, and put that into confusion. And this also is borrowed from David's complaint, Ps. 69:1. The *waters have come in unto my soul.* When *without are fightings* it is no marvel that *within are fears.* Jonah, in the fish's belly, finds the *depths enclosing him round about,* so that if he would get out of his prison, yet he must unavoidably perish in the waters. He feels the *sea-weed* (which the fish sucked in with the water) *wrapped about his head,* so that he has no way left him to help himself, nor hope that any one else can help him. Thus are the people of God sometimes perplexed and entangled, that they may learn not to *trust in themselves, but in God that raises the dead,* 2 Co. 1:8, 9. (3.) How fast he was held (*v.* 6): He *went down to the bottom of the mountains,* to the rocks in the sea, upon which the hills and promontories by the seaside seem to be bottomed; he lay among them, nay, he lay under them; the *earth with her bars was about him,* so close about him that it was likely to be about him for ever. The earth was so shut and locked, so barred and bolted, against him, that he was quite cut off from any hope of ever returning to it. Thus helpless, thus hopeless, did Jonah's case seem to be. Those whom God contends with the whole creation is at war with.

3. He reflects upon the very black and melancholy conclusion he was then ready to make concerning himself, and the relief he obtained against it, *v.* 4, 7. (1.) He began to sink into despair, and to give up himself for gone and undone to all intents and purposes. When the *waters compassed him about even to the soul* no marvel that *his soul fainted within him,* fainted away, so that he had not any comfortable enjoyments or expectations; his spirits quite failed, and he looked upon himself as a dead man. *Then I said, I am cast out of thy sight,* and the apprehension of that was the thing that made his spirit faint within him. He thought God had quite forsaken him, would never return in mercy to him, nor show him any token for good again. He had no example before him of any that were brought alive out of a fish's belly; if he thought of Job upon the dunghill, Joseph in the pit, David in the cave, yet these did not come up to his case. Nor was there any visible way of escape open for him but by miracle; and what reason had he to expect that a miracle of mercy should be wrought for him who was now made a monument of justice? How own conscience told him that he had wickedly *fled from the presence of the Lord,* and therefore he might justly *cast him away from his presence,* and, in token of that, *take away his Holy Spirit from him,* never to visit him more. What hopes could he have of deliverance out of a trouble which his *own ways and doings* had *procured to himself?* Observe, When Jonah would say the worst he could of his case he says this, *I am cast out of thy sight;* those, and those only, are miserable, whom God has cast out of his sight, whom he will no longer own and favour. What is the misery of the damned in hell but this, that they are cast out of God's sight? For what is the happiness of heaven but the vision and fruition of God? Sometimes the condition of God's people may be such in this world that they may think themselves quite excluded from God's presence, so as no more to see him, or to be regarded by him. Jacob and Israel said, *My way is hidden from the Lord, and my judgment is passed over from my God,* Isa. 40:27. *Zion said, The Lord has forsaken me, my God has forgotten me,* Isa. 49:14. But it is only the surmise of unbelief, for God has not *cast away his people whom he has chosen.* (2.) Yet he recovered himself from sinking into despair, with some comfortable prospects of deliverance. Faith corrected and controlled the surmises of fear and distrust. Here was a fierce struggle between sense and faith, but faith had the last word and came off a conqueror. In trying times, the issue will be good at last, providing our faith do not fail; it was therefore the continuance of that in its vigour that Christ secured to Peter. *I have prayed for thee, that thy faith fail not,* Lu. 22:32. David would have fainted if he had not *believed,* Ps. 27:13. Jonah's faith said, *Yet I will look again towards thy holy temple.* Thus, though he was *perplexed,* yet *not in despair;* in the depth of the sea he had this hope in him, as an *anchor of the soul, sure and stedfast.* That which he supports himself with the hope of is that he shall yet *look again towards God's holy temple.* [1.] That he shall live; he shall look again heavenward, shall again see the light of the sun, though now he seems to be cast into utter darkness. Thus *against hope he believed in hope.* [2.] That he shall *live, and praise God;* and a good man does not desire to live for any other purpose, Ps. 119:175. That he shall enjoy communion with God again in holy ordinances, shall *look towards,* and go up to, *the holy temple,* there *to enquire,* there to *behold the beauty of the Lord.* When Hezekiah desired that he might be assured of his recovery, he asked, *What is the sign that I shall go up to the house of the Lord?* (Isa. 38:22), as if that were the only thing for the sake of which he wished for health; so Jonah here hopes he shall *look again towards the temple;* that way he had looked many a time with pleasure, rejoicing when he was called *to go up to the house of the Lord;* and the remembrance of it was his comfort, that, when he had opportunity, he was no stranger to the holy temple. But now he could not so much as look towards it; in the fish's belly he could not tell which way it lay, but he hopes he shall be again able to look towards it, to look on it, to look into it. Observe, How modestly Jonah expresses himself; as one conscious to himself of guilt and unworthiness, he dares not speak of dwelling in God's house, as David, knowing that he is *no more worthy to be called a son,* but he hopes that he may be admitted to look towards it. He calls it the *holy temple,* for the holiness of it was, in his eye, the beauty of it, and that for the sake of which he loved and looked towards it. The temple was a type of heaven; and he promises himself that though being now a *captive exile,* he should never be *loosed,* but *die in the pit,* yet he should look towards the heavenly temple, and be brought safely thither. Though he die in the fish's belly, in the bottom of the sea, yet thence he hopes his soul shall be carried by angels into Abraham's bosom. Or these words may be taken as Jonah's vow when he was in distress, and he speaks (*v.* 9) of paying what he vowed; his vow is that if God deliver him he will praise him *in the gates of the daughter of Zion,* Ps. 9:13, 14. His sin for which God pursued him was *fleeing from the presence of the Lord,* the folly of which he is now convinced of, and promises not only that he will never again look towards Tarshish, but that he will again look towards the temple, and will go *from strength to strength* till he appear before God there. And thus we see how faith and hope were his relief in his desponding condition. To these he added prayer to God (*v.* 7): *"When my soul fainted within me,* then *I remembered* the Lord, I betook myself to that cordial." He remembered what he is, how nigh to those that seem to be thrown at the greatest distance by trouble, how merciful to those that seem to have thrown themselves at a distance from him by sin. He remembered what he had done for him, what he had done for others, what he could do, what he had promised to do; and this kept him from fainting. Remembering God, he made his addresses to him: *"My prayer came in unto thee;* I sent it in, and expected to receive an answer to it." Note, Our afflictions should put us in mind of God, and thereby put us upon prayer to him. When our souls faint we must remember God; and, when we remember God, we must send up a prayer to him, a pious ejaculation at least; when we think on his name we should call on his name.

4. He reflects upon the favour of God to him when thus in his distress he sought to God and trusted him. (1.) He graciously accepted his prayer, and gave admission and au-

dience to it (*v.* 7): *My prayer,* being sent to him, *came in unto him,* even *into his holy temple;* it was heard in the highest heavens, though it was prayed in the lowest deeps. (2.) He wonderfully wrought deliverance for him, and, when he was in the depth of his misery, gave him the earnest and assurance of it (*v.* 6): *Yet hast thou brought up my life from corruption, O Lord my God!* Some think he said this when he was vomited up on dry ground; and then it is the language of thankfulness, and he sets it over-against the great difficulty of his case, that the power of God might be the more magnified in his deliverance: *The earth with her bars was about me for ever,* and yet *thou hast brought up my life from the pit,* from the *bars of the pit.* Or, rather, we may suppose it spoken while he was yet in the fish's belly, and then it is the language of his faith: "Thou hast kept me alive here, in the pit, and therefore thou canst, thou wilt, *bring up my life from the pit;*" and he speaks of it with as much assurance as if it were done already: *Thou has brought up my life.* Though he has not an express promise of deliverance, he has an earnest of it, and on that he depends: he has life, and therefore believes his life shall be *brought up from corruption;* and this assurance he addresses to God: *Thou has done it, O Lord my God!* Thou art the Lord, and therefore *canst* do it for me, my God, and therefore wilt do it. Note, If the Lord be our God, he will be to us the *resurrection and the life,* will redeem our lives from destruction, from the power of the grave.

5. He gives warning to others, and instructs them to keep close to God (*v.* 8): *Those that observe lying vanities forsake their own mercy,* that is, (1.) Those that worship other gods, as the heathen mariners did, and call upon them, and expect relief and comfort from them, *forsake their own mercy;* they stand in their own light; they turn their back upon their own happiness, and go quite out of the way of all good. Note, Idols are *lying vanities,* and those that pay that homage to them which is due to God only act as contrarily to their interests as to their duty. Or, (2.) Those that follow their own inventions, as Jonah himself had done when he *fled from the presence of the Lord* to go to Tarshish, *forsake their own mercy,* that mercy which they might find in God, and might have such a covenant-right and title to it as to be able to call it their own, if they would but keep close to God and their duty. Those that think to go any where to be from under the eye of God, as Jonah did — that think to better themselves by deserting his service, as Jonah did — and that grudge his mercy to any poor sinners, and pretend to be wiser than he in judging who are fit to have prophets sent them and who are not, as Jonah did — they *observe lying vanities,* are led away by foolish groundless fancies, and, like him, they *forsake their own mercy,* and no good can come of it. Note, Those that forsake their own duty forsake their own mercy; those that run away from the work of their place and day run away from the comfort of it.

6. He solemnly binds his soul with a bond that, if God work deliverance for him, the God of his mercies shall be the God of his praises, *v.* 9. He covenants with God, (1.) That he will honour him in his devotions with the *sacrifice of thanksgiving;* and God has said, for the encouragement of those that do so, that those that *offer praise glorify him.* He will, according to the law of Moses, bring *a sacrifice of thanksgiving,* and will offer that according to the law of nature, with the *voice of thanksgiving.* The love and thankfulness of the heart to God are the life and soul of this duty; without these neither the sacrifice of thanksgiving nor the voice of thanksgiving will avail any thing. But gratitude was then, by a divine appointment, to be expressed by a sacrifice, in which the offerer presented the beast slain to God, not in lieu of himself, but in token of himself; and it is now to be expressed by the *voice of thanksgiving,* the *calves of our lips* (Hos. 14:2), the *fruit of our lips* (Heb. 13:15), speaking forth, singing forth, the high praises of our God. This Jonah here promises, that with the sacrifice of thanksgiving he will *mention the lovingkindness of the Lord,* to his glory, and the encouragement of others. (2.) That he will honour him in his conversation by a punctual performance of his vows, which he made in the fish's belly. Some think it was some work of charity that he vowed, or such a vow as Jacob's was, *Of all that thou hast given me I will give the tenth unto thee.* More probably his vow was that if God would deliver him he would readily go wherever he should please to send him, though it were to Nineveh. When we smart for deserting our duty it is time to promise that we will adhere to it, and abound in it. Or, perhaps, the sacrifice of thanksgiving is the thing he vowed, and that is it which he will pay, as David, Ps. 116:17–19.

7. He concludes with an acknowledgment of God as the Saviour of his people: *Salvation is of the Lord;* it *belongs to the Lord,* Ps. 3:8. He is the *God of salvation,* Ps. 68:19, 20. He only can work salvation, and he can do it be the danger and distress ever so great; he has promised salvation to his people that trust in him. All the salvations of his church in general, and of particular saints, were wrought by him; he is the *Saviour of those that believe,* 1 Tim. 4:10. Salvation is still of him, as it has always been; from him alone it is to be expected, and on him we are to depend for it. Jonah's experience shall encourage others, in all ages, to trust in God as the God of their salvation; all that read this story shall say with assurance, say with admiration, that *salvation is of the Lord,* and is sure to all that belongs to him.

Verse 10

We have here Jonah's discharge from his imprisonment, and his deliverance from that death which there he was threatened with — his return, though not to life, for he lived in the fish's belly, yet to the *land of the living,* for from that he seemed to be quite cut off — his resurrection, though not from death, yet from the grave, for surely never man was so buried alive as Jonah was in the fish's belly. His enlargement may be considered, 1. As an instance of God's power over all the creatures. God *spoke to the fish,* gave him orders to return him, as before he had given him orders to receive him. God speaks to other creatures, and *it is done;* they are all his ready obedient servants. But to man he *speaks once, yea, twice, and he perceives it not,* regards it not, but turns a deaf ear to what he says. Note, God has all creatures at his command, makes what use he pleases of them, and serves his own purposes by them. 2. As an instance of God's mercy to a poor penitent, that in his distress prays to him. Jonah had sinned, and had done foolishly, very foolishly; his own backslidings did not correct him, and it appears by his after-conduct that his foolishness was not quite driven from him, no, not by the rod of this correction; and yet, upon his praying, and humbling himself before God, here is a miracle in nature wrought for his deliverance, to intimate what a miracle of grace, free grace, God's reception and entertainment of returning sinners are. When God had him at his mercy he showed him mercy, and did not *contend for ever.* 3. As a type and figure of Christ's resurrection. He died and was buried, to lay in the grave, as Jonah did, three days and three nights, a prisoner for our debt; but the third day he came forth, as Jonah did, by his messengers to preach repentance, and remission of sins, even to the Gentiles. And thus was another scripture fulfilled, *After two days he will receive us, and the third day he will raise us up,* Hos. 6:2. The earth trembled as if full of her burden, as the fish was of Jonah.

CHAPTER 3

In this chapter we have, I. Jonah's mission renewed, and the command a second time given him to go preach at Nineveh (*v.* 1, 2). II. Jonah's message to Nineveh faithfully delivered, by which its speedy overthrow was threatened (*v.* 3, 4). III. The repentance, humiliation, and reformation of the Ninevites hereupon (*v.* 5–9). IV. God's gracious revocation of the sentence passed upon them, and the preventing of the ruin threatened (*v.* 10).

Verses 1–4

We have here a further evidence of the reconciliation between God and Jonah, and that it was a thorough reconciliation, though the controversy between them had run high.

I. Jonah's commission is renewed and readily obeyed.

1. By this it appears that God was perfectly reconciled to Jonah, that he employed him again in his service; and the commission anew given him was an evidence of the remission of his former disobedience. Among men, it has been justly pleaded that the giving of a commission to a criminal convicted is equivalent to a pardon, so it was to Jonah. *The word of the Lord came unto Jonah the second time* (*v.* 1); for, 1. Jonah must be tried, whether he do indeed repent of his former disobedience or no, and whether he have gotten the good designed him both by his strange punishment an by his strange deliverance. He had deserted his work and duty, and had been under arrest for it, had received a *sentence of death within himself;* but, upon his submission, God had released him, had given him his life, had given him his liberty; but it is upon his good behaviour that he is released, and he must again be put upon the trial whether he will follow the will of God or his own will. After he has been thrown into the sea, and thrown out of it again, God comes and asks him, "Jonah, wilt thou go to Nineveh now?" For *when God judges he will overcome,* he will gain his point; he will bring the disobedient stubborn child to his foot at last. Note, When God has afflicted us, and delivered us out of affliction, we must hear his voice, saying to us, Now return to the duties which before you neglected, and which by these providences you are called to. God now said, in effect, to Jonah, as Christ said to the impotent man, when he had healed him, "Now go and sin no more, *lest a worse thing come unto thee* (Jn. 5:14), a worse thing than lying three days and three nights in the whale's belly." God looks upon men, when he has afflicted them and has delivered them out of their affliction, to see whether they will mend of that fault, particularly, for which they were corrected; and therefore in that thing we are concerned to see to it that we receive not the grace of God in vain, neither in the correction nor in the deliverance, for both are designed to be means of grace. (2.) Jonah shall be trusted, in token of God's favour to him. God might justly have said concerning Jonah, as we should concerning one that had cheated us and dealt treacherously with us, that though we would not proceed to the rigour of the law against him, nor ruin him, yet we would never again repose a confidence in him; justly might the Spirit of prophecy, which Jonah had resisted and rebelled against, depart from him, with a resolution never to return to him any more. One would have expected that though his life was spared, yet he would be laid under a disability and incapacity ever to serve the government again in the character of a prophet. But, behold! the word of the Lord comes to him again, to show that when God forgives he forgets, and whom he forgives he gives a new heart and a new spirit to; he receives those into his family again, and restores them to their former estate, that had been prodigal children and disobedient servants. Note, God's making use of us is the best evidence of his being at peace with us. Hereby it will appear that our sins are pardoned, and we have the good-will of God towards us; does his good word come unto us, and do we experience his good work in us! if so, we have reason to admire the riches of free grace and to own our obligations to the Lord Jesus, who received gifts for men, *yea, even for the rebellious also, that the Lord God might dwell* even among them, and employ them in his word, Ps. 68:18.

2. By this it appears that Jonah was well reconciled to God, that he was not now, as he had been before, *disobedient to the heavenly vision,* did not *flee from the presence of the Lord,* as he had done. He neither endeavored to avoid hearing the command, nor did he decline obeying it; he made no objections, as he had done, that the journey was *long,* the errand invidious, the delivery of it perilous, and, if the threatened judgment did come, he should be reproached as a false prophet, and the impenitence of his own nation would be upbraided, which he had objected, *ch.* 4:2. But now, without murmuring and disputing, *Jonah arose, and went unto Nineveh, according to the word of the Lord, v.* 3. See here, (1.) The nature of repentance; it is the change of our mind and way, and a return to our work and duty, from which we had turned aside; it is doing that good which we had left undone. (2.) The benefit of affliction; it reduces those to their place that had deserted it. Jonah might truly say with David, *"Before I was afflicted I went astray, but now have I kept thy word;* and therefore, though it was dreadful, though it was painful to me, and for the present *not joyous, but grievous,* yet *it was good,* very good, *for me, that I was afflicted."* (3.) See the power of divine grace working with affliction, for otherwise affliction of itself would rather drive men from God than bring them to him; but God by his grace can *turn the disobedient to the wisdom of the just,* and make those *willing in the day of his power,* freely willing to come under his yoke, whose *neck* had been *as an iron sinew.* (4.) See the duty of all those to whom the word of the Lord

comes; they must in all points conform themselves to it, and yield a cheerful faithful obedience to the orders God gives them. *Jonah arose,* and did not sit still in sloth or sullenness; he went directly to Nineveh, though it was a great way off, and a place where, it is likely, he never was before; yet thither he took his journey, *according to the word of the Lord.* God's servants must go where he sends them, come when he calls them, and do what he bids them; whatever appears to be the word of the Lord we must conscientiously do according to it.

II. Let us now see what was the command or commission given him, and what he did in prosecution of it.

1. He was sent as a herald at arms, in the name of the God of heaven, to proclaim war with Nineveh (*v.* 2): "Arise, go to Nineveh, that great city," that metropolis, and *preach unto it,* preach *against it,* so the Chaldee. What is against us is preached to us, that we may hear it and take warning; and what is preached to us, if we do not give ear to it, and mix faith with it, will prove to be against us. Jonah is sent to Nineveh, which was at this time the chief city of the Gentile world, as an indication of God's gracious intentions in process of time to make the light of divine revelation to shine in those dark regions. God knew that if Sodom and Gomorrah, Tyre and Sidon, had had the means of grace, they would have repented, and yet he denied them those means, Mt. 11:21, 23. He knew that if Nineveh had now the means of grace they would repent, and he gave them those means, sent Jonah, though not to preach repentance to them expressly (for we find not that he had that in his commission), yet to preach them to repentance, for that was the happy effect of what he had in commission. If God thus in dispensing his favours, in giving the means of grace to some places and not to others, and the spirit of grace to some persons and not to others, acts by prerogative and in a way of sovereignty, who may say unto him, What doest thou? *May he not do what he will with his own?* He is debtor to no man. Go, and preach (says God) *the preaching that I bid thee.* That is, (1.) "The preaching that I did bid thee when I first ordered thee to go thither (*ch.* 1:2); go, *and cry against it;* denounce divine judgments against it; tell the men of Nineveh that their wickedness has come up to God, and God's vengeance is coming down upon them." This was the message Jonah was then very loth to deliver, and therefore flew off and went to Tarshish; but, when he is brought to it the second time, God does not at all alter the message, to gratify him, or make it the more passable with him; no, he must now preach the very same that he was then ordered to preach and would not. Note, The word of God is an unalterable thing, and will not be made to bend to the humours either of its preachers or of its hearers; it shall never comply with their humours and fancies, but they must comply with its truths and laws. See Jer. 15:19. *Let them return unto thee, but return not thou unto them.* Or, (2.) "The preaching that I shall bid thee when thou comest thither." This was an encouragement to him in his undertaking, that God would go along with him, that the Spirit of prophecy should abide upon him, and be ready to him, when he was at Nineveh, to give him all the further instructions that were needed for him. This intimated that he should hear from him again, which would be his great support in this hazardous expedition; as, when God sent Abraham to offer up Isaac, he gave him a similar intimation, by telling him he must do it upon *one of the mountains which he would* afterwards direct *him to. The steps of a good man are ordered by the Lord;* he leads his people step by step, and so he expects they should follow him. Jonah must go with an implicit faith. Though he knows whither he goes, he shall not know, till he come thither, what message he must deliver, but, whatever it is, he must deliver it, be it pleasing or displeasing. Thus God will keep us in a continual dependence upon himself, and the directions of his word and providence. What he does, and what he will have us do, we *know not now,* but we *shall know hereafter.* Admirals, sometimes, when they are sent abroad, are not to open their commission till they have got so many leagues off at sea; so Jonah must go to Nineveh, and, when he comes there, shall be told what to say.

III. He faithfully and boldly delivered his errand. When he came to Nineveh he found his diocese large; it was an *exceedingly great city of three days' journey* (*v.* 3); a city *great to God,* so the Hebrew phrase is, meaning no more than as we render it, *exceedingly great;* this honour that language does to the great God that great things derive their denomination from him. The greatness of Nineveh consisted chiefly in the extent of it; it was much larger than Babylon, such a city, says Diodorus Siculus, as no man ever after built. It was 150 furlongs long and 90 broad, and 480 in compass; the walls 100 feet high, and so thick that three chariots might go a-breast upon them; on them were 1500 towers, each of them 200 feet high. It is here said to be of *three days' journey;* for the compass of the walls, as some relate, was 480 furlongs, which, allowing eight furlongs to a mile, makes sixty miles, which may well be reckoned *three days' journey* for a footman, twenty miles a day. Or, walking slowly and gravely as Jonah must when he went about preaching, it would take him up at least *three days* to go through all the principal streets and lanes of the city, to proclaim his message, that all might have notice of it. When he came thither he lost no time; he did not come to look about him, but applied closely to his work; and, when he began to enter into the city, he did not retire into an inn, to refresh himself after his journey, but opened his commission immediately, according to his instructions, and he *cried, and said, Yet forty days, and Nineveh shall be overthrown.* This, no doubt, he had particular warrant and direction to say; whether he enlarged upon this text, as is most probable, showing them the controversy God had with them, and how provoking their wickedness was, and what reason they had to expect destruction and give credit to this warning, or whether he only repeated those words again and again, is not certain, but this was the purport of his message. 1. He must tell them that this great city shall be overthrown; he meant, and they understood him, that it should be overthrown, not by war, but by some immediate stroke from heaven, either by an earthquake or by fire and brimstone as Sodom was. The wickedness of cities ripens them for destruction, and their wealth and greatness cannot protect them from destruction when the measure of their iniquity is full and the measure of their vengeance has come. Great cities are easily overthrown when the great God comes to reckon with them. 2. He must tell them that it shall shortly be overthrown, at the end of forty days. It has a reprieve granted. So long God will wait to see if, upon this alarm given, they will humble themselves and amend their doings, and so prevent the ruin threatened. See how slow God is to wrath; though Nineveh's wickedness cried for vengeance, yet it shall be spared for forty days, that it may have space to repent and meet God in the way of his judgments. But he will wait no longer; if in that time they turn not, they shall know that he has *whet his sword, and made it ready.* Forty days is a long time for a righteous God to defer his judgments, yet it is but a little time for an unrighteous people to repent and reform in, and so turn away the judgments coming. The fixing of the day thus, with all possible assurance, would help to convince them that it was a message from God, for no man durst be so positive in fixing a time, however he might prognosticate the thing itself; it would also startle them into preparation for it. It may justly awaken secure sinners by a sincere conversion to prevent their own ruin when they see they have but a little time to turn in. And should it not awaken us to get ready for death, to consider that the thing itself is certain, and the time fixed in the counsel of God, but that we are kept in the dark and uncertainty about it in order that we may be always ready? We cannot be so sure that we shall live forty days as Nineveh now was that it should stand forty days; nay, I think it is more probable that we shall die within thirty or forty days than we should live thirty or forty years; and so many years in the day of our security we are apt to promise ourselves.

> Fleres, si scires unum tua tempora mensem;
> Rides, cum non sit forsitan una dies.
>
> We should be alarmed if we were sure not to live a month, and yet we are careless, though we are not sure to live a day.

Verses 5–10

Here is I. A wonder of divine grace in the repentance and reformation of Nineveh, upon the warning given them of their destruction approaching. *Verily I say unto you,* we have not found so great an instance of it, no, not in Israel; and it will *rise up in judgment against the men of* the gospel-*generation, and condemn them; for the Ninevites repented at the preaching of Jonas, but behold, a greater than Jonas is here,* Mt. 12:41. Nay, it did condemn the impenitence and obstinacy of Israel at that time. God sent many prophets to Israel, and those well known among them to be *mighty in word and deed;* but to Nineveh he sent only one, and him a stranger, whose aspect was mean, we may suppose, and his *bodily presence weak,* especially after the fatigue of so long a journey; and yet they repented, but Israel repented not. Jonah preached but one sermon, and we do not find that he gave them any sign or wonder by the accomplishment of which his word might be confirmed; and yet they were wrought upon, while Israel continued obstinate, whose prophets chose out words wherewith to reason with them, and confirmed them by signs following. Jonah only threatened wrath and ruin; we do not find that he gave them any calls to repentance or directions how to repent, much less any encouragements to hope that they should find mercy if they did repent, much less any encouragements to hope that they should find mercy if they did repent, and yet they repented; but Israel persisted in impertinence, though the prophets sent to them drew them *with cords of a man, and with bands of love,* and assured them of great things which God would do for them if they did repent and reform. Now let us see what was the method of Nineveh's repentance, what were the steps and particular instances of it.

1. They *believed God;* they gave credit to the word which Jonah spoke to them in the name of God: they believed that though they had many that they called gods, yet there was but *one living and true God,* the sovereign Lord of all, — that to him they were accountable, — that they had sinned against him and had become obnoxious to his justice, — that this notice sent them of ruin approaching came from him, and consequently that the ruin itself would come from him at a time prefixed if it were not prevented by a timely repentance, — that he is a merciful God, and there might be some hopes of the turning away of the wrath threatened, if they did turn away from the sins for which it was threatened. Note, Those that *come to God,* that come back to him after they have revolted from him, must believe, must believe that he is, that he is reconcilable, that he will be theirs if they take the right course. And observe what great faith God can work by very small, weak, and unlikely means; he can bring even Ninevites by a few threatening words to be *obedient to the faith.* Some think the Ninevites heard, from the mariners or others, or from Jonah himself, of his being cast into the sea and delivered thence by miracle, and that this served for a confirmation of his mission, and brought them the more readily to believe God speaking by him. But of this we have no certainty. However, Christ's resurrection, typified by that of Jonah's, served for the confirmation of his gospel, and contributed abundantly to their great success who in his name *preached repentance and remission of sins to all nations, beginning at Jerusalem.*

2. They brought word to the king of Nineveh, who, some think, was at this time Sardanapalus, others Pul, king of Assyria. Jonah was not directed to go to him first, in respect to his royal dignity; crowned heads, when guilty heads, are before God upon a level with common heads, and therefore Jonah is not sent to the court, but to the streets of Nineveh, to make his proclamation. However, an account of his errand is brought to the king of Nineveh, not by way of information against Jonah, as a disturber of public peace, that he might be silenced and punished, which perhaps would have been done if he had cried thus in the streets of Jerusalem, who *killed God's prophets and stoned those that were sent unto her.* No; the account was brought him of it, not as of a crime, but as a message from heaven, by some that were concerned for the public welfare, and whose hearts trembled for it. Note, Those kings are happy who have such about them as will give them notice of the things that belong to the kingdom's peace, of the warnings both of the word and of the providence of God, and of the tokens of God's displeasure which they are under; and those people are happy who have such kings over them as will take notice of those things.

3. The king set them a good example of humiliation, *v.* 6. When he heard of the *word of God* sent to him he *rose from his throne,* as Eglon the king of Moab, who, when Ehud told him he had a message to him form God, *rose*

up out of his seat. The king of Nineveh *rose from his throne,* not only in reverence to a word from God in general, but in fear of a word of wrath in particular, and in sorrow and shame for sin, by which he and his people had become obnoxious to his wrath. He rose from his royal throne, and laid aside his royal robe, the badge of his imperial dignity, as an acknowledgment that, having not used his power as he ought to have done for the restraining of violence and wrong, and the maintaining of right, he had forfeited his throne and robe to the justice of God, had rendered himself unworthy of the honour put upon him and the trust reposed in him as a king, and that it was just with God to take his kingdom from him. Even the king himself disdained not to put on the garb of a penitent, for he *covered himself with sackcloth, and sat in ashes,* in token of his humiliation for sin and his dread of divine vengeance. It well becomes the greatest of men to abase themselves before the great God.

4. The people conformed to the example of the king, nay, it should seem, they led the way, for they first began to *put on sackcloth, from the greatest of them even to the least of them, v.* 5. The least of them, that had least to lose in the overthrow of the city, did not think themselves unconcerned in the alarm; and the greatest of them, that were accustomed to lie at ease and live in state, did not think it below them to put on the marks of humiliation. The wearing of sackcloth, especially to those who were used to fine linen, was a very uneasy thing, and they would not have done it if they had not had a deep sense of their sin and their danger by reason of sin, which hereby they designed to express. Note, Those that would not be ruined must be humbled, those that would not destroy their souls must afflict their souls; when God's judgments threaten us we are concerned to *humble ourselves under his mighty hand;* and though bodily exercise alone profits nothing, and man's *spreading sackcloth and ashes under him,* if that be all, is but a jest (it is the heart that God looks at, Isa. 58:5), yet on solemn days of humiliation, when God in his providence *calls to mourning and girding with sackcloth,* we must by the outward expressions of inward sorrow *glorify God with our bodies,* at least by laying aside their ornaments.

5. A general fast was proclaimed and observed throughout that great city, *v.* 7–9. It was ordered *by the decree of the king and his nobles;* the whole legislative power concurred in appointing it, and the whole body of the people concurred in observing it, and in both these ways it became a national act, and it was necessary that it should be so when it was to prevent a national ruin. We have here the contents of this proclamation, and it is very observable. See here,

(1.) What it is that is required by it. [1.] That the fast (properly so called) be very strictly observed. On the day appointed for this solemnity, *let neither man or beast taste any thing;* let them not take the least refreshment, no, no so much as *drink water;* let them not plead that they cannot fast so long without prejudice to their health, or that they cannot bear it; let them try for once. What if they do feel it an uneasiness, and feel from it for some time after? It is better to submit to that than be wanting in any act or instance of that repentance which is necessary to save a sinking city. Let them make themselves uneasy in body by *putting on sackcloth,* as well as by fasting, to show how uneasy they are in mind, through sorrow for sin and the fear of divine wrath. Even the *beasts* must do penance as well as man, because they have been made *subject to vanity* as instruments of man's sin, and that, either by their complaints or their silent pining for want of meat, they might stir up their owners, and those that attended them, to the expressions of sorrow and humiliation. Those cattle that were kept within doors must not be fed and watered as usual, because no meat must be stirring on that day. Things of that kind must be forgotten, and not minded. As when the psalmist was intent upon the praises of God he called upon the inferior creatures to join with him therein, so when the Ninevites were full of sorrow for sin, and dread of God's judgments, they would have the inferior creatures concur with them in the expressions of penitence. The beasts that used to be covered with rich and fine trappings, which were the pride of their masters, and theirs too, must now be *covered with sackcloth;* for the great men will (as becomes them) lay aside their equipage. [2.] With their fasting and mourning they must join prayer and supplication to God; for the fasting is designed to fit the body for the service of the soul in the duty of prayer, which is the main matter, and to which the other is but preparatory or subservient. *Let them cry mightily to God;* let even the brute creatures do it according to their capacity; let their cries and moans for want of food be graciously construed as cries to God, as the cries of the *young ravens* are (Job 38:41), and of the *young lions,* Ps. 104:21. But especially let the men, women, and children, *cry to God;* let them *cry mightily* for the pardon of the sins which cry against them. It was time to cry to God when there was but a step between them and ruin — high time to seek the Lord. In prayer we must cry mightily, with a fixedness of thought, firmness of faith, and fervour of pious and devout affections. By crying mightily we wrestle with God; we take hold of him; and we are concerned to do so when he is not only departing from us as a friend, but coming forth against us as an enemy. It therefore concerns us in prayer to stir up all that is within us. Yet this is not all; [3.] They must to their fasting and praying add reformation and amendment of life: *Let them turn every one from his evil way,* the evil way he has chosen, the evil way he is addicted to, and walks in, the evil way of his heart, and the evil way of his conversation, and particularly *from the violence that is in their hands;* let them restore what they had unjustly taken, and make reparation for what wrong they have done, and let them not any more oppress those they have power over nor defraud those they having dealings with; let the men in authority, at the court-end of the town, turn *from the violence that is in their hands,* and not *decree unrighteous decrees,* nor give wrong judgment upon appeals made to them. Let the men of business, at the trading-end of the town, turn *from the violence in their hands,* and use no unjust weights or measures, nor impose upon the ignorance or necessity of those they trade with. Note, It is not enough to fast for sin, but we must fast from sin, and, in order to the success of our prayers, must no more *regard iniquity in our hearts,* Ps. 66:18. This is *the only fast that God has chosen* and will accept, Isa. 58:6; Zec. 7:5, 9. The work of a fast-day is not done with the day; no, then the hardest and most needful part of the work begins, which is to turn from sin, and to live a new life, and not return with the dog to his vomit.

(2.) Upon what inducement this fast is proclaimed and religiously observed (*v.* 9). *Who can tell if God will turn and repent?* Observe, [1.] What it is that they hope for — that God will, upon their repenting and turning, change his way towards them and revoke his sentence against them, that he will *turn from his fierce anger,* which they own they deserve and yet humbly and earnestly deprecate, and that thus their ruin will be prevented, and they perish not. They cannot object against the equity of the judgment, they pretend not to set it aside by appealing to a higher court, but hope in God himself, that he will repent, and that his own mercy (to which they fly) *shall rejoice against judgment.* They believe that God is justly angry with them, that, their sin being very heinous, his anger is very fierce, and that, if he proceed against them, there is no remedy, but they die, they perish, they all perish, and are undone; for who knows the power of his anger? It is not therefore the threatened overthrow that they pray for the prevention of, but the anger of God that they pray for the turning away of. As when we pray for the favour of God we pray for all good, so when we pray against the wrath of God we pray against all evil. [2.] What degree of hope they had of it: *Who can tell if God will turn to us?* Jonah had not told them; they had not among them any other prophets to tell them, so that they could not be so confident of finding mercy upon their repentance as we may be, who have the promise and oath of God to depend upon, and especially the merit and mediation of Christ to trust to, for pardon upon repentance. Yet they had a a general notion of the goodness of God's nature, his mercy to man, and his being pleased with the repentance and conversion of sinners; and from this they raised some hopes that he would spare them; they dare not presume, but they will not despair. Note, Hope of mercy is the great encouragement to repentance and reformation; and though there be but some glimmerings of hope mixed with great fears arising from a sense of our own sinfulness, and unworthiness, and long abuse of divine patience, yet they may serve to quicken and engage our serious repentance and reformation. Let us boldly cast ourselves at the footstool of free grace, resolving that if we perish, we will perish there; yet who knows but God will look upon us with compassion?

II. Here is a wonder of divine mercy in the sparing of these Ninevites upon their repentance (*v.* 10): *God saw their works;* he not only heard their good words, by which they professed repentance, but saw their good works, by which they brought forth *fruits meet for repentance;* he saw that they *turned from their evil way,* and that was the thing he looked for and required. If he had not seen that, their fasting and sackcloth would have been as nothing in his account. He saw there was among them a general conviction of their sins and a general resolution not to return to them, and that for some days they lived better, and there was a new face of things upon the city; and this he was well pleased with. Note, God takes notice of every instance of the reformation of sinners, even those instances that fall not under the cognizance and observation of the world. He sees who turn from their evil way and who do not, and meets those with favour that meet him in a sincere conversion. When they repent of the evil of sin committed by them he repents of the evil of judgment pronounced against them. Thus he spared Nineveh, and *did not the evil which he said he would do against it.* Here were no sacrifices offered to God, that we read of, to make atonement for sin, but the *sacrifice of God is a broken spirit; a broken and contrite heart,* such as the Ninevites now had, it what he *will not despise;* it is what he will give countenance to and put honour upon.

CHAPTER 4

We read, with a great deal of pleasure, in the close of the foregoing chapter, concerning the repentance of Nineveh; but in this chapter we read, with a great deal of uneasiness, concerning the sin of Jonah; and, as there is joy in heaven and earth for the conversion of sinners, so there is grief for the follies and infirmities of saints. In all the book of God we scarcely find a "servant of the Lord" (and such a one we are sure Jonah was, for the scripture calls him so) so very much out of temper as he is here, so very peevish and provoking to God himself. In the first chapter we had him fleeing from the face of God; but here we have him, in effect, flying in the face of God; and, which is more grieving to us, there we had an account of his repentance and return to God; but here, though no doubt he did repent, yet, as in Solomon's case, no account is left us of his recovering himself; but, while we read with wonder of his perverseness, we read with no less wonder of God's tenderness towards him, by which it appeared that he had not cast him off. Here is, I. Jonah's repining at God's mercy to Nineveh, and the fret he was in about it (*v.* 1–3). II. The gentle reproof God gave him for it (*v.* 4). III. Jonah's discontent at the withering of the gourd, and his justifying himself in that discontent (*v.* 5–9). IV. God's improving it for his conviction, that he ought not to be angry at the sparing of Nineveh (*v.* 10–11). Man's badness and God's goodness serve here for a foil to each other, that the former may appear the more exceedingly sinful and the latter the more exceedingly gracious.

Verses 1–4

See here, I. How unjustly Jonah quarrelled with God for his mercy to Nineveh, upon their repentance. This gives us occasion to suspect that Jonah had only delivered the message of wrath against the Ninevites, and had not at all assisted or encouraged them in their repentance, as one would think he should have done; for when they did repent, and found mercy,

1. Jonah grudged them the mercy they found (*v.* 1): *It displeased Jonah exceedingly;* and (would you think it?) *he was very angry,* was in a great heat about it. It was very wrong, (1.) That he had so little government of himself as to be displeased and very angry; he had *no rule over his own spirit,* and therefore, as a city broken down, lay exposed to temptations and snares. (2.) That he had so little reverence of God as to be displeased and angry at what he did, as David was when the Lord had made a breach upon Uzza; whatever pleases God should please us, and, though we cannot account for it, yet we must acquiesce in it. (3.) That he had so little affection for men as to be displeased and very angry at the conversion of the Ninevites and their reception into the divine favour. This was the sin of the scribes and Pharisees, who murmured at our Saviour because he entertained publicans and sinners; but *is our eye evil because his is good?* But why was Jonah so uneasy at it, that the Ninevites repented and were spared? It cannot be expected that we should give any good reason for a thing so very absurd and unreasonable; no, nor any thing that has the face or colour of a reason; but we may conjecture what the provocation was. Hot spir-

its are usually high spirits. *Only by pride comes contention* both with God and man. It was a point of honour that Jonah stood upon and that made him angry. [1.] He was jealous for the honour of his country; the repentance and reformation of Nineveh shamed the obstinacy of Israel that repented not, but *hated to be reformed;* and the favour God had shown to these Gentiles, upon their repentance, was an ill omen to the Jewish nation, as if they should be (as at length they were) rejected and cast out of the church and the Gentiles substituted in their room. When it was intimated to St. Peter himself that he should make no difference between Jews and Gentiles he startled at the thing, and said, *Not so, Lord;* no marvel then that Jonah looked upon it with regret that Nineveh should become a favourite. Jonah herein had *a zeal for God* as the God of Israel in a particular manner, *but not according to knowledge.* Note, Many are displeased with God under pretence of concern for his glory. [2.] He was jealous for his own honour, fearing lest, if Nineveh was not destroyed within forty days, he should be accounted a false prophet, and stigmatized accordingly; whereas he needed not be under any discontent about that, for in the threatening of ruin it was implied that, for the preventing of it, they should repent, and, if they did, it should be prevented. And no one will complain of being deceived by him that is better than his word; and he would rather gain honour among them, by being instrumental to save them, than fall under any disgrace. But melancholy men (and such a one Jonah seems to have been) are apt to make themselves uneasy by fancying evils to themselves that are not, nor are ever likely to be. Most of our frets, as well as our frights, are owing to the power of imagination; and those are to be pitied as perfect bond-slaves that are under the power of such a tyrant.

2. He quarreled with God about it. When his heart was hot within him, he *spoke unadvisedly with his lips;* and here he tells us what he said (*v.* 2, 3): He *prayed unto the Lord,* but it is a very awkward prayer, not like that which he prayed in the fish's belly; for affliction teaches us to pray submissively, which Jonah now forgot to do. Being in discontent, he applied to the duty of prayer, as he used to do in his troubles, but his corruptions got head of his graces, and, when he should have been praying for benefit by the mercy of God himself, he was complaining of the benefit others had by that mercy. Nothing could be spoken more unbecomingly. (1.) He now begins to justify himself in fleeing *from the presence of the Lord,* when he was first ordered to go to Nineveh, for which he had before, with good reason, condemned himself: *"Lord,"* said he, *"was not this my saying when I was in my own country?* Did I not foresee that if I went to preach to Nineveh they would repent, and thou wouldst forgive them, and then thy word would be reflected upon and reproached as yea and nay?" What a strange sort of man was Jonah, to dread the success of his ministry! Many have been tempted to withdraw from their work because they had despaired of doing good by it, but Jonah declined preaching because he was afraid of doing good by it; and still he persists in the same corrupt notion, for, it seems, the whale's belly itself could not cure him of it. It was his saying when he was *in his own country,* but it was a bad saying; yet here he stands to it, and, very unlike the other prophets, *desires the woeful day* which he had foretold and grieves because it does not come. Even Christ's disciples *know not what manner of spirit they are of;* those did not who wished for fire from heaven upon the city that did not receive them, much less did Jonah, who wished for fire from heaven upon the city that did receive him, Lu. 9:55. Jonah thinks he has reason to complain of that, when it is done, which he was before afraid of; so hard is it to get a root of bitterness plucked out of the mind, when once it is fastened there. And why did Jonah expect that God would spare Nineveh? *Because I knew that thou was a gracious God,* indulgent and easily pleased, that *thou wast slow to anger and of great kindness, and repentest thee of the evil.* All this is very true; and Jonah could not but know it by God's proclamation of his name and the experiences of all ages; but it is strange and very unaccountable that that which all the saints had made the matter of their joy and praise Jonah should make the matter of reflection upon God, as if that were an imperfection of the divine nature which is indeed the greatest glory of it — that God *is gracious and merciful.* The servant that said, *I knew thee to be a hard man,* said that which was false, and yet, had it been true, it was not the proper matter of a complaint; but Jonah, though he says what is true, yet, speaking it by way of reproach, speaks very absurdly. Those have a spirit of contention and contradiction indeed that can find in their hearts to quarrel with the goodness of God, and his sparing pardoning mercy, to which we all owe it that we are out of hell. This is making that to be to us *a savour of death unto death* which ought to be *a savour of life unto life.* (2.) In a passion, he wishes for death (*v.* 3), a strange expression of his causeless passion! *"Now, O Lord! take, I beseech thee, my life from me.* If Nineveh must live, let me die, rather than see thy word and mine disproved, rather than see the glory of Israel transferred to the Gentiles," as if there were not grace enough in God both for Jews and Gentiles, or as if his countrymen were the further off from mercy for the Ninevites being taken into favour. When the prophet Elijah had laboured in vain, he wished he might die, and it was his infirmity, 1 Ki. 19:4. But Jonah labours to good purpose, saves a great city from ruin, and yet wishes he may die, as if, having done much good, he were afraid of living to do more; he *sees of the travail of his soul, and is dissatisfied.* What a perverse spirit is mingled with every word he says! When Jonah was brought alive out of the whale's belly, he thought life a very valuable mercy, and was thankful to that God who brought up *his life from corruption,* (*ch.* 2:6), and a great blessing his life had been to Nineveh; yet now, for that very reason, it became a burden to himself and he begs to be eased of it, pleading, *It is better for me to die than to live.* Such a word as this may be the language of grace, as it was in Paul, who desired to depart and be with Christ, *which is far better;* but here it was the language of folly, and passion, and strong corruption; and so much the worse, [1.] Jonah being now in the midst of his usefulness, and therefore fit to live. He was one whose ministry God wonderfully owned and prospered. The conversion of Nineveh might give him hopes of being instrumental to convert the whole kingdom of Assyria; it was therefore very absurd for him to wish he might die when he had a prospect of living to so good a purpose and could be so ill spared. [2.] Jonah being now so much out of temper and therefore unfit to die. How durst he think of dying, and going to appear before God's judgment-seat, when he was actually quarrelling with him? Was this a frame of spirit proper for a man to go out of the world in? But those who passionately desire death commonly have least reason to do it, as being very much unprepared for it. Our business is to get ready to die by doing the work of life, and then to refer ourselves to God to take away our life when and how he pleases.

II. See how justly God reproved Jonah for this heat that he was in (*v.* 4): The Lord said, *Doest thou well to be angry? Is doing well a displeasure to thee?* so some read it. What! dost thou repent of thy good deeds? God might justly have rejected him for this impious heat which he was in, might justly have taken him at his word, and have struck him dead when he wished to die; but he vouchsafes to reason with him for his conviction and to bring him to a better temper, as the father of the prodigal reasoned with his elder son, when, as Jonah here, he murmured at the remission and reception of his brother. *Doest thou well to be angry?* See how mildly the great God speaks to this foolish man, to teach us to restore those that have fallen with a *spirit of meekness,* and with *soft answers* to *turn away wrath.* God appeals to himself and to his own conscience: *"Doest thou well?* Thou knowest thou does not." We should often put this question to ourselves, Is it well to say thus, to do thus? Can I justify it? Must I not unsay it and undo it again by repentance, or be undone forever? Ask, 1. Do I well to be angry? When passion is up, let it meet with this check, "Do I well to be so soon angry, so often angry, so long angry, to put myself into such a heat, and to give others such ill language in my anger? Is this well, that I suffer these headstrong passions to get dominion over me?" 2. "Do I well to be angry at the mercy of God to repenting sinners?" That was Jonah's crime. Do we do well to be angry at that which is so much for the glory of God and the advancement of his kingdom among men — to be angry at that which angels rejoice in and for which abundant thanksgivings will be rendered to God? We do ill to be angry at that grace which we ourselves need and are undone without; if room were not left for repentance, and hope given of pardon upon repentance, what would become of us? Let the conversion of sinners, which is the joy of heaven, be our joy, and never our grief.

Verses 5–11

Jonah persists here in his discontent; for the *beginning of strife* both with God and man *is as the letting forth of waters,* the breach grows wider and wider, and, when passion gets head, bad is made worse; it should therefore be silenced and suppressed at first. We have here,

I. Jonah's sullen expectation of the fate of Nineveh. We may suppose that the Ninevites, giving credit to the message he brought, were ready to give entertainment to the messenger that brought it, and to show him respect, that they would have made him welcome to the best of their houses and tables. But Jonah was out of humour, would not accept their kindness, nor behave towards them with common civility, which one might have feared would have prejudiced them against him and his word; but when there is not only the *treasure* put into *earthen vessels,* but the trust lodged with men *subject to like passions as we are,* and yet the point gained, it must be owned that the *excellency of the power* appears so much the more to be of God *and not of man.* Jonah retires, *goes out of the city,* sits alone, and keeps silence, because he sees the Ninevites repent and reform, *v.* 5. Perhaps he told those about him that he went out of the city for fear of perishing in the ruins of it; but he went to *see what would become of the city,* as Abraham went up to see what would become of Sodom, Gen. 19:27. The forty days were now expiring, or had expired, and Jonah hoped that, if Nineveh was not overthrown, yet some judgement or other would come upon it, sufficient to save his credit; however, it was with great uneasiness that he waited the issue. He would not sojourn in a house, expecting it would fall upon his head, but he *made himself a booth* of the boughs of trees, and sat in that, though there he would lie exposed to wind and weather. Note, It is common for those that have fretful uneasy spirits industriously to create inconveniences themselves, that, resolving to complain, they may still have something to complain of.

II. God's gracious provision for his shelter and refreshment when he thus foolishly afflicted himself and was still adding yet more and more to his own affliction, *v.* 6. Jonah was sitting in his booth, fretting at the cold of the night and the heat of the day, which were both grievous to him, and God might have said, It is his own choice, his own doing, a house of his own building, let him make the best of it; but he looked on him with compassion, as the tender mother does on the froward child, and relieved him against the grievances which he by his own wilfulness created to himself. He *prepared a gourd,* a plant with broad leaves, and full of them, that suddenly grew up, and covered his hut or booth, so as to keep off much of the injury of the cold and heat. It was *a shadow over his head, to deliver him from his grief,* that, being refreshed in body, he might the better guard against the uneasiness of his mind, which outward crosses and troubles are often the occasion and increase of. See how tender God is of his people in their afflictions, yea, though they are foolish and froward, nor is he *extreme to mark what they do amiss.* God had before *prepared a great fish* to secure Jonah from the injuries of the water, and here a great gourd to secure him from the injuries of the air; for he is the protector of his people against evils of every kind, has the command of plants as well as animals, and can soon prepare them, to make them serve his purposes, can make their growth sudden, which, in a course of nature, is slow and gradual. A gourd, one would think, was but a slender fortification at the best, yet Jonah *was exceedingly glad of the gourd;* for, 1. It was really at that time a great comfort to him. A thing in itself small and inconsiderable, yet, coming seasonably, may be to us a very valuable blessing. A gourd in the right place may do us more service than a cedar. The least creatures may be great plagues (as flies and lice were to Pharaoh) or great comforts (as the gourd to Jonah), according as God is pleased to make them. 2. He being now much under the power of imagination took a greater complacency in it than there was cause for. He was exceedingly glad of it, was proud of it, and triumphed in it. Note, Persons of strong passions, as they are apt to be cast down with a trifle that crosses them, so they are apt to be lifted up with a trifle that pleases them. A small toy will serve sometimes to pacify a cross child, as the gourd did Jonah. But wisdom and grace would teach us both to *weep* for our troubles *as though we wept not,* and to *rejoice* in our comforts *as though we rejoiced not.* Creature-comforts we ought to enjoy and be thankful for, but we need not be exceedingly glad of them; it is God only that must be our *exceeding joy,* Ps. 43:4.

III. The sudden loss of this provision which God had made for his refreshment, and the return of his trouble, *v.* 7, 8. God that had provided comfort for him provided also an affliction for him in that very thing which was his comfort; the affliction did not come by chance, but by divine direction and appointment. 1. God *prepared a worm* to destroy the gourd. He that gave took away, and Jonah ought to have *blessed his name* in both; but because, when he took the comfort of the gourd, he did not give God the praise of it, God deprived him of the benefit of it, and justly. See what all our creature-comforts are, and what we may expect them to be; they are gourds, have their root in the earth, are but a thin and slender defence compared with the *rock of ages;* they are withering things; they perish in the using, and we are soon deprived of the comfort of them. The gourd withered the next day after it sprang up; our comforts *come forth like flowers and are soon cut down.* When we please ourselves most with them, and promise ourselves most from them, we are disappointed. A little thing withers them; a small worm at the root destroys a large gourd. Something unseen and undiscerned does it. Our gourds wither, and we know not what to attribute it to. And perhaps those wither first that we have been more exceedingly glad of; that proves least safe that is most dear. God did not send an angel to pluck up Jonah's gourd, but sent a worm to smite it; there it grew still, but it stood him in no stead. Perhaps our creature-comforts are continued to us, but they are embittered; the creature is continued, but the comfort is gone; and the remains, or ruins of it rather, do but upbraid us with our folly in being exceedingly glad of it. 2. He *prepared a wind* to make Jonah feel the want of the gourd, *v.* 8. It was a *vehement east wind,* which drove the heat of the rising sun violently upon the head of Jonah. This wind was not as a fan to abate the heat, but as bellows to make it more intense. Thus poor Jonah lay open to sun and wind.

IV. The further fret that this put Jonah into (*v.* 8): He *fainted, and wished in himself that he might die.* "If the gourd be killed, if the gourd be dead, kill me too, *let me die with the gourd.*" Foolish man, that thinks his life bound up in the life of a weed! Note, It is just that those who love to complain should never be left without something to complain of, that their folly may be manifested and corrected, and, if possible, cured. And see here how the passions that run into an extreme one way commonly run into an extreme the other way. Jonah, who was in transports of joy when the gourd flourished, is in pangs of grief when the gourd has withered. Inordinate affection lays a foundation for inordinate affliction; what we are over-fond of when we have it we are apt to over-grieve for when we lose it, and we may see our folly in both.

V. The rebuke God gave him for this; he again reasoned with him: *Dost thou well to be angry for the gourd? v.* 9. Note, The withering of a gourd is a thing which it does not become us to be angry at. When afflicting providences deprive us of our relations, possessions, and enjoyments, we must bear it patiently, must not be angry at God, must not be angry *for the gourd.* It is comparatively but a small loss, the loss of a shadow; that is the most we can make of it. It was a gourd, a withering thing; we could expect no other than that it should wither. Our being angry for the withering of it will not recover it; we ourselves shall shortly wither like it. If one gourd be withered, another gourd may spring up in the room of it; but that which should especially silence our discontent is that though our gourd be gone our God is not gone, and there is enough in him to make up all our losses.

Let us therefore own that we do ill, that we do very ill, to be angry for the gourd; and let us under such events quiet ourselves *as a child that is weaned from his mother.*

VI. His justification of his passion and discontent; and it is very strange, *v.* 9. He said, *I do well to be angry, even unto death.* It is bad to speak amiss, yet if it be in haste, if what is said amiss be speedily recalled and unsaid again, it is the more excusable; but to speak amiss and stand to it is bad indeed. So Jonah did here, though God himself rebuked him, and by appealing to his conscience expected he would rebuke himself. See what brutish things ungoverned passions are, and how much it is our interest, and ought to be our endeavour, to chain up these roaring lions and ranging bears. *Sin* and *death* are two very dreadful things, yet Jonah, in his heat, makes light of them both. 1. He has so little regard for God as to fly in the face of his authority, and to say that he did well in that which God said was ill done. Passion often over-rules conscience, and forces it, when it is appealed to, to give a false judgment, as Jonah here did. 2. He has so little regard to himself as to abandon his own life, and to think it no harm to indulge his passion even to death, to kill himself with fretting. We read of *wrath* that *kills the foolish man,* and *envy* that *slays the silly one* (Job *v.* 2), and foolish silly ones indeed those are that cut their own throats with their own passions, that fret themselves into consumptions and other weaknesses, and put themselves into fevers with their own intemperate heats.

VII. The improvement of it against him for his conviction that he did ill to murmur at the sparing of Nineveh. Out of his own mouth God will judge him; and we have reason to think it overcame him; for he made no reply, but, we hope, returned to his right mind and recovered his temper, though he could not keep it, and all was well. Now,

1. Let us see how God argued with him (*v.* 10, 11): "*Thou hast had pity on the gourd,* hast *spared* it" (so the word is), "didst what thou couldst, and wouldst have done more, to keep it alive, and saidst, *What a pity it is* that this gourd should ever wither! and *should not I then spare Nineveh?* Should not I have as much compassion upon that as thou hadst upon the gourd, and forbid the earthquake which would ruin that, as thou wouldst have forbidden the worm that smote the gourd? Consider," (1.) "The gourd thou hadst pity on was but one; but the inhabitants of Nineveh, whom I have pity on, are numerous." It is a great city and very populous, as appears by the number of the infants, suppose from two years old and under; there are 120,000 such in Nineveh, that have not come to so much use of understanding as to know *their right hand from their left,* for they are yet but babes. These are taken notice of because the age of infants is commonly looked upon as the age of innocence. So many there were in Nineveh that had not been guilty of any actual transgression, and consequently had not themselves contributed to the common guilt, and yet, if Nineveh had been overthrown, they would all have been involved in the common calamity; "and *shall not I spare* Nineveh then, with an eye to them?" God has a tender regard to little children, and is ready to pity and succour them, nay, here a whole city is spared for their sakes, which may encourage parents to present their children to God by faith and prayer, that though they are not capable of doing him any service (for they cannot discern *between their right hand and their left,* between good and evil, sin and duty), yet they are capable of participating in his favours and of obtaining salvation. The great Saviour discovered a particular kindness for the children that were brought to him, when he *took them up in his arms, put his hands upon them, and blessed them.* Nay, God took notice of the abundance of cattle too that were in Nineveh, which he had more reason to pity and spare than Jonah had to pity and to spare the gourd, inasmuch as the animal life is more excellent than the vegetable. (2.) The gourd which Jonah was concerned for was none of his own; it was that for which he did not labour and which he made not to grow; but the persons in Nineveh whom God had compassion on were all the *work of his own hands,* whose being he was the author of, whose lives he was the preserver of, whom he planted and made to grow; he made them, and his they were, and therefore he had much more reason to have compassion on them, for he cannot *despise the work of his own hands* (Job 10:3); and thus Job there argues with him (*v.* 8, 9), *Thy hands have made me, and fashioned me,* have *made me as the clay;* and *wilt thou destroy* me, *wilt thou bring me into dust again?* And thus he here argues with himself. (3.) The gourd which Jonah had pity on was of a sudden growth, and therefore of less value; it *came up in a night, it was the son of a night* (so the word is); but Nineveh is an ancient city, of many ages standing, and therefore cannot be so easily given up; "the persons I spare have been many years in growing up, not so soon reared as the gourd; and shall not I then have pity on those that have been so many years the care of my providence, so many years my tenants?" (4.) The gourd which Jonah had pity on *perished in a night;* it withered, and there was an end of it. But the precious souls in Nineveh that God had pity on are not so short-lived; they are immortal, and therefore to be carefully and tenderly considered. One soul is of more value than the whole world, and the gain of the world will not countervail the loss of it; surely then one soul is of more value than many gourds, of more value than many sparrows; so God accounts, and so should we, and therefore have a greater concern for the children of men than for any of the inferior creatures, and for our own and others' precious souls than for any of the riches and enjoyments of this world.

2. From all this we may learn, (1.) That though God may suffer his people to fall into sin, yet he will not suffer them to lie still in it, but will take a course effectually to show them their error, and to bring them to themselves and to their right mind again. We have reason to hope that Jonah, after this, was well reconciled to the sparing of Nineveh, and was as well pleased with it as ever he had been displeased. (2.) That God will justify himself in the methods of his grace towards repenting returning sinners as well as in the course his justice takes with those that persist in their rebellion; though there be those that murmur at the mercy of God, because they do not understand it (for his thoughts and ways therein are as far above ours as heaven above the earth), yet he will make it evident that therein he acts like himself, and will be *justified when he speaks.* See what pains he takes with Jonah to convince him that it is very fit that Nineveh should be spared. Jonah had said, *I do well to be angry,* but he could not prove it. God says and proves it, *I do well to be merciful;* and it is a great encouragement to poor sinners to hope that they shall find mercy with him, that he is so ready to justify himself in showing mercy and to triumph in those whom he makes the monuments of it, against those whose eye is evil because his is good. Such murmurers shall be made to understand this doctrine, that, how narrow soever their souls, their principles, are, and how willing soever they are to engross divine grace to themselves and those of their own way, there is one *Lord over all, that is rich in mercy to all that call upon him,* and in *every nation,* in Nineveh as well as in Israel, *he that fears God and works righteousness is accepted of him;* he that repents, and turns from his evil way, shall find mercy with him.

AN EXPOSITION, WITH PRACTICAL OBSERVATIONS, OF

THE PROPHECY OF MICAH

We shall have some account of this prophet in the first verse of the book of his prophecy; and therefore shall here only observe that, being contemporary with the prophet Isaiah (only that he began to prophesy a little after him), there is a near resemblance between that prophet's prophecy and this; and there is a prediction of the advancement and establishment of the gospel-church, which both of them have, almost in the same words, that out of the mouth of two such witnesses so great a word might be established. Compare Isa. 2:2, 3, with Mic. 4:1, 2. Isaiah's prophecy is said to be concerning *Judah and Jerusalem,* but Micah's concerning *Samaria and Jerusalem;* for, though this prophecy be dated only by the reigns of the kings of Judah, yet it refers to the kingdom of Israel, the approaching ruin of which, in the captivity of the ten tribes, he plainly foretels and sadly laments. What we find here in writing was but an abstract of the sermons he preached during the reigns of three kings. The scope of the whole is, I. To convince sinners of their sins, by setting them in order before them, charging both Israel and Judah with idolatry, covetousness, oppression, contempt of the word of God, and their rulers especially, both in church and state, with the abuse of their power; and also by showing them the judgments of God ready to break in upon them for their sins. II. To comfort God's people with promises of mercy and deliverance, especially with an assurance of the coming of the Messiah and of the grace of the gospel through him. It is remarkable concerning this prophecy, and confirms its authority, that we find two quotations out of it made publicly upon very solemn occasions, and both referring to very great events. 1. One is a prediction of the destruction of Jerusalem (3:12), which we find quoted in the Old Testament, by *the elders of the land* (Jer. 26:17, 18), in justification of Jeremiah, when he foretold the judgments of God coming upon Jerusalem, and to stay the proceedings of the court against him. "Micah (say they) foretold that *Zion should be ploughed as a field,* and Hezekiah did not put him to death; why then should we punish Jeremiah for saying the same?" 2. Another is a prediction of the birth of Christ (5:2) which we find quoted in the New Testament, by the *chief priests and scribes of the people,* in answer to Herod's enquiry, *where Christ should be born* (Mt. 2:5, 6); for still we find that to him bear all the prophets witness.

CHAPTER 1

In this chapter we have, I. The title of the book (*v.* 1) and a preface demanding attention (*v.* 2). II. Warning given of desolating judgments hastening upon the kingdoms of Israel and Judah (*v.* 3, 4), and all for sin (*v.* 5). III. The particulars of the destruction specified (*v.* 6, 7). IV. The greatness of the destruction illustrated, 1. By the prophet's sorrow for it (*v.* 8, 9). 2. By the general sorrow that should be for it, in the several places that must expect to share in it (*v.* 10–16). These prophecies of Micah might well be called his lamentations.

Verses 1–7

Here is, I. A general account of this prophet and his prophecy, *v.* 1. This is prefixed for the satisfaction of all that read and hear the prophecy of this book, who will give the more credit to it when they know the author and his authority. 1. The prophecy is the *word of the Lord;* it is a divine revelation. Note, What is written in the Bible, and what is preached by the ministers of Christ according to what is written there, must be heard and received, not as the word of dying men, which we may be judges of, but as the word of the living God, which we must be judged by, for so it is. This word of the Lord came to the prophet, came plainly, came powerfully, came in a preventing way, and he saw it, saw the vision in which it was conveyed to him, saw the things themselves which he foretold, with as much clearness and certainty as if they had been already accomplished. 2. The prophet is Micah the Morasthite; his name *Micah* is a contraction of Micaiah, the name of a prophet some ages before (in Ahab's time, 1 Ki. 22:8); his surname, the *Morasthite,* signifies that he was born, or lived, at Moresheth, which is mentioned here (*v.* 14), or Mareshah, which is mentioned *v.* 15, and Jos. 15:44. The place of his abode is mentioned, that any one might enquire in that place, at that time, and might find there was, or had been, such a one there, who was generally reputed to be a prophet. 3. The date of his prophecy is in the reigns of three kings of Judah — Jotham, Ahaz, and Hezekiah. Ahaz was one of the worst of Judah's kings, and Hezekiah one of the best; such variety of times pass over God's ministers, times that frown and times that smile, to each of which they must study to accommodate themselves, and to arm themselves against the temptations of both. The promises and threatenings of this book are interwoven, by which it appears that even in the wicked reign he preached comfort, and said *to the righteous* then that it should be *well with them;* and that in the pious reign he preached conviction, and said to the wicked then that it should be *ill with them;* for, however the times change, the word of the Lord is still the same. 4. The parties concerned in this prophecy; it is *concerning Samaria and Jerusalem,* the head cities of the two kingdoms of Israel and Judah, under the influence of which the kingdoms themselves were. Though the ten tribes have deserted the houses both of David and Aaron, yet God is pleased to send prophets to them.

II. A very solemn introduction to the following prophecy (*v.* 2), in which, 1. The people are summoned to draw near and give their attendance, as upon a court of judicature: *Hear, all you people,* Note, Where God has a mouth to speak we must have an ear to hear; we all must, for we are all concerned in what is delivered. *"Hear, you people" (all of them,* so the margin reads it), "all you that are now within hearing, and all others that hear it at second hand." It is an unusual construction; but those words with which Micah begins his prophecy are the very same in the original with those wherewith Micaiah ended his, 1 Ki. 22:28. 2. The earth is called upon, with *all that therein is,* to hear what the prophet has to say: *Hearken, O earth!* The earth shall be made to shake under the stroke and weight of the judgments coming; sooner will the earth hear than this stupid senseless people; but God will be heard when he pleads. If the church, and those in it, will not hear, the earth, and those in it, shall, and shame them. 3. God himself is appealed to, and his omniscience, power, and justice, are vouched in testimony against this people: *"Let the Lord God be witness against you,* a witness that you had fair warning given you, that your prophets did their duty faithfully as watchmen, but you would not take the warning; let the accomplishment of the prophecy be a witness against your contempt and disbelief of it, and prove, to your conviction and confusion, that it was the word of God, and no word of his shall fall to the ground." Note, God himself will be a witness, by the judgments of his hand, against those that would not receive his testimony in the judgments of his mouth. He will be a witness *from his holy temple* in heaven, when he comes down to execute judgment (*v.* 3) against those that turned a deaf ear to his oracles, wherein he witnessed to them, out of his holy temple at Jerusalem.

III. A terrible prediction of destroying judgments which should come upon Judah and Israel, which had its accomplishment soon after in Israel, and at length in Judah; for it is foretold, 1. That God himself will appear against them, *v.* 3. They boasted of themselves and their relation to God, as if that would secure them; but, though God never deceives the faith of the upright, he will disappoint the presumption of the hypocrites, for, *behold, the Lord comes forth out of his place,* quits his mercy-seat, where they thought they had him fast, and prepares his throne for judgment; his glory departs, for they drive it from them. God's way towards this people had long been a way of mercy, but now he changes his way, he *comes out of his place,* and will come down. He had seemed to retire, as one regardless of what was done, but now he will show himself, he will *rend the heavens,* and will *come down,* not as sometimes, in surprising mercies, but in surprising judgments, to do things not for them, but against them, which they *looked not for,* Isa. 64:1; 26:21. 2. That when the Creator appears against them it shall be in vain for any creature to appear for them. He will *tread* with contempt and disdain *upon the high places of the* earth, upon all the powers that are advanced in competition with him or in opposition to him; and he will so tread upon them as to tread them down and level them. High places, set up for the worship of idols or for military fortifications, shall all be trodden down and trampled into the dust. Do men trust to the height and strength of the mountains and rocks, as if they were sufficient to bear up their hopes and bear off their fears? They shall be *molten under him,* melted down as *wax before the fire,* Ps. 68:2. Do they trust to the fruitfulness of the valleys, and their products? They *shall be cleft,* or rent, with those *fiery streams* that shall come pouring down from the mountains when they are melted. They shall be ploughed and washed away as the ground is by *the waters that are poured down a steep place.* God is said to *cleave the earth with rivers,* Hab. 3:9. Neither men of *high degree,* as the mountains, nor *men of low degree,* as the valleys, shall be able to secure either themselves or the land from judgments of God, when they are sent with commission to lay all waste, and, like *a sweeping rain,* to *leave no food,* Prov. 28:3. This is applied particularly to the head city of Israel, which they hoped would be a protection to the kingdom (*v.* 6.) I *will make Samaria,* that is now a rich and populous city, as *a heap of the field,* as a heap of dung laid there to be spread, or as a heap of stones gathered together to be carried away, and *as plantings of a vineyard,* as hillocks of earth raised to plant vines in. God will make of that *city a heap,* of that *defenced city a ruin,* Isa. 25:2. Their *altars* had been as *heaps in the furrows of the fields* (Hos. 12:11) and now their houses shall be so, as ruinous heaps. The *stones of the city* are *poured down into the valley* by the fury of the conqueror, who will thus be revenged on those walls that so long held out against him. They shall be quite pulled down, so that the very *foundations* shall be *discovered,* that had been covered by the superstructure; and not one stone shall be left upon another.

IV. A charge of sin upon them, as the procuring cause of these desolating judgments (*v.* 5): *For the transgression of Jacob is all this.* If it be asked, "Why is God so angry, and why are Jacob and Israel thus brought to ruin by his anger?" the answer is ready: Sin has done all the mischief; sin has laid all waste; all the calamities of Jacob and Israel are owing to their transgressions; if they had not gone away from God, he would never have appeared thus against them. Note, External privileges and professions will not secure a sinful people from the judgments of God. If sin be found in the *house of Israel,* if Jacob be guilty of transgression and rebellion, God will not spare them; no, he will punish them first, for their sins are of all others most provoking to him, for they are most reproaching. But it is asked, *What is the transgression of Jacob?* Note, When we feel the smart of sin it concerns us to enquire what the sin is which we smart for, that we may particularly war against that which wars against us. And what is it? 1. It is idolatry; it is the *high places;* that is the transgression, the great transgression which reigns in Israel; that is spiritual whoredom, the violation of the marriage-covenant, which merits a divorce. Even the *high places of Judah,* though not so bad as the transgression of Jacob, were yet offensive enough to God, and a remaining blemish upon some of the good reigns. *Howbeit the high places were not taken away.* 2. It is the idolatry of Samaria and Jerusalem, the royal cities of those two kingdoms. These were the most populous places, and where there were most people there was most wickedness, and they made one another worse. These were the most pompous places; there men lived most in wealth and pleasure, and they forgot God. These were the places that had the greatest influence upon the country, by authority and example; so that from them idolatry and *profaneness went forth throughout all the land,* Jer. 23:15. Note, Spiritual distempers are most contagious in persons and places that are most conspicuous. If the head city of a kingdom, or the chief family in a parish, be vicious and profane, *many will follow their pernicious ways,* and write after a bad copy when great ones set it for them. The vices of leaders and rulers are leading ruling vices, and therefore shall be surely and sorely punished. Those have a great deal to answer for indeed that not only sin, but *make Israel to sin.* Those must expect to be made examples that have been examples of wickedness. If the transgression of Jacob is Samaria, therefore shall *Samaria become a heap.* Let the ringleaders in sin hear this and fear.

V. The punishment made to answer the sin, in the particular destruction of the idols, *v.* 7. 1. The gods they worshipped shall be destroyed: *The graven images shall be beaten to pieces* by the army of the Assyrians, *and all the idols shall be laid desolate. Samaria and her idols* were ruined together by Sennacherib (Isa. 10:11), and *their gods cast into the fire,* for *they were no gods* (Isa. 37:19); and this was the Lord's doing: *I will lay the idols desolate.* Note, If the law of God prevail not to make men in authority destroy idols, God will take the work into his own hands, and will do it himself. 2. The gifts that passed between them and their gods shall be destroyed; for *all the hires thereof shall be burnt with fire,* which may be meant either of the presents they made to their idols for the replenishing of their altars, and the adorning of their statues and temples (these shall become a prey to the victorious army, which shall rifle not only private houses, but the houses of their gods), or of the corn, and wine, and oil, which they called the *rewards,* or *hires,* which *their idols,* their *lovers,* gave them (Hos. 2:12); these shall be taken from them by him whom (by ascribing them to their dear idols) they had defrauded of the honour due to him. Note, That cannot prosper by which men either are hired to sin or hire others to sin; for *the wages of sin* will be *death. She gathered it of the hire of the harlot,* and *it shall return to the hire of a harlot.* They enriched themselves by their leagues with the idolatrous nations, who gave them advantages, to court them into the service of their idols, and their idols' temples were enriched with gifts by those who went a whoring after them. And all this wealth shall become a prey to the idolatrous nations, and so be the *hire of a harlot* again, wages to an army of idolaters, who shall take it as a reward given them by their gods. *It shall be a present to king Jareb,* Hos. 10:6. What they gave to their idols, and what they thought they got by them, shall be as the hire of a harlot; the curse of God shall be upon it, and it shall never prosper, nor do them any good. It is common that what is squeezed out by one lust is squandered away upon another.

Verses 8–16

We have here a long train of mourners attending the funeral of a ruined kingdom.

I. The prophet is himself chief mourner (*v.* 8, 9): *I will wail and howl; I will go stripped and naked,* as a man distracted with grief. The prophets usually expressed their own grief for the public grievances, partly to mollify the predictions of them, and to make it appear that is was not out of ill-will that they denounced the judgments of God (so far were they from desiring the woeful day that they dreaded it more than any thing), partly to show how very dreadful and mournful the calamities would be, and to stir up in the people a holy fear of them, that by repentance they might turn away the wrath of God. Note, We ought to lament the punishments of sinners as well as the sufferings of saints in this world; the weeping prophet did so (Jer. 9:1); so did this prophet. He *makes a wailing like the dragons,* or rather the *jackals,* ravenous beasts that in those countries used to meet in the night, and *howl,* and make *hideous noises;* he mourns *as the owls,* the *screech-owls,* or *ostriches,* as some read it. Two things the prophet here thus dolefully laments: — 1. That Israel's case is desperate: *Her wound is incurable;* it is ruin without remedy; man cannot help her; God will not, because she will not by repentance and reformation help herself. There is indeed balm in Gilead and a physician there; but they will not apply to the physician, nor apply the balm to themselves, and therefore *the wound is incurable.* 2. That Judah likewise is in danger. The cup is going round, and is now put into Judah's hand: *The enemy has come to the gate of Jerusalem.* Soon after the destruction of Samaria and the ten tribes, the Assyrian army, under Sennacherib, laid siege to Jerusalem, came to the gate, but could not force their way any further; however, it was with great concern and trouble that the prophet foresaw the fright, so dearly did he love the peace of Jerusalem.

II. Several places are here brought in mourning, and are called upon to mourn; but with this proviso, that they should not let the Philistines hear them (*v.* 10): *Declare it not in Gath;* this is borrowed from David's lamentation for Saul and Jonathan (2 Sa. 1:20), *Tell it not in Gath,* for the uncircumcised will triumph in Israel's tears. Note, One would not, if it could be helped, gratify those that make themselves and their companions merry with the sins or with the sorrows of God's Israel. David was silent, and stifled his griefs, when *the wicked were before him,* Ps. 39:1. But, though it may be prudent not to give way to a noisy sorrow, yet it is duty to admit a silent one when the church of God is in distress. *"Roll thyself in the dust"* (as great mourners used to do) "and so let the house of Judah and every house in Jerusalem become a *house of Aphrah,* a *house of dust,* covered with dust, crumbled into dust." When God makes the house dust it becomes us to humble ourselves under his mighty hand, and to put our mouths in the dust, thus accommodating ourselves to the providences that concern us. Dust we are; God brings us to the dust, that we may know it, and own it. Divers other places are here named that should be sharers in this universal mourning, the names of some of which we do not find elsewhere, whence it is conjectured that they are names put upon them by the prophet, the signification of which might either indicate or aggravate the miseries coming upon them, thereby to awaken this secure and stupid people to a holy fear of divine wrath. We find Sennacherib's invasion thus described, in the prediction of it, by the impressions of terror it should make upon the several cities that fell in his way, Isa. 10:28, 29, etc. Let us observe the particulars here, 1. *The inhabitants of Saphir,* which signifies *neat* and *beautiful (thou that dwellest fairly,* so the margin reads it), shall *pass away* into captivity, or be forced to flee, stripped of all their ornaments *and having their shame naked.* Note, Those who appear ever so fine and delicate know not what contempt they may be exposed to; and the more grievous will the shame be to those who have been inhabitants of Saphir. 2. *The inhabitants of Zaanan,* which signifies the *country of flocks,* a populous country, where the people are as numerous and thick as flocks of sheep, shall yet be so taken up with their own calamities, felt or feared, that they shall *not come forth in the mourning of Bethezel,* which signifies a *place near,* shall not condole with, nor bring any succour to, their next neighbours in distress; for *he shall receive of you his standing;* the enemy shall encamp among you, O inhabitants of Zaanan! shall take up a station there, shall find footing among you. Those may well think themselves excused from helping their neighbours who find they have enough to do to help themselves and to hold their own. 3. As for *the inhabitants of Maroth* (which, some think, is put for Ramoth, others that it signifies the *rough places*), they *waited carefully for good,* and were grieved for the want of it, but were disappointed; for *evil came from the Lord unto the gate of Jerusalem,* when the Assyrian army besieged it, *v.* 12. The inhabitants of Maroth might well overlook their own particular grievances when they saw the holy city itself in danger, and might well overlook the Assyrian, that was the instrument, when they saw the evil coming *from the Lord.* 4. Lachish was a city of Judah, which Sennacherib laid siege to, Isa. 36:1,2. The inhabitants of that city are called to *bind the chariot to the swift beast,* to prepare for a speedy flight, as having no other way left to secure themselves and their families; or it is spoken ironically: "You have had your chariots and your swift beasts, but where are they now?" God's quarrel with Lachish is that she is *the beginning of sin,* probably the sin of idolatry, *to the daughter of Zion* (*v.* 13); they had learned it from the ten tribes, their near neighbours, and so infected the two tribes with it. Note, Those that help to bring sin into a country do but thereby prepare for the throwing of themselves out of it. Those must expect to be first in the punishment who have been ringleaders in sin. *The transgressions of Israel were found in thee;* when they came to be traced up to their original they were found to take rise very much from that city. God knows at whose door to lay the blame of the transgressions of Israel, and whom to find guilty. Lachish, having been so much accessory to the sin of Israel, shall certainly be reckoned with: *Thou shalt give presents to Moresheth-gath,* a city of the Philistines, which perhaps had a dependence upon Gath, that famous Philistine city; thou shalt send to court those of that city to assist thee, but it shall be in vain, for (*v.* 14) *the houses of Achzib* (a city which joined to Mareshah, or Moresheth, and is mentioned with it, Jos. 15:44) *shall be a lie to the kings of Israel;* though they depend upon their strength, yet they shall fail them. Here there is an allusion to the name. *Achzib* signifies *a lie,* and so it shall prove to those that trust in it. 5. Mareshah, that could not, or would not, help Israel, shall herself be made a prey (*v.* 15): *"I will bring a heir* (that is, an enemy) that shall take possession of thy lands, with as much assurance as if he were heir at law to them, and *he shall come to Adullam,* and *to the glory of Israel,* that is, to Jerusalem the head city;" or *"The glory of Israel* shall come to be as Adullam, a poor despicable place;" or, "The king of Assyria, whom Israel had gloried in, shall come to Adullam, in laying the country waste." 6. The whole land of Judah seems to be spoken to (*v.* 16) and called to weeping and mourning: *"Make thee bald,* by tearing thy hair and shaving thy head; *poll thee for thy delicate children,* that had been tenderly and nicely brought up; *enlarge thy baldness as the eagle* when she casts her feathers and is all over bald; *for they have gone into captivity from thee,* and are not likely to return; and their captivity will be the more grievous to them because they have been brought up delicately and have not been inured to hardship." Or this is directed particularly to the inhabitants of *Mareshah,* as *v.* 15. That was the prophet's own city, and yet he denounces the judgments of God against it; for it shall be an aggravation of its sin that it had such a prophet, and knew not the day of its visitation. Its being thus privileged, since it improved not the privilege, shall not procure favour for it either with God or with his prophet.

CHAPTER 2

In this chapter we have, I. The sins with which the people of Israel are charged — covetousness and oppression, fraudulent and violent practices (*v.* 1, 2), dealing barbarously, even with women and children, and other harmless people (*v.* 8, 9). Opposition of God's prophets and silencing them (*v.* 6, 7), and delighting in false prophets (*v.* 11). II. The judgments with which they are threatened for those sins, that they should be humbled, and impoverished (*v.* 3–5), and banished (*v.* 10). III. Gracious promises of comfort, reserved for the good people among them, in the Messiah (*v.* 12, 13). And this is the sum and scope of most of the chapters of this and other prophecies.

Verses 1–5

Here is, I. The injustice of man contriving the evil of sin, *v.* 1, 2. God was coming forth against this people to destroy them, and here he shows what was the ground of his controversy with them; it is that which is often mentioned as a sin that hastens the ruin of nations and families as much as any, the sin of oppression. Let us see the steps of it. 1. They eagerly desire that which is not their own — that is the *root of bitterness,* the root of all evil, *v.* 2. They *covet fields and houses,* as Ahab did Naboth's vineyard. "Oh that such a one's field and house were mine! It lies convenient for me, and I would manage it better than he does; it is fitter for me than for him." 2. They set their wits on work to invent ways of accomplishing their desire (*v.* 4); they devise iniquity with a great deal of cursed art and policy; they plot how to do it effectually, and yet so as not to expose themselves, or bring themselves into danger, or under reproach, by it. This is called *working evil!* they are working it in their heads, in their families, and are as intent upon it, and with as much pleasure, as if they were doing it, and are as confident of their success (so wisely do they think they have laid the scheme) as if it were assuredly done. Note, It is bad to do mischief upon a sudden thought, but much worse to devise it, to do it with design and deliberation; when the craft and subtlety of the old serpent appear with his poison and venom, it is wickedness in perfection. They devised it *upon their beds,* when they should have been asleep; care to compass a mischievous design held their eyes waking. *Upon their beds,* where they should have been remembering God, and meditating upon him, where they should have been *communing with their own hearts* and examining them, they were *devising iniquity.* It is of great consequence to improve and employ the hours of our retirement and solitude in a proper manner. 3. They employ their power in executing what they have designed and contrived; they practise the iniquity they have devised, *because it is in the power of their hand;* they find that they can compass it by the help of their wealth, and the authority and interest they have, and that none dare control them, or call them to an account for it; and this, they think, will justify them and bear them out in it. Note, It is the mistake of many to think that as they can do they may do; whereas no power is given for destruction, but all for edification. 4. They are industrious and very expeditious in accomplishing the iniquity they have devised; when they have settled the matter in their thoughts, in their beds, they lose no time, but as soon as the *morning is light* they practice it; they are up early in the prosecution of their designs, and what ill their hand finds to do they do it *with all their might,* which shames our slothfulness and dilatoriness in doing good, and should shame us out of them. In the service of God, and our generation, let it never be said that we left that to be done to-morrow which we could do today. 5. They stick at nothing to compass their designs; what they *covet* they *take away,* if they can, and, (1.) They care not what wrong they do, though it be ever so gross and open; they take away men's fields by violence, not only by fraud, and underhand practices and colour of law, but by force and with a high hand. (2.) They care not to whom they do wrong nor how far the iniquity extends which they devise: They *oppress a man and his house;* they rob and ruin those that have numerous families to maintain, and are not concerned though they send them and their wives and children a begging. They *oppress a man and his heritage;* they take away from men that which they have an unquestionable title to, having received it from their ancestors, and which they have but in trust, to transmit it to their posterity; but those oppressors care not how many they impoverish, so they may but enrich themselves. Note, If covetousness reigns in the heart, commonly all compassion is banished from it; and if any man *love this world,* as the *love of the Father,* so the love of his neighbour *is not in him.*

II. The justice of God contriving the evil of punishment for this sin (*v.* 3): *Therefore thus saith the Lord,* the righteous God, that judges between man and man, and is an avenger on those that do wrong, *Behold, against this family do I devise an evil,* that is, against the whole kingdom, the *house of Israel,* and particularly those families in it that were cruel and oppressive. They unjustly devise evil against their brethren, and God will justly devise evil against them. Infinite Wisdom will so contrive the punishment of their sin that it shall be very sure, and such as cannot be avoided, very severe, and such as they cannot bear, very signal and remarkable, and such as shall be universally observed to answer to the sin. The more there appears of a wicked wit in the sin the more there shall appear of a holy wisdom and fitness in the punishment; for the Lord will be *known by the judgments he executes;* he will be owned by them. 1. He finds them very secure, and confident that they shall in some way or other escape the judgment, or, though they fall under it, shall soon throw it off and get clear of it, and therefore he tells them, It is *an evil from which they shall not remove their neck.* They were children of *Belial,* that would not endure the easy yoke of God's righteous commands, but *broke those bonds* asunder, and *cast away those cords from them;* and therefore God will lay upon them the heavy yoke of his righteous judgments, and they shall not be able to withdraw their necks from that; those that will not be overruled shall be overcome. 2. He finds them very proud and stately, and therefore he tells them that they shall not go haughtily, with *stretched-forth necks and wanton eyes, walking and mincing as they go* (Isa. 3:16); for *this time is evil,* and the events of it are very humbling and mortifying, and such as will bring down the stoutest spirit. 3. He finds them very merry and jovial, and therefore tells them their note shall be changed, their laughter shall be turned into mourning and their joy into heaviness (*v.* 4): *In that day,* when God comes to punish you for your oppression, *shall one take up a parable against you,* and *lament with a doleful lamentation,* with *a lamentation of lamentations* (so the word is), a most lamentable lamentation, as a song of songs is a most pleasing song. Their enemies shall insult over them, and make a jest of their griefs, for they shall *take up a parable against them.* Their friends shall mourn over them, and lay to heart their calamities, and this shall be the general cry, *"We are utterly spoiled;* we are all undone." Note, Those that were most haughty and secure in their prosperity are commonly most dejected and most ready to despair in their adversity. 4. He finds them very rich in houses and lands, which they have gained by oppression, and therefore tells them that they shall be stripped of all. (1.) They shall, in their despair, give it all up; they shall say, *We are utterly spoiled; he has changed the portion of my people,* so that it is now no longer theirs, but it is in the possession and occupation of their enemies: *How has he removed it from me!* How suddenly, how powerfully! What is unjustly got by us will not long continue with us; the righteous God will remove it. *Turning away* from us in wrath, he *has divided our fields,* and given them into the hands of strangers. Woe to those from whom God turns away. The margin reads it, *"Instead of restoring, he has divided our fields;* instead of putting us again in the possession of our estates, he has confirmed those in the possession of them that have taken them from us." Note, It is just with God that those who have dealt fraudulently and violently with others should themselves be dealt fraudulently and violently with. (2.) God shall ratify what they say in their despair (*v.* 5); so it shall be: *Thou shalt have none to cast a cord by lot in the congregation of the Lord,* none to divide inheritances, because there shall be no inheritances to divide, no courts to try titles to lands, or determine controversies about them, or cast lots upon them, as in Joshua's time, for all shall be in the enemies' hand. This land, which should be taken from them, they had not only an unquestionable title to, but a very comfortable enjoyment of, for it was *in the congregation of the Lord,* or rather the congregation of the Lord was in it; it was God's land; it was a holy land, and therefore it was the more grievous to them to be turned out of it. Note, Those are to be considered the sorest calamities which cut us off from the congregation of the Lord, or cut us short in the enjoyment of the privileges of it.

Verses 6–11

Here are two sins charged upon the people of Israel, and judgments denounced against them for each, such judgments as exactly answer the sin — persecuting God's prophets and oppressing God's poor.

I. Persecuting God's prophets, suppressing and silencing them, is a sin that provokes God as much as anything, for it not only spits in the face of his authority over us, but spurns at the bowels of his mercy to us; for his sending prophets to us is a sure and valuable token of his goodwill. Now observe here,

1. What the obstruction and opposition were which this people gave to God's prophets: They *said to those that prophesy, Prophesy ye not,* as Isa. 30:10. They *said to the seers, "See not;* do not trouble us with accounts of what you have seen, nor bring us any such frightful messages." They must either not prophesy at all or prophesy only what is pleasing. The word for *prophesying* here signifies *dropping,* for the words of the prophets dropped from heaven as the dew. Note, Those that hate to be reformed hate to be reproved, and do all they can to silence faithful ministers. Amos was forbidden to prophesy, Amos 7:10, etc. *Therefore* persecutors stop their breath, because they have no other way to stop their mouths; for, if they live, they will preach and torment those that dwell on the earth, as the *two witnesses* did, Rev. 11:10. Some read it, *Prophesy not; let these prophesy.* Let not those prophesy that tell us of our faults, and threaten us, but *let those prophesy* that will flatter us in our sins, and cry peace to us. They will not say that they will have no ministers at all, but they will have such as will say just what they would have them and go their way. This they are charged with (*v.* 11), that when they silenced and frowned upon the true prophets they countenanced and encouraged pretenders, and set them up, and made an interest for them, to confront God's faithful prophets: *If a man walk in the spirit of falsehood,* pretend to have the Spirit of God, while really it is a spirit of error, a spirit of delusion, and he himself knows that he has no commission, no instruction, from God, yet, if he says, *I will prophesy unto thee of wine and strong drink,* if he will but assure them that they shall have wine and strong drink enough, that they need not fear the judgments of war and famine which the other prophets threatened them with, that they shall always have plenty of the delights of sense and never know the want of them, and if he will but tell them that it is lawful for them to drink as much as they please of their wine and strong drink, and they need not scruple being drunk, that they *shall have peace though they go on and add drunkenness to thirst,* such a prophet as this is a man after their own heart, who will tell them that there is neither sin nor danger in the wicked course of life they lead: *He shall even be the prophet of this people;* such a man they would have to be their prophet, that will not only associate with them in their rioting and revellings, but will pretend to consecrate their sensualities by his prophecies and so harden them in their security and sensuality. Note, It is not strange if people that are vicious and debauched covet to have ministers that are altogether such as themselves, for they are willing to believe God is so too, Ps. 50:21. But how are sacred things profaned when they are prostituted to such base purposes, when prophecy itself shall be pressed into the services of a lewd and profane crew! But thus that servant who said, *My Lord delays his coming,* by the spirit of falsehood, *smote his fellow servants* and *ate and drank with the drunken.*

2. How they are here expostulated with upon this matter (*v.* 7): *"O thou that art named the house of Jacob,* does it become thee to say and do thus? Wilt thou silence those that prophesy, and forbid them to speak in God's name?" Note, It is an honour and privilege to be *named of the house of Jacob.* Thou art *called a Jew,* Rom. 2:17. But, when those who are called by that worthy name degenerate, they commonly prove the worst of men themselves and the worst enemies to God's prophets. The Jews who were *named of the house of Jacob* were the most violent persecutors of the first preachers of the gospel. Upon this the prophet here argues with these oppressors of the word of God, and shows them, (1.) What an affront they hereby put upon God, the God of the holy prophets: *"Is the Lord's Spirit straitened?* In silencing the Lord's prophets you do what you can to silence his Spirit too; but do you think you can do it? Can you make the Spirit of God your prisoner and your servant? Will you prescribe to him what he shall say, and forbid him to say what is displeasing to you? If you silence the prophets, yet cannot the Spirit of the Lord find out other ways to reach your consciences? Can your unbelief frustrate the divine counsels?" (2.) What a scandal it was to their profession as Jews: "You are *named the house of Jacob,* and this is your honour; but *are these his doings?* Are these the doings of your father Jacob? Do you herein tread in his steps? No; if you were indeed his children you would do his works; but now you seek to kill and silence *a man that tells you the truth,* in God's name; *this did not Abraham* (Jn. 8:39, 40); this did not Jacob." Or, *"Are these God's doings?* Are these the doings that will please him? Are these the doings of his people? No, you know they are not, however some may be so strangely blinded and bigoted as to kill God's ministers and think that therein they *do him service,"* Jn. 16:2. (3.) Let them consider how unreasonable and absurd the thing was in itself: *Do not my words do good to those that walk uprightly?* Yes; certainly they do; it is an appeal to the experiences of the *generation of the upright: "Call now if there be any of them that will answer you, and to which of the saints will you turn?* Turn to which you will, and you will find they all agree in this, that the word of God *does good to those that walk uprightly;* and will you then oppose that which does good, so much good as good preaching does? Herein you wrong God, who owns the words of the prophets to be his words (they are *my words*) and who by them aims and designs to do good to mankind (Ps. 119:68); and will you hinder the great benefactor from doing good? Will

you put the light of the world under a bushel: You might as well say to the sun, Shine not, as *say to the seers, See not.* Herein you wrong the souls of men, and deprive them of the benefit designed them by the word of God." Note, Those are enemies not only to God, but to the world, they are enemies to their country, that silence good ministers, and obstruct the means of knowledge and grace; for it is certainly for the public common good of states and kingdoms that religion should be encouraged. God's words do good to those *that walk uprightly.* It is the character of good people that they *walk uprightly* (Ps. 15:2); and it is their comfort that the words of God are good and do good to them; they find comfort in them. God's words are good words to good people, and speak comfortably to them. But those that opposed the words of God, and silenced the prophets, pleaded, in justification of themselves, that God's words were unprofitable and unpleasant to them, and did them no good, nor prophesied any good concerning them, but evil, as Ahab complained of Micaiah, in answer to which the prophet here tells them that it was their own fault; they might thank themselves. They might find it of good use to them if they were but disposed to make a good use of it; if they would but walk uprightly, as they should, and so qualify themselves for comfort, the word of God would speak comfortably to them. *Do that which is good, and thou shalt have praise for the same.*

3. What they are threatened with for this sin; God also will choose their delusions, and, (1.) They shall be deprived of the benefit of a faithful ministry. Since they say, *Prophesy not,* God will take them at their word, and *they shall not prophesy to them;* their sin shall be their punishment. If men will silence God's ministers, it is just with God to silence them, as he did Ezekiel, and to say, They shall *no more be reprovers* and monitors to them. Let the physician no longer attend the patient that will not be healed, for he will not be ruled. They *shall not prophesy to them,* and then they will not take shame. As it is the work of magistrates, so it is also of ministers, to put men to shame when they do amiss (Jdg. 18:7), that, being made ashamed of their folly, they may not return again to it; but, when God gives men up to be impudent and shameless in sin, he says to his prophets, *They are joined to idols; let them alone.* (2.) They shall be given up to the blind guidance of an unfaithful ministry. We may understand *v.* 11 as a threatening: *If a man be found walking in the spirit of falsehood,* having such a lying spirit as was in the mouth of Ahab's prophets, that will strengthen their hands in their wicked ways, he *shall be the prophet of this people,* that is, God will leave them to themselves to hearken to such; since they will be deceived, let them be deceived; since they will not admit the *truth in the love of it,* God will send them *strong delusions to believe a lie,* 2 Th. 2:10, 11. They shall have prophets that will prophesy to them for *wine and strong drink* (so some read it), that will give you a cast of their office to your mind for a bottle of wine of a flagon of ale, will soothe sinners in their sins if they will but feed them with the gratifications of their lusts; to have such prophets, and to be ridden by them, is as sad a judgment as any people can be under and as bad a preface of ruin approaching as it is to a particular person to be under the influence of a debauched conscience.

II. Oppressing God's poor is another sin they are charged with, as before (*v.* 1, 2), for it is a sin doubly hateful and provoking to God. Observe,

1. How the sin is described, *v.* 8, 9. When they contemned God's prophets and opposed them they broke out into all other wickedness; what bonds will hold those that have no reverence for God's word? Those who formerly rose up against the enemies of the nation, in defence of their country and therein behaved themselves bravely, now of late *rose up as enemies of the nation,* and, instead of defending it, destroyed it, and did it more mischief (as usually such vipers in the bowels of a state do) than a foreign enemy could do. They made a prey of men, women, and children, (1.) Of men, that were travelling on the way, that *pass by securely as men averse from war,* that were far from any bad designs, but went peaceably about their lawful occasions; those they set upon, as if they had been dangerous obnoxious people, and *pulled off the robe with the garment from them,* that is, they stripped them both of the upper and the inner garment, took away *their cloak,* and would have *their coat also;* thus barbarously did they use those that were quiet in the land, who, being harmless, were fearless, and so the more easily make a prey of. (2.) Of women, whose sex should have been their protection (*v.* 9): *The women of my people have you cast out from their pleasant houses. They devoured widows' houses* (Mt. 23:14), and so turned them out of the possession of them, because they were pleasant houses, and such as they had a mind for. It was inhuman to deal thus barbarously with women; but that which especially aggravated it was that they were the women of *God's people,* whom they knew to be under his protection. (3.) Of children, whose age entitles them to a tender usage: *From their children have you taken away my glory for ever.* It was the glory of the Israelites' children that they were free, but they enslaved them — that they were born in God's house, and had a right to the privileges of it, but they sold them to strangers, sent them into idolatrous countries, where they were deprived for ever of that glory; at least the oppressors designed their captivity should be perpetual. Note, The righteous God will certainly reckon for injuries done to the widows and fatherless, who, being helpless and friendless, cannot otherwise expect to be righted.

2. What the sentence is that is passed upon them for it (*v.* 10): *"Arise ye, and depart;* prepare to quit this land, for you shall be forced out of it, as you have forced the women and children of my people out of their possessions; it is not, it shall not, be your rest, as it was intended that Canaan should be, Ps. 95:11. You shall have neither contentment nor continuance in it, *because it is polluted* by your wickedness." Sin is defiling to a land, and sinners cannot expect to rest in a land which they have polluted, but is will spew them out, as this land spewed out the Canaanites of old when they had polluted it with their abominations, Lev. 18:27, 28. "Nay, you shall not only be obliged to depart out of this land, but *it shall destroy you even with a sore destruction;* you shall either be turned out of it or (which is all one) you shall be ruined in it." We may apply this to our state in this present world; it is polluted; there is a great deal of *corruption in the world, through lust,* and therefore we should *arise, and depart out of it,* keep at a distance from the corruption that is in it, and *keep ourselves unspotted* from it. It *is not our rest;* it was never intended to be so; it was designed for our passage, but not for our portion — our inn, but not our home. Here *we have no continuing city;* let us therefore *arise and depart;* let us sit loose to it and live above it, and think of leaving it and seek a continuing city above.

Verses 12–13

After threatenings of wrath, the chapter here concludes, as is usual in the prophets, with promises of mercy, which were in part fulfilled when the Jews returned out of Babylon, and had their full accomplishment in the kingdom of the Messiah. Their grievances shall be all redressed. 1. Whereas they were dispersed, they shall be brought together again, and shall jointly receive the tokens of God's favour to them, and shall have communion with each other and comfort in each other (*v.* 12): *"I will surely assemble, O Jacob! all of thee,* all that belong to thee, all that are *named of the house of Jacob* (*v.* 7) that are now expelled your country, *v.*10. I will bring you together again, and not one of you shall be lost, not one of you shall be missing. *I will surely gather the remnant of Israel,* that remnant that is designed and reserved for salvation; they shall be brought to incorporate in one body. *I will put them together as the sheep of Bozrah."* Sheep are inoffensive and sociable creatures; they shall be *as the flock in the midst of their fold,* where they are safe under the shepherd's eye and care; and *they shall make great noise* (as numerous flocks and herds do, with their bleating and lowing) *by reason of the multitude of men* (for the sheep are *men,* as the prophet explains this comparison, Eze. 34:31), not by reason of their strifes and contentions, but by reason of their great numbers. This was accomplished when Christ by his gospel gathered together in one *all the children of God that were scattered abroad,* and united both Jews and Gentiles in one fold, and under one Shepherd, when all the complaint was that the *place was too strait* for them — that was *the noise, by reason of their multitude* (Isa. 49:19, 20), when there were some added to the church from all parts of the world, and all men were drawn to Christ by the attractive power of his cross, which shall be done yet more and more, and perfectly done, when he shall send forth his angels to *gather in his elect from the four winds.* 2. Whereas God had seemed to desert them, and cast them off, now he will own them, and head them, and help them through all the difficulties that are in the way of their return and deliverance (*v.* 13): *the breaker has come up before them,* to break down all opposition, and clear the road for them; and under his guidance *they have broken up, and have passed through the gate,* the door of escape out of their captivity, and have *gone out by it* with courage and resolution, having Omnipotence for their vanguard. *Their King shall pass before them,* to head them in the way, even Jehovah (he was their king) *on the head of them,* as he was on the head of the armies of Israel when they followed the pillar of cloud and fire through the wilderness and when he appeared to Joshua as *captain of the Lord's host.* Christ is the church's King; he is Jehovah; he heads them, passes before them, brings them out of the land of their captivity, brings them into the land of their rest. He is the *breaker,* that broke through them, that rent the veil, and opened the kingdom of heaven to all believers. The learned bishop Pearson applies it to the resurrection of Christ, by which he obtained the power and became the pattern of our resurrection. *The breaker has gone up before us* out of the grave, and has carried away its gates, as Samson did Gaza's, bar and all, and by that breach we go out. The learned Dr. Pocock mentions, as the sense which some of the ancient Jews give of it, that the breaker is Elias, and their *King* the *Messiah,* the Son of David; and he thinks we may apply it to Christ and his forerunner *John the Baptist.* John was the breaker; he broke the ice, prepared the way of the Lord by the baptism of repentance; in him the gospel began; from his time *the kingdom of heaven suffered violence;* and so the Christian church is introduced, with *Messiah the Prince* before it, on the head of it, going forth *conquering and to conquer.*

CHAPTER 3

What the apostle says of another of the prophets is true of this, who was also his contemporary — "Esaias is very bold," Rom. 10:20. So, in this chapter, Micah is very bold in reproving and threatening the great men that were the ringleaders in sin; and he gives the reason (*v.* 8) why he was so bold, because he had commission and instruction from God to say what he said, and was carried out in it by a higher spirit and power than his own. Magistracy and ministry are two great ordinances of God, for good to his church, but these were both corrupted and the intentions of them perverted; and upon those that abused them, and so abused the church with them, the prophet is very severe, and justly so. I. He gives them their lesson severally, reproving and threatening princes (*v.* 1–4) and false flattering prophets (*v.* 5–7). II. He gives them their lesson jointly, putting them together, as acting in conjunction for the ruin of the kingdom, which they should see the ruins of (*v.* 9–12).

Verses 1–7

Princes and prophets, when they faithfully discharge the duty of their office, are to be highly honoured above other men; but when they betray their trust, and act contrary to it, they should hear of their faults as well as others, and shall be made to know that there is a God above them, to whom they are accountable; at his bar the prophet here, in his name, arraigns them.

I. Let the princes hear their charge and their doom. The *heads of Jacob, and the princes of the house of Israel,* are called upon to *hear* what the prophet has to say to them, *v.* 1. The word of God has reproofs for the greatest of men, which the ministers of that word ought to apply as there is occasion. The prophet here has comfort in the reflection upon it, that, whatever the success was, he had faithfully discharged his trust: *And I said, Hear, O princes!* He had the testimony of his conscience for him that he had not shrunk from his duty for fear of the face of men. He tells them,

1. What was expected from them: *Is it not for you to know judgment?* He means to *do* judgment, for otherwise the knowledge of it is of no avail. "Is it not your business to administer justice impartially, and not to *know faces"* (as the Hebrew phrase for partiality and respect of persons is), "but to *know judgment,* and the merits of every cause?" Or it may be taken for granted that the heads and rulers are well acquainted with the rules of justice, whatever others are; for they have those means of knowledge, and have not those excuses for ignorance, which some others have, that are poor and foolish (Jer. *v.* 4); and, if so, their transgression of the laws of justice is the more pro-

voking to God, for they sin against knowledge. "Is it not for you to know judgment? Yes, it is; therefore stand still, and hear your own judgment, and judge if it be not right, whether any thing can be objected against it."

2. How wretchedly they had transgressed the rules of judgment, though they knew what they were. Their principle and disposition are bad: They *hate the good and love the evil;* they hate good in others, and hate it should have any influence on themselves; they hate to do good, hate to have any good done, and hate those that are good and do good; and they *love the evil,* delight in mischief. This being their principle, their practice is according to it; they are very cruel and severe towards those that are under their power, and whoever lies at their mercy will find that they have none. They barbarously devour those whom they should protect, and, as unfaithful shepherds, fleece the flock they should feed; nay, instead of feeding it, they feed upon it, Eze. 34:2. It is fit indeed that he who feeds a flock should *eat of the milk of the flock* (1 Co. 9:7), but that will not content them: They *eat the flesh of my people.* It is fit that they should be clothed with the wool, but that will not serve: They *flay the skin from off them, v.* 3. By imposing heavier taxes upon them than they can bear, and exacting them with rigour, by mulcts, and fines, and corporal punishments, for pretended crimes, they ruined the estates and families of their subjects, took away from some their lives, from others their livelihoods, and were to their subjects as beasts of prey, rather than shepherds. "They *break their bones* to come at the marrow, and *chop* the flesh *in pieces as for the pot.*" This intimates that they were, (1.) Very ravenous and greedy for themselves, indulging themselves in luxury and sensuality. (2.) Very barbarous and cruel to those that were under them, not caring whom they beggared, so they could but enrich themselves; such evil is the love of money the root of.

3. How they might expect that God should deal with them, since they had been thus cruel to his subjects. The rule is fixed, Those shall have judgment without mercy that have shown no mercy (*v.* 4): *"They shall cry to the Lord, but he will not hear them,* in the day of their distress, as the poor cried to them in the day of their prosperity and they would not hear them." There will come a time when the most proud and scornful sinners will *cry to the Lord,* and sue for that mercy which they once neither valued nor copied out. But it will then be in vain; God will even hide his face from them at that time, that time when they need his favour, and see themselves undone without it. At another time they would have turned their back upon him; but at that time he will turn his back upon them, *as they have behaved themselves ill in their doings.* Note, Men cannot expect to do ill and fare well, but may expect to find, as Adoni-bezek did, that done to them which they did to others; for *he is righteous who takes vengeance. With the froward God will show himself froward,* and he often gives up cruel and unmerciful men into the hands of those who are cruel and unmerciful to them, as they themselves have formerly been to others. This agrees with Prov. 21:13, *Whoso stoppeth his ears at the cry of the poor, he shall cry himself and shall not be heard;* but the merciful have reason to hope that they shall obtain mercy.

II. Let the prophets hear their charge too, and their doom; they were such as prophesied falsely, and the princes bore rule by their means. Observe,

1. What was their sin. (1.) They made it their business to flatter and deceive the people: *They make my people err,* lead them into mistakes, both concerning what they should do and concerning what God would do with them. It is ill with a people when their leaders cause them to err, and those draw them out of the way that should guide them and go before them in it. "They make them to err by crying peace, by telling them that they do well, and that all shall be well with them; whereas they are in the paths of sin, and within a step of ruin. They *cry peace,* but they *bite with their teeth,"* which perhaps is meant of their biting their own lips, as we are apt to do when we would suppress something which we are ready to speak. When they cried *peace* their own hearts gave them the lie, and they were just ready to eat their own words and to contradict themselves, but they bit with their teeth, and kept it in. They were not blind leaders of the blind, for they saw the ditch before them, and yet led their followers into it. (2.) They made it all their aim to glut themselves, and serve their own belly, as the seducers in St. Paul's time (Rom. 16:18), for *their god is their belly,* Phil. 3:19. They *bite with their teeth, and cry peace;* that is, they will flatter and compliment those that will feed them with good bits, will give them something to eat; but as for those that *put not into their mouths,* that are not continually cramming them, they look upon them as their enemies; to them they do not *cry peace,* as they do to those whom they look upon as their benefactors, but they *even prepare war against them;* against them they denounce the judgments of God, but as they are to them, as the crafty priests of the church of Rome, in some places, make their image either to smile or frown upon the offerer according as his offering is. Justly is it insisted on as a necessary qualification of a minister (1 Tim. 3:3, and again Tit. 1:7) that he be not *greedy of filthy lucre.*

2. What is the sentence passed upon them for this sin, *v.* 6, 7. It is threatened, (1.) That they shall be involved in troubles and miseries with those to whom they had cried peace: *Night shall be upon them,* a dark cold night of calamity, such as they, in their flattery, led the people to hope would never come. *It shall be dark unto you,* darker to you than to others; *the sun shall go down over the prophets,* shall go down at noon; all comfort shall depart from them, and they shall be deprived of all hope of it. The *day shall be dark over them,* in which they promised themselves light. Nor shall they be surrounded with outward troubles only, but their mind shall be full of confusion, and they shall be brought to their wits' end; their heads shall be clouded, and their own thoughts shall trouble them; and that is trouble enough. They kept others in the dark, and now God will bring them into the dark. (2.) That thereby they shall be silenced, and all their pretensions to prophecy for ever shamed. They never had any true vision; and now, the event disproving their predictions of peace, it shall be made to appear that they never had any, that there never was an answer of God to them, but it was all a sham, and they were cheats and impostors. Their reputation being thus quite sunk, their confidence would of course fail them. And, their spirits being ruffled and confused, their invention would fail them too; and by reason of this darkness, both without and within too, *they shall not divine,* they shall not have so much as a counterfeit vision to produce, they shall be *ashamed,* and *confounded,* and *cover their lips,* as men that are quite baffled and have nothing to say for themselves. Note, Those who deceive others are but preparing confusion for their own faces.

Verses 8–12

Here, I. The prophet experiences a divine power going along with him in his work, and he makes a solemn profession and protestation of it, as that which would justify him, and bear him out, in his plain dealing with the princes and rulers. He would not, he durst not, make thus bold with the great men, but that he was carried out to do it by a prophetical impulse and impression. It was not he that said it, but God by him, and he could not but speak the word that God put into his mouth. It comes in likewise by way of opposition to the false prophets, who were full of shame when they lived to see themselves proved liars, and who never had courage to deal faithfully with the people, but flattered them in their sins; they were *sensual, not having the Spirit,* but truly (says Micah) *I am full of power by the Spirit of the Lord, v.* 8. Having in himself an assurance of the truth of what he said, he said it with assurance. Compare him with those false prophets, and you will say, There is no comparison between them. *What is the chaff to the wheat?* Jer. 23:28. What is painted fire to real fire? Observe here, 1. What the qualifications were with which this prophet was endured: He was *full of power, and of judgment, and of might;* he had an ardent love to God and to the souls of men, a deep concern for his glory and their salvation, and a flaming zeal against sin. He had likewise courage to reprove it and witness against it, not fearing the wrath either of great men or of great multitudes; whatever difficulties or discouragements he met with, they did not deter him nor drive him from his work; *none of these things moved him.* And all this was guided by judgment and discretion; he was a man of wisdom as well as courage; in all his preaching there was light as well as heat, and a spirit of wisdom as well as of zeal. Thus was this man of God *thoroughly furnished* for every good word he had to say, and every good work he had to do. Those he preached to could not but perceive him to be full both of *power* and *judgment,* for they found both their *understandings opened* and their *hearts* made *to burn within them,* with such evidence and demonstration, and with such power, did the word come from him. 2. Whence he had these qualifications, not from and of himself, but he was *full of power by the Spirit of the Lord.* Knowing that it was indeed the *Spirit of the Lord* that was in him, and spoke by him, that it was a divine revelation that he delivered, he spoke it boldly, and as one having authority, *set his face as a flint,* knowing he should be justified and borne out in what he said, Isa. 50:7, 8. Note, Those who act honestly may act boldly; and those who are sure that they have a commission from God need not be afraid of opposition from men. Nay, he had not only a Spirit of prophecy, which was the ground of his boldness, but the Spirit of sanctification endued him with the boldness and wisdom which were requisite for him. It was not in any strength of his own that he was strong; *for who is sufficient for these things?* but in *the Lord, and in the power of his might;* for *from him* all *our sufficiency* is. Are we full of power at any time, for that which is good? It is purely by *the Spirit of the Lord,* for of ourselves we are weak as water; it is the God of Israel that gives strength and power both to his people and to his ministers. 3. What use he made of these qualifications — this judgment and this power; he *declared to Jacob his transgression and to Israel his sin.* If transgression be found in Jacob and Israel, they must be told of it, and it is the business of God's prophets to tell them of it, to *cry aloud* and *not to spare,* Isa. 58:1. Those who come to hear the word of God must be willing to be told of their faults, and must not only give their ministers leave to deal plainly and faithfully with them, but take it kindly, and be thankful; but, since few have meekness enough to receive reproof, those have need of a great deal of boldness who are to give reproofs, and must pray for a spirit both of wisdom and might.

II. The prophet exerts this power in dealing with the *heads of the house of Jacob,* both the princes and the prophets, whom he had drawn up a high charge against in the former part of the chapter. He repeats the summons of their attendance and attention (*v.* 9), the same that we had *v.* 1, directing himself to *the princes of the house of Israel,* yet he means those of *Judah;* for it appears (Jer. 26:18, 19, where *v.* 12 is quoted) that this was spoken in Hezekiah's kingdom; but, the ten tribes being gone into captivity, Judah is all that is now left of Jacob and Israel. The prophet speaks respectfully to them *(hear, I pray you)* and gives them their titles of *heads* and *princes.* Ministers must be faithful to great men in reproving them for their sins, but they must not be rude and uncivil to them. Now observe here,

1. The great wickedness that these heads of the house of Jacob were guilty of, *princes, priest,* and *prophets;* in short, they were covetous and prostituted their offices to their love of money. (1.) The *princes abhorred all judgment;* they would not be governed by any of its laws, either in their own practice or in passing sentence upon appeals made to them; they *perverted all equity,* and scorned to be under the direction or correction of justice, when it could not be made pliable to their secular interests. When, under pretence of doing right, they did the most palpable wrongs, then they perverted equity, and made it serve a purpose contrary to the intention of the founder of magistracy and fountain of power. It is laid to their charge (*v.* 10) that *they build up Zion with blood.* "They pretend, in justification of their extortion and oppressions, that they build up Zion and Jerusalem; they add new streets and squares to the holy cities, and adorn them; they establish and advance the public interests both in church and state, and think that therein they do God and Israel good service. But it is *with blood* and *with iniquity,* and therefore it cannot prosper; nor will their intentions of good to the city of God justify their contradictions to the law of God." Those mistake who think that a burning zeal for holy church, and the propagating of the faith, will serve to consecrate robberies and murders, massacres and depredations; no, Zion's walls owe those no thanks that build them up with blood and iniquity. The sin of man works not the righteousness of God. "The office of the princes is to judge upon appeals made to them; but *they judge for*

reward (*v.* 11); they give judgment on the side of those that give the bribe; the most righteous cause shall not be carried without a fee, and for a fee the most unrighteous cause shall be carried." Miserable is the people's case when the judge's enquiry upon a cause is not, "What is to be done in it?" but, "What is to be got by it?" (2.) The priests' work was to teach the people, and for that the law had provided them a very honourable comfortable maintenance; but that will not content them, they *teach for hire* over and above, and will be hired to teach any thing, as an oracle of God, which they know will please and gain them an interest. (3.) The prophets, it should seem, had honorary fees given them by way of gratuity (1 Sa. 9:7, 8); but these prophets governed themselves in their prophesying by the prospect of temporal advantage and that was the main thing they had in their eye: They *divine for money.* Their tongues were mercenary; they would either prophesy or let it alone, according as they found it most for their advantage; and a man might have what oracle he would from them if he would but pay them for it. Thus they were fit successors of Balaam, who *loved the wages of unrighteousness.* Note, Though that which is wicked can never be consecrated by a zeal for the church, yet that which is sacred may be, and often is, desecrated, by the love of the world. When men do that which in itself is good, but do it for filthy lucre, it loses its excellency, and becomes an abomination both to God and man.

2. Their vain presumption and carnal confidence, notwithstanding: They *lean upon the Lord,* and because they are, in profession, his people, they think there is neither harm nor danger in these their wicked practices. Faith builds upon the Lord, rests in him, and relies upon him, as the soul's foundation; presumption only *leans upon the Lord* as a prop, makes use of him to serve a turn, while still the world is the foundation that is built upon. They speak with a great deal of confidence, (1.) Of their honour: *"Is not the Lord among us?* Have we not the tokens of his presence with us, his temple, his ark, his lively oracles?" They are *haughty because of the holy mountain* and its dignities (Zep. 3:11), as if their church-privileges would palliate the worst of practices, or as if God's presence with them were intended to make the priests and people rich with the sale of their performances. It was true that the Lord was among them by his ordinances, and this puffed them up with pride; but, if they imagined that he was among them by his favour and love, they were mistaken: but it is a cheat the children of men often put upon themselves to think they have God with them, when they have by their sin provoked him to depart from them. (2.) They are confident of their own safety: *No evil can come upon us.* Many are rocked asleep; in a fatal security by their church-privileges, as if those would protect them in sin, and shelter them from punishment, which are really, and will be, the greatest aggravations both of their sin and of their punishment. If men's having the Lord among them will not restrain them from doing evil, it can never secure them from suffering evil for so doing; and it is very absurd for sinners to think that their impudence will be their impunity.

3. The doom passed upon them for their real wickedness, notwithstanding their imaginary protection (*v.* 12): *Therefore shall Zion for your sake be ploughed as a field.* This is that passage which is quoted as a bold word spoken by Micah (Jer. 26:18), which yet Hezekiah and his princes took well, though in another reign it might have gone near to cost him his head; nay, they repented and reformed, and so the execution of this threatening was prevented, and did not come in those days. (1.) It is the ruin of holy places that is here foretold, places that had been highly honoured with the tokens of God's presence and the performances of his worship; it is Zion that shall be ploughed as a field, the building burnt to the ground and levelled with it. Some observe that this was literally fulfilled in the destruction of Jerusalem by the Romans, when the ground on which the city stood was ploughed up in token of its utter desolation, and that no city should be built upon that ground without the emperor's leave. Even *Jerusalem,* the holy city, shall *become heaps* of ruins, and the *mountain of the house,* on which the temple is built, shall be overgrown with briars and thorns, *as the high places of the forest.* If sacred places be polluted by sin, they must expect to be wasted and ruined by the judgments of God. (2.) It is the wickedness of those who preside in them that brings the ruin: "It is *for your sake* that *Zion shall be ploughed as a field;* you pretend to build up Zion, but, doing it by blood and iniquity, you pull it down." Note, The sin of priests and princes is often the ruin of states and churches. *Delirant reges, plectuntur Achivi — The kings act foolishly and the people suffer for it.*

CHAPTER 4

Comparing this chapter with the close of the foregoing chapter, the comfortable promises here with the terrible threatenings there, we may, with the apostle, "behold the goodness and severity of God," (Rom. 11:22), towards the Jewish church which fell, severity when Zion was ploughed as a field, but towards the Christian church, which was built upon the ruins of it, goodness, great goodness; for it is here promised, I. That it shall be advanced and enlarged by the accession of the nations to it (*v.* 1, 2). II. That it shall be protected in tranquility and peace (*v.* 3, 4). III. That it shall be kept close, and constant, and faithful to God (*v.* 5). IV. That under Christ's government, all its grievances shall be redressed (*v.* 6, 7). V. That it shall have an ample and flourishing dominion (*v.* 8). VI. That its troubles shall be brought to a happy issue at length (*v.* 9, 10). VII. That its enemies shall be disquieted, nay, that they shall be destroyed in and by their attempts against it (*v.* 11–13).

Verses 1–7

It is a very comfortable *but* with which this chapter begins, and very reviving to those who lay the interests of God's church near their heart and are concerned for the welfare of it. When we sometimes see the corruptions of the church, especially of church-rulers, princes, priests, and prophets, seeking their own things and not the things of God, and when we soon after see the desolations of the church, *Zion* for their sakes *ploughed as a field,* we are ready to fear that it will one day perish between both, that the name of Israel shall be no more in remembrance; we are ready to give up all for gone, and to conclude the church will have neither root not branch upon earth. But let not our faith fail in this matter; out of the ashes of the church another phoenix shall arise. In the last words of the foregoing chapter we left *the mountain of the house* as desolate and waste as the *high places of the forest;* and is it possible that such a wilderness should ever become a fruitful field again? Yes, the first words of this chapter bring in *the mountain of the Lord's house* as much dignified by being frequented as ever it had been disgraced by being deserted. Though Zion be ploughed as a field, yet God has not *cast off his people,* but by the fall of the Jews salvation has come to the Gentiles, so that it proves to be the riches of the world, Rom. 11:11, 12. This is the mystery which God by the prophet here shows us, and he says the very same in the first three verses of this chapter which another prophet said by the word of the Lord at the same time (Isa. 2:2–4), that *out of the mouth of these two witnesses* these promises might be established; and very precious promises they are, relating to the gospel-church, which have been in part accomplished, and will be yet more and more, for he is faithful that has promised.

I. That there shall be a church for God set up in the world, after the defection and destruction of the Jewish church, and this in the last days; that is, as some of the rabbin themselves acknowledge, *in the days of the Messiah.* The people of God shall be incorporated by a new charter, a new spiritual way of worship shall be enacted, and a new institution of offices to attend it; better privileges shall be granted by this new charter, and better provision made for enlarging and establishing the kingdom of God among men than had been made by the Old-Testament constitution: *The mountain of the house of the Lord* shall again appear firm ground for God's faithful worshippers to stand, and go, and build upon, in their attendance on him, *v.* 1. And it shall be a centre of unity to them; a church shall be set up in the world, to which the Lord will be daily *adding such as shall be saved.*

II. That this church shall be firmly founded and well-built: It *shall be established in the top of the mountains;* Christ himself will build it upon a rock; it shall be an impregnable fort upon an immovable foundation, so that the gates of hell shall neither overthrow the one nor undermine the other (Mt. 16:18); its foundations are still in the *holy mountains* (Ps. 87:1), the *everlasting mountains,* which cannot, which shall not, be removed. It shall be established, not as the temple, upon one mountain, but upon many; for the foundations of the church, as they are sure, so they are large.

III. That it shall be highly advanced, and become eminent and conspicuous: It *shall be exalted above the hills,* observed with wonder for its growing greatness from small beginnings. The kingdom of Christ shall shine with greater lustre than ever any of the kingdoms of the earth did. It shall be as a *city on a hill, which cannot be hid,* Mt. *v.* 14. The glory of this latter house is greater than that of the former, Hag. 2:9. See 2 Co. 3:7, 8, etc.

IV. That there shall be a great accession of converts to it and succession of converts in it. *People shall flow unto it* as the waters of a river are continually flowing; there shall be a constant stream of believers flowing in from all parts into the church, as the people of the Jews flowed into the temple, while it was standing, to worship there. Then many tribes came to the mountain of the house, to enquire of God's temple; but in gospel-times many nations shall flow into the church, shall *fly like a cloud and as the doves to their windows.* Ministers shall be sent forth to *disciple all nations,* and they shall not *labour in vain;* for, multitudes being wrought upon to believe the gospel and embrace the Christian religion, they shall excite and encourage one another, and shall say, *"Come, and let us go up to the mountain of the Lord* now raised among us, even *to the house of the God of Jacob,* the spiritual temple which we need not travel far to, for it is brought to our doors and set up in the midst of us." Thus shall people be *made willing in the day of his power* (Ps. 110:3), and shall do what they can to make others willing, as Andrew invited Peter, and Philip Nathanael, to be acquainted with Christ. They shall *call the people to the mountain* (Deu. 33:19), for there is in Christ enough for all, enough for each. Now observe what it is, 1. Which these converts expect to find in *the house of the God of Jacob.* They come thither for instruction: *"He will teach us of his ways,* what is the way in which he would have us to walk with him and in which we may depend upon him to meet us graciously." Note, Where we come to worship God we come to be taught of him. 2. Which they engage to do when they are thus taught of God: *We will walk in his paths.* Note, Those may comfortably expect that God will teach them who are firmly resolved by his grace to do as they are taught.

V. That, in order to this, a new revelation shall be published to the world, on which the church shall be founded, and by which multitudes shall be brought into it: *For the law shall go forth of Zion, and the word of the Lord from Jerusalem.* The gospel is here called *the word of the Lord,* for *the Lord gave the word, and great was the company of those that published it,* Ps. 68:11. It was of a divine original, a divine authority; it began to be spoken by the Lord Christ himself, Heb. 2:3. And it is *a law,* a law of faith; we are *under the law to Christ.* This was to go *forth from Jerusalem, from Zion,* the metropolis of the Old-Testament dispensation, where the temple, and altars, and oracles were, and whither the Jews went to worship from all parts; thence the gospel must take rise, to show the connexion between the Old Testament and the New, that the gospel is not set up in opposition to the law, but is an explication and illustration of it, and a *branch growing out of its roots.* It was in Jerusalem that Christ preached and wrought miracles; there he died, rose again, and ascended; there the Spirit was poured out; and those that were to preach repentance and remission of sins to all nations were ordered to *begin at Jerusalem,* so that thence flowed the streams that were to water the desert world.

VI. That a convincing power should go along with the gospel of Christ, in all places where it should be preached (*v.* 3): *He shall judge among many people.* Messiah, the lawgiver (*v.* 2.), is here *the judge,* for to him the Father *committed all judgment,* and *for judgment he came into this world;* his word, the *word of his gospel,* that was to go forth from Jerusalem, was the golden sceptre by which he shall rule and judge when he sits as *king on the holy hill of Zion,* Ps. 2:6. By it he shall *rebuke strong nations afar off;* for the Spirit working with the word shall *reprove the world,* Jn. 16:8. It is promised to the Son of David that he shall *judge among the heathen* (Ps. 110:6), which he does when in the chariot of his everlasting gospel he goes forth, and goes on, *conquering and to conquer.*

VII. That a disposition to mutual peace and love shall be the happy effect of the setting up of the kingdom of the Messiah: *They shall beat their swords into ploughshares;* that is, angry passionate men, that have been fierce and furious, shall be wonderfully sweetened, and made mild and meek, Tit. 3:2, 3. Those who, before their conversion, did injuries, and would bear none, after their conversion can bear injuries, but will do none. As far as the gospel prevails it makes men peaceable, for such is the *wisdom from above;* it is *gentle and easy to be entreated;* and if nations were but leavened by it, there would be universal peace. When Christ was born there was universal peace in the Roman empire; those that were first brought into the gospel church were all of *one heart and of one soul* (Acts 4:32); and it was observed of the primitive Christians how well *they loved one another.* In heaven this will have its full accomplishment. It is promised, 1. That none shall be quarrelsome. The art of war, instead of being improved (which some reckon the glory of a kingdom), shall be forgotten and laid aside as useless. They *shall not learn war any more* as they have done, for they shall have no need to defend themselves nor any inclination to offend their neighbours. *Nation shall no longer lift up sword against nation;* not that the gospel will make men cowards, but it will make men peaceable. 2. That all shall be quiet, both from evil and from the fear of evil (*v.* 4): *They shall sit* safely, and none shall disturb them; they shall sit securely, and shall not disturb themselves, every man *under his vine and under his fig-tree,* enjoying the fruit of them, and needing no other shelter than the leaves of them. *None shall make them afraid;* not only there shall be nothing that is likely to frighten them, but they shall not be disposed to fear. under the dominion of Christ, as that of Solomon, there shall be *abundance of peace.* Though his followers have trouble in the world, in him they enjoy great tranquillity. If this seems unlikely, yet we may depend upon it, *for the mouth of the Lord has spoken it,* and no word of his shall fall to the ground; what he has spoken by his word he will do by his providence and grace. He that is the *Lord of hosts* will be the *God of peace;* and those may well be easy whom *the Lord of hosts,* of all hosts, undertakes the protection of.

VIII. That the churches shall be constant in their duty, and so shall make a good use of their tranquillity and shall not provoke the Lord to deprive them of it, *v.* 5. When *the churches have rest* they shall be edified, and confirmed, and comforted, and shall resolve to be as firm to their God as other nations are to theirs, though they be no gods. Where we find the foregoing promises, Isa. 2:2, etc. it follows (*v.* 5), *O house of Jacob! come ye, and let us walk in the light of the Lord;* and here, *We will walk in the name of the Lord our God.* Note, Peace is a blessing indeed when it strengthens our resolutions to cleave to the Lord. Observe, 1. How constant other nations were to their gods: *All people will walk every one in the name of his god,* will own their god and cleave to him, will worship their god and serve him, will depend upon him and put confidence in him. Whatever men make a god of they will make use of, and take his name along with them in all their actions and affairs. The mariners, in a storm, *cried every man to his god,* Jonah 1:5. And no instance could be found of a nation's changing its gods, Jer. 2:11: If the hosts of heaven were their gods, they loved them, and served them, and *walked after them,* Jer. 8:2. 2. How constant God's people now resolve to be to him: "*We will walk in the name of the Lord our God,* will acknowledge him in all our ways, and govern ourselves by a continual regard to him, doing nothing but what we have warrant from him for, and openly professing our relation to him." Observe, Their resolution is peremptory; it is not a thing that needs be disputed: "*We will walk in the name of the Lord our God.*" It is just and reasonable: He is *our God.* And it is a resolution for a perpetuity: "We will do it *for ever and ever,* and will never leave him. He will be ours for ever, and therefore so we will be his, and never repent our choice."

IX. That notwithstanding the dispersions, distress, and infirmities of the church, it shall be formed and established, and made very considerable, *v.* 6, 7. 1. The state of the church had been low, and weak, and very helpless, in the latter times of the Old Testament, partly through the corruptions of the Jewish nation, and partly through the oppressions under which they groaned. They were like a *flock of sheep* that were *maimed, worried,* and *scattered,* Eze. 34:16; Jer. 50:6. 17. The good people among them, and in other places, that were well inclined, were dispersed, were very infirm, and in a manner lost and cast far off.

2. It is promised that all these grievances shall be redressed and the distemper healed. Christ will come himself (Mt. 15:24), and send his apostles to *the lost sheep of the house of Israel,* Mt. 10:6. From among the Jews that halted, or that for want of strength, could not go upright, God gathered a remnant (*v.* 7), that *remnant according to the election of grace* which is spoken of in Rom. 11:7, which embraced the gospel of Christ. And from among the Gentiles that were cast far off (so the Gentiles are described to be, Eph. 2:13, Acts 2:39) he raised a strong nation; greater numbers of them were brought into the church than of the Jews, Gal. 4:27. And such a strong nation the gospel-church is that the gates of hell shall never be able to prevail against it. The church of Christ is more numerous than any other nation, and *strong in the Lord and in the power of his might.*

X. That the *Messiah* shall be the king of this kingdom, shall protect and govern it, and order all the affairs of it for the best, and this to the end of time. The Lord Jesus *shall reign over them in Mount Zion* by his word and Spirit in his ordinances, and this *henceforth and for ever,* for *of the increase of his government and peace there shall be no end.*

Verses 8–13

These verses relate to Zion and Jerusalem, here called the *tower of the flock* or the *tower of Edor;* we read of such a place (Gen. 35:21) near Bethlehem; and some conjecture it is the same place where the shepherds were keeping their flocks when the angels brought them tidings of the birth of Christ, and some think Bethlehem itself is here spoken of, as *ch.* 5:2. Some think it is a tower at that gate of Jerusalem which is called the *sheep-gate* (Neh. 3:32), and conjecture that through that gate Christ rode in triumph into Jerusalem. However, it seems to be put for Jerusalem itself, or for Zion the *tower of David.* All the sheep of Israel flocked thither three times a year; it was the stronghold (*Ophel,* which is also a name of a place in Jerusalem, Neh. 3:27), or castle, of the *daughter of Zion.* Now here,

I. We have a promise of the glories of the spiritual Jerusalem, the gospel-church, which is; the tower of the flock, that one fold in which all the sheep of Christ are protected under one Shepherd: "*Unto thee shall it come;* that which thou hast long wanted and wished for, *even the first dominion,* a dignity and power equal to that of David and Solomon, by whom Jerusalem was first raised, that *kingdom* shall again *come to the daughter of Jerusalem,* which it was deprived of at the captivity. It shall make as great a figure and shine with as much lustre among the nations, and have as much influence upon them, as ever it had; this is the *first* or *chief* dominion." Now this had by no means its accomplishment in Zerubbabel; his was nothing like the first dominion either in respect of splendour and sovereignty at home or the extent of power abroad; and therefore it must refer to the kingdom of the *Messiah* (and to that the Chaldee-paraphrase refers it) and had its accomplishment when God gave to our Lord Jesus *the throne of his father David* (Lu. 1:32), set him king *upon the holy hill of Zion* and *gave him the heathen for his inheritance* (Ps. 2:6), *made him, his first-born, higher than the kings of the earth,* Ps. 89:27; Dan. 7:14. *David, in spirit, called him Lord,* and (as Dr. Pocock observes) he witnessed of himself, and his witness was true, that he was greater than Solomon, none of their dominions being like his for extent and duration. The common people welcomed Christ into Jerusalem with *hosannas to the son of David,* to show that it was the *first dominion* that came *to the daughter of Zion;* and the evangelist applies it to the promise of Zion's king coming to her, Mt. 21:5; Zec. 9:9. Some give this sense of the words: To Zion, and Jerusalem that tower of the flock, to the nation of the Jews, *came the first dominion;* that is, there the kingdom of Christ was first set up, the *gospel of the kingdom* was first *preached* (Lu. 24:47), there Christ was first called *king of the Jews.*

II. This is illustrated by a prediction of the calamities of the literal Jerusalem, to which some favour and relief should be granted, as a type and figure of what God would do for the gospel-Jerusalem in the last days, notwithstanding its distresses. We have here,

1. Jerusalem put in pain by the providences of God. "She *cries out aloud,* that all her neighbours may take no-

tice of her griefs, because there is *no king in her,* none of that honour and power she used to have. Instead of ruling the nations, as she did when she *sat a queen,* she is ruled by them, and has become a captive. Her *counsellors* have *perished;* she is no longer at her own disposal, but is given up to the will of her enemies, and is governed by their counsellors. *Pangs have taken her.*" (1.) She is carried captive to Babylon, and there is in pangs of grief. "She *goes forth out of the city,* and is constrained to *dwell in the field,* exposed to all manner of inconveniences; she *goes even to Babylon,* and there wears out *seventy tedious* years in a miserable captivity, all that while *in pain, as a woman in travail,* waiting to be delivered, and thinking the time very long." (2.) When she is delivered out of Babylon, and redeemed from the hand of her enemies there, yet still she is in pangs of fear; the end of one trouble is but the beginning of another; for *now also,* when Jerusalem is in the rebuilding, *many nations are gathered against her, v.* 11. They were so in Ezra's and Nehemiah's time, and did all they could to obstruct the building of the temple and the wall. They were so in the time of the Maccabees; they said, *Let her be defiled;* let her be looked upon as a place polluted with sin, and be forsaken and abandoned both of God and man; let her holy places be profaned and all her honours laid in the dust; *let our eye look upon Zion,* and please itself with the sight of its ruins, as it is said of Edom (Obad. 12, *Thou shouldst not have looked upon the day of thy brother);* let our eyes see our desire upon Zion, the day we have long wished for. When they hear the enemies thus combine against them, and insult over them, no wonder that they are in pain, and cry aloud. *Without are fightings, within are fears.*

2. Jerusalem made easy by the promises of God: "*Why dost thou cry out aloud?* Let thy griefs and fears be silenced; indulge not thyself in them, for, though things are bad with thee, they shall end well; thy pangs are great, but they are like those of a *woman in travail* (*v.* 9), that *labours to bring forth* (*v.* 10), the issue of which will be good at last." Jerusalem's pangs are not as dying agonies, but as travailing throes, which after a while will be forgotten, for joy that a child is born into the world. Let the literal Jerusalem comfort herself with this, that, whatever straits she may be reduced to, she shall continue until the coming of the Messiah, for there his kingdom must be first set up, and she shall not be destroyed while that blessing is in her; and when at length she is ploughed as a field, and become heaps (as is threatened, *ch.* 3:12), yet her privileges shall be resigned to the spiritual Jerusalem, and in that the promises made to her shall be fulfilled. Let Jerusalem be easy then, for, (1.) Her captivity in Babylon shall have an end, a happy end (*v.* 10): *There shalt thou be delivered, and the Lord shall redeem thee from the hand of thy enemies there.* This was done by Cyrus, who acted therein as God's servant; and that deliverance was typical of our redemption by Jesus Christ, and the release from our spiritual bondage which is proclaimed in the everlasting gospel, that *acceptable year of the Lord,* in which Christ himself preached *liberty to the captives, and the opening of the prison to those that were bound,* Lu. 4:18, 19. (2.) The designs of her enemies against her afterwards shall be baffled, nay, they shall turn upon themselves, *v.* 12, 13. They promise themselves a day of it, but it shall prove *God's day.* They are *gathered against Zion,* to destroy it, but it shall prove to their own destruction, which Israel and Israel's God shall have the glory of. [1.] Their coming together against Zion shall be the occasion of their ruin. They *associate themselves, and gird themselves,* that they may break Jerusalem in pieces, but it will prove that they shall be broken in pieces, Isa. 8:9. *They know not the thoughts of the Lord.* When they are gathering together, and Providence favours them in it, they little think what God is designing by it, nor do they understand his counsel; they know what they aim at in coming together, but they know not what God aims at in bringing them together; they aim at Zion's ruin, but God aims at theirs. Note, When men are made use of as instruments of Providence in accomplishing its purposes it is very common for them to intend one thing and for God to intend quite the contrary. The king of Assyria is to be a rod in God's hand for the correction of his people, in order to their reformation; *howbeit he means not so, nor does his heart think so,* Isa. 10:7. And thus it is here; the nations are gathered against

Zion, as soldiers into the field, but God gathers them *as sheaves into the floor*, to be beaten to pieces; and they could not have been so easily, so effectually, destroyed, if they had not *gathered together against Zion*. Note, The designs of enemies for the ruin of the church often prove ruining to themselves; and thereby they prepare themselves for destruction and put themselves in the way of it; they are *snared in the work of their own hands*. [2.] Zion shall have the honour of being victorious over them, *v.* 13. When they are *gathered as sheaves into the floor*, to be trodden down, as the corn then was by the oxen, then, *"Arise, and thresh, O daughter of Zion!* instead of fearing them, and fleeing from them, boldly set upon them, and take the opportunity Providence favours thee with of trampling upon them. Plead not thy own weakness, and that thou art not a match for so many confederated enemies; God will make *thy horn iron*, to push them down, and *thy hoofs brass*, to tread upon them when they are down; and thus thou shalt *beat in pieces many people*, that have long been beating thee in pieces." Thus, when God pleases, *the daughter of Babylon is made a threshing floor (it is time to thresh her*, Jer. 51:33), and the *worm Jacob* is made *a threshing instrument*, with which God will *thresh the mountains, and make them as chaff*, Isa. 41:14, 15. How strangely, how happily, are the tables turned, since Jacob was the threshing-floor and Babylon the threshing instrument! Isa. 21:10. Note, When God has conquering work for his people to do he will furnish them with strength and ability for it, will make the horn iron and the hoofs brass; and, when he does so, they must exert the power he gives them, and execute the commission; even the daughter of Zion must arise, and thresh. [3.] The glory of the victory shall redound to God. Zion shall thresh these sheaves in the floor, but the corn threshed out shall be a meat-offering at God's altar: *I will consecrate their gain unto the Lord* (that is, I will have it consecrated) and *their substance unto the Lord of the whole earth*. The spoils gained by Zion's victory shall be brought into the sanctuary, and devoted to God, either in part, as those of Midian (Num. 31:28), or in whole, as those of Jericho, Jos. 6:17. God is Jehovah, the fountain of being; he is the *Lord of the whole earth*, the fountain of power; and therefore he needs not any of our gain or substance, but may challenge and demand it all if he please; and with ourselves we must devote all we have to his honour, to be employed as he directs. Thus far all we have must have *holiness to the Lord* written upon it, all our gain and substance must be *consecrated to the Lord of the whole earth*, Isa. 23:18. And extraordinary successes call for extraordinary acknowledgments, whether they be of spoils in war or gains in trade. It is God that *gives us power to get wealth*, which way soever it is honestly got, and therefore he must be honoured with what we get. Some make all this to point at the defeat of Sennacherib when he besieged Jerusalem, others to the destruction of Babylon, others to the successes of the Maccabees; but the learned Dr. Pocock and others think it had its full accomplishment in the spiritual victories obtained by the gospel of Christ over the powers of darkness that fought against it. The nations thought to ruin Christianity in its infancy, but it was victorious over them; those that persisted in their enmity were *broken to pieces* (Mt. 21:44), particularly the Jewish nation; but multitudes by divine grace were gained to the church, and they and their substance were consecrated to the Lord Jesus, *the Lord of the whole earth*.

CHAPTER 5

In this chapter we have, I. A prediction of the troubles and distresses of the Jewish nation (*v.* 1). II. A promise of the Messiah, and of his kingdom, to support the people of God in the day of these troubles. 1. Of the birth of the Messiah (*v.* 2, 3). 2. Of his advancement (*v.* 4). 3. Of his protection of his people, and his victory over his and their enemies (*v.* 5, 6). 4. Of the great world by it (*v.* 7). 5. Of the destruction of the enemies of the church, both those without, that attack it, and those within, that expose it (*v.* 8–15).

Verses 1–6

Here, as before, we have,

I. The abasement and distress of Zion, *v.* 1. The Jewish nation, for many years before the captivity, dwindled, and fell into disgrace: *Now gather thyself in troops, O daughter of troops!* It is either a summons to Zion's enemies, that had troops at their service, to come and do their worst against her (God will suffer them to do it), or a challenge

to Zion's friends, that had troops too at command, to come and do their best for her; Let them *gather in troops*, yet it shall be to no purpose; for, says the prophet, in the name of the inhabitants of Jerusalem, *He has laid siege against us;* the king of Assyria has, the king of Babylon has, and we know not which way to defend ourselves; so that the enemies shall gain their point, and prevail so far as *to smite the judge of Israel* — the king, the chief justice, and the other inferior judges — *with a rod upon the cheek*, in contempt of them and their dignity; having made them prisoners, they shall use them as shamefully as any of the common captives. Complaint had been made of the judges of Israel (*ch.* 3:11) that they were corrupt and took bribes, and this disgrace came justly upon them for abusing their power; yet it was a great calamity to Israel to have their judges treated thus ignominiously. Some make this the reason why the troops (that is, the Roman army) shall lay siege to Jerusalem, because the Jews *shall smite the judge of Israel upon the cheek*, because of the indignities they shall do to the Messiah, the Judge of Israel, whom they smote on the cheek, saying, *Prophesy, who smote thee*. But the former sense seems more probable, and that it is meant of the besieging of Jerusalem, not by the Romans, but the Chaldeans, and was fulfilled in the indignities done to king Zedekiah, and the princes of the house of David.

II. The advancement of Zion's King. Having shown how low the house of David should be brought, and how vilely the shield of that mighty family should be cast away, as though it had not been anointed with oil, to encourage the faith of God's people, who might be tempted now to think that his covenant with David and his house was abrogated (according to the psalmist's complaint, Ps. 89:38, 39), he adds an illustrious prediction of the Messiah and his kingdom, in whom that covenant should be established, and the honours of that house should be revived, advanced, and perpetuated. Now let us see,

1. How the Messiah is here described. It is he that is to be *ruler in Israel, whose goings forth have been from of old, from everlasting*, from the *days of eternity*, as the word is. Here we have, (1.) His existence from eternity, as God: *his goings forth*, or *emanations*, as the going forth of the beams from the sun, were, or have been, *of old, from everlasting*, which (says Dr. Pocock) is so signal a description of Christ's eternal generation, or his going forth as the Son of God, begotten of his Father before all worlds, that this prophecy must belong only to him, and could never be verified of any other. It certainly speaks of a going forth that was now past, when the prophet spoke, and cannot but be read, as we read it, his *outgoings have been;* and the putting of both these words together, which severally are used to denote eternity, plainly shows that they must here be taken in the strictest sense (the same with Ps. 90:2, *From everlasting to everlasting thou are God),* and can be applied to no other than to him who was able to say, *Before Abraham was, I am,* Jn. 8:58. Dr. Pocock observes that the *going forth* is used (Deu. 8:3) for a *word* which *proceeds out of the mouth*, and is therefore very fitly used to signify the eternal generation of him who is called the *Word of God*, that was *in the beginning with God*, Jn. 1:1, 2. (2.) His office as Mediator; he was to be *ruler in Israel*, king of his church; he was to *reign over the house of Jacob for ever*, Lu. 1:32, 33. The Jews object that our Lord Jesus could not be the Messiah, for he was so far from being ruler in Israel that Israel ruled over him, and put him to death, and would not have him to reign over them; but he answered that himself when he said, *My kingdom is not of this world*, Jn. 18:36. And it is a spiritual Israel that he reigns over, the children of promise, all the followers of believing Abraham and praying Jacob. In the hearts of these he reigns by his Spirit and grace, and in the society of these by his word and ordinances. And was not he *ruler in Israel* whom winds and seas obeyed, to whom legions of devils were forced to submit, and who commanded away diseases from the sick and called the dead out of their graves? None but he whose *goings forth were from of old, from everlasting*, was fit to be *ruler in Israel*, to be head of the church, and *head over all things to the church*.

2. What is here foretold concerning him.

(1.) That Bethlehem should be the place of his nativity, *v.* 2. This was the scripture which the scribes went upon when with the greatest assurance they told Herod *where*

Christ should be born (Mt. 2:6), and hence it was universally known among the Jews that *Christ should come out of the town of Bethlehem where David was*, Jn. 7:42. *Bethlehem* signifies *the house of bread*, the fittest place for him to be born in who is *the bread of life*. And, because it was the city of David, by a special providence it was ordered that he should be born there who was to be the *Son of David*, and his heir and successor for ever. It is called *Bethlehem-Ephratah*, both names of the same city, as appears Gen. 35:19. It was *little among the thousands of Judah*, not considerable either for the number of the inhabitants or the figure they made; it had nothing in it worthy to have this honour put upon it; but God in that, as in other instances, chose to *exalt those of low degree*, Lu. 1:52. Christ would give honour to the place of his birth, and not derive honour from it: *Though thou be little*, yet this shall make thee great, and, as St. Matthew reads it, Thou *art not the least among the princes of Judah*, but upon this account art really honourable above any of them. A relation to Christ will magnify those that are little in the world.

(2.) That in the fulness of time he should be born of a woman (*v.* 3): *Therefore will he give them up;* he will give up his people Israel to distress and trouble, and will defer their salvation, which has been so long promised and expected, *until the time*, the set time, *that she who travails has brought forth*, or (as it should be read) *that she who shall bring forth shall have brought forth*, that the blessed virgin, who was to be the mother of the Messiah, shall have brought him forth at Bethlehem, the place appointed. This Dr. Pocock thinks to be the most genuine sense of the words. Though the out-goings of the Messiah were *from everlasting*, yet the *redemption in Jerusalem*, the *consolation of Israel*, must be *waited for* (Lu. 2:25–38) until the time that *she who should bring forth* (so the virgin Mary is called, as Christ is himself called, *He that shall come*) shall *bring forth;* and in the mean time *he will give them up*. Divine salvations must be waited for until the time fixed for the bringing of them forth.

(3.) That the *remnant of his brethren shall then return to the children of Israel*. The remnant of the Jewish nation shall return to the spirit of the true genuine children of Israel, a people in covenant with God; the hearts of the children shall be turned to the fathers, Mal. 4:6. Some understand it of all believers, Gentiles as well as Jews; they shall all be incorporated into the commonwealth of Israel; and, as they are all brethren to one another, so *he is not ashamed to call them brethren*, Heb. 2:11.

(4.) That he shall be a glorious prince, and his subjects shall be happy under his government (*v.* 4): *He shall stand and feed*, that is, he shall both teach and rule, and continue to do so, as a good shepherd, with wisdom, and care, and love. So it was foretold. *He shall feed his flock like a shepherd*, shall provide green pastures for them, and under-shepherds to lead them into these pastures. He is the *good shepherd* that *goes before the sheep*, and presides among them. He shall do this, not as an ordinary man, but *in the strength of the Lord*, as one clothed with a divine power to go through his work, and break through the difficulties in his way, so as not to *fail*, or be *discouraged;* he shall do it *in the majesty of the name of the Lord his God*, so as plainly to evidence that *God's name was in him* (Ex. 23:21) the majesty of his name, for *he taught as one having authority and not as the scribes*. The prophets prefaced their messages with, *Thus saith the Lord;* but Christ spoke, not as a servant, but as a Son — *Verily, verily, I say unto you*. This was feeding *in the majesty of the name of the Lord his God. All power was given him in heaven and in earth*, a *power over all flesh*, by virtue of which he still rules *in the majesty of the name of the Lord his God*, a name above every name. Christ's government shall be, [1.] Very happy for his subjects, for *they shall abide;* they shall be safe and easy, and continue so for ever. *Because he lives, they shall live also*. They shall lie down in the green pastures to which he shall lead them, *shall abide in God's tabernacle for ever*, Ps. 61:4. His church shall abide, and he in it, and with it, always, even to the end of the world. [2.] It shall be very glorious to himself: *Now shall he be great to the ends of the earth*. Now that he stands and feeds his flock, *now shall he be great*. For Christ reckons it his greatness to do good. Now he shall be *great to the ends of the earth*, for the uttermost parts of the earth shall be given him for his possession, and the ends of the world shall see his salvation.

(5) That he shall secure the peace and welfare of his church and people against all the attempts of his and their enemies (*v.* 5, 6): *This man,* as king and ruler, *shall be the peace when the Assyrians shall come into our land.* This refers to the deliverance of Hezekiah and his kingdom from the power of Sennacherib, who invaded them, in the type; but, under the shadow of that, it is a promise of the safety of the gospel-church and of all believers from the designs and attempts of the powers of darkness, Satan and all his instruments, the dragon and his angels, that seek to devour the church of the first-born and all that belong to it. Observe, [1.] The peril and danger which Christ's subjects are supposed to be in. The Assyrian, a potent enemy, *comes into their land* (*v.* 5, 6), *treads within their borders,* nay, prevails so far as to *tread in their palaces;* it was a time of *treading down and of perplexity* when Sennacherib made a descent upon Judah, took all the defenced cities, and laid siege to Jerusalem, Isa. 36:1; 37:3. This represented the gates of hell fighting against the kingdom of Christ, *encompassing the camp of the saints and of the holy city,* and threatening to bear down all before them. When the terrors of the law set themselves in array against a convinced soul, when the temptations of Satan assault the people of God, and the troubles of the world threaten to rob them of all their comforts, then the *Assyrian comes into their land* and treads in their palaces. *Without are fightings, within are fears.* [2.] The protection and defence which his subjects are then sure to be under. *First,* Christ will himself be *their peace.* When the Assyrian comes with such a force into a land, can there be any other peace than a tame submission and an unresisted desolation? Yes, even then the church's King will be the conservator of the church's peace, will be *for a hiding-place,* Isa. 32:1, 2. Christ is our peace as a priest, making atonement for sin, and reconciling us to God; and he is our peace as a king, conquering our enemies and commanding down disquieting fears and passions; he *creates the fruit of the lips, peace.* Even when the Assyrian comes into the land, when we are in the greatest distress and danger and have received a sentence of death within ourselves, yet *this man may be the peace. In me,* says Christ, *you shall have peace,* when *in the world you have tribulation;* at such a time our souls may dwell at ease in him. *Secondly,* He will find out proper instruments to be employed for their protection and deliverance, and the defeat of their enemies: *Then shall we raise against him seven shepherds and eight principal men,* that is, a competent number of persons, proper to oppose the enemy, and make head against him, and protect the church of God in peace, men that shall have the care and tenderness of shepherds and the courage and authority of *principal men,* or *princes of men. Seven* and *eight* are a certain number for an uncertain. Note, When God has work to do he will not want fitting instruments to do it with; and when he pleases he can do it by a few; he needs not raise thousands, but seven or eight principal men may serve the turn if God be with them. Magistrates and ministers are shepherds and principal men, raised in defence of religion's righteous cause against the powers of sin and Satan in the world. *Thirdly,* The opposition given to the church shall be got over, and the opposers brought down. This is represented by the laying of Assyria and Chaldea waste, which two nations were the most formidable enemies to the Israel of God of any, and the destruction of them signified the making of Christ's enemies his footstool: *They shall waste the land of Assyria with the sword, and the land of Nimrod in the entrances thereof;* they shall make inroads upon the land, and put to the sword all that they find in arms. Note, Those that threaten ruin to the church of God hasten ruin to themselves; and their destruction is the church's salvation: *Thus* shall he *deliver us from the Assyrian.* When *Satan fell as lightning from heaven* before the preaching of the gospel, and Christ's enemies, that would not have him to reign over them, were *slain before him,* then this was fulfilled.

Verses 7–15

Glorious things are here spoken of *the remnant of Jacob,* that remnant which was raised of *her that halted* (*ch.* 4:7), and it seems to be that *remnant which the Lord our God shall call* (Joel 2:32), on whom the Spirit shall be poured out, the remnant that shall be saved, Rom. 9:27. Note, God's people are but a remnant, a small number in comparison with the many that are left to perish, a *little flock;* but they are *the remnant of Jacob,* a people in covenant with God, and in his favour. Now concerning this remnant it is here promised,

I. That they shall be *as a dew* in the midst of the nations, *v.* 7. God's church is dispersed all the world over; it is *in the midst of many people,* as gold in the ore, wheat in the heap. Israel according to the flesh dwelt alone, and was not numbered among the nations; but the spiritual Israel lies scattered *in the midst of many people,* as the *salt of the earth,* or as seed sown in the ground, here a grain and there a grain, Hos. 2:23. Now this remnant shall be *as dew from the Lord.* 1. They shall be of a heavenly extraction; as *dew from the Lord,* who is the *Father of the rain,* and has *begotten the drops of the dew,* Job 38:28. They are *born from above,* and are not of the earth, savouring the things of the earth. 2. They shall be numerous as the drops of dew in a summer's morning. Ps. 110:3, *Thou hast the dew of thy youth.* 3. They shall be pure and clear, not muddy and corrupt, but crystal drops, as the *water of life.* 4. They shall be produced silently and without noise, as the dew that distils insensibly, we know not how; such is the way of the Spirit. 5. They shall live in a continual dependence upon God, and be still deriving from him, as the dew, which *tarries not for man,* not *waits for the sons of men;* they shall not rely upon human aids and powers, but on divine grace, for they are, and own that they are, no more than what the free grace of God makes them every day. 6. They shall be great blessings to those among whom they live, as the dew and the showers are to the grass, to make it grow without the help of man, or the sons of men. Their doctrine, example, and prayers, shall make them as dew, to soften and moisten others, and make them fruitful. Their speech shall *distil as the dew* (Deu. 32:2), and all about them shall *wait for them as for the rain,* Job 29:23. The people among whom they live shall be as the grass, which flourishes only by the blessing of God, and not by the art and care of man; they shall be beneficial to those about them by drawing down God's blessings on them, as Jacob on Laban's house, and by cooling and mitigating God's wrath, which otherwise would burn them up, as the dew preserves the grass from being scorched by the sun; so Dr. Pocock; they shall be mild and gentle in their behaviour, like their Master, who comes down *like rain upon the new-mown grass,* Ps. 72:6.

II. That they shall be *as a lion among the beasts of the forest,* that *treads down and tears in pieces, v.* 8. As they shall be silent, and gentle, and communicative of all good, to those that receive the truth in the love of it, so they shall be bold as a lion in witnessing against the corruptions of the times and places they live in, and strong as a lion, in the strength of God, to resist and overcome their spiritual enemies. The *weapons of their warfare are mighty, through God, to the pulling down of strongholds,* 2 Co. 10:4, 5. They shall have *courage which all their adversaries shall not be able to resist* (Lu. 21:15), as when the lion tears none can deliver. When infidelity is silenced, and all iniquity made *to stop her mouth,* when sinners are convinced and converted by the power of the gospel, in the doctrine of its ministers and the conversation of its professors, then the remnant of Jacob is like a lion. This is explained, *v.* 9, *Thy hand shall be lifted up upon thy adversaries;* the church shall have the upper hand at last of all that oppose her. Her *enemies shall be cut off;* they shall cease to be enemies; their enmity shall be cut off. Christ's arrows of conviction shall be sharp in their hearts, so that they shall fall under him; they shall yield themselves subjects to him (Ps. 45:5) and be happily conquered and subdued, Ps. 110:2.

III. That they shall be brought off from all carnal confidences, which they have relied on, that by the providence of God they shall enjoy such a security that they shall not need them, and by the grace of God they shall be brought to see the folly of them and come off from them. It was the sin of Israel that they furnished themselves extravagantly with *horses and chariots,* and were *soothsayers* and *idolaters;* see Isa. 2:6–8. But here it is promised that they shall not regard them any more. The tranquillity of the kingdom of Christ is intended in that promise, which explains this, Zec. 9:10, *I will cut off the chariot from Ephraim and the horse from Jerusalem.* Note, It is a great mercy to be deprived of those things in which we have reposed a confidence in competition with God, which we have made our arm, and after which we have gone a whoring from God. Let us observe the particulars: — 1. They had trusted in chariots and horses, and multiplied them (Ps. 20:7); but now God will *cut off their horses,* and *destroy their chariots* (*v.* 10), as *David houghed the chariot-horses,* 2 Sa. 8:4. They shall not have them, lest they should be tempted to trust in them. 2. They depended upon their strongholds, and fortified cities, for their security; but God will take care that they be demolished (*v.* 11): *I will cut off the cities of thy land;* I will *throw down thy strongholds.* They shall have them for habitations, but not for garrisons, for God will be their only place of defence, their *high tower,* and *their deliverer.* 3. Many of them depended much upon the conduct and advice of their conjurors, diviners, and fortune-tellers; and those God will cut off, not only as weak things, and insufficient to relieve them, but as wicked things, and sufficient to ruin them (*v.* 12): *"I will cut off witchcrafts out of thy hand,* that thou shalt no more take hold of them, and stay thyself upon them, and *thou shalt have no more soothsayers,* for thou shalt be convinced that all their pretensions are a cheat." The justice of the nation shall cut them off according to law, Lev. 20:27. the preaching of the gospel brought men off from using curious arts, Acts 19:19. 4. Many of them had said to the work of their hands, *You are our gods;* but now idolatry shall be abolished and abandoned (*v.* 13): *"Thy graven images will I cut off, and thy standing images,* both those that were movable and those that were fixed; they shall be destroyed by the power of the law of Moses and deserted by the power of the gospel of Christ, so that *thou shalt no more worship the work of thy hands,* but be ashamed that ever thou hast been so deluded. Among other monuments of idolatry, *I will pluck up thy groves out of the midst of thee," v.* 14. These were planted and preserved in honour of their idols, and used in the worship of them; these they were ordered to burn (Deu. 12:2, 3), and, if they do not, God will, so that they shall not have them to trust to. And so *will I destroy their cities,* meaning the cities that were dedicated to the idols, to some dunghill-deity or other, which they confided in for their protection.

IV. That those who stand it out against the gospel of Christ, and continue in league with their idolatries and witchcrafts, shall fall under the wrath of God, and be consumed by it (*v.* 15): *I will execute vengeance in anger and fury upon the heathen* (that is, upon heathenism), *such as they have not heard;* idolatries shall be done away, and idolaters put to shame. I will execute vengeance upon the heathen *who have not heard* (so some read it), or who would not hear and receive the doctrine of Christ. God will give his Son either the hearts or the necks of his enemies, and make them either his friends or his footstool.

CHAPTER 6

After the precious promises in the two foregoing chapters, relating to the Messiah's kingdom, the prophet is here directed to set the sins of Israel in order before them, for their conviction and humiliation, as necessary to make way for the comfort of gospel-grace. Christ's forerunner was a reprover, and preached repentance, and so prepared his way. Here, I. God enters an action against his people for their base ingratitude, and the bad returns they had made him for his favours (*v.* 1–5). II. He shows the wrong course they should have taken (*v.* 6–8). III. He calls upon them to hear the voice of his judgments, and sets the sins in order for which he still proceeded in his controversy with them (*v.* 9), their injustice (*v.* 10–15), and their idolatry (*v.* 16), for both which ruin was coming upon them.

Verses 1–5

Here, I. The prefaces to the message are very solemn and such as may engage our most serious attention. 1. The people are commanded to give audience: *Hear you now what the Lord says.* What the prophet speaks he speaks from God, and in his name; they are therefore bound to hear it, not as the word of a sinful dying man, but of the holy living God. *Hear now* what he saith, for, first or last, he will be heard. 2. The prophet is commanded to speak in earnest, and to put an emphasis upon what he said: *Arise, contend thou before the mountains,* or *with the mountains,* and *let the hills hear thy voice,* if it were possible; contend with the mountains and hills of Judea, that is, with the inhabitants of those mountains and hills; and, some think, reference is had to those mountains and hills on which they worshipped idols and which were thus polluted. But it is rather to be taken more generally, as appears by his call, not only to the mountains, but to the *strong foundations of the earth,* pursuant to the instructions given him. This is designed, (1.) To excite the earnestness of the prophet; he must speak as vehemently as if he designed to make even the hills and mountains hear him, must *cry aloud, and not spare;* what he had to say in God's name he must proclaim publicly before the mountains, as one that was neither ashamed nor afraid to own his message; he must speak as one concerned, as one that desired to speak to the heart, and therefore appeared to speak from the heart. (2.) To expose the stupidity of the people; *"Let the hills hear thy voice,* for this senseless careless people will not hear it, will not heed it. Let the rocks, the *foundations of the earth,* that have no ears, hear, since Israel, that has ears, will not hear." It is an appeal to the mountains and hills; let them bear witness that Israel has fair warning given them, and good counsel, if they would but take it. Thus Isaiah begins with, *Hear, O heavens! and give ear, O earth!* Let them *judge between God and his vineyard.*

II. The message itself is very affecting. He is to let all the world know that God has a quarrel with his people, good ground for an action against them. Their offences are public, and therefore so are the articles of impeachment exhibited against them. Take notice *the Lord has a controversy with his people and he will plead with Israel,* will plead by his prophets, plead by his providences, to make good his charge. Note, 1. Sin begets a controversy between God and man. The righteous God has an action against every sinner, an action of debt, an action of trespass, an action of slander. 2. If Israel, God's own professing people, provoke him by sin, he will let them know that he has a controversy with them; he sees sin in them, and is displeased with it, nay, their sins are more displeasing to him than the sins of others, as they are a greater grief to his Spirit and dishonour to his name. 3. God will plead with those whom he has a controversy with, will plead with his people Israel, that they may be convinced and that he may be justified. In the close of the foregoing chapter he pleaded with the heathen in anger and fury, to bring them to ruin; but here he pleads with Israel in compassion and tenderness, to bring them to repentance, *Come now, and let us reason together.* God reasons with us, to teach us to reason with ourselves. See the equity of God's cause, it will bear to be pleaded, and sinners themselves will be forced to confess judgment, and to own that *God's ways are equal,* but their *ways are unequal,* Eze. 18:25. Now, (1.) God here challenges them to show what he had done against them which might give them occasion to desert him. They had revolted from God and rebelled against him; but had they any cause to do so? (v. 3): *"O my people! what have I done unto thee? Wherein have I wearied thee?"* If subjects quit their allegiance to their prince, they will pretend (as the ten tribes did when they revolted from Rehoboam), that his yoke is too heavy for them; but can you pretend any such thing? *What have I done to you* that is unjust or unkind? *Wherein have I wearied you* with the impositions of service or the exactions of tribute? *Have I made you to serve with an offering?* Isa. 43:23. *What iniquity have your fathers found in me?* Jer. 2:5. He never deceived us, nor disappointed our expectations from him, never did us wrong, nor put disgrace upon us; why then do we wrong and dishonour him, and frustrate his expectations from us? Here is a challenge to all that ever were in God's service to testify against him if they have found him, in any thing, a hard Master, or if they have found his demands unreasonable. (2.) Since they could not show any thing that he had done against them, he will show them a great deal that he has done for them, which should have engaged them for ever to his service, v. 4, 5. They are here directed, and we in them, to look a great way back in their reviews of the divine favour; let them remember their former days, their first days, when they were formed into a people, and the great things God did for them, [1.] When he brought them out of Egypt, the land of their bondage, v. 4. They were content with their slavery, and almost in love with their chains, for the sake of the garlic and onions they had plenty of; but God *brought them up,* inspired them with an ambition of liberty and animated them with a resolution by a bold effort to shake off their fetters. The Egyptians held them fast, and would not let the people go; but God *redeemed them,*

not by price, but by force, *out of the house of servants,* or, rather, *the house of bondage,* for it is the same word that is used in the preface to the ten commandments, which insinuates that the considerations which are arguments for duty, if they be not improved by us, will be improved against us as aggravations of sin. When he brought them out of Egypt into a vast howling wilderness, as he left not himself without witness, so he left not them without guides, for he sent before them *Moses, Aaron, and Miriam, three prophets* (says the Chaldee paraphrase), Moses the great prophet of the Old Testament, Aaron his prophet (Ex. 7:1), and Miriam a prophetess, Ex. 15:20. Note, When we are calling to mind God's former mercies to us we must not forget the mercy of good teachers and governors when we were young; let those be made mention of, to the glory of God, who went before us, saying, *This is the way, walk in it;* it was God that sent them before us, to prepare the way of the Lord and to prepare a people for him. [2.] When he brought them into Canaan. God no less glorified himself, and honoured them, in what he did for them when he brought them into the land of their rest than in what he did for them when he brought them out of the land of their servitude. When Moses, Aaron, and Miriam, were dead, yet they found God the same. Let them remember now what God did for them, *First,* In baffling and defeating the designs of Balak and Balaam against them, which he did by the power he has over the hearts and tongues of men, v. 5. Let them remember *what Balak the king of Moab consulted,* what mischief he devised and designed to do to Israel, when they encamped in the plains of Moab; that which he consulted was to *curse Israel,* to divide between them and their God, and to disengage him from the protection of them. Among the heathen, when they made war upon any people, they endeavoured by magic charms or otherwise to get from them their tutelar gods, as to rob Troy of its Palladium. Macrobius has a chapter *de ritu evocandi Deos — concerning the solemnity of calling out the gods.* Balak would try this against Israel; but remember *what Balaam the son of Beor answered him,* how contrary to his own intention and inclination; instead of cursing Israel, he blessed them, to the extreme confusion and vexation of Balak. Let them remember the malice of the heathen against them, and for that reason never *learn the way of the heathen,* nor associate with them. Let them remember the kindness of their God to them, how he *turned the curse into a blessing (because the Lord thy God loved thee,* as it is, Deu. 23:5), and for that reason never forsake him. Note, The disappointing of the devices of the church's enemies ought always to be remembered to the glory of the church's protector, who can make *the answer of the tongue* directly to contradict the preparation and consultation of the heart, Prov. 16:1. *Secondly,* In bringing them *from Shittim,* their last lodgment out of Canaan, *unto Gilgal,* their first lodgment in Canaan. There it was, between Shittim and Gilgal, that, upon the death of Moses, Joshua, a type of Christ, was raised up to put Israel in possession of the land of promise and to fight their battles; there it was that they passed over Jordan through the divided waters, and renewed the covenant of circumcision; these mercies of God to their fathers they must now remember, that they may *know the righteousness of the Lord, his righteousness* (so the word is), his justice in destroying the Canaanites, his goodness in giving rest to his people Israel, and his faithfulness to his promise made unto the fathers. The remembrance of what God had done to them might convince them of all this, and engage them for ever to his service. Or they may refer to the controversy now pleaded between God and Israel; let them remember God's many favours to them and their fathers, and compare with them their unworthy ungrateful conduct towards him, *that they may know the righteousness of the Lord* in contending with them, and it may appear that in this controversy he has right on his side; his ways are equal, for he will be *justified when he speaks,* and *clear when he judges.*

Verses 6–8

Here is the proposal for accommodation between God and Israel, the parties that were at variance in the beginning of the chapter. Upon the trial, judgment is given against Israel; they are convicted of injustice and ingratitude towards God, the crimes with which they stood

charged. Their guilt is too plain to be denied, too great to be excused, and therefore,

I. They express their desires to be at peace with God upon any terms (v. 6, 7): *Wherewith shall I come before the Lord?* Being made sensible of the justice of God's controversy with them, and dreading the consequences of it, they were inquisitive what they might do to be reconciled to God and to make him their friend. They apply to a proper person, with this enquiry, to the prophet, the Lord's messenger, by whose ministry they had been convinced. Who so fit to show them their way as he that had made them sensible of their having missed it? And it is observable that each one speaks for himself: *Wherewith shall I come?* Knowing every one the plague of his own heart, they ask, not, *What shall this man do?* But, *What shall I do?* Note, Deep convictions of guilt and wrath will put men upon careful enquiries after peace and pardon, and then, and not till then, there begins to be some hope of them. They enquire *wherewith they may come before the Lord, and bow themselves before the high God.* They believe there is a God, that he is Jehovah, and that he is the *high God,* the *Most High.* Those whose consciences are convinced learn to speak very honourably of God, whom before they spoke slightly of. Now, 1. We know we must *come before God;* he is the God with whom *we have to do;* we must come as subjects, to pay our homage to him, as beggars, to ask alms from him, nay, we must *come before him,* as criminals, to receive our doom from him, must come before him as our Judge. 2. When we come before him we must *bow before him;* it is our duty to be very humble and reverent in our approaches to him; and, when we come before him, there is no remedy but we must submit; it is to no purpose to contend with him. 3. When we come and bow before him it is our great concern to find favour with him, and to be accepted of him; their enquiry is, *What will the Lord be pleased with?* Note, All that rightly understand their own interest cannot but be solicitous what they must do to please God, to avoid his displeasure and to obtain his good-will. 4. In order to God's being pleased with us, our care must be that the sin by which we have displeased him may be taken away, and an atonement made for it. The enquiry here is, *What shall I give for my transgression, for the sin of my soul?* Note, The transgression we are guilty of is the sin of our soul, for the soul acts it (without the soul's act it is not sin) and the soul suffers by it; it is the disorder, disease, and defilement of the soul, and threatens to be the death of it: *What shall I give for my transgressions?* What will be accepted as a satisfaction to his justice, a reparation of his honour? And what will avail to shelter me from his wrath? 5. We must therefore ask, *Wherewith may we come before him?* We must not appear before the Lord empty. What shall we bring with us? In what manner must we come? In whose name must we come? We have not that in ourselves which will recommend us to him, but must have it from another. What righteousness then shall we appear before him in?

II. They make proposals, such as they are, in order to it. Their enquiry was very good and right, and what we are all concerned to make, but their proposals betray their ignorance, though they show their zeal; let us examine them: —

1. They bid high. They offer, (1.) That which is very rich and costly — *thousands of rams.* God required one ram for a sin-offering; they proffer flocks of them, their whole stock, will be content to make themselves beggars, so that they may but be at peace with God. They will bring the best they have, the rams, and the most of them, till it comes to thousands. (2.) That which is very dear to them, and which they would be most loth to part with. They could be content to part with *their first-born for their transgressions,* if that would be accepted as an atonement, and the *fruit of their body for the sin of their soul.* To those that had become *vain in their imaginations* this seemed a probable expedient of making satisfaction for sin, because our children are pieces of ourselves; and therefore the heathen sacrificed their children, to appease their offended deities. Note, Those that are thoroughly convinced of sin, of the malignity of it, and of their misery and danger by reason of it, would give all the world, if they had it, for peace and pardon.

2. Yet they do not bid right. It is true some of these things were instituted by the ceremonial law, as the bring-

ing of burnt-offerings to God's altar, and calves of a year old, rams for sin-offerings, and oil for the meat-offerings; but these alone would not recommend them to God. God had often declared that *to obey is better than sacrifice,* and to *hearken than the fat of rams,* that *sacrifice and offering he would not;* the legal sacrifices had their virtue and value from the institution, and the reference they had to Christ the great propitiation; but otherwise, of themselves, it was *impossible that the blood of bulls and goats should take away sin.* And as to the other things here mentioned, (1.) Some of them are impracticable things, as *rivers of oil,* which nature has not provided to feed men's luxury, but rivers of water to supply men's necessity. All the proposals of peace but those that are according to the gospel are absurd. One stream of the blood of Christ is worth ten thousand rivers of oil. (2.) Some of them are wicked things, as to give our *first-born* and the *fruit of our body* to death, which would but add to the transgression and the *sin of the soul.* He that hates robbery for burnt-offerings much more hates murder, such murder. What right have we to our *first born* and the *fruit of our body?* Do they not belong to God? Are they not his already, and born to him? Are they not sinners by nature, and their lives forfeited upon their own account? How then can they be a ransom for ours? (3.) They are all external things, parts of that bodily exercise which profiteth little, and which could not *make the comers thereunto perfect.* (4.) They are all insignificant, and insufficient to attain the end proposed; they could not answer the demands of divine justice, nor satisfy the wrong done to God in his honour by sin, nor would they serve in lieu of the sanctification of the heart and the reformation of the life. Men will part with any thing rather than their sins, but they part with nothing to God's acceptance unless they part with them.

III. God tells them plainly what he demands, and insists upon, from those that would be accepted of him, *v.* 8. Let their money perish with them that think the pardon of sin and the favour of God may be so purchased; no, *God has shown thee, O man! what is good.* Here we are told,

1. That God has made a discovery of his mind and will to us, for the rectifying of our mistakes and the direction of our practice. (1.) It is God himself that has shown us what we must do. We need not trouble ourselves to make proposals, the terms are already settled and laid down. He whom we have offended, and to whom we are accountable, has told us upon what conditions he will be reconciled to us. (2.) It is to man that he has shown it, not only to thee, *O Israel!* but *to thee, O man!* Gentiles as well as Jews — to men, who are rational creatures, and capable of receiving the discovery, and not to brutes, — to men, for whom a remedy is provided, not to devils, whose case is desperate. What is spoken to *all men every where* in general, must by faith be applied to ourselves in particular, as if it were spoken *to thee, O man!* by name, and to no other. (3.) It is a discovery of *that which is good,* and which *the Lord requires of us.* He has shown us our end, which we should aim at, in showing us what is good, wherein our true happiness does consist; he has shown us our way in which we must walk towards that end in showing us what he requires of us. There is something which God requires we should do for him and devote to him; and it is good. It is good in itself; there is an innate goodness in moral duties, antecedent to the command; they are not, as ceremonial observances, good because they are commanded, but commanded because they are good, consonant to the eternal rule and reason of good and evil, which are unalterable. It has likewise a direct tendency to our good; our conformity to it is not only the condition of our future happiness, but is a great expedient of our present happiness; *in keeping* God's *commandments there is great reward,* as well as after keeping them. (4.) It is shown us. God has not only made it known, but made it plain; he has discovered it to us with such convincing evidence as amounts to a demonstration. *Lo this, we have searched it, so it is.*

2. What that discovery is. The good which God requires of us is not the paying of a price for the pardon of sin and acceptance with God, but doing the duty which is the condition of our interest in the pardon purchased. (1.) We must *do justly,* must *render to all their due,* according as our relation and obligation to them are; we must do wrong to none, but do right to all, in their bodies, goods, and good

name. (2.) We must *love mercy;* we must delight in it, as our God does, must be glad of an opportunity to do good, and do it cheerfully. Justice is put before mercy, for we must not give that in alms which is wrongfully got, or with which our debts should be paid. *God hates robbery for a burnt-offering.* (3.) We must *walk humbly with our God.* This includes all the duties of the first table, as the two former include all the duties of the second table. We must take the Lord for our God in covenant, must attend on him and adhere to him as ours, and must make it our constant care and business to please him. Enoch's walking with God is interpreted (Heb. 11:5) his *pleasing God.* We must, in the whole course of our conversation, conform ourselves to the will of God, keep up our communion with God, and study to approve ourselves to him in our integrity; and this we must do humbly (submitting our understandings to the truths of God and our will to his precepts and providences); we must *humble ourselves to walk with God* (so the margin reads it); every thought within us must be brought down, to be brought into obedience to God, if we would walk comfortably with him. This is that which God requires, and without which the most costly services are *vain oblations;* this is more than *all burnt-offerings and sacrifices.*

Verses 9–16

God, having shown them how necessary it was that they should do justly, here shows them how plain it was that they had done unjustly; and since they submitted not to his controversy, nor went the right way to have it taken up, here he proceeds in it. Observe,

I. How the action is entered against them, *v.* 9. God speaks to *the city,* to Jerusalem, to Samaria. His *voice cries* to it by his servants the prophets who were to *cry aloud and not spare.* Note, The voice of the prophets is *the Lord's voice,* and that *cries to the city,* cries to the country. *Doth not wisdom cry?* Prov. 8:1. When the sin of a city cries to God his voice cries against the city; and, when the judgments of God are coming upon a city, his voice first *cries unto it.* He warns before he wounds, because he is *not willing that any should perish.* Now observe, 1. How the voice of God is discerned by some: *The man of wisdom will see thy name.* When the voice of God cries to us we may by it see his name, may discern and perceive that by which he makes himself known. Yet many see it not, are not aware of it, because they do not regard it. God *speaks once, yea, twice, and they perceive it not* (Job 33:14); but those that are men of wisdom will see it, and perceive it, and make a good use of it. Note, It is a point of true wisdom to discover the name of God in the voice of God, and to learn what he is from what he says. *Wisdom shall see thy name,* for *the knowledge of the holy is understanding.* 2. What this voice of God says to all: *"Hear you the rod, and who hath appointed it.* Hear the rod when it is coming; hear it at a distance, before you see it and feel it; and be awakened to go forth to meet the Lord in the way of his judgments. Hear the rod when it has come, and is actually upon you, and you are sensible of the smart of it; hear what it says to you, what convictions, what counsels, what cautions, it speaks to you." Note, Every rod has a voice, and it is the voice of God that is to be heard in the rod of God, and it is well for those that understand the language of it, which if we would do we must have an eye to *him that appointed it.* Note, Every rod is appointed, of what kind it shall be, where it shall light, and how long it shall lie. God in every affliction *performs the thing that is appointed for us* (Job 23:14), and to him therefore we must have an eye, to him we must have an ear; we must hear what he says to us by the affliction. *Hear it, and know it for thy good,* Job *v.* 6. The work of ministers is to explain the providences of God and to quicken and direct men to learn the lessons that are taught by them.

II. What is the ground of the action, and what are the things that are laid to their charge.

1. They are charged with injustice, a sin against the second table. Are there yet to be found among them the marks and means of fraudulent dealing? What! after all the methods that God has taken to teach them to do justly, will they yet deal unjustly? It seems, they will, *v.* 10. And *shall I count them pure? v.* 11. No; this is a sin which will by no means consist with a profession of purity. Those that are dishonest in their dealings have not the spots of God's

children, and shall never be reckoned pure, whatever shows of devotion they may make. *Be not deceived, God is not mocked.* When a man is suspected of theft, or fraud, the justice of peace will send a warrant to search his house. God here does, as it were, search the houses of those citizens, and there he finds, (1.) *Treasures of wickedness,* abundance of wealth, but it is ill-got, and not likely to prosper; for *treasures of wickedness profit nothing.* (2.) A *scant measure,* by which they sold to the poor, and so exacted upon them and cheated them. (3.) They had *wicked balances and a bag of false weights,* by which, under a pretence of weighing what they sold, and giving the buyer what was right, they did him the greatest wrong, *v.* 11. (4.) Those that had wealth and power in their hands abused it to oppression and extortion; *The rich men thereof are full of violence;* for those that have much would have more, and are in a capacity of making it more by the power which their abundance of wealth gives them. They are *full of violence,* that is, they have their houses full of that which is got by violence. (5.) Those that had not the advantage of doing wrong by their wealth yet found means of defrauding those they dealt with: *The inhabitants thereof have spoken lies;* if they are not able to use force and violence, they use fraud and deceit; the *inhabitants* have *spoken lies, and their tongue is deceitful in their mouth;* they do not stick at a deliberate lie, to make a good bargain. Some understand it of their speaking falsely concerning God, saying, *The Lord seeth not; he hath forsaken the earth,* Eze. 8:12.

2. They are charged with idolatry (*v.* 6): *The statutes of Omri are kept, and all the work of the house of Ahab.* Both these kings were wicked, and *did evil in the sight of the Lord;* but the wickedness which they established by a law, concerning which they made statutes, and which was the peculiar work of that house, was idolatry. Omri walked in the way of Jeroboam, and *in his sin of provoking God to anger with their vanities,* 1 Ki. 16:26, 31. Ahab introduced the worship of Baal. These reigns were some ages before the time when this prophet lived, and yet the wickedness which they established by their laws and examples remained to this day; those statutes were still kept, and that work was still done; and the princes and people still *walked in their counsels,* took the same measures, and governed themselves and the people by the same politics. Observe, (1.) The same wickedness continued from one generation to another. Sin is a *root of bitterness,* soon planted, but not so soon plucked up again. The iniquity of former ages is often transmitted to, and entailed upon, the succeeding ones. Those that make corrupt laws, and bring in corrupt usages, are doing that which perhaps may prove the ruin of the child unborn. (2.) It was not the less evil in itself, provoking to God, and dangerous to the sinners, for its having been established and confirmed by the laws of princes, the examples of great men, and a long prescription. Though the worship of idols is enacted by the statutes of Omri, recommended by the practice of the house of Ahab, and pleads that it has been the usage of many generations, yet it is still displeasing to God and destructive to Israel; for no laws nor customs are of force against the divine command.

III. What is the judgment given upon this. Being found guilty of these crimes, the sentence is that that which God had given them warning of (*v.* 9) shall be brought upon them (*v.* 13): *Therefore also will I make thee sick, in smiting thee.* As they had smitten the poor with the rod of their oppressions, so would God in like manner smite them, so as to make them sick, sick of the gains they had unjustly gotten, so that though they had *swallowed down riches* they should *vomit them up again,* Job 20:15. Their doom is,

1. That what they have they shall not have any comfortable enjoyment of; it shall do them no good. They grasped at more than enough, but, when they have it, it shall not be enough to make them easy and happy. What is got by fraud and oppression cannot be kept or enjoyed with any satisfaction. (1.) Their food shall not nourish them: *Thou shalt eat, but not be satisfied,* either because the food shall not digest, for want of God's blessing going along with it, or because the appetite shall by disease be made insatiable and still craving, the just punishment of those that were greedy of gain and enlarged their desires as hell. Men may be surfeited with the good things of this world and yet not satisfied, Eccl. *v.* 10; Isa. 55:2. (2.) Their country

shall not harbour and protect them: *"Thy casting down shall be in the midst of thee,* that is, thou shalt be broken and ruined by the intestine troubles, mischiefs at home enough to cast thee down, though thou shouldst not be invaded by a foreign force." God can cast a nation down by that which is in the midst of them, can consume them by a fire in their own bowels. (3.) They shall not be able to preserve what they have from a foreign force, nor to recover what they have lost: *"Thou shalt take hold* of what is about to be taken from thee, but thou shalt not hold it fast, shalt catch at it, but *shalt not deliver it,* shalt not retrieve it." It is meant of their wives and children, that were very dear to them, which they took hold of, as resolved not to part with them, but there is no remedy, they must go into captivity. Note, What we hold closest we commonly lose soonest, and that proves least safe which is most dear. (4.) What they save for a time shall be reserved for a future and sorer stroke: *That which thou deliverest* out of the hand of one enemy *will I give up to the sword* of another enemy; for God has many arrows in his quiver; if one miss the sinner, the next shall not. (5.) What they have laboured for they shall not enjoy (*v.* 15): *"Thou shalt sow, but thou shalt not reap;* it shall be blasted and withered, and there shall be nothing to reap, or an enemy shall come and reap it for himself, or thou shalt be carried into captivity, and leave it to be reaped by thou knowest not whom. Thou shalt *tread the olives,* but *thou shalt not anoint thyself with oil,* having no heart to make use of ornaments and refreshments when all is going to ruin. Thou shalt tread out *the sweet wine,* but *shalt not drink wine,* for many things may fall between the cup and the lip." Note, It is very grievous to be disappointed of our expectations, and not to have the pleasure of that which we have taken pains for; and this will be the just punishment of those that frustrate God's expectations from them, and answer not the cost he has been at upon them. See this threatened in the law, Lev. 26:16; Deu. 28:30, 38, etc.; and compare Isa. 62:8, 9.

2. That all they have shall at length be taken from them (*v.* 13): *Thou shalt be made desolate because of thy sins;* and *v.* 16, *a desolation and a hissing.* Sin makes a nation desolate; and when a people that have been famous and flourishing are made desolate it is the astonishment of some and the triumph of others; some lament it, and others hiss at it. Thus *you shall bear the reproach of my people.* Their being the people of God, in name and profession while they kept close to their duty and kept themselves in his love, was an honour to them, and all their neighbours thought it so; but now that they have corrupted and ruined themselves, now that their sins and God's judgments have made their land desolate, their having been once the people of God does but turn so much the more to their reproach; their enemies will say, *These are the people of the Lord,* Eze. 36:20. Note, If professors of religion ruin themselves, their ruin will be the most reproachful of any; and they in a special manner will rise at the last day to everlasting shame and contempt.

CHAPTER 7

In this chapter, I. The prophet, in the name of the church, sadly laments the woeful decay of religion in the age wherein he lived, and the deluge of impiety and immorality which overwhelmed the nation, which levelled the differences, and bore down the fences, of all that is just and sacred (*v.* 1–6). II. The prophet, for the sake of the church, prescribes comforts, which may be of use at such a time, and gives counsel what to do. 1. They must have an eye to God (*v.* 7). 2. They must courageously bear up against the insolences of the enemy (*v.* 8–10). 3. They must patiently lie down under the rebukes of their God (*v.* 9). 4. They must expect no other than that the trouble would continue long, and must endeavour to make the best of it (*v.* 11–13). 5. They must encourage themselves with God's promises, in answer to the prophet's prayers (*v.* 14, 15). 6. They must foresee the fall of their enemies, that now triumphed over them (*v.* 16, 17). 7. They must themselves triumph in the mercy and grace of God, and his faithfulness to his covenant (*v.* 18–20), and with that comfortable word the prophecy concludes.

Verses 1–6

This is such a description of bad times as, some think, could scarcely agree to the times of Hezekiah, when this prophet prophesied; and therefore they rather take it as a prediction of what should be in the reign of Manasseh. But we may rather suppose it to be in the reign of Ahaz (and in that reign he prophesied, *ch.* 1:1) or in the beginning of Hezekiah's time, before the reformation he was instrumental in; nay, in the best of his days, and when he had done his best to purge out corruptions, still there was much amiss. The prophet cries out, *Woe is me!* He bemoans himself that his lot was cast in such a degenerate age, and thinks it his great unhappiness that he lived among a people that were ripening apace for a ruin which many a good man would unavoidably be involved in. Thus David cries out, *Woe is me that I sojourn in Mesech!* He laments, 1. That there were so few good people to be found, even among those that were God's people; and this was their reproach: *The good man has perished out of the earth,* or *out of the land,* the land of Canaan; it was a *good land,* and *a land of uprightness* (Isa. 26:10), but there were few good men in it, none upright among them, *v.* 2. The *good man* is a *godly man* and a *merciful man;* the word signifies both. Those are completely good men that are devout towards God and compassionate and beneficent towards men, that love mercy and walk with God. "These have perished; those few honest men that some time ago enriched and adorned our country are now dead and gone, and there are none risen up *in their stead* that tread in their steps; honesty is banished, and there is no such thing as a good man to be met with. Those that were of religious education have degenerated, and become as bad as the worst; *the godly man ceases,"* Ps. 12:1. This is illustrated by a comparison (*v.* 1): they were *as when they have gathered the summer fruits;* it was as hard a thing to find a good man as to find any of the summer-fruits (which were the choicest and best, and therefore must carefully be gathered in) when the harvest is over. The prophet is ready to say, as Elijah in his time (1 Ki. 19:10), *I, even I only, am left.* Good men, who used to hang in clusters, are now as the *grape-gleanings of the vintage,* here and there a berry, Isa. 17:6. You can find no societies of them as bunches of grapes, but those that are single persons: *There is no cluster to eat;* and the best and fullest grapes are those that grow in large clusters. Some think that this intimates not only that good people were few, but that those few who remained, who went for good people, were good for little, like the small withered grapes, the refuse that were left behind, not only by the gatherer, but by the gleaner. When the prophet observed this universal degeneracy it made him *desire the first-ripe fruit;* he wished to see such worthy good men as were in the former ages, were the ornaments of the primitive times, and as far excelled the best of all the present age as the first and full-ripe fruits do those of the latter growth, that never come to maturity. When we read and hear of the wisdom and zeal, the strictness and conscientiousness, the devotion and charity, of the professors of religion in former ages, and see the reverse of this in those of the present age, we cannot but sit down, and wish, with a sigh, *O for primitive Christianity again!* Where are the plainness and integrity of those that went before us? Where are the Israelites indeed, without guile? Our souls desire them, but in vain. The golden age is gone, and past recall; we must make the best of what is, for we are not likely to see such times as have been. 2. That there were so many wicked mischievous people among them, not only none that did any good, but multitudes that did all the hurt they could: *"They all lie in wait for blood,* and *hunt every man his brother.* To get wealth to themselves, they care not what wrong, what hurt, they do to their neighbours and nearest relations. They act as if mankind were in a state of war, and force were the only right. They are as beasts of prey to their neighbours, for *they all lie in wait for blood* as lions for their prey; they thirst after it, make nothing of taking away any man's life or livelihood to serve a turn for themselves, and lie in wait for an opportunity to do it. Their neighbours are as beasts of prey to them, for they *hunt every man his brother with a net;* they persecute them as noxious creatures, fit to be taken and destroyed, though they are innocent excellent ones." We say of him that is outlawed, *Caput gerit lupinum — He is to be hunted as a wolf.* "Or they hunt them as men do the game, to feast upon it; they have a thousand cursed arts of ensnaring men to their ruin, so that they may but get by it. Thus *they do mischief with both hands earnestly;* their hearts desire it, their heads contrive it, and then *both hands* are ready to put it in execution." Note, The more eager and intent men are upon any sinful pursuit, and the more pains they take in it, the more provoking it is. 3. That the magistrates, who by their office ought to have been the patrons and protectors of right, were the practicers and promoters of wrong: *That they may do evil with both hands earnestly,* to excite and animate themselves in it, *the prince asketh, and the judge asketh, for a reward,* for a bribe, with which they well be hired to exert all their power for the supporting and carrying on of any wicked design *with both hands. They do evil with both hands well* (so some read it); they do evil with a great deal of art and dexterity; they praise themselves for doing it so well. Others read it thus: *To do evil they have both hands* (they catch at an opportunity of doing mischief), *but to do good the prince and the judge ask for a reward;* if they do any good offices they are mercenary in them, and must be paid for them. The great man, who has wealth and power to do good, is not ashamed to utter his mischievous desire in conjunction with the prince and the judge, who are ready to support him and stand by him in it. *So they wrap it up;* they perplex the matter, involve it, and make it intricate (so some understand it), that they may lose equity in a mist, and so make the cause turn which way they please. It is ill with a people when their princes, and judges, and great men are in a confederacy to pervert justice. And it is a sad character that is given of them (*v.* 4), that *the best of them is as a brier, and the most upright is sharper than a thorn-hedge;* it is a dangerous thing to have any thing to do with them; *he that touches them must be fenced with iron* (2 Sa. 23:6,7), he shall be sure to be scratched, to have his clothes torn, and his eyes almost pulled out. And, if this be the character of the best and most upright, what are the worst? And, when things have come to this pass, *the day of thy watchmen comes,* that is, as it follows, *the day of thy visitation,* when God will reckon with thee for all this wickedness, which is called *the day cf the watchmen,* because their prophets, whom God set as watchmen over them, had often warned them of that day. When all flesh have corrupted their way, even the best and the most upright, what can be expected but a day of visitation, a deluge of judgments, as that which drowned the old world when *the earth was filled with violence?* 4. That there was no faith in man; people had grown so universally treacherous that one knew not whom to repose any confidence in, *v.* 5. "Those that have any sense of honour, or spark of virtue, remaining in them, have a firm regard to the laws of friendship; they would not discover what passed in private conversation, nor divulge secrets, to the prejudice of a friend. But those things are now made a jest of; you will not meet with a friend that you dare trust, whose word you dare take, or who will have any tenderness or concern for you; so that wise men shall give it and take it for a rule, *trust you not in a friend,* for you will find him false, you can trust him no further than you can see him; and even him that passes for an honest man you will find to be so only with good looking to. Nay, as for him that undertakes to be *your guide,* to lead you into any business which he professes to understand better than you, you cannot *put a confidence* in him, for he will be sure to mislead you if he can get any thing by it." Some by a guide understand a husband, who is called *the guide of thy youth;* and that agrees well enough with what follows, *"Keep the doors of thy lips from her that lieth in thy bosom,* from thy own wife; take heed what thou sayest before her, lest she betray thee, as Delilah did Samson, lest she be the *bird of the air* that *carries the voice* of that which thou sayest *in thy bed-chamber,"* Eccl. 10:20. It is an evil time indeed when the prudent are obliged even thus far to keep silence. 5. That children were abusive to their parents, and men had no comfort, no satisfaction, in their own families and their nearest relations, *v.* 6. The times are bad indeed when *the son dishonours his father,* gives him bad language, exposes him, threatens him, and studies to do him a mischief, *when the daughter rises up* in rebellion against her own mother, having no sense of duty, or natural affection; and no marvel that then the *daughter-in-law* quarrels with her *mother-in-law,* and is vexatious to her. Either they cannot agree about their property and interest, or their humours and passions clash, or from a spirit of bigotry and persecution, *the brother shall deliver up the brother to death, and the father the child,* Mt. 10:4; Lu. 21:16. It is sad when a man's betrayers and worst enemies are the men of his own house, his own children and servants, that should be his guard and his best friends. Note, The contempt and violation of the laws of domestic duties are a sad symptom of a universal corruption of manners. Those are never likely to come to good that are undutiful to their parents, and study to be provoking to them and cross them.

Verses 7–13

The prophet, having sadly complained of the wickedness of the times he lived in, here fastens upon some considerations for the comfort of himself and his friends, in reference thereunto. The case is bad, but it is not desperate. *Yet now there is hope in Israel concerning this thing.*

I. "Though God be now displeased he shall be reconciled to us, and then all will be well, *v.* 7, 9. We are now under *the indignation of the Lord;* God is angry with us, and justly, because *we have sinned against him.*" Note, It is our sin against God that provokes his indignation against us; and we must see it, and own it, whenever we are under divine rebukes, that we may justify God, and may study to answer his end in afflicting us, by repenting of sin and breaking off from it. Now, at such a time, 1. We must have recourse to God under our troubles (*v.* 7): *Therefore I will look unto the Lord.* When a child of God has ever so much occasion to cry, *Woe is me* (as the prophet here, *v.* 1), yet it may be a comfort to him that he has a God to look to, a God to come to, to fly to, in whom he may rejoice and have satisfaction. All may look bright above him when all looks black and dark about him. The prophet had been complaining that there was no comfort to be had, no confidence to be put, in friends and relations on earth, and this drives him to his God: *Therefore I will look unto the Lord.* The less reason we have to delight in any creature the more reason we have to delight in God. If princes are not to be trusted, we may say, *Happy is the man that has* the God of Jacob for his help, and *happy am I,* even in the midst of my present woes, if he be my help. If men be false, this is our comfort, that God is faithful; if relations be unkind, he is and will be gracious. Let us therefore look above and beyond them, and overlook our disappointment in them, and look unto the Lord. 2. We must submit to the will of God in our troubles: *"I will bear the indignation of the Lord,* will bear it patiently, without murmuring and repining, *because I have sinned against him."* Note, Those that are truly penitent for sin will see a great deal of reason to be patient under affliction. *Wherefore should a man complain for the punishment of his sin?* When we complain to God of the badness of the times we ought to complain against ourselves for the badness of our own hearts. 3. We must depend upon God to work deliverance for us, and put a good issue to our troubles in due time; we must not only look to him, but look for him: "I will *wait for the God of my salvation,* and for his gracious returns to me." In our greatest distresses we shall see no reason to despair of salvation if by faith we eye God as the *God of our salvation,* who is able to save the weakest upon their humble petition, and willing to save the worst upon their true repentance. And, if we depend on God as the God of our salvation, we must wait for him, and for his salvation, in his own way and his own time. Let us now see what the church is here taught to expect and promise herself from God, even when things are brought to the last extremity. (1.) *My God will hear me;* if the Lord be our God, he will hear our prayers, and grant an answer of peace to them. (2.) *"When I fall,* and am in danger of being dashed in pieces by the fall, yet *I shall arise,* and recover myself again. *I fall,* but am not *utterly cast down,"* Ps. 37:24. (3.) *"When I sit in darkness,* desolate and disconsolate, melancholy and perplexed, and not knowing what to do, nor which way to look for relief, yet then *the Lord shall be a light to me,* to comfort and revive me, to instruct and teach me, to direct and guide me, as a light to my eyes, a light to my feet, a light *in a dark place."* (4.) *He will plead my cause, and execute judgment for me, v.* 9. If we heartily espouse the cause of God, the just but injured cause of religion and virtue, and make it our cause, we may hope he will own our cause, and plead it. The church's cause, though it seem for a time to go against her, will at length be pleaded with jealousy, and judgment not only given against, but executed upon, the enemies of it. (5.) "He *will bring me forth to the light,* make me shine eminently out of obscurity, and become conspicuous, will make my righteousness shine evidently from under the dark cloud of calumny, Ps. 37:6; Isa. 58:10. The morning of comfort shall shine forth out of the long and dark night of trouble." (6.) *"I shall behold his righteousness;* I shall see the equity of his proceedings concerning me and the performance of his promises to me."

II. Though enemies triumph and insult, they shall be silenced and put to shame, *v.* 8, 10. Observe here,

1. How proudly the enemies of God's people trample upon them in their distress. They said, *Where is the Lord their God?* As if because they were afflicted God had forsaken them, and they knew not where to find him with their prayers, and he knew not how to help them with his favours. This David's enemies said to him, and it was a sword in his bones, Ps. 42:10, and see Ps. 115:2. Thus, in reproaching Israel as an abandoned people, they reflected on the God of Israel as an unkind unfaithful God.

2. How comfortably the people of God by faith bear up themselves under these insults (*v.* 8): *"Rejoice not against me, O my enemy!* I am now down, but shall not be always so, and when my God appears for me then *she that is my enemy shall see it, and be ashamed"* (not only being disappointed in her expectations of the church's utter ruin, but having the same cup of trembling put into her hand), "then *my eyes shall behold her* in the same deplorable condition that I am now in; *now shall she be trodden down."* Note, The deliverance of the church will be the confusion of her enemies; and their shame shall be double, when, as they have trampled upon God's people, so they shall themselves be trampled upon.

III. Though the land continue a great while desolate, yet it shall at length be replenished again, when the time, even the set time, of its deliverance comes. 1. Its salvation shall not come *till after it has been desolate;* so the margin reads it, *v.* 13. God has a controversy with the land, and it must lie long under his rebukes, *because of those that dwell therein;* it is their iniquity that makes their land desolate (Ps. 107:34); it is *for the fruit of their doings,* their evil doings which they have been themselves guilty of, and the evil fruit of them, the sins of others, which they have been accessory to by their bad influence and example. For this they must expect to smart a great while; for the world shall know that God hates sin even in his own people. 2. When it does come it shall be a complete salvation; and it seems to refer to their deliverance out of Babylon by Cyrus, which Isaiah about this time prophesied of, as a type of our redemption by Christ. (1.) *The decree shall be far removed.* God's decree concerning their captivity, and Nebuchadnezzar's decree concerning the perpetuity of it, his resolution never to release them, "these shall be set aside and revoked, and you shall hear no more of them; they shall no more lie as a yoke upon thy neck." (2.) Jerusalem and the cities of Judah shall be again reared: Then *thy walls shall be built,* walls for habitation, walls for defence, house-walls, town-walls, temple-walls; it is in order to these that the decree is repealed, Isa. 44:28. Though Zion's walls may lie long in ruins, there will come a day when they shall be repaired. (3.) All that belong to the land of Israel, whithersoever dispersed, and howsoever distressed, far and wide over the face of the whole earth, shall come flocking to it again (*v.* 12): *He shall come even to thee,* having liberty to return and a heart to return, from Assyria, whither the ten tribes were carried away, though it lay remote, and *from the fortified cities,* and *from the fortress,* those strongholds in which they thought they had them fast; for when God's time comes, though Pharaoh will not *let the people go,* God will fetch them out with a high hand. They shall come from all the remote parts, *from sea to sea* and *from mountain to mountain,* not turning back for fear of your discouragements, but they shall go from strength to strength till they come to Zion. Thus in the great day of redemption *God will gather his elect from the four winds.*

Verses 14–20

Here is, I. The prophet's prayer to God to take care of his own people, and of their cause and interest, *v.* 14. When God is about to deliver his people he stirs up their friends to pray for them, and pours out *a spirit of grace and supplication,* Zec. 12:10. And when we see God coming towards us in ways of mercy, we must go forth to meet him by prayer. It is a prophetic prayer, which amounts to a promise of the good prayed for; what God directed his prophet to ask no doubt he designed to give. Now, 1. The people of Israel are here called the *flock of God's heritage,* for they are the sheep of his hand, the sheep of his pasture, his little flock in the world; and they are his heritage, his portion in the world. *Jacob is the lot of his inheritance.* 2. This flock *dwells solitarily in the wood,* or *forest, in the midst of Carmel,* a high mountain. Israel was a peculiar people, *that dwelt alone, and was not reckoned among the nations,* like a flock of sheep in a wood. They were now a desolate people (*v.* 13), were in the land of their captivity as sheep in a forest, in danger of being lost and made a prey of to the beasts of the forest. They are *scattered upon the mountains as sheep having no shepherd.* 3. He prays that God would *feed them there with his rod,* that is, that he would take care of them in their captivity, would protect them, and provide for them, and do the part of a good shepherd to them: "Let *thy rod and staff comfort* them, even in that darksome valley; and even there let them want nothing that is good for them. Let them be governed by thy rod, not the rod of their enemies, for they are thy people." 4. He prays that God would in due time bring them back to feed in the plains of Bashan and Gilead, and no longer to be fed in the woods and mountains. *Let them feed* in their own country again, *as in the days of old.* Some apply this spiritually, and make it either the prophet's prayer to Christ or his Father's charge to him, to take care of his church, as the great Shepherd of the sheep, and to go in and out before them while they are here in this world as in a wood, that they may find pasture as in Carmel, as in Bashan and Gilead.

II. God's promise, in answer to this prayer; and we may well take God's promises as real answers to the prayers of faith, and embrace them accordingly, for with him saying and doing are not two things. The prophet prayed that God would feed them, and do kind things for them; but God answers that he *will show them marvellous things* (*v.* 15), will do for them more than they are able to ask or think, will out-do their hopes and expectations; he will *show them his marvellous lovingkindness,* Ps. 17:7. 1. He will do that for them which shall be the repetition of the wonders and miracles of former ages — *according to the days of thy coming out of the land of Egypt.* Their deliverance out of Babylon shall be a work of wonder and grace not inferior to their deliverance out of Egypt, nay, it shall eclipse the lustre of that (Jer. 16:14, 15), much more shall the work of redemption by Christ. Note, God's former favours to his church are patterns of future favours, and shall again be copied out as there is occasion. 2. He will do that for them which shall be matter of wonder and amazement to the present age, *v.* 16, 17. The *nations about* shall take notice of it, and it shall be said *among the heathen, The Lord has done great things for them,* Ps. 126:2. The impression which the deliverance of the Jews out of Babylon shall make upon the neighbouring nations shall be very much for the honour both of God and his church. (1.) Those that had insulted over the people of God in their distress, and gloried that when they had them down they would keep them down, *shall be confounded,* when they see them thus surprisingly rising up; they shall be *confounded at all the might* with which the captives shall now exert themselves, whom they thought for ever disabled. They shall now *lay their hands upon their mouths,* as being ashamed of what they have said, and not able to say more, by way of triumph over Israel. Nay, *their ears shall be deaf* too, so much shall they be ashamed at the wonderful deliverance; they shall stop their ears, as being not willing to hear any more of God's wonders wrought for that people, whom they had so despised and insulted over. (2.) Those that had impudently confronted God himself shall now be struck with a fear of him, and thereby brought, in profession at least, to submit to him (*v.* 17): *They shall lick the dust like a serpent,* they shall be so mortified, as if they were sentenced to the same curse the serpent was laid under (Gen. 3:14), *Upon thy belly shalt thou go, and dust shalt thou eat.* They shall be brought to the lowest abasements imaginable, and shall be so dispirited that they shall tamely submit to them. *His enemies shall lick the dust,* Ps. 72:9. Nay, they shall *lick the dust* of the church's feet, Isa. 49:23. Proud oppressors shall now be made sensible how mean, how little, they are, before the great God, and they shall with trembling and the lowest submission *move out of the holes* into which they had crept (Isa. 2:21), *like worms of the earth* as they are, being ashamed and afraid to *show their heads;* so low shall they be brought, and such abjects shall they be, when they are abased. When God did wonders for his church *many of the people of the land became Jews,* because *the fear of the Jews,* and of their God, *fell upon them,* Esth. 8:17. So it is promised here: *They shall be afraid of the Lord our God, and shall fear because of thee, O Israel!* Forced submissions are often but feigned submissions; yet they redound to the glory of God and the church, though not to the benefit of the dissemblers themselves.

III. The prophet's thankful acknowledgment of God's mercy, in the name of the church, with a believing dependence upon his promise, *v.* 18–20. We are here taught,

1. To give to God the glory of his pardoning mercy, *v.* 18. God having promised to bring back the captivity of his people, the prophet, on that occasion, admires pardoning mercy, as that which was at the bottom of it. As it was their sin that brought them into bondage, so it was God's pardoning their sin that brought them our of it; Ps. 85:1, 2, and Isa. 33:24; 38:17; 60:1,2. The pardon of sin is the foundation of all other covenant-mercies, Heb. 8:12. This the prophet stands amazed at, while the surrounding nations stood amazed only at those deliverances which were but the fruits of this. Note, (1.) God's people, who are the *remnant of his heritage,* stand charged with many transgressions; being but a remnant, a very few, one would hope they should all be very good, but they are not so; God's children have their spots, and often offend their Father. (2.) The gracious God is ready to pass by and pardon the iniquity and transgression of his people, upon their repentance and return to him. God's people are a pardoned people, and to this they owe their all. When God pardons sin, he passes it by, does not punish it as justly he might, nor deal with the sinner according to the desert of it. (3.) Though God may for a time lay his own people under the tokens of his displeasure, yet he will not *retain his anger for ever,* but *though he cause grief he will have compassion;* he is not implacable; yet against those that are not of the remnant of his heritage, that are unpardoned, he will keep his anger for ever. (4.) The reasons why God pardons sin, and keeps not his anger for ever, are all taken from within himself; it is *because he delights in mercy,* and the salvation of sinners is what he has pleasure in, not their death and damnation. (5.) The glory of God in forgiving sin is, as in other things, matchless, and without compare. There is *no God like unto him* for this; no magistrate, no common person, forgives as God does. In this his thoughts and ways are infinitely above ours; in this he is *God, and not man.* (6.) All those that have experienced pardoning mercy cannot but admire that mercy; it is what we have reason to stand amazed at, if we know what it is. Has God forgiven us our transgressions? We may well say, *Who is a God like unto thee?* Our holy wonder at pardoning mercy will be a good evidence of our interest in it.

2. To take to ourselves the comfort of that mercy and all the grace and truth that go along with it. God's people here, as they look back with thankfulness upon God's pardoning their sins, so they look forward with assurance upon what he would yet further do for them. His mercy *endures for ever,* and therefore as he has *shown mercy* so he will, *v.* 19, 20. (1.) He will renew his favours to us: *He will turn again; he will have compassion;* that is, he will again have compassion upon us as formerly he had; his compassions shall be *new every morning;* he seemed to be departing from us in anger, but he will turn again and pity us. He will turn us to himself, and then will *turn to us, and have mercy upon us.* (2.) He will renew us, to prepare and qualify us for his favour: *He will subdue our iniquities;* when he takes away the guilt of sin, that it may not damn us, he will break the power of sin, that it may not have dominion over us, that we may not fear sin, nor be led captive by it. Sin is an enemy that fights against us, a tyrant that oppresses us; nothing less than almighty grace can subdue it, so great is its power in fallen man and so long has it kept possession. But, if God forgive the sin that has been committed by us, he will subdue the sin that dwells in us, and in that there is none like him in forgiving; and all those whose sins are pardoned earnestly desire and hope; to have their corruptions mortified and their iniquities subdued, and please themselves with the hopes of it. If we be left to ourselves, our iniquities will be too hard for us; but God's grace, we trust, shall be sufficient for us to subdue them, so that they shall not rule us, and then they shall not ruin us. (3.) He will confirm this good work, and effectually provide that his act of grace shall never be repealed: *Thou wilt cast all their sins into the depth of the sea,* as when he brought them out of Egypt (to which he has an eye in the promises here, *v.* 15) he subdued Pharaoh and the Egyptians, and cast them into the depth of the sea. It intimates that when God forgives sin he *remembers it no more,* and takes care that it shall never be remembered more against the sinner. Eze. 18:22, *His transgressions shall not be mentioned unto him;* they are *blotted out as a cloud* which never appears more. He casts them into the sea, not near the shore-side, where they may appear again next low water, but into *the depth of the sea,* never to rise again. *All their sins* shall be cast there without exception, for when God forgives sin he forgives all. (4.) He will perfect that which concerns us, and with this good work will do all that for us which our case requires and which he has promised (*v.* 20): *Then wilt thou perform thy truth to Jacob and thy mercy to Abraham.* It is in pursuance of the covenant that our sins are pardoned and our lusts mortified; from that spring all these streams flow, and with these he shall *freely give us all things.* The promise is said to be *mercy to Abraham,* because, as made to him first, it was mere mercy, preventing mercy, considering what state it found him in. But it was *truth to Jacob,* because the faithfulness of God was engaged to make good to him and his seed, as heirs to Abraham, all that was graciously promised to Abraham. See here, [1.] With what solemnity the covenant of grace is ratified to us; it was not only spoken, written, and sealed, but which is the highest confirmation, it was *sworn to our fathers;* nor is it a modern project, but is confirmed by antiquity too; it was sworn *from the days of old;* it is an ancient charter. [2.] With what satisfaction it may be applied and relied upon by us; we may say with the highest assurance, *Thou wilt perform the truth and mercy;* not one iota or tittle of it shall fall to the ground. Faithful is he that has promised, who also will do it.

AN EXPOSITION, WITH PRACTICAL OBSERVATIONS, OF

THE PROPHECY OF NAHUM

The name of this prophet signifies a *comforter;* for it was a charge given to all the prophets, *Comfort you, comfort you, my people:* and even this prophet, though wholly taken up in foretelling the destruction of Nineveh, which speaks terror to the Assyrians, is, even in that, comforter to the ten tribes of Israel, who, it is probable, were now lately carried captives into Assyria. It is very uncertain at what time he lived and prophesied, but it is most probable that he lied in the time of Hezekiah, and prophesied against Nineveh, after the captivity of Israel by the king of Assyria, which was in the ninth year of Hezekiah, and before Sennacherib's invading Judah, which was in the fourteenth year of Hezekiah, for to that attempt, and the defeat of it, it is supposed, the first chapter has reference; and it is probable that it was delivered a little before it, for the encouragement of God's people in that day of treading down and perplexity. It is the conjecture of the learned Huetius that the two other chapters of this book were delivered by Nahum some years after, perhaps in the reign of Manasseh, and in that reign the Jewish chronologies generally place him, somewhat nearer to the time when Nineveh was conquered, and the Assyrian monarchy reduced, by Cyaxares and Nebuchadnezzar, some time before the first captivity of Judah. It is probable that Nahum did by word of mouth prophesy many things concerning Israel and Judah, as it is certain that Jonah did (2 Ki. 14:25), though we have nothing of either of them in writing, but what related to Nineveh, of which though a great and ancient city, yet probably we should never have heard in sacred writ if the Israel of God had not had some concern in it.

CHAPTER 1

In this chapter we have, I. The inscription of the book, (*v.* 1). II. A magnificent display of the glory of God, in a mixture of wrath and justice against the wicked, and mercy and grace towards his people, and the discovery of his majesty and power in both (*v.* 2–8). III. A particular application of this (as most interpreters think) to the destruction of Sennacherib and the Assyrian army, when they besieged Jerusalem, which was a very memorable and illustrious instance of the power both of God's justice and of his mercy, and spoke abundance of terror to his enemies and encouragement to his faithful servants (*v.* 9–16).

Verse 1

This title directs us to consider, 1. The great city against which the word of the Lord is here delivered; it is the *burden of Nineveh,* not only a prophecy, and a weighty one, but a burdensome prophecy, a dead weight to Nineveh, a mill-stone hanged about its neck. Nineveh was the place concerned, and the Assyrian monarchy, which that was the royal seat of. About 100 years before this Jonah had, in God's name, foretold the speedy overthrow of this great city; but then the Ninevites repented and were spared, and that decree did not *bring forth.* The Ninevites then saw clearly how much it was to their advantage to turn from their evil way; it was the saving of their city; and yet, soon after, they returned to it again; it became worse than ever, *a bloody city,* and *full of lies* and *robbery.* They repented of their repentance, returned with the dog to his vomit, and at length grew worse than ever they had been. Then God sent them not this prophet, as Jonah, but this prophecy, to read them their doom, which was now irreversible. Note, The reprieve will not be continued if the repentance be not continued in. If men turn from the good they began to do, they can expect no other than that God should turn from the favour he began to show, Jer. 18:10. 2. The poor prophet by whom the word of the Lord is here delivered: It is *the book of the vision of Nahum the Elkoshite.* The burden of Nineveh was what the prophet plainly foresaw, for it was his vision, and what he left upon record (it is the *book of the vision),* that, when he was gone, the event might be compared with the prediction and might confirm it. All the account we have of the prophet himself is that he was an *Elkoshite,* of the town called *Elkes,* or *Elcos,* which, Jerome says, was in Galilee. Some observe that the scripture ordinarily says little of the prophets themselves, that our faith might not stand upon their authority, but upon that of the blessed Spirit by whom their prophecies were indited.

Verses 2–8

Nineveh knows not God, that God that contends with her, and therefore is here told what a God he is; and it is good for us all to mix faith with that which is here said concerning him, which speaks a great deal of terror to the wicked and comfort to good people; for this glorious description of the Sovereign of the world, like the pillar of cloud and fire, has a bright side towards Israel and a dark side towards the Egyptians. Let each take his portion from it; let sinners read it and tremble; let saints read it and triumph. The wrath of God is here revealed from heaven against him enemies, his favour and mercy are here assured to his faithful loyal subjects, and his almighty power in both, making his wrath very terrible and his favour very desirable.

I. He is a God of inflexible justice, a jealous God, and

will take vengeance on his enemies; let Nineveh know this, and tremble before him. Their idols are insignificant things; there is nothing formidable in them. But the God of Israel is greatly to be feared; for, 1. He resents the affronts and indignities done him by those that deny his being or any of his perfections, that set up other gods in competition with him, that destroy his laws, arraign his proceedings, ridicule his word, or are abusive to his people. Let such know that Jehovah, the one only living and true God, is a *jealous God, and a revenger;* he is jealous for the comfort of his worshippers, *jealous for his land* (Joel 2:18), and will not have that injured. He is a revenger, *and he is furious;* he *has fury* (so the word is), not as man has it, in whom it is an ungoverned passion (so he has said, *Fury is not in me,* Isa. 27:4), but he has it in such a way as becomes the righteous God, to put an edge upon his justice, and to make it appear more terrible to those who otherwise would stand in no awe of it. He is *Lord of anger* (so the Hebrew phrase is for that which we read, *he is furious);* he has anger, but he has it at command and under government. Our anger is often lord over us, as theirs that have *no rule over their own spirits,* but God is always *Lord of his anger* and *weighs a path to it,* Ps. 78:50. 2. He resolves to reckon with those that put those affronts upon him. We are told here, not only that he is a revenger, but that he *will take vengeance;* he has said he will, he has sworn it, Deu. 32:40, 41. Whoever are his adversaries and enemies among men, he will make them feel his resentments; and, though the sentence against his enemies is not executed speedily, yet he reserves wrath for them and reserves them for it in the day of wrath. Against his own people, who repent and humble themselves before him, he keeps *not his anger for ever,* but against his enemies he will for ever let out his anger. *He will not at all acquit the wicked* that sin, and stand to it, and do not repent, *v.* 3. Those *wickedly depart from their God* that depart, and never return (Ps. 18:21), and these he will not acquit. Humble supplicants will find him gracious, but scornful beggars will not find him easy, or that the door of mercy will be opened to a loud, but late, Lord, Lord. This revelation of the wrath of God against his enemies is applied to Nineveh (*v.* 8), and should be applied by all those to themselves who go on still in their trespasses: *With an over-running flood he will make an utter end of the place thereof.* The army of the Chaldeans shall overrun the country of the Assyrians, and lay it all waste. God's judgments, when they come with commission, are like a deluge to any people, which they cannot keep off nor make head against. *Darkness shall pursue his enemies;* terror and trouble shall follow them, whitersoever they go, shall pursue them to utter darkness; if they think to flee from the darkness which pursues them they will but fall into that which is before them.

II. He is a God of irresistible power, and is able to deal with his enemies, be they ever so many, ever so mighty, ever so hardy. He is *great in power* (*v.* 3), and therefore it is good having him our friend and bad having him our enemy. Now here,

1. The power of God is asserted and proved by divers instances of it in the kingdom of nature, where we always find its visible effects in the ordinary course of nature, and sometimes in the surprising alterations of that course. (1.) If we look up into the regions of the air, there we shall find proofs of his power, for *he has his ways in the whirlwind and the storm.* Which way soever God goes he carries a whirlwind and a storm along with him, for the terror of his enemies, Ps. 18:9, etc. And, wherever there is a whirlwind and a storm, God has the command of it, the control of it, makes his way through it, goes on his way in it, and serves his own purposes by it. He spoke to Job out of the whirlwind, and even *stormy winds fulfil his word.* He has *his way in the whirlwind,* that is, he goes on undiscerned, and the methods of his providence are to us unaccountable; as it is said, *His way is in the sea. The clouds are the dust of his feet;* he treads on them, walks on them, raises them when he pleases, as a man with his feet raises a cloud of dust. It is but by permission, or usurpation rather, that the devil is the prince of the power of the air, for that power is in God's hand. (2.) If we cast our eye upon the great deeps, there we find that the sea is his, for he made it; for, when he pleases, *he rebukes the sea and makes it dry, by drying up all the rivers* with which it is continually supplied. He gave those proofs of his power when he divided the Red Sea and Jordan, and can do the same again whenever he pleases. (3.) If we look round us on this earth, we find proofs of his power, when, either by the extreme heat and drought of summer or the cold and frost of winter, *Bashan languishes, and Carmel, and the flower of Lebanon languishes,* the choicest and strongest flower languishes. His power is often seen in earthquakes, which shake the mountains (*v.* 5), melt the hills, and melt them down, and level them with the plains. When he pleases *the earth is burnt at his presence* by the scorching heat of the sun, and he could burn it with fire from heaven, as he did Sodom, and at the end of time he will burn the world *and all that dwell therein.* The earth, and all the works that are therein, shall be burnt up. Thus *great is the Lord* and *of great power.*

2. This is particularly applied to his anger. If God be an almighty God, we may thence infer (*v.* 6), *Who can stand before his indignation?* The Ninevites had once found God *slow to anger* (as he says *v.* 3), and perhaps presumed upon the mercy they had then had experience of, and thought they might make bold with him; but they will find he is just and jealous as well as merciful and gracious, and, having shown the justice of his wrath, in the next he shows the power of it, and the utter insufficiency of his enemies to contend with him. It is in vain for the stoutest and strongest of sinners to think to make their part good against the power of God's anger. (1.) See God here as *a consuming fire,* terrible and mighty. Here is his indignation against sin, and the *fierceness of his anger,* his fury *poured out,* not like water, but *like fire,* like the fire and brimstone rained on Sodom, Ps. 11:6. Hell is the fierceness of God's anger, Rev. 16:19. God's anger is so fierce that it beats down all before it: *The rocks are thrown down by him,* which seemed immovable. Rocks have sometimes been rent by the eruption of subterraneous fires, which is a faint resemblance of the fierceness of God's anger against sinners whose hearts are rocky, for none ever hardened their hearts against him and prospered. (2.) See sinners here are stubble before the fire, weak and impotent, and a very unequal match for the wrath of God. [1.] They are utterly unable to bear up against it, so as to resist it, and put by the strokes of it: *Who can stand before his indignation?* Not the proudest and most daring sinner; not the world of the ungodly; no, not the angels that sinned. [2.] They are utterly unable to bear up under it so as to keep up their spirits, and preserve any enjoyment of themselves: *Who can abide in the fierceness of his anger?* As it is irresistible, so it is intolerable. Some of the effects of God's displeasure in this world a man may bear up under, but the *fierceness of his anger,* when it fastens immediately upon the soul, who can bear? Let us therefore *fear before him;* let us *stand in awe, and not sin.*

III. He is a God of infinite mercy; and in the midst of all this wrath mercy is remembered. *Let the sinners in Zion be afraid,* that go on still in their transgressions, but let not those that trust in God tremble before him. For, 1. He *is slow to anger* (*v.* 3), not easily provoked, but ready to show mercy to those who have offended him and to receive them into favour upon their repentance. 2. When the tokens of his rage against the wicked are abroad he takes care for the safety and comfort of his own people (*v.* 7): *The Lord is good* to those that are *good,* and to them he will be *a stronghold in the day of trouble.* Note, The same almighty power that is exerted for the terror and destruction of the wicked is engaged, and shall be employed, for the protection and satisfaction of his own people; he is able both to save and to destroy. In the day of public trouble, when God's judgments are in the earth, laying all waste, he will be a place of defence to those that by faith put themselves under his protection, those that trust in him in the way of their duty, that live a life of dependence upon him, and devotedness to him; he knows them, he owns them for his, he takes cognizance of their case, knows what is best for them, and what course to take most effectually for their relief. They are perhaps obscure and little regarded in the world, but the Lord knows them, Ps. 1:6.

Verses 9–15

These verses seem to point at the destruction of the army of the Assyrians under Sennacherib, which may well be reckoned a part of the burden of Nineveh, the head city of the Assyrian empire, and a pledge of the destruction of Nineveh itself about 100 years after; and this was an event which Isaiah, with whom probably this prophet was contemporary, spoke much of. Now observe here,

I. The great provocation which the Assyrians gave to God, the just and jealous God, for which, though *slow to anger,* he would take vengeance (*v.* 11): *There is one come out of thee, that imagines evil against the Lord* — Sennacherib, and his spokesman Rabshakeh. They framed an evil letter and an evil speech, not only against Hezekiah and his people, but against God himself, reflecting upon him as level with the gods of the heathen, and unable to protect his worshippers, dissuading his people from putting confidence in him, and urging them rather to put themselves under the protection of the *great king, the king of Assyria.* They contrived to alter the property of Jerusalem, that it should be no longer the city of the Lord, the holy city. This one, this mighty one, so he thinks himself, that comes out of Nineveh, *imagining evil against the Lord,* brings upon Nineveh this burden. Never was the glorious Majesty of heaven and earth more daringly, more blasphemously affronted than by Sennacherib at that time. He was *a wicked counsellor* who counselled them to despair of God's protection, and surrender themselves to the king of Assyria, and endeavour to put them out of conceit with Hezekiah's reformation (Isa. 36:7); with this wicked counsellor he here expostulates (*v.* 9): "*What do you imagine against the Lord?* What a foolish wicked thing it is for you to plot against God, as if you could outwit divine wisdom and overpower omnipotence itself!" Note, There is a great deal imagined against the Lord by the gates of hell, and against the interests of his kingdom in the world; but it will prove a *vain thing,* Ps. 2:1, 2. *He that sits in heaven laughs* at the imaginations of the pretenders to politics against him, and will turn their counsels headlong.

II. The great destruction which God would bring upon them for it, not immediately upon the whole monarchy (the ruin of that was deferred till the measure of their iniquity was full), but,

1. Upon the army; God will *make an utter end* of that; it shall be totally cut off and ruined at one blow; one fatal stroke of the destroying angel shall lay them dead upon the spot; *affliction shall not rise up the second time,* for it shall not need. With some sinners God makes a quick despatch, does their business at once. Divine vengeance goes not by one certain rule, nor in one constant track, but one way or other, by acute diseases or chronical ones, by slow deaths or lingering ones, he will *make an utter end* of all his enemies, who persist in their imaginations against him. We have reason to think that the Assyrian army were mostly of the same spirit, and spoke the same language, with their general, and now God would take them to task, though they did but say as they were taught; and it shall appear that they have laid themselves open to divine wrath by their own act and deed, *v.* 10. (1.) They are *as thorns* that entangle one another, and are *folded together.* They make one another worse, and more inveterate against God and his Israel, harden one another's hearts, and strengthen one another's hands, in their impiety; and therefore God will do with them as the husbandman does with a bush of thorns when he cannot part them: he puts them all into the fire together. (2.) They are *as drunken men,* intoxicated with pride and rage; and such as they shall be irrecoverably overthrown and destroyed. They shall be as drunkards, besotted to their own ruin, and shall stumble and fall, and make themselves a reproach, and be justly laughed at. (3.) They shall be *devoured as stubble fully dry,* which is irresistibly and irrecoverably consumed by the flame. The judgments of God are as devouring fire to those that make themselves as stubble to them. It is again threatened concerning this great army (*v.* 12) that *though they be quiet and likewise many,* very secure, not fearing the sallies out of the besieged upon them, because *they are numerous,* yet *thus shall they be cut down,* or certainly shall they be cut down, as grass and corn are cut down, with as little ado, when *he shall pass through,* even the destroying angel that is commissioned to cut them down. Note, The security of sinners, and their confidence in their own strength, are often presages of ruin approaching.

2. Upon the king. He *imagined evil against the Lord,* and shall he escape? No (*v.* 14): "*The Lord has given a com-*

mandment concerning thee; the decree has gone forth, *that thy name be no more sown,* that thy memory perish, that thou be no more talked of as thou hast been, and that the report of thy mighty actions be dispersed upon the wings of fame and celebrated with her trumpet." Because Sennacherib's son reigned in his stead, some make this to point at the overthrow of the Assyrian empire not long after. Note, Those that *imagine evil against the Lord* hasten evil upon themselves and their own families and interests, and ruin their own names by dishonouring his name. It is further threatened, (1.) That the images he worshipped should be cut off from their temple, the *graven image* and the *molten image out of the house of his gods,* which, some think, was fulfilled when Sennacherib was slain by his *two sons, as he was worshipping in the house of Nisroch his god,* by which barbarous parricide we may suppose the temple was looked upon as defiled, and was therefore disused, and the images were cut off from it, the worshippers of those images no longer attending there. Or it may be taken more generally to denote the utter ruin of Assyria; the army of the enemy shall lay all waste, and not spare even the images of their gods, by which God would intimate to them that one of the grounds of his controversy with them was their idolatry. (2.) That Sennacherib's grave shall be made there, some think in the house of his god; there he is slain, and there he shall be buried, for *he is vile;* he lies under this perpetual mark of disgrace, that he had so far lost his interest in the natural affection of his own children that two of them murdered him. Or it may be meant of the ignominious fall of the Assyrian monarchy itself, upon the ruins of which that of Babylon was raised. What a noise was made about the grave of that once formidable state, but now despicable, is largely described, Eze. 31:3, 11, 15, 16. Note, Those that make themselves vile by scandalous sins God will make vile by shameful punishments.

III. The great deliverance which God would hereby work for his own people and the city that was called by his name. The ruin of the church's enemies is the salvation of the church, and a very great salvation it was that was wrought for Jerusalem by the overthrow of Sennacherib's army.

1. The siege shall hereby be raised: *"Now will I break his yoke from off thee,* by which thou art kept in servitude, and *will burst thy bonds asunder,* by which thou seemest bound over to the Assyrian's wrath." That vast victorious army, when it forced free quarters for itself throughout all the land of Judah, and lived at discretion there, was as yokes and bonds upon them. Jerusalem, when it was besieged, was, as it were, bound and fettered by it; but, when the destroying angel had done his work, Jerusalem's bonds were burst asunder, and it was set at liberty again. This was a figure of the great salvation, by which the Jerusalem that is above is made free, is made free indeed.

2. The enemy shall be so weakened and dispirited that they shall never make any such attempt again, and the end of this trouble shall be so well gained by the grace of God that there shall be no more occasion for such a severe correction. (1.) God will not again afflict Jerusalem; his anger is *turned away,* and he says, *It is enough;* for he has by this fright *accomplished his whole work upon Mount Zion* (Isa. 10:12), and therefore *"though I have afflicted thee, I will afflict thee no more;"* the bitter portion shall not be repeated unless there be need and the patient's case call for it; for God *doth not afflict willingly.* (2.) The enemy shall not dare again to attack Jerusalem (*v.* 15): *The wicked shall no more pass through thee* as they have done, to lay all waste, *for he is utterly cut off* and disabled to do it. His army is cut off, his spirit cut off, and at length he himself is cut off.

3. The tidings of this great deliverance shall be published and welcomed with abundance of joy throughout the kingdom, *v.* 15. While Sennacherib prevailed, and carried all before him, every day brought bad news; but now, *behold, upon the mountains, the feet of him that bringeth good tidings,* the *feet of the evangelist;* he is seen coming at a distance upon the mountains, as fast as his feet will carry him; and how pleasant a sight is it once more to see a messenger of peace, after we have received so many of Job's messengers! We find these words made use of by another prophet to illustrate the mercy of the deliverance of the people of God out of Babylon (Isa. 52:7), not that the prophets stole the word one from another (as those did, Jer. 23:30), but speaking by the same Spirit, they often used the same expressions; and it may be of good use for ministers to testify their consent to wholesome truths (1 Tim. 6:3) by concurring in the same forms of sound words, 2 Tim. 1:13. These words are also quoted by the apostle, both from Isaiah and Nahum, and applied to the great redemption wrought out for us by our Lord Jesus, and the publishing of it to the world by the everlasting gospel, Rom. 10:15. Christ's ministers are those messengers of good tidings, that preach *peace by Jesus Christ. How beautiful are the feet* of those *messengers!* How welcome their message to those that see their misery and danger by reason of sin! And observe, He that brings these good tidings brings with them a call to Judah to *keep her solemn feasts* and *perform her vows.* During the trouble, (1.) The ordinary feasts had been intermitted. *Inter arma silent leges — The voice of law cannot be heard amidst the shouts of battle.* While Jerusalem was *encompassed with armies* they could not go thither to worship; but now that the embargo is taken off they must return to the observance of their feasts; and the feasts of the Lord will be doubly sweet to the people of God when they have been for some time deprived of the benefit of them and God graciously restores them their opportunities again, for we are taught the worth of such mercies by the want of them. (2.) They had made vows to God, that, if he would deliver them out of this distress, they would do something extraordinary in his service, to his honour; and now that the deliverance is wrought they are called upon to perform their vows; the promise they had then made must now be made good, for *better it is not to vow than to vow and not to pay.* And those words, *The wicked shall no more pass through thee,* may be taken as a promise of the perfecting of the good work of reformation which Hezekiah had begun; the wicked shall not, as they have done, walk on every side, but they shall be cut off, and the baffling of the attempts from the wicked enemies abroad is a mercy indeed to a nation when it is accompanied with the restraint and reformation of the wicked at home, who are its more dangerous enemies.

CHAPTER 2

We now come closer to Nineveh, that great city; she took, not warning by the destruction of her armies and the fall of her king, and therefore may expect, since she persists in her enmity to God, that he will proceed in his controversy with her. Here is foretold, I. The approach of the enemy that should destroy Nineveh, and the terror of his military preparations (*v.* 1–5). II. The taking of the city (*v.* 6). III. The captivity of the queen, the flight of the inhabitants, the seizing of all its wealth, and the great consternation it should be in (*v.* 7–10). IV. All this is traced up to its true causes — their sinning against God and God's appearing against them (*v.* 11–13). All this was fulfilled when Nebuchadnezzar, in the first year of his reign, in conjunction with Cyaxares, or Ahasuerus, king of the Medes, conquered Nineveh, and made himself master of the Assyrian monarchy.

Verses 1–10

Here is, I. An alarm of war sent to Nineveh, *v.* 1. The prophet speaks of it as just at hand, for it is neither doubtful nor far distant: "Look about thee, and see, *he that dashes in pieces has come up before thy face.* Nebuchadnezzar, who is noted, and will be yet more so, for dashing nations in pieces, begins with thee, and will dissipate and disperse thee;" so some render the word. Babylon is called the *hammer of the whole earth,* Jer. 1. 23. The attempt of Nebuchadnezzar upon Nineveh is public, bold, and daring: "He *has come up before thy face,* avowing his design to ruin thee; and therefore stand to thy arms, *O Nineveh! keep the munition;* secure thy towers and magazines: *watch the way;* set guards upon all the avenues to the city; *make thy loins strong;* encourage thy soldiers; animate thyself and them; *fortify thy power mightily,* as cities do when an enemy is advancing against them" (this is spoken ironically); "do the utmost thou canst, yet thou shalt not be able to put by the stroke of this judgment, for *there is no counsel or strength against the Lord.*"

II. A manifesto published, showing the causes of the war (*v.* 2): *The Lord has turned away the excellency of Jacob, as the excellency of Israel,* that is, 1. The Assyrians have been abusive to Jacob, the two tribes (have humbled and mortified them), as well as to Israel, the ten tribes, *have emptied them, and marred their vine-branches.* For this God will reckon with them; though done long since, it shall come into the account now against that kingdom, and Nineveh the head-city of it. God's quarrel with them is *for the violence done to Jacob.* Or, (2.) God is now by Nebuchadnezzar about *to turn away the pride of Jacob* by the captivity of the two tribes, as he did the pride of Israel by their captivity; He has determined to do it, to bring *emptiers* upon them, and the enemy that is to do it must begin with Nineveh, and reduce that first, and humble the pride of that. God is looking upon proud cities, and abasing them, even those that are nearest to him. Samaria is humbled, and Jerusalem is to be humbled, and their pride brought low; and shall not Nineveh, that proud city, be brought down too? *Emptiers have emptied* the cities, *and marred the vine-branches* in the country of Jacob and Israel; and must not the excellency of Nineveh, that is so much her pride, be turned away too?

III. A particular account given in of the terrors wherein the invading enemy shall appear against Nineveh; every thing shall contribute to make him formidable. 1. *The shields of his mighty men are made red,* and probably their other arms and array, as if they were already tinctured with the blood they had shed, or intended hereby to signify they would put all to the sword; they hung out a red flag, in token that they would give no quarter. 2. *The valiant men are in scarlet;* not only red clothes, to intimate what bloody work they designed to make, but rich clothes, to intimate the wealth of the army, and that is the sinews of war. 3. *The chariots shall be with flaming torches in the day of his preparation;* when they are making their approaches, they shall fly as swiftly as lightning; the wheels shall strike fire upon the stones, and those that drive them shall drive furiously with a flaming indignation, as Jehu drove. Or they carried flaming torches with them in the open chariots, when they made their approach in the night, as Gideon's soldiers carried lamps in their pitchers, to be both a guide to themselves and a terror to their enemies, and with them to set all on fire wherever they went. 4. *The fir-trees shall be terribly shaken;* the great men of Nineveh, that overtop their neighbours, as the stately firs do the shrubs; or the very standing trees shall be made to shake by the violent concussions of the earth, which that great army shall cause. 5. The chariots of war shall be very terrible (*v.* 4): *They shall rage in the streets,* that is, those that drive them shall rage; you would think the chariots themselves raged; they shall be so numerous, and drive with so much fury, that even *in the broad ways,* where, one would think, there should be room enough, they shall *jostle one another;* and these iron chariots shall be made so bright that in the beams of the sun *they shall seem like torches* in the night; they shall *run like the lightnings,* so swiftly, so furiously. Nebuchadnezzar's commanders are here called his *worthies,* his *gallants* (so the margin reads it), his *heroes;* those *he shall recount,* and order them immediately and without fail to render themselves at their respective posts, for he is entering upon action, is resolved to take the field immediately, and to open the campaign with the siege of Nineveh. *His worthies shall remember* (so some read it); they shall be mindful of the duty of their place, and the charge they have received, and shall thereby be made so intent upon their business that they *shall stumble in their walks,* shall make more haste than good speed; they stumble, but shall not fall; for *they shall make haste to the wall thereof,* shall open the trenches; and the defence, or the covered way, shall be prepared (something to shelter them from the darts of the besieged), and they shall so closely carry on the siege, and with so much vigour, that at length the *gates of the rivers shall be opened* (*v.* 6); those gates of Nineveh which open upon the river Tigris (on which Nineveh was built) shall be first forced by, or betrayed to, the enemy, and by those gates they shall enter. And then the *palace shall be dissolved,* either the king's house or the house of Nisroch his god; the same word signifies both a palace and a temple. When the God of heaven goes forth to contend with a people, neither the palaces nor their kings, neither the temples nor their gods, can protect and shelter them, but must all inevitably fall with them.

IV. A prediction of the consequences of this; and it is easy to guess how dismal those will be. 1. The queen shall fall into the hands of the enemy (*v.* 7): *Huzzab shall be led away captive;* she that was *established* (so some read it), thought herself safe because she was concealed and shut up in secret, shall be *discovered* (so the margin reads it) and shall be led *away captive,* in greater disgrace than that of common prisoners; she shall be *brought up* in a mock state, *and her maids* of honour *shall lead her*, because she is weak and faint, not able to bear such frights and hardships, which are doubly hard and frightful to those that have not been used to them; they shall attend her, not to speak cheerfully to her and to encourage her, but murmuring and moaning themselves, as *with the voice of doves*, the *doves of the valleys* (Eze. 7:16), noted for their *mourning*, Isa. 38:14; 59:11. They shall be *tabering upon their breasts*, beating their own breasts in grief and vexation, as if they were *drumming* upon them, for so the word signifies. 2. The inhabitants, though numerous, shall none of them be able to make head against the invaders, or stand their ground (v. 8): *Nineveh is of old like a pool of water*, replenished with people as a pool with water (and *waters* signify *multitudes*, Rev. 17:15), or as those waters with fish; it was long ago a populous city; in Jonah's time there were 120,000 little children in it (Jonah 4:11), and, ordinarily, cities and countries are increasing in their number every year; but, though they have so many hands to be employed in the public service, yet they shall not be able to inspire one another with courage, but *they shall flee away like cowards*. Their commanders shall do what they can to animate them; they shall cry, *"Stand, stand, have a good heart on it, and we shall do well enough;"* but *none shall* so much as *look back;* they shall not have the least spark of courage remaining, but every one shall think it is his wisest course to make his best of the opportunity to escape; they shall not so much as look back to see who calls for them. Note, God can dispirit the strongest and boldest, in the day of distress, so that they shall not be what one would expect from them, but *like a pool of water*, the water whereof is dried up and gone. 3. The wealth of the city shall become a prey, and all its rich furniture shall fall into the hands of the victorious enemy (v. 9); they shall thus animate and excite one another to plunder: *Take the spoil of silver; take the spoil of gold;* thus the officers shall stir up the soldiers to improve their opportunity; here are silver and gold enough for them, for *there is no end of the store of money and plate.* Nineveh, having been *of old like a pool of water*, has gathered a vast deal of mud; and abundance of glory it has *out of all the pleasant furniture*, all the *vessels of desire*, which they have gloried in and which shall now be a prey and a pride to the conquerors. Note, Those who prepare raiment as the clay, and heap up silver as the dust, know not who may put on the raiment and divide the silver, Job 27:16, 17. Thus this rich city is empty, and void, and waste, *v.* 10. See the vanity of worldly wealth; instead of defending its owners, it does but expose them, and enable their enemies to do them so much the more mischief. 4. The soldiers and people shall have no heart to appear for the defence of the city. Their spirits shall *melt* away like wax before the fire; their *knees shall smite together* (as Belshazzar's did, in his agony, Dan. 5:6), so that they shall not be able to stand their ground, no, nor to make their escape; *much pain* shall be *in all loins*, as is the case in extreme frights, so that they shall not be able to hold up their backs. And the *faces of them all shall gather blackness*, like that of a pot that is every day over the fire; so the word signifies. Note, Guilt in the conscience will fill men with terror in an evil day, and those who place their happiness in the wealth of this world and set their hearts upon it think themselves undone when their silver, and their gold, and their pleasant furniture are taken from them.

Verses 11–13

Here we have Nineveh's ruin, 1. Triumphed in by its neighbours, who now remember against it all the oppressions and abuse of power it had been guilty of in its pomp and prosperity (v. 11, 12): *Where is the dwelling of the lions?* It is gone; there appear no remnants, no footsteps, of it. *Where is the feeding place of the young lions*, where they glutted themselves with prey? The princes of Nineveh had been as lions, as beasts of prey; cruel tyrants are no better, nay, in this respect much worse — that, being men, humanity is expected from them; nay, if they were indeed lions, they would not prey upon those of their own kind. *Savis inter se convenit ursae — Fierce bears agree together.* But in the shape of men they had the cruelty of lions: they walked in Nineveh as a lion in the woods, and *none made them afraid;* every one stood in awe of them, and

they were under no apprehensions of danger from any; though nobody loved them, every body feared them, and that was all they desired. *Oderint, dum metuant — Let them hate, so that they do but fear.* The king himself, as well as every prince, made it his business, by all the arts of violence and extortion, to enrich himself and raise his family; he did *tear in pieces enough for his whelps* (and no little would be enough for them) and he *strangled for his lioness*, killed all that came near him, and seized what they had for his children, for his wives and concubines, and *filled his holes with prey and his dens with ravin*, as lions are wont to do. Note, Many make it an excuse for their rapine and injustice that they have wives and children to provide for, whereas what is so got will never do them any good; those that *fear the Lord*, and get what they have honestly, shall not want a competency for themselves and theirs; *verily they shall be fed*, when *the young lions*, though dens and holes were *filled with prey and ravin* for them, *shall lack, and suffer hunger*, Ps. 34:10. 2. It is avowed by the righteous Judge of heaven and earth; it is his doing, and let all the world take notice that it is so (v. 13): *Behold, I am against thee, saith the Lord of hosts.* And what good can hosts do for her in her defence, when the *Lord of hosts* is against her for her destruction? The oppressors in Nineveh thought they only set their neighbours against them, who were not a match for them, and whom they could easily overpower; but it proved they set God against them, who is, and will be, the asserter of right and the avenger of wrong. God is against the princes of Nineveh, and then, (1.) These military preparations will stand them in no stead: *I will burn their chariots in the smoke;* he does not say *in the fire*, but, in contempt of them, the very *smoke* of God's indignation shall serve to burn their chariots; they shall be consumed as soon as the fire of his indignation is kindled, while as yet it does but smoke, and not flame out. Or, The drivers of the chariots shall be smothered and stifled with the smoke; then the *chariots of their glory* shall be the shame of their families, Isa. 22:18. (2.) Their children, the hopes of their families, shall be cut off: *The sword shall devour the young lions*, whom they were so solicitous to provide for by oppression and extortion. Note, It is just with God to deprive those of their children, or (which is all one) of comfort in them, that take sinful courses to enrich them, and (as has been said of some) damn their souls to make their sons gentlemen. (3.) The wealth they have heaped up by fraud and violence shall neither be enjoyed by them nor employed for them: *I will cut off thy prey from the earth;* not only thou shalt not be the better for it, but no one else shall. Some understand it of the disabling of them for the future to prey upon their neighbours. (4.) Their agents abroad shall not have that respect from their neighbours and that influence upon them which sometimes they had had: *The voice of thy messengers shall no more be heard*, no more be heeded, which some think refers to Rabshakeh, one of Nineveh's messengers, that had blasphemed the living God, an iniquity which was remembered against Nineveh long after. Those are not worthy to be heard again that have once spoken reproachfully of God.

CHAPTER 3

This chapter goes on with the burden of Nineveh, and concludes it. I. The sins of that great city are charged upon it, murder (v. 1), whoredom and witchcraft (v. 4), and a general extent of wickedness (v. 19). II. Judgments are here threatened against it, blood for blood (v. 2, 3), and shame for shameful sins (v. 5–7). III. Instances are given of the like desolations brought upon other places for the like sins (v. 8–11). IV. The overthrow of all those things which they depended upon, and put confidence in, is foretold (v. 12–19).

Verses 1–7

Here is, I. Nineveh arraigned and indicted. It is a high charge that is here drawn up against that great city, and neither her numbers nor her grandeur shall secure her from prosecution. 1. It is a *city of blood*, in which a great deal of innocent blood is shed by unrighteous war, or under colour and pretence of public justice, or by suffering barbarous murders to go unpunished; for this the righteous God will make inquisition. 2. *It is all full of lies;* truth is banished from among them; there is no such thing as honesty; one knows not whom to believe nor whom to trust. 3. It is all full of *robbery* and rapine; no man cares what mischief he does, nor to whom he does it: *The prey departs not*, that is, they never know when they have got

enough by spoil and oppression. They shed blood, and told lies, in pursuit of the prey, that they might enrich themselves. 4. There is a *multitude of whoredoms* in it, that is, idolatries, spiritual whoredoms, by which she defiled herself, and to which she seduced the neighbouring nations, as a well-favoured harlot, and sold and ruined *nations through her whoredoms*. 5. She is a *mistress of witchcrafts*, and by them she *sells families*, v. 4. That which Nineveh aimed at was a universal monarchy, to be the metropolis of the world, and to have all her neighbours under her feet; to compass this, she used not only arms, but arts, compelling some, deluding others, into subjection to her, and wheedling them as a harlot by her charms to lay their necks under her yoke, suggesting to them that it would be for their advantage. She courted them to join with her in her idolatrous rites, to tie them the faster to her interests, and made use of her wealth, power, and greatness, to draw people into alliances with her, by which she gained advantages over them, and made a hand of them. These were her whoredoms, like those of Tyre, Isa. 23:15, 17. These were her witchcrafts, with which she unaccountably gained dominion. And for this that God has a quarrel with her who, having *made of one blood all nations of men*, never designed one to be a nation of tyrants and another of slaves, and who claims it as his own prerogative to be universal Monarch.

II. Nineveh condemned to ruin upon this indictment. Woe to this bloody city! v. 1. See what this woe is.

1. Nineveh had with her cruelties been a terror and destruction to others, and therefore destruction and terror shall be brought upon her. Those that are for overthrowing all that come in their way will, sooner or later, meet with their match. (1.) Hear the alarm with which Nineveh shall be terrified, v. 2. It is a formidable army that advances against it; you may hear them at a distance, the *noise of the whip*, driving the chariot-horses with fury; you may hear the noise of the *rattling of the wheels, the prancing horses, and the jumping chariots;* the very noise is frightful, but much more so when they know that all this force is coming with all this speed against them, and they are not able to make head against it. (2.) See the slaughter with which Nineveh shall be laid waste (v. 3), the sword drawn with which execution shall be done, *the bright sword lifted up and the glittering spear*, the dazzling brightness of which is very terrible to those whom they are lifted up against. See what havoc these make when they are commissioned to slay: *There is a great number of carcases*, for the slain of the land shall be many; *there is no end of their corpses;* there is such a *multitude of slain* that it is in vain to go about to take the number of them; they lie so thick that passengers are ready to stumble *upon their corpses* at every step. The destruction of Sennacherib's army, which, in the morning, were *all dead corpses*, is perhaps looked upon here as a figure of the like destruction that should afterwards be in Nineveh; for those that will not take warning by judgments at a distance shall have them come nearer.

2. Nineveh had with her whoredoms and witchcrafts drawn others to shameful wickedness, and therefore God will load her with shame and contempt (v. 5–7): *The Lord of hosts* is *against her*, and then she shall be exposed to the highest degree of disgrace and ignominy, shall not only lose all her charms, but shall be made to appear very odious. When it shall be seen that while she courted her neighbours it was with design to ruin their liberty and property, when all her wicked artifices shall be brought to light, then her *shame is discovered to the nations*. When her proud pretensions are baffled, and her vain towering hopes of an absolute and universal dominion brought to nought, and she appears not to have been so strong and considerable as she would have been thought to be, then *to see the nakedness of the land do they come*, and it appears ridiculous. Then do they *cast abominable filth upon her*, as upon a carted strumpet, and *make her vile* as the offscouring of all things; that great city, which all nations had made court to and coveted an alliance with, has become a gazing-stock, a laughing stock. Those that formerly looked upon her, and fled to her, in hopes of protection from her, now *look upon her and flee from her*, for fear of being ruined with her. Note, Those that abuse their honour and interest will justly be disgraced and abandoned, and, because miserable, will be made contemptible, and thereby

be made more miserable. When Nineveh is laid waste *who will bemoan her?* Her trouble will be so great, and her sense of it so deep, as not to admit relief from sympathy, or any comforting considerations; or, if it would, none shall do any such good office: *When shall I seek comforters for thee?* Note, Those that showed no pity in the day of their power can expect to find no pity in the day of their fall. When those about Nineveh, that had been deceived by her wiles, come to be undeceived in her ruin, every one shall insult over her, and none bemoan her. This was Nineveh's fate, when she was made a spectacle, or gazing-stock. Note, The greater men's show was in the day of their abused prosperity the greater will their shame be in the day of their deserved destruction. *I will make thee an example;* so Drusus reads it. Note, When proud sinners are humbled and brought down it is designed that others should take example by them not to lift up themselves in security and insolence when they prosper in the world.

Verses 8–19

Nineveh has been told that God is against her, and then none can be for her, to stand her in any stead; yet she sets God himself at defiance, and his power and justice, and says, *I shall have peace.* Threatened folks live long; therefore here the prophet largely shows how vain her confidences would prove and insufficient to ward off the judgment of God. To convince them of this,

I. He shows them that other places, which had been as strong and as secure as they, could not keep their ground against the judgments of God. Nineveh shall fall unpitied and uncomforted (for miserable comforters will those prove who speak peace to those on whom God will fasten trouble), and she shall not be able to help herself: *Art thou better than populous No? v.* 8. He takes them off from their vain confidences by quoting precedents. The city mentioned is *No,* a great city in the land of Egypt (Jer. 46:25), *No-Ammon,* so some read it both there and here. We read of it, Eze. 30:14–16. Some think it was *Diospolis,* others *Alexandria.* As God said to Jerusalem, *Go, see what I did to Shiloh* (Jer. 7:12), so to Nineveh that great city, *Go, see what I did to populous No.* Note, It will help to keep us in a holy fear of the judgments of God to consider that we are not better than those that have fallen under those judgments before us. We deserve them as much, and are as little able to grapple with them. This also should help to reconcile us to afflictions. Are we better than such and such, who were in like manner exercised? Nay, were not they better than we, and less likely to be afflicted? Now, concerning No, observe, 1. How firm her standing seemed to be, *v.* 8. She was fortified both by nature and art, was *situate among the rivers.* Nile, in several branches, not only watered her fields, but guarded her wall. *Her rampart was the sea,* the *lake of Mareotis,* an Egyptian sea, like the sea of Tiberias. Her *wall was from the sea;* it was fenced with a wall which was thought to make the place impregnable. It was also supported by its interests and alliances abroad, *v.* 9. *Ethiopia,* or Arabia, *was her strength,* either by the wealth brought to her in a way of trade or by the auxiliary forces furnished for military service. The whole country of Egypt also contributed to the strength of this populous city; so that it was *infinite, and there was no end of it* (so it might be rendered); She set no bounds to her ambition and knew no end of her wealth and strength; people flocked to her endlessly, and she thought there never would be any end of it; but it is God's prerogative to be infinite. *Put and Lubim were thy helpers,* two neighbouring countries of Africa, Mauritania and Libya, that is, Libya Cyrenica, a country that Egypt had much dependence upon. No, thus helped, seemed to sit as a queen, and was not likely to see any sorrow. But, 2. See how fatal her fall proved to be (v, 10): *Yet was she carried away,* and her strength failed her; even she that was so strong, so secure, yet *went into captivity.* This refers to some destruction of that city which was then well-known, and probably fresh in memory, though not recorded in history; for the destruction of it by Nebuchadnezzar (if we should understand this prophetically) could not be made an example to Nineveh; for the reducing of Nineveh was one of the first of his victories and that of Egypt one of the last. The strength and grandeur of that great city could not be its protection from military execution. (1.) Not from that which was most barbarous; for *her young children* had no compassion shown them, but were *dashed in pieces at the top of all the streets* by the merciless conquerors. (2.) Not from that which was most inglorious and disgraceful: *They cast lots for her honourable men* that were made prisoners of war, who should have them for their slaves. So many had they of them that they knew not what to do with them, but they made sport with throwing dice for them; *all her great men,* that used to be adorned on statedays with chains of gold, *were* now *bound in chains of iron;* they were *pinioned* or *handcuffed* (so the word properly signifies), not only as slaves, but as condemned malefactors. What a mortification was this to *populous No,* to have her honourable men and great men, that were her pride and confidence, thus abused! Now hence he infers against Nineveh (*v.* 11), "Thou also shalt be intoxicated, infatuated; thou also shalt reel and stagger, as drunk with the cup of the Lord's fury, that shall be put into thy hand" (see Jer. 25:17, 27); *"Thou shalt fall and rise no more.* The cup shall go round, and come to thy turn, O Nineveh! to drink off at last, and shall be to thee as the waters of jealousy."

II. He shows them that all those things which they reposed a confidence in should fail them. 1. Did the men of Nineveh trust to their own magnanimity and bravery? Their hearts should sink and fail them. *They shall be hid,* shall abscond for shame, being in disgrace, abscond for fear, being in distress and danger, and not able to face the enemies, because of whose strength and terror, having no strength of their own, they shall *seek strength,* shall come sneaking to their neighbours to beg their assistance in a time of need. Thus God can *cut off the spirit* of princes, and *take away their heart.* 2. Did they depend upon their barrier, the garrisons and strongholds they had, which were regularly fortified and bravely manned? Those shall prove but paper-walls, and *like the first-ripe figs,* which, if you give the tree but a little shake, will *fall into the mouth of the eater* that gapes for them; so easily will all their strongholds be made to surrender to the advancing enemy, upon the first summons, *v.* 12. Note, Strongholds, even the strongest, are no fence against the judgments of God, when they come with commission. *The rich man's wealth is his strong city, and a high wall,* but only *in his own conceit,* Prov. 18:10. They are supposed to make their strongholds as strong as possible, and are challenged to do their utmost to make them tenable, and serviceable to them against the invader (*v.* 14): *Draw thee water for the siege;* lay in great quantities of water, that that which is so necessary to the support of human life may not be wanting; it is put here for all manner of provision, with which Nineveh is ironically told to furnish herself, in expectation of a siege. "Take ever so much care that thou mayest not be starved out, and forced by famine to surrender, yet that shall not avail. *Fortify the strongholds,* by adding out-works to them, or putting men and arms into them," as with us by planting cannon upon them. *"Go into clay, and tread the mortar,* and *make strong the brick-kiln;* take all the pains thou canst in erecting new fortifications; but it shall be all in vain, for (*v.* 15) there shall even *the fire devour thee* if it be taken by storm." It is by fire and sword that in time of war the great devastations are made. 3. Did they put confidence in the multitude of their inhabitants? Were they, from their number and valour, reckoned their strongest walls and fortifications? Alas! these shall stand them in no stead; they shall but sink the sooner under the weight of their own numbers (*v.* 13): *Thy people in the midst of thee are women;* they have no wisdom, no courage; they shall be fickle, feeble, and faint-hearted, as women commonly are in such times of danger and distress; they shall be at their wits' end, adding to their griefs and fears by the power of their own imagination, and utterly unable to do any thing for themselves; the valiant men shall become cowards. *O verè Phrygiae, neque enim Phryges — Phrygian dames, not Phrygian men.* Though they *make themselves many* (*v.* 15), as the *canker-worm* and *as the locust,* that come in vast swarms, *though thou hast multiplied thy merchants above the stars of heaven,* though thy exchange be thronged with wealthy traders, who, having so much money to stand up in defence of and so much to lay out in the means of their defence, should, one would think, give the enemy a warm reception, yet their hearts shall fail them too; though they be numerous as caterpillars, yet the fire and sword shall eat them up easily and irresistibly as the canker-worm, *v.* 15. They are as numerous as those wasting insects, but their enemies shall be mischievous like them. He adds (*v.* 16), *The canker-worm spoils,* or *spreads herself, and flies away.* Both the merchants and the enemies were compared to canker-worms. The enemies shall spoil Nineveh, and carry away the spoil, without opposition, or any hope of recovering it. Or the rich merchants, who have come from abroad to settle in Nineveh, and have raised vast estates there, out of which it was hoped they would contribute largely for the defence of the city, when they see the country invaded and the city likely to be besieged, will send away their effects, and remove to some other place, will *spread their wings* and *fly away* where they may be safe, and Nineveh shall be never the better for them. Note, It is rare to find even those that have shared with us in our joys willing to share with us in our griefs too. The canker-worms will continue upon the field while there is any thing to be had, but they are gone when all is gone. Those that men have got by they do not care to lose by. Nineveh's merchants bid her farewell in her distress. Riches themselves are as the canker-worms, which on a sudden *fly away as the eagle towards heaven,* Prov. 23:5. 4. Did they put a confidence in the strength of their gates and bars? Alas! what fence will those be against the force of the judgments of God? *v.* 13. *The gates of thy land shall be set wide open unto thy enemies,* the gates of thy rivers (*ch.* 2:6), the flood-gates, or the passes and avenues, by which the enemy would make his entrance into the country, or the gates of the cities; these, though ever so strong and well-guarded, shall not answer their end: *The fire shall devour thy bars,* the bars of thy gates, and then they shall fly open. 5. Did they put a confidence in their king and princes? They should do them no service (*v.* 17): *Thy crowned heads are as the locusts;* those that had pomp and power, as crowned heads, were enfeebled, and had no power to make resistance, when the enemy came in like a flood. *"Thy captains,* that should lead thy forces into the field, are great indeed, and look great, but they are as the great *grasshoppers,* the *maximum quod sic — the largest specimens* of that *species;* still they are but grasshoppers, worthless things, that can do no service. *They encamp in the hedges, in the cold day,* the cold weather, *but, when the sun arises, they flee away,* and are gone, nobody knows whither. So these mercenary soldiers that lay slumbering about Nineveh, when any trouble arises, flee away, and shift for their own safety. *The hireling flees, because he is a hireling."* The *king of Assyria* is told, and it is a shame he needs to be told it (who might observe it himself), that *his shepherds slumber;* they have no life or spirit to appear for the flock, and are very remiss in the discharge of the duty of their place and the trust reposed in them: Thy *nobles shall dwell in the dust,* and be buried in silence. 6. Did they hope that they should yet recover themselves and rally again? In this also they should be disappointed; for, when the shepherds are smitten, the *sheep are scattered;* the people are dispersed *upon the mountains* and *no man gathers them,* nor will they ever come together of themselves, but will wander endlessly, as scattered sheep do. The judgment they are under is as a wound, and it is incurable; there is no relief for it, *"no healing of thy bruise,* no possibility that the wound, which is so grievous and painful to thee, should be so much as skinned over; thy case is desperate (*v.* 19) and thy neighbours, instead of lending a hand to help thee, shall *clap their hands over thee,* and triumph in thy fall; and the reason is, because thou hast been one way or other injurious to them all: *Upon whom has not thy wickedness passed continually?* Thou hast been always doing mischief to those about thee; there is none of them but what thou hast abused and insulted; and therefore they shall be so far from pitying thee that they shall be glad to see thee reckoned with." Note, Those that have been abusive to their neighbours will, one time or another, find it come home to them; they are but preparing enemies to themselves against their day comes to fall: and those that dare not lay hands on them themselves will *clap their hands over them,* and upbraid them with their former wickedness, for which they are now well enough served and paid in their own coin. *The troublers shall be troubled* will be the burden of many, as it is here *the burden of Nineveh.*

AN EXPOSITION, WITH PRACTICAL OBSERVATIONS, OF

THE PROPHECY OF HABAKKUK

It is a very foolish fancy of some of the Jewish rabbin that this prophet was the son of the Shunamite woman that was at first miraculously given, and afterwards raised to life, by Elisha (2 Ki. 4), as they say also that the prophet Jonah was the son of the widow of Zarephath, which Elijah raised to life. It is a more probable conjecture of their modern chronologers that he lived and prophesied in the reign of king Manasseh, when wickedness abounded, and destruction was hastening on, destruction by the Chaldeans, whom this prophet mentions as the instruments of God's judgments; and Manasseh was himself carried to Babylon, as an earnest of what should come afterwards. In the apocryphal story of Bel and the Dragon mention is made of Habakkuk the prophet in the land of Judah, who was carried thence by an angel to Babylon, to feed Daniel in the den; those who give credit to that story take pains to reconcile our prophet's living before the captivity, and foretelling it, with that. Huetius thinks that that was another of the same name, a prophet, this of the tribe of Simeon, that of Levi; others that he lived so long as to the end of that captivity, though he prophesied of it before it came. And some have imagined that Habakkuk's feeding Daniel in the den is to be understood mystically, that Daniel then *lived by faith,* as Habakkuk had said *the just should do;* he was *fed* by that word, Hab. 2:4. The prophecy of this book is a mixture of the prophet's addresses to God in the people's name and to the people in God's name; for it is the office of the prophet to carry messages both ways. We have in it a lively representation of the intercourse and communion between a gracious God and a gracious soul. The whole refers particularly to the invasion of the land of Judah by the Chaldeans, which brought spoil upon the people of God, a just punishment of the spoil they had been guilty of among themselves; but it is of general use, especially to help us through that great temptation with which good men have in all ages been exercised, arising from the power and prosperity of the wicked and the sufferings of the righteous by it.

CHAPTER 1

In this chapter, I. The prophet complains to God of the violence done by the abuse of the sword of justice among his own people and the hardships thereby put upon many good people (*v.* 1–4). II. God by him foretels the punishment of that abuse of power by the sword of war, and the desolations which the army of the Chaldeans should make upon them (*v.* 5–11). III. Then the prophet complains of that too, and is grieved that the Chaldeans prevail so far (*v.* 12–17), so that he scarcely knows which is more to be lamented, the sin or the punishment of it, for in both many harmless good people are very great sufferers. It is well that there is a day of judgment, and a future state, before us, in which it shall be eternally well with all the righteous, and with them only, and ill with all the wicked, and them only; so the present seeming disorders of Providence shall be set to rights, and there will remain no matter of complaint whatsoever.

Verses 1–4

We are told no more in the title of this book (which we have, *v.* 1) than that the penman was *a prophet,* a man divinely inspired and commissioned, which is enough (if that be so, we need not ask concerning his tribe or family, or the place of his birth), and that the book itself is *the burden which* he *saw;* he was as sure of the truth of it as if he had seen it with his bodily eyes already accomplished. Here, in these verses, the prophet sadly laments the iniquity of the times, as one sensibly touched with grief for the lamentable decay of religion and righteousness. It is a very melancholy complaint which he here makes to God, 1. That no man could call what he had his own; but, in defiance of the most sacred laws of property and equity, he that had power on his side had what he had a mind to, though he had no right on his side: The land was *full of violence,* as the old world was, Gen. 6:11. The prophet *cries out of violence* (*v.* 2), *iniquity* and *grievance, spoil* and *violence.* In families and among relations, in neighbourhoods and among friends, in commerce and in courts of law, every thing was carried with a high hand, and no man made any scruple of doing wrong to his neighbour, so that he could but make a good hand of it for himself. It does not appear that the prophet himself had any great wrong done him (in losing times it fared best with those that had nothing to lose), but it grieved him to see other people wronged, and he could not but mingle his tears with those of the oppressed. Note, Doing wrong to harmless people, as it is an iniquity in itself, so it is a great grievance to all that are concerned for God's Jerusalem, who *sigh and cry for abominations* of this kind. He complains (*v.* 4) that *the wicked doth compass about the righteous.* One honest man, one honest cause, shall have enemies besetting it on every side; many wicked men, in confederacy against it, run it down; nay, one wicked man (for it is singular) with so many various arts of mischief sets upon a righteous man, that he perfectly besets him. 2. That the kingdom was broken into parties and factions that were continually biting and devouring one another. This is a lamentation to all the sons of peace: *There are that raise up strife and contention* (*v.* 3), that foment divisions, widen breaches, incense men against one another, and sow discord among brethren, by doing the work of him that is the accuser of the brethren. Strifes and contentions that have been laid asleep, and begun to be forgotten, they awake, and industriously raise up again, and blow up the sparks that were hidden under the embers. And, if *blessed are the peace-makers,* cursed are such peace-breakers, that make parties, and so make mischief that spreads further, and lasts longer, than they can imagine. It is sad to see bad men warming their hands at those flames which are devouring all that is good in a nation, and stirring up the fire too. 3. That the torrent of violence and strife ran so strongly as to bid defiance to the restraints and regulations of laws and the administration of justice, *v.* 4. Because God did not appear against them, nobody else would; *therefore the law is slacked,* is silent; it breathes not; *its pulse beats not* (so, it is said, the word signifies); it intermits, *and judgment does not go forth* as it should; no cognizance is taken of those crimes, no justice done upon the criminals; nay, *wrong judgment proceeds;* if appeals be made to the courts of equity, the righteous shall be condemned and the wicked justified, so that the remedy proves the worst disease. The legislative power takes no care to supply the deficiencies of the law for the obviating of those growing threatening mischiefs; the executive power takes no care to answer the good intentions of the laws that are made; the stream of justice is dried up by violence, and has not its free course. 4. That all this was open and public, and impudently avowed; it was barefaced. The prophet complains that this iniquity was shown him; he *beheld it* which way soever he turned his eyes, nor could he look off it: *Spoiling and violence are before me.* Note, The abounding of wickedness in a nation is a very great eye-sore to good people, and, if they did not see it, they could not believe it to be so bad as it is. Solomon often complains of the vexation of this kind which he *saw under the sun;* and the prophet would therefore gladly turn hermit, that he might not see it, Jer. 9:2. But *then we must needs go out of the world,* which *there-fore* we should long to do, that we may remove to that world where holiness and love reign eternally, and no spoiling and violence shall be before us. 5. That he complained of this to God, but could not obtain a redress of those grievances: *"Lord,"* says he, *"why dost thou show me iniquity?* Why hast thou cast my lot in a time and place when and where it is to be seen, and why do I continue to *sojourn in Mesech* and *Kedar? I cry to thee* of this violence; I cry aloud; I have cried long; but *thou wilt not hear, thou wilt not save;* thou dost not take vengeance on the oppressors, nor do justice to the oppressed, as if thy arm were shortened or thy ear heavy." When God seems to connive at the wickedness of the wicked, nay, and to countenance it, by suffering them to prosper in their wickedness, it shocks the faith of good men, and proves a sore temptation to them to say, *We have cleansed our hearts in vain* (Ps. 73:13), and hardens those in their impiety who say, *God has forsaken the earth.* We must not think it strange if wickedness be suffered to prevail far and prosper long. God has reasons, and we are sure they are good reasons, both for the reprieves of bad men and the rebukes of good men; and therefore, though we plead with him, and humbly expostulate concerning his judgments, yet we must say, "He is wise, and righteous, and good, in all," and must believe the day will come, though it may be long deferred, when the cry of sin will be heard against those that do wrong and the cry of prayer for those that suffer it.

Verses 5–11

We have here an answer to the prophet's complaint, giving him assurance that, though God bore long, he would not bear always with this provoking people; for the day of vengeance was in his heart, and he must tell them so, that they might by repentance and reformation turn away the judgment they were threatened with.

I. The preamble to the sentence is very awful (*v.* 5): *Behold, you among the heathen, and regard.* Since they will not be brought to repentance by the long-suffering of God, he will take another course with them. No resentments are so keen, so deep, as those of abused patience. The Lord will inflict upon them, 1. A public punishment, which shall be beheld and regarded among the heathen, which the neighbouring nations shall take notice of and stand amazed at; see Deu. 29:24, 25. This will aggravate the desolations of Israel, that they will thereby be made a spectacle to the world. 2. An amazing punishment, so strange and surprising, and so much out of the common road of Providence, that it shall not be paralleled among the heathen, shall be sorer and heavier than what God has usually inflicted upon the nations that know him not; nay, it shall not be credited even by those that had the prediction of it from God before it comes, or the report of it from those that were eye-witnesses of it when it comes: *You will not believe it, though it be told you;* it will be thought incredible that so many judgments should combine in one, and every circumstance so strangely concur to enforce and aggravate it, that so great and potent a nation should be so reduced and broken, and that God should deal so severely with a people that had been taken into the bond of the covenant and that he had done so much for. The punishment of God's professing people cannot but be the astonishment of all about them. 3. A speedy punishment: *"I will work a work in your days,* now quickly; this generation shall not pass till the judgment threatened be accomplished. The sins of former days shall be reckoned for in your days; for now the measure of the iniquity is full," Mt. 23:36. 4. It shall be a punishment in which much of the hand of God shall appear; it shall be a work of his own working, so that all who see it shall say, *This is the Lord's doing;* and it will be found a fearful thing to fall into his hands; woe to those whom he takes to task! 5. It shall be such a punishment as will typify the destruction to be brought upon the despisers of Christ and his gospel, for to that these words are applied Acts 13:41, *Behold, you despisers, and wonder, and perish.* The ruin of Jerusalem by the Chaldeans for their idolatry was a figure of their ruin by the Romans for rejecting Christ and his gospel, and it is a very marvellous thing, and almost incredible. *Is there not a strange punishment to the workers of iniquity?*

II. The sentence itself is very dreadful and particular (*v.* 6): *Lo, I raise up the Chaldeans.* There were those that raised up a great deal of strife and contention among them, which was their sin; and now God will raise up the Chaldeans against them, who shall strive and contend with them, which shall be their punishment. Note, When God's professing people quarrel among themselves, snarl at, and devour one another, it is just with God to bring the common enemy upon them, that shall make peace by making a universal devastation. The contending parties in Jerusalem were inveterate one against another, when the Romans came and *took away their place and nation.* The Chaldeans shall be the instruments of the destruction threatened, and, though themselves acting unrighteously, they shall *execute the righteousness of the Lord* and punish the unrighteousness of Israel. Now, here we have,

1. A description of the people that shall be raised up against Israel, to be a scourge to them. (1.) They are *a bitter and hasty nation,* cruel and fierce, and what they do is done with violence and fury; they are precipitate in their counsels, vehement in their passions, and push on with resolution in their enterprises; they show no mercy and they spare no pains. Miserable is the case of those that are given up into the hand of these cruel ones. (2.) They are strong, and therefore formidable, and such as there is no standing before, and yet no fleeing from (*v.* 7): *They are terrible and dreadful,* famed for the gallant troops they bring into the field (*v.* 8); *their horses are swifter than leopards* to charge and pursue, and *more fierce* than the *evening wolves;* and wolves are observed to be the most ravenous towards the evening, after they have been kept hungry all day, waiting for that darkness under the protection of which *all the beasts of the forest creep forth,* Ps. 104:20. Their squadrons of horse shall be very numerous: *"Their horse-men shall spread themselves* a great way, for they shall *come from far,* from all parts of their own country, and shall be dispersed into all parts of the country they invade, to plunder it, and enrich themselves with the spoil of it. And, *in making speed to spoil, they shall hasten to the prey* (as those, Isa. 8:1, *margin*), for they shall *fly as the eagle* towards the earth when she *hastens to eat* and strikes at the prey she has an eye upon." (3.) Their own will is a law to them, and, in the fierceness of their pursuits, they will not be governed by any laws of humanity, equity, or honour: *Their judgment and their dignity shall proceed of themselves, v.* 7. Appetite and passion rule them, and not reason nor conscience. Their principle is, *Quicquid libet, licet — My will is my law.* And, *Sic volo, sic jubeo; stat pro ratione voluntas — This is my wish, this is my command; it shall be done because I choose it.* What favour can be hoped for from such an enemy? Note, Those who have been unjust and unmerciful, among whom *the law is slacked, and judgment doth not go forth,* will justly be paid in their own coin and fall into the hands of those who will deal unjustly and unmercifully with them.

2. A prophecy of the terrible execution that shall be made by this terrible nation: *They shall march through the breadth of the earth* (so it may be read); for in a little time the Chaldean forces subdued all the nations in those parts, so that they seemed to have conquered the world; they overran Asia and part of Africa. Or, through the breadth of *the land* of Israel, which was wholly laid waste by them. It is here foretold, (1.) That they shall seize all as their own that they can lay their hands on. They shall come to *possess the dwelling-places that are not theirs,* which they have no right to, but that which their sword gives them. (2.) That they shall push on the war with all possible vigour: *They shall all come for violence* (*v.* 9), not to determine any disputed right by the sword, but, right or wrong, to enrich themselves with the spoil. *Their faces shall sup up as the east wind;* their very countenances shall be so fierce and frightful that a look will serve to make them masters of all they have a mind to; so that they shall *swallow up* all, as the east wind nips and blasts the buds and flowers. *Their faces shall look towards the east* (so some read it); they shall still have an eye to their own country, which lay eastward from Judea, and all the spoil they seize they shall remit thither. (3.) That they shall take a vast number of prisoners, and send them into Babylon: *They shall gather the captivity as the sand* for multitude, and shall never know when they have enough, as long as there are any more to be had. (4.) That they shall make nothing of the opposition that is given to them, *v.* 10. Do the distressed Jews depend upon their great men to make a stand, and with their wisdom and courage to give check to the victorious arms of the Chaldeans? Alas! they will make nothing of them. *They shall scoff* (he shall, so it is in the original, meaning Nebuchadnezzar, who being puffed up with his successes, shall scoff) *at the kings* and commanders of the forces that think to make head against him; and *the princes shall be a scorn to them,* so unequal a match shall they appear to be. Do they depend upon their garrisons and fortified towns? *He shall deride every stronghold,* for to him it shall be weak, and *he shall heap dust, and take it;* a little soil, thrown up for ramparts, shall serve to give him all the advantage against them that he can desire; he shall make but a jest of them, and a sport of taking them. (5.) By all this he shall be puffed up with an intolerable pride, which shall be his destruction (*v.* 11): *Then shall his mind change* for the worse. The spirit both of the people and of the king shall grow more haughty and insolent. Those that will not be content with their own rights will not be content when they have made themselves masters of other people's rights too; but as the condition rises the mind rises too. This victorious king shall *pass over* all the bounds of reason, equity, and modesty, and break through all their bonds, and thereby *he shall offend,* shall make God his enemy, and so prepare ruin for himself by *imputing this his power to his god,* whereas he had it from the God of Israel. *Bel* and *Nebo* were the gods of the Chaldeans, and to them they gave the glory of their successes; they were hardened in their idolatry, and blasphemously argued that because they had conquered Israel their gods were too strong for the God of Israel. Note, It is a great offence (and the common offence of proud people) to take that glory to ourselves, or to give it to gods of our own making, which is due to the living and true God only. These closing words of the sentence give a glimpse of comfort to the afflicted people of God; it is to be hoped that they will change their minds, and grow better, and ripen for deliverance; and they did so. However, their enemies will change their minds, and grow worse, and ripen for destruction, which will inevitably come in God's due time; for a haughty spirit, lifted up against God, *goes before a fall.*

Verses 12–17

The prophet, having received of the Lord that which he was to deliver to the people, now turns to God, and again addresses himself to him for the ease of his own mind under the burden which he saw. And still he is full of complaints. If he look about him, he sees nothing but violence done by Israel; if he look before him, he sees nothing but violence done against Israel; and it is hard to say which is the more melancholy sight. His thoughts of both he pours out before the Lord. It is our duty to be affected both with the iniquities and with the calamities of the church of God and of the times and places wherein we live; but we must take heed lest we grow peevish in our resentments, and carry them too far, so as to entertain any hard thoughts of God, or lose the comfort of our communion with him. The world is bad, and always was so, and will be so; it is out of our power to mend it; but we are sure that God governs the world, and will bring glory to himself out of all, and therefore we must resolve to make the best of it, must be ourselves better, and long for the better world. The prospect of the prevalence of the Chaldeans drives the prophet to his knees, and he takes the liberty to plead with God concerning it. In his plea we may observe,

I. The truths which he lays down, which he resolves to abide by, and with which he endeavours to comfort himself and his friends, under the growing threatening power of the Chaldeans; and they will furnish us with pleasing considerations for our support in the like case.

1. However it be, yet God is *the Lord our God,* and *our Holy One.* The victorious Chaldeans impute their power to their idols, but we are taught to tell them that the *God of Israel is the true God, the living God,* Jer. 10:10, 11. (1.) He is *Jehovah,* the fountain of all being, power, and perfection. *Our rock* is not *as theirs.* (2.) "He is *my God.*" He speaks in the people's name; every Israelite may say, "He is *mine.* Though we are thus sore broken, and *all this has come upon us, yet have we not forgotten the name of our God,* nor quitted our relation to him, yet have we not disowned him, nor hath he disowned us, Ps. 44:17. We are an offending people; he is an offended God; yet he is ours, and we will not entertain any hard thoughts of him, nor of his service, for all this." (3.) "He is *my Holy One.*" This intimates that the prophet loved God as a holy God, loved him for the sake of his holiness. "He is *mine* because he is a *Holy One;* and *therefore* he will be my sanctifier and my Saviour, because he is *my Holy One.* Men are unholy, but *my God is holy.*"

2. Our God is from everlasting. This he pleads with him: *Art thou not from everlasting, O Lord my God?* It is matter of great and continual comfort to God's people, under the troubles of this present life, that their God is from everlasting. This intimates, (1.) The eternity of his nature; if he is from everlasting, he will be to everlasting, and we must have recourse to this first principle, when things seen, which are temporal, are discouraging, that we have hope and help sufficient in a god that is not seen, that is eternal. "Art thou not from everlasting, and then wilt thou not make bare thy everlasting arm, in pursuance of thy everlasting counsels, to make unto thyself an everlasting name?" (2.) The antiquity of his covenant: "Art thou not *from of old,* a God in covenant with thy people" (so some understand it), "and hast thou not done great things for them *in the days of old,* which we have heard with our ears, and which our fathers have told us of; and art thou not the same God still that thou ever wast? Thou art *God, and changest not.*"

3. While the world stands God will have a church in it. Thou art from everlasting, and then *we shall not die.* The Israel of God shall not be extirpated, nor the name of Israel blotted out, though it may sometimes seem to be very near it; like the apostles (2 Co. 6:9), *chastened, and not killed; chastened sorely, but not delivered over to death,* Ps. 118:18. See how the prophet infers the perpetuity of the church from the eternity of God; for Christ has said, *Because I live,* and therefore as long as I live, *you shall live also,* Jn. 14:19. He is the rock on which the church is so firmly built that the *gates of hell shall not, cannot, prevail against it. We shall not die.*

4. Whatever the enemies of the church may do against her, it is according to the counsel of God, and is designed and directed for wise and holy ends: *Thou hast ordained them; thou hast established them.* It was God that gave the Chaldeans their power, made them a formidable people, and in his counsel determined what they should do, nor had they any power against his Israel but what was *given them from above.* He gave them their commission *to take the spoil and to take the prey,* Isa. 10:6. Herein God appears a mighty God, that the power of mighty men is derived from him, depends upon him, and is under his check; he says concerning it, *Hitherto shall it come, and no further.* Those whom God ordains shall do no more than what God has ordained, which is a great comfort to God's suffering people. Men are God's hand, the rod in his hand, Ps. 17:14. And he has *ordained them for judgment,* and *for correction.* God's people need correction, and deserve it; they must expect it; they shall have it; when wicked men are let loose against them, it is not for their destruction, that they may be ruined, but for their correction, that they may be reformed; they are not intended for a sword, to cut them off, but for a rod, to drive out the foolishness that is found in their hearts, though they *mean not so, neither does their heart think so,* Isa. 10:7. Note, It is matter of great comfort to us, in reference to the troubles and afflictions of the church, that, whatever mischief men design to them, God designs to bring good out of them, and we are sure that *his counsel shall stand.*

5. Though the wickedness of the wicked may prosper for a while, yet God is a holy God, and does not approve of that wickedness (*v.* 13): *Thou art of purer eyes than to behold evil.* The prophet, observing how very vicious and impious the Chaldeans were, and yet what great success they had against God's Israel, found a temptation arising from it to say that it was vain to serve God, and that it was indifferent to him what men were. But he soon suppresses the thought, by having recourse to his first principle, That God is not, that he cannot be, the author or patron of sin; as he cannot do iniquity himself, so he is *of purer eyes than to behold it* with any allowance or approbation; no, it is that *abominable thing which the Lord hates.* He sees all the sin that is committed in the world, and it is an offence to him, it is odious in his eyes, and those that commit it are thereby made obnoxious to his justice. There is in the nature of God an antipathy to those dispositions and practices that are contrary to his holy law; and, though an expedient is happily found out for his being

reconciled to sinners, yet he never will, nor can, be reconciled to sin. And this principle we must resolve to abide by, though the dispensations of his providence may for a time, and in some instances, seem to be inconsistent with it. Note, God's connivance at sin must never be interpreted into a giving countenance to it; for *he is not a God that has pleasure in wickedness,* Ps. 5:4, 5. The iniquity which, it is here said, God does not look upon, may be meant especially of the mischief done to God's people by their persecutors; though God sees cause to permit it, yet he does not approve of it; so it agrees with that of Balaam (Num. 23:21), *He has not beheld iniquity against Jacob,* nor *seen,* with allowance, *perverseness against Israel,* which is very comfortable to the people of God, in their afflictions by the rage of men, that they cannot infer God's anger from it; though the instruments of their trouble hate them, it does not therefore follow that God does; nay, he loves them, and it is in love that he corrects them.

II. The grievances he complains of, and finds hard to reconcile with these truths: "Since we are sure that thou art a holy God, why have atheists temptation given them to question whether thou art so or no? *Wherefore lookest thou upon the Chaldeans* that *deal treacherously* with thy people, and givest them success in their attempts upon us? Why dost thou suffer thy sworn enemies, who blaspheme thy name, to deal thus cruelly, thus perfidiously, with thy sworn subjects, who desire to fear thy name? What shall we say to this?" This was a temptation to Job (*ch.* 21:7; 24:1), to David (Ps. 73:2, 3), to Jeremiah, *ch.* 12:1, 2. 1. That God permitted sin, and was patient with the sinners. He *looked upon them;* he saw all their wicked doings and designs, and did not restrain nor punish them, but suffered them to speed in their purposes, to go on and prosper, and to carry all before them. Nay, his looking upon them intimates that he not only gave them no check or rebuke, but that he gave them encouragement and assistance, as if he smiled upon them and favoured them. He *held his tongue* when they went on in their wicked courses, said nothing against them, gave no orders to stop them. *These things thou hast done, and I kept silence.* 2. That his patience was abused, and, *because sentence* against these evil works and workers *was not executed speedily,* therefore *their hearts* were the more *fully set in them to do evil.* (1.) They were false and deceitful, and there was no credit to be given them, nor any confidence to be put in them. They deal *treacherously;* under colour of peace and friendship, they prosecute and execute the most mischievous designs, and make no conscience of their word in any thing. (2.) They hated and persecuted men because they were better than themselves, as Cain hated Abel because *his own works were evil and his brother's righteous. The wicked devours the man that is more righteous than he,* for that very reason, because he shames him; they have an ill will to the image of God, and *therefore* devour good men, because they bear that image. Though many of the Jews were as bad as the Chaldeans themselves, and worse, yet there were those among them that were much more righteous, and yet were devoured by them. (3.) They made no more of killing men that of catching fish. The prophet complains that, Providence having delivered up the weaker to be prey to the stronger, they were, in effect, made as *the fishes of the sea, v.* 14. So they had been among themselves, preying upon one another as the greater fishes do upon the less (*v.* 3), and they were made so to the common enemy. They were *as the creeping things,* or *swimming* things (for the word is used for *fish,* Gen. 1:20), *that have no ruler* over them, either to restrain them from devouring one another or to protect them from being devoured by their enemies. They are given up to the Chaldeans as fish to the fishermen. Those proud oppressors make no conscience of killing them, any more than men do of pulling fish out of the water, so small account do they make of human lives. They make no difficulty of killing them, but do it with as much ease as men catch fish, that make no resistance, but are unguarded and unarmed, and it is rather a pastime than any pains to take them. They make no distinction among them, but all is fish that comes to their net; and they reckon every thing their own that they can lay their hands on. They have various ways of spoiling and destroying, as men have of taking fish. Some they *take up with the angle* (*v.* 15), one by one; others *they catch* in shoals, and by wholesale, *in their net,* and *gather them in their drag,* their enclosing net. Such variety of methods have they to destroy those by whom they hope to enrich themselves. (4.) They gloried in what they got, and pleased themselves with it, though it was got dishonestly: *Their portion is fat, and their meat plenteous;* they prosper in their oppression and fraud; they have a great deal, and it is of the best; their land is good, and they have abundance of it. And therefore, [1.] They have great complacency in themselves, and are very pleasant; they live merrily (*v.* 15): *Therefore they rejoice and are glad,* because their wealth is great, and their projects succeed for the increase of it, Job 31:25. *Soul, take thy ease,* Lu. 12:19. [2.] They have a great conceit of themselves, and are great admirers of their own ingenuity and management: They *sacrifice to their own net, and burn incense to their own drag;* they applaud themselves for having got so much money, though ever so dishonestly. Note, There is a proneness in us to take the glory of our outward prosperity to ourselves, and to say, *My might, and the power of my hands, have gotten me this wealth,* Deu. 8:17. This is idolizing ourselves, sacrificing to the dragnet, because it is our own, which is as absurd a piece of idolatry as sacrificing to Neptune or Dagon. That which makes them adore their net thus is because by it *their portion is fat.* Those that make a god of their money will make a god of their drag-net, if they can but get money by it.

III. The prophet, in the close, humbly expresses his hope that God will not suffer these destroyers of mankind always to go on and prosper thus, and expostulates with God concerning it (*v.* 17): *"Shall they therefore empty their net?* Shall they enrich themselves, and fill their own vessels, with that which they have by violence and oppression taken away from their neighbours? Shall they empty their net of what they have caught, that they may cast it into the sea again, to catch more? And wilt thou suffer them to proceed in this wicked course? Shall they not *spare continually to slay the nations?* Must the numbers and wealth of nations be sacrificed to their net? As if it were a small thing to rob men of their estates, shall they rob God of his glory? Is not God the king of nations, and will he not assert their injured rights? Is he not jealous for his own honour, and will he not maintain that?" The prophet lodges the matter in God's hand, and leaves it with him, as the psalmist does. Ps. 74:22, *Arise, O God! Plead thy own cause.*

CHAPTER 2

In this chapter we have an answer expected by the prophet (*v.* 1), and returned by the Spirit of God, to the complaints which the prophet made of the violences and victories of the Chaldeans in the close of the foregoing chapter. The answer is, I. That after God has served his own purposes by the prevailing power of the Chaldeans, has tried the faith and patience of his people, and distinguished between the hypocrites and the sincere among them, he will reckon with the Chaldeans, will humble and bring down, not only that proud monarch Nebuchadnezzar, but that proud monarchy, for their boundless and insatiable thirst after dominion and wealth, for which they themselves should at length be made a prey (*v.* 2–8). II. That not they only, but all other sinners like them, should perish under a divine woe. 1. Those that are covetous, are greedy of wealth and honours (*v.* 9, 11). 2. Those that are injurious and oppressive, and raise estates by wrong and rapine (*v.* 12–14). 3. Those that promote drunkenness that they may expose their neighbours to shame (*v.* 15–17). 4. Those that worship idols (*v.* 18–20).

Verses 1–4

Here, I. The prophet humbly gives his attendance upon God (*v.* 1): *"I will stand upon my watch,* as a sentinel on the walls of a besieged city, or on the borders of an invaded country, that is very solicitous to gain intelligence. I will look up, will look round, will look within, *and watch to see what he will say unto me,* will listen attentively to the words of his mouth and carefully observe the steps of his providence, that I may not lose the least hint of instruction or direction. *I will watch to see what he will say in me"* (so it may be read), "what the Spirit of prophecy in me will dictate to me, by way of answer to my complaints." Even in a ordinary way, God not only speaks to us by his word, but speaks in us by our own consciences, whispering to us, *This is the way, walk in it;* and we must attend to the voice of God in both. The prophet's standing upon his *tower,* or high place, intimates his prudence, in making use of the helps and means he had within his reach to know the mind of God, and to be instructed concerning it. Those that expect to hear from God must withdraw from the world, and get above it, must raise their attention, fix their thought, study the scriptures, consult experiences and the experienced, continue instant in prayer, and thus set themselves *upon the tower.* His standing upon his watch intimates his patience, his constancy and resolution; he will wait the time, and weather the point, as a watchman does, but he will have an answer; he will know what God will *say to him,* not only for his own satisfaction, but to enable him as a prophet to give satisfaction to others, and answer their exceptions, when he is reproved or argued with. Herein the prophet is an example to us. 1. When we are tossed and perplexed with doubts concerning the methods of Providence, are tempted to think that it is fate, or fortune, and not a wise God, that governs the world, or that the church is abandoned, and God's covenant with his people cancelled and laid aside, then we must take pains to furnish ourselves with considerations proper to clear this matter; we must stand upon our watch against the temptation, that it may not get ground upon us, must set ourselves upon the tower, to see if we can discover that which will silence the temptation and solve the objected difficulties, must do as the psalmist, *consider the days of old* and make *a diligent search* (Ps. 77:6), must go into the sanctuary of God, and there labour to understand the end of these things (Ps. 73:17); we must not give way to our doubts, but struggle to make the best of our way out of them. 2. When we have been at prayer, pouring out our complaints and requests before God, we must carefully observe what answers God gives by his word, his Spirit, and his providences, to our humble representations; when David says, *I will direct my prayer unto thee,* as an arrow to the mark, he adds, *I will look up,* will look after my prayer, as a man does after the arrow he has shot, Ps. 5:3. We must *hear what God the Lord will speak,* Ps. 85:8. 3. When we go to read and hear the word of God, and so to consult the lively oracles, we must set ourselves to observe what God will thereby *say unto us,* to suit our case, what word of conviction, caution, counsel, and comfort, he will bring to our souls, that we may receive it, and submit to the power of it, and may consider what we shall answer, what returns we shall make to the word of God, when we are reproved by it. 4. When we are attacked by such as quarrel with God and his providence as the prophet here seems to have been — beset, besieged, as in a tower, by hosts of objectors — we should consider how to answer them, fetch our instructions from God, hear what he says to us for our satisfaction, and have that ready to say to others, *when we are reproved,* to satisfy them, as a *reason of the hope that is in us* (1 Pt. 3:15), and beg of God *a mouth and wisdom,* and that it may be *given us in that same hour what we shall speak.*

II. God graciously gives him the meeting; for he will not disappoint the believing expectations of his people that wait to hear what he will say unto them, but will *speak peace,* will *answer them with good words and comfortable words,* Zec. 1:13. The prophet had complained of the prevalence of the Chaldeans, which God had given him a prospect of; now, to pacify him concerning it, he here gives him a further prospect of their fall and ruin, as Isaiah, before this, when he had foretold the captivity in Babylon, foretold also the destruction of Babylon. Now, this great and important event being made known to him by a vision, care is taken to publish the vision, and transmit it to the generations to come, who should see the accomplishment of it.

1. The prophet must *write the vision, v.* 2. Thus, when St. John had a vision of the New Jerusalem, he was ordered to *write,* Rev. 21:5. He must write it, that he might imprint it on his own mind, and make it more clear to himself, but especially that it might be notified to those in distant places and transmitted to those in future ages. What is handed down by tradition is easily mistaken and liable to corruption; but what is written is reduced to a certainty, and preserved safe and pure. We have reason to bless God for written visions, that God has written to us the great things of his prophets as well as of his law. He must *write the vision,* and *make it plain upon tables,* must write it legibly, in large characters, so that *he who runs may read it,* that those who will not allow themselves leisure to read it deliberately may not avoid a *cursory* view of it. Probably, the prophets were wont to write some of the most remarkable of their predictions in tables, and to hang them up in the temple, Isa. 8:1. Now the prophet is told to *write this* very *plain.* Note, Those who are employed in preach-

ing the word of God should study plainness as much as may be, so as to make themselves intelligible to the meanest capacities. The things of our everlasting peace, which God has written to us, are made plain, *they are all plain to him that understands* (Prov. 8:9), and they are published with authority; God himself has prefixed his *imprimatur* to them; he has said, *Make them plain.*

2. The people must wait for the accomplishment of the *vision* (v. 3): "*The vision is yet for an appointed time* to come. You shall now be told of your deliverance by the breaking of the Chaldeans' power, and that the time of it is fixed in the counsel and decree of God. *There is an appointed time,* but it is not near; it is yet to be deferred a great while;" and that comes in here as a reason why it must be written, that it may be reviewed afterwards and the event compared with it. Note, God has an appointed time for his appointed work, and will be sure to do the work when the time comes; it is not for us to anticipate his appointments, but to wait his time. And it is a great encouragement to wait with patience, that, though the promised favour be deferred long, it will come at last, and be an abundant recompence to us for our waiting: *At the end it shall speak and not lie.* We shall not be disappointed of it, for it will come at the time appointed; nor shall we be disappointed in it, for it will fully answer our believing expectations. The promise may seem silent a great while, but at the end it shall speak; and therefore, *though it tarry* longer than we expected, yet we must continue *waiting for it,* being assured it will come, and willing to tarry until it does come. The day that God has set for the deliverance of his people, and the destruction of his and their enemies, is a day, (1.) That will surely come at last; it is never adjourned *sine die* — *without fixing another day,* but it will without fail come at the fixed time and the fittest time. (2.) It *will not tarry,* for God is *not slack, as some count slackness* (2 Pt. 3:9);* though it tarry* past our time, yet *it does not tarry* past God's time, which is always the best time.

3. This vision, the accomplishment of which is so long waited for, will be such an exercise of faith and patience as will try and discover men what they are, v. 4. (1.) There are some who will proudly disdain this vision, whose hearts are so lifted up that they scorn to take notice of it; if God will work for them immediately, they will thank him, but they will not give him credit; their hearts are lifted up towards vanity, and, since God puts them off, they will shift for themselves and not be beholden to him; they think *their own hands sufficient for them,* and God's promise is to them an insignificant thing. That man's soul that is thus *lifted up is not upright in him;* it is not right with God, is not as it should be. Those that either distrust or despise God's all-sufficiency will not walk uprightly with him, Gen. 17:1. But, (2.) Those who are truly good, and whose hearts are upright with God, will value the promise, and venture their all upon it; and, in confidence of the truth of it, will keep close to God and duty in the most difficult trying times, and will then live comfortably in communion with God, dependence on him, and expectation of him. *The just shall live by faith;* during the captivity good people shall support themselves, and live comfortably, by faith in these precious promises, while the performance of them is deferred. *The just shall live by his faith,* by that faith which he acts upon the word of God. This is quoted in the New Testament (Rom. 1:17; Gal. 3:11; Heb. 10:38), for the proof of the great doctrine of justification by faith only and of the influence which the grace of faith has upon the Christian life. Those that are made *just by faith shall live,* shall be happy here and for ever; while they are here, they live by it; when they come to heaven faith shall be swallowed up in vision.

Verses 5–14

The prophet having had orders to *write the vision,* and the people to wait for the accomplishment of it, the vision itself follows; and it is, as divers other prophecies we have met with, the burden of Babylon and Babylon's king, the same that was said to *pass over* and *offend,* ch. 1:11. It reads the doom, some think, of Nebuchadnezzar, who was principally active in the destruction of Jerusalem, or of that monarchy, or of the whole kingdom of the Chaldeans, or of all such proud and oppressive powers as bear hard upon any people, especially upon God's people. Observe,

I. The charge laid down against this enemy, upon which the sentence is grounded, v. 5. The *lusts of the flesh, the lusts of the eye,* and *the pride of life,* are the entangling snares of men, and great men especially; and we find him that led Israel captive himself led captive by each of these. For, 1. He is sensual and voluptuous, and given to his pleasures: *He transgresses by wine.* Drunkenness is itself a transgression, and is the cause of abundance of transgression. We read of those that *err through wine,* Isa. 28:7. Belshazzar (in whom particularly this prophecy had its accomplishment) was in the height of his transgression by wine when the hand-writing upon the wall signed the warrant for his immediate execution, pursuant to this sentence, Dan. 5:1. 2. He is haughty and imperious: *He is a proud man,* and his pride is a certain presage of his fall coming on. If great men be proud men, the great God will make them know he is above them. His transgressing by wine is made the cause of his arrogance and insolence: therefore *he is a proud man.* When a man is drunk, though he makes himself as mean as a beast, yet he thinks himself as great as a king, and prides himself in that by which he shames himself. We find *the crown of pride* upon the head of the *drunkards of Ephraim,* and a *woe* to both, Isa. 28:1. 3. He is covetous and greedy of wealth, and this is the effect of his pride; he thinks himself worthy to enjoy all, and therefore makes it his business to engross all. The Chaldean monarchy aimed to be a universal one. He *keeps not at home,* is not content with his own, which he has an incontestable title to, but thinks it too little, and so enjoys it not, nor takes the comfort he might in his own palace, in his own dominion. His sin is his punishment, his ambition is his perpetual uneasiness. Though the home be a palace, yet to a discontented mind it is a prison. He *enlarges his desire as hell,* or *the grave,* which daily receives the body of the dead, and yet still cries, *Give, give;* he is *as death,* which continues to devour, and *cannot be satisfied.* Note, It is the sin and folly of many who have a great deal of the wealth of this world that they do not know when they have enough, but the more they have the more they would have, and the more eager they are for it. And it is just with God that the desires which are insatiable should still be unsatisfied; it is the doom passed on those that *love silver* that they shall never be *satisfied with it,* Eccl. 5:10. Those that will not be content with their allotments shall not have the comfort of their achievements. This proud prince is still *gathering to him all nations, and heaping to him all people,* invading their rights, seizing their properties, and they must not be unless they will be his, and under his command. One nation will not satisfy him unless he has another, and then another, and all at last; as those in a lower sphere, to gratify the same inordinate desire, lay *house to house, and field to field, that they may be placed alone in the earth,* Isa. 5:8. And it is hard to say which is more to be pitied, the folly of such ambitious princes as place their honour in enlarging their dominions, and not in ruling them well, or the misery of those nations that are harassed and pulled to pieces by them.

II. The sentence passed upon him (v. 6): *Shall not all these take up a parable against him?* His doom is,

1. That, since pride has been his sin, disgrace and dishonour shall be his punishment, and he shall be loaded with contempt, shall be laughed at and despised by all about him, as those that look big, and aim high, deserve to be, and commonly are, when they are brought down and baffled.

2. That, since he has been abusive to his neighbours, those very persons whom he has abused shall be the instruments of his disgrace: *All those shall take up a taunting proverb against him.* They shall have the pleasure of insulting over him and he the shame of being trampled upon by them. Those that shall triumph in the fall of this great tyrant are here furnished with a *parable,* and a *taunting proverb,* to take up against him. *He shall say* (he that draws up the insulting ditty shall say thus), *Ho, he that increases that which is not his! Aha!* what has become of him now? So it may be read in a taunting way. Or, *He shall say,* that is, *the just,* who *lives by his faith,* he to whom the vision is written and made plain, with the help of that shall say this, shall foretel the enemy's fall, even when he sees him flourishing, and *suddenly curse his habitation,*

even when he is *taking root,* Job 5:3. He shall indeed denounce woes against him.

(1.) Here is a woe against him for increasing his own possessions by invading his neighbour's rights, v. 6–8. He *increases that which is not his,* but other people's. Note, No more of what we have is to be reckoned ours than what we came honestly by; nor will it long be ours, for *wealth gotten by vanity will be diminished.* Let not those that thrive in the world be too forward to bless themselves in it, for, if they do not thrive lawfully, they are under a woe. See here, [1.] What this prosperous prince is doing; he is *lading himself with thick clay.* Riches are but clay, thick clay; what are gold and silver but white and yellow earth? Those that travel through thick clay are both retarded and dirtied in their journey; so are those that go through the world in the midst of an abundance of the wealth of it; but, as if that were not enough, what fools are those that *load themselves with it,* as if this trash would be their treasure! They burden themselves with continual care about it, with a great deal of guilt in getting, saving, and spending it, and with a heavy account which they must give of it another day. They overload their ship with this thick clay, and so sink it and themselves *into destruction and perdition.* [2.] See what people say of him, while he is thus increasing his wealth; they cry, "*How long? How long will it be ere he has enough?*" They cry to God, "How long wilt thou suffer this proud oppressor to trouble the nations?" Or they say to one another, "See how long it will last, how long he will be able to keep what he gets thus dishonestly." They dare not speak out, but we know what they mean when they say, *How long?* [3.] See what will be in the end hereof. What he has got by violence from others, others shall take by violence from him. The Medes and Persians shall make a prey of the Chaldeans, as they have done of other nations, v. 7, 8. "There shall be those that will *bite thee* and *vex thee;* those from whom thou didst not fear any danger, that seemed *asleep,* shall *rise up* and *awake* to be a plague to thee. They shall rise up *suddenly* when thou are most secure, and least prepared to receive the shock and ward off the blow. *Shall they not rise up suddenly?* No doubt they shall, and thou thyself hast reason to expect it, to be dealt with as thou hast dealt with others, that *thou shalt be for booties unto them,* as others have been unto thee, that, according to the law of retaliation, as *thou hast spoiled many nations* so thou shalt thyself be *spoiled* (v. 8); *all the remnant of the people shall spoil thee.*" The king of Babylon thought he had brought all the nations round about him so low that none of them would be able to make reprisals upon him; but though they were but a remnant of people, a very few left, yet these shall be sufficient to spoil him, when God has such a controversy with him, *First,* For *men's blood,* and the thousands of lives that have been sacrificed to his ambition and revenge, especially for the blood of Israelites, which is in a special manner precious to God. *Secondly,* For *the violence of the land,* his laying waste so many countries, and destroying the fruits of the earth, especially in the land of Israel. *Thirdly,* For the violence *of the city,* the many cities that he had turned into ruinous heaps, especially Jerusalem the holy city, and of *all that dwelt therein,* who were ruined by him. Note, The violence done by proud men to advance and enrich themselves will be called over again (and must be accounted for) another day, by him *to whom vengeance belongs.*

(2.) Here is a woe against him for coveting still more, and aiming to be still higher, v. 9–11. The crime for which this woe is denounced is much the same with that in the foregoing article — an insatiable desire of wealth and honour; it is *coveting an evil covetousness to his house,* that is, grasping at an abundance for his family. Note, Covetousness is a very evil thing in a family; it brings disquiet and uneasiness into it *(he that is greedy of gain troubles his own house),* and, which is worse, it brings the curse of God upon it and upon all the affairs of it. *Woe to him that gains an evil gain;* so the margin reads it. There is a lawful gain, which by the blessing of God may be a comfort to a house *(a good man leaves an inheritance to his children's children),* but what is got by fraud and injustice is ill-got, and will be poor gain, will not only do no good to a family, but will bring poverty and ruin upon it. Now observe, [1.] What this covetous wretch aims at; it is *to set his nest on high,* to raise his family to some greater dignity than it had before arrived at, or to set it, as he apprehends, out of the reach of danger, that he may be *delivered from the power of evil*, that it may not be in the power of the worst of his enemies to do him a mischief nor so much as to disturb his repose. Note, It is common for men to pretend it as an excuse for their covetousness and ambition that they only consult their own safety, and aim to secure themselves; and yet they do but deceive themselves when they think *their wealth* will be a *strong city* to them, *and a high wall*, for it is so only in *their own conceit*, Prov. 18:11. [2.] What he will get by it: *Thou hast consulted*, not safety, but *shame, to thy house, by cutting off many people, v.* 10. Note, An estate raised by iniquity is a scandal to a family. Those that cut off, or undermine, others, to make room for themselves, that impoverish others to enrich themselves, do but consult shame to their houses, and fasten upon them a mark of infamy. Yet that is not the worst of it: *"Thou hast sinned against thy own soul*, hast brought that under guilt and wrath, and endangered that." Note, Those that do wrong to their neighbour do a much greater wrong to their own souls. But if the sinner pleads, Not guilty, and thinks he has managed his frauds and violence with so much art and contrivance that they cannot be proved upon him, let him know that if there be no other witnesses against him *the stone shall cry out of the wall* against him, and *the beam out of the timber* in the roof *shall answer it*, shall second it, shall witness it, that the money and materials wherewith he built the house were unjustly gotten, *v.* 11. The stones and timber cry to heaven for vengeance, as *the whole creation groans under* the sin of man and waits to be delivered from that *bondage of corruption.*

(3.) Here is a woe against him for building a town and a city by blood and extortion (*v.* 12): He *builds a town*, and is him-self lord of it; he *establishes a city*, and makes it his royal seat. So Nebuchadnezzar did (Dan. 4:30): *Is not this great Babylon that I have built for the house of the kingdom?* But it is built with the blood of his own subjects, whom he has oppressed, and the blood of his neighbours, whom he has unjustly invaded; it is *established by iniquity*, by the unrighteous laws that are made for the security of it. *Woe* to him that does so; for the towns and cities thus built can never be established; they will fall, and their founders be buried in the ruins of them. Babylon, which was built by blood and iniquity, did not continue long; its day soon came to fall; and then this woe took effect, when that prophecy, which is expressed as a history (Isa. 21:9), proved a history indeed: *Babylon has fallen, has fallen!* And the destruction of that city was, [1.] The shame of the Chaldeans, who had taken so much pains, and were at such a vast expense, to fortify it (*v.* 13): *Is it not of the Lord of hosts that the people* who have laboured so hard to defend that city shall *labour in the very fire*, shall see the out-works which they confided in the strength of set on fire, and shall labour in vain to save them? Or they, in their pursuits of worldly wealth and honour, put themselves to great fatigue, and ran a great hazard, as those that *labour in the fire* do. The worst that can be said of the labourers in God's vineyards is that *they have borne the burden and heat of the day* (Mt. 20:12); but those that are eager in their worldly pursuits *labour in the very fire*, make themselves perfect slaves to their lusts. There is not a greater drudge in the world than he that is under the power of reigning covetousness. And what comes of it? Though they take a world of pains they are but poorly paid for it; for, after all, *they weary themselves for very vanity;* they were told it was vanity, and when they find themselves disappointed of it, and disappointed in it, they will own it is worse than vanity, it is *vexation of spirit*. [2.] It was the honour of God, as a God of impartial justice and irresistible power; for by the ruin of the Chaldean monarchy (which all the world could not but take notice of) *the earth was filled with the knowledge of the glory of the Lord, v.* 14. *The Lord is known by* these *judgments which he executes*, especially when he is pleased to *look upon proud men and abase them*, for he thereby proves himself to be *God alone*, Job 40:11, 12. See what good God brings out of the staining and sinking of earthly glory; he thereby manifests and magnifies his own glory, and *fills the earth* with the knowledge of it as plentifully as the *waters cover the sea*, which lie deep, spread far, and shall not be dried up until time shall be no more. Such is the *knowledge of the glory of*

God *in the face of Jesus Christ* given by the gospel (2 Co. 4:6), and such was the knowledge of his glory by the miraculous ruin of Babylon. Note, Such as will not be taught the knowledge of God's glory by the judgments of his mouth shall be made to know and acknowledge it by the judgments of his hand.

Verses 15–20

The three foregoing articles, upon which the woes here are grounded, are very near akin to each other. The criminals charged by them are oppressors and extortioners, that raise estates by rapine and injustice; and it is mentioned here again (*v.* 17), the very same that was said *v.* 8, for that is the crime upon which the greatest stress is laid; it is *because of men's blood*, innocent blood, barbarously and unjustly shed, which is a provoking crying thing; it is *for the violence of the land, of the city, and of all that dwell therein*, which God will certainly reckon for, sooner or later, as the asserter of right and the avenger of wrong.

But here are two articles more, of a different nature, which carry a *woe* to all those in general to whom they belong, and particularly to the Babylonian monarchs, by whom the people of God were taken and held captives.

I. The promoters of drunkenness stand here impeached and condemned. Belshazzar was one of those; he was so, remarkably that very night that the prophecy of this chapter was fulfilled in the period of his life and kingdom, when he *drank wine before a thousand* of his lords (Dan. 5:1), began the healths, and forced them to pledge him. And perhaps it was one reason why the succeeding monarchs of Persia made it a law of their kingdom that *in drinking none should compel*, but *they should do according to every man's pleasure* (as we find, Esth. 1:8), because they had seen in the kings of Babylon the mischievous consequences of forcing healths and making people drunk. But the woe here stands firm and very fearful against all those, whoever they are, who are guilty of this sin at any time, and in any place, from the stately palace (where that was) to the paltry ale-house. Observe,

1. Who the sinner is that is here articled against; it is he that *makes his neighbour drunk, v.* 15. To give a neighbour drink who is in want, who is thirsty and poor, though it be but a cup of cold water to a disciple, in the name of a disciple, to give drink to weary traveller, nay, and to give strong drink to him that is ready to perish, and wine to those that are heavy of heart, is a piece of charity which is required of us, and shall be recompensed to us. *I was thirsty, and you gave me drink*. But to give a neighbour drink who has enough already, and more than enough, with design to intoxicate him, that he may expose himself, may talk foolishly, and make himself ridiculous, may disclose his own secret concerns, or be drawn in to agree to a bad bargain for himself — this is abominable wickedness; and those who are guilty of it, who make a practice of it, and take a pride and pleasure in it, are rebels against God in heaven, and his sacred laws, factors for the devil in hell, and his cursed interests, and enemies to men on earth, and their honour and welfare; they are like the son of Nebat, who *sinned and made Israel to sin*. To entice others to drunkenness, to *put the bottle to them*, that they may be allured to it by its charms, by *looking on the wine when it is red and gives its colour in the cup*, or to force them to it, obliging them by the rules of the club (and club-laws indeed they are) to drink so many glasses, and so filled, is to do what we can, and perhaps more than we know of, towards the murder both of soul and body; and those that do so have a great deal to answer for.

2. What the sentence is that is here passed upon him. There is a woe to him (*v.* 15), and a punishment (*v.* 16) that shall answer to the sin. (1.) Does he put the cup of drunkenness into the hand of his neighbour? The cup of fury, the cup of trembling, the *cup of the Lord's right hand*, shall be *turned unto him;* the power of God shall be armed against him. That cup which had gone round among the nations, to make them *a desolation, an astonishment, and a hissing*, which had made them stumble and *fall*, so that they could *rise no more*, shall at length be put into the hand of the king of Babylon, as was foretold, Jer. 25:15, 16, 18, 26, 27. Thus the New-Testament Babylon, which had made the nations drunk with the cup of her fornications, shall *have blood given her to drink, for she is worthy*, Rev. 18:3, 6. (2.) Does he take a pleasure in putting his neigh-

bour to shame? He shall himself be loaded with contempt: *"Thou art filled with shame for glory, with shame instead of glory*, or art filled now with shame more than ever thou wast with glory; and the glory thou hast been filled with shall but serve to make thy shame the more grievous to thyself, and the more ignominious in the eyes of others. Thou *also shalt drink* of the cup of trembling, and shalt expose thyself by thy fear and cowardice, which shall be as the *uncovering of thy nakedness*, to thy shame; and all about thee shall load thee with disgrace, for *shameful spewing shall be on thy glory*, on that which thou hast most prided thyself in, thy dignity, wealth, and dominion; those whom thou hast made drunk shall themselves spew upon it. For *the violence of Lebanon shall cover thee, and the spoil of beasts* (*v.* 17); thou shalt be hunted and run down with as much violence as ever any wild beasts in Lebanon were, shall be spoiled as they are, and thy fall made a sport of; for thou art as one of the beasts that made them afraid, and therefore they triumph when they have got the mastery of thee." Or, "It is because of the violence thou hast done to Lebanon, that is, the land of Israel (Deu. 3:25) and the temple (Zec. 11:1), that God now reckons with thee; that is the sin that now covers thee."

II. The promoters of idolatry stand here impeached and condemned; and this also was a sin that Babylon was notoriously guilty of; it was the *mother of harlots*. Belshazzar, in his revels, *praised his idols*. And for this, here is a woe against them, and in them against all others that do likewise, particularly the New-Testament Babylon. Now see here,

1. What they do to promote idolatry; they are *mad upon their idols;* so the Chaldeans are said to be, Jer. 50:38. For, (1.) They have a great variety of idols, their *graven images* and *molten images*, that people may take their choice, which they like best. (2.) They are very nice and curious in the framing of them: The *maker of the work* has performed his part admirably well, the *fashioner of his fashion* (so it is in the margin), that contrived the model in the most significant manner. (3.) They are at great expense in beautifying and adorning them: *They lay them over with gold and silver*; because these are things people love and dote upon wherever they meet with them, they dress up their idols in them, the more effectually to court the adoration of the children of this world. (4.) They have great expectations from them: *The maker of the work trusts therein* as his god, puts a confidence in it, and gives honour to it as his god. The worshippers of God give honour to him, by offering up their prayers to him, and waiting to receive instructions and directions from him; and these honours they give to their idols. [1.] They pray to them: *They say to the wood, Awake* for our relief, "awake to hear our prayers;" and to the dumb stone, *"Arise*, and save us," as the church prays to her God, *Awake, O Lord! arise*, Ps. 44:23. They own their image to be a god by praying to it. *Deliver me, for thou art my God*, Isa. 44:17. *Deos qui rogat ille facit — That to which a man addresses petitions is to him a god.* [2.] They consult them as oracles, and expect to be directed and dictated to by them: *They say to the dumb stone*, though it cannot speak, *yet it shall teach.* What the wicked demon, or no less wicked priest, speaks to them from the image, they receive with the utmost veneration, as of divine authority, and are ready to be governed by it. Thus is idolatry planted and propagated under the specious show of religion and devotion.

2. How the extreme folly of this is exposed. God, by Isaiah, when he foretold the deliverance of his people out of Babylon, largely showed the shameful stupidity and sottishness of idolaters, and so he does here by the prophet, on the like occasion. (1.) Their images, when they have made them, are but mere matter, which is the meanest lowest rank of being; and all the expense they are at upon them cannot advance them one step above that. They are wholly void both of sense and reason, lifeless and speechless (the idol is a *dumb idol*, a *dumb stone*, and there is *no breath at all in the midst of it*), so that the most minute animal, that has but breath and motion, is more excellent then they. They have not so much as the spirit of a beast. (2.) It is not in their power to do their worshippers any good (*v.* 18): *What profits the graven image?* Though it be mere matter, if it were cast into some other form it might be serviceable to some purpose or other of human life; but, as it is made a god of, it is of no profit at all, nor can do

its worshippers the least kindness. Nay, (3.) It is so far from profiting them that it puts a cheat upon them, and keeps them under the power of a strong delusion; they say, *It shall teach*, but it is a *teacher of lies;* for it represents God as having a body, as being finite, visible, and dependent, whereas he is a Spirit, infinite, invisible, and independent, and it confirms those that become vain in their imaginations in the false notions they have of God, and makes the idea of God to be a precarious thing, and what every man pleases. If we may say to the *works of our hands, You are our gods,* we may say so to any of the creatures of our own fancy, though the chimera be ever so extravagant. An image is a *doctrine of vanities;* it is *falsehood,* and a *work of errors,* Jer. 10:8, 14, 15. It is therefore easy to see what the religion of those is, and what they aim at, who recommend those teachers of lies as laymen's books, which they are to study and govern themselves by, when they have locked up from them the book of the scriptures in an unknown tongue.

3. How the people of God triumph in him, and therewith support themselves, when the idolaters thus shame themselves (*v.* 20): *But the Lord is in his holy temple.* (1.) *Our rock is not as their rock,* Deu. 32:31. Theirs are dumb idols; ours is Jehovah, a living God, who is what he is, and not, as theirs, what men please to make him. He is in his holy temple in heaven, the residence of his glory, where we have access to him in the way, not which we have invented, but which he himself has instituted. Compare Ps. 115:3, *But our God is in the heavens,* and Ps. 11:4. (2.) The multitude of their gods which they set up, and take so much pains to support, cannot thrust out our God; he is, and will be, in his holy temple still, and glorious in holiness. They have laid waste his temple at Jerusalem; but he has a temple above that is out of the reach of their rage and malice, but within the reach of his people's faith and prayers. (3.) Our God will make all the world silent before him, will strike the idolaters as dumb as their idols, convincing them of their folly, and covering them with shame. He will silence the fury of the oppressors, and check their rage against his people. (4.) It is the duty of his people to attend him with silent adorings (Ps. 65:1), and patiently to wait for his appearing to save them in his own way and time. *Be still, and know that he is God,* Zec. 2:13.

CHAPTER 3

Still the correspondence is kept up between God and his prophet. In the first chapter he spoke to God, then God to him, and then he to God again; in the second chapter God spoke wholly to him by the Spirit of prophecy; now, in this chapter, he speaks wholly to God by the Spirit of prayer, for he would not let the intercourse drop on his side, like a genuine son of Abraham, who "returned not to his place until God had left communing with him." Gen. 18:33. The prophet's prayer, in this chapter, is in imitation of David's psalms, for it is directed "to the chief musician," and is set to musical instruments. The prayer is left upon record for the use of the church, and particularly of the Jews in their captivity, while they were waiting for their deliverance, promised by the vision in the foregoing chapter. I. He earnestly begs of God to relieve and succour his people in affliction, to hasten their deliverance, and to comfort them in the mean time (*v.* 2). II. He calls to mind the experiences which the church formerly had of God's glorious and gracious appearances on her behalf, when he brought Israel out of Egypt through the wilderness to Canaan, and there many a time wrought wonderful deliverances for them (*v.* 3-15). III. He affects himself with a holy concern for the present troubles of the church, but encourages himself and others to hope that the issue will be comfortable and glorious at last, though all visible means fail (*v.* 16-19).

Verses 1-2

This chapter is entitled *a prayer of Habakkuk.* It is a meditation with himself, an intercession for the church. Prophets were praying men; this prophet was so (*He is a prophet, and he shall pray for thee,* Gen. 20:7); and sometimes they prayed for even those whom they prophesied against. Those that were intimately acquainted with the mind of God concerning future events knew better than others how to order their prayers, and what to pray for, and, in the foresight of troublous times, could lay up a stock of prayers that might then receive a gracious answer, and so be serving the church by their prayers when their prophesying was over. This prophet had found God ready to answer his requests and complaints before, and therefore now repeats his applications to him. Because *God has inclined his ear to us,* we must resolve that *therefore we* will *call upon him as long as we live.* 1. The prophet owns the receipt of God's answer to his former representation, and the impression it made upon him (*v.* 2): *"O Lord! I have heard thy speech, thy hearing"* (so some read it), "that which thou

wouldst have us hear, the decree that has gone forth for the afflicting of thy people. *I received thine,* and it is before me." Note, Those that would rightly order their speech to God must carefully observe, and lay before them, his speech to them. He had said (*ch.* 2:1), *I will watch to see what he will say;* and now he owns, *Lord, I have heard thy speech;* for, if we turn a deaf ear to God's word, we can expect no other than that he should turn a deaf ear to our prayers, Prov. 28:9. I heard it, *and was afraid.* Messages immediately from heaven commonly struck even the best and boldest men into a consternation; Moses, Isaiah, and Daniel, did *exceedingly fear and quake.* But, besides that, the matter of this message made the prophet afraid, when he heard how low the people of God should be brought, under the oppressing power of the Chaldeans, and how long they should continue under it; he was afraid lest their spirits should quite fail, and lest the church should be utterly rooted out and run down, and, being kept low so long, should be lost at length. 2. He earnestly prays that *for the elect's sake* these *days of trouble* might be *shortened,* or the trouble of these days mitigated and moderated, or the people of God supported and comforted under it. He thinks it very long to wait till the *end of the years;* perhaps he refers to the seventy years fixed for the continuance of the captivity, and therefore, "Lord," says he, "do something on our behalf *in the midst of the years,* those years of our distress; though we be not delivered, and our oppressors destroyed, yet let us not be abandoned and cast off." (1.) "Do something for thy own cause: *Revive thy work,* thy church" (that is the *work of God's own hand,* formed by him, formed for him); "*revive* that, even when it *walks in the midst of trouble,* Ps. 138:7, 8. Grant thy people *a little reviving in their bondage,* Ezra 9:8; Ps. 85:6. *Preserve alive thy work*" (so some read it); "though thy church be chastened, let it not be killed; though it have not its liberty, yet continue its life, save a remnant alive, to be a seed of another generation. *Revive the work of thy grace* in us, by sanctifying the trouble to us and supporting us under it, though the time be not yet come, *even the set time,* for our deliverance out of it. Whatever becomes of us, though we be as dead and dry bones, Lord, let *thy work be revived,* let not that sink, and go back, and come to nothing." (2.) "Do something for thy own honour: *In the midst of the years make known,* make thyself known, for now *verily thou art a God that hidest thyself* (Isa. 45:15), make known thy power, thy pity, thy promise, thy providence, in the government of the world, for the safety and welfare of thy church. Though we be buried in obscurity, yet, Lord, make thyself known; whatever becomes of Israel, let not the God of Israel be forgotten in the world, but discover himself even in the midst of the dark years, before thou art expected to appear." When *in the midst of the years* of the captivity God miraculously owned the three children in the fiery furnace, and humbled Nebuchadnezzar, this prayer was answered, *In the midst of the years make known.* (3.) "Do something for thy people's comfort: *In wrath remember mercy,* and *make that known. Show us thy mercy, O Lord!*" Ps. 85:7. They see God's displeasure against them in their troubles, and that makes them grievous indeed. There is wrath in the bitter cup; that therefore they deprecate, and are earnest in begging that he is a merciful God and they are vessels of his mercy. Note, Even those that are under the tokens of God's wrath must not despair of his mercy; and mercy, mere mercy, is that which we must flee to for refuge, and rely upon as our only plea. He does not say, Remember our merit, but, Lord, *remember thy own mercy.*

Verses 3-15

It has been the usual practice of God's people, when they have been in distress and ready to fall into despair, to help themselves by recollecting their experiences, and reviving them, *considering the days of old,* and *the years of ancient times* (Ps. 77:5), and pleading with God in prayer, as he is pleased sometimes to plead them with himself. Isa. 63:11, *Then he remembered the days of old.* This is that which the prophet does here, and he looks as far back as the first forming of them into a people, when they were brought by miracles out of Egypt, *a house of bondage,* through the wilderness, *a land of drought,* into Canaan, then possessed by *mighty nations.* He that thus brought them at first into Canaan, through so much difficulty, can

now bring them thither again out of Babylon, how great soever the difficulties are that lie in the way. Those works of wonder, wrought of old, are here most magnificently described, for the greater encouragement to the faith of God's people in their present straits.

I. God appeared in his glory, so as he never did before or since (*v.* 3, 4): *He came from Teman, even the Holy One from Mount Paran.* This refers to the visible display of the glory of God when he gave the law upon Mount Sinai, as appears by Deu. 33:2 whence these expressions are borrowed. Then *the Lord came down* upon Mount Sinai in a cloud (Ex. 19:20) and his glory was *as the devouring fire,* not only to enforce the law he then gave them, but to avow the deliverance he had wrought for them and to magnify it; for the first word he said there was, *"I am the Lord thy God, that brought thee out of the land of Egypt.* I that appear in this glory am the author of that work." Then *his glory covered the heavens,* which shone with the reflection of that glorious appearance of his; the *earth also* was *full of his praise,* or of his *splendour,* as some read it. People at a distance saw the cloud and fire on the top of Mount Sinai, and praised the God of Israel. Or the earth was full of those works of God which were to be praised. *His brightness was as the light,* as the light of the sun when he goes forth in his strength; *he had horns,* or *bright beams* (so it should be rendered), *coming out of his side* or hand. Rays of glory were darted forth around him; and with some rays borrowed thence it was that Moses's face shone when he *came down from* that *mount* of glory. Some by the horns, the *two horns* (for the word is dual), *coming out of his hand,* understand the *two tables of the law,* which perhaps, when God delivered them to Moses, though they were tables of stone, had a glory round them; those books were gilt with beams, and so it agrees with Deu. 33:2, *From his right hand went a fiery law for them.* It is added, *And there was the hiding of his power;* there was his hidden power, in the rays that came out of his hand. The operations of his power, compared with what he could have done, were rather the hiding of it than the discovery of it; the secrets of his power, as well as of his wisdom, are *double to that which is,* Job 11:6.

II. God sent plagues on Egypt, for the humbling of proud Pharaoh, and the obliging of him to let the people go (*v.* 5): *Before him went the pestilence,* which slew all the first-born of Egypt in one night; and *burning coals went forth at his feet,* when, in the plague of hail, there was *fire mingled with hail — burning diseases* (so the margin reads it), some think those that wasted Egypt, others those with which the number of the Canaanites was diminished before Israel was brought in upon them. These were *at his feet,* that is, at his coming, for they are at his command; he says to them, Go, and they go, Come, and they come, Do this, and they do it.

III. He divided the land of Canaan to his people Israel, and expelled the heathen from before them (*v.* 6): *He stood, and measured the earth,* measured that land, to assign it for an inheritance to Israel his people, Deu. 32:8, 9. *He beheld, and drove asunder the nations* that were in possession of it; though they combined together against Israel, God dispersed and discomfited them before Israel. Or he exerted such a mighty power as was enough to shake in pieces all the nations of the earth. Then *the everlasting mountains were scattered, and the perpetual hills did bow;* the mighty princes and potentates of Canaan, that seemed as high, as strong, and as firmly fixed, as the mountains and hills, were broken to pieces; they and their kingdoms were totally subdued. Or the power of God was so exerted as to shake the mountains and hills; nay, and Sinai did tremble, and the adjacent hills; see Ps. 68:7, 8. To this he adds, *His ways are everlasting,* that is, all the motions of his providence are according to his eternal counsels; and he is the same for ever, that which he was yesterday and to-day. His covenant is unchangeable, and *his mercy endures for ever.* When he *drove asunder the nations of Canaan* one might have seen the *tents of Cushan in affliction, the curtains of the land of Midian trembling,* and all the inhabitants of the neighbouring countries taking the alarm; and though they were not in the commission given to Israel to destroy, nor their land within the warrant given to Israel to possess, yet they thought their own house in danger when their neighbour's house was on fire, and therefore they were in a great fright, *v.* 7. Balak the king of Moab was so, Num. 22:3, 4. Some make the tents of Cushan to be in affliction when, in the days of judge Othniel, God delivered Cushan-rishathaim into his hand (Jdg. 3:8), and the *curtains of the land of Midian to tremble* when, in the days of judge Gideon, a barley cake, in a dream, overthrew the tent of Midian, Jdg. 7:13.

IV. He divided the Red Sea and Jordan, when they stood in the way of Israel's progress, and yet fetched a river out of a rock when Israel wanted it, *v.* 8. One would have thought that God was *displeased with the rivers,* and that *his wrath* was *against the sea,* for he made them give way and flee before him when he *rode upon his horses and chariots of salvation,* as a general at the head of his forces, mighty to save. Note, God's chariots are not so much chariots of state to himself as chariots of salvation to his people; it is his glory to be Israel's Saviour. This seems to be referred to again (*v.* 15): *"Thou didst walk through the sea,* through the Red Sea, *with thy horses,* in the pillar of cloud and fire (that was his chariot drawn by angels); thus thou didst walk secure, and so as to accommodate thyself to the slow pace that Israel could go, as Jacob tenderly drove, in consideration of his children and cattle: *Thou didst walk through the heap,* or mud, *of great waters;* and Israel likewise was led *through the deep as a horse through the wilderness,"* Isa. 63:13, 14. When they came to enter Canaan the *overflowing of the water passed by,* that is, Jordan, which at that time overflowed all his banks, was divided, Jos. 3:15. Note, When the difficulties in the way of perfecting the salvation of Israel seem most insuperable, when they rise to the height, and overflow, yet then God can put them by, break through them, and get over them. Then *the deep uttered his voice,* when, the Red Sea and Jordan being divided, the waters roared and made a noise, as if they were sensible of the restraint they were under from proceeding in their natural course, and complained of it. They *lifted up their hands,* or sides, *on high* (for the waters *stood up on a heap,* Jos. 3:16), as if they would have made opposition to the orders given them. They *lifted up their voice, lifted up their waves;* but in vain. *The Lord on high was mightier than they,* Ps. 93:3, 4. With the dividing of the sea and Jordan, notice is again taken of the trembling of the mountains, as if the stop given to the waters gave a shock to the adjacent hills; they are put together, Ps. 114:3, 4. When *the sea saw it and fled,* and *Jordan was driven back, the mountains skipped like rams and the little hills like lambs.* The whole creation yielded; earth and waters trembled *at the presence of the Lord, at the presence of the mighty God of Jacob.* But (as Mr. Cowley paraphrases it)

> Fly where thou wilt, thou sea; and, Jordan's current, cease.
> Jordan, there is no need of thee;
> For at God's word, whene'er he please,
> The rocks shall weep new waters forth instead of these.

So here, *Thou didst cleave the earth with rivers;* channels were made in the wilderness, such as seemed to cleave the earth, for the waters to run in, which issued out of the rock, to supply the camp of Israel, and which followed them in all their removes. Note, The God of nature can alter and control the powers of nature, which way he pleases, can turn waters into crystal rocks and rocks into crystal streams.

V. He arrested the motion of the sun and moon, to befriend and complete Israel's victories (*v.* 11): *The sun and moon stood still* at the prayer of Joshua, that the Canaanites might not have the benefit of the night to favour their escape; they *stood still in their habitation* in the heaven (Ps. 19:4), but with an eye to Gibeon and the *valley of Ajalon,* where God's work was in the doing, and of which they, though at so vast a distance, attended the motions. *At the light,* at the direction, *of thy arrows, they went,* and at *the shining of thy glittering spear;* they followed Israel's arms, to favour them; according to the intimation of the arrows God shot (as Jonathan's arrows, 1 Sa. 20:20), and which way soever his spear pointed (the glittering light of which they acknowledged to outshine theirs) that way they directed their influences, benign to Israel and malignant against their enemies, as when *the stars in their courses fought against Sisera.* Note, The heavenly bodies, as well as earth and seas, are at God's command, and, when he pleases, at Israel's service too.

VI. He carried on and completed Israel's victories over the nations of Canaan and their kings; he *slew great kings* and *famous,* Ps. 136:17, 18. This is largely insisted upon here, as a proper plea with God to enforce the present petition, that he would restore them again to that land which they were, at the expense of so many lives, so many miracles, first put in possession of.

1. Many expressions are here used to set forth the conquest of Canaan. (1.) God's *bow was made quite naked,* taken out of the case, to be employed for Israel; we should say, his *sword was quite unsheathed,* not drawn out a little way, to frighten the enemy, and then put up again, but quite drawn out, not to be returned till they are all cut off. (2.) He *marched through the land* from end to end, *in indignation,* as scorning to let that wicked generation of Canaanites any longer possess so good a land. He marched *cum fastidio — with distaste* (so some), despising their confederacies. (3.) He *threshed the heathen in anger,* trod them down, nay, he trod them out, as corn in the floor, to give them, and what they had, to be meat to his people Israel, Mic. 4:13. (4.) He *wounded the heads out of the house of the wicked;* he destroyed the families of the Canaanites, and wounded their princes, the heads of their families; nay, he cut off the heads, and so *discovered the foundations of them,* even *to the neck.* Are they a building? They are razed even to the foundation. Are they a body? They are plunged into deep mire even to the neck, so that they cannot get out, or help themselves. He *broke the heads of leviathan in pieces,* Ps. 74:14. Some apply this to Christ's victories over Satan and the powers of darkness, in which he *wounded the heads over many countries,* Ps. 110:6. (5.) He *struck through with his staves the head of the villages* (*v.* 14); with Israel's staves God *struck through* the *head of the villages* of the enemies, whether Egypt or Canaan. Staves shall do the same execution as swords when God pleases to make use of them. The enemy came out with the utmost force and fury, *as a whirlwind to scatter me* (says Israel); for *many a time have they thus afflicted me,* thus attacked me, *from my youth,* Ps. 129:1. Pharaoh, when he pursued Israel to the Red Sea, *came out as a whirlwind;* so did the kings of Canaan in their confederacies against Israel. *Their rejoicing was as to devour the poor secretly;* they were as confident of success in their enterprise as ever any great man was of devouring a poor man, that was no way a match for him; and his design against him was carried on with secrecy. But God disappointed them, and their pride did but make their fall the more shameful and God's care of his poor the more illustrious. (6.) He *walked to the sea with his horses* (so some read it, *v.* 15), that is, he carried Israel's victories to the Great Sea, which was opposite to that side of Canaan at which they entered, so that they went quite through it, and made themselves masters of it all, or rather God made them so, for they *got it not by their own sword,* Ps. 44:3. Now,

2. There were three things that God had a eye to, in giving Israel so many bloody victories over the Canaanites: — (1.) He would hereby make good his promise to the fathers; it was *according to the oaths of the tribes, even his word, v.* 9. He had sworn to give this land to the *tribes of Israel;* it was his oath *to Isaac confirmed to Jacob,* and repeated many a time to *the tribes of Israel, Unto thee will I give the land of Canaan.* This word God will accomplish, though Israel be ever so unworthy (Deu. 9:5) and their enemies ever so many and mighty. Note, What God does for his tribes is according to the oaths of the tribes, according to what he has said and sworn to them; *for he is faithful that has promised.* (2.) He would hereby show his kindness to *his people,* because of their relation to him, and his interest in them: *Thou wentest forth for the salvation of thy people, v.* 13. All the powers of nature are shaken, and the course of nature changed, and every thing seems to be thrown into disorder, and all is *for the salvation of God's people.* There are a people in the world who are God's people, and their salvation is that which he has in his eye in all the operations of his providence. Heaven and earth shall sooner come together than any of the links in the golden chain of their salvation shall be broken; and even that which seems most unlikely shall by an overruling hand be made to work for their salvation, Phil. 1:19. (3.) He would hereby give a type and figure of the redemption of the world by Jesus Christ. It is *for salvation with thy anointed,* with Joshua, who led the armies of Israel and was a figure of him whose name he bore, even Jesus our Joshua. What God did for his Israel of old was done with an eye to his anointed, for the sake of the Mediator, who was both the founder and foundation of the covenant made with them. It was salvation *with him,* for in all the salvations wrought for them, *God looked upon the face of the anointed,* and did them by him.

Verses 16–19

Within the compass of these few lines we have the prophet in the highest degree both of trembling and triumphing, such are the varieties both of the state and of the spirit of God's people in this world. In heaven there shall be no more trembling, but everlasting triumphs.

I. The prophet had foreseen the prevalence of the church's enemies and the long continuance of the church's troubles; and the sight made him tremble, *v.* 16. Here he goes on with what he had said *v.* 2, *"I have heard thy speech and was afraid. When I heard* what sad times were coming upon the church *my belly trembled, my lips quivered at the voice;* the news made such an impression that it put me into a perfect ague fit." The blood retiring to the heart, to succour that when it was ready to faint, the extreme parts were left destitute of spirits, so that *his lips quivered.* Nay, he was so weak, and so unable to help himself, that he was as if *rottenness* had *entered into his bones;* he had no strength left in him, could neither stand nor go; he *trembled in himself,* trembled all over him, trembled within him; he yielded to his trembling, and *troubled himself,* as our Savior did; his *flesh trembled for fear of God* and *he was afraid of his judgments,* Ps. 119:120. He was touched with a tender concern for the calamities of the church, and trembled for fear lest they should end at length in ruin, and the *name of Israel be blotted out.* Nor did he think it any disparagement to him, nor any reproach to his courage, but freely owned he was one of those that *trembled at God's word,* for to them he will look with favour: *I tremble in myself, that I might rest in the day of trouble.* Note, When we see a day of trouble approaching it concerns us to provide accordingly, and to lay up something in store, by the help of which we may rest in that day; and the best way to make sure rest for ourselves in the day of trouble is to tremble within ourselves at the word of God and the threatenings of that word. He that has joy in store for those that *sow in tears* has rest in store for those that tremble before him. *Good hope through grace* is founded in a *holy fear.* Noah, who was *moved with fear,* trembled within himself at the warning given him of the deluge coming, had the ark for his resting place in the day of that trouble. The prophet tells us what he said in his trembling. His fear is that, *when he comes up to the people,* when the *Chaldean comes up to the people* of Israel, *he will invade them,* will surround them, will break in upon them, nay (as it is in the margin), He will *cut them in pieces with his troops;* he cried out, We are all undone; the whole nation of the Jews is lost and gone. Note, When things look bad we are too apt to aggravate them, and make the worst of them.

II. He had looked back upon the experiences of the church in former ages, and had observed what great things God had done for them, and so he recovered himself out of his fright, and not only retrieved his temper, but fell into a transport of holy joy, with an express *non obstante — notwithstanding* to the calamities he foresaw coming, and this not for himself only, but in the name of every faithful Israelite.

1. He supposes the ruin of all his creature comforts and enjoyments, not only of the delights of this life, but even of the necessary supports of it, *v.* 17. Famine is one of the ordinary effects of war, and those commonly feel it first and most that sit still and are quiet; the prophet and his pious friends, when the Chaldean army comes, will be plundered and stripped of all they have. Or he supposes himself deprived of all by blasting and unseasonable weather, or some other immediate hand of God. Or though the captives in Babylon have not that plenty of all good things in their own land. (1.) He supposes the fruit-tree to be withered and become barren; the *fig-tree* (which used to furnish them with much of their food; hence we often read of *cakes of figs*) shall not so much as *blossom, nor shall fruit be in the vine,* from which they had their drink, that made glad the heart: he supposes *the labour of the olive*

to *fail,* their oil, which was to them as butter is to us; the *labour of the olive shall lie* (so it is in the margin); their expectations from it shall be disappointed. (2.) He supposes the bread-corn to fail; *the fields shall yield no meat;* and, since *the king himself is served of the field,* if the productions of that be withdrawn, every one will feel the want of them. (3.) He supposes the cattle to perish for want of the food which the field should yield and does not, or by disease, or being destroyed and carried away by the enemy: *The flock is cut off from the fold, and there is no herd in the stall.* Note, When we are in the full enjoyment of our creature comforts we should consider that there may come a time when we shall be stripped of them all, and use them accordingly, as not abusing them, 1 Co. 7:29, 30.

2. He resolves to delight and triumph in God notwithstanding; when all is gone his God is not gone (*v.* 18): *"Yet will I rejoice in the Lord;* I shall have him to rejoice in, and will rejoice in him." *Destroy the vines and the fig-trees,* and you make all the mirth of a carnal heart to cease, Hos. 2:11, 12. But those who, when they were full, enjoyed God in all, when they are emptied and impoverished can *enjoy all in God,* and can sit down upon a melancholy heap of the ruins of all their creature comforts and even then can sing to the praise and glory of God, as the God of their salvation. This is the principal ground of our joy in God, that he is the God of our salvation, our eternal salvation, the salvation of the soul; and, if he be so, we may rejoice in him as such in our greatest distresses, since by them our salvation cannot be hindered, but may be furthered. Note, Joy in God is never out of season, nay, it is in a special manner seasonable when we meet with losses and crosses in the world, that it may then appear that our hearts are not set upon these things, nor our happiness bound up in them. See how the prophet triumphs in God: *The Lord God is my strength, v.* 19. He that is the *God of our salvation* in another world will be our strength in this world, to carry us on in our journey thither, and help us over the difficulties and oppositions we meet with in our way. Even when provisions are cut off, to make it appear that *man lives not by bread alone,* we may have the want of bread supplied by the graces and comforts of God's Spirit and with the supplies of them. (1.) We shall be strong for our spiritual warfare and work: *The Lord God is my strength,* the strength of my heart. (2.) We shall be swift for our spiritual race: *"He will make my feet like hinds' feet,* that with enlargement of heart I may run the way of his commands and outrun my troubles." (3.) We shall be successful in our spiritual enterprises: *"He will make me to walk upon my high places;* that is, I shall gain my point, shall be restored unto my own land, and tread upon the high places of the enemy," Deu. 32:13; 33:29. Thus the prophet, who began his prayer with fear and trembling, concludes it with joy and triumph, for prayer is heart's ease to a gracious soul. When Hannah had prayed she *went her way, and did eat, and her countenance was no more sad.* This prophet, finding it so, publishes his experience of it, and puts it into the hand of the *chief singer* for the use of the church, especially in the day of our captivity. And, though then the harps were hung upon the willow-trees, yet in the hope that they would be resumed, and their right hand retrieve its cunning, which it had forgotten, he set his song upon *Shigionoth* (*v.* 1), wandering tunes, *according to the variable songs,* and upon *Neginoth* (*v.* 19), *the stringed instruments.* He that is afflicted, and has prayed aright, may then be so easy, may then be so merry, as to sing psalms.

AN EXPOSITION, WITH PRACTICAL OBSERVATIONS, OF

THE PROPHECY OF ZEPHANIAH

This prophet is placed last, as he was last in time, of all the minor prophets before the captivity, and not long before Jeremiah, who lived at the time of the captivity. He foretels the general destruction of Judah and Jerusalem by the Chaldeans, and sets their sins in order before them, which had provoked God to bring their ruin upon them, calls them to repentance, threatens the neighbouring nations with the like destructions, and gives encouraging promises of their joyful return out of captivity in due time, which have a reference to the grace of the gospel. We have, in the first verse, an account of the prophet and the date of his prophecy, which supersedes our enquiry concerning them here.

CHAPTER 1

After the title of the book (*v.* 1) here is, I. A threatening of the destruction of Judah and Jerusalem, an utter destruction, by the Chaldeans (*v.* 2–4). II. A charge against them for their gross sin, which provoked God to bring that destruction upon them (*v.* 5, 6); and so he goes on in the rest of the chapter, setting both the judgments before them, that they might prevent them or prepare for them, and the sins that destroy them, that they might judge themselves, and justify God in what was brought upon them. 1. They must hold their peace because they had greatly sinned (*v.* 7–9). But, 2, They shall howl because the trouble will be great. The day of the Lord is near, and it will be a terrible day (*v.* 10–18). Such fair and timely warning as this did God give to the Jews of the approaching captivity; but they hardened their neck, which made their destruction remediless.

Verses 1–6

Here is, I. The title-page of this book (*v.* 1), in which we observe, 1. What authority it has, and who gave it that authority; it is from heaven, and not of men: It is *the word of the Lord.* 2. Who was the instrument of conveying it to the church. His name was Zephaniah, which signifies the *servant of the Lord,* for God *revealed his secrets to his servants the prophets.* The pedigree of other prophets, whose extraction we have an account of, goes no further back than their father, except Zecharias, whose grandfather also is named. But this of Zephaniah goes back four generations, and the highest mentioned is *Hizkiah;* it is the very same name in the original with that of Hezekiah king of Judah (2 Ki. 18:1), and refers probably to him; if so, our prophet, being lineally descended from that pious prince, and being of the royal family, could with the better grace reprove the folly of the king's children as he does, *v.* 8. 3. When this prophet prophesied — *in the days of Josiah king of Judah,* who reigned well, and in the twelfth year of his reign began vigorously, and carried on a work of reformation, in which he destroyed idols and idolatry. Now it does not appear whether Zephaniah prophesied in the beginning of his reign; if so, we may suppose his prophesying had a great and good influence on that reformation. When he, as God's messenger, reproved the idolatries of Jerusalem, Josiah, as God's vice-gerent, removed them; and reformation is likely to go on and prosper when both magistrates and ministers do their part towards it. If it were towards the latter end of his reign that he prophesied, we sadly see how a corrupt people relapse into their former distempers. The idolatries Josiah had abolished, it should seem, returned in his own time, when the heat of the reformation began a little to abate and wear off. What good can the best reformers do with a people that hate to be reformed, as if they longed to be ruined?

II. The summary, or contents, of this book. The general proposition contained in it is, That utter destruction is coming apace upon Judah and Jerusalem for sin. Without preamble, or apology, he begins abruptly (*v.* 2): *By taking away I will make an end of all things from off the face of the land, Saith the Lord.* Ruin is coming, utter ruin, destruction from the Almighty. He has said it who can, and will, make good what he has said: *"I will utterly consume all things.* I will *gather* all things" (so some); "I will recall all the blessings I have bestowed, because they have abused them and so forfeited them." The consumption determined shall take away, 1. The inferior creatures: *I will consume the beasts, the fowls of the heaven, and the fishes of the sea* (*v.* 3), as, in the deluge, *every living substance was destroyed that was upon the face of the ground,* Gen. 7:23. The creatures were made for man's use, and therefore when he has perverted the use of them, and made them *subject to vanity,* God, to show the greatness of his displeasure against the sin of man, involves them in his punishment. The expressions are figurative, denoting universal desolation. Those that fly ever so high, as the fowls of heaven, and think themselves out of the reach of the enemies' hand — those that hide ever so close, as the fishes of the sea, and think themselves out of the reach of the enemies' eye — shall yet become a prey to them, and be utterly consumed. 2. The children of men: *"I will consume man; I will cut off man from the land.* The land shall be dispeopled and left uninhabited; I will destroy, not only Israel, but *man.* The land shall enjoy her sabbaths. I will cut off, not only the wicked men, but all men; even the few among them that are good shall be involved in this common calamity. Though they shall not be cut off from the Lord, yet they shall be *cut off from the land."* It is with Judah and Jerusalem that God has this quarrel, both city and country, and upon them he will *stretch out his hand,* the hand of his power, the hand of his wrath; and *who knows the power of his anger? v.* 4. Those that will not humble themselves under God's mighty hand shall be humbled and brought down by it. Note, Even Judah, where God is known, and Jerusalem, where his dwelling-place is, if they revolt from him and rebel against him, shall have his hand stretched out against them. 3. All wicked people, and all those things that are the matter of their wickedness (*v.* 3): *"I will consume the stumbling-blocks with the wicked,* the idols with the idolaters, the offences with the offenders." Josiah had taken away the stumbling-blocks, and, as far as he could, had purged the land of the monuments of idolatry, hoping that there would be no more idolatry; but *the wicked will do wickedly,* the dog will return to his vomit, and therefore, since the sin will not otherwise be cured, the sinners must themselves be consumed, even the *wicked with the stumbling-blocks* of their iniquity, Eze. 14:3. Since it was not done by the sword of justice, it shall be done by the sword of war. See who the sinners are that shall be consumed. (1.) The professed idolaters, who avowed idolatry, and were wedded to it. The *remnant of Baal* shall be *cut off,* the images of Baal, and the worshippers of those images. Josiah cut off a great deal of Baal; but that which was so close as to escape the eye, or so bold as to escape the hand, of his justice, God will cut off, even all the remains of it. The Chaldeans would spare none of the images of Baal, or the worshippers of those images. The *Chemarim* shall be *cut off;* we read of them in the history of Josiah's reformation. 2 Ki. 23:5, *He put down the idolatrous priests:* the word is the *Chemarim.* The word signifies *black men,* some think because they wore black clothes, affecting to appear grave, others because their faces were black with attending the altars, or the fires in which they burnt their children to Moloch. They seem to have been immediate attendants upon the service of Baal. They shall be *cut off with the priests,* the regulars with the seculars. The very name of them shall be cut off; the order shall be quite abolished, so as to be forgotten, or remembered with detestation. And, among other idolaters, the *worshippers of the host of heaven upon the house-tops* shall be cut off (*v.* 5), who justified themselves in their idolatry with those that did not worship images, the work of their own hands, but offered their sacrifices and burnt their incense to the sun, moon, and stars, immediately upon the tops of their houses. But God will let them know that he is a jealous God, and will not endure any rival; and, though some have thought that the most specious and plausible idolatry, yet it will appear as great an offence to God to give divine honours to a star as to give them to a stone or a stock. Even the worshippers of the host of heaven shall be consumed as well as the worshippers of the beasts of the earth or the fiends of hell. The sin of the adulteress is not the less sinful for the gaiety of the adulterer. (2.) Those also shall be consumed that think to compound the matter between God and idols, and keep an even hand between them, that halt between God and Baal, and worship between Jehovah and Moloch, and *swear by both;* or, as it might better be read, swear *to the Lord and to Malcham.* They bind themselves by oath and covenant to the service both of God and idols. They have a good opinion of the worship of the God of Israel; it is the religion of their country, and has been long so, and therefore they will by no means quit it; but they think it will be very much improved and beautified if they join with it the worship of Moloch, for that also is much used in other countries, and travellers admire it; there is a great deal of good fancy and strong flame in it. They cannot keep always to the worship of a God whom they have no visible representation of, and therefore they must have an image; and what better than the image of *Moloch — a king?* They think they shall effectually atone for their sin if they *swear to Moloch,* and, pursuant to that oath, burn their children in sacrifice to that idol; and yet, if they do amiss in that, they hope to atone for it in worshipping the God of Israel too. Note, Those that think to divide their affections and adorations between God and idols will not only come short of acceptance with God, but will have their doom with the worst of idolaters; for what communion can there be between light and darkness, Christ and Belial, God and mammon? She whose own the child is not pleads for the dividing of it, for, if Satan have half, he will have all; but the true mother says, *Divide it not,* for, if God have but half, he will have none. Such waters will not be long sweet, if they come from a fountain that sends forth bitter water too; what have those to do to swear by the Lord that swear by Malcham? (3.) Those also shall be consumed that have apostatized from God, together with those that never gave up their names to him, *v.* 6. I will cut off, [1.] Those *that are turned back from the Lord,* that were well taught, and began well, that had given up their names to him, and set out at first in the worship of him, but have flown off, and turned aside, and fallen in with idolaters, and deserted those good ways of God which they were brought up in, and despised them. Those God will be sure to reckon with who are renegadoes from his service, who began in the Spirit and ended in the flesh; they shall be treated as deserters, to whom no mercy is shown. [2.] Those that *have not sought the Lord,* nor ever *enquired for him,* never made any profession of religion, and think to excuse themselves with that, shall find that this will not excuse them; nay, this is the thing laid to their charge; they are atheistical careless people, that *live without God in the world;* and those that do so are certainly unworthy to live upon God in the world.

Verses 7-13

Notice is here given to Judah and Jerusalem that God is coming forth against them, and will be with them shortly; his *presence,* as a just avenger, *his day,* the day of his judgment and his wrath, are not far off, *v.* 7. Those that improve not the presence of God with them as a Father, but sin away that presence, may expect his presence with them as a Judge, to call them to an account for the contempt put upon his grace. The *day of the Lord* will come. Men have their day now, when they take a liberty to do what they please; but *God's day is at hand;* it is here called his *sacrifice,* a sacrifice of his preparing, for the punishing of presumptuous sinners is a sacrifice to the justice of God, some reparation to his injured honour. Those that brought their offerings to other gods were themselves justly made victims to the true God. On a day of sacrifice great slaughter was made; so shall there be in Jerusalem; men shall be killed up as fast as lambs for the altar, with as little regret, with as much pleasure: *The slain of the Lord shall be many.* On a day of sacrifice great feasts were made upon the sacrifices; so the inhabitants of Judah and Jerusalem shall be feasted upon by their enemies the Chaldeans; these are the guests God has prepared and invited to come and glut themselves — their revenge with slaughter and their covetousness with plunder. Now observe,

I. Who those are that are marked to be sacrificed, that shall be visited and punished in this day of reckoning, and

what it is they shall be called to an account for. 1. The royal family, because of the dignity of their place, shall be first reckoned with for their pride, and vanity, and affectation (*v.* 8): *I will punish the princes, and the king's children,* who think themselves accountable to God, and that, high as they are, he is above them. They shall be punished, and all such as, like them, are clothed *with strange apparel,* such as, in contempt of their own country (where, probably, it was the custom to go in a very plain dress, as became the seed of Jacob that *plain man),* affected to appear in the fashion of other nations and introduced their modes in apparel, studying to resemble those from whom God had appointed them, even in their clothes, industriously to distinguish themselves. *The princes and the king's children* scorned to wear any home-made stuffs, though God had provided them *fine linen* and *silks* (Eze. 16:10), but they must send abroad to strange countries for their clothes, which would not please unless they were far-fetched and dear-bought; and even those of inferior rank affected to imitate the princes and the king's children. Pride in apparel is displeasing to God, and a symptom of the degeneracy of a people. 2. The noblemen, and their stewards and servants, come next to be reckoned with (*v.* 9): *In the same day will I punish those that leap on the threshold,* a phrase, no doubt, well understood then, and which probably signified the invading of their neighbour's rights. Entering their houses by force and violence, and seizing their possessions, they *leap on the threshold,* as much as to say that the house is their own and they will keep their hold of it; and, accordingly, they make all in it their own that they can lay their hands on, and so *fill their masters' houses* with goods gotten *by violence and deceit* and with all the guilt thereby contracted. Nor shall it suffice them to say that the ill-gotten gains were not for themselves but for their masters, and that what they did was by their order; for the obligations we lie under to keep God's commandments are prior and superior to the obligations we lie under to serve the interests of any master on earth. 3. The trading people, and the rich merchants, are next called to account. Iniquity is found in their end of the town, among *the inhabitants of Maktesh,* a low part of Jerusalem, deep like a mortar (for so the word signifies); the *goldsmiths* lived there (Neh. 3:32) and the merchants; and they are now *cut down* (they are broken, and have shut up their shops, and become bankrupts); nay, *All those that bear silver are cut off,* in the first place, by the invaders, for the sake of the silver they carry, which is so far from being a protection to them that it will expose and betray them. The conquerors aimed at the wealthy men, and carried them off first, while *the poor of the land escaped.* Or it may be meant of a general decay of trade, which was a preface and introduction to the general destruction of the land. It is the token of a declining state when great dealers are cut down, and great bankers are cut off and become bankrupts, who cannot fall alone, but with themselves ruin many. 4. All the secure and careless people, the sons of pleasure, that live a loose idle life, are next reckoned with (*v.* 12); they come from all parts of the country, to take up their quarters in the head-quarters of the kingdom, where they take private lodgings, and indulge themselves in ease and luxury; but God will find them out, and punish them: *At that time I will search Jerusalem with candles,* to discover them, that they may be brought out to condign punishment. This intimates that they conceal themselves, as being either ashamed of the sin or afraid of the punishment of it; when the judgments of God are abroad they hope to escape by absconding and getting out of the way, but God will *search Jerusalem,* as search is made for a malefactor in disguise, that is harboured by his accomplices. God's hand will *find out all his enemies,* wherever they lie hid, and will punish not only the secret idolaters, but the secret epicures and profane; and those are the persons that are here described, and marks are given by which they will be discovered when strict search is made for them. (1.) Their dispositions are sensual: They *are settled on their lees,* intoxicated with their pleasures, strengthening themselves in their wealth and wickedness; they are secure and easy, and, because they have had no changes, they fear none, as Moab, Jer. 48:11. They *have not been emptied from vessel to vessel.* They *fill themselves with wine and strong drink,* and banish all thought, saying, *To-morrow shall be as this day,* Isa. 56:12. Their being *settled on their lees* signifies the same

with being *enclosed in their own fat,* Ps. 17:10. (2.) Their notions are atheistical. They could not live such loose lives but that they say *in their heart, The Lord will not do good, neither will he do evil;* that is, He will do nothing. They deny his providential government of the world: "What good and evil there is in the world comes by the wheel of fortune, and not by the disposal of a wise and supreme director." They deny his moral government, and his dispensing rewards and punishments: *"The Lord will not do good* to those that serve him, nor *do evil* to those that rebel against him; and therefore there is nothing got by religion, nor lost by sin." This was the effect of their sensuality; if they were not drowned in sense, they could not be thus senseless, nor could they be so stupid if they had not stupefied themselves with the love of pleasure. It was also the cause of their sensuality; men would not make a god of their belly if they had not at first become so vain, so vile, in their imaginations, as to think the God that made them *altogether such a one as themselves.* But God will *punish them; their end is destruction,* Phil. 3:19.

II. What the destruction will be with which God will punish these sinners, and what course he will take with them. 1. He will silence them (*v.* 7): *Hold thy peace at the presence of the Lord.* He will force them to hold their peace, will strike them dumb with horror and amazement. They shall be speechless. All the excuses of their sin, and exceptions against the sentence, will be overruled, and they shall not have a word to say for themselves. 2. He will *sacrifice* them, for it is *the day of the Lord's sacrifice* (*v.* 8); he will give them into the hands of their enemies, and glorify himself thereby. 3. He will fill both city and country with lamentation (*v.* 10): *In that day there shall be a noise of a cry from the fish-gate,* so called because near either to the fish-ponds or to the fish-market. It belonged to the city of David (2 Chr. 33:14; Neh. 3:3); perhaps the same with that which is called the *first gate* (Zec. 14:10), and, if so, it will explain what follows here, *And a howling from the second,* that is, the second gate, which was next to that *fish-gate.* The alarm shall go round the walls of Jerusalem from gate to gate; and there shall be *a great crashing from the hills,* a mighty noise from the mountains round about Jerusalem, from the acclamations of the victorious invaders, or from the lamentations of the timorous invaded, or from both. The inhabitants of the city, even of the closest safest part of the city, shall *howl* (*v.* 11), so clamorous shall the grief be. 4. They shall be stripped of all they have; it shall be a prey to the enemy (*v.* 13): *Their household goods,* and *shop-goods,* shall *become a booty,* and a rich booty they shall be; *their houses shall be* levelled with the ground and be *a desolation;* those of them that have *built* new houses *shall not inherit them,* but the invaders shall get and keep possession of them. And the *vineyards* they have planted they shall not *drink the wine of,* but, instead of having it for the relief of their friends that faint among them, they shall part with it for the animating of their foes that fight against them, Deu. 28:30.

Verses 14-18

Nothing could be expressed with more spirit and life, nor in words more proper to startle and awaken a secure and careless people, than the warning here given to Judah and Jerusalem of the approaching destruction by the Chaldeans. That is enough to make the sinners in Zion tremble — that it is *the day of the Lord,* the day in which he will manifest himself by taking vengeance on them. It is *the great day of the Lord,* a specimen of the day of judgment, a kind of doom's-day, as the last destruction of Jerusalem by the Romans is represented to be in our Saviour's prediction concerning it, Mt. 24:27.

I. This *day of the Lord* is here spoken of as very near. The vision is not *for a great while to come,* as those imagine who *put the evil day far from them.* Those deceive themselves who look upon it as a thing at a distance, for *it is near — it is near — it hastens greatly.* The prophet gives the alarm like one that is in earnest, like one that awakens a family with the cry of *Fire! fire!* when it is at the next door that the danger is: *"It is near! it is near!* and therefore it is high time to bestir yourselves, and do what you can for your own safety before it be too late." It is madness for those to slumber whose *damnation slumbers not,* and to linger when it hastens.

II. It is spoken of as a very dreadful day. The very *voice* of this *day of the Lord,* the noise of it, when it is coming, shall be so terrible as to make *the mighty men cry there bitterly,* cry for fear as children do. *It shall be a vexation* to *hear the report* of it. In the last great day of the Lord the mighty men shall cry bitterly to rocks and mountains to shelter them; but in vain. Observe how emphatically the prophet speaks of this day approaching (*v.* 15): It is *a day of wrath,* God's wrath, wrath in perfection, wrath to the utmost. It will be a day of *trouble and distress* to the sinners; they shall be in pain, and shall see no ways of easing or helping themselves. The miseries of the damned are summed up (perhaps with reference to this) in the *indignation and wrath of God,* which are the cause, and the *tribulation and anguish* of the sinner's *soul,* which are the effect, Rom. 2:8, 9. It will be a day of *trouble and distress* to the inhabitants, and a day of *wasteness and desolation* to the whole land; that fruitful land shall be turned into a wilderness. It shall be *a day of darkness and gloominess;* every thing shall look dismal, and there shall not be the least gleam of comfort, or glimpse of hope; look round, and it is all black. It is *a day of clouds and thick darkness;* there is not only nothing encouraging, but every thing threatening; the thick clouds are big with storms and tempests.

III. It is spoken of as a destroying day, *v.* 16, 17. It shall be destroying, 1. To places, even the strongest and best fortified: *A day of the trumpet and alarm against the fenced cities,* to break into them, and against the *high towers,* to bring them down; for what forts, what fences, can hold out against the wrath of God? 2. To persons (*v.* 17): *"I will bring distress upon men,* the strongest and stoutest of men; their hearts and hands shall fail them; they shall *walk like blind men,* wandering endlessly, *because they have sinned against the Lord."* Note, Those that walk as bad men will justly be left to walk as blind men, always in the dark, in doubt and danger, without any guide or comfort, and falling at length into the ditch. Because they have *sinned against the Lord* he will deliver them into the hands of cruel enemies, that shall *pour out their blood as dust,* so profusely, and with as little regret, and *their flesh* shall be thrown *as dung* upon the dunghill.

IV. The destruction of that day will be unavoidable and universal, *v.* 18. 1. There shall be no escaping it by ransom: *Neither their silver nor their gold,* which they have hoarded up so covetously against the evil day, or which they have spent so prodigally to make friends for such a time, *shall be able to deliver them in the day of the Lord's wrath.* Another prophet borrowed these words from this, with reference to the same event, Eze. 7:19. Note, Riches profit not in the day of wrath, Prov. 11:4. Nay, riches expose to the wrath of men (Eccl. 5:13.), and riches abused to the wrath of God. 2. There shall be no escaping it by flight or concealment; for the *whole land shall be devoured by the fire of his jealousy,* and where then can a hiding-place be found? See what the fire of God's jealousy is, and what the force of it; it will devour whole lands; how then can particular persons stand before it? He shall make riddance, *a speedy riddance, of all those that dwell in the land,* as the husbandman, when he rids his ground, cuts up all the briers and thorns for the fire. Note, Sometimes the judgments of God make riddance, even utter riddance, with sinful nations, a speedy riddance; their destruction is effected, is completed, in a little time. Let not sinners be laid asleep by the patience of God, for when the measure of their iniquity is full his justice will both overtake and overcome, will make quick work and thorough work.

CHAPTER 2

In this chapter we have, I. An earnest exhortation to the nation of the Jews to repent and make their peace with God, and so to prevent the judgments threatened before it was too late (*v.* 1–3), and this inferred from the revelation of God's wrath against them in the foregoing chapter. II. A denunciation of the judgments of God against several of the neighbouring nations that had assisted, or rejoiced in, the calamity of Israel. 1. The Philistines (*v.* 4–7). 2. The Moabites and Ammonites (*v.* 8–11). 3. The Ethiopians and Assyrians (*v.* 12–15). All these shall drink of the same cup of trembling that is put into the hands of God's people, as was also foretold by other prophets before and after.

Verses 1–3

Here we see what the prophet meant in that terrible description of the approaching judgments which we had in the foregoing chapter. From first to last his design was, not to drive the people to despair, but to drive them to God and to their duty — not to frighten them out of their wits, but to frighten them out of their sins. In pursuance of that he here calls them to repentance, national repentance, as the only way to prevent national ruin. Observe,

I. The summons given them to a national assembly (*v.* 1): *Gather yourselves together.* He had told them, in the last words of the foregoing chapter, that God would make a *speedy riddance of all that dwelt in the land,* upon which, one would think, it should follow, "Disperse yourselves, and flee for shelter where you can find a place." When the decree had absolutely gone forth for the last destruction of Jerusalem by the Romans, that was the advice given (Mt. 24:16), *Then let those who are in Judea flee into the mountains;* but here it is otherwise. God warns, that he may not wound, threatens, that he may not strike, and therefore calls to the people to use means for the turning away of his wrath. The summons is given to a *nation not desired.* The word signifies either, 1. *Not desiring,* that has not any desires towards God or the remembrance of his name, is not desirous of his favour or grace, but very indifferent to it, has no mind to repent and reform. "Yet *come together,* and see if you can stir up desires in one another." Thus God is often *found of those that sought him not,* nor *asked for him,* Isa. 65:1. Or, 2. *Not desirable,* no ways lovely, nor having any thing in them amiable, or which might recommend them to God. The land of Israel had been a *pleasant land, a land of delight* (Dan. 11:41); but now it is unlovely, it is a *nation not desired,* to which God might justly say, *Depart from me;* but he says, *"Gather together to me,* and let us see if any expedient can be found out for the preventing of the ruin. *Gather together,* that you may in a body humble yourselves before God, may fast, and pray, and seek his face. *Gather together,* to consult among yourselves what is to be done in this critical juncture, that every one may consider of it, may give and take advice, and speak his mind, and that what is done may be done by consent and so may be a national act." Some read it, *"Enquire into yourselves,* yea, *enquire into yourselves;* examine your consciences; look into your hearts; search and try your ways; *enquire into yourselves,* that you may find out the sin by which God has been provoked to this displeasure against you, and may find out the way of returning to him." Note, When God is contending with us it concerns us to enquire into ourselves.

II. Arguments urged to press them to the utmost seriousness and expedition herein (*v.* 2): "Do it in earnest; do it with all speed before it is too late, *before the decree bring forth, before the day pass."* The manner of speaking here is very lively and awakening, designed to make them apprehensive, as all sinners are concerned to be, 1. That their danger is very great, that their all lies at stake, that it is a matter of life and death, which therefore well requires and well deserves the closest application of mind that can be. It is not a trifle, and therefore is not a thing to be trifled about. It is the *fierce anger of the Lord* that is kindled against them, and is just ready to kindle upon them, that *devouring fire* which none can *dwell with,* which none can make head against or hold up their head under. "It is tne *day of the Lord's anger,* the day set for the pouring out of the full vials of it, that you are threatened with, that *great day of the Lord"* spoken of, *ch.* 1:14. "Are you not concerned to prepare for that day?" 2. That it is very imminent: "Bestir yourselves now quickly, *before the decree bring forth,* and then it will be too late, the opportunity will be lost and never retrieved. The decree is as it were big with child, and it will *bring forth the day,* the terrible day, which shall *pass as chaff,* which shall hurry you away into captivity as chaff before the wind." *We know not what a day may bring forth* (Prov. 27:1), but we do know what the decree will bring forth against impenitent sinners, whom therefore it highly concerns to repent in time, in *the accepted time.* Note, It is the wisdom of those whom God has a controversy with to agree with him quickly, while they are in the way, before his fierce anger comes upon them, not to be turned away. In a case of this nature delays are highly dangerous and may be fatal; they will be so if by them the heart is hardened. How solicitous should we all be to make our peace with God before the Spirit withdraw from us, or cease to strive with us, before the day of grace be over or the day of life, before our everlasting state shall be determined on the other side of the great gulf fixed!

III. Directions prescribed for the doing of this effectually. It is not enough to gather together in a consternation, but they must seriously and calmly apply to the duty of the day (*v.* 3): *Seek you the Lord.* That they might find mercy with God, they are here put upon seeking; for so is the rule – *Seek, and you shall find.* A general call was given to the whole nation to *gather together,* but little good is to be expected from the far greater part of them; if the land be saved, it must be by the interest and intercession of the pious few, and therefore to them the exhortation here is particularly directed. And observe, 1. How they are described – they are *the meek of the earth,* or of *the land.* It is the distinguishing character of the people of God that they are the *meek ones of the earth;* this is their badge; it is their livery. They are modest, and humble, and low in their own eyes; they are mild, and gentle, and yielding to others, not soon angry, not very angry, not long angry; they are the *quiet in the land,* Ps. 35:20. And they are subject and submissive to their God, to all his precepts and all his providences. Actuated by this principle and disposition, they have *wrought his judgments,* that is, have obeyed his laws, observed his institutions, have made conscience of their duty to him, and have laid out themselves for the advancement of his honour and interest in the world. 2. What they are required to do; they must *seek,* which denotes both a careful enquiry and a constant endeavour, that they may know and do their duty. (1.) They must *seek the Lord,* seek his favour and grace, address him upon all occasions, ask of him what they need, seek him early, seek him diligently, and continue seeking him. (2.) They must *seek righteousness.* "Seek to God for the performance of his promises to you, and see to it that you abound yet more in duty to him; seek for the righteousness of Christ to be imputed to you, for the graces of God's Spirit to be implanted in you; hunger and thirst after them." (3.) They must *seek meekness.* This is a grace they were so eminent for that they were denominated *the meek of the land,* and yet this they must *seek.* Note, Those that are ever so good must still strive to be better, those that have ever so much grace must be still praying and labouring for more. Nay, those that excel in any particular grace must still seek to excel yet more in that, because in that most assaults will be made upon them by their enemies, in that most is expected from them by their friends, and in that they are most apt to be themselves secure. *Si dixisti, Sufficit, periisti — Say but, I am all that I ought to be, and you are undone.* In the difficult trying times approaching, the meek will find exercise for all the meekness they have, and all little enough, and therefore should seek it earnestly, and pray that when God in his providence gives them occasion for it he would by his grace enable them to exercise it, *to show all meekness to all men,* in all instances, that, *as the day is, so may the strength be.*

IV. Encouragements given to take these directions: *It may be, you shall be hid in the day of the Lord's anger.* 1. "You particularly that are the *meek of the earth.* Though the day of the Lord's anger do come upon the land, yet you shall be safe, you shall be taken under special protection. *Verily it shall be well with thy remnant,* Jer. 15:11. *Thy life will I give unto thee for a prey,* Jer. 45:5. *I will deliver thee in that day,* Jer. 39:17. *It may be, you shall be hid;* if any be hid, you shall." Good men cannot be sure of temporal preservation, for *all things come alike to all,* but they are most likely to be hid, and stand fairest for a distinguishing care of Providence. It is expressed thus doubtfully to try if they will trust the goodness of God's nature, though they have but the *it may be* of a promise, and to keep up in them a holy fear and watchfulness lest they should seem to come short, and should do any thing to throw themselves out of the divine protection. Note, those that hold fast their integrity, in times of common iniquity, have reason to hope that God will find out a hiding-place for them, where they shall be safe and easy, in times of common calamity. They shall be hid (as Luther says) *aut in coelo, aut sub coelo — either in heaven or under heaven,* either in the possession of heaven or under the protection of heaven. Or, 2. "You of this nation, though it be a *nation not desired,* yet, in the day of the Lord's anger with the neighbouring nations, when his judgments are abroad, *you shall be hid;* your land shall be preserved for the sake of those few meek ones that stand in the gap to *turn away the wrath of God."* It concerns us all to make it sure to ourselves that we shall be hid in the great day of God's wrath; and, if we hide ourselves in the chambers of duty, God will hide us in chambers of safety, Isa. 26:20. If we prepare an ark, that shall be our hiding-place, Gen. 7:1.

Verses 4–7

The prophet here comes to foretel what share the neighbouring nations should have in the destruction made upon those parts of the world by Nebuchadnezzar and his victorious Chaldees, as others of the prophets did at that time, which is designed, 1. To awaken the people of the Jews, by making them sensible how strong, how deep, how large, the inundation of calamities should be, that the *day of the Lord,* which was near, might appear the more dreadful, and they might thereby be quickened to prepare for it as for a general deluge. 2. To comfort them with this thought, that their case, though sad, should not be singular *(Solamen miseris socios habuisse doloris — The wretched find it consolatory to have companions of their woe),* and much more with this, that though God had seemed to be their enemy, and to fight against them, yet he was still so far their friend, and an enemy to their enemies, that he resented, and would revenge, the indignities done them.

In these verses we have the doom of the Philistines, who were near neighbours, and old enemies, to the people of Israel. Five lordships there were in that country; only four are here named — *Gaza* and *Ashkelon, Ashdod* and *Ekron;* Gath, the fifth, is not named, some think because it was now subject to Judah. They were the *inhabitants of the sea-coasts* (*v.* 5), for their country lay upon the Great Sea. The *nation of the Cherethites* is here joined with them, which bordered upon them (1 Sa. 30:14) and fell with them, as is foretold also, Eze. 25:16. The Philistines' land is here called Canaan, for it belonged to that country which God gave to his people Israel, and was inserted in the grant made to them, Jos. 13:3. This land is yet to be possessed *(five lords of the Philistines),* so that they wrongfully kept Israel out of the possession of it (Jdg. 3:3), which is now remembered against them. For, though the rights of others may be long detained unjustly, the righteous God will at length avenge the wrong.

I. It is here foretold that the Philistines, the usurpers, shall be dispossessed and quite extirpated. In general, here is a woe to them (*v.* 5), which, coming from God, denotes all misery: *The word of the Lord is against them* — the word of the former prophets, which, though not yet accomplished, will be in its season, Isa. 14:31. This word, now by this prophet, is against them. Note, Those are really in a woeful condition that have the word of the Lord against them, for no word of his shall fall to the ground. Those that rebel against the precepts of God's word shall have the *threatenings* of the word against them. The effect will be no less than their destruction, 1. God himself will be the author of it: *"I will even destroy thee,* who can make good what I say and will." 2. It shall be a universal destruction; it shall extend itself to all parts of the land, both city and country: *Gaza shall be forsaken,* though now a populous city. It was foretold (Jer. 47:6) that *baldness* should come upon Gaza; Alexander the Great razed that city, and we find (Acts 8:26) that Gaza was a desert. *Ashkelon* shall be *a desolation,* a pattern of desolation. *Ashdod shall be driven out at noon-day;* in the extremity of the scorching heat they shall have no shade, no shelter to protect them; but then, when most incommoded by the weather, they shall be forced away into captivity, which will be an aggravating circumstance of it. *Ekron* likewise shall be *rooted up,* that had been long taking root. The land of the Philistines shall be dispeopled; there *shall be no inhabitant, v.* 5. God made the earth *to be inhabited* (Isa. 45:18), otherwise he would have made it in vain; but, if men do not answer the end of their creation in serving God, it is just with God that the earth should not answer the end of its creation in serving them for a habitation; man's sin has sometimes subjected it to this vanity. 3. It shall be an utter destruction. The sea-coast, which used to be a harbour for ships and a habitation for merchants, shall now be deserted, and be only *cottages for shepherds* and *folds for flocks* (*v.* 6), and then perhaps put to better use than when it was possessed by the lords of the Philistines.

II. It is here foretold that the house of Judah, the rightful owners, shall recover the possession of it, *v.* 7. The remnant of those that shall *return out of captivity,* when God visits them, shall be made to *lie down* in safety *in the houses of Ashkelon,* to lie down *in the evening,* when they are weary and sleepy. There *they shall feed* themselves and their flocks. Note, God will at length restore his people to their rights, though they may be long kept out from them.

Verses 8–11

The Moabites and Ammonites were both of the posterity of Lot; their countries joined, and, both adjoining to Israel, they are here put together in the prophecy against them.

I. They are both charged with the same crime, and that was reproaching and reviling the people of God and triumphing in their calamities (*v.* 8): *They have reproached my people;* while God's people kept close to their duty it is probable that they reproached them for the singularities of their religion; and now that they had revolted from God, and fallen under his displeasure, they reproached them for that too. It has been the common lot of God's people in all ages to be reproached and reviled upon one account or other. Thus the old serpent spits his venom; and pride is at the bottom of it; it is in their pride that they have *magnified themselves against the people of the Lord of hosts,* thinking themselves as good as they, as great, and every way as happy. It is the *contempt of the proud* that God's people are filled with, Ps. 123:4. They have *spoken big* (so some read it, *magna locuti sunt — they have spoken great things) against their border* (*v.* 8), against those of them that bordered upon their country, whom upon all occasions they insulted, or against the property they claimed, which they disputed, or the protection they boasted of, which they ridiculed; they *spoke big against the people of the Lord of hosts* as a deserted abandoned people. *Great swelling words of vanity* are the genuine language of the church's enemies. "But *I have heard them"* (says God), "and will let you know that I have heard them. I have heard, and I will reckon for them," Jude 15. And, if God hears the reproaches and revilings we are under, it is a good reason why we should be as a *deaf man that hears not,* Ps. 38:14, 15. Nay, God not only takes notice of, but interests himself in the reproaches cast on his people, because they are his; and it is certain that those who look with disdain upon the people of the Lord of hosts thereby dishonour the Lord of hosts himself. See this very thing charged on Moab and Ammon, Eze. 25:3, 8.

II. They are both laid under the same doom. Associates in iniquity may expect to be such in desolation. See with what solemnity sentence is pronounced upon them, *v.* 9. It is *the Lord of hosts,* the sovereign Lord of all, who has authority to pass this sentence and ability to execute it; it is *the God of Israel,* who is jealous for their honour; it is he that has said it, nay, he has sworn it, *As I live, saith the Lord.* The sentence is, 1. That the Moabites and Ammonites shall be quite destroyed; they *shall be as Sodom and Gomorrah,* the marks of whose ruins in the Dead Sea lay near adjoining to the countries of Moab and Ammon; they shall, though not by the same means (even fire from heaven), Yet almost in the same manner, be laid waste; not again to be inhabited, or not of a long time. The country shall produce nothing but *nettles,* instead of corn; and there shall be *brine-pits,* instead of the pleasant fountains of water with which the country had abounded. 2. That Israel shall be too hard for them, shall *spoil them* of their goods and *possess* their country by lawful war. Note, Proud men sometimes, by the just judgment of God, fall under the mortification of being trampled upon themselves by those whom once they haughtily trampled upon. And *this shall they have for their pride.*

III. Other nations shall in like manner be humbled, that the Lord alone may be exalted (*v.* 11): *The Lord will be terrible* unto the Moabites and Ammonites in particular, who have made themselves a terror to his Israel. For, 1. Heathen gods must be abolished. They have long had possession, and their worshippers have both glorified them and gloried in them. But *the Lord* will *famish all the gods of the earth,* will starve them out of their strong-holds. The Pagans had a fond conceit that their idols were regaled by their offerings, and did *eat the fat of their sacrifices,* Deu. 32:38. *Omnia comesta à Belo — Bel has eaten all.* But it is here promised that when the Christian religion is set up in the world men shall be turned from the service of these dumb idols, shall forsake their altars, and bring no more sacrifices to them, and thus they shall be famished, or *made lean* (as the word is), their priests shall. This intimates the vanity of those idols; it lies in the power of their worshippers to famish them; whereas the true God says, *If I were hungry, I would not tell thee.* It intimates also the victory of the God of Israel over them. *Now know we that he is greater than all gods.* 2. Heathen nations must be converted; when the gospel gets ground, by it men shall be brought to worship him who lives for ever (for that is the command of the everlasting gospel, Rev. 14:7), *every one from his place;* they shall not need to go up to Jerusalem to worship the God of Israel, but wherever they are, they may have access to him. *I will that men pray every where.* God shall be worshipped, not only by all the tribes of Israel and the strangers who join themselves to them, but by all *the isles of the heathen.* This is a promise which looks favourably upon our native country, for it is one of the most considerable of the isles of the Gentiles, by which God will be glorified.

Verses 12–15

The cup is *going round,* when Nebuchadnezzar is going on conquering and to conquer; and not only Israel's near neighbours, but those that lay more remote, must be reckoned with for the wrongs they have done to God's people; the Ethiopians and the Assyrians are here taken to task. 1. The Ethiopians, or Arabians, that had sometimes been a terror to Israel (as in Asa's time, 2 Chr. 14:9), must now be reckoned with: They *shall be slain by my sword, v.* 12. Nebuchadnezzar was God's sword, the instrument in his hand with which these and other enemies were subdued and punished, Ps. 17:14. 2. The Assyrians, and Nineveh the head city of their monarchy, are next set to the bar, to receive their doom: *He* that is God's sword *will stretch out his hand against the north, and destroy Assyria,* and make himself master of it. Assyria had been the rod of God's anger against Israel, and now Babylon is the rod of God's anger against Assyria, Isa. 10:5. He *will make Nineveh a desolation,* as was lately and largely foretold by the prophet Nahum. Observe, (1.) How flourishing Nineveh's state had formerly been (*v.* 15): *This is the rejoicing city that dwelt carelessly.* Nineveh was so strong that she feared no evil, and therefore dwelt carelessly and set danger at defiance; she was so rich that she thought herself sure of all good, and therefore was a rejoicing city, full of mirth and gaiety; and she had such a dominion that she admitted no rival, but said in her heart, *"I am, and there is none besides me* that can compare with me, no city in the world that can pretend to be equal with me." God can with his judgments frighten the most secure, humble the most haughty, and mar the mirth of those that most laugh now. (2.) How complete Nineveh's ruin shall now be; it shall be made *a desolation, v.* 13. Such a heap of ruins shall this once pompous city be that it shall be, [1.] A receptacle for beasts, such a wilderness that *flocks shall lie down in it;* nay, such a waste, desolate, frightful place, that wild beasts, shall take up their abode there; the melancholy birds, as the *cormorant and bittern,* shall make their nests in what remains of the houses, as they sometimes do in old ruinous buildings that are uninhabited and unfrequented. The *lintels,* or chapiters of the pillars, the *windows* and *thresholds,* and all the fine *cedar-work* curiously engraven, shall lie exposed; and on them these rueful ominous birds shall perch, and their *voice shall sing.* How are the songs of mirth turned into hideous horrid noises! What little reason have men to be proud of stately buildings, and rich furniture, when they know not what all the pomp of them may come to at last! [2.] A derision to travellers. Those that had come from far, to gratify their curiosity with the sight of Nineveh's splendour, shall now look on her with as much contempt as ever they looked upon her with admiration (*v.* 15): *Every one that passes by shall hiss* at her, and *wag his hand,* making light of her desolations, nay, and making sport with them — "There is an end of proud Nineveh." They shall not weep, and wring their hands (the adversities of those are unpitied and unlamented who were insolent and haughty in their prosperity), but they shall *hiss and wag their hands,* forgetting that perhaps their own ruin is not far off.

CHAPTER 3

We now return to Jerusalem, and must again hear what God has to say to her, I. By way of reproof and threatening, for the abundance of wickedness that was found in her, of which divers instances are given, with the aggravations of them (v. 1–7). II. By way of promise of mercy and grace, which God had yet in reserve for them. Two general heads of promises here are: — 1. That God would bring in a glorious work of reformation among them, cleanse them from their sins, and bring them home to himself; many promises of this kind here are (v. 8–13). 2. That he would bring about a glorious work of salvation for them, when he had thus prepared them for it (v. 14–20). Thus the "Redeemer shall come to Zion," and to clear his own way, shall "turn away ungodliness from Jacob." These promises were to have their full accomplishment in gospel-times and gospel-graces.

Verses 1–7

One would wonder that Jerusalem, the holy city, where God was known, and his name was great, should be the city of which this black character is here given, that a place which enjoyed such abundance of the means of grace should become so very corrupt and vicious, and that God should permit it to be so; yet so it is, to show that *the law made nothing perfect;* but if this be the true character of Jerusalem, as no doubt it is (for God's judgments will make none worse than they are), it is no wonder that the prophet begins with *woe to her.* For the holy God hates sin in those that are nearest to him, nay, in them he hates it most. A sinful state is, and will be, a woeful state.

I. Here is a very bad character given of the city in general. How has the faithful city become a harlot! 1. She shames herself; she is *filthy and polluted* (v. 1), has made herself *infamous* (so some read it), *the gluttonous* city (so the margin), always cramming, and making provision for the flesh, to fulfil the lusts of it. Sin is the filthiness and pollution of persons and places, and makes them odious in the sight of the holy God. 2. She wrongs her neighbours and inhabitants; she is *the oppressing city.* Never any place had *statutes and judgments so righteous* as this city had, and yet, in the administration of the government, never was more unrighteousness. 3. She is very provoking to her God, and in every respect walks contrary to him, *v.* 2. He had given his law, and spoken to her by his servants the prophets, telling her what was the good she should do and what the evil she should avoid; but *she obeyed not his voice,* nor made conscience of doing as he commanded her, in any thing. He had taken her under an excellent discipline, both of the word and of the rod; but she did not receive the instruction of the one nor the correction of the other, did not submit to God's will nor answer his end in either. He encouraged her to depend upon him, and his power and promise, for deliverance from evil and supply with good; but she *trusted not in the Lord;* her confidence was placed in her alliances with the nations more than in her covenant with God. He gave her tokens of his presence, and instituted ordinances of communion for her with himself; but she *drew not near to her God,* did not meet him where he appointed and where he promised to meet her. She stood at a distance, and *said to the Almighty, Depart.*

II. Here is a very bad character of the leading men in it; those that should by their influence suppress vice and profaneness there are the great patterns and patrons of wickedness, and those that should be her physicians are really her worst disease. 1. *Her princes are* ravenous and barbarous as *roaring lions* that make a prey of all about them, and they are universally feared and hated; they use their power for destruction, and not for edification. 2. *Her judges,* who should be the protectors of injured innocence, *are evening wolves,* rapacious and greedy, and their cruelty and covetousness both insatiable: *They gnaw not the bones till the morrow;* they take so much delight and pleasure in cruelty and oppression that when they have devoured a good man they reserve the bones, as it were, for a sweet morsel, to be gnawed the next morning, Job 31:31. 3. *Her prophets,* who pretend to be special messengers from heaven to them, *are light and treacherous persons,* fanciful, and of a vain imagination, frothy and airy, and of a loose conversation, men of no consistency with themselves, in whom one can put no confidence. They were so given to bantering that it was hard to say when they were serious. Their pretended prophecies were all a sham, and they secretly laughed at those that were deluded by them. 4. *Her priests,* who are teachers by office and have the charge of the holy things, are false to their trust and

betray it. They were to preserve the purity of the *sanctuary,* but they did themselves *pollute* it, and the sacred offices of it, which they were to attend upon — such priests as Hophni and Phinehas, who by their wicked lives *made the sacrifices of the Lord to be abhorred.* They were to expound and apply *the law,* and to judge according to it; but, in their explications and applications of it, they *did violence to the law;* they corrupted the sense of it, and perverted it to the patronising of that which was directly contrary to it. By forced constructions, they made the law to speak what they pleased, to serve a turn, and so, in effect, *made void the law.*

III. We have here the aggravations of this general corruption of all orders and degrees of men in Jerusalem.

1. They had the tokens of God's presence among them, and all the advantages that could be of knowing his will, with the strongest inducements possible to do it, and yet they persisted in their disobedience, *v.* 5. (1.) They had the honour and privilege of the Shechinah, God's dwelling in their land, so as he dwelt not with any other people: "*The just Lord is in the midst of thee,* to take cognizance of all thou doest amiss and give countenance to all thou doest well; he is in the midst of thee as a holy God, and therefore thy pollutions are the more offensive, Deu. 23:14. He is in the midst of you as a just God, and therefore will punish the affronts you put upon him, and the wrongs and injuries you do to one another." (2.) They had God's own example set before them, in the discovery he made of himself to them, that they might conform to it: "*He will not do iniquity,* and therefore you should not;" for this was the great rule of their institution, "*Be you holy, for I am holy.* God will be true to you; be not you then false to him." (3.) He sent to them his prophets, rising up early and sending them: *Every morning he brings his judgment to light,* as duly as the morning comes; *he fails not.* He shows them plainly what the good is which he requires of them, and puts them in mind of it; he *wakens morning by morning* (Isa. 50:4), wakens his prophets with the rising sun, to bring to light the things which belong to their peace. So that, upon the whole matter, what more could have been done to his vineyard, to make it fruitful? Isa. 5:4. And yet, after all, *the unjust know no shame;* those that have been unjust are unjust still, and are not ashamed of their unrighteousness, *neither can they blush.* If they had any sense of honour, any shame left in them, they would not go so directly contrary to their profession and to the instructions given them. But those that are past shame are past cure.

2. God had set before their eyes some remarkable monuments of his justice, which were designed for warning to them (*v.* 6): *I have cut off the nations,* the seven nations of Canaan, which the land spewed out for their wickedness, upon which they had this caution given them, to take heed lest it *spew them out also,* Lev. 18:28. Or it may refer to some of the neighbouring nations that were made desolate for their wickedness, especially to the nations of Israel, the ten tribes. *Their towers were desolate,* their high towers, their strong towers, their pride and power broken; *their streets were wasted,* so that none passed along through them; *their cities* were *destroyed* and laid in ruins; *no man* was to be found in them, *no inhabitant,* all were slain or carried into captivity. The enemies did it, but God avows it: *I cut them off,* says he. And God designed this for an admonition to Jerusalem (Eze. 23:9, 11): "*I said, Surely thou wilt fear me;* surely these judgments upon others will deter thee from the like wicked practices; *surely thou wilt receive instruction* by these providences; it ought to be expected that thou wouldst not continue to sin like the nations when thou seest the ruin which their sin brought upon them." They could not but see their own house in danger when their neighbour's was on fire; and, when we are frightened, God should be feared.

3. He had set before them life and death, good and evil, both in his word and in his providence. (1.) He had assured them of the continuance of their prosperity if they would fear him and receive instruction, for so *their dwelling would not be cut off* as their neighbour's was; if they took the warning given them, and reformed, what was past should be pardoned, and their tranquility lengthened out. (2.) He had made them feel the smart of the rod, though he reprieved them from the sword: *Howsoever I punished them,* that, being chastened, they might not be condemned. Such various methods did God take with them,

to reclaim them, but all in vain; they were not won upon by gentle methods, nor had severe ones any effect, for *they rose early, and corrupted all their doings;* they were more resolute and eager in their wicked courses than ever, more studious and solicitous in making provision for their lusts, and let slip no opportunity for the gratification of them. God *rose up early,* to send them his *prophets,* to reduce and reclaim them, but they were *up before him,* to shut and bolt the door against them. Their wickedness was universal: *All their doings* were corrupted; and it was all owing to themselves; they could not lay the blame upon the tempter, but they alone must bear it; they themselves wilfully and designedly *corrupted all their doings;* for *every man is tempted when he is drawn aside of his own lust and enticed.*

Verses 8–13

Things looked very bad with Jerusalem in the foregoing verses; she has got into a very bad name, and seems to be incorrigible, incurable, mercy-proof and judgment-proof. Now one would think it should follow, Therefore expect no other but that she should be utterly abandoned and rejected as *reprobate silver;* since they will not be wrought upon by prophets or providences, let them be made a desolation as their neighbours have been. But behold and wonder at the riches of divine grace, which takes occasion from man's badness to appear so much the more illustrious. They still grew worse and worse, *therefore wait you upon me, saith the Lord, v.* 8. "Since the *law,* it seems, will *make nothing perfect,* the *bringing in of a better hope shall.* Let those that lament the corruptions of the church *wait upon God,* till he send his Son into the world, to *save his people from their sins,* till he send his gospel to reform and refine his church, and to purify to himself a peculiar people both of Jews and Gentiles." And there were those who, according to this direction and encouragement, *waited for redemption,* for this redemption in Jerusalem; and long-looked-for came at last, Lu. 2:38. *For judgment* Christ will *come into this world,* Jn. 9:39.

I. To avenge what has been done amiss against his church, to bring down and destroy the enemies of it, its spiritual enemies, of which the destruction of Babylon, and other oppressors of God's people, in the Old-Testament times, was a type, and would be a happy presage. He will *rise up to the prey,* to *lead captivity captive* (Ps. 67:18), to conquer and spoil the powers of darkness, and the powers on earth that set themselves *against the Lord and his anointed;* he will *break them with a rod of iron* (Ps. 2:5, 9; 11:5, 6); his *determination is to gather the nations* and to *assemble the kingdoms.* By the gospel of Christ preached to every creature all nations are summoned, as it were, to appear in a body before the Lord Jesus, who is about to set up his kingdom in the world. But, since the greatest part of mankind will not obey the summons, he will *pour upon them his indignation,* for he that *believes not is condemned already.* At the time of the setting up of the kingdom of the Messiah, there shall be on earth *distress of nations with perplexity* (Lu. 21:25), *great tribulation,* such as *never was, nor ever shall be,* Mt. 24:21. Then God pours upon the nations his indignation, even *all his fierce anger,* for their indignation and fierce anger against the Messiah and his kingdom, Ps. 2:1, 2. Then *all the earth shall be devoured with the fire of his jealousy;* both Jews and Gentiles shall be reckoned with for their enmity to the gospel. Principalities and powers shall be spoiled, and *made a show of openly,* and the victorious Redeemer shall triumph over them. The end of those that continue to be of the earth, and to *mind earthly things,* after God has set up the *kingdom of heaven* among men, *shall be destruction* (Phil. 3:19); they shall be *devoured with the fire of God's jealousy.*

II. To amend what he finds amiss in his church. When God intends the restoration of Israel, and the revival of their peace and prosperity, he makes way for the accomplishment of his purpose by their reformation and the revival of their virtue and piety; for this is God's method, both with particular persons and with communities, first to make them holy and then to make them happy. These promises were in part accomplished after the return of the Jews out of Babylon, when by their captivity they were thoroughly cured of their idolatry; and this was all the fruit, even the taking away of sin. But they look further, to the blessed effects of the gospel and the grace of it, to those *times of reformation* in which we live, Heb. 9:10.

1. It is promised that there shall be a reformation in men's discourse, which had been generally corrupt, but should now be with grace seasoned with salt (*v.* 9): *"Then will I turn to the people a pure language;* I will turn the people to such a language from that *evil communication* which has almost ruined all *good manners* among them." Note, Converting grace refines the language, not by making the phrases witty, but the substance wise. Among the Jews, after the captivity, there needed a reformation of the dialect, for they had mingled the language of Canaan with that of Ashdod (Neh. 13:24), and that grievance shall be redressed. But that is not all: their language shall be purified from all profaneness, filthiness, and falsehood. I will turn them to a *choice language* (so some read it); they shall not speak rashly, but with caution and deliberation; they shall *choose out their words.* Note, An air of purity and piety in common conversation is a very happy omen to any people; other graces, other blessings, shall be given where God gives a pure language to those who have been a *people of unclean lips.*

2. That the worship of God, according to his will, shall be more closely applied to, and more unanimously concurred in. Instead of sacrifice and incense, they shall *call upon the name of the Lord.* Prayer is the spiritual offering with which God must be honoured; and, to prepare and fit us for that duty, it is necessary that we have a *pure language.* We are utterly unfit to take God's name into our lips, unless they be pure lips. The purifying of the language in common conversation is necessary to the acceptableness of the words of our mouth and the meditation of our heart on our devotion; for how can *sweet waters and bitter* come *out of the same fountain?* James 3:9–12. It is likewise promised that their language being thus purified they shall serve God *with one consent,* with *one shoulder* (so the word is), alluding to oxen in the yoke, that draw even. When Christians are unanimous in the service of God the work goes on cheerfully. This is the effect of the pure language, purified from passion, envy, and censoriousness. Note, Purity is the way to unity; the reformation of manners is the way to a comprehension. *The wisdom from above is first pure, then peaceable.*

3. That those that were driven from God shall return to him and be accepted of him (*v.* 10): *From beyond the rivers of Ethiopia,* that is, from Egypt (so described, Isa. 18:1) or from some other very remote country — *my suppliants, even the daughter of my dispersed, shall bring my offering.* Those that by reason of their distance had almost forgotten God, their obligations to him, shall be put in mind of him, as the prodigal son was of his father's house, in the far country. Those that by reason of their dispersion, under the tokens of his displeasure, might be afraid of coming to him, yet even they shall be gathered under his wings; the *daughter of his dispersed,* that is *afar off,* will be found among those whom *the Lord our God shall call;* and, though they are dispersed, he will own them for his; his calling them *my dispersed* puts honour upon them, sufficient to counterbalance all the disgrace of their dispersion. These shall come, (1.) With their humble petitions: They are *my suppliants.* Note, True converts are suppliants to God; they do not plead, but *make supplication to their Judge* (Job 9:15); and wherever they are, though *beyond the rivers of Ethiopia,* a great way off from his house of prayer, he has his eye upon them and his ear open to them; they are his suppliants. (2.) With their spiritual sacrifices: *They shall bring my offering,* shall bring themselves as spiritual sacrifices to God (Rom. 12:1); the conversion of the Gentiles is called *the offering up of the Gentiles* (Rom. 15:16); and with themselves they shall bring the gospel-sacrifices of prayer, and praise, and alms, with which God is well pleased.

4. That sin and sinners shall be purged out from among them, *v.* 11. God will take away, (1.) Their just reproach: *In that day shalt thou not be ashamed for all thy doings.* They shall be ashamed as penitents, and shall continue to be so (see Eze. 16:63), but they shall not be ashamed as sinners that return to folly again. *"Thou shalt not be ashamed,* that is, thou shalt no more do a shameful thing, as thou hast done." The guilt of sin being taken away by pardoning mercy, the reproach of it shall be rolled away from the sinner's own conscience, that being *purified,* and *pacified,* and *cleansed from dead works.* When wickedness and wicked people abound in a nation those few in it that are good are ashamed of them and of their land; but when sinners are converted, and the land reformed, that shame and the cause of it are removed. (2.) Their unjust glorying: *"I will take away out of the midst of thee,* not only the profane, who are a shame to thy land, but the hypocrites, who appear beautiful outwardly, and *rejoice in thy pride,* in the holy city, the holy house." These were indeed Israel's glory, but they made them their pride, and rejoiced in them, as if they were an invincible bulwark to secure them in their sinful ways; they relied on them as their righteousness and strength, boasting of *the temple of the Lord, the temple of the Lord* (Jer. 7:4); they were *haughty because of the holy mountain,* were conceited of themselves, scornful of others, and set even the judgments of God at defiance. Note, Church-privileges, when they are not duly improved as they ought to be, are often made the matter of men's pride and the ground of their security. But that haughtiness is the most offensive to God which is supported and fed by the pretensions of holiness. This God will silence and take away.

5. That God will have a remnant of holy, humble, serious people among them, that shall have the comfort of their relation to him and interest in him (*v.* 12): *I will leave in the midst of thee an afflicted and poor people.* When the Chaldeans carried away the Jews into captivity they *left of the poor of the land for vine-dressers and husbandmen,* a type and figure of God's distinguished remnant, whom he sets apart for himself. They are *afflicted* and *poor,* low in the world; such *God has chosen,* James 2:5. The poor are evangelized, low in their own eyes, afflicted for sin, poor in spirit. They are God's leaving, for it is a *remnant according to the election of grace. I have reserved them to myself,* says God (Rom. 11:4, 5), *and they shall trust in the name of the Lord.* Note, Those whom God designs for the glory of his name he enables to trust in his name; and the greater their affliction and poverty in the world are the more reason they see to trust in God, having nothing else to trust to, 1 Tim, 5:5.

6. That this select remnant shall be blessed with purity and peace, *v.* 13. (1.) They shall be blessed with purity, both in words and actions: They *shall neither do iniquity nor speak lies.* Justice and veracity shall command them and govern them, though they be ever so much against their secular interest. They shall not only not speak a direct deliberate lie, but *there shall not be a deceitful tongue found in their mouth,* not in the mouth of any of them; not the least equivocation shall come from them. (2.) They shall be blessed with peace. They shall, as the sheep of God's pasture, *feed* and *lie down, and none shall make them afraid.* They shall not be fearful themselves, nor shall any about them be frightful to them. Note, Those that are careful not to do iniquity need not be afraid of any calamity, for it cannot hurt them, and therefore should not terrify them.

Verses 14–20

After the promises of the taking away of sin, here follow promises of the taking away of trouble; for when the cause is removed the effect will cease. What makes a people holy will make them happy of course. The precious promises here made to the purified people were to have their full accomplishment in the comforts of the gospel, in the hope, and much more in the enjoyment, of which, they are here called upon, 1. To rejoice and sing (*v.* 14): *Sing, O daughter of Zion!* sing for joy; *Shout, O Israel!* in a holy transport and exultation; *be glad and rejoice with all the heart;* let the joy be inward, let it be great. Those that love God with all their heart have occasion with all their heart to rejoice in him. It was promised (*v.* 13) that their sins should be mortified and their fears silenced, and then follows, *Sing* and *rejoice.* Note, Those that reform have cause to rejoice, whereas Israel cannot rejoice for joy as other people, while she goes a whoring from her God. God's promises, applied by faith, furnish the saints with constant and abundant matter for joy; they are filled with joy and peace in believing them. 2. To throw off all their discouragements (*v.* 16): *In that day it shall be said to Jerusalem* (God will say it by his prophets, by his providences, their neighbours shall say it, they shall say it to one another), *"Fear thou not,* be not disposed to fear, do not easily admit the impressions of it; when things are bad, fear not their being worse, but hope they will mend; frighten not thyself upon every occasion. *Let not thy hands be slack* or *faint;* wring not thy hands in despair; drop not thy hands in despondence; disfit not thyself for thy work and warfare by giving way to doubts and fears. Pluck up thy spirits, and, in token of that, lift up thy hands, the *hands that hung down,* Heb. 12:12; Isa. 35:3. Lift up thy hands in prayer to God; lift up thy hands to help thyself." Fear makes the hands slack, but faith and hope make them vigorous, and the joy of the Lord will be our strength both for doing and suffering.

Let us now see what these precious promises are which are here made to the people of God, for the banishing of their griefs and fears and the encouraging of their hopes and joys; and to us are these promises made as well as to them.

I. An end shall be put to all their troubles and distresses (*v.* 15): *"The Lord has taken away thy judgments,* has removed all the calamities thou hast been groaning under, which were the punishments of thy sin; the noise of war shall be silenced, the reproach of famine done away, and the captivity brought back. Though some grievances remain, they shall be only afflictions, and not judgments, for sin shall be pardoned. *He has cast out thy enemy,* that has thrust himself into thy land, and triumphed over thee. He has *swept out thy enemy"* (so some read it), "as dirt is swept out of the house to the dunghill." When they sweep out their sins with the besom of reformation God will sweep out their enemies with the besom of destruction. If they should need correction, they shall fall into the hands of the Lord, whose mercies are great, and shall not again fall into the hands of man, whose tender mercies are cruel: *"Thou shalt not see evil any more,* not such evil days as thou hast seen." Note, The way to get clear of the evil of trouble is to keep clear from the evil of sin; and to those that do so trouble has no real evil in it.

II. God will give them the tokens of his presence with them; though he has long seemed to stand at a distance (they having provoked him to withdraw), he will make it to appear that he is *with them of a truth: "The Lord is in the midst of thee, O Zion!* of thee, *O Jerusalem!* as the sun in the centre of the universe, to diffuse his light and influence upon every part. He is *in the midst of thee,* to preside in all thy affairs and to take care of all thy interests." And, 1. "He is the *King of Israel* (*v.* 15) and is in the midst of thee as a king in the midst of his people." With an eye to this, our Lord Jesus is called the *King of Israel* (Jn. 1:49); and he is, and will be, in the midst of his church always, even to the end of the world, to receive the homage of his subjects, and to give out his favours to them, even *where* but *two or three are gathered together in his name.* 2. "He is the Lord thy God, thine in covenant, and he is in the midst of thee as thy God, whom thou hast an interest in and whose own thou art. He has put himself into dear relations to thee, laid himself by promise under obligations to thee, and, that thou mayest have abundant comfort in both, he *is in the midst of thee,* nigh at hand to answer both." 3. "He that is in the midst of thee as thy God and King is *mighty,* is almighty, is able to do all that for thee that thou needest and canst desire." 4. "He has engaged his power for thy succour: *He will save. He will be Jesus,* will answer the name, for he will save his people from their sins."

III. God will take delight in them, and in doing them good. The expressions of this are very lively and affecting (*v.* 17): *He will rejoice over thee with joy,* will not only be well pleased with thee, upon thy repentance and reformation, and take thee into favour, but will take a complacency in thee, as the bridegroom does in his bride, or the bride in her ornaments, Isa. 62:3–5. The conversion of sinners and the consolation of saints are the joy of angels, for they are the joy of God him-self. The church should be the *joy of the whole earth* (Ps. 48:2), for it is the joy of the whole heaven. He will *rest in his love,* will be *silent in his love,* so the word is. "I will not rebuke thee as I have done, for thy sins; I will acquiesce in thee, and in my relation to thee." I know not where there is the like expression of Christ's love to his church, unless in that song of songs, Cant. 4:9, *Thou hast ravished my heart, my sister, my spouse, with one of thy eyes.* O the condescensions of divine grace! The great God not only loves his saints, but he loves to love them, is pleased that he has pitched upon these objects of his love. He *will joy over them with singing.* He that is grieved for the sin of sinners rejoices in the graces and services of the saints, and is ready to express that joy by singing over them. *The Lord takes plea-sure in those that fear him,* and in them Jesus Christ will shortly be glorified and admired.

IV. God will comfort Zion's mourners, who sympathize with her in her griefs, and will wipe away their tears (*v.* 18): *I will gather those who are sorrowful for the solemn assemblies, to whom the reproach of it was a burden.* See, 1. Who those are whom God will rejoice in and make to rejoice. They are such as are sorrowful. Those only must expect to reap in joy that sow in tears. The sorrowful now shall be for ever joyful. 2. What is the great matter of sorrow to Zion's mourners, when Zion is in mourning. Many are her calamities. The city is ruined, and the palaces are demolished; trade is at an end, and the administration of public justice; but all these are nothing to them in comparison with the desolations of the sanctuary, the destruction of the temple and the altar, to attend on which, in solemn feasts, all Israel used to come together three times a year. It is for those sacred solemn assemblies that they are sorrowful, (1.) Because they are dispersed; there is no temple to come up to, or, if there were, no people to come up to it; so that the *solemn feasts and sabbaths are forgotten in Zion,* Lam. 2:6. Note, The restraining of public assemblies for religious worship, the scattering of them by their enemies, or the forsaking of them by their friends, so that either there are no assemblies or not solemn ones, is a very sorrowful thing to all good people. If *the ways of Zion mourn,* the sons of Zion mourn too. And hereby they make it to appear that they are indeed of Zion, living members of that body with the grievances of which they are so sensibly affected. (2.) Because they are despised; the reproach of the solemn assemblies is a burden to them. It had been the lot of the solemn assemblies to lie under a great deal of reproach. Satan and his instruments having a particular spite at them, as the great support of the interest of God's kingdom among men. Black and odious characters have been put upon those assemblies; and this is a burden to all those that have a cordial concern for the glory of God and the welfare of the souls of men. They reckon that the reproaches of those who reproach the solemn assemblies fall upon them, fall foul upon them.

V. God will recover the captives out of the hands of their oppressors, and bring home the banished that seemed to be expelled, *v.* 19, 20. 1. Their enemies shall be disabled to detain them in bondage: *"At that time I will undo all that afflict thee,* will break their power, and blast their counsels, so that they shall be forced to surrender the prey they have taken." *Conficiam — I will take them to task;* "I will be doing with them shortly, and so as to make an end of them." Note, Those that abuse and oppress God's people take the ready way to undo themselves. 2. They shall be enabled to assert and recover their liberty, and all the difficulties in the way of it shall be surmounted. Is the church weak and wounded? *I will save her that halts,* as was promised, Mic. 4:7. He will help her when she cannot help herself; even *the lame shall take the prey,* Isa. 33:23. Is she dispersed, and not likely to incorporate for her common benefit? I will *gather her that was driven out,* and *bring her again at the time that I gather her.* One act of mercy and grace shall serve both to collect them out of their dispersions and to conduct them to their own land. When the *people's hearts are prepared,* the work will be done suddenly; and who can hinder it if God undertake to effect it? *"I will turn back your captivity before your eyes, saith the Lord;* you shall plainly discern the hand of God in it, and say, *This is the Lord's doing."*

VI. God will by all this put honour upon them and gain them respect from all about them. Israel was at first *made high above all nations in praise and fame,* Deu. 26:19. The reproach brought upon them was therefore one of the sorest of their grievances (nothing cuts deeper to those that are in honour than disgrace does); and therefore when God returns, in mercy, to his church, it is here promised that she shall regain her credit; all the reproach shall be for ever rolled way, as Israel's at Gilgal, Jos. 5:9. The church shall be as honourable as ever she had been despicable. 1. Even those that reproached her shall be made to respect her: *"I will get them praise and fame in every land, where they have been put to shame,* that the same who were the witnesses of their disgrace may see cause to change their mind concerning them." Those that said, "This is Zion whom no man looks after," shall say, "This is Zion whom the great God looks after." And she that was looked upon to be the *offscouring of the earth* now appears to be the darling of heaven. 2. Even those that never knew her shall be brought to honour her (*v.* 20): *I will make you a name and a praise among all people of the earth.* So the Jewish church was when *the fear of the Jews* fell upon their neighbours (Esth. 8:17), and some of all nations said, *we will go with you, for we have heard that God is with you,* Zec. 8:23. So the Christian church was when it was made to flourish in the world, for there is that in it which may justly recommend it to the value and esteem of all the people of the earth. And so the universal church of the firstborn will be in the great day, when the saints shall be brought together to Christ, that he may be admired and glorified in them, and they admired and glorified in him before angels and men. Then will God's Israel be *made a name and a praise* to eternity.

AN EXPOSITION, WITH PRACTICAL OBSERVATIONS, OF

THE PROPHECY OF HAGGAI

The captivity in Babylon gave a very remarkable turn to the affairs of the Jewish church both in history and prophecy. It is made a signal epocha in our Saviour's genealogy, Mt. 1:17. Nine of the twelve minor prophets, whose oracles we have been hitherto consulting, lived and preached before that captivity, and most of them had an eye to it in their prophecies, foretelling it as the just punishment of Jerusalem's wickedness. But the last three (in whom the Spirit of prophecy took its period, until it revived in Christ's forerunner) lived and preached after the return out of captivity, not immediately upon it, but some time after. Haggai and Zechariah appeared much about the same time, eighteen years after the return, when the building of the temple was both retarded by its enemies and neglected by its friends. *Then the prophets, Haggai the prophet and Zechariah the son of Iddo, prophesied unto the Jews that were in Jerusalem, in the name of the God of Israel, even unto them* (so we read Ezra 5:1), to reprove them for their remissness, and to encourage them to revive that good work when it had stood still for some time, and to go on with it vigorously, notwithstanding the opposition they met with in it. Haggai began two months before Zechariah, who was raised up to second him, that out of the mouth of two witnesses the word might be established. But Zechariah continued longer at the work; for all Haggai's prophecies that are recorded were delivered within four months, in the second year of Darius, between the beginning of the sixth month and the end of the ninth. But we have Zechariah's prophecies dated above two years after, Zec. 7:1. Some have the honour to lead, others to last, in the work of God. The Jews ascribe to these two prophets the honour of being members of the great synagogue (as they call it), which was formed after the return out of captivity; we think it more certain, and it was their honour, and a much greater honour, that they prophesied of Christ. Haggai spoke of him as the *glory of the latter house,* and Zechariah as *the man, the branch.* In them the light of that morning star shone more brightly than in the foregoing prophecies, as they lived nearer the time of the rising of the Sun of righteousness, and now began to see his day approaching. The Septuagint makes Haggai and Zechariah to be the penmen of Ps. 138 and Ps. 146, 147, and 148.

CHAPTER 1

In this chapter, after the preamble of the prophecy, we have, I. A reproof of the people of the Jews for their dilatoriness and slothfulness in building the temple, which had provoked God to contend with them by the judgment of famine and scarcity, with an exhortation to them to resume that good work and to prosecute it in good earnest (*v.* 1–11). II. The good success of this sermon, appearing in the people's return and close application to that work, wherein the prophet, in God's name, animated and encouraged them, assuring them that God was with them (*v.* 12–15).

Verses 1–11

It was the complaint of the Jews in Babylon that they *saw not their signs,* and there was *no more prophet* (Ps. 74:9), which was a just judgment upon them for mocking and misusing the prophets. We read of no prophets they had in their return, as they had in their coming out of Egypt, Hos. 12:13. God stirred them up immediately by his Spirit to exert themselves in that escape (Ezra 1:5); for, though God makes use of prophets, he needs them not, he can do his work without them. But the lamp of Old-Testament prophecy shall yet make some bright and glorious efforts before it expire; and Haggai is the first that appears under the character of a special messenger from heaven, when the *word of the Lord* had been long *precious* (as when prophecy began, 1 Sa. 3:1) and *there had been no open vision.* In the reign of Darius Hystaspes, the third of the Persian kings, in the second year of his reign, this prophet was sent; and the word of the Lord came to him, and came by him to the leading men among the Jews, who are here named, *v.* 1. The chief governor, 1. In the state; that was *Zerubbabel, the son of Shealtiel,* of the house of David, who was commander-in-chief of the Jews, in their return out of captivity. 2. In the church; and that was *Joshua the son of Josedech,* who was now *high priest.* They were great men and good men, and yet were to be stirred up to their duty when they grew remiss. What the people also were faulty in they must be told of, that they might use their power and interest for the mending of it. The prophets, who were extraordinary messengers, did not go about to set aside the ordinary institutions of magistracy and ministry, but endeavoured to render both more effectual for the ends to which they were appointed, for both ought to be supported. Now observe,

I. What the sin of the Jews was at this time, *v.* 2. As soon as they came up out of captivity they set up an altar for sacrifice, and within a year after laid the foundations of a temple, Ezra 3:10. They then seemed very forward in it, and it was likely enough that the work would be done suddenly; but, being served with a prohibition some time after from the Persian court, and charged not to go on with it, they not only yielded to the force, when they were actually under it, which might be excused, but afterwards, when the violence of the opposition had abated, they continued very indifferent to it, had no spirit nor courage to set about it again, but seemed glad that they had a pretence to let it stand still. Though those who are employed for God may be driven off from their work by a storm, yet they must return to it as soon as the storm is over. These Jews did not do so, but continued loitering until they were afresh reminded of their duty. And that which they suggested one to another was, *The time has not come, the time that the Lord's house should be built;* that is, 1. "Our time has not come for the doing of it, because we have not yet recovered, after our captivity; our losses are not repaired, nor have we yet got before-hand in the world. It is too great an undertaking for new beginners in the world, as we are; let us first get our own houses up, before we talk of building churches, and in the mean time let a bare altar serve us, as it did our father Abraham." They did not say that they would not build a temple at all, but,

"Not yet; it is all in good time." Note, Many a good work is put by by being put off, as Felix put off the prosecution of his convictions to a more convenient season. They do not say that they will never repent, and reform, and be religious, but, "Not yet." And so the great business we were sent into the world to do is not done, under pretence that it is all in good time to go about it. 2. "God's time has not come for the doing of it; for (say they) the restraint laid upon us by authority in a legal way is not broken off, and therefore we ought not to proceed, though there be a present connivance of authority." Note, There is an aptness in us to misinterpret providential discouragements in our duty, as if they amounted to a discharge from our duty, when they are only intended for the trial and exercise of our courage and faith. It is bad to neglect our duty, but it is worse to vouch Providence for the patronising of our neglects.

II. What the judgments of God were by which they were punished for this neglect, *v.* 6, 9–11. They neglected the building of God's house, and put that off, that they might have time and money for their secular affairs. They desired to be excused from such an expensive piece of work under this pretence, that they must provide for their families; their children must have meat and portions too, and, until they have got before-hand in the world, they cannot think of rebuilding the temple. Now, that the punishment might answer to the sin, God by his providence kept them still behind-hand, and that poverty which they thought to prevent by not building the temple God brought upon them for not building it. They were sensible of the smart of the judgment, and every one complained of the unseasonable weather, the great losses they sustained in their corn and cattle, and the decay of trade; but they were not sensible of the cause of the judgment, and the ground of God's controversy with them. They did not, or would not, see and own that it was for their putting off the building of the temple that they lay under these manifest tokens of God's displeasure; and therefore God here gives them notice that this is that for which he contended with them. Note, We need the help of God's prophets and ministers to expound to us, not only the judgments of God's mouth, but the judgments of his hands, that we may understand his mind and meaning in his rod as well as in his word, to discover to us not only wherein we have offended God, but wherein God shows himself offended at us. Let us observe,

1. How God contended with them. He did not send them into captivity again, nor bring a foreign enemy upon them, as they deserved, but took the correcting of them into his own hands; for his mercies are great. (1.) He that *gives seed to the sower* denied his blessing upon the *seed sown,* and then it never prospered; they had nothing, or next to nothing, from it. *They sowed much* (*v.* 6), kept a great deal of ground in tillage, which, they might expect, would turn to a better advantage than usual, because their land had long *lain fallow* and had *enjoyed its sabbaths.* Having sown much, they looked for much from it, enough to spend and enough to spare too; but they were disappointed: *They bring in little,* very little (*v.* 6); when they have made the utmost of it, *it comes to little* (*v.* 9); it did not yield as they expected. Isa. 5:10, *The seed of a homer shall yield an ephah,* a bushel's sowing shall yield a peck. Note, Our expectations from the creature are often most frustrated when they are most raised; and then, when we look for much, it comes to little, that our expectation may be from God only, in whom it will be outdone. We are here told how they came to be disappointed (*v.* 10): *The heaven over you is stayed from dew;* he that has the key of the clouds in his hands shut them up, and withheld the rain when the ground called for it, the former or the latter rain, and then of course *the earth is stayed from her fruit;* for, if the heaven be as brass, the earth is as iron. The corn perhaps came up very well, and promised a very plentiful crop, but, for want of the dews at earing-time, it never filled, but was parched with the heat of the sun and withered away. The restored captives, who had long been kept bare in Babylon, thought they should never want when they had got their own land in possession again and had that at command. But what the better are they for it, unless they had the clouds at command too? God will make us sensible of our necessary and constant dependence upon him, throughout all the links in the chain of second causes, from first to last; so that we can at no time say, "Now we have no further occasion for God and his providence." See Hos. 2:21. But God not only withheld the cooling rains, but he appointed the scorching heats (*v.* 11): *I called for a drought upon the land,* ordered the weather to be extremely hot, and then the fruits of the earth were burnt up. See how every creature is that to us which God makes it to be, either comfortable or afflictive, serving us or incommoding us. Nothing among the inferior creatures is so necessary and beneficial to the world as the heat of the sun; it is that which puts life into the plants and *renews the face of the earth at* spring. And yet, if that go into an extreme, it undoes all again. Our Creator is our best friend; but, if we make him our enemy, we make the best friends we have among the creatures our enemies too. This drought God called for, and it came at the call; as the winds and the waves, so the rays of the sun, obey him. It was universal, and the ill effects of it were general; it was a drought *upon the mountains,* which, lying high, were first affected with it. The mountains were their pasture-grounds, and used to be *covered over with flocks,* but now there was no grass for them. It was *upon the corn, the new wine, and the oil;* all failed through the extremity of the hot weather, even *all that the ground brought forth;* it all withered. Nay, it had a bad influence upon men; the hot weather enfeebled some, and made them weary and faint, and spent their spirits; it inflamed others, and put them into fevers. It should seem, it brought diseases upon cattle too. In short, it spoiled *all the labour of their hands,* which they hoped to eat of and maintain their families by. Note, Meat for the belly is meat that perishes, and, if we labour for that only, we are in danger of losing our labour; but we are sure *our labour shall not be in vain in the Lord* if we labour for *the meat which endures to eternal life.* For the *hand of the diligent,* in the business of religion, will infallibly *make rich,* whereas, in the business of this life, the most solicitous and the most industrious often lose the labour of their hands. *The race is not to the swift, nor the battle to the strong.* (2.) He that gives *bread to the eater* denied his blessing upon the bread they ate, and then that did not nourish them. The cause of the withering and failing of the corn in the field was visible — it was for want of rain; but, besides that, there was a secret blast and curse attending that which they brought home. [1.] When they had it in the barn they were not sure of it: *I did blow upon it, saith the Lord of hosts* (*v.* 9), and that withered it, as buds are sometimes blasted in the spring by a nipping frost, which we see the effects of, but know not the way of. *I did blow it away;* so the margin reads it. When men have heaped wealth together God can scatter it with the breath of his mouth as easily as we can blow away a feather. Note, We can never be sure of any thing in this world; it is exposed, not only when it is in the field, but when it is housed; for there *moth and rust corrupt,* Mt. 6:19. And, if we would have the comfort and continuance of our temporal enjoyments, we must make God our friend; for, if he bless them to us, they are blessings indeed, but if he blow upon them we can expect no good from them: they *make themselves wings and fly away.* [2.] When they had it upon the board it was not that to them that they expected: *"You eat, but you have not enough,* either because the meat is washy, and not satisfying, or because the stomach is greedy, and not satisfied. You eat, but you have no good digestion, and so are not nourished by it, nor does it answer the end, or you have not enough because you are not content, nor think it enough. *You drink,* but are not cooled and refreshed by it; *you are not filled with drink;* you are stinted, and have not enough to quench your thirst. The *new wine is cut off from your mouth* (Joel 1:5), nay, and you *drink your water* too by *measure and with astonishment;* you have no comfort of it, because you have no plenty of it, but are still in fear of falling short." [3.] That which they had upon their backs did them no good there: *"You clothe yourselves, but there is none warm;* your clothes soon wear out, and wax old, and grow thin, because God blows upon them," contrary to what Israel's did in the wilderness when God blessed them. It is God that *makes our garments warm upon* us, when he *quiets the earth,* Job 37:17. [4.] That which they had in their bags, which was not laid out, but laid up, they were not sure of: *"He that earns wages* by hard labour, and has it paid him in ready current money, *puts it into a bag with holes;* it drops through, and wastes away insensibly. Every thing is so scarce and dear that they spend their money as fast as they get it." Those that lay up their treasure on earth put it into a bag with holes; they lose it as they go along, and those that come after them pick it up. But, if we lay up our treasure in heaven, we provide for ourselves *bags that wax not old,* Lu. 12:33.

2. Observe wherefore God thus contended with them, and stopped the current of the favours promised them at their return (Joel 2:24); they provoked him to do it: *It is because of my house that is waste.* This is the quarrel God has with them. The foundation of the temple is laid, but the building does not go on. "Every man *runs to his own house,* to finish that, and to make that convenient and fine, and no care is taken about the Lord's house; and therefore it is that God crosses you thus in all your affairs, to testify his displeasure against you for that neglect, and to bring you to a sense of your sin and folly." Note, As those who seek first the kingdom of God and the righteousness thereof shall not only find them, but are most likely to have other things added to them, so those who neglect and postpone those things will not only lose them, but will justly have other things taken away from them. And if God cross us in our temporal affairs, and we meet with trouble and disappointment, we shall find this is the cause of it, the work we have to do for God and our own souls is left undone, and we *seek our own things more than the things of Jesus Christ,* Phil. 2:21.

III. The reproof which the prophet gives them for their neglect of the temple-work (*v.* 4): *"Is it time for you, O you! to dwell in your ceiled houses,* to have them beautified and adorned, and your families settled in them?" They were not content with walls and roofs for necessity, but they must have for gaiety and fancy. "It is high time," says one, "that my house were wainscoted." "It is high time," says another, "that mine were painted." And God's house, all this time, *lies waste,* and nothing is done at it. "What!" says the prophet, "is it time that you should have your humour pleased, and not time you should have your God pleased?" How much was their disposition the reverse of David's, who could not be easy in his *house of cedar* while the *ark of God* was *in curtains* (2 Sa. 7:2), and of Solomon's, who built the temple of God before he built a palace for himself. Note, Those are very much strangers to their own interest who prefer the conveniences and ornaments of the temporal life before the absolute necessities of the spiritual life, who are full of care to enrich their own houses, while God's temple in their hearts lies waste, and nothing is done for it or in it.

IV. The good counsel which the prophet gives to those who thus despised God, and whom God was therefore justly displeased with. 1. He would have them reflect: *Now therefore consider your ways, v.* 5 and again *v.* 7. "Be sensible of the hand of God gone out against you, and enquire into the reason; think what you have done that has provoked God thus to break in upon your comforts; and think what you will do to testify your repentance, that God may return in mercy to you." Note, It is the great concern of every one of us to consider our ways, to *set our hearts to our ways* (so the word is), to *think on our ways* (Ps. 119:59), to *search* and *try* them (Lam. 3:40), to *ponder the path of our feet* (Prov. 4:26), to apply our minds with all seriousness to the great and necessary duty of self-examination, and communing with our own hearts concerning our spiritual state, our sins that are past, and our duty for the future; for sin is what we must answer for, duty is what we must do; about these therefore we must be inquisitive, rather than about events, which we must leave to God. Many are quick-sighted to pry into other people's ways who are very careless of their own; whereas our concern is to *prove every one his own work,* Gal. 6:4. 2. He would have them reform (*v.* 8): *"Go up to the mountain,* to Lebanon, *and bring wood,* and other materials that are wanting, *and build the house* with all speed; put it off no longer, but set to it in good earnest." Note, Our considering our ways must issue in the amending of whatever we find amiss in them. If any duty has been long neglected, that is not a reason why it should still be so, but why now at length it should be revived; better late than never. For their encouragement to apply in good earnest to this work, he assures them, (1.) That they should be accepted of him in it: *Build the house, and I will take pleasure in it;* and that was encouragement enough for them to apply to it with alacrity and resolution, and to go through with it, whatever it cost them. Note, Whatever God will take pleasure in, when it is done, we ought to take pleasure in the doing of, and to reckon that inducement enough to set about it, and go on with it in good earnest; for what greater satisfaction can we have in our own bosoms than in contributing any thing towards that which God will take pleasure in? It ought to be the top of our ambition to be *accepted of the Lord,* 2 Co. 5:9. Though they had foolishly neglected the house of God, yet, if at length they will resume the care of it, God will not remember against them their former neglects, but will take pleasure in the work of their hands. Those who have long deferred their return to God, if at length they return with all their heart, must not despair of his favour. (2.) That he would be honoured by them in it: *I will be glorified, saith the Lord.* He will be served and worshipped in the temple when it is built, and sanctified in those that come nigh to him. It is worth while to bestow all possible care, and pains, and cost, upon that by which God may be glorified.

Verses 12–15

As an ear-ring of gold (says Solomon), and *an ornament of fine gold, so* amiable, so acceptable, in the sight of God and man, *is a wise reprover upon an obedient ear,* Prov. 25:12. The prophet here was a wise but faithful reprover, in God's name, and he met with an obedient ear. The foregoing sermon met with the desired success among the people, and their obedience met with due encouragement from God. Observe,

I. How the people returned to God in a way of duty. All those to whom that sermon was preached received the word in the love of it, and were wrought upon by it. Zerubbabel, the chief governor, did not think himself above the check and command of God's word. He was a man that had been eminently useful in his day, and serviceable to the interest of the church, yet did not plead his former merits in answer to this reproof for his present remissness, but submitted to it. Joshua's business, as high priest, was to teach, and yet he was willing himself to be taught, and willingly received admonition and instruction. *The remnant of the people* (and the whole body of them was but a remnant, a very few of the many thousands of Israel) also were very pliable; they all *obeyed the voice of the Lord their God,* and bowed their neck to the yoke of his commands, and it is here recorded to their honour that they did so, *v.* 12. Their father said, *Sons, go work to-day in my vineyard,* in my temple; and they not only said, *We go, sir,* but they went immediately. 1. They looked upon the prophet to be the Lord's messenger, and the word he delivered to be the Lord's message to them; and therefore received it *not as the word of man, but as the word of* Almighty God; they obeyed his words, *as the Lord their God had sent him, v.* 12. Note, In attending to God's ministers we must have an eye to him that sent them, and receive them for his sake, while they act according to their commission. 2. They *did fear before the Lord.* Prophecy was a new thing with them; they had had no special messenger from heaven for a great while, and therefore now that they had one, and but one, they paid an extraordinary regard to him; whereas their fathers, who had many prophets, mocked and misused them. It is sometimes so; when good preaching is most scarce it does most good, whereas the manna that is rained in plenty is loathed as *light bread.* And, because they so readily received this prophet, God, within a month or two after, raised them up another, Zec. 1:1. They *feared before the Lord;* they had a great regard to the divine authority and a great dread of the divine wrath, and were of those that *trembled at God's word.* The judgments of God which they had been under, though very severe, had not prevailed to make them fear before the Lord, until the word of God was sent to expound his providences, and then they feared. Note, A holy fear of God will have a great influence upon our obedience to him. *Serve the Lord with fear;* if we fear him not, we shall not serve him. 3. *The Lord stirred up* their spirits, *v.* 14. (1.) He excited them to their duty, and put it into their hearts to go about it. Note, Then the word of God has its success when God by his grace stirs up our spirits to comply with it; and without that grace we should remain stupid and utterly averse to every thing that is good. It is in the day of a divine power that we are made willing. (2.) He encouraged them in their duty, and with those encouragements enlarged their hearts, Ps. 119:32. When they heard the word they feared; but, lest they should sink under the weight of that fear, God stirred them up, and made them cheerful and bold to encounter the difficulties they might meet with. Note, When God has work to do, he will either find or make men fit to do it, and stir them up to it. 4. They applied to their work with all possible vigour: *They came and did work in the house of the Lord of hosts their God.* Every one, according as his capacity or ability was, lent a hand, some way or other, to further that good work; and this they did with an eye to God as the *Lord of hosts,* and as their God, the God of Israel. The consideration of God's sovereign dominion in the world by his providence, and his covenant-relation to his people by his grace, should stir up our spirits to act for him, and for the advancement of the interest of his kingdom among men, to the utmost of our power. 5. They did this speedily; it was but on the first day of the sixth month that Haggai preached them this sermon, and by the twenty-fourth of the same month, little more than three weeks after, they were all busy working in the house of the Lord their God, *v.* 15. To show that they were ashamed of their delays hitherto, now that they were convinced and called they were resolved to delay no longer, but to strike while the iron was hot, and to set about the work while they were under convictions. Note, Those that have lost time have need to redeem time; and the longer we have loitered in that which is good the more haste we should make when we are convinced of our folly.

II. How God met them in a way of mercy. The same prophet that brought them the reproof brought them a very comforting encouraging word (*v.* 13): *Then spoke Haggai, the Lord's messenger, in the Lord's message,* in his name, and as from him, *saying, I am with you, saith the Lord.* That is all he has to say, and that is enough; as that word of Christ to his disciples is (Mt. 28:20), *"Lo, I am with you always, even to the end of the world. I am with you,* that is, I will forgive your neglects hitherto, and they shall not be remembered against you; I will remove the judgments you have been under for those neglects, and will appear for you, as I have in them appeared against you. *I am with you* to protect you against your enemies that bear ill-will to your work, and to prosper you, and to give you success in it — with you to strengthen your hands, and bless the work of them, without which blessing those labour in vain that build." Note, Those that work for God have God with them; and, if he be for us, who can be against us? If he be with us, what difficulty can stand before us?

CHAPTER 2

In this chapter we have three sermons preached by the prophet Haggai for the encouragement of those that are forward to build the temple. In the first he assures the builders that the glory of the house they were now building should, in spiritual respects, though not in outward, exceed that of Solomon's temple, in which he has an eye to the coming of Christ (*v.* 1–9). In the second he assures them that though their sin, in delaying to build the temple, had retarded the prosperous progress of all their other affairs, yet now that they had set about it in good earnest he would bless them, and give them success (*v.* 10–19). In the third he assures Zerubbabel that, as a reward of his pious zeal and activity herein, he should be a favourite of Heaven, and one of the ancestors of Messiah the Prince, whose kingdom should be set up on the ruins of all opposing powers (*v.* 20–23).

Verses 1–9

Here is, I. The date of this message, *v.* 1. It was sent on the twenty-first day of the seventh month, when the builders had been about a month at work (since the twenty-fourth day of the sixth month), and had got it in some forwardness. Note, Those that are hearty in the service of God shall receive fresh encouragements from him to proceed in it, as their case calls for them. Set the wheels a going, and God will oil them.

II. The direction of this message, *v.* 2. The encouragements here are sent to the same persons to whom the reproofs in the foregoing chapter are directed; for those that are wounded by the convictions of the word shall be healed and bound up by its consolations. *Speak to Zerubbabel, and Joshua, and the residue of the people,* the very same that *obeyed the voice of the Lord* (*ch.* 1:12) and whose spirits God stirred up to do so (*ch.* 1:14); to them are sent these words of comfort.

III. The message itself, in which observe,

1. The discouragements which those laboured under who were employed in this work. That which was such a damp upon them, and an alloy to their joy, when the foundation of the temple was laid, was still a clog upon them — that they could not build such a temple now as Solomon built, not so large, so stately, so sumptuous, a one as that was. This fetched tears from the eyes of many, when the dimensions of it were first laid (Ezra 3:12), and still it made the work go on heavily — that the glory of this house, *in comparison* with that of the former, was *as nothing, v.* 3. It was now about seventy years since Solomon's temple was destroyed (for that was in the nineteenth year of the captivity, and this about the nineteenth after the captivity), so that there might be some yet alive who could remember to have seen it, and still they would be upbraiding themselves and their brethren with the great disparity between this house and that. One could remember the gold with which it was overlaid, another the precious stones with which it was garnished; one could describe the magnificence of the porch, another of the pillars — and where are these now? This weakened the hands of the builders; for, though our gracious God is pleased with us if we do in sincerity as well as we can in his service, yet our proud hearts will scarcely let us be pleased with ourselves unless we do as well as others whose abilities far exceed ours. And it is sometimes the fault of old people to discourage the services of the present age by crying up too much the performances and attainments of the former age, with which others should be provoked to emulation, but not exposed to contempt. *Say not thou that the former days were better than these* (Eccl. 7:10), but thank God that there is any good in these, bad as they are.

2. The encouragement that is given them to go on in the work, notwithstanding (*v.* 4): *Yet now,* though this house is likely to be much inferior to the former, *be strong, O Zerubbabel! and be strong, O Joshua!* Let not these leading men give way to this suggestion, nor be disheartened by it, but do as well as they can, when they cannot do so well as they would; and let *all the people of the land be strong* too, *and work;* and, if the leaders have but a good heart on it, it is hoped that the followers will have the better heart. Note, Those that work for God ought to exert themselves with vigour, and then to encourage themselves with hope that it will end well.

3. The grounds of these encouragements. God himself says to them, *Fear you not* (*v.* 5), and he gives good reasons for it.

(1.) They have God with them, his Spirit and his special presence: *Be strong, for I am with you, saith the Lord of hosts, v.* 4. This he had said before (*ch.* 1:13), *I am with you.* But we need to have these assurances repeated, that we may have strong consolation. The presence of God with us, as the *Lord of hosts,* is enough to silence all our fears and to help us over all the discouragements we may meet with in the way of our duty. The Jews had hosts against them, but they had the Lord of hosts with them, to take their part and plead their cause. He is with them; for, [1.] He adheres to his promise. His covenant is inviolable, and he will be always theirs, and will appear and act for them, *according to the word that he covenanted with them when they came out of Egypt.* Though *he chastens them for their transgressions with the rod,* yet he will not make his faithfulness to fail. [2.] He dwells among them by his Spirit, the Spirit of prophecy. When he first formed them into a people *he gave his good Spirit to instruct them* (Neh. 9:20); and still the Spirit, though often grieved and provoked to withdraw, remained among them. It was the Spirit of God that stirred up their spirits to come out of Babylon (Ezra 1:5), and now to build the temple, Hag. i. 14. Note, We have reason to be encouraged as long as we have the Spirit of God remaining among us to work upon us, for so long we have God with us to work for us.

(2.) They shall have the Messiah among them shortly — *him that should come.* To him bore all the prophets witness and this prophet particularly here, *v.* 6, 7. Here is an intimation of the time of his coming, that it should not be long ere he came: *"Yet once, it is a little while,* and he shall come. The Old-Testament church has but one stage more (if we may say so) to travel; five stages were now past, from Adam to Noah, thence to Abraham, thence to Moses, thence to Solomon's temple, thence to the captivity, and now yet one stage more, its sixth day's journey, and then comes the sabbatism of the Messiah's kingdom. Let the Son of man, when he comes, find faith on the earth, and let the children of promise continue still looking for him, for now it is but *a little while* and he will come; *hold out, faith and patience,* yet awhile, for *he that shall come will come, and will not tarry.*" And, as he then said of his first appearance, so now of his second, *Surely I come quickly.* Now concerning his coming it is here foretold, [1.] That it shall be introduced by a general shaking (*v.* 6): *I will shake the heavens, and the earth, and the sea, and the dry land.* This is applied to the setting up of Christ's kingdom in the world, to make way for which he will *judge among the heathen,* Ps. 110:6. God will once again do for his church as he did when he brought them out of Egypt; he shook the heavens and earth at Mount Sinai, with thunder, and lightnings, and earthquakes; he shook the sea and the dry land when lanes were made through the sea and streams fetched out of the rock. This shall be done again, when, at the sufferings of Christ, the sun shall be darkened, the earth shake, the rocks rend — when, at the birth of Christ, Herod and all *Jerusalem are troubled* (Mt. 2:3), and he is *set for the fall and rising again of many.* When his kingdom was set up it was with a shock to the nations; the oracles were silenced, idols were destroyed, and the powers of the kingdoms were moved and removed, Heb. 12:27. It denotes *the removing of the things that are shaken.* Note, The shaking of the nations is often in order to the settling of the church and the establishing of the things that cannot be shaken. [2.] That it shall issue in a general satisfaction. He shall come as *the desire of all nations* — desirable to all nations, for *in him shall all the families of the earth be blessed* with the best of blessings — long expected and desired by the good people in all nations, that had any intelligence from the Old-Testament predictions concerning him. Balaam in the land of Moab had spoken of a star that should arise out of Jacob, and Job in the land of Uz of his living Redeemer; the concourse of devout men from all parts at Jerusalem (Acts 2:5) was in expectation of the setting up of the Messiah's kingdom about that time. All the nations that are brought in to Christ, and discipled in his name, have called him, and will call him, *all their salvation and all their desire.* This glorious title of Christ seems to refer to Jacob's prophecy (Gen. 49:10), that *to him shall the gathering of the people be.*

(3.) The house they are now building shall be filled with glory to such a degree that its glory shall exceed that of Solomon's temple. The enemies of the Jews followed them with reproach, and cast contempt upon the house they were building; but they might very well endure that when God undertook to fill it with glory. It is God's prerogative to fill with glory; the glory that comes from him is satisfying, and not vain glory. Moses's tabernacle and Solomon's temple were filled with glory when God in a cloud took possession of them; but this house shall be filled with glory of another nature. [1.] Let them not be concerned because this house will not have so much silver and gold about it as Solomon's temple had, *v.* 8. God needs not the silver and gold to adorn his temple, for (says he), *The silver is mine, and the gold is mine.* All the silver and gold in the world are his; all that is hid in the bowels of the earth (for *the earth is the Lord's and the fulness thereof*), all that is laid up in the exchequers, banks, and treasuries of the children of men, and all that circulates for the maintaining of trade and commerce; it is all *the Lord's.* Every penny bears his image as well as Caesar's; and therefore when gold and silver are dedicated to his honour, and employed in his service, no addition is made to him, for it was his before. When David and his princes offered vast sums for the service of the house of God, they acknowledged, *It is all thy own, and of thy own, Lord, have we given thee,* 1 Chr. 29:14, 16. Therefore God needs not sacrifice, for *every beast of the forest is his,* Ps. 50:10. Note, If we have silver and gold, we must serve and honour God with them, for they are all his own, we have but the use of them, the property remains in him; but, if we have not silver and gold to honour him with, we must honour him with such as we have, and he will accept us, for he needs them not; all the *silver and gold* in the world are his already. *The earth is full of his riches,* so *is the great and wide sea also.* [2.] Let them be comforted with this, that, though this temple have less gold in it, it shall have more glory than Solomon's (*v.* 9): *The glory of this latter house shall be greater than of the former.* This was never true in respect of outward glory. This latter house was indeed in its latter times very much beautified and enriched by Herod, and we find the disciples admiring the stones and buildings of the temple, how fine they were (Mk. 13:1); but it was nothing in comparison with Solomon's temple; and, besides, the Jews own that several of the divine glories of the first temple were wanting in this — the *ark,* the *urim* and *thummim,* the *fire from heaven,* and the *Schechinah;* so that we cannot conceive how the glory of this latter house should in any thing exceed that of the former, but in that which would indeed excel all the glories of the first house — the presence of the Messiah in it, the Son of God, his being presented there *the glory of his people Israel,* his attending there at twelve years old, and afterwards his preaching and working miracles there, and his driving the buyers and sellers out of it. It was necessary, then, that the Messiah should come while the second temple stood; but, that being long since destroyed, we must conclude that our Lord Jesus is the Christ, is *he that should come,* and we are to *look for no other.* It was also the *glory of this latter house, First,* That, before the coming of Christ, it was always kept free from idols and idolatries, and was never polluted with those abominable things, as the first temple often was (2 Ki. 23:11, 12), and in this its glory excelled all the glory of that. Note, The purity of the church, and the strict adherence to divine institutions, are much more its glory than external pomp and splendour. *Secondly,* That, after Christ, the gospel was preached in it by the apostles, even all the words of this life, Acts 5:20. In the temple Jesus Christ was daily preached, Acts 5:42. Now the ministration of righteousness and life by the gospel was unspeakably more glorious than the law, which was a *ministration of death and condemnation,* 2 Co. 3:9, 10. Note, That is the most valuable glory which arises from our relation to Christ and our interest in him. As, where Christ is, *behold a greater than Solomon is there,* so the heart in which he dwells, and makes a living temple, behold it is more glorious than Solomon's temple, and will be so to eternity.

(4.) They should see a comfortable end of their present troubles, and enjoy the pleasure of a happy settlement: *In this place will I give peace, saith the Lord of hosts.* Note, God's presence with his people in his ordinances secures to them all good. If God be with us, peace is with us. But the Jews under the latter temple had so much trouble that we must conclude this promise to have its accomplishment in that spiritual peace which Jesus Christ has by his blood purchased for, and by his last will and testament bequeathed to, all believers (Jn. 14:27), that peace which Christ himself preached as the prophet of peace, and gives as the prince of peace. God will *give peace in this place;* he will give his Son to be the peace, Eph. 2:14.

Verses 10–19

This sermon was preached two months after that in the former part of the chapter. The priests and Levites preached constantly, but the prophets preached occasionally; both were good and needful. We have need to be taught our duty *in season and out of season.* The people were now going on vigorously with the building of the temple, and in hopes shortly to have it ready for their use and to be employed in the services of it; and now God sends them a message by his prophet, which would be of use to them.

I. By way of conviction and caution. They were now engaged in a very good work, but they were concerned to see to it, not only that it was good for the matter of it, but that it was done in a right manner, for otherwise it would not be accepted of God. God sees there are many among them that spoil this good work, by going about it with unsanctified hearts and hands, and are likely to gain no advantage to themselves by it; these are here convicted, and all are warned thereby to purify the hands they employ in this work, for *to the pure* only *all things are pure,* and from the pure only that comes which is pure. This matter is here illustrated by the established rules of the ceremonial law, in putting *a difference between the clean and the unclean,* about which many of the appointments of the law were conversant. Hereby it appears that a spiritual use is to be made of the ceremonial law, and that it was intended, not only as a divine ritual to the Jews, but for *instruction in righteousness* to all, even to us upon whom the ends of the world have come, to discover to us both sin and Christ, both our disease and our remedy. Now observe here,

1. What the rule of the law was. The prophet is ordered to enquire of the priests concerning it (*v.* 11); for their *lips* should *keep* this *knowledge,* and the people should *enquire the law at their mouth,* Mal. 2:7. Haggai himself, though a prophet, must *ask the priests concerning the law.* His business, as an extraordinary messenger, was to expound the providences of God, and to give directions concerning particular duties, as he had done, *ch.* 1:8, 9. But he would not take the priests' work out of the hands of those who were the ordinary ministers, and whose business it was to expound the ordinances of God, to teach the people the meaning of them, and to give the general rules for the observance of them. In a case of that nature, Haggai must himself consult them. Note, God has given to his ministers diversities of gifts, and calls them out to do diversities of services, so that they have need one of another, should make use one of another, and be helpful one to another. The prophet, though divinely inspired, cannot say to the priest, *I have no need of thee,* nor can the priest say so to the prophet. Perhaps Haggai was *therefore* ordered to consult the priests, that out of their own mouths he might judge both them and the people committed to their charge, and convict them of worse than ceremonial pollution. See Lev. 10:10, 11. Now the rules of the law, in the cases propounded, are, (1.) That he that has holy flesh in his clothes cannot by the touch of his clothes communicate holiness (*v.* 12): *If one bear holy flesh in the skirt of his garment,* though the garment is thereby so far made a devoted thing as that it is not to be put to common use till it has first been washed in the holy place (Lev. 6:27), yet it shall by no means transmit a holiness to either meat or drink, so as to make it ever the better to those that use it. (2.) That he that is ceremonially unclean by the touch of a dead body does by his touch communicate that uncleanness. The law is express (Num. 19:22), *Whatsoever the unclean person touches shall be unclean;* yet this Haggai will have from the priests' own mouth, for concerning those things that we find very plain in our Bibles yet it is good to have the advice of our ministers. The sum of these two rules is that pollution is more easily communicated than sanctification; that is (says Grotius), There are many ways of vice, but only one of virtue, and that a difficult one. *Bonum oritur ex integris; malum ex quolibet defectu — Good implies perfection; evil commences with the slightest defect.* Let not men think that living among good people will recommend them to God if they are not good themselves, but let them fear that touching the unclean thing will defile them, and therefore let them keep at a distance from it.

2. How it is here applied (*v.* 14): *So is this people, and so is this nation, before me.* He does not call them his people and his nation (they are unworthy to be owned by him), but *this people,* and *this nation.* They have been thus before God; they thought their offering sacrifices on the altar would sanctify them, and excuse their neglect to build the temple, and remove the curse which by that neglect they had brought upon their common enjoyments: "No," says God, "your holy flesh and your altar will be so far from sanctifying your meat and drink, your wine and oil, to you, that your contempt of God's temple will bring a pollution, not only on your common enjoyments, but even on your sacrifices too; so that while you continued in that neglect all was unclean to you, nay, and *so is this people* still; and so they will be; on these terms they will still stand with me, and on no other — that if they be profane, and sensual, and morally impure, if they have wicked hearts, and live wicked lives, though they work ever so hard at the temple while it is building, and though they offer ever so many and costly sacrifices there when it is built, yet that shall not serve to sanctify their meat and drink to them, and to give them a comfortable use of them; nay, the impurity of their hearts and lives shall make even that work of their hands, and all their offerings, unclean, and an abomination to God." And the case is the same with us. Those whose devotions are plausible, but whose conversation is wicked, will find their devotions unable to sanctify their enjoyments, but their wickedness prevailing to pollute them. Note, When we are employed in any good

work we should be jealous over ourselves, lest we render it unclean by our corruptions and mismanagements.

II. By way of comfort and encouragement. If their hearts be right with God, and their eye single in his service, they shall have the benefit of their devotion. God will take away the judgment of famine wherewith they have been corrected for their remissness, and will restore them great plenty. This they are called to consider, and to observe whether God would not be to the utmost as good as his word, and by his providence remarkably countenance and recompense their reformation in this matter. To make this the more signal, let them set down the day when they began to work at the building of the temple, to raise the structure upon the foundations that had been laid some time before. On the twenty-fourth day of the sixth month they began to prepare materials (*ch.* 1:15), and now on the twenty-fourth day of the ninth month they began to *lay a stone upon a stone in the temple of the Lord;* let them take notice of this day, and observe, 1. How they had gone behind-hand in their estates before this day. Let them remember the time when there was a sensible waste and decay in all they had, *v.* 16. A man went to his garner, expecting to find *a heap of twenty measures* of corn, so much he used to have from such a piece of ground, or so much used to be left at that time of the year, or so much he took it for granted there was when he fetched the last from it, but he found it unaccountably diminished, and, when he came to measure it, *there were but ten* measures; it had run in and dried away in the keeping, or vermin had eaten it, or it was stolen. In like manner he went to *the wine-press,* expecting to draw *fifty vessels* of wine, for so much he used to have from such a quantity of grapes, but they did not yield as usual, for he could get *but twenty.* This agrees with what we had, *ch.* 1:9, *You looked for much, and it came to little.* Note, It is our folly that we are apt to raise our expectation from the creature, and to think tomorrow must needs be as this day and much more abundant, but we are commonly disappointed, and the more we expect the more grievous the disappointment is. In the stores and treasures of the new covenant we need not fear being disappointed when we come by faith to draw from them. But this was not all. God did visibly contend with them in the weather (*v.* 17): *I smote you with blastings,* winds and frosts, which made every green thing to wither, *and with mildew,* which choked the corn when it was knitting, *and with hail,* which battered it down and broke it when it had grown to some maturity; thus they were disappointed *in all the labour of their hands,* while they neglected to lay their hand to the work of God and to labour in that. Note, While we take no care of God's interest we cannot expect he should take care of ours. And, when he thus walks contrary to us, he expects that we should return to him and to our duty. But this people either saw not the hand of God in it (imputing it to chance) or saw not their own sin as the provoking cause of it, and therefore turned not to him. They were a long time incorrigible and unhumbled under these rebukes, so that God's hand was *stretched out still,* for *the people turned not to him that smote them,* Isa. 9:12, 13. They might easily observe that as long as they continued in neglect of the temple work all their affairs went backward. But, 2. Let them now observe, and they should find that from this day forward God would bless them (*v.* 18, 19): *"Consider now* whether when you begin to change you way towards God you do not find God changing his way towards you; from *this day,* when you fall to work about the temple, *consider it,* I say, and you shall find a remarkable turn given for the better to all your affairs. *Is the seed yet in the barn?* Yes it is, and not yet thrown into the ground. The fruit-trees do not as yet bud, *the vine, and the fig-tree, and the olive-tree,* have not as *yet brought forth,* so that nothing appears to promise a good harvest or vintage next year. Nature does not promise it; but now that you begin to apply in good earnest to your duty, the God of nature promises it; he has said, *From this day I will bless you.* It is the best day's work you ever did in your lives, for hence you may date the return of your prosperity." He does not say what they shall be, but, in general, *I will bless you;* and those that know what are the fruits flowing from God's blessing know they can desire no more to make them happy. *"I will bless you,* and then you shall soon recover all your losses, shall thrive as fast as before you went backward; for *the blessing of the Lord, that maketh rich,* and those *whom he blesses are blessed indeed."* Note, When we begin to make conscience of our duty to God we may expect his blessing; and this tree of life is so known by its fruits that one may discern almost to a day a remarkable turn of Providence in favour of those that return in a way of duty; so that they and others may say that *from this day they are blessed.* See Mal. 3:10. And *whoso is wise will observe these things, and understand* by them *the lovingkindness of the Lord.*

Verses 20–23

After Haggai's sermon *ad populum — to the people,* here follows one, the same day, *ad magistratum — to the magistrates,* a word directed particularly to *Zerubbabel, the governor of Judah,* who was a leading active man in this good work which the people now set about, and therefore he shall have some particular marks put upon him (*v.* 21): *Speak to Zerubbabel, governor of Judah,* speak to him by himself. He has thoughts in his head far above those of the common people, as wise princes are wont to have, who move in a higher and larger sphere than others. The people of the land are in care about their corn-fields and vineyards; God has assured them that they shall prosper, and we hope that will make them easy; but Zerubbabel is concerned about the community and its interests, about the neighbouring nations, and the revolutions of their governments, and what will become of the few and feeble Jews in those changes and convulsions, and how such a poor prince as he is should be able to keep his ground and serve his country. "Go to him," says God, "and tell him it shall be well with him and his remnant, and let that make him easy."

I. Let him expect to hear of great commotions in the nations of the earth, and let them not be a surprise to him; behold, he is told of them before (*v.* 21, 22): *I will shake the heavens and the earth.* This he had said before (*v.* 6, 7), and now says it again to Zerubbabel; let him expect shaking times, universal concussions. The world is like the sea, like the wheel, always in motion, but sometimes in a special manner turbulent. But, Blessed be God, if the earth be shaken, it is to *shake the wicked out of it,* Job 38:13. In the apocalyptic visions earthquakes bode no ill to the church. Here the heavens and the earth are shaken, that proud oppressors may be broken and brought down: *I will overthrow the throne of kingdoms.* The Chaldean monarchy, which had been the throne of kingdoms a great while, was already overthrown; and the powers that are, and are yet to come, shall in like manner be overthrown; their day will come to fall. 1. Though they be ever so powerful, yet the *strength of their kingdoms* shall be destroyed. They *trust in chariots and horses* (Ps. 20:7), but their *chariots* shall be *overthrown,* and *those that ride in them,* so that they shall not be able to attack the people of God, whom they persecute, not to escape the judgments of God, which persecute them. 2. Though there appear none likely to be the instruments of their destruction, yet God will bring it about, for they shall be brought down *every one by the sword of his brother.* This reads the doom of all the enemies of God's church, that will not repent to give him glory; it seems likewise designed as a promise of Christ's victory over the powers of darkness, his overthrow of Satan's throne, that *throne of kingdoms,* the throne of the god of this world, the taking from him all the armour wherein he trusted and *dividing the spoil.* And all opposing *rule, principality, and power,* shall be put down, that the *kingdom* may be *delivered up to God, even the Father.*

II. Let him depend upon it that he shall be safe under the divine protection in the midst of all these commotions, *v.* 23. Zerubbabel was active to build God a house, and therefore God makes the same promise to him as he did to David on the like occasion — that he would *build him a house,* and establish it, even *in that day* when heaven and earth are shaken. This promise refers to this good man himself and to his family. He honoured God, and God would honour him. His successors likewise in the government of Judah might take encouragement from it; though their authority was very precarious as to men, yet God would confirm it, and this would contribute to the stability of the people over whom God had set them. But this promise has special reference to Christ, who lineally descended from Zerubbabel, and is the sole builder of the gospel-temple. 1. Zerubbabel is here owned as *God's servant,* and it is an honourable mention that is hereby made of him, as Moses and David *my servants.* When God destroys his enemies he will prefer his servants. Our Lord Jesus is his Father's servant in the work of redemption, but faithful as a Son, Isa. 42:1. 2. He is owned as God's elect: *I have chosen thee* to this office; and whom God makes choice of he will make use of. Our Lord Jesus is chosen of God, 1 Pt. 2:4. And he is the head of the chosen remnant; in him they are chosen. 3. It is promised that, being chosen, God will make him *as a signet.* Jeconiah had been as the *signet on God's right hand,* but was *plucked thence* (Jer. 22:24); and now Zerubbabel is substituted in the room of him. He shall be near and dear to God, precious in his sight, and honourable, and his family shall continue till the Messiah spring out of it, who is *the signet on God's right hand.* This intimates, (1.) The delight the Father has in him. In him he once and again declared himself to be *well pleased.* He is set as a *seal upon his heart, a seal upon his arm,* is brought near unto him (Dan. 7:13), is *hidden in the shadow of his hand,* Isa. 49:2. (2.) The dominion the Father has entrusted him with. Princes sign their edicts, grants, and commissions, with their signet-rings, Esth. 3:10. Our Lord Jesus is the signet on God's right hand, for all power is given to him and derived from him. By him the great charter of the gospel is signed and ratified, and it is in him that all the promises of God are yea and amen.

AN EXPOSITION, WITH PRACTICAL OBSERVATIONS, OF

THE PROPHECY OF ZECHARIAH

This prophet was colleague with the prophet Haggai, and a worker together with him in forwarding the building of the second temple (Ezra 5:1); for two are better than one. Christ sent forth his disciples two and two. Zechariah began to prophesy some time after Haggai. But he continued longer, soared higher in visions and revelations, wrote more, and prophesied more particularly concerning Christ, than Haggai had done; so *the last shall be first:* the last in time sometimes proves first in dignity. He begins with a plain practical sermon, expressive of that which was the scope of his prophesying, in the first five verses; but afterwards, to the end of *ch.* 6, he relates the visions he saw, and the instructions he received immediately from heaven by them. At *ch.* 7, from an enquiry made by the Jews concerning fasting, he takes occasion to show them the duty of their present day, and to encourage them to hope for God's favour, to the end of *ch.* 8, after which there are two sermons, which are both called *burdens of the word of the Lord* (one begins with *ch.* 9, the other with *ch.* 12), which probably were preached some time after; the scope of them is to reprove for sin, and threaten God's judgments against the impenitent, and to encourage those that feared God with assurances of the mercy God had in store for his church, and especially of the coming of the Messiah and the setting up of his kingdom in the world.

CHAPTER 1

In this chapter, after the introduction (*v.* 1), we have, I. An awakening call to a sinful people to repent of their sins and return to God (*v.* 2–6). II. Great encouragement given to hope for mercy. 1. By the vision of the horses (*v.* 7–11). 2. By the prayer of the angel for Jerusalem, and the answer to that prayer (*v.* 12–17). 3. By the vision of the four carpenters that were employed to cut off the four horns with which Judah and Jerusalem were scattered (*v.* 18–21).

Verses 1–6

Here is, I. The foundation of Zechariah's ministry; it is laid in a divine authority: *The word of the Lord came to him.* He received a divine commission to be God's mouth to the people and with it instructions what to say. He received of the Lord that which also he delivered unto them. *The word of the Lord was to him;* it came in the evidence and demonstration of the Spirit, as a real thing, and not a fancy. For the ascertaining of this, we have here, 1. The time when the word of the Lord came first to him, or when the word that next follows came to him: it was *in the second year of Darius.* Before the captivity the prophets dated their writings by the reigns of the kings of Judah and Israel; but now by the reigns of the kings of Persia, to whom they were subjects. Such a melancholy change had sin made of their circumstances. Zerubbabel took not so much state upon him as to have public acts dated by the years of his government, and in things of this nature the prophets, as is fit, complied with the usage of the time, and scrupled not to reckon by the years of the heathen kings, as Dan. 7:1; 8:1. Zechariah preached his first sermon in the *eighth month* of this *second year* of Darius; Haggai preached his in the sixth month of the same year, Hag. 1:1. The people being readily obedient to the word of the Lord in the mouth of Haggai, God blessed them with another prophet; for to him that has, and uses well what he has, more shall be given. 2. The name and family of the prophet to whom the word of the Lord came; He was *Zechariah, the son of Barachiah, the son of Iddo,* and he was *the prophet,* as Haggai is called *the prophet,* Hag. 1:1. For, though in former ages there was one Iddo a prophet (2 Chr. 12:15), yet we have no reason to think that Zechariah was of his progeny, or should be denominated from him. The learned Mr. Pemble is decidedly of opinion that this Zechariah, the son of Barachiah, is the same that our Saviour says was *slain between the temple and the altar,* perhaps many years after the rebuilding of the temple (Mt. 23:35), and that our Saviour does not mean (as is commonly thought) Zechariah the son of Jehoiada, for why should Jehoiada be called Barachiah? And he thinks the manner of Christ's account persuades us to think so; for, reckoning up the innocent blood shed by the Jews, he begins at Abel, and ends even in the last of the holy prophets. Whereas, after Zechariah the son of Jehoiada, many prophets and righteous men were put to death by them. It is true there is no mention made in any history of their slaying this Zechariah, but Josephus might industriously conceal that shame of his nation. Perhaps what Zechariah spoke in his prophesying concerning Christ of his being sold, his being wounded in the house of his friends, and the shepherd being smitten, was verified in the prophet himself, and so he became a type of Christ. Probably, being assaulted by his persecutors, he took sanctuary in the court of the priests (and some think he was himself a priest), and so was slain between the porch and the altar.

II. The first-fruits of Zechariah's ministry. Before he came to visions and revelations, and delivered his prophetic discourses, he preached that which was plain and practical; for it is best to begin with that. Before he published the promises of mercy, he published calls to repentance, for thus *the way of the Lord* must be *prepared.* Law must be first preached, and then gospel. Now,

1. The prophet here puts them in mind of the controversy God had had with their fathers (*v.* 2): *"The Lord has been sorely displeased with your fathers,* and has laid them under the tokens of his displeasure. You have heard with your ears, and your fathers have told you of it; you have seen with your eyes the woeful remains of it. God's quarrel with you has been of long standing, and therefore it is time for you to think of taking it up." Note, The judgments of God, which those that went before us were under, should be taken as warnings to us not to tread in their steps, and calls to repentance, that we may cut off the entail of the curse and get it turned into a blessing.

2. He calls them, in God's name, to return to him, and make their peace with him, *v.* 3. God by him says that to this backsliding people which he had often said by his servants the prophets: *"Turn you to me* in a way of faith and repentance, duty and obedience, and *I will turn to you* in a way of favour and mercy, peace and reconciliation." Let the rebels return to their allegiance, and they shall be taken under the protection of the government and enjoy all the privileges of good subjects. Let them change their way, and God will change his. See Mal. 3:7. But that which is most observable here is that God is called here the *Lord of hosts* three times: *"Thus saith the Lord of hosts.* It is he that speaks, and therefore you are bound to regard what he says." *Turn you to me, saith the Lord of hosts* (this intimates the authority and obligation of the command), *and I will turn to you, saith the Lord of hosts* — this intimates the validity and value of the promise; so that it is no vain repetition. Note, The consideration of God's almighty power and sovereign dominion should both engage and encourage sinners to repent and turn to him. It is very desirable to have the Lord of hosts our friend and very dreadful to have him our enemy.

3. He warns them not to persist in their impenitence, as their fathers had done (*v.* 4): *Be you not as your fathers.* Instead of being hardened in their evil courses by the example of their fathers' sins, let them rather be deterred from them by the example of their fathers' punishment. We are apt to be governed very much by precedent, and we are well or ill governed according to the use we make of the precedents before us. The same examples to some are a savour of life unto life, to others a savour of death unto death. Some argued, "Shall we be wiser than our fathers? They never minded the prophets, and why then should we mind them? They made laws against them, and why should we tolerate them?" But they are here taught how they should argue: "Our fathers slighted the prophets, and God was sorely displeased with them for it; therefore let us the more carefully regard what God says to us by his prophets." "Review what is past, and observe,"

(1.) "What was the message that God sent by his servants the prophets to your fathers: *The former prophets cried to your fathers.* cried aloud, and did not spare, not spare themselves, not spare your fathers; they cried as men in earnest, as men that would be heard; they spoke not as from themselves, but in the name of *the Lord of hosts;* and this was the substance of what they said, the burden of every song, the application of every sermon — *Turn you now from your evil ways, and from your evil doings;* the very same that we now preach to you. Be persuaded to leave your sins; resolve to have no more to do with them. A speedy reformation is the only way to prevent an approaching ruin: *Turn you now* from sin to God without delay."

(2.) "How little this message was regarded by your fathers: *But they did not hear,* they did not heed. They turned a deaf ear to these calls: *They would not hearken unto me, saith the Lord.* They would not be reclaimed, would not be ruled, by the word I sent them; say not then that you will do as your fathers did, for they did amiss;" see Jer. 44:17. Note, We must not follow the examples of our dear fathers unless they were God's dear children, nor any further than they were dutiful and obedient to him.

(3.) "What has become both of your fathers and of the prophets that preached to them? They are all dead and gone," *v.* 5. [1.] *Your fathers, where are they?* The whole generation of them is swept away, and their place knows them no more. Note, When we think of our ancestors, that have gone through the world and gone out of it before us, we should think, *Where are they?* Here they were, in the towns and countries where we live, passing and repassing in the same streets, dwelling in the same houses, trading in the same shops and exchanges, worshipping God in the same churches. But where are they? They are somewhere still; when they died there was not an end of them. They are in eternity, in the world of spirits, the unchangeable world, to which we are hastening apace. Where are they? Those of them that lived and died in sin are in torment, and we are warned by Moses and the prophets, Christ and his apostles, to look to it that we *come not to that place of torment,* Lu. 16:28, 29. Those of them that lived and died in Christ are in paradise; and, if we live and die as they did, we shall be with them shortly, with them eternally. [2.] *The prophets* also, *did they live for ever?* No, they are gone too. The treasure is put into earthen vessels, the water of life into earthen pitchers, often cracked, and brought home broken at last. Christ is a prophet that lives for ever, but all other prophets have a period put to their office. Note, Ministers are dying men, and live not for ever in this world. They are to look upon themselves as such, and to preach accordingly, as those that must be silenced shortly, and know not which sermon may be the last. People are to look upon them as such, and to hear accordingly, as those that yet a little while have the *light with them,* that they may walk and work *while they have the light.* Oh that this weighty consideration had its due weight given it, that we are dying ministers dealing with dying people about the concerns of immortal souls and an awful eternity, which both they and we are standing upon the brink of! It concerns us to think of the prophets that are gone, that were *before us of old,* Jer. 28:8. Those that were the glory of men withered and fell; but the *word of the Lord endures for ever,* 1 Pt. 1:24, 25. The prophets that are now, do *we live for ever?* (so some read it); no, Haggai and Zechariah will not be long with you, and prophecy itself shall shortly cease. In another world both we and our prophets shall live for ever; and to prepare for that world ought to be our great care and business in this.

(4.) "What were the effects of the word which God spoke to them by his prophets, *v.* 6. The preachers died, and the hearers died, but the word of God died not; that took effect, and not one iota or tittle of it fell to the ground." As the *rain* and *snow* from heaven, *it shall not return void,* Isa. 55:11. He appealed to themselves; they knew very well, [1.] That the judgments God had threatened were executed upon their fathers, and they were made to feel what they would not believe and fear: *"My statutes which I commanded my servants the prophets,* the precepts with the penalties annexed, which I charged them with the delivery of, *did they not take hold of your fathers?"* Though God's prophets could not fasten convictions upon them, the calamities threatened overtook them, and they could not escape them, nor get out of the reach of them. God's words took hold of them as the bailiff arrests the debtor, and takes him in execution for contempt. Note, The unbelief of man cannot make the threatenings of God's word of no effect, but, sooner or later, they will take place, if the prescribed course be not taken to prevent the execution of them. God's anger will certainly take hold of those that will not be taken hold of by his authority; for when he judges he will overcome. [2.] That they themselves could not but own the accomplishment of the word of God in the judgments of God that were upon them, and that therein he was righteous, and had done them no wrong: *They returned, and said* (they changed their mind, and when it was too late to prevent the ruin of their nation they acknowledged), *Like as the Lord of hosts thought to do unto us according to our ways and doings,* to reckon with us for them, *so has he dealt with us,* and we must acknowledge both his truth and his justice, must blame ourselves only, and have no blame to lay to him. *Sero sapiunt Phryges — It is late before the Phrygians become wise.* This afterwit, as it is a proof of the truth of God, so it is a proof of the folly of men, who will look no further than they can see. They would never be persuaded to say in time, "God will be as good as his word, for he is faithful; he will deal with us according to our deserts, for he is righteous." But now they see both plainly enough when the sentence is executed; now he that runs may read, and publish the exact agreement that appears between the present providences and the former predictions which then were slighted, between the present punishments and the former sins which then were persisted in. Now they cannot but say, *The Lord is righteous,* Dan. 9:11–13.

Verses 7–17

We not come to visions and revelations of the Lord; for in that way God chose to speak by Zechariah, to awaken the people's attention, and to engage their humble reverence of the word and their humble enquiries into it, and to fix it the more in their minds and memories. Most of the following visions seem designed for the comfort of the

Jews, now newly returned out of captivity, and their encouragement to go on with the building of the temple. The scope of this vision (which is as an introduction to the rest) is to assure the Jews of the care God took of them, and the eye of his providence that was upon them for good, now in their present state, when they seem to be deserted, and their case deplorable. The vision is dated (*v.* 7) *the twenty-fourth day of the eleventh month,* three months after he preached that sermon (*v.* 1), in which he calls them to repentance from the consideration of God's judgments. Finding that that sermon had a good effect, and that they returned to God in a way of duty, the assurances he had given them are confirmed, that God would return to them in a way of mercy. Now observe here,

I. What the prophet saw, and the explication of that. 1. He saw a grove of *myrtle-trees,* a dark shady grove, down *in a bottom,* hidden by the adjacent hills, so that you were not aware of it till you were just upon it. This represented the low, dark, solitary, melancholy condition of the Jewish church at this time. They were over-topped by all their neighbours, buried in obscurity; what friends they had were hidden, and there appeared no way of relief and succour for them. Note, The church has not been always visible, but sometimes hidden, as the *woman in the wilderness,* Rev. 12:6. 2. He saw *a man* mounted upon *a red horse,* standing in the midst of this shady myrtle-grove. This man is no other than the *man Christ Jesus,* the same that appeared to Joshua with *his sword drawn in his hand* as *captain of the host of the Lord* (Jos. 5:13, 14) and to John with his *bow* and his *crown,* Rev. 6:2. Though the church was in a low condition, yet Christ was present in the midst of it. Was it hidden by the hills? He was much more hidden in the myrtle-grove, yet hidden as in an ambush, ready to appear for the seasonable relief of his people, to their happy surprise. Compare Isa. 45:15, *Verily thou art a God that hidest thyself,* and yet *Israel's God and Saviour* at the same time, their *Holy One in the midst of them.* He was *riding,* as a man of war, as a man in haste, *riding on the heavens for the help* of his people, Deu. 33:26. He rode on a *red horse,* either naturally so or dyed red with the blood of war, as this same victorious prince appeared *red in his apparel,* Isa. 63:1, 2. Red is a fiery colour, denoting that he is *jealous for Jerusalem* (*v.* 14) and very angry at her enemies. Christ, under the law, appeared on a red horse, denoting the terror of that dispensation, and that he had yet his conflict before him, when he was to *resist unto blood.* But, under the gospel, he appears on *a white horse* (Rev. 6:2. and again *ch.* 19:11), denoting that he has now gained the victory, and rides in triumph, and hangs out the white, not the bloody flag. 3. He saw a troop of horse attending him, ready to receive and obey his orders: *Behind him there were some red horses, and* some *speckled, and* some *white,* angels attending the Lord Jesus, ready to be employed by him for the service of his church, some in acts of judgment, others of mercy, others in mixed events. Note, The King of the church has angels at command, not only to do him honour, but to minister for the good of those that are his. 4. He enquired into the signification of this vision. He had an angel talking with him, as his instructor, besides those he saw in the vision; so had Ezekiel (*ch.* 40:3), and Daniel, *ch.* 8:16. Zechariah asked him (*v.* 9), *O my Lord! what are these?* And, it should seem this *angel that talked with him* was Christ himself, the *man on the red horse,* whom the rest were attendants on; to him immediately Zechariah addresses himself. Would we be acquainted with the mysteries of the kingdom of heaven, we must make our application, not to angels (they are themselves learners), but to Christ himself, who is alone *able to take the book, and open the seals,* Rev. 5:7. The prophet's question implies a humble acknowledgment of his own ignorance and an earnest desire to be informed. O let me know what these are! This he desired, not for the satisfying of his curiosity, but that he might be furnished with something proper for the comfort and encouragement of the people of God, in their present distress. 5. He received from the *angel that talked with* him (*v.* 9), and from *the man that stood among the myrtle-trees* (*v.* 10), the interpretation of this vision. Note, Jesus Christ is ready to instruct those that are humbly desirous to be taught the things of God. He immediately said, *I will show thee what these are.* What knowledge we have, or may have, concerning the world of spirits, we are indebted to Christ for. The account given him was, *These are those whom the Lord has sent:* they are his messengers, his envoys, appointed (as his eyes are said to do, 2 Chr. 16:9) to *walk,* to *run,* to fly swiftly *through the earth,* to observe what is done in it and to execute the divine commands. God needs them not, but he is pleased to employ them, and we need the comfort arising from the doctrine of their administration.

II. What the prophet heard, and what instructions were thereby given him. Faith comes by hearing, and, generally, in visions there was something said.

1. He heard the report or representation which the angels made to Christ of the present state of the world, *v.* 11. They had been out abroad, as flying posts *(being hastened by the King of kings' commandment,* Esth. 3:15), and, having returned, they give this account to the *Angel that stood among the myrtle-trees* (for to the Lord Jesus angels themselves are accountable): *We have walked to and fro through the earth, and, behold all the earth sits still and is at rest.* We are taught to pray that the will of God may be done by men on earth as it is done by the angels in heaven; and here we see what need we have to pray so, for it is far from being so. For, (1.) We find the world of angels here very busy. Those that are employed in the court above rest not day nor night from praising God, which is their business there; and those that are employed in the camp below are never idle, nor lose time; they are still *ascending and descending* upon *the Son of man* (Jn. 1:51, as on Jacob's ladder, Gen. 28:12); they are still *walking to and fro through the earth.* Thus active, thus industrious, *Satan* owns himself to be in doing mischief, Job 1:7. It is well for us that good angels bestir themselves as much to do good, and that here in this earth we have guardians going about continually seeking to do us a kindness, as we have adversaries which, as roaring lions, go about continually, seeking to devour us. Though holy angels in this earth meet with a great deal that is disagreeable, yet, while they are going on God's errands, they hesitate not to *walk to and fro through it.* Their own habitation, which those that fell liked not, they will like the better when they return. (2.) We find the world of mankind here very careless: *All the earth sits still, and is at rest,* while all the church is made uneasy, *tossed with tempests and not comforted.* Those that are strangers to the church are secure; those that are enemies to it are successful. The Chaldeans and Persians dwell at ease, while the poor Jews are continually alarmed; as when *the king and Haman sat down to drink, but the city Shushan was perplexed.* The children of men are merry and jovial, but *none grieve for the affliction* of God's children. Note, It is sad to think what a deep sleep the world is cast into, what a spirit of slumber has seized the generality of mankind, that are under God's wrath and Satan's power, and yet secure and unconcerned! They sit still and are at rest, Lu. 17:26, etc.

2. He heard Christ's intercession with the Father for his afflicted church, *v.* 12. The angels related the posture of affairs in this lower world, but we read not of any prayers they made for the redress of the grievances they had made a remonstrance of. No; it is *the Angel among the myrtle-trees* that is the great intercessor. Upon the report of the angels he immediately turned heavenward, and said, *Lord, wilt thou not have mercy* on thy church? (1.) The thing he intercedes for is *mercy;* as Ps. 85:7, *Show us thy mercy, O Lord!* Note, God's mercy is all in all to the church's comfort; and all his mercy must be hoped for through Christ's mediation. (2.) The thing he complains of is the delay of this mercy: *How long wilt thou not have mercy!* He knows that *mercies* through him *shall be built up for ever* (Ps. 89:2), but thinks it long that the building is deferred. (3.) The objects of compassion recommended to the divine mercies are, Jerusalem, the holy city, and the other cities of Judah that were now in ruins; for God had had *indignation against them* now *threescore and ten years.* He mentions seventy years because that was the time fixed in the divine councils for the continuance of the captivity; so long the indignation lasted, and though *now for a little space grace* had been *shown them from the Lord their God,* to *give them some reviving* (Ezra 9:8), yet the scars of those seventy years' captivity still remained so deep, so painful, that this is the melancholy string they still harp upon — the divine indignation during those seventy years. Dr. Lightfoot thinks that whereas the seventy years of the captivity were reckoned from Jehoiakim's fourth year, and ended in the first of Cyrus, these seventy years are to be computed from the eleventh of Zedekiah, when Jerusalem and the temple were burnt, about nineteen years after the first captivity, and which ended in this second year of Darius Hystaspes, about seventeen years after Cyrus's proclamation, as that seventy years mentioned *ch.* 7:5 was about nineteen years after; the captivity went off, as it came on, gradually. "Lord, we are still under the burden of the seventy years' wrath, *and wilt thou be angry with us for ever?"*

3. He heard a gracious reply given to this intercession of Christ's for his church; for it is a prevailing intercession, always acceptable, *and him the Father heareth always* (*v.* 13): *The Lord answered the angel,* this angel of the covenant, *with good words and comfortable words,* with promises of mercy and deliverance, and the perfecting of what he had begun in favour to them. These were comfortable words to Christ, who is grieved in the grievances of his church, and comfortable to all that mourn with Zion. God often answers prayer with good words, when he does not immediately appear in great works; and those good words are real answers to prayer. Men's good words will not feed the body (Jam. 2:16), but God's good words will feed the faith, for saying and doing with him are not two things, though they are with us.

4. He heard that reply which was given to the angel repeated to himself, with a commission to publish it to the children of his people, for their comfort. *The revelation of Jesus Christ which God gave to him* he *signified to his servant John,* and by him *to the churches,* Rev. 1:1, 4. Thus all the good words and comfortable words of the gospel we receive from Jesus Christ, as he received them from the Father, in answer to the prayer of his blood, and his ministers are appointed to preach them *to all the world.* Now that God would *speak comfortably to Jerusalem,* Zechariah is *the voice of one crying in the wilderness, Prepare you the way of the Lord. The voice said, Cry. Cry then.* The prophets must now cry as loudly to show God's people their comforts as ever they did formerly to show them *their transgressions,* Isa. 40:2, 3, 6. And if he ask, *What shall I cry?* he is here instructed. (1.) He must proclaim the wrath God has in store for the enemies of Jerusalem. He is *jealous for Zion with great jealousy, v.* 14. He takes himself to be highly affronted by the injuries and indignities that are done to his church, as he had been formerly by the iniquities found in his church. The earth *sat still and was at rest* (*v.* 11), not relenting at all, nor showing the least remorse, for all the mischief they had done to Jerusalem, as Joseph's brethren, who, when they had sold him, sat down to eat bread; and this God took very ill (*v.* 15): *I am very sorely displeased with the heathen, that are at ease,* and have no concern for the afflicted church. Much more will he be displeased with those that are *at ease in Zion* (Amos 6:1), with Zion's own sons, that sympathize not with her in her sorrows. But this was not all; they were not only not concerned for her, but they were concerned against her: *I was but a little displeased* with my people, and designed to correct them moderately, but those that were employed as instruments of the correction cast off all pity, and with the greatest rage and malice *helped forward the affliction* and added to it, *persecuting those whom God had smitten* (Ps. 69:26) and insulting over those whom he had troubled. See Isa. 47:6; 10:5; Eze. 25:12, 15. Note, God is displeased with those who help forward the affliction even of such as suffer justly; for true humanity, in such a case, is good divinity. (2.) He must proclaim the mercy God has in store for Jerusalem and the *cities of Judah, v.* 16. He must cry, *"Thus saith the Lord, I have returned to Jerusalem with mercies.* I was going away in wrath, but I am now returning in love. *Cry yet* to the same purport," *v.* 17. There must now be line upon line for consolation, as formerly there had been for conviction. *The Lord,* even the Lord of hosts, assures them, [1.] That the temple shall be built that is now but in the building. This good work which they are now about, though it meet with much discouragement, shall be perfected, and they shall have the tokens of God's presence, and opportunities of conversing with him, and worshipping him, as formerly. Note, It is good news indeed to any place to hear that God will build his house in it. [2.] That Jerusalem shall again be *built as a city compact together,* which had formerly been its glory, Ps. 122:3. *A line shall be stretched*

forth upon Jerusalem, in order to the rebuilding of it with great exactness and uniformity. [3.] That the nation shall again become populous and rich, though now diminished and impoverished. Not only Jerusalem, but other cities that are reduced and lie in a little compass, shall yet *spread abroad,* or be diffused; their suburbs shall extend far, and colonies shall be transplanted from them; and this *through prosperity:* they shall be so numerous, and so wealthy, that there shall not be room for them; they shall complain that *the place is too strait,* Isa. 49:20. As they had been scattered and spread abroad, through their calamities, so they should now be through their prosperity. *Let thy fountains be dispersed,* Prov. 5:16. The cities that should thus increase God calls his cities; they are *blessed* by him, and they are *fruitful and multiply, and replenish the land.* [4.] That all their present sorrows should not only be balanced, but for ever silenced, by divine consolations: *The Lord shall yet comfort Zion.* Yet at length, though her griefs and grievances may continue long, God has comforts in reserve for Zion and all her mourners. [5.] That all this will be the fruit of God's preventing distinguishing favour: He shall yet *choose Jerusalem,* shall renew his choice, renew his covenant, shall make it appear that he has chosen Jerusalem. As he first built them up into a people when he brought them out of Egypt, so he will now rebuild them, when he brings them out of Babylon, not for any worthiness of theirs, but in pursuance of his own choice, Deu. 7:7, 8. Jerusalem is the city he has chosen, and he will not cast it off.

Verses 18–21

It is the comfort and triumph of the church (Isa. 59:19) that *when the enemy shall come in like a flood,* with mighty force and fury, then the *Spirit of the Lord shall lift up a standard against him.* Now, in this vision (the second which this prophet had), we have an illustration of that, God's Spirit making a stand, and making head, against the formidable power of the church's adversaries.

I. We have here the enemies of the church bold and daring, and threatening to be its death, to *cut off the name of Israel;* such the people of God had lately been insulted by: *I looked and behold four horns* (*v.* 18), which are explained *v.* 19. They *are the horns which have scattered Judah, Israel, and Jerusalem,* that is, the Jews both in the country and in the city, because they were the Israel of God. They have *tossed them* (so some read it), as furious bulls with their horns toss that which they are enraged at. They have scattered them, *so that no man did lift up his head, v.* 21. No man durst show his face for fear of them, much less give them any opposition, or make head against them. They are *horns,* denoting their dignity and dominion — *horns exalted,* denoting also their strength, and power, and violence. They are *four horns,* for the Jews are surrounded with them on every side; when they avoid one horn that pushes at them they run upon another. The men of Judah and the inhabitants of Jerusalem, and many of Israel that joined themselves to them, set about the building of the temple; but the enemies of that work from all sides pushed at them, and drove them from it. Rehum, and Shimshai, and the other Samaritans that opposed the building of the temple, were these horns, Ezra 4:8. So were Sanballat and Tobiah, and the Ammonites and Arabians, that opposed the building of the wall, Neh. 4:7. Note, The church's enemies have horns, and use them to the hindrance of every good work. The great enemy of the New-Testament church has *seven heads and ten horns* (Rev. 17:3), so that those who endeavour to do the church any service must expect to be pushed at.

II. We have here the friends of the church active and prevailing. The prophet did himself lift up his eyes and see the four horns, and saw them so formidable that he began to despair of the safety of every good man, and the success of every good work; but *the Lord* then *showed him four carpenters,* or *smiths,* who were empowered to cut off these horns, *v.* 20, 21. With an eye of sense we see the power of the enemies of the church; look which way we will, the world shows us that. But it is with an eye of faith that we see it safe, notwithstanding; it is the Lord that shows us that, as he opened the eyes of the prophet's servant to see the angelic guards round about his master, 2 Ki. 6:17. Observe, Those that were to fray or break the horns of the Gentiles, and to cast them out, were, 1. *Carpenters* or *smiths* (for they are supposed by some to have been horns of iron), men who had skill and ability to do it, whose proper business it was, and who understood their business and had tools at hand to do it with. Note, God calls those to serve the interests of his church whom he either finds, or makes, fit for it. If there be horns (which denote the force and fury of beasts) against the church, there are carpenters (which denote the wisdom and forecast of men) for the church, by which they find ways to master the strongest beasts, for *every kind of beasts is tamed, and has been tamed, of mankind,* Jam. 3:7. 2. They were *four carpenters,* as many horns so many hands to saw them off. Note, Which way soever the church is threatened with mischief, and opposition given to its interests, God can find out ways and means to check the force, to restrain the wrath, and make it turn to his praise. Some by these four carpenters understand Zerubbabel and Joshua, Ezra and Nehemiah, who carried on the work of God in spite of the opposition given to it. Those horned beasts broke into God's vineyard to tread it down; but the good magistrates and the good ministers whom God raised up, though they had not power to *cut off the horns of the wicked* (as David did, Ps. 75:5, 10), yet frightened them and cast them out. Note, When God has work to do he will raise up some to do it and others to defend it and protect those that are employed in the doing of it.

CHAPTER 2

In this chapter we have, I. Another vision which the prophet saw, not for his own entertainment, but for his satisfaction and the edification of those to whom he was sent (*v.* 1, 2). II. A sermon upon it, in the rest of the chapter, 1. By way of explication of the vision, showing it to be a prediction of the replenishing of Jerusalem and of its safety and honour (*v.* 3–5). 2. By way of application. Here is, (1.) A use of exhortation to the Jews that were yet in Babylon, pressing them to hasten their return to their own land, (*v.* 6–9). (2.) A use of consolation tot hose that were returned, in reference to the many difficulties they had to struggle with (*v.* 10–12). (3.) A use of caution to all not to prescribe to God, or limit him, but patiently to wait for him (*v.* 13).

Verses 1–5

This prophet was ordered, in God's name, to assure the people (*ch.* 1:16) that a *line should be stretched forth upon Jerusalem.* Now here we have that promise illustrated and confirmed, that the prophet might deliver that part of his message to the people with the more clearness and assurance.

I. He sees, in a vision, a man going to measure Jerusalem (*v.* 1, 2): *He lifted up his eyes again, and looked.* God had shown him that which was very encouraging to him, (*ch.* 1:20), and therefore now he *lifted up his eyes again and looked.* Note, The comfortable sights which by faith we have had of God's goodness made to pass before us should engage us to lift up our eyes again, and to search further into the discoveries made to us of the divine grace; for there is still more to be seen. In the close of the foregoing chapter he had seen Jerusalem's enemies baffled and broken, so that now he begins to hope she shall not be ruined. But that is not enough to make her happy, and therefore that is not all that is promised. Here is more carpenter's work to be done. When David had resolved to *cut off the horns of the wicked* he engaged likewise that the *horns of the righteous* should be *exalted,* Ps. 75:10. And so does the *Son of David* here; for he is *the man,* even *the man Christ Jesus,* whom the prophet sees *with a measuring line in his hand;* for he is the master builder of his church (Heb. 3:3), and he builds exactly by line and level. Zechariah took the boldness to ask him *whither he was going* and what he designed to do with that measuring line. And he readily told him that he was going to *measure Jerusalem,* to take a particular account of the dimensions of it each way, that it might be computed what was necessary for the making of a wall about it, and that it might appear, by comparing its dimensions with the vast numbers that should inhabit it, what additions were necessary to be made for the receiving and containing of them; when multitudes flock to Jerusalem (Isa. 60:4) it is time for her to *enlarge the place of her tent,* Isa. 54:2. Note, God takes notice of the extent of his church, and will take care that, when ever so many guests are brought in to the wedding supper, still there *shall be room,* Lu. 14:22. *In* the New Jerusalem, *my Father's house* above, *there are many mansions.*

II. He is informed that this vision means well to Jerusalem, that the measuring line he saw was not a *line of confusion* (as that Isa. 34:11), not a line to mete out for destruction, as when God *purposed to destroy the wall of the daughter of Zion he stretched out a line* (Lam. 2:8); but it is as when he *divided the inheritance by line,* Ps. 78:55. The *angel that talked with* the prophet *went forth,* as he designed, *to measure Jerusalem,* but *another angel went out to meet him,* to desire that he would first explain this vision to the prophet, that it might not occasion him any uneasy speculations: *Run, and speak to this young man* (for, it seems, the prophet entered upon his prophecy when he was young, yet no man ought to despise his youth when God thus highly honoured it); he is a young man, not experienced, and may be ready to fear the worst; therefore bid him hope the best; tell him that Jerusalem shall be both safe and great, 1. As safe and great as numbers of men can make it (*v.* 4): *Jerusalem shall be inhabited as towns without walls;* the inhabitants of it shall increase, and multiply, and replenish it to admiration, so that it shall extend itself far beyond the present dimensions which now there is an account taken of. The walls of a city, as they defend it, so they straiten and confine it, and keep its inhabitants from multiplying beyond such a pitch; but Jerusalem, even when it is walled, to keep off the enemy, shall be inhabited *as towns without walls.* The city shall be in a manner lost in the suburbs, as London is, where the out-parishes are more populous than those within the walls. So shall it be with Jerusalem; it shall be extended as freely as if it had no walls at all, and yet shall be as safe as if it had the strongest walls, such a *multitude of men* (which are the best walls of a city) *shall there be therein,* and of *cattle too,* to be not only food, but wealth too, for those men. Note, The increase of the numbers of a people is a great blessing, is a fruit of God's blessing on them and an earnest of further blessings, Ps. 107:38. *They are multiplied, for he blesses them.* 2. As safe and great as the presence of God can make it, *v.* 5. (1.) It shall be safe, for God himself will be a *wall of fire round about it.* Jerusalem had no walls about it at this time, but lay naked and exposed; formerly, when it had walls, the enemies not only broke through them, but broke them down; but now God will be unto her a wall of fire. Some think it alludes to shepherds that made fires about their flocks, or travellers that made fires about their tents in desert places, to frighten wild beasts from them. God will not only *make a hedge* about them as he did about Job (*ch.* i. 10), not only make walls and bulwarks about them, Isa. 26:1 (those may be battered down), not only be as the mountains round about them, Ps. 125:2 (mountains may be got over), but he will be a wall of fire round them, which cannot be broken through, nor scaled, nor undermined, nor the foundations of it sapped, nor can it be attempted, or approached, without danger to the assailants. God will not only make a wall of fire about her, but he will himself be such a wall; for *our God is a consuming fire* to his and his church's enemies. He is a wall of fire, not on one side only, but round about on every side. (2.) It shall be great, for God himself *will be the glory in the midst of it.* His temple, his altar, shall be set up and attended there, and his institutions observed, and there then shall the tokens of his special presence and favour be, which will be the glory in the midst of them, will make them truly admirable in the eyes of all about them. God will have honour from them, and put honour upon them. Note, Those that have God for their God have him for their glory; those that have him in the midst of them have glory in the midst of them, and thence the church is said to be *all glorious within.* And those persons and places that have God to be the glory in the midst of them have him for a wall of fire round about them, for *upon all that glory there is,* and shall be, *a defence,* Isa. 4:5. Now all this was fulfilled in part in Jerusalem, which in process of time became a very flourishing city, and made a very great figure in those parts of the world, much beyond what could have been expected, considering how low it was brought and how long it was ere it recovered itself; but it was to have its full accomplishment in the gospel-church, which is extended far, as towns without walls, by the admission of the Gentiles into it, and which has God, the Son of God, for its prince and protector.

Verses 6–9

One would have thought that Cyrus's proclamation, which gave liberty to the captive Jews to return to their own land, would suffice to bring them all back, and that, as when Pharaoh gave them leave to quit Egypt and their house of bondage there, they would not leave a hoof behind; but it seems it had not that effect. There were about 40,000 whose spirits God stirred up to go, and they went; but many, perhaps the greater part, staid behind. The land of their captivity was to most of them the land of their nativity; they had taken root there, had gained a settlement, and many of them a very comfortable one; some perhaps had got estates and preferments there, and they did not think they could better themselves by returning to their own land. *Patria est ubicunque bene est — My country is every spot where I feel myself happy.* They had no great affection to their own land, and apprehended the difficulties in their way to it insuperable. This proceeded from a bad cause — a distrust of the power and promise of God, a love of ease and worldly wealth, and an indifference to the religion of their country and to the God of Israel himself; and it had a bad effect, for it was a tacit censure of those as foolish, rash, and given to change, that did return, and a weakening of their hands in the work of God. Such as these could not sing (Ps. 137) in their captivity, for they had *forgotten thee, O Jerusalem!* and were so far from preferring thee before their chief joy that they preferred any joy before thee. Here is therefore another proclamation issued out by the God of Israel, strictly charging and commanding all his free-born subjects, wherever they were dispersed, speedily to return into their own land and render themselves at their respective posts there. They are loudly summoned (*v.* 6): *Ho! ho! come forth, and flee from the land of the north, saith the Lord.* This fitly follows upon the promise of the rebuilding and enlarging of Jerusalem. If God will build it for them and their comfort, they must come and inhabit it for him and his glory, and not continue sneaking in Babylon. Note, The promises and privileges with which God's people are blessed should engage us, whatever it cost us, to join ourselves to them and *cast in our lot among them.* When Zion is enlarged, to make room for all God's Israel, it is the greatest madness imaginable for any of them to stay in Babylon. The captivity of a sinful state is by no means to be continued in, though a man be ever so easy upon temporal accounts. No: *Come forth and flee* with all speed, and lose no time. *Escape for thy life; look not behind thee.* To induce them to hasten their return, let them consider, 1. They are now dispersed, and are concerned to incorporate themselves for their mutual common defence (*v.* 6): *"I have spread you abroad as the four winds of heaven,* sent some into one corner of the world and some into another; this has been your condition a long time, and therefore you should now think of coming together again, to help one another." God owns that his scattering them was in wrath, and therefore they must take this invitation as a token of God's being willing to be reconciled to them again, so that they kicked at his kindness in refusing to accept the call. 2. They are now in bondage, and are concerned to assert their own liberty; and therefore, *"Deliver thyself, O Zion!* flee from the oppressor, and make the best of thy way. Let us see some such bold efforts and struggles to help thyself as become the generous gracious seed of Abraham." *v.* 7. Note, When Christ has proclaimed that deliverance to the captives which he has himself wrought out it then concerns each of us to *deliver ourselves,* to *loose ourselves from the bands of our necks* (Isa. 52:2), and, since we are under grace, to resolve that *sin shall not have dominion over us,* Zion herself is here said to *dwell with the daughter of Babylon,* because many of the *precious sons of Zion* dwelt there, and where the people of God are there the church of God is, for it is not tied to places. Now it is not fit that Zion should dwell with the daughter of Babylon; what communion can light have with darkness? Zion will be in danger of partaking with the daughter of Babylon both *in her sins* and *in her plagues;* and therefore, *"Come out of her, my people,* Rev. 18:4. *Deliver thyself, O Zion!* by a speedy return to thy own land, and do not destroy thyself by continuing in that polluted devoted land." Those that would be found among the generation of God's children must *save themselves from* the *untoward generation* of this world; it was St. Peter's charge to his new converts, Acts 2:40. 3. They have seemed to be forsaken and forgotten of God, but God will now make it to appear that he espouses their cause and will plead it with jealousy, *v.* 8,9. It was a discouragement to those who remained in Babylon to hear of the difficulties and oppositions which their brethren met with that had returned, by which they were still in danger of being crushed and overpowered. "And we might as well sit still" (think they) "as rise up and fall." In answer to this objection, the *angel that talked with* the prophet (that is, Jesus Christ) tells him what he had commission to do for their protection and the perfecting of their salvation, and herein he has an eye to the great redemption which, in the fulness of time, he was to be the author of. Christ, who is Jehovah, and the *Lord of hosts,* of all the hosts of heaven and earth, in both which he has a sovereign power, *says, He* (that is, the Father) *has sent me.* Note, What Jesus has done, and does, for his church against his enemies, he was sent and commissioned by the Father to do. With great satisfaction he often speaks of *the Father that sent him.* (1.) He is sent *after the glory.* After the glorious beginning of their deliverance he is sent to perfect it, for he is the finisher of that work which he is the author of. Christ is sent, in the first place, to the nation and people of the Jews, *to whom pertained the glory,* Rom. 9:4. And he was himself the *glory of his people Israel.* But *after the glory,* after his care of them, he is *sent to the nations, to be a light to lighten the Gentiles,* by the power of his gospel to captivate them, and bring them, and every high thought among them, into obedience to himself. (2.) He is *sent to the nations that spoiled them,* to take vengeance on them for the wrongs done to Zion, when the year of his redeemed comes and the *year of recompences for the controversy of Zion,* Isa. 34:8. He is sent to *shake his hand upon them,* to lift up his mighty hand against them and to lay upon them his heavy hand, to *bruise them with a rod of iron* and *dash them in pieces like a potter's vessel,* Ps. 2:9. Some think it intimates how easily God can subdue and humble them with the turn of his hand; it is but shaking his hand over them and the work is done. *They shall be a spoil to their servants,* shall be enslaved to those whom they had enslaved, and be plundered by those whom they had plundered. In Esther's time this was fulfilled, when the *Jews had rule over those that hated them* (Esth. 9:1), and often in the time of the Maccabees. The promise is further fulfilled in Christ's victory over our spiritual enemies, his *spoiling principalities and powers and making a show of them openly,* Col. 2:15. And it is still in force to the gospel-church. Christ will reckon with all that are enemies to it, and sooner or later will make them *his footstool,* Ps. 110:1; Rev. 3:9. (3.) What he will do for his church shall be an evident proof of God's tender care of it and affection to it: *He that touches you touches the apple of his eye.* This is a high expression of God's love to his church. By his resentment of the injuries done to her it appears how dear she is to him, how he interests himself in all her interests, and takes what is done against her, not only as done against himself, but as done against the very apple of his eye, the tenderest part, which nature has made very fine, has put a double guard upon, and taught us to be in a special manner careful of, and which the least touch is a great offence to. This encourages the people of God to pray with David (Ps. 17:8), *Keep me as the apple of thy eye;* and engages them to do as Solomon directs (Prov. 7:2), to *keep his law as the apple of their eye.* Some understand it thus: *"He that touches you touches the apple of his own eye;* whoever do you any injury will prove, in the issue, to have done the greatest injury to themselves." (4.) It shall be an evident proof of Christ's mission: *You shall know that the Lord of hosts has sent me* to be the protector of his church, that the promises made to the church are yea and amen in him. Christ's victory over our spiritual enemies proves that the Father sent him and was with him.

Verses 10–13

Here is, I. Joy proclaimed to the church of God, to the *daughter of Zion,* that had separated herself from the *daughter of Babylon.* The Jews that had returned were in distress and danger, their enemies in the neighbourhood were spiteful against them, their friends that remained in Babylon were cool towards them, shy of them, and declined coming in to their assistance; and yet they are directed to *sing,* and to *rejoice* even in tribulation. Note, Those that have recovered their purity, and integrity, and spiritual liberty, though they have not yet recovered their outward prosperity, have reason to sing and rejoice, to give glory to God and take comfort to themselves.

I. God will have a people among them. If their brethren in Babylon will not come to them, those of other nations shall, and shall replenish Jerusalem and the cities of Judah: *Many nations shall be joined to the Lord in that day* that are now at a distance from him and strangers to him. The Jewish nation, after the captivity, multiplied very much, by the accession of proselytes to it, that were naturalized, and were entitled to all the privileges of native Israelites, and perhaps they were equal in number; and therefore Paul mentions it as an honour to him which many Jews had not, that he was of *the tribe of Benjamin, a Hebrew of the Hebrews,* Phil. 3:5. And this was an earnest of the bringing in of the Gentiles into the christian church and in that this and other similar promises were to have their full accomplishment. It was therefore strange that that should be so great an offence to the Jews, as we find it was in the apostles' times, which was promised them as a blessing in the prophets' times — that *many nations* should be *joined to the Lord.* And, as there had been one law, so should there be one gospel *for the stranger and for those born in the land;* whatever nation they come from, when they *join themselves to the Lord, they shall be my people,* as dear to God as ever Israel had been. Note, God will own those for his people who with purpose of heart join themselves to him; and, when many do so, we ought to look upon them, not with a jealous eye, but with a joyful one. Angels rejoice, and therefore so should the daughter of Zion, when many nations are joined to the Lord.

II. They shall have his presence among them: *Sing and rejoice, for I come.* Those to whom God comes have reason to rejoice, for he will be to them their chief joy. God will come, not to make them a visit only, but to reside with them and preside over them: *I will dwell in the midst of thee* (*v.* 10), and it is repeated (*v.* 11), because it was to have a double accomplishment, 1. In the dedication of the temple, in their regularly observing all God's institutions there and God's owning them therein. Those have God *dwelling in the midst of them* that have his ordinances administered in their purity, and a divine power going along with them; with these tokens of God's presence the Jewish church was blessed, after this, as much as ever. 2. In the incarnation of Christ. He that here promises to dwell among them is that *Lord whom the Lord of hosts has sent* (*v.* 11), and therefore must be the *Lord Jesus,* who came and dwelt in the midst of the Jewish nation, the eternal *Word,* that was *made flesh, and dwelt among us.* This was the great honour reserved for that nation in its last days; the promise of it effectually secured their continuance till it was accomplished. They could not be destroyed while that blessing was in them; and the prospect of it, according to the promise, was the great support and comfort of those who *looked for redemption in Jerusalem.* It is promised that when Christ comes and dwells among them *they shall know that the Lord of hosts has sent him;* all that were Israelites indeed were made to know it; sufficient proofs were given of it by the miracles Christ wrought, so that they might have known it, and yet there were those that perished in ignorance and unbelief, that would not know it, for, *if they had known it, they would not have crucified the Lord of glory.*

III. They shall have all their ancient dignities and privileges restored to them again, *v.* 12. 1. Canaan shall be a holy land again, not polluted by sin as it had been formerly, not profaned by the enemies as it had been of late; it shall be an enclosure again, and not laid in common. 2. Judah shall be in this holy land, shall inhabit it, and enjoy the comfort of it, and no longer be lost and scattered in Babylon. 3. Judah shall be God's portion, which he will delight in, which shall be dear to him, by which he will be served, and in which he will be glorified. *The Lord's portion is his people.* 4. God will *inherit Judah* again as *his portion,* will claim his interest, and recover the possession out of the hands of those that had invaded his right. He will protect his people and govern them as a man does his inheritance, and will be at home among them. 5. He will *choose Jerusalem again,* as he had chosen it formerly, to *put his name there;* he will renew and confirm the choice, and continue it a chosen place, till it must resign its honours to the Jerusalem that is from above. Though the election seemed to be set aside for a while, yet it *shall obtain.*

II. Here is silence proclaimed to all the world besides, *v.* 13. The daughter of Zion must sing, but *all flesh* must *be silent.* Observe here, 1. A very awful description of God's appearances for the relief of his people. He is *raised up out of his holy habitation;* as a man out of sleep (Ps. 44:23; 78:65), or as a man entering with resolution upon a business that he will go through with. Heaven is his holy habitation above; thence we must expect him to appear, Isa. 64:1. His temple is so in this lower world; thence from *between the cherubim* he will *shine forth,* Ps. 80:1. He is about to do something unusual, unexpected, and very surprising, and to plead his people's cause, which had long seemed neglected. 2. A seasonable caution and direction at such a time: *Be silent, O all flesh! before the Lord* — before Christ and his grace (let not flesh object against the methods he takes) — before God and his providence; the enemies of the church shall be silenced; all iniquity shall stop her mouth. The friends of the church also must be silent. Leave it to God to take his own way, and neither prescribe to him what he should do nor quarrel with him whatever he does. *Be still, and know that he is God. Stand still, and see his salvation.* See Hab. 2:20; Zep. 1:7. Silently acquiesce in his holy will, and patiently wait the issue, as those who are assured that when God is *raised up out of his holy habitation* he will not retreat, nor sit down again, till he has accomplished his whole work.

CHAPTER 3

The vision in the foregoing chapter gave assurances of the re-establishing of the civil interests of the Jewish nation, the promises of which terminated in Christ. Now the vision in this chapter concerns their church-state, and their ecclesiastical interests, and assures them that they shall be put into a good posture again; and the promises of this also have an eye to Christ, who is not only our prince, but the high priest of our profession, of whom Joshua was a type. Here is, I. A vision relating to Joshua, as the representative of the church in his time, representing the disadvantages he laboured under, and the people in him, with the redress of the grievances of both. 1. He is accused by Satan, but is brought off by Christ (*v.* 1, 2). 2. He appears in filthy garments, but has them changed (*v.* 3–5). 3. He is assured of being established in his office if he conduct himself well (*v.* 6, 7). II. A sermon relating to Christ, who is here called "The branch," who should be endued with all perfections for his undertaking, should be carried triumphantly through it, and by whom we should have pardon and peace (*v.* 8–10).

Verses 1–7

There was a Joshua that was a principal agent in the first settling of Israel in Canaan; here is another of the same name very active in their second settlement there after the captivity; Jesus is the same name, and it signifies *Saviour;* and they were both figures of him that was to come, our chief captain and our chief priest. The angel that talked with *Zechariah showed him Joshua the high priest;* it is probable that the prophet saw him frequently, that he spoke to him, and that there was a great intimacy between them; but, in his common views, he only saw how he appeared before men; if he must know how he stands before the Lord, it must be shown him in vision; and so it is shown him. And men are really as they are with God, not as they appear in the eye of the world. He stood *before the angel of the Lord,* that is, before Christ, the Lord of the angels, to whom even the high priests themselves, of Aaron's order, were accountable. He *stood before the angel of the Lord* to execute his office, to minister to God under the inspection of the angels. He stood to consult the oracle on the behalf of Israel, for whom, as high priest, he was agent. Guilt and corruption are our two great discouragements when we stand before God. By the guilt of the sins committed by us we have become obnoxious to the justice of God; by the power of the sin that dwells in us we have become odious to the holiness of God. All God's Israel are in danger upon these two accounts. Joshua was so here, for *the law made men priests that had infirmity,* Heb. 7:28. And, as to both, we have relief from Jesus Christ, who is made of God to us both *righteousness and sanctification.*

I. Joshua is accused as a criminal, but is justified. 1. A violent opposition is made to him. *Satan stands at his right hand to resist him* to be a *Satan to him, a law-adversary.* He stands at his right hand, as the prosecutor, or witness, at the right hand of the prisoner. Note, The devil is the accuser of the brethren, that *accuses them before God day and night,* Rev. 12:10. Some think the chief priest was accused for the sin of many of the inferior priests, in marrying strange wives, which they were much guilty of after their return out of captivity, Ezra 9:1, 2; Neh. 13:28. When God is about to reestablish the priesthood Satan objects the sins that were found among the priests, as rendering them unworthy the honour designed them. It is by our own folly that we give Satan advantage against us and furnish him with matter for reproach and accusation; and if any thing be amiss, especially with the priests, Satan will be sure to aggravate it and make the worst of it. He *stood to resist him,* that is, to oppose the service he was doing for the public good. He stood *at his right hand,* the hand of action, to discourage him, and raise difficulties in his way. Note, When we stand before God to minister to him, or stand up for God to serve his interests, we must expect to meet with all the resistance that Satan's subtlety and malice can give us. Let us then resist him that resists us and he shall flee from us. 2. A victorious defence is made for him (*v.* 2): *The Lord* (that is, the Lord Christ) *said unto Satan, The Lord rebuke thee.* Note, It is the happiness of the saints that the Judge is their friend; the same that they are accused to is their patron and protector, and an advocate for them, and he will be sure to bring them off. (1.) Satan is here checked by one that has authority, that has conquered him, and many a time silenced him. *The accuser of the brethren,* of the ministers and the ministry, *is cast out;* his indictments are quashed, and his suggestions against them as well as his suggestions to them, are shown to be malicious, frivolous, and vexatious. *The Lord rebuke thee, O Satan! The Lord said* (that is, the Lord our Redeemer), *The Lord rebuke thee,* that is, the Lord the Creator. The power of God is engaged for the making of the grace of Christ effectual. "*The Lord* restrain thy malicious rage, reject thy malicious charge, and revenge upon thee thy enmity to a servant of his" Note, those that belong to Christ have him ready to appear vigorously for them when Satan appears most vehement against them. He does not parley with him, but stops his mouth immediately with this sharp reprimand: *The Lord rebuke thee, O Satan!* This is the best way of dealing with that furious enemy. *Get thee behind me, Satan.* (2.) Satan is here argued with. He resists the priest, but let him know that his resistance, [1.] Will be fruitless; it will be to no purpose to attempt any thing against Jerusalem, for *the Lord has chosen* it, and he will abide by his choice. Whatever is objected against God's people, God saw it; he foresaw it when he chose them and yet he chose them, and therefore that can be no inducement to him now to reject them; he knew the worst of them when he chose them; and his election shall obtain. [2.] It is unreasonable; for *is not this a brand plucked out of the fire?* Joshua is so, and the priesthood, and the people, whose representative he is. Christ has not that to say for them for which they are to be praised, but that for which they are to be pitied. Note, Christ is ready to make the best of his people, and takes notice of every thing that is pleadable in excuse of their infirmities, so far is he from being extreme to mark what they do amiss. They have been lately in the fire; no wonder that they are black and smoked, and have the smell of fire upon them, but they are therefore to be excused, not to be accused. One can expect no other than that those who but the other day were captives in Babylon should appear very mean and despicable. They have been lately brought out of great affliction; and is Satan so barbarous as to desire to have them thrown into affliction again? They have been wonderfully delivered out of the fire, that God might be glorified in them; and will he then cast them off and abandon them? No, he will not quench the smoking flax, the smoking fire-brand; for he snatched it out of the fire because he intended to make use of it. Note, Narrow escapes from imminent danger are happy presages and powerful pleas for more eminent favours. A converted soul is a *brand plucked out of the fire* by a miracle of free grace, and therefore shall not be left to be a prey to Satan.

II. Joshua appears as one polluted, but is purified; for he represents the Israel of God, who are all *as an unclean thing,* till they are washed and sanctified *in the name of the Lord Jesus* and *by the Spirit of our God.* Now observe here, 1. The impurity wherein Joshua appeared (*v.* 3): *He was clothed,* not only in coarse, but in *filthy garments,* such as did very ill become the dignity of his office and the sanctity of his work. By the law of Moses the garments of the high priest were to be *for glory and for beauty,* Ex. 28:2. But Joshua's garments were a shame and reproach to him; yet in them *he stood before the angel of the Lord;* he had no clean linen wherein to minister and to do the duty of his place. Now this intimates, not only that the priesthood was poor and despised, and loaded with contempt, but that there was a great deal of iniquity cleaving to the holy things. The returned Jews were so taken up with their troubles that they thought they needed not complain of their sins, and were not aware that those were the great hindrances of the progress of God's work among them; because they were free from idolatry they thought themselves chargeable with no iniquity. But God showed them there were many things amiss in them, which retarded the advances of God's favours towards them. There were spiritual enemies warring against them, more dangerous than any of the neighbouring nations. The Chaldee paraphrase says, *Joshua had sons who took unto them wives which were not lawful for the priests to take;* and we find it was so, Ezra 10:18. And, no doubt, there were other things amiss in the priesthood, Mal. 2:1. Yet Joshua was permitted to *stand before the angel of the Lord.* Though his children did not as they should, yet the covenant of priesthood was not broken. Note, Christ bears with his people, whose hearts are upright with him, and admits them into communion with himself, notwithstanding their manifold infirmities. 2. The provision that was made for his cleansing. Christ gave orders to the angels that attended him, and were ready to do his pleasure, to put Joshua into a better state. Joshua presented himself before the Lord in his filthy garments, as an object of his pity; and Christ graciously looked upon him with compassion, and not, as justly he might have done, with indignation. Christ loathed the filthiness of Joshua's garments, yet did not put him away, but put them away. Thus God by his grace does with those whom he chooses to be priests to himself; he parts between them and their sins, and so prevents their sins parting between them and their God; he reconciles himself to the sinner, but not to the sin. Two things are here done for Joshua, representing a double work of divine grace wrought in and for believers: — (1.) His filthy garments are taken from him, *v.* 4. The meaning of this is given us in what Christ said, and he said it as one having authority, *Behold, I have caused thy iniquity to pass from thee.* The guilt of it is taken away by pardoning mercy, the stench and stain of it by peace spoken to the conscience, and the power of it broken by renewing grace. When God forgives our sins he *causes our iniquity to pass from us,* that it may not appear against us, to condemn us; it passes from us *as far as the east is from the west.* When he sanctifies the nature he enables us to *put off the old man,* to cast away from us the filthy rags of our corrupt affections and lusts, as things we will never have any thing more to do with, will never gird to us or appear in. Thus Christ *washes those from their sins in his own blood* whom he *makes to our God kings and priests,* Rev. 1:5, 6. Either we must be cleansed from the pollutions of sin or we shall, *as polluted, be put from* that *priesthood,* Ezra 2:62. (2.) He is clothed anew, has not only the shame of his filthiness removed, but the shame of his nakedness covered: *I will clothe thee with change of raiment.* Joshua had no clean linen of his own, but Christ will provide for him, for he will not let a priesthood of his own instituting be lost, be either contemptible before men or unacceptable before God. The change of raiment here is rich costly raiment, such as is worn on high days. Joshua shall appear as lovely as ever he appeared loathsome. Those that minister in holy things shall not only cease to do evil, but learn to do well; God will make them wise, and humble, and diligent, and faithful, and examples of every thing that is good; and then Joshua is clothed with change of raiment. Thus those whom Christ makes spiritual priests are clothed with the spotless robe of his righteousness and appear before God in that, and with the graces of his Spirit, which are ornaments to them. *The righteousness of saints,* both imputed and implanted, is the fine linen, clean and white, with which *the bride, the Lamb's wife,* is arrayed, Rev. 19:8.

III. Joshua is in danger of being turned out of office; but, instead of that, he is reinstalled and established in his office. He not only has his sins pardoned, and is furnished with grace sufficient for himself, but, as *rectus in curia — acquitted in court,* he is restored to his former honours and trusts. 1. The crown of the priesthood is put upon him, *v.* 5.

This was done at the special instance and request of the prophet: I said, *"Let them set a fair mitre upon his head,* as a badge of his office. Now that he looks clean, let him also look great; let him be dressed up in all the garments of the high priest." Note, When God designs the restoring or reviving of religion he stirs up his prophets and people to pray for it, and does it in answer to their prayers. Zechariah prayed that the angels might be ordered to set the mitre on Joshua's head, and they did it immediately, and *clothed him with* the priestly *garments;* for no man took this honour to himself, *but he that was called of God* to it. *The angel of the Lord stood by,* as having the oversight of the work which the created angels were employed in. He stood by, as one well pleased with it, and resolved to stand by the orders he had given for the doing of it and to continue his presence with that priesthood. 2. The covenant of the priesthood is renewed with him, which is called God's *covenant of peace,* Num. 25:12. Mr. Pemble calls it *the patent of his office,* which is here declared and delivered to him before witnesses, *v.* 6, 7. The angel of the Lord, having taken care to make him fit for his office (and all that God calls to any office he either finds fit or makes so), invests him in it. And though he is not *made a priest with an oath* (that honour is reserved for him who is a priest after the order of Melchisedek, Heb. 7:21), yet, being a type of him, he is inaugurated with a solemn declaration of the terms upon which he held his office. The angel of the Lord protested to Joshua that, if he would be sure to do the duty of his place, he should enjoy the dignity and reward of it. Now see, (1.) What the conditions are upon which he enters into his office. Let him know that he is upon his good behaviour; he must *walk in God's ways,* that is, he must live a good life and be holy in all manner of conversation; he must go before the people in the paths of God's commandments, and walk circumspectly. He must also *keep God's charge,* must carefully do all the services of the priesthood, and must see to it that the inferior priests performed the duties of their place decently and in order. He must *take heed to himself, and* to *all the flock,* Acts 20:28. Note, Good ministers must be good Christians; yet that is not enough: they have a trust committed to them, they are charged with it, and they must keep it with all possible care, that they may give up their account of it with joy, 1 Tim. 6:14. (2.) What the privileges are which we may expect, and be assured of, in the due discharge of his office. His patent runs, *Quamdiu se bene gesserit — During good behaviour.* Let him be sure to do his part, and God will own him. [1.] *"Thou shalt judge my house;* thou shalt preside in the affairs of the temple, and the inferior priests shall be under thy direction." Note, The power of the church, and of church rulers, is not a legislative, but only a judicial power. The high priest might not make any new laws for God's house, nor ordain any other rites of worship than what God had ordained; but he must judge God's house, that is, he must see to it that God's laws and ordinances were punctually observed, must protect and encourage those that did observe them, and enquire into and punish the violation of them. [2.] *"Thou shalt also keep my courts;* thou shalt have oversight of what is done in all the courts of the temple, and shalt keep them pure and in good order for the worship to be performed in them." Note, Ministers are God's stewards, and they are to keep his courts, in honour of him who is the chief Lord and for the preserving of equity and good order among his tenants. [3.] *"I will give thee places to walk among those that stand by,* among these angels that are inspectors and assistants in this instalment." They shall stand by while Joshua is at work for God, and shall be as a guard to him, or he shall be highly honoured and respected as an *angel of God,* Gal. 4:14. Ministers are called *angels,* Rev. 1. 20. Those that *walk in God's ways* may be said to *walk among the angels* themselves, for they do the will of God as the angels do it that are in heaven, and are their *fellow-servants,* Rev. 19:10. Some make it a promise of eternal life, and of a reward of his fidelity in the future state. Heaven is not only a palace, a place to repose in, but a paradise, a garden, a place to walk in; and there are walks among the angels, in society with that holy and glorious company. See Eze. 28:14.

Verses 8–10

As the promises made to David often slide insensibly into promises of the Messiah, whose kingdom David's was a type of, so the promises here made to Joshua immediately rise as far upward, and look as far forward, as to Christ, whose priesthood Joshua's was now a shadow of, not only in general, as it kept up the line of Aaron's priesthood, but especially as it was the reviving of that happy method of correspondence between heaven and earth, to which a great interruption had been given by the iniquity and captivity of Israel. Christ is a high priest, as Joshua was, for sinners and sufferers, to mediate for those that have been under guilt and wrath. And it was fit that Joshua should understand the priesthood of Christ, because all the virtue of his priesthood, its value and usefulness to the church, depended upon and was derived from the priesthood of Christ. See,

I. To whom this promise of Christ is directed (*v.* 8): *"Hear now, O Joshua!* Thou hast heard with pleasure what belongs to thyself; but, behold, a greater than Joshua is at hand. *Hear now* concerning him, *thou* and the rest of the priests, *thy fellows, who sit before thee,* at thy feet, as learners, but whom thou art to look upon as *thy fellows,* for all you are brethren; let the high priest, and all the inferior priests, take notice of this, for they are *men wondered at."* They are set *for signs,* for types and figures of Christ's priesthood. What God now did for Joshua and his fellows was a happy omen of the coming of the Messiah promised, and would be so interpreted, with a pleasing wonder, by all that had understanding of the times. Or they are men *wondered at* for their singularity, hooted at as strange sort of people, because they *run not with others to the same excess of riot* (1 Pt. 4:4), or for their strange afflictions and surprising deliverance out of them, as Ps. 71:7, *I am as a wonder unto many.* They are *men of wonder;* they are a wonder to themselves, are amazed to think how happily their condition is altered. God's people and ministers are, upon many accounts, men wondered at. The high priest and his fellows here (as the prophet and his children, Isa. 8:18) are for signs and for wonders. But men's wonder at them will cease when the Messiah comes, as the stars are eclipsed by the light of the sun; for *his name shall be called Wonderful.*

II. The promise itself, which consists of several parts, all designed for the comfort and encouragement of Joshua and his friends in that great good work of building the temple, which they were now engaged in. An eye to Christ, and a believing dependence upon the promises relating to him and his kingdom, would carry them through the difficulties they met with in that and their other services. 1. The Messiah shall come: *Behold, I will bring forth my servant the branch.* He has been long hid, but the fulness of time is now at hand, when he shall be brought forth into the world, brought forth among his people Israel. God himself undertakes to bring him forth, and therefore, no doubt, he will own him and stand by him. He is God's servant, employed in his work, obedient to his will, and entirely devoted to his honour and glory. He is the branch; so he was called Isa. 4:2, *The branch of the Lord.* Isa. 11:1, *A branch out of the roots of Jesse.* Jer. 23:5, *A righteous branch;* and Jer. 23:15, *The branch of righteousness.* His beginning was small, as a tender branch, but in time he should become a great tree and fill the earth, Isa. 53:2. He is the branch from which all our fruit must be gathered. 2. Many eyes shall be upon him. He is *the stone laid before Joshua,* alluding to the foundation or chief cornerstone, of the temple, which probably was laid, with great solemnity, in the presence of Joshua. Christ is not only the branch, which is the beginning of a tree, but the foundation, which is the beginning of a building; and, when he shall be brought forth, *seven eyes shall be upon him.* The eye of his Father was upon him, to take care of him, and protect him, especially in his sufferings; when he was buried in the grave, as the foundation-stones are under ground, the eyes of Heaven were still upon him, buried out of men's sight, but not out of God's. The eyes of all the prophets and Old-Testament saints were upon this one stone; Abraham rejoiced to see Christ's day, and he *saw it and was glad.* The eyes of all believers are upon him; they look unto him and are saved, as the eyes of the stung Israelites were upon the brazen serpent. Some understand this *one stone* to have the seven eyes in it as the wheels had in Ezekiel's vision, and think it denotes that perfection of wisdom and knowledge which Jesus Christ was endued with, for the good of his church. *His eyes run to and fro through the earth.* 3. God himself will beautify him, and put honour upon him: *I will engrave the graving thereof, saith the Lord of hosts.* This stone the builders refused, as rough and unsightly; but God undertakes to smooth and polish it, nay, and to carve it so that it shall be the *head stone of the corner,* the most beautiful in all the building. Christ was God's workmanship; and abundance of his wisdom appears in the contrivance of our redemption, which will appear when the engraving is perfected. This stone is a *precious stone,* though laid for a *foundation;* and the *graving* of it seems to allude to the precious stones in the breast-plate of the high priest, which had the names of the tribes *graven* upon them, as the *engraving of a signet,* Ex. 28:21, 22. In that breast-plate there were twelve stones laid before Aaron, and for aught that appears those were lost; but there shall be one worth them all laid before Joshua, and that is Christ himself. This precious stone shall sparkle as if it had seven eyes; there shall appear a perfection of wisdom and prudence in the oracles that proceed from the breast-plate of judgment. And God will *engrave the engraving thereof;* he will entrust Christ with all his elect, and he shall appear as their representative, and agent for them, as the high priest did when he went in before the Lord with the names of all Israel engraven in the precious stones of his breast-plate. When God gave a remnant to Christ, to be brought through grace to glory, then he *engraved the graving* of this *precious stone.* 4. By him sin shall be taken away, both the guilt and the dominion of it: *I will remove the iniquity of that land in one day.* When the high priest had the names of Israel engraven on the precious stones he was adorned with he is said to *bear the iniquity of the holy things* (Ex. 28:38); but the law *made nothing perfect,* Heb. 10:1. He bore the iniquity of the land, as a type of Christ; but he could not remove it; the doing of that was reserved for Christ, that blessed *Lamb of God, that takes away the sin of the world;* and he did it *in one day,* that day in which he suffered and died; that was done by the sacrifice offered that day which could not be done by the sacrifices of ages before, no, not by all the days of atonement which from Moses to Christ returned every year. This agrees with the angel's prediction (Dan. 9:24): He shall *finish transgression and make an end of sin.* And some make the engravings wherewith God engraved him to signify the wounds and stripes which were given to his blessed body, which he underwent for our *transgression,* for our *iniquity,* and *by which we are healed.* 5. The effect of all this shall be the sweet enjoyment which all believers shall have of themselves, and the sweet communion they shall have with one another (*v.* 10): *In that day you shall call every man his neighbour under the vine and the fig-tree,* which yield most pleasant fruit, and whose leaves also afford a refreshing shade for arbours. When iniquity is taken away, (1.) We reap precious benefits and privileges from our justification, more precious than the products of the vine or the fig-tree, Rom. 5:1. (2.) We repose in a sweet tranquillity and are quiet from the fear of evil. What should terrify us when iniquity is taken away, when nothing can hurt us? We sit down under Christ's shadow with delight, and by it are sheltered from the scorching heat of the curse of the law. We live as Israel in the peaceable reign of Solomon (1 Ki. 4:24, 25); for he is the prince of peace. (3.) We ought to invite others to come to partake with us in the enjoyment of these privileges, to *call every man his neighbour* to come and sit with him, for mutual converse, under the vine and fig-tree, and to share with him in the fruits he is surrounded with. Gospel-grace, as far as it comes with power, makes men neighbourly; and those that have the comfort of acquaintance with Christ themselves, and communion with God through him, will be forward to court others to it. *Let us go unto the house of the Lord.*

CHAPTER 4

In this chapter we have another comfortable vision, which, as it was explained to the prophet, had much in it for the encouragement of the people of God in their present straits, which were so great that they thought their case helpless, that their temple could never be rebuilt nor their city replenished; and therefore the scope of the vision is to show that God would, by his own power, perfect the work, though the assistance given to it by its friends were ever so weak, and the resistance given to it by its enemies were ever so strong. Here is, I. The awakening of the prophet to observe the vision (*v.* 1). II. The vision itself, of a candlestick with seven lamps, which were supplied with oil, and kept burning, immediately from two olive-trees that grew by it, one on either side (v. 2, 3). III. The general encouragement hereby intended to be given to the builders of the temple to go on in that good work, assuring them that it should be brought to perfection at last (v. 4–10). IV. The particular explication of the vision, for the illustration of these assurances (v. 11–14).

Verses 1–10

Here is, I. The prophet prepared to receive the discovery that was to be made to him: *The angel that talked with him came and waked him,* v. 1. It seems, though he was in conference with an angel, and about matters of great and public concern, yet he grew dull and fell asleep, as it should seem, while the angel was yet talking with him. Thus the disciples, when they saw Christ transfigured, were *heavy with sleep,* Lu. 9:32. The prophet's spirit, no doubt, was willing to attend to that which was to be seen and heard, but the flesh was weak; his body could not keep pace with his soul in divine contemplations; the strangeness of the visions perhaps stupefied him, and so he was overcome with sleep, or perhaps the sweetness of the visions composed him and even sung him asleep. Daniel was in a *deep sleep when he heard the voice of the angel's words,* Dan. 10:9. We shall never be fit for converse with spirits till we have got clear of these bodies of flesh. It should seem, the angel let him lose himself a little, that he might be fresh to receive new discoveries, but then *waked him,* to his surprise, *as a man that is wakened out of his sleep.* Note, We need the Spirit of God, not only to make known to us divine things, but to make us take notice of them. *He wakens morning by morning, he wakens my ear,* Isa. 50:4. We should beg of God that, whenever he speaks to us, he would awaken us, and we should then *stir up ourselves.*

II. The discovery that was made to him when he was thus prepared. The angel asked him, *What seest thou?* v. 2. When he was awake perhaps he would not have taken notice of what was presented to his view if he had not thus been excited to look about him. When he observed he saw a *golden candlestick,* such a one as was in the temple formerly, and with the like this temple should in due time be furnished. The church is a candlestick, set up for the enlightening of this dark world and the holding forth of the light of divine revelation to it. The candle is God's; the church is but the candlestick, but all of gold, denoting the great worth and excellence of the church of God. This golden candlestick had *seven lamps* branching out from it, so many sockets, in each of which was a burning and shining light. The Jewish church was but one, and though the Jews that were dispersed, it is probable, had synagogues in other countries, yet they were but as so many lamps belonging to one candlestick; but now, under the gospel, Christ is the centre of unity, and not Jerusalem, or any one place; and therefore seven particular churches are represented, not as *seven lamps,* but as seven several *golden candlesticks,* Rev. 1:20. This candlestick had one *bowl,* or common receiver, on the top, into which oil was continually dropping, and from it, by seven secret pipes, or passages, it was diffused to the seven lamps, so that, without any further care, they received oil as fast as they wasted it (as in those which we call *fountain-ink-horns,* or *fountainpens);* they never wanted, nor were ever glutted, and so kept always burning clear. And the bowl too was continually supplied, without any care or attendance of man; for (v. 3) he saw *two olive-trees,* one on each side the candlestick, that were so fat and fruitful that of their own accord they poured plenty of oil continually into the bowl, which by two larger pipes (v. 12) dispersed the oil to smaller ones and so to the lamps; so that nobody needed to attend this candlestick, to furnish it with oil (it tarried not for man, nor waited for the sons of men), the scope of which is to show that God easily can, and often does, accomplish his gracious purposes concerning his church by his own wisdom and power, without any art or labour of man, and that though sometimes he makes use of instruments, yet he neither needs them nor is tied to them, but can do his work without them, and will rather than it shall be undone.

III. The enquiry which the prophet made concerning the meaning of this, and the gentle reproof given him for his dulness (v. 4): *I answered and spoke to the angel,* saying, *What are these, my lord?* Observe how respectfully he speaks to the angel; he calls him *my lord.* Those that would be taught must give honour to their teachers. He

saw what these *were,* but asked what these *signified.* Note, It is very desirable to know the meaning of God's manifestations of himself and his mind both in his word and by his ordinances and providences. *What mean you by these* services, by these signs? And those that would understand the mind of God must be inquisitive. *Then shall we know if we follow on to know,* if we not only *hear,* but, as Christ, *ask questions* upon what we hear, Lu. 2:46. The angel answered him with a question, *Knowest thou not what these be?* intimating that if he had considered, and compared spiritual things with spiritual, he might have guessed at the meaning of these things; for he knew that there was a golden candlestick in the tabernacle, which it was the priests' constant business to supply with oil and to keep burning, for the use of the tabernacle; when therefore he saw, in vision, such a candlestick, with lamps always kept burning, and yet no priests to attend it, nor any occasion for them, he might discern the meaning of this to be that though God had set up the priesthood again, yet he could carry on his own work for and in his people without them. Note, We have reason to be ashamed of ourselves that we do not more readily apprehend the meaning of divine discoveries. The angel asked the prophet this question, to draw from him an acknowledgment of his own dulness, and darkness, and slowness to understand, and he had it immediately: *"I said, No, my lord; I know not what these are."* Visions had their significance, but often dark and hard to be understood, and the prophets themselves were not always aware of it at first. But those that would be taught of God must see and acknowledge their own ignorance, and their need to be taught, and must apply to God for instruction. To him that gave us the cabinet we must apply for the key wherewith to unlock it. God will teach the meek and humble, not those that are conceited of themselves and lean on the broken reed of their own understanding.

IV. The general intention of this vision. Without a critical descant upon every circumstance of the vision, the design of it is to assure the prophet, and by him the people, that this good work of building the temple should, by the special care of divine Providence, and the immediate influence of divine grace, be brought to a happy issue, though the enemies of it were many and mighty and the friends and furtherers of it few and feeble. Note, In the explication of visions and parables, we must look at the principal scope of them, and be satisfied with that, if that be clear, though we may not be able to account for every circumstance, or accommodate it to our purpose. The angel lets the prophet know, in general, that this vision was designed to illustrate a word which the Lord had to say to Zerubbabel, to encourage him to go on with the building of the temple. Let him know that he is a worker together with God in it, and that it is a work which God will own and crown.

1. God will carry on and complete this work, as he had begun their deliverance from Babylon, not by external force, but by secret operations and internal influences upon the minds of men. *He* says this who is the *Lord of hosts,* and could do it *vi et armis — by force,* has legions at command; but he will do it, *not by human might or power,* but *by his own Spirit.* What is done by his Spirit is done by might and power, but it stands in opposition to visible force. Israel was brought out of Egypt, and into Canaan, by might and power; in both these works of wonder great slaughter was made. But they were brought out of Babylon, and into Canaan the second time, *by the Spirit of the Lord of hosts* working upon the spirit of Cyrus, and inclining him to proclaim liberty to them, and working upon the spirits of the captives, and inclining them to accept the liberty offered them. It was by the *Spirit of the Lord of hosts* that the people were excited and animated to build the temple; and *therefore* they are said to be *helped by the prophets of God,* because they, as the Spirit's mouth, spoke to their hearts, Ezra 5:2. It was by the same Spirit that the heart of Darius was inclined to favour and further that good work and that the sworn enemies of it were infatuated in their councils, so that they could not hinder it as they designed. Note, The work of God is often carried on very successfully when yet it is carried on very silently, and without the assistance of human force; the gospel-temple is built, not by might or power (for *the weapons of our warfare are not carnal),* but by the *Spirit of the Lord of*

hosts, whose work on men's consciences is mighty to the pulling down of strong-holds; thus the excellency of the power is of God, and not of man. When instruments fail, let us therefore leave it to God to do his work himself by his own Spirit.

2. All the difficulties and oppositions that lie in the way shall be got over and removed, even those that seem insuperable (v. 7): *Who art thou, O great mountain? Before Zerubbabel thou shalt become a plain.* See here, (1.) How the difficulty is represented; it is a *great mountain,* impassable and immovable, a heap of rubbish, like a great mountain, which must be got away, or the work cannot go on. The enemies of the Jews are proud and hard as great mountains; but, when God has work to do, the mountains that stand in the way of it shall dwindle into mole-hills; for see here, (2.) How these difficulties are despised: *"Who art thou, O great mountain!* that thou shouldst stand in God's way and think to stop the progress of his work? Who art thou that lookest so big, that thus threatenest, and art thus feared? *Before Zerubbabel,* when he is God's agent, *thou shalt become a plain.* All the difficulties shall vanish, and all the objections be got over. *Every mountain and hill* shall be *brought low* when the *way of the Lord* is to be *prepared,"* Isa. 40:4. Faith will remove mountains and make them plains. Christ is our Zerubbabel; mountains of difficulty were in the way of his undertaking, but before him they were all levelled; nothing is too hard for his grace to do.

3. The same hand that has begun this good work will perform it: *He shall bring forth the head-stone* (v. 7); and again (v. 9), *The hands of Zerubbabel have laid the foundation of this house,* be it spoken to his honour (perhaps with his own hands he laid the first stone), and though it has been long retarded, and is still much opposed, yet it shall be finished at last; he shall live to see it finished, nay, and *his hands shall also finish it;* herein he is a type of Christ, who is both the *author* and the *finisher of our faith;* and his being the *author* of it is an assurance to us that he will be the *finisher,* for, *as for God, his work is perfect;* has he begun and shall he not make an end? Zerubbabel shall himself *bring forth the head-stone with shoutings,* and loud acclamations of joy, among the spectators. The acclamations are not *huzzas,* but *Grace, grace;* that is the burden of the triumphant songs which the church sings. It may be taken, (1.) As magnifying free grace, and giving to that all the glory of what is done. When the work is finished it must be thankfully acknowledged that it was not by any policy or power of our own that it was brought to perfection, but that it was grace that did it — God's goodwill towards us and his good work in us and for us. *Grace, grace,* must be cried, not only to the head-stone, but to the foundation-stone, the corner-stone, and indeed to every stone in God's building; from first to last it is nothing of works, but all of grace, and all our crowns must be cast at the feet of free grace. *Not unto us, O Lord! not unto us.* (2.) As depending upon free grace, and desiring the continuance of it, for what is yet to be done. *Grace, grace,* is the language of prayer as well as of praise; now that this building is finished, all happiness attend it! Peace be within its walls, and, in order to that, *grace.* Let the beauty of the Lord our God be upon it! Note, What comes from the grace of God may, in faith, and upon good grounds, be committed to the grace of God, for God will not forsake the work of his own hands.

4. This shall be a full ratification of the prophecies which went before concerning the Jews' return, and their settlement again. When the temple is finished then *thou shalt know that the Lord of hosts has sent me unto you.* Note, The exact accomplishment of scripture prophecies is a convincing proof of their divine original. Thus God *confirms the word of his servant,* by saying to Jerusalem, *Thou shalt be built,* Isa. 44:26. No word of God shall fall to the ground, nor shall there fail one iota or tittle of it. Zechariah's prophecies of the approaching day of deliverance to the church would soon appear, by the accomplishment of them, to be of God.

5. This shall effectually silence those that looked with contempt upon the beginning of this work, v. 10. Who, where, is he now that despised the day of small things, and thought this work would never come to any thing? The Jews themselves despised the foundation of the second temple, because it was likely to be so far inferior to

the first, Ezra 3:12. Their enemies despised the wall when it was in the building, Neh. 2:19; 4:2, 3. But let them not do it. Note, In God's work the day of small things is not to be despised. Though the instruments be weak and unlikely, God often chooses such, by them to bring about great things. As a great mountain becomes a plain before him when he pleases, so a little stone, cut out of a mountain without hands, comes to fill the earth, Dan. 2:35. Though the beginnings be small, God can make the latter end greatly to increase; a grain of mustard-seed may become a great tree. Let not the dawning light be despised, for it will shine more and more to the perfect day. The day of small things is the day of precious things, and will be the day of great things.

6. This shall abundantly satisfy all the hearty well-wishers to God's interest, who will be glad to see themselves mistaken in *despising the day of small things.* Those that despaired of the finishing of the work shall rejoice when they *see the plummet in the hand of Zerubbabel,* when they see him busy among the builders, giving orders and directions what to do, and taking care that the work be done with great exactness, that it may be both fine and firm. Note, It is matter of great rejoicing to all good people to see magistrates careful and active for the edifying of the house of God, to see the plummet in the hand of those who have power to do much, if they have but a heart according to it; we see not Zerubbabel with the trowel in his hand (that is left to the workmen, the ministers), but we see him with the plummet in his hand, and it is no disparagement, but an honour to him. Magistrates are to inspect ministers' work, and to speak comfortably to the Levites that do their duty.

7. This shall highly magnify the wisdom and care of God's providence, which is always employed for the good of his church. Zerubbabel does his part, does as much as man can do to forward the work, but it is *with those seven, those seven eyes of the Lord* which we read of *ch.* 3:9. He could do nothing if the watchful, powerful, gracious providence of God did not go before him and go along with him in it. Except the Lord had built this house, Zerubbabel and the rest would have *laboured in vain,* Ps. 127:1. These *eyes of the Lord* are those that *run to and fro through the whole earth,* that take cognizance of all the creatures and all their actions (2 Chr. 16:9), and inspire and direct all, according to the divine counsels. Note, We must not think that God is so taken up with the affairs of his church as to neglect the world; but it is a comfort to us that the same all-wise almighty Providence that governs the nations of the earth is in a particular manner conversant about the church. Those *seven eyes* that *run through the earth* are all *upon the stone* that Zerubbabel is laying straight with his plummet, to see that it be well laid. And those that have the plummet in their hand must look up to *those eyes of the Lord,* must have a constant regard to divine Providence, and act in dependence upon its guidance and submission to its disposals.

Verses 11–14

Enough is said to Zechariah to encourage him, and to enable him to encourage others, with reference to the good work of building the temple which they were now about, and that was the principal intention of the vision he saw; but still he is inquisitive about the particulars, which we will ascribe, not to any vain curiosity, but to the value he had for divine discoveries and the pleasure he took in acquainting himself with them. Those that know much of the things of God cannot but have a humble desire to know more. Now observe,

I. What his enquiry was. He understood the meaning of the candlestick with its lamps: It is Jerusalem, it is the temple, and their salvation that is to *go forth as a lamp that burns;* but he wants to know what are these *two olive-trees* (*v.* 11), these *two olive-branches? v.* 12. Observe here, 1. He asked. Note, Those that would be acquainted with the things of God must be inquisitive concerning those things. Ask, and you shall be told. 2. He asked twice, his first question having no reply given to it. Note, If satisfactory answers be not given to our enquiries and requests quickly, we must renew them, and repeat them, and continue instant and importunate in them, and the vision shall at length *speak, and not lie.* 3. His second query varied somewhat from the former. He first asked, What are *these two olive-trees,* but afterwards, *What are these two olive-branches?* that is, those boughs of the tree that hung over the bowl and distilled oil into it. When we enquire concerning the grace of God, it must be rather as it is communicated to us by the fruitful boughs of the word and ordinances (for that is one of the *things revealed,* which *belong to us and to our children)* than as it is resident in the good olive where all our springs are, for that is one of the *secret things,* which *belong not to us.* 4. In his enquiry he mentioned the observations he had made upon the vision; he took notice not only of what was obvious at first sight, that the two olive-trees grew, one *on the right side and the other on the left side of the candlestick* (so nigh, so ready, is divine grace to the church), but he observed further, upon a more narrow inspection, that the *two olive-branches,* from which in particular the candlestick did receive of *the root and fatness of the olive* (as the apostle says of the church, Rom. 11:17), did empty the *golden oil* (that is, the clear bright oil, the best in its kind, and of great value, as if it were *aurum potabile — liquid gold) out of themselves through the two golden pipes,* or (as the margin reads it) which *by the hand of the two golden pipes empty out of themselves oil into the gold,* that is, into the *golden bowl* on the head of the candlestick. Our Lord Jesus emptied himself, to fill us; his precious blood is the golden oil in which we are supplied with all we need.

II. What answer was given to his enquiry. Now again the angel obliged him expressly to own his ignorance, before he informed him (*v.* 13): *"Knowest thou not what these are?* If thou knowest the church to be the candlestick, canst thou think the olive-trees, that supply it with oil, to be any other than the grace of God?" But he owned he either did not fully understand it or was afraid he did not rightly understand it: *I said, No, my Lord, how should I, except some one guide me?* And then he told him (*v.* 14): *These are the two sons of oil* (so it is in the original), *the two anointed ones* (so we read it), rather, *the two oily ones.* That which we read (Isa. 5:1) a *very fruitful hill* is in the original *the horn of the son of oil,* a fat and fattening soil. 1. If by the candlestick we understand the visible church, particularly that of the Jews at that time, for whose comfort it was primarily intended, these *sons of oil,* that *stand before the Lord of the whole earth,* are the two great ordinances and offices of the magistracy and ministry, at that time lodged in the hands of those two great and good men Zerubbabel and Joshua. Kings and priests were anointed; this prince, this priest, were *oily ones,* endued with the gifts and graces of God's Spirit, to qualify them for the work to which they were called. They *stood before the Lord of the whole earth,* to minister to him, and to receive direction from him; and a great influence they had upon the affairs of the church at that time. Their wisdom, courage, and zeal, were continually emptying themselves into the golden bowl, to keep the lamps burning; and, when they are gone, others shall be raised up to carry on the same work; Israel shall no longer be without prince and priest. Good magistrates and good ministers that are themselves anointed with the grace of God and *stand by the Lord of the whole earth,* as faithful adherents to his cause, contribute very much to the maintaining and advancing of religion and the shining forth of the word of life. 2. If by the candlestick we understand the church of the first-born, of true believers, these sons of oil may be meant of Christ and the Spirit, the Redeemer and the Comforter. Christ is not only the Messiah, the *Anointed One* himself, but he is the *good olive* to his church; and *from his fulness we receive,* Jn. 1:16. And the Holy Spirit is the *unction or anointing* which we have received, 1 Jn. 2:20, 27. From Christ, the *olive tree,* by the *Spirit, the olive branch,* all the golden oil of grace is communicated to believers, which keeps their lamps burning, and without a constant supply of which they would soon go out. They *stand by the Lord of the whole earth,* who is in a special manner the church's Lord; for the Son was to be sent by the Father, and so was the Holy Ghost, in the time appointed, and they stand by him ready to go.

CHAPTER 5

Hitherto we have seen visions of peace only, and all the words we have heard have been good words and comfortable words. But the pillar of cloud and fire has a black and dark side towards the Egyptians, as well as a bright and pleasant side towards Israel; so have Zechariah's visions; for God's prophets are not only his ambassadors, to treat of peace with the sons of peace, but heralds, to proclaim war against those that delight in war, and persist in their rebellion. In this chapter we have two visions, by which "the wrath of God is revealed from heaven against all ungodliness and unrighteousness of men." God will do great and kind things for his people, which the faithful sons of Zion shall rejoice in; but "let the sinners in Zion be afraid;" for, I. God will reckon severely with those particular persons among them that are wicked and profane, and that hated to be reformed in these times of reformation; while God is showing kindness to the body of the nation, and loading that with his blessings, they and their families shall, notwithstanding that, lie under the curse, which the prophet sees in a flying roll (*v.* 1–4). II. If the body of the nation hereafter degenerate, and wickedness prevail among them, it shall be carried off and hurried away with a swift destruction, under the pressing weight of divine wrath, represented by a talent of lead upon the mouth of an ephah, carried upon the wing I know not where (*v.* 5–11).

Verses 1–4

We do not find that the prophet now needed to be awakened, as he did *ch.* 4:1. Being awakened then, he kept wakeful after; nay, now he needs not be so much as called to look about him, for of his own accord he *turns and lifts up his eyes.* This good men sometimes get by their infirmities, they make them the more careful and circumspect afterwards. Now observe,

I. What it was that the prophet saw; he looked up into the air, and *behold a flying roll.* A vast large scroll of parchment which had been rolled up, and is therefore called a *roll,* was now unrolled and expanded; this roll was flying upon the wings of the wind, carried swiftly through the air in open view, as an eagle that shoots down upon her prey; it was a *roll,* like Ezekiel's that was *written within and without* with *lamentations, and mourning, and woe,* Eze. 2:9, 10. As the command of the law is in writing, for certainty and perpetuity, so is the *curse of the law;* it *writes bitter things* against the sinner. "What I have written I have written and what is written remains." The angel, to engage the prophet's attention, and to raise in him a desire to have it explained, asks him *what he sees?* And he gives him this account of it: *I see a flying roll,* and as near as he can guess by his eye it is *twenty cubits long* (that is, ten yards) and *ten cubits broad,* that is, five yards. The scriptures of the Old Testament and the New are *rolls,* in which God has *written to us the great things of his law* and gospel. Christ is the Master of the rolls. They are large rolls, have much in them. They are *flying* rolls; the angel that had *the everlasting gospel to preach flew in the midst of heaven,* Rev. 14:6. God's word *runs very swiftly,* Ps. 147:15. Those that would be let into the meaning of these rolls must first tell what they see, must go as far as they can themselves. *"What is written in the law? how readest thou?* Tell me that, and then thou shalt be made to *understand what thou readest."*

II. How it was expounded to him, 5:3,4. This flying roll is a *curse;* it contains a declaration of the righteous wrath of God against those sinners especially who by swearing affront God's majesty or by stealing invade their neighbour's property. Let every Israelite rejoice in the blessings of his country with trembling; for if he swear, if he steal, if he live in any course of sin, he shall see them with his eyes, but shall not have the comfort of them, for against him the curse has gone forth. *If I be wicked, woe to me* for all this. Now observe here,

1. The extent of this curse; the prophet sees it flying, but which way does it steer its course? It *goes forth over the face of the whole earth,* not only of the land of Israel, but the *whole world;* for those that have sinned against the *law written in their hearts* only shall by that law be judged, though they have not the book of the law. Note, All mankind are liable to the judgment of God; and, wherever sinners are, any where upon the face of the whole earth, the curse of God can and will find them out and seize them. Oh that we could with an eye of faith see the flying roll of God's curse hanging over the guilty world as a thick cloud, not only keeping off the sun-beams of God's favour from them, but big with thunders, lightnings, and storms, ready to destroy them! How welcome then would the tidings of a Saviour be, who came to *redeem us from the curse of the law* by being himself *made a curse for us,* and, like the prophet, *eating this roll!* The vast length and breadth of this roll intimate what a multitude of curses sinners lie exposed to. God will make their plagues wonderful, if *they turn not.*

2. The criminals against whom particularly this curse is levelled. The world is full of sin in great variety: so was

the Jewish church at this time. But two sorts of sinners are here specified as the objects of this curse: — (1.) Thieves; it is *for every one that steals,* that by fraud or force takes that which is not his own, especially that robs God and converts to his own use what was devoted to God and his honour, which was a sin much complained of among the Jews at this time, Mal. 3:8; Neh. 13:10. Sacrilege is, without doubt, the worst kind of thievery. He also that *robs his father or mother, and saith, It is no transgression* (Prov. 28:24), let him know that against him this curse is directed, for it is against *every one that steals.* The letter of the eighth commandment has no penalty annexed to it; but the curse here is a sanction to that command. (2.) Swearers. Sinners of the former class offend against the second table, these against the first; for the curse meets those that break either table. He that swears rashly and profanely shall not be held guiltless, much less he that swears falsely (*v.* 4); he imprecates the curse upon himself by his perjury, and so shall his doom be; God will say *Amen* to his imprecation, and turn it upon his own head. He has appealed to God's judgment, which is always according to truth, for the confirming of a lie, and to that judgment he shall go which he has so impiously affronted.

3. The enforcing of this curse, and the equity of it: *I will bring it forth, saith the Lord of hosts,* 5:4. He that pronounces the sentence will take care to see it executed. His bringing it forth denotes, (1.) His giving it commission. It is a righteous curse, for he is a righteous God that warrants it. (2.) His giving it the setting on. He brings it forth with power, and orders what execution it shall do; and who can put by or resist the curse which a God of almighty power brings forth?

4. The effect of this curse; it is very dreadful, (1.) Upon the sinner himself: *Every one that steals shall be cut off,* not corrected, but destroyed, cut off from the land of the living. The curse of God is a cutting thing, a killing thing. He shall be cut off *as on this side* (cut off from this place, that is, from Jerusalem), and so he that swears from *this side* (it is the same word), from this place. God will not spare the sinners he finds among his own people, nor shall the holy city be a protection to the unholy. Or they shall be cut off *from hence,* that is, from the face of the whole earth, over which the curse flies. Or he that steals shall be *cut off on this side,* and he that swears *on that side;* they shall all be cut off, one as well as another, and both according to the curse, for the judgments of God's hand are exactly agreeable with the judgments of his mouth. (2.) Upon his family: *It shall enter into the house of the thief and of him that swears.* God's curse comes with a warrant to break open doors, and cannot be kept out by bars or locks. There where the sinner is most secure, and thinks himself out of danger, — there where he promises himself refreshment by food and sleep, — there, in his own house, shall the curse of God seize him; nay, it shall fall not upon him only, but upon all about him for his sake. *Cursed shall be his basket and his store, and cursed the fruit of his body,* Deu. 28:17, 18. The *curse of the Lord is in the house of the wicked,* Prov. 3:33. It shall not only beset his house, or he at the door, but *it shall remain in the midst of his house,* and diffuse its malignant influences to all the parts of it. *It shall dwell in his tabernacle because it is none of his,* Job 18:15. It shall dwell where he dwells, and be his constant companion at bed and board, to make both miserable to him. Having got possession, it shall keep it, and, unless he repent and reform, there is no way to throw it out or cut off the entail of it. Nay, it shall so remain in it as to *consume it with the timber thereof, and the stones thereof,* which, though ever so strong, though the timber be heart of oak and the stones hewn out of the rocks of adamant, yet they shall not be able to stand before the curse of God. We heard the stone and the timber complaining of the owner's extortion and oppression, and groaning under the burden of them, Hab. 2:11. Now here we have them delivered *from that bondage of corruption.* While they were in their strength and beauty they supported, sorely against their will, the sinner's pride and security; but, when they are consumed, their ruins will, to their satisfaction, be standing monuments of God's justice and lasting witnesses of the sinner's injustice. Note, Sin is the ruin of houses and families, especially the sins of injury and perjury. *Who knows the power of God's anger,* and the operations of his curse? Even timber and stones have been consumed by them; let us therefore stand in awe and not sin.

Verses 5–11

The foregoing vision was very plain and easy, but in this are things *dark and hard to be understood;* and some think that the scope of it is to foretel the final destruction of the Jewish church and nation and the dispersion of the Jews, when, by crucifying Christ and persecuting his gospel, they should have filled up the measure of their iniquities; therefore it is industriously set out in obscure figures and expressions, "lest the plain denunciation of the second overthrow of temple and state might discourage them too much from going forward in the present restoration of both." So Mr. Pemble.

The prophet was contemplating the power and terror of the curse which consumes the houses of thieves and swearers, when he was told to turn and he should see greater desolations than these made by the curse of God for the sin of man: *Lift up thy eyes now,* and see what is here, *v.* 5. *What is this that goeth forth?* Whether over the face of the whole earth, as the flying roll (*v.* 3), or only over Jerusalem, is not certain. But, it seems, the prophet now, through either the distance or the dimness of his sight, could not well tell what it was, but asked, *What is it? v.* 6. And the angel tells him both what it is and what it means.

I. He sees an *ephah,* a measure wherewith they measured corn; it contained *ten omers* (Ex. 16:36) and was the tenth part of a *homer* (Eze. 45:11); it is put for any measure used in commerce, Deu. 25:14. And *this is their resemblance,* the resemblance of the Jewish nation *over all the earth,* wherever they are now dispersed, or at least it will be so when their ruin draws near. They are filling up the measure of their iniquity, which God has set them; and when it is full, as the ephah of corn, they shall be delivered into the hands of those to whom God has sold them for their sins; they are *meted* to destruction, as an ephah of corn measured to the market or to the mill. And some think that the mentioning of an ephah, which is used in buying and selling, intimates that fraud, and deceit, and extortion in commerce, were sins abounding much among them, as that people are known to be notoriously guilty of them at this day. This is a proper representation of them *through all the earth.* There is a measure set them, and they are filling it up apace. See Mt. 23:32; 1 Th. 2:16.

II. He sees a *woman sitting in the midst of the ephah,* representing the sinful church and nation of the Jews in their latter and degenerate age, when *the faithful city became a harlot.* He that weighs the mountains in scales and the hills in a balance measures nations and churches as in an ephah; so exact is he in his judicial dealings with them. God's people are called *the corn of his floor,* Isa. 21:10. And here he puts this corn into the bushel, in order to his parting with it. The angel says of the woman in the *ephah, This is wickedness;* it is a wicked nation, else God would not have rejected it thus; it is as wicked as *wickedness* itself, it is abominably wicked. *How has the gold become dim! Israel was holiness to the Lord* (Jer. 2:3); but now *this is wickedness,* and wickedness is nowhere so scandalous, so odious, and, in many instances, so outrageous, as when it is found among professors of religion.

III. He sees the woman thrust down into the ephah, and a *talent,* or large weight, *of lead,* cast upon the *mouth* of it, by which she is secured, and made a close prisoner in the *ephah,* and utterly disabled to get out of it. This is designed to show that the wrath of God against impenitent sinners is, 1. Unavoidable, and what they cannot escape; they are bound over to it, concluded under sin, and shut up under the curse, as this woman in the ephah; *he would fain flee out of his hand* (Job 27:22), but he cannot. 2. It is insupportable, and what they cannot bear up under. Guilt is upon the sinner as a talent of lead, to sink him to the lowest hell. When Christ said of the things of Jerusalem's peace, *Now they are hidden from thy eyes,* that threw a talent of lead upon them.

IV. He sees the ephah, with the woman thus pressed to death in it, carried away into some far country. 1. The instruments employed to do it were *two women,* who had *wings like* those *of a stork,* large and strong, and, to make them fly the more swiftly, they had the *wind in their wings,* denoting the great violence and expedition with which the Romans destroyed the Jewish nation. God has not only winged messengers in heaven, but he can, when he pleases, give wings to those also whom he employs in this lower world; and, when he does so, he forwards them with the wind in their wings; his providence carries them on with a favourable gale. 2. They bore it up in the air, denoting the terrors which pursued the wicked Jews, and their being a public example of God's vengeance to the world. They *lifted it up between the earth and the heaven,* as unworthy of either and abandoned by both; for the Jews, when this was fulfilled, *pleased not God and* were *contrary to all men,* 1 Th. 2:15. *This is wickedness,* and this comes of it; heaven thrust out wicked angels, and earth spewed out wicked Canaanites. 3. When the prophet enquired whither they carried their prisoner whom they had now in execution (*v.* 10) he was told that they designed *to build it a house in the land of Shinar.* This intimates that the punishment of the Jews should be a final dispersion; they should be hurried out of their own country, *as the chaff which the wind drives away,* and should be forced to dwell in far countries, particularly in the country of Babylon, whither many of the scattered Jews went after the destruction of their country by the Romans, as they did also to other countries, especially in the Levant parts, not to sojourn, as in their former captivity, for seventy years, but to be nailed down for perpetuity. There the *ephah* shall *be established, and set upon her own base.* This intimates, (1.) That their calamity shall continue from generation to generation, and that they shall be so dispersed that they shall never unite or incorporate again; they shall settle in a perpetual unsettlement, and Cain's doom shall be theirs, to dwell in the land of shaking. (2.) That their iniquity shall continue too, and their hearts shall be hardened in it. *Blindness* has *happened* unto Israel, and they are settled upon the lees of their own unbelief; their wickedness is established upon its *own basis.* God has given them a *spirit of slumber* (Rom. 11:8), *lest at any time they should convert, and be healed.*

CHAPTER 6

The two kingdoms of providence and grace are what we are all very nearly interested in, and therefore are concerned to acquaint ourselves with, all our temporal affairs being in a necessary subjection to divine Providence, and all our spiritual and eternal concerns in a necessary dependence upon divine grace; and these two are represented to us in this chapter — the former by a vision, the latter by a type. Here is, I. God, as King of nations, ruling the world by the ministry of angels, in the vision of the four chariots (*v.* 1–8). II. God, as King of saints, ruling the church by the mediation of Christ, in the figure of Joshua the high priest crowned, the ceremony performed, and then explained concerning Christ (*v.* 9–15).

Verses 1–8

The prophet is forward to receive this vision, and, as if he expected it, he *turned and lifted up his eyes and looked.* Though this was the seventh vision he had had, yet he did not think he had had enough; for the more we know of God and his will, if we know it aright, the more desirous we shall be to get a further acquaintance with God. Now observe here the sight that the prophet had of *four chariots* drawn by horses of divers colours, together with the explication of the sight, *v.* 1–5. He did not look long before he discovered that which was worth seeing, and which would serve very much for the encouraging of himself and his friends in this dark day. We are very much in the dark concerning the meaning of this vision. Some by the *four chariots* understand the four monarchies; and then they read (*v.* 5), *These are the four winds of the heavens,* and suppose that therein reference is had to Dan. 7:2, where Daniel saw, in vision, the *four winds of the heavens striving upon the great sea,* representing the four monarchies. The Babylonian monarchy, they think, is here represented by the *red horses,* which are not afterwards mentioned, because that monarchy was now extinct. The second chariot with the *black horses* is the Persian monarchy, which went forth northward against the Babylonians, and *quieted God's Spirit in the north country,* by executing his judgments on Babylon and freeing the Jews from their captivity. The *white,* the Grecians, go *forth after them* in the north, for they overthrow the Persians. The *grizzled,* the Romans, who conquered the Grecian empire, are said to *go forth towards the south country,* because Egypt, which lay southward, was the last branch of the Grecian empire that was subdued by the Romans. The *bay horses* had been with the *grizzled,* but afterwards went forth by themselves; and by these they understand the Goths and Vandals, who with their victorious arms walked to and fro through the earth, or the Seleucidae and Lagidae, the two branches of the Grecian empire. Thus Grotius and others.

But I incline rather to understand this vision more generally, as designing to represent the administration of the kingdom of Providence in the government of this lower world. The *angels* are often called the *chariots of God,* as Ps. 68:17; 18:10. The various providences of God concerning nations and churches are represented by the different colours of horses, Rev. 6:2, 4, 5, 8. And so we may observe here, 1. That the counsels and decrees of God are the spring and original of all events, and they are immovable, as *mountains of brass.* The *chariots* came *from between the two mountains;* for God *performs the thing that is appointed for us:* his appointments are the originals, and his performances are but copies from them; he does all *according to the counsel of his will.* We could as soon grasp the mountains in our arms as comprehend the divine counsels in our finite understandings, and as soon remove *mountains of brass* as alter any of God's purposes; for *he is in one mind, and who can turn him?* Whatever the providences of God are concerning us, as to public or private affairs, we should see them all coming from *between the mountains of brass,* and therefore see it as much our folly to quarrel with them as it is our duty to acquiesce in them. Who may say to God, *What doest thou, or why doest thou so?* Acts 2:23; 4:28. 2. That God executes his decrees in the works of Providence, which are as chariots, in which he rides as a prince in an open chariot, to show his glory to the world, in which, as in chariots of war, he rides forth *conquering and to conquer,* and triumphing over all the enemies of his glory and government. God is great and terrible in his doings (Ps. 66:3), and in them we *see the goings of our God, our King,* Ps. 68:24. His providences move swiftly and strongly as chariots, but all directed and governed by his infinite wisdom and sovereign will, as chariots by their drivers. 3. That the holy angels are the ministers of God's providence, and are employed by him, as *the armies of heaven,* for the executing of his counsels among *the inhabitants of the earth;* they are the *chariots,* or, which comes all to one, they are the horses that draw the chariots, great in power and might, and who, like the horse that God himself describes (Job 39:19, etc.), are clothed with thunder, are terrible, but cannot be *terrified* nor *made afraid;* they are *chariots of fire, and horses of fire,* to carry one prophet to heaven and guard another on earth. They are as observant of and obsequious to the will of God as well-managed horses are to their rider or driver. Not that God needs them or their services, but he is pleased to make use of them, that he may put honour upon them, and encourage our trust in his providence. 4. That the events of Providence have different aspects and the face of the times often changes. The *horses* in the *first chariot* were *red,* signifying war and bloodshed, *blood to the horse-bridles,* Rev. 14:20. Those in the *second chariot* were *black,* signifying the dismal melancholy consequences of war; it puts all into mourning, lays all waste, introduces famines, and pestilences, and desolations, and makes whole lands to languish. Those in the *third chariot* were *white,* signifying the return of comfort, and peace, and prosperity, after these dark and dismal times: though God cause grief to the children of men, yet will he have compassion. Those in the *fourth chariot* were of a mixed colour, *grizzled* and *bay;* some *speckled* and *spotted,* and *ash-coloured,* signifying events of different complexions interwoven and counter-changed, a day of prosperity and a day of adversity set *the one over-against the other.* The cup of Providence in the hand of the Lord is *full of mixture,* Ps. 75:8. 5. That all the instruments of Providence, and all the events of it, come from God, and from him they receive their commissions and instructions (*v.* 5): *These are the four spirits of heaven, the four winds* (so some), which seem to blow as they list, from the various points of the compass; but God has them *in his fists* and brings them out of *his treasuries.* Or, rather, These are the *angels* that *go forth from standing before the Lord of all the earth,* to attend upon him and minister to him, to behold his glory in the upper world, which is their blessedness, and to serve his glory in their blessedness, and to serve his glory in this lower world, which is their business. They *stand before him* as the *Lord of the whole earth,* to receive orders from him and give up their accounts to him concerning their serv-

ices on this earth, for it is all within his jurisdiction. But, when he appoints, they *go forth* as messengers of his counsels and ministers of his justice and mercy. Those secret motions and impulses upon the spirits of men by which the designs of Providence are carried on, some think, are these *four spirits of the heavens,* which *go forth from God* and fulfil what he appoints, who is *the God of the spirits of all flesh.* 6. That there is an admirable beauty in Providence, and one event serves for a balance to another (*v.* 6): *The black horses went forth,* carrying with them very dark and melancholy events, such as made every person and every thing look black; but presently *the white went forth after them,* carrying joy to those that mourned, and, by a new turn given to affairs, making them to look pleasant again. Such are God's dealings with his church and people: if the black horses go forth, the white ones presently go after them; for *as affliction abounds consolation much more abounds.* 7. That the common general aspect of providence is mixed and compounded. The *grizzled* and *bay horses* were both in the *fourth chariot* (*v.* 3), and though they went forth, at first, towards the *south country,* yet afterwards they *sought to walk to and fro through the earth* and were directed to do so, *v.* 7. If we go to and fro through the earth, we shall find the events of Providence neither all black nor all white, but ash-coloured, or gray, mixed of black and white. Such is the world we live in; that before us is unmixed. Here we are singing, at the same time, of *mercy and judgment,* and we must *sing unto God* of both (Ps. 101:1) and labour to accommodate ourselves to God's will and design in the mixtures of Providence, rejoicing in our comforts as though we rejoiced not, because they have their allays, and weeping for our afflictions as though we wept not, because there is so much mercy mixed with them. 8. That God is well-pleased with all the operations of his own providence (*v.* 8): *These have quieted my spirit,* these *black horses* which denote extraordinary judgments, and the *white* ones which denote extraordinary deliverances, both which *went towards the north country,* while the common mixed providences went all the world over. These have *quieted my spirit in the north-country,* which had of late been the most remarkable scene of action with reference to the church; that is, by these uncommon appearances and actings of providence God's wrath is executed upon the enemies of the church, and his favours are conferred upon the church, both which had long been deferred, and in both God had fulfilled his will, accomplished his word, and so *quieted his Spirit. The Lord is well-pleased for his righteousness' sake;* and, as he speaks, Isa. 1:24, made himself easy.

Verses 9–15

God did not only at *sundry times,* but *in divers manners,* speak in time past by the prophets to his church. In the former part of this chapter he spoke by a vision, which only the prophet himself saw; here, in this latter part, he speaks by a sign, or type, which many saw, and which, as it was explained, was an illustrious prediction of the Messiah as the priest and king of his church. Here is,

I. The significant ceremony which God appointed, and that was the *coronation of Joshua* the high priest, *v.* 10, 11. It is observable that there should be two eminent types of Christ in the Old Testament that were both named *Joshua* (the same name with *Jesus,* and by the Septuagint, and in the New Testament, rendered *Jesus,* Acts 7:45) — Joshua the chief captain, a type of Christ the captain of our salvation, and Joshua the chief priest, a type of Christ the high priest of our profession, and both in their day saviours and leaders into Canaan. And this is peculiar to Joshua the high priest, that here was something done to him by the divine appointment on purpose that he might be a type of Christ, a priest after the order of Melchizedek, who was both a king and a priest. Joshua was far from being ambitious of a crown, and the people of having a crowned head over them; but the prophet, to the great surprise of both, is ordered to crown Joshua as if he had been a king. And, as Zerubbabel's prudence and piety kept this from being any affront to him (as the setting up of a rival with him), so God's providence kept the kings of Persia from taking umbrage at it, as raising a rebellion against them. In doing what we are sure is God's pleasure, as this was, we may well venture men's displeasure. 1. Here were some Jews come from Babylon that brought an offering

to the house of God, *some of the captivity,* here named to their honour, that *came from Babylon* on a visit to Jerusalem. They ought to have bidden a final farewell to Babylon, and to have come and settled with their brethren in their own land, and for their remissness and indifference in not doing so they thought to atone by this visit. Perhaps they came as ambassadors from the body of the Jews that were in Babylon, who lived there in ease and fulness; and, hearing that the building of the temple went on slowly for want of money, they sent them with an offering of gold and silver for the service of the house of God. Note, Those that by reason of distance, or otherwise, cannot forward a good work by their persons, must, as they are able, forward it by their purses; if some find hands, let others fill them. 2. Time and place are appointed for the prophet to meet them. They thought to bring their present to the priest, God's ordinary minister; but God has a prophet, an extraordinary one, ready to receive them and it, which would be an encouragement to them, who, in their captivity, had so often complained, *We see not our signs, there is no more any prophet,* and would invite them and others to re-settle in their own land, which then began to look like itself, like a holy land, when the Spirit of prophecy was revived in it. Zechariah was ordered to give them the meeting *the same day* they came (for when they had arrived they would *lose no time,* but present their offering immediately), and to bid them welcome, assuring them that God now accepted their gifts. He was to meet them in the house of Josiah, the son of Zephaniah, who probably was receiver-general for the temple, and kept the treasures of it. They brought their gold and silver, to be employed about the temple, but God ordered it to be used in honour of One *greater than the temple,* Mt. 12:6. 3. Crowns are to be *made,* and *put upon the head of Joshua, v.* 11. It is supposed that there were two crowns provided, one of silver and the other of gold; the former (as some think) denoting his priestly dignity, the latter his kingly dignity. Or, rather, he being a priest already, and having a crown of gold, of pure gold, already, to signify his honour and power as a priest, these crowns of silver and gold both signify the *royal dignity,* the crown of silver being perhaps designed to typify the kingdom of the Messiah when he was here on earth, for then he was the *King of Israel* (Jn. 1:49), but the crown of gold his kingdom in his exalted state, the glory of which as far exceeded that of the former as gold does silver. The sun shines as gold, when he *goes forth in his strength;* and the beams of the moon, when she *walks in brightness,* we call *silver beams.* Those that had worshipped the sun and moon shall now fall down before the golden and silver crowns of the exalted Redeemer, before whom the sun shall be ashamed and the moon confounded, being both out-shone.

II. The signification which God gave of this ceremony. Every one would be ready to ask, "What is the meaning of Joshua's being crowned thus?" And the prophet is as ready to tell them the meaning of it. Upon this speaking sign is grafted a prediction, and the sign was used to make it the more taken notice of and the better remembered. Now the promise is,

1. That God will, in the fulness of time, raise up a great high priest, like Joshua. Tell Joshua that he is but the figure of one that is to come, a faint shadow of him (*v.* 12): *Speak unto him* in the name of *the Lord of hosts,* that *the man whose name is The BRANCH* shall *grow up out of his place,* out of Bethlehem the city of David, the place appointed for his birth; though the family be a root in a dry ground, yet this branch shall spring out of it, as in the spring, when the sun returns, the flowers spring out of the roots, in which they lay buried out of sight and out of mind. He shall *grow up for himself* (so some read it) *propria virtute — by his own vital energy,* shall be exalted *in his own strength.*

2. That, as Joshua was an active useful instrument in building the temple, so *the man, the branch,* shall be the master-builder, the sole builder of the spiritual temple, the gospel-church. He *shall build the temple of the Lord;* and it is repeated (*v.* 13), *Even he shall build the temple of the Lord.* He shall grow up to do good, to be an instrument of God's glory and a great blessing to mankind. Note, The gospel-church is the *temple of the Lord,* a *spiritual house* (1 Pt. 2:5), a *holy temple,* Eph. 2:21. In the temple God made discoveries of himself to his people, and there he

received the service and homage of his people; so, in the gospel-church, the light of divine revelation shines by the word, and the spiritual sacrifices of prayer and praise are offered. Now Christ is not only the foundation, but the founder, of this temple, by his Spirit and grace.

3. That Christ shall bear the glory. Glory is a burden, but not too heavy for him to bear who upholds all things. The cross was his glory, and he bore that; so was the crown *an exceeding weight of glory,* and he bears that. The *government* is *upon his shoulders,* and in it *he bears the glory,* Isa. 9:6. *They shall hang upon him all the glory of his Father's house,* Isa. 22:24. It becomes him, and he is *par negotio — well able to bear it.* The glory of the priesthood and royalty had been divided between the house of Aaron and that of David; but now he alone shall bear all the glory of both. That which he shall bear, which he shall undertake, shall be indeed the *glory of Israel;* and they must wait for that, and, in prospect of it, must be content in the want of that external glory which they formerly had. He shall bear such a glory as shall make the glory of this latter house greater than that of the former. He shall *lift up the glory* (so it may be read); the glory of Israel had been thrown down and depressed, but he shall raise it out of the dust.

4. That he shall have a throne, and be both priest and king upon his throne. A throne denotes both dignity and dominion, an exalted honour with an extensive power. (1.) This priest shall be a king, and his office as a priest shall be no diminution to his dignity as a king: *He shall sit and rule upon his throne.* Christ, as a priest, ever lives to make intercession for us; but he does it sitting at his Father's right hand, as one having authority, Heb. 8:1. We have *such a high priest* as Israel never had, for he is *set on the right hand of the throne of the Majesty in the heavens,* which puts a prevailing virtue into his mediation; he that appears for us within the veil is one that sits and rules there. Christ, who is ordained to offer sacrifices for us, is authorized to give law to us. He will not save us unless we be willing that he should govern us. God has prepared him a throne *in the heavens;* and, if we would have any benefit by that, we must prepare him a throne in our hearts, and be willing and glad that he should *sit and rule upon that throne;* and to him every thought within us must be brought into obedience. (2.) This king shall be a priest, a *priest upon his throne.* With the majesty and power of a king, he shall have the tenderness and simplicity of a priest, who, being *taken from among men,* is *ordained for men,* and *can have compassion on the ignorant,* Heb. 5:1, 2. In all the acts of his government as a king he prosecutes the intentions of his grace as a priest. Let not therefore those that are his look upon his throne, though a throne of glory and a throne of judgment, with terror and amazement; for, as there is a *rainbow about the throne,* so he is a *priest upon the throne.*

5. That *the counsel of peace shall be between them both.* That is, (1.) Between *Jehovah* and the *man the branch,* between the Father and the Son; the counsels concerning the peace to be made between God and man, by the mediation of Christ, shall be concerted (that is, shall *appear to have been* concerted) by Infinite Wisdom in the covenant of redemption; the Father and the Son understood one another perfectly well in that matter. Or, rather, (2.) Between the priest and the throne, between the priestly and kingly office of Jesus Christ. *The man the branch* must grow up to carry on a *counsel of peace,* peace on earth, and, in order to that, peace with heaven. God's thoughts towards us were *thoughts of peace,* and, in prosecution of them, he exalted his Son Christ Jesus to be *both a prince* and a *Saviour;* he gave him a throne, but with this proviso, that he should be a priest upon his throne, and by executing the two offices of a priest and king should bring about that great undertaking of man's reconciliation to God and happiness in God. Some think it alludes to the former government of the Jews' state, wherein the king and priest, separate officers, did take counsel one with another, for the maintenance of peace and prosperity in church and state, as did Zerubbabel and Joshua now. I may add, the *prophets of God helping them.* So shall the peace and welfare of the gospel-church, and of all believers, be wrought, though not by two separate persons, yet by virtue of two separate offices meeting in one — Christ purchasing all peace by his priesthood and maintaining and defending it by his kingdom; so Mr. Pemble. And his prophetic office is serviceable to both in this great design.

6. That there shall be a happy coalition between Jews and Gentiles in the gospel-church, and they shall both meet in Christ, the priest upon his throne, as the centre of their unity (*v.* 15): *Those that are far off shall come and build in the temple of the Lord.* Some understand it of the Jews that were now afar off in Babylon, that staid behind in captivity, to the great discouragement of their brethren that had returned, who wanted their help in building the temple. Now God promises that many of them, and some of other nations too, proselyted to the Jewish religion, should come in, and lend a helping hand to the building of the temple, and many hands would make light work. The kings of Persia contributed to the building of the temple (Ezra 6:8) and the furnishing of it, Ezra 7:19, 20. And, in aftertimes, Herod the Great, and others that were strangers, helped to beautify and enrich the temple. But it has a further reference to that *temple of the Lord* which *the man the branch* was to build. The Gentiles, *strangers afar off,* shall help to build it, for from among them God will raise up ministers that shall be workers together with Christ about that building; and all the Gentile converts shall be stones added to this building, so that it shall *grow up to a holy temple,* Eph. 2:20–22. When God's temple is to be built he can fetch in those that are afar off and employ them in the building of it.

7. That the accomplishment of this will be a strong confirmation of the truth of God's word: *You shall know that the Lord of hosts has sent me unto you.* That promise, that those that were afar off should come and assist them in *building the temple of the Lord,* was as it were the *giving of them a sign;* by this they might be assured that the other promises should be fulfilled in due time. This should be fulfilled now very speedily; it was so, for those that had been their enemies and accusers, in obedience to the king's edict, became their helpers and did speedily what they were ordered to do for the furtherance of the work, and by that means the work went on and was finished; see Ezra 6:13, 14. Now, by this surprising assistance which they had from afar off in building the temple, they might know that Zechariah, who told them of it before, was sent of God, and that therefore his word concerning the man the branch should be fulfilled.

8. That these promises were strong obligations to obedience: *"For this shall come to pass* (you shall have help in building the temple) *if you will diligently obey the voice of the Lord your God.* You shall have the help of foreigners in building the temple, if you will but set about it in good earnest yourselves." The assistance of others, instead of being an excuse for our slothfulness, should be a spur to our industry. "You shall have the benefit and comfort of all those promises if you make conscience of your duty." They must know that they are upon their good behaviour; and, though their God is coming towards them in a way of mercy, they cannot expect him to proceed in it unless they conform to his laws. Note, That which God requires of us, to qualify us for his favour, is obedience to his revealed will; and it must be a diligent obedience. We cannot *obey the voice of God* without a great deal of care and pains, nor will our obedience be accepted of God unless it be laboured by us.

III. The provision that was made to preserve the remembrance of this. *The crowns* that were used in this solemnity were not given to Joshua, but must be *kept for a memorial in the temple of the Lord, v.* 14. Either they were laid up in the temple treasury or (as the Jews' tradition is) they were hung up in the windows of the temple, in the view of all, *in perpetuam rei memoriam — for a perpetual memorial,* for a traditional evidence of the promise of the Messiah and this typical transaction used for the confirmation of that promise. The crowns were delivered to those who found the materials (and some think their names were engraven on the crowns), to be preserved as a public testimony of their pious liberality and an encouragement to others in like manner to bring presents to the house of God. Note, Various means were used for the support of the faith of the Old-Testament saints, who waited for the consolation of Israel, till the time, the set time, for it came.

CHAPTER 7

We have done with the visions, but not with the revelations of this book; the prophet sees no more such signs as he had seen, but still "the word of the Lord came to him." In this chapter we have, I. A case of conscience proposed to the prophet by the children of the captivity concerning fasting, whether they should continue their solemn fasts which they had religiously observed during the seventy years of their captivity (*v.* 1–3). II. The answer to this question, which is given in this and the next chapter; and this answer was given not all at once, but by piece-meal, and, it should seem, at several times, for here are four distinct discourses which have all of them reference to this case, each of them prefaced with "the word of the Lord came," (*v.* 4–8 and 8:1, 18). The method of them is very observable. In this chapter, 1. The prophet sharply reproves them for the mismanagements of their fasts (*v.* 4–7). 2. He exhorts them to reform their lives, which would be the best way of fasting, and to take heed of those sins which brought those judgments upon them which they kept these fasts in memory of (*v.* 8–14). And then in the next chapter, having searched the wound, he binds it up, and heals it, with gracious assurances of great mercy God had yet in store for them, by which he would turn their fasts into feasts.

Verses 1–7

This occasional sermon, which the prophet preached, and which is recorded in this and the next chapter, was above two years after the former, in which he gave them an account of his visions, as appears by comparing the date of this (*v.* 1), in the *ninth month* of the *fourth year* of Darius, with the date of that (*ch.* 1:1), in the eighth month of the second year of Darius; not that Zechariah was idle all that while (it is expressly said that he and Haggai continued *prophesying* till the temple was finished in the sixth year of Darius; Ezra 6:14, 15), but during that time he did not preach any sermon that was afterwards published, and left upon record, as this is. God may be honoured, his work done, and his interest served, by word of mouth as well as by writing; and by inculcating and pressing what has been taught, as well as by advancing something new. Now here we have,

I. A case proposed concerning fasting. Some persons were sent to enquire of the priests and prophets whether they should continue to observe their yearly fasts, particularly that in the fifth month, as they had done. It is uncertain whether the case was put by those that yet remained in Babylon, who, being deprived of the benefit of the solemn feasts which God's ordinance appointed them, made up the want by the solemn fasts which God's providences called them to; or by those that had returned, but lived in the country, as some rather incline to think, because they are called the *people of the land, v.* 5. But, as to that, the answer given to the messengers of the captive Jews might be directed, not to them only, but to *all the people.* Observe,

1. Who they were that came with this enquiry — *Sherezer* and *Regem-melech,* persons of some rank and figure, for they came *with their men,* and did not think it below them, or any disparagement to them, to be sent on this errand, but rather an addition to their honour to be, (1.) Attendants in God's house, there to do duty and receive orders. The greatest of men are less than the least of the ordinances of Jesus Christ. (2.) Agents for God's people, to negotiate their affairs. Men of estates, having more leisure than men of business, ought to employ their time in the service of the public, and by doing good they make themselves truly great; the *messengers of the churches* were the *glory of Christ,* 2 Co. 8:23.

2. What the errand was upon which they came. They were sent perhaps not with *gold and silver* (as those, *ch.* 6:10, 11), or, if they were, that is not mentioned, but upon the two great errands which should bring us all to the house of God, (1.) to intercede with God for his mercy. They were sent to *pray before the Lord,* and, some think (according to the usage then), to *offer sacrifice,* with which they offered up their prayers. The Jews, in captivity, prayed towards the temple (as appears Dan. 6:10); but now that it was in a fair way to be rebuilt they sent their representatives to pray in it, remembering that God had said that his house should be called *a house of prayer for all people,* Isa. 56:7. In prayer we must set ourselves as *before the Lord,* must see his eye upon us and have our eye up to him. (2.) To enquire of God concerning his mind. Note, When we offer up our requests to God it must be with a readiness to receive instructions from him; for, if we turn away our ear from hearing his law, we cannot expect that our prayers should be acceptable to him. We must therefore desire to dwell in the house of the Lord all the days

of our life *that we may enquire* there (Ps. 27:4), asking, not only, Lord, what wilt thou do for me? but, Lord *what wilt thou have me to do?*

3. Whom they consulted. They spoke *to the priests that were in the house of the Lord and to the prophets;* the former were an oracle for ordinary cases, the latter for extraordinary; they were blessed with both, and would try if either could acquaint them with the mind of God in this case. Note, God having given diversities of gifts to men, and all to profit with, we should make use of all as there is occasion. They were not so wedded to the priests, their stated ministers, as to distrust the prophets, who appeared, by the gifts given them, well qualified to serve the church; nor yet were they so much enamoured with the prophets as to despise the priests, but they spoke both to the priests and to the prophets, and, in consulting both, gave glory to the God of Israel, and that one Spirit who *works all in all.* God might speak to them either by *urim* or *by prophets* (1 Sa. 28:6), and therefore they would not neglect either. The priests and the prophets were not jealous one of another, nor had any difference among themselves; let not the people then make differences between them, but thank God they had both. The prophets did indeed reprove what was amiss in the priests, but at the same time told the people that the *priest's lips* should *keep knowledge,* and they must *enquire the law at his mouth,* for *he is the messenger of the Lord of hosts,* Mal. 2:7. Note, Those that would know God's mind should consult God's ministers, and in doubtful cases ask advice of those whose special business it is to *search the scriptures.*

4. What the case was which they desired satisfaction in (*v.* 3): *Should I weep in the fifth month, separating myself, as I have done these so many years.* Observe, (1.) What had been their past practice, not only during the seventy years of the captivity but to this time, which was twenty years after the liberty proclaimed them; they kept up solemn stated fasts for humiliation and prayer, which they religiously observed, according as their opportunities were, in their closets, families, or such assemblies for worship as they had. In the case here, they mention only one, that of the fifth month; but it appears, by *ch.* 8:19, that they observed four anniversary fasts, one in the fourth month (*June* 17), in remembrance of the breaking up of the wall of Jerusalem (Jer. 52:6), another in the fifth month (*July* 4), in remembrance of the burning of the temple (Jer. 52:12, 13), another in the seventh month (*September* 3), in remembrance of the killing of Gedaliah, which completed their dispersion, and another in the tenth month (*December* 10), in remembrance of the beginning of the siege of Jerusalem, 2 Ki. 25:1. Now it was very commendable in them to keep those fasts, thus to humble themselves under those humbling providences, by which God called them to weeping and mourning, thus to accommodate themselves to their troubles, and prepare themselves for deliverance. It would likewise be a means of possessing their children betimes with a due sense of the hand of the Lord gone out against them. (2.) What was their present doubt — whether they should continue these fasts or no. The case is put as by a single person: *Should I weep?* But it was the case of many, and the satisfaction of one would be a satisfaction to the rest. Or perhaps many had left it off, but the querist will not be determined by the practice of others; if God will have him continue it, he will, whatever others do. His fasting is described by his *weeping, separating himself.* A religious fast must be solemnized, not only by abstinence, here called a separating ourselves from the ordinary lawful comforts of life, but by a godly sorrow for sin, here expressed by weeping. "Should I still keep such *days to afflict the soul* as *I have done these so many years?*" It is said (*v.* 5) to be seventy years, computed from the last captivity, as before, *ch.* 1:12. The enquiry intimates a readiness to continue it, if God so appoint, though it be a mortification to the flesh. [1.] Something is to be said for the continuance of these fasts. Fasting and praying are good work at any time, and do good; we have always both cause enough and need enough to humble ourselves before God. To throw off these fasts would be an evidence of their being too secure, and a cause of their being more so. They were still in distress, and under the tokens of God's displeasure; and it is unwise for the patient to break off his course of physic while he is sensible of such remains of his distemper. But, [2.] There is something to be said for the letting fall of these fasts. God had changed the method of his providences concerning them, and returned in ways of mercy to them; and ought not they then to change the method of their duties? Now that the bridegroom has returned, why should the *children of the bride-chamber fast?* Every thing is beautiful in its season. And as to the fast of the fifth month (which is that they particularly enquire about), that, being kept in remembrance of the burning of the temple, might seem to be superseded rather than any of the other, because the temple was now in a fair way to be rebuilt. But, having long kept up this fast, they would not leave it off without advice, and without asking and knowing God's mind in the case. Note, A good method of religious services, which we have found beneficial to ourselves and others, ought not to be altered without good reason, and therefore not without mature deliberation.

II. An answer given to this case. It should seem that, though the question looked plausible enough, those who proposed it were not conscientious in it, for they were more concerned about the ceremony than about the substance; they seemed to boast of their fasting, and to upbraid God Almighty with it, that he had not sooner returned in mercy to them; "for we have done it *these so many years.*" As those, Isa. 58:3, *Wherefore have we fasted, and thou seest not?* And some think that unbelief, and distrust of the promises of God, were at the bottom of their enquiry; for, if they had given them the credit that was due to them, they needed not to doubt but that their fasts ought to be laid aside, now that the occasion of them was over. And therefore the first answer to their enquiry is a very sharp reproof of their hypocrisy, directed, not only to the *people of the land,* but to *the priests,* who had set up these fasts, and perhaps some of them were for keeping them up, to serve some purpose of their own. Let them all take notice that, whereas they thought they had made God very much their debtor by these fasts, they were much mistaken, for they were not acceptable to him, unless they had been observed in a better manner and to better purpose.

1. What they did that was good was not done aright (*v.* 5): *You fasted and mourned.* They were not chargeable with the omission or neglect of the duty, though it was displeasing to the body (thy fasts were *continually before me,* Ps. 50:8), but they had not managed them aright. Note, Those that come to enquire of their duty must be willing first to be told of their faults. And those that seem zealous for the outside of a duty ought to examine themselves faithfully whether they have the regard they ought to have to the inside of it. (1.) They had not an eye to God in their fasting: *Did you at all fast unto me, even to me?* He appeals to their own consciences; they will witness against them that they had not been sincere in it, much more will God, who is greater than the heart and knows all things. You know very well that *you did not at all fast to me; in fasting did you fast to me?* There was the carcase and form of the duty, but none of the life, and soul, and power of it. Was it *to me, even to me?* The repetition intimates what a great deal of stress is laid upon this as the main matter, in that and other holy exercises, that they be done to God, even to him, with an eye to his word as our rule, and his glory as our end, in them, seeking to please him and to obtain his favour, and studious by the sincerity of our intention to approve ourselves to him. When this was wanting every fast was but a jest. To fast, and not fast to God, was to mock him and provoke him, and could not be pleasing to him. Those that make fasting a cloak for sin, as Jezebel's fast, or by it make their court to men for their applause, as the Pharisees, or that rest in outward expressions of humiliation while their hearts are unhumbled, as Ahab, do they *fast to God, even to him? Is this the fast that God has chosen?* Isa. 58:5. If the solemnities of our fasting, though frequent, long, and severe, do not serve to put an edge upon devout affections, to quicken prayer, to increase godly sorrow, and to alter the temper of our minds and the course of our lives for the better, they do not at all answer the intention, and God will not accept them as performed to him, even to him. (2.) They had the same eye to themselves in their fasting that they had in their eating and drinking (*v.* 6): *"When you did eat, and when you did drink,* on other days (nay, perhaps on your fast-days, in the observation of which you could, when you saw cause, dispense with yourselves, and take a liberty to eat and drink), did you not *eat for yourselves and drink for yourselves?* Have you not always done as you had a mind yourselves? Why then do you now pretend a desire to know the mind of God? In your religious feasts and thanksgivings you have had no more an eye to God than in your fasts." Or, rather, it refers to their common meals; they did no more design the honour of God in their fasting and praying than they did in their eating and drinking; but self was still the centre in which the lines of all their actions, natural, civil, and religious, met. They needed not be in such care about the continuance of their fasts, unless they had kept them better. Note, We miss our end in eating and drinking when we eat to ourselves and drink to ourselves, whereas we should *eat and drink to the glory of God* (1 Co. 10:31), that our bodies may be fit to serve our souls in his service.

2. The principal good thing they should have done was left undone (*v.* 7): *"Should you not hear the words which the Lord has cried by the former prophets?* Yes, that you should have done on your fast-days; it was not enough to *weep* and *separate yourselves* on your fast-days, in token of your sorrow for the judgments you were under, but you should have *searched the scriptures* of the prophets, that you might have seen what was the ground of God's controversy with your fathers, and might have taken warning by their miseries not to tread in the steps of their iniquities. You ask, Shall we do as we have done, in fasting? No, you must do that which you have not yet done; you must repent of your sins and reform you lives. This is what we now call you to, and it is the same that the former prophets called your fathers to." To affect them the more with the mischief that sin had done them, that they might be brought to repent of it, he puts them in mind of the former flourishing state of their country: Jerusalem *was* then *inhabited and in prosperity,* that is now desolate and in distress. The *cities round about,* that are now in ruins, were then inhabited too and *in peace.* The country likewise was very populous: *Men inhabited the south of the plain,* which was not at all fortified, and yet they lived safely, and which was fruitful, and so they lived plentifully. But then God *by the prophets cried* to them, as one in earnest, and importunate with them, to amend their ways and doings, or else their prosperity would soon be at an end. "Now," says the prophet, "you should have taken notice of that, and have inferred that what was required of them for the preventing of the judgments, and which they did not, is required of you for the removal of the judgments; and, if you do it not, all your fasting and weeping signify nothing." Note, The words of the later prophets agree with those of the former; and, whether people are in prosperity or adversity, they must be called upon to leave their sins and do their duty; this must still be the burden of every song.

Verses 8–14

What was said *v.* 7, that they *should have heard the words of the former prophets,* is here enlarged upon, for warning to these hypocritical enquirers, who continued their sins when they asked with great preciseness whether they should continue their fasts. This prophet had before put them in mind of their fathers' disobedience to the calls of the prophets, and what was the consequence of it (*ch.* 1:4–6), and now here again; for others' harms should be our warnings. God's judgments upon Israel of old for their sins were written for admonition to us Christians (1 Co. 10:11), and the same use we should make of similar providences in our own day.

I. This prophet here repeats the heads of the sermons which the former prophets preached to their fathers (*v.* 9, 10), because the very same things were required of them now. "Thus does the *Lord of hosts speak* to you now, and thus he did speak to your fathers, saying, *Execute true judgment."* The duties here required of them, which would have been the lengthening of the tranquillity of their fathers and must be the restoring of their tranquillity, are not keeping fasts and offering sacrifices, but *doing justly* and *loving mercy,* duties which they were bound to by the light and law of nature, though there had been no prophets sent to insist upon them, duties which had a direct tendency to the public welfare and peace, and which they themselves would be the gainers by, and not God. 1. Magistrates must administer justice impartially, according to the maxims of the law and the merits of the cause, without respect of persons: "*Judge judgment of truth,* and execute it when you have judged it." 2. Neighbours must have a tender concern for one another, and must not only do one another no wrong, but must be ready to do one another all the good offices that lie in their power. They must *show mercy and compassion every man to his brother,* as the case called for it. The infirmities of others, as well as their calamities, are to be looked upon with compassion. *Hanc veniam petimusque damusque vicissim — This kindness we ask and exercise.* 3. They must not bear hard upon those whom they have advantage against, and who, they know, are not able to help themselves. They must not, either in commerce or in course of law, oppress *the widow, the fatherless, the stranger, and the poor, v.* 10. The weakest must not be thrust to the wall because they are weakest. No thanks to men not to deny right to those who are in a capacity to demand it and recover it; but we must, not only for wrath, but also for conscience' sake, give those their own who have not power to force it from us. Or it intimates that that which is but exactness with others is exaction upon the widows and the fatherless; nay, that not relieving and helping them as we ought is, in effect, oppressing them. 4. They must not only not do wrong to any, but they must not so much as desire it nor think of it: "*Let none of you imagine evil against his brother in your heart.* Do not project it; do not wish it; nay do not so much as please yourself with the fancy of it." The law of God lays a restraint upon the heart, and forbids the entertaining, forbids the admitting, of a malicious, spiteful, ill-natured thought. Deu. 15:9, *Beware that there be not a thought in thy Belial heart against thy brother.*

II. He describes the wilfulness and disobedience of their fathers, who persisted in all manner of wickedness and injustice, notwithstanding these exhortations and admonitions frequently given them in God's name; various expressions to this purport are here heaped up (*v.* 11, 12), setting forth the stubbornness of that carnal mind which is *enmity against God, and is not in subjection to the law of God, neither indeed can be.* They were obstinate and refractory, and persisted in their transgressions of the law purely from a spirit of contradiction to the law. 1. They would not, if they could help it, come within hearing of the prophets, but kept at a distance; or, if they could not avoid hearing what they said, yet they resolved they would not heed it: *They refused to hearken,* and looked another way as if they had not been spoken to. 2. If they did hear what was said to them, and, as it seemed, inclined at first to comply with it, yet they flew off when it came to the setting to, and, like a bullock unaccustomed to the yoke, *they pulled away the shoulder,* and would not submit to the *easy yoke* and the *light burden* of God's commandments. *They gave a withdrawing shoulder* (so the word is); they seemed to lay their shoulder to the work, but they presently withdrew it again, as those Jer. 34:10, 11. They were like a deceitful bow, as that son that said, *I go, sir, but went not.* 3. They filled their own minds with prejudices against the word of God, and had some objection or other ready wherewith to fortify themselves against every sermon they heard. *They stopped their ears, that they should not hear,* as the deaf adder (Ps. 58:4), and none are so deaf as those that will not hear, that *make their own ear heavy,* as the word is. 4. They resolved that nothing which was said to them, for the enforcing of these injunctions, should make any impression upon them: *They made their hearts as an adamant-stone,* as a *diamond,* the hardest of stones to be wrought upon, or as a *flint,* which the mason cannot hew into shape as he can other stone out of the quarry. Nothing is so hard, so unmalleable, so inflexible, as the heart of a presumptuous sinner; and those whose hearts are hard may thank themselves; they are of their own hardening, and it is just with God to give them over to a reprobate sense, to the hardness and impenitence of their own hearts. These stubborn sinners hardened their hearts on purpose *lest they should hear* what God said to them by the written word, *by the law of Moses,* and by the *words of the prophets* that preached to them; they had *Moses and the prophets,* but resolved they would hear neither, nor would they have been persuaded though one had been sent to them from the dead. The *words of the prophet* were not regarded by them, though they were words which the Lord of hosts sent and directed to them, though he sent them immediately *by his Spirit* in the proph-

ets; so that in despising them they affronted God himself and *resisted the Holy Ghost.* Note, The reason why men are not good is because they will not be so; they will not consider, will not comply; and therefore, *if thou scornest, thou alone shalt bear it.*

III. He shows the fatal consequences of it to their fathers: *Therefore came great wrath from the Lord of hosts.* God was highly displeased with them, and justly; he required nothing of them but what was reasonable in itself and beneficial to them; and yet they refused, and in a most insolent manner too. What master could bear to be so abused by his own servant? Such an implacable enmity to the gospel as this was to the law and the prophets was that which brought *wrath to the uttermost* upon the last generation of the Jewish church, 1 Th. 2:16. Great sins against *the Lord of hosts,* whose authority is incontestable, bring *great wrath from the Lord of hosts,* whose power is irresistible. And the effect was, 1. As they had turned a deaf ear to God's word, so God turned a deaf ear to their prayers, *v.* 13. *As he cried* to them in their prosperity to leave their sins, *and they would not hear,* but persisted in their iniquities, so *they cried to him* in the day of their trouble to remove his judgments, and he would not hear, but lengthened out their calamities. Those that set God at defiance, in the height of their pride, when pangs came upon them cried unto him. *Lord, in trouble have they visited thee.* But God has said it, and will abide by it, *He that turns away his ear from hearing the law, even his prayer shall be an abomination,* Prov. 28:9; 1:24, etc. Iniquity, regarded in the heart, will certainly spoil the success of prayer, Ps. 66:18. 2. As they flew off from their duty and allegiance to God, and were of desultory and unsettled spirits, so God dissipated them and threw them about as chaff before a whirlwind: *He scattered them among all the nations whom they knew not,* and whom therefore they could not expect to receive any kindness from, *v.* 14. 3. As they violated all the laws of their land, so God took away all the glories of it: *Their land was desolate after them, and no man passed through or returned.* All that country that was the kingdom of the two tribes, after the dispersion of the remaining Jews, upon the slaughter of Gedaliah, was left utterly uninhabited; there was not man, woman, or child, in it, till the Jews returned at the end of seventy years' captivity; nay, it should seem, the very roads that lay through the country were deserted (none passed or repassed), which, as it had an intimation of mercy in it (though they were cast out of it, yet it was kept empty for their return), so for the present it made the judgment appear much the more dismal; for what a horrid wilderness must a land be that had been so many years uninhabited! And they might thank themselves; it was they that by their own wickedness laid *the pleasant land desolate.* It was not so much the Chaldeans that did it. No; they did it themselves. The desolations of a land are owing to the wickedness of its inhabitants, Ps. 107:34. This came of their wilful disobedience to the law of God. And the present generation saw how desolate sin had made that pleasant land, and yet would not take warning.

CHAPTER 8

The work of ministers is rightly to divide the word of truth and to give every one his portion. So the prophet is here instructed to do, in the further answer he gives to the case of conscience proposed about continuing the public fasts. His answer, in the foregoing chapter, is by way of reproof to those that were disobedient and would not obey the truth. But here he is ordered to change his voice, and to speak by way of encouragement to the willing and obedient. Here are two words from the Lord of hosts, and they are both good words and comfortable words. In the former of these messages (*v.* 1) God promises that Jerusalem shall be restored, reformed, replenished (*v.* 2–8), that the country shall be rich, and the affairs of the nation shall be successful, their reputation retrieved, and their state in all respects the reverse of what it had been for many years past (*v.* 9–15); he then exhorts them to reform what was amiss among them, that they might be ready for these favours designed them (*v.* 16, 17). In the latter of these messages (*v.* 18) he promises that their fasts should be superseded by the return of mercy (*v.* 19), and that thereupon they should be replenished, enriched, and strengthened, by the accession of foreigners to them (*v.* 20–23).

Verses 1–8

The prophet, in his foregoing discourses, had left his hearers under a high charge of guilt and a deep sense of wrath; he had left them in a melancholy view of the desolations of their pleasant land, which was the effect of their fathers' disobedience; but because he designed to bring

them to repentance, not to drive them to despair, he here sets before them the great things God had in store for them, encouraging them hereby to hope that their case of conscience would shortly determine itself and that God's providence would as loudly call them to *joy and gladness* as ever it called them to *fasting and mourning.* It is here promised,

I. That God will appear for Jerusalem, and will espouse and plead her cause. 1. He will be revenged on Zion's enemies (*v.* 2): *I was jealous for Zion,* or *of* Zion; that is, "I have of late been heartily concerned for her honour and interests, *with great jealousy.* The great wrath that was against her (*ch.* 7:12) now turns against her adversaries. I am now *jealous for her with great fury,* and can no more bear to have her abused in her afflictions than I could bear to be abused by her provocations." This he had said before (*ch.* 1:14, 15), that they might promise themselves as much from the power of his anger, when it was turned for them, as they had felt from it when it was against them. The sins of Zion were her worst enemies, and had done her the most mischief; and therefore God, in his jealousy for her honour and comfort, will *take away her sins,* and then, whatever other enemies injured her, it was at their peril. 2. He will be resident in Zion's palaces (*v.* 3): "*I have returned to Zion,* after I had seemed so long to stand at a distance, and I will again *dwell in the midst of Jerusalem* as formerly." This secures to them the tokens of his presence in his ordinances and the instances of his favour in his providences.

II. That there shall be a wonderful reformation in Jerusalem, and religion, in the power of it, shall prevail and flourish there. "*Jerusalem,* that has dealt treacherously both with God and man, shall become so famous for fidelity and honesty that it *shall be called* and known by the name of *a city of truth,* and the inhabitants of it shall be called *children that will not lie.* The *faithful city* has become a *harlot* (Isa. 1:21), but shall now become a *faithful city* again, faithful to the *God of Israel* and to the worship of him only." This was fulfilled; for the Jews after the captivity, though there was much amiss among them, were never guilty of idolatry. Jerusalem shall be called *the mountain of the Lord of hosts,* owning him and owned by him, and therefore *the holy mountain,* cleared from idols and consecrated to God, and not, as it had been, the *mount of corruption,* 2 Ki. 23:13. Note, The city of God ought to be *a city of truth* and the *mountain of the Lord of hosts a holy mountain.* Those that profess religion, and relation to God, must study to adorn their profession by all instances of godliness and honesty.

III. That there shall be in Jerusalem a great increase of people, and all the marks and tokens of a profound tranquillity. When it has become a *city of truth* and a *mountain of holiness,* it is then peaceable and prosperous, and every thing in it looks bright and pleasant. 1. You may look with pleasure upon the generation that is going off the stage, and see them fairly quitting it in the ordinary course of nature, and not driven off from it by war, famine, or pestilence (*v.* 4): *In the streets of Jerusalem,* that had been filled with the bodies of the slain, or deserted and left desolate, shall now dwell *old men* and *old women,* who have not been cut off by untimely deaths (either through their own intemperance or God's vengeance), but have the even thread of their days spun out to a full length; they shall feel no distemper but the decay of nature, and go to their grave in a full age, as a *shock of corn in his season.* They shall have *every one his staff in his hand, for very age,* to support him, as Jacob, who *worshipped, leaning upon the top of his staff,* Heb. 11:21. Old age needs a support, and should not be ashamed to use it, but should furnish itself with divine graces, which will be the strength of the heart and a better support than a staff in the hand. Note, The hoary head, as it is a crown of glory to those that wear it, so it is to the places where they live. It is a graceful thing to a city to see abundance of old people in it; it is a sign, not only of the healthfulness of the air, but of the prevalence of virtue and the suppression and banishment of those many vices which cut off the number of men's months in the midst; it is a sign, not only that the climate is temperate, but that the people are so. 2. You may look with as much pleasure upon the generation that is rising up in their room (*v.* 5): *The streets of the city shall be full of boys and girls playing in the streets.* This intimates, (1.)

That they shall be blessed with a multitude of children; their families shall increase and multiply, and replenish the city, which was an early product of the divine blessing, Gen. 1:28. Happy the man, happy the nation, whose quiver is full of these arrows! They shall have of both sexes, *boys and girls,* in whom their families shall afterwards be joined, and another generation raised up. (2.) That their children shall be healthful, and strong, and active; their boys and girls shall not lie sick in bed, or sit pining in the corner, but (which is a pleasant sight to parents) shall be hearty and cheerful, and play in the streets. It is their pleasant playing age; let us not grudge it to them; much good may it do them and no harm. *Evil days* will come time enough, and *years* of which they will *say* that they have *no pleasure in them,* in consideration of which they are concerned not to spend all their time in play, but to remember their Creator. (3.) That they shall have great plenty, meat enough for all their mouths. In time of famine we find the children *swooning as the wounded, in the streets of the city,* Lam. 2:11, 12. If they are playing in the streets, it is a good sign that they want for nothing. (4.) That they shall not be terrified with the alarms of war, but enjoy a perfect security. There shall be *no breaking* in of invaders, *no going out* of deserters, *no complaining in the streets* (Ps. 144:14); for, when there is playing in the streets, it is a sign that there is little care or fear there. Time was when the enemy hunted their steps so closely that they could not go in their streets (Lam. 4:18), but now they shall *play in the streets* and fear no evil. (5.) That they shall have love and peace among themselves. The boys and girls shall not be fighting in the streets, as sometimes in cities that are divided into factions and parties the children soon imbibe and express the mutual resentments of the parents; but they shall be innocently and lovingly *playing in the streets,* not devouring, but diverting, one another. (6.) That the sports and diversions used shall be all harmless and inoffensive; the boys and girls shall have no other play than what they are willing that persons should see *in the streets,* no play that seeks corners, no playing the fool, or playing the wanton, for it is the mountain of the Lord, the *holy mountain,* but honest and modest recreations, which they have no reason to be ashamed of. (7.) That childish youthful sports shall be confined to the age of childhood and youth. It is pleasing to see the *boys and girls playing in the streets,* but it is ill-favoured to see men and women playing there, who should fill up their time with work and business. It is well enough for *children* to be *sitting in the market-place,* crossing questions (Mt. 11:16, 17), but it is no way fit that men, who are able to *work in the vineyard,* should *stand all the day idle* there, Mt. 20:3.

IV. That the scattered Israelites shall be brought together again from all parts whither they were dispersed (*v.* 7): *"I will save my people from the east country, and from the west;* I will save them from being lost, or losing themselves, in Babylon, or in Egypt, or in any other country whither they were driven." They shall neither be detained by the nations among whom they sojourn nor shall they incorporate with them; but I will *save them,* will separate them, and will bring them to their own land again; by the prosperity of their land I will invite them back, and at the same time incline them to return; and *they shall dwell in the midst of Jerusalem,* shall choose to dwell there, because it is the holy city, though, upon many other accounts, it was more eligible to dwell in the country; and therefore we find (Neh. 11:2) that *the people blessed all the men who willingly offered themselves to dwell at Jerusalem.*

V. That God would renew his covenant with them, would be faithful to them and make them so to him: *They shall be my people and I will be their God.* That is the foundation and crown of all these promises, and is inclusive of all happiness. They shall obey God's laws, and God will secure and advance all their interests. This contract shall be made, shall be new-made, *in truth* and *in righteousness.* Some think that the former denotes God's part of the covenant (he will be *their God in truth,* he will make good all his promises of favour to them) and the latter man's part of the covenant — they shall be his people in *righteousness,* they shall be a righteous people and shall abound in the *fruits of righteousness,* and shall not, as they have done, deal treacherously and unjustly with their God. See Hos. 2:19, 20. God will never leave nor forsake them in a way of mercy, as he has promised them; and they shall never leave nor forsake him in a way of duty, as they have promised him. These promises were fulfilled in the flourishing state of the Jewish church, for some ages, between the captivity and Christ's time; they were to have a further and a fuller accomplishment in the gospel-church, that *heavenly Jerusalem,* which is from above, is free, and is the *mother of us all;* but the fullest accomplishment of all will be in the future state.

All these precious promises are here ratified, and the doubts of God's people silenced, with that question (*v.* 6): *"If it be marvellous in the eyes of this people, should it be marvellous in my eyes?* If it seem unlikely to you that ever Jerusalem should be thus repaired, should be thus replenished, is it therefore impossible with God?" The *remnant of this people* (and God's people in this world are but a remnant), being few and feeble, thought all this was too good news to be true, especially *in these days,* these difficult days, these cloudy and dark days. Considering how bad the times are, it is highly improbable, it is morally impossible, they should ever come to be so good as the prophet speaks. How can these things be? How can dry bones live? But should it therefore appear so in the eyes of God? Note, We do both God and ourselves a deal of wrong if we think that, when we are *nonplussed,* he is so, and that he cannot get over the difficulties which to us seem insuperable. *With men this is impossible; but with God all things are possible;* so far are God's thoughts and ways above ours.

Verses 9–17

God, by the prophet, here gives further assurances of the mercy he had in store for Judah and Jerusalem. Here is line upon line for their comfort, as before there was for their conviction. These verses contain strong encouragements with reference to the difficulties they now laboured under. And we may observe,

I. Who they were to whom these encouragements did belong — to those who, in obedience to the call of God by his prophets, applied in good earnest to the building of the temple (*v.* 9): *"Let your hands be strong,* that are busy at work for God, *you that hear in these days these words by the mouth of the prophets,* and are not disobedient to them *as your fathers were,* in the former days, to the words of those prophets that were sent to them. You may take the comfort of the promises, and shall have the benefit of them, who have obeyed the precepts given you *in the day that the foundation of the house of the Lord was laid,* when you were told that, having begun with it, you must go on, *that the temple might be built;* God told you that you must go on with it, and you have laboured hard at it for some time, in obedience to the heavenly vision. Now you are those whose hands must be strengthened and whose hearts must be comforted, with these precious promises; to you is the word of this consolation sent." Note, Those, and those only, that are employed for God, may expect to be encouraged by him; those who lay their hands to the plough of duty shall have them strengthened with the promises of mercy; and those who avoid their fathers' faults, not only cut off the entail of the curse, but have it turned into a blessing.

II. What the discouragements were which they had hitherto laboured under, *v.* 10. These are mentioned as a foil to the blessings God was now about to bestow upon them, to make them appear the more strange, to the glory of God, and the more sweet, to their comfort. The truth was the times had long been very bad, and the calamities and difficulties of them were many and great. 1. Trade was dead; there was nothing to be done and therefore nothing to be got. *Before these days* of reformation began *there was no hire for man, nor any hire for beasts.* The fruits of the earth (though it had long lain fallow, and therefore, one would think, should have been the more fertile) were thin and poor, so that the husbandman had no occasion to hire harvest people to reap his corn, nor teams to carry it home, for he could be scarcely said to have any. Merchants had no goods to import or export, so that they needed not to hire either men or beasts; hence the poor people, who lived by their labour, had no way of getting bread for themselves and their families. 2. Travelling was dangerous, so that all commerce both by sea and land was cut off; nay, none durst stir abroad so much as to visit their friends, for *their was no peace to him that went out, or came in, because of the affliction.* The Samaritans, and Ammonites, and their other evil neighbours, made inroads upon them in small parties, and seized all they could lay their hands on; the roads were infested with highwaymen, and both city and country with housebreakers; so that neither men's persons nor their goods were safe at home or abroad. 3. There was no such thing as friendship or good neighbourship among them: *I set all men every one against his neighbour.* In this there was a great deal of sin, for these wars and fightings came from men's lust, and this God was not the author of; but there was in it a great deal of misery also, and so God was in it a just avenger of their disobedience to him; because they were of an *evil spirit* towards him, a spirit of contradiction to his laws, God sent among them an evil spirit, to make them vexatious one to another. Those that throw off the love of God forfeit the comfort of brotherly love.

III. What encouragement they shall now have to proceed in the good work they are about, and to hope that it shall yet be well with them: "Thus and thus you have been harassed and afflicted, but now God will change his way towards you, *v.* 11. Now that you return to your duty God will comfort you according to the time that he has afflicted you; the ebbing tide shall flow again." 1. God will not proceed in his controversy with them; *I will not be to them as in the former days.* Note, It is with us well or ill according as God is to us; for every creature is that to us which he makes it to be. And, if we walk not contrary to God as in the former days, he will not walk contrary to us as in the former days; for it is only *with the froward* that he will *wrestle.* 2. They shall have great plenty and abundance of all goods things (*v.* 12): *The seed* sown *shall be prosperous,* and yield a great increase; *the vine shall give her fruit,* which makes glad the heart, and *the ground* its products, which strengthen the heart; they shall have all they can desire, not only for necessity, but for ornament and delight. The *heavens shall give their dew,* without which the earth would not yield her increase, which is a constant intimation to us of the beneficence of the God of heaven to men on earth and of their dependence on him. It is said of a *sweeping rain* that it *leaves no food* (Prov. 28:3); but here the *gentle dew* waters the earth, that it may give *seed to the sower and bread to the eater.* And thus God will *cause the remnant of this people to possess all these things.* They are but a *remnant,* a *residue,* very few, one would think scarcely worth looking after; but, now that they are at work for God, he will take care that they shall want nothing which is fit for them. This confirms what the prophet's colleague had said, a little before (Hag. 2:16, 19), *From this day will I bless you.* Note, God's people, that serve him faithfully, have great possessions. *"All* is yours, for you are Christ's." 3. They shall recover their credit among their neighbours (*v.* 13): *You were a curse among the heathen.* Every one censured and condemned them, spoke ill of them, and wished ill to them, upon the account of the great disgrace that they were under; some think that they were made a form of execration, so that if a man would load his enemy with the heaviest curse he would say, *God make thee like a Jew!* "But now, *I will save you, and you shall be a blessing.* Your restoration shall be as much taken notice of to your honour as ever your desolation and dispersion were to your reproach; you shall be applauded and admired as much as ever you were vilified and run down, shall be courted and caressed as much as ever you were slighted and abandoned." Most men smile or frown upon their neighbours according as Providence smiles or frowns upon them; but those whom God plainly blesses as his own, shows favour to and puts honour upon, we ought also to respect and be kind to. The blessed of the Lord are the blessing of the land, and should be so accounted by us. This is here promised to the house both of Israel and Judah; for many of the ten tribes returned out of captivity with the two tribes, and shared with them in those blessings; and, it is probable, besides what came at first, many, very many, flocked to them afterwards, when they saw their affairs take this turn. 4. God himself will determine to do them good, *v.* 14, 15. All their comforts take rise from the thoughts of the love that God had towards them, Jer. 29:11. Compare these promises with the former threatenings. (1.) When they *provoked him* to anger with *their sins,* he said that he would *punish them,* and so he did; it was his declared purpose to bring destroying judgments upon them, and, because they repented not of their rebellions against him, he repented not of his threatenings against them, but let the sentence of the law take its course. Note, God's punishing sinners is never a sudden and hasty resolve, but is always the product of thought, and there is a counsel in that part of the will of God. If the sinner turn not, God will not turn. (2.) Now that they pleased him with their services; he said that he would *do them good;* and will he not be as true to his promises as he was to his threatenings? No doubt he will: *"So again have I thought to do well to Jerusalem in those days,* when you begin to hearken to the voice of God speaking to you by his prophets; and these thoughts also shall be performed."

IV. The use they are to make of these encouragements.

1. Let them take the comfort which these promises give to them: *Fear you not* (*v.* 15); *let your hands be strong* (*v.* 9); and both together (*v.* 13), *Fear not, but let your hands be strong.* (1.) The difficulties they met with in their work must not drive them from it, nor make them go on heavily in it, for the issue would be good and the reward great. Let this therefore animate them to proceed with vigour and cheerfulness. (2.) The dangers they were exposed to from their enemies must not terrify them; those that have God for them, engaged to do them good, need not fear *what man can do against them.*

2. Let them do the duty which those promises call for from them, *v.* 16, 17. The very same duties which the former prophets pressed upon their fathers from the consideration of the wrath threatened (*ch.* 7:9, 10) this prophet presses upon them from the consideration of the mercy promised: "Leave it to God, to perform for you what he has promised, in his own way and time, but upon condition that you make conscience of your duty. *These are the things then that you shall do;* this is your part of the covenant; these are the articles which you are to perform, fulfil, and keep, that you may not put a bar in your own door and stop the current of God's favours." (1.) "You must never tell a lie, but always speak as you think, and as the matter is, to the best of your knowledge: *Speak you every man the truth to his neighbour,* both in bargains and in common converse; dread every word that looks like a lie." This precept the apostle quotes (Eph. 4:25), and backs it with this reason, *We are members one of another.* (2.) Those that are entrusted with the administration of public justice must see to it, not only that none be wronged by it, but that those who are wronged be righted by it: *Execute the judgment of truth and peace in your gates.* Let the judges that sit in the gates in all their judicial proceedings have regard both to truth and to peace; let them take care to do justice, to accommodate differences, and to prevent vexatious suits. it must be a judgment of truth in order to peace, and making those friends that were at variance, and a judgment of peace as far as is consistent with truth, and no further. (3.) No man must bear malice against his neighbour upon any account; this is the same with what we had *ch.* 7:10. We must not only keep our hands from doing evil, but we must watch over our hearts, that they *imagine not any evil* against our neighbour, Prov. 3:29. Injury and mischief must be crushed in the thought, in the embryo. (4.) Great reverence must be had for an oath, and conscience made of it: "Never take a false oath, nay, *love no false oath;* that is, hate it, dread it, keep at a distance from it. Love not to impose oaths upon others, lest they swear falsely; love not that any should take a false oath for your benefit, and forswear themselves to do you a kindness." A very good reason is annexed against all these corrupt and wicked practices: "For *all these are things that I hate,* and therefore you must hate them if you expect to have God your friend." These things here forbidden are all of them found among the *seven things which the Lord hates,* Prov. 6:16–19. Note, We must forbear sin, not only because God is angry at it, and therefore it is dangerous to us, but because he hates it, and therefore it ill becomes us and is a very ungrateful thing.

Verses 18–23

These verses contain two precious promises, for the further encouragement of those pious Jews that were hearty in building the temple.

I. That a happy period should be put to their fasts, and there should be no more occasion for them, but they should be converted into thanksgiving days, *v.* 19. This is a direct answer to the enquiry concerning their fasts, *ch.* 7:3. Those of them that fasted in hypocrisy had their doom in the foregoing chapter, but those that in sincerity humbled themselves before God, and sought his face, have here a comfortable assurance given them of a large share in the happy times approaching. The four *yearly fasts* which they had religiously observed should be *to the house of Judah joy and gladness, and solemn feasts,* and those cheerful ones. Note, Joyous times will come to the church after troublous times; if weeping endure for more than a night, and joy come not next morning, yet the morning will come that will introduce it at length. And, when God comes towards us in ways of mercy, we must meet him with joy and thankfulness; when God turns judgments into mercies we must turn fasts into festivals, and thus *walk after the Lord.* And those who *sow in tears* with Zion shall *reap in joy* with her; those who submit to the restraints of her solemn fasts while they continue shall share in the triumphs of her cheerful feasts when they come, Isa. 66:10. The inference from this promise is, *"Therefore love the truth and peace;* be faithful and honest in all your dealings, and let it be a pleasure to you to be so, though thereby you cut yourselves short of those gains which you see others get dishonestly; and, as much as in you lies, live peaceably with all men, and be in your element when you are in charity. Let the truths of God rule in your heads, and let the peace of God rule in your hearts."

II. That a great accession should be made to the church by the conversion of many foreigners, *v.* 20–23. This was fulfilled but in part when, in the latter times of the Jewish church, there were abundance of proselytes from all the countries about, and some that lay very remote, who came yearly to worship at Jerusalem, which added very much both to the grandeur and wealth of that city, and contributed greatly to the making of it so considerable as it came to be before our Saviour's time, though now it was but just peeping out of its ruins. But it would be accomplished much more fully in the conversion of the Gentiles to the faith of Christ, and the incorporating of them with the believing Jews in one great body, under Christ the head, a *mystery* which is *made manifest* by the *scriptures of the prophets* (Rom. 16:26), and by this among the rest, which makes it strange that when it was accomplished it was so great a surprise and stumbling-block to the Jews. Observe,

1. Who they are that shall be added to the church — *people, and the inhabitants of many cities* (*v.* 20); not only a few ignorant country people that may be easily imposed upon, or some idle people that have nothing else to do, but intelligent inquisitive citizens, men of business and acquaintance with the world, shall embrace the gospel of Christ; *yea, many people and strong nations* (*v.* 22), some of *all languages, v.* 23. By this it appears that they are brought into the church, not by human persuasion, for they are of different languages, not by external force, for they are strong nations, able to have kept their ground if they had been so attacked, but purely by the effectual working of divine truth and grace. Note, God has his remnant in all parts; and in the general assembly of the church of the first-born some will be found *out of all nations and kindreds,* Rev. 7:9.

2. How their accession to the church is described: They shall come *to pray before the Lord and to seek the Lord of hosts* (*v.* 21); and, to show that this is the main matter in which their conversion consists, it is repeated (*v.* 22): They *shall come to seek the Lord of hosts in Jerusalem, and to pray before the Lord.* No mention is made of their offering sacrifices, not only because these were not expected from the proselytes of the gate, but because, when the Gentiles should be brought in, sacrifice and offering should be quite abolished. See who are to be accounted converts to God and members of the church: and all that are converts to God are members of the church. (1.) They are such as *seek the Lord of hosts,* such as enquire for *God their Maker,* covet and court his favour, and are truly desirous to know his mind and will and sincerely devoted to his honour and glory. *This is the generation of those that seek him.* (2.) They are such as *pray before the Lord,* — such as make conscience, and make a business, of the duty of prayer, — such as dare not, would not, for all the world, live without it, — such as by prayer pay their homage to God, own their dependence upon him, maintain their communion with him, and fetch in mercy and grace from him. (3.) They are such as herein have an eye to the divine revelation and institution, which is signified by their doing this *in Jerusalem,* the place which God had chosen, where his word was, where his temple was, which was a type of Christ and his mediation, which all faithful worshippers will have a believing regard to.

3. How unanimous they shall be in their accession to the church, and how zealous in exciting one another to it (*v.* 21): *The inhabitants of one city shall go to another,* as formerly when they went up from all parts of the country to worship at the yearly feasts; and they shall say, *Let us go speedily to pray before the Lord; I will go also.* This intimates, (1.) That those who are brought into an acquaintance with Christ themselves should do all they can to bring others acquainted with him; thus Andrew invited Peter to Christ and Philip invited Nathanael. True grace hates monopolies. (2.) That those who are duly sensible of their need of Christ, and of the favour of God through him, will stir up themselves and others without delay to hasten to him: *"Let us go speedily to pray;* it is for our lives, and the lives of our souls, that we are to petition, and therefore it concerns us to lose no time; in a matter of such moment delays are dangerous." (3.) That our communion with God is very much assisted and furthered by the communion of saints. It is pleasant to go *to the house of God in company* (Ps. 55:14), *with the multitude* (Ps. 42:4), and it is of good use to those that do so to excite one another to go speedily and lose no time; we should be glad when it is said to us, *Let us go,* Ps. 122:1. As iron sharpens iron, so may good men sharpen the countenances and spirits one of another in that which is good. (4.) That those who stir up others to that which is good must take heed that they do not turn off, or tire, or draw back themselves; he that says, *Let us go,* says, *I will go also.* What good we put others upon doing we must see to it that we do ourselves, else we shall be judged out of our own mouths. Not, "Do you go, and I will stay at home;" but, "Do you go, and I will go with you." "A singular pattern (says Mr. Pemble) of zealous charity, that neither leaves others behind nor turns others before it."

4. Upon what inducement they shall join themselves to the church, not for the church's sake, but for his sake who dwells in it (*v.* 23): *Ten men* of different nations and languages *shall take hold of the skirt of him that is a Jew,* begging of him not to outgo them, but to take them along with him. This intimates the great honour they have for a Jew, as one of the chosen people of God, and therefore well worthy their acquaintance; they cannot all come to take him by the hand, or embrace him in their arms, but are ambitious to take hold of the skirt of his robe, to touch the hem of his garment, saying, *We will go with you, for we have heard that God is with you.* The gospel was preached to the Jews first (for of that nation the apostles were) and by them it was carried to the Gentiles. St. Paul was a Jew whose skirt many took hold of when they welcomed him as *an angel of God,* and begged him to take them along with him to Christ; thus the Greeks took hold of Philip's skirt, saying, *Sir, we would see Jesus,* Jn. 12:21. Note, It is the privilege of the saints that they have God with them, have him among them — the knowledge, and fear, and worship of him; they have his favour and gracious presence, and this should invite us into communion with them. It is good being with those who have God with them, and those who *join themselves to the Lord* must *join themselves to his disciples;* if we take God for our God, we must take his people for our people, cast in our lot among them, and be willing to take our lot with them.

CHAPTER 9

At this chapter begins another sermon, which is continued to the end of *ch.* 11. It is called, "The burden of the word of the Lord," for every word of God has weight in it to those who regard it, and will be a heavy weight upon those who do not, a dead weight. Here is, I. A prophecy against the Jews' unrighteous neighbours — the Syrians, Tyrians, Philistines, and others (*v.* 1–6), with an intimation of mercy to some of them, in their conversion (*v.* 7), and a promise of mercy to God's people, in their protection (*v.* 8). II. A prophecy of their righteous King, the Messiah, and his coming, with a description of him (*v.* 9) and of his kingdom, the nature and extent of it (*v.* 10). III. An account of the obligation the Jews lay under to Christ for their deliverance out of their captivity in Babylon (*v.* 11, 12). IV. A prophecy of the victories and successes God would grant to the Jews over their enemies, as typical of our great deliverance by Christ (*v.* 13–15). V. A promise of great plenty, and joy, and honour, which God had in reserve for his people (*v.* 16, 17), which was written for their encouragement.

Verses 1–8

After the precious promises we had in the foregoing chapter of favour to God's people, their persecutors, who hated them, come to be reckoned with, those particularly that bordered close upon them.

I. The Syrians had been bad neighbours to Israel, and God had a controversy with them. The word of the Lord shall be a *burden in the land of Hadrach,* that is, of *Syria,* but it does not appear why it was so called. That that kingdom is meant is plain, because Damascus, the metropolis of that kingdom, is said to be the *rest* of this burden; that is, the judgments here threatened shall light and lie upon that city. Those are miserable upon whom the burden of the word of the Lord rests, upon whom *the wrath of God abides* (Jn. 3:36); for it is a weight that they can neither shake off nor bear up under. There are those whom God *causes his fury to rest* upon. Those whom the wrath of God makes its mark it will be sure to hit; those whom it makes its rest it will be sure to sink. And the reason of this burden's resting on Damascus is because *the eyes of man, as of all the tribes of Israel* (or rather, *even of all the tribes of Israel),* are *towards the Lord,* because the people of God by faith and prayer look up to him for succour and relief and depend upon him to take their part against their enemies. Note, It is a sign that God is about to appear remarkably for his people when he raises their believing expectations from him and dependence upon him, and when by his grace he turns them from idols to himself. Is. 17:7, 8, *At that day shall a man look to his Maker.* It may be read thus, *for the Lord has an eye upon man, and upon all the tribes of Israel;* he is King of nations as well as King of saints; he governs the world as well as the church, and therefore will punish the sins of other people as well as those of his own people. God is *Judge of all,* and therefore all must give account of themselves to him. When St. Paul was converted at Damascus, and preached there, and disputed with the Jews, then the word of the Lord might be said to rest there, and then *the eyes of men,* of other men besides *the tribes of Israel,* began to be *towards the Lord;* see Acts 9:22. Hamath, a country which lay north of Damascus, and which we often read of, *shall border thereby* (*v.* 2); it joins to Syria, and shall share in the *burden of the word of the Lord* that rests upon Damascus. The Jews have a proverb, *Woe to the wicked man, and woe to his neighbour,* who is in danger of partaking in his sins and in his plagues. Woe to *the land of Hadrach,* and woe to *Hamath that borders thereby.*

II. Tyre and Zidon come next to be called to an account here, as in other prophecies, *v.* 2–4. Observe here,

1. Tyrus flourishing, thinking herself very safe, and ready to set God's judgments, not only at a distance, but at defiance: for, (1.) She is *very wise.* It is spoken ironically; she thinks herself very wise, and able to outwit even the wisdom of God. It is granted that her king is a great politician, and that her statesmen are so, Eze. 28:3. But with all their wit and policy they shall not be able to evade the judgments of God when they come with commission; there is no *wisdom* nor *counsel against the Lord;* nay, it is his honour to take the wise in their own craftiness. (2.) She is very strong, and well fortified both by nature and art: *Tyrus did build herself a strong-hold,* which she thought could never be brought down nor got over. (3.) She is very rich; and *money is a defence;* it is the sinews of war, Eccl. 7:12. By her vast trade she has *heaped up silver as the dust, and fine gold as the mire of the streets,* that is, she has an abundance of them, heaps of silver as common as heaps of sand, Job 27:16. Solomon made silver to be in Jerusalem as the *stones of the streets;* but Tyre went further, and made *fine gold* to be as *the mire of the streets.* It were well if we could all learn so to look upon it, in comparison with the merchandise of wisdom and grace and the gains thereof.

2. Tyrus falling, after all. Her wisdom, and wealth, and strength, shall not be able to secure her (*v.* 4): *The Lord will cast her out* of that strong-hold wherein she has fortified herself, will *make her poor* (so some read it); there have been instances of those that have fallen from the height of plenty to the depth of poverty, and great riches have come to nothing. God will *smite her power in the sea;* her being surrounded by the water shall not secure her, but *she shall be devoured with fire,* and burnt down to the ground. Tyrus, being seated in the midst of the water, was, one would have thought, in danger of being some time or other overflowed or washed away by that; yet God chooses to destroy it by the contrary element. Sometimes he brings ruin upon his enemies by those means which they least suspect. Water enough was nigh at hand to quench the flames of Tyre, and yet by them she shall be devoured; for who can put out the fire which the breath of the Almighty blows up?

III. God next contends with the Philistines, with their great cities and great lords, that bordered southward upon Israel.

1. They shall be alarmed and affrighted by the word of the Lord lighting and resting upon Damascus (*v.* 5); the disgraces of Israel had many a time been *published in the streets of Ashkelon,* and they had triumphed in them; but now *Ashkelon shall see* the ruin of her friends and allies, and shall *fear; Gaza also shall see it, and be very sorrowful, and Ekron,* concluding that their own turns come next, now that the cup of trembling goes round. What will become of their house when their neighbour's is on fire? They had looked upon Tyre and Zidon as a barrier to their country; but, when those strong cities were ruined, their *expectations* from them *were ashamed,* as our expectation from all creatures will be in the issue.

2. They shall themselves be ruined and wasted. (1.) The government shall be dissolved: *The king shall perish from Gaza,* not only the present king shall be cut off, but there shall be no succession, no successor, (2.) The cities shall be dispeopled: *Ashkelon shall not be inhabited;* the rightful owners shall be expelled, either slain or carried into captivity. (3.) Foreigners shall take possession of their land and become masters of all its wealth (*v.* 6): *A bastard shall dwell in Ashdod;* a spurious brood of strangers shall enter upon the inheritances of the natives, which they have no more right to than a bastard has to the estates of the legitimate children. And thus God will *cut off the pride of the Philistines,* all the strength and wealth which they prided themselves in, and which were the ground of their confidence in themselves and their contempt of the Israel of God. This prophecy of the destruction of the Philistines, and of Damascus, and Tyre, was accomplished, not long after this, by Alexander the Great, who ravaged all these countries with his victorious army, took the cities, and planted colonies in them, which Quintus Curtius gives a particular account of in the history of his conquests. And some think he is meant by the bastard that shall dwell in Ashdod, for his mother Olympia owned him begotten in adultery, but pretended it was by Jupiter. The Jews afterwards got ground of the Philistines, Syrians, and others of their neighbours, took some of their cities from them and possessed their countries, as appears by the histories of Josephus and the Maccabees, and this was foretold before, Zep. 2:4, etc.; Obad. 20.

3. Some among them shall be converted, and brought home to God, by his gospel and grace; so some understand *v.* 7, as a promise, (1.) That God would take away the sins of these nations — *their blood* and *their abominations,* their cruelties and their idolatries. God will part between them and these sins which they have rolled under their tongue as a sweet morsel, and are as loth to part with as men are to part with the meat out of their mouths, and which they hold fast between their teeth. Nothing is too hard for the grace of God to do. (2.) That he would accept of a remnant of them for his own: *He that remains shall be for our God.* God would preserve a remnant even of these nations, that should be the monuments of his mercy and grace and be set apart for him; and the disadvantages of their birth shall be no bar to their acceptance with God, but a Philistine shall be as acceptable to God, upon gospel-terms, as one of Judah, nay, as a governor, or chief one, in Judah, and a man of Ekron shall be as a Jebusite, or a man of Jerusalem, as a proselyted Jebusite, as Araunah the Jebusite, 2 Sa. 24:16. In Christ Jesus there is no distinction of nations, but all are one in him, all alike welcome to him.

IV. In all this God intends mercy for Israel, and it is in kindness to them that God will deal thus with the neighbouring nations, to avenge their quarrel for what is past and to secure them for the future.

1. Thus some understand the seventh verse, as intimating, (1.) That thus God would deliver his people from their bloody adversaries, who hated them, and to whom they were an abomination, when they were just ready to devour them and make a prey of them: I will *take away his blood* (that is, the blood of Israel) out of the mouth of the Philistines and *from between their teeth* (Amos 3:12), when, in their hatred of them and enmity to them, they were greedily devouring them. (2.) That lie would thus give them victory and dominion over them: And *he that remains* (that is, the remnant of Israel) *shall be for our God,* shall be taken into his favour, shall own him and be owned by him, and *he shall be as a governor in Judah;* though the Jews have been long in servitude, they shall recover their ancient dignity, and be victorious, as David and other governors in Judah formerly were; and Ekron (that is, the Philistines) shall be as the Jebusites, and the rest of the devoted nations, who were brought into subjection under them.

2. However, this is plainly the sense of *v.* 8, that God will take his people under his special protection, and *therefore* will weaken their neighbours, that it may not be in their power to do them a mischief: *I will encamp about my house because of the army.* Note, God's house lies in the midst of an enemy's country, and his church is as a lily among thorns; and therefore God's power and goodness are to be observed in the special preservation of it. The *camp of the saints,* being a little flock in comparison with the numerous armies of the powers of darkness that are set against it round about, would certainly be swallowed up if the angels of God did not encamp about it, as they did about Elisha, to deliver it, Rev. 20:9; Ps. 34:7. When the times are unusually perilous, when armies are marching and counter-marching, and all bearing ill-will to Zion, then Providence will as it were double its guards upon the church of God, *because of him that passes by and because of him that returns,* that whether he return a conqueror or conquered he may do it no harm. And, as none that pass by shall hurt them, so *no oppressor shall pass through them any more;* they shall have no enemy within themselves to rule them with rigour, and *to make their lives bitter* to them *with sore bondage,* as of old in Egypt. This was fulfilled when, for some time after the struggles of the Maccabees, Judea was a free and flourishing state, or perhaps when Alexander the Great, struck with an awe of Jaddus the high priest, favoured the Jews, and took them under his protection, at the same time when he wasted the neighbouring countries. And the reason given for all this is, *"For now have I seen with my eyes,* now have I carefully distinguished between my people and other people, with whom before they seemed to have their lot in common, and have made it to appear that I know those that are mine," This agrees with Ps. 34:15, *The eyes of the Lord are upon the righteous;* now his eyes, which *run to and fro through the earth,* shall fix upon them, that he may show himself tender of them, and *strong on their behalf,* 2 Chr. 16:9.

Verses 9–11

That here begins a prophecy of the Messiah and his kingdom is plain from the literal accomplishment of the ninth verse in, and its express application to, Christ's riding in triumph into *Jerusalem,* Mt. 21:5; Jn. 12:15.

I. Here is notice given of the approach of the Messiah promised, as matter of great joy to the Old-Testament church: *Behold, thy king cometh unto thee.* Christ is a king, invested with regal powers and prerogatives, a sovereign prince, an absolute monarch, having all power both in heaven and on earth. He is Zion's king. God has *set him upon his holy hill of Zion,* Ps. 2:6. In Zion his glory as a king shines; thence *his law went forth,* even the *word of the Lord.* In the gospel-church his spiritual kingdom is administered; it is by him that the ordinances of the church are instituted, and its officers commissioned; and it is taken under his protection; he fights the church's battles and secures its interests, as its king. "This King has been long in coming, but now, *behold, he cometh;* he is at the door. There are but a few ages more to run out, and he that shall come will come. He *cometh unto thee;* the Word will shortly be made flesh, and dwell within thy borders; he will *come to his own.* And therefore *rejoice,* rejoice *greatly,* and *shout for joy;* look upon it as *good news,* and be assured it is true; please thyself to think that he is coming, that he is on his way towards thee; and be ready to go forth to meet him with acclamations of joy, as one not able to conceal it, it is so great, nor ashamed to own it, it is so just; cry *Hosanna* to him." Christ's approaches ought to be the church's applauses.

II. Here is such a description of him as renders him very amiable in the eyes of all his loving subjects, and his coming to them very acceptable. 1. He is a righteous ruler; all his acts of government will be exactly according to the rules of equity, for *he is just.* 2. He is a powerful protector to all those that bear faith and true allegiance to him, for he *has salvation;* he has it in his power; he has it to bestow upon all his subjects. He is the *God of salvation;* treasures of salvation are in him. He is *servatus — saving himself* (so some read it), rising out of the grave by his own power and so qualifying himself to be our Saviour. (3.) He is a *meek, humble, tender Father* to all his subjects as his children; he is *lowly;* he is *poor* and *afflicted* (so the word signifies), so it denotes the meanness of his condition; having *emptied himself,* he was *despised and rejected of men.* But the evangelist translates it so as to express the temper of his spirit: he is *meek,* not taking state upon him, nor resenting injuries, but *humbling himself* from first to last, condescending to the mean, compassionate to the miserable; this was a bright and excellent character of him as a prophet (Mt. 11:29, *Learn of me, for I am meek and lowly in heart),* and no less so *as a king.* It was a proof of this that, when he made his public entry into his own city (and it was the only passage of his life that had any thing in it magnificent in the eye of the world), he chose to ride, not upon a stately horse, or in a chariot, as great men used to ride, but *upon an ass,* a beast of service indeed, but a poor silly and contemptible one, low and slow, and in those days ridden only by the meaner sort of people; nor was it an ass fitted for use, but an *ass's colt,* a little foolish unmanageable thing, that would be more likely to disgrace his rider than be any credit to him; and that not his own neither, nor helped off, as sometimes a sorry horse is, by good furniture, for he had no saddle, no housings, no trappings, no equipage, but his disciples' clothes thrown upon the colt;' for he *made himself of no reputation* when he visited us in great humility.

III. His kingdom is here set forth in the glory of it. This king has, and will have, a kingdom, not of this world, but a spiritual kingdom, a *kingdom of heaven.* 1. It shall not be set up and advanced by external force, by an arm of flesh or carnal weapons of warfare. No; he *will cut off the chariot from Ephraim and the horses from Jerusalem* (*v.* 10), for he shall have no occasion for them while he himself rides upon an ass. He will, in kindness to his people, cut off their horses and chariots, that they may not cut themselves off from God by putting that confidence in them which they should put in the power of God only. He will himself undertake their protection, will himself be *a wall of fire about Jerusalem* and give his angels charge concerning it (those *chariots of fire and horses of fire),* and then the chariots and horses they had in their service shall be discarded and cut off as altogether needless. 2. It shall be propagated and established by the preaching of the gospel, the *speaking of peace to the heathen;* for Christ *came and preached peace to those that were afar off and to those that were nigh;* and so established his kingdom by proclaiming *on earth peace,* and *good-will towards men.* 3. His kingdom, as far as it prevails in the minds of men and has the ascendant over them, will make them peaceable, and slay all enmities; it will cut off the battle-bow, and *beat swords into plough-shares.* It will not only command the peace, but will *create the fruit of the lips, peace.* 4. It shall extend itself to all parts of the world, in defiance of the opposition given to it. "The chariot and horse that come against Ephraim and Jerusalem, to oppose the progress of Zion's King, shall be cut off; his gospel shall be preached to the world, and be received among the heathen, so that *his dominion shall be from sea to sea, and from the river even to the ends of the earth,* as was foretold by David," Ps. 72:8. The preachers of the gospel shall carry it from one country, one island, to another, till some of the remotest corners of the world are enlightened and reduced by it.

IV. Here is an account of the great benefit procured for mankind by the Messiah, which is redemption from extreme misery, typified by the deliverance of the Jews out of their captivity in Babylon (*v.* 11): *"As for thee also* (thee, O daughter of Jerusalem! or thee, O Messiah the Prince!) *by the blood of thy covenant,* by force and virtue of the covenant made with Abraham, sealed with the blood of circumcision, and the covenant made with Israel at Mount Sinai, sealed with the blood of sacrifices, in pursuance and performance of that covenant, *I have* now of late *sent forth thy prisoners,* thy captives out of Babylon, which was to them a most uncomfortable place, as *a pit* in which was *no water."* It was part of the covenant that, if in the land of their captivity, they sought the Lord, he would be found of them, Lev. 26:42, 44, 45; Deu. 30:4. It was *by the blood of that covenant,* typifying the blood of Christ, in whom all God's covenants with man are yea and amen, that they were released out of captivity; and this was but a shadow of the great salvation wrought out by *thy King, O daughter of Zion!* Note, A sinful state is a state of bondage; it is a spiritual prison; it is a pit, or a dungeon, in which *there is no water,* no comfort at all to be had. We are all by nature prisoners in this pit; the *scripture has concluded* us all *under sin,* and bound us over to the justice of God. God is pleased to deal upon new terms with these prisoners, to enter into another covenant with them; the blood of Christ is the blood of that covenant, purchased it for us and all the benefits of it; by that blood of the covenant effectual provision is made for the sending forth of these prisoners upon easy and honourable terms, and proclamation made of *liberty to the captives and the opening of the prison to those that were bound,* like Cyrus's proclamation to the Jews in Babylon, which all those whose spirits God stirs up will come and take the benefit of.

Verses 12–17

The prophet, having taught those that had returned out of captivity to attribute their deliverance to the *blood of the covenant* and to the promise of the Messiah (for they were so wonderfully helped because that blessing was in them, was yet in the womb of their nation), now comes to encourage them with the prospect of a joyful and happy settlement, and of glorious times before them; and such a happiness they did enjoy, in a great measure, for some time; but these promises have their full accomplishment in the spiritual blessings of the gospel which we enjoy by Jesus Christ.

I. They are invited to look unto Christ, and flee unto him as their city of refuge (*v.* 12): *Turn you to the strong-hold, you prisoners of hope.* The Jews that had returned out of captivity into their own land were yet, in effect, but *prisoners (We are servants this day,* Neh. 9:36), yet *prisoners of hope,* or *expectation,* for God had given them a *little reviving in their bondage,* Ezra 9:8, 9. Those that yet continued in Babylon, detained by their affairs there, yet lived in hope some time or other to see their own land again. Now both these are directed to turn their eyes upon the Messiah, set before them in the promise as their strong-hold, to shelter themselves in him, and stay themselves upon him, for the perfecting of the mercy which by his grace, and for his sake, was so gloriously begun. *Look unto him, and be you saved,* Isa. 45:22. The promise of the Messiah was the strong-hold of the faithful long before his coming; they saw his day at a distance and were glad, and the believing expectation of the *redemption in Jerusalem* was long the support and *consolation of Israel,* Lu. 2:25, 38. They, in their dangers and distresses, were ready to turn towards this and the other creature for relief; but the prophets directed them still to turn to Christ, and to comfort themselves with the joy of their king coming to them with salvation. But, as their deliverance was typical of our redemption by Christ (*v.* 11), so this invitation to the strong-hold speaks the language of the gospel-call. Sinners are prisoners, but they are prisoners of hope; their case is sad, but it is not desperate; yet now there is hope in Israel concerning them. Christ is a strong-hold for them, a strong tower, in whom they may be safe and quiet from the fear of the wrath of God, the curse of the law, and the assaults of their spiritual enemies. To him they must turn by a lively faith; to him they must flee, and trust in his name.

II. They are assured of God's favour to them: *"Even to day do I declare,* when things are at the worst, and you think your case deplorable to the last degree, yet I solemnly promise that *I will render double unto thee,* to thee, O Jerusalem! to every one of you prisoners of hope. I will give you comforts double to the sorrows you have experienced, or blessings double to what I ever bestowed upon your fathers, when their condition was at the best; the glory of your latter state, as well as of your latter house, shall be greater, shall be twice as great as that of your former." And so it was no otherwise than by the coming of the Messiah, the preaching of his gospel, and the setting up of his kingdom; these spiritual blessings in heavenly things were double to what they had ever enjoyed in their most prosperous state. As a pledge of this, in the fulness of time God here promises to the Jews victory, plenty, and joy, in their own land, which yet should be but a type and shadow of more glorious victories, riches, and joys, in the kingdom of Christ.

1. They shall triumph over their enemies. The Jews, after their return, were surrounded with enemies on all sides. They were *as a speckled bird;* all the birds of the field were against them. Their land lay between the two potent kingdoms of Syria and Egypt, branches of the Grecian monarchy, and what frequent dangers they should be in between them was foretold, Dan. 11. But it is here promised that out of them all the Lord would deliver them; and this promise had its primary accomplishment in the times of the Maccabees, when the Jews made head against their enemies, kept their head above water, and, after many struggles and difficulties, came to be head over them. It is promised, (1.) That they shall be instruments in God's hand for the defeating and baffling of their persecutors: "I *have bent Judah for me,* as my bow of steel; that *bow I have filled with Ephraim* as my arrows, have drawn it up to its full bent, till the arrow be at the head;" for some think that this is signified by the phrase of *filling the bow.* The expressions here are very fine, and the figures lively. Judah had been *taught the use of the bow* (2 Sa. 1:18), and Ephraim had been famous for it, Ps. 78:9. But let them not think that they gain their successes by their own bow, for they themselves are no more than God's bow and his arrows, tools in his hands, which he makes use of and manages as he pleases, which he holds as his bow and directs to the mark as his arrows. The best and bravest of men are but what God makes them, and do no more service than he enables them to do. The preachers of the gospel were the bow in Christ's hand, with which he went forth, he went on, *conquering and to conquer,* Rev. 6:2. The following words explain this: *I have raised up* and animated *thy sons, O Zion! against thy sons, O Greece!* This was fulfilled when *against Antiochus,* one of the kings of the Grecian monarchy, the people that knew their God were *strong* and *did exploits,* Dan. 11:32. And they in the hand of an almighty God were made *as the sword of a mighty man,* which none can stand before. Wicked men are said to be God's sword (Ps. 17:13), and sometimes good men are made so; for he employs both as he pleases. (2.) That God will be captain, and commander-in-chief, over them, in every expedition and engagement (*v.* 14): *The Lord shall be seen over them;* he shall make it appear that he presides in their affairs, and that in all their motions they are under his direction, as apparently, though not as sensibly, as he was *seen over Israel* in the pillar of cloud and fire when he led them through the wilderness. [1.] Is their army to be raised, or mustered, and brought into the field? *The Lord shall blow the trumpet,* to gather the forces together, to proclaim the war, to sound the alarm, and to give directions which way to march, which way to move; for, if God blow the trumpet, it shall not give an uncertain sound, nor a feeble ineffectual one. [2.] Is the army taking the field, and entering upon action? Whatever enterprise the campaign is opened with, God shall go forth at the head of their forces, *with whirlwinds of the south,* which were of incredible swiftness and fierceness; and before these whirlwinds thy sons, O Greece! shall be as chaff. [3.] Is the army actually engaged? God's *arrows shall go forth as lightning,* so strongly, so suddenly, so irresistibly; his *lightnings* shall go forth *as arrows* and *scattered them,* that is, he *shot out his lightnings and discomfited them.* This alludes to that which God had done for Israel of old when he brought them out of Egypt, and into Canaan, and had its accomplishment partly in the wonderful successes which the Jews had against their neighbours that attacked them in the time of the Maccabees, by the special appearances of the divine Providence for them, and perfectly in the glorious victories gained by the cross of Christ and the preaching of the cross over Satan and all the powers of darkness, whereby we are made more than conquerors. [4.] Are they

in danger of being overpowered by the enemy? *The Lord of hosts shall defend them* (*v.* 15); *The Lord their God shall save them* (*v.* 16); so that their enemies shall not prevail over them, nor prey upon them. God shall be unto them for defence as well as offence, *the shield of their help* as well as *the sword of their excellency,* and this as *the Lord of hosts,* who has power to defend them, and as *their God,* who is engaged by promise to defend them, and by the property he has in them. He shall save them in *that day,* that critical dangerous day, *as the flock of his people,* with the same care and tenderness that the shepherd protects his sheep with. Those are safe whom God saves. [5.] Did their enemies hope to swallow them up? It shall be turned upon them, and they shall *devour* their enemies, and shall *subdue with sling-stones,* for want of better weapons, those that come forth against them. The *stones of the brook,* when God pleases, shall do as great execution as the best train of artillery; for the *stars in their courses* shall fight on the same side. Goliath was subdued with a sling-stone. Having subdued, they shall *devour, shall drink* the blood of their enemies, as it were, and, as conquerors are wont to do, they shall *make a noise as through wine.* It is usual for conquerors with loud huzzas and acclamations to glory in their victories and proclaim them. We read of those that *shout for mastery,* and of the *shout of a king* among God's people. They shall be filled with blood and spoil, as the bowls and basins of the temple, or the *corners of the altar,* were wont to be filled with the blood of the sacrifices; for their enemies shall fall as victims to divine justice.

2. They shall triumph in their God. They shall take the comfort and give God the glory of their successes. So some read *v.* 15. *They shall eat* (that is, they shall quietly enjoy) what they have got; God will give them power to eat it *after they have subdued the sling-stones* (that is, their enemies that slung stones at them), and *they shall drink and make a noise,* a joyful noise, before the Lord their maker and protector, *as through wine,* as men are merry at a banquet of wine. *Being not drunk with wine, wherein is excess,* but *filled with the Spirit,* they shall *speak* to themselves and one another *in psalms, and hymns, and spiritual songs,* as those that are drunk do with vain and foolish songs, Eph. *v.* 18, 19. And, in the fulness of their joy, they shall offer abundance of sacrifices to the honour of God, so that *they shall fill both the bowls and the corners of the altar* with the fat and blood of their sacrifices. And, when they thus triumph in their successes, their joy shall terminate in God as their God, the God of their salvation. They shall triumph, (1.) In the love he has for them, and the relation wherein they stand to him, that they are *the flock of his people* and he is their Shepherd, and that they are to him *as the stones of a crown,* which are very precious and of great value, and which are kept under a strong guard. Never was any king so pleased with the jewels of his crown as God is, and will be, with his people, who are near and dear unto him, and in whom he glories. They are a *crown of glory* and a *royal diadem* in his hand, Isa. 62:2, 3. And *they shall be mine, saith the Lord, in that day when I make up my jewels,* Mal. 3:17. And *they shall be lifted up as an ensign upon his land,* as the royal standard is displayed in token of triumph and joy. God's people are his glory; so he is pleased to make them, so he is pleased to reckon them. He sets them up as a banner upon his own land, waging war against those who hate him, to whom it is a flag of defiance, while it is a centre of unity to all that love him, to all the children of God, that are scattered abroad, who are invited to come and enlist themselves under this banner, Isa. 11:10, 12. (2.) In the provision he makes for them, *v.* 15. This is the matter of their triumph (*v.* 17): *For how great is his goodness and how great is his beauty!* This is the substance, this the burden, of the songs wherewith they shall *make a noise* before the Lord. We are here taught, [1.] To admire and praise the amiableness of God's being: *How great is his beauty!* All the perfections of God's nature conspire to make him infinitely lovely in the eyes of all that know him. They are to him as the *stones of a crown;* but what is he to them? Our business in the temple is to *behold the beauty of the Lord* (Ps. 27:4), and *how great is that beauty!* How far does it transcend all other beauties, particularly the *beauty of his holiness.* This may refer to the Messiah, to Zion's *King* that *cometh.* See *that king in his beauty* (Isa. 33:17), who is *fairer than the children of men,* the *fairest of ten thousand,* and *altogether lovely.* Though, in the eye of the world, he had no form or comeliness, in the eye of faith how great is his beauty! [2.] To admire and give thanks for the gifts of God's favour and grace, his bounty as well as his beauty; for *how great is his goodness!* How rich in mercy is he! How deep, how full, are its springs! How various, how plenteous, how precious, are its streams! What a great deal of good does God do! How rich in mercy is he! Here is an instance of his goodness to his people: *Corn shall make the young men cheerful and new wine the maids;* that is, God will bless his people with an abundance of the fruits of the earth. Whereas they had been afflicted with scarcity to such a degree that the *young men* and the *maidens* were ready to swoon and faint away for hunger and thirst (Lam. 2:12, 21; 4:7, 8; 5:10), now they shall have bread enough and to spare, not water only, but *wine, new wine,* which shall make the young people grow and be cheerful, and (which some have observed to be the effect of plenty and the cheapness of corn) the poor will be encouraged to marry, and re-people the land, when they shall have wherewithal to maintain their families. Note, What good gifts God bestows upon us we must serve him cheerfully with, and must race the streams up to the fountain, and, when we are refreshed with corn and wine, must say, *How great is his goodness!*

CHAPTER 10

The scope of this chapter is much the same with that of the foregoing chapter — to encourage the Jews that had returned with hopes that though they had been under divine rebukes for their negligence in rebuilding the temple, and were now surrounded with enemies and dangers, yet God would do them good, and make them prosperous at home and victorious abroad. Now, I. They are here directed to eye the great God in all events that concerned them, and, both in the evils they suffered and in the comforts they desired, to acknowledge his hand (*v.* 1–4). II. They are encouraged to expect strength and success from him in all their struggles with the enemies of their church and state, and to hope that the issue would be glorious at last (*v.* 5–12).

Verses 1–4

Gracious things and glorious ones, very glorious and very gracious, were promised to this poor afflicted people in the foregoing chapter; now here God intimates to them that he will *for these things be enquired of* by them, and that he expects they should acknowledge him in all their ways and in all his ways towards them — and not idols that were rivals with him for their respects.

I. The prophet directs them to apply to God by prayer for rain in the season thereof. He had promised, in the close of the foregoing chapter, that there should be great plenty of corn and wine, whereas for several years, by reason of unseasonable weather, there had been great scarcity of both; but the earth will not yield its fruits unless the heavens water it, and therefore they must look up to God for the *dew of heaven,* in order to the fatness and fruitfulness of the earth (*v.* 1): *"Ask you of the Lord rain.* Do not pray to the clouds, nor to the stars, for rain, but *to the Lord;* for he it is that *hears the heavens,* when they *hear the earth,"* Hos. 2:21. Seasonable rain is a great mercy, which we must *ask of God, rain in the time of the latter rain,* when there is most need of it. The former rain fell at the seed-time, in autumn, the latter fell in the spring, between March and May, which brought the corn to an ear and filled it. If either of these rains failed, it was very bad with that land; for from the end of May to September they never had any rain at all. Jerome, who lived in Judea, says that he never saw any rain there in June or July. They are directed to ask for it *in the time* when it used to come. Note, We must, in our prayers, dutifully attend the course of Providence; we must ask for mercies in their proper time, and not expect that God should go out of his usual way and method for us. But, since sometimes God denied rain in the usual time as a token of his displeasure, they must pray for it then as a token of his favour, and they shall not pray in vain. *Ask and it shall be given you. So the Lord shall make bright clouds* (which, though they are without rain themselves, are yet presages of rain) — *lightnings* (so the margin reads it), for *he maketh lightnings for the rain.* He will *give them showers of rain* in great abundance, and so give to *every one grass in the field;* for God is universally good, and *makes his rain to fall upon the just and the unjust.*

II. He shows them the folly of making their addresses to idols as their fathers had done (*v.* 2): *The idols have spoken vanity;* the teraphim, which they courted and consulted in their distress, were so far from being able to command rain for them that they could not so much as tell them when they should have rain. They pretended to promise them rain at such a time, but it did not come. *The diviners,* who were the prophets of those idols, *have seen a lie* (their visions were all a cheat and a sham); and *they have told false dreams,* such as the event did not answer, which proved that they were not from God. Thus they *comforted in vain* those that consulted the lying oracles; all the *vanities of the heathen* put together could not *give rain,* Jer. 14:22. Yet this was not the worst of it; they not only got nothing by the false gods, but they lost the favour of the true God, for *therefore they went their way* into captivity *as a flock* driven into the fold, and *they were troubled* with one vexation after another, as scattered sheep are, *because there was no shepherd,* no prince to rule them, no priest to intercede for them, none to take care of them and keep them together. Those that wandered after strange gods were made to wander, into strange nations.

III. He shows them the hand of God in all the events that concerned them, both those that made against them and those that made for them, *v.* 3. Let them consider, 1. When every thing went cross it was God that walked contrary to them (*v.* 3): *"My anger was kindled against the shepherds* that should have fed the flock, but neglected it, and starved it. I was displeased at the wicked magistrates and ministers, the idol-shepherds." The captivity in Babylon was a token of God's anger against them; in it likewise he *punished the goats,* those of the flock that were filthy and mischievous; they were set on the left hand, to go away into punishment. Though the body of the nation suffered in the captivity, yet it was only the goats and the shepherds that God was angry with, and that he punished; the same affliction to others came from the love of God, and was but a fatherly chastisement, which to them came from his wrath, and was a judicial punishment. 2. When things began to change for the better it was God that gave them the happy turn. "He has now *visited his flock* with favour, to enquire after them, and provides what he finds proper for them, and he has made them *as his goodly horse in the battle,* has beautified them, taken care of them, managed and made use of them, as a man does the horse he rides on, has made them valuable in themselves and formidable to those about them, *as his goodly horse."* It is God that makes us what we are, and it is with us as he appoints.

IV. He shows them that every creature is to them what God makes it to be (*v.* 4): *Out of him came forth the corner, out of him the nails.* 1. All the power that was engaged against them was from God. *Out of him* came all the combined force of their enemies; every *oppressor together* (and the oppressors of Israel were not a few) did but what his hand and his counsel determined before to be done; nor could they have had such power against them unless it had been given them from above. 2. All the power likewise that was engaged for them was derived from him and depended on him. Out of him came forth *the cornerstone* of the building, the power of magistrates, which keeps the several parts of the state together. Princes are often called the *corners of the people,* as 1 Sa. 14:38, marg. Out of him came forth *the nail* that fixed the state, the *nail in the sure place* (Isa. 22:23), the *nail in his holy place,* Ezra 9:8. Out of him came forth *the battle-bow,* the military power, and out of him *every oppressor,* or exactor, that had the civil power in his hand; and therefore to God, the fountain of power, we must always have an eye, and see every man's judgment proceeding from him.

Verses 5–12

Here are divers precious promises made to the people of God, which look further than to the state of the Jews in the latter days of their church, and have certain reference to the spiritual Israel of God, the gospel-church, and all true believers.

I. They shall have God's favour and presence, and shall be owned and accepted of him. This is the foundation of all the rest: *The Lord is with them, v.* 5. He espouses their cause, takes their part, is on their side; and, if he be for them, who can be against them? Again (*v.* 6), *I have mercy upon them.* All their dignity and joy are owing purely to God's mercy; and mercy, as it supposes misery, so it excludes merit. They had been cast off, the effect of which could not but be misery; they had been justly cast off, and therefore could pretend to merit nothing at God's hand but wrath and the curse; yet it is promised, *They shall be as though I had not cast them off.* The transgressions of their fathers, for which they had been rejected, shall not only not be visited upon them, but shall not be so much as remembered against them. God will be as perfectly reconciled to them as if he had never contended with them, and the falling out of these lovers shall rather be the renewing than the weakening of love. They shall have such a full assurance of God's being reconciled to them, and upon that shall be so well reconciled to themselves, that they shall be as easy as if they had never been cast off; and their condition, after their restoration to the divine favour, shall be so very happy that there shall not remain the least scar from the wounds which were given them by their being cast off. Such favour does God show to returning repenting sinners, who were by nature at a distance, and children of wrath; such fellowship are they admitted into, and such freedom does he use with them, that they are *as though they had never been cast off.* 1. The covenant they are admitted into is the same that ever it was: *I am the Lord their God,* according to the original contract, the covenant made with their fathers. 2. The communion they are admitted into is the same that ever it was: *I will hear them.* They shall be as welcome as ever to speak to him, and as sure as ever to receive from him an answer of peace; for, as he never did, so he never will, say to Jacob's seed, *Seek you me in vain.*

II. They shall be victorious over their enemies, that would draw them from either their duty to God or their comfort in God (*v.* 5): *They shall be as mighty men,* that are both strong in body and bold in spirit, men of vigour, men of valour, effective men. *Those of Ephraim,* as well as those of Judah, shall be *like a mighty man* (*v.* 7), that dares to go about a difficult enterprise and is able to go through with it. They shall, as mighty men, *tread down their enemies in the battle,* as the dirt that is thrown out of the houses is trodden with other dirt *in the mire of the streets.* And *they shall* therefore *fight, because the Lord is with them.* Some would argue that they may *therefore* sit still, and do nothing, because the Lord is with them, who can and will do all. No; God's gracious presence with us to help us must not supersede, but quicken and animate, our endeavours to help ourselves; and we must therefore *work out our salvation with fear and trembling,* because *it is God that works in us both to will and to do.* They shall fight with readiness and resolution because, if God be with them, they are sure to be conquerors, more than conquerors. For then *the riders on horses shall be confounded.* The cavalry of the enemies shall be routed, and put into disorder, by the infantry of the Jews. The preachers of the gospel of Christ went forth to war a good warfare; they charged bravely, because God was with them; and the *riders on horses* that opposed them *were confounded,* for God chose the *weak* and *foolish things of the world to confound the wise and mighty.* But whence have they all this might? How come they to be so able, so active? It is in the Lord, and in the power of his might, that they are so (*v.* 6): *I will strengthen the house of Judah,* and *so I will save the house of Joseph.* Note, God saves us by strengthening us, and works out our happiness by working in us to do our duty. And thus we are engaged to the utmost diligence in using the strength God gives us; and yet, when all is done, God must have the glory of all. God is our strength, and so becomes both our song and our salvation.

III. Those of them that are dispersed shall be gathered together into one body (*v.* 6): *I will bring them again to place them,* bring them from other lands to place them in their own land. This was a token of their being perfectly restored to all their other ancient privileges — they shall be restored to the possession of their own land. This was fulfilled when the *children of God that were scattered abroad* were by faith in Christ incorporated in the gospel-chruch, and Jews and Gentiles became *one fold,* Jn. 10:16. In order to this (*v.* 8) *I will hiss for them,* or, rather, *whistle* for them, as the shepherd with his pipe calls his sheep together, that *know his voice;* and so *I will gather them.* The preaching of the gospel was, as it were, God's hissing for souls to come to Jesus Christ, his calling in his scattered sheep to the green pastures. *I will gather them, for I have redeemed them.* Note, Those whom Christ has redeemed by his blood God will gather by his grace, as a *hen gathers her brood under her wings.* This promise is enlarged upon *v.* 10, *I will bring them again also out of the land of Egypt.* Some think this was literally fulfilled when Ptolemaeus Philadelphus king of Egypt sent 120,000 Jews out of his country into their own land, as was the promise of gathering them out of Assyria by Alexander the son of Antiochus Epiphanes. But it has its spiritual accomplishment in the gathering in of precious souls out of a bondage worse than that in Egypt or Assyria, and the bringing of them into the glorious liberties of the children of God and their enjoyments, which are as the beautiful fruitful pastures in *the land of Gilead and Lebanon.* All the land of promise is theirs, even Gilead, the utmost border of it eastward, and Lebanon, the utmost border northward. But how shall this be? How shall a people so dispersed be got together? How shall those that are set at such a distance from their own country be brought to it again? It is true the difficulties seem insuperable, but they shall be got over as easily, as effectually as those that lay in the way of their deliverance out of Egypt and their entrance into Canaan: *He shall pass through the sea with affliction,* as of old through the Red Sea, to the sore affliction of Pharaoh and his hosts, or to the sore affliction of the sea, the waves whereof *he shall smite,* so that it shall be *driven back,* as when *the sea saw and fled,* Ps. 114:3. And *all the deeps of the river* (all the rivers, though ever so deep) *shall dry up,* as Jordan did, to make way for Israel's passage into that good land which God had given them. Does *the pride of Assyria* stand in the way of their deliverance? He shall give check to it who sets bounds to the *proud waves of the sea,* and it *shall be brought down.* Does the sceptre of Egypt oppose it? That shall *depart away,* so that it shall not be able to obstruct the gathering in of God's Israel when his time shall come for the doing of it. When the gospel-chruch was to be gathered out of all nations by the preaching of the gospel great opposition was given to it by the enraged combined powers of earth and hell. Insuperable difficulties seemed to be in the way of it. But, by a divine power going along with the doctrine of Christ, it became *mighty to the pulling down of strong holds,* and the conversion and salvation of thousands. Then the sea fled, and Jordan was *driven back at the presence of the Lord.*

IV. They shall greatly multiply, and the church, that new world, shall be replenished (*v.* 8): *They shall increase as they have increased* formerly in Egypt, and great additions shall be made to their numbers, as in the days of David and Solomon. When God gathers his redeemed ones to himself they shall help to gather in others with them, and their motion homeward shall be like that of a snow-ball. *Crescit eundo — The further it goes the larger it grows by accretion. I will gather them, and they shall increase.* Note, The church of Christ is a growing body, as long as it is in the present state of minority, till it comes *to the measure of the stature of the fulness of Christ.* There are added to it *daily such as shall be saved.* 1. It shall spread to distant places. It shall fill Canaan, even to the lands of Gilead and Lebanon, so that no more place, no more room, shall be found for it there, *v.* 10. *In Judah* only *God* had been *known,* and his *name was great in Israel* only; here only he revealed his *statutes* and *judgments.* But in gospel-times that place shall be much too strait; the church's tent must be enlarged, and its *cords lengthened:* Then *I will sow them among the people, v.* 9. Their scattering shall be like the scattering of seed in the ground, not to bury it, but to increase it, that it may bring forth much fruit. The Jews are said to be dispersed *into every nation under heaven* (Acts 2:5); and, as it was their troubles that dispersed some of them, so perhaps others transplanted themselves into colonies because the land of Israel was too strait for them; and many were natives of other nations, but proselyted to the Jewish religion. Now these were *sown among the people,* Hos. 2:23. And this contributed very much to the spreading of the gospel. The Jews that came from all parts to worship at Jerusalem fetched thence the gospel light and fire to their own countries, as those Acts 2, and the eunuch, Acts 8. And their own synagogues in the several cities of the Gentiles were the first receptacles of the apostles and their preaching, wherever they came. Thus when God *sowed them among the people,* that they might not get hurt by the Gentiles, but do good to them, he took care that they should *remember him,* and make mention of his name *in far countries;* and, by keeping up the knowledge of God among them as he had revealed himself in the Old Testament, they would be the more ready to admit the knowledge of Christ as he has revealed himself in the New Testament. 2. It shall last to future *ages.* The church shall not be *res unius aetatis — a temporary thing,* but a seed in it shall *serve the Lord, v.* 7. Yea, their children shall see it and be glad; and *they shall live with their children, and turn again, v.* 9. Converts to Christ shall have their children about them, whom they shall teach the knowledge of the Lord, and bring with them when they turn again to the holy land and the way of holiness. It was said to those to whom the gospel was first preached, *The promise is to you and to your children,* Acts 2:39. They shall be *so sown among the people* as never to be extirpated. Christ's family upon earth shall never be extinct, nor his purchased possession lost for want of heirs.

V. God himself will be both their strength and their song. 1. In him they shall be comforted, and shall have abundant satisfaction (*v.* 7): *Their heart shall rejoice as through wine;* for Christ's *love,* which is their joy, is *better than wine.* They shall be *like a mighty man,* and *their heart shall rejoice.* When we resolutely resist, and so overcome, our spiritual enemies, then our hearts shall rejoice. But we ruin our own joy if our resistance be feeble and we yield to the temptations of Satan. Their *heart shall rejoice,* and then they shall be as a *mighty man;* for the *joy of the Lord* will be *our strength.* And with their graces their joys shall be propagated: *Their children shall see it and be glad, and their hearts* also *shall rejoice in the Lord.* It is good to acquaint children betimes with the delights of religion, and to make the services of it as pleasant as may be to them, that, learning betimes to rejoice in the Lord, they may with purpose of heart cleave to him. 2. By him they shall be carried on with vigour, and enlargement of heart, in his service (*v.* 12): *I will strengthen them in the Lord,* strengthen them for their walk and work, as well as for their warfare. It is the God of Israel that *gives strength and power unto his people,* that strengthens all their powers and faculties for spiritual performances, above what they are by nature and against what they are by the corruption of nature. Now observe, (1.) How they are thus enabled and invigorated for their duty: *I* the Lord *will strengthen them in the Lord,* in the *Messiah,* who is *Jehovah our strength,* as well as *Jehovah our righteousness.* Strength is treasured up for us in Christ, and from him it is communicated to us. It is *through Christ strengthening* us that we can *do all things,* and *without him we can do nothing.* His *strength is commanded* him *for this* purpose, Ps. 68:28. (2.) What good use they shall make of this strength given unto them: *They shall walk up and down in his name.* If God strengthen us, we must bestir ourselves, must *walk up and down* in all the duties of the Christian life, must be active and busy in the work of God, must walk up and down as industrious men do, losing no time, and letting slip no opportunity. But still we must *walk up and down in the name of Christ,* must do all by warrant from him and in dependence on him, with an eye to his word as our rule and his glory as our end. To us to live must be Christ; and, *whatever we do in word or deed,* we must *do all in the name of the Lord Jesus,* that we receive not the strengthening grace of God in vain. See Ps. 80:17, 18.

CHAPTER 11

God's prophet, who, in the chapters before, was an ambassador sent to promise peace, is here a herald sent to declare war. The Jewish nation shall recover its prosperity, and shall flourish for some time and become considerable; it shall be very happy, at length, in the coming of the long-expected Messiah, in the preaching of his gospel, and in the setting up of his standard there. But, when thereby the chosen remnant among them are effectually called in and united to Christ, the body of the nation, persisting in unbelief, shall be utterly abandoned and given up to ruin, for rejecting Christ; and it is this that is foretold here in this chapter — the Jews rejecting Christ, which was their measure-filling sin, and the wrath which for that sin came upon them to the uttermost. Here is, I. A prediction of the destruction itself that should come upon the Jewish nation (*v.* 1–3). II. The putting of it into the hands of the Messiah. 1. He is charged with the custody of that flock (*v.* 4–6). 2. He undertakes it, and bears rule in it (*v.* 7, 8). 3. Finding it perverse, he gives it up (*v.* 9), breaks his shepherd's staff (*v.* 10, 11), resents the indignities done him and the contempt put upon him (*v.* 12, 13), and then breaks his other staff (*v.* 14). 4. He turns them over into the hands of foolish shepherds, who, instead of preventing, shall complete their ruin, and both the blind leaders and the blind followers shall fall together into the ditch (*v.* 15–17). This is foretold to the poor of the flock before it comes to pass, that, when it does come to pass, they may not be offended.

Verses 1–3

In dark and figurative expressions, as is usual in the scripture predictions of things at a great distance, that destruction of Jerusalem and of the Jewish church and nation is here foretold which our Lord Jesus, when the time was at hand, prophesied of very plainly and expressly. We have here, 1. Preparation made for that destruction (*v.* 1): *"Open thy doors, O Lebanon!* Thou wouldst not open them to let thy king in — he *came to his own and his own received him not;* now thou must open them to let thy ruin in. Let the gates of the forest, and all the avenues to it, be thrown open, and let the fire come in and devour its glory." Some by Lebanon here understand the temple, which was built of cedars from Lebanon, and the stones of it white as the snow of Lebanon. It was burnt with fire by the Romans, and its gates were forced open by the fury of the soldiers. To confirm this, they tell a story, that forty years before the destruction of the second temple the gates of it opened of their own accord, upon which prodigy Rabbi Johanan made this remark (as it is found in one of the Jewish authors), "Now I know," said he, "that the destruction of the temple is at hand, according to the prophecy of Zechariah, *Open thy doors, O Lebanon! that the fire may devour thy cedars."* Others understand it of Jerusalem, or rather of the whole land of Canaan, to which Lebanon was an inlet on the north. All shall lie open to the invader, and the cedars, the mighty and eminent men, shall be devoured, which cannot but alarm those of an inferior rank, *v.* 2. If *the cedars* have *fallen* (if *all the mighty are spoiled,* and brought to ruin), let the *fir-tree howl.* How can the slender fir-trees stand if stately cedars fall? If cedars are devoured by fire, it is time for the fir-trees to howl; for no wood is so combustible as that of the fir. And let the *oaks of Bashan,* that lie exposed to every injury, *howl, for the forest of the vintage* (or the *flourishing vineyard,* that used to be guarded with a particular care) has come down, or (as some read it) when the *defenced forests,* such as Lebanon was, have come down. Note, The falls of the wise and good into sin, and the falls of the rich and great into trouble, are loud alarms to those that are every way their inferiors not to be secure. 2. Lamentation made for the destruction (*v.* 3): *There is a voice of howling.* Those who have fallen howl for grief and shame, and those who see their own turn coming howl for fear. But the great men especially receive the alarm with the utmost confusion. Those who were roaring in the day of their revels and triumphs are howling in the day of their terrors; *for now they are tormented* more than others. Those great men were by office shepherds, and such should have protected God's flock committed to their charge; it is the duty both of princes and priests. But they were as *young lions,* that made themselves a terror to the flock with their roaring and the flock a prey to themselves with their tearing. Note, It is sad with a people when those who should be as shepherds to them are as young lions to them. But what is the issue? The shepherds *howl,* for *their glory is spoiled.* Their pastures, and the flocks which covered them, which were the glory of the swains, are laid waste. The *young lions howl,* for *the pride of Jordan is spoiled.* The pride of Jordan was the thickets on the banks, in which the lions reposed themselves; and therefore, when the river overflowed and spoiled them, the lions came up from them (as we read Jer. 49:19), and they came up roaring. Note, When those who have power proudly abuse their power, and, instead of being shepherds, are as young lions, they may expect that the righteous God will humble their pride and break their power.

Verses 4–14

The prophet here is made a type of Christ, as the prophet Isaiah sometimes was; and the scope of these verses is to show that *for judgment Christ came into this world* (Jn. 9:39), for judgment to the Jewish church and nation, which were, about the time of his coming, wretchedly corrupted and degenerated by the worldliness and hypocrisy of their rulers. Christ would have healed them, but they would not be healed; they are therefore left desolate, and abandoned to ruin. Observe here,

I. The desperate case of the Jewish church, under the tyranny of their own governors. Their slavery in their own country made them as miserable as their captivity in strange countries had done: *Their possessors slay them and sell them, v.* 5. In Zechariah's time we find the rulers and the nobles justly rebuked for *exacting usury of their brethren;* and the governors, even by their servants, oppressive to the people, Neh. 5:7, 15. In Christ's time the *chief priests* and the *elders,* who were the possessors of the flock, by their traditions, the commandments of men, and their impositions on the consciences of the people, became perfect tyrants, devoured their houses, engrossed their wealth, and fleeced the flock instead of feeding it. The Sadducees, who were deists, corrupted their judgments. The Pharisees, who were bigots for superstition, corrupted their morals, by making void the commandments of God, Mt. 15:16. Thus they slew the sheep of the flock, thus they sold them. They cared not what became of them so they could but gain their own ends and serve their own interests. And, 1. In this they justified themselves: They *slay them* and *hold themselves not guilty.* They think that there is no harm in it, and that they shall never be called to an account for it by the chief Shepherd; as if their power were given them for destruction, which was designed only for edification, and as if, because they sat in Moses's seat, they were not under the obligation of Moses's law, but might dispense with it, and with themselves in the breach of it, at their pleasure. Note, Those have their minds woefully blinded indeed who do ill and justify themselves in doing it; but God will not hold those guiltless who hold themselves so. 2. In this they affronted God, by giving him thanks for the gain of their oppression: They said, *Blessed be the Lord, for I am rich,* as if, because they prospered in their wickedness, got money by it, and raised estates, God had made himself patron of their unjust practices, and Providence had become *particeps criminis — the associate of their guilt.* What is got honestly we ought to give God thanks for, and to bless him whose blessing *makes rich and adds no sorrow with it.* But with what face can we go to God either to beg a blessing upon the unlawful methods of getting wealth or to return him thanks for success in them? They should rather have gone to God to confess the sin, to take shame to themselves for it, and to vow restitution, than thus to mock him by making the gains of sin the gift of God, who *hates robbery for burnt-offerings,* and reckons not himself praised by the thanksgiving if he be dishonoured either in the getting or the using of that which we give him thanks for. 3. In this they put contempt upon the people of God, as unworthy their regard or compassionate consideration: *Their own shepherds pity them not;* they make them miserable, and then do not commiserate them. Christ had *compassion on the multitude because they fainted and were scattered abroad, as if they had no shepherd* (as really they had worse than none); but *their own shepherds pitied them not,* nor showed any concern for them. Note, It is ill for a church when its pastors have no tenderness, no compassion for precious souls, when they can look upon the ignorant, the foolish, the wicked, the weak, without pity.

II. The sentence of God's wrath passed upon them for their senselessness and stupidity in this condition. There was a general decay, nay, a destruction, of religion among them, and it was all one to them; they regarded it not. *My people love to have it so,* Jer. 5:31. Though they were *oppressed and broken in judgment,* yet they *willingly walked after the commandment,* Hos. 5:11. And, as their shepherds pitied them not, so they did not bemoan themselves; therefore God says (*v.* 6), *"I will no more pity the inhabitants of the land.* They have courted their own destruction, and so let their doom be." But those are truly miserable whom the God of mercy himself will no more have compassion upon. Those who are willing to have their consciences oppressed by those who *teach for doctrines the commandments of men* (as the Jews were, who called those *Rabbi, Rabbi,* that did so, Mt. 15:9; 23:7), are often punished by oppression in their civil interests, and justly, for those forfeit their own rights who tamely give up God's rights. The Jews did so; the Papists do so; and who can pity them if they be ruled with rigour? God here threatens them, 1. That he will deliver them into the hand of oppressors, *every one into his neighbour's hand,* so that they shall use one another barbarously. The several parties in Jerusalem did so; the *zealots,* the *seditious,* as they were called, committed greater outrages than the common enemy did, as Josephus relates in his history of the wars of the Jews. They shall be delivered every one *into the hand of his king,* that is, the Roman emperor, whom they chose to submit to rather than to Christ, saying, *We have no king but Caesar.* Thus they thought to ingratiate themselves with their lords and masters. But for this God brought the Romans upon them, who *took away their place and nation.* 2. That he will not deliver them out of their hands: *They shall smite the land,* the whole land, and *out of their hand I will not deliver them;* and, if the Lord do not help them, none else can, nor can they help themselves.

III. A trial yet made whether their ruin might be prevented by sending Christ among them as a shepherd; God had sent his servants to them in vain, *but last of all he sent unto them his Son, saying, They will reverence my Son,* Mt. 21:37. Divers of the prophets had spoken of him as the *Shepherd of Israel,* Isa. 40:11; Eze. 34:23. he himself told the Pharisees that he was the *Shepherd of the sheep,* and that those who pretended to be shepherds were *thieves and robbers* (Jn. 10:1, 2, 11), apparently referring to this passage, where we have, 1. The charge he received from his Father to try what might be done with this flock (*v.* 4): *Thus saith the Lord my God* (Christ called his Father *his God* because he acted in compliance with his will and with an eye to his glory in his whole undertaking), *Feed the flock of the slaughter.* The Jews were God's flock, but they were *the flock of slaughter,* for their enemies had killed them all the day long and *accounted them as sheep for the slaughter;* their own *possessors slew them,* and God himself had doomed them to the slaughter. Yet *"feed them* by reproof instruction, and comfort; provide wholesome food for those who have so long been soured with the leaven of the scribes and Pharisees." *Other sheep he had, which were not of this fold,* and which afterwards must be *brought;* but he is first *sent to the lost sheep of the house of Israel,* Mt. 15:24. 2. His acceptance of this charge, and his undertaking pursuant to it, *v.* 7. He does as it were say, *Lo, I come to do thy will, O my God!* and, since this is thy will, it is mine: *I will feed the flock of slaughter.* Christ will care for these lost sheep; he will go about among them, *teaching* and *healing even you, O poor of the flock!* Christ did not neglect the meanest, nor overlook them for their meanness. The shepherds that made a prey of them regarded not the poor; they were conversant with those only that they could get by; but Christ preached his gospel *to the poor,* Mt. 11:5. It was an instance of his humiliation that his converse was mostly with the inferior sort of people; his disciples, who were his constant attendants, were of the poor of the flock. 3. His furnishing himself with tools proper for the charge he had undertaken: I *took unto me two staves,* pastoral staves; other shepherds have but one crook, but Christ had two, denoting the double care he took of his flock, and what he did both for the souls and for the bodies of men. David speaks of God's *rod* and his *staff* (Ps. 23:4), a correcting rod and a supporting staff. One of these staves was called *Beauty,* denoting the temple, which is called *the beauty of holiness* and one of its gates *beautiful,* which Christ called his Father's house, and for which he showed a great zeal when he cleared it of the *buyers and sellers;* the other he called *Bands,* denoting their civil state, and the incorporate society of that nation, which Christ also took care of by preaching love and peace among them. Christ, in his gospel, and in all he did among them, consulted the advancement both of their civil and of their sacred interests. 4. His execution of his office, as the chief Shepherd. *He fed the flock* (*v.* 7), and he displaced those under-shepherds that were false to their trust (*v.* 8): *Three shepherds I cut off in one month.* Through the deficiency and uncertainty of the history of the Jewish church, in its latter ages, we know not what particular event this had its accomplishment in; in general, it seems to be an act of power and justice for the punishment of the sinful shepherds and the redress of the grievances of the abused flock. Some understand it of the three orders of princes, priests, and scribes or prophets, who, when Christ had finished his work, were laid aside for their unfaithfulness. Others understand it of the three sects among the Jews, of Pharisees, Sadducees, and Herodians, all whom Christ silenced in dispute (Mt. 22) and soon after *cut off,* all in a little time.

IV. Their enmity to Christ, and making themselves odious to him. He came to his own, the sheep of his own pasture; it might have been expected that between them and him there would be an entire affection, as between the shepherd and his sheep; but they conducted themselves so ill that *his soul loathed them,* was *straitened* towards them (so it may be read); he intended them kindness, but could not do them the kindness he intended them, *because of their unbelief,* Mt. 13:58. He was disappointed in them, discouraged concerning them, *grieved* for them, not only for the shepherds, whom he cut off, but for the people, whom Christ often looked upon with grief in his heart and tears in his eyes. Their provocations even wore out his patience, and he was weary of that *faithless and perverse generation. Their soul also it abhorred me;* and therefore it was that his soul loathed them; for, whatever estrangement there is between God and man, it begins on man's side. The Jewish shepherds rejected this chief Shepherd, as the Jewish builders rejected this chief corner stone. They *had indignation* at Christ's doctrine and miracles, and his interest in the people, to whom they did all they could to render him odious, as they had made themselves odious to him. Note, There is a mutual enmity between God and wicked people; they are hateful to God and haters of God. Nothing speaks more the sinfulness and misery of an unregenerate state than this does. The carnal mind, the friendship of the world, are enmity to God, and God hates all the workers of iniquity; and it is easy to foresee what this will end in, if the quarrel be not taken up in time, Isa. 27:4, 5.

V. Christ's rejecting them as incurable, and leaving them their house desolate, Mt. 23:38. The things of their peace are now hidden from their eyes, because they knew not the day of their visitation. Here we have,

1. The sentence of their rejection passed (*v.* 9): *"Then said I, I will not feed you.* I will take no further care of you; *you shall not see me again;* take your own course. As I will not feed you, so I will not cure you; *that that dieth, let it die* (the Shepherd will do nothing to save its forfeited life); *that that is to be cut off, let it be cut off;* that which will make itself a prey to the wolf, let it be a prey, and let the rest so far forget their own mild and gentle nature as to *eat the flesh of one another;* let these sheep fight like dogs." Those that reject Christ will be certainly and justly rejected by him, and then are miserable of course.

2. A sign of it given (*v.* 10): *I took my staff, even Beauty, and cut it asunder,* in token of this, that he would be no longer a shepherd to them, as the lord high steward determines his commission by breaking his white staff, and as Moses's breaking the tables of the law put a stop, for the present, to the treaty between God and Israel. The breaking of this staff signified the breaking of God's covenant which he had *made with all the people,* the covenant of peculiarity made with all the tribes of *Israel,* and all other people who, by being proselyted to their religion, were incorporated into their nation. The Jewish church was now stripped of all its glory; its crown was profaned and cast to the ground, and all its honour laid in the dust; for God departed from it, and would no more own it for his. When Christ told them plainly that the *kingdom of God* should be *taken from them,* and *given to another people,* then be broke the *staff of Beauty,* Mt. 21:43. And *it was broken in that day,* though Jerusalem and the Jewish nation held up forty years longer, yet from that day we may reckon the staff of Beauty broken, *v.* 11. And though the great men did not, or would not, understand it as a divine sentence, but thought to put it by with a cold *God forbid* (Lu. 20:16), yet the *poor of the flock,* the disciples of Christ, that *waited on him,* and understood with what authority he spoke, and could distinguish the voice of their Shepherd from that of a stranger, *knew that it was the word of the Lord,* and trembled at it, and were confident that it should not fall to the ground. Note, Christ is waited on by the poor of the flock; he chose them to be with him, to be his pupils, to be his witnesses; the poor received him and his gospel, when those that had great possessions turned their backs upon him. And those that wait upon Christ, that sit at his feet, to hear and receive his words, shall *know of the doctrine whether it be of God,* Jn. 7:17.

3. A further reason given for their rejection. It was said before, *Their souls abhorred him;* and here we have an instance of it, their buying and selling him for thirty pieces of silver, either thirty Roman pence, or rather thirty Jewish shekels; this is here foretold in somewhat obscure expressions, as it is fit that such particular prophecies should be delivered, lest otherwise the plainness of the prophecy might prevent the accomplishment of it. Here, (1.) The Shepherd comes to them for his wages (*v.* 12): *"If you think good, give me my price;* you are weary of me, pay me off and discharge me; *and, if not, forbear;* if you be willing to continue me longer in your service, I will continue, or, if to turn me off without wages, I am content." Christ was no hireling, and yet the labourer is worthy of his hire. Compare with this what Christ said to Judas when he was going to sell him, *"What thou doest do quickly;* be at a word with the chief priests; let them either take the bargain or leave it," Jn. 13:27. Those that betray Christ are not forced to it; they might have chosen. (2.) They value him at *thirty pieces of silver.* Many years' service he had done them as a Shepherd, yet this is all they will now turn him off with — *"A goodly price that I* with all my care and pains *was valued at by them."* If Judas fixed this sum in his demand, it is observable that his name was *Judah,* the same name with that of the body of the people, for it was a national act; or, if (as it rather seems) the chief priests pitched upon this sum in their proffers, they were the representatives of the people; it was part of the priest's office to *put a value* upon the *devoted things* (Lev. 27:8), and thus they valued the Lord Jesus. it was the ordinary price of a slave, Ex. 21:32. Making light of Christ, and undervaluing the love of that great and good Shepherd, are the ruin of multitudes, and justly so. (3.) The silver being no way proportionable to his worth, it is *thrown to the potter* with disdain: "Let him take it to buy clay with, or for any use that a little money will serve to, for it is not worth hoarding; it may be enough for a potter's stock, but not for the pay of such a shepherd, much less for his purchase." So the prophet *cast the thirty pieces of silver to the potter in the house of the Lord:* "Let him take them, and do what he will with them." Now we find a particular accomplishment of this in the history of Christ's sufferings, and reference is had to this prophecy, Mt. 27:9, 10. *Thirty pieces of silver* was the very sum for which Christ was sold to the chief priests; the money, when Judas would not keep it, and the chief priests would not take it back was laid out in the purchase of *the potter's field.* Even that sudden resolve of the chief priests was according to an ancient prophecy and the more ancient counsel and foreknowledge of God.

4. The completing of their rejection in the cutting asunder of the other staff, *v.* 14. The former denoted the ruin of their church, by breaking the covenant between God and them — that defaced their *beauty;* this denotes the ruin of their state, by breaking the brotherhood between Judah and Israel, by reviving animosities and contention among them, such as were of old between Judah and Israel, the writing of whom as *one stick in the hand of the Lord* was one of the blessings promised after their return out of captivity, Eze. 37:19. But that union shall now be dissolved; they shall be crumbled into parties and factions, exasperated one against another; and their kingdom, being thus divided, shall be *brought to desolation.* (1.) Nothing ruins a people so certainly, so inevitably, as the breaking of *the staff of Bands,* and the weakening of the brotherhood among them; for hereby they become an easy prey to the common enemy. (2.) This follows upon the dissolving of the covenant between God and them, and the decay of religion among them. When iniquity abounds love waxes cold. No wonder if those fall out among themselves that have provoked God to fall out with them. When the staff of Beauty is broken the staff of Bands will not hold long. An unchurched people will soon be an undone people.

Verses 15–17

God, having shown the misery of this people in their being justly abandoned by the good Shepherd, here shows their further misery in being shamefully abused by a foolish shepherd. The prophet is himself to personate and represent this pretended shepherd (*v.* 15): *Take unto thee the instruments* or accoutrements *of a foolish shepherd,* that are no way fit for the business, such a shepherd's coat, and bag, and staff, as a foolish shepherd would appear in; for such a shepherd shall be set over them (*v.* 16), who, instead of protecting them, shall oppress them and do them mischief. 1. They shall be under the inspection of unfaithful ministers. Their scribes, and priests, and doctors of their law, shall bind heavy burdens upon them, and grievous to be borne, and, with their traditions imposed, shall make the ceremonial law much more a yoke than God had made it. The description here given of the foolish shepherd suits very well with the character Christ gives of the scribes and Pharisees, Mt. 23:2. They shall be under the tyranny of unmerciful princes, that shall rule them with rigour, and make their own land as much a house of bondage to them as ever Egypt or Babylon was. When they had rejected him *by whom princes decree justice* it was just that they should be turned over to those who *decree unrighteous decrees.* 3. They shall be imposed upon and deluded by false Christs and false prophets, as our Saviour foretold, Mt. 24:5. Many such there were, who by their seditious practices provoked the Romans, and hastened the ruin of the Jewish nation; but it is observable that they were never cheated by a counterfeit Messiah till they had refused and rejected the true Messiah. Now observe,

I. What a curse this foolish shepherd should be to the people, *v.* 16. God will, for their punishment, *raise up a* foolish *shepherd,* who will not do the duty of a shepherd; he will not *visit those that are cut off,* nor go after those that go astray, nor seek those that are missing, to find them out and bring them home, as the good shepherd does, Mt. 18:12, 13. Their shepherds take no care of the *young ones,* that need their care and are well worthy of it, as Christ does, Isa. 40:11. They do not *heal that* which was *broken,* which was worried and torn, but let it die of its bruises, when a little thing, in time, would have saved it. They do not *feed* those who, through weakness, *stand still,* and are ready to faint, and cannot get forward, but leave them behind, let who will take them up; they do not *carry* that which *stands still* (so some read it); they never do any thing to *support the weak* and comfort the *feeble-minded;* but, on the contrary, 1. They are luxurious themselves: They *eat of the flesh of the fat;* they will have of the best for themselves; and, like that *wicked servant* that said, *My lord delays his coming,* they *eat and drink with the drunken,* and *serve their own bellies.* 2. They are barbarous to the flock. Their passions are as ill-governed as their appetites, for, when they are in a rage against any of the flock, they *tear their* very *claws in pieces* by over-driving them; they beat their hoofs; they *smite their fellow servants. Woe unto thee, O land! when thy king is* such *a child!*

II. What a curse this foolish shepherd should bring upon himself (*v.* 17): *Woe to the idol-shepherd,* who, like an idol, has eyes and sees not, who, like an idol, receives abundance of respect and homage from the people and the chief of their offerings, but neither can nor will do them any kindness. He *leaves the flock* when they most need his care, leaves them destitute, and flees, *because he is a hireling;* his doom is that *the sword* of God's justice shall be *upon his arm* and *his right eye,* so that he shall quite lose the use of both. *His arm shall* wither and *be dried up,* so that he who would not help his friends when it was required shall not know how to help himself; *his right eye shall be utterly darkened,* that he shall not discern the danger that his flock is in, nor know which way to look for relief. This was fulfilled when Christ said to the Pharisees, *I have come that those who see may be made blind,* Jn. 9:39. Those that have gifts which qualify them to do good, if they do not do good with them, shall be deprived of them; those that should have been workmen, but were slothful and would do nothing, will justly have their arm dried up; and those that should have been watchmen, but were sleepy and would never look about them, will justly have their eye blinded.

CHAPTER 12

The apostle (Gal. 4:25, 26) distinguishes between "Jerusalem which now is, and is in bondage with her children" — the remaining carcase of the Jewish church that rejected Christ, and "Jerusalem that is from above, that is free, and is the mother of us all" — the Christian church, the spiritual Jerusalem, which God has chosen to put his name there; in the foregoing chapter we read the doom of the former, and left that carcase to be a prey to the eagles that should be gathered to it. Now, in this chapter, we have the blessings of the latter, many precious promises made to the gospel-Jerusalem by him who (*v.* 1) declares his power to make them good. It is promised, I. That the attempts of the church's enemies against her shall be to their own ruin, and they shall find that it is at their peril if they do her any hurt (*v.* 2–4, 6). II. That the endeavours of the church's friends and patrons for her good shall be pious, regular, and successful (*v.* 5). III. That God will protect and strengthen the meanest and weakest that belong to his church, and work salvation for them (*v.* 7, 8). IV. That as a preparative for all this mercy, and a pledge of it, he will pour upon them a spirit of prayer and repentance, the effect of which shall be universal and very particular (*v.* 9–14). These promises were of use then to the pious Jews that lived in the troublous times under Antiochus, and other persecutors and oppressors; and they are still to be improved in every age for the directing of our prayers and the encouraging of our hopes with reference to the gospel-church.

Verses 1–8

Here is, I. The title of this charter of promises made to God's Israel; it is the *burden of the word of the Lord,* a divine prediction; it is of weight in the delivery of it; it is to be pressed upon people, and will be very pressing in the accomplishment of it; it is a *burden,* a heavy burden, to all the church's enemies, like that *talent of lead, ch. v.* 7, 8. But it is *for Israel;* it is for their comfort and benefit. As even the *fiery law* (Deu. 33:2), so the fiery prophecies and fiery providences that come from God's right hand, come for them; the word that speaks terror to their enemies speaks peace to them, as the pillar of cloud and fire, which turned a bright side towards the Israelites, to direct and encourage them, but a black side towards the Egyptians, to terrify and dispirit them. Happy are those that have even the burdens of God's word for them, as well as the blessings of it.

II. The title of him that grants this charter, which is prefixed to it to show that he has both authority to make these promises and ability to make them good, for he is the Creator of the world and our Creator, and therefore has an incontestable irresistible dominion. 1. He *stretches out the heavens;* not only he did so at the first, when he said, *Let there be a firmament,* and he *made the firmament,* but he does so still; he keeps them stretched out *like a curtain,* keeps them from running in, and will do so till the end come, when *the heavens shall be rolled together as a scroll.* No bounds can be set to his power who stretches out the heavens, nor can any thing be too hard for him. 2. He *lays the foundation of the earth,* and keeps it firm and fixed on its own basis, or rather on its own axis, though it is *founded on the seas* (Ps. 24:1, 2), nay, though it is *hung upon nothing,* Job 26:7. The founder of this earth is no doubt the ruler of it, and judges in it, and those deceive themselves who say, *The Lord has forsaken the earth,* for, if he had, it would have sunk, since it is he that not only did lay its foundations at first, but does still lay them, still uphold them. 3. He *forms the spirit of man within him.* He *made us these souls,* Jer. 38:16. He not only breathed into the first man, but still breathes into every man the breath of life; the body is derived from the *fathers of our flesh,* but the soul is infused by the *Father of spirits,* Heb. 12:9. He *fashions men's hearts;* they are *in his hand,* and he turns them *as the rivers of water,* and casts them into what mould he pleases, so as to serve his own purposes with them; and he can therefore save his church by inspiriting his friends and dispiriting his enemies, and will eternally save all his chosen by forming their spirits anew.

III. The promises themselves that are here made them, by which the church shall be secured, and in which all its friends may enjoy a holy security.

1. It is promised that, whatever attacks the enemies of the church may make upon her purity or peace, they will certainly issue in their own confusion. The enemies of God and of his kingdom bear a great deal of malice and ill-will to Jerusalem, and form designs for its destruction; but it will prove, at last, that they are but preparing ruin for themselves; Jerusalem is in safety, and those are in all the danger who fight against it. This is here illustrated by three comparisons: —

(1.) *Jerusalem* shall be *a cup of trembling* to all that lay siege to it, *v.* 2. They promise themselves that it shall be to them a cup of wine, which they shall easily and with pleasure drink off, and they thirst for its spoils, nay, they thirst for its blood, as for such a cup; but it shall prove a *cup of slumber,* nay, a *cup of poison,* to them, which, when they take it into their hands, and think it is all their own, they shall not be able to drink off: the fumes of it shall give them enough. When *the kings were assembled* against her, and saw how *God was known in her palaces for a refuge,* they *trembled and hasted away; fear took hold upon them,* as we find, Ps. 48:3–6. Thus Alexander the Great was struck with amazement when he met Jaddus the high priest, and was deterred thereby from offering any violence to Jerusalem. When Sennacherib laid siege *against Judah* and *Jerusalem* he found them such a cup of stupifying wine as laid all his mighty men asleep, Ps. 76:5, 6. Some read it, *I will make Jerusalem a post of contrition* or *breaking.* Those that make any attempts upon Jerusalem do but run their heads against a post, which they cannot move, but are sure to hurt themselves. The *blast of the terrible ones* is *as a storm against the wall* (Isa. 25:4), broken by it, but not shaking it. God's church is a cup of consolation to all her friends (Isa. 66:11), but a cup of trembling to all that would either debauch her by errors and corruptions or destroy her by wars and persecutions. See Isa. 51:22, 23.

(2.) *Jerusalem* shall be *a burdensome stone* to all that attempt to remove it or carry it away, *v.* 3. All *the people of the earth* are here supposed to be *gathered together against it,* some one time and some another; there has been a succession of enemies, from age to age, making war upon the church. But though they were all at once in a confederacy against it, and had formed a resolution to *cut off the name of Israel, that it should be no more in remembrance* (Ps. 83:4), they will find it a task too hard for them. Those that are for keeping up and advancing the kingdom of sin in the world look upon Jerusalem, even the church of God, as the great obstacle to their designs, and they must have it out of the way; but they will find it heavier than they think it is; so that, [1.] They cannot remove it. God will have a church in the world, in spite of them; it is *built upon a rock,* and is as *Mount Zion, that abides for ever,* Ps. 125:1. This *stone, cut out of the mountain without hands,* will not only keep its ground, but fill the earth, Dan. 2:35. Nay, [2.] It will *break in pieces all that burden themselves* with it, as that stone *smote the image,* Dan. 2:45. All that think themselves a match for it shall be *cut in pieces* by it. Some think it is an allusion to a sport which Jerome, upon this place, says was in use among the Jews, as among us: young men tried their strength, and strove for mastery, by heaving up great stones, which, if they proved too heavy for them, fell upon them, and bruised them. Those that make a jest of religion, and banter sacred things, will find them a burdensome stone, that it is ill-jesting with edged-tools, and though they make light of it (saying, *Am not I in sport?*) they bring upon themselves an insupportable sinking load of guilt. Our Saviour seems to allude to these words when he speaks of himself as a burdensome stone to those that will not have him for their foundation-stone, which shall *fall upon them and grind them to powder,* Mt. 21:44.

(3.) The governors of Judah shall be among their enemies like *a hearth of fire among the wood, and a torch of fire in a sheaf, v.* 6. Not that their own passions shall make them incendiaries and firebrands to all about them; no; Zion's King is *meek and lowly,* and all subordinate governors must be like him; but God's justice will make them avengers of his cause, and theirs, upon their enemies. Those that contend with them will find it is like an opposition given by briers and thorns to a consuming fire, Isa. 27:4. It will go through them, and burn them together. It is God's wrath, and not theirs, that is the fire which devours the adversaries. God's fire is said to be *in Zion,* and *his furnace in Jerusalem.* Isa. 31:9. The enemies thought to be as water to this fire, to extinguish it and put it quite out; but God will make them as wood, nay, as a sheaf of corn (which is more combustible), to this fire, not only to be consumed by it, but to be made thereby to burn the more strongly. When God would make Abimelech and the men of Shechem one another's destroyers fire is said to *come out from the one to devour the other,* Jdg. 9:20. So here, Fire shall come out from the *governors of Judah* to *devour all the people round about,* as from the mouth of God's witnesses to consume those who offer to hurt them, Rev. 11:5. The persecutors of the primitive church found this fulfilled in it, witness Lactantius's history of God's judgments upon the primitive persecutors, and the confession of Julian the apostate at last. *Thou hast overcome me, O thou Galilean!* The church's motto may be, *Nemo me impune lacesset — He that assails me does it at his peril. If you are weary of your life, persecute the Christians,* was once a proverb.

2. It is promised that God will infatuate the counsels and enfeeble the courage of the church's enemies (*v.* 4): *"In that day,* when the people of the earth are gathered together against Jerusalem, *I will smite every horse with astonishment, and his rider with madness;"* and again, *"I will smite every horse of the people with blindness,* so that they shall be no way serviceable to them; blinding the horses will be as bad as houghing them." The horses and their horsemen shall both forget the military exercise to which they were trained, and, instead of keeping ranks and observing the rules of their discipline, they shall both grow mad, and ruin themselves. The church's infantry shall be too hard for the enemy's cavalry; and those who were upbraided with trusting in horses shall be baffled by those who were forbidden to multiply horses.

3. It is promised that Jerusalem shall be re-peopled and replenished (*v.* 6): *Jerusalem shall be inhabited again in her own place, even in Jerusalem.* The natives of Jerusalem shall not incorporate in a colony in some other country, and build a city there, and call that *Jerusalem,* and see the promises fulfilled in that, as those in New England called their towns by the names of towns in Old England. No; they shall have a new Jerusalem upon the same foundation, the same spot of ground, with the old one. They had so after their return out of captivity, but this was to have its full accomplishment in the gospel-church, which is a Jerusalem inhabited *in its own place;* for, the gospel being to be preached to all the world, it may call every place its own.

4. It is promised that the inhabitants of Jerusalem shall be enabled to defend themselves, and yet shall be taken under the divine protection, *v.* 8. See here in what method God preserves his church, and those that are his, from the gates of hell to and through the gates of heaven. (1.) He does himself secure them: *In that day shall the Lord defend the inhabitants of Jerusalem,* not only Jerusalem itself from being taken and destroyed, but every inhabitant of it from being any way damaged. God will not only be a *wall of fire* about the city, to fortify that, but he will encompass particular persons with his favour *as with a shield,* so that no dart of the besiegers shall touch them. (2.) He does it by giving them strength and courage to help themselves. What God works in his people by his grace contributes more to their preservation and defence than what he works for them by his providence. *The God of Israel gives strength and power to his people,* that they may do their part, and then he will not be wanting to do his. it is the glory of God to strengthen the weak, that most need his help, that see and own their need of it, and will be the most thankful for it. [1.] In that day the feeblest of the inhabitants of Jerusalem *shall be as David,* shall be men of war, as bold and brave, as skilful and strong, as David himself, shall attempt and accomplish great things, as David did, and become as serviceable to Jerusalem in guarding it as David himself was in founding it, and as formidable as he was to the enemies of it. See what divine grace does; it makes children not only men, but champions, makes weak saints to be not only good soldiers, but great soldiers, like David. And see how God often does his own work as easily and effectually, and more to his own glory, by weak and obscure instruments than by the most illustrious. [2.] *The house of David shall be as God,* that is, *as the angel of the Lord, before them.* Zerubbabel was now the top-branch of the house of David; he shall be endued with wisdom and grace for the service to which he is called, and shall go before the people as an angel, as that angel (so some think) which went before the people of Israel through the wilderness, which was God himself, Ex. 23:20. God will increase the gifts and abilities both of the people and princes, in proportion to the respective services for which they are designed. It was said of David that he was *as an angel of God, to discern good and bad,* 2 Sa. 14:17. Such shall the house of David now be. The inhabitants of Jerusalem shall be as strong and fit for action as nature made David, and their magistrates as wise and fit for counsel as grace made him. But this was to have its full accomplishment in Christ; now the house of David looked little and mean, and its glory was eclipsed, but in Christ the house of David shone more brightly than ever, and its countenance was as that of an angel; in him it became more blessed, and more a blessing, than ever it had been.

5. It is promised that there shall be a very good understanding between the city and the country, and that the balance shall be kept even between them; there shall be no mutual envies or jealousies between them; they shall not keep up any separate interests, but shall heartily unite in their counsels, and act in concert for the common good;

and this happy agreement between the city and the country, the head and the body, is very necessary to the health, welfare, and safety of any nation. (1.) *The governors of Judah,* the magistrates and gentry of the country, shall think honourably of the citizens, *the inhabitants of Jerusalem,* the merchants and tradesmen; they shall not run them down, and contrive how to keep them under, but they *shall say in their hearts,* not in compliment but in sincerity, *The inhabitants of Jerusalem shall be my strength,* the strength of my country, of my family, *in the Lord of hosts their God, v.* 5. They will therefore, upon all occasions, pay respect and deference to Jerusalem, as the mother-city, the ruling-city, and the city that is to be first served, because they look upon it to be the bulwark of the nation and its strongest fortification in times of public danger and distress, which therefore they would all come in to the assistance of and come under the protection of, and this not so much because it was a rich city, and money is the sinews of war, nor because it was a populous city and could bring the greatest numbers into the field, nor because its inhabitants were generally the most ingenious active men, the best soldiers and the best commanders *(of Zion it shall be said, This and that* brave *man were born there),* but because it was a *holy city,* where God's house and household, the temple and the priests, were, where his worship was kept up and his feasts were observed, and because it should now be more than ever a praying city, for *upon the inhabitants of Jerusalem* God will *pour a spirit of supplication* (*v.* 10); therefore the governors of Judah shall say, *These are my strength;* they are so upon the account of their relation to, their interest in, and their communion with, *the Lord of hosts, their God.* Because *the Lord of hosts* is in a particular manner *their God* (for *in Salem is his tabernacle and his dwelling-place in Zion),* therefore *they shall be my strength.* Note, It is well with a kingdom when its great men know how to value its good men, when its governors look upon religion and religious people to be their strength, and consider it their interest to support them, and learn to call godly praying people, and skilful faithful ministers, *the chariots and horsemen of Israel,* as Joash called Elisha, and not the troublers of the land, as Ahab called Elijah. (2.) The court and the city shall not despise, nor look with contempt upon, the inhabitants of the country; no, not the meanest of them, much less upon the governors of Judah; for God will put signal honour upon Judah, and so save them from the contempt of their brethren. As Jerusalem was dignified by special ordinances, so Judah shall be dignified with special providences. God says (*v.* 4), *I will open my eyes upon the house of Judah,* upon the poor country people. Proud men scornfully overlook them, but the great God will graciously look upon them and look after them. Nay, (*v.* 7), *the Lord shall save the tents of Judah first.* Those that dwell in tents lie most exposed; but God will remarkably protect and deliver them before those that dwell in Jerusalem. He will appear glorious in what he does for the *inhabitants of his villages in Israel,* Jdg. 5:11. Thus, in the mystical body, God *gives more abundant honour to that part which lacked, that there may be no schism in the body* (see 1 Co. 12:22–25), which is the reason here given why *the glory of the house of David,* which has great power, and *the glory of the inhabitants of Jerusalem,* who have great wealth, and both which live in great pomp and pleasure, *may not magnify themselves against Judah* and the *tents of Judah,* the dwellers in which work hard, and fare hard, and perhaps are not so well bred. Note, Courtiers and citizens ought not to despise country people, nor look with disdain upon those whom God *opens his eyes upon* and who are *first saved,* while it is so hard for the rich and great to *enter the kingdom of God.* If God by his grace has magnified the dwellers in the tents of Judah, having chosen the weak and foolish things of the world and chosen to employ them, we affront him if we vilify them, or magnify ourselves against them, Jam. 2:5, 6. This promise has a further reference to the gospel-church, in which no difference shall be made between high and low, rich and poor, bond and free, circumcision and uncircumcision, but all shall be alike welcome to Christ, and partake of his benefits, Col. 3:11. Jerusalem shall not then be thought, as it had been, more holy than other parts of the land of Israel.

Verses 9–14

The *day* here spoken of is the day of Jerusalem's defence and deliverance, that glorious day when God will appear for the salvation of his people, which, if it do refer to the successes which the Jews had against their enemies in the time of the Maccabees, yet certainly looks further, to the *gospel-day,* to Christ's victories over the powers of darkness and the great salvation he has wrought for his chosen. Now we have here an account of two remarkable works designed *in that day.*

I. A glorious work of God to be wrought for his people: *"I will seek to destroy all the nations that come against Jerusalem, v.* 9. Nations come against Jerusalem, many and mighty nations; but they shall all be destroyed, their power shall be broken, and their attempts baffled; the mischief they intend shall return upon their own head." God will seek to destroy them, not as if he were at a loss for ways and means to bring it about (Infinite Wisdom was never nonplussed), but his seeking to do it intimates that he is very earnest and intent upon it (he is jealous for Zion with great jealousy, and has the *day of vengeance* in his heart) and that he overrules means and instruments, and all the motions and operations of second causes, in order to it. He is *framing evil* against them; when he seems to be setting them up he is seeking to destroy them. In Christ's first coming, he *sought to destroy him that had the power of death,* and did destroy him, bruised the serpent's head, and broke all the *powers of darkness* that fought against God's kingdom among men and against the faithful friends and subjects of that kingdom; he *spoiled* them, and *made a show of them openly.* In his second coming, he will complete their destruction, when he shall *put down all* opposing *rule, principality, and power,* and *death* itself shall be *swallowed up in* that *victory. The last enemy shall be destroyed* of all that *fought against Jerusalem.*

II. A gracious work of God to be wrought in his people, in order to the work that is to be wrought for them. When he seeks to destroy their enemies he will *pour upon them the Spirit of grace and supplication.* Note, When God intends great mercy for his people the first thing he does is to set them a praying; thus he seeks to destroy their enemies by stirring them up to seek to him that he would do it for them; because, though he has proposed it and promised it, and it is for his own glory to do it, yet he will *for this be enquired of by the house of Israel,* Eze. 36:37. *Ask, and it shall be given.* This honour will he have to himself, and this honour will he put upon prayer and upon praying people. And it is a happy presage to the distressed church of deliverance approaching, and is, as it were, the dawning of its day, when his people are stirred up to cry mightily to him for it. But this promise has reference to, and is performed in, the graces of the Spirit given to all believers, as that Isa. 44:3, *I will pour my Spirit upon thy seed,* which was fulfilled when *Jesus was glorified,* Jn. 7:39. It is a promise of the Spirit, and with him of all *spiritual blessings in heavenly things by Christ.* Now observe here,

1. On whom these blessings are poured out. (1.) *On the house of David,* on the great men; for they are no more, and no better, than the grace of God makes them. It was promised (*v.* 8) that *the house of David* should be *as the angel of the Lord.* Now, in order to that, the Spirit of grace is poured upon them; for the more the saints have of the Spirit of grace the more like they are to the holy angels. When God was about to appear for the land, he poured his Spirit of grace upon the house of David, the leading men of the land. It bodes well to a people when princes and great men go before the rest in that which is good, as 2 Chr. 20:5. The house of David is all summed up in Jesus Christ, *the Son of David;* and upon him, as the head, the Spirit of grace is poured out, from him to be diffused to all his members; *from his fulness we receive, and grace for grace. (2.) On the inhabitants of Jerusalem,* the common people; for the operations of the Spirit are the same upon the mean and weak Christians that they are upon the strong and more grown. The inhabitants of Jerusalem cannot influence public affairs by their powers and policies, as the great men of the house of David may, yet they may do good service by their prayers, and therefore upon them the Spirit shall be poured out. The church is Jerusalem, the heavenly Jerusalem; all true believers, that have their conversation in the heaven, are inhabitants of this Jerusalem, and to them this promise belongs. God will *pour his Spirit upon them.* This is the earnest which all that *believe in Christ shall receive;* thus they are sanctified; thus they are sealed.

2. What these blessings are: *I will pour upon them the Spirit.* That includes all good things, as it qualifies us for the favour of God, and all his other gifts. He will pour out the Spirit, (1.) As a *Spirit of grace,* to sanctify us and to make us gracious. (2.) As a *Spirit of supplications,* inclining us to, instructing and assisting us in, the duty of prayer. Note, Wherever the Spirit is given as a Spirit of grace, he is given as a Spirit of sanctification. Wherever he is a Spirit of adoption, he *teaches to cry, Abba, Father.* As soon as ever Paul was converted, *Behold, he prays,* Acts 9:11. You may as soon find a living man without breath as a living saint without prayer. There is a more plentiful effusion of the Spirit of prayer now under the gospel than was under the law; and the further the work of sanctification is carried in us the better is the work of supplication carried on by us.

3. What the effect of them will be: *I will pour upon them the Spirit of grace.* One would think that it should follow, "And they shall look on him whom they have believed, and shall rejoice" (and it is true that that is one of the fruits of the pouring out of the Spirit, whence we read of *the joy of the Holy ghost),* but it follows, *They shall mourn;* for there is a holy mourning, that is the effect of the pouring out of the Spirit, a mourning for sin, which is of use to quicken faith in Christ and qualify for joy in God. It is here made the matter of a promise that they shall mourn, for there is a mourning that will end in rejoicing and has a blessing entailed upon it. This mourning is a fruit of the Spirit of grace, an evidence of a work of grace in the soul, and a companion of the Spirit of supplication, as it expresses lively affections working in prayer; hence prayers and tears are often put together, 2 Ki. 20:5. Jacob, that wrestler with God, *wept and made supplication.* But here it is a mourning for sin that is the effect of the pouring out of the Spirit.

(1.) It is a mourning grounded upon a sight of Christ: *They shall look on me whom they have pierced, and shall mourn for him.* Here, [1.] It is foretold that Christ should be pierced, and this scripture is quoted as that which was fulfilled when Christ's side was pierced upon the cross; see Jn. 19:37. [2.] He is spoken of as one whom we have pierced; it is spoken primarily of the Jews, who persecuted him to death (and we find that *those who pierced him* are distinguished from the other *kindreds of the earth* that shall *wail because of him,* Rev. 1:7); yet it is true of us all as sinners, we have pierced Christ, inasmuch as our sins were the cause of his death, for he was *wounded for our transgressions,* and they are the *grief of his soul;* he is *broken with the whorish heart* of sinners, who *therefore* are said to *crucify him afresh* and put him to open shame. [3.] Those that truly repent of sin look upon Christ as one whom they have pierced, who was pierced for their sins and is pierced by them; and this engages them to *look unto him,* as those that are deeply concerned for him. [4.] This is the effect of their looking to Christ; it makes them mourn. This was particularly fulfilled in those to whom Peter preached Christ crucified; when they heard it those who had had a hand in piercing him were *pricked to the heart,* and cried out, *What shall we do?* It is fulfilled in all those who sorrow for sin after a godly sort; they look to Christ, and *mourn for him,* not so much for his sufferings as for their own sins that procured them. Note, The genuine sorrows of a penitent soul flow from the believing sight of a pierced Saviour. Looking by faith upon the cross of Christ will set us a mourning for sin after a godly sort.

(2.) It is a great mourning. [1.] it is like the mourning of a parent for the death of a beloved child. They shall mourn for sin *as one mourns for an only son,* in whose grave the hopes of his family are buried, and shall be inwardly *in bitterness as one that is in bitterness for his first-born,* as the Egyptians were when there was a cry throughout all their land for the death of their first-born. The sorrow of children for the death of their parents is sometimes counterfeited, is often small, and soon wears off and is forgotten; but the sorrow of parents for a child, for a son, for an only son, for a first-born, is natural, sincere, unforced, and unaffected, it is secret and lasting; such are the sorrows of a true penitent, flowing purely from love to Christ above any other. [2.] It is like the mourning of a people for the death of a wise and good prince. It shall be *like the mourning of Hadadrimmon in the valley of Megiddon,* where good king Josiah was slain, for whom there was a general lamentation (*v.* 11), and perhaps the greater because they were told that it was their sin that provoked God to deprive them of so great a blessing; therefore they cried out, *The crown has fallen from our head. Woe unto us, for we have sinned!* Lam. 5:16. Christ is our King; our sins were his death, and, for that reason, ought to be our grief.

(3.) It is a general universal mourning (*v.* 12): *The land shall mourn.* The land itself put on mourning at the death of Christ, for there was then *darkness over all the land,* and the earth trembled; but this is a promise that, in consideration of the death of Christ, multitudes shall be effectually brought to sorrow for sin and turn to God; it shall be such a universal gracious mourning as was when *all the house of Israel lamented after the Lord,* 1 Sa. 7:2. Some think this is yet to have its complete accomplishment in the general conversion of the Jewish nation.

(4.) It is also a private particular mourning. There shall be not only a mourning of the land, by its representatives in a general assembly (as Jdg. 2:5, when the place was called *Bochim — A place of weepers),* but it shall spread itself into all corners of the land: *Every family apart shall mourn* (*v.* 12), *all the families that remain, v.* 14. All have contributed to the guilt, and therefore all shall share in the grief. Note, The exercises of devotion should be performed by private families among themselves, besides their joining in public assemblies for religious worship. National fasts must be observed, not only in our synagogues, but in our houses. In the mourning here foretold the wives mourn apart by themselves, in their own apartment, as Esther and her maids. And some think it intimates their denying themselves the use even of lawful delights in a time of general humiliation 1 Co. 7:5. Four several families are here specified as examples to others in this mourning: — [1.] Two of them are royal families: the *house of David,* in Solomon, and the *house of Nathan,* another son of David, brother to Solomon, from whom Zerubbabel descended, as appears by Christ's genealogy, Lu. 3:27–31. The house of David, particularly that of Nathan, which is now the chief branch of that house, shall go before in this good work. The greatest princes must not think themselves exempted from the law of repentance, but rather obliged most solemnly to express it, for the exciting of others, as Hezekiah humbled himself (2 Chr. 32:26), the princes and the king (2 Chr. 12:6), and the king of Nineveh, Jonah 3:6. [2.] Two of them are sacred families (*v.* 13), *the family of the house of Levi,* which was God's tribe, and in it particularly the family of Shimei, which was a branch of the tribe of Levi (1 Chr. 6:17), and probably some of the descendants of that family were now of note for preachers to the people or ministers to the altar. As the princes must mourn for the sins of the magistracy, so must the priests for the *iniquity of the holy things.* In times of general tribulation and humiliation the Lord's ministers are concerned to *weep between the porch and the altar* (Joel 2:17), and not only there, but in their houses apart; for in what families should godliness, both in the form and in the power of it, be found, if not in ministers' families?

CHAPTER 13

In this chapter we have, I. Some further promises relating to gospel-times. Here is a promise of the remission of sins (*v.* 1), of the reformation of manners (*v.* 2), and particularly of the convicting and silencing of false prophets (*v.* 2–6). II. A clear prediction of the sufferings of Christ and the dispersion of his disciples thereupon (*v.* 7), of the destruction of the greater part of the Jewish nation not long after (*v.* 8), and of the purifying of a remnant of them, a peculiar people to God (*v.* 9).

Verses 1–6

Behold the Lamb of God *taking away the sin of the world,* the sin of the church; for *therefore* was the Son of God manifested, to *take away our sin,* 1 Jn. 3:5.

I. He takes away the guilt of sin by the blood of his cross (*v.* 1): *In that day,* in the gospel-day, *there shall be a fountain opened,* that is, provision made for the cleansing of all those from the pollutions of sin who truly repent and are sorry for them. *In that day,* when the Spirit of grace is poured out to set them a mourning for their sins, they shall not mourn as those who have no hope, but they shall

have their sins pardoned, and the comfort of their pardon in their bosoms. Their consciences shall be purified and pacified by the *blood of Christ, which cleanses from all sin,* 1 Jn. 1:7. For Christ is exalted to give both repentance and remission of sins; and where he gives the one no doubt he gives the other. This *fountain opened* is the pierced side of Jesus Christ, spoken of just before (*ch.* 12:10), for thence came there out *blood and water,* and both for cleansing. And those who *look upon Christ pierced,* and mourn for their sins that pierced him, and are therefore in bitterness for him, may look again upon Christ pierced and rejoice in him, because it pleased the Lord thus to smite this rock, that it might be to us a *fountain of living waters.* See here, 1. How we are polluted; we are all so; we have sinned, and sin is uncleanness; it defiles the mind and conscience, renders us odious to God and uneasy in ourselves, unfit to be employed in the service of God and admitted into communion with him, as those who were ceremonially unclean were shut out of the sanctuary. The *house of David* and the *inhabitants of Jerusalem* are under *sin,* which is uncleanness. The truth is, we are all *as an unclean thing,* and deserve to have our portion with the unclean. 2. How we may be purged. Behold, there is fountain opened for us to wash in, and there are streams flowing to us from that fountain, so that, if we be not made clean, it is our own fault. The blood of Christ, and God's pardoning mercy in that blood, revealed in the new covenant, are, (1.) A fountain; for there is in them an inexhaustible fulness. There is mercy enough in God, and merit enough in Christ, for the forgiving of the greatest sins and sinners, upon gospel-terms. *Such were some of you, but you are washed,* 1 Co. 6:11. Under the law there were a brazen laver and a brazen sea to wash in; those were but vessels, but we have a fountain to ourselves, overflowing, ever-flowing. (2.) *A fountain opened;* for, whoever will, may come and take the benefit of it; it is opened, not only to *the house of David,* but to *the inhabitants of Jerusalem,* to the poor and mean as well as to the rich and great; or it is opened for all believers, who, as the spiritual seed of Christ, are of the house of David, and, as living members of the church, are inhabitants of Jerusalem. Through Christ all that believe are justified, are *washed from their sins in his blood,* that they may be *made to our God kings and priests,* Rev. 1:5, 6.

II. He takes away the dominion of sin by the power of his grace, even of beloved sins. This evermore accompanies the former; those that are washed in the fountain opened, as they are justified, so they are sanctified; the water came with the blood out of the pierced side of Christ. It is here promised that in that day, 1. Idolatry shall be quite abolished and the people of the Jews shall be effectually cured of their inclination to it (*v.* 2): *I will cut off the names of the idols out of the land.* The worship of the idols of their fathers shall be so perfectly rooted out that in one generation or two it shall be forgotten that ever there were such idols among them; they shall either not be named at all or not with any respect; *they shall no more be remembered,* as was promised, Hos. 2:17. This was fulfilled in the rooted aversion which the Jews had, after the captivity, to idols and idolatry, and still retain to this day; it was fulfilled also in the ready conversion of many to the faith of Christ, by which they were taken off from making an idol of the ceremonial law, as the unbelieving Jews did; and it is still in the fulfilling when souls are brought off from the world and the flesh, those two great idols, that they may cleave to God only. 2. False prophecy shall also be brought to an end: *I will cause the prophets and the unclean spirit,* the prophets that are under the influence of the unclean spirit, to *pass out of the land.* The devil is an *unclean spirit;* sin and uncleanness are from him; he has his prophets, that serve his interests and receive their instructions from him. Take away the unclean spirit, and the prophets would not deceive as they do; take away the false prophets that produce sham commissions, and the unclean spirit could not do the mischief he does. When God designs the silencing of the false prophets he banishes the unclean spirit out of the land, that wrought in them, and was a rival with him for the throne in the heart. The church of the Jews, when they were addicted to idols, did also dote much upon false prophets, who flattered them in their sins with promises of impunity and peace; but here it is promised, as a blessed effect of the promised reformation, that they should be very much set against false

prophets, and zealous to clear the land of them; they were so after the captivity, till, through the blindness of their zeal against false prophets, they had put Christ to death under that character, and, after that, there arose many *false Christs and false prophets, and deceived many,* Mt. 24:11. It is here foretold, (1.) That false prophets, instead of being indulged and favoured, should be brought to condign punishment even by their nearest relations, which would be as great an instance as any of flagrant zeal against those deceivers (*v.* 3): *When any shall* set up for a prophet, and shall *speak lies in the name of the Lord,* shall preach that which tends to draw people from God and to confirm them in sin, his own parents shall be the first and most forward to prosecute him for it, according to the law. Deu. 13:6–11, *"If thy son entice thee secretly* from God, *thou shalt surely kill him.* Show thy indignation against him, and prevent any further temptation from him." His *father and his mother shall thrust him through when he prophesies.* Note, We ought to conceive, and always to retain, a very great detestation and dread of every thing that would draw us out of the way of our duty into by-paths, as those who cannot *bear that which is evil,* Rev. 2:2. And holy zeal for God and godliness will make us hate sin, and dread temptation, most in those whom naturally we love best, and who are nearest to us; there our danger is greatest, as Adam's from Eve, Job's from his wife; and there it will be the most praiseworthy to show our zeal, as Levi, who, in the cause of God, did not *acknowledge his brethren,* nor *know his own children,* Deu. 33:9. Thus we must hate and forsake our nearest relations when they come in competition with our duty to God, Lu. 14:26. Natural affections, even the strongest, must be over-ruled by gracious affections. (2.) That false prophets should be themselves convinced of their sin and folly, and let fall their pretensions (*v.* 4): *"The prophets shall be ashamed every one of his vision;* they shall not repeat it, or insist upon it, but desire that it may be forgotten and no more said of it, being ready themselves to own it was a sham, because God has by his grace awakened their consciences and shown them their error, or because the event disproves their predictions, and gives them the lie, or because their prophecies do not meet with such a favourable reception as they used to meet with, but are generally despised and distasted; they perceive the people ashamed of them, which makes them begin to be ashamed of themselves. And therefore they shall no longer *wear a rough garment,* or *garment of hair,* as the true prophets used to do, in imitation of Elijah, and in token of their being mortified to the pleasures and delights of sense." The pretenders had appeared in the habit of true prophets; but, their folly being now made manifest, they shall lay it aside, no more to deceive and impose upon unthinking unwary people by it. A modest dress is a very good thing, if it be the genuine indication of a humble heart, and is to instruct; but it is a bad thing if it be the hypocritical disguise of a proud ambitious heart, and is to deceive. Let men be really as good as they seem to be, but not seem to be better than really they are. This pretender, as a true penitent, [1.] Shall undeceive those whom he had imposed upon: He shall say, *"I am no prophet,* as I have pretended to be, was never designed nor set apart to the office, never educated nor brought up for it, never conversant among the sons of the prophets. *I am a husbandman,* and was bred to that business; I was never taught of God to prophesy, but *taught of man to keep cattle"* Amos was originally such a one too, and yet was afterwards called to be a prophet, Amos 7:14, 15. But this deceiver never had any such call. Note, Those who sorrow after a godly sort for their having deceived others will be forward to confess their sin, and will be so just as to rectify the mistakes which they have been the cause of. Thus those who had *used curious arts,* when they were converted *showed their deeds,* and by what fallacies they had cheated the people, Acts 19:18. [2.] He shall return to his own proper employment, which is the fittest for him: *I will be a husbandman* (so it may be read); "I will apply myself to my calling again, and meddle no more with things that belong not to me; for *man taught me to keep cattle from my youth,* and cattle I will again keep, and never set up for a preacher any more." Note, When we are convinced that we have gone out of the way of our duty we must evince the truth of our repentance by returning to it again, though it be the severest mortification to us. [3.] He shall acknowledge those to be his friends who by a severe discipline were instrumental to bring him to a sight of his error, *v.* 6. When he who with the greatest assurance had asserted himself so lately to be a prophet suddenly drops his claims, and says, I am no prophet, every body will be surprised at it, and some will ask, *"What are these wounds,* or marks of stripes, *in thy hands?* how camest thou by them? Hast thou not been *examined by scourging?* And is not that it that has brought thee to thyself?" *(Vexatio dat intellectum — Vexation sharpens the intellect.)* "Hast thou not been beaten into this acknowledgment? Was it not the rod and reproof that gave thee this wisdom?" And he shall own, "Yes, it was; these are the *wounds with which I was wounded in the house of my friends,* who bound me, and used me hardly and severely, as a distracted man, and so brought me to my senses." By this it appears that those parents of the false prophet that *thrust him through* (*v.* 3) did not do it till they had first tried to reclaim him by correction, and he would not be reclaimed; for so was the law concerning a disobedient son — his parents must first have chastened him in vain before they were allowed to bring him forth to be stoned, Deu. 21:18, 19. But here is another who was reduced by stripes, and so prevented the capital punishment; and he had the sense and honesty to own that they were his friends, his real friends, who thus wounded him, that they might reclaim him; for *faithful are the wounds of a friend,* Prov. 27:6. Some good interpreters, observing how soon this comes after the mention of Christ's being pierced, think that these are the words of that great prophet, not of the false prophet spoken of before. Christ was wounded in his hands, when they were nailed to the cross, and, after his resurrection, he had the marks of these wounds; and here he tells how he came by them; he received them as a false prophet, for the chief priests called him a deceiver, and upon that account would have him crucified; but he received them in the house of his friends — the Jews, who should have been his friends; for *he came to his own,* and, though they were his bitter enemies, yet he was pleased to call them his *friends,* as he did Judas *(Friend, wherefore hast thou come?)* because they forwarded his sufferings for him; as he called Peter *Satan — an adversary,* because he dissuaded him from them.

Verses 7–9

Here is a prophecy,

I. Of the sufferings of Christ, of him who was to be pierced, and was to be the fountain opened. *Awake, O sword! against my Shepherd, v.* 7. These are the words of God the Father, giving order and commission to the sword of his justice to awake against his Son, when he had voluntarily made his soul an offering for sin; for *it pleased the Lord to bruise him* and *put him to grief;* and *he was stricken, smitten of God, and afflicted,* Isa. 53:4, 10. Observe, 1. How he calls him. "As God, he is *my fellow;"* for he thought it *no robbery to be equal with God.* He and *the Father* are *one.* He was from eternity by him, as one brought up with him, and, in the work of man's redemption, he was his elect, in whom his soul delighted, and the counsel of peace was between them both. "As Mediator, he is *my Shepherd,* that great and good Shepherd that undertook to feed the flock," *ch.* 11:7. He is the Shepherd that was to lay down his life for the sheep. 2. How he uses him: *Awake, O sword! against him.* If he will be a sacrifice, he must be slain, for without the shedding of blood, the life-blood, there was no remission. men thrust him through as the good Shepherd (compare *v.* 3), that he might *purchase the flock of God* with *his own blood,* Acts 20:28. It is not a charge given to a rod to correct him, but to a sword to slay him; for *Messiah the prince must be cut off, but not for himself,* Dan. 9:26. It is not the sword of war that receives this charge, that he may die in the bed of honour, but the sword of justice, that he may die as a criminal, upon an ignominious tree. This sword must awake against him; he having no sin of his own to answer for, the sword of justice had nothing to say to him of itself, till, by particular order from the Judge of all, it was warranted to brandish itself against him. he was the Lamb *slain from the foundation of the world,* in the decree and counsel of God; but the sword designed against him had long slumbered, till now at length it is called upon to awake, not, "Awake, and smite him; strike home; not with a drowsy blow, but an awakened one;" for God *spared not his own Son.*

II. Of the dispersion of the disciples thereupon: *Smite the Shepherd, and the sheep shall be scattered.* This our Lord Jesus himself declares to have been fulfilled when *all his disciples were offended because of him* in the night wherein he was betrayed, Mt. 26:31; Mk. 14:27. They all *forsook him and fled.* The smiting of the Shepherd is the scattering of the sheep. They were *scattered every one to his own, and left him alone,* Jn. 16:32. Herein they were like timorous sheep; yet the Shepherd thus provided for their safety, for he said, *If you seek me, let these go their way.* Some make another application of this; Christ was the *Shepherd* of the Jewish nation; he was smitten; they themselves smote him, and therefore they were justly scattered abroad, and dispersed among the nations, and remain so at this day. These words, *I will turn my hand upon the little ones,* may be understood either as a threatening (as Christ suffered, so shall his disciples, they shall *drink of the cup that he drank of* and be *baptized with the baptism that he was baptized* with) or as a promise that God would gather Christ's scattered disciples together again, and he should give them the meeting in Galilee. Though the little ones among Christ's soldiers may be dispersed, they shall rally again; the lambs of his flock, though frightened by the beasts of prey, shall recover themselves, shall be gathered in his arms and laid in his bosom. Sometimes, when the sheep are scattered and lost in the wilderness, yet the little ones, which, it was feared, would be a prey (Num. 14:31), are brought in, are brought home, and God turns his hand upon them.

III. Of the rejection and ruin of the unbelieving Jews (*v.* 8); and this word has, and shall have, its accomplishment, in the destruction of the corrupt and hypocritical part of the church. *It shall come to pass that in all the land of Israel two parts shall be cut off and die.* The Roman army laid the country waste, and slew at least two-thirds of the Jews. Some understand by the *cutting off,* and *dying,* or *two parts* in all *the earth,* the abolishing of heathenism and Judaism, that Christianity, the third part, might be left to reign alone. The Jewish worship was quite taken away by the destruction of Jerusalem and the temple. And, some time after, Pagan idolatry was in a manner extirpated, when the empire became Christian.

IV. Of the reformation and preservation of the chosen remnant, those of them that believed, and the Christian church in general (*v.* 9): *The third part shall be left.* When Jerusalem and Judea were destroyed, all the Christians in that country, having among them the warning Christ gave them to *flee to the mountains,* shifted for their own safety, and were sheltered in a city called *Pella,* on the other side Jordan. We have here first the trials and then the triumphs of the Christian church, and of all the faithful members of it. 1. Their trials: *I will bring* that *third part through the fire* of affliction. *and will refine* and *try them* as *silver and gold are refined and tried.* This was fulfilled in the persecutions of the primitive church, the *fiery trial* which tried the people of God then, 1 Pt. 4:12. Those whom God sets apart for himself must pass through a probation and purification in this world; they must be *tried* that *their faith* may be *found to praise and honour* (1 Pt. 1:6, 7), as Abraham's faith was when it was tried by the command given him to offer up Isaac, *Now know I that thou fearest me.* They must be tried, that both those that are perfect and those that are not may be *made manifest.* They must be refined from their dross; their corruption must be purged out; they must be brightened and bettered. 2. Their triumphs. (1.) Their communion with God is their triumph: *They shall call on my name, and I will hear them.* They write to God by prayer, and receive from him answers of peace, and thus keep up a comfortable communion with him. *This honour have all his saints.* (2.) Their covenant with God is their triumph: *"I will say, It is my people,* whom I have chosen and loved, and will own; *and they shall say, the Lord is my God,* and a God all-sufficient to me; and in me they shall boast every day and all the day long. *This God is our God for ever and ever."*

CHAPTER 14

Divers things were foretold, in the two foregoing chapters, which should come to pass "in that day;" this chapter speaks of a "day of the Lord that cometh," a day of his judgment, and ten times in the foregoing chapters, and seven times in this, it is repeated, "in that day;" but what that day is that is here meant is uncertain, and perhaps will be so (as the Jews speak) till Elias comes; whether it refer to the whole period of time from the prophet's days to the days of the Messiah, or to some particular events in that time, or to Christ's coming, and the setting up of his kingdom upon the ruins of the Jewish polity, we cannot determine, but divers passages here seem to look as far forward as gospel-times. Now the "day of the Lord" brings with it both judgment and mercy, mercy to his church, judgment to her enemies and persecutors. I. The gates of hell are here threatening the church (*v.* 1, 2) and yet not prevailing. II. The power of Heaven appears here for the church and against the enemies of it (*v.* 3, 5). III. The events concerning the church are here represented as mixed (*v.* 6, 7), but issuing well at last. IV. The spreading of the means of knowledge is here foretold, and the setting up of the gospel-kingdom in the world (*v.* 8, 9), which shall be the enlargement and establishment of another Jerusalem (*v.* 10, 11). V. Those shall be reckoned with that fought against Jerusalem (*v.* 12–15) and those that neglect his worship there (*v.* 17–19). VI. It is promised that there shall be great resort to the church, and great purity and piety in it (*v.* 16, 20, 21).

Verses 1–7

God's providences concerning his church are here represented as strangely changing and strangely mixed.

I. As strangely changing. Sometimes the tide runs high and strong against them, but presently it turns, and comes to be in favour of them; and God has, for wise and holy ends, set the one over against the other.

1. God here appears against Jerusalem; judgment begins at the house of God. When the *day of the Lord comes* (*v.* 1) Jerusalem must pass through the fire to be refined. God himself *gathers all nations against Jerusalem to battle* (*v.* 2); he gives them a charge, as he did Sennacherib, to *take the spoil* and to *take the prey* (Isa. 10:6), for the people of Jerusalem have now become the *people of his wrath.* And who can stand before him or before nations gathered by him? Where he gives commission he will give success. The *city shall be taken by the* Romans, who have *nations* at command; the houses shall be rifled, and all the riches of them taken away, by the enemy; and, to gratify an insatiable lust of uncleanness as well as avarice, *the women* shall *be ravished,* as if victory were a license to the worst of villanies, *jusque datum sceleri — and crimes were sanctioned by law. One-half of the city* shall then be carried *into captivity,* to be sold or enslaved, and shall not be able to help itself, such is the destruction that shall be made in the great and terrible *day of the Lord.*

2. He presently changes his way, and appears for Jerusalem; for, though judgment begin at the house of God, yet, as it shall not end there, so it shall not make a full end there, Jer. 4:27; 30:11.

(1.) A remnant shall be spared, the same with that *third part* spoken of, *ch.* 13:8. *One-half shall go into captivity,* whence they may hereafter be fetched back, *and the residue of the people shall not* be cut off, as one would have feared, *from the city.* Many of the Jews shall receive the gospel, and so shall prevent their being cut off from the city of God, his church upon earth. *In it shall be a tenth,* Isa. 6:13; See Eze. 5:3.

(2.) Their cause shall be pleaded against their enemies (*v.* 3): *Then,* when God has made use of these nations as a scourge to his people, he shall *go forth* and *fight against them* by his judgments, *as when he fought* against the enemies of his church formerly *in the day of battle,* with the Egyptians, Canaanites, and others. Note, The instruments of God's wrath will themselves be made the objects of it; for it will come to their turn to drink of the cup of trembling; and whom God fights against he will be sure to overcome and be too hard for. And every former *day of battle,* which God has made to his people a *day of triumph,* as it is an engagement to God to appear for his people, because he is the same, so it is an encouragement to them to trust in him. It is observable that the Roman empire never flourished, after the destruction of Jerusalem as it had done before, but in many instances God fought against it.

(3.) Though Jerusalem and the temple be destroyed, yet God will have a church in the world, into which Gentiles shall be admitted, and with whom the believing Jews shall be incorporated, *v.* 4, 5. These verses are dark and hard to be understood; but divers good expositors take this to be the meaning of them. [1.] God will carefully inspect Jerusalem, even then when the enemies of it are laying it waste: *His feet shall stand in that day upon the mount of Olives,* whence he may take a full view of the city and temple, Mk. 13:3. When the refiner puts his gold into the furnace he stands by it, and has his eye upon it, to see that it receive no damage; so when Jerusalem, God's gold, is to be refined, he will have the oversight of it. He will stand by *upon the mount of Olives;* this was literally fulfilled when our Lord Jesus was often upon this mountain, especially when thence he *ascended up into heaven,* Acts 1:12. It was the last place on which his feet stood on this earth, the place from which he took rise. [2.] The partition-wall between Jews and Gentiles shall be taken away. The *mountains about Jerusalem,* and particularly this, signified it to be an enclosure, and that it stood in the way of those who would approach to it. Between the Gentiles and Jerusalem this *mountain of Bether,* of *division,* stood, Cant. 2:17. But by the destruction of Jerusalem this mountain shall be made to *cleave in the midst,* and so the Jewish pale shall be taken down, and the church laid in common with the Gentiles, who were made one with the Jews by the breaking down of this *middle wall of partition,* Eph. 2:14. *Who art thou, O great mountain?* And a great mountain the ceremonial law was in the way of the Jews' conversion, which, one would think, could never have been got over; yet before Christ and his gospel it was made plain. This *mountain departs,* this *hill removes,* but the *covenant of peace* cannot be *broken;* for peace is still *preached to him that is afar off and to those that are nigh.* [3.] A new and living way shall be opened to the new Jerusalem, both to see it and to come into it. The mountain being divided, one-half *towards the north* and the other half *towards the south,* there shall be *a very great valley,* that is, a broad way of communication opened between Jerusalem and the Gentile world, by which the Gentiles shall have free admission into the gospel-Jerusalem, and the word of the Lord, that *goes forth from Jerusalem,* shall have a *free course* into the Gentile world. Thus the *way of the Lord* is prepared, for *every mountain and hill shall be brought low,* and plain and pleasant valleys shall come in the room of them, Isa. 40:4. [4.] Those of the Jews that believe shall come in, and join themselves to the Gentiles, and incorporate with them in the gospel-church: *You shall flee to the valley of the mountains,* that valley that is opened between the divided halves of the mount of Olives; they shall hasten into the church with the Gentiles, as formerly the Gentiles with them, *ch.* 8:23. The *valley of the mountains* is the gospel-church, to which there were added of the Jews daily *such as should be saved,* who fled to that valley as to their refuge. This *valley of the mountains* is said to *reach unto Azal,* or *to the separate place,* that is, to all those whom God has *set apart for himself.* When God *makes his mountains a way* (Isa. 49:11), by making them a valley, the way shall be opened to all the *way-faring men* (Isa. 35:8), and, *though fools,* they *shall not err therein.* Or, to those that are now separated from God this valley shall reach; for the Gentiles, who are afar off, shall be made nigh, with the Jews, who are a *people near unto him,* and both have *an access,* a mutual access to each other and a joint access to God as a Father by one Spirit, Eph. 2:18. [5.] They shall flee to *the valley of the mountains,* to the gospel-church, under dreadful apprehensions of their danger from the curse of the law. They shall *flee from the wrath to come,* from the avenger of blood, who is in pursuit of them, to the church as to a *city of refuge,* or *as doves to their windows,* as they *fled from before the earthquake in the days of Uzziah,* Amos 1:1. *Therefore* the gospel reveals the wrath of God from heaven (Rom. 1:18) that we might be awakened to *escape for our lives,* to flee as from an earthquake, for we feel the earth ready to sink under us, and we can find no firm footing in it, and therefore must flee to Christ, in whom alone we can stand fast and be easy.

(4.) God shall appear in his glory for the accomplishing of all this: *The Lord my God shall come, and all the saints with thee,* which may refer to his coming to destroy Jerusalem, or to destroy the enemies of Jerusalem, or his coming to set up his kingdom in the world, which is called the *coming of the Son of man* (Mt. 24:37), or to his last coming, at the end of time; however, it teaches us, [1.] That the Lord will come; it has been the faith of all the saints, *Behold, the Lord comes* to fulfil every word that he has spoken in its season. [2.] When he comes all his saints come with him; they attend his motions and are ready to serve his interests. Christ will come at the end of time with *ten thousands of his saints,* as when he came to give the law upon Mount Sinai. [3.] Every particular believer, being related to God as his God, may triumph in the expectation of his coming and speak of it with pleasure, *The Lord my God shall come,* shall come to the comfort of all that are his; for, "Blessed Lord, *all the saints shall be with thee,* and it shall be their everlasting happiness to dwell in thy presence; and therefore *come, Lord Jesus.*" And some think that this may be read as a prayer, *Yet, O Lord my God! come, and bring all the saints with thee.*

II. God's providences appear here strangely mixed (*v.* 6, 7): *In that day* of the Lord the *light shall not be clear nor dark, not day* nor *night;* but *at evening time it shall be light.* Some refer this to all the time from hence to the coming of the Messiah; the Jewish church had neither perfect peace nor constant trouble, but a cloudy day, neither rain nor sunshine. But it may be taken more generally, as designed to represent the method God usually takes in the administration of the kingdom both of providence and grace. Here is, 1. An idea of the usual course and tenour of God's dispensations; the day of his grace and the day of his providence are *neither clear nor dark, not day nor night.* It is so with the church of God in this world; where the Sun of righteousness has risen it cannot be dark night, and yet short of heaven it will not be clear day. It is so with particular saints; they are not darkness, but *light in the Lord,* and yet, while there is so much error and corruption remaining in them, it is not perfect day. So it is as to the providences of God that relate to his church; in general the affairs of the church are neither good nor bad in any extremity, but there is a mixture of both; we are singing both of mercy and judgment, and are uncertain which will prevail, whether it be an evening or a morning twilight. We are between hope and fear, not knowing what to make of things. 2. An intimation of comfort with reference hereunto: *It shall be one day which shall be known to the Lord.* This intimates, (1.) The beauty and harmony of such mixed events; there is one and the same design and tendency in all; all the wheels make but one wheel, all the revolutions but one day. (2.) The brevity of them; it is, as it were, but for one day, for a little moment; the cloud that darkens the light will soon blow over. (3.) The eye God has upon all these events, and the hand he has in them all; they are *known to the Lord;* he takes notice of them, and orders and disposes of all for the best, according to the counsel of his will. 3. An issue very joyful secured at last: *At evening-time it shall be light:* it shall be clear light, and no longer dark; we are sure of it in the other world, and we hope for it in this world — at *evening-time,* when our hopes are quite spent with waiting all day to no purpose, nay, when we fear it will be quite dark, when things are at the worst and the case of the church is most deplorable. As to the church's enemies *the sun goes down at noon,* so to the church it rises at night; unto the upright springs *light out of darkness* (Ps. 112:4); deliverance comes when the tale of bricks is doubled, and when God's people have done looking for it, and so it comes with a pleasing surprise.

Verses 8–15

Here are, I. Blessings promised to Jerusalem, the gospel-Jerusalem, in the day of the Messiah, and to all the earth, by virtue of the blessings poured out on Jerusalem, especially to the land of Israel.

1. Jerusalem shall be a spring of living waters to the world; it was made so when there the Spirit was poured out upon the apostles, and thence the word of the Lord diffused itself to the nations about (*v.* 8): *Living waters shall go out from Jerusalem;* for there they began, and thence those set out who were to preach *repentance* and *remission* of sins *unto all nations,* Lu. 24:47. Note, Where the gospel goes, and the graces of God's Spirit go along with it, there living waters go; those streams that *make glad the city of our God* make glad the country also, and make it like paradise, like the *garden of the Lord,* which was *well watered.* It was the honour of Jerusalem that *thence the word of the Lord went forth* (Isa. 2:3); and thus far, even in its worst and most degenerate age, for old acquaintance-sake, it was made a blessing, and to be so is to be blessed. Half of these waters shall go *towards the former sea* and *half towards the hinder sea,* as all rivers bend their course towards some sea or other, some eastward, others westward. The gospel shall spread into all parts of the world, into some that lie remote from Jerusalem one way and others that lie as far off another way; for the dominion of the Redeemer, which was thereby to be set up, must be *from sea to sea* (Ps. 72:8), and the earth must be *full of the knowledge of the Lord, as the waters cover the sea,* and as the waters that in various channels run to the sea. The knowledge of God shall diffuse itself, (1.) Every way. These living waters shall produce both eastern churches and western churches, that shall each of them in its turn be illustrious. (2.) Every day: In *summer and in winter it shall be.* Note, Those who are employed in spreading the gospel may find themselves work both *winter* and *summer,* and are to serve the Lord therein at all seasons, Acts 20:18. And such a divine power goes along with these living waters that they shall not be dried up, nor the course of them be obstructed, either by the droughts in summer or by the frosts in winter.

2. The kingdom of God among men shall be a universal and united kingdom, *v.* 9. (1.) It shall be a universal kingdom: *The Lord shall be King over all the earth.* He is, and ever was, so of right, and in the sovereign disposals of his providence his kingdom does *rule over all* and none are exempt from his jurisdiction; but it is here promised that he shall be so by actual possession of the hearts of his subjects; he shall be acknowledged King by all in all places; his authority shall be owned and submitted to, and allegiance sworn to him. This will have its accomplishment with that word (Rev. 11:15), *The kingdoms of this world have become the kingdoms of our Lord and of his Christ.* (2.) It shall be a united kingdom: *There shall be one Lord, and his name one.* All shall worship one God only, and not idols, and shall be unanimous in the worship of him. All false gods shall be abandoned, and all false ways of worship abolished; and as God shall be the centre of their unity, in whom they shall all meet, so the scripture shall be the rule of their unity, by which they shall all walk.

3. The land of Judea, and Jerusalem, its mother-city, shall be repaired and replenished, and taken under the special protection of Heaven, *v.* 10, 11. Some think this denotes particular favour to the people of the Jews, and points at their conversion and restoration in the latter days; but it is rather to be understood figuratively of the gospel-church, typified by Judah and Jerusalem, and it signifies the abundant graces with which the church shall be crowned, and the fruitfulness of its members, and the vast numbers of them. (1.) The church shall be like a fruitful country, abounding in all the rich products of the soil. The whole land of Judea, which is naturally uneven and hilly, shall be *turned as a plain;* it shall become a smooth level valley, from Geba, or Gibeah, its utmost border north, to Rimmon, which lay *south of Jerusalem* and was the utmost southern limit of Judea. The gospel of Christ, where it comes in its power, levels the ground; mountains and hills are brought low by it, that the Lord alone may be exalted. (2.) It shall be like a populous city. As the holy land shall be levelled, so the holy city shall be peopled, shall be rebuilt and replenished. *Jerusalem shall be lifted* up out of its low estate, shall be raised out of its ruins; when *the land is turned as a plain,* and not only the *mount of Olives* removed (*v.* 4), but other mountains too, then Jerusalem shall be *lifted up,* that is, shall appear the more conspicuous; she *shall be inhabited in her place,* even *in Jerusalem, ch.* 12:6. The whole city shall be inhabited in the utmost extent of it, and no part of it left to lie waste. The utmost limits of it are here mentioned, between which there shall be no ground lost, but all built upon, from *Benjamin's-gate* north-east to the *corner-gate* north-west, and *from the tower of Hananeel* in the south to the *king's wine-presses* in the north; when the churches of Christ in all places are replenished with great numbers of holy, humble, serious Christians, and many such are daily added to it, then this promise is fulfilled. (3.) This country and this city shall both be safe, both the meat in the country and the mouths in the city: *Those that dwell in it* shall dwell securely, and there shall be none to make them afraid; there shall be no more of that utter destruction that has laid both town and country waste, no more anathema (as some read it), no more cutting off, no more curse, or separation from God to evil, no more such desolating judgments as you have been groaning under, but Jerusalem *shall be safely inhabited;* there shall be no danger, nor any apprehension of it; neither shall its friends be fearful to disquiet themselves nor its enemies formidable to disquiet

them. That promise of Christ explains this — that *the gates of hell shall not prevail against the church;* and so do the holy security and serenity of mind which believers enjoy in relying on the divine protection.

II. Here are judgments threatened against the enemies of the church, that *have fought,* or do fight, against Jerusalem; and the *threatening of these* judgments is in order to the preservation of the church in safety. Men that read and hear of these plagues will be afraid of fighting against Jerusalem, much more when these threatenings are fulfilled in some will others hear and fear. Those that fight against the city of God, and his people, will be found fighting against God, against whom none ever hardened his heart and prospered (*v.* 12): *This shall be the plague wherewith the Lord will smite all the people that have fought against Jerusalem;* whoever they are, God will punish them for the affront done to him, and avenge Jerusalem upon them. 1. They shall waste away under grievous and languishing diseases: *Their flesh shall consume away,* and they shall be miserably emaciated, even *while they stand on their feet,* so that they shall be walking skeletons; nothing shall remain but skin and bones. The flesh which they pampered and indulged, and made provision for, when they were fed to the full with the spoils of God's people, shall now *consume away, that it cannot be seen, and the bones that were not seen shall stick out,* Job 33:21. They *keep their feet,* and hope to *keep their ground,* crawling about as long as they can; but they must yield at last. The organs of sight, the outlets of sin, *their eyes, shall consume away in their holes,* shall sink into their heads or perhaps start out of them; their envious malicious, adulterous eyes, the eyes they had so often fed with spectacles of misery, these shall consume, which shall make not only their countenances ghastly, but their lives wretched. The organs of speech, the outlets of sin, *their tongue, shall consume away in their mouth,* whereby God will reckon with them for all their blasphemies against himself and invectives against his people. Thus *their own tongues shall fall upon them,* and their punishment shall be legible in their sin, as his was whose tongue was tormented in hell-flames. Thus Antiochus and Herod consumed away. 2. They shall be dashed in pieces one against another (*v.* 13): *A great tumult from the Lord shall be among them.* But are tumults from the Lord, who is the *God of order, and not of confusion?* As they are the sin of those that raise them they are not from the Lord, but from the wicked one, and from men's own lusts; but, as they are the punishment of those that suffer by them, they are from the Lord, who serves his own purposes, and carries on his intentions, by the sins, and follies, and restless spirits, of men. It is of themselves that they *bite and devour one another,* but it is of the Lord, the righteous Judge, that thus they are *consumed one of another* (Gal. 5:15); as Ahab was deceived by a lying spirit from the Lord, so Abimelech and the men of Shechem were *divided,* and so *destroyed,* by an *evil spirit from the Lord,* Jdg. 9:23. Note, Those that are confederate and combined against the church will justly be separated, and set against one another; and their tumults raised against God will be avenged in tumults among themselves. And they shall *lay hold every one on the hand of his neighbour,* to hold him from striking, or to bind him as his prisoner; nay, *his hand shall rise up against the hand of his neighbour,* to strike and wound him. Note, Those that aim to destroy the church are often made to destroy one another; and every man's sword is sometimes set against his fellow, by him whose sword they all are. Some think this was fulfilled in the factions and dissensions that were among the Jews, when the Romans were destroying them all; for they had fought against the spiritual Jerusalem, the gospel-church; and to that well enough agrees *v.* 14, *Thou also, O Judah! shalt fight against Jerusalem;* the Jewish nation shall be ruined by itself, shall die by its own hands; the city and country shall be at war with each other, and so both shall be destroyed. *Suis et ipsa Roma viribus ruit — Rome was urged into ruin by its very strength.* 3. The plunder of their camp shall greatly enrich the people of God, or the spoils of their country (*v.* 14): *Judah also shall eat at Jerusalem* (so one learned interpreter reads it); people shall come from all parts to share in the prey; as when Sennacherib's army was routed before Jerusalem there was *the prey of a great spoil divided* (Isa. 33:23), so it shall be now; the *wealth of all the heathen round about,* that had spoiled *Jerusalem, shall be gathered together, gold, and silver, and apparel, in great abundance,* that an equal dividend may be made among all the parties entitled to a share of the prize. Note, The *wealth of the sinner is* often *laid up for the just,* and the Israel of God enriched with the spoil of the Egyptians. 4. The very cattle shall share in the plague with which the enemies of God's church shall be cut off, as they did in divers of the plagues of Egypt (*v.* 15): All *the beasts* that *shall be in the tents* of these wicked men, when God comes to contend with them, shall perish with them, not only beasts used in war, as the horse, but those used for travel, or in the plough, as the *mule,* the *camel,* and the *ass.* Note, The inferior creatures often suffer for the sin of man and in his plagues. Thus God will show his indignation against sin, and will make the creature that is thus *subject to vanity* groan to be *delivered* into the glorious liberty of the children of God, Rom. 8:21, 22.

Verses 16–21

Three things are here foretold: —

I. That a gospel-way of worship being set up in the church there shall be a great resort to it and a general attendance upon it. Those that were left of the enemies of religion shall be so sensible of the mercy of God to them in their narrow escape that they shall apply themselves to the worship of the God of Israel, and pay their homage to him, *v.* 16. Those that were not consumed shall be converted, and this makes their deliverance a mercy indeed, a double mercy. It is a great change that the grace of God makes upon them; those that had *come against Jerusalem,* finding their attempts vain and fruitless, shall become as much her admirers as ever they had been her adversaries, and shall *come to Jerusalem* to worship there, and go in concurrence with those whom they had gone contrary to. Note, As some of Christ's foes shall be made his footstool, so others of them shall be made his friends; and, when the principle of enmity is slain in them, their former acts of hostility are pardoned to them, and their services are admitted and accepted, as though they had never *fought against Jerusalem.* They shall *go up to worship* at Jerusalem, because that was the place which God had chosen, and there the temple was, which was a type of Christ and his mediation. Converting grace sets us right, 1. In the object of our worship. *They shall* no longer *worship* the Molochs and Baals, the *kings* and *lords,* that the Gentiles worship, the creatures of their own imagination, but *the King,* the *Lord of hosts,* the everlasting King, the King of kings, the sovereign Lord of all. 2. In the ordinances of worship, those which God himself has appointed. Gospel-worship is here represented by the *keeping of the feast of tabernacles,* for the sake of those two great graces which were in a special manner *acted* and *signified* in that feast — contempt of the world, and joy in God, Neh. 8:17. The life of a good Christian is a constant *feast of tabernacles,* and, in all acts of devotion, we must retire from the world and rejoice in the Lord, must worship as in that feast. 3. In the *Mediator* of our worship; we must go to Christ our temple with all our offerings, for in him only our *spiritual sacrifices* are acceptable to God, 1 Pt. 2:5. If we rest in ourselves, we come short of pleasing God; we must go up to him, and mention his righteousness only. 4. In the time of it; we must be constant. They shall go up *from year to year,* at the times appointed for this solemn feast. Every day of a Christian's life is a day of the *feast of tabernacles,* and every Lord's day especially (that is the *great day of the feast);* and therefore every day we must worship the Lord of hosts and every Lord's day with a peculiar solemnity.

II. That those who neglect the duties of gospel-worship shall be reckoned with for their neglect. God will compel them to come and worship before him, by suspending his favours from those that keep not his ordinances: *Upon them there shall be no rain, v.* 17. Some understand it figuratively; the rain of heavenly doctrine shall be withheld, and of the heavenly grace, which should accompany that doctrine. God will *command the clouds that they rain no rain upon them.* Note, It is a righteous thing with God to withhold the blessings of grace from those that do not attend the means of grace, to deny the *green pastures* to those that attend not the *shepherd's tents.* Or we may take it literally: *On them there shall be no rain,* to make their ground fruitful. Note, The gifts of common providence are justly denied to those that neglect and despise instituted ordinances. Those that neglected to build the temple were punished with the want of rain (Hag. 2:17), and so were those that neglected to attend there when it was built. If we be barren and unfruitful towards God, justly is the earth made so to us. Many are crossed, and go backward, in their affairs, and this is at the bottom of it — they do not keep close to the worship of God as they should; they go off from God, and then he walks contrary to them. If we omit or postpone the duties he expects from us, it is just with him to deny the favours we expect from him. But what shall be done to the defaulters of the land of Egypt, to whom the threatening of the want of rain is no threatening, for they have no rain at any time; they need none; they desire none; the river Nilus is to them instead of the clouds of heaven, waters their land, and makes it fruitful, so that what is a punishment to others is none to them? *v.* 18, 19. It is threatened that *if the family of Egypt go not up, that have no rain,* yet God will find out a way to meet with them, for there shall be, in effect, the same plague wherewith other nations are smitten for their neglect. God can, and often did, restrain the overflowing of the river, which was equivalent to the shutting up of the clouds; or if the river did its part, and rose as high as it used to do, God had other ways of bringing famine upon them, and destroying the fruits of their ground, as he did by several of the ten plagues of Egypt, so that *this* (that is, the same) shall be *the punishment of Egypt* that is the punishment of other *nations* who come not up to *keep the feast of tabernacles.* Note, Those who think themselves least indebted to, and depending on, the mercy of heaven, cannot *therefore* think themselves guarded against the justice of Heaven. It does not follow that those who can live without rain can therefore live without God; for not the heavens only, but all other creatures, are that to us that God makes them to be, and no more; nor can any man's way of living enable him to set light by the judgments of God. This shall be the *punishment* — margin, *This shall be the sin of Egypt, and the sin of all nations, that come not up to keep the feast of tabernacles.* The same word signifies both *sin* and the *punishment* of sin, so close and inseparable is the connexion between them (as Gen. 4:7), and sin is often its own punishment. Note, Omissions are sins, and we must come into judgment for them; those contract guilt that *go not up to worship* at the times appointed, as they have opportunity; and it is a sin that is its own *punishment,* for those who forsake the duty forfeit the privilege of communion with God.

III. That those who perform the duties of gospel-worship shall have grace to adorn their profession by the duties of a gospel-conversation too. This is promised (*v.* 20, 21), and it is necessary to the completing of the beauty and happiness of the church. In general, all shall be *holiness to the Lord.*

1. The name and character of holiness shall not be so confined as formerly. *Holiness to the Lord* had been written only upon the high priest's forehead, but now it shall not be so appropriated. All Christians shall be *living temples,* and *spiritual priests,* dedicated to the honour of God and employed in his service.

2. Real holiness shall be more diffused than it had been, because there shall be more powerful means of sanctification, more excellent rules, more cogent arguments, and brighter patterns of holiness, and because there shall be a more plentiful effusion of the Spirit of holiness and sanctification, after Christ's ascension than ever before.

(1.) There shall be holiness introduced into common things; and those things shall be devoted to God that seemed very foreign. [1.] The furniture of the horses shall be consecrated to God. *"Upon the bells of the horses* shall be engraven *Holiness to the Lord,* or upon the *bridles* of the horses (so the margin) or the *trappings.* The horses used in war shall no longer be used against God and his people, as they have been, but for him and them. Even their wars shall be holy wars, their troopers serving under God's banner. Their great men, who ride in state with a pompous retinue, shall reckon it their greatest ornament to honour God with their honours. *Holiness to the Lord* shall be written on the harness of their chariot-horses, as great men have sometimes their coat of arms with their motto painted on their coaches; every gentleman shall take the high priest's motto for his, and glory in it, and make it a memento to himself not to do any thing unworthy of it. Travellers shall have it upon their bridles, with which they guide their horses, as those who desire always to be put in mind of it, by having it continually before them, and to guide themselves in all their motions by this rule. The *bells of the horses,* which are designed to quicken them in their journey and to give notice of their approach, shall have *Holiness to the Lord* upon them," to signify that this is that which we ought to be influenced by ourselves, and make profession of to others, wherever we go. [2.] The furniture of their houses too shall be consecrated to God, to be employed in his service. *First,* The furniture of the priests' houses, or apartments adjoining to the house of the Lord. The common drinking cups they used shall be *like the bowls before the altar,* that were used either to receive the blood of the sacrifices or to present the wine and oil in, which were for the *drink-offerings.* The vessels which they used for their own tables shall be used in such a religious manner, with such sobriety and temperance, such devotedness to the glory of God, and such a mixture of pious thoughts and expressions, that their meals shall look like sacrifices; they shall eat and drink, not to themselves, but to him that spreads their tables and fills their cups. And thus, in ministers' families especially, should common actions be done after a godly sort, however they are done in other families. *Secondly,* The furniture of other houses, those of the common people: *"Every pot in Jerusalem and in Judah shall be holiness to the Lord.* The pots in which they boil their meat, the cups out of which they drink their wine (Jer. 35:5), in these God's good creatures shall never be abused to excess, nor that made the food and fuel of lust which should be oil to the wheels of obedience," as had formerly been, when *all tables were full of vomit and filthiness,* Isa. 28:8. "What they eat and drink out of these shall nourish their bodies for the service of God; and out of these they shall give liberally for the relief of the poor;" then are they *Holiness to the Lord,* as the merchandise and the hire of the converted Tyrians are said to be (Isa. 23:18); for both in our gettings and in our spendings we must have an eye to the will of God as our rule and the glory of God as our end. *Thirdly,* When there shall be such an abundance of real holiness people shall not be nice and curious about ceremonial holiness: *"Those that sacrifice shall come and take* of these common vessels, *and seethe* their sacrifices *therein,* making no distinction between them and the *bowls before the altar."* In gospel-times the true worshippers shall worship God *in spirit and in truth,* and *neither in this mountain nor yet at Jerusalem,* Jn. 4:21. One place shall be as acceptable to God as another *(I will that men pray every where);* and one vessel shall be as acceptable as another. Little regard shall be had to the circumstance, provided there be nothing indecent or disorderly, while the substance is religiously preserved and adhered to. Some think it intimates that there should be greater numbers of sacrifices offered than the vessels of the sanctuary would serve for; but, rather than any should be turned back or deferred. they shall make no difficulty at all of using common vessels, as the Levites in a case of necessity helped the priests to kill the sacrifices, 2 Chr. 29:34.

(2.) There shall be no unholiness introduced into their sacred things, to corrupt them: *In that day there shall be no more the Canaanite in the house of the Lord of hosts.* Some read it, There shall be no more *the merchant,* for so a Canaanite sometimes signifies; and they think it was fulfilled when Christ once and again drove the buyers and sellers out of the temple. Or though those that were Canaanites, strangers and foreigners, shall be brought into the house of the Lord, yet they shall cease to be Canaanites; they shall have nothing of the spirit or disposition of Canaanites in them. Or it intimates that though in gospel-times people should grow indifferent as to holy vessels, yet they should be very strict in church-discipline, and careful not to admit the profane to special ordinances, but to separate between the precious and the vile, between Israelites and Canaanites. Yet this will not have its full accomplishment short of the heavenly Jerusalem, that *house of the Lord of hosts,* into which *no unclean thing shall enter;* for at the end of time, and not before, Christ shall gather out of his kingdom every thing that offends, and the tares and wheat shall be perfectly and eternally separated.

AN EXPOSITION, WITH PRACTICAL OBSERVATIONS, OF

THE PROPHECY OF MALACHI

God's prophets were his witnesses to his church, each in his day, for several ages, witnesses for him and his authority, witnesses against sin and sinners, attesting the true intents of God's providences in his dealings with his people then and the kind intentions of his grace concerning his church in the days of the Messiah, to whom all the prophets bore witness, for they all agreed in their testimony; and now we have only one witness more to call, and we have done with our evidence; and though he be the last, and in him prophecy ceased, yet the Spirit of prophecy shines as clearly, as strongly, as brightly in him as in any that went before, and his testimony challenges an equal regard. The Jews say, Prophecy continued forty years under the second temple, and this prophet they call the *seal of prophecy,* because in him the series or succession of prophets broke off and came to a period. God wisely ordered it so that divine inspiration should cease for some ages before the coming of the Messiah, that that great prophet might appear the more conspicuous and distinguishable and be the more welcome. Let us consider, I. The person of the prophet. We have only his name, *Malachi,* and no account of his country or parentage. *Malachi* signifies *my angel,* which has given occasion for a conjecture that this prophet was indeed an angel from heaven and not a man, as that Judges 2:1. But there is no just ground for the conjecture. Prophets were messengers, God's messengers; this prophet was so; his name is the very same with that which we find in the original (3:1) for *my messenger;* and perhaps from that word he might (though, probably, he had another name) be called *Malachi.* The Chaldee paraphrase, and some of the Jews, suggest that Malachi was the same with Ezra; but that also is groundless. Ezra was a scribe, but we never read that he was a prophet. Others, yet further from probability, make him to be Mordecai. But we have reason to conclude he was a person whose proper name was that by which he is here called; the tradition of some of the ancients is that he was of the tribe of Zebulun, and that he died young. II. The scope of the prophecy. Haggai and Zechariah were sent to reprove the people for delaying to build the temple; Malachi was sent to reprove them for the neglect of it when it was built, and for their profanation of the temple-service (for from idolatry and superstition they ran into the other extreme of impiety and irreligion), and the sins he witnesses against are the same that we find complained of in Nehemiah's time, with whom, it is probable, he was contemporary. And now that prophecy was to cease he speaks more clearly of the Messiah, as nigh at hand, than any other of the prophets had done, and concludes with a direction to the people of God to keep in remembrance the law of Moses, while they were in expectation of the gospel of Christ.

CHAPTER 1

This prophet is sent first to convince and then to comfort, first to discover sin and to reprove for that and then to promise the coming of him who shall take away sin. And this method the blessed Spirit takes in dealing with souls, Jn. 16:8. He first opens the wound and then applies the healing balm. God had provided (and one would think effectually) for the engaging of Israel to himself by providences and ordinances; but it seems, by the complaints here made of them, that they received the grace of God in both these in vain. I. They were very ungrateful to God for his favours to them, and rendered not again according to the benefit they received (*v.* 1–5). II. They were very careless and remiss in the observance of his institutions; the priests especially were so, who were in a particular manner charged with them (*v.* 6–14). And what shall we say of those whom neither providences nor ordinances work upon, and who affront God in those very things wherein they should honour him?

Verses 1–5

The prophecy of this book is entitled, *The burden of the word of the Lord* (*v.* 1), which intimates, 1. That it was of great weight and importance; what the false prophets said was light as the chaff, what the true prophets said was ponderous as the wheat, Jer. 23:28. 2. That it ought to be often repeated to them and by them, as the burden of a song. 3. That there were those to whom it was a burden and a reproach; they were weary of it, and found themselves so aggrieved by it that they were not able to bear it. 4. That to them it would prove a burden indeed, to sink them to the lowest hell, unless they repented. 5. That to those who loved it and embraced it, and bade it welcome, though it was a light burden, as our Saviour calls it (Mt. 11:30), yet it was a burden.

This *burden of the word of the Lord* was sent, 1. To Israel, for to them pertained the lively oracles of prophecy as well as those of the written word. Many prophets God had sent to Israel, and now he will try them with one more. 2. *By Malachi, by the hand of Malachi,* as if it were not a message by word of mouth, but a letter put into his hand, for the greater certainty.

In these verses, they are charged with ingratitude, in that they were not duly sensible of God's distinguishing goodness to them; and such a charge as this may well be called a burden, for it is a heavy one.

I. God asserts the great kindness he had, and had often expressed, for them (*v.* 2): *I have loved you, saith the Lord.* Thus abruptly does the sermon begin, as if God intended, whatever reproofs should be given them, to reconcile them to his love, and to take care that they should still have good thoughts of him. *As many as I love I rebuke and chasten.* Thus kindly does the sermon begin. God will have his people satisfied that he loves them and is ever mindful of his love. This is the same with what he said of old to the virgin of Israel, that he might engage her affections to himself (Jer. 31:3, 4): *Yea I have loved thee with an everlasting love.* In this one word God sums up all his gracious dealings with them; love was the spring of all; he loved them because he would *love them* (Deu. 7:7, 8), loved them in their childhood, Hos. 11:1. His delight was in them, Isa. 62:4. *"I have loved you,* but you have not loved me, nor made any suitable returns for my love." Note, God's people need to be often reminded of his love to them.

II. They question his love, and diminish the instances of it, and seem to quarrel with him for telling them of it: *Yet you say, Wherein hast thou loved us?* As God traces up all his favours to them to the fountain, which was his love, so he traces up all their sins against him to the fountain, which was their contempt of his love. Instead of acknowledging his kindness, and studying what they shall render, they scorn to own that they have been beholden to him, challenge him to produce proofs of his love that are material, and think and speak very slightly of the instances they have had of his kindness, as if they were so few, so small, as not to be worth taking notice of, and no more than what they had sufficiently made returns for, or at least than he had sufficiently balanced with instances of his wrath. "Have we not been wasted, impoverished, and carried captive; and wherein then *hast thou loved us?"* Note, God justly takes it very ill to have his favours slighted, as not worth speaking of; and it is very absurd for us to ask wherein he has loved us, when, which way soever we look, we meet with the proofs and instances of his love to us.

III. He makes it out, beyond contradiction, that he has loved them, loved them in a distinguishing way, which was in a special manner obliging. For proof of this he shows the difference he had made, and would still make, between

Jacob and Esau, between Israelites and Edomites. Some read their question, *Wherefore hast thou loved us?* as if they did indeed own that he had loved them, but withal insinuate that there was a reason for it — that he loved them because their father Abraham had loved him, so that it was not a free love, but a love of debt, to which he replies, *"Was not Esau* as near akin to Abraham as you are? Was he not *Jacob's own brother,* his elder brother? And therefore, if there were any right to a recompence for Abraham's love, Esau had it, and yet *I hated Esau* and *loved Jacob."*

1. Let them see what a difference God had made between Jacob and Esau. Esau was Jacob's brother, his twin-brother: *"Yet I loved Jacob* and *I hated Esau,* that is, took Jacob into covenant, and entailed the blessing on him and his, but refused and rejected Esau." Note, Those that are taken into covenant with God, that have the lively oracles and the means of grace committed to them, have reason to look upon these as tokens of his love. Jacob is loved, for he has these, Esau hated, for he has not. The apostle quotes this (Rom. 9:13), and compares it with what the oracle said to Rebecca concerning her twins (Gen. 25:23), *The elder shall serve the younger,* to illustrate the doctrine of God's sovereignty in dispensing his favours; for *may he not do what he will with his own?* Esau was justly hated, but Jacob freely loved; even so, Father, *because it seemed good in thy eyes,* and it is not for us to ask why or wherefore.

2. Let them see what he was now doing and would do with them, pursuant to this original difference.

(1.) The Edomites shall be made the monuments of God's justice, and he will be glorified in their utter destruction: For *Esau have I hated;* I *laid his mountains waste,* the mountains of Seir, which were *his heritage.* When all that part of the world was ravaged by the Chaldean army the country of Edom was, among the rest, laid in ruins, and became a habitation *for the dragons of the wilderness,* so perfectly desolate was it; as was foretold, Isa. 34:6, 11. The Edomites had triumphed in Jerusalem's overthrow (Ps. 137:7), and therefore it was just with God to put the same cup of trembling into their hands. And, though Edom's ruins were last, yet they were lasting, and the desolation perpetual; and in this the difference was made between Jacob and Esau, and is made between the righteous and the wicked, to whom otherwise all things come alike, and there seems to be one event. Jacob's cities are laid waste, but they are rebuilt; Edom's are laid waste, and never rebuilt. The sufferings of the righteous will have an end and will end well; all their grievances will be redressed, and their sorrow turned into joy; but the sufferings of the wicked will be endless and remediless, as Edom's desolations, *v.* 4. Observe here, [1.] The vain hopes of the Edomites, that they shall have their ruins repaired as well as Israel, though they had no promise to build their hope upon. They say, "It is true, *we are impoverished;* it is the common chance, and there is no remedy; but *we will return and build the desolate places;* we are resolved we will" (not so much as asking God leave); *"we will* whether he will or no; nay, we will do it in defiance of God's curse, and that sentence pronounced upon Edom (Isa. 34:10), *From generation to generation it shall lie waste."* They build presumptuously, as Hiel built Jericho in direct contradiction to the word of God (1 Ki. 16:34), and it shall speed accordingly. Note, It is common for those whose hearts are unhumbled under humbling providences to think to make their part good against God himself, and to build, and plant, and flourish again as much as ever, though God has said that they shall be impoverished. But see, [2.] The dashing of these hopes and the disappointment of them: They say, *We will build;* but what says *the Lord of hosts?* For we are sure his word shall stand, and not theirs; and he says, *First,* Their attempts shall be baffled: *They shall build, but I will throw down.* Note, Those that walk contrary to God will find that he will walk contrary to them; for *who ever hardened his heart against God and prospered?* When the Jews had rejected Christ and his gospel they became Edomites, and this word was fulfilled in them; for when, in the time of the emperor Adrian, they attempted to rebuild Jerusalem, God by earthquakes and eruptions of fire threw down what they built, so that they were forced to quit the enterprise. *Secondly,* They shall be looked upon by all as abandoned to utter ruin. All that see them shall call them *the border of wickedness,* a sinful nation, incurably so, and therefore *the people against whom the Lord has indignation for ever.* Since their wickedness is such as will never be reformed, their desolations shall be such as are never to be repaired. Against Israel God was a *little displeased* (Zec. 1:15), but against Edom he has indignation, and will have for ever, for they are *the people of his curse,* Isa. 34:5.

(2.) The Israelites shall be made the monuments of his mercy, and he will be glorified in their salvation, *v.* 5. "The Edomites shall be stigmatized as a people hated of God, *but your eyes shall see* your doubts concerning his love to you for ever silenced; for you shall say, and have cause to say, *The Lord* is and *will be magnified from the border of Israel,* from every part and border of the land of Israel." The border of Edom is a *border of wickedness,* and therefore the Lord will have *indignation against it for ever;* but the *border of Israel* is a *border of holiness,* the *border of the sanctuary* (Ps. 78:54), and therefore God will make it to appear (though it may for a time lie desolate) that he has mercy in store for it, and thence *he will be magnified;* he will give his people Israel both cause, and hearts, to praise him. When the border of Edom still remains desolate, and the border of Israel is repaired and replenished, then it will appear that God has loved Jacob. Note, [1.] Those who doubt of God's love to his people shall, sooner or later, have convincing and undeniable proofs given them of it: *"your* own *eyes shall see* what you will not believe." [2.] Deliverances out of trouble are to be reckoned proofs of God's good-will to his people, though they may be suffered to fall into trouble, Ps. 34:19. [3.] Distinguishing favours are very obliging. If God rear up again the border of Israel, but leave the border of Edom in ruins, let no Israelite ask, for shame, *Wherein hast thou loved us?* [4.] The dignifying of Israel is the magnifying of the God of Israel, and, one way or other, God will have honour from his professing people. [5.] God's goodness being his glory, when he does us good we must proclaim him great, for that is magnifying him. It is an instance of his goodness that he has *pleasure in the prosperity of his servants,* and for this those that love his salvation say, *The Lord be magnified,* Ps. 35:27.

Verses 6–14

The prophet is here, by a special commission, calling the priests to account, though they were themselves appointed judges, to call the people to an account. Let the rulers in the house of God know that there is one above them, who will reckon with them for their maladministrations. Thus *saith the Lord of hosts to you, O priests! v.* 6. God will have a saying to unfaithful ministers; and it concerns those who speak from God to his people to hear and heed what he says to them, that they may *save themselves* in the first place, otherwise how should they help to *save those that hear them?* It is a severe, and no doubt a just reproof, that is here given to the *priests,* for the profanation of the holy things of God, with which they were entrusted; and, if this was the crime of the priests, we have reason to fear the people also were guilty of it: so that what is said to *the priests* is *said to all,* nay, it is *said to us,* who, as Christians, profess ourselves, not only the people of God, but priests to him. Observe here,

I. What it was that God expected from them, and with what good reason he expected it (*v.* 6): *A son honours his father,* because he is his father; nature has written this law in the hearts of children, before God wrote it at Mount Sinai; nay, *a servant,* though his obligation to his master is not natural, but by voluntary compact, yet thinks it his duty to honour him, to be observant of his orders, and true to his interests. Children and servants pay respect to their parents and masters; every one cries out shame on them if they do not, and their own hearts cannot but reproach them too; the order of families is thus kept up, and it is their beauty and advantage. But the priests, who are God's children and his servants, do not fear and honour him. They were *fathers* and *masters* to the people, and expected to be called so (Judges 18:19, Mt. 22:7, 10) and to be reverenced and obeyed as such; but they forgot their Father and Master in heaven, and the duty they owed to him. We may each of us charge upon ourselves what is here charged upon the priests. Note, 1. We are every one of us to look upon God as our Father and Master, and upon ourselves as his children and servants. 2. Our relation to God as our Father and Master strongly obliges us to fear and honour him. If we honour and fear the fathers of our flesh, much more the Father and Master of our spirits, Heb. 12:9. 3. It is a thing to be justly complained of, and lamented, that God is so little feared and honoured even by those that own him for their Father and Master. *Where is his honour? Where is his fear?*

II. What the contempt was which the priests put upon God.

1. This is that, in general, which is charged upon them: — (1.) They despised God's name; their familiarity with it, as priests, bred contempt of it, and served them only to gain a veneration by it for themselves and their own name, while God's name was of small account with them. God's name is all that whereby he has made himself known — his word and ordinances; these they had low thoughts of, and vilified that which it was their business to magnify; and no wonder that when they despised it themselves they did that which made it despicable to others, causing even the *sacrifices of the Lord to be abhorred,* as Eli's sons did. (2.) They *profaned* God's name, *v.* 12. They *polluted* it, *v.* 7. They not only made no account of sacred things, but they made an ill use of them, and perverted them to the service of the worst and vilest purposes — their own pride, covetousness, and luxury. There cannot be a greater provocation to God than the profanation of his name; for it is holy and reverend. His purity cannot be polluted by us, for he is unspotted, but his name may be profaned; and nothing profanes it more than the misconduct of priests, whose business it is to do honour to it. This is the general charge exhibited against them. To this they plead *Not guilty,* and challenge God to prove it upon them, and to make good the charge, which added daring impudence to their daring impiety: *You say, Wherein have we despised thy name?* (*v.* 6), and *wherein have we polluted thee? v.* 7. It is common with proud sinners, when they are reproved, to stand thus upon their own justification. These priests had most horridly profaned sacred things, and yet, like the *adulterous woman,* they said that they had *done no wickedness;* they were so inobservant of themselves that they remembered not or reflected not upon their own acts, or they were so ignorant of the divine law that they thought there was no harm in them, and that what they did could not be construed into despising God's name, or they were so atheistical as to imagine that though they knew their own guilt yet God did not, or they were so scornful in their conduct towards God and his prophets that they took a pride in bantering a serious and just reproof, and turning it off with a jest. They either laugh at the reproof, as those that despise it, and harden their hearts against it, or they laugh it off, as those that resolve they will not be touched by it, or will not seem to be so. Which way soever we take it, their defence was their offence, and, in justifying themselves, their own tongues condemned them, and their saying, *Wherein have we despised thy name?* proved them proud and perverse. Had they asked this question with a humble desire to be told more particularly wherein they had offended, it would have been an evidence of their repentance, and would have given hopes of their reformation; but to ask it thus in disdain and defiance of the word of God argues their hearts *fully set in them to do evil.* Note, Sinners ruin themselves by studying to baffle their own convictions; but they will find it *hard to kick against the pricks.*

2. Justly might they have been convicted and condemned upon the general charge, and their plea thrown out as frivolous; but God will not only overcome, but will be clear, will be justified when he judges, and therefore he shows them very particularly wherein they had despised his name, and what the contempt was that they cast upon him. As formerly, when he charged them with idolatry, so now, when he charges them with profaneness, he bids them *see their way in the valley* and *know what they have* done, Jer. 2:23.

(1.) They despised God's name in what they said, in the low opinion they had of his institutions: *"You say* in your hearts, and perhaps speak it out when you priests get together over your cups. out of the hearing of the people, *The table of the Lord is contemptible"* (*v.* 7), and again (*v.* 12), "You say, *The table of the Lord is polluted;* it is to be no more regarded than any other table." Either the table in the temple, on which the show-bread was placed, is that which they reflect upon (not understanding the mystery of it, they despised it as an insignificant thing), or rather the altar of burnt-offerings is here called the table, for there God, and his priests, and his people, did, as it were, feast together upon the sacrifices, in token of friendship. This they thought was contemptible. Formerly, in the days of superstition, it was thought contemptible in comparison with the idolatrous alters that the heathen had, and was set aside to make room for a new-fashioned one (2 Ki. 16:14, 15); now it is thought contemptible in comparison with their own tables, and those of their great men: *The fruit thereof, even his meat, is contemptible.* Those who served at the altar were to live upon the altar; but they complained that they lived poorly and meanly, and that it was not worth while to attend the service of the altar for the fruit and meat of it, for it was very ordinary and always the same again; they had no dainties, no varieties, no nice dishes. Nay, that part of the sacrifices which was given to God, the blood and the fat, they looked upon with contempt, as not worthy the multitude of laws God had made about it; they asked, "What need is there of so much ado about burning the fat and pouring out the blood?" Note, Those greatly profane and pollute God's name who despise the business of religion, though it is very honourable, as not worth taking pains in, and the advantages of religion, though highly valuable, as not worth taking pains for. Those who live in a careless neglect of holy ordinances, who come to them and attend on them irreverently, and go away from them never the better and under no concern, do in effect say, *"The table of the Lord is contemptible;* there is neither virtue nor value in it, neither credit nor comfort from it."

(2.) They despised God's name in what they did, which was of a piece with what they said, and flowed from it; corrupt principles and notions are roots of bitterness, which bear the gall and wormwood of corrupt practices. They looked upon the table and altar of the Lord as contemptible, and then, [1.] They thought any thing would serve for a sacrifice, though ever so coarse and mean, and were so far from bringing the best, as they ought to have done, that they picked out the worst they had, which was fit neither for the market nor for their own tables, and offered that at God's altar. With every sacrifice they were to bring a meat-offering of *fine flour mingled with oil;* but they brought *polluted bread* (*v.* 7), coarse bread, servants' bread, perhaps it was dry and mouldy, or made of the refuse of the wheat, which they thought good enough to be burnt upon the altar; for had it been better they would have said, *To what purpose is this waste?* And as to the beasts they offered, though the law was express that what was offered in sacrifice should not have a blemish, yet they brought *the blind, and the lame, and the sick* (*v.* 8), and again (*v.* 13), *the torn, and the lame, and the sick,* that was ready to die of itself. They looked no further than the burning of the sacrifice, and they pleaded that it was a pity to burn it if it was good for any thing else. The people were so far convinced of their duty that they would bring sacrifices; they durst not wholly omit the duty, but they brought vain oblations, mocked God, and deceived themselves, by bringing the worst they had; and the priests, who should have taught them better, accepted the gifts brought to the altar and offered them up there, because, if they should refuse them, the people would bring none at all, and then they would lose their perquisites; and therefore, having more regard to their own profit than to God's honour, they accepted that which they knew he would not accept. Some make *v.* 8 to be a continuation of what the priests profanely said *v.* 7, *You say* to the people, *If you offer the blind for sacrifice, it is not evil; or the lame and the sick, it is not evil.* Note, It is a very evil thing, whether men think so or no, to offer the blind and the lame, the torn and the sick, in sacrifice to God. If we worship God ignorantly, and without understanding, we bring the blind for sacrifice; if we do it carelessly, and without consideration, if we are cold, and dull, and dead, in it, we bring the sick; if we rest in the bodily exercise, and do not make heart-work of it, we bring the *lame;* and, if we suffer vain thoughts and distractions to lodge within us, we bring the torn. And *is not this evil?* Is it not a great affront to God and a great wrong and injury to our own souls? Do not our books tell us, nay, do not our own hearts tell us, that *this is evil?* for God, who is the best, ought to be served with the best we have. [2.] They would do no more of their work than what they were paid for. The priests would offer the sacrifices that were brought to the altar, because they had their share of them; but as for any other service of the temple, that had not a particular fee belonging to it, they would not stir a step, nor lend a hand, to it; and this was the general temper of them, *v.* 10. There is not a man among the priests that would *shut the doors,* or *kindle a fire, for nought.* If he were required to do the smallest piece of service, he would ask, how shall I be paid for it? They would do nothing *gratis,* but were all for what they could get, *every one for his gain, from his quarter,* Isa. 56:11. Note, Though God has given order that his servants be well paid in this world, yet those are no acceptable servants to him who are mercenary, and would never do the work but for the wages. [3.] Their work was a perfect drudgery to them (*v.* 13): *You said also, Behold, what a weariness is it!* Both priests and people were of this mind, that they thought God imposed too hard a task upon them; the people grudged the charge of providing the sacrifice and the priests grudged the pains of offering it; they thought the feasts of the Lord came too thick, and they were forced to attend too often, and too long, in the courts of the Lord; the priests thought it a severe penance imposed upon them to purify themselves as was required when they attended the altar and ate of the holy things; they thought the duty of their office toilsome and troublesome, and *snuffed at it* as unreasonable, and bearing hard upon them; they did it, but it was grudgingly and with reluctance. God speaks of it, in justification of his law, that he had not *made them to serve with an offering, nor wearied them with incense,* Isa. 43:23. *Wherein have I wearied thee?* Mic. 6:3. But their own wicked hearts made it a weariness; and they were, as Doeg, *detained before the Lord;* they would rather have been any where else. Note, Those are highly injurious, both to God and themselves, who are weary of his service and worship, and snuff at it.

III. Observe how God expostulates and reasons the case with them, for their conviction and humiliation. 1. Would they, durst they, affront an earthly prince thus? "You offer to God *the lame and the sick; offer it now unto thy governor* (*v.* 8), either as tribute or as a present, when thou art entreating his favour, or in gratitude for some favour received; *will he be pleased with thee?* Or, rather, will he not take himself to be affronted by it?" Note, Those who are careless and irreverent in the duties of religious worship should consider what a shame it is to offer that to their God which they would scorn to offer to their governor, to be more observant of the laws of breeding and good manners than of the laws of religion, and more afraid of being rude than of being profane. 2. Could they imagine that such sacrifices as these would be pleasing to God, or answer the end of sacrifices? *"Should I accept this at your hand, saith the Lord? v.* 13. Have you any reason to think I should either not discern or not resent the affront, that I should connive at the violation of my own laws? No (*v.* 10); *I have no pleasure in you,* and therefore, *I will not accept an offering,* such an offering, *at your hand."* If God has no pleasure in the person, if the person be not in a justified state, if he be not sanctified, God will not accept the offering. God had respect to Abel first and then to his sacrifice. Note, In order to our acceptance with God it is not enough to do that which, for the matter of it, is good, but we must do it from a right principle, in a right manner, and for a right end. It was the ancient rule laid down (Gen. 4:7), *If thou doest well, shalt thou not be accepted?* Now, if we be not accepted of God, in vain do we worship him; it is all lost labour; nay, we are all undone, for ever undone, if we come short of God's acceptance. Those therefore make a bad bargain for themselves who, to save charges in their religion, miss all the ends of it, and, by thinking to go the nearest way to work, bring nothing to pass. Those who make it the top of their ambition, as we all ought to do, *whether present or absent, to be accepted of the Lord,* will not dare to bring the *torn, and the lame, and the sick, for sacrifice.* 3. How could they expect to prevail with God in their intercessions for the people when they thus affronted God in their sacrifices? So some understand *v.* 9, as spoken ironically, *"And now* if you will do the duty of priests, and stand in the gap to turn away the judgments of God that you see ready to pour in upon us, *I pray you, beseech God that he will be gracious to us,* and to our land which is almost eaten up with locusts and caterpillars," as appears *ch.* 3:11. "Try now what interest you have at the throne of grace; improve it for the removing of this plague, for *it has been by your means;* you have provoked God to send it. But as you go on thus to profane his sacred things *will he regard your persons* or your prayers? No, you cannot prevail with him to command it away." For, *if we regard iniquity in our hearts, God will not hear us,* either for ourselves or for others. 4. Had God deserved this at their hands? No, he had provided comfortably for them, and had given them such encouragement in their work as might have engaged them to do it cheerfully and well; so some understand *v.* 10, *"Who is there among you that shall shut a door, or kindle a fire, for nought?* No, God does not expect you should serve him for nothing; you are well paid for it, and shall be so; not a cup of cold water, given for the honour of God, shall *lose its reward."* Note, The consideration of our constant receivings from God, and the present rewards of obedience in obedience, very much aggravates our slothfulness and niggardliness in our returns of duty to God.

IV. He calls them to repentance for their profanations of his holy name. So we may understand *v.* 9, *"Now, I pray you, beseech God that he will be gracious to us.* Humble yourselves for your sin, cry mightily to God for pardon, and make up in the faith and fervency of your prayers what has been wanting in the worth and value of your sacrifices; for all the rebukes of Providence we are under *are by your means."* Note, Those who have by their sins helped to kindle a fire are highly concerned by their repentance, prayers, and the personal reformation, to help to quench it. We must see how much God's judgments are by our means, and be awakened thereby to be earnest with him to return in mercy; and, if we take not this course, how can we think he should regard our persons?

V. He declares his resolution both to secure the glory of his own name and to reckon with those who profane it. Those who put contempt upon God and religion, and think to run down sacred things, let them know,

1. That they shall not gain their point. God will magnify his law and make it honourable, though they vilify it and make it contemptible; for (*v.* 11) *from the rising of the sun to the going down of the same my name shall be great among the Gentiles.* It might be said, "If these are not the worshippers whom God will accept, then he has no worshippers." As if he must make the best of their service, or else he would have no service done him; and then *what will he do for his great name?* But let him alone for that; *though Israel* be not faithful, *be not gathered,* yet God will be *glorious.* Though these priests provoke him to take down the ceremonial economy, and to abolish that *law of commandments,* which *could not make the comers thereunto perfect,* yet he will be no loser by that, at the long run; for, (1.) Instead of those carnal ordinances, which they profaned, a spiritual way of worship shall be introduced and established: *Incense shall be offered to God's name* (which signifies prayer and praise, Ps. 141:2; Rev. 8:3), instead of the blood and fat of bulls and goats. And it shall be a *pure offering,* refined, not only from the corruptions that were in the priests' practice, but from the mere bodily exercise that was in the institutions themselves, which are called *carnal ordinances, imposed till the time of reformation,* Heb. 9:10. When the hour came in which *the true worshippers worshipped the Father in spirit and in truth,* then this *incense* was *offered,* even this *pure offering.* (2.) Instead of his being worshipped and served among the Jews only, a small people in a corner of the world, he will be served and worshipped in all places, *from the rising of the sun to the going down of the same; in every place,* in every part of the world, *incense shall be offered to his name;* nations shall be discipled, and shall speak of the wonderful works of God, and have them spoken to them in their own language. This is a plain prediction of that great revolution in the kingdom of grace by which the Gentiles, who had been *strangers and foreigners,* came to be *fellow-citizens with the saints and of the household of God,* and as welcome to the throne of grace as ever the Jews had been. It is twice said (for the thing was certain), *My name shall be great among the Gentiles,* whereas hitherto in Judah only he was *known,* and *his name was great,* Ps. 76:1. God's name shall be declared to them, the declaration of it shall be received and believed, and there

shall be those among the Gentiles who shall magnify and glorify the name of God better than ever the Jews had done, even the priests themselves.

2. That they shall not go unpunished, *v.* 14. Here is the doom of those who do like these priests, for the sentence on them is a sentence on all such. Observe, (1.) The description of profane and careless worshippers. They are such as *vow and sacrifice to the Lord a corrupt thing* when they have *in their flock a male.* They have of the best, wherewith to serve and honour him, so bountiful has be been in his gifts to them, but they put him off with the worst, and think that good enough for him, so ungrateful are they in their returns to him. This was the fault of the people, but the priests connived at it, and indulged them in it. We find a distinction in the law which allowed *that* to be *offered for a free-will offering* which would *not be accepted for a vow,* Lev. 22:23. But the priests would accept it, though God would not, pretending to be more indulgent than he was, for which he will give them no thanks another day. (2.) The character given of such worshippers. They are *deceivers;* they deal falsely and fraudulently with God; they play the hypocrite with him; they pretend to honour him, in making the vow, but, when it comes to be performed, they put an affront upon him, to such a degree that it would have been *better not to have vowed than to vow* and *thus to pay;* but let not such be themselves deceived, for *God is not mocked.* Those who think to put a cheat upon God will prove, in the end, to have put a damning cheat upon their own souls. Hypocrites are deceivers, and they will prove self-deceivers, and so self-destroyers. (3.) The doom passed upon them: They are *cursed;* they expect a blessing, but will meet with a curse, the tokens of God's wrath, according to the judgment written. (4.) The reason of this doom: *"For I am a great King, saith the Lord of hosts,* and therefore will reckon with those who deal with me but as a man like themselves; *my name is dreadful among the heathen,* and therefore I will not bear that it should be contemptible among my own people." The heathen paid more respect to their gods, though idols, than the Jews did to theirs, though the only true and living God. Note, The consideration of God's universal dominion, and the universal acknowledgment of it, should restrain us from all irreverence in his service.

CHAPTER 2

There are two great ordinances which divine wisdom has instituted, the wretched profanation of both of which is complained of and sharply reproved in this chapter. I. The ordinance of the ministry, which is peculiar to the church, and is designed for the maintaining and keeping up of that; this was profaned by those who were themselves dignified with the honour of it and entrusted with the business of it. The priests profaned the holy things of God; this they are here charged with; their sin is aggravated, and they are severely threatened for it (*v.* 1–9). II. The ordinance of marriage, which is common to the world of mankind, and was instituted for the maintaining and keeping up of that; this was profaned both by the priests and by the people, in marrying strangers (*v.* 11, 12), treating their wives unkindly (*v.* 13), putting them away (*v.* 16), and herein dealing treacherously (*v.* 10, 14, 15). And that which was at the bottom of this and other instances of profaneness and downright atheism, thinking God altogether such a one as themselves, which was, in effect, to say, There is no God (*v.* 17). And these reproofs to them are warnings to us.

Verses 1–9

What was said in the foregoing chapter was directed to the priests (*ch.* 1:6): *Thus saith the Lord of hosts to you, O priests! that despise my name.* But the crimes there charged upon them they were guilty of as sacrificers, and for those they might think it some excuse that they offered what the people brought, and therefore that, if they were not so good as they should be, it was not their fault, but the people's; and therefore here the corruptions there complained of are traced to the source and spring of them — the faults the priests were guilty of as teachers of the people, as expositors of the law and the lively oracles; and this is a part of their office which still remains in the hands of gospel-ministers (who are appointed to be pastors and teachers, like the priests under the law, though not sacrificers, like them), and therefore by them the admonition here is to be particularly regarded. If the priests had given the people better instructions, the people would have brought better offerings; and therefore the blame returns upon the priests: *"And now, O you priests! this commandment is* purely *for you* (*v.* 1), who should have taught the people the good knowledge of the Lord, and how to worship him aright." Note, The governors of the churches are under God's government, and to him they are accountable. Even for those who command God has commandments. Nay (*v.* 4), *you shall know that I have sent these commandments for you.* They should know it either, 1. By the power of the Spirit working with the word for their conviction and reformation: "You shall know its original by its efficacy, whence it comes by what it does." When the word of God to us brings about, and carries on, the work of God in us, then we cannot but know that he sent it to us, that it is not the word of *Malachi — God's messenger,* but it is indeed the word of God, and is sent, not only in general to all, but in particular to us. Or, 2. By the accomplishment of the threatenings denounced against them: *"You shall know,* to your cost, *that I have sent this commandment to you,* and it shall not return void."

Let us now see what this commandment is which is for the priests, which, they must know, was sent to them; and let us put into method the particulars of the charge.

I. Here is a recital of the covenant God made with that sacred tribe, which was their commission for their work and the patent of their honour: The *Lord of hosts sent a commandment* to them, for the establishing of this covenant (*v.* 4), for his covenant is said to be the *word which he commanded* (Ps. 105:8); and he sent *this commandment* by the prophet at this time for the re-establishing of it, that it might not be cut off for their persisting in the violation of it. Let the sons of Levi know then (and particularly the sons of Aaron) what honour God put upon their family, and what a trust he reposed in them (*v.* 5): *My covenant was with him of life and peace.* Besides the covenant of peculiarity made with all the house of Israel, there was a covenant of priesthood made with one family, that they should do the services, and, upon condition of that, should enjoy all the privileges, of the priest's office — that, as Israel was a peculiar nation, a *kingdom of priests,* so the house of Aaron should be a family of priests, set apart for the service and honour of God, to bear up his name in that nation, as they were to bear up his name among the nations; both the one and the other, in different degrees, were to *give glory unto God's name, v.* 2. God covenanted with them as his menial servants, obliged them to do his work and promised to own and accept them in it. This is called *his covenant of life and peace,* because it was intended for the support of religion, which brings life and peace to the souls of men — life to the dead, peace to the distressed, or because life and peace were by this covenant promised to those priests that faithfully and conscientiously discharged their duty; they shall have peace, which implies security from all evil, and life, which comprises the summary of all good. What is here said of the covenant of priesthood is true of the covenant of grace made with all believers, as spiritual priests; it is a covenant of life and peace; it assures all believers of life and peace, everlasting peace, everlasting life, all happiness both in this world and in that to come. This covenant was made with the whole tribe of Levi when they were distinguished from the rest of the tribes, were not numbered with them, but were *taken from among* them and *appointed over the tabernacle of testimony* (Num. 1:49, 50), by virtue of which appointment God says (Num. 3:12), *The Levites shall be mine.* It was made with Aaron when he and his sons were taken to *minister unto the Lord in the priest's office,* Ex. 28:1. Aaron is therefore called *the saint of the Lord,* Ps. 106:16. It was made with Phinehas and his family, a branch of Aaron's, upon a particular occasion, Num. 25:12, 13. And there the covenant of priesthood is called, as here, the *covenant of peace,* because by it peace was made and kept between God and Israel. These great blessings of life and peace, contained in that covenant, God *gave to him,* to Levi, to Aaron, to Phinehas; he promised life and peace to them and their posterity, entrusted them with these benefits for the use and behoof of God's Israel; they received that they might give, as Christ himself did, Ps. 68:18. now, for the further opening of this covenant, observe, 1. The considerations upon which it was grounded: It was *for the fear wherewith he feared me, and was afraid before my name.* The tribe of Levi gave a signal proof of their holy fear of God, and their reverence for his name, when they appeared so bravely against the worshippers of the golden calf (Ex. 32:26); and for their zeal in that matter God bestowed this blessing upon them and invited them to consecrate themselves unto him. Phinehas also showed himself zealous in the fear of God and his judgments when, to stay the plague, he stabbed *Zimri and Cozbi,* Ps. 106:30, 31. Note, Those, and those only, who fear God's name, can expect the benefit of the *covenant of life and peace;* and those who give proofs of their zeal for God shall without fail be recompensed in the glorious privileges of the Christian priesthood. Some read this, not as the consideration of the grant, but as the condition of it: *I gave them to him, provided* that he should *fear before me.* If God grant us life and peace, he expects we should fear before him. 2. The trust that was lodged in the priests by this covenant, *v.* 7. They were hereby made *the messengers of the Lord of hosts,* messengers of that covenant of life and peace, not mediators of it, but only messengers, or ambassadors, employed to treat of the terms of peace between God and Israel. The priests were *God's mouth* to his people, from whom they must receive instructions according to the lively oracles. This was the office to which Levi was advanced; because, in his zeal for God, he *did not acknowledge his brethren, nor know his own children,* therefore *they shall teach Jacob God's judgments,* Deu. 33:9, 10. Note, It is an honour to God's servants to be employed as his messengers and to be sent on his errands. Angels have their name thence. Haggai was called *the Lord's messenger.* This being their office, observe, (1.) What is the duty of ministers: *The priests' lips should keep knowledge,* not keep it from the people, but keep it for them. Ministers must be men of knowledge; for how are those able to teach others the things of God who are themselves unacquainted with those things or unready in them? They must keep knowledge, must furnish themselves with it and retain what they have got, that they may be like the *good householder,* who *brings out of his treasury things new and old.* Not only their heads, but their lips, must keep knowledge; they must not only have it, but they must have it ready, must have it at hand, must have it (as we say) at their tongue's end, to be communicated to others as there is occasion. Thus we read of *wisdom in the lips of him that has understanding,* with which they *feed many,* Prov. 10:13, 21. (2.) What is the duty of the people: *They should seek the law at his mouth;* they should consult the priests as God's messengers, and not only hear the message, but ask questions upon it, that they may the better understand it and that mistakes concerning it may be prevented and rectified. We are all concerned fully to know *what the will of the Lord is,* to know it distinctly and certainly; we should be desirous to know it and therefore inquisitive concerning it. *Lord, what wilt thou have me to do?* We must not only consult the written word *(to the law and to the testimony),* but must have recourse to God's messengers, and desire instruction and advice from them in the affairs of our souls as we do from physicians and lawyers concerning our bodies and estates. Not but that ministers ought to lay down the law of God to those who do not enquire concerning it, or desire the knowledge of it (they must *instruct those that oppose themselves,* 2 Tim. 2:25, as well as those that offer themselves), but it is people's duty to apply to them for instruction, not only to hear, but to ask questions. *Watchman, what of the night?* Thus *if you will enquire, enquire you;* see Isa. 21:8, 11, 12. People should not only seek comfort at the mouth of their ministers, but should seek the law there; for, if we found in the way of duty, we shall find it the way of comfort.

II. Here is a memorial of the fidelity and zeal of many of their predecessors in the priest's office, which are mentioned as an aggravation of their sin in degenerating from such honourable ancestors and deserting such illustrious examples, and as a justification of God in withdrawing from them those tokens of his presence which he had granted to those that kept close to him. See here (*v.* 6) how good the godly priest was, whose steps they should have trod in, and what good he did, God's grace working with him. 1. See how good he was. He was ready and mighty in the scriptures: *The law of truth was in his mouth,* for the use of those that *asked the law at his mouth;* and in all his discourses there appeared more or less of the law of truth. Every thing he said was under the government of that law, and with it he governed others. He spoke as one having authority (every word was *a law),* and as one that had both wisdom and integrity — it was a *law of truth,* and truth is a law, it has a commanding power. It is by truth that Christ rules. *The law of truth was in his mouth,* for his resolutions of cases of conscience proposed to him were such as might be depended upon; his opinion was good law. *Iniquity was not found in his lips;* he did not *handle the word of God deceitfully,* to please men, to serve a turn, or to make an interest for himself, but told all that consulted him what the law was, whether it were pleasing or displeasing. He did not pronounce that unclean which was clean, nor that clean which was unclean, as one of the rabbin expounds it. And his conversation was of a piece with his doctrine. God himself gives him this honourable testimony: *He walked with me in peace and equity.* He did not think it enough to talk of God, but he walked with him. The temper of his mind, and the tenour of his life, were of a piece with his doctrine and profession; he lived a life of communion with God, and made it his constant care and business to please him; he lived like a priest that was chosen to *walk before God,* 1 Sa. 2:30. His conversation was quiet; he was meek and *gentle towards all men,* was a pattern and promoter of love; he walked with God in peace, was himself peaceable and a great peace-maker. His conversation was also honest; he did no wrong to any, but made conscience of rendering to all their due: *He walked with me in equity,* or rectitude. We must not, for peace-sake, transgress the rules of equity, but must keep the peace as far as is consistent with justice. *The wisdom from above is first pure, then peaceable.* Ministers, of all men, are concerned to *walk with God in peace and equity,* that they may be *examples to the flock.* 2. See what good he did; he answered the ends of his advancement to that office: *He did turn many away from iniquity;* he made it his business to do good, and God crowned his endeavours with wonderful success; he helped to save many a soul from death, and there are multitudes now in heaven blessing God that ever they knew him. Ministers must lay out themselves to the utmost for the conversion of sinners, and even among those that have the name of Israelites there is need of conversion-work, there are many to be turned from iniquity; and they must reckon it an honour, and a rich reward of their labour, if they may but be instrumental herein. It is God only that by his grace can turn men from iniquity, and yet it is here said of a pious laborious minister that he turned men from iniquity as a worker together with God, and an instrument in his hand; and *those that turn many to righteousness shall shine as the stars,* Dan. 12:3. Note, Those ministers, and those only, are likely to turn men from iniquity, that preach sound doctrine and live good lives, and both according to the scripture; for, as one of the rabbin observes here, *When the priest is upright many will be upright.*

III. Here is a high charge drawn up against the priests of the present age, who violated the covenant of the priesthood and went directly contrary both to the rules and to the examples that were set before them. Many particulars of their sins we had in the foregoing chapter, and we find (Neh. 13) that many corruptions had crept into the church of the Jews at this time, mixed marriages, admitting strangers into the house of God, profanation of the sabbath-day, which were all owing to the carelessness and unfaithfulness of the priests; here it is charged upon them in general, 1. That they transgressed the rule: *You have departed out of the way* (*v.* 8), out of the good way which God has prescribed to you, and which your godly ancestors walked before you in. It is ill with a people when those whose office it is to guide them in the way do themselves depart out of it: *"You have not kept my ways,* not kept in them yourselves, nor done your part to keep others in them," *v.* 9. 2. That they betrayed their trust: *"You have corrupted the covenant of Levi,* have violated it, have contradicted the great intentions of it, and have done what in you lay to frustrate and defeat them; you have managed your office as if it were designed only to feed you fat and make you great; and not for the glory of God and the good of the souls of men." This was a corrupting of the covenant of Levi; it was perverting the ends of the office, and making it subservient to those sensual secular things over which it ought always to have dominion. And thus they forfeited the benefit of that covenant, and corrupted it to themselves; they *made it void,* and lost the life and peace which were by it settled upon them. We have no reason to expect God should perform his part of the covenant if we do not make conscience of performing ours. Another instance of their betraying their trust was that they were *partial in the law, v.* 9. In the law given to them they would pick and choose their duty; this they would do and that they would not do, just as they pleased; this is the fashion of hypocrites, while those whose hearts are upright with God have a *respect to all his commandments.* Or, rather, in the law they were to lay down to the people; in this they *knew faces* (so the word is); they *accepted persons;* they wilfully misinterpreted and misapplied the law, either to cross those they had a spleen against or to countenance those they had a kindness for; they would wink at those sins in some which in others they would be sharp upon, according as their interest or inclination led them. God is *no respecter of persons* in making his law, nor will he in reckoning for the breach of it; he *regards not the rich more than the poor,* and therefore his priests, his ministers, misrepresent him, and do him a great deal of dishonour, if, in doctrine or discipline, they be respecters of persons. See 1 Tim. 5:21. 3. That they did a great deal of mischief to the souls of men, which they should have helped to save: *You have caused many to stumble at the law,* not only to *fall in the law* (as the margin reads it) by transgressing it, taught and encouraged to do so by the examples of the priests, but to *stumble at the law,* by contracting prejudices against it, as if the law were the minister of sin and gave countenance to it. Thus Hophni and Phinehas by their wickedness *made the sacrifices of the Lord to be abhorred,* 1 Sa. 2:17. There are many to whom the law of God is a *stumbling-block,* the gospel of Christ *a savour of death unto death,* and Christ himself *a rock of offence;* and nothing contributes more to this than the vicious lives of those that make a profession of religion, by which men are tempted to say, "It is all a jest." This is properly a *scandal, a stone of stumbling;* there is no good reason why it should be so to any, but *woe to those by whom this offence comes.* 4. That, when they were under the rebukes both of the word and of the providence of God for it, they *would not hear,* that is, they would not heed, they *would not lay it to heart;* they were not at all grieved or shamed for their sin, nor affected with the tokens of God's displeasure which they were under. What we hear does us no good unless we lay it to heart and admit the impressions of it: *You will not lay it to heart, to give glory unto my name,* by repentance and reformation. *Therefore* we should lay to heart the things of God, that we may give glory to the name of God, may praise him in and for all that whereby he has made himself known. It is bad in any to rob God of his honour, but worst in ministers, whose office and business it is to bear up his name and to give him the glory due to it.

IV. Here is a record of the judgments God had brought upon these priests for their profaneness, and their profanation of holy things. 1. They had lost their comfort (*v.* 2): *I have already cursed your blessings.* They had not the comfort of their work, which is the satisfaction of doing good; for the blessings with which they, as priests, blessed the people, God was so far from saying *Amen* to that he turned them into curses, as he did Balaam's curses into blessings. That profane people should not have the favour of receiving God's blessings, nor those profane priests the honour of conferring and conveying them, but both should lie under the tokens of his wrath. Nor had they the comfort of their wages, for the blessings with which God blessed them were turned into a curse to them by their abuse of them; they could not receive them as the gifts of his favour when they had made themselves so obnoxious to his displeasure by not laying to heart the reproofs given them. 2. They had lost their credit (*v.* 9): *Therefore have I also made you contemptible and base before all the people.* While they glorified God he dignified them and supported their reputation, and a great interest they had in the love and esteem of the people while they did their duty and *walked with God in peace and equity;* every one had a value and veneration for them; they were truly styled *the reverend, the priests;* but when they forsook the ways of God, and corrupted the covenant of Levi, they thereby made themselves not only mean, but vile, in the eyes even of the common people, who, the more they honoured the order, the more they hated the men that were a dishonour to it. Their conduct, their misconduct, had a direct tendency to this, and God owns his hand in it, and will have it looked upon as a just judgment of his upon them, and not only produced by their sin but answering to it; they put dishonour upon God, and made *his table and the fruit thereof contemptible* (*ch.* 1:12), and therefore God justly put dishonour upon them and made them contemptible; they exposed themselves, and therefore God exposed them. Note, As sin is a reproach to any people, so especially to priests; there is not a more despicable animal upon the face of the earth than a profane, wicked, scandalous minister.

V. Here is a sentence of wrath passed upon them; and this the prophet begins with, *v.* 2, 3. But it is conditional: *If you will not lay it to heart,* implying, "If you will, God's anger shall be turned away, and all shall be well; but, if you persist in these wicked courses, hear your doom — Your sin will be your ruin." 1. They shall fall and lie under the curse of God: *I will send a curse upon you.* The wrath of God shall be revealed against them, according to the threatenings of the written word. Note, Those who violate the commands of the law lay themselves under the curses of the law. 2. Neither their employments nor their enjoyments, as priests, shall be clean to them: *"I will curse your blessings,* so that you shall neither be blessed yourselves nor blessings to the people, but even your plenty shall be a plague to you and you shall be plagues to your generation." 3. The fruits of the earth, which they had the tithe of, should be no comfort to them: *"Behold, I will corrupt your seed;* the corn you sow shall rot under ground and never come up again, the consequence of which must needs be famine and scarcity of provisions; so that no meat-offerings shall be brought to the altar, which the priests will soon have a loss of." Or it may be understood of the seed of the word which they preached; God threatens to deny his blessing to the instructions they gave the people, so that their labour shall be lost, as that of the husbandman is when the seed is corrupt; and so it agrees with that threatening (Jer. 23:32), *They shall not profit this people at all.* 4. They and their services shall be rejected of God; he will be so far from taking any pleasure in them that he will loathe and detest them: *I will spread dung in your faces, even the dung of your solemn feasts.* He refers to the sacrifices that were offered at those feasts. Instead of being himself pleased with the fat of their sacrifices, he will show himself displeased by throwing the dung of them in their faces, which he does, in effect, when he says, *Bring no more vain oblations;* your *incense is an abomination* to me. Note, Those who rest in their external performances of religion, which they should count but *dung, that they may win Christ,* shall not only come short of acceptance with God in them, but shall be filled with shame and confusion for their folly. 5. All will end, at last, in their utter ruin: *One shall take you away with it.* They shall be so overspread with the dung of their sacrifices that they shall be carried away with it to the dunghill, as a part of it. Any one shall serve to take you away, the common scavenger. *Reprobate silver shall men call them,* and treat them accordingly, *because the Lord has rejected them.*

Verses 10–17

Corrupt practices are the genuine fruit and product of corrupt principles; and the badness of men's hearts and lives is owing to some loose atheistical notions which they have got and which they govern themselves by. Now, in these verses, we have an instance of this; we here find men dealing falsely with one another, and it is because they think falsely of their God. Observe,

I. How corrupt their practices were. In general, they *dealt treacherously every man against his brother, v.* 10. It cannot be expected that he who is false to his God should be true to his friend. They had dealt treacherously with God in his tithes and offerings, and had defrauded him, and thus conscience was debauched, its bonds and cords were broken, a door was opened to all manner of injustice and dishonesty, and the bonds of relation and natural affection are broken through likewise and no difficulty made of it. Some think that the treacherous dealings here reproved are the same with those instances of oppression and extortion which we find complained of to Nehemiah about this time, Neh. 5:3–7. Therein they forgot the God of their fathers, and the covenant of their fathers, and rendered their offerings unacceptable, Isa. 1:11. But it seems rather to refer to what was amiss in their marriages, which was likewise complained of, Neh. 13:23. Two things they are here charged with, as very provoking to God in this matter — taking strange wives of heathen nations, and abusing and putting away the wives they had of their own nation; in both these they dealt treacherously and violated a sacred covenant; the former was in contempt of the covenant of peculiarity, the latter of the marriage-covenant.

1. In contempt of the covenant God made with Israel, as a peculiar people to himself, they married strange wives, which was expressly prohibited, and provided against, in that covenant, Deu. 7:3. Observe here,

(1.) What good reason they had to deal faithfully with God and one another in this covenant, and not to make marriages with the heathen. [1.] They were expressly bound out from such marriages by covenant. God engaged to do them good upon this condition, that they should not mingle with the heathen; this was the *covenant of their fathers,* the covenant made with their fathers, denoting the antiquity and the authority of it, and its being the great charter by which that nation was incorporated. They lay under all possible obligations to observe it strictly, yet they profaned it, as if they were not bound by it. Those profane the covenant of their fathers who live in disobedience to the command of the God of their fathers. [2.] They were a peculiar people, united in one body, and therefore ought to have united for the preserving of the honour of their peculiarity: *Have we not all one Father?* Yes, we have, for *has not one God created us?* Are we not all *his offspring?* And are we not *made of one blood?* Yes, certainly we are. God is a common Father to all mankind, and, upon that account, *all we are brethren,* members one of another, and therefore ought to *put away lying* (Eph. 4:25), and not to *deal treacherously,* no, not *any man against his brother.* But here it seems to refer to the Jewish nation: *Have we not all one father,* Abraham, or Jacob? This they prided themselves in, *We have Abraham to our father;* but here it is turned upon them as an aggravation of their sin in betraying the honour of their nation by intermarrying with heathens: *"Has not one God created us,* that is, formed us into a people, made us a nation by ourselves, and put a life into us, distinct from that of other nations? And should not this oblige us to maintain the dignity of our character?" Note, The consideration of the unity of the church in Christ, its founder and Father, should engage us carefully to preserve the purity of the church and to guard against all corruptions. [3.] They were dedicated to God, as well as distinguished from the neighbouring nations. *Israel was holiness to the Lord* (Jer. 2:3), taken into covenant with him, set apart by him for himself, to be to him for a name and a praise, and upon this account he *loved them* and delighted in them; the sanctuary set up among them was the *holiness of the Lord, which he loved,* of which he said, It is *my rest for ever, here will I dwell, for I have desired it;* but by marrying strange wives they profaned this holiness, and laid the honour of it in the dust. Note, Those who are devoted to God, and beloved of him, are concerned to preserve their integrity, that they may not throw themselves out of his love, nor lose the honour, or defeat the end, of their dedication to him.

(2.) How treacherously they dealt, notwithstanding, They profaned themselves in that very thing which was prescribed to them for the preserving of the honour of their singularity: *Judah has married the daughter of a strange god.* The harm was not so much that she was the daughter of a strange nation (God has made *all nations of men,* and is himself *King of nations),* but that she was the daughter of a strange god, trained up in the service and worship of false gods, at their disposal, as a daughter at her father's disposal, and having a dependence upon them; hence some of the rabbin (quoted by Dr. Pocock) say, *He that marries a heathen woman is as if he made himself son-in-law to an idol.* The corruption of the old world began with the intermarriages of the *sons of God* with the *daughters of men,* Gen. 6:2. It is the same thing that is here complained of, but as it is expressed it sounds worse: The *sons of God married the daughters of a strange god.* Herein Judah is said to have *dealt treacherously,* for they basely betrayed their own honour and *profaned* that *holiness of the Lord* which they *should have loved* (so some read it); and it is said to be *an abomination committed in Israel and in Jerusalem;* it was hateful to God, and very unbecoming those that were called by his name. Note, it is an abominable thing for those who profess the holiness of the Lord to profane it, particularly by yoking themselves unequally with unbelievers.

(3.) How severely God would reckon with them for it (*v.* 12): *The Lord will cut off the man that doeth this,* that marries the daughter of a strange god. He has, in effect, cut himself off from the holy nation, and joined in with foreigners and *aliens to the commonwealth of Israel,* and so shall his doom be; *God will cut him off, him and all that belongs to him;* so the original intimates. He shall be cut off from Israel and from Jerusalem, and not be *written among the living* there. The Lord will cut off both *the master and the scholar,* that are guilty of this sin, both the teachers and the taught. The blind leaders and the blind followers shall fall together into the ditch, *both him that wakeneth* and *him that answereth* (so it is in the margin), for the master calls up his scholar to his business, and stirs him up in it. They shall be cut off together *out of the tabernacles of Jacob.* God will no more own them as belonging to his nation; nay, and the priest that *offers an offering to the Lord,* if he marry a strange wife (as we find many of the priests did, Ezra 10:18), shall not escape; the offering he offers shall not atone for him, but he shall be cut off from the temple of the Lord, as others from the tabernacles of Jacob. *Nehemiah chased away from him,* and from the priesthood, one of the sons of the high priest, whom he found guilty of this sin, Neh. 13:28.

2. In contempt of the marriage-covenant, which God instituted for the common benefit of mankind, they abused and put away the wives they had of their own nation, probably to make room for those strange wives, when it was all the fashion to marry such (*v.* 13): *This also have you done;* this is the second article of the charge. For the way of sin is down-hill, and one violation of the covenant is an inlet to another.

(1.) Let us see what it is that is here complained of. they did not behave as they ought to have done towards their wives. [1.] They were cross with them, froward and peevish, and made their lives bitter to them, so that when they came with their wives and families to worship God at the solemn feasts, which they should have done with rejoicing, they were all out of humour; the poor wives were ready to break their hearts, and, not daring to make their case known to any other, they complained to God, and *covered the altar of the Lord with tears, with weeping, and with crying.* This is illustrated by the instance of Hannah, who, upon the account of her husband's having another wife (though otherwise a kind husband), and the discontent thence arising, whenever they went up to the house of the Lord to worship *fretted and wept,* and was in *bitterness of soul,* and *would not eat,* 1 Sa. 1:6, 7, 10. So it was with these wives here; and this was so contrary to the cheerfulness which God requires in his worshippers that it spoiled the acceptableness of their devotions: God *regards not their offering any more.* See here what a good Master we serve, who will not have his altar covered with tears, but compassed with songs. This condemns those who left his worship for that of idols, among the rites of which we find *women weeping for Tammuz* (Eze. 8:14), and the blood of the worshippers gushing out upon the altar, 1 Ki. 18:28. See also what a wicked thing it is to put others out of frame for the cheerful worship of God; though it is their fault by their fretfulness to indispose themselves for their duty, yet it is much more the fault of those who *provoked them to make them to fret.* It is a reason given why yokefellows should live in holy love and joy — *that their prayers may not be hindered,* 1 Pt. 3:7. [2.] They dealt treacherously with them, *v.* 14–16. They did not perform their promises to them, but defrauded them of their maintenance or dower, or took in concubines, to share in the affection that was due to their wives only. [3.] They *put them away,* gave them a bill of divorce, and turned them off, nay, perhaps they did it without the ceremony that the law of Moses prescribed, *v.* 16. [4.] In all this *they covered violence with their garment;* they abused their wives, and were vexatious to them, and yet, in the sight of others, they pretended to be very loving to them and tender of them, and to cast a skirt over them. It is common for those who do violence to advance some specious pretence or other wherewith to cover it as with a garment.

(2.) Let us see the proof and aggravations of the charge. [1.] It is sufficiently proved by the testimony of God himself: *"The Lord has been witness between thee and the wife of thy youth* (*v.* 14), has been witness to the marriage-covenant between thee and her, for to him you appealed concerning your sincerity in it and fidelity to it; he has been a witness to all the violations of it, and all thy treacherous dealings in contempt of it, and is ready to judge between thee and her." Note, This should engage us to be faithful both to God and to all with whom we have to do, that God himself is a witness both to all our covenants and to all our covenant-breaches; and he is a witness against whom there lies no exception. [2.] It is highly aggravated by the consideration of the person wronged and abused. *First,* "She is *thy wife;* thy own, bone of thy bone and flesh of thy flesh, the nearest to thee of all the relations thou hast in the world, and to cleave to whom thou must quit the rest." *Secondly,* "She is *the wife of thy youth,* who had thy affections when they were at the strongest, was thy first choice, and with whom thou hast lived long. Let not the darling of thy youth be the scorn and loathing of thy age." *Thirdly,* "She is *thy companion;* she has long been an equal sharer with thee in thy cares, and griefs, and joys." The wife is to be looked upon, not as a servant, but as a companion to the husband, with whom he should freely converse and *take sweet counsel,* as with a friend, and in whose company he should take delight more than in any other's; for *is she not* appointed to be *thy companion? Fourthly,* "She is *the wife of thy covenant,* to whom thou art so firmly bound that, while she continues faithful, thou canst not be loosed from her, for it was a covenant for life. It is the wife with whom thou hast covenanted, and who has covenanted with thee; there is an oath of God between you, which is not to be trifled with, is not to be played fast and loose with." Married people should often call to mind their marriage-vows, and review them with all seriousness, as those that make conscience of performing what they promised.

(3.) Let us see the reasons given why man and wife should continue together, to their lives' end, in holy love and peace, and neither quarrel with each other nor separate from each other. [1.] Because god has joined them together (*v.* 15): *Did not he make one,* one Eve for one Adam, that Adam might never *take another to her to vex her* (Lev. 18:18), nor put her away to make room for another? It is great wickedness to complain of the law of marriage as a confinement, when Adam in innocency, in honour, in Eden, in the garden of pleasure, was confined to one. Yet *God had the residue of the Spirit;* he could have made another Eve, as amiable as that he did make, but, designing *Adam a help meet for him,* he made him *one wife;* had he made him more, he would not have had a *meet help.* And wherefore did he make but one woman for one man? It was *that he might seek a godly seed — a seed of God* (so the word is), a seed that should bear the image of God, be employed in the service of God, and be devoted to his glory and honour, — that *every man having his own wife,* and *but one,* according to the law, (1 Co. 7:2), they might live in chaste and holy love, under the directions and restraints of the divine law, and not, as brute beasts, under the dominion of lust, and thus might propagate the nature of man in such a way as might make it most likely to participate of a divine nature, — that the children, being born in holy matrimony, which is an ordinance of God, and by which the inclinations of nature are kept under the regulations of God's command, might thus be made a *seed to serve him,* and be bred, as they are born, under his direction and dominion. Note, The raising up of a godly seed, which shall be *accounted to the Lord for a generation,* is one great end of the institution of marriage; but that is a good reason why the marriage-bed should be kept undefiled and the marriage bond inviolable. Husbands and wives must *therefore* live in the fear of God, that their seed may be a godly seed, else were they *unclean,* but *now they are holy, as children of the covenant,* the marriage-covenant, which was a type of the covenant of grace, and the conjugal union, when thus preserved entire, of the mystical union between Christ and his church, in which he seeks and secures to himself a godly seed; see Eph. 5:25, 32. [2.] Because he is much displeased with those who go about to put asunder *what he has joined together* (*v.* 16): *The God of Israel saith that he hateth putting away.* He hath indeed permitted it to the Jews, *for the hardness of their hearts,* or, rather, limited and clogged it (Mt. 19:8); but *he hated* it, especially as those practised it who *put away their wives for every cause,* Mt. 19:3. Let those wives that elope from their husbands and put themselves away, those husbands that are cruel to their wives and turn them away, or take their affections off from their wives and place them upon others, yea, and those husbands and wives that live asunder by consent, for want of love to each other, let such as these know that the God of Israel hates such practices, however vain men may make a jest of them.

(4.) Let us see the caution inferred from all this. We have it twice (*v.* 15): *Therefore take heed to your spirit, and let none deal treacherously against the wife of his youth;* and again, *v.* 16. Note, Those that would be kept from sin must *take heed to their spirits,* for there all sin begins; they must keep their hearts with all diligence, must keep a jealous eye upon them and a strict hand, and must watch against the first risings of sin there. We shall act as we are spirited; and therefore, that we may regulate our actions, we must consider *what manner of spirit we are of;* we must *take heed to our spirits* with reference to our particular relations, and see that we stand rightly affected to them and be of a good temper, for otherwise we shall be in danger of dealing treacherously. If our own hearts deal treacherously with us, whom will they not deal treacherously with?

II. Observe how corrupt their principles were, to which were owing all these corrupt practices. Let us trace up the streams to the fountain (*v.* 17): *You have wearied the Lord with your words.* They thought to evade the convictions of the word, and to justify themselves by cavilling with God's proceedings; but their defence was their offence, and their vindication of themselves was the aggravation of their crime; they affronted the Lord with their words, and repeated them so often, and persisted so long in their contradictions, that they even *wearied him;* see Isa. 7:13. They made him weary of doing them good as he had done, and stopped the current of his favours; or they represented him as weary of governing the world, and willing to quit it and lay aside the care of it. Note, It is a wearisome thing, even to God himself, to hear people insist upon their own justification in their corrupt and wicked practices, and plead their atheistical principles in vindication of them. But, as if God by his prophet had done them wrong, see how impudently they ask, *Wherein have we wearied him?* What are those vexatious words whereby we have wearied him? Note, Sinful words are more offensive to the God of heaven than they are commonly thought to be. But God has his proofs ready; two things they had said, at least in their hearts (and thoughts are words to God), with which they had wearied him: — 1. They had denied him to be a holy God, and had asserted that concerning him which is directly contrary to the doctrine of his holiness. As he is a holy God, he hates sin, *is of purer eyes than to behold it,* and *cannot endure to look upon it,* Hab. 1:13. He *is not a God that has pleasure in wickedness,* Ps. 5:4. And yet they had the impudence to say, in direct contradiction to this, *Every one that does evil is good in the sight of the Lord, and he delights in them.* This wicked inference they drew, without any reason, from the prosperity of sinners in their sinful courses (see *ch.* 3:15), as if God's love or hatred were to be known by that which is before us, and those must be concluded *good in the sight of the Lord* who are rich in the world. Or this they said because they wished it might be so; they were resolved to *do evil,* and yet to think themselves *good in the sight of the Lord,* and to believe that *he delighted in them,* notwithstanding; and therefore, under pretence of making God not so severe as he was commonly represented, they said as they would have it, and thought he was *altogether such a one as themselves.* Note, Those who think God a friend to sin affront him and deceive themselves. 2. They had denied him to be the righteous governor of the world. If he did not delight in sin and sinners, yet it would serve their turn to believe that he would never punish it or them. They said, *"Where is the God of judgment?* That God who, we have been so often told, would call us to an account, and reckon with us for what we have said and done — where is he? He has forsaken the earth, and takes no notice of what is said and done there; he has said that he will *come to judgment;* but *where is the promise of his coming?* We may do what we please; he sees us not, nor will regard us." It is such a challenge to the Judge of the whole earth as bids defiance to his justice, and, in effect, dares him to *do his worst.* Such scoffers as these there were in the latter days of the Jewish church, and such there shall be in the latter days of the Christian church; but their unbelief shall not make the promise of God of no effect; for the day of the Lord will come. *Behold, the Judge stands before the door;* the God of judgment *is at hand.*

CHAPTER 3

In this chapter we have, I. A promise of the coming of the Messiah, and of his forerunner; and the errand he comes upon is here particularly described, both the comfort which his coming brings to his church and people and the terror which it will bring to the wicked (*v.* 1–6). II. A reproof of the Jews for their corrupting God's ordinances and sacrilegiously robbing him of his dues, with a charge to them to amend this matter, and a promise that, if they did, God would return in mercy to them (*v.* 7–12). III. A description of the wickedness of the wicked that speak against God (*v.* 13–15), and of the righteousness of the righteous that speak for him, with the precious promises made to them (*v.*16–18).

Verses 1–6

The first words of this chapter seem a direct answer to the profane atheistical demand of the scoffers of those days which closed the foregoing chapter: *Where is the God of judgment?* To which it is readily answered, "Here he is; he is just at the door; the long-expected Messiah is ready to appear; and he says, *For judgment have I come into this world,* for that judgment which you have so impudently bid defiance to." One of the rabbin says that the meaning of this is, That God will raise up a righteous King, to set things in order, even *the king Messiah.* And the *beginning of the gospel of Christ* is expressly said to be the accomplishment of this promise, with which the Old Testament concludes, Mk. 1:1, 2. So that by this the two Testaments are, as it were, tacked together, and made to answer one another. Now here we have,

I. A prophecy of the appearing of his forerunner John the Baptist, which the prophet Isaiah had foretold (*ch.* 40:3), as the *preparing* of the *way of the Lord,* to which this seems to have a reference, for the words of the latter prophets confirmed those of the former: *Behold, I will send my messenger,* or *I do send him,* or *I am sending* him. "I am determined to send him; he will now shortly come, and will not come unsent, though to a careless generation he comes unsent for." Observe, 1. He is *God's messenger;* that is his office; he is *Malachi* (so the word is), the same with the name of this prophet; he is *my angel,* my *ambassador.* John Baptist had his commission *from heaven, and not of men.* All held John Baptist for a prophet, for he was God's messenger, as the prophets were, and came on the same errand to the world that they were sent upon — to call men to repentance and reformation. 2. He is Christ's harbinger: He *shall prepare the way before me,* by calling men to those duties which qualify them to receive the comforts of the Messiah and his coming, and by taking them off from a confidence in their relation to Abraham *as their father* (which, they thought, would serve their turn without a saviour), and by giving notice that the Messiah was now at hand, and so raising men's expectations of him, and making them readily to go into the measures he would take for the setting up of his kingdom in the world. Note, God observes a method in his work, and, before he comes, takes care to have his way prepared. This is like the giving of a sign. The church was told, long before, that the Messiah would come; and here it is added that, a little before he appears, there shall be a signal given; a great prophet shall arise, that shall give notice of his approach, and call to the everlasting gates and doors to *lift up their heads* and give him admission. The accomplishment of this is a proof that *Jesus is the Christ,* is he that *should come,* and we are to *look for no other;* for there was such a messenger sent before him, who *made ready a people prepared for the Lord,* Lu. 1:17. The Jewish writers run into gross absurdities to evade the conviction of this evidence; some of them say that this messenger is the *angel of death,* who shall take the wicked out of this life, to be sent into hell torments; others of them say that it is Messiah the son of Joseph, who shall appear before Messiah the son of David; others, this prophet himself; others, an angel from heaven: such mistakes do those run into that will not receive the truth.

II. A prophecy of the appearing of the Messiah himself: *"The Lord, whom you seek, shall suddenly come to his temple,* even *the God of judgment,* who, you think, has forsaken the earth, and you *wot not what has become of him.* The Messiah has been long called *he that should come,* and you may assure yourselves that now shortly he will come." 1. He is *the Lord — Adonai,* the basis and foundation on which the world is founded and fastened, the ruler and governor of all, that one *Lord over all* (Acts 10:36) that has all power committed to him (Mt. 28:18) and is to *reign over the house of Jacob for ever,* Lu. 1:33. 2. He is the *Messenger of the covenant,* or the *angel of the covenant,* that *blessed one* that was *sent* from heaven to negotiate a peace, and settle a correspondence, between God and man. He is the *angel,* the *archangel,* the Lord of the angels, who received commission from the Father to bring man home to God by a covenant of grace, who had revolted from him by the violation of the covenant of innocency. Christ is the *angel of this covenant,* by whose mediation it is brought about and established as God's covenant with Israel was made by the *disposition of angels,* Acts 7:53; Gal. 3:19. Christ, as a prophet, is the *messenger* and *mediator* of the covenant; nay, he is *given for a covenant,* Isa. 49:8. That covenant which is all our *salvation began to be spoken by the Lord,* Heb. 2:3. Though he is the *prince of the covenant* (as some read this) yet he condescended to be the *messenger of it,* that we might have full assurance of God's good-will towards man, upon his word. 3. He it is *whom you seek, whom you delight in,* whom the pious Jews expect and desire, and whose coming they think of with a great deal of pleasure. In looking and waiting for him, they *looked for redemption in Jerusalem* and *waited for the consolation of Israel,* Lu. 2:25, 38. Christ was to be the *desire of all nations,* desirable to all (Hag. 2:7); but he was *the desire* of the Jewish nation actually, because they had the promise of his coming made to them. Note, Those that seek Jesus shall find pleasure in him. If he be our heart's desire he will be our heart's delight; and we have reason to delight in him who is the *messenger of the covenant,* and to bid him welcome who came to us on so kind an errand. 4. He *shall suddenly come;* his coming draws nigh, and we see it not at so great a distance as the patriarchs saw it at. Or, He shall come immediately after the appearing of John Baptist, shall even tread on the heels of his forerunner; when that *morning-star* appears, believe that the *Sun of righteousness* is not far off. Or, He *shall come suddenly,* that is, he shall come when by many he is not looked for; as his second coming will be, so his first coming was, *at midnight,* when some had done looking for him, for *shall he find faith on the earth?* Lu. 18:8. The Jews reckon the Messiah among the things that come *unawares;* so Dr. Pocock. And the coming of the Son of man in his day is said to be *as the lightning,* which is very surprising, Lu. 17:24. 5. He *shall come to his temple,* this temple at Jerusalem, which was lately built, that *latter house* which he was to be the glory of. It is his temple, for it is *his Father's house,* Jn. 2:16. Christ, at forty days old, was presented in the temple, and thither Simeon went *by the Spirit,* according to the direction of this prophecy, to see him, Lu. 2:27. At twelve years old he was in the temple *about his Father's business,* Lu. 2:49. When he rode in triumph into Jerusalem, it should seem that he went directly *to the temple* (Mt. 21:12), and (*v.* 14) thither the *blind and the lame came to him to be healed;* there he often preached, and often disputed, and often wrought miracles. By this it appears that the Messiah was to come while *that temple* was standing; that, therefore, being long since destroyed, we must conclude that he has come, and we are to look for no other. Note, Those that would be acquainted with Christ and obtain his favour must meet him in his temple, for there he *records his name* and there he will bless his people. There we must receive his oracles and there we must pay our homage. 6. The promise of this coming is repeated and ratified: *Behold, he shall come, saith the Lord of hosts;* you may depend upon his word, who cannot lie, he *shall come,* he *will come,* he *will not tarry.*

III. An account given of the great ends and intentions of his coming, *v.* 2. He is one whom they seek, and one whom they delight in; and yet *who may abide the day of his coming?* It is a thing to be thought of with great seriousness, and with a holy awe and reverence; for who *shall stand when he appears,* though he comes not to condemn the world, but that the world through him might have life? This may refer,

1. To the terrors of his appearance. Even in the days of his flesh there were some emanations of his glory and

power, such as none could stand before, witness his transfiguration, and the prodigies that attended his death; and we read of some that trembled before him, as Mk. 5:33.

2. To the troublous times that should follow soon after. The Jewish doctors speak of the *pangs* or *griefs* of the Messiah, meaning (they say) the great afflictions that should be to Israel at the time of his coming; he himself speaks of great tribulation then approaching, *such as was not since the beginning of the world, nor ever shall be,* Mt. 24:21.

3. To the trial which his coming would make of the children of men. *He shall be like a refiner's fire,* which separates between the gold and the dross by melting the ore, or *like fuller's soap,* which with much rubbing fetches the spots out of the cloth. Christ came to discover men, *that the thoughts of many hearts might be revealed* (Lu. 2:35), to distinguish men, to separate between the precious and the vile, for *his fan in his hand* (Mt. 3:12), to *send fire on the earth, not peace, but rather division* (Lu. 12:49, 51), to *shake heaven and earth,* that the *wicked* might be *shaken out* (Job 38:13) and *that the things which cannot be shaken might remain,* Heb. 12:27. See what the effect of the trial will be that shall be made by the gospel.

(1.) The gospel shall work good upon those that are disposed to be good, to them it shall be a savour of life unto life (*v.* 3): *He shall sit as a refiner.* Christ by his gospel shall purify and reform his church, and by his Spirit working with it shall regenerate and cleanse particular souls; for to this end he gave himself for the church, *that he might sanctify and cleanse it with the washing of water by the word* (Eph. 5:26) and *purify to himself a peculiar people,* Tit. 2:14. Christ is the great refiner. Observe, [1.] Who they are that he will purify — *the sons of Levi,* all those that are devoted to his praise and employed in his service, as the tribe of Levi was, and whom he designs to make unto our God spiritual priests (Rev. 1:6), a *holy priesthood,* 1 Pt. 2:5. Note, All true Christians are sons of Levi, set apart for God, to do the service of his sanctuary, and to *war the good warfare.* [2.] How he will purify them; he will *purge them as gold and silver,* that is, he will sanctify them inwardly; he will not only wash away the spots they have contracted from without, but will take away the dross that is found in them; he will separate from them their indwelling corruptions, which rendered their faculties worthless and useless, and so make them like gold refined, both valuable and serviceable. *He will purge them* with fire, *as gold and silver are purged,* for *he baptizes with the Holy Ghost and with fire* (Mt. 3:11), with the Holy Ghost working like fire. He will purge them by *afflictions and manifold temptations,* that the *trial of their faith* may be *found to praise and honour,* 1 Pt. 1:6, 7. He will purge them so as to make them a precious people to himself. [3.] What will be the effect of it: *That they may offer unto the Lord an offering in righteousness,* that is, that they may be in sincerity converted to God and consecrated to his praise (hence we read of the *offering up,* or *sacrificing, of the Gentiles* to God, when they were *sanctified by the holy Ghost,* Rom. 15:16), and that they may in a spiritual manner worship God according to his will, may *offer the sacrifices of righteousness,* (Ps. 4:5), the offering of prayer, and praise, and holy love, that they may be the *true worshippers,* who *worship the Father in spirit and in truth,* Jn. 4:23, 24. Note, We cannot offer unto the Lord any right performances in religion unless our persons be justified and sanctified. Till we ourselves be refined and purified by the grace of God, we cannot do any thing that will redound to the glory of God. God had respect to Abel first, and then to his offering; and *therefore* God purges his people, that they may offer their offerings to him in righteousness, Zep. 3:9. He makes the tree good that the fruit may be good. And then it follows (*v.* 4), *The offering of Judah and Jerusalem shall be pleasant unto the Lord.* It shall no longer be offensive, as it has been, when, in the former days, they worshipped other gods with the God of Israel, or when, in the present days, they brought the torn, and the lame, and the sick, for sacrifice; but it shall be *acceptable;* he will be pleased with the offerers, and their offerings, *as in the days of old and as in former years,* as in the primitive times of the church, as when God had respect to Abel's sacrifice and smelled a savour of rest from Noah's, and when he kindled Aaron's sacrifice with fire from heaven. When the Messiah comes, *First,* He will, by his grace in them, make them acceptable; when he has purified and refined them, then they

shall offer such sacrifices as God requires and will accept. *Secondly,* He will, by his intercession for them, make them accepted; he will recommend them and their performances to God, so that their prayers, being perfumed with the incense of his intercession, shall be pleasant unto the Lord; for he has *made us accepted in the Beloved,* and in him is well pleased with those that are in him (Mt. 3:17) and bring forth fruit in him.

(2.) It shall turn for a testimony against those that are resolved to go on in their wickedness, *v.* 5. This is the direct answer to their challenge, *"Where is the God of judgment?* You shall know where he is, and shall know it to your terror and confusion, for *I will come near to you to judgment;* to you that set divine justice at defiance." To them the gospel of Christ will be a *savour of death unto death;* it will bind them over to condemnation and will judge them in the great day, Jn. 12:48. Let us see here, [1.] Who the sinners are that must appear to be judged by the gospel of Christ. They are the *sorcerers,* who died in spiritual wickedness, that forsake the oracles of the God of truth to consult the father of lies; and the *adulterers,* who wallow in the lusts of the flesh, those adulterers who were charged with *dealing treacherously* (ch. 2:15); and the *false swearers,* who profane God's name and affront his justice, by calling him to witness to a lie; and the oppressors, who barbarously injure and trample upon those who lie at their mercy, and are not able to help themselves: they *defraud the hireling in his wages* and will not give him what he agreed for; they crush *the widow and fatherless,* and will not pay them their just debts, because they cannot prove them, or have not wherewithal to sue for them; the poor *stranger* too, who has no friend to stand by him and is ignorant of the laws of the country, they *turn aside from his right,* so that he cannot keep or cannot recover his own. That which is at the bottom of all this is, *They fear not me, saith the Lord of hosts.* The transgression of the wicked plainly declares *that there is no fear of God before his eyes.* Where no fear of God is no good is to be expected. [2.] Who will appear against them: *I will come near,* says God, *and will be a swift witness against* them. They justify themselves, and, their sins having been artfully concealed, hope to escape punishment for want of proof; but God, who sees and knows all things, will himself be witness against them, and his omniscience is instead of a thousand witnesses, for to it the sinner's own conscience shall be made to subscribe, and so *every mouth shall be stopped.* He will be a swift witness; though they reflect upon him as slow and dilatory, and ask, *Where is the God of judgment,* and where the promise of his coming? they will find that *he is not slack* concerning his threatenings any more than he is concerning his promises. Judgment against those sinners shall not be put off for want of evidence, for he will be a swift witness. His judgment shall overtake them, and it shall be impossible for them to outrun it. *Evil pursues sinners.*

IV. The ratification of all this (*v.* 6): *For I am the Lord; I change not; therefore you sons of Jacob are not consumed.* Here we have, 1. God's immutability asserted by Himself, and glorified in: *"I am the Lord; I change not;* and therefore no word that I have spoken shall fall to the ground." Is God a just revenger of those that rebel against him? Is he the bountiful rewarder of those that diligently seek him? In both these he is unchangeable. Though the sentence passed against evil works (*v.* 5) be not executed speedily, yet it will be executed, for he is *the Lord;* he *changes not;* he is as much an enemy to sin as ever he was, and impenitent sinners will find him so. There needs no *scire facias* — *a writ calling one to show cause,* to revive God's judgment, for it is never antiquated, or out of date, but against those that go on still in their trespasses the curse of his law still remains *in full force, power, and virtue.* 2. A particular proof of it, from the comfortable experience which the people of Israel had had of it. They had reason to say that he was an unchangeable God, for he had been faithful to his covenant with them and their fathers; if he had not adhered to that, they would have been consumed long ago and cut off from being a people; they had been false and fickle in their conduct to him, and he might justly have abandoned them, and then they would soon have been consumed and ruined; but because he *remembered his covenant,* and would not violate that, nor alter the thing that had gone forth out of his lips, they were preserved

from ruin and recovered from the brink of it. It was purely because he would be as good as his word, Deu. 7:8; Lev. 26:42. Now as God had kept them from ruin, while the covenant of peculiarity remained in force, purely because he would be faithful to that covenant, and would show that *he is not a man that he should lie* (Num. 23:19), so, when that covenant should be superseded and set aside by the New Testament, and they, by rejecting the blessings of it, lay themselves open to the curses, he will show that in the determinations of his wrath, as well as in those of his mercy, *he is not a man, that he should repent,* but will then be as true to his threatenings as hitherto he had been to his promises; see 1 Sa. 15:29. We may all apply this very sensibly to ourselves; because we have to do with a God that *changes not,* therefore it is that *we are not consumed,* even *because his compassions fail not; they are new every morning; great is his faithfulness,* Lam. 3:22, 23.

Verses 7–12

We have here God's controversy with the men of that generation, for deserting his service and robbing him — wicked servants indeed, that not only run away from their Master, but run away with their Master's goods.

I. They had run away from their Master, and quitted the work he gave them to do (*v.* 7): *You have gone away from my ordinances and have not kept them.* The ordinances of God's worship were the business which as servants they must mind, the talents which they must trade with, and the trust which was committed to them to keep; but they went away from them, grew weary of them, and withdrew their neck from that yoke; they deviated from the rule that God had prescribed to them, and betrayed the trust lodged with them. They had revolted from God, not only in worship, but in conversation; they had not *kept his ordinances.* This disobedience they were chargeable with, and had been guilty of, even *from the days of their fathers;* either as in the days of their fathers of old, who were sent into captivity for their disobedience, or, "Now, for some generations past, you have fallen off from what you were, when first you came back out of captivity." Ezra owns it in one particular instance: *Since the days of our fathers have we been in a great trespass unto this day,* Ezra 9:7. Now observe, 1. What a gracious invitation God gives them to return and repent: *"Return unto me,* and to your duty, return to your service, return to your allegiance, return as a traveller that has missed his way, as a soldier that has run his colours, as a treacherous wife that has gone away from her husband; return, thou backsliding Israel, return to me; and then *I will return unto you* and be reconciled, will remove the judgments you are under and prevent those you fear." This had been of old the burden of the song (Zec. 1:3), and is still. 2. What a peevish answer they return to this gracious invitation: *"But you said* with disdain, said it to the prophets that called you, said it to one another, said it to your own hearts, to stifle the convictions you were under; you said, *Wherein shall we return?"* Note, God takes notice what returns our hearts make to the calls of his word, what we say and what we think when we have heard a sermon, what answer we give to the message sent us. When God calls us to *return,* we should answer as those did Jer. 3:22, *Behold, we come.* But not as these here, *Wherein shall we return?* (1.) They take it as an affront to be *told of their faults,* and called upon to amend them; they are ready to say, "What ado do these prophets make about returning and repenting; why are we disgraced and disturbed thus, our own consciences and our neighbours stirred up against us?" It is ill with those who thus count reproofs reproaches, and *kick against the pricks.* (2.) They are so ignorant of themselves, and of the strictness, extent, and spiritual nature, of the divine law, that they see nothing in themselves to be repented of, or reformed; they are pure in their own eyes, and think they need no repentance. (3.) They are so firmly resolved to go on in sin that they will find a thousand foolish frivolous excuses to shift off their repentance, and turn away the calls that are given them to repent. They seem to speak only as those that wanted something to say; it is a mere evasion, a banter upon the prophet, and a challenge to him to descend to particulars. Note, Many ruin their own souls by baffling the calls that are given them to repent of their sins.

II. They had robbed their Master, and embezzled his

goods. They had asked, *"Wherein shall we return? What have we done amiss?"* And he soon tells them. Observe, 1. The prophet's high charge exhibited, in God's name, against the people. They stand indicted for robbery, for sacrilege, the worst of robberies: *You have robbed me.* He expostulates with them upon it: *Will a man be so daringly impudent as to rob God?* Man, who is a weak creature, and cannot contend with God's power, will he think to rob him *vi et armis — forcibly?* Man, who lies open to God's knowledge, and cannot conceal himself from that, will he think to rob him *clam et secreto — privily?* Man, who depends upon God, and derives his all from him, will he rob him that is his benefactor? This is ungrateful, unjust, and unkind, indeed; and it is very unwise thus to provoke him from whom our judgment proceeds. *Will a man do violence to God?* so some read it. *Will a man do violence to God?* so some read it. *Will a man stint or straiten him?* so others read it. Robbing God is a heinous crime. 2. The people's high challenge in answer to that charge: *But you say, Wherein have we robbed thee?* They plead *Not guilty,* and put God upon the proof of it. Note, Robbing God is such a heinous crime that those who are guilty of it are not willing to own themselves guilty. They rob God, and know not what they do. They rob him of his honour, rob him of that which is devoted to him, to be employed in his service, rob him of themselves, rob him of sabbath-time, rob him of that which is given for the support of religion, and give him not his dues out of their estates; and yet they ask, *Wherein have we robbed thee?* 3. The plain proof of the charge, in answer to this challenge; it is *in tithes and offerings.* Out of these the priests and Levites had maintenance for themselves and their families; but they detained them, defrauded the priests of them, would not pay their tithes, or not in full, or not of the best; they brought not the offerings which God required, or brought the torn, and lame, and sick, which were not fit for use. They were all guilty of this sin, even *the whole nation,* as if they were in confederacy against God, and all combined to rob him of his dues and to stand by one another in it when they had done. For this they were *cursed with a curse, v.* 9. God punished them with famine and scarcity, through unseasonable weather, or insects that ate up the fruits of the earth. God had thus punished them for neglecting to build the temple (Hag. 1:10, 11), and now for not maintaining the temple-service. Note, Those that deny God his part of their estates may justly expect a curse upon their own part of them: *"You are cursed with a curse for robbing me, and yet you go on to do it."* Note, It is a great aggravation of sin when men persist in it notwithstanding the rebukes of Providence which they are under for it. Nay, it should seem, because God had punished them with scarcity of bread, they made that a pretence for robbing him — that now, being impoverished, they could not afford to bring their tithes and offerings, but must save them, that they might have bread for their families. Note, It argues great perverseness in sin when men make those afflictions excuses for sin which are sent to part between them and their sins. When they had but little they should have done the more good with that little, and that would have been the way to make it more; but it is ill with the patient when that which should cure the disease serves only to palliate it, and prevent its being searched into. 4. An earnest exhortation to reform in this matter, with a promise that if they did the judgments they were under should be quickly removed. (1.) Let them take care to do their duty (*v.* 10): *Bring you all the tithes into the storehouse.* They had brought some; but, like Ananias and Sapphira, had *kept back part of the price,* pretending they could not spare so much as was required, and *necessity has no law;* but even necessity must have this law, and it would redress the grievance of their necessity: "Bring in the full tithes to the utmost that the law requires, *that there may be meat in God's house* for those that serve at the altar, whether there be meat in your houses or no." Note, God must be served in the first place, and our quota must be contributed for the support of religion in the place where we live, that God's name may be sanctified, and his kingdom may come, and his will be done, even before we provide our daily bread; for the interests of our souls ought to be preferred before those of our bodies. (2.) Let them then trust God to provide for them and their comfort "Let God be first served, and then *prove me herewith, saith the Lord of hosts, wheth-*

er I will not open the windows of heaven." They said, "Let God give us our plenty again, as formerly, and try us whether we will not then bring him his tithes and offerings, as we did formerly." "No," says God, "do you first bring in all your tithes as they become due, and all the arrears of what is past, and try me, whether I will not then restore you your plenty." Note, Those that will deal with God must deal upon trust; and we may all venture to do so, for, though many have been losers for him, never any were losers by him in the end. It is fit that we should venture first, for *his reward* is *with him,* but *his work is before him;* we must first do the work which is our part, and then try him and trust him for the reward. Elijah put the widow of Zarephath into this method when he said (1 Ki. 17:13), *"Make me a little cake first,* and then prove me whether there shall not be enough afterwards *for thee and thy son."* That which discourages people from the expenses of charity is the weakness of their faith concerning the gains and advantages of charity; they cannot think that they shall get by it. But it is a reasonable demand that God here makes: *"Prove me now;* is any thing to be got by charity? *Come and see;"* Nothing venture, nothing win. Trust upon honour, "And you shall find," [1.] "That, whereas the heavens have been shut up, and there has been no rain, now God will *open* to you *the windows of heaven,* for in his hand the key of the clouds is, and you shall have seasonable rain." Or the expression is figurative; every good gift coming from above, thence God will plentifully pour out upon them the bounties of his providence. Very sudden plenty is expressed by *opening the windows of heaven,* 2 Ki. 7:2. We find the *windows of heaven opened,* to pour down a deluge of wrath, in Noah's flood, Gen. 7:11. But here they are opened to *pour down blessings,* to such a degree that there should not be *room enough to receive* them. So plentifully shall their ground bring forth that they shall be tempted to *pull down their barns and build greater,* for want of room, Lu. 12:18. Or, as Dr. Pocock explains it, "I will pour out on you such a blessing as shall be not *enough only,* and such as shall be sufficient, but *more and more than enough;"* that is, a great addition. The oil that is multiplied shall not be stayed as long as there are vessels to receive it, 2 Ki. 4:6. Note, God will not only be reconciled to sinners that repent and reform, but he will be a benefactor, a bountiful benefactor, to them. We are never straitened in him, but often straitened in our own bosoms. God has blessings ready to bestow upon us, but, through the weakness of our faith and narrowness of our desires, we have not room to receive them. [2.] That, whereas the fruits of their ground had been eaten up by locusts and caterpillars God would now remove that judgment (*v.* 11): *"I will rebuke the devourer for your sakes,* and will check the progress of those destroying animals, that they shall no more destroy the products of the earth and the fruits of the trees." God has all creatures at his beck, can command them and remand them at his pleasure. *Neither shall the vine cast her fruit before the time;* it shall not be blasted or blown off. Or, as some read it, *Neither shall the devourer make your vine barren,* as the locusts did, Joel 1:7. [3.] That, whereas their neighbours had upbraided them with their scarcity, and they had lain under the *reproach of famine,* which was the more grievous because their country used to be boasted of for its plenty, now *all nations shall call them blessed,* shall speak honourably of them, and own them to be a happy people. [4.] That whereas their sin had made their land unpleasing to God (even their temple, and altars, and offerings were so, *ch.* 2:13), and whereas his judgments had made their land unpleasant to them, and very melancholy, "Now *you shall be a delightsome land,* your country shall be acceptable to God and comfortable to yourselves." Note, The reviving of religion in a land will make it indeed a delightsome land both to God and to all good people; he will say, It is *my rest for ever; here will I dwell;* and they will say the same, Isa. 62:4; Deu. 11:12. It should seem that this charge to bring in the tithes had its good effect, for we find (Neh. 13:12) that *all Judah did bring in their tithe into the treasuries,* and, no doubt, they had the benefit of these promises, in the return of their plenty, immediately upon their return to their duty, that they might plainly discern for what cause the evil had been upon them (for when the cause was removed the evil was removed), and that they might see how perfectly reconciled God was to them upon their repen-

tance, and how their transgression was remembered no more, for the curse was not only taken away, but turned into an abundant blessing.

Verses 13–18

Among the people of the Jews at this time, though they all enjoyed the same privileges and advantages, there were men of very different characters (as ever were, and ever will be, in the world and in the church), like Jeremiah's figs, some very good and others very bad, some that plainly appeared to be the children of God and others that as plainly discovered themselves to be the children of the wicked one. There are tares and wheat in the same field, chaff and corn in the same floor; and here we have an account of both.

I. Here is the angry notice God takes of the impudent blasphemous talk of the sinners in Zion and his just resentments of it. Probably there was a club of them that were in league against religion, that set up for wits, and set their wits on work to run it down and ridicule it, and herein strengthened one another's hands. Here is,

1. An indictment found against them, for treasonable words spoken against the King of kings: *Your words have been stout against me, saith the Lord.* They spoke *against God,* in reflection upon him, in contradiction to him, as their fathers *in the wilderness* (Ps. 70:19); *yea, they spoke against God.* What he said, and what he designed, they opposed, as if they had been retained of counsel against him and his cause. Their words against God were *stout;* they came from their pride, and haughtiness, and contempt of God. What they said against God they spoke loudly, as if they cared not who heard them; they were not themselves ashamed to say it, and they desired to propagate their atheistical notions and to infect the minds of others with them. They spoke it boldly, as those that were resolved to stand to it, and were in no fear of being called to an account. They spoke it proudly, and with insolence and disdain, scorning to be under the divine check and government. They *strengthened themselves;* they would be valiant *against the Almighty,* Job 15:25.

2. Their plea to this indictment. They said, *What have we spoken so much against thee?* They deny the words, and put the prophet to prove them; or, if they spoke the words, they did not design them against God, and therefore will not own there was any harm in them; at least they extenuate the matter: *What have we spoken so much against thee,* so much that there needs all this ado about it? They cannot deny that they have spoken against God, but they make a light matter of it, and wonder it should be taken notice of: *"Words"* (say they) *"are but wind;* others have said more and done worse; if we are not so good as we should be, yet we hope we are not so bad as we are represented to be." Note, It is common for sinners that are unconvinced and unhumbled to deny or extenuate the faults they are justly charged with, and to insist upon their own justification, against the reproofs of the word and of their own consciences. But it will be to no purpose.

3. The words themselves which they are charged with. God keeps an account of what men say, as well as of what they do, and will let them know that he does so. We quickly forget what we have said, and are ready to deny what we have said amiss; but God can say, *You have said* so and so. They had said it as their deliberate judgment.

(1.) That there is nothing to be got in the service of God, thought it is a service that subjects men to labour and sorrow. They said, *It is vain to serve God,* or, *"He is vain that serves God,* that is, he labours in vain and to no purpose; he has his labour for his pains, and therefore is a fool for his labour. *What profit is it that we have kept his ordinance,* or *his observation,* that we have observed what he has appointed us to observe?" *What mammon,* or *wealth,* have we gained, says the Chaldee, intimating (says Dr. Pocock) that it was for mammon's sake only that they served God, and so indeed not God at all, but mammon. "We have walked *mournfully,* or *in black,* with great gravity and great grief, *before the Lord of hosts,* have afflicted our souls at the times appointed for that purpose, and yet we are never the better." Perhaps this comes in as a reason why they would not trust God to prosper them upon their *bringing in the tithes* (*v.* 10); "For," say they, "we have tried him in other things, and have lost by him." This is a very unjust and unreasonable reflection upon the service of God, and we can call witnesses enough to confront the slander. [1.] They would have it thought that they had served God and had kept his ordinances, whereas it was only the external observance of them that they had kept up, while they were perfect strangers to the inward part of the duty, and therefore might say, It is *in vain.* God says so (Mt. 15:9), *In vain do those worship me* whose *hearts are far from me* while they *draw near with their mouth;* but whose fault is that? Not God's, who is the rewarder of those that seek him diligently, but theirs who seek him carelessly. [2.] They insisted much upon it that they had *walked mournfully* before God, whereas God had required them to serve him with gladness, and to walk cheerfully before him. They by their own superstitions made the service of God a task and drudgery to themselves, and then complained of it as a hard service. The yoke of Christ is easy; it is the yoke of antichrist that is heavy. [3.] They complained that they had got nothing by their religion; they were still in poverty and affliction, and behindhand in the world. This is an old piece of impiety. Job 21:14, 15, *What profit shall we have if we pray unto him?* Elihu charges Job with saying something like this. Job 34:9, *It profits a man nothing that he should delight himself with God.* The enemies of religion do but set up against it the old cavils that have been long since answered and exploded. Perhaps this refers to the errors of the sect of the Sadducees, which was the scandal of the Jewish church in its latter days; they denied a future state, and then said, It is *vain to serve God,* which has indeed some colour in it, for, *if in this life only we had hope in Christ, we were of all men most miserable,* 1 Co. 15:19. Note, Those do a great deal of wrong to God's honour who say that religion is either an unprofitable or an unpleasant thing; for the matter is not so: wisdom's *ways are pleasantness,* and wisdom's gains better than that of *fine gold.*

(2.) They maintained that wickedness was the way to prosperity, for they had observed that the *workers of wickedness* were set up in the world, and those that *tempted God* were *delivered, v.* 15. The outward prosperity of sinners in their sins, as it has weakened the hands of the godly in their godliness (Ps. 73:13), so it has strengthened the hands of the wicked in their wickedness. Note, [1.] Those that work wickedness tempt God by presumptuous sins; they do, as it were, try God, whether he can and will punish them as he has said in his word, and, in effect, challenge him to do his worst, by provoking him in the highest degree. [2.] Those that tempt God by their wicked works are many times both delivered out of the adversity into which they were justly brought and advanced to the prosperity which they were utterly unworthy of. They are not only set up once, but when we thought their day had come to fall, and they were in trouble, they were delivered and set up again; so strangely did Providence seem to smile upon them. [3.] Though it be thus, yet it will not warrant us to *call the proud happy.* For they may be delivered and set up for a while, but it will appear that God resists them, and that their pride is a preface to their fall; and, if so, they are truly miserable, and it is folly to call them happy, and to bless those whom the Lord abhors. Wait awhile, and you shall see *those that work wickedness set up* as a mark to the arrows of God's vengeance, and *those that tempt God delivered* to the tormentors. Judge of things as they will appear shortly, when the doom of these proud sinners (which follows here, *ch.* 4:1) comes to be executed to the utmost.

II. Here is the gracious notice God takes of the pious talk of the saints in Zion, and the gracious recompence of it. Even in this corrupt and degenerate age, when there was so great a decay, nay, so great a contempt, of serious godliness, there were yet some that retained their integrity and zeal for God; and let us see,

1. How they distinguished themselves, and what their character was; it was the reverse of theirs that spoke so much against God; for, (1.) They *feared the Lord* — that is the beginning of wisdom and the root of all religion; they reverenced the majesty of God, submitted to his authority, and had a dread of his wrath in all they thought and said; they humbly complied with God, and never spoke any stout words against him. In every age there has been a remnant that feared the Lord, though sometimes but a little remnant. (2.) They *thought upon his name;* they seriously considered and frequently mediated upon the discoveries God has made of himself in his word and by his providences, and their *mediation of him* was *sweet* to them and influenced them. They *thought on his name;* they consulted the honour of God and aimed at that as their ultimate end in all they did. Note, Those that know the name of God should often think of it and dwell upon it in their thoughts; it is a copious curious subject, and frequent thoughts of it will contribute very much to our communion with God and the stirring up of our devout affections to him. (3.) They *spoke often one to another* concerning the God they feared, and that name of his which they thought so much of; for out of the abundance of the heart the mouth will speak, and a good man, out of a *good treasure* there, will *bring forth good things. Those that feared the Lord* kept together as those that were company for each other; they spoke kindly and endearingly one to another, for the preserving and promoting of mutual love, that that might not *wax cold* when *iniquity* did thus *abound.* They spoke intelligently and edifyingly to one another, for the increasing and improving of faith and holiness; they *spoke one to another* in the language of those that fear the Lord and think on his name — the language of Canaan. When profaneness had come to so great a height as to trample upon all that is sacred, *then* those that feared the Lord *spoke often one to another.* [1.] Then, when iniquity was bold and barefaced, the people of God took courage, and stirred up themselves, *the innocent against the hypocrite,* Job 17:8. The worse others are the better we should be; when vice is daring, let not virtue be sneaking. [2.] Then, when religion was reproached and misrepresented, its friends did all they could to support the credit of it and to keep it in countenance. It had been suggested that the ways of God are melancholy unpleasant ways, solitary and sorrowful; and therefore then those that feared God studied to evince the contrary by their cheerfulness in mutual love and converse, that they might *put to silence the ignorance of foolish men.* [3.] Then, when seducers were busy to deceive and to possess unwary souls with prejudices against religion, those that feared God were industrious to arm themselves and one another against the contagion by mutual instructions, excitements, and encouragements, and to strengthen one another's hands. As evil communication corrupts good minds and manners, so good communication confirms them.

2. How God dignified them, and what further honour and favour he intended for them. Those who spoke stoutly against God, no doubt looked with disdain and displeasure upon those that feared him, hectored and bantered them; but they had little reason to regard that, or be disturbed at it, when God countenanced them.

(1.) He took notice of their pious discourses, and was graciously present at their conferences: *The Lord hearkened and heard it,* and was well pleased with it. God says (Jer. 8:6) that he *hearkened and heard* what bad men would say, and they *spoke not aright;* here he hearkened and heard what good men did say, for they spoke aright. Note, The gracious God observes all the gracious words that proceed out of the mouths of his people; they need not desire that men may hear them, and commend them; let them not seek praise from men by them, nor affect to be taken notice of by them; but let it satisfy them that, be the conference ever so private, God sees and hears in secret and will *reward openly.* When the two disciples, going to Emmaus, were discoursing concerning Christ, he hearkened and heard, and joined himself to them, and made a third, Lu. 24:15.

(2.) He kept an account of them: *A book of remembrance was written before him.* Not that the Eternal Mind needs to be reminded of things by books and writings, but it is an expression after the manner of men, intimating that their pious affections and performances are kept in remembrance as punctually and particularly as if they were written in a book, as if journals were kept of all their conferences. Great kings had books of remembrance written, and read before them, in which were entered all the services done them, when, and by whom, as Esther 2:23. God, in like manner, remembers the services of his people, that, in the review of them, he may say, *Well done; enter thou into the joy of thy Lord.* God has a book for the sighs and tears of his mourners (Ps. 56:8), much more for the pleadings of his advocates. Never was any good word spoken of God, or for God, from an honest heart, but it was registered, that it might be recompensed in the resurrection of the just, and, in no wise lose its reward.

(3.) He promises them a share in his glory hereafter (*v.* 17): *They shall be mine, saith the Lord of hosts, in that day when I make up my jewels.* When God utterly cuts off the Jewish church and nation for their infidelity, the remnant among them, that believed his word, and, having waited for the consolation of Israel, welcome him when he comes, shall be admitted into the Christian church, and shall become a peculiar people to God; God will take care of them, that they *perish not with those that believe not;* but that they be *hidden in the day of the Lord's anger* against that nation. *They shall be my segullah* — *my peculiar treasure* (it is the word used, Ex. 19:5), *in the day when I make* or *do* what I have said and designed to do; so some read it. These pious ones shall have all the glorious privileges of God's Israel appropriated to them and centering in them; they shall now be his peculiar treasure, when the rest are rejected; they shall now be the vessels of mercy and honour, when the rest are made vessels of wrath and dishonour, vessels in which is no pleasure. This may be applied to all the faithful people of God, and the distinction he will put between them and others in the great day. Note,[1.] The saints are God's jewels; they are highly esteemed by him and are dear to him; they are comely with the comeliness that he puts upon them, and he is pleased to glory in them; they are a *royal diadem* in his hand, Isa. 62:3. He looks upon them as his own proper goods, his choice goods, his treasure, laid up in his cabinet, and the furniture of his closet, Ps. 135:4. The rest of the world is but lumber, in comparison with them. [2.] There is a day coming when God will *make up his jewels.* They shall be gathered up out of the dirt into which they are now thrown, and gathered together from all places to which they are now scattered; he shall *send forth his angels* to *gather his elect,* who are his jewels, *from the four winds of heaven* (Mt. 24:31), to gather his jewels into his jewel-house, as the wheat from several fields into the barn. All the saints will then be gathered to Christ, and none but saints, and saints made perfect; then God's jewels will be made up, as stones into a crown, as stars into a constellation. [3.] Those who now own God for theirs, he will then own for his, will publicly confess them before angels and men: *"They shall be mine;"* their sanctification shall be completed, and so they shall be perfectly and entirely mine, without any remaining interests of the world and the flesh." Their relation to God shall be acknowledged, and his property in them. He will separate them from those that are not his, and give them their portion with those that are his; for to them it shall be said, *Come, you blessed of my Father, inherit the kingdom prepared for you.* They were in doubt, sometimes, whether they were belonging to God or no; but the matter shall then be put out of doubt. God himself will say unto them, *You are mine. Now* their relation to God is what they are reproached with, but it will then be gloried in; God himself will glory in it.

(4.) He promises them a share in his grace now: *I will spare them as a man spares his own son that serves him.* God had promised to own them as his and take them to be with him; but it might be a discouragement to them to think that they had offended God, and that he might justly disown them, and cast them off; but, as to that, he says, *"I will spare them;* I will not deal with them as they deserve. *I will rejoice over them"* (so some expound it) "as the bridegroom over his bride," Isa. 62:5; Zep. 3:17. But the word usually signifies to spare with commiseration and compassion, *as a father pities his children,* Ps. 103:13. Note, [1.] It is our duty to serve God with the disposition of children. We must be his sons, must by a new birth partake of a divine nature, must consent to the covenant of adoption and partake of the spirit of adoption. And we must be his servants; God will not have his children trained up in idleness; they must do him service, and they must do it from a principle of love, with cheerfulness and delight, and as those that are therein serving their own true interest, and this is serving as *a son with the father,* Phil. 2:22. [2.] If we serve God with the disposition of children, he will spare us with the tenderness and compassion of a Father. Even God's children that serve him stand in need of sparing mercy, that mercy to which we owe it that we are not consumed, that mercy which keeps us out of hell. Nehemiah, when he had done much good, yet, knowing there is not a *just man on earth,* that *does good and sins not,* and that every sin deserves God's wrath, prays, *Lord, spare me according to the greatness of thy mercy;* see Neh. 13:22. And God, as a Father, will show them this mercy. He will not be extreme to mark what we do amiss, but will make the best of us and our poor performances; he will mitigate the afflictions his children are exercised with, and save them from the ruin they deserve. The father continues to spare the son, and does it with complacency, because he is his own; thus God will spare humble penitents and petitioners, *as a man spares his son that serves him,* though we do him so little service, nay, though we do him so much disservice.

3. How they will thus be distinguished from the children of this world (*v.* 18): *"Then shall you return, and discern between the righteous and the wicked,* between sinners and saints, between those that *serve God* and make conscience of their duty to him and those that *serve him not,* but put contempt upon his service. You that now speak against God as making no difference between good and bad, and therefore say, *It is in vain to serve him* (*v.* 14), you shall be made to see your error; you that would speak for God, but know not what to say as to this, that there seems to be *one event to the righteous and to the wicked,* and *all things come alike to all,* will then have the matter set in a true light, and will see, to your everlasting satisfaction, the difference between the righteous and the wicked. Then *you shall return,* that is, you shall *change you mind,* and come to a right understanding of the thing." This primarily respects the manifest difference that was made by the divine Providence between the believing Jews and those that persisted in their infidelity, at the time of the destruction of Jerusalem, and of the Jewish church and nation, by the Romans. But it is to have its full accomplishment at the second coming of Jesus Christ, and on that great discriminating day when it shall be easy enough to *discern between the righteous* and *the wicked.* Note, (1.) All the children of men are either righteous or wicked, either such as serve God or such as serve him not. This is that division of the children of men which will last for ever, and by which their eternal state will be determined; all are going either to heaven or to hell. (2.) In this world it is often hard to *discern between the righteous and the wicked.* They are mingled together, good fish and bad in the same net. The righteous are so distempered, and the wicked so disguised, that we are often deceived in our opinions concerning both the one and the other. There are many who, we think, serve God, who, having not their hearts right with him, will be found none of his servants; and, on the other hand, many will be found his faithful servants, who, because they followed not with us, did not, as we thought, serve him. But that which especially raised the difficulty here was that the divine Providence seemed to make no difference between the righteous and the wicked; you could not know wicked men by God's frowning upon them, for they commonly prospered in the world, nor righteous men by his smiling upon them, for they were involved with others in the same common calamity. None now knows God's *love or hatred* by *all that is before him,* Eccl. 9:1. (3.) At the bar of Christ, in the last judgment, it will be easy to *discern between the righteous and the wicked;* for then every man's character will be both perfected and perfectly discovered, every man will then appear in his true colours, and his disguises will be taken off. Some men's sins indeed go beforehand, and you may now tell who is wicked, but others follow after; however, in the great day, we shall see who was righteous and who wicked. Every man's condition likewise will be both perfected and everlastingly determined; the righteous will then be perfectly happy and the wicked perfectly miserable, without mixture or allay. When the righteous are all set on the right hand of Christ, and invited to come for a blessing, and all the wicked on his left hand, and are told to depart with a curse, then it will be easy to discern between them. As to ourselves, therefore, we are concerned to think among which we shall have our lot, and, as to others, we must *judge nothing before the time.*

CHAPTER 4

We have here proper instructions given us (very proper to close the canon of the Old Testament with), I. Concerning the state of recompence and retribution that is before us, the misery of the wicked and the happiness of the righteous in that state (*v.* 1–3). And this is represented to us under a prophecy of the destruction of Jerusalem, and the unbelieving Jews with it, and of the comforts and triumphs of those among them that received the gospel. II. Concerning the state of trial and preparation we are now in, in which we are directed to have an eye to divine revelation, and to follow that; they then must keep to the law of Moses (*v.* 4) and expect a further discovery of God's will by Elijah the prophet, that is, by John Baptist, the harbinger of the Messiah (*v.* 5, 6). The last chapter of the New Testament is much to the same purport, setting before us heaven and hell in the other world, and obliging us to adhere to the word of God in this world.

Verses 1–3

The great and terrible day of the Lord is here prophesied of. This, like the pillar of cloud and fire, shall have a dark side turned towards the Egyptians that fight against God, and a bright side towards the faithful Israelites that follow him: *The day cometh,* that is, the Lord cometh, the day of the Lord; and it has reference both to the first and to the second coming of Jesus Christ; the day of both was fixed, and should answer the character here given of it.

I. In both Christ is a consuming fire to those that rebel against him. The day of his coming *shall burn as an oven;* it shall be a day of wrath, of *fiery indignation.* This was foretold concerning the Messiah, Ps. 21:9, *Thy hand shall find out all thy enemies,* and *shall make them as a fiery oven in the time of thy anger.* It will be a day of terror and destruction like the burning of a city, or rather of a wood, the trees whereof are withered and dried, for to that the allusion seems to be, as Isa. 10:17, 18, *The light of Israel shall be for a fire, and his Holy One for a flame, and it shall consume the glory of his forest and of his fruitful field.* Now observe here, 1. Who shall be fuel to this fire — all *the proud* in heart, whose words have been stout against God, and their necks stiff and unapt to yield to the yoke of his commandments (all those that *in the pride of their countenances will not seek after God,* nor submit to the grace and government of Jesus Christ — all that proudly say they *will not have Christ to reign over them),* and all those that *do wickedly* in their affections and conversations, that wilfully persist in sin, in contempt of and contradiction to the law of God; they are such as *do wickedly against the covenant,* as another prophet had lately expressed it, Dan. 11:32. God, that has perfect knowledge of every one's character, knows who are *the proud,* and of every one's actions, knows who they are that *do wickedly;* and they shall be as *stubble* to this fire; they shall be consumed by it, easily consumed, utterly consumed, and it is wholly owing to themselves that they shall be so, for they make themselves stubble, that is, combustible matter, to this fire. If they were not stubble, it would not burn them; for the fire will be to every man according as he and his works are found; if they be *wood, hay,* and *stubble,* they will be *consumed;* but if they be *gold, solver, and precious stones,* they will *abide the fire* and be purified by it, 1 Co. 3:13–15. Those that by their unbelief oppose Christ thereby set themselves as *briers and thorns* before a *devouring fire,* Isa. 27:4, 5. 2. What shall be the force and what the fruit of this fire: *The day that cometh shall burn them up,* shall both terrify and ruin them, and shall *leave them neither root nor branch,* neither *son* nor *nephew* (so the Chaldee paraphrase): neither they nor their posterity shall be spared; they shall be wholly extirpated and cut off. *Who knows the power of God's anger? The proud and those that do wickedly* will not fear it, but they shall be made to feel it. Where are those now that *called the proud happy,* when thus they are made completely miserable, when there remains no branch of their happiness to be enjoyed for the present, nor any root of it out of which it might again spring up? Now this was fulfilled, (1.) When Christ, in his doctrine, spoke terror and condemnation to the proud Pharisees and the other Jews that did wickedly, when he sent that fire on the earth which burnt up the chaff of the traditions of the elders and the corrupt glosses they had put upon the law of God. (2.) When Jerusalem was destroyed by the Romans, and the nation of the Jews, as a nation, quite blotted out from under heaven, and neither root nor branch left them. This seems to be principally intended here; our Saviour says that those should be the *days of vengeance,* when all the things that were written to that purport should be fulfilled, Lu. 21:22. Then the unbelieving Jews were as stubble to the devouring fire of God's judgments, which gathered together to them as the eagles to the carcase. (3.) It is certainly applicable, and is to be applied, to the day of judgment, to the particular judgment at death (some of the Jewish doctors refer it the *punishment that seizes on the souls of the wicked immediately after they go out of the body*), but especially to the general judgment, at the end of time, when Christ shall be *revealed in flaming fire,* to execute judgment on *the proud, and all that do wickedly.* The whole world shall then *burn as an oven,* and all the children of this world, that set their hearts upon it and choose their portion in it, shall take their ruin with it, and the fire then kindled shall never be quenched.

II. In both Christ is a rejoicing light to those who serve him faithfully, to those who fear his name and give him the glory due to it (*v.* 2), who stand in awe of that name of his which the wicked profane and trample upon. Here are mercy and comfort kept in store for all those who fear the Lord and think on his name. Observe,

1. Whence this mercy and comfort shall flow to them: *To you that fear my name shall the Sun of righteousness arise, with healing in his wings.* The day that comes, as it will be a stormy day to the wicked, a day in which God will rain upon them *fire and brimstone, and a horrible tempest,* as he did on Sodom (Ps. 11:6), a *day of clouds and thick darkness* (Amos 5:18, 20), so it will be a fair and bright day to those who fear God, and reviving as the rising sun is to the earth; and particular notice is taken of the rising of the sun upon Zoar when that was mercifully distinguished from the cities of the plain, which the fire *consumed;* see Gen. 19:23. So to those that fear God is comfort spoken. When the hearts of others *fail for fear* let them *lift up their heads for joy,* for *their redemption draws nigh,* Lu. 21:28. But by the *Sun of righteousness* here we are certainly to understand Jesus Christ, who would undertake to secure the believing remnant, in the day of the general destruction of the Jews, from falling with the rest, and to comfort them in that day of distress and perplexity with his consolations; he directed those that were in Judea to *flee to the mountains* (Mt. 24:16), and they did so, and were all safe and easy in Pella. But it is to be applied more generally, (1.) To the coming of Christ in the flesh to seek and save those that were lost; then the *Sun of righteousness* arose upon this dark world. Christ is the *light of the world,* the true light, the great light that makes day and rules the day (Jn. 8:12), as the sun. He is the *light of men* (Jn. 1:4), is to men's souls as the sun is to the visible world, which without the sun would be a dungeon; so would mankind be darkness itself without the *light of the glory of God* shining *in the face of Christ.* Christ is the Sun that has light in himself, and is the fountain of light (Ps. 19:4–6); he is the *Sun of righteousness,* for he is himself a righteous Saviour. Righteousness is both the light and the heat of this Sun; the word of his righteousness is so; it guides, instructs, and quickens; so is the *everlasting righteousness* he has brought in. He is *made of God to us righteousness;* he is the *Lord our righteousness,* and therefore is fitly called *the Sun of righteousness.* Through him we are justified and sanctified, and so are brought to see light. This Sun of righteousness, in the fulness of time, arose upon the world, and with him *light came into the world* (Jn. 3:19), a *great light,* Mt. 4:16. In him *the day-spring from on high visited us, to give light to those that sit in darkness,* Lu. 1:78, 79. Righteousness sometimes signifies mercy or benignity, and it was in Christ that the *tender mercy of our God* visited us. (2.) It is applicable to the graces and comforts of the Holy Spirit, brought into the souls of men. Grotius understands it of Christ's giving the Spirit to those that are his, to shine in their hearts, and to be a *comforter* to them, a *sun and a shield.* Those that are possessed and governed by a holy fear of God and a dread of his majesty shall have his *love* also *shed abroad in their hearts by the Holy Ghost;* and then the sun may be said to arise there, and to bring both a delightful day and a fruitful spring along with it. (3.) Christ's second coming will be a glorious and welcome sunrising to all that *fear his name;* it will be that morning of the resurrection in which *the upright shall have dominion,* Ps. 49:14. That day which to the wicked will *burn as an oven* will to the righteous be bright as the morning; and it is what they wait for, *more than those that wait for the morning.*

2. What this mercy and comfort shall bring to them: He *shall arise with healing under his wings,* or in his *rays* or *beams,* which are as the wings of the sun. Christ came,

as *the sun,* to bring not only light to a dark world, but health to a diseased distempered world. The Jews (says Dr. Pocock) have a proverbial saying, *As the sun riseth, infirmities decrease;* the flowers which drooped and languished all night revive in the morning. Christ came into the world to be the great physician, yea, and the great medicine too, both the balm in Gilead and the physician there. When he was upon earth, he went about as the sun in his circuit, doing this good; he *healed all manner of sicknesses and diseases among the people;* he healed by wholesale, as the sun does. He shall arise *with healing in his skirts;* so some read it, and they apply it to the story of the woman's touching *the hem of his garment,* and being thereby *made whole,* and his finding that *virtue went out of him,* Mk. 5:28–30. But his healing bodily diseases was a specimen of his great design in coming into the world to heal the diseases of men's souls, and to put them into a good state of health, that they may serve and enjoy both God and themselves.

3. What good effect it shall have upon them. (1.) It shall make them vigorous in themselves: *"You shall go forth,* as those that are healed go abroad and return to their business." The souls shall go forth out of their bodies at death, and the bodies out of their graves at the resurrection, as prisoners out of their dungeons, and both to see the light and be set at liberty. *"You shall go forth* as plants out of the earth, when in the spring the sun returns." Some make it to mean the going forth of the Christians from Jerusalem, and the escape they thereby made from its destruction. And thus the souls on whom the Sun of righteousness arises go forth out of the world, go forth out of Babylon, as those that are made *free indeed.* "You shall likewise *grow up;* being restored to health and liberty, you shall increase in knowledge, and grace, and spiritual strength." The souls on which the Sun of righteousness arises are growing up towards *the perfect man;* those that by the grace of God are made wise and good are by the same grace made wiser and better; and their path, like that of the rising sun, *shines more and more to the perfect day,* Prov. 4:18. Their growth is compared to that of *the calves of the stall,* which is a quick, strong, and useful growth. "You shall grow up, not as the *flower of the field,* which is slender, and weak, and of little use, and withers soon after it has grown up, but as the *calves of the stall,"* that, as one of the rabbin expounds it, *grow great in flesh and fatness,* with which both God's altars and men's tables are replenished; so the growth of the saints, on whom the Sun of righteousness arises, honours both God and man. Some read it, instead of *You shall grow up,* You shall *move yourselves,* or *leap for joy,* shall be as frolicsome as calves of the stall, when they are let loose in the open field; it denotes the joy of the saints, who rejoice in Christ Jesus; they shall even leap for joy; they are *always caused to triumph.*

(2.) It shall make them victorious over their enemies (*v.* 3): *You shall tread down the wicked.* Time was when the wicked trod them down, said to their souls, *Bow down, that we may go over;* but the day will come when they shall *tread down the wicked.* The wicked, being made Christ's footstool, are made theirs also (Ps. 110:1), and come and *worship before the feet* of the church, Rev. 3:9. *The elder shall serve the younger.* When believers by faith *overcome the world,* when they suppress their own corrupt appetites and passions, when the God of peace bruises Satan under their feet, then they *tread down the wicked.* When it came to the turn of the Christians to triumph over the Jews that had insulted over them, then this promise was fulfilled: *They shall be ashes under the soles of your feet;* they shall not only be *trodden down,* but trodden to *dirt.* When the day that comes shall have *burnt them up,* they shall trample upon them as ashes. When the righteous shall rise to *everlasting life,* the wicked shall rise to *everlasting contempt;* and, though they shall not triumph over them, they shall triumph in that God whose justice is glorified in their destruction. The saints in glory are said to have power given them over the nations, to *rule them with a rod of iron,* Rev. 2:26, 27. This *you shall do, in the day that I shall do this.* Note, The saints' triumphs are all owing to God's victories; it is not they that do this, but God that does it for them, that says, *Come set your feet on the necks of these kings.* Some read it, *"In the day that I make,* or shall make, the *great day* that I shall make remarkable, of which you will say with joy, *This is the day which the Lord has made."* The day of the destruction of Jerusalem is called the *great and notable day of the Lord* (Acts 2:20), and our Saviour in foretelling that destruction made use of such expressions as, like these, might be applied likewise to the *end of the world* and the *last judgment;* for it was such a terrible revelation of the wrath of God from heaven, and caused such a scene of horror upon this earth, that it might fitly serve for a type of that glorious transaction which will be an outlet to the days of time and an inlet to the days of eternity. By the accomplishment of these prophecies in the ruin of the Jewish nation, we should have our faith confirmed in the assurances Christ has given us concerning the dissolution of all things. *Surely I come quickly;* so says Christ, *the Lord of hosts,* to whom all power in heaven and earth is committed.

Verses 4–6

This is doubtless intended for a solemn conclusion, not only of this prophecy, but of the canon of the Old Testament, and is a plain information that they were not to expect any more sayings nor writing by divine inspiration, any more of the dictates of the Spirit of prophecy, till the beginning of the gospel of the Messiah, which sets aside the Apocrypha as no part of holy writ, and which therefore the Jews never received.

Now that prophecy ceases, and is about to be sealed up, there are two things required of the people of God, that lived then: —

I. They must keep up an obedient veneration for the law of Moses (*v.* 4): *Remember the law of Moses my servant,* and observe to do according to it, even that law which *I commanded unto him in Horeb,* that fiery law which was intended *for all Israel, with the statutes and judgments,* not only the law of the ten commandments, but all the other appointments, ceremonial and judicial, then and there given. Observe here, 1. The honourable mention that is made of *Moses,* the first writer of the Old Testament, in *Malachi,* the last writer. God by him calls him *Moses my servant;* for the righteous shall be had in everlasting remembrance. See how the penmen of scripture, though they lived in several ages at a great distance from each other (it was above 1200 years from Moses to Malachi), all concurred in the same thing, and supported one another, being all actuated and guided by one and the same Spirit. 2. The honourable mention that is made of the *law of Moses;* it was what God himself *commanded;* he owns it for his law, and he commanded it *for all Israel,* as the municipal law of their kingdom. Thus will God *magnify his law and make it honourable.* Note, We are concerned to keep the law because God has commanded it and commanded it for us, for we are the spiritual Israel; and, if we expect the benefit of the covenant with Israel (Heb. 8:10), we must observe the commands given to Israel, those of them that were intended to be of perpetual obligation. 3. The summary of our duty, with reference to the law. We must remember it. Forgetfulness of the law is at the bottom of all our transgressions of it; if we would rightly remember it, we could not but conform to it. We should remember it when we have occasion to use it, remember both the commands themselves and the sanctions wherewith they are enforced. The office of conscience is to bid us *remember the law.* But how does this charge to remember the law of Moses come in here? (1.) This prophet had reproved them for many gross corruptions and irregularities both in worship and conversation, and now, for the reforming and amending of what was amiss, he only charges them to *remember the law of Moses:* "Keep to that rule, and you will do all you should do." He will *lay upon them no other burden* than what they *have received; hold that fast,* Rev. 2:24, 25. Note, Corrupt churches are to be reformed by the written word, and reduced into order by being reduced to the standard of *the law and the testimony,* see 1 Co. 11:23. (2.) The church had long enjoyed the benefit of prophets, extraordinary messengers from God, and now they had a whole book of their prophecies put together, and it was a finished piece; but they must not think that hereby the *law of Moses* was superseded, and had become as an almanac out of date, as if now they were advanced to a higher form and might forget that. No; the prophets do but confirm and apply the law, and press the observance of that; and therefore still *Remember the law.* Note, Even when we have made considerable advances in knowledge we must still retain the first principles of practical religion and resolve to abide by them. Those that study the writings of the prophets, and the apocalypse, must still remember the law of Moses and the four gospels. (3.) Prophecy was now to cease in the church for some ages, and the Spirit of prophecy not to return till the *beginning of the gospel,* and now they are told to *remember the law of Moses;* let them live by the rules of that, and live upon the promises of that. Note, We need not complain for want of visions and revelations as long as we have the written word, and the canon of scripture complete, to be our guide; for that is the most *sure word of prophecy,* and the touchstone by which we are to *try the spirits.* Though we have not prophets, yet, as long as we have Bibles, we may keep our communion with God, and keep ourselves in his way. (4.) They were to expect the coming of the Messiah, the preaching of his gospel, and the setting up of his kingdom, and in that expectation they must *remember the law of Moses,* and live in obedience to that, and then they might expect the comforts that the Messiah would bring to *the willing and obedient.* Let them observe the law of Moses, and live up to the light which that gave them, and then they might expect the benefit of the gospel of Christ, for *to him that has,* and uses what he has well, *more shall be given, and he shall have abundance.*

II. They must keep up a believing expectation of the gospel of Christ, and must look for the beginning of it in the appearing of Elijah the prophet (*v.* 5, 6): *"Behold, I send you Elijah the prophet.* Though the Spirit of prophecy cease for a time, and you will have only the law to consult, yet it shall revive again in one that shall be sent *in the spirit and power of Elias,"* Lu. 1:17. The *law and the prophets were until John* (Lu. 16:16); they continued to be the only lights of the church till that morning-star appeared. Note, As God never *left himself without witness* in the world, so neither in the church, but, as there was occasion, carried the light of divine revelation further and further to the perfect day. They had now Moses and the prophets, and might hear them; but God will go further: he will send them Elijah. Observe,

1. Who this prophet is that shall be sent; it is *Elijah.* The Jewish doctors will have it to be the same Elijah that prophesied in Israel in the days of Ahab — that he shall come again to be the forerunner of the Messiah; yet others of them say not the same person, but another of the same spirit. It should seem, those different sentiments they had when they asked John, *"Art thou Elias,* or *that prophet* that should bear his name?" Jn. 1:19–21. But we Christians know very well that John Baptist was the Elias that was to come, Mt. 17:10–13; and very expressly, Mt. 11:14, *This is Elias that was to come;* and *v.* 10, the same of whom it is written, *Behold, I send my messenger, ch.* 3:1. Elijah was a man of great austerity and mortification, zealous for God, bold in reproving sin, and active to reduce an apostate people to God and their duty; John Baptist was animated by the same spirit and power, and preached repentance and reformation, as Elias had done; and all held him for a prophet, as they did Elijah in his day, and that his baptism was *from heaven,* and not *of men.* Note, When God has such work to do as was formerly to be done he can raise up such men to do it as he formerly raised up, and can put into a John Baptist the spirit of an Elias.

2. When he shall be sent — before the appearing of the Messiah, which, because it was the judgment of this world, and introduced the ruin of the Jewish church and nation, is here called the *coming of the great and dreadful day of the Lord.* John Baptist gave them fair warning of this when he told them of the *wrath to come* (that *wrath to the uttermost* which was hastening upon them) and put them into a way of escape from it, and when he told them of the *fan in Christ's hand,* with which Christ would thoroughly purge his floor; see Mt. 3:7, 10, 12. That day of Christ, when he came first, was as that day will be when he comes again — though a great and joyful day to those that embrace him, yet a *great and dreadful day* to those that oppose him. John Baptist was sent before the coming of this day, to give people notice of it, that they might get ready for it, and go forth to meet it.

3. On what errand he shall be sent: *He shall turn the heart of the fathers to their children, and the heart of the children to their fathers;* that is, "he shall be employed in this work; he shall attempt it; his doctrine and baptism shall

have a direct tendency to it, and with many shall be successful: he shall be an instrument in God's hand of *turning* many *to righteousness,* to *the Lord their God,* and so *making ready a people prepared for him,"* Lu. 1:16, 17. Note, The turning of souls to God and their duty is the best preparation of them for the great and dreadful day of the Lord. It is promised concerning John, (1.) That he shall give a turn to things, shall make a bold stand against the strong torrent of sin and impiety which he found in full force among the children of his people, and beating down all before it. This is called his *coming to restore all things* (Mt. 17:11), to set them to rights, that they may again go in the right channel. (2.) That he shall preach a doctrine that shall reach men's hearts, and have an influence upon them, and work a change in them. God's word, in his mouth, shall be *quick* and *powerful,* and a *discerner of the thoughts and intents of the heart.* Many had their consciences awakened by his ministry who yet were not thoroughly wrought upon, such a spirit and power was there in it. (3.) That he shall turn the hearts of the fathers with the children, and of the children with the fathers (for so some read it), to God and to their duty. He shall call

upon young and old to repent, and shall not labour in vain, for many of the fathers that are going off, and many of the children that are growing up, shall be wrought upon by his ministry. (4.) That thus he shall be an instrument to revive and confirm love and unity among relations, and shall bring them closer and bind them faster to each other, by bringing and binding them all to their God. He shall prepare the way for that kingdom of heaven which will make all its faithful subjects of *one heart* and *one soul* (Acts 4:32), which will be a kingdom of love, and will slay all enmities.

4. With what view he shall be sent on this errand: *Lest I come and smite the earth,* that is, the land of Israel, the body of the Jewish nation (that were of the earth earthy), *with a curse.* They by their impiety and impenitence in it had laid themselves open to the curse of God, which is a separation to all evil. God was ready to smite them with that curse, to bring utter ruin upon them, to strike home, to strike dead, with the curse; but he will yet once more try them, whether they will repent and return, and so prevent it; and therefore he sends John Baptist to preach repentance to them, that their conversion might prevent their

confusion; so unwilling is God that any should perish, so willing to have his anger turned away. Had they universally repented and reformed, their repentance would have had this desired effect; but, they generally rejecting the counsel of God in John's baptism, it proved against themselves (Lu. 7:30) and their land was smitten with the curse which both it and they lie under to this day. Note, Those must expect to be smitten with a sword, with a curse, who *turn not to him that smites them* with a rod, with a cross, Isa. 9:13. Now the *axe is laid to the root of the tree,* says John Baptist, and it is ready to be smitten, to be cut down, *with a curse;* therefore *bring forth fruit meet for repentance.* Some observe that the last word of the Old Testament is a curse, which threatens the earth (Zec. 5:3), our desert of which we must be made sensible of, that we may bid Christ welcome, who comes with a blessing; and it is with a blessing, with the choicest of blessings, that the New Testament ends, and with it let us arm ourselves, or rather let God arm us, against this curse. *The grace of our Lord Jesus Christ be with us all. Amen.*

NEW TESTAMENT

MATTHEW TO REVELATION

:

AN EXPOSITION, WITH PRACTICAL OBSERVATIONS, OF

THE GOSPEL ACCORDING TO ST. MATTHEW

We have now before us, I. *The New Testament of our Lord and Savior Jesus Christ;* so this second part of the holy Bible is entitled: The *new covenant;* so it might as well be rendered; the word signifies both. But, when it is (as here) spoken of as Christ's act and deed, it is most properly rendered a *testament,* for he is the testator, and it becomes of force *by his death* (Heb. 9:16, 17); nor is there, as in covenants, a previous treaty between the parties, but what is granted, though an estate upon condition, is owing to the will, the free-will, the good-will, of the Testator. All the grace contained in this book is owing to Jesus Christ as our Lord and Saviour; and, unless we consent to him as our Lord, we cannot expect any benefit by him as our Saviour. This is called a *new* testament, to distinguish it from that which was given by Moses, and was not antiquated; and to signify that it should be always new, and should never wax old, and grow out of date. These books contain, not only a full discovery of that grace *which has appeared to all men, bringing salvation,* but a legal instrument by which it is conveyed to, and settled upon, all believers. How carefully do we preserve, and with what attention and pleasure do we read, the last will and testament of a friend, who has therein left us a fair estate, and, with it, high expressions of his love to us! How precious then should this testament of our blessed Saviour be to us, which secures to us all his unsearchable riches! It is *his* testament; for though, as is usual, it was written by others (we have nothing upon record that was of Christ's own writing), yet he dictated it; and the night before he died, in the institution of his supper, he signed, sealed, and published it, in the presence of twelve witnesses. For, though these books were not written for some years after, for the benefit of posterity, *in perpetuam rei memoriam — as a perpetual memorial,* yet the New Testament of our Lord Jesus was settled, confirmed, and declared, from the time of his death, as a nuncupative will, with which these records exactly agree. The things which St. Luke wrote were *things which were most surely believed,* and therefore well known, before he wrote them; but, when they were written, the oral tradition was superseded and set aside, and these writings were the repository of that New Testament. This is intimated by the title which is prefixed to many Greek Copies, *Tēs kainēs Diathēkēs Hapanta — The whole of the New Testament,* or *all the things of it.* In it is declared *the whole counsel of God* concerning our salvation, Acts 20:27. As *the law of the Lord is perfect,* so is the gospel of Christ, and nothing is to be added to it. We have it all, and are to look for no more.

II. We have before us *The Four Gospels. Gospel* signifies good news, or glad tidings; and this history of Christ's coming *into the world to save sinners* is, without doubt, the best news that ever came from heaven to earth; the angel gave it this title (Lu. 2:10), *Euangelizomai hymin — I bring you good tidings; I bring the gospel to you.* And the prophet foretold it, Isa. 52:7; 61:1. It is there foretold that in the days of the messiah *good tidings* should be preached. *Gospel* is an old Saxon word; it is *God's spell* or *word;* and God is so called because he is good, *Deus optimus — God most excellent,* and therefore it may be a good spell, or word. If we take *spell* in its more proper signification for a *charm (carmen),* and take that in a good sense, for what is moving and affecting, which is apt *lenire dolorem — to calm the spirits,* or to raise them in admiration or love, as that which is very amiable we call charming, it is applicable to the gospel; for in it the charmer *charmeth wisely,* though to *deaf adders,* Ps. 58:4, 5. Nor (one would think) can any charms be so powerful as those of the beauty and love of our Redeemer. The whole New Testament is the gospel. St. Paul calls it *his* gospel, because he was one of the preachers of it. Oh that we may each of us make it ours by our cordial acceptance of it and subjection to it! But the four books which contain the history of the Redeemer we commonly call *the four gospels,* and the inspired penmen of them *evangelists,* or *gospel-writers;* not, however, very properly, because that title belongs to a particular order of ministers, that were assistants to the apostles (Eph. 4:11): *He gave some apostles, and some evangelists.* It was requisite that the doctrine of Christ should be interwoven with, and founded upon, the narrative of his birth, life, miracles, death, and resurrection; for then it appears in its clearest and strongest light. As in nature, so in grace, the most happy discoveries are those which take rise from the certain representations of matters of fact. Natural history is the best philosophy; and so is the sacred history, both of the Old and New Testament, the most proper and grateful vehicle of sacred truth. These four gospels were early and constantly received by the primitive church, and read in Christian assemblies, as appears by the writings of Justin Martyr and Irenaeus, who lived little more than a hundred years after the ascension of Christ; they declared that neither more nor fewer than four were received by the church. A Harmony of these four evangelists was compiled by Tatian about that time, which he called, *To dia tessarōn — The Gospel out of the four.* In the third and fourth centuries there were gospels forged by divers sects, and published, one under the name of St. Peter, another of St. Thomas, another of St. Philip, etc. But they were never owned by the church, nor was any credit given to them, as the learned Dr. Whitby shows. And he gives this good reason why we should adhere to these written records, because, whatever the pretences of tradition may be, it is not sufficient to preserve things with any certainty, as appears by experience. For, whereas Christ said and did many memorable things, which *were not written* (Jn. 20:30; 21:25), tradition has not preserved any one of them to us, but all is lost except what was written; that therefore is what we must abide by; and blessed by God that we have it to abide by; it is the sure word of history.

III. We have before us *the Gospel according to St. Matthew.* The penman was by birth a Jew, by calling a publican, till Christ commanded his attendance, and then he left *the receipt of custom,* to follow him, and was one of those that accompanied him *all the time that the Lord Jesus went in and out, beginning from the baptism of John unto the day that he was taken up,* Acts 1:21, 22. He was therefore a competent witness of what he has here recorded. He is said to have written this history about eight years after Christ's ascension. Many of the ancients say that he wrote it in the Hebrew or Syriac language; but the tradition is sufficiently disproved by Dr. Whitby. Doubtless, it was written in Greek, as the other parts of the New Testament were; not in that language which was peculiar to the Jews, whose church and state were near a period, but in that which was common to the world, and in which the knowledge of Christ would be most effectually transmitted to the nations of the earth; yet it is probable that there might be an edition of it in Hebrew, published by St. Matthew himself, at the same time that he wrote it in Greek; the former for the Jews, the latter for the Gentiles, when he left Judea, to preach among the Gentiles. Let us bless God that we have it, and have it in a language we understand.

CHAPTER 1

This evangelist begins with the account of Christ's parentage and birth, the ancestors from whom he descended, and the manner of his entry into the world, to make it appear that he was indeed the Messiah promised, for it was foretold that he should be the son of David, and should be born of a virgin; and that he was so is here plainly shown; for here is, I. His pedigree from Abraham in forty-two generations, three fourteens (*v.* 1–17). II. An account of the circumstances of his birth, so far as was requisite to show that he was born of a virgin (*v.* 18–25). Thus methodically is the life of our blessed Saviour written, as lives should be written, for the clearer proposing of the example of them.

Verses 1–17

Concerning this genealogy of our Saviour, observe,

I. The title of it. It is *the book* (or the account, as the Hebrew word *sepher, a book,* sometimes signifies) *of the generation of Jesus Christ,* of his ancestors according to the flesh; or, It is the narrative of his birth. It is *Biblos Geneseōs — a book of Genesis.* The Old Testament begins with the book of the generation of the world, and it is its glory that it does so; but the glory of the New Testament *herein* excelleth, that it begins with *the book of the generation of* him that made the world. As God, *his outgoings were of old, from everlasting* (Mic. 5:2), and none can declare that generation; but, as man, he was *sent forth in the fulness of time, born of a woman,* and it is that generation which is here declared.

II. The principal intention of it. It is not an endless or needless genealogy; it is not a vain-glorious one, as those of great men commonly are. *Stemmata, quid faciunt? — Of what avail are ancient pedigrees?* It is like a pedigree given in evidence, to prove a title, and make out a claim; the design is to prove that our Lord Jesus is *the son of David,* and *the son of Abraham,* and therefore of that nation and family out of which the Messiah was to arise. Abraham and David were, in their day, the great trustees of the promise relating to the Messiah. *The promise* of the *blessing was made to Abraham and his seed,* of the *dominion to David and his seed;* and they who would have an interest in Christ, as *the son of Abraham, in whom all the families of the earth are to be blessed,* must be faithful, loyal subjects to him as *the son of David,* by whom *all the families of the earth* are to be ruled. It was promised to Abraham that Christ should descend from him (Gen. 12:3; 22:18), and to David that he should descend from him (2 Sa. 7:12; Ps. 89:3, etc.; 132:11); and therefore, unless it can be proved that Jesus is a *son of David,* and a *son of Abraham,* we cannot admit him to be the Messiah. Now this is here proved from the authentic records of the heralds' offices. The Jews were very exact in preserving their pedigrees, and there was a providence in it, for the clearing up of the descent of the Messiah from the fathers; and since his coming that nation is so dispersed and confounded that it is a question whether any person in the world can legally prove himself to be *a son of Abraham;* however, it is certain that none can prove himself to either a son of Aaron or a *son of David,* so that the priestly and kingly office must either be given up, as lost for ever, or be lodged in the hands of our Lord Jesus. Christ is here first called *the son of David,* because under that title he was commonly spoken of, and expected, among the Jews. They who owned him to be *the Christ,* called him *the son of David, ch.* 15:22; 20:31; 21:15. Thus, therefore, the evangelist undertakes to make out, that he is not only a *son of David,* but that *son of David* on whose *shoulders the government was to be;* not only *a son of Abraham,* but that *son of Abraham* who was to be *the father of many nations.*

In calling Christ the *son of David,* and *the son of Abraham,* he shows that God is faithful to his promise, and will make good every word that he has spoken; and this. 1. Though the performance be long deferred. When God promised Abraham a son, who should be the great blessing of the world, perhaps he expected it should be his immediate son; but it proved to be one at the distance of forty-two generations, and about 2000 years: so long before can God foretel what shall be done, and so long after, sometimes, does God fulfil what has been promised. Note, Delays of promised mercies, though they exercise our patience, do not weaken God's promise. 2. Though it begin to be despaired of. This *son of David,* and *son of Abraham,* who was to be the glory of his Father's house, was born when the seed of Abraham was a despised people, recently become tributary to the Roman yoke, and when the house of David was buried in obscurity; for Christ was to be *a root out of a dry ground.* Note, God's time for the performance of his promises is when it labours under the greatest improbabilities.

III. The particular series of it, drawn in the direct line from Abraham downward, according to the genealogies recorded in the beginning of the books of Chronicles (as far as those go), and which here we see the use of.

Some particulars we may observe in the genealogy.

1. Among the ancestors of Christ who had brethren, generally he descended from a younger brother; such Abraham himself was, and Jacob, and Judah, and David, and Nathan, and Rhesa; to show that the pre-eminence of Christ came not, as that of earthly princes, from the primogeniture of his ancestors, but from the will of God, who, according to the method of his providence, *exalteth them of low degree,* and puts *more abundant honour upon that part which lacked.*

2. Among the sons of Jacob, besides Judah, from whom Shiloh came, notice is here taken of *his brethren: Judas and his brethren.* No mention is made of Ishmael the son of Abraham, or of Esau the son of Isaac, because they were shut out of the church; whereas all the children of Jacob were taken in, and, though not fathers of Christ, were yet patriarchs of the church (Acts 7:8), and therefore are mentioned in the genealogy, for the encouragement of the *twelve tribes that were scattered abroad,* intimating to them that they have an interest in Christ, and stand in relation to him as well as Judah.

3. Phares and Zara, the twin-sons of Judah, are likewise both named, though Phares only was Christ's ancestor, for the same reason that the brethren of Judah are taken notice of; and some think because the birth of Phares and Zara had something of an allegory in it. Zara put out his hand first, as the first-born, but, drawing it in, Phares got the birth-right. The Jewish church, like Zara, reached first at the birthright, but through unbelief, withdrawing the hand, the Gentile church, like Phares, broke forth and went away with the birthright; and thus *blindness is in part happened unto Israel, till the fulness of the Gentiles become in,* and then Zara shall be born — *all Israel shall be saved,* Rom. 11:25, 26.

4. There are four women, and but four, named in this genealogy; two of them were originally *strangers to the commonwealth of Israel,* Rachab a Canaanitess, and a harlot besides, and Ruth the Moabitess; for *in Jesus Christ there is neither Greek, nor Jew;* those that are *strangers and foreigners* are welcome, in Christ, to *the citizenship of the saints.* The other two were adulteresses, Tamar and Bathsheba; which was a further mark of humiliation put upon our Lord Jesus, that not only he descended from such, but that is decent from them is particularly remarked in his genealogy, and no veil drawn over it. He took upon him *the likeness of sinful flesh* (Rom. 8:3), and takes even great sinners, upon their repentance, into the nearest relation to himself. Note, We ought not to upbraid people with the scandals of their ancestors; it is what they cannot help, and has been the lot of the best, even of our Master himself. *David's begetting Solomon of her that had been the wife of Urias* is taken notice of (says Dr. Whitby) to show that the crime of David, being repented to, was so far from hindering the promise made to him, that it pleased God by this very woman to fulfil it.

5. Though divers kings are here named, yet none is expressly called a king but David (*v.* 6), *David the king;* because with him the covenant of royalty was made, and to him the promise of the kingdom of the Messiah was given, who is therefore said to inherit *the throne of his father David,* Lu. 1:32.

6. In the pedigree of the kings of Judah, between Joram and Ozias (*v.* 8), there are three left out, namely, Ahaziah, Joash, and Amaziah; and therefore when it is said, *Joram begat Ozias,* it is meant, according to the usage of the Hebrew tongue, that Ozias was lineally descended from him, as it is said to Hezekiah that *the sons which he should beget should be carried to Babylon,* whereas they were removed several generations from him. It was not through mistake or forgetfulness that these three were omitted, but, probably, they were omitted in the genealogical tables that the evangelist consulted, which yet were admitted as authentic. Some give this reason for it: — It being Matthew's design, for the sake of memory, to reduce the number of Christ's ancestors to three fourteens, it was requisite that in this period three should be left out, and none more fit than they who were the immediate progeny of cursed Athaliah, who introduced the idolatry of Ahab into the house of David, for which this brand is set upon the family and the iniquity thus visited *to the third and fourth generation.* Two of these three were apostates; and such God commonly sets a mark of his displeasure upon in this world: they all three had their heads brought to the grave with blood.

7. Some observe what a mixture there was of good and bad in the succession of these kings; as for instance (*v.* 7, 8), wicked *Roboam begat* wicked *Abia;* wicked *Abia begat* good *Asa;* good *Asa begat* good *Josaphat;* good *Josaphat begat* wicked *Joram.* Grace does not run in the blood, neither does reigning sin. God's grace is his own, and he gives or withholds it as he pleases.

8. The captivity of Babylon is mentioned as a remarkable period in this line, *v.* 11, 12. All things considered, it was a wonder that the Jews were not lost in that captivity, as other nations have been; but this intimates the reason why the streams of that people were kept to run pure through that dead sea, because from them, as *concerning the flesh, Christ* was to *come. Destroy it not, for a blessing is in it,* even that blessing of blessings, Christ himself, Isa. 65:8, 9. It was with an eye to him that they were restored, and the desolations of the sanctuary were looked upon with favour *for the Lord's sake,* Dan. 9:17.

9. *Josias* is said to *beget Jechonias and his brethren* (*v.* 11); by Jechonias here is meant Jehoiakim, who was the first-born of Josias; but, when it is said (*v.* 12) that *Jechonias begat Salathiel,* that Jechonias was the son of that Jehoiakim who was carried into Babylon, and there begat *Salathiel* (as Dr. Whitby shows), and, when Jechonias is said to have been written *childless* (Jer. 22:30), it is explained thus: *No man of his seed shall prosper. Salathiel* is here said to *beget Zorobabel,* whereas Salathiel begat Pedaiah, and he begat Zorobabel (1 Chr. 3:19): but, as before, the grandson is often called the son; Pedaiah, it is likely, died in his father's lifetime, and so his son Zorobabel was called the *son of Salathiel.*

10. The line is brought down, not to Mary the mother of our Lord, but to *Joseph the husband of Mary* (*v.* 16); for the Jews always reckoned their genealogies by the males: yet Mary was of the same tribe and family with Joseph, so that, both by his mother and by his supposed father, he was of the house of David; yet his interest in that dignity is derived by Joseph, to whom really according to the flesh he had no relation, to show that the kingdom of the Messiah is not founded in a natural descent from David.

11. The centre in whom all these lines meet is *Jesus, who is called Christ, v.* 16. This is he that was so importunately desired, so impatiently expected, and to whom the patriarchs had an eye when they were so desirous of children, that they might have the honour of coming into the sacred line. Blessed be God, we are not now in such a dark and cloudy state of expectation as they were then in, but see clearly what these prophets and kings saw as through a glass darkly. And we may have, if it be not our own fault, a greater honour than that of which they were so ambitious: for they who do the will of God are in a more honourable relation to Christ than those who were akin to him according to the flesh, *ch.* 12:50. *Jesus* is called *Christ,* that is, the *Anointed,* the same with the *Hebrew* name *Messiah.* He is called *Messiah the Prince* (Dan. 9:25), and often God's *Anointed* (Ps. 2:2). Under this character he was expected: *Art thou the Christ* — the *anointed one?* David, the king, was anointed (1 Sa. 16:13); so was Aaron, the priest (Lev. 8:12), and Elisha, the prophet (1 Ki. 19:16), and Isaiah, the prophet (Isa. 61:1). Christ, being appointed to, and qualified for, all these offices, is therefore called the *Anointed — anointed with the oil of gladness above his fellows;* and from this name of his, which is as ointment poured forth, all his followers are called *Christians,* for they also have *received the anointing.*

Lastly. The general summary of all this genealogy we have, *v.* 17, where it is summed up in three fourteens, signalized by remarkable periods. In the first fourteen, we have the family of David rising, and looking forth as the morning; in the second, we have it flourishing in its meridian lustre; in the third, we have it declining and growing less and less, dwindling into the family of a poor carpenter, and then Christ *shines forth* out of it, the *glory of his people Israel.*

Verses 18–25

The mystery of Christ's incarnation is to be adored, not pried into. If we *know not the way of the Spirit* in the formation of common persons, nor *how the bones are formed in the womb of* any one *that is with child* (Eccles. 11:5), much less do we know how the blessed Jesus was formed in the womb of the blessed virgin. When David admires how he himself was *made in secret,* and *curiously wrought* (Ps. 139:13–16), perhaps he speaks in the spirit of Christ's incarnation. Some circumstances attending the birth of Christ we find here which are not in Luke, though it is more largely recorded here. Here we have,

I. Mary's espousal to Joseph. Mary, the mother of our Lord, *was espoused to Joseph,* not completely married, but contracted; a purpose of marriage solemnly declared in words *de futuro — that regarding the future,* and a promise of it made if God permit. We read of a man who *has betrothed a wife and has not taken her,* Deu. 20:7. Christ was born of a virgin, but a betrothed virgin, 1. To put respect upon the marriage state, and to recommend it *as honourable among all,* against that doctrine of devils which *forbids to marry,* and places perfection in the single state. Who more highly favoured than Mary was in her espousals? 2. To save the credit of the blessed virgin, which otherwise would have been exposed. It was fit that her conception should be protected by a marriage, and so justified in the eye of the world. One of the ancients says, It was better it should be asked, Is not this the *son of a carpenter?* than, Is not this the *son of a harlot?* 3. That the blessed virgin might have one to be the guide of her youth, the companion of her solitude and travels, a partner in her cares, and a help meet for her. Some think that Joseph was now a widower, and that those who are called the *brethren of Christ* (*ch.* 13:55), were Joseph's children by a former wife. This is the conjecture of many of the ancients. Joseph was *just man,* she a *virtuous woman.* Those who are *believers* should not be *unequally yoked with unbelievers:* but let those who are religious choose to marry with those who are so, as they expect the comfort of the relation, and God's blessing upon them in it. We may also learn, from this example, that it is good to enter into the married state with deliberation, and not hastily — to preface the nuptials with a contract. It is better to *take* time to consider before than to *find* time to repent after.

II. Her pregnancy of the promised seed; *before they came together,* she *was found with child,* which really was *of the Holy Ghost.* The marriage was deferred so long after the contract that she appeared to be *with child* before the time came for the solemnizing of the marriage, though she was contracted before she conceived. Probably, it was after her return from her cousin Elizabeth, with whom she continued *three months* (Lu. 1:56), that she was perceived by Joseph to be with child, and did not herself deny it. Note, Those in whom Christ is formed will show it: it will be *found to be* a work of God which he will own. Now we may well imagine, what a perplexity this might justly occasion to the blessed virgin. She herself knew the divine original of this conception; but how could she prove it? She would be *dealt with as a harlot.* Note, After great and high advancements, lest we should be puffed up with them, we must expect something or other to humble us, some reproach, *as a thorn in the flesh,* nay, as *a sword in the bones.* Never was any daughter of Eve so dignified as the Virgin Mary was, and yet in danger of falling under the imputation of one of the worse crimes; yet we do not find that she tormented herself about it; but, being conscious of her own innocence, she kept her mind calm and easy, and committed her cause to *him that judgeth righteously.* Note, those who take care to keep a good conscience may cheerfully trust God with the keeping of their good names, and have reason to hope that he will clear up, not only their integrity, but their honour, as the sun at noon day.

III. Joseph's perplexity, and his care what to do in this case. We may well imagine what a great trouble and disappointment it was to him to find one he had such an opinion of, and value for, come under the suspicion of such a heinous crime. *Is this Mary?* He began to think, "How may we be deceived in those we think best of! How may we be disappointed in what we expect most from!" He is loth to believe so ill a thing of one whom he believed to be so good a woman; and yet the matter, as it is too bad to be excused, is also too plain to be denied. What a struggle does this occasion in his breast between that jealousy which is the rage of man, and is cruel as the grave, on the one hand, and that affection which he has for Mary on the other!

Observe, 1. The extremity which he studied to avoid. He was *not willing to make her a public example.* He might have done so; for, by the law, a *betrothed virgin,* if she played the harlot, was to be stoned to death, Deu. 22:23, 24. But he *was not willing* to take the advantage of the law against her; if she be guilty, yet it is not known, nor shall it be known from him. How different was the spirit which Joseph displayed from that of Judah, who in a similar case hastily passed that severe sentence, *Bring her forth and let her be burnt!* Gen. 38:24. How good it is to *think on things,* as Joseph did here! Were there more of deliberation in our censures and judgments, there would be more of mercy and moderation in them. Bringing her to punishment is here called *making her a public example;* which shows what is the end to be aimed at in punishment — the giving of warning to others: it is *in terrorem — that all about may hear and fear. Smite the scorner,* and the simple will beware.

Some persons of a rigorous temper would blame Joseph for his clemency: but it is here spoken of to his praise; because *he was a just man,* therefore he was not willing to expose her. He was a *religious, good man;* and therefore inclined to be merciful as God is, and to *forgive* as one that was *forgiven.* In the case of the betrothed damsel, if she were defiled in the field, the law charitably supposed that she *cried out* (Deu. 22:26), and she was not to be punished. Some charitable construction or other Joseph will put upon this matter; and herein he is a *just man,* tender of the good name of one who never before had done anything to blemish it. Note, It becomes us, in many cases, to be gentle towards those that come under suspicion of having offended, to hope the best concerning them, and make the best of that which at first appears bad, in hopes that it may prove better. *Summum just summa injuria — The rigour of the law is* (sometimes) *the height of injustice.* That court of conscience which moderates the rigour of the law we call a *court of equity.* Those who are found faulty were perhaps *overtaken in the fault,* and are therefore to be *restored with the spirit of meekness;* and threatening, even when just, must be moderated.

2. The expedient he found out for avoiding this extremity. He was *minded to put her away privily,* that is, to give a bill of divorce into her hand before two witnesses, and so to hush up the matter among themselves. Being a *just man,* that is, a strict observer of the law, he would not proceed to marry her, but resolved to *put her away;* and yet, in tenderness for her, determined to do it as privately as possible. Note, The necessary censures of those who have offended ought to be managed without noise. The *words of the wise are heard in quiet.* Christ himself *shall not strive nor cry.* Christian love and Christian prudence will *hide a multitude of sins,* and great ones, as far as may be done without having fellowship with them.

IV. Joseph's discharge from this perplexity by an express sent from heaven, *v.* 20, 21. *While he thought on these things* and knew not what to determine, God graciously directed him what to do, and made him easy. Note, Those who would have direction from God must *think on things* themselves, and consult with themselves. It is the *thoughtful,* not the *unthinking,* whom God will guide. When he was at a loss, and had carried the matter as far as he could in his own thoughts, then God came in with advice. Note, God's time to come in with instruction to his people is when they are *nonplussed* and at a stand. God's comforts most delight the soul *in the multitude* of its perplexed *thoughts.* The message was sent to Joseph by an *angel of the Lord,* probably the same angel that brought Mary the tidings of the conception — the angel Gabriel. Now the intercourse with heaven, by angels, with which the patriarchs had been dignified, but which had been long disused, begins to be revived; for, when the *First-begotten* is to be *brought into the world,* the angels are ordered to attend his motions. How far God may now, in an invisible way, make use of the ministration of angels, for extricating his people out of their straits, we cannot say; but this we are sure of, they are all *ministering spirits* for their good. This angel appeared to Joseph *in a dream* when he was asleep, as God sometimes spoke unto the fathers. When we are most quiet and composed we are in the best frame to receive the notices of the divine will. The Spirit moves on the calm waters. This dream, no doubt, carried its own evidence along with it that it was of God, and not the production of a vain fancy. Now,

1. Joseph is here *directed* to proceed in his intended marriage. The angel calls him, *Joseph, thou son of David;* he puts him in mind of his relation to David, that he might be prepared to receive this surprising intelligence of his relation to the Messiah, who, every one knew, was to be a descendant from David. Sometimes, when great honours devolve upon those who have small estates, they care not for accepting them, but are willing to drop them; it was therefore requisite to put this poor carpenter in mind of his high birth: "Value thyself. Joseph, thou art that *son of David* through whom the line of the Messiah is to be drawn." We may thus say to every true believer, "Fear not, thou son of Abraham, thou child of God; forget not the dignity of thy birth, thy new birth." *Fear not to take Mary for thy wife;* so it may be read. Joseph, sus-

pecting she was with child by whoredom, was afraid of *taking her,* lest he should bring upon himself either guilt or reproach. No, saith God, *Fear not;* the matter is not so. Perhaps Mary had told him that she was with child by the Holy Ghost, and he might have heard what Elizabeth said to her (Lu. 1:43), when she called her the *mother of her Lord;* and, if so, he was afraid of presumption in marrying one so much above him. But, from whatever cause his fears arose, they were all silenced with this word, *Fear not to take unto thee Mary thy wife.* Note, It is a great mercy to be delivered from our fears, and to have our doubts resolved, so as to proceed in our affairs with satisfaction.

2. He is here *informed* concerning that *holy thing* with which his espoused wife was now pregnant. That which is conceived in her is of a divine original. He is so far from being in danger of sharing in an impurity by marrying her, that he will thereby share in the highest dignity he is capable of. Two things he is told,

(1.) That she had conceived *by the power of the Holy Ghost;* not by the power of nature. The Holy Spirit, who produced the world, now produced the Saviour of the world, and *prepared him a body,* as was promised him, when he said, Lo, I come, Heb. 10:5. Hence he is said to be *made of a woman* (Gal. 4:4), and yet to be that second *Adam* that is the *Lord from heaven,* 1 Co. 15:47. He is the *Son of God,* and yet so far partakes of the substance of his mother as to be called the *fruit of her womb,* Lu. 1:42. It was requisite that is conception should be otherwise than by ordinary *generation,* that so, so though he partook of the human nature, yet he might escape the corruption and pollution of it, and not be *conceived* and *shapen* in iniquity. Histories tell us of some who vainly pretended to have conceived by a divine power, as the mother of Alexander; but none ever really did so, except the mother of our Lord. His name in this, as in other things, is *Wonderful.* We do not read that the virgin Mary did herself proclaim the honour done to her; but she hid it in her heart, and therefore God sent an angel to attest it. Those who seek not their own glory shall have the honour that comes from God; it is reserved for the humble.

(2.) That she should bring forth *the Saviour of the world* (*v.* 21). *She shall bring forth a Son;* what he shall be is intimated,

[1.] In the name that should be given to her Son: *Thou shalt call his name Jesus, a Saviour.* Jesus is the same name with Joshua, the termination only being changed, for the sake of conforming it to the Greek. Joshua is called *Jesus* (Acts 7:45; Heb. 4:8), from the Seventy. There were two of that name under the Old Testament, who were both illustrious types of Christ, Joshua who was Israel's captain at their first settlement in Canaan, and Joshua who was their high priest at their second settlement after the captivity, Zec. 6:11, 12. Christ is our Joshua; both the *Captain of our salvation,* and the *High Priest of our profession,* and, in both, our Saviour — a Joshua who comes in the stead of Moses, and does that for us which the *law could not do, in that it was weak.* Joshua had been called *Hosea,* but Moses prefixed the first syllable of the name Jehovah, and so made it *Jehoshua* (Num. 13:16), to intimate that the Messiah, who was to bear that name, should be *Jehovah;* he is therefore *able to save to the uttermost,* neither is there *salvation in any other.*

[2.] In the reason of that name: *For he shall save his people from their sins;* not the nation of the Jews only (he came to *his own,* and they *received him not*), but all who were given him by *the Father's choice,* and all who had given themselves to him by *their own.* He is a king who *protects* his subjects, and, as the judges of Israel of old, *works salvation* for them. Note, those whom Christ saves he saves *from their sins;* from the guilt of sin by the *merit of his death,* from the dominion of sin by the *Spirit of his grace.* In saving them from sin, he saves them from wrath and the curse, and all misery here and hereafter. Christ came to save his people, not *in their sins,* but *from* their sins; to purchase for them, not a liberty *to sin,* but a liberty *from sins, to redeem them from all iniquity* (Tit. 2:14); and so to redeem them *from among men* (Rev. 14:4) to himself, who is *separate from sinners.* So that those who leave their sins, and give up themselves to Christ as *his people,* are interested in the Saviour, and the great salvation which he has *wrought out,* Rom. 11:26.

V. The fulfilling of the scripture in all this. This evangelist, writing among the Jews, more frequently observes this than any other of the evangelists. Here the Old Testament prophecies had their accomplishment in our Lord Jesus, by

which it appears that this was he that should come, and we are to look for no other; for this was he *to whom all the prophets bore witness.* Now the scripture that was fulfilled in the birth of Christ was that promise of a sign which God gave to king Ahaz (Isa. 7:14), *Behold a virgin shall conceive;* where the prophet, encouraging the people of God to hope for the promised deliverance from Sennacherib's invasion, directs them to look forward to the Messiah, who was to come of the people of the Jews, and the house of David; whence it was easy to infer, that though that people and that house were afflicted, yet neither the one nor the other could be abandoned to ruin, so long as God had such an honour, such a blessing, in reserve for them. The deliverances which God wrought for the Old-Testament church were types and figures of the great salvation by Christ; and, if God will do the greater, he will not fail to do the less.

The prophecy here quoted is justly ushered in with a *Behold,* which commands both attention and admiration; for we have here the mystery of godliness, which is, without controversy, great, that God *was manifested in the flesh.*

1. The sign given is that the Messiah shall be *born of a virgin. A virgin shall conceive,* and, by her, he shall be manifested *in the flesh.* The word *Almah* signifies a *virgin* in the strictest sense, such as Mary professes herself to be (Lu. 1:34), *I know not a man;* nor had it been any such wonderful sign as it was intended for, if it had been otherwise. It was intimated from the beginning that the Messiah should be born of a virgin, when it was said that he should be the *seed of the woman;* so the seed of the woman as not to be the seed of any man. Christ was born of a virgin not only because his birth was to be *supernatural,* and altogether extraordinary, but because it was to be *spotless,* and pure, and without any stain of sin. Christ would be born, not of an *empress* or *queen,* for he appeared not in outward pomp or splendour, but of a virgin, to teach us spiritual purity, to die to all the delights of sense, and so to *keep ourselves unspotted* from the world and the flesh that we may be presented *chaste virgins to Christ.*

2. The truth proved by this sign is, that he is the Son of God, and the Mediator between God and man: for *they shall call his name Immanuel;* that is, he shall be *Immanuel;* and when it is said, *He shall be called,* it is meant, he shall *be, the Lord our righteousness. Immanuel* signifies *God with us;* a mysterious name, but very precious; God *incarnate* among us, and so God *reconcilable* to us, at peace with us, and taking us into covenant and communion with himself. The people of the Jews had *God with them,* in types and shadows, dwelling between the cherubim; but never so as when the *Word was made flesh* — that was the blessed *Shechinah.* What a happy step is hereby taken toward the settling of a peace and correspondence between God and man, that the two natures are thus brought together in the person of the Mediator! by this he became an unexceptionable referee, a daysman, fit to *lay his hand upon them both,* since he partakes of the nature of both. Behold, in this, the deepest mystery, and the richest mercy, that ever was. By the light of *nature,* we see God as a God *above us;* by the light of the *law,* we see him as a God *against us;* but by the light of the gospel, we see him as *Immanuel,* God *with us,* in our own nature, and (which is more) in our interest. Herein the Redeemer *commended his love.* With Christ's name, *Immanuel,* we may compare the name given to the gospel church (Eze. 48:35). *Jehovah Shammah — The Lord is there;* the Lord of hosts is with us.

Nor is it improper to say that the prophecy which foretold that he should be called *Immanuel* was fulfilled, in the design and intention of it, when he was called *Jesus;* for if he had not been *Immanuel — God with us,* he could not have been *Jesus — a Saviour;* and herein consists the salvation he wrought out, in the *bringing of God and man together;* this was what he designed, to bring *God* to be *with us,* which is our great happiness, and to bring *us* to be *with God,* which is our great duty.

VI. Joseph's obedience to the divine precept (*v.* 24). *Being raised from sleep* by the impression which the dream made upon him, *he did as the angel of the Lord had bidden him,* though it was contrary to his former sentiments and intentions; *he took unto him his wife;* he did is speedily, without delay, and cheerfully, without dispute; he was not disobedient to the heavenly vision. Extraordinary direction like this we are not now to expect; but God has still ways of making known his mind in doubtful cases, by hints of providence, debates of conscience, and advice of faithful friends; by each of these, applying the general rules of the written word, we should, therefore, in all the steps of our life, particularly the great turns of it, such as this of Joseph's, take direction from God, and we shall find it safe and comfortable to do as he bids us.

VII. The accomplishment of the divine promise (*v.* 25). *She brought forth her first-born* son. The circumstances of it are more largely related, Lu. 2:1, etc. Note, That which is *conceived of the Holy Ghost* never proves *abortive,* but will certainly be *brought forth* in its season. What is *of the will of the flesh,* and *of the will of man,* often miscarries; but, if Christ be *formed* in the soul, God himself has begun the good work which he will perform; what is *conceived* in grace will no doubt be *brought forth* in glory.

It is here further observed, 1. That Joseph, though he solemnized the marriage with Mary, his espoused wife, kept at a distance from her while she was with child of this Holy thing; he *knew her not till she had brought him forth.* Much has been said concerning the perpetual virginity of our Lord: Jerome was very angry with Helvidius for denying it. It is certain that it cannot be proved from scripture. Dr. *Whitby* inclines to think that when it is said, *Joseph knew her not till she had brought forth her first-born,* it is intimated that, afterwards, the reason ceasing, he lived with her, according to the law, Ex. 21:10. 2. That Christ was the *first-born;* and so he might be called though his mother had not any other children after him, according to the language of scripture. Nor is it without a mystery that Christ is called her *first-born,* for he is the *first-born of every creature,* that is, the Heir of all things; and he is the *first-born among many brethren,* that in all things he may have the pre-eminence. 3. That *Joseph called his name Jesus,* according to the direction given him. God having *appointed* him to be the Saviour, which was intimated in his giving him the name *Jesus,* we must *accept* of him to be our Saviour, and, in concurrence with that appointment, we must call him *Jesus, our Saviour.*

CHAPTER 2

In this chapter, we have the history of our Saviour's infancy, where we find how early he began to suffer, and that in him the word of righteousness was fulfilled, before he himself began to fulfil all righteousness. Here is, I. The wise men's solicitous enquiry after Christ (*v.* 1–8). II. Their devout attendance on him, when they found out where he was (*v.* 9–12). III. Christ's flight into Egypt, to avoid the cruelty of Herod (*v.* 13–15). IV. The barbarous murder of the infants of Bethlehem (*v.* 16–18). V. Christ's return out of Egypt into the land of Israel again (*v.* 19–23).

Verses 1–8

It was a *mark of humiliation* put upon the Lord Jesus that, though he was the *Desire of all nations,* yet his coming into the world was little observed and taken notice of, his birth was obscure and unregarded: herein he emptied himself, and made himself of no reputation. If the Son of God must be brought into the world, one might justly expect that he should be received with all the ceremony possible, that crowns and sceptres should immediately have been laid at his feet, and that the high and mighty princes of the world should have been his humble servants; such a Messiah as this the Jews expected, but we see none of all this; he *came into the world,* and the *world knew him not;* nay, he *came to his own,* and *his own received him not;* for having undertaken to make satisfaction to his Father for the wrong done him *in his honour* by the sin of man, he did it by denying himself in, and despoiling himself of, the honours undoubtedly due to an incarnate Deity; yet, as afterward, so in his birth, some rays of glory darted forth in the midst of the greatest instances of his abasement. Though *there was the hiding of his power,* yet he had *horns coming out of his hand* (Hab. 3:4) enough to condemn the world, and the Jews especially, for their stupidity.

The first who took notice of Christ after his birth were the shepherds (Lu. 2:15, etc.), who saw and heard glorious things concerning him, and *made them known abroad,* to the amazement of all that heard them, *v.* 17, 18. After that, Simeon and Anna spoke of him, by the Spirit, to all that were disposed to heed what they said, Lu. 2:38. Now, one would think, these hints should have been taken by the men of Judah and the *inhabitants of Jerusalem,* and they should with both arms have embraced the long-looked-for Messiah; but, for aught that appears, he continued nearly two years after at Bethlehem, and no further notice was taken of him till these wise men came. Note, Nothing will awaken those that are resolved to be regardless. Oh the amazing stupidity of these Jews! And no less that of many who are called Christians! Observe,

I. When this enquiry was made concerning Christ. It was *in the days of Herod the king.* This Herod was an Edomite, made king of Judea by Augustus and Antonius, the then chief rulers of the Roman state, a man made up of falsehood and cruelty; yet he was complimented with the title of *Herod the Great.* Christ was born in the 35th year of his reign, and notice is taken of this, to show that the *sceptre* had now *departed from Judah,* and *the lawgiver from between his feet;* and therefore now was the time for Shiloh to come, and *to him shall the gathering of the people be:* witness these wise men, Gen. 49:10.

II. Who and what these *wise men* were; they are here called *Magoi — Magicians.* Some that it in a good sense; the *Magi* among the *Persians* were their philosophers and their priests; nor would they admit any one for their king who had not first been enrolled among the *Magi;* others think they dealt in unlawful arts; the word is used of Simon, the sorcerer (Acts 8:9, 11), and of Elymas, the sorcerer (Acts 13:6), nor does the scripture use it in any other sense; and then it was an early instance and presage of Christ's victory over the devil, when those who had been so much his devotees became the early adorers even of the infant Jesus; so soon were trophies of his victory over the powers of darkness erected. Well, whatever sort of wise men they were before, now they began to be *wise men* indeed when they set themselves to enquire after Christ.

This we are sure of, 1. That they were Gentiles, and not belonging to the commonwealth of Israel. The Jews regarded not Christ, but these Gentiles enquired him out. Note, Many times those who are nearest to the means, are furthest from the end. See *ch.* 8:11, 12. The respect paid to Christ by these Gentiles was a happy presage and specimen of what would follow when those who were *afar off* should be *made nigh by Christ.* 2. That they were *scholars.* They dealt in arts, curious arts; good scholars should be good Christians, and *then* they complete their *learning* when they *learn Christ.* 3. That they were *men of the east,* who were noted for their *soothsaying,* Isa. 2:6. Arabia is called the land of *the east* (Gen. 25:6), and the *Arabians* are called *men of the east,* Jdg. 6:3. The presents they brought were the products of that country; the Arabians had done homage to David and Solomon as types of Christ. Jethro and Job were of that country. More than this we have not to say of them. The traditions of the Romish church are frivolous, that they were in number three (though one of the ancients says that they were fourteen), that they were kings, and that they lie buried in Colen, thence called the *three kings of Colen;* we covet not to be wise above what is written.

III. What induced them to make this enquiry. They, in their country, which was in the *east,* had seen an *extraordinary star,* such as they had not seen before; which they took to be an indication of an extraordinary person born in the land of *Judea,* over which land this star was seen to hover, in the nature of a comet, or a meteor rather, in the lowers regions of the air; this differed so much from any thing that was common that they concluded it to signify something uncommon. Note, Extraordinary appearances of God in the creatures should put us upon enquiring after his mind and will therein; Christ foretold *signs in the heavens.* The birth of Christ was notified to the Jewish shepherds by *an angel,* to the Gentile philosophers by a *star:* to both God spoke in their own language, and in the way they were best acquainted with. Some think that the light which the shepherds saw shining round about them, the night after Christ was born, was the very same which to the wise men, who lived at such a distance, appeared as a star; but this we cannot easily admit, because the same star which they had seen in the *east* they saw a great while after, leading them to the house where Christ lay; it was a candle set up on purpose to guide them to Christ. The idolaters worshipped the stars as the *host of heaven,* especially the *eastern* nations, whence the planets have the names of their idol-gods; we read of a particular *star* they had in veneration, Amos 5:26. Thus the stars that had been misused came to be put to the right use, to lead men to Christ; the gods of the heathen became his servants. Some think this star put them in mind of Balaam's prophecy, that a star should come out of Jacob, pointing at a *sceptre,* that shall *rise out of Israel;* see Num. 24:17. Balaam came from the *mountains of the east,* and was one of their *wise men.* Others impute their enquiry to the general expectation entertained at that time, in those *eastern* parts, of some great prince to appear. Tacitus, in his history (*lib.* 5), takes notice of it; *Pluribus persuasio inerat, antiquis sacerdotum literis contineri, eo ipso tempore fore, ut valesceret oriens, profectique Judaea rerum potirentur — A persuasion existed in the minds of many that some ancient writings of the priests contained a prediction that about that time an eastern power would prevail, and that persons proceeding from Judea would obtain dominion. Suetonius* also, in the life of *Vespasian,* speaks of it; so that this extraordinary phenomenon was construed as pointing to *that king;* and we may suppose a divine impression made upon their minds, enabling them to interpret this star as a signal given by Heaven of the birth of Christ.

IV. How they prosecuted this enquiry. *They came from the* east to Jerusalem, in further quest of this prince. Wither shall they come to enquire for the king of the Jews, but to Jerusalem, the mother-city, *whither the tribes go up, the tribes of the Lord?* They might have said, "If such a prince be born, we shall hear of him shortly in our own country, and it will be time enough then to pay our homage to him." But so impatient were they to be better acquainted with him, that they took a long journey on purpose to enquire after him. Note, Those who truly desire to know Christ, and find him, will not regard pains or perils in seeking after him. *Then shall we know, if we follow on to know the Lord.*

Their question is, *Where is he that is born king of the Jews?* They do not ask, *whether there were such a one born?* (they are sure of that, and speak of it with assurance, so strongly was it set home upon their hearts); but, *Where is he born?* Note, Those who know *something* of Christ cannot but covet to *know more* of him. They call Christ the *King of the Jews,* for so the Messiah was expected to be: and he is Protector and Ruler of all the spiritual Israel, he is *born a King.*

To this question they doubted not but to have a ready answer, and to find all Jerusalem worshipping at the feet of this new king; but they come from door to door with this question, and no man can give them any information. Note, There is more gross ignorance in the world, and in the church too, than we are aware of. Many that we think should direct us to Christ are themselves strangers to him. They ask, as the spouse of the daughters of Jerusalem, *Saw ye him whom my soul loveth?* But they are never the wiser. However, like the spouse, they pursue the enquiry, *Where is he that is born king of the Jews?* Are they asked, "Why do ye make this enquiry?" It is because they have *seen his star in the east.* Are they asked, "What business have ye with him? What have the men of the *east* to do with the *King of the Jews?"* They have their answer ready, *We are come to worship him.* They conclude he will, in process of time, be *their king,* and therefore they will betimes ingratiate themselves with him and with those about him. Note, Those in whose hearts the day-star is risen, to give them any thing of the knowledge of Christ, must make it their business to worship him. Have we seen Christ's star? Let us study to give him honour.

V. How this enquiry was treated at Jerusalem. News of it at last came to court; and *when Herod heard it he was troubled, v.* 3. He could not be a stranger to the prophecies of the *Old Testament,* concerning the Messiah and his kingdom, and the times fixed for his appearing by Daniel's weeks; but, having himself reigned so long and so successfully, he began to hope that those promises would for ever fail, and that his kingdom would be established and perpetuated in spite of them. What a damp therefore must it needs be upon him, to hear talk of this King being born, now, when the time fixed for his appearing had come! Note, Carnal wicked hearts dread nothing so much as the fulfilling of the scriptures.

But though Herod, an Edomite, was troubled, one would have thought Jerusalem should rejoice greatly to hear that her King comes; yet, it seems, *all Jerusalem,* except the few there that *waited for the consolation of Israel, were troubled with* Herod, and were apprehensive of I know not what ill consequences of the birth of this new king, that it would involve them in war, or restrain their lusts; they, for their parts, desired no king but Herod; no, not the Messiah himself. Note, The slavery of sin is foolishly preferred by many to the glorious liberty of the children of God, only because they apprehend some present difficulties attending that necessary revolution of the government in the soul. Herod and Jerusalem were thus troubled, from a mistaken notion that the kingdom of the Messiah would clash and interfere with the secular powers; whereas the star that proclaimed him king plainly intimated that his kingdom was heavenly, and not of this lower world. Note, The reason why the kings of the earth, and the people, oppose the kingdom of Christ, is because they do not know it, but err concerning it.

VI. What assistance they met with in this enquiry from the scribes and the priests, *v.* 4–6. Nobody can pretend to tell where the King of the Jews is, but Herod enquires where it was expected *he should be born.* The persons he consults are, the chief priests, who were teachers by office; and the scribes, who made it their business to study the law; their *lips must keep knowledge,* but then the people must *enquire the law at their mouth,* Mal. 2:7. It was generally known that Christ should be *born at Bethlehem* (Jn. 7:42); but Herod would have counsel's opinion upon it, and therefore applies himself to the proper persons; and, that he might be the better satisfied, he has them altogether, *all the chief priests, and all the scribes;* and *demands of them* what was the place, according to the scriptures of the Old Testament, *where Christ should be born?* Many a good question is put with an ill design, so was this by Herod.

The priests and scribes need not take any long time to give an answer to this query; nor do they differ in their opinion, but all agree that the Messiah must be *born in Bethlehem, the city of David,* here called *Bethlehem of Judea,* to distinguish it from another city of the same name in the land of Zebulun, Jos. 19:15. *Bethlehem* signifies the *house of bread;* the fittest place for him to be born in who is the true manna, *the bread which came down from heaven,* which was *given for the life of the world.* The proof they produce is taken from Mic. 5:2, where it is foretold that though *Bethlehem be little among the thousands of Judah* (so it is in *Micah*), no very populous place, yet it shall be found *not the least among the princes of Judah* (so it is here); for Bethlehem's honour lay not, as that of other cities, in the multitude of the people, but in the magnificence of the princes it produced. Though, upon some accounts, Bethlehem was little, yet herein it had the pre-eminence above all the cities of Israel, that *the Lord shall count, when he writes up the people, that this man,* even *the man Christ Jesus, was born there,* Ps. 87:6. *Out of thee shall come a Governor,* the *King of the Jews.* Note, Christ will be a *Saviour* to those only who are willing to take him for their *Governor.* Bethlehem was the *city of David,* and David the glory of Bethlehem; there, therefore, must David's son and successor be born. There was a famous well at *Bethlehem,* by the gate, which David longed to drink of (2 Sa. 23:15); in Christ we have not only bread enough and to spare, but may come and take also *of the water of life freely.* Observe here how Jews and Gentiles compare notes about Jesus Christ. The Gentiles know the time of his birth by a star; the Jews know the place of it by the scriptures; and so they are capable of informing one another. Note, It would contribute much to the increase of knowledge, if we did thus mutually communicate what we know. Men grow rich by bartering and exchanging; so, if we have knowledge to communicate to others, they will be ready to communicate to us; thus many shall discourse, shall *run to and fro, and knowledge shall be increased.*

VII. The bloody project and design of Herod, occasioned by this enquiry, *v.* 7, 8. Herod was now an old man, and had reigned thirty-five years; this king was but newly born, and not likely to enterprise any thing considerable for many years; yet Herod is jealous of him. Crowned heads cannot endure to think of successors, much less of rivals; and therefore nothing less than the blood of this infant king will satisfy him; and he will not give himself liberty to think that, if this new-born child should be indeed the Messiah, in opposing him, or making any attempts upon him, he would *be found fighting against God,* than which nothing is more vain, nothing more dangerous. Passion has got the mastery of reason and conscience.

Now, 1. See how cunningly he laid the project (*v.* 7, 8). *He privily called the wise men,* to talk with them about this matter. He would not openly own his fears and jealousies; it would be his disgrace to let the wise men know them, and dangerous to let the people know them. Sinners are often tormented with secret fears, which they keep to themselves. Herod learns of the wise men the *time when the star appeared,* that he might take his measures accordingly; and then employs them to enquire further, and bids them bring him an account. All this might look suspicious, if he had not covered it with a show of religion: *that I may come and worship him also.* Note, The greatest wickedness often conceals itself under a mask of piety. Absalom cloaks his rebellious project with a vow.

2. See how strangely he was befooled and infatuated in this, that he trusted it with the wise men, and did not choose some other managers, that would have been true to his interests. It was but seven miles from Jerusalem; how easily might he have sent spies to watch the wise men, who might have been as soon there to destroy the child as they to worship him! Note, God can hide from the eyes of the church's enemies those methods by which they might easily destroy the church; when he intends to *lead princes away spoiled,* his way is to *make the judges fools.*

Verses 9–12

We have here the wise men's humble attendance upon this new-born *King of the Jews,* and the honours they paid him. From Jerusalem they went to Bethlehem, resolving to *seek till they should find;* but it is very strange that they went alone; that not one person of the court, church, or city, should accompany them, if not in conscience, yet in civility to them, or touched with a curiosity to see this young prince. As *the queen of the south,* so *the wise men of the east,* will *rise up in judgment against* the men of that generation, and of this too, *and will condemn them;* for they *came from a far country,* to worship Christ; while the Jews, his kinsmen, would not stir a step, would not go to the next town to bid him welcome. It might have been a discouragement to these wise men to find him whom they sought thus neglected at home. Are we come so far to honour *the King of the Jews,* and do the Jews themselves put such a slight upon him and us? Yet they persist in their resolution. Note, We must continue our attendance upon Christ, though we be alone in it; whatever others do, we must *serve the Lord;* if they will not go to heaven with us, yet we must not go to hell with them. Now,

I. See how they found out Christ by the same star that they had seen in their own country, *v.* 9, 10. Observe, 1. How graciously God directed them. By the first appearance of the star they were given to understand where they might enquire for this King, and then it disappeared, and they were left to take the usual methods for such an enquiry. Note, Extraordinary helps are not to be expected where ordinary means are to be had. Well, they had traced the matter as far as they could; they were upon their journey to Bethlehem, but that is a populous town, where shall they find him when they come thither? Here they were at a loss, at their wit's end, but not at their faith's end; they believed that God, who had brought them thither by his word, would not leave them there; nor did he; for, behold, *the star which they saw in the east went before them.* Note, If we go on as far as we can in the way of duty, God will direct and enable us to do that which of ourselves we cannot do; *Up, and be doing, and the Lord will be with thee. Vigilantibus, non dormientibus, succurit lex — The law affords its aid, not to the idle, but to the active.* The star had left them a great while, yet now returns. They who follow God in the dark shall find that light is sown, is reserved, for them. Israel was led by a pillar of fire to *the promised land,* the wise men by a star to *the promised Seed,* who is himself *the bright and morning Star,* Rev. 22:16. God would rather *create a new thing* than leave those at a loss who diligently and faithfully sought him. This star was the token of God's presence with them; for he is light, and goes before his people as their Guide. Note, If we by faith eye God in all our ways, we may see ourselves under his conduct; he *guides with his eye* (Ps. 32:8), and said to them, *This is the way, walk in it:* and there is a day-star that arises in the hearts of those that enquire after Christ, 2 Pt. 1:19. 2. Observe how joyfully they followed God's direction (*v.* 10). *When they saw the star, they rejoiced with exceeding great joy.* Now they saw they were not deceived, and had not taken this long journey in vain. *When the desire cometh, it is a tree of life.* Now they were sure that God was with them, and the tokens of his presence and favour cannot but fill with joy unspeakable the souls of those that know how to value them. Now they could laugh at the Jews in Jerusalem, who, probably, had laughed at them as coming on a fool's errand. The watchmen can give the spouse no tidings of her beloved; yet it *is but a little that she passes from them, and she finds him,* Cant. 3:3, 4. We cannot expect too little from man, nor too much from God. What a transport of joy these wise men were in upon this sight of the star; none know so well as those who, after a long and melancholy night of temptation and desertion, under the power of a *Spirit of bondage,* at length *receive the spirit of adoption, witnessing with their spirits that they are the children of God;* this is light out of darkness; it is life from the dead. Now they had reason to hope for a sight of *the Lord's Christ* speedily, of the *Sun of righteousness,* for they see *the Morning Star.* Note, We should be glad of every thing that will show us the way to Christ. This star was sent to meet the wise men, and to conduct them into the presence chamber of the King; by this master of ceremonies they were introduced, to have their audience. Now God fulfills his promise of meeting those that are disposed to *rejoice and work righteousness* (Isa. 64:5), and they fulfill his precept. *Let the hearts of those rejoice that seek the Lord,* Ps. 105:3. Note, God is pleased sometimes to favour young converts with such tokens of his love as are very encouraging to them, in reference to the difficulties they meet with at their setting out of the ways of God.

II. See how they made their address to him when they had found him, *v.* 11. We may well imagine their expectations were raised to find this royal babe, though slighted by the nation, yet honourably attended at home; and what a disappointment it was to them when they found a cottage was his palace, and his own poor mother all the retinue he had! Is this *the Saviour of the world?* Is this *the King of the Jews,* nay, and *the Prince of the kings of the earth?* Yes, this is he, who, *though he was rich,* yet, *for our sakes, became* thus *poor.* However, these wise men were so wise as to see through this veil, and in this despised babe to discern *the glory as of the Only-begotten of the Father;* they did not think themselves balked or baffled in their enquiry; but, as having found the King they sought, they presented themselves first, and then their gifts, to him.

1. They presented themselves to him: *they fell down, and worshipped him.* We do not read that they gave such honour to Herod, though he was in the height of his royal grandeur; but to this babe they gave this honour, not only as to a king (then they would have done the same to Herod), but as to a God. Note, All that have found Christ fall down before him; they adore him, and submit themselves to him. *He is thy Lord, and worship thou him.* It will be the wisdom of the wisest of men, and by this it will appear they know Christ, and understand themselves and their true interests, if they be humble, faithful worshippers of the Lord Jesus.

2. *They presented their gifts to him.* In the eastern nations, when they did homage to their kings, they made them presents; thus the subjection of the kings of Sheba to Christ is spoken of (Ps. 72:10), *They shall bring presents, and offer gifts.* See Isa. 60:6. Note, With ourselves, we must give up all that we have to Jesus Christ; and if we be sincere in the surrender of ourselves to him, we shall not be unwilling to part with what is dearest to us, and most valuable, to him and for him; nor are our gifts accepted, unless we first present ourselves to him living sacrifices. *God had respect to Abel, and* then to *his offering.* The gifts they presented were, *gold, frankincense, and myrrh,* money, and money's-worth. Providence sent this for a seasonable relief to Joseph and Mary in their present poor condition. These were the products of their own country; what God favours us with, we must honour him with. Some think there was a significancy in their gifts; they offered him *gold,* as a king, paying him tribute, *to Caesar, the things that are Caesar's; frankincense,* as God, for they honoured God with the smoke of incense; and *myrrh,* as a Man that should die, for *myrrh* was used in embalming dead bodies.

III. See how they left him when they had made their address to him, *v.* 12. Herod appointed them to *bring him word* what discoveries they had made, and, it is probable, they would have done so, if they had not been countermanded, not suspecting their being thus made his tools in a wicked design. Those that mean honestly and well themselves are easily made to believe that others do so too, and cannot think the world is as bad as it really is; but *the Lord knows how to deliver the godly out of temptation.* We do not find that the wise men promised to come back to Herod, and, if they had, it must have been with the usual proviso, *If God permit;* God did not permit them, and prevented the mischief Herod designed to the Child Jesus, and the trouble it would have been to the wise men to have been made involuntarily accessory to it. They were *warned of God, chrēmatisthentes — oraculo vel responso accepto — by an oracular intimation.* Some think it intimates that they asked counsel of God, and that this was the answer. Note, Those that act cautiously, and are afraid of sin and snares, if they apply themselves to God for direction, may expect to be led in the right way. They were *warned not to return to Herod*, nor to Jerusalem; those were unworthy to have reports brought them concerning Christ, that might have seen with their own eyes, and would not. *They departed into their own country another way*, to bring the tidings to their countrymen; but it is strange that we never hear any more of them, and that they or theirs did not afterwards attend *him* in the temple, whom they had worshipped in the cradle. However, the direction they had from God in their return would be a further confirmation of their faith in this Child, *as the Lord from heaven*.

Verses 13–15

We have here Christ's flight into Egypt to avoid the cruelty of Herod, and this was the effect of the wise men's enquiry after him; for, before that, the obscurity he lay in was his protection. It was but little respect (compared with what should have been) that was paid to Christ in his infancy: yet even that, instead of honouring him among his people, did but expose him.

Now here observe, 1. The command given to Joseph concerning it, *v.* 13. Joseph knew neither the danger the child was in, nor how to escape it; but God by *an angel*, tells him both in *a dream*, as before he directed him in like manner what to do, *ch.* 1:20. Joseph, before his alliance to Christ, had not been wont to converse with angels as now. Note, those that are spiritually related to Christ by faith have that communion and correspondence with Heaven which before they were strangers to.

1. Joseph is here told what their danger was: *Herod will seek the young child to destroy him*. Note, God is acquainted with all the cruel projects and purposes of the enemies of his church. *I know thy rage against me*, saith God to Sennacherib, Isa. 37:28. How early was the blessed Jesus involved in trouble! Usually, even those whose riper years are attended with toils and perils have a peaceable and quiet infancy; but it was not so with the blessed Jesus: his life and sufferings began together; he was born *a man striven with*, as Jeremiah was (Jer. 15:10), who was *sanctified from the womb*, Jer. 1:5. Both Christ the head, and the church his body, agree in saying, *Many a time have they afflicted me, from my youth up*. Pharaoh's cruelty fastens upon the Hebrews' children, and a great red dragon stands ready to *devour the man-child as soon as it should be born*, Rev. 12:4.

2. He is directed what to do, to escape the danger; *Take the young child, and flee into Egypt*. Thus early must Christ give an example to his own rule (*ch.* 10:23): *When they persecute you in one city, flee to another*. He that came to die for us, when *his hour was not yet come*, fled for his own safety. Self-preservation, being a branch of the law of nature, is eminently a part of the law of God. *Flee;* but why *into Egypt?* Egypt was infamous for idolatry, tyranny, and enmity to the people of God; it had been a house of bondage to Israel, and particularly cruel to the infants of Israel; in Egypt, as much as in Ramah, *Rachel had been weeping for her children;* yet that is appointed to be a place of refuge to the hold child Jesus. Note, God, when he pleases, can make the worst of places serve the best of purposes; for *the earth is the Lord's*, he makes what use he pleases of it: sometimes the earth *helps the woman* Rev. 12:16. God, who made Moab a shelter to his outcasts, makes Egypt a refuge for his Son. This may be considered,

(1.) As a trial of faith of Joseph and Mary. They might be tempted to think, "If this child be the Son of God, as we are told he is, has he no other way to secure himself from a man that is a worm, than by such a mean and inglorious retreat as this? Cannot he summon legions of angels to be his life-guard, or cherubim with flaming swords to keep this *tree of life?* Cannot he strike Herod dead, or wither the hand that is stretched out against him, and so save us the trouble of this remove?" They had been lately told that he should be *the glory of his people Israel;* and is the land of Israel so soon become too hot for him? But we find not that they made any such objections; their faith, being tried, was found firm, they believe *this is the Son of God,* though they see no miracle wrought for his preservation; but they are put to the use of ordinary means. Joseph had great honour put upon him in being the husband of the blessed virgin; but that honour has trouble attending it, as all honours have in this world; Joseph must *take the young child,* and carry him *into Egypt;* and now it appeared how well God had provided for *the young child and his mother*, in appointing Joseph to stand

in so near a relation to them; now the gold which the wise men brought would stand them in stead to bear their charges. God foresees his people's distresses, and provides against them beforehand. God intimates the continuance of his care and guidance, when he saith, *Be thou there until I bring thee word*, so that he must expect to hear from God again, and not stir without fresh orders. Thus God will keep his people still in a dependence upon him.

(2.) As an instance of the humiliation of our Lord Jesus. As there was no room for him in the inn in Bethlehem, so there was no quiet room for him in the land of Judea. Thus was he banished from the earthly Canaan, that we, who for sin were banished from the heavenly Canaan, might not be for ever expelled. If we and our infants be at any time in straits, let us remember the straits Christ in his infancy was brought into, and be reconciled to them.

(3.) As a token of God's displeasure against the Jews, who took so little notice of him; justly does he leave those who have slighted him. We have also here an earnest of his favour to the Gentiles, to whom the apostles were to bring the gospel when the Jews rejected it. If Egypt entertain Christ when he is forced out of Judea, it will not be long ere it be said, *Blessed be Egypt my people,* Isa. 19:25.

II. Joseph's obedience to this command, *v.* 14. The journey would be inconvenient and perilous both to the young child and to his mother; they were but poorly provided for it, and were likely to meet with cold entertainment in Egypt: yet Joseph *was not disobedient to the heavenly vision,* made no objection, nor was dilatory in his disobedience. As soon as he had received his orders, he immediately *arose*, and went away *by night,* the same night, as it should seem, that he received the orders. Note, Those that would make *sure* work of their obedience must make *quick* work of it. Now Joseph went out, as his father Abraham did, with an implicit dependence upon God, *not knowing whither he went,* Heb. 11:8. Joseph and his wife, having little, had little to care of in this remove. An abundance encumbers a necessary flight. If rich people have the advantage of the poor while they possess what they have, the poor have the advantage of the rich when they are called to part with it.

Joseph took the young child and his mother. Some observe, that *the young child* is put first, as the principal person, and Mary is called, not *the wife of Joseph,* but, which was her great dignity, *the mother of the young child.* This was not the first Joseph that was driven from Canaan to Egypt for a shelter from the anger of his brethren; this Joseph ought to be welcome there for the sake of that.

If we may credit tradition, at their entrance into Egypt, happening to go into a temple, all the images of their gods were overthrown by an invisible power, and fell, like Dagon before the ark, according to that prophecy, *The Lord shall come into Egypt, and the idols of Egypt shall be moved at his presence,* Isa. 19:1. They continued in Egypt till the death of Herod, which, some think, was seven years, others think, not so many months. There they were at a distance from the temple and the service of it, and in the midst of idolaters; but God sent them thither, and will *have mercy, and not sacrifice.* Though they were far from the temple of the Lord, they had with them the Lord of the temple. A forced absence from God's ordinances, and a forced presence with wicked people, may be the lot, are not the sin, yet cannot but be the grief, of good people.

III. The fulfilling of the scripture in a this — that scripture (Hos. 11:1), *Out of Egypt have I called my son.* Of all the evangelists, Matthew takes most notice of the fulfilling of the scripture in what concerned Christ, because his gospel was first published among the Jews, with whom that would add much strength and lustre to it. Now this word of the prophet undoubtedly referred to the deliverance of Israel out of Egypt, in which God owned them for his son, his first-born (Ex. 4:22); but it is here applied, by way of analogy, to Christ, the Head of the church. Note, The scripture has many accomplishments, so full and copious is it, and so well ordered in all things. God is every day fulfilling the scripture. Scripture is not of private interpretation: we must give it its full latitude. "When Israel was a child, then I loved him; and, though *I loved him,* I suffered him to be a great while in Egypt; but, because *I loved him,* in due time I called him out of Egypt." They that read this must, in their thoughts, not only look back, but look forward; *that which has been shall be again* (Eccl. 1:9); and the manner of expression intimates this; for it is not said, I called *him,* but I called *my son,* out of Egypt.

Note, It is no new thing for God's sons to be in Egypt, in a strange land, in a house of bondage; but they shall be fetched out. They may be hid in Egypt, but they shall not be left there. All the elect of God, being by nature children of wrath, are born in a spiritual Egypt, and in conversion are effectually called out. It might be objected against Christ that he had been in Egypt. Must *the Sun of righteousness* arise out of that land of darkness! But this shows that to be no strange thing; Israel was brought out of Egypt, to be advanced to the highest honours; and this is but doing the same thing.

Verses 16–18

Here is, I. Herod's resentment of the departure of the wise men. He waited long for their return; he hopes, though they be slow, they will be sure, and he shall crush this rival at his first appearing; but he hears, upon enquiry, that they are gone off another way, which increases his jealousy, and makes him suspect they are in the interest of this new King, which made him *exceedingly wroth;* and he is the more desperate and outrageous for his being disappointed. Note, Inveterate corruption swells the higher for the obstructions it meets with in a sinful pursuit.

II. His political contrivance, notwithstanding this, to take off him that is *born King of the Jews.* If he could not reach him by a particular execution, he doubted not but to involve him in a general stroke, which, like the sword of war, should *devour one as well as another.* This would be sure work; and thus those that would destroy *their own* iniquity must be sure to destroy *all* their iniquities. Herod was an Edomite, enmity to Israel was bred in the bone with him. Doeg was an Edomite, who, for David's sake, *slew all the priests of the Lord.* It was strange that Herod could find any so inhuman as to be employed in such a bloody and barbarous piece of work; but wicked hands never want wicked tools to work with. Little children have always been taken under the special protection, not only of human laws, but of human nature; yet these are sacrificed to the rage of this tyrant, under whom, as under Nero, innocence is the least security. Herod was, throughout his reign, a bloody man; it was not long before, that he destroyed the whole Sanhedrim, or bench of judges; but blood to the blood-thirsty is like drink to those in a dropsy; *Quo plus sunt potae, plus sitiuntur aquae — The more they drink, the more thirsty they become.* Herod was now about seventy years old, so that an infant, at this time *under two years old,* was not likely ever to give him any disturbance. Nor was he a man over fond of his own children, or of their preferment, having formerly slain two of his own sons, Alexander and Aristobulus, and his son Antipater after this, but five days before he himself died; so that it was purely to gratify his own brutish lusts of pride and cruelty that he did this. All is fish that comes to his net.

Observe, What large measures he took, 1. As to time; He *slew all from two years old and under.* It is probable that the blessed Jesus was at this time not a year old; yet Herod took in all the infants *under two years old,* that he might be sure not to miss of his prey. He cares not how many heads fall, which he allows to be innocent, provided that escape not which he supposes to be guilty. 2. As to place; He kills all the male children, not only *in Bethlehem,* but *in all the coasts thereof,* in all the villages of that city. This was being *overmuch wicked,* Eccl. 7:17. Hate, an unbridled wrath, armed with an unlawful power, often transports men to the most absurd and unreasonable instances of cruelty. It was no unrighteous thing for God to permit this; every life is forfeited to his justice as soon as it commences; that sin which entered by one man's disobedience, introduced death with it; and we are not to suppose any thing more than that common guilt, we are not to suppose that these children *were sinners above all that were in Israel,* because they suffered such things. *God's judgments are a great deep.* The diseases and deaths of little children are proofs of original sin. But we must look upon this murder of the infants under another character: it was their martyrdom. How early did persecution commence against Christ and his kingdom! *Think ye that he came to send peace on the earth?* No, *but a sword,* such a sword as this, *ch.* 10:34, 35. A passive testimony was hereby given to the Lord Jesus. As when he was in the womb, he was witnessed to by a child's leaping in the womb for joy at his approach, so now, at *two years old,* he had contemporary witnesses to him of the same age. They shed their blood for him, who afterwards shed his for them. These were the infantry of *the noble army of martyrs.* If these infants were thus baptized with blood, though it were their own, into the church triumphant, it could not be said but that, with what they got in heaven, they were abundantly recompensed for what they lost on earth. *Out of the mouths of these babes and sucklings God did perfect his praise;* otherwise, *it is not good to the Almighty that he should thus afflict.*

The tradition of the Greek church (and we have it in the Aethiopic missal) is, that the number of the children slain was 14,000; but that is very absurd. I believe, if the births of the male children in the weekly bills were computed, there would not be found so many *under two years old,* in one of the most populous cities in the world, that was not near a fortieth part of it. But it is an instance of the vanity of tradition. It is strange that Josephus does not relate this story; but he wrote long after St. Matthew, and it is probable that he *therefore* would not relate it, because he would not so far countenance the Christian history; for he was a zealous Jew; but, to be sure, if it had not been true and well attested, he would have contested it. Macrobius, a heathen writer, tells us, that when Augustus Caesar heard that Herod, among the children he order to be slain *under two years old,* slew his own son, he passed this jest upon him, That it was better to be Herod's swine than his son. The usage of the country forbade him to kill a swine, but nothing could restrain him from killing his son. Some think that he had a young child at nurse in Bethlehem; others think that, through mistake, two events are confounded — the murder of the infants, and the murder of his son Antipater. But for the church of Rome to put the Holy Innocents, as they call them, into their calendar, and observe a day in memory of them, while they have so often, by their barbarous massacres, justified, and even out-one Herod, is but to do as their predecessors did, who built the tombs of the prophets, while they themselves filled up the same measure.

Some observe another design of Providence in the murder of the infants. By all the prophecies of the Old Testament it appears that Bethlehem was the place, and this the time, of the Messiah's nativity; now all the children of Bethlehem, born at this time, being murdered, and Jesus only escaping, none but Jesus could pretend to be the Messiah. Herod now thought he had baffled all the Old Testament prophecies, had defeated the indications of the star, and the devotions of the wise men, by ridding the country of this new King; having burnt the hive, he concludes he had killed the master bee; but God in heaven *laughs* at him, *and has* him *in derision.* Whatever crafty cruel devices are in men's hearts, *the counsel of the Lord shall stand.*

III. The fulfilling of scripture in this (*v.* 17, 18); *Then was fulfilled* that prophecy (Jer. 31:15), *A voice was heard in Ramah.* See and adore the fulness of the scripture! That prediction was accomplished in Jeremiah's time, when Nebuzaradan, after he had destroyed Jerusalem, brought all his prisoners to Ramah (Jer. 40:1), and there disposed of them as he pleased, for the sword, or for captivity. Then was the cry *in Ramah heard* to Bethlehem (for those two cities, the one in Judah's lot, and the other in Benjamin's, were not far asunder); but now the prophecy is again fulfilled in the great sorrow that was for the death of these infants. The scripture was fulfilled,

1. In the place of this mourning. The noise of it was heard from Bethlehem to Ramah; for Herod's cruelty extended itself to *all the coasts of Bethlehem,* even into the lot of Benjamin, among the children of Rachel. Some think the country about Bethlehem was called *Rachel,* because there she died, and was buried. Rachel's sepulchre was hard by Bethlehem, Gen. 35:16, 19. Compare 1 Sa. 10:2. Rachel had her heart much set upon children: the son she died in travail of she called *Benoni — the son of her sorrow.* These mothers were like Rachel, lived near Rachel's grave, and many of them descended from Rachel; and therefore their lamentations are elegantly represented by *Rachel's weeping.*

2. In the degree of this mourning. It was *lamentation and mourning, and great mourning;* all little enough to express the sense they had of this aggravated calamity. There was a great cry in Egypt when the first-born were slain, and so there was here when the youngest was slain; for whom we naturally have a particular tenderness. Here was a representation of this world we live in. We hear in it *lamentation, and weeping, and mourning,* and see *the tears of the oppressed,* some upon one account, and some upon another. Our ways lie through a *vale of tears.* This sorrow was so great, that they *would not be comforted.* They hardened themselves in it, and took a pleasure in their grief. Blessed be God, there is no occasion of grief in this world, no, not that which is supplied by sin itself, that will justify us in refusing to *be comforted!* They *would not be comforted, because they are not,* that is, *they are not* in the land of the living, *are not* as they were, in their mothers' embraces. If, indeed, *they were not,* there might be some excuse for sorrowing as though we had no hope; but we know they are not lost, but gone before; if we forget that *they are,* we lose the best ground of our comfort, 1 Th. 4:13. Some make this grief of the Bethlehemites to be a judgment upon them for their contempt of Christ. They that would not rejoice for the birth of the Son of God, are justly made to weep for the death of their own sons; for they only *wondered* at the tidings the shepherds brought them, but did not *welcome* them.

The quoting of this prophecy might serve to obviate an objection which some would make against Christ, upon this sad providence. "Can the Messiah, who is to be the Consolation of Israel, be introduced with all this lamentation?" Yes, for so it was foretold, and the scripture must be accomplished. And besides, if we look further into this prophecy, we shall find that *the bitter weeping* in Ramah was but a prologue to the greatest joy, for it follows, *Thy work shall be rewarded, and there is hope in thy end.* The worse things are, the sooner they will mend. Unto them a child was born, sufficient to repair their losses.

Verses 19–23

We have here Christ's return out of Egypt into the *land of Israel* again. Egypt may serve to sojourn in, or take shelter in, for a while, but not to abide in. Christ was *sent to the lost sheep of the house of Israel,* and therefore to them he must return. Observe,

I. What it was that made way for his return — the death of Herod, which happened not long after the murder of the infants; some think not above three months. Such quick work did divine vengeance make! Note, Herods must die; proud tyrants, that were the terror of the mighty, and the oppressors of the godly, *in the land of the living,* their day must come to fall, and down to the pit they must go. *Who art thou then, that thou shouldest be afraid of a man that shall die?* (Isa. 51:12, 13) especially considering that at death, not only their envy and hatred are perished (Eccl. 9:6), and they cease from troubling (Job 3:17), but they are punished. Of all sins, the guilt of innocent blood fills the measure soonest. It is a dreadful account which Josephus gives of the death of this same Herod (*Antiq.* 17.146–199), that he was seized with a disease which burned him inwardly with an inexpressible torture; that he was insatiably greedy of meat; had the colic, and gout, and dropsy; such an intolerable stench attended his disease, that none could come near him: and so passionate and impatient was he, that he was a torment to himself, and a terror to all that attended him: his innate cruelty, being thus exasperated, made him more barbarous than ever; having ordered his own son to be put to death, he imprisoned many of the nobility and gentry, and ordered that as soon as he was dead they should be killed; but that execution was prevented. See what kind of men have been the enemies and persecutors of Christ and his followers! Few have opposed Christianity but such as have first divested themselves of humanity, as Nero and Domitian.

II. The orders given from heaven concerning their return, and Joseph's obedience to those orders, *v.* 19–21. God had sent Joseph into Egypt, and there he staid till the same that brought him thither ordered him thence. Note, In all our removes, it is good to see our way plain, and God going before us; we should not move either one way or the other without order. These orders were sent him by an angel. Note, Our intercourse with God, if it be kept up on our part, shall be kept up on his, wherever we are. No place can exclude God's gracious visits. Angels come to Joseph in Egypt, to Ezekiel in Babylon, and to John in Patmos. Now, 1. The angel informs him of the death of Herod and his accomplices: *They are dead, which sought the young Child's life.* They are dead, but the young Child lives. Persecuted saints sometimes live to tread upon the graves of their persecutors. Thus did the church's King weather the storm, and many a one has the church in like manner weathered. *They are dead,* to wit, Herod and his son Antipater, who, though there were mutual jealousies between them, yet, probably, concurred in seeking the destruction of this new King. If Herod first kill Antipater, and then die himself, the coasts are cleared, and *the Lord is known by the judgments which he executes,* when one wicked instrument is in the ruin of another. 2. He directs him what to do. He must *go* and return *to the land of Israel;* and he did so without delay; not pleading the tolerably good settlement he had in Egypt, or the inconveniences of the journey, especially if, as is supposed, it was in the beginning of winter that Herod died. God's people follow his direction whithersoever he leads them, wherever he lodges them. Did we but look upon the world as our Egypt, the place of our bondage and banishment, and heaven only as our Canaan, our home, our rest, we should as readily *arise,* and depart thither, when we are called for, as Joseph did out of Egypt.

III. The further direction he had from God, which way to steer, and where to fix in the land of Israel, *v.* 22, 23. God could have given him these instructions with the former, but God reveals his mind to his people by degrees, to keep them still waiting on him, and expecting to hear further from him. These orders Joseph received *in a dream,* probably, as those before, by the ministration of an angel. God could have signified his will to Joseph by the Child Jesus, but we do not find that in those removes he either takes notice, or gives notice, of any thing that occurred; surely it was because *in all things it behoved him to be made like his brethren;* being *a Child,* he *spake as a child,* and did *as a child,* and drew a veil over his infinite knowledge and power; as a child he *increased in wisdom.*

Now the direction given this holy, royal family, is, 1. That it might not settle in Judea, *v.* 22. Joseph might think that Jesus, being *born in Bethlehem,* must be brought up there; yet he is prudently *afraid* for *the young Child,* because *he hears that Archelaus reigns in* Herod's stead, not over all the kingdom as his father did, but only over Judea, the other provinces being put into other hands. See what a succession of enemies there is to fight against Christ and his church! If one drop off, another presently appears, to keep up the old enmity. But for this reason Joseph must not take the young Child into Judea. Note, God will not thrust his children into the mouth of danger, but when it is for his own glory and their trial; for *precious in the sight of the Lord are the* life and the death *of his saints; precious is their blood* to him.

2. That it must settle in Galilee, *v.* 22. There Philip now ruled, who was a mild, quiet, man. Note, The providence of God commonly so orders it, that his people shall not want a quiet retreat from the storm and from the tempest; when one climate becomes hot and scorching, another shall be kept more cool and temperate. Galilee lay far north; Samaria lay between it and Judea; thither they were sent, to Nazareth, a city upon a hill, in the centre of the lot of Zebulun; there the mother of our Lord lived, when she conceived that *holy thing;* and, probably, Joseph lived there too, Lu. 1:26, 27. Thither they were sent, and there they were well known, and were among their relations; the most proper place for them to be in. There they continued, and from thence our Saviour was called *Jesus of Nazareth,* which was to *the Jews a stumbling-block,* for, *Can any good thing come* out of *Nazareth?*

In this is said to be fulfilled what was *spoken by the prophets, He shall be called a Nazarene.* Which may be looked upon, (1.) As a man of honour and dignity, though primarily it signifies no more than *a man of Nazareth;* there is an allusion or mystery in speaking it, speaking Christ to be, [1.] The *Man, the Branch,* spoken of, Isa. 11:1. The word there is *Netzar,* which signifies either a *branch,* or *the city of Nazareth;* in being denominated from that *city,* he is declared to be that Branch. [2.] It speaks him to be the *great Nazarite;* of whom the legal Nazarites were a type and figure (especially Samson, Jdg. 13:5), and Joseph, who is called a *Nazarite among his brethren* (Gen. 49:26), and to whom that which was prescribed concerning the Nazarites, has reference, Num. 6:2, etc. Not that Christ was, *strictly, a Nazarite,* for he drank wine, and touched dead bodies; but he was *eminently* so, both as he was singularly holy, and as he was by a solemn designation and dedication set apart to the honour of God in the work of our redemption, as Samson was to save Israel. And it is a name we have all reason to rejoice in, and to know him by. Or, (2.) As a name of reproach and contempt. To be called a *Nazarene,* was to be called a *despicable man,* a man from whom no good was to be expected, and to whom no respect was to be paid. The devil first fastened this name upon Christ, to render him mean, and prejudice people against him, and it stuck as a nickname to him and his followers. Now this was not particularly foretold by any one prophet, but, in general, it was *spoken by the prophets,* that he should be *despised and rejected of men* (Isa. 53:2, 3), a *Worm, and no man* (Ps. 22:6, 7), that he should be an *Alien to his brethren* Ps. 69:7, 8. Let no name of reproach for religion's sake seem hard to us, when our Master was himself called a *Nazarene.*

CHAPTER 3

At the start of this chapter, concerning the baptism of John, begins the gospel (Mk. 1:1); what went before is but preface or introduction; this is "the beginning of the gospel of Jesus Christ." And Peter observes the same date, Acts 1:22, beginning from the baptism of John, for then Christ began first to appear in him, and then to appear to him, and by him to the world. Here is, I. The glorious rising of the morning-star — John the Baptist (*v.* 1). 1. The doctrine he preached (*v.* 2). 2. The fulfilling of the scripture in him (*v.* 3). 3. His manner of life (*v.* 4). 4. The resort of multitudes to him, and their submission to his baptism (*v.* 5, 6). 5. His sermon that he preached to the Pharisees and Sadducees, wherein he endeavours to bring them to repentance (*v.* 7–10), and so to bring them to Christ (*v.* 11, 12). II. The more glorious shining forth of the Sun of righteousness, immediately after: where we have, 1. The honour done by him to the baptism of John (*v.* 13–15). 2. The honour done to him by the descent of the Spirit upon him, and a voice from heaven (*v.* 16, 17).

Verses 1–6

We have here an account of the preaching and baptism of John, which were the dawning of the gospel-day. Observe,

I. The time when he appeared. *In those days* (*v.* 1), or, *after those days,* long after what was recorded in the foregoing chapter, which left the child Jesus in his infancy. *In those days,* in the time appointed of the Father for the beginning of the gospel, when the *fulness of time* was come, which was often thus spoken of in the *Old Testament, In those days.* Now the last of Daniel's weeks began, or rather, the latter half of the week, when the Messiah was to *confirm the covenant with many,* Dan. 9:27. Christ's appearances are all in their season. Glorious things were spoken both of John and Jesus, at and before their births, which would have given occasion to expect some extraordinary appearances of a divine presence and power with them when they were very young; but it is quite otherwise. Except Christ's disputing with the doctors at twelve years old, nothing appears remarkable concerning either of them, till they were about thirty years old. Nothing is recorded of their childhood and youth, but the greatest part of their life is *tempus, adēlon — wrapt up in darkness and obscurity:* these children differ little in outward appearance from other children, as the heir, while he is under age, differs nothing from a servant, though he be *lord of all.* And this was to show, 1. That even when God is acting as the God of Israel, the *Saviour,* yet *verily he is a God that hideth himself* (Isa. 45:15). *The Lord is in this place and I knew it not,* Gen. 28:16. Our beloved stands behind the wall long before he *looks forth at the windows,* Cant. 2:9. 2. That our faith must principally have an eye to Christ in his office and undertaking, for there is the *display* of his power; but in his person is the *hiding* of his power. All this while, Christ was god-man; yet we are not told what he said or did, till he appeared as a prophet; and then, *Hear ye him.* 3. That young men, though well qualified, should not be forward to put forth themselves in public service, but be humble, and modest, and self-diffident, *swift to hear, and slow to speak.*

Matthew says nothing of the conception and birth of John the Baptist, which is largely related by St. Luke, but finds him at full age, as if dropt from the clouds to preach in the wilderness. For above three hundred years the church had been without prophets; those lights had been long put out, that *he* might be the more desired, who was to be the great prophet. After Malachi there was no prophet, nor any pretender to prophecy, till John the Baptist, to whom therefore the prophet Malachi points more directly than any of the Old Testament prophets had done (Mal. 3:1); *I send my messenger.*

II. The place where he appeared first. *In the wilderness of Judea.* It was not an uninhabited desert, but a part of the country not so thickly peopled, nor so much enclosed into fields and vineyards, as other parts were; it was such a wilderness as had six cities and their villages in it, which are named, Jos. 15:61, 62. In these cities and villages John preached, for thereabouts he had hitherto lived, being born hard by, in Hebron; the scenes of his action began there, where he had long spent his time in contemplation; and even when he showed himself to Israel, he showed how well he loved retirement, as far as would consist with his business. The *word of the Lord* found John here in a *wilderness.* Note, No place is so remote as to shut us out from the visits of divine grace; nay, commonly the sweetest intercourse the saints have with Heaven, is when they are withdrawn furthest from the noise of this world. It was in this *wilderness* of Judah that David penned the 63rd Psalm, which speaks so much of the sweet communion he then had with God, Hos. 2:14. In a wilderness the law was given; and as the *Old Testament,* so the *New Testament Israel* was first found in the desert land, and there God *led him about and instructed him,* Deu. 32:10. John Baptist was a priest of the order of Aaron, yet we find him preaching in a *wilderness,* and never officiating in the *temple;* but Christ, who was not a son of Aaron, is yet often found in the temple, and sitting there as one having authority; so it was foretold, Mal. 3:1. *The Lord whom ye seek shall suddenly come to his temple;* not the *messenger* that was to prepare his way. This intimated that the priesthood of Christ was to thrust out that of Aaron, and drive it into a wilderness.

The beginning of the gospel in a wilderness, speaks comfort to the deserts of the Gentile world. Now must the prophecies be fulfilled, *I will plant in the wilderness the cedar,* Isa. 41:18, 19. The wilderness shall be *a fruitful field,* Isa. 32:15. And the *desert shall rejoice,* Isa. 35:1, 2. The Septuagint reads, *the deserts of Jordan,* the very wilderness in which John preached. In the Romish church there are those who call themselves *hermits,* and pretend to follow John; but when they say of Christ, *Behold, he is in the desert, go not forth, ch.* 24:26. There was a seducer that led his followers *into the wilderness,* Acts 21:38.

III. His preaching. This he made his business. He came, not fighting, nor disputing, but *preaching* (*v.* 1); for by the foolishness of preaching, Christ's kingdom must be set up.

1. The doctrine he preached was that of repentance (*v.* 2); *Repent ye.* He preached this in *Judea,* among those that were called *Jews,* and made a profession of religion; for even they needed repentance. He preached it, not in Jerusalem, but in the wilderness of Judea, among the plain country people; for even those who think themselves most out of the way of temptation, and furthest from the vanities and vices of the town, cannot wash their hands in innocency, but must do it in repentance. John Baptist's business was to call men to *repent* of their sins; *Metanoeite — Bethink yourselves;* "Admit a second *thought,* to correct the errors of the first — an *afterthought.* Consider your ways, *change your minds;* you have thought amiss; *think again,* and *think aright.*" Note, True penitents have *other thoughts* of God and Christ, and sin and holiness, and this world and the other, than they have had, and stand otherwise affected toward them. The change of the *mind* produces a change of the *way.* Those who are truly sorry for what they have done amiss, will be careful to do so no more. This repentance is a necessary duty, in obedience to the command of God (Acts 17:30); and a necessary preparative and qualification for the comforts of the gospel of Christ. If the heart of man had continued upright and unstained, divine consolations might have been received without this painful operation preceding; but, being sinful, it must be first pained before it can be laid at ease, must *labour* before it can be at rest. The sore must be searched, or it cannot be cured. *I wound* and *I heal.*

2. The argument he used to enforce this call was, *For the kingdom of heaven is at hand.* The prophets of the *Old Testament* called people to *repent,* for the obtaining and securing of temporal national mercies, and for the preventing and removing of temporal national judgments: but now, though the duty pressed is the same, the reason is new, and purely evangelical. Men are now considered in their personal capacity, and not so much as then in a social and political one. Now repent, for the *kingdom of heaven is at hand;* the gospel dispensation of the covenant of grace, the opening of the kingdom of heaven to all believers, by the death and resurrection of Jesus Christ. It is a *kingdom* of which Christ is the Sovereign, and we must be the willing, loyal subjects of it. It is a kingdom of *heaven,* not of this world, a spiritual kingdom: its original from heaven, its tendency to heaven. John preached this as *at hand;* then it was at the door; to us it is come, by the pouring out of the Spirit, and the full exhibition of the riches of gospel-grace. Now, (1.) This is a great *inducement* to us *to repent.* There is nothing like the consideration of divine grace to break the heart, both *for sin* and *from sin.* That is evangelical repentance, that flows from a sight of Christ, from a sense of his love, and the hopes of pardon and forgiveness through him. Kindness is conquering; abused kindness, humbling and melting. What a wretch was I to sin against such grace, against the law and love of such a kingdom! (2.) It is a *great encouragement* to us *to repent;* "Repent, for your sins shall be pardoned upon your repentance. Return to God in a way of duty, and he will, through Christ, return to you in a way of mercy." The proclamation of pardon discovers, and fetches in, the malefactor who before fled and absconded. Thus we are drawn to it with the cords of man, and the bands of love.

IV. The *prophecy* that was fulfilled in him, *v.* 3. This is he that was spoken of in the beginning of that part of the prophecy of Esaias, which is mostly evangelical, and which points at gospel-times and gospel-grace; see Isa. 40:3, 4. John is here spoken of,

1. As the *voice of one crying in the wilderness.* John owned it himself (Jn. 1:23); *I am the voice,* and that is all, God is the Speaker, who makes known his mind by John, as a man does by his voice. The word of God must be received as such (1 Th. 2:13); what else is Paul, and what is Apollos, but the voice! John is called the *voice, phōnē boōntos — the voice of one crying* aloud, which is startling and awakening. Christ is called *the Word,* which, being distinct and articulate, is more instructive. John as the *voice,* roused men, and then Christ, as the *Word,* taught them; as we find, Rev. 14:2. The voice of many waters, and of a great thunder, made way for the melodious voice of *harpers* and the *new song, v.* 3. Some observe that, as Samson's mother must drink no *strong drink,* yet he was designed to be a *strong man;* so John Baptist's father was struck dumb, and yet he was designed to be the *voice of one crying.* When the crier's voice is begotten of a dumb father, it shows the *excellency of the power to be of God, and not of man.*

2. As one whose business it was to *prepare the way of the Lord, and to make his paths straight;* so it was said of him before he was born, that he should *make ready a people prepared for the Lord* (Lu. 1:17), as Christ's harbinger and forerunner: he was such a one as intimated the nature of Christ's kingdom, for he came not in the gaudy dress of a herald at arms, but in the homely one of a hermit. Officers were sent before great men to clear the way; so John prepares the way of the Lord. (1.) He himself did so among the men of that generation. In the Jewish church and nation, at that time, all was out of course; there was a great decay of piety, the vitals of religion were corrupted and eaten out by the traditions and injunctions of the elders. The *Scribes* and *Pharisees,* that is, the greatest hypocrites in the world, had the key of knowledge, and the key of government, at their girdle. The people were, generally, extremely proud of their privileges, confident of justification by their own righteousness, insensible of sin; and, though now under the most *humbling* providences, being lately made a province of the Roman Empire, yet they were *unhumbled;* they were much in the same temper as they were in Malachi's time, insolent and haughty, and ready to contradict the word of God: now John was sent to level these mountains, to take down their high opinion of themselves, and to show them their sins, that the doctrine of Christ might be the more acceptable and effectual. (2.) His doctrine of repentance and humiliation is still as necessary as it was then to prepare the way of the Lord. Note, There is a great deal to be done, to make way for Christ into a soul, to *bow the heart* for the reception of the Son of David (2 Sa. 19:14); and nothing is more needful, in order to this, than the discovery of sin, and a conviction of the insufficiency of our own righteousness. That which lets will let, until it be taken out of the way; prejudices must be removed, high thoughts brought down, and captivated to the obedience of Christ. Gates of brass must be broken, and bars of iron cut asunder, ere the everlasting doors be opened for the King of glory to come in. The way of sin and Satan is a *crooked way;* to prepare a way for Christ, the paths must be *made straight,* Heb. 12:13.

V. The garb in which he appeared, the figure he made, and the manner of his life, *v.* 4. They, who expected the Messiah as a temporal prince, would think that his forerunner must come in great pomp and splendour, that his equipage should be very magnificent and gay; but it proves quite contrary; he shall be *great in the sight of the Lord,* but mean in the eyes of the world; and, as Christ himself, having *no form or comeliness;* to intimate betimes, that the glory of Christ's kingdom was to be spiritual, and the subjects of it such as ordinarily were either *found* by *it,* or *made* by it, poor and despised, who derived their honours, pleasures, and riches, from another world.

1. His *dress* was *plain.* This same John had *his raiment of camel's hair, and a leathern girdle about his loins;* he did not go in *long clothing,* as the *scribes,* or *soft clothing,* as the

courtiers, but in the clothing of a country husbandman; for he lived in a country place, and suited his *habit* to his *habitation.* Note, It is good for us to accommodate ourselves to the place and condition which God, in his providence, has put us in. John appeared in this dress, (1.) To show that, like Jacob, he was a *plain man,* and mortified to this world, and the delights and gaieties of it. *Behold an Israelite indeed!* Those that are *lowly in heart* should show it by a holy negligence and indifference in their attire; and not make the putting on of apparel their adorning, nor value others by their attire. (2.) To show that he was a *prophet,* for prophets wore *rough garments,* as mortified men (Zec. 13:4); and, especially, to show that he was the Elias promised; for particular notice is taken of Elias, that he was a *hairy man* (which, some think, is meant of the hairy garments he wore), and that *he was girt with a girdle of leather about his loins,* 2 Ki. 1:8. John Baptist appears no way inferior to him in mortification; this therefore is *that* Elias *that was to come.* (3.) To show that he was a man of resolution; his girdle was not *fine,* such as were then commonly worn, but it was *strong,* it was a *leathern girdle;* and blessed is that servant, whom his Lord, when he comes, finds with *his loins girt,* Lu. 12:35; 1 Pt. 1:13.

2. His *diet* was *plain;* his *meat* was *locusts* and *wild honey;* not as if he never ate any thing else; but these he frequently fed upon, and made many meals of them, when he retired into solitary places, and continued long there for contemplation. *Locusts* were a sort of flying insect, very good for food, and allowed as clean (Lev. 11:22); they required little dressing, and were light, and easy of digestion, whence it is reckoned among the infirmities of old age, that the *grasshopper,* or *locust,* is then *a burden* to the stomach, Eccl. 12:5. *Wild honey* was that which *Canaan* flowed with, 1 Sa. 14:26. Either it was gathered immediately, as it fell in the dew, or rather, as it was found in the hollows of trees and rocks, where bees built, that were not, like those in hives, under the care and inspection of men. This intimates that he ate *sparingly,* a little served his turn; a man would be long ere he filled his belly with locusts and wild honey: *John Baptist* came *neither eating nor drinking* (*ch.* 11:18) — not with the curiosity, formality, and familiarity that other people do. He was so entirely taken up with spiritual things, that he could seldom find time for a set meal. Now, (1.) This agreed with the doctrine he preached of *repentance,* and *fruits meet for repentance.* Note, Those whose business it is to call others to mourn for sin, and to mortify it, ought themselves to live a serious life, a life of self-denial, mortification, and contempt of the world. John Baptist thus showed the deep sense he had of the badness of the time and place he lived in, which made the preaching of repentance needful; every day was a *fast-day* with him. (2.) This agreed with his office as Christ's *forerunner;* by this practice he showed that he knew what the *kingdom of heaven* was, and had experienced the powers of it. Note, Those that are acquainted with divine and spiritual pleasures, cannot but look upon all the delights and ornaments of sense with a holy indifference; they know better things. By giving others this example he made way for Christ. Note, A conviction of the vanity of the world, and everything in it, is the best preparative for the entertainment of the kingdom of heaven in the heart. *Blessed are the poor in spirit.*

VI. The people who attended upon him, and flocked after him (*v.* 5); *Then went out to him Jerusalem, and all Judea.* Great multitudes came to him from the city, and from all parts of the country; some of all sorts, men and women, young and old, rich and poor, Pharisees and publicans; they *went out to him,* as soon as they heard his preaching the *kingdom of heaven,* that they might hear what they heard so much of. Now, 1. This was a great *honour* put upon John, that so many attended him, and with so much respect. Note, Frequently those have most real honour done them, who least court the shadow of it. Those who live a mortified life, who are humble and self-denying, and dead to the world, command respect; and men have a secret value and reverence for them, more than they would imagine. 2. This gave John a great opportunity of doing good, and was an evidence that God was with him. Now people began to crowd and *press into the kingdom of heaven* (Lu. 16:16); and a blessed sight it was, to see the *dew of the youth* dropping *from the womb* of the gospel-morning (Ps. 110:3), to see the net cast where there were so many fish. 3. This was an evidence, that it was now a time of great expectation; it was generally thought that the *kingdom of God* would presently *appear* (Lu. 19:11), and therefore, when John showed himself to Israel, lived and preached at this rate, so very different from the Scribes and Pharisees, they were ready to say of him, that he was *the Christ* (Lu. 3:15); and this occasioned such a confluence of people about him. 4. Those who would have the benefit of John's ministry must *go out* to him in the wilderness, sharing in his reproach. Note, They who truly desire the sincere milk of the word, it if be not brought to them, will seek out for it: and they who would learn the doctrine of repentance must *go out* from the hurry of this world, and be still. 5. It appears by the issue, that of the many who came to John's Baptism, there were but few that adhered to it; witness the cold reception Christ had in Judea, and about Jerusalem. Note, There may be a multitude of forward hearers, where there are but a few true believers. Curiosity, and affectation of novelty and variety, may bring many to attend upon good preaching, and to be affected with it for a while, who yet are never subject to the power of it, Eze. 33:31, 32.

VII. The rite, or ceremony, by which he admitted disciples, *v.* 6. Those who received his doctrine, and submitted to his discipline, were *baptized of him in Jordan,* thereby professing their repentance, and their belief that the kingdom of the Messiah was at hand. 1. They testified their repentance by *confessing their sins;* a general confession, it is probable, they made to John that they were *sinners,* that they were polluted by sin, and needed cleansing; but to God they made a confession of particular sins, for he is the party offended. The Jews had been taught to *justify* themselves; but John teaches them to *accuse* themselves, and not to rest, as they used to do, in the general confession of sin made for all Israel, once a year, upon the day of atonement; but to make a particular acknowledgment, every one, of the *plague of his own heart.* Note, A penitent confession of sin is required in order to peace and pardon; and those only are ready to receive Jesus Christ as their Righteousness, who are brought with sorrow and shame to their own guilt, 1 Jn. 1:9. 2. The benefits of the *kingdom of heaven,* now *at hand,* were thereupon sealed to them by baptism. He washed them with water, in token of this — that from all their iniquities God would *cleanse them.* It was usual with the Jews to baptize those whom they admitted proselytes to their religion, especially those who were only *Proselytes of the gate,* and were not circumcised, as the *Proselytes of righteousness* were. Some think it was likewise a custom for persons of eminent religion, who set up for leaders, by baptism to admit pupils and disciples. Christ's question concerning John's Baptism, Was it *from heaven,* or *of men?* implied, that there were baptisms of men, who pretended not to a divine mission; with this usage John complied, but *his* was from heaven, and was distinguished from all others by this character, It was *the baptism of repentance,* Acts 19:4. All Israel were baptized unto Moses, 1 Co. 10:2. The *ceremonial law* consisted in *divers washings or baptisms* (Heb. 9:10); but John's baptism refers to the remedial law, the law of repentance and faith. He is said to baptize them in Jordan, that river which was famous for Israel's passage through it, and Naaman's cure; yet it is probable that John did not baptize in that river at first, but that afterward, when the people who came to his baptism were numerous, he removed Jordan. By baptism he obliged them to live a holy life, according to the profession they took upon themselves. Note, Confession of sin must always be accompanied with holy resolutions, in the strength of divine grace, not to return to it again.

Verses 7–12

The doctrine John preached was that of repentance, in consideration of the *kingdom of heaven* being *at hand;* now here we have the use of that doctrine. Application is the life of preaching, so it was of John's preaching.

Observe, 1. To whom he applied it; to the Pharisees and Sadducees that came to his baptism, *v.* 7. To others he thought it enough to say, *Repent, for the kingdom of heaven is at hand;* but when he saw these Pharisees and Sadducees come about him, he found it necessary to explain himself, and deal more closely. These were two of the three noted sects among the Jews at that time, the third was that of the Essenes, whom we never read of in the gospels, for they affected retirement, and declined busying themselves in public affairs. The Pharisees were zealots for the ceremonies, for the power of the church, and the traditions of the elders; the Sadducees ran into the other extreme, and were little better than deists, denying the existence of spirits and a future state. It was strange that they came to John's baptism, but their curiosity brought them to be hearers; and some of them, it is probable, submitted to be baptized, but it is certain that the generality of them did not; for Christ says (Lu. 7:29, 30), that *when the publicans justified God, and were baptized of John, the Pharisees and lawyers rejected the counsel of God against themselves, being not baptized of him.* Note, Many come to ordinances, who come not under the power of them. Now to them John here addresses himself with all faithfulness, and what he said to them, he said to the multitude (Lu. 3:7), for they were all concerned in what he said. 2. What the application was. It is plain and home, and directed to their consciences; he speaks as one that came not to preach *before* them, but to preach *to* them. Though his education was private, he was not bashful when he appeared in public, nor did he fear the face of man, for he was full of the Holy Ghost, and of power.

I. Here is a word of conviction and awakening. He begins harshly, calls them not Rabbi, gives them not the titles, much less the applauses, they had been used to. 1. The *title* he gives them is, *O generation of vipers.* Christ gave them the same title; *ch.* 12:34; 23:33. They were as *vipers;* though specious, yet venomous and poisonous, and full of malice and enmity to every thing that was good; they were a *viperous brood,* the seed and offspring of such as had been of the same spirit; it was bred in the bone with them. They gloried in it, that they were the seed of Abraham; but John showed them that they were the serpent's seed (compare Gen. 3:15); of their father the Devil, Jn. 8:44. They were a *viperous gang,* they were all alike; though enemies to one another, yet confederate in mischief. Note, A wicked generation is a *generation of vipers,* and they ought to be told so; it becomes the ministers of Christ to be bold in showing sinners their true character. 2. The *alarm* he gives them is, *Who has warned you to flee from the wrath to come?* This intimates that they were in danger of the wrath to come; and that their case was so nearly desperate, and their hearts so hardened in sin (the Pharisees by their parade of religion, and the Sadducees by their arguments against religion), that it was next to a miracle to effect anything hopeful among them. "What brings you hither? Who thought of seeing you here? What fright have you been put into, that you enquire after the kingdom of heaven?" Note, (1.) There is a *wrath to come;* besides present wrath, the vials of which are poured out now, there is future wrath, the stores of which are treasured up for hereafter. (2.) It is the great concern of every one of us to flee from this wrath. (3.) It is wonderful mercy that we are fairly warned to flee from this wrath; think — *Who has warned us?* God has warned us, who delights not in our ruin; he warns by the written word, by ministers, by conscience. (4.) These warnings sometime startle those who seemed to have been very much hardened in their security and good opinion of themselves.

II. Here is a word of *exhortation* and *direction* (*v.* 8); *"Bring forth therefore fruits meet for repentance. Therefore,* because you are *warned to flee from the wrath to come,* let the terrors of the Lord persuade you to a holy life." Or, *"Therefore,* because you profess repentance, and attend upon the doctrine and baptism of repentance, evidence that you are true penitents." Repentance is seated in the heart. There it is as a root; but in vain do we pretend to have it there, if we do not *bring forth the fruits* of it in a universal reformation, forsaking all sin, and cleaving to that which is good; these are fruits, *axious tēs metanoias — worthy of repentance.* Note, Those are not worthy the name of penitents, or their privileges, who say they are sorry for their sins, and yet persist in them. They that profess repentance, as all that are baptized do, must be and act as becomes penitents, and never do any thing unbecoming a penitent sinner. It becomes penitents to be humble and low in their own eyes, to be thankful for the least mercy, patient under the greatest affliction, to be watchful against all appearances of sin, and approaches towards it, to abound in every duty, and to be charitable in judging others.

III. Here is a word of caution, not to trust to their external privileges, so as with them to shift off these calls to repentance (*v.* 9); *Think not to say within yourselves, We have Abraham to our father.* Note, There is a great deal which carnal hearts are apt to say within themselves, to put by the convincing, commanding power of the word of God, which ministers should labour to meet with and anticipate; vain thoughts which lodge within those who are called to *wash their hearts,* Jer. 4:14. *Mē doxēte — Pretend not, presume not,* to say within yourselves; be not of the opinion that this will save you; harbour not such a conceit. "*Please not yourselves* with saying this" (so some read); "rock not yourselves asleep with this, nor flatter yourselves into a fool's paradise." Note, God takes notice of what we say *within* ourselves, which we dare not speak out, and is acquainted with all the false rests of the soul, and the fallacies with which it deludes itself, but which it will not discover, lest it should be undeceived. Many hide the lie that ruins them, in *their right hand,* and roll it *under their tongue,* because they are ashamed to own it; they keep in the Devil's interest, by keeping the Devil's counsel. Now John shows them,

1. What their pretense was; "*We have Abraham to our father;* we are not sinners of the Gentiles; it is fit indeed that *they* should be called to repent; but we are Jews, a holy nation, a peculiar people, what is this to us?" Note, The word does us no good, when we will not take it as it is spoken to us, and belonging to us. "Think not that because you are the seed of Abraham, therefore," (1.) "You *need not repent,* you have nothing to repent of; your relation to Abraham, and your interest in the covenant made with him, denominate you so holy, that there is no occasion for you to change your mind or way." (2.) "That therefore you shall *fare well enough,* though you do not *repent.* Think not that this will bring you off in the judgment, and secure you from the wrath to come; that God will connive at your impenitence, because you are Abraham's seed." Note, It is vain presumption to think that our having good relations will save us, though we be not good ourselves. What though we be descended from pious ancestors; have been blessed with a religious education; have our lot cast in families where the fear of God is uppermost; and have good friends to advise us, and pray for us; what will all this avail us, if we do not repent, and live a life of repentance? We have Abraham to our father, and therefore are entitled to the privileges of the covenant made with him; being his seed, we are *sons of the church, the temple of the Lord,* Jer. 7:4. Note, Multitudes, by resting in the honours and advantages of their visible church-membership, take up short of heaven.

2. How foolish and groundless this pretence was; they thought that being the seed of Abraham, they were the only people God had in the world, and therefore that, if they were cut off, he would be at a loss for a church; but John shows them the folly of this conceit; *I say unto you* (whatever you say within yourselves), that *God is able of these stones to raise up children unto Abraham.* He was now baptizing in Jordan at Bethabara (Jn. 1:28), *the house of passage,* where the children of *Israel passed over;* and there were the twelve stones, one for each tribe, which Joshua set up for a memorial, Jos. 4:20. It is not unlikely that he pointed to those stones, which God could raise to be, more than in representation, the *twelve tribes of Israel.* Or perhaps he refers to Isa. 51:1, where Abraham is called *the rock out of which they were hewn.* That God who raised Isaac out of such a rock, can, if there be an occasion, do as much again, for with him *nothing is impossible.* Some think he pointed to those *heathen soldiers* that were present, telling the Jews that God would raise up a church for himself among the Gentiles, and entail the blessing of Abraham upon them. Thus when our first parents fell, God could have left them to perish, and out of stones have raised up another Adam and another Eve. Or, take it thus, "Stones themselves shall be owned as Abraham's seed, rather than such hard, dry, barren sinners as you are." Note, As it is lowering to the confidence of the sinners in Zion, so it is encouraging to the hopes of the sons of Zion, that, whatever comes of the present generation, God will never want a church in the world; if the Jews fall off, the Gentiles shall be grafted in, *ch.* 21:43; Rom. 11:12, etc.

IV. Here is a word of terror to the careless and secure Pharisees and Sadducees, and other Jews, that knew not the signs of the times, nor the day of their visitation, *v.* 10. "Now look about you, now that *the kingdom of God is at hand,* and be made sensible."

1. How strict and short your trial is; *Now the axe* is carried before you, now it is *laid to the root of the tree,* now you are upon *your good behavior,* and are to be so but a *while;* now you are marked for ruin, and cannot avoid it but by a speedy and sincere repentance. Now you must expect that God will make quicker work with you by his judgments than he did formerly, and that they will *begin at the house of God:* "where God allows more means, he allows less time." *Behold, I come quickly.* Now they were put upon their last trial; now or never.

2. "How sore and severe your doom will be, if you do not improve this." It is now declared with the axe at the root, to show that God is in earnest in the declaration, that *every tree,* however *high* in gifts and honours, however *green* in external professions and performances, if it *bring not forth good fruit,* the fruits meet for repentance, is *hewn down,* disowned as a tree in God's vineyard, unworthy to have room there, and is *cast into the fire* of God's wrath — the fittest place for barren trees: what else are they good for? If not fit for fruit, they are fit for fuel. Probably this refers to the destruction of Jerusalem by the Romans, which was not, as other judgments had been, like the lopping off of the branches, or cutting down of the body of the tree, leaving the root to bud again, but it would be the total, final, and irrecoverable extirpation of that people, in which all those should perish that continued impenitent. Now God would make a full end, wrath was coming on them to the utmost.

V. A word of instruction concerning Jesus Christ, in whom all John's preaching centered. Christ's ministers preach, not themselves, but him. Here is,

1. The dignity and pre-eminence of Christ above John. See how meanly he speaks of himself, that he might magnify Christ (*v.* 11); "*I indeed baptize you with water,* that is the utmost I can do." Note, Sacraments derive not their efficacy from those who administer them; they can only apply the sign; it is Christ's prerogative to give the thing signified, 1 Co. 3:6; 2 Ki. 4:31. But *he that comes after me is mightier than I.* Though John had much power, for he came in the *spirit and power of Elias,* Christ has more; though John was truly great, great in the sight of the Lord (not a greater was born of woman), yet he thinks himself unworthy to be in the meanest place of attendance upon Christ, *whose shoes I am not worthy to bear.* He sees, (1.) How mighty Christ is, in comparison with him. Note, It is a great comfort to the faithful ministers, to think that Jesus Christ is mightier than they, can do that *for* them, and that *by* them, which they cannot do; his strength is perfected in their weakness. (2.) How mean he is in comparison with Christ, not worthy to carry his shoes after him! Note, Those whom God puts honour upon, are thereby made very humble and low in their own eyes; willing to be abased, so that Christ may be magnified; to be any thing, to be nothing, so that Christ may be all.

2. The design and intention of Christ's appearing, which they were now speedily to expect. When it was prophesied that John should be sent as Christ's forerunner (Mal. 3:1, 2), it immediately follows, *The Lord, whom ye seek, shall suddenly come,* and shall *sit as a refiner, v.* 3. And after the coming of Elijah, *the day comes that shall burn as an oven* (Mal. 4:1), to which the Baptist seems here to refer. Christ will come to make a distinction,

(1.) By the powerful working of his grace; *He shall baptize you,* that is, some of you, *with the Holy Ghost and with fire.* Note, [1.] It is Christ's prerogative to baptize *with the Holy Ghost.* This he did in the extraordinary gifts of the Spirit conferred upon the apostles, to which Christ himself applies these words of John, Acts 1:5. This he does in the graces and comforts of the Spirit given to them that ask him, Lu. 11:13; Jn. 7:38, 39; See Acts 11:16. [2.] They who are baptized with the Holy Ghost are baptized as *with fire;* the seven spirits of God appear as *seven lamps of fire,* Rev. 4:5. Is fire enlightening? So the Spirit is a Spirit of illumination. Is it warming? And do not their hearts burn within them? Is it consuming? And does not the Spirit of judgment, as a *Spirit of burning,* consume the dross of their corruptions? Does fire make all it seizes like itself? And does it move upwards? So does the Spirit make the soul holy like itself, and its tendency is heavenward. Christ says *I am come to send fire,* Lu. 12:49.

(2.) By the final determinations of his judgment (*v.* 12); *Whose fan is in his hand.* His ability to distinguish, as the eternal wisdom of the Father, who sees all by a true light, and his authority to distinguish, as the Person to whom all judgment is committed, is the *fan* that is *in his hand,* Jer. 15:7. Now he sits as a Refiner. Observe here [1.] The visible church is Christ's floor; *O my threshing, and the corn of my floor,* Isa. 21:10. The temple, a type of church, was built upon a threshing-floor. [2.] In this floor there is a mixture of wheat and chaff. True believers are as wheat, substantial, useful, and valuable; hypocrites are as chaff, light, and empty, useless and worthless, and carried about with every wind; these are now mixed, good and bad, under the same external profession; and in the same visible communion. [3.] There is a day coming when the floor shall be purged, and the wheat and chaff shall be separated. Something of this kind is often done in this world, when God calls his people out of Babylon, Rev. 18:4. But it is the day of the last judgment that will be the great winnowing, distinguishing day, which will infallibly determine concerning doctrines and works (1 Co. 3:13), and concerning persons (*ch.* 25:32, 33), when saints and sinners shall be parted for ever. [4.] Heaven is the garner into which Jesus Christ will shortly gather all his wheat, and not a grain of it shall be lost: he will gather them as the ripe fruits were gathered in. Death's scythe is made use of to gather them to their people. In heaven the saints are brought together, and no longer scattered; they are safe, and no longer exposed; separated from corrupt neighbours without, and corrupt affections within, and there is no chaff among them. They are not only gathered into *the barn* (*ch.* 13:30), but into *the garner,* where they are thoroughly purified. [5.] Hell is the *unquenchable fire,* which will burn up the chaff, which will certainly be the portion and punishment, and everlasting destruction, of hypocrites and unbelievers. So that here are life and death, good and evil, set before us; according as we now are in the *field,* we shall be then in the *floor.*

Verses 13–17

Our Lord Jesus, from his childhood till now, when he was almost thirty years of age, had lain hid in Galilee, as it were, buried alive; but now, after a long and dark night, behold, *the Sun of righteousness* rises in glory. *The fulness of time was come* that Christ should enter upon his prophetical office; and he chooses to do it, not at Jerusalem (though it is probable that he went thither at the three yearly feasts, as others did), but there *where John was baptizing;* for to him resorted those who *waited for the consolation of Israel,* to whom alone he would be welcome. John the Baptist was six months older than our Saviour, and it is supposed that he began to preach and baptize about six months before Christ appeared; so long he was employed in preparing his way, *in the region round about Jordan;* and more was done towards it in these six months than had been done in several ages before. Christ's coming from Galilee *to Jordan, to be baptized,* teaches us not the shrink from pain and toil, that we may have an opportunity of drawing nigh to God in ordinance. We should be willing to go far, rather than come short of communion with God. Those who will find must seek.

Now in this story of Christ's baptism we may observe,

I. How hardly John was persuaded to admit of it, *v.* 14, 15. It was an instance of Christ's great humility, that he would offer himself *to be baptized of John;* that he *who knew no sin* would submit to the baptism of repentance. Note, As soon as ever Christ began to preach, he preached humility, preached it by his example, preached it to all, especially the young ministers. Christ was designed for the highest honours, yet in his first step he thus abases himself. Note, Those who would rise high must begin low. *Before honour is humility.* It was a great piece of respect done to John, for Christ thus to come to him; and it was a return for the service he did him, in giving notice of his approach. Note, Those that honour God he will honour. Now here we have,

1. The objection that John made against baptizing Jesus, *v.* 14. *John forbade him,* as Peter did, when Christ went about to wash his feet, Jn. 13:6, 8. Note, Christ's gracious condescensions are so surprising, as to appear at first incredible to the strongest believers; so deep and mysterious, that even they who know his mind well cannot soon find out the meaning of them, but, *by reason of darkness,* start objections against the will of Christ. John's modesty thinks this an honour too great for him to receive, and he expresses himself to Christ, just as his mother had done to Christ's mother (Lu. 1:43); *Whence is this to me, that the mother of my Lord should come to me?* John had now obtained a great name, and was universally respected: yet see how humble he is still! Note, God has further honours in reserve for those whose spirits continue low when their reputation rises.

(1.) John thinks it necessary that he should be baptized of Christ; *I have need to be baptized of thee* with the baptism of the Holy Ghost, as of fire, for that was Christ's baptism, *v.* 11. [1.] Though *John was filled with the Holy Ghost from the womb* (Lu. 1:15), yet he acknowledges he had need to be baptized with that baptism. Note, They who have much of the Spirit of God, yet, while here, in this imperfect state, see that they have need of more, and need to apply themselves to Christ for more. [2.] *John has need to be baptized,* though he was the *greatest that ever was born of woman;* yet, being born of a woman, he is polluted, as others of Adam's seed are, and owns he had need of cleansing. Note, The purest souls are most sensible of their own remaining impurity, and seek most earnestly for spiritual washing. [3.] *He has need to be baptized of Christ,* who can do that for us, which no one else can, and which must be done for us, or we are undone. Note, The best and holiest of men *have need* of Christ, and the better they are, the more they see of that need. [4.] This was said before the multitude, who had a great veneration for John, and were ready to embrace him for the Messiah; yet he publicly owns that he had *need to be baptized of* Christ. Note, It is no disparagement to the greatest of men, to confess that they are undone without Christ and his grace. [5.] John was Christ's forerunner, and yet owns that he had *need to be baptized of* him. Note, Even they who were born before Christ in time depended on him, received from him, and had an eye to him. [6.] While John was dealing with others about their souls, observe how feelingly he speaks of the case of his own soul, *I have need to be baptized of thee.* Note, Ministers, who preach to others, and baptize others, are concerned to look to it that they preach to themselves, and be themselves baptized with the Holy Ghost. Take heed to thyself first; *save thyself,* 1 Tim. 4:16.

(2.) He therefore thinks it very preposterous and absurd, that Christ should be baptized by him; *Comest thou to me?* Does the holy Jesus, that is separated from sinners, come to be baptized by a sinner, as a sinner, and among sinners? How can this be? Or what account can we give of it? Note, Christ's coming to us may well be wondered at.

2. The overruling of this objection (*v.* 15); *Jesus said, Suffer it to be so now.* Christ accepted his humility, but not his refusal; he will have the thing done; and it is fit that Christ should take his own method, though we do not understand it, nor can give a reason for it. See,

(1.) How Christ insisted upon it; It must *be so now.* He does not deny that *John had need to be baptized of* him, yet he will now be *baptized of John. Aphes arti — Let it be yet so; suffer it to be so now.* Note, Every thing is beautiful in its season. But why *now?* Why yet? [1.] Christ is *now* in a state of humiliation: he has emptied himself, and *made himself of no reputation.* He is not only *found in fashion as a man,* but is *made in the likeness of sinful flesh,* and therefore now let him be *baptized of John;* as if he needed to be washed, though perfectly pure; and thus he *was made sin for us,* though he *knew no sin.* [2.] John's baptism is now in reputation, it is that by which God is now doing his work; that is the present dispensation, and therefore Jesus will now be baptized with water; but his baptizing with the Holy Ghost is reserved for hereafter, *many days hence,* Acts 1:5. John's baptism has *now* its day, and therefore honour must *now* be put upon that, and they who attend upon it must be encouraged. Note, They who are of greatest attainments in gifts and graces, should yet, in their place, bear their testimony to instituted ordinances, by a humble and diligent attendance on them, that they may give a good example to others. What we see God owns, and while we see he does so, we must own. John was now increasing, and therefore it must be thus yet; shortly he will decrease, and then it will be otherwise. [3.] It must *be so now,* because now is the time for Christ's appearing in public, and this will be a fair opportunity for it, See Jn. 1:31–34. Thus he must be made manifest to Israel, and be signalized by wonders from heaven, in that act of his own, which was most condescending and self-abasing.

(2.) The reason he gives for it; *Thus it becomes us to fulfil all righteousness.* Note, [1.] There was a propriety in every thing that Christ did for us; it was all graceful (Heb. 2:10; 7:26); and we must study to do not only that which behoves us, but that which becomes us; not only that which is indispensably necessary, but that which is *lovely, and of good report.* [2.] Our Lord Jesus looked upon it as a thing well becoming him, *to fulfil all righteousness,* that is (as Dr. Whitby explains it), to own every divine institution, and to show his readiness to comply with all God's righteous precepts. *Thus it becomes* him to justify God, and approve his wisdom, in sending John to prepare his way by the baptism of repentance. *Thus it becomes us* to countenance and encourage every thing that is good, by pattern as well as precept. Christ often mentioned John and his baptism with honour, which that he might do the better, he was himself baptized. Thus Jesus began *first to do, and then to teach;* and his ministers must take

the same method. Thus *Christ filled up the righteousness of the ceremonial law,* which consisted in divers washings; thus he recommended the gospel-ordinance of baptism to his church, put honour upon it, and showed what virtue he designed to put into it. It became Christ to submit to John's washing with water, because it was a divine appointment; but it became him to oppose the Pharisees' washing with water, because it was a human invention and imposition; and he justified his disciples in refusing to comply with it.

With the will of Christ, and this reason for it, John was entirely satisfied, and *then he suffered him.* The same modesty which made him at first decline the honour Christ offered him, now made him do the service Christ enjoined him. Note, No pretence of humility must make us decline our duty.

II. How solemnly Heaven was pleased to grace the baptism of Christ with a special display of glory (*v.* 16, 17); *Jesus when he was baptized, went up straightway out of the water.* Others that were baptized staid to *confess their sins* (*v.* 6); but Christ, having no sins to confess, *went up* immediately *out of the water;* so we read it, but not right: for it is *apo tou hydatos — from the water;* from the brink of the river, to which he went down to be washed with water, that is, to have his head or face washed (Jn. 13:9); for here is no mention of the putting off, or putting on, of his clothes, which circumstance would not have omitted, if he had been baptized naked. *He went up straightway,* as one that entered upon his work with the utmost cheerfulness and resolution; he would lose no time. *How was he straitened till it was accomplished!*

Now, when he was coming *up out of the water,* and all the company had their eye upon him,

1. *Lo! the heavens were opened unto him,* so as to discover something above and beyond the starry firmament, at least, to him. This was, (1.) To encourage him to go on in his undertaking, with the prospect of the glory and *joy that were set before him.* Heaven is opened to receive him, when he has finished the work he is now entering upon. (2.) To encourage us to receive him, and submit to him. Note, In and through Jesus Christ, the heavens are opened to the children of men. Sin shut up heaven, put a stop to all friendly intercourse between God and man; but now Christ *has opened the kingdom of heaven to all believers.* Divine light and love are darted down upon the children of men, and *we have boldness to enter into the holiest.* We have receipts of mercy from God, we make returns of duty to God, and all by Jesus Christ, who is the ladder that had its foot on earth and its top in heaven, by whom alone it is that we have any comfortable correspondence with God, or any hope of getting to heaven at last. *The heavens were opened* when Christ was baptized, to teach us, that when we duly attend on God's ordinances, we may expect communion with him, and communications from him.

2. *He saw the Spirit of God descending like a dove, or as a dove, and* coming or *lighting upon him.* Christ saw it (Mk. 1:10), and John saw it (Jn. 1:33, 34), and it is probable that all the standers-by saw it; for this was intended to be his public inauguration. Observe,

(1.) *He saw the Spirit of God descended, and lighted on him.* In the beginning of the old world, *the Spirit of God moved upon the face of the waters* (Gen. 1:2), *hovered* as a bird upon the nest. So here, in the beginning of this new world, Christ, as God, needed not to receive the Holy Ghost, but it was foretold that *the Spirit of the Lord should rest upon him* (Isa. 11:2; 61:1), and here he did so; for, [1.] He was to be a Prophet; and prophets always spoke by the Spirit of God, who came upon them. Christ was to execute the prophetic office, not by his divine nature (says Dr. Whitby), but by the afflatus of the Holy Spirit. [2.] He was to be the Head of the church; and *the Spirit descended upon him,* by him to be derived to all believers, in his gifts, graces, and comforts. *The ointment on the head ran down to the skirts;* Christ *received gifts for men,* that he might give *gifts to men.*

(2.) He *descended on him like a dove;* whether it was a real, living dove, or, as was usual in visions, the representation or similitude of a dove, is uncertain. If there must be a bodily shape (Lu. 3:22), it must not be that of a man, for the being seen *in fashion as a man* was peculiar to the second person: none therefore was more fit than the shape of one of the fowls of heaven (heaven being now opened), and of all fowl none was so significant as the dove. [1.] The Spirit of Christ is a dove-like spirit; not like *a silly dove, without heart* (Hos. 7:11), but like an innocent dove, without gall. *The Spirit descended,* not in the shape of an eagle, which is,

though a royal bird, yet a bird of prey, but *in the shape of a dove,* than which no creature is more harmless and inoffensive. Such was the Spirit of Christ: *He shall not strive, nor cry;* such must Christians be, *harmless as doves.* The dove is remarkable for her eyes; we find that both the eyes of Christ (Cant. 5:12), and the eyes of the church (Cant. 1:15; 4:1), are compared to *doves' eyes,* for they have the same spirit. The dove mourns much (Isa. 38:14). Christ wept oft; and penitent souls are compared to *doves of the valleys.* [2.] The dove was the only fowl that was offered in sacrifice (Lev. 1:14), and Christ by the Spirit, *the eternal Spirit, offered himself without spot to God.* [3.] The tidings of the decrease of Noah's flood were brought by a dove, with an olive-leaf in her mouth; fitly therefore are the glad tidings of peace with God brought by the Spirit as *a dove.* It speaks God's *good will towards men;* that his thoughts towards us are *thoughts of good, and not evil.* By *the voice of the turtle heard in our land* (Cant. 2:12), the Chaldee paraphrase understands, *the voice of the Holy Spirit.* That God is in Christ reconciling the world unto himself, is a joyful message, which comes to us upon the wing, *the wings of a dove.*

3. To explain and complete this solemnity, *there came a voice from heaven,* which, we have reason to think, was heard by all that were present. The Holy Spirit manifested himself in the likeness of a *dove,* but God the Father by a *voice;* for when the law was given they *saw no manner of similitude, only they heard a voice* (Deu. 4:12); and so this gospel came, and gospel indeed it is, the best news that ever came from heaven to earth; for it speaks plainly and fully God's favour to Christ, and us in him.

(1.) See here how God owns our Lord Jesus; *This is my beloved Son.* Observe, [1.] The relation he stood in to him; He *is my Son.* Jesus Christ is the Son of God, *by eternal generation,* as he was *begotten of the Father before all the worlds* (Col. 1:15; Heb. 1:3); and by supernatural conception; he was *therefore* called *the Son of God,* because he *was conceived by the power of the Holy Ghost* (Lu. 1:35); yet this is not all; he is the Son of God by special designation to the work and office of the world's Redeemer. He was sanctified and sealed, and sent upon that errand, *brought up with* the Father for it (Prov. 8:30), appointed to it; *I will make him my First-born,* Ps. 89:27. [2.] The affection the Father had for him; He *is my beloved Son;* his dear Son, *the Son of his love* (Col. 1:13); he has lain in his bosom from all eternity (Jn. 1:18), had been *always his delight* (Prov. 8:30), but particularly as Mediator, and in undertaking the work of man's salvation, he was his *beloved Son.* He is *my Elect, in whom my soul delights.* See Isa. 42:1. Because he consented to the covenant of redemption, and delighted to do that *will of God, therefore the Father loved him.* Jn. 10:17; 3:35. *Behold,* then, *behold,* and wonder, *what manner of love the Father has bestowed on us,* that he should deliver up him that was the Son of his love, to suffer and die for those that were the generation of his wrath; nay, and that he *therefore* loved him, *because he laid down his life for the sheep!* Now know we that he loved us, *seeing he has not withheld his Son, his only Son, his Isaac whom he loved,* but *gave him to be a sacrifice for our sin.*

(2.) See here how ready he is to own us in him: He *is my beloved Son,* not only *with* whom, but *in* whom, I am well pleased. He is pleased with all that are in him, and are united to him by faith. Hitherto God had been displeased with the children of men, but now his anger is turned away, and he has made us *accepted in the Beloved,* Eph. 50:6. Let all the world take notice, that this is the Peace-maker, the Daysman, who has laid his hand upon us both, and that *there is no coming to God* as a Father, *but by* him as Mediator, Jn. 14:6. *In him our spiritual sacrifices are acceptable,* for his the Altar that *sanctifies every gift,* 1 Pt. 2:5. Out of Christ, God *is a consuming Fire,* but, in Christ, a reconciled Father. This is the sum of the whole gospel; it *is a faithful saying, and worthy of all acceptation, that* God has declared, *by a voice from heaven,* that Jesus Christ is his *beloved Son, in whom he is well pleased,* with which we must by faith cheerfully concur, and say, that he *is our beloved* Saviour, *in whom we are well pleased.*

CHAPTER 4

John Baptist said concerning Christ, He must increase, but I must decrease; and so it proved. For, after John had baptized Christ, and borne his testimony to him, we hear little more of his ministry; he had done what he came to do, and thenceforward there is as much talk of Jesus as ever there had been of John. As the rising Sun advances, the morning star disappears. Concerning Jesus Christ we have in this chapter, I. The temptation he underwent, the triple assault the tempter made upon him, and the repulse he gave to each assault (*v.* 1–11). II. The teaching work he undertook, the places he preached in (*v.* 12–16), and the subject he preached on (*v.* 17). III. His calling of disciples, Peter and Andrew, James and John (*v.* 18–22). IV. His curing diseases (*v.* 23, 24), and the great resort of the people to him, both to be taught and to be healed.

Verses 1–11

We have here the story of a famous duel, fought hand to hand, between Michael and the dragon, the Seed of the woman and the seed of the serpent, nay, the serpent himself; in which the seed of the woman suffers, being *tempted,* and so has his heel bruised; but the serpent is quite baffled in his temptations, and so has his head broken; and our Lord Jesus comes off a Conqueror, and so secures not only comfort, but conquest at last, to all his faithful followers. Concerning Christ's temptation, observe,

I. The time when it happened: *Then;* there is an emphasis laid upon that. Immediately after *the heavens were opened* to him, and *the Spirit descended on him,* and he was declared to be the Son of God, and the Saviour of the world, the next news we hear of him is, he is *tempted;* for *then* he is best able to grapple with the temptation. Note, 1. Great privileges, and special tokens of divine favour, will not secure us from being *tempted.* Nay, 2. After great honours put upon us, we must expect something that is humbling; as Paul has a messenger of Satan sent to buffer him, after he had been in the third heavens. 3. God usually prepares his people for temptation before he calls them to it; he *gives strength according to the day,* and, before a sharp trial, gives more than ordinary comfort. 4. The assurance of our sonship is the best preparative for temptation. If the good Spirit witness to our adoption, that will furnish us with an answer to all the suggestions of the evil spirit, designed either to debauch or disquiet us.

Then, when he was newly come from a solemn ordinance, when he was baptized, *then* he was *tempted.* Note, After we have been admitted into the communion of God, we must expect to be set upon by Satan. The enriched soul must double its guard. *When thou has eaten and art full, then beware. Then,* when he began to show himself publicly to Israel, *then* he was *tempted,* so as he never had been while he lived in privacy. Note, The Devil has a particular spite at useful persons, who are not only good, but given to do good, especially at their first setting out. It is the advice of the Son of Sirach (Ecclesiasticus 2:1), *My son, if thou come to serve the Lord, prepare thyself for temptation.* Let young ministers know what to expect, and arm accordingly.

II. The place where it was; *in the wilderness;* probably in the great wilderness of *Sinai,* where Moses and Elijah *fasted forty days,* for no part of *the wilderness* of Judea was so abandoned to wild beasts as this is said to have been, Mk. 1:13. When Christ was baptized, he did not go to Jerusalem, there to publish the glories that had been put upon him, but retired into a wilderness. After communion with God, it is good to be private awhile, lest we lose what we have received, in the crowd and hurry of worldly business. Christ withdrew into the wilderness, 1. To gain advantage to himself. Retirement gives an opportunity for meditation an communion with God; even they who are called to the most active life must yet have their contemplative hours, and must first find time to be alone with God. Those are not fit to speak of the things of God in public to others, who have not first conversed with those things in secret by themselves. When Christ would appear as *a Teacher come from God,* it shall not be said of him, "He is newly come from travelling, he has been abroad, and has seen the world;" but, "He is newly come out of the desert, he has been alone conversing with God and his own heart." 2. To give advantage to the tempter, that he might have a readier access to him than he could have had in company. Note, Though solitude is a friend to a good heart, yet Satan knows how to improve it against us. *Woe to him that is alone.* Those who, under pretence of sanctity and devotion, retire into dens and deserts, find that they are not out of reach of their spiritual enemies, and that there they want the benefit of the communion with saints. Christ retired, (1.) To make his victory the more illustrious, he gave the enemy sun and wind on his side, and yet baffled him. He might give the Devil advantage, for *the prince of this world had nothing* in him; but he has in us, and therefore we must pray not to be *led into temptation,* and must keep out of harm's way. (2.) That he might have an opportunity to do his best himself, that he might be exalted in his own strength; for so it was written, *I have trod the wine-press alone,* and of the people there was none with me. Christ entered the lists without a second.

III. The preparatives for it, which were two.

1. He was directed to the combat; he did not wilfully thrust himself upon it, but he *was led up of the Spirit to be tempted of the Devil.* The Spirit that *descended upon him like a dove* made him meek, and yet made him bold. Note, Our care must be, not to enter into temptation; but if God, by his providence, order us into circumstances of temptation for our trial, we must not think it strange, but double our guard. *Be strong in the Lord, resist stedfast in the faith,* and all shall be well. If we presume upon our own strength, and tempt the devil to tempt us, we provoke God to leave us to ourselves; but, whithersoever God leads us, we may hope he will go along with us, and bring us off *more than conquerors.*

Christ was *led to be tempted of the Devil,* and of him only. Others are tempted, *when they are drawn aside of their own lust and enticed* (Jam. 1:14); the Devil takes hold of that handle, and ploughs with that heifer; but our Lord Jesus had no corrupt nature, and therefore he was led securely, without any fear or trembling, as a champion into the field, *to be tempted* purely by *the Devil.*

Now Christ's temptation is, (1.) An instance of his own condescension and humiliation. Temptations are *fiery darts, thorns in the flesh, buffetings, siftings, wrestlings, combats,* all which denote hardship and suffering; *therefore* Christ submitted to them, because he would humble himself, *in all things to be made like unto his brethren;* thus he *gave his back to the smiters.* (2.) An occasion of Satan's confusion. There is no conquest without a combat. Christ was tempted, that he might overcome the tempter. Satan tempted the first Adam, and triumphed over him; but he shall not always triumph, the second Adam shall overcome him and *lead captivity captive.* (3.) Matter of comfort to all the saints. In the temptation of Christ it appears, that our enemy is subtle, spiteful, and very daring in his temptations; but it appears withal, that he is not invincible. Though he is *a strong man armed,* yet the Captain of our salvation is *stronger than he.* It is some comfort to us to think that Christ suffered, being *tempted;* for thus it appears that temptations, if not yielded to, are not sins, they are afflictions only, and such as may be pleased. And we have a High Priest who knows, by experience, what it is to be *tempted,* and who therefore is the more tenderly touch with *the feelings of our infirmities* in an hour of temptation, Heb. 2:18; 4:15. But it is much more a comfort to think that Christ conquered, being *tempted,* and conquered for us; not only that the enemy we grapple with is a conquered, baffled, disarmed enemy, but that we are interested in Christ's victory over him, and through him are *more than conquerors.*

2. He was dieted for the combat, as wrestlers, who are *temperate in all things* (1 Co. 9:25); but Christ beyond any other, for he *fasted forty days and forty nights,* in compliance with the type and example of Moses the great lawgiver, and of Elias, the great reformer, of the Old Testament. John Baptist came as Elias, in those things that were moral, but not in such things as were miraculous (Jn. 10:41); that honour was reserved for Christ. Christ needed not to fast for mortification (he had no corrupt desires to be subdued); yet he *fasted,* (1.) That herein he might humble himself, and might seem as one abandoned, *whom no man seeketh after.* (2.) That he might give Satan both occasion and advantage against him; and so make his victory over him the more illustrious. (3.) That he might sanctify and recommend fasting to us, when God in his providence calls to it, or when we are reduced to straits, and are destitute of daily food, or when it is requisite for the keeping under of the body, or the quickening of prayer, those excellent preparatives for temptation. If good people are brought low, if they want friends and succours, this may comfort them, that their Master himself was in like manner exercised. A man may want bread, and yet be a favourite of heaven, and under the conduct of the Spirit. The reference which the Papists make of their lent-fast to this fasting of Christ *forty days,* is a piece of foppery and superstition which the law of our land witnesses against, Stat. 5 Eliz. chap. 5 sect. 39, 40. *When he fasted forty days he was* never hungry; converse with heaven was instead of meat and drink to him, but *he was afterwards an hungred,* to show that he was really and truly Man; and he took upon him our natural infirmities, that he might atone for us. Man fell by eating, and that way we often sin, and therefore Christ *was an hungred.*

IV. The temptations themselves. That which Satan aimed at, in all his temptations, was, to bring him to *sin against God,* and so to render him for ever incapable of being a Sacrifice for the sins of others. Now, whatever the colours were, that which he aimed at was, to bring him, 1. To despair of his Father's goodness. 2. To presume upon his Father's power. 3. To alienate his Father's honour, by giving it to Satan. In the two former, that which he tempted him *to,* seemed innocent, and therein appeared the subtlety of the tempter; in the last, that which he tempted him *with,* seemed desirable. The two former are artful temptations, which there was need of great wisdom to discern; the last was a strong temptation, which there was need of great resolution to resist; yet he was baffled in them all.

1. He tempted him to despair of his Father's goodness, and to distrust his Father's care concerning him.

(1.) See how the temptation was managed (*v.* 3); *The tempter came to him.* Note, The Devil is *the tempter,* and therefore he is *Satan — an adversary;* for those are our worst enemies, that entice us to sin, and are Satan's agents, are doing his work, and carrying on his designs. He is called emphatically *the tempter,* because he was so to our first parents, and still is so, and all other tempters are set on work by him. *The tempter came* to Christ in a visible appearance, not terrible and affrighting, as afterward in his agony in the garden; no, if ever the Devil *transformed himself into an angel of light,* he did so now, and pretended to be a good genius, a guardian angel.

Observe the subtlety of *the tempter,* in joining this first temptation with what went before to make it the stronger. [1.] Christ began to be hungry, and therefore the motion seemed very proper, to turn *stones* into *bread* for his necessary support. Note, It is one of the wiles of Satan to take advantage of our outward condition, in that to plant the battery of his temptations. He is an adversary no less watchful than spiteful; and the more ingenious he is to take advantage against us, the more industrious we must be to give him none. When he began to be hungry, and that in a *wilderness,* where there was nothing to be had, then the Devil assaulted him. Note, Want and poverty are a great temptation to discontent and unbelief, and the use of unlawful means for our relief, under pretence that necessity has no law; and it is excused with this that hunger will break through stone walls, which yet is no excuse, for the law of God ought to be stronger to us than stone walls. Agur prays against poverty, not because it is an affliction and reproach, but because it is a temptation; *lest I be poor, and steal.* Those therefore who are reduced to straits, have need to double their guard; it is better to starve to death, than live and thrive by sin. [2.] Christ was lately declared to be *the Son of God,* and here the Devil tempts him to doubt of that; *If thou be the Son of God.* Had not the Devil known that the Son of God was to come into the world, he would not have said this; and had he not suspected that this was he, he would not have said it to him, nor durst he have said it if Christ had not now drawn a veil over his glory, and if the Devil had not now put on an impudent face.

First, "Thou has now an occasion to question whether *thou be the Son of God* or no; for can it be, that *the Son of God,* who is *Heir of all things,* should be reduced to such straits? If God were thy Father, he would not see thee starve, for *all the beasts of the forest are his,* Ps. 50:10, 12. It is true there *was a voice from heaven, This is my beloved Son,* but surely it was delusion, and thou was imposed upon by it; for either God is not thy Father, or he is a very unkind one." Note, 1. The great thing Satan aims at, in tempting good people, is to overthrow their relation to God as a Father, and so to cut off their dependence on him, their duty to him, and their communion with him. The good Spirit, as the Comforter of the brethren, witnesses that they are the *children of God;* the evil spirit, as the accuser of the brethren, does all he can to shake that testimony. 2. Outward afflictions, wants and burdens, are the great arguments Satan uses to make the people of God question their sonship; as if afflictions could not consist with, when really they proceed from, God's fatherly love. They know how to answer this temptation, who can say with holy Job, *Though he slay me, though he* starve me, *yet I will trust in him,* and love him as a Friend, even when he seems to come forth against me as an Enemy. 3. The Devil aims to shake our faith in the word of God, and bring us to question the truth of that. Thus he began with our first parents; *Yea, has God said* so and so? Surely he has not. So here,

Has God said that thou art his *beloved Son?* Surely he did not say so; or if he did it is not true. We then *give place to the Devil,* when we question the truth of any word that God has spoken; for his business, as the father of lies, is to oppose the true sayings of God. 4. The Devil carries on his designs very much by possessing people with hard thoughts of God, as if he were unkind, or unfaithful, and had forsaken or forgotten those who had ventured their all with him. He endeavored to beget in our first parents a notion that God forbade them the tree of knowledge, because he grudged them the benefit of it; and so here he insinuates to our Saviour, that his Father had cast him off, and left him to shift for himself. But see how unreasonable this suggestion was, and how easily answered. If Christ seemed to be a mere Man now, because he was hungry, why was he not confessed to be more than a Man, even the *Son of God,* when for *forty days he fasted,* and was not hungry?

Secondly, "Thou hast now an opportunity to show that thou art *the son of God. If thou art the Son of God,* prove it by this, *command these stones"* (a heap of which, probably, lay now before him) *"be made bread, v.* 3. John Baptist said but the other day, that God *can out of stone raise up children to Abraham,* a divine power therefore can, no doubt, out of stones, make bread for those children; if there thou has that power, exert it now in a time of need for thyself." He does not say, *Pray to thy Father* that he would turn them into *bread;* but *command* it to be done; thy Father hath forsaken thee, set up for thyself, and be not beholden to him. The Devil is for nothing that is humbling, but ever thing that is assuming; and gains his point, if he can but bring men off from their dependence upon God, and possess them with an opinion of their self-sufficiency.

(2.) See how this temptation was resisted and overcome. [1.] Christ refused to comply with it. He would not *command these stones to be made bread;* not because he could not; his power, which soon after this turned *stones* into *bread;* but he would not. And why would he not? At first view, the thing appears justifiable enough, and the truth is, the more plausible a temptation is, and the greater appearance there is of good in it, the more dangerous it is. This matter would bear a dispute, but Christ was soon aware of the snake in the grass, and would not do any thing, *First,* That looked like questioning the truth of the voice he heard from heaven, or putting that upon a new trial which was already settled. *Secondly,* That looked like distrusting his Father's care of him, or limiting him to one particular way of providing for him. *Thirdly,* That looked like setting up for himself, and being his own carver; or, *Fourthly,* That looked like gratifying Satan, by doing a thing at his motion. Some would have said, To give the Devil his due, this was good counsel; but for those *who wait upon God,* to consult *him,* is more than his due; it is like enquiring of the god Ekron, when there is a God in Israel.

[2.] He was ready to reply to it (*v.* 4); *He answered and said, It is written.* This is observable, that Christ answered and baffled all the temptations of Satan with, *It is written.* He is himself the eternal Word, and could have produced the mind of God without having recourse to the writings of Moses; but he put honour upon the scripture, and, to set us an example, he appealed to what was written in the law; and he says this to Satan, taking it for granted that he knew well enough what was written. It is possible that those who are the Devil's children may yet know very well what is written in God's book; *The devils believe and tremble.* This method we must take when at any time we are tempted to sin; resist and repel the temptation with, *It is written.* The Word of God is *the sword of the Spirit,* the only offensive weapon in all the Christian armoury (Eph. 6:17); and we may say of it as David of Goliath's sword, *None is like that* in our spiritual conflicts.

This answer, as all the rest, is taken out of the book of *Deuteronomy,* which signifies *the second law,* and in which there is very little ceremonial; the Levitical sacrifices and purifications could not drive away Satan, though of divine institution, much less holy water and the sign of the cross, which are of human invention; but moral precepts and evangelical promises, mixed with faith, these are *mighty, through God,* for the vanquishing of Satan. This is here quoted from Deu. 8:3, where the reason given why God fed the Israelites with manna is, because he would teach them that *man shall not live by bread alone.* This Christ applies to his own case. Israel was God's son, whom he *called out of Egypt* (Hos. 11:1),

so was Christ (*ch.* 2:15); Israel was then in a wilderness, Christ was so now, perhaps the same wilderness. Now, *First,* The Devil would have him question his sonship, because he was in straits; no, says he, Israel was God's son, and a son he was very tender of and whose manners he bore (Acts 13:18); and yet he brought them into straits; and it follows there (Deu. 8:5), *As a man chasteneth his son, so the Lord thy God chasteneth thee.* Christ, *being a Son,* thus *learns obedience. Secondly,* The Devil would have him distrust his Father's love and care. "No," says he, "that would be to do as Israel did, who, when they were in want, said, *Is the Lord among us?* and, *Can he furnish a table in the wilderness? Can he give bread?"* *Thirdly,* The Devil would have him, as soon as he began to be hungry, immediately looking out for supply; whereas God, for wise and holy ends, suffered Israel to hunger before he fed them; to humble them, and prove them. God will have his children, when they want, not only to wait on him, but to wait for him. *Fourthly,* The Devil would have him to supply himself with bread. "No," says Christ, "what need is there of that? It is a point long since settled, and incontestably proved, that man may live without bread, as Israel in the wilderness lived forty years upon manna." It is true, God in his providence ordinarily maintains men by *bread out of the earth* (Job 28:5); but he can, if he please, make use of other means to keep men alive; *any word proceeding out of the mouth of God,* any thing that God shall order and appoint for that end, will be a good a livelihood for man as bread, and will maintain him as well. As we may *have bread,* and yet not be nourished, if God deny his blessing (Hag. 1:6, 9; Mic. 6:14; for though bread is *the staff of life,* it is God's blessing that is *the staff of bread),* so we may *want bread,* and yet be nourished some other way. God sustains Moses and Elias without bread, and Christ himself just now for forty days; he sustained Israel with bread from heaven, angels' food; Elijah with bread sent miraculously by ravens, and another time with the widow's meal miraculously multiplied; therefore Christ need not turn stones into bread, but trust God to keep him alive some other way now that he is hungry, as he had done forty days before he hungred. Note, As in our great abundance we must not think to live *without* God, so in our greatest straits we must learn to live *upon* God; and when the *fig-tree does not blossom,* and *the field yields no meat,* when all ordinary means of succour and support are cut off, yet then we must *rejoice in the Lord;* then we must not think to command what we will, though contrary to his command, but must humbly pray for what he thinks fit to give us, and be thankful for the bread of our allowance, though it be a short allowance. Let us learn of Christ here to be at God's finding, rather than at our own; and not to take any irregular courses for our supply, when our wants are ever so pressing (Ps. 37:3). *Jehovah-jireh;* some way or other *the Lord will provide.* It is better to live poorly upon the fruits of God's goodness, than live plentifully upon the products of our own sin.

2. He tempted him to presume upon his Father's power and protection. See what a restless unwearied adversary the Devil is! If he fail in one assault, he tries another.

Now in this second attempt we may observe,

(1.) What the temptation was, and how it was managed. In general, finding Christ so confident of his Father's care of him, in point of nourishment, he endeavors to draw him to presume upon that care in point of safety. Note, We are in danger of missing our way, both on the right hand and on the left, and therefore must take heed, lest, when we avoid one extreme, we be brought by the artifices of Satan, to run into another; lest, by overcoming our prodigality, we fall into covetousness. Nor are any extremes more dangerous than those of despair and presumption, especially in the affairs of our souls. Some who have obtained a persuasion that Christ is able and willing to save them *from* their sins, are then tempted to presume that he will save them *in* their sins. Thus when people begin to be zealous in religion, Satan hurries them into bigotry and intemperate heats.

Now in this temptation we may observe,

[1.] How he made way for it. He took Christ, not by force against his will, but moved him to go, and went along with him, to Jerusalem. Whether Christ went upon the ground, and so went up the stairs to the top of the temple, or whether he went in the air, is uncertain; but so it was, that he was *set upon a pinnacle,* or spire; *upon the fane* (so some), *upon the battlements* (so others), *upon the wing* (so the word is), *of the temple.* Now observe, *First,* How submissive Christ was,

in suffering himself to be hurried thus, that he might let Satan do his worst and yet conquer him. The patience of Christ here, as afterward in his sufferings and death, is more wonderful than the power of Satan or his instruments; for neither he nor they could have any power against Christ but *what was given them from above.* How comfortable is it, that Christ, who let loose this power of Satan against himself, does not in like manner let it loose against us, but restrains it, for he *knows our frame! Secondly,* How subtle the Devil was, in the choice of the place for his temptations. Intending to solicit Christ to an ostentation of his own power, and a vainglorious presumption upon God's providence, he fixes him on a public place in Jerusalem, a populous city, and *the joy of the whole earth;* in the temple, one of the wonders of the world, continually gazed upon with admiration by some one or other. There he might make himself remarkable, and be taken notice of by every body, and prove himself the Son of God; not, as he was urged in the former temptation, in the obscurities of a wilderness, but before multitudes, upon the most eminent stage of action.

Observe, 1. That Jerusalem is here called the *holy city;* for so it was in name and profession, and there was in it a *holy seed,* that was the *substance thereof.* Note, There is no city on earth so holy as to exempt and secure us from the Devil and his temptations. The first *Adam* was tempted in the *holy garden,* the second in the *holy city.* Let us not, therefore, in any place, be off our watch. Nay, the *holy city* is the place where he does, with great advantage and success, tempt men to pride and presumption; but, blessed be God, into the Jerusalem above, that holy city, no unclean thing shall enter; there we shall be for ever out of temptation. 2. That he set him *upon a pinnacle of the temple,* which (as Josephus describes it, *Antiq.* 15.412) was so very high, that it would make a man's head giddy to look down to the bottom. Note, Pinnacles of the temple are places of temptation; I mean, (1.) High places are so; they are slippery places; advancement in the world makes a man a fair mark for Satan to shoot his fiery darts at. God casts down, that he may raise up; the Devil raises up, that he may cast down: therefore they who would take heed of *falling,* must take heed of *climbing.* (2.) High places *in the church* are, in a special manner, dangerous. They who excel in gifts, who are in eminent stations, and have gained great reputation, have need to keep humble; for Satan will be sure to aim at them, to puff them up with pride, that they may *fall into the condemnation of the Devil.* Those that *stand high* are concerned to *stand fast.*

[2.] How he moved it; *"If thou be the Son of God,* now show thyself to the world, and prove thyself to be so; *cast thyself down,* and then," *First,* "Thou wilt be admired, as *under the special protection of heaven.* When they see thee receive no hurt by a fall from such a precipice, they will say" (as the barbarous people did of Paul) "that thou art a God." Tradition says, that *Simon Magnus* by this very thing attempted to prove himself a god, but that his pretensions were disproved, for he fell down, and was miserably bruised. "Nay," *Secondly,* "Thou wilt be received, as coming *with a special commission from heaven.* All Jerusalem will see and acknowledge, not only that thou art more than a man, but that thou art that *Messenger,* that *Angel of the covenant,* that should *suddenly come to the temple* (Mal. 3:1), and from thence descend into the streets of the holy city; and thus the work of convincing the Jews will be cut short, and soon done."

Observe, The Devil said, *Cast thyself down.* The Devil could not cast him down, though a little thing would have done it, from the top of a spire. Note, The power of Satan is a limited power; *hitherto he shall come, and no further.* Yet, if the Devil *had cast him down,* he had not gained his point; that had been his suffering only, not his sin. Note, Whatever real mischief is done us, it is of *our own doing;* the Devil can but persuade, he cannot compel; he can but say, *Cast thyself down;* he cannot cast us down. Every man is tempted, when he is drawn away of his own lust, and not forced, but enticed. Therefore let us not *hurt ourselves,* and then, blessed be God, no one else can hurt us, Prov. 9:12.

[3.] How he backed this motion with a scripture; *For it is written, He shall give his angels charge concerning thee.* But *is Saul also among the prophets?* Is Satan so well versed in scripture, as to be able to quote it so readily? It seems, he is. Note, It is possible for a man to have his head full of scripture-notions, and his mouth full of scripture-expressions, while his heart is full of reigning enmity to God and all goodness. The knowledge which the devils have of the scripture, increases both their mischievousness and their torment. Never did the devil speak with more vexation to himself, than when he said to Christ, *I know thee who thou art.* The devil would persuade Christ to *throw himself down,* hoping that he would be his own murderer, and that there would be an end of him and his undertaking, which he looked upon with a jealous eye; to encourage him to do it, he tells them, that there was no danger, that the good angels would protect him, for so was the promise (Ps. 91:11), *He shall give his angels charge over thee.* In this quotation,

First, There was *something right.* It is true, there is such a promise of the ministration of the angels, for the protection of the saints. The devil knows it by experience; for he finds his attempts against them fruitless, and he frets and rages at it, as he did at the hedge about Job, which he speaks of so sensibly, Job 1:10. He was also right in applying it to Christ, for to him all the promises of the protection of the saints primarily and eminently belong, and to them, in and through him. That promise, that *not a bone of theirs shall be broken* (Ps. 34:20), was fulfilled in Christ, Jn. 19:36. The angels guard the saints for Christ's sake, Rev. 7:5, 11.

Secondly, There was a great deal *wrong in it;* and perhaps the devil had a particular spite against this promise, and perverted it, because it often stood in his way, and baffled his mischievous designs against the saints. See here, 1. How he *misquoted* it; and that was *bad.* The promise is, They shall *keep thee;* but how? *In all thy ways;* not otherwise; if we *go out of our way,* out of the way of our duty, we forfeit the promise, and put ourselves out of God's protection. Now this word made against the tempter, and therefore he industriously left it out. If Christ had *cast himself down,* he had been *out of his way,* for he had no call so to expose himself. It is good for us upon all occasions to consult the scriptures themselves, and not to take things upon trust, that we may not be imposed upon by those that maim and mangle the word of God; we must do as the noble *Bereans,* who searched the scriptures daily. 2. How he *misapplied* it; and that was *worse.* Scripture is abused when it is pressed to patronize sin; and when men thus wrest it to their own temptation, they do it to *their own destruction* 2 Pt. 3:16. This promise is firm, and stands good; but the devil made an ill use of it, when he used it as an encouragement to presume upon the divine care. Note, It is no new thing for the *grace of God* to be *turned into wantonness;* and for men to take encouragement in sin from the discoveries of God's good will to sinners. But *shall we continue in sin, that grace may abound?* throw ourselves down, that the angels may bear us up? God forbid.

(2.) How Christ overcame this temptation; he resisted and overcame it, as he did the former, with, *It is written.* The devil's *abusing* of scripture did not prevent Christ from using it, but he presently urges, Deu. 6:16, *Thou shalt not tempt the Lord thy God.* The meaning of this is not, Therefore thou must not tempt me; but, Therefore I *must not tempt* my Father. In the place whence it is quoted, it is in the plural number, *You shall not tempt;* here it is singular, *Thou shalt not.* Note, We are *then* likely to get good by the word of God, when we hear and receive general promises as speaking to us in particular. Satan said, *It is written;* Christ says, *It is written;* not that one scripture contradicts another. God is one, and his word one, and he is one mind, but that is a promise, this is a precept, and therefore that is to be explained and applied by this; for scripture is the best interpreter of scripture; and they who prophesy, who expound scripture, must do it according to the proportion of faith (Rom. 12:6), consistently with practical godliness.

If Christ should *cast himself down,* it would be the tempting of God, [1.] As it would be *requiring a further confirmation* of that which was so well confirmed. Christ was abundantly satisfied that God was already his Father, and took care of him, and gave his angels a charge concerning him; and therefore to put it upon a new experiment, would be to tempt him, as the Pharisees tempted Christ; when they had so many signs on earth, they demanded a *sign from heaven.* This is limiting the *Holy One of Israel.* [2.] As it would be *requiring a special preservation* of him, in doing that which he had no call to. If we expect that because God has promised not to forsake us, therefore he should follow us out of the way of our duty; that because he has promised to supply our wants, therefore he should humour us, and please our fancies; that because he has promised to keep us, we may wilfully thrust ourselves into danger, and may expect the desired end, without using the appointed means; this is presumption, this is tempting God. And it is an aggravation of the sin, that he is the Lord our God; it is an abuse of the privilege we enjoy, in having him for our God; he has thereby encouraged us to trust him, but we are very ungrateful, if therefore we tempt him; it is contrary to our duty to him as our God. This is to affront him whom we ought to honour. Note, We must never promise ourselves any more than God has promised us.

3. He tempted him to the most *black and horrid idolatry,* with the proffer of the *kingdoms of the world, and the glory of them.* And here we may observe,

(1.) How the devil made this push at our Saviour, *v.* 8, 9. The worst temptation was reserved for the last. Note, Sometimes the saint's last encounter is with the sons of *Anak,* and the parting blow is the sorest; therefore, whatever temptation we have been assaulted by, still we must prepare for worse; must be armed for all attacks, with the armour of righteousness on the right hand and on the left.

In this temptation, we may observe,

[1.] What he *showed him — all the kingdoms of the world.* In order to do this, he took him to an *exceeding high mountain;* in hopes of prevailing, as Balak with Balaam, he changed his ground. The pinnacle of the temple is not high enough; the prince of the power of the air must have him further up into his territories. Some think this high mountain was on the other side of Jordan, because there we find Christ next after the temptation, Jn. 1:28, 29. Perhaps it was *mount Pisgah,* whence Moses, in communion with God, had all the kingdoms of Canaan shown him. Hither the blessed Jesus was carried for the advantage of a prospect; as if the devil could show him more of the world than he knew already, who made and governed it. Thence he might discover some of the kingdoms situate about Judea, though not *the glory of them;* but there was doubtless a juggle and a delusion of Satan's in it; it is probable that that which he showed him, was but a landscape, an airy representation in a cloud, such as that great deceiver could easily frame and put together; setting forth, in proper and lively colours, the glories and the splendid appearances of princes; their robes and crowns, their retinue, equipage, and lifeguards; the pomp of thrones, and courts, and stately palaces, the sumptuous buildings in cities, the gardens and fields about the country-seats, with the various instances of their wealth, pleasure, and gaiety; so as might be most likely to strike the fancy, and excite the admiration and affection. Such was this show, and his taking him up into a high mountain, was but to *humour the thing,* and to colour the delusion; in which yet the blessed Jesus did not suffer himself to be imposed upon, but saw through the cheat, only he permitted Satan to take his own way, that his victory over him might be the more illustrious. Hence observe, concerning *Satan's temptations,* that, *First,* They often *come in at the eye,* which is blinded to the things it should see, and dazzled with the vanities it should be turned from. The first sin began in the eye, Gen. 3:6. We have therefore need to make a covenant with our eyes, and to pray that God would *turn them away from beholding vanity. Secondly,* That temptations commonly take rise from the world, and the things in it. The *lust of the flesh,* and of *the eye,* with the *pride of life,* are the topics from which the devil fetches most of his arguments. *Thirdly,* That it is a *great cheat* which the devil puts upon poor souls, in his temptations. He deceives, and so destroys; he imposes upon men with shadows and fast colours; shows the world and the glory of it, and hides from men's eyes the sin and sorrow and death which stain the pride of all this glory, the cares and calamities which attend great possessions, and the thorns which crowns themselves are lined with. *Fourthly,* That the *glory of the world* is the most *charming* temptation to the *unthinking* and *unwary,* and that by which men are most imposed upon. *Laban's* sons grudge *Jacob all this glory;* the *pride of life* is the most dangerous snare.

(2.) What he *said to him* (*v.* 9); *All these things I will give thee, if thou wilt fall down and worship me.* See,

First, How *vain the promise* was. *All these things I will give thee.* He seems to take it for granted, that in the former temptations he had in part gained his point, and proved that Christ was not the *Son of God,* because he had not given him those evidences of it which he demanded; so that here he looks upon him as a mere man. "Come," says he, "it seems that God whose Son thou thinkest thyself to be deserts thee, and starves thee — a sign that he is not thy Father; but if thou wilt be ruled by me, I will provide better for thee than so; own me for thy father, and ask my blessing, and *all this will I give thee.*" Note, Satan makes an easy prey of men, when he can persuade them to think themselves abandoned of God. The fallacy of this promise lies in that, *All this will I give thee.* And what was *all that?* It was but a map, a picture, a mere phantasm, that had nothing in it real or solid, and this he would give him; a goodly prize! Yet such are Satan's proffers. Note, Multitudes lose the sight of that which is, by setting their eyes on that which is not. The devil's baits are all a sham; they are shows and shadows with which he deceives them, or rather they deceive themselves. The *nations of the earth* had been, long before, promised to the Messiah; if he be *the Son of God,* they belong to him; Satan pretends now to be a good angel, probably one of those that were set over kingdoms, and to have received a commission to deliver possession to him according to promise. Note, We must take heed of receiving even that which God hath promised, out of the devil's hand; we do so when we precipitate the performance, by catching at it in a sinful way.

Secondly, How *vile* the *condition* was; *If thou will fall down, and worship me.* All the worship which the heathen performed to their gods, was directed to the devil (Deu. 32:17), who is therefore called the *god of this world,* 2 Co. 4:4; 1 Co. 10:20. And fain would he draw Christ into his interests, and persuade him, now that he set up for a Teacher, to preach up the Gentile idolatry, and to introduce it again among the Jews, and then the nations of the earth would soon flock in to him. What temptation could be more hideous, more black? Note, The best of saints may be tempted to the worst of sins, especially when they are under the power of melancholy; as, for instance, to atheism, blasphemy, murder, self-murder, and what not. This is their affliction, but while there is no consent to it, nor approbation of it, it is not their sin; Christ was tempted to worship Satan.

(2.) See how Christ warded off the thrust, baffled the assault, and came off a conqueror. He rejected the proposal,

[1.] With *abhorrence* and *detestation; Get thee hence, Satan.* The two former temptations had something of colour, which would admit a consideration, but this was so gross as not to bear a parley; it appears abominable at the first sight, and therefore is immediately rejected. If the best friend we have in the world suggests such a thing as this to us, *Go, serve other gods,* he must not be heard with patience, Deu. 13:6, 8. Some temptations have their wickedness written in their forehead, they are open before-hand; they are not to be disputed with, but rejected; *"Get thee hence, Satan.* Away with it, I cannot bear the thought of it!" While Satan tempted Christ to do himself a mischief, by casting himself down, though he yielded not, yet he heard it; but now that the temptation flies in the face of God, he cannot bear it; *Get thee hence, Satan.* Note, It is a just indignation, which rises at the proposal of any thing that reflects on the honour of God, and strikes at his crown. Nay, whatever is an abominable thing, which we are sure the Lord hates, we must thus abominate it; far be it from us that we should have any thing to do with it. Note, It is good to be *peremptory* in resisting temptation, and to *stop our ears* to Satan's charms.

[2.] With an argument fetched from scripture. Note, In order to the strengthening of our resolutions against sin, it is good to see what a great deal of reason there is for those resolutions. The argument is very suitable, and exactly to the purpose, taken from Deu. 6:13, and 10:20. *Thou shalt worship the Lord thy God, and him only shalt thou serve.* Christ does not dispute whether he were an angel of light, as he pretended, or not; but though he were, yet he must not be worshipped, because that is an honour due to God only. Note, It is good to make our answers to temptation as full and as brief as may be, so as not to leave room for objections. Our Saviour has recourse to the fundamental law in this case, which is indispensable, and universally obligatory. Note, Religious worship is due to God only, and must not be given to any creature; it is a flower of the crown which cannot be alienated, a branch of God's glory which he will not give to another, and which he would not give to his own Son, by obliging all men to *honour the Son, even as they honour the Father,* if he had not been God, *equal to him,* and *one with him.* Christ quotes this law concerning religious worship, and quotes it with application to himself; *First,* To show that in his estate of humiliation he was himself *made under this law:* though, as God, he was worshipped, yet, as Man, he did worship God, both publicly and privately. He obliges us to no more than what he was first pleased to oblige himself to. Thus it became him to fulfil all righteousness. *Secondly,* To show that the law of religious worship is of eternal obligation:

though he abrogated and altered many institutions of worship, yet this fundamental law of nature — That God only is to be worshipped, he came to ratify, and confirm, and enforce upon us.

V. We have here the end and issue of this combat, *v.* 11. Though the children of God may be exercised with many and great temptations, yet God will not suffer them to be tempted above the strength which either they have, or he will put into them, 1 Co. 10:13. It is but for a season that they are in heaviness, through manifold temptations.

Now the issue was glorious, and much to Christ's honour: for,

1. The devil was baffled, and quitted the field; *Then the devil leaveth him,* forced to do so by the power that went along with that word of command, *Get thee hence, Satan.* He made a shameful and inglorious retreat, and came off with disgrace; and the more daring his attempts had been, the more mortifying was the foil that was given him. *Magnis tamen excidit ausis — The attempt, however, in which he failed, was daring.* Then, when he had done his worst, had tempted him with *all the kingdoms of the world, and the glory of them,* and found that he was not influenced by that bait, that he could not prevail with that temptation with which he had overthrown so many thousands of the children of men, then he leaves him; then he gives him over as more than a man. Since this did not move him, he despairs of moving him, and begins to conclude, that he is the *Son of God,* and that it is in vain to tempt him any further. Note, If we resist the devil, he will flee from us; he will yield, if we keep our ground; as when *Naomi* saw that *Ruth was steadfastly resolved, she left off speaking to her.* When the devil left our Saviour, he owned himself fairly beaten; his head was broken by the attempt he made to *bruise Christ's heel.* He left him because he had *nothing in him,* nothing to take hold of; he saw it was to no purpose, and so gave over. Note, The devil, though he is an enemy to all saints, is a conquered enemy. The Captain of our salvation has defeated and disarmed him; we have nothing to do but to *pursue the victory.*

2. The holy angels came and attended upon our victorious Redeemer; *Behold, angels came and ministered unto him.* They came in a visible appearance, as the devil had done in the temptation. While the devil was making his assaults upon our Saviour, the angels stood at a distance, and their immediate attendance and administration were suspended, that it might appear that he vanquished Satan in his own strength, and that his victory might be the more illustrious; and that afterward, when *Michael* makes use of *his angels* in fighting with the *dragon and his angels,* it might appear, that it is not because he *needs them,* or could not do his work without them, but because he is pleased to honour them so far as to employ them. One angel might have served to bring him food, but here are many attending him, to testify their respect to him, and their readiness to receive his commands. Behold this! It is worth taking notice of; (1.) That as there is a world of wicked, malicious spirits that fight against Christ and his church, and all particular believers, so there is a world of holy, blessed spirits engaged and employed for them. In reference to our *war with devils,* we may take abundance of comfort from our *communion with angels.* (2.) That Christ's victories are the angels' triumphs. The angels came to congratulate Christ on his success, to rejoice with him, and to give him the glory due to his name; for that was sung with a loud voice in heaven, when the great dragon was cast out (Rev. 12:9, 10), *Now is come salvation and strength.* (3.) That the angels ministered to the Lord Jesus, not only food, but whatever else he wanted after this great fatigue. See how the instances of Christ's condescension and humiliation were balanced with tokens of his glory. As when he was *crucified in weakness,* yet he *lived by the power of God;* so when in weakness he was tempted, was hungry and weary, yet by his divine power he commanded the ministration of angels. Thus the Son of man did eat angels' food, and, like Elias, is fed by an angel in the wilderness, 1 Ki. 19:4, 7. Note, Though God may suffer his people to be brought into wants and straits, yet he will take effectual care for their supply, and will rather send angels to feed them, than see them perish. *Trust in the Lord, and verily thou shalt be fed,* Ps. 37:3.

Christ was thus succoured after the temptation, [1.] For his encouragement to go on in his undertaking, that he might see the powers of heaven siding with him, when he saw the powers of hell set against him. [2.] For our encouragement to trust in him; for as he knew, by experience, what it was to *suffer, being tempted,* and how hard that was, so he knew what it was to be succoured, being tempted, and how comfortable that was; and therefore we may expect, not only that he will sympathize with his tempted people, but that he will come in with seasonable relief to them; as our great Melchizedec, who met Abraham when he returned from the battle, and as the angels here ministered to him.

Lastly, Christ, having been thus signalized and made great in the invisible world by the voice of the Father, the descent of the Spirit, his victory over devils, and his dominion over angels, was doubtless qualified to appear in the visible world as the Mediator between God and man; for *consider how great this man was!*

Verses 12–17

We have here an account of Christ's preaching in the synagogues of Galilee, for he came into the world to be a Preacher; the great salvation which he wrought out, he himself began to publish (Heb. 2:3) to show how much his heart *was* upon it, and ours *should* be.

Several passages in the other gospels, especially in that of St. John, are supposed, in the order of the story of Christ's life, to intervene between his temptation and his preaching in Galilee. His first appearance after his temptation, was when John Baptist pointed to him, saying, *Behold the Lamb of God,* Jn. 1:29. After that, he went up to Jerusalem, to the passover (Jn. 2), discoursed with Nicodemus (Jn. 3), with the woman of Samaria (Jn. 4), and then returned into Galilee, and preached there. But Matthew, having had his residence in Galilee, begins his story of Christ's public ministry with his preaching there, which here we have an account of. Observe,

I. The time; *When Jesus had heard that John was cast into prison,* then he *went into Galilee, v.* 12. Note, The cry of the saints' sufferings comes up into the ears of the Lord Jesus. If John be cast into prison, Jesus hears it, takes cognizance of it, and steers his course accordingly: *he remembers the bonds* and afflictions that abide his people. Observe, 1. Christ did *not* go into the country, *till he heard of* John's imprisonment; for he must have time given him to *prepare the way of the Lord,* before the Lord himself appear. Providence wisely ordered it, that John should be *eclipsed* before Christ *shone forth;* otherwise the minds of people would have been distracted between the two; one would have said, *I am of John,* and another, *I am of Jesus.* John must be Christ's harbinger, but not his rival. The moon and stars are lost when the sun rises. John had done his work by the baptism of repentance, and then he was laid aside. The witnesses were slain when they had finished their testimony, and not before, Rev. 11:7. 2. He *did* go into the country as soon as he heard of John's imprisonment; not only to provide for his own safety, knowing that the Pharisees in Judea were as much enemies to him as Herod was to John, but to supply the want of John Baptist, and to build upon the good foundation he had laid. Note, God will not leave himself without witness, nor his church without guides; when he removes one useful instrument, he can raise up another, for he has the residue of the Spirit, and he will do it, if he has work to do. *Moses my servant is dead,* John is cast into prison; now, therefore, Joshua, arise; Jesus, arise.

II. The place where he preached; in Galilee, a remote part of the country, that lay furthest from Jerusalem, as was there looked upon with contempt, as rude and boorish. The inhabitants of that country were reckoned stout men, fit for soldiers, but not polite men, or fit for scholars. Thither Christ went, there he set up the standard of his gospel; and in this, as in other things, he humbled himself. Observe,

1. The particular city he chose for his residence; not Nazareth, where he had been bred up; no, he left Nazareth; particular notice is taken of that, *v.* 13. And with good reason did he leave Nazareth; for the men of that city *thrust him out* from among them, Lu. 4:29. He made them his first, and a very fair, offer of his service, but they rejected him and his doctrine, and were filled with indignation at him and it; and therefore he left Nazareth, and shook off the dust of his feet for a testimony against those there, who would not have him to teach them. Nazareth was the first place that refused Christ, and was therefore refused by him. Note, It is just with God, to take the gospel and the means of grace from those that slight them, and thrust them away. Christ will not stay long where he is not welcome. Unhappy Nazareth! *If thou hadst known* in this thy day the things that belong to thy peace, how well had it been for thee! *But now they are hid from thine eyes.*

But he *came and dwelt in Capernaum,* which was a city of Galilee, but many miles distant from Nazareth, a great city and of much resort. It is said here to be *on the sea coast,* not the *great sea,* but the sea of Tiberias, an inland water, called also *the lake of Gennesaret.* Close by the falling of Jordan into the sea stood Capernaum, in the tribe of Naphtali, but bordering upon Zebulun; hither Christ came, and here he dwelt. Some think that his father Joseph had a habitation here, others that he took a house or lodgings at least; and some think it more than probable, that he dwelt in the house of Simon Peter; however, here he fixed not constantly, for he went about doing good; but this was for some time his head quarters: what little rest he had, was here; here he had a place, though not a place of his own, to lay his head on. And at Capernaum, it should seem, he was welcome, and met with better entertainment than he had at Nazareth. Note, If some reject Christ, yet others will receive him, and bid him welcome. Capernaum is glad of Nazareth's leavings. If Christ's own countrymen be not gathered, yet he will be glorious. "And thou, Capernaum, has now a day of it; thou art now lifted up to heaven; be wise for thyself, and know the time of thy visitation."

2. The prophecy that was fulfilled is this, *v.* 14–16. It is quoted from Isa. 9:1, 2, but with some variation. The prophet in that place is foretelling a greater darkness of affliction to befal the contemners of Immanuel, than befel the countries there mentioned, either in their first captivity under Benhadad, which was but light (1 Ki. 15:20), or in their second captivity under the Assyrian, which was much heavier, 2 Ki. 15:29. The punishment of the Jewish nation for rejecting the gospel should be sorer than either (see Isa. 8:21, 22); for those captivated places had some reviving in their bondage, and saw a great light again, *ch.* 9:2. This is Isaiah's sense; but the Scripture has many fulfillings; and the evangelist here takes only the latter clause, which speaks of the return of the light of liberty and prosperity to those countries that had been in the darkness of captivity, and applies it to the appearing of the gospel among them.

The places are spoken of, *v.* 15. *The land of Zebulun is* rightly said to be *by the sea coast,* for *Zebulun* was a *haven of ships,* and *rejoiced* in her *going out,* Gen. 49:13; Deu. 33:18. Of Naphtali, it had been said, that he should *give goodly words* (Gen. 49:21), and should be *satisfied with favour* (Deu. 33:23), for from him began the gospel; goodly words indeed, and such as bring to a soul God's satisfying favour. The country beyond Jordan is mentioned likewise, for there we sometimes find Christ preaching, and Galilee of the Gentiles, the upper Galilee to which the Gentiles resorted for traffic, and where they were mingled with the Jews; which intimates a kindness in reserve for the poor Gentiles. When Christ came to Capernaum, the gospel came to all those places round about; such diffusive influences did the Sun of righteousness cast.

Now, concerning the inhabitants of these places, observe, (1.) The posture they were in before the gospel came among them (*v.* 16); they were *in darkness.* Note, Those that are without Christ, are in the dark, nay, they are darkness itself; as the darkness that was upon the *face of the deep.* Nay, they were *in the region and shadow of death;* which denotes not only *great darkness,* as the grave is a *land of darkness,* but *great danger.* A man that is desperately sick, and not likely to recover, is in the *valley of the shadow of death,* though not quite dead; so the poor people were on the borders of damnation, though not yet damned — dead in law. And, which is worst of all, they were *sitting* in this condition. Sitting in a continuing posture; where we sit, we mean to stay; they were in the dark, and likely to be so, despairing to find the way out. And it is a contented posture; they were in the dark, and they loved darkness, they chose it rather than light; they were willingly ignorant. Their condition was sad; it is still the condition of many great and mighty nations, which are to be thought of, and prayed for, with pity. But *their* condition is more sad, who sit in darkness in the midst of gospel-light. He that is in the dark because it is night, may be sure that the sun will shortly arise; but he that is in the dark because he is blind, will not so soon have his eyes opened. We have the light, but what will that avail us, if we be not the light in the Lord? (2.) The privilege they enjoyed, when Christ and his gospel came among them; it was as great a reviving as ever light was to a benighted traveller. Note, When the gospel comes, light comes; when it comes to any place, when it comes to any soul, it makes day there, Jn. 3:19; Lu. 1:78, 79. Light is discovering, it is directing; so is the gospel.

It is a *great* light; denoting the clearness and evidence of gospel-revelations; not like the light of a candle, but the light of the sun when he goes forth in his strength. *Great* in comparison with the light of the law, the shadows of which were now done away. It is a *great light,* for it discovers great things and of vast consequence; it will last long, and spread far. And it is a *growing light,* intimated in that word, It is *sprung up.* It was but *spring of day* with them; now the day dawned, which afterward *shone more and more.* The gospel-kingdom, like a grain of mustard-seed or the morning light, was small in its beginnings, gradual in its growth, but great in its perfection.

Observe, the light *sprang up to them;* they did not go to seek it, but were prevented with the blessings of this goodness. It came upon them ere they were aware, at the time appointed, by the disposal of him who *commandeth the morning,* and *causes the day-spring to know its place, that it may take hold of the ends of the earth,* Job 38:12, 13.

III. The text he preached upon (*v.* 17): *From that time,* that is, from the time of his coming into Galilee, into the land of Zebulun and Naphtali, from that time, he began to preach. He had been preaching, before this, in Judea, and had made and baptized many disciples (Jn. 4:1); but his preaching was no so public and constant as now it began to be. The work of the ministry is so great and awful, that it is fit to be entered upon by steps and gradual advances.

The subject which Christ dwelt upon now in his preaching (and it was indeed the sum and substance of all his preaching), was the very same John has preached upon (*ch.* 3:2); *Repent, for the kingdom of heaven is at hand;* for the gospel is the same for substance under various dispensations; the commands the same, and the reasons to enforce them the same; an *angel from heaven* dares not preach any other gospel (Gal. 1:8), and will preach this, for it is the *everlasting gospel. Fear God, and,* by repentance, *give honour to him,* Rev. 14:6, 7. Christ put a great respect upon John's ministry, when he preached to the same purport that John had preached before him. By this he showed that John was his messenger and ambassador; for when he brought the errand himself, it was the same that he had sent by him. Thus did God confirm the word of his messenger, Isa. 44:26. The Son came on the same errand that the servants came on (*ch.* 21:37), to *seek fruit,* fruits meet for repentance. Christ had lain in the bosom of the Father, and could have preached sublime notions of divine and heavenly things, that should have alarmed and amused the learned world, but he pitches upon this old, plain text, *Repent, for the kingdom of heaven is at hand.* [1.] This he preached *first* upon; he began with this. Ministers must not be ambitious of broaching new opinions, framing new schemes, or coining new expressions, but must content themselves with plain, practical things, with the word that is *nigh us,* even *in our mouth,* and *in our heart.* We need not go up to heaven, nor down to the deep, for matter or language in our preaching. As John prepared Christ's way, so Christ prepared his own, and made way for the further discoveries he designed, with the doctrine of repentance. *If any man* will do this part of *his will, he shall know* more of *his doctrine,* Jn. 7:17. [2.] This is preached *often* upon; wherever he went, this was his subject, and neither he nor his followers ever reckoned it worn threadbare, as those would have done, that have *itching ears,* and are fond of novelty and variety more than that which is truly edifying. Note, That which has been preached and heard before, may yet very profitably be preached and heard again; but then it should be preached and heard better, and with new affections; what Paul had said before, he said again, *weeping,* Phil. 3:1, 18. [3.] This he preached as gospel; "Repent, review your ways, and return to yourselves." Note, The doctrine of repentance is right gospel-doctrine. Not only the austere Baptist, who was looked upon as a melancholy, morose man, but the sweet and gracious Jesus, whose lips dropped as a honey-comb, preached repentance; for it is an unspeakable privilege that room is left for repentance. [4.] The reason is still the same; The *kingdom of heaven is at hand;* for it was not reckoned to be fully come, till that pouring out of the Spirit after Christ's ascension. John had preached the kingdom of heaven at hand above a year before this; but now it was so much the stronger; now is the *salvation nearer,* Rom. 13:11. We should be so much the more quickened to our duty, *as we see the day approaching,* Heb. 10:25.

Verses 18–22

When Christ began to preach, he began to *gather disciples,* who should now be the *hearers,* and hereafter the *preachers,* of his doctrine, who should now be witnesses *of* his miracles, and hereafter *concerning* them. Now, in these verses, we have an account of the first disciples that he called into fellowship with himself.

And this was an instance, 1. Of *effectual calling* to Christ. In all his preaching he gave a common call to all the country, but in this he gave a special and particular call to those that were given him by the Father. Let us see and admire the power of Christ's grace, own his word to be the rod of his strength, and wait upon him for those powerful influences which are necessary to the efficacy of the gospel call — those distinguishing influences. All the country was *called,* but these were *called out,* were *redeemed from among them.* Christ was so manifested to them, as he was not manifested unto the world. 2. It was an instance of *ordination,* and appointment to the work of the ministry. When Christ, as a Teacher, set up his great school, one of his first works was to appoint ushers, or under masters, to be employed in the work of instruction. Now he began to give gifts unto men, to put the treasure into earthen vessels. It was an early instance of his care for the church.

Now we may observe here,

I. *Where* they were called — by the *sea of Galilee,* where Jesus was walking, Capernaum being situated near that sea. Concerning this sea of Tiberias, the Jews have a saying, That of all the seven seas that God made, he made choice of none but the sea of Gennesaret; which is very applicable to Christ's choice of it, to honour it, as he often did, with his presence and his miracles. Here, on the banks of the sea, Christ was walking for contemplation, as Isaac in the field; hither he went to call his disciples; not to Herod's court (for few mighty or noble are called), not to Jerusalem, among the chief priests and the elders, but to the sea of Galilee; surely Christ sees not as man sees. Not but that the same power which effectually called Peter and Andrew would have wrought upon Annas and Caiaphas, for with God nothing is impossible; but, as in other things, so in his converse and attendance, he would humble himself, and show that God ha *chosen the poor of this world.* Galilee was a remote part of the nation, the inhabitants were less cultivated and refined, their very language was broad and uncouth to the curious, their *speech betrayed them.* They who were picked up at the sea of Galilee, had not the advantages and improvements, no, not of the more polished Galileans; yet thither Christ went, to call his apostles that were to be the prime ministers of state in his kingdom, for he *chooses the foolish things of this world, to confound the wise.*

II. *Who* they were. We have an account of the call of two pair of brothers in these verses — Peter and Andrew, James and John; the two former, and, probably, the two latter also, had had acquaintance with Christ before (Jn. 1:40, 41), but were not till now called into a close and constant attendance upon him. Note, Christ brings poor souls by degrees into fellowship with himself. They had been disciples of John, and so were the better disposed to follow Christ. Note, Those who have submitted to the discipline of repentance, shall be welcome to the joys of faith. We may observe concerning them,

1. That they were *brothers.* Note, It is a blessed thing, when they who are *kinsmen according to the flesh* (as the apostle speaks, Rom. 9:3), are brought together into a spiritual alliance to Jesus Christ. It is the honour and comfort of a house, when those that are of the *same* family, are of *God's* family.

2. That they were *fishers.* Being fishers, (1.) They were *poor men:* if they had had estates, or any considerable stock in trade, they would not have made fishing their trade, however, they might have made it their recreation. Note, Christ does not despise the poor, and therefore we must not; the poor are evangelized, and the Fountain of honour sometimes gives more abundant honour to that part which most lacked. (2.) The were *unlearned men,* not bred up to books or literature as Moses was, who was conversant with all the learning of the Egyptians. Note, Christ sometimes chooses to endow those with the gifts of grace who have least to show of the gifts of nature. Yet this will not justify the bold intrusion of ignorant and unqualified men into the work of the ministry: extraordinary gifts of knowledge and utterance are not now to be expected, but requisite abilities must be obtained in an ordinary way, and without a competent measure of these, none are to be admitted to that service. (3.) They were *men of business,* who had been bred up to labour. Note, Diligence in an honest calling is pleasing to Christ, and no hindrance to a holy life. Moses was called from keeping sheep, and David from following the ewes, to eminent employments. Idle people lie more open to the temptations of Satan than to the calls of God. (4.) They were men that were accustomed to *hardships* and hazards; the fisher's trade, more than any other, is laborious and perilous; fishermen must be often wet and cold; they must watch, and wait, and toil, and be often in *perils by waters.* Note, Those who have learned to bear hardships, and run hazards, are best prepared for the fellowship and discipleship of Jesus Christ. Good soldiers of Christ must endure hardness.

III. *What they were doing.* Peter and Andrew were then using their nets, they were fishing; and James and John were *mending their nets,* which was an instance of their industry and good husbandry. They did not go to their father for money to buy new nets, but took pains to mend their old ones. It is commendable to make what we have go as far, and last as long, as may be. James and John were *with their father Zebedee,* ready to assist him, and make his business easy to him. Note, It is a happy and hopeful presage, to see children careful of their parents, and dutiful to them. Observe, 1. They were *all* employed, all very busy, and none idle. Note, When Christ comes, it is good to be found doing. "Am I in Christ?" is a very needful question for us to ask ourselves; and, next to that, "Am I in my calling?" 2. They were *differently* employed; two of them were fishing, and two of them *mending their nets.* Note, Ministers should be always employed, either in teaching or studying; they may always find themselves something to do, if it be not their own fault; and *mending their nets,* is, in its season, as necessary work as fishing.

IV. *What the call was* (*v.* 19); *Follow me, and I will make you fishers of men.* They had followed Christ before, as ordinary disciples (Jn. 1:37), but so they might follow Christ, and follow their calling too; therefore they were called to a more close and constant attendance, and must leave their calling. Note, Even they who had been called to follow Christ, have need to be called to follow on, and to follow nearer, especially when they are designed for the work of the ministry. Observe,

1. What Christ intended them for; *I will make you fishers of men;* this alludes to their former calling. Let them be not proud of the new honour designed them, they are still but fishers; let them not be afraid of the new work cut out for them, for they have been used to fishing, and fishers they are still. It was usual with Christ to speak of spiritual and heavenly things under such allusions, and in such expressions, as took rise from common things that offered themselves to his view. David was called from feeding sheep to feed God's Israel; and when he is a king, is a shepherd. Note, (1.) Ministers are *fishers of men,* not to destroy them, but to save them, by bringing them into another element. They must fish, not for wrath, wealth, honour, and preferment, to gain them to themselves, but for souls, to gain them to Christ. *They watch for your souls* (Heb. 13:17), *and seek not yours, but you,* 2 Co. 12:14, 16. (2.) It is Jesus Christ that makes them so; *I will make you fishers of men.* It is he that qualifies men for this work, calls them to it, authorizes them in it, gives them commission to fish for souls, and wisdom to win them. Those ministers are likely to have comfort in their work, who are thus made by Jesus Christ.

2. What they must do in order to this; *Follow me.* They must separate themselves to a diligent attendance on him, and set themselves to a humble imitation of him; must follow him as their Leader. Note, (1.) Those whom Christ employs in any service for him, must first be fitted and qualified for it. (2.) Those who would *preach Christ,* must first *learn* Christ, and learn of him. How can we expect to bring others to the knowledge of Christ, if we do not know him well ourselves? (3.) Those who would get an acquaintance with Christ, must be diligent and constant in their attendance on him. The apostles were prepared for their work, by *accompanying Christ all the time that he went in and out among them,* Acts 1:21. There is no learning comparable to that which is got by following Christ. Joshua, by ministering to Moses, is fitted to be his successor. (4.) Those who are to fish for men, must therein follow Christ, and do it as he did, with diligence, faithfulness, and tenderness. Christ is the great pat-

tern for preachers, and they ought to be *workers together with him.*

V. What was the *success* of this call. Peter and Andrew *straightway left their nets* (*v.* 20); and James and John *immediately left the ship and their father* (*v.* 22); *and they* all *followed him.* Note, Those who would follow Christ aright, must *leave all* to follow him. Every Christian must leave all in affection, set loose to all, must *hate father and mother* (Lu. 14:26), must love them less than Christ, must be ready to part with his interest in them rather than with his interest in Jesus Christ; but those who are devoted to the work of the ministry are, in a special manner, concerned to disentangle themselves from all the affairs of this life, that they may give themselves wholly to that work which requires the whole man. Now,

1. This instance of the power of the Lord Jesus gives us good encouragement to depend upon the sufficiency of his grace. How strong and effectual is his word! *He speaks, and it is done.* The same power goes along with this word of Christ, *Follow me,* that went along with that word, *Lazarus, come forth;* a power *to make willing,* Ps. 110:3.

2. This instance of the pliableness of the disciples, gives us a good example of obedience to the command of Christ. Note, It is the good property of all Christ's faithful servants to come when they are called, and to follow their Master wherever he leads them. They objected not their present employments, their engagements to their families, the difficulties of the service they were called to, or their own unfitness for it; but, being called, they obeyed, and, like Abraham, *went out not knowing whither they went,* but knowing very well whom they followed. James and John *left their father:* it is not said what became of him; their mother Salome was a constant follower of Christ; no doubt, their father Zebedee was a believer, but the call to follow Christ fastened on the young ones. Youth is the learning age, and the labouring age. The priests ministered in the prime of their life.

Verses 23–25

See here, I. What an industrious preacher Christ was; He *went about all Galilee, teaching in their synagogues, and preaching the gospel of the kingdom.* Observe, 1. *What* Christ preached — *the gospel of the kingdom. The kingdom of heaven,* that is, of grace and glory, is emphatically *the kingdom, the kingdom* that was now to come; that kingdom which shall survive, as it doth surpass, all the kingdoms of the earth. *The gospel* is the charter of that kingdom, containing the King's coronation oath, by which he has graciously obliged himself to pardon, protect, and save the subjects of that kingdom; it contains also their oath of allegiance, by which they oblige themselves to observe his statutes and seek his honour; this is *the gospel of the kingdom;* this Christ was himself the Preacher of, that our faith in it might be confirmed. 2. *Where* he preached — *in the synagogues;* not there only, but there chiefly, because those were *the places of concourse,* where *wisdom* was to *lift up her voice* (Prov. 1:21); because they were *places of concourse* for religious worship, and there, it was to be hoped, the minds of the people would be prepared to receive *the gospel;* and there the scriptures of the Old Testament were read, the exposition of which would easily introduce *the gospel of the kingdom.* 3. *What pains he took* in preaching; He *went about all Galilee, teaching.* He might have issued out a proclamation to summon all to come to him; but, to show his humility, and the condescensions of his grace, he goes to them; for he *waits to be gracious,* and comes *to seek and save.* Josephus says, There were above two hundred cities and towns in Galilee, and all, or most of them, Christ visited. He *went about doing good.* Never was there such an itinerant preacher, such an indefatigable one, as Christ was; he went from town to town, to beseech poor sinners to be reconciled to God. This is an example to ministers, to lay themselves out to do good, and to *be instant,* and constant, in *season, and out of season,* to preach the word.

II. What a powerful physician Christ was; he *went about* not only *teaching,* but *healing,* and both with his word, that he might magnify that above all his name. *He sent his word, and healed them.* Now observe,

1. What diseases he cured — all without exception. He *healed all manner of sickness, and all manner of disease.* There are diseases which are called *the reproach of physicians,* being obstinate to all the methods they can prescribe; but even those were the glory of this Physician, for *he healed them* all, however inveterate. His word was the true *panpharmacon — all-heal.*

Three general words are here used to intimate this; he healed every sickness, *noson,* as blindness, lameness, fever, dropsy; every *disease,* or languishing, *malakian,* as fluxes and consumptions; and all *torments, basanous,* as gout, stone, convulsions, and such like torturing distempers; whether the disease was acute or chronical; whether it was a racking or a wasting disease; none was too bad, none too hard, for Christ to heal with a word's speaking.

Three particular diseases are specified; *the palsy,* which is the greatest weakness of the body; *lunacy,* which is the greatest malady of the mind, and *possession of the Devil,* which is the greatest misery and calamity of both, yet Christ healed all: for he is the sovereign Physician both of soul and body, and has command of all diseases.

2. What patients he had. A physician who was so easy of access, so sure of success, who cured immediately, without either a painful suspense and expectation, or such painful remedies as are worse than the disease; who cured gratis, and took no fees, could not but have abundance of patients. See here, what flocking there was to him from all parts; great multitudes of people came, not only *from Galilee* and the country about, but even *from Jerusalem* and *from Judea,* which lay a great way off; for *his fame went throughout all Syria,* not only among all the people of the Jews, but among the neighbouring nations, which, by the report that now spread far and near concerning him, would be prepared to receive his gospel, when afterwards it should be brought them. *This* is given as the reason why such multitudes came to him, because his fame had spread so widely. Note, What we hear of Christ from others, should invite us to him. The queen of Sheba was induced, by the fame of Solomon, to pay him a visit. The voice of fame is "Come, and see." Christ both *taught and healed.* They who came for cures, met with instruction concerning *the things that belonged to their peace.* It is well if any thing will bring people to Christ; and they who come to him will find more in him than they expected. These Syrians, like Naaman the Syrian, coming to be healed of their diseases, many of them being converts, 2 Kings *v.* 15, 17. They sought health for the body, and obtained the salvation of the soul; like Saul, who sought the asses, and found the kingdom. Yet it appeared, by the issue, that many of those who rejoiced in Christ as a Healer, forgot him as a Teacher.

Now concerning the cures which Christ wrought, let us, once for all, observe the *miracle,* the *mercy,* and the *mystery,* of them.

(1.) The *miracle* of them. They were wrought in such a manner, as plainly spake them to be the immediate products of a divine and supernatural power, and they were God's seal to his commission. Nature could not do these things, it was the God of nature; the cures were many, of diseases incurable by the art of the physician, of persons that were strangers, of all ages and conditions; the cures were wrought openly, before many witnesses, in mixed companies of persons that would have denied the matter of fact, if they could have had any colour for so doing; no cure ever failed, or was afterwards called in question; they were wrought speedily, and not (as cures by natural causes) gradually; they were perfect cures, and wrought with a word's speaking; all which proves him *a Teacher come from God,* for, otherwise, none could have done the works that he did, Jn. 3:2. He appeals to these as credentials, *ch.* 11:4, 5; Jn. 5:36. It was expected that the Messiah should work miracles (Jn. 7:31); miracles of this nature (Isa. 35:5, 6); and we have this indisputable proof of his being the Messiah; never was there any man that did thus; and therefore his healing and his preaching generally went together, for the former confirmed the latter; thus here he *began to* do *and to* teach, Acts 1:1.

(2.) The *mercy* of them. The miracles that Moses wrought, to prove his mission, were most of them plagues and judgments, to intimate the terror of that dispensation, though from God; but the miracles that Christ wrought, were most of them cures, and all of them (except the cursing of the barren fig tree) blessings and favours; for the gospel dispensation is founded, and built up in love, and grace, and sweetness; and the management is such as tends not to affright but to allure us to obedience. Christ designed by his cures to win upon people, and to ingratiate himself and his doctrine into their minds, and so to draw them with the bands of love, Hos. 11:4. The miracle of them proved his doctrine *a faithful saying,* and convinced men's judgments; the mercy of them proved it *worthy of all acceptation,* and wrought upon their affections. They were not only *great* works, but *good works,* that he *showed them from his Father* (Jn. 10:32); and this goodness was intended to *lead men to repentance* (Rom. 2:4), as also to show that kindness, and beneficence, and doing good to all, to the utmost of our power and opportunity, are essential branches of that holy religion which Christ came into the world to establish.

(3.) The *mystery* of them. Christ, by curing *bodily diseases,* intended to show, that his great errand into the world was to cure *spiritual maladies.* He is the *Sun of righteousness,* that *arises with this healing under his wings.* As the Converter of sinners, he is the *Physician of souls,* and has taught us to call him so, *ch.* 9:12, 13. Sin is the *sickness, disease,* and *torment* of the soul; Christ *came to take away sin,* and so to heal these. And the particular stories of the cures Christ wrought, may not only be applied spiritually, by way of allusion and illustration, but, I believe, are very much intended to reveal to us spiritual things, and to set before us the way and method of Christ's dealing with souls, in their conversion and sanctification; and those cures are recorded, that were most significant and instructive this way; and they are therefore so to be explained and improved, to the honour and praise of that glorious Redeemer, *who forgiveth all our iniquities, and so healeth all our diseases.*

CHAPTER 5

This chapter, and the two that follow it, are a sermon; a famous sermon; the sermon upon the mount. It is the longest and fullest continued discourse of our Saviour that we have upon record in all the gospels. It is a practical discourse; there is not much of the credenda of Christianity in it — the things to be believed, but it is wholly taken up with the agenda — the things to be done; these Christ began with in his preaching; for if any man will do his will, he shall know of the doctrine, whether it be of God. The circumstances of the sermon being accounted for (*v.* 1, 2), the sermon itself follows, the scope of which is, not to fill our heads with notions, but to guide and regulate our practice. I. He proposes blessedness as the end, and gives us the character of those who are entitled to blessedness (very different from the sentiments of a vain world), in eight beatitudes, which may justly be called paradoxes (*v.* 3–12). II. He prescribes duty as the way, and gives us standing rules of that duty. He directs his disciples, 1. To understand what they are — the salt of the earth, and the lights of the world (*v.* 13–16). 2. To understand what they have to do — they are to be governed by the moral law. Here is, (1.) A general ratification of the law, and a recommendation of it to us, as our rule (*v.* 17–20). (2.) A particular rectification of divers mistakes; or, rather, a reformation of divers wilful, gross corruptions, which the scribes and Pharisees had introduced in their exposition of the law; and an authentic explication of divers branches which most needed to be explained and vindicated (*v.* 20). Particularly, here is an explication, [1.] Of the sixth commandment, which forbids murder (*v.* 21–26). [2.] Of the seventh commandment, against adultery (*v.* 27–32). [3.] Of the third commandment (*v.* 33–37). [4.] Of the law of retaliation (*v.* 38–42). [5.] Of the law of brotherly love (*v.* 43–48). And the scope of the whole is, to show that the law is spiritual.

Verses 1–2

We have here a general account of this sermon.

I. *The Preacher* was our Lord Jesus, the Prince of preachers, the great Prophet of his church, who *came into the world,* to be *the Light of the world.* The prophets and John had *done virtuously* in preaching, *but* Christ *excelled them all.* He is the eternal Wisdom, *that lay in the bosom of the Father, before all worlds,* and perfectly knew his will (Jn. 1:18); and he is the eternal Word, by whom he *has in these last days spoken to us.* The many miraculous cures wrought by Christ in Galilee, which we read of in the close of the foregoing chapter, were intended to make way for this sermon, and to dispose people to receive instructions from one in whom there appeared so much of a divine power and goodness; and, probably, this sermon was the summary, or rehearsal, of what he had preached up and down in the synagogues of Galilee. His text *was, Repent, for the kingdom of heaven is at hand.* This is a sermon on the former part of that text, showing what it is to *repent;* it is to reform, both in judgment and practice; and here he tells us wherein, in answer to that question (Mal. 3:7), *Wherein shall we return?* He afterward preached upon the latter part of the text, when, in divers parables, he showed what the kingdom of heaven is like, *ch.* 13.

II. *The place* was a mountain in Galilee. As in other things, so in this, our Lord Jesus was but ill accommodated; he had no convenient place to preach in, any more than *to lay his head* on. While the scribes and Pharisees had Moses' chair to sit in, with all possible ease, honour, and state, and there corrupted the law; our Lord Jesus, the great Teacher of truth, is driven out to the desert, and finds no better a pulpit than *a mountain* can afford; and not one of the *holy mountains* neither, not one of *the mountains of Zion,* but a common *mountain;* by which Christ would intimate that there is no such distinguishing holiness of places now, under the gospel, as there was under the law; but that it is *the will of God that men should pray* and preach *every where,* any where, provided it be decent and convenient. Christ preached this sermon, which was an exposition of the law, upon a mountain, because upon a *mountain* the law was given; and this was also a solemn promulgation of the Christian law. But observe the difference: when *the law was given,* the Lord *came down* upon the *mountain;* now the Lord *went up:* then, he spoke *in thunder and lightning;* now, *in a still small voice:* then the people were ordered to keep their distance; now they are invited to draw near: a blessed change! If God's grace and goodness are (as they certainly are) his glory, then the glory of the gospel is the glory that excels, for *grace and truth came by Jesus Christ,* 2 Co. 3:7; Heb. 12:18, etc. It was foretold of Zebulun and Issachar, two of the tribes of Galilee (Deu. 33:19), that *they shall call the people to the mountain;* to this *mountain* we are called, to learn *to offer the sacrifices of righteousness.* Now was this *the mountain of the Lord,* where he *taught us his ways,* Isa. 2:2, 3; Mic. 4:1, 2.

III. *The auditors* were *his disciples,* who *came unto him;* came at his call, as appears by comparing Mk. 3:13, Lu. 6:13. To them he directed his speech, because they followed him for love and learning, while others attended him only for cures. *He taught them,* because they were willing to be *taught (the meek will he teach his way);* because they would *understand* what he taught, which to others was foolishness; and because they were to teach others; and it was therefore requisite that they should have a clear and distinct knowledge of these things themselves. The duties prescribed in this sermon were to be conscientiously performed by all those that would *enter into that kingdom of heaven* which they were sent to set up, with hope to have the benefit of it. But though this discourse was directed to the disciples, it was in the hearing of *the multitude;* for it is said (*ch.* 7:28), *The people were astonished.* No bounds were set about *this mountain,* to keep the people off, as were about *mount Sinai* (Ex. 19:12); for, through Christ, we have access to God, not only to speak to him, but to hear from him. Nay, he had an eye to the *multitude,* in preaching this sermon. When the fame of his miracles had brought a vast crowd together, he took the opportunity of so great a confluence of people, to instruct them. Note, It is an encouragement to a faithful minister to cast the net of the gospel where there are a great many fishes, in hope that some will be caught. The sight of a *multitude* puts life into a preacher, which yet must arise from a desire of their profit, not his own praise.

IV. *The solemnity* of his sermon is intimated in that word, *when he was set.* Christ preached many times occasionally, and by interlocutory discourses; but this was a set sermon, *kathisantos autou,* when he had placed himself so as to be best heard. He sat down as a Judge or Lawgiver. It intimates with what sedateness and composure of mind the things of God should be spoken and heard. *He sat,* that *the scriptures might be fulfilled* (Mal. 3:3), *He shall sit as a refiner,* to purge away the dross, the corrupt doctrines of the sons of Levi. He *sat* as *in the throne, judging right* (Ps. 9:4); for *the word he spoke shall judge us.* That phrase, *He opened his mouth,* is only a Hebrew periphrasis of speaking, as Job 3:1. Yet some think it intimates the solemnity of this discourse; the congregation being large, he raised his voice, and spoke louder than usual. He had spoken long *by his servants the prophets,* and *opened their mouths* (Eze. 3:27; 24:27; 33:22); but now *he opened his* own, and spoke with freedom, *as one having authority.* One of the ancients has this remark upon it; Christ *taught* much without *opening his mouth.* that is, by his holy and exemplary life; nay, he *taught,* when, being *led as a lamb to the slaughter, he opened not his mouth,* but now *he opened his mouth, and taught,* that *the scriptures might be fulfilled,* Prov. 8:1, 2, 6. *Doth not wisdom cry — cry on the top of high places?* And *the opening of her lips shall be right things. He taught them,* according to the promise (Isa. 54:13), *All thy children shall be taught of the Lord;* for this purpose he had *the tongue of the learned* (Isa. 50:4), and *the Spirit of the Lord,* Isa. 61:1. *He taught them,* what was the evil they should abhor, and what was the good they should abide and abound in; for Christianity is not a matter of speculation, but is designed to regulate the temper of our minds and the tenour of our conversations; gospel-time is a time of reformation (Heb. 9:10); and by the gospel we must be reformed, must be made good, must be made better. *The truth, as it is in Jesus,* is *the truth which is according to godliness,* Tit. 1:1.

Verses 3–12

Christ begins his sermon with blessings, for *he came into the world to bless us* (Acts 3:26), as *the great High Priest of our profession;* as *the blessed Melchizedec;* as He *in whom all the families of the earth should be blessed,* Gen. 12:3. He came not only to purchase blessings for us, but to pour out and pronounce blessings on us; and here he does it *as one having authority,* as one that can *command the blessing, even life for evermore,* and that is the blessing here again and again promised to the good; his pronouncing them happy makes them so; for those whom he blesses, are blessed indeed. The Old Testament ended with a curse (Mal. 4:6), the gospel begins with a blessing; for *hereunto are we called, that we should inherit the blessing.* Each of the blessings Christ here pronounces has a double intention: 1. To show who they are that are to be accounted truly happy, and what their characters are. 2. What that is wherein true happiness consists, in the promises made to persons of certain characters, the performance of which will make them happy. Now,

1. This is designed to rectify the ruinous mistakes of a blind and carnal world. Blessedness is the thing which men pretend to pursue; *Who will make us to see good?* Ps. 4:6. But most mistake the end, and form a wrong notion of happiness; and then no wonder that they miss the way; they choose their own delusions, and court a shadow. The general opinion is, *Blessed are they* that are rich, and great, and honourable in the world; they spend their days in mirth, and their years in pleasure; they eat the fat, and drink the sweet, and carry all before them with a high hand, and have every sheaf bowing to their sheaf; *happy the people that is in such a case;* and their designs, aims, and purposes are accordingly; they *bless the covetous* (Ps. 10:3); they *will be rich.* Now our Lord Jesus comes to correct this fundamental error, to advance a new hypothesis, and to give us quite another notion of blessedness and blessed people, which, however paradoxical it may appear to those who are prejudiced, yet is in itself, and appears to be to all who are savingly enlightened, a rule and doctrine of eternal truth and certainty, by which we must shortly be judged. If this, therefore, be the beginning of Christ's doctrine, the beginning of a Christian's practice must be to take his measures of happiness from those maxims, and to direct his pursuits accordingly.

2. It is designed to remove the discouragements of the weak and poor who receive the gospel, by assuring them that his gospel did not make those only happy that were eminent in gifts, graces, comforts, and usefulness; but that even *the least in the kingdom of heaven,* whose heart was upright with God, was happy in the honours and privileges of that kingdom.

3. It is designed to invite souls to Christ, and to make way for his law into their hearts. Christ's pronouncing these blessings, not at the end of his sermon, to dismiss the people, but at the beginning of it, to prepare them for what he had further to say to them, may remind us of mount Gerizim and mount Ebal, on which the blessings and cursings of the law were read, Deu. 27:12, etc. *There* the curses are expressed, and the blessings only implied; *here* the blessings are expressed, and the curses implied: in both, *life and death are set before us;* but the law appeared more as a ministration of death, to deter us from sin; the gospel as a dispensation of life, to allure us to Christ, in whom alone all good is to be had. And those who had seen the gracious cures wrought by his hand (*ch.* 4:23, 24), and now heard *the gracious words proceeding out of his mouth,* would say that he was all of a piece, made up of love and sweetness.

4. It is designed to settle and sum up the articles of agreement between God and man. The scope of the divine revelation is to let us know what God expects from us, and what we may then expect from him; and no where is this more fully set forth in a few words than here, nor with a more exact reference to each other; and this is that gospel which we are required to believe; for what is faith but a conformity to these characters, and a dependence upon these promises? The way to happiness is here opened, and made a *highway* (Isa. 35:8); and this coming from the mouth of Jesus Christ, it is intimated that from him, and by him, we are to receive both the seed and the fruit, both the grace required, and the glory promised. Nothing passes between God and fallen man, but through his hand. Some of the wiser heathen had notions of blessedness different from the rest of mankind, and looking toward this of our Saviour. Seneca, undertaking to describe a blessed man, makes it out, that it is only an honest, good man that is to be so called: *De Vitâ Beatâ.* cap. 4. *Cui nullum bonum malumque sit, nisi bonus malusque animus — Quem nec extollant fortuita, nec frangant — Cui vera voluptas erit voluptatum comtemplio — Cui unum bonum honestas, unum malum turpitudo. — In whose estimation nothing is good or evil, but a good or evil heart — Whom no occurrences elate or deject — Whose true pleasure consists in a contempt of pleasure — To whom the only good is virtue, and the only evil vice.*

Our Saviour here gives us eight characters of blessed people; which represent to us the principal graces of a Christian. On each of them a present blessing is pronounced; *Blessed are* they; and to each a future blessing is promised, which is variously expressed, so as to suit the nature of the grace or duty recommended.

Do we ask then who are happy? It is answered,

I. *The poor in spirit* are happy, *v.* 3. There is a poor-spiritedness that is so far from making men blessed that it is a sin and a snare — cowardice and base fear, and a willing subjection to the lusts of men. But this poverty of spirit is a gracious disposition of soul, by which we are emptied of self, in order to our being filled with Jesus Christ. To be *poor in spirit* is, 1. To be contentedly poor, willing to be emptied of worldly wealth, if God orders that to be our lot; to bring our mind to our condition, when it is a low condition. Many are poor in the world, but high in spirit, poor and proud, murmuring and complaining, and blaming their lot, but we must accommodate ourselves to our poverty, must *know how to be abased,* Phil. 4:12. Acknowledging the wisdom of God in appointing us to poverty, we must be easy in it, patiently bear the inconveniences of it, be thankful for what we have, and make the best of that which is. It is to sit loose to all worldly wealth, and not set our hearts upon it, but cheerfully to bear losses and disappointments which may befal us in the most prosperous state. It is not, in pride or pretence, to make ourselves poor, by throwing away what God has given us, especially as those in the church of Rome, who vow poverty, and yet engross the wealth of the nations; but if we be rich in the world we must be *poor in spirit,* that is, we must condescend to the poor and sympathize with them, as being touched with the feeling of their infirmities; we must expect and prepare for poverty; must not inordinately fear or shun it, but must bid it welcome, especially when it comes upon us for keeping a good conscience, Heb. 10:34. Job was *poor in spirit,* when he blessed God in *taking away,* as well as giving. 2. It is to be humble and lowly in our own eyes. To be *poor in spirit,* is to think meanly of ourselves, of what we are, and have, and do; the poor are often taken in the Old Testament for the humble and self-denying, as opposed to those that are at ease, and the proud; it is to be as little children in our opinion of ourselves, weak, foolish, and insignificant, *ch.* 18:4; 19:14. Laodicea was *poor in spirituals,* wretchedly and miserably poor, and yet *rich in spirit,* so well increased with goods, as to *have need of nothing,* Rev. 3:17. On the other hand, Paul was rich in *spirituals,* excelling most in gifts and graces, and yet *poor in spirit, the least of the apostles,* less than the least of all saints, and *nothing* in his own account. It is to look with a holy contempt upon ourselves, to value others and undervalue ourselves in comparison of them. It is to be willing to make ourselves cheap, and mean, and little, to do good; to *become all things to all men.* It is to acknowledge that God is great, and we are mean; that he is holy and we are sinful; that he is all and we are nothing, less than nothing, worse than nothing; and to humble ourselves before him, and under his mighty hand. 3. It is to come off from all confidence in our own righteousness and strength, that we may depend only upon the merit of Christ for our justification, and the spirit and grace of Christ for our sanctification. That *broken and contrite spirit* with which the publican cried for mercy to a poor sinner, is that poverty of spirit. We must call ourselves poor, because always in want of God's grace, always begging at God's door, always hanging on in his house.

Now, (1.) This poverty in spirit is put first among the Christian graces. The philosophers did not reckon humility among their moral virtues, but Christ puts it first. Self-denial is the first lesson to be learned in his school, and poverty of spirit entitled to the first beatitude. The foundation of all other graces is laid in humility. Those who would build high must begin low; and it is an excellent preparative for the entrance of gospel-grace into the soul; it fits the soil to receive the seed. Those *who are weary and heavy laden,* are *the poor in spirit,* and they shall find rest with Christ.

(2.) They are *blessed.* Now they are so, in this world. God looks graciously upon them. They are his little ones, and have their angels. To them he gives more grace; they live the most comfortable lives, and are easy to themselves and all about them, and nothing comes amiss to them; while high spirits are always uneasy.

(3.) *Theirs is the kingdom of heaven.* The kingdom of *grace* is composed of such; they only are fit to be members of Christ's church, which is called *the congregation of the poor* (Ps. 74:19); the kingdom of *glory* is prepared for them. Those who thus humble themselves, and comply with God when he humbles them, shall be thus exalted. The great, high spirits go away with the glory of *the kingdoms of the earth;* but the humble, mild, and yielding souls obtain the glory of *the kingdom of heaven.* We are ready to think concerning those who are rich, and do good with their riches, that, no doubt, *theirs is the kingdom of heaven;* for they can thus lay up in store a good security *for the time to come;* but what shall the poor do, who have not wherewithal to do good? Why, the same happiness is promised to those who are contentedly poor, as to those who are usefully rich. If I am not able to *spend* cheerfully for his sake, if I can but *want* cheerfully for his sake, even that shall be recompensed. And do not we serve a good master then?

II. *They that mourn* are happy (*v.* 4); *Blessed are they that mourn.* This is another strange blessing, and fitly follows the former. The poor are accustomed to mourn, the graciously poor mourn graciously. We are apt to think, Blessed are the *merry;* but Christ, who was himself a great mourner, says, Blessed are the *mourners.* There is a sinful mourning, which is an enemy to blessedness — *the sorrow of the world;* despairing melancholy upon a spiritual account, and disconsolate grief upon a temporal account. There is a natural mourning, which may prove a friend to blessedness, by the grace of God working with it, and sanctifying the afflictions to us, for which we mourn. But there is a gracious mourning, which qualifies for blessedness, an habitual seriousness, the mind mortified to mirth, and an actual sorrow. 1. A penitential mourning for our own sins; this is *godly sorrow,* a sorrow according to God; sorrow for sin, with an eye to Christ, Zec. 12:10. Those are God's mourners, who live a life of repentance, who lament the corruption of their nature, and their many actual transgressions, and God's withdrawings from them; and who, out of regard to God's honour, mourn also for the sins of others, and *sigh and cry for their abominations,* Eze. 9:4. 2. A sympathizing mourning for the afflictions of others; the mourning of those who *weep with them that weep,* are sorrowful *for the solemn assemblies, for the desolations of Zion* (Zep. 3:18; Ps. 137:1), especially who look with compassion on perishing souls, and *weep over* them, as Christ *over Jerusalem.*

Now these gracious mourners, (1.) *Are blessed.* As in vain and sinful *laughter the heart is sorrowful,* so in gracious mourning *the heart* has a serious joy, a secret satisfaction, which a *stranger does not intermeddle with.* They are *blessed,* for they are like the Lord Jesus, who *was a man of sorrows,* and of whom we never read that he laughed, but often that he wept. The are armed against the many temptations that attend vain mirth, and are prepared for the comforts of a sealed pardon and a settled peace. (2.) *They shall be comforted.* Though perhaps they are not immediately comforted, yet plentiful provision is made for their comfort; light is sown for them; and in heaven, it is certain, *they shall be comforted,* as Lazarus, Lu. 16:25. Note, The happiness of heaven consists in being perfectly and eternally comforted, and in the *wiping away of all tears from their eyes.* It *is the joy of our Lord; a fulness of joy and pleasures for evermore;* which will be doubly sweet to those who have been prepared for them by this *godly sorrow.* Heaven will be a heaven indeed to those who go mourning thither; it will be a harvest of joy, the return of a seed-time of tears (Ps. 126:5, 6); a mountain of joy, to which our way lies through a vale of tears. See Isa. 66:10.

III. *The meek* are happy (*v.* 5); *Blessed are the meek.* The meek are those who quietly submit themselves to God, to his word and to his rod, who follow his directions, and comply with his designs, and are *gentle towards all men* (Tit. 3:2); who can bear provocation without being inflamed by it; are either silent, or return a soft answer; and who can show their displeasure when there is occasion for it, without being transported into any indecencies; who can be cool when others are hot; and in their patience keep possession of their own souls, when they can scarcely keep possession of any thing else. *They* are the meek, who are rarely and hardly provoked, but quickly and easily pacified; and who would rather forgive twenty injuries than revenge one, having the rule of their own spirits.

These meek ones are here represented as happy, even in this world. 1. They are *blessed,* for they are like the blessed Jesus, in that wherein particularly they are to learn of him, *ch.* 11:29. They are like the blessed God himself, who is Lord of his anger, and in whom fury is not. They are *blessed,* for they have the most comfortable, undisturbed enjoyment of themselves, their friends, their God; they are fit for any relation, and condition, any company; fit to live, and fit to die. 2. *They shall inherit the earth;* it is quoted from Ps. 37:11, and it is almost the only express temporal promise in all the New Testament. Not that they shall always have much of *the earth,* much less that they shall be put off with that only; but this branch of godliness has, in a special manner, *the promise of life that now is.* Meekness, however ridiculed and run down, has a real tendency to promote our health, wealth, comfort, and safety, even in this world. *The meek* and quiet are observed to live the most easy lives, compared with the froward and turbulent. Or, *They shall inherit the land* (so it may be read), *the land of Canaan,* a type of heaven. So that all the blessedness of heaven above, and all the blessings of earth beneath, are the portion of the meek.

IV. *They that hunger and thirst after righteousness* are happy, *v.* 6. Some understand this as a further instance of our outward poverty, and a low condition in this world, which not only exposes men to injury and wrong, but makes it in vain for them to seek to have justice done to them; they *hunger and thirst after* it, but such is the power on the side of their oppressors, that they cannot have it; they desire only that which is just and equal, but it is denied them by those that *neither fear God nor regard men.* This is a melancholy case! Yet, *blessed are they,* if they suffer these hardships for and with a good conscience; let them hope in God, who will see justice done, right take place, and will deliver the poor from their oppressors, Ps. 103:6. Those who contentedly bear oppression, and quietly refer themselves to God to plead their cause, shall in due time be satisfied, abundantly satisfied, in the wisdom and kindness which shall be manifested in his appearances for them. But it is certainly to be understood spiritually, of such a desire as, being terminated on such an object, is gracious, and the work of God's grace in the soul, and qualifies for the gifts of the divine favour. 1. *Righteousness* is here put for all spiritual blessings. See Ps. 24:5; *ch.* 6:33. They are purchased for us by *the righteousness of Christ;* conveyed and secured by the imputation of that righteousness to us; and confirmed by the faithfulness of God. To have Christ *made of God to us righteousness,* and to be *made the righteousness of God in him;* to have *the whole man renewed in righteousness,* so as to become *a new man,* and to bear the image of God; to have an interest in Christ and the promises — this is *righteousness.* 2. These we must *hunger and thirst after.* We must truly and really desire them, as one who is hungry and thirsty desires meat and drink, who cannot be satisfied with any thing but meat and drink, and will be satisfied with them, though other things be wanting. Our desires of spiritual blessings must be earnest and importunate; "*Give me these, or else I die;* every thing else is dross and chaff, unsatisfying; give me these, and I have enough, though I had nothing else." *Hunger and thirst* are appetites that return frequently, and call for fresh satisfactions; so these holy desires rest not in any thing attained, but are carried out toward renewed pardons, and daily fresh supplies of grace. The quickened soul calls for constant meals of righteousness, grace to do the work of every day in its day, as duly as the living body calls for food. Those who *hunger and thirst* will labour for supplies; so we must not only desire spiritual blessings, but take pains for them in the use of the appointed means. Dr. Hammond, in his practical Catechism, distinguishes between *hunger and thirst. Hunger* is a desire of food to sustain, such as *sanctifying righteousness. Thirst* is the desire of drink to refresh, such as justifying *righteousness,* and the sense of our pardon.

Those who *hunger and thirst* after spiritual blessings, *are blessed* in those desires, and *shall be filled* with those blessings. (1.) They are *blessed* in those desires. Though all desires of grace are not grace (feigned, faint desires are not), yet such a desire as this is; it is an *evidence* of something *good,* and an *earnest* of something *better.* It is a desire of God's own raising, and he will not forsake the work of his own hands. Something or other the soul will be *hungering* and *thirsting* after; therefore *they* are blessed who fasten upon the right object, which is satisfying, and not deceiving; and do not *pant after the dust of the earth,* Amos 2:7; Isa. 55:2. (2.) They *shall be filled* with those blessings. God will give them what they desire to complete their satisfaction. It is God only who can *fill a soul,* whose grace and favour are adequate to its just desires; and he will fill those with *grace for grace,* who, in a sense of their own emptiness, have recourse to his fulness. He *fills the hungry* (Lu. 1:53), *satiates* them, Jer. 31:25. The happiness of heaven will certainly fill the soul; their righteousness shall be complete, the favour of God and his image, both in their full perfection.

V. The *merciful* are happy, *v.* 7. This, like the rest, is a paradox; for the merciful are not taken to be the wisest, nor are likely to be the richest; yet Christ pronounces them *blessed.* Those are the *merciful,* who are piously and charitably inclined to pity, help, and succour persons in misery. A man may be truly *merciful,* who has not wherewithal to be bountiful or liberal; and then God accepts the willing mind. We must not only bear our own afflictions patiently, but we must, by Christian sympathy, partake of the afflictions of our brethren; pity must be shown (Job 6:14), and *bowels of mercy put on* (Col. 3:12); and, being put on, they must put forth themselves in contributing all we can for the assistance of those who are any way in misery. We must have compassion on the souls of others, and help them; pity the ignorant, and instruct them; the careless, and warn them; those who are in a state of sin, and snatch them as *brands out of the burning.* We must have compassion on those who are melancholy and in sorrow, and comfort them (Job 16:5); on those whom we have advantage against, and not be rigorous and severe with them; on those who are in want, and supply them; which if we refuse to do, whatever we pretend, we *shut up the bowels of our compassion,* James 2:15, 16; 1 Jn. 3:17. *Draw out they soul* by *dealing thy bread* to the hungry, Isa. 58:7, 10. Nay, a *good man is merciful to his beast.*

Now as to the merciful. 1. They are *blessed;* so it was said in the Old Testament; *Blessed is he that considers the poor,* Ps. 41:1. Herein they resemble God, whose goodness is his glory; in being *merciful as he is merciful,* we are, in our measure, *perfect as he is perfect.* It is an evidence of love to God; it will be a satisfaction to ourselves, to be any way instrumental for the benefit of others. One of the purest and most refined delights in this world, is that of *doing good.* In this word, *Blessed are the merciful,* is included that saying of Christ, which otherwise we find not in the gospels, *It is more blessed to give than to receive,* Acts 20:35. 2. *They shall obtain mercy;* mercy *with men,* when they need it; *he that watereth, shall be watered also himself* (we know not how soon we may stand in need of kindness, and therefore should be kind); but especially mercy *with God,* for *with the merciful he will show himself merciful,* Ps. 18:25. The most *merciful* and charitable cannot pretend to *merit,* but must fly to mercy. The merciful shall find with God *sparing* mercy (*ch.* 6:14), *supplying* mercy (Prov. 19:17), *sustaining* mercy (Ps. 41:2), mercy in that day (2 Tim. 1:18); may, they shall *inherit the kingdom prepared for them* (*ch.* 25:34, 35); whereas *they* shall have *judgment without mercy* (which can be nothing short of *hell-fire*) who have *shown no mercy.*

VI. The *pure in heart* are happy (*v.* 8); *Blessed are the poor in heart, for they shall see God.* This is the most comprehensive of all the beatitudes; here holiness and happiness ar fully described and put together.

1. Here is the most *comprehensive character* of the blessed: they are *pure in heart.* Note, True religion consists in heart-purity. Those who are inwardly pure, show themselves to be under the power of *pure and undefiled* religion. True Christianity lies in the heart, in the *purity of heart;* the *washing* of that *from wickedness,* Jer. 4:14. We must lift up to God, not only clean hands, but a pure heart, Ps. 24:4, 5; 1 Tim. 1:5. The heart must be *pure,* in opposition to *mixture* — an honest heart that aims well; and pure, in opposition to *pollution* and *defilement;* as wine *unmixed,* as water *unmuddied.* The heart must be kept *pure* from *fleshly lusts,* all unchaste thoughts and desires; and from *worldly lusts;* cov-

etousness is called *filthy lucre;* from all filthiness of flesh and spirit, all that which come *out of the heart,* and *defiles the man.* The heart must be *purified by faith,* and entire for God; must be presented and preserved a chaste virgin to Christ. *Create in me such a clean heart, O God!*

2. Here is the most *comprehensive comfort* of the blessed; They shall see God. Note, (1.) It is the perfection of the soul's happiness to *see God; seeing him,* as we may by faith in our present state, is a *heaven upon earth;* and seeing him as we shall in the future state, in the *heaven of heaven.* To see him *as he is,* face to face, and no longer through a glass darkly; to see him as ours, and to see him and enjoy him; to see him and be like him, and be satisfied with that likeness (Ps. 17:15); and to see him for ever, and never lose the sight of him; this is heaven's happiness. (2.) The happiness of seeing God is promised to those, and those only, who are *pure in heart.* None but the *pure* are capable of *seeing* God, nor would it be a felicity to the impure. What pleasure could an unsanctified soul take in the vision of a holy God? As *he* cannot endure to look upon their iniquity, *so they* cannot endure to look upon his purity; nor shall any unclean thing enter into the new Jerusalem; but all that are *pure in heart,* all that are truly sanctified, have desires wrought in them, which nothing but the sight of God will sanctify; and divine grace will not leave those desires unsatisfied.

VII. The *peace-makers* are happy, *v.* 9. The wisdom that is from above is first *pure,* and then *peaceable;* the blessed ones are *pure* toward God, and *peaceable* toward men; for with reference to both, conscience must be kept *void of offence.* The *peace-makers* are those who have, 1. *A peaceable disposition:* as, to *make a lie,* is to be given and addicted to lying, so, to *make peace,* is to have a strong and hearty affection to peace. *I am for peace,* Ps. 120:7. It is to love, and desire, and delight in peace; to be put in it as in our element, and to study to be quiet. 2. A *peaceable conversation;* industriously, as far as we can, to preserve the peace that it be not broken, and to recover it when it is broken; to hearken to proposals of peace ourselves, and to be ready to make them to others; where distance is among brethren and neighbours, to do all we can to accommodate it, and to be *repairers of the breaches. The making of peace* is sometimes a *thankless office,* and it is the lot of him who parts a fray, to have *blows on both sides;* yet it is a good office, and we must be forward to it. Some think that this is intended especially as a lesson for ministers, who should do all they can to reconcile those who are at variance, and to promote Christian love among those under their charge.

Now, (1.) Such persons are *blessed;* for they have the satisfaction of *enjoying themselves,* by keeping the peace, and of being truly serviceable to others, by disposing them to peace. They are working together with Christ, who came into the world to *slay all enmities,* and to proclaim *peace on earth.* (2.) *They shall be called the children of God;* it will be an evidence to themselves that they are so; God will own them as such, and herein they will resemble him. He is the God of peace; the Son of God is the Prince of peace; the Spirit of adoption is a Spirit of peace. Since God has declared himself reconcilable to us all, he will not own those for his children who are implacable in their enmity to one another; for if the peacemakers are blessed, woe to the peace-breakers! Now by this it appears, that Christ never intended to have his religion propagated by fire and sword, or penal laws, or to acknowledge bigotry, or intemperate zeal, as the mark of his disciples. The children of this world love to fish in troubled waters, but the children of God are the peace-makers, the *quiet in the land.*

VIII. Those who are *persecuted for righteousness' sake,* are happy. This is the greatest paradox of all, and peculiar to Christianity; and therefore it is put last, and more largely insisted upon than any of the rest, *v.* 10–12. This beatitude, like Pharaoh's dream, is doubled, because hardly credited, and yet *the thing is certain;* and in the latter part there is change of the person, "Blessed are *ye* — ye my disciples, and immediate followers. This is that which you, who excel in virtue, are more immediately concerned in; for you must reckon upon hardships and troubles more than other men." Observe here,

1. The case of suffering saints described; and it is a hard case, and a very piteous one.

(1.) They are persecuted, hunted, pursued, run down, as noxious beasts are, that are sought for to be destroyed; as if a Christian did *caput gerere lupinum — bear a wolf's head,* as an outlaw is said to do — any one that finds him may slay him; they are abandoned as the *offscouring of all things;* fined, imprisoned, banished, stripped of their estates, excluded from all places of profit and trust, scourged, racked, tortured, always delivered to death, and accounted as sheep for the slaughter. This has been the effect of the enmity of the serpent's seed against the holy seed, ever since the time *of righteous Abel.* It was so in *Old-Testament* times, as we find, Heb. 11:35, etc. Christ has told us that it would much more be so with the Christian church, and we are not to think it strange, 1 Jn. 3:13. He has left us an example.

(2.) The are *reviled, and have all manner of evil said against them falsely.* Nicknames, and names of reproach, are fastened upon them, upon particular persons, and upon the generation of the righteous in the gross, to render them odious; sometimes to make them formidable, that they may be powerfully assailed; things are laid to their charge that they knew not, Ps. 35:11; Jer. 20:18; Acts 17:6, 7. Those who have had no power in their hands to do them any other mischief, could yet do this; and those who have had power to *persecute,* had found it necessary to *do this too,* to justify themselves in their barbarous usage of them; they could not have baited them, if they had not dressed them in bear-skins; nor have given them the worst of treatment, if they had not first represented them as the worst of men. They will *revile you, and persecute you.* Note, *Reviling* the saints is *persecuting* them, and will be found so shortly, when *hard speeches* must be accounted for (Jude 15), and *cruel mockings,* Heb. 11:36. They will say *all manner of evil of you falsely;* sometimes before the *seat of judgment,* as witnesses; sometimes in the *seat of the scornful,* with *hypocritical mockers at feasts;* they are the *song of the drunkards;* sometimes to face their faces, as Shimei cursed David; sometimes behind their backs, as the enemies of Jeremiah did. Note, There is no evil so black and horrid, which, at one time or other, has not been said, falsely, of Christ's disciples and followers.

(3.) All this is *for righteousness' sake* (*v.* 10); *for my sake, v.* 11. If for *righteousness' sake,* then for *Christ's sake,* for he is nearly interested in the work of righteousness. Enemies to righteousness are enemies to Christ. This precludes those from the blessedness who suffer *justly,* and are evil spoken of *truly* for their real crimes; let such be ashamed and confounded, it is part of their punishment; it is not the suffering, but the cause, that makes the martyr. Those suffer for *righteousness' sake,* who suffer because they will not sin against their consciences, and who suffer for doing that which is good. Whatever pretence persecutors have, it is the power of godliness that they have an enmity to; it is really Christ and his righteousness that are maligned, hated, and persecuted; *For thy sake I have borne reproach,* Ps. 69:9; Rom. 8:36.

2. The comforts of suffering saints laid down.

(1.) They *are blessed;* for they now, in their life-time, receive *their evil things* (Lu. 16:25), and receive them upon a good account. They are *blessed;* for it is an honour to them (Acts 5:41); it is an opportunity of glorifying Christ, of doing good, and of experiencing special comforts and visits of grace and tokens of his presence, 2 Co. 1:5; Dan. 3:25; Rom. 8:29.

(2.) They shall be *recompensed;* Theirs is *the kingdom of heaven.* They have at present a sure title to it, and sweet foretastes of it; and shall ere long be in possession of it. Though there be nothing in those sufferings that can, in strictness, merit of God (for the sins of the best deserve the worst), yet this is here promised as a *reward* (*v.* 12); *Great is your reward in heaven:* so great, as far to transcend the service. It is *in heaven,* future, and out of sight; but well secured, out of the reach of chance, fraud, and violence. Note, God will provide that those who lose *for* him, though it be life itself, shall not lose *by* him in the end. Heaven, at last, will be an abundant recompence for all the difficulties we meet with in our way. This is that which has borne up the suffering saints in all ages — this *joy set before them.*

(3.) *"So persecuted they the prophets that were before you, v.* 12. They were *before you* in excellency, above what you are yet arrived at; they were *before you* in time, that they might be examples to you of *suffering affliction* and *of patience,* James 5:10. They were in like manner persecuted and abused; and can you expect to go to heaven in a way by yourself? Was not Isaiah mocked for his *line upon line? Elisha* for his *bald head?* Were not all the prophets thus treated? Therefore *marvel not* at it as a *strange* thing, *murmur not* at it as a *hard* thing; it is a comfort to see the way of suffering a beaten road, and an honour to follow such leaders. That grace which was *sufficient for them,* to carry them through their sufferings, shall not be *deficient to you.* Those who are your enemies are the seed and successors of them who of old mocked the messengers of the Lord," 2 Chr. 36:16; *ch.* 23:31; Acts 7:52.

(4.) Therefore *rejoice and be exceeding glad, v.* 12. It is not enough to be patient and content under these sufferings as under common afflictions, and not to render railing for railing; but we must rejoice, because the honour and dignity, the pleasure and advantage, of suffering for Christ, are much more considerable than the pain or shame of it. Not that we must take a *pride* in our sufferings, (that spoils all), but we must take a *pleasure* in them, as Paul (2 Co. 12:10); as knowing that Christ is herein *before-hand* with us, and that he will not be *behind-hand* with us, 1 Pt. 4:12, 13.

Verses 13–16

Christ had lately called his disciples, and told them that they should be *fishers of men;* here he tells them further what he designed them to be — *the salt of the earth,* and *lights of the world,* that they might be indeed what it was expected they should be.

I. *Ye are the salt of the earth. This* would encourage and support them under their sufferings, that, though they should be treated with contempt, yet they should really be blessings to the world, and the more so for their suffering thus. The prophets, who went before them, were the salt of the land of Canaan; but the apostles were the salt of *the whole earth,* for they must *go into all the world to preach the gospel.* It was a discouragement to them that they were so *few* and so *weak.* What could they do in so large a province as *the whole earth?* Nothing, if they were to work by force of arms and dint of sword; but, being to work silent as salt, one handful of that salt would diffuse its savour far and wide; would go a great way, and work insensibly and irresistibly as leaven, *ch.* 13:33. The doctrine of the gospel is as *salt;* it is penetrating, *quick,* and *powerful* (Heb. 4:12); it reaches *the heart* Acts 2:37. It is cleansing, it is relishing, and preserves from putrefaction. We read of the *savour of the knowledge of Christ* (2 Co. 2:14); for all other learning is insipid without that. An everlasting covenant is called a *covenant of salt* (Num. 18:19); and the gospel is an everlasting gospel. Salt was required in all the sacrifices (Lev. 2:13), in Ezekiel's mystical temple, Eze. 43:24. Now Christ's disciples having themselves learned the doctrine of the gospel, and being employed to teach it to others, were as salt. Note, Christians, and especially ministers, are the salt of the earth.

1. If they be as they should be they are *as good salt,* white, and small, and broken into many grains, but very useful and necessary. Pliny says, *Sine sale, vita humana non potest degere — Without salt human life cannot be sustained.* See in this, (1.) What they are to be in themselves — seasoned with the gospel, with the salt of grace; thoughts and affections, words and actions, all seasoned with grace, Col. 4:6. *Have salt in yourselves,* else you cannot diffuse it among others, Mk. 9:50. (2.) What they are to be to others; they must not only *be* good but *do* good, must insinuate themselves into the minds of the people, not to serve any secular interest of their own, but that they might transform them into the taste and relish of the gospel. (3.) What great blessings they are to the world. Mankind, lying in ignorance and wickedness, were a vast heap of unsavoury stuff, ready to putrefy; but Christ sent forth his disciples, by their lives and doctrines, to season it with knowledge and grace, and so to render it acceptable to God, to the angels, and to all that relish divine things. (4.) How they must expect to be disposed of. They must not be laid on a heap, must not continue always together at Jerusalem, but must be scattered as salt upon the meat, here a grain and there a grain; as the Levites were dispersed in Israel, that, wherever they live, they may communicate their savour. Some have observed, that whereas it is foolishly called an ill omen to have the salt fall towards us, it is really an ill omen to have the salt fall from us.

2. If they be not, they are as *salt* that has *lost its savour.* If you, who should season others, are yourselves unsavoury, void of spiritual life, relish, and vigour; if a Christian be so, especially if a minister be so, his condition is very sad; for, (1.) He is *irrecoverable: Wherewith shall it be salted?* Salt is a remedy for *unsavoury meat,* but there is no remedy for *unsavoury salt.* Christianity will give a man a relish; but if a man can take up and continue the profession of it, and yet remain flat and foolish, and graceless and insipid, no other

doctrine, no other means, can be applied, to make him savoury. If Christianity do not do it, nothing will. (2.) He is *unprofitable: It is thenceforth good for nothing;* what use can it be put to, in which it will not do more hurt than good? As a man without reason, so is a Christian without grace. A wicked man is the worst of creatures; a wicked Christian is the worst of men; and a wicked minister is the worst of Christians. (3.) He is doomed to ruin and rejection; He shall be *cast out* — expelled the church and the communion of the faithful, to which he is a blot and a burden; and he shall be *trodden under foot of men.* Let God be glorified in the shame and rejection of those by whom he has been reproached, and who have made themselves fit for nothing but to be trampled upon.

II. *Ye are the light of the world, v.* 14. This also bespeaks them useful, as the former *(Sole et sale nihil utilius — Nothing more useful than the sun and salt),* but more glorious. All Christians are *light in the Lord* (Eph. 5:8), and must *shine as lights* (Phil. 2:15), but ministers in a special manner. Christ call himself *the Light of the world* (Jn. 8:12), and they are *workers together with him,* and have some of his honour put upon them. Truly *the light is sweet,* it is welcome; the light of the first day of the world was so, when it *shone out of darkness;* so is the morning light of every day; so is the gospel, and those that spread it, to all sensible people. The *world sat in darkness,* Christ raised up his disciples to shine in it; and, that they may do so, from him they borrow and derive their light.

This similitude is here explained in two things:

1. As *the lights of the world,* they are illustrious and conspicuous, and have many eyes upon them. A city that is *set on a hill cannot be hid.* The disciples of Christ, especially those who are forward and zealous in his service, become remarkable, and are taken notice of as beacons. They are for *signs* (Isa. 7:18), *men wondered at* (Zec. 3:8); all their neighbours have any eye upon them. Some admire them, commend them, rejoice in them, and study to imitate them; others envy them, hate them, censure them, and study to blast them. They are concerned therefore to *walk circumspectly,* because of *their observers;* they are as *spectacles to the world,* and must take heed of every thing that *looks ill,* because they are so much *looked at.* The disciples of Christ were obscure men before he called them, but the character he put upon them dignified them, and as preachers of the gospel they made a figure; and though they were reproached for it by some, they were respected for it by others, advanced to thrones, and made judges (Lu. 22:30); for Christ will honour those that honour him.

2. As the *lights of the world,* they are intended to illuminate and give light to others (*v.* 15), and therefore, (1.) They shall be *set up* as lights. Christ has lighted these candles, they shall not be put under a bushel, not confined always, as they are now, to the cities of Galilee, or the lost sheep of the house of Israel, but they shall be sent into all the world. The churches are the candlesticks, the golden candlesticks, in which these lights are placed, that they light may be diffused; and the gospel is so strong a light, and carries with it so much of its own evidence, that, *like a city on a hill, it cannot be hid,* it cannot but appear to be from God, to all those who do not wilfully shut their eyes against it. It will *give light to all that are in the house,* to all that will draw near to it, and come where it is. Those to whom it does not give light, must thank themselves; they will not be in the house with it; will not make a diligent and impartial enquiry into it, but are prejudiced against it. (2.) They must *shine* as lights, [1.] By their *good preaching.* The knowledge they have, they must communicate for the good of others; not put it *under a bushel,* but spread it. The talent must not be buried in a napkin, but traded with. The disciples of Christ must not muffle themselves up in privacy and obscurity, under pretence of contemplation, modesty, or self-preservation, but, *as they have received the gift,* must *minister the same,* Lu. 12:3. [2.] By their *good living.* They must be *burning and shining lights* (Jn. 5:35); must evidence, in their whole conversation, that they are indeed followers of Christ, James 3:13. They must be to others for instruction, direction, quickening, and comfort, Job 29:11.

See here, *First, How* our light must shine — by doing such *good works* as men *may see,* and may approve of; such works as are of *good report* among them that are without, and as will therefore give them cause to think well of Christianity. We must do good works *that may be seen* to the edification of others, but not *that they may be seen* to our own ostentation; we are bid to pray in secret, and what lies between God and our souls, must be kept to ourselves; but that which is of itself open and obvious to the sight of men, we must study to make *congruous* to our profession, and praiseworthy, Phil. 4:8. Those about us must not only *hear* our good words, but *see* our good works; that they may be convinced that religion is more than a bare name, and that we do not only make a profession of it, but abide under the power of it.

Secondly, For what *end* our light must shine — "That those who see your good works may be brought, not to glorify *you* (which was the things the Pharisees aimed at, and it spoiled all their performances), but to *glorify your Father which is in heaven."* Note, The glory of God is the great thing we must aim at in every thing we do in religion, 1 Pt. 4:11. In this centre the lines of all our actions must meet. We must not only endeavor to glorify God ourselves, but we must do all we can to bring others to glorify him. The sight of our *good works* will do this, by furnishing them, 1. With *matter for praise.* "Let them see *your good works,* that they may see the power of God's grace in you, and may thank him for it, and give him the glory of it, who has given such power unto men." 2. With *motives of piety.* "Let them see your good works, that they may be convinced of the truth and excellency of the Christian religion, may be provoked by a holy emulation to imitate your good works, and so may glorify God." Note, The holy, regular, and exemplary conversation of the saints, may do much towards the conversion of sinners; those who are unacquainted with religion, may hereby be brought to know what it is. Examples teach. And those who are prejudiced against it, may hereby by brought in love with it, and thus there is a winning virtue in a godly conversation.

Verses 17–20

Those to whom Christ preached, and for whose use he gave these instructions to his disciples, were such as in their religion had an eye, 1. To the *scriptures* of the *Old Testament* as their rule, and therein Christ here shows them they were in the right: 2. To the scribes and the Pharisees as their *example,* and therein Christ here shows them they were in the wrong; for,

I. The rule which Christ came to establish exactly agreed with the scriptures of the Old Testament, here called *the law* and *the prophets.* The *prophets* were commentators upon the law, and both together made up that rule of faith and practice which Christ found upon the throne in the Jewish church, and here he keeps it on the throne.

1. He protests against the thought of cancelling and weakening the *Old Testament; Think not that I am come to destroy the law and the prophets.* (1.) "Let not the pious Jews, who have an affection for the *law and the prophets, fear* that I come to *destroy* them." Let them be not prejudiced against Christ and his doctrine, from a jealousy that this kingdom he came to set up, would derogate from the honour of the scriptures, which they had embraced as coming from God, and of which they had experienced the power and purity; no, let them be satisfied that Christ has no ill design upon the law and the prophets. "Let not the profane Jews, who have a disaffection to the law and the prophets, and are weary of that yoke, hope that I am come to destroy them." Let not carnal libertines imagine that the Messiah is come to discharge them from the obligation of divine precepts and yet to secure to them divine promises, to make the happy and yet to give them leave to live as they list. Christ commands nothing now which was forbidden either by the law of nature or the moral law, nor forbids any thing which those laws had enjoined; it is a great mistake to think he does, and he here takes care to rectify the mistake; *I am not come to destroy.* The Saviour of souls is the *destroyer* of nothing but the *works of the devil,* of nothing that comes from God, much less of those excellent dictates which we have from Moses and the prophets. No, he came to *fulfil* them. That is, [1.] To obey the commands of the law, for he was *made under the law,* Gal. 4:4. He in all respects yielded obedience to the law, honoured his parents, sanctified the sabbath, prayed, gave alms, and did that which never any one else did, obeyed perfectly, and never broke the law in any thing. [2.] To make good the promises of the law, and the predictions of the prophets, which did all bear witness to him. The covenant of grace is, for substance, the same now that it was then, and Christ the Mediator of it. [3.] To answer the types of the law; thus (as bishop Tillotson expresses it), he did not make *void,* but make *good,* the ceremonial law, and manifested himself to be the Substance of all those shadows. [4.] To fill up the defects of it, and so to complete and perfect it. Thus the word *plērōsai* properly signifies. If we consider the law as a vessel that had some water in it before, he did not come to pour out the water, but to fill the vessel up to the brim; or, as a picture that is first rough-drawn, displays some outlines only of the piece intended, which are afterwards filled up; so Christ made an improvement of the law and the prophets by his additions and explications. [5.] To carry on the same design; the Christian institutes are so far from thwarting and contradicting that which was the main design of the Jewish religion, that they promote it to the highest degree. The gospel is the *time of reformation* (Heb. 9:10), not the repeal of the law, but the amendment of it, and, consequently, its establishment.

2. He asserts the perpetuity of it; that not only he designed not the abrogation of it, but that it never should be abrogated (*v.* 18); *"Verily I say unto you,* I, the *Amen,* the faithful Witness, solemnly declare it, that *till heaven and earth pass,* when time shall be no more, and the unchangeable state of recompences shall supersede all laws, *one jot, or one tittle,* the least and most minute circumstance, *shall in no wise pass from the law till all be fulfilled;"* for what is it that God is doing in all the operations both of providence and grace, but fulfilling the scripture? Heaven and earth shall come together, and all the fulness thereof be wrapped up in ruin and confusion, rather than any word of God shall fall to the ground, or be in vain. *The word of the Lord endures for ever,* both that of the law, and that of the gospel. Observe, The care of God concerning his law extends itself even to those things that seem to be of least account in it, the iotas and the tittles; for whatever belongs to God, and bears his stamp, be it ever so little, shall be preserved. The laws of men are conscious to themselves of so much imperfection, that they allow it for a maxim, *Apices juris non sunt jura — The extreme points of the law are not the law,* but God will stand by and maintain every iota and every tittle of his law.

3. He gives it in charge to his disciples, carefully to preserve the law, and shows them the danger of the neglect and contempt of it (*v.* 19); *Whosoever therefore shall break one of the least commandments of the law of Moses,* much more any of the greater, as the Pharisees did, who neglected the weightier matters of the law, and shall teach men so as they did, who made void the commandment of God with their traditions (*ch.* 15:3), *he shall be called the least in the kingdom of heaven.* Though the Pharisees be cried up for such teachers as should be, they shall not be employed as teachers in Christ's kingdom; but *whosoever shall do and teach them,* as Christ's disciples would, and thereby prove themselves better friends to the *Old Testament* than the Pharisees were, they, though despised by men, shall be *called great in the kingdom of heaven.* Note, (1.) Among the commands of God there are some less than others; none absolutely little, but comparatively so. The Jews reckon the least of the commandments of the law to be that of the bird's nest (Deu. 22:6, 7); yet even that had a significance and an intention very great and considerable. (2.) It is a dangerous thing, in doctrine or practice, to disannul the least of God's commands; to break them, that is, to go about either to *contract the extent,* or *weaken the obligation* of them; whoever does so, will find it is at his peril. Thus to vacate any of the ten commandments, is too bold a stroke for the jealous God to pass by. it is something more than transgressing the law, it is making void the law, Ps. 119:126. (3.) That the further such corruptions as they spread, the worse they are. It is impudence enough to break the command, but is a greater degree of it to teach men so. This plainly refers to those who at this time sat in Moses' seat, and by their comments corrupted and perverted the text. Opinions that tend to the destruction of serious godliness and the vitals of religion, by corrupt glosses on the scripture, are bad when they are held, but worse when they are propagated and taught, as the word of God. He that does so, shall be called *least in the kingdom of heaven,* in the kingdom of glory; he shall never come thither, but be eternally excluded; or, rather, in the kingdom of the gospel-church. He is so far from deserving the dignity of a teacher in it, that he shall not so much as be accounted a member of it. The prophet that teaches these lies shall be the tail in that kingdom (Isa. 9:15); when truth shall appear in its own evidence, such corrupt teachers, though cried up as the Pharisees, shall be of no account with the wise and good. Noth-

ing makes ministers more contemptible and base than corrupting the law, Mal. 2:8, 11. Those who extenuate and encourage sin, and discountenance and put contempt upon strictness in religion and serious devotion, are the dregs of the church. But, on the other hand, Those are truly honourable, and of great account in the church of Christ, who lay out themselves by their life and doctrine to promote the purity and strictness of practical religion; who both do and teach that which is good; for those who do not as they teach, pull down with one hand what they build up with the other, and give themselves the lie, and tempt men to think that all religion is a delusion; but those who speak from experience, who live up to what they preach, are truly great; they honour God, and God will honour them (1 Sa. 2:30), and hereafter they shall shine as the *stars in the kingdom of our Father.*

II. The righteousness which Christ came to establish by this rule, must exceed that of the scribes and Pharisees, *v.* 20. This was strange doctrine to those who looked upon the scribes and Pharisees as having arrived at the highest pitch of religion. The scribes were the most noted teachers of the law, and the Pharisees the most celebrated professors of it, and they both sat in Moses' chair (*ch.* 23:2), and had such a reputation among the people, that they were looked upon as super-conformable to the law, and people did not think themselves obliged to be as good as they; it was therefore a great surprise to them, to hear that they must be better than they, or they should not go to heaven; and therefore Christ here avers it with solemnity; *I say unto you,* It is so. The scribes and Pharisees were enemies to Christ and his doctrine, and were great oppressors; and yet it must be owned, that there was something commendable in them. They were much in fasting and prayer, and giving of alms; they were punctual in observing the ceremonial appointments, and made it their business to teach others; they had such an interest in the people that they ought, if but two men went to heaven, one would be a Pharisee; and yet our Lord Jesus here tells his disciples, that the religion he came to establish, did not only exclude the badness, but excel the goodness, of the scribes and Pharisees. We must do more than they, and better than they, or we shall come short of heaven. They were *partial in the law,* and laid most stress upon the ritual part of it; but we must be *universal,* and not think it enough to give the priest his tithe, but must give God our hearts. They minded only the *outside,* but we must make conscience of *inside* godliness. They aimed at the *praise* and *applause of men,* but we must aim at *acceptance with God:* they were *proud* of what they did in religion, and trusted to it as a *righteousness;* but we, when we have done all, must *deny ourselves,* and say, We are *unprofitable servants,* and trust only to the *righteousness of Christ;* and thus we may go beyond the scribes and Pharisees.

Verses 21–26

Christ having laid down these principles, that Moses and the prophets were still to be their rulers, but that the scribes and Pharisees were to be no longer their rulers, proceeds to expound the law in some particular instances, and to vindicate it from the corrupt glosses which those expositors had put upon it. He adds not any thing new, only limits and restrains some permissions which had been abused: and as to the precepts, shows the breadth, strictness, and spiritual nature of them, adding such explanatory statutes as made them more clear, and tended much toward the perfecting of our obedience to them. In these verses, he explains the law of the sixth commandment, according to the true intent and full extent of it.

I. Here is the *command itself* laid down (*v.* 12); *We have heard it,* and remember it; he speaks *to them who know the law,* who had Moses read to them in their synagogues every sabbath-day; you have heard that it was said *by them,* or rather as it is in the margin, *to them of old time,* to your forefathers the Jews, *Thou shalt not kill.* Note, The laws of God are not novel, upstart laws, but were delivered to them of old time; they are ancient laws, but of that nature as never to be *antiquated* nor grow *obsolete.* The moral law agrees with the law of nature, and the eternal rules and reasons of good and evil, that is, the rectitude of the eternal Mind. *Killing* is here forbidden, killing ourselves, killing any other, directly or indirectly, or being any way accessory to it. The law of God, the God of life, is a hedge of protection about our lives. It was one of the precepts of Noah, Gen. 9:5, 6.

II. The exposition of this command which the Jewish teachers contended themselves with; their comment upon it was, *Whosoever shall kill, shall be in danger of the judgment.* This was all they had to say upon it, that wilful murderers were liable to the sword of justice, and casual ones to the judgment of the city of refuge. The courts of judgment sat in the gate of their principal cities; the judges, ordinarily, were in number twenty-three; these tried, condemned, and executed murderers; so that whoever killed, was in danger of their judgment. Now this gloss of theirs upon this commandment was faulty, for it intimated, 1. That the law of the sixth commandment was only external, and forbade no more than the act of murder, and laid to restraint upon the inward lusts, from which *wars and fightings come.* This was indeed the *prōton pseudos — the fundamental error* of the Jewish teachers, that the divine law prohibited only the sinful act, not the sinful thought; they were disposed *haerere in cortice — to rest in the letter* of the law, and they never enquired into the spiritual meaning of it. Paul, while a Pharisee, did not, till, by the key of the tenth commandment, divine grace let him into the knowledge of the spiritual nature of all the rest, Rom. 7:7, 14. 2. Another mistake of theirs was, that this law was merely *political* and *municipal,* given for them, and intended as a directory for their courts, and no more; as if they only were the people, and the wisdom of the law must die with them.

III. The exposition which Christ gave of this commandment; and we are sure that according to his exposition of it we must be judged hereafter, and therefore ought to be ruled now. *The commandment is exceeding broad,* and not to be limited by the will of the flesh, or the will of men.

1. Christ tells them that *rash anger is heart-murder* (*v.* 22); *Whosoever is angry with his brother without a cause,* breaks the sixth commandment. By our *brother* here, we are to understand any person, though ever so much our inferior, as a child, a servant, for we are all *made of one blood.* Anger is a natural passion; there are cases in which it is lawful and laudable; but it is then *sinful,* when we are angry without cause. The word is *eikē,* which signifies, *sine causâ, sine effectu, et sine modo — without cause, without any good effect, without moderation;* so that the anger is then sinful, (1.) When it is without any just provocation given; either for no cause, or no good cause, or no great and proportionable cause; when we are angry at children or servants for that which could not be helped, which was only a piece of forgetfulness or mistake, that we ourselves might easily have been guilty of, and for which we should not have been angry at ourselves; when we are angry upon groundless surmises, or for trivial affronts not worth speaking of. (2.) When it is without any good end aimed at, merely to show our authority, to gratify a brutish passion, to let people know our resentments, and excite ourselves to revenge, then it is in vain, it is to do hurt; whereas if we are at any time angry, it should be to awaken the offender to repentance, and prevent his doing so again; to clear ourselves (2 Co. 7:11), and to give warning to others. (3.) When it exceeds due bounds; when we are hardy and headstrong in our anger, violent and vehement, outrageous and mischievous, and when we seek the hurt of those we are displeased at. This is a breach of the sixth commandment, for he that is thus angry, would kill if he could and durst; he has taken the first step toward it; Cain's killing his brother began in anger; he is a murderer in the account of God, who knows his heart, whence murder proceeds, *ch.* 15:19.

2. He tells them, that given opprobrious language to our brother is tongue-murder, calling him, *Raca,* and, *Thou fool.* When this is done with mildness and for a good end, to convince others of their vanity and folly, it is not sinful. Thus James says, *O vain man;* and Paul, *Thou fool;* and Christ himself, *O fools, and slow of heart.* But when it proceeds from anger and malice within, it is the smoke of that fire which is kindled from hell, and falls under the same character. (1.) *Raca* is a scornful word, and comes from pride, "Thou empty fellow;" it is the language of that which Solomon calls *proud wrath* (Prov. 21:24), which tramples upon our brother — disdains *to set him even with the dogs of our flock. This people who knoweth not the law, is cursed,* is such language, Jn. 7:49. (2.) *Thou fool,* is a spiteful word, and comes from hatred; looking upon him, not only as mean and not to be honoured, but as vile and not to be loved; "Thou wicked man, thou reprobate." The former speaks a man without sense, this (in scripture language) speaks a man without grace; the more the reproach touches his spiritual condition, the worse it is; the former is a haughty taunting of our brother, this is a malicious censuring and condemning of him, as abandoned of God. Now this is a breach of the sixth commandment; malicious slanders and censures are *poison under the tongue,* that kills secretly and slowly; *bitter words* are as *arrows* that would suddenly (Ps. 64:3), or as a sword in the bones. The good name of our neighbour, which is better than life, is thereby stabbed and murdered; and it is an evidence of such an ill-will to our neighbour as would strike at his life, if it were in our power.

3. He tells them, that how light soever they made of these sins, they would certainly be reckoned for; he *that is angry with is brother shall be in danger of the judgment* and anger of God; he that calls him *Raca, shall be in danger of the council,* of being punished by the Sanhedrim for reviling an Israelite; *but whosoever saith, Thou fool,* thou profane person, thou child of hell, *shall be in danger of hell-fire,* to which he condemns his brother; so the learned Dr. Whitby. Some think, in allusion to the penalties used in the several courts of judgment among the Jews, Christ shows that the sin of rash anger exposes men to lower or higher punishments, according to the degrees of its proceeding. The Jews had three capital punishments, each worse than the other; beheading, which was inflicted by the judgment; stoning, by the council or chief Sanhedrim; and burning *in the valley of the son of Hinnom,* which was used only in extraordinary cases: it signifies, therefore, that rash anger and reproachful language are damning sins; but some are more sinful than others, and accordingly there is a greater damnation, and a sorer punishment reserved for them: Christ would thus show which sin was most sinful, by showing which it was the punishment whereof was most dreadful.

IV. From all this it is here inferred, that we ought carefully to preserve Christian love and peace with our brethren, and that if at any time a breach happens, we should labour for a reconciliation, by confessing our fault, humbling ourselves to our brother, begging his pardon, and making restitution, or offering satisfaction for wrong done in word or deed, according as the nature of the thing is; and that we should do this quickly for two reasons:

1. Because, till this be done, we are utterly unfit for communion with God in holy ordinances, *v.* 23, 24. The case supposed is, *"That thy brother have* somewhat *against thee,"* that thou has injured and offended him, either really or in his apprehension; if thou are the party offended, there needs not this delay; if thou *have aught against thy brother,* make short work of it; no more is to be done but to forgive him (Mk. 11:25), and forgive the injury; but if the quarrel began on thy side, and the fault was either at first or afterwards thine, so *that thy brother* has a controversy with *thee, go* and *be reconciled to* him before thou *offer thy gift at the altar,* before thou approach solemnly to God in the gospel-services of prayer and praise, hearing the word or the sacraments. Note, (1.) When we are addressing ourselves to any religious exercises, it is good for us to take that occasion of serious reflection and self-examination: there are many things to be *remembered,* when we *bring our gift to the altar,* and this among the rest, whether *our brother hath aught against us;* then, if ever, we are disposed to be serious, and therefore should then call ourselves to an account. (2.) Religious exercises are not acceptable to God, if they are performed when we are in wrath; envy, malice, and uncharitableness, are sins so displeasing to God, that nothing pleases him which comes from a heart wherein they are predominant, 1 Tim. 2:8. Prayers made in wrath are written in gall, Isa. 1:15; 58:4. (3.) Love or charity is so much *better than all burnt-offerings and sacrifice,* that God will have reconciliation made with an offended brother before the gift be offered; he is content to stay for the gift, rather than have it offered while we are under guilt and engaged in a quarrel. (4.) Though we are unfitted for communion with God, by a continual quarrel with a brother, yet that can be no excuse for the omission or neglect of our duty: *"Leave there thy gift before the altar,* lest otherwise, when thou has gone away, thou be tempted not to come again." Many give this as a reason why they do not come to church or to the communion, because they are at variance with some neighbour; and whose fault is that? One sin will never excuse another, but will rather double the guilt. Want of charity cannot justify the want of piety. The difficulty is easily got over; those who have wronged us, we must forgive; and those whom we have wronged, we must make satisfaction to, or at least make a tender of it, and desire a re-

newal of the friendship, so that if reconciliation be not made, it may not be our fault; *and then come,* come and welcome, *come and offer thy gift,* and it shall be accepted. *Therefore* we must *not let the sun go down upon our wrath* any day, because we must go to prayer before we go to sleep; much less let the sun rise *upon our wrath* on a sabbath-day, because it is a day of prayer.

2. Because, till this be done, we lie exposed to much danger, *v.* 25, 26. It is at our peril if we do not labour after an agreement, and that quickly, upon two accounts:

(1.) Upon a temporal account. If the offence we have done to our brother, in his body, goods, or reputation, be such as will bear action, in which he may recover considerable damages, it is our wisdom, and it is our duty to our family, to prevent that by a humble submission and a just and peaceable satisfaction; lest otherwise he recover it by law, and put us to the extremity of a prison. In such a case it is better to compound and make the best terms we can, than to stand it out; for it is in vain to contend with the law, and there is danger of our being crushed by it. Many ruin their estates by an obstinate persisting in the offences they have given, which would soon have been pacified by a little yielding at first. Solomon's advice in case of suretyship is, *Go, humble thyself,* and so secure *and deliver thyself,* Prov. 6:1–5. It is good to agree, for the law is costly. Though we must be merciful to those we have advantage against, yet we must be just to those that have advantage against us, as far as we are able. "Agree, and compound *with thine adversary quickly,* lest he be exasperated by thy stubbornness, and provoked to insist upon the utmost demand, and will not make thee the abatement which at first he would have made." A prison is an uncomfortable place to those who are brought to it by their own pride and prodigality, their own wilfulness and folly.

(2.) Upon a spiritual account. "Go, and be *reconciled to thy brother,* be just to him, be friendly with him, because while the quarrel continues, as thou art unfit to *bring thy gift to the altar,* unfit to come to *the table of the Lord,* so thou art unfit to die: if thou persist in this sin, there is danger lest thou be suddenly snatched away by the wrath of God, whose judgment thou canst not escape nor except against; and if that iniquity be laid to thy charge, thou art undone for ever." Hell is a prison for all that live and die in malice and uncharitableness, for all that are *contentious* (Rom. 2:8), and out of that prison there is no rescue, no redemption, no escape, to eternity.

This is very applicable to the great business of our reconciliation to God through Christ; *Agree with him quickly, whilst thou art in the way.* Note, [1.] The great God is an Adversary to all sinners, *antidikos — a law-adversary;* he has a controversy with them, an action against them. [2.] It is our concern to *agree with him,* to acquaint ourselves with him, that we may *be at peace,* Job 22:21; 2 Co. 5:20. [3.] It is our wisdom to do this *quickly, while we are in the way.* While we are alive, *we are in the way;* after death, it will be too late to do it; therefore *give not sleep to thine eyes* till it be done. [4.] They who continue in a state of enmity to God, are continually exposed to the arrests of his justice, and the most dreadful instances of his wrath. Christ is the Judge, to whom impenitent sinners will be delivered; for *all judgment is committed to the Son;* he that was rejected as a Saviour, cannot be escaped as a Judge, Rev. 6:16, 17. It is a fearful thing to be thus turned over to the Lord Jesus, when the Lamb shall become the Lion. Angels are the officers to whom Christ will deliver them (*ch.* 13:41, 42); devils are so too, having the *power of death* as executioners to all unbelievers, Heb. 2:14. Hell is the prison, into which those will be cast that continue in a state of enmity to God, 2 Pt. 2:4. [5.] Damned sinners must remain in it to eternity; they shall not *depart till they have paid the uttermost farthing,* and that will not be to the utmost ages of eternity: divine justice will be for ever in the satisfying, but never satisfied.

Verses 27–32

We have here an exposition of the seventh commandment, given us by the same hand that made the law, and therefore was fittest to be the interpreter of it: it is the law against uncleanness, which fitly follows upon the former; *that* laid a restraint upon sinful passions, *this* upon sinful appetites, both which ought always to be under the government of reason and conscience, and if indulged, are equally pernicious.

I. The command is here laid down (*v.* 27), *Thou shalt not commit adultery;* which includes a prohibition of all other acts of uncleanness, and the desire of them: but the Pharisees, in their expositions of this command, made it to extend no further than the act of adultery, suggesting, that if the iniquity was only *regarded in the heart,* and went no further, God could not hear it, would not regard it (Ps. 66:18), and therefore they thought it enough to be able to say that they were *no adulterers,* Lu. 18:11.

II. It is here explained in the strictness of it, in three things, which would seem new and strange to those who had been always governed by the tradition of the elders, and took all for oracular that they taught.

1. We are here taught, that there is such a thing as *heart-adultery,* adulterous thoughts and dispositions, which never proceed to the act of adultery or fornication; and perhaps the defilement which these give to the soul, that is here so clearly asserted, was not only included in the seventh commandment, but was signified and intended in many of those ceremonial pollutions under the law, for which they were to *wash their clothes, and bathe their flesh in water. Whosoever looketh on a woman* (not only another man's wife, as some would have it, but any woman), *to lust after her, has committed adultery with her in his heart, v.* 28. This command forbids not only the acts of fornication and adultery, but, (1.) All appetites to them, all lusting after the forbidden object; this is the beginning of the sin, *lust conceiving* (James 1:15); it is a bad step towards the sin; and where the lust is dwelt upon and approved, and the wanton desire is rolled under the tongue as a sweet morsel, it is the commission of sin, as far as the heart can do it; there wants nothing but convenient opportunity for the sin itself. *Adultera mens est — The mind is debauched.* Ovid. Lust is conscience baffled or biassed: biassed, if it say nothing against the sin; baffled, if it prevail not in what is says. (2.) All approaches toward them; feeding the eye with the sight of the forbidden fruit; not only looking for that end, that I may lust; but looking till I do lust, or looking to gratify the lust, where further satisfaction cannot be obtained. The eye is both the inlet and outlet of a great deal of wickedness of this kind, witness Joseph's mistress (Gen. 39:7), Samson (Jdg. 16:1), David, 2 Sa. 11:2. We read the *eyes full of adultery, that cannot cease from sin,* 2 Pt. 2:14. What need have we, therefore, with holy Job, to *make a covenant with our eyes,* to make this bargain with them that they should have the pleasure of beholding the light of the sun and the works of God, provided they would never fasten or dwell upon any thing that might occasion impure imaginations or desires; and under this penalty, that if they did, they must smart for it in penitential tears! Job 31:1. What have we the covering of the eyes for, but to restrain corrupt glances, and to keep out of their defiling impressions? This forbids also the using of any other of our senses to stir up lust. If ensnaring looks are forbidden fruit, much more unclean discourses, and wanton dalliances, the fuel and bellows of this hellish fire. These precepts are hedges about the law of heart-purity, *v.* 8. And if looking be lust, they who dress and deck, and expose themselves, with design to be looked at and lusted after (like Jezebel, that *painted her face and tired her head, and looked out at the window*) are no less guilty. Men sin, but devils tempt to sin.

2. That such looks and such dalliances are so very dangerous and destructive to the soul, that it is better to lose the eye and the hand that thus offend then to give way to the sin, and perish eternally in it. This lesson is here taught us, *v.* 29, 30. Corrupt nature would soon object against the prohibition of heart-adultery, that it is impossible to governed by it; *"It is a hard saying, who can bear it?* Flesh and blood cannot but look with pleasure upon a beautiful woman; and it is impossible to forbear lusting after and dallying with such an object." Such pretences as these will scarcely be overcome by reason, and therefore must be argued against with *the terrors of the Lord,* and so they are here argued against.

(1.) It is a severe operation that is here prescribed for the preventing of these fleshly lusts. *If thy right eye offend thee,* or *cause thee to offend,* by wanton glances, or wanton gazings, upon forbidden objects; *if thy right hand offend thee,* or *cause thee to offend,* by wanton dalliances; and if it were indeed impossible, as is pretended, to govern the eye and the hand, and they have been so accustomed to these wicked practices, that they will not be withheld from them; if there be no other way to restrain them (which, blessed be God, through his grace, there is), it were better for us to *pluck out the eye,* and *cut off the hand,* though the *right eye,* and *right hand,* the more honourable and useful, than to indulge them in sin to the ruin of the soul. And if this must be submitted to, at the thought of which nature startles, much more must we resolve to *keep under the body, and to bring it into subjection;* to live a life of mortification and self-denial; to keep a constant watch over our own hearts, and to suppress the first rising of lust and corruption there; to avoid the occasions of sin, to resist the beginnings of it, and to decline the company of those who will be a snare to us, though ever so pleasing; to keep out of harm's way, and abridge ourselves in the use of lawful things, when we find them temptations to us; and to seek unto God for his grace, and depend upon that grace daily, and so to *walk in the Spirit,* as that we may not *fulfil the lusts of the flesh;* and this will be as effectual as *cutting off a right hand* or *pulling out a right eye;* and perhaps as much against the grain to flesh and blood; it is the destruction of the old man.

(2.) It is a startling argument that is made use of to enforce this prescription (*v.* 29), and it is repeated in the same words (*v.* 30), because we are loth to hear such rough things; Isa. 30:10. *It is profitable for thee that one of thy members should perish,* though it be an eye or a hand, which can be worse spared, *and not that thy whole body should be cast into hell.* Note, [1.] It is not unbecoming a minister of the gospel to preach of hell and damnation; nay, he *must* do it, for Christ himself did it; and we are unfaithful to our trust, if we give not warning of *the wrath to come.* [2.] There ar some sins from which we need to be *saved with fear,* particularly *fleshly lusts,* which are such *natural brute beasts* as cannot be checked, but by being frightened; cannot be kept from a forbidden tree, but by *cherubim, with a flaming sword.* [3.] When we are tempted to think it hard to *deny ourselves,* and to *crucify fleshly lusts,* we ought to consider how much harder it will be to lie for ever in *the lake that burns with fire and brimstone;* those do not know or do not believe what hell is, that will rather venture their eternal ruin in those flames, than deny themselves the gratification of a base and brutish lust. [4.] In hell there will be torments for the body; the *whole body* will be *cast into hell,* and there will be torment in every part of it; so that if we have a care of our own bodies, we shall *possess them in sanctification and honour,* and *not in the lusts of uncleanness.* [5.] Even those duties that are most unpleasant to flesh and blood, are *profitable for us;* and our Master requires nothing from us but what he knows to be for our advantage.

3. That men's divorcing of their wives upon dislike, or for any other cause except adultery, however tolerated and practised among the Jews, was a violation of the seventh commandment, as it opened a door to adultery, *v.* 31, 32. Here observe,

(1.) How the matter now stood with reference to divorce. *It hath been said* (he does not say as before, *It hath been said by them of old time,* because this was not a precept, as those were, though the Pharisees were willing so to understand it, *ch.* 19:7, but only a permission), *"Whosoever shall put away his wife, let him give her a bill of divorce;* let him not think to do it by word of mouth, when he is in a passion; but let him do it deliberately, by a legal instrument in writing, attested by witnesses; if he will dissolve the matrimonial bond, let him do it solemnly." Thus the law had prevented rash and hasty divorces; and perhaps at first, when writing was not so common among the Jews, that made divorces rare things; but in process of time it became very common, and this direction of how to do it, when there was just cause for it, was construed into a permission of it for any cause, *ch.* 19:3.

(2.) How this matter was rectified and amended by our Saviour. He reduced the ordinance of marriage to its primitive institution: *They two shall be one flesh,* not to be easily separated, and therefore divorce is not to be allowed, except in case of adultery, which breaks the marriage covenant; but he that puts away his wife upon any other pretence, *causeth her to commit adultery,* and him also that shall marry her when she is thus divorced. Note, Those who lead others into temptation to sin, or leave them in it, or expose them to it, make themselves guilty of their sin, and will be accountable for it. This is one way of being *partaker with adulterers* Ps. 50:18.

Verses 33–37

We have here an exposition of the third commandment, which we are the more concerned right to understand, because it is particularly said, that *God will not hold him guilt-*

less, however he may hold himself, who breaks this commandment, by *taking the name of the Lord in vain.* Now as to this command,

I. It is agreed on all hands that it forbids perjury, forswearing, and the violation of oaths and vows, *v.* 33. This was said to them of old time, and is the true intent and meaning of the third commandment. *Thou shalt not* use, or *take up, the name of God* (as we do by an oath) *in vain,* or *unto vanity,* or *a lie.* He *hath not lift up his soul unto vanity,* is expounded in the next words, *nor sworn deceitfully,* Ps. 24:4. Perjury is a sin condemned by the light of nature, as a complication of impiety toward God and injustice toward man, and as rendering a man highly obnoxious to the divine wrath, which was always judged to follow so infallibly upon that sin, that the forms of swearing were commonly turned into execrations or imprecations; as that, *God do so to me, and more also;* and with us, *So help me God;* wishing I may never have any help from God, if I swear falsely. Thus, by the consent of nations, have men cursed themselves, not doubting but that God would curse them, if they lied against the truth then, when they solemnly called God to witness to it.

It is added, from some other scriptures, *but shalt perform unto the Lord thine oaths* (Num. 30:2); which may be meant, either, 1. Of those promises to which God is a party, vows made to God; these must be punctually paid (Eccl. 5:4, 5): or, 2. Of those promises made to our brethren, to which God was a Witness, he being appealed to concerning our sincerity; these must be *performed to the Lord,* with an eye to him, and for his sake: for to him, by ratifying the promises with an oath, we have made ourselves debtors; and if we break a promise so ratified, *we have not lied unto men* only, *but unto God.*

II. It is here added, that the commandment does not only forbid false swearing, but all rash, unnecessary swearing: *Swear not at all, v.* 34; Compare Jam. 5:12. Not that all swearing is sinful; so far from that, if rightly done, it is a part of religious worship, and we in it *give unto God the glory due to his name.* See Deu. 6:13; 10:20; Isa. 45:23; Jer. 4:2. We find Paul confirming what he said by such solemnities (2 Co. 1:23), when there was a necessity for it. In swearing, we pawn the truth of something known, to confirm the truth of something doubtful or unknown; we appeal to a greater knowledge, to a higher court, and imprecate the vengeance of a righteous Judge, if we swear deceitfully.

Now the mind of Christ in this matter is,

1. That we must *not swear at all,* but when we are duly called to it, and justice or charity to our brother, or respect to the commonwealth, make it necessary for *the end of strife* (Heb. 6:16), of which necessity the civil magistrate is ordinarily to be the judge. We may be sworn, but we must now swear; we may be adjured, and so obliged to it, but we must not thrust ourselves upon it for our own worldly advantage.

2. That we must not swear lightly and irreverently, in common discourse: it is a very great sin to make a ludicrous appeal to the glorious Majesty of heaven, which, being a sacred thing, ought always to be very serious: it is a gross profanation of God's holy name, and of one of the holy things which the *children of Israel sanctify to the Lord:* it is a sin that has no cloak, no excuse for it, and therefore a sign of a graceless heart, in which enmity to God reigns: *Thine enemies take thy name in vain.*

3. That we must in a special manner avoid promissory oaths, of which Christ more particularly speaks here, for they are oaths that are to be performed. The influence of an affirmative oath immediately ceases, when we have faithfully discovered the truth, and the whole truth; but a promissory oath binds so long, and may be so many ways broken, by the surprise as well as strength of a temptation, that it is not to be used but upon great necessity: the frequent requiring and using of oaths, is a reflection upon Christians, who should be of such acknowledged fidelity, as that their sober words should be as sacred as their solemn oaths.

4. That we must not swear by any other creature. It should seem there were some, who, in civility (as they thought) to the name of God, would not make use of that in swearing, but would swear *by heaven or earth, etc.* This Christ forbids here (*v.* 34) and shows that there is nothing we can swear by, but it is some way or other related to God, who is the Fountain of all beings, and therefore that it is as dangerous to swear by them, as it is to swear by God himself: it is the verity of the creature that is laid at stake; now that cannot be an instrument of testimony, but as it has regard to God, who is the *summum verum — the chief Truth.* As for instance,

(1.) *Swear not by the heaven;* "As sure as there is a heaven, this is true;" *for it is God's throne,* where he resides, and in a particular manner manifests his glory, as a Prince upon his throne: this being the inseparable dignity of the upper world, you cannot *swear by heaven,* but you swear by God himself.

(2.) *Nor by the earth, for it is his footstool.* He governs the motions of this lower world; as he rules in heaven, so he rules over the earth; and though under his feet, yet it is also under his eye and care, and stands in relation to him as his, Ps. 24:1. *The earth is the Lord's;* so that in swearing by it, you swear by its Owner.

(3.) *Neither by Jerusalem,* a place for which the Jews had such a veneration, that they could not speak of any thing more sacred to *swear by;* but beside the common reference Jerusalem has to God, as part of the earth, it is in special relation to him, *for it is the city of the great King* (Ps. 48:2), *the city of God* (Ps. 46:4), he is therefore interested in it, and in every oath taken by it.

(4.) "*Neither shalt thou swear by the head;* though it be near thee, and an essential part of thee, yet it is more God's than thine; for he made it, and formed all the springs and powers of it; whereas thou thyself canst not, from any natural intrinsic influence, change the colour of *one hair,* so as to make *it white or black;* so that thou canst not *swear by thy head,* but thou swearest by him who is the *Life of thy head,* and *the Lifter up of it.*" Ps. 3:3.

5. That therefore in all our communications we must content ourselves with, *Yea, yea,* and *nay, nay, v.* 37. In ordinary discourse, if we affirm a thing, let us only say, *Yea,* it is so; and, if need be, to evidence our assurance of a thing, we may double it, and say, *Yea, yea,* indeed it is so: *Verily, verily,* was our Saviour's *yea, yea.* So if we deny a thing, let is suffice to say, No; or if it be requisite, to repeat the denial, and say, No, no; and if our fidelity be known, that will suffice to gain us credit; and if it be questioned, to back what we say with swearing and cursing, is but to render it more suspicious. They who can *swallow* a profane oath, will not *strain at a* lie. It is a pity that this, which Christ puts in the mouths of all his disciples, should be fastened, as a name of reproach, upon a sect faulty enough other ways, when (as Dr. Hammond says) we are not forbidden any more than *yea* and *nay,* but are in a manner directed to the use of that.

The reason is observable; *For whatsoever is more than these cometh of evil,* though it do not amount to the iniquity of an oath. It comes *ek tou Diabolou*; so an ancient copy has it: it comes *from the Devil,* the evil one; it comes from the corruption of men's nature, from passion and vehemence; from a reigning vanity in the mind, and a contempt of sacred things: it comes from that deceitfulness which is in men, *All men are liars;* therefore men use these protestations, because they are distrustful one of another, and think they cannot be believed without them. Note, Christians should, for the credit of their religion, avoid not only that which is in itself evil, but *that which cometh of evil,* and has *the appearance of* it. That may be suspected as a bad thing, which comes from a bad cause. An oath is physic, which supposes a disease.

Verses 38–42

In these verses the law of retaliation is expounded, and in a manner repealed. Observe,

I. What the *Old-Testament permission* was, in case of injury; and here the expression is only, *Ye have heard that is has been said;* not, as before, concerning the commands of the decalogue, *that it has been said by,* or to, *them of old time.* It was a command, that every one should of necessity require such satisfaction; but they might lawfully insist upon it, if they pleased; *an eye for an eye, and a tooth for a tooth.* This we find, Ex. 21:24; Lev. 24:20; Deu. 19:21; in all which places it is appointed to be done by the magistrate, who *bears not the sword in vain,* but is *the minister of God, an avenger to execute wrath,* Rom. 13:4. It was a direction to the judges of the Jewish nation what punishment to inflict in case of maims, for terror to such as would do mischief on the one hand, and for a restraint to such as have mischief done to them on the other hand, that they may not insist on a greater punishment than is proper: it is not *a life for an eye,* nor *a limb for a tooth,* but observe a proportion; and it is intimated (Num. 35:31), that the forfeiture in this case might be redeemed with money; for when it is provided that *no ransom shall be taken for the life of a murderer,* it is supposed that for maims a pecuniary satisfaction was allowed.

But some of the Jewish teachers, who were not the most compassionate men in the world, insisted upon it as necessary that such revenge should be taken, even by private persons themselves, and that there was no room left for remission, or the acceptance of satisfaction. Even now, when they were under the government of the Roman magistrates, and consequently the judicial law fell to the ground of course, yet they were still zealous for any thing that looked harsh and severe.

Now, so far this is in force with us, as a direction to magistrates, to use the sword of justice according to the good and wholesome laws of the land, for the terror of evil-doers, and the vindication of the oppressed. That judge *neither feared God nor regarded man,* who would not *avenge* the poor widow *of her adversary,* Lu. 18:2, 3. And it is in force as a rule to lawgivers, to provide accordingly, and wisely to apportion punishments to crimes, for the restraint of rapine and violence, and the protection of innocency.

II. What the *New-Testament precept* is, as to the complainant himself, his duty is, to *forgive the injury* as done to himself, and no further to insist upon the punishment of it than is necessary to the public good: and this precept is consonant to the meekness of Christ, and the gentleness of his yoke.

Two things Christ teaches us here:

1. We must not be revengeful (*v.* 39); *I say unto you, that ye resist not evil;* — the evil person that is injurious to you. The resisting of any ill attempt upon us, is here as generally and expressly forbidden, as *the resisting of the higher powers* is (Rom. 13:2); and yet this does not repeal the law of self-preservation, and the care we are to take of our families; we may *avoid evil,* and may *resist* it, so far as is necessary to our own security; but we must not *render evil for evil,* must not bear a grudge, nor avenge ourselves, nor study to be even with those that have treated us unkindly, but we must go beyond them by forgiving them, Prov. 20:22; 24:29; 25:21, 22; Rom. 12:7. The law of retaliation must be made consistent with the law of love: nor, if any have injured us, is our recompence in our own hands, but in the hands of God, to whose wrath we must give place; and sometimes in the hands of his viceregents, where it is necessary for the preservation of the public peace; but it will not justify us in hurting our brother to say that he began, for it is the second blow that makes the quarrel; and when we were injured, we had an opportunity not to justify our injuring him, but to show ourselves the true disciples of Christ, by forgiving him.

Three things our Saviour specifies, to show that Christians must patiently yield to those who bear hard upon them, rather than contend; and these include others.

(1.) A blow on the cheek, which is an injury to me in my body; "*Whosoever shall smite thee on thy right cheek,*" which is not only a hurt, but an affront and indignity (2 Co. 11:20), if a man in anger or scorn thus abuse thee, "*turn to him the other cheek;*" that is, "instead of avenging that injury, prepare for another, and bear it patiently: give not the rude man as good as he brings; do not challenge him, nor enter an action against him; if it be necessary to the public peace that he be bound to his good behaviour, leave that to the magistrate; but for thine own part, it will ordinarily be the wisest course to pass it by, and take no further notice of it: there are no bones broken, no great harm done, forgive it and forget it; and if proud fools think the worse of thee, and laugh at thee for it, all wise men will value and honour thee for it, as a follower of the blessed Jesus, who, though he was the Judge of Israel, did not smite those who smote him on the cheek," Micah 5:1. Though this may perhaps, with some base spirits, expose us to the like affront another time, and so it is, in effect, to *turn the other cheek,* yet let not that disturb us, but let us trust God and his providence to protect us in the way of our duty. Perhaps, the forgiving of one injury may prevent another, when the avenging of it would but draw on another; some will be overcome by submission, who by resistance would but be the more exasperated, Prov. 25:22. However, our recompence is in Christ's hands, who will reward us with eternal glory for the shame we thus patiently endure; and though it be not directly inflicted, it if be quietly borne for conscience' sake, and in conformity to Christ's example, it shall be put upon the score of suffering for Christ.

(2.) The loss of a coat, which is a wrong to me in my estate (*v.* 40); *If any man will sue thee at the law, and take away thy coat.* It is a hard case. Note, It is common for legal processes to be made use of for the doing of greatest injuries. Though judges be just and circumspect, yet it is possible for bad men who make no conscience of oaths and forgeries, by course of law to force off the coat from a man's back. *Marvel not at the matter* (Eccl. 5:8), but, in such a case, rather than go to the law by way of revenge, rather than exhibit a cross bill, or stand out to the utmost, in defence of that which is thy undoubted right, *let him* even take *thy cloak also.* If the matter be small, which we may lose without an considerable damage to our families, it is good to submit to it for peace' sake. "It will not cost thee so much to buy another cloak, as it will cost thee by course of law to recover that; and therefore unless thou canst get it again by fair means, it is better to let him take it."

(3.) The going a mile by constraint, which is a wrong to me in my liberty (*v.* 41); "*Whosoever shall compel thee to go a mile,* to run an errand for him, or to wait upon him, grudge not at it, but *go with him two miles* rather than fall out with him:" say not, "I would do it, if I were not compelled to it, but I hate to be forced;" rather say, "Therefore I will do it, for otherwise there will be a quarrel;" and it is better to serve him, than to serve thy own lusts of pride and revenge. Some give this sense of it: The Jews taught that the disciples of the wise, and the students of the law, were not to be pressed, as others might, by the king's officers, to travel upon the public service; but Christ will not have his disciples to insist upon this privilege, but to comply rather than offend the government. The sum of all is, that Christians must not be litigious; small injuries must be submitted to, and no notice taken of them; and if the injury be such as requires us to seek reparation, it must be for a good end, and without thought of revenge: though we must not invite injuries, yet we must meet them cheerfully in the way of duty, and make the best of them. If any say, Flesh and blood cannot pass by such an affront, let them remember, that *flesh and blood shall not inherit the kingdom of God.*

2. We must be charitable and beneficent (*v.* 42); must not only do no hurt to our neighbours, but labour to do them all the good we can. (1.) We must be ready to give; "*Give to him that asketh thee.* If thou has an ability, look upon the request of the poor as giving thee an opportunity for the duty of almsgiving." When a real object of charity presents itself, we should give at the first word: *Give a portion to seven, and also to eight;* yet the affairs of our charity must be *guided with discretion* (Ps. 112:5), lest we give that to the idle and unworthy, which should be given to those that are necessitous, and deserve well. What God says to us, we should be ready to say to our poor brethren, Ask, and it shall be given you. (2.) We must be ready to lend. This is sometimes as great a piece of charity as giving; as it not only relieves the present exigency, but obliges the borrower to providence, industry, and honesty; and therefore, "*From him that would borrow of thee* something to live on, or something to trade on, *turn not thou away:* shun not those that thou knowest have such a request to make of thee, nor contrive excuses to shake them off." Be easy of access to him *that would borrow:* though he be bashful, and have not confidence to make known his case and beg the favour, yet thou knowest both his need and his desire, and therefore offer him the kindness. *Exorabor antequam rogor; honestis precibus occuram — I will be prevailed on before I am entreated; I will anticipate the becoming petition.* Seneca, *De Vitâ Beatâ.* It becomes us to be thus forward in acts of kindness, for before we call, God hears us, and *prevents us with the blessings of his goodness.*

Verses 43–48

We have here, lastly, an exposition of that great fundamental law of the second table, *Thou shalt love thy neighbour,* which was the fulfilling of the law.

I. See here how this law was corrupted by the comments of the Jewish teachers, *v.* 43. God said, *Thou shalt love thy neighbour;* and by *neighbour* they understood those only of their own country, nation, and religion; and those only that they were pleased to look upon as their friends: yet this was not the worst; from this command, *Thou shalt love thy neighbour,* they were willing to infer what God never designed; *Thou shalt hate thine enemy;* and they looked upon whom they pleased as their enemies, thus making void the great command of God by their traditions, though there were express laws to the contrary, Ex. 23:4, 5; Deu. 23:7. *Thou shalt not abhor an Edomite, nor an Egyptian,* though these nations had been as much enemies to Israel as any whatso-

ever. It was true, God appointed them to destroy the seven devoted nations of Canaan, and not to make leagues with them; but there was a particular reason for it — to make room for Israel, and that they might not be *snares to them;* but it was very ill-natured from hence to infer, that they must hate all their enemies; yet the moral philosophy of the heathen then allowed this. It is Cicero's rule, *Nemini nocere nisi prius lacessitum injuriâ — To injure no one, unless previously injured. De Offic.* See how willing corrupt passions are to fetch countenance from the word of God, and to *take occasion by the commandment* to justify themselves.

II. See how it is cleared by the command of the Lord Jesus, who teaches us another lesson: "*But I say unto you, I,* who come to be the great Peace-Maker, the general Reconciler, who loved you when you were strangers and enemies, *I say, Love your enemies,*" *v.* 44. Though men are ever so bad themselves, and carry it ever so basely towards us, yet that does not discharge us from the great debt we owe them, of love to our kind, love to our kin. We cannot but find ourselves very prone to wish the hurt, or at least very coldly to desire the good, of those *that hate* us, and have been abusive to us; but that which is at the bottom hereof is a root of bitterness, which must be plucked up, and a remnant of corrupt nature which grace must conquer. Note, it is the great duty of Christians to *love their enemies;* we cannot have complacency in one that is openly wicked and profane, nor put a confidence in one that we know to be deceitful; nor are we to love all alike; but we must pay respect to the human nature, and so far *honour all men:* we must take notice, with pleasure, of that even in our enemies which is amiable and commendable; ingenuousness, good temper, learning, and moral virtue, kindness to others, profession of religion, etc., and love that, though they are our enemies. We must have a compassion for them, and a good will toward them. We are here told,

1. That we must *speak* well of them: *Bless them that curse you.* When we speak to them, we must answer their revilings with courteous and friendly words, and *not render railing for railing;* behind their backs we must commend that in them which is commendable, and when we have said all the good we can of them, not be forward to say any thing more. See 1 Pt. 3:9. They, in whose tongues is *the law of kindness,* can give good words to those who give bad words to them.

2. That we must *do* well to them: "*Do good to them that hate you,* and that will be a better proof of love than good words. Be ready to do them all the real kindness that you can, and glad of an opportunity to do it, in their bodies, estates, names, families; and especially to do good to their souls." It was said of Archbishop Cranmer, that the way to make him a friend was to do him an ill turn; so many did he serve who had disobliged him.

3. We must *pray for them: Pray for them that despitefully use you, and persecute you.* Note, (1.) It is no new thing for the most excellent saints to be hated, and cursed, and persecuted, and despitefully used, by wicked people; Christ himself was so treated. (2.) That when at any time we meet with such usage, we have an opportunity of showing our conformity both to the precept and to the example of Christ, by praying for them who thus abuse us. If we cannot otherwise testify our love to them, yet this way we may without ostentation, and it is such a way as surely we durst not dissemble in. We must pray that God will forgive them, that they may never fare the worse for any thing they have done against us, and that he would make them to be at peace with us; and this is one way of making them so. Plutarch, in his Laconic Apophthegms, has this of Aristo; when one commended Cleomenes's saying, who, being asked *what a good king should do,* replied, *Tous men philous euergetein, tous de echthrous kakōs poiein — Good turns to his friends, and evil to his enemies;* he said, How much better is it *tous men philous euergetein, tous de echthrous philous poiein —* to do good to our friends, and make friends of our enemies. This is *heaping coals of fire on their heads.*

Two reasons are here given to enforce this command (which sounds so harsh) of *loving our enemies.* We must do it,

[1.] That we may be *like God our Father;* "that ye may be, may approve yourselves to be, *the children of your Father which is in heaven.*" Can we write a better copy? It is a copy in which love to the worst of enemies is reconciled to, and consistent with, infinite purity and holiness. God *maketh his sun to rise,* and *sendeth rain,* on *the just and the un-*

just, *v.* 45. Note, *First, Sunshine* and *rain* are great blessings to the world, and they come from God. It is *his sun* that *shines,* and the rain is sent by him. They do not come of course, or by chance, but from God. *Secondly,* Common mercies must be valued as instances and proofs of the goodness of God, who in them shows himself a bountiful Benefactor to the world of mankind, who would be very miserable without these favours, and are utterly unworthy of the least of them. *Thirdly,* These gifts of common providence are dispensed indifferently to *good* and *evil, just* and *unjust;* so that we cannot know *love* and *hatred* by what is *before us,* but by what is *within us;* not by the shining of the sun on our heads, but by the rising of the Sun of Righteousness in our hearts. *Fourthly,* The worst of men partake of the comforts of this life in common with others, though they abuse them, and fight against God with his own weapons; which is an amazing instance of God's patience and bounty. It was but once that God forbade his sun to shine on the Egyptians, when the Israelites had *light in their dwellings;* God could make such a distinction every day. *Fifthly,* The gifts of God's bounty to wicked men that are in rebellion against him, teach us to *do good to those that hate us;* especially considering, that though there is in us a carnal mind which is enmity to God, yet we share in his bounty. *Sixthly,* Those only will be accepted as the children of God, who study to resemble him, particularly in his goodness.

[2.] That we may herein *do more than others, v.* 46, 47. *First, Publicans love their friends.* Nature inclines them to it; interest directs them to it. To do good to them who do good to us, is a common piece of humanity, which even those whom the Jews hated and despised could give as good proofs as of the best of them. The publicans were men of no good fame, yet they were grateful to such as had helped them to their places, and courteous to those they had a dependence upon; and shall we be no better than they? In doing this we serve ourselves and consult our own advantage; and what reward can we expect for that, unless a regard to God, and a sense of duty, carrying us further than our natural inclination and worldly interest? *Secondly,* We must therefore love our enemies, that we may exceed them. If we must go beyond scribes and Pharisees, much more beyond publicans. Note, Christianity is something more than humanity. It is a serious question, and which we should frequently put to ourselves, "*What do we more than others? What excelling thing do we do?* We *know* more than others; we *talk* more of the things of God than others; we *profess,* and have *promised,* more than others; God has done more for us, and therefore justly expects more from us than from others; the glory of God is more concerned in us than in others; but *what do we more than others?* Wherein do we live above the rate of the children of this world? *Are we not carnal,* and do we not walk as men, below the character of Christians? In this especially we must do more than others, that while every one will render *good for good,* we must render *good for evil;* and this will speak a nobler principle, and is consonant to a higher rule, than the most of men act by. Others *salute their brethren,* they embrace those of their own party, and way, and opinion; but we must not so confine our respect, but *love our enemies,* otherwise *what reward have we?* We cannot expect the reward of Christians, if we rise no higher than the virtue of publicans." Note, Those who promise themselves a reward above others must study to *do more than others.*

Lastly, Our Saviour concludes this subject with this exhortation (*v.* 48), *Be ye therefore perfect, as your Father which is in heaven is perfect.* Which may be understood, 1. In general, including all those things wherein we must be *followers of God as dear children.* Note, It is the duty of Christians to desire, and aim at, and press toward a perfection in grace and holiness, Phil. 3:12–14. And therein we must study to conform ourselves to the example of our heavenly Father, 1 Pt. 1:15, 16. Or, 2. In this particular before mentioned, of *doing good to our enemies;* see Lu. 6:36. It is God's perfection to *forgive injuries* and to *entertain strangers,* and to do good to the evil and unthankful, and it will be ours to be like him. We that owe *so much,* that owe *our all,* to the divine bounty, ought to copy it out as well as we can.

CHAPTER 6

Christ having, in the former chapter, armed his disciples against the corrupt doctrines and opinions of the scribes and Pharisees, especially in their expositions of the law (that was called their leaven, 16:12), comes in this chapter to warn them against their corrupt practices, against the two sins which, though in their doctrine they did not justify, yet in their conversation they were notoriously guilty of, and so as even to recommend them to their admirers: these were hypocrisy and worldly-mindedness, sins which, of all others, the professors of religion need most to guard against, as sins that most easily beset those who have escaped the grosser pollutions that are in the world through lust, and which are therefore highly dangerous. We are here cautioned, I. Against hypocrisy; we must not be as the hypocrites are, nor do as the hypocrites do. 1. In the giving of alms (*v.* 1–4). 2. In prayer (*v.* 5–8). We are here taught what to pray for, and how to pray (*v.* 9–13); and to forgive in prayer (*v.* 14, 15). 3. In fasting (*v.* 16–18). II. Against worldly-mindedness, 1. In our choice, which is the destroying sin of hypocrites (*v.* 19–24). 2. In our cares, which is the disquieting sin of many good Christians (*v.* 25–34).

Verses 1–4

As we must do better than the scribes and Pharisees in avoiding heart-sins, heart-adultery, and heart-murder, so likewise in maintaining and keeping up heart-religion, doing what we do from an inward, vital principle, that we may be approved of God, not that we may be applauded of men; that is, we must watch against hypocrisy, which was the leaven of the Pharisees, as well as against their doctrine, Lu. 12:1. *Almsgiving, prayer,* and *fasting,* are three great Christian duties — the three foundations of the law, say the Arabians: by them we do homage and service to God with our three principal interests; by *prayer* with our *souls,* by *fasting* with our *bodies,* by *alms-giving* with our *estates.* Thus we must not only *depart from evil,* but *do good,* and do it well, and so *dwell for evermore.*

Now in these verses we area cautioned against hypocrisy in giving alms. *Take heed* of it. Our being bid to *take heed* of it intimates that it is sin. 1. We are in *great danger of;* it is a subtle sin; vain-glory insinuates itself into what we do ere we are aware. The disciples would be tempted to it by the power they had to do many wondrous works, and their living with some that admired them and others that despised them, both which are temptations to covet to make a fair show in the flesh. 2. It is a sin we are *in great danger by.* Take heed of hypocrisy, for if it reign in you, it will ruin you. It is the dead fly that spoils the whole box of precious ointment.

Two things are here supposed,

I. The *giving of alms* is a great duty, and a duty which all the disciples of Christ, according to their ability, must abound in. It is prescribed by the law of nature and of Moses, and great stress is laid upon it by the prophets. Divers ancient copies here for *tēn eleēmosynēn — your alms,* read *tēn dikaiosynēn — your righteousness,* for *alms* are *righteousness,* Ps. 112:9; Prov. 10:2. The Jews called the *poor's box* the *box of righteousness.* That which is given to the poor is said to be their due, Prov. 3:27. The duty is not the less necessary and excellent for its being abused by hypocrites to serve their pride. If superstitious papists have placed a merit in works of charity, that will not be an excuse for covetous protestants that are barren in such good works. It is true, our alms-deeds do not deserve heaven; but it is as true that we cannot go to heaven without them. It is *pure religion* (Jam. 1:27), and will be the test at the great day; Christ here takes it for granted that his disciples *give alms,* nor will he own those that do not.

II. That it is such a duty as has a great reward attending it, which is lost if it be done in hypocrisy. It is sometimes rewarded in temporal things with *plenty* (Prov. 11:24, 25; 19:17); *security from want* (Prov. 28:27; Ps. 37:21, 25); *succour in distress* (Ps. 41:1, 2); *honour and a good* name, which follow those most that least covet them, Ps. 112:9. However, it shall be recompensed in the resurrection of the just (Lu. 14:14), in *eternal riches.*

> *Quas dederis, solas semper habebis, opes.*
>
> *The riches you impart form the only wealth you will always retain.* — Martial.

This being supposed, observe now,

1. What was the *practice of the hypocrites* about this duty. They did it indeed, but not from any principle of obedience to God, or love to man, but in pride and vain-glory; not in compassion to the poor, but purely for ostentation, that they might be extolled as good men, and so might gain an interest in the esteem of the people, with which they knew how to serve their own turn, and to get a great deal more than they gave. Pursuant to this intention, they chose to give their alms *in the synagogues, and in the streets,* where there was the greatest concourse of people to observe them, who applauded their liberality because they shared in it, but were so ignorant as not to discern their abominable pride. Probably they had collections for the poor in the synagogues, and the common beggars haunted the streets and highways, and upon these public occasions they chose to give their alms. Not that it is unlawful to give alms *when men see us;* we may do it; but not *that men may see us;* we should rather choose those objects of charity that are less observed. The hypocrites, if they gave alms to their own houses, *sounded a trumpet,* under pretence of calling the poor together to be served, but really to proclaim their charity, and to have that taken notice of and made the subject of discourse.

Now the doom that Christ passes upon this is very observable; *Verily I say unto you, they have their reward.* At first view this seems a promise — If they have their reward they have enough, but two words in it make it a threatening.

(1.) It is a reward, but it is *their* reward; not the reward which God promises to them that do good, but the reward which they promise themselves, and a poor reward it is; they did it to be *seen of men,* and they *are* seen of men; they *chose their own delusions* with which they cheated themselves, and they shall have what they chose. Carnal professors stipulate with God for preferment, honour, wealth, and they shall have their bellies filled with those things (Ps. 17:14); but let them expect no more; these are their consolation (Lu. 6:24), their good things (Lu. 16:25), and they shall be put off with these. *"Didst thou not agree with me for a penny?* It is the bargain that thou art likely to abide by."

(2.) It is a reward, but it is a *present reward,* they *have* it; and there is none reserved for them in the future state. They now have all that they are likely to have from God; they have their reward here, and have none to hope for hereafter. *Apechousi ton misthon.* It signifies a *receipt in full.* What rewards the godly have in this life are but *in part of payment;* there is more behind, much more; but hypocrites have their *all* in this world, so shall their doom be; themselves have decided it. The world is but for *provision* to the saints, it is their spending-money; but it is *pay* to hypocrites, it is their portion.

2. What is the *precept of our Lord Jesus* about it, *v.* 3, 4. He that was himself such an example of humility, pressed it upon his disciples, as absolutely necessary to the acceptance of their performances. *"Let not thy left hand know what thy right hand doeth* when thou givest alms." Perhaps this alludes to the placing of the Corban, the poor man's box, or the chest into which they cast their free-will offerings, *on the right hand* of the passage into the temple; so that they put their gifts into it with the *right-hand.* Or the giving of alms with the *right hand,* intimates readiness to it and resolution in it; do it dexterously, not awkwardly nor with a sinister intention. The *right hand* may be used in helping the poor, lifting them up, writing for them, dressing their sores, and other ways besides giving to them; but, "whatever kindness thy right hand doeth to the poor, *let not thy left hand know it:* conceal it as much as possible; industriously keep it private. Do it because it is a good work, not because it will give thee a good name." *In omnibus factis, re, non teste, moveamur — In all our actions, we should be influenced by a regard to the object, not to the observer.* Cic. de Fin. It is intimated, (1.) That we must not let *others* know what we do; no, not those that stand *at our left hand,* that are very near us. Instead of acquainting them with it, keep it from them if possible; however, appear so desirous to keep it from them, as that in civility they may seem not to take notice of it, and keep it to themselves, and let it go no further. (2.) That we must not observe it too much *ourselves:* the left hand is a part of ourselves; we must not within ourselves take notice too much of the good we do, must not applaud and admire ourselves. Self-conceit and self-complacency, and an adoring of our own shadow, are branches of pride, as dangerous as vain-glory and ostentation before men. We find those had their good works remembered to their honour, who had themselves forgotten them: *When saw we thee an hungered, or athirst?*

3. What is the *promise to those who are thus sincere and humble* in their alms-giving. Let *thine alms be in secret,* and then *thy Father who seeth in secret* will observe them. Note, When we take least notice of our good deeds ourselves, God takes most notice of them. As God hears the wrongs done to us when we do not hear them (Ps. 38:14, 15), so he sees the good done by us, when we do not see it. As it is a terror to hypocrites, so it is a comfort to sincere Christians, that God *sees in secret.* But this is not all; not only the observation and praise, but the recompence is of God, *himself shall reward thee openly.* Note, They who in their alms-giving study to approve themselves to God, only turn themselves over to him as their Paymaster. The hypocrite catches at the shadow, but the upright man makes sure of the substance. Observe how emphatically it is expressed; *himself shall reward,* he will himself be the Rewarder, Heb. 11:6. Let him alone to make it up in kind or kindness; nay, he will *himself be the Reward* (Gen. 15:1), thine *exceeding great reward.* He will reward thee as thy Father, not as a master who gives his servant just what he earns and no more, but as a father who gives abundantly more, and without stint, to his son that serves him. Nay, he shall reward thee *openly,* if not in the present day, yet in the great day; *then shall every man have praise of God,* open praise, thou shall be confessed *before men.* If the work be not open, the reward shall, and that is better.

Verses 5–8

In *prayer* we have more immediately to do with God than in *giving alms,* and therefore are yet more concerned to be *sincere,* which is what we are here directed to. *When thou prayest* (*v.* 5). It is taken for granted that all the disciples of Christ *pray.* As soon as ever Paul was converted, *behold he prayeth.* You may as soon find a living man that does not breathe, as a living Christian that does not pray. *For this shall every one that is godly pray.* If prayerless, then graceless. *"Now, when thou prayest,* thou shalt not be *as the hypocrites are,* nor do as they do," *v.* 2. Note, Those who would not do as the hypocrites do in their ways and actions must not be as the hypocrites are in their frame and temper. He names nobody, but it appears by *ch.* 23:13, that by the hypocrites here he means especially the scribes and Pharisees.

Now there were two great faults they were guilty of in prayer, against each of which we are here cautioned — vain-glory (*v.* 5, 6); and vain repetitions, *v.* 7, 8.

I. We must not be *proud* and *vain-glorious* in prayer, nor aim at the praise of men. And here observe,

1. What was the *way and practice of the hypocrites.* In all their exercises of devotion, it was plain, the chief thing they aimed at was to be commended by their neighbours, and thereby to make an interest for themselves. When they seemed to *soar upwards* in prayer (and if it be right, it is the soul's ascent toward God), yet even then their eye was *downwards* upon this as their *prey.* Observe,

(1.) What the *places* were which they chose for their devotions; they prayed in the *synagogues,* which were indeed proper places for public prayer, but not for personal. They pretended hereby to do honour to the place of their assemblies, but intended to do honour to themselves. They prayed in *the corners of the streets,* the broad streets (so the word signifies), which were most frequented. They withdrew thither, as if they were under a pious impulse which would not admit delay, but really it was to cause themselves to be taken notice of. There, where two streets met, they were not only within view of both, but every passenger turning close upon them would observe them, and hear what they said.

(2.) The *posture* they used in prayer; they prayed standing; this is a lawful and proper posture for prayer (Mk. 11:25, *When ye stand praying*), but kneeling being the more humble and reverent gesture, Lu. 22:41; Acts 7:60; Eph. 3:14, their standing seemed to savour of pride and confidence in themselves (Lu. 18:11), *The Pharisee stood and prayed.*

(3.) Their *pride* in choosing these public places, which is expressed in two things: [1.] They *love* to pray there. They did not love prayer for its own sake, but they loved it when it gave them an opportunity of making themselves noticed. Circumstances may be such, that our good deeds must needs be done openly, so as to fall under the observation of others, and be commended by them; but the sin and danger is when we love it, and are pleased with it, because it feeds the proud humour. [2.] It is that they may be *seen of men;* not that God might accept them, but that men might admire and applaud them; and that they might easily get the estates of widows and orphans into their hands (who would not trust such devout, praying men?) and that, when they had them, they might devour them without being suspected (*ch.* 23:14); and effectually carry on their public designs to enslave the people.

(4.) The *product* of all this, *they have their reward;* they have all the recompence they must ever expect from God for their service, and a poor recompence it is. What will it avail us to have the good word of our fellow-servants, if our Master do not say, *Well done?* But if in so great a transaction as is between us and God, when we are at prayer, we can take in so poor a consideration as the praise of men is, it is just that that should be all our reward. They did it to be *seen of men,* and they are so; and much good may it do them. Note, Those that would approve themselves to God by their integrity in their religion, must have to regard to the praise of men; it is not to men that we pray, nor from them that we expect an answer; they are not to be our judges, they are dust and ashes like ourselves, and therefore we must not have our eye to them: what passes between God and our own souls must be out of sight. In our synagogue-worship, we must avoid every thing that tends to make our personal devotion remarkable, as they that caused their *voice to be heard on high,* Isa. 58:4. Public places are not proper for private solemn prayer.

2. What is the *will of Jesus Christ* in opposition to this. Humility and sincerity are the two great lessons that Christ teaches us; *Thou, when thou prayest,* do so and so (*v.* 6); *thou* in particular by thyself, and for thyself. Personal prayer is here supposed to be the duty and practice of all Christ's disciples.

Observe, (1.) The directions here given about it.

[1.] Instead of praying in *the synagogues* and in the *corners of the streets, enter into thy closet,* into some place of privacy and retirement. Isaac went into the field (Gen. 24:63), Christ to a mountain, Peter to a housetop. No place amiss in point of ceremony, if it do but answer the end. Note, Secret prayer is to be performed in retirement, that we may be unobserved, and so may avoid ostentation; undisturbed, and so may avoid distraction; unheard, and so may use greater freedom; yet if the circumstances be such that we cannot possibly avoid being taken notice of, we must not therefore neglect the duty, lest the omission be a greater scandal than the observation of it.

[2.] Instead of doing it to be *seen of men, pray to thy Father who is in secret; to me, even to me,* Zec. 7:5, 6. The Pharisees prayed rather to men than to God; whatever was the form of their prayer, the scope of it was to beg the applause of men, and court their favours. "Well, do thou pray to God, and let that be enough for thee. Pray to him as a Father, as thy Father, ready to hear and answer, graciously inclined to pity, help, and succour thee. Pray to thy Father *who is in secret."* Note, In secret prayer we must have an eye to God, as present in all places; he is there in thy closet when no one else is there; there especially nigh to thee in what thou *callest upon him for.* By *secret* prayer we give God the glory of his universal presence (Acts 17:24), and may take to ourselves the comfort of it.

(2.) The encouragements here given us to it.

[1.] Thy Father *seeth in secret;* his eye is upon thee to accept thee, when the eye of no man is upon thee to applaud thee; *under the fig-tree, I saw thee,* said Christ to Nathaniel, Jn. 1:48. He saw Paul at prayer in such a street, at such a house, Acts 9:11. There is not a secret, sudden breathing after God, but he observes it.

[2.] He *will reward thee openly;* they have their reward that do it openly, and thou shalt not lose thine for thy doing it in secret. It is called a *reward,* but it is of *grace,* not of *debt;* what merit can there be in begging? The reward will be open; they shall not only have it, but have it honourably: the open reward is that which hypocrites are fond of, but they have not patience to stay for it; it is that which the sincere are dead to, and they shall have it over and above. Sometimes secret prayers are rewarded openly in this world by signal answers to them, which manifests God's praying people in the consciences of their adversaries; however, at the great day there will be an open reward, when all praying people shall *appear in glory* with the great Intercessor. The Pharisees had their reward *before all the town,* and it was a *mere flash and shadow;* true Christians shall have theirs *before all the world,* angels and men, and it shall be a *weight of glory.*

II. We must not *use vain repetitions* in prayer, *v.* 7, 8. Though the life of prayer lies in *lifting up the soul and pouring out the heart,* yet there is some interest which words have in prayer, especially in joint prayer; for in that, words are necessary, and it should seem that our Saviour speaks here especially of that; for before he said, *when thou prayest,* he here, when *ye pray;* and the Lord's prayer which follows is a joint prayer, and in that, he that is the mouth of others is most tempted to an ostentation of language and expression, against which we are here warned; *use not vain repetitions,* either alone or with others: the Pharisees affected this, *they made long prayers* (*ch.* 23:14), all their care was to make them long. Now observe,

1. What the *fault* is that is here reproved and condemned;

it is making a mere lip-labour of the duty of prayer, the service of the tongue, when it is not the service of the soul. This is expressed here by two words, *Battologia, polylogia.* (1.) *Vain repetitions* — tautology, battology, idle babbling over the same words again and again to no purpose, like *Battus, Sub illis montibus erant, erant sub montibus illis;* like that imitation of the wordiness of a fool, Eccl. 10:14, *A man cannot tell what shall be; and what shall be after him who can tell?* which is indecent and nauseous in any discourse, much more in speaking to God. It is not all repetition in prayer that is here condemned, but vain repetitions. Christ himself prayed, saying the same words (*ch.* 26:44), out of more than ordinary fervour and zeal, Lu. 22:44. So Daniel, *ch.* 9:18, 19. And there is a very elegant repetition of the same words, Ps. 136. It may be of use both to express our own affections, and to excite the affections of others. But the superstitious rehearsing of a tale of words, without regard to the sense of them, as the papists saying by their beads so many Ave-Marys and Paternosters; or the barren and dry going over of the same things again and again, merely to drill out the prayer to such a length, and to make a show of affection when really there is none; these are the vain repetitions here condemned. When we would fain say much, but cannot say much to the purpose; this is displeasing to God and all wise men. (2.) *Much speaking,* an affectation of prolixity in prayer, either out of pride or superstition, or an opinion that God needs either to be informed or argued with by us, or out of mere folly and impertinence, because men love to *hear themselves talk.* Not that all long prayers are forbidden; Christ prayed all night, Lu. 6:12. Solomon's was a long prayer. There is sometimes need of long prayers when our errands and our affections are extraordinary; but merely to prolong the prayer, as if it would make it more pleasing or more prevailing with God, is that which is here condemned; it is not much *praying* that is condemned; no, we are bid to *pray always,* but much *speaking;* the danger of this error is when we only *say* our prayers, and not when we *pray* them. This caution is explained by that of Solomon (Eccl. 5:2), *Let thy words be few,* considerate and well weighed; *take with you words* (Hos. 14:2), *choose out words* (Job 9:14), and do not say every thing that comes uppermost.

2. What reasons are given against this.

(1.) This is the way of the heathen, *as the heathen do;* and it ill becomes Christians to worship their God as the Gentiles worship theirs. The heathen were taught by the light of nature to worship God; but becoming vain in their imaginations concerning the object of their worship, no wonder they became so concerning the manner of it, and particularly in this instance; thinking God altogether such a one as themselves, they thought he needed many words to make him understand what was said to him, or to bring him to comply with their requests; as if he were weak and ignorant, and hard to be entreated. Thus Baal's priests were hard at it from morning till almost night with their *vain repetitions; O Baal, hear us; O Baal, hear us;* and vain petitions they were; but Elijah, in a grave, composed frame, with a very concise prayer, prevailed for fire from heaven first, and then water, 1 Ki. 18:26, 36. *Lip-labour* in prayer, though ever so well *laboured,* if that be all, is but *lost labour.*

(2.) "It need not be your way, *for your Father* in heaven *knoweth what things ye have need of before ye ask him,* and therefore there is no occasion for such abundance of words. It does not follow that therefore ye need not pray; for God requires you by prayer to own your need of him and dependence on him, and to please his promises; but therefore you are to open your case, and pour out your hearts before him, and then leave it with him." Consider, [1.] The God we pray to is our Father by creation, by covenant; and therefore our addresses to him should be easy, natural, and unaffected; children do not use to make long speeches to their parents when they want any thing; it is enough to say, *my head, my head.* Let us come to him with the disposition of children, with love, reverence, and dependence; and then they need not say many words, that are taught by the Spirit of adoption to say that one aright, *Abba, Father.* [2.] He is a Father that knows our case and knows our wants better than we do ourselves. *He knows what things we have need of;* his eyes run to and fro through the earth, to observe the necessities of his people (2 Chr. 16:9), and he often gives *before we call* (Isa. 65:24), and *more than we ask for* (Eph. 3:20), and if he do not give his people what they ask, it is because he knows they do not need it, and that it is not for their good; and of that he is

fitter to judge for us than we for ourselves. We need not be long, nor use many words in representing our case; God knows it better than we can tell him, only he will know it *from us (what will ye that I should do unto you?);* and when we have told him what it is, we must refer ourselves to him, *Lord, all my desire is before thee,* Ps. 38:9. So far is God from being wrought upon by the length or language of our prayers, that the most powerful intercessions are those which are made with *groanings that cannot be uttered,* Rom. 8:26. We are not to *pre*scribe, but *sub*scribe to God.

Verses 9–15

When Christ had condemned what was amiss, he directs to do better; for his are reproofs of instruction. Because we know not what to pray for as we ought, he here helps our infirmities, by putting words into our mouths; *after this manner therefore pray ye, v.* 9. So many were the corruptions that had crept into this duty of prayer among the Jews, that Christ saw it needful to give a new directory for prayer, to show his disciples what must ordinarily be the matter and method of their prayer, which he gives in words that may very well be used as a form; as the summary or contents of the several particulars of our prayers. Not that we are tied up to the use of this form only, or of this always, as if this were necessary to the consecrating of our other prayers; we are here bid to pray after this manner, with these words, or to this effect. That in Luke differs from this; we do not find it used by the apostles; we are not here taught to pray in the name of Christ, as we are afterward; we are here taught to pray that the kingdom might come which did come when the Spirit was poured out: yet, without doubt, it is very good to use it as a form, and it is a pledge of the communion of saints, it having been used by the church in all ages, at least (says Dr. Whitby) from the third century. It is our Lord's prayer, it is of his composing, of his appointing; it is very compendious, yet very comprehensive, in compassion to our infirmities in praying. The matter is choice and necessary, the method instructive, and the expression very concise. It has much in a little, and it is requisite that we acquaint ourselves with the sense and meaning of it, for it is used acceptably no further than it is used with understanding and without vain repetition.

The Lord's prayer (as indeed every prayer) is a letter sent from earth to heaven. Here is the inscription of the letter, the person to whom it is directed, *our Father;* the where, *in heaven;* the contents of it in several errands of request; the close, *for thine is the kingdom;* the seal, *Amen;* and if you will, the date too, *this day.*

Plainly thus: there are three parts of the prayer.

I. *The preface, Our Father who art in heaven.* Before we come to our business, there must be a solemn address to him with whom our business lies; *Our Father.* Intimating, that we must pray, not only alone and for ourselves, but with and for others; for we are members one of another, and are called into fellowship with each other. We are here taught to *whom to pray,* to God only, and not to saints and angels, for they are ignorant of us, are not to have the high honours we give in prayer, nor can give favours we expect. We are taught how to address ourselves to God, and what title to give him, that which speaks him rather beneficent than magnificent, for we are to come boldly to the throne of grace.

1. We must address ourselves to him as *our Father,* and must call him so. He is a common Father to all mankind by creation, Mal. 2:10; Acts 17:28. He is in a special manner a Father to the saints, by adoption and regeneration (Eph. 1:5; Gal. 4:6); and an unspeakable privilege it is. Thus we must eye him in prayer, keep up good thoughts of him, such as are encouraging and not affrighting; nothing more pleasing to God, nor pleasant to ourselves, than to call God *Father.* Christ in prayer mostly called God *Father.* If he be our Father, he will pity us under our weaknesses and infirmities (Ps. 103:13), will spare us (Mal. 3:17), will make the best of our performances, though very defective, will deny us nothing that is good for us, Lu. 11:11–13. We have access with boldness to him, as to a father, and have an *advocate with the Father,* and the Spirit of adoption. When we come repenting of our sins, we must eye God as a Father, as the prodigal did (Lu. 15:18; Jer. 3:19); when we come begging for grace, and peace, and the inheritance and blessing of sons, it is an encouragement that we come to God, not as an unreconciled, avenging Judge, but as a loving, gracious, reconciled Father in Christ, Jer. 3:4.

2. As our Father *in heaven:* so in heaven as to be every where else, for the heaven cannot contain him; yet so in heaven as there to manifest his glory, for it is his throne (Ps. 103:19), and it is to believers a throne of grace: thitherward we must direct our prayers, for Christ the Mediator is now in heaven, Heb. 8:1. Heaven is out of sight, and a world of spirits, therefore our converse with God in prayer must be spiritual; it is on high, therefore in prayer we must be raised above the world, and lift up our hearts, Ps. 5:1. Heaven is a place of perfect purity, and we must therefore lift up pure hands, must study to sanctify his name, who is the Holy One, and dwells in that holy place, Lev. 10:3. From heaven God beholds the children of men, Ps. 33:13, 14. And we must in prayer see his eye upon us: thence he has a full and clear view of all our wants and burdens and desires, and all our infirmities. It is the firmament of his power likewise, as well as of his prospect, Ps. 150:1. He is not only, as a Father, able to help us, able to do great things for us, more than we can ask or think; he has wherewith to supply our needs, for every good gift is from above. He is a Father, and therefore we may come to him with boldness, but a Father in heaven, and therefore we must come with reverence, Eccl. *v.* 2. Thus all our prayers should correspond with that which is our great aim as Christians, and that is, to be with God in heaven. God and heaven, the end of our whole conversation, must be particularly eyed in every prayer; there is the centre to which we are all tending. By prayer, we send before us thither, where we profess to be going.

II. *The petitions,* and those are six; the three first relating more immediately to God and his honour, the three last to our own concerns, both temporal and spiritual; as in the ten commandments, the four first teach us our duty toward God, and the last six our duty toward our neighbour. The method of this prayer teaches us to seek first the *kingdom of God and his righteousness,* and then to hope that *other things shall be added.*

1. *Hallowed be thy name.* It is the same word that in other places is translated *sanctified.* But here the old word *hallowed* is retained, only because people were used to it in the Lord's prayer. In these words, (1.) We give glory to God; it may be taken not as a petition, but as an adoration; as that, *the Lord be magnified,* or *glorified,* for God's holiness is the greatness and glory of all his perfections. We must begin our prayers with praising God, and it is very fit he should be first served, and that we should give glory to God, before we expect to receive mercy and grace from him. Let him have praise of his perfections, and then let us have the benefit of them. (2.) We fix our end, and it is the right end to be aimed at, and ought to be our chief and ultimate end in all our petitions, that God may be glorified; all our other requests must be in subordination to this, and in pursuance of it. *"Father, glorify thyself* in giving me my daily bread and pardoning my sins," etc. Since all is of him and through him, all must be to him and for him. In prayer our thoughts and affections should be carried out most to the glory of God. The Pharisees made their own name the chief end of their prayers (*v.* 5, *to be seen of men*), in opposition to which we are directed to make the name of God our chief end; let all our petitions centre in this and be regulated by it. "Do so and so for me, *for the glory of thy name,* and as far as is for the glory of it." (3.) We desire and pray that the name of God, that is, God himself, in all that whereby he has made himself known, may be sanctified and glorified both by us and others, and especially by himself. "Father, let thy name be glorified as a Father, and a Father in heaven; glorify thy goodness and thy highness, thy majesty and mercy. *Let thy name be sanctified,* for it is a holy name; no matter what becomes of our polluted names, but, Lord, *what wilt thou do to thy great name?"* When we pray that God's name may be glorified, [1.] We make a virtue of necessity; for God will *sanctify his own name,* whether we desire it or not; *I will be exalted among the heathen,* Ps. 46:10. [2.] We ask for that which we are sure shall be granted; for when our Saviour prayed, *Father glorify thy name,* it was immediately answered, *I have glorified it, and will glorify it again.*

2. *Thy kingdom come.* This petition has plainly a reference to the doctrine which Christ preached at this time, which John Baptist had preached before, and which he afterwards sent his apostles out to preach — *the kingdom of heaven is at hand.* The kingdom of your Father who is in heaven, the kingdom of the Messiah, this is at hand, pray that it may come. Note, We should turn the word we hear into prayer, our hearts should echo to it; does Christ promise, *surely I come quickly?* our hearts should answer, *Even so, come.* Ministers should pray over the word: when they preach, *the kingdom of God is at hand,* they should pray, *Father, thy kingdom come.* What God has promised we must pray for; for promises are given, not to supersede, but to quicken and encourage prayer; and when the accomplishment of a promise is near and at the door, when the kingdom of heaven is at hand, we should then pray for it the more earnestly; *thy kingdom come;* as Daniel set his face to pray for the deliverance of Israel, when he understood that the time of it was at hand, Dan. 9:2. See Lu. 19:11. It was the Jews' daily prayer to God, *Let him make his kingdom reign, let his redemption flourish, and let his Messiah come and deliver his people.* Dr. Whitby, *ex Vitringa. "Let thy kingdom come,* let the gospel be preached to all and embraced by all; let all be brought to subscribe to the record God has given in his word concerning his Son, and to embrace him as their Saviour and Sovereign. Let the bounds of the gospel-church be enlarged, the kingdom of the world be made Christ's kingdom, and all men become subjects to it, and live as becomes their character."

3. *Thy will be done in earth as it is in heaven.* We pray that God's kingdom being come, we and others may be brought into obedience to all the laws and ordinances of it. By this let it appear that Christ's kingdom is come, *let God's will be done;* and by this let is appear that it is come as a *kingdom of heaven,* let it introduce a *heaven upon earth.* We make Christ but a titular Prince, if we call him King, and do not do his will: having prayed that he may rule us, we pray that we may in every thing be ruled by him. Observe, (1.) The thing prayed for, *thy will be done;* "Lord, do what thou pleasest with me and mine; 1 Sa. 3:18. I refer myself to thee, and am well satisfied that all thy counsel concerning me should be performed." In this sense Christ prayed, *not my will, but thine be done.* "Enable me to do what is pleasing to thee; give me that grace that is necessary to the right knowledge of thy will, and an acceptable obedience to it. Let thy will be done conscientiously by me and others, not our own will, the will of the flesh, or the mind, not the will of men (1 Pt. 4:2), much less Satan's will (Jn. 8:44), that we may neither displease God in any thing we do *(ut nihil nostrum displiceat Deo),* nor be displeased at any thing God does" *(ut nihil Dei displiceat nobis).* (2.) The pattern of it, that it might be *done on earth,* in this place of our trial and probation (where our work must be done, or it never will be done), *as it is done in heaven,* that place of rest and joy. We pray that earth may be made more like heaven by the observance of God's will (this earth, which, through the prevalency of Satan's will, has become so near akin to hell), and that saints may be made more like the holy angels in their devotion and obedience. We are *on earth,* blessed be God, not yet *under the earth;* we pray for the *living* only, not for *the dead that have gone down into silence.*

4. *Give us this day our daily bread.* Because our natural being is necessary to our spiritual well-being in this world, therefore, after the things of God's glory, kingdom, and will, we pray for the necessary supports and comforts of this present life, which are the gifts of God, and must be asked of him, *Ton arton epiousion — Bread for the day approaching,* for all the remainder of our lives. *Bread for the time to come, or bread for our being and subsistence,* that which is agreeable to our condition in the world (Prov. 30:8), *food convenient for us* and our families, according to our rank and station.

Every word here has a lesson in it: (1.) We ask for *bread;* that teaches us sobriety and temperance; we ask for *bread,* not dainties, not superfluities; that which is wholesome, though it be not nice. (2.) We ask for *our* bread; that teaches us honesty and industry: we do not ask for the bread out of other people's mouths, not the *bread of deceit* (Prov. 20:17), not the *brad of idleness* (Prov. 31:27), but the bread honestly gotten. (3.) We ask for our *daily* bread; which teaches us not to *take thought for the morrow* (*v.* 34), but constantly to depend upon divine Providence, as those that live from hand to mouth. (4.) We beg of God to *give* it us, not sell it us, nor lend it us, but *give* it. The greatest of men must be beholden to the mercy of God for their *daily bread,* (5.) We pray, "Give it to *us;* not to me only, but to others in common with me." This teaches us charity, and a compassionate concern for the poor and needy. It intimates also, that we ought to pray with our families; we and our households eat together, and therefore ought to pray together. (6.) We pray that God would give us *this day;* which teaches us to renew the desire of our souls toward God, as the wants of our bodies are renewed; as duly as the day comes, we must pray to our heavenly Father, and reckon we could as well go a day without meat, as without prayer.

5. *And forgive us our debts, as we forgive our debtors,* This is connected with the former; and *forgive,* intimating, that unless our sins be pardoned, we can have no comfort in life, or the supports of it. *Our daily bread* does but feed us *as lambs for the slaughter,* if our sins be not pardoned. It intimates, likewise, that we must pray for daily *pardon,* as duly as we pray for daily *bread. He that is washed, needeth to wash his feet.* Here we have,

(1.) A petition; *Father in heaven forgive us our debts,* our debts to thee. Note, [1.] Our sins are our debts; there is a debt of duty, which, as creatures, we owe to our Creator; we do not pray to be discharged from that, but upon the non-payment of that there arises a debt of punishment; in default of obedience to the will of God, we become obnoxious *to the wrath of God;* and for not observing the precept of the law, we stand obliged to the penalty. A debtor is liable to process, so are we; a malefactor is a debtor to the law, so are we. [2.] Our hearts' desire and prayer to our heavenly Father every day should be, that he would *forgive us our debts;* that the obligation to punishment may be cancelled and vacated, that we may *not come into condemnation;* that we may be discharged, and have the comfort of it. In suing out the pardon of our sins, the great plea we have to rely upon is the satisfaction that was made to the justice of God for the sin of man, by the dying of the Lord Jesus our Surety, or rather Bail to the action, that undertook our discharge.

(2.) An argument to enforce this petition; *as we forgive our debtors.* This is not a plea of merit, but a plea of grace. Note, Those that come to God for the forgiveness of their sins against him, must make conscience of forgiving those who have offended them, else they curse themselves when they say the Lord's prayer. Our duty is to *forgive our debtors;* as to debts of money, we must not be rigorous and severe in exacting them from those that cannot pay them without ruining themselves and their families; but this means debt of injury; our debtors are those that *trespass against us,* that *smite us (ch.* 5:39, 40), and in strictness of law, might be prosecuted for it; we must forbear, and forgive, and forget the affronts put upon us, and the wrongs done us; and this is a moral qualification for pardon and peace; it encourages to hope, that God will *forgive us;* for if there be in us this gracious disposition, it is wrought of God, and therefore is a perfection eminently and transcendently in himself; it will be an evidence to us that he has forgiven us, having wrought in us the condition of forgiveness.

6. *And lead us not into temptation, but deliver us from evil.* This petition is expressed,

(1.) Negatively: *Lead us not into temptation.* Having prayed that the guilt of sin may be removed, we pray, as it is fit, that we may never return again to folly, that we may not be tempted to it. It is not as if God tempted any to sin; but, "Lord, do not let Satan loose upon us; chain up that *roaring lion,* for he is subtle and spiteful; Lord, do not leave us to ourselves (Ps. 19:13), for we are very weak; Lord, do not *lay stumbling-blocks* and snares before us, nor put us into circumstances that may be *an occasion of falling."* Temptations are to be prayed against, both because of the discomfort and trouble of them, and because of the danger we are in of being overcome by them, and the guilt and grief that then follow.

(2.) Positively: *But deliver us from evil; apo tou ponērou — from the evil one,* the devil, the tempter; "keep us, that either we may not be assaulted by him, or we may not be overcome by those assaults:" Or *from the evil thing,* sin, the worst of evils; an evil, an only evil; that evil thing which God hates, and which Satan tempts men to and destroys them by. "Lord, deliver us from the evil of the world, the corruption that is in the world through lust; from the evil of every condition in the world; from the evil of death; from the *sting of death, which is sin:* deliver us from ourselves, from our own evil hearts: deliver us from evil men, that they may not be a snare to us, nor we a prey to them."

III. The conclusion: *For thine is the kingdom, and the power and the glory, for ever. Amen.* Some refer this to David's doxology, 1 Chr. 29:11. *Thine, O Lord, is the greatness.* It is,

1. A form of plea to enforce the foregoing petitions. It is our duty to plead with God in prayer, to fill our mouth with

arguments (Job 23:4) not to move God, but to affect ourselves; to encourage the faith, to excite our fervency, and to evidence both. Now the best pleas in prayer are those that are taken from God himself, and from that which he has made known of himself. We must wrestle with God in his own strength, both as to the nature of our pleas and the urging of them. The plea here has special reference to the first three petitions; *"Father in heaven, thy kingdom come, for thine is the kingdom; thy will be done, for thine is the power; hallowed be thy name, for thine is the glory."* And as to our own particular errands, these are encouraging: *"Thine is the kingdom;* thou hast the government of the world, and the protection of the saints, thy willing subjects in it;" God gives and saves like a king. *"Thine is the power,* to maintain and support that kingdom, and to make good all thine engagements to thy people." *Thine is the glory,* as the end of all that which is given to, and done for, the saints, in answer to their prayers; for their *praise waiteth* for him. This is matter of comfort and holy confidence in prayer.

2. It is a form of praise and thanksgiving. The best pleading with God is praising of him; it is the way to obtain further mercy, as it qualifies us to receive it. In all our addresses to God, it is fit that praise should have a considerable share, for *praise becometh the saints;* they are to be our God *for a name and for a praise.* It is just and equal; we praise God, and give him glory, not because he needs it — he is praised by a world of angels, but because he deserves it; and it is our duty to give him glory, in compliance with his design in revealing himself to us. Praise is the work and happiness of heaven; and all that would go to heaven hereafter, must begin their heaven now. Observe, how full this doxology is, *The kingdom, and the power, and the glory,* it is all thine. Note, It becomes us to be copious in praising God. A true saint never thinks he can speak honourably enough of God: here there should be a gracious fluency, and this *for ever.* Ascribing glory to God *for ever,* intimates an acknowledgement, that it is eternally due, and an earnest desire to be eternally doing it, with angels and saints above, Ps. 71:14.

Lastly, To all this we are taught to affix our *Amen,* so be it. God's *Amen* is a grant; his *fiat* is, it shall be so; our *Amen* is only a summary desire; our *fiat* is, let it be so: it is in the token of our desire and assurance to be heard, that we say *Amen. Amen* refers to every petition going before, and thus, in compassion to our infirmities, we are taught to knit up the whole in one word, and so to gather up, in the general, what we have lost and let slip in the particulars. It is good to conclude religious duties with some warmth and vigour, that we may go from them with a sweet savour upon our spirits. It was of old the practice of good people to say, *Amen,* audibly at the end of every prayer, and it is a commendable practice, provided it be done with understanding, as the apostle directs (1 Co. 14:16), and uprightly, with life and liveliness, and inward expressions, answerable to that outward expression of desire and confidence.

Most of the petitions in the Lord's prayer had been commonly used by the Jews in their devotions, or words to the same effect: but that clause in the fifth petition, *As we forgive our debtors,* was perfectly new, and therefore our Saviour here shows for what reason he added it, not with any personal reflection upon the peevishness, litigiousness, and ill nature of the men of that generation, though there was cause enough for it, but only from the necessity and importance of the thing itself. God, in forgiving us, has a peculiar respect to our forgiving those that have injured us; and therefore, when we pray for pardon, we must mention our making conscience of that duty, not only to remind ourselves of it, but to bind ourselves to it. See that parable, *ch.* 18:23–35. Selfish nature is loth to comply with this, and therefore it is here inculcated, *v.* 14, 15.

1. In a promise. *If ye forgive, your heavenly Father will also forgive.* Not as if this were the only condition required; there must be repentance and faith, and new obedience; but as where other graces are in truth, there will be this, so this will be a good evidence of the sincerity of our other graces. He that relents toward his brother, thereby shows that he repents toward his God. Those which in the prayer are called *debts,* are here called *trespasses, debts* of injury, wrongs done to us in our bodies, goods, or reputation: *trespasses* is an extenuating term for offences, *paraptōmata — stumbles, slips, falls.* Note, It is a good evidence, and a good help of our forgiving others, to call the injuries done us by a mollifying, excusing name. Call them not *treasons,* but *trespasses;* not wilful injuries, but casual inadvertencies; *peradventure it was an oversight* (Gen. 43:12), therefore make the best of it. We must forgive, as we hope to be forgiven; and therefore must not only bear no malice, nor mediate revenge, but must not upbraid our brother with the injuries he has done us, nor rejoice in any hurt that befals him, but must be ready to help him and do him good, and if he repent and desire to be friends again, we must be free and familiar with him, as before.

2. In a threatening. *"But if you forgive not* those that have injured you, that is a bad sign you have not the other requisite conditions, but are altogether unqualified for pardon: and therefore *your Father,* whom you call Father, and who, as a father, offers you his grace upon reasonable terms, will nevertheless *not forgive you.* And if other grace be sincere, and yet you be defective greatly in forgiving, you cannot expect the comfort of your pardon, but to have your spirit brought down by some affliction or other to comply with this duty." Note, Those who would have found mercy with God must show mercy to their brethren; no can we expect that he should stretch out the hands of his favour to us, unless we lift up to him *pure hands, without wrath,* 1 Tim. 2:8. If we pray in anger, we have reason to fear God will answer in anger. It has been said, Prayers made in wrath are written in gall. What reason is it that God should forgive us the talents we are indebted to him, if we forgive not our brethren the pence they are indebted to us? Christ *came into the world* as the great Peace-Maker, and not only *to reconcile us to God,* but one to another, and in this we must comply with him. It is great presumption and of dangerous consequence, for any to make a light matter of that which Christ here lays such a stress upon. Men's passions shall not frustrate God's word.

Verses 16–18

We are here cautioned against hypocrisy in fasting, as before in almsgiving, and in prayer.

I. It is here supposed that religious fasting is a duty required of the disciples of Christ, when God, in his providence, calls to it, and when the case of their own souls upon any account requires it; *when the bridegroom is taken away, then shall they fast, ch.* 9:15. Fasting is here put last, because it is not so much a duty for its own sake, as a means to dispose us for other duties. Prayer comes in between almsgiving and fasting, as being the life and soul of both. Christ here speaks especially of private fasts, such as particular persons prescribe to themselves, as free-will offerings, commonly used among the pious Jews; some fasted one day, some two, every week; others seldomer, as they saw cause. On those days they did not eat till sun-set, and then very sparingly. It was not the Pharisee's fasting *twice in the week,* but his boasting of it, that Christ condemned, Lu. 18:12. It is a laudable practice, and we have reason to lament it, that is so generally neglected among Christians. Anna was much in fasting, Lu. 2:37. Cornelius fasted and prayed, Acts 10:30. The primitive Christians were much in it, see Acts 13:3; 14:23. Private fasting is supposed, 1 Co. 7:5. It is an act of self-denial, and mortification of the flesh, a holy revenge upon ourselves, and humiliation under the hand of God. The most grown Christians must hereby own, they are so far from having any thing to be proud of, that they are unworthy of their daily bread. It is a means to curb the flesh and the desires of it, and to make us more lively in religious exercises, as fulness of bread is apt to make us drowsy. Paul was *in fastings often,* and so he *kept under this body, and brought it into subjection.*

II. We are cautioned not to do this *as the hypocrites* did it, lest we lose the reward of it; and the more difficulty attends the duty, the greater loss it is to lose the reward of it.

Now, 1. The *hypocrites* pretended fasting, when there was nothing of that contrition or humiliation of soul in them, which is the life and soul of the duty. Theirs were mock-fasts, the show and shadow without the substance; they took on them to be more humbled than really they were, and so endeavored to put a cheat upon God, than which they could not put a greater affront upon him. The fast that God has chosen, is *a day to afflict the soul, not to hang down the head like a bulrush,* nor for a man *to spread sackcloth and ashes under him;* we are quite mistaken if we call this a fast, Isa. 58:5. Bodily exercise, if that be all, profits little, since that is not fasting to God, even to him.

2. They proclaimed their fasting, and managed it so that all who saw them might take notice that it was a fasting-day with them. Even on these days they appeared in the streets, whereas they should have been in their closets; and the affected a downcast look, a melancholy countenance, a slow and solemn pace; and perfectly disfigured themselves, that men might see how often they fasted, and might extol them as devout, mortified men. Note, It is sad that men, who have, in some measure, mastered their pleasure, which is sensual wickedness, should be ruined by their pride, which is spiritual wickedness, and no less dangerous. Here also *they have their reward,* that praise and applause of men which they court and covet so much; *they have* it, and it is their all.

III. We are directed how to manage a private fast; we must keep it in private, *v.* 17, 18. He does not tell us how often we must fast; circumstances vary, and wisdom is profitable therein to direct; the Spirit in the word has left that to the Spirit in the heart; but take this for a rule, whenever you undertake this duty, study therein to approve yourselves to God, and not to recommend yourselves to the good opinion of men; humility must evermore attend upon our humiliation. Christ does not direct to abate any thing of the reality of the fast; he does not say,"take a little meat, or a little drink, or a little cordial;" no, "let the body suffer, but lay aside the show and appearance of it; appear with thy ordinary countenance, guise, and dress; and while thou deniest thyself thy bodily refreshments, do it so as that it may not be taken notice of, no, not by those that are nearest to thee; look pleasant, *anoint thine head and wash thy face,* as thou dost on ordinary days, on purpose to conceal thy devotion; and thou shalt be no loser in the praise of it at last; for though it be not of men, it shall be of God." Fasting is the humbling of the soul (Ps. 35:13), that is the inside of the duty; let that therefore be thy principal care, and as to the outside of it, covet not to let it be seen. If we be sincere in our solemn fasts, and humble, and trust God's omniscience for our witness, and his goodness for our reward, we shall find, both that he did *see in secret,* and will *reward openly.* Religious fasts, if rightly kept, will shortly be recompensed with an everlasting feast. Our acceptance with God in our private fasts should make us dead, both to the applause of men (we must not do the duty in hopes of this), and to the censures of men too (we must not decline the duty for fear of them). David's fasting was turned to his reproach, Ps. 69:10; and yet, *v.* 13, *As for me,* let them say what they will of me, *my prayer is unto thee in an acceptable time.*

Verses 19–24

Worldly-mindedness is as common and as fatal a symptom of hypocrisy as any other, for by no sin can Satan have a surer and faster hold of the soul, under the cloak of a visible and passable profession of religion, than by this; and therefore Christ, having warned us against coveting *the praise of men,* proceeds next to warn us against coveting the wealth of the world; in this also we must take heed, lest we be as the hypocrites are, and do as they do: the fundamental error that they are guilty of is, that they choose the world for *their reward;* we must therefore take heed of hypocrisy and worldly-mindedness, in the choice we make of our treasure, our end, and our masters.

I. In choosing the *treasure* we *lay up.* Something or other every man has which he makes his *treasure,* his portion, which his heart is upon, to which he carries all he can get, and which he depends upon for futurity. It is *that good,* that chief good, which Solomon speaks of with such an emphasis, Eccl. 2:3. Something the soul will have, which it looks upon as the best thing, which it has a complacency and confidence in above other things. Now Christ designs not to deprive us of our treasure, but to direct us in the choice of it; and here we have,

1. A *good caution* against making *the things that are seen,* that *are temporal,* our best things, and placing our happiness in them. *Lay not up for yourselves treasures upon earth.* Christ's disciples had left all to follow him, let them still keep in the same good mind. A *treasure* is an abundance of something that is in itself, at least in our opinion, precious and valuable, and likely to stand us in stead hereafter. Now we must *not lay up our treasures on earth,* that is, (1.) We must not count these things the best things, nor the most valuable in themselves, nor the most serviceable to us: we must not call them glory, as Laban's sons did, but see and own that they have no glory in comparison with *the glory that excelleth.* (2.) We must not covet an abundance of these things, nor be still grasping at more and more of them, and adding to them, as men do to that which is their treasure, as never

knowing when we have enough. (3.) We must not confide in them for futurity, to be our security and supply in time to come; we must not say to the gold, *Thou art my hope.* (4.) We must not content ourselves with them, as all we need or desire: we must be content with a little for our passage, but not with all for our portion. These things must not be made *our consolation* (Lu. 6:24), our *good things,* Lu. 16:25. Let us consider we are laying up, not for our *posterity* in this world, but for *ourselves* in the other world. We are put to our choice, and made in a manner our own carvers; that is ours which *we lay up for ourselves.* It concerns thee to choose wisely, for thou art choosing for thyself, and shalt have as thou choosest. If we know and consider ourselves what we are, what we are made for, how large our capacities are, and how long our continuance, and that our souls are ourselves, we shall see it is foolish thing to *lay up our treasures on earth.*

2. Here is a *good reason* given why we should not look upon any thing *on earth* as our *treasure,* because it is liable to loss and decay: (1.) From corruption within. That which is treasure *upon earth moth and rust do corrupt.* If the *treasure* be laid up in fine clothes, the *moth* frets them, and they are gone and spoiled insensibly, when we thought them most securely laid up. If it be in corn or other eatables, as his was who had his barns full (Lu. 12:16, 17), *rust* (so we read it) *corrupts* that: *brōsis* — *eating,* eating by men, for *as goods are increased they are increased that eat them* (Eccl. 5:11); eating by mice or other vermin; manna itself bred worms; or it grows mouldy and musty, is struck, or smutted, or blasted; fruits soon rot. Or, if we understand it of silver and gold, they tarnish and canker; they grow less with using, and grow worse with keeping (Jam. 5:2, 3); the *rust and the moth* breed in the metal itself and in the garment itself. Note, Worldly riches have in themselves a principal of corruption and decay; they wither of themselves, and *make themselves wings.* (2.) From violence without. *Thieves break through and steal.* Every hand of violence will be aiming at the house where *treasure* is laid up; nor can any thing be laid up so safe, but we may be spoiled of it. *Numquam ego fortunae credidi, etiam si videretur pacem agere; omnia illa quae in me indulgentissime conferebat, pecuniam, honores, gloriam, eo loco posui, unde posset ea, since metu meo, repetere — I never reposed confidence in fortune, even if she seemed propitious: whatever were the favours which her bounty bestowed, whether wealth, honours, or glory, I so disposed of them, that it was in her power to recall them without occasioning me any alarm.* Seneca. *Consol. ad Helv.* It is folly to make that our *treasure* which we may so easily be robbed of.

3. *Good counsel,* to make the joys and glories of the other world, those *things not seen* that are *eternal,* our best things, and to place our happiness in them. *Lay up for yourselves treasures in heaven.* Note, (1.) There are *treasures in heaven,* as sure as there are on this earth; and those in heaven are the only true *treasures,* the riches and glories and pleasures that are at God's right hand, which those that are sanctified truly arrive at, when they come to be sanctified perfectly. (2.) It is our wisdom to *lay up* our *treasure* in those treasures; to give all diligence to make sure our title to eternal life through Jesus Christ, and to depend upon that as our happiness, and look upon all things here below with a holy contempt, as not worthy to be compared with it. We must firmly believe there is such a happiness, and resolve to be content with that, and to be content with nothing short of it. If we thus make those *treasures* ours, they are laid up, and we may trust God to keep them safe for us; thither let us then refer all our designs, and extend all our desires; thither let us send before our best efforts and best affections. Let us not burthen ourselves with the cash of this world, which will but load and defile us, and be liable to sink us, but lay up in store good securities. The promises are bills of exchange, by which all true believers return their *treasure to heaven,* payable in the future state: and thus we make that sure that will be made sure. (3.) It is a great encouragement to us to *lay up* our *treasure in heaven,* that there it is safe; it will not decay of itself, no *moth* nor *rust* will *corrupt* it; nor can we be by force or fraud deprived of it; *thieves do not break through and steal.* It is a happiness above and beyond the changes and chances of time, *an inheritance incorruptible.*

4. A *good reason* why we should thus choose, and an evidence that we have done so (*v.* 21), *Where your treasure is,* on earth or in heaven, *there will you heart be.* We are therefore concerned to be right and wise in the choice of our *treasure,* because the temper of our minds, and consequently the tenor of our lives, will be accordingly either carnal or spiritual, earthly or heavenly. The *heart* follows the *treasure,* as the needle follows the loadstone, or the sunflower the sun. *Where the treasure is there* the value and esteem are, *there* the love and affection are (Col. 3:2), that way the desires and pursuits go, thitherward the aims and intents are levelled, and all is done with that in view. *Where the treasure is, there* our cares and fears are, lest we come short of it; about that we are most solicitous; *there* our hope and trust are (Prov. 18:10, 11); *there* our joys and delights will be (Ps. 119:111); and *there* our thoughts will be, there the *inward* thought will be, the *first* thought, the *free* thought, the *fixed* thought, the *frequent,* the *familiar* thought. The *heart* is God's due (Prov. 23:26), and that he may have it, our *treasure* must be laid up with him, and then our souls will be lifted up to him.

This direction about laying up our *treasure,* may very fitly be applied to the foregoing caution, of not doing what we do in religion *to be seen of men.* Our *treasure* is our alms, prayers, and fastings, and the reward of them; if we have done these only to gain the applause of men, we have *laid up this treasure on earth,* have lodged it in the hands of men, and must never expect to hear any further of it. Now it is folly to do this, for *the praise of men* we covet so much is liable to corruption: it will soon be rusted, and moth-eaten, and tarnished; a little folly, like a dead fly, will spoil it all, Eccl. 10:1. Slander and calumny are *thieves that break through and steal* it away, and so we lose all the *treasure* of our performances; we have run in vain, and laboured in vain, because we misplaced our intentions in doing of them. Hypocritical services lay up nothing in heaven (Isa. 58:3); the gain of them is gone, when the soul is called for, Job 27:8. But if we have prayed and fasted and given alms in truth and uprightness, with an eye to God and to his acceptance, and have approved ourselves to him therein, we have laid up that treasure *in heaven; a book of remembrance is written there* (Mal. 3:16), and being there recorded, they shall be there rewarded, and we shall meet them again with comfort on the other side death and the grave. Hypocrites are *written in the earth* (Jer. 17:13), but God's faithful ones have their names *written in heaven,* Lu. 10:20. Acceptance with God is *treasure in heaven,* which can neither be corrupted nor stolen. His *well done* shall stand for ever; and if we have thus laid up our *treasure* with him, with him our *hearts* will be; and where can they be better?

II. We must take heed of hypocrisy and worldly-mindedness in choosing the *end we look at.* Our concern as to this is represented by two sorts of eyes which men have, a *single eye* and an *evil eye, v.* 22, 23. The expressions here are somewhat dark because concise; we shall therefore take them in some variety of interpretation. *The light of the body is the eye,* that is plain; *the eye* is discovering and directing; the *light of the world* would avail us little without this *light of the body;* it is *the light of the eye* that *rejoiceth the heart* (Prov. 15:30), but what is that which is here compared to the *eye* in the *body.*

1. *The eye,* that is, *the heart* (so some) if that *be single — haplous — free and bountiful* (so the word is frequently rendered, as Rom. 12:8; 2 Co. 8:2, 9:11, 13; Jam. 1:5, and we read of a *bountiful eye,* Prov. 22:9). If the heart be liberally affected and stand inclined to goodness and charity, it will direct the man to Christian actions, the whole conversation *will be full of light,* full of evidences and instances of true Christianity, that *pure religion and undefiled before God and the Father* (Jam. 1:27), *full of light,* of good works, which are our *light shining before men;* but *if the heart be evil,* covetous, and hard, and envious, griping and grudging (such a temper of mind is often expressed by an *evil eye, ch.* 20:15; Mk. 7:22; Prov. 23:6, 7), *the body will be full of darkness,* the whole conversation will be heathenish and unchristian. *The instruments of the churl are* and always will be *evil,* but *the liberal deviseth liberal things,* Isa. 32:5–8. *If the light that is in us,* those affections which should guide us to that which is good, *be darkness,* if these be corrupt and worldly, if there be not so much as good nature in a man, not so much as a kind disposition, *how great is* the corruption of a man, and the *darkness* in which he sits! This sense seems to agree with the context; we must *lay up treasure in heaven* by liberality in giving alms, and that not grudgingly but with cheerfulness, Lu. 12:33; 2 Co. 9:7. But these words in the parallel place do not come in upon any such occasion, Lu. 11:34, and therefore the coherence here does not determine that to be the sense of them.

2. *The eye,* that is, *the understanding* (so some); the practical judgment, the conscience, which is to the other faculties of the soul, as *the eye* is to the *body,* to guide and direct their motions; now *if this eye be single,* if it make a true and right judgment, and discern things that differ, especially in the great concern of *laying up the treasure* so as to choose aright in that, it will rightly guide the affections and actions, which will all be *full of the light* of grace and comfort; *but if this be evil* and corrupt, and instead of leading the inferior powers, is led, and bribed, and biassed by them, if this be erroneous and misinformed, the heart and life must needs be *full of darkness,* and the whole conversation corrupt. They that *will not understand,* are said to *walk on in darkness,* Ps. 82:5. It is sad when the spirit of a man, that should be *the candle of the Lord,* is an *ignis fatuus:* when the *leaders of the people,* the leaders of the faculties, *cause them to err,* for then *they that are led of them are destroyed,* Isa. 9:16. An error in the practical judgment is fatal, it is that which calls *evil good and good evil* (Isa. 5:20); therefore it concerns us to understand things aright, to get our eyes anointed with eye-salve.

3. *The eye,* that is, *the aims* and *intentions; by the eye* we set our end before us, the mark we shoot at, the place we go to, we keep that in view, and direct our motion accordingly; in every thing we do in religion; there is something or other that we have in our *eye;* now *if our eye be single,* if we aim honestly, fix right ends, and move rightly towards them, if we aim purely and only at the glory of God, seek his honor and favour, and direct all entirely to him, then *the eye is single;* Paul's was so when he said, *To me to live is Christ;* and if we be right here, *the whole body will be full of light,* all the actions will be regular and gracious, pleasing to God and comfortable to ourselves; *but if this eye be evil,* if, instead of aiming only at the glory of God, and our acceptance with him, we look aside at the applause of men, and while we profess to honour God, contrive to honour ourselves, and seek our own things under colour of *seeking the things of Christ,* this spoils all, the whole conversation will be perverse and unsteady, and the foundations being thus out of course, there can be nothing but *confusion and every evil work* in the superstructure. Draw the lines from the circumference to any other point but the centre, and they will cross. *If the light that is in thee be* not only dim, but *darkness* itself, it is a fundamental error, and destructive to all that follows. The end specifies the action. It is of the last importance in religion, that we be right in our aims, and make *eternal things,* not *temporal,* our scope, 2 Co. 4:18. The hypocrite is like the waterman, that looks one way and rows another; the true Christian like the traveller, that has his journey's end in his eye. The hypocrite soars like the kite, with his eye upon the prey below, which he is ready to come down to when he has a fair opportunity; the true Christian soars like the lark, higher and higher, forgetting the things that are beneath.

III. We must take heed of hypocrisy and worldly-mindedness in choosing the master we serve, *v.* 24. *No man can serve two masters.* Serving *two masters* is contrary to the *single eye;* for *the eye* will be to the master's hand, Ps. 123:1, 2. Our Lord Jesus here exposes the cheat which those put upon their own souls, who think to divide between God and the world, to have a *treasure on earth,* and a *treasure in heaven* too, to please God and please men too. Why not? says the hypocrite; it is good to have two strings to one's bow. They hope to make their religion serve their secular interest, and so turn to account both ways. The pretending mother was for dividing the child; the Samaritans will compound between God and idols. No, says Christ, this will not do; it is but a supposition that *gain is godliness,* 1 Tim. 6:5. Here is,

1. A general maxim laid down; it is likely it was a proverb among the Jews, *No man can serve two masters,* much less two gods; for their commands will some time or other cross or contradict one another, and their occasions interfere. While *two masters* go together, a servant may follow them both; but when they part, you will see to which he belongs; he cannot love, and observe, and cleave to both as he should. If to the one, not to the other; either this or that must be comparatively hated and despised. This truth is plain enough in common cases.

2. The application of it to the business in hand. *Ye cannot serve God and Mammon. Mammon* is a Syriac word, that signifies gain; so that whatever in this world is, or is accounted by us to be, *gain* (Phil. 3:7), is *mammon. Whatever is in the world, the lust of the flesh, the lust of the eye, and the pride of life,* is *mammon.* To some their belly is their *mammon,*

and they serve that (Phil. 3:19); to others their ease, their sleep, their sports and pastimes, are their *mammon* (Prov. 6:9); to others worldly riches (James 4:13); to others honours and preferments; the praise and applause of men was the Pharisees' *mammon;* in a word, self, the unity in which the world's trinity centres, sensual, secular self, is the *mammon* which cannot be served in conjunction with *God;* for if it be served, it is in competition with him and in contradiction to him. He does not say, We *must* not or we *should* not, but we *cannot serve God and Mammon;* we *cannot* love both (1 Jn. 2:15; Jam. 4:4); or hold to both, or hold by both in observance, obedience, attendance, trust, and dependence, for they are contrary the one to the other. *God* says, *"My son, give me thy heart." Mammon* says, "No, give it me." *God* says, *"Be content with such things as ye have." Mammon* says, "Grasp at all that ever thou canst. *Rem, rem, quocunque modo rem — Money, money; by fair means or by foul, money." God* says, "Defraud not, never lie, be honest and just in all thy dealings." *Mammon* says "Cheat thine own Father, if thou canst gain by it." *God* says, "Be charitable." *Mammon* says, "Hold thy own: this giving undoes us all." *God* says, *"Be careful for nothing." Mammon* says, "Be careful for every thing." *God* says, *"Keep holy thy sabbath-day." Mammon* says, "Make use of that day as well as any other for the world." Thus inconsistent are the commands of *God and Mammon,* so that we *cannot serve* both. Let us not then *halt between God and Baal, but choose ye this day whom ye will serve,* and abide by our choice.

Verses 25–34

There is scarcely any one sin against which our Lord Jesus more largely and earnestly warns his disciples, or against which he arms them with more variety of arguments, than the sin of disquieting, distracting, distrustful cares about the things of life, which are a bad sign that both the *treasure* and the heart are *on the earth;* and therefore he thus largely insists upon it. Here is,

I. The prohibition laid down. It is the counsel and command of the Lord Jesus, that we *take no thought* about the things of this world; *I say unto you.* He says it as our Lawgiver, and the Sovereign of our hearts; he says it as our Comforter, and the Helper of our joy. What is it that he says? It is this, and *he that hath ears to hear, let him hear it. Take no thought for your life, nor yet for your body* (*v.* 25). *Take no thought, saying, What shall we eat?* (*v.* 31) and again (*v.* 34), *Take no thought, mē merimnate — Be not in care.* As against hypocrisy, so against worldly cares, the caution is thrice repeated, and yet no vain repetition: *precept* must be *upon precept, and line upon line,* to the same purport, and all little enough; it is a *sin which doth so easily beset us.* It intimates how pleasing it is to Christ, and of how much concern it is to ourselves, that we should live without carefulness. It is the repeated command of the Lord Jesus to his disciples, that they should not divide and pull in pieces their own minds with care about the world. There is a *thought* concerning the things of this life, which is not only lawful, but duty, such as is commended in the virtuous woman. See Prov. 27:23. The word is used concerning Paul's care of the churches, and Timothy's care for the state of souls, 2 Co. 11:28; Phil. 2:20.

But the *thought* here forbidden is, 1. A disquieting, tormenting *thought,* which hurries the mind hither and thither, and hangs it in suspense; which disturbs our joy in God, and is a damp upon our hope in him; which breaks the sleep, and hinders our enjoyment of ourselves, of our friends, and of what God has given us. 2. A distrustful, unbelieving *thought.* God has promised to provide for those that are his all things needful for life as well as godliness, *the life that now is,* food and a covering: not dainties, but necessaries. He never said, "They shall be feasted," but, *"Verily, they shall be fed."* Now an inordinate care for time to come, and fear of wanting those supplies, spring from a disbelief of these promises, and of the wisdom and goodness of Divine Providence; and that is the evil of it. As to present sustenance, we may and must use lawful means to get it, else we tempt God; we must be diligent in our callings, and prudent in proportioning our expenses to what we have, and we must pray for *daily bread;* and if all other means fail, we may and must ask relief of those that are able to give it. He was none of the best of men that said, *To beg I am ashamed* (Lu. 16:3); as he was, who (*v.* 21) *desired to be fed with the crumbs;* but for the future, we must *cast our care upon God,* and *take no thought,* because it looks like a jealousy of God, who knows how to give what we want when we know not now to get it. Let our souls dwell at ease in him! This gracious carelessness is the same with that sleep which God gives to his beloved, in opposition to the worldling's toil, Ps. 127:2. Observe the cautions here,

(1.) *Take no thought for your life.* Life is our greatest concern for this world; *All that a man has will he give for his life;* yet take no thought about it. [1.] Not about the *continuance* of it; refer it to God to *lengthen* or *shorten* it as he pleases; *my times are in thy hand,* and they are in a good hand. [2.] Not about the *comforts* of this life; refer it to God to embitter or sweeten it as he pleases. We must not be solicitous, no not about the necessary support of this life, *food* and *raiment;* these God has promised, and therefore we may more confidently expect; say not, *What shall we eat?* It is the language of one at a loss, and almost despairing; whereas, though many good people have the prospect of little, yet there are few but have present support.

(2.) *Take no thought for the morrow,* for the time to come. Be not solicitous for the future, how you shall live next year, or when you are old, or what you shall leave behind you. As we must not *boast* of to-morrow, so we must not *care for* to-morrow, or the events of it.

II. The reasons and arguments to enforce this prohibition. One would think the command of Christ was enough to restrain us from this foolish sin of disquieting, distrustful care, independently of the comfort of our own souls, which is so nearly concerned; but to show how much the heart of Christ is upon it, and what *pleasures he takes* in those that *hope in his mercy,* the command is backed with the most powerful arguments. If reason may but rule us, surely we shall ease ourselves of these thorns. To free us from anxious thoughts, and to expel them, Christ here suggests to us *comforting* thoughts, that we may be filled with them. It will be worth while to take pains with our own hearts, to argue them out of their disquieting cares, and to make ourselves ashamed of them. They may be weakened by right reason, but it is by an active faith only that they can be overcome. Consider then,

1. *Is not the life more than meat, and the body than raiment? v.* 25. Yes, no doubt it is; so he says who had reason to understand the true value of present things, for he made them, he supports them, and supports us by them; and the thing speaks for itself. Note, (1.) Our *life* is a greater blessing than our *livelihood.* It is true, life cannot subsist without a livelihood; but the meat and raiment which are here represented as inferior to the life and body are such as are for ornament and delight; for about such as are for ornament ad delight; for about such we are apt to be solicitous. Meat and raiment are in order to life, and the *end* is more noble and excellent than the *means.* The daintiest food and finest raiment are from the *earth,* but life from the *breath of God.* Life is the *light of men;* meat is but the *oil* that feeds that light: so that the difference between rich and poor is very inconsiderable, since, in the greatest things, they stand on the same level, and differ only in the less. (2.) This is an encouragement to us to trust God for *food* and *raiment,* and so to ease ourselves of all perplexing cares about them. God has given us life, and given us the body; it was an act of power, it was an act of favour, it was done without our care: what cannot he do for us, who did that? — what will he not? If we take care about our souls and eternity, which are more than the body, and its life, we may leave it to God to provide for us food and raiment, which are less. God has maintained our lives hitherto; if sometimes with pulse and water, that has answered the end; he has protected us and kept us alive. He that guards us against the evils we are exposed to, will supply us with the *good things* we are in need of. If he had been pleased to kill us, to starve us, he would not so often have *given his angels a charge concerning us* to keep us.

2. *Behold the fowls of the air,* and *consider the lilies of the field.* Here is an argument taken from God's common providence toward the inferior creatures, and their dependence, according to their capacities, upon that providence. A fine pass fallen man has come to, that he must be sent to school to the *fowls of the air,* and that they must *teach him!* Job 12:7, 8.

(1.) Look upon the *fowls,* and learn to trust God *for food* (*v.* 26), and disquiet not yourselves with thoughts *what you shall eat.*

[1.] Observe the providence of God concerning them. Look upon them, and receive instruction. There are various sorts of fowls; they are numerous, some of them ravenous, but they are all fed, and fed with food convenient for them; it is rare that any of them perish for want of food, even in winter, and there goes no little to feed them all the year round. The fowls, as they are least serviceable to man, so they are least within his care; men often feed upon them, but seldom feed them; yet they are fed, we know not how, and some of them fed best in the hardest weather; and it is *your heavenly Father that feeds them;* he *knows all the wild fowls of the mountains,* better than you know the tame ones at your own barn-door, Ps. 50:11. Not a sparrow lights to the ground, to pick up a grain of corn, but by the providence of God, which extends itself to the meanest creatures. But that which is especially observed here is, that they are fed without any care or project of their own; *they sow not, neither do they reap, nor gather into barns.* The ant indeed does, and the bee, and they are set before us as examples of prudence and industry; but the fowls of the air do not; they make no provision for the future themselves, and yet every day, as duly as the day comes, provision is made for them, and their *eyes wait on God,* that great and good Housekeeper, who *provides food for all flesh.*

[2.] Improve this for your encouragement to trust in God. *Are ye not much better than they?* Yes, certainly you are. Note, The *heirs* of heaven are much better than the *fowls* of heaven; nobler and more excellent beings, and, by faith, they soar higher; they are of a better nature and nurture, *wiser than the fowls of heaven* (Job 35:11): though the children of this world, that *know not the judgment of the Lord,* are not so wise as *the stork, and the crane, and the swallow* (Jer. 8:7), you are dearer to God, and nearer, though they fly in the open firmament of heaven. He is their Master and Lord, their Owner and Master; but besides all this, he is your Father, and in his account *ye are of more value than many sparrows;* you are his children, his first-born; now he that feeds his birds surely will not starve his babes. They trust your Father's providence, and will not you trust it? In dependence upon that, they are careless for the morrow; and being so, they live the merriest lives of all creatures; they *sing among the branches* (Ps. 104:12), and, to the best of their power, they praise their Creator. If we were, by faith, as unconcerned about the morrow as they are, we should sing as cheerfully as they do; for it is worldly care that mars our mirth and damps our joy, and silences our praise, as much as any thing.

(2.) Look upon the *lilies,* and learn to trust God for *raiment.* That is another part of our care, *what we shall put on;* for decency, to cover us; for defence, to keep us warm; yea, and, with many, for dignity and ornament, to make them look great and fine; and so much concerned are they for gaiety and variety in their clothing, that this care returns almost as often as that for their daily bread. Now to ease us of this care, let us *consider the lilies of the field;* not only *look upon* them (every eyes does that with pleasure), but *consider* them. Note, There is a great deal of good to be learned from what we see every day, if we would but consider it, Prov. 6:6; 24:32.

[1.] Consider how *frail* the lilies are; they are the *grass of the field.* Lilies, though distinguished by their colours, are still but *grass.* Thus *all flesh is grass:* though some in the endowments of body and mind are as lilies, much admired, still they are grass; the grass of the field in nature and constitution; they stand upon the same level with others. Man's days, at best, are *as grass,* as the *flower of the grass* 1 Pt. 1:24. This grass *to-day is,* and *to-morrow is cast into the oven;* in a little while the place that *knows us* will *know us no more.* The grave is the oven into which we shall be cast, and in which we shall be consumed as grass in the fire, Ps. 49:14. This intimates a reason why we should not take thought for the morrow, what we shall put on, because perhaps, by to-morrow, we may have occasion for our grave-clothes.

[2.] Consider how *free from care* the lilies are: they *toil not* as men do, to earn clothing; as servants, to earn their liveries; *neither do they spin,* as women do, to make clothing. It does not follow that we must therefore neglect, or do carelessly, the proper business of this life; it is the praise of the virtuous woman, that *she lays her hand to the spindle, makes fine linen and sells it,* Prov. 31:19, 24. Idleness *tempts* God, instead of *trusting* him; but he that provides for inferior creatures, without their labour, will much more provide for us, by blessing our labour, which he has made our duty. And if we should, through sickness, be unable to *toil* and *spin,* God can furnish us with what is necessary for us.

[3.] Consider how *fair,* how *fine* the lilies are; *how they grow;* what they *grow from.* The root of the lily or tulip, as other bulbous roots, is, in winter, lost and buried under ground, yet, when spring returns, it appears, and starts up in a little time; hence it is promised to God's Israel, that they should grow *as the lily,* Hos. 14:5. Consider what they *grow to.* Out of that obscurity in a few weeks they come to be so very gay, that even *Solomon, in all his glory, was not arrayed like one of these.* The array of Solomon was very splendid and magnificent: he that had the peculiar treasure of kings and provinces, and studiously affected pomp and gallantry, doubtless had the richest clothing, and the best made up, that could be got; especially when he appeared in his glory on high days. And yet, let him dress himself as fine as he could, he comes far short of the beauty of the lilies, and a bed of tulips outshines him. Let us, therefore, be ambitious of the *wisdom* of Solomon, in which he was outdone by none (wisdom to do our duty in our places), rather than the *glory* of Solomon, in which he was outdone by the lilies. Knowledge and grace are the perfection of man, not beauty, much less fine clothes. Now God is here said thus to *clothe the grass of the field.* Note, All the excellences of the creature flow from God, the Fountain and spring of them. It was he that gave the horse his strength, and the lily its beauty; every creature is in itself, as well as to us, what he makes it to be.

[4.] Consider how instructive all this is to us, *v.* 30.

First, As to *fine* clothing, this teaches us not to care for it at all, not to covet it, nor to be proud of it, not to make the *putting on of apparel* our *adorning,* for after all our care in this the lilies will far outdo us; we cannot dress so fine as they do, why then should we attempt to vie with them? Their adorning will soon perish, and so will ours; they fade — *are to-day,* and *to-morrow are cast,* as other rubbish, *into the oven;* and the clothes we are proud of are wearing out, the gloss is soon gone, the color fades, the shape goes out of fashion, or in awhile the garment itself is worn out; such is man in all his pomp (Isa. 40:6, 7), especially rich men (Jam. 1:10); they *fade away in their ways.*

Secondly, As to *necessary* clothing; this teaches us to cast the care of it upon God — Jehovah-jireh; trust him that clothes the lilies, to provide for you what you shall *put on.* If he give such fine clothes to the grass, much more will he give fitting clothes to his own children; clothes that shall be warm upon them, not only *when he quieteth the earth with the south wind,* but when he disquiets it with the *north wind,* Job 37:17. He shall much more clothe you: for you are nobler creatures, of a more excellent being; if so he clothe the short-lived grass, much more will he clothe you that are made for immortality. Even the children of Nineveh are preferred before the gourd (Jonah 4:10, 11), much more the sons of Zion, that are in covenant with God. Observe the title he gives them (*v.* 30), *O ye of little faith.* This may be taken, 1. As an encouragement to truth faith, though it be but weak; it entitles us to the divine care, and a promise of suitable supply. Great faith shall be commended, and shall procure great things, but little faith shall not be rejected, even that shall procure food and raiment. *Sound* believers shall be provided for, though they be not *strong* believers. The babes in the family are fed and clothed, as well as those that are grown up, and with a special care and tenderness; say not, I am but a child, but a dry tree (Isa. 56:3, 5), for though *poor and needy* yet *the Lord thinketh on thee.* Or, 2. It is rather a rebuke to weak faith, though it be true, *ch.* 14:31. It intimates what is at the bottom of all our inordinate care and thoughtfulness; it is owing to the weakness of our faith, and the remains of unbelief in us. If we had but more faith, we should have less care.

3. *Which of you,* the wisest, the strongest of you, *by taking thought, can add one cubit to his stature?* (*v.* 27) to *his age,* so some; but the measure of a cubit denotes it to be meant of the stature, and the age at longest is but a span, Ps. 39:5. Let us consider, (1.) We did not arrive at the stature we are of by our own care and thought, but by the providence of God. An infant of a span long has grown up to be a man of six feet, and how was one cubit after another added to his stature? not by his own forecast or contrivance; he grew he knew not how, by the power and goodness of God. Now he that made our bodies, and made them of such size, surely will take care to provide for them. Note, God is to be acknowledged in the increase of our bodily strength and stature, and to be trusted for all needful supplies, because he has made it to appear, that he is mindful for the body. The growing age is the thoughtless, careless age, yet we grow; and shall not he who reared us to this, provide for us now we are reared? (2.) We cannot alter the stature we are of, if we would: what a foolish and ridiculous thing would it be for a man of low stature to perplex himself, to break his sleep, and beat his brains, about it, and to be continually taking thought how he might be a cubit higher; when, after all, he knows he cannot effect it, and therefore he had better be content and take it as it is! We are not all of a size, yet the difference in stature between one and another is not material, nor of any great account; a little man is ready to wish he were as tall as such a one, but he knows it is to no purpose, and therefore does as well as he can with it. Now as we do in reference to our bodily stature, so we should do in reference to our worldly estate. [1.] We should not covet an abundance of the wealth of this world, any more than we would covet the addition of a cubit to one's stature, which is a great deal in a man's height; it is enough to grow by inches; such an addition would but make one unwieldy, and a burden to one's self. [2.] We must reconcile ourselves to our state, as we do to our stature; we must set the conveniences against the inconveniences, and so make a virtue of necessity: what cannot be remedied must be made the best of. We cannot alter the disposals of Providence, and therefore must acquiesce in them, accommodate ourselves to them, and relieve ourselves, as well as we can, against inconveniences, as Zaccheus against the inconvenience of his stature, by climbing into the tree.

4. *After all these things do the Gentiles seek, v.* 32. Thoughtfulness about the world is a *heathenish* sin, and unbecoming *Christians.* The *Gentiles* seek *these things,* because they know not *better things;* they are eager for this world, because they are strangers to a better; they seek these things with care and anxiety, because they are *without God in the world,* and understand not his providence. They fear and worship their idols, but know not how to trust them for deliverance and supply, and, therefore, are themselves full of care; but it is a shame for Christians, who build upon nobler principles, and profess a religion which teaches them not only that there is a Providence, but that there are promises made to the good of the life that now is, which teaches them a confidence in God and a contempt of the world, and gives such reasons for both; it is a shame for them to walk as Gentiles walk, and to fill their heads and hearts with these things.

5. *Your heavenly Father knows ye have need of all these things;* these necessary things, food and raiment; he knows our wants better than we do ourselves; though he be in heaven, and his children on earth, he observes what the least and poorest of them has occasion for (Rev. 2:9), *I know thy poverty.* You think, if such a good friend did not but know your wants and straits, you would soon have relief: your God knows them; and he is your Father that loves you and pities you, and is ready to help you; your heavenly Father, who has wherewithal to supply all your needs: away, therefore, with all disquieting thoughts and cares; go to thy Father; tell him, *he knows that thou has need of such and such things;* he asks you, *Children, have you any meat?* Jn. 21:5. Tell him whether you have or have not. Though he knows our wants, he will know them from us; and when we have opened them to him, let us cheerfully refer ourselves to his wisdom, power, and goodness, for our supply. Therefore, we should ease ourselves of the burthen of care, by casting it upon God, because it is he *that careth for us* (1 Pt. 5:7), and what needs all this ado? If he care, why should be care?

6. *Seek first the kingdom of God, and his righteousness, and all these things shall be added unto you. v.* 33. Here is a double argument against the sin of *thoughtfulness; take no thought* for your life, the life of the body; for, (1.) You have greater and better things to take thought about, the life of your soul, your eternal happiness; that is the *one thing needful* (Lu. 10:42), about which you should employ your thoughts, and which is commonly neglected in those hearts wherein worldly cares have the ascendant. If we were but more careful to please God, and to work out our own salvation, we should be less solicitous to please ourselves, and work out an estate in the world. Thoughtfulness for our souls in the most effectual cure of thoughtfulness for the world. (2.) You have a surer and easier, a safer and more compendious way to obtain the necessaries of this life, than by carking, and caring, and fretting about them; and that is, by *seeking first the kingdom of God,* and making religion your business: say not that this is the way to starve, no, it is the way to be well provided for, even in this world. Observe here,

[1.] The great duty required: it is the sum and substance of our whole duty: "*Seek first the kingdom of God,* mind religion as your great and principle concern." Our duty is to seek; to desire, pursue, and aim at these things; it is a word that has in it much of the constitution of the new covenant in favour of us; *though we have not attained,* but in many things fail and come short, sincere seeking (a careful concern and an earnest endeavor) is accepted. Now observe, *First,* The object of this seeking; *The kingdom of God, and his righteousness;* we must mind heaven as our end, and holiness as our way. "Seek the comforts of the kingdom of grace and glory as your felicity. Aim at the *kingdom of heaven;* press towards it; give diligence to make it sure; resolve not to take up short of it; seek for this glory, honour, and immortality; prefer heaven and heavenly blessings far before earth and earthly delights." We make nothing of our religion, if we do not make heaven of it. And with the *happiness* of this kingdom, seek the *righteousness* of it; *God's righteousness,* the righteousness which he requires to be wrought *in* us, and wrought *by* us, such as exceeds that of the scribes and Pharisees; we must *follow peace and holiness,* Heb. 12:14. *Secondly,* The order of it. *Seek first the kingdom of God.* Let your care for your souls and another world take the place of all other cares: and let all the concerns of this life be made subordinate to those of the life to come: we must seek the things of Christ more than our own things; and if every they come in competition, we must remember to which we are to give the preference. "Seek these things *first;* first in thy days: let the morning of thy youth be dedicated to God. Wisdom must be sought early; it is good beginning betimes to be religious. Seek the first every day; let waking thoughts be of God." Let this be our principle, to do that first which is most needful, and let him that is the First, have the first.

[2.] The gracious promise annexed; *all these things,* the necessary supports of life, *shall be added unto you;* shall be *given over and above;* so it is in the margin. You shall have what you seek, the *kingdom of God and his righteousness,* for never any sought *in vain,* that sought *in earnest;* and besides that, you shall have food and raiment, by way of overplus; as he that buys goods has paper and packthread given him in the bargain. *Godliness has the promise of the life that now is,* 1 Tim. 4:8. Solomon asked wisdom, and had that and other things added to him, 2 Chr. 1:11, 12. O what a blessed change would it make in our hearts and lives, did we but firmly believe this truth, that the best way to be comfortably provided for in this world, is to be most intent upon another world! We then begin at the right end of our work, when we begin with God. If we give diligence to make sure to ourselves the kingdom of God and the righteousness thereof, as to all the things of this life, Jehovah-jireh — the Lord will provide as much of them as he sees good for us, and more we would not wish for. Have we trusted in him for the *portion of our inheritance* at our end, and shall we not trust him for the *portion of our cup,* in the way to it? God's Israel were not only brought to Canaan at last, but had their charges borne through the wilderness. O that we were more thoughtful about the things that are not seen, that are eternal, and then the less thoughtful we should be, and the less thoughtful we should need to be, about the things that are seen, that are temporal! *Also regard not your stuff,* Gen. 45:20, 23.

7. *The morrow shall take thought for the things of itself: sufficient unto the day is the evil thereof, v.* 34. We must not perplex ourselves inordinately about future events, because every day brings along with it its own burthen of cares and grievances, as, if we look about us, and suffer not our fears to betray the succours which grace and reason offer, it brings along with it its own strength and supply too. So that we are here told,

(1.) That *thoughtfulness* for the morrow is *needless; Let the morrow take thought for the things of itself.* If wants and troubles be renewed with the day, there are aids and provisions renewed likewise; *compassions,* that are *new every morning,* Lam. 3:22, 23. The saints have a Friend that is *their arm every morning,* and gives out fresh supplies daily (Isa. 33:2), according *as the business of every day requires* (Ezra 3:4), and so he keeps his people in constant dependence upon him. Let us refer it therefore to the morrow's strength, to do the morrow's work, and bear the morrow's burthen. Tomorrow, and the things of it, will be provided for without us; why need we anxiously care for that which is so wisely cared for already? This does not forbid a prudent foresight, and preparation accordingly, but a perplexing solicitude, and a prepossession of difficulties and calamities, which may perhaps never come, or if they do, may be easily borne, and the evil of them guarded against. The meaning is, let us *mind present duty,* and then *leave events to God;* do the *work of the day in its day,* and then let *to-morrow bring its work along with it.*

(2.) That thoughtfulness for the morrow is one of those *foolish and hurtful lusts,* which those that will be rich fall into, and one of the *many sorrows,* wherewith they *pierce themselves through. Sufficient unto the day is the evil thereof.* This present day has trouble enough attending it, we need not *accumulate* burthens by *anticipating* our trouble, nor borrow perplexities from to-morrow's evils to add to those of this day. It is uncertain what to-morrow's evils may be, but whatever they be, it is time enough to take thought about them when they come. What a folly it is to take that trouble upon ourselves this day by care and fear, which belongs to another day, and will be never the lighter when it comes? Let us not pull that upon ourselves all together at once, which Providence has wisely ordered to be borne by parcels. The conclusion of this whole matter then is, that it is the will and command of the Lord Jesus, that his disciples should not be their own tormentors, nor make their passage through this world more dark and unpleasant, by their apprehension of troubles, than God has made it by the troubles themselves. By our daily prayers we may procure strength to bear us up under our daily troubles, and to arm us against the temptations that attend them, and then let none of these things move us.

CHAPTER 7

This chapter continues and concludes Christ's sermon on the mount, which is purely practical, directing us to order our conversation aright, both toward God and man; for the design of the Christian religion is to make men good, every way good. We have, I. Some rules concerning censure and reproof (*v.* 1–6). II. Encouragements given us to pray to God for what we need (*v.* 7–11). III. The necessity of strictness in conversation urged upon us (*v.* 12–14). IV. A caution given us to take heed of false prophets (*v.* 15–20). V. The conclusion of the whole sermon, showing the necessity of universal obedience to Christ's commands, without which we cannot expect to be happy (*v.* 21–27). VI. The impression which Christ's doctrine made upon his hearers (*v.* 28, 29).

Verses 1–6

Our Saviour is here directing us how to conduct ourselves in reference to the faults of others; and his expressions seem intended as a reproof to the scribes and Pharisees, who were very rigid and severe, very magisterial and supercilious, in condemning all about them, as those commonly are, that are proud and conceited in justifying themselves. We have here,

I. A caution *against judging v.* 1, 2. There are those whose office it is to judge — magistrates and ministers. Christ, though he made not himself a Judge, yet came not to unmake them, for by him *princes decree justice;* but this is directed to private persons, to his disciples, who shall hereafter *sit on thrones judging,* but not now. Now observe,

1. The prohibition; *Judge not.* We must judge ourselves, and judge our own acts, but we must not judge our brother, not magisterially assume such an authority over others, as we allow not them over us: since our rule is, to be *subject to one another. Be not many masters,* Jam. 3:1. We must not sit in the judgment-seat, to make our word a law to every body. We must not judge our brother, that is, we must not *speak evil* of him, so it is explained, Jam. 4:11. We must not *despise him,* nor *set him at nought,* Rom. 14:10. We must not judge rashly, nor pass such a judgment upon our brother as has no ground, but is only the product of our own jealousy and ill nature. We must not make the worst of people, nor infer such invidious things from their words and actions as they will not bear. We must not judge uncharitably, unmercifully, nor with a spirit of revenge, and a desire to do mischief. We must not judge of a man's state by a single act, nor of what he is in himself by what he is to us, because in our own cause we are apt to be partial. We must not judge the hearts of others, nor their intentions, for it is God's prerogative to try the heart, and we must not step into his throne; nor must we judge of their eternal state, nor call them *hypocrites, reprobates,* and *castaways;* that is stretching beyond our line; what have we to do, thus to judge another man's servant? Counsel him, and help him, but do not judge him.

2. The reason to enforce this prohibition. *That ye be not judged.* This intimates, (1.) That if we presume to judge others, we may expect to be ourselves judged. He who usurps the bench, shall be called to the bar; he shall be judged of men; commonly none are more censured, than those who are most censorious; every one will have a stone to throw at them; he who, like Ishmael, has his hand, his tongue, *against every man,* shall, like him, have *every man's* hand and tongue *against him* (Gen. 16:12); and no mercy shall be shown to the reputation of those that show no mercy to the reputation of others. Yet that is not the worst of it; they shall be judged of God; from him they shall receive the *greater condemnation,* Jam. 3:1. Both parties must appear before him (Rom. 14:10), who, as he will relieve the *humble sufferer,* will also resist the *haughty scorner,* and give him enough of judging. (2.) That if we be modest and charitable in our censures of others, and decline judging them, and judge ourselves rather, *we shall not be judged of the Lord.* As God will forgive those that forgive their brethren; so he will not judge those that will not judge their brethren; the *merciful shall find mercy.* It is an evidence of humility, charity, and deference to God, and shall be owned and rewarded by him accordingly. See Rom. 14:10.

The judging of those that judge others is according to the law of retaliation; *With what judgment ye judge, ye shall be judged, v.* 2. The righteous God, in his judgments, often observes a rule of proportion, as in the case of Adonibezek, Jdg. 1:7. See also Rev. 13:10; 18:6. Thus will he be both justified and magnified in his judgments, and all flesh will be silenced before him. *With what measure ye mete, it shall be measured to you again;* perhaps in this world, so that men may read their sin in their punishment. Let this deter us from all severity in dealing with our brother. *What shall we do when God rises up?* Job 31:14. What would become of us, if God should be as exact and severe in judging us, as we are in judging our brethren; if he should weigh us in the same balance? We may justly expect it, if we be extreme to mark what our brethren do amiss. In this, as in other things, the violent dealings of men return upon their own heads.

II. Some cautions *about reproving.* Because we must not judge others, which is a great sin, it does not therefore follow that we must not reprove others, which is a great duty, and may be a means of *saving a soul from death;* however, it will be a means of saving our souls from sharing in their guilt. Now observe here,

1. It is not every one who is fit to reprove. Those who are themselves guilty of the same faults of which they accuse others, or of worse, bring shame upon themselves, and are not likely to do good to those whom they reprove, *v.* 3–5. Here is,

(1.) A just reproof to the censorious, who quarrel with their brother for small faults, while they allow themselves in great ones; who are quick-sighted to spy *a mote* in his eye, but are not sensible of *a beam in their own;* nay, and will be very officious to *pull out the mote out of his eye,* when they are as unfit to do it as if they were themselves quite blind. Note, [1.] There are degrees in sin: some sins are comparatively but as *motes,* others as *beams;* some as a *gnat,* others as a *camel:* not that there is any sin little, for there is no little God to sin against; if it be a *mote* (or *splinter,* for so it might better be read), it is in the eye; if a *gnat,* it is in the throat; both painful and perilous, and we cannot be easy or well till they are got out. [2.] Our own sins ought to appear greater to us than the same sins in others: that which charity teaches us to call but a *splinter in our brother's eye,* true repentance and godly sorrow will teach us to call a *beam in our own;* for the sins of others must be extenuated, but our own aggravated. [3.] There are many that have *beams in their own eyes,* and yet do not consider it. They are under the guilt and dominion of very great sins, and yet are not aware of it, but justify themselves, as if they needed no repentance nor reformation; it is as strange that a man can be in such a sinful, miserable condition, and not be aware of it, as that a man should have a beam in him eye, and not consider it; but the god of this world so artfully blinds their minds, that notwithstanding, with great assurance, they say, *We see.* [4.] It is common for those who are most sinful themselves, and least sensible of it, to be most forward and free in judging and censuring others: the Pharisees, who were most haughty in justifying themselves, were most scornful in condemning others. They were severe upon Christ's disciples for *eating with unwashen hands,* which was scarcely a *mote,* while they encouraged men in a contempt of their parents, which was a *beam.* Pride and uncharitableness are commonly *beams* in the eyes of those that pretend to be critical and nice in their censures of others. Nay, many are guilty of that secret, which they have the face to punish in others when it is discovered. *Cogita tecum, fortasse vitium de quo quereris, si te diligenter excusseris, in sinu invenies; inique publico irasceris crimini tuo — Reflect that perhaps the fault of which you complain, might, on a strict examination, be discovered in yourself; and that it would be unjust publicly to express indignation against your own crime.* Seneca, *de Beneficiis.* But, [5.] Men's being so severe upon the faults of others, while they are indulgent of their own, is a mark of hypocrisy. *Thou hypocrite, v.* 5. Whatever such a one may pretend, it is certain that he is no enemy to sin (if he were, he would be an enemy to his own sin), and therefore he is not worthy of praise; nay, it appears that he is an enemy to his brother, and therefore worthy of blame. This spiritual charity must begin at home; *"For how canst thou say,* how canst thou for shame say, to thy brother, *Let me help to reform thee,* when thou takest no care to reform thyself? Thy own heart will upbraid thee with the absurdity of it; thou wilt do it with an ill grace, and thou wilt expect every one to tell thee, that *vice corrects sin: physician, heal thyself;" I prae, sequar — Go you before, I will follow.* See Rom. 2:21. [6.] The consideration of what is amiss in ourselves, though it ought not to keep us from administering friendly reproof, ought to keep us from magisterial censuring, and to make us very candid and charitable in judging others. "Therefore *restore with the spirit of meekness, considering thyself* (Gal. 6:1); what thou has been, what thou art, and what thou wouldst be, if God should leave thee to thyself."

(2.) Here is a good rule for reprovers, *v.* 5. Go in the right method, *first cast the beam out of thine own eye.* Our own badness is so far from excusing us in not reproving, that our being by it rendered unfit to reprove is an aggravation of our badness; I must not say, "I have *a beam in my own eye,* and therefore I will not help my brother with the *mote out of his."* A man's *of*fence will never be his *de*fence: but I must first reform myself, that I may thereby help to reform my brother, and may qualify myself to reprove him. Note, Those who blame others, ought to be blameless and harmless themselves. Those who are *reprovers in the gate,* reprovers by office, magistrates and ministers, are concerned to *walk circumspectly,* and to be very regular in their conversation: an *elder must have a good report,* 1 Tim. 3:2, 7. The snuffers of the sanctuary were to be of pure gold.

2. It is not every one that is fit to be reproved; *Give not that which is holy unto the dogs, v.* 6. This may be considered, either, (1.) As a rule to the disciples in preaching the gospel; not that they must not preach it to any one who were wicked and profane (Christ himself preached to publicans and sinners), but the reference is to such as they found obstinate after the gospel was preached to them, such as blasphemed it, and persecuted the preachers of it; let them not spend much time among such, for it would be lost labour, but let them turn to others, Acts 13:41. So Dr. Whitby. Or, (2.) As a rule to all in giving reproof. Our zeal against sin must be guided by discretion, and we must not go about to give instructions, counsels, and rebukes, much less comforts, to hardened scorners, to whom it will certainly do no good, but who will be exasperated and enraged at us. Throw a pearl to a swine, and he will resent it, as if you threw a stone at him; *reproofs* will be called *reproaches,* as they were (Lu. 11:45; Jer. 6:10), therefore give not to dogs and swine (unclean creatures) holy things. Note, [1.] Good counsel and reproof are a holy thing, and a pearl: they are ordinances of God, they are precious; as an *ear-ring of gold, and an ornament of fine gold,* so is the wise reprover (Prov. 25:12), and a wise reproof is *like an excellent oil* (Ps. 141:5); it is *a tree of life* (Prov. 3:18). [2.] Among the generation of the wicked, there are some that have arrived at such a pitch of wickedness, that they are looked upon as dogs and swine; they are impudently and notoriously vile; they have so long *walked in the way of sinners,* that they have sat down *in the seat of the scornful;* they professedly hate and despise instruction, and set it at defiance, so that they are irrecoverably and irreclaimably wicked; they return with *the dog to his vomit,* and with the *sow to her wallowing in the mire.* [3.] Reproofs of instruction are ill bestowed upon such, and expose the reprover to all the contempt and mischief that may be expected from dogs and swine. One can expect no other than that they will trample the reproofs under their feet, in scorn of them, and rage against them; for they are impatient of control and contradiction; and they will turn again and rend the reprovers; rend their good names with their revilings, return them wounding words for their healing ones; rend them with persecution; Herod rent John Baptist for his faithfulness. See here what is the evidence of men's being *dogs* and *swine.* Those

are to be reckoned such, who *hate reproofs* and reprovers, and fly in the face of those who, in kindness to their souls, show them their sin and danger. These sin against the remedy; who shall heal and help those that will not be healed and helped? It is plain that God has determined to destroy such. 2 Chr. 25:16. The rule here given is applicable to the distinguishing, sealing ordinances of the gospel; which must not be prostituted to those who are openly wicked and profane, lest holy things be thereby rendered contemptible, and unholy persons be thereby hardened. *It is not meet to take the children's bread, and cast it to the dogs.* Yet we must be very cautious whom we condemn as dogs and swine, and not do it till after trial, and upon full evidence. Many a patient is lost, by being thought to be so, who, if means had been used, might have been saved. As we must take heed of calling the *good, bad,* by judging all professors to be hypocrites; so we must take heed of calling the *bad, desperate,* by judging all the wicked to be *dogs* and *swine.* [4.] Our Lord Jesus is very tender of the safety of his people, and would not have them needlessly to expose themselves to the fury of those that will *turn again and rend* them. Let them not be *righteous over much,* so as to destroy themselves. Christ makes the law of self-preservation one of his own laws, and *precious is the blood* of his subjects to him.

Verses 7–11

Our Saviour, in the foregoing chapter, had spoken of prayer as a commanded duty, by which God is honoured, and which, if done aright, shall be rewarded; here he speaks of it as the appointed means of obtaining what we need, especially grace to obey the precepts he had given, some of which are so displeasing to flesh and blood.

I. Here is a precept in three words to the same purport, *Ask, Seek, Knock* (*v.* 7); that is, in one word, "Pray; pray often; pray with sincerity and seriousness; pray, and pray again; make conscience of prayer, and be constant in it; make a business of prayer, and be earnest in it. *Ask,* as a beggar asks alms." Those that would be rich in grace, must betake themselves to the poor trade of begging, and they shall find it a thriving trade. *"Ask;* represent your wants and burthens to God, and refer yourselves to him for support and supply, according to his promise. *Ask* as a traveller asks the way; to pray is to *enquire of God,* Eze. 36:37. *Seek,* as for a thing of value that we have lost, or as the merchantman that *seeks goodly pearls. Seek by prayer,* Dan. 9:3. *Knock,* as he that desires to enter into the house knocks at the door." We would be admitted to converse with God, would be taken into his love, and favour, and kingdom; sin has shut and barred the door against us; by prayer, we knock; *Lord, Lord, open to us.* Christ knocks at our door (Rev. 3:20; Cant. 5:2); and allows us to knock at his, which is a favour we do not allow to common beggars. Seeking and knocking imply something more than asking and praying. 1. We must not only *ask* but *seek;* we must second our prayers with our endeavors; we must, in the use of the appointed means, *seek* for that which we *ask* for, else we tempt God. When the dresser of the vineyard asked for a year's respite for the barren fig-tree, he added, *I will dig about it,* Lu. 13:7, 8. God gives knowledge and grace to those that search the scriptures, and wait at Wisdom's gates; and power against sin to those that avoid the occasions of it. 2. We must not only *ask,* but *knock;* we must come to God's door, must *ask* importunately; not only pray, but plead and wrestle with God; we must *seek* diligently; we must continue knocking; must persevere in prayer, and in the use of means; must endure to the end in the duty.

II. Here is a promised annexed: *our labour* in prayer, if indeed we do labour in it, *shall not be in vain:* where God finds a praying heart, he will be found a prayer-hearing God; *he shall give thee an answer of peace.* The precept is threefold, *ask, seek, knock;* there is *precept upon precept;* but the promise is sixfold, *line upon line,* for our encouragement; because a firm belief of the promise would make us cheerful and constant in our obedience. Now here,

1. The promise is made, and made so as exactly to answer the precept, *v.* 7. *Ask, and it shall be given you;* not lent you, not sold you, but *given you;* and what is more free than gift? Whatever you pray for, according to the promise, whatever you *ask, shall be given you,* if God see it fit for you, and what would you have more? It is but *ask* and have; *ye have not, because ye ask not,* or *ask* not aright: what is not worth asking, is not worth having, and then it is worth nothing. *Seek,* and *ye shall find,* and then you do not lose your labour; God is himself *found of those that seek* him, and if we find him we have enough. *"Knock, and it shall be opened;* the door of mercy and grace shall no longer be shut against you as enemies and intruders, but opened to you as friends and children. It will be asked, *who is at the door?* If you be able to say, a friend, and have the ticket of promise ready to produce in the hand of faith, doubt not of admission. If the door be not *opened* at the first *knock, continue instant in prayer;* it is an affront to a friend to *knock* at his door, and then go away; though he tarry, yet wait."

2. It is repeated, *v.* 8. It is to the same purport, yet with some addition. (1.) It is made to extend to all that pray aright; "Not only you my disciples shall receive what you pray for, but *every one that asketh, receiveth,* whether Jew or Gentile, young or old, rich or poor, high or low, master or servant, learned or unlearned, they are all alike welcome to *the throne of grace,* if they come in faith: *for God is no respecter of persons."* (2.) It is made so as to amount to a grant, in words of the present tense, which is more than a promise for the future. *Every one that asketh,* not only *shall* receive, but *receiveth;* by faith, applying and appropriating the promise, we are actually interested and invested in the good promised: so sure and inviolable are the promises of God, that they do, in effect, give present possession: an active believer enters immediately, and makes the blessings promised his own. What have we in hope, according to the promise, is as sure, and should be as sweet, as what we have in hand. *God hath spoken in his holiness,* and then *Gilead is mine, Manasseh mine* (Ps. 108:7, 8); it is all mine own, if I can but make it so by believing it so. Conditional grants become absolute upon the performance of the condition; so here, *he that asketh, receiveth.* Christ hereby puts his *fiat* to the petition; and he having all power, that is enough.

3. It is illustrated, by a similitude taken from earthly parents, and their innate readiness to give their children what they ask. Christ appeals to his hearers, *What man is there of you,* though never so morose and ill-humoured, *whom if his son ask bread, will he give him a stone? v.* 9, 10. Whence he infers (*v.* 11), *If ye then, being evil,* yet grant your children's requests, *much more will your heavenly Father give you the good things you ask.* Now this is of use,

(1.) To *direct* our prayers and expectations. [1.] We must come to God, as children to a *Father in heaven,* with reverence and confidence. How naturally does a child in want or distress run to the father with its complaints; *My head, my head;* thus should the new nature send us to God for supports and supplies. [2.] We must come to him for *good things,* for those he *gives to them that ask him;* which teaches us to refer ourselves to him; we know not what is good for ourselves (Eccl. 6:12), but he knows what is good for us, we must therefore leave it with him; *Father, thy will be done.* The child is here supposed to *ask bread,* that is necessary, and *a fish,* that is wholesome; but if the child should foolishly ask for *a stone,* or *a serpent,* for unripe fruit to eat, or a sharp knife to play with, the father, though kind, is so wise as to deny him. We often ask that of God which would do us harm if we had it; he knows this, and therefore does not give it to us. Denials in love are better than grants in anger; we should have been undone ere this if we had had all we desired; this is admirably well expressed by a heathen, Juvenal, *Sat.* 10.

Permittes ipsis expendere numinibus, quid
Conveniat nobis, rebusque sit utile nostris,
Nam pro jucundis aptissima quaeque dabunt dii.
Carior est illis homo, quam sibi: nos animorum
Impulsu, et caeca, magnaque cupidine ducti,
Conjugium petimus, partumque uxoris; at illis
Notum est, qui pueri, qualisque futura sit uxor.

Entrust thy fortune to the powers above.
Leave them to manage for thee, and to grant
What their unerring wisdom sees thee want:
In goodness, as in greatness, they excel;
Ah, that we lov'd ourselves but half so well!
We, blindly by our headstrong passions led,
Seek a companion, and desire to wed;
Then wish for heirs: but to the gods alone
Our future offspring and our wives are known.

(2.) To *encourage* our prayers and expectations. We may hope that we shall not be denied and disappointed: we shall not have *a stone* for *bread,* to break our teeth (though we have a hard crust to employ our teeth), nor *a serpent* for *a fish,* to sting us; we have reason indeed to fear it, because we deserve it, but God will be better to us than the desert of our sins. The world often gives *stones for bread,* and *serpents for fish,* but God never does; nay, we shall be heard and answered, for children are by their parents. [1.] God has put into the hearts of parents a compassionate inclination to succour and supply their children, according to their need. Even those that have had little conscience of duty, yet have done it, as it were by instinct. No law was ever thought necessary to oblige parents to maintain their legitimate children, nor, in Solomon's time, their illegitimate ones. [2.] He has assumed the relation of a Father to us, and owns us for his children; that from the readiness we find in ourselves to relieve our children, we may be encouraged to apply ourselves to him for relief. What love and tenderness fathers have are from him; not from nature but from the God of nature; and therefore they must needs be infinitely greater in himself. He compares his concern for his people to that of a father for his children (Ps. 103:13), nay, to that of a mother, which is usually more tender, Isa. 66:13; 49:14, 15. But here it is supposed, that his love, and tenderness, and goodness, far excel that of any earthly parent; and therefore it is argued with a *much more,* and it is grounded upon this undoubted truth, that God is a better Father, infinitely better than any earthly parents are; *his thoughts are above theirs.* Our earthly fathers have taken care of us; we have taken care of our children; much more will God take care of his; for they are evil, originally so; the degenerate seed of fallen Adam; they have lost much of the good nature that belonged to humanity, and among other corruptions, have that of crossness and unkindness in them; yet they *give good things to their children,* and they *know how to give,* suitably and seasonably; *much more will* God, for he takes up when they forsake, Ps. 27:10. And, *First,* God is more knowing; parents are often foolishly fond, but God is wise, infinitely so; he knows what we need, what we desire, and what is fit for us. *Secondly,* God is more kind. If all the compassions of all the tender fathers in the world were crowded into the bowels of one, yet compared *with the tender mercies of our God,* they would be but as a candle to the sun, or a drop to the ocean. God is more rich, and more ready to give to his children than the fathers of our flesh can be; for he is the Father of our spirits, an ever-loving, ever-living Father. The bowels of Fathers yearn even towards undutiful children, towards prodigals, as David's toward Absalom, and will not all this serve to silence disbelief?

Verses 12–14

Our Lord Jesus here presses upon us that righteousness towards men which is an essential branch of true religion, and that religion towards God which is an essential branch of universal righteousness.

I. We must make righteousness our rule, and be ruled by it, *v.* 12. *Therefore,* lay this down for your principle, to do as you would be done by; therefore, that you may conform to the foregoing precepts, which are particular, that you may not judge and censure others, go by this rule in general; (you would not be censured, therefore do not censure), Or that you may have the benefit of the foregoing promises. Fitly is the law of justice subjoined to the law of prayer, for unless we be honest in our conversation, God will not hear our prayers, Isa. 1:15–17; 58:6, 9; Zec. 7:9, 13. We cannot expect to receive *good things* from God, if we do not *fair* things, and that which is *honest,* and *lovely, and of good report* among men. We must not only be devout, but honest, else our devotion is but hypocrisy. Now here we have,

1. The rule of justice laid down; *Whatsoever ye would that men should do to you, do you even so to them.* Christ came to teach us, not only what we are to know and believe, but what we are to do; what we are to do, not only toward God, but toward men; not only towards our fellow-disciples, those of our party and persuasion, but towards men in general, all with whom we have to do. The golden rule of equity is, to do to others as we would they should do to us. Alexander Severus, a heathen emperor, was a great admirer of this rule, had it written upon the walls of his closet, often quoted it in giving judgment, honoured Christ, and favoured Christians for the sake of it. *Quod tibi, hoc alteri — do to others as you would they should do to you.* Take it negatively *(Quod tibi fieri non vis, ne alteri feceris),* or positively, it comes all to the same. We must not do to others the evil they have done us, nor the evil which they would do to us, if it were in their power; nor may we do that which we think, if it were done to us, we could bear contentedly, but what we desire should be done to us. This is grounded upon that great commandment, *Thou shalt love thy neighbor as thyself.* As we must

bear the same affection to our neighbour that we would have borne to ourselves, so we must do the same good offices. The meaning of this rule lies in three things. (1.) We must do that to our neighbour which we ourselves acknowledge to be fit and reasonable: the appeal is made to our own judgment, and the discovery of our judgment is referred to that which is our own will and expectation, when it is our own case. (2.) We must put other people upon the level with ourselves, and reckon we are as much obliged to them, as they to us. We are as much bound to the duty of justice as they, and they as much entitled to the benefit of it as we. (3.) We must, in our dealings with men, suppose ourselves in the same particular case and circumstances with those we have to do with, and deal accordingly. If I were making such a one's bargain, labouring under such a one's infirmity and affliction, how should I desire and expect to be treated? And this is a just supposition, because we know not how soon their case may really be ours: at least we may fear, lest God by his judgments should do to us as we have done to others, if we have not done as we would be done by.

2. A reason given to enforce this rule; *This is the law and the prophets.* It is the summary of that second great commandment, which is one of the two, *on which hang all the law and the prophets, ch.* 22:40. We have not this in so many words, either in *the law* or *the prophets,* but it is the concurring language of the whole. All that is there said concerning our duty towards our neighbour (and that is no little) may be reduced to this rule. Christ has here adopted it into this law; so that both the Old Testament and the New agree in prescribing this to us, to do as we would be done by. By this rule the law of Christ is commended, but the lives of Christians are condemned by comparing them with it. *Aut hoc non evangelium, aut hi non evangelici. — Either this is not the gospel, or these are not Christians.*

II. We must make religion our business, and be intent upon it; we must be strict and circumspect in our conversation, which is here represented to us as entering in at a *strait gate,* and walking on in a *narrow way, v.* 13, 14. Observe here,

1. The account that is given of the bad way of sin, and the good way of holiness. There are but two ways, right and wrong, good and evil; the way to heaven, and the way to hell; in the one of which we are all of us walking: no middle place hereafter, no middle way now: the distinction of the children of men into saints and sinners, godly and ungodly, will swallow up all to eternity.

Here is, (1.) An account given us of the way of sin and sinners; both what is the best, and what is the worst of it.

[1.] That which allures multitudes into it, and keeps them in it; *the gate is wide, and the way broad,* and there are many travellers in that way. *First,* "You will have abundance of liberty in that way; *the gate is wide,* and stands wide open to tempt those that go right on their way. You may go in at this gate with all your lusts about you; it gives no check to your appetites, to your passions: you may *walk in the way of your heart, and in the sight of your eyes;* that gives room enough." It is a *broad way,* for there is nothing to hedge in those that walk in it, but they wander endlessly; a *broad way,* for there are many paths in it; there is choice of sinful ways, contrary to each other, but all paths in this *broad way. Secondly,* "You will have abundance of company in that way: *many there be that go in* at this gate, and walk in this way." If we *follow the multitude,* it will be *to do evil:* if we go with the crowd, it will be the wrong way. It is natural for us to incline to go down the stream, and do as the most do; but it is too great a compliment, to be willing to be damned for company, and to go to hell with them, because they will not go to heaven with us: if many perish, we should be the more cautious.

[2.] That which should affright us all from it is, that it *leads to destruction.* Death, eternal death, is at the end of it (and the way of sin tends to it), — everlasting *destruction from the presence of the Lord.* Whether it be the high way of open profaneness, or the back way of close hypocrisy, if it be a way of sin, it will be our ruin, if we repent not.

(2.) Here is an account given us of the way of holiness.

[1.] What there is in it that frightens many from it; let us know the worst of it, that we may sit down and count the cost. Christ deals faithfully with us, and tells us,

First, That *the gate is strait.* Conversion and regeneration are *the gate,* by which we enter into this way, in which we begin a life of faith and serious godliness; out of a state of sin into a state of grace we must pass, by the new birth, Jn. 3:3, 5. This is a *strait gate,* hard to find, and hard to get through; like a passage between two rocks, 1 Sa. 14:4. There must be *a new heart, and a new spirit,* and *old things must pass away.* The bent of the soul must be changed, corrupt habits and customs broken off; what we have been doing all our days must be undone again. We must swim against the stream; much opposition must be struggled with, and broken through, from without, and from within. It is easier to set a man against all the world than against himself, and yet this must be in conversion. It is a *strait gate,* for we must stoop, or we cannot go in at it; we must become as little children; high thoughts must be brought down; nay, we must strip, must deny ourselves, put off the world, *put off the old man;* we must be willing to forsake all for our interest in Christ. *The gate is strait* to all, but to some straiter than others; as to the rich, to some that have been long prejudiced against religion. *The gate is strait;* blessed be God, it is not shut up, nor locked against us, nor kept with a flaming sword, as it will be shortly, *ch.* 25:10.

Secondly, That *the way is narrow.* We are not in heaven as soon as we have got through the *strait gate,* nor in Canaan as soon as we have got through the Red Sea; no, we must go through a wilderness, must travel a *narrow way,* hedged in by the divine law, which *is exceedingly broad,* and that makes *the way narrow;* self must be denied, the body kept under, corruptions mortified, that are as a *right eye* and a *right hand;* daily temptations must be resisted; duties must be done that are against our inclination. We must endure hardness, must wrestle and be in an agony, must watch in all things, and walk with care and circumspection. We must go *through much tribulation.* It is *hodos tethlimmenē — an afflicted way,* a way hedged about with thorns; blessed be God, it is not hedged up. The bodies we carry about with us, and the corruptions remaining in us, make the way of our duty difficult; but, as the understanding and will grow more and more sound, it will open and enlarge, and grow more and more pleasant.

Thirdly, The gate being so *strait and the way so narrow,* it is not strange that there are but *few that find it,* and choose it. Many pass it by, through carelessness; they will not be at the pains to find it; they are well as they are, and see no need to change their way. Others look upon it, but shun it; they like not to be so limited and restrained. Those that are going to heaven are but few, compared to those that are going to hell; a remnant, a little flock, like the grape-gleanings of the vintage; as the eight that were saved in the ark, 1 Pt. 3:20. *In vitia alter alterum trudimus; Quomodo ad salutem revocari potest, quum nullus retrahit, et populus impellit — In the ways of vice men urge each other onward: how shall any one be restored to the path of safety, when impelled forwards by the multitude, without any counteracting influence?* Seneca, *Epist.* 29. This discourages many: they are loth to be singular, to be solitary; but instead of stumbling at this, say rather, If so few are going to heaven, there shall be one the more for me.

[2.] Let us see what there is in this way, which, notwithstanding this, should invite us all to it; it *leads to life,* to present comfort in the favour of God, which is the life of the soul; to eternal bliss, the hope of which, at the end of our way, should reconcile us to all the difficulties and inconveniences of the road. Life and godliness are put together (2 Pt. 1:3); *The gate is strait and the way narrow* and up-hill, but one hour in heaven will make amends for it.

2. The great concern and duty of every one of us, in consideration of all this; *Enter ye in at the strait gate.* The matter is fairly stated; life and death, good and evil, are set before us; both the ways, and both the ends: now let the matter be taken entire, and considered impartially, and then choose you this day which you will walk in; nay, the matter determines itself, and will not admit of a debate. No man, in his wits, would choose to go to the gallows, because it is a smooth, pleasant way to it, nor refuse the offer of a palace and a throne, because it is a rough, dirty way to it; yet such absurdities as these are men guilty of, in the concerns of their souls. Delay not, therefore; deliberate not any longer, but *enter ye in at the strait gate; knock* at it by sincere and constant prayers and endeavors, *and it shall be opened;* nay, a wide door shall be opened, and an effectual one. It is true, we can neither go in, nor go on, without the assistance of divine grace; but it is as true, that grace is freely offered, and shall not be wanting to those that seek it, and submit to it. Conversion is hard work, but it is needful, and, blessed be God, it is not impossible if we strive, Lu. 13:24.

Verses 15–20

We have here a caution against *false prophets,* to take heed that we be not deceived and imposed upon by them. *Prophets* are properly such as foretel things to come; there are some mentioned in the Old Testament, who pretended to that without warrant, and the event disproved their pretensions, as Zedekiah, 1 Ki. 22:11, and another Zedekiah, Jer. 29:21. But *prophets* did also teach the people their duty, so that *false prophets* here are false teachers. Christ being a Prophet and *a Teacher come from God,* and designing to send abroad teachers under him, gives warning to all to take heed of counterfeits, who, instead of healing souls with wholesome doctrine, as they pretend, would poison them.

They are false teachers and *false prophets,* 1. Who produce false commissions, who pretend to have immediate warrant and direction from God to set up for *prophets,* and to be divinely inspired, when they are not so. Though their doctrine may be true, we are to *beware* of them as *false prophets.* False apostles are those who *say they are apostles, and are not* (Rev. 2:2); such are *false prophets.* "Take heed of those who pretend to revelation, and admit them not without sufficient proof, lest that one absurdity being admitted, a thousand follow." 2. Who preach false doctrine in those things that are essential to religion; who teach that which is contrary to *the truth as it is in Jesus,* to *the truth which is accordingly to godliness.* The former seems to be the proper notion of *pseudo-propheta,* a *false* or pretending *prophet,* but commonly the latter falls in with it; for who would hang out false colours, but with design, under pretence of them, the more successfully to attack the truth. "Well, beware of them, suspect them, try them, and when you have discovered their falsehood, avoid them, have nothing to do with them. Stand upon your guard against this temptation, which commonly attends the days of reformation, and the breakings out of divine light in more than ordinary strength and splendour." When God's work is revived, Satan and his agents are most busy. Here is,

I. A good reason for this caution, *Beware of* them, for they are *wolves in sheep's clothing, v.* 15.

1. We have need to be very cautious, because their pretences are very fair and plausible, and such as will deceive us, if we be not upon our guard. They *come in sheep's clothing,* in the habit of *prophets,* which was plain and coarse, and unwrought; they *wear a rough garment to deceive,* Zec. 13:4. Elijah's mantle the Septuagint calls *hē mēlotē — a sheepskin* mantle. We must take heed of being imposed upon by men's dress and garb, as by that of the scribes, who *desire to walk in long robes,* Lu. 20:46. Or it may be taken figuratively; they pretend to be sheep, and outwardly appear so innocent, harmless, meek, useful, and all that is good, as to be excelled by none; they feign themselves to be just men, and for the sake of their clothing are admitted among the sheep, which gives them an opportunity of doing them a mischief ere they are aware. They and their errors are gilded with the specious pretences of sanctity and devotion. Satan turns himself *into an angel of light,* 2 Co. 11:13, 14. The enemy has *horns like a lamb* (Rev. 13:11); *faces of men,* Rev. 9:7, 8. Seducers in language and carriage are *soft as wool,* Rom. 16:18; Isa. 30:10.

2. Because under these pretensions their designs are very malicious and mischievous; *inwardly they are ravening wolves.* Every *hypocrite* is a *goat* in sheep's clothing; not only not a sheep, but the worst enemy the sheep has, that comes not but to tear and devour, to *scatter the sheep* (Jn. 10:12), to drive them from God, and from one another, into crooked paths. Those that would cheat us of any truth, and possess us with error, whatever they pretend, design mischief to our souls. Paul calls them *grievous wolves,* Acts 20:29. They raven for themselves, *serve their own belly* (Rom. 16:18), make a prey of you, make a gain of you. Now since it is so easy a thing, and withal so dangerous, to be cheated, *Beware of false prophets.*

II. Here is a good rule to go by in this caution; we must *prove all things* (1 Th. 5:21), *try the spirits* (1 Jn. 4:1), and here we have a touchstone; *ye shall know them by their fruits,* 16–20. Observe,

1. The illustration of this comparison, of the fruit's being the discovery of the tree. You cannot always distinguish them by their bark and leaves, nor by the spreading of their boughs, but *by their fruits ye shall know them.* The fruit is according to the tree. Men may, in their professions, put a force upon their nature, and contradict their inward principles, but the

stream and bent of their practices will agree with them. Christ insists upon this, the agreeableness between the fruit and the tree, which is such as that, (1.) If you know what the tree is, you may know what fruit to expect. Never look to gather *grapes from thorns, nor figs from thistles;* it is not in their nature to produce such fruits. An apple may be stuck, or a bunch of grapes may hang, upon a thorn; so may a good truth, a good word or action, be found in a bad man, but you may be sure it never grew there. Note, [1.] Corrupt, vicious, unsanctified hearts are like thorns and thistles, which came in with sin, are worthless, vexing, and for the fire at last. [2.] Good works are *good fruit,* like grapes and figs, pleasing to God and profitable to men. [3.] This *good fruit* is never to be expected from bad men, and more than *a clean thing out of an unclean:* they want an influencing acceptable principle. *Out of* an *evil treasure* will be brought forth *evil things.* (2.) On the other hand, if you know what the fruit is, you may, by that, perceive what the tree is. *A good tree cannot bring forth evil fruit;* and *a corrupt tree cannot bring forth good fruit,* nay, it cannot but *bring forth evil fruit.* But then that must be reckoned the fruit of the tree which it brings forth naturally and which is its genuine product — which it brings forth plentifully and constantly and which is its usual product. Men are known, not by particular acts, but by the course and tenour of their conversation, and by the more frequent acts, especially those that appear to be free, and most their own, and least under the influence of external motives and inducements.

2. The application of this to the false prophets.

(1.) By way of terror and threatening (*v.* 19); *Every tree that brings not forth good fruit is hewn down.* This very saying John the Baptist had used, *ch.* 3:10. Christ could have spoken the same sense in other words; could have altered it, or given it a new turn; but he thought it no disparagement to him to say the same that John had said before him; let not ministers be ambitious of coining new expressions, nor people's ears itch for novelties; to write and speak the same things must not be grievous, for it is safe. Here is, [1.] The description of barren trees; they are trees that do *not bring forth good fruit;* though there be fruit, if it be not *good fruit* (though that be done, which for the matter of it is good, if it be not done well, in a right manner, and for a right end), the tree is accounted barren. [2.] The doom of barren trees; *they are,* that is, certainly they shall be, *hewn down, and cast into the fire;* God will deal with them as men use to deal with dry trees that cumber the ground: he will mark them by some signal tokens of his displeasure, he will bark them by stripping them of their parts and gifts, and will cut them *down* by death, *and cast* them *into the fire* of hell, a fire blown with the bellows of God's wrath, and fed with the wood of barren trees. Compare this with Eze. 31:12, 13; Dan. 4:14; Jn. 15:6.

(2.) By way of trial; *By their fruits ye shall know them.*

[1.] *By the fruits* of their persons, their words and actions, and the course of their conversation. If you would know whether they be right or not, observe how they live; their works will testify for them or against them. The scribes and Pharisees sat in Moses's chair, and taught the law, but they were proud, and covetous, and false, and oppressive, and therefore Christ warned him disciples to *beware of* them and of their *leaven,* Mk. 12:38. If men pretend to be prophets and are immoral, that disproves their pretensions; those are no true friends *to the cross of Christ,* whatever they profess, *whose God is their belly,* and *whose mind earthly things,* Phil. 3:18, 19. Those are not taught nor sent of the holy God, whose lives evidence that they are led by the unclean spirit. God puts the treasure into earthen vessels, but not into such corrupt vessels: they may declare God's statutes, but what have they to do to declare them?

[2.] *By the fruits* of their doctrine; their fruits as prophets: not that this is the only way, but it is one way, of trying doctrines, *whether they be of God* or not. What do they tend to do? What affections and practices will they lead those into, that embrace them? If *the doctrine be of God,* it will tend to promote serious piety, humility, charity, holiness, and love, with other Christian graces; but if, on the contrary, the doctrines these prophets preach have a manifest tendency to make people proud, worldly, and contentious, to make them loose and careless in their conversations, unjust or uncharitable, factious or disturbers of the public peace; if it indulge carnal liberty, and take people off from governing themselves and their families by the strict rules of *the narrow way,* we may conclude, that *this persuasion comes not of him that calleth us,* Gal. 5:8. *This wisdom is from above,* James 3:15. *Faith and a good conscience* are held together, 1 Tim. 1:19; 3:9. Note, *Doctrines of doubtful disputation* must be tried by graces and duties of confessed certainty: those opinions come not from God that lead to sin: but if we cannot *know them by their fruits,* we must have recourse to the great touchstone, to the law, and to the testimony; do they speak according to that rule?

Verses 21–29

We have here the conclusion of this long and excellent sermon, the scope of which is to show the indispensable necessity of obedience to the commands of Christ; this is designed to clench the nail, that it might fix in a sure place: he speaks this to his disciples, that sat at his feet whenever he preached, and followed him wherever he went. Had he sought his own praise among men, he would have said, that was enough; but the religion he came to establish is in power, not in word only (1 Co. 4:20), and therefore something more is necessary.

I. He shows, by a plain remonstrance, that an outward profession of religion, however remarkable, will not bring us to heaven, unless there be a correspondent conversation, *v.* 21–23. All judgment is committed to our Lord Jesus; the keys are put into his hand; he has power to prescribe new terms of life and death, and to judge men according to them: now this is a solemn declaration pursuant to that power. Observe here,

1. Christ's law laid down, *v.* 21. *Not every one that saith, Lord, Lord, shall enter into the kingdom of heaven, into the kingdom of* grace and glory. It is an answer to that question, Ps. 15:1. *Who shall sojourn in thy tabernacle?* — the church militant; *and who shall dwell in thy holy hill?* — the church triumphant. Christ here shows,

(1.) That it will not suffice to say, *Lord, Lord;* in word and tongue to own Christ for our Master, and to make addresses to him, and professions of him accordingly: in prayer to God, in discourse with men, we must call Christ, *Lord, Lord;* we *say well,* for *so he is* (Jn. 13:13); but can we imagine that this is enough to bring us to heaven, that such a piece of formality as this should be so recompensed, or that he who knows and requires the heart should be so put off with shows for substance? Compliments among men are pieces of civility that are returned with compliments, but they are never paid as real services; and can they then be of an account with Christ? There may be a seeming importunity in prayer, *Lord, Lord:* but if inward *im*pressions be not answerable to outward *ex*pressions, we are but *as sounding brass and a tinkling cymbal.* This is not to take us off from saying, *Lord, Lord;* from praying, and being earnest in prayer, from professing Christ's name, and being bold in professing it, but from resting in these, in the *form of godliness,* without *the power.*

(2.) That it is necessary to our happiness that we *do the will of* Christ, which is indeed *the will of* his *Father in heaven. The will of* God, as Christ's *Father,* is his will in the gospel, for there he is made known, as *the Father of our Lord Jesus Christ:* and in him our Father. Now this is his will, that we believe in Christ, that we repent of sin, that we live a holy life, that we *love one another. This is his will, even our sanctification.* If we comply not with the will of God, we mock Christ in calling him *Lord,* as those did who put on him a gorgeous robe, and said, *Hail, King of the Jews.* Saying and doing are two things, often parted in conversation of men: he that said, *I go, sir,* stirred never a step (*ch.* 21:30); but these two things *God has joined* in his command, and *let no man* that *puts* them *asunder* think to *enter into the kingdom of heaven.*

2. The hypocrite's plea against the strictness of this law, offering other things in lieu of obedience, *v.* 22. The plea is supposed to be *in that day,* that great day, when every man shall appear in his own colours; *when the secrets of all hearts shall be* manifest, and among the rest, the secret pretences with which sinners now support their vain hopes. Christ knows the strength of their cause, and it is but weakness; what they now harbour in their bosoms, they will then produce in arrest of judgment to stay the doom, but is will be in vain. They put in their plea with great importunity, *Lord, Lord;* and with great confidence, appealing to Christ concerning it; *Lord,* does thou not know, (1.) That *we have prophesied in thy name?* Yes, it may be so; Balaam and Caiaphas were overruled to prophesy, and Saul was against his will *among the prophets,* yet that did not save them. These *prophesied in* his *name,* but he did not send them; they only made use of his name to serve a turn. Note, A man may be a preacher, may have gifts for the ministry, and an external call to it, and perhaps some success in it, and yet be a wicked man; may help others to heaven, and yet come short himself. (2.) That *in thy name we have cast out devils?* That may be too; Judas *cast out devils,* and yet was a *son of perdition.* Origen says, that in his time so prevalent was the name of Christ to *cast out devils,* that sometimes it availed when named by wicked Christians. A man might *cast devils out* of others, and yet have a devil, nay, be a devil himself. (3.) That *in thy name we have done many wonderful works.* There may be a faith of miracles, where there is no justifying faith; none of that *faith which works by love* and obedience. Gifts of tongues and healing would recommend men to the world, but it is real holiness or sanctification that is accepted of God. Grace and love are *a more excellent way* than *removing mountains,* or *speaking with the tongues of men and of angels,* 1 Co. 13:1, 2. Grace will bring a man to heaven without working miracles, but working miracles will never bring a man to heaven without grace. Observe, That which their heart was upon, in doing these works, and which they confided in, was the wonderfulness of them. Simon Magus wondered at the miracles (Acts 8:13), and therefore would give any money for power to do the like. Observe, They had not many good works to plead: they could not pretend to have done many gracious works of piety and charity; one such would have passed better in their account than *many wonderful works,* which availed not at all, while they persisted in disobedience. Miracles have now ceased, and with them this plea; but do not carnal hearts still encourage themselves in their groundless hopes, with the like vain supports? They think they shall go to heaven, because they have been of good repute among professors of religion, have kept fasts, and given alms, and have been preferred in the church; as if this would atone for their reigning pride, worldliness, and sensuality; and want of love to God and man. *Bethel is their confidence* (Jer. 48:13), they are *haughty because of the holy mountain* (Zep. 3:11); and boast that they are *the temple of the Lord,* Jer. 7:4. Let us take heed of resting in external privileges and performances, lest *we deceive ourselves,* and perish eternally, as multitudes do, *with a lie in our right hand.*

3. The rejection of this plea as frivolous. The same that is the Law-Maker (*v.* 21) is here the Judge according to that law (*v.* 23), and he will overrule the plea, will overrule it publicly; he *will profess to them* with all possible solemnity, as sentence is passed by the Judge, *I never knew you,* and therefore *depart from me, ye that work iniquity.* — Observe, (1.) Why, and upon what ground, he rejects them and their plea — because they were *workers for iniquity.* Note, It is possible for men to have a great name for piety, and yet to be *workers of iniquity;* and those that are so will *receive the greater damnation.* Secret haunts of sin, kept under the cloak of a visible profession, will be the ruin of the hypocrites. Living in known sin nullifies men's pretensions, be they ever so specious. (2.) How it is expressed; *I never knew you;* "I never owned you as my servants, no, not when you *prophesied in* my *name,* when you were in the height of your profession, and were most extolled." This intimates, that if he had ever known them, as *the Lord knows them that are his,* had ever owned them and loved them as his, he would have known them, and owned them, and *loved them, to the end;* but he *never* did *know* them, for he always knew them to be hypocrites, and rotten at heart, as he did Judas; therefore, says he, *depart from me.* Has Christ need of such guests? When he came in the flesh, he called sinners *to* him (*ch.* 9:13), but *when he shall come again in glory,* he will drive sinners *from* him. They that would not *come to* him to be saved, must *depart from* him to be damned. To *depart from* Christ is the very hell of hell; it is the foundation of all the misery of the damned, to be cut off from all hope of benefit from Christ and he mediation. Those that go no further in Christ's service than a bare profession, he does not accept, nor will he own them in the great day. See from what a height of hope men may fall into the depth of misery! How they may go to hell, by the gates of heaven! This should be an awakening word to all Christians. If a preacher, one that *cast out devils,* and wrought miracles, be disowned of Christ for *working iniquity;* what will become of us, if we be found such? And if we *be* such, we shall certainly be found such. At God's bar, a profession of religion will not bear out any man in the prac-

tice and indulgence of sin; therefore *let every one that names the name of Christ, depart from all iniquity.*

II. He shows, by a parable, that hearing these sayings of Christ will not make us happy, if we do not make conscience of doing them; but that if we hear them and do them, we are *blessed in our deed, v.* 24–27.

1. The hearers of Christ's word are here divided into two sorts; some that hear, and do what they hear; others that hear and do not. Christ preached now to a mixed multitude, and he thus *separates them, one from the other,* as he will at the great day, when *all nations shall be gathered before him.* Christ is still speaking from heaven by his word and Spirits, speaks by ministers, by providences, and of those that hear him there are two sorts.

(1.) Some that *hear his sayings and do them:* blessed be God that there are any such, though comparatively few. To hear Christ is not barely to give him the hearing, but to obey him. Note, It highly concerns us all to do what we *hear* of the saying of Christ. It is a mercy that we *hear* his *sayings: Blessed are those ears, ch.* 13:16, 17. But, if we practise not what we hear, we *receive* that *grace in vain.* To *do* Christ's *sayings* is conscientiously to abstain from the sins that he forbids, and to perform the duties that he requires. Our thoughts and affections, our words and actions, the temper of our minds, and the tenour of our lives, must be conformable to the gospel of Christ; that is the doing he requires. All the *sayings* of Christ, not only the laws he has enacted, but the truths he has revealed, must be done by us. *They are a light,* not only to *our eyes,* but *to our feet,* and are designed not only to *in*form our judgments, but to *re*form our hearts and lives: nor do we indeed believe them, if we do not live up to them. Observe, It is not enough to *hear* Christ's *sayings,* and understand them, *hear* them, and remember them, *hear* them, and talk of them, repeat them, dispute for them; but we must *hear, and do* them. *This do, and thou shalt live.* Those only *that hear, and do,* are *blessed* (Lu. 11:28; Jn. 13:17), and are akin to Christ. *ch.* 12:50.

(2.) There are others who *hear* Christ's *sayings and do them not;* their religion rests in bare hearing, and goes no further; like children that have the rickets, their heads swell with empty notions, and indigested opinions, but their joints are weak, and they heavy and listless; they neither can stir, nor care to stir, in any good duty; *they hear* God's *words,* as if they desired to *know his ways,* like a people *that did righteousness, but they will not do them,* Eze. 33:30, 31; Isa. 58:2. Thus they deceive themselves, as Micah, who thought himself happy, because he had a Levite to be his priest, though he had not the Lord to be his God. The seed is sown, but it never comes up; they see their spots in the glass of the word, but wash them off, Jam. 1:22, 24. Thus they put a cheat upon their own souls; for it is certain, if our hearing be not the means of our obedience, it will be the aggravation of our disobedience. Those who only *hear* Christ's *sayings, and do them not,* sit down in the midway to heaven, and that will never bring them to their journey's end. They are akin to Christ only by the half-blood, and our law allows not such to inherit.

2. These two sorts of hearers are here represented in their true characters, and the state of their case, under the comparison of two builders; one was *wise,* and *built upon a rock,* and his building stood in a storm; the other *foolish,* and *built upon the sand,* and his building fell.

Now, (1.) The general scope of this parable teaches us that the only way to make sure work for our souls and eternity is, to *hear and do the sayings of* the Lord Jesus, *these sayings of* his in this sermon upon the mount, which is wholly practical; some of them seem hard sayings to flesh and blood, but they must be done; and thus we *lay up in store a good foundation for the time to come* (1 Tim. 6:19); a *good bond,* so some read it; a bond of God's making, which secures salvation upon gospel-terms, that is *a good bond;* not one of our own devising, which brings salvation to our own fancies. They make sure the *good part,* who, like Mary, when they hear the word of Christ, *sit at his feet* in subjection to it: *Speak, Lord, for thy servant heareth.*

(2.) The particular parts of it teach us divers good lessons.

[1.] That we have every one of us a house to build, and that house is our hope for heaven. It ought to be our chief and constant care, to *make our calling and election sure,* and so we make our salvation sure; to secure a title to heaven's happiness, and then to get the comfortable evidence of it; to make it sure, and sure to ourselves, *that when we fail, we* shall *be received into everlasting habitations.* Many never mind this: it is the furthest thing from their thoughts; they are building for this world, as if they were to be here always, but take no care to build for another world. All who take upon them a profession of religion, profess to enquire, what they shall *do to be saved;* how they may get to heaven at last, and may have a well-grounded hope of it in the mean time.

[2.] That there is *a rock* provided for us to build this house upon, *and that rock is Christ.* He is *laid for a foundation,* and *other foundation can no may lay,* Isa. 28:16; 1 Co. 3:11. He *is our Hope,* 1 Tim. 1:1. Christ in us is so; we must ground our hopes of heaven upon the fulness of Christ's merit, for the pardon of sin, the power of his Spirit, for the sanctification of our nature, and the prevalency of his intercession, for the conveyance of all that good which he has purchased for us. There is that in him, as *he is made known,* and made over, *to us in the gospel,* which is sufficient to redress all our grievances, and to answer all the necessities of our case, so that he is *a Saviour to the uttermost.* The church is *built upon this Rock,* and so is every believer. He is strong and immovable as a *rock;* we may venture our all upon him, and shall not be made *ashamed of our hope.*

[3.] That there is a remnant, who by hearing and doing the *sayings of* Christ, build their hopes *upon this Rock;* and it is their wisdom. Christ is our only *Way to the Father,* and the obedience of faith is our only *way* to Christ: for *to them that obey him,* and to *them* only, he *becomes the Author of eternal salvation.* Those *build upon* Christ, who having sincerely consented to him, as their Prince and Saviour, make it their constant care to conform to all the rules of his holy religion, and therein depend entirely upon him for assistance from God, and acceptance with him, *and count* every *thing but loss and dung that they may win Christ,* and be found in him. Building *upon a rock* requires care and pains: they that would make their *calling and election sure,* must *give diligence.* They are wise builders who *begin to build* so as they may be *able to finish* (Lu. 14:30), and therefore lay a firm foundation.

[4.] That there are many who profess that they hope to go to heaven, but despise this *Rock,* and build their hopes *upon the sand;* which is done without much pains, but it is their folly. Every thing besides Christ is sand. Some build their hopes upon their worldly prosperity, as if they were a sure token of God's favour, Hos. 12:8. Others upon their external profession of religion, the privileges they enjoy, and the performances they go through in that profession, and the reputation they have got by it. They are called Christians, were baptized, go to church, hear Christ's word, say their prayers, and do nobody any harm, and, if they perish, God help a great many! This is the light of their own fire, which they walk in; this is that, upon which, with a great deal of assurance, they venture; but it is all sand, took weak to bear such a fabric as our hopes of heaven.

[5.] That there is a storm coming, that will try what our hopes are bottomed on; *will try every man's work* (1 Co. 3:13); *will discover the foundation,* Hab. 3:13. *Rain, and floods, and wind, will beat upon the house;* the trial is sometimes in this world; *when tribulation and persecution arise because of the word,* then it will be seen, who only heard the word, and who heard and practiced it; then when we have occasion to use our hopes, it will be tried whether they were right, and well-grounded, or not. However, when death and judgment come, then the storm comes, and it will undoubtedly come, how calm soever things may be with us now. Then every thing else will fail us but these hopes, and then, if ever, they will be turned into everlasting fruition.

[6.] That those hopes which are built upon Christ the Rock will stand, and will stand the builder in stead when the storm comes; they will be his preservation, both from desertion, and from prevailing disquiet. His profession will not wither; his comforts will not fail; they will be his strength and song, *as an anchor of the soul, sure and steadfast.* When he comes to the last encounter, those hopes will take off the terror of death and the grave; will carry him cheerfully through that dark valley; will be approved by the Judge; will stand the test of the great day; and will be crowned with endless glory, 2 Co. 1:12; 2 Tim. 4:7, 8. *Blessed is that servant, whom his Lord, when he comes, finds so doing,* so hoping.

[7.] That those hopes which foolish builders ground upon any thing but Christ, will certainly fail them on a stormy day; will yield them no true comfort and satisfaction in trouble, in the hour of death, and in the day of judgment; will be no fence against temptations to apostacy, in a time of persecution. *When God takes away the soul, where is the hope of the hypocrite?* Job 27:8. It is as *the spider's web,* and as *the giving up of the ghost.* He shall *lean upon his house, but it shall not stand,* Job 8:14, 15. It fell in the storm, when the builder had most need of it, and expected it would be a shelter to him. It fell when it was too late to build another: *when a wicked man dies, his expectation perishes;* then, when he thought it would have been turned into fruition, *it fell, and great was the fall of it.* It was a great disappointment to the builder; the shame and loss were great. The higher men's hopes have been raised, the lower they fall. It is the sorest ruin of all that attends formal professors; witness Capernaum's doom.

III. In the two last verses, we are told what impressions Christ's discourse made upon the auditory. It was an excellent sermon; and it is probable that he said more than is here recorded; and doubtless the delivery of it from the mouth of him, into whose lips grace was poured, did mightily set it off. Now, 1. *They were astonished at this doctrine;* it is to be feared that few of them were brought by it to follow him: but for the present, they were filled with wonder. Note, It is possible for people to admire good preaching, and yet to remain in ignorance and unbelief; to be astonished, and yet not sanctified. 2. The reason was because he taught them *as one having authority, and not as the scribes.* The scribes pretended to as much authority as any teachers whatsoever, and were supported by all the external advantages that could be obtained, but their preaching was mean, and flat, and jejune: they spake as those what were not themselves masters of what they preached: the word did not come from them with any life or force; they delivered it as a school-boy says his lesson; but Christ delivered his discourse, as a judge gives his charge. He did indeed, *dominari in conscionibus — deliver his discourses with a tone of authority;* his lessons were law; his word a word of command. Christ, upon the mountain, showed more true authority, than the scribes in Moses's seat. Thus when Christ teaches by his Spirit in the soul, he teaches with authority. He says, *Let there be light, and there is light.*

CHAPTER 8

The evangelist having, in the foregoing chapters, given us a specimen of our Lord's preaching, proceeds now to give some instances of the miracles he wrought, which prove him a Teacher come from God, and the great Healer of a diseased world. In this chapter we have, I. Christ's cleansing of a leper (*v.* 1–4). II. His curing a palsy and fever (*v.* 5–18). III. His communing with two that were disposed to follow him (*v.* 19–22). IV. His controlling the tempest (*v.* 23–27). V. His casting out devils (*v.* 28–34).

Verses 1–4

The first verse refers to the close of the foregoing sermon: the people that heard him were *astonished at his doctrine;* and the effect was, that *when he came down from the mountain, great multitudes followed him;* though he was so strict a Lawgiver, and so faithful a Reprover, they diligently attended him, and were loth to disperse, and go from him. Note, They to whom Christ has manifested himself, cannot but desire to be better acquainted with him. They who know much of Christ should covet to know more; and *then shall we know, if we* thus *follow on to know the Lord.* It is pleasing to see people so well affected to Christ, as to think they can never hear enough of him; so well affected to the best things, as thus to flock after good preaching, and to *follow the Lamb* withersoever he goes. Now was Jacob's prophecy concerning the Messiah fulfilled, that *unto him shall the gathering of the people be;* yet they who gathered to him did not cleave to him. They who followed him closely and constantly were but few, compared with the multitudes that were but followers at large.

In these verses we have an account of Christ's *cleansing a leper.* It should seem, by comparing Mk. 1:40, and Lu. 5:12, that this passage, though placed, by St. Matthew, after the sermon on the mount, because he would give account of his doctrine first, and then of his miracles, happened some time before; but that is not at all material. This is fitly recorded with the first of Christ's miracles, 1. Because the leprosy was looked upon, among the Jews, as a particular mark of God's displeasure: hence we find Miriam, Gehazi, and Uzziah, smitten with leprosy for some one particular sin; and therefore Christ, to show that he came to turn away the wrath of God, by taking away sin, began with the cure of a leper. 2. Because this disease, as it was supposed to come immediately from the hand of God, so also it was supposed to be removed immediately by his hand, and therefore it was not attempted to be cured by physicians, but was put under the inspection of the priests, the Lord's ministers, who waited to see what God would do. And its being in a garment, or in the walls of a house, was altogether supernatural: and it should seem to be a disease of a quite different nature from what we now call the leprosy. The king of Israel said, *Am I God,* that I am sent to, to *recover a man of a leprosy?* 2 Ki. 5:7. Christ proved himself God, by recovering many from the leprosy, and authorizing his disciples, in his name, to do so too (*ch.* 10:8), and it is put among the proofs of his being the Messiah, *ch.* 11:5. He also showed himself to be the Saviour of his people from their sins; for though every disease is both the fruit of sin, and a figure of it, as the disorder of the soul, yet the leprosy was in a special manner so; for it contracted such a pollution, and obliged to such a separation from holy things, as no other disease did; and therefore in the laws concerning it (Lev. 13 and 14), it is treated, not as a sickness, but as an uncleanness; the priest was to pronounce the party clean or unclean, according to the indications: but the honour of making the lepers clean was reserved for Christ, who was to do it as the *High Priest of our profession;* he comes to do that which the *law could not do, in that it was weak through the flesh,* Rom. 8:3. The law discovered sin (for by the law is the knowledge of sin), and pronounced sinners unclean; it shut them up (Gal. 3:23), as the priest did the leper, but could go no further; it could not *make the comers thereunto perfect.* But Christ takes away sin; cleanses us from it, and so *perfecteth for ever them that are sanctified.* Now here we have,

I. The leper's address to Christ. If this happened, as it is here placed, after the sermon on the mount, we may suppose that the leper, though shut out by his disease from the cities of Israel, yet got within hearing of Christ's sermon, and was encouraged by it to make his application to him; for he that taught *as one having authority,* could heal so; and therefore he *came and worshipped him,* as one clothed with a divine power. His address is, *Lord, if thou wilt, thou canst make me clean.* The cleaning of him may be considered,

1. As a temporal mercy; a mercy to the body, delivering it from a disease, which, though it did not threaten life, embittered it. And so it directs us, not only to apply ourselves to Christ, who has power over bodily diseases, for the cure of them, but it also teaches us in what manner to apply ourselves to him; with an assurance of his power, believing that he is as able to cure diseases now, as he was when on earth, but with a submission to his will; *Lord, if thou wilt, thou canst.* As to temporal mercies, we cannot be so sure of God's *will* to bestow them, as we may of his *power,* for his *power* in them is unlimited by a regard to his glory and our good: when we cannot be sure of his will, we may be sure of his wisdom and mercy, to which we may cheerfully refer ourselves; *Thy will be done:* and this makes the expectation easy, and the event, when it comes, comfortable.

2. As a typical mercy. Sin is the leprosy of the soul; it shuts us out from communion with God, to which that we maybe restored, it is necessary that we be cleansed from this leprosy, and this ought to be our great concern. Now observe, It is our comfort when we apply ourselves to Christ, as the great Physician, that if he will, he can make us clean; and we should, with an humble, believing boldness, go to him and tell him so. That is, (1.) We must rest ourselves upon his power; we must be confident of this, that Christ *can* make us clean. No guilt is so great but that there is a sufficiency in his righteousness to atone for it; no corruption so strong, but there is a sufficiency in his grace to subdue it. God would not appoint a physician to his hospital that is not *par negotio — every way qualified for the undertaking.* (2.) We must recommend ourselves to his pity; we cannot demand it as a debt, but we must humbly request it as a favour; *"Lord, if thou wilt.* I throw myself at thy feet, and if I perish, I will perish there."

II. Christ's answer to this address, which was very kind, *v.* 3.

1. *He put forth his hand and touched him.* The leprosy was a noisome, loathsome disease, yet Christ touched him; for he did not disdain to converse with publicans and sinners, to do them good. There was a ceremonial pollution contracted by the touch of a leper; but Christ would show, that when he conversed with sinners, he was in no danger of being infected by them, for the prince of this world had nothing in him. If we touch pitch, we are defiled; but Christ was *separate from sinners,* even when he lived among them.

2. He said, *I will, be thou clean.* He did not say, as Elisha to Naaman, *Go, wash in Jordan;* did not put him upon a tedious, troublesome, chargeable course of a physic, but spake the word and healed him. (1.) Here is a word of kindness, *I will;* I am as willing to help thee, as thou art to be helped. Note, They who by faith apply themselves to Christ for mercy and grace, may be sure that he is willing, freely willing, to give them the mercy and grace they come to him for. Christ is a Physician, that does not need to be sought for, he is always in the way; does not need to be urged, while we are yet speaking, he hears; does not need to be feed, he heals freely, not for price nor reward. he has given all possible demonstration, that he is as willing as he is able to save sinners. (2.) A word of power, *Be thou clean.* Both a power of authority, and a power of energy, are exerted in this word. Christ heals by a word of command to us; *Be thou clean;* "Be willing to be clean, and use the means; cleanse thyself from all filthiness;" but there goes along with this a word of command concerning us, a word that does the work; *I will that thou be clean.* Such a word as this is necessary to the cure, and effectual for it; and the Almighty grace which speaks it, shall not be wanting to those who truly desire it.

III. The happy change hereby wrought: *Immediately his leprosy was cleansed.* Nature works gradually, but the God of nature works immediately; he speaks it, it is done; and yet he works effectually; he *commands, and it stands fast.* One of the first miracles Moses wrought, was curing himself of a leprosy (Ex. 4:7), for the priests under the law offered sacrifices first for their own sin; but one of Christ's first miracles was curing another of leprosy, for he had no sin of his own to atone for.

IV. The after-directions Christ gave him. It is fit that they who are cured by Christ should ever after be ruled by him.

1. *See thou tell no man;* "Tell no man till thou has shown thyself to the priest, and he has pronounced thee clean; and so thou hast a legal proof, both that thou wast before a leper, and art now thoroughly cleansed." Christ would have his miracles to appear in their full light and evidence, and not to be published till they could appear so. Note, They that preach the truths of Christ should be able to prove them; to defend what they preach, and *convince gainsayers. "Tell no man, till thou hast showed thyself to the priest,* lest if he hear who cured thee, he should out of spite deny to give thee a certificate of the cure, and so keep thee under confinement." Such were the priests in Christ's time, that they who had any thing to do with them had need to have been as wise as serpents.

2. *Go show thyself to the priest,* according to the law, Lev. 14:2. Christ took care to have the law observed, lest he should give offence, and to show that he will have order kept up, and good discipline and respect paid to those that are in office. It may be of use to those that are cleansed of their spiritual leprosy, to have recourse to Christ's ministers, and to open their case to them, that they may assist them in their enquiries into their spiritual state, and advise, and comfort, and pray for them.

3. *Offer the gift that Moses commanded,* in token of thankfulness to God, and recompence to the priest for his pains; and this *for a testimony unto them;* either, (1.) Which *Moses commanded for a testimony:* the ceremonial laws were testimonies of God's authority over them, care of them, and of that grace which should afterwards be revealed. Or, (2.) "Do thou offer it for a testimony, and let the priest know who cleansed thee, and how; and it shall be a testimony, that there is one among them who does that which the high priest cannot do. Let it remain upon record as a witness of my power, and a testimony for me *to* them, if they will use it and improve it; but *against* them, if they will not:" for so Christ's word and works are testimonies.

Verses 5–13

We have here an account of Christ's curing the centurion's servant of a palsy. This was done at Capernaum, where Christ now dwelt, *ch.* 4:13. Christ went about doing good, and came home to do good too; every place he came to was the better for him.

The persons Christ had now to do with were,

1. A *centurion;* he was a supplicant, a Gentile, a Roman, an officer of the army; probably commander-in-chief of that part of the Roman army which was quartered at Capernaum, and kept garrison there. (1.) Though he was a soldier (and a little piety commonly goes a great way with men of that profession), yet he was a godly man; he was eminently so. Note, God has his remnant among all sorts of people. No man's calling or place in the world will be an excuse for his unbelief and impiety; none shall say in the great day, I had been religious, if I had not been a soldier; for such there are among the *ransomed of the Lord.* And sometimes where grace conquers the unlikely, it is more than a conqueror; this soldier that was good, was very good. (2.) Though he was a Roman soldier, and his very dwelling among the Jews was a badge of their subjection to the Roman yoke, yet Christ, who was *King of the Jews,* favoured him; and therein has taught us to do good to our enemies, and not needlessly to interest ourselves in national enmities. (3.) Though he was a Gentile, yet Christ countenanced him. It is true, he went not to any of the Gentile towns (it was the land of Canaan that was Immanuel's land, Isa. 8:8), yet he received addresses from Gentiles; now good old Simeon's word began to be fulfilled, that he should be *a light to lighten the Gentiles,* as well as *the glory of his people Israel.* Matthew, in annexing this cure to that of the leper, who was a Jew, intimates this; the leprous Jews Christ touched and cured, for he preached personally to them; but the paralytic Gentiles he cured at a distance; for to them he did not go in person, but *sent his word and healed them;* yet in them he was more magnified.

2. *The centurion's servant;* he was the patient. In this also it appears, that there is no respect of persons with God; for *in Christ Jesus,* as there is *neither circumcision nor uncircumcision,* so there is *neither bond nor free.* He is as ready to heal the poorest servant, as the richest master; for himself *took upon him the form of a servant,* to show his regard to the meanest.

Now in the story of the cure of this servant, we may observe an intercourse or interchanging of graces, very remarkable between Christ and the centurion. See here,

I. The grace of the centurion working towards Christ. Can any good thing come out of a Roman soldier? any thing tolerable, much less any thing laudable? Come and see, and you will find abundance of good coming out of this centurion that was eminent and exemplary. Observe, 1. His affectionate address to Jesus Christ, which speaks,

(1.) A pious regard to our great Master, as one able and willing to succour and relieve poor petitioners. He came to him *beseeching him,* not as Naaman the Syrian (a centurion too) came to Elisha, demanding a cure, taking state, and standing upon points of honour; but with cap in hand as a humble suitor. By this it seems that he saw more in Christ than appeared at first view; saw that which commanded respect, though to those who looked no further, his visage was marred more than any man's. The officers of the army, being comptrollers of the town, no doubt made a great figure, yet he lays by the thoughts of his post of honour, when he addresses himself to Christ, and comes *beseeching him.* Note, the greatest of men must turn beggars, when they have to do with Christ. He owns Christ's sovereignty, in calling him Lord, and referring the case to him, and to his will, and wisdom, by a modest remonstrance, without any formal and express petition. He knew he had to do with a wise and gracious Physician, to whom the opening of the malady was equivalent to the most earnest request. A humble confession of our spiritual wants and diseases shall not fail of an answer of peace. Pour out thy complaint, and mercy shall be poured out.

(2.) A charitable regard to his poor servant. We read of many that came to Christ for their children, but this is the only instance of one that came to him for a servant: *Lord, my servant lieth at home sick.* Note, it is the duty of masters to concern themselves for their servants, when they are in affliction. The palsy disabled the servant for his work, and made him as troublesome and tedious as any distemper could, yet he did not turn him away when he was sick (as that Amalekite did his servants, 1 Sa. 30:13), did not send him to his friends, not let him lie by neglected, but sought out the best relief he could for him; the servant could not have done more for the master, than the master did here for the servant. The centurion's servants were very dutiful to him (*v.* 9), and here we see what made them so; he was very kind to them, and that made them the more cheerfully obedient to him. As we must not despise the *cause of our servants, when they contend with us* (Job 31:13, 15), so we must not despise their case when God contends with them; for we are made in the same mould, by the same hand, and stand upon the same level with them before God, and must not set them *with the dogs of our flock.* The centurion applies not to witches or wizards for his servant, but to Christ. The palsy is a disease in which the physician's skill commonly fails; it was therefore a great evidence of his faith in the power of Christ, to come to him for a cure, which was above the power of natural means to effect. Observe, How pathetically he represents his servant's case as very sad; he is *sick of the palsy,* a disease which commonly makes the patient senseless of pain, but this person was *grievously tormented;* being young, nature was strong to struggle with the stroke, which made it painful. (It was not *paralysis simplex,* but *scorbutica*). We should thus concern ourselves for the souls of our children, and servants, that are spiritually sick of the palsy, the dead-palsy, the dumb palsy; senseless of spiritual evils, inactive in that which is spiritually good, and bring them to the means of healing and health.

2. Observe his great humility and self-abasement. After Christ had intimated his readiness to come and heal his servants (*v.* 7), he expressed himself with the more humbleness of mind. Note, Humble souls are made more humble, by Christ's gracious condescensions to them. Observe what was the language of his humility; *Lord, I am not worthy that thou shouldest come under my roof* (*v.* 8), which speaks mean thought of himself, and high thoughts of our Lord Jesus. He does not say, "My servant is not worthy that thou shouldest come into his chamber, because it is in the garret;" But *I am not worthy that thou shouldest come into my house.* The centurion was a great man, yet he owned his unworthiness before God. Note, Humility very well becomes persons of quality. Christ now made but a mean figure in the world, yet the centurion, looking upon him as a prophet, *yea, more than a prophet,* paid him this respect. Note, We should have a value and veneration for what we see of God, even in those who, in outward condition, are every way our inferiors. The centurion came to Christ with a petition, and therefore expressed himself thus humbly. Note, In all our approaches to Christ, and to God through Christ, it becomes us to abase ourselves, and to lie low in the sense of our own unworthiness, as mean creatures and as vile sinners, to do any thing for God, to receive any good from him, or to have any thing to do with him.

3. Observe his great faith. The more humility the more faith; the more diffident we are of ourselves, the stronger will be our confidence in Jesus Christ. He had an assurance of faith not only that Christ could cure his servant, but,

(1.) That he could cure him at a distance. There needed not any physical contact, as in natural operations, nor any application to the part affected; but the cure, he believed, might be wrought, without bringing the physician and patient together. We read afterwards of those, who brought the *man sick of the palsy to Christ,* through much difficulty, and set him before him; and Christ commended their faith for a *working* faith. This centurion did not bring his man *sick of the palsy,* and Christ commended his faith for a *trusting* faith: true faith is accepted of Christ, though variously appearing: Christ puts the best construction upon the different methods of religion that people take, and thereby has taught us to do so too. This centurion believed, and it is undoubtedly true, that the power of Christ knows no limits, and therefore nearness and distance are alike to him. Distance of place cannot obstruct either the knowing or working of him that *fills all places. Am I a God at hand, says the Lord, and not a God afar off?* Jer. 23:23.

(2.) That he could cure him with a *word,* not send him a medicine, much less a charm; but *speak the word only,* and I do not question but *my servant shall be healed.* Herein he owns him to have a divine power, an authority to command all the creatures and powers of nature, which enables him to do whatsoever he pleases in the kingdom of nature; as at first he raised that kingdom by an almighty word, when he said, *Let there be light.* With men, saying and doing are two things; but not so with Christ, who is therefore the *Arm of the Lord,* because he is the *eternal Word.* His saying, *Be ye warmed and filled* (Jam. 2:16), and healed, warms, and fills and heals.

The centurion's faith in the power of Christ he here illustrates by the dominion he had, as a centurion, over his soldiers, as a master over his servants; he says to one, *Go, and he goes, etc.* They were all at his beck and command, so as that he could by them execute things at a distance; his word was a law to them — *dictum factum;* well-disciplined soldiers know that the commands of their officers are not to be disputed, but obeyed. Thus could Christ speak, and it is done; such a power had he over all bodily diseases. The centurion had this command over his soldiers, though he was himself a *man under authority;* not a commander-in-chief, but a subaltern officer; much more had Christ this power, who is the supreme and sovereign Lord of all. The centurion's servants were very obsequious, would go and come at every the least intimation of their master's mind. Now, [1.] Such servants we all should be to God: we must go and come at his bidding, according to the directions of his word, and the disposals of his providence; run where he sends us, return when he remands us, and do what he appoints. *What saith my Lord unto his servant?* When his will crosses our own, his must take place, and our own be set aside. [2.] Such servants bodily diseases are to Christ. They seize us when he sends them; they leave us when he calls them back; they have that effect upon us, upon our bodies, upon our souls, that he orders. It is a matter of comfort to all that belong to Christ, for whose good his power is exerted and engaged, that every disease has his commission, executes his command, is under his control, and is made to serve the intentions of his grace. They need not fear sickness, nor what it can do, who see it in the hand of so good a Friend.

II. Here is the grace of Christ appearing towards this centurion; for to the gracious he will show himself gracious.

1. He complies with his address at the first word. He did but tell him his servant's case, and was going on to beg a cure, when Christ prevented him, with this good word, and comfortable word, *I will come and heal him* (*v.* 7); not *I will come and see him* — that had evinced him a kind Saviour; but, *I will come and heal him* — that shows him a mighty, an almighty Saviour; it was a great word, but no more than he could make good; for he has *healing under his wings;* his coming is healing. They who wrought miracles by a derived power, did not speak thus positively, as Christ did, who wrought them by his own power, as one that had authority. When a minister is sent for to a sick friend, he can but say, *I will come and pray for him;* but Christ says, *I will come and heal him:* it is well that Christ can do more for us than our ministers can. The centurion desired he would heal his servant; he says, *I will come and heal him;* thus expressing more favour than he did either ask or think of. Note, Christ often outdoes the expectations of poor supplicants. See an instance of Christ's humility, that he would make a visit to a poor soldier. He would not go down to see a nobleman's sick child, who insisted upon his coming down (Jn. 4:47–49), but he proffers to go down to see a sick servant; thus does he regard *the low estate* of his people, and give *more abundant honour to that part which lacked.* Christ's humility, in being willing to come, gave an example to him, and occasioned his humility, in owning himself unworthy to have him come. Note, Christ's gracious condescensions to us, should make us the more humble and self-abasing before him.

2. He commends his faith, and takes occasion from it to speak a kind word of the poor Gentiles, *v.* 10–12. See what great things a strong but self-denying faith can obtain from Jesus Christ, even of general and public concern.

(1.) As to the centurion himself; he not only approved him and accepted him (that honour have all true believers), but he admired him and applauded him: that honour great believers have, as Job; there is *none like unto him in the earth.*

[1.] Christ admired him, not for his greatness, but for his graces. *When Jesus heard it, he marvelled;* not as if it were to him new and surprising, he knew the centurion's faith, for he wrought it; but it was great and excellent, rare and uncommon, and Christ spoke of it as wonderful, to teach us what to admire; not worldly pomp and decorations, but the beauty of holiness, and the ornaments which are *in the sight of God of great price.* Note, The wonders of grace should affect us more than the wonders of nature or providence, and spiritual attainments more than any achievements in this world. Of those that are *rich in faith,* not of those that are *rich in gold and silver,* we should say that they have *gotten all this glory,* Gen. 30:1. But whatever there is admirable in the faith of any, it must redound to the glory of Christ, who will shortly be himself *admired in all them that believe,* as having done in and for them *marvellous things.*

[2.] He *applauded* him in what he said to *them that followed.* All believers shall be, *in the other world,* but some believers are, *in this world,* confessed and acknowledged by Christ before men, in his eminent appearances for them and with them. *Verily, I have not found so great faith, no, not in Israel.* Now this speaks, *First, Honour to the centurion;* who, though not a son of Abraham's loins, was an heir of Abraham's faith, and Christ found it so. Note, The thing that Christ seeks is *faith,* and wherever it is, he finds it, though but *as a grain of mustard-seed.* He had not found *so great faith,* all things considered, and in proportion to the means; as the poor widow is said to *cast in more than they all,* Lu. 21:3. Though the centurion was a Gentile, yet he was thus commended. Note, We must be so far from grudging, that we must be forward, to give those their due praise, that are not within our denomination or pale. *Secondly,* It speaks *shame to Israel,* to whom pertained *the adoption, the glory, the covenants,* and all the assistances and encouragements of faith. Note, When *the Son of man comes,* he *finds* little *faith,* and, therefore, he finds so little *fruit.* Note, the attainments of some, who have had but little helps for their souls, will aggravate the sin and ruin of many, that have had great plenty of the means of grace, and have not made a good improvement of them. Christ said this *to those that followed* him, if by any means he might provoke them to a holy emulation, as Paul speaks, Rom. 11:14. They were Abraham's seed; in jealousy for that honour, let them not suffer themselves to be outstripped by a Gentile, especially in that grace for which Abraham was eminent.

(2.) As to others. Christ takes occasion from hence to make a comparison between Jews and Gentiles, and tells them two things, which could not but be very surprising to them who had been taught that *salvation was of the Jews.*

[1.] That *a great many of the Gentiles should be saved, v.* 11. The faith of the centurion was but a specimen of the conversion of the Gentiles, and a preface to their adoption into the church. This was a topic our Lord Jesus touched often upon; he speaks it with assurance; *I say unto you,* "I that know all men;" and he could not say any thing more pleasing to himself, or more displeasing to the Jews; an intimation of this kind enraged the Nazarenes against him, Lu. 4:27. Christ gives us here an *idea, First,* of the *persons* that shall be *saved;* many *from the east and the west:* he had said (*ch.* 7:14), *Few there be that find the way of life;* and yet here *many shall come.* Few at one time, and in one place; yet, when they come altogether, they will be a great many. We now see but here and there one brought to grace; but we shall shortly see the Captain of our salvation *bringing many sons to glory,* Heb. 2:10. He will come with *ten thousands of his saints* (Jude 14), with such a company as *no man can number* (Rev. 7:9); *with nations of them that are saved,* Rev. 21:24. They shall come *from the east* and *from the west;* places far distant from each other; and yet they shall all meet at the right hand of Christ, the Centre of their unity. Note, God has his remnant in all places; *from the rising of the sun, to the going down of the same,* Mal. 1:11. The elect will be gathered from the four winds, *ch.* 24:31. They are *sown in the earth,* some scattered in every corner of the field. The Gentile world lay *from east to west,* and they are especially meant here; though they were *strangers to the covenant of promise* now, and had been long, yet who knows what *hidden ones* God had among them then? As in Elijah's time in Israel (1 Ki. 19:14), soon after which they flocked into the church in great multitudes, Isa. 60:3, 4. Note, When we come to heaven, as we shall miss a great many there, that we thought had been going thither, so we shall meet a great many there, that we did not expect. *Secondly,* Christ gives us an idea of the *salvation itself.* They shall come, shall come together, shall come together to Christ, 2 Th. 2:1. 1. They shall be admitted *into the kingdom of grace* on earth, into the covenant of grace made with Abraham, Isaac, and Jacob; they shall be *blessed with faithful Abraham,* whose blessing comes upon the Gentiles, Gal. 3:14. This makes Zaccheus a son of Abraham, Lu. 19:9. 2. They shall be admitted into the *kingdom of glory in heaven.* They shall come cheerfully, flying *as doves to their windows;* they shall sit down to rest from their labours, as having done their day's work; sitting denotes *continuance:* while we *stand,* we are *going;* where we *sit,* we mean to *stay;* heaven is a *remaining* rest, it is a *continuing* city; they shall *sit down,* as upon a throne (Rev. 3:21); as *at a table;* that is the metaphor here; they shall sit down to be *feasted;* which denotes both *fulness* of *communication,* and *freedom* and familiarity of communion, Lu. 22:30. They shall *sit down with Abraham.* They who in this world were ever so far distant from each other in time, place, or outward condition, shall all meet together in heaven; ancients and moderns, Jews and Gentiles, rich and poor.

The rich man in hell *sees* Abraham, but Lazarus *sits down with him,* leaning on his breast. Note, Holy society is a part of the felicity of heaven; and they on whom the ends of the world are come, and who are most obscure, shall share in glory with the renowned patriarchs.

[2.] That a great many of the Jews should perish, *v.* 12. Observe,

First, A strange sentence passed; *The children of the kingdom shall be cast out;* the Jews that persist in unbelief, though they were by birth *children of the kingdom,* yet shall be cut off from being members of the visible church: *the kingdom of God,* of which they boasted that they were *the children,* shall be taken from them, and they shall become *not a people,* not *obtaining mercy,* Rom. 11:20; 9:31. In the great day it will not avail men to have been *children of the kingdom,* either as Jews or as Christians; for men will then be judged, not by what they were *called,* but by what they *were. If children* indeed, *then heirs;* but many are children in profession, in the family, but not of it, that will come short of the inheritance. Being born of professing parents denominates us *children of the kingdom;* but if we rest in that, and have nothing else to show for heaven but that, we shall be *cast out.*

Secondly, A strange punishment for *the workers of iniquity* described; *They shall be cast into outer darkness,* the darkness of those that are without, of the Gentiles that were out of the church; into that the Jews were cast, and into worse; they were blinded, and hardened, and filled with terrors, as the apostle shows, Rom. 11:8–10. A people so unchurched and given up to spiritual judgments, are in *utter darkness* already: but it looks further, to the state of damned sinners in hell, to which the other is a dismal preface. *They shall be cast out* from God, and all true comfort, and *cast into darkness.* In hell there is fire, but no light; it is *utter darkness;* darkness in extremity; the highest degree of darkness, without any remainder, or mixture, or hope, of light; not the least gleam or glimpse of it; it is darkness that results from their being shut out of heaven, the land of light; they who are *without,* are *in the regions of darkness;* yet that is not the worst of it, *there shall be weeping and gnashing of teeth.* 1. In hell there will be great grief, floods of tears shed to no purpose; anguish of spirit preying eternally upon the vitals, in the sense of the wrath of God, is the torment of the damned. 2. Great indignation: damned sinners will *gnash their teeth* for spite and vexation, *full of the fury of the Lord;* seeing with envy the happiness of others, and reflecting with horror upon the former possibility of their own being happy, which is now past.

3. He cures his servant. He not only commends his application to him, but grants him that for which he applied, which was a real answer, *v.* 13. Observe,

(1.) What Christ said to him: he said that which made the cure as great a favour to him as it was to his servant, and much greater; *As thou hast believed, so be it done to thee.* The servant got a cure of his disease, but the master got the confirmation and approbation of his faith. Note, Christ often gives encouraging answers to his praying people, when they are interceding for others. It is kindness to us, to be heard for others. God turned the captivity of Job, when he prayed for his friends, Job 42:10. It was a great honour which Christ put upon this centurion, when he gave him a blank, as it were; *Be it done as thou believest.* What could he have more? Yet what was said to him is said to us all, *Believe, and ye shall receive; only believe.* See here the power of Christ, and the power of faith. As Christ can *do* what he will, so an active believer may *have* what he will from Christ; the oil of grace multiplies, and stays not till the vessels of faith fail.

(2.) What was the effect of this saying: the prayer of faith was a prevailing prayer, it ever was so, and ever will be so; it appears, by the suddenness of the cure, that it was *miraculous:* and by its coincidence with Christ's saying, that the miracle was *his; he spake, and it was done;* and this was a proof of his omnipotence, that he has a long arm. It is the observation of a learned physician, that the diseases Christ cured were chiefly such as were the most difficult to be cured by any natural means, and particularly the palsy. *Omnis paralysis, praesertim vetusta, aut incurabilis est, aut difficilis curatu, etiam pueris: atque soleo ego dicere, morbos omnes qui Christo curandi fuerunt propositi, difficillimos sua matura curatu esse — Every kind of palsy, especially of long continuance, is either incurable, or is found to yield with the utmost difficulty to medical skill, even in young subjects; so that I have frequently remarked, that all the diseases which were referred to Christ for cure appear to have been of the most obstinate and hopeless kind.* Mercurialis *De Morbis Puerorum,* lib. 2. cap. 5.

Verses 14–17

They who pretend to be critical in the Harmony of the evangelists, place this passage, and all that follows to the end of *ch.* 9 before the sermon on the mount, according to the order which Mark and Luke observe in placing it. Dr. Lightfoot places only this passage before the sermon on the mount, and *v.* 18, etc. after. Here we have,

I. A particular account of the cure of *Peter's wife's mother,* who was ill *of a fever;* in which observe,

1. The *case,* which was nothing extraordinary; fevers are the most common distempers; but, the patient being a near relation of Peter's, it is recorded as an instance of Christ's peculiar care of, and kindness to, the families of his disciples. Here we find, (1.) That Peter had a *wife,* and yet *was called to be an apostle of Christ;* and Christ countenanced the marriage state, by being thus kind to his *wife's* relations. The church of Rome, therefore, which forbids ministers to marry, goes contrary to that apostle from whom they pretend to derive an infallibility. (2.) That Peter had a *house,* though Christ had not, *v.* 20. Thus was the disciple better provided for than his Lord. (3.) That he had a house at Capernaum, though he was originally of Bethsaida; it is probably, he removed to Capernaum, when Christ removed thither, and made that his principal residence. Note, It is worth while to change our quarters, that we may be near to Christ, and have opportunities of converse with him. When the ark removes, Israel must remove and go after it. (4.) That he had his *wife's mother* with him in his family, which is an example to yoke-fellows to be kind to one another's relations as their own. Probably, this good woman was old, and yet was respected and taken care of, as old people ought to be, with all possible tenderness. (5.) That she lay ill *of a fever.* Neither the strength of youth, nor the weakness and coldness of age, will be a fence against diseases of this kind. The palsy was a chronical disease, the fever an acute disease, but both were brought to Christ.

2. The *cure, v.* 15. (1.) How it was *effected; He touched her hand;* not to know the disease, as the physicians do, by the pulse, but to heal it. This was an intimation of his kindness and tenderness; he is *himself touched with the feeling of our infirmities;* it likewise shows the way of spiritual healing, by the exerting of the power of Christ with his word, and the application of Christ to ourselves. The scripture *speaks the word,* the Spirit gives the touch, touches the heart, touches the hand. (2.) How it was *evidenced:* this showed that the *fever left her, she arose, and ministered to them.* By this it appears, [1.] That the mercy was perfected. They that recover from fevers by the power of nature are commonly weak and feeble, and unfit for business a great while after; to show therefore that this cure was above the power of nature, she was immediately so well as to go about the business of the house. [2.] That the mercy was sanctified; and the mercies that are so are indeed perfected. Though she was thus dignified by a peculiar favour, yet she does not assume importance, but is as ready to wait at table, if there be occasion, as any servant. They must be humble whom Christ has honoured; being thus delivered, she studies what she shall render. It is very fit that they whom Christ hath healed should minister unto him, as his humble servants, all their days.

II. Here is a general account of the many cures that Christ wrought. This cure of Peter's mother-in-law brought him abundance of patients. "He healed such a one; why not me? Such a one's friend, why not mine?" Now we are here told,

1. What he did, *v.* 16. (1.) *He cast out devils; cast out the* evil *spirits with his word.* There may be much of Satan's agency, by the divine permission, in those diseases of which natural causes may be assigned, as in Job's boils, especially in the diseases of the mind; but, about the time of Christ's being in the world, there seems to have been more than ordinary letting loose of the devil, to possess and vex the bodies of people; he came, *having great wrath, for he knew that his time was short;* and God wisely ordered it so, that Christ might have the fairer and more frequent opportunities of showing his power over Satan, and the purpose and design of his coming into the world, which was to disarm and dispossess Satan, to break his power, and to destroy his works; and his success was as glorious as his design was gracious. (2.) *He healed all that were sick;* all without exception, though the patient was ever so mean, and the case ever so bad.

2. How the scripture was herein fulfilled, *v.* 17. The accomplishment of the Old-Testament prophecies was the great thing Christ had in his eye, and the great proof of his being the Messiah: among other things, it was written of him (Isa. 53:4), *Surely he hath borne our griefs, and carried our sorrows:* it is referred to, 1 Pt. 2:24, and there it is construed, *he hath borne our sins;* here it is referred to, and is construed, *he hath borne our sicknesses;* our sins make our sicknesses our griefs; Christ bore away sin by the merit of his death, and bore away sickness by the miracles of his life; nay, though those miracles are ceased, we may say, that *he bore our sicknesses* then, *when he bore our sins in his own body upon the tree;* for sin is both the cause and the sting of sickness. Many are the diseases and calamities to which we are liable in the body: and there is more, in this one line of the gospels, to support and comfort us under them, than in all the writings of the philosophers — that Jesus Christ *bore our sicknesses, and carried our sorrows;* he bore them before us; though he was never sick, yet he was hungry, and thirsty, and weary, and troubled in spirit, sorrowful and very heavy; he bore them for us in his *passion,* and bears them with us in *compassion,* being *touched with the feeling of our infirmities:* and thus he bears them off from us, and makes them sit light, if it be not our own fault. Observe how emphatically it is expressed here: *Himself took our infirmities, and bare our sicknesses;* he was both able and willing to interpose in that matter, and concerned to deal with *our infirmities and sicknesses,* as our Physician; that part of the calamity of the human nature was his particular care, which he evidenced by his great readiness to cure diseases; and he is no less powerful, no less tender now, for we are sure that never were any the worse for going to heaven.

Verses 18–22

Here is, I. Christ's removing to *the other side of the sea of Tiberias,* and his ordering his disciples, whose boats attended him, to get their transport-vessels ready, in order to it, *v.* 18. The influences of this Sun of righteousness were not to be confined to one place, but diffused all the country over; he must go about to do good; the necessities of souls called to him, *Come over, and help us* (Acts 16:9); he removed *when he saw great multitudes about him.* Though by this it appeared that they were desirous to have him there, he knew there were others as desirous to have him with them, and they must have their share of him: his being acceptable and useful in one place was no objection against, but a reason for, his going to another. Thus he would try the multitudes that were *about him,* whether their zeal would carry them to follow him, and attend on him, when his preaching was removed to some distance. Many would be glad of such helps, if they could have them at next door, who will not be at the pains to follow them to *the other side;* and thus Christ shook off those who were less zealous, and the perfect were made manifest.

II. Christ's communication with two, who, upon his remove to *the other side,* were loth to stay behind, and had a mind to follow him, not as others, who were his followers at large, but to come into close discipleship, which the most were shy of; for it carried such a face of strictness as they could not like, nor be well reconciled to; but here is an account of two who seemed desirous to come into communion, and yet were not right; which is here given as a specimen of the hindrances by which many are kept from closing with Christ, and cleaving to him; and a warning to us, to set out in following Christ, so as that we may not come short; to lay such a foundation, as that our building may stand.

We have here Christ's managing of two different tempers, one quick and eager, the other dull and heavy; and his instructions are adapted to each of them, and designed for our use.

1. Here is one that was *too hasty in promising;* and he was *a certain scribe* (*v.* 19), a scholar, a learned man, one of those that studied and expounded the law; generally we find them in the gospels to be men of no good character; usually coupled with the Pharisees, as enemies to Christ and his doctrine. *Where is the scribe?* 1 Co. 1:20. He is very seldom following Christ; yet here was one that bid pretty fair for discipleship, a *Saul among the prophets.* Now observe,

(1.) How he expressed his forwardness; *Master, I will follow thee, whithersoever thou goest.* I know not how any man could have spoken better. His profession of a self-dedication to Christ is, [1.] Very ready, and seems to be *ex mero motu*

— *from his unbiased inclination:* he is not called to it by Christ, nor urged by any of the disciples, but, of his own accord, he proffers himself to be a close follower of Christ; he is not a pressed man, but a volunteer. [2.] Very resolute; he seems to be at a point in this matter; he does not say, "I have a mind to *follow thee;*" but, "I am determined, *I will* do it." [3.] It was unlimited and without reserve; *"I will follow thee whithersoever thou goest;* not only to *the other side* of the country, but if it were to the utmost regions of the world." Now we should think ourselves sure of such a man as this; and yet it appears, by Christ's answer, that his resolution was rash, his ends low and carnal: either he did not consider at all, or not that which was to be considered; he saw the miracles Christ wrought, and hoped he would set up a temporal kingdom, and he wished to apply betimes for a share in it. Note, There are many resolutions for religion, produced by some sudden pangs of conviction, and taken up without due consideration, that prove abortive, and come to nothing: soon ripe, soon rotten.

(2.) How Christ tried his forwardness, whether it were sincere or not, *v.* 20. He let him know that this *Son of man,* whom he is so eager to follow, *has not where to lay his head, v.* 20. Now from this account of Christ's deep poverty, we observe,

[1.] That it is strange in itself, that the Son of God, when he came into the world, should put himself into such a very low condition, as to want the convenience of a certain resting-place, which the meanest of the creatures have. If he would *take our nature upon him,* one would think, he should have taken it in its best estate and circumstances: no, he takes it in its worst. See here, *First,* How well provided for the inferior creatures are: *The foxes have holes;* though they are not only not useful, but hurtful, to man, yet God provides holes for them in which they are earthed: man endeavours to destroy them, but thus they are sheltered; their holes are their castles. *The birds of the air,* though they take no care for themselves, yet are taken care of, and *have nests* (Ps. 104:17); *nests* in the field; some of them *nests* in the house; in God's courts, Ps. 84:3. *Secondly,* How poorly the Lord Jesus was provided for. it may encourage us to trust God for necessaries, that the beasts and birds have such good provision; and may comfort us, if we want necessaries, that our Master did so before us. Note, Our Lord Jesus, when he was here in the world, submitted to the disgraces and distresses of extreme poverty; *for our sakes he became poor,* very poor. He had not a settlement, had not a place of repose, not a house of his own, to put his head in, not a pillow of his own, to lay his head on. he and his disciples lived upon the charity of well-disposed people, that *ministered to him of their substance,* Lu. 8:2. Christ submitted to this, not only that he might in all respects humble himself, and fulfil the scriptures, which spake of him as *poor and needy,* but that he might show us the vanity of worldly wealth, and teach us to look upon it with a holy contempt; that he might purchase better things for us, and so *make us rich,* 2 Co. 8:9.

[2.] It is strange that such a declaration should be made on this occasion. When a scribe offered to follow Christ, one would think he would have encouraged him, and said, *Come, and I will take care of thee;* one scribe might be capable of doing him more credit and service than twelve fishermen: but Christ saw his heart, and answered to the thoughts of that, and therein teaches us all how to come to Christ. *First,* The scribe's resolve seems to have been sudden; and Christ would have us, when we take upon us a profession of religion, to *sit down and count the cost* (Lu. 14:28), to do it intelligently, and with consideration, and choose the way of godliness, not because we know no other, but because we know no better. It is no advantage to religion, to take men by surprise, ere they are aware. They that take up a profession *in a pang,* will throw it off again *in a fret;* let them, therefore, *take time,* and they will have *done the sooner:* let him that will follow Christ know the worst of it, and expect to lie hard, and fare hard. *Secondly,* His resolve seems to have been from a worldly, covetous principle. He saw what abundance of cures Christ wrought, and concluded that he had large fees, and would get an estate quickly, and therefore he would follow him in hopes of growing rich with him; but Christ rectifies his mistake, and tells him, he was so far from growing rich, that he had not a place to *lay his head on;* and that if he follow him, he cannot expect to fare better than he fared. Note, Christ will accept none for his followers that aim at worldly advantages in following him, or design to make any thing but heaven of their religion. We have reason to think that this scribe, hereupon, *went away sorrowful,* being disappointed in a bargain which he thought would turn to account; he is not for following Christ, unless he can *get by him.*

2. Here is another that was too *slow in performing.* Delay in execution is as bad, on the one hand, as precipitancy in resolution is on the other hand; when we have taken time to consider, and then have determined, let it never be said, we left that to be done to-morrow, which we could do to-day. This candidate for the ministry was one of Christ's disciples already (*v.* 21), a follower of him at large. Clemens Alexandrinus tells us, from an ancient tradition, that this was Philip; he seems to be better qualified and disposed than the former; because not so confident and presumptuous: a bold, eager, over-forward temper is not the most promising in religion; sometimes the last are first, and the first last. Now observe here,

(1.) The excuse that this disciple made, to defer an immediate attendance on Christ (*v.* 21); *"Lord, suffer me first to go and bury my father.* Before I come to be a close and constant follower of thee, let me be allowed to perform this last office of respect to my father; and in the mean time, let it suffice to be a hearer of thee now and then, when I can spare time." His father (some think) was now sick, or dying, or dead; others think, he was only aged, and not likely in a course of nature, to continue long; and he desired leave to attend upon him in his sickness, at his death, and to his grave, and then he would be at Christ's service. This seemed a reasonable request, and yet it was not right. He had not the zeal he should have had for the work, and therefore pleaded this, because it seemed a plausible plea. Note, An unwilling mind never wants an excuse. The meaning of *Non vacat* is, *Non placet — The want of leisure is the want of inclination.* We will suppose it to come from a true filial affection and respect for his father, yet still the preference should have been given to Christ. Note, Many are hindered *from* and *in* the way of serious godliness, by an over-concern for their families and relations; these lawful things undo us all, and our duty to God is neglected, and postponed, under colour of discharging our debts to the world; here therefore we have need to double our guard.

(2.) Christ's disallowing of this excuse (*v.* 22); *Jesus said to him, Follow me;* and, no doubt, power accompanied this word to him, as to others, and he did *follow Christ,* and cleaved to him, as Ruth to Naomi, when the scribe, in the verses before, like Orpah, took leave of him. That said, *I will follow thee;* to this Christ said, *Follow me;* comparing them together, it is intimated that we are brought to Christ by the force of his call to us, not of our promises to him; it is *not of him that willeth, nor of him that runneth, but of God that showeth mercy;* he calls whom he will, Rom. 9:16. And further, Note, Though chosen vessels may make excuses, and delay their compliance with divine calls a great while, yet Christ will at length answer their excuses, conquer their unwillingness, and bring them to his feet; when Christ calls, he will overcome, and make the call effectual, 1 Sa. 3:10. His excuse is laid aside as insufficient; *Let the dead bury their dead.* It is a proverbial expression; "Let one dead man bury another: rather let them lie unburied, than that the service of Christ should be neglected. *Let the dead* spiritually *bury the dead* corporally; let worldly offices be left to worldly people; do not thou encumber thyself with them. Burying the dead, and especially a dead father, is a good work, but it is not thy work at this time: it may be done as well by others, that are not called and qualified, as thou art, to be employed for Christ; thou hast something else to do, and must not defer that." Note, Piety to God must be preferred before piety to parents, though that is a great and needful part of our religion. The Nazarites, under the law, were not to mourn for their own parents, because they were *holy to the Lord* (Num. 6:6–8); nor was the high priest to *defile himself for the dead,* no, not for *his own father,* Lev. 21:11, 12. And Christ requires of those who would follow him, that they *hate father and mother* (Lu. 14:26); love them less than God; we must comparatively neglect and disesteem our nearest relations, when they come in competition with Christ, and either our doing for him, or our suffering for him.

Verses 23–27

Christ had given sailing orders to his disciples (*v.* 18), that they should *depart to the other side of the sea of Tiberias,* into the country of Gadara, in the tribe of Gad, which lay east of Jordan; thither he would go to rescue a poor creature that was possessed *with a legion of devils,* though he foresaw how he should be affronted there. Now. 1. He chose to go by water. It had not been much about, if he had gone by land; but he chose to cross the lake, that he might have occasion to manifest himself the God *of the sea* as well as of *the dry land,* and to show that *all power is his, both in heaven and in earth.* It is a comfort to those *who go down to the sea in ships,* and are often in perils there, to reflect that they have a Saviour to trust in, and pray to, who knows what it is to be at sea, and to be in storms there. But observe, when he went to sea, he had no yacht or pleasure-boat to attend him, but made use of his disciples' fishing-boats; so poorly was he accommodated in all respects. 2. *His disciples followed him;* the twelve kept close to him, when others staid behind upon the *terra firma,* where there was sure footing. Note, They, and they only, will be found the true disciples of Christ, that are willing to go to sea with him, to follow him into dangers and difficulties. Many would be content to go the land-way to heaven, that will rather stand still, or go back, than venture upon a dangerous sea; but those that would rest with Christ hereafter must follow him now wherever he leads them, into a ship or into a prison, as well as into a palace. Now observe here,

I. The peril and perplexity of the disciples in this voyage; and in this appeared the truth of what Christ had just now said, that those who follow him must count upon difficulties, *v.* 20.

1. *There arose a very great storm, v.* 24. Christ could have prevented this storm, and have ordered them a pleasant passage, but that would not have been so much for his glory and the confirmation of their faith as their deliverance was: this storm was *for their sakes,* as Jn. 11:4. One would have expected, that having Christ with them, they should have had a very favourable gale, but it is quite otherwise; for Christ would show that they who are passing with him over the ocean of this world to the other side, must expect storms by the way. The church is *tossed with tempests* (Isa. 54:11); it is only the upper region that enjoys a perpetual calm, this lower one is ever and anon disturbed and disturbing.

2. Jesus Christ *was asleep in this storm.* We never read of Christ's sleeping but at this time; he was in watchings often, and continued all night in prayer to God: this was a sleep, not of security, like Jonah's in a storm, but of holy serenity, and dependence upon his Father: he slept to show that he was really and truly man, and subject to the sinless infirmities of our nature: his work made him weary and sleepy, and he had no guilt, no fear within, to disturb his repose. Those that can lay their heads upon the pillow of a clear conscience, may sleep quietly and sweetly in a storm (Ps. 4:8), as Peter, Acts 12:6. He slept at this time, to try the faith of his disciples, whether they could trust him when he seemed to slight them. He slept not so much with a desire to be refreshed, as with a design to be awaked.

3. The poor disciples, though used to the sea, were in a great fright, and in their fear *came to* their Master, *v.* 25. Whither else should they go? It was well they had him so near them. They *awoke him* with their prayers; *Lord, save us, we perish.* Note, They who would learn to pray must go to sea. Imminent and sensible dangers will drive people to him who alone can help in time of need. Their prayer has life in it, *Lord, save us, we perish.* (1.) Their petition is, *Lord, save us.* They believed he *could* save them; they begged he *would,* Christ's errand into the world was *to save,* but those only *shall be saved that call on the name of the Lord,* Acts 2:21. They who by faith are interested in the eternal salvation wrought out by Christ, may with a humble confidence apply themselves to him for temporal deliverances. Observe, They call him, *Lord,* and then pray, *Save us.* Note, Christ will save none but those that are willing to take him for their Lord; for he is a Prince and a Saviour. (2.) Their plea is, *We perish;* which was, [1.] The language of their fear; they looked upon their case as desperate, and gave up all for lost; they had received a sentence of death within themselves, and this they plead, *"We perish,* if thou dost not save us; look upon us therefore with pity." [2.] It was the language of their fervency; they pray as men in earnest, that beg for their lives; it becomes us thus to strive and wrestle in prayer; *therefore* Christ slept, that he might draw out this importunity.

II. The power and grace of Jesus Christ put forth for their succour: then the Lord Jesus awaked, as one refreshed, Ps.

78:65. Christ may sleep when his church is in a storm, but he will not outsleep himself: the time, the set time to favour his distressed church, will come, Ps. 102:13.

1. He rebuked the disciples (*v.* 26); *Why are ye fearful, O ye of little faith?* He does not chide them for disturbing him with their prayers, but for disturbing themselves with their fears. Christ reproved them first, and then delivered them; this is his method, to prepare us for a mercy, and then to give it us. Observe, (1.) His dislike of their fears; *"Why are ye fearful?* Ye, my disciples? Let the sinners in Zion be afraid, let heathen mariners tremble in a storm, but you shall not be so. Enquire into the reasons of your fear, and weigh them." (2.) His discovery of the cause and spring of their fears; *O ye of little faith.* Many that have true faith are weak in it, and it does but little. Note, [1.] Christ's disciples are apt to be disquieted with fears in a stormy day, to torment themselves with jealousies that things are bad with them, and dismal conclusions that they will be worse. [2.] The prevalence of our inordinate fears in a stormy day is owing to the weakness of our faith, which would be as an anchor to the soul, and would ply the oar of prayer. By faith we might see through the storm to the quiet shore, and encourage ourselves with hope that we shall weather our point. [3.] The fearfulness of Christ's disciples in a storm, and their unbelief, the cause of it, are very displeasing to the Lord Jesus, for they reflect dishonour upon him, and create disturbance to themselves.

2. He *rebukes the wind;* the former he did as the God of *grace,* and the Sovereign of the heart, who can do what he pleases *in* us; this he did as the God of *nature,* the Sovereign of the world, who can do what he pleases *for* us. It is the same *power that stills the noise of the sea,* and the tumult of fear, Ps. 65:7. See, (1.) How *easily* this was done, with a word's speaking. Moses commanded the waters with a rod; Joshua, with the ark of the covenant; Elisha, with the prophet's mantle; but Christ with a word. See his absolute dominion over all the creatures, which bespeaks both his honour, and the happiness of those that have him on their side. (2.) How *effectually* it was done? *There was a great calm,* all of a sudden. Ordinarily, after a storm, there is such a fret of the waters, that it is a good while ere they can settle; but if Christ speak the word, not only the storm ceases, but all the effects of it, all the remains of it. Great storms of doubt, and fear in the soul, under the power of the spirit of bondage, sometimes end in a wonderful calm, created and spoken by the Spirit of adoption.

3. This excited their astonishment (*v.* 27); *The men marvelled.* They had been long acquainted with the sea, and never saw a storm so immediately turned into a perfect calm, in all their lives. It has all the marks and signatures of a miracle upon it; *it is the Lord's doing, and is marvellous in their eyes.* Observe, (1.) Their admiration of Christ; *What manner of man is this!* Note, Christ is a Nonsuch; every thing in him is admirable: none so wise, so mighty, so amiable, as he. (2.) The reason of it; *Even the winds and the sea obey him.* Upon this account, Christ is to be admired, that he has a commanding power even over *winds and seas.* Others pretended to cure diseases, but he only undertook to command *the winds.* We know not the way of *the wind* (Jn. 3:8), much less can we control it; but he that *bringeth forth the wind out of his treasury* (Ps. 135:7), when it is out, gathers it into his fists, Prov. 30:4. He that can do this, can do any thing, can do enough to encourage our confidence and comfort in him, in the most stormy day, within or without, Isa. 26:4. The Lord *sits upon the floods,* and is *mightier than the noise of many waters.* Christ, by commanding *the seas,* showed himself to be the same that *made the world, when, at his rebuke, the waters fled* (Ps. 104:7, 8), as now, *at his rebuke,* they fell.

Verses 28–34

We have here the story of Christ's casting the devils out of two men that were possessed. The scope of this chapter is to show the divine power of Christ, by the instances of his dominion over bodily diseases, which to us are irresistible; over winds and waves, which to us are yet more uncontrollable; and lastly, over devils, which to us are most formidable of all. Christ has not only all *power in heaven and earth* and all deep places, but has the keys of hell too. *Principalities and powers were made subject to him,* even while he was in his estate of humiliation, as an earnest of what should be at his entrance into his glory (Eph. 1:21); he spoiled them, Col. 2:15. It was observed in general (*v.* 16), that Christ *cast out the spirits with his word;* here we have a particular instance of it, which have some circumstances more remarkable than the rest. This miracle was wrought in the country of the Gergesenes; some think, they were the remains of the old Girgashites, Deu. 7:1. Though Christ was sent chiefly *to the lost sheep of the house of Israel,* yet some sallies he made among the borderers, as here, to gain this victory over Satan, which was a specimen of the conquest of his legions in the Gentile world.

Now, besides the general instance which this gives us of Christ's power over Satan, and his design against him to disarm and dispossess him, we have here especially discovered to us the way and manner of evil spirits in their enmity to man. Observe, concerning this legion of devils, What work they made where they *were,* and where they *went.*

I. What work they made where they *were;* which appears in the miserable condition of these two that were possessed by them; and some think, these two were man and wife, because the other Evangelists speak but of one.

1. They dwelt among *the tombs;* thence they came when the met Christ. The devil having *the power of death,* not as judge, but as executioner, he delighted to converse among the trophies of his victory, the dead bodies of men; but there, where he thought himself in the greatest triumph and elevation, as afterwards in Golgotha, the place of a skull, did Christ conquer and subdue him. Conversing among the graves increased the melancholy and frenzy of the poor possessed creatures, and so strengthened the hold he had of them by their bodily distemper, and also made them more formidable to other people, who generally startle at any thing that stirs among *the tombs.*

2. They were *exceeding fierce;* not only ungovernable themselves, but mischievous to others, frightening many, having hurt some; *so that no man durst pass that way.* Note, The devil bears malice to mankind, and shows it by making men spiteful and malicious one to another. Mutual enmities, where they should be mutual endearments and assistances, are effects and evidences of Satan's enmity to the whole race; he makes one man a wolf, a bear, a devil, to another — *Homo homini lupus.* Where Satan rules in a man spiritually, by those lusts that war in the members, pride, envy, malice, revenge, they make him as unfit for human society, as unworthy of it, and as much an enemy to the comfort of it, as these poor possessed creatures were.

3. They bid defiance to Jesus Christ, and disclaimed all interest in him, *v.* 29. It is an instance of the power of God over the devils, that, notwithstanding the mischief they studied to do *by* and *to* these poor creatures, yet they could not keep them from meeting Jesus Christ, who ordered the matter so as to meet them. It was his overpowering hand that dragged these unclean spirits into his presence, which they dreaded more than any thing else: his chains could hold them, when the chains that men made for them could not. But being brought before him, they protested against his jurisdiction, and broke out into a rage, *What have we to do with thee, Jesus, thou Son of God?* Here is,

(1.) *One* word that the devil spoke like a *saint;* he addressed himself to Christ as *Jesus the Son of God;* a *good* word, and at this time, when it was a truth but in the proving, it was a *great* word too, what flesh and blood did not reveal to Peter, *ch.* 16:17. Even the devils know, and believe, and confess Christ to be the *Son of God,* and yet they are devils still, which makes their enmity to Christ so much the more wicked, and indeed a perfect torment to themselves; for how can it be otherwise, to oppose one they know to be the *Son of God?* Note, It is not knowledge, but love, that distinguishes saints from devils. He is the first-born of hell, that knows Christ and yet hates him, and will not be subject to him and his law. We may remember that not long since the devil made a doubt whether Christ were *the Son of God* or not, and would have persuaded him to question it (*ch.* 4:33), but now he readily owns it. Note, Though God's children may be much disquieted in an hour of temptation, by Satan's questioning their relation to God as a Father, yet the Spirit of adoption shall at length clear it up to them so much to their satisfaction, as to set it even above the devil's contradiction.

(2.) *Two* words that he said like a *devil,* like himself.

[1.] A word of defiance; *What have we to do with thee?* Now, *First,* It is true that the devils have nothing to do with Christ as a Saviour, *for he took not on him the nature of the angels* that fell, nor did he lay hold on them (Heb. 2:16); they are in no relation to him, they neither have, nor hope for, any benefit by him. O the depth of this mystery of divine love, that fallen man hath so much *to do with Christ,* when fallen angels have nothing *to do with* him! Surely here was torment enough before the time, to be forced to own the excellency *that is in Christ,* and yet that he has no interest in him. Note, It is possible for me to call Jesus *the Son of God,* and yet have nothing to do with him. *Secondly,* It is as true, that the devils desire not to have any thing *to do with Christ* as a Ruler; they hate him, they are filled with enmity against him, they stand in opposition to him, and are in open rebellion against his crown and dignity. See whose language they speak, that will have nothing *to do with the* gospel of Christ, with his laws and ordinances, that throw off his yoke, that *break his bands in sunder,* and *will not have him to reign over them;* that say *to the Almighty* Jesus, *Depart from us: they are of their father the devil, they do his lusts,* and speak his language. *Thirdly,* But it is not true, that the devils have nothing *to do with Christ* as a Judge, for they have, and they know it. These devils could not say, *What hast thou to do with us?* could not deny that the Son of God is the Judge of devils; to his judgment they are bound over in chains of darkness, which they would fain shake off, and shake off the thought of.

[2.] A word of dread and deprecation; *"Art thou come hither to torment us* — to cast us out from these men, and to restrain us from doing the hurt we would do?" Note, To be turned out, and tied up, from doing mischief, is a torment to the devil, all whose comfort and satisfaction are man's misery and destruction. Should not we then count it our heaven to be doing well, and reckon that our torment, whether within or without, that hinders us from well-doing? Now must we be tormented by thee *before the time;* Note, *First,* There is a time in which devils will be more tormented than they are, and they know it. The great assize at the last day is the time fixed for their complete torture, in that Tophet which is ordained of old *for the king, for the prince of the devils, and his angels* (Isa. 30:33; Mt. 25:41); *for the judgment of that day* they are *reserved,* 2 Pt. 2:4. Those malignant spirits that are, by the divine permission, prisoners *at large,* walking to and fro through the earth (Job 1:7), are even now in a chain; hitherto shall their power reach, and no further; they will then be made *close* prisoners: they have now some ease; they will then be in torment without ease. This they here take for granted, and ask not never to be tormented (despair of relief is the misery of their case), but they beg that they may not be tormented *before the time;* for though they knew not when the day of judgment should be, they knew it should not be yet. *Secondly,* The devils have *a certain fearful looking for of that judgment and fiery indignation,* upon every approach of Christ, and every check that is given to their power and rage. The very sight of Christ and his word of command to come out of the man, made them thus apprehensive of their torment. Thus *the devils believe, and tremble,* Jam. 2:19. It is their own enmity to God and man that puts them upon the rack, and *torments them before the time.* The most desperate sinners, whose damnation is sealed, yet cannot quite harden their hearts against the surprise of fearfulness, *when they see the day approaching.*

II. Let us now see what work they made where they *went,* when they were turned out of the men possessed, and that was into *a herd of swine,* which *was a good way off, v.* 30. These Gergesenes, though living on the other side Jordan, were Jews. What had they to do with *swine,* which by the law were unclean, and not to be eaten nor touched? Probably, lying in the outskirts of the land, there were many Gentiles among them, to whom this *herd of swine* belonged: or they kept them to be sold, or bartered, to the Romans, with whom they had now great dealings, and who were admirers of *swine's* flesh. Now observe,

1. How the devils seized the *swine.* Though they were *a good way off,* and, one would think, out of danger, yet the devils had an eye upon them, to do them a mischief: for they *go up and down, seeking to devour,* seeking an opportunity; and they seek not long but they find. Now here,

(1.) They *asked* leave to enter *into the swine* (*v.* 31); *they besought him,* with all earnestness, *If thou cast us out, suffer us to go away into the herd of swine.* Hereby, [1.] They discover their own inclination to do mischief, and what a pleasure it is to them; those, therefore, are their children, and resemble them, *whose sleep departeth from them, except they cause some to fall,* Prov. 4:16. "Let us go *into the herd of swine,* any where rather than into the place of torment, any where to do mischief." If they might not be suffered to hurt men in their bodies, they would hurt them in their goods, and in that too they intend hurt to their souls, by making Christ a burthen to them: such malicious devices hath that old subtle serpent! [2.] They own Christ's power over them; that, without his sufferance and permission, they could not so much as hurt a *swine.* This is comfortable to all the Lord's people, that, though the devil's power be very great, yet it is limited, and not equal to his malice (what would become of us, if it were?) especially that it is under the control of our Lord Jesus, our most faithful, powerful friend and Saviour; that Satan and his instruments can go no further than he is pleased to permit; *here shall their proud waves be stayed.*

(2.) They *had* leave. Christ said unto them, *Go* (*v.* 32), as God did to Satan, when he desired leave to afflict Job. Note, God does often, for wise and holy ends, permit the efforts of Satan's rage, and suffer him to do the mischief he would, and even by it serve his own purposes. The devils are not only Christ's captives, but his vassals; his dominion over them appears in the harm they do, as well as in the hindrance of them from doing more. Thus even their wrath is made to praise Christ, and the remainder of it he does and will restrain. Christ permitted this, [1.] For the conviction of the Sadducees that were then among the Jews, who denied the existence of spirits, and would not own that there were such beings, because they could not see them. Now Christ would, by this, bring it as near as might be to an ocular demonstration of the being, multitude, power, and malice, of evil spirits, that, if they were not hereby convinced, they might be left inexcusable in their infidelity. We see not the wind, but it would be absurd to deny it, when we see trees and houses blown down by it. [2.] For the punishment of the Gadarenes, who perhaps, though Jews, took a liberty to eat *swine's* flesh, contrary to the law: however, their keeping *swine* bordered upon evil; and Christ would also show what a hellish crew they were delivered from, which, if he had permitted it, would soon have choked them, as they did their *swine.* The devils, in obedience to Christ's command, came out of the men, and having permission, *when they were come out, immediately they went into the herd of swine.* See what an industrious enemy Satan is, and how expeditious; he will lose no time in doing mischief. Observe,

2. *Whither they hurried them,* when they had seized them. They were not bid to *save their lives,* and, therefore, they were made to *run violently down a steep place into the sea,* where they all perished, to the number of about *two thousand,* Mk. 5:13. Note, The possession which the devil gets is for destruction. Thus the devil hurries people to sin, hurries them to that which they have resolved against, and which they know will be shame and grief to them: with what a force doth the evil spirit *work in the children of disobedience,* when by so many foolish and hurtful lusts they are brought to act in direct contradiction, not only to religion, but to right reason, and their interest in this world! Thus, likewise, he hurries them to ruin, for he is Apollyon and Abaddon, the great destroyer. By his lusts which men do, they are *drowned in destruction and perdition.* This is Satan's will, to *swallow up* and to *devour;* miserable then is the condition of those that are led *captive by him at his will.* They are hurried into a worse lake than this, a lake that *burns with fire and brimstone.* Observe,

3. *What effect this had upon the owners.* The report of it was soon brought them by the swine-herds, who seemed to be more concerned for the loss of the swine than any thing else, for they went not to tell *what was befallen to the possessed of the devils,* till the swine were lost, *v.* 33. Christ went not *into the city,* but the news of his being there did, by which he was willing to feel how their pulse beat, and what influence it had upon them, and then act accordingly.

Now, (1.) Their curiosity brought them out to see Jesus. The *whole city came out to meet him,* that they might be able to say, they had seen a man who did such wonderful works. Thus many go out, in profession, to meet Christ for company, that have no real affection for him, nor desire to know him.

(2.) Their covetousness made them *willing to be rid of him.* Instead of inviting him into their city, or bringing their sick to him to be healed, they desired him *to depart out of their coasts,* as if they had borrowed the words of the devils, *What have we to do with thee, Jesus thou Son of God?* And now the devils had what they aimed at in drowning the swine; *they* did it, and then made the people believe that *Christ* had done it, and so prejudiced them against him. He seduced our first parents, by possessing them with hard thoughts of God, and kept the Gadarenes from Christ, by suggesting that he came into their country to destroy their cattle, and that he would do more hurt than good; for though he had cured two men, yet he had drowned two thousand swine. Thus the devil sows tares in God's field, does mischief in the Christian church, and then lays the blame upon Christianity, and incenses men against that. They besought him that he would depart, lest, like Moses in Egypt, he should proceed to some other plague. Note, There are a great many who prefer their swine before their Saviour, and so come short of Christ, and salvation by him. They desire Christ to depart out of their hearts, and will not suffer his word to have a place in them, because he and his word will be the destruction of their brutish lusts — those swine which they give up themselves to feed. And justly will Christ forsake those that thus are weary of him, and say to them hereafter, *Depart, ye cursed,* who now say to the Almighty, *Depart from us.*

CHAPTER 9

We have in this chapter remarkable instances of the power and pity of the Lord Jesus, sufficient to convince us that he is both able to save to the uttermost all that come to God by him, and as willing as he is able. His power and pity appear here in the good offices he did, I. To the bodies of people, in curing the palsy (*v.* 2–8); raising to life the ruler's daughter, and healing the bloody issue (*v.* 18–26); giving sight to two blind men (*v.* 27–31); casting the devil out of one possessed (*v.* 32–34); and healing all manner of sickness (*v.* 35). II. To the souls of people; in forgiving sins (*v.* 2); calling Matthew, and conversing freely with publicans and sinners (*v.* 9–13); considering the frame of his disciples, with reference to the duty of fasting (*v.* 14–17); preaching the gospel, and, in compassion to the multitude, providing preachers for them (*v.* 35–38). Thus did he prove himself to be, as undoubtedly he is, the skilful, faithful Physician, both of soul and body, who has sufficient remedies for all the maladies of both: for which we must, therefore, apply ourselves to him, and glorify him both with our bodies and with our spirits, which are his, in return to him for his kindness to both.

Verses 1–8

The first words of this chapter oblige us to look back to the close of that which precedes it, where we find the Gadarenes so resenting the loss of their swine, that they were disgusted with Christ's company, and besought him to *depart out of their coasts.* Now here it follows, *He entered into a ship, and passed over.* They bid him begone, and he took them at their word, and we never read that he came into their coasts again. Now here observe, 1. His justice — that he left them. Note, Christ will not tarry long where he is not welcome. In righteous judgment, he forsakes those places and persons that are weary of him, but abides with those that covet and court his stay. *If the unbeliever will depart* from Christ, *let him depart;* it is at his peril, 1 Co. 7:15. 2. His patience — that he did not leave some destroying judgment behind him, to punish them, as they deserved, for their contempt and contumacy. How easily, how justly, might he have sent them after their swine, who were already so much under the devil's power. The provocation, indeed, was very great: but he put it up, and passed it by; and, without any angry resentments or upbraidings, he *entered into a ship, and passed over.* This was the day of his patience; he came not to *destroy men's lives,* but to save them; not to kill, but to cure. Spiritual judgments agree more with the constitution of gospel times; yet some observe, that in those bloody wars which the Romans made upon the Jews, which began not many years after this, they first besieged the town of Gadara, where these Gadarenes dwelt. Note, Those that drive Christ from them, draw all miseries upon them. Woe unto us, if God depart from us.

He came *into his own city, Capernaum,* the principal place of his residence at present (Mk. 2:1), and therefore called *his own city.* He had himself testified, that a prophet it least honoured in *his own country* and *city,* yet thither he came; for he *sought not his own honour;* but, being in a state of humiliation, he was content to be despised of the people. At Capernaum all the circumstances recorded in this chapter happened, and are, therefore, put together here, though, in the harmony of the evangelists, other events intervened. When the Gadarenes desired Christ to depart, they of Capernaum received him. If Christ be affronted by some, there are others in whom he will be glorious; if one will not, another will.

Now the first occurrence, after Christ's return to Capernaum, as recorded in these verses, was the cure of the man sick of the palsy. In which we may observe,

I. The *faith of his friends* in bringing him to Christ. His distemper was such, that he could not come to Christ himself, but as he was carried. Note, Even the halt and the lame may be brought to Christ, and they shall not be rejected by him. If we do as well as we can, he will accept of us. Christ had an eye to their faith. Little children cannot go to Christ themselves, but he will have an eye to the faith of those that bring them, and it shall not be in vain. *Jesus saw their faith,* the faith of the paralytic himself, as well as of them that brought him; Jesus saw the habit of faith, though his distemper, perhaps, impaired his intellect, and obstructed the actings of it. Now their faith was, 1. A strong faith; they firmly believed that Jesus Christ both could and would heal him; else they would not have brought the sick man to him so publicly, and through so much difficulty. 2. A humble faith; though the sick man was unable to stir a step, they would not ask Christ to make him a visit, but brought him to attend on Christ. It is fitter than we should wait on Christ, than he on us. 3. An active faith: in the belief of Christ's power and goodness, they brought the sick man to him, *lying on a bed,* which could not be done without a deal of pains. Note, A strong faith regards no obstacles in pressing after Christ.

II. The *favour of Christ,* in what he said to him; *Son, be of good cheer, thy sins be forgiven thee.* This was a sovereign cordial to a sick man, and was enough to *make all his bed in his sickness;* and to make it easy to him. We read not of any thing said to Christ; probably the poor sick man could not speak for himself, and they that brought him chose rather to speak by actions than words; they set him before Christ; that was enough. Note, It is not in vain to present ourselves and our friends to Christ, as the objects of his pity. Misery cries as well as sin, and mercy is no less quick of hearing than justice. Here is, in what Christ said, 1. A kind compellation; *Son.* Note, Exhortations and consolations to the afflicted speak to them as to sons, for afflictions are fatherly discipline, Heb. 12:5. 2. A gracious encouragement; *"Be of good cheer. Have a good heart on it;* cheer up thy spirits." Probably the poor man, when let down among them all in his bed, was put out of countenance, was afraid of a rebuke for being brought in so rudely: but Christ does not stand upon ceremony; he bids him *be of good cheer;* all would be well, he should not be laid before Christ in vain. Christ bids him *be of good cheer;* and then cures him. He would have those to whom he deals his gifts, to be cheerful in seeking him, and in trusting in him; to be of good courage. 3. A good reason for that encouragement; *Thy sins are forgiven thee.* Now this may be considered, (1.) as an introduction to the cure of his bodily distemper; "Thy sins are *pardoned,* and therefore thou shalt be healed." Note, As sin is the cause of sickness, so the remission of sin is the comfort of recovery from sickness; not but that sin may be pardoned, and yet the sickness not removed; not but that the sickness may be removed, and yet the sin not pardoned: but if we have the comfort of our reconciliation to God, with the comfort of our recovery from sickness, this makes it a mercy indeed to us, as to Hezekiah, Isa. 38:17. Or, (2.) As a reason of the command to *be of good cheer,* whether he were cured of his disease or not; "Though I should not heal thee, wilt thou not say thou hast not sought in vain, if I assure thee that *thy sins are pardoned;* and wilt thou not look upon that as a sufficient ground of comfort, though thou shouldst continue *sick of the palsy?"* Note, They who, through grace, have some evidence of the forgiveness of their sins, have reasons to be of good cheer, whatever outward troubles or afflictions they are under; see Isa. 33:24.

III. The *cavil of the scribes* at that which Christ said (*v.* 3); They *said within themselves,* in their hearts, *among themselves,* in their secret whisperings, *This man blasphemeth.* See how the greatest instance of heaven's power and grace is branded with the blackest note of hell's enmity; Christ's pardoning sin is termed blasphemy; nor had it been less, if he had not had commission from God for it. They, therefore, are guilty of blasphemy, that have no such commission, and yet pretend to pardon sin.

IV. The conviction which Christ gave them of the unreasonableness of this cavil, before he proceeded.

1. He *charged them with it.* Though they did but say it within themselves, he *knew their thoughts.* Note, Our Lord Jesus has the perfect knowledge of all that we say within ourselves. Thoughts are secret and sudden, yet naked and open before Christ, the eternal Word (Heb. 4:12, 13), and he *understands them afar off,* Ps. 139:2. He could say to them (which no mere man could), *Wherefore think ye evil in your hearts?*

Note, There is a great deal of evil in sinful thoughts, which is very offensive to the Lord Jesus. He being the Sovereign of the heart, sinful thoughts invade his right, and disturb his possession; therefore he takes notice of them, and is much displeased with them. In them lies the *root of bitterness,* Gen. 6:5. The sins that begin and end in the heart, and go no further, are as dangerous as any other.

2. He *argued them out of it, v.* 5, 6. Where observe,

(1.) How he *asserts* his authority in the *kingdom of grace.* He undertakes to make out, that the *Son of man,* the Mediator, has *power on earth to forgive sins;* for *therefore* the Father has *committed all judgment to the Son,* and has given him this authority, *because he is the Son of man,* Jn. 5:22, 27. If he has *power to give eternal life,* as he certainly has (Jn. 17:2), he must have power to forgive sin; for guilt is a bar that must be removed, or we can never get to heaven. What an encouragement is this to poor sinners to repent, that the power of pardoning sin is put into the hands of the *Son of man,* who is bone of our bone! And if he had this *power on earth,* much more now that he is exalted to the Father's right hand, to give *repentance and remission of sins,* and so to be both *a Prince and a Saviour,* Acts 5:31.

(2.) How he *proves* it, by his power in the kingdom of nature; his power to cure diseases. Is it not as easy to say, *Thy sins are forgiven thee,* as to say, *Arise and walk?* He that can cure the disease, whether *declaratively* as a Prophet, or *authoritatively* as God, can, in like manner, forgive the sin. Now, [1.] This is a general argument to prove that Christ had a divine mission. His miracles, especially his miraculous cures, confirm what he said of himself, that he was the Son of God; the *power* that appeared in his cures proved him *sent of God;* and the *pity* that appeared in them proved him sent of God *to heal and save.* The God of truth would not set his seal to a lie. [2.] It had a particular cogency in this case. The palsy was but a symptom of the disease of sin; now he made it to appear, that he could effectually cure the original disease, by the immediate removal of that symptom; so close a connection was there between the sin and the sickness. He that had power to remove the punishment, no doubt, had power to remit the sin. The scribes stood much upon a legal righteousness, and placed their confidence in that, and made no great matter of the *forgiveness of sin,* the doctrine upon which Christ hereby designed to put honour, and to show that his great errand to the world was to *save his people from their sins.*

V. The immediate cure of the sick man. Christ turned from disputing with them, and spake healing to him. The most necessary arguings must not divert us from doing the good that our *hand finds to do.* He saith to *the sick of the palsy, Arise, take up thy bed, and go to thine house;* and a healing, quickening, strengthening power accompanied this word (*v.* 7): *he arose and departed to his house.* Now, 1. Christ bid him *take up his bed,* to show that he was *perfectly cured,* and that not only he had no more occasion to be *carried* upon his bed, but that he had strength to *carry it.* 2. He sent him to *his house,* to be a blessing to his family, where he had been so long a burden; and did not take him along with him for a show, which those would do in such a case who seek the honour that comes from men.

VI. The impression which this made upon the multitude (*v.* 8); they *marvelled,* and *glorified God.* Note, All our wonder should help to enlarge our hearts in *glorifying God,* who alone does marvellous things. They glorified God for what he had done for this poor man. Note, Others' mercies should be our praises, and we should give him thanks for them, for we are members one of another. Though few of this multitude were so convinced, as to be brought to believe in Christ, and to follow him, yet they admired him, not as God, or the Son of God, but as a *man* to whom God *had given such power.* Note, God must be glorified in all the power that is *given to men* to do good. For all power is originally his; it is in him, as the Fountain, in men, as the cisterns.

Verses 9–13

In these verses we have an account of the grace and favour of Christ to poor publicans, particularly to Matthew. What he did to the bodies of people was to make way for a kind design upon their souls. Now observe here,

I. The call of Matthew, the penman of this gospel. Mark and Luke call him Levi; it was ordinary for the same person to have two names: perhaps Matthew was the name he was most known by as a publican, and, therefore, in his humility, he called himself by that name, rather than by the more honourable name of Levi. Some think Christ gave him the name of Matthew when he called him to be an apostle; as Simon, he surnamed Peter. Matthew signifies, *the gift of God,* Ministers are God's gifts to the church; their ministry, and their ability for it, are God's gifts to them. Now observe,

1. The posture that Christ's call found Matthew in. He was *sitting at the receipt of custom,* for he was a publican, Lu. 5:27. He was a custom-house officer at the port of Capernaum, or an exciseman, or collector of the land-tax. Now, (1.) He was in his calling, as the rest of them whom Christ called, *ch.* 4:18. Note, As Satan chooses to come, with his temptations, to those that are idle, so Christ chooses to come, with his calls, to those that are employed. But, (2.) It was a calling of ill fame among serious people; because it was attended with so much corruption and temptation, and there were so few in that business that were honest men. Matthew himself owns what he was before his conversion, as does St. Paul (1 Tim. 1:13), that the grace of Christ in calling him might be the more magnified, and to show, that God has his remnant among all sorts of people. None can justify themselves in their unbelief, by their calling in the world; for there is no *sinful* calling, but some have been saved *out of it,* and no *lawful calling,* but some have been saved *in it.*

2. The preventing power of this call. We find not that Matthew looked after Christ, or had any inclination to follow him, though some of his kindred were already disciples of Christ, but Christ prevented him with the blessings of his goodness. He is found of those that seek him not. Christ *spoke first;* we have not chosen him, but he hath chosen us. He said, *Follow me;* and the same divine, almighty power accompanied this word to convert Matthew, which attended that word (*v.* 6), *Arise and walk,* to cure the man sick of the palsy. Note, A saving change is wrought in the soul by Christ as the *Author,* and his word as the *means.* His gospel is the *power of God unto salvation,* Rom. 1:16. The call was effectual, for he came at the call; *he arose, and* followed him immediately; neither denied, nor deferred his obedience. The power of divine grace soon answers and overcomes all objections. Neither his commission for his place, nor his gains by it, could detain him, when Christ called him. *He conferred not with flesh and blood,* Gal. 1:15, 16. He quitted his post, and his hopes of preferment in that way; and, though we find the disciples that were fishers occasionally fishing again afterwards, we never find Matthew at the receipt of custom again.

II. Christ's converse with publicans and sinners upon this occasion; Christ called Matthew, to introduce himself into an acquaintance with the people of that profession. *Jesus sat at meat in the house, v.* 10. The other evangelists tell us, that Matthew made a *great feast,* which the poor fishermen, when they were called, were not able to do. But when he comes to speak of this himself, he neither tells us that it was his own house, nor that it was a feast, but only that he *sat at meat in the house;* preserving the remembrance of Christ's favours to the publicans, rather than of the respect he had paid to Christ. Note, It well becomes us to speak sparingly of our own good deeds.

Now observe, 1. When Matthew invited Christ, he invited his disciples to *come along with him.* Note, They that welcome Christ, must welcome all that are his, for his sake, and let them have a room in their hearts. 2. He invited many publicans and sinners to *meet him.* This was the chief thing Matthew aimed at in this treat, that he might have an opportunity of bringing his old associates acquainted with Christ. He knew by experience what the grace of Christ could do, and would not despair concerning them. Note, They who are effectually brought to Christ themselves, cannot but be desirous that others also may be brought to him, and ambitious of contributing something towards it. True grace will not contentedly eat its morsels alone, but will invite others. When by the conversion of Matthew the fraternity was broken, presently his house was filled with publicans, and surely some of them will *follow him,* as he *followed Christ.* Thus did Andrew and Philip, Jn. 1:41, 45; 4:29. See Judges 14:9.

III. The displeasure of the Pharisees at this, *v.* 11. They cavilled at it; *why eateth your Master with publicans and sinners?* Here observe, 1. That Christ was quarrelled with. It was not the least of his sufferings, that he *endured the contradiction of sinners against himself.* None was more quarrelled with by men, than he that came to take up the great quarrel between God and man. Thus he denied himself the honour due to an incarnate Deity, which was to be justified in what he spake, and to have all he said readily subscribed to: for though he never spoke or did anything amiss, every thing he said and did was found fault with. Thus he taught us to expect and prepare for reproach, and to bear it patiently. 2. They that quarrelled with him were the Pharisees; a proud generation of men, conceited of themselves, and censorious of others; of the same temper with those in the prophet's time, who said, *Stand by thyself, come not near me; I am holier than thou:* they were very strict in avoiding *sinners,* but not in avoiding *sin;* none greater zealots than they for the *form* of godliness, nor greater enemies to the *power* of it. They were for keeping up the traditions of the elders to a nicety, and so propagating the same spirit that they were themselves governed by. 3. They brought their cavil, not to Christ himself; they had not the courage to face him with it, but to his disciples. The disciples were in the same company, but the quarrel is with the Master: for they would not have done it, if he had not; and they thought it worse in him who was a prophet, than in them; his dignity, they thought, should set him at a greater distance from such company than others. Being offended at the Master, they quarrel with the disciples. Note, It concerns Christians to be able to vindicate and justify Christ, and his doctrines and laws, and to be *ready always to give an answer to those that ask them a reason of the hope that is in them,* 1 Pt. 3:15. While he is an Advocate for us in heaven, let us be advocates for him on earth, and make his reproach our own. 4. The complaint was his *eating with publicans and sinners:* to be intimate with wicked people is against the law of God (Ps. 119:115; 1:1); and perhaps by accusing Christ of this to his disciples, they hoped to tempt them from him, to put them out of conceit with him, and so to bring them over to themselves to be their disciples, who kept better company; for they *compassed sea and land to make proselytes.* To be intimate with publicans was against the *tradition of the elders,* and, therefore, they looked upon it as a heinous thing. They were angry with Christ for this, (1.) Because they *wished ill to him,* and sought occasion to misrepresent him. Note, It is an easy and very common thing to put the worst constructions upon the best words and actions. (2.) Because they *wished no good to* publicans and sinners, but envied Christ's favour to them, and were grieved to see them brought to repentance. Note, It may justly be suspected, that they have not the grace of God themselves, who grudge others a share in that grace, who are not pleased with it.

IV. The defence that Christ made for himself and his disciples, in justification of their converse with publicans and sinners. The disciples, it should seem, being yet weak, had to seek for an answer to the Pharisees' cavil, and, therefore, bring it to Christ, and he heard it (*v.* 12), or perhaps overheard them whispering it to his disciples. Let him alone to vindicate himself and to plead his own cause, to answer for himself and for us too. Two things he urges in his defence,

1. The necessity and exigence of the case of the publicans, which called aloud for his help, and therefore justified him in conversing with them for their good. It was the extreme necessity of poor, lost sinners, that brought Christ from the pure regions above, to these impure ones; and the same was it, that brought him into this company which was thought impure. Now,

(1.) He proves the necessity of the case of the publicans: *they that be whole need not a physician, but they that are sick.* The publicans are sick, and they need one to help and heal them, which the Pharisees think they do not. Note,

[1.] Sin is the sickness of the soul; sinners are spiritually sick. Original corruptions are the diseases of the soul, actual transgressions are its wounds, or the eruptions of the disease. It is deforming, weakening, disquieting, wasting, killing, but, blessed be God, not incurable. [2.] Jesus Christ is the great Physician of souls. His curing of bodily diseases signified this, that he arose with *healing under his wings.* He is a skilful, faithful, compassionate Physician, and it is his office and business to heal the sick. Wise and good men should be as physicians to all about them; Christ was so. *Hunc affectum versus omnes habet sapiens, quem versus aegros suos medicus — A wise man cherishes towards all around him the feelings of a physician for his patient.* Seneca *De Const.* [3.] Sin-sick souls have need of this Physician, for their disease is dangerous; nature will not help itself; no man can help us; such need have we of Christ, that we are undone, eternally undone, without him. Sensible sinners see their need, and apply themselves to him accordingly. [4.] There are multitudes who fancy themselves to be sound and whole, who think they have *no need of Christ,* but that they can shift for themselves well enough without him, as Laodicea, Rev. 3:17. Thus the Pharisees desired not the knowledge of Christ's word and ways, not because they had no need of him, but because they thought they had none. See Jn. 9:40, 41.

(2.) He proves, that their necessity did sufficiently justify his conduct, in conversing familiarly with them, and that he ought not to be blamed for it; for that necessity made it *an act of charity,* which ought always to be preferred before the formalities of a religious profession, in which *bene*ficence and *muni*ficence are far better than *magni*ficence, as much as substance is better than shows or shadows. Those duties, which are of moral and natural obligation, are to take place even of those divine laws which are positive and ritual, much more of those impositions of men, and traditions of the elders, which make God's law stricter than he has made it. This he proves (*v.* 13) by a passage quoted out of Hos. 6:6, *I will have mercy and not sacrifice.* That morose separation from the society of publicans, which the Pharisees enjoined, was *less than sacrifice;* but Christ's conversing with them was more than an act of common mercy, and therefore to be preferred before it. If to do well ourselves is better than sacrifice, as Samuel shows (1 Sa. 15:22, 23), much more to do good to others. Christ's conversing with sinners is here called mercy: to promote the conversion of souls is the greatest act of mercy imaginable; it is *saving a soul from death,* Jam. 5:20. Observe how Christ quotes this, *Go ye and learn what that meaneth.* Note, It is not enough to be acquainted with the letter of scripture, but we must learn to understand the meaning of it. And they have best learned the meaning of the scriptures, that have learned how to apply them as a reproof to their own faults, and a rule for their own practice. This scripture which Christ quoted, served not only to vindicate him, but, [1.] To show wherein true religion consists; not in external observances: not *in meats and drinks* and shows of sanctity, not in little particular opinions and doubtful disputations, but in doing all the good we can to the bodies and souls of others; in righteousness and peace; in *visiting the fatherless and widows.* [2.] To condemn the Pharisaical hypocrisy of those who place religion in rituals, more than in morals, *ch.* 23:23. They espouse those forms of godliness which may be made consistent with, and perhaps subservient to, their pride, covetousness, ambition, and malice, while they hate that power of it which is mortifying to those lusts.

2. He urges the nature and end of his own commission. He must keep to his orders, and prosecute that for which he was appointed to be the great Teacher; now, says he, *"I am not come to call the righteous, but sinners to repentance,* and therefore must converse with publicans."* Observe, (1.) What his errand was; it was to *call to repentance.* This was his first text (*ch.* 4:17), and it was the tendency of all his sermons. Note, The gospel call is a call to repentance; a call to us to change our mind and to change our way. (2.) With whom his errand lay; not with *the righteous,* but with *sinners.* That is, [1.] If the children of men had not been *sinners,* there had been no occasion for Christ's coming among them. He is the Saviour, not of man as *man,* but of man as *fallen.* Had the first Adam continued in his original *righteousness,* we had not needed a second Adam. [2.] Therefore his *greatest business* lies with the *greatest sinners;* the more dangerous the sick man's case is, the more occasion there is for the physician's help. Christ came into the world to *save sinners,* but especially *the chief* (1 Tim. 1:15); to call not those so much, who, though sinners, are comparatively righteous, but the worst of sinners. [3.] The more sensible any sinners are of their sinfulness, the more welcome will Christ and his gospel be to them; and every one chooses to go where his company is desired, not to those who would rather have his room. Christ came not with an expectation of succeeding among *the righteous,* those who conceit themselves so, and therefore will sooner be sick of their Saviour, than sick of their sins, but among the convinced humble *sinners;* to them Christ will come, for to them he will be welcome.

Verses 14–17

The objections which were made against Christ and his disciples gave occasion to some of the most profitable of his discourses; thus are the interests of truth often served, even by the opposition it meets with from gainsayers, and thus the wisdom of Christ brings good out of evil. This is the third instance of it in this chapter; his discourse of his power to

forgive sin, and his readiness to receive sinners, was occasioned by the cavils of the scribes and Pharisees; so here, from a reflection upon the conduct of his family, arose a discourse concerning his tenderness for it. Observe,

I. The objection which the disciples of John made against Christ's disciples, for not fasting so often as they did; which they are charged with, as another instance of the looseness of their profession, besides that of eating with publicans and sinners; and it is therefore suggested to them, that they should change that profession for another more strict. It appears by the other evangelists (Mk. 2:18 and Lu. 5:33) that the disciples of the Pharisees joined with them, and we have reason to suspect that they instigated them, making use of John's disciples as their spokesmen, because they, being more in favour with Christ and his disciples, could do it more plausibly. Note, It is no new thing for bad men to set good men together by the ears; if the people of God differ in their sentiments, designing men will take that occasion to sow discord, and to incense them one against another, and alienate them one from another, and so make an easy prey of them. If the disciples of John and of Jesus clash, we have reason to suspect the Pharisees have been at work underhand, blowing the coals. Now the complaint is, *Why do we and the Pharisees fast often, but thy disciples fast not?* It is pity the duties of religion, which ought to be the confirmations of holy love, should be made the occasions of strife and contention; but they often are so, as here; where we may observe,

1. How they boasted of their own fasting. *We and the Pharisees fast often.* Fasting has in all ages of the church been consecrated, upon special occasions, to the service of religion; the Pharisees were much in it; many of them kept two fast-days in a week, and yet the generality of them were hypocrites and bad men. Note, False and formal professors often excel others in outward acts of devotion, and even of mortification. The disciples of John *fasted often,* partly in compliance with their master's practice, for he came *neither eating nor drinking* (ch. 11:18); and people are apt to imitate their leaders, though not always from the same inward principle; partly in compliance with their master's doctrine of repentance. Note, The severer part of religion is often most *minded* by those that are yet under the discipline of the Spirit, as a *Spirit of bondage,* whereas, though these are good in their place, we must pass through them to that life of delight in God and dependence on him, to which these should lead. Now they come to Christ to tell him that they *fasted often,* at least they thought it often. Note, *Most men will proclaim every one his own goodness,* Prov. 20:6. There is a proneness in professors to brag of their own performance in religion, especially if there by any thing extraordinary in them; nay, and not only to boast of them before men, but to plead them before God, and confide in them as a righteousness.

2. How they blamed Christ's disciples for not fasting so often as they did. *Thy disciples fast not.* They could not but know, that Christ had instructed his disciples to keep their fasts private, and to manage themselves so as that they might not *appear unto men to fast;* and, therefore, it was very uncharitable in them to conclude they did *not fast,* because they did not proclaim their fasts. Note, We must not judge of people's religion by that which falls under the eye and observation of the world. But suppose it was so, that Christ's disciples did not *fast* so often or so long as they did, why truly, they would therefore have it thought, that they had more religion in them than Christ's disciples had. Note, It is common for vain professors to make themselves a standard in religion, by which to try and measure persons and things, as if all who differed from them were so far in the wrong; as if all that did less than they, did too little, and all that did more than they, did too much, which is a plain evidence of their want of humility and charity.

3. How they brought this complaint to Christ. Note, If Christ's disciples, either by omission or commission, give offence, Christ himself will be sure to hear of it, and be reflected upon for it. *O, Jesus, are these thy Christians?* Therefore, as we tender the honour of Christ, we are concerned to conduct ourselves well. Observe, The quarrel with Christ was brought to the disciples (*v.* 11), the quarrel with the disciples was brought to Christ (*v.* 14), this is the way of sowing discord and killing love, to set people against ministers, ministers against people, and one friend against another.

II. The apology which Christ made for his disciples in this matter. Christ might have upbraided John's disciples with the former part of their question, *Why do ye fast often?* "Nay,

you know best why you do it; but the truth is, many abound in external instances of devotion, that scarcely do themselves know why and wherefore." But he only vindicates the practice of his disciples; whey they had nothing to say for themselves, he had something ready to say for them. Note, As it is wisdom's honour to be justified of all her children, so it is her children's happiness to be all justified of wisdom. What we do according to the precept and pattern of Christ, he will be sure to bear us out in, and we may with confidence leave it to him to clear up our integrity.

But thou shalt answer, Lord, for me. — Herbert
Two things Christ pleads in defence of their *not fasting.*

1. That it was not a season proper for that duty (*v.* 15): *Can the children of the bride-chamber mourn, as long as the bridegroom is with them?* Observe, Christ's answer is so framed, as that it might sufficiently justify the practice of his own disciples, and yet not condemn the institution of John, or the practice of his disciples. When the Pharisees fomented this dispute, they hoped Christ would cast blame, either on his own disciples, or on John's, but he did neither. Note, When at any time we are unjustly censured, our care must be only to clear ourselves, not to recriminate, or throw dirt upon others; and such a variety may there be of circumstances, as may justify us in our practice, without condemning those that practise otherwise.

Now his argument is taken from the common usage of joy and rejoicing during the continuance of marriage solemnities; when all instances of melancholy and sorrow are looked upon as improper and absurd, as it was at Samson's wedding, Judges 14:17. Now, (1.) The disciples of Christ were the *children of the bride-chamber,* invited to the wedding-feast, and welcome there; the disciples of the Pharisees were not so, but *children of the bond-woman* (Gal. 4:25, 31), continuing under a dispensation of darkness and terror. Note, The faithful followers of Christ, who have the Spirit of adoption, have a continual feast, while they who have the spirit of bondage and fear, cannot rejoice for joy, as other people, Hos. 9:1. (2.) The disciples of Christ had the *bridegroom with them,* which the disciples of John had not; their master was now cast into prison, and lay there in continual danger of his life, and therefore it was seasonable for them to *fast often.* Such a day would come upon the disciples of Christ, when the bridegroom should be taken from them, when they should be deprived of his bodily presence, and *then should they fast.* The thoughts of parting grieved them when he was going, Jn. 16:6. Tribulation and affliction befel them when he was gone, and gave them occasion of *mourning* and *praying,* that is, of religious fasting. Note, [1.] Jesus Christ is the Bridegroom of his Church, and his disciples are the *children of the bride-chamber.* Christ speaks of himself to John's disciples under this similitude, because that John had used it, when he called himself a friend of the bridegroom, Jn. 3:29. And if they would by this hint call to mind what their master then said, they would answer themselves. [2.] The condition of those who are the children of the bride-chamber is liable to many changes and alterations in this world; they sing of mercy and judgment. [3.] It is merry or melancholy with the children of the bride-chamber, according as they have more or less of the bridegroom's presence. When he is with them, the candle of God shines upon their head, and all is well; but when he is withdrawn, though but for a small moment, *they are troubled,* and walk heavily; the presence and nearness of the sun makes day and summer, his absence and distance, night and winter. Christ is all in all to the church's joy. [4.] Every duty is to be done in its proper season. See Eccles. 7:14; Jam. 5:13. There is a time to mourn and a time to laugh, to each of which we should accommodate ourselves, and bring forth fruit in due season. In fasts, regard is to be had to the methods of God's grace towards us; when he *mourns to us,* we must *lament;* and also to the dispensations of his providence concerning us; there are times when *the Lord God calls to weeping and mourning;* regard is likewise to be had to any special work before us, *ch.* 17:21; Acts 13:2.

2. That they had not strength sufficient for that duty. This is set forth in two similitudes, one of putting *new cloth into an old garment,* which does but pull the old to pieces (*v.* 16); the other of putting *new wine into old bottles,* which does but burst the bottles, *v.* 17. Christ's disciples were not able to bear these severe exercises so well as those of John and of the Pharisees, which the learned Dr. Whitby gives this reason for: There were among the Jews not only sects of the Pharisees and Essenes, who led an austere life, but also

schools of the prophets, who frequently lived in mountains and deserts, and were many of them Nazarites; they had also private academies to train men up in a strict discipline; and possibly from these many of John's disciples might come, and many of the Pharisees; whereas Christ's disciples, being taken immediately from their callings, had not been used to such religious austerities, and were unfit for them, and would by them be rather unfitted for their other work. Note, (1.) Some duties of religion are harder and more difficult than others, like *new cloth* and *new wine,* which require most intenseness of mind, and are most displeasing to flesh and blood; such are religious fasting and the duties that attend it. (2.) The best of Christ's disciples pass through a state of infancy; all the trees in Christ's garden are not of a growth, nor all his scholars in the same form; there are *babes in Christ* and grown men. (3.) In the enjoining of religious exercises, the weakness and infirmity of young Christians ought to be considered: as the food provided for them must be such as is proper for their age (1 Co. 3:2; Heb. 5:12), so must the work be that is cut out for them. Christ would not speak to his disciples that which they could not then bear, Jn. 16:12. Young beginners in religion must not be put upon the hardest duties at first, lest they be discouraged. Such as was God's care of his Israel, when he brought them out of Egypt, not to lead them by the way of the Philistines (Ex. 13:17, 18), and such as was Jacob's care of his children and cattle, not to overdrive them (Gen. 33:13), such is Christ's care of the little ones of his family, and the lambs of his flock: he gently leads them. For want of this care, many times, *the bottles break,* and *the wine is spilled;* the profession of many miscarries and comes to nothing, through indiscretion at first. Note, There may be *over*-doing even in *well*-doing, a being *righteous over-much;* and such an *over*-doing as may prove an *un*doing through the subtlety of Satan.

Verses 18–26

We have here two passages of history put together; that of the raising of Jairus's daughter to life, and that of the curing of the woman that had *the bloody issue,* as he was going to Jairus's house, which is introduced in a parenthesis, in the midst of the other; for Christ's miracles were thick sown, and interwoven; *the work of him that sent* him was his daily work. He was called to do these good works from speaking the things foregoing, in answer to the cavils of the Pharisees, *v.* 18: *While he spake these things;* and we may suppose it is a pleasing interruption given to that unpleasant work of disputation, which, though sometimes needful, a good man will gladly leave, to go about a work of devotion or charity. Here is,

I. The ruler's address to Christ, *v.* 18. *A certain ruler,* a ruler of the synagogue, *came and worshipped him. Have any of the rulers believed on him?* Yes, here was one, a church ruler, whose faith condemned the unbelief of the rest of the rulers. This ruler had a little daughter, of twelve years old, just dead, and this breach made upon his family comforts was the occasion of his coming to Christ. Note, In trouble we should visit God: the death of our relations should drive us to Christ, who is our life; it is well if any thing will do it. When affliction is in our families, we must not sit down astonished, but, as Job, *fall down and worship.* Now observe,

1. His humility in this address to Christ. He came with his errand to Christ himself, and did not send his servant. Note, It is no disparagement to the greatest rulers, personally to attend on the Lord Jesus. He *worshipped him,* bowed the knee to him, and gave him all imaginable respect. Note, They that would receive mercy from Christ must give honour to Christ.

2. His faith in this address; *"My daughter is even now dead,"* and though any other physician would now come too late (nothing more absurd than *post mortem medicina — medicine after death*), yet Christ comes not too late; he is a Physician after death, for he is *the resurrection and the life; "O come* then, *and lay thy hand upon her, and she shall live."* This was quite above the power of nature *(a privatione ad habitum non datur regressus — life once lost cannot be restored),* yet within the power of Christ, who has *life in himself, and quickeneth whom he will.* Now Christ works in an ordinary, *by* nature and not *against* it, and, therefore, we cannot in faith bring him such a request as this; while there is life, there is hope, and room for prayer; but when our friends are dead, the case is determined; *we shall go to them, but they shall not return to us.* But while Christ was here upon earth working miracles, such a confidence as this was not only allowable but very commendable.

II. The readiness of Christ to comply with his address, *v.* 19. *Jesus* immediately *arose,* left his company, *and followed him;* he was not only willing to grant him what he desired, in raising his daughter to life, but to gratify him so far as to come to his house to do it. Surely *he never said to the seed of Jacob, Seek ye me in vain.* He denied to go along with the nobleman, who said, *Sir, come down, ere my child die* (Jn. 4:48–50), yet he went along with the ruler of the synagogue, who said, *Sir, come down, and my child shall live.* The variety of methods which Christ took in working his miracles is perhaps to be attributed to the different frame and temper of mind which they were in who applied to him, which he *who searcheth the heart* perfectly knew, and accommodated himself to. He knows what is in man, and what course to take with him. And observe, when *Jesus followed him, so did his disciples,* whom he had chosen for his constant companions; it was not for state, or that he might come with observation, that he took his attendants with him, but that they might be the witnesses of his miracles, who were hereafter to be the preachers of his doctrine.

III. The healing of the poor woman's bloody issue. I call her a poor woman, not only because her case was piteous, but because, she had *spent it all upon physicians,* for the cure of her distemper, and was never the better; which was a double aggravation of the misery of her condition, that she had been full, but was now empty; and that she had impoverished herself for the recovery of her health, and yet had not her health neither. This *woman was diseased with a constant issue of blood twelve years* (*v.* 20); a disease, which was not only weakening and wasting, and under which the body must needs languish; but which also rendered her ceremonially unclean, and shut her *out from the courts of the Lord's house;* but it did not cut her off from approaching to Christ. She applied herself to Christ, and received mercy from him, by the way, as he followed the ruler, whose daughter was dead, to whom it would be a great encouragement, and a help to keep up his faith in the power of Christ. So graciously does Christ consider the frame, and consult the case, of weak believers. Observe,

1. The woman's great faith in Christ, and in his power. Her disease was of such a nature, that her modesty would not suffer her to speak openly to Christ for a cure, as others did, but by a peculiar impulse of the Spirit of faith, she believed him to have such an overflowing fulness of healing virtue, that the very *touch of his garment* would be her cure. This, perhaps, had something of fancy mixed with faith; for she had no precedent for this way of application to Christ, unless, as some think, she had an eye to the raising of the dead man by the touch of Elisha's bones, 2 Ki. 13:21. But what *weakness of understanding* there was in it, Christ was pleased to overlook, and to accept the sincerity and strength of her faith; for he *eateth the honey-comb with the honey,* Cant. 4:11. She believed she should be healed if she did but *touch the* very *hem of his garment,* the very extremity of it. Note, There is virtue in every thing that belongs to Christ. The holy oil with which the high priest was anointed, *ran down to the skirts of his garments,* Ps. 133:2. Such a fulness of grace is there in Christ, that *from it we may all receive,* Jn. 1:16.

2. Christ's great favour to this woman. He did not suspend (as he might have done) his healing influences, but suffered this bashful patient to steal a cure unknown to any one else, though she could not think to do it unknown to him. And now she was well content to be gone, for she had what she came for, but Christ was not willing to let he to so; he will not only have his power magnified in her cure, but his grace magnified in her comfort and commendation: the triumphs of her faith must be to her praise and honour. He *turned about* to see for her (*v.* 22), and soon discovered her. Note, It is great encouragement to humble Christians, that they who hide themselves from men are known to Christ, who sees in secret their applications to heaven when most private. Now here,

(1.) He *puts gladness into her heart,* by that word, *Daughter, be of good comfort.* She feared being chidden for coming clandestinely, but she is encouraged. [1.] He calls her *daughter,* for he spoke to her with the tenderness of a father, as he did *to the man sick of the palsy* (*v.* 2), whom he called *son.* Note, Christ has comforts ready for *the daughters of Zion,* that are of a sorrowful spirit, as Hannah was, 1 Sa. 1:15. Believing women are Christ's *daughters,* and he will own them as such. [2.] He bids her *be of good comfort:* she has reason to be so, if Christ own her for a *daughter.* Note, The saints' consolation is founded in their adoption. His bidding her *be comforted,* brought comfort with it, as his saying, *Be ye whole,* brought health with it. Note, It is the will of Christ that his people should be comforted, and it is his prerogative to command comfort to troubled spirits. He *creates the fruit of the lips, peace,* Isa. 57:19.

(2.) He puts honour upon her faith. That grace of all others gives most honour to Christ, and therefore he puts most honour upon it; *Thy faith has made thee whole.* Thus *by faith she obtained a good report.* And as of all graces Christ puts the greatest honour upon faith, so of all believers he puts the greatest honour upon those that are most humble; as here on this woman, who had more faith than she thought she had. She had reason to *be of good comfort,* not only because she was *made whole,* but because her *faith had made her whole;* that is, [1.] She was spiritually healed; that cure was wrought in her which is the proper fruit and effect of faith, the pardon of sin and the work of grace. Note, We may then be abundantly comforted in our temporal mercies when they are accompanied with those spiritual blessings that resemble them; our food and raiment will be comfortable, when by faith we are fed with *the bread of life,* and *clothed with the righteousness of Jesus Christ;* our rest and sleep will be comfortable, when by faith we repose in God, and dwell at ease in him; our health and prosperity will be comfortable, when by faith our souls prosper, and are in health. See Isa. 38:16, 17. [2.] Her bodily cure was the fruit of faith, of her faith, and that made it a happy, comfortable cure indeed. They out of whom the devils were cast, were helped by Christ's sovereign power; some by the faith of others (as *v.* 2); but it is *thy faith that has made thee whole.* Note, Temporal mercies are then comforts indeed to us, when they are received by faith. If, when in pursuit of mercy, we prayed for it in faith, with an eye to the promise, and in dependence upon that, if we desired it for the sake of God's glory, and with a resignation to God's will, and have our hearts enlarged by it in faith, love, and obedience, we may then say, it was received by faith.

IV. The posture in which he found the ruler's house, *v.* 23. — He *saw the people and the minstrels,* or musicians, *making a noise.* The house was in a hurry: such work does death make, when it comes into a family; and, perhaps, the necessary cares that arise at such a time, when our dead is to be decently buried out of our sight, give some useful diversion to that grief which is apt to prevail and play the tyrant. The people in the neighbourhood came together to condole on account of the loss, to comfort the parents, to prepare for, and attend on, the funeral, which the Jews were not wont to defer long. The musicians were among them, according to the custom of the Gentiles, with their doleful, melancholy tunes, to increase the grief, and stir up the lamentations of those that attended on this occasion; as (they say) is usual among the Irish, with their Ahone, Ahone. Thus they indulged a passion that is apt enough of itself to grow intemperate, and affected to *sorrow as those that had no hope.* See how religion provides cordials, where irreligion administers corrosives. Heathenism aggravates that grief which Christianity studies to assuage. Or perhaps these musicians endeavoured on the other hand to divert the grief and exhilarate the family; but, *as vinegar upon nitre, so is he that sings songs to a heavy heart.* Observe, The parents, who were immediately touched with the affliction, were silent, while *the people and minstrels,* whose lamentations were forced, made such a noise. Note, The loudest grief is not always the greatest; rivers are most noisy where they run shallow. *Ille dolet vere, qui sine teste dolet — That grief is most sincere, which shuns observation.* But notice is taken of this, to show that the girl was really dead, in the undoubted apprehension of all about her.

V. The rebuke that Christ gave to this hurry and noise, *v.* 24. He said, *Give place.* Note, Sometimes, when *the sorrow of the world* prevails, it is difficult for Christ and his comforts to enter. They that harden themselves in sorrow, and, like Rachel, *refuse to be comforted,* should think they hear Christ saying to their disquieting thoughts, *Give place:* "Make room for him who is *the Consolation of Israel,* and brings with him *strong consolations,* strong enough to overcome the confusion and tyranny of these worldly griefs, if he may but be admitted into the soul." He gives a good reason why they should not thus disquiet themselves and one another; *The maid is not dead but sleepeth.* 1. This was eminently true of this maid, that was immediately to be raised to life; she was really dead, but not so to Christ, who knew within himself what he would do, and could do, and who had determined to make her death but as a sleep. There is little more difference between sleep and death, but in continuance; whatever other difference there is, it is but a dream. This death must be but of short continuance, and therefore is but a sleep, like one night's rest. He that quickens the dead, may well call the things which be not as though they were, Rom. 4:17. 2. It is in a sense true of all that die, chiefly of them *that die in the Lord.* Note, (1.) Death is a sleep. All nations and languages, for the softening of that which is so dreadful, and withal so unavoidable, and the reconciling of themselves to it, have agreed to call it so. It is said, even of the wicked kings, that they *slept with their fathers;* and of those that shall arise to everlasting contempt, that they *sleep in the dust,* Dan. 12:2. It is not the sleep of the soul; its activity ceases not; but the sleep of the body, which lies down in the grave, still and silent, regardless and disregarded, wrapt up in darkness and obscurity. Sleep is a short death, and death a long sleep. But *the death of the righteous* is in a special manner to be looked upon as a sleep, Isa. 57:2. They sleep in Jesus (1 Th. 4:14); they not only rest from the toils and labours of the day, but *rest in hope* of a joyful waking again in the morning of the resurrection, when they shall wake refreshed, wake to a new life, wake to be richly dressed and crowned, and *wake to sleep no more.* (2.) The consideration of this should moderate our grief at the death of our dear relations: "say not, They *are* lost; no, they are but *gone before:* say not, They are *slain;* no, they are but *fallen asleep;* and the apostle speaks of it as an absurd thing to imagine that *they that are fallen asleep in Christ are perished* (1 Co. 15:18); *give place,* therefore, to those comforts which the covenant of grace ministers, fetched from the future *state, and the glory to be revealed.*"

Now could it be thought that such a comfortable word as this, from the mouth of our Lord Jesus, should be ridiculed as it was? *They laughed him to scorn.* These people lived in Capernaum, knew Christ's character, that he never spake a rash or foolish word; they knew how many mighty works he had done; so that if they did not understand what he meant by this, they might at least have been silent in expectation of the issue. Note, The words and works of Christ which cannot be understood, yet are not therefore to be despised. We must adore the mystery of divine sayings, even when they seem to contradict what we think ourselves most confident of. Yet even this tended to the confirmation of the miracle: for it seems she was so apparently dead, that it was thought a very ridiculous thing to say otherwise.

VI. The raising of the damsel to life by the power of Christ, *v.* 25. *The people were put forth.* Note, Scorners that laugh at what they see and hear that is above their capacity, are not proper witnesses of the wonderful works of Christ, the glory of which lies not in pomp, but in power. The widow's son at Nain, and Lazarus, were raised from the dead openly, but this damsel privately; for Capernaum, that had slighted the lesser miracles of restoring health, was unworthy to see the greater, of restoring life; these *pearls were not* to be *cast before* those that would *trample them under their feet.*

Christ went in and *took her by the hand,* as it were to awake her, and to help her up, prosecuting his own metaphor of her being asleep. The high priest, that typified Christ, was not to come near the dead (Lev. 21:10, 11), but Christ *touched the dead.* The Levitical priesthood leaves the dead in their uncleanness, and therefore keeps at a distance from them, because it cannot remedy them; but Christ, having power to raise the dead, is above the infection, and therefore is not shy of touching them. He *took her by the hand, and the maid arose.* So easily, so effectually was the miracle wrought; not by prayer, as Elijah did (1 Ki. 17:21), and Elisha (2 Ki. 4:33), but by a touch. They did it as servants, he as a Son, as a God, *to whom belong the issues from death.* Note, Jesus Christ is the Lord of souls, he commands them forth, and commands them back, when and as he pleases. Dead souls are not raised to spiritual life, unless Christ *take them by the hand:* it is done in the *day of his power.* He helps us up, or we lie still.

VII. The general notice that was taken of this miracle, though it was wrought privately; *v.* 26. *The fame thereof went abroad into all that land:* it was the common subject of discourse. Note, Christ's works are more talked of than considered and improved. And doubtless, they that heard only the report of Christ's miracles, were accountable for that as well as they that were eye-witnesses of them. Though we at this distance have not seen Christ's miracles, yet having an authentic history of them, we are bound, upon the credit of that, to receive his doctrine; and blessed *are they that have not seen, and yet have believed,* Jn. 20:29.

Verses 27–34

In these verses we have an account of two more miracles wrought together by our Saviour.

I. The giving of sight to two blind men, *v.* 27–31. Christ is the Fountain of light as well as life; and as, by raising the dead, he showed himself to be the same that at first *breathed into man the breath of life,* so, by giving sight to the blind, he showed himself to be the same that at first *commanded the light to shine out of darkness.* Observe,

1. The importunate address of the blind men to Christ. He was returning from the ruler's house to his own lodgings, and these *blind men followed him,* as beggars do, with their incessant cries, *v.* 27. He that cured diseases so easily, so effectually, and, withal, at so cheap a rate, shall have patients enough. As for other things, so he is famed for an Oculist. Observe,

(1.) The title which these blind men gave to Christ; *Thou Son of David, have mercy on us.* The promise made to David, that of his loins the Messiah should come, was well known, and the Messiah was therefore commonly called *the Son of David.* At this time there was a general expectation of his appearing; these blind men know, and own, and proclaim it in the streets of Capernaum, that he is come, and that this is he; which aggravates the folly and sin of the chief priests and Pharisees who denied and opposed him. They could not see him and his miracles, but *faith comes by hearing.* Note, They who, by the providence of God, are deprived of bodily sight, may yet, by the grace of God, have *the eyes of their understanding so enlightened,* as to discern those great things of God, *which are hid from the wise and prudent.*

(2.) Their petition, *Have mercy on us.* It was foretold that the *Son of David* should be *merciful* (Ps. 72:12, 13), and in him *shines the tender mercy of our God,* Lu. 1:78. Note, Whatever our necessities and burthens are, we need no more for supply and support, than a share in the *mercy of our Lord Jesus.* Whether he heal us or no, if he *have mercy on us,* we have enough; as to the particular instances and methods of mercy, we may safely and wisely refer ourselves to the wisdom of Christ. They did not each of them say for himself, *Have mercy on me,* but both for one another, *Have mercy on us.* Note, It becomes those that are under the same affliction, to concur in the same prayers for relief. Fellow-sufferers should be joint-petitioners. In Christ there is enough for all.

(3.) Their importunity in this request; they *followed him, crying.* It seems, he did not take notice of them at first, for he would try their faith, which he knew to be strong; would quicken their prayers, and make his cures the more valued, when they did not always come at the first word; and would teach us to *continue instant in prayer, always to pray, and not to faint:* and, though the answer do not come presently, yet to wait for it, and to follow providence, even in those steps and outgoings of it which seem to neglect or contradict our prayers. Christ would not heal them publicly in the streets, for this was a cure he would have kept private (*v.* 30), but *when he came into the house,* they *followed him* thither, and *came to him.* Note, Christ's doors are always open to believing and importunate petitioners; it seemed rude in them to rush into the house after him, when he desired to retire; but, such is the tenderness of our Lord Jesus, that they were not more bold than welcome.

2. The confession of faith, which Christ drew from them upon this occasion. When they came to him for mercy, he asked them, *Believe ye that I am able to do this?* Note, Faith is the great condition of Christ's favours. They who would receive the *mercy* of Christ, must firmly believe the *power* of Christ. What we would have him do for us, we must be fully assured that he is *able to do.* They followed Christ, and followed him crying, but the great question is, *Do ye believe?* Nature may work fervency, but it is only grace that can work faith; spiritual blessings are obtained only by faith. They had intimated their faith in the office of Christ as *Son of David,* and in his mercy; but Christ demands likewise a profession of faith in his power. *Believe ye that I am able to do this;* to bestow this favour; to give sight to the blind, as well as to cure the palsy and raise the dead? Note, It is good to be particular in the exercise of faith, to apply the general assurances of God's power and good will, and the general promises, to our particular exigencies. *All shall work for good,* and if all, then this. *"Believe ye that I am able,* not only to prevail with God for it, as a prophet, but *that I am able to do it* by my own power?" This will amount to their belief of his being not only *the Son of David,* but *the Son of God;* for it is God's prerogative to *open the eyes of the blind* (Ps. 146:8); he makes *the seeing eye,* Ex. 4:11. Job *was eyes to the blind* (Job 29:15); was to them instead of eyes, but he could not *give* eyes to the blind. Still it is put to us, *Believe we that Christ is able to do for us,* by the power of his merit and intercession in heaven, of his Spirit and grace in the heart, and of his providence and dominion in the world? To believe the power of Christ is not only to assure ourselves of it, but to commit ourselves to it, and encourage ourselves in it.

To this question they give an immediate answer, without hesitation: they said, *Yea, Lord.* Though he had kept them in suspense awhile, and had not helped them at first, they honestly imputed that to his wisdom, not to his weakness, and were still confident of his ability. Note, The treasures of mercy that are laid up in the power of Christ, are *laid out and wrought for those that trust in him,* Ps. 31:19.

3. The cure that Christ wrought on them; *he touched their eyes, v.* 29. This he did to encourage their faith, which, by his delay, he had tried, and to show that he gives sight to blind souls by the operations of his grace accompanying the word, *anointing the eyes with eye-salve:* and he put the cure upon their faith, *According to your faith be it unto you.* When they begged for a cure, he enquired into their faith (*v.* 28), *Believe ye that I am able?* He did not enquire into their wealth, whether they were able to pay him for a cure; nor into their reputation, should he get credit by curing them; but into their faith; and now they had professed their faith he referred the matter to that: "I know you do believe, and the power you believe in shall be exerted for you; *According to your faith be it unto you."* This speaks, (1.) His knowledge of the sincerity of their faith, and his acceptance and approbation of it. Note, It is a great comfort to true believers, that Jesus Christ knows their faith, and is well pleased with it. Though it be weak, though others do not discern it, though they themselves are ready to question it, it is known to him. (2.) His insisting upon their faith as necessary; "If you believe, take what you come for." Note, They who apply themselves to Jesus Christ, shall be dealt with *according to their faith;* not according to their *fancies,* nor according to their *profession,* but *according to their faith;* that is, unbelievers cannot expect to find any favour with God, but true believers may be sure to find all that favour which is offered in the gospel; and our comforts ebb or flow, according as our faith is stronger or weaker; we are not straitened in Christ, let us not then be straitened in ourselves.

4. The charge he gave them to keep it private (*v.* 30), *See that no man know it.* He gave them this charge, (1.) To set us an example of that humility and lowliness of mind, which he would have us to learn of him. Note, In the good we do, we must not seek our own praise, but only the glory of God. It must be more our care and endeavour to be useful, than to be known and observed to be so, Prov. 20:6; 25:27. Thus Christ seconded the rule he had given, *Let not thy left hand know what thy right hand doeth.* (2.) Some think that Christ, in keeping it private, showed his displeasure against the people of Capernaum, who had seen so many miracles, and yet believed not. Note, The silencing of those who should proclaim the works of Christ is a judgment to any place or people: and it is just in Christ to deny the means of conviction to those that are obstinate in their infidelity; and to shroud the light from those that shut their eyes against it. (3.) He did it in discretion, for his own preservation; because the more he was proclaimed, the more jealous would the rulers of the Jews be of his growing interest among the people. (4.) Dr. Whitby gives another reason, which is very considerable, why Christ sometimes concealed his miracles, and afterwards forbid the publishing of his transfiguration; because he would not indulge that pernicious conceit which obtained among the Jews, that their Messiah should be a temporal prince, and so give occasion to the people to attempt the setting up of his kingdom, by tumults and seditions, as they offered to do, Jn. 6:15. But when, after his resurrection (which was the full proof of his mission), his spiritual kingdom was set up, then that danger was over, and they must be published to all na-

tions. And he observes, that the miracles which Christ wrought among the Gentiles and the Gadarenes, were ordered to be published, because with them there was not that danger.

But honour is like the shadow, which, as it flees from those that follow it, so it follows those that flee from it (*v.* 31); *They spread abroad his fame.* This was more an act of zeal, than of prudence; and though it may be excused as honestly meant for the honour of Christ, yet it cannot be justified, being done against a particular charge. Whenever we profess to direct our intention to the glory of God, we must see to it that the action be according to the will of God.

II. The healing of a *dumb man,* that was *possessed with a devil.* And here observe,

1. His case, which was very sad. He was under the power of the devil in this particular instance, that he was disabled from speaking, *v.* 32. See the calamitous state of this world, and how various the afflictions of the afflicted are! We have no sooner dismissed *two blind men,* but we meet with a *dumb man.* How thankful should we be to God for our sight and speech! See the malice of Satan against mankind, and in how many ways he shows it. This man's dumbness was the effect of his being *possessed with a devil;* but it was better he should be unable to say any thing, than be forced to say, as those demoniacs did (*ch.* 8:29), *What have we to do with thee?* Of the two, better a dumb devil than a blaspheming one. When the devil gets possession of a soul, it is made silent as to any thing that is good; dumb in prayers and praises, which the devil is a sworn enemy to. This poor creature *they brought to Christ,* who entertained not only those that came of themselves in their own faith, but those that were *brought to him* by their friends in the faith of others. Though *the just shall live* eternally *by his faith,* yet temporal mercies may be bestowed on us with an eye to their faith who are intercessors on our behalf. They brought him in just as *the blind man went out.* See how unwearied Christ was in doing good; how closely one good work followed another! Treasures of mercy, wondrous mercy, are hid in him; which may be continually communicated, but can never be exhausted.

2. His cure, which was very sudden (*v.* 33), *When the devil was cast out, the dumb spake.* Note, Christ's cures strike at the root, and remove the effect by taking away the cause; they open the lips, by breaking Satan's power in the soul. In sanctification he heals the waters by casting salt into the spring. When Christ, by his grace, *casts the devil out* of a soul, presently *the dumb speaks.* When Paul was converted, *behold, he prays;* then *the dumb spake.*

3. The consequences of this cure.

(1.) *The multitudes marvelled;* and well they might; though *few believed, many wondered.* The admiration of the common people is sooner raised than any other affection. It was foretold, that the new song, the New-Testament song, should be sung for *marvellous works,* Ps. 98:1. They said, *It was never so seen in Israel,* and therefore never so seen any where; for no people experienced such wonders of mercy as Israel did. There had been those in Israel that were famous for working miracles, but Christ excelled them all. The miracles Moses wrought had reference to Israel as a people, but Christ's were brought home to particular persons.

(2.) *The Pharisees* blasphemed, *v.* 34. When they could not gainsay the convincing evidence of these miracles, they fathered them upon the devil, as if they had been wrought by compact and collusion: *he casteth out devils* (say they) by *the prince of the devils* — a suggestion horrid beyond expression; we shall hear more of it afterwards, and Christ's answer to it (*ch.* 12:25); only observe here, how *evil men and seducers wax worse and worse* (2 Tim. 3:13), and it is both their sin and their punishment. Their quarrels with Christ for taking upon him to *forgive sin* (*v.* 3), for *conversing with publicans and sinners,* (*v.* 11), for *not fasting* (*v.* 14), though spiteful enough, yet had some colour of piety, purity, and devotion in them; but this (which they are left to, to punish them for those) breathes nothing but malice and falsehood, and hellish enmity in the highest degree; it is diabolism all over, and was therefore justly pronounced unpardonable. Because the people marvelled, they must say something to diminish the miracle, and this was all they could say.

Verses 35–38

Here is, I. A conclusion of the foregoing account of Christ's preaching and miracles (*v.* 35); *He went about all the cities teaching and healing.* This is the same we had before, 4:23. There it ushers in the more particular record of Christ's preaching (*ch.* 5, 6 and 7) and of his cures (*ch.* 8 and 9), and here it is elegantly repeated in the close of these instances, as the *quod erat demonstrandum — the point to be proved;* as if the evangelist should say, "Now I hope I have made it out, by an induction of particulars, that Christ preached and healed; for you have had the heads of his sermons, and some few instances of his cures, which were wrought to confirm his doctrine: and *these were written that you might believe."* Some think that this was a second perambulation in Galilee, like the former; he visited again those whom he had before preached to. Though the Pharisees cavilled at him and opposed him, he went on with his work; he *preached the gospel of the kingdom.* He told them of a kingdom of grace and glory, now to be set up under the government of a Mediator: this was gospel indeed, *good news, glad tidings of great joy.*

Observe how Christ in his preaching had respect,

1. To the private towns. He visited not only the great and wealthy cities, but the poor, obscure villages; there he preached, there he healed. The souls of those that are meanest in the world are as precious to Christ, and should be to us, as the souls of those that make the greatest figure. *Rich and poor meet together* in him, citizens and boors: his *righteous acts towards the inhabitants of his villages* must be *rehearsed,* Jdg. 5:11.

2. To the public worship. He taught *in their synagogues,* (1.) That he might bear a testimony to solemn assemblies, even then when there were corruptions in them. We *must not forsake the assembling of ourselves together, as the manner of some is.* (2.) That he might have an opportunity of preaching there, where people were gathered together, with an expectation to hear. Thus, even where the gospel church was founded, and Christian meetings erected, the apostles often *preached in the synagogues of the Jews.* It is the wisdom of the prudent, to make the best of that which is.

II. A preface, or introduction, to the account in the following chapter, of his sending forth his apostles. *He* took notice of *the multitude* (*v.* 36); not only of the crowds that *followed him,* but of the vast numbers of people with whom (as he passed along) he observed the country to be replenished; he noticed what nests of souls the towns and cities were, and how thick of inhabitants; what abundance of people there were in every synagogue, and what places of concourse the openings of the gates were: so very populous was that nation now grown; and it was the effect of God's blessing on Abraham. Seeing this,

1. He pities them, and was concerned for them (*v.* 36); *He was moved with compassion on them;* not upon a temporal account, as he pities the blind, and lame, and sick; but upon a spiritual account; he was concerned to see them ignorant and careless, and ready to perish for lack of vision. Note, Jesus Christ is a very compassionate friend to precious souls; here his bowels do in a special manner yearn. It was pity to souls that brought him from heaven to earth, and there to the cross. Misery is the object of mercy; and the miseries of sinful, self-destroying souls, are the greatest miseries: Christ pities those most that pity themselves least; so should we. The most Christian compassion is compassion to souls; it is most Christ-like.

See what moved this pity. (1.) *They fainted;* they were destitute, vexed, wearied. *They strayed,* so some; were loosed one from another; *The staff of bands was broken,* Zec. 11:14. They wanted help for their souls, and had none at hand that was good for any thing. The scribes and Pharisees filled them with vain notions, burthened them with the traditions of the elders, deluded them into many mistakes, while they were not instructed in their duty, nor acquainted with the extent and spiritual nature of the divine law; therefore *they fainted;* for what spiritual health, and life, and vigour can there be in those souls, that are fed with husks and ashes, instead of *the bread of life?* Precious souls *faint* when duty is to be done, temptations to be resisted, afflictions to be borne, being not nourished up with the word of truth. (2.) *They were scattered abroad, as sheep having no shepherd.* That expression is borrowed from 1 Ki. 22:17, and it sets forth the sad condition of those that are destitute of faithful guides to go before them in the things of God. No creature is more apt to go astray than a sheep, and when gone astray more helpless, shiftless, and exposed, or more unapt to find the way home again: sinful souls *are as lost sheep;* they need the care of shepherds to bring them back. The teachers the Jews then had pretended to be *shepherds,* yet Christ says they had not *shepherds,* for they were worse than none; idle shepherds that led them away, instead of leading them back, and fleeced the flock, instead of feeding it: such shepherds as were described, Jer. 23:1, etc. Eze. 34:2, etc. Note, The case of those people is very pitiable, who either have no ministers at all, or those that are as bad as none; that seek their own things, not *the things of Christ* and souls.

2. He excited his disciples to pray for them. His pity put him upon devising means for the good of these people. It appears (Lu. 6:12, 13) that upon this occasion, before he sent out his apostles, he did himself spend a great deal of time in prayer. Note, Those we pity we should pray for. Having spoken to God for them he turns to his disciples, and tells them,

(1.) How the case stood; *The harvest truly is plenteous, but the labourers are few.* People desired good preaching, but there were few good preachers. There was a great deal of work to be done, and a great deal of good likely to be done, but there wanted hands to do it. [1.] It was an encouragement, that *the harvest* was so *plenteous.* It was not strange, that there were multitudes that needed instruction, but it was what does not often happen, that they who needed it, desired it, and were forward to receive it. They that were ill taught were desirous to be better taught; people's expectations were raised, and there was such a moving of affections, as promised well. Note, It is a blessed thing, to see people in love with good preaching. The valleys are then covered over with corn, and there are hopes it may be well gathered in. That is a gale of opportunity, that calls for a double care and diligence in the improvement of it; a harvest-day should be a busy day. [2.] It was a pity when it was so that *the labourers* should be so *few;* that the corn should shed and spoil, and rot upon the ground for want of reapers; loiterers many, but *labourers* very *few.* Note, It is ill with the church, when good work stands still, or goes slowly on, for want of good workmen; when it is so, the *labourers* that there are have need to be very busy.

(2.) What was their duty in this case (*v.* 38); *Pray ye therefore the Lord of the harvest.* Note, The melancholy aspect of the times and the deplorable state of precious souls, should much excite and quicken prayer. When things look discouraging, we should pray more, and then we should complain and fear less. And we should adapt our prayers to the present exigencies of the church; such an understanding we ought to have of the times, as to know, not only what Israel ought to do, but what Israel ought to pray for. Note, [1.] God is *the Lord of the harvest; my Father is the Husbandman,* Jn. 15:1. It is *the vineyard of the Lord of hosts,* Isa. 5:7. It is for him and to him, and to his service and honour, that *the harvest* is gathered in. *Ye are God's husbandry* (1 Co. 3:9); *his threshing, and the corn of his floor,* Isa. 21:10. He orders every thing concerning *the harvest* as he pleases; when and where *the labourers* shall work, and how long; and it is very comfortable to those who wish well to *the harvest-work,* that God himself presides in it, who will be sure to order all for the best. [2.] Ministers are and should be *labourers* in God's *harvest;* the ministry is a *work* and must be attended to accordingly; it is *harvest-work,* which is needful work; work that requires every thing to be done in its season, and diligence to do it thoroughly; but it is pleasant work; they *reap in joy,* and the joy of the preachers of the gospel is likened to the *joy of harvest* (Isa. 9:2, 3); and *he that reapeth receiveth wages; the hire of the labourers* that reap down God's field, shall not be *kept back,* as theirs was, Jam. 5:4. [3.] It is God's work to *send forth labourers;* Christ makes ministers (Eph. 4:11); the office is of his appointing, the qualifications of his working, the call of his giving. They will not be owned nor paid as *labourers,* that run without their errand, unqualified, uncalled. *How shall they preach except they be sent?* [4.] All that love Christ and souls, should show it by their earnest prayers to God, especially when *the harvest is plenteous, that he would send forth* more skillful, faithful, wise, and industrious *labourers into his harvest;* that he would raise up such as he will own in the conversion of sinners and the edification of saints; would give them a spirit for the work, call them to it, and succeed them in it; *that he would* give them *wisdom to win souls; that he would thrust forth labourers,* so some; intimating unwillingness to go forth, because of their own weakness and the people's badness, and opposition from men, that endeavour to thrust them out of *the harvest;* but we should pray that all contradiction from within and from without, may be conquered and got over. Christ puts his friends upon praying this, just before he sends apostles forth to labour in *the harvest.*

Note, It is a good sign God is about to bestow some special mercy upon a people, when he stirs up those that have an interest at the throne of grace, to pray for it, Ps. 10:17. Further observe, that Christ said this to his disciples, who were to be employed as *labourers.* They must pray, First, That God *would send them forth. Here am I, send me,* Isa. 6:8. Note, Commissions, given in answer to prayer, are most likely to be successful; Paul is a chosen vessel, for *behold he prays,* Acts 9:11, 15. Secondly, That he would send others forth. Note, Not the people only, but those who are themselves ministers, should pray for the increase of ministers. Though self-interest makes those that seek their own things desirous to be placed alone (the fewer ministers the more preferments), yet those that *seek the things of Christ,* desire more workmen, that more work may be done, though they be eclipsed by it.

CHAPTER 10

This chapter is an ordination sermon, which our Lord Jesus preached, when he advanced his twelve disciples to the degree and dignity of apostles. In the close of the foregoing chapter, he had stirred up them and others to pray that God would send forth labourers, and here we have an immediate answer to that prayer: while they are yet speaking he hears and performs. What we pray for, according to Christ's direction, shall be given, Now here we have, I. The general commission that was given them (*v.* 1). II. The names of the persons to whom this commission was given (*v.* 2–4). III. The instructions that were given them, which are very full and particular; 1. Concerning the services they were to do; their preaching; their working miracles; to whom they must apply themselves; how they must behave themselves; and in what method they must proceed (*v.* 5–15). 2. Concerning the sufferings they were to undergo. They are told what they should suffer, and from whom; counsels are given them what course to take when persecuted, and encouragements to bear up cheerfully under their sufferings (*v.* 16–42). These things, though primarily intended for direction to the apostles, are of use to all Christ's ministers, with whom, by his word, Christ, and will be always to end the world.

Verses 1–4

Here we are told, I. Who they were that Christ ordained to be his apostles or ambassadors; they were his disciples, *v.* 1. He had called them some time before to be disciples, his immediate followers and constant attendants, and he then told them that they should be made fishers of men, which promise he now performed. Note, Christ commonly confers honours and graces by degrees; the light of both, like that of the morning, *shines more and more.* All this while Christ had kept these twelve,

1. In a state of probation. Though he knows what is in man, though he knew from the first what was in them (Jn. 6:70), yet he took this method to give an example to his church. Note, The ministry being a great trust, it is fit that men should be tried for a time, before they are entrusted with it. Let them *first be proved,* 1 Tim. 3:10. Therefore, hands must not be laid suddenly on any man, but let him first be observed as a candidate and probationer, a proposant (that is the term the French churches use), because some men's sins go before, others follow, 1 Tim. 5:22.

2. In a state of preparation. All this while he had been fitting them for this great work. Note, Those whom Christ intends for, and calls to, any work, he first prepares and qualifies, in some measure, for it. He prepared them, (1.) By *taking them to be with him.* Note, The best preparative for the work of the ministry, is an acquaintance and communion with Jesus Christ. They that would *serve Christ,* must first be *with him* (Jn. 12:26). Paul had Christ revealed, not only *to him,* but *in him,* before he went to preach him among the Gentiles, Gal. 1:16. By the lively acts of faith, and the frequent exercise of prayer and meditation, that fellowship with Christ must be maintained and kept up, which is a requisite qualification for the work of the ministry. (2.) By *teaching them;* they were with him as scholars or pupils, and he taught them privately, besides the benefit they derived from his public preaching; he opened the scriptures to them, and opened their understandings to understand the scriptures: to them it was given to *know the mysteries of the kingdom of heaven,* and to them they were *made plain.* Note, They that design to be teachers must first be learners; they must receive, that they may give; they must be *able to teach others,* 2 Tim. 2:2. Gospel truths must be first committed to them, before they be commissioned to be gospel ministers. To give men *authority* to teach others, that have not an *ability,* is but a mockery to God and the church; it is *sending a message by the hand of a fool,* Prov. 26:6. Christ *taught his disciples* before he sent them forth (*ch.* 5:2), and afterwards, when he enlarged their commission, he gave them more ample instructions, Acts 1:3.

II. What the commission was that he gave them.

1. He *called them to him, v.* 1. He had called them to come *after* him before; now he calls them to come *to* him, admits them to a greater familiarity, and will not have them to keep at such a distance as they had hitherto observed. They that *humble themselves* shall thus be *exalted.* The priests under the law were said to *draw near* and *approach* unto God, nearer than the people; the same may be said of gospel ministers; they are called to draw near to Christ, which, as it is an honour, so should strike an awe upon them, remembering that Christ will be sanctified in those that *come nigh unto him.* It is observable, that when the disciples were to be *instructed,* they *came unto* him of their own accord, *ch.* 5:1. But now they were to be *ordained,* he *called them.* Note, It well becomes the disciples of Christ to be more forward to learn than to teach. In the sense of our own ignorance, we must seek opportunities to be taught; and in the same sense we must *wait for a call,* a clear call, ere we take upon us to *teach others;* for *no man ought to take this honour to himself.*

2. He *gave them power, exousian, authority* in his name, to command men to obedience, and for the confirmation of that authority, to command devils too into a subjection. Note, All rightful authority is derived from Jesus Christ. All power is given to him without limitation, and the subordinate powers that be are ordained of him. Some of his honour he put on his ministers, as Moses put some of his on Joshua. Note, It is an undeniable proof of the fulness of power which Christ used as Mediator, that he could impart his power to those he employed, and enable them to work the same miracles that he wrought in his name. He gave them *power over unclean spirits,* and over *all manner of sickness.* Note, The design of the gospel was to *conquer the devil* and to *cure the world.* These preachers were sent out destitute of all external advantages to recommend them; they had no wealth, nor learning, nor titles of honour, and they made a very mean figure; it was therefore requisite that they should have some extraordinary power to advance them above the scribes.

(1.) He gave them power *against unclean spirits, to cast them out.* Note, The power that is committed to the ministers of Christ, is directly levelled against the devil and his kingdom. The devil, as an *unclean spirit,* is working both in doctrinal errors (Rev. 16:13), and in practical debauchery (2 Pt. 2:10); and in both these, ministers have a charge against him. Christ gave them power to cast him out of the bodies of people; but that was to signify the destruction of his *spiritual kingdom,* and all the works of the devil; for which purpose the *Son of God* was *manifested.*

(2.) He gave them power to *heal all manner of sickness.* He authorized them to work miracles for the confirmation of their doctrine, to prove that it was of God; and they were to work useful miracles for the illustration of it, to prove that it is not only faithful, but well *worthy of all acceptation;* that the design of the gospel is to heal and save. Moses's miracles were many of them for destruction; those Mahomet pretended to, were for ostentation; but the miracles Christ wrought, and appointed his apostles to work, were all for edification, and evince him to be, not only the great Teacher and Ruler, but the great Redeemer, of the world. Observe what an emphasis is laid upon the extent of their power to *all manner of sickness,* and *all manner of disease,* without the exception even of those that are reckoned incurable, and the reproach of physicians. Note, In the grace of the gospel there is a salve for every sore, a remedy for every malady. There is no spiritual disease so malignant, so inveterate, but there is a sufficiency of power in Christ, for the cure of it. Let none therefore say there is no hope, or that the breach is wide as the sea, that cannot be healed.

III. The number and names of those that were commissioned; they are made apostles, that is, messengers. An angel, and an apostle, both signify the same thing — one *sent on an errand,* an ambassador. All faithful ministers are sent of Christ, but they that were first, and immediately, sent by him, are eminently called *apostles,* the prime ministers of state in his kingdom. Yet this was but the infancy of their office; it was when Christ *ascended on high* that he *gave some apostles,* Eph. 4:11. Christ himself is called an apostle (Heb. 3:1), for he was *sent by the Father,* and so sent them, Jn. 20:21. The prophets were called God's messengers.

1. Their number was twelve, referring to the number of the tribes of Israel, and the sons of Jacob that were the patriarchs of those tribes. The gospel church must be the Israel of God; the Jews must be first invited into it; the apostles must be spiritual fathers, to beget a seed to Christ. Israel after the flesh is to be rejected for their infidelity; these twelve, therefore, are appointed to be the fathers of another Israel. These twelve, by their doctrine, were to judge the twelve tribes of Israel, Lu. 22:30. These were the twelve stars that made up the church's crown (Rev. 12:1): the twelve foundations of the new Jerusalem (Rev. 21:12, 14), typified by the twelve precious stones in Aaron's breast-plate, the twelve loaves on the table of show-bread, the twelve wells of water at Elim. This was that famous jury (and to make it a grand jury, Paul was added to it) that was impanelled to enquire between the King of kings, and the body of mankind; and, in this chapter, they have their charge given them, by him to whom *all judgment was committed.*

2. Their names are here left upon record, and it is their honour; yet in this they had more reason to rejoice, that their names were *written in heaven* (Lu. 10:20), while the high and mighty names of the great ones of the earth are *buried in the dust.* Observe,

(1.) There are some of these twelve apostles, of whom we know no more, from the scripture, than their names; as Bartholomew, and Simon the Canaanite; and yet they were faithful servants to Christ and his church. Note, all the good ministers of Christ are not alike famous, nor their actions alike celebrated.

(2.) They are names by couples; for at first they were sent forth *two and two,* because *two are better than one;* they would be serviceable to each other, and the more serviceable jointly to Christ and souls; what one forgot the other would remember, and *out of the mouth of two witnesses every word would be established.* Three couple of them were brethren; Peter and Andrew, James and John, and the other James and Lebbeus. Note, Friendship and fellowship ought to be kept up among relations, and to be made serviceable to religion. It is an excellent thing, when brethren by nature are brethren by grace, and those two bonds strengthen each other.

(3.) Peter is named first, because he was first called; or because he was the most forward among them, and upon all occasions made himself the mouth of the rest, and because he was to be the apostle of the circumcision; but that gave him no power over the rest of the apostles, nor is there the least mark of any supremacy that was given to him, or ever claimed by him, in this sacred college.

(4.) Matthew, the penman of this gospel, is here joined with Thomas (*v.* 3), but in two things there is a variation from the accounts of Mark and Luke, Mk. 3:18; Lu. 6:15. There, Matthew is put first; in that order it appears he was ordained before Thomas; but here, in his own catalogue, Thomas is put first. Note, It well becomes the disciples of Christ in honour to prefer one another. There, he is only called Matthew, here Matthew the publican, the toll-gatherer or collector of the customs, who was called from that infamous employment to be an apostle. Note, It is good for those who are advanced to honour with Christ, to look *unto the rock whence they were hewn;* often to remember what they were before Christ called them, that thereby they may be kept humble, and divine grace may be the more glorified. Matthew the apostle was Matthew the publican.

(5.) Simon is called the Canaanite, or rather the Canite, from Cana of Galilee, where probably he was born; or Simon the Zealot, which some make to be the signification of *Kanitēs.*

(6.) Judas Iscariot is always named last, and with that black brand upon his name, *who also betrayed him;* which intimates that from the first, Christ knew what a wretch he was, that he had a devil, and would prove a traitor; yet Christ took him among the apostles, that it might not be a surprise and discouragement to his church, if, at any time, the vilest scandals should break out in the best societies. Such spots there have been in our feasts of charity; tares among the wheat, wolves among the sheep; but there is a day of discovery and separation coming, where hypocrites shall be unmasked and discarded. Neither the apostleship, nor the rest of the apostles, were ever the worse for Judas's being one of the twelve, while his wickedness was concealed and did not break out.

Verses 5–15

We have here the instructions that Christ gave to his disciples, when he gave them their commission. Whether this charge was given them in a continued discourse, or the several articles of it hinted to them at several times, is not material; in this he *commanded them.* Jacob's blessing his sons, is called his *commanding* them, and with these commands Christ commanded a blessing. Observe,

I. The people to whom he sent them. These ambassadors are directed what places to go to.

1. Not to the Gentiles nor the Samaritans. They must not *go into the way of the Gentiles,* nor into any road out of the land of Israel, whatever temptations they might have. The Gentiles must not have the gospel brought them, till the Jews have first refused it. As to the Samaritans, who were the posterity of the mongrel people that the king of Assyria planted about Samaria, their country lay between Judea and Galilee, so that they could not avoid *going into the way* of the Samaritans, but they must *not enter into any of their cities.* Christ had declined manifesting himself to the Gentiles or Samaritans, and therefore the apostles must not preach to them. If the gospel be hid from any place, Christ thereby hides himself from that place. This restraint was upon them only in their first mission, afterwards they were appointed to go *into all the world,* and teach *all nations.*

2. But *to the lost sheep of the house of Israel.* To them Christ appropriated his own ministry (*ch.* 15:24), for he was a *minister of the circumcision* (Rom. 15:8): and, therefore, to them the apostles, who were but his attendants and agents, must be confined. The first offer of salvation must be made to the Jews, Acts 3:26. Note, Christ had a particular and very tender concern for the *house of Israel;* they were *beloved for the fathers' sakes,* Rom. 11:28. He looked with compassion upon them as *lost sheep,* whom he, as a shepherd, was to gather out of the by-paths of sin and error, into which they were gone astray, and in which, if not brought back, they would wander endlessly; see Jer. 2:6. The Gentiles also had been as lost sheep, 1 Pt. 2:25. Christ gives this description of those to whom they were sent, to quicken them to diligence in their work, they were sent to the house of Israel (of which number they themselves lately were), whom they could not but pity, and be desirous to help.

II. The preaching work which he appointed them. He did not send them forth without an errand; no, *As ye go, preach, v.* 7. They were to be itinerant preachers: wherever they come they must proclaim the beginning of the gospel, saying, *The kingdom of heaven is at hand.* Not that they must say nothing else, but this must be their text; on this subject they must enlarge: let people know, that the kingdom of the Messiah, who is the Lord from heaven, is now to be set up according to the scriptures; from whence it follows, that men must *repent* of their sins and forsake them, that they might be admitted to the privileges of that kingdom. It is said (Mk. 6:12), *they went out, and preached that men should repent;* which was the proper use and application of this doctrine, concerning the approach of the *kingdom of heaven.* They must, therefore, expect to hear more of this long-looked-for Messiah shortly, and must be ready to receive his doctrine, to believe in him, and to submit to his yoke. The preaching of this was like the morning light, to give notice of the approach of the rising sun. How unlike was this to the preaching of Jonah, which proclaimed ruin at hand! Jonah 3:4. This proclaims salvation at hand, *nigh them that fear God; mercy and truth meet together* (Ps. 85:9, 10), that is, *the kingdom of heaven at hand:* not so much the personal presence of the king; that must not be doated upon; but a spiritual kingdom which is to be set up, when his bodily presence is removed, in the hearts of men.

Now this was the same that John the Baptist and Christ had preached before. Note, People need to have good truths pressed again and again upon them, and if they be preached and heard with new affections, they are as if they were fresh to us. Christ, in the gospel, is *the same yesterday, to-day, and for ever,* Heb. 13:8. Afterwards, indeed, when the Spirit was poured out, and the Christian church was formed, this *kingdom of heaven came,* which was now spoken of as *at hand;* but the *kingdom of heaven* must still be the subject of our preaching: now it is come, we must tell people it is come to them, and must lay before them the precepts and privileges of it; and there is a kingdom of glory yet to come, which we must speak of as at hand, and quicken people to diligence from the consideration of that.

III. The power he gave them to work miracles for the confirmation of their doctrine, *v.* 8. When he sent them to preach the same doctrine that he had preached, he empowered them to confirm it, by the same divine seals, which could never be set to a lie. This is not necessary now the kingdom of God is come; to call for miracles now is to lay again the foundation when the building is reared. The point being settled, and the doctrine of Christ sufficiently attested, by the miracles which Christ and his apostles wrought, it is tempting God to ask for more signs. They are directed here,

1. To use their power in doing good: not "Go and remove mountains," or "fetch fire from heaven," but, *Heal the sick, cleanse the lepers.* They are sent abroad as public blessings, to intimate to the world, that love and goodness were the spirit and genius of that gospel which they came to preach, and of that kingdom which they were employed to set up. By this it would appear, that they were the servants of that God who is good and does good, and whose mercy is *over all his works;* and that the intention of the doctrine they preached, was to heal sick souls, and to *raise* those that were *dead in sin;* and therefore, perhaps, that of *raising the dead* is mentioned; for though we read not of their raising any to life before the *resurrection of Christ,* yet they were instrumental to raise many to *spiritual life.*

2. In *doing good freely; Freely ye heave received, freely give.* Those that had power to heal all diseases, had an opportunity to enrich themselves; who would not purchase such easy certain cures at any rate? Therefore they are cautioned not to make a gain of the power they had to work miracles: they must cure *gratis,* further to exemplify the nature and complexion of the gospel kingdom, which is made up, not only of grace, but of free grace. *Gratia gratis data* (Rom. 3:24), *freely by his grace,* Buy medicines *without money, and without price,* Isa. 55:1. And the reason is, because *freely you have received.* Their power to heal the sick cost them nothing, and, therefore, they must not make any secular advantage to themselves of it. Simon Magus would not have offered money for the gifts of the Holy Ghost, if he had not hoped to get money by them; Acts 8:18. Note, The consideration of Christ's freeness in doing good to us, should make us free in doing good to others.

IV. The provision that must be made for them in this expedition; it is a thing to be considered in sending an ambassador, who must bear the charge of the embassy. As to that,

1. They must make no provision for it themselves, *v.* 9, 10. *Provide neither gold nor silver.* As, on the one hand, they shall not raise estates by their work, so, on the other hand, they shall not spend what little they have of their own upon it. This was confined to the present mission, and Christ would teach them, (1.) To act *under the conduct of human prudence.* They were now to make but a short excursion, and were soon to return to their Master, and to their head-quarters again, and, therefore, why should they burthen themselves with that which they would have no occasion for? (2.) To act in *dependence upon Divine Providence.* They must be taught to live, without *taking thought for life, ch.* 6:25, etc. Note, They who go upon Christ's errand, have, of all people, most reason to trust him for *food convenient.* Doubtless he will not be wanting to those that are working for him. Those whom he employs, as they are taken under special protection, so they are entitled to special provisions. Christ's hired servants shall have *bread enough and to spare;* while we abide faithful to God and our duty, and are in care to do our work well, we may cast all our other care upon God; Jehovah-jireh, let the Lord provide for us and ours as he thinks fit.

2. They might expect that those to whom they were sent would *provide for them* what was necessary, *v.* 10. The *workman is worthy of his meat.* They must not expect to be fed by miracles, as Elijah was: but they might depend upon God to incline the hearts of those they went among, to be kind to them, and provide for them. Though they who *serve at the altar* may not expect to grow rich by the altar, yet they may expect to live, and to live comfortably upon it, 1 Co. 9:13, 14. It is fit they should have their maintenance from their work. Ministers are, and must be, workmen, labourers, and they that are so are *worthy of their meat,* so as not to be forced to any other labour for the earning of it. Christ would have his disciples, as not to distrust their God, so not to distrust their countrymen, so far as to doubt of a comfortable subsistence among them. If you preach to them, and endeavour to do good among them, surely they will give you meat and drink enough for your necessities: and if they do, never desire dainties; God will pay you your wages hereafter, and it will be running on in the mean time.

V. The proceedings they were to observe in dealing with any place, *v.* 11–15. They went abroad they knew not whither, uninvited, unexpected, knowing none, and known of none; the land of their nativity was to them a strange land; what rule must they go by? what course must they take? Christ would not send them out without full instructions, and here they are.

1. They are here directed how to conduct themselves toward those that were *strangers to them;* How to do,

(1.) In *strange towns and cities:* when you come to a town, *enquire who* in it *is worthy.* [1.] It is supposed that there were some such in every place, as were better disposed than others to receive the gospel, and the preachers of it; though it was a time of general corruption and apostasy. Note, In the worst of times and places, we may charitably hope that there are some who distinguish themselves, and are better than their neighbours; some who swim against the stream, and are as wheat among the chaff. There were saints in Nero's household. Enquire who is worthy, who there are that have some fear of God before their eyes, and have made a good improvement of the light and knowledge they have. The best are far from meriting the favour of a gospel offer; but some would be more likely than others to give the apostles and their message a favourable entertainment, and would not trample these pearls under their feet. Note, Previous dispositions to that which is good, are both directions and encouragements to ministers, in dealing with people. There is most hope of the word being profitable to those who are already so well inclined, as that it is acceptable to them; and there is here and there one such. [2.] They must enquire out such; not enquire for the best inns; public houses were no proper places for them that neither took money with them (*v.* 9), nor expected to receive any (*v.* 8); but they must look out for accommodations in private houses, with those that would entertain them well, and expect no other recompence for it but a prophet's reward, an apostle's reward, their praying and preaching. Note, They that entertain the gospel, must neither grudge the expense of it, nor promise themselves to get by it in this world. They must enquire, not who is rich, but who is worthy; not who is the best gentleman, but who is the best man. Note, Christ's disciples, wherever they come, should ask for the good people of the place, and be acquainted with them; when we took God for our God, we took his people for our people, and like will rejoice in its like. Paul in all his travels found out the brethren, if there were any, Acts 28:14. It is implied, that if they did enquire who was worthy, they might discover them. They that were better than their neighbours would be taken notice of, and any one could tell them, there lives an honest, sober, good man; for this is a character which, like the ointment of the right hand, betrays itself and fills the house with its odours. Every body knew where the seer's house was, 1 Sa. 9:18. [3.] In the house of those they found worthy, they must continue; which intimates that they were to make so short a stay at each town, that they needed not change their lodging, but whatever house providence brought them to at first, there they must continue till they left that town. They are justly suspected, as having no good design, that are often changing their quarters. Note, It becomes the disciples of Christ to make the best of that which is, to abide by it, and not be for shifting upon every dislike or inconvenience.

(2.) In strange houses. When they had found the house of one they thought worthy, they must at their entrance salute it. "In those common civilities, be beforehand with people, in token of your humility. Think it not a disparagement, to invite yourselves into a house, nor stand upon the *punctilio* of being invited. Salute the family, [1.] To draw on further discourse, and so to introduce your message." (From matters of common conversation, we may insensibly pass into that communication which is good to the use of edifying.) [2.] "To try whether you are welcome or not; you will take notice whether the salutation be received with shyness and coldness, or with a ready return. He that will not receive your salutation kindly, will not receive your message kindly; for he that is unskilful and unfaithful in a little, will also be in much, Lu. 16:10. [3.] To insinuate yourselves into their good opinion. *Salute the family,* that they may see that though you are serious, you are not morose." Note, Religion teaches us to be courteous and civil, and obliging to all with whom we have to do. Though the apostles went out backed with the authority of the Son of God himself, yet their instructions were, when they came into a house, not to *command it,* but to *salute* it; for *love's sake rather to beseech,* is the evangelical way, Philemon 8, 9. Souls are first drawn to Christ with the *cords of a man,* and kept to him by the *bands of love,* Hos. 11:4. When Peter made the first offer of the gospel to Cornelius, a Gentile, Peter was first saluted; see Acts 10:25, for the Gentiles courted that which the Jews were courted to.

When they had saluted the family after a godly sort, they must by the return, judge concerning the family, and proceed accordingly. Note, The eye of God is upon us, to observe what entertainment we give to good people and good ministers; if *the house be worthy, let your peace come and rest upon it; if not, let it return to you, v.* 13. It seems then, that after they had enquired for the *most worthy* (v. 11), it was possible they might light upon those that were unworthy. Note, Though it is wisdom to hearken to, yet it is folly to rely upon, common report and opinion; we ought to use a judgment of discretion, and to see with our own eyes. *The wisdom of the prudent is* himself to *understand his* own *way.* Now this rule is intended,

First, For satisfaction to the apostles. The common salutation was, *Peace be unto you;* this, as they used it, was turned into gospel; it was the *peace of God,* the peace of the kingdom of heaven, that they wished. Now lest they should make a scruple of pronouncing this blessing upon all promiscuously, because many were utterly unworthy of it, this is to clear them of that scruple; Christ tells them that this gospel prayer (for so it was now become) should be put up for all, as the gospel proffer was made to all indefinitely, and that they should leave it to God who knows the heart, and every man's true character, to determine the issue of it. If the house be worthy, it will reap the benefit of your blessing; if now, there is no harm done, you will not lose the benefit of it; *it shall return to you,* as David's prayers for his ungrateful enemies did, Ps. 35:13. Note, It becomes us to judge charitably of *all,* to pray heartily *for all,* and to conduct ourselves courteously *to all,* for that is our part, and then to leave it with God to determine what effect it shall have upon them, for that is his part.

Secondly, For direction to them. "If, upon your salutation, it appear that they are indeed worthy, let them have more of your company, and so *let your peace come upon them;* preach the gospel to them, peace by Jesus Christ; but if otherwise, if they carry it rudely to you, and shut their doors against you, *let your peace,* as much as in you lies, *return to you.* Retract what you have said, and turn your backs upon them; by slighting this, they have made themselves unworthy of the rest of your favours, and cut themselves short of them." Note, Great blessings are often lost by a neglect seemingly small and inconsiderable, when men are in their probation and upon their behaviour. Thus Esau lost his birthright (Gen. 25:34), and Saul his kingdom, 1 Sa. 13:13, 14.

2. They are here directed how to carry it towards those that were refusers of them. The case is put (v. 14) of those that *would not receive them, nor hear their words.* The apostles might think, that now they had such a doctrine to preach, and such a power to work miracles for the confirmation of it, no doubt but they should be universally entertained and made welcome: they are, therefore, told before, that there would be those that would slight them, and put contempt on them and their message. Note, The best and most powerful preachers of the gospel must expect to meet with some, that will not so much as give them the hearing, nor show them any token of respect. Many turn *a deaf ear,* even to the *joyful sound,* and will not *hearken to the voice of the charmers, charm they never so wisely.* Observe, "They will not *receive you,* and they will not *hear your words.*" Note, Contempt of the gospel, and contempt of gospel ministers, commonly go together, and they will either of them be construed into a contempt of Christ, and will be reckoned for accordingly.

Now in this case we have here,

(1.) The directions given to the apostles what to do. They must *depart out of that house or city.* Note, The gospel will not tarry long with those that put it away from them. At their departure they must *shake off the dust of their feet,* [1.] In detestation of their wickedness; it was so abominable, that it did even pollute the ground they went upon, which must therefore be *shaken off* as a filthy thing. The apostles must have no fellowship nor communion with them; must not so much as carry away the dust of their city with them. *The work of them that turn aside* shall *not cleave to me,* Ps. 101:3. The prophet was not to *eat or drink* in Bethel, 1 Ki. 13:9. [2.] As a denunciation of wrath against them. It was to signify, that they were base and vile as dust, and that God would *shake*

them *off.* The dust of the apostles' feet, which they left behind them, would witness against them, and be brought in as evidence, that the gospel had been preached to them, Mk. 6:11. Compare Jam. 5:3. See this practised, Acts 13:51, 18:6. Note, They who *despise* God and his gospel shall be *lightly esteemed.*

(2.) The *doom passed* upon such *wilful recusants, v.* 15. It shall be *more tolerable, in the day of judgment, for the land of* Sodom, as wicked a place as it was. Note, [1.] There is a day of judgment coming, when all those that refused the gospel will certainly be called to account for it; however they now make a jest of it. They that would not hear the doctrine that would save them, shall be made to hear the sentence that will ruin them. Their judgment is respited till *that day.* [2.] There are different degrees of punishment in that day. All the pains of hell will be *intolerable;* but some will be more so than others. Some sinners sink deeper into hell than others, and are beaten with more stripes. [3.] The condemnation of those that reject the gospel, will in that day be severer and heavier than that of Sodom and Gomorrah. Sodom is said to suffer the vengeance of eternal fire, Jude 7. But that *vengeance* will come with an aggravation upon those that despise the great salvation. Sodom and Gomorrah were exceedingly wicked (Gen. 13:13), and that which filled up the measure of their iniquity was, that they *received not* the angels that were sent to them, but abused them (Gen. 19:4, 5), and *hearkened not to their words, v.* 14. And yet it will be more tolerable for them than for those who receive not Christ's ministers and hearken not to their words. God's wrath against them will be more flaming, and their own reflections upon themselves more cutting. *Son, remember I* will sound most dreadfully in the ears of such as had a fair offer made them of *eternal life,* and chose death rather. The iniquity of Israel, when God sent them his servants the prophets, is represented as, upon that account, more heinous than the iniquity of Sodom (Eze. 16:48, 49), much more now he sent them his Son, the great Prophet.

Verses 16–42

All these verses relate to the sufferings of Christ's ministers in their work, which they are here taught to expect, and prepare for; they are directed also how to bear them, and how to go on with their work in the midst of them. This part of the sermon looks further than to their present mission; for we find not that they met with any great hardships or persecutions while Christ was with them, nor were they well able to bear them; but they are here forewarned of the troubles they should meet with, when after Christ's resurrection, their commission should be *enlarged,* and the kingdom of heaven, which was not *at hand,* should be actually set up; they dreamed of nothing then, but outward pomp and power; but Christ tells them, they must expect greater sufferings than they were yet called to; that they should then be made prisoners, when they expected to be made princes. It is good to be told what troubles we may hereafter meet with, that we may provide accordingly, and may not boast, as if we had put off the harness, when we are yet but girding it on.

We have here intermixed, I. Predictions of trouble: and, II. Prescriptions of counsel and comfort, with reference to it.

I. We have here predictions of trouble; which the disciples should meet with in their work: Christ foresaw *their* sufferings as well as his own, and yet will have them go on, as he went on himself; and he foretold them, not only that the troubles might not be a surprise to them, and so a shock to their faith, but that, being the accomplishment of a prediction, they might be a confirmation to their faith.

He tells them what they should suffer, and from whom.

1. *What they should suffer:* hard things to be sure; for, *Behold, I send you forth as sheep in the midst of wolves, v.* 16. And what may a flock of poor, helpless, unguarded sheep expect, in the midst of a herd of ravenous wolves, but to be worried and torn? Note, Wicked men are like wolves, in whose nature it is to devour and destroy. God's people, and especially his ministers, are like sheep among them, of a contrary nature and disposition, exposed to them, and commonly an easy prey to them. It looked unkind in Christ to expose them to so much danger, who had left all to follow him; but he knew that the glory reserved for his sheep, when in the great day they shall be set on his right hand, would be a recompence sufficient for sufferings as well as services. They are as *sheep among wolves,* that is frightful; but Christ

sends them forth, that is comfortable; for he that sends them forth will protect them, and bear them out. But that they might know the worst, he tells them particularly what they must expect.

(1.) They must expect to be hated, *v.* 22. *Ye shall be hated for my name's sake:* that is the root of all the rest, and a bitter root it is. Note, Those whom Christ loves, the world hates; as whom the court blesses the country curses. *If the world hated Christ without a cause* (Jn. 15:25), no marvel if it hated those that bore his image and served his interests. We hate what is nauseous, and they *are counted as the offscouring of all things,* 1 Co. 4:13. We hate what is noxious, and they are counted *the troublers of the land* (1 Ki. 18:17), and the tormentors of their neighbours, Rev. 11:10. It is grievous to be *hated,* and to be the object of so much ill-will, but it is *for thy name's sake;* which, as it speaks the true reason of the hatred, whatever is pretended, so it speaks comfort to them who are thus hated; it is for a good cause, and they have a good friend that shares with them in it, and takes it to himself.

(2.) They must expect to be apprehended and arraigned as malefactors. Their restless malice is resistless malice, and they will not only attempt, but will prevail, to *deliver you up to the councils* (v. 17, 18), to the bench of aldermen or justices, that take care of the public peace. Note, A deal of mischief is often done to good men, under colour of law and justice. In *the place of judgment there is wickedness,* persecuting wickedness, Eccl. 3:16. They must look for trouble, not only from inferior magistrates in the councils, but from governors and kings, the supreme magistrates. To be brought before them, under such black representations as were commonly made of Christ's disciples, was dreadful and dangerous; for *the wrath of a king is as the roaring of a lion.* We find this often fulfilled in the *acts of the apostles.*

(3.) They must expect to be put to death (v. 21); *They shall deliver them to death,* to death in state, with pomp and solemnity, when it shows itself most as *the king of terrors.* The malice of the enemies rages so high as to inflict this; it is *the blood of the saints* that they thirst after: the faith and patience of the saints stand so firm as to expect this; *Neither count I my life dear to myself:* the wisdom of Christ permits it, knowing how to make the blood of the martyrs *the seal of the truth,* and *the seed of the church.* By this noble army's not loving *their lives to the death,* Satan has been vanquished, and the kingdom of Christ and its interests greatly advanced, Rev. 11:11. They were put to death as criminals, so the enemies meant it, but really as sacrifices (Phil. 2:17; 2 Tim. 4:6); as burnt offerings, sacrifices of acknowledgement to the honour of God, and in his truth and cause.

(4.) They must expect, in the midst of these sufferings, to be branded with the most odious and ignominious names and characters that could be. Persecutors would be ashamed in this world, if they did not first dress up those in bear-skins whom they thus bait, and represent them in such colours as may serve to justify such cruelties. The blackest of all the ill characters they give them is here stated; they call them Beelzebub, the name of the prince of the devils, *v.* 25. They represent them as ringleaders of the interest of the kingdom of darkness, and since every one thinks he hates the devil, thus they endeavour to make them odious to all mankind. See, and be amazed to see, how this world is imposed upon: [1.] Satan's sworn enemies are represented as his friends; the apostles, who pulled down the devil's kingdom, were called devils. Thus *men laid to their charge,* not only *things which they knew not,* but *things which* they abhorred, and were directly contrary to, and the reverse of. [2.] Satan's sworn servants would be thought to be his enemies, and they never more effectually do his work, than when they pretend to be fighting against him. Many times they who themselves are nearest akin to the devil, are most apt to father others upon him; and those that paint him on others' clothes have him reigning in their own hearts. It is well there is a day coming, when (as it follows here, *v.* 26) that which is hid will be brought to light.

(5.) These sufferings are here represented by a sword and division, *v.* 34, 35. *Think not that I am come to send peace,* temporal peace and outward prosperity; they thought Christ came to give all his followers wealth and power in the world; "no," says Christ, "I did not come with a view to give them *peace; peace* in heaven they may be sure of, but not *peace* on earth." Christ came to give us *peace* with God, *peace* in our consciences, *peace* with our brethren, but *in the world ye shall have tribulation.* Note, They mistake the design of the gospel, who think their profession of it will secure them from, for it will certainly expose them to, trouble in this world. If all the world would receive Christ, there would then follow a universal *peace,* but while there are and will be so many that reject him (and those not only *the children of this world,* but *the seed of the serpent*), the children of God, that are called out of the world, must expect to feel the fruits of their enmity.

[1.] Look not for *peace, but a sword,* Christ came to give *the sword of the word,* with which his disciples fight against the world, and *conquering* work this sword has made (Rev. 6:4; 19:21), and *the sword of persecution,* with which the world fights against the disciples, being *cut to the heart* with *the sword of the word* (Acts 7:54), and tormented by the testimony of Christ's witnesses (Rev. 11:10), and *cruel* work this sword made. Christ sent that gospel, which gives occasion for the drawing of this sword, and so may be said to send this sword; he orders his church into a suffering state for the trial and praise of his people's graces, and *the filling up of the measure of their* enemies' sins.

[2.] Look not for *peace,* but division (v. 35), *I am come to set men at variance.* This effect of the preaching of the gospel is not the fault of the gospel, but of those who do not receive it. When some *believe the things that are spoken, and others believe them not,* the faith of those that believe condemns those that believe not, and, therefore, they have an enmity against them that believe. Note, the most violent and implacable feuds have ever been those that have arisen from difference in religion; no enmity like that of the persecutors, no resolution like that of the persecuted. Thus Christ tells his disciples what they should suffer, and these were hard sayings; if they could bear these, they could bear any thing. Note, Christ has dealt fairly and faithfully with us, in telling us the worst we can meet with in his service; and he would have us deal so with ourselves, in sitting down and counting the cost.

2. They are here told from whom, and by whom, they should suffer these hard things. Surely hell itself must be let loose, and devils, those desperate and despairing spirits, that *have no part nor lot in* the great salvation, must become incarnate, ere such spiteful enemies could be found to a doctrine, the substance of which was *good will toward men,* and *the reconciling of the world to God;* no, would you think it? all this mischief arises to the preachers of the gospel, from those to whom they came to preach salvation. Thus *the bloodthirsty hate the upright, but the just seek his soul* (Prov. 29:10), and therefore heaven is so much opposed on earth, because earth is so much under the power of hell, Eph. 2:2.

These hard things Christ's disciples must suffer,

(1.) From men (v. 17). *"Beware of men;* you will have need to stand upon your guard, even against those who are of the same nature with you" — such is the depravity and degeneracy of that nature *(homo homini lupus,* — *man is a wolf to man),* crafty and politic as men, but cruel and barbarous as beasts, and wholly divested of the thing called humanity. Note, Persecuting rage and enmity turn men into brutes, into devils. Paul at Ephesus fought with beasts in the shape of men, 1 Co. 15:32. It is a sad pass that the world is come to, when the best friends it has, have need to *beware of men.* It aggravates the troubles of Christ's suffering servants, that they arise from those who *are bone of their bone,* made of the same blood. Persecutors are, in this respect, worse than beasts, that they prey upon those of their own kind: *Saevis inter se convenit ursis — Even savage bears agree among themselves.* It is very grievous to have *men rise up against us* (Ps. 124), from whom we might expect protection and sympathy; *men,* and no more: mere *men; men,* and not saints; *natural men* (1 Co. 2:14); *men of this world,* Ps. 17:14. Saints are more than *men,* and are *redeemed from among men,* and therefore are *hated by them.* The nature of man, if it be not sanctified, is the worst nature in the world next to that of devils. *They are men,* and therefore subordinate, dependent, dying creatures; *they are men,* but *they are but men* (Ps. 9:20), and *who art thou, that thou shouldst be afraid of a man that shall die?* Isa. 51:12. *Beware of the men,* so Dr. Hammond; those you are acquainted with, the men of the Jewish sanhedrim, which disallowed Christ, 1 Pt. 2:4.

(2.) From professing men, men that *have a form of godliness,* and make a show of religion. *They will scourge you in their synagogues,* their places of meeting for the worship of God, and for the exercise of their church-discipline: so that

they looked upon the scourging of Christ's ministers to be a branch of their religion. Paul was *five times scourged in the synagogues,* 2 Co. 11:24. The Jews, under colour of zeal for Moses, were the most bitter persecutors of Christ and Christianity, and placed those outrages to the score of their religion. Note, Christ's disciples have suffered much from conscientious persecutors, that *scourge them in their synagogues,* cast them out and kill them, and *think they do God good service* (Jn. 16:2), and say, *Let the Lord be glorified,* Isa. 66:5; Zec. 11:4, 5. But the synagogue will be so far from consecrating the persecution, that the persecution, doubtless, profanes and desecrates the synagogue.

(3.) From great men, and men in authority. The Jews did not only scourge them, which was the utmost their remaining power extended to, but when they could go no further themselves, they delivered them up to the Roman powers, as they did Christ, Jn. 18:30. *Ye shall be brought before governors and kings* (v. 18), who, having more power, are in a capacity of doing the more mischief. *Governors and kings* receive their power from Christ (Prov. 8:15), and should be his servants, and his church's protectors and nursing-fathers, but they often use their power against him, and are rebels to Christ, and oppressors of his church. *The kings of the earth* set themselves against his kingdom, Ps. 2:1, 2; Acts 4:25, 26. Note, It has often been the lot of good men to have great men for their enemies.

(4.) From all men (v. 22). *Ye shall be hated of all men,* of all wicked men, and these are the generality of men, *for the whole world lies in wickedness.* So few are there that love, and own, and countenance Christ's righteous cause, that we may say, the friends of it are *hated of all men;* they *are all gone astray,* and, therefore, *eat up my people,* Ps. 14:3. As far as the apostasy from God goes, so far the enmity against the saints goes; sometimes it appears more general than at other times, but there is something of this poison lurking in the hearts of all *the children of disobedience. The world hates you,* for it *wonders after the beast,* Rev. 13:3. *Every man is a liar,* and therefore a hater of truth.

(5.) From those of their own kindred. *The brother shall deliver up the brother to death,* v. 21. *A man shall be,* upon this account, *at variance with his own father;* nay, and those of the weaker and tenderer sex too shall become persecutors and persecuted; *the persecuting daughter will be against the believing mother,* where natural affection and filial duty, one would think, should prevent or soon extinguish the quarrel; and then, no marvel *if the daughter-in-law be against the mother-in-law;* where, too often, the coldness of love seeks occasion of contention, v. 35. In general, *a man's foes shall be they of his own household* (v. 36). They who should be his friends will be incensed against him for embracing Christianity, and especially for adhering to it when it comes to be persecuted, and will join with his persecutors against him. Note, The strongest bonds of relative love and duty have often been broken through, by an enmity against Christ and his doctrine. Such has been the power of prejudice against the true religion, and zeal for a false one, that all other regards, the most natural and sacred, the most engaging and endearing, have been sacrificed to these Molochs. They who *rage against the Lord, and his anointed ones,* break even *these bonds in sunder, and cast away* even *these cords from them,* Ps. 2:2, 3. Christ's spouse suffers hard things from the anger of *her own mother's children,* Cant. 1:6. Sufferings from such are more grievous; nothing cuts more than this, *It was thou, a man, mine equal* (Ps. 55:12, 13); and the enmity of such is commonly most implacable; *a brother offended is harder to be won than a strong city,* Prov. 18:19. The martyrologies, both ancient and modern, are full of instances of this. Upon the whole matter, it appears, that *all that will live godly in Christ Jesus, must suffer persecution; and through* many *tribulations we must* expect to *enter into the kingdom of God.*

II. With these predictions of trouble, we have here prescriptions of counsels and comforts for a time of trial. He sends them out exposed to danger indeed, and expecting it, but well armed with instructions and encouragements, sufficient to bear them up, and bear them out, in all these trials. Let us gather up what he says,

1. By way of counsel and direction in several things.

(1.) *Be ye wise as serpents,* v. 16. "You may be so" (so some take it, only as a permission); "you may be as wary as you please, provided you be harmless as doves." But it is rather to be taken as a precept, recommending to us that wisdom of the prudent, which is to understand his way, as useful at

all times, but especially in suffering times. *"Therefore,* because you are exposed, as sheep among wolves; *be ye wise as serpents;* not wise as foxes, whose cunning is to deceive others; but as *serpents,* whose policy is only to defend themselves, and to shift for their own safety." The disciples of Christ are hated and persecuted as *serpents,* and their ruin is sought, and, therefore, they need the *serpent's* wisdom. Note, It is the will of Christ that his people and ministers, being so much exposed to troubles in this world, as they usually are, should not needlessly expose themselves, but use all fair and lawful means for their own preservation. Christ gave us an example of this wisdom, *ch.* 21:24, 25; 22:17, 18, 19; Jn. 7:6, 7; besides the many escapes he made out of the hands of his enemies, till his hour was come. See an instance of Paul's wisdom, Acts 23:6, 7. In the cause of Christ we must sit loose to life and all its comforts, but must not be prodigal of them. It is the wisdom of the *serpent* to secure his head, that it may not be broken, to *stop his ear to the voice of the charmer* (Ps. 58:4, 5), and to *take shelter in the clefts of the rocks;* and herein we may *be wise as serpents.* We must *be wise,* not to pull trouble upon our own heads; *wise* to keep silence in an evil time, and not to give offence, if we can help it.

(2.) *Be ye harmless as doves.* "Be mild, and meek, and dispassionate; not only do nobody any hurt, but bear nobody any ill will; be without gall, *as doves* are; this must always go along with the former." They are *sent forth among wolves,* therefore must *be as wise as serpents,* but they are *sent forth as sheep,* therefore must *be harmless as doves.* We must *be wise,* not to wrong ourselves, but rather so than wrong any one else; must use the harmlessness of the *dove* to bear twenty injuries, rather than the subtlety of the *serpent* to offer or to return one. Note, It must be the continual care of all Christ's disciples, to be innocent and inoffensive in word and deed, especially in consideration of the enemies they are in the midst of. We have need of a *dove-like* spirit, when we are beset with birds of prey, that we may neither provoke them nor be provoked by them: David coveted *the wings of a dove,* on which to fly away and be at rest, rather than the wings of a hawk. *The Spirit descended on Christ as a dove,* and all believers partake of *the Spirit of Christ, a dove-like* spirit, made for love, not for war.

(3.) *Beware of men,* v. 17. "Be always upon your guard, and avoid dangerous company; take heed what you say and do, and presume not too far upon any man's fidelity; be jealous of the most plausible pretensions; *trust not in a friend,* no, not *in the wife of thy bosom,"* Micah 7:5. Note, It becomes those who are gracious to be cautious, for we are taught to *cease from man.* Such a wretched world do we live in, that we know not whom to trust. Ever since our Master was betrayed with a kiss, by one of his own disciples, we have need to *beware of men,* of false brethren.

(4.) *Take no thought how or what ye shall speak,* v. 19. "When you are brought before magistrates, conduct yourselves decently, but afflict not yourselves with care how you shall come off. A prudent thought there must be, but not an anxious, perplexing, disquieting thought; let this *care be cast upon God,* as well as that — *what you shall eat and what you shall drink.* Do not study to make fine speeches, *ad captandam benevolentiam — to ingratiate yourselves;* affect not quaint expressions, flourishes of wit, and laboured periods, which only serve to gild a bad cause; the gold of a good one needs it not. It argues a diffidence of your cause, to be solicitous in this matter, as if it were not sufficient to speak for itself. You know upon what grounds you go, and then *verbaque praevisam rem non invita sequentur — suitable expressions will readily occur."* Never any spoke better before governors and kings than those three champions, who took *no thought before, what they should speak: O Nebuchadnezzar, we are not careful to answer thee in this matter,* Dan. 3:16. See Ps. 119:46. Note, The disciples of Christ must be more thoughtful how to *do* well than how to *speak* well; how to *keep* their integrity than how to *vindicate* it. *Non magna loquimur, sed vivimus — Our lives, not boasting words,* form the best apology.

(5.) *When they persecute you in this city, flee to another,* v. 23. "Thus reject them who reject you and your doctrine, and try whether others will not receive you and it. Thus shift for your own safety." Note, In case of imminent peril, the disciples of Christ may and must secure themselves by flight, when God, in his providence, opens to *them a door of escape.* He that flies may fight again. It is no inglorious thing for Christ's soldiers to quit their ground, provided they do not quit their colours: they may go out of the way of *danger,* though they must not go out of the way of *duty.* Observe Christ's care of his disciples, in providing places of retreat and shelter for them; ordering it so, that persecution rages not in all places at the same time; but *when one city* is made too hot for them, *another* is reserved for a cooler shade, and *a little sanctuary;* a favour to be used and not to be slighted; yet always with this proviso, that no sinful, unlawful means be used to make the escape; for then it is not a door of God's opening. We have many examples to this rule in the history both of Christ and his apostles, in the application of all which to particular cases *wisdom* and integrity are *profitable to direct.*

(6.) *Fear them not* (*v.* 26), because *they can but kill the body* (*v.* 28). Note, it is the duty and interest of Christ's disciples, not to fear the greatest of their adversaries. They who truly fear God, need not fear man; and they who are afraid of the least sin, need not be afraid of the greatest trouble. *The fear of man brings a snare,* a perplexing snare, that disturbs our peace; an entangling snare, by which we are drawn into sin; and, therefore, it must be carefully watched, and striven, and prayed against. Be the times never so difficult, enemies never so outrageous, and events never so threatening, yet need we not fear, *yet will we not fear, though the earth be removed,* while we have so good a God, so good a cause, and so *good a hope through grace.*

Yes, this is soon said; but when it comes to the trial, racks and tortures, dungeons and galleys, axes and gibbets, fire and faggot, are terrible things, enough to make the stoutest heart to tremble, and to start back, especially when it is plain, that they may be avoided by a few declining steps; and therefore, to fortify us against this temptation, we have here,

[1.] A good reason against this fear, taken from the limited power of the enemies; they *kill the body,* that is the utmost their rage can extend to; hitherto they can go, if God permit them, but no further; *they are not able to kill the soul,* nor to do it any hurt, and the soul is the man. By this it appears, that the soul does not (as some dream) fall asleep at death, nor is deprived of thought and perception; for then the killing of the body would be the killing of the soul too. The soul is killed when it is separated from God and his love, which is its life, and is made a vessel of his wrath; now this is out of the reach of their power. *Tribulation, distress, and persecution* may separate us from all the world, but cannot part between us and God, cannot make us either not to love him, or not to be loved by him, Rom. 8:35, 37. If, therefore, we were more concerned about our souls, as our jewels, we should be less afraid of men, whose power cannot rob us of them; they can but *kill the body,* which would quickly die of itself, *not the soul,* which will enjoy itself and its God in spite of them. They can but crush the cabinet: a heathen set the tyrant at defiance with this, *Tunde capsam Anaxarchi, Anaxarchum nom laedis — you may abuse the case of Anaxarchus, you cannot injure Anaxarchus himself.* The pearl of price is untouched. Seneca undertakes to make it out, that you cannot hurt a wise and good man, because death itself is no real evil to him. *Si maximum illud ultra quod nihil habent iratae leges, aut saevissimi domini minantur, in quo imperium suum fortuna consumit, aequo placidoque animo accipimus, et scimus mortem malum non esse ob hoc, ne injuriam quidem — If with calmness and composure we meet that last extremity, beyond which injured laws and merciless tyrants have nothing to inflict, and in which fortune terminates her dominion, we know that death is not an evil, because it does not occasion the slightest injury.* Seneca *De Constantiâ.*

[2.] A good remedy against it, and that is, to fear God. *Fear him who is able to destroy both soul and body in hell.* Note, First, *Hell* is the destruction both of *soul and body;* not of the *being* of either, but the *well*-being of both; it is the ruin of the whole man; if the soul be lost, the body is lost too. They sinned together; the body was the soul's tempter to sin, and its tool in sin, and they must eternally suffer together. Secondly, This destruction comes from the power of God: he *is able to destroy;* it is a destruction from his *glorious power* (2 Th. 1:9); *he will* in it *make his power known;* not only his authority to sentence, but his ability to execute the sentence, Rom. 9:22. Thirdly, God *is therefore to be feared,* even by the best saints in this world. *Knowing the terrors of the Lord, we persuade men* to *stand in awe of him. If according to his fear so is his wrath,* then *according to his wrath so* should *his fear* be, especially because *none knows the power of his anger,* Ps. 90:11. When Adam, in innocency, was awed by a threatening, let none of Christ's disciples think that they need not the restraint of a holy fear. *Happy is the man that fears always.* The *God of Abraham,* who was then dead, is called the *Fear of Isaac,* who was yet alive, Gen. 31:42, 53. Fourthly, The fear of God, and of his power reigning in the soul, will be a sovereign antidote against the fear of man. It is better to fall under the frowns of all the world, than under God's frowns, and therefore, as it is most right in itself, so it is most safe for us, *to obey God rather than men,* Acts 4:19. They who *are afraid of a man that shall die, forget the Lord their Maker,* Isa. 51:12, 13; Neh. 4:14.

(7.) *What I tell you in darkness, that speak ye in light* (*v.* 27); "whatever hazards you run, go on with your work, publishing and proclaiming the everlasting gospel to all the world; that is your business, mind that. The design of the enemies is not merely to destroy *you,* but to suppress *that,* and, therefore, whatever be the consequence, publish *that.*" *What I tell you, that speak ye.* Note, That which the apostles have delivered to us is the same that *they received from Jesus Christ,* Heb. 2:3. They spake what he told them — *that, all that,* and *nothing but that.* Those ambassadors received their instructions in private, *in darkness,* in the ear, in corners, in parables. *Many things Christ spake openly, and nothing in secret* varying from what he preached in public, Jn. 18:20. But the particular instructions which he gave his disciples after his resurrection, concerning *the things pertaining to the kingdom of God,* were whispered in the ear (Acts 1:3), for then *he never showed himself openly.* But they must deliver their embassy publicly, *in the light,* and *upon the house-tops;* for the doctrine of the gospel is what all are concerned in (Prov. 1:20, 21; 8:2, 3), therefore *he that hath ears to hear, let him hear.* The first indication of the reception of the Gentiles into the church, was *upon a house-top,* Acts 10:9. Note, There is no part of Christ's gospel that needs, upon any account, to be concealed; *the whole counsel of God must be revealed,* Acts 20:27. In never so mixed a multitude let it be plainly and fully delivered.

2. By way of comfort and encouragement. Here is very much said to that purpose, and all little enough, considering the many hardships they were to grapple with, throughout the course of their ministry, and their present weakness, which was such, as that, without some powerful support, they could scarcely bear even the prospect of such usage; Christ therefore shows them why they should be of good cheer.

(1.) Here is one word peculiar to their present mission, *v.* 23. *Ye shall not have gone over the cities of Israel, till the Son of man be come.* They were to preach that *the kingdom of the Son of man,* the Messiah, was *at hand;* they were to pray, *Thy kingdom come:* now they should *not have gone over all the cities of Israel,* thus praying and thus preaching, before that kingdom should come, in the exaltation of Christ, and the pouring out of the Spirit. It was a comfort, [1.] That what they said should be made good: they said *the Son of man* is coming, and *behold, he comes.* Christ *will confirm the word of his messengers,* Isa. 44:26. [2.] That it should be made good quickly. Note, It is matter of comfort to Christ's labourers, that their working time will be short, and soon over; the hireling has his day; the work and warfare will in a little time be accomplished. [3.] That then they should be advanced to a higher station. *When the Son of man comes, they shall be endued with greater power from on high;* now they were sent forth as agents and envoys, but in a little time their commission should be enlarged, and they should be sent forth as plenipotentiaries into all the world.

(2.) Here are many words that relate to their work in general, and the troubles they were to meet with in it; and *they are good words and comfortable words.*

[1.] That their sufferings were *for a testimony against them and the Gentiles, v.* 18. When the Jewish consistories transfer you to the Roman governors, that they may have you put to death, your being hurried thus from one judgment-seat to another, will help to make your testimony the more public, and will give you an opportunity of bringing the gospel to the Gentiles, as well as to the Jews; nay, you will testify to them, and against them, by the very troubles you undergo. Note, God's people, and especially God's ministers, are his witnesses (Isa. 43:10), not only in their *doing* work, but in their *suffering* work. Hence they are called martyrs — *witnesses* for Christ, that his truths are of undoubted certainty and value; and, being witnesses for him, they are witnesses against those who oppose him and his gospel. The sufferings of the martyrs, as they witness to the truth of the gospel they profess, so they are testimonies of the enmity of their persecutors, and both ways they are a testimony against them, and will be produced in evidence in the great day, when *the saints shall judge the world;* and the reason of the sentence will be, *Inasmuch as ye did it unto these, ye did it unto me.* Now if their sufferings be a testimony, how cheerfully should they be borne! for the testimony is not finished till those come, Rev. 11:7. If they be Christ's witnesses, they shall be sure to have their charges borne.

[2.] That upon all occasions they should have God's special presence with them, and the immediate assistance of his Holy Spirit, particularly when they should be called out to bear their testimony *before governors and kings; it shall be given you* (said Christ) *in that same hour what ye shall speak.* Christ's disciples were chosen *from among the foolish of the world,* unlearned and ignorant men, and, therefore, might justly distrust their own abilities, especially when they were called before great men. When Moses was sent to Pharaoh, he complained, *I am not eloquent,* Ex. 4:10. When Jeremiah was set over the kingdoms, he objected, *I am but a child,* Jer. 1:6, 10. Now, in answer to this suggestion, First, they are here promised that *it should be given them,* nor some time before, but *in that same hour, what they should speak.* They shall speak *extempore,* and yet shall speak as much to the purpose, as if it had been never so well studied. Note, When God calls us out to speak for him, we may depend upon him to teach us what to say; even then, when we labour under the greatest disadvantages and discouragements. Secondly, They are here assured, that the blessed Spirit should draw up their plea for them. *It is not ye that speak, but the Spirit of your Father, which speaketh in you, v.* 20. They were not left to themselves upon such an occasion, but God undertook for them; his Spirit of wisdom spoke *in* them, as sometimes his providence wonderfully spoke *for* them, and by both together they were manifested in the consciences even of their persecutors. God gave them an ability, not only to speak to the purpose, but what they did say, to say it with holy zeal. The same Spirit that assisted them in the pulpit, assisted them at the bar. They cannot but come off well, who have such an advocate; to whom God says, as he did to Moses (Ex. 4:12), *Go, and I will be with thy mouth, and with thy heart.*

[3.] That *he that endures to the end shall be saved, v.* 22. Here it is very comfortable to consider, First, that there will be an *end* of these troubles; they may last long, but will not last always. Christ comforted himself with this, and so may his followers; *The things concerning me have an end,* Lu. 22:37. *Dabit Deus his quoque finem — These also will God bring to a termination.* Note, A believing prospect of the period of our troubles, will be of great use to support us under them. *The weary will be at rest, when the wicked cease from troubling,* Job 3:17. God will give an expected *end,* Jer. 29:11. The troubles may seem tedious, *like the days of a hireling,* but, blessed be God, they are not everlasting. Secondly, That while they continue, they may be *endured;* as they are not *eternal,* so they are not *intolerable;* they may be borne, and borne *to the end,* because the sufferers shall be borne up under them, in everlasting arms: *The strength shall be according to the day,* 1 Co. 10:13. Thirdly, Salvation will be the eternal recompence of all those *that endure to the end.* The weather stormy, and the way foul, but the pleasure of home will make amends for all. A believing regard to the crown of glory has been in all ages the cordial and support of suffering saints, 2 Co. 4:16; 17, 18; Heb. 10:34. This is not only an encouragement to us to *endure,* but an engagement to *endure to the end.* They who *endure but awhile, and in time of temptation fall away,* have run in vain, and lose all that they have attained; but they who persevere, are sure of the prize, and they only. *Be faithful unto death,* and then thou shalt have *the crown of life.*

[4.] That whatever hard usage the disciples of Christ meet with, it is no more than what their Master met with before (*v.* 24, 25). *The disciple is not above his master.* We find this given them as a reason, why they should not hesitate to perform the meanest duties, no, not washing one another's feet. Jn. 13:16. Here it is given as a reason, why they should not stumble at the hardest sufferings. They are reminded of this saying, Jn. 15:20. It is a proverbial expression, *The servant is not better than his master,* and, therefore, let him not expect to fare *better.* Note, First, Jesus Christ is our *Master,* our teaching *Master,* and we are his disciples, to learn of him; our ruling *master,* and we are his servants to obey him: He is *Master* of the house, *oikodespotēs*, has a despotic power in the church, which is his family. Secondly, Jesus Christ our Lord and Master met with very hard usage from the world; they called him Beelzebub, the god of flies, the name of the chief of the devils, with whom they said he was in league. It is hard to say which is here more to be wondered at, the wickedness of men who thus abused Christ, or the patience of Christ, who suffered himself to be thus abused; that he who was the God of glory should be stigmatized as the god of flies; the King of Israel, as the god of Ekron; the Prince of light and life, as the prince of the powers of death and darkness; that Satan's greatest Enemy and Destroyer should be run down as his confederate, and yet *endure such contradiction of sinners.* Thirdly, The consideration of the ill treatment which Christ met with in the world, should engage us to expect and prepare for the like, and to bear it patiently. Let us not think it strange, if they who hated him hate his followers, for his sake; nor think it hard if they who are shortly to be made *like him in glory,* be now made *like him in sufferings.* Christ began in the *bitter cup,* let us be willing to pledge him; his bearing the cross made it easy for us.

[5.] That *there is nothing covered that shall not be revealed, v.* 26. We understand this, First, Of the revealing of the gospel to all the world. "Do you *publish* it (*v.* 27), for it shall be published. The truths which are now, as mysteries, hid from the children of men, shall all be made known, to all nations, in their own language," Acts 2:11. The *ends of the earth must see this salvation.* Note, It is a great encouragement to those who are doing Christ's work, that it is a work which shall certainly be done. It is a plough which God will speed. Or, Secondly, Of the clearing up of the innocency of Christ's suffering servants, that are called Beelzebub; their true character is now invidiously disguised with false colours, but however their innocency and excellency are now *covered,* they *shall be revealed;* sometimes it is in a great measure done in this world, when the righteousness of the saints is made, by subsequent events, to *shine forth as the light:* however it will be done at the great day, when their glory shall be manifested to all the world, angels and men, to whom they are now *made spectacles,* 1 Co. 4:9. All their reproach shall be rolled away, and their graces and services, that are now *covered, shall be revealed,* 1 Co. 4:5. Note, It is matter of comfort to the people of God, under all the calumnies and censures of men, that there will be a resurrection of *names* as well as of *bodies,* at the last day, when *the righteous shall shine forth as the sun.* Let Christ's ministers faithfully reveal his truths, and then leave it to him, in due time, to reveal their integrity.

[6.] That the providence of God is in a special manner conversant about the saints, in their suffering, *v.* 29–31. It is good to have recourse to our first principles, and particularly to the doctrine of God's universal providence, extending itself to all the creatures, and all their actions, even the smallest and most minute. The light of nature teaches us this, and it is comfortable to all men, but especially to all good men, who can in faith call this God their Father, and for whom he has a tender concern. See here,

First, The general extent of providence to all the creatures, even the least, and least considerable, to the *sparrows, v.* 29. These little animals are of so small account, that one of them is not valued; there must go two to be worth a *farthing* (nay, you shall have five for a halfpenny, Lu. 12:6), and yet they are not shut out of the divine care; *One of them shall not fall to the ground without your Father:* That is, 1. They do not light on the *ground* for food, to pick up a grain of corn, but *your* heavenly *Father,* by his providence, laid it ready for them. In the parallel place, Lu. 12:6, it is thus expressed, *Not one of them is forgotten before God,* forgotten to be provided for; *he feedeth them,* ch. 6:26. Now he that feeds the sparrows, will not starve the saints. 2. They do *not fall to the ground* by death, either a natural or a violent death, without the notice of God: though they are so small a part of the creation, yet even their death comes within the notice of the divine providence; much more does the death of his disciples. Observe, The birds that soar above, when they die, *fall to the ground;* death brings the highest to the earth. Some think that Christ here alludes to the *two sparrows* that were used in cleansing the leper (Lev. 14:4–6); the two birds in the margin are called *sparrows;* of these one was killed, and so *fell to the ground,* the other was let go. Now it seemed a casual thing which of the two was killed; the persons employed took which they pleased, but God's providence designed, and

determined which. Now this God, who has such an eye to the sparrows, because they are his creatures, much more will have an eye to you, who are his children. If a sparrow die not *without your Father,* surely a man does not, — a Christian, — a minister, — my friend, my child. A bird falls not into the fowler's net, nor by the fowler's shot, and so comes not to be sold in the market, but according to the direction of providence; your enemies, like subtle fowlers, *lay snares for* you, and *privily shoot at* you, but they cannot take you, they cannot hit you, unless God give them leave. Therefore be not afraid of death, for your enemies have no power against you, but what is *given them from above.* God can break their bows and snares (Ps. 38:12–15; 64:4, 7), and make our souls to *escape as a bird* (Ps. 124:7); *Fear ye not, therefore, v.* 31. Note, There is enough in the doctrine of God's providence to silence all the fears of God's people: *Ye are of more value than many sparrows.* All men are so, for the other creatures were made for man, and *put under his feet* (Ps. 8:6–8); much more the disciples of Jesus Christ, who are the excellent ones of the earth, however contemned, as if not worth one sparrow.

Secondly, The particular cognizance which providence takes of the disciples of Christ, especially in their sufferings (*v.* 30), *But the very hairs of your head are all numbered.* This is a proverbial expression, denoting the account which God takes and keeps of all the concernments of his people, even of those that are most minute, and least regarded. This is not to be made a matter of curious enquiry, but of encouragement to live in a continual dependence upon God's providential care, which extends itself to all occurrences, yet without disparagement to the infinite glory, or disturbance to the infinite rest, of the Eternal Mind. If God numbers their hairs, much more does he number their heads, and take care of their lives, their comforts, their souls. It intimates, that God takes more care of them, than they do of themselves. They who are solicitous to number their money, and goods, and cattle, yet were never careful to number their hairs, which fall and are lost, and they never miss them: but God *numbers the hairs of* his people, and *not a hair of their head shall perish* (Lu. 21:18); not the least hurt shall be done them, but upon a valuable consideration: so precious to God are his saints, and their lives and deaths!

[7.] That he will shortly, in the day of triumph, own those who now own him, in the day of trial, when those who deny him shall be for ever disowned and rejected by him, *v.* 32, 33. Note, First, It is our duty, and if we do it, it will hereafter be our unspeakable honour and happiness, to *confess Christ before men.* 1. It is our duty, not only to believe in Christ, but to profess that faith, in suffering for him, when we are called to it, as well as in serving him. We must never be ashamed of our relation to Christ, our attendance on him, and our expectations from him: hereby the sincerity of our faith, is evidenced, his name glorified, and others edified. 2. However this may expose us to reproach and trouble now, we shall be abundantly recompensed for that, *in the resurrection of the just,* when it will be our unspeakable honour and happiness to hear Christ say (what would we more?) "*Him will I confess,* though a poor worthless worm of the earth; this is one of mine, one of my friends and favourites, who loved me and was beloved by me; the purchase of my blood, the workmanship of my Spirit; *I will confess him before my Father,* when it will do him the most service; I will speak a good word for him, when he appears before *my Father* to receive his doom; I will present him, will represent him to *my Father.*" Those who honour Christ he will thus honour. They honour him *before men;* that is a *poor* thing: he will honour them *before his Father;* that is a *great* thing. Secondly, It is a dangerous thing for any to deny and disown *Christ before men;* for they who so do will be disowned by him *in the great day,* when they have most need of him: he will not own them for his servants who would not own him for their master: *I tell you, I know you not,* ch. 7:23. In the first ages of Christianity, when for a man to *confess Christ* was to venture all that was dear to him in this world, it was more a trial of sincerity, than it was afterwards, when it had secular advantages attending it.

[8.] That the foundation of their discipleship was laid in such a temper and disposition, as would make sufferings very light and easy to them; and it was upon the condition of a preparedness for suffering, that Christ took them to be his followers, *v.* 37–39. He told them at first, that they were *not worthy of* him, if they were not willing to part with all for

him. Men hesitate not at those difficulties which necessarily attend their profession, and which they counted upon, when they undertook that profession; and they will either cheerfully submit to those fatigues and troubles, or disclaim the privileges and advantages of their profession. Now, in the Christian profession, they are reckoned unworthy the dignity and felicity of it, that put not such a value upon their interest in Christ, as to prefer that before any other interests. They cannot expect the gains of a bargain, who will not come up to the terms of it. Now thus the terms are settled; if religion be worth *any* thing, it is worth *every* thing: and, therefore, all who believe the truth of it, will soon come up to the price of it; and they who make it their business and bliss, will make every thing else to yield to it. They who like not Christ on these terms, may leave him at their peril. Note, It is very encouraging to think, that whatever we leave, or lose, or suffer for Christ, we do not make a hard bargain for ourselves. Whatever we part with for this pearl of price, we may comfort ourselves with this persuasion, that it is well worth what we give for it. The terms are, that we must prefer Christ.

First, Before our nearest and dearest relations; *father or mother, son or daughter.* Between these relations, because there is little room left for envy, there is commonly more room for love, and, therefore, these are instanced, as relations which are most likely to affect us. Children must love their parents, and parents must love their children; but if they love them better than Christ, they are unworthy of him. As we must not be *deterred* from Christ by the hatred of our relations which he spoke of (*v.* 21, 35, 36), so we must not be *drawn* from him, by their love. Christians must be as Levi, who *said to his father, I have not seen him,* Deu. 33:9.

Secondly, Before our ease and safety. We must *take up our cross and follow him,* else we are *not worthy* of him. Here observe, 1. They who would *follow Christ,* must expect *their cross and take it up.* 2. In taking *up the cross,* we must *follow Christ's* example, and bear it as he did. 3. It is a great encouragement to us, when we meet with crosses, that in bearing them we *follow Christ,* who has showed us the way; and that if we follow him faithfully, he will lead us through sufferings like him, to glory with him.

Thirdly, Before life itself, *v.* 39. *He that findeth his life shall lose it;* he that thinks he had found it when he has saved it, and kept it, by denying Christ, *shall lose it* in an eternal death; but *he that loseth his life for Christ's sake,* that will part with it rather than deny Christ, *shall find it,* to his unspeakable advantage, an eternal life. They are best prepared for the life to come, that sit most loose to this present life.

[9.] That Christ himself would so heartily espouse their cause, as to show himself a friend to all their friends, and to repay all the kindnesses that should at any time be bestowed upon them, *v.* 40–42. *He that receiveth you, receiveth me.*

First, It is here implied, that though the generality would reject them, yet they should meet with some who would receive and entertain them, would bid the message welcome to their hearts, and the messengers to their houses, for the sake of it. Why was the gospel market made, but that if some will not, others will. In the worst of times there is a remnant according to the election of grace. Christ's ministers shall not *labour in vain.*

Secondly, Jesus Christ takes what is done to his faithful ministers, whether in kindness or in unkindness, as done to himself, and reckons himself *treated* as they are *treated. He that receiveth you, receiveth me.* Honour or contempt put upon an ambassador reflects honour or contempt upon the prince that sends him, and ministers are *ambassadors for Christ.* See how Christ may still be entertained by those who would testify their respects to him; his people and ministers we have always with us; and he is *with them always,* even to the end of the world. Nay, the honour rises higher, *He that receiveth me, receiveth him that sent me.* Not only Christ takes it as done to himself, but through Christ God does so too. By entertaining Christ's ministers, they entertain not *angels unawares,* but Christ, nay, and God himself, and *unawares* too, as appears, ch. 25:37. *When saw we thee an hungered?*

Thirdly, That though the kindness done to Christ's disciples be never so small, yet if there be occasion for it, and ability to do no more, it shall be accepted, though it be *but a cup of cold water given to one of these little ones, v.* 42. They are *little ones,* poor and weak, and often stand in need of refreshment, and glad of the least. The extremity may be such, that a *cup of cold water* may be a great favour. Note, Kindnesses shown to Christ's disciples are valued in Christ's books, not according to the cost of the gift, but according to the love and affection of the giver. On that score the widow's mite not only passed current, but was stamped high, Lu. 21:3, 4. Thus they who are truly rich in graces may be rich in good works, though poor in the world.

Fourthly, That kindness to Christ's disciples which he will accept, must b done with an eye to Christ, and for his sake. A prophet must be received *in the name of a prophet,* and a *righteous man* in the name of a *righteous man,* and one of those *little ones* in *the name of a disciple;* not because they are learned, or witty, nor because they are our relations or neighbours, but because they are righteous, and so bear Christ's image; because they are prophets and disciples, and so are sent on Christ's errand. It is a believing regard to Christ that puts an acceptable value upon the kindnesses done to his ministers. Christ does not interest himself in the matter, unless we first interest him in it. *Ut tibi debeam aliquid pro eo quod praestas, debes non tantum mihi praestare, sed tanquam mihi — If you wish me to feel an obligation to you for any service you render, you must not only perform the service, but you must convince me that you do it for my sake.* Seneca.

Fifthly, That kindnesses shown to Christ's people and ministers, shall not only be accepted, but richly and suitably rewarded. There is a great deal to be gotten, by doing good offices to Christ's disciples. If it be done to the Lord, he will repay them again with interest; for he is *not unrighteous to forget any labour of love,* Heb. 6:10. 1. They shall *receive a reward,* and in no wise *lose it.* He does not say, that they *deserve* a reward; we cannot merit any thing as wages, from the hand of God; but they shall *receive a reward* from the free gift of God; and they shall *in no wise lose it,* as good services often do among men; because they who should reward them are either false or forgetful. The reward may be deferred, the full reward will be deferred, till the resurrection of the just; but it shall in no wise be *lost,* nor shall they be any *losers* by the delay. 2. This is a *prophet's reward,* and a *righteous man's.* That is, either, (1.) The reward that God gives to prophets and righteous men; the blessings conferred upon them shall distil upon their friends. Or, (2.) The reward he gives by prophets and righteous men; in answer to their prayers (Gen. 20:7), *He is a prophet, and he shall pray for thee,* that is a prophet's reward; and by their ministry; when he gives the instructions and comforts of the word, to those who are kind to the preachers of the word, then he sends a *prophet's reward.* Prophets' rewards are spiritual blessings in heavenly things, and if we know how to value them, we shall reckon them good payment.

CHAPTER 11

In this chapter we have, I. The constant and unwearied diligence of our Lord Jesus in his great work of preaching the gospel (*v.* 1). II. His discourse with the disciples of John concerning his being the Messiah (*v.* 2–6). III. The honourable testimony that Christ bore to John Baptist (*v.* 7–15). IV. The sad account he gives of that generation in general, and of some particular places with reference to the success, both of John's ministry and of his own (*v.* 16–24). V. His thanksgiving to his Father for the wise and gracious method he had taken in revealing the great mysteries of the gospel (*v.* 25, 26). VI. His gracious call and invitation of poor sinners to come to him, and to be ruled, and taught, and saved by him (*v.* 27–30). No Where have we more of the terror of gospel woes for warning to us, or of the sweetness of gospel grace for encouragement to us, than in this chapter, which sets before us life and death, the blessing and the curse.

Verses 1–6

The first verse of this chapter some join to the foregoing chapter, and make it (not unfitly) the close of that.

1. The ordination sermon which Christ preached to his disciples in the foregoing chapter is here called his commanding them. Note, Christ's commissions imply commands. Their preaching of the gospel was not only permitted them, but it was enjoined them. It was not a thing respecting which they were left at their liberty, but *necessity was laid upon them,* 1 Co. 9:16. The promises he made them are included in these commands, for the covenant of grace is a *word which he hath commanded,* Ps. 105:8. He *made an end of commanding, etelesendiatassōn.* Note, The instructions Christ gives are full instructions. He goes through with his work.

2. When Christ had said what he had to say to his disciples, he *departed thence.* It should seem they were very loth to leave their Master, till *he departed* and separated himself from them; as the nurse withdraws the hand, that the child may learn to go by itself. Christ would now teach them how to live, and how to work, without his bodily presence. It was *expedient for them,* that Christ should thus go away for awhile, that they might be prepared for his long departure, and that, by the help of the Spirit, their own hands might be *sufficient for them* (Deu. 33:7), and they might not be always children. We have little account of what they did now pursuant to their commission. They went abroad, no doubt; probably into Judea (for in Galilee the gospel had been mostly preached hitherto), publishing the doctrine of Christ, and working miracles in his name: but still in a more immediate dependence upon him, and not being long from him; and thus they were trained up, by degrees, for their great work.

3. Christ departed, *to teach and preach* in the cities whither he sent his disciples before him to *work miracles* (*ch.* 10:1–8), and so to raise people's expectations, and to make way for his entertainment. Thus was the *way of the Lord prepared;* John prepared it by bringing people to *repentance,* but he did *no miracles.* The disciples go further, they *work miracles* for confirmation. Note, Repentance and faith prepare people for the blessings of the kingdom of heaven, which Christ gives. Observe, When Christ empowered them to *work miracles,* he employed himself in *teaching* and *preaching,* as if that were the more honourable of the two. That was but in order to do this. Healing the sick was the *saving of bodies,* but preaching the gospel was to the *saving of souls.* Christ had directed his disciples to preach (*ch.* 10:7), yet he did not leave off preaching himself. He set them to work, not for his own ease, but for the ease of the country, and was not the less busy for employing them. How unlike are they to Christ, who yoke others only that they may themselves be idle! Note, the increase and multitude of labourers in the Lord's work should be made not an excuse for our negligence, but an encouragement to our diligence. The more busy others are, the more busy we should be, and all little enough, so much work is there to be done. Observe, he went to preach *in their cities,* which were populous places; he cast the net of the gospel where there were most fish to be enclosed. Wisdom cries in *the cities* (Prov. 1:21), *at the entry of the city* (Prov. 8:3), in *the cities of the Jews,* even of them who made light of him, who notwithstanding had the first offer.

What he preached we are not told, but it was probably to the same purpose with his sermon on the mount. But here is next recorded a message which John Baptist sent to Christ, and his return to it, *v.* 2–6. We heard before that Jesus heard of John's sufferings, *ch.* 4:12. Now we are told that John, in prison, hears of Christ's doings. He *heard in the prison the works of Christ;* and no doubt he was glad to hear of them, for he was a true friend of the Bridegroom, Jn. 3:29. Note, When one useful instrument is laid aside, God knows how to raise up many others in the stead of it. The work went on, though John was in prison, and it added no affliction, but a great deal of consolation, to his bonds. Nothing more comfortable to God's people in distress, than to *hear of the works of Christ;* especially to experience them in their own souls. This turns a prison into a palace. Some way or other Christ will convey the notices of his love to those that are in trouble for conscience sake. John could not see the works of Christ, but he heard of them with pleasure. And blessed are they who *have not seen,* but only heard, and yet *have believed.*

Now John Baptist, hearing of Christ's works, sent two of his disciples to him; and what passed between them and him we have here an account of. Here is,

I. The question they had to propose to him: *Art thou he that should come, or do we look for another?* This was a serious and important question; *Art thou the Messiah promised, or not? Art thou the Christ? Tell us.* 1. It is taken for granted that the Messiah should come. It was one of the names by which he was known to the Old-Testament saints, *he that cometh or shall come,* Ps. 118:26. He is now come, but there is another coming of his which we still expect. 2. They intimate, that if this be not *he,* they would *look for another.* Note, We must not be weary of looking for him that is to come, nor ever say, we will not more expect him till we come to enjoy him. Though he tarry, wait for him, for he that shall come will come, though not in our time. 3. They intimate likewise, that if they be convinced that this is he, they will not be sceptics, they will be satisfied, and will look *for no other.* 4. They therefore ask, *Art thou he?* John had said for his part, *I am not the Christ,* Jn. 1:20. Now, (1.) Some think that John sent this question for his own satisfaction. It is true he had borne a noble testimony to Christ; he had declared him to be the *Son of God* (Jn. 1:34), the Lamb of God (*v.* 29), and he that *should baptize with the Holy Ghost* (*v.* 33), and *sent of God* (Jn. 3:34), which were great things. But he desired to be further and more fully assured, that he was the Messiah that had been so long promised and expected. Note, In matters relating to Christ and our salvation by him, it is good to be sure. Christ appeared not in that external pomp and power in which it was expected he should appear; his own disciples stumbled at this, and perhaps John did so; Christ saw something of this at the bottom of this enquiry, when he said, *blessed is he who shall not be offended in me.* Note, It is hard, even for good men, to bear up against vulgar errors. (2.) John's doubt might arise from his own present circumstances. He was a prisoner, and might be tempted to think, if Jesus be indeed the Messiah, whence is it that I, his friend and forerunner, am brought into this trouble, and am left to be so long in it, and he never looks after me, never visits me, nor sends to me, enquires not after me, does nothing either to sweeten my imprisonment or hasten my enlargement? Doubtless there was a good reason why our Lord Jesus did not go to John in prison, lest there should seem to have been a compact between them: but John construed it into a neglect, and it was perhaps a shock to his faith in Christ. Note, [1.] Where there is true faith, yet there may be a mixture of unbelief. The best are not always alike strong. [2.] Troubles for Christ, especially when they continue long unrelieved, are such trials of faith as sometimes prove too hard to be borne up against. [3.] The remaining unbelief of good men may sometimes, in an hour of temptation, strike at the root, and call in question the most fundamental truths which were thought to be well settled. *Will the Lord cast off for ever?* But we will hope that John's faith did not fail in this matter, only he desired to have it strengthened and confirmed. Note, The best saints have need of the best helps they can get for the strengthening of their faith, and the arming of themselves against temptations to infidelity. Abraham believed, and yet desired a sign (Gen. 15:6, 8), so did Gideon, Jdg. 6:36, 37. But, (3.) Others think that John sent his disciples to Christ with this question, not so much for his own satisfaction as for theirs. Observe, Though he was a prisoner they adhered to him, attended on him, and were ready to receive instructions from him; they loved him, and would not leave him. Now, [1.] They were weak in knowledge, and wavering in their faith, and needed instruction and confirmation; and in this matter they were somewhat prejudiced; being jealous *for their* master, they were jealous *of our* Master; they were loth to acknowledge Jesus to be the Messiah, because he eclipsed John, and are loth to believe their own master when they think he speaks against himself and them. Good men are apt to have their judgments blessed by their interest. Now John would have their mistakes rectified, and wished them to be as well satisfied as he himself was. Note, The strong ought to consider the infirmities of the weak, and to do what they can to help them: and such as we cannot help ourselves we should send to those that can. *When thou art converted, strengthen thy brethren.* [2.] John was all along industrious to turn over his disciples to Christ, as from the grammar-school to the academy. Perhaps he foresaw his death approaching, and therefore would bring his disciples to be better acquainted with Christ, under whose guardianship he must leave them. Note, Ministers' business is to direct every body to Christ. And those who would know the certainty of the doctrine of Christ, must apply themselves to him, who is come to give an understanding. They who would grow in grace must be inquisitive.

II. Here is Christ's answer to this question, *v.* 4–6. It was not so direct and express, as when he said, *I that speak unto thee am he;* but it was a real answer, an answer in fact. Christ will have us to spell out the convincing evidences of gospel truths, and to take pains in digging for knowledge.

1. He points them to what they heard and saw, which they must tell John, that he might from thence take occasion the more fully to instruct and convince them out of their own mouths. Go and tell him *what you hear and see.* Note, Our senses may and ought to be appealed to in those things that are their proper objects. Therefore the popish doctrine of the real presence agrees not with the truth *as it is in Jesus;* for Christ refers us to the things we *hear and see. Go and tell John,*

(1.) *What you see* of the *power of Christ's miracles;* you see how, by the word of Jesus, *the blind receive their sight,* the *lame walk,* etc. Christ's miracles were done openly, and in the view of all; for they feared not the strongest and most impartial scrutiny. *Veritas no quaerit angulos — Truth seeks not concealment.* They are to be considered, [1.] As the *acts of a divine power.* None but the God of nature could thus overrule and outdo the power of nature. It is particularly spoken of as God's prerogative to *open the eyes of the blind,* Ps. 146:8. Miracles are therefore the broad seal of heaven, and the doctrine they are affixed to must be of God, for his power will never contradict his truth; nor can it be imagined that he should set his seal to a lie; however *lying wonders* may be vouched for in proof of *false doctrines, true miracles* evince a divine commission; such Christ's were, and they leave no room to doubt that he was sent of God, and that his doctrine was his that *sent him.* [2.] As the *accomplishment of a divine prediction.* It was foretold (Isa. 35:5, 6), that our God should come, and that then *the eyes of the blind should be opened.* Now if the works of Christ agree with the words of the prophet, as it is plain they do, then no doubt but this is our God whom we have waited for, who shall *come with a recompence;* this is he who is so much wanted.

(2.) Tell him *what you hear* of the *preaching of his gospel,* which accompanies his miracles. Faith, though confirmed by seeing, comes by hearing. Tell him, [1.] That *the poor preach the gospel;* so some read it. It proves Christ's divine mission, that those whom he employed in founding his kingdom were poor men, destitute of all secular advantages, who, therefore, could never have carried their point, if they had not been carried on by a divine power. [2.] That *the poor have the gospel preached to them.* Christ's auditory is made up of such as the scribes and Pharisees despised, and looked upon with contempt, and the *rabbies* would not instruct, because they were notable to pay them. The *Old-Testament* prophets were sent mostly to kings and princes, but Christ preached to the *congregations of the poor.* It was foretold that the *poor of the flock* should *wait upon him,* Zec. 11:11. Note, Christ's gracious condescensions and compassions to *the poor,* are an evidence that it was he that should bring to the world the tender mercies of our God. It was foretold that the *Son of David* should be the *poor man's King,* Ps. 72:2, 4, 12, 13. Or we may understand it, not so much of the *poor of the world,* as the *poor in spirit,* and so that scripture is fulfilled, Isa. 61:1, *He hath anointed me to preach glad tidings to the meek.* Note, It is a proof of Christ's divine mission that his doctrine is gospel indeed; good news to those who are truly humbled in sorrow for their sins, and truly humble in the denial of self; to them it is accommodated, for whom God always declared he had mercy in store. [3.] That the *poor receive the gospel,* and are wrought upon by it, they are evangelized, they receive and entertain the gospel, are leavened by it, and delivered into it as into a mould. Note, The wonderful efficacy of the gospel is a proof of its divine original. The poor are *wrought upon* by it. The prophets complained of *the poor,* that they *knew not the way of the Lord,* Jer. 5:4. They could do no good upon them; but the gospel of Christ made its way into their untutored minds.

2. He pronounces a *blessing* on those that *were not offended in him, v.* 6. So clear are these evidences of Christ's mission, that they who are not wilfully prejudiced against him, and scandalized in him (so the word is), cannot but receive his doctrine, and so be *blessed in him.* Note, (1.) There are many things in Christ which they who are ignorant and unthinking are apt to be offended at, some circumstances for the sake of which they reject the substance of his gospel. The meanness of his appearance, his education at Nazareth, the poverty of his life, the despicableness of his followers, the slights which the great men put upon him, the strictness of his doctrine, the contradiction it gives to flesh and blood, and the sufferings that attend the profession of his name; these are things that keep many from him, who otherwise cannot but see much of God in him. Thus he is set *for the fall of many,* even in Israel (Lu. 2:34), a *Rock of offence,* 1 Pt. 2:8. (2.) They are happy who get over these offences. *Blessed are they.* The expression intimates, that it is a difficult thing to conquer these prejudices, and a dangerous thing not to conquer them; but as to those, who, notwithstanding this opposition, to believe in Christ, their faith will be found so much the more, to *praise, and honour, and glory.*

Verses 7–15

We have here the high encomium which our Lord Jesus gave of John the Baptist; not only to revive his honour, but to revive his work. Some of Christ's disciples might perhaps take occasion from the question John sent, to reflect upon him, as weak and wavering, and inconsistent with himself, to prevent which Christ gives him this character. Note, It is our duty to consult the reputation of our brethren, and not only to remove, but to obviate and prevent, jealousies and ill thoughts of them; and we must take all occasions, especially such as discover any thing of infirmity, to speak well of those who are praiseworthy, and to give them that *fruit of their hands.* John the Baptist, when he was upon the stage, and Christ in privacy and retirement, bore testimony to Christ; and now that Christ appeared publicly, and John was under a cloud, he bore testimony to John. Note, They who have a confirmed interest themselves, should improve it for the helping of the credit and reputation of others, whose character claims it, but whose temper or present circumstances put them out of the way of it. This is giving honour to whom honour is due. John had abased himself to honour Christ (Jn. 3:20, 30, *ch.* 3:11), had made himself nothing, that Christ might be All, and now Christ dignifies him with this character. Note, They who humble themselves shall be exalted, and those that honour Christ he will honour; those that confess him before men, he will confess, and sometimes *before men* too, even in this world. John had now *finished his testimony,* and now Christ commends him. Note, Christ reserves honour for his servants when they *have done their work,* Jn. 12:26.

Now concerning this commendation of John, observe,

I. That Christ spoke thus honourably of John, not in the hearing of John's disciples, but *as they departed,* just after they were gone, Lu. 7:24. He would not so much as seem to flatter John, nor have these praises of him reported to him. Note, Though we must be forward to give to all their due praise for their encouragement, yet we must avoid every thing that looks like flattery, or may be in danger of puffing them up. They who in other things are mortified to the world, yet cannot well bear their own praise. Pride is a corrupt humour, which we must not feed either in others or in ourselves.

II. That what Christ said concerning John, was intended not only for his praise, but for the people's profit, to revive the remembrance of John's ministry, which had been well attended, but which was now (as other such things used to be) strangely forgotten: they did for a season, and but *for a season, rejoice in his light,* Jn. 5:35. "Now, consider, *what went ye out into the wilderness to see?* Put this question to yourselves." 1. John preached *in the wilderness,* and thither people flocked in crowds to him, though in a *remote* place, and an *inconvenient* one. If teachers be removed into corners, it is better to go after them than to be without them. Now if his preaching was worth taking so much pains to hear it, surely it was worth taking some care to recollect it. The greater the difficulties we have broken through to hear the word, the more we are concerned to profit by it. 2. They went out to him to see him; rather to feed their eyes with the unusual appearance of his person, than to feed their souls with his wholesome instructions; rather for curiosity than for conscience. Note, Many that attend on the word come rather to see and be seen, than to learn and be taught, to have something to talk of, than to be made wise to salvation. Christ puts it to them, *what went ye out to see?* Note, They who attend on the word will be called to an account, what their intentions and what their improvements were. We think when the sermon is done, the care is over; no, then the greatest of the care begins. It will shortly be asked, "What business had you such a time at such an ordinance? *What brought you thither?* Was it custom or company, or was it a desire to honour God and get good? *What have you brought thence?* What knowledge, and grace, and comfort? *What went you to see?"* Note, When we go to read and hear the word, we should see that we aim right in what we do.

III. Let us see what the commendation of John was. They know not what answer to make to Christ's question; well, says Christ, "I will tell you what a man John the Baptist was."

1. "He was a firm, resolute man, and not *a reed shaken with the wind; you* have been so in your thoughts of him, but *he* was not so. He was not wavering in his principles, nor uneven in his conversation; but was remarkable for his steadiness and constant consistency with himself." They who are *weak* as reeds will be *shaken* as reeds; but John was *strong in spirit,* Eph. 4:14. When the wind of popular applause on the one hand blew fresh and fair, when the storm of Herod's rage on the other hand grew fierce and blustering, John was still the same, the same in all weathers. The testimony he had borne to Christ was not the testimony of *a reed,* of a man who was of one mind to-day, and of another to-morrow; it was not a weather-cock testimony; no, his constancy in it is intimated (Jn. 1:20); he *confessed and denied not, but confessed,* and stood to it afterwards, Jn. 3:28. And therefore this question sent by his disciples was not to be construed into any suspicion of the truth of what he had formerly said: therefore the people flocked to him, because he was not as a reed. Note, There is nothing lost in the long run by an unshaken resolution to go on with our work, neither courting the smiles, nor fearing the frowns of men.

2. He was a *self-denying* man, and *mortified* to this world. "Was he a man *clothed in soft raiment?* If so, you would not have gone *into the wilderness* to see him, but to the *court.* You went to see one that had *his raiment of camel's hair,* and a *leathern girdle about his loins;* his mien and habit showed that he was dead to all the pomps of the world and the pleasures of sense; his clothing agreed with the *wilderness* he lived in, and the doctrine he preached there, that of repentance. Now you cannot think that he who was such a stranger to the pleasures of a court, should be brought to change his mind by the terrors of a prison, and now to question whether Jesus be the Messiah or not!" Note, they who have lived a life of mortification, are least likely to be driven off from their religion by persecution. He was not a man clothed in *soft raiment;* such *there are,* but they are *in kings' houses.* Note, It becomes people in all their appearances to be consistent with their character and their situation. They who are preachers must not affect to look like courtiers; nor must they whose lot is cast in common dwellings, be ambitious of the soft clothing which they wear who are in kings' houses. Prudence teaches us to be *of a piece.* John appeared rough and unpleasant, yet they flocked after him. Note, The remembrance of our former zeal in attending on the word of God, should quicken us to, and in, our present work: let it not be said that we have done and suffered so many things *in vain,* have *run in vain* and *laboured in vain.*

3. His greatest commendation of all was his office and ministry, which was more his honour than any personal endowments or qualifications could be; and therefore this is most enlarged upon in a full encomium.

(1.) He was *a prophet,* yea, and *more than a prophet* (*v.* 9); so he said of him who was the great Prophet, to whom all the prophets bear witness. John said of himself, he was not *that prophet,* that great prophet, the Messiah himself; and now Christ (a very competent Judge) says of him, that he was *more than a prophet.* He owned himself inferior to Christ, and Christ owned him superior to all other prophets. Observe, The forerunner of Christ was not a king, but a prophet, lest it should seem that the kingdom of the Messiah had been laid in earthly power; but his immediate forerunner was, as such, a *transcendent* prophet, more than an *Old-Testament prophet;* they all *did virtuously,* but John excelled them all; they *saw Christ's day* at a distance, and their vision was yet for a great while to come; but John saw the day dawn, he saw the sun rise, and told the people of the Messiah, as one that stood among them. They spake of Christ, but he pointed to him; they said, *A virgin shall conceive:* he said, *Behold the Lamb of God!*

(2.) He was the same that was predicted to be Christ's forerunner (*v.* 10); *This is he of whom it is written.* He was prophesied of by the other prophets, and therefore was greater than they. Malachi prophesied concerning John, *Behold, I send my messenger before thy face.* Herein some of Christ's honour was put upon him, that the *Old-Testament* prophets spake and wrote of him; and this honour have all the saints, that their *names* are *written in the Lamb's book of life.* It was great preferment to John above all the prophets, that he was Christ's harbinger. He was a *messenger* sent on a great errand; a messenger, *one among a thousand,* deriving his honour from his whose messenger he was: he is *my messenger* sent *of God.* His business was to *prepare Christ's way,* to dispose people to receive the Saviour, by discovering to them their sin and misery, and their need of a Saviour. This he had said of himself (Jn. 1:23) and now Christ said it of him; intending hereby not only to put an honour upon John's ministry, but to revive people's regard to it, as making way for the Messiah. Note, Much of the beauty of God's dispensations lies in their mutual connection and coherence, and the reference they have one to another. That which advanced John above the

Old-Testament prophets was, that he went immediately before Christ. Note, The nearer any are to Christ, the more truly honourable they are.

(3.) There *was not a greater born of women* than John the Baptist, *v.* 11. Christ knew how to value persons according to the degrees of their worth, and he prefers John before all that went before him, before all that were *born of women* by ordinary generation. Of all that God had raised up and called to any service in his church, John is the most eminent, even beyond Moses himself; for he began to preach the gospel doctrine of remission of sins to those who are truly penitent; and he had more signal revelations from heaven than any of them had; for he *saw heaven opened,* and the *Holy Ghost descend.* He also had great success in his ministry; almost the whole nation flocked to him: none rose on so great a design, or came on so noble an errand, as John did, or had such claims to a welcome reception. Many had been born of women that made a great figure in the world, but Christ prefers John before them. Note, Greatness is not to be measured by appearances and outward splendour, but they are the greatest men who are the greatest saints, and the greatest blessings, who are, as John was, *great in the sight of the Lord,* Lu. 1:15.

Yet this high encomium of John has a surprising limitation, *notwithstanding, he that is least in the kingdom of heaven is greater than he.* [1.] In the kingdom of *glory.* John was a *great* and *good* man, but he was yet in a state of infirmity and imperfection, and therefore came short of glorified saints, and the *spirits of just men made perfect.* Note, First, There are degrees of glory in heaven, some that are less than others there; though every vessel is alike full, all are not alike large and capacious. Secondly, The least saint in heaven is *greater,* and knows more, and loves more, and does more in praising God, and receives more from him, than the greatest in this world. The saints on earth are excellent ones (Ps. 16:3), but those in heaven are much more excellent; the best in this world are *lower than the angels* (Ps. 8:5), the least there are *equal with the angels,* which should make us long for that blessed state, where the *weak shall be as David,* Zec. 12:8. [2.] By the *kingdom of heaven* here, is rather to be understood the *kingdom of grace,* the gospel dispensation in the perfection of its power and purity; and ho mikroteros — *he that is less* in that is *greater than John.* Some understand it of Christ himself, who was younger than John, and, in the opinion of some, less than John, who always spoke diminishingly of himself; *I am a worm, and no man,* yet greater than John; so it agrees with what John the Baptist said (Jn. 1:15), *He that cometh after me is preferred before me.* But it is rather to be understood of the apostles and ministers of the *New Testament,* the evangelical prophets; and the comparison between them and John is not with respect to their personal sanctity, but to their office; John preached Christ coming, but they preached Christ not only come, but *crucified* and *glorified.* John came to the dawning of the gospel-day, and therein excelled the foregoing prophets, but he was taken off before the noon of that day, before the rending of the veil, before Christ's death and resurrection, and the pouring out of the Spirit; so that the least of the apostles and evangelists, having greater discoveries made to them, and being employed in a greater embassy, is *greater than John.* John did no miracles; the apostles wrought many. The ground of this preference is laid in the preference of the *New*-Testament dispensation to that of the *Old* Testament. Ministers of the New Testament therefore excel, because their ministration does so, 2 Co. 3:6, etc. John was a *maximum quod sic — the greatest of his order;* he went to the utmost that the dispensation he was under would allow; but *minimum maximi est majus maximo minimi — the least of the highest order is superior to the first of the lowest;* a dwarf upon a mountain sees further than a giant in the valley. Note, All the true greatness of men is derived from, and denominated by, the gracious manifestation of Christ to them. The best men are no better than he is pleased to make them. What reason have we to be thankful that our lot is cast in the days of the *kingdom of heaven,* under such advantages of light and love! And the greater the advantages, the greater will the account be, if we *receive the grace of God in vain.*

(4.) The great commendation of John the Baptist was, that God owned his ministry, and made it wonderfully successful for the breaking of the ice, and the preparing of people for the *kingdom of heaven. From the days of* the first appearing of *John the Baptist,* until now (which was not much above

two years), a great deal of good was done; so quick was the motion when it came near to Christ the Centre; *The kingdom of heaven suffereth violence — biazetai — vim patitur,* like the violence of an army taking a city by storm, or of a crowd bursting into a house, so the *violent take it by force.* The meaning of this we have in the parallel place, Lu. 16:16. Since that time *the kingdom of God is preached, and every man presseth into it.* Multitudes are wrought upon by the ministry of John, and become his disciples. And it is

[1.] An *improbable* multitude. Those strove for a place in this kingdom, that one would think had no right nor title to it, and so seemed to be intruders, and to make a *tortuous* entry, as our law calls it, a wrongful and forcible one. When the *children of the kingdom* are excluded out of it, and many come into it *from the east and the west,* then it *suffers violence.* Compare this with *ch.* 21:31, 32. The publicans and harlots believed John, whom the scribes and Pharisees rejected, and so went into the kingdom of God before them, *took it over their heads,* while they trifled. Note, It is no breach of good manners to go to heaven before our betters: and it is a great commendation of the gospel from the days of its infancy, that it has brought many to holiness that were very unlikely.

[2.] An *importunate* multitude. This violence denotes a strength, and vigour, and earnestness of desire and endeavour, in those who followed John's ministry, else they would not have come so far to attend upon it. It shows us also, what fervency and zeal are required of all those who design to make heaven of their religion. Note, They who would *enter into the kingdom of heaven* must *strive to enter;* that kingdom suffers a holy violence; self must be denied, the bent and bias, the frame and temper, of the mind must be altered; there are hard sufferings to be undergone, a force to be put upon the corrupt nature; we must run, and wrestle, and fight, and be *in an agony,* and all little enough to win such a prize, and to get over such opposition from without and from within. *The violent take it by force.* They who will have an interest in the great salvation are carried out towards it with a strong desire, will have it *upon any terms,* and not think them hard, nor quit their hold without a blessing, Gen. 32:26. They who will make their calling and election sure must give diligence. The kingdom of heaven was never intended to indulge the ease of triflers, but to be the rest of them that labour. It is a blessed sight; Oh that we could see a greater number, not with an *angry* contention thrusting others out of the kingdom of heaven, but with a *holy* contention thrusting themselves into it!

(5.) The ministry of John was the *beginning of the gospel,* as it is reckoned, Mk. 1:1; Acts 1:22. This is shown here in two things:

[1.] In John the Old Testament dispensation began to die, *v.* 13. So long that ministration continued in full force and virtue, but then it began to decline. Though the obligation of the law of Moses was not removed till Christ's death, yet the discoveries of the Old Testament began to be superseded by the more clear manifestation of the *kingdom of heaven* as *at hand.* Because the *light of the gospel* (as that of nature) was to precede and make way for its *law,* therefore the prophecies of the Old Testament came to an end (*finis perficiens,* not *interficiens — an end of completion, not of duration*), before the precepts of it; so that when Christ says, *all the prophets and the law prophesied until John,* he shows us, First, How the light of the Old Testament was set up; it was set up in *the law and the prophets,* who spoke, though darkly, of Christ and his kingdom. Observe, The *law* is said to prophesy, as well as the *prophets,* concerning him that was to come. Christ *began at Moses* (Lu. 24:27); Christ was foretold by the dumb signs of the Mosaic work, as well as by the more articulate voices of the prophets, and was exhibited, not only in the verbal predictions, but in the personal and real types. Blessed be God that we have both the New-Testament doctrine to explain the Old-Testament prophecies, and the Old-Testament prophecies to confirm and illustrate the New-Testament doctrine (Heb. 1:1); like the two cherubim, they look at each other. The law was given by Moses long ago, and there had been no prophets for three hundred years before John, and yet they are both said to *prophecy until John,* because the law was still observed, and Moses and the prophets still read. Note, The scripture is teaching to this day, though the penmen of it are gone. Moses and the prophets are dead; the apostles and evangelists are dead (Zec. 1:5), but the *word of the Lord endures for ever* (1 Pt. 1:25); the *scrip-*

ture is speaking expressly, though the writers are silent in the dust. Secondly, How this light was *laid aside:* when he says, they *prophesied until John,* he intimates, that their glory was eclipsed by the glory which excelled; their predictions superseded by John's testimony, *Behold the Lamb of God!* Even before the sun rises, the morning light makes candles to shine dim. Their prophecies of a Christ to come became out of date, when John said, *He is come.*

[2.] In him the New-Testament day began to dawn; for (*v.* 14) *This is Elias, that was for to come.* John was as the loop that coupled the two Testaments; as Noah was *Fibula utriusque mundi — the link connecting both worlds,* so was he *utriusque Testamenti — the link connecting both Testaments.* The concluding prophecy of the Old Testament was, *Behold, I will send you Elijah,* Mal. 4:5, 6. Those words prophesied until John, and then, being turned into a history, they ceased to prophecy. First, Christ speaks of it as a great truth, that John the Baptist is the Elias of the New Testament; not Elias *in propria persona — in his own person,* as the carnal Jews expected; he denied that (Jn. 1:21), but one that should come in the spirit and power of Elias (Lu. 1:17), like him in temper and conversation, that should press repentance with terrors, and especially as it is in the prophecy, that should *turn the hearts of the fathers to the children.* Secondly, He speaks of it as a truth, which would not be easily apprehended by those whose expectations fastened upon the temporal kingdom of the Messiah, and introductions to it agreeable. Christ suspects the welcome of it, *if ye will receive it.* Not but that it was true, whether they would receive it or not, but he upbraids them with their prejudices, that they were backward to receive the greatest truths that were opposed to their sentiments, though never so favourable to their interests. Or, "If *you will receive him,* or if you will receive the ministry of John as that of the promised Elias, he will be an Elias to you, to turn you and prepare you for the Lord," Note, Gospel truths are as they are received, a savour of life or death. Christ is a Saviour, and John an Elias, to those who will receive the truth concerning them.

Lastly, Our Lord Jesus closes this discourse with a solemn demand of attention (*v.* 15): *He that hath ears to hear, let him hear;* which intimates, that those things were dark and hard to be understood, and therefore needed attention, but of great concern and consequence, and therefore well deserved it. "Let all people take notice of this, if John be the Elias prophesied of, then certainly here is a great revolution on foot, the Messiah's kingdom is at the door, and the world will shortly be surprised into a happy change. These are things which require your serious consideration, and therefore you are all concerned to hearken to what I say." Note, The things of God are of great and common concern: every one that has *ears to hear* any thing, is concerned to hear this. It intimates, that God requires no more from us but the right use and improvement of the faculties he has already given us. He requires those to hear that have ears, those to use their reason that have reason. Therefore people are ignorant, not because they want power, but because they want will; therefore they do not hear, because, like the deaf adder, they *stop their ears.*

Verses 16–24

Christ was going on in the praise of John the Baptist and his ministry, but here stops on a sudden, and turns that to the reproach of those who enjoyed both that, and the ministry of Christ and his apostles too, in vain. As to that generation, we may observe to whom he *compares them* (*v.* 16–19), and as to the particular places he instances in, we may observe with whom he *compares them, v.* 20–24.

I. As to that *generation,* the body of the Jewish people at that time. There were many indeed that pressed into the kingdom of heaven; but the generality continued in unbelief and obstinacy. John was a great and good man, but the generation in which his lot was cast was as barren and unprofitable as could be, and unworthy of him. Note, The badness of the places where good ministers live serves for a foil to their beauty. It was Noah's praise that he was *righteous in his generation.* Having commended John, he condemns those who had him among them, and did not profit by his ministry. Note, The more praise-worthy the people are, if they slight him, and so it will be found in the day of account.

This our Lord Jesus here sets forth in a parable, yet speaks as if he were at a loss to find out a similitude proper to represent this, *Whereunto shall I liken this generation?* Note,

There is not a greater absurdity than that which they are guilty of who have good preaching among them, and are never the better for it. It is hard to say *what they are like.* The similitude is taken from some common custom among the Jewish children at their play, who, as is usual with children, imitated the fashions of grown people at their marriages and funerals, *rejoicing and lamenting;* but being all a jest, it made no impression; no more did the ministry either of John the Baptist or of Christ upon that generation. He especially reflects on the scribes and Pharisees, who had a proud conceit of themselves; therefore to humble them he compares them to children, and their behaviour to children's play.

The parable will be best explained by opening it and the illustration of it together in these five observations.

Note, 1. The God of heaven uses a variety of proper means and methods for the conversion and salvation of poor souls; he would *have all men to be saved,* and therefore leaves no stone unturned in order to it. The great thing he aims at, is the *melting* of our *wills* into a compliance with the will of God, and in order to this the affecting of us with the discoveries he has made of himself. Having various affections to be wrought upon, he uses various ways of working upon them, which though differing one from another, all tend to the same thing, and God is in them all carrying on the same design. In the parable, this is called his *piping* to us, and his *mourning* to us; he hath *piped to us* in the precious promises of the gospel, proper to work upon hope, and mourned to us in the dreadful threatenings of the law, proper to work upon fear, that he might frighten us out of our sins and allure us to himself. He had *piped to us* in gracious and merciful providences, *mourned to us* in calamitous, afflicting providences, and has set the one over against the other. He has taught his ministers to *change their voice* (Gal. 4:20); sometimes to speak in thunder from *mount Sinai,* sometimes in a still small voice from *mount Sion.*

In the explanation of the parable is set forth the different temper of John's ministry and of Christ's, who were the two great lights of that generation.

(1.) On the one hand, John came *mourning to them, neither eating nor drinking;* not conversing familiarly with people, nor ordinarily eating in company, but alone, in his cell in the wilderness, where *his meat was locusts and wild honey.* Now this, one would think, should work upon them; for such an austere, mortified life as this, was very agreeable to the doctrine he preached: and that minister is most likely to do good, whose conversation is according to his doctrine; and yet the preaching even of such a minister is not always effectual.

(2.) On the other hand, *the Son of man came eating and drinking,* and so he *piped unto them.* Christ conversed familiarly with all sorts of people, not affecting any peculiar strictness or austerity; he was affable and easy of access, not shy of any company, was often at feasts, both with Pharisees and publicans, to try if this would win upon those who were not wrought upon by John's reservedness: those who were not awed by John's frowns, would be allured by Christ's smiles; from whom St. Paul learned to be come *all things to all men,* 1 Co. 9:22. Now our Lord Jesus, by his freedom, did not at all condemn John, any more than John did condemn him, though their deportment was so very different. Note, Though we are never so clear in the goodness of our own practice, yet we must not judge of others by it. There may be a *great diversity of operations,* where *it is the same God that worketh all in all* (1 Co. 12:6), and this *various manifestation of the Spirit is given to every man to profit withal, v.* 7. Observe especially, that God's ministers are variously gifted: the ability and genius of some lie one way, of others, another way: some are Boanerges — *sons of thunder;* others, Barnabeses — *sons of consolation;* yet *all these worketh that one and the self-same Spirit* (1 Co. 12:11), and therefore we ought not to condemn either, but to praise both, and praise God for both, who thus tries various ways of dealing with persons of various tempers, that sinners may be either made pliable or left inexcusable, so that, whatever the issue is, God will be glorified.

Note, 2. The various methods which God takes for the conversion of sinners, are with many fruitless and ineffectual: *"Ye have not danced, ye have not lamented;* you have not been suitably affected either with the one or with the other." Particular means have, as in medicine, their particular intentions, which must be answered, particular impressions, which must be submitted to, in order to the success of the great and general design; now if people will be neither bound by laws, nor invited by promises, nor frightened by threatenings, will neither be awakened by the *greatest* things, nor allured by the *sweetest* things, nor startled by the most *terrible* things, nor be made sensible by the *plainest* things; if they will hearken to the voice neither of scripture, nor reason, nor experience, nor providence, nor conscience, nor interest, what more can be done? *The bellows are burned, the lead is consumed, the founder melteth in vain; reprobate silver shall men call them,* Jer. 6:29. Ministers' labour is bestowed in vain (Isa. 49:4), and, which is a much greater loss, *the grace of God received in vain,* 2 Co. 6:1. Note, It is some comfort to faithful ministers, when they see little success of their labours, that it is no new thing for the best preachers and the best preaching in the world to come short of the desired end. *Who has believed our report?* If from *the blood of the slain,* from *the fat of the mighty,* the bow of those great commanders, Christ and john, returned so often empty (2 Sa. 1:22), no marvel if ours do so, and we prophecy to so little purpose upon dry bones.

Note, 3. That commonly those persons who do not profit by the means of grace, are perverse, and reflect upon the ministers by whom they enjoy those means; and because they do not get good themselves, they do all the hurt they can to others, by raising and propagating prejudices against the word, and the faithful preachers of it. Those who will not comply with God, and walk after him, confront him, and walk contrary to him. So *this generation* did; because they were resolved not to believe Christ and john, and to own them, as they ought to have done, for the best of men, they set themselves to abuse them, and to represent them as the worst. (1.) As for John the Baptist, they say, *He has a devil.* They imputed his strictness and reservedness to melancholy, and some kind or degree of a possession of Satan. "Why should we heed him? he is a poor hypochondriacal man, full of fancies, and under the power of a crazed imagination." (2.) As for Jesus Christ, they imputed his free and obliging conversation to the more vicious habit of luxury and flesh-pleasing: *Behold a gluttonous man and a wine-bibber.* No reflection could be more foul and invidious; it is the charge against the rebellious son (Deu. 21:20), *He is a glutton and a drunkard;* yet none could be more false and unjust; for Christ *pleased not himself* (Rom. 15:3), nor did ever any man live such a life of self-denial, mortification, and contempt of the world, as Christ lived: he that was *undefiled, and separate from sinners,* is here represented as in league with them, and polluted by them. Note, The most unspotted innocency, and the most unparalleled excellency, will not always be a fence *against the reproach of tongues:* nay, a man's best gifts and best actions, which are both well intended and well calculated for edification, may be made the matter of his reproach. The best of our actions may become the worst of our accusations, as David's fasting, Ps. 69:10. It was true in some sense, that Christ was *a Friend to publicans and sinners,* the best Friend they ever had, for he *came into the world to save sinners,* great sinners, even the chief; so he said very feelingly, who had been himself not a *publican and sinner,* but a Pharisee and sinner; but this is, and will be to eternity, Christ's praise, and they forfeited the benefit of it who thus turned it to his reproach.

Note, 4. That the cause of this great unfruitfulness and perverseness of people under the means of grace, is that they are *like children sitting in the markets;* they are foolish as children, froward as children, mindless and playful as children; would they but *show themselves men* in understanding, there would be some hopes of them. *The market-place they sit in* is to some a place of idleness (*ch.* 20:3); to others a place of worldly business (James 4:13); to all a place of noise or diversion; so that if you ask the reason why people get so little good by the means of grace, you will find it is because they are slothful and trifling, and do not love to take pains; or because their heads, and hands, and hearts are full of the world, the cares of which *choke the word,* and choke their souls at last (Eze. 33:31; Amos 8:5); and they study to divert their own thoughts from every thing that is serious. Thus *in the markets* they are, and there they *sit;* in these things their hearts rest, and by them they resolve to abide.

Note, 5. Though the means of grace be thus slighted and abused by many, by the most, yet there is a remnant that through grace do improve them, and answer the designs of them, to the glory of God, and the good of their own souls. *But wisdom is justified of her children.* Christ is *Wisdom;* in him *are hid treasures of wisdom;* the saints are the *children God has given* him, Heb. 2:13. The gospel is *wisdom,* it is *the wisdom from above:* true believers are begotten again by it, and born from above too; they are wise *children,* wise for themselves, and their true interests; not *like the foolish children that sat in the markets.* These *children of wisdom justify wisdom;* they comply with the designs of Christ's grace, answer the intentions of it, and are suitably affected with, and impressed by, the various methods it takes, and so evidence the wisdom of Christ in taking these methods. This is explained, Lu. 7:29. *The publicans justified God, being baptized with the baptism of John,* and afterwards embracing the gospel of Christ. Note, The success of the means of grace justifies the wisdom of God in the choice of these means, against those who charge him with folly therein. The cure of every patient, that observes the physician's orders, justifies the wisdom of the physician: and therefore Paul is *not ashamed of the gospel of Christ,* because, whatever it is to others, *to them that believe it is the power of God unto salvation,* Rom. 1:16. When *the cross of Christ,* which to others is *foolishness* and *a stumbling-block,* is *to them that are called the wisdom of God and the power of God* (1 Co. 1:23, 24), so that they make the knowledge of that the summit of their ambition (1 Co. 2:2), and the efficacy of that the crown of their glorying (Gal. 6:14), here is *wisdom justified of her children. Wisdom's children* are *wisdom's* witnesses in the world (Isa. 43:10), and shall be produced as witnesses in that day, when *wisdom,* that is now *justified* by *the saints,* shall *be glorified in the saints,* and *admired in all them that believe,* 2 Th. 1:10. If the unbelief of some reproach Christ by giving him the lie, the faith of others shall honour him by setting to its seal that he is true, and that *he also is wise,* 1 Co. 1:25. Whether we do it or not, it will be done; not only God's equity, but his *wisdom, will be justified when he speaks, when he judges.*

Well, this is the account Christ gives of that *generation,* and that *generation is not passed away,* but remains in a succession of the like; for as it was then, it has been since and is still; *some believe the things which are spoken, and some believe not,* Acts 28:24.

II. As to the particular *places* in which Christ was most conversant. What he said in general of that *generation,* he applied in particular to those *places,* to affect them. *Then began he to upbraid them, v.* 20. He began to preach to them long before (*ch.* 4:17), but he did not *begin to upbraid* till now. Note, Rough and unpleasing methods must not be taken, till gentler means have first been used. Christ is not apt *to upbraid; he gives liberally, and upbraideth not,* till sinners by their obstinacy extort it from him. *Wisdom* first invites, but when her invitations are slighted, then she *upbraids,* Prov. 1:20, 24. Those do not go in Christ's method, who begin with upbraidings. Now observe,

1. The sin charged upon them; not any against the moral law, then an appeal would have lain to the gospel, which would have relieved, but a sin against the gospel, the remedial law, and that is impenitency: this was it he upbraided them with, or reproached them for, as the most shameful, ungrateful thing that could be, that *they repented not.* Note, Wilful impenitency is the great damning sin of multitudes that enjoy the gospel, and which (more than any other) sinners will be upbraided with to eternity. The great doctrine that both John the Baptist, and Christ, and the apostles preached, was repentance; the great thing designed, both in the *piping* and in the *mourning,* was to prevail with people to change their minds and ways, to leave their sins and turn to God; and this they would not be brought to. He does not say, because they *believed* not (for some king of faith many of them had) that Christ was a *Teacher come from God;* but because *they repented not:* their faith did not prevail to the transforming of their hearts, and the reforming of their lives. Christ reproved them for their other sins, that he might *lead them to repentance;* but when *they repented not, He upbraided them* with that, as their refusal *to be healed: He upbraided them* with it, that they might upbraid themselves, and might at length see the folly of it, as that which alone makes the sad case a desperate one, and the wound incurable.

2. The aggravation of the sin; they were *the cities in which most of his mighty works were done;* for thereabouts his principal residence had been for some time. Note, Some places enjoy the means of grace in greater plenty, power, and purity, than other places. God is a free agent, and acts so in all his disposals, both as the God of nature and as the God of grace, common and distinguishing grace. By Christ's *mighty*

works they should have been prevailed with, not only to receive his doctrine, but to obey his law; the curing of bodily diseases should have been the healing of their souls, but it had not that effect. Note, The stronger inducements we have to repent, the more heinous is the impenitency and the severer will the reckoning be, for Christ keeps account of the *mighty works done* among us, and of the gracious works done for us too, by which also we should be *led to repentance,* Rom. 2:4.

(1.) Chorazin and Bethsaida are here instanced (*v.* 21, 22), they have each of them their woe: *Woe unto thee, Chorazin, woe unto thee, Bethsaida.* Christ came *into the world to bless us;* but if that blessing be slighted, he has woes in reserve, and his woes are of all others the most terrible. These two cities were situate upon *the sea of Galilee,* the former on the east side, and the latter on the west, rich and populous places; Bethsaida was lately advanced to a city by Philip the tetrarch; out of it Christ took at least three of his apostles: thus highly were these places favoured! Yet because they *knew not the day of their visitation,* they fell under these woes, which stuck so close to them, that soon after this they decayed, and dwindled into mean, obscure villages. So fatally does sin ruin cities, and so certainly does the word of Christ take place!

Now Chorazin and Bethsaida are here compared with Tyre and Sidon, two maritime cities we read much of in the Old Testament, that had been brought to ruin, but began to flourish again; these cities bordered upon Galilee, but were in a very ill name among the Jews for idolatry and other wickedness. Christ sometimes went *into the coasts of Tyre and Sidon* (*ch.* 15:21), but never thither; the Jews would have taken it very heinously if he had; therefore Christ, to convince and humble them, here shows,

[1.] That Tyre and Sidon would not have been so bad as Chorazin and Bethsaida. If they had had the same word preached, and the same miracles wrought among them, *they would have repented,* and that *long ago,* as Nineveh did, in *sackcloth and ashes.* Christ, who knows the hearts of all, knew that if he had gone and lived among them, and preached among them, he should have done more good there than where he was; yet he continued where he was for some time, to encourage his ministers to do so, though they see not the success they desire. Note, Among the children of disobedience, some are more easily wrought upon than others; and it is a great aggravation of the impenitency of those who plentifully enjoy the means of grace, not only that there are many who sit under the same means that are wrought upon, but that there are many more that would have been wrought upon, if they had enjoyed the same means. See Eze. 3:6, 7. Our repentance is slow and delayed, but theirs would have been speedy; they would have repented long ago. Ours has been slight and superficial; theirs would have been deep and serious, in *sackcloth and ashes.* Yet we must observe, with an awful adoration of the divine sovereignty, that the Tyrians and Sidonians will justly perish in their sin, though, if they had had the means of grace, they would have repented; for God is a *debtor to no man.*

[2.] That therefore Tyre and Sidon shall not be so miserable as Chorazin and Bethsaida, but it shall be *more tolerable* for them in the *day of judgment, v.* 22. Note, First, At the *day of judgment* the everlasting state of the children of men will, by an unerring and unalterable doom, be determined; happiness or misery, and the several degrees of each. Therefore it is called the *eternal judgment* (Heb. 6:2), because decisive of the eternal state. Secondly, In that judgment, all the means of grace that were enjoyed in the state of probation will certainly come into the account, and it will be enquired, not only how bad we were, but how much better we might have been, had it not been our own fault, Isa. 5:3, 4. Thirdly, Though the damnation of all that perish will be intolerable, yet the damnation of those who had the fullest and clearest discoveries made them of the power and grace of Christ, and yet repented not, will be of all others the most intolerable. The gospel light and sound open the faculties, and enlarge the capacities of all that see and hear it, either to receive the riches of *divine grace,* or (if that grace be slighted) to take in the more plentiful effusions of *divine wrath.* If self-reproach be the torture of hell, it must needs be hell indeed to those who had such a fair opportunity of getting to heaven. *Son, remember that.*

(2.) Capernaum is here condemned with an emphasis (*v.* 23), *"And thou, Capernaum,* hold up thy hand, and hear they doom," Capernaum, above all the cities of Israel, was dignified with Christ's most usual residence; it was like Shiloh of old, the place which he chose, to put his name there, and it fared with it as with Shiloh, Jer. 7:12, 14. Christ's miracles here were *daily bread,* and therefore, as the manna of old, were despised and called light bread. Many a sweet and comfortable lecture of grace Christ had read them to little purpose, and therefore he reads them a dreadful lecture of wrath: those who will not hear the former shall be made to feel the latter.

We have here Capernaum's doom,

[1.] Put absolutely; Thou *which art exalted to heaven shalt be brought down to hell* Note, First, Those who enjoy the gospel in power and purity, are thereby *exalted to heaven;* they have therein a great honour for the present, and a great advantage for eternity; they are lifted up toward *heaven;* but if, notwithstanding, they still *cleave to the earth,* they may thank themselves that they are not lifted up *into heaven.* Secondly, Gospel advantages and advancements abused will sink sinners so much lower into hell. Our external privileges will be so far from saving us, that if our hearts and lives be not agreeable to them, they will but inflame the reckoning: the higher the precipice is, the more fatal is the fall from it: Let us *not therefore be high-minded, but fear;* not slothful, but diligent. See Job 20:6, 7.

[2.] We have it here put in comparison with the doom of Sodom — a place more remarkable, both for sin and ruin, than perhaps any other; and yet Christ here tells us,

First, That Capernaum's means would have saved Sodom. If these miracles had been done among the Sodomites, as bad as they were, they would have repented, and *their city would have remained unto this day* a monument of sparing mercy, as now it is of destroying justice, Jude 7. Note, Upon true repentance through Christ, even the greatest sin shall be pardoned and the greatest ruin prevented, that of Sodom not excepted. Angels were sent to Sodom, and yet it remained not; but if Christ had been sent thither, it *would have remained;* how well is it for us, then, that the world to come is *put in subjection to Christ,* and *not to angels!* Heb. 2:5. Lot would not have *seemed as one that mocked,* if he had wrought miracles.

Secondly, That Sodom's ruin will therefore be less at the great day than Capernaum's. Sodom will have many things to answer for, but not the sin of neglecting Christ, as Capernaum will. If the gospel prove *a savour of death,* a killing savour, it is doubly so; it is *of death unto death,* so great a death (2 Co. 2:16); Christ had said the same of all other places that receive not his ministers nor bid his gospel welcome (*ch.* 10:15); *It shall be more tolerable for the land of Sodom than for that city.* We that have now the written word in our hands, the gospel preached, and the gospel ordinances administered to us, and live under the dispensation of the Spirit, have advantages not inferior to those of Chorazin, and Bethsaida, and Capernaum, and the account in the great day will be accordingly. It has therefore been justly said, that the professors of this age, whether they go to heaven or hell, will be the greatest debtors in either of these places; if to heaven, the greatest debtors to divine mercy for those rich means that brought them thither; if to hell, the greatest debtors to divine justice, for those rich means that would have kept them from thence.

Verses 25–30

In these verses we have Christ looking up to heaven, with thanksgiving to his Father for the sovereignty and security of the covenant of redemption; and looking around him upon this earth, with an offer to all the children of men, to whom these presents shall come, of the privileges and benefits of the covenant of grace.

I. Christ here returns thanks to God for his favour to those *babes* who had the mysteries of the gospel *revealed to them* (*v.* 25, 26). *Jesus answered and said.* It is called an answer, though no other words are before recorded but his own, because it is so comfortable a reply to the melancholy considerations preceding, and is aptly set in the balance against them. The sin and ruin of those woeful cities, no doubt, was a grief to the Lord Jesus; he could not but *weep over* them, as he did *over Jerusalem* (Lu. 19:41); with this thought therefore he refreshes himself; and to make it the more refreshing, he puts it into a thanksgiving; that for all this, *there is a remnant,* though but *babes,* to whom the things of the gospel are *revealed. Though Israel be not gathered, yet shall he be glorious.* Note, We may take great encouragement in looking upward to God, when round about us we see nothing but what is discouraging. It is sad to see how regardless most men are of their own happiness, but it is comfortable to think that the wise and faithful God will, however, effectually secure the interests of his own glory. *Jesus answered and said, I thank thee.* Note, Thanksgiving is a proper answer to dark and disquieting thoughts, and may be an effectual means to silence them. Songs of praise are sovereign cordials to drooping souls, and will help to cure melancholy. When we have no other answer ready to the suggestions of grief and fear, we may have recourse to this, *I thank thee, O Father;* let us bless God that it is not worse with us than it is.

Now in this thanksgiving of Christ, we may observe,

1. The titles he gives to God; *O Father, Lord of heaven and earth.* Note, (1.) In all our approaches to God, by praise as well as by prayer, it is good for us to eye him as a Father, and to fasten on that relation, not only when we ask for the mercies we want, but when we give thanks for the mercies we have received. Mercies are then doubly sweet, and powerful to enlarge the heart in praise, when they are received as tokens of a Father's love, and gifts of a Father's hand; *Giving thanks to the Father,* Col. 1:12. It becomes children to be grateful, and to say, *Thank you, father,* as readily as, *Pray, father.* (2.) When we come to God as a Father, we must withal remember, that he is *Lord of heaven and earth;* which obliges us to come to him with reverence, as to the sovereign Lord of all, and yet with confidence, as one able to do for us whatever we need or can desire; to defend us from all evil and to supply us with all good. Christ, in Melchizedec, had long since *blessed God* as the Possessor, or *Lord of heaven and earth;* and in all our thanksgivings for mercies in the stream, we must give him the glory of the all-sufficiency that is in the fountain.

2. The thing he gives thanks for: *Because thou has hid these things from the wise and prudent, and* yet *revealed them to babes. These things;* he does not say what things, but means the great things of the gospel, *the things that belong to our peace,* Lu. 19:42. he spoke thus emphatically of them, *these things,* because they were things that filled him, and should fill us: all other things are as nothing to *these things.*

Note (1.) The great things of the everlasting gospel have been and are hid from many that were *wise and prudent,* that were eminent for learning and worldly policy; some of the greatest scholars and the greatest statesmen have been the greatest strangers to gospel mysteries. *The world by wisdom knew not God,* 1 Co. 1:21. Nay, there is an opposition given to the gospel, by a *science falsely so called,* 1 Tim. 6:20. Those who are most expert in things sensible and secular, are commonly least experienced in spiritual things. Men may dive deeply into the mysteries of nature and into the mysteries of state, and yet be ignorant of, and mistake about, the mysteries of *the kingdom of heaven,* for want of an experience of the power of them.

(2.) While *the wise and prudent men* of the world are in the dark about gospel mysteries, even the *babes in Christ* have the sanctifying saving knowledge of them: *Thou hast revealed them unto babes.* Such the disciples of Christ were; men of mean birth and education; no scholars, no artists, no politicians, unlearned and ignorant men, Acts 4:13. Thus are the secrets of wisdom, which are double to that which is (Job 11:6), made known *to babes and sucklings,* that *out of their mouth strength* might be *ordained* (Ps. 8:2), and God's *praise* thereby *perfected.* The learned men of the world were not made choice of to be the preachers of the gospel, but *the foolish things of the world* (1 Co. 2:6, 8, 10).

(3.) This difference between *the prudent* and the *babes* is of God's own making. [1.] It is he that has *hid these things from the wise and prudent;* he gave them parts, and learning, and much of human understanding above others, and they were proud of that, and rested in it, and looked no further; and therefore God justly denies them the Spirit of wisdom and revelation, and then, though they hear the sound of the gospel tidings, they are to them as a *strange thing.* God is not the Author of their ignorance and error, but he leaves them to themselves, and their sin becomes their punishment, and the Lord is righteous in it. See Jn. 12:39, 40; Rom. 11:7, 8; Acts 28:26, 27. Had they honoured God with the wisdom and prudence they had, he would have given them the knowledge of these better things; but because they served their lusts with them, he has *hid their hearts from this understanding.* [2.] It is he that has *revealed them unto babes.* Things revealed belong to our children (Deu. 29:29), and to them he *gives an understanding* to receive these things, and the impressions of them. Thus *he resists the proud,* and *gives grace to the humble,* Jam. 4:6.

(4.) This dispensation must be resolved into the divine sovereignty. Christ himself referred it to that; *Even so, Father, for so it seemed good in thy sight.* Christ here subscribes to the will of his Father in this matter; *Even so.* Let God take what ways he pleases to glorify himself, and make us of what instruments he pleases for the carrying on of his own work; his grace is his own, and he may give or withhold it as he pleases. We can give no reason why Peter, a fisherman, should be made an apostle, and not Nicodemus, a Pharisee, and a ruler of the Jews, though he also believed in Christ; but *so it seemed good in God's sight.* Christ said this in the hearing of his disciples, to show them that it was not for any merit of their own that they were thus dignified and distinguished, but purely from God's good pleasure; he made them to differ.

(5.) This way of dispensing divine grace is to be acknowledged by us, as it was by our Lord Jesus, with all thankfulness. We must thank God, [1.] That *these things* are *revealed;* the mystery hid from ages and generations is manifested; that they are *revealed,* not to a few, but to be published to all the world. [2.] That they are *revealed to babes;* that the meek and humble are beautified with this salvation; and this honour put upon those whom the world pours contempt upon. [3.] It magnifies the mercy to them, that *these things* are *hid from the wise and prudent:* distinguishing favours are the most obliging. As Job adored *the name of the Lord* in *taking away* as well as in *giving,* so may we in *hiding these things from the wise and prudent,* as well as in *revealing them unto babes;* not as it is their misery, but as it is a method by which self is abased, proud thoughts brought down, all flesh silenced, and divine power and wisdom made to shine the more bright. See 1 Co. 1:27, 31.

II. Christ here makes a gracious offer of the benefits of the gospel to all, and these are the things which are *revealed to babes, v.* 25, etc. Observe here,

1. The solemn preface which ushers in this call or invitation, both to command our attention to it, and to encourage our compliance with it. That we *might have strong consolation,* in flying for refuge to this *hope set before us,* Christ prefixes his authority, produces his credentials; we shall see he is empowered to make this offer.

Two things he here lays before us, *v.* 27.

(1.) His commission from the Father: *All things are delivered unto me of my Father.* Christ, as God, is equal in power and glory with the Father; but as Mediator he receives his power and glory from the Father; has *all judgment committed to him.* He is authorized to settle a new covenant between God and man, and to offer peace and happiness to the apostate world, upon such terms as he should think fit: he was sanctified and sealed to be the sole Plenipotentiary, to concert and establish this great affair. In order to this, he has *all power* both *in heaven and in earth, (ch.* 28:18); power over all flesh (Jn. 17:2); authority to execute judgment, Jn. 5:22, 27. This encourages us to come to Christ, that he is commissioned to receive us, and to give us what we come for, and has *all things delivered to him* for that purpose, by him who is *Lord of all.* All powers, all treasures are in his hand. Observe, The Father has delivered his all into the hands of the Lord Jesus; let us but deliver our all into his hand and the work is done; God has made him the great Referee, the blessed Daysman, to lay his hand upon us both; that which we have to do is to agree to the reference, to submit to the arbitration of the Lord Jesus, for the taking up of this unhappy controversy, and to enter into bonds to stand to his award.

(2.) His intimacy with the Father: *No man knoweth the Son but the Father, Neither knoweth any man the Father save the Son.* This gives us a further satisfaction, and an abundant one. Ambassadors use to have not only their commissions, which they produce, but their instructions, which they reserve to themselves, to be made use of as there is occasion in their negotiations; our Lord Jesus had both, not only authority, but ability, for his undertaking. In transacting the great business of our redemption, the Father and the Son are the parties principally concerned; *the counsel of peace is between them,* Zec. 6:13. It must therefore be a great encouragement to us to be assured, that they understood one another very well in this affair; that the Father knew the Son, and the Son knew the Father, and both perfectly (a mutual consciousness we may call it, between the Father and the Son), so that there could be no mistake in the settling of this matter; as often there is among men, to the overthrow of contracts, and the breaking of the measures taken, through their misunderstanding one another. The Son had *lain in the bosom of the Father* from eternity; he was *a secretioribus — of the cabinet-council,* Jn. 50:18. He was *by him, as one brought up with him* (Prov. 8:30), so that *none knows the Father save the Son,* he adds, *and he to whom the Son will reveal him.* Note, [1.] The happiness of men lies in an acquaintance with God; it *is life eternal,* it is the perfection of rational beings. [2.] Those who would have an acquaintance with God, must apply themselves to Jesus Christ; for the light of the knowledge of the glory of God shines in the face of Christ, 2 Co. 4:6. We are obliged to Christ for all the revelation we have of God the Father's will and love, ever since Adam sinned; there is no comfortable intercourse between a holy God and sinful man, but in and by a Mediator, Jn. 14:6.

2. Here is the offer itself that is made to us, and an invitation to accept of it. After so solemn a preface, we may well expect something very great; and it is *a faithful saying,* and well *worthy of all acceptation; words whereby we may be saved.* We are here invited to Christ as our Priest, Prince, and Prophet, to be saved, and, in order to that, to be ruled and taught by him.

(1.) We must come to Jesus Christ as our Rest, and repose ourselves in him (*v.* 28), *Come unto me all ye that labour.* Observe, [1.] The character of the persons invited; *all that labour, and are heavy laden.* This is a word in season to him that is weary, Isa. 50:4. Those who complain of the burthen of the ceremonial law, which was an intolerable yoke, and was made much more so by the tradition of the elders (Lu. 11:46), let them come to Christ, and they shall be made easy; he came to free his church from this yoke, to cancel the imposition of those carnal ordinances, and to introduce a purer and more spiritual way of worship; but it is rather to be understood of the burthen of sin, both the guilt and the power of it. Note, All those, and those only, are invited to rest in Christ, that are sensible of sin as a burthen, and groan under it; that are not only convinced of the evil of sin, of their own sin, but are contrite in soul for it; that are really sick of their sins, weary of the service of the world and of the flesh; that see their state sad and dangerous by reason of sin, and are in pain and fear about it, as Ephraim (Jer. 31:18–20), the prodigal (Lu. 15:17), the publican (Lu. 18:13), Peter's hearers (Acts 2:37), Paul (Acts 9:4, 6, 9), the jailor (Acts 16:29, 30). This is a necessary preparative for pardon and peace. The Comforter must first convince (Jn. 16:8); I have torn and then will heal. [2.] The invitation itself: *Come unto me.* That glorious display of Christ's greatness which we had (*v.* 27), as Lord of all, might frighten us from him, but see here how he holds out *the golden sceptre,* that we may touch the top of it and may live. Note, It is the duty and interest of weary *and heavy laden* sinners to *come to Jesus Christ.* Renouncing all those things which stand in opposition to him, or in competition with him, we must accept of him, as our Physician and Advocate, and give up ourselves to his conduct and government; freely willing to be saved by him, in his own way, and upon his own terms. *Come* and *cast that burden upon* him, under which thou art *heavy laden.* This is the gospel call, *The Spirit saith, Come;* and *the bride saith, Come; let him that is athirst come; Whoever will, let him come.*

[3.] The blessing promised to those that do come: *I will give you rest.* Christ is our Noah, whose name signifies *rest,* for *this same shall give us rest.* Gen. 5:29; 8:9. Truly *rest is good* (Gen. 49:15), especially to those *that labour and are heavy laden,* Eccl. 5:12. Note, Jesus Christ will give assured rest to those weary souls, that by a lively faith come to him for it; *rest* from the terror of sin, in a well-grounded peace of conscience; *rest* from the power of sin, in a regular order of the soul, and its due government of itself; a *rest* in God, and a complacency of soul, in his love. Ps. 11:6, 7. This is that *rest which remains for the people of God* (Heb. 4:9), begun in grace, and perfected in glory.

(2.) We must come to Jesus Christ as our Ruler, and submit ourselves to him (*v.* 29). *Take my yoke upon you.* This must go along with the former, for Christ is exalted to be both a *Prince and a Saviour,* a *Priest upon his throne.* The *rest* he promises is a release from the drudgery of sin, not from the service of God, but an obligation to the duty we owe to him. Note, Christ has a *yoke* for our necks, as well as a *crown* for our heads, and this *yoke* he expects we should *take upon* us and draw in. To call those who are weary *and heavy laden,* to *take a yoke upon* them, looks like adding *affliction to the afflicted;* but the pertinency of it lies in the word *my:* "You are under a *yoke* which makes you weary: shake that off and try mine, which will make you easy." Servants are said to be *under the yoke* (1 Tim. 6:1), and subjects, 1 Ki. 12:10. To take Christ's *yoke upon* us, is to put ourselves into the relation to servants and subjects to him, and then of conduct ourselves accordingly, in a conscientious obedience to all his commands, and a cheerful submission to all his disposals: it is to *obey the gospel of Christ, to yield ourselves to the Lord:* it is Christ's *yoke;* the *yoke* he has appointed; a *yoke* he has himself drawn in before us, for *he learned obedience,* and which he does by his Spirit draw in with us, for *he helpeth our infirmities,* Rom. 8:26. A *yoke* speaks some hardship, but if the beast must draw, the *yoke* helps him. Christ's commands are all in our favour: we must take this *yoke upon* us to draw in it. We are yoked to work, and therefore must be diligent; we are yoked to submit, and therefore must be humble and patient: we are yoked together with our fellow-servants, and therefore must keep up the communion of saints: and *the words of the wise are as goads,* to those who are thus yoked.

Now this is the hardest part of our lesson, and therefore it is qualified (*v.* 30). *My yoke is easy and my burden is light;* you need not be afraid of it.

[1.] The *yoke* of Christ's commands is an *easy yoke;* it is *chrēstos,* not only *easy,* but gracious, so the word signifies; it is sweet and pleasant; there is nothing in it to gall the yielding neck, nothing to hurt us, but, on the contrary, must to refresh us. It is a *yoke* that is lined with love. Such is the nature of all Christ's commands, so reasonable in themselves, so profitable to us, and all summed up in one word, and that a sweet word, love. So powerful are the assistances he gives us, so suitable the encouragements, and so strong the consolations, that are to be found in the way of duty, that we may truly say, it is a *yoke* of pleasantness. It is easy to the new nature, very *easy to him that understandeth,* Prov. 14:6. It may be a little hard at first, but it is easy afterwards; the love of God and the hope of heaven will make it *easy.*

[2.] The *burden* of Christ's cross is a *light burden,* very *light:* afflictions from Christ, which befal us as men; afflictions for Christ, which befal us as Christians; the latter are especially meant. This *burden* in itself is *not joyous, but grievous;* yet as it is Christ's, it is *light.* Paul knew as much of it as any man, and he calls it a *light affliction,* 2 Co. 4:17. God's presence (Isa. 43:2), Christ's sympathy (Isa. 73:9, Dan. 3:25), and especially the Spirit's aids and comforts (2 Co. 1:5), make suffering for Christ *light* and *easy.* As afflictions abound, and are prolonged, consolations abound, and are prolonged too. Let this therefore reconcile us to the difficulties, and help us over the discouragements, we may meet with, both in doing work and suffering work; though we may lose *for* Christ, we shall not lose *by him.*

(3.) We must come to Jesus Christ as our Teacher, and set ourselves to learn of him, *v.* 29. Christ has erected a great school, and has invited us to be his scholars. We must enter ourselves, associate with his scholars, and daily attend the instructions he gives by his word and Spirit. We must converse much with what he said, and have it ready to use upon all occasions; we must conform to what he did, and follow his steps, 1 Pt. 2:21. Some make the following words, *for I am meek and lowly in heart,* to be the particular lesson we are required to learn from the example of Christ. We must learn of him to be *meek* and *lowly,* and must mortify our pride and passion, which render us so unlike to him. We must so *learn of Christ* as to *learn Christ* (Eph. 4:20), for he is both Teacher and Lesson, Guide and Way, and All in All.

Two reasons are given why we must *learn of Christ.*

[1.] *I am meek and lowly in heart,* and therefore fit to teach you.

First, He is *meek,* and can have *compassion on the ignorant,* whom others would be in a passion with. Many able teachers are hot and hasty, which is a great discouragement to those who are dull and slow; but Christ knows how to bear with such, and to open their understandings. His carriage towards his twelve disciples was a specimen of this; he was mild and gentle with them, and made the best of them; though they were heedless and forgetful, he was not extreme to mark their follies. Secondly, *He is lowly in heart.* He condescends to teach poor scholars, to teach novices; he chose disciples, not from the court, nor the schools, but from the seaside. He teaches the first principles, such things as are milk for babes;

he stoops to the meanest capacities; he taught Ephraim to go, Hos. 11:3. Who teaches like him? It is an encouragement to us to put ourselves to school to such a Teacher. This humility and meekness, as it qualifies him to be a Teacher, so it will be the best qualification of those who are to be taught by him; *for the meek will he guide in judgment*, Ps. 25:9.

[2.] *You shall find rest to your souls.* This promise is borrowed from Jer. 6:16, for Christ delighted to express himself in the language of the prophets, to show the harmony between the two Testaments. Note, First, Rest for the soul is the most desirable rest; to have the soul to *dwell at ease.* Secondly, The only way, and a sure way to find *rest for our souls* is, to sit at Christ's feet and hear his word. The way of duty is the way of rest. The *understanding* finds *rest* in the *knowledge of* God and Jesus Christ, and is there abundantly satisfied, finding *that* wisdom in the gospel which has been sought for in vain throughout the whole creation, Job 28:12. The truths Christ teaches are such as we may venture our souls upon. The affections find rest in the love of God and Jesus Christ, and meet with that in them which gives them an abundant satisfaction; quietness and assurance for ever. And those satisfactions will be perfected and perpetuated in heaven, where we shall see and enjoy God immediately, shall see him as he is, and enjoy him as he is ours. This rest is to be had with Christ for all those who learn of him.

Well, this is the sum and substance of the gospel call and offer: we are here told, in a few words, what the Lord Jesus requires of us, and it agrees with what God said of him once and again. *This is my beloved Son, in whom I am well pleased, hear ye him.*

CHAPTER 12

In this chapter, we have, I. Christ's clearing of the law of the fourth commandment concerning the sabbath-day, and vindicating it from some superstitious notions advanced by the Jewish teachers; showing that works of necessity and mercy are to be done on that day (*v.* 1–13). II. The prudence, humility, and self-denial of our Lord Jesus in working his miracles (*v.* 14–21). III. Christ's answer to the blasphemous cavils and calumnies of the scribes and Pharisees, who imputed his casting out devils to a compact with the devil (*v.* 22–37). IV. Christ's reply to a tempting demand of the scribes and Pharisees, challenging him to show them a sign from heaven (*v.* 38–45). V. Christ's judgment about his kindred and relations (*v.* 46–50).

Verses 1–13

The Jewish teachers had corrupted many of the commandments, by interpreting them more loosely than they were intended; a mistake which Christ discovered and rectified (*ch.* 5) in his sermon on the mount: but concerning the fourth commandment, they had erred in the other extreme, and interpreted it too strictly. Note, it is common for men of corrupt minds, by their zeal in rituals, and the external services of religion, to think to atone for the looseness of their morals. But they are cursed who *add to,* as well as they who *take from, the words of this book,* Rev. 22:16, 19; Prov. 30:6.

Now that which our Lord Jesus here lays down is, that the works of necessity and mercy are lawful on the sabbath day, which the Jews in many instances were taught to make a scruple of. Christ's industrious explanation of the fourth commandment, intimates its perpetual obligation to the religious observation of *one day in seven,* as a *holy sabbath.* He would not expound a law that was immediately to expire, but doubtless intended hereby to settle a point which would be of use to his church in all ages; and so it is to teach us, that our Christian sabbath, though under the direction of the fourth commandment, is not under the injunctions of the Jewish elders.

It is usual to settle the meaning of a law by judgments given upon cases that happen in fact, and in like manner is the meaning of this law settled. Here are two passages of story put together for this purpose, happening at some distance of time from each other, and of a different nature, but both answering this intention.

I. Christ, by justifying his disciples in plucking the ears of corn on the sabbath-day, shows that *works of necessity* are *lawful* on that day. Now here observe,

1. What it was that the disciples did. They were following their Master one sabbath day through a corn-field; it is likely they were going to the synagogue (*v.* 9), for it becomes not Christ's disciples to take *idle walks* on that day, and *they were hungry;* let it be no disparagement to our Master's housekeeping. But we will suppose they were so intent upon the sabbath work, that they forgot to eat bread; had spent so much time in their morning worship, that they had no time for their morning meal, but came out fasting, because they would not come late to the synagogue. Providence ordered it that they *went through the corn,* and there they were supplied. Note, God has many ways of bringing suitable provision to his people when they need it, and will take particular care of them when they are going to the synagogue, as of old for them that went up to Jerusalem to worship (Ps. 84:6, 7), for whose use the rain filled the pools: while we are in the way of duty, *Jehovah-jireh,* let God alone to provide for us. Being in the corn-fields, they began to *pluck the ears of corn;* the law of God allowed this (Deu. 23:25), to teach people to be neighbourly, and not to insist upon property in a small matter, whereby another may be benefited. This was but slender provision for Christ and his disciples, but it was the best they had, and they were content with it. The famous Mr. Ball, of Whitmore, used to say he had two dishes of meat to his sabbath dinner, a dish of hot milk, and a dish of cold, and he had enough and enough.

2. What was the offence that the Pharisees took at this. It was but a dry breakfast, yet the Pharisees would not let them eat that in quietness. They did not quarrel with them for taking another man's corn (they were no great zealots for justice), but for doing it *on the sabbath day;* for plucking and rubbing the ears of corn of that day was expressly forbidden by the tradition of the elders, for this reason, because it was *a kind of reaping.*

Note, It is no new thing for the most harmless and innocent actions of Christ's disciples to be evil spoken of, and reflected upon as unlawful, especially by those who are zealous for their own inventions and impositions. The Pharisees complained of them to their Master for doing that which it was not *lawful to do.* Note, Those are no friends to Christ and his disciples, who make that to be unlawful which God has not made to be so.

3. What was Christ's answer to this cavil of the Pharisees. The disciples could say little for themselves, especially because those who quarrelled with them seemed to have the strictness of the sabbath sanctification on their side; and it is safest to err on that hand: but Christ came to free his followers, not only from the corruptions of the Pharisees, but from their unscriptural impositions, and therefore has something to say for them, and justifies what they did, though it was a transgression of the canon.

(1.) He justifies them by precedents, which were allowed to be good by the Pharisees themselves.

[1.] He urges an ancient instance of David, who in a case of necessity did that which otherwise he ought not to have done (*v.* 3, 4); *"Have ye not read* the story (1 Sa. 21:6) of David's eating the show-bread, which by the law was appropriated to the priest?" (Lev. 24:5–9). *It is most holy to Aaron and his sons;* and (Ex. 29:33) *a stranger shall not eat of it;* yet the priest gave it to David and his men; for though the exception of a case of necessity was not expressed, yet it was implied in that and all other ritual institutions. That which bore out David in eating the show-bread was not his dignity (Uzziah, that invaded the priest's office in the pride of his heart, though a king, was struck with a leprosy for it, 2 Chr. 26:16, etc.), but his hunger. The greatest shall not have their lusts indulged, but the meanest shall have their wants considered. Hunger is a natural desire which cannot be mortified, but must be gratified, and cannot be put off with any thing but meat; therefore we say, It will *break through stone walls.* Now the *Lord is for the body,* and allowed his own appointment to be dispensed with in a case of distress; much more might the tradition of the elders be dispensed with. Note, That may be done in a case of necessity which may not be done at another time; there are laws which necessity has not, but it is a law to itself. *Men do not despise,* but pity, *a thief that steals to satisfy his soul when he is hungry,* Prov. 6:30.

[2.] He urges a daily instance of the priests, which they likewise *read in the law,* and according to which was the constant usage, *v.* 5. *The priests in the temple* did a great deal of servile work on the sabbath day; killing, flaying, burning the sacrificed beasts, which in a common case would *have been profaning the sabbath;* and yet it was never reckoned any transgression of the fourth commandment, because the temple-service required and justified it. This intimates, that those labours are lawful on the sabbath day which are necessary, not only to the *support of life,* but to the *service of the day;* as tolling a bell to call the congregation together, travelling to church, and the like. Sabbath rest is to promote, not to hinder, sabbath worship.

(2.) He justifies them by arguments, three cogent ones.

[1.] *In this place is one greater than the temple, v.* 6. If the temple-service would justify what the priests did in their ministration, the service of Christ would much more justify the disciples in what they did in their attendance upon him. The Jews had an extreme veneration for the temple: it *sanctified the gold;* Stephen was accused for *blaspheming that holy place* (Acts 6:13); but Christ, in a corn-field, was *greater than the temple,* for in him dwelt not the *presence of God* symbolically, but *all the fulness of the Godhead bodily.* Note, If whatever we do, we do it *in the name of Christ,* and *as unto him,* it shall be graciously accepted of God, however it may be censured and cavilled at by men.

[2.] *God will have mercy and not sacrifice, v.* 7. Ceremonial duties must give way to moral, and the natural, royal law of love and self-preservation must take place of ritual observances. This is quoted from Hos. 6:6. It was used before, *ch.* 9:13, in vindication of mercy to the souls of men; here, of mercy to their bodies. The rest of the sabbath was ordained for man's good, in favour of the body, Deu. *v.* 14. Now no law must be construed so as to contradict its own end. *If you had known what this means,* had known what it is to be of a merciful disposition, you would have been sorry that they were forced to do this to satisfy their hunger, and would *not have condemned the guiltless.* Note, *First,* Ignorance is the cause of our rash and uncharitable censures of our brethren. *Secondly,* It is not enough for us to know the scriptures, but we must labour to *know the meaning* of them. *Let him that readeth understand. Thirdly,* Ignorance of the meaning of the scripture is especially shameful in those who take upon them to teach others.

[3.] *The Son of man is Lord even of the sabbath day, v.* 8. That law, as all the rest, is put into the hand of Christ, to be altered, enforced, or dispensed with, as he sees good. It was by *the Son* that God *made the world,* and by him he instituted the sabbath in innocency; by him he gave the ten commandments at mount Sinai, and as Mediator he is entrusted with the institution of ordinances, and to make what changes he thought fit; and particularly, as being *Lord of the sabbath,* he was authorized to make such an alteration of that day, as that it should become the Lord's day, the Lord Christ's day. And if Christ be the *Lord of the sabbath,* it is fit the day and all the work of it should be dedicated to him. By virtue of this power Christ here enacts, that works of necessity, if they be really such, and not a pretended and self-created necessity, are lawful on the sabbath day; and this explication of the law plainly shows that it was to be perpetual. *Exceptio firmat regulam — The exception confirms the rule.*

Christ having thus silenced the Pharisees, and got clear of them (*v.* 9), *departed,* and *went into their synagogue,* the synagogue of these Pharisees, in which they presided, and toward which he was going, when they picked this quarrel with him. Note, *First,* We must take heed lest any thing that occurs in our way to holy ordinances unfit us for, or divert us from, our due attendance on them. Let us proceed in the way of our duty, notwithstanding the artifices of Satan, who endeavours, by the *perverse disputings of men of corrupt minds,* and many other ways, to ruffle and discompose us. *Secondly,* We must not, for the sake of private feuds and personal piques, draw back from public worship. Though the Pharisees had thus maliciously cavilled at Christ, yet he *went into their synagogue.* Satan gains this point, if, by sowing discord among brethren, he prevail to drive them, or any of them, from the synagogue, and the communion of the faithful.

II. Christ, by *healing the man that had the withered hand on the sabbath day,* shows that works of mercy are lawful and proper to be done on that day. The work of necessity was done by the disciples, and justified by him; the work of mercy was done by himself; the works of mercy were his works of necessity; it was his *meat and drink to do good. I must preach,* says he, Lu. 4:43. This cure is recorded for the sake of the time when it was wrought, on the sabbath.

Here is, 1. The affliction that this poor man was in; his hand was withered so that he was utterly disabled to get his living by *working with his hands.* St. Jerome says, that the gospel of Matthew in Hebrew, used by the Nazarenes and Ebionites, adds this circumstance to this story of the man with the withered hand, that he was *Caementarius — a bricklayer,* and applied himself to Christ thus; "Lord, I am a bricklayer, and *have got my living by my labour (manibus victum quaeritans);* I beseech thee, O Jesus, restore me the use of my hand, *that I may not be obliged to beg my bread" (ne turpiter mendicem cibos).* Hieron. *in loc.* This poor man was in the synagogue. Note, Those who can do but little, or have but little to do for the world, must do so much the more for their souls; as the rich, the aged, and the infirm.

2. A spiteful question which the Pharisees put to Christ upon the sight of this man. *They asked him, saying, Is it lawful to heal?* We read not here of any address this poor man made to Christ for a cure, but they observed Christ began to take notice of him, and knew it was usual for him to be *found of those that sought him not,* and therefore with their badness they anticipated his goodness, and started this case as a stumbling-block in the way of doing good; *Is it lawful to heal on the sabbath-day?* Whether it was lawful for *physicians to heal* on that day or not, which was the thing disputed in their books, one would think it past dispute, that it is lawful for *prophets to heal,* for him to heal who discovered a divine power and goodness in all he did of this kind, and manifested himself to be *sent of God.* Did ever any ask, whether it is lawful for God to heal, to send his word and heal? It is true, Christ was now *made under the law,* by a voluntary submission to it, but he was never made under the precepts of the elders. *Is it lawful to heal?* To enquire into the lawfulness and unlawfulness of actions is very good, and we cannot apply ourselves to any with such enquiries more fitly than to Christ; but they asked here, not that they might be instructed by him, but *that they might accuse him.* If he should say that it was lawful to heal on the sabbath day, they would accuse him of a contradiction to the fourth commandment; to so great a degree of superstition had the Pharisees brought the sabbath rest, that, unless in peril of life, they allowed not any medicinal operations on the sabbath day. If he should say that it was not lawful, they would accuse him of partiality, having lately justified his disciples in plucking the ears of corn on that day.

3. Christ's answer to this question, by way of appeal to themselves, and their own opinion and practice, *v.* 11, 12. In case a *sheep* (though but one, of which the loss would not be very great) should fall into a pit on the sabbath day, *would they not lift it out?* No doubt they might do it, the fourth commandment allows it; they must do it, for a *merciful man regardeth the life of his beast,* and for their parts they would do it, rather than lose a sheep; does Christ take care for sheep? Yes, he does; he preserves and provides for both man and beast. But here he says it for our sakes (1 Co. 9:9, 10), and hence argues, *How much then is a man better than a sheep?* Sheep are not only harmless but useful creatures, and are prized and tended accordingly; yet a man is here preferred far before them. Note, Man, in respect of his being, is a great deal better, and more valuable, than the best of the brute creatures: man is a reasonable creature, capable of knowing, loving, and glorifying God, and therefore is better than a sheep. The sacrifice of a sheep could therefore not atone for the sin of a soul. They do not consider this, who are more solicitous for the education, preservation, and supply of their horses and dogs than of God's poor, or perhaps their own household.

Hence Christ infers a truth, which, even at first sight, appears very reasonable and good-natured; that *it is lawful to do well on the sabbath days;* they had asked, *Is it lawful to hear?* Christ proves it is lawful to *do well,* and let any one judge whether healing, as Christ healed, was not *doing well.* Note, There are more ways of *doing well* upon sabbath days, than by the duties of God's immediate worship; attending the sick, relieving the poor, helping those who are fallen into sudden distress, and call for speedy relief; this is *doing good:* and this must be done from a principle of love and charity, with humility and self-denial, and a heavenly frame of spirit, and this is *doing well,* and it *shall be accepted,* Gen. 4:7.

4. Christ's curing of the man, notwithstanding the offence which he foresaw the Pharisees would take at it, *v.* 13. Though they could not answer Christ's arguments, they were resolved to persist in their prejudice and enmity; but Christ went on with his work notwithstanding. Note, Duty is not to be left undone, nor opportunities of doing good neglected, for fear of giving offence. Now the manner of the cure is observable; he said to the man, *"Stretch forth thy hand,* exert thyself as well as thou canst;" and he did so, *and it was restored whole.* This, as other cures Christ wrought, had a spiritual significancy. (1.) By nature our hands are withered, we are utterly unable of ourselves to doing any thing that is good. (2.) It is Christ only, by the power of his grace, that cures us; he heals the withered hand by putting life into the dead soul, works in us both to will and to do. (3.) In order to our cure, he commands us to *stretch forth our hands,* to improve our natural powers, and do as well as we can; to stretch them out in prayer to God, to stretch them out to lay hold on Christ by faith, to stretch them out in holy endeavours. Now this man could not stretch forth his withered hand of himself, any more than the impotent man could arise and carry his bed, or Lazarus come forth out of his grave; yet Christ bid him do it. God's commands to us to do the duty which of ourselves we are not able to do are no more absurd or unjust, than this command to the man with the withered hand, *to stretch it forth;* for with the command, there is a promise of grace which is given by the word. *Turn ye at my reproof, and I will pour out my Spirit,* Prov. 1:23. Those who perish are as inexcusable as this man would have been, if he had not attempted to stretch forth his hand, and so had not been healed. But those who are saved have no more to boast of than this man had of contributing to his own cure, by stretching forth his hand, but are as much indebted to the power and grace of Christ as he was.

Verses 14–21

As in the midst of Christ's greatest humiliations, there were proofs of his dignity, so in the midst of his greatest honours, he gave proofs of his humility; and when the mighty works he did gave him an opportunity of making a figure, yet he made it appear that *he emptied himself,* and *made himself of no reputation.* Here we have,

I. The cursed malice of the Pharisees against Christ (*v.* 14); being enraged at the convincing evidence of his miracles, they *went out, and held a council against him, how they might destroy him.* That which vexed them was, not only that by his miracles his honour eclipsed theirs, but that the doctrine he preached was directly opposite to their pride, and hypocrisy, and worldly interest; but they pretended to be displeased at his breaking the sabbath day, which was by the law a capital crime, Ex. 35:2. Note, it is no new thing to see the vilest practices cloaked with the most specious pretences. Observe their policy; they took counsel about it, considered with themselves which way to do it effectually; they took counsel together in a close cabal about it, that they might both animate and assist one another. Observe their cruelty; they took counsel, not to imprison or banish him, but to destroy him, to be the death of him who came *that we might have life.* What an indignity was hereby put upon our Lord Jesus, to run him down as an outlaw *(qui caput gerit lupinum — carries a wolf's head),* and the plague of his country, who was the greatest blessing of it, the Glory of his people Israel!

II. Christ's absconding upon this occasion, and the privacy he chose, to decline, not his work, but his danger; because *his hour was not yet come* (*v.* 15), *he withdrew himself from thence.* He could have secured himself by miracle, but chose to do it in the ordinary way of flight and retirement; because in this, as in other things, he would submit to the sinless infirmities of our nature. Herein he humbled himself, that he was driven to the common shift of those who are most helpless; thus also he would give an example to his own rule, *When they persecute you in one city, flee to another.* Christ had said and done enough to convince those Pharisees, if reason or miracles would have done it; but instead of yielding to the conviction, they were hardened and enraged, and therefore he left them as incurable, Jer. 51:9.

Christ did not retire for his own ease, nor seek an excuse to leave off his work; no, his retirements were filled up with business, and he was even then doing good, when he was forced to flee for the same. Thus he gave an example to his ministers, to do what they can, when they cannot do what they would, and to continue teaching, even when they are removed into corners. When the Pharisees, the great dons and doctors of the nation, drove Christ from then, and forced him to withdraw himself, yet the common people crowded after him; *great multitudes followed him* and found him out. This some would turn to his reproach, and call him the ringleader of the mob; but it was really his honour, that all who were unbiased and unprejudiced, and not blinded by the pomp of the world, were so hearty, so zealous for him, that they would follow him whithersoever he went, and whatever hazards they ran with him; as it was also the honour of his grace, that the poor were evangelized; that when they received him, he received them and healed them all. Christ came into the world to be a Physician-general, as the sun to the lower world, *with healing under his wings.* Though the Pharisees persecuted Christ for doing good, yet he went on in it, and did not let the people fare the worse for the wickedness of their rulers. Note, Though some are unkind to us, we must not on that account be unkind to others.

Christ studied to reconcile usefulness and privacy; he *healed them all,* and yet (*v.* 16), *charged them that they should not make him known;* which may be looked upon, 1. As an act of prudence; it was not so much the miracles themselves, as the public discourse concerning them, that enraged the Pharisees (*v.* 23, 24); therefore Christ, though he would not omit doing good, yet would do it with as little noise as possible, to avoid offence to them and peril to himself. Note, Wise and good men, though they covet to do good, yet are far from coveting to have it talked of when it is done; because it is God's acceptance, not men's applause, that they aim at. And in suffering times, though we must boldly go on in the way of duty, yet we must contrive the circumstances of it so as not to exasperate, more than is necessary, those who seek occasion against us; *Be ye wise as serpents, ch.* 10:16. 2. It may be looked upon as an act of righteous judgment upon the Pharisees, who were unworthy to hear of any more of his miracles, having made so light of those they had seen. By shutting their eyes against the light, they had forfeited the benefit of it. 3. As an act of humility and self-denial. Though Christ's intention in his miracles was to prove himself the Messiah, and so to bring men to believe on him, in order to which it was requisite that they should be known, yet sometimes he charged the people to conceal them, to set us an example of humility, and to teach us not to proclaim our own goodness or usefulness, or to desire to have it proclaimed. Christ would have his disciples to be the reverse of those who did all their works *to be seen of men.*

III. The fulfilling of the scriptures in all this, *v.* 17. Christ retired into privacy and obscurity, that though he was eclipsed, the word of God might be fulfilled, and so illustrated and glorified, which was the thing his heart was upon. The scripture here said to be fulfilled is Isa. 42:1–4, which is quoted at large, *v.* 18–21. The scope of it is to show how mild and quiet, and yet how successful, our Lord Jesus should be in his undertaking; instances of both which we have in the foregoing passages. observe here,

1. The pleasure of the Father in Christ (*v.* 18); *Behold, my Servant whom I have chosen, my Beloved in whom my soul is well pleased.* Hence we may learn,

(1.) That our Saviour was God's Servant in the great work of our redemption. He therein submitted himself to the Father's will (Heb. 10:7), and set himself to serve the design of his grace and the interests of his glory, in repairing the breaches that had been made by man's apostasy. As a *Servant,* he had a great work appointed him, and a great trust reposed in him. This was a part of his humiliation, that though he *thought it not robbery to be equal with God,* yet that in the work of our salvation he took upon him the form of a servant, received a law, and came into bonds. *Though he were a son, yet learned he this obedience,* Heb. 5:8. The motto of this Prince is, *Ich dien — I serve.*

(2.) That Jesus Christ was chosen of God, as the only fit and proper person for the management of the great work of our redemption. He is *my Servant whom I have chosen,* as *par negotio — equal to the undertaking.* None but he was able to do the Redeemer's work, or fit to wear the Redeemer's crown. He was *one chosen out of the people* (Ps. 89:19), chosen by Infinite Wisdom to that post of service and honour, for which neither man nor angel was qualified; none but Christ, that he might in all things have the pre-eminence. Christ did not thrust himself upon this work, but was duly chosen into it; Christ was so God's Chosen as to be the head of election, and of all other the Elect, for we are *chosen in him,* Eph. 1:4.

(3.) That Jesus Christ is God's Beloved, his beloved Son; as God, he lay from eternity in his bosom (Jn. 1:18); he was *daily his delight,* (Prov. 8:30). Between the Father and the Son there was before all time an eternal and inconceivable intercourse and interchanging of love, and thus *the Lord possessed him in the beginning of his way,* Prov. 8:22. As Mediator, the Father loved him; then when it pleased the Lord to bruise him, and he submitted to it, *therefore did the Father love him,* Jn. 10:17.

(4.) That Jesus Christ is one in whom the Father is well

pleased, in whom his soul is pleased; which denotes the highest complacency imaginable. God declared, by a voice from heaven, that he was his beloved Son in whom he is well pleased; well pleased *in him,* because he was the ready and cheerful Undertaker of that work of wonder which God's heart was so much upon, and he is well pleased with us in him; for he had *made us accepted in the Beloved,* Eph. 1:6. All the interest which fallen man has or can have in God is grounded upon and owing to God's *well-pleasedness* in Jesus Christ; for there is *no coming to the Father but by him,* Jn. 14:6.

2. The promise of the Father to him in two things.

(1.) That he should be every way well qualified for his undertaking; *I will put my Spirit upon him,* as a Spirit of *wisdom and counsel,* Isa. 11:2, 3. Those whom God calls to any service, he will be sure to fit and qualify for it; and by that it will appear that he called them to it, as Moses, Ex. 4:12. Christ, as God, was equal in power and glory with the Father; as Mediator, he received from the Father power and glory, and received that he might give: and all that the Father gave him, to qualify him for his undertaking, was summed up in this, he *put his Spirit upon him:* this was that *oil of gladness* with which he was *anointed above his fellows,* Heb. 1:9. He received the Spirit, not by measure, but *without measure,* Jn. 3:34. Note, Whoever they be that God has chosen, and in whim he is well pleased, he will be sure to *put his Spirit upon them.* Wherever he confers his love, he confers somewhat of his likeness.

(2.) That he should be abundantly successful in his understanding. Those whom God sends he will certainly own. It was long since secured by promise to our Lord Jesus, that the *good pleasure of the Lord should prosper in his hand,* Isa. 53:10. And here we have an account of that prospering good pleasure.

[1.] He shall *show judgment to the Gentiles.* Christ in his own person preached to those who bordered upon the heathen nations (see Mk. 3:6–8), and by his apostle showed his gospel, called here his *judgment,* to the Gentile world. The way and method of salvation, the *judgment* which is *committed to the Son,* is not only wrought out by him as our great High Priest, but showed and published by him as our great Prophet. The gospel, as it is a rule of practice and conversation, which has a direct tendency to the reforming and bettering of men's hearts and lives, shall be showed to the Gentiles. God's judgments had been the Jews' peculiar (Ps. 147:19), but it was often foretold, by the Old-Testament prophets, that they should be *showed to the Gentiles,* which therefore ought not to have been such a surprise as it was to the unbelieving Jews, much less a vexation.

[2.] *In his name shall the Gentiles trust, v.* 21. He shall so show judgment to them, that they shall heed and observe what he shows them, and be influenced by it to depend upon him, to devote themselves to him, and conform to that judgment. Note, The great design of the gospel, is to bring people to trust in the name of Jesus Christ; his name Jesus, a Saviour, that precious name whereby he is called, and which is as ointment poured forth; *The Lord our Righteousness.* The evangelist here follows the Septuagint (or perhaps the latter editions of the Septuagint follow the evangelist); the Hebrew (Isa. 42:4) is, *The isles shall wait for his law.* The isles of the Gentiles are spoken of (Gen. 10:5), as peopled by the sons of Japhet, of whom it was said (Gen. 9:27), *God shall persuade Japhet to dwell in the tents of Shem;* which was now to be fulfilled, when *the isles* (says the prophet), *the Gentiles* (says the evangelist), *shall wait for his law,* and *trust in his name:* compare these together, and observe, that they, and they only, can with confidence *trust in Christ's name,* that *wait for his law* with a resolution to be ruled by it. Observe also, that the law we wait for is the law of faith, the law of trusting in his name. This is now his great commandment, that we *believe in Christ,* 1 Jn. 3:23.

3. The prediction concerning him, and his mild and quiet management of his undertaking, *v.* 19, 20. It is chiefly for the sake of this that it is here quoted, upon occasion of Christ's affected privacy and concealment.

(1.) That he should carry on his undertaking without noise or ostentation. *He shall not strive, or make an outcry.* Christ and his kingdom *come not with observation,* Lu. 17:20, 21. When the First-begotten was brought into the world, it was not with state and ceremony; he made no public entry, had no harbingers to proclaim him King. He *was in the world and the world knew him not.* Those were mistaken who fed themselves with hopes of a pompous Saviour. *His voice was not heard in the streets;* "Lo, here is Christ;" or, "Lo, he is there:" he spake in a still small voice, which was alluring to all, but terrifying to none; he did not affect to make a noise, but came down silently like the dew. What he spake and did was with the greatest possible humility and self-denial. His kingdom was spiritual, and therefore not to be advanced by force or violence, or by high pretensions. No, *the kingdom of God is not in word, but in power.*

(2.) That he should carry on his undertaking without severity and rigour (*v.* 20). *A bruised reed shall he not break.* Some understand this of his patience in bearing with the wicked; he could as easily have broken these Pharisees as a bruised reed, and have quenched them as soon as smoking flax; but he will not do it till the judgment-day, when all his enemies shall be made his footstool. Others rather understand it of his power and grace in bearing up the weak. In general, the design of his gospel is to establish such a method of salvation as encourages sincerity, though there be much infirmity; it does not insist upon a sinless obedience, but accepts an upright, willing mind. As to particular persons, that follow Christ in meekness, and in fear, and in much trembling, observe, [1.] How their case is here described — they are like *a bruised reed,* and *smoking flax.* Young beginners in religion are weak as a bruised reed, and their weakness offensive like smoking flax; some little life they have, but it is like that of a bruised reed; some little heat, but like that of smoking flax. Christ's disciples were as yet but weak, and many are so that have a place in his family. The grace and goodness in them are as a bruised reed, the corruption and badness in them are as smoking flax, as the wick of a candle when it is put out and is yet smoking. [2.] What is the compassion of our Lord Jesus toward them? He will not discourage them, much less reject them or cast them off; the reed that is bruised shall not be broken and trodden down, but shall be supported, and made as strong as a cedar or flourishing palm-tree. The candle newly lighted, though it only smokes and does not flame, shall not be blown out, but blown up. The *day of small things* is the day of *precious* things, and therefore he will not despise it, but make it *the day of great things,* Zec. 4:10. Note, Our Lord Jesus deals very tenderly with those who have true grace, though they be weak in it, Isa. 40:11; Heb. 5:2. He remembers not only that we are dust, but that we are flesh. [3.] The good issue and success of this, intimated in that, *till he send forth judgment unto victory.* That judgment which he showed to the Gentiles shall be victorious, he will go on conquering and to conquer, Rev. 6:2. Both the preaching of the gospel in the world, and the power of the gospel in the heart, shall prevail. Grace shall get the upper hand of corruption, and shall at length be perfected in glory. Christ's judgment will be brought forth to victory, for when he judges he will overcome. He shall *bring forth judgment unto truth;* so it is, Isa. 42:3. Truth and victory are much the same, for *great is the truth, and will prevail.*

Verses 22–37

In these verses we have,

I. Christ's glorious conquest of Satan, in the gracious cure of one who, by the divine permission, was under his power, and in his possession, *v.* 22. Here observe,

1. The man's case was very sad; he was *possessed with a devil.* More cases of this kind occurred in Christ's time than usual, that Christ's power might be the more magnified, and his purpose the more manifested, in opposing and dispossessing Satan; and that it might the more evidently appear, that he *came to destroy the works of the devil.* This poor man that was possessed was blind and dumb; a miserable case! he could neither see to help himself, nor speak to others to help him. A soul under Satan's power, and led captive by him, is blind in the things of God, and dumb at the throne of grace; sees nothing, and says nothing to the purpose. Satan blinds the eye of faith, and seals up the lips of prayer.

2. His cure was very strange, and the more so, because sudden; *he healed him.* Note, The conquering and dispossessing of Satan is the healing of souls. And the cause being removed, immediately the effect ceased; the *blind and dumb both spake and saw.* Note, Christ's mercy is directly opposite to Satan's malice; his favours, to the devil's mischiefs. When Satan's power is broken in the soul, the eyes are opened to see God's glory, and the lips opened to speak his praise.

II. The conviction which this gave to the people to *all the people:* they *were amazed.* Christ had wrought divers miracles of this kind before; but his works are not the less wonderful, nor the less to be wondered at, for their being often repeated. They inferred from it, *"Is not this the Son of David?* The Messiah promised, that was to spring from the loins of David? Is not this he that should come?" We may take this, 1. As an *enquiring* question; they asked, *Is not this the Son of David?* But they did not stay for an answer: the impressions were cogent, but they were transient. It was a good question that they started; but, it should seem, it was soon lost, and was not prosecuted. Such convictions as these should be brought to a head, and then they are likely to be brought to the heart. Or, 2. as an *affirming* question; *Is not this the Son of David?* "Yes, certainly it is, it can be no other; such miracles as these plainly evince that the kingdom of the Messiah is now setting up." And they were the people, the vulgar sort of the spectators, that drew this inference from Christ's miracles. Atheists will say, "That was because they were less prying than the Pharisees;" no, the matter of fact was obvious, and required not much search: but it was because they were less prejudiced and biassed by worldly interest. So plain and easy was the way made to this great truth of Christ being the Messiah and Saviour of the world, that the common people could not miss it; the *wayfaring men, though fools, could not err therein.* See Isa. 35:8. It was found of them that sought it. It is an instance of the condescensions of divine grace, that the things that were *hid from the wise and prudent* were *revealed unto babes.* The world by wisdom knew not God, and by the foolish things the wise were confounded.

III. The blasphemous cavil of the Pharisees, *v.* 24. The Pharisees were a sort of men that pretended to more knowledge in, and zeal for, the divine law, than other people; yet they were the most inveterate enemies to Christ and his doctrine. They were proud of the reputation they had among the people; *that* fed their pride, supported their power, and filled their purses; and when they heard the people say, *Is not this the Son of David?* they were extremely irritated, more at that than at the miracle itself; this made them jealous of our Lord Jesus, and apprehensive, that as *his* interest in the people's esteem increased, *theirs* must of course be eclipsed and diminished; therefore they envied him, as Saul did his father David, because of what the women sang of him, 1 Sa. 18:7, 8. Note, Those who bind up their happiness in the praise and applause of men, expose themselves to a perpetual uneasiness upon every favourable word that they hear said of any other. The shadow of honour followed Christ, who fled from it, and fled from the Pharisees, who were eager in the pursuit of it. They said, *"This fellow does not cast out devils, but by Beelzebub the prince of the devils,* and therefore is not the Son of David." Observe,

1. How scornfully they speak of Christ, *this fellow;* as if that precious name of his, which is *as ointment poured forth,* were not worthy to be taken into their lips. It is an instance of their pride and superciliousness, and their diabolical envy, that the more people magnified Christ, the more industrious they were to vilify him. It is a bad thing to speak of good men with disdain because they are poor.

2. How blasphemously they speak of his miracles; they could not deny the matter of fact; it was as plain as the sun, that devils were cast out by the word of Christ; nor could they deny that it was an extraordinary thing, and supernatural. Being thus forced to grant the premises, they had no other way to avoid the conclusion, that *this is the Son of David,* than by suggesting that *Christ cast out devils by Beelzebub;* that there was a compact between Christ and the devil; pursuant to that, the devil was not cast out, but did voluntarily retire, and give back by consent and with design: or as if, by an agreement with the ruling devil, he had power to cast out the inferior devils. No surmise could be more palpably false and vile than this; that he, who is Truth itself, should be in combination with the father of lies, to cheat the world. This was the last refuge, or subterfuge rather, or an obstinate infidelity, that was resolved to stand it out against the clearest conviction. Observe, Among the devils there is a prince, the ringleader of the apostasy from God and rebellion against him; but this prince is Beelzebub — the god of a fly, or a dunghill god. How art thou fallen, O Lucifer! from an anger of light, to be a lord of flies! Yet this is the prince of the devils too, the chief of the gang of infernal spirits.

IV. Christ's reply to this base insinuation, *v.* 25–30. *Jesus knew their thoughts.* Note, Jesus Christ knows what we are thinking at any time, knows what is in man; he *understands our thoughts afar off.* It should seem that the Pharisees could not for shame speak it out, but kept it in their minds; they could not expect to satisfy the people with it; they therefore reserved it for the silencing of the convictions of their own consciences. Note, Many are kept off from their duty by that which they are ashamed to own, but which they cannot hide from Jesus Christ: yet it is probable that the Pharisees had whispered what they thought among themselves, to help to harden one another; but Christ's reply is said to be to their thoughts, because he knew with what mind, and from what principle, they said it; that they did not say it in their haste, but that it was the product of a rooted malignity.

Christ's reply to this imputation is copious and cogent, that *every mouth may be stopped* with sense and reason, before it be stopped with fire and brimstone. Here are three arguments by which he demonstrates the unreasonableness of this suggestion.

1. It would be very strange, and highly improbably, that Satan should be cast out by such a compact, because then Satan's *kingdom would be divided against itself;* which, considering his subtlety, is not a thing to be imagined, *v.* 25, 26.

(1.) Here is a known rule laid down, that in all societies a common ruin is the consequence of mutual quarrels: *Every kingdom divided against itself is brought to desolation;* and every family too: *Quae enim domus tam stabilis est, quae tam firma civitas, quae non odiis atque dissidiis funditus everti possit? — For what family is so strong, what community so firm, as not to be overturned by enmity and dissension?* Cic. *Lael.* 7. Divisions commonly end in desolations; if we clash, we break; if we divide one from another, we become an easy prey to a common enemy; much more *if we bite and devour one another,* shall *we be consumed one of another,* Gal. 5:15. Churches and nations have known this by sad experience.

(2.) The application of it to the case in hand (*v.* 26), *If Satan cast out Satan;* if the prince of the devils should be at variance with the inferior devils, the whole kingdom and interest would soon be broken; nay, if Satan should come into a compact with Christ, it must be to his own ruin; for the manifest design and tendency of Christ's preaching and miracles was to overthrow the kingdom of Satan, as a kingdom of darkness, wickedness, and enmity to God; and to set up, upon the ruins of it, a kingdom of light, holiness, and love. *The works of the devil,* as a rebel against God, and a tyrant over the souls of men, were destroyed by Christ; and therefore it was the most absurd thing imaginable, to think that Beelzebub should at all countenance such a design, or come into it: if he should fall in with Christ, *how should then his kingdom stand?* He would himself contribute to the overthrow of it. Note, The devil has a kingdom, a common interest, in opposition to God and Christ, which, to the utmost of his power, he will make to stand, and he will never come into Christ's interests; he must be conquered and broken by Christ, and therefore cannot submit and bend to him. *What concord or communion can there be between light and darkness, Christ and Belial, Christ and Beelzebub?* Christ will destroy the devil's kingdom, but he needs not do it by any such little arts and projects as that of a secret compact with Beelzebub; no, this victory must be obtained by nobler methods. Let the prince of the devils muster up all his forces, let him make use of all his powers and politics, and keep his interests in the closest confederacy, yet Christ will be too hard for his united force, and his kingdom shall not stand.

2. It was not at all strange, or improbable, that devils should be cast out by the Spirit of God; for,

(1.) *How otherwise do your children cast them out?* There were those among the Jews who, by invocation of the name of the most high God, or the God of Abraham, Isaac, and Jacob, did sometimes cast out devils. Josephus speaks of some in his time that did it; we read of *Jewish exorcists* (Acts 19:13), and of some that *in Christ's name cast out devils,* though they did not follow him (Mk. 9:38), or were not faithful to him, *ch.* 7:22. These the Pharisees condemned not, but imputed what they did to the Spirit of God, and valued themselves and their nation upon it. It was therefore merely from spite and envy to Christ, that they would own that others cast out devils by the Spirit of God, but suggest that he did it by compact with Beelzebub. Note, It is the way of malicious people, especially the malicious persecutors of Christ and Christianity, to condemn the same thing in those they hate, which they approve of and applaud in those they have a kindness for: the judgments of envy are made, not by things, but persons; not by reason, but prejudice. But those were very unfit to

sit in Moses's seat, who knew faces, and knew nothing else in judgment: *Therefore they shall be your judges;* "This contradicting of yourselves will rise up in judgment against you at the last great day, and will condemn you." Note, In the last judgment, not only every sin, but every aggravation of it, will be brought into the account, and some of our notions that were right and good will be brought in evidence against us, to convict us of partiality.

(2.) This casting out of devils was a certain token and indication of the approach and appearance of the kingdom of God (*v.* 28); "But if it be indeed that *I cast out devils by the Spirit of God,* as certainly I do, then you must conclude, that though you are unwilling to receive it, yet the kingdom of the Messiah is now about to be set up among you." Other miracles that Christ wrought proved him *sent of God,* but this proved him sent of God to destroy the devil's kingdom and his works. Now that great promise was evidently fulfilled, that *the seed of the woman should break the serpent's head,* Gen. 3:15. "Therefore that glorious dispensation of the kingdom of God, which has been long expected, is now commenced; slight it at your peril." Note, [1.] The destruction of the devil's power is wrought by the Spirit of God; that Spirit who works to the obedience of faith, overthrows the interest of that spirit who *works in the children of* unbelief and *disobedience.* [2.] The casting out of devils is a certain introduction to the kingdom of God. If the devil's interest in a soul be not only checked by custom or external restraints, but sunk and broken by the Spirit of God, as a Sanctifier, no doubt but *the kingdom of God is come* to that soul, the kingdom of grace, a blessed earnest of the kingdom of the glory.

3. The comparing of Christ's miracles, particularly this of casting out devils, with his doctrine, and the design and tendency of his holy religion, evidenced that he was so far from being in league with Satan, that he was at open enmity and hostility against him (*v.* 29); *How can one enter into a strong man's house, and plunder his goods,* and carry them away, *except he first bind the strong man? And then he* may do what he pleases with his goods. The world, that sat in darkness, and lay in wickedness, was in Satan's possession, and under his power, as a house in the possession and under the power of a strong man; so is every unregenerate soul; there Satan resides, there he rules. Now, (1.) The design of Christ's gospel was to spoil the devil's house, which, as a strong man, he kept in the world; *to turn the people from darkness to light,* from sin to holiness, from this world to a better, *from the power of Satan unto God* (Acts 26:18); to alter the property of souls. (2.) Pursuant to this design, he bound the strong man, when he cast out unclean spirits by his word: thus he wrested the *sword* out of the devil's hand, that he might wrest the *sceptre* out of it. The doctrine of Christ teaches us how to construe his miracles, and when he showed how easily and effectually he could cast the devil out of people's bodies, he encouraged all believers to hope that, whatever power Satan might usurp and exercise in the souls of men, Christ by his grace would break it: he will spoil him, for it appears that he can bind him. When nations were turned *from the service of idols to serve the living God,* when some of the worst of sinners were sanctified and justified, and became the best of saints, then Christ spoiled the devil's house, and will spoil it more and more.

4. It is here intimated, that this holy war, which Christ was carrying on with vigour against the devil and his kingdom, was such as would not admit of a neutrality (*v.* 30), *He that is not with me is against me.* In the little differences that may arise between the disciples of Christ among themselves, we are taught to lessen the matters in variance, and to seek peace, by accounting those who *are not against us, to be with us* (Lu. 9:50); but in the great quarrel between Christ and the devil, no peace is to be sought, nor any such favourable construction to be made of any indifference in the matter; he that is not hearty *for* Christ, will be reckoned with as really *against* him: he that is cold in the cause, is looked upon as an enemy. When the dispute is between God and Baal, there is no halting between two (1 Ki. 18:21), there is no trimming between Christ and Belial; for the kingdom of Christ, as it is eternally opposite to, so it will be eternally victorious over, the devil's kingdom; and therefore in this cause there is no sitting still with *Gilead beyond Jordan, or Asher on the seashore,* (Jdg. 4:16, 17), we must be entirely, faithfully, and immovably, on Christ's side; it is the *right* side, and will at last be the *rising* side. See Ex. 32:26.

The latter clause is to the same purport: *He that gath-*

ereth not with me scattereth. Note, (1.) Christ's errand into the world was to gather, to gather in his harvest, to gather in those whom the Father had given him, Jn. 11:52; Eph. 1:10. (2.) Christ expects and requires from those who are with him, that they gather with him; that they not only gather to him themselves, but do all they can in their places to gather others to him, and so to strengthen his interest. (3.) Those who will not appear, and act, as furtherers of Christ's kingdom, will be looked upon, and dealt with, as hinderers of it; if we *gather not with Christ, we scatter;* it is not enough, not to do hurt, but we must do good. Thus is the breach widened between Christ and Satan, to show that there was no such compact between them as the Pharisees whispered.

V. Here is a discourse of Christ's upon this occasion, concerning tongue-sins; *Wherefore I say unto you.* He seems to turn from the Pharisees to the people, from disputing to instructing; and from the sin of the Pharisees he warns the people concerning three sorts of tongue-sins; for others' harms are admonitions to us.

1. Blasphemous words against the Holy Ghost are the worst kind of tongue-sins, and unpardonable, *v.* 31, 32.

(1.) Here is a gracious assurance of the pardon of all sin upon gospel terms: this Christ says to us, and it is a comfortable saying, that the greatness of sin shall be no bar to our acceptance with God, if we truly repent and believe the gospel: *All manner of sin and blasphemy shall be forgiven unto men.* Though the sin has been as *scarlet and crimson* (Isa. 1:18), though ever so heinous in its nature, ever so much aggravated by its circumstances, and ever so often repeated, though it *reach up to the heavens,* yet *with the Lord there is mercy, that reacheth beyond the heavens;* mercy will be extended even to blasphemy, a sin immediately touching God's name and honour. Paul obtained mercy, who had *been a blasphemer,* 1 Tim. 1:13. Well may we say, *Who is a God like unto thee, pardoning iniquity?* Micah 7:18. Even *words spoken against the Son of man shall be forgiven;* as theirs were who reviled him at his death, many of whom repented and found mercy. Christ herein has set an example to all the sons of men, to be ready to forgive words spoken against them: *I, as a deaf man, heard not.* Observe, *They shall be forgiven unto men,* not to devils; this is love to the whole world of mankind, above the world of fallen angels, that all sin is pardonable to them.

(2.) Here is an exception of *the blasphemy against the Holy Ghost,* which is here declared to be the only unpardonable sin. See here,

[1.] What this sin; it is *speaking against the Holy Ghost.* See what malignity there is in tongue-sins, when the only unpardonable sin is so. *But Jesus knew their thoughts, v.* 25. It is not all speaking against the person or essence of the Holy Ghost, or some of his more private operations, or merely the resisting of his internal working in the sinner himself, that is here meant; for *who then should be saved?* It is adjudged in our law, that an act of indemnity shall always be construed in favour of that grace and clemency which is the intention of the act; and therefore the exceptions in the act are not to be extended further than needs must. The gospel is an act of indemnity; none are excepted by name, nor any by description, but those only *that blaspheme the Holy Ghost;* which therefore must be construed in the narrowest sense: all presuming sinners are effectually cut off by the conditions of the indemnity, faith and repentance; and therefore the other exceptions must not be stretched far: and this blasphemy is excepted, not for any defect of mercy in God or merit in Christ, but because it inevitably leaves the sinner in infidelity and impenitency. We have reason to think that none are guilty of this sin, who believe that Christ is *the Son of God,* and sincerely desire to have part in his merit and mercy: and those who fear they have committed this sin, give a good sign that they have not. The learned Dr. Whitby very well observes, that Christ speaks not of what should be (Mk. 3:28; Lu. 12:10); *Whosoever shall blaspheme.* As for those who blasphemed Christ when he was here upon earth, and called him a Winebibber, a Deceiver, a Blasphemer, and the like, they had some colour of excuse, because of the meanness of his appearance, and the prejudices of the nation against him; and the proof of his divine mission was not perfected till after his ascension; and therefore, upon their repentance, they shall be pardoned: and it is hoped that they may be convinced by the pouring out of the Spirit, as many of them were, who had been his betrayers and murderers. But if, when the Holy Ghost is given, in his inward gifts of revelation, speaking with tongues, and the like, such as were the distributions of the Spirit among the apostles, if they continue to blaspheme the Spirit likewise, as an evil spirit, there is no hope of them that they will ever be brought to believe in Christ; for *First,* Those gifts of the Holy Ghost in the apostles were the last proof that God designed to make use of for the confirming of the gospel, and were still kept in reserve, when other methods preceded. *Secondly,* This was the most powerful evidence, and more apt to convince than miracles themselves. *Thirdly,* Those therefore who blaspheme this dispensation of the Spirit, cannot possibly be brought to believe in Christ; those who shall impute them to a collusion with Satan, as the Pharisees did the miracles, what can convince them? This is such a strong hold of infidelity as a man can never be beaten out of, and is therefore unpardonable, because hereby repentance is hid from the sinner's eyes.

[2.] What the sentence is that is passed upon it; *It shall not be forgiven, neither in this world, nor in the world to come.* As in the then present state of the Jewish church, there was no sacrifice of expiation for *the soul that sinned presumptuously;* so neither under the dispensation of gospel grace, which is often in scripture called *the world to come,* shall there be any pardon to *such as tread underfoot the blood of the covenant, and do despite to the Spirit of grace:* there is no cure for a sin so directly against the remedy. It was a rule in our old law, No sanctuary for sacrilege. Or, *It shall be forgiven neither now,* in the sinner's own conscience, *nor in the great day,* when the pardon shall be published. Or, this is a sin that exposes the sinner both to temporal and eternal punishment, both to present wrath and *the wrath to come.*

2. Christ speaks here concerning other wicked words, the products of corruption reigning in the heart, and breaking out thence, *v.* 33–35. It was said (*v.* 25) that *Jesus knew their thoughts,* and here he spoke with an eye to them, showing that it was not strange that they should speak so ill, when their hearts were so full of enmity and malice; which yet they often endeavoured to cloak and cover, by feigning themselves just men. Our Lord Jesus therefore points to the springs and heals them; let the heart be sanctified and it will appear in our words.

(1.) The heart is the *root,* the language is the *fruit* (*v.* 33); if the nature of the tree be good, it will bring forth fruit accordingly. Where grace is the reigning principle in the heart, the language will be the language of Canaan; and, on the contrary, whatever lust reigns in the heart it will break out; diseased lungs make an offensive breath: men's language discovers what country they are of, so likewise *what manner of spirit they are of: "Either make the tree good, and then the fruit will be good;* get pure hearts and then you will have pure lips and pure lives; or else *the tree will be corrupt, and the fruit* accordingly. you may make a crab-stock to become a good tree, by grafting into it a shoot from a good tree, and then the fruit will be good; but if the tree be still the same, plant it where you will, and water it how you will, the fruit will be still corrupt." Note, Unless the heart be *trans*formed, the life will never be thoroughly *re*formed. These Pharisees were shy of speaking out their wicked thoughts of Jesus Christ; but Christ here intimates, how vain it was for them to seek to hide that root of bitterness in them, that bore this gall and wormwood, when they never sought to mortify it. Note, It should be more our care to be good really, than to seem good outwardly.

(2.) The heart is the *fountain,* the words are the streams (*v.* 34); *Out of the abundance of the heart the mouth speaks,* as the streams are the overflowings of the spring. A wicked heart is said to *send forth wickedness, as a fountain casts forth her waters,* Jer. 6:7. *A troubled fountain, and a corrupt spring,* such as Solomon speaks of (Prov. 25:26), must needs *send forth muddy and unpleasant streams.* Evil words are the natural, genuine product of an evil heart. Nothing but the salt of grace, cast into the spring, will heal the waters, *season the speech,* and purify the *corrupt communications.* This they wanted, they were evil; *and how can ye, being evil, speak good things?* They were *a generation of vipers;* John Baptist had called them so (*ch.* 3:7), and they were still the same; for *can the Ethiopian change his skin?* The people looked upon the Pharisees as a generation of saints, but Christ calls them *a generation of vipers, the seed of the serpent,* that had an enmity to Christ and his gospel. Now what could be expected from *a generation of vipers,* but that which is poisonous and malignant? Can the viper be otherwise than venomous? Note, Bad things may be expected from bad people, as said the proverb of the ancients, *Wickedness proceedeth from the wicked,* 1 Sa. 24:13. *The vile person will speak villany,* Isa. 32:6. Those who are themselves evil, have neither skill nor will to speak good things, as they should be spoken. Christ would have his disciples know what sort of men they were to live among, that they might know what to look for. They are as Ezekiel *among scorpions* (Eze. 2:6), and must not think it strange if they be stung and bitten.

(3.) The heart is the *treasury,* the words are the things brought out of that treasury (*v.* 35); and from hence men's characters may be drawn, and may be judged of.

[1.] It is the character of a *good man,* that he has a *good treasure in his heart,* and from thence *brings forth good things,* as there is occasion. Graces, comforts, experiences, good knowledge, good affections, good resolutions, these are a *good treasure in the heart;* the word of God hidden there, the law of God written there, divine truths dwelling and ruling thee, are a treasure there, valuable and suitable, kept safe and kept secret, as the stores of the good householder, but ready for use upon all occasions. *A good man,* thus furnished, will *bring forth,* as Joseph out of his stores; will be speaking and doing that which is good, for God's glory, and the edification of others. See Prov. 10:11, 13, 14, 20, 21, 31, 32. This is *bringing forth good things.* Some pretend to good expenses that have not a *good treasure* — such will soon be bankrupts: some pretend to have a good treasure within, but give no proof of it: they hope they have it in them, and thank God, whatever their words and actions are, they have good hearts; but *faith without works is dead:* and some have a *good treasure* of wisdom and knowledge, but they are not communicative, they do not *bring forth* out of it: they have a talent, but know not how to trade with it. The complete Christian in *this* bears the image of God, that he both *is good, and does good.*

[2.] It is the character of *an evil man,* that he has an *evil treasure in his heart,* and out of it *bringeth forth evil things.* Lusts and corruptions dwelling and reigning in the heart are an evil treasure, out of which the sinner brings forth bad words and actions, to the dishonour of God, and the hurt of others. See Gen. 6:5, 12; Mt. 15:18–20; Jam. 1:15. But *treasures of wickedness* (Prov. 10:2) will be *treasures of wrath.*

3. Christ speaks here concerning *idle words,* and shows what evil there is in them (*v.* 36, 37); much more is there in such wicked words as the Pharisees spoke. It concerns us to think much of the day of judgment, that *that* may be a check upon our tongues; and let us consider,

(1.) How particular the account will be of tongue-sins in that day: even *for every idle words,* or discourse, *that men speak, they shall give account.* This intimates, [1.] That God takes notice of every word we say, even that which we ourselves do not notice. See Psalm 139:4. *Not a word in my tongue but thou knowest it:* though spoken without regard or design, God takes cognizance of it. [2.] That vain, idle, impertinent talk is displeasing to God, which tends not to any good purpose, is not good to any use of edifying; it is the product of a vain and trifling heart. These *idle words* are the same with that *foolish talking and jesting* which is forbidden, Eph. 5:4. This is that sin which is seldom wanting in *the multitude of words, unprofitable talk,* Job 15:3. [3.] We must shortly account for these idle words; they will be produced in evidence against us, to prove us unprofitable servants, that have not improved the faculties of reason and speech, which are part of the talents we are entrusted with. If we repent not of our idle words, and our account for them be not balanced by the blood of Christ, we are undone.

(2.) How strict the judgment will be upon that account (*v.* 37); *By thy words thou shall be justified or condemned;* a common rule in men's judgments, and here applied to God's. Note, The constant tenour of our discourse, according as it is gracious or not gracious, will be an evidence for us, or against us, at the great day. Those who seemed to be religious, but bridled not their tongue, will then be found to have put a cheat upon themselves with a vain religion, Jam. 1:26. Some think that Christ here refers to that of Eliphaz (Job 15:6), *Thine own mouth condemneth thee, and not I;* or, rather, to that of Solomon (Prov. 18:21), *Death and life are in the power of the tongue.*

Verses 38–45

It is probable that these Pharisees with whom Christ is here in discourse were not the same that cavilled at him (*v.* 24), and would not credit the signs he gave; but another set of them, who saw that there was no reason to discredit them, but would not content themselves with the signs he gave, nor admit the evidence of them, unless he would give them such further proof as they should demand. Here is,

I. Their address to him, *v.* 38. They compliment him with the title of *Master,* pretending respect for him, when they intended to abuse him; all are not indeed Christ's servants, who call him *Master.* Their request is, *We would see a sign from thee.* It was highly reasonable that they should see a sign, that he should by miracles prove his divine mission: see Ex. 4:8, 9. He came to take down a model of religion that was set up by miracles, and therefore it was requisite he should produce the same credentials; but it was highly unreasonable to demand a sign now, when he had given so many signs already, that did abundantly prove him *sent of God.* Note, It is natural to proud men to *pre*scribe to God, and then to make that an excuse for not *sub*scribing to him; but a man's *offence* will never be his *de*fence.

II. His answer to this address, this insolent demand,

1. He condemns the demand, as the language of *an evil and adulterous generation, v.* 39. He fastens the charge, not only on *the scribes and Pharisees,* but the whole nation of the Jews; they were all like their leaders, a seed and succession of evil-doers: they were an evil generation indeed, that not only hardened themselves against the conviction of Christ's miracles, but set themselves to abuse him, and put contempt on his miracles. They were *an adulterous generation,* (1.) As an adulterous brood; so miserably degenerated from the faith and obedience of their ancestors, that Abraham and Israel acknowledged them not. See Isa. 57:3. Or, (2.) As an adulterous wife; they departed from that God, to whom by covenant they had been espoused: they were not guilty of the whoredom of idolatry, as they had been before the captivity, but they were guilty of infidelity, and all iniquity, and that is whoredom too: they did not look after gods of their own making, but they looked for signs of their own devising; and that was adultery.

2. He refuses to give them any other sign than he has already given them, but *that of the prophet Jonas.* Note, Though Christ is always ready to hear and answer holy desires and prayers, yet he will not gratify corrupt lusts and humours. Those who *ask amiss, ask, and have not.* Signs were granted to those who desired them for the confirmation of their faith, as to Abraham and Gideon; but were denied to those who demanded them for the excuse of their unbelief.

Justly might Christ have said, They shall never see another miracle: but see his wonderful goodness; (1.) They shall have the same signs still repeated, for their further benefit, and more abundant conviction. (2.) They shall have one sign of a different kind from all these, and that is, *the resurrection of Christ from the dead by his own power,* called here *the sign of the prophet Jonas* this was yet reserved for their conviction, and was intended to be the great proof of Christ's being the Messiah; for by that he was *declared to be the Son of God with power,* Rom. 1:4. That was such a sign as surpassed all the rest, completed and crowned them. *"If they will not believe* the former signs, they will believe this (Ex. 4:9), and if this will not convince them, nothing will." And yet the unbelief of the Jews found out an evasion to shift off that too, by saying, *His disciples came and stole him away;* for none are so incurably blind as those who are resolved they will not see.

Now this sign of the prophet Jonas he further explains here; (*v.* 40) *As Jonas was three days and three nights in the whale's belly,* and then came out again safe and well, thus Christ shall be so long in the grave, and then shall rise again. [1.] The grave was to Christ as the belly of the fish was to Jonah; thither he was thrown, as a Ransom for lives ready to be lost in a storm; there he lay, as *in the belly of hell* (Jonah 2:2), and seemed to be cast out of God's sight. [2.] He continued in the grave just as long as Jonah continued in the fish's belly, *three days and three nights;* not three whole days and nights: it is probable, Jonah did not lie so long in the whale's belly, but part of three natural days (*nychthēmerai,* the Greeks called them); he was buried in the afternoon of the sixth day of the week, and rose again in the morning of the first day; it is a manner of speech very usual; see 1 Ki. 20:29; Esth. 4:16; 5:1; Lu. 2:21. So long Jonah was a prisoner for his own sins, so long Christ was a Prisoner for ours. [3.] As Jonah in the whale's belly comforted himself with an assurance that yet he should look again *toward God's holy temple* (Jonah 2:4), so Christ when he lay in the grave, is expressly said to *rest in hope,* as one assured he should *not see corruption,* Acts 2:26, 27. [4.] As Jonah on the third day was discharged from his prison, and came to the land of the living again, from *the congregation of the dead* (for dead things are said to be *formed from under the waters,* Job 26:5), so Christ on the third day should return to life, and rise out of his grave to send abroad the gospel to the Gentiles.

3. Christ takes this occasion to represent the sad character and condition of that generation in which he lived, a generation that would not be reformed, and therefore could not but be ruined; and he gives them their character, as it would stand in the day of judgment, under the full discoveries and final sentences of that day. Persons and things now appear under false colours; characters and conditions are here changeable: if therefore we would make a right estimate, we must take our measures from the last judgment; things are really, what they are eternally.

Now Christ represents the people of the Jews,

(1.) As a generation that would be condemned by the *men of Nineveh,* whose *repenting at the preaching of Jonas* would *rise up in judgment* against them, *v.* 41. Christ's resurrection will be the sign of the prophet Jonas to them: but it will not have so happy an effect upon them, as that of Jonas had upon the Ninevites, for they were by it brought to such a repentance as prevented their ruin; but the Jews will be hardened in an unbelief that shall hasten their ruin; and in the day of judgment, the repentance of the Ninevites will be mentioned as an aggravation of the sin, and consequently the condemnation of those to whom Christ preached then, and of those to whom Christ is preached now; for this reason, because Christ is greater than Jonah. [1.] Jonah was but a man, subject to like passions, to like sinful passions, as we are; but Christ is the Son of God. [2.] Jonah was a stranger in Nineveh, he came among the strangers that were prejudiced against his country; but Christ came to his own, when he preached to the Jews, and much more when he is preached among professing Christians, that are called by his name. [3.] Jonah preached but one short sermon, and that with no great solemnity, but as he passed along the streets; Christ renews his calls, sat and taught, taught in the synagogues. [4.] Jonah preached nothing but wrath and ruin within forty days, gave no instructions, directions, or encouragements, to repent: but Christ, besides the warning given us of our danger, has shown wherein we must repent, and assured us of acceptance upon our repentance, because *the kingdom of heaven is at hand.* [5.] Jonah wrought no miracle to confirm his doctrine, showed no good will to the Ninevites; but Christ wrought abundance of miracles, and all miracles of mercy: yet the Ninevites *repented at the preaching of Jonas,* but the Jews were not wrought upon by Christ's preaching. Note, The goodness of some, who have less helps and advantages for their souls, will aggravate the badness of those who have much greater. Those who by the twilight discover *the things that belong to their peace,* will shame those who grope at noon-day.

(2.) As a generation that would be condemned by the queen of the south, the queen of Sheba, *v.* 42. The Ninevites would shame them for not repenting, the queen of Sheba for not believing in Christ. She came from a far country to hear the wisdom of Solomon; yet people will not be persuaded to come and hear the wisdom of Christ, though he is in every thing greater than Solomon. [1.] The queen of Sheba had no invitation to come to Solomon, nor any promise of being welcome; but we are invited to Christ, to sit at his feet and hear his word. [2.] Solomon was but a wise man, but Christ is wisdom itself, *in whom are hid all the treasures of wisdom.* [3.] The queen of Sheba had many difficulties to break through; she was a woman, unfit for travel, the journey long and perilous; she was a queen, and what would become of her own country in her absence? We have no such cares to hinder us. [4.] She could not be sure that it would be worth her while to go so far on this errand; fame uses to flatter men, and perhaps she might have in her own country or court wise men sufficient to instruct her; yet, having heard of Solomon's fame, she would see him; but we come not to Christ upon such uncertainties. [5.] *She came from the uttermost parts of the earth,* but we have Christ among us, and his word nigh us: *Behold he stands at the door, and knocks.* [6.] It should seem the wisdom the queen of Sheba came for was only philosophy and politics; but the wisdom that is to be had with Christ is wisdom to salvation. [7.] She could only *hear* Solomon's wisdom; he could not *give* her wisdom: but Christ will give wisdom to those who come to him; nay, he will himself be *made*

of God to them Wisdom; so that, upon all these accounts, if we do not hear the wisdom of Christ, the forwardness of the queen of Sheba to come and hear the wisdom of Solomon will rise up in judgment against us and condemn us; for Jesus Christ is greater than Solomon.

(3.) As a generation that were resolved to continue in the possession, and under the power, of Satan, notwithstanding all the methods that were used to dispossess him and rescue them. They are compared to one out of whom the devil is gone, but returns with double force, *v.* 43–45. The devil is here called *the unclean spirit,* for he has lost all his purity, and delights in and promotes all manner of impurity among men. Now,

[1.] The parable represents his possessing men's bodies: Christ having lately cast out a devil, and they having said *he had a devil,* gave occasion to show how much they were under the power of Satan. This is a further proof that Christ did not cast out devils by compact with the devil, for then he would soon have returned again; but Christ's ejectment of him was final, and such as barred a re-entry: we find him charging the evil spirit to *go out, and enter no more,* Mk. 9:25. Probably the devil was wont sometimes thus to sport with those he had possession of; he would go out, and then return again with more fury; hence the lucid intervals of those in that condition were commonly followed with the more violent fits. When the devil is gone out, he is uneasy, for *he sleeps not except he have done mischief* (Prov. 4:16); *he walks in dry places,* like one that is very melancholy; he *seeks rest but finds none,* till he returns again. When Christ cast the legion out of the man, they begged leave to enter into the swine, where they went not long in dry places, but into the lake presently.

[2.] The application of the parable makes it to represent the case of the body of the Jewish church and nation: *So shall it be with this wicked generation,* that now resist, and will finally reject, the gospel of Christ. The devil, who by the labours of Christ and his disciples had been cast out of many of the Jews, sought for rest among the heathen, from whose persons and temples the Christians would every where expel him: so Dr. Whitby: or finding no where else in the heathen world such pleasant, desirable habitations, to his satisfaction, as here in the heart of the Jews: so Dr. Hammond: he shall therefore enter again into them, for Christ had not found admission among them, and they, by their prodigious wickedness and obstinate unbelief, were still more ready than ever to receive him; and then he shall take a durable possession here, and the state of this people is likely to be more desperately damnable (so Dr. Hammond) than it was before Christ came among them, or would have been if Satan had never been cast out.

The body of that nation is here represented, *First,* As an apostate people. After the captivity in Babylon, they began to reform, left their idols, and appeared with some face of religion; but they soon corrupted themselves again: though they never relapsed into idolatry, they fell into all manner of impiety and profaneness, grew worse and worse, and added to all the rest of their wickedness a wilful contempt of, and opposition to, Christ and his gospel. *Secondly,* As a people marked for ruin. A new commission was passing the seals against that hypocritical nation, the people of God's wrath (like that, Isa. 10:6), and their destruction by the Romans was likely to be greater than any other, as their sins had been more flagrant: then it was *that wrath came upon them to the uttermost,* 1 Th. 2:15, 16. Let this be a warning to all nations and churches, to take heed of leaving their first love, of letting fall a good work of reformation begun among them, and returning to that wickedness which they seemed to have forsaken; *for the last state of such will be worse than the first.*

Verses 46–50

Many excellent, useful sayings came from the mouth of our Lord Jesus upon particular occasions; even his digressions were instructive, as well as his set discourses: as here, Observe, I. How Christ was interrupted in his preaching by *his mother and his brethren,* that *stood without, desiring to speak with him* (*v.* 40, 47); which desire of theirs was conveyed to him through the crowd. It is needless to enquire which of his brethren they were that came along with his mother (perhaps they were those *who did not believe in him,* Jn. 7:5); or what their business was; perhaps it was only designed to oblige him to break off, for fear he should fatigue

himself, or to caution him to take heed of giving offence by his discourse to the Pharisees, and or involving himself in a difficulty; as if they could teach *him* wisdom.

1. He was as yet talking to the people. Note, Christ's preaching was talking; it was plain, easy, and familiar, and suited to their capacity and case. What Christ had delivered had been cavilled at, and yet he went on. Note, The opposition we meet with in our work, must not drive us from it. He left off talking with the Pharisees, for he saw he could do no good with them; but continued to talk to the common people, who, not having such a conceit of their knowledge as the Pharisees had, were willing to learn.

2. His mother and brethren stood without, desiring to speak with him, when they should have been standing within, desiring to hear him. They had the advantage of his daily converse in private, and therefore were less mindful to attend upon his public preaching. Note, Frequently those who are nearest to the means of knowledge and grace, are most negligent. Familiarity and easiness of access breed some degree of contempt. We are apt to neglect *that* this day, which we think we may have any day, forgetting that it is only the present time we can be sure of; tomorrow is none of ours. There is too much truth in that common proverb, "The nearer the church, the further from God;" it is pity it should be so.

3. They not only would not hear him themselves, but they interrupted others that *heard him gladly.* The devil was a sworn enemy to our Saviour's preaching. He had sought to baffle his discourse by the unreasonable cavils of the scribes and Pharisees, and when he could not gain his point that way, he endeavoured to break it off by the unseasonable visits of relations. Note, We often meet with hindrances and obstructions in our work, by our friends that are about us, and are taken off by civil respects from our spiritual concerns. Those who really wish well to us and to our work, may sometimes, by their indiscretion, prove our back-friends, and impediments to us in our duty; as *Peter* was offensive to Christ, with his, *"Master, spare thyself,"* when he thought himself very officious. The mother of our Lord desired to speak with him; it seemed she had not then learned to command her Son, as the iniquity and idolatry of the church of Rome has since pretended to teach her: nor was she so free from fault and folly as they would make her. It was Christ's prerogative, and not his mother's, to do every thing wisely, and well, and in its season. Christ once said to his mother, *How is it that ye sought me? Wist he not, that I must be about my Father's business?* And it was then said, she *laid up that saying in her heart* (Lu. 2:49); but if she had remembered it now, she would not have given him this interruption when he was about his Father's business. Note, There is many a good truth that we thought was well laid up when we heard it, which yet is out of the way when we have occasion to use it.

II. How he resented this interruption, *v.* 48–50.

1. He would not hearken to it; he was so intent upon his work, that no natural or civil respects should take him off from it. *Who is my mother and who are my brethren?* Not that natural affection is to be put off, or that, under pretence of religion, we may be disrespectful to parents, or unkind to other relations; but *every thing is beautiful in its season,* and the less duty must stand by, while the greater is done. When our regard to our relations comes in competition with the service of God, and the improving of an opportunity to *do good,* in such a case, we must *say to our Father, I have not seen him,* as Levi did, Deu. 33:9. The nearest relations must be comparatively hated, that is, we must love them less than Christ (Lu. 14:26), and our duty to God must have the preference. This Christ has here given us an example of; *the zeal of God's house* did so far *eat him up,* that it made him not only forget himself, but forget his dearest relations. And we must not take it ill of our friends, nor put it upon the score of their wickedness, if they prefer the pleasing of God before the pleasing of us; but we must readily forgive those neglects which may be easily imputed to a pious zeal for God's glory and others' good. Nay, we must deny ourselves and our own satisfaction, rather than do that which may any way divert our friends from, or distract them in, their duty to God.

2. He took that occasion to prefer his disciples, who were his spiritual kindred, before his natural relations as such: which was a good reason why he would not leave preaching to speak with his brethren. He would rather be profiting his disciples, than pleasing his relations. Observe,

(1.) The description of Christ's disciples. They are such as *do the will of his Father;* not only hear it, and know it, and talk of it, but *do it;* for doing the will of God is the best preparative for discipleship (Jn. 7:17), and the best proof of it (*ch.* 7:21); *that* denominates us his disciples indeed. Christ does not say, "Whosoever shall do my will," for he came not to seek or do his own will distinct from his Father's: his will and his Father's are the same; but he refers us to his Father's will, because now in his present state and work he referred himself to it, Jn. 6:38.

(2.) The dignity of Christ's disciples: *The same is my brother, and sister, and mother.* His disciples, that had left all to follow him, and embraced his doctrine, were dearer to him than any that were akin to him according to the flesh. They had preferred Christ before their relations; they *left their father* (*ch.* 4:22; 10:37); and now to make them amends, and to show that there was no love lost, he preferred them before his relations. Did not they hereby receive, in point of honour, *a hundred fold? ch.* 19:29. It was very endearing and very encouraging for Christ to say, *Behold my mother and my brethren;* yet it was not *their* privilege alone, *this honour have all the saints.* Note, All obedient believers are near akin to Jesus Christ. They wear his name, bear his image, have his nature, are of his family. He loves them, converses freely with them as his relations. He bids them welcome to his table, takes care of them, provides for them, sees that they want nothing that is fit for them: when he died he left them rich legacies, now he is in heaven he keeps up a correspondence with them, and will have them all with him at last, and will in nothing fail to *do the kinsman's part* (Ruth 3:13), nor will ever be ashamed of his poor relations, but will confess them before men, before the angels, and before his Father.

CHAPTER 13

In this chapter, we have, I. The favour which Christ did to his countrymen in preaching the kingdom of heaven to them (*v.* 1–2). He preached to them in parables, and here gives the reason why he chose that way of instructing (*v.* 10–17). And the evangelist gives another reason (*v.* 34, 35). There are eight parables recorded in this chapter, which are designed to represent the kingdom of heaven, the method of planting the gospel kingdom in the world, and of its growth and success. The great truths and laws of that kingdom are in other scriptures laid down plainly, and without parables: but some circumstances of its beginning and progress are here laid open in parables. 1. Here is one parable to show what are the great hindrances of people's profiting by the word of the gospel, and in how many it comes short of its end, through their own folly, and that is the parable of the four sorts of ground, delivered (*v.* 3–9). and expounded (*v.* 18–23). 2. Here are two parables intended to show that there would be a mixture of good and bad in the gospel church, which would continue till the great separation between them in the judgment day: the parable of the tares put forth (*v.* 24–30), and expounded at the request of the disciples (*v.* 36–43); and that of the net cast into the sea (*v.* 47–50). 3. Here are two parables intended to show that the gospel church should be very small at first, but that in process of time it should become a considerable body: that of the grain of mustard-seed (*v.* 31, 32), and that of the leaven (*v.* 33). 4. Here are two parables intended to show that those who expect salvation by the gospel must be willing to venture all, and quit all, in the prospect of it, and that they shall be no losers by the bargain; that of the treasure hid in the field (*v.* 44), and that of the pearl of great price (*v.* 45, 46). 5. Here is one parable intended for direction to the disciples, to make use of the instructions he had given them for the benefit of others; and that is the parable of the good householder (*v.* 51, 52). II. The contempt which his countrymen put upon him on account of the meanness of his parentage (*v.* 53–58).

Verses 1–23

We have here Christ preaching, and may observe,

1. *When* Christ preached this sermon; it was the same day that he preached the sermon in the foregoing chapter: so unwearied was he in doing good, and working the works of him that sent him. Note, Christ was for preaching both ends of the day, and has by his example recommended that practice to his church; we must *in the morning sow our seed, and in the evening not withhold our hand,* Eccl. 11:6. An afternoon sermon well heard, will be so far from driving out the morning sermon, that it will rather clench it, and fasten the nail in a sure place. Though Christ had been in the morning opposed and cavilled at by his enemies, disturbed and interrupted by his friends, yet he went on with his work; and in the latter part of the day, we do not find that he met with such discouragements. Those who with courage and zeal break through difficulties in God's service, will perhaps find them not so apt to recur as they fear. Resist them, and they will flee.

2. *To whom* he preached; there were *great multitudes gathered together to him,* and they were the auditors; we do not find that any of the scribes or Pharisees were present. They were willing to hear him when he preached in the synagogue (*ch.* 12:9, 14), but they thought it below them to hear

a sermon by the sea-side, though Christ himself was the preacher: and truly he had better have their room than their company, for now they were absent, he went on quietly and without contradiction. Note, Sometimes there is most of the *power* of religion where there is least of the *pomp* of it: *the poor receive the gospel.* When Christ went to the *sea-side, multitudes* were presently *gathered together to him.* Where the king is, there is the court; where Christ is, there is the church, though it be by the sea-side. Note, Those who would get good by the word, must be willing to follow it in all its removes; when the ark shifts, shift after it. The Pharisees had been labouring, by base calumnies and suggestions, to drive the people off from following Christ, but they still flocked after him as much as ever. Note, Christ will be glorified in spite of all opposition; he will be followed.

3. *Where* he preached this sermon.

(1.) His meeting-place was the sea-side. He went out of the house (because there was no room for the auditory) into the open air. It was pity but such a Preacher should have had the most spacious, sumptuous, and convenient place to preach in, that could be devised, like one of the Roman theatres; but he was now in his state of humiliation, and in this, as in other things, he denied himself the honours due to him; as he had not a house of his own to live in, so he had not a chapel of his own to preach in. By this he teaches us in the external circumstances of worship not to covet that which is stately, but to make the best of the conveniences which God in his providence allots to us. When Christ was born, he was crowded into the stable, and now to the sea-side, upon the strand, where all persons might come to him with freedom. He that was truth itself sought no corners (no *adyta*), as the pagan mysteries did. *Wisdom crieth without,* Prov. 1:20; Jn. 13:20.

(2.) His pulpit was a ship; not like Ezra's pulpit, that was *made for the purpose* (Neh. 8:4); but converted to this use for want of a better. No place amiss for such a Preacher, whose presence dignified and consecrated any place: let not those who preach Christ be ashamed, though they have mean and inconvenient places to preach in. Some observe, that the people stood upon dry ground and firm ground, while the Preacher was upon the water in more hazard. Ministers are most exposed to trouble. Here was a true rostrum, a ship pulpit.

4. *What* and *how* he preached. (1.) He spake many things *unto them.* Many more it is likely than are here recorded, but all excellent and necessary things, things that belong to our peace, things pertaining to the kingdom of heaven: they were not trifles, but things of everlasting consequence, that Christ spoke of. It concerns us to give a more earnest heed, when Christ has so many things to say to us, that we miss not any of them. (2.) What he spake was in parables. A parable sometimes signifies any wise, weighty saying that is instructive; but here in the gospels it generally signifies a continued similitude or comparison, by which spiritual or heavenly things were described in language borrowed from the things of this life. It was a way of teaching used very much, not only by the Jewish rabbin, but by the Arabians, and the other wise men of the east; and it was found very profitable, and the more so from its being pleasant. Our Saviour used it much, and in it condescended to the capacities of people, and lisped to them in their own language. God had long *used similitudes by his servants the prophets* (Hos. 12:10), and to little purpose; now he uses similitudes by his Son; surely they will reverence him who speaks from heaven, and of heavenly things, and yet clothes them with expressions borrowed from things earthly. See Jn. 3:12. So descending in a cloud. Now,

I. We have here the general reason why Christ taught in parables. The disciples were a little surprised at it, for hitherto, in his preaching, he had not much used them, and therefore they ask, *Why speakest thou to them in parables?* Because they were truly desirous that the people might hear with understanding. They do not say, Why speakest thou to *us?* (they knew how to get the parables explained) but to *them.* Note, We ought to be concerned for the edification of others, as well as for our own, by the word preached; and if ourselves be *strong,* yet to *bear the infirmities of the weak.*

To this question Christ answers largely, *v.* 11–17, where he tells them, that *therefore* he preached by parables, because thereby the things of God were made more plain and easy to them who were willingly ignorant; and thus the gospel would be *a savour of life* to some, and *of death* to others.

A parable, like the pillar of cloud and fire, turns a dark side towards Egyptians, which confounds them, but a light side towards Israelites, which comforts them, and so answers a double intention. The same light directs the eyes of some, but dazzles the eyes of others. Now,

1. This reason is laid down (*v.* 11): *Because it is given unto you to know the mysteries of the kingdom of heaven, but to them it is not given.* That is, (1.) The disciples had knowledge, but the people had not. You know already something of these mysteries, and need not in this familiar way to be instructed; but the people are ignorant, are yet but babes, and must be taught as such by plain similitudes, being yet incapable of receiving instruction in any other way: for though they have eyes, they know not how to use them; so some. Or, (2.) The disciples were well inclined to the knowledge of gospel mysteries, and would search into the parables, and by them would be led into a more intimate acquaintance with those mysteries; but the carnal hearers that rested in bare hearing, and would not be at the pains to look further, nor to ask the meaning of the parables, would be never the wiser, and so would justly suffer for their remissions. A parable is a shell that keeps good fruit *for* the diligent, but keeps it *from* the slothful. Note, There are mysteries in the kingdom of heaven, and *without controversy, great is the mystery of godliness:* Christ's incarnation, satisfaction, intercession, our justification and sanctification by union with Christ, and indeed the whole work of redemption, from first to last, are *mysteries,* which could never have been discovered but by divine revelation (1 Co. 15:51), were at this time discovered but in part to the disciples, and will never be fully discovered till the veil shall be rent; but the mysteriousness of gospel truth should not discourage us from, but quicken us in, our enquiries after it and searches into it. [1.] It is graciously given to the disciples of Christ to be acquainted with these mysteries. Knowledge is the first gift of God, and it is a distinguishing gift (Prov. 2:6); it was given to the apostles, because they were Christ's constant followers and attendants. Note, The nearer we draw to Christ, and the more we converse with him, the better acquainted we shall be with gospel mysteries. [2.] It is given to all true believers, who have an experimental knowledge of the gospel mysteries, and that is without doubt the best knowledge: a principle of grace in the heart, is that which makes men of quick understanding in *the fear of the Lord,* and in the faith of Christ, and so in the meaning of parables; and for want of that, Nicodemus, a master in Israel, talked of the *new birth* as a blind man of colours. [3.] There are those to *whom this knowledge is not given,* and a man can *receive nothing unless it be given him from above* (Jn. 3:27); and be it remembered that God is debtor to no man; his grace is his own; he gives or withholds it at pleasure (Rom. 11:35); the difference must be resolved into God's sovereignty, as before, *ch.* 11:25, 26.

2. This reason is further illustrated by the rule God observes in dispensing his gifts; he bestows them on those who improve them, but takes them away from those who bury them. It is a rule among men, that they will rather entrust their money with those who have increased their estates by their industry, than with those who have diminished them by their slothfulness.

(1.) Here is a promise to him that has, that has true grace, pursuant to the election of grace, that has, and uses what he has; he shall have more abundance: God's favours are earnests of further favours; where he lays the foundation, he will build upon it. Christ's disciples used the knowledge they now had, and they had more abundance at the pouring out of the Spirit, Acts 2. They who have the *truth* of grace, shall have the *increase* of grace, even to an abundance in glory, Prov. 4:18. *Joseph — he will add,* Gen. 30:24.

(2.) Here is a threatening to him that has not, that has no desire of grace, that makes no right use of the gifts and graces he has: has not root, no solid principle; that has, but uses not what he has; from him shall be *taken away* that which he has or seems to have. His leaves shall wither, his gifts decay; the means of grace he has, and makes no use of, shall be taken from him; God will *call in* his talents out of their hands that are likely to become bankrupts quickly.

3. This reason is particularly explained, with reference to the two sorts of people Christ had to do with.

(1.) Some were willingly ignorant; and such were amused by the parables (*v.* 13); *because they seeing, see not.* They had shut their eyes against the clear light of Christ's plainer preaching, and therefore were now left in the dark. Seeing

Christ's person, they see not his glory, see no difference between him and another man; seeing his miracles, and hearing his preaching, they see not, they hear not with any concern or application; they understand neither. Note, [1.] There are many that see the gospel light, and hear the gospel sound, but it never reaches their hearts, nor has it any place in them. [2.] It is just with God to take away the light from those who shut their eyes against it; that such as will be ignorant, may be so; and God's dealing thus with them magnifies his distinguishing grace to his disciples.

Now in this the scripture would be fulfilled, *v.* 14, 15. It is quoted from Isa. 6:9, 10. The evangelical prophet that spoke most plainly of gospel grace, foretold the contempt of it, and the consequences of that contempt. It is referred to no less than six times in the New Testament, which intimates, that in gospel times spiritual judgments would be most common, which make least noise, but are most dreadful. That which was spoken of the sinners in Isaiah's time was fulfilled in those in Christ's time, and it is still fulfilling every day; for while the wicked heart of man keeps up the same sin, the righteous hand of God inflicts the same punishment. Here is,

First. A description of sinners' wilful blindness and hardness, which is their sin. *This people's heart is waxed gross;* it is *fattened*, so the word is; which denotes both sensuality and senselessness (Ps. 119:70); secure under the word and rod of God, and scornful as Jeshurun, that *waxed fat and kicked*, Deu. 32:15. And when the heart is thus heavy, no wonder that the ears are dull of hearing; the whispers of the Spirit they hear not at all; the loud calls of the word, though the word be nigh them, they regard not, nor are at all affected by them: *they stop their ears*, Ps. 58:4, 5. And because they are resolved to be ignorant, they shut both the learning senses; for their eyes also they have closed, resolved that they would not see light come into the world, when the Son of Righteousness arose, but they shut their windows, because they *loved darkness rather than light*, Jn. 3:19; 2 Pt. 3:5.

Secondly, A description of that judicial blindness, which is the just punishment of this. *"By hearing, ye shall hear, and shall not understand;* what means of grace you have, shall be to no purpose to you; though, in mercy to others, they are continued, yet in judgment to you, the blessing upon them is denied." The saddest condition a man can be in on this side hell, is to sit under the most lively ordinances with a dead, stupid, untouched heart. To hear God's word, and see his providences, and yet not to understand and perceive his will, either in the one or in the other, is the greatest sin and the greatest judgment that can be. Observe, It is God's work to *give an understanding heart*, and he often, in a way of righteous judgment, denies it to those to whom he has given the hearing ear, and the seeing eye, in vain. Thus does God choose sinners' delusions (Isa. 66:4),. and bind them over to the greatest ruin, by giving them up to their own hearts' lusts (Ps. 81:11, 12); *let them alone* (Hos. 4:17); *my Spirit shall not always strive*, Gen. 6:3.

Thirdly, The woeful effect and consequence of this; *Lest at any time they should see.* They will not see because they will not turn; and God says that they shall not see, because they shall not turn: *lest they should be converted, and I should heal them.*

Note, 1. That seeing, hearing, and understanding, are necessary to conversion; for God, in working grace, deals with men as men, as rational agents; he draws with the cords of a man, changes the heart by opening the eyes, and turns *from the power of Satan unto God,* by turning first *from darkness to light,* (Acts 26:18). 2. All those who are truly converted to God, shall certainly be healed by him. "If they be converted I shall heal them, I shall save them:" so that if sinners perish, it is not to be imputed to God, but to themselves; they foolishly expected to be healed, without being converted. 3. It is just with God to deny his grace to those who have long and often refused the proposals of it, and resisted the power of it. Pharaoh, for a good while, hardened his own heart (Ex. 8:15, 32), and afterwards God hardened it, *ch.* 9:12; 10:20. Let us therefore fear, lest by sinning against the divine grace, we sin it away.

(2.) Others were effectually called to be the disciples of Christ, and were truly desirous to be taught of him; and they were instructed, and made to improve greatly in knowledge, by these parables, especially when they were expounded; and by them the things of God were made more plain and easy, more intelligible and familiar, and more apt to be remembered (*v.* 16, 17). *Your eyes see, your ears hear.* They saw the

glory of God in Christ's person; they heard the mind of God in Christ's doctrine; they saw much, and were desirous to see more, and thereby were prepared to receive further instruction; they had opportunity for it, by being constant attendants on Christ, and they should have it from day to day, and grace with it. Now this Christ speaks of,

[1.] As a blessing; *"Blessed are your eyes for they see, and your ears for they hear;* it is your happiness, and it is a happiness for which you are indebted to the peculiar favour and blessing of God." It is a promised blessing, that in the days of the Messiah *the eyes of them that see shall not be dim,* Isa. 32:3. The eyes of the meanest believer that knows experimentally the grace of Christ, are more blessed than those of the greatest scholars, the greatest masters in experimental philosophy, that are strangers to God; who, like the other gods they serve, *have eyes, and see not. Blessed are your eyes.* Note, True blessedness is entailed upon the right understanding and due improvement of the mysteries of the kingdom of God. The hearing ear and the seeing eye are God's work in those who are sanctified; they are the work of his grace (Prov. 20:12), and they are a blessed work, which shall be fulfilled with power, when those who *now see through a glass darkly, shall see face to face.* It was to illustrate this blessedness that Christ said so much of the misery of those who are left in ignorance; *they have eyes and see not;* but *blessed are your eyes.* Note, The knowledge of Christ is a distinguishing favour to those who have it, and upon that account it lays under the greater obligations; see Jn. 14:22. The apostles were to teach others, and therefore were themselves blessed with the clearest discoveries of divine truth. *The watchmen shall see eye to eye,* Isa. 52:8.

[2.] As a transcendent blessing, desired by, but not granted to, many prophets and righteous men, *v.* 17. The Old-Testament saints, who had some glimpses, some glimmerings of gospel light, coveted earnestly further discoveries. They had the types, shadows, and prophecies, of those things but longed to see the Substance, that glorious end of those things which they could not steadfastly look unto; that glorious inside of those things which they could not look into. They desired to see the great Salvation, the Consolation of Israel, but did not see it, because the fulness of time was not yet come. Note, *First,* Those who know something of Christ, cannot but covet to know more. *Secondly,* The discoveries of divine grace are made, even to prophets and righteous men, but according to the dispensation they are under. Though they were the favourites of heaven, with whom God's secret was, yet they have not seen the things which they desired to see, because God had determined not to bring them to light yet; and his favours shall not anticipate his counsels. There was then, as there is still, a *glory to be revealed;* something in reserve, *that they without us should not be made perfect,* Heb. 11:40. *Thirdly,* For the exciting of our thankfulness, and the quickening of our diligence, it is good for us to consider what means we enjoy, and what discoveries are made to us, now under the gospel, above what they had, and enjoyed, who lived under the Old-Testament dispensation, especially in the revelation of the atonement for sin; see what are the advantages of the New Testament above the Old (2 Co. 3:7, etc. Heb. 12:18); and see that our improvements be proportionable to our advantages.

II. We have, in these verses, one of the parables which our Saviour put forth; it is that of the *sower and the seed;* both the parable itself, and the explanation of it. Christ's parables are borrowed from common, ordinary things, not from any philosophical notions or speculations, or the unusual phenomena of nature, though applicable enough to the matter in hand, but from the most obvious things, that are of every day's observation, and come within the reach of the meanest capacity; many of them are fetched from the husbandman's calling, as this of the sower, and that of the tares. Christ chose to do thus, 1. That spiritual things might hereby be made more plain, and, by familiar similitudes, might be made the more easy to slide into our understandings. 2. That common actions might hereby be spiritualized, and we might take occasion from those things which fall so often under our view, to meditate with delight on the things of God; and thus, when our hands are busiest about the world, we may not only notwithstanding that, but even with the help of that, be led to have our hearts in heaven. Thus the word of God shall talk with us, talk familiarly with us, Prov. 6:22.

The parable of the sower is plain enough, *v.* 3–9. The exposition of it we have from Christ himself, who knew best

what was his own meaning. The disciples, when they asked, *Why speakest thou unto them in parables?* (*v.* 10), intimated a desire to have the parable explained for the sake of the people; nor was it any disparagement to their own knowledge to desire it for themselves. Our Lord Jesus kindly took the hint, and gave the sense, and caused them to understand the parable, directing his discourse to the disciples, but in the hearing of the multitude, for we have not the account of his dismissing them till *v.* 36. *"Hear ye therefore the parable of the sower* (*v.* 18); you have heard it, but let us go over it again." Note, It is of good use, and would contribute much to our understanding the word and profiting by it, to hear over again what we have heard (Phil. 3:1); "You have heard it, but hear the interpretation of it." Note, *Then* only we hear the word aright, and to good purpose, when we understand what we hear; it is no hearing at all, if it be not with understanding, Neh. 8:2. It is God's grace indeed that gives the understanding, but it is our duty to give our minds to understand.

Let us therefore compare the parable and the exposition.

(1.) The seed sown is the word of God, here called *the word of the kingdom* (*v.* 19): the kingdom of heaven, that is the kingdom; the kingdoms of the world, compared with that, are not to be called kingdoms. The gospel comes *from* that kingdom, and conducts *to* that kingdom; the word of the gospel is the word of the kingdom; it is the word of the King, and where that is, *there is power;* it is a law, by which we must be ruled and governed. This word is the seed sown, which seems a dead, dry thing, but all the product is virtually in it. It is *incorruptible seed* (1 Pt. 1:23); it is the gospel that *brings forth fruit* in souls, Col. 1:5, 6.

(2.) The sower that scatters the seed is our Lord Jesus Christ, either by himself, or by his ministers; see *v.* 37. The people are God's husbandry, his tillage, so the word is; and ministers are *labourers together with God,* 1 Co. 3:9. Preaching to a multitude is sowing the corn; we know not where it must light; only see that it be good, that it be clean, and be sure to give it seed enough. The sowing of the word is the sowing of a people for God's field, the *corn of his floor,* Isa. 21:10.

(3.) The ground in which this seed is sown is the hearts of the children of men, which are differently qualified and disposed, and accordingly the success of the word is different. Note, Man's heart is like soil, capable of improvement, of bearing good fruit; it is pity it should lie fallow, or be like the field of the slothful, Prov. 24:30. The soul is the proper place for the word of God to dwell, and work, and rule in; its operation is upon conscience, it is to light that candle of the Lord. Now according as we are, so the word is to us: *Recipitur ad modum recipientis — The reception depends upon the receiver.* As it is with the earth; some sort of ground, take ever so much pains with it, and throw ever so good seed into it, yet it brings forth no fruit to any purpose; while the good soil brings forth plentifully: so it is with the hearts of men, whose different characters are here represented by four sorts of ground, of which *three* are bad, and but *one* good. Note, The number of fruitless hearers is very great, even of those who heard Christ himself. *Who has believed our report?* It is a melancholy prospect which this parable gives us of the congregations of those who hear the gospel preached, that scarcely one in four brings forth fruit to perfection. Many are called with the common call, but in few is the eternal choice evidenced by the efficacy of that call, *ch.* 20:16.

Now observe the characters of these four sorts of ground.

[1.] The highway ground, *v.* 4–10. They had pathways through their corn-fields (*ch.* 12:1), and the seed that fell on them never entered, and so the birds picked it up. The place where Christ's hearers now stood represented the characters of most of them, the sand on the sea-shore, which was to the seed like the highway ground.

Observe *First,* What kind of hearers are compared to *the highway ground;* such as *hear the word and understand it not;* and it is their own fault that they do not. They take no heed to it, take no hold of it; they do not come with any design to get good, as the highway was never intended to be sown. They *come before God as his people come, and sit before his as his people sit;* but it is merely for fashion-sake, to see and be seen; they mind not what is said, it comes in at one ear and goes out at the other, and makes no impression.

Secondly, How they come to be unprofitable hearers. The *wicked one,* that is, the devil, *cometh and catcheth away that which was sown.* — Such mindless, careless, trifling hearers are an easy prey to Satan; who, as he is the great murderer of souls, so he is the great thief of sermons, and will be sure to rob us of the word, if we take not care to keep it: as the birds pick up the seed that falls on the ground that is neither ploughed before nor harrowed after. If we break not up the fallow ground, by preparing our hearts for the word, and humbling them to it, and engaging our own attention; and if we cover not the seed afterwards, by meditation and prayer; if we give not a *more earnest heed to the things which we have heard,* we are as the highway ground. Note, The devil is a sworn enemy to our profiting by the word of God; and none do more befriend his design than heedless hearers, who are thinking of something else, when they should be thinking of the things that belong to their peace.

[2.] The *stony ground. Some fell upon stony places* (*v.* 5, 6), which represents the case of hearers that go further than the former, who receive some good impressions of the word, but they are not lasting, *v.* 20, 21. Note, It is possible we may be a great deal better than some others, and yet not be so good as we should be; may go beyond our neighbours, and yet come short of heaven. Now observe, concerning these hearers that are represented by the stony ground,

First, How far they went. 1. They *hear the word;* they turn neither their backs upon it, nor a deaf ear to it. Note, hearing the word, though ever so frequently, ever so gravely, if we rest in that, will never bring us to heaven. 2. They are *quick in hearing,* swift to hear, *he anon receiveth it, euthys,* he is ready to receive it, *forthwith it sprung up* (*v.* 5), it sooner appeared above ground than that which was sown in the good soil. Note, Hypocrites often get the start of true Christians in the shows of profession, and are often too hot to hold. He *receiveth it straightway,* without trying it; swallows it without chewing, and then there can never be a good digestion. Those are most likely to *hold fast that which is good,* that *prove all things,* 1 Th. 5:21. 3. They receive it with joy. Note, There are many that are very glad to hear a good sermon, that yet do not profit by it; they may be pleased with the word, and yet not changed and ruled by it; the heart may melt under the word, and yet not be melted down by the word, much less into it, as into a mould. Many *taste the good word of God* (Heb. 6:5), and say they find sweetness in it, but some beloved lust is *rolled under the tongue,* which it would not agree with, and so they spit it out again. 4. They *endure for awhile,* like a violent motion, which continues as long as the impression of the force remains, but ceases when that has spent itself. Note, Many endure for awhile, that do not endure to the end, and so come short of the happiness which is promised to them only that persevere (*ch.* 10:22); they did run well, but something hindered them, Gal. 5:7.

Secondly, How they fell away, so that no fruit was brought to perfection; no more than the corn, that having no depth of earth from which to draw moisture, is scorched and withered by the heat of the sun. And the reason is,

1. They have *no root in themselves,* no settled, fixed principles in their judgments, no firm resolution in their wills, nor any rooted habits in their affections: nothing firm that will be either the sap or the strength of their profession. Note, (1.) It is possible there may be the green blade of a profession, where yet there is not the root of grace; hardness prevails in the heart, and what there is of soil and softness is only in the surface; inwardly they are no more affected than a stone; they have no root, they are not by faith united to Christ who is our Root; they derive not from him, they depend not on him. (2.) Where there is not a principle, though there be a profession, we cannot expect perseverance. Those who have no root will endure but awhile. A ship without ballast, though she may at first out-sail the laden vessel, yet will certainly fail in stress of weather, and never make her port.

2. Times of trial come, and then they come to nothing. *When tribulation and persecution arise because of the word, he is offended;* it is a stumbling-block in his way which he cannot get over, and so he flies off, and this is all his profession comes to. Note, (1.) After a fair gale of opportunity usually follows a storm of persecution, to try who have received the word in sincerity, and who have not. When the word of Christ's kingdom comes to be the word of Christ's patience (Rev. 3:10), then is the trial, who keeps it, and who does not, Rev. 1:9. It is wisdom to prepare for such a day. (2.) When trying times come, those who have no root are soon offended; they first quarrel with their profession, and then quit it; first find fault with it, and then throw it off. Hence we read of *the offence of the cross,* Gal. 5:11. Observe, Persecution is represented in the parable by *the scorching sun,* (*v.* 6); the same sun which warms and cherishes that which was well rooted, withers and burns up that which wanted root. As the word of Christ, so the cross of Christ, is to some *a savour of life unto life,* to others *a savour of death unto death:* the same tribulation which drives some to apostasy and ruin, works for others *a far more exceeding and eternal weight of glory.* Trials which shake some, confirm others, Phil. 1:12. Observe how soon they fall away, by and by; as soon rotten as they were ripe; a profession taken up without consideration is commonly let fall without it: "Lightly come, lightly go."

[3.] The thorny ground, *Some fell among thorns* (which are a good guard to the corn when they are in the hedge, but a bad inmate when they are in the field); *and the thorns sprung up,* which intimates that they did not appear, or but little, when the corn was sown, but afterwards they proved choking to it, *v.* 7. This went further than the former, for it had root; and it represents the condition of those who do not quite cast off their profession, and yet come short of any saving benefit by it; the good they gain by the word, being insensibly overcome and overborne by the things of the world. Prosperity destroys the word in the heart, as much as persecution does; and more dangerously, because more silently: the stones spoiled the root, the thorns spoil the fruit.

Now what are these choking thorns?

First, The cares of this world. Care for another world would quicken the springing of this seed, but care for this world chokes it. Worldly cares are fitly compared to thorns, for they came in with sin, and are a fruit of the curse; they are good in their place to stop a gap, but a man must be well armed that deals much in them (2 Sa. 23:6, 7); they are entangling, vexing, scratching, and *their end is to be burned,* Heb. 6:8. These thorns choke the good seed. Note, Worldly cares are great hindrances to our profiting by the word of God, and our proficiency in religion. They eat up that vigour of soul which should be spent in divine things; divert us from duty, distract us in duty, and do us most mischief of all afterwards; quenching the sparks of good affections, and bursting the cords of good resolutions; those who *are careful and cumbered about many things,* commonly neglect *the one thing needful.*

Secondly, The deceitfulness of riches. Those who, by their care and industry, have raised estates, and so the danger that arises from care seems to be over, and they *continue hearers of the word,* yet are still in a snare (Jer. 5:4, 5); it is *hard for them to enter into the kingdom of heaven:* they are apt to promise themselves that in riches which is not in them; to rely upon them, and to take an inordinate complacency in them; and this chokes the word as much as care did. Observe, It is not so much riches, as *the deceitfulness of riches,* that does the mischief: now they cannot be said to be deceitful to us unless we put our confidence in them, and raise our expectations from them, and then it is that they choke the good seed.

[4.] The good ground (*v.* 18); *Others fell into good ground,* and it is pity but that good seed should always meet with good soil, and then there is no loss; such are *good hearers of the word, v.* 23. Note, Though there are many that *receive the grace of God,* and the word of his grace, *in vain,* yet God has a remnant by whom it is received to good purpose; for God's *word shall not return empty,* Isa. 55:10, 11.

Now that which distinguished this good ground from the rest, was, in one word, fruitfulness. By *this* true Christians are distinguished from hypocrites, that they *bring forth the fruits of righteousness; so shall ye be my disciples,* Jn. 15:8. He does not say that this good ground has no stones in it, or no thorns; but there were none that prevailed to hinder its fruitfulness. Saints, in this world, are not perfectly free from the remains of sin; but happily freed from the reign of it.

The hearers represented by the good ground are,

First, Intelligent hearers; they *hear the word and understand it;* they understand not only the sense and meaning of the word, but their own concern in it; they understand it as a man of business understands his business. God in his word deals with men as men, in a rational way, and gains possession of the will and affections by opening the understanding: whereas Satan, who is *a thief and a robber, comes not in by* that *door, but climbeth up another way.*

Secondly, Fruitful hearers, which is an evidence of their good understanding: which *also beareth fruit.* Fruit is to every seed its own body, a substantial product in the heart and life, agreeable to the seed of the word received. We *then* bear fruit, when we practise according to the word; when the temper of our minds and the tenour of our lives are conformable to the gospel we have received, and we do as we are taught.

Thirdly, Not all alike fruitful; *some a hundred-fold, some sixty, some thirty.* Note, Among fruitful Christians, some are more fruitful than others: where there is true grace, yet there are degrees of it; some are of greater attainments in knowledge and holiness than others; all Christ's scholars are not in the same form. We should aim at the highest degree, to bring *forth a hundred-fold,* as Isaac's ground did (Gen. 26:12), *abounding in the work of the Lord,* Jn. 15:8. But if the ground be good, and the fruit right, the heart honest, and the life of a piece with it, those who bring forth but thirty-fold shall be graciously accepted of God, and it will be fruit abounding to their account, for *we are under grace, and not under the law.*

Lastly, He closes the parable with a solemn call to attention (*v.* 9), *Who hath ears to hear, let him hear.* Note, The sense of hearing cannot be better employed than in hearing the word of God. Some are for hearing sweet melody, their ears are only *the daughters of music* (Eccl. 12:4): there is no melody like that of the word of God: others are for hearing *new things,* (Acts 17:21); no news like that.

Verses 24–43

In these verses, we have, I. Another reason given why Christ preached by parables, *v.* 34, 35. *All these things he spoke in parables,* because the time was not yet come for the more clear and plain discoveries of the mysteries of the kingdom. Christ, to keep the people attending and expecting, preached in *parables, and without a parable spake he not unto them;* namely, at this time and in this sermon. Note, Christ tries all ways and methods to do good to the souls of men, and to make impressions upon them; if men will not be instructed and influenced by plain preaching, he will try them with parables; and the reason here given is, *That the scripture might be fulfilled.* The passage here quoted for it, is part of the preface to that historical Psalm, 78:2, *I will open my mouth in a parable.* What the Psalmist David, or Asaph, says there of his narrative, is accommodated to Christ's sermons; and that great precedent would serve to vindicate this way of preaching from the offence which some took at it. Here is, 1. The matter of Christ's preaching; he preached *things which had been kept secret from the foundation of the world.* The mystery of the gospel had been *hid in God,* in his councils and decrees, *from the beginning of the world.* Eph. 3:9. Compare Rom. 16:25; 1 Co. 2:7; Col. 1:26. If we delight in the records of ancient things, and in the revelation of secret things, how welcome should the gospel be to us, which has in it such antiquity and such mystery! It was *from the foundation of the world* wrapt up in types and shadows, which are *now done away;* and those secret things are now become such things revealed *as belong to us and to our children,* Deu. 29:29. 2. The manner of Christ's preaching; he preached by parables; wise sayings, but figurative, and which help to engage attention and a diligent search. Solomon's sententious dictates, which are full of similitudes, are called *proverbs,* or *parables;* it is the same word; but in this, as in other things, *Behold a greater than Solomon is here, in whom are hid treasures of wisdom.*

II. The parable of the *tares,* and the exposition of it; they must be taken together, for the exposition explains the parable and the parable illustrates the exposition.

Observe, 1. The disciples' request to their Master to have this parable expounded to them (*v.* 36); *Jesus sent the multitude away;* and it is to be feared many of them went away no wiser than they came; they had heard a sound of words, and that was all. It is sad to think how many go away from sermons with the word of grace in their hearts. Christ *went into the house,* not so much for his own repose, as for particular converse with his disciples, whose instruction he chiefly intended in all his preaching. He was ready to do good in all places; the disciples laid hold on the opportunity, and *they came to him.* Note, Those who would be wise for every thing else, must be wise to discern and improve their opportunities, especially of converse with Christ, of converse with him alone, in secret meditation and prayer. It is very good, when we return from the solemn assembly, to talk over what we have heard there, and by familiar discourse to help one another to understand and remember it, and to be affected with it; for we lose the benefit of many a sermon by vain and unprofitable discourse after it. See Lu. 24:32; Deu. 6:6, 7. It is especially good, if it may be, to ask of the ministers of the word the meaning of the word, for *their lips should keep knowledge,* Mal. 2:7. Private conference would contribute much to our profiting by public preaching. Nathan's *Thou art the man,* was that which touched David to the heart.

The disciples' request to their Master was, *Declare unto us the parable of the tares.* This implied an acknowledgement of their ignorance, which they were not ashamed to make. It is probable they apprehended the general scope of the parable, but they desired to understand it more particularly, and to be assured that they took it right. Note, Those are rightly disposed for Christ's teaching, that are sensible of their ignorance, and sincerely desirous to be taught. He will *teach the humble* (Ps. 25:8, 9), but *will for this be enquired of. If any man lack* instruction, *let him ask it of God.* Christ had expounded the foregoing parable unasked, but for the exposition of this they ask him. Note, The mercies we have received must be improved, both for direction what to pray for, and for our encouragement in prayer. The first light and the first grace are given in a preventing way, further degrees of both which must be daily prayed for.

2. The exposition Christ gave of the parable, in answer to their request; so ready is Christ to answer such desires of his disciples. Now the drift of the parable is, to represent to us the present and future state of the kingdom of heaven, the gospel church: Christ's care of it, the devil's enmity against it, the mixture that there is in it of good and bad in the other world. Note, The visible church is the kingdom of heaven; though there be many hypocrites in it, Christ rules in it as a King; and there is a remnant in it, that are the subjects and heirs of heaven, from whom, as the better part, it is denominated: the church is *the kingdom of heaven* upon earth.

Let us go over the particulars of the exposition of the parable.

(1.) *He that sows the good seed is the Son of man.* Jesus Christ is the Lord of the field, *the Lord of the harvest,* the Sower of good seed. When *he ascended on high, he gave gifts to* the world; not only good ministers, but other good men. Note, Whatever good seed there is in the world, it all comes from the hand of Christ, and is of his sowing: truths preached, graces planted, souls sanctified, are good seed, and all owing to Christ. Ministers are instruments in Christ's hand to sow good seed; are employed by him and under him, and the success of their labours depends purely upon his blessing; so that it may well be said, It is Christ, and no other, that sows the good seed; he *is the Son of man,* one of us, that his terror might not make us afraid; *the Son of man,* the Mediator, and that has authority.

(2.) *The field is the world;* the world of mankind, a large field, capable of bringing forth good fruit; the more is it to be lamented that it brings forth so much bad fruit: the world here is the visible church, scattered all the world over, not confined to one nation. Observe, In the parable it is called *his field; the world* is Christ's *field,* for *all things are delivered unto him of the Father:* whatever power and interest the devil has in the world, it is usurped and unjust; when Christ comes to take possession, he comes whose right it is; it is his field, and because it is his he took care to sow it with good seed.

(3.) *The good seed are the children of the kingdom,* true saints. They are, [1.] The *children of the kingdom;* not in profession only, as the Jews were (*ch.* 8:12), but in sincerity; Jews inwardly, Israelites indeed, incorporated in faith and obedience to Jesus Christ the great King of the church. [2.] They are the good seed, precious as seed, Ps. 126:6. The seed is the substance of the field; so the holy seed, Isa. 6:13. The seed is scattered, so are the saints; dispersed, here one and there another, though in some places thicker sown than in others. The seed is that from which fruit is expected; what fruit of honour and service God has from this world he has from the saints, whom he has *sown unto himself in the earth,* Hos. 2:23.

(4.) *The tares are the children of the wicked one.* Here is the character of sinners, hypocrites, and all profane and wicked people. [1.] They are the children of the devil, as a wicked one. Though they do not own his name, yet they bear his image, do his lusts, and from him they have their education; he rules over them, he works in them, Eph. 2:2; Jn. 8:44. [2.] They are tares in the field of this world; they do no good, they do hurt; unprofitable in themselves, and hurt-

ful to *the good seed,* both by temptation and persecution: they are weeds in the garden, have the same rain, and sunshine, and soil, with the good plants, but are good for nothing: the *tares are among the wheat.* Note, God has so ordered it, that good and bad should be mixed together in this world, that the good may be exercised, the bad left inexcusable, and a difference made between earth and heaven.

(5.) *The enemy that sowed the tares is the devil;* a sworn enemy to Christ and all that is good, to the glory of the good God, and the comfort and happiness of all good men. He is an enemy to the field of the world, which he endeavours to make his own, by sowing his tares in it. Ever since he became a wicked spirit himself, he has been industrious to promote wickedness, and has made it his business, aiming therein to counterwork Christ.

Now concerning the sowing of the tares, observe in the parable,

[1.] That they were sown *while men slept.* Magistrates slept, who by their power, ministers slept, who by their preaching, should have prevented this mischief. Note, Satan watches all opportunities, and lays hold of all advantages, to propagate vice and profaneness. The prejudice he does to particular persons is when reason and conscience sleep, when they are off their guard; we have therefore need to *be sober, and vigilant.* It was in the night, for that is the sleeping time. Note, Satan rules in *the darkness of this world;* that gives him an opportunity to sow tares, Ps. 104:20. It was *while men slept;* and there is no remedy but men must have some sleeping time. Note, It is as impossible for us to prevent hypocrites being in the church, as it is for the husbandman, when he is asleep, to hinder an enemy from spoiling his field.

[2.] The enemy, when he had sown the tares, *went his way* (*v.* 25), that it might not be known who did it. Note, When Satan is doing the greatest mischief, he studies most to conceal himself; for his design is in danger of being spoiled if he be seen in it; and therefore, when he comes to sow tares, he *transforms himself into an angel of light,* 2 Co. 11:13, 14. He *went his way,* as if he had done no harm; *such is the way of the adulterous woman,* Prov. 30:20. Observe, Such is the proneness of fallen man to sin, that if the enemy sow the tares, he may even go his way, they will spring up of themselves and do hurt; whereas, when good seed is sown, it must be tended, watered, and fenced, or it will come to nothing.

[3.] The tares appeared not till *the blade sprung up, and brought forth fruit, v.* 26. There is a great deal of secret wickedness in the hearts of men, which is long hid under the cloak of a plausible profession, but breaks out at last. As the good seed, so the tares, lie a great while under the clods, and at first springing up, it is hard to distinguish them; but when a trying time comes, when fruit is to be brought forth, when good is to be done that has difficulty and hazard attending it, then you will return and discern between the sincere and the hypocrite: then you may say, This is wheat, and that is tares.

[4.] The servants, when they were aware of it, complained to their master (*v.* 27); *Sir, didst thou not sow good seed in thy field?* No doubt he did; whatever is amiss in the church, we are sure it is not of Christ: considering the seed which Christ sows, we may well ask, with wonder, *Whence should these tares come?* Note, The rise of errors, the breaking out of scandals, and the growth of profaneness, are matter of great grief to all the servants of Christ; especially to his faithful ministers, who are directed to complain of it to him whose the field is. It is sad to see such tares, such weeds, in the garden of the Lord; to see the good soil wasted, the good seed choked, and such a reflection cast on the name and honour of Christ, as if his field were no better than *the field of the slothful, all grown over with thorns.*

[5.] The Master was soon aware whence it was (*v.* 28); *An enemy has done this.* He does not lay the blame upon the servants; they could not help it, but had done what was in their power to prevent it. Note, The ministers of Christ, that are faithful and diligent, shall not be judged of Christ, and therefore should not be reproached by men, for the mixtures of bad with good, hypocrites with the sincere, in the field of the church. *It must needs be that such offences will come;* and they shall not be laid to our charge, if we do our duty, though it have not the desired success. Though they sleep, if they do not love sleep; though tares be sown, if they do not sow them nor water them, nor allow of them, the blame shall not lie at their door.

[6.] The servants were very forward to have these tares

rooted up. *"Wilt thou that we go* and do it presently?" Note, The over-hasty and inconsiderate zeal of Christ's servants, before they have consulted with their Master, is sometimes ready, with the hazard of the church, to root out all that they presume to be tares: Lord, wilt thou that we call for fire from heaven?

[7.] The Master very wisely prevented this (*v.* 29); *Nay, lest while ye gather up the tares, ye root up also the wheat with them.* Note, It is not possible for any man infallibly to distinguish between tares and wheat, but he may be mistaken; and therefore such is the wisdom and grace of Christ, that he will rather permit the tares, than any way endanger the wheat. It is certain, scandalous offenders are to be censured, and we are to withdraw from them; those who are openly *the children of the wicked one,* are not to be admitted to special ordinances; yet it is possible there may be a discipline, either so mistaken in its rules, or so over-nice in the application of them, as may prove vexatious to many that are truly godly and conscientious. Great caution and moderation must be used in inflicting and continuing church censures, lest the wheat be trodden down, if not plucked up. The *wisdom from above,* as it *is pure,* so it is *peaceable,* and those who oppose themselves must not be cut off, but instructed, and *with meekness,* 2 Tim. 2:25. The tares, if continued under the means of grace, may become good corn; therefore have patience with them.

(6.) *The harvest is the end of the world, v.* 39. This world will have an end; though it continue long, it will not continue always; time will shortly be swallowed up in eternity. At the end of the world, there will be a great harvest-day, a day of judgment; at harvest all is ripe and ready to be cut down: both good and bad are ripe at the great-day, Rev. 6:11. It is *the harvest of the earth,* Rev. 14:15. At harvest the reapers cut down all before them; not a field, not a corner, is left behind; so at the great day all must be judged (Rev. 20:12, 13); God has *set a harvest* (Hos. 6:11), and it shall not fail, Gen. 8:22. At harvest every man reaps as he sowed; every man's ground, and seed, and skill, and industry, will be manifested: see Gal. 6:7, 8. Then they who *sowed precious seed, will come again with rejoicing* (Ps. 126:5, 6), with *the joy of harvest* (Isa. 9:3); when *the sluggard, who would not plough by reason of cold, shall beg, and have nothing* (Prov. 20:4); shall cry, *Lord, Lord,* but in vain; when the harvest of those who sowed to the flesh, shall *be a day of grief, and of desperate sorrow,* Isa. 17:11.

(7.) *The reapers are the angels:* they shall be employed, in the great day, in executing Christ's righteous sentences, both of approbation and condemnation, as ministers of his justice, *ch.* 25:31. The angels are skilful, strong, and swift, obedient servants to Christ, holy enemies to the wicked, and faithful friends to all the saints, and therefore fit to be thus employed. *He that reapeth receiveth wages,* and the angels will not be unpaid for their attendance; for *he that soweth, and he that reapeth, shall rejoice together* (Jn. 4:36); that is *joy in heaven in the presence of the angels of God.*

(8.) Hell-torments are the *fire,* into which the *tares* shall then be cast, and in which they shall be burned. At the great day a distinction will be made, and with it a vast difference; it will be a notable day indeed.

[1.] The tares will then be gathered out: *The reapers* (whose primary work it is to gather in the corn) shall be charged first to *gather out the tares.* Note, Though good and bad are together in this world undistinguished, yet at the great day they shall be parted; no tares shall then be among the wheat; no sinners among the saints: then you shall plainly discern *between the righteous and the wicked,* which here sometimes it is hard to do, Mal. 3:18; 4:1. Christ will not bear always, Ps. 50:1, etc. They shall *gather out of his kingdom all wicked things that offend, and all wicked persons that do iniquity: when he begins, he will make a full end.* All those corrupt doctrines, worships, and practices, which have offended, have been scandals to the church, and stumbling-blocks to men's consciences, shall be condemned by the righteous Judge in that day, and consumed by the *brightness of his coming;* all *the wood, hay, and stubble* (1 Co. 3:12); and then *woe to them that do iniquity,* that make a trade of it, and persist in it; not only those in the last age of Christ's kingdom upon earth, but those in every age. Perhaps here is an allusion to Zep. 1:3, *I will consume the stumbling-blocks with the wicked.*

[2.] They will then be *bound in bundles, v.* 30. Sinners of the same sort will be bundled together in the great day: a bundle of atheists, a bundle of epicures, a bundle of persecutors, and a great bundle of hypocrites. Those who have been associates in sin, will be so in shame and sorrow; and it will be an aggravation of their misery, as the society of glorified saints will add to their bliss. Let us pray, as David, *Lord, gather not my soul with sinners* (Ps. 26:9), but let it be bound in *the bundle of life, with the Lord our God,* 1 Sa. 25:29. [3.] They will *be cast into a furnace of fire;* such will be the end of wicked, mischievous people, that are in the church as *tares in the field;* they are fit for nothing but fire; to it they shall go, it is the fittest place for them. Note, Hell is a furnace of fire, kindled by the wrath of God, and kept burning by the bundles of tares cast into it, who will be ever in the consuming, but never consumed. But he slides out of the metaphor into a description of those torments that are designed to be set forth by it: *There shall be weeping, and gnashing of teeth;* comfortless sorrow, and an incurable indignation at God, themselves, and one another, will be the endless torture of damned souls. Let us therefore, *knowing these terrors of the Lord,* be persuaded not to do iniquity.

(9.) Heaven is the *barn* into which all God's wheat shall be gathered in that harvest-day. *But gather the wheat into my barn:* so it is in the parable, *v.* 30. Note, [1.] In the field of this world good people are the wheat, the most precious grain, and the valuable part of the field. [2.] This wheat shall shortly be gathered, gathered from among the tares and weeds: all *gathered together in a general assembly,* all the Old-Testament saints, all the New-Testament saints, not one missing. *Gather my saints together unto me,* Ps. 50:5. [3.] All God's wheat shall be lodged together in God's barn: particular souls are housed at death as a shock of corn (Job 5:26), but the general in-gathering will be at the end of time: God's wheat will then be put together, and no longer scattered; there will be sheaves of corn, as well as bundles of tares: they will then be secured, and no longer exposed to wind and weather, sin and sorrow: no longer afar off, and at a great distance, in the field, but near, in the barn. Nay, heaven is a *garner* (*ch.* 3:12), in which the wheat will not only be separated from the tares of ill companions, but sifted from the chaff of their own corruptions.

In the explanation of the parable, this is gloriously represented (*v.* 43); *Then shall the righteous shine forth as the sun in the kingdom of their Father. First,* It is their present honour, that God is their Father. *Now are we the sons of God* (1 Jn. 3:2); *our Father in heaven* is King there. Christ, when he went to heaven, went to his *Father, and our Father,* Jn. 20:17. It is our *Father's house,* nay, it is *our Father's* palace, his throne, Rev. 3:21. *Secondly,* The honour in reserve for them is, that they *shall shine forth as the sun in that kingdom.* Here they are obscure and hidden (Col. 3:3), their beauty is eclipsed by their poverty, and the meanness of their outward condition; their own weaknesses and infirmities, and the reproach and disgrace cast upon them, cloud them; but then they shall shine forth as the sun from behind a dark cloud; at death they shall shine forth to themselves; at the great day they will shine forth publicly before all the world, *their bodies will be made like Christ's glorious body:* they shall shine by reflection, with a light borrowed from the Fountain of light; their sanctification will be perfected, and their justification published; God will own them for his children, and will produce the record of all their services and sufferings for his name: they shall shine as the sun, the most glorious of all visible beings. The glory of the saints is in the Old Testament compared to that of the firmament and the stars, but here to that of the sun; *for life and immortality are brought to* a much clearer *light by the gospel,* than under the law. Those who shine as lights in this world, that God may be glorified, shall shine as the sun in the other world, that *they* may be glorified. Our Saviour concludes, as before, with a demand of attention; *Who hath ears to hear, let him hear.* These are things which it is our happiness to hear of, and our duty to hearken to.

III. Here is the parable of the *grain of mustard-seed, v.* 31, 32. The scope of this parable is to show, that the beginnings of the gospel *would be small, but that its latter end would greatly increase.* In this way the gospel church, *the kingdom of God among us,* would be *set up in the world;* in this way the work of grace in the heart, *the kingdom of God within us,* would be carried on in particular persons.

Now concerning the work of the gospel, observe,

1. That it is commonly very weak and small at first, *like a grain of mustard-seed, which is one of the least of all seeds.* The kingdom of the Messiah, which was now in the setting up, made but a small figure; Christ and the apostles, compared with the grandees of the world, appeared *like a grain of mustard-seed, the weak things of the world.* In particular places, the first breaking out of the gospel light is but as *the dawning of the day;* and in particular souls, it is at first *the day of small things,* like a bruised reed. Young converts are like *lambs* that must be *carried in his arms,* Isa. 40:11. There is a little faith, but there is much lacking in it (1 Th. 3:10), and the *groanings* such as *cannot be uttered,* they are so small; a principle of spiritual life, and some motion, but scarcely discernible.

2. That yet it is growing and coming on. Christ's kingdom strangely got ground; great accessions were made to it; nations were born at once, in spite of all the oppositions it met with from hell and earth. In the soul where grace is true it will grow really, though perhaps insensibly. *A grain of mustard-seed* is small, but however it is seed, and has in it a disposition to grow. Grace will be getting ground, shining more and more, Prov. 4:18. Gracious habits confirmed, actings quickened, and knowledge more clear, faith more confirmed, love more inflamed; here is the seed growing.

3. That it will at last come to a great degree of strength and usefulness; *when it is grown to* some maturity, *it becomes a tree,* much larger in those countries than in ours. The church, like *the vine brought out of Egypt,* has taken root, and *filled the earth,* Ps. 80:9–11. The church is like a great tree, in which the fowls of the air do lodge; God's people have recourse to it for food and rest, shade and shelter. In particular persons, the principle of grace, if true, will persevere and be perfected at last: growing grace will be strong grace, and will bring much to pass. Grown Christians must covet to be useful to others, as the mustard-seed when grown is to the birds; that those who dwell near or under their shadow may be the better for them, Hos. 14:7.

IV. Here is the parable of the *leaven, v.* 33. The scope of this is much the same with that of the foregoing parable, to show that the gospel should prevail and be successful by degrees, but silently and insensibly; the preaching of the gospel is like leaven, and works like leaven in the hearts of those who receive it.

1. *A woman took* this *leaven;* it was her work. Ministers are employed in leavening places, in leavening souls, with the gospel. *The woman is the weaker vessel,* and we have this treasure in such vessels.

2. The leaven was *hid in three measures of meal.* The heart is, as the meal, soft and pliable; it is the tender heart that is likely to profit by the word: leaven among corn unground does not work, nor does the gospel in souls unhumbled and unbroken for sin: the law grinds the heart, and then the gospel leavens it. It is *three measures of meal,* a great quantity, for *a little leaven leaveneth the whole lump.* The meal must be kneaded, before it receive the leaven; our hearts, as they must be broken, so they must be moistened, and pains taken with them to prepare them for the word, that they may receive the impressions of it. The leaven must be *hid in the heart* (Ps. 119:11), not so much for secrecy (for it will show itself) as for safety; our inward thought must be upon it, we must lay it up, as Mary laid up the sayings of Christ, Lu. 2:51. When the woman hides the leaven in the meal, it is with an intention that it should communicate its taste and relish to it; so we must treasure up the word in our souls, that we may be sanctified by it, Jn. 17:17.

3. The leaven thus hid in the dough, works there, it ferments; *the word is quick and powerful,* Heb. 4:12. The leaven works speedily, so does the word, and yet gradually. What a sudden change did Elijah's mantle make upon Elisha! 1 Ki. 19:20. It works silently and insensibly (Mk. 4:26), yet strongly and irresistibly: it does its work without noise, for so is *the way of the Spirit,* but does it without fail. Hide but the leaven in the dough, and all the world cannot hinder it from communicating its taste and relish to it, and yet none sees how it is done, but by degrees *the whole is leavened.*

(1.) Thus it was in the world. The apostles, by their preaching, hid a handful of leaven in the great mass of mankind, and it had a strange effect; it put the world into a ferment, and in a sense turned it *upside down* (Acts 17:6), and by degrees made a wonderful change in the taste and relish of it: the savour of the gospel was *manifested in every place,* 2 Co. 2:14; Rom. 15:19. It was thus effectual, not by outward force, and therefore not by any such force resistible and conquerable, but by *the Spirit of the Lord of hosts, who works, and none can hinder.*

(2.) Thus it is in the heart. When the gospel comes into the soul, [1.] It works a change, not in the substance; the dough is the same, but in the quality; it makes us to savour otherwise than we have done, and other things to savour with us otherwise than they used to do, Rom. 8:5. [2.] It works a universal change; it diffuses itself into all the powers and faculties of the soul, and alters the property even of the members of the body, Rom. 6:13. [3.] This change is such as makes the soul to partake of the nature of the word, as the dough does of the leaven. We are delivered into it as into a mould (Rom. 6:17), changed into the same image (2 Co. 3:18), like the impression of the seal upon the wax. The gospel savours of God, and Christ, and free grace, and another world, and these things now relish with the soul. It is a word of faith and repentance, holiness and love, and these are wrought in the soul by it. This savour is communicated insensibly, for *our life is hid;* but inseparably, for grace is a *good part that shall never be taken away* from those who have it. When the dough is leavened, then to the oven with it; trials and afflictions commonly attend this change; but thus saints are fitted to be bread for our Master's table.

Verses 44–52

We have four short parables in these verses.

I. That of the *treasure hid in the field.* Hitherto he had compared *the kingdom of heaven* to small things, because its beginning was small; but, lest any should thence take occasion to think meanly of it, in this parable and the next he represents it as of great value in itself, and of great advantage to those who embrace it, and are willing to come up to its terms; it is here likened *to a treasure hid in the field,* which, if we will, we may make our own.

1. Jesus Christ is the true Treasure; in him there is an abundance of all that which is rich and useful, and will be a portion for us: *all fulness* (Col. 1:19; Jn. 1:16): *treasures of wisdom and knowledge* (Col. 2:3), of righteousness, grace, and peace; these are laid up for us in Christ; and, if we have an interest in him, it is all our own.

2. The gospel is the field in which this treasure is hid: it is hid in the word of the gospel, both the Old-Testament and the New-Testament gospel. In gospel ordinances it is hid as the milk in the breast, the marrow in the bone, the manna in the dew, the water in the well (Isa. 12:3), *the honey in the honey-comb.* It is hid, not *in a garden enclosed,* or *a spring shut up,* but *in a field,* an open field; *whoever will, let him come, and search the scriptures;* let him dig in *this field* (Prov. 2:4); and whatever royal mines we find, they are all our own, if we take the right course.

3. It is a great thing to discover the treasure hid in this field, and the unspeakable value of it. The reason why so many slight the gospel, and will not be at the expense, and run the hazard, of entertaining it, is because they look only upon the surface of the field, and judge by that, and so see no excellency in the Christian institutes above those of the philosophers; nay, the richest mines are often in grounds that appear most barren; and therefore they will not so much as bid for the field, much less come up to the price. *What is thy beloved more than another beloved?* What is the Bible more than other good books? The gospel of Christ more than Plato's philosophy, or Confucius's morals: but those who have *searched the scriptures,* so as in them to find Christ and *eternal life* (Jn. 5:39), have discovered such a treasure in this field as makes it infinitely more valuable.

4. Those who discern this treasure in the field, and value it aright, will never be easy till they have made it their own upon any terms. He that has found this treasure, hides it, which denotes a holy jealousy, *lest we come short* (Heb. 4:1), *looking diligently* (Heb. 12:15), lest Satan come between us and it. He rejoices in it, though as yet the bargain be not made; he is glad there is such a bargain to be had, and that he is in a fair way to have an interest in Christ; that the matter is in treaty: their *hearts* may *rejoice,* who are yet *but seeking the Lord,* Ps. 105:3. He resolves to *buy this field:* they who embrace gospel offers, upon gospel terms, buy this field; they make it their own, for the sake of the unseen treasure in it. It is Christ in the gospel that we are to have an eye to; we need not go up to heaven, but Christ in the word is nigh us. And so intent he is upon it, *that he sells all to buy this field:* they who would have saving benefit by Christ, must be willing to part with all, that they may make it sure to themselves; must *count every thing but loss, that they may win Christ, and be found in him.*

II. That of *the pearl of price* (*v.* 45, 46), which is to the same purport with the former, of the treasure. *The dream is thus doubled, for the thing is certain.*

Note, 1. All the children of men are busy, *seeking goodly pearls:* one would be rich, another would be honourable, another would be learned; but the most are imposed upon, and take up with counterfeits for pearls.

2. Jesus Christ is a *Pearl of great price,* a Jewel of inestimable value, which will make those who have it rich, truly rich, rich toward God; in having him, we have enough to make us happy here and for ever.

3. A true Christian is a spiritual *merchant,* that seeks and finds this pearl of price; that does not take up with any thing short of an interest in Christ, and, as one that is resolved to be spiritually rich, trades high: *He went and bought that pearl;* did not only bid for it, but purchased it. What will it avail us to know Christ, if we do not know him as ours, *made to us wisdom?* 1 Co. 1:30.

4. Those who would have a saving interest in Christ, must be willing to part with all for him, leave all to follow him. Whatever stands in opposition to Christ, or in competition with him for our love and service, we must cheerfully quit it, though ever so dear to us. A man may buy gold too dear, but not this pearl of price.

III. That of the *net cast into the sea, v.* 47–49.

1. Here is the parable itself. Where note, (1.) The world is a vast sea, and the children of men *are things creeping innumerable, both small and great,* in that sea, Ps. 104:25. Men in their natural state are *like the fishes of the sea* that have no ruler over them, Hab. 1:14. (2.) The preaching of the gospel is the casting of a net into this sea, to catch something out of it, for his glory who has the sovereignty of the sea. Ministers are *fishers of men,* employed in casting and drawing this net; and *then* they speed, when at Christ's word they let down the net; otherwise, they *toil and catch nothing.* (3.) This net gathers of every kind, as large dragnets do. In the visible church there is a deal of trash and rubbish, dirt and weeds and vermin, as well as fish. (4.) There is a time coming when this net will be full, and drawn to the shore; a set time when the gospel shall have fulfilled that for which it was sent, and we are sure it shall not return void, Is. 55:10, 11. The net is now filling; sometimes it fills faster than at other times, but still it fills, and will be drawn to shore, when the *mystery of God shall be finished.* (5.) When the net is full and drawn to the shore, there shall be a separation between the good and bad that were gathered in it. Hypocrites and true Christians shall then be parted; the good shall be gathered into vessels, as valuable, and therefore to be carefully kept, but the bad shall be cast away, as vile and unprofitable; and miserable is the condition of those who are cast away in that day. While the net is in the sea, it is not known what is in it, the fishermen themselves cannot distinguish; but they carefully draw it, and all that is in it, to the shore, for the sake of the good that is in it. Such is God's care for the visible church, and such should ministers' concern be for those under their charge, though they are mixed.

2. Here is the explanation of the latter part of the parable, the former is obvious and plain enough: we see gathered in the visible church, *some of every kind:* but the latter part refers to that which is yet to come, and is therefore more particularly explained, *v.* 49, 50. *So shall it be at the end of the world;* then, and not till then, will the dividing, discovering day be. We must not look for the net full of all good fish; the vessels will be so, but in the net they are mixed. See here, (1.) The distinguishing of the wicked from the righteous. The angels of heaven shall come forth to do that which the angels of the churches could never do; they shall *sever the wicked from among the just;* and we need not ask how they will distinguish them when they have both their commission and their instructions from him that knows all men, and particularly knows them that are *his,* and them that are *not,* and we may be sure there shall be no mistake or blunder either way. (2.) The doom of the wicked when they are thus severed. They shall be *cast into the furnace,* Note, Everlasting misery and sorrow will certainly be the portion of those who live among sanctified ones, but themselves die unsanctified. This is the same with what we had before, *v.* 42. Note, Christ himself preached often of hell-torments, as the everlasting punishment of hypocrites; and it is good for us to be often reminded of this awakening, quickening truth.

IV. Here is the parable of the *good householder,* which is intended to rivet all the rest.

1. The occasion of it was the good proficiency which the disciples had made in learning, and their profiting by this sermon in particular. (1.) He asked them, *Have ye understood all these things?* Intimating, that if they had not, he was ready to explain what they did not understand. Note, It is the will of Christ, that all those who read and hear the word should understand it; for otherwise how should they get good by it? It is therefore good for us, when we have read or heard the word, to examine ourselves, or to be examined, whether we have understood it or not. It is no disparagement to the disciples of Christ to be catechised. Christ invites us to seek to him for instruction, and ministers should proffer their service to those who have any good question to ask concerning what they have heard. (2.) They answered him, *Yea, Lord:* and we have reason to believe they said true, because, when they did not understand, they asked for an explication, *v.* 36. And the exposition of that parable was a key to the rest. Note, The right understanding of one good sermon, will very much help us to understand another; for good truths mutually explain and illustrate one another; and *knowledge is easy to him that understandeth.*

2. The scope of the parable itself was to give his approbation and commendation of their proficiency. Note, Christ is ready to encourage willing learners in his school, though they are but weak; and to say, *Well done, well said.*

(1.) He commends them as *scribes instructed unto the kingdom of heaven.* They were now learning that they might teach, and the teachers among the Jews were the scribes. Ezra, who *prepared his heart to teach in Israel,* is called *a ready scribe,* Ezra 7:6, 10. Now a skilful, faithful minister of the gospel is a scribe too; but for distinction, he is called a scribe *instructed unto the kingdom of heaven,* well versed in the things of the gospel, and well able to teach those things. Note, [1.] Those who are to instruct others, have need to be well instructed themselves. If the priest's lips must keep knowledge, his head must first have knowledge. [2.] The instruction of a gospel minister must be in the *kingdom of heaven,* that is it about which his business lies. A man may be a great philosopher and politician, and yet if not instructed to the kingdom of heaven, he will make but a bad minister.

(2.) He compares them to a good householder, who *brings forth out of his treasure things new and old;* fruits of last year's growth and this year's gathering, abundance and variety, for the entertainment of his friends, Cant. 7:13. See here, [1.] What should be a minister's furniture, *a treasure of things new and old.* Those who have so many and various occasions, have need to stock themselves well in their gathering days with truths new and old, out of the Old Testament and out of the new; with ancient and modern improvements, *that the man of God may be thoroughly furnished,* 2 Tim. 3:16, 17. Old experiences, and new observations, all have their use; and we must not content ourselves with old discoveries, but must be adding new. Live and learn. [2.] What use he should make of this furniture; he should *bring forth:* laying up is in order to laying out, for the benefit of others. *Sic vox non vobis — You are to lay up, but not for yourselves.* Many are full, but they have no vent (Job 32:19); have a talent, but they bury it; such are unprofitable servants; Christ himself received that he might give; so must we, and we shall have more. In bringing forth, things new and old do best together; old truths, but new methods and expressions, especially new affections.

Verses 53–58

We have here Christ in his own country. He went about doing good, yet left not any place till he had finished his testimony there at that time. His own countrymen had rejected him once, yet he came to them again. Note, Christ does not take refusers at their first word, but repeats his offers to those who have often repulsed them. In this, as in other things, Christ was like his brethren; he had a natural affection to his own country; *Patriam quisque amat, non quia pulchram, sed quia suam — Every one loves his country, not because it is beautiful, but because it is his own.* Seneca. His treatment this time was much the same as before, scornful and spiteful. Observe,

I. How they expressed their contempt of him. When he *taught them in their synagogue, they were astonished;* not that they were taken with his preaching, or admired his doctrine in itself, but only that it should be his; looking upon him as unlikely to be such a teacher. Two things they upbraided him with.

1. His want of academical education. They owned that he had wisdom, and did mighty works; but the question was, Whence he had them: for they knew that he was not brought up at the feet of the rabbin: he had never been at the university, nor taken his degree, nor was called of men, *Rabbi, Rabbi.* Note, Mean and prejudiced spirits are apt to judge of men by their education, and to enquire more into their rise than into their reasons. *"Whence has this man these mighty works?* Did he come honestly by them? Has he not been studying the black art?" Thus they turned that against him which was really for him; for if they had not been wilfully blind, they must have concluded him to be divinely assisted and commissioned, who without the help of education gave such proofs of extraordinary wisdom and power.

2. The meanness and poverty of his relations, *v.* 55, 56.

(1.) They upbraid him with his father. *Is not this the carpenter's son?* Yes, it is true he was reputed so: and what harm in that? No disparagement to him to be the son of an honest tradesman. They remember not (though they might have known it) that this carpenter was *of the house of David* (Lu. 1:27), *a son of David* (*ch.* 1:20); though a carpenter, yet a person of honour. Those who are willing to pick quarrels will overlook that which is worthy and deserving, and fasten upon that only which seems mean. Some sordid spirits regard no branch, no not the Branch from the stem of Jesse (Isa. 11:1), if it be not the top branch.

(2.) They upbraid him with his mother; and what quarrel have they with her? Why, truly, *his mother is called Mary,* and that was a very common name, and they all knew her, and knew her to be an ordinary person; she *was called Mary,* not *Queen Mary,* nor *Lady Mary,* nor so much as *Mistress Mary,* but plain *Mary;* and this is turned to his reproach, as if men had nothing to be valued by but foreign extraction, noble birth, or splendid titles; poor things to measure worth by.

(3.) They upbraid him with his brethren, whose names they knew, and had them ready enough to serve this turn; James, and Joses, and Simon, and Judas, good men but poor men, and therefore despised; and Christ for their sakes. These brethren, it is probable, were Joseph's children by a former wife; or whatever their relation was to him, they seem to have been brought up with him in the same family. And therefore of the calling of three of these, who were of the twelve, to that honour (James, Simon, and Jude, the same with Thaddeus), we read not particularly, because they needed not such an express call into acquaintance with Christ who had been the companions of his youth.

(4.) His sisters too are all with us; they should therefore have loved him and respected him the more, because he was one of themselves, but therefore they despised him. They were *offended in him:* they stumbled at these stumbling-stones, for he was set for *a sign that should be spoken against,* Lu. 2:34; Isa. 8:14.

II. See how he resented this contempt, *v.* 57, 58.

1. It did not trouble his heart. It appears he was not much concerned at it; he *despised the shame,* Heb. 12:2. Instead of aggravating the affront, or expressing an offence at it, or returning such an answer to their foolish suggestions as they deserved, he mildly imputes it to the common humour of the children of men, to undervalue excellences that are cheap, and common, and home-bred. It is usually so. *A prophet is not without honour, save in his own country.* Note, (1.) Prophets should have honour paid them, and commonly have; men of God are great men, and men of honour, and challenge respect. It is strange indeed if prophets have not honour. (2.) Notwithstanding this, they are commonly least regarded and reverenced in their own country, nay, and sometimes are most envied. Familiarity breeds contempt.

2. It did for the present (to speak with reverence), in effect, tie his hands: *He did not many mighty works there, because of their unbelief.* Note, Unbelief is the great obstruction to Christ's favours. *All things are* in general *possible to God* (*ch.* 19:26), but then it is *to him that believes* as to the particulars, Mk. 9:23. The gospel is *the power of God unto salvation,* but then it is to *every one that believes,* Rom. 1:16. So that if mighty works be not wrought in us, it is not for want of power or grace in Christ, but for want of faith in us. *By grace ye are saved,* and that is a mighty work, but it is *through faith,* Eph. 2:8.

CHAPTER 14

John the Baptist had said concerning Christ, He must increase, but I must decrease, Jn. 3:30. The morning-star is here disappearing, and the

Sun of righteousness rising to its meridian lustre. Here is, I. The martyrdom of John; his imprisonment for his faithfulness to Herod (*v.* 1–5), and the beheading of him to please Herodias (*v.* 6–12). II. The miracles of Christ. 1. His feeding five thousand men that came to him to be taught, with five loaves and two fishes (*v.* 13–21). 2. Christ's walking on the waves to his disciples in a storm (*v.* 22–23). 3. His healing the sick with the touch of the hem of his garment (*v.* 34–36). Thus he went forth, thus he went on, conquering and to conquer, or rather, curing and to cure.

Verses 1–12

We have here the story of John's martyrdom. Observe,

I. The occasion of relating this story here, *v.* 1, 2. Here is,

1. The account brought to Herod of the miracles which Christ wrought. Herod the tetrarch or chief governor of Galilee *heard of the fame of Jesus.* At that time, when his countrymen slighted him, upon the account of his meanness and obscurity, he began to be famous at court. Note, God will honour those that are despised for his sake. And the gospel, like the sea, gets in one place what it loses in another. Christ had now been preaching and working miracles above two years; yet, it should seem, Herod had not heard of him till now, and now only heard the fame of him. Note, It is the unhappiness of the great ones of the world, that they are most out of the way of hearing the best things (1 Co. 2:8). *Which none of the princes of this world knew,* 1 Co. 1:26. Christ's disciples were now sent abroad to preach, and to work miracles in his name, and this spread the fame of him more than ever; which was an indication of the spreading of the gospel by their means after his ascension.

2. The construction he puts upon this (*v.* 2); *He said to his servants* that told him of the fame of Jesus, as sure as we are here, *this is John the Baptist; he is risen from the dead.* Either the leaven of Herod was not Sadducism, *for the Sadducees say, There is no resurrection* (Acts 23:8); or else Herod's guilty conscience (as is usual with atheists) did at this time get the mastery of his opinion, and now he concludes, whether there be a general resurrection or no, that *John Baptist is certainly risen,* and therefore *mighty works do show forth themselves in him.* John, while he lived, *did no miracle* (Jn. 10:41); but Herod concludes, that, being risen from the dead, he is clothed with a greater power than he had while he was living. And he very well calls the miracles he supposed him to work, not *his mighty works,* but *mighty works showing forth themselves in him.* Observe here concerning Herod,

(1.) How he was disappointed in what he intended by beheading John. He thought if he could get that troublesome fellow out of the way, he might go on in his sins, undisturbed and uncontrolled; yet no sooner is that effected, than he hears of Jesus and his disciples preaching the same pure doctrine that John preached; and, which is more, even the disciples confirming it by miracles in their Master's name. Note, Ministers may be silenced, and imprisoned, and banished, and slain, but the word of God cannot be run down. The prophets *live not for ever, but the word takes hold,* Zec. 1:5, 6. See 2 Tim. 2:9. Sometimes God raises up many faithful ministers out of the ashes of one. This *hope* there is of God's trees, *though they be cut down,* Job 14:7–9.

(2.) How he was filled with causeless fears, merely from the guilt of his own conscience. Thus *blood cries,* not only *from the earth* on which it was shed, but from the heart of him that shed it, and makes him *Magor-missabib — A terror round about,* a terror to himself. A guilty conscience suggests every thing that is frightful, and, like a whirlpool, gathers all to itself that comes near it. Thus *the wicked flee when none pursue* (Prov. 28:1); are in *great fear, where no fear is,* Ps. 14:5. Herod, by a little enquiry, might have found out that this Jesus was in being long before John Baptist's death, and therefore could not be *Johannes redivivus — John restored to life;* and so he might have undeceived himself; but God justly left him to this infatuation.

(3.) How, notwithstanding this, he was hardened in his wickedness; for though he was convinced that John was a prophet, and one owned of God, yet he does not express the least remorse or sorrow for his sin in putting him to death. The devils believe and tremble, but they never believe and repent. Note, There may be the terror of strong convictions, where there is not the truth of a saving conversion.

II. The story itself of the imprisonment and martyrdom of John. These extraordinary sufferings of him who was the first preacher of the gospel, plainly show that bonds and afflictions will abide the professors of it. As the first Old-Testament saint, so the first New-Testament minister, died a martyr. And if Christ's forerunner was thus treated, let not his followers expect to be caressed by the world. Observe here,

1. John's faithfulness in reproving Herod, *v.* 3, 4. Herod was one of John's hearers (Mk. 6:20), and therefore John might be the more bold with him. Note, Ministers, who are reprovers by office, are especially obliged to reprove those that are under their charge, and *not to suffer sin upon them;* they have the fairest opportunity of dealing with them, and with them may expect the most favourable acceptance.

The particular sin he reproved him for was, marrying his brother Philip's wife, not his widow (that had not been so criminal), but his wife. Philip was now living, and Herod inveigled his wife from him, and kept here for his own. Here was a complication of wickedness, adultery, incest, besides the wrong done to Philip, who had had a child by this woman; and it was an aggravation of the wrong, that he was his brother, his half-brother, by the father, but not by the mother. See Ps. 50:20. For this sin John reproved him; not by tacit and oblique allusions, but in plain terms, *It is not lawful for thee to have her.* He charges it upon him as a sin; not, It is not honourable, or, It is not safe, but, It is not *lawful;* the *sinfulness* of sin, as it is the *transgression of the law,* is the worst thing in it. This was Herod's own iniquity, his beloved sin, and therefore John Baptist tells him of this particularly. Note, (1.) That which by the law of God is unlawful to other people, is by the same law unlawful to princes and the greatest of men. They who rule over men must not forget that they are themselves but men, and subject to God. "*It is not lawful for thee,* any more than for the meanest subject thou hast, to debauch another man's wife." There is no prerogative, no, not for the greatest and most arbitrary kings, to break the laws of God. (2.) If princes and great men break the law of God, it is very fit they should be told of it by proper persons, and in a proper manner. As they are not above the commands of God's word, so they are not above the reproofs of his ministers. *It is not fit* indeed, *to say to a king, Thou art Belial* (Job 34:18), any more than to call a brother *Raca,* or, *Thou fool:* it is not fit, while they keep within the sphere of their own authority, to arraign them. But it is fit that, by those whose office it is, they should be told what is unlawful, and told with application, *Thou art the man;* for it follows there (*v.* 19), that God (whose agents and ambassadors faithful ministers are) *accepteth not the persons of princes, nor regardeth the rich more than the poor.*

2. The imprisonment of John for his faithfulness, *v.* 3. *Herod laid hold on John* when he was going on to preach and baptize, put an end to his work, *bound him, and put him in prison;* partly to gratify his own revenge, and partly to please Herodias, who of the two seemed to be most incensed against him; it was *for her sake* that he did it. Note, (1.) Faithful reproofs, if they do not profit, usually provoke; if they do not do good, they are resented as affronts, and they that will not bow to the reproof, will fly in the face of the reprover and hate him, as Ahab hated Micaiah, 1 Ki. 22:8. See Prov. 9:8; 15:10, 12. *Veritas odium parit — Truth produces hatred.* (2.) It is no new thing for God's ministers to suffer ill for doing well. Troubles abide those most that are most diligent and faithful in doing their duty, Acts 20:20. Perhaps some of John's friends would blame him as indiscreet in reproving Herod, and tell him he had better be silent than provoke Herod, whose character he knew very well, thus to deprive him of his liberty; but away with that discretion that would hinder men from doing their duty as magistrates, ministers, or Christian friends; I believe John's own heart did not reproach him for it, but this testimony of his conscience for him made his bonds easy, that he suffered for well-doing, and not as a *busy-body in other men's matters,* 1 Pt. 4:15.

3. The restraint that Herod lay under from further venting of his rage against John, *v.* 5.

(1.) He would have put him to death. Perhaps that was not intended at first when he imprisoned him, but his revenge by degrees boiled up to that height. Note, The way of sin, especially the sin of persecution, is down-hill; and when once a respect to Christ's ministers is cast off and broken through in one instance, that is at length done, which the man would sooner have thought himself a dog than to have been guilty of, 2 Ki. 8:13.

(2.) That which hindered him was his *fear of the multitude, because they counted John as a prophet.* It was not because he feared God (if the fear of God had been before his eyes he would not have imprisoned him), nor because he feared John, though formerly he had had a reverence for him (his lusts had overcome that), but because he feared the people; he was afraid for himself, his own safety, and the safety of his government, his abuse of which he knew had already rendered him odious to the people, whose resentments being so far heated already would be apt, upon such a provocation as the putting of a prophet to death, to break out into a flame. Note, [1.] Tyrants have their fears. Those who are, and affect to be, *the terror of the mighty,* are many times the greatest terror of all to themselves; and when they are most ambitious to be feared by the people, are most afraid of them. [2.] Wicked men are restrained from the most wicked practices, merely by their secular interest, and not by any regard to God. A concern for their ease, credit, wealth, and safety, being their reigning principle, as it keeps them from many duties, so it keeps them from many sins, which otherwise they would not be restrained from; and this is one means by which sinners are kept from being overmuch wicked, Eccl. 7:17. The danger of sin that appears to sense, or to fancy only, influences men more than that which appears to faith. Herod feared that the putting of John to death might raise a mutiny among the people, which it did not; but he never feared it might raise a mutiny in his own conscience, which it did, *v.* 2. Men fear being hanged for that which they do not fear being damned for.

4. The contrivance of bringing John to his death. Long he lay in prison; and, against the liberty of the subject (which, blessed be God, is secured to us of this nation by law), might neither be tried nor bailed. It is computed that he lay a year and a half a close prisoner, which was about as much time as he had spent in his public ministry, from his first entrance into it. Now here we have an account of his release, not by any other discharge than death, the period of all a good man's troubles, that brings the prisoners to rest together, so that *they hear not the voice of the oppressor,* Job 3:18.

Herodias laid the plot; her implacable revenge thirsted after John's blood, and would be satisfied with nothing less. Cross the carnal appetites, and they turn into the most barbarous passions; it was a woman, a whore, and the mother of harlots, that was *drunk with the blood of the saints,* Rev. 17:5, 6. Herodias contrived how to bring about the murder of John so artificially as to save Herod's credit, and so to pacify the people. A sorry excuse is better than none. But I am apt to think, that if the truth were known, Herod was himself in the plot; and with all his pretences of surprise and sorrow, was privy to the contrivance, and knew before what would be asked. And his pretending his oath, and respect to his guests, was all but sham and grimace. But if he were trepanned into it ere he was aware, yet because it was the thing he might have prevented, and would not, he is justly found guilty of the whole contrivance. Though Jezebel bring Naboth to his end, yet if Ahab take possession, *he hath killed.* So, though Herodias contrive the beheading of John, yet if Herod consent to it, and take pleasure in it, he is not only an accessary, but a principal murderer. Well, the scene being laid behind the curtain, let us see how it was acted upon the stage, and in what method. Here we have,

(1.) The humouring of Herod by the damsel's dancing upon a birth-day. It seems, Herod's birth-day was kept with some solemnity; in honour of the day, there must needs be, as usual, a ball at court; and, to grace the solemnity, the daughter of Herodias danced before them; who being the queen's daughter, it was more than she ordinarily condescended to do. Note, Times of carnal mirth and jollity are convenient times for carrying on bad designs against God's people. When the king was *made sick with bottles of wine, he stretched out his hand with scorners* (Hos. 7:5), for it is part of the *sport of a fool* to do mischief, Prov. 10:23. The Philistines, when their heart was merry, called for Samson to abuse him. The Parisian massacre was at a wedding. This young lady's dancing pleased Herod. We are not told who danced with her, but none pleased Herod like her dancing. Note, A vain and graceless heart is apt to be greatly in love with the lusts of the flesh and of the eye, and when it is so, it is entering into further temptation; for by that Satan gets and keeps possession. See Prov. 23:31–33. Herod was now in a mirthful mood, and nothing was more agreeable to him than that which fed his vanity.

(2.) The rash and foolish promise which Herod made to this wanton girl, to give her whatsoever she would ask: and this promise confirmed with an oath, *v.* 7. It was a very extravagant obligation which Herod here entered into, and no way becoming a prudent man that is afraid of being *snared in the words of his mouth* (Prov. 6:2), much less a good man that fears an oath, Eccl. 9:2. To put this blank into her hand, and enable her to draw upon him at pleasure, was too great a recompense for such a sorry piece of merit; and, I am apt to think, Herod would not have been guilty of such an absurdity, if he had not been instructed of Herodias, as well as the damsel. Note, Promissory oaths are ensnaring things, and, when made rashly, are the products of inward corruption, and the occasion of many temptations. Therefore, swear not so at all, lest thou have occasion to say, *It was an error,* Eccl. 5:6.

(3.) The bloody demand the young lady made of John the Baptist's head, *v.* 8. She was before instructed of her mother. Note, The case of those children is very sad, whose parents are *their counsellors to do wickedly,* as Ahaziah's (2 Chr. 22:3); who instruct them and encourage them in sin, and set them bad examples; for the corrupt nature will sooner be quickened by bad instructions than restrained and mortified by good ones. Children ought not to *obey their parents* against *the Lord,* but if they command them to sin, must say, as Levi did to *father and mother,* they *have not seen them.*

Herod having given her her commission, and Herodias her instructions, she requires John the Baptist's head in a charger. Perhaps Herodias feared lest Herod should grow weary of her (as lust useth to nauseate and be cloyed), and then would make John Baptist's reproof a pretence to dismiss her; to prevent which she contrives to harden Herod in it by engaging him in the murder of John. John must be beheaded then; that is the death by which he must glorify God; and because it was *his* who died first after the beginning of the gospel, though the martyrs died various kinds of deaths, and not so easy and honourable as this, yet this is put for all the rest, Rev. 20:4, where we read of *the souls of those that were beheaded for the witness of Jesus.* Yet this is not enough, the thing must be humoured too, and not only a revenge, but a fancy must be gratified; it must be *given her here in a charger,* served up in blood, as a dish of meat at the feast, or sauce to all the other dishes; it is reserved for the third course, to come up with the rarities. He must have no trial, no public hearing, no forms of law or justice must add solemnity to his death; but he is tried, condemned, and executed, in a breath. It was well for him he was so mortified to the world that death could be no surprise to him, though ever so sudden. It must be given her, and she will reckon it a recompence for her dancing, and desire no more.

(4.) Herod's grant of this demand (*v.* 9); *The king was sorry,* at least took on him to be so, but, *for the oath's sake, he commanded it to be given her.* Here is,

[1.] A pretended concern for John. *The king was sorry.* Note, Many a man sins with regret, that never has any true regret for his sin; is sorry to sin, yet is utterly a stranger to godly sorrow; sins with reluctancy, and yet goes on to sin. Dr. Hammond suggests, that one reason of Herod's sorrow was, because it was his birth-day festival, and it would be an ill omen to shed blood on that day, which, as other days of joy, used to be graced with acts of clemency; *Natalem colimus, tacete lites — We are celebrating the birth-day, let there be no contentions.*

[2.] Here is a pretended conscience of his oath, with a specious show of honour and honesty; he must needs do something, for the oath's sake. Note, It is a great mistake to think that a wicked oath will justify a wicked action. It was implied so necessarily, that it needed not be expressed, that he would do any thing for her that was lawful and honest; and when she demanded what was otherwise, he ought to have declared, and he might have done it honourably, that the oath was null and void, and the obligation of it ceased. No man can lay himself under an obligation to sin, because God has already so strongly obliged every man against sin.

[3.] Here is a real baseness in compliance with wicked companions. Herod yielded, not so much for the sake of the oath, but because it was public, and in compliment to *them that sat at meat with him;* he granted the demand that he might not seem, before them, to have broken his engagement. Note, A point of honour goes much further with many than a point of conscience. Those who sat at meat with him, probably, were as well pleased with the damsel's dancing as he, and therefore would have her by all means to be gratified in a frolic, and perhaps were as willing as she to see John the Baptist's head off. However, none of them had the honesty to interpose, as they ought to have done, for the preventing of it, as Jehoiakim's princes did, Jer. 36:25. If some of the common people had been here, they would have rescued this Jonathan, as 1 Sa. 14:45.

[4.] Here is a real malice to John at the bottom of this concession, or else he might have found out evasions enough to have got clear of his promise. Note, Though a wicked mind never wants an excuse, yet the truth of the matter is, that *every man is tempted when he is drawn aside of his own lust, and enticed,* Jam. 1:14. Perhaps Herod presently reflecting upon the extravagance of his promise, on which she might ground a demand of some vast sum of money, which he loved a great deal better than John the Baptist, was glad to get clear of it so easily; and therefore immediately issues out a warrant for the beheading of John the Baptist, it should seem not in writing, but only by word of mouth; so little account is made of that precious life; *he commanded it to be given her.*

(5.) The execution of John, pursuant to this grant (*v.* 10); *He sent and beheaded John in the prison.* It is probable the prison was very near, at the gate of the palace; and thither an officer was sent to cut off the head of this great man. He must be beheaded with expedition, to gratify Herodias, who was in a longing condition till it was done. It was done in the night, for it was at supper-time, after supper, it is likely. It was done in the prison, not at the usual place of execution, for fear of an uproar. A great deal of innocent blood, of martyr's blood, has thus been huddled up in corners, which, when God comes to make inquisition for blood, the earth shall disclose, and shall no more cover, Isa. 26:21; Ps. 9:12.

Thus was that voice silenced, that burning and shining light extinguished; thus did that prophet, that Elias, of the new Testament, fall a sacrifice to the resentments of an imperious, whorish woman. Thus did he, who was great in the sight of the Lord, *die as a fool dieth, his hands were bound, and his feet put into fetters; and as a man falleth before wicked men,* so he fell, a true martyr to all intents and purposes: dying, though not for the professions of his faith, yet for the performance of his duty. However, though his work was soon done, *it was done and his testimony finished,* for till then none of God's witnesses are slain. And God brought this good out of it, that hereby his disciples, who while he lived, though in prison, kept close to him, now after his death heartily closed with Jesus Christ.

5. The disposal of the poor remains of this blessed saint and martyr. The head and body being separated,

(1.) The damsel brought the head in triumph to her mother, as a trophy of the victories of her malice and revenge, *v.* 11. *Jerome ad Rufin,* relates, that when Herodias had John the Baptist's head brought her, she gave herself the barbarous diversion of pricking the tongue with a needle, as Fulvia did Tully's. Note, Bloody minds are pleased with bloody sights, which those of tender spirits shrink and tremble at. Sometimes the insatiable rage of bloody persecutors has fallen upon the dead bodies of the saints, and made sport with them, Ps. 79:2. When the witnesses are slain, they that *dwell on the earth rejoice over them, and make merry,* Rev. 11:10; Ps. 14:4, 5.

(2.) The disciples *buried the body,* and brought the news in tears to our Lord Jesus. The disciples of John had fasted often whole their master was in prison, their *bridegroom was taken away from them,* and they prayed earnestly for his deliverance, as the church did for Peter's, Acts 12:5. They had free access to him in prison, which was a comfort to them, but they wished to see him at liberty, that he might preach to others; but now on a sudden all their hopes are dashed. Disciples weep and lament, when the world rejoices. Let us see what they did.

[1.] *They buried the body.* Note, There is a respect owing to the servants of Christ, not only while they live, but in their bodies and memories when they are dead. Concerning the first two New-Testament martyrs, it is particularly taken notice of, that they were decently buried, John the Baptist by his disciples, and Stephen by devout men (Acts 8:2); yet there was no enshrining of their bones or other relics, a piece of superstition which sprung up long after, when the enemy had sowed tares. That over-doing, in respect to the bodies of the saints, is undoing; though they are not to be vilified, yet they are not to be deified.

[2.] *They went and told Jesus;* not so much that he might shift for his own safety (no doubt he heard it from others, the country rang of it), as they might receive comfort from him, and be taken in among his disciples. Note, *First,* When any thing ails us at any time, it is our duty and privilege to make Christ acquainted with it. It will be a relief to our burthened spirits to unbosom ourselves to a friend we may be free with. Such a relation dead or unkind, such a comfort lost or embittered, go and tell Jesus who knows already, but will know from us, the trouble of *our souls in adversity. Secondly,* We must take heed, lest our religion and the profession of it die with our ministers; when John was dead, they did not return every man to his own, but resolved to abide by it still. When the shepherds are smitten, the sheep need not be scattered while they have the great Shepherd of the sheep to go to, who is still the same, Heb. 13:8, 20. The removal of ministers should bring us nearer to Christ, into a more immediate communion with him. *Thirdly,* Comforts otherwise highly valuable, are sometimes *therefore* taken from us, because they come between us and Christ, and are apt to carry away that love and esteem which are due to him only: John had long since directed his disciples to Christ, and turned them over to him, but they could not leave their old master while he lived; therefore he is removed that they may go to Jesus, whom they had sometimes emulated and envied for John's sake. It is better to be drawn to Christ by want and loss, than not to come to him at all. If our masters be taken from our head, this is our comfort, we have a Master in heaven, who himself is our Head.

Josephus mentions this story of the death of John the Baptist (*Antiq.* 18.116–119), and adds, that a fatal destruction of Herod's army in his war with Aretas, king of Petrea (whose daughter was Herod's wife, whom he put away to make room for Herodias), was generally considered by the Jews to be a just judgment upon him, for putting John the Baptist to death. Herod having, at the instigation of Herodias, disobliged the emperor, was deprived of his government, and they were both banished to Lyons in France; which, says Josephus, was his just punishment for hearkening to her solicitations. And, lastly, it is storied of this daughter of Herodias, that going over the ice in winter, the ice broke, and she slipt in up to her neck, which was cut through by the sharpness of the ice. God requiring her head (says Dr. Whitby) for that of the Baptist; which, if true, was a remarkable providence.

Verses 13–21

This passage of story, concerning Christ's feeding *five thousand men with five loaves and two fishes,* is recorded by all the four Evangelists, which very few, if any, of Christ's miracles are: this intimates that there is something in it worthy of special remark. Observe,

I. The great resort of people to Christ, when he was retired *into a desert place, v.* 13. He withdrew into privacy when he heard, not of John's death, but of the thoughts Herod had concerning him, that he was *John the Baptist risen from the dead,* and therefore so feared by Herod as to be hated; he departed further off, to get out of Herod's jurisdiction. Note, In times of peril, when God opens a door of escape, it is lawful to flee for our own preservation, unless we have some special call to expose ourselves. Christ's *hour was not yet come,* and therefore he would not thrust himself upon suffering. He could have secured himself by divine power, but because his life was intended for an example, he did it by human prudence; *he departed by ship.* But *a city on a hill cannot be hid; when the people heard it, they followed him on foot* from all parts. Such an interest Christ had in the affections of the multitude, that his withdrawing from them did but draw them after him with so much the more eagerness. Here, as often, *the scripture was fulfilled,* that *unto him shall the gathering of the people be.* It should seem, there was more crowding to Christ after John's martyrdom than before. Sometimes *the suffering of the saints* are made to further the gospel (Phil. 1:12), and "the blood of the martyrs is the seed of the church." Now John's testimony was finished, it was recollected, and more improved than ever. Note, 1. When Christ and his word withdraw from us, it is best for us (whatever flesh and blood may object to the contrary) to follow it, preferring opportunities for our souls before any secular advantages whatsoever. *When the ark removes, ye shall remove, and go after it,* Jos. 3:3. 2. *Those that truly desire the sincere milk of the word,* will not stick at the difficulties they may meet with in their attendance on it. The presence of Christ and his gospel makes a desert place not only tolerable, but desirable; it makes the wilderness an Eden, Isa. 51:3; 41:19, 20.

II. The tender compassion of our Lord Jesus towards those who thus followed him, *v.* 14. 1. He went forth, and appeared publicly among them. Though he retired for his own security, and his own repose, yet he went forth from his retirement, when he saw people desirous to hear him, as one willing both to toil himself, and to expose himself, for the good of souls; for *even Christ pleased not himself.* 2. *When he saw the multitude, he had compassion on them.* Note, The sight of a great multitude may justly move compassion. To see a great multitude, and to think how many precious, immortal souls here are, the greatest part of which, we have reason to fear, are neglected and ready to perish, would grieve one to the heart. None like Christ for pity to souls; *his compassions fails not.* 3. He did not only pity them, but he helped them; many of them were *sick, and he, in compassion to them, healed them;* for he came into the world to be the great Healer. After awhile, they were all hungry, *and he, in compassion to them, fed them.* Note, In all the favours Christ shows to us, he is *moved with compassion,* Isa. 63:9.

III. The motion which the disciples made for the dismissing of the congregation, and Christ's setting aside the motion. 1. The *evening* drawing on, the disciples moved it to Christ to send the multitude away; they thought there was a good day's work done, and it was time to disperse. Note, Christ's disciples are often more careful to show their discretion, than to show their zeal; and their abundant affection in the things of God. 2. Christ would not dismiss them hungry as they were, nor detain them longer without meat, nor put them upon the trouble and charge of buying meat for themselves, but orders his disciples to provide for them. Christ all along expressed more tenderness toward the people than his disciples did; for what are the compassions of the most merciful men, compared with *the tender mercies of God in Christ?* See how loth Christ is to part with those who are resolved to cleave to him! *They need not depart.* Note, Those who have Christ have enough, and need not depart to seek a happiness and livelihood in the creature; they that have made sure of *the one thing needful,* need not be *cumbered about much serving:* nor will Christ put his willing followers upon a needless expense, but will make their attendance cheap to them.

But if they be hungry, they have need to depart, for that is a necessity which has no law, therefore, *give you them to eat.* Note, *The Lord is for the body;* it is *the work of his hands,* it is part of his purchase; he was himself clothed with a body, that he might encourage us to depend upon him for the supply of our bodily wants. But he takes a particular care of the body, when it is employed to serve the soul in his more immediate service. If we *seek first the kingdom of God,* and make that our chief care, we may depend upon God to *add other things to us,* as far as he sees fit, and may *cast all care* of them *upon him.* These followed Christ but for a trial, in a present fit of zeal, and yet Christ took this care of them; much more will he provide for those who follow him fully.

IV. The slender provision that was made for this great multitude; and here we must compare the number of invited guests with the bill of fare.

1. The number of the guests was *five thousand of men, besides women and children;* and it is probable the women and children might be as many as the men, if not more. This was a vast auditory that Christ preached to, and we have reason to think an attentive auditory; and, yet it should seem, far the greater part, notwithstanding all this seeming zeal and forwardness, came to nothing; they went off and followed him no more; *for many are called, but few are chosen.* We would rather perceive the acceptableness of the word by the conversion, than by the crowds, of its hearers; though that also is a good sight and a good sign.

2. The bill of fare was very disproportionable to the number of the guests, but *five loaves and two fishes.* This provision the disciples carried about with them for the use of the family, now they *were retired into the desert.* Christ could have fed them by miracle, but to set us an example of providing for those of our own households, he will have their own camp victualled in an ordinary way. Here is neither plenty, nor variety, nor dainty; a dish of fish was no rarity to them that were fishermen, but it was food convenient for the twelve; two fishes for their supper, and bread to serve them perhaps for a day or two: here was no wine or strong drink; fair water from the rivers in the desert was the best they had to drink with their meat; and yet out of this Christ will have the multitude fed. Note, Those who have but a little, yet when the necessity is urgent, must relieve others out of that little, and that is the way to make it more. *Can God*

furnish a table in the wilderness? Yes, he can, when he pleases, a plentiful table.

V. The liberal distribution of this provision among the multitude (v. 18, 19); *Bring them hither to me.* Note, The way to have our creature-like comforts, comforts indeed to us, is to bring them to Christ; for every thing is sanctified by his word, and by prayer to him: that is likely to prosper and do well with us, which we put into the hands of our Lord Jesus, that he may dispose of it as he pleases, and that we may take it back from his hand, and then it will be doubly sweet to us. What we give in charity, we should bring to Christ first, that he may graciously accept it from us, and graciously bless it to those to whom it is given; this is *doing it as unto the Lord.*

Now at this miraculous meal we may observe,

1. The seating of the guests (v. 19); *He commanded them to sit down;* which intimates, that while he was preaching to them, they were standing, which is a posture of reverence, and readiness for motion. But what shall we do for chairs for them all? Let them *sit down on the grass.* When Ahasuerus would *show the riches of his glorious kingdom, and the honour of his excellent majesty, in a royal feast for the great men of all his provinces,* the beds or couches they sat on *were of gold and silver, upon a pavement of red, and blue, and white, and black marble,* Esther 1:6. Our Lord Jesus did now show, in a divine feast, the riches of a more glorious kingdom than that, and the honour of a more excellent majesty, even a dominion over nature itself; but here is not so much as a cloth spread, no plates or napkins laid, no knives or forks, nor so much as a bench to sit down on; but, as if Christ intended indeed to reduce the world to the plainness and simplicity, and so to the innocency and happiness, of Adam in paradise, *he commanded them to sit down on the grass.* By doing every thing thus, without any pomp or splendour, he plainly showed *that his kingdom was not of this world,* nor *cometh with observation.*

2. The craving of a blessing. He did not appoint one of his disciples to be his chaplain, but he himself *looked up to heaven, and blessed, and gave thanks;* he praised God for the provision they had, and prayed to God to bless it to them. His craving a blessing, was commanding a blessing; for as he preached, so he prayed, *like one having authority;* and in this prayer and thanksgiving, we may suppose, he had special reference to the multiplying of this food; but herein he has taught us that good duty of craving a blessing and giving thanks at our meals: God's good creatures must be *received with thanksgiving,* 1 Tim. 4:4. Samuel *blessed* the feast, 1 Sa. 9:13; Acts 2:46, 47; 27:34, 35. This is *eating and drinking to the glory of God* (1 Co. 10:31); *giving God thanks* (Rom. 14:6); *eating before God,* as Moses, and his father-in-law, Ex. 18:12, 15. When Christ *blessed,* he *looked up to heaven,* to teach us, in prayer, to eye God as a *Father in heaven;* and when we receive our creature-comforts to look thitherward, as taking them from God's hand, and depending on him for a blessing.

3. The carving of the meat. The Master of the feast was himself head-carver, for *he brake, and gave the loaves to the disciples, and the disciples to the multitude.* Christ intended hereby to put honour upon his disciples, that they might be respected *as workers together with him;* as also to signify in what way the spiritual food of the word should be dispensed to the world; from Christ, as the original Author, by his ministers. What Christ designed for *the churches he signified to his servant John* (Rev. 1:1, 4); *they delivered all that,* and that only, *which they received from the Lord,* 1 Co. 11:23. Ministers can never fill the people's hearts, unless Christ first fill their hands: and what he has given to the disciples, they must give to the multitude; for they are *stewards, to give to every one his portion of meat,* ch. 24:45. And, blessed be God, be the multitude ever so great, there is enough for all, enough for each.

4. The increase of the meat. This is taken notice of only in the effect, not in the cause or manner of it; here is no mention of any word that Christ spoke, by which the food was multiplied; the purposes and intentions of his mind and will shall take effect, though they be not spoken out: but this is observable, that the meat was multiplied, not in the heap at first, but in the distribution of it. As the widow's oil increased in the pouring out, so here the bread in the breaking. Thus grace grows by being acted, and, while other things perish in the using, spiritual gifts increase in the using. God ministers seed to the sower, and multiplies not the seed hoarded

up, but *the seed sown,* 2 Co. 9:10. Thus *there is that scattereth and yet increaseth;* that scattereth, and so increaseth.

VI. The plentiful satisfaction of all the guests with this provision. Though the disproportion was so great, yet there was enough and to spare.

1. There was enough: *They did all eat, and were filled.* Note, Those whom Christ feeds, he fills; so runs the promise (Ps. 37:19), *They shall be satisfied.* As there was enough for all, *they did all eat,* so there was enough for each, *they were filled;* though there was but little, there was enough, and that is as good as a feast. Note, The blessing of God can make a little go a great way; as, if God blasts what we have, *we eat, and have not enough,* Hag. 1:6.

2. There was to spare; *They took up of the fragments that remained, twelve baskets full,* one basket for each apostle: thus what they gave they had again, and a great deal more with it; and they were so far from being nice, that they could make this broken meat serve another time, and be thankful. This was to manifest and magnify the miracle, and to show that the provision Christ makes for those who are his is not bare and scanty, but rich and plenteous; *bread enough, and to spare* (Lu. 15:17), an overflowing fulness. Elisha's multiplying the loaves was somewhat like this, but far short of it; and then it was said, *They shall eat and leave,* 2 Ki. 4:43.

It is the same divine power, though exerted in an ordinary way, which multiplies *the seed sown in the ground* every year, and makes *the earth yield her increase;* so that what was brought out by handfuls, is brought home in sheaves. *This is the Lord's doing;* it is *by Christ* that all natural things consist, and *by the word of his power* that they are upheld.

Verses 22–33

We have here the story of another miracle which Christ wrought for the relief of his friends and followers, his *walking upon the water to his disciples.* In the foregoing miracle he acted as the Lord of nature, improving its powers for the supply of those who were in want; in this, he acted as the Lord of nature, correcting and controlling its powers for the succour of those who were in danger and distress. Observe,

I. Christ's dismissing of his disciples and *the multitude,* after he had fed them miraculously. He constrained his disciples to get into a ship, and to go before him unto the other side, v. 22. St John gives a particular reason for the hasty breaking up of this assembly, because the people were so affected with the miracle of the loaves, that they were about *to take him by force, and make him a king* (Jn. 6:15); to avoid which, he immediately scattered the people, sent away the disciples, lest they should join with them, and he himself withdrew, Jn. 6:15.

When they had *sat down to eat and drink, they* did not *rise up to play,* but each went to his business.

1. Christ sent the people away. It intimates somewhat of solemnity in the dismissing of them; he sent them away with a blessing, with some parting words of caution, counsel, and comfort, which might abide with them.

2. He *constrained the disciples to go into a ship* first, for till they were gone the people would not stir. The disciples were loth to go, and would not have gone, if he had not constrained them. They were loth to go to sea without him. *If thy presence go not with us, carry us not up hence.* Ex. 33:15. They were loth to leave him alone, without any attendance, or any ship to wait for him; but they did it in pure obedience.

II. Christ's retirement hereupon (v. 23); *He went up into a mountain apart to pray.* Observe here,

1. That he was alone;; *he went apart into a solitary place, and was there all alone.* Though he had so much work to do with others, yet he chose sometimes to be alone, to set us an example. Those are not Christ's followers that do not care for being alone; that cannot enjoy themselves in solitude, when they have none else to converse with, none else to enjoy, but God and their own hearts.

2. That he was alone at prayer; that was his business in this solitude, to pray. Though Christ, as God, was Lord of all, and was prayed to, yet Christ, as Man, had *the form of a servant,* of a beggar, and prayed. Christ has herein set before us an example of secret prayer, and the performance of it secretly, according to the rule he gave, ch. 6:6. Perhaps in this mountain there was some private oratory or convenience, provided for such an occasion; it was usual among the Jews to have such. Observe, When the disciples went to sea, their Master went to prayer; when Peter was to be *sifted as wheat, Christ prayed for him.*

3. That he was long alone; *there he was when the evening was come,* and, for aught that appears, there he was till towards morning, *the fourth watch of the night. The night* came on, and it was a stormy, tempestuous night, yet he continued *instant in prayer.* Note, It is good, at least sometimes, upon special occasions, and when we find our hearts enlarged, to continue long in secret prayer, and to take full scope in *pouring out our hearts before the Lord.* We must not *restrain prayer,* Job 15:4.

III. The condition that the poor disciples were in at this time: *Their ship was now in the midst of the sea, tossed with waves, v.* 24. We may observe here,

1. That they were got into the midst of the sea when the storm rose. We may have fair weather at the beginning of our voyage, and yet meet with storms before we arrive at the port we are bound for. Therefore, *let not him that girdeth on the harness boast as he that puts it off,* but after a long calm expect some storm or other.

2. The disciples were now where Christ sent them, and yet met with this storm. Had they been flying from their Master, and their work, as Jonah was, when he was arrested by the storm, it had been a dreadful one indeed; but they had a special command from their Master to go to sea at this time, and were going about their work. Note, It is no new thing for Christ's disciples to meet with storms in the way of their duty, and to be sent to sea then when their Master foresees a storm; but let them not take it unkindly; what he does they *know not now, but they shall know hereafter,* that Christ designs hereby to manifest himself with the more wonderful grace to them and for them. 3. It was a great discouragement to them now that they had not Christ with them, as they had formerly when they were in a storm; though he was then asleep indeed, yet he was soon awaked (*ch.* 8:24), but now he was not with them at all. Thus Christ used his disciples first to less difficulties, and then to greater, and so trains them up by degrees to live *by faith, and not by sense.*

4. Though *the wind was contrary,* and they were tossed with waves, yet being ordered by their Master *to the other side,* they did not tack about and come back again, but made the best of their way forward. Note, Though troubles and difficulties may disturb us in our duty, they must not drive us from it; but through the midst of them we must press forwards.

IV. Christ's approach to them in this condition (*v.* 25); and in this we have an instance,

1. Of his goodness, that he went unto them, as one that took cognizance of their case, and was under a concern about them, as a father about his children. Note, The extremity of the church and people of God is Christ's opportunity to visit them and appear for them: but he came not till *the fourth watch,* toward three o'clock in the morning, for then the fourth watch began. It was *in the morning-watch* that the Lord appeared for Israel in the Red sea (Ex. 14:24), so was this. *He that keepeth Israel neither slumbers nor sleeps,* but, when there is occasion, *walks in darkness* for their succour; helps, and that right early.

2. Of his power, that he *went unto them, walking on the sea.* This is a great instance of Christ's sovereign dominion over all the creatures; they are all under his feet, and at his command; they forget their natures, and change the qualities that we call essential. We need not enquire how this was done, whether by condensing the surface of the water (when God pleases, *the depths are congealed in the heart of the sea,* Ex. 15:8), or by suspending the gravitation of his body, which was transfigured as he pleased; it is sufficient that it proves his divine power, for it is God's prerogative to *tread upon the waves of the sea* (Job 9:8), as it is *to ride upon the wings of the wind.* He *that made the waters of the sea a wall for the redeemed of the Lord* (Isa. 51:10), here makes them a walk for the Redeemer himself, who, as Lord of all, appears with one foot on the sea and the other on dry land, Rev. 10:2. The same power that made iron to swim (2 Ki. 6:6), did this. *What ailed thee, O thou sea?* Ps. 114:5. *It was at the presence of the Lord. Thy way, O God, is in the sea,* (Ps. 77:19). Note, Christ can take what way he pleases to save his people.

V. Here is an account of what passed between Christ and his distressed friends upon his approach.

1. Between him and all the disciples. We are here told,

(1.) How their fears were raised (*v.* 26); *When they saw him walking on the sea, they were troubled, saying, It is a spirit; phantasma esti — It is an apparition;* so it might much better be rendered. it seems, the existence and appearance of spirits were generally believed in by all except the Sadducees, whose doctrine Christ had warned his disciples against; yet, doubtless, many supposed apparitions have been merely the creatures of men's own fear and fancy. These disciples said, *It is the Lord;* it can be no other. Note, [1.] Even the appearances and approaches of deliverance are sometimes the occasions of trouble and perplexity to God's people, who are sometimes most frightened when they are least hurt; nay, when they are most favoured, as the Virgin Mary, Lu. 1:29; Ex. 3:6, 7. The comforts of *the Spirit of adoption* are introduced by the terrors of *the spirit of bondage,* Rom. 8:15. [2.] The appearance of a spirit, or the fancy of it, cannot but be frightful, and strike a terror upon us, because of the distance of the world of spirits from us, the just quarrel good spirits have with us, and the inveterate enmity evil spirits have against us: see Job 4:14, 15. The more acquaintance we have with God, the Father of spirits, and the more careful we are to keep ourselves in his love, the better able we shall be to deal with those fears. [3.] The perplexing, disquieting fears of good people, arise from their mistakes and misapprehensions concerning Christ, his person, offices, and undertaking; the more clearly and fully we know his name, with the more assurance we shall trust in him, Ps. 9:10. [4.] A little thing frightens us in a storm. When *without are fightings,* no marvel that *within are fears.* Perhaps the disciples fancied it was some evil spirit that raised the storm. Note, Most of our danger from outward troubles arises from the occasion they give for inward trouble.

(2.) How these fears were silenced, *v.* 27. He straightway relieved them, by showing them their mistake; when they were wrestling *with the waves,* he delayed his succour for some time; but he hastened his succour against their fright, as much the more dangerous; he straightway laid that storm with his word, *Be of good cheer; it is I; be not afraid.*

[1.] He rectified their mistake, by making himself known to them, as Joseph to his brethren; *It is I.* He does not name himself, as he did to Paul, *I am Jesus;* for Paul as yet knew him not: but to these disciples it was enough to say, *It is I;* they *knew his voice, as his sheep* (Jn. 10:4), as Mary Magdalene, Jn. 20:16. They need not ask, *Who art thou, Lord? Art thou for us or for our adversaries?* They could say with the spouse, *It is the voice of my beloved,* Cant. 2:8; *v.* 2. True believers know it by a good token. It was enough to make them easy, to understand who it was they saw. Note, A right knowledge opens the door to true comfort, especially the knowledge of Christ.

[2.] He encouraged them against their fright; *It is I,* and therefore, *First, Be of good cheer; tharseite — "Be courageous;* pluck up your spirits, and be courageous." If Christ's disciples be not cheerful in a storm, it is their own fault, he would have them so. *Secondly, Be not afraid;* 1. "Be not afraid of me, now that you know it is I; surely you will not fear, for you know I mean you no hurt." Note, Christ will not be a terror to those to whom he manifests himself; when they come to understand him aright, the terror will be over. 2. *"Be not afraid* of the tempest, of the winds and waves, though noisy and very threatening; fear them not, while I am so near you. I am he that concerns himself for you, and will not stand by and see you perish." Note, Nothing needs be a terror to those that have Christ near them, and know he is theirs; no, not death itself.

2. Between him and Peter, *v.* 28–31, where observe,

(1.) Peter's courage, and Christ's countenancing that.

[1.] It was very bold in Peter, that he would venture to come to Christ *upon the water* (*v.* 28); *Lord, if it be thou, bid me come unto thee.* Courage was Peter's master grace; and that made him so forward above the rest to express his love to Christ, though others perhaps loved him as well.

First, It is an instance of Peter's affection to Christ, that he desired to come to him. When he sees Christ, whom, doubtless, during the storm, he had many a time wished for, he is impatient to be with him. He does not say, *Bid me walk on the waters,* as desiring it for the miracle sake; but, *Bid me come to thee,* as desiring it for Christ's sake; "Let me come to thee, no matter how." Note, True love will break through fire and water, if duly called to it, to come to Christ. Christ was coming to them, to succour and deliver them. *Lord,* said Peter, *bid me come to thee.* Note, When Christ is coming towards us in a way of mercy, we must go forth to meet him in a way of duty; and herein we must be willing and bold to venture with him and venture for him. Those that would have benefit by Christ as a Saviour, must thus by faith come to him. Christ had been now, for some time, absent, and hereby it appears why he absented himself; it was to endear himself so much the more to his disciples at his return, to make it highly seasonable and doubly acceptable. Note, When, for a small amount, Christ has forsaken his people, his returns are welcome, and most affectionately embraced; when gracious souls, after long seeking, find their Beloved at last, they *hold him, and will not let him go,* Cant. 3:4.

Secondly, It is an instance of Peter's caution and due observance of the will of Christ, that he would not come without a warrant. Not, "If it be thou, I will come;" but *If it be thou, bid me come.* Note, The boldest spirits must wait for a call to hazardous enterprizes, and we must not rashly and presumptuously thrust ourselves upon them. Our will to services and sufferings is interpreted, not willingness, but wilfulness, if it have not a regard to the will of Christ, and be not regulated by his call and command. Such extraordinary warrants as this to Peter we are not now to expect, but must have recourse to the general rules of the word, in the application of which to particular cases, with the help of providential hints, *wisdom is profitable to direct.*

Thirdly, It is an instance of Peter's faith and resolution, that he ventured upon the water when Christ bid him. To quit the safety of the ship, and throw himself into the jaws of death, to despise the threatening waves he so lately dreaded, argued a very strong dependence upon the power and word of Christ. What difficulty or danger could stand before such a faith and such a zeal?

[2.] It was very kind and condescending in Christ, that he was pleased to own him in it, *v.* 29. He might have condemned the proposal as foolish and rash; nay, and as proud and assuming; "Shall Peter pretend to do as his Master does?" But Christ knew that it came from a sincere and zealous affection to him, and graciously accepted of it. Note, Christ is well pleased with the expressions of his people's love, though mixed with manifold infirmities, and makes the best of them.

First, He bid him *come.* When the Pharisees asked a sign, they had not only a repulse, but a reproof, for it, because they did it with a design to tempt Christ; when Peter asked a sign, he had it, because he did it with a resolution to trust Christ. The gospel call is, *"Come, come,* to Christ; venture all in his hand, and commit the keeping of your souls to him; venture through a stormy sea, a troublesome world, to Jesus Christ."

Secondly, He bore him out when he did come; Peter *walked upon the water.* The communion of true believers with Christ is represented by their being *quickened with him, raised up with him, made to sit with him,* (Eph. 2:5, 6), and being *crucified with him,* Gal. 2:20. Now, methinks, it is represented in this story by their *walking with him on the water.* Through the strength of Christ we are borne up above the world, enabled to trample upon it, kept from sinking into it, from being overwhelmed by it, obtain a victory over it (1 John *v.* 4), by faith in Christ's victory (Jn. 16:33), and with him are *crucified to it,* Gal. 6:14. See blessed Paul walking upon the water with Jesus, and *more than a conqueror through him,* and treading upon all the threatening waves, as *not able to separate him from the love of Christ,* Rom. 8:35, etc. Thus the sea of the world is become like a sea of glass, congealed so as to bear; and they that have gotten the victory, stand upon it and sing, Rev. 15:2, 3.

He walked upon the water, not for diversion or ostentation, but to go to Jesus; and in that he was thus wonderfully borne up. Note, When *our souls are following hard after God,* then it is that his *right hand upholds us;* it was David's experience, Ps. 63:8. Special supports are promised, and are to be expected, only in spiritual pursuits. When God bears his Israel upon eagles' wings, it is *to bring them to himself* (Ex. 19:4); nor can we ever come to Jesus, unless we be upheld by his power; it is in his own strength that we wrestle with him, that we reach after him, that we *press forward toward the mark,* being *kept by the power of God,* which power we must depend upon, as Peter when he *walked upon the water:* and there is no danger of sinking while *underneath are the everlasting arms.*

(2.) Here is Peter's cowardice, and Christ's reproving him and succouring him. Christ bid him come, not only that he might walk upon the water, and so know Christ's power, but that he might sink, and so know his own weakness; for as he would encourage his faith, so he would check his confidence, and make him ashamed of it. Observe then,

[1.] Peter's great fear (*v.* 30); *He was afraid.* The strongest faith and the greatest courage have a mixture of fear. Those that can say, *Lord, I believe;* must say, *Lord, help my unbelief.* Nothing but *perfect love* will quite *cast out fear.* Good men often fail in those graces which they are most eminent for, and which they have then in exercise; to show that they have not yet attained. Peter was very stout at first, but afterwards his heart failed him. The lengthening out of a trial discovers the weakness of faith.

Here is, *First,* The cause of this fear; *He saw the wind boisterous.* While Peter kept his eye fixed upon Christ, and upon his word and power, he *walked upon the water* well enough; but when he took notice withal of the danger he was in, and observed how *the floods lift up their waves,* then he feared. Note, Looking at difficulties with an eye of sense more than at precepts and promises with an eye of faith is at the bottom of all our inordinate fears, both as to public and personal concerns. Abraham was strong in faith, because he *considered not his own body* (Rom. 4:19); he minded not the discouraging improbabilities which the promise lay under, but kept his eye on God's power; and so, *against hope, believed in hope, v.* 18. Peter, *when he saw the wind boisterous,* should have remembered what he had seen (*ch.* 8:27), when the winds and the sea obeyed Christ; but *therefore we fear continually every day,* because *we forget the Lord our Maker,* Isa. 51:12, 13.

Secondly, The effect of this fear; *He began to sink.* While faith kept up, he kept up above water: but when faith staggered, *he began to sink.* Note, The sinking of our spirits is owing to the weakness of our faith; we are upheld (but it is as we are saved) *through faith* (1 Pt. 1:5); and therefore, when our *souls are cast down and disquieted,* the sovereign remedy is, *to hope in God,* Ps. 43:5. It is probable that Peter, being bred a fisherman, could swim very well (Jn. 21:7); and perhaps he trusted in part to that, when he cast himself into the sea; if he could not walk, he could swim; but Christ let him begin to sink, to show him that it *was Christ's right hand and his holy arm,* not any skill of his own, that was his security. It was Christ's great mercy to him, that, upon the failing of his faith, he did not leave him to sink outright, to sink to the *bottom as a stone* (Ex. 15:5), but gave him time to cry, *Lord, save me.* Such is the care of Christ concerning true believers; though weak, they do but begin to sink! A man is never sunk, never undone, till he is in hell. Peter *walked* as he *believed;* to him, as to others, the rule held good, *According to your faith be it unto you.*

Thirdly, The remedy he had recourse to in this distress, the old, tried, approved remedy, and that was prayer: he cried, *Lord, save me.* Observe, 1. The manner of his praying; it is fervent and importunate; *He cried.* Note, When faith is weak, prayer should be strong. Our Lord Jesus has taught us in the day of our fear to *offer up strong cries,* Heb. 5:7. Sense of danger will make us cry, sense of duty and dependence on God should make us cry to him. 2. The matter of his prayer was pertinent and to the purpose; *He cried, Lord, save me.* Christ is the great Saviour, he came to save; those that would be saved, must not only *come* to him, but *cry* to him for salvation; but we are never brought to this, till we find ourselves sinking; sense of need will drive us to him.

[2.] Christ's great favour to Peter, in this fright. Though there was a mixture of presumption with Peter's faith in his first adventure, and of unbelief with his faith in his after-fainting, yet Christ did not cast him off; for,

First, He saved him; *he answered him with the saving strength of his right hand* (Ps. 20:6), for immediately *he stretched forth his hand, and caught him.* Note, Christ's time to save is, when we sink (Ps. 18:4–7): he helps at a dead lift. Christ's hand is still stretched out to all believers, to keep them from sinking. Those whom he hath once apprehended as his own, and hath snatched as *brands out of the burning,* he will catch out of the water too. Though he may seem to have left his hold, he doth but seem to do so, for they shall *never perish, neither shall any man pluck them out of his hand,* Jn. 10:28. Never fear, he will hold his own. Our deliverance from our own fears, which else would overwhelm us, is owing to the hand of his power and grace, Ps. 34:4.

Secondly, He rebuked him; for as many as he loves and saves, he reproves and chides; *O thou of little faith, wherefore didst thou doubt?* Note, 1. Faith may be true, and yet weak; at first, like a grain of mustard-seed. Peter had faith enough to bring him upon the water, yet, because not enough to carry him through, Christ tells him he had but *little.* 2. Our discouraging doubts and fears are all owing to the weakness of our faith: *therefore we doubt,* because we are but *of little faith.* It is the business of faith to resolve doubts, the doubts of sense, in a stormy day, so as even then to keep the head above water. Could we but believe more, we should doubt less. 3. The weakness of our faith, and the prevalence of our doubts, are very displeasing to our Lord Jesus. It is true, he doth not cast off weak believers, but it is as true, that he is not pleased with weak faith, no, not in those that are nearest to him. *Wherefore didst thou doubt?* What reason was there for it? Note, Our doubts and fears would soon vanish before a strict enquiry into the cause of them; for, all things considered, there is no good reason why Christ's disciples should be of a doubtful mind, no, not in a stormy day, because he is ready to them *a very present Help.*

VI. The *ceasing of the storm, v.* 32. When Christ was come into the ship, they were presently at the shore. Christ *walked upon the water* till he came to the ship, and then went into that, when he could easily have walked to the shore; but when ordinary means are to be had, miracles are not to be expected. Though Christ needs not instruments for the doing of his work, he is pleased to use them. Observe, when Christ came into the ship, Peter came in with him. Companions with Christ in his patience, shall be companions in his kingdoms, Rev. 1:9. Those that walk with him shall reign with him; those that are exposed, and that suffer with him, shall triumph with him.

When they were come into the ship, immediately the storm ceased, for it had done its work, its trying work. He that has *gathered the winds into his fists, and bound the waters in a garment,* is the same that *ascended and descended;* and *his word* even *stormy winds fulfil,* Ps. 148:8. When Christ comes into a soul, he makes winds and storms to cease there, and commands peace. Welcome Christ, and the *noise of her waves will soon be quelled.* The way to be still is, to know that he is God, that he is the *Lord with us.*

VII. The adoration paid to Christ hereupon (*v.* 33); *They that were in the ship came and worshipped him, and said, Of a truth, thou art the Son of God.* Two good uses they made of this distress, and this deliverance.

1. It was a confirmation of their faith in Christ, and abundantly convinced them that *the fulness of the Godhead dwelt in him;* for none but the world's Creator could multiply the loaves, none but its Governor could tread upon the waters of the sea; they therefore yield to the evidence, and make confession of their faith; *Thou truly art the Son of God.* They knew before that he was the Son of God, but now they know it better. Faith, after a conflict with unbelief, is sometimes the more active, and gets to greater degrees of strength by being exercised. Now they *know it of a truth.* Note, It is good for us to know more and more of *the certainty of those things wherein we have been instructed,* Lu. 1:4. Faith *then* grows, when it arrives at a full assurance, when it sees clearly, and saith, *Of a truth.*

2. They took occasion from it to *give him the glory due unto his name.* They not only owned that great truth, but were suitable affected by it; *they worshiped Christ.* Note, When Christ manifests his glory for us, we ought to return it to him (Ps. 50:15); *I will deliver thee, and thou shalt glorify me.* Their worship and adoration of Christ were thus expressed, *Of a truth thou art the Son of God.* Note, The matter of our creed may and must be made the matter of our praise. Faith is the proper principle of worship, and worship the genuine product of faith. *He that comes to God must believe;* and he that *believes* in God, will come, Heb. 9:6.

Verses 34–36

We have here an account of miracles by wholesale, which Christ wrought on the other side of the water, in the land of Gennesaret. Whithersoever Christ went, he was doing good. Gennesaret was a tract of land that lay between Bethsaida and Capernaum, and either gave the name to, or took the name from, this sea, which is called (Lu. 5:1) *The Lake of Gennesaret;* it signifies the valley of branches. Observe here,

I. The forwardness and faith of *the men of that place.* These were more noble than the Gergesenes, their neighbours, who were borderers upon the same lake. Those *besought Christ to depart* from them, they had no occasion for him; these besought him to help them, they had need of him. Christ reckons it the greatest honour we can do him, to make use of him. Now here we are told,

1. How *the men of that place* were brought to Christ; they *had knowledge of him.* It is probable that his miraculous passage over the sea, which they that were in the ship would industriously spread the report of, might help to make way for his entertainment in those parts; and perhaps it was one thing Christ intended in it, for he has great reaches in what he does. This they had knowledge of, and of the other miracles Christ had wrought, and therefore they flocked to him. Note, They that know Christ's name, will make their application to him: if Christ were better known, he would not be neglected as he is; he is trusted as far as he is known.

They *had knowledge of him,* that is, of his being among them, and that he would be put awhile among them. Note, The discerning of the day of our opportunities is a good step toward the improvement of it. This was *the condemnation of the world,* that Christ *was in the world, and the world knew him not* (Jn. 1:10); Jerusalem knew him not (Lu. 19:42), but there were some who, when he was among them, *had knowledge of him.* It is better to know that there *is* a prophet among us than that there *has been* one, Eze. 2:5.

2. How they brought others to Christ, by giving notice to their neighbours of Christ's being come into those parts; *They sent out into all that country.* Note, those that have got the knowledge of Christ themselves, should do all they can to bring others acquainted with him too. We must not eat these spiritual morsels alone; there is in Christ enough for us all, so that there is nothing got by monopolizing. When we have opportunities of getting good to our souls, we should bring as many as we can to share with us. More than we think of would close with opportunities, if they were but called upon and invited to them. *They sent into their own country,* because it was their own, and they desired the welfare of it. Note, We can no better testify our love to our country than by promoting and propagating the knowledge of Christ in it. Neighbourhood is an advantage of doing good which must be improved. Those that are near to us, we should contrive to do something for, at least by our example, to bring them near to Christ.

3. What their business was with Christ; not only, perhaps not chiefly, if at all, to be taught, but to have their sick healed; *They brought unto him all that were diseased.* If love to Christ and his doctrine will not bring them to him, yet self-love would. Did we but rightly seek our own things, the things of our own peace and welfare, we should seek the things of Christ. We should do him honour, and please him, by deriving grace and righteousness from him. Note, Christ is the proper Person to bring the diseased to; whither should they go but to the Physician, to *the Sun of Righteousness, that hath healing under his wings?*

4. How they made their application to him; *They besought him that they might only touch the hem of his garment, v.* 36. They applied themselves to him, (1.) With great importunity; they besought him. Well may we beseech to be healed, when God by his ministers beseecheth us that we will be healed. Note, The greatest favours and blessings are to be obtained from Christ by entreaty; *Ask, and it shall be given.* (2.) With great humility; they came to him as those that were sensible of their distance, humbly beseeching him to help them; and their desiring to touch the hem of his garment, intimates that they thought themselves unworthy that he should take any particular notice of them, that he should so much as speak to their case, much less touch them for their cure; but they will look upon it as a great favour, if he will give them leave to *touch the hem of his garment.* The eastern nations show respect to their princes, by kissing their sleeve, or skirt. (3.) With great assurance of the all-sufficiency of his power, not doubting but that they should be healed, even by touching the hem of his garment; that they should receive abundant communications from him by the smallest token of symbol of communion with him. They did not expect the formality of striking his hand over the place or persons diseased, as Naaman did (2 Ki. 5:11); but they were sure that there was in him such an overflowing fulness of healing virtue, that *they* could not fail of a cure, who were but admitted near him. It was in this country and neighbourhood that the woman with the bloody issue was cured by *touching the hem of his garment,* and was commended for her faith (*ch.* 9:20–22); and thence, probably, they took occasion to ask this. Note, The experiences of others in their attendance upon Christ may be of use both to direct and to encourage us in our attendance on him. It is good using those means and methods which others before us have sped well in the use of.

II. The fruit and success of this their application to Christ.

It was not in vain that these seed of Jacob sough him, for as *many as touched, were made perfectly whole.* Note, 1. Christ's cures are perfect cures. Those that he heals, he heals perfectly. He doth not do his work by halves. Though spiritual healing be not perfected at first, yet, doubtless, *he that has begun the good work will perform it,* Phil. 1:6. 2. There is an abundance of healing virtue in Christ for all that apply themselves to him, be they ever so many. That *precious ointment* which was poured on his head, *ran down to the skirts of his garment,* Ps. 133:2. The least of Christ's institutions, like the hem of his garment, is replenished with the overflowing fulness of his grace, and he is able to *save to the uttermost.* 3. The healing virtue that is in Christ, is put forth for the benefit of those that by a true and lively faith touch him. Christ is in heaven, but his word is nigh us, and he himself in that word. When we mix faith with the word, apply it to ourselves, depend upon it, and submit to its influences and commands, then we touch the hem of Christ's garment. It is but thus touching, and we are made whole. On such easy terms are spiritual cures offered by him, that he may truly be said to heal *freely;* so that if our souls die of their wounds, it is not owing to our Physician, it is not for want of skill or will in him; but it is purely owing to ourselves. He *could* have healed us, he *would* have healed us, but we *would not be healed;* so that our blood will lie upon our own heads.

CHAPTER 15

In this chapter, we have our Lord Jesus, as the great Prophet teaching, as the great Physician healing, and as the great Shepherd of the sheep feeding; as the Father of spirits instructing them; as the Conqueror of Satan dispossessing him; and as concerned for the bodies of his people, providing for them. Here is, I. Christ's discourse with the scribes and Pharisees about human traditions and injunctions (*v.* 1–9). II. His discourse with the multitude, and with his disciples, concerning the things that defile a man (*v.* 10–20). III. His casting of the devil out of the woman of Canaan's daughter (*v.* 21–28). IV. His healing of all that were brought to him (*v.* 29–31). V. His feeding of four thousand men, with seven loaves and a few little fishes (*v.* 32–30).

Verses 1–9

Evil manners, we say, beget good laws. The intemperate heat of the Jewish teachers for the support of their hierarchy, occasioned many excellent discourses of our Saviour's for the settling of the truth, as here.

I. Here, is the cavil of the scribes and Pharisees at Christ's disciples, for *eating with unwashen hands.* The scribes and Pharisees were the great men of the Jewish church, men whose gain was godliness, great enemies to the gospel of Christ, but colouring their opposition with a pretence of zeal for the law of Moses, when really nothing was intended but the support of their own tyranny over the consciences of men. They were men of learning and men of business. These scribes and Pharisees here introduced were of Jerusalem, the holy city, the head city, whither *the tribes went up,* and where *were set the thrones of judgment;* they should therefore have been better than others, but they were worse. Note, External privileges, if they be not duly improved, commonly swell men up the more with pride and malignity. Jerusalem, which should have been a pure spring, was now become a poisoned sink. *How is the faithful city become a harlot!*

Now if these great men be the accusers, pray what is the accusation? What articles do they exhibit against the disciples of Christ? Why, truly, the thing laid to their charge, is, nonconformity to the canons of their church (*v.* 2); *Why do thy disciples transgress the tradition of the elders?* This charge they make good in a particular instance; *They wash not their hands when they eat bread.* A very high misdemeanor! It was a sign that Christ's disciples conducted themselves inoffensively, when this was the worst thing they could charge them with.

Observe, 1. What was the *tradition of the elders* — That people should often wash their hands, and always at meat. This they placed a great deal of religion in, supposing that the meat they touched with unwashen hands would be defiling to them. The Pharisees practiced this themselves, and with a great deal of strictness imposed it upon others, not under civil penalties, but as matter of conscience, and making it a sin against God if they did not do it. Rabbi Joses determined, "that to eat with unwashen hands is as great a sin as adultery." And Rabbi Akiba being kept a close prisoner, having water sent him both to wash his hands with, and to drink with his meat, the greatest part being accidentally shed, he washed his hands with the remainder, though he left himself none to drink, saying he would rather die than transgress the tradition of the elders. Nay, they would not eat meat with one that did not wash before meat. This mighty zeal in so small a matter would appear very strange, if we did not still see it incident to church-oppressors, not only to be fond of practising their own inventions, but to be furious in pressing their own impositions.

2. What was the transgression of this tradition or injunction by the disciples; it seems, they did not wash their hands when they ate bread, which was the more offensive to the Pharisees, because they were men who in other things were strict and conscientious. The custom was innocent enough, and had a decency in its civil use. We read of the water for purifying at the marriage where Christ was present (Jn. 2:6), though Christ turned it into wine, and so put an end to that use of it. But when it came to be practised and imposed as a religious rite and ceremony, and such a stress laid upon it, the disciples, though weak in knowledge, yet were so well taught as not to comply with it, or observe it; no not when the scribes and Pharisees had their eye upon them. They had already learned St. Paul's lesson, *All things are lawful for me;* no doubt, it is lawful to wash before meat; but I will not be brought under the power of any; especially not those who *said to their souls, Bow down, that we may go over.* 1 Co. 6:12.

3. What was the complaint of the scribes and Pharisees against them. They quarrel with Christ about it, supposing that he allowed them in it, as he did, no doubt, by his own example; *"Why do thy disciples transgress* the canons of the church? And why dost thou suffer them to do it?" It was well that the complaint was made to Christ; for the disciples themselves, though they knew their duty in this case, were perhaps not so well able to give a reason for what they did as were to be wished.

II. Here is Christ's answer to this cavil, and his justification of the disciples in that which was charged upon them as a transgression. Note, While we stand fast in the liberty wherewith Christ has made us free, he will be sure to bear us out in it.

Two ways Christ replies upon them;

1. By way of recrimination, *v.* 3–6. They were spying motes in the eyes of his disciples, but Christ shows them a beam in their own. But that which he charges upon them is not barely a recrimination, for it will be no vindication of ourselves to condemn our reprovers; but it is such a censure of their tradition (and the authority of that was what they built their charge upon) as makes not only a non-compliance lawful, but an opposition a duty. That human authority must never be submitted to, which sets up in competition with divine authority.

(1.) The charge in general is, *You transgress the commandment of God by your tradition.* They called it the *tradition of the elders,* laying stress upon the antiquity of the usage, and the authority of them that imposed it, as the church of Rome does upon fathers and councils; but Christ calls it *their* tradition. Note, Illegal impositions will be laid to the charge of those who support and maintain them, and keep them up, as well of those who first invented and enjoined them; Mic. 4:16. *You transgress the commandment of God.* Note, Those who are most zealous of their own impositions, are commonly most careless of God's commands; which is a good reason why Christ's disciples should stand upon their guard against such impositions, lest, though at first they seem only to infringe the liberty of Christians, they come at length to confront the authority of Christ. Though the Pharisees, in this command of washing before meat, did not entrench upon any command of God; yet, because in other instances they did, he justifies his disciples' disobedience to this.

(2.) The proof of this charge is in particular instance, that of their transgressing the fifth commandment.

[1.] Let us see what the command of God is (*v.* 4), what the precept, and what the sanction of the law is.

The precept is, *Honour thy father and thy mother;* this is enjoined by the common Father of mankind, and by paying respect to them whom Providence has made the instruments of our being, we give honour to him who is the Author of it, who has thereby, as to us, put some of his image upon them. The whole of children's duty to their parents is included in this of honouring them, which is the spring and foundation of all the rest, *If I be a father, where is my honour?* Our Saviour here supposes it to mean the duty of children's maintaining their parents, and ministering to their wants, if there be occasion, and being every way serviceable to their comfort. *Honour widows,* that is, maintain them, 1 Tim. 5:3.

The sanction of this law in the fifth commandment, is, a promise, *that thy days may be long;* but our Saviour waives that, lest any should thence infer it to be only a thing commendable and profitable, and insists upon the penalty annexed to the breach of this commandment in another scripture, which denotes the duty to be highly and indispensably necessary; *He that curseth father or mother, let him die the death:* this law we have, Ex. 21:17. The sin of cursing parents is here opposed to the duty of honouring them. Those who speak ill of their parents, or wish ill to them, who mock at them, or give them taunting and opprobrious language, break this law. If to call a brother *Raca* be so penal, what is it to call a father so? By our Saviour's application of this law, it appears, that denying service or relief to parents is included in cursing them. Though the language be respectful enough, and nothing abusive in it, yet what will that avail, if the deeds be not agreeable? it is but like him that said, *I go, Sir, and went not, ch.* 21:30.

[2.] Let us see what was the contradiction which the tradition of the elders gave to this command. It was not direct and downright, but implicit; their casuists gave them such rules as furnished them with an easy evasion from the obligation of this command, *v.* 5, 6. You hear what God saith, *but ye say* so and so. Note, That which men say, even great men, and learned men, and men in authority, must be examined by that which God saith; and if it be found either contrary or inconsistent, it may and must be rejected, Acts 4:19. Observe,

First, What their tradition was; That a man could not in any case bestow his worldly estate better than to give it to the priests, and devote it to the service of the temple: and that when any thing was so devoted, it was not only unlawful to alienate it, but all other obligations, though ever so just and sacred, were thereby superseded, and a man was thereby discharged from them. And this proceeded partly from their ceremoniousness, and the superstitious regard they had to the temple, and partly from their covetousness, and love of money: for what was given to the temple they were gainers by. The former was, in pretence, the latter was, in truth, at the bottom of this tradition.

Secondly, How they allowed the application of this to the case of children. When their parents' necessities called for their assistance, they pleaded, that all they could spare from themselves and their children, they had devoted to the treasury of the temple; *It is a gift, by whatsoever thou mightest be profited by me,* and therefore their parents must expect nothing from them; suggesting withal, that the spiritual advantage of what was so devoted, would redound to the parents, who must live upon that air. This, they taught, was a good and valid plea, and many undutiful, unnatural children made use of it, and they justified them in it, and said, *He shall be free;* so we supply the sense. Some go further, and supply it thus, *"He doth well, his days shall be long in the land,* and he shall be looked upon as having duly observed the fifth commandment." The pretence of religion would make his refusal to provide for his parents not only passable but plausible. But the absurdity and impiety of this tradition were very evident: for revealed religion was intended to improve, not to overthrow, natural religion; one of the fundamental laws of which is this of honouring our parents; and had they known what that meant, *I will have justice, and mercy, and not sacrifice,* they had not thus made the most arbitrary rituals destructive of the most necessary morals. This was *making the command of God of no effect.* Note, Whatever leads to, or countenances, disobedience, does, in effect, make void the command; and they that take upon them to dispense with God's law, do, in Christ's account, repeal and disannul it. To break the law is bad, but to *teach men so,* as the scribes and Pharisees did, is much worse, *ch.* 5:19. To what purpose is the command given, if it be not obeyed? The rule is, as to us, of none effect, if we be not ruled by it. *It is time for thee, Lord, to work;* high time for the great Reformer, the great Refiner, to appear; for they have *made void thy law* (Ps. 119:126); not only sinned *against* the commandment, but, as far as in them lay, sinned *away* the commandment. But, thanks be to God, in spite of them and all their traditions, the command stands in full force, power, and virtue.

2. The other part of Christ's answer is by way of reprehension; and that which he here charges them with, is hypocrisy; *Ye hypocrites, v.* 7. Note, It is the prerogative of him who searcheth the heart, and knows what is in man, to pronounce who are hypocrites. The eye of man can perceive

open profaneness, but it is only the eye of Christ that can discern hypocrisy, Lu. 16:15. And as it is a sin which his eye discovers, so it is a sin which of all others his soul hates.

Now Christ fetches his reproof from Isa. 29:13. *Well did Esaias prophesy of you.* Isaiah spoke it of the men of that generation to which he prophesied, yet Christ applies it to these scribes and Pharisees. Note, The reproofs of sin and sinners, which we find in scripture, were designed to reach the like persons and practices to the end of the world; for they are not of private interpretation, 2 Pt. 1:20. The sinners of the latter days are prophesied of, 1 Tim. 4:1; 2 Tim. 3:1; 2 Pt. 3:3. Threatenings directed against others, belong to us, if we be guilty of the same sins. Isaiah prophesied not of them only, but of all other hypocrites, against whom that word of his is still levelled, and stands in force. The prophecies of scripture are every day in the fulfilling.

This prophecy exactly deciphers a hypocritical nation, Isa. 9:17; 10:6. Here is,

(1.) The description of hypocrites, in two things.

[1.] In their own performances of religious worship, *v.* 8, when they *draw nigh to God with their mouth, and honour him with their lips, their heart is far from him.* Observe,

First, How far a hypocrite goes; he draws nigh to God, and honours him; he is, in profession, a worshipper of God. The *Pharisee went up to the temple, to pray;* he does not stand at that distance which those are at, who *live without God in the world,* but has a name among the people near unto him. They honour him; that is, they take on them to honour God, they join with those that do so. Some honour God has even from the services of hypocrites, as they help to keep up the face and form of godliness in the world, whence God fetches honour to himself, though they intend it not to him. When God's enemies submit themselves but feignedly, when *they lie unto him,* so the word is (Ps. 66:3), it redounds to his honour, and he *gets himself a name.*

Secondly, Where he rests and takes up; this is done gut with his mouth and with his lips. It is piety but from the teeth outwards; he shows much love, and that is all, there is in his heart no true love; *they make their voices to be heard* (Isa. 58:4), mention the name of the Lord, Isa. 48:1. Hypocrites are those that only make a lip-labour of religion and religious worship. In word and tongue, the worst hypocrites may do as well as the best saints, and speak as fair with Jacob's voice.

Thirdly, What that is wherein he comes short; it is in the main matter; *Their heart is far from me,* habitually alienated and estranged (Eph. 4:18), actually wandering and dwelling upon something else; no serious thoughts of God, no pious affections toward him, no concern about the soul and eternity, no thoughts agreeable to the service. God is *near in their mouth, but far from their reins,* Jer. 12:2; Eze. 33:31. The heart, with the *fool's eyes, is in the ends of the earth.* It is a silly dove that is without a heart, and so it is a *silly duty,* Hos. 7:11. A hypocrite says one thing, but thinks another. The great thing that God looks at and requires is the heart (Prov. 23:26); if that be far from him, it is not a reasonable service and therefore not an acceptable one; it is the sacrifice of fools, Eccl. 5:1.

[2.] In their prescriptions to others. This is an instance of their hypocrisy, that *they teach for doctrines the commandments of men.* The Jews then, as the papists since, paid the same respect to oral tradition that they did to the word of God, receiving it *pari pietatis affectu ac reverentiâ* — *with the same pious affection and reverence.* Conc. Trident. *Sess.* 4. *Decr.* 1. When men's inventions are tacked to God's institutions, and imposed accordingly, this is hypocrisy, a mere human religion. The commandments of men are properly conversant about the things of men, but God will have his own work done by his own rules, and accepts not that which he did not himself appoint. That only cones *to* him, that comes *from* him.

(2.) The doom of hypocrites; it is put in a little compass; *In vain do they worship me.* Their worship does not attain the end for which it was appointed; it will neither please God, nor profit themselves. If it be not *in spirit,* it is not *in truth,* and so it is all nothing. That man who only *seems* to be religious, but is not so, his *religion is vain* (James 1:26); and if our religion be a vain oblation, a vain religion, *how great is that vanity!* How sad is it to live in an age of prayers and sermons, and sabbaths and sacraments, *in vain,* to *beat the air in* all these; it is so, if the heart be not with God in them. Lip-labour is lost labour, Isa. 1:11. Hypocrites sow the wind

and reap the whirlwind; they trust in vanity, and vanity will be their recompence.

Thus Christ justified his disciples in their disobedience to the traditions of the elders; and this the scribes and Pharisees got by their cavilling. We read not of any reply they made; if they were not satisfied, yet they were silenced, and could not resist the power wherewith Christ spake.

Verses 10–20

Christ having proved that the disciples, in eating with unwashen hands, were not to be blamed, as transgressing the traditions and injunctions of the elders, comes here to show that they were not to be blamed, as having done any thing that was in itself evil. In the former part of his discourse he overturned the authority of the law, and in this the reason of it. Observe,

I. The solemn introduction to this discourse (*v.* 10); *He called the multitude.* They were withdrawn while Christ discoursed with the scribes and Pharisees; probably those proud men ordered them to withdraw, as not willing to talk with Christ in their hearing; Christ must favour them at their pleasure with a discourse in private. But Christ had a regard to the multitude; he soon despatched the scribes and Pharisees, and then turned them off, invited the mob, the multitude, to be his hearers: thus the poor are evangelized; and the foolish things of the world, and things that are despised hath Christ chosen. The humble Jesus embraced those whom the proud Pharisees looked upon with disdain, and to them he designed it for a mortification. He turns from them as wilful and unteachable, and turns to the multitude, who, though weak, were humble, and willing to be taught. To them he said, *Hear and understand.* Note, What we hear from the mouth of Christ, we must give all diligence to understand. Not only scholars, but even the multitude, the ordinary people, must apply their minds to understand the words of Christ. He *therefore* calls upon them to understand, because the lesson he was now about to teach them, was contrary to the notions which they had sucked in with their milk from their teachers; and overturned many of the customs and usages which they were wedded to, and laid stress upon. Note, There is need of a great attention of mind and clearness of understanding to free men from those corrupt principles and practices which they have been bred up in and long accustomed to; for in that case the understanding is commonly bribed and biassed by prejudice.

II. The truth itself laid down (*v.* 11), in two propositions, which were opposite to the vulgar errors of that time, and were therefore surprising.

1. *Not that which goes into the mouth defileth the man.* It is not the kind or quality of our food, nor the condition of our hands, that affects the soul with any moral pollution or defilement. *The kingdom of God is not meat and drink,* Rom. 14:17. That defiles the man, by which guilt is contracted before God, and the man is rendered offensive to him, and disfitted for communion with him; now what we eat, if we do not eat unreasonably and immoderately, does not this; for *to the pure all things are pure,* Tit. 1:15. The Pharisees carried the ceremonial pollutions, by eating such and such meats, much further than the law intended, and burdened it with additions of their own, which our Saviour witnesses against; intending hereby to pave the way to a repeal of the ceremonial law in that matter. He was now beginning to teach his followers to call *nothing common or unclean;* and if Peter, when he was bid to *kill and eat,* had remembered this word, he would not have said, *Not so, Lord,* Acts 10:13–15, 28.

2. *But that which comes out of the mouth, this defiles a man.* We are polluted, not by the meat we eat with unwashen hands, but by the words we speak from an unsanctified heart; thus it is that *the mouth causeth the flesh to sin,* Eccl. 5:6. Christ, in a former discourse, had laid a great stress upon our *words* (ch. 12:36, 37); and that was intended for reproof and warning to those that cavilled at him; this here is intended for reproof and warning to those that cavilled at the disciples, and censured them. It is not the disciples that defile themselves with what they eat, but the Pharisees that defile themselves with what they speak spitefully and censoriously of them. Note, Those who charge guilt upon others for transgressing the commandments of men, many times bring greater guilt upon themselves, by transgressing the law of God against rash judging. Those most defile themselves, who are most forward to censure the defilements of others.

III. The offence that was taken at this truth and the ac-

count brought to Christ of that offence (*v.* 12); *"The disciples said unto him, Knowest thou that the Pharisees were offended,* and didst thou not foresee that they would be so, *at this saying,* and would think the worse of thee and of thy doctrine for it, and be the more enraged at thee?"

1. It was not strange that the Pharisees should be offended at this plain truth, for they were men made up of error and enmity, mistakes and malice. Sore eyes cannot bear clear light; and nothing is more provoking to proud imposers than the undeceiving of those whom they have first blindfolded, and then enslaved. It should seem that the Pharisees, who were strict observers of the traditions, were more offended than the scribes, who were the teachers of them; and perhaps they were as much galled with the latter part of Christ's doctrine, which taught a strictness in the government of our tongue, as with the former part, which taught an indifference about washing our hands; great contenders for the formalities of religion, being commonly as great contemners of the substantials of it.

2. The disciples thought it strange that their Master should say that which he knew would give so much offence; he did not use to do so: surely, they think, if he had considered how provoking it would be, he would not have said it. But he knew what he said, and to whom he said it, and what would be the effect of it; and would teach us, that though in indifferent things we must be tender of giving offence, yet we must not, for fear of that, evade any truth or duty. Truth must be owned, and duty done; and if any be offended, it is his own fault; it is scandal, not given, but taken.

Perhaps the disciples themselves stumbled at the word Christ said, which they thought bold, and scarcely reconcileable with the difference that was put by the law of God between *clean* and *unclean* meats; and therefore objected this to Christ, that they might themselves be better informed. They seem likewise to have a concern upon them for the Pharisees, though they had quarrelled with them; which teaches us to forgive, and seek the good, especially the spiritual good, of our enemies, persecutors, and slanderers. They would not have the Pharisees go away displeased at any thing Christ had said; and therefore, though they do not desire him to retract it, they hope he will explain, correct, and modify it. Weak hearers are sometimes more solicitous than they should be not to have wicked hearers offended. But if we please men with the concealment of truth, and the indulgence of their errors and corruptions, we are not the servants of Christ.

IV. The doom passed upon the Pharisees and their corrupt traditions; which comes in as a reason why Christ cared not though he offended them, and therefore why the disciples should not care; because they were a generation of men that hated to be reformed, and were marked out for destruction. Two things Christ here foretels concerning them.

1. The rooting out of them and their traditions (*v.* 13); *Every plant which my heavenly Father hath not planted, shall be rooted up.* Not only the corrupt opinions and superstitious practices of the Pharisees, but their sect, and way, and constitution, were plants not of God's planting. The rules of their profession were no institutions of his, but owed their origin to pride and formality. The people of the Jews were planted *a noble vine;* but now that they are become the degenerate plant of a strange vine, God disowned them, as not of his planting. Note, (1.) In the visible church, it is no strange thing to find plants that our heavenly Father has not planted. It is implied, that whatever is good in the church is of God's planting, Isa. 41:19. But let the husbandman be ever so careful, his ground will cast forth weeds of itself, more or less, and there is an enemy busy sowing tares. What is corrupt, though of God's permitting, is not of his planting; he sows nothing bur *good seed in his field.* Let us not therefore be deceived, as if all must needs be right that we find in the church, and all those persons and things our Father's plants that we find in our Father's garden. *Believe not every spirit, but try the spirits;* see Jer. 19:5; 23:31, 32. (2.) Those that are of the spirit of the Pharisees, proud, formal, and imposing, what figure soever they make, and of what denomination soever they be, God will not own them as of his planting. *By their fruit you shall know them.* (3.) Those plants that are not of God's planting, shall not be of his protecting, but shall undoubtedly be rooted up. What is not of God shall not stand, Acts 5:38. What things are unscriptural, will wither and die of themselves, or be justly exploded by the churches; however in the great day these tares that offend will be bundled

for the fire. What is become of the Pharisees and their traditions? They are long since abandoned; but the gospel of truth is great, and will remain. It cannot be rooted up.

2. The ruin of them; and their followers, who had their persons and principles in admiration, *v.* 14. Where,

(1.) Christ bids his disciples *let them alone.* "Have no converse with them or concern for them; neither court their favour, nor dread their displeasure; care not though they be offended, they will take their course, and let them take the issue of it. They are wedded to their own fancies, and will have every thing their own way; let them alone. Seek not to please a generation of men that please not God (1 Th. 2:15), and will be pleased with nothing less than absolute dominion over your consciences. They are *joined to idols,* as Ephraim (Hos. 4:17), the idols of their own fancy; *let them alone, let them be filthy still,*" Rev. 22:11. The case of those sinners is sad indeed, whom Christ orders his ministers to let alone.

(2.) He gives them two reasons for it. *Let them alone;* for,

[1.] They are proud and ignorant; two bad qualities that often meet, and render a man incurable in his folly, Prov. 26:12. *They are blind leaders of the blind.* They are grossly ignorant in the things of God, and strangers to the spiritual nature of the divine law; and yet so proud, that they think they see better and further than any, and therefore undertake to be leaders of others, to show others the way to heaven, when they themselves know not one step of the way; and, accordingly, they prescribe to all, and proscribe those who will not follow them. Though they were blind, if they had owned it, and come to Christ for eye-salve, they might have seen, but they disdained the intimation of such a thing (Jn. 9:40); *Are we blind also?* They were confident that *they themselves were guides of the blind* (Rom. 2:19, 20), were appointed to be so, and fit to be so; that every thing they said was an oracle and a law; "Therefore *let them alone,* their case is desperate; do not meddle with them; you may soon provoke them, but never convince them." How miserable was the case of the Jewish Church now when their leaders were blind, so self-conceitedly foolish, as to be peremptory in their conduct, while the people were so sottishly foolish as to follow them with an implicit faith and obedience, and *willingly walk after the commandment,* Hos. 5:11. Now the prophecy was fulfilled, Isa. 29:10, 14. And it is easy to imagine *what will be in the end hereof,* when *the prophets prophesy falsely, and the priests bear rule by their means, and the people love to have it so,* Jer. 5:31.

[2.] They are posting to destruction, and will shortly be plunged into it; *Both shall fall into the ditch.* This must needs be the end of it, if both be so blind, and yet both so bold, venturing forward, and yet not aware of danger. Both will be involved in the general desolation coming upon the Jews, and both drowned in eternal destruction and perdition. The blind leaders and the blind followers will perish together. We find (Rev. 22:15), that hell is the portion of those that *make a lie,* and of those that *love* it when it is made. *The deceived and the deceiver* are obnoxious to the judgment of God, Job 12:16. Note, *First,* Those that by their cunning craftiness draw others to sin and error, shall not, with all their craft and cunning, escape ruin themselves. If *both fall together into the ditch,* the blind leaders will fall undermost, and have the worst of it; see Jer. 14:15, 16. *The prophets shall be consumed first,* and then the *people to whom they prophesy,* Jer. 20:6; 27:15, 16. *Secondly,* The sin and ruin of the deceivers will be no security to those that are deceived by them. Though the leaders of this people *cause them to err,* yet they that are *led of them are destroyed* (Isa. 9:16), because they shut their eyes against the light which would have rectified their mistake. Seneca, complaining of most people's being led by common opinion and practice *(Unusquisque mavult credere quam judicare — Things are taken upon trust, and never examined),* concludes, *Indeista tanta coacervatio aliorum super alios ruentium — Hence crowds fall upon crowds, in vast confusion. De Vitâ Beatâ.* The falling of both together will aggravate the fall of both; for they that have thus mutually increased each other's sin, will mutually exasperate each other's ruin.

V. Instruction given to the disciples concerning the truth Christ had laid down, *v.* 10. Though Christ rejects the wilfully ignorant who care not to be taught, he can have compassion on the ignorant who are willing to learn, Heb. 5:2. If the Pharisees, who made void the law, be offended, let them be offended: but this *great peace have they who love the law,* that *nothing shall offend them,* but, some way or other, the offence shall be taken off, Ps. 119:165.

Here is, 1. Their desire to be better instructed in this matter (*v.* 15); in this request as in many others, Peter was their speaker; the rest, it is probable, putting him on to speak, or intimating their concurrence; *Declare unto us this parable.* What Christ said was plain, but, because it agreed not with the notions they had imbibed, though they would not contradict it, yet they call it a parable, and cannot understand it. Note, (1.) Weak understandings are apt to turn plain truths into parables, and to seek for a knot in a bulrush. The disciples often did so, as Jn. 16:17. Even the grasshopper is a burthen to a weak stomach, and babes in understanding cannot bear and digest strong meat. (2.) Where a weak head doubts concerning any word of Christ, an upright heart and a willing mind will seek for instruction. The Pharisees were offended, but kept it to themselves; hating to be reformed, they hated to be informed; but the disciples, though offended, sought for satisfaction, imputing the offence, not to the doctrine delivered, but to the shallowness of their own capacity.

2. The reproof Christ gave them for their weakness and ignorance (*v.* 16); *Are ye also yet without understanding?* As many as Christ loves and teaches, he thus rebukes. Note, They are very ignorant indeed, who understand not that moral pollutions are abundantly worse and more dangerous than ceremonial ones. Two things aggravate their dulness and darkness.

(1.) That they were the disciples of Christ; "Are *ye* also without understanding? Ye whom I have admitted into so great a degree of familiarity with me, are ye so unskilful in the word of righteousness?" Note, The ignorance and mistakes of those that profess religion, and enjoy the privileges of church-membership, are justly a grief to the Lord Jesus. "No wonder that the Pharisees understand not this doctrine, who know nothing of the Messiah's kingdom: but ye that have heard of it, and embraced it yourselves, and preached it to others, are ye also such strangers to the spirit and genius of it?"

(2.) That they had been a great while Christ's scholars; "Are ye *yet* so, after ye have been so long under my teaching?" Had they been but of yesterday in Christ's school, it had been another matter, but to have been for so many months Christ's constant hearers, and yet to be without understanding, was a great reproach to them. Note, Christ expects from us some proportion of knowledge, and grace, and wisdom, according to the time and means we have had. See Jn. 14:9; Heb. 5:12; 2 Tim. 3:7, 8.

3. The explication Christ gave them of this doctrine of pollutions. Though he chid them for their dulness, he did not cast them off, but pitied them, and taught them, as Lu. 24:25–27. He here shows us,

(1.) What little danger we are in of pollution from that which *entereth in at the mouth, v.* 17. An inordinate appetite, intemperance, and excess in eating, come out of the heart, and are defiling; but meat in itself is not so, as the Pharisees supposed. What there is of dregs and defilement in our meat, nature (or rather God of nature) has provided a way to clear us of it; *it goes in at the belly, and is cast out into the draught,* and nothing remains to us but pure nourishment. So *fearfully* and *wonderfully are we made* and preserved, and our souls held in life. The expulsive faculty is as necessary in the body as any other, for the discharge of that which is superfluous, or noxious; so happily is nature enabled to help itself, and shift for its own good: by this means nothing defiles; if we eat with unwashen hands, and so any thing unclean mix with our food, nature will separate it, and cast it out, and it will be no defilement to us. It may be a piece of cleanliness, but it is not point of conscience, to wash before meat; and we go upon a great mistake if we place religion in it. It is not the practice itself, but the opinion it is built upon, that Christ condemns, as if meat commended us to God (1 Co. 8:8); whereas Christianity stands not in such observances.

(2.) What great danger we are in of pollution from that which *proceeds out of the mouth* (*v.* 18), out of the abundance of the heart: compare *ch.* 12:34. There is no defilement in the products of God's bounty; the defilement arises from the products of out corruption. Now here we have,

[1.] The corrupt fountain of that which proceeds out of the mouth; it comes from the heart; that is the spring and source of all sin, Jer. 8:7. It is the heart that is so desperately wicked (Jer. 17:9); for there is no sin in a word or deed, which was not first in the heart. There is the root of bitterness, which *bears gall and wormwood.* It is the inward part of a sinner, that is very wickedness, Ps. 5:9. All evil speakings come forth from the heart, and are defiling; from the corrupt heart comes the corrupt communication.

[2.] Some of the corrupt streams which flow from this fountain, specified; though they do not all *come out of the mouth,* yet they all come out of the man, and are the fruits of that wickedness which is in the heart, and is wrought there, Ps. 58:2.

First, Evil thoughts, sins against all the commandments. Therefore David puts vain thoughts in opposition to the whole law, Ps. 119:113. These are the first-born of the corrupt nature, the beginning of its strength, and do most resemble it. These, as the son and heir, *abide in the house, and lodge within us.* There is a great deal of sin that begins and ends in the heart, and goes no further. Carnal fancies and imaginations are evil thoughts, wickedness in the contrivance (*dialogismoi ponēroi*), wicked plots, purposes, and devices of mischief to others, Mic. 2:1.

Secondly, Murders, sins against the sixth commandment; these come from a malice in the heart against our brother's life, or a contempt of it. Hence he *that hates his brother,* is said to be a *murderer;* he is so at God's bar, 1 Jn. 3:15. *War is in the heart,* Ps. 4:21; James 4:1

Thirdly, Adulteries and fornications, sins against the seventh commandment; these come from the wanton, unclean, carnal heart; and the lust that reigns there, is conceived there, and brings forth these sins, James 1:15. There is adultery in the heart first, and then in the act, *ch.* 5:28.

Fourthly, Thefts, sins against the eighth commandment; cheats, wrongs, rapines, and all injurious contracts; the fountain of all these is in the heart, that is it that is *exercised in these covetous practices* (2 Pt. 2:14), that is set upon riches, Ps. 62:10. *Achan coveted, and then took,* Joshua 7:20, 21.

Fifthly, False witness, against the ninth commandment; this comes from a complication of falsehood and covetousness, or falsehood and covetousness, or falsehood and malice in the heart. If truth, holiness, and love, which God *requires in the inward parts,* reigned as they ought, there would be no false witness bearing, Ps. 64:6: Jer. 9:8.

Sixthly, Blasphemies, speaking evil of God, against the third commandment; speaking evil of our neighbour, against the ninth commandment; these come from a contempt and disesteem of both in the heart; thence *the blasphemy against the Holy Ghost* proceeds (*ch.* 12:31, 32); these are the overflowing of the gall within.

Now *these are the things which defile a man, v.* 20. Note, Sin is defiling to the soul, renders it unlovely and abominable in the eyes of a pure and holy God; unfit for communion with him, and for the enjoyment of him in the new Jerusalem, into which nothing shall enter that defileth or worketh iniquity. The mind and conscience are defiled by sin, and that makes every thing else so, Tit. 1:15. This defilement by sin was signified by the ceremonial pollutions which the Jewish doctors added to, but understood not. See Heb. 9:13, 14; 1 Jn. 1:7.

These therefore are the things we must carefully avoid, and all approaches toward them, and not lay stress upon the washing of the hands. Christ doth not yet repeal the law of the distinction of meats (that was not done till Acts 10), but the tradition of the elders, which was tacked to that law; and therefore he concludes, *To eat with unwashen hands* (which was the matter now in question), *this defileth not a man.* If he wash, he is not the better before God; if he wash not, he is not the worse.

Verses 21–28

We have here that famous story of Christ's *casting the devil out of the woman of Canaan's daughter;* it has something in it singular and very surprising, and which looks favourably upon the poor Gentiles, and is an earnest of the mercy which Christ had in store for them. Here is a gleam of that *light* which was *to lighten the Gentiles,* Lu. 2:32. Christ *came to his own, and his own received him not;* but many of them quarrelled with him, and were offended in him; and observe what follows, *v.* 21.

I. *Jesus went thence.* Note, Justly is the light taken from those that either play by it, or rebel against it. When Christ and his disciples could not be quiet among them, he left them, and so left an example to his own rule (*ch.* 10:14), *Shake off the dust of your feet.* Though Christ endure long, he will not always *endure, the contradiction of sinners against himself.* He had said (*v.* 14), *Let them alone,* and he did so. Note, Wilful prejudices against the gospel, and cavils at it, often provoke Christ to withdraw, and *to remove the candlestick out of its place.* Acts 13:46, 51.

II. When he went thence, he *departed into the coasts of Tyre and Sidon;* not to those cities (they were excluded from any share in *Christ's mighty works, ch.* 11:21, 22), but into that part of the land of Israel which lay that way: thither he went, as Elias *to Sarepta, a city of Sidon* (Lu. 4:26); thither he went to look after this poor woman, whom he had mercy in reserve for. While he went about doing good, he was never out of his way. The dark corners of the country, which lay most remote, shall have their share of his benign influences; and as now *the ends of the land,* so afterward *the ends of the earth, shall see his salvation,* Isa. 49:6. Here it was, that this miracle was wrought, in the story of which we may observe,

1. The address of the woman of Canaan to Christ, *v.* 22. She was a Gentile, *a stranger to the commonwealth of Israel;* probably one of the posterity of those accursed nations that were devoted by that word, *Cursed be Canaan.* Note, The doom of political bodies doth not always reach every individual member of them. God will have his remnant out of all nations, chosen vessels in all coasts, even the most unlikely: she came out of the same coasts. If Christ had not now made a visit to these coasts, though the mercy was worth travelling far for, it is probable that she had never come to him. Note, It is often an excitement to a dormant faith and zeal, to have opportunities of acquaintance with Christ brought to our doors, to have the word nigh us.

Her address was very importunate, she *cried* to Christ, as one in earnest; cried, as being at some distance from him, not daring to approach too near, being a Canaanite, lest she should give offence. In her address,

(1.) She relates her misery; *My daughter is grievously vexed with a devil, kakōs daimonizetai — She is ill-bewitched,* or *possessed.* There were degrees of that misery, and this was the worst sort. It was common case at that time, and very calamitous. Note, The vexations of children are the trouble of parents, and nothing should be more so than their being under the power of Satan. Tender parents very sensibly feel the miseries of those that are pieces of themselves. "Though vexed with the devil, yet she is my daughter still." The greatest afflictions of our relations do not dissolve our obligations to them, and therefore ought not to alienate our affections from them. It was the distress and trouble of her family, that now brought her to Christ; she came to him, not for teaching, but for healing; yet, because she came in faith, he did not reject her. Though it is need that drives us to Christ, yet we shall not therefore be driven from him. It was the affliction o her daughter, that gave her this occasion of applying to Christ. It is good to make the afflictions of others our own, in sense and sympathy, that we may make them our own, in improvement and advantage.

(2.) She requests for mercy; *Have mercy on me, O Lord, thou Son of David,* she owns him to be the Messiah: that is the great thing which faith should fasten upon, and fetch comfort from. From the Lord we may expect acts of power: he can command deliverances; from the Son of David we may expect all the mercy and grace which were foretold concerning him. Though a Gentile, she owns *the promise made to the fathers* of the Jews, and the honour of the house of David. The Gentiles must receive Christianity, not only as an improvement of natural religion, but as the perfection of the Jewish religion, with an eye to the Old Testament.

Her petition is, *Have mercy on me.* She does not limit Christ to this or that particular instance of mercy, but mercy, mercy is the thing she begs: she pleads not merit, but depends upon mercy; *Have mercy upon me.* Mercies to the children are mercies to the parents; favours to ours are favours to us, and are so to be accounted. Note, It is the duty of parents to pray for their children, and to be earnest in prayer for them, especially for their souls; "I have a son, a daughter, grievously vexed with a proud will, an unclean devil, a malicious devil, led captive by him at his will; *Lord, help them.*" This is a case more deplorable than that of a bodily possession. Bring them to Christ by faith and prayer, who alone is able to heal them. Parents should look upon it as a great mercy to themselves, to have Satan's power broken in the souls of their children.

2. The discouragement she met with in this address; in all the story of Christ's ministry we do not meet with the like. He was wont to countenance and encourage all that came to him, and either *to answer before they called,* or *to hear while they were yet speaking;* but here was one otherwise treated: and what could be the reason of it? (1.) Some think that Christ showed himself backward to gratify this poor woman, because he would not give offence to the Jews, by being as free and forward in his favour to the Gentiles as to them. He had bid his disciples *not go into the way of the Gentiles* (*ch.* 10:5), and therefore would not himself seem so inclinable to them as to others, but rather more shy. Or rather, (2.) Christ treated her thus, to try her; he knows what is in the heart, knew the strength of her faith, and how well able she was, by his grace, to break through such discouragements; he *therefore* met her with them, *that the trial of her faith might be found unto praise, and honour, and glory,* 1 Pt. 1:6, 7. This was like God's tempting Abraham (Gen. 22:1), like the angel's wrestling with Jacob, only to put him upon wrestling, Gen. 32:24. Many of the methods of Christ's providence, and especially of his grace, in dealing with his people, which are dark and perplexing, may be explained with the key of this story, which is for that end left upon record, to teach us that there may be love in his face, and to encourage us, therefore, *though he slay us, yet to trust in him.*

Observe the particular discouragements given her:

[1.] When she cried after him, *he answered her not a word, v.* 23. His ear was wont to be always open and attentive to the cries of poor supplicants, and his lips, which dropped as the honeycomb, always ready to give an answer of peace; but to this poor woman he turned a deaf ear, and she could get neither an alms nor an answer. It was a wonder that she did not fly off in a fret, and say, "Is this he that is so famed for clemency and tenderness? Have so many been heard and answered by him, as they talk, and must I be the first rejected suitor? Why so distant to me, if it be true that he hath stooped to so many?" But Christ knew what he did, and *therefore* did not answer, that she might be the more earnest in prayer. He heard her, and was pleased with her, and *strengthened her with strength in her soul* to prosecute her request (Ps. 138:3; Job 23:6), though he did not immediately give her the answer she expected. By seeming to draw away the desired mercy from her, he drew her on to be so much the more importunate for it. Note, Every accepted prayer is not immediately an answered prayer. Sometimes God seems not to regard his people's prayers, like a man asleep or astonished (Ps. 44:23; Jer. 14:9; Ps. 22:1, 2); nay, to be angry at them (Ps. 80:4; Lam. 3:8, 44); but it is to prove, and so to *improve,* their faith, and to make his after-appearances for them the more glorious to himself, and the more welcome to them; for *the vision, at the end, shall speak, and shall not lie,* Heb. 2:3. See Job 35:14

[2.] When the disciples spake a good word for her, he gave a reason why he refused her, which was yet more discouraging.

First, It was some little relief, that the disciples interposed on her behalf; they said, *Send her away, for she crieth after us.* It is desirable to have an interest in the prayers of good people, and we should be desirous of it. But the disciples, though wishing she might have what she came for, yet therein consulted rather their own ease than the poor woman's satisfaction; *"Send her away* with a cure, *for she cries,* and is in good earnest; *she cries after us,* and is troublesome to us, and shames us." Continued importunity may be uneasy to men, even to good men; but Christ loves to be cried after.

Secondly, Christ's answer to the disciples quite dashed her expectations; *"I am not sent, but to the lost sheep of the house of Israel;* you know I am not, she is none of them, and would you have me go beyond by commission?" Importunity seldom conquers the settled reason of a wise man; and those refusals are most silencing, which are so backed. He doth not only not answer her, but he argues against her, and stops her mouth with a reason. It is true, she is a *lost sheep,* and hath as much need of his care as any, but she is not *of the house of Israel,* to whom he was first sent (Acts 3:26), and therefore not immediately interested in it, and entitled to it. Christ was *a Minister of the circumcision* (Rom. 15:8); and though he was intended for *a Light to the Gentiles, yet the fulness of time* for that *was* not now *come, the veil was* not yet *rent,* nor *the partition-wall taken down.* Christ's personal ministry was *to be the glory of his people Israel;* "If I am sent to them, what have I to do with those that are none of them." Note, It is a great trial, when we have occasion given us to question whether we be of those to whom Christ was sent. But, blessed be God, no room is left for that doubt; the distinction between Jew and Gentile is taken away; we are sure that he *gave his life a ransom for many,* and if for many, why not for me?

Thirdly, When she continued her importunity, he insisted upon the unfitness of the thing, and gave her not only a repulse, but a seeming reproach too (*v.* 26); *It is not meet to take the children's bread and to cast it to dogs.* This seems to cut her off from all hope, and might have driven her to despair, if she had not had a very strong faith indeed. Gospel grace and miraculous cures (the appurtenances of it), were children's bread; they belonged to them *to whom pertained the adoption* (Rom. 9:4), and lay not upon the same level with that rain from heaven, and those fruitful seasons, which God gave to the nations whom he suffered *to walk in their own ways* (Acts 14:16, 17); no, these were peculiar favours, appropriated to the peculiar people, the garden enclosed. Christ preached to the Samaritans (Jn. 4:41), but we read not of any cures he wrought among them; *that salvation was of the Jews:* it is not meet therefore to alienate these. The Gentiles were looked upon by the Jews with great contempt, were called and counted *dogs;* and, in comparison with the house of Israel, who were so dignified and privileged, Christ here seems to allow it, and therefore thinks it not meet that the Gentiles should share in the favours bestowed on the Jews. But see how the tables are turned; after the bringing of the Gentiles into the church, the Jewish zealots for the law are called *dogs,* Phil. 3:2.

Now this Christ urgeth against this woman of Canaan; "How can she expect to eat of the children's bread, who is not of the family?" Note, 1. Those whom Christ intends most signally to honour, he first humbles and lays low in a sense of their own meanness and unworthiness. We must first see ourselves to be as dogs, *less than the least of all God's mercies,* before we are fit to be dignified and privileged with them. 2. Christ delights to exercise great faith with great trials, and sometimes reserves the sharpest for the last, that, *being tried, we may come forth like gold.* This general rule is applicable to other cases for direction, though here used only for trial. Special ordinances and church-privileges are children's bread, and must not be prostituted to the grossly ignorant and profane. Common charity must be extended to all, but spiritual dignities are appropriated to the household of faith; and therefore promiscuous admission to them, without distinction, wastes the children's bread, and is the *giving of that which is holy to the dogs, ch.* 7:6. *Procul hinc, procul inde, profani — Off, ye profane.*

3. Here is the strength of her faith and resolution, in breaking through all these discouragements. Many a one, thus tried, would either have sunk into silence, or broken out into passion. "Here is cold comfort," might she have said, "for a poor distressed creature; as good for me to have staid at home, as come hither to be taunted at and abused at this rate; not only to have a piteous case slighted, but to be called a *dog!*" A proud, unhumbled heart would not have borne it. The reputation of the house of Israel was not now so great in the world, but that this slight put upon the Gentiles was capable of being retorted, had the poor woman been so minded. It might have occasioned a reflection upon Christ, and might have been a blemish upon his reputation, as well as a shock to the good opinion, she had entertained of him; for we re apt to judge of persons as we ourselves find them; and think that they are what they are to us. *"Is this the Son of David?"* (might she have said): "Is this he that has such a reputation for kindness, tenderness, and compassion? I am sure I have no reason to give him that character, for I was never treated so roughly in my life; he might have done as much for me as for others; or, if not, he needed not to have *set me with the dogs of his flock.* I am not a dog, I am a woman, and an honest woman, and a woman in misery; and I am sure it is not meet to call me a *dog.*" No, here is not a word of this. Note, A humble, believing soul, that truly loves Christ, takes every thing in good part that he saith and doeth, and puts the best construction upon it.

She breaks through all these discouragements,

(1.) With a holy earnestness of desire in prosecuting her petition. This appeared upon the former repulse (*v.* 25); *Then came she, and worshipped him, saying, Lord, help me.* [1.] She continued to pray. What Christ said, silenced the disciples; you hear no more of them; they took the answer, but the woman did not. Note, The more sensibly we feel the burthen, the more resolutely we should pray for the removal of it. *And it is the will of God that we should continue instant in prayer, should always pray, and not faint.* [2.] She improved in prayer. Instead of blaming Christ, or charging him with unkindness, she seems rather to suspect herself, and lay the fault upon herself. She fears lest, in her first address, she had not been humble and reverent enough, and therefore now *she came, and worshipped him,* and paid him more respect than she had done; or she fears that she had not been earnest enough, and therefore now she cries, *Lord, help me.* Note, When the answers of prayer are deferred, God is thereby teaching us to pray more, and pray better. It is then time to enquire wherein we have come short in our former prayers, that what has been amiss may be amended for the future. Disappointments in the success of prayer, must be excitements to the duty of prayer. Christ, in his agony, *prayed more earnestly.* [3.] She waives the question, whether she was of those to whom Christ was sent or no; she will not argue that with him, though perhaps she might have claimed some kindred to the house of Israel; but, "Whether an Israelite or no, I come to the Son of David for mercy, and *I will not let him go, except he bless me.*" Many weak Christians perplex themselves with questions and doubts about their election, whether they are of the house of Israel or no; such had better mind their errand to God, and continue instant in prayer for mercy and grace; throw themselves by faith at the feet of Christ, and say, *If I perish, I will perish here;* and then that matter will by degrees clear itself. If we cannot *reason* down our unbelief, let us *pray* it down. A fervent, affectionate *Lord, help me,* will help us over many of the discouragements which are sometimes ready to bear us down and overwhelm us. [4.] Her prayer is very short, but comprehensive and fervent, *Lord, help me.* Take this, *First,* As lamenting her case; "If the Messiah be sent only to the house of Israel, the *Lord help me,* what will become of me and mine," Note, It is not in vain for broken hearts to bemoan themselves; God looks upon them then, Jer. 31:18. Or, *Secondly,* As begging grace to insist her in this hour of temptation. She found it hard to keep up her faith when it was thus frowned upon, and therefore prays, *"Lord, help me;* Lord, strengthen my faith now; *Lord, let thy right hand uphold me,* while my soul is *following hard after thee,"* Ps. 63:8. Or, *Thirdly,* As enforcing her original request, *"Lord, help me;* Lord, give me what I come for." She believed that Christ could and would help her, though she was not of the house of Israel; else she would have dropt her petition. Still she keeps up good thoughts of Christ, and will not quit her hold. *Lord, help me,* is a good prayer, if well put up; and it is pity that it should be turned into a byword, and that we should take God's name in vain in it.

(2.) With a holy skilfulness of faith, suggesting a very surprising plea. Christ had placed the Jews with the children, *as olive-plants round about* God's *table,* and had put the Gentiles with the dogs, under the table; and she doth not deny the aptness of the similitude. Note, There is nothing got by contradicting any word of Christ, though it bear ever so hard upon us. But this poor woman, since she cannot object against it, resolves to make the best of it (*v.* 27); *Truth, Lord, yet the dogs eat of the crumbs.* Now, here,

[1.] Her acknowledgment was very humble: *Truth, Lord.* Note, You cannot speak so meanly and slightly of a humble believer, but he is ready to speak as meanly and slightly of himself. Some that seem to dispraise and disparage themselves, will yet take it as an affront if others do so too; but one that is humbled aright, will subscribe to the most abasing challenges, and not call them abusing ones. *"Truth, Lord;* I cannot deny it; I am a dog, and have no right to the children's bread." David, *Thou hast done foolishly, very foolishly; Truth, Lord.* Asaph, Thou *hast been as a beast before God; Truth, Lord.* Agur, Thou art *more brutish than any man; Truth, Lord.* Paul, Thou hast been *the chief of sinners, art less than the least of saints, not meet to be called an apostle; Truth, Lord.*

[2.] Her improvement of this into a plea was very ingenious; *Yet the dogs eat of the crumbs.* It was by a singular acumen, and spiritual quickness and sagacity, that she discerned matter of argument in that which looked like a slight. Note, A lively, active faith will make that to be for us, which seems to be against us; will fetch *meat out of the eater, and sweetness out of the strong.* Unbelief is apt to mistake recruits for enemies, and to draw dismal conclusions even from comfortable premises (Judges 13:22, 23); but faith can find encouragement even in that which is discouraging, and get nearer to God by taking hold on that hand which is stretched out to push it away. So good a thing it is to be of *quick understanding in the fear of the Lord,* Isa. 11:3.

Her plea is, *Yet the dogs eat of the crumbs.* It is true, the full and regular provision is intended for the children only, but the small, casual, neglected crumbs are allowed to the dogs, and are not grudged them; that is to the dogs under the table, that attend there expecting them. We poor Gentiles cannot expect the stated ministry and miracles of the Son of David, that belongs to the Jews; but they begin now to be weary of their meat, and to play with it, they find fault with it, and crumble it away; surely then some of the broken meat may fall to a poor Gentile; "I beg a cure by the by, which is but a crumb, though of the same precious bread, yet but a small inconsiderable piece, compared with the loaves which they have." Note, When we are ready to surfeit on the children's bread, we should remember how many there are, that would be glad of the crumbs. Our broken meat in spiritual privileges, would be a feast to many a soul; Acts 13:42. Observe here,

First, Her humility and necessity made her glad of crumbs. Those who are conscious to themselves that they deserve nothing, will be thankful for any thing; and *then* we are prepared for the greatest of God's mercies, when we see ourselves less than the least of them. The least of Christ is precious to a believer, and the very crumbs of the bread of life.

Secondly, Her faith encouraged her to expect these crumbs. Why should it not be at Christ's table as at a great man's, where the dogs are fed as sure as the children? Observe, She calls it their *master's* table; if she were a dog, she was *his* dog, and it cannot be ill with us, if we stand but in the meanest relation to Christ; "Though unworthy to be called children, yet *make me as one of thy hired servants:* nay, rather let me be set with the dogs than turned out of the house; for *in my Father's house there is not only bread enough, but to spare,"* Lu. 15:17–19. It is good lying in God's house, though we lie at the threshold there.

4. The happy issue and success of all this. She came off with credit and comfort from this struggle; and, though a Canaanite, approved herself a true daughter of Israel, who, *like a prince, had power with God, and prevailed.* Hitherto Christ hid his face from her, but now *gathers her with everlasting kindness, v.* 28. *Then Jesus said, O woman, great is thy faith.* This was like Joseph's making himself know to his brethren, *I am Joseph;* so here, in effect, *I am Jesus.* Now he begins to speak like himself, and to put on his own countenance. *He will not contend for ever.*

(1.) He commended her faith. *O woman, great is thy faith.* Observe, [1.] It is her faith that he commends. There were several other graces that shone bright in her conduct of this affair — wisdom, humility, meekness, patience, perseverance in prayer; but these were the product of her faith, and therefore Christ fastens upon that as most commendable; because of all graces faith honours Christ most, therefore of all graces Christ honours faith most. [2.] It is the greatness of her faith. Note, *First,* Though the faith of all the saints is alike precious, yet it is not in all alike strong; all believers are not of the same size and stature. *Secondly,* The greatness of faith consists much in a resolute adherence to Jesus Christ as an all-sufficient Saviour, even in the face of discouragements; to love him, and trust him, as a Friend, even then when he seems to come forth against us as an Enemy. This is *great faith! Thirdly,* Though weak faith, if true, shall not be rejected, yet great faith shall be commended, and shall appear greatly well-pleasing to Christ; for in them that thus believe he is most admired. Thus Christ commended the faith of the centurion, and he was a Gentile too, he had a strong faith in the power of Christ, this woman in the good-will of Christ; both were acceptable.

(2.) He cured her daughter; *"Be it unto thee even as thou wilt:* I can deny thee nothing, take what thou camest for." Note, Great believers may have what they will for the asking. When our will conforms to the will of Christ's precept, his will concurs with the will of our desire. Those that will deny Christ nothing, shall find that he will deny them nothing at last, though for a time he seems to hide his face from them. "Thou wouldst have thy sins pardoned, thy corruptions mortified, thy nature sanctified; *be it unto thee even as thou wilt.* And what canst thou desire more?" When we come, as this poor woman did, to pray against Satan and his kingdom, we concur with the intercession of Christ, and it shall be accordingly. Though Satan may *sift* Peter, and *buffet* Paul, yet, through Christ's prayer and the sufficiency of his grace, *we shall be more than conquerors,* Lu. 22:31, 32; 2 Co. 12:7–9; Rom. 16:20.

The event was answerable to the word of Christ; *Her daughter was made whole from that very hour;* from thenceforward was never vexed with the devil any more; the mother's faith prevailed for the daughter's cure. Though the patient was at a distance, that was no hindrance to the efficacy of Christ's word. *He spake, and it was done.*

Verses 29–39

Here is, I. A general account of Christ's cures, his curing by wholesale. The tokens of Christ's power and goodness are neither scarce nor scanty; for there is in him an overflowing fulness. Now observe,

1. The place where these cures were wrought; it was *near the sea of Galilee,* a part of the country Christ was much conversant with. We read not of any thing he did in the coasts of Tyre and Sidon, but the casting of the devil out of the woman of Canaan's daughter, as if he took that journey on purpose, with that in prospect. Let not ministers grudge their pains to do good, though but to few. He that knows the worth of souls, would go a great way to help to save one from death and Satan's power.

But *Jesus departed thence.* Having let fall that crumb under table, he here returns to make a full feast for the children. We may do that occasionally for one, which we may not make a constant practice of. Christ steps into the coast of Tyre and Sidon, but he *sits down by the sea of Galilee* (*v.* 29), sits down not on a stately throne, or tribunal of judgment, but on a mountain: so mean and homely were his most solemn appearances in the days of his flesh! He *sat down on a mountain,* that all might see him, and have free access to him; for he is an open Saviour. He sat down there, as one tired with his journey, and willing to have a little rest; or rather, as one waiting to be gracious. He sat, expecting patients, as Abraham at his tent-door, ready to entertain strangers. He settled himself to this good work.

2. The multitudes and maladies that were healed by him (*v.* 30); *Great multitudes came to him;* that the scripture might be fulfilled, *Unto him shall the gathering of the people be,* Gen. 49:10. If Christ's ministers could cure bodily diseases as Christ did, there would be more flocking to them than there is; we are soon sensible of bodily pain and sickness, but few are concerned about their souls and their spiritual diseases.

Now, (1.) Such was the goodness of Christ, that he admitted all sorts of people; the poor as well as the rich are welcome to Christ, and with him there is room enough for all comers. He never complained of crowds or throngs of seekers, or looked with contempt upon the vulgar, the *herd,* as they are called; for the souls of peasants are as precious with him as the souls of princes.

(2.) Such was the power of Christ, that he healed all sorts of diseases; those that came to him, brought their sick relations and friends along with them, and *cast them down at Jesus' feet, v.* 30. We read not of any thing they said to him, but they laid them down before him as objects of pity, to be looked upon by him. Their calamities spake more for them than the tongue of the most eloquent orator could. *David showed before God his trouble,* that was enough, he then left it with him, Ps. 142:2. Whatever our case is, the only way to find ease and relief, is, to lay it at Christ's feet, to spread it before him, and refer it to his cognizance, and then submit it to him, and refer it to his disposal. Those that would have spiritual healing from Christ, must lay themselves at his feet, to be ruled and ordered as he pleaseth.

Here were *lame, blind, dumb, maimed, and many others,* brought to Christ. See what work sin has made! It has turned the world into a hospital: what various diseases are human bodies subject to! See what work the Saviour makes! He conquers those hosts of enemies to mankind. Here were such diseases as a flame of fancy could contribute neither to the cause of nor to the cure of; as lying not in the humours, but in the members of the body; and yet these were subject to the commands of Christ. *He sent his word, and healed them.* Note, All diseases are at the command of Christ, to go and come as he bids them. This is an instance of Christ's power, which may comfort us in all our weaknesses; and of his pity, which may comfort us in all our miseries.

3. The influence that this had upon the people, *v.* 31.

(1.) They *wondered,* and well they might. Christ's works should be our wonder. *It is the Lord's doing, and it is mar-*

vellous, Ps. 118:23. The spiritual cures that Christ works are wonderful. When blind souls are made to see by faith, *the dumb to speak* in prayer, *the lame to walk* in holy obedience, it is to be wondered at. *Sing unto the Lord a new song, for thus he has done marvellous things.*

(2.) *They glorified the God of Israel,* whom the Pharisees, when they saw these things, blasphemed. Miracles, which are the matter of our wonder, must be the matter of our praise; and mercies, which are the matter of our rejoicing, must be the matter of our thanksgiving. Those that were healed, glorified God; if he heal our diseases, all that is within us must bless his holy name; and if we have been graciously preserved from blindness, and lameness, and dumbness, we have as much reason to bless God as if we had been cured of them; nay, and the standers-by glorified God. Note, God must be acknowledged with praise and thankfulness in the mercies of others as in our own. *They glorified* him as *the God of Israel,* his church's God, a God in covenant with his people, who hath sent the Messiah promised; and this is he. See Lu. 1:68. *Blessed be the Lord God of Israel.* This was done by the power of the God of Israel, and no other could do it.

II. Here is a particular account of his feeding *four thousand men* with *seven loaves, and a few little fishes,* as he had lately fed *five thousand with five loaves.* The guests indeed were now not quite so many as then, and the provision a little more; which does not intimate that Christ's arm was shortened, but that he wrought his miracles as the occasion required, and not for ostentation, and therefore he suited them to the occasion: both then and now he took as many as were to be fed, and made use of all that was at hand to feed them with. When once the utmost powers of nature are exceeded, we must say, *This is the finger of God;* and it is neither here nor there how far they are outdone; so that this is no less a miracle than the former.

Here is, 1. Christ's pity (*v.* 32); *I have compassion on the multitude.* He tells his disciples this, both to try and to excite their compassion. When he was about to work this miracle, he called them to him, and made them acquainted with his purpose, and discoursed with them about it; not because he needed their advice, but because he would give an instance of his condescending love to them. He called them not *servants,* for *the servant knows not what his Lord doeth,* but treated them as his friends and counsellors. *Shall I hide from Abraham the thing that I do?* Gen. 18:17. In what he said to them, Observe,

(1.) The case of the multitude; *They continue with me now three days, and have nothing to eat.* This is an instance of their zeal, and the strength of their affection to Christ and his word, that they not only left their callings, to attend upon him on week-days, but underwent a deal of hardship, to continue with him; they wanted their natural rest, and, for aught that appeared, lay like soldiers in the field; they wanted necessary food, and had scarcely enough to keep life and soul together. In those hotter countries they could better bear long fasting than we can in these colder climates: but though it could not but be grievous to the body, and might endanger their health, yet *the zeal of God's house thus ate them up,* and they esteemed the words of Christ more than their necessary food. We think three hours too much to attend upon public ordinances; but these people staid together three days, and yet snuffed not at it, nor said, *Behold, what a weariness is it!* Observe, With what tenderness Christ spoke of it; *I have compassion on them.* It had become them to have compassion on him, who took so much pains with them for three days together, and was so indefatigable in teaching and healing; so much virtue had gone out of him, and yet for aught that appears he was fasting too: but he prevented them with his compassion. Note, Our Lord Jesus keeps an account how long his followers continue their attendance on him, and takes notice of the difficulty they sustain in it (Rev. 2:2); *I know thy works, and thy labour, and thy patience:* and it shall *in no wise lose its reward.*

Now the exigence the people were reduced to serves to magnify. [1.] The mercy of their supply: he fed them when they were hungry; and then food was doubly welcome. He treated them as he did Israel of old; *he suffered them to hunger, and then fed them* (Deu. 8:3); for that is *sweet to the hungry soul,* which *the full soul loathes.* [2.] The miracle of their supply: having been so long fasting, their appetites were the more craving. If two hungry meals make the third a glutton, what would three hungry days do? And yet *they did all eat and were filled.* Note, There are mercy and grace enough with

Christ, to give the most earnest and enlarged desire an abundant satisfaction; *Open thy mouth wide, and I will fill it. He replenisheth even the hungry soul.*

(2.) The care of our master concerning them; *I will not send them away fasting, lest they should faint by the way;* which would be a discredit to Christ and his family, and a discouragement both to them and to others. Note, It is the unhappiness of our present state, that when our souls are in some measure elevated and enlarged, our bodies cannot keep pace with them in good duties. The weakness of the flesh is a great grievance to the willingness of the spirit. It will not be so in heaven, where the body shall be made spiritual, where *they rest not, day and night, from praising God,* and yet faint not; where *they hunger no more, nor thirst any more,* Rev. 7:16.

Here is, 2. Christ's power. His pity of their wants sets his power on work for their supply. Now observe,

(1.) How his power was distrusted by his disciples (*v.* 23); *whence should we have so much bread in the wilderness?* A proper question, one would think, like that of Moses (Num. 11:22). *Shall the flocks and the herds be slain to suffice them?* But it was here an improper question, considering not only the general assurance the disciples had of the power of Christ, but the particular experience they lately had of a seasonable and sufficient provision by miracle in a like case; they had been not only the witnesses, but the ministers, of the former miracle; the multiplied bread went through their hands; so that it was an instance of great weakness for them to ask, *Whence shall we have bread?* Could they be at a loss, while they had their Master with them? Note, Forgetting former experiences leaves us under present doubts.

Christ knew how slender the provision was, but he would know it from them (*v.* 34); *How many loaves have ye?* Before he would work, he would have it seen how little he had to work on, that his power might shine the brighter. What they had, they had for themselves, and it was little enough for their own family; but Christ would have them bestow it all upon the multitude, and trust Providence for more. Note, it becomes Christ's disciples to be generous, their Master was so: what we have, we should be free of, as there is occasion; *given to hospitality;* not like Nabal (1 Sa. 25:11), but like Elisha, 2 Ki. 4:42. Niggardliness to-day, out of thoughtfulness for to-morrow, is a complication of corrupt affection that ought to be mortified. If we be prudently kind and charitable with what we have, we may piously hope that God will send more. *Jehovah-jireh, The Lord will provide.* The disciples asked, *Whence should we have bread?* Christ asked, *How many loaves have ye?* Note, When we cannot have what we would, we must make the best of what we have, and do good with it as far as it will go; we must not think so much of our wants as of our havings. Christ herein went according to the rule he gave to Martha, not to be *troubled about many things, nor cumbered about much serving.* Nature is content with little, grace with less, but lust with nothing.

(2.) How his power was discovered to the multitude, in the plentiful provision he made for them; the manner of which is much the same as before, *ch.* 14:18, etc. Observe here,

[1.] The provision that was at hand; *seven loaves, and a few fishes:* the fish not proportionable to the bread, for bread is the staff of life. It is probable that the fish was such as they had themselves taken; for they were fishers, and were now near the sea. Note, It is comfortable to *eat the labour of our hands* (Ps. 128:2), and to enjoy that which is any way the product of our own industry, Prov. 12:27. And what we have got by God's blessing on our labour we should be free of; for *therefore* we must labour, *that we may have to give,* Eph. 4:28.

[2.] The putting of the people in a posture to receive it (*v.* 35); *He commanded the multitude to sit down on the ground.* They saw but very little provision, yet they must sit down, in faith that they should have a meal's meat out of it. They who would have spiritual food from Christ, must sit down at his feet, to hear his word, and expect it to come in an unseen way.

[3.] The distributing of the provision among them. He first *gave thanks — eucharistēsas.* The word used in the former miracle was *eulogēse — he blessed.* It comes all to one; giving thanks to God is a proper way of craving a blessing from God. And when we come to ask and receive further mercy, we ought to give thanks for the mercies we have received. He then *broke the loaves* (for it was in the breaking that the bread multiplied) *and gave to his disciples, and they to the*

multitude. Though the disciples had distrusted Christ's power, yet he made use of them now as before; he is not provoked, as he might be, by the weakness and infirmities of his ministers, to lay them aside; but still he gives to them, and they to his people, of the word of life.

[4.] The plenty there was among them (*v.* 37). *They did all eat, and were filled.* Note, Those whom Christ feeds, he fills. While we labour for the world, we labour for that which satisfieth not (Isa. 55:2); but those that duly wait on Christ shall be *abundantly satisfied with the goodness of his house,* Ps. 65:4. Christ thus fed people once and again, to intimate that though he was called Jesus of Nazareth, yet he was *of Bethlehem, the house of bread;* or rather, that he was himself *the Bread of Life.*

To show that they had all enough, there was a great deal left — *seven baskets full of broken meat;* not so much as there was before, because they did not gather after so many eaters, but enough to show that with Christ *there is bread enough, and to spare;* supplies of grace for more than seek it, and for those that seek more.

[5.] The account taken of the guests; not that they might pay their share (here was no reckoning to be discharged, they were fed gratis), but that they might be witnesses to the power and goodness of Christ, and that this might be some resemblance of that universal providence that *gives food to all flesh,* Ps. 136:25. Here were four thousand men fed; but what were they to that great family which is provided for by the divine care every day? God is a great Housekeeper, on whom *the eyes of all the creatures wait, and he giveth them their food in due season,* Ps. 104:27; 145:15.

[6.] The dismission of the multitude, and Christ's departure to another place (*v.* 39). He *sent away* the people. Though he had fed them twice, they must not expect miracles to be their daily bread. Let them now go home to their callings, and to their own tables. And he himself departed by ship to another place; for, being the *Light of the world,* he must be still *in motion,* and go about to do good.

CHAPTER 16

None of Christ's miracles are recorded in this chapter, but four of his discourses. Here is, I. A conference with the Pharisees, who challenged him to show them a sign from heaven (*v.* 1–4). II. Another with his disciples about the leaven of the Pharisees (*v.* 5–12). III. Another with them concerning himself, as the Christ, and concerning his church built upon him (*v.* 13–20). IV. Another concerning his sufferings for them, and theirs for him (*v.* 21–28). And all these are written for our learning.

Verses 1–4

We have here Christ's discourse with the Pharisees and Sadducees, men at variance among themselves, as appears Acts 23:7, 8, and yet unanimous in their opposition to Christ; because his doctrine did equally overthrow the errors and heresies of the Sadducees, who denied the existence of spirits and a future state; and the pride, tyranny, and hypocrisy of the Pharisees, who were the great imposters of the traditions of the elders. Christ and Christianity meet with opposition on all hands. Observe,

I. Their demand, and the design of it.

1. The demand was of a sign from heaven; this they desired him to show them; pretending they were very willing to be satisfied and convinced, when really they were far from being so, but sought excuses from an obstinate infidelity. That which they pretended to desire was,

(1.) Some other sign than what they had yet had. They had great plenty of signs; every miracle Christ wrought was a sign, for *no man could do what he did unless God were with him.* But this will not serve, they must have a sign of their own choosing; they despised those signs which relieved the necessity of the sick and sorrowful, and insisted upon some sign which gratify the curiosity of the proud. It is fit that the proofs of divine revelation should be chosen by the wisdom of God, not by the follies and fancies of men. The evidence that is given is sufficient to satisfy an unprejudiced understanding, but was not intended to please a vain humour. Ant it is an instance of the deceitfulness of the heart, to think that we should be wrought upon by the means and advantages which we have not, while we slight those which we have. *If we hear not Moses and the prophets,* neither would we be wrought upon *though one rose from the dead.*

(2.) It must be a sign from heaven. They would have such miracles to prove his commission, as were wrought at the giving of the law upon mount Sinai: thunder, and lightening, and the voice of words, were the sign from heaven they required. Whereas the sensible signs and terrible ones were not agreeable to the spiritual and comfortable dispensation of the gospel. Now the word comes more nigh us (Rom. 10:8), and therefore the miracles do so, and do not oblige us to keep such a distance as these did, Heb. 12:18.

2. The design was to tempt him; not to be taught by him, but to ensnare him. If he should show them a sign from heaven, they would attribute it to a confederacy with the *prince of the power of the air;* if he should not, as they supposed he would not, they would have that to say for themselves, *why they did not believe on him.* They now tempted Christ as Israel did, 1 Co. 10:9. And observe their perverseness; *then,* when they had signs from heaven, they tempted Christ, saying, *Can he furnish a table in the wilderness?* Now that he had furnished a table in the wilderness, they tempted him, saying, *Can he give us a sign from heaven?*

II. Christ's reply to this demand; lest they should be *wise in their own conceit,* he *answered these fools according to their folly,* Prov. 26:5. In his answer,

1. He condemns their overlooking of the signs they had, *v.* 2, 3. They were seeking for the signs of the kingdom of God, when it was already among them. *The Lord was in this place,* and they *knew it not.* Thus their unbelieving ancestors, when miracles were their daily bread, asked, *Is the Lord among us, or is he not?*

To expose this, he observes to them,

(1.) Their skilfulness and sagacity in other things, particularly in natural prognostications of the weather; "You know that a red sky over-night is a presage of fair weather, and a red sky in the morning of foul weather." There are common rules drawn from observation and experience, by which it is easy to foretel very probably what weather it will be. When second causes have begun to work, we may easily guess at their issue, so uniform is nature in its motions, and so consistent with itself. We *know not the balancing of the clouds* (Job 37:16), but we may spell something from the faces of them. This gives no countenance at all to the wild and ridiculous predictions of *the astrologers, the star-gazers, and the monthly prognosticators* (Isa. 47:13) concerning the weather long before, with which weak and foolish people are imposed upon; we are sure, in general, that *seed-time and harvest, cold and heat, summer and winter, shall not cease.* But as to the particulars, till, by the weather-glasses, or otherwise, we perceive the immediate signs and harbingers of the change of weather, it is not for us to know, no, not *that* concerning the times and seasons. Let it suffice, that it shall be what weather pleases God; and that which pleases God, should not displease us.

(2.) Their sottishness and stupidity in the concerns of their souls; *Can ye not discern the signs of the times?*

[1.] "Do you not see that the Messiah is come?" The sceptre was departed from Judah, Daniel's weeks were just expiring, and yet they regarded not. The miracles Christ wrought, and the gathering of the people to him, were plain indications that the *kingdom of heaven was at hand,* that this was *the day of their visitation.* Note, *First,* There are signs of the times, by which wise and upright men are enabled to make moral prognostications, and so far to understand the motions and methods of Providence, as from thence to take their measures, and to know what Israel ought to do, as the men of Issachar, as the physician from some certain symptoms finds a crisis formed. *Secondly,* There are many who are skilful enough in other things, and yet cannot or will not discern the day of their opportunities, are not aware of the wind when it is fair for them, and so let slip the gale. See Jer. 8:7; Isa. 1:3. *Thirdly,* It is great hypocrisy, when we slight the signs of God's ordaining, to seek for signs of our own prescribing.

[2.] "Do not you foresee your own ruin coming for rejecting him? You will not entertain the gospel of peace, and can you not evidently discern that hereby you pull an inevitable destruction upon your own heads?" Note, It is the undoing of multitudes, that they are not aware what will be the end of their refusing Christ.

2. He refuses to give them any other sign (*v.* 4), as he had done before in the same words, *ch.* 12:39. Those that persist in the same iniquities, must expect to meet with the same reproofs. Here, as there, (1.) He calls them *an adulterous generation;* because, while they professed themselves of the true church and spouse of God, they treacherously departed from him, and brake their covenants with him. The Pharisees were *a generation pure in their own eyes,* having the way of the adulterous woman, that thinks she has done no wickedness, Prov. 30:20. (2.) He refuses to gratify their desire. Christ will not be prescribed to; *we ask, and have not, because we ask amiss.* (3.) He refers them to the sign of the prophet Jonas, which should yet be given them; his resurrection from the dead, and his preaching by his apostles to the Gentiles; these were reserved for the last and highest evidences of his divine mission. Note, Though the fancies of proud men shall not be humoured, yet the faith of the humble shall be supported, and the unbelief of them that perish left for ever inexcusable, and *every mouth shall be stopped.*

This discourse broke off abruptly; *he left them and departed.* Christ will not tarry long with those that tempt him, but justly withdraws from those that are disposed to quarrel with him. He left them as irreclaimable; *Let them alone.* He left them to themselves, left them in the hand of their own counsels; *so he gave them up to their own hearts' lust.*

Verses 5–12

We have here Christ's discourse with his disciples concerning bread, in which, as in many other discourses, he speaks to them of spiritual things under a similitude, and they misunderstand him of carnal things. The occasion of it was, their forgetting to victual their ship, and to take along with them provisions for their family on the other side of the water; usually they carried bread along with them, because they were sometimes in desert places; and when they were not, yet they would not be burthensome. But now they forgot; we will hope it was because their minds and memories were filled with better things. Note, Christ's disciples are often such as have no great forecast for the world.

I. Here is the caution Christ gave them, to *beware of the leaven of the Pharisees.* He had now been discoursing with the Pharisees and Sadducees, and saw them to be men of such a spirit, that it was necessary to caution his disciples to have nothing to do with them. Disciples are in most danger from hypocrites; against those that are openly vicious they stand upon their guard, but against Pharisees, who are great pretenders to devotion, and Sadducees, who pretend to a free and impartial search after truth, they commonly lie unguarded: and therefore the caution is doubted, *Take heed, and beware.*

The corrupt principles and practices of the Pharisees and Sadducees are compared to leaven; they were souring, and swelling, and spreading, like leaven; they fermented wherever they came.

II. Their mistake concerning this caution, *v.* 7. They thought Christ hereby upbraided them with their improvidence and forgetfulness, that they were so busy attending to his discourse with the Pharisees, that *therefore* they forgot their private concerns. Or, because having no bread of their own with them, they must be beholden to their friends for supply, he would not have them to ask it of the Pharisees and Sadducees, nor to receive of *their* alms, because he would not so far countenance them; or, for fear, lest, under pretence of feeding them, they should do them a mischief. Or, they took it for a caution, not to be familiar with the Pharisees and Sadducees, not to eat with them (Prov. 23:6), whereas the danger was not in their bread (Christ himself did eat with them, Lu. 7:36; 11:37; 14:1), but in their principles.

III. The reproof Christ gave them for this.

1. He reproves their distrust of his ability and readiness to supply them in this strait (*v.* 8); *"O ye of little faith,* why are ye in such perplexity because ye have *taken no bread,* that ye can mind nothing else, that ye think your Master is as full of it as you, and apply every thing he saith to that?" He does not chide them for their little forecast, as they expected he would. Note, Parents and masters must not be angry at the forgetfulness of their children and servants, more than is necessary to make them take more heed another time; we are all apt to be forgetful of our duty. This should serve to excuse a fault, *Peradventure it was an oversight.* See how easily Christ forgave his disciples' carelessness, though it was in such a material point as taking bread; and do likewise. But that which he chides them for is their little faith.

(1.) He would have them to depend upon him for supply, though it were in a wilderness, and not to disquiet themselves with anxious thoughts about it. Note, Though Christ's disciples be brought into wants and straits, through their own carelessness and incogitancy, yet he encourages them to trust in him for relief. We must not therefore use this as an excuse for our want of charity to those who are really poor, that they should have minded their own affairs better, and then they would not have been in need. It may be so, but they must not therefore be left to starve when they are in need.

(2.) He is displeased at their solicitude in this matter. The weakness and shiftlessness of good people in their worldly affairs is that for which men are apt to condemn them; but it is not such an offence to Christ as their inordinate care and anxiety about those things. We must endeavour to keep the mean between the extremes of carelessness and carefulness; but of the two, the excess of thoughtfulness about the world worst becomes Christ's disciples. *"O ye of little faith,* why are ye disquieted for want of bread?" Note, To distrust Christ, and to disturb ourselves when we are in straits and difficulties, is an evidence of the weakness of our faith, which, if it were in exercise as it should be, would ease us of the burthen of care, by casting it on the Lord, who *careth for us.*

(3.) The aggravation of their distrust was the experience they had so lately had of the power and goodness of Christ in providing for them, *v.* 9, 10. Though they had no bread with them, they had him with them who could provide bread for them. If they had not the cistern, they had the Fountain. *Do ye not yet understand, neither remember?* Note, Christ's disciples are often to be blamed for the shallowness of their understandings, and the slipperiness of their memories. "Have ye forgot those repeated instances of merciful and miraculous supplies; five thousand fed with five loaves, and four thousand with seven loaves, and yet they had enough and to spare? Remember *how many baskets ye took up.*" These baskets were intended for memorials, by which to keep the mercy in remembrance, as the pot of manna which was preserved in the ark, Ex. 16:32. The fragments of those meals would be a feast now; and he that could furnish them with such an overplus then, surely could furnish them with what was necessary now. That meat for their bodies was intended to be meat or their faith (Ps. 74:14), which therefore they should have lived upon, now that they had forgotten to take bread. Note, We are *therefore* perplexed with present cares and distrusts, because we do not duly remember our former experiences of divine power and goodness.

2. He reproves their misunderstanding of the caution he gave them (*v.* 11); *How is it that you do not understand?* Note, Christ's disciples may well be ashamed of the slowness and dulness of their apprehensions in divine things; especially when they have long enjoyed the means of grace; *I spake it not unto you concerning bread.* He took it ill, (1.) That they should think him as thoughtful about bread as they were; whereas his *meat and drink were to do his Father's will.* (2.) That they should be so little acquainted with his way of preaching, as to take that literally which he spoke by way of parable; and should thus make themselves like the multitude, who, when Christ spoke to them in parables, seeing, saw not, and hearing, heard not, *ch.* 13:13.

IV. The rectifying of the mistake by this reproof (*v.* 12); *Then understood they* what he meant. Note, Christ *therefore* shows us our folly and weakness, that we may stir up ourselves to take things right. He did not tell them expressly what he meant, but repeated what he had said, that they should beware of the leaven; and so obliged them, by comparing this with his other discourses, to arrive at the sense of it in their own thoughts. Thus Christ teaches by the Spirit of wisdom in the heart, opening the understanding to the Spirit of revelation in the word. And those truths are most precious, which we have thus digged for, and have found out after some mistakes. Though Christ did not tell them plainly, yet now they were aware that by the leaven of the Pharisees and Sadducees, he meant their doctrine and way, which were corrupt and vicious, but, as they managed them, very apt to insinuate themselves into the minds of men like leaven, and to *eat like a canker.* They were leading men, and were had in reputation, which made the danger of infection by their errors the greater. In our age, we may reckon atheism and deism to be the leaven of the Sadducees, and popery to be the leaven of the Pharisees, against both which it concerns all Christians to stand upon their guard.

Verses 13–20

We have here a private conference which Christ had with his disciples concerning himself. It was in the coasts of Cesarea Philippi, the utmost borders of the land of Canaan northward; there in that remote corner, perhaps, there was less flocking after him than in other places, which gave him leisure for this private conversation with his disciples. Note,

When ministers are abridged in their public work, they should endeavour to do the more in their own families.

Christ is here catechising his disciples.

I. He enquires what the opinions of others were concerning him; *Who do men say that I, the Son of man, am?*

1. He calls himself the *Son of man;* which may be taken either, (1.) As a title common to him with others. He was called, and justly, *the Son of God,* for so he was (Lu. 1:35); but he called himself the Son of man; for he is really and truly "Man, made of a woman." In courts of honour, it is a rule to distinguish men by their highest titles; but Christ, having now emptied himself, though he was the Son of God, will be known by the style and title of the Son of man. Ezekiel was often so called to *keep* him humble; Christ called himself so, to show that he *was* humble. Or, (2.) As a title peculiar to him as Mediator. He is made known, in Daniel's vision, as the *Son of man,* Dan. 7:13. I am the Messiah, that Son of man that was promised. But,

2. He enquires what people's sentiments were concerning him: *"Who do men say that I am? The Son of man?"* (So I think it might better be read). "Do they own me for the Messiah?" He asks not, "Who do the *scribes* and *Pharisees* say that I am?" They were prejudiced against him, and said that he was a deceiver and in league with Satan; but, "Who do *men* say that I am?" He referred to the common people, whom the Pharisees despised. Christ asked this question, not as one that knew not; for if he knows what men think, much more what they say; nor as one desirous to hear his own praises, but to make the disciples solicitous concerning the success of their preaching, by showing that he himself was so. The common people conversed more familiarly with the disciples than they did with their Master, and therefore from them he might better know what they said. Christ had not plainly said who he was, but left people to infer it from his works, Jn. 10:24, 25. Now he would know what inferences the people drew from *them,* and from the miracles which his apostles wrought in his name.

3. To this question the disciples have him an answer (*v.* 14),*Some say, thou art John the Baptist, etc.* There were some that said, he was the *Son of David* (*ch.* 12:23), and the great Prophet, Jn. 6:14. The disciples, however, do not mention that opinion, but only such opinions as were wide of the truth, which they gathered up from their countrymen. Observe,

(1.) They are different opinions; some say one thing, and others another. Truth is one; but those who vary from that commonly vary one from another. Thus Christ came eventually to send division, Lu. 12:51. Being so noted a Person, every one would be ready to pass his verdict upon him, and, "Many men, many minds;" those that were not willing to own him to be the Christ, wandered in endless mazes, and followed the chase of every uncertain guess and wild hypothesis.

(2.) They are honourable opinions, and bespeak the respect they had for him, according to the best of their judgment. These were not the sentiments of his enemies, but the sober thoughts of those that followed him with love and wonder. Note, It is possible for men to have good thoughts of Christ, and yet not right ones, a high opinion of him, and yet not high enough.

(3.) They all suppose him to be *one risen from the dead;* which perhaps arose from a confused notion they had of the resurrection of the Messiah, before his public preaching, as of Jonas. Or their notions arose from an excessive value for antiquity; as if it were not possible for an excellent man to be produced in their own age, but it must be one of the ancients returned to life again.

(4.) They are all false opinions, built upon mistakes, and wilful mistakes. Christ's doctrines and miracles bespoke him to be an extraordinary Person; but because of the meanness of his appearance, so different from what they expected, they would not own him to be the Messiah, but will grant him to be any thing rather than that.

[1.] *Some say, thou art John the Baptist.* Herod said so (*ch.* 14:2), and those about him would be apt to say as he said. This notion might be strengthened by an opinion they had, that those who died as martyrs, should rise again before others; which some think the second of the seven sons refers to, in his answer to Antiochus, 2 Macc. 7:9, *The King of the world shall raise us up, who have died for his laws, unto everlasting life.*

[2.] *Some Elias;* taking occasion, no doubt, from the prophecy of Malachi (*ch.* 4:5), *Behold, I will send you Elijah.* And the rather, because Elijah (as Christ) did many miracles, and was himself, in his translation, the greatest miracle of all.

[3.] *Others Jeremias:* they fasten upon him, either because he was the weeping prophet, and Christ was often in tears; or because God had *set him over the kingdoms and nations* (Jer. 1:10), which they thought agreed with their notion of the Messiah.

[4.] *Or, one of the prophets.* This shows what an honourable idea they entertained of the prophets; and yet they were *the children of them that persecuted and slew them, ch.* 23:29. Rather than they would allow Jesus of Nazareth, one of their own country, to be such an extraordinary Person as his works bespoke him to be, they would say, "It was not he, but *one of the old prophets.*"

II. He enquires what *their* thoughts were concerning him; *"But who say ye that I am? v.* 15. Ye tell me what other people say of me; can ye say better?" 1. The disciples had themselves been better taught than others; had, by their intimacy with Christ, greater advantages of getting knowledge than others had. Note, It is justly expected that those who enjoy greater plenty of the means of knowledge and grace than others, should have a more clear and distinct knowledge of the things of God than others. Those who have more acquaintance with Christ than others, should have truer sentiments concerning him, and be able to give a better account of him than others. 2. The disciples were trained up to teach others, and therefore it was highly requisite that they should understand the truth themselves: "Ye that are to preach the gospel of the kingdom, what are your notions of him that sent you?" Note, Ministers must be examined before they be sent forth, especially what their sentiments are of Christ, and who they say that he is; for how can they be owned as ministers of Christ, that are either ignorant or erroneous concerning Christ? This is a question we should every one of us be frequently putting to ourselves, *"Who* do we say, *what* kind of one do we say, that *the Lord Jesus is?* Is he precious to us? Is he in our eyes the chief of ten thousand? Is he the Beloved of our souls?" It is well or ill with us, according as our thoughts are right or wrong concerning Jesus Christ.

Well, this is the question; now let us observe,

(1.) Peter's answer to this question, *v.* 16. To the former question concerning the opinion others had of Christ, several of the disciples answered, according as they had heard people talk; but to this Peter answers in the name of all the rest, they all consenting to it, and concurring in it. Peter's temper led him to be forward in speaking upon all such occasions, and sometimes he spoke well, sometimes amiss; in all companies there are found some warm, bold men, to whom a precedency of speech falls of course; Peter was such a one: yet we find other of the apostles sometimes speaking as the mouth of the rest; as *John* (Mk. 9:38), *Thomas, Philip,* and *Jude,* Jn. 14:5, 8, 22. So that this is far from being a proof of such primacy and superiority of Peter above the rest of the apostles, as the church of Rome ascribes to him. They will needs advance him to be a judge, when the utmost they can make of him, is, that he was but foreman of the jury, to speak for the rest, and that only *pro hâc vice — for this once;* not the perpetual dictator or speaker of the house, only chairman upon this occasion.

Peter's answer is short, but it is full, and true, and to the purpose; *Thou art the Christ, the Son of the Living God.* Here is a confession of the Christian faith, addressed to Christ, and so made an act of devotion. Here is a confession of the true God as the living God, in opposition to dumb and dead idols, and of *Jesus Christ, whom he hath sent,* whom to know is *life eternal.* This is the conclusion of the whole matter.

[1.] The people called him *a Prophet, that Prophet* (Jn. 6:14); but the disciples own him to be the Christ, the anointed One; the great Prophet, Priest, and King of the church; the true Messiah promised to the fathers, and depended on by them as *He that shall come.* It was a great thing to believe this concerning one whose outward appearance was so contrary to the general idea the Jews had of the Messiah.

[2.] He called himself the *Son of Man;* but they owned him to be *the Son of the living God.* The *people's* notion of him was, that he was the ghost of a dead man, Elias, or Jeremias; but *they* know and believe him to be *the Son of the living God,* who has life in himself, and has given to his Son to have life in himself, and to be the *Life of the world.* If he be *the Son of the living God,* he is of the same nature with him: and though his divine nature was now veiled with the cloud of flesh, yet there were those who looked through it, and *saw his glory, the glory as of the Only-Begotten of the Father, full of grace and truth.* Now can we with an assurance of faith subscribe to this confession? Let us then, with a fervency of affection and adoration, go to Christ, and tell him so; Lord Jesus, *thou art the Christ, the Son of the living God.*

(2.) Christ's approbation of his answer (*v.* 17–19); in which Peter is replied to, both as a believer and as an apostle.

[1.] As a believer, *v.* 17. Christ shows himself well pleased with Peter's confession, that it was so clear and express, without *ifs* or *ands,* as we say. Note, The proficiency of Christ's disciples in knowledge and grace is very acceptable to him; and Christ shows him whence he received the knowledge of this truth. At the first discovery of this truth in the dawning of the gospel day, it was a mighty thing to believe it; *all men had not this knowledge,* had not this faith. But,

First, Peter had the happiness of it; *Blessed art thou, Simon Bar-jona.* He reminds him of his rise and original, the meanness of his parentage, the obscurity of his extraction; he was *Bar-jonas — The son of a dove;* so some. Let him remember *the rock out of which he was hewn,* that he may see he was not born to this dignity, but preferred to it by the divine favour; it was free grace that made him to differ. Those that have received the Spirit must remember who is their Father, 1 Sa. 10:12. Having reminded him of this, he makes him sensible of his great happiness as a believer; *Blessed art thou.* Note, True believers are truly blessed, and those are blessed indeed whom Christ pronounces blessed; his saying they are so, makes them so. "Peter, thou art a happy man, who thus *knowest the joyful sound,"* Ps. 89:15 *Blessed are your eyes, ch.* 13:16. All happiness attends the right knowledge of Christ.

Secondly, God must have the glory of it; *"For flesh and blood have not revealed it to thee.* Thou hadst this neither by the invention of thy own wit and reason, nor by the instruction and information of others; this light sprang neither from nature nor from education, but from my Father who is in heaven." Note, 1. The Christian religion is a revealed religion, has its rise in heaven; it is a religion from above, given by inspiration of God, not the learning of philosophers, nor the politics of statesmen. 2. Saving faith is the gift of God, and, wherever it is, is wrought by him, as the Father of our Lord Jesus Christ, for his sake, and upon the score of his mediation, Phil. 1:29. *Therefore* thou art blessed, because *my Father has revealed it to thee.* Note, The revealing of Christ to us and in us is a distinguishing token of God's good will, and a firm foundation of true happiness; and blessed are they that are thus highly favoured.

Perhaps Christ discerned something of pride and vainglory in Peter's confession; a subtle sin, and which is apt to mingle itself even with our good duties. It is hard for good men to compare themselves with others, and not to have too great a conceit of themselves; to prevent which, we should consider that our preference to others is no achievement of our own, but the free gift of God's grace too us, and not to others; so that we have nothing to boast of, Ps. 115:1; 1 Co. 4:7.

[2.] Christ replies to him as an apostle or minister, *v.* 18, 19. Peter, in the name of the church, had confessed Christ, and to him therefore the promise intended for the church is directed. Note, There is nothing lost by being forward to confess Christ; for those who honour him, he will honour.

Upon occasion of this great confession made of Christ, which is the church's homage and allegiance, he signed and published this royal, this divine charter, by which that body politic is incorporated. Such is the communion between Christ and the church, the Bridegroom and the spouse. God had a church in the world from the beginning, and it was built upon the rock of the promised Seed, Gen. 3:15. But now, that promised Seed being come, it was requisite that the church should have a new charter, as Christian, and standing in relation to a Christ already come. Now here we have that charter; and a thousand pities it is, that this word, which is the great support of the kingdom of Christ, should be wrested and pressed into the service of antichrist. But the devil has employed his subtlety to pervert it, as he did that promise, Ps. 91:11, which he perverted to his own purpose, *ch.* 4:6, and perhaps both that scripture and this he thus perverted because they stood in his way, and therefore he owed them a spite.

Now the purport of this charter is,

First, To establish the being of the church; *I say also unto thee.* It is Christ that makes the grant, he who is the church's Head, and Ruler, to whom all judgment is committed, and from whom all power is derived; he who makes it pursuant to the authority received from the Father, and his undertaking for the salvation of the elect. The grant is put into Peter's hand; "I say it to *thee*." The Old Testament promises relating to the church were given immediately to particular persons, eminent for faith and holiness, as to Abraham and David; which yet gave no supremacy to them, much less to any of their successors; so the New-Testament charter is here delivered to Peter as an agent, but to the use and behoof of the church in all ages, according to the purposes therein specified and contained. Now it is here promised,

1. That Christ would build his church upon a rock. This body politic is incorporated by the style and title of *Christ's church*. It is a number o the children of men called out of the world, and set apart from it, and dedicated to Christ. It is not *thy* church, but *mine*. Peter remembered this, when he cautioned ministers *not to lord it over God's heritage*. The church is Christ's peculiar, appropriated to him. The world is God's, and they that dwell therein; but the church is a chosen remnant, that stands in relation to God through Christ as Mediator. It bears him image and superscription.

(1.) The Builder and Maker of the church is Christ himself; *I will build it*. The church is a temple which Christ is the Builder of, Zec. 6:11–13. Herein Solomon was a type of Christ, and Cyrus, Isa. 44:28. The materials and workmanship are his. By the working of his Spirit with the preaching of his word he adds souls to his church, and so builds it up with living stones, 1 Pt. 2:5. *Ye are God's building*; and building is a progressive work; the church in this world is but *in fieri — in the forming*, like a house in the building. It is a comfort to all those who wish well to the church, that Christ, who has divine wisdom and power, undertakes to build it.

(2.) The foundation on which it is built is, *this Rock*. Let the architect do his part ever so well, if the foundation be rotten, the building will not stand; let us therefore see what the foundation is, and it must be meant of Christ, for *other foundation can no man lay*. See Isa. 28:16.

[1.] The church is built upon a *rock*; a firm, strong, and lasting foundation, which time will not waste, nor will it sink under the weight of the building. Christ would not build his house upon the sand, for he knew that storms would arise. A rock is high, Ps. 61:2. Christ's church does not stand upon a level with this world; a rock is large, and extends far, so does the church's foundation; and the more large, the more firm; those are not the church's friends that narrow its foundation.

[2.] It is built upon *this* rock; thou art *Peter*, which signifies *a stone or rock;* Christ gave him that name when he first called him (Jn. 1:42), and here he confirms it; "Peter, thou dost answer thy name, thou art a solid, substantial disciple, fixed and stayed, and one that there is some hold of. Peter is thy name, and strength and stability are with thee. Thou art not shaken with the waves of men's fluctuating opinions concerning me, but established in the present truth," 2 Pt. 1:12. From the mention of this significant name, occasion is taken for this metaphor of *building upon a rock*.

First, Some by this rock understand Peter himself as an apostle, the chief, though not the prince, of the twelve, senior among them, but not superior over them. The church is built upon the foundation of the apostles, Eph. 2:20. The first stones of that building were laid in and by their ministry; hence their names are said to be *written in the foundations* of the new Jerusalem, Rev. 21:14. Now Peter being that apostle by whose hand the first stones of the church were laid, both in Jewish converts (Acts 2), and in the Gentile converts (Acts 10), he might in some sense be said to be the rock on which it was built. *Cephas* was one that seemed to be a pillar, Gal. 2:9. But it sounds very harsh, to call a man that only lays the first stone of a building, which is a transient act, the foundation on which it is built, which is an abiding thing. Yet if it were so, this would not serve to support the pretensions of the Bishop of Rome; for Peter had no such headship as he claims, much less could he derive it to his successors, least of all to the Bishops of Rome, who, whether they are so in place or no, is a question, but that they are not so in the truth of Christianity, is past all question.

Secondly, Others, by this *rock*, understand Christ; "Thou art *Peter*, thou hast the name of a *stone*, but *upon this rock*, pointing to himself, *I will build my church*." Perhaps he laid his hand on his breast, as when he said, *Destroy this temple* (Jn. 2:19), when he *spoke of the temple of his body*. Then he took occasion from the temple, where he was, so to speak of himself, and gave occasion to some to misunderstand him

of that; so here he took occasion from Peter, to speak of himself as the Rock, and gave occasion to some to misunderstand him of Peter. But this must be explained by those many scriptures which speak of Christ as the only Foundation of the church; see 1 Co. 3:11; 1 Pt. 2:6. Christ is both its Founder and its Foundation; he draws souls, and draws them to himself; to him they are united, and on him they rest and have a constant dependence.

Thirdly, Others by this *rock* understand this confession which Peter made of Christ, and this comes all to one with understanding it of Christ himself. It was a good confession which Peter witnessed, *Thou art the Christ, the Son of the living God;* the rest concurred with him in it. "Now," saith Christ, "this is that great truth *upon which I will build my church*." 1. Take away this truth itself, and the universal church falls to the ground. If Christ be not the Son of God, Christianity is a cheat, and the church is a mere chimera; *our preaching is vain, your faith is vain, and you are yet in your sins*, 1 Co. 15:14–17. If Jesus be not the Christ, those that own him are not of the church, but deceivers and deceived. 2. Take away the faith and confession of this truth from any particular church, and it ceases to be a part of Christ's church, and relapses to the state and character of infidelity. This is *articulus stantis et cadentis ecclesia — that article, with the admission or the denial of which the church either rises or falls;* "the main hinge on which the door of salvation turns;" those who let go this, do not hold the foundation; and though they may call themselves Christians, they give themselves the lie; for the church is a sacred society, incorporated upon the certainty and assurance of this great truth; and great it is, and has prevailed.

2. Christ here promises to preserve and secure his church, when it is built; *The gates of hell shall not prevail against it;* neither against this truth, nor against the church which is built upon it.

(1.) This implies that the church has enemies that fight against it, and endeavour its ruin overthrow, here represented by *the gates of hell, that is*, the city of hell; (which is directly opposite to this heavenly city, this *city of the living God*), the devil's interest among the children of men. The gates of hell are the powers and policies of the devil's kingdom, the dragon's head and horns, by which he *makes war with the Lamb;* all that comes out of hell-gates, as being hatched and contrived there. These fight against the church by opposing gospel truths, corrupting gospel ordinances, persecuting good ministers and good Christians; drawing or driving, persuading by craft or forcing by cruelty, to that which is inconsistent with the purity of religion; this is the design of the gates of hell, to root out the name of Christianity (Ps. 83:4), *to devour the man-child* (Rev. 12:9), to raze this city to the ground.

(2.) This assures us that the enemies of the church shall not gain their point. While the world stands, Christ will have a church in it, in which his truths and ordinances shall be owned and kept up, in spite of all the opposition of the powers of darkness; *They shall not prevail against it*, Ps. 129:1, 2. This gives no security to any particular church, or church-governors that they shall never err, never apostatize or be destroyed; but that somewhere or other the Christian religion shall have a being, though not always in the same degree of purity and splendour, yet so as that the entail of it shall never be quite cut off. The *woman lives, though in a wilderness* (Rev. 12:14), *cast down but not destroyed* (2 Co. 4:9). Corruptions grieving, persecutions grievous, but neither fatal. The church may be foiled in particular encounters, but in the main battle it shall come off *more than a conqueror*. Particular believers are *kept by the power of God, through faith, unto salvation*, 1 Pt. 1:5.

Secondly, The other part of this charter is, to settle the order and government of the church, *v*. 19. When a city or society is incorporated, officers are appointed and empowered to act for the common good. A city without government is a chaos. Now this constituting of the government of the church, is here expressed by the delivering of the keys, and, with them, a power to bind and loose. This is not to be understood of any peculiar power that Peter was invested with, as if he were sole door-keeper of the kingdom of heaven, and had that key of David which belongs only to the Son of David; no, this invests all the apostles and their successors with a ministerial power to guide and govern the church of Christ, as it exists in particular congregations or churches, according to the rules of the gospel. *Claves regni caelorum in B. Petro apostolo cuncti suscepimus sacerdotes — All we*

that are priests, received, in the person of the blessed apostle Peter, the keys of the kingdom of heaven; so Ambrose *De Dignit. Sacerd*. Only the keys were first put into Peter's hand, because he was the first *that opened the door of faith to the Gentiles*, Acts 10:28. As the king, in giving a charter to a corporation, empowers the magistrates to hold courts in his name, to try matters of fact, and determine therein according to law, confirming what is so done regularly as if done in any of the superior courts; so Christ, having incorporated his church, hath appointed the office of the ministry for the keeping up of order and government, and to see that his laws be duly served; *I will give thee the keys*. He doth not say, "I *have* given them," or "I *do* now;" but "I *will* do it," meaning after his resurrection; *when he ascended on high, he gave those gifts*, Ephes. 4:8; then this power was actually given, not to Peter only, but to all the rest, *ch*. 28:19, 20; Jn. 20:21. He doth not say, The keys *shall* be given, but, *I will give* them; for ministers derive their authority from Christ, and all their power is to be used in his name, 1 Co. 5:4.

Now, 1. The power here delegated is a spiritual power; it is a power *pertaining to the kingdom of heaven*, that is, to the church, that part of it which is militant here on earth, to the gospel dispensation; that is it about which the apostolical and ministerial power is wholly conversant. It is not any civil, secular power that is hereby conveyed, Christ's *kingdom is not of this world;* their instructions afterward were *in things pertaining to the kingdom of God*, Acts 1:3.

2. It is the *power* of the keys that is given, alluding to the custom of investing men with authority in such a place, by delivering to them the keys of the place. Or as the master of the house gives the keys to the steward, the keys of the stores where the provisions are kept, that he may give to every one in the house *his portion of meat in due season* (Lu. 12:42), and deny it as there is occasion, according to the rules of the family. Ministers are *stewards*, 1 Co. 4:1; Tit. 1:7. Eliakim, who had *the key* of the house of David, *was over the household*, Isa. 22:22.

3. It is a power to *bind and loose*, that is (following the metaphor of the keys), to shut and open. Joseph, who was lord of Pharaoh's house, and steward of the stores, had power *to bind his princes, and to teach his senators wisdom*, Ps. 105:21, 22. When the stores and treasures of the house are shut up from any, they are bound, *interdico tibi aquâ et igne — I forbid thee the use of fire and water;* when they are opened to them again, they are loosed from that bond, are discharged from the censure, and restored to their liberty.

4. It is a power which Christ has promised to own the due administration of; he will ratify the sentences of his stewards with his own approbation; *It shall be bound in heaven, and loosed in heaven:* not that Christ hath hereby obliged himself to confirm all church-censures, right or wrong; but such as are duly passed according to the word, *clave non errante — the key turning the right way*, such are sealed in heaven; that is, the word of the gospel, in the mouth of faithful ministers, is to be looked upon, not as the word of man, but as the word of God, and to be received accordingly, 1 Th. 2:13; Jn. 12:20.

Now *the keys of the kingdom of heaven are*,

(1.) The key of *doctrine*, called the key of *knowledge*. "Your business shall be to explain to the world the will of God, both as to truth and duty; and for this you shall have your commissions, credentials, and full instructions to bind and loose:" these, in the common speech of the Jews, at that time, signified to prohibit and permit; to teach or declare a thing to be unlawful was to *bind;* to be lawful, was to *loose*. Now the apostles had an extraordinary power of this kind; some things forbidden by the law of Moses were now to be allowed, as the eating of such and such meats; some things allowed there were now to be forbidden, as divorce; and the apostles were empowered to declare this to the world, and men might take it upon their words. When Peter was first taught himself, and then taught others, *to call nothing common or unclean*, this power was exercised. There is also an ordinary power hereby conveyed to all ministers, to preach the gospel as appointed officers; to tell people, in God's name, and according to the scriptures, *what is good, and what the Lord requires of them:* and they who *declare the whole counsel of God*, use these keys well, Acts 20:27.

Some make the giving of the keys to allude to the custom of the Jews in creating a doctor of the law, which was to put into his hand the keys of the chest where the book of the law was kept, denoting his being authorized to take and read it; and *the binding and loosing,* to allude to the fashion about their books, which were in rolls; they shut them by binding them up with a string, which they untied when they opened them. Christ gives his apostles power to shut or open the book of the gospel to people, as the case required. See the exercise of this power, Acts 13:46; 18:6. When ministers preach pardon and peace to the penitent, wrath and the curse to the impenitent, in Christ's name, they act then pursuant to this authority of binding and loosing.

(2.) The key of *discipline,* which is but the application of the former to particular persons, upon a right estimate of their characters and actions. It is not legislative power that is hereby conferred, but judicial; the judge doth not make the law, but only declares what is law, and upon an impartial enquiry into the merits of the cause, gives sentence accordingly. Such is *the power of the keys,* wherever it is lodged, with reference to church-membership and the privileges thereof. [1.] Christ's ministers have a power to admit into the church; "*Go, disciple all nations, baptizing them;* those who profess faith in Christ, and obedience to him, admit them and their seed members of the church by baptism." Ministers are to let in to *the wedding-feast those that are bidden;* and to keep out such as are apparently unfit for so holy a communion. [2.] They have a power to expel and cast out such as have forfeited their church-membership, that is binding; refusing to unbelievers the application of gospel promises and the seals of them; and declaring to such as appear to be *in the gall of bitterness and bond of iniquity,* that *they have no part or lot in the matter,* as Peter did to Simon Magus, though he had been baptized; and this is a binding over to the judgment of God. [3.] They have a power to restore and to receive in again, upon their repentance, such as had been thrown out; to loose those whom they had bound; declaring to them, that, if their repentance be sincere, the promise of pardon belongs to them. The apostles had a miraculous gift of *discerning spirits;* yet even *they* went by the rule of outward appearances (as Acts 8:21; 1 Co. 5:1; 2 Co. 2:7; 1 Tim. 1:20), which ministers may still make a judgment upon, if they be skilful and faithful.

Lastly, Here is the charge which Christ gave his disciples, to keep this private for the present (*v.* 20); *They must tell no man that he was Jesus the Christ.* What they had professed to him, they must not yet publish to the world, for several reasons; 1. Because this was the time of preparation for his kingdom; the great thing now preached, was, that the *kingdom of heaven was at hand;* and therefore those things were now to be insisted on, which were proper to make way for Christ; as the doctrine of repentance; not this great truth, in and with which *the kingdom of heaven* was to be actually set up. Every thing is beautiful in its season, and it is good advice, *Prepare thy work, and afterwards build,* Prov. 24:27. 2. Christ would have his Messiahship proved by his works, and would rather *they* should testify of him than that his *disciples* should, because their testimony was but as his own, which he insisted not on. See Jn. 5:31, 34. He was so secure of the demonstration of his miracles, that he waived other witnesses, Jn. 10:25, 38. 3. If they had known *that he was Jesus the Christ, they would not have crucified the Lord of glory,* 1 Co. 2:8. 4. Christ would not have the apostles preach this, till they had the most convincing evidence ready to allege in confirmation of it. Great truths may suffer damage by being asserted before they can be sufficiently proved. Now the great proof of Jesus being the Christ was his resurrection: by that *he was declared to be the Son of God, with power;* and therefore the divine wisdom would not have this truth preached, till that could be alleged for proof of it. 5. It was requisite that the preachers of so great a truth should be furnished with greater measures of the Spirit than the apostles as yet had; therefore the open asserting of it was adjourned till the Spirit should be poured out upon them. But when Christ was glorified and the Spirit poured out, we find Peter proclaiming upon the house-tops what was here spoken in a corner (Acts 2:36), *That God hath made this same Jesus both Lord and Christ;* for, as there is a time to keep silence, so there is a time to speak.

Verses 21–23

We have here Christ's discourse with his disciples concerning his own sufferings; in which observe,

I. Christ's foretelling of his sufferings. Now he *began* to do it, and from this time he frequently spake of them. Some hints he had already given of his sufferings, as when he said,

Destroy this temple: when he spake of *the Son of man being lifted up,* and of *eating his flesh, and drinking his blood:* but now he *began* to show it, to speak plainly and expressly of it. Hitherto he had not touched upon this, because the disciples were weak, and could not well bear the notice of a thing so very strange, and so very melancholy; but now that they were more ripe in knowledge, and strong in faith, he began to tell them this. Note, Christ reveals his mind to his people gradually, and lets in light as they can bear it, and are fit to receive it.

From that time, when they had made that full confession of Christ, that he was the Son of God, then he began to show them this. When he found them knowing in one truth, he taught them another; *for to him that has, shall be given.* Let them first be established in the principles of the doctrine of Christ, and then go on to perfection, Heb. 6:1. If they had not been well grounded in the belief of Christ's being the Son of God, it would have been a great shaking to their faith. All truths are not to be spoken to all persons at all times, but such as are proper and suitable to their present state. Now observe,

1. What he foretold concerning his sufferings, the particulars and circumstances of them, and all surprising.

(1.) The place where he should suffer. He must go to Jerusalem, the head city, the holy city, and suffer there. Though he lived most of his time in Galilee, he must die at Jerusalem; there all the sacrifices were offered, there therefore *he* must die, *who is the great sacrifice.*

(2.) The persons by whom he should suffer; *the elders, and chief priests, and scribes;* these made up the great sanhedrim, which sat at Jerusalem, and was had in veneration by the people. Those that should have been most forward in owning and admiring Christ, were the most bitter in persecuting him. It was strange that men of knowledge in the scripture, who professed to expect the Messiah's coming, and pretended to have something sacred in their character, should use him thus barbarously when he did come. It was the Roman power that condemned and crucified Christ, but he lays it at the door of *the chief priests and scribes,* who were the first movers.

(3.) What he should suffer; *he must suffer many things, and be killed.* His enemies' insatiable malice, and his own invincible patience, appear in the variety and multiplicity of his sufferings (he suffered many things) and in the extremity of them; nothing less than his death would satisfy them, he must be killed. The suffering of many things, if not unto death, is more tolerable; for while there is life, there is hope; and death, without such prefaces, would be less terrible; but *he must* first *suffer many things, and then be killed.*

(4.) What should be the happy issue of all his sufferings; he shall *be raised again the third day.* As the prophets, so Christ himself, when he testified beforehand his sufferings, testified withal the glory that should follow, 1 Pt. 1:11. His rising again the third day proved him to be the Son of God, notwithstanding his sufferings; and therefore he mentions that, to keep up their faith. When he spoke of the cross and the shame, he spoke in the same breath of *the joy set before him,* in the prospect of which *he endured the cross, and despised the shame.* Thus we must look upon Christ's suffering for us, trace in it the way to his glory; and thus we must look upon our suffering for Christ, look through it to the recompence of reward. *If we suffer with him, we shall reign with him.*

2. Why he foretold his sufferings. (1.) To show that they were the product of an eternal counsel and consent; were agreed upon between the Father and the Son from eternity; *Thus is behoved Christ to suffer.* The matter was settled in *the determinate counsel and foreknowledge,* in pursuance of his own voluntary susception and undertaking for our salvation; his sufferings were no surprise to him, did not come upon him as a snare, but he had a distinct and certain foresight of them, which greatly magnifies his love, Jn. 18:4. (2.) To rectify the mistakes which his disciples had imbibed concerning the external pomp and power of his kingdom. Believing him to be the Messiah, they counted upon nothing but dignity and authority in the world; but here Christ reads them another lesson, tells them of the cross and sufferings; nay, that the chief priests and the elders, whom, it is likely, they expected to be the supports of the Messiah's kingdom, should be its great enemies and persecutors; this would give them quite another idea of that kingdom which they themselves had preached the approach of; and it was requisite that this mistake should be rectified. Those that follow Christ must

be dealt plainly with, and warned not to expect great things in this world. (3.) It was to prepare them for the share, at least, of sorrow and fear, which they must have in his sufferings. When he suffered many things, the disciples could not but suffer some; if their Master be killed, they will be seized with terror; let them know it before, that they may provide accordingly, and, being fore-*warned,* may be fore-*armed.*

II. The offence which Peter took at this he said, *Be it far from thee, Lord:* probably he spake the sense of the rest of the disciples, as before, for he was chief speaker. *He took him, and began to rebuke him.* Perhaps Peter was a little elevated with the great things Christ had how said unto him, which made him more bold with Christ than did become him; so hard is it to keep the spirit low and humble in the midst of great advancements!

1. It did not become Peter to contradict his Master, or take upon him to advise him; he might have wished, *that, if it were possible, this cup might pass away,* without saying so peremptorily, *This shall not be,* when Christ had said, It must be. Shall any teach God knowledge? *He that reproveth God, let him answer it.* Note, When God's dispensations are either intricate or cross to us, it becomes us silently to acquiesce in, and not to prescribe to, the divine will; God knows what he has to do, without our teaching. Unless we know the mind of the Lord, it is not for us to be his counsellors, Rom. 11:34.

2. It savoured much of fleshly wisdom, for him to appear so warmly against suffering, and to startle thus at the offence of the cross. It is the corrupt part of us, that is thus solicitous to sleep in a whole skin. We are apt to look upon sufferings as they relate to this present life, to which they are uneasy; but there are other rules to measure them by, which, if duly observed, will enable us cheerfully to bear them, Rom. 8:18. See how passionately Peter speaks: *"Be it far from thee, Lord. God forbid, that thou shouldst suffer and be killed; we cannot bear the thoughts of it." Master, spare thyself:* so it might be read; *hileōs soi, kyrie* — *"Be merciful to thyself,* and then no one else can be cruel to thee; pity thyself, and then *this shall not be to thee."* He would have Christ to dread suffering as much as he did; but we mistake, if we measure Christ's love and patience by our own. He intimates, likewise, the improbability of the thing, humanly speaking; *"This shall not be unto thee.* It is impossible that one who hath so great an interest in the people as thou hast, should be crushed by the elders, who fear the people: this can never be; we that have followed thee, will fight for thee, if occasion be; and there are thousands that will stand by us."

III. Christ's displeasure against Peter for this suggestion of his, *v.* 23. We do not read of any thing said or done by any of his disciples, at any time, that he resented so much as this, though they often offended.

Observe, 1. How he expressed his displeasure: He turned upon Peter, and (we may suppose) with a frown said, *Get thee behind me, Satan.* He did not so much as take time to deliberate upon it, but gave an immediate reply to the temptation, which was such as made it to appear how ill he took it. Just now, he had said, *Blessed art thou, Simon,* and had even laid him in his bosom; but here, *Get thee behind me, Satan;* and there was cause for both. Note, A good man may by a surprise of temptation soon grow very unlike himself. He answered him as he did Satan himself, ch. 4:10. Note, (1.) It is the subtlety of Satan, to send temptations to us by the unsuspected hands of our best and dearest friends. Thus he assaulted Adam by Eve, Job by his wife, and here Christ by his beloved Peter. It concerns us therefore not to be ignorant of his devices, but to stand against his wiles and depths, by standing always upon our guard against sin, whoever moves us to it. Even the kindnesses of our friends are often abused by Satan, and made use of as temptations to us. (2.) Those who have their spiritual senses exercised, will be aware of the voice of Satan, even in a friend, a disciple, a minister, that dissuades them from their duty. We must not regard who speaks, so much as what is spoken; we should learn to know the devil's voice when he speaks in a saint as well as when he speaks in a serpent. Whoever takes us off from that which is good, and would have us afraid of doing too much for God, speaks Satan's language. (3.) We must be free and faithful in reproving the dearest friend we have, that saith or doth amiss, though it may be under colour of kindness to us. We must not compliment, but rebuke, mistaken courtesies. *Faithful are the wounds of a friend.* Such smitings must be accounted kindnesses, Ps. 141:5. (4.) Whatever appears to be a temptation to sin, must be resisted with abhorrence, and not parleyed with.

2. What was the ground of this displeasure; why did Christ thus resent a motion that seemed not only harmless, but kind? Two reasons are given:

(1.) *Thou art an offence to me — Skandalon mou ei — Thou art my hindrance* (so it may be read); "thou standest in my way." Christ was hastening on in the work of our salvation, and his heart was so much upon it, that he took it ill to be hindered, or tempted to start back from the hardest and most discouraging part of his undertaking. So strongly was he engaged for our redemption, that they who but indirectly endeavoured to divert him from it, touched him in a very tender and sensible part. Peter was not so sharply reproved for disowning and denying his Master in his sufferings as he was for dissuading him from them; though that was the defect, this the excess, of kindness. It argues a very great firmness and resolution of mind in any business, when it is *an offence* to be dissuaded, and a man will not endure to hear any thing to the contrary; like that of Ruth, *Entreat me not to leave thee.* Note, Our Lord Jesus preferred our salvation before his own ease and safety; for *even Christ pleased not himself* (Rom. 15:3); he came into the world, not to spare himself, as Peter advised, but to spend himself.

See why he called Peter *Satan,* when he suggested this to him; because, whatever stood in the way of our salvation, he looked upon as coming from the devil, who is a sworn enemy to it. The same Satan that afterward entered into Judas, maliciously to destroy him in his undertaking, here prompted Peter plausibly to divert him from it. Thus *he changes himself into an angel of light.*

Thou art an offence to me. Note, [1.] Those that engage in any great good work must expect to meet with hindrance and opposition from friends and foes, from within and from without. [2.] Those that obstruct our progress in any duty must be looked upon as an offence to us. *Then* we do the will of God as Christ did, *whose meat and drink it was to do it,* when it is a trouble to us to be solicited from our duty. Those that hinder us from doing or suffering for God, when we are called to it, whatever they are in other things in that they are *Satans, adversaries* to us.

(2.) *Thou savourest not the things that are of God, but those that are of men.* Note, [1.] *The things that are of God,* that is, the concerns of his will and glory, often clash and interfere with *the things that are of men,* that is, with our own wealth, pleasure, and reputation. While we mind Christian duty as out way and work, and the divine favour as our end and portion, we *savour the things of God;* but if these be minded, the flesh must be denied, hazards must be run and hardships borne; and here is the trial which of the two we savour. [2.] Those that inordinately fear, and industriously decline suffering for Christ, when they are called to it, savour more of the things of man than of the things of God; they relish those things more themselves, and make it appear to others that they do so.

Verses 24–28

Christ, having shown his disciples that *he* must suffer, and that he was ready and willing to suffer, here shows them that *they* must suffer too, and must be ready and willing. It is a weighty discourse that we have in these verses.

I. Here is the law of discipleship laid down, and the terms fixed, upon which we may have the honour and benefit of it, *v.* 24. He said this to his disciples, not only that they might instruct others concerning it, but that by this rule they might examine their own security. Observe,

1. What it is to be a disciple of Christ; it is to come after him. When Christ called his disciples, this was the word of command, *Follow me.* A true disciple of Christ is one that doth follow him in duty, and shall follow him to glory. He is one that comes after Christ, not one that prescribes to him, as Peter now undertook to do, forgetting his place. A disciple of Christ comes after him, as the sheep after the shepherd, the servant after his master, the soldiers after their captain; he is one that aims at the same end that Christ aimed at, the glory of God, and the glory of heaven: and one that walks in the same way that he walked in, is led by his Spirit, treads in his steps, submits to his conduct, and *follows the Lamb, whithersoever he goes,* Rev. 14:4.

2. What are the great things required of those that will be Christ's disciples; *If any man will come, ei tis thelei — If any man be willing* to come. It denotes a deliberate choice, and cheerfulness and resolution in that choice. Many are disciples more by chance or the will of others than by any act of their own will; but Christ will have his people volunteers, Ps. 110:3. It is as if Christ had said, "If any of the people that are not my disciples, be steadfastly minded to come to me, and if you that are, be in like manner minded to adhere to me, it is upon these terms, these and no other; you must *follow me* in sufferings as well as in other things, and therefore when you sit down to count the cost, reckon upon it."

Now what are these terms?

(1.) *Let him deny himself.* Peter had advised Christ to spare himself, and would be ready, in the like case, to take the advice; but Christ tells them all, they must be so far from *sparing* themselves, that they must *deny* themselves. Herein they must come after Christ, for his birth, and life, and death, were all a continued act of self-denial, a self-emptying, Phil. 2:7, 8. If self-denial be a hard lesson, and against the grain to flesh and blood, it is no more than what our Master learned and practised before us and for us, both for our redemption and for our instruction; and *the servant is not above his lord.* Note, All the disciples and followers of Jesus Christ must deny themselves. It is the fundamental law of admission into Christ's school, and the first and great lesson to be learned in this school, to deny ourselves; it is both the *strait* gate, and the *narrow* way; it is necessary in order to our learning all the other good lessons that are there taught. We must deny ourselves absolutely, we must not admire our own shadow, nor gratify our own humour; we must not lean to our own understanding, nor seek our own things, nor be our own end. We must deny ourselves comparatively; we must deny ourselves for Christ, and his will and glory, and the service of his interest in the world; we must deny ourselves for our brethren, and for their good; and we must deny ourselves for ourselves, deny the appetites of the body for the benefit of the soul.

(2.) *Let him take up his cross.* The cross is here put for all sufferings, as men or Christians; providential afflictions, persecutions for righteousness' sake, every trouble that befals us, either for doing well or for not doing ill. The troubles of Christians are fitly called *crosses,* in allusion to the death of the cross, which Christ was obedient to; and it should reconcile us to troubles, and take off the terror of them, that they are what we bear in common with Christ, and such as he hath borne before us. Note, [1.] Every disciple of Christ hath his cross, and must count upon it; as each hath his special duty to be done, so each hath his special trouble to be borne, and every one feels most from his own burthen. Crosses are the common lot of God's children, but of this common lot of God's children, but of this common lot each hath his particular share. That is our cross which Infinite Wisdom has appointed for us, and a Sovereign Providence has laid on us, as fittest for us. It is good for us to call the cross we are under *our own,* and entertain it accordingly. We are apt to think we could bear such a one's cross better than our own; but that is best which is, and we ought to make the best of it. [2.] Every disciple of Christ must take up that which the wise God hath made his cross. It is an allusion to the Roman custom of compelling those that were condemned to be crucified, to carry their cross: when Simon carried Christ's cross after him, this phrase was illustrated. *First,* It is supposed that the cross lies in our way, and is prepared for us. We must not make crosses to ourselves, but must accommodate ourselves to those which God has made for us. Our rule is, not to go a step out of the way of duty, either to meet a cross, or to miss one. We must not by our rashness and indiscretion pull crosses down upon our own heads, but must take them up when they are laid in our way. We must so manage an affliction, that it may not be a stumbling-block or hindrance to us in any service we have to do for God. We must take it up out of our way, by getting over *the offence of the cross; None of these things move me;* and we must then go on with it in our way, though it lie heavy. *Secondly,* That which we have to do, is, not only to bear the cross (that a stock, or a stone, or a stick may do), not only to be silent under it, but we must *take up* the cross, must improve it to some good advantage. We should not say, "This is an evil, and I must bear it, because I cannot help it;" but, "This is an evil, and I will bear it, because it shall work for my good." When we *rejoice in our afflictions, and glory in them,* then we take up the cross. This fitly follows upon denying ourselves; for he that will not deny himself the pleasures of sin, and the advantages of this world for Christ, when it comes to the push, will never have the heart to take up his cross. "He that cannot take up the resolution to live a saint, has a demonstration within himself, that he is never likely to die a martyr;" so Archbishop Tillotson.

(3.) *Let him follow me,* in this particular of taking up the cross. Suffering saints must look unto Jesus, and take from him both direction and encouragement in suffering. Do we bear the cross? We therein follow Christ, who bears it *before* us, bears it *for* us, and so bears it *from* us. He bore the heavy end of the cross, the end that had the curse upon it, that was a heavy end, and so made the other light and easy for us. Or, we may take it in general, we must follow Christ in all instances of holiness and obedience. Note, The disciples of Christ must study to imitate their Master, and conform themselves in every thing to his example, and continue in well-doing, whatever crosses lie in their way. To do well and to suffer ill, is to follow Christ. *If any man will come after me, let him follow me;* that seems to be *idem per idem — the same thing over again.* What is the difference? Surely it is this, *"If any man will come after me,* in profession, and so have the name and credit of a disciple, *let him follow me in truth,* and so do the work and duty of a disciple." Or thus, *"If any man will set out after me,* in good beginnings, *let him* continue to *follow me* with all perseverance." That is *following the Lord fully,* as Caleb did. Those that come after Christ, must follow after him.

II. Here are arguments to persuade us to submit to these laws, and come up to these terms. Self-denial, and patient suffering, are hard lessons, which will never be learned if we consult with flesh and blood; let us therefore consult with our Lord Jesus, and see what advice he gives us; and here he gives us,

1. Some considerations proper to engage us to these duties of self-denial and suffering for Christ. Consider,

(1.) The weight of that eternity which depends upon our present choice (*v.* 25); *Whosoever will save his life,* by denying Christ, *shall lose it: and whosoever* is content to *lose his life,* for owning Christ, *shall find it.* Here are *life and death, good and evil, the blessing and the curse, set before us.* Observe,

[1.] The misery that attends the most plausible apostasy. *Whosoever will save his life* in this world, if it be by sin, he *shall lose it* in another; he that forsakes Christ, to preserve a temporal life and avoid a temporal death, will certainly come short of eternal life, and will be hurt of the second death, and eternally held by it. There cannot be a fairer pretence for apostasy and iniquity than saving the life by it, so cogent is the law of self-preservation; and yet even that is folly, for it will prove in the end self-destruction; the life saved is but for a moment, the death shunned is but as a sleep; but the life lost is everlasting, and the death run upon is the depth and complement of all misery, and an endless separation from all good. Now, let any rational man consider of it, take advice and speak his mind, whether there is any thing got, at long run, by apostasy, though a man save his estate, preferment, or life, by it.

[2.] The advantage that attends the most perilous and expensive constancy; *Whosoever will lose his life for Christ's sake* in this world, *shall find it* in a better, infinitely to his advantage. Note, *First,* Many a life is lost, for Christ's sake, in doing his work, by labouring fervently for his name; in suffering work, by choosing rather to die than to deny him or his truths and ways. Christ's holy religion is handed down to us, sealed with the blood of thousands, that have *not known their own souls,* but have *despised their lives* (as Job speaks in another case), though very valuable ones, when they have stood in competition with their duty and *the testimony of Jesus,* Rev. 20:4. *Secondly,* Though many have been losers for Christ, even of life itself, yet never any one was, or will be, a loser by him in the end. The loss of other comforts, for Christ, may possibly be made up in this world (Mk. 10:30); the loss of life cannot, but it shall be made up in the other world, in an eternal life; the believing prospect of which hath been the great support of suffering saints in all ages. An assurance of the life they should find, in lieu of the life they hazarded, hath enabled them to triumph over death in all its terrors; to go smiling to a scaffold, and stand singing at a stake, and to call the utmost instances of their enemies' rage but *a light affliction.*

[3.] The worth of the soul which lies at stake, and the worthlessness of the world in comparison of it (*v.* 26). *What is a man profited, if he gain the whole world and lose his own soul? tēn psychēn autou;* the same word which is translated *his life* (*v.* 25), for the *soul* is the *life*, Gen. 2:7. This alludes to that common principle, that, whatever a man gets, if he lose his life, it will do him no good, he cannot enjoy his gains. But it looks higher, and speaks of the soul as immortal, and a loss of it beyond death, which cannot be compensated by the gain of the whole world. Note, *First,* Every man has a soul of his own. The soul is the spiritual and immortal part of man, which thinks and reasons, has a power of reflection and prospect, which actuates the body now, and will shortly act in a separation from the body. Our souls are our own not in respect of dominion and property (for we are not our *own, All souls are mine,* saith God), but in respect of nearness and concern; our souls are our own, for they are ourselves. *Secondly,* It is possible for the soul to be lost, and there is danger of it. The soul is lost when it is eternally separated from all the good to all the evil that a soul is capable of; when it dies as far as a soul can die; when it is separated from the favour of God, and sunk under his wrath and curse. A man is never undone till he is in hell. *Thirdly,* If the soul be lost, it is of the sinner's own losing. The *man loses his own soul,* for he does that which is certainly destroying to it, and neglects that which alone would be saving, Hos. 13:9. The sinner dies because he will die; *hes blood is on his own head. Fourthly,* One soul is worth more than all the world; our own souls are of greater value to us than all the wealth, honour, and pleasures of this present time, if we had them. Here is *the whole world* set in the scale against *one soul,* and *Tekel* written upon it; it is weighed in the balance, and found too light to weigh it down. This is Christ's judgment upon the matter, and he is a competent Judge; he had reason to know the price of *souls,* for he redeemed them; nor would he underrate the world, for he made it. *Fifthly,* The winning of the world is often the losing of the soul. Many a one has ruined his eternal interest by his preposterous and inordinate care to secure and advance his temporal ones. It is *the love of the world,* and the eager pursuit of it, *that drowns men in destruction and perdition. Sixthly,* The loss of the soul is so great a loss, that the gain of the whole world will not countervail it, or make it up. He that loses his soul, though it be to gain the world, makes a very bad bargain for himself, and will sit down at last an unspeakable loser. When he comes to balance the account, and to compare profit and loss, he will find that, instead of the advantage he promised himself, he is ruined to all intents and purposes, is irreparably broken.

What shall a man give in exchange for his soul? Note, If once the soul be lost, it is lost for ever. There is no *antallagma — counter-price,* that can be paid,, or will be accepted. It is a loss that can never be repaired, never be retrieved. If, after that great price which Christ laid down to redeem our souls, and to restore us to the possession of them, they be so neglected for the world, that they come to be lost, that new mortgage will never be taken off; there remains no more sacrifice for sins, nor price for souls, but the equity of redemption is eternally precluded. Therefore it is good to be wise in time, and do well for ourselves.

2. Here are some considerations proper to encourage us in self-denial and suffering for Christ.

(1.) The assurance we have of Christ's glory, at his second coming to judge the world, *v.* 27. If we look to the end of all these things, the period of the world, and the posture of souls then, we shall thence form a very different idea of the present state of things. If we see things as the *will* appear then, we shall see them as they *should* appear now.

The great encouragement to steadfastness in religion is taken from the second coming of Christ, considering it,

[1.] As his honour; *The Son of man shall come in the glory of his Father, with his angels.* To look upon Christ in his state of humiliation, so abased, so abused, *a reproach of men, and despised of the people,* would discourage his followers from taking any pains, or running any hazards for him; but with an eye of faith to see the Captain of our salvation coming in his glory, in all the pomp and power of the upper world, will animate us, and make us think nothing too much to do, or too hard to suffer, or him. *The Son of man shall come.* He here gives himself the title of his humble state (he is the *Son of man),* to show that he is not ashamed to own it. His first coming was in the meanness of his children, who being partakers of flesh, he took part of the same; but his second coming will be in the glory of his Father. At his first coming, he was attended with poor disciples; at his second coming,

he will be attended with glorious angels; and *if we suffer with him, we shall be glorified with him,* 2 Tim. 2:12.

[2.] As our concern; *Then he shall reward every man according to his works.* Observe, *First,* Jesus Christ will come as a Judge, to dispense rewards and punishments, infinitely exceeding the greatest that any earthly potentate has the dispensing of. The terror of men's tribunal (*ch.* 10:18) will be taken off by a believing prospect of the glory of Christ's tribunal. *Secondly,* Men will then be rewarded, not according to their gains in this world, but according to their works, according to what they were and did. In that day, the treachery of backsliders will be punished with eternal destruction, and the constancy of faithful souls recompensed with a crown of life. *Thirdly,* The best preparative for that day is to *deny ourselves, and take up our cross, and follow Christ;* for so we shall make the Judge our Friend, and these things will then pass well in the account. *Fourthly,* The rewarding of men according to their works is deferred till that day. Here good and evil seem to be dispensed promiscuously; we see not apostasy punished with immediate strokes, nor fidelity encouraged with immediate smiles, from heaven; but in that day all will be set to rights. Therefore *judge nothing before the time,* 2 Tim. 4:6–8.

(2.) The near approach of his kingdom in this world, *v.* 28. It was so near, that there were some attending him who should live to see it. As Simeon was assured that he should not see death till he had seen the Lord's Christ come in the flesh; so some here are assured that they shall not taste death (death is a sensible thing, its terrors are seen, its bitterness is tasted) till they had seen the Lord's Christ coming in his kingdom. At the end of time, he shall come in his Father's glory; but now, in the fulness of time, he was to come in his own kingdom, his mediatorial kingdom. Some little specimen was given of his glory a few days after this, in his transfiguration (*ch.* 17:1); then he tried his robes. But this points at Christ's coming by the pouring out of his Spirit, the planting of the gospel church, the destruction of Jerusalem, and the taking away of the place and nation of the Jews, who were the most bitter enemies to Christianity. Here was *the Son of man coming in his kingdom.* Many then present lived to see it, particularly John, who lived till after the destruction of Jerusalem, and saw Christianity planted in the world. Let *this* encourage the followers of Christ to suffer for him, [1.] That their undertaking shall be succeeded; the apostles were employed in setting up Christ's kingdom; let them know, for their comfort, that whatever opposition they meet with, yet they shall carry their point, shall *see of the travail of their soul.* Note, It is a great encouragement to suffering saints to be assured, not only of the safety, but of the advancement of Christ's kingdom among men; not only *notwithstanding* their sufferings, but *by* their sufferings. A believing prospect of the success of the kingdom of grace, as well as of our share in the kingdom of glory, may carry us cheerfully through our sufferings. [2.] That their cause shall be pleaded; their deaths shall be revenged, and their persecutors reckoned with. [3.] That this shall be done shortly, in the present age. Note, The nearer the church's deliverances are, the more cheerful should we be in our sufferings for Christ. *Behold the Judge standeth before the door.* It is spoken as a favour to those that should survive the present cloudy time, that they should see better days. Note, It is desirable to share with the church in her joys, Dan. 12:12. Observe, Christ saith, *Some* shall live to see those glorious days, not *all;* some shall enter into the promised land, but others shall fall in the wilderness. He does not tell them *who* shall live to see this kingdom, lest if they had known, they should have put off the thoughts of dying, but *some* of them shall; *Behold, the Lord is at hand. The Judge standeth before the door; be patient, therefore, brethren.*

CHAPTER 17

In this chapter we have, I. Christ in his pomp and glory transfigured (*v.* 1–13). II. Christ in his power and grace, casting the devil out of a child (*v.* 14–21). And, III. Christ in his poverty and great humiliation, 1. Foretelling his own sufferings (*v.* 22, 23). 2. Paying tribute (*v.* 24–27). So that here is Christ, the Brightness of his Father's glory, by himself purging our sins, paying our debts, and destroying for us him that had the power of death, that is, the devil. Thus were the several indications of Christ's gracious intentions admirable interwoven.

Verses 1–13

We have here thee story o Christ's transfiguration; he ha said that the *Son of man should* shortly *come in his kingdom,* with which promise all the three evangelists industri-

ously connect this story; as if Christ's transfiguration were intended for a specimen and an earnest of the kingdom of Christ, and of that light and love of his, which therein appears to his select and sanctified ones. Peter speaks of this as *the power and coming of our Lord Jesus* (2 Pt. 1:16); because it was an emanation of his power, and a previous notice of his coming, which was fitly introduced by such prefaces.

When Christ was here in his humiliation, though his state, in the main, was a state of abasement and afflictions, there were some glimpses of his glory intermixed, that he himself might be the more encouraged in his sufferings, and others the less offended. His birth, his baptism, his temptation, and his death, were the most remarkable instances of his humiliation; and these were each of them attended with some signal points of glory, and the smiles of heaven. But the series of his public ministry being a continued humiliation, here, just in the midst of that, comes in this discovery of his glory. As, now that he is in heaven, he has his condescensions, so, when he was on earth, he had his advancements.

Now concerning Christ's transfiguration, observe,

I. The circumstances of it, which are here noted, *v.* 1.

1. The time; *six days* after he had the solemn conference with his disciples, *ch.* 16:21. St Luke saith, *It was about eight days after,* six whole days intervening, and this the eighth day, that day seven-night. Nothing is recorded to be said or done by our Lord Jesus for six days before his transfiguration; thus, before some great appearances, *there was silence in heaven for the space of half an hour,* Rev. 8:1. *Then* when Christ seems to be doing nothing for his church, expect, ere long, something more than ordinary.

2. The place; it was *on top of a high mountain apart.* Christ chose a mountain, (1.) As a secret place. He went apart; for though a city upon a hill can hardly be hid, two or three persons upon a hill can hardly be found; therefore their private oratories were commonly on mountains. Christ chose a retired place to be transfigured in, because his appearing publicly in his glory was not agreeable to his present state; and thus he would show his humility, and teach us that privacy much befriends our communion with God. Those that would maintain intercourse with Heaven, must frequently withdraw from the converse and business of this world; and they will find themselves never less alone than when alone, for the Father is with them. (2.) Though a sublime place, elevated above things below. Note, Those that would have a transforming fellowship with God, must not only retire, but ascend; lift up their hearts, and *seek things above.* The call is, *Come up hither,* Rev. 4:1.

3. The witnesses of it. He took with him Peter and James and John. (1.) He took three, a competent number to testify what they should see; for *out of the mouth of two or three witnesses shall every word be established.* Christ makes his appearances certain enough, but not too common; *not to all the people, but to witnesses* (Acts 10:41), that they might be blessed, who have not seen, and yet have believed. (2.) He took these three because they were the chief of his disciples, the first three of the worthies of the Son of David; probably they excelled in gifts and graces; they were Christ's favourites, singled out to be the witnesses of his retirements. They were present when he raised the damsel to life, Mk. 5:37. They were afterward to be the witnesses of his agony, and this was to prepare them for that. Note, A sight of Christ's glory, while we are here in this world, is a good preparative for our sufferings with him, as these are preparatives for the sight of his glory in the other world. Paul, who had abundance of trouble, had abundance of revelations.

II. The manner of it (*v.* 2); *He was transfigured before them.* The substance of his body remained the same, but the accidents and appearances of it were greatly altered; he was not turned into a spirit, but his body, which had appeared in weakness and dishonour, now appeared in power and glory. *He was transfigured, metamorphōthē — he was metamorphosed.* The profane poets amused and abused the world with idle extravagant stories of metamorphoses, especially the metamorphoses of their gods, such as were disparaging and diminishing to them, equally false and ridiculous; to these some think Peter has an eye, when, being about to mention this transfiguration of Christ, he saith, *We have not followed cunningly devised fables when we made it known unto you,* 2 Pt. 1:16. Christ was both God and man; but, in the days of his flesh, he took on him the *form of a servant — morphēn doulou,* Phil. 2:7. He drew a veil over the glory of his godhead; but now, in his transfiguration, he put by that veil, appeared *en morphē theou* — in the form of God (Phil. 2:6), and gave his disciples a glimpse of his glory, which could not but change his form.

The great truth which we declare, is, that *God is light* (1 Jn. 1:5), *dwells in the light* (1 Tim. 6:16), *covers himself with light,* Ps. 104:2. And therefore when Christ would appear in the *form of God,* he appeared *in light,* the most glorious of all visible beings, the first-born of the creation, and most nearly resembling the eternal Parent. Christ is *the Light;* while he was in the world, he *shined in darkness,* and therefore *the world knew him not* (Jn. 1:5, 10); but, at this time, that Light shined out of the darkness.

Now his transfiguration appeared in two things:

1. *His face did shine as the sun.* The face is the principal part of the body, by which we are known; therefore such a brightness was put on Christ's face, that face which afterward *he hid not from shame and spitting.* It shone as the sun when he goes forth in his strength, so clear, so bright; for he is the Sun of righteousness, the Light of the world. The face of Moses shone but as the moon, with a borrowed reflected light, but Christ's shone as the sun, with an innate inherent light, which was the more sensibly glorious, because it suddenly broke out, as it were, from behind a black cloud.

2. *His raiment was white as the light.* All his body was altered, as his face was; so that beams of light, darting from every part through his clothes, made them white and glittering. The shining of the face of Moses was so weak, that it could easily be concealed by a thin veil; but such was the glory of Christ's body, that his clothes were enlightened by it.

III. The companions of it. He will come, at last, *with ten thousands of his saints;* and, as a specimen of that, there now *appeared unto them Moses and Elias talking with him, v.* 3. Observe, 1. There were glorified saints attending him, that, when there were *three to bear record on earth,* Peter, James, and John, there might be some to bear record from heaven too. Thus here was a lively resemblance of Christ's kingdom, which is made up of saints in heaven and saints on earth, and to which belong *the spirits of just men made perfect.* We see here, that they who are fallen asleep in Christ are not perished, but exist in a separate state, and shall be forthcoming when there is occasion. 2. These two were Moses and Elias, men very eminent in their day. They had both fasted forty days and forty nights, as Christ did, and wrought other miracles, and were both remarkable at their going out of the world as well as in their living in the world. Elias was carried to heaven in a fiery chariot, and died not. The body of Moses was never found, possibly it was preserved from corruption, and reserved for this appearance. The Jews had great respect for the memory of Moses and Elias, and therefore they came to witness of him, they came to carry tidings concerning him to the upper world. In them the law and the prophets honoured Christ, and bore testimony to him. Moses and Elias appeared to the disciples; they saw them, and heard them talk, and, either by their discourse or by information from Christ, they knew them to be Moses and Elias; glorified saints shall know one another in heaven. They talked with Christ. Note, Christ has communion with the blessed, and will be no stranger to any of the members of that glorified corporation. Christ was now to be sealed in his prophetic office, and therefore these two great prophets were fittest to attend him, as transferring all their honour and interest to him; for *in these last days God speaks to us by his Son,* Heb. 1:1.

IV. The great pleasure and satisfaction that the disciples took in the sight of Christ's glory. Peter, as usual, spoke or the rest; *Lord, it is good for us to be here.* Peter here expresses,

1. The delight they had in this converse; *Lord, it is good to be here.* Though upon a high mountain, which we may suppose rough and unpleasant, bleak and cold, yet *it is good to be here.* He speaks the sense of his fellow-disciples; It is good not only for *me,* but for *us.* He did not covet to monopolize this favour, but gladly takes them in. He saith this to Christ. Pious and devout affections love to pour out themselves before the Lord Jesus. The soul that loves Christ, and loves to be with him, loves to go and tell him so; *Lord, it is good for us to be here.* This intimates a thankful acknowledgment of his kindness in admitting them to this favour. Note, Communion with Christ is the delight of Christians. All the disciples of the Lord Jesus reckon it is good for them to be with him in the holy mount. It is good to be here where Christ is, and whither he brings us along with him by his appointment; it is good to be here, retired and alone with Christ; to be here, where we may behold the beauty of the Lord Jesus, Ps. 27:4. It is pleasant to hear Christ compare notes with Moses and the prophets, to see how all the institutions of the law, and all the predictions of the prophets, pointed at Christ, and were fulfilled in him.

2. The desire they had of the continuance of it; *Let us make here three tabernacles.* There was in this, as in many other of Peter's sayings, a mixture of weakness and of goodwill, more zeal than discretion.

(1.) Here was a zeal for this converse with heavenly things, a laudable complacency in the sight they had of Christ's glory. Note, Those that by faith *behold the beauty of the Lord* in his house, cannot but desire to *dwell there all the days of their life.* It is good having a nail in God's holy place (Ezra 9:8), a constant abode; to be in holy ordinances as a man at home, not as a wayfaring man. Peter thought this mountain was a fine spot of ground to build upon, and he was for making tabernacles there; as Moses in the wilderness made a tabernacle for the Shechinah, or divine glory.

It argued great respect for his Master and the heavenly guests, with some commendable forgetfulness of himself and his fellow-disciples, that he would have tabernacles for Christ, and Moses, and Elias, but none for himself. He would be content to lie in the open air, on the cold ground, in such good company; if his Master have but where to lay his head, no matter whether he himself has or no.

(2.) Yet in this zeal he betrayed a great deal of weakness and ignorance. What need had Moses and Elias of tabernacles? They belonged to that blessed world, *where they hunger no more, nor doth the sun light upon them.* Christ had lately foretold his sufferings, and bidden his disciples expect the like; Peter forgets this, or, to prevent it, will needs be building tabernacles in the mount of glory, out of the way of trouble. Still he harps upon, *Master, spare thyself,* though he had been so lately checked for it. Note, There is a proneness in good men to expect the crown without the cross. Peter was for laying hold of this as the prize, though he had not yet fought his fight, nor finished his course, as those other disciples, *ch.* 20:21. We are out in our aim, if we look for a heaven here upon earth. It is not for strangers and pilgrims (such as we are in our best circumstances in this world), to talk of building, or to expect a continuing city.

Yet it is some excuse for the incongruity of Peter's proposal, not only that *he knew not what he said* (Lu. 9:33), but also that he submitted the proposal to the wisdom of Christ; *If thou wilt, let us make tabernacles.* Note, Whatever tabernacles we propose to make to ourselves in this world, we must always remember to ask Christ's leave.

Now to this which Peter said, there was no reply made; the disappearing of the glory would soon answer it. They that promise themselves great things on earth will soon be undeceived by their own experience.

V. The glorious testimony which God the Father gave to our Lord Jesus, in which *he received from him honour and glory* (2 Pt. 1:17), when *there came this voice from the excellent glory.* This was like proclaiming the titles of honour or the royal style of a prince, when, at his coronation, he appears in his robes of state; and be it known, to the comfort of mankind, the royal style of Christ is taken from his mediation. Thus, in vision, he appeared with a rainbow, the seal of the covenant, about his throne (Rev. 4:3); for it is his glory to be our Redeemer.

Now concerning this testimony from heaven to Christ, observe.

1. How it came, and in what manner it was introduced.

(1.) There was a cloud. We find often in the Old Testament, that a cloud was the visible token of God's presence; he came down upon mount Sinai in a cloud (Ex. 19:9), and so to Moses, Ex. 34:5; Num. 11:25. He took possession of the tabernacle in a cloud, and afterwards of the temple; where Christ was in his glory, the temple was, and there God showed himself present. We know not the balancing of the clouds, but we know that much of the intercourse and communication between heaven and earth is maintained by them. By the clouds vapours *as*cend, and rains *de*scend; therefore God is said to make *the clouds his chariots;* so he did here when he descended upon this mount.

(2.) It was a bright cloud. Under the law it was commonly a thick and dark cloud that God made the token of his presence; he came down upon mount Sinai in a thick cloud (Ex. 19:16), and said he would *dwell in thick darkness;* see 1 Ki. 8:12. But *we are now come, not to the mount that was covered with thick blackness and darkness* (Heb. 12:18), but to the mount that is crowned with a bright cloud. Both the Old-Testament and the New-Testament dispensation had tokens of God's presence; but that was a dispensation of darkness, and terror, and bondage, this of light, love, and liberty.

(3.) It overshadowed them. This cloud was intended to break the force of that great light which otherwise would have overcome the disciples, and have been intolerable; it was like the veil which Moses put upon his face when it shone. God, in manifesting himself to his people, considers their frame. This cloud was to their eyes as parables to their understandings, to convey spiritual things by things sensible, as they were able to bear them.

(4.) *There came a voice out of the cloud,* and it was the voice of God, who now, as of old, *spake in the cloudy pillar,* Ps. 99:7. Here was no thunder, or lightning, or voice of a trumpet, as there was when the law was given by Moses, but only a voice, a still small voice, and that not ushered in with a strong wind, or an earthquake, or fire, as when God spake to Elias, 1 Ki. 19:11, 12. Moses then and Elias were witnesses, that *in these last days God hath spoken to us by his Son,* in another way than he spoke formerly to them. This voice came from the excellent glory (2 Pt. 1:17), the glory which excelleth, in comparison of which the former had no glory; though the excellent glory was clouded, yet thence came a voice, for *faith comes by hearing.*

2. What this testimony from heaven was; *This is my beloved Son, hear ye him.* Here we have,

(1.) The great gospel mystery revealed; *This is my beloved Son, in whom I am well pleased.* This was the very same that was spoken from heaven at his baptism (*ch.* 3:17); and it was the best news that ever came from heaven to earth since man sinned. It is to the same purport with that great doctrine (2 Co. 5:19), *That God was in Christ, reconciling the world unto himself.* Moses and Elias were great men, and favourites of Heaven, yet they were but servants, and servants that God was not always well pleased in; for Moses spoke unadvisedly, and Elias was a man subject to passions; but Christ is *a Son,* and in him God was always well pleased. Moses and Elias were sometimes instruments of reconciliation between God and Israel; Moses was a great intercessor, and Elias a great reformer; but in Christ God is reconciling the world; his intercession is more prevalent than that of Moses, and his reformation more effectual than that of Elias.

This repetition of the same voice that came from heaven at his baptism was no vain repetition; but, like the doubling of Pharoah's dream, was to show the thing was established. What God hath thus spoken once, yea twice, no doubt he will stand to, and he expects we should take notice of it. It was spoken at his baptism, because then he was entering upon his temptation, and his public ministry; and now it was repeated, because he was entering upon his sufferings, which are to be dated from hence; for now, and not before, he began to foretel them, and immediately after his transfiguration it is said (Lu. 9:51), that *the time was come that he should be received up;* this therefore was then repeated, to arm him against the terror, and his disciples against the offence, of the cross. When sufferings begin to abound, consolations are given in more abundantly, 2 Co. 1:5.

(2.) The great gospel duty required, and it is the condition of our benefit by Christ; *Hear ye him.* God is well pleased with none in Christ but those that hear him. It is not enough to give him the hearing (what will that avail us?) but we must hear him and believe him, as the great Prophet and Teacher; hear him, and be ruled by him, as the great Prince and Lawgiver; hear him, and heed him. Whoever would know the mind of God, must hearken to Jesus Christ; for by him God has in these last days spoken to us. This voice from heaven has made all the sayings of Christ as authentic as if they had been thus spoken out of a cloud. God does here, as it were, turn us over to Christ for all the revelations of his mind; and it refers to that prediction concerning *the Prophet God would raise up like unto Moses* (Deu. 18:18); *him shall ye hear.*

Christ now appeared in glory; and the more we see of Christ's glory, the more cause we shall see to hearken to him: but the disciples were gazing on that glory of his which they saw; they are therefore bid not to look at him, but to hear him. Their sight of his glory was soon intercepted by the cloud, but their business was to hear him. We walk *by faith,* which *comes by hearing,* not *by sight,* 2 Co. 5:7.

Moses and Elias were now with him; the law and the prophets; hitherto it was said, *Hear them,* Lu. 16:29. The disciples were ready to equal them with Christ, when they must have tabernacles for them as well as for him. They had been talking with Christ, and probably the disciples were very desirous to know what they said, and to hear something more from them; No, saith God, *hear him,* and that is enough; him, and not Moses and Elias, who were present, and whose silence gave consent to this voice; they had nothing to say to the contrary; whatever interest they had in the world as prophets, they were willing to see it all transferred to Christ, that in *all things he might have the pre-eminence.* Be not troubled that Moses and Elias make so short a stay with you; hear Christ, and you will not want them.

IV. The fright which the disciples were put into by this voice, and the encouragement Christ gave them.

1. The disciples *fell on their faces, and were sore afraid.* The greatness of the light, and the surprise of it, might have a natural influence upon them, to dispirit them. But that was not all, ever since man sinned, and heard God's voice in the garden, extraordinary appearances of God have ever been terrible to man, who, knowing he has no reason to expect any good, has been afraid to hear any thing immediately from God. Note, even then when *fair weather* comes *out of the secret place,* yet *with God* is *terrible majesty,* Job 37:22. See what dreadful work *the voice of the Lord makes,* Ps. 29:4. It is well for us that God speaks to us by men like ourselves, whose terror shall not make us afraid.

2. Christ graciously raised them up with abundance of tenderness. Note, The glories and advancements of our Lord Jesus do not at all lessen his regard to, and concern for, his people that are compassed about with infirmity. It is comfortable to think, that now, in his exalted state, he has a compassion for, and condescends to, the meanest true believer. Observe here, (1.). What he did; *he came, and touched them.* His approaches banished their fears; and when they apprehended that they were apprehended of Christ, there needed no more to make them easy. Christ laid his right hand upon John is a like case, and upon Daniel, Rev. 1:17; Dan. 8:18; 10:18. Christ's touches were often healing, and here they were strengthening and comforting. (2.) What he said; *Arise, and be not afraid.* Note, Though a fear of reverence in our converse with Heaven is pleasing to Christ, yet a fear of amazement is not so, but must be striven against. Christ said, *Arise.* Note, It is Christ by his word, and the power of his grace going along with it, that raises up good men from their dejections, and silences their fears; and none but Christ can do it; *Arise, be not afraid.* Note, causeless fears would soon vanish, if we would not yield to them, and lie down under them, but get up, and do what we can against them. considering what they had seen and heard, they had more reason to rejoice than to fear, and yet, it seems, they needed this caution. Note, Through the infirmity of the flesh, we often frighten ourselves with that wherewith we should encourage ourselves. Observe, After they had an express command from heaven to hear Christ, the first word they had from him was, *Be not afraid,* hear that. Note, Christ's errand into the world was to give comfort to good people, that, being delivered out of the hands of their enemies, they might *serve God without fear,* Lu. 1:74, 75.

VII. The disappearing of the vision (*v.* 8); *They* lift up themselves, and then *lift up their eyes,* and *saw no man, save Jesus only.* Moses and Elias were gone, the rays of Christ's glory were laid aside, or veiled again. They hoped this had been the day of Christ's entrance into his kingdom, and his public appearance in that external splendour which they dreamed of; but see how they are disappointed. Note, It is not wisdom to raise our expectations high in this world, for the most valuable of our glories and joys here are vanishing, even those of near communion with God are so, not a continual feast, but a running banquet. If sometimes we are favoured with special manifestations of divine grace, glimpses and pledges of future glory, yet they are withdrawn presently; two heavens are too much for those to expect that never deserve one. Now *they saw no man, save Jesus only.* Note, Christ will tarry with us when Moses and Elias are gone. The *prophets do not live for ever* (Zec. 1:5), and we see the period of our ministers' conversation; but *Jesus Christ is the same yesterday, today, and for ever,* Heb. 13:7, 8.

VIII. The discourse between Christ and his disciples as they came down from the mountain, *v.* 9–13.

Observe, 1. *They came down from the mountain.* Note, We must come down from the holy mountains, where we have communion with God, and complacency in that communion, and of which we are saying. *It is good to be here;* even there we have no continuing city. Blessed be God, there is a mountain of glory and joy before us, whence we shall never come down. But observe, When the disciples came down, Jesus came with them. Note, When we return to the world again after an ordinance, it must be our care to take Christ with us, and then it may be our comfort that he is with us.

2. As they came down, they talked of Christ. Note, When we are returning from holy ordinance, it is good to entertain ourselves and one another with discourse suitable to the work we have been about. That communication which is good to the use of edifying is then in a special manner seasonable; as, on the contrary, that which is corrupt, is worse then than at another time.

Here is, (1.) The charge that Christ gave the disciples to keep the vision very private for the present (*v.* 9); *Tell it to no man till the Son of man is risen.* If they had proclaimed it, the credibility of it would have been shocked by his sufferings, which were now hastening on. But let the publication of it be adjourned till after his resurrection, and then that and his subsequent glory will be a great confirmation of it. Note, Christ observed a method in the manifestation of himself; he would have his works put together, mutually to explain and illustrate each other, that they might appear in their full strength and convincing evidence. Every thing is beautiful in its season. Christ's resurrection was properly the beginning of the gospel state and kingdom, to which all before was but preparatory and by way of preface; and therefore, though this was transacted before, it must not be produced as evidence till then (and then it appears to have been much insisted on by 2 Pt. 1:16–18), when the religion it was designed for the confirmation of was brought to its full consistence and maturity. Christ's time is the best and fittest for the manifesting of himself and must be attended to by us.

(2.) An objection which the disciples made against something Christ had said (*v.* 10); *"Why then say the scribes that Elias must first come?* If Elias make so short a stay, and is gone so suddenly, and we must say nothing of him; why have we been taught out of the law to expect his public appearance in the world immediately before the setting up of the Messiah's kingdom? Must the coming of Elias be a secret, which every body looks for?" or thus; "If the resurrection of the Messiah, and with it the beginning of his kingdom, be at hand, what becomes of that glorious preface and introduction to it, which we expect in the coming of Elias?" The scribes, who were the public expositors of the law, said this according to the scripture (Mal. 4:5); *Behold I send you Elijah the prophet.* The disciples spoke the common language of the Jews, who made that the saying of the scribes which was the saying of the scripture, whereas of that which ministers speak to us according to the word of God, we should say, *"God* speaks to us, not the *ministers;"* for we must not receive it *as the word of men,* 1 Th. 2:13. Observe, When the disciples could not reconcile what Christ said with what they had heard out of the Old Testament, they desired him to explain it to them. Note, When we are puzzled with scripture difficulties, we must apply ourselves to Christ by prayer for his Spirit to open our understandings and to lead us into all truth.

(3.) The solving of this objection. *Ask, and it shall be given,* ask instruction, and it shall be given.

[1.] Christ allows the prediction (*v.* 11); *"Elias truly shall first come, and restore all things;* so far you are in the right." Christ did not come to alter or invalidate any thing foretold in the Old Testament. Note, Corrupt and mistaken glosses may be sufficiently rejected and exploded, without diminishing or derogating from the authority or dignity of the sacred text. New-Testament prophecies are true and good, and are to be received and improved, though some hot foolish men may have misinterpreted them and drawn wrong inferences from them. He shall come, and restore all things; not restore them to their former state (John Baptist went not about to do that), but he shall accomplish all things (so it may be read), all things that were written of him, all the predictions of the coming of Elias. John Baptist came to restore things spiritually, to revive the decays of religion, to *turn the hearts of the fathers to the children;* which means the same with this, *he shall restore all things.* John preached repentance, and that restores all things.

[2.] He asserts the accomplishment. The scribes say true, that *Elias is come, v.* 12. Note, God's promises are often fulfilled, and men perceive it not, but enquire, *Where is the promise?* when it is already performed. *Elias is come, and they knew him not;* they knew him not to be the Elias promised, the forerunner of the Messiah. The scribes busied themselves in criticizing upon the scripture, but understood not by the signs of the times the fulfilling of the scripture. Note, It is easier to explain the word of God than to apply it and make a right use of it. But it is no wonder that the morning star was not observed, when he who is the Sun itself, was *in the world, and the world knew him not.*

Because they knew him not, *they have done to him whatsoever they listed;* if they had known, they would not have crucified Christ, or beheaded John, 1 Co. 2:8. They ridiculed John, persecuted him, and at last put him to death; which was Herod's doing, but is here charged upon the whole generation of unbelieving Jews, and particularly the scribes, who, though they could not prosecute John themselves, were pleased with what Herod did. He adds, *Likewise also shall the Son of man suffer of them.* Marvel not that Elias should be abused and killed by those who pretended, with a great deal of reverence, to expect him, when the Messiah himself will be in like manner treated. Note, The sufferings of Christ took off the strangeness of all other sufferings (Jn. 15:18); when they had imbrued their hands in the blood of John Baptist, they were ready to do the like to Christ. Note, As men deal with Christ's servants, so they would deal with him himself; and they that are drunk with the blood of the martyrs still cry, *Give, give,* Acts 12:1–3.

(4.) The disciples' satisfaction in Christ's reply to their objection (*v.* 13); *They understood that he spake unto them of John the Baptist.* He did not name John, but gives them such a description of him as would put them in mind of what he had said to them formerly concerning him; *This is Elias.* This is a profitable way of teaching; it engages the learners' own thoughts, and makes them, if not their own teachers, yet their own remembrancers; and thus knowledge becomes easy to him that understands. When we diligently use the means of knowledge, how strangely are mists scattered and mistakes rectified!

Verses 14–21

We have here the miraculous cure of a child that was lunatic and vexed with a devil. Observe,

I. A melancholy representation of the case of this child, made to Christ by the afflicted father. This was immediately upon his coming down from the mountain where he was transfigured. Note, Christ's glories do not make him unmindful of us and of our wants and miseries. Christ, when he came down from the mount, where had conversation with Moses and Elias, did not take state upon him, but was as easy of access, as ready to poor beggars, and as familiar with the multitude, as ever he used to be. This poor man's address was very importunate; he came kneeling to Christ. Note, Sense of misery will bring people to their knees. Those who see their need of Christ will be earnest, will be in good earnest, in their applications to him; and he delights to be thus wrestled with.

Two things the father of the child complains of.

1. The distress of his child (*v.* 15); *Lord have mercy on my son.* The affliction of the children cannot but affect the tender parents, for they are pieces of themselves. And the case of afflicted children should be presented to God by faithful and fervent prayer. This child's distemper, probably, disabled him to pray for himself. Note, Parents are doubly concerned to pray for their children, not only that are weak and cannot, but much more that are wicked and will not, pray for themselves. Now, (1.). The nature of this child's disease was very sad; *He was lunatic and sore vexed.* A lunatic is properly one whose distemper lies in the brain, and returns with the change of the moon. The devil, by the divine permission, either caused this distemper, or at least concurred with it, to heighten and aggravate it. The child had the falling-sickness, and the hand of Satan was in it; by it he tormented then, and made it much more grievous than ordinarily it is. Those whom Satan got possession of, he afflicted by those diseases of the body which do most affect the mind; for it is the soul that he aims to do mischief to. The father, in his complain, saith, *He is lunatic,* taking notice of the effect; but Christ, in the cure, rebuked the devil, and so struck at the cause. Thus he doth in spiritual cures. (2.) The effects of the disease were very deplorable; *He oft falls into the fire, and into the water.* If the force of the disease made him to fall,

the malice of the devil made him to fall into the fire or water; so mischievous is he where he gains possession and power in any soul. He *seeks to devour,* 1 Pt. 5:8.

2. The disappointment of his expectation from the disciples (*v.* 16); *I brought him to thy disciples, and they could not cured him.* Christ gave his disciples power to cast out devils (*ch.* 10:1, 8), and therein they were successful (Lu. 10:17); yet at this time they failed in the operation, though there were nine of them together, and before a great multitude. Christ permitted this, (1.) To keep them humble, and to show their dependence upon him, that without him they could do nothing. (2.) To glorify himself and his own power. It is for the honour of Christ to come in with help at a dead-lift, when other helpers cannot help. Elisha's staff in Gehazi's hand will not raise the child: he must come himself. Note, There are some special favours which Christ reserves the bestowment of to himself; and sometimes he keeps the cistern empty; that he may bring us to himself, the Fountain. But the failures of instruments shall not hinder the operations of his grace, which will work, if not *by* them, yet *without* them.

II. The rebukes that Christ gave to the people first, and then to the devil.

1. He chid those about him (*v.* 17); *O faithless and perverse generation!* This is not spoken to the disciples, but to the people, and perhaps especially to the scribes, who are mentioned in Mk. 9:14, and who, as it should seem, insulted over the disciples, because they had now met with a case that was too hard for them. Christ himself could not do many mighty works among a people in whom unbelief reigned. It was here owing to the faithlessness of this generation, that they could not obtain those blessings from God, which otherwise they might have had; as it was owing to the weakness of the disciples' faith, that they could not do those works for God, which otherwise they might have done. They were faithless and perverse. Note, Those that are faithless will be perverse; and perverseness is sin in its worst colours. Faith is compliance with God, unbelief is opposition and contradiction to God. Israel of old was perverse, because faithless (Ps. 95:9), forward, for in them is no faith, Deu. 32:20.

Two things he upbraids them with. (1.) His presence with them so long; *"How long shall I be with you?* Will you always need my bodily presence, and never come to such maturity as to be fit to be left, the people to the conduct of the disciples, and the disciples to the conduct of the Spirit and of their commission? Must the child be always carried, and will it never learn to go alone?" (2.) His patience with them so long; *How long shall I suffer you?* Note, [1.] The faithlessness and perverseness of those who enjoy the means of grace are a great grief to the Lord Jesus. Thus did he suffer the manners of Israel of old, Acts 13:18. [2.] The longer Christ has borne with a perverse and faithless people, the more he is displeased with their perverseness and unbelief; and he is God, and not man, else he would not suffer so long, nor bear so much, as he doth.

2. He cured the child, and set him to-rights again. He called, *Bring him hither to me.* Though the people were perverse, and Christ was provoked, yet care was taken of the child. Note, Though Christ may be angry, he is never unkind, nor doth he, in the greatest of his displeasure, shut up the bowels of his compassion from the miserable; *Bring him to me.* Note, When all other helps and succours fail, we are welcome to Christ, and may be confident in him and in his power and goodness.

See here an emblem of Christ's undertaking as our Redeemer.

(1.) He breaks the power of Satan (*v.* 18); *Jesus rebuked the devil,* as one having authority, who could back with force his word of command. Note, Christ's victories over Satan are obtained by the power of his word, the sword that comes out of his mouth, Rev. 19:21. Satan cannot stand before the rebukes of Christ, though his possession has been ever so long. It is comfortable to those who are wrestling with principalities and powers, that Christ hath spoiled them, Colos. 2:15. The lion of the tribe of Judah will be too hard for the roaring lion that seeks to devour.

(2.) He redresses the grievances of the children of men; *The child was cured from that very hour.* It was an immediate cure, and a perfect one. This is an encouragement to parents to bring their children to Christ, whose souls are under Satan's power; he is able to heal them, and as willing as he is able. Not only bring them to Christ by prayer, but bring them to the word of Christ, the ordinary means by which Satan's strongholds are demolished in the soul. Christ's rebukes, brought home to the heart, will ruin Satan's power there.

III. Christ's discourse with his disciples hereupon.

1. They ask the reason why they could not cast out the devil at this time (*v.* 19); *They came to Jesus apart.* Note, Ministers, who are to deal for Christ in public, have need to keep up a private communion with him, that they may in secret, where no eye sees, bewail their weakness and straitness, their follies and infirmities, in their public performances, and enquire into the cause of them. We should make use of the liberty of access we have to Jesus apart, where we may be free and particular with him. Such questions as the disciples put to Christ, we should put to ourselves, in communing with our own hearts upon our beds; Why were we so dull and careless at such a time? Why came we so much short in such a duty? That which is amiss may, when found out, be amended.

2. Christ gives them two reasons why they failed.

(1.) It was *because of their unbelief, v.* 20. When he spake to the father of the child and to the people, he charged it upon their unbelief; when he spake to his disciples, he charged it upon theirs; for the truth was, there were faults on both sides; but we are more concerned to hear of our own faults than of other people's, and to impute what is amiss to ourselves than to others. When the preaching of the word seems not to be so successful as sometimes it has been, the people are apt to lay all the fault upon the ministers, and the ministers upon the people; whereas, it is more becoming for each to own his own faultiness, and to say, "It is owing to me." Ministers, in reproving, must learn thus to give to each his portion of the word; and to take people off from judging others, by teaching all to judge themselves; *It is because of your unbelief.* Though they had faith, yet that faith was weak and ineffectual. Note, [1.] As far as faith falls short of its due strength, vigour, and activity, it may truly be said, "There is unbelief." Many are chargeable with unbelief, who yet are not to be called *unbelievers.* [2.] It is because of our unbelief, that we bring so little to pass in religion, and so often miscarry, and come short, in that which is good.

Our Lord Jesus takes this occasion to show them the power of faith, that they might not be defective in that, another time, as they were now; *If ye have faith as a grain of mustard-seed,* ye shall do wonders, *v.* 20. Some make the comparison to refer to the quality of the mustard-seed, which is, when bruised, sharp and penetrating; "If you have an active growing faith, not dead, flat, or insipid, you will not be baffled thus." But it rather refers to the quantity; "If you had but a grain of true faith, though so little that it were like that which is the least of all seeds, you would do wonders." Faith in general is a firm assent to, a compliance with, and a confidence in, all divine revelation. The faith here required, is that which had for its object that particular revelation by which Christ gave his disciples power to work miracles in his name, for the confirmation of the doctrine they preached. It was a faith in this revelation that they were defective in; either doubting the validity of their commission, or fearing that it expired with their first mission, and was not to continue when they were returning to their Master; or that it was some way or other forfeited or withdrawn. Perhaps their Master's absence with the three chief of his disciples, with a charge to the rest not to follow them, might occasion some doubts concerning their power, or rather the power of the Lord with them, to do this; however, there were not, at present, such a strong actual dependence upon, and confidence in, the promise of Christ's presence with them, as there should have been. It is good for us to be diffident of ourselves and of our own strength; but it is displeasing to Christ, when we distrust any power derived from him or granted by him.

If ye have ever so little of this faith in sincerity, if ye truly rely upon the powers committed to you, *ye shall say to this mountain, Remove.* This is a proverbial expression, denoting that which follows, and no more, *Nothing shall be impossible to you.* They had a full commission, among other things, to cast out devils without exception; but, this devil being more than ordinarily malicious and inveterate, they distrusted the power they had received, and so failed. To convince them of this, Christ shows them what they might have done. Note, An active faith can remove mountains, not of itself, but in the virtue of a divine power engaged by a divine promise, both which faith fastens upon.

(2.) Because there was something in the kind of the malady, which rendered the cure more than ordinarily difficult (*v.* 21); *"This kind goes not out but by prayer and fasting.* This possession, which works by a falling-sickness, or this kind of devils that are thus furious, is not cast out ordinarily but by great acts of devotion, and wherein ye were defective." Note, [1.] Though the adversaries we wrestle, be all principalities and powers, yet some are stronger than others, and their power more hardly broken. [2.] The extraordinary power of Satan must not discourage our faith, but quicken us to a greater intenseness in the acting of it, and more earnestness in praying to God for the increase of it; so some understand it here; "This kind of faith (which removeth mountains) doth not proceed, is not obtained, from God, nor is it carried up to its full growth, nor drawn out into act and exercise, but by earnest prayer." [3.] Fasting and prayer are proper means for the bringing down of Satan's power against us, and the fetching in of divine power to our assistance. Fasting is of use to put an edge upon prayer; it is an evidence and instance of humiliation which is necessary in prayer, and is a means of mortifying some corrupt habits, and of disposing the body to serve the soul in prayer. When the devil's interest in the soul is confirmed by the temper and constitution of the body, fasting must be joined with prayer, to keep under the body.

Verses 22–23

Christ here foretels his own sufferings; he began to do it before (*ch.* 16:21); and, finding that it was to his disciples a hard saying, he saw it necessary to repeat it. There are some things which *God speaketh once, yea twice, and yet man perceiveth it not.* Observe here,

1. What he foretold concerning himself — that he should be betrayed and killed. He perfectly knew, before, all things that should come to him, and yet undertook the work of our redemption, which greatly commends his love; nay, his clear foresight of them was a kind of ante-passion, had not his love to man made all easy to him.

(1.) He tells them that he should *be betrayed into the hands of men.* He *shall be delivered up* (so it might be read and understood of his Father's delivering him up *by his determined counsel and fore-knowledge,* Acts 2:23; Rom. 8:32); but as we render it, it refers to Judas's betraying him into the hands of the priests, and their betraying him into the hands of the Romans. He was *betrayed into the hands of men;* men to whom he was allied by nature, and from whom therefore he might expect pity and tenderness; men whom he had undertaken to save, and from whom therefore he might expect honour and gratitude; yet these are his persecutors and murderers.

(2.) That *they should kill him;* nothing less than that would satisfy their rage; it was his blood, his precious blood, that they thirsted after. *This is the heir, come, let us kill him.* Nothing less would satisfy God's justice, and answer his undertaking; if he be a Sacrifice of atonement, he must be killed; without blood no remission.

(3.) That *he shall be raised again the third day.* Still, when he spoke of his death, he gave a hint of his resurrection, *the joy set before him,* in the prospect of which *he endured the cross, and despised the shame.* This was an encouragement, not only to him, but to his disciples; for if he rise the third day, his absence from them will not be long, and his return to them will be glorious.

2. How the disciples received this; *They were exceedingly sorry.* Herein appeared their love to their Master's person, but with all their ignorance and mistake concerning his undertaking. Peter indeed durst not say any thing against it, as he had done before (*ch.* 16:22), having then been severely chidden for it; but he, and the rest of them, greatly lamented it, as it would be their own loss, their Master's grief, and the sin and ruin of them that did it.

Verses 24–27

We have here an account of Christ's paying tribute.

I. Observe how it was demanded, *v.* 24. Christ was now at Capernaum, his headquarters, where he mostly resided; he did not keep from thence, to decline being called upon for his dues, but rather came thither, to be ready to pay them.

1. The tribute demanded was not any civil payment to the Roman powers, that was strictly exacted by the publicans, but the church-duties, the half shekel, about fifteen pence, which were required from every person or the service of the temple, and the defraying of the expenses of the worship there; it is called *a ransom for the soul,* Ex. 30:12,

etc. This was not so strictly exacted now as sometimes it had been, especially not in Galilee.

2. The demand was very modest; the collectors stood in such awe of Christ, because of his mighty works, that they durst not speak to him about it, but applied themselves to Peter, whose house was in Capernaum, and probably in his house Christ lodged; he therefore was fittest to be spoken to as the housekeeper, and they presumed he knew his Master's mind. Their question is, *Doth not your master pay tribute?* Some think that they sought an occasion against him, designing, if he refused, to represent him as disaffected to the temple-service, and his followers as lawless people, that would pay *neither toll, tribute, nor custom,* Ezra 4:13. It should rather seem, they asked this with respect, intimating, that if he had any privilege to exempt him from this payment, they would not insist upon it.

Peter presently his word for his Master; *"Yes,* certainly; my *Master pays tribute;* it is his principle and practice; you need not fear moving it to him." (1.) *He was made under the law* (Gal. 4:4); therefore under this law he was paid for at forty days old (Lu. 2:22), and now he paid for himself, as one who, in his state of humiliation, *had taken upon him the form of a servant,* Phil. 2:7, 8. (2.) *He was made sin for us,* and was *sent forth in the likeness of sinful flesh,* Rom. 8:3. Now this tax paid to the temple is called *an atonement for the soul,* Ex. 30:15. Christ, that in every thing he might *appear in the likeness of sinners,* paid it though he had no sin to atone for. (3.) *Thus it became him to fulfil all righteousness, ch.* 3:15. He did this to set an example, [1.] Of *rendering to all their due, tribute to whom tribute is due,* Rom. 13:7. The kingdom of Christ not being of this world, the favourites and officers of it are so far from having a power granted them, as such, to tax other people's purses, that theirs are made liable to the powers that are. [2.] Of contributing to the support of the public worship of God in the places where we are. If we reap spiritual things, it is fit that we should return carnal things. The temple was now made a den of thieves, and the temple-worship a pretence for the opposition which the chief priests gave to Christ and his doctrine; and yet Christ paid this tribute. Note, Church-duties, legally imposed, are to be paid, notwithstanding church-corruptions. We must take care not to use *our liberty as a cloak of covetousness or maliciousness,* 1 Pt. 2:16. If Christ pay tribute, who can pretend an exemption?

II. How it was disputed (*v.* 25), not with the collectors themselves, lest they should be irritated, but with Peter, that he might be satisfied in the reason why Christ paid tribute, and might not mistake about it. He brought the collectors into the house; but Christ anticipated him, to give him a proof of his omniscience, and that no thought can be withholden from him. The disciples of Christ are never attacked without his knowledge.

Now, 1. He appeals to the way of the kings of the earth, which is, to take tribute of strangers, of the subjects of their kingdom, or foreigners that deal with them, but not of their own children that are of their families; there is such a community of goods between parents and children, and a joint-interest in what they have, that it would be absurd for the parents to levy taxes upon the children, or demand any thing from them; it is like one hand taxing the other.

2. He applies this to himself; *Then are the children free.* Christ is the Son of God, and Heir of all things; the temple is his temple (Mal. 3:1), his Father's house (Jn. 2:16), in it *he is faithful as a Son in his own house* (Heb. 3:6), and therefore not obliged to pay this tax for the service of the temple. Thus Christ asserts his right, lest his paying this tribute should be misimproved to the weakening of his title as the Son of God, and the King of Israel, and should have looked like a disowning of it himself. These immunities of the children are to be extended no further than our Lord Jesus himself. God's children are freed by grace and adoption from the slavery of sin and Satan, but not from their subjection to civil magistrates in civil things; here the law of Christ is express; *Let every soul* (sanctified souls not excepted) *be subject to the higher powers. Render to Caesar the things that are Caesar's.*

III. How it was paid, notwithstanding, *v.* 27.

1. For what reason Christ waived his privilege, and paid this tribute, though he was entitled to an exemption — *Lest we should offend them.* Few knew, as Peter did, that he was *the Son of God;* and it would have been a diminution to the honour of that great truth, which was yet a secret, to advance it now, to serve such a purpose as this. Therefore Christ drops that argument, and considers, that if he should refuse this payment, it would increase people's prejudice against him and his doctrine, and alienate their affections from him, and therefore he resolves to pay it. Note, Christian prudence and humility teach us, in many cases, to recede from our right, rather than give offence by insisting upon it. We must never decline our duty for fear of giving offence (Christ's preaching and miracles offended them, yet he went on with him, *ch.* 15:12, 13, better offend men than God); but we must sometimes deny ourselves in that which is our secular interest, rather than give offence; as Paul, 1 Co. 8:13; Rom. 14:13.

2. What course he took for the payment of this tax; he furnished himself with money for it out of the mouth of a fish (*v.* 27), wherein appears,

(1.) The poverty of Christ; he had not fifteen pence at command to pay his tax with, though he cured so many that were diseased; it seems, he did all gratis; *for our sakes he became poor,* 2 Co. 8:9. In his ordinary expenses, he lived upon alms (Lu. 8:3), and in extraordinary ones, he lived upon miracles. He did not order Judas to pay this out of the bag which he carried; that was for subsistence, and he would not order that for his particular use, which was intended for the benefit of the community.

(2.) The power of Christ, in fetching money out of a fish's mouth for this purpose. Whether his omnipotence put it there, or his omniscience knew that it was there, it comes all to one; it was an evidence of his divinity, and that he is Lord of hosts. Those creatures that are most remote from man are at the command of Christ, even the fishes of the sea are under his feet (Ps. 8:5); and to evidence his dominion in this lower world, and to accommodate himself to his present state of humiliation, he chose to take it out of a fish's mouth, when he could have taken it out of an angel's hand. Now observe,

[1.] Peter must catch the fish by angling. Even in miracles he would use means to encourage industry and endeavour. Peter has something to do, and it is in the way of his own calling too; to teach us diligence in the employment we are called *to,* and called *in.* Do we expect that Christ should give to us? Let us be ready to work for him.

[2.] The fish came up, with money in the mouth of it, which represents to us the reward of obedience in obedience. What work we do at Christ's command brings its own pay along with it: *In* keeping God's commands, as well as *after* keeping them, *there is great reward,* Ps. 19:11. Peter was made a fisher of men, and those that he caught thus, came up; where the heart is opened to entertain Christ's word, the hand is open to encourage his ministers.

[3.] The piece of money was just enough to pay the tax for Christ and Peter. Thou shalt find *a stater,* the value of a Jewish shekel, which would pay the poll-tax for two, for it was half a shekel, Ex. 30:13. Christ could as easily have commanded a bag of money as a piece of money; but he would teach us not to covet superfluities, but, having enough for our present occasions, therewith to be content, and not to distrust God, though we live but from hand to mouth. Christ made the fish his cash-keeper; and why may not we make God's providence our storehouse and treasury? If we have a competency for today, *let to-morrow take thought for the things of itself.* Christ paid for himself and Peter, because it is probable that here *he* only was assessed, and of him it was at this time demanded; perhaps the rest had paid already, or were to pay elsewhere. The papists make a great mystery of Christ's paying for Peter, as if this made him the head and representative of the whole church; whereas the payment of tribute for him was rather a sign of subjection than of superiority. His pretended successors pay no tribute, but exact it. Peter fished for this money, and therefore part of it went for his use. Those that are *workers together with Christ* in winning souls shall shine with him. *Give it for thee and me.* What Christ paid for himself was looked upon as a debt; what he paid for Peter was a courtesy to him. Note, it is a desirable thing, if God so please, to have wherewithal of this world's goods, not only to be just, but to be kind; not only to be charitable to the poor, but obliging to our friends. What is a great estate good for, but that it enables a man to do so much the more good?

Lastly, Observe, The evangelist records here the orders Christ gave to Peter, the warrant; the effect is not particularly mentioned, but taken for granted, and justly; for, with Christ, saying and doing are the same thing.

CHAPTER 18

The gospels are, in short, a record of what Jesus began both to do and to teach. In the foregoing chapter, we had an account of his doings, in this, of his teachings; probably, not all at the same time, in a continued discourse, but at several times, upon divers occasions, here put together, as near akin. We have here, I. Instructions concerning humility (*v.* 1–6). II. Concerning offences in general (*v.* 7), particularly offences given, 1. By us to ourselves (*v.* 8, 9). 2. By us to others, (*v.* 10–14). 3. By others to us; which are of two sorts, (1.) Scandalous sins, which are to be reproved (*v.* 15–20). (2.) Personal wrongs, which are to be forgiven (*v.* 21–35). See how practical Christ's preaching was; he could have revealed mysteries, but he pressed plain duties, especially those that are most displeasing to flesh and blood.

Verses 1–6

As there never was a greater pattern of humility, so there never was a greater preacher of it, than Christ; he took all occasions to command it, to commend it, to his disciples and followers.

I. The occasion of this discourse concerning humility was an unbecoming contest among the disciples for precedency; they *came to him, saying,* among themselves (for they were ashamed to ask him, Mk. 9:34), *Who is the greatest in the kingdom of heaven?* They mean not, *who* by character (then the question had been good, that they might know what graces and duties to excel in), but *who* by name. They had heard much, and preached much, of the kingdom of heaven, the kingdom of the Messiah, his church in this world; but ass yet they were so far from having any clear notion of it, that they dreamt of a temporal kingdom, and the external pomp and power of it. Christ had lately foretold his sufferings, and the glory that should follow, that he should rise again, from whence they expected his kingdom would commence; and now they thought it was time to put in for their places in it; it is good, in such cases, to speak early. Upon other discourses of Christ to that purport, debates of this kind arose (*ch.* 20:19, 20; Lu. 22:22, 24); he spoke many words of his sufferings, but only one of his glory; yet they fasten upon that, and overlook the other; and, instead of asking how they might have strength and grace to suffer with him, they ask him, "Who shall be highest in reigning with him." Note, Many love to hear and speak of privileges and glory, who are willing to pass by the thoughts of work and trouble. They look so much at the crown, that they forget the yoke and the cross. So the disciples here did, when they asked, *Who is the greatest in the kingdom of heaven?*

1. They suppose that all who have a place in that kingdom are great, for it is a kingdom of priests. Note, Those are truly great who are truly good; and they will appear so at last, when Christ shall own them as his, though ever so mean and poor in the world.

2. They suppose that there are degrees in this greatness. All the saints are honourable, but not all alike so; *one star differs from another star in glory.* All David's officers were not worthies, nor all his worthies of the first three.

3. They suppose it must be some of them, that must be prime ministers of state. To whom should King Jesus delight to do honour, but to them who had left all for him, and were now his companions in patience and tribulation?

4. They strive who it should be, each having some pretence or other to it. Peter was always the chief speaker, and already had the keys given him; he expects to be lord-chancellor, or lord-chamberlain of the household, and so to be the greatest. Judas had the bag, and therefore he expects to be lord-treasurer, which, though now he come last, he hopes, will then denominate him the greatest. Simon and Jude are nearly related to Christ, and they hope to take place of all the great officers of state, as princes of the blood. John is the beloved disciple, the favourite of the Prince, and therefore hopes to be the greatest. Andrew was first called, and why should not he be first preferred? Note, We are very apt to amuse and humour ourselves with foolish fancies of things that will never be.

II. The discourse itself, which is a just rebuke to the question, *Who shall be greatest?* We have abundant reason to think, that if Christ ever intended that Peter and his successors at Rome should be heads of the church, and his chief vicars on earth, having so fair an occasion given him, he would now have let his disciples know it; but so far is he from this, that his answer disallows and condemns the thing itself. Christ will not lodge such an authority or supremacy any where in his church; whoever pretend to it are usurpers; instead of settling any of the disciples in this dignity, he warns them all not to put in for it.

Christ here teacheth them to be humble,

1. By a sign (*v.* 2); *He called a little child to him, and set him in the midst of them.* Christ often taught by signs or sensible representations (comparisons to the eye), as the prophets of old. Note, Humility is a lesson so hardly learned, that we have need by all ways and means to be taught it. When we look upon a little child, we should be put in mind of the use Christ made of this child. Sensible things must be improved to spiritual purposes. *He set him in the midst of them;* not that they might play with him, but that they might learn by him. Grown men, and great men, should not disdain the company of little children, or think it below them to take notice of them. They may either speak to them, and give instruction to them; or look upon them, and receive instruction from them. Christ himself, when a child, was *in the midst of the doctors,* Lu. 2:46.

2. By as sermon upon this sign; in which he shows them and us,

(1.) The necessity of humility, *v.* 3. His preface is solemn, and commands both attention and assent; *Verily I say unto you, I, the Amen, the faithful Witness,* say it, *Except ye be converted, and become as little children, ye shall not enter into the kingdom of heaven.* Here observe,

[1.] What it is that he requires and insists upon.

First, "You must be converted, you must be of another mind, and in another frame and temper, must have other thoughts, both of yourselves and of the kingdom of heaven, before you be fit for a place in it. The pride, ambition, and affectation of honour and dominion, which appear in you, must be repented of, mortified, and reformed, and you must come to yourselves." Note, Besides the first conversion of a soul from a state of nature to a state of grace, there are after-conversions from particular paths of backsliding, which are equally necessary to salvation. Every step out of the way by sin, must be a step into it again by repentance. When Peter repented of his denying his Master, he was converted. *Secondly,* You must *become as little children.* Note, Converting grace makes us like little children, not foolish as children (1 Co. 14:20), nor fickle (Eph. 4:14), nor playful (*ch.* 11:16); but, *as children,* we must *desire the sincere milk of the word* (1 Pt. 2:2); as children, we must be careful for nothing, but leave it to our heavenly Father to care for us (*ch.* 6:31); we must, as children, be harmless and inoffensive, and void of malice (1 Co. 14:20), governable, and under command (Gal. 4:2); and (which is here chiefly intended) we must be humble as little children, who do not take state upon them, nor stand upon the punctilios of honour; the child of a gentleman will play with the child of a beggar (Rom. 12:16), the child in rags, if it have the breast, is well enough pleased, and envies not the gaiety of the child in silk; little children have no great aims at great places, or projects to raise themselves in the world; they *exercise not themselves in things too high for them;* and we should in like manner *behave, and quiet ourselves,* Ps. 131:1, 2. As children are little in body and low in stature, so we must be little and low in spirit, and in our thoughts of ourselves. This is a temper which leads to other good dispositions; the age of childhood is the learning age.

[2.] What stress he lays upon this; Without this, *you shall not enter into the kingdom of heaven.* Note, Disciples of Christ have need to be kept in awe by threatenings, that they may fear *lest they seem to come short,* Heb. 4:1. The disciples, when they put that question (*v.* 1), thought themselves sure of the kingdom of heaven; but Christ awakens them to be jealous of themselves. They were ambitious of being *greatest in the kingdom of heaven;* Christ tells them, that, except they came to a better temper, they should never come thither. Note, many that set up for great ones in the church, prove not only little, but nothing, and are found to *have no part or lot in the matter.* Our Lord designs here to show the great danger of pride and ambition; whatever profession men make, if they allow themselves in this sin, they will be rejected both from God's tabernacle and from his holy hill. Pride threw the angels that sinned out of heaven, and will keep us out, if we be not converted from it. They that are lifted up with pride, *fall into the condemnation of the devil;* to prevent this, we must become as little children, and, in order to do that, *must be born again, must put on the new man,* must be like the *holy child Jesus;* so he is called, even after his ascension, Acts 4:27.

(2.) He shows the honour and advancement that attend humility (*v.* 4), thus furnishing a direct but surprising answer to their question. He that humbles himself as a little child, though he may fear that hereby he will render himself contemptible, as men of timid minds, who thereby throw themselves out of the way of preferment, yet *the same is greatest in the kingdom of heaven.* Note, The humblest Christians are the best Christians, and most like to Christ, and highest in his favour; are best disposed for the communications of divine grace, and fittest to serve God in this world, and enjoy him in another. They are great, for God overlooks heaven and earth, to look on such; and certainly those are to be most respected and honoured in the church that are most humble and self-denying; for, though they least seek it, they best deserve it.

(3.) The special care Christ takes for those that are humble; he espouses their cause, protects them, interests himself in their concerns, and will see that they are not wronged, without being righted.

Those that thus humble themselves will be afraid,

[1.] That nobody will receive them; but (*v.* 5), *Whoso shall receive one such little child in my name, receiveth me.* Whatever kindnesses are done to such, Christ takes as done to himself. Whoso entertains a meek and humble Christian, keeps him in countenance, will not let him lose by his modesty, takes him into his love and friendship, and society and care, and studies to do him a kindness; and doth this in Christ's name, for his sake, because he bears the image of Christ, serves Christ, and because Christ has received him; this shall be accepted and recompensed as an acceptable piece of respect to Christ. Observe, Though it be but one such little child that is received in Christ's name, it shall be accepted. Note, The tender regard Christ has to his church extends itself to every particular member, even the meanest; not only to the whole family, but to every child of the family; the less they are in themselves, to whom we show kindness, the more there is of good will in it to Christ; the less it is for their sakes, the more it is for his; and he takes it accordingly. If Christ were personally among us, we think we should never do enough to welcome him; *the poor, the poor in spirit, we have always with us,* and they are his receivers. See *ch.* 25:35–40.

[2.] They will be afraid that every body will abuse them; the basest men delight to trample upon the humble; *Vexat censura columbas — Censure pounces on doves.* This objection he obviates (*v.* 6), where he warns all people, as they will answer it at their utmost peril, not to offer any injury to one of Christ's little ones. This word makes a wall of fire about them; he that touches them, touches the apple of God's eye.

Observe, *First,* The crime supposed; *offending one of these little ones that believe in Christ.* Their believing in Christ, though they be little ones, unites them to him, and interests him in their cause, so that, as they partake of the benefit of his sufferings, he also partakes in the wrong of theirs. Even the little ones that believe have the same privileges with the great ones, for they have all obtained like precious faith. There are those that offend these little ones, by drawing them to sin (1 Co. 8:10, 11), grieving and vexing their righteous souls, discouraging them, taking occasion from their mildness to make a prey of them in their persons, families, goods, or good name. Thus the best men have often met with the worst treatment in this world.

Secondly, The punishment of this crime; intimated in that word, *Better for him that he were drowned in the depth of the sea.* The sin is so heinous, and the ruin proportionably so great, that he had better undergo the sorest punishments inflicted on the worst of malefactors, which can only kill the body. Note, 1. Hell is worse than the depth of the sea; for it is a bottomless pit, and it is a burning lake. The depth of the sea is only killing, but hell is tormenting. We meet with one that had comfort in the depth of the sea, it was Jonah (*ch.* 2:2, 4, 9); but never any had the least grain or glimpse of comfort in hell, nor will have to eternity. 2. The irresistible irrevocable doom of the great Judge will sink sooner and surer, and bind faster, than *a mill-stone hanged about the neck.* It fixes a great gulf, which can never be broken through, Lu. 16:26. Offending Christ's little ones, though by omission, is assigned as the reason of that dreadful sentence, *Go ye cursed,* which will at last be the doom of proud persecutors.

Verses 7–14

Our Savior here speaks of offences, or scandals,

I. In general, *v.* 7. Having mentioned the offending of little ones, he takes occasion to speak more generally of offences. That is an offence, 1. Which occasions guilt, which by enticement or affrightment tends to draw men from that which is good to that which is evil. 2. Which occasions grief, which *makes the heart of the righteous sad.* Now, concerning offences, Christ here tells them,

(1.) That they were certain things; *It must needs be, that offences come.* When we are sure there is danger, we should be the better armed. Not that Christ's word necessitates any man to offend, but it is a prediction upon a view of the causes; considering the subtlety and malice of Satan, the weakness and depravity of men's hearts, and the foolishness that is found there, it is morally impossible but that there should be offences; and God has determined to permit them for wise and holy ends, that both *they which are perfect, and they which are not, may be made manifest.* See 1 Co. 11:19; Dan. 11:35. Being told, before, that there will be seducers, tempters, persecutors, and many bad examples, let us stand upon our guard, *ch.* 24:24; Acts 20:29, 30.

(2.) That they would be woeful things, and the consequence of them fatal. Here is a double woe annexed to offences:

[1.] A woe to the careless and unguarded, to whom the offence is given; *Woe to the world because of offences.* The obstructions and oppositions given to faith and holiness in all places are the bane and plague of mankind, and the ruin of thousands. This present world is an evil world, it is so full of offences, of sins, and snares, and sorrows; a dangerous road we travel, full of stumbling-blocks, precipices, and false guides. Woe to the world. As for those whom God hath chosen and called out of the world, and delivered from it, they are preserved by the power of God from the prejudice of these offences, are helped over all these stones of stumbling. *They that love God's law have great peace, and nothing shall offend them,* Ps. 119:165.

[2.] A woe to the wicked, who wilfully give the offence; *But woe to that man by whom the offence comes.* Though it must needs be, that the offence will come, that will be no excuse for the offenders. Note, Though God makes the sins of sinners to serve his purposes, that will not secure them from his wrath; and the guilt will be laid at the door of those who give the offence, though they also fall under a woe who take it. Note, They who any way hinder the salvation of others, will find their own condemnation the more intolerable, like *Jeroboam, who sinned, and made Israel to sin.* This woe is the moral of that judicial law (Ex. 21:33, 21:34–22:6), that he who opened the pit, and kindled the fire, was accountable for all the damage that ensued. The antichristian generation, by whom came the great offence, will fall under this woe, for their delusion of sinners (2 Th. 2:11, 12), and their persecutions of saints (Rev. 17:1, 2, 6), for the righteous God will reckon with those who ruin the eternal interests of precious souls, and the temporal interests of precious saints; for *precious in the sight of the Lord is* the blood of souls and *the blood of saints;* and men will be reckoned with, not only for their doings, but for the fruit of their doings, the mischief done by them.

II. In particular, Christ here speaks of offences given,

1. By us to ourselves, which is expressed by our hand or foot offending us; in such a case, it must be *cut off, v.* 8, 9. This Christ had said before (*ch.* 5:29, 30), where it especially refers to seventh-commandment sins; here it is taken more generally. Note, Those hard sayings of Christ, which are displeasing to flesh and blood, need to be repeated to us again and again, and all little enough. Now observe,

(1.) What it is that is here enjoined. We must part with an *eye,* or a *hand,* or a *foot,* that is, that, whatever it is, which is dear to us, when it proves unavoidably an occasion of sin to us. Note, [1.] Many prevailing temptations to sin arise from within ourselves; our own eyes and hands offend us; if there were never a devil to tempt us, we should be drawn away of our own lust: nay, those things which in themselves are good, and may be used as instruments of good, even those, through the corruptions of our hearts, prove snares to us, incline us to sin, and hinder us in duty. [2.] In such a case, we must, as far as lawfully we may, part with that which we cannot keep without being entangled in sin by it. *First,* It is certain, the inward lust must be mortified, though it be dear to us as an eye, or a hand. *The flesh, with its affections and lusts, must be mortified,* Gal. 5:24. *The body of sin must be destroyed;* corrupt inclinations and appetites must be checked and crossed; the beloved lust, that has been rolled under the tongue as a sweet morsel, must be abandoned with abhorrence. *Secondly,* The outward occasions of sin must be avoided, though we thereby put as great a violence upon ourselves as it would be to cut off a hand, or pluck out an eye. When Abraham quitted his native country, for fear of being ensnared in the idolatry of it, and when Moses quitted Pharoah's court, for fear of being entangled in the sinful pleasures of it, there was a right hand cut off. We must think nothing too dear to part with, for the keeping of a good conscience.

(2.) Upon what inducement this is required; *It is better for thee to enter into life maimed, than, having two hands, to be cast into hell.* The argument is taken from the future state, from heaven and hell; thence are fetched the most cogent dissuasives from sin. The argument is the same with that of the apostle, Rom. 8:13. [1.] *If we live after the flesh, we shall die;* having two eyes, no breaches made upon the body of sin, inbred corruption like Adonijah never displeased, we shall *be cast into hell-fire.* [2.] *If we through the Spirit mortify the deeds of the body, we shall live;* that is meant by our *entering into life maimed,* that is, the body of sin maimed; and it is but maimed at the best, while we are in this world. If the right hand of the old man be cut off, and its right eye be plucked out, its chief policies blasted and powers broken, it is well; but there is still an eye and a hand remaining, with which it will struggle. They that are Christ's have nailed the flesh to the cross, but it is not yet dead; its life is prolonged, but its *dominion taken away* (Dan. 7:12), and the deadly wound given it, that shall not be healed.

1. Concerning offences given by us to others, especially Christ's little ones, which we are here charged to take heed of, pursuant to what he had said, *v.* 6. Observe,

(1.) The caution itself; *Take heed that ye despise not one of these little ones.* This is spoken to the disciples. As Christ will be displeased with enemies of his church, if they wrong any of the members of it, even the least, so he will be displeased with the great ones of the church, if they despise the little ones of it. "You that are striving who shall be greatest, take heed lest in this contest you despise the little ones." We may understand it literally of little children; of them Christ was speaking, *v.* 2, 4. The infant seed of the faithful belong to the family of Christ, and are not to be despised. Or, figuratively; true but weak believers are these little ones, who in their outward condition, or the frame of their spirits, are like little children, the lambs of Christ's flock.

[1.] We must not despise them, not think meanly of them, as lambs despised, Job 12:5. We must not make a jest of their infirmities, not look upon them with contempt, not conduct ourselves scornfully or disdainfully toward them, as if we cared not what became of them; we must not say, "Though they be offended, and grieved, and stumble, what is that to us?" Nor should we make a slight matter of doing that which will entangle and perplex them. This despising of the little ones is what we are largely cautioned against, Rom. 14:3, 10, 15, 20, 21. We must not impose upon the consciences of others, nor bring them into subjection to our humours, as they do who say to men's souls, *Bow down, that we may go over.* There is a respect owing to the conscience of every man who appears to be conscientious.

[2.] We must take heed that we do not despise them; we must be afraid of the sin, and be very cautious what we say and do, lest we should through inadvertency give offence to Christ's little ones, lest we put contempt upon them, without being aware of it. There were those that hated them, and cast them out, and yet said, *Let the Lord be glorified.* And we must be afraid of the punishment; "Take heed of despising them, for it is at your peril if you do."

(2.) The reasons to enforce the caution. We must not look upon these little ones as contemptible, because really they are considerable. Let not earth despise those whom heaven respects; let not *those* be looked upon by us with respect, as his favourites. To prove that the little ones which believe in Christ are worthy to be respected, consider,

[1.] The ministration of the good angels about them; *In heaven their angels always behold the face of my Father.* This Christ saith to us, and we may take it upon *his* word, who came from heaven to let us know what is done there by the world of angels. Two things he lets us know concerning them,

First, That they are the little ones' angels. God's angels are theirs; for all his is ours, if we be Christ's. 1 Co. 3:22. They are theirs; for they have a charge concerning them to minister for their good (Heb. 1:14), to pitch their tents about them, and bear them up in their arms. Some have imagined that every particular saint has a guardian angel; but why should we suppose this, when we are sure that every particular saint, when there is occasion, has a guard of angels? This is particularly applied here to the little ones, because they are most despised and most exposed. They have but little that they can call their own, but they can look by faith on the heavenly hosts, and call them theirs. While the great ones of the world have honourable men for their retinue and guards, the little ones of the church are attended with glorious angels; which bespeaks not only their dignity, but the danger those run themselves upon, who despise and abuse them. It is bad being enemies to those who are so guarded; and it is good having God for our God, for then we have his angels for our angels.

Secondly, That *they always behold the face of the Father in heaven.* This bespeaks, 1. The angels' continual felicity and honour. The happiness of heaven consists in the vision of God, seeing him face to face as he is, beholding his beauty; this the angels have without interruption; when they are ministering to us on earth, yet even then by contemplation they behold the face of God, for they are *full of eyes within.* Gabriel, when speaking to Zecharias, yet stands in the presence of God, Rev. 4:8; Lu. 1:19. The expression intimates, as some think, the special dignity and honour of the little ones' angels; the prime ministers of state are said to *see the king's face* (Esth. 1:14), as if the strongest angels had the charge of the weakest saints. 2. It bespeaks their continual readiness to minister to the saints. They behold the face of God, expecting to receive orders from him what to do for the good of the saints. *As the eyes of the servant are to the hand of his master,* ready to go or come upon the least beck, so the eyes of the angels are upon the face of God, waiting for the intimations of his will, which those winged messengers fly swiftly to fulfil; they *go and return like a flash of lightning,* Eze. 1:14. If we would behold the face of God in glory hereafter, as the angels do (Lu. 20:36), we must behold the face of God now, in readiness to our duty, as they do, Acts 9:6.

[2.] The gracious design of Christ concerning them (*v.* 11); *For the Son of man is come to save that which was lost.* This is a reason, *First,* Why the little ones' angels have such a charge concerning them, and attend upon them; it is in pursuance of Christ's design to save them. Note, The ministration of angels is founded in the mediation of Christ; through him angels are reconciled to us; and, when they celebrated God's goodwill toward men, to it they annexed their own. *Secondly,* Why they are not to be despised; because Christ came to save them, to save them that are lost, the little ones that are lost in their own eyes (Isa. 66:3), that are at a loss within themselves. Or rather, the children of men. Note, 1. Our souls by nature are lost souls; as a traveller is lost, that is out of his way, as a convicted prisoner is lost. God lost the service of fallen man, lost the honour he should have had from him. 2. Christ's errand into the world was to *save that which was lost,* to reduce us to our allegiance, restore us to our work, reinstate us in our privileges, and so to put us into the right way that leads to our great end; to save those that are spiritually lost from being eternally so. 3. This is a good reason why the least and weakest believers should not be despised or offended. If Christ put such a value upon them, let us not undervalue them. If he denied himself so much for their salvation, surely we should deny ourselves for their edification and consolation. See this argument urged, Rom. 14:15; 1 Co. 8:11, 12. Nay, if Christ came into the world to save souls, and his heart is so much upon that work, he will reckon severely with those that obstruct and hinder it, by obstructing the progress of those that are setting their faces heavenward, and so thwart his great design.

[3.] The tender regard which our heavenly Father has to these little ones, and his concern for their welfare. This is illustrated by a comparison, *v.* 12–14. Observe the gradation of the argument; the angels of God are their servants, the Son of God is their Saviour, and, to complete their honour, God himself is their Friend. *None shall pluck them out of my Father's hand,* Jn. 10:28.

Here is, *First,* The comparison, *v.* 12, 13. The owner that had lost one sheep out of a hundred, does not slight it, but diligently enquires after it, is greatly pleased when he has found it, and has in that a sensible and affecting joy, more than in the ninety and nine that wandered not. The fear he was in of losing that one, and the surprise of finding it, add to the joy. Now this is applicable, 1. To the state of fallen man in general; he is strayed like a lost sheep, the angels that stood were as the ninety-nine that never went astray; wandering man is sought upon the mountains, which Christ, in great fatigue, traversed in pursuit of him, and he is found; which is a matter of joy. Greater joy there is in heaven for returning sinners than for remaining angels. 2. To particular believers, who are offended and put out of their way by the stumbling-blocks that are laid in their way, or the wiles of those who seduce them out of the way. Now though but one of a hundred should hereby be driven off, as sheep easily are, yet that one shall be looked after with a great deal of care, the return of it welcomed with a great deal of pleasure; and therefore the wrong done to it, no doubt, will be reckoned for with a great deal of displeasure. If there be joy in heaven for the finding of one of these little ones, there is wrath in heaven for the offending of them. Note, God is graciously concerned, not only for his flock in general, but for every lamb, or sheep, that belongs to it. Though they are many, yet out of those many he can easily miss one, for he is a *great* Shepherd, but not so easily lose it, for he is a *good* Shepherd, and takes a more particular cognizance of his flock than ever any did; for he *calls his own sheep by name,* Jn. 10:3. See a full exposition of this parable, Eze. 34:2, 10, 16, 19.

Secondly, The application of this comparison (*v.* 14); *It is not the will of your Father, that one of these little ones should perish.* More is implied than is expressed. It is not his will that any should perish, but, 1. It is his will, that these little ones should be saved; it is the will of his design and delight: he has designed it, and set his heart upon it, and he will effect it; it is the will of his precept, that all should do what they can to further it, and nothing to hinder it. 2. This care extends itself to every particular member of the flock, even the meanest. We think if but *one* or *two* be offended and ensnared, it is no great matter, we need not mind it; but God's thoughts of love and tenderness are above ours. 3. It is intimated that those who do any thing by which any of these little ones are brought into danger of perishing, contradict the will of God, and highly provoke him; and though they cannot prevail in it, yet they will be reckoned with for it by him, who, in his saints, as in other things, is jealous of his honour, and will not bear to have it trampled on. See Isa. 3:15, *What mean ye, that ye beat my people?* Ps. 76:8, 9.

Observe, Christ called God, *v.* 19, *my Father which is in heaven;* he calls him, *v.* 14, *your Father which is in heaven;* intimating that he is not ashamed to call his poor disciples *brethren;* for have not he and they one Father? *I ascend to my Father and your Father* (Jn. 20:17); therefore ours because his. This intimates likewise the ground of the safety of his little ones; that God is their Father, and is therefore inclined to succour them. A father takes care of all his children, but is particularly tender of the little ones, Gen. 33:13. He is their Father in heaven, a place of prospect, and therefore he sees all the indignities offered them; and a place of power, therefore he is able to avenge them. This comforts offended little ones, that their Witness is in heaven (Job 16:19), their Judge is there, Ps. 68:5.

Verses 15–20

Christ, having cautioned his disciples not to give offence, comes next to direct them what they must do in case of offences given them; which may be understood either of personal injuries, and then these directions are intended for the preserving of the peace of the church; or of public scandals, and then they are intended for the preserving of the purity and beauty of the church. Let us consider it both ways.

I. Let us apply it to the quarrels that happen, upon any account, among Christians. If thy brother trespass against thee, by grieving thy soul (1 Co. 8:12), by affronting thee, or putting contempt or abuse upon thee; if he blemish thy good name by false reports or tale-bearing; if he encroach on thy rights, or be any way injurious to thee in thy estate; if he be guilty of any of those trespasses that are specified, Lev. 6:2, 3; if he transgress the laws of justice, charity, or relative duties; these are trespasses against us, and often happen among Christ's disciples, and sometimes, for want of prudence, are of very mischievous consequence. Now observe what is the rule prescribed in this case,

1. *Go, and tell him his fault between thee and him alone.* Let this be compared with, and explained by, Lev. 19:17, *Thou shalt not hate thy brother in thy heart;* that is, "If thou hast conceived a displeasure at thy brother for any injury he hath done thee, do not suffer thy resentments to ripen into a secret malice (like a wound, which is most dangerous when it bleed inwardly), but give vent to them in a mild and grave

admonition, let them so spend themselves, and they will expire the sooner; do not go and rail against him behind his back, but *thou shalt in any ways reprove him.* If he has indeed done thee a considerable wrong, endeavour to make him sensible of it, but let the rebuke be private, between thee and him alone; if thou wouldest convince him, do not expose him, for that will but exasperate him, and make the reproof look like a revenge." this agrees with Prov. 25:8, 9, *"Go not forth hastily to strive,* but *debate thy cause with thy neighbour himself,* argue it calmly and amicably; and *if he shall hear thee,* well and good, *thou hast gained thy brother,* there is an end of the controversy, and it is a happy end; let no more be said of it, but let the falling out of friends be the renewing of friendship."

2. *"If he will not hear thee,* if he will not own himself in a fault, nor come to an agreement, yet do not despair, but try what he will say to it, if thou take *one or two or more,* not only to be witnesses of what passes, but to reason the case further with him; he will be the more likely to hearken to them because they are disinterested; and if reason will rule him, the word of reason in the mouth of two or three witnesses will be better spoken to him" *(Plus vident oculi quam oculus — Many eyes see more than one),* "and more regarded by him, and perhaps it will influence him to acknowledge his error, and to say, *I repent."*

3. "If *he shall neglect to hear them,* and will not refer the matter to their arbitration, then *tell it to the church,* to the ministers, elders, or other officers, or the most considerable persons in the congregation you belong to, make them the referees to accommodate the matter, and do not presently appeal to the magistrate, or fetch a writ for him." This is fully explained by the apostle (1 Co. 6), where he reproves those that went to law before the unjust, and not before the saints (*v.* 1), and would have the saints to judge those small matters (*v.* 2) that pertain to this life, *v.* 3. If you ask, "Who is *the church* that must be told?" the apostle directs there (*v.* 5), *Is there not a wise man among you?* Those of the church that are presumed to be most capable of determining such matters; and he speaks ironically, when he says (*v.* 4), *"Set them to judge who are least esteemed in the church;* those, if there be no better, those, rather than suffer an irreconcileable breach between two church members." This rule was then in a special manner requisite, when the civil government was in the hands of such as were not only aliens, but enemies.

4. "If he will not *hear the church,* will not stand to their award, but persists in the wrong he has done thee, and proceeds to do thee further wrong, *let him be to thee as a heathen man, and a publican;* take the benefit of the law against him, but let that always be the last remedy; appeal not to the courts of justice till thou hast first tried all other means to compromise the matter in variance. Or thou mayest, if thou wilt, break off thy friendship and familiarity with him; though thou must by no means study revenge, yet thou mayest choose whether thou wilt have any dealings with him, at least, in such a way as may give him an opportunity of doing the like again. Thou wouldest have healed him, wouldest have preserved his friendship, but he would not, and so has forfeited it." If a man cheat and abuse me once, it is his fault; if twice, it is my own.

II. Let us apply it to scandalous sins, which are an offence to the little ones, of bad example to those that are weak and pliable, and of great grief to those that are weak and timorous. Christ, having taught us to indulge the weakness of our brethren, here cautions us not to indulge their wickedness under pretence of that. Christ, designing to erect a church for himself in the world, here took care for the preservation, 1. Of its purity, that it might have an expulsive faculty, a power to cleanse and clear itself, like a fountain of living waters, which is necessary as long as the net of the gospel brings up both good fish and bad. 2. Of its peace and order, that every member may know his place and duty, and the purity of it may be preserved in a regular way and not tumultuously. Now let us see,

(1.) What is the case supposed? *If thy brother trespass against thee.* [1.] "The offender is a brother, one that is in Christian communion, that is baptized, that hears the word, and prays with thee, with whom thou joinest in the worship of God, statedly or occasionally." Note, Church discipline is for church members. *Them that are without God judges,* 1 Co. 5:12, 13. When any trespass is done against us, it is good to remember that the trespasser is a brother, which furnishes us with qualifying consideration. [2.] "The offense is a trespass against thee; if thy brother sin against thee (so the word is), if he do any thing which is offensive to thee as a Christian." Note, A gross sin against God is a trespass against his people, who have a true concern for his honour. Christ and believers have twisted interests; what is done against them Christ takes as done against himself, and what is done against him they cannot but take as done against themselves. *The reproaches of them that reproached thee are fallen upon me,* Ps. 69:9.

(2.) What is to be done in this case. We have here,

[1.] The rules prescribed, *v.* 15–17. Proceed in this method:

First, "Go and tell him his fault between thee and him alone. Do not stay till he comes to thee, but go to him, as the physician visits the patient, and the shepherd goes after the lost sheep." Note, We should think no pains too much to take for the recovering of a sinner to repentance. *"Tell him his fault,* remind him of what he has done, and of the evil of it, *show him his abominations."* Note, People are loth to see their faults, and have need to be told of them. Though the fact is plain, and the fault too, yet they must be put together with application. Great sins often amuse conscience, and for the present stupify and silence it; and there is need of help to awaken it. David's own heart smote him, when he had cut off Saul's skirt, and when he had numbered the people; but (which is very strange) we do not find that it smote him in the matter of Uriah, till Nathan told him, *Thou art the man.*

"Tell him his fault, elenxon auton — argue the case with him" (so the word signifies); "and do it with reason and argument, not with passion." Where the fault is plain and great, the person proper for us to deal with, and we have an opportunity for it, and there is no apparent danger of doing more hurt than good, we must with meekness and faithfulness tell people of what is amiss in them. Christian reproof is an ordinance of Christ for the bringing of sinners to repentance, and must be managed as an ordinance. "Let the reproof be private, between thee and him alone; that it may appear you seek not his reproach, but his repentance." Note, It is a good rule, which should ordinarily be observed among Christians, not to speak of our brethren's faults to others, till we have first spoken of them to themselves, this would make less reproaching and more reproving; that is, less sin committed, and more duty done. It will be likely to work upon an offender, when he sees his reprover concerned not only for his salvation, in telling him his fault, but for his reputation in telling him of it privately.

"If he shall hear thee" — that is, "heed thee — if he be wrought upon by the reproof, it is well, *thou hast gained thy brother;* thou hast helped to save him from sin and ruin, and it will be thy credit and comfort," James 5:19, 20. Note, The converting of a soul is the winning of that soul (Prov. 11:30); and we should covet it, and labour after it, as gain to us; and, if the loss of a soul be a great loss, the gain of a soul is sure no small gain.

Secondly, If that doth not prevail, *then take with thee one or two more, v.* 16. Note, We must not be weary of well-doing, though we see not presently the good success of it. "If he will not hear thee, yet do not give him up as in a desperate case; say not, It will be to no purpose to deal with him any further; but go on in the use of other means; even those that harden their necks must be often reproved, and those that oppose themselves instructed in meekness." In work of this kind we must *travail in birth again* (Gal. 4:19); and it is after many pains and throes that the child is born.

"Take with thee one or two more; 1. To assist thee; they may speak some pertinent convincing word which thou didst not think of, and may manage the matter with more prudence than thou didst." note, Christians should see their need of help in doing good, and pray in the aid one of another; as in other things, so in giving reproofs, that the duty may be done, and may be done well. 2. "To affect him; he will be the more likely to be humbled for his fault, when he sees it witnessed against by *two or three."* Deu. 19:15. Note, Those should think it high time to repent and reform, who see their misconduct become a general offence and scandal. Though in such a world as this it is rare to find one good whom *all men speak well of,* yet it is more rare to find one good whom *all men speak ill of.* 3. "To be witnesses of his conduct, in case the matter should afterward be brought before the church." None should come under the censure of the church as obstinate and contumacious, till it be very well proved that they are so.

Thirdly, If he neglect to hear them, and will not be humbled, *then tell it to the church, v.* 17. There are some stubborn spirits to whom the likeliest means of conviction prove ineffectual; yet such must not be given over as incurable, but let the matter be made more public, and further help called in. Note, 1. Private admonitions must always go before public censures; if gentler methods will do the work, those that are more rough and severe must not be used, Tit. 3:10. Those that will be reasoned out of their sins, need not be shamed out of them. Let God's work be done effectually, but with as little noise as may be; his kingdom comes with power, but not with observation. But, 2. Where private admonition does not prevail, there public censure must take place. The church must receive the complaints of the offended, and rebuke the sins of the offenders, and judge between them, after an impartial enquiry made into the merits of the cause.

Tell it to the church. It is a thousand pities that this appointment of Christ, which was designed to end differences, and remove offences, should itself be so much a matter of debate, and occasion differences and offences, through the corruption of men's hearts. What church must be told — is the great question. The civil magistrate, say some; The Jewish sanhedrim then in being, say others; but by what follows, *v.* 18, it is plain that he means a Christian church, which, though not yet formed, was now in the embryo. *"Tell it to the church,* that particular church in the communion of which the offender lives; make the matter known to those of that congregation who are by consent appointed to receive informations of that kind. Tell it to the guides and governors of the church, the minister or ministers, the elders or deacons, or (if such the constitution of the society be) tell it to the representatives or heads of the congregation, or to all the members of it; let them examine the matter and, if they find the complaint frivolous and groundless, let them rebuke the complainant; if they find it just, let them rebuke the offender, and call him to repentance, and this will be likely to put an edge and an efficacy upon the reproof, because given," 1. "With greater solemnity," and, 2. "With greater authority." It is an awful thing to receive a reproof from a church, from a minister, a reprover by office; and therefore it is the more regarded by such as pay any deference to an institution of Christ and his ambassadors.

Fourthly, "If he neglect to hear the church, if he slight the admonition, and will neither be ashamed of his faults, nor amend them, *let him be unto thee as a heathen man and publican;* let him be cast out of the communion of the church, secluded from special ordinances, degraded from the dignity of a church member, let him be put under disgrace, and let the members of the society be warned to withdraw from him, that he may be ashamed of his sin, and they may not be infected by it, or made chargeable with it." Those who put contempt on the orders and rules of a society, and bring reproach upon it, forfeit the honours and privileges of it, and are justly laid aside till they repent and submit, and reconcile themselves to it again. Christ has appointed this method for the vindicating of the church's honour, the preserving of its purity, and the conviction and reformation of those that are scandalous. But observe, he doth not say, "Let him be to thee as a devil or damned spirit, as one whose case is desperate," but "as a heathen and a publican, as one in a capacity of being restored and received in again. Count him not as an enemy, but admonish him as a brother." The directions given to the church of Corinth concerning the incestuous person, agree with the rules here; he must be *taken away from among them* (1 Co. 5:2), must be *delivered to Satan;* for if he be cast out of Christ's kingdom, he is looked upon as belonging to Satan's kingdom; they must not keep company with him, *v.* 11, 13. But when by this he is humbled and reclaimed, he must be welcomed into communion again, and all shall be well.

[2.] Here is a warrant signed for the ratification of all the church's proceedings according to these rules, *v.* 18. What was said before to Peter is here said to all the disciples, and in them to all the faithful office-bearers in the church, to the world's end. While ministers preach the word of Christ faithfully, and in their government of the church strictly adhere to his laws *(clave non errante — the key not turning the wrong way),* they may be assured that he will own them, and stand by them, and will ratify what they say and do, so that it shall be taken as said and done by himself. He will own them,

First, In their sentence of suspension; *Whatsoever ye shall bind on earth shall be bound in heaven.* If the censures of the church duly follow the institution of Christ, his judgments will follow the censures of the church, his spiritual judgments, which are the sorest of all other, such as the rejected Jews fell under (Rom. 11:8), a *spirit of slumber;* for Christ will not suffer his own ordinances to be trampled upon, but will say *amen* to the righteous sentences which the church passes on obstinate offenders. How light soever proud scorners may make of the censures of the church, let them know that they are confirmed in the court of heaven; and it is in vain for them to appeal to that court, for judgment is there already given against them. They that are shut out from the *congregation of the righteous* now shall not *stand in it* in the great day, Ps. 1:5. Christ will not own those as his, nor receive them to himself, whom the church has duly delivered to Satan; but, if through error or envy the censures of the church be unjust, Christ will graciously find those who are so cast out, Jn. 9:34, 35.

Secondly, In their sentence of absolution; *Whatsoever ye shall loose on earth shall be loosed in heaven.* Note, 1. No church censures bind so fast, but that, upon the sinner's repentance and reformation, they may and must be loosed again. Sufficient is the punishment which has attained its end, and the offender must then be forgiven and comforted, 2 Co. 2:6. There is no unpassable gulf fixed but that between hell and heaven. 2. Those who, upon their repentance, are received by the church into communion again may take the comfort of their absolution in heaven, if their hearts be upright with God. As suspension is for the terror of the obstinate, so absolution is for the encouragement of the penitent. St. Paul speaks in the person of Christ, when he saith, *To whom ye forgive any thing, I forgive also,* 2 Co. 2:10.

Now it is a great honour which Christ here puts upon the church, that he will condescend not only to take cognizance of their sentences, but to confirm them; and in the following verses we have two things laid down as ground of this.

(1.) God's readiness to answer the church's prayers (*v.* 19); *If two of you shall agree* harmoniously, *touching any thing that they shall ask, it shall be done for them.* Apply this,

[1.] In general, to all the requests of the faithful praying seed of Jacob; they shall not *seek God's face in vain.* Many promises we have in scripture of a gracious answer to the prayers of faith, but this gives a particular encouragement to the joint-prayer; "the requests which two of you agree in, much more which many agree in." No law of heaven limits the number of petitioners. Note, Christ has been pleased to put an honour upon, and to allow a special efficacy in, the joint-prayers of the faithful, and the common supplications they make to God. If they join in the same prayer, if they meet by appointment to come together to the throne of grace on some special errand, or, though at a distance, agree in some particular matter of prayer, they shall speed well. Besides the general regard God has to the prayers of the saints, he is particularly pleased with their union and communion in those prayers. See 2 Chr. 5:13; Acts 4:31.

[2.] In particular, to those requests that are put up to God about binding and loosing; to which this promise seems more especially to refer. Observe, *First,* That the power of church discipline is not here lodged in the hand of a single person, but two, at least, are supposed to be concerned in it. When the incestuous Corinthian was to be cast out, the church was gathered together (1 Co. 5:4), and it was a punishment inflicted of many, 2 Co. 2:6. In an affair of such importance, *two are better than one, and in the multitude of counsellors there is safety. Secondly,* It is good to see those who have the management of church discipline, agreeing in it. Heats and animosities, among those whose work it is to remove offences, will be the greatest offence of all. *Thirdly,* Prayer must evermore go along with church discipline. Pass no sentence, which you cannot in faith ask God to confirm. The binding and loosing spoken of (*ch.* 16:19) was done by preaching, this by praying. Thus the whole power of gospel ministers is resolved into the word and prayer, to which they must wholly give themselves. He doth not say, "If you shall agree to sentence and decree a thing, it shall be done" (as if ministers were judges and lords); but, "If you agree to ask it of God, from him you shall obtain it." Prayer must go along with all our endeavours for the conversion of sinners; see Jas. 5:16. *Fourthly,* The unanimous petitions of the church of God, for the ratification of their just censures, shall be heard in heaven, and obtain an answer; "*It shall be done,* it shall be bound and loosed in heaven; God will set his fiat to the appeals and applications you make to him." If Christ (who here speaks as one having authority) say, "It shall be done," we may be assured that it is done, though we see not the effect in the way that we look for it. God doth especially own and accept us, when we are praying for those that have offended him and us. *The Lord turned the captivity of Job,* not when he prayed for himself, but when he prayed for his friends who had trespassed against him.

(2.) The presence of Christ in the assemblies of Christians, *v.* 20. Every believer has the presence of Christ with him; but the promise here refers to the meetings where two or three are gathered in his name, not only for discipline, but for religious worship, or any act of Christian communion. Assemblies of Christians for holy purposes are hereby appointed, directed, and encouraged.

[1.] They are hereby appointed; the church of Christ in the world exists most visibly in religious assemblies; it is the will of Christ that these should be set up, and kept up, for the honour of God, the edification of men, and the preserving of a face of religion upon the world. When God intends special answers to prayer, he calls for a solemn assembly, Joel 2:15, 16. If there be no liberty and opportunity for large and numerous assemblies, yet then it is the will of God that two or three should gather together, to show their good-will to the great congregation. Note, When we cannot do what we would in religion, we must do as we can, and God will accept us.

[2.] They are hereby directed to gather together in Christ's name. In the exercise of church discipline, they must *come together in the name of Christ,* 1 Co. 5:4. That name gives to what they do an authority on earth, and an acceptableness in heaven. In meeting or worship, we must have an eye to Christ; must come together by virtue of his warrant and appointment, in token of our relation to him, professing faith in him, and in communion with all that in every place call upon him. When we come together, to worship God in a dependence upon the Spirit and grace of Christ as Mediator for assistance, and upon his merit and righteousness as Mediator for acceptance, having an actual regard to him as our Way to the Father, and our Advocate with the Father, then we are met together in his name.

[3.] They are hereby encouraged with an assurance of the presence of Christ; *There am I in the midst of them.* By his common presence he is in all places, as God; but this is a promise of his special presence. Where his saints are, his sanctuary is, and there he will dwell; it is his rest (Ps. 132:14), it is his walk (Rev. 2:1); he is in the midst of them, to quicken and strengthen them, to refresh and comfort them, as the sun in the midst of the universe. He is in the midst of them, that is, in their hearts; it is a spiritual presence, the presence of Christ's Spirit with their spirits, that is here intended. *There am I,* not only *I will be* there, but *I am there;* as if he came first, is ready before them, they shall find him there; he repeated this promise at parting (*ch.* 28:20), *Lo, I am with you always.* Note, The presence of Christ in the assemblies of Christians is promised, and may in faith be prayed for and depended on; *There am I.* This is equivalent to the Shechinah, or special presence of God in the tabernacle and temple of old, Ex. 40:34; 2 Chr. 5:14.

Though but two or three are met together, Christ is among them; this is an encouragement to the meeting of a few, when it is either, *First,* of choice. Besides the secret worship performed by particular persons, and the public services of the whole congregation, there may be occasion sometimes for two or three to come together, either for mutual assistance in conference or joint assistance in prayer, not in contempt of public worship, but in concurrence with it; there Christ will be present. Or, *Secondly,* By constraint; when there are not more than two or three to come together, or, if there be, they dare not, *for fear of the Jews,* yet Christ will be *in the midst of them,* for it is not the multitude, but the faith and sincere devotion, of the worshippers, that invites the presence of Christ; and though there be but two or three, the smallest number that can be, yet, it Christ make one among them, who is the principal one, their meeting is as honourable and comfortable as if they were two or three thousand.

Verses 21–35

This part of the discourse concerning offences is certainly to be understood of personal wrongs, which is in our power to forgive. Now observe,

I. Peter's question concerning this matter (*v.* 21); *Lord, how oft shall my brother trespass against me, and I forgive him?* Will it suffice to do it *seven times?*

1. He takes it for granted that he must forgive; Christ had before taught his disciples this lesson (*ch.* 6:14, 14), and Peter has not forgotten it. He knows that he must not only not bear a grudge against his brother, or meditate revenge, but be as good a friend as ever, and forget the injury.

2. He thinks it is a great matter to forgive till seven times; he means not *seven times a day,* as Christ said (Lu. 17:4), but seven times in his life; supposing that if a man had any way abused him seven times, though he were ever so desirous to be reconciled, he might then abandon his society, and have no more to do with him. Perhaps Peter had an eye to Prov. 24:16. *A just man falleth seven times;* or to the mention of *three transgressions,* and *four,* which God would no more pass by, Amos 2:1. Note, There is a proneness in our corrupt nature to stint ourselves in that which is good, and to be afraid of doing too much in religion, particularly of forgiving too much, though we have so much forgiven us.

II. Christ's direct answer to Peter's question; *I say not unto thee, Until seven times* (he never intended to set up any such bounds), but, *Until seventy times seven;* a certain number for an indefinite one, but a great one. Note, It does not look well for us to keep count of the offences done against us by our brethren. There is something of ill-nature in scoring up the injuries we forgive, as if we would allow ourselves to be revenged when the measure is full. God keeps an account (Deu. 32:34), because he is the Judge, and vengeance is his; but we must not, lest we be found stepping into his throne. It is necessary to the preservation of peace, both within and without, to pass by injuries, without reckoning how often; to forgive, and forget. God multiplies his pardons, and so should we, Ps. 77:38, 40. It intimates that we should make it our constant practice to forgive injuries, and should accustom ourselves to it till it becomes habitual.

III. A further discourse of our Saviour's, by way of parable, to show the necessity of forgiving the injuries that are done to us. Parables are of use, not only for the pressing of Christian duties; for they make and leave an impression. The parable is a comment upon the fifth petition of the Lord's prayer, *Forgive us our trespasses, as we forgive them that trespass against us.* Those, and those only, may expect to be forgiven of God, who forgive their brethren. The parable represents the *kingdom of heaven,* that is, the church, and the administration of the gospel dispensation in it. The church is God's family, it is his court; there he dwells, there he rules. God is our master; his servants we are, at least in profession and obligation. In general, the parable intimates how much provocation God has from his family on earth, and how untoward his servants are.

There are three things in the parable.

1. The master's wonderful clemency to his servant who was indebted to him; he forgave him ten thousand talents, out of pure compassion to him, *v.* 23–27. Where observe,

(1.) Every sin we commit is a debt to God; not like a debt to an equal, contracted by buying or borrowing, but to a superior; like a debt to a prince when a recognizance is forfeited, or a penalty incurred by a breech of the law or a breach of the peace; like the debt of a servant to his master, by withholding his service, wasting his lord's goods, breaking his indentures, and incurring the penalty. We are all debtors; we owe satisfaction, and are liable to the process of the law.

(2.) There is an account kept of these debts, and we must shortly be reckoned with for them. This king *would take account of his servants.* God now reckons with us by our own consciences; conscience is an auditor for God in the soul, to call us to account, and to account with us. One of the first questions that an awakened Christian asks, is, *How much owest thou unto my Lord?* And unless it be bribed, it will tell the truth, and not write fifty for a hundred. There is another day of reckoning coming, when these accounts will be called over, and either passed or disallowed, and nothing but the blood of Christ will balance the account.

(3.) The debt of sin is a very great debt; and some are more in debt, by reason of sin, than others. When he *began to reckon,* one of the first defaulters appeared to owe *ten thousand talents.* There is no evading the enquiries of divine justice; your sin will be sure to find you out. The debt was ten thousand talents, a vast sum, amounting by computation to one million eight hundred and seventy-five thousand pounds sterling; a king's ransom or a kingdom's subsidy, more likely than a servant's debt; see what our sins are, [1.] For the heinousness of their nature; they are talents, the greatest denomination that ever was used in the account of money or weight. Every sin is the load of a talent, *a talent of lead, this is wickedness,* Zec. 5:7, 8. The trusts committed to us, as stewards of the grace of God, are each of them a talent (*ch.* 25:15), a talent of gold, and for every one of them buried, much more for every one of them wasted, we are a talent in debt, and this raises the account. [2.] For the vastness of their number; they are ten thousand, a myriad, more than *the hairs on our head,* Ps. 40:12. Who can understand *the number of his errors, or tell how oft he offends?* Ps. 19:12.

(4.) The debt of sin is so great, that we are not able to pay it; *He had not to pay.* Sinners are insolvent debtors; the scripture, *which concludes all under sin,* is a statute of bankruptcy against us all. Silver and gold would not pay our debt, Ps. 49:6, 7. Sacrifice and offering would not do it; our good works are but God's work in us, and cannot make satisfaction; we are without strength, and cannot help ourselves.

(5.) If God should deal with us in strict justice; we should be condemned as insolvent debtors, and God might exact the debt by glorifying himself in our utter ruin. Justice demands satisfaction, *Currat, lex — Let the sentence of the law be executed.* The servant had contracted this debt by his wastefulness and wilfulness, and therefore might justly be left to lie by it. *His lord commanded him to be sold,* as a bond-slave into the galleys, sold to grind in the prison-house; *his wife and children to be sold, and all that he had, and payment to be made.* See here what every sin deserves; this is *the wages of sin.* [1.] To be sold. Those that *sell themselves to work wickedness,* must be sold, to make satisfaction. Captives to sin are captives to wrath. He that is sold for a bond-slave is deprived of all his comforts, and has nothing left him but his life, that he may be sensible of his miseries; which is the case of damned sinners. [2.] Thus he would have *payment to be made,* that is, something done towards it; though it is impossible that the sale of one so worthless should amount to the payment of so great a debt. By the damnation of sinners divine justice will be to eternity in the satisfying, but never satisfied.

(6.) Convinced sinners cannot but humble themselves before God, and pray for mercy. *The servant,* under this charge, and this doom, *fell down* at the feet of his royal master, *and worshipped him;* or, as some copies read it, *he besought him;* his address was very submissive and very importunate; *Have patience with me, and I will pay thee all, v.* 26. The servant knew before that he was so much in debt, and yet was under no concern about it, till he was called to an account. Sinners are commonly careless about the pardon of their sins, till they come under the arrests of some awakening word, some startling providence, or approaching death, and then, *Wherewith shall I come before the Lord?* Mic. 6:6. How easily, how quickly, can God bring the proudest sinner to his feet; Ahab to his sackcloth, Manasseh to his prayers, Pharaoh to his confessions, Judas to his restitution, Simon Magus to his supplication, Belshazzar and Felix to their tremblings. The stoutest heart will fail, when God sets the sins in order before it. This servant doth not deny the debt, nor seek evasions, nor go about to abscond.

But, [1.] He begs time; *Have patience with me.* Patience and forbearance are a great favour, but it is folly to think that these alone will save us; reprieves are not pardons. Many are borne with, who are not thereby *brought to repentance* (Rom. 2:4), and then their being borne with does them no kindness.

[2.] He promises payment; *Have patience* awhile, *and I will pay thee all.* Note, It is the folly of many who are under convictions of sin, to imagine that they can make God satisfaction for the wrong they have done him; as those who, like a compounding bankrupt, would discharge the debt, by giving their *first-born for their transgressions* (Mic. 6:7), who *go about to establish their own righteousness,* Rom. 10:3. He that *had nothing to pay* with (*v.* 25) fancied he could pay *all.* See how close pride sticks, even to awakened sinners; they are convinced, but not humbled.

(7.) The God of infinite mercy is very ready, out of pure compassion, to forgive the sins of those that humble themselves before him (*v.* 27); *The lord of that servant,* when he might justly have ruined him, mercifully released him; and, since he could not be satisfied by the payment of the debt, he would be glorified by the pardon of it. The servant's prayer was, *Have patience with me;* the master's grant is a discharge in full. Note, [1.] The pardon of sin is owing to the mercy of God, to his tender mercy (Lu. 1:77, 78); *He was moved with compassion.* God's reasons of mercy are fetched from within himself; he has mercy *because he will have mercy.* God looked with pity on mankind in general, because miserable, and sent his Son to be a Surety for them; he looks with pity on particular penitents, because sensible of their misery (their hearts broken and contrite), and accepts them in the Beloved. [2.] There is forgiveness with God for the greatest sins, if they be repented of. Though the debt was vastly great, he *forgave it all, v.* 32. Though our sins be very numerous and very heinous, yet, upon gospel terms, they may be pardoned. [3.] The forgiving of the debt is the loosing of the debtor; *He loosed him.* The obligation is cancelled, the judgment vacated; we never walk at liberty till our sins are forgiven. But observe, Though he discharged him from the penalty as a debtor, he did not discharge him from his duty as a servant. The pardon of sin doth not slacken, but strengthen, our obligations to obedience; and we must reckon it a favour that God is pleased to continue such wasteful servants as we have been in such a gainful service as his is, and should therefore *deliver us, that we might serve him,* Lu. 1:74. *I am thy servant, for thou hast loosed my bonds.*

2. The servant's unreasonable severity toward his fellow-servant, notwithstanding his lord's clemency toward him, *v.* 28–30. This represents the sin of those who, though they are not unjust in demanding that which is not their own, yet are rigorous and unmerciful in demanding that which is their own, to the utmost of right, which sometimes proves a real wrong. *Summum jus summa injuria — Push a claim to an extremity, and it becomes a wrong.* To exact satisfaction for debts of injury, which tends neither to reparation nor to the public good, but purely for revenge, though the law may allow it, *in terrorem — in order to strike terror,* and for the hardness of men's hearts, yet savours not of a Christian spirit. To sue for money-debts, when the debtor cannot possibly pay them, and so let him perish in prison, argues a greater love of money, and a less love of our neighbour, than we ought to have, Neh. 5:7.

See here, (1.) How small the debt was, how very small, compared with the *ten thousand talents* which his lord forgave him; *He owed him a hundred pence,* about three pounds and half a crown of our money. Note, Offences done to men are nothing to those which are committed against God. Dishonours done to a man like ourselves are but as *peace, motes, gnats;* but dishonours done to God are as *talents, beams, camels.* Not that *therefore* we may make light of wronging our neighbour, for that is also a sin against God; but *therefore* we should make light of our neighbour's wronging us, and not aggravate it, or study revenge. David was unconcerned as the indignities done to him; *I, as a deaf man, heard not;* but laid much to heart the sins committed against God; for them, *rivers of tears ran down his eyes.*

(2.) How severe the demand was; *He laid hands on him, and took him by the throat.* Proud and angry men think, if the matter of their demand be just, that will bear them out, though the manner of it be ever so cruel and unmerciful; but it will not hold. What needed all this violence? The debt might have been demanded without taking the debtor by the throat; without sending for a writ, or setting the bailiff upon him. How lordly is this man's carriage, and yet how base and servile is his spirit! If he had been himself going to prison for his debt to his lord, his occasions would have been so pressing, that he might have had some pretence for going to this extremity in requiring his own; but frequently pride and malice prevail more to make men severe than the most urgent necessity would do.

(3.) How submissive the debtor was; *His fellow servant,* though his equal, yet knowing how much he lay at his mercy, *fell down at his feet,* and humbled himself to him for this trifling debt, as much as he did to his lord for that great debt; for *the borrower is servant to the lender,* Prov. 22:7. Note, Those who cannot pay their debts ought to be very respectful to their creditors, and not only give them good words, but do them all the good offices they possibly can: they must not be angry at those who claim their own, nor speak ill of them for it, no, not though they do it in a rigorous manner, but in that case leave it to God to plead their cause. The poor man's request is, *Have patience with me;* he honestly confesses the debt, and puts not his creditor to the charge of proving it, only begs time. Note, Forbearance, though it be no acquittance, is sometimes a piece of needful and laudable charity. As we must not be hard, so we must not be hasty, in our demands, but think how long God bears with us.

(4.) How implacable and furious the creditor was (*v.* 30); *He would not have patience with him,* would not hearken to his fair promise, but without mercy *cast him into prison.* How insolently did he trample upon one as good as himself, that submitted to him! How cruelly did he use one that had done him no harm, and though it would be no advantage to himself! In this, as in a glass, unmerciful creditors may see their own faces, who take pleasure in nothing more than to swallow up and destroy (2 Sa. 20:19), and glory in having their poor debtors' bones.

(5.) How much concerned the rest of the servants were; *They were very sorry* (*v.* 31), sorry for the creditor's cruelty, and for the debtor's calamity. Note, The sins and sufferings of our fellow-servants should be a matter of grief and trouble to us. It is sad that any of our brethren should either make themselves beast of prey, by cruelty and barbarity; or be made beasts of slavery, by the inhuman usage of those who have power over them. To see a fellow-servant, either raging like a bear or trampled on like a worm, cannot but occasion great regret to all that have any jealousy for the honour either of their nature of their religion. See with what eye Solomon looked both upon *the tears of the oppressed,* and *the power of the oppressors,* Eccl. 4:1.

(6.) How notice of it was brought to the master; *They came, and told their lord.* They durst not reprove their fellow-servant for it, he was so unreasonable and outrageous *(let a bear robbed of her whelps meet a man, rather than such a fool in his folly);* but they went to their lord, and besought him to appear for the oppressed against the oppressor. Note, That which gives us occasion for sorrow, should give us occasion for prayer. Let our complaints both of the wickedness of the wicked and of the afflictions of the afflicted, be brought to God, and left with him.

3. The master's just resentment of the cruelty his servant was guilty of. If the servants took it so ill, much more would the master, whose compassions are infinitely above ours. Now observe here,

(1.) How he reproved his servant's cruelty (*v.* 32, 33); *O thou wicked servant.* Note, Unmercifulness is wickedness, it is great wickedness. [1.] He upbraids him with the mercy he had found with his master; *I forgive thee all that debt.* Those that will use God's favours, shall never be upbraided with them, but those that abuse them, may expect it, *ch.* 11:20. Consider, It was *all that debt,* that great debt. Note, The greatness of sin magnifies the riches of pardoning mercy: we should think *how much has been forgiven us,* Lu. 7:47. [2.] He thence shows him the obligation he was under to be merciful to his fellow-servant; *Shouldst not thou also have had compassion on thy fellow-servant, even as I had pity on thee?* Note, It is justly expected, that such as have received mercy, should show mercy. *Dat ille veniam facile, cui venia est opus — He who needs forgiveness, easily bestows it.* Senec. Agamemn. He shows him, *First,* That he should have been more compassionate to the distress of his fellow servant, because he had himself experienced the same distress. What we have had the feeling of ourselves, we can the better have the fellow feeling of with our brethren. *The Israelites knew the heart of a stranger, for they were strangers;* and this servant should have better known the heart of an arrested debtor, than to have been thus hard upon such a one. *Secondly,* That he should have been more conformable to the example of his master's tenderness, having himself experienced it, so much to his advantage. Note, The comfortable sense of pardoning mercy tends much to the disposing of our hearts to forgive our brethren. It was in the close of the day o atonement that the jubilee trumpet sounded *a release of debts* (Lev. 25:9); for we must have compassion on our brethren, as God has on us.

(2.) How he revoked his pardon and cancelled the acquittance, so that the judgment against him revived (*v.* 34); *He delivered him to the tormentors, till he should pay all that was due unto him.* Though the wickedness was very great, his lord laid upon him no other punishment than the payment of his own debt. Note, Those that will not come up to the terms of the gospel need be no more miserable than to be left open to the law, and to let that have its course against them. See how the punishment answers the sin; he that would not forgive shall not be forgiven; *He delivered him to the tormentors;* the utmost he could do to his fellow servant was but to cast him into prison, but he was himself delivered to the tormentors. Note, The power of God's wrath to ruin us, goes far beyond the utmost extent of any creature's strength and wrath. The reproaches and terrors of his own conscience would be his tormentors, for that is a worm that dies not; devils, the executioners of God's wrath, that are sinners' tempters now, will be their tormentors for ever. He was sent to Bridewell till he should pay all. Note, Our debts to God are never compounded; either all is forgiven or all is exacted; glorified saints in heaven are pardoned all, through Christ's complete satisfaction; damned sinners in hell are paying all, that is, are punished for all. The offence done to God by sin is in point of honour, which cannot be compounded for without such a diminution as the case will by no means admit, and therefore, some way or other, by the sinner or by his surety, it must be satisfied.

Lastly, Here is the application of the whole parable, (*v.* 35). *So likewise shall my heavenly Father do also unto you.* The title Christ here gives to God was made use of, *v.* 19, in a comfortable promise; *It shall be done for them of my Father which is in heaven;* here it is made use of in a terrible threatening. If God's governing be fatherly, it follows thence, that it is righteous, but it does not therefore follow that it is not rigorous, or that under his government we must not be kept in awe by the fear of the divine wrath. When we pray to God as *our Father in heaven,* we are taught to ask for *the forgiveness of sins, as we forgive our debtors.* Observe here,

1. The duty of forgiving; we must *from our hearts* forgive. Note, We do not forgive our offending brother aright, nor acceptably, if we do not forgive from the heart; for that is it that God looks at. No malice must be harboured there, nor ill will to any person, one or another; no projects of revenge must be hatched there, nor desires of it, as there are in many who outwardly appear peaceable and reconciled. Yet this is not enough; we must from the heart desire and seek the welfare even of those that have offended us.

2. The danger of not forgiving; *So shall your heavenly Father do.* (1.) This is not intended to teach us that God reverses his pardons to any, but that he denies them to those that are unqualified for them, according to the tenour of the gospel; though having seemed to be humbled, like Ahab, they thought themselves, and others thought them, in a pardoned state, and they made bold with the comfort of it. Intimations enough we have in scripture of the forfeiture of pardons, for caution to the presumptuous; and yet we have security enough of the continuance of them, for comfort to those that are sincere, but timorous; that the one may fear, and the other may hope. Those that do not *forgive their brother's trespasses,* did never truly repent of their own, nor ever truly believe the gospel; and therefore that which is *taken away* is only what *they seemed to have,* Lu. 8:18. (2.) This is intended to teach us, that *they shall have judgment without mercy, that have showed no mercy,* Jam. 2:13. It is indispensably necessary to pardon and peace, that we not only *do justly,* but *love mercy.* It is an essential part of that religion which is *pure and undefiled before God and the Father,* of that *wisdom from above,* which is *gentle, and easy to be entreated.* Look how *they* will answer it another day, who, though they bear the Christian name, persist in the most rigorous and unmerciful treatment of their brethren, as if the strictest laws of Christ might be dispensed with for the gratifying of their unbridled passions; and so they curse themselves every time they say the Lord's prayer.

CHAPTER 19

In this chapter, we have, I. Christ changing his quarters, leaving Galilee, and coming into the coasts of Judea (*v.* 1, 2). II. His dispute with the Pharisees about divorce, and his discourse with his disciples upon occasion of it (*v.* 3–12). III. The kind entertainment he gave to some little children which were brought to him (*v.* 13–15). IV. An account of what passed between Christ and a hopeful young gentleman that applied himself to him (*v.* 16–22). V. His discourse with his disciples upon that occasion, concerning the difficulty of the salvation of those that have much in the world, and the certain recompence of those that leave all for Christ (*v.* 23–30).

Verses 1–2

We have here an account of Christ's removal. Observe, 1. He left Galilee. There he had been brought up, and had spent the greatest part of his life in that remote despicable part of the country; it was only upon occasion of the feasts, that he *came up to Jerusalem, and manifested himself there;* and, we may suppose, that, having no constant residence there when he did come, his preaching and miracles were the more observable and acceptable. But it was an instance

of his humiliation, and in this, as in other things, he appeared in a mean state, that he would go under the character of a Galilean, a north-countryman, the least polite and refined part of the nation. Most of Christ's sermons hitherto had been preached, and most of his miracles wrought, in Galilee; but now, having *finished these sayings, he departed from Galilee,* and it was his final farewell; for (unless his *passing through the midst of Samaria and Galilee,* Lu. 17:11, was after this, which yet was but a visit *in transitu — as he passed through the country*) he never came to Galilee again till after his resurrection, which makes this transition very remarkable. Christ did not take his leave of Galilee till he had done his work there, and then he departed thence. Note, As Christ's faithful ministers are not taken out of the world, so they are not removed from any place, till they have finished their testimony in that place, Rev. 11:7. This is very comfortable to those that follow not their own humours, but God's providence, in their removals, that their sayings shall be finished before they depart. And who would desire to continue any where longer than he has work to do for God there?

2. *He came into the coasts of Judea, beyond Jordan,* that *they* might have their day of visitation as well as Galilee, for they also belonged to *the lost sheep of the house of Israel.* But still Christ kept to those parts of Canaan that lay towards other nations: Galilee is called *Galilee of the Gentiles;* and the Syrians dwelt beyond Jordan. Thus Christ intimated, that, while he kept within the confines of the Jewish nation, he had his eye upon the Gentiles, and his gospel was aiming and coming toward them.

3. *Great multitudes followed him.* Where Shiloh is, there will *the gathering of the people be.* The *redeemed of the Lord* are such as *follow the Lamb whithersoever he goes,* Rev. 14:4. When Christ departs, it is best for us to follow him. It was a piece of respect to Christ, and yet it was a continual trouble, to be thus crowded after, wherever he went; but he sought not his own ease, nor, considering how mean and contemptible this mob was (as some would call them), his own honour much, in the eye of the world; he *went about doing good;* for so it follows, *he healed them there.* This shows what they followed him for, to have their sick healed; and they found him as able and ready to help here, as he had been in Galilee; for, wherever this *Sun of righteousness arose,* it was *with healing under his wings. He healed them there,* because he would not have them follow him to Jerusalem, lest it should give offence. *He shall not strive, nor cry.*

Verses 3–12

We have here the law of Christ in the case of divorce, occasioned, as some other declarations of his will, by a dispute with *the Pharisees.* So patiently did he endure the contradiction of sinners, that he turned it into instructions to his own disciples! Observe, here

I. The case proposed by the Pharisees (*v.* 3); *Is it lawful for a man to put away his wife?* This they asked, tempting him, not desiring to be taught by him. Some time ago, he had, in Galilee, declared his mind in this matter, against that which was the common practice (*ch.* 5:31, 32); and if he would, in like manner, declare himself now against divorce, they would make use of it for the prejudicing and incensing of the people of this country against him, who would look with a jealous eye upon one that attempted to cut them short in a liberty they were fond of. They hoped he would lose himself in the affections of the people as much by this as by any of his precepts. Or, the temptation might be designed this: If he should say that divorces were not lawful, they would reflect upon him as an enemy to the law of Moses, which allowed them; if he should say that they were, they would represent his doctrine as not having that perfection in it which was expected in the doctrine of the Messiah; since, though divorces were tolerated, they were looked upon by the stricter sort of people as not of good report. Some think, that, though the law of Moses did permit divorce, yet, in assigning the just causes for it, there was a controversy between the Pharisees among themselves, and they desired to know what Christ said to it. Matrimonial cases have been numerous, and sometimes intricate and perplexed; made so not by the law of God, but by the lusts and follies of men; and often in these cases people resolve, before they ask, what they will do.

Their question is, *Whether a man may put away his wife for every cause.* That it might be done for some cause, even for that of fornication, was granted; but may it be done, as

now it commonly was done, by the looser sort of people, for every cause; for any cause that a man shall think fit to assign, though ever so frivolous; upon every dislike or displeasure? The toleration, in this case, permitted it, *in case she found no favour in his eyes, because he hath found some uncleanness in her,* Deu. 24:1. This they interpreted so largely as to make any disgust, though causeless, the ground of a divorce.

II. Christ's answer to this question; though it was proposed to tempt him, yet, being a case of conscience, and a weighty one, he gave a full answer to it, not a direct one, but an effectual one; laying down such principles as undeniably prove that such arbitrary divorces as were then in use, which made the matrimonial bond so very precarious, were by no means lawful. Christ himself would not give the rule without a reason, nor lay down his judgment without scripture proof to support it. Now his argument is this; "If husband and wife are by the will and appointment of God joined together in the strictest and closest union, then they are not to be lightly, and upon every occasion, separated; if the know be sacred, it cannot be easily untied." Now, to prove that there is such a union between man and wife, he urges three things.

1. The creation of Adam and Eve, concerning which he appeals to their own knowledge of the scriptures; *Have ye not read?* It is some advantage in arguing, to deal with those that own, and have read, the scriptures; *Ye have read* (but have not considered) *that he which made them at the beginning, made them male and female,* Gen. 1:27; 5:2. Note, It will be of great use to us often to think of our creation, how and by whom, what and for what, we were created. *He made them male and female,* one female for one male; so that Adam could not divorce his wife, and take another, for there was no other to take. It likewise intimated an inseparable union between them; Eve was a rib out of Adam's side, so that he could not put her away, but he must put away a piece of himself, and contradict the manifest indications of her creation. Christ hints briefly at this, but, in appealing to what they had read, he refers them to the original record, where it is observable, that, though the rest of the living creatures were made male and female, yet it is not said so concerning any of them, but only concerning mankind; because between man and woman the conjunction is rational, and intended for nobler purposes than merely the pleasing of sense and the preserving of a seed; and it is therefore more close and firm than that between male and female among the brutes, who were not capable of being such help-meets for one another as Adam and Ever were. Hence the manner of expression is somewhat singular (Gen. 1:27), *In the image of God created he him, male and female created he them; him* and *them* are used promiscuously; being one by creation before they were two, when they became one again by marriage-covenant, that oneness could not but be closer and indissoluble.

2. The fundamental law of marriage, which is, that *a man shall leave father and mother, and shall cleave to his wife, v.* 5. The relation between husband and wife is nearer than that between parents and children; now, if the filial relation may not easily be violated, much less may the marriage union be broken. May a child desert his parents, or may a parent abandon his children, for any cause, for every cause? No, by no means. Much less may a husband put away his wife, betwixt whom, though not by nature, yet by divine appointment, the relation is nearer, and the bond of union stronger, than between parents and children; for that is in a great measure superseded by marriage, when a man must leave his parents, to cleave to his wife. See here the power of a divine institution, that the result of it is a union stronger than that which results from the highest obligations of nature.

3. The nature of the marriage contract; it is a union of persons; *They twain shall be one flesh,* so that (*v.* 6) *they are no more twain, but one flesh.* A man's children are pieces of himself, but his wife is himself. As the conjugal union is closer than that between parents and children, so it is in a manner equivalent to that between one member and another in the natural body. As this is a reason why husbands should love their wives, so it is a reason why they should not put away their wives, for *no man ever yet hated his own flesh,* or cut it off, *but nourishes and cherishes it,* and does all he can to preserve it. They two shall be one, therefore there must be but one wife, for God made but one Eve for one Adam, Mal. 2:15.

From hence he infers, *What God hath joined together, let*

not man put asunder. Note, (1.) Husband and wife are of God's joining together; *synezeuxen — he hath yoked them together,* so the word is, and it is very significant. God himself instituted the relation between husband and wife in the state of innocence. Marriage and the sabbath are the most ancient of divine ordinances. Though marriage be not peculiar to the church, but common to the world, yet, being stamped with a divine institution, and here ratified by our Lord Jesus, it ought to be managed *after a godly sort, and sanctified by the word of God, and prayer.* A conscientious regard to God in this ordinance would have a good influence upon the duty, and consequently upon the comfort, of the relation. (2.) Husband and wife, being joined together by the ordinance of God, are not to be put asunder by any ordinance of man. Let not man put them asunder; not the husband himself, nor any one for him; not the magistrate, God never gave him authority to do it. The God of Israel hath said, that *he hateth putting away,* Mal. 2:16. It is a general rule that man must not go about to *put asunder what God hath joined together.*

III. An objection started by the Pharisees against this; an objection not destitute of colour and plausibility (*v.* 7); *"Why did Moses command to give a writing of divorcement,* in case a man did put away his wife?" He urged scripture reason against divorce; they allege scripture authority for it. Note, The seeming contradictions that are in the word of God are great stumbling-blocks to men of corrupt minds. It is true, *Moses was faithful to him that appointed him,* and commanded nothing but *what he received from the Lord;* but as to the thing itself, what they call a *command* was only as *allowance* (Deu. 24:1), and designed rather to restrain the exorbitances of it than to give countenance to the thing itself. The Jewish doctors themselves observe such limitations in that law, that it could not be done without great deliberation. A particular reason must be assigned, the bill of divorce must be written, and, as a judicial act, must have all the solemnities of a deed, executed and enrolled. It must be given into the hands of the wife herself, and (which would oblige men, if they had any consideration in them, to consider) they were expressly forbidden ever to come together again.

IV. Christ's answer to this objection, in which,

1. He rectifies their mistake concerning the law of Moses; they called it a *command,* Christ calls it but a *permission, a toleration.* Carnal hearts will take an ell if but an inch be given them. The law of Moses, in this case, was a political law, which God gave, as the Governor of that people; and it was for reasons of state, that divorces were tolerated. The strictness of the marriage union being the result, not of a natural, but of a positive law, the wisdom of God dispensed with divorces in some cases, without any impeachment of his holiness.

But Christ tells them there was a reason for this toleration, not at all for their credit; *It was because of the hardness of your hearts,* that you were permitted to *put away your wives.* Moses complained of the people of Israel in his time, that *their hearts were hardened* (Deu. 9:6; 31:27), hardened against God; this is here meant of their being hardened against their relations; they were generally violent and outrageous, which way soever they took, both in their appetites and in their passions; and therefore if they had not been allowed to put away their wives, when they had conceived a dislike of them, they would have used them cruelly, would have beaten and abused them, and perhaps have murdered them. Note, There is not a greater piece of hard-heartedness in the world, than for a man to be harsh and severe with his own wife. The Jews, it seems, were infamous for this, and therefore were allowed to put them away; better divorce them than do worse, than that *the altar of the Lord should be covered with tears,* Mal. 2:13. A little compliance, to humour a madman, or a man in a frenzy, may prevent a greater mischief. Positive laws may be dispensed with for the preservation of the law of nature, for God *will have mercy and not sacrifice;* but then those are hard-hearted wretches, who have made it necessary; and none can wish to have the liberty of divorce, without virtually owning the hardness of their hearts. Observe, He saith, It is for the hardness of *your* hearts, not only theirs who lived then, but all their seed. Note, God not only sees, but foresees, the hardness of men's hearts; he suited both the ordinances and providences of the Old Testament to the temper of that people, both in terror. Further observe, The law of Moses considered the hardness of men's hearts, but the gospel of Christ cures it; and his grace *takes away the heart of stone, and gives a heart of flesh.* By the law was the knowledge of sin, but by the gospel was the conquest of it.

2. He reduces them to the original institution; *But from the beginning it was not so.* Note, Corruptions that are crept into any ordinance of God must be purged out by having recourse to the primitive institution. If the copy be vicious, it must be examined and corrected by the original. Thus, when St. Paul would redress the grievances in the church of Corinth about the Lord's supper, he appealed to the appointment (1 Co. 11:23), So and so *I received from the Lord.* Truth was from the beginning; we must therefore enquire for *the good old way* (Jer. 6:16), and must reform, mot by later patterns, but by ancient rules.

3. He settles the point by an express law; *I say unto you* (*v.* 9); and it agrees with what he said before (*ch.* 5:32); there it was said in preaching, here in dispute, but it is the same, for Christ is constant to himself. Now, in both these places,

(1.) He allows divorce, in case of adultery; the reason of the law against divorce being this, *They two shall be one flesh.* If the wife play the harlot, and make herself one flesh with an adulterer, the reason of the law ceases, and so does the law. By the law of Moses adultery was punished with death, Deu. 22:22. Now our Saviour mitigates the rigour of that, and appoints divorce to be the penalty. Dr. Whitby understands this, not of adultery, but (because our Saviour uses the word *porneia — fornication*) of uncleanness committed before marriage, but discovered afterward; because, if it were committed after, it was a capital crime, and there needed no divorce.

(2.) He disallows it in all other cases: *Whosoever puts away his wife, except for fornication, and marries another, commits adultery.* This is a direct answer to their query, that it is not lawful. In this, as in other things, gospel times are *times of reformation,* Heb. 9:10. The law of Christ tends to reinstate man in his primitive integrity; the law of love, conjugal love, is no new commandment, but was from the beginning. If we consider what mischiefs to families and states, what confusions and disorders, would follow upon arbitrary divorces, we shall see how much this law of Christ is for our own benefit, and what a friend Christianity is to our secular interests.

The law of Moses allowing divorce for the hardness of men's hearts, and the law of Christ forbidding it, intimate, that Christians being under a dispensation of love and liberty, tenderness of heart may justly be expected among them, that they will not be hard-hearted, like Jews, *for God has called us to peace.* There will be no occasion for divorces, if we *forbear one another, and forgive one another, in love,* as those that are, and hope to be, forgiven, and have found God not forward to *put us away,* Isa. 50:1. No need of divorces, if *husbands love their wives, and wives be obedient to their husbands,* and they live together as heirs of the grace of life: and these are the laws of Christ, such as we find not in all the law of Moses.

V. Here is a suggestion of the disciples against this law of Christ (*v.* 10); *If the case of the man be so with his wife, it is better not to marry.* It seems, the disciples themselves were loth to give up the liberty of divorce, thinking it a good expedient for preserving comfort in the married state; and therefore, like sullen children, if they have not what they would have, they will throw away what they have. If they may not be allowed to put away their wives when they please, they will have no wives at all; though, from the beginning, when no divorce was allowed, God said, *It is not good for man to be alone, and blessed them,* pronounced them blessed who were thus strictly joined together; yet, unless they may have a liberty of divorce, they think it is good for a man not to marry. Note, 1. Corrupt nature is impatient of restraint, and would fain break Christ's bonds in sunder, and have a liberty for its own lusts. 2. It is a foolish, peevish thing for men to abandon the comforts of this life, because of the crosses that are commonly woven in with them, as if we must needs go out of the world, because we have not every thing to our mind in the world; or must enter into no useful calling or condition, because it is made our duty to abide in it. No, whatever our condition is, we must bring our minds to it, be thankful for its comforts, submissive to its crosses, and, as God has done, *set the one over against the other,* and make the best of that which is, Eccl. 7:14. If the yoke of marriage may not be thrown off at pleasure, it does not follow that *therefore* we must not come under it; but *therefore,* when we do come under it, we must resolve to comport with it, by love, and meekness, and patience, which will make divorce the most unnecessary undesirable thing that can be.

VI. Christ's answer to this suggestion (*v.* 11, 12), in which,

1. He allows it good for some not to marry; *He that is able to receive it, let him receive it.* Christ allowed what the disciples said, *It is good not to marry;* not as an objection against the prohibition of divorce, as they intended it, but as giving them a rule (perhaps no less unpleasing to them), that they who have the gift of continence, and are not under any necessity of marrying, do best if they continue single (1 Co. 7:1); for they that are unmarried have opportunity, if they have but a heart, to care more *for the things of the Lord, how they may please the Lord* (1 Co. 7:32–34). being less encumbered with the cares of this life, and having a greater vacancy of thought and time to mind better things. The increase of grace is better than the increase of the family, and fellowship with the Father and with his Son Jesus Christ is to be preferred before any other fellowship.

2. He disallows it, as utterly mischievous, to forbid marriage, because *all men cannot receive this saying;* indeed few can, and therefore the crosses of the married state must be borne, rather than that men should run themselves into temptation, to avoid them; *better marry than burn.*

Christ speaks here of a twofold unaptness to marriage.

(1.) That which is a calamity by the providence of God; such as those labour under who are born eunuchs, or made so by men, who, being incapable of answering one great end of marriage, ought not to marry. But to that calamity let them oppose the opportunity that there is in the single state of serving God better, to balance it.

(2.) That which is a virtue by the grace of God; such is theirs who *have made themselves eunuchs for the kingdom of heaven's sake.* This is meant of an unaptness for marriage, not in body (which some, through mistake of this scripture, have foolishly and wickedly brought upon themselves), but in mind. Those have thus made themselves eunuchs who have attained a holy indifference to all the delights of the married state, have a fixed resolution, in the strength of God's grace, wholly to abstain from them; and by fasting, and other instances of mortification, have subdued all desires toward them. These are they that *can receive* this saying; and yet these are not to bind themselves by a vow that they will never marry, only that, in the mind they are now in, they purpose not to marry.

Now, [1.] This affection to the single state must be given of God; for none can receive it, *save they to whom it is given.* Note, Continence is a special gift of God to some, and not to others; and when a man, in the single state, finds by experience that he has this gift, he may determine with himself, and (as the apostle speaks, 1 Co. 7:37), stand steadfast in his heart, having no necessity, but having power over his own will, that he will keep himself so. But men, in this case, must take heed lest they boast of a false gift, Prov. 25:14.

[2.] The single state must be chosen for the kingdom of heaven's sake; in those who resolve never to marry, only that they may save charges, or may gratify a morose selfish humour, or have a greater liberty to serve other lusts and pleasures, it is so far from being a virtue, that it is an ill-natured vice; but when it is for religion's sake, not as in itself a meritorious act (which papists make it), but only as a means to keep our minds more entire for, and more intent upon, the services of religion, and that, having no families to provide for, we may do the more works of charity, then it is approved and accepted of God. Note, That condition is best for us, and to be chosen and stuck to accordingly, which is best for our souls, and tends most to the preparing of us for, and the preserving of us to, the kingdom of heaven.

Verses 13–15

We have here the welcome which Christ gave to some little children that were brought to him. Observe,

I. The faith of those that brought them. How many they were, that were brought, we are not told; but they were so little as to be taken up in arms, a year old, it may be, or two at most. The account here given of it, is, that *there were brought unto him little children, that he should put his hands on them, and pray, v.* 13. Probably they were their parents, guardians, or nurses, that brought them; and herein, 1. They testified their respect to Christ, and the value they had for his favour and blessing. Note, Those who glorify Christ by coming to him themselves, should further glorify him by bringing all they have, or have influence upon, to him likewise. Thus give him the honour of his unsearchable riches of grace, his overflowing, never-failing, fulness. We cannot better honour Christ than by making use of him. 2. They did a kindness to their children, not doubting but they would fare the better, in this world and the other, for the blessing and prayers of the Lord Jesus, whom they looked upon at least as an extraordinary person, as a prophet, if not as a priest and king; and the blessings of such were valued and desired. Others brought their children to Christ, to be healed when they were sick; but these children were under no present malady, only they desired a blessing for them. Note, It is a good thing when we come to Christ ourselves, and bring our children to him, before we are driven to him (as we say) by woe-need; not only to visit him when we are in trouble, but to address ourselves to him in a sense of our general dependence on him, and of the benefit we expect by him, this is pleasing to him.

They desired that he would put his hands on them, and pray. Imposition of hands was a ceremony used especially in paternal blessings; Jacob used it when he blessed and adopted the sons of Joseph, Gen. 48:14. It intimates something of love and familiarity mixed with power and authority, and bespeaks an efficacy in the blessing. Whom Christ prays for in heaven, he *puts his hand upon* by his Spirit. Note, (1.) Little children may be brought to Christ as needing, and being capable of receiving, blessings from him, and having an interest in his intercession. (2.) Therefore they should be brought to him. We cannot do better for our children than to commit them to the Lord Jesus, to be wrought upon, and prayed for, by him. We can but beg a blessing for them, it is Christ only that can command the blessing.

II. The fault of the disciples in rebuking them. They discountenanced the address as vain and frivolous, and reproved them that made it as impertinent and troublesome. Either they thought it below their Master to take notice of little children, except any thing in particular ailed them; or, they thought he had toil enough with his other work, and would not have him diverted from it; or, they thought if such an address as this were encouraged, all the country would bring their children to him, and they should never see an end of it. Note, It is well for us, that Christ has more love and tenderness in him than the best of his disciples have. And let us learn of him not to discountenance any willing well-meaning souls in their enquiries after Christ, though they are but weak. If *he* do not break the bruised reed, *we* should not. Those that seek unto Christ, must not think it strange if they meet with opposition and rebuke, even from good men, who think they know the mind of Christ better than they do.

III. The favour of our Lord Jesus. See how he carried it here.

1. He rebuked the disciples (*v.* 14); *Suffer little children, and forbid them not;* and he rectifies the mistake they went upon, *Of such is the kingdom of heaven.* Note, (1.) The children of believing parents belong to the kingdom of heaven, and are members of the visible church. Of such, not only of such in *disposition and affection* (that might have served for a reason why doves or lambs should be brought to him), but of such, *in age,* is the kingdom of heaven; to them pertain the privileges of visible church-membership, as among the Jews of old. *The promise is to you, and to your children. I will be a God to thee and thy seed.* (2.) That for this reason they are welcome to Christ, who is ready to entertain those who, when they cannot come themselves, are brought to him. And this, [1.] In respect to the little children themselves, whom he has upon all occasions expressed a concern for; and who, having participated in the malignant influences of the first Adam's sin, must needs share in the riches of the second Adam's grace, else what would become of the apostle's parallel? 1 Co. 15:22; Rom. 5:14, 15, etc. Those who are given to Christ, as part of his purchase, he will in no wise cast out. [2.] With an eye to the faith of the parents who brought them, and presented them as living sacrifices. Parents are trustees of their children's wills, are empowered by nature to transact for their benefit; and therefore Christ accepts their dedication of them as their act and deed, and will own these dedicated things in the day he makes up his jewels. [3.] Therefore he takes it ill of those who forbid them, and exclude those whom he has received: who cast them out from the inheritance of the Lord, and say, *Ye have no part in the Lord* (see Jos. 22:27); and who forbid water, that they should be baptized, who, if that promise be fulfilled (Isa. 44:3), *have received the Holy Ghost as well as we,* for aught we know.

2. *He received the little children,* and did as he was desired; *he laid his hands on them,* that is, *he blessed them.* The strongest believer lives not so much by apprehending Christ as by being apprehended of him (Phil. 3:12), not so much by knowing God as by being known of him (Gal. 4:9); and this the least child is capable of. If they cannot stretch out their hands to Christ, yet he can lay his hands on them, and so make them his own, and own them for his own.

Methinks it has something observable in it, that, when he had done this, he departed thence, *v.* 15. As if he reckoned he had done enough there, when he had thus asserted the rights of the lambs of his flock, and made this provision for a succession of subjects in his kingdom.

Verses 16–22

Here is an account of what passed between Christ and a hopeful young gentleman that addressed himself to him upon a serious errand; he said to be a *young man* (*v.* 20); and I called him a *gentleman,* not only because he had great possessions, but because he was a ruler (Lu. 18:18), a magistrate, a justice of peace in his country; it is probable that he had abilities beyond his years, else his youth would have debarred him from the magistracy.

Now concerning this young gentleman, we are told how fair he bid for heaven and came short.

I. How fair he bid for heaven, and how kindly and tenderly Christ treated him, in favour to good beginnings. Here is,

1. The gentleman's serious address to Jesus Christ (*v.* 16); *Good Master, what good thing shall I do, that I may have eternal life?* Not a better question could be asked, not more gravely.

(1.) He gives Christ an honourable title, *Good Master — didaskale agathe.* It signifies not a ruling, but a teaching Master. His calling him *Master,* bespeaks his submissiveness, and willingness to be taught; and *good Master,* his affection and peculiar respect to the Teacher, like that of Nicodemus, *Thou art a Teacher come from God.* We read not of any that addressed themselves to Christ more respectfully than that Master in Israel and this ruler. It is a good thing when men's quality and dignity increase their civility and courtesy. It was gentleman-like to give this title of respect to Christ, notwithstanding the present meanness of his appearance. It was not usual among the Jews to accost their teachers with the title of *good;* and therefore this bespeaks the uncommon respect he had for Christ. Note, Jesus Christ is a good Master, the best of teachers; none teaches like him; he is distinguished for his goodness, for *he can have compassion on the ignorant; he is meek and lowly in heart.*

(2.) He comes to him upon an errand of importance (none could be more so), and he came not to tempt him, but sincerely desiring to be taught by him. His question is, *What good thing shall I do, that I may have eternal life?* By this it appears, [1.] That he had a firm belief of eternal life; he was no Sadducee. He was convinced that there is a happiness prepared for those in the other world, who are prepared for it in this world. [2.] That he was concerned to make it sure to himself that he should live eternally, and was desirous of that life more than any of the delights of this life. It was a rare thing for one of his age and quality to appear so much in care about another world. The rich are apt to think it below them to make such an enquiry as this; and young people think it time enough yet; but here was a young man, and a rich man, solicitous about his soul and eternity. [3.] That he was sensible something must be done, some good thing, for the attainment of this happiness. It is *by patient continuance in well-doing* that *we seek for immortality,* Rom. 2:7. We must be doing, and doing that which is good. The blood of Christ is the only purchase of eternal life (he merited it for us), but obedience to Christ is the appointed way to it, Heb. 5:9. [4.] That he was, or at least thought himself, willing to do what was to be done for the obtaining of this eternal life. Those that know what it is to have eternal life, and what it is to come short of it, will be glad to accept of it upon any terms. Such a holy violence does the kingdom of heaven suffer. Note, While there are many that say, *Who will show us any good?* our great enquiry should be, *What shall we do, that we may have eternal life?* What shall we do, to be for ever happy, happy in another world? For this world has not that in it that will make us happy.

2. The encouragement that Jesus Christ gave to this address.. It is not his manner to send any away without an answer, that come to him on such an errand, for nothing pleases him more, *v.* 17. In his answer,

(1.) He tenderly assists his faith; for, doubtless, he did not mean it for a reproof, when he said, *Why callest thou me good?* But he would seem to find that faith in what he said, when he called him *good Master,* which the gentleman perhaps was not conscious to himself of; he intended no more than to own and honour him as a good man, but Christ would lead him to own and honour him as a good God; for *there is none good but one, that is God.* Note, As Christ is graciously ready to make the best that he can of what is said or done amiss; so he is ready to make the most that can be of what is well said and well done. His constructions are often better than our intentions; as in that, *"I was hungry, and you gave me meat,* though you little thought it was to me." Christ will have this young man either know him to be God, or not call him *good;* to teach us to transfer to God all the praise that is at any time given to us. Do any call us *good?* Let us tell them all goodness is from God, and therefore not to us, but to him give glory. All crowns must lie before his throne. Note, God only is good, and there is none essentially, originally, and unchangeably, good, but God only. His goodness is of and from himself, and all the goodness in the creature is from him; he is the Fountain of goodness, and whatever the streams are, *all the springs are in him,* Jam. 1:17. He is the great Pattern and Sample of goodness; by him all goodness is to be measured; that is good which is like him, and agreeable to his mind. We in our language call him *God,* because he is good. In this, as in other things, our Lord Jesus was *the Brightness of his glory* (and his goodness is his glory), and *the express image of his person,* and therefore fitly called *good Master.*

(2.) He plainly directs his practice, in answer to his question. He started that thought of his being good, and therefore God, but did not stay upon it, lest he should seem to divert from, and so to drop, the main question, as many do in needless disputes and strifes of words. Now Christ's answer is, in short, this, *If thou wilt enter into life, keep the commandments.*

[1.] The end proposed is, entering into life. The young man, in his question, spoke of eternal life. Christ, in his answer, speaks of *life;* to teach us, that eternal life is the only true life. The words concerning that are the words of *this life,* Acts 5:20. The present life scarcely deserves the name of life, for *in the midst of life we are in death.* Or into *life,* that spiritual life which is the beginning and earnest of eternal life. He desired to know how he might *have* eternal life; Christ tells him how he might *enter into it;* we *have* it by the merit of Christ, a mystery which was not as yet fully revealed, and therefore Christ waives that; but the way of *entering into it,* is, by obedience, and Christ directs us in that. By the former we *make* our title, by this, as by our evidence, we *prove* it; it is *by adding to faith virtue,* that an *entrance* (the word here used) is *ministered to us into the everlasting kingdom,* 2 Pt. 1:5, 11. Christ, who is our Life, is the Way to the Father, and to the vision and fruition of him; he is the only Way, but duty, and the obedience of faith, are the way to Christ. There is an entrance into life hereafter, at death, at the great day, a complete entrance, and those only shall then enter into life, that do their duty; it is the diligent faithful servant that shall then *enter into the joy of his Lord,* and that joy will be his eternal life. There is an entrance into life now; *we who have believed, do enter into rest,* Heb. 4. 3. We have peace, and comfort, and joy, in the believing prospect of the glory to be revealed, and to this also sincere obedience is indispensably necessary.

[2.] The way prescribed is, keeping the commandments. Note, Keeping the commandments of God, according as they are revealed and made known to us, is the only way to life and salvation; and sincerity herein is accepted through Christ as our gospel perfection, provision being made of pardon, upon repentance, wherein we come short. Through Christ we are delivered from the condemning power of the law, but the commanding power of it is lodged in the hand of the Mediator, and under that, in that hand, we still are *under the law to Christ* (1 Co. 9:21), under it as a rule, though not as a covenant. *Keeping the commandments* includes *faith in Jesus Christ,* for that is the great commandment (1 Jn. 3:23), and it was one of the laws of Moses, that, when the great Prophet should be raised up, they should hear him. Observe, In order to our happiness here and for ever, it is not enough for us to *know* the commandments of God, but we must *keep* them, keep in them as our way, keep to them as our rule, keep them as our treasure, and with care, as the apple of our eye.

[3.] At his further instance and request, he mentions some particular commandments which he must keep (*v.* 18, 19); *The young man saith unto him, Which?* Note, Those that would do the commandments of God, must seek them diligently, and enquire after them, what they are. Ezra set himself to seek the law, and to *do it,* Ezra 7:10. "There were many commandments in the law of Moses; good Master, let me know which those are, the keeping o which is necessary to salvation."

In answer to this, Christ specifies several, especially the commandments of the second table. *First,* That which concerns our own and our neighbour's life; *Thou shalt do no murder. Secondly,* Our own and our neighbour's chastity, which should be as dear to us as life itself; *Thou shalt not commit adultery. Thirdly,* Our own and our neighbour's wealth and outward estate, as hedged about by the law of property; *Thou shalt not steal. Fourthly,* That which concerns truth, and our own and our neighbour's good name; *Thou shalt not bear false witness,* neither *for thyself,* nor *against thy neighbour;* for so it is here left at large. *Fifthly,* That which concerns the duties of particular relations; *Honour thy father and mother. Sixthly,* That comprehensive law of love, which is the spring and summary of all these duties, whence they all flow, on which they are all founded, and in which they are all fulfilled; *Thou shalt love thy neighbour as thyself* (Gal. 5:14; Rom. 13:9), that *royal* law, Jas. 2:8. Some think this comes in here, not as the sum of the second table, but as the particular import of the tenth commandment; *Thou shalt not covet,* which Mark is, *Defraud not;* intimating that it is not lawful for me to design advantage or gain to myself by the diminution or loss of another; for that is to covet, and to love myself better than my neighbour, whom I ought to love a myself, and to treat as I would myself be treated.

Our Saviour here specifies second-table duties only; not as if the first were of less account, but, 1. Because they that now sat in Moses's seat, either wholly neglected, or greatly corrupted, these precepts in their preaching. While they pressed the tithing of *mint, anise, and cummin, — judgment, and mercy, and faith,* the summary of second-table duties, were overlooked, *ch.* 23:23. Their preaching ran out all in rituals and nothing in morals; and therefore Christ pressed that most, which they least insisted on. As one truth, so one duty, must not jostle out another, but each must know its place, and be kept in it; but equity requires that that be helped up, which is most in danger of being thrust out. That is the present truth which we are called to bear our testimony to, not only which is opposed, but which is neglected. 2. Because he would teach him, and us all, that moral honesty is a necessary branch of true Christianity, and to be minded accordingly. Though a mere moral man comes short of being a complete Christian, yet an immoral man is certainly no true Christian; for the grace of God teaches us to live soberly and righteously, as well as godly. Nay, though first-table duties have in them more of the essence of religion, yet second-table duties have in them more of the evidence of it. Our light *burns* in love to God, but it *shines* in love to our neighbour.

II. See here how he came short, though he bid thus fair, and wherein he failed; he failed by two things.

1. By pride, and a vain conceit of his own merit and strength; this is the ruin of thousands, who keep themselves miserable by fancying themselves happy. When Christ told him what commandments he must keep, he answered very scornfully, *All these things have I kept from my youth up, v.* 20.

Now, (1.) According as he understood the law, as prohibiting only the outward acts of sin, I am apt to think that he said true, and Christ knew it, for he did not contradict him; nay, it is said in Mark, *He loved him;* so far was very good and pleasing to Christ. St. Paul reckons it a privilege, not contemptible in itself, though it was dross in comparison with Christ, that he was, *as toughing righteousness that is in the law, blameless,* Phil. 3:6. His observance of these commands was universal; *All these have I kept:* it was early and constant; *from my youth up.* Note, A man may be free from gross sin, and yet come short of grace and glory. His hands may be clean from external pollutions, and yet he may perish eternally in his heart-wickedness. What shall we think then of those who do not attain to this; whose fraud and injustice, drunkenness and uncleanness, witness against them, that all these they have broken from their youth up, though they have named the name of Christ? Well, it is sad to come short of those that come short of heaven.

It was commendable also, that he desired to know further what his duty was; *What lack I yet?* He was convinced that he wanted something to fill up his works before God, and was therefore desirous to know it, because, if he was not mistaken in himself, he was willing to do it. Having not yet attained, he thus seemed to press forward. And he applied himself to Christ, whose doctrine was supposed to improve and perfect the Mosaic institution. He desired to know what were the peculiar precepts of his religion, that he might have all that was in them to polish and accomplish him. Who could bid fairer?

But, (2.) Even in this that he said, he discovered his ignorance and folly. [1.] Taking the law in its spiritual sense, as Christ expounded it, no doubt, in many things he had offended against all these commands. Had he been acquainted with the extent and spiritual meaning of the law, instead of saying, *All these have I kept; what lack I yet?* he would have said, with shame and sorrow, "All these have I broken, what shall I do to get my sins pardoned?" [2.] Take it how you will, what he said savoured of pride and vain-glory, and had in it too much of that boasting which is excluded by the law of faith (Rom. 3:27), and which excludes from justification, Lu. 18:11, 14. He valued himself too much, as the Pharisees did, upon the plausibleness of his profession before men, and was proud of that, which spoiled the acceptableness of it. That word, *What lack I yet?* perhaps was not so much a desire of further instruction as a demand of the praise of his present fancied perfection, and a challenge to Christ himself to show him any one instance wherein he was deficient.

2. He came short by an inordinate love of the world, and his enjoyments in it. This was the fatal rock on which he split. Observe,

(1.) How he was tried in this matter (*v.* 21); *Jesus said unto him, If thou wilt be perfect, go and sell that thou hast.* Christ waived the matter of his boasted obedience to the law, and let that drop, because this would be a more effectual way of discovering him than a dispute of the extent of the law. "Come," saith Christ, "if thou wilt be perfect, if thou wilt approve thyself sincere in thine obedience" (for sincerity is our gospel perfection), "if thou wilt come up to that which Christ has added to the law of Moses, if thou wilt be perfect, if thou wilt *enter into life,* and so be perfectly happy;" for that which Christ here prescribes, is not a thing of supererogation, or a perfection we may be saved without; but, in the main scope and intendment of it, it is our necessary and indispensable duty. What Christ said to him, he thus far said to us all, that, if we would approve ourselves Christians indeed, and would be found at last the heirs of eternal life, we must do these two things:

[1.] We must practically prefer the heavenly treasures before all the wealth and riches in this world. That glory must have the pre-eminence in our judgment and esteem before this glory. No thanks to us to prefer heaven before hell, the worst man in the world would be glad of that Jerusalem for a refuge when he can stay no longer here, and to have it in reserve; but to make it our choice, and to prefer it before this earth — that is to be a Christian indeed. Now, as an evidence of this, *First,* We must dispose of what we have in this world, for the honour of God, and in his service: *"Sell that thou hast, and give to the poor.* If the occasions of charity be very pressing, sell thy possessions that thou mayest have to give to them that need; as the first Christians did, with an eye to this precept, Acts 4:34. Sell what thou canst spare for pious uses, all thy superfluities; if thou canst not otherwise do good with it, sell it. Sit loose to it, be willing to part with it for the honour of God, and the relief of the poor." A gracious contempt of the world, and compassion of the poor and afflicted ones in it, are in all a necessary condition of salvation; and in those that have wherewithal, giving of alms is as necessary an evidence of that contempt of the world, and compassion to our brethren; by this the trial will be at the great day, *ch.* 25:35. Though many that call themselves Christians, do not act as if they believed it; it is certain, that, when we embrace Christ, we must let go the world, for we cannot serve God and mammon. Christ knew that covetousness was the sin that did most easily beset this young man, that, though what he had he had got honestly, yet he could not cheerfully part with it, and by this he discovered his insincerity. This command was like the call to Abraham, *Get thee out of thy country, to a land that I will show thee.* As God tries believers by their strongest graces, so hypocrites by their strongest corruptions. *Secondly,* We must depend upon what we hope for in the other world as an abundant recompence for all we have left, or lost, or laid out, for God in this world; *Thou shalt have treasure in heaven.* We must, in the way of chargeable duty, trust God for a happiness out of sight, which will make us rich amends for all our expenses in God's service. The precept sounded hard and harsh; "Sell that thou hast, and give it away;" and the objection against it would soon arise, that "Charity begins at home;" therefore Christ immediately annexes this assurance of a treasure in heaven. Note, Christ's promises make his precepts easy, and his yoke not only tolerable, but pleasant, and sweet, and very comfortable; yet this promise was as much a trial of this young man's faith as the precept was of his charity, and contempt of the world.

[2.] We must devote ourselves entirely to the conduct and government of our Lord Jesus; *Come, and follow me.* It seems here to be meant of a close and constant attendance upon his person, such as the selling of what he had in the world was as necessary to as it was to the other disciples to quit their callings; but of us it is required that we follow Christ, that we duly attend upon his ordinances, strictly conform to his pattern, and cheerfully submit to his disposals, and by upright and universal obedience observe his statutes, and keep his laws, and all this from a principle of love to him, and dependence on him, and with a holy contempt of every thing else in comparison of him, and much more in competition with him. This is to *follow Christ fully.* To sell all, and give to the poor, will not serve, unless we come, and follow Christ. If I give all my goods to feed the poor, and have not love, it profits me nothing. Well, on these terms, and on no lower, is salvation to be had; and they are very easy and reasonable terms, and will appear so to those who are brought to be glad of it upon any terms.

(2.) See how he was discovered. This touched him in a tender part (*v.* 22); *When he heard that saying, he went away sorrowful, for he had great possessions.*

[1.] He was a rich man, and loved his riches, and therefore went away. He did not like eternal life upon these terms. Note, *First,* Those who have much in the world are in the greatest temptation to love it, and to set their hearts upon it. Such is the bewitching nature of worldly wealth, that those who want it least desire most; when riches increase, then is the danger of setting the heart upon them, Ps. 62:10. If he had had but two mites in all the world, and had been commanded to give them to the poor, or but one handful of meal in the barrel, and a little oil in the cruse, and had been bidden to make a cake of that for a poor prophet, the trial, one would think, had been much greater, yet those trials have been overcome (Lu. 21:4, and 1 Ki. 17:14); which shows that the love of the world draws stronger than the most pressing necessities. *Secondly,* The reigning love of this world keeps many from Christ, who seem to have some good desires toward him. A great estate, as to those who are got above it, is a great furtherance, so to those who are entangled in the love of it, it is a great hindrance, in the way to heaven.

Yet something of honesty there was in it, that, when he did not like the terms, he went away, and would not pretend to that, which he could not find in his heart to come up to the strictness of; better so than do as Demas did, who, *having known the way of righteousness,* afterward turned aside, out of love to this present world, to the greater scandal of his profession; since he could not be a complete Christian, he would not be a hypocrite.

[2.] Yet he was a thinking man, and well-inclined, and therefore *went away sorrowful.* He had a leaning toward Christ, and was loth to part with him. Note, Many a one is ruined by the sin he commits with reluctance; leaves Christ sorrowfully, and yet is never truly sorry for leaving him, for, if he were, he would return to him. Thus this man's wealth was *vexation of spirit* to him, then when it was his temptation. What then would the sorrow be afterward, when his possessions would be gone, and all hopes of eternal life gone too?

Verses 23–30

We have here Christ's discourse with his disciples upon occasion of the rich man's breaking with Christ.

I. Christ took occasion from thence to show the difficulty of the salvation of the rich people, *v.* 23–26.

1. That it is a very hard thing for a rich man to get to heaven, such a rich man as this here. Note, From the harms and falls of others it is good for us to infer that which will be of caution to us.

Now, (1.) This is vehemently asserted by our Saviour, *v.* 23, 24. He said this to his disciples, who were poor, and had but little in the world, to reconcile them to their condition with this, that the less they had of worldly wealth, the less hindrance they had in the way to heaven. Note, It should be a satisfaction to them who are in a low condition, that they are not exposed to the temptations of a high and prosperous condition: If they live more hardy in this world than the rich, yet, if withal they get more easily to a better world, they have no reason to complain. This saying is ratified, *v.* 23. *Verily I say unto you.* He that has reason to know what the way to heaven is, for he has laid it open, he tells us that this is one of the greatest difficulties in that way. It is repeated, *v.* 24. *Again I say unto you.* Thus he speaks once, yea, twice that which man is loth to perceive and more loth to believe.

[1.] He saith that it is a hard thing for a rich man to be a good Christian, and to be saved; to enter into the kingdom of heaven, either here or hereafter. The way to heaven is to all a narrow way, and the gate that leads into it, a strait gate; but it is particularly so to rich people. More duties are expected from them than from others, which they can hardly do; and more sins do easily beset them, which they can hardly avoid. Rich people have great temptations to resist, and such as are very insinuating; it is hard not to be charmed with a smiling world; very hard, when we are filled with these hid treasures, not to take up with them for a portion. Rich people have a great account to make up for their estates, their interest, their time, and their opportunities of doing and getting good, above others. It must be a great measure of divine grace that will enable a man to break through these difficulties.

[2.] He saith that the conversion and salvation of a rich man is so extremely difficult, that *it is easier for a camel to go through the eye of a needle, v.* 24. This is a proverbial expression, denoting a difficulty altogether unconquerable by the art and power of man; nothing less than the almighty grace of God will enable a rich man to get over this difficulty. The difficulty of the salvation of apostates (Heb. 6:4), and of old sinners (Jer. 13:23), is thus represented as an impossibility. The salvation of any is so very difficult (even *the righteous scarcely are saved*), that, where there is a peculiar difficulty, it is fitly set forth thus. It is very rare for a man to be rich, and not to set his heart upon his riches; and it is utterly impossible for a man that sets his heart upon his riches, to get to heaven; for *if any man love the world, the love of the Father is not in him,* 1 Jn. 2:15; James 4:4. *First,* The way to heaven is very fitly compared to a *needle's eye,* which is hard to hit and hard to get through. *Secondly,* A rich man is fitly compared to a *camel,* a beast of burthen, for he has riches, as a camel has his load, he carries it, but it is another's, he has it from others, spends it for others, and must shortly leave it to others; it is a burthen, for *men load themselves with thick clay,* Hab. 2:6. A camel is a large creature, but unwieldy.

(2.) This truth is very much wondered at, and scarcely credited by the disciples (*v.* 25); *They were exceedingly amazed, saying, Who then can be saved?* Many surprising truths Christ told them, which they ere astonished at, and knew not what to make of; this was one, but their weakness was the cause of their wonder. It was not in contradiction to Christ, but for awakening to themselves, that they said, *Who then can be saved?* Note, Considering the many difficulties that are in the way of salvation, it is really strange that any are saved. When we think how good God is, it may seem a wonder that so *few* are his; but when we think how bad man is, it is more a wonder that so *many* are, and Christ will be eternally admired in them. *Who then can be saved?* Since so many are rich, and have great possessions, and so many more would be rich, and are well affected to great possessions; who can be saved? If riches are a hindrance to rich people, are not price and luxury incident to those that are not rich, and as dangerous to them? and who then can get to heaven? This is a good reason why rich people should strive against the stream.

2. That, though it be hard, yet it is not impossible, for the rich to be saved (*v.* 26); *Jesus beheld them,* turned and looked wistfully upon his disciples, to shame them out of their fond conceit of the advantages rich people had in spiritual things. He beheld them as men that had got over this difficulty, and were in a fair way for heaven, and the more so because poor in this world; *and he said unto them, with men this is impossible, but with God all things are possible.* This is a great truth in general, that God is able to do that which quite exceeds all created power; that nothing is too hard for God, Gen. 18:14; Num. 11:23. When men are at a loss, God is not, for his power is infinite and irresistible; but this truth is here applied, (1.) To the salvation of any. *Who can be saved?* say the disciples. None, saith Christ, by any created power. *With men this is impossible:* the wisdom of man would soon be nonplussed in contriving, and the power of man baffled in effecting, the salvation of a soul. No creature can work the change that is necessary to the salvation of a soul, either in itself or in any one else. With men it is impossible that so strong a stream should be turned, so hard a heart softened, so stubborn a will bowed. It is a creation, it is a resurrection, and with men this is impossible; it can never be done by philosophy, medicine, or politics; but *with God all things are possible.* Note, The beginning, progress, and perfection, of the work of salvation, depend entirely upon the almighty power of God, to which all things are possible. Faith is wrought by that power (Eph. 1:19), and is kept by it, 1 Pt. 1:5. Job's experience of God's convincing, humbling grace, made him acknowledge more than any thing else, *I know that thou canst do every thing,* Job 42:2. (2.) To the salvation of rich people especially; it is impossible with men that such should be saved, but with God even this is possible; not that rich people should be saved *in* their worldliness, but that they should be saved *from* it. Note, The sanctification and salvation of such as are surrounded with the temptations of this world are not to be despaired of; it is possible; it may be brought about by the all-sufficiency of the divine grace; and when such are brought to heaven, they will be there everlasting monuments of the power of God. I am willing to think that in this word of Christ there is an intimation o mercy Christ had yet in store for this young gentleman, who was now gone away sorrowful; it was not impossible to God yet to recover him, and bring him to a better mind.

II. Peter took occasion from hence to enquire what *they* should get by it, who had come up to these terms, upon which this young man broke with Christ, and had left all to follow him, *v.* 27, etc. We have here the disciples' expectations from Christ, and his promises to them.

1. We have their expectations from Christ; Peter, in the name of the rest, signifies that they depended upon him for something considerable in lieu of what they had left for him; *Behold, we have forsaken all, and have followed thee; what shall we have therefore?* Christ had promised the young man, that, if he would sell all, and come and follow him, he should *have treasure in heaven;* now Peter desires to know,

(1.) Whether they had sufficiently come up to those terms: they had not sold all (for they had many of them wives and families to provide for), but they had *forsaken all;* they had not given it to the poor, but they had renounced it as far as it might be any way a hindrance to them in serving Christ. Note, When we hear what are the characters of those that shall be saved, it concerns us to enquire whether we, through grace, answer those characters. Now Peter hopes that, as to the main scope and intendment of the condition, they had come up to it, for God had wrought in them a holy contempt of the world and the things that are seen, in comparison with Christ and the things that are not seen; and how this must be evidenced, no certain rule can be given, but according as we are called.

Lord, saith Peter, *we have forsaken all.* Alas! it was but a poor *all* that they had forsaken; one of them had indeed quitted a place in the custom-house, but Peter and the most of them had only left a few boats and nets, and the appurtenances of a poor fishing-trade; and yet observe how Peter there speaks of it, as it had been some mighty thing; *Behold, we have forsaken all.* Note, We are too apt to make the most of our services and sufferings, our expenses and losses, for Christ, and to think we have made him much our debtor. However, Christ does not upbraid them with this; though it was but little that they had forsaken, yet it was their *all,* like the widow's two mites, and was as dear to them as if it had been more, and therefore Christ took it kindly that they left it to follow him; for he accepts *according to what a man hath.*

(2.) Whether therefore they might expect *that treasure* which the young man shall have if he will sell all. "Lord," saith Peter, "shall *we* have it, who have left all?" All people are for what they can get; and Christ's followers are allowed to consult their own true interest, and to ask, *What shall we have?* Christ *looked at the joy set before him,* and Moses *at the recompence of reward.* For this end it is set before us, that *by a patient continuance in well-doing* we may seek for it. Christ encourages us to ask what we shall gain by leaving all to follow him; that we may see he doth not call us to our prejudice, but unspeakably to our advantage. As it is the language of an obediential faith to ask, "What shall we *do?*" with an eye to the precepts; so it is of a hoping, trusting faith, to ask, "What shall we *have?*" with an eye to the promises. But observe, The disciples had long since left all to engage themselves in the service of Christ, and yet never till now asked, *What shall we have?* Though there was no visible prospect of advantage by it, they were so well assured of his goodness, that they knew they should not lose by him at last, and therefore referred themselves to him, in what way he would make up their losses to them; minded their work, and asked not what should be their wages. Note, It honours Christ, to trust him and serve him, and not to bargain with him. Now that this young man was gone from Christ to his possessions, it was time for them to think which they should take to, what they should trust to. When we see what others keep by their hypocrisy and apostasy, it is proper for us to consider what we hope, through grace, to gain, not *for,* but *by,* our sincerity and constancy, and then we shall see more reason to pity them than to envy them.

2. We have here Christ's promises to them, and to all others that tread in the steps of their faith and obedience. What there was either of vain-glory or of vain hopes in that which Peter said, Christ overlooks, and is not extreme to mark it, but takes this occasion to give the bond of a *promise,*

(1.) To his immediate followers, *v.* 28. They had signalized their respect to him, as the first that followed him, and to them he promises not only *treasure,* but *honour,* in heaven; and here they have a grant or patent for it from him who is the fountain of honour in that kingdom; *Ye which have followed me in the regeneration shall sit upon twelve thrones.* Observe,

[1.] The *preamble* to the patent, or the *consideration* of the grant, which, as usual, is a recital of their services; "You have followed me in the regeneration, and therefore this will I do for you." The time of Christ's appearing in this world was a time of regeneration, of reformation (Heb. 9:10), when old things began to pass away, and all things to look new. The disciples had followed Christ when the church was yet in the embryo state, when the gospel temple was but in the framing, when they had more of the work and service of the apostles than of the dignity and power that belonged to their office. Now they followed Christ with constant fatigue, when few did; and therefore on them he will put particular marks of honour. Note, Christ hath special favour for those who begin early with him, who trust him further than they can see him, as they did who *followed him in the regeneration.* Observe, Peter spoke of their forsaking *all,* to follow him, Christ only speaks of their *following him,* which was the main matter.

[2.] The *date* of their honour, which fixes the time when it should commence; not immediately from the day of the date of *these presents,* no, they must continue a while in obscurity, as they were. But *when the Son of man shall sit in the throne of his glory;* and to this some refer that, *in the regeneration;* "You who now have followed me, shall, in the regeneration, be thus dignified." Christ's second coming will be a regeneration, when there shall be *new heavens, and a new earth, and the restitution of all things.* All that partake of the regeneration in grace (Jn. 3:3) shall partake of the regeneration in glory; for as grace is the first resurrection (Rev. 20:6), so glory is the second regeneration.

Now their honour being adjourned till the Son of man's sitting in the throne of his glory, intimates, *First,* That they must stay for their advancement till then. Note, As long as our Master's glory is delayed, it is fit that ours should be so too, and that we should wait for it with an earnest expectation, as of a *hope not seen.* Rom. 8:19. We must live, and work, and suffer, in faith, and hope, and patience, which therefore must be tried by these delays. *Secondly,* That they must share with Christ in his advancement; their honour must be a communion with him in his honour. They, having suffered with a suffering Jesus, must reign with a reigning Jesus, for both here and hereafter Christ will be *all in all;* we must *be where he is* (Jn. 12:26), must *appear with him* (Col. 3:4);

and this will be an abundant recompence not only for our loss, but for the delay; and when our Lord comes, we shall receive not only *our own,* but our own *with usury.* The longest voyages make the richest returns.

[3.] The honour itself hereby granted; *Ye also shall sit upon twelve thrones, judging the twelve tribes of Israel.* It is hard to determine the particular sense of this promise, and whether it was not to have many accomplishments, which I see no harm in admitting. *First,* When Christ is ascended to the right hand of the Father, and sits on the throne of his glory, then the apostles shall receive power by the Holy Ghost (Acts 1:8); shall be so much advanced above themselves as they are now, that they shall think themselves upon thrones, in promoting the gospel; they shall deliver it with authority, as a judge from the bench; they shall then have their commission enlarged, and shall publish the laws of Christ, by which the church, God's spiritual Israel (Gal. 6:16), shall be governed, and *Israel according to the flesh,* that continues in infidelity, with all others that do likewise, shall be condemned. The honour and power given them, may be explained by Jer. 1:19, *See, I have set thee over the nations;* and Ezek; 20:4, *Wilt thou judge them?* and Dan. 7:18, *The saints shall take the kingdom;* and Rev. 12:1, where the doctrine of Christ is called *a crown of twelve stars. Secondly,* When Christ appears for the destruction of Jerusalem (*ch.* 24:31), then shall he send the apostles to judge the Jewish nation, because in that destruction their predictions, according to the word of Christ, would be accomplished. *Thirdly,* Some think it has reference to the conversion of the Jews, which is yet to come, at the latter end of the world, after the fall of antichrist; so Dr. Whitby; and that "it respects the apostles' government or *the twelve tribes of Israel,* not by a resurrection of their persons, but by a reviviscence of that Spirit which resided in them, and of that purity and knowledge which they delivered to the world, and, chiefly, by admission of their gospel to be the standard of their faith and the direction of their lives." *Fourthly,* It is certainly to have its full accomplishment at the second coming of Jesus Christ, when *the saints* in general *shall judge the world,* and the twelve apostles especially, as assessors with Christ, *in the judgment of the great day,* when all the world shall receive their final doom, and they shall ratify and applaud the sentence. But the *tribe* of Israel are named, partly because the number of the apostles was designedly the same with the number of the tribes; partly because the apostles were Jews, befriended them most, but were most spitefully persecuted by them; and it intimates that the saints will judge their acquaintance and kindred according to the flesh, and will, in the great day, judge those they had a kindness for; will judge their persecutors, who in this world judged them.

But the general intendment of this promise is, to show the glory and dignity reserved for the saints in heaven, which will be an abundant recompence for the disgrace they suffered here in Christ's cause. There are higher degrees of glory for those that have done and suffered most. The apostles in this world were hurried and tossed, there they shall sit down at rest and ease; here *bonds, and afflictions, and deaths, did abide them,* but there they *shall sit on thrones of glory;* here they were dragged to the bar, there they shall be advanced to the bench; here the twelve tribes of Israel trampled upon them, there they shall tremble before them. And will not this be recompence enough to make up all their losses and expenses for Christ? Lu. 22:29.

[4.] The ratification of this grant; it is firm, it is inviolably immutably sure; for Christ hath said, *"Verily I say unto you, I the Amen, the faithful Witness,* who am empowered to make this grant, I have said it, and it cannot be disannulled."

(2.) Here is a promise to all others that should in like manner leave all to follow Christ. It was not peculiar to the apostles, to be thus preferred, but *this honour have all his saints.* Christ will take care they shall none of them lose by him (*v.* 29); *Every one that has forsaken* any thing for Christ, *shall receive.*

[1.] Losses for Christ are here supposed. Christ had told them that his disciples must deny themselves in all that is done to them in this world; now here he specifies particulars; for it is good to count upon the worst. If they have not forsaken all, as the apostles did, yet they have forsaken a great deal, houses suppose, and have turned themselves out, to wander in deserts; or dear relations, that would not go with them, to follow Christ; these are particularly mentioned, as hardest for a tender gracious spirit to part with; *brethren, or sisters, or father, or mother, or wife, or children;* and *lands* are added in the close; the profits of which were the support of the family.

Now, *First,* the loss of these things is supposed to be *for Christ's name's sake;* else he doth not oblige himself to make it up. Many forsake brethren, and wife, and children, in humour and passion, as *the bird that wanders from her nest;* that is a sinful desertion. But if we forsake them *for Christ's sake,* because we cannot keep them and keep a good conscience, we must either quit them, or quit our interest in Christ; if we do not quit our concern for them, or our duty to them, but our comfort in them, and will do it rather than deny Christ, and this with an eye to him, and to his will and glory, this is that which shall be thus recompensed. It is not the suffering, but the cause, that makes both the martyr and the confessor.

Secondly, It is supposed to be a great loss; and yet Christ undertakes to make up, for he is able to do it, be it ever so great. See the barbarity of the persecutors, that they stripped innocent people of all they had, for no other crime than their adherence to Christ! See the patience of the persecuted; and the strength of their love to Christ, which was such as all these waters could not quench!

[2.] A recompence of these losses is here secured. Thousands have dealt with Christ, and have trusted him far; but never any one lost by him, never any one but was an unspeakable gainer by him, when the account came to be balanced. Christ here gives his word for it, that he will not only indemnify his suffering servants, and save them harmless, but will abundantly reward them. Let them make a schedule of their losses for Christ, and they shall be sure to receive,

First, A hundred-fold in this life; sometimes in *kind,* in the things themselves which they have parted with. God will raise up for his suffering servants more friends, that will be so to them for Christ's sake, than they have left that were so for their own sakes. The apostles, wherever they came, met with those that were kind to them, and entertained them, and opened their hearts and doors to them. However, they *shall receive a hundred-fold,* in *kindness,* in those things that are abundantly better and more valuable. Their graces shall increase, their comforts abound, they shall have tokens of God's love, more free communion with him, more full communications from him, clearer foresights, and sweeter foretastes, of *the glory to be revealed;* and then they may truly say, they have received a hundred times more comfort in God and Christ than they could have had in *wife, or children.*

Secondly, Eternal life at last. The former is reward enough, if there were no more; cent. per cent. is great profit; what then is a hundred to one? But this comes in over and above, as it were, into the bargain. The *life* here promised includes in it all the comforts of life in the highest degree, and all *eternal.* Now if we could but mix faith with the promise, and trust Christ for the performance of it, surely we should think nothing too much to do, nothing too hard to suffer, nothing too dear to part with, for him.

Our Saviour, in the last verse, obviates a mistake of some, as if pre-eminence in glory went by precedence in time, rather than the measure and degree of grace. No; *Many that are first, shall be last, and the last, first, v.* 30. God will cross his hands; will *reveal that to babes,* which he *hid from the wise and prudent;* will reject unbelieving Jews and receive believing Gentiles. The heavenly inheritance is not given as earthly inheritances commonly are, by seniority of age, and priority of birth, but according to God's pleasure. This is the text of another sermon, which we shall meet with in the next chapter.

CHAPTER 20

We have four things in this chapter. I. The parable of the labourers in the vineyard (*v.* 1–16). II. A prediction of Christ's approaching sufferings (*v.* 17–19). III. The petition of two of the disciples, by their mother, reproved (*v.* 20–28). IV. The petition of the two blind men granted, and their eyes opened (*v.* 29–34).

Verses 1–16

This parable of the labourers in the vineyard is intended,

I. To represent to us *the kingdom of heaven* (*v.* 1), that is, the way and method of the gospel dispensation. The laws of that kingdom are not wrapt up in parables, but plainly set down, as in the sermon upon the mount; but the mysteries of that kingdom are delivered in parables, in sacraments, as here and *ch.* 13. The duties of Christianity are more necessary to be known than the notions of it; and yet the notions of it are more necessary to be illustrated than the duties of it; which is that which parables are designed for.

II. In particular, to represent to us that concerning the kingdom of heaven, which he had said in the close of the foregoing chapter, that *many that are first shall be last, and the last, first;* with which this parable is connected; that truth, having in it a seeming contradiction, needed further explication.

Nothing was more a mystery in the gospel dispensation than the rejection of the Jews and the calling in of the Gentiles; so the apostle speaks of it (Eph. 3:3–6); that the Gentiles should be fellow-heirs: nor was any thing more provoking to the Jews than the intimation of it. Now this seems to be the principal scope of this parable, to show that the Jews should be first called into the vineyard, and many of them should come at the call; but, at length, the gospel should be preached to the Gentiles, and they should receive it, and be admitted to equal privileges and advantages with the Jews; should be *fellow-citizens with the saints,* which the Jews, even those of them that believed, would be very much disgusted at, but without reason.

But the parable may be applied more generally, and shows us, 1. That God is debtor to no man; a great truth, which the contents in our Bible give as the scope of this parable. 2. That many who begin last, and promise little in religion, sometimes, by the blessing of God, arrive at greater attainments in knowledge, grace, and usefulness, than others whose entrance was more early, and who promised fairer. Though Cushi gets the start of Ahimaaz, yet Ahimaaz, choosing *the way of the plain,* outruns Cushi. John is swifter of foot, and comes *first to the sepulchre:* but Peter has more courage, and goes *first into it.* Thus *many that are last shall be first.* Some make it a caution to the disciples, who had boasted of their timely and zealous embracing of Christ; they had left all, to follow him; but let them look to it, that they keep up their zeal; let them press forward and persevere; else their good beginnings will avail them little; they that seemed to be *first,* would be *last.* Sometimes those that are converted later in their lives, outstrip those that are converted earlier. Paul was *as one born out of due time, yet came not behind the chiefest of the apostles,* and outdid those that were in Christ before him. Something of affinity there is between this parable and that of the prodigal son, where he that returned from his wandering, was as dear to his father as he was, that never went astray; *first and last alike.* 3. That *the recompence of reward* will be given to the saints, not according to the time of their conversion, but according to the preparations for it by grace in this world; not according to the seniority (Gen. 43:33), but *according to the measure of the stature of the fulness of Christ.* Christ had promised the apostles, who followed him *in the regeneration,* at the beginning of the gospel dispensation, great glory (*ch.* 19:38); but he now tells them that those who are in like manner faithful to him, even in the latter end of the world, shall have the same reward, shall *sit with Christ on his throne,* as well as the apostles, Rev. 2:26–3:21. Sufferers for Christ in the latter days, shall have the same reward with the martyrs and confessors of the primitive times, though they are more celebrated; and faithful ministers now, the same with the first fathers.

We have two things in the parable; the *agreement* with the labourers, and the *account* with them.

(1.) Here is the agreement made with the labourers (*v.* 1–7); and here it will be asked, as usual,

[1.] Who hires them? *A man that is a householder.* God is the great Householder, *whose we are, and whom we serve;* as a householder, he has work that he will have to be done, and servants that he will have to be doing; he has a great family in heaven and earth, which is named from Jesus Christ (Eph. 3:15), which he is Owner and Ruler of. God hires labourers, not because he needs them or their services (for, *if we be righteous, what do we unto him?*), but as some charitable generous householders keep poor men to work, in kindness to them, to save them from idleness and poverty, and pay them for working for themselves.

[2.] Whence they are hired? Out of *the market-place,* where, till they are hired into God's service, they *stand idle* (*v.* 3), *all the day idle* (*v.* 6). Note, *First,* The soul of man stands ready to be hired into some service or other; it was (as all the creatures were) created to work, and is either a *servant to iniquity,* or a *servant to righteousness,* Rom. 6:19. The devil, by his temptations, is *hiring labourers* into his field, to *feed swine.* God, by his gospel, is *hiring labourers into his vine-*

yard, to dress it, and keep it, paradise-work. We are put to our choice; for hired we must be (Jos. 24:15); *Choose ye this day whom ye will serve. Secondly,* Till we are hired into the service of God, we are standing all the day idle; a sinful state, though a state of drudgery to Satan, may really be called *a state of idleness;* sinners are doing nothing, nothing to the purpose, nothing of the great work they were sent into the world about, nothing that will pass well in the account. *Thirdly,* The gospel call is given to those that *stand idle in the market-place.* The market-place is *a place of concourse,* and there *Wisdom cries* (Prov. 1:20, 21); it is a place of sport, there the *children are playing* (*ch.* 11:16); and the gospel calls us from vanity to seriousness; it is a place of business, of noise and hurry; and from that we are called to retire. "Come, come from this market-place."

[3.] What are they hired to do? To labour in his vineyard. Note, *First,* The church is God's vineyard; it is of his planting, watering, and fencing; and the fruits of it must be to his honour and praise. *Secondly,* We are all called upon to be labourers in this vineyard. The work of religion is vineyard-work, pruning, dressing, digging, watering, fencing, weeding. We have each of us our own vineyard to keep, our own soul; and it is God's and to be kept and dressed for him. In this work we must not be slothful, not loiterers, but *labourers,* working, and *working out our own salvation.* Work for God will not admit of trifling. A man may go idle to hell; but he that will go to heaven, must be busy.

[4.] What shall be their wages? He promises, *First, A penny, v.* 2. The Roman penny was, in our money, of the value of a sevenpence half-penny, a day's wages for a day's work, and the wages sufficient for a day's maintenance. This doth not prove that the reward of our obedience to God is *of works,* or *of debt* (no, it is *of grace, free grace,* Rom. 4:4), or that there is any proportion between our services and heaven's glories; no, when we have done all, *we are unprofitable servants;* but it is to signify that there is a reward set before us, and a sufficient one. *Secondly, Whatsoever is right, v.* 4–7. Note, God will be sure not to be behind-hand with any for the service they do him: never any lost by working for God. The crown set before us is *a crown of righteousness, which the righteous Judge shall give.*

[5.] For what term are they hired? For *a day.* It is but a day's work that is here done. The time of life is the day, in which *we must work the works of him that sent us* into the world. It is a short time; the reward is for eternity, the work is but for *a day;* man is said *to accomplish, as a hireling, his day,* Job 14:6. This should quicken us to expedition and diligence in our work, that we have but a little time to work in, and *the night* is hastening on, *when no man can work;* and if our great work be undone when our day is done, we are undone for ever. It should also encourage us in reference to the hardships and difficulties of our work, that it is but *for a day;* the approaching *shadow, which the servant earnestly desireth,* will bring with it both rest, and *the reward of our work,* Job 7:2. Hold out, faith, and patience, yet a little while.

[6.] Notice is taken of the several hours of the day, at which the labourers were hired. The apostles were sent forth at *the first and third hour* of the gospel day; they had a first and a second mission, while Christ was on earth, and their business was to call in the Jews; after Christ's ascension, about *the sixth and ninth hour,* they went out again on the same errand, *preaching the gospel to the Jews only, to them in Judea first,* and afterward to them of the dispersion; but, at length, as it were *about the eleventh hour,* they called the Gentiles to the same work and privilege with the Jews, and told them that in Christ Jesus there should be *no difference* made *between Jew and Greek.*

But this may be, and commonly is, applied to the several ages of life, in which souls are converted to Christ. The common call is promiscuous, to come and work in the vineyard; but the effectual call is particular, and it is *then* effectual when we come at the call.

First, Some are effectually called, and begin to work in the vineyard when they are very young; are sent in early in the morning, whose tender years are seasoned with grace, and the remembrance of their Creator. John the Baptist was *sanctified from the womb,* and therefore great (Lu. 1:15); Timothy *from a child* (2 Tim. 3:15); Obadiah *feared the Lord from his youth.* Those that have such a journey to go, had need set out betimes, the sooner the better.

Secondly, Others are savingly wrought upon in middle age;

Go work in the vineyard, at the third, sixth, or ninth hour. The power of divine grace is magnified in the conversion of some, when they are in the midst of their pleasures and worldly pursuits, as Paul. God has work for all ages; no time amiss to turn to God; none can say, "It is all in good time;" for, whatever hour of the day it is with us, the time past of our life may suffice that we have served sin; *Go ye also into the vineyard.* God turns away none that are willing to be hired, for *yet there is room.*

Thirdly, Others are hired into the vineyard in old age, at *the eleventh hour,* when *the day of life is far spent,* and there is but *one hour* of the twelve remaining. None are hired at the twelfth hour; when life is done, opportunity is done; but "while there is life, there is hope." 1. There is hope *for* old sinners; for if, in sincerity, they turn to God, they shall doubtless be accepted; true repentance is never too late. And, 2. There is hope of *old* sinners, that they may be brought to true repentance; nothing is too hard for Almighty grace to do, it *can change the Ethiopian's skin, and the leopard's spots;* can set those to work, who have contracted a habit of idleness. Nicodemus may *be born again when he is old,* and *the old man may be put off, which is corrupt.*

Yet let none, upon this presumption, put off their repentance till they are old. These were *sent into the vineyard,* it is true, *at the eleventh hour;* but nobody had hired them, or offered to hire them, before. The Gentiles came in *at the eleventh hour,* but it was because the gospel had not been before preached to them. those that have had gospel offers made them *at the third, or sixth hour,* and have resisted and refused them, will not have that to say for themselves at the eleventh hour, that these had; *No man has hired us;* nor can they be sure that any man will hire them at the ninth or eleventh hour; and therefore not to discourage any, but to awaken all, be it remembered, that *now is the accepted time; if we will hear his voice,* it must be *to-day.*

(2.) Here is the account with the labourers. Observe,

[1.] When the account was taken; *when the evening was come,* then, as usual, the day-labourers were called and paid. Note, Evening time is the reckoning time; the particular account must be given up in the evening of our life; for after death cometh the judgment. Faithful labourers shall receive their reward when they die; it is deferred till then, that they may wait with patience for it, but no longer; for God will observe his own rule, *The hire of the labourers shall not abide with thee all night, until the morning.* See Deu. 24:15. When Paul, that faithful labourer, departs, he is with Christ presently. The payment shall not be wholly deferred till *the morning of the resurrection;* but then, in the evening of the world, will be the general account, when *every one shall receive according to the things done in the body.* When time ends, and with it the world of work and opportunity, then the state of retribution commences; then call the labourers, and give them their hire. Ministers call them into the vineyard, to do their work; death calls them out of the vineyard, to receive their penny: and those to whom the call into the vineyard is effectual, the call out of it will be joyful. Observe, They did not come for their pay till they were called; we must with patience wait God's time for our rest and recompence; go by our master's clock. *The last trumpet, at the great day,* shall call the labourers, 1 Th. 4:16. *Then shalt thou call,* saith the good and faithful servant, *and I will answer.* In calling the labourers, they must begin from the last, and so to the first. Let not those that come in at the eleventh hour, be put behind the rest, but, lest they should be discouraged, call them first. *At the great day,* though *the dead in Christ shall rise first,* yet *they which are alive and remain, on whom the ends of the world* (the eleventh hour of its day) *comes, shall be caught up together with them in the clouds;* no preference shall be given to seniority, but every man *shall stand in his own lot at the end of the days.*

[2.] What the account was; and in that observe,

First, The general pay (*v.* 9, 10); *They received every man a penny.* Note, *All that by patient continuance in well-doing, seek for glory, honour, and immortality,* shall undoubtedly *obtain eternal life* (Rom. 2:7), not as *wages* for the value of their work, but as the *gift* of God. Though there be degrees of glory in heaven, yet it will be to all a complete happiness. They that come from the east and west, and so come in late, that are picked up out of *the highways and the hedges, shall sit down with Abraham, Isaac, and Jacob,* at the same feast, *ch.* 7:11. In heaven, every vessel will be full, brimful, though every vessel is not alike large and capacious. In the distri-

bution of future joys, as it was in the gathering of the manna, he that shall gather much, will have nothing over, and he that shall gather little, will have no lack, Ex. 16:18. Those whom Christ fed miraculously, though of different sizes, *men, women, and children, did all eat, and were filled.*

The giving of a whole day's wages to those that had not done the tenth part of a day's work, is designed to show that God distributes his rewards by *grace* and *sovereignty,* and not of *debt.* The best of the labourers, and those that begin soonest, having so many empty spaces in their time, and their works not being filled up before God, may truly be said to labour in the vineyard scarcely one hour of their twelve; but because *we are under grace,* and *not under the law,* even such defective services, done in sincerity, shall not only be accepted, but by free grace richly rewarded. Compare Lu. 17:7, 8, with Lu. 12:37.

Secondly, The particular pleading with those that were offended with this distribution in gavel-kind. The circumstances of this serve to adorn the parable; but the general scope is plain, that *the last shall be first.* We have here,

1. The offence taken (*v.* 11, 12); *They murmured at the good man of the house;* not that there is, or can be, any discontent or murmuring in heaven, for that is both guilt and grief, and in heaven there is neither; but there may be, and often are, discontent and murmuring concerning heaven and heavenly things, while they are in prospect and promise in this world. This signifies the jealousy which the Jews were provoked to by the admission of the Gentiles into the kingdom of heaven. As the elder brother, in the parable of the prodigal, repined at the reception of his younger brother, and complained of his father's generosity to him; so these labourers quarrelled with their master, and found fault, not because they had not enough, so much as because others were made equal with them. They boast, as the prodigal's elder brother did, of their good services; *We have borne the burthen and heat of the day;* that was the most they could make of it. Sinners are said to *labour in the very fire* (Hab. 2:13), whereas God's servants, at the worst, do but labour in the sun; not in the heat of the iron furnace, but only in the heat of the day. Now *these last have worked but one hour,* and that too in the cool of the day; and yet *thou hast made them equal with us.* The Gentiles, who are newly called in, have as much of the privileges of the kingdom of the Messiah as the Jews have, who have so long been labouring in the vineyard of the Old-Testament church, under the yoke of the ceremonial law, in expectation of that kingdom. Note, There is a great proneness in us to think that we have too little, and other too much, of the tokens of God's favour; and that we do too much, and others too little, in the work of God. Very apt we all are to undervalue the deserts of others, and to overvalue our own. Perhaps, Christ here gives an intimation to Peter, not to boast too much, as he seemed to do, of his having *left all to follow Christ;* as if, because he and the rest of them had borne the burthen and heat of the day thus, they must have a heaven by themselves. It is hard for those that do or suffer more than ordinary for God, not to be elevated too much with the thought of it, and to expect to merit by it. Blessed Paul guarded against this, when, though *the chief of the apostles,* he owned himself to be *nothing,* to be *less than the least of all saints.*

2. The offence removed. Three things the master of the house urges, in answer to this ill-natured surmise.

(1.) That the complainant had no reason at all to say he had any wrong done to him, *v.* 13, 14. Here he asserts his own justice; *Friend, I do thee no wrong.* He calls him *friend,* for in reasoning with others we should use soft words and hard arguments; if our inferiors are peevish and provoking, yet we should not thereby be put into a passion, but speak calmly to them. [1.] It is incontestably true, that God can do no wrong. This is the prerogative of the King of kings. *Is there unrighteousness with God?* The apostle startles at the thought of it; *God forbid!* Rom. 3:5, 6. His word should silence all our murmurings, that, whatever God does to us, or withholds from us, he does us no wrong. [2.] If God gives that grace to others, which he denies to us, it is kindness to them, but no injustice to us; and bounty to another, while it is no injustice to us, we ought not to find fault with. Because it is free grace, that is given to those that have it, boasting is for ever excluded; and because it is free grace, that is withheld from those that have it not, murmuring is for ever excluded. Thus *shall every mouth be stopped, and all flesh be silent before God.*

To convince the murmurer that he did no wrong, he refers him to the bargain: *"Didst not thou agree with me for a penny?* And if thou hast what thou didst agree for, thou hast no reason to cry out of wrong; thou shalt have what we agreed for." Though God is a debtor to none, yet he is graciously pleased to make himself a debtor by his own promise, for the benefit of which, through Christ, believers agree with him, and he will stand to his part of the agreement. Note, It is good for us often to consider what it was that we agreed with God for. *First,* Carnal worldlings agree with God for their penny in this world; they choose *their portion in this life* (Ps. 17:14); in these things they are willing to *have their reward* (*ch.* 6:2, 5), *their consolation* (Lu. 6:24), *their good things* (Lu. 16:25); and with these they shall be put off, shall be cut off from spiritual and eternal blessings; and herein God does them no wrong; they have what they chose, the penny they agreed for; *so shall their doom be, themselves have decided it;* it is conclusive against them. *Secondly,* Obedient believers agree with God for their penny in the other world, and they must remember that they have so agreed. Didst not thou agree to take God's word for it? Thou didst; and wilt thou go and agree with the world? Didst not thou agree to take up with heaven as thy portion, thy all, and to take up with nothing short of it? And wilt thou seek for a happiness in the creature, or think from thence to make up the deficiencies of thy happiness in God?

He therefore, 1. Ties him to his bargain (*v.* 14); *Take that thine is, and go thy way.* If we understand it of that which is ours by debt or absolute propriety, it would be a dreadful word; we are all undone, if we be put off with that only which we can call our *own.* The highest creature must go away into nothing, if he must go away with that only which is his own: but if we understand it of that which is ours by *gift,* the free gift of God, it teaches us *to be content with such things as we have.* Instead of repining that we have no more, let us take what we have, and be thankful. If God be better in any respect to others than to us, yet we have no reason to complain while he is so much better to us than we deserve, in giving us our penny, though we are unprofitable servants. 2. He tells him that those he envied should fare as well as he did; *"I will give unto this last, even as unto thee;* I am resolved I will." Note, The unchangeableness of God's purposes in dispensing his gifts should silence our murmurings. If he will do it, it is not for us to gainsay; for *he is in one mind, and who can turn him? Neither giveth he an account of any of his matters;* nor is it fit he should.

(2.) He had no reason to quarrel with the master; for what he gave was absolutely his own, *v.* 15. As before he asserted his justice, so here his sovereignty; *Is it not lawful for me to do what I will with my own?* Note, [1.] God is the Owner of all good; his propriety in it is absolute, sovereign, and unlimited. [2.] He may therefore give or withhold his blessings, as he pleases. What we have, is not our *own,* and therefore *it is not lawful for us to do what we will with* it; but what God has, is his own; and this will justify him, *First,* In all the disposals of his providence; when God takes from us that which was dear to us, and which we could ill spare, we must silence our discontents with this; *May he not do what he will with his own? Abstulit, sed et dedit — He hath taken away; but he originally gave.* It is not for such depending creatures as we are to quarrel with our Sovereign. *Secondly,* In all the dispensations of his grace, God gives or withholds the means of grace, and the Spirit of grace, as he pleases. Not but that there is a counsel in every will of God, and what seems to us to be done arbitrarily, will appear at length to have been done wisely, and for holy ends. But this is enough to silence all murmurs and objectors, that God is sovereign Lord of all, and *may do what he will with his own.* We are in his hand, as clay in the hands of a potter; and it is not for us to prescribe to him, or strive with him.

(3.) He had no reason to envy his fellow servant, or to grudge at him; or to be angry that he came into the vineyard no sooner; for he was not sooner called; he had no reason to be angry that the master had given him wages for the whole day, when he had idled away the greatest part of it; for *Is thine eye evil, because I am good?* See here,

[1.] The nature of envy; It is an evil eye. The eye is often both the inlet and the outlet of this sin. *Saul saw that David prospered, and he eyed him,* 1 Sa. 18:9, 15. It is an evil eye, which is displeased at the good of others, and desires their hurt. What can have more evil in it? It is grief to ourselves, anger to God, and ill-will to our neighbour; and it is a sin that has neither pleasure, profit, nor honour, in it; *it is an evil, an only evil.*

[2.] The aggravation of it; "It is because I am good." Envy is unlikeness to God, who is good, and doeth good, and delighteth in doing good; nay, it is an opposition and contradiction to God; it is a dislike of his proceedings, and a displeasure at what he does, and is pleased with. It is a direct violation of both the two great commandments at once; both that of love to God, in whose will we should acquiesce, and love to our neighbour, in whose welfare we should rejoice. Thus man's badness takes occasion from God's goodness to be more exceedingly sinful.

Lastly, Here is the application of the parable (*v.* 16), in that observation which occasioned it (*ch.* 19:30); *So the first shall be last, and the last first.* There were many that followed Christ now in the regeneration, when the gospel kingdom was first set up, and these Jewish converts seemed to have got the start of others; but Christ, to obviate and silence their boasting, here tells them,

1. That they might possibly be outstripped by their successors in profession, and, though they were before others in profession, might be found inferior to them in knowledge, grace, and holiness. The Gentile church, which was as yet unborn, the Gentile world, which as yet stood *idle in the market-place,* would produce greater numbers of eminent, useful Christians, than were found among the Jews. More and more excellent shall be *the children of the desolate than those of the married wife,* Isa. 54:1. Who knows but that the church, in its old age, may be more fat and flourishing than ever, to show that the Lord is upright? Though primitive Christianity had more of the purity and power of that holy religion than is to be found in the degenerate age wherein we live, yet what *labourers* may be *sent into the vineyard in the eleventh hour of the church's day,* in the Philadelphian period, and what plentiful effusions of the Spirit may then be, above what has been yet, who can tell?

2. That they had reason to fear, lest they themselves should be found hypocrites at last; for *many are called but few chosen.* This is applied to the Jews (*ch.* 22:14); it was so then, it is too true still; many are called with a common call, that are not chosen with a saving choice. All that are chosen from eternity, are effectually called, *in the fulness of time* (Rom. 8:30), so that in making our effectual calling sure we *make sure our election* (2 Pt. 1:10); but it is not so as to the outward call; *many are called,* and yet refuse (Prov. 1:24), nay, as they are called to God, so they go *from* him (Hos. 11:2, 7), by which it appears that they were not chosen, for *the election will obtain,* Rom. 11:7. Note, There are but few *chosen* Christians, in comparison with the many that are only *called* Christians; it therefore highly concerns us to build our hope for heaven upon the rock of an eternal choice, and not upon the sand of an external call; and we should fear lest we be found but seeming Christians, and so should really come short; nay, lest we be found blemished Christians, and so should *seem to come short,* Heb. 4:1.

Verses 17–19

This is the third time that Christ gave his disciples notice of his approaching sufferings; he was not going up to Jerusalem to celebrate the passover, and to offer up himself the great Passover; both must be done at Jerusalem: there *the passover must be kept* (Deu. 12:5), and there a prophet must perish, because there the great Sanhedrim sat, who were judges in that case, Lu. 13:33. Observe,

I. The privacy of this prediction; *He took the twelve disciples apart in the way.* This was one of those things which were told to them in *darkness,* but which they were afterward to *speak in the light, ch.* 10:27. His secret was with them, as his friends, and this particularly. It was a hard saying, and, if any could bear it, they could. They would be more immediately exposed to peril with him, and therefore it was requisite that they should know of it, that, being fore-warned, they might be fore-armed. It was not fit to be spoken publicly as yet, 1. Because many that were cool toward him, would hereby have been driven to turn their backs upon him; the scandal of the cross would have frightened them from following him any longer. 2. Because many that were hot for him, would hereby be driven to take up arms in his defense, and it might have occasioned *an uproar among the people* (*ch.* 26:5), which would have been laid to his charge, if he had told them of it publicly before: and, besides that such methods are utterly disagreeable to the genius of his kingdom, which is not of this world, he never countenanced any thing which had a tendency to prevent his sufferings. This discourse was not in the synagogue, or in the house, but *in the way,* as they travelled along; which teaches us, in our walks or travels with our friends, to keep up such discourse as *is good, and to the use of edifying.* See Deu. 16:7.

II. The prediction itself, *v.* 18, 19. Observe,

1. It is but a repetition of what he had once and again said before, *ch.* 16:21; 17:22, 23. This intimates that he not only saw clearly what troubles lay before him, but that his heart was upon his suffering-work; it filled him, not with fear, then he would have studied to avoid it, and could have done it, but with desire and expectation; he spoke thus frequently of his sufferings, because through them he was to enter into his glory. Note, It is good for us to be often thinking and speaking of our death, and of the sufferings which, it is likely, we may meet with betwixt this and the grave; and thus, by making them more familiar, they would become less formidable. This is one way of dying daily, and of taking up our cross daily, to be daily speaking of the cross, and of dying; which would come neither the sooner nor the surer, but much the better, for our thoughts and discourses of them.

2. He is more particular here in foretelling his sufferings than any time before. He had said (*ch.* 16:21), that he *should suffer many things, and be killed;* and (*ch.* 17:22), that he should *be betrayed into the hands of men, and they should kill him;* but here he adds; that he shall be *condemned, and delivered to the Gentiles,* that *they shall mock him, and scourge him, and crucify him.* These are frightful things, and the certain foresight of them was enough to damp an ordinary resolution, yet (as was foretold concerning him, Isa. 42:4) *he did not fail, nor was discouraged;* but the more clearly he foresaw his sufferings, the more cheerfully he went forth to meet them. He foretels by whom he should suffer, by *the chief priests and the scribes;* so he had said before, but here he adds, *They shall deliver him to the Gentiles,* that he might be the better understood; for the chief priests and scribes had no power to put him to death, nor was crucifying a manner of death in use among the Jews. Christ suffered from the malice both of Jews and Gentiles, because he was to suffer for the salvation both of Jews and Gentiles; both had a hand in his death, because he was to reconcile both by his cross, Eph. 2:16.

3. Here, as before, he annexes the mention of his resurrection and his glory to that of his death and sufferings; *The third day he shall rise again.* He still brings this in, (1.) To encourage himself in his sufferings, and to carry him cheerfully through them. *He endured the cross for the joy set before him;* he foresaw he should rise again, and rise quickly, the third day. He shall be straightway glorified, Jn. 13:32. The reward is not only sure, but very near. (2.) To encourage his disciples, and comfort them, who would be overwhelmed and greatly terrified by his sufferings. (3.) To direct us, under all *the sufferings of this present time,* to keep up a believing prospect of *the glory to be revealed,* to look at *the things that are not seen, that are eternal,* which will enable us to call the present afflictions light, and but for a moment.

Verses 20–28

Here, is first, the request of the two disciples to Christ, and the rectifying of the mistake upon which that was grounded, *v.* 20–23. The sons of Zebedee were James and John, two of the first three of Christ's disciples; Peter and they were his favourites; John was the disciple whom Jesus loved; yet none were so often reproved as they; whom Christ loves best he reproves most, Rev. 3:19.

I. Here is the ambitious address they made to Christ — that they might sit, the one on his right hand, and the other on his left, in his kingdom, *v.* 20, 21. It was a great degree of faith, that they were confident of his kingdom, though now he appeared in meanness; but a great degree of ignorance, that they still expected a temporal kingdom, with worldly pomp and power, when Christ had so often told them of sufferings and self-denial. In this they expected to be grandees. They ask not for employment in this kingdom, but for honour only; and no place would serve them in this imaginary kingdom, but the highest, next to Christ, and above every body else. It is probable that the last word in Christ's foregoing discourse gave occasion to this request, that *the third day he should rise again.* They concluded that his resurrection would be his entrance upon his kingdom, and therefore were resolved to put in betimes for the best place; nor would they lose it for want of speaking early. What Christ said to comfort them, they thus abused, and were puffed up with. Some cannot bear comforts, but they turn them to a wrong purpose; as sweetmeats in a foul stomach produce bile. Now observe,

1. There was policy in the management of this address, that they put their mother on to present it, that it might be looked upon as her request, and not theirs. Though proud people think well of themselves, they would not be thought to do so, and therefore affect nothing more than *a show of humility* (Col. 2:18), and others must be put on to court that honour for them, which they are ashamed to court for themselves. The mother of James and John was Salome, as appears by comparing *ch.* 27:61, with Mk. 15:40. Some think she was daughter of Cleophas or Alpheus, and sister or cousin german to Mary the mother of our Lord. She was one of those women that attended Christ, and ministered to him; and they thought she had such an interest in him, that he could deny her nothing, and therefore they made her their advocate. Thus when Adonijah had reasonable request to make to Solomon, he put Bathsheba on to speak for him. It was their mother's weakness thus to become that tool of their ambition, which she should have given a check to. Those that are wise and good, would not be seen in an ill-favoured thing. In gracious requests, we should learn this wisdom, to desire the prayers of those that have an interest at the throne of grace; we should beg of our praying friends to pray for us, and reckon it a real kindness.

It was likewise policy to ask first for a general grant, that he would do a *certain* thing for them, not in faith, but in presumption, upon that general promise; *Ask, and it shall be given you;* in which is implied this qualification of our request, that it be according to the revealed will of God, otherwise we *ask and have not,* if we ask to *consume it upon our lusts,* Jam. 4:3.

2. There was pride at the bottom of it, a proud conceit of their own merit, a proud contempt of their brethren, and a proud desire of honour and preferment; pride is a sin that most easily besets us, and which it is hard to get clear of. It is a holy ambition to strive to excel others in grace and holiness; but it is a sinful ambition to covet to exceed others in pomp and grandeur. *Seekest thou great things for thyself,* when thou hast just now heard of thy Master's being mocked, and scourged, and crucified? For shame! *Seek them not,* Jer. 45:5.

II. Christ's answer to this address (*v.* 22, 23), directed not to the mother, but to the sons that set her on. Though others be our mouth in prayer, the answer will be given to us according as we stand effected. Christ's answer is very mild; they were overtaken in the fault of ambition, but Christ *restored them with the spirit of meekness.* Observe,

1. How he reproved the ignorance and error of their petition; *Ye know not what ye ask.* (1.) They were much in the dark concerning the kingdom they had their eye upon; they dreamed of a temporal kingdom, whereas Christ's kingdom is not of this world. They knew not what it was to sit on his right hand, and on his left; they talked of it as blind men do of colours. Our apprehensions of that glory which is yet to be revealed, are like the apprehensions which a child has of the preferments of grown men. If at length, through grace, we arrive at perfection, we shall then put away such childish fancies: when we come to see face to face, we shall know what we enjoy; but now, alas, we know not what we ask; we can but ask for the good as it lies in the promise, Tit. 1:2. What it will be in the performance, eye has not seen, nor ear heard. (2.) They were much in the dark concerning the way to that kingdom. *They* know not what they ask, who ask for the end, but overlook the means, and so put asunder what God has joined together. The disciples thought, when they had left what little *all* they had for Christ, and had gone about the country awhile preaching the gospel of the kingdom, all their service and sufferings were over, and it was now time to ask, *What shall we have?* As if nothing were now to be looked for but crowns and garlands; whereas there were far greater hardships and difficulties before them than they had yet met with. They imagined their warfare was accomplished when it was scarcely begun, and they had yet but run with the footmen. They dream of being in Canaan presently, and consider not what they shall do in the swellings of Jordan. Note, [1.] We are all apt, when we are but *girding on the harness, to boast* as though we *had put it off.* [2.] We know not what we ask, when we ask for the glory of wearing the crown, and ask not for grace to bear the cross in our way to it.

2. How he repressed the vanity and ambition of their request. They were pleasing themselves with the fancy of sitting on his right hand, and on his left, in great state; now, to check this, he leads them to the thoughts of their sufferings, and leaves them in the dark about their glory.

(1.) He leads them to the thoughts of their sufferings, which they were not so mindful of as they ought to have been. They looked so earnestly upon the crown, the prize, that they were ready to plunge headlong and unprepared into the foul way that led to it; and therefore he thinks it necessary to put them in mind of the hardships that were before them, that they might be no surprise or terror to them.

Observe, [1.] How fairly he puts the matter to them, concerning these difficulties (*v.* 22); "You would stand candidates for the first post of honour in the kingdom; but *are you able to drink of the cup that I shall drink of?* You talk of what great things you must have when you have done your work; but are you able to hold out to the end of it?" Put the matter seriously to yourselves. These same two disciples once knew not what manner of spirit they were of, when they were disturbed with anger, Lu. 9:55; and now they were not aware what was amiss in their spirits when they were lifted up with ambition. Christ sees that pride in us which we discern not in ourselves.

Note, *First,* That to suffer for Christ is *to drink of a cup,* and *to be baptized with a baptism.* In this description of sufferings, 1. It is true, that affliction doth abound. It is supposed to be a bitter cup, that is drunk of, wormwood and gall, those waters of a full cup, that are wrung out to God's people (Ps. 43:10); a cup of trembling indeed, but not of fire and brimstone, the portion of the cup of wicked men, Ps. 11:6. It is supposed to be a baptism, a washing with the waters of affliction; some are dipped in them; the waters compass them about even to the soul (Jonah 2:5); others have but a sprinkling of them; both are baptism, some are overwhelmed in them, as in a deluge, others ill wet, as in a sharp shower. But, 2. Even in this, *consolation doth more abound.* It is but a cup, not an ocean; it is but a draught, bitter perhaps, but we shall see the bottom of it; it is a cup in the hand of a Father (Jn. 18:11); and it is full of mixture, Ps. 75:8. It is but a baptism; if dipped, that is the worst of it, not drowned; perplexed, but not in despair. Baptism is an ordinance by which we join ourselves to the Lord in covenant and communion; and so is suffering for Christ, Eze. 20:37; Isa. 48:10. Baptism is "an outward and visible sign of an inward and spiritual grace;" and so is suffering for Christ, for *unto us it is given,* Phil. 1:29.

Secondly, It is to drink of the same cup that Christ drank of, and to be baptized with the same baptism that he was baptized with. Christ is beforehand with us in suffering, and in that as in other things left us an example. 1. It bespeaks the condescension of a suffering Christ, that he would drink of such a cup (Jn. 18:11), nay, and such a brook (Ps. 110:7), and drink so deep, and yet so cheerfully; that he would be baptized with such a baptism, and was so forward to it, Lu. 12:50. It was much that he would be baptized with water as a common sinner, much more with blood as an uncommon malefactor. But in all this he was made *in the likeness of sinful flesh,* and *was made sin for us.* 2. It bespeaks the consolation of suffering Christians, that they do but pledge Christ in the bitter cup, are *partakers of his sufferings,* and *fill up that which is behind* of them; we must therefore arm ourselves with the same mind, and *go to him without the camp.*

Thirdly, It is good for us to be often putting it to ourselves, whether we are able to drink of this cup, and to be baptized with this baptism. We must expect suffering, and not look upon it as a hard thing to suffer well and as becomes us. Are we able to suffer cheerfully, and in the worst of times still to hold fast our integrity? What can we afford to part with for Christ? How far will we give him credit? Could I find in my heart to drink of a bitter cup, and to be baptized with a bloody baptism, rather than let go my hold of Christ? The truth is, Religion, if it be worth any thing, is worth every thing; but it is worth little, if it be not worth suffering for. Now let us sit down, and count the cost of dying for Christ rather than denying him, and ask, Can we take him upon these terms?

[2.] See how boldly they engage for themselves; they said, *We are able,* in hopes of sitting on his right hand, and on his left; but at the same time they fondly hoped that they should never be tried. As before they knew not what they asked, so now they knew not what they answered. *We are able;* they would have done well to put in, *"Lord, by thy strength,* and *in thy grace, we are able,* otherwise we are not." But the same that was Peter's temptation, to be confident of his own sufficiency, and presume upon his own strength, was here the temptation of James and John; and it is a sin we are all prone to. They knew not what Christ's cup was, nor what his baptism, and therefore they were thus bold in promising for themselves. But those are commonly most confident, that are least acquainted with the cross.

[3.] See how plainly and positively their sufferings are here foretold (*v.* 23); *Ye shall drink of my cup.* Sufferings foreseen will be the more easily borne, especially if looked upon under a right notion, as drinking of his cup, and being baptized with his baptism. Christ began in suffering for us, and expects we should pledge him in suffering for him. Christ will have us know the worst, that we may make the best of our way to heaven; *Ye shall drink;* that is, ye shall suffer. James drank the bloody cup first of all the apostles, Acts 12:2. John, though at last he died in his bed, if we may credit the ecclesiastical historians, yet often drank of this bitter cup, as when he was banished into the isle of Patmos (Rev. 1:9), and when (as they say) at Ephesus he was put into a caldron of boiling oil, but was miraculously preserved. He was, as the rest of the apostles, in deaths often. He took the cup, offered himself to the baptism, and it was accepted.

(2.) He leaves them in the dark about the degrees of their glory. To carry them cheerfully through their sufferings, it was enough to be assured that they should have *a place in his kingdom.* The lowest seat in heaven is an abundant recompence for the greatest sufferings on earth. But as to the preferments there, it was not fit there should be any intimation given for whom they were intended; for the infirmity of their present state could not bear such a discovery with any evenness; *"To sit on my right hand and on my left is not mine to give,* and therefore it is not for you to ask it or to know it; *but it shall be given to them for whom it is prepared of my Father."* Note, [1.] It is very probable that there are degrees of glory in heaven; for our Saviour seems to allow that there are some that shall sit on his right hand and on his left, in the highest places. [2.] As the future glory itself, so the degrees of it, are purposed and prepared in the eternal counsel of God; as the common salvation, so the more peculiar honours, are appointed, the whole affair is long since settled, and there is a certain measure of the stature, both in grace and glory, Eph. 4:13. [3.] Christ, in dispensing the fruits of his own purchase, goes exactly by the measures of his Father's purpose; *It is not mine to give, save to them* (so it may be read) *for whom it is prepared.* Christ has the sole power of giving eternal life, but then it is *to as many as were given him,* Jn. 17:2. *It is not mine to give,* that is, *to promise* now; that matter is already settled and concerted, and the Father and Son understand one another perfectly well in this matter. "It is not mine to give to those that seek and are ambitious of it, but to those that by great humility and self-denial are prepared for it."

III. Here are the reproof and instruction which Christ gave to the other ten disciples for their displeasure at the request of James and John. He had much to bear with in them all, they were so weak in knowledge and grace, yet he bore their manners.

1. The fret that the ten disciples were in (*v.* 24). *They were moved with indignation against the two brethren;* not because they were desirous to be preferred, which was their sin, and for which Christ was displeased with them, but because they were desirous to be preferred *before them,* which was a reflection upon them. Many seem to have indignation at sin; but it is not because it is sin, but because it touches them. They will inform against a man that swears; but it is only if he swear at them, and affront them, not because he dishonours God. These disciples were angry at their brethren's ambition, though they themselves, bay *because* they themselves, were as ambitious. Note, It is common for people to be angry at those sins in others which they allow of and indulge in themselves. Those that are proud and covetous themselves do not care to see others so. Nothing makes more mischief among brethren, or is the cause of more indignation and contention, than ambition, and desire of greatness. We never find Christ's disciples quarreling, but something of this was at the bottom of it.

2. The check that Christ gave them, which was very gentle, rather by way of instruction what they should be, than by way of reprehension for what they were. He had reproved

this very sin before (*ch.* 18:3), and told them they must be humble as little children; yet they relapsed into it, and yet he reproved them for it thus mildly.

He called them unto him, which intimates great tenderness and familiarity. He did not, in anger, bid them get out of his presence, but called them, in love, to come into his presence: for *therefore* he is fit to teach, and we are invited to learn of him, because *he is meek and lowly in heart.* What he had to say concerned both the two disciples and the ten, and therefore he will have them all together. And he tells them, that, whereas they were asking which of them should have dominion a temporal kingdom, there was really no such dominion reserved for any of them. For,

(1.) They must not be *like the princes of the Gentiles.* Christ's disciples must not be like Gentiles, no not like princes of the Gentiles. Principality doth no more become ministers than Gentilism doth Christians.

Observe, [1.] What is the way of the princes of the Gentiles (*v.* 25); to *exercise dominion and authority* over their subjects, and (if they can but win the upper hand with a strong hand) over one another too. That which bears them up in it is, that they are great, and great men think they may do any thing. Dominion and authority are the great things which the princes of the Gentiles pursue, and pride themselves in; they would bear sway, would carry all before them, have every body truckle to them, and every sheaf bow to theirs. They would have it cried before them, *Bow the knee;* like Nebuchadnezzar, who slew, and kept alive, at pleasure.

[2.] What is the will of Christ concerning his apostles and ministers, in this matter.

First, "*It shall not be so among you.* The constitution of the spiritual kingdom is quite different from this. You are to teach the subjects of this kingdom, to instruct and beseech them, to counsel and comfort them, to take pains with them, and suffer with them, not to exercise dominion or authority over them; you are not to *lord it over God's heritage* (1 Pt. 5:3), but to labour in it." This forbids not only tyranny, and abuse of power, but the claim or use of any such secular authority as the princes of the Gentiles lawfully exercise. So hard is it for vain men, even good men, to have such authority, and not to be puffed up with it, and do more hurt than good with it, that our Lord Jesus saw fit wholly to banish it out of his church. Paul himself disowns dominion over the faith of any, 2 Co. 1:24. The pomp and grandeur of the princes of the Gentiles ill become Christ's disciples. Now, if there were no such power and honour intended to be in the church, it was nonsense for them to be striving who should have it. *They knew not what they asked.*

Secondly, How then shall it be among the disciples of Christ? Something of greatness among them Christ himself had intimated, and here he explains it; *"He that will be great among you,* that *will be chief,* that would really be so, and would be found to be so at last, *let him be your minister, your servant," v.* 26, 27. Here observe, 1. That it is the duty of Christ's disciples to serve one another, for mutual edification. This includes both humility and usefulness. The followers of Christ must be ready to stoop to the meanest offices of love for the good one of another, must *submit one to another* (1 Pt. 5:5; Eph. 5:21), and *edify one another* (Rom. 14:19), *please one another* for good, Rom. 15:2. The great apostle made himself every one's servant; see 1 Co. 9:19. 2. It is the dignity of Christ's disciples faithfully to discharge this duty. The way to be great and chief is to be humble and serviceable. Those are to be best accounted of, and most respected, in the church, and will be so by all that understand things aright; not those that are dignified with high and mighty names, like the names of the great ones of the earth, that appear in pomp, and assume to themselves a power proportionable, but those that are most humble and self-denying, and lay out themselves most to do good, though to the diminishing of themselves. These honour God most, and those he will honour. As he must become a fool that would be wise, so he must become a servant that would be chief. St. Paul was a great example of this; he *laboured more abundantly than they all,* made himself (as some would call it) a drudge to his work; and is not he chief? Do we not by consent call him the *great* apostle, though he called himself *less than the least?* And perhaps our Lord Jesus had an eye to him, when he said, There were *last* that should be *first;* for Paul was *one born out of due time* (1 Co. 15:8); not only the youngest child of the family of the apostles, but a posthumous one, yet he became greatest. And perhaps he it was for whom the first post of honour in Christ's kingdom was reserved and prepared of his Father, not for James who sought it; and therefore just before Paul began to be famous as an apostle, Providence ordered it so that James was cut off (Acts 12:2), that in the college of the twelve Paul might be substituted in his room.

(2.) They must be like the Master himself; and it is very fit that they should, that, while they were in the world, they should be as he was when he was in the world; for to both the present state is a state of humiliation, the crown and glory were reserved for both in the future state. Let them consider that the *Son of Man came not to be ministered to, but to minister, and to give his life a ransom for many, v.* 28. Our Lord Jesus here sets himself before his disciples as a pattern of those two things before recommended, humility, and usefulness.

[1.] Never was there such an example of humility and condescension as there was in the life of Christ, who came not to be *ministered unto, but to minister.* When the Son of God came into the world, his Ambassador to the children of men, one would think he should have been ministered to, should have appeared in an equipage agreeable to his person and character; but he did not so; he made no figure, had no pompous train of state-servants to attend him, nor was he clad in robes of honour, for he took upon him the *form of a servant.* He was indeed ministered to as a poor man, which was a part of his humiliation; there were those that *ministered to him of their substance* (Lu. 8:2, 3); but he was never ministered to as a great man; he never took state upon him, was not waited on at table; he once washed his disciples' feet, but we never read that they washed his feet. He came to minister help to all that were in distress; he made himself a servant to the sick and diseased; was as ready to their requests as ever any servant was at the beck of his master, and took as much pains to serve them; he attended continually to this very thing, and denied himself both food and rest to attend to it.

[2.] Never was there such an example of beneficence and usefulness as there was in the death of Christ, who *gave his life a ransom for many.* He lived as a servant, and went about doing good; but he died as a sacrifice, and in that he did the greatest good of all. He came into the world on purpose to give his life a ransom; it was first in his intention. The aspiring princes of the Gentiles make the lives of many a ransom for their own honour, and perhaps a sacrifice to their own humour. Christ doth not do so; his subjects' blood is precious to him, and he is not prodigal of it (Ps. 72:14); but on the contrary, he gives his honour and life too ransom for his subjects. Note, *First,* Jesus Christ laid down his life for a ransom. Our lives were forfeited into the hands of divine justice by sin. Christ, by parting with his life, made atonement for sin, and so rescued ours; *he was made sin, and a curse for us,* and died, not only *for our good, but in our stead,* Acts 20:28; 1 Pt. 1:18, 19. *Secondly,* It was a ransom for many, sufficient for all, effectual for many; and, if for many, then, saith the poor doubting soul, "Why not for me?" It was for many, that by him many may be made righteous. These many were his seed, for which his soul travailed (Isa. 53:10, 11); for many, so they will be when they come all together, though now they appear but a little flock.

Now this is a good reason why we should not strive for precedency, because the cross is our banner, and our Master's death is our life. It is a good reason why we should study to do good, and, in consideration of the love of Christ in dying for us, not hesitate *to lay down our lives for the brethren,* 1 Jn. 3:16. Ministers should be more forward than others to serve and suffer for the good of souls, as blessed Paul was, Acts 20:24; Phil. 2:17. The nearer we are all concerned in, and the more we are advantaged by, the humility and humiliation of Christ, the more ready and careful we should be to imitate it.

Verses 29–34

We have here an account of the cure of two poor blind beggars; in which we may observe,

I. Their address to Christ, *v.* 29, 30. And in this,

1. The circumstances of it are observable. It was as Christ and his disciples departed from Jericho; of that devoted place, which was rebuilt under a curse, Christ took his leave with this blessing, for he received gifts even for the rebellious. It was in the presence of *a great multitude that followed him;* Christ had a numerous, though not a pompous, attendance, and did good to them, though he did not take state to himself. This multitude that followed him for loaves, and some for love, some for curiosity, and some in expectation of his temporal reign, which the disciples themselves dreamed of, very few with desire to be taught their duty; yet, for the sake of those few, he confirmed his doctrine by miracles wrought in the presence of great multitudes; who, if they were not convinced by them, would be the more inexcusable. Two blind men concurred in their request; for joint-prayer is pleasing to Christ, *ch.* 18:19. These joint-sufferers were joint-suitors; being companions in the same tribulation, they were partners in the same supplication. Note, It is good for those that are labouring under the same calamity, or infirmity of body or mind, to join together in the same prayer to God for relief, that they may quicken one another's fervency, and encourage one another's faith. There is mercy enough in Christ for all the petitioners. These blind men were *sitting by the way-side,* as blind beggars used to do. Note, Those that would receive mercy from Christ, must place themselves there where his out-goings are; where he manifests himself to those that seek him. It is good thus to way-lay Christ, to be in his road.

They heard that Jesus passed by. Though they were blind, they were not deaf. Seeing and hearing are the learning senses. It is a great calamity to want either; but the defect of one may be, and often is, made up in the acuteness of the other; and therefore it has been observed by some as an instance of the goodness of Providence, that none were ever known to be born both blind and deaf; but that, one way or other, all are in a capacity of receiving knowledge. These blind men had heard of Christ by the hearing of the ear, but they desired that their eyes might see him. *When they heard that Jesus passed by,* they asked no further questions, who were with him, or whether he was in haste, but immediately *cried out.* Note, It is good to improve the present opportunity, to make the best of the price now in the hand, because, if once let slip, it may never return; these blind men did so, and did wisely; for we do not find that Christ ever came to Jericho again. *Now is the accepted time.*

2. The address itself is more observable; *Have mercy on us, O Lord, thou Son of David,* repeated again, *v.* 31. Four things are recommended to us for an example in this address; for, though the eye of the body was dark, the eye of the mind was enlightened concerning truth, duty, and interest.

(1.) Here is an example of importunity in prayer. They cried out as men in earnest; men in want are earnest, of course. Cold desires do but beg denials. Those that would prevail in prayer, must stir up themselves to take hold on God in duty. When they were discountenanced in it, they cried the more. The stream of fervency, if it be stopped, will rise and swell the higher. This wrestling with God in prayer, and makes us the fitter to receive mercy; for the more it is striven for, the more it will be prized and thankfully acknowledged.

(2.) Of humility in prayer; in that word, *Have mercy on us,* not specifying the favour, or prescribing what, much less pleading merit, but casting themselves upon, and referring themselves cheerfully to, the Meditator's mercy, in what way he pleases; "Only have mercy." They ask not for silver and gold, though they were poor, but mercy, mercy. This is that which our hearts must be upon, when we come to *the throne of grace, that we may find mercy,* Heb. 4:16; Ps. 130:7.

(3.) Of faith in prayer; in the title they gave to Christ, which was in the nature of a plea; *O Lord, thou Son o David;* they confess that *Jesus Christ is Lord,* and therefore had authority to command deliverance for them. Surely it was by the Holy Ghost that they called Christ *Lord,* 1 Co. 12:3. Thus they take their encouragement in prayer from his power, as in calling him the Son of David they take encouragement from his goodness, as Messiah, of whom so many kind and tender things had been foretold, particularly his compassion to the poor and needy, Ps. 72:12, 13. It is of excellent use, in prayer, to eye Christ in the grace and glory of his Messiahship; to remember that he is the Son of David, whose office it is to help, and save, and to plead it with him.

(4.) Of perseverance in prayer, notwithstanding discouragement. *The multitude rebuked them,* as noisy, clamorous, and impertinent, and bid them *hold their peace,,* and not disturb the Master, who perhaps at first himself seemed not to regard them. In following Christ with our prayers, we must expect to meet with hindrances and manifold discouragements from within and from without, something or other that bids us hold our peace. Such rebuke are permitted, that faith and fervency, patience and perseverance, may be tried. These poor blind men were rebuked by the multitude that followed Christ. Note, the sincere and serious beggars at Christ's door commonly meet with the worst rebukes from those that follow him but in pretence and hypocrisy. But they would not be beaten off so; when they were in pursuit of such a mercy, it was no time to compliment, or to practise a timid delicacy; no, *they cried the more.* Note, *Men ought always to pray, and not to faint;* to *pray with all perseverance* (Lu. 18:1); to continue in prayer with resolution, and not to yield to opposition.

II. The answer of Christ to this address of theirs. The multitude rebuked them; but Christ encouraged them. It were sad for us, if the Master were not more kind and tender than the multitude; but he loves to countenance those with special favour, that are under frowns, and rebukes, and contempts from men. He will not suffer his humble supplicants to be run down, and put out of countenance.

1. *He stood still, and called them, v.* 32. He was now going up to Jerusalem, and was straitened till his work there was accomplished; and yet he stood still to cure these blind men. Note, When we are ever so much in haste about any business, yet we should be willing to stand still to do good. *He called them,* not because he could not cure them at a distance, but because he would do it in the most obliging and instructive way, and would countenance weak but willing patients and petitioners. Christ not only enjoins us to pray, but invites us; holds out the golden sceptre to us, and bids us come touch the top of it.

2. He enquired further into their case; *What will ye that I shall do unto you?* This implies, (1.) A very fair offer; "Here I am; let me know what you would have, and you shall have it." What would we more? He is able to do for us, and as willing as he is able; *Ask, and it shall be given you.* (2.) A condition annexed to this offer, which is a very easy and reasonable one — that they should tell him what they would have him do for them. One would think this a strange question, any one might tell what they would have. Christ knew well enough; but he would know it from them, whether they begged only for alms, as from a common person, or for a cure, as from the Messiah. Note, It is the will of God that we should in every thing make our requests known to him by prayer and supplication; not to inform or move him, but to qualify ourselves for the mercy. The waterman in the boat, who with his hook takes hold of the shore, does not thereby pull the shore to the boat, but the boat to the shore. So in prayer we do not draw the mercy to ourselves, but ourselves to the mercy.

They soon made known their request to him, such a one as they never made to any one else; *Lord, that our eyes may be opened.* The wants and burthens of the body we are soon sensible of, and can readily relate; *Ubi dolor, ubi digitus — The finger promptly points to the seat of pain.* O that we were but as apprehensive of our spiritual maladies, and could as feelingly complain of them, especially our spiritual blindness! Lord, that the eyes of our mind may be opened! Many are spiritually blind, and yet say they see, Jn. 9:41. Were we but sensible of our darkness, we should soon apply ourselves to him, who alone has the eye-salve, with this request, *Lord, that our eyes may be opened.*

3. He cured them; when he encouraged them to seek him, he did not say, *Seek in vain.* What he did was an instance,

(1.) Of his pity; *He had compassion on them.* Misery is the object of mercy. They that are poor and blind are *wretched and miserable* (Rev. 3:17), and the objects of compassion. It was the tender mercy of our God, that gave light and sight to them that sat in darkness, Lu. 1:78, 79. We cannot help those that are under such calamities, as Christ did; but we may and must pity them, as Christ did, and draw out our soul to them.

(2.) Of his power; *He that formed the eye, can he not heal it?* Yes, he can, he did, he did it easily, he touched their eyes; he did it effectually, *Immediately their eyes received sight.* Thus he not only proved that he was sent of God, but showed on what errand he was sent — to give sight to those that are spiritually blind, *to turn them from darkness to light.*

Lastly, These blind men, when they had received sight, *followed him.* Note, None follow Christ blindfold. He first by his grace opens men's eyes, and so draws their hearts after him. They followed Christ, as his disciples, to learn of him, and as his witnesses, eye-witnesses, to bear their testimony to him and to his power and goodness. The best evidence of spiritual illumination is a constant inseparable adherence to Jesus Christ as our Lord and Leader.

CHAPTER 21

The death and resurrection of Jesus Christ are the two main hinges upon which the door of salvation turns. He came into the world on purpose to give his life a ransom; so he had lately said, *ch.* 20, 28. And therefore the history of his sufferings, even unto death, and his rising again, is more particularly recorded by all the evangelists than any other part of his story; and to that this evangelist now hastens apace. For at this chapter begins that which is called the passion-week. He had said to his disciples more than once, Behold, we go up to Jerusalem, and there the Son of man must be betrayed. A great deal of good work he did by the way, and now at length he is come up to Jerusalem; and here we have, I. The public entry which he made into Jerusalem, upon the first day of the passion-week (*v.* 1–11). II. The authority he exercised there, in cleansing the temple, and driving out of it the buyers and sellers (*v.* 12–16). III. The barren fig-tree, and his discourse with his disciples thereupon (*v.* 17–22). IV. His justifying his own authority, by appealing to the baptism of John (*v.* 23–27). V. His shaming the infidelity and obstinacy of the chief priests and elders, with the repentance of the publicans, illustrated by the parable of the two sons (*v.* 29–32). VI. His reading the doom of the Jewish church for its unfruitfulness, in the parable of the vineyard let out to unthankful husbandmen (*v.* 33–46).

Verses 1–11

All the four evangelists take notice of this passage of Christ's *riding in triumph into Jerusalem,* five days before his death. The passover was on the fourteenth day of the month, and this was the tenth; on which day the law appointed that the paschal lamb should be taken up (Ex. 12:3), and set apart for that service; on that day therefore Christ our Passover, who was to be sacrificed for us, was publicly showed. So that this was the prelude to his passion. He had lodged at Bethany, a village not far from Jerusalem, for some time; at a supper there the night before Mary had *anointed his feet,* Jn. 12:3. But, as usual with ambassadors, he deferred his public entry till some time after his arrival. Our Lord Jesus travelled much, and his custom was to travel on foot from Galilee to Jerusalem, some scores of miles, which was both humbling and toilsome; many a dirty weary step he had when *he went about doing good.* How ill does it become Christians to be inordinately solicitous about their own ease and state, when their Master had so little of either! Yet once in his life he rode in triumph; and it was now when he went into Jerusalem, to suffer and die, as if that were the pleasure and preferment he courted; and then he thought himself begin to look great.

Now here we have,

I. The provision that was made for this solemnity; and it was very poor and ordinary, and such as bespoke his *kingdom* to be *not of this world.* Here were no heralds at arms provided, no trumpet sounded before him, no chariots of state, no liveries; such things as these were not agreeable to his present state of humiliation, but will be far outdone at his second coming, to which his magnificent appearance is reserved, when the last trumpet shall sound, the glorious angels shall be his heralds and attendants, and the clouds his chariots. But in this public appearance,

1. The preparation was sudden and offhand. for his glory in the other world, and ours with him, preparation was made before the foundation of the world, for that was the glory his heart was upon; his glory in this world he was dead to, and therefore, though he had it in prospect, did not forecast for it, but took what came next. They were come to Bethphage, which was the suburb of Jerusalem, and was accounted (say the Jewish doctors) in all things, as Jerusalem, a long scattering street that lay toward the mount of Olives; when he entered upon that, *he sent two of his disciples,* some think Peter and John, to fetch him an ass, for he had none ready for him.

2. It was very mean. He sent only for an ass and her colt, *v.* 2. Asses were much used in that country for travel; horses were kept only by great men, and for war. Christ could have summoned a cherub to carry him (Ps. 18:10); but though *by his name Jah,* which speaks him God, *he rides upon the heavens,* yet now by his name Jesus, *Immanuel, God with us,* in his state of humiliation, he *rides upon an ass.* Yet some think that he had herein an eye to the custom in Israel for the judges to ride upon white asses (Jdg. 5:10), and their sons on ass-colts, Jdg. 12:14. And Christ would thus enter, not as a Conqueror, but as the Judge of Israel, *who for judgment came into this world.*

3. It was not his own, but borrowed. Though he had not a house of his own, yet, one would think, like some wayfaring men that live upon their friends, he might have had an ass of his own, to carry him about; but for our sakes he became in all respects poor, 2 Co. 8:9. It is commonly said, "They that live on borrowing, live on sorrowing;" in this therefore, as in other things, Christ *was a man of sorrows* — that he had nothing of this world's goods but what was given him or lent him.

The disciples who were sent to borrow this ass are directed to say, *The Lord has need of him.* Those that are in need, must not be ashamed to own their need, nor say, as the unjust steward, *To beg I am ashamed,* Lu. 16:3. On the other hand, none ought to impose upon the kindness of their friends, by going to beg or borrow when they have not need. In the borrowing of this ass,

(1.) We have an instance of Christ's knowledge. Though the thing was altogether contingent, yet Christ could tell his disciples where they should find an ass tied, and a colt with her. His omniscience extends itself to the meanest of his creatures; asses and their colts, and their being bound or loosed. *Doth God take care for oxen?* (1 Co. 9:9.) No doubt he doth, and would not see Balaam's ass abused. He knows all the creatures, so as to make them serve his own purpose.

(2.) We have an instance of his power over the spirits of men. The hearts of the meanest subjects, as well as of kings, *are in the hand of the Lord.* Christ asserts his right to use the ass, in bidding them bring it to him; the fulness of the earth is the Lord Christ's; but he foresees some hindrance which disciples might meet with in this service; they must not take them *clam et secreto — privily,* but in the sight of the owner, much less *vi et armis — with force and arms,* but with the consent of the owner, which he undertakes they shall have; *If any man say aught to you, ye shall say, The Lord hath need of him.* Note, What Christ sets us to do, he will bear us out in the doing of, and furnish us with answers tot he objections we may be assaulted with, and make them prevalent; as here, *Straightway he will send them.* Christ, in commanding the ass into his service, showed that he is Lord of hosts; and, in inclining the owner to send him without further security, showed that he is the *God of the spirits of all flesh,* and can bow men's hearts.

(3.) We have an example of justice and honesty, in not using the ass, though for so small a piece of service as riding the length of a street or two, without the owner's consent. As some read the latter clause, it gives us a further rule of justice; *"You shall say the Lord hath need of them, and he"* (that is, *the Lord) "will presently send them back,* and take care that they be safely delivered to the owner, as soon as he has done with them." Note, What we borrow we must restore in due time and in good order; for *the wicked borrows and pays not again.* Care must be taken of borrowed goods, that they be not damaged. *Alas, Master, for it was borrowed!*

II. The prediction that was fulfilled in this, *v.* 4, 5. Our Lord Jesus, in all that he did and suffered, had very much his eye upon this, *That the scriptures might be fulfilled.* As the prophets looked forward to him (to him they all bare witness), so he looked upon them, that all things which were written of the Messiah, might be punctually accomplished in him. This particularly which was written of him, Zec. 9:9, where it ushers in a large prediction of the kingdom of the Messiah, *Tell ye the daughter of Sion, Behold, thy King cometh,* must be accomplished. Now observe here,

1. How the coming of Christ is foretold; *Tell ye the daughter of Sion,* the church, the holy mountain, *Behold, thy King cometh unto thee.* Note, (1.) Jesus Christ is the church's King, one of our brethren like unto us, according to the law of the kingdom, Deu. 17:15. He is appointed King over the church, Ps. 2:6. He is accepted King by the church; the daughter of Sion swears allegiance to him, Hos. 1:11. (2.) Christ, the King of his church, came to his church, even in this lower world; he comes to thee, to rule thee, to rule in thee, to rule for thee; he is *Head over all things to the church. He came to Sion* (Rom. 11:26), that out of Sion the law might go forth; for the church and its interests were all in all with the Redeemer. (3.) Notice was given to the church beforehand of the coming of her King; *Tell the daughter of Sion.* Note, Christ will have his coming looked for, and waited for, and his subjects big with expectation of it; *Tell the daughters of Sion,* that they may *go forth, and behold King Solomon,* Cant. 3:11. Notices of Christ's coming are usually ushered in with a *Behold!* A note commanding both attention and admiration; *Behold thy King cometh;* behold, and wonder at him, behold, and welcome him. Here is a royal progress truly admirable. Pilate,

like Caiaphas, said he knew not what, in that great word (Jn. 19:14), *Behold your King.*

2. How his coming is described. When a king comes, something great and magnificent is expected, especially when he comes to take possession of his kingdom. The King, the Lord of hosts, was seen *upon a throne, high and lifted up* (Isa. 6:1); but there is nothing of that here; *Behold, he cometh to thee, meek, and sitting upon an ass.* When Christ would appear in his glory, it is in his meekness, not in his majesty.

(1.) His temper is very mild. He comes not in wrath to take vengeance, but in mercy to work salvation. He is meek to suffer the greatest injuries and indignities for Sion's cause, meek to bear with the follies and unkindness of Sion's own children. He is easy of access, easy to be entreated. He is meek not only as a Teacher, but as a Ruler; he rules by love. His government is mild and gentle, and his laws not written in the blood of his subjects, but in his own. His yoke is easy.

(2.) As an evidence of this, his appearance is very mean, sitting upon an ass, as creature made not for state, but service, not for battles, but for burthens; slow in its motions, but sure, and safe, and constant. The foretelling of this so long before, and the care taken that it should be exactly fulfilled, intimate it to have a peculiar significancy, for the encouragement of poor souls to apply themselves to Christ. Sion's King comes riding, not on a prancing horse, which the timorous petitioner dares not come near, or a running horse, which the slow-footed petitioner cannot keep pace with, but on a quiet ass, that the poorest of his subjects may not be discouraged in their access to him. Mention is made in the prophecy of *a colt, the foal of an ass;* and *therefore* Christ sent for the colt with the ass, that the scripture might be fulfilled.

III. The procession itself, which was answerable to the preparation, both being destitute of worldly pomp, and yet both accompanied with a spiritual power.

Observe, 1. His equipage; *The disciples did as Jesus commanded them* (*v.* 6); they went to fetch the ass and the colt, not doubting but to find them, and to find the owner willing to lend them. Note, Christ's commands must not be disputed, but obeyed; and those that sincerely obey them, shall not be balked or baffled in it; *They brought the ass and the colt.* The meanness and contemptibleness of the beast Christ rode on, might have been made up with the richness of the trappings; but those were, like all the rest, such as came next to hand; they had not so much as a saddle for the ass, but the disciples threw some of their clothes upon it, and that must serve for want of better accommodations. Note, We ought not to be nice or curious, or to affect exactness, in outward conveniences. A holy indifference or neglect well becomes us in these things: it will evidence that our heart is not upon them, and that we have learned the apostle's rule (Rom. 12:16, margin), *to be content with mean things.* Any thing will serve travellers; and there is a beauty in some sort of carelessness, a noble negligence; yet the disciples furnished him with the best they had, and did not object the spoiling of their clothes when *the Lord had need of them.* Note, We must not think the clothes on our backs too der to part with for the service of Christ, for the clothing of his poor destitute and afflicted members. *I was naked, and you clothed me, ch.* 25:36. Christ stripped himself for us.

2. His retinue; there was nothing in this stately or magnificent. Sion's King comes to Sion, and the daughter of Sion was told of his coming long before; yet he is not attended by the gentlemen of the country, nor met by the magistrates of the city in their formalities as one might have expected; he should have had the keys of the city presented to him, and should have been conducted with all possible convenience to *the thrones of judgment, the thrones of the house of David;* but here is nothing of all this; yet he has his attendants, *a very great multitude;* they were only the common people, the mob (the *rabble* we should have been apt to call them), that graced the solemnity of Christ's triumph, and none but such. The chief priests and the elders afterward herded themselves with the multitude that abused him upon the cross; but we find none of them here joining with the multitude that did him honour. Ye see here your calling, brethren, *not many mighty, or noble,* attend on Christ, but *the foolish things of this world and base things, which are despised,* 1 Co. 1:26, 28. Note, Christ is honoured by the multitude, more than by the magnificence, of his followers; for he values men by their souls, not by their preferments, names, or titles of honour.

Now, concerning this great multitude, we are here told,

(1.) What they did; according to the best of their capacity, they studied to do honour to Christ. [1.] *They spread their garments in the way,* that he might ride upon them. When Jehu was proclaimed king, the captains put their garments under him, in token of their subjection to him. Note, Those that take Christ for their King must lay their all under his feet; the clothes, in token of the heart; for when Christ comes, though not when any one else comes, it must be *said to the soul, Bow down, that he may go over.* Some think that these garments were spread, not upon the ground, but on the hedges or walls, to adorn the roads; as, to beautify a cavalcade, the balconies are hung with tapestry. This was but a poor piece of state, yet Christ accepted their good-will; and we are hereby taught to contrive how to make Christ welcome, Christ and his grace, Christ and his gospel, into our hearts and houses. How shall we express our respects to Christ? What honour and what dignity shall be done to him? [2.] *Others cut down branches from the trees, and strewed them in the way,* as they used to do at the feast of tabernacles, in token of liberty, victory, and joy; for the mystery of that feast is particularly spoken of as belonging to gospel times, Zec. 14:16.

(2.) What they said; *They that went before, and they that followed,* were in the same tune; both those that gave notice of his coming, and those that attended him with their applauses, *cried, saying, Hosanna to the Son of David, v.* 9. When they carried branches about at the feast of tabernacles, they were wont to cry *Hosanna,* and from thence to call their bundles of branches their *hosannas. Hosanna* signifies, *Save now, we beseech thee;* referring to Ps. 118:25, 26, where the Messiah is prophesied of as the *Head-stone of the corner,* though *the builders refused him;* and all his loyal subjects are brought in triumphing with him, and attending him with hearty good wishes to the prosperity of all his enterprises. *Hosanna to the Son of David* is, "This we do in honour of the Son of David."

The hosannas with which Christ was attended bespeak two things:

[1.] Their welcoming his kingdom. *Hosanna* bespeaks the same with, *Blessed is he that cometh in the name of the Lord.* It was foretold concerning this Son of David, that *all nations shall call him blessed* (Ps. 72:17); these here began, and all true believers in all ages concur in it, and call him blessed; it is the genuine language of faith. Note, *First,* Jesus Christ *comes in the name of the Lord;* he is sanctified, and sent into the world, as Mediator; *him hath God the Father sealed. Secondly,* The coming of Christ in the name of the Lord, is *worthy of all acceptation;* and we all ought to say, *Blessed is he that cometh;* to praise him, and be pleased in him. Let his coming in the name of the Lord be mentioned with strong affections, to our comfort, and joyful acclamations, to his glory. Well may we say, *Blessed is he;* for it is in him that we are blessed. Well may we follow *him* with our blessings, who meets us with his.

[2.] Their wishing well to his kingdom; intimated in their *Hosanna;* earnestly desiring that prosperity and success may attend it, and that it may be a victorious kingdom; *"Send now prosperity* to that kingdom." If they understood it of a temporal kingdom, and had their hearts carried out thus toward that, it was their mistake, which a little time would rectify; however, their good-will was accepted. Note, It is our duty earnestly to desire and pray for the prosperity and success of Christ's kingdom in the world. Thus *prayer must be made for him continually* (Ps. 72:15), that all happiness may attend his interest in the world, and that, though he may ride on an ass, yet in his majesty he may *ride prosperously, because* of that *meekness,* Ps. 45:4. This we mean when we pray, *Thy kingdom come.* They add, *Hosanna in the highest:* Let prosperity in the highest degree attend him, let him have a name above every name, a throne above every throne; or, Let us praise him in the best manner for his church ascend to heaven, to the highest heavens, and fetch in peace and salvation from thence. See Ps. 20:6. *The Lord saveth his Anointed, and will hear from his* high, his *holy heaven.*

3. We have here his entertainment in Jerusalem (*v.* 10); *When he was come into Jerusalem, all the city was moved;* every one took notice of him, some were moved with wonder at the novelty of the thing, others with laughter at the meanness of it; some perhaps were moved with joy, *who waited for the Consolation of Israel;* others, of the Pharisaical class, were moved with envy and indignation. So various are the motions in the minds of men upon the approach of Christ's kingdom!

Upon this commotion we are further told,

(1.) What the citizens said; *Who is this?* [1.] They were, it seems, ignorant concerning Christ. Though he was *the Glory of his people Israel,* yet *Israel knew him not;* though he had distinguished himself by the many miracles he wrought among them, yet *the daughters of Jerusalem* knew him not *from another beloved,* Cant. 5:9. The Holy One unknown in the holy city! In places where the clearest light shines, and the greatest profession of religion is made, there is more ignorance than we are. [2.] Yet they were inquisitive concerning him. Who is this that is thus cried, and comes with so much observation? *Who is this King of glory,* that demands admission into our hearts? Ps. 24:8; Isa. 63:1.

(2.) How the multitude answered them; *This is Jesus, v.* 11. The multitude were better acquainted with Christ than the great ones. *Vox populi — The voice of the people,* is sometimes *Vox Dei — the voice of God.* Now, in the account they give of him, [1.] They were right in calling him *the Prophet, that great Prophet.* Hitherto he had been known as a Prophet, teaching and working miracles; now they attend him as a King; Christ's priestly office was, of all the three, last discovered. [2.] Yet they missed it, in saying he was *of Nazareth;* and it helped to confirm some in their prejudices against him. Note, Some that are willing to honour Christ, and bear their testimony to him, yet labour under mistakes concerning him, which would be rectified if they would take pains to inform themselves.

Verses 12–17

When Christ came into Jerusalem, he did not go up to the court or the palace, though he came in as a King, but *into the temple;* for his kingdom is spiritual, and *not of this world;* it is in holy things that he rules, in the temple of God that he exercises authority. Now, what did he do there?

I. Thence he drove the buyers and sellers. Abuses must first be purged out, and the plants not of God's planting be plucked up, before that which is right can be established. The great Redeemer appear as a great Reformer, that turns away ungodliness, Rom. 11:26. Here we are told,

1. What he did (*v.* 12); *He cast out all them that sold and bought;* he had done this once before (Jn. 2:14, 15), but there was occasion to do it again. Note, Buyers and sellers driven out of the temple, will return and nestle there again, if there be not a continual care and oversight to prevent it, and if the blow be not followed, and often repeated.

(1.) The abuse was, buying and selling, and changing money, in the temple. Note, Lawful things, ill timed and ill placed, may become sinful things. That which was decent enough in another place, and not only lawful, but laudable, on another day, *defiles the sanctuary,* and *profanes the sabbath.* This buying and selling, and changing money, though secular employments, yet had the pretence of being *in ordine ad spiritualia — for spiritual purposes.* They sold beasts for sacrifice, for the convenience of those that could more easily bring their money with them than their beast; and they changed money for those that wanted the half shekel, which was their yearly poll, or redemption-money; or, upon the bills of return; so that this might pass for the outward business of the house of God; and yet Christ will not allow of it. Note, Great corruptions and abuses come into the church by the practices of those whose *gain is godliness,* that is, who make worldly gain the end of their godliness, and counterfeit godliness their way to worldly gain (1 Tim. 6:5); *from such withdraw thyself.*

(2.) The purging out of this abuse. Christ *cast them out that sold.* He did it before *with a scourge of small cords* (Jn. 2:15); now he did it with a look, with a frown, with a word of command. Some reckon this none of the least of Christ's miracles, that he should himself thus clear the temple, and not be opposed in it by them who by this craft got their living, and were backed in it by the priests and elders. It is an instance of his power over the spirits of men, and the hold he has of them by their own consciences. This was the only act of regal authority and coercive power that Christ did in the days of his flesh; he began with it, Jn. 2 and here ended with it. Tradition says, that his face shone, and beams of light darted from his blessed eyes, which astonished these market-people, and compelled them to yield to his command; if so, the scripture was fulfilled, Prov. 20:8, *A King that sitteth in the throne of judgment scattereth away all evil with his eyes.*

He overthrew the tables of the money-changers; he did not take the money to himself, but scattered it, threw it to the ground, the fittest place for it. The Jews, in Esther's time, *on the spoil laid not their hand,* Esther 9:10.

2. What he said, to justify himself, and to convict them (*v.* 13); *It is written.* Note, In the reformation of the church, the eye must be upon the scripture, and that must be adhered to as the rule, the pattern in the mount; and we must go no further than we can justify ourselves with, *It is written.* Reformation is *then* right, when corrupted ordinances are reduced to their primitive institution.

(1.) He shows, from a scripture prophecy, what the temple should be, and was designed to be; *My house shall be called the house of prayer;* which is quoted from Isa. 56:7. Note, All the ceremonial institutions were intended to be subservient to moral duties; the house of sacrifices was to be a house of prayer, for that was the substance and soul of all those services; the temple was in a special manner sanctified to be a house of prayer, for it was not only the place of that worship, but the medium of it, so that the prayers made in or toward that house had a particular promise of acceptance (2 Chr. 6:21), as it was a type of Christ; therefore Daniel looked that way in prayer; and in this sense no house or place is now, or can be, a house of prayer, for Christ is our Temple; yet in some sense the appointed places of our religious assemblies may be so called, as *places where prayer is wont to be made,* Acts 16:13.

(2.) He shows, from a scripture reproof, how they had abused the temple, and perverted the intention of it; *Ye have made it a den of thieves.* This is quoted from Jer. 7:11, *Is this house become a den of robbers in your eyes?* When dissembled piety is made the cloak and cover of iniquity, it may be said that *the house of prayer* is become *a den of thieves,* in which they lurk, and shelter themselves. Markets are too often dens of thieves, so many are the corrupt and cheating practices in buying and selling; but markets in the temple are certainly so, for they rob God of his honour, the worst of thieves, Mal. 3:8. The priests lived, and lived plentifully, upon the altar; but, not content with that, they found other ways and means to squeeze money out of the people; and therefore Christ here calls them *thieves,* for they exacted that which did not belong to them.

II. There, in the temple, *he healed the blind and the lame, v.* 14. When he had driven the buyers and sellers out of the temple, he invited the blind and lame into it; for *he fills the hungry with good things, but the rich he sends empty away.* Christ, in the temple, by his word there preached, and in answer to the prayers there made, heals those that are spiritually blind and lame. It is good coming to the temple, when Christ is there, who, as he shows himself jealous for the honour of his temple, in expelling those who profane it, so he shows himself gracious to those who humbly seek him. *The blind and the lame* were debarred David's palace (2 Sa. 5:8), but were admitted into God's house; for the state and honour of his temple lie not in those things wherein the magnificence of princes' palaces is supposed to consist; from them blind and lame must keep their distance, but from God's temple only the wicked and profane. The temple was profane and abused when it was made a market-place, but it was graced and honoured when it was made an hospital; to be doing good in God's, is more honourable, and better becomes it, than to be getting money there. Christ's healing was a real answer to that question, *Who is this?* His works testified of him more than the *hosannas;* and his healing in the temple was the fulfilling of the promise, that *the glory of the latter house should be greater than the glory of the former.*

There also he silenced the offence which the chief priests and scribes took at the acclamations with which he was attended, *v.* 15, 16. They that should have been most forward to give him honour, were his worst enemies.

1. They were inwardly vexed at the wonderful things that he did; they could not deny them to be true miracles, and therefore were cut to the heart with indignation at them, as Acts 4:16; 5:33. The works that Christ did, recommended themselves to every man's conscience. If they had any sense, they could not but own the miracle of them; and if any good nature, could not but be in love with the mercy of them: yet, because they were resolved to oppose him, for these they envied him, and bore him a grudge.

2. They openly quarrelled at the children's hosannas; they thought that hereby an honour was given him, which did not belong to him, and that it looked like ostentation. Proud men cannot bear that honour should be done to any but to themselves, and are uneasy at nothing more than at the just praises of deserving men. Thus Saul envied David the women's songs; and "Who can stand before envy?" When Christ is most honoured, his enemies are most displeased.

Just now we had Christ preferring the blind and the lame before the buyers and sellers; now here we have him (*v.* 16), taking part with the children against priests and scribes.

Observe, (1.) The children were in the temple, perhaps playing there; no wonder, when the rulers make it a *market-place,* that the children make it a place of pastime; but we are willing to hope that many of them were worshipping there. Note, It is good to bring children betimes to the house of prayer, *for of such is the kingdom of heaven.* Let children be taught to keep up the form of godliness, it will help to lead them to the power of it. Christ has a tenderness for the lambs of his flock.

(2.) They were there *crying Hosanna to the Son of David.* This they learned from those that were grown up. Little children say and do as they hear others say, and see others do; so easily do they imitate; and therefore great care must be taken to set them good examples, and no bad ones. *Maxima debetur puero reverentia — Our intercourse with the young should be conducted with the most scrupulous care.* Children will learn of those that are with them, either to curse and swear, or to pray and praise. The Jews did betimes teach their children to carry branches at the feast of tabernacles, and to cry *Hosanna;* but God taught them here to apply it to Christ. Note, *Hosanna to the Son of David* well becomes the mouths of little children, who should learn young the language of Canaan.

(3.) Our Lord Jesus not only allowed it, but was very well pleased with it, and quoted a scripture which was fulfilled in it (Ps. 8:2), or, at least, may be accommodated to it; *Out of the mouth of babes and sucklings thou hast perfected praise;* which, some think, refers to the children's joining in the acclamations of the people, and the women's songs with which David was honoured when he returned from the slaughter of the Philistine, and therefore is very fitly applied here to the hosannas with which the Son of David was saluted, now that he was entering upon his conflict with Satan, that Goliath. Note, [1.] Christ is so far from being ashamed of the services of little children, that he takes particular notice of them (and children love to be taken notice of), and is well pleased with them. If God may be honoured by babes and sucklings, who are made to hope at the best, much more by children who are grown up to maturity and some capacity. [2.] Praise is perfected out of the mouth of such; it has a peculiar tendency to the honour and glory of God for little children to join in his praises; the praise would be accounted defective and imperfect, if they had not their share in it; which is an encouragement for children to be good betimes, and to parents to teach them to be so; the labour neither of the one nor of the other shall be in vain. In the psalm it is, *Thou hast ordained strength.* Note, God *perfecteth praise,* by *ordaining strength out of the mouths of babes and sucklings.* When great things are brought about by weak and unlikely instruments, God is thereby much honoured, for his *strength is perfected in weakness,* and the infirmities of the babes and sucklings serve for a foil to the divine power. That which follows in the psalm, *That thou mightest still the enemy and the avenger,* was very applicable to the priests and scribes; but Christ did not apply it to them, but left it to them to apply it.

Lastly, Christ, having thus silenced them, forsook them, *v.* 17. *He left them,* in prudence, lest they should now have seized him before his hour was come; in justice, because they had forfeited the favour of his presence. By repining at Christ's praises we drive him from us. *He left them* as incorrigible, and he *went out of the city to Bethany,* which was a more quiet retired place; not so much that he might *sleep* undisturbed as that he might *pray* undisturbed. *Bethany was but two little miles from Jerusalem;* thither he went on foot, to show that, when he rode, it was only to *fulfil the scripture.* He was not lifted up with the hosannas of the people; but, as having forgot them, soon returned to his mean and toilsome way of travelling.

Verses 18–22

Observe,

I. Christ *returned in the morning to Jerusalem, v.* 18. Some think that he went out of the city over-night, because none of his friends there durst entertain him, for fear of the great men; yet, having work to do there, he returned. Note, We must never be driven off from our duty either by the malice of our foes, or the unkindness of our friends. Though he knew that in this city *bonds and afflictions did abide him, yet none of these things moved* him. Paul followed him when he *went bound in the spirit to Jerusalem,* Acts 30:22.

II. *As he went, he hungered.* He was a Man, and submitted to the infirmities of nature; he was an active Man, and was so intent upon his work, that he neglected his food, and came out, fasting; for *the zeal of God's house* did even *eat him up,* and his *meat and drink was to do his Father's will.* He was a poor Man, and had no present supply; he was a Man that pleased not himself, for he would willingly have taken up with green raw figs for his breakfast, when it was fit that he should have had something warm.

Christ *therefore* hungered, that he might have occasion to work this miracle, in cursing and so withering the barren fig-tree, and therein might give us an instance of his justice and his power, and both instructive.

1. See his *justice, v.* 19. He went to it, expecting fruit, because it had leaves; but, finding none, he sentenced it to a perpetual barrenness. The miracle had its significance, as well as others of his miracles. All Christ's miracles hitherto were wrought for the good of men, and proved the power of his grace and blessing (the sending the devils into the herd of swine was but a permission); all he did was for the benefit and comfort of his friends, none for the terror or punishment of his enemies; but now, at last, to show that *all judgment is committed to him,* and that *he is able* not only *to save, but to destroy,* he would give a specimen of the power of his wrath and curse; yet this not on any man, woman, or child, because *the great day of his wrath is not yet come,* but on an inanimate tree; that is set forth for an example; *Come, learn a parable of the fig-tree, ch.* 24:32. The scope of it is the same with *the parable of the fig-tree,* Lu. 13:6.

(1.) This cursing of the barren fig-tree, represents the state of hypocrites in general; and so it teaches us, [1.] That the fruit of fig-trees may justly be expected from those that have the leaves. Christ looks for the power of religion from those that make profession of it; the favour of it from those that have the show of it; grapes from the vineyard that is planted in a fruitful hill: he hungers after it, his soul *desires the first ripe fruits.* [2.] Christ's just expectations from flourishing professors are often frustrated and disappointed; he comes to many, seeking fruit, and finds leaves only, and he discovers it. Many have a name to live, and are not alive indeed; dote on the form of godliness, and yet deny the power of it. [3.] The sin of barrenness is justly punished with the curse and plague of barrenness; *Let no fruit grow on thee henceforward for ever.* As one of the chiefest blessings, and which was the first, is, *Be fruitful;* so one of the saddest curses is, *Be no more fruitful.* Thus the sin of hypocrites is made their punishment; they *would* not do good, and therefore they *shall* do none; he that is fruitless, let him be fruitless still, and lose his honour and comfort. [4.] A false and hypocritical profession commonly withers in this world, and it is the effect of Christ's curse; the fig-tree that had no fruit, soon lost its leaves. Hypocrites may look plausible for a time, but, having no principle, *no root in themselves,* their profession will soon come to nothing; the gifts wither, common graces decay, the credit of the profession declines and sinks, and the falseness and folly of the pretender are manifested to all men.

(2.) It represents the state of the nation and people of the Jews in particular; they were a fig-tree planted in Christ's way, as a church. Now observe, [1.] The disappointment they gave to our Lord Jesus. He came among them, expecting to find some fruit, something that would be pleasing to him; he hungered after it; not that he *desired a gift,* he needed it not, *but fruit that might abound to a good account.* But his expectations were frustrated; he found nothing but leaves; they called *Abraham their father, but did not do the works of Abraham;* they professed themselves expectants of the promised Messiah, but, when he came, they did not receive and entertain him. [2.] The doom he passed upon them, *that never any fruit should grow upon them* or be gathered from them, as a church or as a people, *from henceforward for ever.* Never any good came from them (except the particular persons among them that believe), after they rejected Christ; they became worse and worse; blindness and hardness happened to them, and grew upon them, till they were unchurched, unpeopled, and undone, and their place and nation rooted up; their beauty was defaced, their privileges and ornaments, their temple, and priesthood, and sacrifices, and festivals, and all the glories of their church and state, fell like leaves in autumn. How soon did their fig-tree wither away, after they said, *His blood be on us, and our children!* And the Lord was righteous in it.

2. See the *power* of Christ; the former is wrapped up in the figure, but this more fully discoursed of; Christ intending thereby to direct his disciples in the use of their powers.

(1.) The disciples admired the effect of Christ's curse (*v.* 20); *They marvelled;* no power could do it but his, *who spake, and it was done.* They marvelled at the suddenness of the thing; *How soon is the fig-tree withered away!* There was no visible cause of the fig-tree's withering, but it was a secret blast, a worm at the root; it was not only the leaves of it that withered, but the body of the tree; it withered away in an instant and became like a dry stick. Gospel curses are, upon this account, the most dreadful — that they work insensibly and silently, by a fire not blown, but effectually.

(2.) Christ empowered them by faith to do the like (*v.* 21, 22); as he said (Jn. 14:12), *Greater works than these shall ye do.*

Observe, [1.] The description of this wonder-working faith; *If ye have faith, and doubt not.* Note, Doubting of the power and promise of God is the great thing that spoils the efficacy and success of faith. "If you have faith, and dispute not" (so some read it), "dispute not with yourselves, dispute not with the promise of God; if you *stagger not at the promise*" (Rom. 4:20); for, as far as we do so, our faith is deficient; as certain as the promise is, so confident our faith should be.

[2.] The power and prevalence of it expressed figuratively; *If ye shall say to this mountain,* meaning the mount of Olives, *Be thou removed, it shall be done.* There might be a particular reason for his saying so of this mountain, for there was a prophecy, that *the mount of Olives, which is before Jerusalem, should cleave in the midst, and then remove,* Zec. 14:4. Whatever was the intent of that word, the same must be the expectation of faith, how impossible soever it might appear to sense. But this is a proverbial expression; intimating that we are to believe that nothing is impossible with God, and therefore that what he has promised shall certainly be performed, though to us it seem impossible. It was among the Jews a usual commendation of their learned Rabbin, that they were removers of mountains, that is, could solve the greatest difficulties; now this may be done by faith acted on the word of God, which will bring great and strange things to pass.

[3.] The way and means of exercising this faith, and of doing that which is to be done by it; *All things whatsoever ye shall ask in prayer, believing, ye shall receive.* Faith is the soul, prayer is the body; both together make a complete man for any service. Faith, if it be right, will excite prayer; and prayer is not right, if it do not spring from faith. This is the condition of our receiving — we must *ask in prayer, believing.* The requests of prayer shall not be denied; the expectations of faith shall not be frustrated. We have many promises to this purport from the mouth of our Lord Jesus, and all to encourage faith, the principal grace, and prayer, the principal duty, of a Christian. It is but ask and have, believe and receive; and what would we more? Observe, How comprehensive the promise is — *all things whatsoever ye shall ask;* this is like all and every the premises in a conveyance. *All things,* in general; *whatsoever,* brings it to particulars; though generals include particulars, yet such is the folly of our unbelief, that, though we think we assent to promises in the general, yet we fly off when it comes to particulars, and therefore, *that we might have strong consolation,* it is thus copiously expressed, *All things whatsoever.*

Verses 23–27

Our Lord Jesus (like St. Paul after him) preached his gospel *with much contention;* his first appearance was in a dispute with *the doctors in the temple, when he was twelve years old;* and here, just before he died, we have him engaged in controversy. In this sense, he was like Jeremiah, *a man of contention; not striving, but striven with.* The great contenders with him, were, *the chief priests and the elders,* the judges of two distinct courts: the chief priests presided in the ecclesiastical court, in all matters of the Lord, as they are called; the elders of the people were judges of the civil courts, in temporal matters. See an idea of both, 2 Chr. 19:5, 8, 11. These joined to attack Christ thinking they should find or make him obnoxious either to the one or to the other. See how woefully degenerate that generation was, when the governors both in church and state, who should have been the great promoters of the Messiah's kingdom, were the great opposers of it! Here we have them disturbing him when he was preaching, *v.* 23. They would neither receive his instructions themselves, nor let others receive them. Observe,

I. As soon as he came into Jerusalem, he went to the temple, though he had been affronted there the day before, was there in the midst of enemies and in the mouth of danger; yet thither he went, for there he had a fairer opportunity of doing good to souls than any where else in Jerusalem. Though he came hungry to the city, and was disappointed of a breakfast at the barren fig-tree, yet, for aught that appears, he went straight to the temple, as one that *esteemed the words of God's mouth,* the preaching of them, *more than his necessary food.*

II. In the temple he was teaching; he had called it *a house of prayer* (*v.* 13), and here we have him preaching there. Note, In the solemn assemblies of Christians, praying and preaching must go together, and neither must encroach upon, or jostle out, the other. To make up communion with God, we must not only speak to him in prayer, but hear what he has to say to us by his word; ministers must *give themselves both to the word and to prayer,* Acts 6:4. Now that Christ *taught in the temple,* that scripture was fulfilled (Isa. 2:3), *Let us go up to the house of the Lord, and he will teach us his ways.* The priests of old often taught there *the good knowledge of the Lord;* but they never had such a teacher as this.

III. When Christ was teaching the people, the priests and elders came upon him, and challenged him to produce his orders; the hand of Satan was in this, to hinder him in his work. Note, It cannot but be a trouble to a faithful minister, to be taken off, or diverted from, plain and practical preaching, by an unavoidable necessity of engaging in controversies, yet good was brought out of this evil, for hereby occasion was given to Christ to dispel the objections that were advanced against him, to the greater satisfaction of his followers; and, while his adversaries thought by their power to have silenced him, he by his wisdom silenced them.

Now, in this dispute with them, we may observe,

1. How he was assaulted by their insolent demand; *By what authority doest thou these things, and who gave thee this authority?* Had they duly considered his miracles, and the power by which he wrought them, they needed not to have asked this question; but they must have something to say for the shelter of an obstinate infidelity. "Thou ridest in triumph into Jerusalem, receivest the hosannas of the people, controllest in the temple, drivest out such as had license to be there, from the rulers of the temple, and paid them rent; thou are here preaching a new doctrine; whence hadst thou a commission to do all this? Was it from Caesar, or from the high priest, or from God? Produce thy warrant, thy credentials. Dost not thou take too much upon thee?" Note, It is good for all that take upon them to act with authority, to put this question to themselves, "Who gave us that authority?" For, unless a man be clear in his own conscience concerning that, he cannot act with any comfort or hope of success. They who run before their warrant, run without their blessing, Jer. 23:21, 22.

Christ had often said it, and proved it beyond contradiction, and Nicodemus, a master in Israel, had owned it, that he was *a teacher sent of God* (Jn. 3:2); yet, at this time of day, when that point had been so fully cleared and settled, they come to him with this question. (1.) In the ostentation of their own power, as chief priests and elders, which they thought authorized them to call him to an account in this manner. How haughtily do they ask, *Who gave thee this authority?* Intimating that he could have no authority, because he had none from them, 1 Ki. 22:24; Jer. 20:1. Note, It is common for the greatest abusers of their power to be the most rigorous assertors of it, and to take a pride and pleasure in any thing that looks like the exercise of it. (2.) It was to ensnare and entangle him. Should he refuse to answer this question, they would enter judgment against him upon *Nihil dicit — He says nothing;* would condemn him as standing mute; and would insinuate to the people, that his silence was a tacit confessing of himself to be a usurper: should he plead an authority from God, they would, as formerly, demand a sign from heaven, or make his *de*fence his *of*fence, and accuse him of blasphemy for it.

2. How he answered this demand with another, which would help them to answer it themselves (*v.* 24, 25); *I also will ask you one thing.* He declined giving them a direct answer, lest they should take advantage against him; but answers them with a question. Those that are *as sheep in the midst of wolves,* have need to *be wise as serpents: the heart of the wise studieth to answer.* We must *give a reason of the hope that is in us,* not only *with meekness, but with fear* (1 Pt. 3:15), with prudent caution, lest truth be damaged, or ourselves endangered.

Now this question is concerning John's baptism, here put for his whole ministry, preaching as well as baptizing; "Was this *from heaven, or of men?* One of the two it must be; either what he did was of his own head, or he was sent of God to do it." Gamaliel's argument turned upon this hinge (Acts 5:38, 39); either *this counsel is of men or of God.* Though that which is manifestly bad cannot be of God, yet that which is seemingly good may be of men, nay of Satan, when *he transforms himself into an angel of light.* This question was not at all shuffling, to evade theirs; but,

(1.) If they answered this question, it would answer theirs: should they say, against their consciences, that John's baptism was of men, yet it would be easy to answer, *John did no miracle* (Jn. 10:41), Christ did many; but should they say, as they could not but own, that John's baptism was from heaven (which was supposed in the questions sent him, Jn. 1:21, *Art thou Elias, or that prophet?*) then their demand was answered, for he bare testimony to Christ. Note, Truths appear in the clearest light when they are taken in their due order; the resolving of the *previous* questions will be a key to the *main* question.

(2.) If they refused to answer it, that would be a good reason why he should not offer proofs of his authority to men that were obstinately prejudiced against the strongest conviction; it was but to cast pearls before swine. Thus *he taketh the wise in their own craftiness* (1 Co. 3:19); and those that would not be convinced of the plainest truths, shall be convicted of the vilest malice, against John first, then against Christ, and in both against God.

3. How they were hereby baffled and run aground; they knew the truth, but would not own it, and so were taken in the snare they laid for our Lord Jesus. Observe,

(1.) How *they reasoned with themselves,* not concerning the merits of the cause, what proofs there were of the divine original of John's baptism; no, their care was, how to make their part good against Christ. Two things they considered and consulted, in this reasoning with themselves — their credit, and their safety; the same things which *they* principally aim at, who *seek their own things.*

[1.] They consider their own credit, which they would endanger if they should own John's baptism to be of God; for then Christ would ask them, before all the people. *Why did ye not believe him?* And to acknowledge that a doctrine is from God, and yet not to receive and entertain it, is the greatest absurdity and iniquity that a man can be charged with. Many that will not be kept by the fear of sin from neglecting and opposing that which they know to be true and good are kept by the fear of shame from owning that to be true and good which they neglect and oppose. Thus they *reject the counsel of God against themselves,* in not submitting to John's baptism, and are left without excuse.

[2.] They consider their own safety, that they would expose themselves to the resentments of the people, if they should say that John's baptism was of men; *We fear the people, for all hold John as a prophet.* It seems, then, *First,* That the people had truer sentiments of John than the chief priests and the elders had, or, at least, were more free and faithful in declaring their sentiments. This people, of whom they said in their pride that they *knew not the law, and were cursed* (Jn. 7:49), it seems, knew the gospel, and were blessed. *Secondly,* That the chief priests and elders stood in awe of the common people, which is an evidence that things were in disorder among them, and that mutual jealousies were at a great height; that the government was become obnoxious to the hatred and scorn of the people, and the scripture was fulfilled, *I have made you contemptible and base,* Mal. 2:8, 9. If they had kept their integrity, and done their duty, they had kept up their authority, and needed not to fear the people. We find sometimes that the people feared them, and it served them for a reason why they did not confess Christ, Jn. 9:22, 12:42. Note, Those could not but fear the people, who studied only how to make the people fear them. *Thirdly,* That it is usually the temper even of common people to be zealous for the honour of that which they account sacred and divine. If they *account John as a prophet,* they will not endure that it should be said, *His baptism was of men;* hence the hottest contests have been about holy things. *Fourthly,* That the chief priests and elders were kept from an open denial of the truth, even against the conviction of their own minds, not by the fear of God, but purely by the fear of the people; as the *fear of man* may *bring* good people into *a snare* (Prov. 29:25), so sometimes it may keep bad people from being *overmuch wicked, lest they should die before their time,* Eccl. 7:17. Many bad people would be much worse than they are, if they durst.

(2.) How they replied to our Saviour, and so dropped the question. They fairly confessed *We cannot tell;* that is, "We will not;" *ouk oi damen — We never knew.* The more shame for them, while they pretended to be leaders of the people, and by their office were obliged to take cognizance of such things; when they would not confess their knowledge, they were constrained to confess their ignorance. And observe, by the way, when they said, *We cannot tell,* they told a lie, for they knew that John's baptism was of God. Note, There are many who are more afraid of the *shame* of lying than of the *sin,* and therefore scruple not to speak that which they know to be false concerning their own thoughts and apprehensions, their affections and intentions, or their remembering or forgetting of things, because in those things they know nobody can disprove them.

Thus Christ avoided the snare they laid for him, and justified himself in refusing to gratify them; *Neither tell I you by what authority I do these things.* If they be so wicked and base as either not to believe, or not to confess, that the baptism of John was from heaven (though it obliged to repentance, that great duty, and sealed the kingdom of God at hand, that great promise), they were not fit to be discoursed with concerning Christ's authority; for men of such a disposition could not be convinced of the truth, nay, they could not but be provoked by it, and therefore *he that is thus ignorant, let him be ignorant still.* Note, Those that imprison the truths they know, in unrighteousness (either by not professing them, or by not practising according to them), are justly denied the further truths they enquire after, Rom. 1:18, 19. Take away the talent from him that buried it; those that *will not* see, *shall not* see.

Verses 28–32

As Christ instructed his disciples by parables, which made the instructions the more easy, so sometimes he convinced his adversaries by parables, which bring reproofs more close, and make men, or ever they are aware, to reprove themselves. Thus Nathan convinced David by a parable (2 Sa. 22:1), and the woman of Tekoa surprised him in like manner, 2 Sa. 14:2: Reproving parables are appeals to the offenders themselves, and judge them out of their own mouths. This Christ designs here, as appears by the first words (*v.* 28), *But what think you?*

In these verses we have the parable of the *two sons* sent to work in the vineyard, the scope of which is to show that they who knew not John's baptism to be of God, were shamed even by the publicans and harlots, who knew it, and owned it. Here is,

I. The parable itself, which represents two sorts of persons; some that prove better than they promise, represented by the first of those sons; others that promise better than they prove represented by the second.

1. They had both one and the same father, which signifies that God is a common Father to all mankind. There are favours which all alike receive from him, and obligations which all alike lie under to him; *Have we not all one Father?* Yes, and yet there is a vast difference between men's characters.

2. They had both the same command given them; *Son, go work to-day in my vineyard.* Parents should not breed up their children in idleness; nothing is more pleasing, and yet nothing more pernicious, to youth than that. Lam. 3:27. God sets his children to work, though they are all heirs. This command is given to every one of us. Note, (1.) The work of religion, which we are called to engage in, is vineyard work, creditable, profitable, and pleasant. By the sin of Adam we were turned out to work upon the common, and to eat the herb of the field; but by the grace of our Lord Jesus we are called to work again in the vineyard. (2.) The gospel call to work in the vineyard, requires present obedience; *Son, go work* to-day, while it is called to-day, because *the night comes when no man can work.* We were not sent into the world to be idle, nor had we daylight given us to play by; and therefore, if ever we mean to do any thing for God and our souls, why not now? Why not to-day? (3.) The exhortation to go *work to-day in the vineyard,* speaketh unto us *as unto children* (Heb. 12:5); *Son, go work.* It is the command of a Father, which carries with it both authority and affection, a Father that pities his children, and considers their frame, and will not overtask them (Ps. 103:13, 14), a Father that is very tender of *his Son that serves him,* Mal. 3:17. If we work in our Father's vineyard, we work for ourselves.

3. Their conduct was very different.

(1.) One of the sons did better than he said, proved better than he promised. His answer was bad, but his actions were good.

[1.] Here is the untoward answer that he gave to his father; he said, flat and plain *I will not.* See to what a degree of impudence the corrupt nature of man rises, to say, *I will not,* to the command of a Father; such a command of such a Father; they are impudent children, and stiff-hearted. Those that will not bend, surely they cannot blush; if they had any degree of modesty left them, they could not say, *We will not.* Jer. 2:25. Excuses are bad, but downright denials are worse; yet such peremptory refusals do the calls of the gospel often meet with. *First,* Some love their ease, and will not work; they would live in the world as leviathan in the waters, to play therein (Ps. 104:26); they do not love working. *Secondly,* Their hearts are so much upon their own fields, that they are not for working in God's vineyard. They love the business of the world better than the business of their religion. Thus some by the delights of sense, and others by the employments of the world, are kept from doing that great work which they were sent into the world about, and so *stand all the day idle.*

[2.] Here is the happy change of his mind, and of his way, upon second thought; *Afterward he repented, and went.* Note, There are many who in the beginning are wicked and wilful, and very unpromising, who afterward repent and mend, and come to something. Some that God hath chosen, are suffered for a great while to run to a great excess of riot; *Such were some of you,* 1 Co. 6:11. These are set forth for *patterns of long-suffering,* 1 Tim. 1:16. *Afterward he repented.* Repentance is *metanoia — an after-wit:* and *metameleia — an after-care.* Better late than never. Observe, When he repented he went; that was the *fruit meet for repentance.* The only evidence of our repentance for our former resistance, is, immediately to comply, and set to work; and then what is past, shall be pardoned, and all shall be well. See what a kind Father God is; he resents not the affront of our refusals, as justly he might. He that told his father to his face, that he *would not* do as he bid him, deserved to be turned out of doors, and disinherited; but our God *waits to be gracious,* and, not withstanding our former follies, if we repent and mend, will favourably accept of us; blessed be God, we are under a covenant that leaves room for such a repentance.

(2.) The other son said better than he did, promised better than he proved; his answer was good but his actions bad. To him the father *said likewise, v.* 30. The gospel call, though very different, is, in effect, the same to all, and is carried on with an even tenour. We have all the same commands, engagements, encouragements, though to some they are a savour of life unto life, to others of death unto death. Observe,

[1.] How fairly this other son promised; *He said, I go, sir.* He gives his father a title of respect, *sir.* Note, It becomes children to speak respectfully to their parents. It is one branch of that honour which the fifth commandment requires. He professes a ready obedience, *I go;* not, "I will go by and by," but, "Ready, sir, you may depend upon it, I go just now." This answer we should give from the heart heartily to all the calls and commands of the word of God. See Jer. 3:22; Ps. 27:8.

[2.] How he failed in the performance; *He went not.* Note, There are many that give good words, and make fair promises, in religion, and those from some good motions for the present, that rest there, and go no further, and so come to nothing. Saying and doing are two things; and many there are that say, and do not; it is particularly charged upon the Pharisees, *ch.* 23:3. Many with their mouth show much love, but their heart goes another way. They had a good mind to be religious, but they met with something to be done, that was too hard, or something to be parted with, that was too dear, and so their purposes are to no purpose. Buds and blossoms are not fruit.

II. A general appeal upon the parable; *Whether of them twain did the will of his father? v.* 31. They both had their faults, one was rude and the other was false, such variety of exercises parents sometimes have in the different humours of their children, and they have need of a great deal of wisdom and grace to know what is the best way of managing them. But the question is, Which was the better of the two, and the less faulty? And it was soon resolved; the first, because his actions were better than his words, and his latter end than his beginning. This they had learned from the common sense of mankind, who would much rather deal with one that will be better than his word, than with one that will be false to his word. And, in the intention of it, they had learned from the account God gives of the rule of his judgment (Eze. 18:21–24), that if *the sinner turn from his wickedness,* he shall be pardoned; and*if the righteous man turn from his righteousness,* he shall be rejected. The tenour of the whole scripture gives us to understand that those are accepted as doing their Father's will, who, wherein they have missed it, are sorry for it, and do better.

III. A particular application of it to the matter in hand, *v.* 31, 32. The primary scope of the parable is, to show how the publicans and harlots, who never talked of the Messiah and his kingdom, yet entertained the doctrine, and submitted to the discipline, of John the Baptist, his forerunner, when the priests and elders, who were big with expectations of the Messiah, and seemed very ready to go into his measures, slighted John the Baptist, and ran counter to the designs of his mission. But it has a further reach; the Gentiles were *sometimes disobedient,* had been long so, children of disobedience, like the elder son (Tit. 3:3, 4); yet, when the gospel was preached to them, they became obedient to the faith; whereas the Jews who said, *I go, sir,* promised fair (Ex. 24:7; Jos. 24:24); yet went not; they did but flatter God with their mouth. Ps. 78:36.

In Christ's application of this parable, observe.

1. How he proves that John's baptism was *from heaven, and not of men.* "If you *cannot* tell," saith Christ, "you *might* tell,"

(1.) By the scope of his ministry; *John came unto you in the way of righteousness.* Would you know whether John had his commission from heaven, remember the rule of trial, *By their fruits ye shall know them;* the fruits of their doctrines, the fruits of their doings. Observe but their way, and you may trace out both their rise and their tendency. Now it was evident that John came *in the way of righteousness.* In his ministry, he taught people to repent, and to work the works of righteousness. In his conversation, he was a great example of strictness, and seriousness, and contempt of the world, denying himself, and doing good to every body else. Christ *therefore* submitted to the baptism of John, because it *became him to fulfil all righteousness.* Now, if John thus came in the way of righteousness, could they be ignorant that his baptism was from heaven, or make any doubt of it?

(2.) By the success of his ministry; *The publicans and the harlots believed him;* he did abundance of good among the worst sort of people. St. Paul proves his apostleship by the seals of his ministry, 1 Co. 9:2. If God had not sent John the Baptist, he would not have crowned his labours with such wonderful success, nor have made him so instrumental as he was for the conversion f souls. If publicans and harlots believe his report, surely the arm of the Lord is with him. The people's profiting is the minister's best testimonial.

2. How he reproves them for their contempt of John's baptism, which yet, for fear of the people, they were not willing to own. To shame them for it, he sets before them the faith, repentance, and obedience, of the publicans and harlots, which aggravated their unbelief and impenitence. As he shows, *ch.* 11:21, that the less likely would have repented, so here that the less likely did repent.

(1.) The publicans and harlots were like the first son in the parable, from whom little of religion was expected. They promised little good, and those that knew them promised themselves little good from them. Their disposition was generally rude, and their conversation profligate and debauched; and yet many of them were wrought upon the by the ministry of John, who came in the spirit and power of Elias. See Lu. 7:29. These fitly represented the Gentile world; for, as Dr. Whitby observes, the Jews generally ranked the publicans with the heathen; nay, and the heathen were represented by the Jews as harlots, and born of harlots, Jn. 8:41.

(2.) The scribes and Pharisees, the chief priests and elders, and indeed the Jewish nation in general, were like the other son that gave good words; they made a specious profession of religion, and yet, when the kingdom of the Messiah was brought among them by the baptism of John, they slighted it, they turned their back upon it, nay they *lifted up the heel against it.* A hypocrite is more hardly convinced and converted than a gross sinner; the form of godliness, if that be rested in, becomes one of Satan's strongholds, by which he opposes the power of godliness. It was an aggravation of their unbelief, [1.] That John was such an excellent person, that he came, and came to them, in *the way of righteousness.* The better the means are, the greater will the account be, if not improved. [2.] That, when they saw the publicans and harlots go before them into the kingdom of heaven, they did not afterward repent and believe; were not thereby provoked to a holy emulation, Rom. 11:14. Shall publicans and harlots go away with grace and glory; and shall not we put in for a share? Shall our inferiors be more holy and more happy than we? They had not the wit and grace that Esau had, who was moved to take other measures than he had done, by the example of his younger brother, Gen. 28:6. These proud priests, that set up for leaders, scorned to follow, though it were into the kingdom of heaven, especially to follow publicans; through the pride of their countenance, they would not seek after God, after Christ, Ps. 10:4.

Verses 33–46

This parable plainly sets forth the sin and ruin of the Jewish nation; they and their leaders are the husbandmen here; and what is spoken for conviction to them, is spoken for caution to all that enjoy the privileges of the visible church, not to be high-minded, but fear.

I. We have here the privileges of the Jewish church, represented by the letting out of a vineyard to the husbandmen; they were as tenants holding by, from, and under, God the great Householder. Observe,

1. How God established a church for himself in the world. The kingdom of God upon earth is here compared to a vineyard, furnished with all things requisite to an advantageous management and improvement of it. (1.) He planted this vineyard. The church is *the planting of the Lord,* Isa. 61:3. The forming of a church is a work by itself, like the planting of a vineyard, which requires a great deal of cost and care. It is *the vineyard which his right hand has planted* (Ps. 80:15), planted with the *choicest vine* (Isa. 5:2), *a noble vine,* Jer. 2:21. The earth of itself produces thorns and briars; but vines must be planted. The being of a church is owing to God's distinguishing favour, and his manifesting himself to some, and not to others. (2.) He hedged it round about. Note, God's church in the world is taken under his special protection. It is *a hedge round about,* like that about Job on every side (Job 1:10), a wall of fire, Zec. 2:5. Wherever God has a church, it is, and will always be, his peculiar care. The covenant of circumcision and the ceremonial law were a hedge or a wall of partition about the Jewish church, which is taken down by Christ; who yet has appointed a gospel order and discipline to be the hedge of his church. He will not have his vineyard to lie in common, that those who are without, may thrust in at pleasure; not to lie at large, that those who are within, may lash out at pleasure; but care is taken to set bounds about this holy mountain. (3.) He *digged a wine-press and built a tower.* The altar of burnt-offerings was the wine-press, to which all the offerings were brought. God instituted ordinances in his church, for the due oversight of it, and for the promoting of its fruitfulness. What could have been done more to make it every way convenient?

2. How he entrusted these visible church-privileges with the nation and people of the Jews, especially their chief priests and elders; he let it out to them as husbandmen, not because he had need of them as landlords have of their tenants, but because he would try them, and be honoured by them. When in Judah God was known, and his name was great, when they were taken to be to God *for a people, and for a name, and for a praise* (Jer. 13:11), when he *revealed his word unto Jacob* (Ps. 147:19), when the *covenant of life and peace* was made with Levi (Mal. 2:4, 5), then this vineyard was let out. See an abstract of the lease, Cant. 8:11, 12. The Lord of the vineyard was to have *a thousand pieces of silver* (compare Isa. 7:13); the main profit was to be his, but the keepers were to have two hundred, a competent and comfortable encouragement. And then he *went into a far country.* When God had in a visible appearance settled the Jewish church at mount Sinai, he did in a manner withdraw; they had no more such open vision, but were left to the written word. Or, they imagined that he was gone into a far country, as Israel, when they made the calf, fancied that Moses was gone. They put far from them the evil day.

II. God's expectation of rent from these husbandmen, *v.* 34. It was a reasonable expectation; for *who plants a vineyard, and eats not of the fruit thereof?* Note, From those that enjoy church-privileges, both ministers and people, God looks for fruit accordingly. 1. His expectations were not hasty; he did not demand a fore-rent, though he had been at such expense upon it; but staid *till the time of the fruit drew near,* as it did now that John preached the *kingdom of heaven is at hand.* God waits to be gracious, that he may give us time. 2. They were not high; he did not require them to come at their peril, upon penalty of forfeiting their lease if they ran behind-hand; but he sent his *servants to them,* to remind them of their duty, and of the rent-day, and to help them in gathering in the fruit, and making return of it. These servants were the prophets of the Old Testament, who were sent, and sometimes directly, to the people of the Jews, to reprove and instruct them. 3. They were not hard; it was only to *receive the fruits.* He did not demand more than they could make of it, but some fruit of that which he himself planted — an observance of the laws and statutes he gave them. What could have been done more reasonable? Israel was an empty vine, nay it was become the degenerate plant of a strange vine, and brought forth wild grapes.

III. The husbandmen's baseness in abusing the messengers that were sent to them.

1. When he sent them his servants, they abused them, though they represented the master himself, and spoke in his name. Note, The calls and reproofs of the word, if they do not engage, will but exasperate. See here what hath all along been the lot of God's faithful messengers, more or less; (1.) To suffer; *so persecuted they the prophets,* who were hated with a cruel hatred. They not only despised and reproached them, but treated them as the worst of malefactors — they beat them, and killed them, and stoned them. They beat Jeremiah, killed Isaiah, stoned Zechariah the son of Jehoiada in the temple. If they that *live godly in Christ Jesus* themselves shall *suffer persecution,* much more they that press others to it. This was God's old quarrel with the Jews, misusing his prophets, 2 Chr. 36:16. (2.) It has been their lot to suffer from their Master's own tenants; they were the husbandmen that treated them thus, the chief priests and elders that *sat in Moses's chair,* that professed religion and relation to God; these were the most bitter enemies of the Lord's prophets, that cast them out, and killed them, and said, *Let the Lord be glorified,* Isa. 66:5 See Jer. 20:1, 2; 26:11.

Now see, [1.] How God persevered in his goodness to them. He sent other servants, more than the first; though the first sped not, but were abused. He had sent them John the Baptist, and him they had beheaded; and yet he sent them his disciples, to prepare his way. O the riches of the patience and forbearance of God, in keeping up in his church a despised, persecuted ministry! [2.] How they persisted in their wickedness. They *did unto them likewise.* One sin makes way for another of the same kind. They that are drunk with the blood of the saints, add drunkenness to thirst, and still cry, Give, give.

2. At length, he sent them his Son; we have seen God's goodness in sending, and their badness in abusing, the servants; but in the latter instance both these exceed themselves.

(1.) Never did grace appear more gracious than in *sending the Son.* This was done *last of all.* Note, All the prophets were harbingers and forerunners to Christ. He was sent last; for if nothing else would work upon them, surely this would; it was therefore served for the *ratio ultima — the last expedient. Surely they will reverence my Son,* and therefore I will send him. Note, It might reasonably be expected that the Son of God, when he came to his own, should be reverenced; and reverence to Christ would be a powerful and effectual principle of fruitfulness and obedience, to the glory of God; if they will but reverence the Son, the point is gained. *Surely they will reverence my Son,* for he comes with more authority than the servants could; judgment is committed to him, that *all men should honour him.* There is greater danger in refusing him than in despising Moses's law.

(2.) Never did sin appear more sinful than in the abusing of him, which was now to be done in two or three days. Observe,

[1.] How it was plotted (*v.* 38); *When they saw the Son:* when he came, whom the people owned and followed as the Messiah, who would either have the rent paid, or distrain for it; this touched their copyhold, and they were resolved to make one bold push for it, and to preserve their wealth and grandeur by taking *him* out of the way, who was the only hindrance to it, and rival with them. *This is the heir, come, let us kill him.* Pilate and Herod, the princes of this world, *knew not;* for *if they had known, they would not have crucified the Lord of glory,* 1 Co. 2:8. But the *chief priests and elders* knew that *this was the heir,* at least some of them; and therefore *Come, let us kill him.* Many are killed for what they have. The chief thing they envied him, and for which they hated and feared him, was his interest in the people, and their hosannas, which, if he was taken off, they hope to engross securely to themselves. They pretended that he must die, to save the people from the Romans (Jn. 11:50); but really he must die, to save their hypocrisy and tyranny from that reformation which the expected kingdom of the Messiah would certainly bring along with it. He drives the buyers and sellers out of the temple; and therefore *let us kill him;* and then, as if the premises must of course go to the occupant, *let us seize on his inheritance.* They thought, if they could but get rid of this Jesus, they should carry all before them in the church without control, might impose what traditions, and force the people to what submissions, they pleased. Thus they *take counsel against the Lord and his Anointed;* but he that *sits in heaven,* laughs to see them *outshot in their own bow;* for, while they thought to kill him, and so to seize on his inheritance, he went by his cross to his crown, and they were broken pieces with a rod of iron, and their inheritance seized. Ps. 2:2, 3, 6, 9.

[2.] How this plot was executed, *v.* 39. While they were so set upon killing him, in pursuance of their design to secure their own pomp and power, and while he was so set upon dying, in pursuance of his design to subdue Satan, and save his chosen, no wonder if they soon *caught him, and slew him,* when his hour was come. Though the Roman power condemned him, yet it is still charged upon the chief priests and elders; for they were not only the prosecutors, but the principal agents, and had *the greater sin. Ye have taken,* Acts 2:23. Nay looking upon him to be as unworthy to live, as they were unwilling he should, *they cast him out of the vineyard,* out of the holy church, which they supposed themselves to have the key of, and out of the holy city for he was crucified *without the gate,* Heb. 13:12. As if *He* had been the shame and reproach, who was the greatest glory of his people Israel. Thus they who persecuted the servants, persecuted the Son; as men treat God's ministers, they would treat Christ himself, if he were with them.

IV. Here is their doom read out of their own mouths, *v.* 40, 41. He puts it to them, *When the Lord of the vineyard cometh, what will he do unto these husbandmen?* He puts it to themselves, for their stronger conviction, that *knowing the judgment of God* against them which do such things, they might be the more inexcusable. Note, God's proceedings are so unexceptionable, that there needs but an appeal to sinners themselves concerning the equity of them. God will be *justified when he speaks.* They could readily answer, *He will miserably destroy those wicked men.* Note, Many can easily prognosticate the dismal consequences of other people's sins, that see not what will be the end of their own.

1. Our Saviour, in his question, supposes that *the lord of the vineyard will come,* and reckon with them. God is the Lord of the vineyard; the property is his, and he will make *them* know it, who now *lord it over his heritage,* as if it were all their own. The Lord of the vineyard will come. Persecutors say in their hearts, He *delays his coming,* he *doth not see,* he *will not require;* but they shall find, though he bear long with them, he will not bear always. It is comfort to abused saints and ministers, that *the Lord is at hand,* the *Judge stands before the door.* When he comes, what will he do to carnal professors? What will he do to cruel persecutors? They must be called to account, they have their day now; but he *sees that his day is coming.*

2. They, in their answer, suppose that it will be a terrible reckoning; the crime appearing so very black, you may be sure,

(1.) That he will *miserably destroy those wicked men;* it is destruction that is their doom. *Kakous kakōs apolesei — Malos male perdet.* Let men never expect to do ill, and fare well. This was fulfilled upon the Jews, in that miserable destruction which was brought upon them by the Romans, and was completed about forty years after this; and unparalleled ruin, attended with all the most dismal aggravating circumstances. It will be fulfilled upon all that tread in the steps of their wickedness; hell is everlasting destruction, and it will be the most miserable destruction to them of all others, that have enjoyed the greatest share of church privileges, and have not improved them. The hottest place in hell will be the portion of hypocrites and persecutors.

(2.) That he will *let out his vineyard to other husbandmen.* Note, God will have a church in the world, notwithstanding the unworthiness and opposition of many that abuse the privileges of it. The unbelief and frowardness of man shall not make the word of God of no effect. If one will not, another will. The Jews' leavings were the Gentiles' feast. Persecutors may destroy the ministers, but cannot destroy the church. The Jews imagined that no doubt *they were the people,* and wisdom and holiness must *die with them;* and if they were cut off, what would God do for a church in the world? But when God makes use of any to bear up his name, it is not because he needs them, nor is he at all beholden to them. If we were made a desolation and an astonishment, God could build a flourishing church upon our ruins; for he is never at a loss what to do for his great name, whatever becomes of us, and of our place and nation.

V. The further illustration and application of this by Christ himself, telling them, in effect, that they had rightly judged.

1. He illustrates it by referring to a scripture fulfilled in this (*v.* 42); *Did ye never read in the scriptures?* Yes, no doubt, they had often read and sung it, but had not considered it. We lose the benefit of what we read for want of meditation. The scripture he quotes is Ps. 118:22, 23, the same context out of which the children fetched their hosannas. The same word yields matter of praise and comfort to Christ's friends and followers, which speaks conviction and terror to his enemies. Such a two-edged sword is the word of God. That scripture, the *Stone which the builders refused is become the headstone of the corner,* illustrates the preceding parable, especially that part of it which refers to Christ.

(1.) The builders' rejecting of the stone is the same with the husbandmen's abusing of the son that was sent to them. The chief priests and the elders were the builders, had the oversight of the Jewish church, which was God's building: and they would not allow Christ a place in their building, would not admit his doctrine or laws into their constitution; they threw him aside as a despised broken vessel, a stone that would serve only for a stepping-stone, to be trampled upon.

(2.) The advancing of this stone to be the head of the corner is the same with *letting out the vineyard to other husbandmen.* He who was rejected by the Jews was embraced by the Gentiles; and to that church where there is no difference of circumcision or uncircumcision, *Christ is all, and in all.* His authority over the gospel church, and influence upon it, his ruling it as the Head, and uniting it as the Cornerstone, are the great tokens of his exhaltation. Thus, in spite of the malice of the priests and elders, he *divided a portion with the great,* and received *his kingdom,* though they would not have him to reign over them.

(3.) The hand of God was in all this; *This is the Lord's doing.* Even the rejecting of him by the Jewish builders was by the determinate counsel and foreknowledge of God; he permitted and overruled it; much more was his advancement to the Head of the corner; his right hand and his holy arm brought it about; it was God himself that *highly exalted him,* and gave him *a name above every name; and it is marvellous in our eyes.* The wickedness of the Jews that rejected him is marvellous,; that men should be so prejudiced against their own interest! See Isa. 29:9, 10, 14. The honour done him by the Gentile world, notwithstanding the abuses done him by his own people, is marvellous; that he whom men despised and abhorred, should be adored by kings! Isa. 49:7. But *it is the Lord's doing.*

2. He applies it to them, and application is the life of preaching.

(1.) He applies the sentence which they had passed (*v.* 41), and turns it upon themselves; not the former part of it, concerning the miserable destruction of the husbandmen (he could not bear to speak of that), but the latter part, of *letting out the vineyard to others;* because though it looked black upon the Jews, it spoke good to the Gentiles. Know then,

[1.] That the Jews shall be unchurched; *The kingdom of God shall be taken from you.* This turning out of the hus-

bandmen speaks the same doom with that of dismantling the vineyard, and laying it common. Isa. 5:5. To the Jews had long pertained *the adoption and the glory* (Rom. 9:4); to them were committed the *oracles of God* (Rom. 3:2), and the sacred trust of revealed religion, and bearing up of God's name in the world (Ps. 76:1, 2); but now it shall be so no longer. They were not only unfruitful in the use of their privileges, but, under pretence of them, opposed the gospel of Christ, and so forfeited them, and it was not long ere the forfeiture was taken. Note, It is a righteous thing with God to remove church privileges from those that not only sin against them, but sin with them, Rev. 2:4, 5. The kingdom of God was taken from the Jews, not only by the temporal judgments that befel them, but by the spiritual judgments they lay under, their blindness of mind, hardness of heart, and indignation at the gospel, Rom. 11:8–10; 1 Th. 2:15.

[2.] That the Gentiles shall be taken in. God needs not ask us leave whether he shall have a church in the world; though his vine be plucked up in one place, he will find another to plant it in. He will give it *ethnei — to the Gentile world,* that will *bring forth the fruit of it.* They who had been not a people, and had not obtained mercy, became favourites of Heaven. This is the mystery which blessed Paul was so much affected with (Rom. 11:30, 33), and which the Jews were so much affronted by, Acts 22:21. 22. At the first planting of Israel in Canaan, the *fall of the Gentiles was the riches of Israel* (Ps. 135:10, 11), so, at their extirpation, the fall of Israel was the riches of the Gentiles, Rom. 11:12. It shall go to *a nation bringing forth the fruits thereof.* Note, Christ knows beforehand who will bring forth gospel fruits in the use of gospel means; because our fruitfulness is all the work of his own hands, and *known unto God are all his works.* They shall bring forth the fruits better than the Jews had done; God has had more glory from the New Testament church than from that of the Old Testament; for, when he changes, it shall not be to his loss.

(2.) He applies the scripture which he had quoted (*v.* 42), to their terror, *v.* 44. This *Stone,* which the *builders refused, is set for the fall of many in Israel;* and we have here the doom of two sorts of people, for whose fall it proves that Christ is set.

[1.] Some, through ignorance, stumble at Christ in his estate of humiliation; when this Stone lies on the earth, where the builders threw it, they, through their blindness and carelessness, fall on it, fall over it, and *they shall be broken.* The offence they take at Christ, will not hurt him, any more than he that stumbles, hurts the stone he stumbles at; but it will hurt themselves; they will fall, and be broken, and snared, Isa. 8:14; 1 Pt. 2:7, 8. The unbelief of sinners will be their ruin.

[2.] Others, through malice, oppose Christ, and bid defiance to him in his estate of exaltation, when this Stone is advanced to the head of the corner; and on them *it shall fall,* for they pull it on their own heads, as the Jews did by that challenge, *His blood be upon us and upon our children,* and *it will grind them to powder.* The former seems to bespeak the sin and ruin of all unbelievers; this is the greater sin, and sorer ruin, of persecutors, that *kick against the pricks,* and persist in it. Christ's kingdom will be a burthensome stone to all those that attempt to overthrow it, or heave it out of its place; see Zec. 12:3. This Stone cut out of the mountain without hands, will break in pieces all opposing power, Dan. 2:34, 35. Some make this an allusion to the manner of stoning to death among the Jews. The malefactors were first thrown down violently from a high scaffold upon a great stone, which would much bruise them; but then they threw another great stone upon them, which would crush them to pieces: one way or other, Christ will utterly destroy all those that fight against him. If they be so stout-hearted, that they are not destroyed by falling on this stone, yet it shall fall on them, and so destroy them. He will *strike through kings,* he will *fill the places with dead bodies,* Ps. 110:5, 6. None ever hardened his heart against God and prospered.

Lastly, The entertainment which this discourse of Christ met with among the chief priests and elders, that heard his parables.

1. *They perceived that he spake of them* (*v.* 45), and that in what they said (*v.* 41) they had but read their own doom. Note, A guilty conscience needs no accuser, and sometimes will save a minister the labour of saying, *Thou art the man. Mutato nomine, de te fabula narratur — Change but the name, the tale is told of the.* So quick and powerful is the word of God, and such a discerner of the thoughts and in-

tents of the heart, that it is easy for bad men (if conscience be not quite seared) to perceive that it speaks of them.

2. *They sought to lay hands on him.* Note, When those who hear the reproofs of the word, perceive that it speaks of them, if it do not do them a great deal of good, it will certainly do them a great deal of hurt. If they be not pricked to the heart with conviction and contrition, as they were Acts 2:37, they will be cut to the heart with rage and indignation, as they were Acts 5:33.

3. They durst not do it, *for fear of the multitude, who took him for a prophet,* though not for the Messiah; this served to keep the Pharisees in awe. The fear of the people restrained them from speaking ill of John (*v.* 26), and here from doing ill to Christ. Note, God has many ways of restraining the remainders of wrath, as he has of making that which breaks out redound to his praise, Ps. 76:10.

CHAPTER 22

This chapter is a continuation of Christ's discourses in the temple, two or three days before he died. His discourses then are largely recorded, as being of special weight and consequence. In this chapter, we have, I. Instruction given, by the parable of the marriage-supper, concerning the rejection of the Jews, and the calling of the Gentiles (*v.* 1–10), and, by the doom of the guest that had not the wedding-garment, the danger of hypocrisy in the profession of Christianity (*v.* 11–14). II. Disputes with the Pharisees, Sadducees, and scribes, who opposed Christ, 1. Concerning paying tribute to Caesar (*v.* 15–22). 2. Concerning the resurrection of the dead, and the future state (*v.* 23–33). 3. Concerning the great commandment of the law (*v.* 34–40). 4. Concerning the relation of the Messiah to David (*v.* 41–46).

Verses 1–14

We have here the parable of the guests invited to *the wedding-feast.* In this it is said (*v.* 1), *Jesus answered,* not to what his opposers *said* (for they were put to silence), but to what they *thought,* when they were wishing for an opportunity to *lay hands on him,* ch. 21:46. Note, Christ knows how to answer men's thoughts, for he is a Discerner of them. Or, He *answered,* that is, he continued his discourse to the same purport; for this parable represents the gospel offer, and the entertainment it meets with, as the former, but under another similitude. The parable of the vineyard represents the sin of the rulers that persecuted the prophets; it shows also the sin of the people, who generally neglected the message, while their great ones were persecuting the messengers.

I. Gospel preparations are here represented by a feast which a king made *at the marriage of his son;* such is *the kingdom of heaven,* such the provision made for precious souls, in and by the new covenant. The *King* is God, *a great King, King of kings.* Now,

1. Here is *a marriage made for his son,* Christ is the Bridegroom, the church is the bride; the gospel-day is *the day of his espousals,* Cant. 3:11. Behold by faith *the church of the first-born, that are written in heaven,* and were given to Christ by him whose they were; and in them you see the bride, the *Lamb's wife,* Rev. 21:9. The gospel covenant is a marriage covenant betwixt Christ and believers, and it is a marriage of God's making. This branch of the similitude is only mentioned, and not prosecuted here.

2. Here is a *dinner prepared for this marriage, v.* 4. All the privileges of church-membership, and all the blessings of the new covenant, pardon of sin, the favour of God, peace of conscience, the promises of the gospel, and all the riches contained in them, access to the throne of grace, the comforts of the Spirit, and a well-grounded hope of eternal life. These are the preparations for this feast, a heaven upon earth now, and a heaven in heaven shortly. God has prepared it in his counsel, in his covenant. It is a dinner, denoting present privileges in the midst of our day, beside the supper at night in glory.

(1.) It is a *feast.* Gospel preparations were prophesied of as a *feast* (Isa. 25:6), a *feast of fat things,* and were typified by the many festivals of the ceremonial law (1 Co. 5:8); *Let us keep the feast.* A *feast is a good day* (Esth. 7:17); so is the gospel; it is a continual feast. *Oxen and fatlings are killed* for this feast; no niceties, but substantial food; enough, and enough of the best. The day of a feast is a *day of slaughter,* or sacrifice, Jam. 5:5. Gospel preparations are all founded in the death of Christ, his sacrifice of himself. A feast was made for love, it is a reconciliation feast, a token of God's goodwill toward men. It was made *for laughter* (Eccl. 10:19), it is a rejoicing feast. It was made for fulness; the design of the gospel was to fill every *hungry soul with good things.* It was made for fellowship, to maintain an intercourse between heaven and earth. We are sent for *to the banquet of wine, that we may tell what is our petition, and what is our request.*

(2.) It is a *wedding feast.* Wedding feasts are usually rich, free, and joyful. The first miracle Christ wrought, was, to make plentiful provision for a wedding feast (Jn. 2:7); and surely then he will not be wanting in provision for his own wedding feast, when *the marriage of the Lamb is come, and the bride hath made herself ready,* a victorious triumphant feast, Rev. 19:7, 17, 18.

(3.) It is a *royal wedding feast;* it is *the feast of a king* (1 Sa. 25:36), at the marriage, not of a servant, but of a son; and then, if ever, he will, like Ahasuerus, show *the riches of his glorious kingdom,* Esth. 1:4. The provision made for believers in the covenant of grace, is not such as worthless worms, like us, had any reason to expect, but such as it becomes *the King of glory* to give. He gives like himself; for he gives himself to be to them *El shaddai — a God that is enough,* a feast indeed for a soul.

II. Gospel calls and offers are represented by an invitation to this feast. Those that make a feast will have guests to grace the feast with. God's guests are the children of men. *Lord, what is man,* that he should be thus dignified! *The guests* that were first invited were the Jews; wherever the gospel is preached, this invitation is given; ministers are the *servants* that are sent to invite, (Prov. 9:4, 5)

Now, 1. The guests *are called, bidden* to the wedding. All that are within hearing of the joyful sound of the gospel, to them is the word of this invitation sent. The servants that bring the invitation do not set down their names in a paper; there is no occasion for that, since none are excluded but those that exclude themselves. *Those that are bidden to the dinner are bidden to the wedding;* for all that partake of gospel privileges are to give a due and respectful attendance on the Lord Jesus, as the faithful friends and humble servants of the Bridegroom. They are *bidden to the wedding,* that they may *go forth to meet the bridegroom;* for it is the Father's will that *all men should honour the Son.*

2. The guests are called upon; for in the gospel there are not only gracious proposals made, but gracious persuasives. *We persuade men, we beseech them in Christ's stead,* 2 Co. 5:11, 20. See how much Christ's heart is set upon the happiness of poor souls! He not only provides for them, in consideration of their want, but sends to them, in consideration of their weakness and forgetfulness. When the invited guests were slack in coming, the king *sent forth other servants, v.* 4. When the prophets of the Old Testament prevailed not, nor John the Baptist, nor Christ himself, who told them the entertainment was almost ready *(the kingdom of God was at hand),* the apostles and ministers of the gospel were sent after Christ's resurrection, to tell them it was come, it was quite ready; and to persuade them to accept the offer. One would think it had been enough to give men an intimation that they had leave to come, and should be welcome; that, during the solemnity of the wedding, the king kept open house; but, because *the natural man discerns not,* and therefore desires not, *the things of the Spirit of God,* we are pressed to accept the call by the most powerful inducements, *drawn with the cords of a man, and all the bonds of love.* If the repetition of the call will move us, *Behold, the Spirit saith, Come; and the bride saith, Come; let him that heareth say, Come; let him that is athirst come,* Rev. 22:17. If the reason of the call will work upon us, *Behold, the dinner is prepared, the oxen and fatlings are killed, and all things are ready;* the Father is ready to accept of us, the Son to intercede for us, the Spirit to sanctify us; pardon is ready; peace is ready, comfort is ready; the promises are ready, as *wells of living water* for supply; ordinances are ready, as golden pipes for conveyance; angels are ready to attend us, creatures are ready to be in league with us, providences are ready to work for our good, and heaven, at last, is ready to receive us; it is *a kingdom prepared, ready to be revealed in the last time.* Is all this ready; and shall we be unready? Is all this preparation made for us; and is there any room to doubt of our welcome, if we come in a right manner? Come, therefore, O *come to the marriage; we beseech you, receive not* all this *grace of God in vain,* 2 Co. 6:1.

III. The cold treatment which the gospel of Christ often meets with among the children of men, represented by the cold treatment that this message met with and the hot treatment that the messengers met with, in both which the king himself and the royal bridegroom are affronted. This reflects primarily upon the Jews, who rejected the counsel of God against themselves; but it looks further, to the contempt that would, by many in all ages, be put upon, and the opposition that would be given to, the gospel of Christ.

1. The message was basely slighted (*v.* 3); *They would not come.* Note, The reason why sinners come not to Christ and salvation by him is, not because they *cannot,* but because *they will not* (Jn. 5:40); *Ye will not come to me.* This will aggravate the misery of sinners, that they might have had happiness for the coming for, but it was their own act and deed to refuse it. *I would, and ye would not.* But this was not all (*v.* 5); *they made light of it;* they thought it not worth coming for; thought the messengers made more ado than needs; let them magnify the preparations ever so much, they could feast as well at home. Note, Making light of Christ, and of the great salvation wrought out by him, is the damning sin of the world. *Amelēsantes — They were careless.* Note, Multitudes perish eternally through mere carelessness, who have not any direct aversion, but a prevailing indifference, to the matters of their souls, and an unconcernedness about them.

And the reason why *they made light of the marriage feast* was, because they had other things that they minded more, and had more mind to; *they went their ways, one to his farm, and another to his merchandise.* Note, The business and profit of worldly employments prove to many a great hindrance in closing with Christ: none turn their back on the feast, but with some plausible excuse or other, Lu. 14:18. The country people have their farms to look after, about which there is always something or other to do; the town's people must tend their shops, and be constant upon the exchange; they must *buy, and sell, and get gain.* It is true, that both farmers and merchants must be diligent in their business but not so as to keep them from making religion their main business. *Licitis perimus omnes — These lawful things undo us,* when they are unlawfully managed, when we are so *careful and troubled about many things* as to neglect the *one thing needful.* Observe, Both the city and the country have their temptations, the merchandise in the one, and the farms in the other; so that, whatever we have of the world in our hands, our care must be to keep it out of our hearts, lest it come between us and Christ.

2. The messengers were basely abused; *The remnant,* or the rest of them, that is, those who did not go the *farms,* or *merchandise,* were neither husbandmen nor tradesmen, but ecclesiastics, *the scribes, and Pharisees, and chief priests;* these were the persecutors, these *took the servants, and treated them spitefully, and slew them.* This, in the parable, is unaccountable, never any could be so rude and barbarous as this, to servants that came to invite them to a feast; but, in the application of the parable, it was matter of fact; they whose *feet* should have been *beautiful,* because they brought *the glad tidings of the solemn feasts* (Nahum 1:15), were *treated as the offscouring of all things,* 1 Co. 4:13. The prophets and John the Baptist had been thus abused already, and the apostles and ministers of Christ must count upon the same. The Jews were, either directly or indirectly, agents in most of the persecutions of the first preachers of the gospel; witness the history of *the Acts,* that is, the sufferings *of the apostles.*

IV. The utter ruin that was coming upon the Jewish church and nation is here represented by the revenge which the king, in wrath, took on these insolent recusants (*v.* 7); *He was wroth.* The Jews, who had been the people of God's love and blessing, by rejecting the gospel became the generation of his wrath and curse. *Wrath came upon them to the uttermost,* 1 Th. 2:16. Now observe here,

1. What was the crying sin that brought the ruin; it was their being *murderers.* He does not say, he destroyed those *despisers of his call,* but *those murderers of his servants;* as if God were more jealous for the lives of his ministers than for the honour of his gospel; he that *toucheth them, toucheth the apple of his eye.* Note, Persecution of Christ's faithful ministers fills the measure of guilt more than any thing. *Filling Jerusalem with innocent blood* was that sin of Manasseh which *the Lord would not pardon,* 2 Ki. 24:4.

2. What was the ruin itself, that was coming; *He sent forth his armies.* The Roman armies were his armies, of his raising, of his sending against the people of his wrath; and he *gave them a charge to tread them down,* Isa. 10:6. God is the Lord of men's host, and makes what use he pleases of them, to serve his own purposes, though they *mean not so, neither doth their heart think so,* Isa. 10:7. See Mic. 4:11, 12. *His armies destroyed those murderers, and burnt up their city.* This points out very plainly the destruction of the Jews, and the burning of Jerusalem, by the Romans, forty years after this. No age ever saw a greater desolation than that, nor more of the direful effects of fire and sword. Though Jerusalem had been a *holy city, the city that God had chosen, to put his name there, beautiful for situation, the joy of the whole earth;* yet that city being now *become a harlot, righteousness being no longer lodged in it, but murderers, the worst of murderers* (as the prophet speaks, Isa. 1:21), judgment came upon it, and ruin without remedy; and it is set forth for an example to all that should oppose Christ and his gospel. It was the Lord's doing, to avenge the quarrel of his covenant.

V. The replenishing of the church again, by the bringing in of the Gentiles, is here represented by the furnishing of the feast with guests *out of the high-ways, v.* 8–10.

Here is, 1. The complaint of the master of the feast concerning those that were first bidden (*v.* 8), *The wedding is ready,* the covenant of grace ready to be sealed, a church ready to be founded; *but they which were bidden,* that is, the Jews, *to whom pertained the covenant and the promises,* by which they were of old invited to the *feast of fat things,* they *were not worthy,* they were utterly unworthy, and, by their contempt of Christ, had forfeited all the privileges they were invited to. Note, It is not owing to God, that sinners perish, but to themselves. Thus, when Israel of old was within sight of Canaan, the land of promise was ready, the milk and honey ready, but their unbelief and murmuring, and contempt of that pleasant land, shut them out, and their carcases were left to perish in the wilderness; and *these things happened to them for ensamples.* See 1 Co. 10:11; Heb. 3:16–4:1.

2. The commission he gave to the servants, to invite other guests. The inhabitants of the *city* (*v.* 7) had refused; *Go into the high-ways* then; into *the way of the Gentiles,* which at first they were to decline, *ch.* 10:5. Thus by the fall of the Jews salvation is come to the Gentiles, Rom. 11:11, 12; Eph. 3:8. Note, Christ will have a *kingdom in the world,* though many reject the grace, and resist the power, of that kingdom. *Though Israel be not gathered, he will be glorious.* The offer of Christ and salvation to the Gentiles was, (1.) Unlooked for and unexpected; such a surprise as it would be to wayfaring men upon the road to be met with an invitation to a wedding feast. The Jews had notice of the gospel, long before, and expected the Messiah and his kingdom; but to the Gentiles it was all new, what they had never heard of before (Acts 17:19, 20), and, consequently, what they could not conceive of as belonging to them. See Isa. 65:1, 2. (2.) It was universal and undistinguishing; *Go, and bid as many as you find.* The highways are public places, and there *Wisdom cries,* Prov. 1:20. "Ask them that go by the way, ask any body (Job 21:29), high and low, rich and poor, bond and free, young and old, Jew and Gentile; tell them all, that they shall be welcome to gospel-privileges upon gospel-terms; whoever will, let him come, without exception."

3. The success of this second invitation; if some will not come, others will (*v.* 10); *They gathered together all, as many as they found.* The servants obeyed their orders. Jonah was sent *into the high-ways,* but was so tender of the honour of his country, that he avoided the errand; but Christ's apostles, though Jews, preferred the service of Christ before their respect to their nation; and St. Paul, though sorrowing for the Jews, yet magnifies his office as the apostle of Gentiles. *They gathered together all.* The design of the gospel is, (1.) To gather souls together; not the nation of the Jews only, but *all the children of God* who were *scattered abroad* (Jn. 11:52), *the other sheep that were not of that fold,* Jn. 10:16. They were gathered into one body, one family, one corporation. (2.) To gather them together to the wedding-feast, to pay their respect to Christ, and to partake of the privileges of the new covenant. Where the dole is, there will the poor be gathered together.

Now the guests that were gathered were, [1.] A multitude, *all, as many as they found;* so many, that the guest-chamber was filled. The sealed ones of the Jews were numbered, but those of other nations *were without number, a very great multitude,* Rev. 7:9. See Isa. 60:4, 8. [2.] A mixed multitude, *both bad and good;* some that before their conversion were sober and well-inclined, as the devout Greeks (Acts 17:4) and Cornelius; others that had run to an excess of riot, as the Corinthians (1 Co. 6:11); *Such were some of you;* or, some that after their conversion proved bad, that *turned not to the Lord with all their heart,* but feignedly; others that were upright and sincere, and proved of the right class. Ministers, in casting the net of the gospel, enclose *both good* fish *and bad; but the Lord knows them that are his.*

VI. The case of hypocrites, who are *in* the church, but not *of* it, who have a name to live, but are not alive indeed, is represented by *the guest that had not on a wedding garment;* one of the bad that were gathered in. Those come short of salvation by Christ, not only who refuse to take upon them the profession of religion, but who are not sound at heart in that profession. Concerning this hypocrite observe,

1. His discovery, how he was found out, *v.* 11.

(1.) *The king came in to see the guests,* to bid those welcome who came prepared, and to turn those out who came otherwise. Note, The God of heaven takes particular notice of those who profess religion, and have a place and name in the visible church. Our Lord Jesus *walks among the golden candlesticks* and therefore *knows their works.* See Rev. 2:1, 2; Cant. 7:12. Let this be a warning to us against hypocrisy, that disguises will shortly be stripped off, and every man will appear in his own colours; and an encouragement to us in our sincerity, that God is a witness to it.

Observe, This hypocrite was never discovered to be without *a wedding garment,* till *the king himself came in to see the guests.* Note, It is God's prerogative to know who are sound at heart in their profession, and who are not. We may be deceived in men, either one way or other; but He cannot. The day of judgment will be the great discovering day, when all the guests will be presented to the King: then *he will separate between the precious and the vile* (*ch.* 25:32), *the secrets of all hearts will then be made manifest,* and we shall infallibly discern *between the righteous and the wicked,* which now it is not easy to do. It concerns all the guests, to prepare for the scrutiny, and to consider how they will pass the piercing eye of the heart-searching God.

(2.) As soon as he came in, he presently espied the hypocrite; *He saw there a man which had not on a wedding garment;* though but one, he soon had his eye upon him; there is no hope of being hid in a crowd from the arrests of divine justice; he had not on a wedding garment; he was not dressed as became a nuptial solemnity; he had not his best clothes on. Note, Many come to the wedding feast without a wedding garment. If the gospel be the wedding feast, then the wedding garment is a frame of heart, and a course of life agreeable to the gospel and our profession of it, *worthy of the vocation wherewith we are called* (Eph. 4:1), *as becomes the gospel of Christ,* Phil. 1:27. *The righteousness of saints,* their real holiness and sanctification, and Christ, *made Righteousness to them, is the clean linen,* Rev. 19:8. This man was not naked, or in rags; some raiment he had, but not a wedding garment. Those, and those only, who *put on the Lord Jesus,* that have a Christian temper of mind, and are adorned with Christian graces, who live by faith in Christ, and to whom he is all in all, have the wedding garment.

2. His trial (*v.* 12); and here we may observe,

(1.) How he was arraigned (*v.* 12); *Friend, how camest thou in hither, not having a wedding garment?* A startling question to one that was priding himself in the place he securely possessed at the feast. *Friend!* That was a cutting word; a seeming friend, a pretended friend, a friend in profession, under manifold ties and obligations to be a friend. Note, There are many in the church who are false friends to Jesus Christ, who say that they love him while their hearts are not with him. *How camest thou in hither?* He does not chide the servants for letting him in (the wedding garment is an inward thing, ministers must go according to that which falls within their cognizance); but he checks his presumption in crowding in, when he knew that his heart was not upright; "How durst thou claim a share in gospel benefits, when tho hadst no regard to gospel rules? *What has thou to do to declare my statutes?*" Ps. 50:16, 17 Such are spots in the feast, dishonour the bridegroom, affront the company, and disgrace themselves; and therefore, *How camest thou in hither?* Note, The day is coming, when hypocrites will be called to an account for all their presumptuous intrusion into gospel ordinances, and usurpation of gospel privileges. *Who hath required this at your hand?* Isa. 1:12. Despised sabbaths and abused sacraments must be reckoned for, and judgment taken out upon an action of waste against all those who *received the grace of God in vain.* "How camest thou to the Lord's table, at such a time, unhumbled and unsanctified? What brought thee to sit before God's prophets, as his people do, when thy heart went after thy covetousness? *How cames thou in?* Not by the door, but *some other way, as a thief and a robber.* It was a tortuous entry, a possession without colour of a title." Note, It is good for those that have a place in the church, often to put it to themselves, "How came I in hither? Have I a wedding-garment?" If we would thus *judge ourselves, we should not be judged.*

(2.) How he was convicted; *he was speechless: ephimōthē — he was muzzled* (so the word is used, 1 Co. 9:9); the man stood mute, upon his arraignment, being convicted and condemned by his own conscience. They who live within the church, and die without Christ, will not have one word to say for themselves in the judgment of the great day, they will be without excuse; should they plead, *We have eaten and drunk in thy presence,* as they do, Lu. 13:26, that is to plead guilty; for the crime they are charged with, is thrusting themselves into the presence of Christ, and to his table, before they were called. They who never heard a word of this wedding feast will have more to say for themselves; their sin will be more excusable, and their condemnation more tolerable, than theirs who came to the feast without the wedding garment, and so sin against the clearest light and dearest love.

3. His sentence (*v.* 13); *Bind him hand and foot,* etc.

(1.) He is ordered to be pinioned, as condemned malefactors are, to be manacled and shackled. Those that will not work and walk as they should, may expect to be bound hand and foot. There is a binding in this world by the servants, the ministers, whose suspending of persons that walk disorderly, to the scandal of religion, is called binding of them, *ch.* 18:18. "Bind them up from partaking of special ordinances, and the peculiar privileges of their church-membership; bind them over to the righteous judgment of god." *In the day of judgment,* hypocrites will be bound; *the angels shall bind up these tares in bundles for the fire, ch.* 13:41. Damned sinners are bound hand and foot by an irreversible sentence; this signifies the same with the fixing of the great gulf; they can neither resist nor outrun their punishment.

(2.) He is ordered to be carried off from the wedding feast; *Take him away.* When the wickedness of hypocrites appears, they are to be taken away from the communion of the faithful, to be cut of as withered branches. This bespeaks the punishment of loss in the other world; they shall be taken away from the king, from the kingdom, from the wedding feast, *Depart from me, ye cursed.* It will aggravate their misery, that (like the unbelieving lord, 2 Ki. 7:2), *they shall see all this plenty with their eyes, but shall not taste of it.* Note, Those that walk unworthy of their Christianity, forfeit all the happiness they presumptuously laid claim to, and complimented themselves with a groundless expectation of.

(3.) He is ordered into a doleful dungeon; *Cast him into utter darkness.* Our Saviour here insensibly slides out of this parable into that which it intimates — the damnation of hypocrites in the other world. Hell is utter darkness, it is darkness out of heaven, the land of light; or it is extreme darkness, darkness to the last degree, without the least ray or spark of light, or hope of it, like that of Egypt; *darkness which might be felt; the blackness of darkness, as darkness itself,* Job 10:22. Note, Hypocrites go by the light of the gospel itself down to utter darkness; and hell will be hell indeed to such, a condemnation more intolerable; *there shall be weeping, and gnashing of teeth.* This our Saviour often uses as part of the description of hell-torments, which are hereby represented, not so much by the misery itself, as by the resentment sinners will have of it; there shall be *weeping,* an expression of great sorrow and anguish; not a gush of tears, which gives present ease, but constant weeping, which is constant torment; and the *gnashing of teeth* is an expression of the greatest rage and indignation; they will be *like a wild bull in a net, full of the fury of the Lord,* Isa. 51:20; 8:21, 22. Let us therefore hear and fear.

Lastly, The parable is concluded with that remarkable saying which we had before (*ch.* 20:16), *Many are called, but few are chosen, v.* 14. Of the many that are called to the wedding feast, if you set aside all those as unchosen that make light of it, and avowedly prefer other things before it; if then you set aside all that make a profession of religion, but the temper of whose spirits and the tenour of whose conversation are a constant contradiction to it; if you set aside all the profane, and all the hypocritical, you will find that they are few, very few, that are chosen; many called to the wedding feast, but few chosen to the wedding garment, that is, to *salvation, by sanctification of the Spirit.* This is *the strait gate, and narrow way,* which *few find.*

Verses 15–22

It was not the least grievous of the sufferings of Christ, that *he endured the contradiction of sinners against himself,* and had snares laid for him by those that sought how to take him off with some pretence. In these verses, we have him attacked by the Pharisees and Herodians with a question about paying tribute to Caesar. Observe,

I. What the design was, which they proposed to themselves; *They took counsel to entangle him in his talk.* Hitherto, his encounters had been mostly with the chief priests and the elders, men in authority, who trusted more to their power than to their policy, and examined him concerning his commission (*ch.* 21:23); but now he is set upon from another quarter; the Pharisees will try whether they can deal with him by their learning in the law, and in casuistical divinity, and they have a *tentamen novum — a new trial* for him. Note, It is in vain for the best and wisest of men to think that, by their ingenuity, or interest, or industry, or even by their innocence and integrity, they can escape the hatred and ill will of bad men, or screen themselves from *the strife of tongues.* See how unwearied the enemies of Christ and his kingdom are in their opposition!

1. *They took counsel.* It was foretold concerning him, that *the rulers* would *take counsel against him* (Ps. 2:2); and *so persecuted they the prophets. Come, and let us devise devices against Jeremiah.* See Jer. 18:18; 20:10. Note, The more there is of contrivance and consultation about sin, the worse it is. There is a particular *woe to them that devise iniquity,* Mic. 2:1. The more there is of the wicked wit in the contrivance of a sin, the more there is of the wicked will in the commission of it.

2. That which they aimed at was *to entangle him in his talk.* They saw him free and bold in speaking his mind, and hoped by that, if they could bring him to some nice and tender point, to get an advantage against him. It has been the old practice of Satan's agents and emissaries, to make a man an offender for a word, a word misplaced, or mistaken, or misunderstood; a word, though innocently designed, yet perverted by strained inuendos: thus they lay a snare for him that *reproveth in the gate* (Isa. 29:21), and represent the greatest teachers as the greatest troublers of Israel: thus *the wicked plotteth against the just,* Ps. 37:12, 13.

There are two ways by which the enemies of Christ might be revenged on him, and be rid of him; either by law or by force. By law they could not do it, unless they could make him obnoxious to the civil government; for *it was not lawful for them to put any man to death* (Jn. 18:31); and the Roman powers were not apt to concern themselves about *questions of words, and names, and their law,* Acts 18:15. By force they could not do it, unless they could make him obnoxious to the people, who were always the hands, whoever were the heads, in such acts of violence, which they call the beating of the rebels; but the people took Christ for a Prophet, and therefore his enemies could not raise the mob against him. Now (as the old serpent was from the beginning *more subtle than any beast of the field),* the design was, to bring him into such a dilemma, that he must make himself liable to the displeasure either of the Jewish multitude, or of the Roman magistrates; let him take which side of the question he will, he shall run himself into a premunire; and so they will gain their point, and make his own tongue to fall upon him.

II. The question which they put to him pursuant to this design, *v.* 16, 17. Having devised this iniquity in secret, in a close cabal, behind the curtain, when they went abroad without loss of time they practised it. Observe,

1. The persons they employed; they did not go themselves, lest the design should be suspected and Christ should stand the more upon his guard; but they sent their disciples, who would look less like tempters, and more like learners. Note, Wicked men will never want wicked instruments to be employed in carrying on their wicked counsels. Pharisees have their disciples at their beck, who will go any errand for them, and say as they say; and they have this in their eyes, when they are so industrious to make proselytes.

With them they sent the Herodians, a party among the Jews, who were for a cheerful and entire subjection to the Roman emperor, and to Herod his deputy; and who made it their business to reconcile people to that government, and pressed all to pay their tribute. Some think that they were the collectors of the land tax, as the publicans were of the customs, and that they went with the Pharisees to Christ, with this blind upon their plot, that while the Herodians demanded the tax, and the Pharisees denied it, they were both willing to refer it to Christ, as a proper Judge to decide the quarrel. Herod being obliged, by the charter of the sovereignty, to take care of the tribute, these Herodians, by assisting him in that, helped to endear him to his great friends at Rome. The Pharisees, on the other hand, were zealous for the liberty of the Jews, and did what they could to make them impatient of the Roman yoke. Now, if he should countenance the paying of tribute, the Pharisees would incense the people against him; if he should discountenance or disallow it, the Herodians would incense the government against him. Note, It is common for those that oppose one another, to continue in an opposition to Christ and his kingdom. Samson's foxes looked several ways, but met in one firebrand. See Ps. 83:3, 5, 7, 8. If they are unanimous in opposing, should not we be so in maintaining, the interests of the gospel?

2. The preface, with which they were plausibly to introduce the question; it was highly complimentary to our Saviour (*v.* 16); *Master, we know that thou art true, and teachest the way of God in truth.* Note, It is a common thing for the most spiteful projects to be covered with the most specious pretences. Had they come to Christ with the most serious enquiry, and the most sincere intention, they could not have expressed themselves better. Here is *hatred covered with deceit,* and a *wicked heart with burning lips* (Prov. 26:23); as Judas, who kissed, and betrayed, as Joab, who kissed, and killed.

Now, (1.) What they said of Christ was right, and whether they knew it or no, blessed be God, we know it.

[1.] That Jesus Christ was a faithful Teacher; *Thou art true, and teachest the way of God in truth.* For himself, *he is true, the Amen, the faithful Witness;* he is the Truth itself. As for his doctrine, the matter of his teaching was the way of God, the way that God requires us to walk in, the way of duty, that leads to happiness; that is the way of God. The manner of it was in truth; he showed people *the right way, the way in which they should go.* He was a skilful Teacher, and knew the way of God; and a faithful Teacher, that would be sure to let us know it. See Prov. 8:6–9. This is the character of a good teacher, to preach the truth, the whole truth, and nothing but the truth, and not to suppress, pervert, or stretch, any truth, for favour or affection, hatred or good will, either out of a desire to please, or a fear to offend, any man.

[2.] That he was a bold Reprover. In preaching, he *cared not for any;* he valued no man's frowns or smiles, he did not court, he did not dread, either the great or the many, for he *regarded not the person of man.* In his evangelical judgment, he did not know faces; that *Lion of the tribe of Judah, turned not away for any* (Prov. 30:30), turned not a step from the truth, nor from his work, for fear of the most formidable. He *reproved with equity* (Isa. 11:4), and never with partiality.

(2.) Though what they said was true for the matter of it, yet there was nothing but flattery and treachery in the intention of it. They called him *Master,* when they were contriving to treat him as the worst of malefactors; they pretended respect for him, when they intended mischief against him; and they affronted his wisdom as Man, much more his omniscience as God, of which he had so often given undeniable proofs, when they imagined that they could impose upon him with these pretences, and that he could not see through them. It is the grossest atheism, that is the greatest folly in the world, to think to put a cheat upon Christ, who searches the heart, Rev. 2:23. Those that mock God do but deceive themselves. Gal. 6:7.

3. The proposal of the case; *What thinkest thou?* As if they had said, "Many men are of many minds in this matter; it is a case which relates to practice, and occurs daily; let us have thy thought freely in the matter, *Is it lawful to give tribute to Caesar or not?"* This implies a further question; Has Caesar a right to demand it? The nation of the Jews was lately, about a hundred years before this, conquered by the Roman sword, and so, as other nations, made subject to the Roman yoke, and became a province of the empire; accordingly, toll, tribute, and custom, were demanded from them, and sometimes poll-money. By this it appeared that *the sceptre was departed from Judah* (Gen. 49:10); and therefore, if they had understood the signs of the times, they must have concluded that *Shiloh was come,* and either that this was he, or they must find out another more likely to be so.

Now the question was, Whether it was lawful to pay these taxes voluntarily, or, Whether they should not insist upon the ancient liberty of their nation, and rather suffer themselves to be distrained upon? The ground of the doubt was, that they *were Abraham's seed,* and should not by consent be *in bondage to any man,* Jn. 8:33. God had given them a law, that they should not *set a stranger over them.* Did not that imply, that they were not to yield any willing subjection to any prince, state, or potentate, that was not of their own nation and religion? This was an old mistake, arising from that *pride and thathaughty spirit* which bring *destruction and a fall.* Jeremiah, in his time, though he spoke in God's name, could not possibly beat them off it, nor persuade them to submit to the king of Babylon; and their obstinacy in that matter was then their ruin (Jer. 27:12, 13): and now again they stumbled at the same stone; and it was the very thing which, in a few years after, brought final destruction upon them by the Romans. They quite mistook the sense both of the precept and of the privilege, and, under colour of God's word, contended with his providence, when they should have kissed the rod, and accepted the punishment of their iniquity.

However, by this question they hoped to entangle Christ, and, which way soever he resolved it, to expose him to the fury either of the jealous Jews, or of the jealous Romans; they were ready to triumph, as Pharaoh did over Israel, that *the wilderness had shut him in,* and his doctrine would be concluded either injurious to the rights of the church, or hurtful to kings and provinces.

III. The breaking of this snare by the wisdom of the Lord Jesus.

1. He discovered it (*v.* 18); *He perceived their wickedness;* for, *surely in vain is the net spread in the sight of any bird,* Prov. 1:17. A temptation perceived is half conquered, for our greatest danger lies from snakes under the green grass; *and he said, Why tempt ye me, ye hypocrites?* Note, Whatever vizard the hypocrite puts on, our Lord Jesus sees through it; he perceives all the wickedness that is in the hearts of pretenders, and can easily convict them of it, and set it in order before them. He cannot be imposed upon, as we often are, by flatteries and fair pretences. He that searches the heart can call hypocrites by their own name, as Ahijah did the wife of Jeroboam (1 Ki. 14:6)__, *Why feignest thou thyself to be another? Why tempt ye me, ye hypocrites?* Note, Hypocrites tempt Jesus Christ; they try his knowledge, whether he can discover them through their disguises; they try his holiness and truth, whether he will allow of them in this church; but if they that of old *tempted Christ,* when he was but darkly revealed, *were destroyed of serpents, of how much sorer punishment shall they be thought worthy* who tempt him now in the midst of gospel light and love! Those that presume to tempt Christ will certainly find him too hard for them, and that he is of more piercing eyes than not to see, and more pure eyes than not to hate, the disguised wickedness of hypocrites, that dig deep to hide their counsel from him.

2. He evaded it; his convicting them of hypocrisy might have served for an answer (such captious malicious questions deserve a reproof, not a reply): but our Lord Jesus gave a full answer to their question, and introduced it by an argument sufficient to support it, so as to lay down a rule for his church in this matter, and yet to avoid giving offence, and to break the snare.

(1.) He forced them, ere they were aware, to confess Caesar's authority over them, *v.* 19, 20. In dealing with those that are captious, it is good to give our reasons, and, if possible, reasons of confessed cogency, before we give our resolutions. Thus the evidence of truth may silence gainsayers by surprise, while they only stood upon their guard against the truth itself, not against the reason of it; *Show me the tribute-money.* He had none of his own to convince them by; it should seem, he had not so much as one piece of money about him, for for our sakes he emptied himself, and became poor; he despised the wealth of this world, and thereby taught us not to over-value it; silver and gold he had none; why then should we covet to load ourselves with the thick clay? The Romans demanded their tribute in their own money, which was current among the Jews at that time: that therefore is called the *tribute-money;* he does not name what piece but the *tribute money,* to show that he did not mind things of that nature, nor concern himself about them; his heart was upon better things, the kingdom of God and the riches and righteousness thereof, and ours should be so too. They presently *brought him a penny,* a Roman penny in silver, in value about sevenpence half-penny of our money, the most common piece then in use: it was stamped with the emperor's image and superscription, which was the warrant of the public faith for the value of the pieces so stamped; a method agreed on by most nations, for the more easy circulation of money with satisfaction. The coining of money has always been looked upon as a branch of the prerogative, a flower of the crown, a royalty belonging to the sovereign powers; and the admitting of that as the good and lawful money of a country is an implicit submission to those powers, and an owning of them in money matters. How happy is our constitution, and how happy we, who live in a nation where, though the image and superscription be the sovereign's, the property is the subject's, under the protection of the laws, and what we have we can call our own!

Christ asked them, *Whose image is this?* They owned it to be Caesar's, and thereby convicted those of falsehood who said, *We were never in bondage to any;* and confirmed what afterward they said, *We have no king but Caesar.* It is a rule in the Jewish Talmud, that "he is the king of the country whose coin is current in the country." Some think that the superscription upon this coin was a memorandum of the conquest of Judea by the Romans, *anno post captam Judaeam — the year after that event;* and that they admitted that too.

(2.) From thence he inferred the lawfulness of paying tribute to Caesar (*v.* 21); *Render therefore to Caesar the things that are Caesar's;* not, *"Give* it him" (as they expressed it, *v.* 17), but, *"Render* it; Return," or "Restore it; if Caesar fill the purses, let Caesar command them. It is too late now to dispute paying tribute to Caesar; for you are become a province of the empire, and, when once a relation is admitted, the duty of it must be performed. *Render to all their due,* and particularly *tribute to whom tribute is due."* Now by this answer,

[1.] No offence was given. It was much to the honour of Christ and his doctrine, that he did not interpose as a Judge or a Divider in matters of this nature, but left them as he found them, for *his kingdom is not of this world;* and in this he hath given an example to his ministers, who deal in sacred things, not to meddle with disputes about things secular, not to wade far into controversies relating to them, but to leave that to those whose proper business it is. Ministers that would mind their business, and please their master, must not *entangle themselves in the affairs of this life:* they forfeit the guidance of God's Spirit, and the convoy of his providence when they thus to out of their way. Christ discusses not the emperor's title, but enjoins a peaceable subjection to *the powers that be.* The government therefore had no reason to take offence at his determination, but to thank him, for it would strengthen Caesar's interest with the people, who held him for a Prophet; and yet such was the impudence of his prosecutors, that, though he had expressly charged them to *render to Caesar the things that are Caesar's,* they laid the direct contrary in his indictment, that he *forbade to give tribute to Caesar,* Lu. 23:2. As to the people, the Pharisees could not accuse him to them, because they themselves had, before they were aware, yielded the premises, and then it was too late to evade the conclusion. Note, Though truth seeks not a fraudulent concealment, yet it sometimes needs a prudent management, to prevent the offence which may be taken at it.

[2.] His adversaries were reproved. *First,* Some of them would have had him make it unlawful to give tribute to Caesar, that they might have a pretence to save their money. Thus many excuse themselves from that which they must do, by arguing whether they may do it or no. *Secondly,* They all withheld from God his dues, and are reproved for that: while they were vainly contending about their civil liberties, they had lost the life and power of religion, and needed to be put in mind of their duty to God, with that to Caesar.

[3.] His disciples were instructed, and standing rules left to the church.

First, That the Christian religion is no enemy to civil government, but a friend to it. Christ's kingdom doth not clash or interfere with the kingdoms of the earth, in any thing that pertains to their jurisdiction. By Christ kings reign.

Secondly,, It is the duty of subjects to render to magistrates that which, according to the laws of their country, is their due. The higher powers, being entrusted with the public welfare, the protection of the subject, and the conservation of the peace, are entitled, in consideration thereof, to a just proportion of the public wealth, and the revenue of the nation. *For this cause pay we tribute,* because *they attend continually to this very thing* (Rom. 13:6); and it is doubtless a greater sin to cheat the government than to cheat a private person. Though it is the constitution that determines what is Caesar's, yet, when that is determined, Christ bids us render it to him; my coat is my coat, by the law of man; but he is a thief, by the law of God, that takes it from me.

Thirdly, When we render to Caesar the things that are Caesar's, we must remember withal to render to God the things that are God's. If our purses be Caesar's, our consciences are God's; he hath said, *My son, give me thy heart:* he must have the innermost and uppermost place there; we must render to God that which is his due, out of our time and out of our estates; from them he must have his share as well as Caesar his; and if Caesar's commands interfere with God's *we must obey God rather than men.*

Lastly, Observe how they were nonplussed by this answer; they *marvelled, and left him, and went their way, v.* 22. They admired his sagacity in discovering and evading a snare which they thought so craftily laid. Christ is, and will be, the Wonder, not only of his beloved friends, but of his baffled enemies. One would think they should have marvelled and followed him, marvelled and submitted to him; no, they marvelled and left him. Note, There are many in whose eyes Christ is marvellous, and yet not precious. They admire his wisdom, but will not be guided by it, his power, but will not submit to it. *They went their way,* as persons ashamed, and made an inglorious retreat. The stratagem being defeated, they quitted the field. Note, There is nothing got by contending with Christ.

Verses 23–33

We have here Christ's dispute with the Sadducees concerning the resurrection; it was the same day on which he was attacked by the Pharisees about paying tribute. Satan was now more busy than ever to ruffle and disturb him; it was *an hour of temptation,* Rev. 3:10. The truth as it is in Jesus will still meet with contradiction, in some branch or other of it. Observe here,

I. The opposition which the Sadducees made to a very great truth of religion; they say, *There is no resurrection,* as there are some fools who say, *There is no God.* These heretics were called *Sadducees* from one Sadoc, a disciple of Antigonus Sochaeus, who flourished about two hundred and eighty-four years before our Saviour's birth. They lie under heavy censures among the writers of their own nation, as men of base and debauched conversations, which their principles led them to. They were the fewest in number of all the sects among the Jews, but generally persons of some rank. As the Pharisees and Essenes seemed to follow Plato and Pythagoras, so the Sadducees were much of the genius of the Epicureans; they denied the resurrection, they said, There is no future state, no life after this; that, when the body dies, the soul is annihilated, and dies with it; that there is no state of rewards or punishments in the other world; no judgment to come in heaven or hell. They maintained, that, except God, there is not spirit (Acts 23:8), nothing but matter and motion. They would not own the divine inspiration of the prophets, nor any revelation from heaven, but what God himself spoke upon mount Sinai. Now the doctrine of Christ carried that great truth of the resurrection and a future state much further than it had yet been revealed, and therefore the Sadducees in a particular manner set themselves against it. The Pharisees and Sadducees were contrary to each other, and yet confederates against Christ. Christ's gospel hath always suffered between superstitious ceremonious hypocrites and bigots on the one hand, and profane deists and infidels on the other. The former abusing, the latter despising, the *form* of godliness, but both denying the *power* of it.

II. The objection they made against the truth, which was taken from a supposed case of a woman that had seven husbands successively; now they take it for granted, that, if there be a resurrection, it must be a return to such a state as this we are now in, and to the same circumstances, like the imaginary Platonic year; and if so, it is an invincible absurdity for this woman in the future state to have seven husbands, or else an insuperable difficulty which of them should have her, he whom she had first, or he whom she had last, or he whom she loved best, or he whom she lived longest with.

1. They suggest the law of Moses in this matter (*v.* 24), that the next of kin should marry the widow of him that died childless (Deu. 25:5); we have it practised Ruth 4:5. It was a political law, founded in the particular constitution of the Jewish commonwealth, to preserve the distinction of families and inheritances, of both which there was special care taken in that government.

2. They put a case upon this statute, which, whether it were a *case in fact* or only a *moot case,* is not at all material; if it had not really occurred, yet possibly it might. It was of seven brothers, who married the same woman, *v.* 25–27. Now this case supposes,

(1.) The desolations that death sometimes makes in families when it comes with commission; how it often sweeps away a whole fraternity in a little time;: seldom (as the case is put) according to seniority (the land of darkness is without any order,) but *heaps upon heaps;* it diminishes families that had multiplied greatly, Ps. 107:38, 39. When there were seven brothers grown up to man's estate, there was a family very likely to be built up; and yet this numerous family leaves *neither son nor nephew, nor any remaining in their dwellings,* Job 18:19. Well may we say then, *Except the Lord build the house, they labour in vain that build it.* Let none be sure of the advancement and perpetuity of their names and families, unless they could *make a covenant* of peace *with death,* or be at an *agreement with the grave.*

(2.) The obedience of these seven brothers to the law, though they had a power of refusal under the penalty of a reproach, Deu. 25:7. Note, Discouraging providences should not keep us from doing our duty because we must be governed by the rule, not by the event. The seventh, who ventured last to marry the widow (many a one would say) was a*bold* man. I would say, if he did it purely in obedience to God, he was a *good* man, and one that made conscience of his duty.

But, *last of all, the woman died also.* Note, Survivorship is but a reprieve; they that live long, and bury their relations and neighbours one after another, do not thereby acquire an immortality; no, their day will come to fall. Death's bitter cup goes round, and, sooner or later, we must all pledge in it, Jer. 25:26.

3. They propose a doubt upon this case (*v.* 28); *"In the resurrection, whose wife shall she be of the seven?* You cannot tell whose; and therefore we must conclude *there is no resurrection."* The Pharisees, who professed to believe a resurrection, had very gross and carnal notions concerning it, and concerning the future state; expecting to find there, as the Turks in their paradise, the delights and pleasures of the animal life, which perhaps drove the Sadducees to deny the thing itself; for nothing gives greater advantage to atheism and infidelity than the carnality of those that make religion, either in its professions or in its prospects, a servant to their sensual appetites and secular interests; while those that are erroneous deny the truth, those that are superstitious betray it to them. Now they, in this objection, went upon the Pharisees' hypothesis. Note, It is not strange that carnal minds have very false notions of spiritual and eternal things. The natural man receiveth not these things, *for they are foolishness to him.* 1 Co. 2:14. Let truth be set in a clear light, and then it appears in its full strength.

III. Christ's answer to this objection; by reproving their ignorance, and rectifying their mistake, he shows the objection to be fallacious and unconcluding.

1. He reproves their ignorance (*v.* 29); *Ye do err.* Note, Those do greatly err, in the judgment of Christ, who deny the resurrection and a future state. Here Christ reproves with the meekness of wisdom, and is not so sharp upon them (whatever was the reason) as sometimes he was upon the chief priests and elders; *Ye do err, not knowing.* Note, Ignorance is the cause of error; those that are in the dark, miss their way. The patrons of error do *therefore* resist the light, and do what they can to take away the key of knowledge; *Ye do err* in this matter, *not knowing.* Note, Ignorance is the cause of error about the resurrection and the future state. *What* it is in its particular instances, the wisest and best know not; it doth not yet appear what we shall be, it is a glory that is to be revealed: when we speak of the state of separate souls, the resurrection of the body, and of eternal happiness and misery, we are soon at a loss; we cannot order our speech, by reason of darkness, but that it *is* a thing about which we are not left in the dark; blessed be God, we are not; and those who deny it are guilty of a willing and affected ignorance. It seems, there were some Sadducees, some such monsters, among professing Christians, *some among you, that say, There is no resurrection of the dead* (1 Co. 15:12) and some that did in effect deny it, by turning it into an allegory, saying, The *resurrection is past already.* Now observe,

(1.) *They know not the power of God;* which would lead men to infer that there *may be* a resurrection and a future state. Note, The ignorance, disbelief, or weak belief, of God's power, is at the bottom of many errors, particularly theirs who deny the resurrection. When we are told of the soul's existence and agency in a state of separation from the body, and especially that a dead body, which had lain many ages in the grave, and is turned into common and indistinguished dust, that this shall be raised the same body that it was, and live, move, and act, again; we are ready to say, *How can these things be?* Nature allows it for a maxim, *A privatione ad habitum non datur regressus — The habits attaching to a state of existence vanish irrecoverably with the state itself.* If a man die, shall he live again? And vain men, because they cannot comprehend the *way* of it, question the *truth* of it; whereas, if we firmly believe in God the Father Almighty, that nothing is impossible with God, all these difficulties vanish. This therefore we must fasten upon, in the first place, that God is omnipotent, and can do what he will; and then no room is left for doubting but that he will do what he has promised; and, if so, *why should it be thought a thing incredible with you that God should raise the dead?* Acts 26:8. His power far exceeds the power of nature.

(2.) *They know not the scriptures,* which decidedly affirm that there shall be a resurrection and a future state. The power of God, determined and engaged by his promise, is the foundation for faith to build upon. Now the scriptures speak plainly, that the soul is immortal, and there is another life after this; it is the scope both of the law and of the prophets, *that there shall be a resurrection of the dead, both of the just and of the unjust,* Acts 24:14, 15. Job knew it (Job 19:26), Ezekiel foresaw it (Eze. 37), and Daniel plainly foretold it, Dan. 12:2. Christ rose again *according to the scriptures* (1 Co. 15:3); and so shall we. Those therefore who deny it, either have not conversed with the Scriptures, or do not believe them, or do not take the true sense and meaning of them. Note, Ignorance of the scripture is the rise of abundance of mischief.

2. He rectifies their mistake, and (*v.* 30) corrects those gross ideas which they had of the resurrection and a future state, and fixes these doctrines upon a true and lasting basis. Concerning that state, observe,

(1.) It is not like the state we are now in upon earth; *They neither marry, nor are given in marriage.* In our present state marriage is necessary; it was instituted in innocency; whatever intermission or neglect there has been of other institutions, this was never laid aside, nor will be till the end of time. In the old world, they were *marrying, and giving in marriage;* the Jews in Babylon, when cut off from other ordinances, yet were bid to *take them wives,* Jer. 29:6. All civilized nations have had a sense of the obligation of the marriage covenant; and it is requisite for the gratifying of the desires, and recruiting the deficiencies, of the human nature. But, in the resurrection, there is no occasion for marriage; whether in glorified bodies there will be any distinction of sexes some too curiously dispute (the ancients are divided in their opinions about it); but, whether there will be a distinction or not, it is certain that there will be no conjunction; where God will be *all in all,* there needs no other *meet-help;* the body will be *spiritual,* and there will be in it no carnal desires to be gratified: when the mystical body is completed, there will be no further occasion to *seek a godly seed,* which was one end of the institution of marriage, Mal. 2:15. In heaven there will be no decay of the individuals, and therefore no eating and drinking; no decay of the species, and therefore no marrying; *where there shall be no more deaths* (Rev. 21:4), there need be no more births. The married state is a composition of joys and cares; those that enter upon it are taught to look upon it as subject to changes, *richer and poorer, sickness and health;* and therefore it is fit for this mixed, changing world; but as in hell, where there is no joy, the voice of the bridegroom and the voice of the bride shall be heard no more at all, so in heaven, where there is all joy, and no care or pain or trouble, there will be no marrying. The joys of that state are pure and spiritual, and arise from the marriage of all of them to the Lamb, not of any of them to one another.

(2.) It is like the state angels are now in in heaven; *They are as the angels of God in heaven;* they *are* so, that is, undoubtedly they shall be so. They are so already in Christ their Head, who has made them *sit with him in heavenly places,* Eph. 2:6. The spirits of just men already made perfect are of the same corporation with the innumerable company of angels, Heb. 12:22, 23. Man in his creation was *made a little lower than the angels* (Ps. 8:5); but in his complete redemption and renovation will be as the angels; pure and spiritual as the angels, knowing and loving as those blessed seraphim, ever praising God like them and with them. The bodies of the saints shall be raised incorruptible and glorious, like the uncompounded vehicles of those pure and holy spirits (1 Co. 15:42, etc.), swift and strong, like them. We should *therefore* desire and endeavour to do the will of God now as the angels do it in heaven, because we hope shortly to be like the angels who always behold our Father's face. He saith nothing of the state of the wicked in the resurrection; but, by consequence, they shall be like the devils, whose lusts they have done.

IV. Christ's argument to confirm this great truth of the resurrection and a future state; the matters being of great concern, he did not think it enough (as in some other disputes) to discover the fallacy and sophistry of the objection, but backed the truth with a solid argument; for Christ *brings forth judgment to truth* as well as victory, and enables his followers to give a reason of the hope that is in them. Now observe,

1. Whence he fetched his argument — from the scripture; that is the great magazine or armoury whence we may be furnished with spiritual weapons, offensive and defensive. *It is written* is Goliath's sword. *Have ye not read that which was spoken to you by God?* Note, (1.) What the scripture speaks God speaks. (2.) What was spoken to Moses was spoken to us; it was spoken and *written for our learning.* (3.) It concerns us to read and hear what God hath spoken, because it is spoken to us. It was spoken to you Jews in the first place, for to them were committed the oracles of God. The argument is fetched from the books of Moses, because the Sadducees received *them* only, as some think, or, at least, them chiefly, for canonical scriptures; Christ therefore fetched his proof from the most indisputable fountain. The latter prophets have more express proofs of a future state than the law of Moses has; for though the law of Moses supposes the immortality of the soul and a future state, as principles of what is called natural religion, yet no express revelation of it is made by the law of Moses; because so much of that law was peculiar to that people, and was therefore guarded as municipal laws used to be with temporal promises and threatenings, and the more express revelation of a future state was reserved for the latter days; but our Saviour finds a very solid argument for the resurrection even in the writings of Moses. Much scripture lies under ground, that must be digged for.

2. What his argument was (*v.* 32); *I am the God of Abraham.* This was not an express proof, *totidem verbis — in so many words;* and yet it was really a conclusive argument. Consequences from scripture, if rightly deduced, must be received as scripture; for it was written for those that have the use of reason.

Now the drift of the argument is to prove,

(1.) That there is a future state, another life after this, in which the righteous shall be truly and constantly happy. This is proved from what God said; *I am the God of Abraham.*

[1.] For God to be any one's God supposes some very extraordinary privilege and happiness; unless we know fully what God is, we could not comprehend the riches of that word, *I will be to thee a God,* that is, a Benefactor like myself. The God *of* Israel is a God *to* Israel (1 Chr. 17:24), a spiritual Benefactor; for he is the Father of spirits, and blesseth with spiritual blessings: it is to be an all-sufficient Benefactor, a God that is enough, a complete Good, and an eternal Benefactor; for he is himself an everlasting God, and will be to those that are in covenant with him an everlasting Good. This great word God had often said to Abraham, Isaac, and Jacob; and it was intended as a recompence for their singular faith and obedience, in quitting the country at God's call. The Jews had a profound veneration for those three patriarchs, and would extend the promise God made them to the uttermost.

[2.] It is manifest that these good men had no such extraordinary happiness, in *this* life, as might look any thing like the accomplishment of so great a word as that. They were strangers in the land of promise, wandering, pinched with famine; they had not a foot of ground of their own but a burying-place, which directed them to look for something beyond this life. In present enjoyments they came far short of their neighbours that were strangers to this covenant. What was there in this world to distinguish them and the heirs of their faith from other people, any whit proportionable to the dignity and distinction of this covenant? If no happiness had been reserved for these great and good men on the other side of death, that melancholy word of poor Jacob's, when he was old (Gen. 47:9), *Few and evil have the days of the years of my life been,* would have been an eternal reproach to the wisdom, goodness, and faithfulness, of that God who had so often called himself *the God of Jacob.*

[3.] Therefore there must certainly be a future state, in which, as God will ever live to be eternally rewarding, so Abraham, Isaac, and Jacob, will ever live to be eternally rewarded. That of the apostle (Heb. 11:16), is a key to this argument, where, when he had been speaking of the faith and obedience of the patriarchs in the land of their pilgrimage, he adds, *Wherefore God is not ashamed to be called their God;* because *he has provided for them a city,* a heavenly city; implying, that if he had not provided so well for them in the other world, considering how they sped in this, he would have been ashamed to have called himself *their God;* but now he is not, having done that for them which answers it in its true intent and full extent.

(2.) That the soul is immortal, and the body shall rise again, to be united; if the former point be gained, these will follow; but they are likewise proved by considering the time when God spoke this; it was to Moses at the bush, long after Abraham, Isaac, and Jacob, were dead and buried; and yet God saith, not, "*I was,*" or "*have been,*" but *I am the God of Abraham.* Now *God is not God of the dead, but of the living.* He is a living God, and communicates vital influences to those to whom he is a God. If, when Abraham died, there had been an end of him, there had been an end likewise of God's relation to him as his God; but at that time, when God spoke to Moses, he was the God of Abraham, and therefore Abraham must be then alive; which proves the immortality of the soul in a state of bliss; and that, by consequence, infers the resurrection of the body; for there is such an inclination in the human soul to its body, as would make a final and eternal separation inconsistent with the bliss of those that have God for *their God.* The Sadducees' notion was, that the union between body and soul is so close, that, when the body dies, the soul dies with it. Now, upon the same hypothesis, if the soul lives, as it certainly does, the body must some time or other live with it. And besides, the Lord is for the body, it is an essential part of the man; there is a covenant with the dust, which will be remembered, otherwise *the man* would not be happy. The charge which the dying patriarchs gave concerning their bones, and that *in faith,* was an evidence that they had some expectation of the resurrection of their bodies. But this doctrine was reserved for a more full revelation after the resurrection of Christ, who *was the first-fruits of them that slept.*

Lastly, We have the issue of this dispute. The Sadducees were *put to silence* (*v.* 34), and so put to shame. They thought by their subtlety to put Christ to shame, when they were preparing shame for themselves. But the multitude *were astonished at this doctrine, v.* 33. 1. Because it was new to them. See to what a sad pass the exposition of scripture was come among them, when people were astonished at it as a miracle to hear the fundamental promise applied to this great truth; they had sorry scribes, or this had been no news to them. 2. Because it had something in it very good and great. Truth often shows the brighter, and is the more admired, for its being opposed. Observe, Many gainsayers are silenced, and many hearers astonished, without being savingly converted; yet even in the silence and astonishment of unsanctified souls God magnifies his law, magnifies his gospel, and makes both honourable.

Verses 34–40

Here is a discourse which Christ had with a Pharisee-lawyer, about the great commandment of the law. Observe,

I. The combination of the Pharisees against Christ, *v.* 34. They heard *that he had put the Sadducees to silence,* had stopped their mouths, though their understandings were not opened; and they were *gathered together,* not to return him the thanks of their party, as they ought to have done, for his effectually asserting and confirming of the truth against the Sadducees, the common enemies of their religion, but to *tempt him,* in hopes to get the reputation of puzzling him who had puzzled the Sadducees. They were more vexed that Christ was honoured, than pleased that the Sadducees were silenced; being more concerned for their own tyranny and traditions, which Christ opposed, than for the doctrine of the resurrection and a future state, which the Sadducees opposed. Note, It is an instance of Pharisaical envy and malice, to be displeased at the maintaining of a confessed truth, when it is done by those we do not like; to sacrifice a public good to private piques and prejudices. Blessed Paul was otherwise minded, Phil. 1:18.

II. The lawyer's question, which he put to Christ. The lawyers were students in, and teachers of, the law of Moses, as the scribes were; but some think that in *this* they differed, that they dealt more in practical questions than the scribes; they studied and professed casuistical divinity. This lawyer *asked him a question, tempting him;* not with any design to ensnare him, as appears by St. Mark's relation of the story, where we find that this was he to whom Christ said, *Thou are not far from the kingdom of God,* Mk. 12:34, but only to see what he would say, and to draw on discourse with him, to satisfy his own and his friends' curiosity.

1. The question was, *Master, which is the greatest commandment of the law?* A needless question, when all the things of God's law are great things (Hos. 8:12), and the wisdom from above is without partiality, partiality in the law (Mal. 2:9), and hath respect to them all. Yet it is true, there are some commands that are the principles of the oracles of God, more extensive and inclusive than others. Our Saviour speaks of the *weightier matters of the law,* ch. 23:23.

2. The design was to try him, or tempt him; to try, not so much his knowledge as his judgment. It was a question disputed among the critics in the law. Some would have the law of circumcision to be the great commandment, others the law of the sabbath, others the law of sacrifices, according as they severally stood affected, and spent their zeal; now they would try what Christ said to this question, hoping to incense the people against him, if he should not answer according to the vulgar opinion; and if he should magnify one commandment, they would reflect on him as vilifying the rest. The question was harmless enough; and it appears by comparing Lu. 10:27, 28, that it was an adjudged point among the lawyers, that the *love of God* and our *neighbour* is the great commandment, and the sum of all the rest, and Christ had there approved it; so the putting of it to him here seems rather a scornful design to catechise him as a child, than spiteful design to dispute with him as an adversary.

III. Christ's answer to this question; it is well for us that such a question was asked him, that we might have his answer. It is no disparagement to great men to answer plain questions. Now Christ recommends to us those as the great commandments, not which are so exclusive of others, but which are *therefore* great because inclusive of others. Observe,

1. Which these great commandments are (*v.* 37–39); not the judicial laws, those could not be the greatest now that the people of the Jews, to whom they pertained, were so little; not the ceremonial laws, those could not be the greatest, now that they were waxen old, and were ready to vanish away; nor any particular moral precept; but the love of God and our neighbour, which are the spring and foundation of all the rest, which (these being supposed) will follow of course.

(1.) All the law is fulfilled in one word, and that is, *love.* See Rom. 13:10. All obedience begins in the affections, and nothing in religion is done right, that is not done there first. Love is the leading affection, which gives law, and gives ground, to the rest; and therefore that, as the main fort, is to be first secured and garrisoned for God. Man is a creature cut out for love; thus therefore is the law written in the heart, that it is a *law of love.* Love is a short and sweet word; and, if that be *the fulfilling of the law,* surely the yoke of the command is very easy. Love is the rest and satisfaction of the soul; if we walk in this good old way, we shall find rest.

(2.) The *love of God* is the first and great commandment of all, and the summary of all the commands of the first table. The proper act of love being complacency, good is the proper object of it. Now God, being good infinitely, originally, and eternally, is to be loved in the first place, and nothing loved beside him, but what is loved for him. *Love* is the first and great thing that God demands from us, and therefore the first and great thing that we should devote to him.

Now here we are directed,

[1.] To love God as ours; *Thou shalt love the Lord they God* as thine. The first commandment is, *Thou shalt have no other God;* which implies that we must have him for our God, and that will engage our love to him. Those that made the sun and moon their gods, loved them, Jer. 8:2; Judges 18:24. To love God as ours is to love him because he is ours, our Creator, Owner, and Ruler, and to conduct ourselves to him as ours, with obedience to him, and dependence on him. We must love God as reconciled to us, and made ours by covenant; that is the foundation of this, *Thy God.*

[2.] To love him *with all our heart, and soul, and mind.* Some make these to signify one and the same thing, to love him with all our powers; others distinguish them; the heart, soul, and mind, are the will, affections, and understanding; or the vital, sensitive, and intellectual faculties. Our love of God must be a sincere love, and not in word and tongue only, as theirs is who say they love him, but their hearts are not with him. It must be a strong love, we must love him in the most intense degree; as we must *praise* him, so we must *love* him, with *all that is within us,* Ps. 103:1. It must be a singular and superlative love, we must love him more than any thing else; this way the stream of our affections must entirely run. The heart must be united to love God, in opposition to a divided heart. All our love is too little to bestow upon him, and therefore all the powers of the soul must be engaged for him, and carried out toward him. *This is the first and great commandment;* for obedience to this is the spring of obedience to all the rest; which is *then* only acceptable, when it flows from love.

(3.) To *love our neighbour as ourselves* is the *second* great commandment (v. 39); *It is like unto that first;* it is inclusive of all the precepts of the second table, as that is of the first. It is *like* it, for it is founded upon it, and flows from it; and a right love to our brother, whom we have seen, is both an instance and an evidence of our *love to God, whom we have not seen,* 1 Jn. 4:20.

[1.] It is implied, that we do, and should, love ourselves. There is a self-love which is corrupt, and the root of the greatest sins, and it must be put off and mortified: but there is a self-love which is natural, and the rule of the greatest duty, and it must be preserved and sanctified. We must love ourselves, that is, we must have a due regard to the dignity of our own natures, and a due concern for the welfare of our own souls and bodies.

[2.] It is prescribed, that we *love our neighbour as ourselves.* We must honour and esteem all men, and must wrong and injure none; must have a good will to all, and good wishes for all, and, as we have opportunity, must do good to all. We must love our neighbour as ourselves, as truly and sincerely as we love ourselves, and in the same instances; nay, in many cases we must deny ourselves for the good of our neighbour, and must make ourselves servants to the true welfare of others, and be willing to *spend and be spent for them,* to *lay down our lives for the brethren.*

2. Observe what the weight and greatness of these commandments is (v. 40); *On these two commandments hang all the law and the prophets;* that is, This is the sum and substance of all those precepts relating to practical religion which were written in men's hearts by nature, revived by Moses, and backed and enforced by the preaching and writing of the prophets. All hang upon the law of love; take away this, and all falls to the ground, and comes to nothing. Rituals and ceremonials must give way to these, as must all spiritual gifts, for love is the more excellent way. This is the spirit of the law, which animates it, the cement of the law, which joins it; it is the root and spring of all other duties, the compendium of the whole Bible, not only of the law and the prophets, but of the gospel too, only supposing this love to be the fruit of faith, and that we love God in Christ, and our neighbour for his sake. All hangs on these two commandments, as the effect doth both on its efficient and on its final cause; for *the fulfilling of the law is love* (Rom. 13:10) and *the end of the law is love,* 1 Tim. 1:5. The law of love is the nail, is the *nail in the sure place, fastened by the masters of assemblies* (Eccl. 12:11), on which is hung all *the glory of the law and the prophets* (Isa. 22:24), a nail that shall never be drawn; for on this nail all the glory of the new Jerusalem shall eternally hang. *Love never faileth.* Into these two great commandments therefore let our hearts be delivered as into a mould; in the defence and evidence of these let us spend our zeal, and not in notions, names, and strifes of words, as if those were the mighty things on which the law and the prophets hung, and to them the love of God and our neighbour must be sacrificed; but to the commanding power of these let every thing else be made to bow.

Verses 41–46

Many questions the Pharisees had asked Christ, by which, though they thought to pose him, they did but *expose them-*

selves; but now let him ask them a question; and he will do it when they are gathered together, v. 41. He did not take some one of them apart from the rest *(ne Hercules contra duos — Hercules himself may be overmatched),* but, to shame them the more, he took them all together, when they were in confederacy and consulting against him, and yet puzzled them. Note, God delights to baffle his enemies when they most strengthen themselves; he gives them all the advantages they can wish for, and yet conquers them. *Associate yourselves, and you shall be broken in pieces,* Isa. 3:9, 10. Now here,

I. Christ proposes a question to them, which they could easily answer; it was a question in their own catechism; *"What think ye of Christ? Whose Son is He?* Whose Son do you expect the Messiah to be, who was promised to the fathers?"* This they could easily answer, *The Son of David.* It was the common periphrasis of the Messiah; they called him *the Son of David.* So the scribes, who expounded the scripture, had taught them, from Ps. 89:35, 36, *I will not lie unto David; his seed shall endure for ever* (Isa. 9:7), *upon the throne of David.* And Isa. 11:1, *A rod out of the stem of Jesse.* The covenant of royalty made with David was a figure of the covenant of redemption made with Christ, who as David, was made King *with an oath,* and was first humbled and then advanced. If Christ was the Son of David, he was really and truly Man. Israel said, *We have ten parts in David;* and Judah said, *He is our bone and our flesh;* what part have we then in the Son of David, who took our nature upon him?

What think ye of Christ? They had put questions to him, one after another, out of the law; but he comes and puts a question to them upon the promise. Many are so full of the law, that they forget Christ, as if their duties would save them without his merit and grace. It concerns each of us seriously to ask ourselves, What think we of Christ? Some think not of him at all, he is not in all, not in any, of their thoughts; some think meanly, and some think hardly, of him; but *to them that believe he is precious;* and *how precious then are the thoughts of him!* While *the daughters of Jerusalem* think no more of Christ than of *another beloved;* the spouse thinks of him as the *Chief of ten thousands.*

II. He starts a difficulty upon their answer, which they could not easily solve, v. 43–45. Many can so readily affirm the truth, that they think they have knowledge enough to be proud of, who, when they are called to confirm the truth, and to vindicate and defend it, show they have ignorance enough to be ashamed of. The objection Christ raised was, *If Christ be David's son, how then doth David, in spirit, call him Lord?* He did not hereby design to ensnare them, as they did him, but to instruct them in a truth they were loth to believe — that the expected Messiah is God.

1. It is easy to see that David calls Christ *Lord,* and this in spirit being divinely inspired, and actuated therein by a spirit of prophecy; for it was *the Spirit of the Lord that spoke by him,* 2 Sa. 23:1, 2. David was one of those *holy men that spoke as* they were *moved by the Holy Ghost,* especially in calling Christ *Lord;* for it was then, as it is still (1 Co. 12:3) that *no man can say that Jesus is the Lord, but by the Holy Ghost.* Now, to prove that David, in spirit, called Christ *Lord,* he quotes Ps. 110:1, which psalm the scribes themselves understood of Christ; of him, it is certain, the prophet there speaks, of him and of no other man; and it is a prophetical summary of the doctrine of Christ, it describes him executing the offices of a Prophet, Priest, and King, both in his humiliation and also in his exaltation.

Christ quotes the whole verse, which shows the Redeemer in his exaltation; (1.) *Sitting at the right hand of God.* His sitting denotes both rest and rule; his sitting at God's right hand denotes superlative honour and sovereign power. See in what great words this is expressed (Heb. 8:1); *He is set on the right hand of the throne of the Majesty.* See Phil. 2:9; Eph. 1:20. He did not take this honour to himself, but was entitled to it by covenant with his Father, and invested in it by commission from him, and here is that commission. (2.) Subduing his enemies. There he shall sit, till they be all made either his friends or his footstool. *The carnal mind,* wherever it is, *is enmity to Christ;* and that is subdued in the *conversion of the willing people that are called to his foot* (as the expression is, Isa. 41:2), and in the confusion of his impenitent adversaries, who shall be brought under his foot, as the kings of Canaan were under the feet of Joshua.

But that which this verse is quoted for is, that David calls the Messiah *his Lord; the Lord,* Jehovah, *said unto my Lord.*

This intimates to us, that in expounding scripture we must take notice of, and improve, not only that which is the main scope and sense of a verse, but of the words and phrases, by which they Spirit chooses to express that sense, which have often a very useful and instructive significance. Here is a good note from that word, *My Lord.*

2. It is not so easy for those who believe not the Godhead of the Messiah, to clear this from an absurdity, if Christ b David's son. It is incongruous for the father to speak of his son, the predecessor of his successor, as his *Lord.* If David call him *Lord,* that is laid down (v. 45) as the *magis notum — the more evident truth;* for whatever is said of Christ's humanity and humiliation must be construed and understood in consistency with the truth of his divine nature and dominion. We must hold this fast, that he is David's Lord, and by that explain his being David's son. The seeming differences of scripture, as here, may not only be accommodated, but contribute to the beauty and harmony of the whole. *Amicae scripturarum lites, utinam et nostrae — The differences observable in the scriptures are of a friendly kind; would to God that our differences were of the same kind!*

III. We have here the success of this gentle trial which Christ made of the Pharisees' knowledge, in two things.

1. It puzzled them (v. 46); *No man was able to answer him a word.* Either it was their ignorance that they did not know, or their impiety that they would not own, the Messiah to be God; which truth was the only key to unlock this difficulty. What those Rabbies could not then answer, blessed be God, the plainest Christian that is led into the understanding of the gospel of Christ, can now account for; that Christ, as God, was David's *Lord;* and Christ, as Man, was David's *son.* This he did not now himself explain, but reserved it till the proof of it was completed by his resurrection; but we have it fully explained by him in his glory (Rev. 22:16); *I am the root and the offspring of David.* Christ, as God, was David's *Root;* Christ, as Man, was David's *Offspring.* If we hold not fast this truth, that Jesus Christ is over all God blessed for ever, we run ourselves into inextricable difficulties. And well might David, his remote ancestor, call him *Lord,* when Mary, his immediate mother, after she had conceived him, *called him, Lord and God, her Saviour,* Lu. 1:46, 47.

2. It silenced them, and all others that sought occasion against him; *Neither durst any man, from that day forth, ask him any more* such captious, tempting, ensnaring *questions.* Note, God will glorify himself in the silencing of many whom he will not glorify himself in the salvation of. Many are convinced, that are not converted, by the word. Had these been converted, they would have asked him more questions, especially that great question, *What must we do to be saved?* But since they could not gain their point, they would have no more to do with him. But, thus all that strive with their Master shall be convinced, as these Pharisees and lawyers here were, of the inequality of the match.

CHAPTER 23

In the foregoing chapter, we had our Saviour's discourses with the scribes and Pharisees; here we have his discourse concerning them, or rather against them. I. He allows their office (v. 2, 3). II. He warns his disciples not to imitate their hypocrisy and pride (v. 4–12). III. He exhibits a charge against them for divers high crimes and misdemeanors, corrupting the law, opposing the gospel, and treacherous dealing both with God and man; and to each article he prefixes a woe (v. 13–33). IV. He passes sentence upon Jerusalem, and foretels the ruin of the city and temple, especially for the sin of persecution (v. 34–49).

Verses 1–12

We find not Christ, in all his preaching, so severe upon any sort of people as upon these *scribes and Pharisees;* for the truth is, nothing is more directly opposite to the spirit of the gospel than the temper and practice of that generation of men, who were made up of pride, worldliness, and tyranny, under a cloak and pretence of religion; yet these were the idols and darlings of the people, who thought, if but two men went to heaven, one would be a Pharisee. Now Christ directs his discourse here *to the multitude, and to his disciples* (v. 1) to rectify their mistakes concerning these scribes and Pharisees, by painting them out in their true colours, and so to take off the prejudice which some of the multitude had conceived against Christ and his doctrine, because it was opposed by those men of their church, that called themselves the people's guides. Note, It is good to know the true characters of men, that we may not be imposed upon by great and mighty names, titles, and pretensions to power. People must be told of *the wolves* (Acts 20:29, 30), *the dogs* (Phil. 3:2), *the deceitful workers* (2 Co. 11:13), that they may know here to stand upon their guard. And not only the mixed multitude, but even the disciples, need these cautions; for good men are apt to have their eyes dazzled with worldly pomp.

Now, in this discourse,

I. Christ allows their office as expositors of the law; *The scribes and Pharisees* (that is, the whole Sanhedrim, who sat at the helm of church government, who were all called *scribes,* and were some of them Pharisees), they *sit in Moses' seat* (*v.* 2), as public teachers and interpreters of the law; and, the law of Moses being the municipal law of their state, they were as judges, or a bench of justices; teaching and judging seem to be equivalent, comparing 2 Chr. 17:7, 9, with 2 Chr. 19:5, 6, 8. They were not the itinerant judges that rode the circuit, but the standing bench, that determined on appeals, special verdicts, or writs of error by the law; they sat in Moses's seat, not as he was Mediator between God and Israel, but only as he was chief justice, Ex. 18:26. Or, we may apply it, not to the Sanhedrim, but to the other Pharisees and scribes, that expounded the law, and taught the people how to apply it to particular cases. *The pulpit of wood,* such as was made for Ezra, *that ready scribe in the law of God* (Neh. 8:4), is here called *Moses's seat,* because Moses had those in every city (so the expression is, Acts 15:21), who in those pulpits preached him; this was their office, and it was just and honourable; it was requisite that there should be some at whose mouth the people might *enquire the law,* Mal. 2:7. Note, 1. Many a good place is filled with bad men; it is no new thing for the vilest men to be exalted even to *Moses's seat* (Ps. 12:8); and, when it is so, the men are not so much honoured by the seat as the seat is dishonoured by the men. Now they that sat in Moses's seat were so wretchedly degenerated, that it was time for the great Prophet to arise, like unto Moses, to erect another seat. 2. Good and useful offices and powers are not *therefore* to be condemned and abolished, because they fall sometimes into the hands of bad men, who abuse them. We must not *therefore* pull down Moses's seat, because scribes and Pharisees have got possession of it; rather than so, *let both grow together until the harvest, ch.* 13:30.

Hence he infers (*v.* 3), *"Whatsoever they bid you observe, that observe and do* As far as they *sit in Moses's seat,* that is, read and preach the law that was given by Moses" (which, as yet, continued in full force, power, and virtue), "and judge according to that law, so far you must hearken to them, as remembrances to you of the written word." The scribes and Pharisees made it their business to study the scripture, and were well acquainted with the language, history, and customs of it, and its style and phraseology. Now Christ would have the people to make use of the helps they gave them for the understanding of the scripture, and do accordingly. As long as their comments did illustrate the text and not pervert it; did make plain, and not *make void, the commandment of God;* so far they must be observed and obeyed, but with caution and a judgment of discretion. Note, We must not think the worse of good truths for their being preached by bad ministers; nor of good laws for their being executed by bad magistrates. Though it is most desirable to have our food brought by angels, yet, if God send it to us by ravens, if it be good and wholesome, we must take it, and thank God for it. Our Lord Jesus promiseth this, to prevent the cavil which some would be apt to make at this following discourse; as if, by condemning the scribes and Pharisees, he designed to bring the law of Moses into contempt, and to draw people off from it; whereas he *came not to destroy, but to fulfil.* Note, It is wisdom to obviate the exceptions which may be taken at just reproofs, especially when there is occasion to distinguish between officers and their offices, *that the ministry be not blamed* when the ministers are.

II. He condemns the men. He had ordered the multitude to do as they taught; but here he annexeth a caution not to do as they did, to beware of their leaven; *Do not ye after their works.* Their traditions were their works, were their idols, the works of their fancy. Or, "Do not according to their example." Doctrines and practices are spirits that must be tried, and where there is occasion, must be carefully separated and distinguished; and as we must not swallow corrupt doctrines for the sake of any laudable practices of those that teach them, so we must not imitate any bad examples for the sake of the plausible doctrines of those that set them. The scribes and Pharisees boasted as much of the goodness of their works as of the orthodoxy of their teaching, and hoped to be justified by them; it was the plea they put in (Lu. 18:11, 12); and yet these things, which they valued themselves so much upon, were an abomination in the sight of God.

Our Saviour here, and in the following verses, specifies divers particulars of their works, wherein we must not imitate them. In general, they are charged with hypocrisy, dissimulation, or double-dealing in religion; a crime which cannot be enquired of at men's bar, because we can only judge according to outward appearance; but God, who searcheth the heart, can convict of hypocrisy; and nothing is more displeasing to him, for he desireth truth.

Four things are in these verses charged upon them.

1. Their saying and doing were two things.

Their practice was no way agreeable either to their preaching or to their profession; for *they say, and do not;* they teach out of the law that which is good, but their conversation gives them the lie; and they seem to have found another way to heaven for themselves than what they show to others. See this illustrated and charged home upon them, Rom. 2:17–24. Those are of all sinners most inexcusable that allow themselves in the sins they condemn in others, or in worse. This doth especially touch wicked ministers, who will be sure to have their portion appointed them with hypocrites (*ch.* 24:51); for what greater hypocrisy can there be, than to press that upon others, to be believed and done, which they themselves disbelieve and disobey; pulling down in their practice what they build up in their preaching; when in the pulpit, preaching so well that it is a pity they should ever come out; but, when out of the pulpit, living so ill that it is a pity they should ever come in; like bells, that call others to church, but hang out of it themselves; or Mercurial posts, that point the way to others, but stand still themselves? Such will *be judged out of their own mouths.* It is applicable to all others that say, and do not; that make a plausible profession of religion, but do not live up to that profession; that make fair promises, but do not perform their promises; are full of good discourse, and can lay down the law to all about them, but are empty of good works; great talkers, but little doers; *the voice is Jacob's voice, but the hands are the hands of Esau. Vox et praeterea nihil — mere sound.* They speak fair, *I go, sir;* but there is no trusting them, for *there are seven abominations in their heart.*

2. They were very severe in imposing upon others those things which they were not themselves willing to submit to the burthen of (*v.* 4); *They bind heavy burthens, and grievous to be borne;* not only insisting upon the minute circumstances of the law, which is called *a yoke* (Acts 15:10), and pressing the observation of them with more strictness and severity than God himself did (whereas the maxim of the lawyers, is *Apices juris son sunt jura — Mere points of law are not law*), but by adding to his words, and imposing their own inventions and traditions, under the highest penalties. They loved to show their authority and to exercise their domineering faculty, lording it over God's heritage, and saying to men's souls, *Bow down, that we may go over;* witness their many additions to the law of the fourth commandment, by which they made the sabbath a burthen on men's shoulders, which was designed to be the joy of their hearts. Thus with force and cruelty did those shepherds *rule the flock,* as of old, Eze. 34:4.

But see their hypocrisy; *They themselves will not move them with one of their fingers.* (1.) They would not exercise themselves in those things which they imposed upon others; they pressed upon the people a strictness in religion which they themselves would not be bound by; but secretly transgressed their own traditions, which they publicly enforced. They indulged their pride in giving law to others; but consulted their ease in their own practice. Thus it has been said, to the reproach of the popish priests, that they fast with wine and sweetmeats, while they force the people to fast with bread and water; and decline the penances they enjoin the laity. (2.) They would not ease the people in these things, nor put a finger to lighten their burthen, when they saw it pinched them. They could find out loose constructions to put upon God's law, and could dispense with that, but would not bate an ace of their own impositions, nor dispense with a failure in the least punctilio of them. They allowed no chancery to relieve the extremity of their common law. How contrary to this was the practice of Christ's apostles, who would allow to others that use of Christian liberty which, for the peace and edification of the church, they would deny themselves in! They would lay no other burthen than necessary things, and those easy, Acts 15:28. How carefully doth Paul spare those to whom he writes! 1 Co. 7:28; 9:12.

3. They were all for show, and nothing for substance, in religion (*v.* 5); *All their works they do, to be seen of men.* We must do such good works, that they who see them may glorify God; but we must not proclaim our good works, with design that others may see them, and glorify us; which our Saviour here chargeth upon the Pharisees in general, as he had done before in the particular instances of prayer and giving of alms. All their end was to be praised of men, and therefore all their endeavour was to be seen of men, to *make a fair show in the flesh.* In those duties of religion which fall under the eye of men, none ere so constant and abundant as they; but in what lies between God and their souls, in the retirement of their closets, and the recesses of their hearts, they desire to be excused. The *form* of godliness will get them a name to live, which is all they aim at, and therefore they trouble not themselves with the *power* of it, which is essential to a life indeed. He that does all to be seen does nothing to the purpose.

He specifies two things which they did to be seen of men.

(1.) *They made broad their phylacteries.* Those were little scrolls of paper or parchment, wherein were written, with great niceness, these four paragraphs of the law, Ex. 13:2–11; 13:11–16; Deu. 6:4–9; 11:13–21. These were sewn up in leather, and worn upon their foreheads and left arms. It was a tradition of the elders, which had reference to Ex. 13:9, and Prov. 7:3, where the expressions seem to be figurative, intimating no more than that we should bear the things of God in our minds as carefully as if we had them bound between our eyes. Now the Pharisees made broad these phylacteries, that they might be thought more holy, and strict, and zealous for the law, than others. It is a gracious ambition to covet to be really more holy than others, but it is a proud ambition to covet to appear so. It is good to excel in real piety, but not to exceed in outward shows; for overdoing is justly suspected of design, Prov. 27:14. It is the guise of hypocrisy to make more ado than needs in external service, more than is needful either to prove, or to *im*prove, the good affections and dispositions of the soul.

(2.) *They enlarged the borders of their garments.* God appointed the Jews to make borders or fringes upon their garments (Num. 15:38), to distinguish them from other nations, and to be a memorandum to them of their being a peculiar people; but the Pharisees were not content to have these borders like other people's, which might serve God's design in appointing them; but they must be larger than ordinary, to answer their design of making themselves to be taken notice of; as if they were more religious than others. But those who thus enlarge their phylacteries, and the borders of their garments, while their hearts are straitened, and destitute of the love of God and their neighbour, though they may now deceive others, will in the end deceive themselves.

4. They much affected pre-eminence and superiority, and prided themselves extremely in it. Pride was the darling reigning sin of the Pharisees, *the sin that did most easily beset them* and which our Lord Jesus takes all occasions to witness against.

(1.) He describes their pride, *v.* 6, 7. They courted, and coveted,

[1.] Places of honour and respect. In all public appearances, as *at feasts, and in the synagogues,* they expected, and had, to their hearts' delight, *the uppermost rooms, and the chief seats.* They took place of all others, and precedency was adjudged to them, as persons of the greatest note and merit; and it is easy to imagine what a complacency they took in it; *they loved to have the preeminence,* 3 Jn. 9. It is not possessing the uppermost rooms, nor sitting in the chief seats, that is condemned (somebody must sit uppermost), but *loving* them; for men to value such a little piece of ceremony as sitting highest, going first, taking the wall, or the better hand, and to value themselves upon it, to seek it, and to feel resentment if they have it not; what is that but making an idol of ourselves, and then falling down and worshipping it — the worst kind of idolatry! It is bad any where, but especially in the synagogues. *There* to seek honour to ourselves, where we appear in order to give glory to God, and to humble ourselves before him, is indeed to mock God instead of serving him. David would willingly lie at the threshold in God's house; so far was he from coveting *the chief seat* there, Ps. 84:10. It savours much of pride and hypocrisy, when people do not care for going to church, unless they can look fine and make a figure there.

[2.] Titles of honour and respect. They *loved greetings in the markets,* loved to have people put off their hats to them, and show them respect when they met them in the streets. O how it pleased them, and fed their vain humour, *digito monstrari et dicier, Hic est — to be pointed out, and to have it said, This be he,* to have way made for them in the crowd of market people; "Stand off, here is a Pharisee coming!" and to be complimented with the high and pompous title of *Rabbi, Rabbi!* This was meat and drink and dainties to them; and they took as great a satisfaction in it as Nebuchadnezzar did in his palace, when he said, *Is not this great Babylon that I have built?* The *greetings* would not have done them half so much good, if they had not been in the markets, where every body might see how much they were respected, and how high they stood in the opinion of the people. It was but a little before Christ's time, that the Jewish teachers, the masters of Israel, had assumed the title of *Rabbi, Rab,* or *Rabban,* which signifies *great or much;* and was construed as *Doctor,* or *My lord.* And they laid such a stress upon it, that they gave it for a maxim that "he who salutes his teacher, and does not call him Rabbi, provokes the divine Majesty to depart from Israel;" so much religion did they place in that which was but a piece of good manners! For him that is taught in the word to give respect to him that teaches is commendable enough in him that gives it; but for him that teaches to love it, and demand it, and affect it, to be puffed up with it, and to be displeased if it be omitted, is sinful and abominable; and, instead of teaching, he has need to learn the first lesson in the school of Christ, which is humility.

(2.) He cautions his disciples against being herein like them; herein they must not do after their works; "But be not ye called so, for ye shall not be of such a spirit," *v.* 8, etc.

Here is, [1.] A prohibition of pride. They are here forbidden,

First, To challenge titles of honour and dominion to themselves, *v.* 8–10. It is repeated twice; *Be not called Rabbi, neither be ye called Master or Guide:* not that it is unlawful to give civil respect to *those that are over us in the Lord,* nay, it is an instance of the honour and esteem which it is our duty to show them; but, 1. Christ's ministers must not affect the name of *Rabbi* or *Master,* by way of distinction from other people; it is not agreeable to the simplicity of the gospel, for them to covet or accept the honour which they have that are in kings' palaces. 2. They must not assume the authority and dominion implied in those names; they must not be magisterial, nor domineer over their brethren, or over God's heritage, as if they had dominion over the faith of Christians: what they received of the Lord, all must receive from them; but in other things they must not make their opinions and wills a rule and standard to all other people, to be admitted with an implicit obedience. The reasons for this prohibition are,

(1.) *One is your Master, even Christ, v.* 8, and again, *v.* 10. Note, [1.] Christ is our Master, our Teacher, our Guide. Mr. George Herbert, when he named the name of *Christ,* usually added, *My Master.* [2.] Christ only is our Master, ministers are but ushers in the school. Christ only is the Master, the great Prophet, whom we must hear, and be ruled and overruled by; whose word must be an oracle and a law to us; *Verily I say unto you,* must be enough to us. And if he only be our Master, then for his ministers to set up for dictators, and to pretend to a supremacy and an infallibility, is a daring usurpation of that honour of Christ which he will not give to another.

(2.) *All ye are brethren.* Ministers are brethren not only to one another, but to the people; and therefore it ill becomes them to be masters, when there are none for them to master it over but their brethren; yea, and we are all younger brethren, otherwise the eldest might claim an *excellency of dignity and power,* Gen. 49:3. But, to preclude that, Christ himself is *the first-born among many brethren,* Rom. 8:29. Ye are brethren, as ye are all disciples of the same Master. Schoolfellows are brethren, and, as such, should help one another in getting their lesson; but it will by no means be allowed that one of the scholars step into the master's seat, and give law to the school. If we are all brethren, we must not be *many masters.* Jam. 3:1.

Secondly, They are forbidden to ascribe such titles to others (*v.* 9); *"Call no man your father upon the earth;* constitute no man the father of your religion, that is, the founder, author, director, and governor, of it." The fathers of our flesh must be called *fathers,* and as such we must *give them reverence;* but God only must be allowed as *the Father of our spirits,* Heb. 12:9. Our religion must not be derived from, or made to depend upon, any man. We are born again to the spiritual and divine life, *not of corruptible seed, but by the word of God; not of the will of the flesh, or the will of man, but of God.* Now the will of man, not being the rise of our religion, must not be the rule of it. We must not *jurare in verba magistri — swear to the dictates of any creature,* not the wisest or best, nor pin our faith on any man's sleeve, because we know not whither he will carry it. St. Paul calls himself *a Father* to those whose conversion he had been an instrument of (1 Co. 4:15; Phil. 10); but he pretends to no dominion over them, and uses that title to denote, not authority, but affection: therefore he calls them not his *obliged,* but his *beloved,* sons, 1 Co. 4:14.

The reason given is, *One is your Father, who is in heaven.* God is our Father, and is All in all in our religion. He is the Fountain of it, and its Founder; the Life of it, and its Lord; from whom alone, as the Original, our spiritual life is derived, and on whom it depends. He is *the Father of* all *lights* (Jam. 1:17), that *one Father, from whom are all things, and we in him,* Eph. 4:6. Christ having taught us to say, *Our Father, who art in heaven;* let us *call no man Father upon earth;* no man, because *man is a worm, and the son of man is a worm,* hewn out of the same rock with us; especially not upon earth, for man upon earth is a sinful worm; *there is not a just man upon earth, that doeth good, and sinneth not,* and therefore no one is fit to be called *Father.*

[2.] Here is a precept of humility and mutual subjection (*v.* 11); *He that is greatest among you shall be your servant;* not only call himself so (we know of one who styles himself *Servus servorum Dei — Servant of the servants of God,* but acts as Rabbi, and father, and master, and *Dominus Deus noster — The Lord our God,* and what not), but he shall be so. Take it as a promise; *"He* shall be accounted greatest, and stand highest in the favour of God, that is most submissive and serviceable;" or as a precept; "He that is advanced to any place of dignity, trust, and honour, in the church, *let him be your servant"* (some copies read *estō* for *estai*), "let him not think that his patent of honour is a writ of ease; no; *he that is greatest* is not a lord, but a minister." St. Paul, who knew his privilege as well as duty, though *free from all, yet made himself servant unto all* (1 Co. 9:19); and our Master frequently pressed it upon his disciples to be humble and self-denying, mild and condescending, and to abound in all offices of Christian love, though mean, and to the meanest; and of this he hath set us an example.

[3.] Here is a good reason for all this, *v.* 12. Consider,

First, The punishment intended for the proud; *Whosoever shall exalt himself shall be abased.* If God give them repentance, they will be abased in their own eyes, and will abhor themselves for it; if they repent not, sooner or later they will be abased before the world. Nebuchadnezzar, in the height of his pride, was turned to be a fellow-commoner with the beasts; Herod, to be a feast for the worms; and Babylon, that sat as a queen, to be the scorn of nations. God made the proud and aspiring priests contemptible and base (Mal. 2:9), and the lying prophet to be *the tail,* Isa. 9:15. But if proud men have not marks of humiliation set upon them in this world, there is a day coming, when they shall *rise to everlasting shame and contempt* (Dan. 12:2); *so plentifully will he reward the proud doer!* Ps. 31:23.

Secondly, The preferment intended for the humble; *He that shall humble himself shall be exalted.* Humility is that *ornament which is in the sight of God of great price.* In this world the humble have the honour of being accepted with the holy God, and respected by all wise and good men; of being qualified for, and often called out to, the most honourable services; for honour is like the shadow, which flees from those that pursue it, and grasp at it, but follows those that flee from it. However, in the other world, they that have humbled themselves in contrition for their sin, in compliance with their God, and in condescension to their brethren, shall be exalted to inherit the throne of glory; shall be not only owned, but crowned, before angels and men.

Verses 13–33

In these verses we have eight woes levelled directly against the scribes and Pharisees by our Lord Jesus Christ, like so many claps of thunder, or flashes of lightning, from mount Sinai. *Three* woes are made to look very dreadful (Rev. 8:13; 9:12); but here are *eight* woes, in opposition to the eight beatitudes, Mt. 5:3. The gospel has its woes as well as the law, and gospel curses are of all curses the heaviest. These woes are the more remarkable, not only because of the authority, but because of the meekness and gentleness, of him that denounced them. He came to bless, and loved to bless; but, if his wrath be kindled, there is surely cause for it: and who shall entreat for him that the great Intercessor pleads against? A woe from Christ is a remediless woe.

This is here the burthen of the song, and it is a heavy burthen; *Woe unto you, scribes and Pharisees, hypocrites.* Note, 1. The scribes and Pharisees were hypocrites; that is it in which all the rest of their bad characters are summed up; it was the leaven which gave the relish to all they said and did. A hypocrite is a stage-player in religion (that is the primary signification of the word); he personates or acts the part of one that he neither is nor may be, or perhaps the he neither is nor would be. 2. That hypocrites are in a woeful state and condition. *Woe to hypocrites;* so *he* said whose saying that their case is miserable makes it so: while they live, their religion is vain; when they die, their ruin is great.

Now each of these woes against the scribes and Pharisees has a reason annexed to it containing a separate crime charged upon them, proving their hypocrisy, and justifying the judgment of Christ upon them; for his woes, his curses, are never causeless.

I. They were sworn enemies to the gospel of Christ, and consequently to the salvation of the souls of men (*v.* 13); *They shut up the kingdom of heaven against men,* that is, they did all they could to keep people from believing in Christ, and so entering into his kingdom. Christ came to *open the kingdom of heaven,* that is, to lay open for us *a new and living way* into it, to bring men to be subjects of that kingdom. Now the scribes and Pharisees, who sat in Moses's seat, and pretended to the key of knowledge, ought to have contributed their assistance herein, by opening those scriptures of the Old Testament which pointed at the Messiah and his kingdom, in their true and proper sense; they that undertook to expound Moses and the prophets should have showed the people how they testified of Christ; that Daniel's weeks were expiring, *the sceptre was departed from Judah,* and therefore now was the time for the Messiah's appearing. Thus they might have facilitated that great work, and have helped thousands to heaven; but, instead of this, they shut up the kingdom of heaven; they made it their business to press the ceremonial law, which was now in the vanishing, to suppress the prophecies, which were now in the accomplishing, and to beget and nourish up in the minds of the people prejudices against Christ and his doctrine.

1. They would not go in themselves; *Have any of the rulers,* or *of the Pharisees, believed on him?* Jn. 7:48. No; they were to proud to stoop to his meanness, too formal to be reconciled to his plainness; they did not like a religion which insisted so much on humility, self-denial, contempt of the world, and spiritual worship. Repentance was the door of admission into this kingdom, and nothing could be more disagreeable to the Pharisees, who justified and admired themselves, than to repent, that is, to accuse and abase and abhor themselves; therefore they *went not in themselves;* but that was not all.

2. They would not *suffer them that were entering to go in.* It is bad to keep away from Christ ourselves, but it is worse to keep others from him; yet that is commonly the way of hypocrites; they do not love that any should go beyond them in religion, or be better than they. Their not going in themselves was a hindrance to many; for, they having so great an interest in the people, multitudes rejected the gospel only because their leaders did; but, besides that, they opposed both Christ's entertaining of sinners (Lu. 7:39), and sinners' entertaining of Christ; they perverted his doctrine, confronted his miracles, quarrelled with his disciples, and represented him, and his institutes and economy, to the people in the most disingenuous, disadvantageous manner imaginable; they thundered out their excommunications against those that confessed him, and used all their wit and power to serve their malice against him; and thus they *shut up the kingdom of heaven,* so that *they who would enter* into it must *suffer violence* (*ch.* 11:12), and *press into it* (Lu. 16:16), through a crowd of scribes and Pharisees, and all the obstructions and difficulties they could contrive to lay in their way. How well is it for us that our salvation is not entrusted in the hands of

any man or company of men in the world! If it were, we should be undone. They that shut out of the church would shut out of heaven if they could; but the malice of men cannot *make the promise of God* to his chosen *of no effect;* blessed be God, it cannot.

II. They made religion and the form of godliness a cloak and stalking-horse to their covetous practices and desires, *v.* 14. Observe here,

1. What their wicked practices were; they *devoured widows' houses,* either by quartering themselves and their attendants upon them for entertainment, which must be of the best for men of their figure; or by insinuating themselves into their affections, and so getting to be the trustees of their estates, which they could make an easy prey of; for who could presume to call such as they were to an account? The thing they aimed at was to enrich themselves; and, this being their chief and highest end, all considerations of justice and equity were laid aside, and even widows' houses were sacrificed to this. Widows are of the weaker sex in its weakest state, easily imposed upon; and therefore they fastened on them, to make a prey of. They devoured those whom, by the law of God, they were particularly obliged to protect, patronise, and relieve. There is a woe in the Old Testament to those that *made widows their prey* (Isa. 10:1, 2); and Christ here seconded it with his woe. God is the judge of the widows; they are his peculiar care, he *establisheth their border* (Prov. 15:25), and *espouseth their cause* (Ex. 22:22, 23); yet these were they whose houses the Pharisees devoured by wholesale; so greedy were they to get *their bellies filled with the treasures of wickedness!* Their devouring denotes not only covetousness, but cruelty in their oppression, described Mic. 3:3, *They eat the flesh, and flay off the skin.* And doubtless they did all this under colour of law; for they did it so artfully that it passed uncensured, and did not at all lessen the people's veneration for them.

2. What was the cloak with which they covered this wicked practice; *For a pretence they made long prayers;* very long indeed, if it be true which some of the Jewish writers tell us, that they spent three hours at a time in the formalities of meditation and prayer, and did it thrice every day, which is more than an upright soul, that makes a conscience of being inward with God in the duty, dares pretend ordinarily to do; but to the Pharisees it was easy enough, who never made a business of the duty, and always made a trade of the outside of it. By this craft they got their wealth, and maintained their grandeur. It is not probable that these long prayers were extemporary, for then (as Mr. Baxter observes) the Pharisees had much more the gift of prayer than Christ's disciples had; but rather that they were stated forms of words in use among them, which they said over by tale, as the papists drop their beads. Christ doth not here condemn long prayers, as in themselves hypocritical; nay if there were not a great appearance of good in them, they would not have been used for a pretence; and the cloak must be very thick which was used to cover such wicked practices. Christ himself *continued all night in prayer to God,* and we are commanded to *pray without ceasing* too soon; where there are many sins to be confessed, and many wants to pray for the supply of, and many mercies to give thanks for, there is occasion for long prayers. But the Pharisees' long prayers were made up of vain repetitions, and (which was the end of them) they were for a *pretence;* by them they got the reputation of pious devout men, that loved prayer, and were the favourites of Heaven; and by this means people were made to believe it was not possible that such men as they should cheat them;, and, therefore, happy the widow that could get a Pharisee for her trustee, and guardian to her children! Thus, while they seemed to soar heaven-ward, upon the wings of prayer, their eye, like the kite's, was all the while upon their prey on the earth, some widow's house or other that lay convenient for them. Thus circumcision was the cloak of the Shechemites' covetousness (Gen. 34:22, 23), the payment of a vow in Hebron the cover of Absalom's rebellion (2 Sa. 15:7), a fast in Jezreel must patronise Naboth's murder, and the extirpation of Baal is the footstool of Jehu's ambition. Popish priests, under pretence of long prayers for the dead, masses and dirges, and I know not what, enrich themselves by devouring the house of the widows and fatherless. Note, It is no new thing for the show and form of godliness to be made a cloak to the greatest enormities. But dissembled piety, however it passeth now, will be reckoned for as double iniquity, *in the day when God shall judge the secrets of men.*

3. The doom passed upon them for this; *Therefore ye shall receive the greater damnation.* Note, (1.) There are degrees of damnation; there are some whose sin is more inexcusable, *and whose ruin will therefore be more intolerable.* (2.) The pretences of religion, with which hypocrites disguise or excuse their sin now, will aggravate their condemnation shortly. Such is the deceitfulness of sin, that the very thing by which sinners hope to expiate and atone for their sins will come against them, and make their sins more exceedingly sinful. But it is sad for the criminal, when his defence proves his offence, and his pleas (*We have prophesied in thy name, and in thy name* made long prayers) heightens the charge against him.

III. While they were such enemies to the conversion of souls to Christianity, they were very industrious in the perversion of them to their faction. They shut up the kingdom of heaven against those that would turn to Christ, but at the same time *compassed sea and land to make proselytes* to themselves, *v.* 15. Observe here,

1. Their commendable industry in making proselytes to the Jewish religion, not only proselytes of *the gate,* who obliged themselves to no more than the observance of the seven precepts of the sons of Noah, but proselytes of *righteousness,* who addicted themselves wholly to all the rites of the Jewish religion, for that was the game they flew at; for this, for one such, though but one, they compass sea and land, had many a cunning reach, and laid many a plot, rode and run, and sent and wrote, and laboured unweariedly. And what did they aim at? Not the glory of God, and the good of souls; but that they might have the credit of making them proselytes, and the advantage of making a prey of them when they were made. Note, (1.) The making of proselytes, if it be to the truth and serious godliness, and be done with a good design, is a good work, well worthy of the utmost care and pains. Such is the value of souls, that nothing must be thought too much to do, to save a soul from death. The industry of the Pharisees herein may show the negligence of many who would be thought to act from better principles, but will be at no pains or cost to propagate the gospel. (2.) To make a proselyte, sea and land must be compassed; all ways and means must be tried; first one way, and then another, must be tried, all little enough; but all well paid, if the point be gained. (3.) Carnal hearts seldom shrink from the pains necessary to carry on their carnal purposes; when a proselyte is to be made to serve a turn for themselves, they will compass sea and land to make him, rather than be disappointed.

2. Their cursed impiety in abusing their proselytes when they were made; "Ye make him the disciple of a Pharisee presently, and he sucks in all a Pharisee's notions; and so *ye make him twofold more the child of hell than yourselves.*" Note, (1.) Hypocrites, while they fancy themselves heirs of heaven, are, in the judgment of Christ, the children of hell. The rise of their hypocrisy is from hell, for the devil is the father of lies; and the tendency of their hypocrisy is toward hell, that is the country they belong to, the inheritance they are heirs to; they are called *children of hell,* because of their rooted enmity to the kingdom of heaven, which was the principle and genius of Pharisaism. (2.) Though all that maliciously oppose the gospel are children of hell, yet some are twofold more so than others, more furious and bigoted and malignant. (3.) Perverted proselytes are commonly the greatest bigots; the scholars outdid their masters, [1.] In fondness of ceremony; the Pharisees themselves saw the folly of their own impositions, and in their hearts smiled at the obsequiousness of those that conformed to them; but their proselytes were eager for them. Note, Weak heads commonly admire those shows and ceremonies which wise men (however for public ends they countenance them) cannot but think meanly of. [2.] In fury against Christianity; the proselytes readily imbibed the principles which their crafty leaders were not wanting to possess them with, and so became extremely hot against the truth. The most bitter enemies the apostles met with in all places were the Hellenist Jews, who were mostly proselytes, Acts 13:45; 14:2–19; 17:5; 18:6. Paul, a disciple of the Pharisees, was *exceedingly mad against the Christians* (Acts 26:11), when his master, Gamaliel, seems to have been more moderate.

IV. Their seeking their own worldly gain and honour more than God's glory put them upon coining false and unwarrantable distinction, with which they led the people into dangerous mistakes, particularly in the matter of oaths; which,

as an evidence of a universal sense of religion, have been by all nations accounted sacred (*v.* 16); *Ye blind guides.* Note, 1. It is sad to think how many are under the guidance of such as are themselves blind, who undertake to show others that way which they are themselves willingly ignorant of. *His watchmen are blind* (Isa. 56:10); and too often the people love to have it so, and say to the seers, *See not.* But the case is bad, when the leaders of the people *cause them to err,* Isa. 9:16. 2. Though the condition of those whose guides are blind is very sad, yet that of the blind guides themselves is yet more woeful. Christ denounces a woe to the blind guides that have the blood of so many souls to answer for.

Now, to prove their blindness, he specifies the matter of swearing, and shows what corrupt casuists they were.

(1.) He lays down the doctrine they taught.

[1.] They allowed swearing by creatures, provided they were consecrated to the service of God, and stood in any special relation to him. They allowed swearing by the temple and the altar, though they were the work of men's hands, intended to be the servants of God's honour, not sharers in it. An oath is an appeal to God, to his omniscience and justice; and to make this appeal to any creature is to put that creature in the place of God. See Deu. 6:13.

[2.] They distinguished between an oath by *the temple* and an oath by *the gold of the temple;* an oath by *the altar* and an oath by *the gift upon the altar;* making the latter binding, but not the former. Here was a double wickedness; *First,* That there were some oaths which they dispensed with, and made light of, and reckoned a man was not bound by to assert the truth, or perform a promise. They ought not to have sworn by the temple or the altar; but, when they had so sworn, they were taken in the words of their mouth. That doctrine cannot be of the God of truth which gives countenance to the breach of faith in any case whatsoever. Oaths are edge-tools and are not to be jested with. *Secondly,* That they preferred the gold before the temple, and the gift before the altar, to encourage people to bring gifts to the altar, and gold to the treasures of the temple, which they hoped to be gainers by. Those who had made gold their hope, and whose eyes were blinded by gifts in secret, were great friends to the Corban; and, gain being their godliness, by a thousand artifices they made religion truckle to their worldly interests. Corrupt church-guides make things to be sin or not sin as it serves their purposes, and lay a much greater stress on that which concerns their own gain than on that which is for God's glory and the good of souls.

(2.) He shows the folly and absurdity of this distinction (*v.* 17–19); *Ye fools, and blind.* It was in the way of a necessary reproof, not an angry reproach, that Christ called them *fools.* Let it suffice us from the word of wisdom to show the folly of sinful opinions and practices: but, for the fastening of the character upon particular persons, leave that to Christ, who knows what is in man, and has forbidden us to say, *Thou fool.*

To convict them of folly, he appeals to themselves, *Whether is greater, the gold* (the golden vessels and ornaments, or the gold in the treasury) *or the temple that sanctifies the gold; the gift, or the altar that sanctifies the gift?* Any one will own, *Propter quod aliquid est tale, id est magis tale — That, on account of which any thing is qualified in a particular way, must itself be much more qualified in the same way.* They that sware by the gold of the temple had an eye to it as holy; but what was it that made it holy but the holiness of the temple, to the service of which it was appropriated? And therefore the temple cannot be less holy than the gold, but must be more so; for the less is blessed and sanctified of the better, Heb. 7:7. The temple and altar were dedicated to God fixedly, the gold and gift but secondarily. Christ is our altar (Heb. 13:10), our temple (Jn. 2:21); for it is he that sanctifies all our gifts, and puts an acceptableness in them, 1 Pt. 2:5. Those that put their own works into the place of Christ's righteousness in justification are guilty of the Pharisees' absurdity, who preferred the gift before the altar. Every true Christian is a living temple; and by virtue thereof common things are sanctified to him; *unto the pure all things are pure* (Tit. 1:15), and *the unbelieving husband is sanctified by the* believing *wife,* 1 Co. 7:14.

(3.) He rectifies the mistake (*v.* 20–22), by reducing all the oaths they had invented to the true intent of an oath, which is, By the name of the Lord: so that though an oath by the temple, or the altar, or heaven, be formally bad, yet it is binding. *Quod fieri non debuit, factum valet — Engagements which ought not to have been made, are yet, when made, binding.* A man shall never take advantage of his own fault.

[1.] He that swears by the altar, let him not think to shake off the obligation of it by saying, "The altar is but wood, and stone, and brass;" for his oath shall be construed most strongly against himself; because he was culpable, and so as that the obligation of it may be preserved, *ut res potius valeat quam pereat — the obligation being hereby strengthened rather than destroyed.* And therefore an oath by the altar shall be interpreted by it and by all things thereon; for the appurtenances pass with the principal. And, the things thereon being offered up to God, to swear by it and them was, in effect, to call God himself to witness: for it was the altar of God; and he that went to that, went to God, Ps. 43:4; 26:6.

[2.] He that swears by the temple, if he understand what he does, cannot but apprehend that the ground of such a respect to it, is, not because it is a fine house, but because it is the house of God, dedicated to his service, the place which he has chosen to put his name there; and therefore he swears *by it, and by him that dwells therein;* there he was pleased in a peculiar manner to manifest himself, and give tokens of his presence; so that whoso swears by it, swears by him who had said, *This is my rest, here will I dwell.* Good Christians are God's temples, and the Spirit of God dwells in them (1 Co. 3:16; 6:19), and God takes what is done to them as done to himself; he that grieves a gracious soul, grieves it and the Spirit that dwells in it. Eph. 4:30.

[3.] If a man swears by heaven, he sins (*ch.* 5:34); yet he shall not therefore be discharged from the obligation of his oath; no, God will make him know that the heaven he swears by, is his throne (Isa. 66:1); and he that swears by the throne, appeals to him that sits upon it; who, as he resents the affront done to him in the form of the oath, so he will certainly revenge the greater affront done to him by the violation of it. Christ will not countenance the evasion of a solemn oath, though ever so plausible.

V. They were very strict and precise in the smaller matters of the law, but as careless and loose in the weightier matters, *v.* 23, 24. They were *partial in the law* (Mal. 2:9), would pick and choose their duty, according as they were interested or stood affected. Sincere obedience is universal, and he that from a right principle obeys any of God's precepts, will have respect to them all, Ps. 119:6. But hypocrites, who act in religion for themselves, and not for God, will do no more in religion than they can serve a turn by for themselves. The partiality of the scribes and Pharisees appears here, in two instances.

1. They observed smaller duties, but omitted greater; they were very exact in paying tithes, till it came to *mint, anise,* and *cummin,* their exactness in tithing of which would not cost them much, but would be cried up, and they should buy reputation cheap. The Pharisee boasted of this, *I give tithes of all that I possess,* Lu. 18:12. But it is probable that they had ends of their own to serve, and would find their own account in it; for the priests and Levites, to whom the tithes were paid, were in their interests, and knew how to return their kindness. Paying tithes was their duty, and what the law required; Christ tells them they ought not to leave it undone. Note, All ought in their places to contribute to the support and maintenance of a standing ministry: withholding tithes is called *robbing God,* Mal. 2:8–10. They that *are taught in the word,* and do not *communicate to them that teach them* that love a cheap gospel, come short of the Pharisee.

But that which Christ here condemns them for, is, that they *omitted the weightier matters of the law, judgment, mercy, and faith;* and their niceness in paying tithes, was, if not to atone before God, yet at least to excuse end palliate to men the omission of those. All the things of God's law are weighty, but those are most weighty, which are most expressive of inward holiness in the heart; the instances of self-denial, contempt of the world, and resignation to God, in which lies the life of religion. Judgment and mercy toward men, and faith toward God, are the weightier matters of the law, the *good things* which the *Lord our God requires* (Mic. 6:8); to do justly, and love mercy, and humble ourselves by faith to walk with God. This is the obedience which is better than sacrifice or tithe; judgment is preferred before sacrifice, Isa. 1:11. To be just to the priests in their tithe, and yet to cheat and defraud every body else, is but to mock God, and deceive ourselves. Mercy also is preferred before sacrifice, Hos. 6:6. To feed those who *made themselves fat with the offering of the Lord,* and at the same time to shut up the bowels of compassion from a brother or a sister that is naked, and destitute of daily food, to pay tithe-mint to the priest, and to deny a crumb to Lazarus, is to lie open to that judgment without mercy, which is awarded to those who pretended to judgment, and showed no mercy; nor will judgment and mercy serve without faith in divine revelation; for God will be honoured in his truths as well as in his laws.

2. They avoided lesser sins, but committed greater (*v.* 24); *Ye blind guides;* so he had called them before (*v.* 16), for their corrupt teaching; here he calls them so for their corrupt living, for their example was leading as well as their doctrine; and in this also they were blind and partial; they *strained at a gnat, and swallowed a camel.* In their doctrine they strained at gnats, warned people against every the least violation of the tradition of the elders. In their practice they strained at gnats, heaved at them, with a seeming dread, as if they had a great abhorrence of sin, and were afraid of it in the least instance; but they made no difficulty of those sins which, in comparison with them, were as a camel to a gnat; when they devoured widows' houses, they did indeed *swallow a camel;* when they gave Judas the price of innocent blood, and yet scrupled to put the returned money into the treasury (*ch.* 27:6); when they would not go into the judgment-hall, for fear of being defiled, and yet would stand at the door, and cry out against the holy Jesus (Jn. 18:28); when they quarrelled with the disciples for eating with unwashen hands, and yet, for the filling of the Corban, taught people to break the fifth commandment, they strained at gnats, or lesser things, and yet swallowed camels. It is not the scrupling of a little sin that Christ here reproves; if it be a sin, though but a gnat, it must be strained at, but the doing of that, and then swallowing a camel. In the smaller matters of the law to be superstitious, and to be profane in the greater, is the hypocrisy here condemned.

VI. They were all for the outside, and not at all for the inside, of religion. They were more desirous and solicitous to appear pious to men than to approve themselves so toward God. This is illustrated by two similitudes.

1. They are compared to a vessel that is clean washed on the outside, but all dirt within, *v.* 25, 26. The Pharisees placed religion in that which at best was but a point of decency — the *washing of cups,* Mk. 7:4. They were in care to eat their meat in clean cups and platters, but made no conscience of getting their meat by extortion, and using it to excess. Now what a foolish thing would it be for a man to wash only the outside of a cup, which is to be looked at, and to leave the inside dirty, which is to be used; so they do who only avoid scandalous sins, that would spoil their reputation with men, but allow themselves in heart-wickedness, which renders them odious to the pure and holy God. In reference to his, observe,

(1.) The practice of the Pharisees; they made clean the outside. In those things which fell under the observation of their neighbours, they seemed very exact, and carried on their wicked intrigues with so much artifice, that their wickedness was not suspected; people generally took them for very good men. But within, in the recesses of their hearts and the close retirements of their lives, they were *full of extortion and excess;* of *violence and incontinence* (so Dr. Hammond); that is, of injustice and intemperance. While they would seem to be godly, they were neither sober nor righteous. Their *inward part was very wickedness* (Ps. 5:9); and that we are really, which we are inwardly.

(2.) The rule Christ gives, in opposition to this practice, *v.* 26. It is addressed to the blind Pharisees. They thought themselves the *seers of the land,* but (Jn. 9:39) Christ calls them *blind.* Note, those are blind, in Christ's account who (how quick-sighted soever they are in other things) are strangers, and no enemies, to the wickedness of their own hearts; who see not, and hate not, the secret sin that lodgeth there. Self-ignorance is the most shameful and hurtful ignorance, Rev. 3:17. The rule is, *Cleanse first that which is within.* Note, the principal care of every one of us should be to wash our hearts from wickedness, Jer. 4:14. The main business of a Christian lies within, to get cleansed from the *filthiness of the spirit.* Corrupt affections and inclinations, the secret lusts that lurk in the soul, unseen and unobserved, these must first be mortified and subdued. Those sins must be conscientiously abstained from, which the eye of God only is a witness to, who searcheth the heart.

Observe the method prescribed; *Cleanse first that which is within* not that *only,* but that *first;* because, if due care be taken concerning that, the outside will be clean also. External motives and inducements may keep the outside clean, while the inside is filthy; but if renewing, sanctifying grace make clean the inside, that will have an influence upon the outside, for the commanding principle is within. If the heart be well kept, all is well, for *out of it are the issues of life;* the eruptions will vanish of course. If the heart and spirit be made new, there will be a newness of life; here therefore we must begin with ourselves; first cleanse that which is within; we then make sure work, when this is our first work.

2. They are compared to *whited sepulchres, v.* 27, 28.

(1.) They were fair without, like sepulchres, *which appear beautiful outward.* Some make it to refer to the custom of the Jews to whiten graves, only for the notifying of them, especially if they were in unusual places, that people might avoid them, because of the ceremonial pollution contracted by the touch of a grave, Num. 19:16. And it was part of the charge of the overseers of the highways, to repair that whitening when it was decayed. Sepulchres were thus made remarkable, 2 Ki. 23:16, 17. The formality of hypocrites, by which they study to recommend themselves to the world, doth but make all wise and good men the more careful to avoid them, for fear of being defiled by them. *Beware of the scribes,* Lu. 20:46. It rather alludes to the custom of whitening the sepulchres of eminent persons, for the beautifying of them. It is said here (*v.* 29), that they *garnished the sepulchres of the righteous;* as it is usual with us to erect monuments upon the graves of great persons, and to strew flowers on the graves of dear friends. Now the righteousness of the scribes and Pharisees was like the ornaments of a grave, or the dressing up of a dead body, only for show. The top of their ambition was to *appear righteous before men,* and to be applauded and had in admiration by them. But,

(2.) They were *foul* within, like sepulchres, *full of dead men's bones, and all uncleanness:* so vile are our bodies, when the soul has deserted them! Thus were they full of hypocrisy and iniquity. Hypocrisy is the worst iniquity of all other. Note, It is possible for those that have their hearts full of sin, to have their lives free from blame, and to appear very good. But what will it avail us, to have the good word of our fellow-servants, if our Master doth not say, *Well done*? When all other graves are opened, these whited sepulchres will be looked into, and the dead men's bones, and all the uncleanness, shall be *brought out,* and be *spread before all the host of heaven,* Jer. 8:1, 2. For it is the day when God shall judge, not the shows, but the secrets, of men. And it will then be small comfort to them who shall have their portion with hypocrites, to remember how creditably and plausibly they went to hell, applauded by all their neighbours.

VII. They pretended a deal of kindness for the memory of the prophets that were dead and gone, while they hated and persecuted those that were present with them. This is put last, because it was the blackest part of their character. God is jealous for his honour in his laws and ordinances, and resents it if they be profaned and abused; but he has often expressed an equal jealousy for his honour in his prophets and ministers, and resents it worse if they be wronged and persecuted: and therefore, when our Lord Jesus comes to this head, he speaks more fully than upon any of the other (*v.* 29–37); for that toucheth his ministers, *toucheth his Anointed,* and toucheth the *apple of his eye.* Observe here,

1. The respect which the scribes and Pharisees pretend for the prophets that were gone, *v.* 29, 30. This was the varnish, and that in which they outwardly appeared righteous.

(1.) They honoured the relics of the prophets, they built their tombs, and garnished their sepulchres. It seems, the places of their burial were known, David's sepulchre was with them, Acts 2:29. There was a title upon the sepulchre of *the man of God* (2 Ki. 23:17), and Josiah thought it respect enough not to *move his bones, v.* 18. But they would do more, rebuild and beautify them. Now consider this, [1.] As an instance of honour done to deceased prophets, who, while they lived, were counted as the off-scouring of all things, and had all manner of evil spoken against them falsely. Note, God can extort, even from bad men, an acknowledgment of the honour of piety and holiness. Them that honour God he will honour, and sometimes with those from whom contempt is expected, 2 Sa. 6:22. *The memory of the just is blessed,* when the names of those that hated and persecuted them shall be covered with shame. The honour of constancy and resolution in the way of duty will be a lasting honour; and those that are manifest to God, will be manifest in the consciences of those about them. [2.] As an instance of the hypocrisy of the scribes and Pharisees, who paid their respect to them. Note, Carnal people can easily honour the memories of faithful ministers that are dead and gone, because they do not reprove them, nor disturb them, in their sins. Dead prophets are *seers that see not,* and those they can bear well enough; they do not torment them, as the living witnesses do, that bear their testimony *viva voce — with a living voice,* Rev. 11:10. They can pay respect to the writings of the dead prophets, which tell them what they *should* be; but not the reproofs of the living prophets, which tell them what they *are. Sit divus, modo non sit vivus — Let there be saints; but let them not be living here.* The extravagant respect which the church of Rome pays to the memory of saints departed, especially the martyrs, dedicating days and places to their names, enshrining their relics, praying to them, and offering to their images, while they make themselves drunk with the blood of the saints of their own day, is a manifest proof that they not only *succeed,* but *exceed,* the scribes and Pharisees in a counterfeit hypocritical religion, which builds the prophets' tombs, but hates the prophets' doctrine.

(2.) They protested against the murder of them (*v.* 30); *If we had been in the days of our fathers, we would not have been partakers with them.* They would never have consented to the silencing of Amos, and the imprisonment of Micaiah, to the putting of Hanani in the stocks, and Jeremiah in the dungeon, to the stoning of Zechariah, the mocking of all the messengers of the Lord, and the abuses put upon his prophets; no, not they, they would sooner have lost their right hands than have done any such thing. *What, is thy servant a dog?* And yet they were at this time plotting to murder Christ, *to whom all the prophets bore witness.* They think, if they had lived in the days of the prophets, they would have heard them gladly and obeyed; and yet they rebelled against the light that Christ brought into the world. But it is certain, a Herod and an Herodias to John the Baptist, would have been an Ahab and a Jezebel to Elijah. Note, The deceitfulness of sinners' hearts appears very much in this, that, while they go down the stream of the sins of their own day, they fancy they should have swum against the stream of the sins of the former days; that, if they had had other people's opportunities, they should have improved them more faithfully; if they had been in other people's temptations, they should have resisted them more vigorously; when yet they improve not the opportunities they have, nor resist the temptations they are in. We are sometimes thinking, if we had lived when Christ was upon earth, how constantly we would have followed him; we would not have despised and rejected him, as they then did; and yet Christ in his Spirit, in his word, in his ministers, is still no better treated.

2. Their enmity and opposition to Christ and his gospel, notwithstanding, and the ruin they were bringing upon themselves and upon that generation thereby, *v.* 31–33. Observe here,

(1.) The indictment proved; *Ye are witnesses against yourselves.* Note, Sinners cannot hope to escape the judgment of Christ for want of proof against them, when it is easy to find them witnesses against themselves; and their very pleas will not only be overruled, but turned to their conviction, and *their own tongues* shall be made to *fall upon them,* Ps. 64:8.

[1.] By their own confession, it was the great wickedness of their forefathers, to kill the prophets; so that they knew the fault of it, and yet were themselves guilty of the same fact. Note, They who condemn sin in others, and yet allow the same or worse in themselves, are of all others most inexcusable, Rom. 1:32–2:1. They knew they ought not to have been partakers with persecutors, and yet were the followers of them. Such self-contradictions now will amount to self-condemnations in the great day. Christ puts another construction upon their building of the tombs of the prophets than what they intended; as if by beautifying their graves they justified their murderers (Lu. 11:48), for they persisted in the sin.

[2.] By their own confession, these notorious persecutors were their ancestors; *Ye are the children of them.* They meant no more than that they were their children by blood and nature; but Christ turns it upon them;, that they were so by spirit and disposition; *You are of those fathers, and their lusts you will do.* They are, as you say, *your* fathers, and you *patrizare — take after your fathers;* it is the sin that runs in the blood among you. *As your fathers did, so do ye,* Acts 7:51. They came of a persecuting race, were *a seed of evil doers* (Isa. 1:4), *risen up in their fathers' stead,* Num. 32:14. Malice,

envy, and cruelty, were bred in the bone with them, and they had formerly espoused it for a principle, to *do as their fathers did,* Jer. 44:17. And it is observable here (*v.* 30) how careful they are to mention the relation; "They were *our* fathers, that killed the prophets, and they were men in honour and power, whose sons and successors we are." If they had detested the wickedness of their ancestors, as they ought to have done, they would not have been so fond to call them *their fathers;* for it is no credit to be akin to persecutors, though they have ever so much dignity and dominion.

(2.) The sentence passed upon them. Christ here proceeds,

[1.] To give them up to sin as irreclaimable (*v.* 32); *Fill ye up then the measure of your fathers.* If Ephraim be joined to idols, and hate to be reformed, *let him alone. He that is filthy, let him be filthy still.* Christ knew they were now contriving his death, and in a few days would accomplish it; "Well," saith he, "go on with your plot, take your curse, walk in the way of your heart and in the sight of your eyes, and see what will come of it. *What thou doest, do quickly.* You will but fill up the measure of guilt, which will then overflow in a deluge of wrath." Note, *First,* There is a measure of sin to be filled up, before utter ruin comes upon persons and families, churches and nations. God will bear long, but the time will come when he can *no longer forbear,* Jer. 44:22. We read of the measure of the Amorites that was to be filled (Gen. 15:16), of the *harvest of the earth being ripe for the sickle* (Rev. 14:15–19), and of sinners *making an end to deal treacherously,* arriving at a full stature in treachery, Isa. 33:1. *Secondly,* Children fill up the measure of their fathers' sins whey they are gone, if they persist in the same or the like. That national guilt which brings national ruin is made up of the sin of many in several ages, and in the successions of societies there is a score going on; for God justly visits the iniquity of the fathers upon the children that tread in the steps of it. *Thirdly,* Persecuting Christ, and his people and ministers, is a sin that fills the measure of a nation's guilt sooner than any other. This was it that brought wrath without remedy upon the fathers (2 Chr. 36:16), and wrath to the utmost upon the children too, 1 Th. 2:16. This was that fourth transgression, of which, when added to the other three, the Lord *would not turn away the punishment,* Amos 1:3, 6, 9, 11, 13. *Fourthly,* It is just with God to give those up to their own heart's lusts, who obstinately persist in the gratification f them. Those who will run headlong to ruin, let the reins be laid on their neck, and it is the saddest condition a man can be in on this side hell.

[2.] He proceeds to give them up to ruin as irrecoverable, to a personal ruin in the other world (*v.* 33); *Ye serpents, ye generation of vipers, how can ye escape the damnation of hell?* These are strange words to come from the mouth of Christ, into whose lips grace was poured. But he can and will speak terror, and in these words he explains and sums up the *eight* woes he had denounced against the scribes and Pharisees.

Here is, *First,* Their description; *Ye serpents.* Doth Christ call names? Yes, but this doth not warrant us to do so. He infallibly knew what was in man, and knew them to be subtle as serpents, cleaving to the earth, feeding on dust; they had a specious outside, but were within malignant, had poison under their tongues, the seed of the old serpent. They were a *generation of vipers;* they and those that went before them, they and those that joined with them, were a generation of envenomed, enraged, spiteful adversaries to Christ and his gospel. They loved to be called of men, *Rabbi, rabbi,* but Christ calls them *serpents* and *vipers;* for he gives men their true characters, and delights to put contempt upon the proud.

Secondly, Their doom. He represents their condition as very sad, and in a manner desperate; *How can ye escape the damnation of hell?* Christ himself preached hell and damnation, for which his ministers have often been reproached by those that care not to hear of it. Note, 1. The damnation of hell will be the fearful end of all impenitent sinners. This doom coming from Christ, was more terrible than coming from all the prophets and ministers that ever were, for he is the Judge, into whose hands the keys of hell and death are put, and his saying they were damned, made them so. 2. There is a way of escaping this damnation, this is implied here; some are *delivered from the wrath to come.* 3. Of all sinners, those who are of the spirit of the scribes and Pharisees, are least likely to escape this damnation; for repentance and faith are necessary to that escape; and how will *they* be

brought to these, who are so conceited of themselves, and so prejudiced against Christ and his gospel, as they were? How could *they* be healed and saved, who could not bear to have their wound searched, nor the balm of Gilead applied to it? Publicans and harlots, who were sensible of their disease and applied themselves to the Physician, were more likely to escape the damnation of hell than those who, though they were in the high road to it, were confident they were in the way to heaven.

Verses 34–39

We have left the blind leaders fallen into the ditch, under Christ's sentence, into the damnation of hell; let us see what will become of the blind followers, of the body of the Jewish church, and particularly Jerusalem.

I. Jesus Christ designs yet to try them with the means of grace; *I send unto you prophets, and wise men, and scribes.* The connection is strange; *"You are a generation of vipers,* not likely to *escape the damnation of hell;"* one would think it should follow, "Therefore you shall never have a prophet sent to you any more;" but no, *"Therefore I will send unto you prophets,* to see if you will yet at length be wrought upon, or else to leave you inexcusable, and to justify God in your ruin." It is therefore ushered in with a note of admiration, behold! Observe,

1. It is Christ that sends them; *I send.* By this he avows himself to be God, having power to gift and commission prophets. It is an act of kingly office; he sends them as ambassadors to treat with us about the concerns of our souls. After his resurrection, he made this word good, when he said, *So send I you,* Jn. 20:21. Though now he appeared mean, yet he was entrusted with this great authority.

2. He sends them to the Jews first; "I send them to *you."* They began at Jerusalem; and, wherever they went, they observed this rule, to make the first tender of gospel grace *to the Jews,* Acts 13:46.

3. Those he sends are called *prophets, wise men,* and *scribes,* Old-Testament names for New-Testament officers; to show that the ministers sent to them now should not be inferior to the prophets of the Old Testament, to Solomon the wise, or Ezra the scribe. The extraordinary ministers, who in the first ages were divinely inspired, were as the prophets commissioned immediately from heaven; the ordinary settled ministers, who were then, and continue in the church still, and will do to the end of time, are as the wise men and scribes, to guide and instruct the people in the things of God. Or, we may take the apostles and evangelists for the prophets and wise men, and the pastors and teachers for the scribes, *instructed to the kingdom of heaven* (*ch.* 13:52); for the office of a scribe was honourable till the men dishonoured it.

II. He foresees and foretels the ill usage that his messengers would meet with among them; *"Some of them ye shall kill and crucify,* and yet I will send them." Christ knows beforehand how ill his servants will be treated, and yet sends them, and appoints them their measure of sufferings; yet he loves them never the less for his thus exposing them, for he designs to glorify himself by their sufferings, and them after them; he will counter-balance them, though not prevent them. Observe,

1. The cruelty of these persecutors; *Ye shall kill and crucify them.* It is no less than the blood, the life-blood, that they thirst after; their lust is not satisfied with any thing short of their destruction, Ex. 15:9. They killed the two James's, crucified Simon the son of Cleophas, and scourged Peter and John; thus did the members partake of the sufferings of the Head, he was killed and crucified, and so were they. Christians must expect to resist unto blood.

2. Their unwearied industry; *Ye shall persecute them from city to city.* As the apostles went from city to city, to preach the gospel, the Jews dodged them, and haunted them, and stirred up persecution against them, Acts 14:19; 17:13. They that *did not believe in Judea* were more bitter enemies to the gospel than any other unbelievers, Rom. 15:31.

3. The pretence of religion in this; they scourged them in their synagogues, their place of worship, where they kept their ecclesiastical courts; so that they did it as a piece of service to the church; cast them out, and said, *Let the Lord be glorified,* Isa. 66:5; Jn. 16:2.

III. He imputes the sin of their fathers to them, because they imitated it; *That upon you may come all the righteous blood shed upon the earth, v.* 35, 36. Though God bear long with a persecuting generation, he will not bear always; and patience abused, turns into the greatest wrath. The longer sinners have been heaping up treasures of wickedness, the deeper and fuller will the treasures of wrath be; and the breaking of them up will be like breaking up the fountains of the great deep.

Observe, 1. The extent of this imputation; it takes in *all the righteous blood shed upon the earth,* that is, the blood shed for righteousness' sake, which has all been laid up in God's treasury, and not a drop of it lost, for *it is precious.* Ps. 72:14. He dates the account *from the blood of righteous Abel,* thence this *aera martyrum — age of martyrs —* commences; he is called *righteous* Abel, for he obtained witness from heaven, that he was *righteous, God testifying of his gifts.* How early did martyrdom come into the world! The first that died, died for his religion, and, *being dead, he yet speaketh.* His blood not only cried against Cain, but continues to cry against all that walk in the way of Cain, and hate and persecute their brother, *because their works are righteous.* He extends it *to the blood of Zacharias, the son of Barachias* (*v.* 36), not Zecharias the prophet (as some would have it), though he was *the son of Barachias* (Zec. 1:1.) nor Zecharias the father of John Baptist, as others say; but, as is most probable, *Zechariah the son of Jehoiada,* who was *slain in the court of the Lord's house,* 2 Chr. 24:20, 21. His father is called *Barachias,* which signifies much the same with Jehoiada; and it was usual among the Jews for the same person to have two names; *whom ye slew,* ye of this nation, though not of this generation. This is specified, because the requiring of that is particularly spoken of (2 Chr. 24:22), as that of Abel's is. The Jews imagined that the captivity had sufficiently atoned for the guilt; but Christ lets them know that it was not yet fully accounted for, but remained upon the score. And some think that this is mentioned with a prophetical hint, for there was one Zecharias, the son of Baruch, whom Josephus speaks of (*War* 4.335), who was a just and good man, who was killed in the temple a little before it was destroyed by the Romans. Archbishop Tillotson thinks that Christ both alludes to the history of the former Zecharias in *Chronicles,* and foretels the death of this latter in Josephus. Though the latter was not yet slain, yet, before this destruction comes, it would be true that they had slain him; so that all shall be put together from first to last.

2. The effect of it; *All these things shall come;* all the guilt of this blood, all the punishment of it, it shall *all come upon this generation.* The misery and ruin that are coming upon them, shall be so very great, that, though, considering the evil of their own sins, it was less that even those deserved; yet, comparing it with other judgments, it will seem to be a general reckoning for all the wickedness of their ancestors, especially their persecutions, to all which God declared this ruin to have special reference and relation. The destruction shall be so dreadful, as if God had once for all arraigned them for all the righteous blood shed in the world. It shall *come upon this generation;* which intimates, that it shall come quickly; some here shall live to see it. Note, The sorer and nearer the punishment of sin is, the louder is the call to repentance and reformation.

IV. He laments the wickedness of Jerusalem, and justly upbraids them with the many kind offers he had made them, *v.* 37. See with what concern he speaks of that city; *O Jerusalem, Jerusalem!* The repetition is emphatical, and bespeaks abundance of commiseration. A day or two before Christ had wept over Jerusalem, now he sighed and groaned over it. Jerusalem, *the vision of peace* (so it signifies), must now be the seat of war and confusion. Jerusalem, that had been *the joy of the whole earth,* must now be *a hissing, and an astonishment, and a by-word;* Jerusalem, that has been *a city compact together,* shall now be shattered and ruined by its own intestine broils. Jerusalem, *the place that God has chosen to put his name there,* shall now be abandoned to the spoil and the robbers, Lam. 1:1, 4:1. But wherefore will the Lord do all this to Jerusalem? Why? *Jerusalem hath grievously sinned,* Lam. 1:8.

1. She persecuted God's messengers; *Thou that killest the prophets, and stonest them that are sent unto thee.* This sin is especially charged upon Jerusalem; because there the Sanhedrim, or great council, sat, who took cognizance of church matters, and therefore a prophet could not perish but in Jerusalem, Lu. 13:33. It is true, they had not now a power to put any man to death, but they killed the prophets in popular tumults, mobbed them, as Stephen, and put the Roman powers on to kill them. At Jerusalem, where the gospel was first preached, it was first persecuted (Acts 8:1), and that place was the head-quarters of the persecutors; thence warrants were issued out to other cities, and thither the saints were brought bound, Acts 9:2. *Thou stonest them:* that was a capital punishment, in use only among the Jews. By the law, false prophets and seducers were to *be stoned* (Deu. 13:10), under colour of which law, they put the true prophets to death. Note, It has often been the artifice of Satan, to turn that artillery against the church, which was originally planted in the defence of it. Brand the true prophets as seducers, and the true professors of religion as heretics and schismatics, and then it will be easy to persecute them. There was abundance of other wickedness in Jerusalem; but this was the sin that made the loudest cry, and which God had an eye to more than any other, in bringing that ruin upon them, as 2 Ki. 24:4; 2 Chr. 36:16. Observe, Christ speaks in the present tense; *Thou killest, and stonest;* for all they had done, and all they would do, was present to Christ's notice.

2. She refused and rejected Christ, and gospel offers. The former was a sin *without* remedy, this *against* the remedy. Here is, (1.) The wonderful grace and favour of Jesus Christ toward them; *How often would I have gathered thy children together, as a hen gathers her chickens under her wings!* Thus kind and condescending are the offers of gospel grace, even to Jerusalem's children, bad as she is, the inhabitants, the little ones not excepted. [1.] The favour proposed was the gathering of them. Christ's design is to gather poor souls, gather them in from their wanderings, gather them home to himself, as the Centre of unity; for *to him must the gathering of the people be.* He would have taken the whole body of the Jewish nation into the church, and so gathered them all (as the Jews used to speak of proselytes) *under the wings of the Divine Majesty.* It is here illustrated by a humble similitude; *as a hen* clucks *her chickens together.* Christ would have gathered them, *First,* With such a tenderness of affection as the hen does, which has, by instinct, a peculiar concern for her young ones. Christ's gathering of souls, comes from his love, Jer. 31:3. *Secondly,* For the same end. *The hen gathered her chickens under her wings,* for protection and safety, and for warmth and comfort; poor souls have in Christ both refuge and refreshment. The chickens naturally run to the hen for shelter, when they are threatened by the birds of prey; perhaps Christ refers to that promise (Ps. 91:4), *He shall cover thee with his feathers.* There is *healing under Christ's wings* (Mal. 4:2); that is more than the hen has for her chickens.

[2.] The forwardness of Christ to confer this favour. His offers are, *First,* Very free; *I would have done it.* Jesus Christ is truly willing to receive and save poor souls that come to him. He desires not their ruin, he delights in their repentance. *Secondly,* Very frequent; *How often!* Christ often came up to Jerusalem, preached, and wrought miracles there; and the meaning of all this, was, he would have gathered them. He keeps account how often his calls have been repeated. As often as we have heard the sound of the gospel, as often as we have felt the strivings of the Spirit, so often Christ would have gathered us.

[3.] Their wilful refusal of this grace and favour; *Ye would not.* How emphatically is their obstinacy opposed to Christ's mercy! I would, and *ye would not.* He was willing to save them, but they were not willing to be saved by him. Note, It is wholly owing to the wicked wills of sinners, that they are not gathered under the wings of the Lord Jesus. They did not like the terms upon which Christ proposed to gather them; they loved their sins, and yet trusted to their righteousness; they would not submit either to the grace of Christ or to his government, and so the bargain broke off.

V. He reads Jerusalem's doom (*v.* 38, 39); *Therefore behold your house is left unto you desolate.* Both the city and the temple, God's house and their own, all shall be laid waste. But it is especially meant of the temple, which they boasted of, and trusted to; that holy mountain because of which they were so haughty. Note, they that will not be gathered by the love and grace of Christ shall be consumed and scattered by his wrath; *I would, and you would not. Israel would none of me, so I gave them up,* Ps. 81:11, 12.

1. Their house shall be *deserted; It is left unto you.* Christ was now departing from the temple, and never came into it again, but by this word abandoned it to ruin. They doated on it, would have it to themselves; Christ must have no room or interest there. "Well," saith Christ, "it is left to you; take it, and make your best of it; I will never have any thing more to do with it." They had made it *a house of merchandise, and a den of thieves,* and so it is left to them. Not long after this, the voice was heard in the temple, "Let us depart hence." When Christ went, *Ichabod, the glory departed.* Their city also was left to them, destitute of God's presence and grace; he was no longer *a wall of fire about them,* nor *the glory in the midst of them.*

2. It shall be *desolate; It is left unto you desolate;* it is left *erēmos — a wilderness.* (1.) It was immediately, when Christ left it, in the eyes of all that understood themselves, a very dismal melancholy place. Christ's departure makes the best furnished, best replenished place a wilderness, though it be the temple, the chief place of concourse; for what comfort can there be where Christ is not? Though there may be a crowd of other contentments, yet, if Christ's special spiritual presence be withdrawn, that soul, that place, is *become a wilderness, a land of darkness, as darkness itself.* This comes of men's rejecting Christ, and driving him away from them. (2.) It was, not long after, destroyed and ruined, and *not one stone left upon another.* The lot of Jerusalem's enemies will now become Jerusalem's lot, *to be made of a city a heap, of a defenced city a ruin* (Isa. 25:2), *a lofty city laid low, even to the ground,* Isa. 26:5. The temple, that holy and beautiful house, became desolate. When God goes out, all enemies break in.

Lastly, Here is the final farewell that Christ took of them and their temple; *Ye shall not see me henceforth, till ye shall say, Blessed is he that cometh.* This bespeaks,

1. His departure from them. The time was at hand, when *he should leave the world, to go to his Father,* and be seen no more. *After his resurrection, he was seen only by a few chosen witnesses,* and they saw him not long, but he soon removed to the invisible world, and there will be *till the time of the restitution of all things,* when his welcome at his first coming will be repeated with loud acclamations; *Blessed is he that cometh in the name of the Lord.* Christ will not be seen again till he *come in the clouds, and every eye shall see him* (Rev. 1:7); and then, even they, who, when time was, rejected and pierced him, will be glad to come in among his adorers; then every knee shall bow to him, even those that had bowed to Baal; and even the workers of iniquity will then cry, *Lord, Lord,* and will own, when his wrath is kindled, that *blessed are all they that put their trust in him.* Would we have our lot in that day with those that say, *Blessed is he that cometh?* let us be with them now, with them that truly worship, and truly welcome, Jesus Christ.

2. Their continued blindness and obstinacy; *Ye shall not see me,* that is, not see me to be the Messiah (for otherwise they did see him upon the cross), not see the light of the truth concerning me, nor *the things that belong to your peace, till ye shall say, Blessed is he that cometh.* They will never be convinced, till Christ's second coming convince them, when it will be too late to make an interest in him, and nothing will remain *but a fearful looking for of judgment.* Note, (1.) Wilful blindness is often punished with judicial blindness. If they *will* not see, they *shall* not see. With this word he concludes his public preaching. *After his resurrection,* which was *the sign of the prophet Jonas,* they should have no other sign given them, till they should *see the sign of the Son of man, ch.* 24:30. (2.) When *the Lord comes with ten thousand of his saints,* he will convince all, and will force acknowledgments from the proudest of his enemies, of his being the Messiah, and even *they shall be found liars to him.* They that would not now come at his call, shall then be forced to depart with his curse. The chief priests and scribes were displeased with the children for crying *hosanna* to Christ; but the day is coming, when proud persecutors would gladly be found in the condition of the meanest and poorest they now trample upon. They who now reproach and ridicule the hosannas of the saints will be of another mind shortly; it were therefore better to be of that mind now. Some make this to refer to the conversion of the Jews to the faith of Christ; then they shall see him, and own him, and *say, Blessed is he that cometh;* but it seems rather to look further, for the complete manifestation of Christ, and conviction of sinners, are reserved to be the glory of the last day.

CHAPTER 24

Christ's preaching was mostly practical; but, in this chapter, we have a prophetical discourse, a prediction of things to come; such however as had a practical tendency, and was intended, not to gratify the curiosity of his disciples, but to guide their consciences and conversations, and it is therefore concluded with a practical application. The church has always had particular prophecies, besides general promises, both for direction and for encouragement to believers; but it is observable, Christ preached this prophetical sermon in the close of his ministry, as the Apocalypse is the last book of the New Testament, and the prophetical books of the Old Testament are placed last, to intimate to us, that we must be well grounded in plain truths and duties, and those must first be well digested, before we dive into those things that are dark and difficult; many run themselves into confusion by beginning their Bible at the wrong end. Now, in this chapter, we have, I. The occasion of this discourse (v. 1–3). II. The discourse itself, in which we have, 1. The prophecy of divers events, especially referring to the destruction of Jerusalem, and the utter ruin of the Jewish church and nation, which were not hastening on, and were completed about forty years after; the prefaces to that destruction, the concomitants and consequences of it; yet looking further, to Christ's coming at the end of time, and the consummation of all things, of which that was a type and figure (v. 4–31). 2. The practical application of this prophecy for the awakening and quickening of his disciples to prepare for these great and awful things (v. 32–51).

Verses 1–3

Here is,

I. Christ's quitting *the temple,* and his public work there. He had said, in the close of the foregoing chapter, *Your house is left unto you desolate;* and here he made his words good; *He went out, and departed from the temple.* The manner of expression is observable; he not only went out of the temple, but departed from it, took his final farewell of it; he departed from it, never to return to it any more; and then immediately follows a prediction of its ruin. Note, That house is left desolate indeed, which Christ leaves. *Woe unto them when I depart,* Hos. 9:12; Jer. 6:8. It was now time to groan out their *Ichabod, The glory is departed, their defence is departed.* Three days after this, the veil of the temple was rent; when Christ left it, all became *common and unclean;* but Christ departed not till they drove him away; did not reject them, till they first rejected him.

II. His private discourse with his disciples; he left the temple, but he did not leave the twelve, who were the seed of the gospel church, which the casting off of the Jews was the enriching of. When he left the temple, his disciples left it too, and came to him. Note, It is good being where Christ is, and leaving that which he leaves. They came to him, to be instructed in private, when his public preaching was over; for *the secret of the Lord is with them that fear him.* He had spoken of the destruction of the Jewish church to the multitude in parables, which here, as usual, he explains to his disciples. Observe,

1. *His disciples came to him, to show him the buildings of the temple,* It was a stately and beautiful structure, one of the wonders of the world; no cost was spared, no art left untried, to make it sumptuous. Though it came short of Solomon's temple, and *its beginning was small,* yet *its latter end did greatly increase.* It was richly furnished with gifts and offerings, to which there were continual additions made. They showed Christ these things, and desired him to take notice of them, either,

(1.) As being greatly pleased with them themselves, and expecting he should be so too. They had lived mostly in Galilee, at a distance from the temple, had seldom seen it, and therefore were the more struck with admiration at it, and thought he should admire as much as they did *all this glory* (Gen. 31:1); and they would have him divert himself (after his preaching, and from his sorrow which they saw him perhaps almost overwhelmed with) with looking about him. Note, Even good men are apt to be too much enamoured with outward pomp and gaiety, and to overvalue it, even in the things of God; whereas we should be, as Christ was, dead to it, and look upon it with contempt. The temple was indeed glorious, but, [1.] Its glory was sullied and stained with the sin of the priests and people; that wicked doctrine of the Pharisees, which preferred the gold before the temple that sanctified it, was enough to deface the beauty of all the ornaments of the temple. [2.] Its glory was eclipsed and outdone by the presence of Christ in it, who was *the glory of this latter house* (Hag. 2:9), so that the buildings had no glory, in comparison with that glory which excelled.

Or, (2.) As grieving that this house should be left desolate; they showed him the buildings, as if they would move him to reverse the sentence; "Lord, let not this holy and beautiful house, where our fathers praised thee, be made a desolation." They forgot how many providences, concerning Solomon's temple, had manifested how little God cared for that outward glory which they had so much admired, when the people were wicked, 2 Chr. 7:21. *This house, which is high,*

sin will bring low. Christ had lately looked upon *the precious souls, and wept for them,* Lu. 19:41. The disciples look upon the pompous buildings, and are ready to weep for them. In this, as in other things, *his thoughts are not like ours.* It was weakness, and meanness of spirit, in the disciples, to be so fond of fine buildings; it was a childish thing. *Animo magno nihil magnum — To a great mind nothing is great.* Seneca.

2. Christ, hereupon, foretels the utter ruin and destruction that were coming upon this place, v. 2. Note, A believing foresight of the defacing of all worldly glory will help to take us off from admiring it, and overvaluing it. The most beautiful body will be shortly worms' meat, and the most beautiful building a ruinous heap. And shall we then set our eyes upon that which so soon is not, and look upon that with so much admiration which ere long we shall certainly look upon with so much contempt? *See ye not all these things?* They would have Christ look upon them, and be as much in love with them as they were; he would have them look upon them, and be as dead to them as he was. There is such a sight of these things as will do us good; so to see them as to see through them and see to the end of them.

Christ, instead of reversing the decree, ratifies it; *Verily, I say unto you, there shall not be left one stone upon another.*

(1.) He speaks of it as a certain ruin; "*I say unto you. I, that know what I say, and know how to make good what I say; take my word for it,* it shall be so; *I, the Amen, the true Witness, say it to you.*" All judgment being committed to the Son, the threatenings, as well as the promises, are all *yea, and amen,* in him. Heb. 6:17, 18.

(2.) He speaks of it as an utter ruin. The temple shall not only be stripped, and plundered, and defaced, but utterly demolished and laid waste; *Not one stone shall be left upon another.* Notice is taken, in the *building* of the second temple, of the *laying of one stone upon another* (Hag. 2:15); and here, in the *ruin,* of *not leaving one stone upon another.* History tells us, that this was fulfilled in the latter; for though Titus, when he took the city, did all he could to preserve the temple, yet he could not restrain the enraged soldiers from destroying it utterly; and it was done to that degree, that Turnus Rufus ploughed up the ground on which it had stood: thus that scripture was fulfilled (Mic. 3:12), *Zion shall, for your sake, be ploughed as a field.* And afterward, in Julian the Apostate's time, when the Jews were encouraged by him to rebuild their temple, in opposition to the Christian religion, what remained of the ruins was quite pulled down, to level the ground for a new foundation; but the attempt was defeated by the miraculous eruption of fire out of the ground, which destroyed the foundation they laid, and frightened away the builders. Now this prediction of the final and irreparable ruin of the temple includes a prediction of the period of the Levitical priesthood and the ceremonial law.

3. The disciples, not disputing either the truth or the equity of this sentence, nor doubting of the accomplishment of it, enquire more particularly of the time when it should come to pass, and the signs of its approach, v. 3. Observe,

(1.) Where they made this enquiry; privately, *as he sat upon the mount of Olives;* probably, he was returning to Bethany, and there sat down by the way, to rest him; the mount of Olives directly faced the temple, and from thence he might have a full prospect of it at some distance; there he sat as a Judge upon the bench, the temple and city being before him as at the bar, and thus he passed sentence on them. We read (Eze. 11:23) of the removing of the glory of the Lord from the temple to the mountain; so Christ, the great Shechinah, here removes to this mountain.

(2.) What the enquiry itself was; *When shall these things be; and what shall be the sign of thy coming, and of the end of the world?* Here are three questions.

[1.] Some think, these questions do all point at one and the same thing — the destruction of the temple, and the period of the Jewish church and nation, which Christ had himself spoken of as his coming (ch. 16:28), and which would be the consummation of the age (for so it may be read), the finishing of that dispensation. Or, they thought the destruction of the temple must needs be the end of the world. If that house be laid waste, the world cannot stand; for the Rabbin used to say that the house of the sanctuary was one of the seven things for the sake of which the world was made; and they think, if so, the world will not survive the temple.

[2.] Others think their question, *When shall these things be?* refers to the destruction of Jerusalem, and the other two to the end of the world; or Christ's coming may refer to his

setting up his gospel kingdom, and the end of the world to the day of judgment. I rather incline to think that their question looked no further than the event Christ now foretold; but it appears by other passages, that they had very confused thoughts of future events; so that perhaps it is not possible to put any certain construction upon this question of theirs.

But Christ, in his answer, though he does not expressly rectify the mistakes of his disciples (that must be done by the pouring out of the Spirit), yet looks further than their question, and instructs his church, not only concerning the great events of that age, the destruction of Jerusalem, but concerning his second coming at the end of time, which here he insensibly slides into a discourse of, and of that it is plain he speaks in the next chapter, which is a continuation of this sermon.

Verses 4–31

The disciples had asked concerning the times, *When shall these things be?* Christ gives them no answer to that, after what number of days and years his prediction should be accomplished, for *it is not for us to know the times* (Acts 1:7); but they had asked, *What shall be the sign?* That question he answers fully, for we are concerned to *understand the signs of the times, ch.* 16:3. Now the prophecy primarily respects the events near at hand — the destruction of Jerusalem, the period of the Jewish church and state, the calling of the Gentiles, and the setting up of Christ's kingdom in the world; but as the prophecies of the Old Testament, which have an immediate reference to the affairs of the Jews and the revolutions of their state, under the figure of them do certainly look further, to the gospel church and the kingdom of the Messiah, and are so expounded in the New Testament, and such expressions are found in those predictions as are peculiar thereto and not applicable otherwise; so this prophecy, under the type of Jerusalem's destruction, looks as far forward as the general judgment; and, as is usual in prophecies, some passages are most applicable to the type, and others to the antitype; and toward the close, as usual, it points more particularly to the latter. It is observable, that what Christ here saith to his disciples tends more to engage their caution than to satisfy their curiosity; more to prepare them for the events that should happen than to give them a distinct idea of the events themselves. This is that good understanding of the time which we should all covet, thence to infer what Israel ought to do: and so this prophecy is of standing lasting use to the church, and will be so to the end of time; for *the thing that hath been, is that which shall be* (Eccl. 1:5, 6, 7, 9), and the series, connection, and presages, of events, are much the same still that they were then; so that upon the prophecy of this chapter, pointing at that event, moral prognostications may be made, and such constructions of the signs of the times as the wise man's heart will know how to improve.

I. Christ here foretels the going forth of deceivers; he begins with a caution, *Take heed that no man deceive you.* They expected to be told when these things should be, to be let into that secret; but this caution is a check to their curiosity, *"What is that to you?* Mind you your duty, follow me, and be not seduced from following me." Those that are most inquisitive concerning the secret things which belong not to them are most easily imposed upon by seducers, 2 Th. 2:3. The disciples, when they heard that the Jews, their most inveterate enemies, should be destroyed, might be in danger of falling into security; "Nay," saith Christ, "you are more exposed other ways." Seducers are more dangerous enemies to the church than persecutors.

Three times in this discourse he mentions the appearing of *false prophets,* which was, 1. A presage of Jerusalem's ruin. Justly were they who killed the true prophets, left to be ensnared by false prophets; and they who crucified the true Messiah, left to be deceived and broken by false Christs and pretended Messiahs. The appearing of these was the occasion of dividing that people into parties and factions, which made their ruin the more easy and speedy; and the sin of the many that were led aside by them, helped to fill the measure. 2. It was a trial to the disciples of Christ, and therefore agreeable to their state of probation, *that they which are perfect, may be made manifest.*

Now concerning these deceivers, observe here,

(1.) The pretences they should come under. Satan acts most mischievously, when he appears as an angel of light: the colour of the greatest good is often the cover of the greatest evil.

[1.] There should appear *false prophets* (*v.* 11–24); the deceivers would pretend to divine inspiration, an immediate mission, and a spirit of prophecy, when it was all a lie. Such they had been formerly (Jer. 23:16; Eze. 13:6), as was foretold, Deu. 13:3. Some think, the seducers here pointed to were such as had been settled teachers in the church, and had gained reputation as such, but afterward betrayed the truth they had taught, and revolted to error; and from such the danger is the greater, because least suspected. One false traitor in the garrison may do more mischief than a thousand avowed enemies without.

[2.] There should appear *false Christs, coming in Christ's name* (*v.* 5), assuming to themselves the name peculiar to him, and saying, *I am Christ, pseudo-christs, v.* 24. There was at that time a general expectation of the appearing of the Messiah; they spoke of him; as *he that should come;* but when he did come, the body of the nation rejected him; which those who were ambitious of making themselves a name, took advantage of, and set up for Christ. Josephus speaks of several such impostors between this and the destruction of Jerusalem; one Theudas, that was defeated by Cospius Fadus; another by Felix, another by Festus. Dosetheus said he was the Christ foretold by Moses. *Origen adversus Celsum.* See Acts 5:36, 37. Simon Magus pretended to be *the great power of God,* Acts 8:10. In after-ages there have been such pretenders; one about a hundred years after Christ, that called himself *Bar-cochobas — The son of a star,* but proved *Bar-cosba — The son of a lie.* About fifty years ago Sabbati-Levi set up for a Messiah in the Turkish empire, and was greatly caressed by the Jews; but in a short time *his folly was made manifest.* See Sir Paul Rycaut's *History.* The popish religion doth, in effect, set up a false Christ; the Pope comes, in Christ's name, as his vicar, but invades and usurps all his offices, and so is a rival with him, and, as such, an enemy to him, a deceiver, and an antichrist.

[3.] These false Christs and false prophets would have their agents and emissaries busy in all places to draw people in to them. *v.* 23. *Then* when public troubles are great and threatening, and people will be catching at any thing that looks like deliverance, then Satan will take the advantage of imposing on them; they will say, *Lo, here is a Christ, or there* is one; but do not mind them: the true Christ did not strive, nor cry; nor was it said of him, *Lo, hère! or Lo, there!* (Lu. 17:21), therefore if any man say so concerning him, look upon it as a temptation. The hermits, who place religion in a monastical life, say, *He is in the desert;* the priests, who made the consecrated wafer to be Christ, say, "He is *en tois tameiois — in the cupboards, in the secret chambers:* lo, he is in this shrine, in that image." Thus some appropriate Christ's spiritual presence to one party or persuasion, as if they had the monopoly of Christ and Christianity; and the kingdom of Christ must stand and fall, must live and die, with them; "Lo, he is in this church, in that council:" whereas Christ is All in all, not here or there, but meets his people with a blessing *in every place where he records his name.*

(2.) The proof they should offer for the making good of these pretences; *They shall show great signs and wonders* (*v.* 24), not true miracles, those are a divine seal, and with those the doctrine of Christ stands confirmed; and therefore if any offer to draw us from that by signs and wonders, we must have recourse to that rule given of old (Deu. 13:1–3), *If the sign or wonder come to pass,* yet follow not him that would draw you *to serve other gods,* or believe in other Christs, *for the Lord your God proveth you.* But these were *lying wonders* (2 Th. 2:9), wrought by Satan (God permitting him), who is *the prince of the power of the air.* It is not said, *They shall work miracles,* but, *They shall show great signs;* they are but a show; either they impose upon men's credulity by false narratives, or deceive their senses by tricks of legerdemain, or arts of divination, as the magicians of Egypt by their enchantments.

(3.) The success they should have in these attempts,

[1.] *They shall deceive many* (*v.* 5), and again, *v.* 11. Note, The devil and his instruments may prevail far in deceiving poor souls; few find the strait gate, but many are drawn into the broad way; many will be imposed upon by their signs and wonders, and many drawn in by the hopes of deliverance from their oppressions. Note, Neither miracles nor multitudes are certain signs of a true church; for *all the world wonders after the beast,* Rev. 13:3.

[2.] *They shall deceive, if it were possible, the very elect, v.* 24. This bespeaks, *First,* The strength of the delusion; it is such as many shall be carried away by (so strong shall the stream be), even those that were thought to stand fast. Men's knowledge, gifts, learning, eminent station, and long profession, will not secure them; but, notwithstanding these, many will be deceived; nothing but the almighty grace of God, pursuant to his eternal purpose, will be a protection. *Secondly,* The safety of the elect in the midst of this danger, which is taken for granted in that parenthesis, *If it were possible,* plainly implying that it is not possible, for they are *kept by the power of God,* that *the purpose of God, according to the election, may stand.* It is possible for those that have been enlightened to fall away (Heb. 6:4, 5, 6), but not for those that were elected. If God's chosen ones should be deceived, God's choice would be defeated, which is not to be imagined, *for whom he did predestinate, he called, justified, and glorified,* Rom. 8:30. They were given to Christ; and of all that were given to him, he will lose none, Jn. 10:28. Grotius will have this to be meant of the great difficulty of drawing the primitive Christians from their religion, and quotes it as used proverbially by Galen; when he would express a thing very difficult and morally impossible, he saith, "You may sooner draw away a Christian from Christ."

(4.) The repeated cautions which our Saviour gives to his disciples to stand upon their guard against them; *therefore* he gave them warning, that they might watch (*v.* 25); *Behold, I have told you before.* He that is told before where he will be assaulted, may save himself, as the king of Israel did, 2 Ki. 6:9, 10. Note, Christ's warnings are designed to engage our watchfulness; and though the elect shall be preserved from delusion, yet they shall be preserved by the use of appointed means, and a due regard to the cautions of the word; we are kept through faith, faith in Christ's word, which he has told us before.

[1.] We must not believe those who say, *Lo, here is Christ;* or, *Lo, he is there, v.* 23. We believe that the true Christ is at the right hand of God, and that his spiritual presence is *where two or three are gathered together in his name;* believe not those therefore who would draw you off from a Christ in heaven, by telling you he is any where on earth; or draw you off from the catholic church on earth, by telling you he is here, or he is there; believe it not. Note, There is not a greater enemy to true faith than vain credulity. The simple believeth every word, and runs after every cry. *Memnēso apistein — Beware of believing.*

[2.] We must not go forth after those that say, *He is in the desert,* or, *He is in the secret chambers, v.* 26. We must not hearken to every empiric and pretender, nor follow every one that puts up the finger to point us to a new Christ, and a new gospel; "Go not forth, for if you do, you are in danger of being taken by them; therefore keep out of harm's way, *be not carried about with every wind;* many a man's vain curiosity to go forth hath led him into a fatal apostasy; your strength at such a time is to sit still, to have the heart established with grace."

II. He foretels wars and great commotions among the nations, *v.* 6, 7. When Christ was born, there was a universal peace in the empire, the temple of Janus was shut; but *think not that Christ came to send,* or continue such a *peace* (Lu. 12:51); no, his city and his wall are to be built even in troublesome times, and even wars shall forward his work. From the time that the Jews rejected Christ, and he *left their house desolate, the sword did never depart from their house, the sword of the Lord* was never quiet, because he had given it a charge against a hypocritical nation and the people of his wrath, and by it brought ruin upon them.

Here is, 1. A prediction of the event of the day; You will now shortly *hear of wars, and rumours of wars.* When wars are, they will be heard; for *every battle of the warrior is with confused noise,* Isa. 9:5. See how terrible it is (Jer. 4:19), *Thou hast heard, O my soul, the alarm of war!* Even the quiet in the land, and the least inquisitive after new things, cannot but hear the rumours of war. See what comes of refusing the gospel! Those that will not hear the messengers of peace, shall be made to hear the messengers of war. God has a sword ready to avenge the quarrel of his covenant, his new covenant. *Nation shall rise up against nation,* that is, one part or province of the Jewish nation against another, one city against another (2 Chr. 15:5, 6); and in the same province and city one party or faction shall rise up against another, so that they shall be devoured by, and dashed in pieces against one another, Isa. 9:19–21.

2. A prescription of the duty of the day; *See that ye be not troubled.* Is it possible to hear such sad news, and not be troubled? Yet, where the heart is fixed, trusting in God, it is kept in peace, and is not afraid, no not of the evil tidings of wars, and rumours of wars; no not the noise of *Arm, arm. Be not troubled; Mē throeithe — Be not put into confusion or commotion;* not put into throes, as a woman with child by a fright; *see that ye be not orate.* Note, There is need of constant care and watchfulness to keep trouble from the heart when there are wars abroad; and it is against the mind of Christ, that his people should have troubled hearts even in troublous times.

We must not be troubled, for two reasons.

(1.) Because we are bid to expect this: the Jews must be punished, ruin must be brought upon them; by this the justice of God and the honour of the Redeemer must be asserted; and therefore *all those things must come to pass;* the word is gone out of God's mouth, and it shall be accomplished in its season. Note, The consideration of the unchangeableness of the divine counsels, which govern all events, should compose and quiet our spirits, whatever happens. God is but performing the thing that is appointed for us, and our inordinate trouble is an interpretative quarrel with that appointment. Let us therefore acquiesce, because *these things must come to pass;* not only *necessitate decreti — as the product of the divine counsel,* but *necessitate medii — as a means in order to a further end.* The old house must be taken down (though it cannot be done without noise, and dust, and danger), ere the new fabric can be erected: the things that are shaken (and ill shaken they were) *must be removed, that the things which cannot be shaken may remain,* Heb. 12:27.

(2.) Because we are still to expect worse; *The end is not yet;* the end of time is not, and, while time lasts, we must expect trouble, and that the end of one affliction will be but the beginning of another; or, "The end of these troubles is not yet; there must be more judgments that one made use of to bring down the Jewish power; more vials of wrath must yet be poured out; there is but one woe past, more woes are yet to come, more arrows are yet to be spent upon them out of God's quiver; therefore be not troubled, do not give way to fear and trouble, sink not under the present burthen, but rather gather in all the strength and spirit you have, to encounter what is yet before you. Be not troubled to hear of wars and rumours of wars; for then what will become of you when the famines and pestilences come?" If it be to us a vexation but to *understand the report* (Isa. 28:19), what will it be to feel the stroke when it *toucheth the bone and the flesh?* If running with the footmen weary us, how shall we contend with horses? And if we be frightened at a little brook in our way, *what shall we do in the swellings of Jordan?* Jer. 12:5.

III. He foretels other judgments more immediately sent of God — *famines, pestilences, and earthquakes.* Famine is often the effect of war, and pestilence of famine. These were the three judgments which David was to choose one out of; and he was in a great strait, for he knew not which was the worst: but what dreadful desolations will they make, when they all pour in together upon a people! Beside war (and that is enough), there shall be,

1. *Famine,* signified by the *black horse* under the *third seal,* Rev. 6:5, 6. We read of a famine in Judea, not long after Christ's time, which was very impoverishing (Acts 11:28); but the sorest famine was in Jerusalem during the siege. See Lam. 4:9, 10.

2. *Pestilences,* signified by the *pale horse, and death upon him,* and *the grave at his heels,* under the *fourth seal,* Rev. 6:7, 8. This destroys without distinction, and in a little time lays heaps upon heaps.

3. *Earthquakes in divers places,* or from place to place, pursuing those that flee from them, as they did from the earthquake *in the days of Uzziah,* Zec. 14:5. Great desolations have sometimes been made by earthquakes, of late and formerly; they have been the death of many, and the terror of more. In the apocalyptic visions, it is observable, that earthquakes bode good, and no evil, to the church, Rev. 6:12. Compare Rev. 6:15; 11:12, 13, 19; 16:17–19. When God *shakes terribly the earth* (Isa. 2:21), it is to *shake the wicked out of it* (Job 38:13), and to introduce *the desire of all nations,* Hag. 2:6, 7. But here they are spoken of as dreadful judgments, and yet but *the beginning of sorrows, ōdinōn — of travailing pains,* quick, violent, yet tedious too. Note, When God judgeth, he will overcome; *when he begins* in wrath, *he will make* a full *end,* 1 Sa. 3:12. When we look forward to the eternity of misery that is before the obstinate refusers of Christ and

his gospel, we may truly say, concerning the greatest temporal judgments, "They are but the beginning of sorrows; bad as things are with them, there are worse behind."

IV. He foretells the persecution of his own people and ministers, and a general apostasy and decay in religion thereupon, *v.* 9, 10, 12. Observe,

1. The *cross* itself foretold, *v.* 9. Note, Of all future events we are as much concerned, though commonly as little desirous, to know of our own sufferings as of any thing else. *Then,* when famines and pestilences prevail, then they shall impute them to the Christians, and make that a pretence for persecuting them; *Christianos ad leones — Away with Christians to the lions.* Christ had told his disciples, when he first sent them out, what hard things they should suffer; but they had hitherto experienced little of it, and therefore he reminds them again, that the less they had suffered, the more there was behind to be filled up, Col. 1:24.

(1.) They shall be *afflicted* with bonds and imprisonments, *cruel mockings and scourgings,* as blessed Paul (2 Co. 11:23–25;) not killed outright, but *killed all the day long, in deaths often,* killed so as to feel themselves die, *made a spectacle to the world,* 1 Co. 4:9, 11.

(2.) They shall be *killed;* so cruel are the church's enemies, that nothing less will satisfy them than the blood of the saints, which they thirst after, suck, and shed, like water.

(3.) They shall be *hated of all nations for Christ's name's sake,* as he had told them before, *ch.* 10:22. The world was generally leavened with enmity and malignity to Christians: the Jews, though spiteful to the Heathen, were never persecuted by them as the Christians were; they were hated by the Jews that were dispersed among the nations, were the common butt of the world's malice. What shall we think of this world, when the best men had the worst usage in it? It is the cause that makes the martyr, and comforts him; it was for Christ's sake that they were thus hated; their professing and preaching his name incensed the nations so much against them; the devil, finding a fatal shock thereby given to his kingdom, and that his time was likely to be short, *came down, having great wrath.*

2. *The offence of the cross, v.* 10-12. Satan thus carries on his interest by force of arms, though Christ, at length, will bring glory to himself out of the sufferings of his people and ministers. Three ill effects of persecution are here foretold.

(1.) The *apostasy* of some. When the profession of Christianity begins to cost men dear, *then shall many be offended,* shall first fall out with, and then fall off from, their profession; they will begin to pick quarrels with their religion, sit loose to it, grow weary of it, and at length revolt from it. Note, [1.] It is no new thing (though it is a strange thing) for those that have known the way of righteousness, to turn aside out of it. Paul often complains of deserters, who began well, but something hindered them. They were with us, but went out from us, because never truly of us, 1 Jn. 2:19. We are told of it before. [2.] Suffering times are shaking times; and those fall in the storm, that stood in fair weather, like the *stony ground hearers, ch.* 13:21. Many will follow Christ in the sunshine, who will shift for themselves, and leave him to do so to, in the cloudy dark day. They like their religion while they can have it cheap, and sleep with it in a whole skin; but, if their profession cost them any thing, they quit it presently.

(2.) The *malignity* of others. When persecution is in fashion, envy, enmity, and malice, are strangely diffused into the minds of men by contagion: and charity, tenderness, and moderation, are looked upon as singularities, which make a man like a speckled bird. Then *they shall betray one another,* that is,"Those that have treacherously deserted their religion, shall hate and betray those who adhere to it, for whom they have pretended friendship." Apostates have commonly been the most bitter and violent persecutors. Note, Persecuting times are discovering times. Wolves in sheep's clothing will then throw off their disguise, and appear wolves: they shall *betray one another, and hate one another.* The times must needs be perilous, when treachery and hatred, two of the worst things that can be, because directly contrary to two of the best (truth and love), shall have the ascendant. This seems to refer to the barbarous treatment which the several contending factions among the Jews gave to one another; and justly were they who ate up God's people as they ate bread, left thus to bite and devour one another till they were *consumed one of another;* or, it may refer to the mischiefs done to Christ's disciples by those that were nearest to them, as *ch.* 10:21. *The brother shall deliver up the brother to death.*

(3.) The general *declining* and *cooling* of most, *v.* 12. In seducing times, when false prophets arise, in persecuting times, when the saints are hated, expect these two things,

[1.] The *abounding* of iniquity; though the world always lies in wickedness, yet there are some times in which it may be said, that *iniquity doth* in a special manner abound; as when it is more extensive than ordinary, as in the old world, when *all flesh had corrupted their way;* and when it is more *excessive* than ordinary, when *violence is risen up to a rod of wickedness* (Eze. 7:11), so that hell seems to be broke loose in blasphemies against God, and enmities to the saints.

[2.] The *abating* of love; this is the consequence of the former; *Because iniquity shall abound, the love of many shall wax cold.* Understand it in general of true serious godliness, which is all summed up in *love;* it is too common for professors of religion to grow cool in their profession, when the wicked are hot in their wickedness; as the church of Ephesus in bad times *left her first love,* Rev. 2:2–4. Or, it may be understood more particularly of brotherly love. When iniquity abounds, seducing iniquity, persecuting iniquity, this grace commonly waxes cold. Christians begin to be shy and suspicious one of another, affections are alienated, distances created, parties made, and so love comes to nothing. The devil is the accuser of the brethren, not only to their enemies, which makes persecuting iniquity abound, but one to another, which makes the love of many to wax cold.

This gives a melancholy prospect of the times, that there shall be such a great decay of love; but, *First,* It is of the love of *many,* not of *all.* In the worst of times, God has his remnant that hold fast their integrity, and retain their zeal, as in Elijah's days, when he thought himself left alone. *Secondly,* This love is grown cold, but not dead; it abates, but is not quite cast off. There is life in the root, which will show itself when the winter is past. The new nature may *wax cold,* but shall not *wax old,* for then it would decay and vanish away.

3. Comfort administered in reference to this offence of the cross, for the support of the Lord's people under it (*v.* 13); *He that endures to the end, shall be saved.* (1.) It is comfortable to those who wish well to the cause of Christ in general, that, though many are offended, yet some shall endure to the end. When we see so many drawing back, we are ready to fear that the cause of Christ will sink for want of supporters, and his name be left and forgotten for want of some to make profession of it; but even at this time there is *a remnant according to the election of grace,* Rom. 11:5. It is spoken of the same time that this prophecy has reference to; a remnant who are not of *them that draw back unto perdition,* but believe and persevere *to the saving of the soul;* they endure to the end, to the end of their lives, to the end of their present state of probation, or to the end of these suffering trying times, to the last encounter, though they should be called to resist unto blood. (2.) It is comfortable to those who do thus endure to the end, and suffer for their constancy, that they shall be saved. Perseverance wins the crown, through free grace, and shall wear it. *They shall be saved:* perhaps they may be delivered out of their troubles, and comfortably survive them in this world; but it is eternal salvation that is here intended. They that endure to the end of their days, shall then receive the end of their faith and hope, *even the salvation of their souls,* 1 Pt. 1:9; Rom. 2:7; Rev. 3:20. The crown of glory will make amends for all; and a believing regard to that will enable us to choose rather to die at a stake with the persecuted, than to live in a palace with the persecutors.

V. He foretells the preaching of the gospel in all the world (*v.* 14); *This gospel shall be preached, and then shall the end come.* Observe here, 1. It is called the *gospel of the kingdom,* because it reveals the kingdom of grace, which leads to the kingdom of glory; sets up Christ's kingdom in this world; and secures ours in the other world. 2. This gospel, sooner or later, is to be preached in all the world, to every creature, and all nations are to be discipled by it; for in it Christ is to be *Salvation to the ends of the earth;* for this end the gift of tongues was the *first-fruits of the Spirit.* 3. The gospel is preached *for a witness to all nations,* that is, a faithful declaration of the mind and will of God concerning the duty which God requires from man, and the recompence which man may expect from God. It is a *record* (1 Jn. 5:11), it is a *witness,* for those who believe, that they shall be saved, and against those who persist in unbelief, that they shall be damned. See Mk. 16:16. But how does this come in here?

(1.) It is intimated that the gospel should be, if not heard, yet at least heard of, throughout the then known world,

before the destruction of Jerusalem; that the Old-Testament church should not be quite dissolved till the New Testament was pretty well settled, had got considerable footing, and began to make some figure. Better is the face of a corrupt degenerate church than none at all. Within forty years after Christ's death, the *sound of the gospel was gone forth to the ends of the earth,* Rom. 10:18. St. Paul *fully preached the gospel from Jerusalem, and round about unto Illyricum;* and the other apostles were not idle. The persecuting of the saints at Jerusalem helped to disperse them, so that they *went every where, preaching the word,* Acts 8:1–4. And when the tidings of the Redeemer are sent over all parts of the world, then shall come the end of the Jewish state. Thus, that which they thought to prevent, by putting Christ to death, they thereby procured; all men *believed on him, and the Romans came, and took away their place and nation,* Jn. 11:48. Paul speaks of the gospel being *come to all the world, and preached to every creature,* Col. 1:6–23.

(2.) It is likewise intimated that even in times of temptation, trouble, and persecution, the gospel of the kingdom shall be preached and propagated, and shall force its way through the greatest opposition. Though the enemies of the church grow very *hot,* and many of her friends very *cool,* yet the gospel shall be preached. And even *then,* when many fall by the sword and by flame, and many do wickedly, and are corrupted by flatteries, yet then the people that do know their God, shall be strengthened to do the greatest exploits of all, in instructing many; see Dan. 11:32, 33; and see an instance, Phil. 1:12–14.

(3.) That which seems chiefly intended here, is, that the end of the world shall be *then,* and not till then, when the gospel has done its work in the world. The gospel shall be preached, and that work carried on, when you are dead; so that all nations, first or last, shall have either the enjoyment, or the refusal, of the gospel; and *then cometh the end,* when the kingdom *shall be delivered up to God, even the Father;* when the mystery of God shall be finished, the mystical body completed, and the nations either converted and saved, or convicted and silenced, by the gospel; *then shall the end come,* of which he had said before (*v.* 6, 7), *not yet,* not till those intermediate counsels be fulfilled. The world shall stand as long as any of God's chosen ones remain uncalled; but, when they are all gathered in, it will be set on fire immediately.

VI. He foretells more particularly the ruin that was coming upon the people of the Jews, their city, temple, and nation, *v.* 15, etc. Here he comes more closely to answer their questions concerning the desolation of the temple; and what he said here, would be of use to his disciples, both for their conduct and for their comfort, in reference to that great event; he describes the several steps of that calamity, such as are usual in war.

1. The Romans *setting up the abomination of desolation in the holy place, v.* 15. Now, (1.) Some understand by this an image, or statue, set up in the temple by some of the Roman governors, which was very offensive to the Jews, provoked them to rebel, and so brought the desolation upon them. The image of Jupiter Olympius, which Antiochus caused to be set upon the altar of God, is called *Bdelygma erēmōseōs — The abomination of desolation,* the very word here used by the historian, 1 Mac. 1:54. Since the captivity in Babylon, nothing was, nor could be, more distasteful to the Jews than an image in the holy place, as appeared by the mighty opposition they made when Caligula offered to set up his statue there, which had been of fatal consequence, if it had not been prevented, and the matter accommodated, by the conduct of Petronius; but Herod did set up an eagle over the temple-gate; and, some say, the statue of Titus was set up in the temple. (2.) Others choose to expound it by the parallel place (Lu. 21:20), *when ye shall see Jerusalem compassed with armies.* Jerusalem was the holy city, Canaan the holy land, the Mount Moriah, which lay about Jerusalem, for its nearness to the temple was, they thought in a particular manner holy ground; on the country lying round about Jerusalem the Roman army was encamped, that was the abomination that made desolate. The land of an enemy is said to be *the land which thou abhorrest* (Isa. 7:16); so an enemy's army to a weak but wilful people may well be called *the abomination.* Now this is said to be *spoken of by Daniel, the prophet,* who spoke more plainly of the Messiah and his kingdom than any of the Old-Testament prophets did. He speaks of an abomination making desolate, which should be set up

by Antiochus (Dan. 11:31; 12:11); but this that our Saviour refers to, we have in the message that the angel brought him (Dan. 9:27), of what should come at the end of seventy weeks, long after the former; *for the overspreading of abominations,* or, as the margin reads it, *with the abominable armies* (which comes home to the prophecy here), *he shall make it desolate.* Armies of idolaters may well be called *abominable armies;* and some think, the tumults, insurrections, and abominable factions and seditions, in the city and temple, may at least be taken in as part of the abomination making desolate. Christ refers them to that prophecy of Daniel, that they might see how the ruin of their city and temple was spoken of in the Old Testament, which would both confirm his prediction, and take off the odium of it. They might likewise from thence gather the time of it — soon after the cutting off of Messiah the prince; the sin that procured it — their rejecting him, and the certainty of it — *it is a desolation determined.* As Christ by his precepts confirmed the law, so by his predictions he confirmed the prophecies of the Old Testament, and it will be of good use to compare both together.

Reference being here had to a prophecy, which is commonly dark and obscure, Christ inserts this memorandum, "*Whoso readeth, let him understand;* whoso readeth the prophecy of Daniel, let him understand that it is to have its accomplishment now shortly in the desolations of Jerusalem." Note, Those that read the scriptures, should labour to understand the scriptures, else their reading is to little purpose; we cannot use that which we do not understand. See Jn. 5:39; Acts 8:30. The angel that delivered this prophecy to Daniel, stirred him up to *know and understand,* Dan. 9:25. And we must not despair of understanding even dark prophecies; the great New-Testament prophecy is called a *revelation,* not a *secret.* Now *things revealed belong to us,* and therefore must be humbly and diligently searched into. Or, *Let him understand,* not only the scriptures which speak of those things, but by the scriptures let him *understand the times,* 1 Chr. 12:32. Let him observe, and take notice; so some read it; let him be assured, that, notwithstanding the vain hopes with which the deluded people feed themselves, the abominable armies will make desolate.

2. The means of preservation which thinking men should betake themselves to (*v.* 16, 20); *Then let them which are in Judea, flee.* Then conclude there is no other way to help yourselves than by flying for the same. We may take this,

(1.) As a prediction of the ruin itself; that it should be irresistible; that it would be impossible for the stoutest hearts to make head against it, or contend with it, but they must have recourse to the last shift, getting out of the way. It bespeaks that which Jeremiah so much insisted upon, but in vain, when Jerusalem was besieged by the Chaldeans, that it would be to no purpose to resist, but that it was their wisdom to yield and capitulate; so Christ here, to show how fruitless it would be to stand it out, bids every one make the best of his way.

(2.) We may take it as a direction to the followers of Christ what to do, not to *say, A confederacy* with those who fought and warred against the Romans for the preservation of their city and nation, only that they might consume the wealth of both upon their lusts (for to this very affair, the struggles of the Jews against the Roman power, some years before their final overthrow, the apostle refers, Jam. 4:1-3); but let them acquiesce in the decree that was gone forth, and with all speed quit the city and country, as they would quit a falling house or a sinking ship, as Lot quitted Sodom, and Israel the tents of Dathan and Abiram; he shows them,

[1.] Whither they must flee — from Judea *to the mountains;* not the mountains round about Jerusalem, but those in the remote corners of the land, which would be some shelter to them, not so much by their strength as by their secrecy. Israel is said to be *scattered upon the mountains* (2 Chr. 18:16); and see Heb. 11:38. It would be safer among the lions' dens, and the mountains of the leopards, than among the seditious Jews or the enraged Romans. Note, In times of imminent peril and danger, it is not only lawful, but our duty, to seek our own preservation by all good and honest means; and if God opens a door of escape, we ought to make our escape, otherwise we do not trust God but tempt him. There may be a time when even *those that are in Judea,* where God is known, and his name is great, must *flee to the mountains;* and while we only go out of the way of danger, not out of the way of duty, we may trust God to provide *a dwelling for his outcasts,* Isa. 16:4, 5. In times of public calamity, when it is manifest that we cannot be serviceable at home and may be safe abroad, Providence calls us to make our escape. He that flees, may fight again.

[2.] What haste they must make, *v.* 17, 18. The life will be in danger, in imminent danger, the scourge will slay suddenly; and therefore he *that is on the house-top,* when the alarm comes, let him not *come down into the house,* to look after his effects there, but go the nearest way down, to make his escape; and so he that shall be *in the field,* will find it his wisest course to run immediately, and not return to fetch his clothes or the wealth of his house, for two reasons, *First,* Because the time which would be taken up in packing up his things, would delay his flight. Note, When death is at the door, delays are dangerous; it was the charge to Lot, *Look not behind thee.* Those that are convinced of the misery of a sinful state, and the ruin that attends them in that state, and, consequently, of the necessity of their fleeing to Christ, must take heed, lest, after all these convictions, they perish eternally by delays. *Secondly,* Because the carrying of his clothes, and his other movables and valuables with him, would but burthen him, and clog his flight. The Syrians, in their flight, *cast away their garments,* 2 Ki. 7:15. At such a time, we must be thankful *if our lives be given us for a prey,* though we can save nothing, Jer. 45:4, 5. *For the life is more than meat, ch.* 6:25. Those who carried off least, were safest in their flight. *Cantabit vacuus coram latrone viator — The pennyless traveller can lose nothing by robbers.* It was to his own disciples that Christ recommended this forgetfulness of their house and clothes, who had a habitation in heaven, treasure there, and durable clothing, which the enemy could not plunder them of. *Omnia mea mecum porto — I have all my property with me,* said Bias the philosopher in his flight, empty-handed. He that has grace in his heart carries his all along with him, when tripped of all.

Now those to whom Christ said this immediately, did not live to see this dismal day, none of all the twelve but John only; they needed not to be hidden in the mountains (Christ hid them in heaven), but they left the direction to their successors in profession, who pursued it, and it was of use to them; for when the Christians in Jerusalem and Judea saw the ruin coming on, they all retired to a town called *Pella,* on the other side Jordan, where they were safe; so that of the many thousands that perished in the destruction of Jerusalem, there was not so much as one Christian. See *Euseb. Eccl. Hist.* lib. 3, cap. 5. Thus *the prudent man foresees the evil, and hides himself,* Prov. 22:3; Heb. 11:7. This warning was not kept private. St. Matthew's gospel was published long before that destruction, so that others might have taken the advantage of it; but their perishing through their unbelief of this, was a figure of their eternal perishing through their unbelief of the warnings Christ gave concerning the wrath to come.

[3.] Whom it would go hard with at that time (*v.* 19); *Woe to them that are with child, and to them that give suck.* To this same event that saying of Christ at his death refers (Lu. 23:29), They shall say, *Blessed are the wombs that never bare, and the paps that never gave suck.* Happy are they that have no children to see the murder of; but most unhappy they whose wombs are then bearing, their paps then giving suck: they of all others will be in the most melancholy circumstances. *First,* To them the famine would be most grievous, when they should see the *tongue of the sucking child cleaving to the roof of his mouth for thirst,* and themselves by the calamity made more cruel than the sea monsters, Lam. 4:3, 4. *Secondly,* To them the sword would be most terrible, when in the hand of worse than brutal rage. It is a direful midwifery, when the women with child come to be ripped up by the enraged conqueror (2 Ki. 15:16; Hos. 13:16; Amos 1:13), or the children *brought forth to their murderer,* Hos. 9:13. *Thirdly,* To them also the flight would be most afflictive,; the women with child cannot make haste, or go far; the sucking child cannot be left behind, or, if it should, *can a woman forget it, that she should not have compassion on it?* If it be carried along, it retards the mother's flight, and so exposes her life, and is in danger of Mephibosheth's fate, who was lamed by a fall he got in his nurse's flight. 2 Sa. 4:4.

[4.] What they should pray against at that time — *that your flight be not in the winter, nor on the sabbath day, v.* 20. Observe, in general, it becomes Christ's disciples, in times of public trouble and calamity, to be much in prayer; that is a salve for every sore, never out of season, but in a special manner seasonable when we are distressed on every side. There is no remedy but you must flee, the decree is gone forth, so that God will not be entreated to take away his wrath, no, not if *Noah, Daniel, and Job, stood before him. Let it suffice thee, speak no more of that matter,* but labour to make the best of that which is; and when you cannot in faith pray that you may not be forced to flee, yet pray that the circumstances of it may be graciously ordered, that, though the cup may not pass from you, yet the extremity of the judgment may be prevented. Note, God has the disposing of the circumstances of events, which sometimes make a great alteration one way or other; and therefore in those our eyes must be ever toward him. Christ's bidding them pray for this favour, intimates his purpose of granting it to them; and in a general calamity we must not overlook a circumstantial kindness, but see and own wherein it might have been worse. Christ still bids his disciples to pray for themselves and their friends, that, whenever they were forced to flee, it might be in the most convenient time. Note, When trouble is in prospect, at a great distance, it is good to lay in a stock of prayers beforehand; they must pray, *First, That their flight,* if it were the will of God, *might not be in the winter,* when the days are short, the weather cold, the ways dirty, and therefore travelling very uncomfortable, especially for whole families. Paul hastens Timothy to come to him before winter, 2 Tim. 4:21. Note, Though the ease of the body is not to be *mainly* consulted, it ought to be *duly* considered; though we must take what God sends, and when he sends it, yet we may pray against bodily inconveniences, and are encouraged to do so, in that *the Lord is for the body. Secondly,* That it might not be *on the sabbath day;* not on the Jewish sabbath, because travelling then would give offence to them who were angry with the disciples for plucking the ears of corn on the day; not on the Christian sabbath, because being forced to travel on the day would be a grief to themselves. This intimates Christ's design, that a weekly sabbath should be observed in his church after the preaching of the gospel to all the world. We read not of any of the ordinances of the Jewish church, which were purely ceremonial, that Christ ever expressed any care about, because they were all to vanish; but for the sabbath he often showed a concern. It intimates likewise that the sabbath is ordinarily to be observed as a day of rest from travel and worldly labour; but that, according to his own explication of the fourth commandment, works of necessity were lawful on the sabbath day, as this of fleeing from an enemy to save our lives: had it not been lawful, he would have said, "Whatever becomes of you, do not flee on the sabbath day, but abide by it, though you die by it." For we must not commit the least sin, to escape the greatest trouble. But it intimates, likewise, that it is very uneasy and uncomfortable to a good man, to be taken off by any work of necessity from the solemn service and worship of God on the sabbath day. We should pray that we may have quiet undisturbed sabbaths, and may have no other work than sabbath work to do on sabbath days; that we may attend upon the Lord without distraction. It was desirable, that, if they must flee, they might have the benefit and comfort of one sabbath more to help to bear their charges. To flee in the winter is uncomfortable to the body; but to flee on the sabbath day is so to the soul, and the more so when it remembers former sabbaths, as Ps. 42:4.

3. The greatness of the troubles which should immediately ensue (*v.* 21); *Then shall be great tribulation;* then when the measure of iniquity is full; then when the servants of God are sealed and secured, then come the troubles; nothing can be done against Sodom till Lot is entered into Zoar, and then look for fire and brimstone immediately. *There shall be great tribulation.* Great, indeed, when within the city plague and famine raged, and (worse than either) faction and division, so that every man's sword was against his fellow; then and there it was that the hands of the pitiful women flayed their own children. Without the city was the Roman army ready to swallow them up, with a particular rage against them, not only as Jews, but as rebellious Jews. War was the only one of the three sore judgments that David excepted against; but that was it by which the Jews were ruined; and there were famine and pestilence in extremity besides. Josephus's *History of the Wars of the Jews,* has in it more tragical passages than perhaps any history whatsoever.

(1.) It was a desolation unparalleled, such as *was not since the beginning of the world, nor ever shall be.* Many a city and kingdom has been made desolate, but never any with a desolation like this. Let not daring sinners think that God has done his worst, he can heat the furnace seven times and yet seven times hotter, and will, when he sees greater and still greater abominations. The Romans, when they destroyed Jerusalem, were degenerated from the honour and virtue of their ancestors, which had made even their victories easy to the vanquished. And the wilfulness and obstinacy of the Jews themselves contributed much to the increase of the tribulation. No wonder that the ruin of Jerusalem was an unparalleled ruin, when the sin of Jerusalem was an unparalleled sin — even their crucifying Christ. The nearer any people are to God in profession and privileges, the greater and heavier will his judgments be upon them, if they abuse those privileges, and be false to that profession, Amos 3:2.

(2.) It was a desolation which, if it should continue long, would be intolerable, so that *no flesh should be saved, v.* 22. So triumphantly would death ride, in so many dismal shapes, and with such attendants, that there would be no escaping, but, first or last, all would be cut off. He that escaped one sword, would fall by another, Isa. 24:17, 18. The computation which Josephus makes of those that were slain in several places, amounts to above two millions. *No flesh shall be saved;* he doth not say, "No *soul* shall be saved," for the destruction of the flesh may be for *the saving of the spirit in the day of the Lord Jesus;* but temporal lives will be sacrificed so profusely, that one would think, if it last awhile, it would make a full end.

But here is one word of comfort in the midst of all this terror — that *for the elects' sake these days shall be shortened,* not made shorter than what God had determined (for *that which is determined, shall be poured upon the desolate,* Dan. 9:27), but shorter than what he might have decreed, if he had dealt with them according to their sins; shorter than what the enemy designed, who would have cut all off, if God who made use of them to serve his own purpose, had not set bounds to their wrath; shorter than one who judged by human probabilities would have imagined. Note, [1.] In times of common calamity God manifests his favour to the elect remnant; his jewels, which he will then make up; his peculiar treasure, which he will secure when the lumber is abandoned to the spoiler. [2.] The shortening of calamities is a kindness God often grants for the elects' sake. Instead of complaining that our afflictions last so long, if we consider our defects, we shall see reason to be thankful that they do not last always; when it is bad with us, it becomes us to say, "Blessed be God that it is no worse; blessed be God that it is not hell, endless and remediless misery." It was a lamenting church that said, *It is of the Lord's mercies that we are not consumed;* and it is for the sake of the elect, lest their spirit should fail before them, if he should contend for ever, and lest they should be tempted to put forth, if not their heart, yet their hand, to iniquity.

And now comes in the repeated caution, which was opened before, to take heed of being ensnared by false Christs, and false prophets; (*v.* 23, etc.), who would promise them deliverance, as the lying prophets in Jeremiah's time (Jer. 14:13; 23:16, 17; 27:16; 28:2), but would delude them. Times of great trouble are times of great temptation, and therefore we have need to double our guard then. If they shall say, *Here is a Christ, or there is one,* that shall deliver us from the Romans, do not heed them, it is all but talk; such a deliverance is not to be expected, and therefore not such a deliverer.

VII. He foretels the sudden spreading of the gospel in the world, about the time of these great events (*v.* 27, 28); *As the lightning comes out of the east, so shall the coming of the Son of man be.* It comes in here as an antidote against the poison of those seducers, that said, *Lo, here is Christ,* or, *Lo, he is there;* compare Lu. 17:23, 24. Hearken not to them, for the coming of the Son of man will be as the lightning.

1. It seems primarily to be meant of his coming to set up his spiritual kingdom in the world; where the gospel came in its light and power, there the Son of man came, and in a way quite contrary to the fashion of the seducers and false Christs, who came creeping *in the desert,* or the *secret chambers* (2 Tim. 3:6); whereas Christ comes not with such a *spirit of fear,* but *of power, and of love, and of a sound mind.* The gospel would be remarkable for two things.

(1.) Its swift spreading; it shall fly as the lightning; so shall the gospel be preached and propagated. The gospel is light (Jn. 3:19); and it is not in this as the lightning, that it is a sudden flash, and away, for it is sun-light, and day-light; but it is as lightning in these respects:

[1.] It is light from heaven, as the lightning. It is God, and not man, that sends the lightnings, and summons them, that they may go, and say, *Here we are,* Job 38:35. It is God that directs it (Job 37:3); to man it is one of nature's miracles, above his power to effect, and of nature's mysteries, above his skill to account for: but it is from above; *his lightnings enlightened the world,* Ps. 97:4.

[2.] It is visible and conspicuous as the lightning. The seducers carried on their depths of Satan in the desert and the secret chambers, shunning the light; heretics were called *lucifugae — light-shunners.* But truth seeks no corners, however it may sometimes be forced into them, as the *woman in the wilderness,* though *clothed with the sun,* Rev. 12:1, 6. Christ preached his gospel openly (Jn. 18:20), and his apostles on *the housetop* (*ch.* 10:27), not *in a corner,* Acts 26:26. See Ps. 98:2.

[3.] It was sudden and surprising to the world as the lightning; the Jews indeed had predictions of it, but to the Gentiles it was altogether unlooked for, and came upon them with unaccountable energy, or ever they were aware. It was *light out of darkness, ch.* 4:16; 2 Co. 4:6. We read of the discomfiting of armies by lightning, 2 Sa. 22:15; Ps. 144:6. The powers of darkness were dispersed and vanquished by the gospel lightning.

[4.] It spread far and wide, and that quickly and irresistibly, like the lightning, which comes, suppose, out of the east (Christ is said to ascend *from the east,* Rev. 7:2; Isa. 41:2), and lighteneth to the west. The propagating of Christianity to so many distant countries, of divers languages, by such unlikely instruments, destitute of all secular advantages, and in the face of so much opposition, and this in so short a time, was one of the greatest miracles that was ever wrought for the confirmation of it; here was Christ upon his white horse, denoting speed as well as strength, and *going on conquering and to conquer,* Rev. 6:2. Gospel light rose with the sun, and went with the same, so that the beams of it reached to the ends of the earth, Rom. 10:18. Compare with Ps. 19:3, 4. Though it was fought against, it could never be cooped up in a desert, or in a secret place, as the seducers were; but by this, according to Gamaliel's rule, proved itself to be *of God,* that it *could not be overthrown,* Acts 5:38, 39. Christ speaks of *shining into the west,* because it spread most effectually into those countries which lay west from Jerusalem, as Mr. Herbert observes in his *Church-militant.* How soon did the gospel lightning reach this island of Great Britain! Tertullian, who wrote in the second century, takes notice of it, *Britannorum in accessa Romanis loca, Christo tamen subdita — The fastnesses of Britain, though inaccessible to the Romans, were occupied by Jesus Christ.* This was the Lord's doing.

(2.) Another thing remarkable concerning the gospel, was, its strange success in those places to which is was spread; it gathered in multitudes, not by external compulsion, but as it were by such a natural instinct and inclination, as brings the birds of prey to their prey; for *wheresoever the carcase is, there will the eagles be gathered together* (*v.* 28), where Christ is preached, souls will be gathered in to him. The *lifting up of Christ from the earth,* that is, the preaching of Christ crucified, which, one would think, should drive all men from him, will *draw all men to him* (Jn. 12:32), according to Jacob's prophecy, that *to him shall the gathering of the people be,* Gen. 49:10. See Isa. 60:8. The eagles will be where the carcase is, for it is food for them, it is a feast for them; *where the slain are, there is she,* Job 39:30. Eagles are said to have a strange sagacity and quickness of scent to find out the prey, and they fly swiftly to it, Job 9:26. So those whose spirits God shall stir up, will be effectually drawn to Jesus Christ, to feed upon him; whither should the eagle go but to the prey? Whither should the soul go but to Jesus Christ, who *has the words of eternal life?* The eagles will distinguish what is proper for them from that which is not; so those who have spiritual senses exercised, will know the voice of the good Shepherd from that of a thief and a robber. Saints will be where the true Christ is, not the false Christs. This is applicable to the desires that are wrought in every gracious soul after Christ, and communion with him. Where he is in his ordinances, there will his servants choose to be. A living principle of grace is a kind of natural instinct in all the saints, drawing them to Christ to live upon him.

2. Some understand these verses of the coming of the Son of man *to destroy Jerusalem,* Mal. 3:1, 2, 5. So much was there of an extraordinary display of divine power and justice in that event, that it is called *the coming of Christ.*

Now here are two things intimated concerning it.

(1.) That to the most it would be as unexpected as a flash of lightning, which indeed gives warning of the clap of thunder which follows, but is itself surprising. The seducers say, *Lo, here is Christ* to deliver us; or there is one, a creature of their own fancies; but ere they are aware, the wrath of the Lamb, the true Christ, will arrest them, and they shall not escape.

(2.) That it might be as justly expected as that the eagle should fly to the carcases; though they put far from them the evil day, yet the desolation will come as certainly as the birds of prey to a dead carcase, that lies exposed in the open field. [1.] The Jews were so corrupt and degenerate, so vile and vicious, that they were become a carcase, obnoxious to the righteous judgment of God; they were also so factious and seditious, and every way so provoking to the Romans, that they had made themselves obnoxious to their resentments, and an inviting prey to them. [2.] The Romans were as an eagle, and the ensign of their armies was an eagle. The army of the Chaldeans is said *to fly as the eagle that hasteth to eat,* Hab. 1:8. The ruin of the New-Testament Babylon is represented by a call to the birds of prey to come and feast upon the slain, Rev. 19:17, 18. Notorious malefactors have their eyes eaten out by *the young eagles* (Prov. 30:17); the Jews were hung up in chains, Jer. 7:33; 16:4. [3.] The Jews can no more preserve themselves from the Romans than the carcase can secure itself from the eagles. [4.] The destruction shall find out the Jews wherever they are, as the eagle scents the prey. Note, When a people do by their sin make themselves carcases, putrid and loathsome, nothing can be expected but that God should send eagles among them, to devour and destroy them.

3. It is very applicable to the day of judgment, the coming of our Lord Jesus Christ in that day, and *our gathering together unto him,* 2 Th. 2:1. Now see here,

(1.) How he shall come; *as the lightning,* The time was now at hand, when he should *depart out of the world, to go to the Father.* Therefore those that enquire after Christ must not go into the desert or the secret place, nor listen to every one that will put up the finger to invite them to a sight of Christ; but let them look upward, for the heavens must contain him, and thence *we look for the Saviour* (Phil. 3:20); he shall *come in the clouds,* as the lightning doth, and *every eye shall see him,* as they say it is natural for all living creatures to turn their faces towards the lightning, Rev. 1:7. Christ will appear to all the world, from one end of heaven to the other; nor shall any thing be hid from the light and heat of that day.

(2.) How the saints shall be gathered to him; as the eagles are to the carcase by natural instinct, and with the greatest swiftness and alacrity imaginable. Saints, when they shall be fetched to glory, will be carried as on eagles' wings (Ex. 19:4), as on angels' wings. *They shall mount up with wings, like eagles,* and like them renew their youth.

VIII. He foretels his second coming at the *end of time, v.* 29–31. *The sun shall be darkened,* etc.

1. Some think this is to be understood only of the destruction of Jerusalem and the Jewish nation; the darkening of the sun, moon, and stars, denotes the eclipse of the glory of that state, its convulsions, and the general confusion that attended that desolation. Great slaughter and devastation are in the Old Testament thus set forth (as Isa. 13:10; 34:4; Eze. 32:7; Joel 2:31); or by the sun, moon, and stars, may be meant the temple, Jerusalem, and the cities of Judah, which should all come to ruin. The *sign of the Son of man* (*v.* 30) means a signal appearance of the power and justice of the Lord Jesus in it, avenging his own blood on them that imprecated the guilt of it upon themselves and their children; and the gathering *of his elect* (*v.* 31) signifies the delivering of a remnant from this sin and ruin.

2. It seems rather to refer to Christ's second coming. The destruction of the particular enemies of the church was typical of the complete conquest of them all; and therefore what will be done really at the great day, may be applied metaphorically to those destructions: but still we must attend to the principal scope of them; and while we are all agreed to expect Christ's second coming, what need is there to put such strained constructions as some do, upon these verses, which speak of it so clearly, and so agreeably to other scriptures, especially when Christ is here answering an enquiry con-

cerning his coming at the end of the world, which Christ was never shy of speaking of to his disciples?

The only objection against this, is, that it is said to be *immediately after the tribulation of those days;* but as to that, (1.) It is usual in the prophetical style to speak of things great and certain as near and just at hand, only to express the greatness and certainty of them. Enoch spoke of Christ's second coming as within ken, *Behold, the Lord cometh,* Jude 14. (2.) *A thousand years are* in God's sight *but as one day,* 2 Pt. 3:8. It is there urged, with reference to this very thing, and so it might be said to be immediately after. The tribulation of those days includes not only the destruction of Jerusalem, but all the other tribulations which the church must pass through; not only its share in the calamities of the nations, but the tribulations peculiar to itself; while the nations are torn with wars, and the church with schisms, delusions, and persecutions, we cannot say that the tribulation of those days is over; the whole state of the church on earth is militant, we must count upon that; but when the church's tribulation is over, her warfare accomplished, and what is behind of the sufferings of Christ filled up, then look for the end.

Now concerning Christ's second coming, it is here foretold,

[1.] That there shall be then a great and amazing change of the creatures, and particularly the *heavenly bodies* (*v.* 29). *The sun shall be darkened, and the moon shall not give her light.* The moon shines with a borrowed light, and therefore if the sun, from whom she borrows her light, is turned into darkness, she must fail of course, and become bankrupt. *The stars shall fall;* they shall lose their light, and disappear, and be as if they were fallen; and *the powers of heaven shall be shaken.* This intimates,

First, That there shall be a great change, in order to the making of all things new. Then shall be *the restitution of all things,* when the heavens shall not be cast away as a rag, but *changed as a vesture,* to be worn in a better fashion, Ps. 102:26. They shall *pass away with a great noise,* that there may be *new heavens,* 2 Pt. 3:10–13.

Secondly, It shall be a visible change, and such as all the world must take notice of; for such the darkening of the sun and moon cannot but be: and it would be an amazing change; for the heavenly bodies are not so liable to alteration as the creatures of this lower world are. The days of heaven, and the continuance of the sun and moon, are used to express that which is lasting and unchangeable (As Ps. 89:29; 36:37); yet they shall thus be shaken.

Thirdly, It shall be a universal change. If the sun be turned into darkness, and the powers of heaven be shaken, the earth cannot but be turned into a dungeon, and its foundation made to tremble. *Howl, fir trees, if the cedars be shaken.* When the stars of heaven drop, no marvel if the *everlasting mountains melt,* and the *perpetual hills bow.* Nature shall sustain a general shock and convulsion, which yet shall be no hindrance to the joy and rejoicing of heaven and earth *before the Lord, when he cometh to judge the world* (Ps. 96:11, 13); they shall as it were *glory in the tribulation.*

Fourthly, The darkening of the sun, moon, and stars, which were *made to rule over the day, and over the night* (which is the first dominion we find of any creature, Gen. 1:16–18), signifies the *putting down of all rule, authority, and power* (even that which seems of the greatest antiquity and usefulness), *that the kingdom may be delivered up to God, even the Father,* and he may be *All in all,* 1 Co. 15:24, 28. The sun was darkened at the death of Christ, for then was in one sense *the judgment of this world* (Jn. 12:31), an indication of what would be at the general judgment.

Fifthly, The glorious appearance of our Lord Jesus, who will then show himself as the *Brightness of his Father's glory, and the express Image of his person,* will darken the sun and moon, as a candle is darkened in the beams of the noon-day sun; they will have no glory, *by reason of the glory that excelleth,* 2 Co. 3:10. Then *the sun shall be ashamed, and the moon confounded,* when God shall appear, Isa. 24:23.

Sixthly, The sun and moon shall be then darkened, because there will be no more occasion for them. To sinners, that choose their portion in this life, all comfort will be eternally denied; as they shall not have a drop of water, so not a ray of light. Now God causeth his sun to rise on the earth, but then *Interdico tib sole et luna — I forbid thee the light of the sun and the moon.* Darkness must be their portion. To the saints that had their treasure above, such light of joy and comfort will be given as shall supersede that of the sun and moon, and render it useless. What need is there of vessels of light, when we come to *the Fountain and Father of light*? See Isa. 60:19; Rev. 22:5.

[2.] That *then shall appear the sign of the Son of man in heaven* (*v.* 30), the Son of man himself, as it follows here, *They shall see the Son of man coming in the clouds.* At his first coming, he was *set for a Sign that should be spoken against* (Lu. 2:34), but at his second coming, a sign that should be admired. Ezekiel was *a son of man set for a sign,* Eze. 12:6. Some make this a prediction of the harbingers and forerunners of his coming, giving notice of his approach; *a light shining before him, and the fire devouring* (Ps. 50:3; 1 Ki. 19:11, 12), *the beams coming out of his hand, where had long been the hiding of his power,* Hab. 3:4. It is a groundless conceit of some of the ancients, that this sign of the Son of man, will be the sign of the cross displayed as a banner. It will certainly be such a clear convincing sign as will dash infidelity quite out of countenance, and fill their faces with shame, who said, *Where is the promise of his coming?*

[3.] That *then all the tribes of the earth shall mourn, v.* 30. See Rev. 1:7. *All the kindreds of the earth shall then wail because of him;* some of all the tribes and kindreds of the earth shall mourn; for the greater part will tremble at his approach, while the chosen remnant, one of a family and two of a tribe, shall lift up their heads with joy, knowing that their redemption draws nigh, and their Redeemer. Note, Sooner or later, all sinners will be mourners; penitent sinners look to Christ, and mourn after a godly sort; and they who sow in those tears, shall shortly reap in joy; impenitent sinners *shall look unto him whom they have pierced,* and, though they laugh now, shall mourn and weep after a devilish sort, in endless horror and despair.

[4.] That *then they shall see the Son of man coming in the clouds of heaven, with power and great glory.* Note, *First,* The judgment of the great day will be committed to the Son of man, both in pursuance and in recompence of his great undertaking for us as Mediator, Jn. 5:22, 27. *Secondly,* The Son of man will at that day come in the clouds of heaven. Much of the sensible intercourse between heaven and earth is by the clouds; they are betwixt them, as it were, the *medium participationis — the medium of participation,* drawn by heaven from the earth, distilled by heaven upon the earth. Christ went to heaven in a cloud, and *will in like manner come again,* Acts 1:9, 11. *Behold, he cometh in the clouds,* Rev. 1:7. A cloud will be the Judge's chariot (Ps. 104:3), his robe (Rev. 10:1), his pavilion (Ps. 18:11), his throne, Rev. 14:14. When the world was destroyed by water, the judgment came in the clouds of heaven, for the windows of heaven were opened; so shall it be when it shall be destroyed by fire. Christ went before Israel in a cloud, which had a bright side and a dark side;; so will the cloud have in which Christ will come at the great day, it will bring both comfort and terror. *Thirdly,* He will *come with power and great glory:* his first coming was in weakness and great meanness (2 Co. 13:4); but his second coming will be with power and glory, agreeable both to the dignity of his person and to the purposes of his coming. *Fourthly,* He will be seen with bodily eyes in his coming: *therefore* the Son of man will be the Judge, that he may be seen, that sinners thereby may be the more confounded, who shall see him as Balaam did, *but not nigh* (Num. 24:17), see him, but not as theirs. It added to the torment of that damned sinner, that *he saw Abraham afar off.* "Is this he whom we have slighted, and rejected, and rebelled against; whom we have crucified to ourselves afresh; who might have been our Saviour, but is our Judge, and will be our enemy for ever?" *The Desire of all nations* will then be their dread.

[5.] That *he shall send his angels with a great sound of a trumpet, v.* 31. Note, *First,* The angels shall be attendants upon Christ at his second coming; they are called *his* angels, which proves him to be God, and Lord of the angels; they shall be obliged to wait upon him. *Secondly,* These attendants shall be employed by him as officers of the court in the judgment of that day; they are now ministering spirits sent forth by him (Heb. 1:14), and will be so then. *Thirdly,* Their ministration will be ushered in with a great sound of a trumpet, to awaken and alarm a sleeping world. This trumpet is spoken of, 1 Co. 15:52, and 1 Th. 4:16. At the giving of the law on mount Sinai, the sound of the trumpet was remarkably terrible (Ex. 19:13, 16); but much more will it be so in the great day. By the law, trumpets were to be sounded for the calling of assemblies (Num. 10:2), in praising God (Ps. 81:3), in offering sacrifices (Num. 10:10), and in proclaiming the year of jubilee, Lev. 25:9. Very fitly therefore shall there be the sound of a trumpet at the last day, when the general assembly shall be called, when the praises of God shall be gloriously celebrated, when sinners shall fall as sacrifices to divine justice, and when the saints shall enter upon their eternal jubilee.

[6.] That *they shall gather together his elect from the four winds.* Note, At the second coming of Jesus Christ, there will be a general meeting of all the saints. *First,* The *elect* only will be gathered, the chosen remnant, who are but few in comparison with the many that are only *called.* This is the foundation of the saints' eternal happiness, that they are God's elect. The gifts of love to eternity follow the thought of love from eternity; and *the Lord knows them that are his. Secondly,* The angels shall be employed to bring them together, as Christ's servants, and as the saints' friends; we have the commission given them, Ps. 50:5 *Gather my saints together unto me;* nay, it will be said to them, *Habetis fratres — These are your brethren;* for the elect will then *be equal to the angels,* Lu. 20:36. *Thirdly,* They *shall be gathered from one end of heaven to the other;* the elect of God are scattered abroad (Jn. 11:52), there are some in all places, in all nations (Rev. 7:9); but when that great gathering day comes, there shall not one of them be missing; distance of place shall keep none out of heaven, if distance of affection do not. *Undique ad coelos tantundem est viae — Heaven is equally accessible from every place.* See *ch.* 8:11; Isa. 43:6; 49:12.

Verses 32–51

We have here the practical application of the foregoing prediction; in general, we must expect and prepare for the events here foretold.

I. We must expect them; *"Now learn a parable of the fig-tree, v.* 32, 33. Now learn what use to make of the things you have heard; so observe and understand the signs of the times, and compare them with the predictions of the word, as from thence to foresee what is at the door, that you may provide accordingly." The parable of the fig-tree is no more than this, that its budding and blossoming are a presage of summer; for as the *stork* in the heaven, so the trees of the field, *know their appointed time.* The beginning of the working of second causes assures us of the progress and perfection of it. Thus when God begins to fulfil prophecies, he will make an end. There is a certain series in the works of providence, as there is in the works of nature. The signs of the times are compared with the prognostics of *the face of the sky* (*ch.* 16:3), so here with those of *the face of the earth;* when that is renewed, we foresee that summer is coming, not immediately, but at some distance; after *the branch grows tender,* we expect the March winds, and the April showers, before the summer comes; however, we are sure it is coming; "so likewise ye, when the gospel day shall dawn, count upon it, that through this variety of events which I have told you of, the perfect day will come. *The things revealed must shortly come to pass* (Rev. 1:1); they must come in their own order, in the order appointed for them. *Know that it is near."* He does not here say what, but it is that which the hearts of his disciples are upon, and which they are inquisitive after, and long for; *the kingdom of God is near,* so it is expressed in the parallel place, Lu. 21:31. Note, When the trees of righteousness begin to bud and blossom, when God's people promise faithfulness, it is a happy presage of good times. In them God begins his work, first prepares their heart, and then he will go on with it; for, *as for God, his work is perfect;* and he will *revive it in the midst of their years.*

Now touching the events foretold here, which we are to expect,

1. Christ here assures us of the certainty of them (*v.* 35); *Heaven and earth shall pass away;* they continue this day indeed, according to God's ordinance, but they shall not continue for ever (Ps. 102:25, 26; 2 Pt. 3:10); *but my words shall not pass away.* Note, The word of Christ is more sure and lasting than heaven and earth. *Hath he spoken? And shall he not do it?* We may build with more assurance upon the word of Christ than we can upon the pillars of heaven, or the strong foundations of the earth; for, when they shall be made to tremble and totter, and shall be no more, the word of Christ shall remain, and be in full force, power, and virtue. See 1 Pt. 1:24, 25. *It is easier for heaven and earth to pass,* than the word of Christ; so it is expressed, Lu. 16:17. Compare Isa. 54:10. The accomplishment of these prophecies might seem to be delayed, and intervening events might seem to disagree with them, but do not think that therefore

the word of Christ is fallen to the ground, for that shall never pass away: though it be not fulfilled, either in the time or in the way that we have prescribed; yet, in God's time, which is the best time, and in God's way, which is the best way, it shall certainly be fulfilled. Every word of Christ is very pure, and therefore very sure.

2. He here instructs us as to the time of them, *v.* 34, 36. As to this, it is well observed by the learned Grotius, that there is a manifest distinction made between the *tauta* (*v.* 34), and the *ekeinē* (*v.* 36), *these things,* and *that day and hour;* which will help to clear this prophecy.

(1.) As to *these things,* the wars, seductions, and persecutions, here foretold, and especially the ruin of the Jewish nation; *"This generation shall not pass away, till all these things be fulfilled* (*v.* 34); there are those now alive, that shall see Jerusalem destroyed, and the Jewish church brought to an end." Because it might seem strange, he backs it with a solemn asseveration; *"Verily, I say unto you.* You may take my word for it, these things are at the door." Christ often speaks of the nearness of that desolation, the more to affect people, and quicken them to prepare for it. Note, There may be greater trials and troubles yet before us, in our own day, than we are aware of. They that are old, know not what sons of Anak may be reserved for their last encounters.

(2.) But as to *that day and hour* which will put a period to time, *that knoweth no man, v.* 36. Therefore take heed of confounding these two, as *they* did, who, from the words of Christ and the apostles; letters, inferred that *the day of Christ was at hand,* 2 Th. 2:2. No, it was not; *this generation,* and many another, *shall pass,* before *that day and hour* come. Note, [1.] There is a certain day and hour fixed for the judgment to come; it is called *the day of the Lord,* because so unalterably fixed. None of God's judgments are adjourned *sine die — without the appointment of a certain day.* [2.] That day and hour are a great secret.

Prudens futuri temporis exitum
Caliginosa nocte premit Deus.

But Heaven has wisely hid from human sight
The dark decrees of future fate,
And sown their seeds in depth of nights. — Horace.

No man knows it; not the wisest by their sagacity, not the best by any divine discovery. We all know that there shall be such a day; but none knows when it shall be, no, not the angels; though their capacities for knowledge are great, and their opportunities of knowing this advantageous (they dwell at the fountain-head of light), and though they are to be employed in the solemnity of that day, yet they are not told when it shall be: none *knows but my Father only.* This is one of those *secret things* which *belong to the Lord our God.* The uncertainty of the time of Christ's coming, is, to those who are watchful, *a savour of life unto life,* and makes them more watchful; but to those who are careless, it is *a savour of death unto death,* and makes them more careless.

II. To this end we must expect these events, that we may prepare for them; and here we have a caution against security and sensuality, which will make it a dismal day indeed to us, *v.* 37–41. In these verses we have such an idea given us of the judgment day, as may serve to startle and awaken us, that we may not sleep as others do.

It will be a surprising day, and a separating day.

1. It will be a surprising day, as the deluge was to the old world, *v.* 37–39. That which he here intends to describe, is, the posture of the world at the coming of the Son of man; besides his first coming, to save, he has other comings to judge. He saith (Jn. 9:39), *For judgment I am come;* and for judgment he will come; for all judgment is committed to him, both that of the word, and that of the sword.

Now this here is applicable,

(1.) To *temporal judgments,* particularly that which was now hastening upon the nation and people of the Jews; though they had fair warning given them of it, and there were many prodigies that were presages of it, yet it found them secure, crying, *Peace and safety,* 1 Th. 5:3. The siege was laid to Jerusalem by Titus Vespasian, when they were met at the passover in the midst of their mirth; like the men of Laish, they dwelt careless when the ruin arrested them, Jdg. 18:7, 27. The destruction of Babylon, both that in the Old Testament and that in the New, comes when she saith, *I shall be a lady for ever,* Isa. 47:7–9; Rev. 18:7. Therefore the plagues come in a moment, in one day. Note, Men's unbelief shall not make God's threatenings of no effect.

(2.) To *the eternal judgment;* so the judgment of the great day is called, Heb. 6:2. Though notice has been given of it from Enoch, yet, when it comes, it will be unlooked for by the most of men; the latter days, which are nearest to that day, will produce scoffers, that say, *Where is the promise of his coming?* 2 Pt. 3:3, 4; Lu. 18:8. Thus it will be when the world that now is shall be destroyed by fire; for thus it was when the old world, being overflowed by water, perished, 2 Pt. 3:6, 7. Now Christ here shows what were the temper and posture of the old world when the deluge came.

[1.] They were sensual and worldly; *they were eating and drinking, marrying and giving in marriage.* It is not said, They were killing and stealing, and whoring and swearing (these were indeed the horrid crimes of some of the worst of them; *the earth was full of violence*); but they were all of them, except Noah, over head and ears in the world, and regardless of the word of God, and this ruined them. Note, Universal neglect of religion is a more dangerous symptom to any people than particular instances here and there of daring irreligion. *Eating and drinking* are necessary to the preservation of man's life; *marrying and giving in marriage* are necessary to the preservation of mankind; but, *Licitus perimus omnes — These lawful things undo us,* unlawfully managed. *First,* They were unreasonable in it, inordinate and entire in the pursuit of the delights of sense, and the gains of the world; they were wholly taken up with these things, *ēsan trōgontes — they were eating;* they were in these things as in their element, as if they had their being for no other end than *to eat and drink,* Isa. 56:12. *Secondly,* They were unreasonable in it; they were entire and intent upon the world and the flesh, when the destruction was at the door, which they had had such fair warning of. They were eating and drinking, when they should have been repenting and praying; when God, by the ministry of Noah, called to *weeping and mourning, then joy and gladness.* This was to them, as it was to Israel afterwards, the unpardonable sin (Isa. 22:12, 14), especially, because it was in defiance of those warnings by which they should have been awakened. *"Let us eat and drink, for tomorrow we die;* if it must be a short life, let it be a merry one." The apostle James speaks of this as the general practice of the wealthy Jews before the destruction of Jerusalem; when they should have been *weeping for the miseries that were coming upon them, they were living in pleasure, and nourishing their hearts as in a day of slaughter,* Jam. 5:1, 5.

[2.] They were secure and careless; *they knew not, until the flood came, v.* 39. *Knew not!* Surely they could not but know. Did not God, by Noah, give them fair warning of it? Did he not call them to repentance, while his long-suffering waited? 1 Pt. 3:19, 20. But they knew not, that is, they believed not; they might have known, but would not know. Note, What we know of *the things that belong to our everlasting peace,* if we do not mix faith with it, and improve it, is all one as if we did not know it at all. Their *not knowing* is joined with their *eating, and drinking, and marrying;* for, *First, Therefore* they were sensual, because they were secure. Note, the reason why people are so eager in the pursuit, and so entangled in the pleasures of this world, is, because they do not know, and believe, and consider, the eternity which they are upon the brink of. Did we know aright that all these things must shortly be dissolved, and we must certainly survive them, we should not set our eyes and hearts so much upon them as we do. *Secondly, Therefore* they were secure, because they were sensual; *therefore* they knew not that the flood was coming, because they were eating and drinking; were so taken up with things seen and present, that they had neither time nor heart to mind the things not seen as yet, which they were warned of. Note, As security bolsters men up in their brutal sensuality; so sensuality rocks them asleep in their carnal security. *The knew not, until the flood came.* 1. The flood did come, though they would not foresee it. Note, Those that will not know by faith, shall be made to know by feeling, *the wrath of God revealed from heaven against their ungodliness and unrighteousness.* The evil day is never the further off for men's putting it far off from them. 2. They did not know it till it was too late to prevent it, as they might have done if they had known it in time, which made it so much the more grievous. Judgments are most terrible and amazing to the secure, and those that have made a jest of them.

The application of this, concerning the old world, we have in these words; *So shall the coming of the Son of man be;* that is, (1.) In such a posture shall he find people, eating and drinking, and not expecting him. Note, Security and sensuality are likely to be the epidemical diseases of the latter days. All *slumber and sleep, and at midnight the bridegroom comes.* All are off their watch, and at their ease. (2.) With such a power, and for such a purpose, will he come upon them. As the flood took away the sinners of the old world, irresistibly and irrecoverably; so shall secure sinners, that mocked at Christ and his coming, be taken away by *the wrath of the Lamb, when the great day of his wrath comes,* which will be like the coming of the deluge, a destruction which there is no fleeing from.

2. It will be a separating day (*v.* 40, 41); *Then shall two be in the field.* Two ways this may be applied.

(1.) We may apply it to the success of the gospel, especially at the first preaching of it; it divided the world; *some believed the things which were spoken,* and were taken to Christ; *others believed not,* and were left to perish in their unbelief. Those of the same age, place, capacity, employment, and condition, in the world, *grinding in the same mill,* those of the same family, nay, those that were joined in the same bond of marriage, were, one effectually called, the other passed by, and left in the gall of bitterness. This is that division, that separating fire, which Christ *came to send,* Lu. 12:49, 51. *This* renders free grace the more obliging, that it is distinguishing; *to us, and not to the world* (Jn. 14:22), nay to us, and not to those in the same field, the same mill, the same house.

When ruin came upon Jerusalem, a distinction was made by Divine Providence, according to that which had been before made by divine grace; for all the Christians among them were saved from perishing in that calamity, by the special care of Heaven. If two were at work in the field together, and one of them was a Christian, he was taken into a place of shelter, and had his life given him for a prey, while the other was left to the sword of the enemy. Nay, if but two women were grinding at the mill, if one of them belonged to Christ, though but a woman, a poor woman, a servant, she was taken to a place of safety, and the other abandoned. Thus *the meek of the earth are hid in the day of the Lord's anger* (Zep. 2:3), either in heaven, or *under* heaven. Note, Distinguishing preservations, in times of general destruction, are special tokens of God's favour, and ought so to be acknowledged. If we are safe when thousands fall on our right hand and our left, are not consumed when others are consumed round about us, so that we are as brands plucked out of the fire, we have reason to say, *It is of the Lord's mercies,* and it is a great mercy.

(2.) We may apply it to the second coming of Jesus Christ, and the separation which will be made in that day. He had said before (*v.* 31), that the elect will be *gathered together.* Here he tells us, that, in order to that, they will be distinguished from those who were nearest to them in this world; the choice and chosen ones taken to glory, the other left to perish eternally. Those who sleep in the dust of the earth, two in the same grave, their ashed mixed, shall yet arise, one to be taken to everlasting life, the other left *to shame and everlasting contempt,* Dan. 12:2. Here it is applied to them who shall be found alive. Christ will come unlooked for, will find people busy at their usual occupations, *in the field, at the mill;* and then, according as they are vessels of mercy prepared for glory, or vessels of wrath prepared for ruin, accordingly it will be with them; the one taken *to meet the Lord and his angels in the air, to be for ever with him and them;* the other left to the devil and his angels, who, when Christ has gathered out his own, will sweep up the residue. This will aggravate the condemnation of sinners that others shall be taken from the midst of them to glory, and they left behind. And it speaks abundance of comfort to the Lord's people. [1.] Are they mean and despised in the world, as the man-servant in the field, or the maid at the mill (Ex. 11:5)? Yet they shall not be forgotten or overlooked in that day. The poor in the world, if rich in faith, are *heirs of the kingdom.* [2.] Are they dispersed in distant and unlikely places, where one would not expect to find the heirs of glory, *in the field, at the mill?* Yet the angels will find them there (hidden as Saul among the stuff, when they are to be enthroned), and fetch them thence; and well may they be said to be *changed,* for a very great change it will be to go to heaven from ploughing and grinding. [3.] Are they weak, and unable of themselves to move heavenward? They shall be taken, or *laid hold of,* as Lot was taken out of Sodom by a gracious violence, Gen. 19:16. Those whom Christ has once apprehended and laid hold on, he will never lose his hold of. [4.] Are they intermixed with others, linked with them in the same habitations, societies, employments? Let not that discourage any true Christian; God knows how to separate between the precious and the vile, the gold and dross in the same lump, the wheat and chaff in the same floor.

III. Here is a general exhortation to us, *to watch, and be ready* against that day comes, enforced by divers weighty considerations, *v.* 42, etc. Observe,

1. The duty required; *Watch, and be ready, v.* 42, 44.

(1.) *Watch therefore, v.* 42. Note, It is the great duty and interest of all the disciples of Christ to watch, to be awake and keep awake, that they may mind their business. As a sinful state or way is compared to *sleep,* senseless and inactive (1 Th. 5:6), so a gracious state or way is compared to *watching* and *waking.* We must watch for our Lord's coming, to us in particular at our death, *after which is the judgment,* that is *the great day* with us, the end of our time; and his coming at the end of all time to judge the world, the *great day* with all mankind. To watch implies not only to believe that our Lord will come, but to desire that he would come, to be often thinking of his coming, and always looking for it as sure and near, and the time of it uncertain. To watch for Christ's coming, is to maintain that gracious temper and disposition of mind which we should be willing that our Lord, when he comes, should find us in. To watch is to be aware of the first notices of his approach, that we may immediately attend his motions, and address ourselves to the duty of meeting him. Watching is supposed to be in the night, which is sleeping time; while we are in this world, it is *night* with us, and we must take pains to keep ourselves awake.

(2.) *Be ye also ready.* We wake in vain, if we do not get ready. It is not enough to *look* for such things; but we must therefore *give diligence,* 2 Pt. 3:11, 14. We have then our Lord to attend upon, and we must have our lamps ready trimmed; a cause to be tried, and we must have our plea ready drawn and signed by our Advocate; a reckoning to make up, and we must have our accounts ready stated and balanced; there is an inheritance which we then hope to enter upon, and we must have ourselves ready, made meet to partake of it, Col. 1:12.

2. The reasons to induce us to this watchfulness and diligent preparation for that day; which are two.

(1.) Because the time of our Lord's coming is very uncertain. This is the reason immediately annexed to the double exhortation (*v.* 42, 44); and it is illustrated by a comparison, *v.* 43. Let us consider then,

[1.] That *we know not what hour he will come, v.* 42. We know not *the day of our death,* Gen. 27:2. We may know that we have but *a little time to live (The time of my departure is at hand,* 2 Tim. 4:6); but we cannot know that we have a long time to live, for our souls are continually in our hands; nor can we know how little a time we have to live, for it may prove less than we expect; much less do we know the time fixed for the general judgment. Concerning both we are kept at uncertainty, that we may, every day, expect that which may come any day; may never boast of a year's continuance (James 4:13), no, nor of tomorrow's return, as if it were ours, Prov. 27:1; Lu. 12:20.

[2.] That he may *come at such an hour as we think not, v.* 44. Though there be such uncertainty in the time, there is none in the thing itself: though we know not *when* he will come, we are sure he *will* come. His parting word was, *Surely I come quickly;* his saying, "I come *surely,*" obliges us to expect him: his saying "I come *quickly.*" obliges us to be always expecting him; for it keeps us in a state of expectancy. *In such an hour as you think not,* that is, such an hour as they who are unready and unprepared, think not (*v.* 50); nay, such an hour as the most lively expectants perhaps thought least likely. The bridegroom came when the wise were slumbering. It is agreeable to our present state, that we should be under the influence of a constant and general expectation, rather than that of particular presages and prognostications, which we are sometimes tempted vainly to desire and wish for.

[3.] That the children of this world are thus wise in their generation, that, when they know of a danger approaching, they will keep awake, and stand on their guard against it. This he shows in a particular instance, *v.* 43. If the master of a house had notice that a thief would come such a night, and such a watch of the night (for they divided the night into four watches, allowing three hours to each), and would make an attempt upon his house, though it were the midnight-watch, when he was most sleepy, yet he would be up, and listen to every noise in every corner, and be ready to give him a warm reception. Now, though we know not *just when* our Lord will come, yet, knowing that he *will* come, and come quickly, and without any other warning than what he hath given in his word, it concerns us to watch always. Note, *First,* We have every one of us a house to keep, which lies exposed, in which all we are worth is laid up: that house is our own souls, which we must *keep with all diligence. Secondly,* The day of the Lord comes *by surprise, as a thief in the night.* Christ chooses to come when he is least expected, that the triumphs of his enemies may be turned into the greater shame, and the fears of his friends into the greater joy. *Thirdly,* If Christ, when he comes, finds us asleep and unready, our house will be broken up, and we shall lose all we are worth, not as by a thief unjustly, but as by a just and legal process; death and judgment will seize upon all we have, to our irreparable damage and utter undoing. Therefore be ready, *be ye also ready;* as ready at all times as the good man of the house would be at the hour when he expected the thief: we must put on the armour of God, that we may not only stand in that evil day, but, as more than conquerors, may divide the spoil.

(2.) Because the issue of our Lord's coming will be very happy and comfortable to those that shall be found ready, but very dismal and dreadful to those that shall not, *v.* 45, etc. This is represented by the different state of good and bad servants, when their lord comes to reckon with them. It is likely to be well or ill with us to eternity, according as we are found ready or unready at that day; for Christ comes *to render to every man according to his works.* Now this parable, with which the chapter closes, is applicable to all Christians, who are in profession and obligation God's servants; but it seems especially intended as a warning to ministers; for the servant spoken of is a *steward.* Now observe what Christ here saith,

[1.] Concerning the *good servant;* he shows here what he is — *a ruler of the household;* what, being so, he should be — *faithful* and *wise;* and what, if he be so, he shall be eternally — *blessed.* Here are good instructions and encouragements to the ministers of Christ.

First, We have here his place and office. He is one *whom the Lord has made ruler over his household, to give them meat in due season.* Note, 1. The church of Christ is his household, or family, standing in relation to him as the Father and Master of it. It is *the household of God,* a family named from Christ, Eph. 3:15. 2. Gospel ministers are appointed *rulers* in this household; not at princes (Christ has entered a caveat against that), but as stewards, or other subordinate officers; not as lords, but as guides; not to prescribe new ways, but to show and lead in the ways that Christ has appointed: that is the signification of the *hēgoumenoi,* which we translate, *having rule over you* (Heb. 13:17); as *overseers,* not to cut out new work, but to direct in, and quicken to, the work which Christ has ordered; that is the signification of *episkopoi — bishops.* They are rulers by Christ; what power they have is derived from him, and none may take it from them, or abridge it to them; he is one whom *the Lord has made ruler;* Christ has the *making* of ministers. They are rulers *under* Christ, and act in subordination to him; and rulers *for* Christ, for the advancement of his kingdom. 3. The work of gospel ministers is to give to Christ's household their meat in due season, as stewards, and therefore they have the keys delivered to them. (1.) Their work is *to give,* not take to themselves (Eze. 34:8), but give to the family what the Master has bought, to *dispense* what Christ has *purchased.* And to ministers it is said, that *it is more blessed to give than to receive,* Acts 20:35. (2.) It is to give *meat;* not to give *law* (that is Christ's work), but to deliver those doctrines to the church which, if duly digested, will be nourishment to souls. They must give, not the poison of false doctrines, not the stones of hard and unprofitable doctrines, but the meat that is *sound* and *wholesome.* (3.) It must be given *in due season, en kairō — while there is time for it;* when eternity comes, it will be too late; we must *work while it is day:* or *in time,* that is, whenever any opportunity offers itself; or in the stated time, time after time, according as the duty of every day requires.

Secondly, His right discharge of this office. The good servant, if thus preferred, will be a good *steward;* for,

1. He is *faithful;* stewards must be so, 1 Co. 4:2. He that is *trusted,* must be trusty; and the greater the trust is, the more is expected from them. It is a great good thing that is committed to *ministers* (2 Tim. 1:14); and they must be faithful, as Moses was, Heb. 3:2. Christ counts those ministers, and those only, that are *faithful,* 1 Tim. 1:12. A faithful minister of Jesus Christ is one that sincerely designs his master's honour, not his own; delivers *the whole counsel of God,* not his own fancies and conceits; follows Christ's institutions and adheres to them; regards the meanest, reproves the greatest, and doth not respect persons.

2. He is wise to understand his duty and the proper season of it; and in guiding of the flock there is need, not only of the integrity of the heart, but the skilfulness of the hands. Honesty may suffice for a good *servant,* but wisdom is necessary to a *good steward;* for it is profitable to direct.

3. He is doing; *so doing* as his office requires. The ministry is a good work, and they whose office it is, have always something to do; they must not indulge themselves in ease, nor leave the work undone, or carelessly turn it off to others, but be doing, and doing to the purpose — *so doing,* giving meat to the household, minding their own business, and not meddling with that which is foreign; *so doing* as the Master has appointed, as the office imports, and as the case of the family requires; not *talking,* but *doing.* It was the motto Mr. Perkins used, *Minister verbi es — You are a minister of the word.* Not only *Age — Be doing;* but *Hoc age — Be so doing.*

4. He is *found doing* when his Master comes; which intimates, (1.) Constancy at his work. At what hour soever his Master comes, he is found busy at the work of the day. Ministers should not leave empty spaces in their time, lest their Lord should come in one of those empty spaces. As with a good God the end of one mercy is the beginning of another, so with a good man, a good minister, the end of one duty is the beginning of another. When Calvin was persuaded to remit his ministerial labours, he answered, with some resentment, "What, would you have my Master find me idle?" (2.) Perseverance in his work till the Lord come. *Hold fast till then,* Rev. 2:25. *Continue in these things,* 1 Tim. 4:16; 6:14. Endure to the end.

Thirdly, The recompence of reward intended him for this, in three things.

1. He shall be taken notice of. This is intimated in these words, Who then is that *faithful and wise servant?* Which supposes that there are but few who answer this character; such an interpreter is *one of a thousand,* such a faithful and wise *steward.* Those who thus distinguish themselves now by humility, diligence, and sincerity in their work, Christ will in the great day both dignify and distinguish by the glory conferred on them.

2. He shall be blessed? *Blessed is that servant;* and Christ's pronouncing him blessed makes him so. All the dead that die n the Lord are blessed, Rev. 14:13. But there is a peculiar blessedness secured to them that approve themselves faithful stewards, and are found so doing. Next to the honour of those who die in the field of battle, suffering for Christ as the martyrs, is the honour of those that die in the field of service, ploughing, and sowing, and reaping, for Christ.

3. He shall be preferred (*v.* 47); *He shall make him ruler over all his goods.* The allusion is to the way of great men, who, if the stewards of their house conduct themselves well in that place, commonly prefer them to be the managers of their estates; thus Joseph was preferred in the house of Potiphar, Gen. 29:4, 6. But the greatest honour which the kindest master ever did to his most tried servants in this world, is nothing to that weight of glory which the Lord Jesus will confer upon his faithful watchful servants in the world to come. What is here said by a similitude, is the same that is said more plainly, Jn. 11:26, *Him will my Father honour.* And God's servants, when thus preferred; shall be perfect in wisdom and holiness to bear that weight of glory, so that there is no danger from these servants when they reign.

[2.] Concerning the *evil* servant. Here we have,

First, His description given (*v.* 48, 49); where we have the wretch drawn in his own colours. The vilest of creatures is a wicked man, the vilest of men is a wicked Christian, and the vilest of them a wicked minister. *Corruptio optimi est pessima — What is best, when corrupted, becomes the worst.* Wickedness in the prophets of Jerusalem is a *horrible* thing indeed, Jer. 23:14. Here is,

1. The cause of his wickedness; and that is, a practical disbelief of Christ's second coming; He hath *said in his heart, My Lord delays his coming;* and therefore he begins to think he will never come, but has quite forsaken his church. Ob-

serve, (1.) Christ knows that *they* say in their hearts, who with their lips cry, *Lord, Lord,* as this servant here. (2.) The delay of Christ's coming, though it is a gracious instance of his patience, is greatly abused by wicked people, whose hearts are thereby hardened in their wicked ways. When Christ's coming is looked upon as doubtful, or a thing at an immense distance, the hearts of *men are fully set to do evil,* Eccl. 8:11. See Eze. 12:27. They that walk by sense, are ready to say of the unseen Jesus, as the people did of Moses when he tarried in the mount upon their errand, *We wot not what is become of him,* and therefore *up, make us gods,* the world a god, the belly a god, any thing but him that should be.

2. The particulars of his wickedness; and they are sins of the first magnitude; he is a slave to his passions and his appetites.

(1.) Persecution is here charged upon him. He begins to *smite his fellow servants.* Note, [1.] Even the stewards of the house are to look upon all the servants of the house as their fellow servants, and therefore are forbidden to *lord it over them.* If the angel call himself *fellow servant* to John (Rev. 19:10), no marvel if John have learned to call himself *brother* to the Christians of the churches of Asia, Rev. 1:9. [2.] It is no new thing to see evil servants smiting their fellow servants; both private Christians and faithful ministers. He smites them, either because they reprove him, or because they will not bow, and do him reverence; will not say as he saith, and do as he doeth, against their consciences: he smites them with the tongue, as they smote the prophet, Jer. 18:18. And if he get power into his hand, or can press those into his service that have, as the ten horns upon the head of the beast, it goes further. Pashur the priest smote Jeremiah, and put him in the stocks, Jer. 20:2. The revolters have often been of all others most *profound to make slaughter,* Hos. 5:2. The steward, when he smites his fellow servants, does it under colour of his Master's authority, and in his name; he says, *Let the Lord be glorified* (Isa. 66:5); but he shall know that he could not put a greater affront upon his Master.

(2.) Profaneness and immorality; *He begins to eat and drink with the drunken.* [1.] He associates with the worst of sinners, has fellowship with them, is intimate with them; he walks in their counsel, stands in their way, sits in their seat, and sings their songs. The drunken are the merry and jovial company, and those he is for, and thus he hardens them in their wickedness. [2.] He does like them; *eats, and drinks, and is drunken;* so it is in Luke. This is an inlet to all manner of sin. Drunkenness is a leading wickedness; they who are slaves to that, are never masters of themselves in any thing else. The persecutors of God's people have commonly been the most vicious and immoral men. Persecuting consciences, whatever the pretensions be, are commonly the most profligate and debauched consciences. What will not *they* be drunk with, that will be *drunk with the blood of the saints?* Well, this is the description of a wicked minister, who yet may have the common gifts of learning and utterance above others; and, as hath been said of some, may preach so well in the pulpit, that it is a pity he should ever come out, and yet live so ill out of the pulpit, that it is a pity he should ever come in.

Secondly, His doom read, *v.* 50, 51. The coat and character of wicked ministers will not only not secure them from condemnation, but will greatly aggravate it. They can plead no exemption from Christ's jurisdiction, whatever they pretend to, in the church of Rome, from that of the civil magistrate; there is no benefit of clergy at Christ's bar. Observe,

1. The surprise that will accompany his doom (*v.* 50); *The Lord of that servant will come.* Note, (1.) Our putting off the thoughts of Christ's coming will not put off his coming. Whatever fancy he deludes himself with, his Lord will come. The unbelief of man shall not make that great promise, or threatening (call it which you will), of no effect. (2.) The coming of Christ will be a most dreadful surprise to secure and careless sinners, especially to wicked ministers; *He shall come in a day when he looketh not for him.* Note, Those that have slighted the warnings of the word, and silenced those of their own consciences concerning the judgment to come, cannot expect any other warnings; these will be adjudged sufficient legal notice given, whether taken or no; and no unfairness can be charged on Christ, if he come suddenly, without giving other notice. Behold, he has told us before.

2. The severity of his doom, *v.* 51. It is not more severe than righteous, but it is a doom that carries in it utter ruin, wrapt up in two dreadful words, *death* and *damnation.*

(1.) Death. His Lord shall *cut him asunder, dikotomēsei auton,* "he shall cut him off from the land of the living," from the congregation of the righteous, shall separate him unto evil; which is the definition of a *curse* (Deu. 29:21), shall cut him down, as a tree that cumbers the ground; perhaps it alludes to the sentence often used in the law, *That soul shall be cut off from his people;* denoting an utter extirpation. Death cuts off a good man, as a choice imp is cut off to be grafted in a better stock; but it cuts off a wicked man, as a withered branch is cut off for the fire — cuts him off from this world, which he set his heart so much upon, and was, as it were, one with. Or, as we read it, *shall cut him asunder,* that is, part body and soul, send the body to the grave to be a prey for worms, and the soul to hell to be a prey for devils, and there is the sinner cut asunder. The soul and body of a godly man at death part fairly, the one cheerfully lifted up to God, the other left to the dust; but the soul and body of a wicked man at death are cut asunder, torn asunder, for to them death is the *king of terrors,* Job 18:14. The wicked servant divided himself between God and the world, Christ and Belial, his profession and his lusts, justly therefore will he thus be divided.

(2.) Damnation. He *shall appoint him his portion with the hypocrites,* and a miserable portion it will be, for *there shall be weeping.* Note, [1.] There is a place and state of everlasting misery in the other world, where there is nothing but *weeping and gnashing of teeth;* which speaks the soul's tribulation and anguish under God's indignation and wrath. [2.] The divine sentence will appoint this place and state as the portion of those who by their own sin were fitted for it. Even he of whom he said, that he was *his* Lord, shall thus appoint him his portion. He that is now *the Saviour,* will then be *the Judge,* and the everlasting state of the children of men will be as he appoints. They that choose the world for their portion in this life, will have hell for their portion in the other life. *This is the portion of a wicked man from God,* Job 20:29. [3.] Hell is the proper place of hypocrites. This wicked servant has *his portion with the hypocrites.* They are, as it were, the freeholders, other sinners are but as inmates with them, and have but a portion of their misery. When Christ would express the most severe punishment in the other world, he calls it *the portion of hypocrites.* If there be any place in hell hotter than other, as it is likely there is, it will be the allotment of those that have the form, but hate the power of godliness. [4.] Wicked ministers will have their portion in the other world with the worst of sinners, even with the hypocrites, and justly, for they are the worst of hypocrites. The blood of Christ, which they have by their profaneness trampled under their feet, and the blood of souls, which they have by their unfaithfulness brought upon their heads, will bear hard upon them in that *place of torment. Son, remember,* will be as cutting a word to a minister if he perish as to any other sinner whatsoever. Let them therefore who preach to others, fear, lest they themselves should be cast-aways.

CHAPTER 25

This chapter continues and concludes our Saviour's discourse, which began in the foregoing chapter, concerning his second coming and the end of the world. This was his farewell sermon of caution, as that, Jn. 14:15, 16, was of comfort to his disciples; and they had need of both in a world of so much temptation and trouble as this is. The application of that discourse, was, Watch therefore, and be ye also ready. Now, in prosecution of these serious awakening cautions, in this chapter we have three parables, the scope of which is the same — to quicken us all with the utmost care and diligence to get ready for Christ's second coming, which, in all his farewells to his church, mention was made of, as in that before he died (Jn. 14:2), in that at his ascension (Acts 1:11), and in that at the shutting up of the canon of the scriptures, Rev. 22:20. Now it concerns us to prepare for Christ's coming; I. That we may then be ready to attend upon him; and this is shown in the parable of the ten virgins (*v.* 1–13). II. That we may then be ready to give u our account to him; and this is shown in the parable of the three servants (*v.* 14–30). III. That we may then be ready to receive from him our final sentence, and that it may be to eternal life; and this is shown in a more plain description of the process of the last judgment (*v.* 31–46). These are things of awful consideration, because of everlasting concern to every one of us.

Verses 1–13

Here,

I. That in general which is to be illustrated is, *the kingdom of heaven,* the state of things under the gospel, the external kingdom of Christ, and the administration and success of it. Some of Christ's parables had shown us what it is like now in the present reception of it, as *ch.* 13. This tells us what it shall be like, when the mystery of God shall be finished, and that kingdom delivered up to the Father. The administration of Christ's government, towards the ready and the unready in the great day, may be illustrated by this similitude; or the kingdom is put for the subjects of the kingdom. The professors of Christianity shall then be likened to these ten virgins, and shall be thus distinguished.

II. That by which it is illustrated, is, a marriage solemnity. It was a custom sometimes used among the Jews on that occasion, that the bridegroom came, attended with his friends, late in the night, to the house of the bride, where she expected him, attended with her bride-maids; who, upon notice given of the bridegrooms' approach, were to go out with lamps in their hands, to light him into the house with ceremony and formality, in order to the celebrating of the nuptials with great mirth. And some think that on these occasions they had usually *ten virgins;* for the Jews never held a synagogue, circumcised, kept the passover, or contracted marriage, but ten persons at least were present. Boaz, when he married Ruth, had *ten witnesses,* Ruth 4:2. Now in this parable,

1. The *Bridegroom* is our Lord Jesus Christ; he is so represented in the 45th Psalm, Solomon's Song, and often in the New Testament. It bespeaks his singular and superlative love to, and his faithful and inviolable covenant with, his spouse the church. Believers are now betrothed to Christ (Hos. 2:19); but the solemnizing of the marriage is reserved for the great day, when the bride, the Lamb's wife, will have made herself completely ready, Rev. 19:7, 9.

2. The virgins are the professors of religion, members of the church; but here represented as *her companions* (Ps. 45:14), as elsewhere her *children* (Isa. 54:1), her *ornaments,* Isa. 49:18. They that follow the Lamb, are said to be *virgins* (Rev. 14:4); this denotes their beauty and purity; they are to be presented as chaste *virgins to Christ,* 2 Co. 11:2. The bridegroom is a king; so these virgins are *maids of honour,* virgins *without number* (Cant. 6:8), yet here said to be *ten.*

3. The office of these virgins is to meet the bridegroom, which is as much their happiness as their duty. They come to wait *upon* the bridegroom when he appears, and in the mean time to wait *for* him. See here the nature of Christianity. As Christians, we profess ourselves to be, (1.) Attendants upon Christ, to do him honour, as the glorious Bridegroom, to be to him for a name and a praise, especially then when he shall come to be glorified in his saints. We must follow him as honorary servants do their masters, Jn. 12:26. Hold up the name, and hold forth the praise of the exalted Jesus; this is our business. (2.) Expectants of Christ, and of his second coming. As Christians, we profess, not only to believe and look for, but to love and long for, the appearing of Christ, and to act in our whole conversation with a regard to it. The second coming of Christ is the centre in which all the lines of our religion meet, and to which the whole of the divine life hath a constant reference and tendency.

4. Their chief concern is to have lights in their hands, when they attend the bridegroom, thus to do him honour and do him service. Note, Christians are children of light. The gospel is light, and they who receive it must not only be enlightened by it themselves, but must *shine as lights,* must *hold it forth,* Phil. 2:15, 16. This in general.

Now concerning these ten virgins, we may observe,

(1.) Their different character, with the proof and evidence of it.

[1.] Their character was that *five were wise, and five foolish* (*v.* 2); and *wisdom excelleth folly, as far as light excelleth darkness;* so saith Solomon, a competent judge, Eccl. 2:13. Note, Those of the same profession and denomination among men, may yet be of characters vastly different in the sight of God. Sincere Christians are the *wise* virgins, and hypocrites the *foolish ones,* as in another parable they are represented by wise and foolish builders. Note, Those are wise or foolish indeed, that are so in the affairs of their souls. True religion is true wisdom; sin is folly, but especially the sin of hypocrisy, for those are the greatest fools, that are *wise in their own conceit,* and those the worst of sinners, that *feign themselves just men.* Some observe from the equal number of the wise and foolish, what a charitable decorum (it is Archbishop Tillotson's expression) Christ observes, as if he would hope that the number of true believers was nearly equal to that of hypocrites, or, at least, would teach us to hope the best concerning those that profess religion, and to think of them with a bias to the charitable side. Though, in judging of ourselves, we ought to remember that the gate is strait, and few find it; yet, in judging of others, we ought to remember that the Captain of our salvation brings many sons to glory.

[2.] The evidence of this character was in the very thing which they were to attend to; by that they are judged of.

First, It was the folly of the foolish virgins, that they *took their lamps, and took no oil with them, v.* 3. They had just the oil enough to make their lamps burn for the present, to make a show with, as if they intended to meet the bridegroom; but no cruse or bottle of oil with them for a recruit if the bridegroom tarried; thus hypocrites.

1. They have no principle within. They have a lamp of profession in their hands, but have not in their hearts that stock of sound knowledge, rooted dispositions, and settled resolutions, which is necessary to carry them through the services and trials of the present state. They act under the influence of external inducements, but are void of spiritual life; like a tradesman, that sets up without a stock, or the seed on the stony ground, that wanted root.

2. They have no prospect of, nor make provision for, what is to come. They took lamps for a present show, but not oil for after use. This incogitancy is the ruin of many professors; all their care is to recommend themselves to their neighbours, whom they now converse with, not to approve themselves to Christ, whom they must hereafter appear before; as if any thing will serve, provide it will but serve for the present. Tell them of things not seen as yet, and you are like Lot to his sons-in-law, as one that mocked. They do not provide for hereafter, as the ant does, nor *lay up for the time to come,* 1 Tim. 6:19.

Secondly, It was the wisdom of the wise virgins, that *they took oil in their vessels with their lamps, v.* 4. They had a good principle within, which would maintain and keep up their profession. 1. The heart is the vessel, which it is our wisdom to get furnished; for, out of a good treasure there, good things must be brought; but if that root be rottenness, the blossom will be dust. 2. Grace is the *oil* which we must have in this *vessel;* in the tabernacle there was constant provision made of *oil for the light,* Ex. 35:14. Our light must shine before men in good works, but this cannot be, or not long, unless there be a fixed active principle in the heart, of faith in Christ, and love to God and our brethren, from which we must act in every thing we do in religion, with an eye to what is before us. They that took oil in their vessels, did it upon supposition that perhaps the bridegroom might tarry. Note, In looking forward it is good to prepare for the worst, to lay in for a long siege. But remember that this oil which keeps the lamps burning, is derived to the candlestick from Jesus Christ, the great and good *Olive,* by the *golden pipes* of the ordinances, as it is represented in that vision (Zec. 4:2, 3, 12), which is explained Jn. 1:16, *Of his fulness have all we received, and grace for grace.*

(2.) Their common fault, during the bridegroom's delay; *They all slumbered and slept, v.* 5. Observe here,

[1.] The bridegroom tarried, that is, he did not come out so soon as they expected. What we look for as certain, we are apt to think is very near; many in the apostles' times imagined that the *day of the Lord was at hand,* but it is not so. Christ, as to us, *seems* to tarry, and yet really *does not,* Hab. 2:3. There is good reason for the Bridegroom's tarrying; there are many intermediate counsels and purposes to be accomplished, the elect must all be called in, God's patience must be manifested, and the saints' patience tried, the harvest of the earth must be ripened, and so must the harvest of heaven too. But though Christ tarry past *our* time, he will not tarry past the *due* time.

[2.] While he tarried, those that waited for him, grew careless, and forgot what they were attending; *They all slumbered and slept;* as if they had given over looking for him; for *when the Son of man cometh,* he will *not find faith,* Lu. 18:8. Those that inferred the suddenness of it from its certainty, when that answered not their expectation, were apt from the delay to infer its uncertainty. The wise virgins slumbered, and the foolish slept; so some distinguish it; however, they were both faulty. The wise virgins kept their lamps burning, but did not keep themselves awake. Note, Too many good Christians, when they have been long in profession, grow remiss in their preparations for Christ's second coming; they intermit their care, abate their zeal, their graces are not lively, nor their works found perfect before God; and though all *love* be not lost, yet the *first* love is left. If it was hard to the disciples to watch with Christ *an hour,* much more to watch with him *an age. I sleep,* saith the spouse, *but my heart wakes,*

Observe, *First,* They slumbered, and then they slept. Note, One degree of carelessness and remissness makes way for another. Those that allow themselves in slumbering, will scarcely keep themselves from sleeping; therefore dread the beginning of spiritual decays; *Venienti occurrite morbo — Attend to the first symptoms of disease.* The ancients generally understood the virgins' slumbering and sleeping of their dying; they all died, wise and foolish (Ps. 49:10), before judgment-day. So Ferus, *Antequam veniat sponsus omnibus obdormiscendum est, hoc est, moriendum — Before the Bridegroom come, all must sleep, that is, die.* So Calvin. But I think it is rather to be taken as we have opened it.

(3.) The surprising summons given them, to attend the bridegroom (*v.* 6); *At midnight there was a cry made, Behold, the bridegroom cometh.* Note, [1.] Though Christ tarry long, he will come at last; though he seem slow, he is sure. In his first coming, he was thought long by those that waited for the consolation of Israel; yet in the *fulness of time* he came; so his second coming, though long deferred, is not forgotten; his enemies shall find, to their cost, that forbearance is no acquittance; and his friends shall find, to their comfort, that *the vision is for an appointed time, and at the end it shall speak, and not lie.* The year of the redeemed is fixed, and it will come. [2.] Christ's coming will be at our midnight, when we least look for him, and are most disposed to take our rest. His coming for the relief and comfort of his people, often is when the good intended seems to be at the greatest distance; and his coming to reckon with his enemies, is when they put the evil day furthest from them. It was at midnight that the first-born of Egypt were destroyed, and Israel delivered, Ex. 12:29. Death often comes when it is least expected; the soul is *required this night,* Lu. 12:20. Christ will come when he pleases, to show his sovereignty, and will not let us know when, to teach us our duty. [3.] When Christ comes, we must *go forth to meet him.* As Christians we are bound to attend all the motions of the Lord Jesus, and meet him in all his outgoings. When he comes to us at death, we must go forth out of the body, out of the world, to meet him with affections and workings of soul suitable to the discoveries we then expect him to make of himself. *Go ye forth to meet him,* is a call to those who are habitually prepared, to be actually ready. [4.] The notice given of Christ's approach, and the call to meet him, will be awakening; *There was a cry made.* His first coming was not with any observation at all, nor did they say, *Lo, here is Christ,* or *Lo, he is there; he was in the world, and the world knew him not;* but his second coming will be with the observation of all the world; *Every eye shall see him.* There will be a cry from heaven, for he shall *descend with a shout, Arise, ye dead, and come to judgment;* and a cry from the earth too, a *cry to rocks and mountains,* Rev. 6:16.

(4.) The address they all made to answer this summons (*v.* 7); *They all arose, and trimmed their lamps,* snuffed them and supplied them with oil and went about with all expedition to put themselves in a posture to receive the bridegroom. Now, [1.] This, in the wise virgins, bespeaks an actual preparation for the Bridegroom's coming. Note, even those that are best prepared for death, have, upon the immediate arrests of it, work to do, to get themselves actually ready, that they may be *found in peace* (2 Pt. 3:14), *found doing* (ch. 24:46), and not *found naked,* 2 Co. 5:3. It will be a day of search and enquiry; and it concerns us to think how we shall then be found. When we see the day approaching, we must address ourselves to our dying work with all seriousness, renewing our repentance for sin, our consent to the covenant, our farewells to the world; and our souls must be carried out toward God in suitable breathings. [2.] In the foolish virgins, it denotes a vain confidence, and conceit of the goodness of their state, and their readiness for another world. Note, Even counterfeit graces will serve a man to make a show of when he comes to die, as well as they have done all his life long; the hypocrite's hopes blaze when they are just expiring, like a lightening before death.

(5.) The distress which the foolish virgins were in, for want of *oil, v.* 8, 9. This bespeaks, [1.] The apprehensions which some hypocrites have of the misery of their state, even on this side death, when God opens their eyes to see their folly, and themselves perishing *with a lie in their right hand.* Or, however, [2.] The real misery of their state on the other side death, and in the judgment; how far their fair, but false, profession of religion will be from availing them any thing in the great day; see what comes of it.

First, Their lamps are gone out. The lamps of hypocrites

often go out in this life; when they who have begun in the spirit, end in the flesh, and the hypocrisy breaks out in an open apostasy, 2 Pt. 2:20. The profession withers, and the credit of it is lost; the hopes fail, and the comfort of them is gone; how often is *the candle of the wicked* thus *put out?* Job 21:17. Yet many a hypocrite keeps up his credit, and the comfort of his profession, such as it is, to the last; but what is it when *God taketh away his soul?* Job 27:8. If his candle be not put out *before* him, it is put out *with* him, Job 18:5, 6. He shall *lie down in sorrow,* Isa. 50:11. The gains of a hypocritical profession will not follow a man to judgment, *ch.* 7:22, 23. The lamps are gone out, when the hypocrite's hope proves *like the spider's web* (Job 8:11, etc.), and like the *giving up of the ghost* (Job 11:20), like Absalom's mule that left him in the oak.

Secondly, They wanted oil to supply them when they were going out. Note, Those that take up short of true grace, will certainly find the want of it one time or other. An external profession well humoured may carry a man far, but it will not carry him through; it may light him along this world, but the damps of the valley of the shadow of death will put it out.

Thirdly, They would gladly be beholden to the wise virgins for a supply out of their vessels; *Give us of your oil.* Note, The day is coming, when carnal hypocrites would gladly be found in the condition of true Christians. Those who now hate the strictness of religion, will, at death and judgment, wish for the solid comforts of it. Those who care not to live the life, yet would die the death, of the righteous. The day is coming when those who now look with contempt upon humble contrite saints, would gladly get an interest in them, and would value those as their best friends and benefactors, whom now they *set with the dogs of their flock. Give us of your oil;* that is, "Speak a good word for us;" so some; but there is no occasion for vouchers in the great day, the Judge knows what is every man's true character. But is it not well that they are brought to say, *Give us of your oil?* It is so; but, 1. This request was extorted by sensible necessity. Note, Those will see their need of grace hereafter, when it should save them, who will not see their need of grace now, when it should sanctify and rule them. (2.) It comes too late. God would have given them oil, had they asked in time; but there is no buying when the market is over, no bidding when the inch of candle is dropped.

Fourthly, They were denied a share in their companions' oil. It is a sad presage of a repulse with God, when they were thus repulsed by good people. *The wise answered, Not so;* that peremptory denial is not in the original, but supplied by the translators: these wise virgins would rather give a reason without a positive refusal, than (as many do) give a positive refusal without a reason. They were well inclined to help their neighbours in distress; but, We must not, we cannot, we dare not, do it, *lest there be not enough for us and you;* charity begins at home; but *go, and buy for yourselves.* Note, 1. Those that would be saved, must have grace of their own. Though we have benefit by the communion of saints, and the faith and prayers of others may now redound to our advantage, yet our own sanctification is indispensably necessary to our own salvation. The just shall live by his faith. Every man shall give account of himself, and therefore let every man *prove his own work;* for he cannot get another to muster for him in that day. 2. Those that have most grace, have none to spare; all we have, is little enough for ourselves to appear before God in. The best have need to borrow from Christ, but they have none to lend to any of their neighbours. The church of Rome, which dreams of works of supererogation and the imputation of the righteousness of saints, forgets that it was the wisdom of the wise virgins to understand that they had but oil enough for themselves, and none for others. But observe, These wise virgins do not upbraid the foolish with their neglect, nor boast of their own forecast, nor torment them with suggestions tending to despair, but give them the best advice the case will bear, *Go ye rather to them that sell.* Note, Those that deal foolishly in the affairs of their souls, are to be pitied, and not insulted over; for who made thee to differ? When ministers attend such as have been mindless of God and their souls all their days, but are under death-bed convictions; and, because true repentance is never too late, direct them to repent, and turn to God, and close with Christ; yet, because late repentance is seldom true, they do but as these wise virgins did by the foolish, even made the best of bad. They can but tell them what is to be done, if it be not too late, but whether the door may not be shut before it is done, is an unspeakable hazard. It is good advice now, if it be taken in time, *Go to them that sell, and buy for yourselves.* Note, Those that would have grace, must have recourse to, and attend upon, the means of grace. See Isa. 55:1

(6.) The coming of the bridegroom, and the issue of all this different character of the wise and foolish virgins. See what came of it.

[1.] *While they went out to buy, the bridegroom came.* Note, With regard to those that put off their great work to the last, it is a thousand to one, that they have not time to do it then. Getting grace is a work of time, and cannot be done in a hurry. While the poor awakened soul addresses itself, upon a sick bed, to repentance and prayer, in awful confusion, it scarcely knows which end to begin at, or what to do first; and presently death comes, judgment comes, and the work is undone, and the poor sinner undone for ever. This comes of having oil to buy when we should burn it, and grace to get when we should use it.

The bridegroom came. Note, Our Lord Jesus will come to his people, at the great day, as a Bridegroom; will come in pomp and rich attire, attended with his friends: now that the Bridegroom is taken away from us, *we fast* (*ch.* 9:15), but then will be an everlasting feast. Then the Bridegroom will fetch home his bride, to be *where he is* (Jn. 17:24), and will *rejoice over his bride,* Isa. 62:5.

[2.] *They that were ready, went in with him to the marriage.* Note, *First,* To be eternally glorified is to go in with Christ to the marriage, to be in his immediate presence, and in the most intimate fellowship and communion with him in a state of eternal rest, joy, and plenty. *Secondly,* Those, and those only, shall go to heaven hereafter, that are made ready for heaven here, that are *wrought to the self-same thing,* 2 Co. 5:5. *Thirdly,* The suddenness of death, and of Christ's coming to us then, will be no obstruction to our happiness, if we have been habitually prepared.

[3.] *The door was shut,* as is usual when all the company is come, that are to be admitted. The door was shut, *First,* To secure those that were within; that, being now made *pillars in the house of our God, they may go no more out,* Rev. 3:12. Adam was put into paradise, but the door was left open and so he went out again; but when glorified saints are put into the heavenly paradise, they are shut in. *Secondly,* To exclude those that were out. The state of saints and sinners will then be unalterably fixed, and those that are shut out then, will be shut out for ever. Now the gate is strait, yet it is open; but then it will be shut and bolted, and *a great gulf fixed.* This was like the shutting of the door of the ark when Noah was in; as he was thereby preserved, so all the rest were finally abandoned.

[4.] The foolish virgins came when it was *too late* (*v.* 11); *Afterward came also the other virgins.* Note, *First,* There are many that will seek admission into heaven when it is too late; as profane Esau, who *afterward would have inherited the blessing.* God and religion will be glorified by those late solicitations, though sinners will not be saved by them; it is for the honour of *Lord, Lord,* that, of fervent and importunate prayer, that those who slight it now, will flee to it shortly, and it will not be called whining and canting then. *Secondly,* The vain confidence of hypocrites will carry them very far in their expectations of happiness. They go to heaven-gate, and demand entrance, and yet are shut out; lifted up to heaven in a fond conceit of the goodness of their state, and yet thrust down to hell.

[5.] They were *rejected,* as Esau was (*v.* 12); *I know you not.* Note, We are all concerned to *seek the Lord while he may be found;* for there is a time coming when he will not be found. Time was, when, *Lord, Lord, open to us,* would have sped well, by virtue of that promise, *Knock, and it shall be opened to you;* but now it comes too late. The sentence is solemnly bound on with, *Verily I say unto you,* which amounts to no less than *swearing in his wrath, that they shall never enter into his rest.* It bespeaks him resolved, and them silenced by it.

Lastly, Here is a practical inference drawn from this parable (*v.* 13); *Watch therefore,* We had it before (*ch.* 24:42), and here it is repeated as the most needful caution. Note, 1. Our great duty is to watch, to attend to the business of our souls with the utmost diligence and circumspection. Be awake, and be wakeful. 2. It is a good reason for our watching, that the time of our Lord's coming is very uncertain; *we know neither the day nor the hour.* Therefore every day and every hour we must be ready, and not off our watch any day in the year, or any hour in the day. Be thou *in the fear of the Lord* every day and *all the day long.*

Verses 14–30

We have here the parable of the *talents* committed to three servants; this implies that we are in a state of work and business, as the former implies that we are in a state of expectancy. *That* showed the necessity of habitual preparation, *this* of actual diligence in our present work and service. In *that* we were stirred up to do well for our own souls; in *this* to lay out ourselves for the glory of God and the good of others.

In this parable, 1. The *Master* is Christ, who is the absolute Owner and Proprietor of all persons and things, and in a special manner of his church; into his hands all things are delivered. 2. The *servants* are Christians, his own servants, so they are called; born in his house, bought with his money, devoted to his praise, and employed in his work. It is probable that *ministers* are specially intended here, who are more immediately attending on him, and sent by him. St. Paul often calls himself a *servant of Jesus Christ.* See 2 Tim. 2:24.

We have three things, in general, in this parable.

I. The trust committed to these servants; Their master *delivered to them his goods:* having appointed them to work (for Christ keeps no servants to be idle), he left them something to work upon. Note, 1. Christ's servants have and receive their all from him; for they are of themselves worth nothing, nor have any thing they can call their own but sin. 2. Our receiving from Christ is in order to our working for him. Our privileges are intended to find us with business. The *manifestation of the Spirit* is given to every man to *profit withal.* 3. Whatever we receive to be made use of for Christ, still the property is vested in him; we are but tenants upon his land, *stewards of his manifold grace,* 1 Pt. 4:10. Now observe here,

(1.) On what occasion this trust was committed to these servants: The master was *travelling into a far country.* This is explained, Eph. 4:8. *When he ascended on high, he gave gifts to men.* Note, [1.] When Christ went to heaven, he was as a man *travelling into a far country;* that is, he went with a purpose to be away a great while. [2.] When he went, he took care to furnish his church with all things necessary for it during his personal absence. For, and in consideration of, his departure, he committed to his church truths, laws, promises and powers; these were the *parakathēkē — the great depositum* (as it is called, 1 Tim. 6:20; 2 Tim. 1:14), the *good thing* that is committed to us; and he sent his Spirit to enable his servants to teach and profess those truths, to press and observe those laws, to improve and apply those promises, and to exercise and employ those powers, ordinary or extraordinary. Thus Christ, at his ascension, left his goods to his church.

(2.) In what proportion this trust was committed. [1.] He gave *talents;* a talent of silver is computed to be in our money three hundred and fifty-three pounds eleven shillings and ten pence halfpenny; so the learned Bishop Cumberland. Note, Christ's gifts are rich and valuable, the purchases of his blood inestimable, and none of them mean. [2.] He gave to some more, to others less; to one *five* talents, to another *two,* to another *one;* to every one according to his several ability. When Divine Providence has made a difference in men's ability, as to mind, body, estate, relation, and interest, divine grace dispenses spiritual gifts accordingly, but still the ability itself is from him. Observe, *First,* Every one had some one talent at least, and that is not a despicable stock for a poor servant to begin with. A *soul* of our own is the *one* talent we are every one of us entrusted with, and it will find us with work. *Hoc nempe ab homine exigiture, ut prosit hominibus; si fieri potest, multis; si minus, paucis; si minus, proximis, si minus, sibi: nam cum se utilem caeteris efficit, commune agit negotium. Et si quis bene de se meretur, hoc ipso aliis prodest quod aliis profuturum parat — It is the duty of a man to render himself beneficial to those around him; to a great number if possible; but if this is denied him, to a few; to his intimate connections; or, at least, to himself. He that is useful to others, may be reckoned a common good. And whoever entitles himself to his own approbation, is serviceable to others, as forming himself to those habits which will result in their favour.* Seneca de Otio Sapient. *Secondly,* All had not alike, for they had not all alike abilities and opportunities. God is a free Agent, *dividing to every man severally as he will;* some are cut out for service in one kind, others in another, as the members of the natural body. When the householder had thus settled his affairs, he *straightway took his journey.* Our Lord Jesus, when he had given commandments to his apostles, as one in haste to be gone, went to heaven.

II. The different management and improvement of this trust, which we have an account of, *v.* 16–18.

1. Two of the servants did well.

(1.) They were diligent and faithful; *They went, and traded;* they put the money they were entrusted with, to the use for which it was intended — laid it out in goods, and made returns of it; as soon as ever their master was gone, they immediately applied themselves to their business. Those that have so much work to do, as every Christian has, need to set about it quickly, and lose not time. *They went, and traded.* Note, A true Christian is a spiritual tradesman. Trades are called *mysteries,* and *without controversy great is the mystery of godliness;* it is a manufacture trade; there is something to be done by upon our own hearts, and for the good of others. It is a merchant-trade; things of less value to us are parted with for things of greater value; *wisdom's merchandize,* Prov. 3:15; Mt. 13:45. A tradesman is one who, having made his trade his choice, and taken pains to learn it, makes it his business to follow it, lays out all he has for the advancement of it, makes all other affairs bend to it, and lives upon the gain of it. Thus does a true Christian act in the work of religion; we have no stock of our *own* to trade with, but trade as factors with our master's stock. The endowments of the mind — reason, wit, learning, must be used in subserviency to religion; the enjoyments of the world — estate, credit, interest, power, preferment, must be improved for the honour of Christ. The ordinances of the gospel, and our opportunities of attending them, bibles, ministers, sabbaths, sacraments, must be improved for the end for which they were instituted, and communion with God kept up by them, and the gifts and graces of the Spirit must be exercised; and this is trading with our talents.

(2.) They were successful; they doubled their stock, and in a little time made *cent. per cent.* of it: he that had *five talents,* soon made them *other five.* Trading with our talents is not alway successful with others, but, however, it shall be so to ourselves, Isa. 49:4. Note, The hand of the diligent makes rich in graces, and comforts, and treasures of good works. There is a great deal to be got by industry in religion.

Observe, The returns were in proportion to the receivings. [1.] From those to whom God hath given five talents, he expects the improvement of five, and to reap plentifully where he sows plentifully. The greater gifts any have, the more pains they ought to take, as those must that have a large stock to manage. [2.] From those to whom he has given but two talents, he expects only the improvement of two, which may encourage those who are placed in a lower and narrower sphere of usefulness; if they lay out themselves to do good according to the best of their capacity and opportunity, they shall be accepted, though they do not so much good as others.

2. The third did ill (*v.* 18); *He that had received one talent, went, and hid his lord's money.* Though the parable represents but one in three unfaithful, yet in a history that answers this *parable,* we find the disproportion quite the other way, when *ten lepers were cleansed, nine* of *ten* hid the talent, and *only one returned to give thanks,* Lu. 17:17, 18. The unfaithful servant was he that had but *one* talent: doubtless there are many that have five talents, and bury them all; great abilities, great advantages, and yet do no good with them: but Christ would hint to us, (1.) That if he that had but one talent, be reckoned with thus for burying that one, much more will they be accounted offenders, that have more, that have many, and bury them. If he that was but of small capacity, was cast into utter darkness because he did not improve what he had as he might have done, *of how much sorer punishment, suppose ye, shall he be thought worthy, that tramples underfoot the greatest advantages?* (2.) That those who have least to do for God, frequently do least of what they have to do. Some make it an excuse for their laziness, that they have not the opportunities of serving God that others have; and because they have not wherewithal to do what they say they would, they will not do what we are sure they can, and so sit down and do nothing; it is really an aggravation of their sloth, that when they have but one talent to take care about, they neglect that one.

He digged in the earth, and hid the talent, for fear it should be stolen; he did not misspend or misemploy it, did not embezzle it or squander it away, but he *hid it.* Money is like manure (so my Lord Bacon used to say,) good for nothing in the heap, but it must be spread; yet it is an evil which we have often seen under the sun, *treasure heaped together* (Jam. 5:3; Eccl. 6:1, 2), which does good to nobody; and so it is in spiritual gifts; many have them, and make no use of them for the end for which they were given them. Those that have estates, and do not lay them out in works of piety and charity; that have power and interest, and do not with it promote religion in the places where they live; ministers that have capacities and opportunities of doing good, but do not stir up the gift that is in them, are those slothful servants that seek their own things more than Christ's.

He hid his *lord's* money; had it been his *own,* he might have done as he pleased; but, whatever abilities and advantages we have, they are not our *own,* we are but stewards of them, and must give account to our Lord, whose goods they are. It was an aggravation of his slothfulness, that his fellow-servants were busy and successful in trading, and their zeal should have provoked his. Are others active, and shall we be idle?

III. The account of this improvement, *v.* 19. 1. The account is deferred; it is not *till after a long time* that they are reckoned with; not that the master neglects his affairs, or that God is *slack concerning his promise* (2 Pt. 3:9); no, he is *ready to judge* (1 Pt. 4:5); but every thing must be done in its time and order. 2. Yet the day of account comes at last; *The lord of those servants reckoneth with them.* Note, The stewards of the manifold grace of God must shortly *give account of their stewardship.* We must all be reckoned with — what good we have got to our own souls, and what good we have done to others by the advantages we have enjoyed. See Rom. 14:10, 11. Now here is,

(1.) The good account of the faithful servants; and here observe,

[1.] The servants *giving up the account* (*v.* 20, 22); "*Lord, thou deliveredst to me five talents,* and to me *two;* behold, *I have gained five talents,* and I *two* talents *more.*"

First, Christ's faithful servants acknowledge with thankfulness his vouchsafements to them; *Lord, thou deliveredst to me* such and such things. Note, 1. It is good to keep a particular account of our receivings from God, to remember what we have received, that we may know what is expected from us, and may render according to the benefit. 2. We must never look upon our improvements but with a general mention of God's favour to us, of the honour he has put upon us, in entrusting us with his goods, and of that grace which is the spring and fountain of all the good that is in us or is done by us. For the truth is, the more we do for God, the more we are indebted to him for making use of us, and enabling us, for his service.

Secondly, They produce, as an evidence of their faithfulness, what they have gained. Note, God's good stewards have something to show for their diligence; *Show me thy faith by thy works.* He that is a good man, *let him show it,* Jam. 3:13. If we be careful in our spiritual trade, it will soon be seen by us, and *our works will follow us,* Rev. 14:13. Not that the saints will in the great day make mention of their own good deeds; no, Christ will do that for them (*v.* 35); but it intimates that they who faithfully improve their talents, *shall have boldness in the day of Christ,* 1 Jn. 2:28–4:17. And it is observable that he who had but *two* talents, gave up his account as cheerfully as he who had *five;* for our comfort, in the day of account, will be according to our faithfulness, not according to our usefulness; our sincerity, not our success; according to the uprightness of our hearts, not according to the degree of our opportunities.

[2.] The master's acceptance and approbation of their account, *v.* 21, 23.

First, He commended them; *Well done, good and faithful servant.* Note, The diligence and integrity of those who approve themselves the good and faithful servants of Jesus Christ, will certainly be *found to praise, and honour, and glory, at his appearing,* 1 Pt. 1:7. Those that own and honour God now, he will own and honour shortly. 1. Their persons will be accepted; *Thou good and faithful servant.* He that knows the integrity of his servants now, will witness to it in the great day; and they that are found faithful, shall be called so. Perhaps they were censured by men, as *righteous overmuch;* but Christ will give them their just characters, of *good and faithful.* 2. Their performances will be accepted; *Well done.* Christ will call those, and those only, *good servants,* that have done well; for it is *by patient continuance in well-doing* that we seek for this glory and honour; and if we seek, we shall find; if we do that which is good, and do it well, we shall have *praise of the same.* Some masters are so morose, that they will not commend their servants, though they do their work ever so well; it is thought enough not to chide: but Christ will commend his servants that do well; whether their praise be of men or not, it is of him; and if we have the good word of our Master, the matter is not great what our fellow-servants say of us; if he saith, *Well done,* we are happy, and it should then be a small thing to us to be judged of men's judgment; as, on the contrary, not he who commendeth himself, or whom his neighbours commend, is approved, but whom the Lord commends.

Secondly, He rewards them. The faithful servants of Christ shall not be put off with bare commendation; no, all their work and labour of love shall be rewarded.

Now this reward is here expressed two ways.

1. In one expression agreeable to the parable; *Thou hast been faithful over a few things, I will make thee ruler over many things.* It is usual in the courts of princes, and families of great men, to advance those to higher offices, that have been faithful in lower. Note, Christ is a master that will prefer his servants who acquit themselves well. Christ has honour in store for those that honour him — *a crown* (2 Tim. 4:8), *a throne* (Rev. 3:21), *a kingdom, ch.* 25:34. Here they are beggars; in heaven they shall be rulers. The upright shall have dominion: Christ's servants are all princes.

Observe the disproportion between the work and the reward; there are but few things in which the saints are serviceable to the glory of God, but there are many things wherein they shall be glorified with God. What charge we receive from God, what work we do for God in this world, is but little, very little, compared with *the joy set before us.* Put together all our service, all our sufferings, all our improvements, all the good we do to others, all we get to ourselves, and they are but a few things, next to nothing, not worthy to be compared, not fit to be named the same day with the glory to be revealed.

2. In another expression, which slips out of the parable into the thing signified by it; *Enter thou into the joy of thy Lord.* Note, (1.) The state of the blessed is a state of joy, not only because all tears shall then be wiped away, but all the springs of comfort shall be opened to them, and the fountains of joy broken up. Where there are the vision and fruition of God, a perfection of holiness, and the society of the blessed, there cannot but be a fulness of joy. (2.) This joy is the *joy of their Lord;* the joy which he himself has purchased and provided for them; the joy of the redeemed, bought with the sorrow of the Redeemer. It is the joy which he himself is in the possession of, and which he had his eye upon when he *endured the cross, and despised the shame,* Heb. 12:2. It is the joy of which he himself is the fountain and centre. It is the joy of our Lord, for it is *joy in the Lord,* who is our exceeding joy. Abraham was not willing that the *steward of his house,* though *faithful,* should be *his heir* (Gen. 15:3); but Christ admits his faithful stewards into his own joy, to be joint-heirs with him. (3.) Glorified saints shall enter into this joy, shall have a full and complete possession of it, as the heir when he comes of age enters upon his estate, or as they that were ready, *went* in to the marriage feast. Here the joy of our Lord enters into the saints, in the earnest of the Spirit; shortly they shall enter into it, shall be in it to eternity, as in their element.

(2.) The bad account of the slothful servant. Observe,

[1.] His apology for himself, *v.* 24, 25. Though he had received but *one* talent, for that one he is called to account. The smallness of our receiving will not excuse us from a reckoning. None shall be called to an account for more than they have received; but for what we have, we must all account.

Observe, *First,* What he confides in. He comes to the account with a deal of assurance, relying on the plea he had to put in, that he was able to say, "*Lo, there thou hast that is thine;* if I have not made it more, as the others have done, yet this I can say, I have not made it less." This, he thinks, may serve to bring him off, if not with praise, yet with safety.

Note, Many a one goes very securely to judgment, presuming upon the validity of a plea that will be overruled as vain and frivolous. Slothful professors, that are afraid of doing too much for God, yet hope to come off as well as those that take so much pains in religion. Thus *the sluggard is wiser in his own conceit than seven men that can render a reason,* Prov. 26:16. This servant thought that his account would pass well enough, because he could say, *There thou hast that is thine.* "Lord, I was no spendthrift of my estate, no prodigal of my time, no profaner of my sabbaths, no opposer of good ministers and good preaching; Lord, I never ridiculed my bible, nor set my wits to work to banter religion, nor abused my power to persecute any good man; I never drowned my parts, nor wasted God's good creatures in drunkenness and gluttony, nor ever to my knowledge did I injury to any body." Many that are called Christians, build great hopes for heaven upon their being able to make such an account; yet all this amounts to no more than *there thou hast that is thine;* as if no more were required, or could be expected.

Secondly, What he confesses. He owns the burying of his talent; *I hid thy talent in the earth.* He speaks as if that were no great fault; nay, as if he deserved praise for his prudence in putting it in a safe place, and running no hazards with it. Note, It is common for people to make a very light matter of that which will be their condemnation in the great day. Or, if he was conscious to himself that it was his fault, it intimates how easily slothful servants will be convicted in the judgment; there will need no great search for proof, for *their own tongues shall fall upon them.*

Thirdly, What he makes his excuse; *I knew that thou were a hard man, and I was afraid.* Good thought of God would beget love, and that love would make us diligent and faithful; but hard thoughts of God beget fear, and that fear makes us slothful and unfaithful. His excuse bespeaks,

1. The sentiments of an enemy; *I knew thee, that thou art a hard man.* This was like that wicked saying of the house of Israel, *The way of the Lord is not equal,* Eze. 18:25. Thus his *defence* is his *offence. The foolishness of man perverteth his way,* and then, as if that would mend the matter, *his heart fretteth against the Lord.* This is covering the transgression, as Adam, who implicitly laid the fault on God himself; *The woman which thou gavest me.* Note, Carnal hearts are apt to conceive false and wicked opinions concerning God, and with them to harden themselves in their evil ways. Observe how confidently he speaks; *I knew thee to be so.* How could he know him to be so? *What iniquity have we or our fathers found in him?* Jer. 2:5. Wherein has he wearied us with his work, or deceived us in his wages? Mic. 6:3. Has he *been a wilderness to us, or a land of darkness?* Thus long God has governed the world, and may ask with more reason than Samuel himself could, *Whom have I defrauded? or whom have I oppressed?* Does not all the world know the contrary, that he is so far from being a hard master, that *the earth is full of his goodness,* so far from reaping where he sowed not, that he sows a great deal where he reaps nothing? For he *causes the sun to shine, and his rain to fall, upon the evil and unthankful, and fills their hearts with food and gladness* who say to the Almighty, *Depart from us.* This suggestion bespeaks the common reproach which wicked people cast upon God, as if all the blame of their sin and ruin lay at his door, for denying them his grace; whereas it is certain that never any who faithfully improved the common grace they had, perished for want of special grace; nor can any show what could in reason have been done more for an unfruitful vineyard than God has done in it. God does not demand brick, and deny straw; no, whatever is required in the covenant, is promised in the covenant; so that if we perish, it is owing to ourselves.

2. The spirit of a slave; *I was afraid,* This ill affection toward God arose from his false notions of him; and nothing is more unworthy of God, nor more hinders our duty to him, than slavish fear. This has bondage and torment, and is directly opposite to that entire love which the great commandment requires. Note, Hard thoughts of God drive us from, and cramp us in his service. Those who think it impossible to please him, and in vain to serve him, will do nothing to purpose in religion.

[2.] His Lord's answer to this apology. His plea will stand him in no stead, it is overruled, nay, it is made to turn against him, and he is struck speechless with it; for here we have his conviction and his condemnation.

First, His conviction, *v.* 26, 27. Two things he is convicted of.

1. Slothfulness; *Thou wicked and slothful servant.* Note, Slothful servants are wicked servants, and will be reckoned with as such by their master, for he that is *slothful in his work,* and neglects the good that God has commanded, *is brother to him that is a great waster,* by doing the evil that God has

forbidden, Prov. 18:9. He that is careless in God's work, is near akin to him that is busy in the devil's work. *Satis est mali nihil fecisse boni — To do no good is to incur very serious blame.* Omissions are sins, and must come into judgment; slothfulness makes way for wickedness; all become *filthy,* for *there is none that doeth good,* Ps. 14:3. When the house is empty, the unclean spirit takes possession. Those that are idle in the affairs of their souls, are not only idle, but something worse, 1 Tim. 5:13. When men sleep, the enemy sows tares.

2. Self-contradiction (*v.* 26, 27); *Thou knewest that I reap where I sowed not: thou oughtest therefore to have put my money to the exchangers.* Note, The hard thoughts which sinners have of God, though false and unjust, will be so far from justifying their wickedness and slothfulness, that they will rather aggravate and add to their guilt. Three ways this may be taken; (1.) "Suppose I had been so hard a master, shouldest not thou therefore have been the more diligent and careful to please me, if not for *love,* yet for *fear,* and for that reason oughtest not thou to have minded thy work?" If our God is a consuming fire, in consideration of that let us study how to serve him. Or thus, (2.) "If thou didst think me to be a hard master, and therefore durst not trade with the money thyself, for fear of losing by it, and being made to stand to the loss, yet thou mightest have put it into the hands of the exchangers, or goldsmith, mightest have brought it into the bank, and then at my coming, if I could not have had the greater improvement, by trade and merchandize (as of the other talents), yet I might have had the less improvement, of bare interest, and should have received *my own with usury;"* which, it seems, was a common practice at that time, and not disallowed by our Saviour. Note, If we could not, or durst not, do what we would, yet that excuse will not serve, when it will be made to appear that we did not do what we could and durst. If we could not find in our hearts to venture upon more difficult and hazardous services, yet will that justify us in shrinking from those that were more safe and easy? Something is better than nothing; if we fail of showing our courage in bold enterprises, yet we must not fail to testify our goodwill in honest endeavours; and our Master *will not despise the day of small things.* Or thus, (3.) "Suppose I did reap *where I sowed not,* yet that is nothing to thee, for I had sowed upon thee, and the talent was my money which thou wast entrusted with, not only to keep, but to improve." Note, In the day of account, wicked and slothful servants will be left quite without excuse; frivolous pleas will be overruled, and every mouth will be stopped; and those who now stand so much upon their own justification will not have one word to say for themselves.

Secondly, His condemnation. The slothful servant is sentenced,

1. To be deprived of his talent (*v.* 28, 29); *Take therefore the talent from him.* The talents were first disposed of by the Master, as an absolute Owner, but this was now disposed of by him as a Judge; he takes it from the unfaithful servant, to punish him, and gives it to him that was eminently faithful, to reward him. And the meaning of this part of the parable we have in the reason of the sentence (*v.* 29), *To every one that hath shall be given.* This may be applied, (1.) To the blessings of this life — worldly wealth and possessions. These we are entrusted with, to be used for the glory of God, and the good of those about us. Now *he that hath* these things, and useth them for these ends, he *shall have abundance;* perhaps abundance of the things themselves, at least, abundance of comfort in them, and of better things; but *from him that hath not,* that is, that hath these things as if he had them not, had not power to eat of them, or to do good with *(Avaro deest, tam quod habet, quam quod non habet — The miser may be considered as destitute of what he has, as well as of what he has not), they shall be taken away.* Solomon explains this, Prov. 11:24. *There is that scattereth, and yet increaseth; and there is that withholdeth more than is meet, and it tendeth to poverty.* Giving to the poor is trading with what we have, and the returns will be rich; it will multiply the meal in the barrel, and the oil in the cruse: but those that are sordid, and niggardly, and uncharitable, will find that those riches which are so got, *perish by evil travail,* Eccl. 5:13, 14. Sometimes Providence strangely transfers estates from those that do no good with them to those that do; they are *gathered for him that will pity the poor,* Prov. 28:8. See Prov. 13:22; Job 27:16, 17; Eccl. 2:26. (2.) We may apply it to the means of grace. They who are diligent in improving the opportunities they have, God will enlarge them, will *set before them an open door* (Rev. 3:8); but they who know not the day of their visitation, shall have the things that belong to their peace hid from their eyes. For proof of this, *go see what God did to Shiloh,* Jer. 7:12. (3.) We may apply it to the common gifts of the Spirit. He that hath these, and doeth good with them, shall have abundance; these gifts improve by exercise, and brighten by being used; the more we do, the more we may do, in religion; but those who stir not up the gift that is in them, who do not exert themselves according to their capacity, their gifts rust, and decay, and go out like a neglected fire. From his that hath not a living principle of grace in his soul, shall be taken away the common gifts which he hath, as the lamps of the foolish virgins went out for want of oil, *v.* 8. Thus the arm of the *idle shepherd,* which he had sluggishly folded up in his bosom, comes to be dried up, and his right eye, which he had carelessly or wilfully shut, becomes utterly darkened, as it is threatened, Zec. 11:17.

2. He is sentenced to be *cast into outer darkness, v.* 30. Here,

(1.) His character is that of an *unprofitable servant.* Note, Slothful servants will be reckoned with as unprofitable servants, who do nothing to the purpose of their coming into the world, nothing to answer the end of their birth or baptism, who are no way serviceable to the glory of God, the good of others, or the salvation of their own souls. A slothful servant is a withered member in the body, a barren tree in the vineyard, an idle drone in the hive, he is good for nothing. In one sense, we are all *unprofitable servants* (Lu. 17:10); we cannot *profit God,* Job 22:2. But to others, and to ourselves, it is required that we be profitable; if we be not, Christ will not own us as his servants: it is not enough not to do hurt, but we must do good, must bring forth fruit, and though thereby God is not profited, yet he is glorified, Jn. 15:8.

(2.) His doom is, to be *cast into outer darkness.* Here, as in what was said to the faithful servants, our Saviour slides insensibly out of the parable into the thing intended by it, and it serves as a key to the whole; for, *outer darkness, where there is weeping and gnashing of teeth,* is, in Christ's discourses, the common periphrasis of the miseries of the damned in hell. Their state is, [1.] Very dismal; it is outer darkness. Darkness is uncomfortable and frightful: it was one of the plagues of Egypt. In hell there are *chains of darkness,* 2 Pt. 2:4. In the dark *no man can work,* a fit punishment for a slothful servant. It is *outer* darkness, *out* from the light of heaven, *out* from the joy of their Lord, into which the faithful servants were admitted; *out* from the feast. Compare *ch.* 8:12; 22:13. [2.] Very doleful; there is weeping, which bespeaks great sorrow, and gnashing of teeth, which bespeaks great vexation and indignation. This will be the portion of the slothful servant.

Verses 31–46

We have here a description of the process of the last judgment in the great day. There are some passages in it that are parabolical; as the separating between the sheep and the goats, and the dialogues between the judge and the persons judged: but there is no thread of similitude carried through the discourse, and therefore it is rather to be called a draught or delineation of the final judgment, than a parable; it is, as it were, the explanation of the former parables. And here we have,

I. The placing of the judge upon the judgment-seat (*v.* 31); *When the Son of man shall come.* Observe here,

1. That there is a judgment to come, in which every man shall be sentenced to a state of everlasting happiness, or misery, in the world of recompence or retribution, according to what he did in this world of trial and probation, which is to be judged of by the rule of the everlasting gospel.

2. The administration of the judgment of the great day is committed to the Son of man; for by him God will judge the world (Acts 17:31), and to him all judgment is committed, and therefore the judgment of that day, which is the centre of all. Here, as elsewhere, when the last judgment is spoken of, Christ is called *the son of man,* because he is to judge the sons of men (and, being himself of the same nature, he is the more unexceptionable); and because his wonderful condescension to take upon him our nature, and to become the son of man, will be recompensed by this exaltation in that day, and an honour put upon the human nature.

3. Christ's appearing to judge the world will be splendid and glorious. Agrippa and Bernice came to the judgment-seat with *great pomp* (Acts 25:23); but that was (as the original word is) *great fancy.* Christ will come to the judgment-seat in real glory: the Sun of righteousness shall then shine in his meridian lustre, and the Prince of the kings of the earth shall show the riches of his glorious kingdom, and the honours of his excellent majesty; and all the world shall see what the saints only do now believe — that he is the brightness of his Father's glory. He shall come not only in the glory of his Father, but in his own glory, as mediator: his first coming was under a black cloud of obscurity; his second will be in a bright cloud of glory. The assurance Christ gave his disciples of his future glory, might help to take off the offence of the cross, and his approaching disgrace and suffering.

4. When Christ comes in his glory to judge the world, he will bring all his holy angels with him. This glorious person will have a glorious retinue, his holy myriads, who will be not only his attendants, but ministers of his justice; they shall come with him both for state and service. They must come to call the court (1 Th. 4:16), to gather the elect (*ch.* 24:31), to bundle the tares (*ch.* 13:40), to be witnesses of the saints' glory (Lu. 12:8), and of sinners' misery, Rev. 14:10.

5. He will then sit upon the throne of his glory. He is *now* set down with the Father upon his throne; and it is a throne of grace, to which we may come boldly; it is a throne of government, the throne of his father David; he is a priest upon that throne: but *then* he will sit upon the throne of glory, the throne of judgment. See Dan. 7:9, 10. Solomon's throne, though there was not its like in any kingdom, was but a dunghill to it. Christ, in the days of his flesh, was arraigned as a prisoner at the bar; but at his second coming, he will sit as a judge upon the bench.

II. The appearing of all the children of men before him (*v.* 32); *Before him shall be gathered all nations.* Note, The judgment of the great day will be a general judgment. All must be summoned before Christ's tribunal; all of every age of the world, from the beginning to the end of time; all of every place on earth, even from the remotest corners of the world, most obscure, and distant from each other; all nations, all those nations of men that are made of one blood, to dwell on all the face of the earth.

III. The distinction that will then be made between the precious and the vile; *He shall separate them one from another,* as the tares and wheat are separated at the harvest, the good fish and the bad at the shore, the corn and chaff in the floor. Wicked and godly here dwell together in the same kingdoms, cities, churches, families, and are not certainly distinguishable one from another; such are the infirmities of saints, such the hypocrisies of sinners, and one event to both: but in that day they will be separated, and parted for ever; *Then shall ye return, and discern between the righteous and the wicked,* Mal. 3:18. They cannot separate themselves one from another in this world (1 Co. 5:10), nor can any one else separate them (*ch.* 13:29); but the Lord knows them that are his, and he can separate them. This separation will be so exact, that the most inconsiderable saints shall not be lost in the crowd of sinners, nor the most plausible sinner hid in the crowd of saints (Ps. 1:5), but every one shall go to his own place. This is compared to a shepherd's dividing between the sheep and the goats; it is taken from Eze. 34:17, *Behold, I judge between cattle and cattle.* Note, 1. Jesus Christ is the great Shepherd; he now feeds his flock like a shepherd, and will shortly distinguish between those that are his, and those that are not, as Laban divided his sheep from Jacob's, and set three days' journey between them, Gen. 30:35, 36. 2. The godly are like sheep — innocent, mild, patient, useful: the wicked are like goats, a baser kind of animal, unsavoury and unruly. The sheep and goats are here feeding all day in the same pasture, but will be coted at night in different folds. Being thus divided, he will set the *sheep on his right hand,* and the *goats on his left, v.* 33. Christ puts honour upon the godly, as we show respect to those we set on our right hand; but the wicked shall rise to everlasting shame, Dan. 12:2. It is not said that he shall put the rich on his right hand, and the poor on his left; the learned and noble on his right hand, and unlearned and despised on his left; but the godly on his right hand, and the wicked on his left. All other divisions and subdivisions will then be abolished; but the great distinction of men into saints and sinners, sanctified and unsanctified, will remain for ever, and men's eternal state will be determined by it. The wicked took up with left-handed blessings, riches and honour, and so shall their doom be.

IV. The process of the judgement concerning each of these.

1. Concerning the godly, on the right hand. Their cause must be first despatched, that they may be assessors with Christ in the judgement of the wicked, whose misery will be aggravated by their seeing Abraham, and Isaac, and Jacob, admitted into the kingdom of heaven, Lu. 13:28. Observe here,

(1.) The *glory* conferred upon them; the sentence by which they shall be not only acquitted, but preferred and rewarded (*v.* 34); *The king shall say unto them.* He that was the Shepherd (which bespeaks the care and tenderness wherewith he will make this disquisition), is here the King, which bespeaks the authority wherewith he will then pronounce the sentence: where the word of this King is, there is power. Here are two things in this sentence:

[1.] The acknowledging of the saints to be the blessed of the Lord; *Come, ye blessed of my Father. First,* He pronounces them *blessed;* and his saying they are blessed, makes them so. The law curses them for their many discontinuances; but Christ having redeemed them from the curse of the law, and purchased a blessing for them, commands a blessing on them. *Secondly, Blessed of his Father;* reproached and cursed by the world, but blessed of God. As the Spirit glorifies the Son (Jn. 16:14), so the Son glorifies the Father by referring the salvation of the saints to him as the First Cause; all our blessings in heavenly things flow to us from God, as the Father of our Lord Jesus Christ, Eph. 1:3. *Thirdly,* He calls them *to come:* this *come* is, in effect, "*Welcome,* ten thousand welcomes, to the blessings of my father; come to me, come to be for ever with me; you that followed me bearing the cross, now come along with me wearing the crown. The blessed of my Father are the beloved of my soul, that have been too long at a distance from me; come, now, come into my bosom, come into my arms, come into my dearest embraces!" O with what joy will this fill the hearts of the saints in that day! We now come boldly to the throne of grace, but we shall then come boldly to the throne of glory; and this word holds out the golden sceptre, with an assurance that our requests shall be granted to more than the half of the kingdom. Now the Spirit saith, *Come,* in the word; and the bride saith, *Come,* in prayer; and the result hereof is a sweet communion: but the perfection of bliss will be, when *the King shall say, Come.*

[2.] The admission of the saints into the blessedness and kingdom of the Father; *Inherit the kingdom prepared for you.*

First, the happiness they shall be possessed of is very rich; we are told what it is by him who had reason to know it, having purchased it for them, and possessed it himself.

1. It is a *kingdom;* which is reckoned the most valuable possession on earth, and includes the greatest wealth and honour. Those that inherit kingdoms, wear all the glories of the crown, enjoy all the pleasures of the court, and command the peculiar treasures of the provinces; yet this is but a faint resemblance of the felicities of the saints in heaven. They that here are beggars, prisoners, accounted as the offscouring of all things, shall then inherit a kingdom, Ps. 113:7; Rev. 2:26, 27.

2. It is a kingdom *prepared:* the happiness must needs be great, for it is the product of the divine counsels. Note, There is great preparation made for the entertainment of the saints in the kingdom of glory. The Father designed it for them in his thoughts of love, and provided it for them in the greatness of his wisdom and power. The Son purchased it for them, and is entered as the fore-runner to prepare a place, Jn. 14:2. And the blessed Spirit, in preparing them for the kingdom, in effect, is preparing it for them.

3. It is prepared *for them.* This bespeaks, (1.) The suitableness of this happiness; it is in all points adapted to the nature of a soul, and to the new nature of a a sanctified soul. (2.) Their property and interest in it. It is prepared on purpose for them; not only for such as you, but for you, you by name, you personally and particularly, who were chosen to salvation through sanctification.

4. It is prepared *from the foundation of the world.* This happiness was designed for the saints, and they for it, before time began, from all eternity, Eph. 1:4. The end, which is last in execution, is first in intention. Infinite Wisdom had an eye to the eternal glorification of the saints, from the first founding of the creation: *All things are for your sakes,* 2 Co. 4:15. Or, it denotes the preparation of the place of this happiness, which is to be the seat and habitation of the blessed, in the very beginning of the work of creation, Gen. 1:1. There in the heaven of heavens the morning stars were singing together, when the foundations of the earth were fastened, Job 38:4–7.

Secondly, The tenure by which they shall hold and possess it is very good, they shall come and *inherit it.* What we come to by inheritance, is not got by any procurement of our own, but purely, as the lawyers express it, *by the act of God.* It is God that makes heirs, heirs of heaven. We come to an inheritance by virtue of our sonship, our adoption; *if children, then heirs.* A title by inheritance is the sweetest and surest title; it alludes to possessions in the land of Canaan, which passed by inheritance, and would not be alienated longer than to the year of Jubilee. Thus is the heavenly inheritance indefeasible, and unalienable. Saints, in this world, are as heirs under age, tutored and governed till the time appointed of the Father (Gal. 4:1, 2); and then they shall be put in full possession of that which now through grace they have a title to; *Come,* and inherit it.

(2.) The ground of this (*v.* 35, 36), *For I was an hungered, and ye gave me meat.* We cannot hence infer that any good words of ours merit the happiness of heaven, by any intrinsic worth or excellency in them: our goodness extends not unto God; but it is plain that Jesus Christ will judge the world by the same rule by which he governs it, and therefore will reward those that have been obedient to that law; and mention will be made of their obedience, not as their title, but as their evidence of an interest in Christ, and his purchase. This happiness will be adjudged to obedient believers, not upon a *quantum meruit — an estimate of merit,* which supposes a proportion between the work and the reward, but upon the promise of God purchased by Jesus Christ, and the benefit of it secured under certain provisos and limitations; and it is the purchase and promise that give the title, the obedience is only the qualification of the person designed. An estate made by deed or will upon condition, when the condition is performed according to the true intent of the donor or testator, becomes absolute; and then, though the title be built purely upon the deed or will, yet the performing of the condition must be given in evidence: and so it comes in here; for Christ is the Author of eternal salvation to those only that obey him, and who patiently continue in well doing.

Now the good works here mentioned are such as we commonly call works of charity to the poor: not but that many will be found on the right hand who never were in a capacity to feed the hungry, or clothe the naked, but were themselves fed and clothed by the charity of others; but one instance of sincere obedience is put for all the rest, and it teaches us this in general, that faith working by love is all in all in Christianity; *Show me thy faith by thy works;* and nothing will abound to a good account hereafter, but the fruits of righteousness in a good conversation now. The good works here described imply three things, which must be found in all that are saved.

[1.] Self-denial, and contempt of the world; reckoning the things of the world no further good things, than as we are enabled to do good with them: and those who have not wherewithal to do good, must show the same disposition, by being contendedly and cheerfully poor. Those are fit for heaven that are mortified to the earth.

[2.] Love to our brethren; which is the second great commandment, the fulfilling of the law, and an excellent preparative for the world of everlasting love. We must give proof of this love by our readiness to do good, and to communicate; good wishes are but mockeries without good works, Jam. 2:15, 16; 1 Jn. 3:17. Those that have not to give, must show the same disposition some other way.

[3.] A believing regard to Jesus Christ. That which is here rewarded is the relieving of the poor for Christ's sake, out of love to him, and with an eye to him. *This* puts an excellency upon the good work, when in it we serve the Lord Christ, which those may do that work for their own living, as well as those that help to keep others alive. See Eph. 6:5–7. Those good works shall then be accepted which are done in the name of the Lord Jesus, Col. 3:17.

I was hungry, that is, my disciples and followers were so, either by the persecutions of enemies for well-doing, or by the common dispensations of Providence; for in these things there is one event to the righteous and wicked: and *you gave them meat.* Note, *First,* Providence so variously orders and disposes of the circumstances of his people in this world, as that while some are in a condition to give relief, others need it. It is no new thing for those that are feasted with the dainties of heaven to be hungry and thirsty, and to want daily food; for those that are at home in God, to be strangers in a strange land; for those that have put on Christ, to want clothes to keep them warm; for those that have healthful souls, to have sickly bodies; and for those to be in prison, that Christ has made free. *Secondly,* Works of charity and beneficence, according as our ability is, are necessary to salvation; and there will be more stress laid upon them in the judgment of the great day, than is commonly imagined; these must be the proofs of our love, and of our professed subjection to the gospel of Christ, 2 Co. 9:13. But they that show no mercy, shall have judgment without mercy.

Now this reason is modestly excepted against by the righteous, but is explained by the Judge himself.

1. It is questioned by the righteous, *v.* 37–39. Not as if they were loth to inherit the kingdom, or were ashamed of their good deeds, or had not the testimony of their own consciences concerning them: but, (1.) The expressions are parabolical, designed to introduce and impress these great truths, that Christ has a mighty regard to works of charity, and is especially pleased with kindnesses done to his people for his sake. Or, (2.) They bespeak the humble admiration which glorified saints will be filled with, to find such poor and worthless services, as theirs are, so highly celebrated, and richly rewarded: *Lord, when saw we thee an hungered, and fed thee?* Note, Gracious souls are apt to think meanly of their own good deeds; especially as unworthy to be compared with the glory that shall be revealed. Far from this is the temper of those who said, *Wherefore have we fasted, and thou seest not?* Isa. 58:3. Saints in heaven will wonder what brought them thither, and that God should so regard them and their services. It even put Nathanael to the blush, to hear Christ's encomium of him: *Whence knowest thou me?* Jn. 1:47, 48. See Eph. 3:20. "*When saw we thee an hungered?* We have seen the poor in distress many a time; but when saw we thee?" Note, Christ is more among us than we think he is; surely the Lord is in this place, by his word, his ordinances, his ministers, his Spirit, yea, and his poor, and we know it not: *When thou wert under the fig-tree, I saw thee,* Jn. 1:48.

2. It is explained by the Judge himself (*v.* 40); *Inasmuch as ye have done it to these my brethren,* to the least, to one of the least of them, *ye have done it unto me.* The good works of the saints, when they are produced in the great day, (1.) Shall all be remembered; and not the least, not one of the least, overlooked, no not a cup of cold water. (2.) They shall be interpreted most to their advantage, and the best construction that can be put upon them. As Christ makes the best of their infirmities, so he makes the most of their services.

We see what recompences Christ has for those that feed the hungry, and clothe the naked; but what will become of the godly poor, that had not wherewithal to do so? Must they be shut out? No, [1.] Christ will own them, even the least of them, as his brethren; he will not be ashamed, nor think it any disparagement to him, *to call them brethren,* Heb. 2:11. In the height of his glory, he will not disown his poor relations; Lazarus is there laid in his bosom, as a friend, as a brother. Thus he will confess them, *ch.* 10:32. [2.] He will take the kindness done to them, as done to himself; *Ye have done it unto me;* which shows a respect to the poor that were relieved, as well as to the rich that did relieve them. Note, Christ espouses his people's cause, and interests himself in their interests, and reckons himself received, and love, and owned in them. If Christ himself were among us in poverty, how readily would we relieve him? In prison, how frequently would we visit him? We are ready to envy the honour they had, who ministered to him of their substance, Lu. 8:3. Wherever poor saints and poor ministers are, there Christ is ready to receive our kindnesses in them, and they shall be put to his account.

2. Here is the process concerning the wicked, those on the left hand. And in that we have,

(1.) The sentence passed upon them, 5:41. It was a disgrace to be set on the left hand; but that is not the worst of it, he shall say to them, *Depart from me, ye cursed.* Every word has terror in it, like that of the trumpet at mount Sinai, waxing louder and louder, every accent more and more doleful, and exclusive of comfort.

[1.] To be so near to Christ was some satisfaction, though under his frowns; but that will not be allowed, *Depart from me.* In this world they were often called to come to Christ, to come for life and rest, but they turned a deaf ear to his calls; justly therefore are they bid to depart from Christ, that would not come to him. "Depart from me the Fountain of all good, from me the Saviour, and therefore from all hope of salvation; I will never have any thing more to say to you, or do with you." Here they said to the Almighty, *Depart from us;* then he will *choose their delusions,* and say to them, *Depart from me.* Note, It is the hell of hell to depart from Christ.

[2.] If they must depart, and depart from Christ, might they not be dismissed with a blessing, with one kind and compassionate word at least? No, *Depart, ye cursed,* They that would not come to Christ, to inherit a blessing, must depart from him under the burthen of a curse, that curse of the law on every one that breaks it, Gal. 3:10. *As they loved cursing, so it shall come unto them.* But observe, The righteous are called *the blessed of my Father;* for their blessedness is owing purely to the grace of God and his blessing, but the wicked are called only *ye cursed,* for their damnation is of themselves. Hath God sold them? No, they have sold themselves, have laid themselves under the curse, Isa. 50:1.

[3.] If they must depart, and depart with a curse, may they not go into some place of ease and rest? Will it not be misery enough for them to bewail their loss? No, there is a punishment of sense as well as loss; they must depart into *fire,* into torment as grievous as that of fire is to the body, and much more. This fire is the wrath of the eternal God fastening upon the guilty souls and consciences of sinners that have made themselves fuel for it. Our God is a consuming fire, and sinners fall immediately into his hands, Heb. 10:31; Rom. 2:8, 9.

[4.] If into fire, may it not be some light or gentle fire? No, it is *prepared* fire; it is a torment *ordained of old,* Isa. 30:33. The damnation of sinners is often spoken of as an act of the divine power; *he is able to cast into hell.* In the vessels of wrath he makes his power known; it is a *destruction from the presence of the Lord, and from the glory of his power.* In it shall be seen what a provoked God can do to make a provoking creature miserable.

[5.] If into fire, prepared fire, O let it be but of short continuance, let them but pass *through* fire; no, the fire of God's wrath will be an *everlasting* fire; a fire, that, fastening and preying upon immortal souls, can never go out for want of fuel; and, being kindled and kept burning by the wrath of an immortal God, can never go out for want of being blown and stirred up; and, the streams of mercy and grace being for ever excluded, there is nothing to extinguish it. If a drop of water be denied to cool the tongue, buckets of water will never be granted to quench this flame.

[6.] If they must be doomed to such a state of endless misery, yet may they not have some good company there? No, none but *the devil and his angels,* their sworn enemies, that helped to bring them to this misery, and will triumph over them in it. They served the devil while they lived, and therefore are justly sentenced to be where he is, as those that served Christ, are taken to be with him where he is. It is terrible to lie in a house haunted with devils; what will it be then to be companions with them for ever? Observe here, *First,* Christ intimates that there is one that is the prince of the devils, the ring-leader of the rebellion, and that the rest are his angels, his messengers, by whose agency he supports his kingdom. Christ and his angels will in that day triumph over the dragon and his, Rev. 12:7, 8. *Secondly,* The fire is said to be prepared, not primarily for the wicked, as the kingdom is prepared for the righteous; but it was originally intended for *the devil and his angels.* If sinners make themselves associates with Satan by indulging their lusts, they may thank themselves if they become sharers in that misery which was prepared for him and his associates. Calvin notes upon this, that *therefore* the torment of the damned is said to be *prepared for the devil and his angels,* to cut off all hope of escaping it; the devil and his angels are already made prisoners in the pit, and can worms of the earth think to escape?

(2.) The reason of this sentence assigned. God's judgments are all just, and he will be justified in them. He is Judge himself, and therefore *the heavens shall declare his righteousness.*

Now, [1.] All that is charged upon them, on which the sentence is grounded, is, omission; as, before, the servant was condemned, not for wasting his talent, but for burying it; so here, he doth not say, "I was hungry and thirsty, for you took my meat and drink from me; I was a stranger, for you banished me; naked, for you stripped me; in prison, for you laid me there:" but, "When I was in these distresses, you were

so selfish, so taken up with your own ease and pleasure, made so much of your labour, and were so loth to part with your money, that you did not *minister* as you might have done to my relief and succour. You were like those epicures that were at ease in Zion, and were not *grieved for the affliction of Joseph,*" Amos 6:4–6. Note, Omissions are the ruin of thousands.

[2.] It is the omission of works of charity to the poor. They are not sentenced for omitting their sacrifices and burnt-offerings (they abounded in these, Ps. 50:8), but for omitting the weightier matter of the law, *judgment, mercy, and faith.* The Ammonites and Moabites were excluded the sanctuary, because they *met not Israel with bread and water,* Deu. 23:3, 4. Note, Uncharitableness to the poor is a damning sin. If we will not be brought to works of charity by the hope of reward, let us be influenced by fear of punishment; for *they shall have judgment without mercy, that have showed no mercy.* Observe, He doth not say, "I was sick, and you did not cure me; in prison, and you did not release me" (perhaps that was more than they could do); but, "You *visited me not,* which you might have done." Note, Sinners will be condemned, at the great day, for the omission of that good which it was in the power of their hand to do. But if the doom of the uncharitable be so dreadful, how much more intolerable will the doom of the cruel be, the doom of persecutors! Now this reason of the sentence is.

First, Objected against by the prisoners (v. 44); *Lord, when saw we thee an hungered, or athirst?* Condemned sinners, though they have no plea that will bear them out, will yet in vain offer at excuses. Now. 1. The manner of their pleading bespeaks their present precipitation. They cut it short, as men in haste; *when saw we thee hungry, or thirsty, or naked?* They care not to repeat the charge, as conscious to themselves of their own guilt, and unable to bear the terrors of the judgment. Nor will they have time allowed them to insist upon such frivolous pleas; for it is all (as we say) but "trifling with the court." 2. The matter of their plea bespeaks their former inconsideration of that which they might have known, but would not till now that it was too late. They that had slighted and persecuted poor Christians, would not own that they had slighted and persecuted Christ: no, they never intended any affront to him, nor expected that so great a matter would have been made of it. They imagined it was only a company of poor, weak, silly, and contemptible people, who made more ado than needed about religion, that they put those slights upon; but they who do so, will be made to know, either in the day of their conversion, as Paul, or of their condemnation, as these here, that it was *Jesus whom they persecuted.* And, if they say, *Behold, we knew it not: doth not he that pondereth the heart consider it?* Prov. 24:11, 12.

Secondly, Justified by the Judge, who will convince all the ungodly of the hard speeches spoken against him in those that are his, Jude 15. He goes by this rule (v. 45); *Inasmuch as ye did it not to one of the least of these, ye did it not to me.* Note, What is done against the faithful disciples and followers of Christ, even the least of them, he takes as done against himself. He is reproached and persecuted in them, for they are reproached and persecuted for his sake, and *in all their afflictions he is afflicted.* He that touches them, touches him in a part no less tender than the apple of his eye.

Lastly, Here is the execution of both these sentences, v. 46. Execution is the life of the law, and Christ will take care that that be done according to the sentence.

1. *The wicked shall go away into everlasting punishment.* Sentence will then be executed speedily, and no reprieve granted, nor any time allowed to move in arrest of judgment. The execution of the wicked is first mentioned; for first the tares are gathered and burned. Note, (1.) The punishment of the wicked in the future state will be an everlasting punishment, for that state is an unalterable state. It can neither be thought that sinners should change their own natures, nor that God should give his grace to change them, when in this world the day of grace was misspent, the Spirit of grace resisted, and the means of grace abused and baffled. (2.) The wicked shall be made to *go* away into that punishment; not that they will go voluntarily, no, they are *driven* from light into darkness; but it bespeaks an irresistible conviction of guilt, and a final despair of mercy.

2. *The righteous shall go away into life eternal;* that is, they shall *inherit the kingdom,* v. 34. Note, (1.) Heaven is life, it is all happiness. The life of the soul results from its union with God by the mediation of Jesus Christ, as that of the body from its union with the soul by the animal spirits. The heav-

enly life consists in the vision and fruition of God, in a perfect conformity to him, and an immediate uninterrupted communion with him. (2.) It is *eternal* life. There is no death to put a period to the life itself, nor old age to put a period to the comfort of it, or any sorrow to embitter it. Thus life and death, good and evil, the blessing and the curse, are set before us, that we may choose our way; and so shall our end be. Even the heathen had some notion of these different states of good and bad in the other world. Cicero in his *Tusculan Questions,* lib. 1, brings in Socrates thus speaking, *Duae sunt viae, duplicesque cursus è corpore exeuntium: nam qui se vitiis humanis contaminarunt, et libidinibus se tradiderunt, iis devium quoddam iter est, seclusum à consilio deorum; qui autem se integros castosque servarunt, quibusque fuerit minima cum corporibus contagio, suntque in corporibus humanis vitam imitati deorum, iis ad illos a quibus sunt profecti facile patet reditus — Two paths open before those who depart out of the body. Such as have contaminated themselves with human vices, and yielded to their lusts, occupy a path that conducts them far from the assembly and council of the gods; but the upright and chaste, such as have been least defiled by the flesh, and have imitated, while in the body, the gods, these find it easy to return to the sublime beings from whom they came.*

CHAPTER 26

The narrative of the death and sufferings of Christ is more particularly and fully recorded by all the four evangelists than any part of his history; for what should be determine, and desire to know, but Christ, and him crucified? And this chapter begins that memorable narrative. The year of the redeemed was now come, the seventy weeks determined were now accomplished, when transgression must be finished, reconciliation made, and an everlasting righteousness brought in, by the cutting off of Messiah the Prince, Dan. 9:24, 26. That awful scene is here introduced, to be read with reverence and holy fear. In this chapter, we have, I. The preliminaries, or prefaces, to Christ's sufferings. 1. The previous notice given by him to his disciples (v. 1, 2). 2. The rulers' conspiracy against him (v. 3–5). 3. The anointing of his head at a supper in Bethany (v. 6–13). 4. Judas's bargain with the priests to betray him (v. 14–16). 5. Christ eating the passover with his disciples (v. 17–25). 6. His instituting the Lord's supper, and his discourse with his disciples after it (v. 26–35). II. His entrance upon them, and some of the particulars of them. 1. His agony in the garden (v. 36–46). 2. The seizing of him by the officers, with Judas's help (v. 47–56). 3. His arraignment before the chief priest, and his condemnation in his court (v. 57–68). 4. Peter's denying him (v. 69–75).

Verses 1–5

Here is, 1. The notice Christ gave his disciples of the near approach of his sufferings, v. 1, 2. While his enemies were preparing trouble for him, he was preparing himself and his followers for it. He had often told them of his sufferings at a distance, now he speaks of them as at the door; *after two days,* Note, After many former notices of trouble we still have need of fresh ones. Observe,

(1.) The *time* when he gave this alarm; *when he had finished all these sayings.* [1.] Not till he had finished all he had to say. Note, Christ's witnesses die not till they have finished their testimony. When Christ had gone through his undertaking as a prophet, he entered upon the execution of his office as a priest. [2.] After he had finished these sayings, which go immediately before; he had bid his disciples to expect sad times, bonds and afflictions, and then tells them, *The Son of man is betrayed;* to intimate that they should fare no worse than he should, and that his sufferings should take the sting out of theirs. Note, Thoughts of a suffering Christ are great supports to a suffering Christian, suffering with him and for him.

(2.) The thing itself he gave them notice of; *The Son of man is betrayed.* The thing was not only so sure, but so near, that it was as good as done. Note, It is good to make sufferings that are yet to come, as present to us. He *is* betrayed, for Judas was then contriving and designing to betray him.

2. The plot of the chief priests, and scribes, and elders of the people, against the life of our Lord Jesus, 5:3–5. Many consultations had been held against the life of Christ but this plot was laid deeper than any yet, for the grandees were all engaged in it. The chief priests, who presided in ecclesiastical affairs; the elders, who were judges in civil matters, and the scribes, who, as doctors of the law, were directors to both — these composed the sanhedrim, or great council that governed the nation, and these were confederate against Christ. Observe (1.) The *place* where they met; *in the palace of the high priest,* who was the centre of their unity in this wicked project. (2.) The plot itself; to *take Jesus by subtlety, and kill him;* nothing less than his blood, his life-blood, would serve

their turn. So cruel and bloody have been the designs of Christ's and his church's enemies. (3.) The policy of the plotters; *Not on the feast-day.* Why not? Was it in regard to the holiness of the time, or because they would not be disturbed in the religious services of the day? No, but *lest there should be an uproar among the people.* They knew Christ had a great interest in the common people, of whom there was a great concourse on the feast-day, and they would be in danger of taking up arms against their rulers, if they should offer to lay violent hands on Christ, whom all held for a prophet. They were awed, not by the fear of God, but by the fear of the people; all their concern was for their own safety, not God's honour. They would have it done at the feast; for it was a tradition of the Jews, that malefactors should be put to death at one of the three feasts, especially rebels and impostors, that *all Israel might see and fear;* but *not on the feast-day.*

Verses 6–13

In this passage of story, we have,

I. The singular kindness of a good woman to our Lord Jesus in anointing his head, *v.* 6, 7. It was *in Bethany,* a village hard by Jerusalem, and *in the house of Simon the leper.* Probably, he was one who had been miraculously cleansed from his leprosy by our Lord Jesus, and he would express his gratitude to Christ by entertaining him; nor did Christ disdain to converse with him, to come in to him, and sup with him. Though he was cleansed, yet he was called *Simon the leper.* Those who are guilty of scandalous sins, will find that, though the sin be pardoned, the reproach will cleave to them, and will hardly be wiped away. The woman that did this, is supposed to have been Mary, the sister of Martha and Lazarus. And Dr. Lightfoot thinks it was the same that was called *Mary Magdalene.* She had a *box of ointment very precious,* which she *poured upon the head* of Christ as he sat at meat. This, among us, would be a strange sort of compliment. But it was then accounted the highest piece of respect; for the smell was very grateful, and the ointment itself refreshing to the head. David had his *head anointed,* Ps. 23:5; Lu. 7:46. Now this may be looked upon,

1. As an act of faith in our Lord Jesus, the Christ, the Messiah, the anointed. To signify that she believed in him as God's anointed, whom he had set king, she anointed him, and made him her king. They shall *appoint themselves one head,* Hos. 1:11. This is *kissing the Son.*

2. As an act of love and respect to him. Some think that this was he who *loved much* at first, and *washed Christ's feet with her tears* (Lu. 7:38, 47); and that she had not left her first love, but was now as affectionate in the devotions of a grown Christian as she was in those of a young beginner. Note, Where there is true love in the heart to Jesus Christ, nothing will be thought too good, no, nor good enough, to bestow upon him.

II. The offence which the disciples took at this. They *had indignation* (*v.* 8, 9), were vexed to see this ointment thus spent, which they thought might have been better bestowed.

1. See how they expressed their offence at it. They said, *To what purpose is this waste?* Now this bespeaks,

(1.) Want of tenderness toward this good woman, in interpreting her over-kindness (suppose it was so) to be wastefulness. Charity teaches us to put the best construction upon every thing that it will bear, especially upon the words and actions of those that are *zealously affected in doing a good thing,* though we may think them not altogether so discreet in it as they might be. It is true, there may be over-doing in well-doing; but thence we must learn to be cautious ourselves, lest we run into extremes, but not to be censorious of others; because that which we may impute to the want of prudence, God may accept as an instance of abundant love. We must not say, Those do too much in religion, that do more than we do, but rather aim to do as much as they.

(2.) Want of respect to their Master. The best we can make of it, is, that they knew their Master was perfectly dead to all the delights of sense; he that was so much *grieved for the affliction of Joseph,* cared not for being *anointed with the chief ointments,* Amos 6:6. And therefore they thought such pleasures ill bestowed upon one who took so little pleasure in them. But supposing that, it did not become them to call it *waste,* when they perceived that he admitted and accepted it as a token of his friend's love. Note, We must take heed of thinking any thing waste, which is bestowed upon the Lord Jesus, either by others or by ourselves. We must not think that time waste, that is spent in the service of Christ, or that money waste, which is laid out in any work of piety; for, though it seem to be cast upon the waters, to be thrown down the river, we shall *find it again,* to advantage, *after many days,* Eccl. 11:1.

2. See how they excused their offence at it, and what pretence they made for it; *This ointment might have been sold for much, and given to the poor.* Note, It is no new thing for bad affections to shelter themselves under specious covers; for people to shift off works of piety under colour of works of charity.

III. The reproof Christ gave to his disciples for the offence at this good woman (*v.* 10, 11); *Why trouble ye the woman?* Note, It is a great trouble to good people to have their good works censured and misconstrued; and it is a thing that Jesus Christ takes very ill. He here took part with a good, honest, zealous, well-meaning woman, against all his disciples, though they seemed to have so much reason on their side; so heartily does he espouse the cause of the *offended little ones, ch.* 18:10.

Observe his reason; *You have the poor always with you.* Note,

1. There are some opportunities of doing and getting good which are constant, and which we must give constant attendance to the improvement of. Bibles we have always with us, sabbaths always with us, and so *the poor, we have always with us.* Note, Those who have a heart to do good, never need complain for want of opportunity. The poor never ceased even out of the land of Israel, Deu. 15:11. We cannot but see some in this world, who call for our charitable assistance, who are as God's receivers, some poor members of Christ, to whom he will have kindness shown as to himself.

2. There are other opportunities of doing and getting good, which come but seldom, which are short and uncertain, and require more peculiar diligence in the improvement of them, and which ought to be preferred before the other; *"Me ye have not always,* therefore use me while ye have me." Note, (1.) Christ's constant *bodily* presence was not to be expected here in this world; it was expedient that he should go away; his *real* presence in the eucharist is a fond and groundless conceit, and contradicts what he here said, *Me ye have not always.* (2.) Sometimes special works of piety and devotion should take place of common works of charity. The poor must not rob Christ; we must do good to all, but *especially to the household of faith.*

IV. Christ's approbation and commendation of the kindness of this good woman. The more his servants and their services are cavilled at by men, the more he manifests his acceptance of them. He calls it a *good work* (*v.* 10), and says more in praise of it than could have been imagined; particularly,

1. That the meaning of it was mystical (*v.* 12); *She did it for my burial.* (1.) Some think that she *intended* it so, and that the woman better understood Christ's frequent predictions of his death and sufferings than the apostles did; for which they were recompensed with the honour of being the first witnesses of his resurrection. (2.) However, Christ interpreted it so; and he is always willing to make the best, to make the most of his people's well-meant words and actions. This was as it were the embalming of his body; because the doing of that after his death would be prevented by his resurrection, it was therefore done before; for it was fit that it should be done some time, to show that he was still the Messiah, even when he seemed to be triumphed over by death. The disciples thought the ointment wasted, which was poured upon his head. "But," saith he, "If so much ointment were poured upon a dead body, according to the custom of your country, you would not grudge it, or think it waste. Now this is, in effect, so; the body she anoints is as good as dead, and her kindness is very seasonable for that purpose; therefore rather than call it waste, put it upon that score."

2. That the memorial of it should be honourable (*v.* 13); *This shall be told for a memorial.* This act of faith and love was so remarkable, that the preachers of Christ crucified, and the inspired writers of the history of his passion, could not choose but take notice of this passage, proclaim the notice of it, and perpetuate the memorial of it. And being once enrolled in these records, it was *graven as with an iron pen and lead in the rock for ever,* and could not possibly be forgotten. None of all the trumpets of fame sound so loud and so long as the everlasting gospel. Note, (1.) The story of the death of Christ, though a tragical one, is gospel, glad-tidings, because he died for us. (2.) The gospel was to be preached in the whole world; not in Judea only, but in every nation, to every creature. Let the disciples take notice of this, for their encouragement, that their sound should go to the ends of the earth. (3.) Though the honour of Christ is principally designed in the gospel, yet the honour of his saints and servants is not altogether overlooked. The memorial of this woman was to be preserved, not by dedicating a church to her, or keeping an annual feast in honour of her, or preserving a piece of her broken box for a sacred relic; but by mentioning her faith and piety in the preaching of the gospel, for example to others, Heb. 6:12. Hereby honour redounds to Christ himself, who in this world, as well as in that to come, will be *glorified in his saints, and admired in all them that believe.*

Verses 14–16

Immediately after an instance of the greatness kindness done to Christ, follows an instance of the greatest unkindness; such mixture is there of good and bad among the followers of Christ; he hath some faithful friends, and some false and feigned ones. What could be more base than this agreement which Judas here made with the chief priests, to betray Christ to them?

I. The traitor was Judas Iscariot; he is said to be *one of the twelve,* as an aggravation of his villany. When the *number of the disciples was multiplied* (Acts 6:1), no marvel if there were some among them that were a shame and trouble to them; but when there were but twelve, and one of them was *a devil,* surely we must never expect any society perfectly pure on this side heaven. The twelve were Christ's chosen friends, that had the privilege of his special favour; they were his constant followers, that had the benefit of his most intimate converse, that upon all accounts had reason to love him and be true to him; and yet one of them betrayed him. Note, No bonds of duty or gratitude will hold those that have a devil, Mk. 5:3, 4.

II. Here is the proffer which he made to the chief priests; he *went to them, and said,, What will ye give me? v.* 15. They did not send for him, nor make the proposal to him; they could not have thought that one of Christ's own disciples should be false to him. Note, There are those, even among Christ's followers, that are worse than any one can imagine them to be, and want nothing but opportunity to show it.

Observe, 1. What Judas promised; *"I will deliver him unto you;* I will let you know where he is, and undertake to bring you to him, at such a convenient time and place that you may seize him without noise, or danger of an uproar." In their conspiracy against Christ, this was it they were at a loss about, *v.* 4, 5. They durst not meddle with him in public, and knew not where to find him in private. Here the matter rested, and the difficulty was insuperable; till Judas came, and offered them his service. Note, Those that give up themselves to be led by the devil, find him readier than they imagine to help them at a dead lift, as Judas did the chief priests. Though the rulers, by their power and interest, could kill him when they had him in their hands, yet none but a disciple could betray him. Note, The greater profession men make of religion, and the more they are employed in the study and service of it, the greater opportunity they have of doing mischief, if their hearts be not right with God. If Judas had not been an apostle, he could not have been a traitor; if men had known the way of righteousness, they could not have abused it.

I will deliver him unto you. He did not offer himself, nor did they tamper with him, to be a witness against Christ, though they wanted evidence, *v.* 59. And if there had been any thing to be alleged against him, which had but the colour of proof that he was an impostor, Judas was the likeliest person to have attested it; but this is an evidence of the innocency of our Lord Jesus, that his own disciple, who knew so well his doctrine and manner of life, and was false to him, could not charge him with any thing criminal, though it would have served to justify his treachery.

2. What he asked in consideration of this undertaking; *What will ye give me?* This was the only thing that made Judas betray his Master; he hoped to get money by it: his Master had not given him any provocation, though he knew from the first that he *had a devil;* yet, for aught that appears, he showed the same kindness to him that he did to the rest, and put no mark of disgrace upon him that might disoblige him; he had placed him in a post that pleased him, had made him purse-bearer, and though he had embezzled the common

stock (for he is called *a thief,* Jn. 12:6), yet we do not find he was in any danger of being called to account for it; nor does it appear that he had any suspicion that the gospel was a cheat: no, it was not the hatred of his Master, nor any quarrel with him, but purely the love of money; that, and nothing else, made Judas a traitor.

What will ye give me? Why, what did he want? Neither bread to eat, nor raiment to put on; neither necessaries nor conveniences. Was not he welcome, wherever his Master was? Did he not fare as he fared? Had he not been but just now nobly entertained at a supper in Bethany, in the house of Simon the leper, and a little before at another, where no less a person than Martha herself waited at table? And yet this covetous wretch could not be content, but comes basely cringing to the priests with, *What will ye give me?* Note, It is not the *lack* of money, but the *love* of money, that is the root of all evil, and particularly of apostasy from Christ; witness Demas, 2 Tim. 4:10. Satan tempted our Saviour with this bait, *All these things will I give thee* (*ch.* 4:9); but Judas offered himself to be tempted with it; he asks, *What will ye give me?* as if his Master was a commodity that stuck on his hands.

III. Here is the bargain which the chief priests made with him; *they covenanted with him for thirty pieces of silver;* thirty shekels, which in our money is about three pounds eight shillings, so some; three pounds fifteen shillings, so others. It should seem, Judas referred himself to them, and was willing to take what they were willing to give; he catches at the first offer, lest the next should be worse. Judas had not been wont to trade high, and therefore a little money went a great way with him. By the law (Ex. 21:32), thirty pieces of silver was the price of a slave — a goodly price, at which Christ was valued! Zec. 11:13. No wonder that Zion's sons, though comparable to fine gold, are esteemed as earthen pitchers, when Zion's King himself was thus undervalued. They *covenanted with him; estēsan — appenderunt — they paid it down,* so some; gave him his wages in hand, to secure him and to encourage him.

IV. Here is the industry of Judas, in pursuance of his bargain (*v.* 16); *he sought opportunity to betray him,* his head was still working to find out how he might do it effectually. Note, 1. It is a very wicked thing to seek opportunity to sin, and to devise mischief; for it argues the heart fully set in men to do evil, and a malice prepense. 2. Those that are *in,* think they must *on,* though the matter be ever so bad. After he had made that wicked bargain, he had time to repent, and to revoke it; but now by his covenant the devil has one hank more upon him than he had, and tells him that he must be true to his word, though ever so false to his Master, as Herod must behead John *for his oath's sake.*

Verses 17–25

We have here an account of Christ's keeping the passover. Being made under the law, he submitted to all the ordinances of it, and to this among the rest; it was kept in remembrance of Israel's deliverance out of Egypt, the birthday of that people; it was a tradition of the Jews, that in the days of the Messiah they should be redeemed on the very day of their coming out of Egypt; and it was exactly fulfilled, for Christ died the day after the passover, in which day they began their march.

I. The time when Christ ate the passover, was the usual time appointed by God, and observed by the Jews (*v.* 17); *the first day of the feast of unleavened bread,* which that year happened on the fifth day of the week, which is our Thursday. Some have advanced a suggestion, that our Lord Jesus celebrated the passover at this time of day sooner than other people did; but the learned Dr. Whitby has largely disproved it.

II. The place where, was particularly appointed by himself to the disciples, upon their enquiry (*v.* 17); they asked, *Where wilt thou that we prepare the passover?* Perhaps Judas was one of those that asked this question (where he would eat the passover,) that he might know the better how to lay his train; but the rest of the disciples asked it as usual, that they might do their duty.

1. They took it for granted that their Master would eat the passover, though he was at this time persecuted by the chief priests, and his life sought; they knew that he would not be put by his duty, either by frightenings without or fears within. Those do not follow Christ's example who make it an excuse for their not attending on the Lord's supper, our gospel passover, that they have many troubles and many enemies, are full of care and fear; for, if so, they have the more need of that ordinance, to help to silence their fears, and comfort them under their troubles, to help them in forgiving their enemies, and casting all their cares on God.

2. They knew very well that there must be preparation made for it, and that it was their business, as his servants, to make preparation; *Where wilt thou that we prepare?* Note, Before solemn ordinances there must be solemn preparation.

3. They knew that he had no house of his own wherein to eat the passover; in this, as in other things, *for our sakes he became poor.* Among all Zion's palaces there was none for Zion's King; but his kingdom was not of this world. See Jn. 1:11.

4. They would not pitch upon a place without direction from him, and from him they had direction; he sent them to *such a man* (*v.* 18), who probably was a friend and follower of his, and to his house he invited himself and his disciples.

(1.) Tell him, *My time is at hand;* he means the time of his death, elsewhere called *his hour* (Jn. 8:20; 13:1); the time, the hour, fixed in the counsel of God, which his heart was upon, and which he had so often spoken of. He knew when it was at hand, and was busy accordingly; we *know not our time* (Eccl. 9:12), and therefore must never be off our watch; *our time is always ready* (Jn. 7:6), and therefore we must be always ready. Observe, Because his *time was at hand,* he would *keep the passover* Note, The consideration of the near approach of death should quicken us to a diligent improvement of all our opportunities for our souls. Is our time at hand, and an eternity just before us? *Let us then keep the feast with the unleavened bread of sincerity.* Observe, When our Lord Jesus invited himself to this good man's house, he sent him this intelligence, that his time was at hand. Note, Christ's secret is with them that entertain him in their hearts. Compare Jn. 14:21 with Rev. 3:20.

(2.) Tell him, *I will keep the passover at thy house.* This was an instance of his authority, as *the Master,* which it is likely this man acknowledged; he did not beg, but command, the use of his house for this purpose. Thus, when Christ by his Spirit comes into the heart, he demands admission, as one whose own the heart is and cannot be denied, and he gains admission as one who has all power in the heart and cannot be resisted; if he saith, "I will keep a feast in such a soul," he will do it; for he works, and none can hinder; his people shall be willing, for he makes them so. *I will keep the passover with my disciples.* Note, Wherever Christ is welcome, he expects that his disciples should be welcome too. When we take God for our God, we take his people for our people.

III. The preparation was made by the disciples (*v.* 19); *They did as Jesus had appointed.* Note, Those who would have Christ's presence with them in the gospel passover, must strictly observe his instructions, and do as he directs; *They made ready the passover;* they got the lamb killed in the court of the temple, got it roasted, the bitter herbs provided, bread and wine, the cloth laid, and every thing set in readiness for such a sacred solemn feast.

IV. They ate the passover according to the law (*v.* 20); *He sat down,* in the usual table-gesture, not lying on one side, for it was not easy to eat, nor possible to drink, in that posture, but sitting upright, though perhaps sitting low. It is the same word that is used for his posture at other meals, *ch.* 9:10; Lu. 7:37; *ch.* 26:7. It was only the first passover in Egypt, as most think, that was eaten with *their loins girded, shoes on their feet, and staff in their hand,* though all that might be in a sitting posture. His sitting down, denotes the composedness of his mind, when he addressed himself to this solemnity; *He sat down with the twelve,* Judas not excepted. By the law, they were to *take a lamb for a household* (Ex. 12:3, 4), which were to be not less than ten, nor more than twenty; Christ's disciples were his household. Note, They whom God has charged with families, must have their houses with them in serving the Lord.

V. We have here Christ's discourse with his disciples at the passover-supper. The usual subject of discourse at that ordinance, was the deliverance of Israel out of Egypt (Ex. 12:26, 27); but the great Passover is now ready to be offered, and the discourse of that swallows up all talk of the other, (Jer. 16:14, 15). Here is,

1. The general notice Christ gives his disciples of the treachery that should be among them (*v.* 21); *One of you shall betray me.* Observe, (1.) Christ knew it. We know not what troubles will befal us, nor whence they will arise: but Christ knew all his, which, as it proves his omniscience, so it magnifies his love, that he knew all things that should befal him, and yet did not draw back. He foresaw the treachery and baseness of a disciple of his own, and yet went on; took care of those that were given him, though he knew there was a Judas among them; would pay the price of our redemption, though he foresaw some would *deny the Lord that bought them;* and shed his blood, though he knew it would be *trodden under foot as an unholy thing.* (2.) When there was occasion, he let those about him know it. He had often told them that the Son of man should be betrayed; now he tells them that one of them should do it, that when they saw it, they might not only be the less surprised, but have their faith in him confirmed, Jn. 13:19; 14:29.

2. The disciples' feelings on this occasion, *v.* 22. How did they take it?

(1.) *They were exceeding sorrowful.* [1.] It troubled them much to hear that their Master should be betrayed. When Peter was first told of it, he said, *Be it far from thee;* and therefore it must needs be a great trouble to him and the rest of them, to hear that it was very *near* to him. [2.] It troubled them more to hear that one of them should do it. It would be a reproach to the fraternity, for an apostle to prove a traitor, and this grieved them; gracious souls grieve for the sins of others, especially of those that have made a more than ordinary profession of religion. 2 Co. 11:29. [3.] It troubled them most of all, that they were left at uncertainty which of them it was, and each of them was afraid for himself, lest, as Hazael speaks (2 Ki. 8:13), he was the *dog* that should *do this great thing.* Those that know the strength and subtlety of the tempter, and their own weakness and folly, cannot but be in pain for themselves, when they hear that *the love of many will wax cold.*

(2.) *They began every one of them to say, Lord, is it I?*

[1.] They were not apt to suspect Judas. Though he was *a thief,* yet, it seems, he had carried it so plausibly, that those who were intimate with him, were not jealous of him: none of them so much as looked upon him, much less said, *Lord, is it Judas?* Note, It is possible for a hypocrite to go through the world, not only undiscovered, but unsuspected; like bad money so ingeniously counterfeited that nobody questions it.

[2.] They were apt to suspect themselves; *Lord, is it I?* Though they were not conscious to themselves of any inclination that way (no such thought had ever entered into their mind), yet they feared the worst, and asked Him who knows us better than we know ourselves, *Lord, is it I?* Note, It well becomes the disciples of Christ always to be jealous over themselves with a godly jealousy, especially in trying times. We know not how strongly we may be tempted, nor how far God may leave us to ourselves, and therefore have reason, *not to be high-minded, but fear.* It is observable that our Lord Jesus, just before he instituted the Lord's supper, put his disciples upon this trial and suspicion of themselves, to teach us to examine and *judge ourselves, and so to eat of that bread, and drink of that cup.*

3. Further information given them concerning this matter (*v.* 23, 24), where Christ tells them, (1.) That the traitor was a familiar friend; *He that dippeth his hand with me in the dish,* that is, One of you that are now with me at the table. He mentions this, to make the treachery appear the more exceeding sinful. Note, External communion with Christ in holy ordinances is a great aggravation of our falseness to him. It is base ingratitude to dip with Christ in the dish, and yet betray him. (2.) That this was according to the scripture, which would take off the offence at it. Was Christ betrayed by a disciple? So it was written (Ps. 61:9); *He that did eat bread with me, hath lifted up his heel against me.* The more we see of the fulfilling of the scripture in our troubles, the better we may bear them. (3.) That it would prove a very dear bargain to the traitor; *Woe to that man by whom the Son of man is betrayed.* This he said, not only to awaken the conscience of Judas, and bring him to repent, and revoke his bargain, but for warning to all others to take heed of sinning like Judas; though God can serve his own purposes by the sins of men, that doth not make the sinner's condition the less woeful; *It had been good for that man, if he had not been born.* Note, The ruin that attends those who betray Christ, is so great, that it were more eligible by far not be at all than to be thus miserable.

4. The conviction of Judas, *v.* 25. (1.) He asked, *Is it I?* to avoid coming under the suspicion of guilt by his silence. He knew very well that it was he, and yet wished to appear a stranger to such a plot. Note, Many whose consciences con-

demn them are very industrious to justify themselves before men, and put a good face on it, with, *Lord, is it I?* He could not but know that Christ knew, and yet trusted so much to his courtesy, because he had hitherto concealed it, that he had the impudence to challenge him to tell: or, perhaps, he was so much under the power of infidelity, that he imagined Christ did not know it, as those who said, *The Lord shall not see* (Ps. 94:7), and asked, *Can he judge through the dark clouds?* (2.) Christ soon answered this question; *Thou hast said,* that is, It is as thou hast said. This is not spoken out so plainly as Nathan's *Thou art the man;* but it was enough to convict him, and, if his heart had not been wretchedly hardened, to have broken the neck of his plot, when he saw it discovered to his Master, and discovered by him. Note, They who are contriving to betray Christ, will, some time or other, betray themselves, and *their own tongues will fall upon them.*

Verses 26–30

We have here the institution of the great gospel ordinance of the Lord's supper, which was received of the Lord. Observe,

I. The time when it was instituted — *as they were eating.* At the latter end of the passover-supper, before the table was drawn, because, as a feast upon a sacrifice, it was to come in the room of that ordinance. Christ is to us the Passover-sacrifice by which atonement is made (1 Co. 5:7); *Christ our Passover is sacrificed for us.* This ordinance is to us the passover-supper, by which application is made, and commemoration celebrated, of a much greater deliverance than that of Israel out of Egypt. All the legal sacrifices of propitiation being summed up in the death of Christ, and so abolished, all the legal feasts of rejoicing were summed up in this sacrament, and so abolished.

II. The institution itself. A sacrament must be instituted; it is no part of moral worship, nor is it dictated by natural light, but has both its being and significancy from the institution, from a divine institution; it is his prerogative who established the covenant, to appoint the seals of it. Hence the apostle (1 Co. 11:23, etc), in that discourse of his concerning this ordinance, all along calls Jesus Christ *the Lord,* because, as *Lord,* as Lord of the covenant, Lord of the church, he appointed this ordinance. In which,

1. The body of Christ is signified and represented by bread; he had said formerly (Jn. 6:35), *I am the bread of life,* upon which metaphor this sacrament is built; as the life of the body is supported by bread, which is therefore put for all bodily nourishment (*ch.* 4:4; 6:11), so the life of the soul is supported and maintained by Christ's mediation.

(1.) *He took bread, estēsan — the loaf;* some loaf that lay ready to hand, fit for the purpose; it was, probably, unleavened bread; but, that circumstance not being taken notice of, we are not to bind ourselves to that, as some of the Greek churches do. His taking the bread was a solemn action, and was, probably, done in such a manner as to be observed by them that sat with him, that they might expect something more than ordinary to be done with it. Thus was the Lord Jesus set apart in the counsels of divine love for the working out of our redemption.

(2.) *He blessed it;* set it apart for this use by prayer and thanksgiving. We do not find any set form of words used by him upon this occasion; but what he said, no doubt, was accommodated to the business in hand, that new testament which by this ordinance was to be sealed and ratified. This was like God's *blessing the seventh day* (Gen. 2:3), by which it was separated to God's honour, and made to all that duly observe it, a blessed day: Christ could command the blessing, and we, in his name, are emboldened to beg the blessing.

(3.) *He brake it;* which denotes, [1.] The breaking of Christ's body for us, that it might be fitted for our use; *He was bruised for our iniquities,* as *bread-corn is bruised* (Isa. 28:28); though *a bone of him was not broken* (for all his breaking did not weaken him), yet his flesh was *broken with breach upon breach,* and his wounds were multiplied (Job 9:17; 16:14), and that pained him. God complains that he is broken with the *whorish heart* of sinners (Eze. 6:9); his law broken, our covenants with him broken; now justice requires *breach for breach* (Lev. 24:20), and Christ was broken, to satisfy that demand. [2.] The breaking of Christ's body to us, as the father of the family breaks the bread to the children. The breaking of Christ to us, is to facilitate the application; every thing is made ready for us by the grants of God's word and the operations of his grace.

(4.) *He gave it to his disciples,* as the Master of the family, and the Master of this feast; it is not said, He gave it *to the apostles,* though they were so, and had been often called so before this, but *to the disciples,* because all the disciples of Christ have a right to this ordinance; and those shall have the benefit of it who are his disciples indeed; yet he gave it to them as he did the multiplied loaves, by them to be handed to all his other followers.

(5.) *He said, Take, eat; this is my body, v.* 26. He here tells them,

[1.] What they should do with it; *"Take, eat;* accept of Christ as he is offered to you, receive the atonement, approve of it, consent to it, come up to the terms on which the benefit of it is proposed to you; submit to his grace and to his government." Believing on Christ is expressed by *receiving him* (Jn. 1:12), and *feeding upon him,* Jn. 6:57, 58. Meat looked upon, or the dish ever so well garnished, will not nourish us; it must be fed upon: so must the doctrine of Christ.

[2.] What they should have with it; *This is my body,* not *outos — this bread,* but *touto — this eating and drinking.* Believing carries all the efficacy of Christ's death to our souls. *This is my body,* spiritually and sacramentally; this signifies and represents my body. He employs sacramental language, like that, Ex. 12:11. *It is the Lord's passover.* Upon a carnal and much-mistaken sense of these words, the church of Rome builds the monstrous doctrine of Transubstantiation, which makes the bread to be changed into the substance of Christ's body, only the accidents of bread remaining; which affronts Christ, destroys the nature of a sacrament, and gives the lie to our senses. We partake of the sun, not by having the bulk and body of the sun put into our hands, but the beams of it darted down upon us; so we partake of Christ by partaking of his grace, and the blessed fruits of the breaking of his body.

2. The blood of Christ is signified and represented by the wine; to make it a complete feast, here is not only bread to strengthen, but wine to *make glad the heart* (*v.* 27, 28); *He took the cup,* the grace-cup, which was set ready to be drank, after thanks returned, according to the custom of the Jews at the passover; this Christ took, and made the sacramental-cup, and so altered the property. It was intended for a *cup of blessing* (so the Jews called it), and therefore St. Paul studiously distinguished between the cup of blessing which *we* bless, and that which *they* bless. *He gave thanks,* to teach us, not only in every ordinance, but in every part of the ordinance, to have our eyes up to God.

This cup he gave to the disciples,

(1.) With a command; *Drink ye all of it.* Thus he welcomes his guests to his table, obliges them all to drink of his cup. Why should he so expressly command them all to drink, and to see that none let it pass them, and press that more expressly in this than in the other part of the ordinance? Surely it was because he foresaw how in after-ages this ordinance would be dismembered by the prohibition of the cup to the laity, with an express *non obstante — notwithstanding* to the command.

(2.) With an explication; *For this is my blood of the New Testament.* Therefore drink it with appetite, delight, because it is so rich a cordial. Hitherto the blood of Christ had been represented by the blood of beasts, real blood: but, after it was actually shed, it was represented by the blood of grapes, metaphorical blood; so wine is called in an Old-Testament prophecy of Christ, Gen. 49:10, 11.

Now observe what Christ saith of his blood represented in the sacrament.

[1.] *It is my blood of the New Testament.* The Old Testament was confirmed by the *blood of bulls and goats* (Heb. 9:19, 20; Ex. 24:8); but the New Testament with the blood of Christ, which is here distinguished from that; *It is my blood of the New Testament.* The covenant God is pleased to make with us, and all the benefits and privileges of it, are owing to the merits of Christ's death.

[2.] *It is shed;* it was not shed till next day, but it was now upon the point of being shed, it is as good as done. "Before you come to repeat this ordinance yourselves, it will be shed." He was *now ready to be offered,* and his blood to be poured out, as the blood of the sacrifices which made atonement.

[3.] *It is shed for many.* Christ came to confirm *a covenant with many* (Dan. 9:27), and the intent of his death agreed. The blood of the Old Testament was shed for a few: it confirmed a covenant, which (saith Moses) the Lord has *made with you,* Ex. 24:8. The atonement was made only *for the children of Israel* (Lev. 16:34): but Jesus Christ is a propitiation *for the sins of the whole world,* 1 Jn. 2:2.

[4.] It *is shed for the remission of sins,* that is, to purchase remission of sins for us. The redemption which we have through his blood, is *the remission of sins,* Eph. 1:7. The new covenant which is procured and ratified by the blood of Christ, is a charter of pardon, an act of indemnity, in order to a reconciliation between God and man; for sin was the only thing that made the quarrel, and *without shedding of blood is no remission,* Heb. 9:22. The pardon of sin is that great blessing which is, in the Lord's supper, conferred upon all true believers; it is the foundation of all other blessings, and the spring of everlasting comfort, *ch.* 9:2, 3. A farewell is now bidden to the fruit of the vine, *v.* 29. Christ and his disciples had now feasted together with a deal of comfort, in both an Old Testament and a New Testament festival, *fibula utriusque Testamenti — the connecting tie of both Testaments.* How amiable were these tabernacles! How good to be here! Never such a heaven upon earth as was at this table; but it was not intended for a perpetuity; he now told them (Jn. 16:16), that *yet a little while and they should not see him: and again a little while and they should see him,* which explains this here.

First, He takes leave of such communion; *I will not drink henceforth of this fruit of the vine,* that is, now that I am no more in the world (Jn. 17:11); I have had enough of it, and am glad to think of leaving it, glad to think that this is the last meal. *Farewell this fruit of the vine,* this passover-cup, this sacramental wine. Dying saints take their leave of sacraments, and the other ordinances of communion which they enjoy in this world, with comfort, for the joy and glory they enter into supersede them all; when the sun rises, farewell the candles.

Secondly, He assures them of a happy meeting again at last. It is a long, but not an everlasting, farewell; *until that day when I drink it new with you.* 1. Some understand it of the interviews he had with them after his resurrection, which was the first step of his exaltation *into the kingdom of his Father;* and though during those forty days he did not converse with them so constantly as he had done, yet he *did eat and drink with them* (Acts 10:41), which, as it confirmed their faith, so doubtless it greatly comforted their hearts, for they were overjoyed at it, Lu. 24:41. 2. Others understand it of the joys and glories of the future state, which the saints shall partake of in everlasting communion with the Lord Jesus, represented here by the pleasures of *a banquet of wine.* That will be the kingdom of his Father, for unto him shall the kingdom be then delivered up; *the wine of consolation* (Jer. 16:7) will there be always new, never flat or sour, as wine with long keeping; never nauseous or unpleasant, as wine to those that have drank much; but ever fresh. Christ will himself partake of those pleasures; it was *the joy set before him,* which he had in his eye, and all his faithful friends and followers shall partake with him.

Lastly, Here is the close of the solemnity with a hymn (*v.* 30); *They sang a hymn* or psalm; whether the psalms which the Jews usually sang at the close of the passover-supper, which they called *the great hallel,* that is, Ps. 113 and the five that follow it, or whether some new hymn more closely adapted to the occasion, is uncertain; I rather think the former; had it been new, John would not have omitted to record it. Note, 1. Singing of psalms is a gospel-ordinance. Christ's removing the hymn from the close of the passover to the close of the Lord's supper, plainly intimates that he intended that ordinance should continue in his church, that, as it had not its birth with the ceremonial law, so it should not die with it. 2. It is very proper after the Lord's supper, as an expression of our joy in God through Jesus Christ, and a thankful acknowledgment of that great love wherewith God has loved us in him. 3. It is not unseasonable, no, not in times of sorrow and suffering; the disciples were in sorrow, and Christ was entering upon his sufferings, and yet they could sing a hymn together. Our spiritual joy should not be interrupted by outward afflictions.

When this was done, they *went out into the mount of Olives.* He would not stay in the house to be apprehended, lest he should bring the master of the house into trouble; nor would he stay in the city, lest it should occasion an uproar; but he retired into the adjacent country, the mount of Olives, the same mount that David in his distress went *up the ascent of, weeping,* 2 Sa. 15:30. They had the benefit of moonlight for this walk, for the passover was always at the full moon. Note, After we have received the Lord's supper, it is good for us to retire for prayer and meditation, and to be alone with God.

Verses 31–35

We have here Christ's discourse with his disciples upon the way, as they were going to the mount of Olives. Observe,

I. A prediction of the trial which both he and his disciples were now to go through. He here foretels,

1. A dismal scattering storm just arising, *v.* 31.

(1.) That they should *all be offended because of Christ that very night;* that is, they would all be so frightened with the sufferings, that they would not have the courage to cleave to him in them, but would all basely desert him; *Because of me this night, en emoi en tē nykti tautē — because of me, even because of this night;* so it might be read; that is, because of what happens to me this night. Note, [1.] Offences will come among the disciples of Christ in an hour of trial and temptation; it cannot be but they should, for they are weak; Satan is busy; God permits offences; even they whose hearts are upright may sometimes be overtaken with an offence. [2.] There are some temptations and offences, the effects of which are general and universal among Christ's disciples; *All you shall be offended.* Christ had lately discovered to them the treachery of Judas; but let not the rest be secure; though there will be but one traitor, they will be all deserters. This he saith, to alarm them all, that they might all watch. [3.] We have need to prepare for sudden trials, which may come to extremity in a very little time. Christ and his disciples had eaten their supper well together in peace and quietness; yet that very night proved such a night of offence. How soon may a storm arise! We know not what a day, or a night, may bring forth, nor what great event may be in the teeming womb of a little time, Prov. 27:1. [4.] The cross of Christ is the great stumbling-block to many that pass for his disciples; both the cross he bore for us (1 Co. 1:23), and that which we are called out to bear for him, *ch.* 16:24.

(2.) That herein the scripture would be fulfilled; *I will smite the Shepherd.* It is quoted from Zec. 13:7. [1.] Here is the smiting of the Shepherd in the sufferings of Christ. God awakens the sword of his wrath against the Son of his love, and he is smitten. [2.] The scattering of the sheep, thereupon, in the flight of the disciples. When Christ fell into the hands of his enemies, his disciples ran, one one way and another another; it was each one's care to shift for himself, and happy he that could get furthest from the cross.

2. He gives them the prospect of a comfortable gathering together again after this storm (*v.* 32); *"After I am risen again, I will go before you.* Though you will forsake me, I will not forsake you; though you fall, I will take care you shall not fall finally: we shall have a meeting again in Galilee, *I will go before you,* as the shepherd before the sheep." Some make the last words of that prophecy (Zec. 13:7), a promise equivalent to this here; *and I will bring my hand again to the little ones.* There is no bringing them back but by bringing his hand to them. Note, The captain of our salvation knows how to rally his troops, when, through their cowardice, they have been put into disorder.

II. The presumption of Peter, that he should keep his integrity, whatever happened (*v.* 33); *Though all men be offended, yet will I never be offended.* Peter had a great stock of confidence, and was upon all occasions forward to speak, especially to speak for himself; sometimes it did him a kindness, but at other times it betrayed him, as it did here. Where observe,

1. How he bound himself with a promise, that he would never be offended in Christ; not only not this night, but at no time. If this promise had been made in a humble dependence upon the grace of Christ, it had been an excellent word. Before the Lord's supper, Christ's discourse led his disciples to *examine* themselves with, *Lord, is it I?* For that is our preparatory duty; after the ordinance, his discourse leads them to an *engaging* of themselves to close walking, for that is the subsequent duty.

2. How he fancied himself better armed against temptation than any one else, and this was his weakness and folly; *Though all men shall be offended yet will not I.* This was worse than Hazael's, *What! is thy servant a dog?* For he supposed the thing to be so bad, that no man would do it. But Peter supposes it possible that *some,* nay that *all,* might be offended, and yet he escape better than any. Note, It argues a great degree of self-conceit and self-confidence, to think ourselves either safe from the temptations, or free from the corruptions, that are common to men. We should rather say, If it be possible that others may be offended, there is danger that I may be so. But it is common for those who think too well of themselves, easily to admit suspicions of others. See Gal. 6:1.

III. The particular warning Christ gave Peter of what he would do, *v.* 34. He imagined that in the hour of temptation he should come off better than any of them, and Christ tells him that he should come off worse. The warning is introduced with a solemn asseveration; *"Verily, I say unto thee;* take my word for it, who know thee better than thou knowest thyself." He tells him,

1. That he should deny him. Peter promised that he would not be so much as offended in him, not desert him; but Christ tells him that he will go further, he will disown him. He said, "Though all men, yet not I;" and he did it sooner than any.

2. How quickly he should do it; *this night,* before tomorrow, nay, *before cock-crowing.* Satan's temptations are compared to *darts* (Eph. 6:16), which wound ere we are aware; *suddenly doth he shoot.* As we know not how near we may be to trouble, so we know not how near we may be to sin; if God leave us to ourselves, we are always in danger.

3. How often he should do it; *thrice.* He thought that he should never once do such a thing; but Christ tells him that he would do it again and again; for, when once our feet begin to slip, it is hard to recover our standing again. *The beginnings of sin are as the letting forth of water.*

IV. Peter's repeated assurances of his fidelity (*v.* 35); *Though I should die with thee.* He supposed the temptation strong, when he said, *Though all men do it, yet will not I.* But here he supposeth it stronger, when he puts it to the peril of life; *Though I should die with thee.* He knew what he *should* do — rather die with Christ than deny him, it was the condition of discipleship (Lu. 14:26); and he thought what he *would* do — never be false to his Master whatever it cost him; yet, it proved, he was. It is easy to talk boldly and carelessly of death at a distance; "I will rather die than do such a thing:" but it is not so soon done as said, when it comes to the setting-to, and death shows itself in its own colours.

What Peter said the rest subscribed to; *likewise also said all the disciples.* Note, 1. There is a proneness in good men to be over-confident of their own strength and stability. We are ready to think ourselves able to grapple with the strongest temptations, to go through the hardest and most hazardous services, and to bear the greatest afflictions for Christ; but it is because we do not know ourselves. 2. Those often fall soonest and foulest that are most confident of themselves. Those are least safe that are most secure. Satan is most active to seduce such; they are most off their guard, and God leaves them to themselves, to humble them. See 1 Co. 10:12.

Verses 36–46

Hitherto, we have seen the preparatives for Christ's sufferings; now, we enter upon the bloody scene. In these verses we have the story of his agony in the garden. This was the beginning of sorrows to our Lord Jesus. Now the *sword of the Lord* began to awake against *the man that was his Fellow; and how should it be quiet when the Lord had given it a charge?* The clouds had been gathering a good while, and looked black. He had said, some days before, *Now is my soul troubled,* Jn. 12:27. But now the storm began in good earnest. He put himself into this agony, before his enemies gave him any trouble, to show that he was a Freewill offering; that his life was not forced from him, but he *laid it down of himself.* Jn. 10:18. Observe,

I. The place where he underwent this mighty agony; it was *in a place called Gethsemane.* The name signifies, *torculus olei — an olive-mill,* a press for olives, like a winepress, where they *trod the olives,* Mic. 6:15. And this was the proper place for such a thing, at the foot of the mount of Olives. There our Lord Jesus began his passion; there it pleased the Lord to bruise him, and crush him, that fresh oil might flow to all believers from him, that we might partake of the root and fatness of that *good Olive.* There he trod the wine-press of his Father's wrath, and trod it alone.

II. The company he had with him, when he was in this agony.

1. He took all the twelve disciples with him to the garden, except Judas, who was at this time otherwise employed. Though it was late in the night, near bed-time, yet they kept with him, and took this walk by moonlight with him, as Elisha, who, when he was told that his master should shortly be taken from his head, declared that he *would not leave him,* though he *led him about;* so these follow the Lamb, wheresoever he goes.

2. He took only Peter, and James, and John, with him into that corner of the garden where he suffered his agony. He left the rest at some distance, perhaps at the garden door, with this charge, *Sit ye here, while I go and pray yonder;* like that of Abraham to his *young men* (Gen. 22:5), *Abide ye here, and I will go yonder and worship.* (1.) Christ went to pray alone, though he had lately prayed with his disciples, Jn. 17:1. Note, Our prayers with our families must not excuse us from our secret devotions. (2.) He ordered them to sit here. Note, We must take heed of giving any disturbance or interruption to those who retire for secret communion with God. He took these three with him, because they had been the witnesses of his glory in his transfiguration (*ch.* 17:1, 2), and that would prepare them to be the witnesses of his agony. Note, Those are best prepared to suffer with Christ, that have by faith beheld his glory, and have conversed with the glorified saints upon the holy mount. *If we suffer with Christ, we shall reign with him;* and if we hope to reign with him, why should we not expect to suffer with him?

III. The agony itself that he was in; *He began to be sorrowful, and very heavy.* It is called an agony (Lu. 22:44), a conflict. It was not any bodily pain or torment that he was in, nothing occurred to hurt him; but, whatever it was, it was from within; he troubled himself, Jn. 11:33. The words here used are very emphatical; he began *en emoi en tē nykti tautē — to be sorrowful, and in a consternation.* The latter word signifies such a sorrow as makes a man neither fit for company nor desirous of it. He had like a weight of lead upon his spirits. Physicians use a word near akin to it, to signify the disorder a man is in in a fit of an ague, or beginning of a fever. Now was fulfilled, Ps. 22:14, *I am poured out like water, my heart is like wax, it is melted;* and all those passages in the Psalms where David complains of the sorrows of his soul, Ps. 18:4, 5; 42:7; 55:4, 5; 69:1–3; 88:3; 116:3, and Jonah's complaint, *ch.* 2:4, 5.

But what was the cause of all this? What was it that put him into his agony? *Why art thou cast down,* blessed Jesus, and *why disquieted?* Certainly, it was nothing of despair or distrust of his Father, much less any conflict or struggle with him. As the Father loved him because he laid down his life for the sheep, so he was entirely subject to his Father's will in it. But,

1. He engaged in an encounter with the powers of darkness; so he intimates (Lu. 22:53); *This is your hour, and the power of darkness:* and he spoke of it just before (Jn. 14:30, 31); *"The prince of this world cometh.* I see him rallying his forces, and preparing for a general assault; but *he has nothing in me,* no garrisons in his interest, none that secretly hold correspondence with him; and therefore his attempts, though fierce, will be fruitless: but *as the Father gave me commandment, so I do;* however it be, I must have a struggle with him, the field must be fairly fought; and therefore *arise, let us go hence,* let us hasten to the field of battle, and meet the enemy." Now is the close engagement in single combat between Michael and the dragon, hand to hand; *now is the judgment of this world;* the great cause is now to be determined, and the decisive battle fought, in which the *prince of this world,* will certainly be beaten and *cast out,* Jn. 12:31. Christ, when he works salvation, is described like a champion taking the field, Isa. 59:16–18. Now the serpent makes his fiercest onset on the seed of the woman, and directs his sting, the sting of death, to his very heart; *animamque in vulnere ponit — and the wound is mortal.*

2. He was now *bearing the iniquities* which the Father laid upon him, and, by his sorrow and amazement, he accommodated himself to his undertaking. The sufferings he was entering upon were for our sins; they were all made to meet upon him, and he knew it. As we are obliged to be sorry for our particular sins, so was he grieved for the sins of us all. So Bishop Pearson, p. 191. Now, *in the valley of Jehoshaphat,* where Christ now was, God *gathered all nations,* and *pleaded with them in his* Son, Joel 3:2, 12. He knew the malignity of the sins that were laid upon him, how provoking to God, how ruining to man; and these being all set in order before him, and charged upon him, he was *sorrowful and very heavy.* Now it was that *iniquities took hold on him;* so that he was *not able to look up,* as was foretold concerning him, Ps. 40:7, 12.

3. He had a full and clear prospect of all the sufferings that were before him. He foresaw the treachery of Judas, the unkindness of Peter, the malice of the Jews, and their base ingratitude. He knew that he should now in a few hours be scourged, spit upon, crowned with thorns, nailed to the cross; death in its most dreadful appearances, death in pomp, attended with all its terrors, looked him in the face; and this made him sorrowful, especially because it was the wages of our sin, which he had undertaken to satisfy for. It is true, the martyrs that have suffered for Christ, have entertained the greatest torments, and the most terrible deaths, without any such sorrow and consternation; have called their prisons their delectable orchards, and a bed of flames a bed of roses: but then, (1.) Christ was now denied the supports and comforts which they had; that is, he denied them to himself, and *his soul refused to be comforted,* not in passion, but in justice to his undertaking. Their cheerfulness under the cross was owing to the divine favour, which, for the present, was suspended from the Lord Jesus. (2.) His sufferings were of another nature from theirs. St. Paul, when he is to be offered upon the sacrifice and service of the saints' faith, can *joy and rejoice with them all;* but to be offered a sacrifice, to make atonement for sin, is quite a different case. On the saints' cross there is a blessing pronounced, which enables them to rejoice under it (*ch.* 5:10, 12); but to Christ's cross there was a curse annexed, which made him sorrowful and very heavy under it. And his sorrow under the cross was the foundation of their joy under it.

IV. His complaint of this agony. Finding himself under the arrest of his passion, he goes to his disciples (*v.* 38), and,

1. He acquaints them with his condition; *My soul is exceedingly sorrowful, even unto death.* It gives some little ease to a troubled spirit, to have a friend ready to unbosom itself to, and give vent to its sorrows. Christ here tells them, (1.) What was the seat of his sorrow; it was his soul that was now in an agony. This proves that Christ had a true human soul; for he suffered, not only in his body, but in his soul. We had sinned both against our own bodies, and against our souls; both had been used in sin, and both had been wronged by it; and therefore Christ suffered in soul as well as in body. (2.) What was the degree of his sorrow. He was *exceedingly sorrowful, perilypos — compassed about with sorrow on all hands.* It was sorrow in the highest degree, even unto death; it was a killing sorrow, such sorrow as no mortal man could bear and live. He was ready to die for grief; they were sorrows of death. (3.) The duration of it; it will continue even unto death. "My soul will be sorrowful as long as it is in this body; I see no outlet but death." He now *began* to be sorrowful, and never ceased to be so till he said, *It is finished;* that grief is now finished, which began in the garden. It was prophesied of Christ, that he should be *a Man of sorrows* (Is. 53:3); he was so all along, we never read that he laughed; but all his sorrows hitherto were nothing to this.

2. He bespeaks their company and attendance; *Tarry ye here, and watch with me.* Surely he was destitute indeed of help, when he entreated theirs, who, he knew, would be but miserable comforters; but he would hereby teach us the benefit of the communion of saints. It is good to have, and therefore good to seek, the assistance of our brethren, when at any time we are in an agony; *for two are better than one.* What he said to them, he saith to all, *Watch,* Mk. 13:37. Not only watch for him, in expectation of his future coming, but watch with him, in application to our present work.

V. What passed between him and his Father when he was in this agony; *Being in an agony, he prayed.* Prayer is never out of season, but it is especially seasonable in an agony.

Observe, 1. The place where he prayed; *He went a little further,* withdrew from them, that the scripture might be fulfilled, *I have trod the wine-press alone;* he retired for prayer; a troubled soul finds most ease when it is alone with God, who understands the broken language of sighs and groans. Calvin's devout remark upon this is worth transcribing, *Utile est seorsim orare, tunc enim magis familiariter sese denudat fidelis animus, et simplicius sua vota, gemitus, curas, pavores, spes, et gaudia in Dei sinum exonerat — It is useful to pray apart; for then the faithful soul develops itself more familiarly, and with greater simplicity pours forth its petitions, groans, cares, fears, hopes and joys, into the bosom of God.* Christ has hereby taught us that secret prayer must be made secretly. Yet some think that even the disciples whom he left at the garden door, overheard him; for it is said (Heb. 5:7), they were *strong cries.*

2. His posture in prayer; *He fell on his face;* his lying prostrate denotes, (1.) The agony he was in, and the extremity of his sorrow. Job, in great grief, *fell on the ground;* and great anguish is expressed by *rolling in the dust,* Mic. 1:10. (2.) His humility in prayer. This posture was an expression of his, *eulabeia — his reverential fear* (spoken of Heb. 5:7), with which he offered up these prayers: and it was *in the days of his flesh,* in his estate of humiliation, to which hereby he accommodated himself.

3. The prayer itself; wherein we may observe three things.

(1.) The title he gives to God; *O my Father.* Thick as the cloud was, he could see God as a Father through it. Note, In all our addresses to God we should eye him as a Father, as our Father; and it is in a special manner comfortable to do so, when we are in an agony. It is a pleasing string to harp upon at such a time, *My Father;* whither should the child go, when any thing grieves him, but to his father?

(2.) The favour he begs; *If it be possible, let this cup pass from me.* He calls his sufferings a *cup;* not a river, not a sea, but a cup, which we shall soon see the bottom of. When we are under troubles, we should make the best, the least, of them, and not aggravate them. His sufferings might be called a *cup,* because allotted him, as at feasts a cup was set to every mess. He begs that this cup might *pass from him,* that is, that he might avoid the sufferings now at hand; or, at least, that they might be shortened. This intimates no more than that he was really and truly Man, and as a Man he could not but be averse to pain and suffering. This is the first and simple act of man's will — to start back from that which is sensibly grievous to us, and to desire the prevention and removal of it. The law of self-preservation is impressed upon the innocent nature of man, and rules there till overruled by some other law; therefore Christ admitted and expressed a reluctance to suffer, to show that he was *taken from among men* (Heb. 5:1), was touched with *the feeling of our infirmities* (Heb. 4:15), and *tempted as we are; yet without sin.* Note, A prayer of faith against an affliction, may very well consist with the patience of hope under affliction. When David had said, *I was dumb, I opened not my mouth, because thou didst it;* his very next words were, *Remove thy stroke away from me,* Ps. 39:9, 10. But observe the proviso; *If it be possible.* If God may be glorified, man saved, and the ends of his undertaking answered, without his drinking of this bitter cup, he desires to be excused; otherwise not. What we cannot do with the securing of our great end, we must reckon to be in effect impossible; Christ did so. *Id possumus quod jure possumus — We can do that which we can do lawfully.* We *can* do nothing, not only we *may* do nothing, against the truth.

(3.) His entire submission to, and acquiescence in, the will of God; *Nevertheless, not as I will, but as thou wilt.* Not that the human will of Christ was adverse or averse to the divine will; it was only, in its first act, diverse from it; to which, in the second act of the will, which compares and chooses, he freely submits himself. Note, [1.] Our Lord Jesus, though he had a quick sense of the extreme bitterness of the sufferings he was to undergo, yet was freely willing to submit to them for our redemption and salvation, and *offered himself, and gave himself, for us.* [2.] The reason of Christ's submission to his sufferings, was, his Father's will; *as thou wilt, v.* 39. He grounds his own willingness upon the Father's will, and resolves the matter wholly into that; *therefore* he did what he did, and did it with delight, because it was the will of God, Ps. 40:8. This he had often referred to, as that which put him upon, and carried him through, his whole undertaking; *This is the Father's will,* Jn. 6:39, 40. This he sought (Jn. 5:30); it was his *meat and drink* to do it, Jn. 4:34. [3.] In conformity to this example of Christ, we must drink of the bitter cup which God puts into our hands, be it ever so bitter; though nature struggle, grace must submit. We then are disposed as Christ was, when our wills are in every thing melted into the will of God, though ever so displeasing to flesh and blood; *The will of the Lord be done,* Acts 21:14.

4. The repetition of the prayer; *He went away again the second time, and prayed* (*v.* 42), and again the third time (*v.* 44), and all to the same purport; only, as it is related here, he did not, in the second and third prayer, expressly ask that the cup might pass from him, as he had done in the first. Note, Though we may pray to God to prevent and remove an affliction, yet our chief errand, and that which we should most insist upon, must be, that he will give us grace to bear it well. It should be more our care to get our troubles sanctified, and our hearts satisfied under them, than to get them taken away. *He prayed, saying, Thy will be done.* Note, Prayer is the offering up, not only of our desires, but of our resignations, to God. It amounts to an acceptable prayer, when at any time we are in distress, to refer ourselves to God, and to commit our way and work to him; *Thy will be done.* The third time he *said the same words, eulabeia — the same word,* that is the same matter or argument; he spoke to the same purport. We have reason to think that this was not all he said, for it should seem by *v.* 40 that he continued *an hour* in his agony and prayer; but, whatever more he said, it was to this effect, deprecating his approaching sufferings, and yet resigning himself to God's will in them, in the expressions of which we may be sure he was not straitened.

But what answer had he to this prayer? Certainly it was not made in vain; he that heard him *always,* did not deny him *now.* It is true, the cup did not pass from him, for he withdrew that petition, and did not insist upon it (if he had, for aught I know, the cup had passed away); but he had an answer to his prayer; for, (1.) *He was strengthened with strength in his soul,* in the day when he cried (Ps. 138:3); and that was a real answer, Lu. 22:43. (2.) He was delivered from that which he feared, which was, lest by impatience and distrust he should offend his Father, and so disable himself to go on with his undertaking, Heb. 5:7. In answer to his prayer, God provided that he should not fail or be discouraged.

VI. What passed between him and his three disciples at this time; and here we may observe,

1. The fault they were guilty of; that when he was in his agony, sorrowful and heavy, sweating and wrestling and praying, they were so little concerned, that they could not keep awake; he comes, and *finds them asleep, v.* 40. The strangeness of the thing should have roused their spirits to *turn aside now, and see this great sight — the bush burning, and yet not consumed;* much more should their love to their Master, and their care concerning him, have obliged them to a more close and vigilant attendance on him; yet they were so dull, that they could not keep their eyes open. What had become of us, if Christ had been now as sleepy as his disciples were? It is well for us that our salvation is in the hand of one who *neither slumbers nor sleeps.* Christ engaged them to watch with him, as if he expected some succour from them, and yet they slept; surely it was the unkindest thing that could be. When David wept at this mount of Olives, all his followers wept with him (2 Sa. 15:30); but when the Son of David was here in tears, his followers were asleep. His enemies, who watched for him, were wakeful enough (Mk. 14:43); but his disciples, who should have watched with him, were asleep. Lord, what is man! What are the best of men, when God leaves them to themselves! Note, Carelessness and carnal security, especially when Christ is in his agony, are great faults in any, but especially in those who profess to be nearest in relation to him. The church of Christ, which is his body, is often in an agony, fightings without and fears within; and shall we be asleep then, like Gallio, that *cared for none of these things;* or those (Amos 6:6) that *lay at ease, and were not grieved for the affliction of Joseph?*

2. Christ's favour to them, notwithstanding. Persons in sorrow are too apt to be cross and peevish with those about them, and to lay it grievously to heart, if they but seem to neglect them; but Christ in his agony is as meek as ever, and carries it as patiently toward his followers as toward his Father, and is not apt to take things ill.

When Christ's disciples put this slight upon him,

(1.) *He came to them,* as if he expected to receive some comfort from them; and if they had put him in mind of what they had heard from him concerning his resurrection and glory perhaps it might have been some help to him; but, instead of that, they added grief to his sorrow; and yet he came to them, more careful for them than they were for themselves; when he was most engaged, yet he came to look after them; for those that were given him, were upon his heart, living and dying.

(2.) He gave them a gentle reproof, for as many as he loves he rebukes; he directed it to Peter, who used to *speak* for them; let him now *hear* for them. The reproof was very melting; *What! could ye not watch with me one hour?* He speaks as one amazed to see them so stupid; every word, when closely considered, shows the aggravated nature of the case. Consider, [1.] Who *they* were; "Could not *ye* watch — ye, my disciples and followers? No wonder if others neglect me, if *the earth sit still, and be at rest* (Zec. 1:11); but from you I expected better things." [2.] Who *he* was; "Watch with *me.* If one of yourselves were ill and in an agony, it would be very unkind not to watch with him; but it is undutiful not to watch with your Master, who has long watched over you for good, has led you, and fed you, and taught you, borne you, and borne with you; do ye thus requite him?" He awoke out of his sleep, to help them when they were in distress (*ch.* 8:36); and could not they keep awake, at least to show their good-will to him, especially considering that he was now suffering *for them,* in an agony *for them? Jam tua res agiture — I am suffering in your cause.* [3.] How small a thing it was that he expected from them — only to *watch with him.* If he had bid them do some great thing, had bid them be in an agony with him, or die with him, they thought they could have done it; and yet they could not do it, when he only desired them to *watch with him,* 2 Ki. 5:13. [4.] How short a time it was that he expected it — but *one hour;* they were not set upon the guard whole nights, as the prophet was (Isa. 21:8), only *one hour.* Sometimes he *continued all night in prayer to God,* but did not then expect that his disciples should watch with him; only now, when he had but one hour to spend in prayer.

(3.) He gave them good counsel; *Watch and pray, that ye enter not into temptation, v.* 41. [1.] There was an hour of temptation drawing on, and very near; the troubles of Christ were temptations to his followers to disbelieve and distrust him, to deny and desert him, and renounce all relation to him. [2.] There was danger of their entering into the temptation, as into a snare or trap; of their entering into a parley with it, or a good opinion of it, of their being influenced by it, and inclining to comply with it; which is the first step toward being overcome by it. [3.] He therefore exhorts them to watch and pray; *Watch with me, and pray with me.* While they were sleeping, they lost the benefit of joining in Christ's prayer. "Watch *yourselves,* and pray *yourselves.* Watch and pray against this present temptation to drowsiness and security; *pray* that you may *watch;* beg of God by his grace to keep you awake, now that there is occasion." When we are drowsy in the worship of God, we should pray, as a good Christian once did, "The Lord deliver me from this sleepy devil!" *Lord, quicken thou me in thy way,* Or, "Watch and pray against the further temptation you may be assaulted with; *watch and pray* lest this sin prove the inlet of many more." Note, When we find ourselves entering into temptation, we have need to watch and pray.

(4.) He kindly excused for them; *The spirit indeed is willing, but the flesh is weak.* We do not read of one word they had to say for themselves (the sense of their own weakness stopped their mouth); but then he had a tender word to say on their behalf, for it is his office to be an Advocate; in this he sets us an example of the love *which covers a multitude of sins.* He considered their frame, and did not chide them, for he remembered that they were but flesh; *and the flesh is weak, though the spirit be willing,* Ps. 78:38, 39. Note, [1.] Christ's disciples, as long as they are here in this world, have bodies as well as souls, and a principle of remaining corruption as well as of reigning grace, like Jacob and Esau in the same womb, *Canaanites* and *Israelites* in the same land, Gal. 5:17, 24. [2.] It is the unhappiness and burthen of Christ's disciples, that their bodies cannot keep pace with their souls in works of piety and devotion, but are many a time a cloud and clog to them; that, when the spirit is free and disposed to that which is good, the flesh is averse and indisposed. This St. Paul laments (Rom. 7:25); *With my mind I serve the law of God, but with my flesh the law of sin.* Our impotency in the service of God is the great iniquity and infidelity of our nature, and it arises from these sad remainders of corruption, which are the constant grief and burthen of God's people. [3.] Yet it is our comfort, that our Master graciously considers this, and accepts the willingness of the spirit, and pities and pardons the weakness and infirmity of the flesh; for *we are under grace, and not under the law.*

(5.) Though they continued dull and sleepy, he did not any further rebuke them for it; for, though we daily offend, yet he will not always chide. [1.] When he came to them the second time, we do not find that he said any thing to them (*v.* 43); *he findeth them asleep again.* One would have thought that he had said enough to them to keep them awake; but it is hard to recover from a spirit of slumber. Carnal security, when once it prevails, is not easily shaken off. *Their eyes were heavy,* which intimates that they strove against it as much as they could, but were overcome by it, like the spouse; *I sleep, but my heart waketh* (Cant. 5:2); and therefore their Master looked upon them with compassion. [2.] When he came the third time, he left them to be alarmed with the approaching danger (*v.* 45, 46); *Sleep on now, and take your rest.* This is spoken ironically; "Now sleep if you can, sleep if you dare; I would not disturb you if Judas and his band of men would not." See here how Christ deals with those that suffer themselves to be overcome by security, and will not be awakened out of it. *First,* Sometimes he gives them up to the power of it; *Sleep on now.* He that will sleep, let him sleep still. The curse of spiritual slumber is the just punishment of the sin of it, Rom. 11:8; Hos. 4:17. *Secondly,* Many times he sends some startling judgment, to awaken those that would not be wrought upon by the word; and those who will not be alarmed by reasons and arguments, had better be alarmed by swords and spears than left to perish in their security. Let those that would not believe, be made to feel.

As to the disciples here, 1. Their Master gave them notice of the near approach of his enemies, who, it is likely, were now within sight or hearing, for they came with candles and torches, and, it is likely, made a great noise; *The Son of man is betrayed into the hands of sinners.* And again, *He is at hand that doth betray me.* Note, Christ's sufferings were no surprise to him; he knew what, and when, he was to suffer. By this time the extremity of his agony was pretty well over, or, at least, diverted; while with an undaunted courage he addresses himself to the next encounter, as a champion to the combat. 2. He called them to rise, and be going: not, "Rise, and let us flee from the danger;" but, "Rise, and let us go meet it;" before he had prayed, he feared his sufferings, but now he had got over his fears. But, 3. He intimates to them their folly, in sleeping away the time which they should have spent in preparation; now the event found them unready, and was a terror to them.

Verses 47–56

We are here told how the blessed Jesus was seized, and taken into custody; this followed immediately upon his agony, *while he yet spake;* for from the beginning to the close of his passion he had not the least intermission or breathing-time, but *deep called unto deep.* His trouble hitherto was raised within himself; but now the scene is changed, now the Philistines are upon thee, thou blessed Samson; *the Breath of our nostrils, the Anointed of the Lord is taken in their pits,* Lam. 4:20.

Now concerning the apprehension of the Lord Jesus, observe,

I. Who the persons were, that were employed in it. 1. Here was *Judas, one of the twelve,* at the head of this infamous guard: *he was guide to them that took Jesus* (Acts 1:16); without his help they could not have found him in this retirement. Behold, and wonder; the first that appears with his enemies, is one of his own disciples, who an hour or two ago was eating bread with him! 2. Here was *with him a great multitude;* that the scripture might be fulfilled, *Lord, how are they increased that trouble me!* Ps. 3:1. This multitude was made up partly of a detachment out of the guards, that were posted in the tower of Antonia by the Roman governor; these were Gentiles, *sinners,* as Christ calls them, *v.* 45. The rest were the servants and officers of the High Priest, and they were Jews; they that were at variance with each other, agreed against Christ.

II. How they were armed for this enterprise.

1. What weapons they were armed with; They came *with swords and staves.* The Roman soldiers, no doubt, had swords; the servants of the priests, those of them that had not swords, brought staves or clubs. *Furor arma ministrat — Their rage supplied their arms.* They were not regular troops, but a tumultuous rabble. But wherefore is this ado? If they had been ten times as many, they could not have taken him had he not yielded; and, his hour being come for him to give up himself, all this force was needless. When a butcher goes into the field to take out a lamb for the slaughter, does he raise the militia, and come armed? No, he needs not; yet is there all this force used to seize the Lamb of God.

2. What warrant they were armed with; *They came from the chief priests, and elders of the people;* this armed multitude was sent by them upon this errand. He was taken up by a warrant from the great sanhedrim, as a person obnoxious to them. Pilate, the Roman governor, gave them no warrant to search for him, he had no jealousy of him; but they were men who pretended to religion, and presided in the affairs of the church, that were active in this prosecution, and were the most spiteful enemies Christ had. It was a sign that he was supported by a divine power, for by all earthly powers he was not only deserted, but opposed; Pilate upbraided him with it; *Thine own nation and the chief priests delivered thee to me,* Jn. 18:35.

III. The manner how it was done, and what passed at that time.

1. How Judas betrayed him; he did his business effectually, and his resolution in this wickedness may shame us who fail in that which is good. Observe,

(1.) The instructions he gave to the soldiers (*v.* 48); *He gave them a sign;* as commander of the party in this action, he gives the word or signal. He *gave them a sign,* lest by mistake they should seize one of the disciples instead of him, the disciples having so lately said, in Judas's hearing, that they would be willing to die for him. What abundance of caution was here, not to miss him — *That same is he;* and when they had him in their hands, not to lose him — *Hold him fast;* for he had sometimes escaped from those who thought to secure him; as Lu. 6:30. Though the Jews, who frequented the temple, could not but know him, yet the Roman soldiers perhaps had never seen him, and the sign was to direct them; and Judas by his kiss intended not only to distinguish him, but to detain him, while they came behind him, and laid hands on him.

(2.) The dissembling compliment he gave his Master. He came close up to Jesus; surely now, if ever, his wicked heart will relent; surely when he comes to look him in the face, he will either be awed by its majesty, or charmed by its beauty. Dares he to come into his very sight and presence, to betray him? Peter denied Christ, but when *the Lord turned and looked* upon him, he relented presently; but Judas comes up to his Master's face, and betrays him. *Me mihi (perfide) prodis? me mihi prodis? — Perfidious man, betrayest thou me to thyself?* He said, *Hail, Master; and kissed him.* It should seem, our Lord Jesus had been wont to admit his disciples to such a degree of familiarity with him, as to give them his cheek to kiss after they had been any while absent, which Judas villainously used to facilitate this treason. A kiss is a token of allegiance and friendship, Ps. 2:12. But Judas, when he broke all the laws of love and duty, profaned this sacred sign to serve his purpose. Note, There are many that betray Christ with *a kiss,* and *Hail, Master;* who, under pretence of doing him honour, betray and undermine the interests of his kingdom. *Mel in ore, fel in corde — Honey in the mouth, gall in the heart. Kataphilein ouk esti philein. To embrace is one thing, to love is another. Philo Judaeus.* Joab's kiss and Judas's were much alike.

(3.) The entertainment his Master gave him, *v.* 50.

[1.] He calls him *friend.* If he had called him *villain,* and *traitor, raca, thou fool,* and *child of the devil,* he had not *mis*-called him; but he would teach us under the greatest provocation to forbear bitterness and evil-speaking, and to show all meekness. *Friend,* for a friend he had been, and should have been, and seemed to be. Thus he upbraids him, as Abraham, when he called the rich man in hell, *son.* He calls him *friend,* because he furthered his sufferings, and so *befriended* him; whereas, he called Peter *Satan* for attempting to hinder them.

[2.] He asks him, "*Wherefore art thou come?* Is it peace, Judas? Explain thyself; if thou come as an enemy, what means this kiss? If as a friend, what mean these swords and staves? *Wherefore art thou come?* What harm have I done thee? Wherein have I wearied thee? *eph' hō parei — Wherefore art thou present?* Why hadst thou not so much shame left thee, as to keep out of sight, which thou mightest have done, and yet have given the officer notice where I was?" This was an instance of great impudence, for him to be so forward and barefaced in this wicked transaction. But it is usual for apostates from religion to be the most bitter enemies to it; witness Julian. Thus Judas did his part.

2. How the officers and soldiers secured him; *Then came they, and laid hands on Jesus, and took him;* they made him their prisoner. *How were they not afraid to stretch forth their hands against the Lord's Anointed?* We may well imagine what rude and cruel hands they were, which this barbarous multitude laid on Christ; and how, it is probable, they handled him the more roughly for their being so often disappointed when they sought to lay hands on him. They could not have taken him, if he had not surrendered himself, and been *delivered by the determinate counsel and foreknowledge of God,* Acts 2:23. He who said concerning his anoint-

ed servants, *Touch them not,* and *do them no harm* (Ps. 105:14, 15), *spared not his anointed Son, but delivered him up for us all;* and again, *gave his strength into captivity, his glory into the enemies' hands,* Ps. 78:61. See what was the complaint of Job (*ch.* 16:11), *God hath delivered me to the ungodly,* and apply that and other passages in that book of Job as a type of Christ.

Our Lord Jesus was made a prisoner, because he would in all things be treated as a malefactor, punished for our crime, and as a surety under arrest for our debt. The yoke of our transgressions was bound by the Father's hand upon the neck of the Lord Jesus, Lam. 1:14. He became a prisoner, that he might set us at liberty; for he said, *If ye seek me, let these go their way* (Jn. 18:8); and those are free indeed, whom he makes so.

3. How Peter fought for Christ, and was checked for his pains. It is here only said to be *one of them that were with Jesus in the garden;* but Jn. 18:10, we are told that it was Peter who signalized himself upon this occasion. Observe,

(1.) Peter's rashness (*v.* 51); He *drew his sword.* They had but two swords among them all (Lu. 22:38), and one of them, it seems, fell to Peter's share; and now he thought it was time to draw it, and he laid about him as if he would have done some great matter; but all the execution he did was the cutting off an ear from a servant of the High Priest; designing, it is likely, to cleave him down the head, because he saw him more forward than the rest in laying hands on Christ, he missed his blow. But if he would be striking, in my mind he should rather have aimed at Judas, and have marked him for a rogue. Peter had talked much of what he would do for his Master, he would *lay down his life for him;* yea, that he would; and now he would be as good as his word, and venture his life to rescue his Master: and thus far was commendable, that he had a great *zeal* for Christ, and his honour and safety; but it was not *according to knowledge,* nor guided by discretion; for [1.] He did it without warrant; some of the disciples asked indeed, *Shall we smite with the sword?* (Lu. 22:49) But Peter struck before they had an answer. We must see not only our cause good, but our call clear, before we draw the sword; we must show by what authority we do it, and who gave us that authority. [2.] He indiscreetly exposed himself and his fellow-disciples to the rage of the multitude; for what could they with two swords do against a band of men?

(2.) The rebuke which our Lord Jesus gave him (*v.* 52); *Put up again thy sword into its place.* He does not command the officers and soldiers to put up their swords that were drawn against him, he left them to the judgment of God, who judges them that are without; but he commands Peter to put up his sword, does not chide him indeed for what he had done, because done out of good will, but stops the progress of his arms, and provides that it should not be drawn into a precedent. Christ's errand into the world was to make peace. Note, *The weapons of our warfare are not carnal, but spiritual;* and Christ's ministers, though they are his soldiers, do not *war after the flesh,* 2 Co. 10:3, 4. Not that the law of Christ overthrows either the law of nature of the law of nations, as far as those warrant subjects to stand up in defence of their civil rights and liberties, and their religion, when it is incorporated with them; but it provides for the preservation of public peace and order, by forbidding private persons, *qua tales — as such,* to resist the powers that are; nay, we have a general precept that we *resist not evil* (*ch.* 5:39), nor will Christ have his ministers propagate his religion by force of arms, *Religio cogi non potest; et defendenda non occidendo, sed moriendo — Religion cannot be forced; and it should be defended, not by killing, but by dying.* Lactantii Institut. As Christ forbade his disciples the sword of justice (*ch.* 20:25, 26), so here the sword of war. Christ bade Peter put up his sword, and never bade him draw it again; yet that which Peter is here blamed for is his doing it unseasonably; the hour was come for Christ to suffer and die, he knew Peter knew it, the *sword of the Lord was drawn against him* (Zec. 13:7), and for Peter to draw his sword for him, was like, *Master, spare thyself.*

Three reasons Christ give to Peter for this rebuke:

[1.] His drawing the sword would be dangerous to himself and to his fellow-disciples; *They that take the sword, shall perish with the sword;* they that use violence, fall by violence; and men hasten and increase their own troubles by blustering bloody methods of self-defence. They that take the sword before it is given them, that use it without warrant or call, expose themselves to the sword of war, or public justice. Had it not been for the special care and providence of the Lord Jesus, Peter and the rest of them had, for aught I know, been cut in pieces immediately. Grotius gives another, and a probable sense of this blow, making those that take the sword to be, not Peter, but the officers and soldiers that come with swords *to take Christ;* They shall *perish with the sword.* "Peter, thou needest not draw they sword to punish them. God will certainly, shortly, and severely, reckon with them." They took the Roman sword to seize Christ with, and by the Roman sword, not long after, they and their place and nation were destroyed. *Therefore* we must not *avenge ourselves,* because *God will repay* (Rom. 12:19); and therefore we must suffer with faith and patience, because persecutors will be paid in their own coin. See Rev. 13:10.

[2.] It was needless for him to draw his sword in defence of his Master, how, if he pleased, could summon into his service all the hosts of heaven (*v.* 53); *"Thinkest thou that I cannot now pray to my Father, and he shall send* from heaven effectual succours? Peter, if I would put by these sufferings, I could easily do it without thy hand or thy sword." Note, God has no need of us, of our services, much less of our sins, to bring about his purposes; and it argues our distrust and disbelief of the power of Christ, when we go out of the way of our duty to serve his interests. God can do his work without us; if we look into the heavens, and see how he is attended there, we may easily infer, that, *though we be righteous,* he is not beholden to us, Job 35:5, 7. Though Christ was crucified through weakness, it was a voluntary weakness; he submitted to death, not because he could not, but because he would not contend with it. This takes off the offence of the cross, and proves Christ crucified the power of God; even now in the depth of his sufferings he could call in the aid of legions of angels. *Now, arti — yet;* "Though the business is so far gone, I could yet with a word speaking turn the scale." Christ here lets us know,

First, What a great interest he had in his Father; *I can pray to my Father, and he will send me help from the sanctuary.* I can *parakalesai — demand of my Father these succours.* Christ prayer *as one having authority.* Note, It is a great comfort to God's people, when they are surrounded with enemies on all hands, that they have a way open heavenward; if they can do nothing else, they can pray to him that can do every thing. And they who are much in prayer at other times, have most comfort in praying when troublesome times come. Observe, Christ saith, not only that God could send him such a number of angels, but that, if he insisted upon it, he would do it. Though he had undertaken the work of our redemption, yet, if he had desired to be released, it should seem by this that the Father would not have held him to it. He might yet have gone out free from the service, but he loved it, and would not; so that it was only with the cords of his own love that he was bound to the altar.

Secondly, What a great interest he had in the heavenly hosts; *He shall presently give me more than twelve legions of angels,* amounting to above seventy-two thousand. Observe here, 1. There is an *innumerable company of angels,* Heb. 12:2. A detachment of more than twelve legions might be spared for our service, and yet there would be no miss of them about the throne. See Dan. 7:10. They are marshalled in exact order, like the well-disciplined legions; not a confused multitude, but regular troops; all know their post, and observe the word of command. 2. This innumerable company of angels are all at the disposal of our heavenly Father, and do his pleasure, Ps. 103:20, 21. 3. These angelic hosts were ready to come in to the assistance of our Lord Jesus in his sufferings, if he had needed or desired it. See Heb. 1:6, 14. They would have been to him as they were to Elisha, *chariots of fire, and horses of fire,* not only to secure him, but to consume those that set upon him. 4. Our heavenly Father is to be eyed and acknowledged in all the services of the heavenly hosts; *He shall give them me:* therefore angels are not to be prayed to, but the Lord of the angels, Ps. 91:11. 5. It is matter of comfort to all that wish well to the kingdom of Christ, that there is a world of angels always at the service of the Lord Jesus, that can do wonders. He that has the armies of heaven at his beck, can do what he pleases among the *inhabitants of the earth;* He shall *presently* give them me. See how ready his Father was to hear his prayer, and how ready the angels were to observe his orders; they are willing servants, winged messengers, they *fly swiftly.* This is very encouraging to those that have the honour of Christ, and the welfare of his church, much at heart. Think they that they have more care and concern for Christ and his church, than God and the holy angels have?

[3.] It was no time to make any defence at all, or to offer to put by the stroke; *For how then shall the scripture be fulfilled, that thus it must be? v.* 54. It was written, that Christ should be *led as a lamb to the slaughter,* Isa. 53:7. Should he summon the angels to his assistance, he would not be led to the slaughter at all; should he permit his disciples to fight, he would not be led as a lamb quietly and without resistance; therefore he and his disciples must yield to the accomplishment of the predictions. Note, In all difficult cases, the word of God must be conclusive against our own counsels, and nothing must be done, nothing attempted, against the fulfilling of the scripture. If the easing of our pains, the breaking of our bonds, the saving of our lives, will not consist with the fulfilling of the scripture, we ought to say, "Let God's word and will take place, let his law be magnified and made honourable, whatever becomes of us." Thus Christ checked Peter, when he set up for his champion, and captain of his life-guard.

4. We are next told how Christ argued the case with them that came to take him (*v.* 55); though he did not resist them, yet he did reason with them. Note, It will consist with Christian patience under our sufferings, calmly to expostulate with our enemies and persecutors, as David with Saul, 1 Sa. 24:14; 26:18. *Are ye come out,* (1.) With rage and enmity, *as against a thief,* as if I were an enemy to the public safety, and deservedly suffered this? Thieves draw upon themselves the common odium; every one will lend a hand to stop a thief: and thus they fell upon Christ as the offscouring of all things. If he had been the plague of his country, he could not have been prosecuted with more heat and violence. (2.) With all this power and force, as against the worst of thieves, that dare the law, bid defiance to public justice, and add rebellion to their sin? You are come out as against a thief, with swords and staves, as if there were danger of resistance; whereas ye have *killed the just One, and he doth not resist you,* Jam. 5:6. If he had not been willing to suffer, it was folly to *come with swords and staves, for they could not conquer him;* had he been minded to resist, he would have esteemed their iron as straw, and their swords and staves would have been as briars before a consuming fire; but, being willing to suffer, it was folly to come thus armed, for he would not contend with them.

He further expostulates with them, by reminding them how he had behaved himself hitherto toward them, and they toward him. [1.] Of his public appearance; *I sat daily with you in the temple teaching.* And, [2.] Of their public connivance; *Ye laid no hold on me.* How comes then this change? They were very unreasonable, in treating him as they did. *First,* He had given them no occasion to look upon him as a thief, for he had taught in the temple. And such were the matter, and such the manner of his teaching, that he was manifested in the consciences of all that heard him, not to be a bad man. Such gracious words as came from his mouth, were not the words of a thief, nor of one that had a devil. *Secondly,* Nor had he given them occasion to look upon him as one that absconded, or fled from justice, that they should come in the night to seize him; if they had any thing to say to him, they might find him every day in the temple, ready to answer all challenges, all charges, and there they might do as they pleased with him; for the chief priests had the custody of the temple, and the command of the guards about it; but to come upon him thus clandestinely, in the place of his retirement, was base and cowardly. Thus the greatest hero may be villainously assassinated in a corner, by one that in open field would tremble to look him in the face.

But all this was done (so it follows, *v.* 56) *that the scriptures of the prophets might be fulfilled.* It is hard to say, whether these are the words of the sacred historian, as a comment upon this story, and a direction to the Christian reader to compare it with the scriptures of the Old Testament, which pointed at it; or, whether they are the words of Christ himself, as a reason why, though he could not but resent this base treatment, he yet submitted to it, that the scriptures of the prophets might be fulfilled, to which he had just now referred himself, *v.* 54. Note, The scripture are in the fulfilling every day; and all those scriptures which speak of the Messiah, had their full accomplishment in our Lord Jesus.

5. How he was, in the midst of this distress, shamefully deserted by his disciples; *They all forsook him, and fled, v.* 56.

(1.) This was their sin; and it was a great sin for them who had left all to follow him, now to leave him for they knew not what. There was unkindness in it, considering the relation they stood in to him, the favours they had received from him, and the melancholy circumstances he was now in. There was unfaithfulness in it, for they had solemnly promised to adhere to him, and never to forsake him. He had indented for their safe conduct (Jn. 18:8); yet they could not rely upon that, but shifted for themselves by an inglorious flight. What folly was this, for fear of death to flee from him whom they themselves knew and had acknowledged to be the *Fountain of life?* Jn. 6:67, 68. *Lord, what is man!*

(2.) It was a part of Christ's suffering, it added affliction to his bonds, to be thus deserted, as it did to Job (*ch.* 19:13), *He hath put my brethren far from me;* and to David (Ps. 38:11), *Lovers and friends stand aloof from my sore.* They should have staid with him, to minister to him, to countenance him, and, if need were, to be witnesses for him at his trial; but they treacherously deserted him, as, at St. Paul's *first answer, no man stood with him.* But there was a mystery in this. [1.] Christ, as a sacrifice for sins, stood thus abandoned. The deer that by the keeper's arrow is marked out to be hunted and run down, is immediately deserted by the whole herd. In this he was made a curse for us, being left as one separated to evil. [2.] Christ, as the Saviour of souls, stood thus alone; as he needed not, so he had not the assistance of any other in working out our salvation; he bore all, and did all himself. He *trod the wine-press alone,* and when there was *none to uphold,* then *his own arm wrought salvation,* Isa. 63:3, 5. So *the Lord alone did lead his Israel,* and they *stand still, and only see this great salvation,* Deu. 32:12.

Verses 57–68

We have here the arraignment of our Lord Jesus in the ecclesiastical court, before the great sanhedrim. Observe,

I. The sitting of the court; the scribes and the elders were assembled, though it was in the dead time of the night, when other people were fast asleep in their beds; yet, to gratify their malice against Christ, they denied themselves that natural rest, and sat up all night, to be ready to fall upon the prey which Judas and his men, they hoped, would *seize.*

See, 1. Who they were, that were assembled; the *scribes,* the principal teachers, and *elders,* the principal rulers, of the Jewish church: these were the most bitter enemies to Christ our great teacher and ruler, on whom therefore they had a jealous eye, as one that eclipsed them; perhaps some of these scribes and elders were not so malicious at Christ as some others of them were; yet, in concurrence with the rest, they made themselves guilty. Now the scripture was fulfilled (Ps. 22:16); *The assembly of the wicked have enclosed me.* Jeremiah complains of an assembly of treacherous men; and David of his enemies *gathering themselves together against him,* Ps. 35:15.

2. Where they were assembled; *in the palace of Caiaphas the High Priest;* there they assembled two days before, to lay the plot (*v.* 3), and there they now convened again, to prosecute it. The *High Priest* was *Ab-beth-din — the father of the house of judgment,* but he is now the patron of wickedness; his house should have been the sanctuary of oppressed innocency, but it is become the throne of iniquity; and no wonder, when even God's house of prayer was made a den of thieves.

II. The setting of the prisoner to the bar; they that had *laid hold on Jesus, led him away,* hurried him, no doubt, with violence, led him as a trophy of their victory, led him as a victim to the altar; he was brought into Jerusalem through that which was called the *sheep-gate,* for that was the way into town from the mount of Olives; and it was so called because the sheep appointed for sacrifice were brought that way to the temple; very fitly therefore is Christ led that way, who is the Lamb of God, that takes away the sin of the world. Christ was led first to the High Priest, for by the law all sacrifices were to be first *presented to the priest, and delivered into his hand,* Lev. 17:5.

III. The cowardice and faint-heartedness of Peter (*v.* 58); *But Peter followed afar off.* This comes in here, with an eye to the following story of his denying him. He forsook him as the rest did, when he was seized, and what is here said of his following him is easily reconcilable with his forsaking him; such following was no better than forsaking him; for,

1. He followed him, but it was *afar off.* Some sparks of love and concern for his Master there were in his breast, and therefore he followed him; but fear and concern for his own safety prevailed, and therefore he followed afar off. Note, It

looks ill, and bodes worse, when those that are willing to be Christ's disciples, are not willing to be known to be so. Here began Peter's denying him; for to follow him afar off, is by little and little to go back from him. There is danger in drawing back, nay, in looking back.

2. He followed him, but he *went in, and sat with the servants.* He should have gone up to the court, and attended on his Master, and appeared for him; but he went in where there was a good fire, and sat with the servants, not to silence their reproaches, but to screen himself. It was presumption in Peter thus to thrust himself into temptation; he that does so, throws himself out of God's protection. Christ had told Peter that he could not follow him now, and had particularly warned him of his danger *this night;* and yet he would venture into the midst of this wicked crew. It helped David to walk in his integrity, that he *hated the congregation of evil doers, and would not sit with the wicked.*

3. He followed him, but it was only *to see the end,* led more by his curiosity than by his conscience; he attended as an idle spectator rather than as a disciple, a person concerned. He should have gone in, to do Christ some service, or to get some wisdom and grace to himself, by observing Christ's behaviour under his sufferings: but he went in, only to look about him; it is not unlikely that Peter went in, expecting that Christ would have made his escape miraculously out of the hands of his persecutors; that, having so lately struck them down, who came to seize him, he would now have struck them dead, who sat to judge him; and this he had a mind to see: if so, it was folly for him to think of seeing any other end than what Christ had foretold, that he should be put to death. Note, It is more our concern to prepare for the end, whatever it may be, than curiously to enquire what the end will be. The event is God's, but the duty is ours.

IV. The trial of our Lord Jesus in this court.

1. They examined witnesses against him, though they were resolved, right or wrong, to condemn him; yet, to put the better colour upon it, they would produce evidence against him. The crimes properly cognizable in their court, were, false doctrine and blasphemy; these they endeavoured to prove upon him. And observe here,

(1.) Their search for proof; *They sought false witness against him;* they had seized him, bound him, abused him, and after all have to seek for something to lay to his charge, and can show no cause for his commitment. They tried if any of them could allege seemingly from their own knowledge any thing against him; and suggested one calumny and then another, which, if true, might touch his life. Thus *evil men dig up mischief,* Prov. 16:27. Here they trod in the steps of their predecessors, who *devised devices against Jeremiah,* Jer. 18:18; 20:10. They made p[proclamation, that, if any one could give information against the prisoner at the bar, they were ready to receive it, and presently many bore false witness against him (*v.* 60); for is a *ruler hearken to lies, all his servants are wicked,* and will carry false stories to him, Prov. 29:12. This is an evil often seen under the sun, Eccl. 10:5. If Naboth must be taken off, there are sons of Belial to swear against him.

(2.) Their success in this search; in several attempts they were baffled, they sought false testimonies among themselves, others came in to help them, and yet they found none; they could make nothing of it, could not take the evidence together, or give it any colour of truth or consistency with itself, no, not they themselves being judges. The matters alleged were such palpable lies, as carried their own confutation along with them. This redounded much to the honour of Christ now, when they were loading him with disgrace.

But at last they met with *two* witnesses, who, it seems, agreed in their evidence, and therefore were hearkened to, in hopes that now the point was gained. The words they swore against him, were, that he should say, *I am able to destroy the temple of God, and to build it in three days, v.* 61. Now by this they designed to accuse him, [1.] As an enemy to the temple, and one that sought for the destruction of it, which they could not bear to hear of; for they valued themselves by *the temple of the Lord* (Jer. 7:4), and, when they abandoned other idols, made a perfect idol of that. Stephen was accused for *speaking against this holy place,* Acts 6:13, 14. [2.] As one that dealt in witchcraft, or some such unlawful arts, by the help of which he could rear such a building in three days: they had often suggested that he was in league with Beelzebub. Now, as to this, *First,* The words were misrecited; he said, *Destroy ye this temple* (Jn. 2:19), plainly in-

timating that he spoke of a temple which his enemies would seek to destroy; they come, and swear that he said, *I am able to destroy* this temple, as if the design against it were his. He said, *In Three days I will raise it up — egerō auton,* a word properly used of a living temple; *I will raise it to life.* They come, and swear that he said, *I am able, oikodomēsai — to build it;* which is properly used of a house temple. *Secondly,* The words were misunderstood; *he spoke of the temple of his body* (Jn. 2:21), and perhaps when he said, *this temple,* pointed to, or laid his hand upon, his own body; but they swore that he said the *temple of God,* meaning this holy place. Note, There have been, and still are, such as *wrest* the sayings of Christ *to their own destruction,* 2 Pt. 3:16. *Thirdly,* Make the worst they could of it, it was no capital crime, even by their own law; if it had been, no question but he had been prosecuted for it, when he spoke the words in a public discourse some years ago; nay, the words were capable of a laudable construction, and such as bespoke a kindness for the temple; if it were destroyed, he would exert himself to the utmost to rebuild it. But any thing that looked criminal, would serve to give colour to their malicious prosecution. Now the scriptures were fulfilled, which said, *False witnesses are risen up against me* (Ps. 27:12); and see Ps. 35:11. *Though I have redeemed them, yet they have spoken lies against me,* Hos. 7:13. We stand justly accused, the law *accuseth us,* Deu. 27:26; Jn. 5:45. Satan and our own consciences accuse us, 1 Jn. 3:20. The creatures cry out against us. Now, to discharge us from all these just accusations, our Lord Jesus submitted to this, to be unjustly and falsely accused, that in the virtue of his sufferings we may be enabled to triumph over all challenges; *Who shall lay any thing to the charge of God's elect?* Rom. 8:33, 34. He was accused, that he might not be condemned; and if at any time we suffer thus, have all manner of evil, not only said, but *sworn, against us falsely,* let us remember that we cannot expect to fare better than our Master.

(3.) Christ's silence under all these accusations, to the amazement of the court, *v.* 62. The High Priest, the judge of the court, arose in some heat, and said, *"Answerest thou nothing?* Come, you the prisoner at the bar; you hear what is sworn against you, what have you now to say for yourself? What defence can you make? Or what please have you to offer in answer to this charge?" *But Jesus held his peace* (*v.* 63), not as one sullen, or as one self-condemned, or as one astonished and in confusion; not because he wanted something to say, or knew not how to say it, but that the scripture might be fulfilled (Isa. 53:7); *As the sheep is dumb before the shearer,* and before the butcher, *so he opened not his mouth;* and that he might be the Son of David, who, when his enemies spoke mischievous things against him, was *as a deaf man that heard not,* Ps. 38:12–14. He was silent, because *his hour was come;* he would not deny the charge, because he was willing to submit to the sentence; otherwise, he could as easily have put them to silence and shame now, as he had done many a time before. If God had entered into judgment with us, we had been *speechless* (*ch.* 22:12), not able to *answer for one of a thousand,* Job 9:3. Therefore, when Christ was *made sin for us,* he was silent, and left it to his blood to speak, Heb. 12:24. He stood mute at this bar, that we might have something to say at God's bar.

Well, this way will not do; *aliâ aggrediendum est viâ — recourse must be had to some other expedient.*

2. They examined our Lord Jesus himself upon an oath like that *ex officio;* and, since they could not accuse him, they will try, contrary to the law of equity, to make him accuse himself.

(1.) Here is the interrogatory put to him by the High Priest. Observe, [1.] The question itself; *Whether thou be the Christ, the Son of God?* That is, Whether thou pretend to be so? For they will by no means admit it into consideration, whether he be really so or no; though the Messiah was to *be the Consolation of Israel,* and glorious things were spoken concerning him in the Old Testament, yet so strangely besotted were they with a jealousy of any thing that threatened their exorbitant power and grandeur, that they would never enter into the examination of the matter, whether Jesus was the Messiah or no; never once put the case, suppose he should be so; they only wished him to confess that he called himself so, that they might on that indict him as a deceiver. What will not pride and malice carry men to?

[2.] The solemnity of the proposal of it; *I adjure thee by the living God, that thou tell us.* Not that he had any regard to the living God, but took his name in vain; only thus he hoped to gain his point with our Lord Jesus; "If thou hast any value for the blessed name of God, and reverence for his Majesty, tell us this." If he should refuse to answer when he was thus adjured, they would charge him with contempt of the blessed name of God. Thus the persecutors of good men often take advantage against them by their consciences, as Daniel's enemies did against him in the matter of his God.

(2.) Christ's answer to this interrogatory (*v.* 64), in which,

[1.] He owns himself to be *The Christ the Son of God. Thou hast said;* that is, "It is as thou hast said;" for in St. Mark it is, *I am.* Hitherto, he seldom professed himself expressly to be the Christ, the Son of God; the tenour of his doctrine bespoke it, and his miracles proved it: but now he would not omit to make a confession of it, *First,* Because that would have looked like a disowning of that truth which he came into the world to bear witness to. *Secondly,* It would have looked like declining his sufferings, when he knew the acknowledgment of this would give his enemies all the advantage they desired against him. He thus confessed himself, for example and encouragement to his followers, when they are called to it, to *confess him before men,* whatever hazards they run by it. And according to this pattern the martyrs readily confessed themselves Christians, though they knew they must die for it, as the martyrs at Thebais, *Euseb. Hist.* 50.8, 100.9. That Christ answered out of a regard to the adjuration which Caiaphas had profanely used by the *living God,* I cannot think, any more than that he had any regard to the like adjuration in the devil's mouth, Mk. 5:7.

[2.] He refers himself, for the proof of this, to his second coming, and indeed to his whole estate of exaltation. It is probable that they looked upon him with a scornful disdainful smile, when he said, *"I am;"* "A likely fellow," thought they, "to be the Messiah, who is expected to come in so much pomp and power;" and to that this *nevertheless* refers. "Though now you see me in this low and abject state, and think it a ridiculous thing for me to call myself the Messiah, *nevertheless* the day is coming when I shall appear otherwise." *Hereafter, ap' arti — à modo — shortly;* for his exaltation began in a few days; now shortly his kingdom began to be set up; and *hereafter ye shall see the Son of man sitting on the right hand of power, to judge the world;* of which his coming shortly to judge and destroy the Jewish nation would be a type and earnest. Note, The terrors of the judgment-day will be a sensible conviction to the most obstinate infidelity, not in order to conversion (that will be then too late), but in order to an eternal confusion. Observe, *First,* Whom they should see; *the Son of man.* Having owned himself the Son of God, even now in his estate of humiliation, he speaks of himself as the Son of man, even in his estate of exaltation; for he had these two distinct natures in one person. The incarnation of Christ has made him Son of God and Son of man; for he is *Immanuel,* God with us. *Secondly,* In what posture they should see him; 1. *Sitting on the right hand of power,* according to the prophecy of the Messiah (Ps. 110:1); *Sit thou at my right hand;* which denotes both the dignity and the dominion he is exalted to. Though now he stood at the bar, they should shortly see him sit on the throne. 2. *Coming in the clouds of heaven;* this refers to another prophecy concerning the *Son of man* (Dan. 7:13, 14), which is applied to Christ (Lu. 1:33), when he came to destroy Jerusalem; so terrible was the judgment, and so sensible the indications of the wrath of the Lamb in it, that it might be called *a visible appearance of Christ;* but doubtless it has reference to the general judgment; to this day he appeals, and summons them to an appearance, then and there to answer for what they are now doing. He had spoken of this day to his disciples, awhile ago, for their comfort, and had bid them *lift up their heads* for joy in the prospect of it, Lu. 21:27, 28. Now he speaks of it to his enemies, for their terror; for nothing is more comfortable to the righteous, nor more terrible to the wicked, than Christ's judging the world at the last day.

V. His conviction upon this trial; *The High Priest rent his clothes,* according to the custom of the Jews, when they heard or saw any thing done or said, which they looked upon to be a reproach to God; as Isa. 36:22; 37:1; Acts 14:14. Caiaphas would be thought extremely tender of the glory of God *(Come, see his zeal for the Lord of hosts);* but, while he pretended an abhorrence of blasphemy, he was himself the greatest blasphemer; he now forgot the law which forbade the High Priest in any case to rend his clothes, unless we will suppose this an excepted case.

Observe, 1. The crime he was found guilty of; *blasphemy. He hath spoken blasphemy;* that is, he hath spoken reproachfully of the living God; that is the notion we have of blasphemy; because we by sin had reproached the Lord, therefore Christ, when *he was made Sin for us,* was condemned as a blasphemer for the truth he told them.

2. The evidence upon which they found him guilty; *Ye have heard the blasphemy;* why should we trouble ourselves to examine *witnesses* any further? He owned the fact, that he did profess himself the *Son of God;* and then they made blasphemy of it, and convicted him upon his confession. The High Priest triumphs in the success of the snare he had laid; "Now I think I have done his business for him." *Aha, so would we have it.* Thus was he *judged out of his own mouth* at their bar, because we were liable to be so judged at God's bar. There is no need of witnesses against us; our own consciences are against us instead of a thousand witnesses.

VI. His sentence passed, upon this conviction, *v.* 66.

Here is, 1. Caiaphas's appeal to the bench; *What think ye?* See his base hypocrisy and partiality; when he had already prejudged the cause, and pronounced him a blasphemer, then, as if he were willing to be advised, he asks the judgment of his brethren; but hide malice ever so cunningly under the robe of justice, some way or other it will break out. If he would have dealt fairly, he should have collected the votes of the bench *seriatim — in order,* and begun with the junior, and delivered his own opinion last; but he knew that by the authority of his place he could sway the rest, and therefore declares his judgment, and presumes they are all of his mind; he takes the crime, with regard to Christ, *pro confesso — as a crime confessed;* and the judgment, with regard to the court, *pro concesso — as a judgment agreed to.*

2. Their concurrence with him; they said, *He is guilty of death;* perhaps they did not all concur: it is certain that Joseph of Arimathea, if he was present, dissented (Lu. 23:51); so did Nicodemus, and, it is likely, others with them; however, the majority carried it that way; but, perhaps, this being an extraordinary council, or cabal rather, none had notice to be present but such as they knew would concur, and so it might be voted *nemine contradicente — unanimously.* The judgment was, *"He is guilty of death;* by the law he deserves to die." Though they had not power now to put any man to death, yet by such a judgment as this they made a man an *outlaw* among his people *(qui caput gerit lupinum — he carries a wolf's head;* so our old law describes an outlaw), and so exposed him to the fury either of a popular tumult, as Stephen was, or to be clamoured against before the governor, as Christ was. Thus was the Lord of life condemned to die, that through him there may be *no condemnation to us.*

VII. The abuses and indignities done to him after sentence passed (*v.* 67, 68); *Then,* when he was found guilty, they *spat in his face.* Because they had not power to put him to death, and could not be sure that they should prevail with the governor to be their executioner, they would do him all the mischief they could, now that they had him in their hands. Condemned prisoners are taken under the special protection of the law, which they are to make satisfaction to, and by all civilized nations have been treated with tenderness; sufficient is this punishment. But when they had passed sentence upon our Lord Jesus, he was treated as if hell had broken loose upon him, as if he were not only *worthy of death,* but as if that were too good for him, and he were unworthy of the compassion shown to the worst malefactors. Thus *he was made a curse for us.* But who were they that were thus barbarous? It should seem, the very same that had passed sentence upon him. *They said, He is guilty of death, and then did they spit in his face.* The priests began, and then no wonder if the servants, who would do any thing to make sport to themselves, and curry favour with their wicked masters, carried on the humour. See how they abused him.

1. *They spat in his face.* Thus the scripture was fulfilled (Isa. 50:6), *He hid not his face from shame and spitting.* Job complained of this indignity done to him, and herein was a type of Christ (Job 31:10); *They spare not to spit in my face.* It is an expression of the greatest contempt and indignation possible; looking upon him as more despicable than the very ground they spit upon. When Miriam was under the leprosy, it was looked upon as a disgrace to her, like that of *her father spitting in her face,* Num. 12:14. He that refused to raise up seed to his brother, was to undergo this dishonour, Deu. 25:9. Yet Christ, when he was repairing the decays of the great family of mankind, submitted to it. That face which was *fairer than the children of men,* which was *white and ruddy,* and which angels reverence, was thus filthily abused by the basest and vilest of the children of men. Thus was confusion poured upon his face, that ours might not be filled with everlasting shame and contempt. They who now profane his blessed name, abuse his word, and hate his image in his sanctified ones; what do they better than spit in his face? They would do that, if it were in their reach.

2. *They buffeted him, and smote him with the palms of their hands.* This added pain to the shame, for both came in with sin. Now the scripture was fulfilled (Isa. 50:6), *I gave my cheeks to them that plucked off the hair; and* (Lam. 3:30), *He giveth his cheek to him that smiteth him; he is filled with reproach,* and yet *keepeth silence* (*v.* 28); and (Mic. 5:1), *They shall smite the Judge of Israel with a rod upon the cheek;* here the margin reads it, *They smote him with rods;* for so *errapisan* signifies, and this he submitted to.

3. They challenged him to tell who struck him, having first blindfolded him; *Prophesy unto us, thou Christ, who is he that smote thee?* (1.) They made sport of him, as the Philistines did with Samson; it is grievous to those that are in misery, for people to make merry *about* them, but much more to make merry *with* them and their misery. Here was an instance of the greatest depravity and degeneracy of the human nature that could be, to show that there was need of a religion that should recover men to humanity. (2.) They made sport with his prophetical office. They had heard him called a *prophet,* and that he was famed for wonderful discoveries; this they upbraided him with, and pretended to make a trial of; as if the divine omniscience must stoop to a piece of children's play. *They* put a like affront upon Christ, who profanely jest with the scripture, and make themselves merry with holy things; like Belshazzar's revels in the temple bowls.

Verses 69–75

We have here the story of Peter's denying his Master, and it comes in as a part of Christ's sufferings. Our Lord Jesus was now in the High Priest's hall, not to be tried, but baited rather; and then it would have been some comfort to him to see his friends near him. But we do not find any friend he had about the court, save Peter only, and it would have been better if he had been at a distance. Observe how he fell, and how he got up again by repentance.

I. His sin, which is here impartially related, to the honour of the penmen of scripture, who dealt faithfully. Observe,

1. The immediate occasion of Peter's sin. He sat without in the palace, among the servants of the High Priest. Note, Bad company is to many an occasion of sin; and those who needlessly thrust themselves into it, go upon the devil's ground, venture into his crowds, and may expect either to be tempted and ensnared, as Peter was, or to be ridiculed and abused, as his Master was; they scarcely can come out of such company, without guilt or grief, or both. He that would keep God's commandments and his own covenant, must say to evil-doers, *Depart from me,* Ps. 119:115. Peter spoke from his own experience, when he warned his new converts to *save themselves from that untoward generation;* for he had like to have ruined himself by but going once among them.

2. The temptation to it. He was challenged as a retainer to Jesus of Galilee. First one maid, and then another, and then the rest of the servants, charged it upon him; *Thou also wert with Jesus of Galilee, v.* 69. And again, *This fellow was with Jesus of Nazareth, v.* 71. And again (*v.* 73), *Thou also art one of them, for thy speech betrayeth thee* to be a Galilean; whose dialect and pronunciation differed from that of the other Jews. Happy he whose speech betrays him to be a disciple of Christ, by the holiness and seriousness of whose discourse it appears that he has been with Jesus! Observe how scornfully they speak of Christ — Jesus *of Galilee,* and *of Nazareth,* upbraiding him with the country he was of: and how disdainfully they speak of Peter — *This fellow;* as if they thought it a reproach to them to have such a man in their company, and he was well enough served for coming among them; yet they had nothing to accuse him of, but that he was with Jesus, which, they thought, was enough to render him both a scandalous and a suspected person.

3. The sin itself. When he was charged as one of Christ's disciples, he denied it, was ashamed and afraid to own himself so, and would have all about him to believe that he had no knowledge of him, nor any kindness or concern for him.

(1.) Upon the first mention of it, he said, *I know not what thou sayest.* This was a shuffling answer; he pretended that he did not understand the charge, that he knew not whom she meant by *Jesus of Galilee,* or what she meant by being *with* him; so making strange of that which his heart was now as full of as it could be. [1.] It is a fault thus to misrepresent our own apprehensions, thoughts, and affections, to serve a turn; to pretend that we do not understand, or did not think of, or remember, that which yet we do apprehend, and did think of, and remember; this is a species of lying which we are more prone to than any other, because in this a man is not easily disproved; for *who knows the spirit of a man, save himself?* But God knows it, and we must be restrained from this wickedness by a fear of him, Prov. 24:12. [2.] It is yet a greater fault to be shy of Christ, to dissemble our knowledge of him, and to shift off a confession of him, when we are called to it; it is, in effect, to *deny* him.

(2.) Upon the next attack, he said, flat and plain, *I know not the man,* and backed it with an oath, *v.* 72. This was, in effect, to say, I will not own him, I am no Christian; for Christianity is the knowledge of Christ. Why, Peter? Canst thou look upon yonder Prisoner at the bar, and say thou dost not know him? Didst not thou quit all to follow him? And hast thou not been the man of his counsel? Hast thou not known him better than any one else? Didst thou not confess him to be the Christ, the Son of the Blessed? Hast thou forgotten all the kind and tender looks thou hast had from him, and all the intimate fellowship thou hast had with him? Canst thou look him in the face, and say that thou dost not know him?

(3.) Upon the third assault, *he began to curse and to swear, saying, I know not the man, v.* 74. This was worst of all, for the way of sin is down-hill. He cursed and swore, [1.] To back what he said, and to gain credit to it, that they might not any more call it in question; he did not only *say* it, but *swear* it; and yet what he said, was false. Note, We have reason to suspect the truth of that which is backed with rash oaths and imprecations. None but the devil's sayings need the devil's proofs. He that will not be restrained by the third commandment from mocking his God, will not be kept by the ninth from deceiving his brother. [2.] He designed it to be an evidence for him, that he was none of Christ's disciples, for this was none of their language. Cursing and swearing suffice to prove a man no disciple of Christ; for it is the language of his enemies thus to *take his name in vain.*

This is written for warning to us, that we sin not after the similitude of Peter's transgression; that we never, either directly or indirectly, deny Christ the Lord that bought us, by rejecting his offers, resisting his Spirit, dissembling our knowledge of him, and being ashamed of him and his words, or afraid of suffering for him and with his suffering people.

4. The aggravations of this sin, which it may be of use to take notice of, that we may observe the like transgressions in our own sins. Consider, (1.) Who he was: an apostle, one of the first three, that had been upon all occasions the most forward to speak to the honour of Christ. The greater profession we make of religion, the greater is our sin if in any thing we walk unworthily. (2.) What fair warning his Master had given him of his danger; if he had regarded this as he ought to have done, he would not have run himself into the temptation. (3.) How solemnly he had promised to adhere to Christ in this night of trial; he had said again and again, *"I will never deny thee;* no, I will die with thee first;" yet he broke these bonds in sunder, and his word was yea and nay. (4.) How soon he fell into this sin after the Lord's supper. There to receive such an inestimable pledge of redeeming love, and yet the same night, before morning, to disown his Redeemer, was indeed *turning aside quickly.* (5.) How weak comparatively the temptation was; it was not the judge, nor any of the officers of the court, that charged him with being a disciple of Jesus, but a silly maid or two, that probably designed him no hurt, nor would have done him any if he had owned it. This was but *running with the footmen,* Jer. 12:5. (6.) How often he repeated it; even after the cock had crowed once he continued in the temptation, and a second and third time relapsed into the sin. Is this Peter? *How art thou fallen!*

Thus was his sin aggravated; but on the other hand there is this to extenuate it, that, what he said he said *in his haste,* Ps. 116:11. He fell into the sin by surprise, not as Judas, with design; his heart was against it; he spoke very ill, but it was unadvisedly, and before he was aware.

II. Peter's repentance for this sin, *v.* 75. The former is written for our admonition, that we may not sin; but, if at any time we be overtaken, this is written for our imitation, that we may make haste to repent. Now observe,

1. What it was, that brought Peter to repentance.

(1.) *The cock crew* (*v.* 74); a common contingency; but, Christ having mentioned the crowing of *the cock* in the warning he gave him, that made it a means of bringing him to himself. The word of Christ can put a significancy upon whatever sign he shall please to choose, and by virtue of that word he can make it very beneficial to the souls of his people. The crowing of a cock is to Peter instead of a John Baptist, the voice of one calling to repentance. Conscience should be to us as the crowing of the cock, to put us in mind of what we had forgotten. When *David's heart smote him* the cock crew. Where there is a living principle of grace in the soul, though for the present overpowered by temptation, a little hint will serve, only for a memorandum, when God sets in with it, to recover it from a by-path. Here was the crowing of a cock made a happy occasion of the conversion of a soul. Christ comes sometimes in mercy *at cock-crowing.*

(2.) *He remembered the words of the Lord;* this was it that brought him to himself, and melted him into tears of godly sorrow; a sense of his ingratitude to Christ, and the slight regard he had had to the gracious warning Christ had given him. Note, A serious reflection upon the words of the Lord Jesus will be a powerful inducement to repentance, and will help to break the heart for sin. Nothing grieves a penitent more than that he has sinned against the grace of the Lord Jesus and the tokens of his love.

2. How his repentance was expressed; *He went out, and wept bitterly.*

(1.) His sorrow was secret; he went out, out of the High Priest's hall, vexed at himself that ever he came into it, now that he found what a snare he was in, and got out of it as fast as he could. He went out into the porch before (*v.* 71); and if he had gone quite off then, his second and third denial had been prevented; but then he came in again, now he went out and came in no more. He went out to some place of solitude and retirement, where he might *bemoan* himself, *like the doves of the valleys,* Eze. 7:16; Jer. 9:1, 2. He went out, that he might not be disturbed in his devotions on this sad occasion. We may *then* be most free in our communion with God, when we are most free from the converse and business of this world. In mourning for sin, we find *the families apart, and their wives apart,* Zec. 12:11, 12.

(2.) His sorrow was serious; *He wept bitterly.* Sorrow for sin must not be slight, but great and deep, like that for an only son. Those that have sinned sweetly, must weep bitterly; for, sooner or later, sin will be bitterness. This deep sorrow is requisite, not to satisfy divine justice (a sea of tears would not do that), but to evidence that there is a real change of mind, which is the essence of repentance, to make the pardon the more welcome, and sin for the future the more loathsome. Peter, who wept so bitterly for denying Christ, never denied him again, but *confessed* him often and openly, and in the mouth of danger; so far from ever saying, *I know not the man,* that he made all the house of *Israel know assuredly that this same Jesus was Lord and Christ.* True repentance for any sin will be best evidenced by our abounding in the contrary grace and duty; that is a sign of our weeping, not only bitterly, but sincerely. Some of the ancients say, that as long as Peter lived, he never heard a cock crow but it set him a weeping. Those that have truly sorrowed for sin, will sorrow upon every remembrance of it; yet not so as to hinder, but rather to increase, their joy in God and in his mercy and grace.

CHAPTER 27

It is a very affecting story which is recorded in this chapter concerning the sufferings and death of our Lord Jesus. Considering the thing itself, there cannot be a more tragical story told us; common humanity would melt the heart, to find an innocent and excellent person thus misused. But considering the design and fruit of Christ's sufferings, it is gospel, it is good news, that Jesus Christ was thus delivered for our offences; and there is nothing we have more reason to glory in than the cross of Christ. In this chapter, observe, I. How he was prosecuted. 1. The delivering of him to Pilate (*v.* 1, 2). 2. The despair of Judas (*v.* 3–10). 3. The arraignment and trial of Christ before Pilate (*v.* 11–14). 4. The clamours of the people against him (*v.* 15–25). 5. Sentence passed, and the warrant signed for his execution (*v.* 26). II. How he was executed. 1. He was barbarously used (*v.* 27–30). 2. Led to the place of execution (*v.* 31–33). 3. There he had all possible indignities done him, and reproaches cast upon him (*v.* 34–44). 4. Heaven frowned upon him (*v.* 45–49). 5. Many remarkable things attended his death (*v.* 50–56). He was buried and a watch set on his grave (*v.* 57–66).

Verses 1–10

We left Christ in the hands of the chief priests and elders, condemned to die, but they could only show their teeth; about two years before this the Romans had taken from the Jews the power of capital punishment; they could put no man to death, and therefore early in the morning another council is held, to consider what is to be done. And here we are told what was done in that morning-council, after they had been for two or three hours consulting with their pillows.

I. Christ is delivered up to Pilate, that he might execute the sentence they had passed upon him. Judea having been almost one hundred years before this conquered by Pompey, had ever since been tributary to Rome, and was lately made part of the province of Syria, and subject to the government of the president of Syria, under whom there were several *procurators,* who chiefly attended the business of the *revenues,* but sometimes, as Pilate particularly, had the whole power of the president lodged in them. This was a plain evidence that *the sceptre was departed from Judah,* and that therefore now *the Shilloh must come,* according to Jacob's prophecy, Gen. 49:10. Pilate is characterized by the Roman writers of that time, as a man of a rough and haughty spirit, wilful and implacable, and extremely covetous and oppressive; the Jews had a great enmity to his person, and were weary of his government, and yet they made use of him as the tool of their malice against Christ.

1. They *bound* Jesus. He was bound when he was first seized; but either they took off these bonds when he was before the council, or now they added to them. Having found him guilty, they tied his hands behind him, as they usually do with convicted criminals. He was already bound with the bonds of love to man, and of his own undertaking, else he had soon broken these bonds, as Samson did his. We were fettered with the *bond of iniquity,* held in the cords of our sins (Prov. 10:22); but God had bound the *yoke of our transgressions* upon the neck of the Lord Jesus (Lam. 50:14), that we might be loosed by his bonds, as we are *healed by his stripes.*

2. *They led him away* in a sort of triumph, led him *as a lamb to the slaughter;* so *was he taken from prison and from judgment,* Isa. 53:7, 8. It was nearly a mile from Caiaphas's house to Pilate's. All that way they led him through the streets of Jerusalem, when in the morning they began to fill, to make him a spectacle to the world.

3. They *delivered him to Pontius Pilate;* according to that which Christ had often said, that he should be *delivered to the Gentiles.* Both Jews and Gentiles were obnoxious to the judgment of God, and *concluded under sin,* and Christ was to be the Saviour both of Jews and Gentiles; and therefore Christ was brought into the judgment both of Jews and Gentiles, and both had a hand in his death. See how these corrupt church-rulers abused the civil magistrate, making use of him to execute their unrighteous decrees, and *inflict the grievance which they had prescribed,* Isa. 10:1. Thus have the kings of the earth been wretchedly imposed upon by the papal powers, and condemned to the drudgery of extirpating with the sword of war, as well as that of justice, those whom they have marked for heretics, right or wrong, to the great prejudice of their own interests.

II. The money which they had paid to Judas for betraying Christ, is by him delivered back to them, and Judas, in despair, hangs himself. The chief priests and elders supported themselves with *this,* in prosecuting Christ, that his own disciple betrayed him to them; but now, in the midst of the prosecution, that string failed them, and even *he* is made to them a *witness* of Christ's innocency and a monument of God's justice; which served, 1. For glory to Christ in the midst of his sufferings, and a specimen of his victory over Satan who had entered into Judas. 2. For warning to his persecutors, and to leave them the more inexcusable. If their heart had not been fully set in them to do this evil, what Judas said and did, one would think, should have stopped the prosecution.

(1.) See here how Judas *repented:* not like Peter, who repented, believed, and was pardoned: no, he repented, despaired, and was ruined. Now observe here,

[1.] What induced him to repent. It was *when he saw that he was condemned.* Judas, it is probable, expected that either Christ would have made his escape out of their hands, or would so have pleaded his own cause at their bar as to have come off, and then Christ would have had the honour, the Jews the shame, and he the money, and no harm done.

This he had no reason to expect, because he had so often heard his Master say that he must be *crucified;* yet it is probable that he did expect it, and when the event did not answer his vain fancy, then he fell into this horror, when he saw the stream strong against Christ, and him yielding to it. Note, Those who measure actions by the consequences of them rather than by the divine law, will find themselves mistaken in their measures. The way of sin is down-hill; and if we cannot easily stop ourselves, much less can we stop others whom we have set a going in a sinful way. He *repented himself;* that is, he was filled with grief, anguish, and indignation, at himself, when reflecting upon what he had done. When he was tempted to betray his Master, the thirty pieces of silver looked very fine and glittering, like the *wine, when it is red, and gives its colour in the cup.* But when the thing was done, and the money paid, the silver was become dross, it *bit like a serpent, and stung like an adder.* Now his conscience flew in his face; "What have I done! What a fool, what a wretch, am I, to sell my Master, and all my comfort and happiness in him, for such a trifle! All these abuses and indignities done him are chargeable upon me; it is owing to me, that he is bound and condemned, spit upon and buffeted. I little thought it would have come to this, when I made that wicked bargain; so foolish was I, and ignorant, and so like a beast." Now he curses the bag he carried, the money he coveted, the priests he dealt with, and the day that he was born. The remembrance of his Master's goodness to him, which he had so basely requited, the bowels of mercy he had spurned at, and the fair warnings he had slighted, steeled his convictions, and made them the more piercing. Now he found his Master's words true; *It were better for that man, that he had never been born.* Note, Sin will soon change its taste. Though it be *rolled under the tongue* as a *sweet morsel,* in the bowels it will be turned into the *gall of asps* (Job 20:12–14), like John's book, Rev. 10:9.

[2.] What were the indications of his repentance.

First, He made restitution; *He brought again the thirty pieces of silver to the chief priests,* when they were all together publicly. Now the money burned in his conscience, and he was as sick of it as ever he had been fond of it. Note, That which is ill gotten, will never do good to those that get it, Jer. 13:10; Job 20:15. If he had repented, and brought the money back before he had betrayed Christ, he might have done it with comfort, then he had *agreed while yet in the way;* but now it was too late, now he cannot do it without horror, wishing ten thousand times he had never meddled with it. See Jam. 5:3. He brought it again. Note, what is unjustly gotten, must not be kept; for that is a continuance in the sin by which it was got, and such an avowing of it as is not consistent with repentance. He brought it to those from whom he had it, to let them know that he repented his bargain. Note, Those who have served and hardened others in their sin, when God gives them repentance, should let them know it whose sins they have been partakers in, that it may be a means to bring them to repentance.

Secondly, He made confession (*v.* 4); *I have sinner, in that I have betrayed innocent blood.* 1. To the *honour of Christ,* he pronounces his blood *innocent.* If he had been guilty of any sinful practices, Judas, as his disciple, would certainly have know it, and, as his betrayer, would certainly have discovered it; but he, freely and without being urged to it, pronounces him innocent, to the face of those who had pronounced him *guilty.* 2. To *his own shame,* he confesses that he had sinned, in betraying this blood. He does not lay the blame on any one else; does not say, "You have sinned, in hiring me to do it;" but takes it all to himself; "I have sinned, in doing it." Thus far Judas went toward his repentance, yet it was *not to salvation.* He confessed, but not to God, did not go to him, and say, *I have sinned, Father, against heaven.* He confessed the betraying of innocent blood, but did not confess that wicked love of money, which was the root of this evil. There are those who betray Christ, and yet justify themselves in it, and so come short of Judas.

(2.) See here how the chief priests and elders entertained Judas's penitential confession; they said, *What is that to us? See thou to that.* He made them his confessors, and that was the *absolution* they gave him; more like the priests of devils than like the priests of the holy living God.

[1.] See here how carelessly they speak of the betraying of Christ. Judas had told them that the blood of Christ was innocent blood; and they said, *What is that to us?* Was it nothing to them that they had thirsted after this blood, and hired Judas to betray it, and had now condemned it to be shed unjustly? Is this nothing to them? Does it give no check to the violence of their prosecution, no warning to take need what they do to this just man? Thus do fools make a mock at sin, as if no harm were done, no hazard run, by the commission of the greatest wickedness. Thus light do many make of Christ crucified; what is it to them, that he suffered such things?

[2.] See here how carelessly they speak of the sin of Judas; he said, *I have sinned,* and they said, *"What is that to us?* What are we concerned in thy sin, that thou tellest us of it?" Note, It is folly for us to think that the sins of others are nothing to us, especially those sins that we are any way accessary to, or partakers in. Is it nothing to us, that God is dishonoured, souls wounded, Satan gratified and his interests served, and that we have aided and abetted it? If the elders of Jezreel, to please Jezebel, murder Naboth, is that nothing to Ahab? Yes, *he has killed,* for he has *taken possession,* 1 Ki. 21:19. The guilt of sin is not so easily transferred as some people think it is. If there were guilt in the matter, they tell Judas that he must *look to it,* he must *bear it. First,* Because he had betrayed him to them. His was indeed *the greater sin* (Jn. 19:11); but it did not therefore follow, that theirs was no sin. It is a common instance of the deceitfulness of our hearts, to extenuate our own sin by the aggravation of other people's sins. But the judgment of God is according to truth, not according to comparison. *Secondly,* Because he knew and believed him to be innocent. "If he be innocent, see thou to it, that is more than we know; we have adjudged him *guilty,* and therefore may justly prosecute him as such," Wicked practices are buoyed up by wicked principles, and particularly by this, That sin is sin only to those that think it to be so; that it is no harm to persecute a good man, if we take him to be a bad man; but those who thus think to mock God, will but deceive and destroy themselves.

[3.] See how carelessly they speak of the conviction, terror, and remorse, that Judas was under. They were glad to make use of him in the sin, and were then very fond of him; none more welcome to them than Judas, when he said, *What will ye give me, and I will betray him to you?* They did not say, *What is that to us?* But now that his sin had put him into a fright, now they slighted him, had nothing to say to him, but turned him over to his own terrors; why did he come to trouble them with his melancholy fancies? They had something else to do than to heed him. But why so shy? *First,* Perhaps they were in some fear lest the sparks of his conviction, brought too near, should kindle a fire in their own consciences, and lest his moans, listened to, should give an alarm to their own convictions. Note, Obstinate sinners stand upon their guard against convictions; and those that are resolvedly impenitent, look with disdain upon the penitent. *Secondly,* However, they were in no concern to succour Judas; when they had brought him into the snare, they not only left him, but laughed at him. Note, Sinners, under convictions, will find their old companions in sin but miserable comforters. It is usual for those that love the treason, to hate the traitor.

(3.) Here is the utter despair that Judas was hereby driven into. If the chief priests had promised him to stay the prosecution, it would have been some comfort to him; but, seeing no hopes of that, he grew desperate, *v.* 5.

[1.] *He cast down the pieces of silver in the temple.* The chief priests would not take the money, for fear of taking thereby the whole guilt to themselves, which they were willing that Judas should bear the load of; Judas would not keep it, it was too hot for him to hold, he therefore threw it down in the temple, that, whether they would or no, it might fall into the hands of the chief priests. See what a *drug* money was, when the guilt of *sin* was tacked to it, or was thought to be so.

[2.] *He went, and hanged himself. First, He retired — anechōrēse*; he withdrew into some solitary place, like the possessed man that was drawn by the devil into the wilderness, Lu. 8:29. Woe to him that is in despair, and is alone. If Judas had gone to Christ, or to some of the disciples, perhaps he might have had relief, bad as the case was; but, missing of it with the chief priests, he abandoned himself to despair: and the same devil that with the help of the priests drew him to the sin, with their help drove him to despair. *Secondly,* He became his own executioner; *He hanged himself;* he was *suffocated* with grief, so Dr. Hammond: but Dr. Whitby is clear that our translation is right. Judas had a *sight* and *sense* of sin, but no apprehension of the mercy of God in Christ, and so *he pined away in his iniquity.* His sin, we may suppose, was not in its own nature unpardonable: there were some of those saved, that had been Christ's betrayers and murderers; but he concluded, as Cain, that his iniquity was greater than could be forgiven, and would rather throw himself on the devil's mercy than God's. And some have said, that Judas sinned more in *despairing* of the mercy of God, than in *betraying* his Master's blood. Now the terrors of the Almighty set themselves in array against him. All the curses written in God's book now *came into his bowels like water, and like oil into his bones,* as was foretold concerning him (Ps. 109:18, 19), and drove him to this desperate shift, for the escaping of a *hell* within him, to leap into *that* before him, which was but the perfection and perpetuity of this horror and despair. He throws himself into the fire, to avoid the flame; but miserable is the case when a man must go to hell for ease.

Now, in this story, 1. We have an instance of the wretched end of those into whom Satan enters, and particularly those that are given up to the love of money. This is the destruction in which many are drowned by it, 1 Tim. 6:9, 10. Remember what became of the swine into which, and of the traitor into whom, *the devil enters;* and *give not place to the devil.* 2. We have an instance of the wrath of God revealed from heaven against the ungodliness and unrighteousness of men, Rom. 1:18. As in the story of Peter we behold the goodness of God, and the triumphs of Christ's grace in the conversion of some sinners; so in the story of Judas we behold the severity of God, and the triumphs of Christ's power and justice in the confusion of other sinners. When Judas, into whom Satan entered, was thus *hung up,* Christ made an open show of the principalities and powers he undertook the *spoiling of,* Col. 2:15. 3. We have an instance of the direful effects of despair; it often ends in self-murder. *Sorrow,* even that for sin, if not *according to God, worketh death* (2 Co. 7:10), the worst kind of death; for *a wounded spirit, who can bear?* Let us think as bad as we can of sin, provided we do not think it unpardonable; let us despair of help in ourselves, but not of help in God. He that thinks to ease his conscience by destroying his life, doth, in effect, dare God Almighty to do his worst. And self-murder, though prescribed by some of the heathen moralists, is certainly a remedy worse than the disease, how bad soever the disease may be. Let us watch against the beginnings of melancholy, and pray, Lord, *lead us not into temptation.*

(4.) The disposal of the money which Judas brought back, *v.* 6–10. It was laid out in the purchase of a field, called *the potter's field;* because some potter had owned it, or occupied it, or lived near it, or because broken potters' vessels were thrown into it. And this field was to be a burying-place for strangers, that is, proselytes to the Jewish religion, who were of other nations, and, coming to Jerusalem to worship, happened to die there. [1.] It looks like an instance of their humanity, that they took care for the *burying of strangers;* and it intimates that they themselves allowed (as St. Paul saith, Acts 24:15), *that there shall be a resurrection of the dead, both of the just and of the unjust;* for we *therefore* take care of the dead body, not only because it has been the habitation of a rational soul, but because it must be so again. But, [2.] It was no instance of their humility that they would bury strangers in a place by themselves, as if they were not worthy to be laid in their burying-places; strangers must keep their distance, alive and dead, and that principle must go down to the grace, *Stand by thyself, come not near me, I am holier than thou,* Isa. 65:5. The sons of Seth were better affected towards Abraham, though a stranger among them, when they offered him the choicest of their own sepulchres, Gen. 23:6. But *the sons of the stranger, that have joined themselves to the Lord,* though buried by themselves, shall rise with all that are *dead in Christ.*

This buying of the potter's field did not take place on the day that Christ died (they were then too busy to mind any thing else but hunting him down); but it took place not long after; for Peter speaks of it soon after Christ's ascension; yet it is here recorded.

First, To show the hypocrisy of the chief priests and elders. They were maliciously persecuting the blessed Jesus, and now,

1. They scruple to put that money into the treasury, or *corban,* of the temple, with which they had hired the traitor. Though perhaps they had taken it out of the treasury, pretending it was for the public good, and though they were great sticklers for the *corban,* and laboured to draw all the wealth

of the nation into it, yet they would not put that money into it, which was the price of blood. The hire of a traitor they thought parallel to the hire of a whore, and the price of a malefactor (such a one they made Christ to be) equivalent to the price of a dog, neither of which was to be *brought into the house of the Lord,* Deu. 23:18. They would thus save their credit with the people, by possessing them with an opinion of their great reverence for the temple. Thus they that *swallowed a camel, strained at a gnat.*

2. They think to *atone* for what they had done, by this public good act of providing a burying-place for strangers, though not at their own charge. Thus in times of ignorance people were made to believe that building churches and endowing monasteries would make amends for immoralities.

Secondly, To signify the favour intended by the blood of Christ to *strangers,* and sinners of the Gentiles. Through the price of his blood, a resting place is provided for them after death. Thus many of the ancients apply this passage. The *grave* is the potter's field, where the bodies are thrown as despised broken vessels; but Christ by his blood *purchased* it for those who by confessing themselves *strangers* on earth seek the better country; he has altered the property of it (as a purchaser doth), so that now death is ours, the grave is ours, a bed of rest for us. The Germans, in their language, call burying-places *God's fields;* for in them God *sows* his people as a *corn of wheat,* Jn. 12:24. See Hos. 2:23; Isa. 26:19.

Thirdly, To perpetuate the infamy of those that bought and sold the blood of Christ. This field was commonly called *Aceldama — the field of blood;* not by the chief priests, they hoped in this burying-place to bury the remembrance of their own crime; but by the people; who took notice of Judas's acknowledgment that he had betrayed the innocent blood, though the chief priests made nothing of it. They fastened this name upon the field *in perpetuam rei memoriam — for a perpetual memorial.* Note, Divine Providence has many ways of entailing disgrace upon the wicked practices even of great men, who, though they seek to cover their shame, are *put to a perpetual reproach.*

Fourthly, That we may see how the scripture was fulfilled (*v.* 9, 10); *Then was fulfilled that which was spoken by Jeremy the prophet.* The words quoted are found in the prophecy of Zechariah, *ch.* 11:12. How they are here said to be spoken by Jeremy is a difficult question; but the credit of Christ's doctrine does not depend upon it; for that proves itself perfectly divine, though there should appear something human as to small circumstances in the penmen of it. The Syriac version, which is ancient, reads only, *It was spoken by the prophet,* not naming any, whence some have thought that *Jeremy* was added by some scribe; some think that the whole volume of the prophets, being in one book, and the prophecy of Jeremiah put first, it might not be improper, *currente calamo — for a transcriber* to quote any passage out of that volume, under his name. The Jews used to say, *The spirit of Jeremiah was in Zechariah,* and so they were as one prophet. Some suggest that it was *spoken* by Jeremiah, but written by Zechariah; or that Jeremiah wrote the ninth, tenth, and eleventh chapters of Zechariah. Now this passage in the prophet is a representation of the great contempt of God, that was found among the Jews, and the poor returns they made to him for rich receivings from him. But here that is really acted, which was there but figuratively expressed. The sum of money is the same — *thirty pieces of silver;* this they *weighed for his price,* at this rate they valued him; a goodly price; and this was *cast to the potter in the house of the Lord;* which was here literally accomplished. Note, We should better understand the events of Providence, if we were better acquainted even with the language and expressions of scripture; for even those also are sometimes written upon the dispensations of Providence so plainly, that *he who runs may read them.* What David spoke figuratively (Ps. 42:7), Jonah made a literal application of; *All thy waves and thy billows are gone over me,* Jonah 3:3.

The giving of the price of him that was valued, not for him, but for the *potter's field,* bespeaks, 1. The high value that ought to be put upon Christ. The price was given, not for him; no, when it was given for him, it was soon brought back again with disdain, as infinitely below his worth; he cannot be *valued with the gold of Ophir,* nor this unspeakable Gift *brought with money.* 2. The low value that was put upon him. *They of the children of Israel* did strangely undervalue him, when his price did but reach to buy a potter's field, a pitiful sorry spot of ground, not worth looking upon. It added to the reproach of his being bought and sold, that it was at so low a rate. *Cast it to the potter,* so it is in Zechariah; a contemptible petty chapman, not the merchant that deals in things of value. And observe, *They of the children of Israel* thus *undervalued him;* they who were his own people, that should have known better what estimate to put upon him, they to whom he was first sent, whose glory he was, and whom he had valued so highly, and bought so dear. He gave kings' ransoms for them, and the richest countries (so *precious were they in his sight,* Isa. 43:3, 4), Egypt, and Ethiopia, and Seba; but they gave a slave's ransom for him (see Ex. 21:32), and valued him but at the rate of a potter's field; so was that blood trodden under foot, which bought the kingdom of heaven for us. But all this was *as the Lord appointed;* so the prophetic vision was, which typified this event, and so the event itself, as the other instances of Christ's sufferings, was *by the determinate counsel and foreknowledge of God.*

Verses 11–25

We have here an account of what passed in Pilate's judgment-hall, when the blessed Jesus was brought thither betimes in the morning. Though it was no court-day, Pilate immediately took his case before him. We have there,

I. The trial Christ had before Pilate.

1. His arraignment; *Jesus stood before the governor,* as the prisoner before the judge. We could not stand before God because of our sins, nor lift up our face in his presence, if Christ had not been thus made sin for us. He was arraigned that we might be discharged. Some think that this bespeaks his courage and boldness; he stood *undaunted,* unmoved by all their rage. He thus stood in this judgment, that we might stand in God's judgment. He stood for a *spectacle,* as Naboth, when he was arraigned, was *set on high among the people.*

2. His indictment; *Art thou the king of the Jews?* The Jews were now not only under the government, but under the very jealous inspection, of the Roman powers, which they were themselves to the highest degree disaffected to, and yet now pretended a concern for, to serve this turn; accusing Jesus as an Enemy to Caesar (Lu. 23:2), which they could produce no other proof of, than that he himself had newly owned he was *the Christ.* Now they thought that whoever was the Christ, must be the *king of the Jews,* and must deliver them from the Roman power, and restore to them a temporal dominion, and enable them to trample upon all their neighbours. According to this chimera of their own, they accused our Lord Jesus, as making himself king of the Jews, in opposition to the Roman yoke; whereas, though he said that he was the Christ, he meant not such a Christ as this. Note, Many oppose Christ's holy religion, upon a mistake of the nature of it; they dress it up in false colours, and then fight against it. They assuring the governor that, if he made himself Christ, he made himself king of the Jews, the governor takes it for granted, that he goes about to pervert the nation, and subvert the government. *Art thou a king?* It was plain that he was not so *de facto — actually;* "But dost thou lay any claim to the government, or pretend a right to rule the Jews?" Note, It has often been the hard fate of Christ's holy religion, unjustly to fall under the suspicions of the civil powers, as if it were hurtful to kings and provinces, whereas it tends mightily to the benefit of both.

3. His plea; *Jesus said unto him, "Thou sayest.* It is as thou sayest, though not as thou meanest; I am a king, but not such a king as thou dost suspect me to be." Thus before Pilate he witnessed a good confession, and was not ashamed to own himself a king, though it looked ridiculous, nor afraid, though at this time it was dangerous.

4. The evidence (*v.* 12); He was *accused of the chief priests.* Pilate found *no fault in him;* whatever was said, nothing was proved, and therefore what was wanting in matter they made up in noise and violence, and followed him with repeated accusations, the same as they had given in before; but by the repetition they thought to force a belief from the governor. They had learned, not only *calumniari — to calumniate,* but *fortiter calumniari — to calumniate stoutly.* The best men have often been accused of the worst crimes.

5. The prisoner's silence as to the prosecutors' accusations; *He answered nothing,* (1.) Because there was no occasion; nothing was alleged but what carried its own confutation along with it. (2.) He was now taken up with the great concern that lay between him and his Father, to whom he was offering up himself a Sacrifice, to answer the demands of his justice, which he was so intent upon, that he minded not what they said against him. (3.) His hour was come, and he submitted to his Father's will; *Not as I will, but as thou wilt.* He knew what his Father's will was, and therefore silently *committed himself to him that judgeth righteously. We* must not thus by our silence throw away our lives, because we are not lords of our lives, as Christ was of his; nor can we know, as he did, when our hour is come. But hence we must learn, *not to render railing for railing,* 1 Pt. 2:23.

Now, [1.] Pilate pressed him to make some reply (*v.* 13); *Hearest thou not how many things they witness against thee?* What these things were, may be gathered from Lu. 23:3, 5, and Jn. 19:7. Pilate, having no malice at all against him, was desirous he should clear himself, urges him to it, and believes he could do it; *Hearest thou not?* Yes, he did hear; and still he hears all that is witnessed unjustly against his truths and ways; but he keeps silence, because it is the day of his patience, and doth not answer, as he will shortly, Ps. 50:3. [2.] He wondered at his silence; which was not interpreted so much into a contempt of the court, as a contempt of himself. And therefore Pilate is not said to be angry at it, but to have *marvelled greatly* at it, as a thing very unusual. He believed him to be innocent, and had heard perhaps that *never man spake like him;* and therefore he thought it strange that he had not one word to say for himself. We have,

II. The outrage and violence of the people, in pressing the governor to crucify Christ. The chief priests had a great interest in the people, they called them *Rabbi, Rabbi,* made idols of them, and oracles of all they said; and they made use of this to incense them against him, and by the power of the mob gained the point which they could not otherwise carry. Now here are two instances of their outrage.

1. Their preferring Barabbas before him, and choosing to have him released rather than Jesus.

(1.) It seems it was grown into a custom with the Roman governors, for the honouring of the Jews, to grace the feast of the passover with the release of a prisoner, *v.* 15. This, they thought, did honour to the feast, and was agreeable to the commemoration of their deliverance; but it was an invention of their own, and no divine institution; though some think that it was ancient, and kept up by the Jewish princes, before they became a province of the empire. However, it was a bad custom, an obstruction to justice, and an encouragement to wickedness. But our gospel-passover is celebrated with the release of prisoners, by him who hath *power on earth to forgive sins.*

(2.) The prisoner put in competition with our Lord Jesus was Barabbas; he is here called a *notable* prisoner (*v.* 16); either because by birth and breeding he was of some note and quality, or because he had signalized himself by something remarkable in his crimes; whether he was so *notable* as to recommend himself the more to the favours of the people, and so the more likely to be interceded for, or whether so *notable* as to make himself more liable to their age, is uncertain. Some think the latter, and therefore Pilate mentioned him, as taking it for granted that they would have desired any one's release rather than his. *Treason, murder,* and *felony,* are the three most enormous crimes that are usually punished by the sword of justice; and Barabbas was guilty of all three, Lu. 23:19; Jn. 18:40. A *notable prisoner* indeed, whose crimes were so complicated.

(3.) The proposal was made by Pilate the governor (*v.* 17); *Whom will ye that I release unto you?* It is probable that the judge had the nomination of two, one of which the people were to *choose.* Pilate proposed to them to have Jesus *released;* he was convinced of his innocency, and that the prosecution was malicious; yet had not the courage to acquit him, as he ought to have done, by his own power, but would have him released by the people's election, and so he hoped to satisfy both his own *conscience,* and the *people* too; whereas, finding no fault in him, he ought not to have *put him upon the country,* or brought him *into peril of his life.* But such little tricks and artifices as these, to trim the matter, and to keep in with conscience and the world too, are the common practice of those that seek more to please men than God. *What shall I do then,* saith Pilate, *with Jesus, who is called Christ?* He puts the people in mind of this, that this *Jesus,* whose release he proposed, was looked upon by some among them as the Messiah, and had given pregnant proofs of his being so; "Do not *reject* one of whom your nation has professed such an expectation."

The reason why Pilate *laboured* thus to get Jesus *dis-*

charged was because he knew that *for envy the chief priests had delivered him up* (v. 18); that it was not his *guilt*, but his goodness, that they were provoked at; and for this reason he *hoped* to bring him off by the people's act, and that they would be for his release. When David was *envied* by Saul, he was the *darling of the people;* and any one that heard the *hosannas* with which Christ was but a few days ago brought into Jerusalem, would have thought that he had been so, and that Pilate might safely have referred this matter to the commonalty, especially when so notorious a rogue was set up as a rival with him for their favours. But it proved otherwise.

(4.) While Pilate was thus labouring the matter, he was confirmed in his unwillingness to condemn Jesus, by a message sent him from his wife (v. 19), by way of caution; *Have thou nothing to do with that just man* (together with the reason), *for I have suffered many things this day in a cream because of him.* Probably, this message was delivered to Pilate publicly, in the hearing of all that were present, for it was intended to be a warning not to him only, but to the prosecutors. Observe,

[1.] The special providence of God, in sending this dream to Pilate's wife; it is not likely that she had heard any thing, before, concerning Christ, at least not so as to occasion her dreaming of him, but it was immediately from God: perhaps she was one of the *devout and honourable women,* and had some sense of religion; yet God revealed himself by dreams to some that had not, as to Nebuchadnezzar. She *suffered many things* in this dream; whether she dreamed of the cruel usage of an innocent person, or of the judgments that would fall upon those that had any hand in his death, or both, it seems that it was a frightful dream, and her thoughts *troubled her,* as Dan. 2:1; 4:5. Note, The Father of spirits has many ways of access to the spirits of men, and can *seal their instruction in a dream, or vision of the night,* Job 33:15, 16. Yet to those who have the written word, God more ordinarily speaks by conscience on a waking bed, than by dreams, when *deep sleep falls upon men.*

[2.] The tenderness and care of Pilate's wife, in sending this caution, thereupon, to her husband; *Have nothing to do with that just man. First,* This was an honourable testimony to our Lord Jesus, witnessing for him that he was a *just man,* even then when he was persecuted as the worst of malefactors: when his friends were afraid to appear in defence of him, God made even those that were strangers and enemies, to speak in his favour; when Peter denied him, Judas confessed him; when the chief priests pronounced him guilty of death, Pilate declared he *found no fault* in him; when the women that loved him stood afar off, Pilate's wife, who knew little of him, showed a concern for him. Note, God will not leave himself without witnesses to the truth and equity of his cause, even when it seems to be most spitefully run down by its enemies, and most shamefully deserted by its friends. *Secondly,* It was a fair warning to Pilate; *Have nothing to do with him.* Note, God has many ways of giving checks to sinners in their sinful pursuits, and it is a great mercy to have such checks from Providence, from faithful friends, and from our own consciences; it is also our great duty to hearken to them. *O do not this abominable thing which the Lord hates,* is what we may hear said to us, when we are entering into temptation, if we will but regard it. Pilate's lady sent him this warning, out of the love she had to him; she feared not a rebuke from him for meddling with that which belonged not to her; but, let him take it how he would, she would give him the caution. Note, It is an instance of true love to our friends and relations, to do what we can to keep them from sin; and the nearer any are to us, and the greater affection we have for them, the more solicitous we should be not to suffer sin to come or lie upon them, Lev. 19:17. The best friendship is friendship to the soul. We are not told how Pilate turned this off, probably with a jest; but by his proceeding against the just man it appears that he did not regard it. Thus faithful admonitions are made light of, when they are given as warnings against sin, but will not be so easily made light of, when they shall be reflected upon as aggravations of sin.

(5.) The chief priests and the elders were busy, all this while, to influence the people in favour of Barabbas, v. 20. They *persuaded the multitude,* both by themselves and their emissaries, whom they sent abroad among them, *that they should ask Barabbas, and destroy Jesus;* suggesting that this Jesus was a deceiver, in league with Satan, an enemy to their church and temple; that, if he were let alone, the Romans would come, and take away their place and nation; that Barabbas, though a bad man, yet, having not the interest that Jesus had, could not do so much mischief. Thus they managed the mob, who otherwise were well affected to Jesus, and, if they had not been so much at the beck of their priests, would never have done such a preposterous thing as to prefer Barabbas before Jesus. Here, [1.] We cannot but look upon these wicked priests with indignation; by the law, in *matters of controversy between blood and blood,* the people were to be guided by the priests, and to do as they informed them, Deu. 17:8, 9. This great power put into their hands they wretchedly abused, and the leaders of the people caused them to err. [2.] We cannot but look upon the deluded people with pity; *I have compassion on the multitude,* to see them hurried thus violently to so great wickedness, to see them thus priest-ridden, and falling in the ditch with their *blind leaders.*

(6.) Being thus over-ruled by the priests, at length they made their choice, v. 21. *Whether of the twain* (saith Pilate) *will ye that I release unto you?* He hoped that he had gained his point, to have Jesus released. But, to his great surprise, they said *Barabbas;* as if his *crimes* were *less,* and therefore he less *deserved to die;* or as if his *merits* were *greater,* and therefore he better *deserved to live.* The cry for Barabbas was so universal, one and all, that there was no colour to demand a poll between the candidates. *Be astonished, O heavens, at this, and, thou earth, be horribly afraid!* Were ever men that pretended to reason or religion, guilty of such prodigious madness, such horrid wickedness! This was it that Peter charged so home upon them (Acts 3:14); *Ye desired a murderer to be granted to you;* yet multitudes who choose the world, rather than God, for their ruler and portion, thus *choose their own delusions.*

2. Their pressing earnestly to have Jesus crucified, v. 22, 23. Pilate, being amazed at their choice of Barabbas, was willing to hope that it was rather from a fondness for him than from an enmity to Jesus; and therefore he puts it to them, *"What shall I do then with Jesus?* Shall I release him likewise, for the greater honour of your feast, or will you leave it to me?" No, *they all said, Let him be crucified.* That death they desired he might die, because it was looked upon as the most scandalous and ignominious; and they hoped thereby to make his followers ashamed to own him, and their relation to him. It was absurd for them to prescribe to the judge what sentence he should pass; but their malice and rage made them forget all rules of order and decency, and turned a court of justice into a *riotous, tumultuous,* and *seditious assembly.* Now was truth fallen in the street, and equity could not enter; where one *looked for judgment, behold, oppression,* the worst kind of oppression; for righteousness, behold, a cry, the worse cry that ever was, *Crucify, crucify* the Lord of glory. Though they that cried thus, perhaps, were not the same persons that the other day cried *Hosanna,* yet see what a change was made upon the mind of the populace in a little time: when he *rode in triumph* into Jerusalem, so *general* were the *acclamations of praise,* that one would have thought he had *no enemies;* but now when he was *led in triumph* to Pilate's judgment-seat, so *general* were the *outcries* of enmity, that one would think he had *no friends.* Such revolutions are there in this changeable world, through which our way to heaven lies, as our Master's did, *by honour and dishonour, by evil report, and good report,* counter-changed (2 Co. 6:8); that we may not be lifted up by honour, as if, when we were applauded and caressed, we had *made our nest among the stars,* and should *die in that nest;* nor yet be dejected or discouraged by dishonour, as if, when we were trodden to the lowest hell, from which there is *no redemption. Bides tu istos qui te laudant; omnes aut sunt hostes, aut (quod in aequo est) esse possunt — You observe those who applaud you; either they are all your enemies, or, which is equivalent, they may become so.* Seneca de Vita Beat.

Now, as to this demand, we are further told,

(1.) How Pilate objected against it; *Why, what evil hath he done?* A proper question to ask before we censure any in common discourse, much more for a judge to ask before he pass a sentence of death. Note, It is much for the honour of the Lord Jesus, that, though he suffered as an evil-doer, yet neither his judge nor his prosecutors could find that he had done any evil. Had he done any evil *against God?* No, he *always did those things that pleased him.* Had he done any evil against the *civil government?* No, as he did himself, so he taught others, to *render to Caesar the things that were*

Caesar's. Had he done any evil against the *public peace?* No, he did not *strive or cry,* nor did his kingdom *come with observation.* Had he done any evil to particular persons? *Whose ox had he taken, or whom had he defrauded?* No, so far from that, that he *went about doing good.* This repeated assertion of his unspotted innocency, plainly intimates that he died to satisfy for the sins of others; for if it had not been for our transgressions that he was thus wounded, and for our offences that he was delivered up, and that upon his own voluntary undertaking to atone for them, I see not how these extraordinary sufferings of a person that had never thought, said, or done, any thing amiss, could be reconciled with the justice and equity of that providence that governs the world, and at least *permitted* this to be done in it.

(2.) How they *insisted* upon it; *They cried out the more, Let him be crucified.* They do not go about to show any evil he had done, but, right or wrong, he must be *crucified.* Quitting all pretensions to the proof of the premises, they resolve to hold the conclusion, and what was wanting in evidence to make up in clamour; this unjust judge was wearied by importunity into an unjust sentence, as he in the parable into a just one (Lu. 18:4, 5), and the cause carried purely by noise.

III. Here is the *devolving* of the guilt of Christ's blood upon the *people* and *priests.*

1. Pilate endeavours to transfer it from himself, v. 24.

(1.) He sees it *to no purpose to contend.* What he said, [1.] Would do no good; *he could prevail nothing;* he could not convince them what an unjust unreasonable thing it was for him to condemn a man whom he believed innocent, and whom they could not prove guilty. See how strong the stream of lust and rage sometimes is; neither authority nor reason will prevail to give check to it. Nay, [2.] It was more likely to *do hurt;* he saw that rather a *tumult was made.* This rude and brutish people fell to high words, and began to threaten Pilate what they would do if he did not gratify them; and how great a matter might this fire kindle, especially when the priests, those great incendiaries, blew the coals! Now this turbulent tumultuous temper of the Jews, by which Pilate was awed to condemn Christ against his conscience, contributed more than any thing to the ruin of that nation not long after; for their frequent insurrections provoked the Romans to destroy them, though they had reduced them, and their inveterate quarrels among themselves made them an easy prey to the common enemy. Thus their sin was their ruin.

Observe how easily we may be mistaken in the inclination of the common people; the priests were apprehensive that their endeavours to *seize* Christ would have caused an uproar, especially *on the feast day;* but it proved that Pilate's endeavour to *save* him, caused an uproar, and that on the feast day; so uncertain are the sentiments of the crowd.

(2.) This puts him into a *great strait,* betwixt the peace of his own mind, and the peace of the city; he is loth to condemn an innocent man, and yet loth to *disoblige* the people, and raise a devil that would not be soon laid. Had he steadily and resolutely adhered to the sacred laws of justice, as a judge ought to do, he had not been in any perplexity; the matter was plain and past dispute, that a man in whom was found *no faulty,* ought not to be crucified, upon any pretence whatsoever, nor must an unjust thing be done, to gratify any man or company of men in the world; the cause is soon decided; *Let justice be done, though heaven and earth come together — Fiat justitia, ruat coelum.* If *wickedness proceed from the wicked,* though they be priests, yet *my hand shall not be upon him.*

(3.) Pilate thinks to trim the matter, and to pacify both the people and his own conscience too, by *doing it,* and yet *disowning* it, *acting* the thing, and yet *acquitting* himself from it at the same time. Such absurdities and self-contradictions do *they* run upon, whose convictions are *strong,* but their corruptions *stronger. Happy is he* (saith the apostle, Rom. 14:22) *that condemneth not himself in that thing which he alloweth;* or, which is all one, that *allows* not himself in that thing which he *condemns.*

Now Pilate endeavours to clear himself from the guilt,

[1.] By a *sign;* He *took water, and washed his hands before the multitude;* not as if he thought thereby to cleanse himself from any guilt contracted before God, but to acquit himself before the people, from so much as contracting any guilt in this matter; as if he had said, "If it be done, bear witness that it is none of my doing." He *borrowed* the ceremony from that law which appointed it to be used for the clearing of the country from the guilt of an undiscovered murder (Deu.

21:6, 7); and he used it the more to affect the people with the conviction he was under of the prisoner's innocency; and, probably, such was the noise of the rabble, that, if he had not used some such surprising sign, in the view of them all, he could not have been heard.

[2.] By a *saying;* in which, *First,* He *clears* himself; *I am innocent of the blood of this just person.* What nonsense was this, to condemn him, and yet protest that he was innocent of his blood! For men to protest against a thing, and yet to practise it, is only to proclaim that they sin against their consciences. Though Pilate professed his innocency, God charges him with guilt, Acts 4:27. Some think to justify themselves, by pleading that their *hands* were not in the sin; but David kills by the sword of the children of Ammon, and Ahab by the elders of Jezreel. Pilate here thinks to justify himself, by pleading that his *heart* was not in the action; but this is an averment which will never be admitted. *Protestatio non valet contra factum — In vain does he protest against the deed which at the same time he perpetrates. Secondly,* He casts it upon the priests and people; *"See ye to it;* if it must be done, I cannot help it, do you answer it before God and the world." Note, Sin is a brat that nobody is willing to own; and many deceive themselves with this, that they shall bear no blame if they can but find any to lay the blame upon; but it is not so easy a thing to transfer the guilt of sin as many think it is. The condition of him that is infected with the plague is not the less dangerous, either for his catching the infection from others, or his communicating the infection to others; we may be *tempted* to sin, but cannot be *forced.* The priests threw it upon Judas; *See thou to it;* and now Pilate throws it upon them; *See ye to it; for with what measure ye mete, it shall be measured to you.*

2. The priests and people *consented* to take the guilt *upon themselves;* they all said, *"His blood be on us, and one our children;* we are so well assured that there is neither sin nor danger in putting him to death, that we are willing to run the hazard of it;" as if the guilt would do no harm to them or theirs. They saw that it was the dread of guilt that made Pilate hesitate, and that he was getting over this difficulty by a fancy of transferring it; to prevent the return of his hesitation, and to confirm him in that fancy, they, in the heat of their rage, agreed to it, rather than lose the prey they had in their hands, and cried, *His blood be upon us.* Now,

(1.) By this they designed to indemnify Pilate, that is, to make him think himself indemnified, by becoming bound to divine justice, to save him harmless. But those that are themselves bankrupts and beggars will never be admitted security for others, nor taken as a bail for them. None could bear the sin of others, except him that had none of his own to answer for; it is a bold undertaking, and too big for any creature, to become bound for a sinner to Almighty God.

(2.) But they did really imprecate wrath and vengeance upon themselves and their posterity. What a desperate word was this, and how little did they think what as the direful import of it, or to what an abyss of misery it would bring them and theirs! Christ had lately told them, that upon them would come *all the righteous blood shed upon the earth,* from that of the righteous Abel; but as if that were too little, they here imprecate upon themselves the guilt of that blood which was more precious than all the rest, and the guilt of which would lie heavier. O the daring presumption of wilful sinners, that *run upon God, upon his neck,* and defy his justice! Job 15:25, 26. Observe,

[1.] How *cruel* they were in their *imprecation.* They imprecated the punishment of this sin, not only upon themselves, but upon *their children* too, even those that were yet unborn, without so much as limiting the entail of the curse, as God himself had been pleased to limit it, to the *third and fourth generation.* It was madness to pull it upon themselves, but the height of barbarity to entail it on their posterity. Surely they were like the ostrich; they were *hardened against their young ones,* as though they were not *theirs.* What a dreadful conveyance was this of guilt and wrath to them and their heirs for ever, and this delivered by *joint consent, nemine contradicents — unanimously,* as their own *act and deed;* which certainly amounted to a forfeiture and defeasance of that ancient charter, *I will be a God to thee, and to thy seed.* Their entailing the curse of the Messiah's blood upon their nation, cut off the entail of the blessings of that blood from *their* families, that, according to another promise made to Abraham, in him *all the families of the earth* might be blessed. See what enemies wicked men are to their own children and families; those that damn their own souls, care not how many they take to hell with them.

[2.] How righteous God was, in his retribution according to this imprecation; they said, *His blood be on us, and on our children;* and God said *Amen* to it, so shall thy doom be; as they *loved cursing,* so it came upon them. The wretched remains of that abandoned people feel it to this day; from the time they imprecated this blood upon them, they were followed with one judgment after another, till they were quite laid waste, and made an astonishment, a hissing, and a byword; yet on some of them, and some of theirs, this blood came, not to *condemn* them, but to *save* them; divine mercy, upon their repenting and believing, cut off this entail, and then *the promise* was again *to them, and to their children.* God is better to us and ours than we are.

Verses 26–32

In these verses we have the *preparatives* for, and *prefaces* to, the crucifixion of our Lord Jesus. Here is,

I. The sentence passed, and the warrant signed for his execution; and this *immediately,* the same hour.

1. Barabbas was released, that notorious criminal: if he had not been put in competition with Christ for the favour of the people, it is probable that he had died for his crimes; but that proved the means of his escape; to intimate that Christ was condemned for this purpose, that sinners, even the chief of sinners, might be *released;* he was *delivered up,* that we might be delivered; whereas the *common instance* of divine Providence, is, that *the wicked is a ransom for the righteous, and the transgressor for the upright,* Prov. 21:18; 11:18. In this *unparalleled instance* of divine grace, the *upright* is a *ransom for the transgressors,* the just for the unjust.

2. Jesus was *scourged;* this was an ignominious cruel punishment, especially as is was inflicted by the Romans, who were not under the moderation of the Jewish law, which forbade scourgings, above forty stripes; this punishment was most unreasonably inflicted on one that was sentenced to die: the *rods* were not to introduce the axes, but to supersede them. Thus the scripture was fulfilled, *The ploughers ploughed upon my back* (Ps. 129:3), *I gave my back to the smiters* (Isa. 50:6), and, *By his stripes we are healed,* Isa. 53:5. He was *chastised with whips,* that we might not be for ever *chastised with scorpions.*

3. He was then *delivered to be crucified;* though his chastisement was in order to our peace, yet there is no peace made but by the *blood of his cross* (Col. 1:20); therefore the scourging is not enough, he must be *crucified;* a kind of death used only among the Romans; the manner of it is such, that it seems to be the result of wit and cruelty in combination, each putting forth itself to the utmost, to make death in the highest degree terrible and miserable. A cross was set up in the ground, to which the hands and feet were nailed, on which nails the weight of the body hung, till it died of the pain. This was the death to which Christ was condemned, that he might answer the type of the brazen serpent lifted up upon a pole. It was a bloody death, a painful, shameful, cursed death; it was so miserable a death, that merciful princes appointed those who were condemned to it by the law, to be strangled first, and then nailed to the cross; so Julius Caesar did by some pirates, *Sueton. lib.* 1. Constantine, the first Christian emperor, by an edict abolished the use of that punishment among the Romans, *Sozomen, Hist. lib.* 1. *ch.* 8. *Ne salutare signum subserviret ad perniciem — That the symbol of salvation might not be subservient to the victim's destruction.*

II. The barbarous treatment which the soldiers gave him, while things were getting ready for his execution. When he was condemned, he ought to have had some time allowed him to prepare for death. There was a law made by the Roman senate, in Tiberius's time, perhaps upon complaint of this and the like precipitation, that the execution of criminals should be deferred at least *ten days* after sentence. *Sueton in Tiber. cap.* 25. But there were scarcely allowed so many minutes to our Lord Jesus; nor had he any breathing-time during those minutes; it was a *crisis,* and there were no *lucid intervals* allowed him; *deep called unto deep,* and the storm continued without any intermission.

When he was *delivered* to be *crucified,* that was enough; they that *kill the body,* yield that there is no more that they *can do,* but Christ's enemies will *do more,* and, if it be possible, wrap up a thousand deaths in one. Though Pilate pronounced him innocent, yet his soldiers, his guards, set themselves to abuse him, being swayed more by the fury of the people *against him,* than by their master's testimony *for him;* the Jewish *rabble* infected the Roman soldiery, or perhaps it was not so much in spite to him, as to make *sport* for themselves, that they thus abused him. They understood that he *pretended to a crown; to taunt* him with that gave them some diversion, and an opportunity to make themselves and one another merry. Note, It is an argument of a base, servile, sordid spirit, to insult over those that are in misery, and to make the calamities of any matter of sport and merriment.

Observe, 1. *Where* this was done — in the *common hall.* The *governor's house,* which should have been a shelter to the wronged and abused, is made the theatre of this barbarity. I wonder that the governor, who was so desirous to acquit himself from the blood of this just person, would suffer this to be done in *his* house. Perhaps he did not order it to be done, but he *connived* at it; and those in authority will be accountable, not only for the wickedness which they *do,* or *appoint,* but for that which they do not restrain, when it is in the power of their hands. Masters of families should not suffer their houses to be places of abuse to any, nor their servants to make sport with the sins, or miseries, or religion, of others.

2. *Who* were concerned in it. They gathered the *whole band,* the soldiers that were to attend the execution, would have the whole regiment (at least five hundred, some think twelve or thirteen hundred) to share in the diversion. If Christ was thus made a *spectacle,* let none of his followers think it strange to be so used, 1 Co. 4:9; Heb. 10:33.

3. What particular indignities were done him.

(1.) They *stripped him, v.* 28. The shame of nakedness came in with sin (Gen. 3:7); and therefore Christ, when he came to satisfy for sin, and take it away, was *made naked,* and submitted to *that shame,* that he might prepare for us *white raiment, to cover us,* Rev. 3:18.

(2.) They *put on him a scarlet robe,* some old red cloak, such as the Roman soldiers wore, in imitation of the *scarlet robes* which kings and emperors wore; thus upbraiding him with his being called *a King.* This *sham* of majesty they put upon him in his dress, when nothing but meanness and misery appeared in his countenance, only to expose him to the spectators, as the more *ridiculous;* yet there was something of *mystery* in it; this was he that was *red in his apparel* (Isa. 63:1, 2), that *washed his garments in wine* (Gen. 49:11); therefore he was dressed in a *scarlet robe.* Our sins were as *scarlet and crimson.* Christ being clad in a *scarlet robe,* signified his bearing our sins, to his shame, in his own body upon the tree; that we might wash our robes, and make them white, in the blood of the Lamb.

(3.) They *platted a crown of thorns, and put it upon his head, v.* 29. This was to carry on the humour of making him a *mock-king;* yet, had they intended it only for a *reproach,* they might have *platted a crown of straw,* or *rushes,* but they designed it to be painful to him, and to be *literally,* what crowns are said to be figuratively, lined with thorns; he that invented this abuse, it is likely, valued himself upon the wit of it; but there was a mystery in it. [1.] Thorns came in with sin, and were part of the curse that was the product of sin, Gen. 3:18. Therefore Christ, being made a *curse for us,* and dying to remove the curse from us, felt the pain and smart of those thorns, nay, and *binds them as a crown* to him (Job 31:36); for his sufferings for us were *his glory.* [2.] Now he answered to the type of Abraham's ram that was *caught in the thicket,* and so offered up instead of Isaac, Gen. 22:13. [3.] Thorns signify afflictions, 2 Chr. 33:11. These Christ put into a *crown;* so much did he alter the property of them to them that are his, giving them cause to *glory in tribulation,* and making it to work for them a weight of glory. [4.] Christ was crowned with thorns, to show that *his kingdom was not of this world,* nor the glory of it worldly glory, but is attended here with bonds and afflictions, while the glory of it is *to be revealed.* [5.] It was the custom of some heathen nations, to bring their sacrifices to the altars, crowned with garlands; these thorns were the garlands with which this great Sacrifice was crowned. [6.] these thorns, it is likely, fetched blood from his blessed head, which trickled down his face, *like the previous ointment* (typifying the blood of Christ with which he consecrated himself) *upon the head, which ran down upon the beard, even Aaron's beard,* Ps. 133:2. Thus, when he came to espouse to himself his love, his dove, his undefiled church, his *head was filled with dew,* and his *locks with the drops of the night,* Cant. 5:2.

(4.) They *put a reed in his right hand;* this was intended for a *mock-sceptre,* another of the *insignia* of the majesty they jeered him with; as if this were a sceptre good enough for such a King, as was like *a reed shaken with the wind* (ch. 11:7); like sceptre, like kingdom, both weak and wavering, and withering and worthless; but they were quite mistaken, for his throne is *for ever and ever,* and the *sceptre of his kingdom is a right sceptre,* Ps. 45:6.

(5.) They *bowed the knee before him, and mocked him, saying, Hail, King of the Jews!* Having made him a sham King, they thus make a jest of doing homage to him, thus ridiculing his pretensions to sovereignty, as Joseph's brethren (Gen. 37:8); *Shalt thou indeed reign over us?* But as they were afterward compelled to do obeisance to him, and enrich his dreams, so these here bowed the knee, in scorn to him who was, soon after this, exalted to the right hand of God, that *at his name every knee might bow,* or break before him; it is ill jesting with that which, sooner or later, will come in earnest.

(6.) They *spit upon him;* thus he had been abused in the High Priest's hall, ch. 26:67. In doing homage, the subject kissed the sovereign, in token of his allegiance; thus Samuel kissed Saul, and we are bid to *kiss the Son;* but they, in this mock-homage, instead of kissing him, spit in his face; that blessed face which outshines the sun, and before which the angels cover theirs, was thus polluted. It is strange that the sons of men should ever do such a piece of *villany,* and that the Son of God should ever *suffer* such a piece of *ignominy.*

(7.) They *took the reed, and smote him on the head.* That which they had made the *mock-ensign* of his royalty, they now make the real instrument of *their* cruelty, and *his pain.* They smote him, it is probable, upon the *crown of thorns,* and so struck them into his head, that they might wound it the deeper, which made the more sport for them, to whom his pain was the greatest pleasure. Thus was he *despised and rejected of men; a man of sorrows, and acquainted with grief.* All this misery and shame he underwent, that he might purchase for us everlasting life, and joy, and glory.

III. The conveying of him to the place of execution. After they had mocked and abused him, as long as they thought fit, they then *took the robe off from him;* to signify their divesting him of all the kingly authority they had invested him with, by putting it on him; and they put his own raiment on him, because that was to fall to the soldiers' share, that were employed in the execution. They took off the robe, but no mention is made of their taking off the *crown of thorns,* whence it is commonly supposed (though there is no certainty of it) that he was crucified with that on his head; for as he is a Priest upon his throne, so he was a King upon his cross. Christ was led to be crucified in *his own raiment,* because he himself was to *bear our sins in his own body upon the tree.* And here,

1. They *led him away* to be *crucified;* he was led *as a lamb to the slaughter,* as a sacrifice to the altar. We may well imagine how they hurried him on, and dragged him along, with all the speed possible, lest any thing should intervene to prevent the glutting of their cruel rage with his precious blood. It is probable that they now loaded him with taunts and reproaches, and treated him as the off-scouring of all things. They led him away *out of the city;* for Christ, that he might sanctify the people with his own blood, *suffered without the gate* (Heb. 13:12), as if he that was the glory of them that *waited for redemption* in Jerusalem was not worthy to live among them. To this he himself had an eye, when in the parable he speaks of his being *cast out of the vineyard,* ch. 21:39.

2. They compelled Simon of Cyrene *to bear his cross, v.* 32. It seems, at first he *carried the cross* himself, as Isaac carried the wood for the burnt-offering, which was to burn him. And this was intended, as other things, both for pain and shame to him. But after a while they *took the cross* off from him, either, (1.) In compassion to him, because they saw it was too great a load for him. We can hardly think that they had any consideration of that, yet it teaches us that God *considers the frame* of his people, and will not *suffer them to be tempted above what they are able;* he gives them some breathing-time, but they must expect that the cross will return, and the lucid intervals only give them space to prepare for the next fit. But, (2.) Perhaps it was because he could not, with the cross on his back, go forward so fast as they would have him. Or, (3.) They were afraid, lest he should faint away under the load of his cross, and die, and so prevent what their malice further intended to do against him: thus even the *tender mer-*

cies of the wicked (which seem to be so) *are* really *cruel.* Taking the cross off from him, they *compelled* one Simon of Cyrene to bear it, pressing him to the service by the authority of the governor or the priests. It was a reproach, and none would do it but by compulsion. Some think that this Simon was a disciple of Christ, at least a well-wisher to him, and that they knew it, and therefore put this upon him. Note, All that will approve themselves disciples indeed, must follow Christ, *bearing his cross* (ch. 16:24), *bearing his reproach,* Heb. 13:13. We must know the *fellowship of his sufferings for us,* and patiently submit to all the sufferings for him we are called out to; for those only shall *reign with him,* that *suffer with him;* shall sit with him in his kingdom, that drink of *his cup,* and are baptized with *his baptism.*

Verses 33–49

We have here the crucifixion of our Lord Jesus.

I. The place where our Lord Jesus was put to death.

1. They came to a place called *Golgotha,* near adjoining to Jerusalem, probably the common place of execution. If he had had a house of his own in Jerusalem, probably, for his greater disgrace, they would have crucified him before his own door. But now in the same place where criminals were sacrificed to the justice of the government, was our Lord Jesus sacrificed to the justice of God. Some think that it was called *the place of a skull,* because it was the common charnel-house, where the bones and skulls of dead men were laid together out of the way, lest people should touch them, and be defiled thereby. Here lay the trophies of death's victory over multitudes of the children of men; and when by dying Christ would destroy death, he added this circumstance of honour to his victory, that he triumphed over death upon his own dunghill.

2. There they *crucified* him (*v.* 35), nailed his hands and feet to the cross, and then reared it up, and him hanging on it; for so the manner of the Romans was to crucify. Let our hearts be touched with the feeling of that exquisite pain which our blessed Saviour now endured, and let us look upon him who was thus pierced, and mourn. Was ever sorrow like unto his sorrow? And when we behold what manner of death he died, let us in that behold with *what manner of love he loved us.*

II. The barbarous and abusive treatment they gave him, in which their wit and malice vied which should excel. As if death, so great a death, were not bad enough, they contrived to add to the bitterness and terror of it.

1. By the drink they provided for him before he was nailed to the cross, *v.* 34. It was usual to have a cup of spiced wine for those to drink of, that were to be put to death, according to Solomon's direction (Prov. 31:6, 7), *Give strong drink to him that is ready to perish;* but with that cup which Christ was to drink of, they mingled *vinegar and gall,* to make it sour and bitter. This signified, (1.) The *sin of man,* which is a *root of bitterness, bearing gall and wormwood,* Deu. 29:18. The sinner perhaps rolls it under his tongue as a sweet morsel, but to God it is *grapes of gall,* Deu. 32:32. It was so to the Lord Jesus, when he bare our sins, and sooner or later it will be so to the sinner himself, *bitterness at the latter end, more bitter than death,* Eccl. 7:26. (2.) It signified the *wrath of God,* that cup which is Father *put into his hand,* a bitter cup indeed, like the *bitter water which caused the curse,* Num. 5:18. This drink they offered him, as was literally foretold, Ps. 69:21. And, [1.] He *tasted thereof,* and so had the *worst* of it, took the bitter taste into his mouth; he let no bitter cup go by him untasted, when he was making atonement for all our sinful tasting of forbidden fruit; now he was *tasting* death in its full bitterness. [2.] He *would not drink it,* because he would not have the *best* of it; would have nothing like an opiate to lessen his sense of pain, for he would die so as to *feel himself die,* because he had so much *work* to *do,* as our High Priest, in his suffering work.

2. By the dividing of his garments, *v.* 35. When they nailed him to the cross, they *stripped* him of his garments, at least his *upper garments;* for by sin we were made naked, to our shame, and thus he purchased for us white raiment to cover us. If we be at any time stripped of our comforts for Christ, let us bear it patiently; he was stripped for us. Enemies may strip us of our *clothes,* but cannot strip us of our *best comforts;* cannot take from us the *garments of praise.* The clothes of those that are executed are the executioner's fee: four soldiers were employed in crucifying Christ, and they must each of them have a share: his upper garment, if it were divided,

would be of no use to any of them, and therefore they agreed to *cast lots* for it. (1.) Some think that the garment was so fine and rich, that it was worth contending for; but that agreed not with the poverty Christ appeared in. (2.) Perhaps they had heard of those that had been cured by touching the hem of his garment, and they thought it valuable for some magic virtue in it. Or, (3.) They hoped to get money of his friends for such a sacred relic. Or, (4.) Because, in derision, they would seem to put a value upon it, as royal clothing. Or, (5.) It was for diversion; to pass away the time while they waited for his death, they would play a game at dice for the clothes; but, whatever they designed, the word of God is herein accomplished. In that famous *psalm,* the first words of which Christ made use of upon the cross, it was said, *They parted my garments among them, and cast lots upon my vesture,* Ps. 22:18. This was never true of David, but looks *primarily* at Christ, of whom David, in spirit, spoke. Then is the offence of this part of the cross ceased; for it appears to have been by the *determinate counsel and foreknowledge of God.* Christ stripped himself of his glories, to divide them among us.

They now *sat down, and watched him, v.* 36. The chief priests were careful, no doubt, in setting this guard, lest the people, whom they still stood in awe of, should rise, and rescue him. But Providence so ordered it, that those who were appointed to *watch* him, thereby became unexceptionable witnesses for him; having the opportunity to see and hear that which extorted from them that noble confession (*v.* 54), *Truly this was the Son of God.*

3. By the *title* set up over his head, *v.* 37. It was usual for the vindicating of public justice, and putting the greater shame upon malefactors that were executed, not only by a crier to proclaim before them, but by a writing also over their heads to notify what was the crime for which they suffered; so they set up over Christ's head his accusation written, to give public notice of the charge against him; *This is Jesus the King of the Jews.* This they designed for his reproach, but God so overruled it, that even his accusation redounded to his honour. For, (1.) Here was no crime alleged against him. It is not said that he was a pretended Saviour, or a usurping King, though they would have it thought so (Jn. 19:21); but, *This is Jesus, a Saviour;* surely that was no crime; and, *This is the King of the Jews;* nor was that a crime; for they expected that the Messiah should be so: so that, his enemies themselves being judges, he *did no evil.* Nay, (2.) Here was a very glorious truth asserted concerning him — that he is *Jesus the King of the Jews,* that King whom the Jews expected and ought to have submitted to; so that his accusation amounts to this, That he was the true Messiah and Saviour of the world; as Balaam, when he was sent for to curse Israel, blessed them all together, and that three times (Num. 24:10), so Pilate, instead of accusing Christ as a Criminal, proclaimed him a *King,* and that *three times,* in three inscriptions. Thus God makes men to serve *his* purposes, quite beyond *their own.*

4. By his companions with him in suffering, *v.* 38. There were *two thieves crucified with him* at the same time, in the same place, under the same guard; two highway-men, or robbers upon the road, as the word properly signifies. It is probable that this was appointed to be *execution-day;* and therefore they hurried the prosecution of Christ in the morning, that they might have him ready to be executed with the other criminals. Some think that Pilate ordered it thus, that this piece of necessary justice, in executing these thieves, might atone for his injustice in condemning Christ; others, that the Jews contrived it, to add to the ignominy of the sufferings of our Lord Jesus; however it was, the scripture was fulfilled in it (Isa. 53:12), *He was numbered with the transgressors.*

(1.) It was a reproach to him, that he was *crucified with them.* Though, while he lived, he was *separate from sinners,* yet *in their deaths they were not divided,* but he was made to partake with the vilest malefactors in their plagues, as if he had been a partaker with them in their sins; for he was made sin for us, and took upon him the *likeness of sinful flesh.* He was, at his death, numbered among the transgressors, and had his lot with the wicked, that we, at our death, might be *numbered among the saints,* and have our *lot among the chosen.*

(2.) It was an additional reproach, that he was crucified *in the midst, between them,* as if he had been the worst of the three, the principal malefactor; for among *three* the *middle* is the place for the chief. Every circumstance was contrived to his dishonour, as if the great Saviour were of all others the *greatest sinner.* It was also intended to ruffle and discompose him, in his last moments, with the shrieks, and groans, and blasphemies, of these malefactors, who, it is likely, made a hideous outcry when they were nailed to the cross; but thus would Christ affect himself with the miseries of sinners, when he was suffering for their salvation. Some of Christ's apostles were afterwards crucified, as Peter, and Andrew, but none of them were crucified *with him,* lest it should have looked as if they had been joint undertakers with him, in satisfying for man's sin, and joint purchasers of life and glory; therefore he was crucified between two malefactors, who could not be supposed to contribute any thing to the merit of his death; for he himself bare our sins *in his own body.*

5. By the blasphemies and revilings with which they loaded him when he was hanging upon the cross; though we read not that they cast any reflections on the thieves that were crucified with him. One would have thought that, when they had nailed him to the cross, they had done their worst, and malice itself had been exhausted: indeed if a criminal be put into the pillory, or carted, because it is a punishment less than death, it is usually attended with such expressions of abuse; but a dying man, though an infamous man, should be treated with compassion. It is an insatiable revenge indeed which will not be satisfied with death, *so great a death.* But, to complete the humiliation of the Lord Jesus, and to show that, when he was dying, he was *bearing iniquity,* he was then *loaded with reproach,* and, for aught that appears, not one of his friends, who the other day cried *Hosanna* to him, durst be seen to show him any respect.

(1.) The common *people, that passed by, reviled him.* His extreme misery and exemplary patience under it, did not mollify them, or make them to relent; but they who by their outcries brought him to this, now think to justify themselves in it by their reproaches, as if they *did well to condemn* him. They *reviled* him: *eblasphēmoun — they blasphemed* him; and *blasphemy* it was, in the strictest sense, speaking evil of him who *thought it not robbery to be equal with God.* Observe here,

[1.] The persons that reviled him; *they that passed by,* the travellers that went along the road, and it was a great *road,* leading from Jerusalem to Gibeon; they were possessed with prejudices against him by the reports and clamours of the High Priest's creatures. It is a hard thing, and requires more application and resolution than is ordinarily met with, to keep up a good opinion of persons and things that are *every where* run down, and spoken against. Every one is apt to say as the most say, and to throw a stone at that which is put into an ill name. *Turba Remi sequitur fortunam semper et odit damnatos — The Roman rabble fluctuate with a man's fluctuating fortunes, and fail not to depress those that are sinking.* Juvenal.

[2.] The gesture they used, in contempt of him — *wagging their heads;* which signifies their triumph in his fall, and their insulting over him, Isa. 37:22.; Jer. 18:16; Lam. 2:15. The language of it was, *Aha, so would we have it,* Ps. 35:25. Thus they insulted over him that was the Saviour of their country, as the Philistines did over Samson the destroyer of their country. This very gesture was prophesied of (Ps. 22:7); *They shake the head at me.* And Ps. 109:25.

[3.] The taunts and jeers they uttered. These are here recorded.

First, They upbraided him with his *destroying of the temple.* Though the judges themselves were sensible that what he had said of that was misrepresented (as appears Mk. 14:59), yet they industriously spread it among the people, to bring an *odium* upon him, that he had a design to destroy the temple; than which nothing would more *incense* the people against him. And this was not the only time that the enemies of Christ had laboured to *make others believe* that of religion and the people of God, which they themselves have known to be *false,* and the charge *unjust "Thou that destroyest the temple,* that vast and strong fabric, try thy strength now in plucking up that *cross,* and drawing those *nails,* and so *save thyself;* if thou hast the power thou hast boasted of, this is a proper time to exert it, and give proof of it; for it is supposed that every man will do his utmost to *save himself."* This made the cross of Christ such a *stumbling-block* to the Jews, that they looked upon it to be inconsistent with the *power* of the Messiah; he was *crucified in weakness* (2 Co. 13:4), so it seemed to them; but indeed Christ crucified is the *Power of God.*

Secondly, They upbraided him with his saying that he was *the Son of God;* If thou be so, say they, *come down from the cross.* Now they take the devil's words out of his mouth, with which he tempted him in the wilderness (*ch.* 4:3, 6), and renew the same assault; *If thou be the Son of God.* They think that now, or never, he must prove himself to be the *Son of God;* forgetting that he had proved it by the miracles he wrought, particularly his raising of the dead; and unwilling to wait for the complete proof of it by his own resurrection, to which he had so often referred himself and them; which, if they had observed it, would have anticipated the offence of the cross. This comes of judging things by the present aspect of them, without a due remembrance of what is *past,* and a patient expectation of *what may further be produced.*

(2.) The *chief priests and scribes,* the church rulers, and the *elders,* the state rulers, they mocked him, *v.* 41. They did not think it enough to invite the rabble to do it, but gave Christ the dishonour, and themselves the diversion, or reproaching him in their own proper persons. They should have been in the temple at their devotion, for it was the first day of the feast of unleavened bread, when there was to be a *holy convocation* (Lev. 23:7); but they were here at the place of execution, spitting their venom at the Lord Jesus. How much below the grandeur and gravity of their character was this! Could any thing tend more to make them *contemptible and base before the people?* One would have thought, that, though they neither feared God nor regarded man, yet common prudence should have taught them who had so great a hand in Christ's death, to keep as much as might be behind the curtain, and to play least in sight; but nothing is so mean as that malice may stick at it. Did they disparage themselves thus, to do despite to Christ, and shall we be afraid of disparaging ourselves, by joining with the multitude to *do him honour,* and not rather say, *If this be to be vile, I will be yet more vile?*

Two things the priests and elders upbraided him with.

[1.] That he could not *save himself, v.* 42. He had been before abused in his prophetical and kingly office, and now in his priestly office as a Saviour. *First,* They take it for granted that he *could not* save himself, and therefore had not the power he pretended to, when really he *would not* save himself, because he would die to *save us.* They should have argued, "He *saved others,* therefore he *could* save himself, and if he do not, it is for some good reason." But, *Secondly,* They would insinuate, that, because he did not now save himself, therefore all his pretence to save others was but sham and delusion, and was never really done; though the truth of his miracles was demonstrated beyond contradiction. *Thirdly,* They upbraid him with being *the King of Israel.* They dreamed of the external pomp and power of the Messiah, and therefore thought *the cross* altogether disagreeable to the King of Israel, and inconsistent with that character. Many people would like the *King of Israel* well enough, if he would but *come down from the cross,* if they could have his kingdom without the tribulation through which they must *enter into* it. But the matter is settled; if no cross, then no Christ, no crown. Those that would reign with him, must be willing to suffer with him, for Christ and his cross are *nailed together* in this world. *Fourthly,* They challenged him to *come down from the cross.* And what had become of us then, and the work of our redemption and salvation? If he had been provoked by these scoffs to *come down from the cross,* and so to have left his undertaking *unfinished,* we had been for ever *undone.* But his unchangeable love and resolution set him above, and fortified him against, this temptation, so that he did not *fail,* nor was *discouraged. Fifthly,* They promised that, if he would *come down from the cross, they would believe him.* Let him give them that proof of his being the Messiah, and they will own him to be so. When they had formerly demanded a sign, he told them that the sign he would give them, should be not his *coming down from the cross,* but, which was a greater instance of his power, his *coming up from the grave,* which they had not patience to wait two or three days for. If he had *come down from the cross,* they might with as much reason have said that the soldiers had juggled in nailing him to it, as they said, when he was raised from the dead, that the *disciples came by night, and stole him away.* But to promise ourselves that we would believe, if we had such and such means and motives of faith as we ourselves would prescribe, when we do not improve what God has appointed, is not only a gross instance of the deceitfulness of our hearts, but the sorry *refuge,* or *subterfuge* rather, of an obstinate destroying infidelity.

[2.] That God, *his Father,* would *not save him* (*v.* 43); *He trusted in God,* that is, he pretended to do so; for he said, *I am the Son of God.* Those who call God *Father,* and themselves *his children,* thereby profess to put a confidence in him, Ps. 9:10. Now they suggest, that he did but deceive himself and others, when he made himself so much the *darling of heaven;* for, if he had been the Son of God (as *Job's* friends argued concerning him), he would not have been *abandoned to* all this misery, much less *abandoned in* it. This was a *sword in his bones,* as David complains of the like (Ps. 42:10); and it was a *two-edged* sword, for it was intended, *First,* To *vilify* him, and to make the standers-by think him a deceiver and an impostor; as if his saying, that he was the *Son of God,* were now effectually *disproved. Secondly,* To *terrify* him, and drive him to distrust and despair of his Father's power and love; which some think, was the thing *he feared, religiously feared,* prayed against, and was *delivered from,* Heb. 5:7. David complained more of the endeavours of his persecutors to *shake his faith,* and drive him from his hope in God, than of their attempts to *shake his throne,* and drive him from his kingdom; their saying, There is *no help for him in God* (Ps. 3:2), and, *God has forsaken him,* Ps. 71:11. In this, as in other things, he was a type of Christ. Nay, these very words David, in that famous prophecy of Christ, mentions, as spoken by *his enemies* (Ps. 22:8); He *trusted on the Lord that he would deliver him.* Surely these priests and scribes had forgotten their psalter, or they would not have used the same words, so exactly to answer the type and prophecy: but the *scriptures must be fulfilled.*

(3.) To complete the reproach, the *thieves also that were crucified with him* were not only not reviled as he was, as if they had been saints compared with him, but, though fellow-sufferers with him, joined in with his prosecutors, and *cast the same in his teeth;* that is, one of them did, who said, *If thou be the Christ, save thyself and us,* Lu. 23:39. One would think that of all people this thief had *least cause,* and should have had *least mind,* to banter Christ. Partners in suffering, though for different causes, usually commiserate one another; and few, whatever they have done before, will breathe their last in revilings. But, it seems, the greatest mortifications of the body, and the most humbling rebukes of Providence, will not of themselves mortify the corruptions of the soul, nor suppress the wickedness of the wicked, without the grace of God.

Well, thus our Lord Jesus having undertaken to satisfy the justice of God for the wrong done him in his honour by sin, he did it by suffering *in his honour;* not only by divesting himself of that which was due to him as the Son of God, but by submitting to the utmost indignity that could be done to the worst of men; because he was made sin for us, he was thus made a curse for us, to make reproach easy to us, if at any time we suffer it, and have all manner of evil said against us falsely, for righteousness' sake.

III. We have here the frowns of heaven, which our Lord Jesus was under, in the midst of all these injuries and indignities from men. Concerning which, observe,

1. How this was signified — by an extraordinary and miraculous eclipse of the sun, which continued for *three hours, v.* 45. There was darkness *epi pasan tēn gēn — over all the earth;* so most interpreters understand it, though our translation confines it to *that land.* Some of the ancients appealed to the annals of the nation concerning this extraordinary eclipse at the death of Christ, as a thing well known, and which gave notice to those parts of the world of something great then in doing; as the sun's going back in Hezekiah's time did. It is reported that Dionysius, at Heliopolis in Egypt, took notice of this darkness, and said, *Aut Deus naturae patitur, aut mundi machina dissolvitur — Either the God of nature is suffering, or the machine of the world is tumbling into ruin.* An extraordinary light gave intelligence of the birth of Christ (*ch.* 2:2), and therefore it was proper that an extraordinary darkness should notify his death, for he is the *Light of the world.* The indignities done to our Lord Jesus, made the *heavens astonished,* and *horribly afraid,* and even put them into disorder and confusion; such wickedness as this the sun never saw before, and therefore withdrew, and would not see this. This surprising, amazing, darkness was designed to stop the mouths of those blasphemers, who were reviling Christ as he hung on the cross; and it should seem that, for the present, it struck such a terror upon them, that though their hearts were not changed, yet they were silent, and stood doubting what this should mean, till after *three hours* the

darkness *scattered,* and then (as appears by *v.* 47), like Pharaoh when the plague was over, they hardened their hearts. But that which was principally intended in this darkness, was, (1.) Christ's present *conflict* with the *powers of darkness.* Now the prince of this world, and his forces, the *rulers of the darkness of this world,* were to be cast out, to be spoiled and vanquished; and to make his victory the more illustrious, he fights them on their own ground; gives them all the advantage they could have against him by this darkness, lets them take the *wind* and *sun,* and yet baffles them, and so becomes more than a conqueror. (2.) His present want of heavenly comforts. This darkness signified that dark cloud which the human soul of our Lord Jesus was now under. God makes his sun to shine upon the just and upon the unjust; but even the light of the sun was withheld from our Saviour, when he was *made sin for us.* A pleasant thing it is for the eyes to behold the sun; but because now his soul was exceeding sorrowful, and the cup of divine displeasure was filled to him without mixture, even the light of the sun was suspended. When earth denied him a drop of cold water, heaven denied him a beam of light; having to deliver us from *utter darkness,* he did himself, in the depth of his sufferings, walk in darkness, and had no light, Isa. 50:10. During the *three hours* that this darkness continued, we do not find that he said *one word,* but passed this time in a silent retirement into his own soul, which was now in agony, wrestling with the powers of darkness, and taking in the impressions of his Father's displeasure, not against himself, but the sin of man, which he was now *making his soul an offering for.* Never were there three such hours since the day that God created man upon the earth, never such a dark and awful scene; the *crisis* of that great affair of man's redemption and salvation.

2. How he complained of it (*v.* 46); *About the ninth hour,* when it began to clear up, after a long and silent conflict. *Jesus cried, Eli, Eli, lama sabachthani?* The words are related in the Syriac tongue, in which they were spoken, because worthy of double remark, and for the sake of the perverse construction which his enemies put upon them, in putting *Elias* for *Eli.* Now observe here,

(1.) Whence he borrowed this complaint — from Ps. 22:1. It is not probable (as some have thought) that he repeated the whole psalm; yet hereby he intimated that the whole was to be applied to him, and that David, in spirit, there spoke of his humiliation and exaltation. This, and that other word, *Into thy hands I commit my spirit,* he fetched from David's psalms (though he could have expressed himself in his own words), to teach us of what use the word of God is to us, to direct us in prayer, and to recommend to us the use of scripture-expressions in prayer, which will *help our infirmities.*

(2.) How he uttered it — *with a loud voice;* which bespeaks the extremity of his pain and anguish, the strength of nature remaining in him, and the great earnestness of his spirit in this expostulation. Now the scripture was fulfilled (Joel 3:15, 16); *The sun and the moon shall be darkened. The Lord shall also roar out of Zion, and utter his voice form Jerusalem.* David often speaks of his *crying aloud* in prayer, Ps. 55:17.

(3.) What the complaint was — *My God, My God, why hast thou forsaken me?* A strange complaint to come from the mouth of our Lord Jesus, who, we are sure, was *God's elect, in whom his soul delighted* (Isa. 42:1), and one in whom he was always *well pleased.* The Father now loved him, nay, he knew that *therefore he loved him, because he laid down his life for the sheep;* what, and yet forsaken of him, and in the midst of his sufferings too! Surely never sorrow was like unto that sorrow which extorted such a complaint as this from one who, being perfectly free from sin, could never be a terror to himself; but the heart knows its own bitterness. No wonder that such a complaint as this made the earth to quake, and rent the rocks; for it is enough to make both the *ears of every one that hears it to tingle,* and ought to be spoken of with great reverence.

Note, [1.] That our Lord Jesus was, in his sufferings, for a time, *forsaken by his Father.* So he saith himself, who we are sure was under no mistake concerning his own case. Not that the union between the divine and human nature was in the least weakened or shocked; no, he was *now by the eternal Spirit offering himself:* nor as if there were any abatement of his Father's love to him, or his to his Father; we are sure that there was upon his mind no horror of God, or despair of his favour, nor any thing of the torments of hell; but his Father forsook him; that is, *First,* He delivered him up into the hands of his enemies, and did not appear to deliver him

out of their hands. He let loose the powers of darkness against him, and suffered them to do their worst, worse than against Job. Now was that scripture fulfilled (Job 16:11), *God hath turned me over into the hands of the wicked;* and no angel is sent from heaven to deliver him, no friend on earth raised up to appear for him. *Secondly,* He withdrew from him the present comfortable sense of his complacency in him. When *his soul* was first *troubled,* he had a *voice from heaven* to comfort him (Jn. 12:27, 28); when he was in his agony in the garden, there appeared an angel from heaven strengthening him; but now he had neither the one nor the other. God hid his face from him, and for awhile withdrew his rod and staff in the darksome valley. God *forsook* him, not as he forsook Saul, leaving him to an endless despair, but as sometimes he forsook David, leaving him to a present despondency. *Thirdly,* He let out upon his soul an afflicting sense of his wrath against man for sin. Christ was made *Sin* for us, a *Curse* for us; and therefore, though God loved him as a Son, he frowned upon him as a Surety. These impressions he was pleased to *admit,* and to *waive* that *resistance* of them which he *could have made;* because he would accommodate himself to this part of his undertaking, as he had done to all the rest, when it was in his power to have avoided it.

[2.] That Christ's being *forsaken* of his Father was the most grievous of his sufferings, and that which he complained most of. Here he laid the most doleful accents; he did not say, "Why am I scourged? And why spit upon? And why nailed to the cross?" Nor did he say to his disciples, when they turned their back upon him, *Why have ye forsaken me?* But when his Father stood at a distance, he cried out thus; for this as it that *put wormwood and gall* into the affliction and misery. This brought the *waters into the soul,* Ps. 69:1–3.

[3.] That our Lord Jesus, even when he was thus forsaken of his Father, kept hold of him as his God, notwithstanding; *My God, my God;* though forsaking me, yet *mine.* Christ was God's *servant* in carrying on the work of redemption, to him he was to make satisfaction, and by him to be carried through and crowned, and upon that account he calls him *his God;* for he was now *doing his will.* See Isa. 49:5–9. This supported him, and bore him up, that even in the depth of his sufferings God was his God, and this he resolves to keep fast hold of.

(4.) See how his enemies impiously bantered and ridiculed this complaint (*v.* 47); *They said, This man calleth for Elias.* Some think that this was the ignorant mistake of the Roman soldiers, who had heard talk of Elias, and of the Jews' expectation of the coming of Elias, but knew not the signification of *Eli, Eli,* and so made this blundering comment upon these words of Christ, perhaps not hearing the latter part of what he said, for the noise of the people. Note, Many of the reproaches cast upon the word of God and the people of God, take rise from gross mistakes. Divine truths are often corrupted by ignorance of the language and style of the scripture. Those that hear by the halves, pervert what they hear. But others think that it was the wilful mistake of some of the Jews, who knew very well what he said, but were disposed to abuse him, and make themselves and their companions merry, and to misrepresent him as one who, being forsaken of God, was driven to trust in creatures; perhaps hinting also, that he who had pretended to be himself the Messiah, would now be glad to be beholden to Elias, who was expected to be only the harbinger and forerunner of the Messiah. Note, It is no new thing for the most pious devotions of the best men to be ridiculed and abused by profane scoffers; nor are we to think it strange if what is well said in praying and preaching be misconstrued, and turned to our reproach; Christ's words were so, though he spoke as never man spoke.

IV. The cold comfort which his enemies ministered to him in this agony, which was like all the rest.

1. Some *gave him vinegar to drink* (*v.* 48); instead of some cordial-water to revive and refresh him under this heavy burthen, they tantalized him with that which did not only add to the reproach they were loading him with, but did too sensibly represent that cup of trembling which his Father had *put into his hand. One of them ran* to fetch it, seeming to be officious to him, but really glad of an opportunity to abuse and affront him, and afraid lest any one should take it out of his hands.

2. Others, which the same purpose of disturbing and abusing him, refer him to Elias (*v.* 49); *"Let be, let us see whether Elias will come to save him.* Come, let him alone, his case is desperate, neither heaven nor earth can help him; let us

do nothing either to hasten his death, or to retard it; he has appealed to Elias, and *to Elias let him go.*"

Verses 50–56

We have here, at length, an account of the death of Christ, and several remarkable passages that attended it.

I. The *manner* how he breathed his last (*v.* 50); between the third and the sixth hour, that is, between nine and twelve o'clock, as we reckon, he was nailed to the cross, and soon after the ninth hour, that is, between three and four o'clock in the afternoon, he *died.* That was the time of the offering of the evening sacrifice, and the time when the paschal lamb was killed; and Christ our Passover was sacrificed for us and offered himself in the evening of the world a sacrifice to God of a sweet-smelling savour. It was at that time of the day, that the angel Gabriel delivered to Daniel that glorious prediction of the Messiah, Dan. 9:21, 24, etc. And some think that from that very time when the angel spoke it, to this time when Christ died, was just seventy weeks, that is, four hundred and ninety years to a day, to an hour; as the departure of *Israel* out of Egypt was at the end of the four hundred and thirty years, *even the self-same day,* Ex. 12:41.

Two things are here noted concerning the manner of Christ's dying.

1. That he *cried with a loud voice,* as before, *v.* 46. Now,

(1.) This was a sign, that, after all his pains and fatigues, his life was *whole* in him, and nature *strong.* The voice of dying men is one of the first things that fails; with a panting breath and a faltering tongue, a few broken words are hardly spoken, and more hardly heard. But Christ, just before he expired, spoke like a man *in his full strength,* to show that his life was not forced from him, but was freely *delivered* by him into his Father's hands, as *his own act and deed.* He that had strength to cry thus when he died, could have got loose from the arrest he was under, and have bid defiance to the powers of death; but to show that *by the eternal Spirit he offered himself,* being the Priest as well as the Sacrifice, he *cried with a loud voice.*

(2.) It was significant. This *loud voice* shows that he attacked our spiritual enemies with an undaunted courage, and such a bravery of resolution as bespeaks him hearty in the cause and daring in the encounter. He was now *spoiling principalities and powers,* and in this loud voice he did, as it were, *shout for mastery,* as one *mighty to save,* Isa. 63:1. Compare with this, Isa. 62:13, 14. He now bowed himself with all his might, as Samson did, when he said, *Let me die with the Philistines,* Jdg. 16:30. *Animamque in vulnere ponit — And lays down his life.* His crying with a loud voice when he died, signified that his death should be published and proclaimed to all the world; all mankind being concerned in it, and obliged to take notice of it. Christ's loud cry was like a trumpet blown over the sacrifices.

2. That then he *yielded up the ghost.* This is the usual periphrasis of dying; to show that the Son of God upon the cross did truly and properly die by the violence of the pain he was put to. His *soul* was separated from his *body,* and so his body was left really and truly dead. It was certain that he *did die,* for it was requisite that he should die; *thus it was written,* both in the *close rolls* of the *divine counsels,* and in the *letters patent of* the *divine predictions,* and therefore thus *it behoved him to suffer.* Death being the penalty for the breach of the first covenant *(Thou shalt surely die),* the Mediator of the new covenant must make atonement *by means of death,* otherwise no remission, Heb. 9:15. He had undertaken to make his soul an *offering for sin;* and he did it, when he *yielded up the ghost,* and voluntarily resigned it.

II. The miracles that attended his death. So many miracles being wrought *by him* in his life, we might well expect some to be wrought concerning him at his death, for his name was called *Wonderful.* Had he been fetched away as Elijah in a *fiery chariot,* that had itself been miracle enough; but, being sent for away by an ignominious cross, it was requisite that his humiliation should be attended with some signal emanations of the divine glory.

1. *Behold, the veil of the temple was rent in twain.* This relation is ushered in with *Behold;* "Turn aside, and see this great sight, and be astonished at it." Just as our Lord Jesus expired, at the time of the offering of the evening-sacrifice, and upon a solemn day, when the priests were officiating in the temple, and might themselves be eyewitnesses of it, *the veil of the temple was rent* by an invisible power; that veil which parted between the *holy place* and the *most holy.* They

had condemned him for saying, *I will destroy this temple,* understanding it literally; now by this specimen of his power he let them know that, if he had pleased, he could have made his words good. In this, as in others of Christ's miracles, there was a mystery.

(1.) It was in correspondence with the temple of Christ's body, which was now in the dissolving. This was the true temple, in which dwelt *the fulness of the Godhead;* when Christ *cried with a loud voice, and gave up the ghost,* and so dissolved that temple, the literal temple did, as it were, echo to that cry, and answer the stroke, by *rending its veil.* Note, Death is the rending of the veil of flesh which interposes between us and the holy of holies; the death of Christ was so, the death of true Christians is so.

(2.) It signified the revealing and unfolding of the mysteries of the Old Testament. The veil of the temple was for concealment, as was that on the face of Moses, therefore it was called the *veil of the covering;* for it was highly penal for any person to see the furniture of the most holy place, except the High-Priest, and he but once a year, with great ceremony and through a cloud of smoke; all which signified the darkness of that dispensation; 2 Co. 3:13. But now, at the death of Christ, all was laid open, the mysteries were unveiled, so that now he that runs may read the meaning of them. Now we see that the mercy-seat signified *Christ* the great *Propitiation;* the pot of *manna* signified Christ the Break of life. Thus *we all with open face behold, as in a glass* (which helps the sight, as the veil hindered it), *the glory of the Lord. Our eyes see the salvation.*

(3.) It signified the uniting of Jew and Gentile, by the removing of the partition wall between them, which was the ceremonial law, by which the Jews were distinguished from all other people (as a *garden enclosed*), were brought near to God, while others were made to *keep their distance.* Christ, in his death, repealed the ceremonial law, cancelled that *hand-writing of ordinances,* took it out of the way, nailed it to his cross, and so *broke down the middle wall of partition;* and by abolishing those institutions *abolished the enmity,* and *made in himself of twain one new man* (as two rooms are made one, and that large and lightsome, by taking down the partition), so *making peace,* Eph. 2:14–16. Christ died, to rend all dividing veils, and to make all his one, Jn. 17:21.

(4.) It signified the consecrating and laying open of *a new and living way* to God. The veil kept people off from drawing near to the most holy place, where the *Shechinah* was. But the rending of it signified that Christ by his death opened a way to God, [1.] *For himself.* This was the great *day of atonement,* when our Lord Jesus, as the great *High-Priest,* not *by the blood of goats and calves, but by his own blood, entered once for all into the holy place;* in token of which the veil was rent, Heb. 9:7, etc. Having offered his sacrifice in the outer court, the blood of it was now to be sprinkled upon the mercy-seat within the veil; wherefore *lift up your heads, O ye gates,* and *be ye lift up, ye everlasting doors; for the King of glory,* the Priest of glory, *shall come in.* Now was he caused to draw near, and made to approach, Jer. 30:21. Though he did not personally ascend into the holy place not made with hands till above forty days after, yet he immediately acquired a right to enter, and had a virtual admission. [2.] *For us in him:* so the apostle applies it, Heb. 10:19, 20. We have *boldness to enter into the holiest, by that new and living way which he has consecrated for us through the veil.* He died, to *bring us to God,* and, in order thereunto, to rend that veil of guilt and wrath which interposed between us and him, to take away the *cherubim* and *flaming sword,* and to open the way to *the tree of life.* We have free access through Christ to the throne of grace, or mercy-seat, now, and to the throne of glory hereafter, Heb. 4:16; 6:20. The rending of the veil signified (as that ancient hymn excellently expresses it), that, *when Christ had overcome the sharpness of death, he opened the kingdom of heaven to all believers.* Nothing can obstruct or discourage our access to heaven, for the veil is rent; *a door is opened in heaven,* Rev. 4:1.

2. The *earth did quake;* not only mount Calvary, where Christ was crucified, but the *whole land,* and the adjacent countries. This earthquake signified two things.

(1.) The *horrible* wickedness of *Christ's crucifiers.* The earth, by trembling under such a load, bore its testimony to the innocency of him that was persecuted, and against the impiety of those that persecuted him. Never did the whole creation, before, groan under such a burthen as the Son of God crucified, and the guilty wretches that crucified him. The earth *quaked,* as if it *feared to open its mouth* to *receive* the blood of Christ, so much more precious than that of Abel, which it had received, and was *cursed* for it (Gen. 4:11, 12); and as if it *fain would open its mouth,* to swallow up those rebels that put him to death, as it had swallowed up Dathan and Abiram for a much less crime. When the prophet would express God's great displeasure against the wickedness of the wicked, he asks, *Shall not the land tremble for this?* Amos 8:8.

(2.) The *glorious* achievements of *Christ's cross.* This *earthquake* signified the mighty shock, nay, the fatal blow, now given to the devil's kingdom. So vigorous was the assault Christ now made upon the infernal powers, that (as of old, *when he went out of Seir, when he marched through the field of Edom*) the *earth trembled,* Jdg. 5:4; Ps. 68:7, 8. God shakes all nations, when the Desire of all nations is to come; and there is a *yet once more,* which perhaps refers to this shaking, Hag. 2:6, 21.

3. The *rocks rent;* the hardest and firmest part of the earth was made to feel this mighty shock. Christ had said, that if the children should cease to cry *Hosanna, the stones would immediately cry out;* and now, in effect, they did so, proclaiming the glory of the suffering Jesus, and themselves more sensible of the wrong done him than the hard-hearted Jews were, who yet will shortly be glad to find a *hole in the rocks, and a cleft in the ragged rocks,* to hide them from the face of him that sitteth on the throne. See Rev. 6:16; Isa. 2:21. But when God's *fury is poured out like fire, the rocks are thrown down by him,* Nah. 1:6. Jesus Christ is *the Rock;* and the rending of *these* rocks, signified the rending of *that* rock, (1.) That in the clefts of it was may be *hid,* as Moses in the cleft of the rock at Horeb, that there we may *behold the glory of the Lord,* as he did, Ex. 33:22. Christ's dove is said to be *hid in the clefts of the rock* (Cant. 2:14), that is, as some make the allusion, sheltered in the wounds of our Lord Jesus, the Rock rent. (2.) That from the cleft of it rivers of living water may flow, and follow us in this wilderness, as from the rock which Moses *smote* (Ex. 17:6), and which God clave (Ps. 78:15); and *that rock was Christ,* 1 Co. 10:4. When we celebrate the memorial of Christ's death, our hard and rocky hearts must be *rent* — the heart, and not the garments. That heart is harder than a rock, that will not *yield,* that will not *melt,* where Jesus Christ is *evidently set forth crucified.*

4. The *graves were opened.* This matter is not related so fully as our curiosity would wish; for the scripture was not intended to gratify that; it should seem, that same earthquake that rent the rocks, *opened the graves,* and many bodies of *saints which slept, arose.* Death to the saints is but the *sleep* of the body, and the *grave* the bed it *sleeps in;* they awoke by the power of the Lord Jesus, and (*v.* 53) came *out of the graves after his resurrection, and went into Jerusalem, the holy city, and appeared unto many.* Now here,

(1.) We may raise many enquiries concerning it, which we cannot resolve: as, [1.] *Who* these *saints* were, that *did arise.* Some think, the *ancient patriarchs,* that were in such care to be buried in the land of Canaan, perhaps in the believing foresight of the advantage of this early resurrection. Christ had lately proved the doctrine of the resurrection from the instance of the patriarchs (*ch.* 22:32), and here was a speedy confirmation of his argument. Others think, these that arose were *modern saints,* such as had been Christ in the flesh, but died before him; as his father Joseph, Zecharias, Simeon, John Baptist, and others, that had been known to the disciples, while they lived, and therefore were the fitter to be witnesses to them in an *apparition* after. What if we should suppose that they were the *martyrs,* who in the Old-Testament times had sealed the truths of God with their blood, that were thus *dignified* and *distinguished?* Christ particularly points at them as his forerunners, *ch.* 23:35. And we find (Rev. 20:4, 5), that those who were *beheaded for the testimony of Jesus,* arose *before the rest of the dead.* Sufferers with Christ shall *first* reign with him. [2.] It is uncertain whether (as some think) they arose to life, now at the death of Christ, and disposed of themselves elsewhere, but did not *go into the city* till after his resurrection; or whether (as others think), though *their sepulchres* (which the *Pharisees* had *built* and *varnished, ch.* 23:29), and so made remarkable, were shattered now by the earthquake (so little did God regard that hypocritical respect), yet they did not *revive* and *rise* till after the resurrection; only, for brevity-sake, it is mentioned here, upon the mention of the *opening of the graves,* which seems more probable. [3.] Some think that they arose only to bear witness of Christ's resurrection to those to whom they appeared, and, having finished their testimony, retired to their graves again. But it is more agreeable, both to Christ's honour and theirs, to *suppose,* though we cannot *prove,* that they arose as Christ did, to *die no more,* and therefore ascended with him to glory. Surely on them who did partake of his first resurrection, a *second* death had no power. [4.] To whom they appeared (not *to all the people* it is certain, but to *many*), whether enemies or friends, in what manner they appeared, how often, what they said and did, and how they disappeared, are secret things which belong not to us; we must not covet to be *wise above what is written.* The relating of this matter so briefly, is a plain intimation to us, that we must not look that way for a confirmation of our faith; we have a more sure word of prophecy. See Lu. 16:31.

(2.) Yet we may learn many good lessons from it. [1.] That even those who lived and died before the death and resurrection of Christ, had saving benefit thereby, as well as those who have lived since; for he *was* the same *yesterday* that he is *to-day,* and will be *for ever,* Heb. 13:8. [2.] That Jesus Christ, by dying, conquered, disarmed, and disabled, death. These saints that arose, were the present trophies of the victory of Christ's cross over the powers of *death,* which he thus *made a show of openly.* Having by death destroyed him that had the power of death, he thus *led captivity captive,* and gloried in these *re-taken prizes,* in them fulfilling that scripture, *I will ransom them from the power of the grave.* [3.] That, in virtue of Christ's resurrection, the bodies of all the saints shall, in the fulness of time, *rise again.* This was an earnest of the general resurrection at the last day, when *all that are in the graves shall hear the voice of the Son of God.* And perhaps Jerusalem is *therefore* called here the *holy city,* because the saints, at the general resurrection, shall enter into the *new Jerusalem;* which will be indeed what the other was in name and type only, the *holy city,* Rev. 21:2. [4.] That all the saints do, by the influence of Christ's death, and in conformity to it, rise from the *death of sin* to the *life of righteousness.* They are *raised up with him* to a divine and spiritual life; they go *into the holy city,* become *citizens* of it, have their conversation in it, and *appear to many,* as persons not of this world.

III. The conviction of his enemies that were employed in the execution (*v.* 54), which some make no less than another miracle, all things considered. Observe,

1. The persons convinced; *the centurion, and they that were with him watching Jesus;* a captain and his company, that were set on the guard on this occasion. (1.) They were *soldiers,* whose profession is commonly hardening, and whose breasts are commonly not so susceptible as some others of the impressions either of fear or pity. But there is no spirit too big, too bold, for the power of Christ to break and humble. (2.) They ware *Romans, Gentiles,* who knew not the scriptures which were now fulfilled; yet they only were convinced. A sad presage of the *blindness* that should *happen to Israel,* when the gospel should be sent to the Gentiles, to open their eyes. Here were the Gentiles *softened,* and the Jews *hardened.* (3.) They were the persecutors of Christ, and those that but just before had reviled him, as appears Lu. 23:36. How soon can God, by the power he has over men's consciences, alter their language, and fetch confessions of his truths, to his own glory, out of the mouths of those that have *breathed* nothing but *threatenings, and slaughter,* and blasphemies!

2. The means of their conviction; they perceived *the earthquake,* which frightened them, and saw the other *things that were done.* These were designed to assert the honour of Christ in his sufferings, and had their end on these soldiers, whatever they had on others. Note, The dreadful appearances of God in his providence sometimes work strangely for the conviction and awakening of sinners.

3. The expressions of this conviction, in two things.

(1.) The *terror* that was *struck* upon them; they *feared greatly;* feared lest they should have been buried in the darkness, or swallowed up in the earthquake. Note, God can easily frighten the most daring of his adversaries, and make them know themselves to be but men. Guilt puts men into fear. He that, when iniquity abounds, doth not *fear always,* with a fear of *caution,* when judgments are abroad, cannot but *fear greatly,* with a fear of *amazement;* whereas there are those who will not fear, *though the earth be removed,* Ps. 46:1, 2.

(2.) The *testimony* that was *extorted* from them; they said, *Truly this was the Son of God;* a noble confession; Peter was blessed for it, *ch.* 16:16, 17. It was the great matter now in dispute, the point upon which he and his enemies had *joined issue, ch.* 26:63, 64. His disciples believed it, but at this time durst not confess it; our Saviour himself was tempted to question it, when he said, *Why hast thou forsaken me?* The Jews, now that he was dying upon the cross, looked upon it as plainly determined against him, that he was not the Son of God, because he did not come down from the cross. And yet now this centurion and the soldiers make this voluntary confession of the Christian faith, *Truly this was the Son of God.* The best of his disciples could not have said more at any time, and at this time they had not faith and courage enough to say thus much. Note, God can maintain and assert the honour of a truth then when it seems to be crushed, and run down; for *great is the truth, and will prevail.*

IV. The attendance of his friends, that were witnesses of his death, *v.* 55, 56. Observe,

1. Who they were; *many women who followed him from Galilee.* Not his apostles (only elsewhere we find John by the cross, Jn. 19:26), their hearts failed them, they durst not appear, for fear of coming under the same condemnation. But here were a company of women, some would have called them *silly* women, that *boldly* stuck to Christ, when the rest of his disciples had basely deserted him. Note, Even those of the weaker sex are often, by the grace of God, made strong in faith, that Christ's strength may be made perfect in weakness. There have been women martyrs, famous for courage and resolution in Christ's cause. Now of these women it is said, (1.) That they had *followed Jesus from Galilee,* out of the great love they had to him, and a desire to hear him preach; otherwise, the males only were obliged to come up, to worship at the feast. Now having followed him such a long journey as from Galilee to Jerusalem, eighty or a hundred miles, they resolved not to forsake him now. Note, Our former services and sufferings for Christ should be an argument with us, faithfully to persevere to the end in our attendance on him. Have we followed him *so far* and so long, done so much, and laid out so much for him, and shall we forsake him now? Gal. 3:3, 4. (2.) That they *ministered to him* of their substance, for his necessary subsistence. How gladly would they have ministered to him now, if they might have been admitted! But, being forbidden that, they resolved to *follow him.* Note, When we are restrained from doing what we *would,* we must do what we can, in the service of Christ. Now that he is *in heaven,* though he is out of the reach of our *ministration,* he is not out of the reach of our *believing views.* (3.) Some of them are particularly named; for God will *honour* those that *honour* Christ. They were such as we have several times met with *before,* and it was their praise, that we meet with them *to the last.*

2. What they did; they were *beholding afar off.*

(1.) They stood *afar off.* Whether their own fear or their enemies' fury kept them at a distance, is not certain; however, it was an aggravation of the sufferings of Christ, that his *lovers and friends stood aloof from his sore,* Ps. 38:11; Job 19:13. Perhaps they might have come nearer, if they would; but good people, when they are in sufferings, must not think it strange, if some of their best friends be shy of them. When Paul's danger was imminent, *no man stood by him,* 2 Tim. 4:16. If we be thus looked strangely upon, remember, our Master was so before us.

(2.) They were there *beholding,* in which they showed a concern and kindness for Christ; when they were debarred from doing any other office of love to him, they looked a look of love toward him. [1.] It was a *sorrowful* look; they looked unto him who was now pierced, and *mourned;* and no doubt, were *in bitterness* for him. We may well imagine how it cut them to the heart, to see him in this torment; and what floods of tears it fetched from their eyes. Let us with an eye of faith behold Christ and him crucified, and be affected with that great love wherewith he loved us. But, [2.] It was no more than a look; they beheld him, but they could not *help him.* Note, When Christ was in his sufferings, the best of his friends were but spectators and lookers on, even the *angelic guards stood trembling by,* saith Mr. Norris, for he *trod the winepress alone,* and of the people there was none with him; so *his own arm wrought salvation.*

Verses 57–66

We have here an account of Christ's *burial,* and the manner and circumstances of it, concerning which observe, 1. The *kindness* and *good will* of his friends that *laid him in the grave.* 2. The *malice* and *ill will* of his enemies that were very solicitous to keep him there.

I. His friends gave him a *decent burial.* Observe,

1. In general, that Jesus Christ was *buried;* when his precious soul was gone to paradise, his blessed body was deposited in the chambers of the grave, that he might answer the type of Jonas, and fulfil the prophecy of Isaias; he *made his grave with the wicked.* Thus in all things he must be made *like unto his brethren,* sin only excepted, and, like us, unto dust *he must return.* He was buried, to make his death the more certain, and his resurrection the more illustrious. Pilate would not deliver his body to be buried, till he was well assured that he was really dead; while the witnesses lay *unburied,* there were some hopes concerning them, Rev. 11:8. But Christ, the great Witness, is as one *free among the dead, like the slain that lie in the grave.* He was *buried,* that he might take off the terror of the grave, and make it easy to us, might warm and perfume that cold noisome bed for us, and that we might be *buried with him.*

2. The particular circumstances of his burial here related.

(1.) The time *when* he was buried; *when the evening was come;* the same evening that he died, before sun-set, as is usual in burying malefactors. It was not deferred till the next day, because it was *the sabbath;* for burying the dead is not proper work either for a day of rest or for a day of rejoicing, as the sabbath is.

(2.) The person that took care of the funeral was Joseph of Arimathea. The apostles had all fled, and none of them appeared to show this respect to their Master, which the disciples of John *showed* to him after he was beheaded, who *took up his body, and buried it, ch.* 14:12. The women that followed him durst not move in it; then did God stir up this good man to do it; for what work God has to do, he will find out instruments to do it. Joseph was a fit man, for, [1.] He had wherewithal to do it, being a *rich man.* Most of Christ's disciples were poor men, such were most fit to go about the country to preach the gospel; but here was one that was a *rich man,* ready to be employed in a piece of service which required *a man of estate.* Note, Worldly wealth, though it is to many an objection in religion's way, yet, in some services to be done for Christ, it is an advantage and an opportunity, and it is well for those who have it, if withal they have a heart to use it for God's glory. [2.] He was well affected to our Lord Jesus, for he was himself *his disciple,* believed in him, though he did not openly profess it. Note, Christ has more secret disciples than we are aware of; seven thousand in Israel, Rom. 11:4.

(3.) The grant of the dead body procured from Pilate, *v.* 58. Joseph *went to* Pilate, the proper person to be applied to on this occasion, who had the disposal of the body; for in things wherein the power of the magistrate is concerned, due regard must be had to that power, and nothing done to break in upon it. What we do that is good, must be done peaceably, and not tumultuously. Pilate was willing to give the body to one that would inter it decently, that he might do something towards atoning for the guilt his conscience charged him with in condemning an innocent person. In Joseph's petition, and Pilate's ready grant of it, *honour* was done to Christ, and a testimony borne to his *integrity.*

(4.) The dressing of the body in its grave-clothes (*v.* 59); though he was an honourable counsellor, yet he himself *took the body,* as it should seem, into his own arms, from the infamous and accursed tree (Acts 13:29); for where there is true love to Christ, no service will be thought too mean to stoop to for him. Having taken it, he wrapped it in a *clean linen cloth;* for burying in linen was then the common usage, which Joseph complied with. Note, Care is to be taken of the dead bodies of good men, for there is a glory intended for them at the resurrection, which we must hereby testify our belief of, and wind up the dead body as designed for a better place. This common act of humanity, if done after a *godly sort,* may be made an acceptable piece of Christianity.

(5.) The depositing of it in the sepulchre, *v.* 60. Here there was nothing of that pomp and solemnity with which the grandees of the world are *brought to the grave, and laid in the tomb,* Job 21:32. A private funeral did best befit him whose kingdom came not with observation.

[1.] He was laid in a *borrowed* tomb, in Joseph's burying place; as he had not a house of his own, wherein to *lay his head* while he lived, so he had not a grave of his own, wherein to *lay his body* when he was dead, which was an instance of his poverty; yet in this there might be somewhat of a mystery. The grave is the peculiar heritage of a *sinner,* Job 24:19. There is nothing we can truly call our own but our sins and our graves; he *returneth to his earth,* Psalm 146:4. When we go to the grave, we go to our own place; but our Lord Jesus, who had no sin of his own, had no grave of his own; dying under imputed sin, it was fit that he should be buried in a *borrowed* grave; the Jews designed that he should have *made his grave with the wicked,* should have been buried with the thieves with whom he was crucified, but God overruled it, so as that he should make it *with the rich in his death,* Isa. 53:9.

[2.] He was laid in a *new tomb,* which Joseph, it is likely, designed *for himself;* it would, however, be *never the worse* for *his* lying in it, who was to rise so quickly, but a *great deal the better* for *his* lying in it, who has altered the property of the grave, and made it *anew* indeed, by turning it into a *bed of rest,* nay into a *bed of spices,* for all the saints.

[3.] In a tomb that was *hewn out of a rock;* the ground about Jerusalem was generally rocky. Shebna had his sepulchre hewn out thereabouts *in a rock,* Isa. 22:16. Providence ordered it that Christ's sepulchre should be in a solid entire rock, that no room might be left to suspect his disciples had access to it by some underground passage, or broke through the back wall of it, to steal the body; for there was no access to it but by the door, which was watched.

[4.] A *great stone was rolled to the door of his sepulchre;* this also was according to the custom of the Jews in burying their dead, as appears by the description of the grave of Lazarus (Jn. 11:38), signifying that those who are dead, are *separated* and *cut off from all the living;* if the grave were his prison, now was the prison-door locked and bolted. The rolling of the stone to the grave's mouth, was with them as filling up the grave is with us, it completed the funeral. Having thus in silence and sorrow deposited the previous body of our Lord Jesus in the grave, the house *appointed for all living,* they *departed* without any further ceremony. It is the most melancholy circumstance in the funerals of our Christian friends, when we have laid their bodies in the dark and silent grave, to go home, and leave them behind; but alas, it is not we that *go home,* and *leave them behind,* no, it is they that are gone to the better home, and have left us behind.

(6.) The company that attended the funeral; and that was very *small* and *mean.* Here were none of the relations in mourning, to follow the corpse, no formalities to grace the solemnity, but some good women that were true mourners — *Mary Magdalene, and the other Mary, v.* 56. These, as they had attended him *to the cross,* so they followed him to *the grave;* as if they composed themselves to sorrow, they *sat over against the sepulchre,* not so much to fill their eyes with the sight of what was done, as to empty them in rivers of tears. Note, True love to Christ will carry us through, to the utmost, in following him. Death itself cannot quench that divine fire, Cant. 8:6, 7.

II. His enemies did what they could to prevent his resurrection; what they did herein was *the next day that followed the day of the preparation, v.* 62. That was the seventh day of the week, the Jewish *sabbath,* yet not expressly called so, but described by this periphrasis, because it was now shortly to give way to the Christian sabbath, which began the day after. Now, 1. All that day, Christ lay dead in the grave; having for six days laboured and done all his work, on the seventh day he *rested,* and was *refreshed.* 2. On that day, the *chief priests and Pharisees,* when they should have been at their devotions, asking pardon for the sins of the week past, were dealing with Pilate about securing the sepulchre, and so *adding rebellion to their sin.* They that had so often quarrelled with Christ for works of the greatest mercy on that day, were themselves busied in a work of the greatest malice. Observe here,

(1.) Their address to *Pilate;* they were vexed that the body was given to one that would bury it decently; but, since it must be so, they desire a guard may be set on the sepulchre.

[1.] Their petition sets forth, that *that deceiver* (so they call him who is truth itself) *had said, After three days I will rise again.* He had said so, and his disciples *remembered* those very words for the confirmation of their faith, but his persecutors remember them for the provocation of their rage and malice. Thus the same word of Christ to the one was a savour of life unto life, to the other of death unto death. See how they compliment Pilate with the title of *Sir,* while they reproach Christ with the title of *Deceiver.* Thus the most malicious slanderers of *good men* are commonly the most sordid flatterers of *great men.*

[2.] It further sets forth their jealousy; *lest his disciples come by night, and steal him away, and say, He is risen.*

First, That which *really* they were afraid of, was, his *resurrection;* that which is most Christ's honour and his people's joy, is most the terror of his enemies. That which exasperated Joseph's brethren against him, was the presage of his rise, and of his having dominion over them (Gen. 37:8); and all they aimed at, in what they did against him, was, to prevent that. Come, say they, let us *slay him,* and see *what will become of his dreams.* So the chief priests and Pharisees laboured to defeat the predictions of Christ's resurrection, saying, as David's enemies of him (Ps. 41:8), *Now that he lieth, he shall rise up no more;* if he should rise, that would break all their measures. Note, Christ's enemies, even when they have gained their point, are still in fear of losing it again. Perhaps the priests were surprised at the respect shown to Christ's dead body by Joseph and Nicodemus, two honourable counsellors, and looked upon it as an ill presage; nor can they forget his raising Lazarus from *the dead,* which so confounded them.

Secondly, That which they took on them to be afraid of, was, lest *his disciples should come by night, and steal him away,* which was a very improbable thing; for, 1. They had not the courage to own him while he lived, when they might have done him and themselves real service; and it was not likely that his death should put courage into such cowards. 2. What could they promise themselves by stealing away his body, and making people believe he was risen; when, if he should not rise, and so prove himself a deceiver, his disciples, who had left all for him in this world, in dependence upon a recompence in the other world, would of all others suffer most by the imposture, and would have had reason to throw the first stone at his name? What good would it do them, to carry on a cheat upon themselves, to steal away his body, and say, *He is risen;* when, if he were not risen, their faith was vain, and they were *of all men the most miserable?* The chief priests apprehend that if the doctrine of Christ's resurrection be once preached and believed, the *last error will be worse than the first;* a proverbial expression, intimating no more than this, that we shall all be routed, all undone. They think it was *their error,* that they had so long connived at his preaching and miracles, which *error* they thought they had *rectified* by putting him to death; but if people should be persuaded of his resurrection, that would *spoil all* again, his interest would revive with him, and theirs must needs sink, who had so barbarously murdered him. Note, Those that opposed Christ and his kingdom, will see not only their attempts baffled, but themselves miserably *plunged* and *embarrassed,* their errors each worse than other, and the last worst of all, Ps. 2:4, 5.

[3.] In consideration hereof, they humbly move to have a guard set upon the sepulchre till the third day; *Command that the sepulchre be made sure.* Pilate must still be their drudge, his civil and military power must both be engaged to serve their malice; one would think that death's prisoners needed no other guard, and that the grave were *security* enough to itself; but what will not those fear, who are conscious to themselves both of *guilt* and *impotency,* in opposing the Lord and his anointed?

(2.) Pilate's answer to this address (*v.* 65); *He have a watch, make it sure, as sure as you can.* He was ready to gratify Christ's friends, in allowing them the body, and his enemies, in setting a guard upon it, being desirous to please all sides, while perhaps he laughed in his sleeve at both for making such ado, *pro* and *con,* about the dead body of a man, looking upon the hopes of one side and the fears of the other to be alike ridiculous. *Ye have a watch;* he means the constant guard that was kept in the tower of Antonia, out of which the allows them to detach as many as they pleased for that purpose, but, as if ashamed to be himself seen in such a thing, he leaves the management of it wholly to them. Methinks that word, *Make it as sure as you can,* looks like a banter, either, [1.] Of their *fears;* "Be sure to set a strong guard upon the dead man;" or rather, [2.] Of their *hopes;* "Do your worst, try your wit and strength to the utmost; but if he be of God, he will rise, in spite of you and all your guards." I am apt to think, that by this time Pilate had had some talk with the centurion, his own officer, of whom he would be apt to enquire how that *just man* died, whom he had condemned with such reluctance; and that he gave him such an account of those things as made him conclude that *truly he was the Son of God;* and Pilate would give more credit to him than to a thousand of those spiteful priests that called him a *Deceiver;* and if so, no marvel that he tacitly derides their project, in thinking to secure the sepulchre upon him who had so lately rent the rocks, and made the earth to quake. Tertullion, speaking of Pilate, saith, *Ipse jam pro suâ conscientiâ Christianus — In his conscience he was a Christian;* and it is possible that he might be under such convictions at this time, upon the centurion's report, and yet never be thoroughly persuaded, any more than Agrippa or Felix was, to be a Christian.

(3.) The wonderful care they took, hereupon, to secure the sepulchre (*v.* 66); *They sealed the stone;* probably with the great seal of their *sanhedrim,* whereby they interposed their authority, for who durst break the public seal? But not trusting too much to that, withal they *set a watch,* to keep *his disciples* from coming to *steal him away,* and, if possible, to hinder *him* from coming out of the grave. So they intended, but God brought this good out of it, that they who were set to *oppose* his resurrection, thereby had an opportunity to observe it, and did so, and told the chief priests what they observed, who were thereby rendered the more inexcusable. Here was all the power of earth and hell combined to keep Christ a prisoner, but all in vain, when his hour was come; death, and all those sons and heirs of death, could then no longer hold him, no longer have dominion over him. To guard the sepulchre against the poor weak disciples, was folly, because *needless;* but to think to guard it against the power of God was folly, because *fruitless* and to no purpose; and yet they thought they had *dealt wisely.*

CHAPTER 28

In the foregoing chapters, we saw the Captain of our salvation engaged with the powers of darkness, attacked by them, and vigorously attacking them; victory seemed to hover between the combatants; nay, at length, it inclined to the enemies' side, and our Champion fell before them; behold, God has delivered his strength into captivity, and his glory into the enemies' hand. Christ in the grave is like the ark in Dagon's temple; the powers of darkness seemed to ride masters, but then the Lord awaked as one out of sleep, and like a mighty man that shouteth by reason of wine, Ps. 78:61, 65. The prince of our peace is in this chapter rallying again, coming out of the grave, a Conqueror, yea, more than a conqueror, leading captivity captive; though the ark be a prisoner, Dagon falls before it, and it proves that none is able to stand before the holy Lord God. Now the resurrection of Christ being one of the main foundations of our religion, it is requisite that we should have infallible proofs of it; four of which proofs we have in this chapter, which are but a few of many, for Luke and John give a larger account of the proofs of Christ's resurrection than Matthew and Mark do. Here is, I. The testimony of the angel to Christ's resurrection (*v.* 1–8). II. His appearance himself to the women (*v.* 9, 10). III. The confession of the adversaries that were upon the guard (*v.* 11–15). IV. Christ's appearance to the disciples in Galilee, and the commission he gave them (*v.* 16–20).

Verses 1–10

For the proof of Christ's resurrection, we have here the testimony of *the angel,* and of *Christ* himself, concerning his resurrection. Now we may think that it would have been better, if the matter had been so ordered, that a competent number of witnesses should have been present, and have seen the stone rolled away by the angel, and the dead body reviving, as people saw Lazarus come out of the grave, and then the matter had been past dispute; but let us not prescribe to Infinite Wisdom, which ordered that the witnesses of his resurrection should see him *risen,* but not see him *rise.* His incarnation was a mystery; so was this *second incarnation* (if we may so call it), this *new making* of the body of Christ, for his exalted state; it was therefore *made in secret. Blessed are they that have not seen, and yet have believed.* Christ gave such proofs of his resurrection as were *corroborated* by the scriptures, and by the *word* which he had *spoken* (Lu. 24:6, 7–44; Mk. 16:7); for here we must *walk by faith, not by sight.* We have here,

I. The *coming* of the *good women* to the *sepulchre.*

Observe, 1. *When* they came; *in the end of the sabbath, as it began to dawn toward the first day of the week, v.* 1. This fixes the time of Christ's resurrection.

(1.) He arose the *third day* after his death; that was the time which he had often prefixed, and he kept within it. He was buried in the evening of the sixth day of the week, and arose in the morning of the first day of the following week, so that he lay in the grave about thirty-six or thirty-eight hours. He lay so long, to show that he was really and truly dead; and no longer, that he might not *see corruption.* He arose the third day, to answer the type of the prophet Jonas (*ch.* 12:40), and to accomplish that prediction (Hos. 6:2), *The third day he will raise us up, and we shall live in his sight.*

(2.) He arose *after the Jewish sabbath,* and it was the passover-sabbath; all that day he lay in the grave, to signify the abolishing of the Jewish feasts and the other parts of the ceremonial law, and that his people must be dead to such observances, and take no more notice of them than he did when he *lay in the grave.* Christ on *the sixth day finished* his work; he said, *It is finished;* on the seventh day he rested, and then on the first day of the next week did as it were begin a new world, and enter upon new work. Let no man therefore judge us now in respect of *the new moons,* or of the *Jewish sabbaths,* which were indeed a shadow of good things to come, but the *substance* if of *Christ.* We may further observe, that the time of the saints' lying in the grave, is a sabbath to them (such as the Jewish sabbath was, which consisted chiefly in bodily rest), for there they *rest from their labours* (Job 3:17); and it is owing to Christ.

(3.) He arose upon the *first day of the week;* on the first day of the first week God *commanded the light to shine out of darkness;* on this day therefore did he who was to be the Light of the world, shine out of the darkness of the grave; and the seventh-day sabbath being buried with Christ, it arose again in the first-day sabbath, called the *Lord's day* (Rev. 1:10), and no other day of the week is from henceforward mentioned in all the New Testament than this, and this often, as the day which Christians religiously observed in solemn assemblies, to the honour of Christ, Jn. 20:19, 26; Acts 20:7; 1 Co. 16:2. If the deliverance of Israel out of the land of the north superseded the remembrance of that out of Egypt (Jer. 23:7, 8), much more doth our redemption by Christ eclipse the glory of God's former works. The sabbath was instituted in remembrance of the *perfecting* of the work of creation, Gen. 2:1. Man by his revolt made a breach upon that *perfect* work, which was never perfectly repaired till Christ arose from the dead, and the *heavens and the earth were* again *finished,* and the disordered *hosts of them* modelled anew, and the day on which this was done was justly *blessed and sanctified,* and the seventh day from that. He who on that day arose from the dead, is the same by whom, and for whom, all things were at first created, and now anew created.

(4.) He arose *as it began to dawn* toward that day; as soon as it could be said that the *third day* was come, the time prefixed for his resurrection, he *arose;* after his withdrawings from his people, he returns with all convenient *speed,* and *cuts the work* as *short in righteousness* as may be. He had said to his disciples, that though within a little while they *should not see him,* yet again *a little while,* and they *should see him,* and accordingly he made it as little a while as possible, Isa. 54:7, 8. Christ arose *when the day began to dawn,* because then the day-spring from on high did again visit us, Lu. 1:78. His passion began in the night; when he hung on the cross the sun was darkened; he was laid in the grave in the dusk of the evening; but he arose from the grave when the sun was near rising, for he is the *bright and morning Star* (Rev. 22:16), the *true Light.* Those who address themselves early in the morning to the religious services of the Christian sabbath, that they may take the day before them, therein follow this example of Christ, and that of David, *Early will I seek thee.*

2. Who they were, that came to the sepulchre; *Mary Magdalene and the other Mary,* the same that attended the funeral, and *sat over against the sepulchre,* as before they *sat over against the cross;* still they studied to express their love to Christ; still they were inquiring after him. Then shall we *know,* if we thus *follow on to know.* No mention is made of the Virgin Mary being with them; it is probable that the *beloved disciple,* who had taken her to his own home, hindered her from *going to the grave to weep there.* Their attendance on Christ not only *to* the grave, but *in* the grave, represents his like care for those that are his, when they have *made their bed in the darkness.* As Christ in the grave was beloved of the *saints,* so the saints in the grave are beloved of Christ; for death and the grave cannot slacken that bond of love which is between them.

3. What they *came to do:* the other evangelists say that they came to anoint the body; Matthew saith that they came to *see the sepulchre,* whether it was as they left it; hearing perhaps, but not being sure, that the chief priests had set a guard upon it. They went, to show their good-will in another visit to the dear remains of their beloved Master, and perhaps not without some thoughts of his resurrection, for they

could not have quite forgotten all he had said of it. Note, Visits to the grave are of great use to Christians, and will help to make it familiar to them, and to take off the terror of it, especially visits to the grave of our Lord Jesus, where we may see sin buried out of sight, the pattern of our sanctification, and the great proof of redeeming love shining illustriously even in that *land of darkness.*

II. The appearance of an angel of the Lord to them, *v.* 2–4. We have here an account of the manner of the resurrection of Christ, as far as it was fit that we should know.

1. There was a *great earthquake.* When he died, the earth that *received him,* shook for fear; now that he arose, the earth that *resigned him,* leaped for joy in his exaltation. This earthquake did as it were *loose* the bond of death, and *shake off* the fetters of the grave, and introduce the *Desire of all nations,* Hag. 2:6, 7. It was the *signal* of Christ's victory; notice was hereby given of it, that, when the *heavens rejoiced,* the *earth* also might be *glad.* It was a *specimen* of the *shake* that will be given to the earth at the general resurrection, when mountains and islands shall be removed, that the earth may no longer *cover her slain.* There was a *noise and a shaking* in the valley, when the *bones were to come together, bone to his bone,* Eze. 37:7. The kingdom of Christ, which was now to be set up, made the earth to quake, and *terribly shook it.* Those who are sanctified, and thereby raised to a spiritual life, while it is in the doing find an earthquake in their own bosoms, as Paul, who *trembled* and was *astonished.*

2. The *angel of the Lord descended from heaven.* The angels frequently attended our Lord Jesus, at his birth, in his temptation, in his agony; but upon the cross we find no angel attending him: when his Father *forsook him,* the angels withdrew from him; but now that he is resuming the glory he had before the foundation of the world, now, behold, the *angels of God worship him.*

3. He came, and rolled back the stone from the door, and sat upon it. Our Lord Jesus could have *rolled back the stone* himself by his own power, but he chose to have it done by an angel, to signify that having undertaken to make satisfaction for our sin, imputed to him, and being under arrest pursuant to that imputation, he did not *break prison,* but had a fair and *legal discharge,* obtained from heaven; he did not break prison, but an officer was sent on purpose to *roll away the stone,* and so to open the prison door, which would never have been done, if he had not made a *full satisfaction.* But being delivered for our offences, to complete the deliverance, he was *raised again for our justification;* he died to pay our debt, and rose again to take out our acquittance. The *stone* of our sins was *rolled* to the door of the grave of our Lord Jesus (and we find the rolling of a great stone to signify the *contracting of guilt,* 1 Sa. 14:33); but to demonstrate that divine justice was satisfied, an angel was commissioned to roll back the stone; not that the angel *raised him from the dead,* any more than those that *took away the stone* from Lazarus's grave raised him, but thus he intimated the consent of Heaven to his release, and the joy of Heaven in it. The enemies of Christ had sealed the stone, resolving, like Babylon, not to *open the house of his prisoners; shall the prey be taken from the mighty?* For this was *their hour;* but all the powers of death and darkness are under the control of the God of light and life. An angel from heaven has power to *break the seal,* though it were the *great seal of Israel,* and is able to *roll away the stone,* though ever so great. Thus the *captives of the mighty are taken away.* The angel's *sitting* upon the *stone,* when he had *rolled it away,* is very observable, and bespeaks a secure triumph over all the obstructions of Christ's resurrection. There he sat, defying all the powers of hell to roll the stone to the grave again. Christ erects his seat of rest and seat of judgment upon the opposition of his enemies; *the Lord sitteth upon the floods.* The angel sat as a guard to the grave, having frightened away the enemies' *black* guard; he sat, expecting the women, and ready to give them an account of his resurrection.

4. That his *countenance was like lightning, and his raiment white as snow, v.* 3. This was a visible representation, by that which we call *splendid* and *illustrious,* of the *glories* of the invisible world, which know no *difference of colours.* His look upon the keepers was like *flashes of lightning; he cast forth lightning, and scattered them,* Ps. 144:6. The *whiteness* of his raiment was an emblem not only of purity, but of joy and triumph. When Christ died, the court of heaven *went into keep mourning,* signified by the *darkening of the sun;* but when he arose, they again put on the *garments of praise.* The glory of this angel represented the glory of Christ, to which he was now risen, for it is the same description that was given of him in his transfiguration (*ch.* 17:2); but when he conversed with his disciples after his resurrection, he drew a veil over it, and it bespoke the glory of the saints in their resurrection, when they shall be *as the angels of God in heaven.*

5. That *for fear of him the keepers did shake, and became as dead men, v.* 4. They were *soldiers,* that thought themselves hardened against fear, yet the very sight of an angel struck them with terror. Thus *when* the Son of *God arose to judgment, the stout-hearted were spoiled,* Ps. 76:5, 9. Note, The resurrection of Christ, as it is the joy of his friends, so it is the terror and confusion of his enemies. *They did shake;* the word *eseisthēsan* is the same with that which was used for the earthquake, *v.* 2, *seismos.* When the *earth* shook, these *children of the earth,* that had their portion in it, *shook too;* whereas, those that have their happiness in things above, *though the earth be removed, yet are without fear.* The keepers became *as dead men,* when he whom they kept guard upon became alive, and they whom they kept guard against revived with him. It struck a terror upon them, to see themselves baffled in that which was their business here. They were posted here, to *keep a dead man in his grave* — as easy a piece of service surely as was ever assigned them, and yet it proves too hard for them. They were told that they must expect to be assaulted by a company of feeble faint-hearted disciples, who for fear of them would soon *shake* and become as *dead men,* but are amazed when they find themselves attacked by a *mighty angel,* whom they dare not look in the face. Thus doth God *frustrate* his enemies by *frightening them,* Ps. 9:20.

III. The message which this angel delivered to the women, *v.* 5–7.

1. He *encourages them against their fears, v.* 5. To come near to graves and tombs, especially in silence and solitude, has something in it *frightful,* much more was it so to those women, to find an angel at the sepulchre; but he soon makes them easy with the word, *Fear not ye.* The keepers shook, and became as dead men, but, *Fear not ye.* Let the sinners in Zion be afraid, for there is cause for it; but, *Fear not, Abraham,* nor any of the faithful seed of Abraham; why should the daughters of Sarah, that *do well,* be afraid *with any amazement?* 1 Pt. 3:6. *"Fear not ye.* Let not the news I have to tell you, be any surprise to you, for you were told before that your Master would rise; let it be no terror to you, for his resurrection will be your consolation; fear not any hurt, that I will do you, nor nay evil tidings I have to tell you. *Fear not ye, for I know that ye seek Jesus.* I know you are friends to the cause. I do not come to frighten you, but to encourage you." Note, Those that *seek Jesus,* have no reason to be *afraid;* for, if they seek him diligently they shall *find him,* and shall find him their *bountiful Rewarder.* All our believing enquiries after the Lord Jesus are observed, and taken notice of, in heaven; *I know that ye seek Jesus;* and shall certainly be answered, as these were, *with good words, and comfortable words. Ye seek Jesus that was crucified.* He mentions his being crucified, the more to commend their love to him; "You seek him still, though *he was crucified;* you retain your kindness for him notwithstanding." Note, True believers love and seek Christ, not only *though* he was crucified, but *because* he was so.

2. He *assures them of the resurrection of Christ;* and there was enough in that to silence their fears (*v.* 6); He *is not here, for he is risen.* To be told *He is not here,* would have been no welcome news to those who sought him, if it had not been added, *He is risen.* Note, It is matter of comfort to those who seek Christ, and miss of finding him where they expected, that *he is risen:* if we find him not in sensible comfort, yet *he is risen.* We must not hearken to those who say, *Lo, here is Christ, or, Lo, he is there,* for he is not *here,* he is not *there,* he is *risen.* In all our enquiries after Christ, we must remember that he is *risen;* and we must seek him as one *risen.* (1.) Not with any *gross carnal* thoughts of him. There were those that *knew Christ after the flesh;* but now henceforth know we him so no more, 2 Co. 5:16. It is true, he had a body; but it is now a *glorified body.* They that make pictures and images of Christ, forget that *he is not here, he is risen;* our communion with him must be spiritual, by faith in his word, Rom. 10:6–9. (2.) We must seek him with great *reverence* and *humility,* and an awful regard to his glory, for *he is risen.* God has *highly exalted him,* and *given him a name above every name,* and therefore every knee and every soul must *bow before him.* (3.) We must seek him with a *heavenly mind;* when we are ready to make this world our home, and to say, *It is good to be here,* let us remember our Lord Jesus *is not here, he is risen,* and therefore let not our *hearts* be *here,* but let them *rise too,* and *seek the things that are above,* Col. 3:1–3; Phil. 3:20.

Two things the angel refers these women to, for the confirmation of their faith, touching Christ's resurrection.

[1.] To his *word* now *fulfilled,* which they might *remember; He is risen, as he said.* This he vouches as the proper object of faith; "He said that he *would rise,* and you know that he is the *Truth* itself, and therefore have reason to expect that he *should rise;* why should you be backward to *believe* that which he told you would be?" Let us never think that strange, of which the word of Christ has raised our expectations, whether the *sufferings of this present time,* or the *glory* that is *to be revealed.* If we remember what Christ hath said *to us,* we shall be the less surprised at what he does *with us.* This angel, when he said. *He is not here, he is risen,* makes it to appear that he preaches no other gospel than what they had already received, for he refers himself to the word of Christ as sufficient to bear him out; *He is risen, as he said.*

[2.] To his *grave* now *empty,* which they might *look into; "Come, see the place where the Lord lay.* Compare what you have *heard,* with what you *see,* and, putting both together, you will *believe.* You see that *he is not here,* and, remembering what he said, you may be satisfied that *he is risen;* come, *see the place,* and you will see that he is not there, you will see that he could not be stolen thence, and therefore must conclude that he is risen." Note, It may be of use to affect us, and may have a good influence upon us, to come, and with an eye of faith *see the place where the Lord lay.* See the marks he has there left of his love in condescending so low for us; see how *easy* he has made that *bed,* and how *lightsome,* for us, by lying in it himself; when we look into the grave, where we expect we must lie, to take off the terror of it, let us look into the grave where the Lord lay; the place where *our Lord* lay, so the Syriac. The angels own him for *their* Lord, as well as *we;* for the *whole family,* both in heaven and earth, is *named from him.*

3. He *directs them* to go *carry the tidings* of it to his disciples (*v.* 7); Go *quickly, and tell his disciples.* It is probable that they were for entertaining themselves with the sight of the sepulchre and discourse with the angels. It was good to be here, but they have other work appointed them; *this is a day of good tidings,* and though they have the *premier seisin* of the comfort, the *first taste* of it, yet they must not have the *monopoly* of it, must not hold their peace, any more than those lepers, 2 Ki. 7:9. They must go *tell the disciples.* Note, Public usefulness to others must be preferred before the pleasure of secret communion with God ourselves; for *it is more blessed to give than to receive.* Observe,

(1.) The *disciples* of Christ must first be *told the news;* not, Go, tell the *chief priests* and the *Pharisees,* that they may be *confounded;* but, Tell the disciples, that they may be *comforted.* God anticipates the joy of his friends more than the *shame* of his enemies, though the perfection of both is reserved for hereafter. *Tell his disciples;* it may be they will believe your report, however tell them, [1.] That they may encourage themselves under their present sorrows and dispersions. It was a dismal time with them, between grief and fear; what a cordial would this be to them now, to hear, *their Master is risen!* [2.] That they may enquire further into it themselves. This alarm was sent them, to awaken them from that strange stupidity which had seized them, and to raise their expectations. This was to set them on seeking him, and to prepare them for his appearance to them. General hints excite to closer searches. They shall now hear of him, but shall very shortly see him. Christ discovers himself *gradually.*

(2.) The *women* are sent to tell it to them, and so are made, as it were, the *apostles of the apostles.* This was an honour put upon them, and a recompence for their constant affectionate adherence to him, at the cross, and in the grave, and a rebuke to the disciples who forsook him. Still God chooses the weak things of the world, to confound the mighty, and puts the treasure, not only into *earthen* vessels, but here into the *weaker* vessels; as *the woman, being deceived* by the suggestions of an evil angel, *was first in the transgression* (1 Tim. 2:14), so these women, being duly informed by the instructions of a good angel, were first in the belief of the redemption from transgression by Christ's resurrection, that that reproach of their sex might be rolled away, by putting this in the balance against it, which is their perpetual praise.

(3.) They were bid to *go quickly* upon this errand. Why, what haste was there? Would not the news keep cold, and be welcome to them at any time? Yes, but they were now overwhelmed with grief, and Christ would have this cordial hastened to them; when Daniel was humbling himself before God for sin, the angel Gabriel was caused to fly *swiftly* with a message of comfort, Dan. 9:21. We must always be ready and forward; [1.] To obey the commands of God, Ps. 119:60. [2.] To do good to our brethren, and to carry comfort to them, as those that felt from their afflictions; *Say not, Go, and come again, and to-morrow I will give;* but now quickly.

(4.) They were directed to appoint the disciples to *meet him in Galilee.* There were other appearances of Christ to them before that in *Galilee,* which were sudden and surprising; but he would have one to be solemn and public, and gave them notice of it before. Now this general rendezvous was appointed in Galilee, eighty or a hundred miles from Jerusalem; [1.] *In kindness* to those of his disciples that remained in Galilee, and *did not* (perhaps they *could not*) come up to Jerusalem; into that country therefore he would go, to manifest himself to his friends there. *I know thy works, and where thou dwellest.* Christ knows where his disciples dwell, and will visit there. Note, The exaltation of Christ doth not make him forget the meaner and poorer sort of his disciples, but even to them that are at a distance from the plenty of the means of grave he will graciously *manifest himself.* [2.] In consideration of the weakness of his disciples that were now at Jerusalem, who as yet were *afraid of the Jews,* and durst not appear publicly, and therefore this meeting was adjourned to Galilee. Christ knows our fears, and considers our frame, and made his appointment where there was least danger of disturbance.

Lastly, The angel solemnly affirms upon his word the truth of what he had related to them; *"Lo, I have told you,* you may be assured of it, and depend upon it; *I* have told you, who dare not tell a lie." *The word spoken by angels was stedfast,* Heb. 2:2. God had been wont formerly to make known his mind to his people by the ministration of angels, as at the giving of the law; but as he intended in gospel times to lay aside that way of communication (for *unto the angels hath he not put in subjection the world to come,* nor appointed them to be the preachers of the gospel), this angel was *now* sent to certify the resurrection of Christ to the disciples, and so leave it in their hands to be published to the world, 2 Co. 4:7. In saying, *Lo, I have told you,* he doth, as it were, discharge himself from the blame of their unbelief, if they should not receive this record, and throw it upon them; *"I have done my errand,* I have faithfully delivered my message, now look you to it, believe it at your peril; whether you will hear or whether you will forbear, *I have told you."* Note, Those messengers from God, that discharge their trust faithfully, may take the comfort of that, whatever the success be, Acts 20:26, 27.

IV. The women's *departure* from the *sepulchre,* to bring notice to the disciples, *v.* 8. And observe,

1. What frame and temper of spirit they were in; They *departed with fear and great joy;* a strange mixture, fear and joy at the same time, in the same soul. To hear that Christ was risen, was matter of joy; but to be led into his grave, and to see an angel, and talk with him about it, could not but cause fear. It was good news, but they were *afraid* that it was too *good* to be true. But observe, it is said of their *joy,* I was *great* joy; it is not said so of their fear. Note, (1.) Holy fear has joy attending it. They that serve the Lord with *reverence,* serve him with *gladness.* (2.) Spiritual joy is mixed with trembling, Ps. 2:11. It is only perfect love and joy that will cast out all fear.

2. What haste they made; *They did run.* The fear and joy together quickened their pace, and added wings to their motion; the angel bid them *go quickly,* and they *ran.* Those that are sent on God's errand must not loiter, or lose time; where the *heart* is *enlarged* with the glad tidings of the gospel, the feet will *run the way of God's commandments.*

3. What errand they went upon; They ran, to *bring his disciples word.* Not doubting but it would be joyful news to them, they ran, to comfort them with the same comforts wherewith they themselves were comforted of God. Note, The disciples of Christ should be forward to communicate to each other their experiences of sweet communion with heaven; should tell others what God has *done for their souls,* and spo-

ken to them. Joy in Christ Jesus, like the ointment of the right hand, will betray itself, and fill all places within the lines of its communication with its odours. When Samson found honey, he brought it to his parents.

V. Christ's appearing to the women, to confirm the testimony of the angel, *v.* 9, 10. These zealous good women not only heard the first tidings of him, but had the first sight of him, after his resurrection. The angel directed those that would see him, to go to Galilee, but before that time came, even *here also,* they *looked after him* that lives, and sees them. Note, Jesus Christ is often better than his word, but never worse; often anticipates, but never frustrates, the believing expectations of his people.

Here is, 1. Christ's surprising appearance to the women; *As they went to tell his disciples, behold, Jesus met them.* Note, God's gracious visits usually meet us in the way of duty, and to those who use what they have for others' benefit, more shall be given. This interview with Christ was unexpected, *or ever they were aware,* Cant. 6:12. Note, Christ is nearer to his people than they imagine. They needed not *descend into the deep,* to fetch Christ thence; he *was not there, he was risen;* nor go up to heaven, for he *was not yet ascended:* but Christ was *high them,* and still in *the word is nigh us.*

2. The salutation wherewith he accosted them; *All hail — chairete.* We use the old *English form of salutation,* wishing *all health* to those we meet; for so *All hail* signifies, and is expressive of the Greek form of salutation here used, answering to that of the Hebrew, *Peace be unto you.* And it bespeaks, (1.) The good-will of Christ to us and our happiness, even since he entered upon his state of exaltation. Though he is advanced, he wishes us as well as ever, and is as much concerned for our comfort. (2.) The freedom and holy familiarity which he used in his fellowship with his disciples; for he called them *friends.* But the Greek word signifies, *Rejoice ye.* They were affected both with *fear* and *joy;* what he said to them tended to encourage their joy (*v.* 9), *Rejoice ye,* and to silence their fear (*v.* 10), *Be not afraid.* Note, It is the will of Christ that his people should be a cheerful joyful people, and his resurrection furnishes them with abundant matter for joy.

3. The affectionate respect they paid him; *They came, and held him by the feet, and worshipped him.* Thus they expressed, (1.) The *reverence* and *honour* they had *for* him; they threw themselves at his feet, put themselves into a posture of adoration, and *worshipped him* with humility and godly fear, as the Son of God, and now exalted. (2.) The *love* and *affection* they had to him; they *held him,* and *would not let him go,* Cant. 3:4. How *beautiful* were the *feet of the Lord Jesus* to them! Isa. 52:7. (3.) The *transport of joy* they were in, now that they had this further assurance of his resurrection; they welcomed it with both arms. Thus we must embrace Jesus Christ offered us in the gospel, with *reverence* cast ourselves at his feet, by faith *take hold* of him, and with love and joy lay him near our hearts.

4. The encouraging words Christ said to them, *v.* 10. We do not find that they said any thing to him, their affectionate embraces and adorations spoke plainly enough; and what he said to them was no more than what the angel had said (*v.* 5, 7); for he will *confirm the word of his messengers* (Isa. 44:26); and his way of *comforting* his people, is, by his Spirit to speak over again to their hearts the same that they had heard before from *his angels,* the ministers. Now observe here,

(1.) How he rebukes their fear; *Be not afraid.* They must not fear being imposed upon by these repeated notices of his resurrection, nor fear any hurt from the appearance of one from the dead; for the news, though strange, was both *true* and *good.* Note, Christ arose from the dead, to silence his people's fears, and there is enough in that to silence them.

(2.) How he repeats their message; *"Go, tell my brethren,* that they must prepare for a journey into Galilee, and there *they shall see me."* If there be any communion between our souls and Christ, it is he that *appoints the meeting,* and he will observe the appointment. Jerusalem had forfeited the honour of Christ's presence, it was a *tumultuous* city, therefore he adjourns the meeting to Galilee. *Come, my beloved, let us go forth,* Cant. 7:11. But that which is especially observable here, is, that he calls his disciples *his brethren.* Go, tell *my brethren,* not only those of them that were akin to him, but all the rest, for they are all his brethren (*ch.* 12:50), but he never called them so till after his resurrection, here and Jn. 20:17. Being by the resurrection himself declared to be the *Son of God with power,* all the children of God were

thereby declared to be *his brethren.* Being the *First-begotten from the dead,* he is become the *First-born among many brethren,* even of all that are planted together in the likeness of his resurrection. Christ did not now converse so constantly and familiarly with his disciples as he had done before his death; but, lest they should think him grown strange to them, he gives them this endearing title, *Go to my brethren,* that the scripture might be fulfilled, which, speaking of his entrance upon his exalted state, saith, *I will declare thy name unto my brethren.* They had shamefully *deserted* him in his sufferings; but, to show that he could forgive and forget, and to teach us to do so, he not only continues his purpose to *meet* them, but calls them *brethren.* Being all *his brethren,* they were *brethren* one to another, and must love as brethren. His owning them for his brethren put a great honour upon them, but withal gave them an example of humility in the midst of that honour.

Verses 11–15

For the further proof of the resurrection of Christ, we have here the confession of the adversaries that were upon the guard; and there are two things which strengthen this testimony — that they were *eye-witnesses,* and did themselves see the glory of the resurrection, which none else did — and that they were *enemies,* set there to oppose and obstruct his resurrection. Now observe here,

I. How this testimony was *given in* to the chief priests (*v.* 11); *when* the women *were going* to bring that news to the disciples, which would *fill their hearts with joy,* the soldiers went to bring the same news to the chief priests, which would *fill their faces with shame. Some of the watch,* probably those of them that commanded in chief, *came into the city,* and brought to those who employed them, the report of their disappointment. *They showed to the chief priests all the things that were done;* told them of the earthquake, the descent of the angel, the rolling of the stone away, and the coming of the body of Jesus alive out of the grave. Thus the *sign of the prophet Jonas* was brought to the chief priests with the most clear and incontestable evidence that could be; and so the utmost means of conviction were afforded them; we may well imagine what a mortification it was to them, and that, like the enemies of the Jews, they were *much cast down in their own eyes,* Neh. 6:16. It might justly have been expected that they should now have believed in Christ, and repented their putting him to death; but they were obstinate in their infidelity, and therefore sealed up under it.

II. How it was baffled and stifled by them. They called an assembly, and considered what was to be done. For their own parts, they were resolved not to believe that Jesus was risen; but their care was, to keep others from believing, and themselves from being quite ashamed from their disbelief of it. They had put him to death, and there was no way of standing to what they had done, but by confronting the evidence of his resurrection. Thus they who have sold themselves to work wickedness, find that one sin draws on another, and that they have plunged themselves into a wretched necessity of *adding iniquity to iniquity,* which is part of the curse of Christ's persecutors, Ps. 69:27.

The result of their debate was, that those soldiers must by all means be bribed off, and hired not to tell tales.

1. They *put money into their hands;* and what wickedness is it which men will not be brought to by the love of money? They *gave large money,* probably a great deal more than they gave to Judas, unto *the soldiers.* These chief priests loved their money as well as most people did, and were as loth to part with it; and yet, to carry on a malicious design against the gospel of Christ, they were very prodigal of it; they gave the soldiers, it is likely, as much as they asked, and they knew how to improve their advantages. Here was *large money* given for the advancing of that which they knew to be a lie, yet many grudge a little money for the advancement of that which they know to be the truth, though they have a promise of being reimbursed in the resurrection of the just. Let us never starve a good cause, when we see a bad one so liberally supported.

2. They *put a lie into their mouths* (*v.* 13); *Say ye, His disciples came by night, and stole him away while we slept;* a sorry shift is better than none, but this is a sorry one indeed. (1.) The sham was *ridiculous,* and carried along with it its own confutation. If *they slept,* how could they know any thing of the matter, or say who came? If *any one* of them was awake to *observe it,* no doubt, he would awake them all to *oppose*

it; for that was the only thing they had in charge. It was altogether improbable that a company of poor, weak, cowardly, dispirited men should expose themselves for so inconsiderable an achievement as the rescue of the dead body. Why were not the houses where they lodged diligently searched, and other means used to discover the dead body; but this was so thin a lie as one might easily see through. But had it been ever so plausible, (2.) It was a wicked thing for these priests and elders to hire those soldiers to tell a deliberate lie (if it had been in a matter of ever so small importance), against their consciences. Those know not what they do, who draw others to commit one wilful sin; for that may debauch conscience, and be an inlet to many. But, (3.) Considering this as intended to overthrow the great doctrine of Christ's resurrection, this was a sin against the last remedy, and was, in effect, a blasphemy *against the Holy Ghost,* imputing *that* to the roguery of the disciples, which was done by *the power of the Holy Ghost.*

But lest the soldiers should object the penalty they incurred by the Roman law for *sleeping upon the guard,* which was very severe (Acts 12:19), they promised to interpose with the governor; *"We will persuade him, and secure you.* We will use our own interest in him, to get him not to take notice of it;" and they had lately found how easily they could manage him. If really these soldiers had slept, and so suffered the disciples to steal him away, as they would have the world believe, the priests and elders would certainly have been the forwardest to solicit the governor to punish them for their treachery; so that *their* care for the soldiers' safety plainly gives the lie to the story. They undertook to *secure* them from the sword of Pilate's justice, but could not secure them from the sword of God's justice, which hangs over the head of those that love and make a lie. *They* promise more than they can perform who undertake to save a man harmless in the commission of a wilful sin.

Well, thus was the plot laid; now what success had it?

[1.] Those that were *willing to deceive,* took the money, and did as they were taught. They cared as little for Christ and his religion as the chief priests and elders did; and men that have no religion at all, can be very well pleased to see Christianity run down, and lend a hand to it, if need be, to serve a turn. They *took the money;* that was it they aimed at, and nothing else. Note, Money is a bait for the blackest temptation; mercenary tongues will sell the truth for it.

The great argument to prove Christ to be the Son of God, is, his resurrection, and none could have more convincing proofs of the truth of that than these soldiers had; they saw the angel descend from heaven, saw the stone rolled away, saw the body of Christ come out of the grave, unless the consternation they felt hindered them; and yet they were so far from being convinced by it themselves, that they were hired to belie him, and to hinder others from believing in him. Note, The most sensible evidence will not convince men, without the concurring operation of the Holy Spirit.

[2.] Those that were willing to be deceived, not only credited, but propagated, the story; This *saying is commonly reported among the Jews until this day.* The sham took well enough, and answered the end. The Jews, who persisted in their infidelity, when they were pressed with the argument of Christ's resurrection, had this still ready to reply, *His disciples came, and stole him away.* To this purport was the solemn narrative, which (as Justin Martyr relates in his dialogue with Typho the Jew) the great sanhedrim sent to all the Jews of the dispersion concerning this affair, exciting them to a vigorous resistance of Christianity — that, *when they had crucified, and buried him, the disciples came by night, and stole him out of the sepulchre,* designing thereby not only to overthrow the truth of Christ's resurrection, but to render his disciples odious to the world, as the greatest villains in nature. When once a lie is raised, none knows how far it will spread, nor how long it will last, nor what mischief it will do. Some give another sense of this passage, *This saying is commonly reported,* that is, "Notwithstanding the artifice of the chief priests, thus to impose upon the people, the collusion that was between them and the soldiers, and the money that was given to support the cheat, were commonly *reported* and whispered among the Jews;" for one way or other *truth will out.*

Verses 16–20

This evangelist passes over several other appearances of Christ, recorded by Luke and John, and hastens to this, which was of all other the most solemn, as being promised and appointed again and again before his death, and after his resurrection. Observe,

I. How the disciples attended his appearance, according to the appointment (*v.* 16); *They went into Galilee,* a long journey to go for one sight of Christ, but it was worth while. They had seen him several times at Jerusalem, and yet they went into Galilee, to see him there.

1. Because he appointed them to do so. Though it seemed a needless thing to go into Galilee, to see him whom they might see at Jerusalem, especially when they must so soon come back again to Jerusalem, before his ascension, yet they had learned to obey Christ's commands and not object against them. Note, Those who would maintain communion with Christ, must attend him there where he has appointed. Those who have met him in one ordinance, must attend him in another; those who have seen him at Jerusalem, must go to Galilee.

2. Because that was to be a public and general meeting. They had seen him themselves, and conversed with him in private, but that should not excuse their attendance in a solemn assembly, where many were to be gathered together to see him. Note, Our communion with God in secret must not supersede our attendance on public worship, as we have opportunity; for *God loves the gates of Zion,* and so must we. The place was a *mountain in Galilee,* probably the same mountain on which he was transfigured. There they met, for privacy, and perhaps to signify the exalted state into which he was entered, and his advances toward the upper world.

II. How they were affected with the appearance of Christ to them, *v.* 17. Now was the time that he was *seen of above five hundred brethren at once,* 1 Co. 15:6. Some think that they saw him, at first, at some distance, above in the air, *ephthē epanō — He was seen above, of five hundred brethren* (so they read it); which gave occasion to some to doubt, till he *came nearer* (*v.* 18), and then they were satisfied. We are told,

1. That they *worshipped him;* many of them did so, nay, it should seem, they all did that, they gave divine honour to him, which was signified by some outward expressions of adoration. Note, All that see the Lord Jesus with an eye of faith are obliged to *worship him.*

2. But *some doubted,* some of those that were then present. Note, Even among those that *worship* there are some that *doubt.* The faith of those that are sincere, may yet be very weak and wavering. They *doubted, edistasan — they hung in suspense,* as the scales of the balance, when it is hard to say which preponderates. These doubts were afterward removed, and their faith grew up to a full assurance, and it tended much to the honour of Christ, that the disciples *doubted* before they *believed;* so that they cannot be said to be credulous, and willing to be imposed upon; for they first *questioned,* and *proved all things,* and then *held fast* that which was *true,* and which they found to be so.

III. What Jesus Christ said to them (*v.* 18–20); *Jesus came, and spoke unto them.* Though there were those that doubted, yet, he did not therefore reject them; for he will not *break the bruised reed.* He did not stand at a distance, but *came near,* and gave them such convincing proofs of his resurrection, as turned the wavering scale, and made their faith to triumph over their doubts. *He came, and spoke* familiarly *to them,* as one friend speaks to another, that they might be fully satisfied in the commission he was about to give them. He that *drew near* to God, to speak for us to him, *draws near* to us, to speak from him to us. Christ now delivered to his apostles the great charter of his kingdom in the world, was sending them out as his ambassadors, and here gives them their credentials.

In opening this great charter, we may observe two things.

1. The commission which our Lord Jesus received himself from the Father. Being about to *authorize* his apostles, if any ask by what authority he doeth it, and who gave him that authority, here he tells us, *All power is given unto me in heaven and in earth;* a very great word, and which none but he could say. Hereby he asserts his universal dominion as Mediator, which is the great foundation of the Christian religion. He has *all power.* Observe, (1.) *Whence* he hath this power. He did not assume it, or usurp it, but it was *given* him, he was legally entitled to it, and invested in it, by a grant from him who is the Fountain of all being, and consequently of all power. God *set him King* (Ps. 2:6), inaugurated and enthroned him, Lu. 1:32. As God, equal with the Father, all power was originally and essentially *his;* but as Mediator, as God-man, *all power* was *given him;* partly in *recompence* of his work (because he humbled himself, therefore God thus *exalted him*), and partly in *pursuance* of his design; he had this *power* given him *over all flesh,* that he might *give eternal life to as many as were given him* (Jn. 17:2), for the more effectual carrying on and completing our salvation. This power he was now more signally invested in, upon his resurrection, Acts 13:3. He had power before, *power to forgive sins* (*ch.* 9:6); but now *all power* is given him. He is now going to *receive for himself a kingdom* (Lu. 19:12), to sit down *at the right hand,* Ps. 110:1. Having purchased it, nothing remains but to take possession; it is *his own* for ever. (2.) *Where* he has this power; in *heaven and earth,* comprehending the universe. Christ is the sole universal Monarch, he is *Lord of all,* Acts 10:36. He has all *power in heaven.* He has power of dominion over the angels, they are all his humble servants, Eph. 1:20, 21. He has power of intercession with his Father, in the virtue of his satisfaction and atonement; he intercedes, not as a suppliant, but as a demandant; *Father, I will.* He has *all power on earth* too; having prevailed with God, by the sacrifice of atonement, he prevails with men, and deals with them as one having authority, by the ministry of reconciliation. He is indeed, in all causes and over all persons, supreme Moderator and Governor. *By him kings reign.* All souls are his, and to him *every* heart and *knee must bow,* and *every tongue confess* him to be the *Lord.* This our Lord Jesus tells them, not only to satisfy them of the authority he had to commission them, and to bring them out in the execution of their commission, but to take off the offence of the cross; they had no reason to be ashamed of *Christ crucified,* when they saw him *thus glorified.*

2. The commission he gives to those whom he sent forth; *Go ye therefore.* This commission is given, (1.) To the *apostles* primarily, the chief ministers of state in Christ's kingdom, the architects that laid the foundation of the church. Now those that had followed Christ in the regeneration, were *set on thrones* (Lu. 22:30); *Go ye.* It is not only a word of command, like that, *Son, go work,* but a word of encouragement, *Go,* and *fear not, have I not sent you?* Go, and make a business of this work. They must not *take state,* and issue out summons to the nations to attend upon them; but they must go, and bring the gospel to their doors, *Go ye.* They had doted on Christ's *bodily presence,* and hung upon *that,* and built all their joys and hopes upon *that;* but now Christ discharges them from further attendance on his person, and sends them abroad about other work. *As an eagle stirs up her nest, flutters over her young,* to excite them to fly (Deu. 32:11), so Christ stirs up his disciples, to disperse themselves over all the world. (2.) It is given to their successors, the ministers of the gospel, whose business it is to transmit the gospel from age to age, to the end of the world in time, as it was theirs to transmit it from nation to nation, to the end of the world in place, and no less necessary. The Old-Testament promise of a gospel ministry is made to a succession (Isa. 59:21); and this must be so understood, otherwise how could Christ be with them always to the *consummation of the world?* Christ, at his ascension, gave not only apostles and prophets, but *pastors and teachers,* Eph. 4:11. Now observe,

[1.] How far his commission is extended; to *all nations.* Go, and disciples *all nations.* Not that they must go all together into every place, but by consent disperse themselves in such manner as might best *diffuse* the light of the gospel. Now this plainly signifies it to be the will of Christ, *First,* That the covenant of peculiarity, made with the Jews, should now be cancelled and disannulled. This word broke down the middle wall of partition, which had so long excluded the Gentiles from a visible church-state; and whereas the apostles, when first sent out, were forbidden to go into the way of the Gentiles, now they were sent to *all nations. Secondly,* That salvation by Christ should be offered to all, and none excluded that did not by their unbelief and impenitence exclude themselves. The salvation they were to preach is a *common salvation;* whoever will, let him come, and take the benefit of the *act of indemnity;* for there is no difference of Jew or Greek in Christ Jesus. *Thirdly,* That Christianity should be twisted in with national constitutions, that the kingdoms of the world should become Christ's kingdoms, and their kings the church's nursing-fathers.

[2.] What is the principal intention of this commission; to *disciple* all nations. *Mathēteusate — "Admit them disciples;* do your utmost to make the nations Christian nations;" not,

"Go to the nations, and denounce the judgments of God against them, as Jonah against Nineveh, and as the other Old-Testament prophets" (though they had reason enough to expect it for their wickedness), "but go, and *disciple them.*" Christ the Mediator is setting up a kingdom in the world, bring the nations to be his subjects; setting up a school, bring the nations to be his scholars; raising an army for the carrying on of the war against the powers of darkness, enlist the nations of the earth under his banner. The work which the apostles had to do, was, to set up the Christian religion in all places, and it was honourable work; the achievements of the mighty heroes of the world were nothing to it. They conquered the nations for themselves, and made them miserable; the apostles conquered them for Christ, and made them happy.

[3.] Their instructions for executing this commission.

First, They must *admit disciples* by the *sacred rite of baptism;* "Go into all nations, preach the gospel to them, work miracles among them, and persuade them to come in themselves, and bring their children with them, into the church of Christ, and then admit them and theirs into the church, by washing them with water;" either dipping them in the water, or pouring or sprinkling water upon them, which seems the more proper, because the thing is most frequently expressed so, as Isa. 44:3, *I will pour my Spirit on thy seed.* And, Tit. 3:5, 6, *Which he shed on us abundantly.* And, Eze. 36:25, *I will sprinkle clean water upon you.* And, Isa. 52:15, *So shall he sprinkle many nations;* which seems a prophecy of this commission to *baptize the nations.*

Secondly, This baptism must be administered *in the name of the Father, and of the Son, and of the Holy Ghost.* That is, 1. *By authority from heaven,* and not *of man;* for his ministers act by authority from the three persons in the Godhead, who all concur, as to our *creation,* so to our *redemption;* they have their commission under the great seal of heaven, which puts an honour upon the ordinance, though to a carnal eye, like him that instituted it, it has *no form or comeliness.* 2. *Calling upon the name* of the Father, Son, and Holy Ghost. Every thing is sanctified by prayer, and particularly the waters of baptism. The prayer of faith obtains the presence of God with the ordinance, which is its lustre and beauty, its life and efficacy. But, 3. It is *into the name* (*eis to onoma*) of *Father, Son, and Holy Ghost;* this was intended as the *summary* of the first principles of the Christian religion, and of the new covenant, and according to it the ancient creeds were drawn up. By our being baptized, we solemnly profess, (1.) Our *assent* to the scripture-revelation concerning *God, the Father, Son, and Holy Ghost.* We confess our belief that there is a God, that there is but *one God,* that in the Godhead there is a *Father* that *begets,* a *Son* that is *begotten,* and a Holy *Spirit* of both. We are baptized, not into the *names,* but into the *name,* of Father, Son, and Spirit, which plainly intimates that *these three are one,* and *their name one.* The distinct mentioning of the *three persons* in the Trinity, both in the *Christian baptism* here, and in the *Christian blessing* (2 Co. 13:14), as it is a full proof of the doctrine of the Trinity, so it has done much towards preserving it pure and entire through all ages of the church; for nothing is more great and awful in *Christian assemblies* than these two. (2.) Our *consent* to a covenant-relation to God, *the Father, Son, and Holy Ghost.* Baptism is a *sacrament,* that is, it is *an oath; super sacramentum dicere,* is *to say upon oath.* It is an oath of *abjuration,* by which we renounce the world and the flesh, as rivals with God for the throne in our hearts; and an oath of *allegiance,* by which we resign and give up *ourselves* to God, to be *his,* our own selves, our whole selves, *body, soul, and spirit,* to be governed by his will, and made happy in his favour; *we become his men,* so the form of homage in our law runs. Therefore *baptism* is applied to *the person,* as *livery and seisin* is given of the premises, because it is the person that is *dedicated* to God. [1.] It is into the name of *the Father,* believing him to be the *Father of our Lord Jesus Christ* (for that is principally intended here), by *eternal generation,* and *our Father,* as our Creator, Preserver, and Benefactor, to whom therefore we resign ourselves, as our absolute *owner* and *proprietor,* to actuate us, and dispose of us; as our supreme *rector* and *governor,* to rule us, as free agents, by his law; and as our *chief good,* and *highest* end. [2.] It is into the name of *the Son,* the *Lord Jesus Christ,* the *Son of God,* and *correlate* to the Father. Baptism was in a particular manner

administered *in the name of the Lord Jesus,* Acts 8:16; 19:5. In baptism we *assent,* as Peter did, *Thou art Christ, the Son of the living God* (ch. 16:16), and *consent,* as Thomas did, *My Lord, and my God,* Jn. 20:28. We take Christ to be our Prophet, Priest, and King, and give up ourselves to be taught, and saved, and ruled, by him. [3.] It is into the name of *the Holy Ghost.* Believing the Godhead of the Holy Spirit, and his agency in carrying on our redemption, we give up ourselves to his conduct and operation, as our sanctifier, teacher, guide, and comforter.

Thirdly, Those that are thus baptized, and enrolled among the disciples of Christ, must be taught (*v.* 20); *Teaching them to observe all thing, whatsoever I have commanded you.* This denotes two things.

1. The duty of *disciples,* of all *baptized Christians;* they must observe all things whatsoever Christ has commanded, and, in order to that, must submit to the teaching of those whom he sends. Our admission into the visible church is in order to something further; when Christ hath *discipled* us, he hath not *done with us;* he *enlist* soldiers that he may *train them* up for his service.

All that are baptized, are thereby obliged, (1.) To make the command of Christ their rule. There is a *law of faith,* and we are said to be *under the law to Christ;* we are by baptism *bound,* and must *obey.* (2.) To *observe* what Christ has commanded. Due *obedience* to the commands of Christ requires a diligent observation; we are in danger of missing, if we take not *good heed:* and in all our obedience, we must have an eye to the command, and do what we do as unto the Lord. (3.) To observe *all things,* that he has commanded, without exception; all the *moral* duties, and all the *instituted* ordinances. Our obedience to the laws of Christ is not *sincere,* if it be not universal; we must *stand complete in his whole will.* (4.) To confine themselves to the commands of Christ, and as not to *diminish* from them, so not to *add* to them. (5.) To learn their duty according to the law of Christ, from those whom he has appointed to be teachers in his school, for *therefore* we were entered into his school.

2. The duty of the apostles of Christ, and his ministers; and that is, to *beach* the commands of Christ, to expound them to his disciples, to press upon them the necessity of obedience, and to assist them in applying the general commands of Christ to particular cases. They must teach *them,* not their own inventions, but the institutions of Christ; to them they must religiously adhere, and in the knowledge of *them* Christians must be *trained up.* A *standing* ministry is hereby *settled* in the church, for the *edifying* of the body of Christ, *till we all come to the perfect man,* Eph. 4:11–13. The heirs of heaven, till they come to age, must be *under tutors and governors.*

3. Here is the assurance he gives them of his spiritual presence with them in the execution of this commission; *And lo, I am with you always, even unto the end of the world.* This exceeding great and precious promise is ushered in with a *behold,* to strengthen their faith, and engage their observation of it. "Take notice of this; it is what you may assure yourselves of and venture upon." Observe,

(1.) The favour promised them; *I am with you.* Not, *I will be* with you, but *I am — egō eimi.* As God sent Moses, so Christ sent his apostles, by this name, *I am;* for he is God, to whom past, present, and to come, are the same. See Rev. 1:8. He was now about to leave them; his bodily presence was now to be removed from them, and this grieved them; but he assures them of his *spiritual* presence, which was more expedient for them than his bodily presence could be; *I am with you;* that is, "My Spirit is with you, the Comforter shall *abide with you,* Jn. 16:7. I am *with you,* and not *against you:* with you to take your part, to be on your side, and to *hold* with you, as Michael our prince is said to do, Dan. 10:21. I am *with you,* and not *absent from you,* not at a distance; I am a very *present help,*" Ps. 46:1. Christ was now sending them to set up his kingdom in the world, which was a great undertaking. And then doth he seasonably promise them his presence with them, [1.] To *carry them* on through the difficulties they were likely to meet with. "I am with you, to *bear you up,* to plead your cause; with you in all your services, in all your sufferings, to bring you through them with comfort and honour. *When you go through the fire or water, I will be with you.* In the pulpit, in the prison, *lo, I am with*

you." [2.] To *succeed* this great undertaking; "Lo, *I am with you,* to make your ministry effectual for the discipling of the nations, for the *pulling down* of the strong holds of Satan, and the setting up of stronger for the Lord Jesus." It was an unlikely thing that they should unhinge national constitutions in religion, and turn the stream of so long a usage; that they should *establish* a doctrine so directly contrary to the genius of the age, and persuade people to become the disciples of a *crucified* Jesus; but *lo, I am with you,* and therefore you shall *gain your point.*

(2.) The continuance of the favour, *always, even unto the end of the world.*

[1.] They shall have his *constant* presence; *Always, pasas tas hēmeras — all days,* every day. "I will be with you on sabbath days and week days, fair days and foul days, winter days and summer days." There is no day, no hour of the day, in which our Lord Jesus is not present with his churches and with his ministers; if there were, that day, that hour, they were undone. Since his resurrection he had appeared to them *now and then,* once a week it may be, and scarcely that. But he assures them that they shall have his spiritual presence continued to them without intermission. Wherever we are the word of Christ is nigh us, even *in our mouth,* and the Spirit of Christ nigh us, even *in our hearts.* The *God of Israel,* the *Saviour,* is sometimes *a God that hideth himself* (Isa. 45:15), but never a God that absenteth himself; sometimes *in the dark,* but never *at a distance.*

[2.] They shall have his perpetual presence, even to *the end of the world.* There is a world before us, that will never have an end, but this is hastening towards its period; and even till then the Christian religion shall, in one part of the world or other, be *kept up,* and the presence of Christ continued with his ministers. I am with you *to the end of the world,* not with your persons, they died quickly, but, First, With *you and your writings.* There is a divine power going along with the scripture of the New Testament, not only preserving them in being, but producing strange effects by them, which will continue to the end of time. *Secondly,* With you and *your successors;* with you and all the ministers of the gospel in the several ages of the church; with all to whom this commission extends, with all who, being duly called and sent, thus *baptize* and thus *teach.* When the *end of the world* is come, and the kingdom delivered up to God, even the Father, there will then be no further need of ministers and their ministration; but till then they shall continue, and the great intentions of the institution shall be answered. This is an encouraging word to all the faithful ministers of Christ, that what was said to the apostles, was said to them all, *I will never leave thee, nor forsake thee.*

Two solemn farewells we find our Lord Jesus giving to his church, and his parting word at both of them is very encouraging; one was here, when he closed up his personal converse with them, and then his parting word was, *"Lo, I am with you always;* I leave you, and yet still I am with you;" the other was, when he closed up the canon of the scripture by the pen of his beloved disciple, and then his parting word was, *"Surely, I come quickly.* I leave you for awhile, but I will be with you again shortly," Rev. 22:20. By this it appears that he did not part in anger, but in love, and that it is his will we should keep up both our communion with him and our expectation of him.

There is one word more remaining, which must not be overlooked, and that is *Amen;* which is not a cipher, intended only for a concluding word, like *finis* at the end of a book, but it has its significancy. 1. It bespeaks Christ's confirmation of this promise, *Lo, I am with you.* It is his *Amen,* in whom all the promises are *Yea and Amen, "Verily* I am, and will be, with you; I the Amen, the faithful Witness, do assure you of it." Or, 2. It bespeaks the church's concurrence with it, in their desire, and prayer, and expectation. It is the evangelist's *Amen — So be it,* blessed Lord. Our *Amen* to Christ's promises turns them into prayers. Hath Christ promised to be present with his ministers, present in his word, present in the assemblies of his people, though but two or three are gathered together in his name, and this *always, even to the end of the world?* Let us heartily say *Amen* to it; believe that it *shall be so,* and pray that it *may be so:* Lord, *Remember this word unto thy servants, upon which thou hast caused us to hope.*

AN EXPOSITION, WITH PRACTICAL OBSERVATIONS, OF

THE GOSPEL ACCORDING TO ST. MARK

We have heard the evidence given in by the first witness to the doctrine and miracles of our Lord Jesus; and now here is another witness produced, who calls for our attention. The second *living creature* saith, *Come, and see,* Rev. 6:3. Now let us enquire a little,

I. Concerning *this witness.* His name is *Mark. Marcus* was a Roman name, and a very common one, and yet we have no reason to think, but that he was by birth a Jew; but as Saul, when he went among the nations, took the Roman name of *Paul,* so he of *Mark,* his Jewish name perhaps being *Mardocai;* so Grotius. We read of John whose surname was *Mark,* sister's son to Barnabas, whom Paul was displeased with (Acts 15:37, 38), but afterward had a great kindness for, and not only ordered the churches to receive him (Col. 4:10), but sent for him to be his assistant, with this encomium, *He is profitable to me for the ministry* (2 Tim. 4:11); and he reckons him among his fellow-labourers, Philemon 24. We read of Marcus whom Peter calls his *son,* he having been an instrument of his conversion (1 Pt. 5:13); whether that was the same with the other, and, if not, which of them was the penman of this gospel, is altogether uncertain. It is a tradition very current among the ancients, that St. Mark wrote this gospel under the direction of St. Peter, and that it was confirmed by his authority; so Hieron. Catal. Script. Eccles. *Marcus discipulus et interpres Petri, juxta quod Petrum referentem audierat, legatus Roma à fratribus, breve scripsit evangelium — Mark, the disciple and interpreter of Peter, being sent from Rome by the brethren, wrote a concise gospel;* and Tertullian saith (Adv. Marcion. lib. 4, cap. 5), *Marcus quod edidit, Petri affirmetur, cujus interpres Marcus — Mark, the interpreter of Peter, delivered in writing the things which had been preached by Peter.* But as Dr. Whitby very well suggests, Why should we have recourse to the authority of Peter for the support of this gospel, or say with St. Jerome that Peter approved of it and recommended it by his authority to the church to be read, when, though it is true Mark was no apostle, yet we have all the reason in the world to think that both he and Luke were of the number of the seventy disciples, who *companied with the apostles all along* (Acts 1:21), who had a commission like that of the apostles (Lu. 10:19, compared with Mk. 16:18), and who, it is highly probable, received the Holy Ghost when they did (Acts 1:15; 2:1–4), so that it is no diminution at all to the validity or value of this gospel, that Mark was not one of the twelve, as Matthew and John were? St. Jerome saith that, after the writing of this gospel, he went into Egypt, and was the first that preached the gospel at Alexandria, where he founded a church, to which he was a great example of holy living. *Constituit ecclesiam tantâ doctrinâ et vitae continentiâ ut omnes sectatores Christi ad exemplum sui cogeret — He so adorned, by his doctrine and his life, the church which he founded, that his example influenced all the followers of Christ.*

II. Concerning *this testimony.* Mark's gospel, 1. Is but short, much shorter than Matthew's, not giving so full an account of Christ's sermons as that did, but insisting chiefly on his miracles. 2. It is very much a repetition of what we had in Matthew; many remarkable circumstances being added to the stories there related, but not many new matters. When many witnesses are called to prove the same fact, upon which a judgment is to be given, it is not thought *tedious,* but highly *necessary,* that they should each of them relate it in their own words, again and again, that by the agreement of the testimony the thing may be established; and therefore we must not think this book of scripture needless, for it is written not only to confirm our belief that *Jesus is the Christ the Son of God,* but to put us in mind of things which we have read in the foregoing gospel, that we may *give the more earnest heed to them,* lest at any time we let them slip; and even *pure minds* have need to be *thus stirred up by way of remembrance.* It was fit that such great things as these should be spoken and written, once, yea twice, because man is so *unapt* to *perceive* them, and so *apt* to *forget* them. There is no ground for the tradition, that this gospel was written first in Latin, though it was written at Rome; it was written in Greek, as was St. Paul's epistle to the Romans, the Greek being the more universal language.

CHAPTER 1

Mark's narrative does not take rise so early as those of Matthew and Luke do, from the birth of our Saviour, but from John's baptism, from which he soon passes to Christ's public ministry. Accordingly, in this chapter, we have, I. The office of John Baptist illustrated by the prophecy of him (*v.* 1–3), and by the history of him (*v.* 4–8). II. Christ's baptism, and his being owned from heaven (*v.* 9–11). III. His temptation (*v.* 12, 13). IV. His preaching (*v.* 14, 15, 21, 22, 38, 39). V. His calling disciples (*v.* 16–20). VI. His praying (*v.* 35). VII. His working miracles. 1. His rebuking an unclean spirit (*v.* 23–28). 2. His curing Peter's mother-in-law, who was ill of a fever (*v.* 29–31). 3. His healing all that came to him (*v.* 32, 34). 4. His cleansing a leper (*v.* 40–45).

Verses 1–8

We may observe here,

I. What the New Testament is — the *divine* testament, to which we *adhere* above all that is *human;* the new testament, which we *advance* above that which was old. It is *the gospel of Jesus Christ the Son of God, v.* 1. 1. It is *gospel;* it is God's word, and is *faithful* and *true;* see Rev. 19:9; 21:5; 22:6. It is a *good word,* and well *worthy of all acceptation;* it brings us glad tidings. 2. It is the *gospel of Jesus Christ,* the *anointed Saviour,* the Messiah promised and expected. The foregoing gospel began with the *generation of Jesus Christ* — that was but preliminary, this comes immediately to the business — *the gospel of Christ.* It is called *his,* not only because he is the *Author* of it, and it comes *from him,* but because he is the *Subject of it,* and it treats wholly *concerning him.* 3. This Jesus is the *Son of God.* That truth is the foundation on which the gospel is built, and which it is written to demonstrate; for is Jesus be not *the Son of God,* our *faith is vain.*

II. What the *reference* of the New Testament is to the Old, and its *coherence* with it. The gospel of Jesus Christ *begins,* and so we shall find it *goes on,* just *as it is written in the prophets* (*v.* 2); for it *saith no other things than those which the prophets and Moses said should come* (Acts 26:22), which was most proper and powerful for the conviction of the Jews, who believed the Old-Testament prophets to be sent of God and ought to have *evidenced* that they did so by welcoming the accomplishment of their prophecies in its season; but it is of use to us all, for the confirmation of our faith both in the Old Testament and in the New, for the exact harmony that there is between both shows that they both have the same divine original.

Quotations are here borrowed from two prophecies — that of Isaiah, which was the *longest,* and that of Malachi, which was the *latest* (and there were above three hundred years between them), both of whom spoke to the same purport concerning *the beginning of the gospel of Jesus Christ,* in the ministry of John.

1. Malachi, in whom we had the Old-Testament *farewell,* spoke very plainly (*ch.* 3:1) concerning John Baptist, who was to give the New-Testament *welcome. Behold, I send my messenger before thy face, v.* 2. Christ himself had taken notice of this, and applied it to John (Mt. 11:10), who was God's *messenger,* sent to *prepare Christ's way.*

2. Isaiah, the most evangelical of all the prophets, *begins* the evangelical part of his prophecy with this, which points to the *beginning of the gospel of Christ* (Isa. 40:3); *The voice of him that crieth in the wilderness, v.* 3. Matthew had taken notice of this, and applied it to John, *ch.* 3:3. But from these two put together here, we may observe, (1.) That Christ, in his gospel, *comes among us,* bringing with him a treasure of grace, and a sceptre of government. (2.) Such is the corruption of the world, that there is something to do to *make room* for him, and to remove that which gives not only *obstruction,* but *opposition* to his progress. (3.) When God sent his Son into the world, he *took care,* and when he sends him into the heart, he *takes care,* effectual care, to *prepare his way before him;* for the designs of his grace shall not be *frustrated;* nor may any expect the comforts of that grace, but such as, by conviction of sin and humiliation for it, are *prepared* for those comforts, and disposed to receive them. (4.) When the *paths* that were *crooked,* are *made straight* (the mistakes of the judgment rectified, and the *crooked ways* of the affections), then way is made for Christ's comforts. (5.) It is in a *wilderness,* for such this world is, that *Christ's way* is prepared, and theirs that follow him, like that which Israel passed through to Canaan. (6.) The messengers of conviction and terror, that come to prepare Christ's way, are *God's messengers,* whom he sends and will own, and must be *received* as such. (7.) They that are sent to *prepare the way of the Lord,* in such a vast howling wilderness as this is, have need to *cry aloud,* and not spare, and to *lift up their voice like a trumpet.*

III. What the *beginning* of the New Testament was. The gospel began in John Baptist; for *the law and the prophets were, until John,* the only divine revelation, but then the *kingdom of God began to be preached,* Lu. 16:16. Peter begins *from the baptism of John,* Acts 1:22. The gospel did not begin *so soon* as the *birth* of Christ, for he took time to *increase in wisdom and stature,* not so late as his entering upon his public ministry, but half a year before, when John began to preach the same doctrine that Christ afterward preached. His baptism was the dawning of the *gospel day;* for,

1. In John's way of *living* there was the beginning of a *gospel spirit;* for it bespoke great self-denial, mortification of the flesh, a holy contempt of the world, and nonconformity to it, which may truly be called the *beginning of the gospel of Christ* in any soul, *v.* 6. He was *clothed with camels' hair,* not with soft raiment; was girt, not with a golden, but with a *leathern girdle;* and, in contempt of dainties and delicate things, his meat was *locusts and wild honey.* Note, The more we sit loose to the body, and live above the world, the better we are prepared for Jesus Christ.

2. In John's *preaching* and *baptizing* there was the *beginning* of the *gospel doctrines and ordinances,* and the first fruits of them. (1.) He preached the *remission of sins,* which is the great gospel privilege; showed people their *need* of it, that they were *undone* without it, and that it might be obtained. (2.) He preached *repentance,* in order to it; he told people that there must be a renovation of their hearts and a reformation of their lives, that they must forsake their sins and turn to God, and upon those terms and no other, their sins should be forgiven. *Repentance for the remission of sins,* was what the apostles were commissioned to *preach to all nations,* Lu. 24:27. (3.) He preached Christ, and directed his hearers to *expect him* speedily to appear, and to *expect great things* from him. The preaching of Christ is pure gospel, and that was John Baptist's preaching, *v.* 7, 8. Like a true gospel minister, he preaches, [1.] The great *pre-eminence* Christ is *advanced to;* so high, so great, is Christ, that John, though one of the greatest that was born of women, thinks himself unworthy to be employed in the meanest office about him, even to *stoop down,* and *untie his shoes.* Thus industrious is he to give honour to him, and to bring others to do so too. [2.] The great *power* Christ is *invested with;* He *comes after me* in time, but he is *mightier than I,* mightier than the mighty ones of the earth, for he is able to *baptize with the Holy Ghost;* he can *give* the Spirit of God, and by him *govern* the spirits of men. [3.] The great *promise* Christ makes in his gospel to those who have *repented,* and have had their sins forgiven them; They shall be *baptized with* the Holy Ghost, shall be *purified* by his graces, and *refreshed* by his comforts. And, *lastly,* All those who received his doctrine, and submitted to his institution, he *baptized with water,* as the manner of the Jews was to admit proselytes, in token of their *cleansing themselves* by repentance and reformation (which were the duties required), and of God's *cleansing them* both by remis-

sion and by sanctification, which were the blessings promised. Now this was afterward to be advanced into a gospel ordinance, which John's using it was a preface to.

3. In the success of John's preaching, and the disciples he admitted by baptism, there was the *beginning of a gospel church.* He baptized *in the wilderness,* and declined going into the cities; but *there went out unto him all the land of Judea, and they of Jerusalem,* inhabitants both of city and country, families of them, and *were all baptized of him.* They entered themselves his disciples, and bound themselves to his discipline; in token of which, they *confessed their sins;* he admitted them his disciples, in token of which, he *baptized* them. Here were the stamina of the gospel church, the *dew of its youth* from *the womb of the morning,* Ps. 110:3. Many of these afterward became followers of Christ, and preachers of his gospel, and this grain of mustard-seed became a *tree.*

Verses 9–13

We have here a brief account of Christ's baptism and temptation, which were largely related Mt. 3 and 4.

I. His *baptism,* which was his first public appearance, after he had long lived obscurely *in Nazareth.* O how much *hidden worth* is there, which in this world is either lost in the dust of contempt and *cannot* be known, or wrapped up in the veil of humility and *will not* be known! But sooner or later it *shall be* known, as Christ's was.

1. See how *humbly* he *owned* God, by coming to be *baptized of John;* and thus *it became him to fulfil all righteousness.* Thus he *took upon him the likeness of sinful flesh,* that, though he was perfectly pure and unspotted, yet he was *washed* as if he had been *polluted;* and thus *for our sakes he sanctified himself, that we also might be sanctified,* and be baptized with him, Jn. 17:19.

2. See how *honourably* God owned him, when he submitted to John's *baptism.* Those who *justify God,* and *they* are said to do, who were *baptized with the baptism* of John, he will *glorify,* Lu. 7:29, 30.

(1.) He *saw the heavens opened;* thus he was owned to be the Lord from heaven, and had a glimpse of the glory and joy that were *set before him,* and *secured* to him, as the recompence of his undertaking. Matthew saith, *The heavens were opened to him.* Mark saith, *He saw them opened.* Many have the heavens opened to receive them, but they do not see it; Christ had not only a clear foresight of his sufferings, but of his glory too.

(2.) He *saw the Spirit like a dove descending upon him.* Note, *Then* we may see heaven opened to us, when we perceive the Spirit *descending* and working upon us. God's good work in us is the surest evidence of his good will towards us, and his preparations for us. Justin Martyr says, that *when Christ was baptized, a fire was kindled in Jordan:* and it is an ancient tradition, that *a great light shone round the place;* for the Spirit brings both *light* and *heat.*

(3.) He heard a voice which was intended for his encouragement to proceed in his undertaking, and therefore it is here expressed as directed *to him, Thou art my beloved Son.* God lets him know, [1.] That he *loved him* never the *less* for that *low* and *mean* estate to which he had now *humbled himself;* "Though thus emptied and made of no reputation, yet he is my *beloved Son* still." [2.] That he *loved him* much the *more* for that *glorious* and *kind* undertaking in which he had now *engaged himself.* God is *well pleased* in him, as referee of all matters in controversy between him and man; and so well pleased in him, as to be well pleased *with us* in him.

II. His *temptation.* The *good Spirit* that descended upon him, *led him into the wilderness, v.* 12. Paul mentions it as a proof that he had his doctrine from God, and not from man — that, as soon as he was called, he *went not to Jerusalem,* but *went into Arabia,* Gal. 1:17. Retirement from the world is an opportunity of more free converse with God, and therefore must sometimes be chosen, for a while, even by those that are called to the greatest business. Mark observes this circumstance of his being *in the wilderness* — that he was *with the wild beasts.* It was an instance of his Father's care of him, that he was preserved from being torn in pieces by the wild beasts, which encouraged him the more that his Father would provide for him when he was hungry. Special protections are earnests of seasonable supplies. It was likewise an intimation to him of the inhumanity of the men of that generation, whom he was to live among — no better than *wild beasts* in the *wilderness,* nay abundantly worse. In that wilderness,

1. The *evil spirits* were *busy with him;* he *was tempted of Satan;* not by any inward injections (the prince of this world had *nothing in him* to fasten upon), but by outward solicitations. Solicitude often gives advantages to the tempter, therefore *two are better than one.* Christ himself was tempted, not only to teach us, that *it is no sin to be tempted,* but to direct us whither to go for succour when we are tempted, even to him that *suffered,* being *tempted;* that he might experimentally sympathize with us when we are *tempted.*

2. The *good spirits* were *busy about him;* the *angels ministered to him,* supplied him with what he needed, and dutifully attended him. Note, The ministration of the good angels about us, is matter of great comfort in reference to the malicious designs of the evil angels against us; but much more doth it befriend us, to have the indwelling of the spirit in our hearts, which they that have, are so *born of God,* that, as far as they are so, *the evil one toucheth them not,* much less shall be *triumph* over them.

Verses 14–22

Here is, I. A general account of Christ's preaching in Galilee. John gives an account of his preaching in Judea, before this (*ch.* 2 and 3), which the other evangelists had omitted, who chiefly relate what occurred in Galilee, because that was least known at Jerusalem. Observe,

1. When Jesus began to preach in Galilee; *After that John was put in prison.* When he had *finished* his testimony, then Jesus *began* his. Note, The silencing of Christ's ministers shall not be the suppressing of Christ's gospel; if some be laid aside, others shall be raised up, perhaps mightier than they, to carry on the same work.

2. What he preached; *The gospel of the kingdom of God.* Christ came to set up the kingdom of God among men, that they might be brought into *subjection to it,* and might obtain *salvation in it;* and he set it up by the preaching of his gospel, and a power going along with it.

Observe, (1.) The great *truths* Christ preached; *The time is fulfilled, and the kingdom of God is at hand.* This refers to the Old Testament, in which the kingdom of the Messiah was promised, and the time fixed for the introducing of it. They were not so well versed in those prophecies, nor did they so well observe the signs of the times, as to understand it themselves, and therefore Christ gives them notice of it; "The time prefixed is now *at hand;* glorious discoveries of divine light, life, and love, are now to be made; a new dispensation far more spiritual and heavenly than that which you have hitherto been under, is now to commence." Note, God keeps time; when *the time is fulfilled,* the *kingdom of God is at hand,* for the vision is *for an appointed time,* which will be punctually observed, though it tarry past our time.

(2.) The great *duties* inferred from thence. Christ gave them to *understand the times,* that they might know *what Israel ought to do;* they fondly expected the Messiah to appear in external pomp and power, not only to free the Jewish nation from the Roman yoke, but to make it have dominion over all its neighbours, and therefore thought, when that *kingdom of God* was *at hand,* they must prepare for war, and for victory and preferment, and great things in the world; but Christ tells them, in the prospect of that kingdom approaching, they must *repent, and believe the gospel.* They had broken the *moral law,* and could not be saved by a *covenant of innocency,* for both Jew and Gentile are concluded *under guilt.* They must therefore take the benefit of a *covenant of grace,* must submit to a *remedial law,* and this is it — *repentance towards God, and faith towards our Lord Jesus Christ.* They had not made use of the prescribed preservatives, and therefore must have recourse to the prescribed restoratives. By repentance we must lament and forsake our sins, and by faith we must receive the forgiveness of them. By repentance we must give glory to our Creator whom we have offended; by faith we must give glory to our Redeemer who came to *save us from our sins.* Both these must go together; we must not think either that reforming our lives will save us without trusting in the righteousness and grace of Christ, or that trusting in Christ will save us without the reformation of our hearts and lives. Christ hath joined these two together, and let no man think to put them asunder. They will mutually assist and befriend each other. Repentance will quicken faith, and faith will make repentance evangelical; and the sincerity of both together must be evidenced by a diligent conscientious obedience to all God's commandments. Thus the preaching of the gospel began, and thus it continues; still the call is, Repent, and believe, and live a *life of repentance* and a *life of faith.*

II. Christ appearing as a teacher, here is next his *calling of disciples, v.* 16–20. Observe, 1. Christ will have followers. If he set up a school, he will have scholars; if he set up his standard, he will have soldiers; if he preach, he will have hearers. He has taken an effectual course to secure this; for *all that the Father has given him, shall,* without fail, *come to him.* 2. The instruments Christ chose to employ in setting up his kingdom, were the *weak* and *foolish things of the world;* not called from the great sanhedrim, or the schools of the rabbin, but picked up from among the tarpaulins *by the seaside, that the excellency of the power* might appear to be wholly *of God,* and not at all *of them.* 3. Though Christ needs not the help of man, yet he is pleased to make use of it in setting up his kingdom, that he might deal with us not in a formidable but in a familiar way, and that in his kingdom the *nobles and governors may be of ourselves,* Jer. 31:21. 4. Christ puts honour upon those who, though mean in the world, are *diligent in their business,* and *loving to one another;* so those were, whom Christ called. He found them *employed,* and employed *together. Industry* and unity are *good* and *pleasant,* and there the Lord Jesus commands the blessing, even this blessing, *Follow me.* 5. The business of ministers is to *fish for souls,* and *win them to Christ.* The children of men, in their natural condition, are lost, wander endlessly in the great ocean of this world, and are carried down the stream of its course and way; they are unprofitable. Like leviathan in the waters, they *play therein;* and often, like the fishes of the sea, they devour one another. Ministers, in preaching the gospel, *cast the net* into the waters, Mt. 13:47. Some are enclosed and brought to shore, but far the greater number escape. *Fishermen* take great pains, and expose themselves to great perils, so do *ministers;* and they have need of wisdom. If many a draught brings home nothing, yet they must go on. 6. Those whom Christ called, must *leave all,* to follow him; and by his grace he inclines them to do so. *Not that we must needs go out of the world* immediately, but we must sit loose to the world, and forsake every thing that is inconsistent with our duty to Christ, and that cannot be kept without prejudice to our souls. Mark takes notice of James and John, that they left not only *their father* (which we had in Matthew), but *the hired servants,* whom perhaps they loved as their own brethren, being their *fellow-labourers* and pleasant comrades; not only relations, but companions, must be left for Christ, and old acquaintance. Perhaps it is an intimation of their care for their father; they did not leave him without assistance, they left the *hired servants* with him. Grotius thinks it is mentioned as an evidence that their calling was gainful to them, for it was worth while to keep servants in pay, to help them in it, and their *hands* would be much *missed,* and yet they *left it.*

III. Here is a particular account of his preaching in Capernaum, one of the *cities* of Galilee; for though John Baptist chose to preach *in a wilderness,* and did *well,* and did *good,* yet it doth not therefore follow, that Jesus must do so too; the inclinations and opportunities of ministers may very much differ, and yet both be in the *way of their duty,* and both useful. Observe, 1. When Christ *came into Capernaum,* he *straightway* applied himself to his work there, and took the *first* opportunity of preaching the gospel. Those will think themselves concerned not to *lose time,* who consider what a deal of work they have to do, and what a little time to do it in. 2. Christ religiously observed the sabbath day, though not by tying himself up to the tradition of the elders, in all the niceties of the *sabbath-rest,* yet (which was far better) by applying himself to, and abounding in, the *sabbath-work,* in order to which the sabbath-rest was instituted. 3. Sabbaths are to be sanctified in *religious assemblies,* if we have opportunity; it is a *holy day,* and must be honoured with a *holy convocation;* this was the *good old way,* Acts 13:27; 15:21. On the sabbath-day, *pois sabbasin — on the sabbath-days;* every sabbath-day, as duly as it returned, he *went into the synagogue.* 4. In *religious assemblies* on sabbath-days, the gospel is to be preached, and those to be *taught,* who are willing to learn the *truth as it is in Jesus.* 5. Christ was a nonsuch preacher; he did not preach *as the scribes,* who expounded the law of Moses by rote, as a school-boy says his lesson, but were neither *acquainted* with it (Paul himself, when a Pharisee, was ignorant of the law), nor *affected* with it; it came not *from the heart,* and therefore came not *with authority.*

But Christ taught *as one that had authority,* as one that knew the mind of God, and was commissioned to declare it. 6. There is much in the doctrine of Christ, that is *astonishing;* the more we hear it, the more cause we shall see to *admire it.*

Verses 23–28

As soon as Christ began to preach, he began to work miracles for the confirmation of his doctrine; and they were such as intimated the design and tendency of his doctrine, which were to conquer Satan, and cure sick souls.

In these verses, we have,

I. Christ's *casting the devil* out of a man that was possessed, in the synagogue at Capernaum. This passage was not related in Matthew, but is afterward in Lu. 4:33. *There was in the synagogue a man with an unclean spirit, en pneumati akathartō — in an unclean spirit;* for the spirit had the man in his possession, and led him captive at his will. So the whole world is said to lie *en tō ponerō — in the wicked one.* And some have thought it more proper to say, The *body* is *in the soul,* because it is governed by it, than the soul *in the body.* He was *in the unclean* spirit, as a man is said to be *in a fever,* or in a frenzy, quite overcome by it. Observe, The devil is here called *an unclean spirit,* because he has lost all the purity of his nature, because he acts in direct opposition to the *Holy* Spirit of God, and because with his suggestions he pollutes the spirits of men. This man *was in the synagogue;* he did not come either to be taught or to be healed, but, as some think, to confront Christ and oppose him, and hinder people from believing on him. Now here we have,

1. The rage which the unclean spirit expressed at Christ; *He cried out,* as one in an agony, at the presence of Christ, and afraid of being dislodged; thus the *devils believe and tremble,* have a horror of Christ, but no hope in him, nor reverence for him. We are told what he said, *v.* 24, where he doth not go about to *capitulate* with him, or *make terms* (so far was he from being in league or compact with him), but speaks as one that knew his doom. (1.) He calls him *Jesus of Nazareth;* for aught that appears, he was the first that called him so, and he did it with design to possess the minds of the people with *low thoughts* of him, because no good thing was expected out of Nazareth; and with *prejudices* against him as a Deceiver, because every body knew the Messiah must be of Bethlehem. (2.) Yet a confession is extorted from him — that he is *the holy One of God,* as was from the damsel that had the spirit of divination concerning the apostles — that they were the *servants of the most high God,* Acts 16:16, 17. Those who have only a *notion* of Christ — that he is the *holy One of God,* and have no faith in him, or love to him, go no further than the devil doth. (3.) He in effect acknowledgeth that Christ was too hard for him, and that he could not stand before the power of Christ; *"Let us alone;* for if thou take us to task, we are undone, thou canst *destroy us."* This is the misery of those wicked spirits, that they persist in their rebellion, and yet know it will end in their destruction. (4.) He desires to have *nothing to do* with Jesus Christ; for he *despairs* of being *saved* by him, and *dreads* being *destroyed* by him. *"What have we to do with thee?* If thou wilt let us alone, we will let thee alone." See whose language they speak, that *say to the Almighty, Depart from us.* This, being an *unclean spirit,* therefore hated and dreaded Christ, because he knew him to be a *holy One;* for the *carnal mind is enmity against God,* especially against *his holiness.*

2. The victory which Jesus Christ obtained over the unclean spirit; *for this purpose was the Son of God manifested, that he might destroy the works of the devil,* and so he makes it to appear; nor will he be turned back from prosecuting this war, either by his flatteries or by his menaces. It is in vain for Satan to beg and pray, *Let us alone;* his power must be broken, and the poor man must be relieved; and therefore, (1.) Jesus *commands.* As he taught, so he healed, *with authority.* Jesus *rebuked him;* he chid him and threatened him, imposed silence upon him; *Hold thy peace; phimōthēti — be muzzled.* Christ has a muzzle for that unclean spirit when he *fawns* as well as when he *barks;* such acknowledgments of him as this was, Christ *disdains,* so far is he from *accepting* them. Some confess Christ to be the *holy One of God,* that under the cloak of that profession they may carry on malicious mischievous designs; but their confession is doubly an abomination to the Lord Jesus, as it sues in his name for a license to sin, and shall therefore be put to silence and shame. But this is not all, he must not only *hold his peace,* but he must *come out of the man;* this was it he dreaded — his being restrained from doing further mischief. But, (2.) The unclean spirit *yields,* for there is no remedy (*v.* 26); He *tore him,* put him into a *strong convulsion;* that one could have thought he had been pulled in pieces; when he would not *touch* Christ, in fury at him he grievously disturbed this poor creature. Thus, when Christ by his grace delivers poor souls out of the hands of Satan, it is not without a grievous toss and tumult in the soul; for that spiteful enemy will *disquiet* those whom he cannot *destroy.* He *cried with a loud voice,* to frighten the spectators, and make himself seem terrible, as if he would have it thought that though he was conquered, he was but just conquered, and that he hopes to rally again, and recover his ground.

II. The impression which this miracle made upon the minds of the people, *v.* 27, 28.

1. It astonished them that saw it; *They were all amazed.* It was evident, beyond contradiction, that the man was possessed — witness the tearing of him, and the *loud voice* with which the *spirit cried;* it was evident that he was *forced out* by the authority of Christ; this was surprising to them, and put them upon considering with themselves, and enquiring of one another, *"What is this new doctrine?* For it must certainly be of God, which is thus confirmed. *He* hath certainly an authority to command us, who hath ability to *command even the unclean spirits,* and they cannot resist him, but are forced *to obey him."* The Jewish exorcists pretended by charm or invocation to drive away evil spirits; but this was quite another thing, *with authority he commands them.* Surely it is our interest to make *him* our Friend, who has the control of infernal spirits.

2. It raised his reputation among all that heard it; *Immediately his fame spread abroad into the whole adjacent region of Galilee,* which was a third part of the land of Canaan. The story was presently got into every one's mouth, and people wrote it to their friends all the country over, together with the remark made upon it, *What new doctrine is this?* So that it was universally concluded, that he was a *Teacher come from God,* and under that character he shone more bright than if he had appeared in all the external pomp and power which the Jews expected their Messiah to *appear* in; and thus he *prepared his own way,* now that John, who was his harbinger, was clapped up; and the fame of this miracle spread the further, because as yet the Pharisees, who *envied* his fame, and laboured to *eclipse* it, had not advanced their blasphemous suggestion, that he *cast out devils* by compact with the *prince of the devils.*

Verses 29–39

In these verses, we have,

I. A particular account of one miracle that Christ wrought, in the cure of Peter's wife's mother, who was ill of a fever. This passage we had before, in Matthew. Observe,

1. When Christ had done that which *spread his fame* throughout all parts, he did not then sit still, as some think that they may *lie in bed* when their *name is up.* No, he continued to *do good,* for that was it he aimed at, and not his own honour. Nay, those who are in reputation, had need be busy and careful to keep it up.

2. When he *came out of the synagogue,* where he had taught and healed with a divine authority, yet he conversed familiarly with the poor fishermen that attended him, and did not think it below him. Let the same mind, the same lowly mind, be in us, that was in him.

3. He went into Peter's house, probably invited thither to such entertainment as a poor fisherman could give him, and he accepted of it. The apostles left all for Christ; so far as that what they had should not hinder them from him, yet not so, but that they might use it for him.

4. He cured his mother-in-law, who was sick. Wherever Christ comes, he comes to do good, and will be sure to pay richly for his entertainment. Observe, How complete the cure was; when *the fever left her,* it did not, as usual, leave her *weak,* but the same hand that *healed* her, *strengthened* her, so that she was able to *minister* to them; the cure is in order to that, to fit for action, that we may minister to Christ, and to those that are *his* for his sake.

II. A general account of many cures he wrought — diseases healed, devils expelled. It was on the *evening of the sabbath,* when the *sun did set,* or *was set;* perhaps many scrupled bringing their sick to him, till the sabbath was over, but their weakness therein was no prejudice to them in applying to Christ. Though he proved it *lawful to heal on the sabbath days,* yet, if any stumbled at it, they were welcome at another time. Now observe,

1. How *numerous* the patients were; *All the city was gathered at the door,* as beggars for a dole. That *one cure* in the synagogue occasioned this crowding after him. Others speeding well with Christ should quicken us in our enquiries after him. Now the *Sun of righteousness rises with healing under his wings;* to him shall the *gathering of the people be.* Observe, How Christ was flocked after in a *private house,* as well as in the *synagogue;* wherever he is, there let his servants, his patients, be. And in the *evening of the sabbath,* when the public worship is over, we must continue our attendance upon Jesus Christ; he healed, as Paul preached, publicly, and from house to house.

2. How *powerful* the Physician was; he *healed all* that were brought to him, though ever so many. Nor was it some one particular disease, that Christ set up for the cure of, but he healed those that were *sick of divers* diseases, for his word was a *panpharmacon — a salve for every sore.* And that miracle particularly which he wrought in the synagogue, he *repeated in the house* at night; for he *cast out many devils,* and *suffered not the devils to speak,* for he made them *know who he was,* and that silenced them. Or, He *suffered them not to say that they knew him* (so it may be read); he would not permit any more of them to say, as they did (*v.* 24), *I know thee, who thou art.*

III. His *retirement* to his *private devotion* (*v.* 35); *He prayed,* prayed alone; to set us an example of secret prayer. Though as God he was *prayed to,* as man he *prayed.* Though he was glorifying God, and doing good, in his public work, yet he found time to be alone with his Father; and thus *it became him to fulfil all righteousness.* Now observe,

1. The time *when* Christ prayed. (1.) It was *in the morning,* the morning after the *sabbath day.* Note, When a sabbath day is over and past, we must not think that we may intermit our devotion till the next sabbath: no, though we go not *to the synagogue,* we must go to the *throne of grace,* every day in the week; and the morning after the sabbath particularly, that we may preserve the good impressions of the day. This *morning* was the morning of the *first day of the week,* which afterward he sanctified, and made remarkable, by another sort of *rising early.* (2.) It was early, *a great while before day.* When others were asleep in their beds, he was *praying,* as a genuine Son of David, who seeks God *early,* and *directs his prayer in the morning;* nay, and *at midnight will rise to give thanks.* It has been said, *The morning is a friend to the Muses — Aurora Musis amica;* and it is no less so to the *Graces.* When our spirits are most fresh and lively, then we should take time for *devout* exercises. He that is the *first* and *best,* ought to have the *first* and *best.*

2. The place *where* he prayed; He *departed into a solitary place,* either out of town, or some remote garden or outbuilding. Though he was in no danger of distraction, or of temptation to vain-glory, yet he retired, to set us an example to his own rule, *When thou prayest enter into thy closet.* Secret prayer must be made secretly. Those that have the most business in public, and of the best kind, must sometimes be *alone with God;* must retire into *solitude,* there to converse with God, and keep up communion with him.

IV. His *return* to his *public* work. The disciples thought they were *up early,* but found their Master was up *before them,* and they enquired which way he went, *followed him* to his *solitary place,* and there *found him* at prayer, *v.* 36, 37. They told him that he was much wanted, that there were a great many patients waiting for him; *All men seek for thee.* They were proud that their Master was become so popular already, and would have him appear *in public,* yet more in that place, because it was *their own city;* and we are apt to be partial to the places we know and are interested in. "No," saith Christ, "Capernaum must not have the monopoly of the Messiah's preaching and miracles. *Let us go into the next towns,* the *villages* that lie about here, *that I may preach there also,* and work miracles there, *for therefore came I forth,* not to be constantly resident in one place, but to *go about doing good."* Even the *inhabitants of the villages in Israel* shall *rehearse the righteous acts of the Lord,* Jdg. 5:11. Observe, Christ had still an eye to the end *wherefore he came forth,* and closely pursued that; nor will he be drawn by importunity, or the persuasions of his friends, to decline from that; for (*v.* 39) he *preached in their synagogues throughout all Galilee,* and, to illustrate and confirm his doctrine, *he cast out devils.* Note, Christ's doctrine is Satan's destruction.

Verses 40–45

We have here the story of Christ's *cleansing a leper,* which we had before, Mt. 8:2–4. It teaches us,

1. *How to apply ourselves to Christ;* come as this leper did, (1.) With great *humility;* this leper came *beseeching him, and kneeling down to him* (*v.* 40); whether giving divine honour to him as God, or rather a less degree of respect as a *great Prophet,* it teaches us that those who would receive grace and mercy from Christ, must ascribe honour and glory to Christ, and approach to him with humility and reverence. (2.) With a firm belief of *his power; Thou canst make me clean.* Though Christ's outward appearance was but *mean,* yet he had this faith in his power, which implies his belief that he was *sent of God.* He believes it with application, not only in general, *Thou cast do every thing* (as Jn. 11:22), but, *Thou cast make me clean.* Note, What we believe of the power of Christ we must bring home to our particular case; *Thou canst do this for me.* (3.) With submission to the will of Christ; *Lord, if thou wilt.* Not as if he had any doubt of Christ's readiness in general to help the distressed, but, with the modesty that became a poor petitioner, he refers his own particular case to him.

2. *What to expect from Christ;* that according to our faith it shall be to us. His address is not in the form of prayer, yet Christ answered it as a request. Note, Affectionate professions of faith in Christ, and resignations to him, are the most prevailing petitions for mercy from him, and shall speed accordingly. (1.) Christ was *moved with compassion.* This is added here, in Mark, to show that Christ's power is employed by his pity for the relief of poor souls; that his reasons are fetched from within himself, and we have nothing in us to recommend us to his favour, but our *misery* makes us the objects of his *mercy.* And what he does for us he does with all possible tenderness. (2.) He *put forth his hand, and touched him.* He *exerted* his power, and directed it to *this* creature. In healing souls, Christ *toucheth them,* 1 Sa. 10:26. When the queen toucheth for the evil, she saith, *I touch, God heals;* but Christ *toucheth and healeth too.* (3.) He said, *I will, be thou clean.* Christ's power was put forth in and by a *word,* to signify in what way Christ would ordinarily work spiritual cures; *He sends his word and heals,* Ps. 107:20; Jn. 15:3; 17:17. The poor leper put an *if* upon the will of Christ; *If thou wilt;* but that *doubt* is soon put *out of doubt; I will.* Christ most readily *wills* favours to those that most readily *refer themselves* to his will. He was confident of Christ's *power;* Thou *canst make me clean;* and Christ will show how much his power is drawn out into act by the faith of his people, and therefore speaks the word as one having authority, *Be thou clean.* And power accompanied this word, and the cure was perfect in an instant; *Immediately his leprosy* vanished, and there remained no more sign of it, *v.* 42.

3. *What to do when we have received mercy from Christ.* We must with his favours receive his commands. When Christ had cured him, *he strictly charged him;* the word here is very significant, *embrimēsamenos — graviter interminatus — prohibiting with threats.* I am apt to think that this refers not to the directions he gave him to conceal it (*v.* 44), for those are mentioned by themselves; but that this was such a charge as he gave to the impotent man whom he cured, Jn. 5:14, *Sin no more, lest a worse thing come unto thee;* for the *leprosy* was ordinarily the punishment of some particular sinners, as in Miriam's, Gehazi's, and Uzziah's, case; now, when Christ healed him, he *warned* him, he *threatened* him with the fatal consequence of it if he should *return to sin* again. He also appointed him, (1.) To *show himself to the priest,* that the priest by his own judgment of this leper might be a witness for Christ, that he was the Messiah, Mt. 11:5. (2.) Till he had done that, not to *say any thing* of it *to any man:* this is an instance of the *humility* of Christ and his self-denial, that he did not seek his own honour, *did not strive or cry,* Is. 42:2. And it is an example to us, not to *seek our own glory,* Prov. 25:27. He must not *proclaim* it, because that would much increase the crowd that followed Christ, which he thought was too great already; not as if he were unwilling to *do good to all,* to as many as came; but he would do it with as little *noise* as might be, would have no offence given to the government, no disturbance of the public peace, not any thing done that looked like ostentation, or an affecting of popular applause. What to think of the leper's *publishing* it, and *blazing it abroad,* I know not; the concealment of the good characters and good works of good men better become *them* than *their friends;* nor are we always bound by the modest commands of humble men. The leper ought to have observed his orders; yet, no doubt, it was with a good design that he *proclaimed* the cure, and it had no other ill effect than that it increased the multitudes which followed Christ, to that degree, that he *could no more openly enter into the city;* not upon the account of persecution (there was no danger of that yet,) but because the crowd was so great, that the streets would not hold them, which obliged him to go into *desert places,* to a *mountain* (*ch.* 3:13), to the *sea-side, ch.* 4:1. This shows how *expedient* it was for us, that Christ should *go away,* and *send the Comforter,* for his bodily presence could be but in one place at a time; and those that *came to him from every quarter,* could not get *near him;* but by his spiritual presence he is with his people wherever they are, and comes to them to *every quarter.*

CHAPTER 2

In this chapter, we have, I. Christ's healing a man that was sick of a palsy (*v.* 1–12). II. His calling of Matthew from the receipt of custom, and his eating, upon that occasion, with publicans and sinners, and justifying himself in so doing (*v.* 13–17). III. His justifying his disciples in not fasting so much as those plucking the ears of corn on the sabbath day (*v.* 23–28). All which passages we had before, Mt. 9 and 12.

Verses 1–12

Christ, having been for some time preaching about in the country, here returns to Capernaum his head-quarters, and makes his appearance there, in hopes that by this time the talk and crowd would be somewhat abated. Now observe,

I. The great resort there was to him. Though he was *in the house,* wither Peter's house, or some lodgings of his own which he had taken, yet people came to him as soon as it was *noised* that he was in town; they did not stay till he appeared in the synagogue, which they might be sure he would do on the *sabbath day,* but *straightway many were gathered together to him.* Where the king is, there is the court; where Shiloh is, there *shall the gathering of the people be.* In improving opportunities for our souls, we must take care not to *lose time.* One invited another (Come, let us go see Jesus), so that his house could not contain his visitants. *There was no room to receive them,* they were so numerous, *no not so much as about the door.* A blessed sight, to see people thus flying like a cloud to Christ's house, though it was but a poor one, and *as the doves to their windows!*

II. The good entertainment Christ gave them, the best his house would afford, and better than any other could; he *preached the word unto them, v.* 2. Many of them perhaps came only for cures, and many perhaps only for curiosity, to get a sight of him; but when he had them together he *preached to them.* Though the synagogue-door was open to him at proper times, he thought it not at all amiss to preach in a house, on a week day; though some might reckon it both an improper place and an improper time. *Blessed are ye that sow beside all waters,* Isa. 32:20.

III. The presenting of a poor cripple to him, to be helped by him. The patient was one *sick of the palsy,* it should seem not as that, Mt. 8:6, *grievously tormented,* but perfectly disabled, so that he was *borne of four,* was carried upon *a bed,* as if he had been upon *a bier,* by four persons. It was his misery, that he needed to be so carried, and bespeaks the calamitous state of human life; it was their charity, who did so carry him, and bespeaks the compassion that it is justly expected should be in the children of men toward their fellow-creatures in distress, because we know not how soon the distress may be *our own.* These kind relations or neighbours thought, if they could but carry this poor man once to Christ, they should not need to carry him any more; and therefore made hard shift to get him to him; and when they could not otherwise get to him, they *uncovered the roof where he was, v.* 4. I see no necessity to conclude that Christ was preaching in an *upper room,* though in such the Jews that had stately houses, had their oratories; for then to what purpose should the crowd stand *before the door,* as wisdom's clients used to do? Prov. 8:34. But I rather conjecture that the house he was in, was so little and mean (agreeable to his present state), that it had no *upper room,* but the *ground-floor* was open to the roof: and these petitioners for the poor paralytic, resolving not to be disappointed, when they could not get through the crowd at the door, got their friend by some means or other to the roof of the house, took off some of the tiles, and so let him down upon his bed with cords into the house where Christ was preaching. This bespoke both their *faith* and their *fervency* in this address to Christ. Hereby it appeared that they were in earnest, and would not go away, nor *let Christ go without a blessing.* Gen. 32:26.

IV. The kind word Christ said to this poor patient; *He saw their faith;* perhaps not so much his, for his distemper hindered him from the exercise of faith, but *theirs* that brought him. In curing the centurion's servant, Christ took notice of it as an instance of *his faith,* that he did not bring him to Christ, but believed he could cure him at a distance; here he commended *their faith,* because they did bring their friend through so much difficulty. Note, True faith and strong faith may work variously, conquering sometimes the objections of reason, sometimes those of sense; but, however manifested, it shall be accepted and approved by Jesus Christ. Christ said, *Son, thy sins be forgiven thee.* The *compellation* is very *tender — Son;* intimating a fatherly *care* of him and *concern* for him. Christ owns true believers as his sons: *a son,* and yet sick of the palsy. Herein God *deals with you as with sons.* The *cordial* is very rich; *Thy sins are forgiven thee.* Note, 1. Sin is the procuring cause of all our pains and sicknesses. The word of Christ was to take his thoughts off from the disease, which was the effect, and to lead them to the sin, the cause, that he might be more concerned about that, to get that pardoned. 2. God doth *then* graciously take away the sting and malignity of sickness, when he forgives sin; recovery from sickness is *then* a mercy indeed, when way is made for it by the pardon of sin. See Isa. 38:17; Ps. 103:3. The way to remove the effect, is, to take away the cause. Pardon of sin strikes at the root of all diseases, and either cures them, or alters their property.

V. The cavil of the scribes at that which Christ said, and a demonstration of the unreasonableness of their cavil. They were expositors of the law, and their doctrine was *true* — that it is blasphemy for any creature to undertake the pardon of sin, and that it is God's prerogative, Isa. 43:25. But, as is usual with such teachers, their application was *false,* and was the effect of their ignorance and enmity to Christ. It is *true, None can forgive sins but God only;* but it is false that therefore Christ cannot, who had abundantly proved himself to have a divine power. But Christ *perceived in his spirit that they so reasoned within themselves;* this proves him to be God, and therefore confirmed what was to be proved, that he had authority to *forgive sins;* for he *searched* the heart, and knew *what was in man,* Rev. 2:23. God's royalties are inseparable, and he that could *know thoughts,* could *forgive sins.* This magnifies the grace of Christ, in *pardoning sin,* that he knew men's thoughts, and therefore knows more than any other can know, both of the sinfulness of their sins and the particulars of them, and yet is ready to pardon. Now he proves his power to *forgive sin,* by demonstrating his power to cure the *man sick of the palsy, v.* 9–11. He would not have pretended to do *the one,* if he could not have done *the other; that ye may know that the Son of man,* the Messiah, *has power on earth to forgive sin,* that I have that power, *Thou that art* sick of the palsy, *arise, take up thy bed.* Now, 1. This was a *suitable* argument in itself. He could not have cured the disease, which was the effect, if he could not have taken away the sin, which was the cause. And besides, his curing diseases was a figure of his pardoning sin, for sin is the disease of the soul; when it is pardoned, it is healed. He that could by a word accomplish the sign, could doubtless perform the thing signified, 2. It was suited to them. These carnal scribes would be more affected with such a suitable effect of a pardon as the cure of the disease, and be sooner convinced by it, than by any other more spiritual consequences; therefore it was proper enough to appeal, whether it is easier to say, *Thy sins are forgiven thee,* or to say, *Arise, and walk?* The removing of the punishment as such, was the remitting of the sin; he that could go so far in the cure, no doubt could perfect it. See Isa. 33:24.

VI. The cure of the sick man, and the impression it made upon the people, *v.* 12. He not only *arise* out of his bed, perfectly well, but, to show that he had perfect strength restored to him, *he took up his bed,* because it lay in the way, *and went forth before them all;* and *they were all amazed,* as well they might, and *glorified God,* as indeed they ought; saying, "*We never saw it on this fashion;* never were such wonders as these done before in our time." Note, Christ's works were without precedent. When we see what he does in healing souls, we must own that we *never saw the like.*

Verses 13–17

Here is,

I. Christ preaching by the *sea-side* (*v.* 13), whither he went *for room,* because he found, upon second trial, no house or street large enough to contain his auditory; but upon the strand there might come as many as would. It should seem by this, that our Lord Jesus had a strong voice, and could and did speak loud; for *wisdom crieth without* in the *places of concourse.* Wherever he goes, though it be to the sea-side, *multitudes resort to him.* Wherever the doctrine of Christ is faithfully preached, though it be driven into corners or into deserts, we must follow it.

II. His calling Levi; the same with Matthew, who had a place in the custom-house at Capernaum, from which he was denominated a *publican;* his place fixed him by the water-side, and thither Christ went to meet with him, and to give him an effectual call. This Levi is here said to be *the son of Alpheus* or *Cleophas,* husband to that Mary who was sister or near kinswoman to the virgin Mary and if so, he was own brother to James the less, and Jude, and Simon the Canaanite, so that there were four brothers of them apostles, It is probable that Matthew was but a loose extravagant young man, or else, being a Jew, he would never have been a publican. However, Christ called him to *follow him.* Paul, though a Pharisee, had been one of the chief of sinners, and yet was called to be an apostle. With God, through Christ, there is mercy to pardon the greatest sins, and grace to sanctify the greatest sinners. Matthew, that had been a publican, became an evangelist, the *first* that put pen to paper, and the *fullest* in writing the life of Christ. Great sin and scandal before conversion, are no bar to great gifts, graces, and advancements, after; nay, God may be the more glorified. Christ prevented him with this call; in bodily cures, ordinarily, he was *sought unto,* but in these spiritual cures, he was *found of them that sought him not.* For this is the great evil and peril of the disease of sin, that those who are under it, desire not to be *made whole.*

III. His familiar converse with *publicans and sinners, v.* 15. We are here told, 1. That Christ *sat at meat in Levi's house,* who invited *him and his disciples* to the farewell-feast he made to his friends, when he left all to attend on Christ: such a feast he made, as Elisha did (1 Ki. 19:21), to show, not only with what cheerfulness in himself, but with what thankfulness to God, he quitted all, in compliance with Christ's call. Fitly did he make the *day of his espousals* to Christ a festival day. This was also to testify his respect to Christ, and the grateful sense he had of his kindness, in snatching him from the receipt of custom as a brand out of the burning. 2. That *many publicans and sinners* sat with Christ in Levi's house (for *there were many* belonging to that custom-house); and *they followed him.* They followed Levi; so some understand it, supposing that, like Zaccheus, he was *chief among the publicans,* and was *rich;* and for that reason, the inferior sort of them attended him for what they could get. I rather take it, that they *followed Jesus* because of the report they had heard of him. They did not *for conscience-sake* leave all to follow him, but *for curiosity-sake* they came to Levi's feast, to see him; whatever brought them thither, they were sitting with *Jesus and his disciples.* The publicans are here and elsewhere ranked with *sinners,* the worst of *sinners.* (1.) Because commonly they *were such;* so general were the corruptions in the execution of that office, oppressing, exacting, and taking bribes or fees to extortion, and *accusing falsely,* Lu. 3:13, 14. A faithful fair-dealing publican was so rare, even at Rome, that one Sabinus, who kept a clean reputation in that office, was, after his death, honoured with this inscription, *Kalōs telōnēsanti — Here lies an honest publican.* (2.) Because the Jews had a particular antipathy to them and their office, as an affront to the liberty of their nation and a badge of their slavery, and therefore put them into an ill name, and thought it scandalous to be seen in their company. Such as these our blessed Lord was pleased to converse with, when he appeared *in the likeness of sinful flesh.*

IV. The *offence* which the scribes and Pharisees took at this, *v.* 16. They would not come to hear him preach, which they might have been convinced the edified by; but they would come themselves to *see him* sit with publicans and sinners, which they would be provoked by. They endeavoured to put the disciples out of conceit with their Master, as a man not of such sanctity and severe morals as became his character; and therefore put the question to them. *How is it, that he eateth and drinketh with publicans and sinners?* Note, It is no new thing for that which is both well-*done,* and well-*designed,* to be misrepresented, and turned to the reproach of the wisest and best of men.

V. Christ's justification of himself in it, *v.* 17. He stood to what he did, and would not withdraw, though the Pharisees were offended, as Peter afterwards did, Gal. 2:12. Note, Those are too tender of their own *good name,* who, to preserve it with some nice people, will decline a *good work.* Christ would not do so. They thought the publicans were to be *hated.* "No," saith Christ, "they are to be *pitied,* they are *sick* and *need a physician;* they are sinners, and need a Saviour." They thought Christ's character should separate him from them; "No," saith Christ, "my commission directs me to them; *I came not to call the righteous, but sinners to repentance.* If the world had been *righteous,* there had been no occasion for my coming, either to *preach* repentance, or to *purchase* remission. It is to a *sinful world* that I am sent, and therefore my business lies most with those that are the greatest sinners in it." Or thus; *"I am not come to call the righteous,* the proud Pharisees that think themselves righteous, that ask, *Wherein shall we return?* (Mal. 3:7), Of what shall we repent? But poor publicans, that own themselves to be sinners, and are glad to be invited and encouraged to repent." It is good dealing with those that there is hope of; now there is *more hope of a fool* than of one that is *wise in his own conceit,* Prov. 26:12.

Verses 18–28

Christ had been put to *justify* himself in conversing with *publicans and sinners:* here he is put to justify his disciples; and in what they do according to his will he will justify them, and bear them out.

I. He justifies them in their *not fasting,* which was turned to their reproach by the Pharisees. Why do the Pharisees and the disciples of John fast? They *used to fast,* the Pharisees fasted *twice in the week* (Lu. 18:12), and probably the disciples of John did so too; and, it should seem, this very day, when Christ and his disciples were feasting in Levi's house, was their *fast-day,* for the word is *nēsteuousi — they do fast,* or *are fasting,* which aggravated the offence. Thus apt are strict professors to make their own practice a standard, and to censure and condemn all that do not fully come up to it. They invidiously suggest that if Christ went among sinners to do them *good,* as he had pleaded, yet the disciples went to indulge their appetites, for they never knew what it was to fast, or to deny themselves. Note, Ill-will always suspects the worst.

Two things Christ pleads in excuse of his disciples *not fasting.*

1. That these were *easy days* with them, and fasting was not so *seasonable* now as it would be hereafter, *v.* 19, 20. There is a time for all things. Those that enter into the married state, must expect care and *trouble in the flesh,* and yet, during the nuptial solemnity, they are merry, and think it becomes them to be so; it was very absurd for Samson's bride to *weep before* him, *during the days that the feast lasted,* Jdg. 14:17. Christ and his disciples were but newly married, the bridegroom was *yet with them,* the nuptials were yet in the celebrating (Matthew's particularly); when the bridegroom should be removed from them to the far country, about his business, then would be a proper time to sit as a widow, in solitude and fasting.

2. That these were *early days* with them, and they were not so able for the severe exercises of religion as hereafter they would be. The Pharisees had long accustomed themselves to such austerities; and John Baptist himself came neither eating nor drinking. His disciples from the first inured themselves to hardships, and thus found it easier to bear strict and frequent fasting, but it was not so with Christ's disciples; their Master came *eating and drinking,* and had not bred them up to the difficult services of religion as yet, for it was all in good time. To put them upon such frequent fasting at first, would be a discouragement to them, and perhaps drive them off from following Christ; it would be of as ill consequence as *putting new wine into old casks,* or sewing *new cloth* to that which is worn thin and threadbare, *v.* 21, 22. Note, God graciously *considers the frame* of young Christians, that are *weak* and *tender,* and so must we; nor must we expect more than the *work of the day in its day,* and that day according to the strength, because it is not in our hands to give strength according to the day. Many contract an antipathy to some kind of food, otherwise good, by being surfeited with it when they are young; so, many entertain prejudices against the exercises of devotion by being burthened with them, and *made to serve with an offering,* at their setting out. Weak Christians must take heed of *over-tasking* themselves, and of making the yoke of Christ otherwise than as it is, easy, and sweet, and pleasant.

II. He justifies them in *plucking the ears of corn on the sabbath day,* which, I will warrant you, a disciples of the Pharisees would not dare to have done; for it was contrary to an express tradition of their elders. In this instance, as in that before, they reflect upon the discipline of Christ's school, as if it were not so strict as that of theirs: so common it is for those who deny the *power of godliness,* to be jealous for the *form,* and censorious of those who affect not *their* form.

Observe, 1. What a poor breakfast Christ's disciples had on a sabbath-day morning, when they were going to church (*v.* 23); they *plucked the ears of corn,* and that was the best they had. They were so intent upon spiritual dainties, that they forgot even their *necessary food;* and the word of Christ was to them instead of that; and their zeal for it even *ate them up.* The Jews made it a piece of religion, to eat dainty food on sabbath days, but the disciples were content with any thing.

2. How even this was *grudged them* by the Pharisees, upon supposition that it was not lawful to *pluck the ears of corn* on the sabbath day, that that was as much a servile work as *reaping* (*v.* 24); *Why do they on the sabbath day that which is not lawful?* Note, If Christ's disciples do that which is unlawful, Christ will be reflected upon, and upbraided with it, as he was here, and dishonour will redound to his name. It is observable, that when the Pharisees thought Christ did amiss, they told the disciples (*v.* 16); and now when they thought the disciples did amiss, they spoke to Christ, as makebates, that did what they could to sow discord between Christ and his disciples, and make a breach in the family.

3. How Christ defended them in what they did.

(1.) By example. They had a good precedent for it in David's eating the *show-bread,* when he was hungry, and there was no other bread to be had (*v.* 25, 26); *Have ye never read?* Note, Many of our mistakes would be rectified, and our unjust censures of others corrected, if we would but recollect what *we have read* in the scripture; appeals to that are most convincing. "You have read that David, the man after God's own heart, *when he was hungry,* made no difficulty of eating *the show-bread,* which by the law none might eat of but the priests and their families." Note, Ritual observances must give way to moral obligations; and that may be done in a case of necessity, which otherwise may not be done. This, it is said, David did in the days of *Abiathar the High-Priest;* or *just before* the days of Abiathar, who immediately succeeded Abimelech his father in the pontificate, and, it is probable, was at that time his father's deputy, or assistant, in the office; and he it was that escaped the massacre, and brought the ephod to David.

(2.) By argument. To reconcile them to the disciples' *plucking the ears of corn,* let them consider,

[1.] Whom the sabbath was *made for* (*v.* 27); *it was made for man, and not man for the sabbath.* This we had not in Matthew. The sabbath is a sacred and divine institution; but we must receive and embrace it as a privilege and a benefit, not as a task and a drudgery. *First,* God never designed it to be an *imposition* upon us, and therefore we must not make it so to ourselves. *Man was not made for the sabbath,* for he was made a day before the sabbath was instituted. Man was made *for God,* and for his honour and service, and he just rather die than deny him; but he was not *made for the sabbath,* so as to be tied up by the law of it, from that which is necessary to the support of his life. *Secondly,* God did design it to be an *advantage* to us, and so we must make it, and improve it. He made if *for man.* 1. He had *some* regard to our *bodies* in the institution, that they might rest, and not be tired out with the constant business of this world (Deu. 5:14); *that thy man-servant and thy maid-servant may rest.* Now he that intended the *sabbath-rest* for the *repose* of our bodies, certainly never intended it should restrain us, in a case of necessity, from fetching in the necessary *supports* of the body; it must be construed so as not to contradict itself — for *edification,* and not for *destruction.* 2. He had *much more* regard to our *souls.* The *sabbath* was made a day of rest, only in order to its being a day of holy work, a day of communion with God, a day of praise and thanksgiving; and the rest from worldly business is *therefore* necessary, that we may closely apply ourselves to this work, and spend the whole time in it, in public and in private; but then time is allowed us for that which is necessary to the fitting of our bodies for the service of our souls in God's service, and the enabling of them to *keep pace* with them in that work. See here, (1.) What a *good Master* we serve, all whose institutions are for our own benefit, and if we be so wise as to observe them, we are *wise for ourselves;* it is not he, but we, that are gainers by our service. (2.) What we should aim at in our *sabbath work,* even the good of our own souls. If the sabbath was made for man, we should then ask ourselves at night, "What am I the better for this sabbath day?" (3.) What care we ought to take not to make those exercises of religion burthens to ourselves or others, which God ordained to be blessings; neither adding to the command by unreasonable strictness, nor indulging those corruptions which are adverse to the command, for thereby we make those devout exercises a penance to ourselves, which otherwise would be a pleasure.

[2.] Whom the sabbath was *made by* (*v.* 28); *"The Son of man is Lord also of the sabbath;* and therefore he will not see the kind intentions of the institution of it frustrated by your impositions." Note, The sabbath days are *days of the Son of man;* he is the Lord of the day, and to his honour it must be observed; by him God made the worlds, and so it was by him that the sabbath was first instituted; by him God gave the law at mount Sinai, and so the *fourth* commandment was *his law;* and that little alteration that was shortly to be made, by the shifting of it one day forward to the first day of the week, was to be in remembrance of *his* resurrection, and therefore the Christian sabbath was to be called *the Lord's day* (Rev. 1:10), the Lord Christ's day; and the *Son of man,* Christ, as Mediator, is always to be looked upon as Lord of the sabbath. This argument he largely insists upon in his own justification, when he was charged with having broken the sabbath, Jn. 5:16.

CHAPTER 3

In this chapter, we have, I. Christ's healing a man that had a withered hand, on the sabbath day, and the combination of his enemies against him for it (*v.* 1–6). II. The universal resort of people to him from all parts, to be healed, and the relief they all found with him (*v.* 7–12). III. His ordaining his twelve apostles to be attendants on him, and the preachers of his gospel (*v.* 13–21). IV. His answer to the blasphemous cavils of the scribes, who imputed his power to cast out devils to a confederacy with the prince of the devils (*v.* 22–30). V. His owning his disciples for his nearest and dearest relations (*v.* 31–35).

Verses 1–12

Here, as before, we have our Lord Jesus busy at work *in the synagogue* first, and then by *the sea side;* to teach us that his presence should not be confined either to the one or to the other, but, wherever any are gathered together in his name, whether *in the synagogue* or any where else, there is he in the midst of them. *In every place where he records his name,* he will meet his people, and *bless them;* it is his will that men *pray every where.* Now here we have some account of what he did.

I. When he *entered again into the synagogue,* he improved the opportunity he had there, of doing good, and having, no doubt, preached a sermon there, he wrought a miracle for the confirmation of it, or at least for the confirmation of this truth — that *it is lawful to do good on the sabbath day.* We had the narrative, Mt. 12:9.

1. The patient's case was piteous; he had a *withered hand,* by which he was disabled to work for his living; and those that are so, are the most proper objects of charity; let those be helped that cannot help themselves.

2. The spectators were very unkind, both to the patient and to the Physician; instead of interceding for a poor neighbour, they did what they could to hinder his cure: for they intimated that if Christ cured him now on the sabbath day, they would accuse him as a *Sabbath breaker.* It had been very unreasonable, if they should have opposed a physician or surgeon in helping any poor body in misery, by ordinary methods; but much more absurd was it to oppose him that cured without any labour, but by a word's speaking.

3. Christ dealt very fairly with the spectators, and dealt with them *first,* if possible to *prevent* the offence.

(1.) He laboured to convince their judgment. He bade the man *stand forth* (*v.* 3), that by the sight of him they might be moved with compassion toward him, and might not, for shame, account his cure a crime. And then he appeals to their own consciences; though the thing *speaks itself,* yet *he* is pleased to *speak* it; *"Is it lawful to do good on the sabbath days,* as I design to do, *or to do evil,* as you design to do? Whether is better, to *save life* or to *kill?"* What fairer question could be put? And yet, because they saw it would turn against them, *they held their peace.* Note, Those are obstinate indeed in their infidelity, who, when they can say nothing *against* a truth, will say nothing *to it;* and, when they cannot *resist,* yet will not *yield.*

(2.) When they rebelled against the light, he *lamented their stubbornness* (*v.* 5); *He looked round about on them with anger, being grieved for the hardness of their hearts.* The *sin* he had an eye to, was, the *hardness of their hearts,* their insensibleness of the evidence of his miracles, and their inflexible resolution to persist in unbelief. We hear what is said amiss, and see what is done amiss; but Christ looks at the *root of bitterness* in the heart, the blindness and hardness of *that.* Observe, [1.] How he was *provoked* by the sin; he looked *round upon them;* for they were so many, and had so placed themselves, that they surrounded him: and he looked *with anger;* his anger, it is probable, appeared in his countenance; his anger was, like God's, without the least *perturbation* to himself, but not without great *provocation* from us. Note, The sin of sinners is very displeasing to Jesus Christ; and the way to be angry, and not to sin, is it be angry, as Christ was, at nothing but sin. Let hard-hearted sinners tremble to think of the anger with which he will *look round* upon them shortly, when the *great day of his wrath comes.* [2.] How he *pitied* the sinners; he was *grieved for the hardness of their hearts;* as God was grieved forty years for the hardness of the hearts of their fathers in the wilderness. Note, It is a great grief to our Lord Jesus, to see sinners bent upon their own ruin, and obstinately set against the methods of their conviction and recovery, for he would not that any should perish. This is a good reason why the hardness of our own hearts and of the hearts of others, should be a grief to us.

4. Christ dealt very kindly with the patient; he bade him *stretch forth his hand,* and it was immediately *restored.* Now, (1.) Christ has hereby taught us to go on with resolution in the way of our duty, how violent soever the opposition is, that we meet with in it. We must deny ourselves sometimes in our ease, pleasure, and convenience, rather than give offence even to those who causelessly take it; but we must not deny ourselves the satisfaction of serving God, and doing good, though offence may unjustly be taken at it. None could be more tender of giving offence than Christ; yet, rather than send this poor man away uncured, he would venture offending all the scribes and Pharisees that compassed him about. (2.) He hath hereby given us a *specimen* of the cures wrought by his grace upon *poor souls;* our hands are spiritually *withered,* the powers of our souls weakened by sin, and disabled for that which is good. The great healing day is the *sabbath,* and the healing place the *synagogue;* the healing power is that of Christ. The gospel command is like this recorded here; and the command is rational and just; though our hands are withered, and we cannot of ourselves *stretch them forth,* we must attempt it, must, as well as we can, *lift them up* to God in prayer, *lay hold* on Christ and eternal life, and employ them in good works; and if we do our endeavour, power goes along with the word of Christ, he effects the cure. Though our hands be *withered,* yet, if we will not offer to *stretch them out,* it is our own fault that we are not healed; but if we do, and are healed, Christ and his power and grace must have all the glory.

5. The enemies of Christ dealt very barbarously with him. Such a work of *mercy* should have engaged their love *to him,* and such a work of *wonder* their faith *in him.* But, instead of that, the Pharisees, who pretended to be oracles in the church, and the Herodians, who pretended to be the supporters of the state, though of opposite interests one to another, *took counsel together against him, how they might destroy him.* Note, They that suffer for doing good, do but suffer as their Master did.

II. When he withdrew *to the sea,* he did good there. While his enemies sought to *destroy him,* he quitted the place; to teach us in troublous times to shift for our own safety; but see here,

1. How he was followed into his retirement. When some had such an enmity to him, that they drove him out of their country, others had such a value for him, that they followed him wherever he went; and the enmity of their leaders to Christ did not cool their respect to him. *Great multitudes* followed him from all parts of the nation; as far north, as *from Galilee;* as far south, as from Judea and Jerusalem; nay, and from Idumea; as far east, as from beyond Jordan; and west, as from about Tyre and Sidon, *v.* 7, 8. Observe, (1.) What induced them to follow him; it was the report they heard of the *great things he did* for all that applied themselves to him; some wished *to see* one that had done such *great things,* and others hoped he would do great things *for them.* Note, The consideration of the *great things* Christ has done, should engage us to *come to him.* (2.) What they followed him for (*v.* 10); They *pressed upon him, to touch him, as many as had plagues.* Diseases are here called *plagues, mastigas — corrections, chastisements;* so they are designed to be, to make us *smart* for our sins, that thereby we may be made *sorry* for them, and may be warned not to return to them. Those that were under these *scourgings* came to Jesus; this is the errand on which sickness is sent, to quicken us to enquire after Christ, and apply ourselves to him as our Physician. They *pressed upon him,* each striving which should get *nearest to* him, and which should be *first served.* They *fell down before him* (so Dr. Hammond), as petitioners for his favour; they desired leave but to *touch him,* having faith to be healed, not only by *his* touching *them,* but by *their* touching him; which no doubt they had many instances of. (3.) What provision he made to be ready to attend them (*v.* 9); He *spoke to his disciples,* who were fishermen, and had fisher-boats at command, that a *small ship should* constantly *wait on him,* to carry him from place to place on the same coast; that, when he had despatched the necessary business he had to do in one place, he might easily remove to another, where his presence was requisite, without pressing through the crowds of people that followed him for curiosity. Wise men, as much as they can, decline a crowd.

2. What abundance of good he did in his retirement. He did not withdraw to be idle, nor did he send back those who rudely crowded after him when he withdrew, but took it kindly, and gave them what they came for; for he never said to any that sought him diligently, *Seek ye me in vain.* (1.) Diseases were effectually cured; He *healed many;* divers sorts of patients, ill of divers sorts of diseases; though numerous, though various, he *healed them.* (2.) *Devils* were effectually *conquered;* those whom unclean spirits had got possession of, *when they saw him,* trembled at his presence, and they also *fell down before him,* not to supplicate his favour, but to deprecate his wrath, and by their own terrors were compelled to own that *he was the Son of God, v.* 1.. It is sad that this great truth should be denied by any of the children of men, who may have the benefit of it, when a confession of it has so often been extorted from devils, who are excluded from having benefit by it. (3.) Christ sought not applause to himself in doing those great things, for *he strictly charged* those for whom he did them, *that they should not make him known* (*v.* 12); that they should not be *industrious* to spread the notice of his cures, as it were by advertisements in the newspapers, but let them leave *his own works to praise him,* and let the report of them *diffuse itself,* and make its own way. Let not those that are cured, be forward to divulge it, lest it should feed their pride who are so *highly favoured;* but let the *standers-by* carry away the intelligence of it. When we do that which is *praiseworthy,* and yet covet not to be *praised of men* for it, then *the same mind is in us,* which was *in Christ Jesus.*

Verses 13–21

In these verses, we have,

I. The choice Christ made of the *twelve apostles* to be his constant followers and attendants, and to be sent abroad as there was occasion, to preach the gospel. Observe,

1. The introduction to this *call* or *promotion* of disciples; He *goes up into a mountain,* and his errand thither was *to pray.* Ministers must be set apart with solemn prayer for the pouring out of the Spirit upon them; though Christ had authority to confer the gifts of the Holy Ghost, yet, to set us an example, he prayed for them.

2. The rule he went by in his choice, and that was his own good pleasure; *He called unto him whom he would.* Not such as we should have thought *fittest to be called, looking upon the countenance, and the height of the stature;* but such as he *thought fit* to call, and determined to *make fit* for the service to which he called them: *even so,* blessed Jesus, *because it seemed good in thine eyes.* Christ calls *whom he will;* for he is a free Agent, and his grace is his own.

3. The efficacy of the call; He *called them* to separate

themselves from the crowd, and stand by him, and they *came unto him.* Christ calls those who were *given him* (Jn. 17:6); and *all that the Father gave him, shall come to him,* Jn. 6:37. Those whom it was his *will* to call, he made *willing to come;* his *people shall be willing in the day of his power.* Perhaps they came to him readily enough, because they were in expectation of *reigning with him* in temporal pomp and power; but when afterward they were *undeceived* in that matter, yet they had such a prospect given them of better things, that they would not say they were *deceived* in their Master, nor repented their leaving all to be with him.

4. The end and intention of this call; He *ordained them* (probably by the imposition of hands, which was a ceremony used among the Jews), *that they should be with him* constantly, to be witnesses of *his doctrine, manner of life, and patience,* that they might *fully know it,* and be able to give an account of it; and especially that they might attest the truth of his miracles; they must be *with him* to receive instructions *from him,* that they might be qualified to give instructions *to others.* It would *require time* to fit them for that which he designed them for; for they must be *sent forth to preach;* not to preach till they were *sent,* and not to be *sent* till by a long and intimate acquaintance with Christ they were fitted. Note, Christ's ministers must be much *with him.*

5. The power he gave them to work miracles; and hereby he put a very great honour upon them, beyond that of the great men of the earth. He ordained them to *heal sicknesses and to cast out devils.* This showed that the power which Christ had to work these miracles was an *original* power; that he had it not *as a Servant,* but *as a Son in his own house,* in that he could confer it upon others, and invest them with it: they have a rule in the law, *Deputatus non potest deputare — He that is only deputed himself, cannot depute another;* but our Lord Jesus had *life in himself,* and the Spirit without measure; for he could give this power even to the *weak* and *foolish things* of the world.

6. Their number and names; He *ordained twelve,* according to the number of the twelve tribes of Israel. They are here named not just in the same order as they were in Matthew, nor by couples, as they were there; but as there, so here, Peter is put first and Judas last. Here Matthew is put before Thomas, probably being called in that order; but in that catalogue which Matthew himself drew up, he puts himself after Thomas; so far was he from insisting upon the precedency of his consecration. But that which Mark only takes notice of in this list of the apostles, is, that Christ called James and John *Boanerges,* which is, *The sons of thunder;* perhaps they were remarkable for a loud commanding voice, they were thundering preachers; or, rather, it denotes the zeal and fervency of their spirits, which would make them active for God above their brethren. These two (saith Dr. Hammond) were to be special eminent ministers of the gospel, which is called *a voice shaking the earth,* Heb. 12:26. Yet John, one of those *sons of thunder,* was full of love and tenderness, as appears by his epistles, and was the beloved disciple.

7. Their retirement with their Master, and close adherence to him; *They went into a house.* Now that this jury was impanelled, they *stood together, to hearken to their evidence.* They went together into the house, to settle the orders of their infant college; and now, it is likely, the bag was given to Judas, which pleased him, and made him easy.

II. The continual crowds that attended Christ's motions (*v.* 20); The *multitude cometh together again,* unsent for, and unseasonably pressing upon him, some with one errand and some with another; so that he and his disciples could not get time *so much as to eat bread,* much less for a set and full meal. Yet he did not shut his doors against the petitioners, but bade them welcome, and gave to each of them *an answer of peace.* Note, They whose hearts are enlarged in the work of God, can easily bear with great inconveniences to themselves, in the prosecution of it, and will rather lose a meal's meat at any time than slip an opportunity of doing good. It is happy when zealous *hearers* and zealous *preachers* thus *meet,* and encourage one another. Now the *kingdom of God was preached,* and men pressed into it, Lu. 16:16. This was a gale of opportunity worth improving; and the disciples might well afford to adjourn their meals, to lay hold on it. It is good striking while the iron is hot.

III. The care of his relations concerning him (*v.* 21); *When his friends* in Capernaum heard how he was followed, and what pains he took, they *went out, to lay hold on him,* and fetch him home, for they said, *He is beside himself.* 1. Some understand it of an absurd preposterous care, which had more in it of reproach to him than of respect; and so we must take it as we read it, *He is beside himself;* either they suspected it themselves, or it was suggested to them, and they gave credit to the suggestion, that he was *gone distracted,* and therefore his friends ought to bind him, and put him in a dark room, to bring him to his right mind again. His kindred, many of them, had mean thoughts of him (Jn. 7:5), and were willing to hearken to this ill construction which some put upon his great zeal, and to conclude him crazed in his intellects, and under that pretence to take him off from his work. The prophets were called *mad fellows,* 2 Ki. 9:11. 2. Others understand it of a *well-meaning* care; and then they read *exestē* — *"He fainteth,* he has no time to *eat bread,* and therefore his strength will fail him; he will be stifled with the crowd of people, and will have his spirits quite exhausted with constant speaking, and the virtue that *goes out of him* in his miracles; and therefore let us use a friendly violence with him, and get him a little *breathing-time."* In his preaching-work, as well as his suffering-work, he was attacked with, *Master, spare thyself.* Note, They who go on with vigour and zeal in the work of God, must expect to meet with hindrances, both from the groundless disaffection of their enemies, and the mistaken affections of their friends, and they have need to stand upon their guard against both.

Verses 22–30

I. Here is, The impudent impious brand which the scribes fastened upon Christ's casting out devils, that they might evade and invalidate the conviction of it, and have a poor excuse for not yielding to it. These *scribes came down from Jerusalem, v.* 22. It should seem they came this long journey on purpose to hinder the progress of the doctrine of Christ; such pains did they take to do mischief; and, coming from Jerusalem, where were the most polite and learned scribes, and where they had opportunity of *consulting* together *against the Lord and his Anointed,* they were in the greater capacity to do mischief; the reputation of scribes from Jerusalem would have an influence not only upon the *country people,* but upon the *country scribes;* they had never thought of this base suggestion concerning Christ's miracles till the *scribes from* Jerusalem put it into their heads. They could not deny but that he cast out devils, which plainly bespoke him sent of God; but they insinuated that *he had Beelzebub* on his side, was in league with him, and by *the prince of the devils cast out devils.* There is a trick in the case; Satan is not *cast out,* he only *goes out* by consent. There was nothing in the manner of Christ's *casting out devils,* that gave any cause to suspect this; he did it *as one having authority;* but so they will have it, who resolve not to believe him.

II. The rational answer which Christ gave to this objection, demonstrating the absurdity of it.

1. Satan is so *subtle,* that he will never voluntarily quit his possession; *If Satan cast out Satan, his kingdom is divided against itself,* and it *cannot stand, v.* 23–26. He *called them to him,* as one desirous they should be convinced; he treated them with all the freedom, friendliness, and familiarity that could be; he vouchsafed to reason the case with them, *that every mouth may be stopped.* It was plain that the doctrine of Christ *made war* upon the devil's kingdom, and had a direct tendency to break his power, and crush his interest in the souls of men; and it was as plain that the casting of him out of the bodies of people confirmed that doctrine, and gave it the setting on; and therefore it cannot be imagined that he should come into such a design; every one knows that Satan is no *fool,* nor will act so directly against his own interest.

2. Christ is so *wise,* that, being engaged in war with him, he will attack his forces wherever he meets them, whether in the bodies or souls of people, *v.* 27. It is plain, Christ's design is to *enter into the strong man's house,* to take possession of the interest he has in the world, and to *spoil his goods,* and convert them to his own service; and therefore it is natural to suppose that he will thus *bind the strong man,* will forbid him to *speak* when he would, and to *stay* where he would, and thus show that he has gained a victory over him.

III. The awful warning Christ gave them to take heed how they spoke such dangerous words as these; however they might make light of them, as only conjectures, and the language of *free-thinking,* if they persisted in it, it would be of fatal consequence to them; it would be found a sin against the last remedy, and consequently *unpardonable;* for what could be imagined possible to bring *them* to repentance for their sin in blaspheming Christ, who would set aside such a *strong* conviction with such a *weak* evasion? It is true, the gospel *promiseth,* because Christ hath *purchased,* forgiveness for the greatest sins and sinners, *v.* 28. Many of those who reviled Christ on the cross (which was a *blaspheming of the Son of man,* aggravated to the highest degree), found mercy, and Christ himself prayed, *Father, forgive them;* but this was *blaspheming the Holy Ghost,* for it was by the Holy Spirit that he *cast out* devils, and they said, It was *by the unclean spirit, v.* 30. By this method they would outface the conviction of all the gifts of the Holy Ghost after Christ's ascension, and defeat them all, after which there remained no more proof, and therefore they should *never have forgiveness,* but were *liable to eternal damnation.* They were in imminent danger of that everlasting punishment, from which there was *no redemption,* and in which there was no *intermission,* no *remission.*

Verses 31–35

Here is, 1. The *disrespect* which Christ's *kindred, according to the flesh,* showed to him, when he was preaching (and they knew very well that he was then in his element); they not only *stood without,* having no desire to come in, and hear him, but they sent in a message to *call him out to them* (*v.* 31. 32), as if he must leave his work, to hearken to their *impertinences;* it is probable that they had *no business with him,* only sent for him on purpose to oblige him to *break off,* lest he should *kill himself.* He knew how far his strength would go, and preferred the salvation of souls before his own life, and soon after made it to appear with a witness; it was therefore an *idle thing* for them, under pretence of his sparing himself, to interrupt him; and it was worse, if really they had business with him, when they knew he preferred his business, as a Saviour, so much before any other business.

2. The *respect* which Christ showed to his spiritual kindred upon this occasion. Now, as at other times, he put a *comparative neglect* upon his mother, which seemed purposely designed to obviate the prevent the extravagant respect which men in aftertimes would be apt to pay her. *Our* respect ought to be guided and governed by Christ's; now the virgin Mary, or Christ's mother, is not equalled with, but postponed to, ordinary believers, on whom Christ here puts a *superlative* honour. He looked upon those that *at about* him, and pronounced those of them that not only heard, but did, the will of God, to be to him as *his brother, and sister, and mother;* as much esteemed, loved, and cared for, as his nearest relations, *v.* 33–35. This is a good reason why we should *honour those that fear the Lord,* and choose them for our people; why we should be not hearers of the word only, but doers of the work, that we may share with the saints in this honour, Surely it is good to be akin to those who are thus nearly allied to Christ, and to have fellowship with those that have fellowship with Christ; and woe to those that hate and persecute Christ's kindred, that are *his bone and his flesh,* every one *resembling the children of a king* (see Jdg. 8:18, 19); for he will with jealously plead their cause, and avenge their blood.

CHAPTER 4

In this chapter, we have, I. The parable of the seed, and the four sorts of ground (*v.* 1–9), with the exposition of it (*v.* 10–20), and the application of it (*v.* 21–25). II. The parable of the seed growing gradually, but insensibly (*v.* 26–29). III. The parable of the grain of mustard-seed, and a general account of Christ's parables (*v.* 30–34). IV. The miracle of Christ's sudden stilling a storm at sea (*v.* 35–41).

Verses 1–20

The foregoing chapter began with Christ's *entering into the synagogue* (*v.* 1); this chapter begins with Christ's *teaching again by the sea side.* Thus he changed his method, that if possible all might be reached and wrought upon. To gratify the nice and more genteel sort of people that had seats, *chief seats, in the synagogue,* and did not care for hearing a sermon any where else, he did not preach always by the *sea side,* but, having liberty, went often *into the synagogue,* and taught there; yet, to gratify the poor, the mob, that could not get room in the synagogue, he did not always preach there, but *began again to teach by the sea side,* where they could come *within hearing.* Thus are we *debtors both to the wise and to the unwise,* Rom. 1:14.

Here seems to be a new convenience found out, which had not been used before, though he had before preached by the sea side (*ch.* 2:13), and that was — his standing *in a ship*, while his hearers *stood upon the land;* and that inland sea of Tiberias having no tide, there was no ebbing and flowing of the waters to disturb them. Methinks Christ's carrying his doctrine into a ship, and preaching it thence, was a presage of his sending the gospel to the *isles of the Gentiles*, and the shipping off of the kingdom of God (that rich cargo) from the Jewish nation, to be sent to a people that would bring forth more of the fruits of it. Now observe here,

I. The *way of teaching* that Christ used with the *multitude* (*v.* 2); He *taught them many things*, but it was *by parables* or similitudes, which would *tempt them to hear;* for people love to be spoken to in their own language, and careless hearers will catch at a plain comparison borrowed from common things, and will retain and repeat that, when they have *lost*, or perhaps never *took*, the truth which it was designed to explain and illustrate: but unless they would take pains to search into it, it would but amuse them; *seeing they would see, and not perceive* (*v.* 12); and so, while it gratified their curiosity, it was the punishment of their stupidity; they wilfully shut their eyes against the light, and therefore justly did Christ put it into the dark lantern of a parable, which had a bright side toward those who applied it to themselves, and were willing to be guided by it; but to those who were only *willing for a season to play with it*, it only gave a flash of light now and then, but sent them away in the dark. It is just with God to say of those that *will not see*, that they *shall not see*, and to hide from their eyes, who only look about them with a great deal of carelessness, and never look before them with any concern upon the things that belong to their peace.

II. The *way of expounding* that he used with his *disciples; When he was alone* by himself, not only the *twelve*, but others that were *about him with the twelve*, took the opportunity to *ask him* the meaning of the parables, *v.* 10. They found it good to be *about Christ;* the nearer him the better; good to be *with the twelve*, to be conversant with those that are intimate with him. And he told them what a distinguishing favour it was to them, that they were made acquainted with the *mystery of the kingdom of God, v.* 11. *The secret of the Lord was with them.* That *instructed* them, which others were only *amused* with, and they were made to increase in knowledge by every parable, and understood more of the way and method in which Christ designed to set up his kingdom in the world, while others were dismissed, never the wiser. Note, Those who know the *mystery* of the *kingdom of heaven*, must acknowledge that it is *given to them;* they receive both the light and the sight from Jesus Christ, who, after his resurrection, both *opened the scriptures*, and *opened the understanding*, Lu. 24:27, 45.

In particular, we have here,

1. The parable of the sower, as we had it, Mt. 13:3, etc. He begins (*v.* 3), with, *Hearken*, and concludes (*v.* 9) with, *He that hath ears to hear, let him hear.* Note, The words of Christ demand attention, and those who speak from him, may command it, and should stir it up; even that which as yet we do not *thoroughly* understand, or not *rightly*, we must carefully attend to, believing it to be both intelligible and weighty, that at length we may understand it; we shall find more in Christ's sayings than at first there seemed to be.

2. The exposition of it to the disciples. Here is a question Christ put to them before he expounded it, which we had not in Matthew (*v.* 13); *"Know ye not this parable?* Know ye not the meaning of it? How then will ye know all parables?"* (1.) "If ye know not this, which is so plain, how will ye understand other parables, which will be more dark and obscure? If ye are gravelled and run aground with this, which bespeaks so plainly the different success of the word preached upon those that hear it, which ye yourselves may see easily, how will ye understand the parables which hereafter will speak of the rejection of the Jews, and the calling of the Gentiles, which is a thing ye have no idea of?" Note, This should quicken us both to prayer and pains that we may get knowledge, that there are a great many things which we are concerned to know; and if we understand not the plain truths of the gospel, how shall we master those that are more difficult? *Vita brevis, ars longa — Life is short, art is long. If we have run with the footmen, and they have wearied us*, and run us down, then *how shall we contend with horses?* Jer. 12:5. (2.) "If ye know not this, which is intended for your direction in hearing the word, that ye may profit by it; how shall ye profit by what ye are further to hear? This parable is to teach you to be attentive to the word, and affected with it, that you may

understand it. If ye receive not this, ye will not know how to use the key by which ye must be let into all the rest." If we understand not the rules we are to observe in order to our profiting by the word, how shall we profit by any other rule? Observe, Before Christ expounds the parable, [1.] He shows them how sad *their* case was, who were not let into the meaning of the doctrine of Christ; *To you it is given, but not to them.* Note, It will help us to put a value upon the privileges we enjoy as disciples of Christ, to consider the deplorable state of those who want such privileges, especially that they are out of the ordinary way of conversion; *lest they should be converted, and their sins should be forgiven them. v.* 12. Those only who are *converted*, have *their sins forgiven them:* and it is the misery of *unconverted* souls, that they lie under *unpardoned* guilt. [2.] He shows them what a shame it was, that they needed such particular explanations of the word they heard, and did not apprehend it at first. Those that would improve in knowledge, must be made sensible of their ignorance.

Having thus prepared them for it, he gives them the interpretation of the parable of the sower, as we had it before in Matthew. Let us only observe here,

First, That in the great field of the church, the word of God is dispensed to all promiscuously; *The sower soweth the word* (*v.* 14), sows it at a venture, *beside all waters*, upon all sorts of ground (Isa. 32:20), not knowing where it will light, or what fruit it will bring forth. He *scatters* it, in order to the *increase* of it. Christ was awhile *sowing* himself, when he went about teaching and preaching; now he sends his ministers, and sows by their hand. Ministers are sowers; they have need of the skill and discretion of the husbandman (Isa. 28:24–26); they must not observe winds and clouds (Eccl. 11:4, 6), and must look up to God, who *gives seed to the sower*, 2 Co. 9:10.

Secondly, That of the many that hear the word of the gospel, and read it, and are conversant with it, there are, comparatively, but few that receive it, so as to bring forth the fruits of it; here is but one in four, that comes to good. It is sad to think, how much of the precious seed of the word of God is lost, and *sown in vain;* but there is a day coming when *lost sermons* must be accounted for. Many that have heard Christ himself *preach in their streets*, will hereafter be bidden to depart from him; those therefore who place all their religion in hearing, as if that alone would save them, do but deceive themselves, and build their hope upon the sand, Jam. 1:22.

Thirdly, Many are much affected with the word for the present, who yet receive no abiding benefit by it. The motions of soul they have, answerable to what they hear, are but a mere flash, like the crackling of thorns under a pot. We read of hypocrites, that they *delight to know God's ways* (Isa. 58:2); of Herod, that he heard John gladly (*ch.* 6:20); of others, that they *rejoiced in his light* (Jn. 5:35); of those to whom Ezekiel was a *lovely song* (Eze. 33:32); and those represented here by the stony ground, received the word *with gladness*, and yet came to nothing.

Fourthly, The reason why the word doth not leave commanding, abiding, impressions upon the minds of the people, is, because their hearts are not duly disposed and prepared to receive it; the fault is in themselves, not in the word; some are careless forgetful hearers, and these get *no good at all* by the word; it comes in at one ear, and goes out at the other; others have their convictions overpowered by their corruptions, and they lose the good impressions the word has made upon them, so that they get no *abiding* good by it.

Fifthly, The devil is very busy about loose, careless hearers, as the fowls of the air go about the seed that lies above ground; when the heart, like the *highway*, is unploughed, unhumbled, when it *lies common*, to be trodden on by every passenger, as theirs that are great company-keepers, then the devil is *like the fowls;* he comes swiftly, and carries away the word ere we are aware. When therefore these fowls come down upon the sacrifices, we should take care, as *Abram* did, to *drive them away* (Gen. 15:11); that, though we cannot keep them from hovering over our heads, we may not let them nestle in our hearts.

Sixthly, Many that are not openly *scandalized*, so as to throw off their profession, as they on the stony ground did, yet have the efficacy of it secretly *choked* and stifled, so that it comes to nothing; they continue in a barren, hypocritical profession, which brings nothing to pass, and so go down as certainly, though more plausibly, to hell.

Seventhly, Impressions that are not *keep*, will not be dur-

able, but will wear off in suffering, trying times; like footsteps on the sand of the sea, which are gone the next high tide of persecution; when *that* iniquity doth abound, the love of many to the ways of God waxeth cold; many that keep their profession in fair days, lose it in a storm; and do as those that go to sea only for pleasure, come back again when the wind arises. It is the ruin of hypocrites, that they *have no root;* they do not act from a living fixed principle; they do not mind *heart-work*, and without that religion is nothing; for he is the Christian, that is *one inwardly.*

Eighthly, Many are hindered from profiting by the word of God, by their abundance of the world. Many a good lesson of humility, charity, self-denial, and heavenly-mindedness, is choked and lost by that prevailing complacency in the world, which *they* are apt to have, on whom it smiles. Thus many professors, that otherwise might have come to something, prove like Pharaoh's *lean kine* and *thin ears.*

Ninthly, Those that are not encumbered with the cares of the world, and the deceitfulness of riches, may yet lose the benefit of their profession by the *lusts of other things;* this is added here in Mark; *by the desires which are about other things* (so Dr. Hammond), an inordinate appetite toward those things that are pleasing to sense or to the fancy. Those that have but little of the world, may yet be ruined by an indulgence of the body.

Tenthly, Fruit is the thing that God expects and requires from those that enjoy the gospel: fruit according to the *seed;* a temper of mind, and a course of life, agreeable to the gospel; Christian graces daily exercised, Christian duties duly performed. This is *fruit*, and it will abound to our account.

Lastly, No good fruit is to be expected but from good seed. If the seed be sown on *good ground*, if the heart be humble, and holy, and heavenly, there will be *good fruit*, and it will *abound* sometimes even to a *hundred fold*, such a crop as Isaac reaped, Gen. 26:12.

Verses 21–34

The lessons which our Saviour designs to teach us here by parables and figurative expressions are these: —

I. That those who *are good* ought to consider the obligations they are under to *do good;* that is, as in the parable before, to *bring forth fruit.* God expects a grateful return of his gifts to us, and a useful improvement of his gifts in us; for (*v.* 21), *Is a candle brought to be put under a bushel, or under a bed?* No, but that it may be *set on a candlestick.* The apostles were ordained, to receive the gospel, not for themselves only, but for the good of others, to communicate it to them. All Christians, as they have *received the gift*, must *minister the same.* Note, 1. Gifts and graces make a man *as a candle;* the *candle of the Lord* (Prov. 20:27), lighted by the Father of lights; the most eminent are but candles, poor lights, compared with the *Sun of righteousness.* A candle gives light but a *little way*, and but a *little while*, and is easily blown out, and continually burning down and wasting. 2. Many who are *lighted* as candles, put themselves *under a bed, or under a bushel:* they do not *manifest* grace themselves, nor *minister* grace to others; they have estates, and do no good with them; have their limbs and senses, wit and learning perhaps, but nobody is the better for them; they have spiritual gifts, but do not use them; like a taper in an urn, they burn to themselves. 3. Those who are lighted as candles, should set themselves *on a candlestick;* that is, should improve all opportunities of doing good, as those that were made for the glory of God, and the service of the communities they are members of; we are not born for ourselves.

The reason given for this, is, because *there is nothing hid, which shall not be manifested*, which *should* not be made manifest (so it might better be read), *v.* 22. There is no treasure of gifts and graces lodged in any but with design to be communicated; nor was the gospel made a *secret* to the apostles, to be concealed, but that it should *come abroad*, and be divulged to all the world. Though Christ expounded the parables to his disciples privately, yet it was with design to make them the more publicly useful; they were *taught*, that they might teach; and it is a general rule, that *the ministration of the Spirit is given to every man to profit withal*, not himself only, but others also.

II. It concerns those who hear the word of the gospel, to *mark* what they hear, and to *make a good use* of it, because their *weal* or *woe* depends upon it; what he had said before he saith again, *If any man have ears to hear, let him hear, v.* 23. Let him give the gospel of Christ a fair hearing; but that is not enough, it is added (*v.* 24), *Take heed what ye hear,* and give a due regard to that which ye do hear; *Consider what ye* hear, so Dr. Hammond reads it. Note, What we hear, doth us no good, unless we consider it; those especially that are to teach others must themselves be very observant of the things of God; must take notice of the message they are to deliver, that they may be exact. We must likewise *take heed what we hear,* by *proving* all things, that we may *hold fast that which is good.* We must be *cautious,* and stand upon our guard, lest we be imposed upon. To enforce this caution, consider,

1. As we deal with God, God will deal with us, so Dr. Hammond explains these words, *"With what measure ye mete, it shall be measured to you.* If ye be faithful servants to him, he will be a faithful Master to you: *with the upright he will show himself upright."*

2. As we improve the talents we are entrusted with, we shall increase them; if we make use of the knowledge we have, for the glory of God and the benefit of others, it shall sensibly grow, as stock in trade doth by being turned; *Unto you that hear, shall more be given; to you that have, it shall be given, v.* 25. If the disciples *deliver* that to the church, which they have *received of the Lord,* they shall be *led* more into the *secret of the Lord.* Gifts and graces multiply by being exercised; and God has promised to bless the *hand of the diligent.*

3. If we do not *use,* we *lose,* what we have; *From him that hath not,* that doeth no good with what he hath, and so hath it in vain, is as if he had it not, *shall be taken even that which he hath.* Burying a talent is the betraying of a trust, and amounts to a forfeiture; and gifts and graces *rust* for want of *wearing.*

III. The good seed of the gospel sown in the world, and sown in the heart, doth by degrees produce wonderful effects, but without noise (*v.* 26, etc.); *So is the kingdom of God;* so is the gospel, when it is sown, and received, as seed in good ground.

1. It will *come up;* though it seem lost and buried under the clods, it will find or make its way through them. The seed *cast into the ground will spring.* Let but the word of Christ have the place it ought to have in a soul, and it will show itself, as the *wisdom from above* doth in a *good conversation.* After a field is sown with corn, how soon is the surface of it altered! How gay and pleasant doth it look, when it is covered with green!

2. The husbandman cannot describe how it comes up; it is one of the mysteries of nature; It *springs and grows up, he knows not how, v.* 27. He sees it has grown, but he cannot tell in what manner it grew, or what was the cause and method of its growth. Thus we know not how the Spirit by the word makes a change in the heart, any more than we can account for the blowing of the wind, which we hear the sound of, but cannot tell whence it comes, or whither it goes. Without controversy, great is the mystery of godliness; how *God manifested in the flesh* came to be *believed on in the world,* 1 Tim. 3:16.

3. The husbandman, when he hath sown the seed, doth nothing toward the springing of it up; *He sleeps, and rises, night and day;* goes to sleep *at night,* gets up *in the morning,* and perhaps never so much as thinks of the corn he hath sown, or ever looks upon it, but follows his pleasures or other business, and yet *the earth brings forth fruit of itself,* according to the ordinary course of nature, and by the concurring power of the God of nature. Thus the *word of grace,* when it is received in faith, is in the heart a *work of grace,* and the preachers contribute nothing to it. The Spirit of God is carrying it on when *they sleep,* and can do no business (Job 33:15, 16), or when they rise to go about other business. The prophets do not *live for ever;* but the word which they preached, is doing its work, when they are in their graves, Zec. 1:5, 6. The dew by which the seed is brought up *tarrieth not for man, nor waiteth for the sons of men,* Mic. 5:7.

4. It grows gradually; *first the blade, then the ear, after that the full corn in the ear, v.* 28. When it is sprung up, it will go forward; nature will have its course, and so will grace. Christ's interest, both in the world and in the heart, is, and will be, a *growing* interest; and though *the beginning be small, the latter end will greatly increase.* Though thou sowest not that body that shall be, but *bare grain,* yet God *will give to every seed its own body;* though at first it is but a tender *blade,* which the frost may nip, or the foot may crush, yet it will increase to *the ear,* to the *full corn in the ear. Natura nil facit per saltum — Nature does nothing abruptly.* God carries on his work insensibly and without noise, but insuperably and without fail.

5. It comes to perfection at last (*v.* 29); *When the fruit is brought forth,* that is, when it is *ripe,* and ready to be *delivered* into the owner's hand; then he *puts in the sickle.* This intimates, (1.) That Christ *now accepts* the services which are done to him by an honest heart from a good principle; from the fruit of the gospel taking place and working in the soul, Christ *gathers in* a harvest of honour to himself. See Jn. 4:35. (2.) That he will reward them in eternal life. When those that receive the gospel aright, have finished their course, the harvest comes, when they shall be gathered as *wheat into God's barn* (Mt. 13:30), as a shock of corn *in his season.*

IV. The work of grace is small in its beginnings, but comes to be great and considerable at last (*v.* 30–32); *"Whereunto shall I liken the kingdom of God,* as now to be set up by the Messiah? How shall I make you to understand the designed method of it?" Christ speaks as one considering and consulting with himself, how to illustrate it with an apt similitude; *With what comparison shall we compare it?* Shall we fetch it from the motions of the sun, or the revolutions of the moon? No, the comparison is borrowed from this earth, it is *like a grain of mustard-seed;* he had compared it before to *seed sown,* here to *that seed,* intending thereby to show,

1. That the beginnings of the *gospel kingdom* would be very small, like that which is *one of the least of all seeds.* When a Christian church was *sown in the earth* for God, it was all contained in one room, and the *number of the names* was but one hundred and twenty (Acts 1:15), as the children of Israel, when they went down into Egypt, were but seventy souls. The work of grace in the soul, is, at first, but the *day of small things;* a *cloud* no *bigger than a man's hand.* Never were there such great things undertaken by such an inconsiderable handful, as that of the discipling of the nations by the ministry of the apostles; nor a work that was to end in such great glory, as the work of grace raised from such weak and unlikely beginnings. *Who hath begotten me these?*

2. That the perfection of it will be very great; *When it grows up, it becomes greater than all herbs.* The gospel kingdom in the world, shall increase and spread to the remotest nations of the earth, and shall continue to the latest ages of time. The *church* hath *shot out great branches,* strong ones, spreading far, and fruitful. The *work of grace* in the soul has mighty products, now while it is in its growth; but what will it be, when it is perfected in heaven? The difference between a *grain of mustard seed* and a *great tree,* is nothing to that between a *young convert* on earth and a *glorified saint* in heaven. See Jn. 12:24.

After the parables thus specified the historian concludes with this general account of Christ's preaching — that *with many such parables he spoke the word unto them* (*v.* 33); probably designing to refer us to the larger account of the parables of this kind, which we had before, Mt. 13. He spoke in parables, *as they were able to hear them;* he fetched his comparisons from those things that were familiar to them, and level to their capacity, and delivered them in plain expressions, in condescension to their capacity; though he did not let them into the *mystery* of the parables, yet his manner of expression was easy, and such as they might hereafter recollect to their edification. But, for the present, *without a parable spoke he not unto them, v.* 34. The glory of the Lord was covered with a cloud, and God speaks to us in the language of the *sons of men,* that, though not *at first,* yet *by degrees,* we may understand his meaning; the disciples themselves understood those sayings of Christ afterward, which at first they did not rightly take the sense of. But these parables *he expounded to them, when they were alone.* We cannot but wish we had had that exposition, as we had of the parable of the sower; but it was not so needful; because, when the church should be enlarged, that would *expound* these parables to us, without any more ado.

Verses 35–41

This miracle which Christ wrought for the relief of his disciples, in stilling the storm, we had before (Mt. 8:23, etc.); but it is here more fully related. Observe,

1. It was *the same day* that he had preached out of a ship, *when the even was come, v.* 35. When he had been *labouring in the word and doctrine* all day, instead of reposing himself, he exposeth himself, to teach us not to think of a constant remaining rest till we come to heaven. The end of a toil may perhaps be but the beginning of a toss. But observe, the ship that Christ made his pulpit is taken under his special protection, and, though in danger, cannot sink. What is used for Christ, he will take particular care of.

2. He himself proposed putting to sea at night, because he would lose no time; *Let us pass over to the other side;* for we shall find, in the next chapter, he has work to do there. Christ went about doing good, and no difficulties in his way should hinder him; thus industrious we should be in serving him, and our generation according to his will.

3. They did not put to sea, till *they had sent away the multitude,* that is, had given to each of them that which they came for, and answered all their requests; for he sent none home complaining that they had attended him *in vain.* Or, They sent them away *with a solemn blessing;* for Christ came into the world, not only to pronounce, but to *command,* and to *give,* the blessing.

4. They took him *even as he was,* that is, in the same dress that he was in when he preached, without any cloak to throw over him, which he ought to have had, to keep him *warm,* when he went to sea at night, especially after preaching. We must not hence infer that we may be careless of our health, but we may learn hence not to be over nice and solicitous about the body.

5. The storm was so great, that the ship was *full of water* (*v.* 37), not by springing a leak, but perhaps partly with the shower, for the word here used signifies a *tempest of wind with rain;* however, the ship being little, the waves beat into it so that *it was full.* Note, It is no new thing for that ship to be greatly hurried and endangered, in which Christ and his disciples, Christ and his name and gospel, are embarked.

6. There were *with him other little ships,* which, no doubt, shared in the distress and danger. Probably, these *little ships* carried those who were desirous to go along with Christ, for the benefit of his preaching and miracles on the other side. The *multitude went away* when he put to sea, but some there were, that would venture upon the water with him. Those follow the Lamb aright, that follow him *wherever he goes.* And those that hope for a happiness in Christ, must be willing to take their lot with him, and run the same risks that he runs. One may boldly and cheerfully put to sea in Christ's company, yea though we foresee a storm.

7. Christ was asleep in this storm; and here we are told that it was *in the hinder part of the ship,* the pilot's place: he lay at the helm, to intimate that, as Mr. George Herbert expresses it,

> When winds and waves assault my keel,
> He doth preserve it, he doth steer,
> Ev'n when the boat seems most to reel.
> Storms are the triumph of his art;
> Though he may close his eyes, yet not his heart.

He had a *pillow* there, such a one as a fisherman's ship would furnish him with. And he *slept,* to try the faith of his disciples and to stir up prayer: upon the trial, their faith appeared *weak,* and their prayers *strong.* Note, Sometimes when the church is in a storm, Christ seems as if he were asleep, unconcerned in the troubles of his people, and regardless of their prayers, and doth not presently appear for their relief. *Verily he is a God that hideth himself,* Isa. 45:15. But as, when he tarries, he doth not tarry (Hab. 2:3), so when he sleeps he doth not sleep; the keeper of Israel doth not so much as slumber (Ps. 121:3, 4); he slept, but his heart was awake, as the spouse, Cant. 5:2.

8. His disciples encouraged themselves with their having his presence, and thought it the best way to improve that, and appeal to that, and ply the oar of prayer rather than their other oars. Their confidence lay in this, that they had their Master with them; and the ship that has Christ in it, though it may be *tossed,* cannot *sink;* the bush that has God in it, though it may *burn,* shall not *consume.* Caesar encouraged the master of the ship, that had him on board, with this, *Caesarem vehis, et fortunam Caesaris — Thou hast Caesar on board, and Caesar's fortune.* They *awoke Christ.* Had not the necessity of the case called for it, they would not have *stirred up* or *awoke* their Master, *till he had pleased* (Cant. 2:7); but they knew he would *forgive them this wrong.* When Christ seems as if he slept in a storm, he is awaked by the prayers of his people; when we know not what to do, our eye must be to him (2 Chr. 20:12); we may be at our wits' end, but not at our faith's end, while we have such a Saviour to go to. Their address to Christ is here expressed very emphatically; *Mas-*

ter, carest thou not that we perish? I confess this sounds somewhat harsh, rather like chiding him for sleeping than begging him to awake. I know no excuse for it, but the great familiarity which he was pleased to admit them into, and the freedom he allowed them; and the present distress they were in, which put them into such a fright, that they knew not what they said. *They* do Christ a deal of wrong, who suspect him to be *careless* of his people in distress. The matter is not so; he is not willing that any should perish, much less any of his little ones, Mt. 18:14.

9. The word of command with which Christ rebuked the storm, we have here, and had not in Matthew, *v.* 39. He says, *Peace, be still — Siōpa, pephimōso — be silent, be dumb.* Let not the wind any longer roar, nor the sea rage. Thus he *stills the noise of the sea, the noise of her waves;* a particular emphasis is laid upon the noisiness of them, Ps. 65:7, and 93:3, 4. The noise is threatening and terrifying; let us hear no more of it. This is, (1.) A word of command to us; when our wicked hearts are *like the troubled sea which cannot rest* (Isa. 57:20); when our passions are up, and are unruly, let us think we hear the law of Christ, saying, *Be silent, be dumb.* Think not confusedly, speak not unadvisedly; but *be still.* (2.) A word of comfort to us, that, be the storm of trouble ever so loud, ever so strong, Jesus Christ can lay it with a word's speaking. When without are fightings, and within are fears, and the spirits are in a tumult, Christ can *create the fruit of the lips, peace.* If he say, *Peace, be still,* there is a *great calm* presently. It is spoken of as God's prerogative to command the seas, Jer. 31:35. By this therefore Christ proves himself to be God. He that made the seas, can make them *quiet.*

10. The reproof Christ gave them for their fears, is here carried further than in Matthew. There it is, *Why are ye fearful?* Here, *Why are ye so fearful?* Though there may be cause for some fear, yet not for fear to such a degree as this. There it is, *O ye of little faith.* Here it is, *How is it that ye have no faith?* Not that the disciples were without faith. No, they believed that *Jesus is the Christ, the Son of God;* but at this time their fears prevailed so that they seemed to *have no faith* at all. It was out of the way, when they had occasion for it, and so it was as if they had not had it. *"How is it, that in this matter ye have no faith,* that ye think I would not come in with seasonable and effectual relief?" Those may suspect their faith, who can entertain such a thought as that Christ *careth not* though his *people perish,* and Christ justly takes it ill.

Lastly, The impression this miracle made upon the disciples, is here differently expressed. In Matthew it is said, *The men marvelled;* here it is said, *They feared greatly.* They *feared a great fear;* so the original reads it. Now their fear was rectified by their faith. When they feared the winds and the seas, it was for want of the reverence they ought to have had for Christ. But now that they saw a demonstration of his power over them, they feared *them* less, and *him* more. They *feared* lest they had offended Christ by their unbelieving fears; and therefore studied now to give him honour. They had *feared* the power and wrath of the Creator in the storm, and that fear had torment and amazement in it; but now they feared the power and grace of the Redeemer in the calm; they *feared the Lord and his goodness,* and it had pleasure and satisfaction in it, and by it they gave glory to Christ, as Jonah's mariners, who, when the *sea ceased from her raging, feared the Lord exceedingly, and offered a sacrifice unto the Lord,* Jon. 1:16. This sacrifice they offered to the honour of Christ; they said, *What manner of man is this?* Surely more than a man, *for even the winds and the seas obey him.*

CHAPTER 5

In this chapter, we have, I. Christ's casting the legion of devils out of the man possessed, and suffering them to enter into the swine (*v.* 1–20). II. Christ's healing the woman with the bloody issue, in the way as he was going to raise Jairus's daughter to life (*v.* 21–43). These three miracles we had the story of before (Mt. 8:28, etc. and Mt. 9:18, etc.) but more fully related here.

Verses 1–20

We have here an instance of Christ's dispossessing the strong man armed, and disposing of him as he pleased, to make it appear that he was *stronger than he.* This he did when he was come *to the other side,* whither he went through a storm; his business there was to rescue this poor creature out of the hands of Satan, and when he had done that, he returned. Thus he came from heaven to earth, and returned, in a storm, to redeem a remnant of mankind out of the hands of the devil, though but a *little remnant,* and did not think his pains *ill bestowed.*

In Matthew, they were said to be *two* possessed with devils; here it is said to be a *man* possessed with an unclean spirit. If there were *two,* there was one, and Mark doth not say that there was *but one;* so that this difference cannot give us any just offence; it is probable that one of them was much more remarkable than the other, and said what was said. Now observe here,

I. The miserable condition that this poor creature was in; he was under the power of an *unclean spirit,* the devil got possession of him, and the effect of it was not, as in many, a silent melancholy, but a raging frenzy; he was raving mad; his condition seems to have been worse than any of the possessed, that were Christ's patients.

1. He had *his dwelling among the tombs,* among the graves of dead people. Their tombs were out of the cities, in *desolate places* (Job 3:14); which gave the devil great advantage: for *woe to him that is alone.* Perhaps the devil drove him to *the tombs,* to make people fancy that the souls of the dead were turned into daemons, and did what mischief was done, so to excuse themselves from it. The touch of a grave was polluting, Num. 19:16. The *unclean spirit* drives people into that company that is *defiling,* and so keeps possession of them. Christ, by rescuing souls out of Satan's power, *saves the living from among the dead.*

2. He was very strong and ungovernable; *No man could bind him,* as it is requisite both for their own good, and for the safety of others, that those who are distracted should be. Not only cords would not hold him, but *chains* and *fetters of iron* would not, *v.* 3, 4. Very deplorable is the case of such as *need to be* thus *bound,* and of all miserable people in this world they are most to be pitied; but his case was worst of all, in whom the devil was so strong, that he could not be *bound.* This sets forth the sad condition of those souls in which the devil has dominion; those *children of disobedience,* in whom that unclean spirit works. Some notoriously wilful sinners are like this madman; all are herein *like the horse and the mule,* that they need to be *held in with bit and bridle;* but some are like the *wild ass,* that will not be so held. The commands and curses of the law are as *chains* and *fetters,* to restrain sinners from their wicked courses; but they *break those bands in sunder,* and it is an evidence of the power of the devil in them.

3. He was a terror and torment to himself and to all about him, *v.* 5. The devil is a *cruel* master to those that are *led captive* by him, a perfect tyrant; this wretched creature was *night and day in the mountains and in the tombs, crying, and cutting himself with stones,* either bemoaning his own deplorable case, or in a rage and indignation against heaven. Men in frenzies often wound and destroy themselves; what is a man, when reason is *de*throned and Satan *en*throned? The worshippers of Baal in their fury *cut themselves,* like this madman in his. The voice of God is, *Do thyself no harm;* the voice of Satan is, *Do thyself all the harm thou canst;* yet God's word is despised, and Satan's regarded. Perhaps his *cutting himself with stones* was only cutting his feet with the sharp stones he ran barefoot upon.

II. His application to Christ (*v.* 6); *When he saw Jesus afar off,* coming ashore, he *ran, and worshipped him.* He usually *ran upon* others with *rage,* but he *ran to* Christ with *reverence.* That was done by an invisible hand of Christ, which could not be done with chains and fetters; his fury was all on a sudden curbed. Even the devil, in this poor creature, was forced to tremble before Christ, and bow to him: or, rather, the poor man came, and *worshipped Christ,* in a sense of the need he had of his help, the power of Satan in and over him being, for this instant, suspended.

III. The word of command Christ gave to the unclean spirit, to quit his possession (*v.* 8); *Come out of him, thou unclean spirit.* He made the man desirous to be relieved, when he enabled him to *run, and worship him,* and then put forth his power for his relief. If Christ *work in us* heartily to pray for a deliverance from Satan, he will work for us that deliverance. Here is an instance of the power and authority with which Christ *commanded the unclean spirits, and they obeyed him, ch.* 1:27. He said, *Come out of the man.* The design of Christ's gospel is to *expel* unclean spirits out of the souls of people; *"Come out of the man, thou unclean spirit,* that the Holy Spirit may enter, may take possession of the heart, and have dominion in it."

IV. The dread which the devil had of Christ. The *man ran,* and *worshipped Christ;* but it was the devil in the man, that *cried with a loud voice* (making use of the poor man's tongue), *What have I to do with thee? v.* 7. Just as that other unclean spirit, *ch.* 1:24. 1. He calls God the *most high God,* above all other gods. By the name *Elion — the Most High,* God was *known* among the Phoenicians, and the other nations that bordered upon Israel; and by that name the devil calls him. 2. He owns Jesus to be the *Son of God.* Note, It is no strange thing to hear the best words drop from the worst mouths. There is such a way of saying this as none can attain to but *by the Holy Ghost* (1 Co. 12:3); yet it may be said, after a sort, by the *unclean spirit.* There is no judging of men by their loose sayings; but by their fruits ye shall know them. Piety from the teeth outward is an easy thing. The most fair-spoken hypocrite cannot say better than to call Jesus the Son of God, and yet that the devil did. 3. He disowns any design against Christ; *"What have I to do with thee?* I have no need of thee, I pretend to none; I desire to have nothing to do with thee; I *cannot stand* before thee, and *would not* fall." 4. He deprecates his wrath; I *adjure thee,* that is, "I earnestly beseech thee, by all that is sacred, I beg of thee for God's sake, by whose permission I have got possession of this man, that, though thou drive me out hence, yet that thou *torment me not,* that thou do not restrain me from doing mischief somewhere else; though I know I am *sentenced,* yet let me not be *sent* to the chains of darkness, or hindered from going to and fro, to *devour.*"

V. The account Christ took from this unclean spirit of his name. This we had not in Matthew. Christ asked him, *What is thy name?* Not but that Christ could call all the *fallen* stars, as well as the *morning* stars, by their names; but he demands this, that the standers by might be affected with the vast numbers and power of those malignant infernal spirits, as they had reason to be, when the answer was, *My name is Legion, for we are many;* a *legion* of soldiers among the Romans consisted, some say, of six thousand men, others of twelve thousand and five hundred; but the number of a legion with them, like that of a regiment with us, was not always the same. Now this intimates that the devils, the infernal powers, are, 1. *Military* powers; a legion is a number of soldiers in arms. The devils war against God and his glory, Christ and his gospel, men and their holiness and happiness. They are such as we are to *resist* and *wrestle against,* Eph. 6:12. 2. That they are *numerous;* he *owns,* or rather he *boasts — We are many;* as if he hoped to be *too many* for Christ himself to deal with. What multitudes of apostate spirits were there, and all enemies to God and man; when here were a legion posted to keep garrison in one poor wretched creature against Christ! Many there are that rise up against us. 3. That they are *unanimous;* they are *many* devils, and yet but *one legion* engaged in the same wicked cause; and therefore that cavil of the Pharisees, which supposed Satan to cast out Satan, and to be divided against himself, was altogether groundless. It was not *one* of this legion that betrayed the rest, for they all said, as one man, *What have I to do with thee?* 4. That they are very *powerful;* Who can stand before a *legion?* We are not a match for our spiritual enemies, in our own strength; but *in the Lord, and in the power of his might,* we shall be able to *stand against them,* though there are legions of them. 5. That there is *order* among them, as there is in a *legion;* there are *principalities, and powers, and rulers of the darkness of this world,* which supposes that there are those of a lower rank; the *devil* and his angels; the *dragon* and his; the prince of the devils and his subjects: which makes those enemies the more formidable.

VI. The request of this legion, that Christ would suffer them to go into a herd of swine that was *feeding nigh unto the mountains* (*v.* 11), those mountains which the demoniacs haunted, *v.* 5. Their request was, 1. That he *would not send them away out of the country* (*v.* 10); not only that he would not *commit* them, or *confine* them, to their infernal prison, and so *torment them before the time;* but that he would not *banish* them *that country,* as justly he might, because in this poor man they had been such a terror to it, and done so much mischief. They seem to have had a particular affection for *that country;* or, rather, a particular spite to it; and to have liberty to walk *to and fro through* the rest of *the earth,* will not serve (Job 1:7), unless the *range of those mountains* be allowed them for their pasture, Job 39:8. But why would they abide in *that country?* Grotius saith, Because in *that country* there were many *apostate Jews,* who had thrown themselves out of the covenant of God, and had thereby given Satan power over them. And some suggest, that, having by experience got the knowledge of the dispositions and manners of the people of that country, they could the more effectually do them mischief by their temptations. 2. That he would suffer them to *enter into the swine,* by destroying which they hoped to do more mischief to the souls of all the people in the country, than they could by entering into the body of any particular person, which therefore they did not ask leave to do, for they knew Christ would not grant it.

VII. The permission Christ gave them to enter into the swine, and the immediate destruction of the swine thereby; *He gave them leave* (*v.* 13), he did not forbid or restrain them, he let them do as they had a mind. Thus he would let the Gadarenes see what powerful spiteful enemies devils are, that they might thereby be induced to make him their Friend, who alone was able to control and conquer them, and had made it appear that he was so. Immediately the *unclean spirits entered into the swine,* which by the law were unclean creatures, and naturally love to *wallow in the mire,* the fittest place for them. Those that, like the swine, delight in *the mire* of sensual lusts, are fit habitations for Satan, and are, like Babylon, the *hold of every foul spirit,* and a *cage of every unclean and hateful bird* (Rev. 18:2), as pure souls are habitations of the Holy Spirit. The consequence of the devils entering into the swine, was, that they all *ran mad* presently, and ran headlong into the adjoining sea, where they were all drowned, to the number of *two thousand.* The man they possessed did only *cut himself,* for God had said, *He is in your hands, only save his life.* But thereby it appeared, that, if he had not been so restrained, the poor man would have *drowned himself.* See how much we are indebted to the providence of God, and the ministration of good angels, for our preservation from malignant spirits.

VIII. The report of all this dispersed through the country immediately. They that *fed the swine,* hastened to the owners, to give an account of their charge, *v.* 14. This drew the people together, to see what was done: and, 1. When they saw how wonderfully the poor man was cured, they hence conceived a *veneration for Christ, v.* 15. They saw him that was *possessed with the devil,* and knew him well enough, by the same token that they had many a time been frightened at the sight of him; and were now as much surprised to see him *sitting clothed and in his right mind;* when Satan was cast out, he came to himself, and was his own man presently. Note, Those who are grave and sober, and live by rule and with consideration, thereby make it appear that by the power of Christ the devil's power is broken in their souls. The sight of this *made them afraid;* it astonished them, and forced them to own the power of Christ, and that he is *worthy to be feared.* But, 2. When they found that their swine were lost, they thence conceived a *dislike of Christ,* and wished to have rather his room than his company; they prayed him to *depart out of their coasts,* for they think not any good he can do them sufficient to make them amends for the loss of so many swine, fat swine, it may be, and ready for the market. Now the devils had what they would have; for by no handle do these evil spirits more effectually manage sinful souls than by that of the love of the world. They were afraid of some further punishment, if Christ should tarry among them, whereas, if they would but part with their sins, he had life and happiness for them; but, being loth to quit either their sins or their swine, they chose rather to abandon their Saviour. Thus *they* do, who, rather than let go a base lust, will throw away their interest in Christ, and their expectations from him. They should rather have argued, "If he has such a power as this over devils and all creatures, it is good having him our Friend; if the devils have leave to tarry *in our country* (*v.* 10), let us entreat *him* to tarry in it too, who alone can control them." But, instead of this, they wished him further off. Such strange misconstructions do carnal hearts make of the just judgments of God; instead of being by them driven to him as they ought, they set him at so much the greater distance; though he hath said, *Provoke me not, and I will do you no hurt,* Jer. 25:6.

IX. An account of the conduct of the poor man after his deliverance. 1. He *desired that he might go along with Christ* (*v.* 18), perhaps for fear lest the evil spirit should again seize him; or, rather, that he might receive instruction from him, being unwilling to stay among those heathenish people that desired him to depart. Those that are freed from the evil spirit, cannot but covet acquaintance and fellowship with Christ. 2. Christ *would not suffer him* to go with him, lest it should savour of ostentation, and to let him know that he could both protect and instruct him at a distance. And besides, he had other work for him to do; he must go home to his friends, and tell them what *great things the Lord had done for him,* the Lord Jesus had done; that Christ might be honoured, and his neighbours and friends might be edified, and invited to believe in Christ. He must take particular notice rather of Christ's *pity* than of his *power,* for that is it which especially he glories in; he must tell them what *compassion* the Lord had had on him in his misery. 3. The man, in a transport of joy, proclaimed, all the country over, what *great things Jesus had done for him, v.* 20. This is a debt we owe both to Christ and to our brethren, that he may be glorified and they edified. And see what was the effect of it; *All men did marvel,* but few went any further. Many that cannot but wonder at the works of Christ, yet do not, as they ought, *wonder after him.*

Verses 21–34

The Gadarenes having desired Christ to leave their country, he did not stay to trouble them long, but presently went by water, as he came, back *to the other side* (*v.* 21), and there *much people gathered to him.* Note, If there be some that reject Christ, yet there are others that receive him, and bid him welcome. A despised gospel will *cross the water,* and go where it will have better entertainment. Now among the many that applied themselves to him,

I. Here is one, that comes *openly* to *beg* a cure for a sick child; and it is no less a person than one of the *rulers of the synagogue,* one that presided in the synagogue-worship or, as some think, one of the judges of the consistory court, which was in every city, consisting of *twenty-three.* He was not named in Matthew, he is here, *Jairus,* or *Jair,* Jdg. 10:3. He addressed himself to Christ, though a ruler, with great humility and reverence; *When he saw him, he fell at his feet,* giving honour to him as one really greater than he appeared to be; and with great importunity, he *besought him greatly,* as one in earnest, as one that not only valued the mercy he came for, but that knew he could obtain it no where else. The case is this, He has a *little daughter,* about twelve years old, the darling of the family, and she *lies a dying;* but he believes that if Christ will but come, and *lay his hands upon her,* she will return even from the gates of the grave. He said, at first, when he came, *She lies a dying* (so Mark); but afterward, upon fresh information sent him, he saith, *She is even now dead* (so Matthew); but he still prosecutes his suit; see Lu. 8:42–49. Christ readily agreed, and went with him, *v.* 24.

II. Here is another, that comes *clandestinely* to *steal* a cure (if I may so say) for herself; and she got the relief she came for. This cure was wrought by *the way,* as he was going to raise the ruler's daughter, and was followed by a crowd. See how Christ improved his time, and lost none of the precious moments of it. Many of his discourses, and some of his miracles, are dates *by the way-side;* we should be doing good, not only when we *sit in the house,* but when we *walk by the way,* Deu. 6:7. Now observe,

1. The piteous case of this poor woman. She had a constant *issue of blood* upon her, for *twelve years,* which had thrown her, no doubt, into great weakness, had embittered the comfort of her life, and threatened to be her death in a little time. She had had the best advice of physicians, that she could get, and had made use of the many medicines and methods they prescribed: as long as she had any thing to give them, they had kept her in hopes that they could cure her; but now that she had spent all she had among them, they gave her up as incurable. See here, (1.) That skin for skin, and all that a man has, will be give for life and health; she spent all she had upon physicians. (2.) It is ill with those patients whose physicians are their worst disease; who *suffer* by their physicians, instead of being relieved by them. (3.) Those that are not *bettered* by medicines, commonly *grow worse,* and the disease gets the more ground. (4.) It is usual with people not to apply themselves to Christ, till they have tried in vain all other helpers, and find them, as certainly they will, *physicians of no value.* And he will be found a *sure refuge,* even to those who make him their *last refuge.*

2. The strong faith that she had in the power of Christ to heal her; she said within herself, though it doth not appear that she was encouraged by any preceding instance to say it, *If I may but touch his clothes, I shall be whole, v.* 28. She believed that he cured, not as a prophet, by virtue *derived* from God, but as the Son of God, by a virtue *inherent* in himself. Her case was such as she could not in modesty tell him publicly, as others did their grievances, and therefore a private cure was what she wished for, and her faith was suited to her case.

3. The wonderful effect produced by it; *She came in the* crowd *behind* him, and with much ado got to *touch his garment,* and immediately she felt the cure wrought, *v.* 29. The flux of blood was *dried up,* and she felt herself perfectly well all over her, as well as ever she was in her life, in an instant; by this it appears that the cure was altogether miraculous; for those that in such cases are cured by natural means, recover their strength slowly and gradually, and not *per saltum — all at once;* but *as for God, his work is perfect.* Note, Those whom Christ heals of the disease of sin, that bloody issue, cannot but experience in themselves a universal change for the better.

4. Christ's enquiry after his concealed patient, and the encouragement he gave her, upon the discovery of her; Christ *knew in himself that virtue had gone out of him, v.* 30. He knew it not by any deficiency of spirits, through the exhausting of this virtue, but rather by an agility of spirits, in the exerting of it, and the innate and inseparable pleasure he had in doing good. And being desirous to see his patient, he asked, not in displeasure, as one affronted, but in tenderness, as one concerned, *Who touched my clothes?* The disciples, not without a show of rudeness and indecency, almost ridiculed his question (*v.* 31); *The multitudes throng thee, and sayest thou, Who touched me?* As if it had been an improper question. Christ passed by the affront, and *looks around* to *see her that had done this thing;* not that he might *blame* her for her presumption, but that he might *commend* and *encourage* her faith, and by his own act and deed might *warrant* and *confirm* the cure, and *ratify* to her that which she had *surreptitiously* obtained. He needed not that any should inform him, for he had presently his eye upon her. Note, As secret acts of sin, so secret acts of faith, are known to the Lord Jesus, and are under his eye. If believers derive virtue from Christ ever so closely, he knows it, and is pleased with it. The poor woman, hereupon, presented herself to the Lord Jesus (*v.* 33), *fearing and trembling,* not knowing how he would take it. Note, Christ's patients are often trembling, when they have reason to be triumphing. She might have come boldly, *knowing what was done in her;* yet, *knowing that,* she *fears* and *trembles.* It was a *surprise,* and was not yet, as it should have been, a *pleasing* surprise. However, she *fell down before him.* Note, There is nothing better for those that fear and tremble, than to throw themselves at the feet of the Lord Jesus; to humble themselves before him, and refer themselves to him. And she *told him all the truth.* Note, We must not be ashamed to own the secret transactions between Christ and our souls; but, when called to it, mention, to his praise, and the encouragement of others, what he has done for our souls, and the experience we have had of *healing virtue* derived from him. And the consideration of this, that nothing can be hid from Christ, should engage us to confess all to him. See what an encouraging word he gave her (*v.* 34); *Daughter, thy faith hath made thee whole.* Note, Christ puts honour upon faith, because faith gives honour to Christ. But see how *what is done by faith* on earth is ratified in heaven; Christ saith, *Be whole of thy disease.* Note, If our faith sets the seal of its *amen* to the power and promise of God, saying, "So it is, and so let it be to me;" God's grace will set the seal of its *amen* to the prayers and hopes of faith, saying, "So be it, and so it shall be, to thee." And therefore, *"Go in peace;* be well satisfied that thy cure is honestly come by, is effectually wrought, and take the comfort of it." Note, They that by faith are healed of their spiritual diseases, have reason to *go in peace.*

Verses 35–43

Diseases and deaths came into the world by the sin and disobedience of the first Adam; but by the grace of the second Adam both are conquered. Christ, having healed an incurable disease, here goes on to triumph over death, as in the beginning of the chapter he had triumphed over an outrageous devil.

I. The melancholy news is brought to Jairus, that his *daughter is dead,* and therefore, if Christ be as other physicians, he comes too late. While there is life, there is hope, and room for the use of means; but when life is gone, it is past recall; *Why troublest thou the Master any further? v.* 35. Ordinarily, the proper thought in this case, is, "The matter is determined, the will of God is done, and I submit, I acquiesce; *The Lord gave, and the Lord hath taken away. While the child was alive, I fasted and wept; for I said, Who can tell but God will yet be gracious to me,* and *the child shall live?* But *now that it is dead, wherefore should I weep?* I *shall go to it, but it shall not return to me.*" With such words we should *quiet ourselves* at such a time, that our souls may be *as a child that is weaned from his mother:* but there the case was extraordinary; the death of the child doth not, as usually, put an end to the narrative.

II. Christ encourageth the afflicted father yet to hope that his application to Christ on the behalf of his child should not be in vain. Christ had staid to work a cure by the way, but he shall be no sufferer by that, nor loser by the gain of others; *Be not afraid, only believe.* We may suppose Jairus at a pause, whether he should ask Christ to go on or no; but have we not as much occasion for the grace of God, and his consolations, and consequently of the prayers of our ministers and Christian friends, when death is in the house, as when sickness is? Christ therefore soon determines this matter; "*Be not afraid* that my coming will be to no purpose, only believe that I will make it turn to a good account." Note, 1. We must not despair concerning our relations that are dead, nor *sorrow* for them *as those that have no hope.* See what is said to Rachel, who *refused to be comforted concerning her children,* upon the presumption that they *were not; Refrain thy voice from weeping, and thine eyes from tears; for there is hope in thine end, that thy children shall come again,* Jer. 31:16, 17. Therefore fear not, faint not. 2. Faith is the only remedy against disquieting grief and fear at such a time: let that silence them, *Only believe.* Keep up a confidence in Christ, and a dependence upon him, and he will do what is for the best. Believe the resurrection, and then be not afraid.

III. He went with a select company to the house where the dead child was. He had, by the crowd that attended him, given advantage to the poor woman he last healed, and, having done that, now he shook off the crowd, and *suffered no man to follow him* (to *follow with him,* so the word is), but his three bosom-disciples, Peter, and James, and John; a competent number to be witnesses of the miracle, but not such a number as that his taking them with him might look like vainglory.

IV. He raised the dead child to life; the circumstances of the narrative here are much the same as we had them in Matthew; only here we may observe,

1. That the child was extremely well beloved, for the relations and neighbours *wept and wailed greatly.* It is very afflictive when that which is come forth like a flower is so *soon cut down,* and withereth before it is grown up; when that grieves us, of which we said, *This same shall comfort us.*

2. That it was evident beyond dispute, that the child was really and truly dead. Their *laughing* Christ to *scorn,* for saying, *She is not dead, but sleepeth,* though highly reprehensible, serves for the proof of this.

3. That Christ put those out as unworthy to be witnesses of the miracle, who were noisy in their sorrow, and were so ignorant in the things of God, as not to understand him when he spoke of death as a *sleep,* or so scornful, as to ridicule him for it.

4. That he took the parents of the child to be witnesses of the miracle, because in it he had an eye to *their faith,* and designed it for *their* comfort, who were the *true,* for they were the *silent* mourners.

5. That Christ raised the child to life by a word of power, which is recorded here, and recorded in Syriac, the language in which Christ spoke, for the greater certainty of the thing; *Talitha, cumi; Damsel, I say unto thee, Arise.* Dr. Lightfoot saith, It was customary with the Jews, when they gave physic to one that was *sick,* to say, *Arise from thy disease;* meaning, *We wish* thou mayest arise: but to one that was *dead,* Christ said, *Arise from the dead;* meaning, *I command* that thou arise; nay, there is more in it — the dead have not power to arise, therefore power goes along with this word, to make it effectual. *Da quod jubes, et jube quod vis — Give what thou commandest, and command what thou wilt.* Christ works while he commands, and works by the command, and therefore may command what he pleaseth, even the dead to arise. Such is the gospel call to those that are by nature dead in trespasses and sins, and can no more rise from that death by their own power, than this child could; and yet that word, *Awake, and arise from the dead,* is neither vain, nor in vain, when it follows immediately, *Christ shall give thee light,* Eph. 5:14. It is by the word of Christ that spiritual life is given, *I said unto thee, Live,* Eze. 16:6.

6. That the damsel, as soon as life returned, *arose, and walked, v.* 42. Spiritual life will appear by our *rising* from the bed of sloth and carelessness, and our *walking* in a religious conversation, our walking *up and down* in Christ's name and strength; even from those that are *of the age of twelve years,* it may be expected that they should walk as those whom Christ has *raised to life,* otherwise than in the native *vanity of their minds.*

7. That all who saw it, and heard of it, admired the miracle, and him that wrought it; *They were astonished with a great astonishment.* They could not but acknowledge that there was something in it extraordinary and very great, and yet they knew not what to make of it, or to infer from it. Their wonder should have worked forward to a lively faith, but it rested in a *stupor* or *astonishment.*

8. That Christ endeavoured to conceal it; *He charged them straitly, that no man should know it.* It was sufficiently known to a competent number, but he would not have it as yet *proclaimed* any further; because his own resurrection was to be the great instance of his power over death, and therefore the divulging of other instances must be reserved till that great proof was given: let one part of the evidence be kept private, till the other part, on which the main stress lies, be made ready.

9. That Christ took care something should be *given her to eat.* By this it appeared that she was raised not only to life, but to a good state of health, that she had an appetite to her meat; even the new-born babes in Christ's house desire the sincere milk, 1 Pt. 2:1, 2. And it is observable, that, as Christ, when at first he had made man, presently provided food for him, and food out of the earth of which he was made (Gen. 1:29), so now when he had given a new life, he took care that something should be given to eat; for is he has given *life,* he may be trusted to give *livelihood,* because *the life is more than meat,* Mt. 6:25. Where Christ hath given *spiritual life,* he will provide food for the support and nourishment of it unto life eternal, for he will *never forsake,* or be wanting to, the *work of his own hands.*

CHAPTER 6

A great variety of observable passages we have, in this chapter, concerning our Lord Jesus, the substance of all which we had before in Matthew, but divers circumstances we have, which we did not there meet with. Here is, I. Christ contemned by his countrymen, because he was one of them, and they knew, or thought they knew, his original (*v.* 1–6). II. The just power he gave his apostles over unclean spirits, and an account given of their negotiation (*v.* 7–13). III. A strange notion which Herod and others had of Christ, upon which occasion we have the story of the martyrdom of John Baptist (*v.* 14–29). IV. Christ's retirement into a desert place with his disciples; the crowds that followed him thither to receive instruction from him; and his feeding five thousand of them with five loaves and two fishes (*v.* 30–44). V. Christ's walking upon the sea to his disciples, and the abundance of cures he wrought on the other side of the water (*v.* 45–56).

Verses 1–6

Here, I. Christ makes a visit to *his own country,* the place not of his birth, but of his education; that was *Nazareth;* where his relations were. He had been in danger of his life among them (Lu. 4:29), and yet he came among them again; so strangely doth he wait to be gracious, and seek the salvation of his enemies. Whither he went, though it was into danger, *his disciples followed him* (*v.* 1); for they had left all, to follow him whithersoever he went.

II. There he *preached* in their *synagogue,* on the *sabbath day, v.* 2. It seems, there was not such flocking to him there as in other places, so that he had no opportunity of preaching till they came together on the sabbath day; and then he expounded a portion of scripture with great clearness. In religious assemblies, on sabbath days, the word of God is to be preached according to Christ's example. We *give glory* to God by receiving instruction from him.

III. They could not but own that which was very honourable concerning him. 1. That he spoke with great *wisdom,* and that this wisdom was *given to him,* for they knew he had no learned education. 2. That he did *mighty works,* did them with his own hands, for the confirming of the doctrine he taught. They acknowledged the two great proofs of the divine original of his gospel — the *divine wisdom* that appeared in the contrivance of it, and the *divine power* that was exerted for the ratifying and recommending of it; and yet, though they could not deny the premises, they would not admit the conclusion.

IV. They studied to disparage him, and to raise prejudices in the minds of people against him, notwithstanding. All this *wisdom,* and all these *mighty works,* shall be of no account, because he had a home-education, had never travelled, nor been at any university, or bred up at the feet of any of their doctors (*v.* 3); *Is not this the Carpenter?* In Matthew, they upbraid him with being the carpenter's son, his supposed father Joseph being of that trade. But, it seems, they could say further, *Is not this the Carpenter?* our Lord Jesus, it is probable, employing himself in that business with his father, before he entered upon his public ministry, at least, sometimes in journey-work. 1. He would thus *humble himself,* and make himself of no reputation, as one that had taken upon him the form of a servant, and came to minister. Thus low did our Redeemer stoop, when he came to redeem us out of our low estate. 2. He would thus teach us to *abhor idleness,* and to find *ourselves something to do* in this world; and rather to take up with mean and laborious employments, and such as no more is to be got by than a bare livelihood, than indulge ourselves in sloth. Nothing is more pernicious for young people than to get a *habit of sauntering.* The Jews had a good rule for this — that their young men who were designed for scholars, were yet bred up to some trade, as Paul was a tentmaker, that they might have some business to fill up their time with, and, if need were, to get their bread with. 3. He would thus put an honour upon despised mechanics, and encourage those who eat the labour of their hands, though great men look upon them with contempt.

Another thing they upbraided him with, was, the meanness of his relations; "*He is the son of Mary;* his *brethren* and *sisters* are here *with us;* we know his family and kindred;" and therefore, though they were *astonished* at his doctrine (*v.* 2), yet they were *offended* at his person (*v.* 3), were prejudiced against him, and looked upon him with contempt; and for that reason would not receive his doctrine, though ever so well recommended. May we think that if they had not known his pedigree, but he had dropped among them from the clouds, without father, without mother, and without descent, they would have entertained him with any more respect? Truly, no; for in Judea, where this was not know, that was made an objection against him (Jn. 9:29); *As for this fellow, we know not from whence he is.* Obstinate unbelief will never want excuses.

V. Let us see how Christ bore this contempt.

1. He partly *excused it,* as a common thing, and what might be expected, though not reasonably or justly (*v.* 4); *A prophet is not despised any where but in his own country.* Some exceptions there may be to this rule; doubtless many have got over this prejudice, but ordinarily it holds good, that ministers are seldom so acceptable and successful in their own country as among strangers; *familiarity* in the younger years breeds a contempt, the advancement of one that was an inferior begets *envy,* and men will hardly set those among the guides of their souls whose fathers they were ready to set with the dogs of their flock; in such a case therefore it must not be thought hard, it is common treatment, it was Christ's, and *wisdom is profitable to direct* to other soil.

2. He did *some good* among them, notwithstanding the slights they put upon him, for he is kind even to the evil and unthankful; *He laid his hands upon a few sick folks, and healed them.* Note, It is generous, and becoming the followers of Christ, to content themselves with the pleasure and satisfaction of doing good, though they be unjustly denied the praise of it.

3. Yet he *could there do* no such mighty works, at least not so many, as in other places, because of the unbelief that prevailed among the people, by reason of the prejudices which their leaders instilled into them against Christ, *v.* 5. It is a strange expression, as if unbelief tied the hands of omnipotence itself; he *would have done* as many miracles there as he had done elsewhere, but he could not, because people would not make application to him, nor sue for his favours; he could have wrought them, but they forfeited the honour of having them wrought for them. Note, By unbelief and contempt of Christ men stop the current of his favours to them, and put a bar in their own door.

4. He *marvelled because of their unbelief, v.* 6. We never find Christ wondering but at the *faith* of the Gentiles that were strangers, as the *centurion* (Mt. 8:10), and the woman of Samaria, and at the unbelief of Jews that were his own coun-

trymen. Note, The unbelief of those that enjoy the means of grace, is a most amazing thing.

5. He *went round about the village, teaching.* If we cannot do good where we would, we must do it where we can, and be glad if we may have any opportunity, though but in the villages, of serving Christ and souls. Sometimes the gospel of Christ finds better entertainment in the country villages, where there is less wealth, and pomp, and mirth, and subtlety, than in the populous cities.

Verses 7–13

Here is, I. The commission given to the twelve apostles, to preach and work miracles; it is the same which we had more largely, Mt. 10. Mark doth not name them here, as Matthew doth, because he had named them before, when they were first called into fellowship with him, *ch.* 3:16–19. Hitherto they had been conversant with Christ, and had set at his feet, had heard his doctrine, and seen his miracles; and now he determines to make some use of them; they had *received,* that they might *give,* had *learned,* that they might *teach;* and therefore now he *began to send them forth.* They must not always be studying in the academy, to get knowledge, but they must preach in the country, to do good with the knowledge they have got. Though they were not as yet so well accomplished as they were to be, yet, according to their present ability and capacity, they must be set to work, and make further improvements afterward. Now observe here,

1. That Christ sent them forth *by two and two;* this Mark takes notice of. They went two and two to a place, that out of the mouth of two witnesses every word might be established; and that they might be company for one another when they were among strangers, and might strengthen the hands, and encourage the hearts, one of another; might help one another if any thing should be amiss, and keep one another in countenance. Every common soldier has his comrade; and it is an approved maxim, *Two are better than one.* Christ would thus teach his ministers to associate, and both lend and borrow help.

2. That he *gave them power over unclean spirits.* He commissioned them to attack the devil's kingdom, and empowered them, as a specimen of their breaking his interest in the souls of men by their doctrine, to cast him out of the bodies of those that were possessed. Dr. Lightfoot suggests, that they cured diseases, and cast out devils, by the Spirit, but preached that only which they had learned from the mouth of Christ.

3. That he *commanded them* not to take provisions along with them, neither *victuals* nor *money,* that they might appear, wherever they came, to be poor men, men not of this world, and therefore might with the better grace call people off from it to another world. When afterward he bid them *take purse and scrip* (Lu. 22:36), that did not intimate (as Dr. Lightfoot observes) that his care of them was abated from what it had been; but that they should meet with worse times and worse entertainment than they met with at their first mission. In Matthew and Luke they are forbidden to *take staves* with them, that is, fighting staves; but here in Mark they are bid to take nothing save a *staff only,* that is, a walking staff, such as pilgrims carried. They must not put on *shoes,* but *sandals* only, which were only the soles of shoes tied under their feet, or like pumps, or slippers; they must go in the readiest plainest dress they could, and must not so much as have *two coats;* for their stay abroad would be short, they must return before winter, and what they wanted, those they preached to would cheerfully accommodate them with.

4. He directed them, whatever city they came to, to make that house their head-quarters, which happened to be their first quarters (*v.* 10); *"There abide, till ye depart from that place.* And since ye know ye come on an errand sufficient to make you welcome, have such charity for your friends that first invited you, as to believe they do not think you burthensome."

5. He pronounces a very heavy doom upon those that rejected the gospel they preached (*v.* 11); *"Whosoever shall not receive you,* or will not so much as *hear you, depart thence* (if one will not, another will), and *shake off the dust under your feet, for a testimony against* them. Let them know that they have had a fair offer of life and happiness made them, witness that dust; but that, since they have refused it, they cannot expect ever to have another; let them take up with their own dust, for so shall their doom be." That dust, like the dust of Egypt (Ex. 9:9), shall turn into a plague to them; and their condemnation in the great day, will be more intolerable than *that of Sodom:* for the angels were sent to Sodom, and were abused there; yet that would not bring on so great a guilt and so great a ruin as the contempt and abuse of the apostles of Christ, who bring with them the offers of gospel grace.

II. The apostles' conduct in pursuance of their commission. Though they were conscious to themselves of great weakness, and expected no secular advantage by it, yet, in obedience to their Master's order, and in dependence upon his strength, they *went out* as Abraham, not knowing whither they went. Observe here,

1. The doctrine they preached; *They preached that men should repent* (*v.* 12); that they should change their minds, and reform their lives, in consideration of the near approach of the kingdom of the Messiah. Note, The great design of the gospel preachers, and the great tendency of gospel preaching, should be, to bring people to repentance, to a *new heart* and a *new way.* They did not amuse people with curious speculations, but told them that they must repent of their sins, and turn to God.

2. The miracles they wrought. The power Christ gave them *over unclean spirits,* was not ineffectual, nor did they receive it in vain, but used it, for they *cast out many devils* (*v.* 13); and they *anointed with oil many that were sick, and healed them.* Some think this oil was used *medicinally,* according to the custom of the Jews; but I rather think it was used as a *sign of miraculous* healing, by the appointment of Christ, though not mentioned; and it was afterward used by those *elders of the church,* to whom *by the Spirit* was given the *gift of healing,* Jam. 5:14. It is certain here, and therefore probable there, that *anointing the sick with oil,* is appropriated to that extraordinary power which has long ceased, and therefore that sign must cease with it.

Verses 14–29

Here is, I. The wild notions that the people had concerning our Lord Jesus, *v.* 15. His own countrymen could believe nothing great concerning him, because they knew his poor kindred; but others that were not under the power of that prejudice against him, were yet willing to believe any thing rather than the truth — that he was the Son of God, and the true Messias: they said, He is Elias, whom they expected; or, *He is a prophet,* one of the Old-Testament prophets raised to life, and returned to this world; or *as one of the prophets,* a prophet now newly raised up, equal to those under the Old Testament.

II. The opinion of Herod concerning him. He heard of *his name* and fame, of what he said and what he did; and he said, "It is certainly John Baptist, *v.* 14. As sure as we are here, *It is John, whom I beheaded, v.* 16. He is *risen from the dead;* and though while he was with us *he did no miracle,* yet, having removed for awhile to another world, he is come again with greater power, and *now mighty works do show forth themselves in him."*

Note, 1. Where there is an *idle faith,* there is commonly a *working fancy.* The people said, It is a prophet risen from the dead; Herod said, It is *John Baptist risen from the dead.* It seems by this, that the *rising of a prophet from the dead,* to do *mighty works,* was a thing expected, and was thought neither impossible nor improbable, and it was now readily suspected when it was *not true;* but afterward, when *it was true* concerning Christ, and a truth undeniably evidenced, yet then it was obstinately gainsaid and denied. Those who most wilfully disbelieve the truth, are commonly most credulous of errors and fancies.

2. They who fight against the cause of God, will find themselves baffled, even when they think themselves conquerors; they cannot gain their point, for the word of the Lord endures for ever. They who rejoiced when the witnesses were slain, fretted as much, when in three or four days they *rose again* in their successors, Rev. 11:10, 11. The impenitent unreformed sinner, that escapeth the sword of Jehu, shall Elisha slay.

3. A guilty conscience needs no accuser or tormentor but itself. Herod charges himself with the murder of John, which perhaps no one else dare charge him with; *I beheaded him;* and the terror of it made him imagine that Christ was John risen. He feared John while he lived, and now, when he thought he had got clear of him, fears him ten times worse when he is dead. One might as well be haunted with ghosts and furies, as with the horrors of an accusing conscience; those therefore who would keep an undisturbed peace, must keep an undefiled conscience, Acts 24:16.

4. There may be the terrors of strong conviction, where there is not the truth of a saving conversion. This Herod, who had this notion concerning Christ, afterward sought to kill him (Lu. 13:31), and did set him at nought (Lu. 23:11); so that he will not be persuaded, though it be *by one risen from the dead;* no, not by a John the Baptist risen from the dead.

III. A narrative of Herod's putting John Baptist to death, which is brought in upon this occasion, as it was in Matthew. And here we may observe,

1. The great value and veneration which Herod had some time had for John Baptist, which is related only by this evangelist, *v.* 20. Here we see what a great way a man may go toward grace and glory, and yet come short of both, and perish eternally.

(1.) He *feared John, knowing that he was a just man, and a holy.* It is possible that a man may have a great reverence for good men, and especially for good ministers, yea, and for that in them that is good, and yet himself be a bad man. Observe, [1.] John was a *just man, and a holy;* to make a complete good man, both justice and holiness are necessary; holiness toward God, and justice toward men. John was mortified to this world, and so was a good friend both to justice and holiness. [2.] Herod knew this, not only by common fame, but by personal acquaintance with him. Those that have but little justice and holiness themselves, may yet discern it with respect in others. And, [3.] He therefore *feared* him, he honoured him. Holiness and justice command veneration, and many that are not good themselves, have respect for those that are.

(2.) He *observed* him; he sheltered him from the malice of his enemies (so some understand it); or, rather, he had a regard to his exemplary conversation, and took notice of that in him that was praiseworthy, and commended it in the hearing of those about him; he made it appear that he observed what John said and did.

(3.) He *heard him* preach; which was great condescension, considering how mean John's appearance was. To hear Christ himself preach in our streets will be but a poor plea in the great day, Lu. 13:26.

(4.) He *did many of those things* which John in his preaching taught him. He was not only a *hearer of the word,* but in part a *doer of the work.* Some sins which John in his preaching reproved, he forsook, and some duties he bound himself to; but it will not suffice to do *many* things, unless we have *respect to all* the commandments.

(5.) He *heard him gladly.* He did not hear him with terror as Felix heard Paul, but heard him with pleasure. There is a flashy joy, which a hypocrite may have in hearing the word; Ezekiel was to his hearers as a *lovely song* (Eze. 33:32); and the *stony ground received the word with joy,* Lu. 8:13.

2. John's faithfulness to Herod, in telling him of his faults. Herod had married his brother Philip's wife, *v.* 17. All the country, no doubt, cried shame on him for it, and reproached him for it; but John *reproved* him, told him plainly, *It is not lawful for thee to have thy brother's wife.* This was Herod's own iniquity, which he could not leave, when he did many things that John taught him; and therefore John tells him of this particularly. Though he were a king, he would not spare him, any more than Elijah did Ahab, when he said, *Hast thou killed and also taken possession?* Though John had an interest in him, and he might fear this plain-dealing would destroy his interest, yet he reproved him; for *faithful are the wounds of a friend* (Prov. 27:6); and though there are some swine that will *turn again, and rend* those that *cast pearls* before them, yet, ordinarily, *he that rebuketh a man* (if the person reproved has any thing of the understanding of a man), *afterwards shall find more favour than he that flattereth with his tongue,* Prov. 28:23. Though it was dangerous to offend Herod, and much more to offend Herodias, yet John would run the hazard rather than be wanting in his duty. Note, Those ministers that would be found faithful in the work of God, must not be afraid of the face of man. If we seek to please men, further than is for their spiritual good, we are not the servants of Christ.

3. The malice which Herodias bore to John for this (*v.* 19); She *had a quarrel with him, and would have killed him;* but when she could not obtain that, she got him committed to prison, *v.* 17. Herod respected him, till he touched him in his Herodias. Many that pretend to honour prophesying, are for smooth things only, and love good preaching, if it keep far

enough from their beloved sin; but if that be touched, they cannot bear it. No marvel if the world hate those who testify of it that its works are evil. But it is better that sinners persecute ministers now for their faithfulness, than curse them eternally for their unfaithfulness.

4. The plot laid to take off John's head. I am apt to think that Herod was himself in the plot, notwithstanding his pretences to be displeased and surprised, and that the thing was concerted between him and Herodias; for it is said to be *when a convenient day was come* (v. 21), fit for such a purpose. (1.) There must be a ball at court, upon the king's birth-day, and a supper prepared for *his lords, high captains, and chief estates of Galilee.* (2.) To grace the solemnity, the daughter of Herodias must *dance* publicly, and Herod must take on him to be wonderfully charmed with her dancing; and if he be, they that *sit with him* cannot but, in compliment to him, be so too. (3.) The king hereupon must make her an extravagant promise, to give her *whatever she would ask,* even to the *half of the kingdom;* and yet, that, if rightly understood, would not have reached the end designed, for John Baptist's head was worth more than his *whole kingdom.* This promise is bound with an oath, that no room might be left to fly off from it; *He sware unto her, Whatsoever thou shalt ask, I will give.* I can scarcely think he would have made such an unlimited promise, but that he knew what she would ask. (4.) She, being instructed by Herodias her mother, asked the *head of John Baptist;* and she must have it brought her *in a charger,* as a pretty thing for her to play with (v. 24, 25); and there must be no delay, no time lost, she must have it *by and by.* (5.) Herod granted it, and the execution was done immediately while the company were together, which we can scarcely think the king would have done, if he had not determined the matter before. But he takes on him, [1.] To be very backward to it, and that he would not for all the world have done it, if he had not been surprised into such a promise; The *king was exceeding sorry,* that is, he seemed to be so, he said he was so, he looked as if he had been so; but it was all sham and grimace, he was really pleased that he had found a pretence to get John out of the way. *Qui nescit dissimulare, nescit regnare — The man who cannot dissemble, knows not how to reign.* And yet he was not without sorrow for it; he could not do it but with great regret and reluctancy; natural conscience will not suffer men to sin easily; the very commission of it is vexatious; what then will the reflection upon it be? [2.] He takes on him to be very sensible of the obligation of his oath; whereas if the damsel had asked but a fourth part of his kingdom, I doubt not but he would have found out a way to evade his oath. The promise was rashly made, and could not bind him to do an unrighteous thing. Sinful oaths must be repented of, and therefore not performed; for repentance is the undoing of what we have done amiss, as far as is in our power. When Theodosius the emperor was urged by a suitor with a *promise,* he answered, *I said it,* but did not *promise* it if it be unjust. If we may suppose that Herod knew nothing of the design when he made that rash promise, it is probable that he was hurried into the doing of it by those about him, only to carry on the humour; for he did it *for their sakes who sat with him,* whose company he was proud of, and therefore would do any thing to gratify them. Thus do princes make themselves slave to those whose respect they covet, and both value and secure themselves by. None of Herod's subjects stood in more awe of him than he did of *his lords, high captains, and chief estates.* The king sent an *executioner,* a soldier of his guard. Bloody tyrants have executioners ready to obey their most cruel and unrighteous decrees. Thus Saul has a *Doeg* at hand, to *fall upon the priests of the Lord,* when his own footmen declined it.

5. The effect of this is, (1.) That Herod's wicked court is *all in triumph,* because this prophet tormented them; the head is made a present of *to the damsel,* and by her to her *mother,* v. 28. (2.) That John Baptist's sacred college is *all in tears;* the disciples of John little thought of this; but, when they *heard of it,* they came, and took up the neglected *corpse,* and *laid it in a tomb;* where Herod, if he had pleased, might have found it, when he frightened himself with the fancy that John Baptist was *risen from the dead.*

Verses 30–44

In there verses, we have,

I. The return to Christ of the apostles whom he had sent forth (v. 7), to preach, and work miracles. They had dispersed

themselves into several quarters of the country for some time, but when they had made good their several appointments, by consent they *gathered themselves together,* to compare notes, and came to Jesus, the centre of their unity, to give him an account of what they had done pursuant to their commission: as the servant that was sent to invite to the feast, and had received answers from the guests, came, and *showed his Lord all those things,* so did the apostles here; they *told him all things,* both *what they had done, and what they had taught.* Ministers are accountable both for what they *do,* and for what they *teach;* and must both watch over their own souls, and watch for the souls of others, as those that must *give account,* Heb. 13:17. Let them not either *do* any thing, or *teach* any thing, but what they are willing should be related and repeated to the Lord Jesus. It is a comfort to faithful ministers, when they can appeal to Christ concerning their doctrine and manner of life, both which perhaps have been misrepresented by men; and he gives them leave to be free with him, and to lay open their case before him, to *tell him all things,* what treatment they have met with, what success, and what disappointment.

II. The tender care Christ took for their repose, after the fatigue they had (v. 31); *He said unto them,* perceiving them to be almost spent, and out of breath, *Come ye yourselves apart into a desert place, and rest awhile.* It should seem that John's disciples came to Christ with the mournful tidings of their master's death, much about the same time that his own disciples came to him with the report of their negotiation. Note, Christ takes cognizance of the *frights* of some, and the *toils* of others, of his disciples, and provides suitable relief for both, rest for those that are tired, and refuge for those that are terrified. With what kindness and compassion doth Christ say to them, *Come, and rest!* Note, The most active servants of Christ cannot be always upon the stretch of business, but have bodies that require some relaxation, some breathing-time; we shall not be able to serve God without ceasing, day and night, till we come to heaven, where they *never rest* from praising him, Rev. 4:8. And the Lord is for the body, considers its frame, and not only allows it time for rest, but puts it in mind of resting. *Come, my people, enter thou into thy chambers. Return to thy rest.* And those that work diligently and faithfully, may cheerfully retire to rest. *The sleep of the labouring man is sweet.* But observe, 1. Christ calls them to come *themselves apart;* for, if they had any body with them, they would have something to say, or something to do, for their good; if they must *rest,* they must be *alone.* 2. He invites them not to some pleasant country-seat, where there were fine buildings and fine gardens, but *into a desert place,* where the accommodations were very poor, and which was fitted by nature only, and not by art, for quietness and rest. But it was of a piece with all the other circumstances he was in; no wonder that he who had but a ship for his preaching place, had but a desert for his resting place. 3. He calls them only to rest *awhile;* they must not expect to rest *long,* only to *get breath,* and then to go to work again. There is no *remaining rest* for the people of God till they come to heaven. 4. The reason given for this, is, not so much because they had been in *constant work,* but because they now were in a *constant hurry;* so that they had not their work in any order; *for there were many coming and going, and they had no leisure so much as to eat.* Let but proper time be set, and kept for every thing, and a great deal of work may be done with a great deal of ease; but if people be continually coming and going, and no rule or method be observed, a little work will not be done without a deal of trouble. 5. They withdrew, accordingly, *by ship;* not crossing the water, but making a coasting voyage to the desert of Bethsaida, v. 32. Going *by water* was much less toilsome than going *by land* would have been. They went away *privately,* that they might be by themselves. The most public persons cannot but wish to be private sometimes.

III. The diligence of the people to follow him. It was rude to do so, when he and his disciples were desirous, for such good reason, to *retire;* and yet they are not blamed for it, nor bid to go back, but bid welcome. Note, A failure in good manners will easily be excused in those who follow Christ, if it be but made up in a fulness of good affections. They followed him of their own accord, without being called upon. Here is no time set, no meeting appointed, no bell tolled; yet they thus fly like a cloud, and as the doves to their windows. They followed him *out of the cities,* quitted their houses and shops, their callings and affairs, to hear him preach. They followed

him *afoot,* though he was gone by sea, and so, to try them, seemed to put a slight upon them, and to endeavour to shake them off; yet they stuck to him. They *ran* afoot, and made such haste, that they *out-went* the disciples, and *came together* to him with an appetite to the word of God. Nay they followed him, though it was into a *desert place,* despicable and inconvenient. The presence of Christ will turn a wilderness into a paradise.

IV. The entertainment Christ gave them (v. 34); *When he saw much people,* instead of being moved with displeasure, because they disturbed him when he desired to be private, as many a man, many a good man, would have been, he was *moved with compassion toward them,* and looked upon them with concern, because *they were as sheep having no shepherd,* they seemed to be well-inclined, and manageable as sheep, and willing to be taught, but they had *no shepherd,* none to lead and guide them in the right way, none to feed them with good doctrine: and therefore, in compassion to them, he not only *healed their sick,* as it is in Matthew, but he *taught them many things,* and we may be sure that they were all true and good, and fit for them to learn.

V. The provision he made for them all; all his hearers he generously made his guests, and treated them at a *splendid* entertainment: so it might truly be called, because a *miraculous* one.

1. The disciples moved that they should be *sent home.* When *the day was not far spent,* and night drew on, they said, *This is a desert place,* and *much time is now past; send them away to buy bread,* v. 35, 36. This the disciples suggested to Christ; but we do not find that the multitude themselves did. They did not say, *Send us away* (though they could not but be hungry), for they *esteemed the words of Christ's mouth more than their necessary food,* and forgot themselves when they were hearing him; but the disciples thought it would be a kindness to them to dismiss them. Note, Willing minds will do more, and hold out longer, in that which is good, than one would expect from them.

2. Christ ordered that they should all be fed (v. 37); *Give ye them to eat.* Though their crowding after him and his disciples hindered them from eating (v. 31), yet he would not *therefore,* to be even with them, send them away fasting, but, to teach us to be kind to those who are rude to us, he ordered provision to be made for them; that bread which Christ and his disciples took with them into the desert, that they might make a quiet meal of it for themselves, he will have them to partake of. Thus was he given to hospitality. They attended on the spiritual food of his word, and then he took care that they should not want corporal food. The way of duty, as it is the way of safety, so it is the way to supply. Let God alone to fill the pools with rain from heaven, and so to make a well even in the valley of Baca, for those that are going Zion-ward, from strength to strength, Ps. 84:6, 7. Providence, not *tempted,* but duly *trusted,* never yet failed any of God's faithful servants, but has refreshed many with seasonable and surprising relief. It has often been seen in the *mount of the Lord, Jehovah-jireh,* that *the Lord will provide* for those that wait on him.

3. The disciples objected against it as impracticable; *Shall we go, and buy two hundred penny-worth of bread, and give them to eat?* Thus, through the weakness of their faith, instead of waiting for directions from Christ, they perplex the cause with projects of their own. It was a question, whether they had two hundred pence with them, whether the country would of a sudden afford so much bread if they had, and whether that would suffice so great a company; but thus Moses objected (Num. 11:22), *Shall the flocks and the herds be slain for them?* Christ would let them see their folly in forecasting for themselves, that they might put the greater value upon his provision for them.

4. Christ effected it, to universal satisfaction. They had brought with them *five loaves,* for the victualling of their ship, and *two fishes* perhaps they caught as they came along; and that is the bill of fare. This was but a little for Christ and his disciples, and yet this they must give away, as the widow her *two mites,* and as the church of Macedonia's *deep poverty abounded to the riches of their liberality.* We often find Christ entertained at other people's tables, dining with one friend, and supping with another: but here we have him supping a great many at his own charge, which shows that, when others *ministered to him of their substance,* it was not because he could not supply himself otherwise (if he was *hungry,* he needed not *tell them*); but it was a piece of humiliation, that

he was pleased to submit to, nor was it agreeable to the intention of miracles, that he should work them for himself. Observe,

(1.) The provision was *ordinary.* Here were no rarities, no varieties, though Christ, if he had pleased, could have furnished his table with them; but thus he would teach us to be content with food convenient for us, and not to be desirous of dainties. If we have for necessity, it is no matter though we have not for delicacy and curiosity. God, in love, gives *meat for our hunger;* but, in wrath, gives *meat for our lusts,* Ps. 78:18. The promise to them that fear the Lord, is, that verily they shall be fed; he doth not say, They shall be *feasted.* If Christ and his disciples took up with mean things, surely we may.

(2.) The guests were *orderly;* for they *sat down by companies on the green grass* (*v.* 39), they *sat down in ranks by hundreds and by fifties* (*v.* 40), that the provision might the more easily and regularly be distributed among them; for God is the God of order, and not of confusion. Thus care was taken that every one should have enough, and none be over-looked, nor any have more than was fitting.

(3.) A blessing was craved upon the meat; *He looked up to heaven, and blessed.* Christ did not call one of his disciples to crave a blessing, but did it himself (*v.* 41); and by virtue of this blessing the bread strangely multiplied, and so did the fishes, for they did *all eat, and were filled,* though they were to the number of *five thousand, v.* 42, 44. This miracle was significant, and shows that Christ came into the world, to be the great feeder as well as the great healer; not only to restore, but to preserve and nourish, spiritual life; and in him there is enough for all that come to him, enough to fill the soul, to fill the treasures; none are sent empty away from Christ, but those that come to him full of themselves.

(4.) Care was taken of the fragments that remained, with which they filled *twelve baskets.* Though Christ had bread enough at command, he would hereby teach us, not to make waste of any of God's good creatures; remembering how many there are that do want, and that we know not but we may some time or other want such fragments as we throw away.

Verses 45–56

This passage of story we had Mt. 14:22, etc., only what was there related concerning Peter, is omitted here. Here we have,

I. The dispersing of the assembly; Christ *constrained his disciples* to go before by ship to Bethsaida, intending to follow them, as they supposed, by land. The people were loth to scatter, so that it cost him some time and pains to send them away. For now that they had got a good supper, they were in no haste to leave him. But as long as we are here in this world, we have no continuing city, no not in communion with Christ. The everlasting feast is reserved for the future state.

II. Christ departed *into a mountain, to pray.* Observe, 1. He *prayed;* though he had so much preaching-work upon his hands, yet he was much in prayer; he prayed often, and prayed long, which is an encouragement to us to depend upon the intercession he is making for us at the right hand of the Father, that *continual* intercession. 2. He went *alone,* to pray; though he needed not to retire for the avoiding either of distraction or of ostentation, yet, to set us an example, and to encourage us in our *secret* addresses to God, he prayed *alone,* and, for want of a closet, went up into a mountain, to pray. A good man is never less alone than when alone with God.

III. The disciples were in distress at sea; *The wind was contrary* (*v.* 48), so that they *toiled in rowing,* and could not get forward. This was a specimen of the hardships they were to expect, when hereafter he should send them abroad to preach the gospel; it would be like sending them to sea at this time with the *wind in their teeth:* they must expect to toil in rowing, they must work hard to strive against so strong a stream; they must likewise expect to be tossed with waves, to be persecuted by their enemies; and by exposing them now he intended to train them up for such difficulties, that they might learn to *endure hardness.* The church is often like a ship at sea, *tossed with tempests, and not comforted* we may have Christ for us, and yet wind and tide against us; but it is a comfort to Christ's disciples in a storm, that their Master is in the heavenly mount, interceding for them.

IV. Christ made them a kind visit upon the water. He could have checked the winds, where he was, or have sent an angel to their relief; but he chose to help them in the most endearing manner possible, and therefore came to them himself.

1. He did not come till the *fourth watch of the night,* not till after three o'clock in the morning; but then he came. Note, If Christ's visits to his people be deferred long, yet at length he will come; and their extremity is his opportunity to appear for them so much the more seasonably. Though the salvation tarry, yet we must wait for it; *at the end it shall speak,* in the fourth watch of the night, *and not lie.*

2. He came, walking upon the waters. The sea was now tossed with waves, and yet Christ came, walking upon it; for though the *floods lift up their voice, the Lord on high is mightier,* Ps. 93:3, 4. No difficulties can obstruct Christ's gracious appearances for his people, when the set time is come. He will either find, or force, a way through the most tempestuous sea, for their deliverance, Ps. 42:7, 8,

3. He *would have passed by them,* that is, he set his face and steered his course, as if he would have gone further, and took no notice of them; this he did, to awaken them to call to him. Note, Providence, when it is acting designedly and directly for the succour of God's people, yet sometimes seems as if it were *giving them the go-by,* and regarded not their case. They thought that *he would,* but we may be sure that he would not, *have passed by them.*

4. They were frightened at the sight of him, supposing him to have been an apparition; *They all saw him, and were troubled* (*v.* 50), thinking it had been some daemon, or evil genius, that haunted them, and raised this storm. We often perplex and frighten ourselves with phantasms, the creatures of our own fancy and imagination.

5. He encouraged them, and silenced their fears, by making himself known to them; *he talked* familiarly with them, saying, *Be of good cheer, it is I; be not afraid.* Note, (1.) We know not Christ till he is pleased to reveal himself to us. *"It is I;* I your Master, I your friend, I your Redeemer and Saviour. *It is I,* that came to a troublesome earth, and now to a tempestuous sea, to look after you." (2.) The knowledge of Christ, as he is in himself, and near to us, is enough to make the disciples of Christ cheerful even in a storm, and no longer fearful. *If it be so, why am I thus?* If it is Christ that is with thee, *be of good cheer, be not afraid.* Our fears are soon satisfied, if our mistakes be but rectified, especially our mistakes concerning Christ. See Gen. 21:19; 2 Ki. 6:15–17. Christ's presence with us in a stormy day, is enough to make us of good cheer, though clouds and darkness be round about us. He said, *It is I.* He doth not tell them who he was (there was no occasion), they knew his voice, as the sheep know the voice of their own shepherd, Jn. 10:4. How readily doth the spouse say, once and again, *It is the voice of my beloved!* Cant. 2:8; 5:2. He said, *egō eimi — I am he;* or *I am;* it is God's name, when he comes to deliver Israel, Ex. 3:14. So it is Christ's, now that he comes to deliver his disciples. When Christ said to those that came to apprehend him by force, *I am he,* they were struck down by it, Jn. 18:6. When he saith to those that come to apprehend him by faith, *I am he,* they are raised up by it, and comforted.

6. He *went up to them into the ship,* embarked in the same bottom with them, and so made them perfectly easy. Let them but have their Master with them, and all is well. And as soon as he was come into the ship, *the wind ceased.* In the former storm that they were in, it is said, *He arose, and rebuked the winds, and said to the sea, Peace, be still* (*ch.* 4:39); but here we read of no such formal command given, only the wind ceased all of a sudden. note, Our Lord Jesus will be sure to do his own work always effectually, though not always alike solemnly, and with observation. Though we hear not the command given, yet, if thus the wind cease, and we have the comfort of a calm, say, It is because Christ is in the ship, and his decree is gone forth *or ever we are aware,* Cant. 6:12. When we come with Christ to heaven, the wind ceaseth presently; there are no storms in the upper region.

7. They were more surprised and astonished at this miracle than did become them, and there was that at the bottom of their astonishment, which was really culpable; *They were sore amazed in themselves,* were in a perfect ecstasy; as if it were a new and unaccountable thing, as if Christ had never done the like before, and they had no reason to expect he should do it now; they ought to admire the power of Christ, and to be confirmed hereby in their belief of his being the Son of God: but why all this confusion about it? It was because they *considered not the miracle of the loaves;* had they given that its due weight, they would not have been so much surprised at this; for his multiplying the bread was as great an instance of his power as his walking on the water. They were strangely stupid and unthinking, and their heart was hardened, or else they would not have thought it a thing incredible that Christ should command a calm. It is for want of a right understanding of Christ's former works, that we are transported at the thought of his present works, as if there never were the like before.

V. When they came to the land of Gennesaret, which lay between Bethsaida and Capernaum, the people bid them very welcome; *The men of that place* presently *knew Jesus* (*v.* 54), and knew what mighty works he did wherever he came, what a universal Healer he was; they knew likewise that he used to stay but a little while at a place, and therefore they were concerned to improve the opportunity of this kind visit which he made them; *They ran through that whole region round about,* with all possible expedition, and *began to carry about in beds those that were sick,* and not able to go themselves; there was no danger of their getting cold when they hoped to get a cure, *v.* 55. Let him go where he would, he was crowded with patients — in towns, in the cities, in the villages about the cities; they *laid the sick in the streets,* to be in his way, and begged leave for them to touch if it were but *the border of his garment,* as the woman with the bloody issue did, by whom, it should seem, this method of application was first brought in; *and as many as touched, were made whole.* We do not find that they were desirous to be taught by him, only to be healed. If ministers could not cure people's bodily diseases, what multitudes would attend them! But it is sad to think how much more concerned the most of men are about their bodies than about their souls.

CHAPTER 7

In this chapter we have, I. Christ's dispute with the scribes and Pharisees about eating meat with unwashen hands (*v.* 1–13); and the needful instructions he gave to the people on that occasion, and further explained to his disciples (*v.* 14–23). II. His curing of the woman Canaan's daughter that was possessed (*v.* 24–30). III. The relief of a man that was deaf, and had an impediment in his speech (*v.* 31–37).

Verses 1–23

One great design of Christ's coming, was, to set aside the ceremonial law which God made, and to put an end to it; to make way for which he begins with the ceremonial law which men had made, and added to the law of God's making, and discharges his disciples from the obligation of that; which here he doth fully, upon occasion of the offence which the Pharisees took at them for the violation of it. These Pharisees and scribes with whom he had this argument, are said to *come from Jerusalem* down to Galilee — fourscore or a hundred miles, to pick quarrels with our Saviour there, where they supposed him to have the greatest interest and reputation. Had they come so far to be taught by him, their zeal had been commendable; but to come so far to oppose him, and to check the progress of his gospel, was great wickedness. It should seem that the scribes and Pharisees at Jerusalem pretended not only to a pre-eminence above, but to an authority over, the country clergy, and therefore kept up their visitations and sent inquisitors among them, as they did to John when he appeared, Jn. 1:19.

Now in this passage we may observe,

I. What the tradition of the elders was: by it all were enjoined to *wash their hands* before meat; a cleanly custom, and no harm in it; and yet as such to be over-nice in it discovers too great a care about the body, which is *of the earth;* but they placed religion in it, and would not leave it indifferent, as it was in its own nature; people were at their liberty to do it or not to do it; but they interposed their authority, and commanded all to do it upon pain of excommunication; this they kept up as a *tradition of the elders.* The Papists pretend to a zeal for the authority and antiquity of the church and its canons, and talk much of councils and fathers, when really it is nothing but a zeal for their own wealth, interest, and dominion, that governs them; and so it was with the Pharisees.

We have here an account of the practice of the Pharisees and *all the Jews, v.* 3, 4. 1. They *washed their hands oft;* they washed them, *pygmē;* the critics find a great deal of work about that word, some making it to denote the frequency of their washing (so we render it); others think it signifies the pains they took in washing their hands; they washed with great care, they washed their hands *to their wrists* (so some);

they lifted up their hands when they were wet, that the water might *run to their elbows.* 2. They particularly washed before they *ate bread;* that is, before they sat down to a solemn meal; for that was the rule; they must be sure to wash before they ate the bread on which they begged a blessing. "Whosoever eats the bread over which they recite the benediction, *Blessed be he that produceth bread,* must wash his hands before and after," or else he was thought to be defiled. 3. They took special care, when they came in *from the markets,* to wash their hands; from the *judgment-halls,* so some; it signifies any place of concourse where there were people of all sorts, and, it might be supposed, some heathen or Jews under a ceremonial pollution, by coming near to whom they thought themselves polluted; saying, *Stand by thyself, come not near me, I am holier than thou,* Isa. 65:5. They say, The rule of the rabbies was — That, if they washed their hands well in the morning, the first thing they did, it would serve for all day, provided they kept alone; but, if they went into company, they must not, at their return, either eat or pray till they had washed their hands; thus the elders gained a reputation among the people for sanctity, and thus they exercised and kept up an authority over their consciences. 4. They added to this the washing of *cups,* and *pots,* and *brazen vessels,* which they suspected had been made use of by heathens, or persons polluted; nay, and the very *tables* on which they ate their meat. There were many cases in which, by the law of Moses, washings were appointed; but they *added* to them, and enforced the observation of their own impositions as much as of God's institutions.

II. What the practice of Christ's disciples was; they knew what the law was, and the common usage; but they understood themselves so well that they would not be bound up by it: they ate bread with *defiled,* that is, with *unwashen, hands, v.* 2. Eating with *unwashen hands* they called eating with *defiled* hands; thus men keep up their superstitious vanities by putting every thing into an ill name that contradicts them. The disciples knew (it is probable) that the Pharisees had their eye upon them, and yet they would not humour them by a compliance with their traditions, but took their liberty as at other times, and ate bread with *unwashen* hands; and herein *their righteousness,* however it might seem to come short, did really *exceed, that of the scribes and Pharisees,* Mt. 5:20.

III. The offence which the Pharisees took at this; They *found fault* (*v.* 2); they censured them as profane, and men of a loose conversation, or rather as men that would not submit to the power of the church, to decree rites and ceremonies, and were therefore rebellious, factious, and schismatical. They brought a complaint against them to their Master, expecting that he should check them, and order them to conform; for they that are fond of their own inventions and impositions, are commonly ready to appeal to Christ, as if he should countenance them, and as if his authority must interpose for the enforcing of them, and the rebuking of those that do not comply with them. They do not ask, Why do not thy disciples *do as we do?* (Though that was what they meant, coveting to make themselves the standard.) But, Why do not they *walk according to the tradition of the elders? v.* 5. To which it was easy to answer, that, by receiving the doctrine of Christ, they had *more understanding than all their teachers,* yea *more than the ancients,* Ps. 119:99, 100.

IV. Christ's vindication of them; in which,

1. He argues with the Pharisees concerning the authority by which this ceremony was imposed; and *they* were the fittest to be discoursed with concerning that, who were the great sticklers for it: but this he did not speak of publicly to the multitude (as appears by his *calling the people* to him, *v.* 14) lest he should have seemed to stir them up to faction and discontent at their governors; but addressed it as a reproof to the persons concerned: for the rule is, *Suum cuique — Let every one have his own.*

(1.) He reproves them for their hypocrisy in pretending to honour God, when really they had no such design in their religious observances (*v.* 6, 7); *They honour me with their lips,* they pretend it is for the glory of God that they impose those things, to distinguish themselves from the heathen; but really *their heart is far from God,* and is governed by nothing but ambition and covetousness. They would be thought hereby to appropriate themselves as a holy people to the Lord their God, when really it is the furthest thing in their thought. They rested in the outside of all their religious exercises, and their hearts were not right with God in them, and this was worshipping God in vain; for neither was he pleased with such sham-devotions, nor were they profited by them.

(2.) He reproves them for placing religion in the inventions and injunctions of their elders and rulers; They *taught for doctrines the traditions of men.* When they should have been pressing upon people the great principles of religion, they were enforcing the canons of their church, and judged of people's being Jews or no, according as they did, or did not, conform to them, without any consideration had, whether they lived in obedience to God's laws or no. It was true, there were *divers washings* imposed by the law of Moses (Heb. 9:10), which were intended to signify that inward purification of the heart from worldly fleshly lusts, which God requires as absolutely necessary to our communion with him; but, instead of providing the substance, they presumptuously added to the ceremony, and were very nice in *washing pots and cups;* and observe, he adds, *Many other such like things ye do, v.* 8. Note, Superstition is an endless thing. If one human invention and institution be admitted, though seemingly ever so innocent, as this of washing hands, *behold, a troop comes,* a door is opened for *many other such things.*

(3.) He reproves them for *laying aside the commandment of God,* and overlooking that, not urging that in their preaching, and in their discipline conniving at the violation of that, as if that were no longer of force, *v.* 8. Note, It is the mischief of impositions, that too often they who are zealous for them, have little zeal for the essential duties of religion, but can contentedly see them laid aside. Nay, they *rejected the commandment of God, v.* 9. *He do fairly disannul and abolish the commandment of God;* and even *by* your traditions *make the word of God of no effect, v.* 13. God's statutes shall not only *lie forgotten,* as antiquated obsolete laws, but they shall, in effect, *stand repealed,* that their traditions may take place. They were entrusted to expound the law, and to enforce it; and, under pretence of using that power, they violated the law, and dissolved the bonds of it; destroying the text with the comment.

This he gives them a particular instance of, and a flagrant one — God commanded children to *honour their parents,* not only by the law of Moses, but, antecedent to that, by the law of nature; and whoso *revileth,* or *speaketh evil of,* father or mother, *let him die the death, v.* 10. Hence it is easy to infer, that it is the duty of children, if their parents be poor, to relieve them, according to their ability; and if those children are worthy to die, that curse their parents, much more those that starve them. But if a man will but conform himself in all points to the tradition of the elders, they will find him out an expedient by which he may be discharged from this obligation, *v.* 11. If his parents be in want and he has wherewithal to help them, but has no mind to do it, let him swear by the *Corban,* that is, by the *gold of the temple,* and the *gift upon the altar,* that his parents shall not be profited by him, that he will not relieve them; and, if they ask any thing of him, let him tell them this, and it is enough; as if by the obligation of this wicked vow he had discharged himself from the obligation of God's holy law; thus Dr. Hammond understands it: and it is said to be an ancient canon of the rabbin, That vows take place in things commanded by the law, as well as in things indifferent; so that, if a man make a vow which cannot be ratified without breaking a commandment, the vow must be ratified, and the commandment violated; so Dr. Whitby. Such doctrine as this the Papists teach, discharging children from all obligation to their parents by their monastic vows, and their entrance into religion, as they call it. He concludes, *Any many such like things do ye.* Where will men stop, when once they have made the word of God give way to their tradition? These eager imposers of such ceremonies, at first only *made light* of God's commandments *in comparison* with their traditions, but afterward *made void* God's commandments, if they stood *in competition* with them. All this, in effect, Isaiah prophesied of them; what he said of the hypocrites of his own day, was applicable to the scribes and Pharisees, *v.* 6. Note, When we see, and complain of, the wickedness of the present times, yet we do not *enquire wisely of that matter,* if we say that all *the former days were better than these,* Eccl. 7:10. The worst of hypocrites and evil doers have had their predecessors.

2. He instructs the people concerning the principles upon which this ceremony was grounded. It was requisite that this part of his discourse should be public, for it related to daily practice, and was designed to rectify a great mistake which the people were led into by their elders; he therefore *called the people unto him* (*v.* 14), and bid them *hear and understand.* Note, It is not enough for the common people to *hear,* but they must *understand* what they hear. When Christ would run down the tradition of the Pharisees about washing before meat, he strikes at the opinion which was the root of it. Note, Corrupt customs are best cured by rectifying corrupt notions.

Now that which he goes about to set them right in, is, what the pollution is, which we are in danger of being damaged by, *v.* 15. (1.) Not by the *meat we eat,* though it be eaten with unwashen hands; that is but from without, and goes through a man. But, (2.) It is by the breaking out of the corruption that is in our hearts; the mind and conscience are defiled, guilt is contracted, and we become odious in the sight of God by that which *comes out* of us; our wicked thoughts and affections, words and actions, these defile us, and these only. Our care must therefore be, to *wash our heart from wickedness.*

3. He gives his disciples, in private, an explication of the instructions he gave the people. They *asked* him, when they had him by himself, *concerning the parable* (*v.* 17); for to them, it seems, it was a parable. Now, in answer to their enquiry, (1.) He reproves their dulness; *"Are ye so without understanding also?* Are ye dull *also,* as dull as the people that *cannot* understand, as dull as the Pharisees that *will not?* Are ye *so* dull?" He doth not expect they should understand every thing; "But are ye so weak as not to understand *this?"* (2.) He explains this truth to them, that they might *perceive* it, and then they would *believe* it, for it carried its own evidence along with it. Some truths prove themselves, if they be but rightly explained and apprehended. If we understand the spiritual nature of God and of his law, and what it is that is offensive to him, and disfits us for communion with him, we shall soon perceive, [1.] That that which we eat and drink cannot defile us, so as to call for any religious washing; it *goes into the stomach,* and passes the several digestions and secretions that nature has appointed, and what there may be in it that is defiling is voided and gone; *meats for the belly, and the belly for meats,* but *God shall destroy both it and them.* But, [2.] It is that which *comes out from* the heart, the corrupt heart, that defiles us. As by the ceremonial law, whatsoever (almost) comes out of a man, defiles him (Lev. 15:2; Deu. 23:13), so what comes out from the *mind* of a man is that which defiles him before God, and calls for a religious washing (*v.* 21); *From within, out of the heart of men,* which they boast of the *goodness* of, and think is the best part of them, thence that which defiles proceeds, thence comes all the mischief. As a corrupt fountain sends forth corrupt streams, so doth a corrupt heart send forth corrupt reasonings, corrupt appetites and passions, and all those wicked words and actions which are produced by them. Divers particulars are specified, as in Matthew; we had one there, which is not here, and that is, *false witness-bearing;* but *seven* are mentioned here, to be added to those we had there. *First, Covetousnesses,* for it is plural; *pleonexiai — immoderate desires* of more of the wealth of the world, and the gratifications of sense, and still more, still crying, *Give, give.* Hence we read of a *heart exercised with covetous practices,* 2 Pt. 2:14. *Secondly, Wickedness — ponēriai*; malice, hatred, and ill-will, a desire to do mischief, and a delight in mischief done. *Thirdly, Deceit;* which is wickedness covered and disguised, that it may be the more securely and effectually committed. *Fourthly, Lasciviousness;* that filthiness and foolish talking which the apostle condemns; the eye full of adultery, and all wanton dalliances. *Fifthly,* The *evil eye;* the envious eye, and the covetous eye, grudging others the good we give them, or do for them (Prov. 23:6), or grieving at the good they do or enjoy. *Sixthly, Pride — hyperēphania*; exalting ourselves in our own conceit above others, and looking down with scorn and contempt upon others. *Seventhly, Foolishness — aphrosynē*; imprudence, inconsideration; some understand it especially of vainglorious boasting, which St. Paul calls *foolishness* (2 Co. 11:1, 19), because it is here joined with *pride;* I rather take it for that rashness in speaking and acting, which is the cause of so much evil. *Ill-thinking* is put first, as that which is the spring of all our commissions, and *unthinking* put last, as that which is the spring of all our omissions. Of all these he concludes (*v.* 23), 1. That they *come from within,* from the corrupt nature, the carnal mind, the evil treasure in the heart; justly is it said, that the *inward part is very wickedness,* it must needs be so, when all this comes from within. 2. That they *defile the man;* they render a man unfit for communion with God, they bring a stain upon the con-

science; and, if not mortified and rooted out, will shut men out of the new Jerusalem, into which no *unclean thing shall enter.*

Verses 24–30

See here, I. How *humbly* Christ was pleased to *conceal himself.* Never man was so cried up as he was in Galilee, and therefore, to teach us, though not to decline any opportunity of doing good, yet not to be fond of popular applause, he arose from thence, and *went into the borders* of Tyre and Sidon, where he was little known; and there he entered, not into a synagogue, or place of concourse, but *into a* private *house,* and he *would have no man to know it;* because it was foretold concerning him, *He shall not strive nor cry, neither shall his voice be heard in the streets.* Not but that he was willing to preach and heal here as well as in other places, but for this he would be sought unto. Note, As there is a time to *appear,* so there is a time to *retire.* Or, he would not be known, because he was upon the borders of Tyre and Sidon, among Gentiles, to whom he would not be so forward to show himself as to the tribes of Israel, whose glory he was to be.

II. How *graciously* he was pleased to *manifest himself,* notwithstanding. Though he would not carry a harvest of miraculous cures into those parts, yet, it should seem, he came on purpose to drop a handful, to let fall this one which we have here an account of. *He could not be hid;* for, though a candle may be put under a bushel, the sun cannot. Christ was too well known to be long *incognito — hid,* any where; the oil of gladness which he was anointed with, like ointment of the right hand, would betray itself, and fill the house with its odours. Those that had only heard his fame, could not converse with him, but they would soon say, "This must be Jesus." Now observe,

1. The application made to him by a poor woman in distress and trouble. She was a Gentile, a Greek, *a stranger to the commonwealth of Israel, an alien to the covenant of promise;* she was by extraction a Syrophenician, and not in any degree proselyted to the Jewish religion; she had a *daughter,* a *young* daughter, that was possessed *with the devil.* How many and grievous are the calamities that young children are subject to! Her address was, (1.) Very humble, pressing, and importunate; *She heard of him,* and *came, and fell at his feet.* Note, Those that would obtain mercy from Christ, must throw themselves at his feet; must refer themselves to him, humble themselves before him, and give up themselves to be ruled by him. Christ never put any from him, that fell at his feet, which a poor trembling soul may do, that has not boldness and confidence to throw itself into his arms. (2.) It was very particular; she tells him what she wanted. Christ gave poor supplicants leave to be thus free with him; she besought him that he would *cast forth the devil out of her daughter, v.* 26. Note, The greatest blessing we can ask of Christ for our children is, that he would break the power of Satan, that is, the power of sin, in their souls; and particularly, that he would cast forth the *unclean spirit,* that they may be temples of the Holy Ghost, and he may dwell in them.

2. The discouragement he gave to this address (*v.* 27); He said unto her, *"Let the children first be filled;* let the Jews have all the miracles wrought for them, that they have occasion for, who are in a particular manner God's chosen people; and let not that which was intended for them, be thrown to those who are not of God's family, and who have not that knowledge of him, and interest in him, which they have, and who are as *dogs in comparison of them,* vile and profane, and who are as *dogs to them,* snarling at them, spiteful toward them, and ready to worry them." Note, Where Christ knows the faith of poor supplicants to be strong, he sometimes delights to try it, and put it to the stretch. But his saying, *Let the children first be filled,* intimates that there was mercy in reserve for the Gentiles, and not far off; for the Jews began already to be surfeited with the gospel of Christ, and some of them had desired him to *depart out of their coasts.* The children begin to play with their meat, and their leavings, their loathings, would be a feast for the Gentiles. The apostles went by this rule, *Let the children first be filled,* let the Jews have the first offer; and if their full souls loathe this honeycomb, *Lo, we turn to the Gentiles!*

3. The turn she gave to this word of Christ, which made against her, and her improvement of it, to make for her, *v.* 28. She said, *"Yes, Lord,* I own it is true that the *children's bread* ought not to be cast to the dogs; but they were never denied the *crumbs* of that bread, nay it belongs to them, and they are allowed a place *under the table,* that they may be ready to receive them. I ask not for a *loaf,* no, nor for a *morsel,* only for a *crumb;* do not refuse me that." This she speaks, not as undervaluing the mercy, or making light of it in itself, but magnifying the abundance or miraculous cures with which she heard the Jews were feasted, in comparison with which a single cure was but as a crumb. Gentiles do not come in crowds, as the Jews do; *I come alone.* Perhaps she had heard of Christ's feeding five thousand lately at once, after which, even when they had gathered up the fragments, there could not but be some crumbs left for the dogs.

4. The grant Christ thereupon made of her request. Is she thus humble, thus earnest? For *this saying, Go thy way,* thou shalt have what thou camest for, *the devil is gone out of thy daughter, v.* 29. This encourages us to *pray* and not to *faint,* to continue instant in prayer, not doubting but to prevail at last; the vision at the end shall *speak, and not lie.* Christ's saying that is *was done,* did it effectually, as at other times his saying, *Let it be done;* for (*v.* 30) she *came to her house,* depending upon the word of Christ, that her daughter was healed, and so she *found it,* the *devil was gone out.* Note, Christ can conquer Satan at a distance; and it was not only when the demoniacs *saw him,* that they yielded to his power (as *ch.* 3:11), but when they saw him not, for the Spirit of the Lord is not *bound,* nor *bounded.* She found her daughter not in any toss or agitation, but very quietly *laid on the bed,* and reposing herself; waiting for her mother's return, to rejoice with her, that she was so *finely well.*

Verses 31–37

Our Lord Jesus seldom staid long in a place, for he knew where his work lay, and attended the changes of it. When he had cured the woman of Canaan's daughter, he had done what he had to do in that place, and therefore presently left those parts, and returned *to the sea of Galilee,* whereabout his usual residence was; yet he did not come directly thither, but fetched a compass *through the midst of the coasts of Decapolis,* which lay mostly on the other side Jordan; such long walks did our Lord Jesus take, when he *went about doing good.*

Now here we have the story of a cure that Christ wrought, which is not recorded by any other of the evangelists; it is of one that was *deaf* and *dumb.*

I. His case was sad, *v.* 32. There were those that brought to him one that was *deaf;* some think, born deaf, and then he must be dumb of course; others think that by some distemper or disaster he was become deaf, or, at least, thick of hearing; and he had an *impediment in his speech.* He was *mogilalos*; some think that he was quite dumb; others, that he could not speak but with great difficulty to himself, and so as scarcely to be understood by those that heard him. He was *tongue-tied,* so that he was perfectly unfit for conversation, and deprived both of the pleasure and of the profit of it; he had not the satisfaction either of hearing other people talk, or of telling his own mind. Let us take occasion from hence to give thanks to God for preserving to us the sense of hearing, especially that we may be capable of hearing the word of God; and the faculty of speech, especially that we may be capable of speaking God's praises; and let us look with compassion upon those that are deaf or dumb, and treat them with great tenderness. They that brought this poor man to Christ, besought him that he would *put his hand upon him,* as the prophets did upon those whom they *blessed* in the name of the Lord. It is not said, They besought him to *cure him,* but to *put his hand upon him,* to take cognizance of his case, and put forth his power to do to him as he pleased.

II. His cure was solemn, and some of the circumstances of it were singular.

1. Christ *took him aside from the multitude, v.* 33. Ordinarily, he wrought his miracles publicly before all the people, to show that they would bear the strictest scrutiny and inspection; but this he did privately, to show that he did not seek his own glory, and to teach us to avoid every thing that savours of ostentation. Let us learn of Christ to be humble, and to do good where no eye sees, but his that is *all eye.*

2. He used more significant actions, in the doing of this cure, than usual. (1.) He *put his fingers into his ears,* as if he would *syringe* them, and fetch out that which stopped them up. (2.) He spit upon his own finger, and then *touched his tongue,* as if he would moisten his mouth, and so loosen that with which his tongue was tied; these were no causes that could in the least contribute to his cure, but only signs of the exerting of that power which Christ had in himself to cure him, for the encouraging of his faith, and theirs that brought him. The application was all from himself, it was his own *fingers* that he put into his ears, and his own *spittle* that he put upon his tongue; for he alone heals.

3. He *looked up to heaven,* to give his Father the praise of what he did; for he sought his praise, and did his will, and, as Mediator, acted in dependence on him, and with an eye to him. Thus he signified that it was by a divine power, a power her had as the Lord from heaven, and brought with him thence, that he did this; for the *hearing ear* and the *seeing eye* the *Lord has made,* and can remake even *both of them.* He also hereby directed his patient who could *see,* though he could not *hear,* to look up to heaven for relief. Moses with his stammering tongue is directed to look that way (Ex. 4:11); *Who hath made man's mouth? Or who maketh the dumb or deaf, or the seeing or the blind? Have not I the Lord?*

4. He sighed; not as if he found any difficulty in working this miracle, or obtaining power to do it from his father; but thus he expressed his pity for the miseries of human life, and his sympathy with the afflicted in their afflictions, as one that was himself *touched with the feeling of their infirmities.* And as to this man, he *sighed,* not because he was loth to do him this kindness, or did it with reluctancy; but because of the many temptations which he would be exposed to, and the sins he would be in danger of, the tongue-sins, after the restoring of his speech to him, which before he was free from. He had better be *tongue-tied* still, unless he have grace to *keep his mouth as with a bridle,* Ps. 39:1.

5. He said, *Ephphatha;* that is, *Be opened.* This was nothing that looked like *spell* or *charm,* such as they used, who had *familiar spirits,* who *peeped and muttered,* Isa. 8:19. Christ speaks as one having authority, and power went along with the word. *Be opened,* served both parts of the cure; "Let the *ears* be *opened,* let the *lips* be *opened,* let him hear and speak freely, and let the restraint be taken off;" and the effect was answerable (*v.* 35); *Straightway his ears were opened, and the string of his tongue was loosed,* and all was well: and happy he who, as soon as he had his hearing and speech, had the blessed Jesus so near him to converse with.

Now this cure was, (1.) A proof of Christ's being the Messiah; for it was foretold that by his power the *ears of the deaf should be unstopped,* and the *tongue of the dumb* should be made to *sing,* Isa. 35:5, 6. (2.) It was a specimen of the operations of his gospel upon the minds of men. The great command of the gospel, and grace of Christ to poor sinners, is *Ephphatha — Be opened.* Grotius applies it thus, that the internal impediments of the mind are removed by the Spirit of Christ, as those bodily impediments were by the word of his power. He *opens the heart,* as he did Lydia's, and thereby opens the ear to receive the word of God, and opens the mouth in prayer and praises.

6. He ordered it to be kept very private, but it was made very public (1.) It was his humility, that he *charged them they should tell no man, v.* 36. Most men will proclaim their own goodness, or, at least, desire that others should proclaim it; but Christ, though he was himself in no danger of being puffed up with it, knowing that we are, would thus set us an example of self-denial, as in other things, so especially in praise and applause. We should take pleasure in doing good, but not in its being known. (2.) It was their zeal, that, though he charged them to say nothing of it, yet they published it, before Christ would have had it published. But they meant honestly, and therefore it is to be reckoned rather an act of indiscretion than an act of disobedience, *v.* 36. But they that told it, and they that heard it, were *beyond measure astonished, hyperperissōs — more than above measure;* they were exceedingly affected with it, and this was said by every body, it was the common verdict, *He hath done all things well* (*v.* 37); whereas there were those that hated and persecuted him as an *evil-doer,* they are ready to witness for him, not only that he has done no evil, but that he has done a great deal of good, and has done it well, modestly and humbly, and very devoutly, and all gratis, *without money and without price,* which added much to the lustre of his good works. He *maketh both the deaf to hear, and the dumb to speak;* and that is *well,* it is well for them, it is well for their relations, to whom they had been a burthen; and therefore *they* are inexcusable who speak ill of him.

CHAPTER 8

In this chapter, we have, I. Christ's miraculous feeding of four thousand with seven loaves and a few small fishes (*v.* 1–9). II. His refusing to give the Pharisees a sign from heaven (*v.* 10–13). III. His cautioning his disciples to take heed of the leaven of Pharisaism and Herodianism (*v.* 14–21). IV. His giving of sight to a blind man at Bethsaida (*v.* 22–26). V. Peter's confession of him (*v.* 27–30). VI. The notice he gave his disciples of his own approaching sufferings (*v.* 31–33), and the warning he gave them to prepare for sufferings likewise (*v.* 34–38).

Verses 1–9

We had the story of a miracle very like this before, in this gospel (*ch.* 6:35), and of this same miracle (Mt. 15:32), and here is little or no addition or alternation as to the circumstances. Yet observe,

1. That our Lord Jesus was greatly followed; *The multitude was very great* (*v.* 1); notwithstanding the wicked arts of the scribes and Pharisees to blemish him, and to blast his interest, the common people, who had more honesty, and therefore more true wisdom, than their leaders, kept up their high thoughts of him. We may suppose that this multitude were generally of the meaner sort of people, with such Christ conversed, and was familiar; for thus he humbled himself, and made himself of no reputation, and thus encouraged the meanest to come to him for life and grace.

2. Those that followed him, underwent a great deal of difficulty in following him; *They were with him three days, and had nothing to eat,* that was hard service. Never let the Pharisee say, that *Christ's disciples fast not.* There were those, probably, that brought some food with them from home; but by this time it was all spent, and they had a great way home; and yet they *continued* with Christ, and did not speak of leaving him till he spoke of dismissing them. Note, True zeal makes nothing of hardships in the way of duty. They that have a full feast for their souls may be content with slender provision for their bodies. It was an old saying among the Puritans, *Grown bread and the gospel are good fare.*

3. As Christ has a *compassion* for all that are in wants and straits, so he has a special *concern* for those that are reduced to straits by their zeal and diligence in attending on him. Christ said, *I have compassion on the multitude.* Whom the proud Pharisees looked upon with disdain, the humble Jesus looked upon with pity and tenderness; and thus must we *honour all men.* But that which he chiefly considers, is, *They have been with me three days, and have nothing to eat.* Whatever losses we sustain, or hardships we go through, for Christ's sake, and in love to him, he will take care that they shall be made up to us one way or other. *They that seek the Lord, shall not* long *want any good thing,* Ps. 34:10. Observe with what sympathy Christ saith (*v.* 3), *If I send them away fasting to their own houses, they will faint by the way,* for hunger. Christ knows and considers our frame; and he is *for the body,* if we glorify him, *verily we shall be fed.* He considered that *many of them came from afar,* and had a great way home. When we see *multitudes* attending upon the word preached, it is comfortable to think that Christ knows whence they all come, though we do not. *I know thy works, and where thou dwellest,* Rev. 2:13. Christ would by no means have them go home fasting, for it is not his manner to send those *empty* way from him, that in a right manner attend on him.

4. The doubts of Christians are sometimes made to work for the magnifying of the power of Christ. The disciples could not imagine whence so many men should be *satisfied with bread* here in the wilderness, *v.* 4. That therefore must needs be *wonderful,* and appear so much the more so, which the disciples looked upon as *impossible.*

5. Christ's time to act for the relief of his people, is, when things are brought to the last extremity; when they were ready to *faint,* Christ provided for them. That he might not invite them to follow him for the *loaves,* he did not supply them but when they were utterly reduced, and then he *sent them away.*

6. The bounty of Christ is inexhaustible, and, to evidence that, Christ *repeated* this miracle, to show that he is still the same for the succour and supply of his people that attend upon him. His favours are renewed, as our wants and necessities are. In the former miracle, Christ used all the bread he had, which was *five loaves,* and fed all the guests he had, which were *five thousand,* and so he did now; though he might have said, "If five loaves would feed five thousand, four may feed four thousand;" he took all the seven loaves, and fed with them the four thousand; for he would teach us to take things as they are, and accommodate ourselves to them; to use what we have, and make the best of that which is. Here it was, as in the dispensing of manna, *He that gathered much had nothing over, and he that gathered little had no lack.*

7. In our Father's house, in our Master's house, *there is bread enough, and to spare;* there is a fulness in Christ, which he communicates to all that passes through his hands; so that from it we receive, and *grace for grace,* Jn. 1:16. Those need not fear wanting, that have Christ to live upon.

8. It is good for those that follow Christ, *to keep together;* these followers of Christ continued in a body, *four thousand* of them together, and Christ fed them all. Christ's sheep must abide by the flock, and go forth by their footsteps, and verily they shall be fed.

Verses 10–21

Still Christ is upon motion; now he visits the parts of Dalmanutha, that no corner of the land of Israel might say that they had not had his presence with them. He came thither *by ship* (*v.* 10); but, meeting with occasions of dispute there, and not with opportunities of doing good, he *entered into the ship again* (*v.* 13), and came back. In these verses, we are told,

I. How he refused to gratify the Pharisees, who challenged him to give them a *sign from heaven.* They *came forth* on purpose to *question with him;* not to propose questions to him, that they might learn of him, but to cross question with him, that they might ensnare him.

1. They demanded of him a *sign from heaven,* as if the signs he gave them on earth, which were more familiar to them, and were more capable of being examined and enquired into, were not sufficient. There was a sign *from heaven* at his baptism, in the descent of the dove, and the voice (Mt. 3:16, 17); it was public enough; and if they had attended John's baptism as they ought to have done, they might themselves have seen it. Afterward, when he was nailed to the cross, they prescribed a new sign; *Let him come down from the cross, and we will believe him;* thus obstinate infidelity will still have something to say, though ever so unreasonable. They demanded this sign, *tempting him;* not in hopes that he would give it them, that they might be satisfied, but in hopes that he would not, that they might imagine themselves to have a pretence for their infidelity.

2. He denied them their demand; He *sighed deeply in his spirit, v.* 12. He *groaned* (so some), being grieved for the *hardness of their hearts,* and the little influence that his preaching and miracles had had upon them. The infidelity of those that have long enjoyed the means of conviction, is a great grief to the Lord Jesus; it troubles him, that sinners should thus stand in their own light, and put a bar in their own door. (1.) He expostulates with them upon this demand; *"Why doth this generation seek after a sign;* this generation, that is so unworthy to have the gospel brought to it, and to have any sign accompanying it; *this generation,* that so greedily swallows the traditions of the elders, without the confirmation of any sign at all; *this generation,* into which, by the calculating of the times prefixed in the Old Testament, they might easily perceive that the coming of the Messiah must fall; *this generation,* that has had such plenty of sensible and merciful signs given them in the cure of their sick? What an absurdity is it for them to desire a sign!" (2.) He refuses to answer their demand; *Verily, I say unto you, there shall no sign,* no such sign, *be given to this generation.* When God spoke to particular persons in a particular case, out of the road of his common dispensation, they were encouraged to ask a sign, as Gideon and Ahaz; but when he speaks in general to all, as in the law and the gospel, sending each with their own evidence, it is presumption to prescribe other signs than what he has given. *Shall any teach God knowledge?* He denied them, and then *left them,* as men not fit to be talked with; if they will not be convinced, they shall not; leave them to their strong delusions.

II. How he warned his disciples against the leaven of the Pharisees and of Herod. Observe here,

1. What the caution was (*v.* 15); *"Take heed, beware,* lest ye partake of the *leaven of the Pharisees,* lest ye embrace the tradition of the elders, which they are so wedded to, lest ye be proud, and hypocritical, and ceremonious, like them." Matthew adds, *and of the Sadducees;* Mark adds, *and of Herod:* whence some gather, that Herod, and his courtiers were generally Sadducees, that is, deists, men of no religion. Others give this sense, The Pharisees demanded a *sign from heaven;* and Herod was long *desirous* to see some miracle wrought by Christ (Lu. 23:8); such as he should prescribe, so that the leaven of both was the same; they were unsatisfied with the signs they had, and would have others of their own devising; "Take heed of *this leaven"* (saith Christ), "be convinced by the miracles ye have seen, and covet not to see more."

2. How they misunderstood this caution. It seems, at their putting to sea this time, they had *forgotten to take bread,* and *had not in their ship more than one loaf, v.* 14. When therefore Christ bid them *beware of the leaven of the Pharisees,* they understood it as an intimation to them, not to apply themselves to any of the Pharisees for relief, when they came to the other side, for they had lately been offended at them for eating with *unwashen hands.* They *reasoned among themselves,* what should be the meaning of this caution, and concluded, *"It is because we have no bread;* he saith this, to reproach us for being so careless as to go to sea, and go among strangers, with but one loaf of bread; he doth, in effect, tell us, we must be brought to *short allowance,* and must eat our bread by weight." They *reasoned it — dielogizonto,* they *disputed* about it; one said, "It was owing to you;" and the other said, "It was owing to you, that we are so ill provided for this voyage." Thus distrust of God makes Christ's disciples quarrel among themselves.

3. The reproof Christ gave them for their uneasiness in this matter, as it argued a disbelief of his power to supply them, notwithstanding the abundant experience they had had of it. The reproof is given with some warmth, for he knew their hearts, and knew they needed to be thus soundly chidden; *"Perceive ye not yet, neither understand,* that which you have had so many demonstrations of? *Have ye your hearts yet hardened,* so as that nothing will make any impression upon them, or bring them to compliance with your Master's designs? *Having eyes, see ye not* that which is plain before your eyes? *Having ears, hear ye not* that which you have been so often told? How strangely stupid and senseless are ye! *Do ye not remember* that which was done but the other day, *when I broke the five loaves among the five thousand,* and soon after, the *seven loaves among the four thousand?* Do ye not remember *how many baskets full ye took up* of the fragments?" Yes, they did remember, and could tell that they took up *twelve* baskets full one time, and *seven* another; "Why then," said he, *"how is it that ye do not understand?* As if he that multiplied *five* loaves, and *seven,* could not multiply one." They seemed to suspect that the one was not matter enough to work upon, if he should have a mind to entertain his hearers a third time: and if that was their thought, it was indeed a very senseless one, as if it were not all alike to the Lord, to save by many or few, and as easy to make one loaf to feed five thousand as five. It was therefore proper to remind them, not only of the sufficiency, but of the overplus, of the former meals; and justly were they chidden for not understanding what Christ therein designed, and what they from thence might have learned. Note, (1.) The experiences we have had of God's goodness to us in the way of duty, greatly aggravate our distrust of him, which is *therefore* very provoking to the Lord Jesus. (2.) Our *not understanding* of the true intent and meaning of God's favours to us, is equivalent to our not remembering of them. (3.) We are *therefore* overwhelmed with present cares and distrusts, because we do not *understand,* and remember, what we have known and seen of the power and goodness of our Lord Jesus. It would be a great support to us, to *consider the days of old,* and we are wanting both to God and ourselves if we do not. (4.) When we thus *forgot the works of God,* and distrust him, we should chide ourselves severely for it, as Christ doth his disciples here; "Am I thus without understanding? How is it that my heart is thus hardened?"

Verses 22–26

This cure is related only by this evangelist, and there is something singular in the circumstances.

I. Here is a *blind man* brought to Christ by his friends, with a desire that he would *touch him, v.* 22. Here appears the faith of those that brought him — they doubted not but that one touch of Christ's hand would recover him his sight; but the man himself showed not that earnestness for, or expectation of, a cure that other blind men did. If those that are spiritually blind, do not pray for themselves, yet let their friends and relations pray for them, that Christ would be pleased to *touch them.*

II. Here is Christ *leading* this blind man, *v.* 23. He did not bid his friends lead him, but (which bespeaks his wonderful condescension) he himself *took him by the hand, and led him,* to teach us to be as Job was, *eyes to the blind,* Job 29:15. Never had poor blind man such a Leader. He led him *out of the town.* Had he herein only designed privacy, he might have led him into a house, into an inner chamber, and have cured him there; but he intended hereby to upbraid Bethsaida with the *mighty works* that had *in vain* been done *in her* (Mt. 11:21), and was telling her, in effect, she was unworthy to have any more done within her walls. Perhaps Christ took the blind man *out of the town,* that he might have a larger prospect in the *open fields,* to try his sight with, than he could have in the *close streets.*

III. Here is the cure of the blind man, by that blessed Oculist, who came into the world to *preach the recovering of sight to the blind* (Lu. 4:18), and to *give* what he *preached.* In this cure we may observe, 1. That Christ used a *sign;* he *spat on his eyes* (spat *into* them, so some), and *put his hand upon him.* He could have cured him, as he did others, with a word speaking, but thus he was pleased to assist his faith which was very weak, and to help him against his *unbelief.* And this spittle signified the *eye-salve* wherewith Christ anoints the eyes of those that are spiritually blind, Rev. 3:18. 2. That the cure was wrought *gradually,* which was not usual in Christ's miracles. He *asked him if he saw aught, v.* 23. Let him tell what condition his sight was in, for the satisfaction of those about him. And he *looked up;* so far he *recovered his sight,* that he could open his eyes, and he said, *I see men as trees walking;* he could not distinguish men from trees, otherwise than he could discern them to move. He had some glimmerings of sight, and betwixt him and the sky could perceive a man erect like a tree, but *could not discern the form thereof,* Job 4:16. But, 3. It was soon completed; Christ never doeth *his work* by the halves, nor leaves it till he can say, *It is finished.* He *put his hands again upon his eyes,* to disperse the remaining darkness, and then bade him look up again, and he *saw every man clearly, v.* 25. Now Christ took this way, (1.) Because he would not *tie himself to a method,* but would show with what liberty he acted in all he did. He did not cure by *rote,* as I may say, and in a *road,* but *varied* as he thought fit. Providence gains the same end in different ways, that men may attend its motions with an *implicit faith.* (2.) Because it should be to the patient *according to his faith;* and perhaps this man's faith was at first very weak, but afterward gathered strength, and accordingly his cure was. Not that Christ always went by this rule, but thus he would sometimes put a rebuke upon those who came to him, doubting. (3.) Thus Christ would show how, and in what method, those are healed by his grace, who by nature are *spiritually blind;* at first, their knowledge is confused, they see *men as trees walking;* but, like the light of the morning, it *shines more and more to the perfect day,* and then they *see all things clearly,* Prov. 4:18. Let us enquire then, if we *see aught* of those things which *faith* is the *substance* and *evidence* of; and if through grace we see *any thing* of them, we may hope that we shall see yet *more* and *more,* for Jesus Christ will *perfect* for ever those that are *sanctified.*

IV. The directions Christ gave the man he had cured, not to *tell it to any in the town of Bethsaida,* nor so much as to *go into the town,* where probably there were some expecting him to come back, who had seen Christ lead him out of the town, but, having been eyewitnesses of so many miracles, had not so much as the curiosity to follow him: let not those be gratified with the sight of him when he was cured, who would not show so much respect to Christ as to go a step out of the town, to see this cure wrought. Christ doth not forbid him to tell it to others, but he must not tell it to *any in the town.* Slighting Christ's favours is forfeiting them; and Christ will make those know the worth of their privileges by the want of them, that would not know them otherwise. Bethsaida, in the day of her visitation, would not know the things that belonged to her peace, and now they are *hid from her eyes.* They will not see, and therefore shall not see.

Verses 27–38

We have read a great deal of the doctrine Christ preached, and the miracles he wrought, which were many, and strange, and well-attested, of various kinds, and wrought in several places, to the astonishment of the multitudes that were eyewitnesses of them. It is now time for us to pause a little, and to consider what these things mean; the wondrous works which Christ then forbade the publishing of, being recorded in these sacred writings, are thereby published to all the world, to us, to all ages; now what shall we think of them? Is the record of those things designed only for an amusement, or to furnish us with matter for discourse? No, certainly *these things are written, that we may believe that Jesus is the Christ the Son of God* (Jn. 20:31); and this discourse which Christ had with his disciples, will assist us in making the necessary reflections upon the miracles of Christ, and a right use of them. Three things we are here taught to infer from the miracles Christ wrought.

I. They *prove* that he is *the true Messiah,* the Son of God, and Saviour of the world: this the works he did witnessed concerning him; and this his disciples, who were the eyewitnesses of those works, here profess their belief of; which cannot but be a satisfaction to us in making the same inference from them.

1. Christ enquired of them what the sentiments of the people were concerning him; *Who did men say that I am? v.* 27. Note, Though it is a small thing for us to be judged of men, yet it may sometimes do us good to know what people say of us, not that we may seek our own glory, but that we may hear our faults. Christ asked them, not that he might be informed, but that they might observe it themselves, and inform one another.

2. The account they gave him, was such as plainly intimated the *high opinion* the people had of him. Though they came short of the truth, yet they were convinced by his miracles that he was an extraordinary person, sent from the invisible world with a divine commission. It is probable that they would have acknowledged him to be the Messiah, if they had not been possessed by their teachers with a notion that the Messiah must be a temporal Prince, appearing in external pomp and power, which the figure Christ made, would not comport with; yet (whatever the Pharisees said, whose copyhold was touched by the strictness and spirituality of his doctrine) none of the people said that he was a Deceiver, but some said that *he was John Baptist,* others *Elias,* others *one of the prophets, v.* 28. All agreed that he was one *risen from the dead.*

3. The account they gave him of their own sentiments concerning him, intimated their abundant satisfaction in him, and in their having left all to follow him, which now, after some time of trial, they see no reason to repent; *But whom say ye that I am?* To this they have an answer ready, *Thou art the Christ,* the Messiah often promised, and long expected, *v.* 29. To be a Christian indeed, is, sincerely to believe that Jesus is the Christ, and to act accordingly; and that he is so, plainly appears by his wondrous works. This they knew, and must shortly publish and maintain; but for the present they must keep it secret (*v.* 30), till the proof of it was completed, and they were completely qualified to maintain it, by the pouring out of the Holy Ghost; and then *let all the house of Israel know assuredly that God has made this same Jesus, whom ye crucified, both Lord and Christ,* Acts 2:36.

II. These miracles of Christ *take off the offence of the cross,* and assure us that Christ was, in it, not conquered, but a Conqueror. Now that the disciples are convinced that Jesus is the Christ, they may bear to hear of his sufferings, which Christ now *begins* to give them notice of, *v.* 31.

1. Christ *taught* his disciples that he must *suffer many things,* Though they had got over the vulgar error of the Messiah's being a temporal Prince, so far as to believe their Master to be the Messiah, notwithstanding his present meanness, yet still they retained it, so far as to expect that he would *shortly* appear in outward pomp and grandeur, and *restore the kingdom to Israel;* and therefore, to rectify that mistake, Christ here gives them a prospect of the contrary, that he must be *rejected of the elders, and the chief priests,* and *the scribes,* who, they expected, should be brought to own and prefer him; that, instead of being crowned, *he must be killed,* he must be crucified, and *after three days he must rise again* to a heavenly life, and to be *no more in this world.* This he spoke openly (*v.* 32), *parrēsia.* He said it freely and plainly, and did not wrap it up in ambiguous expressions. The disciples might easily understand it, if they had not been very much under the power of prejudice: or, it intimates that he spoke it cheerfully and without any terror, and would have them to hear it so: he spoke that saying *boldly,* as one that not only knew he *must* suffer and die, but was resolved he *would,* and made it his own act and deed.

2. Peter opposed it; *He took him, and began to rebuke him.* Here Peter showed more love than discretion, a zeal for Christ and his safety, but not according to knowledge. He *took him — proslabomenos.* He took hold of him, as it were to stop and hinder him, took him in his arms, and embraced him (so some understand it); he fell on his neck, as impatient to hear that his dear Master should suffer such hard things; or he took him aside privately, and *began to rebuke* him. This was not the language of the least authority, but of the greatest affection, of that *jealousy* for the welfare of those we love, which is *strong as death.* Our Lord Jesus allowed his disciples to be free with him, but Peter here took too great a liberty.

3. Christ checked him for his opposition (*v.* 33); He *turned about,* as one offended, and *looked on his disciples,* to see if the rest of them were of the same mind, and concurred with Peter in this, that, if they did, they might take the reproof to themselves, which he was now about to give to Peter; and he said, *Get thee behind me, Satan.* Peter little thought to have had such a sharp rebuke for such a kind dissuasive, but perhaps expected as much commendation now for his love as he had lately for his faith. Note, Christ sees that amiss in what we say and do, which we ourselves are not aware of, and knows what manner of spirit we are of, when we ourselves do not. (1.) Peter spoke as one that did not rightly understand, nor had duly considered, the purposes and counsels of God. When he saw such proofs as he every day saw of the *power* of Christ, he might conclude that he could not be *compelled to suffer;* the most potent enemies could not overpower him whom diseases and deaths, whom winds and waves and devils themselves, were forced to obey and yield to: and when he saw so much of the *wisdom* of Christ every day, he might conclude that he would not *choose to suffer* but for some very great and glorious purposes; and therefore he ought not thus to have contradicted him, but to have acquiesced. He looked upon his death only as a *martyrdom,* like that of the prophets, which he thought might be prevented, if either he would take a little care not to provoke the chief priests, or to keep out of the way; but he knew not that the thing was necessary for the glory of God, the destruction of Satan, and the salvation of man, that the Captain of our salvation must be *made perfect through sufferings,* and so must *bring many sons to glory.* Note, The wisdom of man is perfect folly, when it pretends to give measures to the divine counsels. The cross of Christ, the great instance of God's power and wisdom, was to some a stumbling-block, and to others foolishness. (2.) Peter spoke as one that did not rightly understand, nor had duly considered, the nature of Christ's kingdom; he took it to be *temporal* and *human,* whereas it is *spiritual* and *divine. Thou savourest not the things that are of God, but those that are of men; ou phroneis — thou mindest not;* so the word is rendered, Rom. 8:5. Peter seemed to mind more the things that relate to the lower world, and the life that now is, than those which relate to the upper world, and the life to come. Minding the *things of men* more than the *things of God,* our own credit, ease, and safety, more than the *things of God,* and his glory and kingdom, is a very great sin, and the root of much sin, and very common among Christ's disciples; and it will appear in suffering times, those times of temptation, when those in whom the *things of men* have the ascendant, are in danger of falling off. *Non sapis — Thou art not wise* (so it may be read) *in the things of God,* but in the *things of men.* It is important to consider what *generation* we appear *wise in,* Lu. 16:8. It seems policy to shun trouble, but if with that we shun duty, it is fleshly wisdom (2 Co. 1:12), and it will be folly in the end.

III. These miracles of Christ should engage us all to *follow him,* whatever it cost us, not only as they were *confirmations* of his *mission,* but as they were *explications* of his *design,* and the tendency of that grace which he came to bring; plainly intimating that by his Spirit he would do that for our blind, deaf, lame, leprous, diseased, possessed *souls,* which he did for the *bodies* of those many who in those distresses applied themselves to him. Frequent notice had been taken of the great flocking that there was to him for help in various cases: now this is written, that we may believe that he is the great Physician of souls, and may become his patients, and submit to his *regimen;* and here he tells us upon what terms we may be admitted; and he *called all the people to him,* to hear this, who modestly stood at some distance when he was in private conversation with his disciples. This is that which all are concerned to know, and consider, if they expect Christ should heal *their souls.*

1. They must not be *indulgent* of the *ease of the body;* for (*v.* 34), "*Whosoever will come after me* for spiritual cures, as these people do for bodily cures, *let him deny himself,* and live a life of self-denial, mortification, and contempt of the world; let him not pretend to be his own physician, but renounce all confidence in himself and his own righteousness and strength, and let him *take up his cross,* conforming himself to the pattern of a crucified Jesus, and accommodating himself to the will of God in all the afflictions he lies under; and thus let him continue to *follow me;*" as many of those did, whom Christ healed. Those that will be Christ's patients must attend on him, converse with him, receive instruction and reproof from him, as those did that *followed* him, and must resolve they will never forsake him.

2. They must not be *solicitous,* no, not for *the life of the body,* when they cannot keep it without quitting Christ, *v.* 35. Are we invited by the words and works of Christ to follow him? Let us sit down, and count the cost, whether we can prefer our advantages by Christ before life itself, whether we can bear to think of losing our life *for Christ's sake and the gospel's.* When the devil is drawing away disciples and servants after him, he conceals the worst of it, tells them only of the pleasure, but nothing of the peril, of his service; *Ye shall not surely die;* but what there is of trouble and danger in the service of Christ, he tells us of it before, tells us we shall *suffer,* perhaps we shall *die,* in the cause; and represents the discouragements not *less,* but *greater,* than commonly they prove, that it may appear he *deals fairly* with us, and is not afraid that we should know the worst; because the *advantages* of his service abundantly suffice to *balance* the *discouragements,* if we will but impartially set the one over against the other. In short,

(1.) We must *not dread the loss of our lives,* provided it be *in the cause of Christ* (*v.* 35); *Whosoever will save his life,* by declining Christ, and refusing to come to him, or by disowning and denying him after he has in profession come to Christ, he shall *lose it,* shall lose the comfort of his natural life, the root and fountain of his spiritual life, and all his hopes of eternal life; such a bad bargain will he make for himself. But *whosoever shall lose his life,* shall be truly willing to lose it, shall venture it, shall lay it down when he cannot keep it without denying Christ, he shall *save it,* he shall be an unspeakable gainer; for the loss of his life shall be made up to him in a better life. It is looked upon to be some kind of recompence to those who lose their lives in the service of their prince and country, to have their memories honoured and their families provided for; but what is that to the recompence which Christ makes in eternal life to all that die for him?

(2.) We must *dread the loss of our souls,* yea, though we should *gain the whole world* by it (*v.* 36, 37); *For what shall it profit a man, if he should gain the whole world,* and all the wealth, honour, and pleasure, in it, by denying Christ, and *lose his own soul?* "True it is," said Bishop Hooper, the night before he suffered martyrdom, "that *life is sweet,* and *death is bitter,* but *eternal death is more bitter,* and *eternal life is more sweet.*" As the happiness of heaven with Christ, is enough to countervail the loss of life itself for Christ, so the gain of all the world *in sin,* is not sufficient to countervail the ruin of the soul *by sin.*

What that is that men do, to *save their lives,* and *gain the world,* he tells us (*v.* 38), and of what fatal consequence it will be to them; *Whosoever therefore shall be ashamed of me, and of my words, in this adulterous and sinful generation, of him shall the Son of man be ashamed.* Something like this we had, Mt. 10:33. But it is here expressed more fully. Note, [1.] The disadvantage that the cause of Christ labours under this world, is, that it is to be owned and professed in an *adulterous and sinful generation;* such the generation of mankind is, gone a whoring from God, in the impure embraces of the world and the flesh, lying in wickedness; some ages, some places, are more especially adulterous and sinful, as that was in which Christ lived; in such a *generation* the cause of Christ is opposed and run down, and those that own it, are exposed to reproach and contempt, and every where ridiculed and *spoken against.* [2.] There are many, who, though they cannot but own that the cause of Christ is a righteous cause, are *ashamed* of it, because of the reproach that attends the professing of it; they are *ashamed* of their relation to Christ, and *ashamed* of the credit they cannot but give to *his words;* they cannot bear to be frowned upon and despised, and therefore throw off their profession, and go down the stream of a prevailing apostasy. [3.] There is a day coming, when the cause of Christ will appear as bright and illustrious as now it appears mean and contemptible; when the Son of man comes *in the glory of his Father with his holy angels,* as the true Shechinah, the brightness of his Father's glory, and the Lord of angels. [4.] Those that are ashamed of Christ in this world where he is despised, he will be ashamed of in that world where he is eternally adored. *They* shall not share with him in his glory then, that were not willing to share with him in his disgrace now.

CHAPTER 9

In this chapter, we have, I. Christ's transfiguration upon the mount (*v.* 1–13). II. His casting the devil out of a child, when the disciples could not do it (*v.* 14–29). III. His prediction of his own sufferings and death (*v.* 30–32). IV. The check he gave to his disciples for disputing who should be greatest (*v.* 33–37); and to John for rebuking one who cast out devils in Christ's name, and did not follow with them (*v.* 38–41). V. Christ's discourse with his disciples of the danger of offending one of his little ones (*v.* 42), and of indulging that in ourselves, which is an offence and an occasion of sin to us (*v.* 43–50), most of which passages we had before, Mt. 17 and 18.

Verses 1–13

Here is, I. A prediction of Christ's kingdom now near approaching, *v.* 1. That which is foretold, is, 1. That the *kingdom of God* would *come,* and would come so as to be *seen:* the kingdom of the Messiah shall be set up in the world by the utter destruction of the Jewish polity, which stood in the way of it; this was the restoring of the kingdom of God among men, which had been in a manner lost by the woeful degeneracy both of Jews and Gentiles. 2. That it would come *with power,* so as to make its own way, and bear down the opposition that was given to it. It came *with power,* when vengeance was taken on the Jews for crucifying Christ, and when it conquered the idolatry of the Gentile world. 3. That it would come while some now *present were alive;* There are some *standing here, that shall not taste of death,* till they see it; this speaks the same with Mt. 24:34, This *generation shall not pass, till all these things be fulfilled.* Those that were standing here with Christ, should see it, when the others could not discern it to be the kingdom of God, for it came not with observation.

II. A specimen of that kingdom in the transfiguration of Christ, *six days* after Christ spoke that prediction. He had begun to give notice to his disciples of his death and sufferings; and, to prevent their offence at that, he gives them this glimpse of his glory, to show that his sufferings were voluntary, and what a virtue the dignity and glory of his person would put into them, and to prevent the *offence of the cross.*

1. It was on the top of a *high mountain,* like the converse Moses had with God, which was on the top of mount Sinai, and his prospect of Canaan from the top of mount Pisgah. Tradition saith, It was on the top of the mount Tabor that Christ was transfigured; and if so, the scripture was fulfilled, *Tabor and Hermon shall rejoice in thy name,* Ps. 89:12. Dr. Lightfoot, observing that the last place where we find Christ was in the coasts of Caesarea-Philippi, which was far from mount Tabor, rather thinks it was a high mountain which Josephus speaks of, near Caesarea.

2. The witnesses of it were Peter, James, and John; these were the *three* that were to *bear record on earth,* answering to Moses, Elias, and the *voice from heaven,* the three that were to bear record from above. Christ did not take all the disciples with him, because the thing was to be kept very private. As there are distinguishing favours which are given to disciples and not to the world, so there are to some disciples and not to others. All the saints are a people *near to Christ,* but some lie in his bosom. James was the first of all the twelve that died for Christ, and John survived them all, to be the last eyewitness of this glory; he bore record (Jn. 1:14); *We saw his glory:* and so did Peter, 2 Pt. 1:16–18.

3. The manner of it; *He was transfigured before them;* he appeared in another manner than he used to do. This was a change of the accidents, the substance remaining the same, and it was a miracle. But transubstantiation, the change of the substance, all the accidents remaining the same, is not a miracle, but a fraud and imposture, such a work as Christ never wrought. See what a great change human bodies are capable of, when God is pleased to put an honour upon them, as he will upon the bodies of the saints, at the resurrection. He was transfigured *before them;* the change, it is probable, was *gradual,* from glory to glory, so that the disciples, who had their eye upon him all the while, had the clearest and most certain evidence they could have, that this glorious appearance was no other than the blessed Jesus himself, and there was no illusion in it. John seems to refer to this (1 Jn. 1:1), when he speaks of the *word of life,* as that which they had *seen with their eyes, and looked upon.* His *raiment became shining;* so that, though probably, it was sad-coloured, if not black, yet it was now *exceeding white as snow,* beyond what the fuller's art could do toward whitening it.

4. His companions in this glory were Moses and Elias (*v.* 4); They appeared *talking with him,* not to *teach* him, but to *testify* to him, and to be *taught* by him; by which it appears that there are converse and intercourse between glorified saints, they have ways of talking one with another, which we understand not. Moses and Elias lived at a great distance of time one from another, but that breaks no squares in heaven, where the *first shall be last, and the last first,* that is, all one in Christ.

5. The great delight that the disciples took in seeing this sight, and hearing this discourse, is expressed by Peter, the mouth of the rest; *He said, Master, it is good for us to be here, v.* 5. Though Christ was transfigured, and was in discourse with Moses and Elias, yet he gave Peter leave to speak to him, and to be as free with him as he used to be. Note, Our Lord Jesus, in his exaltation and glory, doth not at all abate of his condescending kindness to his people. Many, when they are in their greatness, oblige their friends to keep their distance; but even to the glorified Jesus true believers have access with boldness, and freedom of speech with him. Even in this heavenly discourse there was room for Peter to put in a word; and this is it, *"Lord, it is good to be here,* it is good *for us* to be here; here *let us make tabernacles;* let this be our rest for ever." Note, Gracious souls reckon it *good to be* in communion with Christ, good to be near him, good to be *in the mount* with him, though it be a cold and solitary place; it is good to be here retired from the world, and alone with Christ: and if it is good to be with Christ transfigured only upon a mountain with Moses and Elias, how good it will be to be with Christ glorified in heaven with all the saints! But observe, While Peter was for staying here, he forgot what need there was of the presence of Christ, and the preaching of his apostles, among the people. At this very time, the other disciples wanted them greatly, *v.* 14. Note, When it is well with us, we are apt to be mindless of others, and in the fulness of our *enjoyments* to forget the *necessities* of our brethren; it was a weakness in Peter to prefer private communion with God before public usefulness. Paul is willing to *abide in the flesh,* rather than depart to the mountain of glory (though that be far better), when he sees it needful for the church, Phil. 1:24, 25. Peter talked of making three distinct tabernacles for Moses, Elias, and Christ, which was not well-contrived; for such a perfect harmony there is between the law, the prophets, and the gospel, that one tabernacle will hold them all; they dwell together in unity. But whatever was incongruous in what he said, he may be excused, for they were all *sore afraid;* and he, for his part, *wist not what to say* (*v.* 6), not knowing what would be the end thereof.

6. The voice that came from heaven, was an attestation of Christ's mediatorship, *v.* 7. *There was a cloud that overshadowed them,* and was a shelter to them. Peter had talked of making tabernacles for Christ and his friends; but *while he yet spoke,* see how his project was superseded; this cloud was unto them instead of tabernacles for their shelter (Isa. 4:5); while he *spoke* of his tabernacles, God created his tabernacle *not made with hands.* Now out of this cloud (which was but a shade to *the excellent glory* Peter speaks of, whence *this voice* came) it was said, *This is my beloved Son, hear him.* God owns him, and accepts him, as his beloved Son, and is ready to accept of us in him; we must then own and accept him as our beloved Saviour, and must give up ourselves to be ruled by him.

7. The vision, being designed only to introduce the voice, when that was delivered, disappeared (*v.* 8); *Suddenly when they had looked round about,* as men amazed to see where they were, all was gone, *they saw no man any more.* Elias and Moses were vanished out of sight, and Jesus only remained with them, and he not transfigured, but as he used to be. Note, Christ doth not leave the soul, when extraordinary joys and comforts leave it. Though more sensible and ravishing communications may be withdrawn, Christ's disciples have, and shall have, his ordinary presence with them

always, even to the end of the world, and that is it we must depend upon. Let us thank God for *daily bread* and not expect a continual feast on this side of heaven.

8. We have here the discourse between Christ and his disciples, as they came down from the mount.

(1.) He charged them to keep this matter very private, till he was *risen from the dead,* which would complete the proof of his divine mission, and then this must be produced with the rest of the evidence, *v.* 9. And besides, he, being now in a state of humiliation, would haves nothing publicly taken notice of, that might be seen disagreeable to such a state; for to that he would in every thing accommodate himself. This enjoining of silence to the disciples, would likewise be of use to them, to prevent their boasting of the intimacy they were admitted to, that they might not be *puffed up* with the *abundance of the revelations.* It is a mortification to a man, to be tied up from telling of his advancements, and may help to hide pride from him.

(2.) The disciples were at a loss what the *rising from the dead* should mean; they could not form any notion of the Messiah's dying (Lu. 18:34), and therefore were willing to think that the *rising* he speaks of, was figurative, his rising from his present mean and low estate to the dignity and dominion they were in expectation of. But if so, here is another thing that embarrasses them (*v.* 11); *Why say the Scribes,* that before the appearing of the Messiah in his glory, according to the order settled in the prophecies of the Old Testament, *Elias must first come?* But Elias was gone, and Moses too. Now that which raised this difficulty, was, the scribes taught them to expect the person of Elias, whereas the prophecy intended one *in the spirit and power of Elias.* Note, The misunderstanding of scripture is a great prejudice to the entertainment of truth.

(3.) Christ gave them a key to the prophecy concerning Elias (*v.* 12, 13); "It is indeed prophesied that Elias will come, and will *restore all things,* and set them to rights; and (though you will not understand it) it is also prophesied of the *Son of man,* that he must *suffer many things,* and be *set at nought,* must be a reproach of men, and despised of the people: and though the scribes do not tell you so, the *scriptures* do, and you have as much reason to expect that as the other, and should not *make so strange* of it; but as to Elias, I tell you *he is come;* and if you consider a little, you will understand whom I mean, it is one to whom they have *done whatsoever they listed;*" which was very applicable to the ill usage they had given John Baptist. Many of the ancients, and the Popish writers generally, think, that besides the coming of John Baptist in the spirit of Elias, himself in his own person is to be expected, with Enoch, before the second appearance of Christ, wherein the prophecy of Malachi will have a more full accomplishment than it had in John Baptist. But it is groundless fancy; the true Elias, as well as the true Messiah promised, is come, and we are to look for *no other.* These words *as it is* written of him, refer not to their *doing to him whatever they listed* (that comes in a parenthesis), but only to his coming. He is come, and hath been, and done, according as was *written of him.*

Verses 14–29

We have here the story of Christ casting the devil out of a child, somewhat more fully related than it was in Mt. 17:14, etc. Observe here,

I. Christ's return to his disciples, and the perplexity he found them in. He laid aside his robes of glory, and came to look after his family, and to enquire what was become of them. Christ's glory above does not make him forget the concerns of his church below, which he visits in *great humility,* *v.* 14. And he came very seasonably, when the disciples were embarrassed and run a-ground; the scribes, who were sworn enemies both to him and them, had gained an advantage against them. A child possessed with a devil was brought to them, and they could not cast out the devil, whereupon the scribes insulted over them, and reflected upon their Master, and triumphed as if the day were their own. He *found the scribes questioning with them,* in the hearing of the multitude, some of whom perhaps began to be shocked by it. Thus Moses, when he came down from the mount, found the camp of Israel in great disorder; so soon were Christ and Moses missed. Christ's return was very welcome, no doubt, to the disciples, and *un*welcome to the scribes. But particular notice is taken of its being very surprising to the people, who perhaps were ready to say, *As for this Jesus, we wot not what is become of him;* but when *they beheld him* coming to them again, they were *greatly amazed* (some copies add, *kai exephobēthēsan — and they were afraid*); and *running to him* (some copies for *prostrechontes,* read *proschairontes — congratulating* him, or bidding him welcome), they saluted him. It is easy to give a reason why they should be glad to see him; but why where they *amazed, greatly amazed,* when they beheld him? Probably, there might remain something unusual in his countenance; as Moses's *face shone* when he came down from the mount, which made the people *afraid to come nigh him,* Ex. 34:30. So perhaps did Christ's face, in some measure; at least, instead of seeming *fatigued,* there appeared a wonderful briskness and sprightliness in his looks, which *amazed* them.

II. The case which perplexed the disciples, brought before him. He asked the scribes, who, he knew, were always *vexatious* to his disciples, and *teazing* them upon every occasion, *"What question ye with them?* What is the quarrel now?" The scribes made no answer, for they were confounded at his presence; the disciples made none, for they were comforted, and now left all to him. But the father of the child opened the case, *v.* 17, 18. 1. His child is possessed with a *dumb spirit;* he has the falling-sickness, and in his fits *is speechless;* his case is very sad, for, wheresoever the fit takes him, the spirit *tears* him, throws him into such violent convulsions as almost pull him to pieces; and, which is very grievous to himself, and frightful to those about him, *he foams* at his mouth, and *gnashes with his teeth,* as one in pain and great misery; and though the fits go off presently, yet they leave him so weak, that he *pines away,* is worn to a skeleton; his flesh is *dried* away; so the word signifies, Ps. 102:3–5. This was a constant affliction to a tender father. 2. The disciples cannot give him any relief; "I *desired they would cast him out,* as they had done many, and they would willingly have done it, but *they could not;* and therefore thou couldest never have come in better time; *Master, I have brought him to thee."*

III. The rebuke he gave to them all (*v.* 19); *O faithless generation, how long shall I be with you? How long shall I suffer you?* Dr. Hammond understands this as spoken to the disciples, reproving them for not exerting the power he had given them, and because they did not *fast* and *pray,* as in some cases he had directed them to do. But Dr. Whitby takes it as a rebuke to the scribes, who gloried in this disappointment that the disciples met with, and hoped to run them down with it. Them he calls a *faithless generation,* and speaks as one weary of *being with them,* and of *bearing with* them. We never heard him complaining, "How long shall I be in this low condition, and suffer that?" But, "How long shall I be among these *faithless* people, and suffer them?"

IV. The deplorable condition that the child was actually in, when he was brought to Christ, and the doleful representation which the father made of it. When the child saw Christ, he fell into a fit; *The spirit straightway tore him, boiled within him, troubled him* (so Dr. Hammond); as if the devil would set Christ at defiance, and hoped to be too hard for him too, and to keep possession in spite of him. The child *fell* on the *ground, and wallowed foaming.* We may put another construction upon it — that the devil raged, and had so much the greater wrath, because he *knew* that *his time was short,* Rev. 7:12. Christ asked, *How long since this came to him?* And, it seems, the disease was of long standing; it came to him *of a child* (*v.* 21), which made the case the more sad, and the cure more difficult. We are all by nature *children of disobedience,* and in such the evil spirit *works,* and has done so from our childhood; for *foolishness is bound in the heart of a child,* and nothing but the mighty grace of Christ can cast it out.

V. The pressing instances which the father of the child makes with Christ for a cure (*v.* 22); *Ofttimes it hath cast him into the fire, and into the waters, to destroy him.* Note, The devil aims at the ruin of those in whom he rules and works, and *seeks whom he may devour.* But, *if thou canst do any thing, have compassion on us, and help us.* The leper was confident of Christ's power, but put an *if* upon his will (Mt. 8:2); *If thou wilt, thou canst.* This poor man referred himself to his good-will, but put an *if* upon his power, because his disciples, who cast out devils *in his name,* had been nonplussed in this case. Thus Christ suffers in his honour by the difficulties and follies of his disciples.

VI. The answer Christ gave to his address (*v.* 23); *If thou canst believe, all things are possible to him that believeth.* Here, 1. He tacitly checks the weakness of his faith. The sufferer put it upon Christ's power, *If thou canst do any thing,* and reflected on the want of power in the disciples; but Christ turns it upon him, and puts him upon questioning his own faith, and will have him impute the disappointment to the want of that; *If thou canst believe.* 2. He graciously encourages the strength of his desire; *"All things are possible,* will appear possible, *to him that believes* the almighty power of God, to which all things are possible;" or "That shall be done by the grace of God, for them that believe in the promise of God, which seemed utterly impossible." Note, In dealing with Christ, very much is put upon our believing, and very much promised it. *Canst thou believe?* Darest thou believe? Art thou willing to venture thy all in the hands of Christ? To venture all thy spiritual concerns with him, and all thy temporal concerns for him? Canst thou find in thy heart to do this? If so, it is not impossible but that, though thou has been a great sinner, thou mayest be reconciled; though thou art very mean and unworthy, thou mayest get to heaven. *If thou canst believe,* it is possible that thy hard heart may be softened, thy spiritual diseases may be cured; and that, weak as thou art, thou mayest be able to hold out to the end.

VII. The *profession of faith* which the poor man made hereupon (*v.* 24); He cried out, *"Lord, I believe;* I am fully persuaded both of thy power and of thy pity; my cure shall not be prevented by the want of faith; *Lord, I believe."* He adds a prayer for grace to enable him more firmly to rely upon the assurances he had of the ability and willingness of Christ to save; *Help thou my unbelief.* Note, 1. Even those who through grace can say, *Lord, I believe,* have reason to complain of their unbelief; that they cannot so readily apply to themselves, and their own case, the word of Christ as they should, no so cheerfully depend upon it. 2. Those that complain of unbelief, must look up to Christ for grace to *help* them against it, *and his grace* shall be *sufficient for them. "Help mine unbelief,* help me to a pardon for it, help me with power against it; help out what is wanting in my faith with thy grace, the strength of which is perfected in our weakness."

VIII. The cure of the child, and the conquest of this raging devil in the child. Christ *saw the people come running together,* expecting to see the issue of this trial of skill, and therefore kept them in suspense no longer, but *rebuked the foul spirit;* the *unclean spirit,* so it should be rendered, as in other places. Observe, 1. What the charge was which Christ gave to this unclean spirit; *"Thou dumb and deaf spirit,* that makest the poor child dumb and deaf, but shalt thyself be made to *hear* thy doom, and not be able to *say* any thing against it, *come out of him* immediately, and *enter no more into him.* Let him not only be brought out of this fit, but let his fits never return." Note, Whom Christ cures, he cures effectually. Satan may *go out himself,* and yet recover possession; but if Christ *cast* him out, he will *keep* him out. 2. How the unclean spirit took it; he grew yet more outrageous, he *cried,* and *rent him sore,* gave him such a twitch at parting, that he was *as one dead;* so loth was he to quit his hold, so exasperated at the superior power of Christ, so malicious to the child, and so desirous was he to kill him. *Many said, He is dead.* Thus the toss that a soul is in at the breaking of Satan's power in it may perhaps be frightful for the present, but opens the door to lasting comfort. 3. How the child was perfectly restored (*v.* 27); *Jesus took him by the hand, kratēsas — took fast hold of him,* and strongly bore him up, and he arose and recovered, and all was well.

IX. The reason he gave to the disciples why they could not cast out this devil. They *enquired* of him privately *why they could not,* that wherein they were defective might be made up another time, and they might not again be thus publicly shamed; and he told them (*v.* 29), *This kind can come forth by nothing but prayer and fasting.* Whatever other difference there really might be, none appears between this and other kinds, but that the unclean spirit had had possession of this poor patient *from a child,* and that strengthened his interest, and confirmed his hold. When *vicious habits* are rooted by long usage, and begin to plead prescription, like chronical diseases that are *hardly cured. Can the Aethiopian change his skin?* The disciples must not think to do their work always with a like ease; some services call them to take more than ordinary pains; but Christ can do that with a word's speaking, which they must prevail for the doing of by *prayer and fasting.*

Verses 30–40

Here, I. Christ foretels his own approaching sufferings. He *passed through Galilee* with more expedition than usual, and *would not that any man should know of it* (*v.* 30); because he had done many mighty and good works among them in vain, they shall not be invited to see them and have the benefit of them, as they have been. The time of his sufferings drew nigh, and therefore he was willing to be private awhile, and to converse only with his disciples, to prepare them for the approaching trial, *v.* 31. He said to them, *The Son of man is delivered* by the determinate council and fore-knowledge of God *into the hands of men* (*v.* 31), and *they shall kill him.* He had been delivered into the hands of devils, and they had worried him, it had not been so strange; but that *men,* who have *reason,* and should have *love,* that they should be thus spiteful to the *Son of man,* who came to redeem and save them, is unaccountable. But still it is observable that when Christ spoke of his death, he alway spoke of his resurrection, which took away the reproach of it from himself, and should have taken away the grief of it from his disciples. But they *understood not that saying, v.* 32. The words were plain enough, but they could not be reconciled to the thing, and therefore would suppose them to have some mystical meaning which they did not understand, and they were *afraid to ask him;* not because he was difficult of access, or stern to those who consulted him, but either because they were loth to know the truth, or because they expected to be chidden for their backwardness to receive it. Many remain ignorant because they are ashamed to enquire.

II. He rebukes his disciples for magnifying themselves. When he came to Capernaum, he privately asked his disciples what it was they *disputed among themselves by the way, v.* 33. He knew very well what the dispute was, but he would know it *from them,* and would have them to confess their fault and folly in it. Note, 1. We must all expect to be called to an account by our Lord Jesus, concerning what passes while we are in the way in this state of passage and probation. 2. We must in a particular manner be called to an account about our discourses among ourselves; for by our words we must be justified or condemned. 3. As our other discourses among ourselves by the way, so especially our disputes, will be all called over again, and we shall be called to an account about them. 4. Of all disputes, Christ will be sure to reckon with his disciples for their disputes about precedency and superiority: that was the subject of the debate here, *who should be the greater, v.* 34. Nothing could be more contrary to the two great laws of Christ's kingdom, lessons of his school, and instructions of his example, which are *humility* and *love,* than *desiring* preferment in the world, and *disputing* about it. This ill temper he took all occasions to check, both because it arose from a mistaken notion of his kingdom, as if it were of this world, and because it tended so directly to be debasing of the honour, and the corrupting of the purity, of his gospel, and, he foresaw, would be so much the bane of the church.

Now, (1.) They were willing to *cover this fault* (*v.* 34); they *held their peace.* As they would not *ask* (*v.* 32), because they were ashamed to own their ignorance, so here they would not *answer* because they were ashamed to own their pride. (2.) He was willing to *amend this fault* in them, and to bring them to a better temper; and therefore *sat down,* that he might have a solemn and full discourse with them about this matter; he *called the twelve to him,* and told them, [1.] That ambition and affectation of dignity and dominion, instead of gaining them preferment in his kingdom, would but postpone their preferment; *If any man desire* and aim *to be first,* he *shall be last;* he that exalteth himself, shall be abased, and men's *pride* shall *bring them low.* [2.] That there is no preferment to be had under him, but an opportunity for, and an obligation to, so much the more labour and condescension; *If any man desire to be first,* when he is so, he must be much the more busy and serviceable to every body. *He that desires the office of a bishop, desires a good work,* for he must, as St. Paul did, labour the more abundantly, and make himself the *servant of all.* [3.] That those who are most humble and self-denying, do most resemble Christ, and shall be most tenderly owned by him. This he taught them by a sign; *He took a child in his arms,* that had nothing of pride and ambition in it. "Look you," saith he; *"whosoever shall receive* one like this child, *receives me.* Those of a humble, meek, mild disposition are such as I will own and countenance, and encourage every body else to do so too, and will take what is done to them as done to myself; and so will my Father too, for he who thus *receiveth me, receiveth him that sent me,* and it shall be placed to his account, and repaid with interest."

III. He rebukes them for *vilifying all but themselves;* while they are striving which of them should be greatest, they will not allow those who are not in communion with them to be any thing. Observe,

1. The account which John gave him, of the restraint they had laid upon one from making use of the name of Christ, because he was not of their society. Though they were ashamed to own their contests for preferment, they seem to boast of this exercise of their authority, and expected their Master would not only justify them in it, but commend them for it; and hoped he would not blame them for desiring to be great, when they would thus use their power for maintaining the honour of the sacred college. *Master,* saith John, *we saw one casting out devils in thy name, but he followeth not us, v.* 38. (1.) It was strange that the one who was not a professed disciple and follower of Christ, should yet have power to *cast out devils,* in his name, for that seemed to be peculiar to those whom he called, *ch.* 6:7. But some think that he was a disciple of John, who made use of the name of the Messiah, not as come, but as near at hand, not knowing that Jesus was he. It should rather seem that he made use of the name of Jesus, believing him to be the Christ, as the other disciples did. And why not he receive that power from Christ, whose *Spirit,* like the wind, *blows where it listeth,* without such an outward call as the apostles had? And perhaps there were many more such. Christ's grace is not tied to the visible church. (2.) It was strange that one who *cast out devils* in the name of Christ, did not join himself to the apostles, and follow Christ with them, but should continue to act in *separation* from them. I know of nothing that could hinder him from following them, unless because he was loth to leave all to follow them; and if so, that was an ill principle. The thing did not look well, and therefore the disciples *forbade him* to make use of Christ's name as they did, unless he would follow him as they did. This was like the motion Joshua made concerning Eldad and Medad, that prophesied in the camp, and went not up with the rest to the door of the tabernacle; *"My lord Moses, forbid them* (Num. 11:28); restrain them, silence them, for it is a schism." Thus apt are we to imagine that those do not follow Christ at all, who do not follow him *with us,* and that those do nothing well, who do not just as we do. But the *Lord knows them that are his,* however they are dispersed; and this instance gives us a needful caution, to take heed lest we be carried, by an excess of zeal for the unity of the church, and for that which we are sure is right and good, to oppose that which yet may tend to the enlargement of the church, and the advancement of its true interests another way.

2. The rebuke he gave to them for this (*v.* 39); *Jesus said, "Forbid him not,* nor any other that does likewise." This was like the check Moses gave to Joshua; *Enviest thou for my sake?* Note, That which is good, and doeth good, must not be prohibited, though there be some defect or irregularity in the manner of doing it. *Casting out devils,* and so destroying Satan's kingdom, doing this *in Christ's name,* and so owning him to be sent of God, and giving honour to him as the Fountain of grace, preaching down sin, and preaching up Christ, are good things, very good things, which ought not to be forbidden to any, merely because they *follow not with us.* If Christ be preached, Paul therein doth, and will rejoice, though he be eclipsed by it, Phil. 1:18. Two reasons Christ gives why such should not be forbidden. (1.) Because we cannot suppose that any man who makes use of Christ's name in working miracles, should blaspheme his name, as the scribes and Pharisees did. There were those indeed that did *in Christ's name cast out devils,* and yet in other respects were *workers of iniquity;* but they did not *speak evil of Christ.* (2.) Because those that differed in communion, while they agreed to fight against Satan under the banner of Christ, ought to look upon one another as on the same side, notwithstanding that difference. *He that is not against us is on our part.* As to the great controversy between Christ an Beelzebub, he had said, *He that is not with me is against me,* Mt. 12:30. He that will not own Christ, owns Satan. But as to those that own Christ, though not in the same circumstances, that follow him, though *not with us,* we must reckon that though these differ from us, they are not against us, and therefore are *on our part,* and we must not be any hindrance to their usefulness.

Verses 41–50

Here, I. Christ promiseth a reward to all those that are any way kind to his disciples (*v.* 41); *"Whosoever shall give you a cup of water,* when you need it, and will be a refreshment to you, *because ye belong to Christ,* and are of his family, *he shall not lose his reward."* Note, 1. It is the honour and happiness of Christians, that they *belong to Christ,* they have joined themselves to him, and are owned by him; they wear his livery and retainers to his family; nay, they are more nearly related, they are *members of his body.* 2. They who belong to Christ, may sometimes be reduced to such straits as to be glad of a *cup of cold water.* 3. The relieving of Christ's poor in their distresses, is a good deed, and will turn a good account; he accepts it, and will reward it. 4. What kindness is done to Christ's poor, must be done them *for his sake,* and *because they belong to him;* for that is it that sanctifies the kindness, and puts a value upon it in the sight of God. 5. This is a reason why we must not discountenance and discourage those who are serving the interests of Christ's kingdom, though they are not in every thing of our mind and way. It comes in here as a reason why those must not be hindered, that cast out devils in Christ's name, though they did not follow him; for (as Dr. Hammond paraphrases it) "It is not only the great eminent performances which are done by you my constant attendants and disciples, that are accepted by me, but every the least degree of sincere faith and Christian performance, proportionable but to the expressing the least kindness, as giving a cup of water to a disciple of mine for being such, shall be accepted and rewarded." If Christ reckons *kindness to us* services to *him,* we ought to reckon *services to him* kindnesses to us, and to encourage them, though done by those that follow not with us.

II. He threatens those that *offend* his *little ones,* that wilfully are the occasion of sin or trouble to them, *v.* 42. Whosoever shall grieve any true Christians, though they be of the weakest, shall oppose their *entrance* into the ways of God, or discourage and obstruct their *progress* in those ways, shall either restrain them from doing good, or draw them in to commit sin, it were *better for him that a millstone were hanged about his neck, and he were cast into the sea:* his punishment will be very great, and the death and ruin of his soul more terrible than such a death and ruin of his body would be. See Mt. 18:6.

III. He warns all his followers to take heed of ruining their own souls. This charity must begin at home; if we must take heed of doing any thing to hinder others from good, and to occasion their sin, much more careful must we be to avoid every thing that will take us off from our duty, or lead us to sin; and that which doth so we must part with, though it be ever so dear to us. This we had twice in Matthew, *ch.* 5:29, 30, and *ch.* 18:8, 9. It is here urged somewhat more largely and pressingly; certainly this requires our serious regard, which is so much insisted upon. Observe,

1. The case supposed, that our own *hand,* or *eye,* or *foot, offend us;* that the impure *corruption* we indulge is as dear to us as an eye or a hand, or that that which is to us as an eye or a hand, is become an invisible *temptation* to sin, or *occasion* of it. Suppose the beloved is become a sin, or the sin a beloved. Suppose we cannot keep that which is dear to us, but it will be a snare and a stumbling-block; suppose we must part with it, or part with Christ and a good conscience.

2. The duty prescribed in that case; *Pluck out the eye, cut off the hand and foot,* mortify the darling lust, kill it, crucify it, starve it, make no provision for it. Let the idols that have been *delectable* things, be cast away as *detestable* things; keep at a distance from that which is a temptation, though ever so pleasing. It is necessary that the part which is gangrened, should be taken off for the preservation of the whole. *Immedicabile vulnus ense recidendum est, ne pars sincera trahatur — The part that is incurably wounded must be cut off, lest the parts that are sound be corrupted.* We must put ourselves to pain, that we may not bring ourselves to ruin; self must be denied, that it may not be destroyed.

3. The necessity of doing this. The flesh must be mortified, that we may *enter into life* (*v.* 43, 45), into the kingdom of God, *v.* 47. Though, by abandoning sin, we may, for the present, feel ourselves as if we were *halt* and *maimed* (it may seem to be a force put upon ourselves, and may create us some uneasiness), yet it is for *life;* and all that men have, they will give for their lives: it is for a *kingdom,* the *kingdom of God,* which we cannot otherwise obtain; these *halts* and

maims will be the *marks of the Lord Jesus*, will be in that kingdom *scars of honour.*

4. The danger of not doing this. The matter is brought to this issue, that either sin must die, or we must die. If we will lay this *Delilah* in our bosom, it will betray us; if we be *ruled* by sin, we shall inevitably be *ruined* by it; if we must keep our *two hands*, and *two eyes*, and *two feet*, we must with them be *cast into hell.* Our Saviour often pressed our duty upon us, from the consideration of the torments of hell, which we run ourselves into if we continue in sin. With what an emphasis of terror are those words repeated three times here, *Where their worm dieth not, and the fire is not quenched!* The words are quoted from Isa. 66:24. (1.) The reflections and reproaches of the sinner's own conscience are the *worm that dieth not;* which will cleave to the damned soul as the worms do to the dead body, and prey upon it, and never leave it till it is quite devoured. *Son, remember,* will set this worm gnawing; and how terrible will it bite that word (Prov. 5:12, 23), *How have I hated instruction!* The soul that is food to this worm, dies not; and the worm is bred in it, and one with it, and therefore neither doth that die. Damned sinners will be to eternity accusing, condemning, and upbraiding, themselves with their own follies, which, how much soever they are now in love with them, will at the last *bite like a serpent,* and *sting like an adder.* (2.) The wrath of God fastening upon a guilty and polluted conscience, is the *fire* that is *not quenched;* for it is the wrath of the living God, the eternal God, into whose hands it is a fearful thing to fall. There are no operations of the Spirit of grace upon the souls of the damned sinners, and therefore there is nothing to alter the nature of the fuel, which must remain for ever combustible; nor is there any application of the merit of Christ to them, and therefore there is nothing to appease or quench the violence of the fire. Dr. Whitby shows that the eternity of the torments of hell was not only the constant faith of the Christian church, but had been so of the Jewish church. Josephus saith, The Pharisees held that the souls of the wicked were to be *punished with perpetual punishment;* and that there was appointed for them *a perpetual prison.* And Philo saith, The punishment of the wicked is *to live for ever dying,* and to be *for ever in pains and griefs that never cease.*

The two last verses are somewhat difficult, and interpreters agree not in the sense of them; *for every one* in general, or rather every one *of them* that are cast into hell, shall be *salted with fire,* and every sacrifice shall be *salted with salt.* Therefore *have salt in yourselves.* [1.] It was appointed by the law of Moses, that every sacrifice should be *salted with salt,* not *to preserve* it (for it was to be immediately consumed), but because it was the food of God's table, and no flesh is eaten without salt; it was therefore particularly required in the meat-offerings, Lev. 2:13. [2.] The nature of man, being *corrupt,* and as such being called *flesh* (Gen. 6:3; Ps. 78:39), some way or other must be *salted,* in order to its being a sacrifice to God. The *salting* of fish (and I think of other things) they call the *curing* of it. [3.] Our chief concern is, to present ourselves *living sacrifices* to the grace of God (Rom. 12:1), and, in order to our acceptableness, we must be *salted with salt,* our corrupt affections must be subdued and mortified, and we must have in our souls a savour of grace. Thus the *offering up* or *sacrificing* of the Gentiles is said to be *acceptable, being sanctified by the Holy Ghost,* as the sacrifices were *salted,* Rom. 15:16. [4.] Those that have the salt of grace, must make it appear that they have it; that they *have salt in themselves,* a living principle of grace in their hearts, which works out all corrupt dispositions, and every thing in the soul that tends to *putrefaction,* and would *offend* our God, or our own consciences, as unsavoury meat doth. Our *speech* must be *always with grace seasoned with* this salt, that no *corrupt communication* may *proceed out of our mouth,* but we may loathe it as much as we would to put putrid meat into our mouths. [5.] As this gracious salt will keep our own consciences void of offence, so it will keep our conversation with others so, that we may not offend any of Christ's little ones, but may be *at peace one with another.* [6.] We must not only have this salt of grace, but we must always retain the relish and savour of it; for if this *salt lose its saltiness,* if a Christian revolt from his Christianity, if he loses the savour of it, and be no longer under the power and influence of it, what can recover him, or *wherewith will ye season him?* This was said Mt. 5:13. [7.] Those that present not themselves *living* sacrifices to God's grace, shall be made for ever *dying* sacrifices to his justice, and since they would not give honour to him,

he will get him honour upon them; they would not be *salted with the salt* of divine grace, would not admit that to subdue their corrupt affections, no, they would not submit to the operation, could not bear the corrosives that were necessary to eat out the proud flesh, it was to them like cutting off a hand, or plucking out an eye; and therefore in hell they shall be *salted with fire;* coals of fire shall be *scattered* upon them (Eze. 10:2), as salt upon the meat, and *brimstone* (Job 18:15), as fire and brimstone were rained on Sodom; the pleasures they have lived *in, shall eat their flesh, as it were with fire,* Jam. 5:3. The pain of mortifying the flesh now is no more to be compared with the punishment for not mortifying it, than *salting* with *burning.* And since he had said, that the *fire* of hell *shall not be quenched,* but it might be objected, that the fuel will not last always, he here intimates, that by the power of God it shall be made to last always; for those that are *cast into hell,* will find the fire to have not only the *corroding* quality of salt, but its *preserving* quality; whence it is used to signify that which is *lasting:* a covenant of *salt* is a *perpetual* covenant, and Lot's wife being turned into a *pillar of salt,* made her a remaining monument of divine vengeance. Now since this will certainly be the doom of those that do not crucify the flesh with its affections and lusts, let us, knowing this *terror of the Lord,* be *persuaded* to do it.

CHAPTER 10

In this chapter, we have, I. Christ's dispute with the Pharisees concerning divorce (v. 1–12). II. The kind entertainment he gave to the little children that were brought to him to be blessed (v. 13–16). III. His trial of the rich man that enquired what he must do to get to heaven (v. 17–22). IV. His discourse with his disciples, upon that occasion, concerning the peril of riches (v. 23–27), and the advantage of being impoverished for his sake (v. 28–31). V. The repeated notice he gave his disciples of his sufferings and death approaching (v. 32–34). VI. The counsel he gave to James and John, to think of suffering with him, rather than of reigning with him (v. 15–45). VII. The cure of Bartimeus, a poor blind man (v. 46–52). All which passages of story we had the substance of before, Mt. 19 and 20.

Verses 1–12

Our Lord Jesus was an itinerant Preacher, did not continue long in a place, for the whole land of Canaan was his parish, or diocese, and therefore he would visit every part of it, and give instructions to those in the remotest corners of it. Here we have him in the *coasts* of Judea, by the further side of Jordan eastward, as we found him, not long since, in the utmost borders westward, near Tyre and Sidon. Thus was his circuit like that of the sun, from whose light and heat nothing is hid. Now here we have him,

I. *Resorted to* by the *people, v.* 1. Wherever he was, they flocked after him in crowds; they came to him *again,* as they had done when he had formerly been in these parts, and, *as he was wont, he taught them again.* Note, Preaching was Christ's constant practice; it was what he was used to, and, wherever he came, he did *as he was wont.* In Matthew it is said, *He healed them;* here it is said, *He taught them:* his cures were to confirm his doctrine, and to recommend it, and his doctrine was to explain his cures, and illustrate them. He *taught them again.* Note, Even those whom Christ hath taught, have need to be taught *again.* Such is the fulness of the Christian doctrine, that there is still more to be learned; and such our forgetfulness, that we need to be reminded of what we do know.

II. We have him *disputed with* by the Pharisees, who envied the progress of his spiritual arms, and did all they could to obstruct and oppose it; to divert him, to perplex him, and to prejudice the people against him.

Here is, 1. A question they started concerning divorce (v. 2); *Is it lawful for a man to put away his wife?* This was a good question, if it had been well put, and with a humble desire to know the mind of God in this matter; but they proposed it, *tempting him,* seeking an occasion against him, and an opportunity to expose him, which side soever he should take of the question. Ministers must stand upon their guard, lest, under pretence of being advised with, they be ensnared.

2. Christ's reply to them with a question (v. 3); *What did Moses command you?* This he asked them, to testify his respect to the law of Moses, and to show that he came not to destroy it; and to engage them to a universal impartial respect for Moses's writings and to compare one part of them with another.

3. The fair account they gave of what they found in the law of Moses, expressly concerning divorce, v. 4. Christ asked, *What did Moses command you?* They own that Moses only

suffered, or *permitted,* a man to write his wife a *bill of divorce,* and to put *her away,* Deu. 24:1. "If you *will* do it, you must do it *in writing,* delivered into her own hand, and so put her away, and never return to her again."

4. The answer that Christ gave to their question, in which he abides by the doctrine he had formerly laid down in this case (Mt. 5:32), *That whosoever puts away his wife, except for fornication, causeth her to commit adultery.* And to clear this he here shows,

(1.) That the reason why Moses, in his *law,* permitted divorce, was such, as that they ought not to make use of that permission; for it was only *for the hardness of their hearts* (v. 5), lest, if they were not permitted to divorce their wives, they should murder them; so that none must put away their wives but such as are willing to own that their hearts were so hard as to need this permission.

(2.) That the account which Moses, in this *history, gives* of the institution of marriage, affords such a reason against divorce, as amounts to a prohibition of it. So that if the question be, *What did Moses command?* (v. 3), it must be answered, "Though by a temporary proviso he allowed divorce to the Jews, yet by an eternal reason he forbade it to all the children of Adam and Eve, and that is it which we must abide by."

Moses tells us, [1.] That God made man *male and female,* one male, and *one* female; so that *Adam* could *not* put away his wife and take another, for there was no other to take, which was an intimation to all his sons, that they *must not.* [2.] When this male and this female were, by the ordinance of God, joined together in holy marriage, the law was, That a man must *leave his father and mother, and cleave to his wife* (v. 7); which intimates not only the nearness of the relation, but the perpetuity of it; he shall so cleave to his wife as not to be separated from her. [3.] The result of the relation is, That, though they are *two,* yet they are *one,* they are *one flesh, v.* 8. The union between them is the most intimate that can be, and, as Dr. Hammond expresses it, a sacred thing that must not be violated. [4.] God himself was *joined them together;* he has not only, as Creator, fitted them to be comforts and helps meet for each other, but he has, in wisdom and goodness, appointed them who are thus joined together, to live together in love till death parts them. Marriage is not an invention of men, but a divine institution, and therefore is to be religiously observed, and the more, because it is a figure of the mystical inseparable union between Christ and his church.

Now from all this he infers, that men ought not to *put* their wives *asunder* from them, whom God has put so near them. The bond which God himself has tied, is not to be lightly untied. They who are divorcing their wives for every offence, would do well to consider what would become of them, if God should in like manner deal with them. See Isa. 50:1; Jer. 3:1.

5. Christ's discourse with his disciples, in private, about this matter, *v.* 10–12. It was an advantage to them, that they had opportunity of personal converse with Christ, not only about gospel mysteries, but about moral duties, for further satisfaction. No more is here related of this private conference, that the law Christ laid down in this case — That it is adultery for a man to put away his wife, and marry another; it is adultery *against the wife* he puts away, it is a wrong to her, a breach of his contract with her, v. 11. He adds, *If a woman shall put away her husband,* that is, elope from him, leave him by consent, and *be married to another,* she *commits adultery* (v. 12), and it will be no excuse at all for her to say that it was with the consent of her husband. Wisdom and grace, holiness and love, reigning in the heart, will make those commands easy which to the carnal mind may be as a heavy yoke.

Verses 13–16

It is looked upon as the indication of a kind and tender disposition to take notice of little children, and this was remarkable in our Lord Jesus, which is an encouragement not only to little children to apply themselves to Christ when they are very young, but to grown people, who are conscious to themselves of weakness and childishness, and of being, through manifold infirmities, helpless and useless, like little children. Here we have,

I. Little children brought to Christ, *v.* 13. Their parents, or whoever they were that had the nursing of them, brought them to him, that he should *touch them,* in token of his commanding and conferring a blessing on them. It doth not appear that they needed any bodily *cure,* nor were they capable of being *taught:* but it seems, 1. That they had the care of them were mostly concerned *about their souls,* their better part, which ought to be the principal care of all parents for their children; for that is the principal part, and it is well with them, it if be well with their souls. 2. They believed that Christ's blessing would do their souls good; and therefore to him they brought them, that he might *touch* them, knowing that he could reach their hearts, when nothing their parents could say to them, or do for them, would reach them. We may present our children to Christ, now that he is in heaven, for from thence he can reach them with his blessing, and therein we may act faith upon the fulness and extent of his grace, the kind intimations he hath always given of favour to the seed of the faithful, the tenour of the covenant with Abraham, and the promise *to us and to our children,* especially that great promise of pouring his *Spirit upon our seed,* and his *blessing* upon *our offspring,* Isa. 44:3.

II. The *dis*couragement which the disciples gave to the bringing of children to Christ; *They rebuked them that brought them;* as if they had been sure that they knew their Master's mind in this matter, whereas he had lately cautioned them not to *despise the little ones.*

III. The *en*couragement Christ gave to it. 1. He took it very ill that his disciples should keep them off; *When he saw it, he was much displeased, v.* 14. "What do you mean? Will you hinder me from doing good, from doing good to the rising generation, to the lambs of the flock?" Christ is very angry with his own disciples, if they discountenance any in coming to him themselves, or in bringing their children to him. 2. He ordered that they should be *brought to him,* and nothing said or done to hinder them; suffer *little children,* as soon as they are capable, to *come to me,* to offer up their supplications to me, and to receive instructions from me. Little children are welcome betimes to the throne of grace with their Hosannas. 3. He owned them as members of his church, as they had been of the Jewish church. He came to set up the *kingdom of God* among men, and took this occasion to declare that that kingdom admitted *little children* to be the subjects of it, and gave them a title to the privileges of subjects. Nay, the kingdom of God is to be kept up by such: they must be taken in when they are little children, that they may be secured for hereafter, to bear up the name of Christ. 4. That there must be something of the temper and disposition of little children found in all that Christ will own and bless. We must *receive the kingdom of God as little children* (*v.* 15); that is, we must stand affected to Christ and his grace as little children do to their parents, nurses, and teachers. We must be *inquisitive,* as children, must learn as children (that is the learning age), and in learning must *believe, Oportet discentem credere — A learner must believe.* The mind of a child is white paper *(tabula rose — a mere blank),* you may write upon it what you will; such must our minds be to the pen of the blessed Spirit. Children are under government; so must we be. *Lord, what wilt thou have me to do?* We must receive the kingdom of God as the child Samuel did, *Speak, Lord, for thy servant heareth.* Little children depend upon their parents' wisdom and care, are carried in their arms, go where they send them, and take what they provide for them; and thus must we receive the *kingdom of God,* with a humble resignation of ourselves to Jesus Christ, and an easy dependence upon him, both for strength and righteousness, for tuition, provision, and a portion. 5. He received the children, and gave them what was desired (*v.* 16); *He took them up in his arms,* in token of his affectionate concern for them; *put his hands upon them,* as was desired, and *blessed them.* She how he out-did the desires of these parents; they begged he would touch them, but he did more. (1.) He *took them in his arms.* Now the scripture was fulfilled (Isa. 40:11), *He shall gather the lambs in his arms, and carry them in his bosom.* Time was, when Christ himself was taken up in old Simeon's arms, Lu. 2:28. And now he took up these children, not complaining of the burthen (as Moses did, when he was bid to *carry Israel,* that peevish child, *in his bosom, as a nursing father bears the sucking child,* Num. 11:12), but pleased with it. If we in a right manner bring our children to Christ, he will take them up, not only in the arms of his power and providence, but in the arms of his pity and grace (as Eze. 16:8); underneath them are the *everlasting arms.* (2.) He *put his hands upon them,* denoting the bestowing of his Spirit upon them (for that is the hand of the Lord), and his setting them apart for himself. (3.) He *blessed* them with the spiritual blessings he came to give. Our children are happy, if they have but the *Mediator's blessing* for their portion. It is true, we do not read that he baptized these children, baptism was not fully settled as the door of admission into the church until after Christ's resurrection; but he asserted their visible church-membership, and by another sign bestowed those blessings upon them, which are now appointed to be conveyed and conferred by baptism, the seal of the promise, which is *to us* and *to our children.*

Verses 17–31

I. Here is a *hopeful meeting* between Christ and a *young man;* such he is said to be (Mt. 19:20, 22), and a *ruler* (Lu. 18:18), a person of quality. Some circumstances here are, which we had not in Matthew, which makes his address to Christ very promising.

1. He came *running* to Christ, which was an indication of his humility; he laid aside the gravity and grandeur of a ruler, when he came to Christ: thus too he manifested his earnestness and importunity; he *ran* as one *in haste,* and longing to be in conversation with Christ. He had now an opportunity of consulting this great Prophet, in the things that belonged to his peace, and he would not let slip the opportunity.

2. He came to him when he was *in the way,* in the midst of company: he did not insist upon a private conference with him by night, as Nicodemus did, though like him he was a ruler, but *when he shall find him without,* will *embrace* that opportunity of advising with him, *and not be ashamed,* Cant. 8:1.

3. He *kneeled to him,* in token of the great value and veneration he had for him, as a teacher come from God, and his earnest desire to be taught by him. He bowed the knee to the Lord Jesus, as one that would not only *do obeisance* to him now, but would *yield obedience* to him always; he *bowed the knee,* as one that meant to *bow the soul* to him.

4. His address to him was serious and weighty; *Good Master, what shall I do, that I may inherit eternal life?* Eternal life was an article of his creed, though then denied by the Sadducees, a prevailing party: he asks, What shall he do now that he may be happy for ever. Most men enquire for good to be *had* in this world (Ps. 4:6), *any good;* he asks for *good to be done* in this world, in order to the enjoyment of the greatest good in the other world; not, Who will make us to *see good?* But, "Who will make us to *do good?"* He enquires for *happiness* in the way of *duty;* the *summum bonum — chief good* which Solomon was in quest of, was *that good for the sons of men which they do should do,* Eccl. 2:3. Now this was, (1.) A very serious question in itself; it was about eternal things, and his own concern in those things. Note, *Then* there begins to be some hope of people, when they begin to enquire solicitously, what they shall do to get to heaven. (2.) It was proposed to a right person, one that was every way fit to answer it, being himself *the Way, the Truth,* and *the Life,* the true way to life, to eternal life; who came *from heaven* on purpose, first to *lay open for us,* and then to *lay open to us;* first to make, and then to make known, the way to *heaven.* Note, Those who would know what they shall do to be saved, must apply themselves to Christ, and enquire of him; it is peculiar to the Christian religion, both to show eternal life, and to show the way to it. (3.) It was proposed with a good design — to be instructed. We find this same question put by a lawyer, not *kneeling,* but standing up (Lu. 10:25), with a bad design, to pick quarrels with him; he *tempted him, saying, Master, what shall I do?* It is not so much the good *words* as the good *intention* of them that Christ looks at.

5. Christ encouraged this address, (1.) By *assisting his faith, v.* 18. He called him *good Master;* Christ would have him mean thereby, that he looked upon him to be *God,* since there is none good but *one,* that is *God,* who is one, and his name one, Zec. 14:9. Our English word *God* doubtless hath affinity with *good;* as the Hebrews name God by his power, *Elohim, the strong God;* so we by his goodness, the *good God.* (2.) By directing his practice (*v.* 19); *Keep the commandments;* and thou *knowest* what they are. He mentions the six commandments of the second table, which prescribe our duty to our neighbour; he inverts the order, putting the seventh commandment before the sixth, to intimate that *adultery* is a sin no less heinous than *murder* itself. The fifth commandment is here put last, as that which should especially be remembered and observed, to keep us to all the rest. Instead of the tenth commandment, *Thou shalt not covet,* our Saviour here puts, *Defraud not. Mē aposterēsēs —* that is, saith Dr. Hammond, "Thou shalt not rest contented with thy own, and not seek to increase it by the diminution of other men's." It is a rule of justice not to advance or enrich ourselves by doing wrong or injury to any other.

6. The young man bid fair for heaven, having been free from any open gross violations of the divine commands. Thus far he was able to same in some measure (*v.* 20), *Master, all these have I observed from my youth.* He thought he had, and his neighbours thought so too. Note, Ignorance of the extent and spiritual nature of the divine law, makes people think themselves in a better condition than they really are. Paul was alive *without the law.* But when he saw that to be *spiritual,* he saw himself to be *carnal,* Rom. 7:9, 14. However, he that could say he was free from scandalous sin, went further than many in the way to eternal life. But though we *know nothing by ourselves, yet are we not thereby justified.* 1 Co. 4:4.

7. Christ had a kindness for him; *Jesus, beholding him, loved him, v.* 21. He was pleased to find that he had lived inoffensively, and pleased to see that he was inquisitive how to live better than so. Christ particularly *loves* to see young people, and rich people, *asking the way to heaven, with their faces thitherward.*

II. Here is a *sorrowful parting* between Christ and this young man.

1. Christ gave him a command of trial, by which it would appear whether he did in sincerity aim at eternal life, and press towards it: he seemed to have his heart much upon it, and if so, he is what he should be; but has he indeed his heart upon it? Bring him to the touchstone. (1.) Can he find in his heart *to part with his riches* for the service of Christ? He hath a good estate, and now, shortly, at the first founding of the Christian church, the necessity of the case will require that those who have *lands, sell them, and lay the money at the apostles' feet;* and how will he dispense with that? Acts 4:34, 35. After awhile, tribulation and persecution will arise, because of the word; and he must be forced to sell his estate, or have it taken from him, and how will he like that? Let him know the worst now; if he will not come up to these terms, let him quit his pretensions; as good as the first as at last. *"Sell whatsoever thou hast* over and above what is necessary for thy support;" probably, he had no family to provide for; let him therefore be a *father to the poor,* and make them his heirs. Every man, according to his ability, must relieve the poor, and be content, when there is occasion, to straiten himself to do it. Worldly wealth is given us, not only as *maintenance* to bear our charges through this world, according to our place in it, but as *talent,* to be used and employed for the glory of our great Master in the world, who hath so ordered it, that the poor we should have always with us as his receivers. (2.) Can he find it in his heart to go through the hardest costliest services he may be called to as a disciple of Christ, and depend upon him for a recompence *in heaven?* He asks Christ what he should do more than he has done to obtain *eternal life,* and Christ puts it to him, whether he has indeed that firm belief of, and that high value for, eternal life that he seems to have. Doth he really believe there is a true treasure in heaven sufficient to make up all he can leave, or lose, or lay out, for Christ? Is he willing to deal with Christ *upon trust?* Can he give him credit for all he is worth; and be willing to bear a present cross, in expectation of a future crown?

2. Upon this he flew off (*v.* 22); *He was sad at that saying;* was sorry that he could not be a follower of Christ upon any easier terms than leaving all to follow him; that he could not *lay hold* on eternal life, and *keep hold* of his temporal possessions too. But since he could not come up to the terms of discipleship, he was so fair as not to pretend to it; *He went away grieved.* Here appeared the truth of that (Mt. 6:24), *Ye cannot serve God and mammon;* while he held to mammon he did in effect *despise* Christ, as all those do who prefer the world before him. He bids for what he has a mind for in the market, yet goes away grieved, and leaves it, because he cannot have it at his own price. Two words to a bargain. Motions are not marriages. That which ruined this young man was, *he had great possessions;* thus the *prosperity of fools destroys them,* and those who spend their days in wealth are tempted to say to God, *Depart from us;* or to their hearts, *Depart from God.*

III. Here is Christ's discourse with his disciples. We are

tempted to wish that Christ had *mollified* that saying which frightened this young gentleman from following him, and by an explanation taken off the harshness of it: but he knew all men's hearts; he would not court him to be his follower, because he was a *rich man* and a ruler; but, if he will go, let him go. Christ will keep no man against his will; and therefore we do not find that Christ called him back, but took this occasion to instruct his disciples in two things.

1. The difficulty of the salvation of those who have an abundance of this world; because there are few who have *a deal to leave,* that can be persuaded to *leave it* for Christ, or to lay it out in doing good.

(1.) Christ asserts this here; *He looked about* upon his *disciples,* because he would have them all take notice of what he said, that by it they might have their judgments rightly informed, and their mistakes rectified, concerning worldly wealth, which they were apt to over-rate; *How hardly shall they who have riches enter into the kingdom of God! v.* 23. They have many temptations to grapple with, and many difficulties to get over, which lie not in the way of poor people. But he explains himself, *v.* 24, where he calls the disciples *children,* because as such they should be *taught* by him, and *portioned* by him with better things than this young man left Christ to cleave to; and whereas he had said, *How hardly will those who have riches get to heaven;* here he tells them, that the danger arose not so much from their *having* riches as from their *trusting to them,* and placing their confidence in them, expecting protection, provision, and a portion from them; saying that *to their gold,* which they should say only to their God, *Thou art my hope,* Job 31:24. They have such a value as this for the wealth of the world, will never be brought to put a right value upon Christ and his grace. They that *have* ever so much riches, but do not *trust in them,* that see the vanity of them, and their utter insufficiency to make a soul happy, have got over the difficulty, and can easily part with them for Christ: but they have ever so little, if they set their hearts upon that little, and place their happiness in it, it will keep them from Christ. He enforces this assertion with, *v.* 25, *It is easier for a camel to go through the eye of a needle, than for a rich man,* that *trusts in riches,* or inclines to do so, *to enter into the kingdom of God.* The disproportion here seems so great (though the more it is so the more it answers the intention), that some have laboured to bring the camel and the eye of the needle a little nearer together. [1.] Some imagine there might be some wicket-gate, or door, to Jerusalem, commonly known by the name of *the needle's eye,* for its straitness, through which a camel could not be got, unless he were unloaded, and made to kneel, as those camel, Gen. 24:11. So a rich man cannot get to heaven unless he is willing to part with the burthen of his worldly wealth, and stoop to the duties of a humble religion, and so enter *at the strait gate.* [2.] Others suggest that the word we translate a *camel,* sometimes signifies a cable-rope, which, though not to be got through a needle's eye, yet is of great affinity to it. A rich man, compared with the poor, is as a cable to a single thread, stronger, but not so pliable, and it will not go through the *needle's eye,* unless it be untwisted. So the rich man must be loosed and disentangled from his riches, and then there is some hope of him, that thread by thread he may be got through the eye of the needle, otherwise he is good for nothing but to cast anchor in the earth.

(2.) This truth was very surprising to the disciples; *They were astonished at his words, v.* 24. *They were astonished out of measure, and said among themselves, Who then can be saved?* They knew what were generally the sentiments of the Jewish teachers, who affirmed that the Spirit of God chooses to reside in rich men; nay, they knew what abundance of promises there were, in the Old Testament, of temporal good things; they knew likewise that all either are rich, or fain would be so, and that they who are rich, have so much the larger opportunities of doing good, and therefore were amazed to hear that it should be so hard for rich people to go to heaven.

(3.) Christ reconciled them to it, by referring it to the almighty power of God, to help even rich people over the difficulties that lie in the way of their salvation (*v.* 27); He *looked upon them,* to engage their attention, and said, *"With men it is impossible;* rich people cannot by their own skill or resolution get over these difficulties, but the grace of God can do it, for *with him all things are possible."* If *the righteous scarcely are saved,* much more may we say so of the *rich;* and therefore when any get to heaven, they must give all the glory to God, who worketh in them *both to will and to do.*

2. The greatness of the salvation of those that have but a little of this world, and leave it for Christ. This he speaks of, upon occasion of Peter's mentioning what he and the rest of the disciples had left to follow him; *Behold,* (saith he), *we have left all to follow thee, v.* 28. "You have *done well,"* saith Christ, "and it will prove in the end that you have done well *for yourselves;* you shall be abundantly recompensed, and not only you shall be *reimbursed,* who have left but a little, but those that have ever so much, though it were so much as this young man had, that could not persuade himself to quit it for Christ; yet they shall have much more than an equivalent for it." (1.) The loss is supposed to be very great; he specifies, [1.] Worldly wealth; *houses* are here put first, and *lands* last: if a man quit his *house,* which should be for his habitation, and his *land,* which should be for his maintenance, and so make himself a beggar and an outcast. This has been the choice of suffering saints; farewell houses and lands, though ever so convenient and desirable, through the inheritance of fathers, for the house which is from heaven, and the inheritance of the saints in light, where are many mansions. [2.] Dear relations. *Father and mother, wife and children, brethren and sisters.* In these, as much as in any temporal blessing, the comfort of life is bound up; without these the world would be a wilderness; yet, when we must either forsake these or Christ, we must remember that we stand in nearer relation to Christ than we do to any creature; and therefore to keep in with him, we must be content to break with all the world, and to say to father and mother, as Levi did, *I have not known you.* The greatest trial of a good man's constancy is, when his love to Christ comes to stand in competition with a love that is lawful, nay, that is his duty. It is easy to such a one to forsake a *lust* for Christ, for he hath that within him, that rises against it; but to forsake a *father,* a *brother,* a *wife,* for Christ, that is, to forsake those whom he knows he must love, is hard. And yet he must do so, rather than deny or disown Christ. Thus great is the loss supposed to be; but it is *for Christ's sake,* that he may be honoured, and the *gospel's,* that it may be promoted and propagated. It is not the *suffering,* but the *cause,* that makes the *martyr.* And therefore, (2.) The advantage will be great. [1.] *They shall receive a hundred-fold in this time, houses, and brethren, and sisters;* not *in specie,* but that which is equivalent. He shall have abundance of comfort while he lives, sufficient to make up for all his losses; his relation to Christ, his communion with the saints, and his title to eternal life, shall be to him *brethren,* and *sisters,* and *houses,* and all. God's providence gave Job double to what he had had, but suffering Christians shall have a *hundred-fold* in the comforts of the Spirit sweetening their creature comforts. But observe, It is added here in Mark, *with persecutions.* Even when they are gainers by Christ, let them still expect to be sufferers for him; and not be out of the reach of persecution, till they come to heaven. Nay, The *persecutions* seem to come in here among *the receivings* in this present time; for unto you it is given, not only to believe in Christ, but also to *suffer for his name;* yet this is not all, [2.] They shall have *eternal life in the world to come.* If they receive a hundred-fold in this world, one would think they should not be encouraged to expect any more. Yet, as if that were a small matter, they shall have *life eternal* into the bargain; which is more than ten thousand-fold, ten thousand times told, for all their losses. But because they talked so much, and really more than became them, of *leaving all* for Christ, he tells them, though they were *first called,* that there should be disciples called after them, that should be preferred before them; as St. Paul, who was one *born out of due time,* and yet laboured more abundantly than all the rest of the apostles, 1 Co. 15:10. Then the *first* were *last,* and the last *first.*

Verses 32–45

Here is, I. Christ's prediction of his own sufferings; this string he harped much upon, though in the ears of his disciples it sounded very harsh and unpleasing.

1. See here how bold he was; when they were going up to Jerusalem, *Jesus went before them,* as the *captain of our salvation,* that was now to be *made perfect through sufferings, v.* 32. Thus he showed himself forward to go on with his undertaking, even when he came to the hardest part of it. Now that the time was at hand, he said, *Lo, I come;* so far was he from *drawing back,* that now, more than ever, he *pressed forward. Jesus went before them, and they were amazed.* They began now to consider what imminent danger they ran themselves into, when they went to Jerusalem; how very malicious the Sanhedrim which sat there was against their Master and them; and they were ready to tremble at the thought of it. To hearten them, therefore, Christ *went before them.* "Come," saith he, "surely you will venture where your Master ventures." Note, When we see ourselves entering upon sufferings, it is encouraging to see our Master go before us. Or, *He went before them,* and *therefore* they were *amazed;* they admired to see with what cheerfulness and alacrity he went on, though he knew he was going to suffer and die. Note, Christ's courage and constancy in going on with his undertaking for our salvation, are, and will be, the wonder of all his disciples.

2. See here how timorous and faint-hearted his disciples were; *As they followed, they were afraid,* afraid for themselves, as being apprehensive of their own danger; and justly might they be *ashamed* of their being thus *afraid.* Their Master's courage should have put spirit into them.

3. See here what method he took to silence their fears. He did not go about to make the matter better than it was, nor to feed them with hopes that he might escape the storm, but told them *again* what he had often told them before, the *things that should happen to him.* He knew the worst of it, and therefore went on thus boldly, and he will let them know the worst of it. Come, *be not afraid;* for, (1.) There is no remedy, the matter is determined, and cannot be avoided. (2.) It is only the *Son of man* that shall suffer; their time of suffering was now at hand, he will now provide for their security. (3.) He *shall rise again;* the issue of his sufferings will be glorious to himself, and advantageous to all that are his, *v.* 33, 34. The method and particulars of Christ's sufferings are more largely foretold here than in any other of the predictions — that he shall first be delivered up by Judas to the *chief priests and the scribes;* that they shall condemn him to death, but, not having the power to put him to death, shall *deliver him to the Gentiles,* to the Roman powers, and they shall *mock him,* and *scourge him,* and *spit upon him,* and *kill him.* Christ had a perfect foresight, not only of his own death, but of all the aggravating circumstances of it; and yet he thus went forth to meet it.

II. The check he gave to two of his disciples for their ambitious request. This story is much the same here as we had it Mt. 20:20. Only there they are said to have made their request by their mother, here they are said to make it themselves; she introduced them, and presented their petition, and then they seconded it, and assented to it.

Note, 1. As, on the one hand, there are some that do not *use,* so, on the other hand, there are some that *abuse,* the great encouragements Christ has given us in prayer. He hath said, *Ask, and it shall be given you;* and it is a commendable faith to ask for the great things he has promised; but it was a culpable presumption in these disciples to make such a boundless demand upon their Master; *We would that thou shouldest do for us whatsoever we shall desire.* We had much better leave it to him to do for us what he sees fit, and he will do more than we can desire, Eph. 3:20.

2. We must be cautious how we make general promises. Christ would not engage to do for them whatever they desired, but would know from them what it was they did desire; *What would ye that I should do for you?* He would have them go on with their suit, that they might be made ashamed of it.

3. Many have been led into a snare by false notions of Christ's kingdom, as if it were *of this world,* and like the kingdoms of the potentates of this world. James and John conclude, If Christ *rise again,* he must be a king, and if he be a king, his apostles must be peers, and one of these would willingly be the *Primus par regni — The first peer of the realm,* and the other next him, like Joseph in Pharaoh's court, or Daniel in Darius's.

4. Worldly honour is a glittering thing, with which the eyes of Christ's own disciples have many a time been dazzled. Whereas to *be good* should be more our care than to *look great,* or to have the pre-eminence.

5. Our weakness and short-sightedness appear as much in our prayers as in any thing. We cannot order our speech, when we speak to God, by reason of darkness, both concerning him and concerning ourselves. It is folly to *prescribe* to God, and wisdom to *subscribe.*

6. It is the will of Christ that we should prepare for suf-

ferings, and leave it to him to recompense us for them. He needs not be put in mind, as Ahasuerus did, of the services of his people, nor can he forget their *work of faith and labour of love.* Our care must be, that we may have wisdom and grace to know how to suffer with him, and then we may trust him to provide in the best manner how we shall reign with him, and when, and where, and what, the degrees of our glory shall be.

III. The check he gave to the rest of the disciples, for their uneasiness at it. *They began to be much displeased,* to have indignation *about James and John, v.* 41. They were angry at them for affecting precedency, not because it did so ill become the disciples of Christ, but because each of them hoped to have it himself. When the Cynic trampled on Alexander's foot-cloth, with *Calco fastum Alexandri — Now I tread on Alexander's pride,* he was seasonably checked with *Sed majori fastu — But with a greater pride of thine own.* So these discovered their own ambition, in their displeasure at the ambition of James and John; and Christ took this occasion to warn them against it, and all their successors in the ministry of the gospel, *v.* 42–44. He *called them to him* in a familiar way, to give them an example of condescension, then when he was reproving their ambition, and to teach them never to bid their disciples keep their distance. He shows them,

1. That dominion was generally *abused in the world* (*v.* 42); *That they seemed to rule over the* Gentiles, that have the name and title of rulers, *they exercise lordship over them,* that is all they study and aim at, not so much to protect them, and provide for their welfare, as to *exercise authority upon them;* they *will be obeyed,* aim to be arbitrary, and to have their will in every thing. *Sic volo, sic jubeo, stat pro ratione voluntas — Thus I will, thus I command; my good pleasure is my law.* Their care is, what they shall get by their subjects to support their own pomp and grandeur, not what they shall do for them.

2. That therefore it ought not to be *admitted into the church;* "*It shall not be so among you;* those that shall be put under your charge, must be as sheep under the charge of the *shepherd,* who is to tend them and feed them, and be a servant to them, not as horses under the command of the driver, that works them and beats them, and gets his pennyworths out of them. He that affects to be great and chief, that thrusts himself into a secular dignity and dominion, *he shall be servant of all,* he shall be mean and contemptible in the eyes of all that are wise and good; *he that exalteth himself shall be abased.*" Or rather, "He that would be *truly* great and chief, he must lay out himself to do good to all, must stoop to the meanest services, and labour in the hardest services. Those not only shall be most *honoured* hereafter, but are most *honourable* now, who are most useful." To convince them of this, he sets before them his own example (*v.* 45); "The *Son of man* submits first to the greatest hardships and hazards, and then enters into his glory, and can you expect to come to it any other way; or to have more ease and honour than he has?" (1.) He takes upon him *the form of a servant,* comes not to be *ministered to,* and waited upon, but *to minister,* and wait to be gracious. (2.) He comes *obedient to death,* and to its dominion, for he *gives his life a ransom for many;* did he die for the benefit of good people, and shall not we study to live for their benefit?

Verses 46–52

This passage of story agrees with that, Mt. 20:29, etc. Only that there were told of *two* blind men; here, and Lu. 18:35, only of one: but if there were *two,* there was *one.* This one is named here, being a *blind beggar that* was much talked of; he was called *Bartimeus,* that is, *the son of Timeus;* which, some think, signifies *the son of a blind man;* he was the blind son of a blind father, which made the case worse, and the cure more wonderful, and the more proper to typify the spiritual cures wrought by the grace of Christ, on those that not only are born blind, but are born of those that are blind.

I. This blind man sat *begging;* as they do with us. Note, Those who by the providence of God are disabled to get a livelihood by their own labour, and have not any other way of subsisting, are the most proper objects of charity; and particular care ought to be taken of them.

II. He cried out to the Lord Jesus for *mercy; Have mercy on me, O Lord, thou Son of David.* Misery is the object of mercy, his own miserable case he recommends to the compassion of the *Son of David,* of whom it was foretold, that, when he should come to save us, *the eyes of the blind should*

be opened, Isa. 35:5. In coming to Christ for help and healing, we should have an eye to him as the promised Messiah, the Trustee of mercy and grace.

III. Christ encouraged him to hope that he should find mercy; for he *stood still, and commanded him to be called.* We must never reckon it a hindrance to us in our way, to *stand still,* when it is to do a good work. Those about him, who had discouraged him at first, perhaps were now the persons that signified to him the gracious call of Christ; "*Be of good comfort, rise, he calls thee;* and if he calls thee, he will cure thee." Note, The gracious invitations Christ gives us to come to him, are great encouragements to our hope, that we shall speed well if we come to him, and shall have what we come for. Let the guilty, the empty, the tempted, the hungry, the naked, be of good comfort, for he *calls them* to be pardoned, to be supplied, to be succoured, to be filled, to be clothed, to have all that done for them, which their case calls for.

IV. The poor man, hereupon, made the best of his way to Christ; He *cast away his* loose upper *garment,* and came to Jesus (*v.* 50); he cast away every thing that might be in danger of throwing him down, or might in any way hinder him in coming to Christ, or retard his motion. Those who would come to Jesus, must cast away the garment of their own sufficiency, must strip themselves of all conceit of that, and must free themselves from *every weight,* and the sin that, like long garments, doth *most easily beset them,* Heb. 12:1.

V. The particular favour he begged, was, that his *eyes might be opened;* that so he might be able to work for his living, and might be no longer burthensome to others. It is a very desirable thing to be in a capacity of earning our own bread; and where God has given men their limbs and senses, it is a shame for men by their foolishness and slothfulness to make themselves, in effect, *blind* and *lame.*

VI. This favour he received; his eyes were opened (*v.* 52); and two things Mark here adds, which intimate, 1. How Christ made it a double favour to him, by putting the honour of it upon his faith; "*Thy faith hath made thee whole;* faith in Christ as the Son of David, and in his pity and power; not thy importunity, but *thy faith,* setting Christ on work, or rather Christ setting thy faith on work." Those supplies are most comfortable, that are fetched in by our faith. 2. How he made it a double favour to himself; When he had *received his sight,* he *followed Jesus by the way.* By this he made it appear that he was thoroughly cured, that he no more needed one to lead him, but could go himself; and by this he evidenced the grateful sense he had of Christ's kindness to him, that, when he had his sight, he made this use of it. It is not enough to *come to Christ* for spiritual healing, but, when we are healed, we must continue to follow him; that we may do honour to him, and receive instruction from him. Those that have spiritual eye-sight, see that beauty in Christ, that will effectually draw them to *run after him.*

CHAPTER 11

We are now come to the Passion-Week, the week in which Christ died, and the great occurrences of that week. I. Christ's riding in triumph into Jerusalem (*v.* 1–11). II. His cursing the barren fig-tree (*v.* 12–14). III. His driving those out of the temple that turned it into an exchange (*v.* 15–19). IV. His discourse with his disciples concerning the power of faith and the efficacy of prayer, on occasion of the withering of the fig-tree he cursed (*v.* 20–26). V. His reply to those who questioned his authority (*v.* 27–33).

Verses 1–11

We have here the story of the public entry Christ made into Jerusalem, four or five days before his death. And he came into town thus remarkably, 1. To show that he was not afraid of the power and malice of his enemies in Jerusalem. He did not steal into the city *incognito,* as one that durst not show his face; no, they needed not send spies to search for him, he comes in with observation. This would be an encouragement to his disciples that were timorous, and cowed at the thought of their enemies' power and rage; let them see how bravely their Master sets them all at defiance. 2. To show that he was not cast down or disquieted at the thoughts of his approaching sufferings. He came, not only publicly, but cheerfully, and with acclamations of joy. Though he was now but taking the field, and *girding on the harness,* yet, being fully assured of a complete victory, he thus triumphs as though he had put it off.

I. The *outside* of this triumph was very *mean;* he rode upon an ass's *colt,* which being an ass, looked contemptible, and made no figure; and, being but a *colt, whereon never*

man sat, we may suppose, was rough and untrimmed, and not only so, but rude and ungovernable, and would disturb and disgrace the solemnity. This *colt* was borrowed too. Christ went upon the water in a *borrowed* boat, ate the passover in a *borrowed* chamber, was buried in a *borrowed* sepulchre, and here rode on a *borrowed* ass. Let not Christians scorn to be beholden one to another, and, when need is, to go a borrowing, for our Master did not. He had no rich trappings; they threw their clothes upon the colt, and so he *sat upon him, v.* 7. The persons that attended, were mean people; and all the show they could make, was, by *spreading their garments in the way* (*v.* 8), as they used to do at the feast of tabernacles. All these were marks of his humiliation; even when he would be taken notice of, he would be taken notice of for his meanness; and they are instructions to us, not to *mind high things,* but to *condescend to them of low estate.* How ill doth it become Christians to *take state,* when Christ was so far from affecting it!

II. The *inside* of this triumph was very *great;* not only as it was the fulfilling of the scripture (which is not taken notice of here, as it as in Matthew), but as there were several rays of Christ's glory shining forth in the midst of all this meanness. 1. Christ showed his knowledge of things distant, and his power over the wills of men, when he sent his disciples for the colt, *v.* 1–3. By this it appears that he can *do every thing,* and *no thought can be withholden from him.* 2. He showed his dominion over the *creatures* in riding on *a colt that was never backed.* The subjection of the inferior part of the creation to man is spoken of with application to Christ (Ps. 8:5, 6, compared with Heb. 2:8); for to him it is owing, and to his mediation, that we have any remaining benefit by the grant God made to man, of a sovereignty in this lower world, Gen. 1:28. And perhaps Christ, in riding the ass's colt, would give a shadow of his power over the spirit of man, who is born as the *wild ass's colt,* Job 11:12. 3. The colt was brought from a place *where two ways met* (*v.* 4), as if Christ would show that he came to direct those into the right way, who had *two ways* before them, and were in danger of taking the wrong. 4. Christ received the joyful *hosannas* of the people; that is, both the *welcome* they gave him and their *good wishes* to the prosperity of his kingdom, *v.* 9. It was God that put it into the hearts of these people to cry *Hosanna,* who were not by art and management brought to it, as those were who afterward cried, *Crucify, crucify.* Christ reckons himself honoured by the faith and praises of the multitude, and it is God that brings people to do him this honour beyond their own intentions.

(1.) They *welcomed* his *person* (*v.* 9); *Blessed is he that cometh,* the *ho erchomenos, he that should come,* so often promised, so long expected; he comes *in the name of the Lord,* as God's Ambassador to the world; *Blessed be he:* let him have our applauses, and best affections; he is a *blessed* Saviour, and brings blessings to us, and blessed be he that sent him. Let him be *blessed in the name of the Lord,* and let all nations and ages call him *Blessed,* and think and speak highly and honourably of him.

(2.) They *wished well* to his *intent, v.* 10. They believed that, mean a figure as he made, he had a *kingdom,* which should shortly be set up in the world, that it was the kingdom of *their father David* (that father of his country), the kingdom promised to him and his seed for ever; a kingdom that came *in the name of the Lord,* supported by a divine authority. *Blessed be this kingdom;* let it take place, let it get ground, let it come in the power of it, and let all opposing rule, principality, and power, be put down; let it go on *conquering, and to conquer. Hosanna* to this kingdom; prosperity be to it; all happiness attend it. The proper signification of *hosanna* is that which we find, Rev. 7:10. *Salvation to our God, that sitteth on the throne, and to the Lamb;* success to religion, both *natural* and *revealed, Hosanna in the highest.* Praises be to our God, who is in the *highest heavens* over all, God blessed for ever; or, Let him be praised by his angels, that are *in the highest* heavens, let our *hosannas* be an echo to theirs.

Christ, thus *attended,* thus *applauded,* came into the city, and went directly *to the temple.* Here was no banquet of wine prepared for his entertainment, nor the least refreshment; but he immediately applied himself to his work, for that was his *meat* and *drink.* He went *to the temple,* that the scripture might be fulfilled; "The *Lord whom ye seek, shall suddenly come to his temple,* without sending any immediate notice before him; he shall surprise you with a *day of visitation,* for he shall be *like a refiner's fire, and like fuller's soap,"* Mal. 3:1-3. He came to the temple, and took a view of the present state of it, *v.* 11. He *looked round about upon all things,* but as yet said nothing. He saw many disorders there, but *kept silence,* Ps. 50:21. Though he intended to suppress them, he would not go about the doing of it all *on a sudden,* lest he should seem to have done it *rashly;* he let things be as they were for this night, intending the next morning to apply himself to the necessary reformation, and to take the day before him. We may be confident that God sees all the wickedness that is in the world, though he do not presently reckon for it, nor cast it out. Christ, having make his remarks upon what he saw in the temple, retired in the evening to a friend's house at Bethany, because there he would be more out of the noise of the town, and out of the way of being suspected, a designing to head a faction.

Verses 12–26

Here is, I. Christ's cursing the fruitless fig-tree. He had a convenient resting-place at Bethany, and therefore thither he went at resting-time; but his work lay at Jerusalem, and thither therefore he returned in the morning, at working-time; and so intent was he upon his work, that he went out from Bethany without breakfast, which, before he was gone far, he found the want of, and *was hungry* (*v.* 12), for he was subject to all the sinless infirmities of our nature. Finding himself in want of food, he went to a *fig-tree,* which he saw at some distance, and which being well *adorned* with green leaves he hoped to find *enriched* with some sort of fruit. But he *found nothing but leaves;* he hoped to find some fruit, *for* though *the time of* gathering in *figs* was near, it *was not yet;* so that it could not be pretended that it had had fruit, but that it was gathered and gone; for the season had not yet arrived. Or, He found none, for indeed *it was not a season of figs,* it was no good fig-year. But this was worse than any fig-tree, for there was not so much as one fig to be found upon it, though it was so full of leaves. However, Christ was willing to make an example of it, not to the *trees,* but to the *men,* of that generation, and therefore cursed it with that curse which is the reverse of the first blessing, *Be fruitful;* he said unto it, *Never let any man eat fruit of thee hereafter for ever, v.* 14. *Sweetness and good fruit* are, in Jotham's parable, the honour of the *fig-tree* (Jdg. 9:11), and its serviceableness therein to man, preferable to the preferment of being *promoted over the trees;* now to be deprived of that, was a grievous *curse.* This was intended to be a type and figure of the doom passed upon the Jewish church, to which he came, *seeking fruit, but found none* (Lu. 13:6, 7); and though it was not, according to the doom in the parable, immediately cut down, yet, according to this in the history, *blindness* and *hardness* befel them (Rom. 11:8, 25), so that they were from henceforth *good for nothing.* The *disciples heard* what sentence Christ passed on this tree, and took notice of it. Woes from Christ's mouth are to be observed and kept in mind, as well as blessings.

II. His clearing the temple of the market-people that frequented it, and of those that made it a thoroughfare. We do not find that Christ met with food elsewhere, when he missed of it on the fig-tree; but the zeal of God's house so ate him up, and made him forget himself, that he came, hungry as he was, to Jerusalem, and went straight to the temple, and began to reform those abuses which the day before he had marked out; to show that when the Redeemer came to Zion, his errand was, *to turn away ungodliness from Jacob* (Rom. 11:26), and that he came not, as he was falsely accused, to *destroy* the temple, but to purify and refine it, and reduce his church to its primitive rectitude.

1. He cast out the *buyers* and *sellers, overthrew the tables of the money-changers* (and threw the money to the ground, the fitter place for it), and threw down the *seats of them that sold doves.* This he did as one having authority, as *a Son in his own house.* The filth of the daughter of Zion is purged away, not by might, nor by power, but by *the spirit of judgment, and the spirit of burning.* And he did it without opposition; for what he did, was manifested to be right and good, even in the consciences of those that had connived at it, and countenanced it, because they got money by it. Note, It may be some encouragement to zealous reformers, that frequently the purging out of corruptions, and the correcting of abuses, prove an easier piece of work than was apprehended. Prudent attempts sometimes prove successful beyond expectation, and there are not those lions *found* in the way, that were feared to be.

2. He *would not suffer that any man should carry any vessel,* any sort of goods or wares, *through the temple,* or any of the courts of it, because it was the nearer way, and would save them the labour of going about, *v.* 16. The Jews owned that it was one of the instances of honour due to the temple, not to make the mountain of the house, or the court of the Gentiles, a road, or common passage, or to come into it with any bundle.

3. He gave a good reason for this; because it was written, *My house shall be called of all nations, The house of prayer, v.* 17. So it is written, Isa. 56:7. It shall pass among all people under that character. *It shall be the house of prayer to all nations;* it was so in the first institution of it; when Solomon dedicated it, it was with an eye to the sons of the strangers, 1 Ki. 8:41. And it was prophesied that it should be yet more so. Christ will have the temple, as a type of the gospel-church, to be, (1.) A *house of prayer.* After he had turned out the oxen and doves, which were things for sacrifice, he revived the appointment of it as a *house of prayer,* to teach us that when all sacrifices and offerings should be abolished, the spiritual sacrifices of prayer and praise should continue and remain for ever. (2.) That it should be so *to all nations,* and not to the people of the Jews only; for *whosoever shall call upon the name of the Lord, shall be saved,* though not of the seed of Jacob, according to the flesh. It was therefore insufferable for them to *make it a den of thieves,* which would prejudice those nations against it, whom they should have invited to it. When Christ drove out the buyers and sellers at the beginning of his ministry, he only charged them with making the temple a *house of merchandise* (Jn. 2:16); but now he chargeth them with making it a *den of thieves,* because since then they had twice gone about to stone him in the temple (Jn. 8:59; 10:31), or because the traders there were grown notorious for cheating their customers, and imposing upon the ignorance and necessity of the country people, which is no better than downright thievery. Those that suffer vain worldly thoughts to lodge within them when they are at their devotions, turn the *house of prayer* into a *house of merchandise;* but they that make long prayers for pretence to devour widows' houses, turn it into a *den of thieves.*

4. The scribes and the chief priests were extremely nettled at this, *v.* 18. They hated him, and hated to be reformed by him; and yet they *feared him,* lest he should next overthrow *their* seats, and expel *them,* being conscious to themselves of the profaning and abusing of their power. They found that he had a great interest, that *all the people were astonished at his doctrine,* and that every thing he said, was an oracle and a law to them; and what durst *he* not attempt, what could *he* not effect, being thus supported? They therefore sought, not how he might make their peace with him, but *how they might destroy him.* A desperate attempt, and which, one would think, they themselves could not but fear was *fighting against God.* But they care not what they do, to support their own power and grandeur.

III. His discourse with his disciples, upon occasion of the fig-tree's withering away which he had cursed. At *even,* as usual, he *went out of the city* (*v.* 19), to Bethany; but it is probable that it was in the dark, so that they could not see the fig-tree; but the next morning, as they *passed by,* they observed the *fig-tree dried up from the roots, v.* 20. More is *included* many times in Christ's curses than is *expressed,* as appears by the effects of them. The curse was no more than that it should never bear fruit again, but the effect goes further, *it is dried up from the roots.* If it bear no fruit, it shall bear no leaves to cheat people. Now observe,

1. How the disciples were affected with it. Peter remembered Christ's words, and said, with surprise, *Master, behold, the fig-tree which thou cursedst is withered away, v.* 21. Note, Christ's curses have wonderful effects, and make those to wither presently, that flourished like the green bay-tree. *Those whom he curseth are cursed indeed.* This represented the character and state of the Jewish church; which, from henceforward, was a tree dried up from the roots; no longer fit for food, but for fuel only. The first establishment of the Levitical priesthood was ratified and confirmed by the miracle of a *dry rod,* which in *one night* budded, and blossomed, and brought forth almonds (Num. 17:8), a happy omen of the fruitlessness and flourishing of that priesthood. And now, by a contrary miracle, the expiration of that priesthood was signified by a flourishing tree dried up in a night; the just punishment of those priests that had abused it. And this seemed very strange to the disciples, and scarcely credible, that the Jews, who had been so long God's own, his only professing people in the world, should be thus abandoned; they could not imagine how that *fig-tree* should *so soon wither away:* but this comes of rejecting Christ, and being rejected by him.

2. The good instructions Christ gave them from it; for of *those* even this *withered* tree was *fruitful.*

(1.) Christ teacheth them from hence to *pray in faith* (*v.* 22); *Have faith in God.* They admired the power of Christ's word of command; "Why," said Christ, "a lively active faith would put as great a power into your prayers, *v.* 23, 24. *Whosoever shall say to this mountain,* this mount of Olives, *Be removed, and be cast into the sea;* if he has but any word of God, general or particular, to build his faith upon, and if he *shall not doubt in his heart, but shall believe that those things which he saith,* according to the warrant he has from what God hath said, *shall come to pass, he shall have whatsoever he saith."* Through the strength and power of God in Christ, the greatest difficulty shall be got over, and the thing shall be effected. And therefore (*v.* 24), *"What things soever ye desire, when ye pray believe that ye shall* receive them; nay, believe that ye *do receive them,* and he that has power to give them, saith, *Ye shall have them. I say unto you,* Ye shall, *v.* 24. *Verily* I say unto you, Ye shall," *v.* 23. Now this is to be applied, [1.] To that *faith of miracles* which the apostles and first preachers of the gospel were endued with, which did wonders in *things natural,* healing the sick, raising the dead, casting out devils; these were, in effect, the removing of mountains. The apostles speak of a faith which would do that, and yet might be found where holy love was not, 1 Co. 13:2. [2.] It may be applied to that *miracle of faith,* which all true Christians are endued with, which doeth wonders in *things spiritual. It justifies* us (Rom. 5:1), and so removes the mountains of guilt, and casts them into the *depths of the sea,* never to rise up in judgment against us, Mic. 7:19. It *purifies* the heart (Acts 15:9), and so removes mountains of corruption, and *makes them plains* before the grace of God, Zec. 4:7. It is by faith that the world is conquered, Satan's fiery darts are quenched, a soul is crucified with Christ, and yet lives; by faith we set the Lord always before us, and see him that is invisible, and have him present to our minds; and this is effectual to remove mountains, for at the presence of the Lord, at the presence of the God of Jacob, the mountains were not only moved, but *removed,* Ps. 114:4–7.

(2.) To this is added here that necessary qualification of the prevailing prayer, that we freely forgive those who have been any way injurious to us, and be in charity with all men (*v.* 25, 26); *When ye stand praying,* forgive. Note, Standing is no improper posture for prayer; it was generally used among the Jews; hence they called their prayers, their *standings;* when they would say how the world was *kept up* by prayer, they expressed it thus, *Stationibus stat mundus — The world is held up by standings.* But the primitive Christians generally used more humble and reverent gesture of kneeling, especially on fast days, though not on Lord's days. When we are at prayer, we must remember to pray for others, particularly for our enemies, and those that have wronged us; now we cannot pray sincerely that God would do them good, if we bear malice to them, and wish them ill. If we have injured others before we pray, we must go and *be reconciled to them;* Mt. 5:23, 24. But if they have injured us, we go a nearer way to work, and must immediately from our hearts *forgive* them. [1.] Because this is a *good step* towards obtaining the *pardon* of our own sins: *Forgive,* that *your Father may forgive you;* that is, "that he may be qualified to receive forgiveness, that he may forgive you without injury to his honour, as it would be, if he should suffer those to have such benefit by his mercy, as are so far from being conformable to the pattern of it." [2.] Because the want of this is a certain bar to the obtaining of the pardon of our sins; *"If ye do not forgive* those who have injured you, if he hate their persons, bear them a grudge, meditate revenge, and take all occasion to speak ill of them, *neither will your Father forgive your trespasses."* This ought to be remembered in prayer, because one great errand we have to the throne of grace, is, to pray for the pardon of our sins: and care about it ought to be our daily care, because prayer is a part of our daily work. Our Saviour often insists on this, for it was his great design to engage his disciples to love one another.

Verses 27–33

We have here Christ examined by the great Sanhedrim concerning his authority; for they claimed a power to call prophets to an account concerning their mission. They came to him when he was *walking in the temple,* not for his diversion, but *teaching* the people, first one company and then another. The Peripatetic philosophers were so called from the custom they had of *walking* when they taught. The cloisters, or piazzas, in the courts of the temple, were fitted for this purpose. The great men were vexed to see him followed and heard with attention, and therefore *came to him* with some solemnity, and did as it were arraign him at the bar with this question, *By what authority doest thou these things? v.* 28. Now observe,

I. How they designed hereby to run him aground, and embarrass him. If they could make it out before the people, that he had not a *legal mission,* that he was not duly *ordained,* though he was ever so well qualified, and preached ever so profitably and well, they would tell the people that they *ought not to hear him.* This they made the last refuge of an obstinate unbelief; because they were resolved not to receive his doctrine, they were resolved to find some flaw or other in his commission, and will conclude it invalid, if it be not produced and ratified in their court. Thus the Papists resolve their controversy with us very much into the mission of our ministers, and if they have but any pretence to overthrow that, they think they have gained their point, though we have the scripture ever so much on our side. But this is indeed a question, which all that act either as magistrates or ministers, ought to be furnished with a good answer to, and often put to themselves, *By what authority do I these things?* For *how can men preach except they be sent?* Or how can they act with comfort, or confidence, or hope of success, except they be authorized? Jer. 23:32.

II. How he effectually ran them aground, and embarrassed them, with this question, "What are your thoughts concerning *the baptism of John? Was it from heaven, or of men?* By what authority did John preach, and baptize, and gather disciples? *Answer me, v.* 30. Deal fairly and ingenuously, and give a categorical answer, one way or the other." By this resolve of *their* question into *this,* our Saviour intimates how near akin his doctrine and baptism were to John's; they had the same original, and the same design and tendency — to introduce the gospel kingdom. Christ might with the better grace put this question to *them,* because they had sent a committee of their own house to examine John, Jn. 1:19. "Now," saith Christ, "what was the result of your enquiries concerning him?"

They knew what they *thought* of this question; they could not but think that *John Baptist* was a man sent of God. But the difficulty was, what they should *say to it* now. Men that oblige not themselves to speak *as they think* (which is a certain rule) cannot avoid perplexing themselves thus.

1. If they own the baptism of John to be *from heaven,* as really it was, they *shame themselves;* for Christ will presently turn it upon them, *Why did ye not then believe him,* and receive his baptism? They could not bear that Christ should say this, but they could bear it that their own consciences should say so, because they had an art of stifling and silencing them, and because what conscience said, though it might gall and grate them a little, would not *shame them;* and then *they* would do well enough, who looked no further than Saul's care, when he was convicted, *Honour me now before this people,* 1 Sa. 15:30.

2. If they say, "*It is of men,* he was not sent of God, but his doctrine and baptism were inventions of his own," they *expose themselves,* the people will be ready to do them a mischief, or a least clamour upon them; for *all men counted John that he was a prophet indeed,* and therefore they could not bear that he should be reflected on. Note, There is a carnal slavish fear, which not only wicked subjects but wicked rulers likewise are liable to, which God makes use of as a means to keep the world in some order, and to suppress *violence,* that it shall not always *grow up into a rod of wickedness.* Now by this dilemma to which Christ brought them, (1.) They were confounded and baffled, and forced to make a dishonourable retreat; to pretend ignorance — *We cannot tell* (and that was mortification enough to those proud men), but really to discover the greatest malice and wilfulness. What Christ did by his wisdom, we must labour to do by our well doing — *put to silence the ignorance of foolish men,* 1 Pt. 2:15. (2.) Christ came off with honour, and justified himself in refusing to give them an answer to their imperious demand; *Neither tell I you by what authority I do these things.* They did not deserve to be told; for it was plain that they contended not for truth, but victory; nor did *he* need to *tell them,* for the works which he did, told them plainly that he had authority from God to do what he did; since no man could do those miracles which he did unless God were with him. Let them wait but three or four days, and his resurrection shall tell them who gave him his authority, for by that he will be *declared to be the Son of God with power,* as by their rejecting of him, notwithstanding, they will be declared to be the enemies of God.

CHAPTER 12

In this chapter, we have, I. The parable of the vineyard let out to unthankful husbandmen, representing the sin and ruin of the Jewish church (*v.* 1–12). II. Christ's silencing those who thought to ensnare him with a question about paying tribute Caesar (*v.* 13–17). III. His silencing the Sadducees, who attempted to perplex the doctrine of the resurrection (*v.* 18–27). IV. His conference with a scribe about the first and great command of the law (*v.* 28–34). V. His puzzling the scribes with a question about Christ's being the Son of David (*v.* 35–37). VI. The caution he gave the people, to take heed of the scribes (*v.* 38–40). VII. His commendation of the poor widow that cast her two mites into the treasury (*v.* 41–44).

Verses 1–12

Christ had formerly in parables showed how he designed to set up the gospel church; now he begins in parables to show how he would lay aside the Jewish church, which it might have been grafted into the *stock of,* but was built upon the *ruins of.* This parable we had just as we have it here, Mt. 21:33. We may observe here,

I. They that enjoy the privileges of the visible church, have a vineyard let out to them, which is capable of great improvement, and from the occupiers of which rent is justly expected. When God *showed his word unto Jacob, his statutes and judgments unto Israel* (Ps. 147:19), when he set up his temple among them, his priesthood, and his ordinances, then he *let out* to them the *vineyard* he had *planted;* which he *hedged,* and in which he *built a tower, v.* 1. Members of the church are God's tenants, and they have both a good Landlord and a good bargain, and may live well upon it, if it be not their own fault.

II. Those whom God lets out his vineyard to, he sends his servants to, to put them in mind of his just expectations from them, *v.* 2. He was not *hasty* in his demands, nor *high,* for he did not send for the rent till they could make it, *at the season;* nor did he put them to the trouble of making money of it, but was willing to take it *in specie.*

III. It is sad to think what base usage God's faithful ministers have met with, in all ages, from those that have enjoyed the privileges of the church, and have not brought forth fruit answerable. The Old-Testament prophets were persecuted even by those that went under the name of the Old-Testament church. They *beat them,* and *sent them empty away* (*v.* 3); that was bad: they *wounded them,* and *sent them away shamefully entreated* (*v.* 4); that was worse: nay, at length, they came to such a pitch of wickedness, that they *killed* them, *v.* 5.

IV. It was no wonder if those who abused the prophets, abused Christ himself. God did at length send them his Son, his *well-beloved;* it was therefore so much the greater kindness in him to send him; as in Jacob to send Joseph to visit his brethren, Gen. 37:14. And it might be expected that he whom their Master *loved,* they also should respect and love (*v.* 6); "*They will reverence my son,* and, in reverence to him, will pay their rent." But, instead of *reverencing* him because he was the son and heir, they *therefore* hated him, *v.* 7. Because Christ, in calling to repentance and reformation, made his demands with more authority than the prophets had done, they were the more enraged against him, and determined to put him to death, that they might engross all church power to themselves, and that all the respect and obedience of the people might be paid to them only; "*The inheritance shall be ours,* we will be lords paramount, and bear all the sway." There is an *inheritance,* which, if they had duly *reverenced the Son,* might have been theirs, a heavenly inheritance; but they slighted that, and would have their inheritance in the wealth, and pomp, and powers, of this world. So they *took him, and killed him;* they had not done it yet, but they would do it in a little time; and they *cast him out of the vineyard,* they refused to admit his gospel when he was gone; it would by no means agree with their scheme, and so they threw it out with disdain and detestation.

V. For such sinful and shameful doings nothing can be expected but a fearful doom (*v.* 9); *What shall therefore the Lord of the vineyard do?* It is easy to say what, for nothing could be done more provoking.

1. He will *come, and destroy the husbandmen,* whom he would have saved. When they only denied the fruit, he did not *distrain* upon them for rent, nor *disseize* them and *dispossess* them for *non-payment;* but when they killed his servants, and his Son, he determined to *destroy* them; and this was fulfilled when Jerusalem was laid waste, and the Jewish nation extirpated and made a desolation.

2. He will *give the vineyards to others.* If he have not the rent from them, he will have it from another people, for God will be no loser by any. This was fulfilled in the taking in of the Gentiles, and the abundance of fruit which the *gospel brought forth in all the world,* Col. 1:6. If some from whom we expected well, prove bad, it doth not follow but that others will be better. Christ encouraged himself with this in his undertaking; *Though Israel be not gathered,* not gathered to him, but gathered against him, *yet shall I be glorious* (Isa. 49:5, 6), as a *Light to lighten the Gentiles.*

3. Their opposition to Christ's exaltation shall be no obstruction to it (*v.* 10, 11); *The stone which the builders rejected,* notwithstanding that, is become *the Head of the corner,* is highly advanced as the *Head-stone,* and of necessary use and influence as the *Corner-stone.* God will set Christ as *his King,* upon his *holy hill of Zion,* in spite of *their* project, who would *break his bands asunder.* And all the world shall see and own this to *be the Lord's doing,* in justice to the Jews, and in compassion to the Gentiles. The exaltation of Christ *was the Lord's doing,* and it is *his doing* to exalt him in our hearts, and to set up his throne there; and if it be done, it cannot but be marvellous in our eyes.

Now what effect had this parable upon the chief priests and scribes, whose conviction was designed by it? They knew *he spoke this parable against them, v.* 12. They could not but see their own faces in the glass of it; and one would think it showed them their sin so very heinous, and their ruin so certain and great, that it should have frightened them into a compliance with Christ and his gospel, should have prevailed to bring them to repentance, at least to make them desist from their malicious purpose against him: but, instead of that, (1.) They *sought to lay hold on him,* and make him their prisoner immediately, and so to fulfil what he had just now said they would do to him, *v.* 8. (2.) Nothing restrained them from it but the awe they stood in of the people; they did not *reverence* Christ, nor had an *fear of* God before their eyes, but were afraid, if they should publicly lay hold on Christ, the mob would rise, and lay hold on them, and rescue them. (3.) They *left him, and went their way;* if they could not do hurt to him, they resolved he should not do good to them, and therefore they got out of the hearing of his powerful preaching, *lest they should be converted and healed.* Note, If men's prejudices be not conquered by the evidence of truth, they are but confirmed; and if the corruptions of the heart be not subdued by faithful reproofs, they are but enraged and exasperated. If the gospel be not a *savour of life unto life,* it will be a *savour of death unto death.*

Verses 13–17

When the enemies of Christ, who thirsted for his blood, could not find occasion against him from what he said against them, they tried to ensnare him by putting questions to him. Here we have him tempted, or *at*tempted rather, with a question about the lawfulness of paying tribute to Caesar. We had this narrative, Mt. 22:15.

I. The persons they employed were the *Pharisees* and the *Herodians,* men that in this matter were contrary to one another, and yet concurred against Christ, *v.* 13. The Pharisees were great sticklers for the liberty of the Jews, and, if he should say, It is lawful to give tribute to Caesar, they would incense the common people against him, and the Herodians would, underhand, assist them in it. The Herodians were great sticklers for the Roman power, and, if he should discountenance the paying of tribute to Caesar, they would incense the governor against hum, yea, and the Pharisees, against their own principles, would join with them in it. It is no new thing for those that are at variance in other things, to join in a confederacy against Christ.

II. The pretence they made was, that they desired him to resolve them a case of conscience, which was of great importance in the present juncture; and they take on them to have a high opinion of his ability to resolve it, *v.* 14. They complimented him at a high rate, called him *Master,* owned him for a Teacher of the *way of God,* a Teacher of it *in truth,* one who taught what was good, and upon principles of truth, who would not be brought by smiles or frowns to depart a step from the rules of equity and goodness; *"Thou carest for no man,* nor *regardest the person of men,* thou art not afraid of offending either the jealous prince on one hand, or the jealous people on the other; *thou art right,* and always in the right, and dost in a right manner declare good and evil, truth and falsehood." If they spoke as they thought concerning Christ, when they said, *We know that thou art right,* their persecuting him, and putting him to death, as a deceiver, was sin against knowledge; they knew him, and yet crucified him. However, a man's testimony shall be taken most strongly against himself, and *out of their own mouths are they judged;* they knew that he taught the way of God in truth, and yet rejected the counsel of God against themselves. The professions and pretences of hypocrites will be produced in evidence against them, and they will be self-condemned. But if they did not know or believe it, they *lied unto God with their mouth, and flattered him with their tongue.*

III. The question they put was, *Is it lawful to give tribute to Caesar, or not?* They would be thought desirous to know their duty. *As a nation that did righteousness, they ask of God the ordinances of justice,* when really they desired nothing but to know what he would say, in hopes that, which side soever he took of the question, they might take occasion from it to accuse him. Nothing is more likely to ensnare ministers, than bringing them to meddle with controversies about civil rights, and to settle land-marks between the prince and the subject, which it is fit should be done, while it is not at all fit that they should have the doing of it. They seemed to refer the determining of this matter to Christ; and he indeed was fit to determine it, for *by him kings reign, and princes decree justice;* they put the question fairly, *Shall we give, or shall we not give?* They seemed resolved to stand to his award; "If thou sayest that we must pay tribute, we will do it, thou we be made beggars by it. If thou sayest that we must not, we will not, though we be made traitors for it." Many seemed desirous to do it; as those proud men, Jer. 42:20.

IV. Christ determined the question, and evaded the snare, by referring them to their national concessions already made, by which they were precluded from disputing this matter, *v.* 15–17. He *knew their hypocrisy,* the malice that was in their hearts against him, while *with their mouth they showed all this love.* Hypocrisy, though ever so artfully managed, cannot be concealed from the Lord Jesus. He sees the *potsherd* that is *covered* with the *silver dross.* He knew they intended to ensnare him, and therefore contrived the matter so as to ensnare them, and to oblige them by their own words to do what they were unwilling to do, which was, to pay their taxes honestly and quietly, and yet at the same time to screen himself against their exceptions. He made them acknowledge that the current money of their nation was Roman money, had the emperor's image on one side, and his *superscription* on the reverse; and if so, 1. Caesar might command their money for the public benefit, because he had the custody and conduct of the state, wherein he ought to have his charges borne; *Render to Caesar the things that are Caesar's.* The circulation of the money is from him as the fountain, and therefore it must return to him. As far as it is *his,* so far it must be rendered to him; and how far it is *his,* and may be commanded by him, is to be judged by the constitution of the government, according as it is, and hath settled the prerogative of the prince and the property of the subject. 2. Caesar might not command their consciences, nor did he pretend to it; he offered not to make any alteration in their religion. "Pay your tribute, therefore, without murmuring or disputing, but be sure to *render to God the things that are God's."* Perhaps he referred to the parable he had just now put forth, in which he had condemned them for not *rendering* the fruits to the Lord of the vineyard, *v.* 2. Many that seem careful to give to men their due, are in no care to give God *the glory due to his name;* whereas our hearts and best affections are as much due to him as ever rent was to a landlord, or tribute to a prince. All that heard Christ, *marvelled* at the discretion of his answer, and how ingenuously he avoided the snare; but I doubt none were brought by it, as they ought to be, to render to God themselves and their devotions. Many will commend the wit of a sermon, that will not be commanded by the divine laws of a sermon.

Verses 18–27

The Sadducees, who were the deists of that age, here attack our Lord Jesus, it should seem, not as the scribes, and Pharisees, and chief-priests, with any malicious design upon his person; they were not bigots and persecutors, but sceptics and infidels, and their design was upon his doctrine, to hinder the spreading of that: they denied that there was any resurrection, and world of spirits, any state of rewards and punishments on the other side of death: now those great and fundamental truths which they denied, Christ had made it his business to establish and prove, and had carried the notion of them much further that ever it was before carried; and therefore they set themselves to perplex his doctrine.

I. See here the method they take to entangle it; they quote the ancient law, by which, if a man died without issue, his brother was obliged to marry his widow, *v.* 19. They suppose a case to happen that, according to that law, seven brothers were, successively, the husbands of one woman, *v.* 20. Probably, these Sadducees, according to their wonted profaneness, intended hereby to ridicule that law, and so to bring the whole frame of the Mosaic institution into contempt, as absurd and inconvenient in the practice of it. Those who deny divine truths, commonly set themselves to disparage divine laws and ordinances. But this was only by the by; their design was to expose the doctrine of the resurrection; for they suppose that if there be a future state, it must be such a one as this, and then the doctrine, they think, is clogged either with this invincible absurdity, that a woman in that state must have seven husbands, or else with this insolvable difficulty, whose wife must she be. See with what subtlety these heretics *undermine* the truth; they do not *deny* it, nor say, *There can be* no resurrection; nay, they do not seem to doubt of it, nor say, *If there be a resurrection,* whose wife shall she be? as the devil to Christ, *If thou be the Son of God.* But, as though these beasts of the field were more subtle than the serpent himself, they pretend to own the truth, as if they were not Sadducees, no not they; who said that they denied the resurrection? They take it for granted that there is a resurrection, and would be thought to desire instruction concerning it, when really they are designing to give a fatal stab, and think that they shall do it. Note, It is the common artifice of heretics and Sadducees to perplex and entangle the truth, which they have not the impudence to deny.

II. See here the method Christ takes to clear and establish this truth, which they attempted to darken, and give a shock to. This was a matter of moment, and therefore Christ does not pass it over lightly, but enlarges upon it, that, if they should not be reclaimed, yet others might be confirmed.

1. He charges the Sadducees with *error,* and charges that upon their *ignorance.* They who banter the doctrine of the resurrection as some do in our age, would be thought the only knowing men, because the only *free thinkers,* when really they are the fools in Israel, and the most *enslaved* and, prejudiced thinkers in the world. *Do ye not therefore err?* Ye cannot but be sensible of it yourselves, and that the cause of your error is, (1.) Because ye do not *know the scriptures.* Not but that the Sadducees had read the scriptures, and perhaps were ready in them; yet they might be truly said not to *know the scriptures,* because they did not know the sense and meaning of them, but put false constructions upon them; or they did not receive the scriptures as the word of God, but set up their own corrupt reasonings in opposition to the scripture, and would believe nothing but what they could see. Note, A right knowledge of the scripture, as the fountain whence all revealed religion now flows, and the foundation on which it is built, is the best preservative against error. Keep the truth, the scripture-truth, and it shall keep thee. (2.) Because ye *know not the power of God.* They could not but know that God is almighty, but they would not apply that doctrine to this matter, but gave up the truth to the objections of the impossibility of it, which would all have been answered, if they had but stuck to the doctrine of God's omnipotence, to which *nothing is impossible.* This therefore which God hath spoken once, we are concerned to hear twice, to hear and believe, to hear and apply — that *power belongs to God,* Ps. 62:11; Rom. 4:19–21. The same power that made soul and body and preserved them while they were together, can preserve the body safe, and the soul active, when they are parted, and can unite them together again; for *behold, the Lord's arm is not shortened.* The power of God, seen in the return of the spring (Ps. 104:30), in the reviving of the corn (Jn. 12:24), in the restoring of an abject people to their prosperity (Eze. 37:12–14), in the raising of so many to life, miraculously, both in the Old Testament and in the New, and especially in the resurrection of Christ (Eph. 1:19, 20), are all earnests of our resurrection by the same power (Phil. 3:21); *according to the mighty working whereby he is able to subdue all things to himself.*

2. He sets aside all the force of their objection, by setting the doctrine of the future state in a true light (*v.* 25); *When they shall rise from the dead, they neither marry, nor are given in marriage.* It is a folly to ask, *Whose wife shall she be of the seven?* For the relation between husband and wife, though instituted in the earthly paradise, will not be known in the heavenly one. Turks and infidels expect sensual pleasures in their fools' paradise, but Christians *know* better things — that *flesh and blood shall not inherit the kingdom of God* (1 Co. 15:50); and *expect* better things — even a full satisfaction in God's love and likeness (Ps. 17:15); they are *as the angels of God in heaven,* and we know that they have neither wives nor children. It is no wonder if we confound ourselves with endless absurdities, when we measure our ideas of the world of spirits by the affairs of this world of sense.

III. He builds the doctrine of the future state, and of the blessedness of the righteous in that state, upon the covenant of God with Abraham, which God was pleased to own, being after Abraham's death, *v.* 26, 27. He appeals to the scriptures; *Have ye not read in the book of Moses?* We have some advantage in dealing with those that have *read the scriptures,* though many that have read them, *wrest them,* as these Sadducees did, to *their own destruction.* Now that which he refers them to is, what God says to Moses at the bush, *I am the God of Abraham;* not only, I *was* so, but I *am* so; I am the portion and happiness of Abraham, a God all-sufficient to him. Note, It is absurd to think that God's relation to Abraham should be continued, and thus solemnly recognised, if Abraham was annihilated, or that the *living God* should be the portion and happiness of a man that is dead, and must be for ever so; and therefore you must conclude, 1. That Abraham's soul exists and acts as a state of separation from the body. 2. That therefore, some time or other, the body must rise again; for there is such an innate inclination in a human soul towards its body, as would make a total and everlasting separation inconsistent with the ease and repose, much more with the bliss and joy of those souls that have the Lord for their God. Upon the whole matter, he concludes, *Ye therefore do greatly err.* Those that deny the resurrection, greatly err, and ought to be told so.

Verses 28–34

The scribes and Pharisees were (however bad otherwise) enemies to the Sadducees; now one would have expected that, when they heard Christ argue so well against the Sadducees, they would have countenanced him, as they did Paul when he appeared against the Sadducees (Acts 23:9); but it had not the effect: because he did not fall in with them in the ceremonials of religion, he agreeing with them in the essentials, gained him no manner of respect with them. Only we have here an account of *one* of them, a scribe, who had so much civility in him as to take notice of Christ's answer to the Sadducees, and to own that he had *answered well,* and much to the purpose (*v.* 28); and we have reason to hope that he did not join with the other scribes in persecuting Christ; for here we have his application to Christ for instruction, and it was such as became him; not tempting Christ, but desiring to improve his acquaintance with him.

I. He enquired, *Which is the first commandment of all? v.* 28. He doth not mean the first in *order,* but the first in *weight* and *dignity;* "Which is that command which we ought to have in a special manner an eye to, and our obedience to which will lay a foundation for our obedience to all the rest?" Not that any commandment of God is little (they are all the commands of a great God), but some are greater than others, moral precepts than rituals, and of some we may say, They are the *greatest of all.*

II. Christ gave him a direct answer to this enquiry, *v.* 29–31. Those that sincerely desire to be instructed concerning their duty, Christ will *guide in judgment,* and *teach his way.* He tells him,

1. That the great commandment of all, which is indeed inclusive of all, is, that of *loving God with all our hearts.* (1.) Where there is a commanding principle in the soul, there is a disposition to every other duty. Love is the leading affection of the soul; the love of God is the leading grace in the

renewed soul. (2.) Where this is not, nothing else that is good is done, or done aright, or accepted, or done long. Loving God with all our heart, will effectually take us off from, and arm us against, all those things that are rivals with him for the throne in our souls, and will engage us to every thing by which he may be honoured, and with which he will be pleased; and no commandment will be grievous where this principle commands, and has the ascendant. Now here in, Mark, our Saviour prefixes to this command the great doctrinal truth upon which it is built (*v.* 29);*"Hear, O Israel, The Lord our God is one Lord;* if we firmly believe this, it will follow, that we shall love him *with all our heart.* He is Jehovah, who has all amiable perfections in himself; he is *our God,* to whom we stand related and obliged; and therefore we ought to *love him,* to set our affections on him, let out own desire toward him, and take a delight in him; and he is *one Lord,* therefore he must be loved with our *whole heart;* he has the sole *right to us,* and therefore ought to have the sole *possession of us.* If he be one, our hearts must be one with him, and since there is no God besides, no rival must be admitted with him upon the throne.

2. That the second great commandment is, to *love our neighbour as ourselves* (*v.* 31), as truly and sincerely as we love ourselves, and in the same instances, and we must show it by *doing as we would be done by.* As we must therefore love God better than ourselves, because he is Jehovah, a being infinitely better than we are, and must love him with *all our heart,* because he is *one Lord,* and there is no other like him; so we must *love our neighbour as ourselves,* because he is of the same nature with ourselves; our hearts are fashioned alike, and my neighbour and myself are of one body, of one society, that of the world of mankind; and if a fellow-Christian, and of the same sacred society, the obligation is the stronger. *Hath not one God created us?* Mal. 2:10. Has not one Christ redeemed us? Well might Christ say, *There is no other commandment greater than these;* for in these all the law is fulfilled, and if we make conscience of obedience to these, all other instances of obedience will follow of course.

III. The scribe consented to what Christ said, and descanted upon it, *v.* 32, 33. 1. He commends Christ's decision of this question; *Well, Master, thou hast said the truth.* Christ's assertions needed not the scribe's attestations; but this scribe, being a man in authority, thought it would put some reputation upon what Christ said, to have it commended by him; and it shall be brought in evidence against those who persecuted Christ, as a deceiver, that one of themselves, even a scribe of their own, confessed that he *said the truth,* and said it *well.* And thus must we subscribe to Christ's sayings, must set to our seal that they are true. 2. He comments upon it. Christ had quoted that great doctrine, that *the Lord our God is one Lord;* and this he not only assented to, but added, *"There is none other but he;* and therefore we must have no other God besides." This excludes all rivals with him, and secures the throne in the heart entire for him. Christ had laid down that great law, of loving God *with all our hearts;* and this also he explains — that it is loving him *with the understanding,* as those that know what abundant reason we have to love him. Our love to God, as it must be an *entire,* so it must be an *intelligent,* love; we must love him with *all* the understanding, *ex holēs tēs syneseōs — out of the whole understanding;* our rational powers and faculties must all be set on work to lead out the affections of our souls toward God. Christ has said, "To love God and our neighbour is the greatest commandment of all;" "Yea," saith the scribe, "it is better, it is *more than all whole-burnt-offerings and sacrifices,* more acceptable to God, and will turn to a better account to ourselves." There were those who held, that the law of *sacrifices* was the *greatest commandment* of all; but this scribe readily agreed with our Saviour in this — that the law of love to God and our neighbour is greater than that of *sacrifice,* even than that of *whole-burnt-offerings,* which were intended purely for the honour of God.

IV. Christ approved of what he said, and encouraged him to proceed in his enquiries of him, *v.* 34. 1. He owned that he understood well, as far as he went; so far, so good. *Jesus saw that he answered discreetly,* and was the more pleased with it, because he had of late met with so many even of the scribes, men of letters, that answered *indiscreetly,* as those that had *no understanding,* nor desired to have any. He answered *nounechōs — as one that had a mind;* as a rational intelligent man, as one that had his wits about him; as one whose reason was not blinded, whose judgment was not biassed, and whose forethought was not fettered, by the prejudices which other scribes were so much under the power of. He answered as one that allowed himself liberty and leisure to consider, as one that had considered. 2. He owned that he stood fair for a further advance; *"Thou art not far from the kingdom of God,* the kingdom of grace and glory; thou art in a likely way to be a Christian, a disciple of Christ. For the doctrine of Christ insists most upon these things, and is designed, and has a tendency direct, to bring thee to this." Note, There is hope of those who make a good use of the light they have, and go as far as that will carry them, that by the grace of God they will be led further, by the clearer discoveries God has to make to them. What became of this scribe we are not told, but would willingly hope that he took the hint Christ hereby gave him, and that, having been told by him, so much to his satisfaction, what was the great commandment of the law, he proceeded to enquire of him, or his apostles, what was the great commandment of the gospel too. Yet, if he did not, but took, up here, and went no further, we are not to think it strange; for there are many who are *not far from the kingdom of God,* and yet never come thither. Now, one would think, this should have invited many to consult him: but it had a contrary effect; *No man, after that, durst ask him any question;* every thing he said, was spoken with such authority and majesty, that every one stood in awe of him; those that desired to *learn,* were *ashamed* to ask, and those that designed to *cavil,* were *afraid* to ask.

Verses 35–40

Here, I. Christ shows the people how weak and defective the scribes were in their preaching, and how unable to solve the difficulties that occurred in the scriptures of the Old Testament, which they undertook to expound. Of this he gives an instance, which is not so fully related here as it was in Matthew. Christ was *teaching in the temple:* many things he said, which were not written; but notice is taken of this, because it will stir us up to enquire *concerning Christ,* and to enquire *of him;* for none can have the right knowledge of him but *from himself;* it is not to be had from *the scribes,* for they will soon be run aground.

1. They told the people that the Messiah was to be the *Son of David* (*v.* 35), and they were in the right; he was not only to descend from his loins, but to fill his throne (Lu. 1:32); *The Lord shall give him the throne of his father David.* The scripture said it often, but the people took it as what the scribes said; whereas the truths of God should rather be quoted from our Bibles than from our ministers, for there is the original of them. *Dulcius ex ipso fonte bibuntur aquae — The waters are sweetest when drawn immediately from their source.*

2. Yet they could not tell them how, notwithstanding that it was very proper for David, in spirit, the spirit of prophecy, to call him *his Lord,* as he doth, Ps. 110:1. They had taught the people that concerning the Messiah, which would be for the honour of their nation — that he should be a branch of their royal family; but they had not taken care to teach them that which was for the honour of the Messiah himself — that he should be the Son of God, and, as such, and not otherwise, *David's Lord.* Thus they *held the truth in unrighteousness,* and were *partial* in the gospel, as well as in the law, of the Old Testament. They were able to say it, and prove it — that Christ was to be David's son; but if any should object, *How then doth David himself call him Lord?* they would not know how to avoid the force of the objection. Note, Those are unworthy to sit in Moses's seat, who, though they are able to preach the truth, are not in some measure able to defend it when they have preached it, and to convince gainsayers.

Now this galled the scribes, to have their ignorance thus exposed, and, no doubt, incensed them more against Christ; but the *common people heard him gladly, v.* 37. What he preached was surprising and affecting; and though it reflected upon the scribes, it was instructive to them, and they had never heard such preaching. Probably there was something more than ordinarily commanding and charming in his voice and way of delivery, which recommended him to the affections of the common people; for we do not find that any were wrought upon to *believe* in him, and to *follow* him, but he was to them as a *lovely song of one that could play well on an instrument;* as Ezekiel was to his hearers, Eze. 33:32. And perhaps some of these cried, *Crucify him,* as Herod heard John Baptist gladly, and yet cut off his head.

II. He cautions the people to take heed of suffering themselves to be imposed upon by the scribes, and of being infected with their pride and hypocrisy; *He said unto them in his doctrine, "Beware of the scribes* (*v.* 38); stand upon your guard, that you neither imbibe their peculiar opinions, nor the opinions of the people concerning them." The charge is long as drawn up against them in the parallel place (Mt. 23); it is here contracted.

1. They affect to appear *very great;* for they go in *long clothing,* with vestures *down to their feet,* and in those they walk *about the streets,* as princes, or judges, or gentlemen of the long robe. Their going in such clothing was not sinful, but their *loving* to go in it, priding themselves in it, valuing themselves on it, commanding respect by it, saying to their long clothes, as Saul to Samuel, *Honour me now before this people,* this was a product of pride. Christ would have his disciples go with *their loins girt.*

2. They affect to appear *very good;* for they pray, they make *long prayers,* as if they were very intimate with heaven, and had a deal of business there. They took care it should be known that they prayed, that they prayed long, which, some think, intimates that they prayed not for themselves only, but for others, and therein were very particular and very large; this they did *for a pretence,* that they might seem to love prayer, not only for God's sake, whom hereby they pretended to glorify, but for their neighbour's sake, whom hereby they pretended to be serviceable to.

3. They here aimed to *advance* themselves: they coveted applause, and were fond of it; they loved *salutations in the marketplaces,* and the *chief seats in the synagogues, and the uppermost rooms at feasts;* these pleased a vain fancy; to have these given them, they thought, expressed the value *they* had for them, who did know them, and gained them respect for those who did not.

4. They herein aimed to *enrich* themselves. They *devoured widows' houses,* made themselves masters of their estates by some trick or other; it was to screen themselves from the suspicion of dishonesty, that they put on the mask of piety; and that they might not be thought as bad as the worst, they were studious to seem as good as the best. Let fraud and oppression be thought the worse of for their having *profaned* and *disgraced* long prayers; but let not prayers, no nor *long prayers,* be thought the worse of, if made in humility and sincerity, for their having been by some thus abused. But as iniquity, thus disguised with a show of piety, is *double* iniquity, so its doom will be doubly heavy; *These shall receive great damnation;* greater than those that live without prayer, greater than they would have received for the wrong done to the poor widows, if it had not been thus disguised. Note, The damnation of hypocrites will be of all others the greatest damnation.

Verses 41–44

This passage of story was not in Matthew, but is here and in Luke; it is Christ's commendation of the poor widow, that cast *two mites* into the treasury, which our Saviour, busy as he was in preaching, found leisure to take notice of. Observe,

I. There was a *public fund* for charity, into which contributions were brought, and out of which distributions were made; a poor's-box, and this in *the temple;* for works of charity and works of piety very fitly go together; where God is honoured by our worship, it is proper he should be honoured by the relief of his poor; and we often find *prayers* and *alms* in conjunction, as Acts 10:2, 4. IT is good to erect public receptacles of charity for the inviting and directing of private hands in giving to the poor; nay it is good for those who are of ability to have funds of their own, to *lay by as God has prospered them* (1 Co. 16:2), that they might have something ready to give when an object of charity offers itself, which is before dedicated to such uses.

II. Jesus Christ had *an eye* upon it; *He sat over against the treasury, and beheld now the people cast money into it;* not grudging either that he had none to cast in, or had not the disposal of that which was cast in, but observing what was cast in. Note, Our Lord Jesus takes notice of what we contribute to pious and charitable uses; whether we give liberally or sparingly; whether cheerfully or with reluctance and ill-will; nay, he looks at the heart; he observes what principles we act upon, and what our views are, in giving alms; and whether we do it as unto the Lord, or only to be seen of men.

III. He saw *many that were rich cast in much:* and it was

a good sight to see rich people charitable, to see *many* rich people so, and to see them not only cast in, but cast in *much.* Note, Those that are rich, ought to give richly; if God give abundantly to us, he expects we should give abundantly to the poor; and it is not enough for those that are rich, to say, that they give as much as others do, who perhaps have much less of the world than they have, but they must give in proportion to their estates; and if objects of charity do not present themselves, that require so much, they ought to enquire them out, and to *devise liberal things.*

IV. There was a *poor widow that cast in two mites, which make a farthing* (*v.* 42); and our Lord Jesus highly commended her; *called his disciples* to him, and bid them take notice of it (*v.* 43); told them that she could very ill spare that which she gave, she had scarcely enough for herself, it was *all her living,* all she had to live upon for that day, and perhaps a great part of what she had earned by her labour the day before; and that forasmuch as he knew she did it from a truly charitable disposition, he reckoned it more than all that put together, which the rich people threw in; for they did *cast in of their abundance, but she of her want, v.* 44. Now many would have been ready to censure this *poor widow,* and to think she did ill; why should she give to others, when she had little enough for herself? Charity begins at home; or, if she would give it, why did she not bestow it upon some poor body that she knew? What occasion was there for her bringing it to the *treasury* to be disposed of by the chief priests, who, we have reason to fear, were partial in the disposal of it? It is so rare a thing to find any that would not blame this widow, that we cannot expect to find any that will imitate her; and yet our Saviour commends her, and therefore we are sure that she did very well and wisely. If Christ saith, *Well-done,* no matter who saith otherwise; and we must hence learn, 1. That *giving alms,* is an excellent good thing, and highly pleasing to the Lord Jesus; and if we be humble and sincere in it, he will graciously accept of it, though in some circumstances there may not be all the discretion in the world. 2. Those that have but a *little,* ought to give alms out of *their little.* Those that live by their labour, from hand to mouth, must *give to those that need,* Eph. 4:28. 3. It is very good for us to straiten and deny ourselves, that we may be able to give the more to the poor; to deny ourselves not only superfluities, but even conveniences, for the sake of charity. We should in many cases pinch ourselves, that we may supply the necessities of others; this is loving our neighbours as ourselves. 4. Public charities should be encouraged, for they bring upon a nation public blessings; and though there may be some mismanagement of them, yet that is not a good reason why we should not bring in our *quota* to them. 5. Though we can give but a *little* in charity, yet if it be according to our ability, and be given with an upright heart, it shall be accepted of Christ, who requires *according to what a man has, and not according to what he has not;* two mites shall be put upon the score, and brought to account, if given in a right manner, as if they had been two pounds. 6. It is much to the praise of charity, when we give not only *to our power,* but *beyond our power,* as the Macedonian churches, whose *deep poverty abounded to the riches of their liberality,* 2 Co. 8:2, 3. When we can cheerfully provide for others, out of our own necessary provision, as the widow of Sarepta for Elijah, and Christ for his five thousand guests, and trust God to provide for us some other way, *this is thank-worthy.*

CHAPTER 13

We have here the substance of that prophetical sermon which our Lord Jesus preached, pointing at the destruction of Jerusalem, and the consummation of all things; it was one of the last of his sermons, and not *ad populum* — to the people, but *ad clerum* — to the clergy; it was private, preached only to four of his disciples, with whom his secret was. Here is, I. The occasion of his prediction — his disciples' admiring the building of the temple (*v.* 1, 2), and their enquiry concerning the time of the desolation of them (*v.* 3, 4). II. The predictions themselves, 1. Of the rise of deceivers (*v.* 5, 6, 21–23). 2. Of the wars of the nations (*v.* 7, 8). 3. Of the persecution of Christians (*v.* 9–13). 4. Of the destruction of Jerusalem (*v.* 14–20). 5. Of the end of the world (*v.* 24–27). III. Some general intimations concerning the time of them (*v.* 28–32). IV. Some practical inferences from all (*v.* 33–37).

Verses 1–4

We may here see,

I. How apt many of Christ's own disciples are to idolize things that look *great,* and have been long looked upon as *sacred.* They had heard Christ complain of those who had made the temple a *den of thieves;* and yet, when he quitted it, for the wickedness that remained in it, they court him to be as much in love as they were with the stately structure and adorning of it. One of them said to him, "Look, Master, *what manner of stones, and what buildings are here, v.* 1. We never saw the like in Galilee; O do not leave this fine place."

II. How little Christ values external pomp, where there is not real purity; *"Seest thou these great buildings"* (saith Christ), "and admirest thou them? I tell thee, the time is at hand when *there shall not be left one stone upon another, that shall not be thrown down," v.* 2. And the sumptuousness of the fabric shall be no security to it, no nor move any compassion in the Lord Jesus towards it. He looks with *pity* upon the ruin of precious souls, and weeps over them, for on them he has put great value; but we do not find him look with any pity upon the ruin of a magnificent house, when he is driven out of it by sin, for that is of small value with him. With what little concern doth he say, *Not one stone shall be left on another!* Much of the strength of the temple lay in the largeness of the stones, and if these be thrown down, no footstep, no remembrance, of it will remain. While any part remained standing, there might be some hopes of the repair of it; but what hope is there, when not one stone is *left upon another?*

III. How natural it is to us to desire to know things to come, and the times of them; more inquisitive we are apt to be about that than about our duty. His disciples knew not how to *digest* this doctrine of the ruin of the temple, which they thought must be their Master's royal palace, and in which they expected their preferment, and to have the posts of honour; and therefore they were in pain till they got him alone, and got more out of him concerning this matter. As he was returning to Bethany therefore, he *sat upon the mount of Olives, over against the temple,* where he had a full view of it; and there four of them agreed to *ask him privately,* what he meant by the destroying of the temple, which they understood no more than they did the predictions of his own death, so inconsistent was it with their scheme. Probably, though these four proposed the question, yet Christ's discourse, in answer to it, was in the hearing of the rest of the disciples, yet *privately,* that is, apart from the multitude. Their enquiry is, *When shall these things be?* They will not question, at least not seem to question, whether they shall be or no (for their Master has said that they shall), but are willing to hope it is a great way off. Yet they ask not precisely the day and year (therein they were modest), but say, "Tell us *what shall be the sign, when all these things shall be fulfilled?* What presages shall there be of them, and how may we prognosticate their approach?"

Verses 5–13

Our Lord Jesus, in reply to their question, sets himself, not so much to satisfy their curiosity as to direct their consciences; leaves them still in the dark concerning the *times* and *seasons,* which the father has *kept in his own power,* and which *it was not for them to know;* but gives them the cautions which were needful, with reference to the events that should now shortly come to pass.

I. They must take heed that they be not *deceived* by the *seducers* and *imposters* that should now shortly arise (*v.* 5, 6); *"Take heed lest any man deceive you,* lest, having found the *true Messiah,* you lose him again in the crowd of *pretenders,* or be inveigled to embrace others in rivalship with him. Many shall come *in my name* (not in the name of *Jesus*), but saying, *I am the Christ,* and so claiming the dignities which I only an entitled to." After the Jews had rejected the true Christ, they were imposed upon, and so exposed by many false Christs, but never before; those false Christs *deceived many;* Therefore *take heed lest they deceive you.* Note, When many are deceived, we should thereby be awakened to look to ourselves.

II. They must take heed that they be not *disturbed* at the noise of wars, which they should be alarmed with, *v.* 7, 8. Sin introduced *wars,* and they come *from men's lusts.* But at some times the nations are more distracted and wasted with wars than at other times; so it shall be now; Christ was born into the world when there was a general peace, but soon after he went out of the world there were general wars; *Nation shall rise against nation, and kingdom against kingdom.* And what will become of them then who are to preach the gospel to every nation? *Inter arma silent leges — Amidst the clash of arms, the voice of law is not heard.* "But *be not troubled at it."* 1. "Let it be no *surprise* to you; you are bid to expect it, and *such things must needs be,* for God has appointed them, in order to further accomplishment of his purposes, and by the *wars of the Jews"* (which Josephus has given us a large account of) "God will punish the *wickedness of the Jews."* 2. "Let it be no *terror* to you, as if your interest were in danger of being overthrown, or your work obstructed by these wars; you have no concern in them, and therefore need not be apprehensive of any damage by them." Note, Those that despise the smiles of the world, and do not court and covet them, may despise the frowns of the world, and need not fear them. If we seek not to rise with them that *rise in the world,* why should we dread falling with them that fall in the world? 3. "Let it not be looked upon as an omen of the approaching period of the world, for the *end is not yet, v.* 7. Think not that these *wars* will bring the world to a period; no, there are other intermediate counsels to be fulfilled betwixt that end and the end of all things, which are designed to prepare you for the end, but not to hasten it out of due time." 4. "Let it not be looked upon as if in them God has done his worst; no, he has more arrows in his quiver, and they are *ordained against the persecutors;* be not troubled at the wars you shall hear of, for they are but *the beginnings of sorrows,* and therefore, instead of being disturbed at *them,* you ought to *prepare for worse;* for there shall also be *earthquakes in divers places,* which shall bury multitudes in the ruins of their own houses, and there *shall be famines,* by which many of the poor shall perish for want of bread, and *troubles* and commotions; so that there shall be no peace to him that *goes out* or *comes in.* The world shall be full of *troubles,* but *be not ye troubled;* without are *fightings,* within are *fears,* but *fear not ye their fear."* Note, The disciples of Christ, if it be not their own fault, may enjoy a holy security and serenity of mind, when all about them is in the greatest disorder.

III. They must take heed that they be not *drawn away* from Christ, and from their duty to him, by the sufferings they should meet with for Christ's sake. Again, he saith, *"Take heed to yourselves, v.* 9. Though you may escape the *sword of war,* better than some of your neighbours, because you interest not yourselves in the public quarrels, yet be not secure; you will be exposed to the *sword of justice* more than others, and the parties that contend with one another, will unite against you. *Take heed* therefore lest you *deceive* yourselves with the hopes of outward prosperity, and such a temporal kingdom as you have been dreaming of, when it is *through many tribulations* that *you must enter into the kingdom of God.* Take heed lest you needlessly expose yourselves to trouble, and pull it upon your own head. *Take heed* what you say and do, for you will have many eyes upon you." Observe,

1. What the trouble is which they must expect.

(1.) They shall be *hated of all men;* trouble enough! The thoughts of *being hated* are grievous to a tender spirit, and the fruits of that hatred must needs be a constant vexation; those that are *malicious,* will be *mischievous.* It was not for any thing amiss in them, or done amiss by them, that they were *hated,* but for Christ's name sake, because they were called by his name, called upon his name, preached his name, and wrought miracles in his name. The world hated them because he loved them.

(2.) Their own *relations* shall *betray them,* those to whom they were most nearly allied, and on whom therefore they depended for protection; "They *shall betray you,* shall inform against you, and be your prosecutors." If a father has a child that is a Christian, he shall become void of natural affection, it shall be swallowed up in bigotry, and he shall betray his own child to the persecutors, as if he were a worshipper of other gods, Deu. 13:6–10.

(3.) Their *church-rulers* shall inflict *their censures* upon them; "You shall be *delivered up* to the great Sanhedrim at Jerusalem, and to the inferior courts and consistories in other cities, and shall be *beaten in the synagogues* with forty stripes at a time, as offenders against the law which was read in the synagogue." It is no new thing for the church's artillery, through the treachery of its officers, to be turned against some of its best friends.

(4.) *Governors* and *kings* shall use their power against them. Because the Jews have not power to put them to death, they shall incense the Roman powers against them, as they did Herod against James and Peter; and they shall *cause you to be put to death,* as enemies to the empire. They must resist unto blood, and still resist.

2. What they shall have to comfort themselves with, in the midst of these great and sore troubles.

(1.) That the work they were called to should be carried on and prosper, notwithstanding all this opposition which they should meet with in it (*v.* 10); "*The gospel* shall, for all this, be *published among all nations,* and before the destruction of Jerusalem the *sound* of it shall *go forth into all the earth;* not only through all the nation of the Jews, but to all the nations of the earth." It is comfort to those who suffer for the gospel, that, though they may be crushed and borne down, the gospel cannot; it shall keep its ground, and carry the day.

(2.) That their sufferings, instead of obstructing their work, should forward it; "Your being *brought before governors and kings* shall be for *a testimony of them* (so some read it, *v.* 9); it shall give you an opportunity of preaching the gospel to those before whom you are brought as criminals, to whom otherwise you could not have access." Thus St. Paul's being brought before Felix, and Festus, and Agrippa, and Nero, was a testimony to them concerning Christ and his gospel. Or, as we read it, It shall be for a testimony *against them,* against both the judges and the prosecutors, who pursue those with the utmost rage that appear, upon examination, to be not only innocent but excellent persons. The gospel is a testimony to us concerning Christ and heaven. If we receive it, it will be a testimony for us: it will justify and save us; if not, it will be a testimony *against* us in the great day.

(3.) That, when they were brought before kings and governors for Christ's sake, they should have special assistance from heaven, to plead Christ's cause and their own (*v.* 11); "*Take no thought before-hand what he shall speak,* be not solicitous how to address yourselves to great men, so as to obtain their favour; your cause is just and glorious, and needs not be supported by premeditated speeches and harangues; but *whatsoever shall be given you in that hour,* whatsoever shall be suggested to you, and put into your minds, and into your mouths" *(pro re natâ — on the spur of the occasion),* "that *speak ye,* and fear not the success of it, because it is *off-hand,* for *it is not ye that speak,* purely by the strength of your own wisdom, consideration, and resolution, but it is *the Holy Ghost.*" Note, Those whom Christ calls out to be advocates for him, shall be furnished with full instructions: and when we are engaged in the service of Christ, we may depend upon the aids of the Spirit of Christ.

(4.) That heaven at last would *make amends for all;* "You will meet with a great deal of hardship in your way, but have a good heart on it, your warfare will be accomplished, and your testimony finished, and *he that shall endure to the end, the same shall be saved,*" *v.* 13. Perseverance gains the crown. The salvation here promised is more than a deliverance from evil, it is an everlasting blessedness, which shall be an abundant recompence for all their services and sufferings. All this we have, Mt. 10:17, etc.

Verses 14–23

The Jews, in rebelling against the Romans, and in persecuting the Christians, were hastening to their own ruin apace, both efficiently and meritoriously, were setting both God and man against them; see 1 Th. 2:15. Now here we have a prediction of that ruin which came upon them within less than forty years after this: we had it before, Mt. 24:15, etc. Observe,

I. What is here foretold concerning it.

1. That the Roman *armies* should make a descent upon Judea, and invest Jerusalem, the holy city. These were the *abomination* of *desolation,* which the Jews did *abominate,* and by which they should be made *desolate.* The country of thine enemy is called *the land which thou abhorrest,* Isa. 7:16. *Therefore* it was an abomination, because it brought with it nothing but desolation. They had rejected Christ as an *abomination,* who would have been their *salvation;* and now God brought upon them an abomination that would be their *desolation,* thus spoken of by Daniel *the prophet* (*ch.* 9:27), as that by which this sacrifice and offering should be made to cease. This army stood *where it ought not,* in and about the *holy city,* which the heathen ought not to have approached, nor would have been suffered to approach, if Jerusalem had not first profaned the crown of their holiness. This the church complains of, Lam. 1:10, The *heathen entered into her sanctuary, whom thou didst command that they should not enter into the congregation;* but sin made the breach, at which the glory went out, and the abomination of desolation broke in, *and stood where it ought not.* Now, let *him that readeth* this, *understand it,* and endeavor to take it right. Prophecies should not be too plain, and yet intelligible to those that search them; and they are best understood by comparing them first with one another, and at last with the event.

2. That when the Roman *army* should come into the country, there would be no safety any where but by quitting the country, and that with all possible expedition. It will be in vain to *fight,* the enemies will be too hard for them; in vain to *abscond,* the enemies will find them out; and in vain to *capitulate,* the enemies will give them no quarter; a man cannot have so much as his life given him for a prey, but by *fleeing to the mountains* out of Judea; and let him take the first alarm, and make the best of his way. If he be *on the housetop,* trying from thence to discover the motions of the enemy, and spies them coming, let him not *go down, to take any thing out of the house,* for it will occasion his losing of time, which is more precious than his best goods, and will but encumber him, and embarrass his flight. If he be in the field, and there discover the approach of the enemy, let him get away as he is, and not *turn back again, to take up his garment, v.* 16. If he can save his life, let him reckon it is a good bargain, though he can save nothing else, and be thankful to God, that, though he is cut short, he is not cut off.

3. That it would go very hard at that time with poor mothers and nurses (*v.* 17); "*Woe to them that are with child,* that dare not go into strange places, that cannot shift for themselves, nor make haste as others can. And *woe to them that give suck,* that know not how either to leave the tender infants behind them, or to carry them along with them." Such is the vanity of the creature, that the time may often be, when the greatest comforts may prove the greatest burthens. It would likewise be very uncomfortable, if they should be forced to flee *in the winter* (*v.* 18), when the *weather* and *ways* were bad, when the roads would be scarcely passable, especially in the mountains to which they must flee. If there be no remedy but that trouble must come, yet we may desire and pray that, if it be God's will, the circumstances of it may be so ordered as to be a mitigation of the trouble; and when things are bad, we ought to consider they might have been worse. It is bad to be forced to flee, but it would have been worse if it had been *in the winter.*

4. That throughout all the country of the Jews, there should be such destruction and desolation made, as could not be paralleled in any history (*v.* 19); *In those days shall be affliction, such as was not from the beginning* of time; that is, *of the creation which God created,* for time and the creation are of equal date, *unto this day, neither shall be* to the end of time; such a complication of miseries, and of such continuance. The destruction of Jerusalem by the Chaldeans was very terrible, but this exceeded it. It threatened a universal slaughter of all the people of the Jews; so barbarously did they devour one another, and the Romans devour them all, that, if their wars had continued a little longer, *no flesh could have been saved,* not one Jew could have been left alive; but in the midst of wrath God remembered mercy; and, (1.) He *shortened the days;* he let fall his controversy before he had *made a full end.* As a church and nation the ruin was complete, but many particular persons had their lives given them for a prey, by the storm's subsiding when it did. 2. It was *for the elects' sake* that those days were shortened; *many* among them fared the better for the sake of the *few* among them that believed in Christ, and were faithful to him. There was a promise, that *a remnant* should be saved (Isa. 10:22), and that God would not, for his servants' sakes, *destroy them all* (Isa. 65:8); and these promises must be fulfilled. God's own *elect cry day and night to him,* and their prayers must be answered, Lu. 18:7.

II. What directions are given to the disciples with reference to it.

1. They must shift for the safety of *their lives;* "When you see the country invaded, and the city invested, flatter not yourselves with thoughts that the enemy will retire, or that you may be able to make your part good with them; but, without further deliberation or delay, *let them that are in Judea, flee to the mountains, v.* 14. Meddle not with the strife that *belongs not to you; let the potsherds strive with the potsherds of the earth,* but do you go out of the ship when you see it sinking, that you die not the *death of the uncircumcised* in heart."

2. They must provide for the safety of *their souls;* "*Seducers* will be busy at that time, for they love to fish in troubled waters, and therefore then you must double your guard; *then, if any man shall* say unto you, *Lo, here is Christ,* or, *Lo, he is there,* you know he is in heaven, and will come again at the end of time, to judge the world, and therefore *believe them not;* having received *Christ,* be not drawn into the snares of any *antichrist;* for *false Christs,* and *false prophets, shall arise,*" *v.* 22. When the gospel kingdom was in the setting up, Satan mustered all his force, to oppose it, and made use of all his wiles; and God permitted it, for the trial of sincerity of some, and the discovery of the hypocrisy of others, and the confusion of those who rejected Christ, when he was offered to them. *False Christs* shall *rise,* and false prophets that shall preach them up; or such, as, though they pretend not to be Christs, set up for *prophets,* and undertake to foretel things to come, and they shall *show signs* and lying *wonders;* so early did the *mystery of iniquity* begin to *work,* 2 Th. 2:7. They *shall seduce, if it were possible, the very elect;* so plausible shall their pretences be, and so industrious shall they be to impose upon people, that they shall drawn away many that were forward and zealous professors of religion, many that were very likely to have persevered; for nothing will be effectual to secure men but that foundation of God which stands immovably sure, *The Lord knoweth them that are his,* who shall be preserved when the faith of some is overthrown, 2. Tim. 2:18, 19. They *shall seduce, if it were possible, the very elect;* but it is not possible to seduce them; the *election shall obtain,* whoever are *blinded,* Rom. 11:7. But, in consideration hereof, let the disciples be cautious whom they give credit to (*v.* 23); But *take ye heed.* Christ knew that they were of the *elect,* who could not possibly be *seduced,* and yet he said to them, *Take heed.* An assurance of persevering, and cautions against apostasy, will very well consist with each other. Though Christ said to them, *Take heed,* it doth not therefore follow, that their perseverance was doubtful, for they were kept by the power of God; and though their perseverance was secured, yet it doth not therefore follow, that this caution was needless, because they must be kept in the use of proper means. God will keep them, but they must keep themselves. "*I have foretold you all things;* have foretold you of this danger, that, being *fore-warned,* you may be *fore-armed;* I have foretold *all things* which you needed to have foretold to you, and therefore take heed of hearkening to such as pretend to be prophets, and to foretel more than I have foretold." The sufficiency of the scripture is good argument against listening to such as pretend to inspiration.

Verses 24–27

These verses seem to point at Christ's second coming, to judge the world; the disciples, in their question, had confounded the *destruction* of Jerusalem and the *end of the world* (Mt. 24:3), which was built upon a mistake, as if the temple must needs stand as long as the world stands; this mistake Christ rectifies, and shows that the *end of the world in those days,* those other days you enquire about, the day of Christ's coming, and the day of judgment, shall be *after that tribulation,* and not coincident with it. Let those who live to see the Jewish nation destroyed, take heed of thinking that, because the Son of man doth not visibly come in the clouds *then,* he will never *so* come; no, he will come *after that.* And here he foretels,

1. The final dissolution of the present frame and fabric of the world; even of that part of it which seems least liable to change, the upper part, the pure and more refined part; *The sun shall be darkened,* and the *moon* shall no more *give her light;* for they shall be quite outshone by the glory of the Son of man, Isa. 24:23. The *stars of heaven,* that from the beginning had kept their place and regular motion, shall fall as leaves in autumn; and the *powers that are in heaven,* the heavenly bodies, the fixed stars, *shall be shaken.*

2. The visible appearance of the Lord Jesus, to whom the judgment of that day shall be committed (*v.* 26); *Then shall they see the Son of man coming in the clouds.* Probably he will come over that very place where he sat when he said this; for the clouds are in the lower region of the air. He shall come with *great power and glory,* such as will be suited to the errand on which he comes. *Every eye shall then see him.*

3. The gathering together of all the elect to him (*v.* 27); He shall *send his angels,* and *gather together his elect* to him, to *meet him in the air,* 1 Th. 4:17. They shall be fetched from one end of the world to the other, so that none shall be missing from that *general* assembly; they shall be fetched *from the uttermost part of the earth,* most remote from the places where Christ's tribunal shall be set, and shall be brought to the *uttermost part of heaven;* so sure, so swift, so easy, shall

their conveyance be, that there shall none of them miscarry, though they were to be brought from the uttermost part of the earth one way, to the uttermost part of the heaven another way. A faithful Israelite shall be carried safely, though it were from the utmost border of the land of bondage to the utmost border of the land of promise.

Verses 28–37

We have here the application of this prophetical sermon; *now learn* to look forward in a right manner.

I. "As to the *destruction* of Jerusalem, *expect* it to come very *shortly;* as when the *branch of the fig-tree becomes soft,* and the *leaves sprout forth,* ye expect that summer will come shortly, *v.* 28. When second causes begin to work, ye expect their effects in their proper order and time. So when *ye see these things come to pass,* when ye see the Jewish nation embroiled in wars, distracted by false Christs and prophets, and drawing upon them the displeasure of the Romans, especially when ye see them persecuting you for your Master's sake, and thereby standing to what they did when they put him to death, and repeating it, and so filling up the measure of their iniquity, then say that their *ruin is nigh, even at the door,* and provide for yourselves accordingly." The disciples themselves were indeed all of them, except John, taken away from the evil to come, but the next generation whom they were to train up, would live to see it; and by these instructions which Christ left behind him would be kept from sharing in it; "*This generation* that is now rising up, shall not all be worn off before *all these things* come to pass, which I have told you of, relating to Jerusalem, and they shall begin to take effect now shortly. And as this destruction is near and within ken, so it is sure. The decree is gone forth, it is a *consummation determined,*" Dan. 9:27. Christ doth not speak these things, merely to frighten them; no, they are declarations of God's fixed purpose; "*Heaven and earth shall pass away,* at the end of time; but *my words shall not pass away* (*v.* 31), not one of these predictions shall fail of a punctual accomplishment."

II. "As to the *end of the world,* do not enquire when it will come, for it is not a question fit to be asked, for of *that day,* and *that hour, knoweth no man;* it is a thing at a great distance; the exact time is fixed in the counsel of God, but is not revealed by any word of God, either to *men* on earth, or to *angels in heaven;* the angels shall have timely notice to prepare to attend in that day, and it shall be published, when it comes to the children of men, with sound of trumpet; but, at present, *men* and *angels* are kept in the dark concerning the precise time of it, that they may both attend to their proper services in the present day." But it follows, *neither the Son;* but is there any thing which the Son is ignorant of? We read indeed of a book which was sealed, till the Lamb opened the seals; but did not he know what was in it, before the seals were opened? Was not he privy to the writing of it? There were those in the primitive times, who taught from this text, that there were some things that Christ, as man, was *ignorant* of; and from these were called *Agnoetae;* they said, "It was no more absurd to say so, than to say that his human soul suffered grief and fear;" and many of the orthodox fathers approved of this. Some would evade it, by saying that Christ spoke this in a way of prudential economy, to divert the disciples from further enquiry: but to this one of the ancients answers, *It is not fit to speak too nicely in this matter — ou dei pany akribologein,* so Leontius in Dr. Hammond, "It is certain (says Archbishop Tillotson) that Christ, as God, could not be ignorant of any thing; but the divine wisdom which dwelt in our Saviour, did communicate itself to his human soul, according to the divine pleasure, so that his human nature might sometimes not know some things; therefore Christ is said to grow in wisdom (Lu. 2:52), which he could not be said to do, if the human nature of Christ did necessarily know all things by virtue of its union with the divinity." Dr. Lightfoot explains it thus; Christ calls himself the Son, as Messiah. Now the Messiah, as such, was the father's servant (Isa. 42:1), sent and deputed by him, and as such a one he refers himself often to his Father's will and command, and owns he *did nothing of himself* (Jn. 5:19); in like manner he might be said to *know nothing of himself.* The revelation of Jesus Christ was what *God gave unto him,* Rev. 1:1. He thinks, therefore, that we are to distinguish between those excellencies and perfections of his, which resulted from the personal union between the divine and human nature, and those which flowed from the anointing of the Spirit; from

the former flowed the infinite dignity of his perfect freedom from all sin; but from the latter flowed his power of working miracles, and his foreknowledge of things to come. What therefore (saith he) was to be revealed by him to his church, he was pleased to take, not from the union of the human nature with the divine, but from the revelation of the Spirit, by which he yet knew not this, but *the Father* only knows it; that is, God only, the Deity; for (as Archbishop Tillotson explains it) it is not used here *personally,* in distinction from the Son and the Holy Ghost, but as the Father is, *Fons et Principium Deitatis — The Fountain of Deity.*

III. "As to both, your duty is to *watch and pray.* Therefore the time is kept a secret, that you may be engaged to stand always upon your guard (*v.* 33); *Take ye heed* of every thing that would indispose you for your Master's coming, and would render your accounts *perplexed,* and your spirits so too; *watch* for his coming, that it may not at any time be a surprise to you, and *pray* for that grace which is necessary to qualify you for it, for *ye know not when the time is; and* you are concerned to be ready for that *every day,* which may come *any day.*" This he illustrates, in the close, by a parable.

1. Our Master is gone away, and left us something in trust, in charge, which we must give account of, *v.* 34. He is *as a man taking a far journey;* for he is gone to be away a great while, he has *left his house* on earth, and left his servants in their offices, given *authority* to some, who are to be overseers, and *work* to others, who are to be labourers. They that have *authority* given them, in that had *work* assigned them, for those that have the greatest *power* have the most *business;* and to them to whom he gave *work,* he gave some sort of *authority,* to do that work. And when he took his last leave, he *appointed the porter to watch,* to be sure to be ready to open to him at his return; and in the mean time to take care to whom he opened his gates, not to thieves and robbers, but only to his Master's friends and servants. Thus our Lord Jesus, when he *ascended on high,* left something for all his servants to do, expecting they should all do him service in his absence, and be ready to receive him at his return. *All* are appointed to work, and some authorized to rule.

2. We ought to be always upon our watch, in expectation of his return, *v.* 35–37. (1.) Our Lord *will come,* and will come as the *Master of the house,* to take account of his servants, of their work, and of the improvement they have made. (2.) We know not *when he will come;* and he has very wisely kept us at uncertainty, that we might all be always ready. We know not *when he will come,* just at what precise time; the *Master of the house* perhaps will come *at even,* at nine at night; or it may be *at midnight,* or a *cock-crowing,* at three in the morning, or perhaps not until six. This is applicable to his coming to us in particular, at our death, as well as to the general judgment. Our present life is a *night,* a dark night, compared with the other life; we know not in which watch of the night our Master will come, whether in the days of youth, or middle age, or old age; but, as soon as we are born, we begin to die, and therefore, as soon as we are capable of expecting any thing, we must expect death. (3.) Our great care must be, that, whenever our Lord comes, he do not *find us sleeping,* secure in ourselves, off our guard, indulging ourselves in ease and sloth, mindless of our work and duty, and thoughtless of our Lord's coming; *ready* to say, He will not come, and *unready* to meet him. (4.) His coming will indeed be *coming suddenly;* it will be a great *surprise* and *terror* to those that are careless, and asleep, it will come upon them as a thief in the night. (5.) It is therefore the indispensable duty of all Christ's disciples, to *watch,* to be awake, and keep awake; "*What I say unto you* four (*v.* 37), I *say unto all* the twelve, or rather to *you* twelve, I say unto all my disciples and followers; what I say to you of this generation, I say to all that shall believe in men, through your word, in every age, *Watch, watch,* expect my second coming, prepare for it, that you may be found in peace, without spot, and blameless."

CHAPTER 14

In this chapter begins the account which this evangelist gives of the death and sufferings of our Lord Jesus, which we are all concerned to be acquainted, not only with the history of, but with the mystery of. Here is, I. The plot of the chief priests and scribes against Christ (*v.* 1, 2). II. The anointing of Christ's head at a supper in Bethany, two days before his death (*v.* 3–9). III. The contract Judas made with the chief priests, to betray him (*v.* 10, 11). IV. Christ's eating the passover with his disciples, his instituting the Lord's supper, and his discourse with his disciples, at and after supper (*v.* 12–31). V. Christ's agony in the garden (*v.* 32–42). VI. The betraying of him by Judas, and the apprehending

of him by the chief priests' agents (*v.* 43–52). VII. His arraignment before the high priest, his conviction, and the indignities done him at that bar (*v.* 53–65). VIII. Peter's denying him (*v.* 66–72). Most of which passages we had before, Mt. 26.

Verses 1–11

We have here instances,

I. Of the *kindness of Christ's friends,* and the provision made of respect and honour for him. Some friends he had, even in and about Jerusalem, that loved him, and never thought they could do enough for him, among whom, though Israel be not gathered, he is, and will be, glorious.

1. Here was *one friend,* that was so kind as to *invite him to sup with him;* and he was so kind as to accept the invitation, *v.* 3. Though he had a prospect of his death approaching, yet he did not abandon himself to a melancholy retirement from all company, but conversed as freely with his friends as usual.

2. Here was *another friend,* that was so kind as to *anoint his head* with very precious ointment as he *sat at meat.* This was an extraordinary piece of respect paid him by a good woman that thought nothing too good to bestow upon Christ, and to do him honour. Now the scripture was fulfilled, *When the king sitteth at his table, my spikenard sendeth forth the smell thereof,* Cant. 1:12. Let us *anoint* Christ as our *Beloved,* kiss him with a kiss of *affection;* and anoint him as our *Sovereign,* kiss him with a kiss of *allegiance.* Did he pour out his soul unto death for us, and shall we think any box of ointment too precious to pour out upon him? It is observable that she took care to pour it all out upon Christ's head; she *broke the box* (so we read it); but because it was an *alabaster box,* not easily broken, nor was it necessary that it should be broken, to get out the ointment, some read it, she *shook* the box, or *knocked it to the ground,* to loosen what was in it, that it might be got out the better; or, she *rubbed* and *scraped* out all that stuck tot he sides of it. Christ must have been honoured with *all we* have, and we must not think to keep back any part of the price. Do we give him the *precious ointment* of our best affections? Let him have them *all;* love him *with all the heart.*

Now, (1.) There were those that put a *worse construction* upon this than it *deserved.* They called it a *waste of the ointment, v.* 4. Because they could not have found their hearts to put themselves to such an expense for the honouring of Christ, they thought that she was *prodigal,* who did. Note, As the *vile person* ought to be *called liberal,* nor the *churl* said to be *bountiful* (Isa. 32:5); so the *liberal* and *bountiful* ought not to be called *wasteful.* They pretend it might have been *sold,* and *given to the poor, v.* 5. But as a *common piety* to the *corban* will not excuse from a *particular charity* to a poor parent (*ch.* 7:11), so a common charity to the poor will not excuse from a particular act of piety to the Lord Jesus. What thy hand finds to do, that is good, *do it with thy might.*

(2.) Our Lord Jesus put a *better construction* upon it than, for aught that appears, was *designed.* Probably, she intended no more, than to show the great honour she had for him, before all the company, and to complete his entertainment. But Christ makes it to be an act of *great faith,* as well as *great love* (*v.* 8); "*She is come aforehand, to anoint my body to the burying,* as if she foresaw that my resurrection would prevent her doing it afterward." This funeral rite was a kind of presage of, or prelude to, his death approaching. See how Christ's heart was filled with the thoughts of his death, how every thing was construed with a reference to that, and how familiarly he spoke of it upon all occasions. It is usual for those who are *condemned to die,* to have their coffins prepared, and other provision made for their funerals, while they are yet alive; and *so* Christ accepted *this.* Christ's death and burial were the lowest steps of his humiliation, and therefore, though he cheerfully submitted to them, yet he would have some marks of honour to attend them, which might help to take off the *offence of the cross,* and be an intimation how *precious in the sight of the Lord the death of his saints is.* Christ never rode in triumph into Jerusalem, but when he came thither to suffer; nor had ever his head anointed, but for *his burial.*

(3.) He recommended this piece of heroic piety to the applause of the church in all ages; *Wherever this gospel shall be preached, it shall be spoken of, for a memorial of her, v.* 9. Note, The honour which attends well-doing, even in this world, is sufficient to balance the reproach and contempt that are cast upon it. *The memory of the just is blessed,* and they that had *trial of cruel mockings,* yet *obtained a good report,* Heb. 11:6, 39. Thus was this good woman repaid for her box of ointment, *Nec oleum perdidit nec operam — She lost neither her oil nor her labour.* She got by it that good name which is *better than precious ointment.* Those that *honour* Christ *he will honour.*

II. Of the *malice of Christ's enemies,* and the preparation made by them to do him mischief.

1. The chief priests, his *open enemies,* consulted how they might *put him to death, v.* 1, 2. The feast of the *passover* was now at hand, and at *that* feast he must be crucified, (1.) That his death and suffering might be the more public, and that all *Israel,* even those *of the dispersion,* who came from all parts to the feast, might be witnesses of it, and of the wonders that attended it. (2.) That the Anti-type might answer to the type. Christ, our Passover, was sacrificed for us, and brought us out of the house of bondage, at the same time that the paschal lamb was sacrificed, and Israel's deliverance out of Egypt was *commemorated.*

Now see, [1.] How *spiteful* Christ's enemies were; they did not think it enough to banish or imprison him, for they aimed not only to *silence* him, and *stop* his progress for the future, but to be revenged on him for all the good he had done. [2.] How *subtle* they were; *Not on the feast-day,* when the people are together; they do not say, Lest they should be disturbed in their devotions, and diverted from them, but, *Lest there should be an uproar* (*v.* 2); lest they should rise, and rescue him, and *fall foul* upon those that *attempt* any thing against him. They who *desired* nothing more than the *praise* of men, dreaded nothing more than the rage and displeasure of men.

2. Judas, his *disguised enemy,* contracted with them for the betraying of him, *v.* 10, 11. He is said to be *one of the twelve* that were Christ's family, intimate with him, trained up for the service of the kingdom; and he *went to the chief priests,* to tender his service in this affair.

(1.) That which he proposed to them, was, to *betray Christ* to them, and to give them notice when and where they might find him, and seize him, without making an *uproar among the people,* which they were afraid of, if they should seize him when he appeared *in public,* in the midst of his admirers. Did he know then what help it was they wanted, and where they were run aground in their counsels? It is probable that he did not, for the debate was held in their close *cabal.* Did they know that he had a mind to serve them, and make court to him? No, they could not imagine that any of his intimates should be so base; but Satan, who was entered into Judas, knew what occasion they had for him, and could guide him to be *guide to them,* who were contriving to *take Jesus.* Note, The spirit that works in all the children of disobedience, knows how to bring them in to the assistance one of another in a wicked project, and then to harden them in it, with the fancy that Providence favours them.

(2.) That which he proposed to himself, was, to *get money* by the bargain; he had what he aimed at, when *they promised to give him money.* Covetousness was Judas's master-lust, *his own iniquity,* and that betrayed him to the sin of betraying his Master; the devil suited his temptation to *that,* and so conquered him. It is not said, They promised him *preferment* (he was not ambitious of that), but, they promised him *money.* See what need we have to double our guard against the sin that *most easily besets us.* Perhaps it was Judas's covetousness that brought him at first to *follow Christ,* having a promise that he should be cash-keeper, or purser, to the society, and he loved in his heart to be fingering money; and now that there was money to be got on the other side, he was as ready to betray him as ever he had been to follow him. Note, Where the principle of men's profession of religion is carnal and worldly, and the serving of a secular interest, the very same principle, whenever the wind turns, will be the bitter root of a vile and scandalous apostasy.

(3.) Having secured the money, he set himself to make good his bargain; he sought *how he might conveniently betray him,* how he might *seasonably deliver him up,* so as to answer the intention of those who had hired him. See what need we have to be careful that we do not ensnare ourselves in sinful engagements. If at any time we be so ensnared in the words of our mouths, we are concerned to deliver ourselves by a speedy retreat, Prov. 6:1–5. It is a rule in our law, as well as in our religion, that an *obligation* to do an *evil thing* is *null* and *void;* it binds to repentance, not to performance. See how the way of sin is down-hill — when men are *in,* they must be *on;* and what *wicked* contrivances many have in their sinful pursuits, to compass their designs *conveniently;* but such conveniences will prove mischiefs in the end.

Verses 12–31

In these verses we have,

I. Christ's eating the passover with his disciples, the night before he died, with the joys and comforts of which ordinance he prepared himself for his approaching sorrows, the full prospect of which did not indispose him for that solemnity. Note, No apprehension of trouble, come or coming, should put us by, or put us out of frame for, our attendance on holy ordinances, as we have opportunity for it.

1. Christ ate the passover at the *usual time* when the other Jews did, as Dr. Whitby had fully made out, and not, as Dr. Hammond would have it, the night before. It was on the first day of that feast, which (taking in all the eight days of the feast) was called, *The feast of unleavened bread,* even that day when they *killed the passover, v.* 12.

2. He directed his disciples how to find the place where he intended to eat the passover; and hereby gave such another proof of his infallible knowledge of things distant and future (which to us seem altogether *contingent*), as he had given when he sent them for the ass on which he rode in triumph (*ch.* 11:6); *"Go into the city* (for the *passover* must be *eaten* in Jerusalem), and *there shall meet you a man bearing a pitcher of water* (a servant sent for water to clean the rooms in his master's house); *follow him, go in* where he *goes,* enquire for his master, *the good man of the house* (*v.* 14), and desire him to show you a room." No doubt, the inhabitants of Jerusalem had rooms fitted up to be *let out,* for this occasion, to those that came out of the country to keep the passover, and one of those Christ made use of; not any friend's house, nor any house he had formerly frequented, for then he would have said, "Go to such a friend," or, "You know where we used to be, go thither and prepare." Probably he went where he was not known, that he might be *undisturbed* with his disciples. Perhaps he notified it by *a sign,* to conceal it from Judas, that he might not know till he came to the place; and by *such a sign* to intimate that he will dwell in the *clean heart,* that is, *washed* as with *pure water.* Where he designs to come, a pitcher of water must go before him; see Isa. 1:16–18.

3. He ate the passover in an *upper room furnished, estrōmenon — laid with carpets* (so Dr. Hammond); it would seem to have been a very handsome *dining-room.* Christ was far from affecting any thing that looked stately in eating his common meals; on the contrary, he chose that which was homely, sat down on the grass: but, when he was to keep a sacred feast, in honour of that he would be at the expense of as good a room as he could get. God looks not at *outward pomp,* but he looks at the tokens and expressions of *inward reverence* for a divine institution, which, it is to be feared, those want, who, to save charges, deny themselves decencies in the worship of God.

4. He ate it *with the twelve,* who were his family, to teach those who have the charge of families, not only families of *children,* but families of *servants,* or families of *scholars,* or *pupils,* to keep up religion among them, and worship God with them. If Christ came *with the twelve,* then Judas was with them, though he was at this time contriving to betray his Master; and it is plain by what follows (*v.* 20), that he was there: he did not absent himself, lest he could have been suspected; had his *seat* been *empty* at this feast, they would have said, as Saul of David, *He is not clean, surely he is not clean,* 1 Sa. 20:26. Hypocrites, though they know it is at their peril, yet crowd into special ordinances, to keep up their repute, and palliate their secret wickedness. Christ did not *exclude* him from the feast, though he *knew* his wickedness, for it was not as yet become public and scandalous. Christ, designing to put the *keys of the kingdom of heaven* into the hands of men, who can judge only according to outward appearance, would hereby both direct and encourage them in their admissions to his table, to be satisfied with a justifiable profession, because they cannot discern the *root of bitterness* till it *springs up.*

II. Christ's discourse with his disciples, as they were *eating* the passover. It is probable that they had discourse, according to the custom of the feast, of the deliverance of Israel out of Egypt, and the preservation of the first-born, and were as pleasant as they used to be together on this occasion, till Christ told them that which would mix *trembling* with their *joys.*

1. They were *pleasing* themselves with the society of *their Master;* but he tells them that they must now presently lose him; *The Son of man is betrayed;* and they knew, for he had often told them, what followed — If he be *betrayed,* the next news you will hear of him, is, that he is *crucified* and *slain;* God hath determined it concerning him, and he agrees to it; *The Son of man goes, as it is written of him, v.* 21. It was *written* in the counsels of God, and *written* in the prophecies of the Old Testament, not one jot or tittle of either of which can *fall to the ground.*

2. They were *pleasing* themselves with the society *one of another,* but Christ casts a damp upon the joy of that, by telling them, *One of you that eateth with me shall betray me, v.* 18. Christ said this, if it might be, to startle the conscience of Judas, and to awaken him to repent of his wickedness, and to draw back (for it was not too late) from the brink of the pit. But for aught that appears, he who was *most concerned in* the warning, was *least concerned at* it. All the rest were affected with it. (1.) They began to be *sorrowful.* As the remembrance of our former falls into sin, so the fear of the like again, doth often much embitter the comfort of our spiritual feasts, and damp our joy. Here were the *bitter herbs,* with which this *passover-feast* was taken. (2.) They began to be *suspicious* of themselves; they said *one by one, Is it I? And another said, Is it I?* They are to be commended for their *charity,* that they were more jealous of themselves than of *one another.* It is the law of charity, to *hope the best* (1 Co. 13:5–7), because we assuredly *know,* therefore we may justly *suspect,* more evil by ourselves than by our brethren. They are also to be commended for their acquiescence in what Christ said; they trusted more to *his words* than to *their own hearts;* and therefore do not say, "I am sure *it is not I,*" but, *"Lord, is it I?* see if there be such a *way of wickedness in us,* such a *root of bitterness,* and discover it to us, that we may pluck up that *root,* and stop up that *way."*

Now, in answer to their enquiry, Christ saith that, [1.] Which would make them easy; "It is not *you,* or *you;* it is this that now *dips with me in the dish;* the adversary and enemy is this wicked Judas." [2.] Which, one would think, should make Judas very *uneasy.* If he go on in his undertaking, it is upon the sword's point, for *woe to that many by whom the Son of man is betrayed;* he is undone, for every undone; his sin will soon *find him out;* and it were *better for him that he had never been born,* and had never had a being than such a miserable one as he must have. It is very probable that Judas encouraged himself in it with *this* thought, that his Master had often said he must be betrayed; "And if it must be done, surely God *will not find fault* with him that doth it, for who *hath resisted his will?"* As that objector argues, Rom. 9:19. But Christ tells him that this will be no shelter or excuse to him; *The Son of man indeed goes; as it is written of him,* as a lamb to the slaughter; but *woe to that man by whom he is betrayed.* God's decree to permit the sins of men, and bring glory to himself out of them, do neither necessitate their sins, nor determine to them, nor will they be any *excuse* of the sin, or *mitigation* of the punishment. Christ was delivered indeed by *the determinate counsel and fore-knowledge of God;* but, notwithstanding that, it is *with wicked hands that he is crucified and slain,* Acts 2:23.

III. The institution of the Lord's supper.

1. It was instituted in the close of a *supper,* when they were sufficiently fed with the *paschal lamb,* to show that in the Lord's supper there is no *bodily repast* intended; to preface it with such a thing, is to revive Moses again. But it is food for *the soul* only, and therefore a very little of that which is for the body, as much as will serve for a *sign,* is enough. It was at the close of the *passover-supper,* which by this was evangelized, and then superseded and set aside. Much of the doctrine and duty of the eucharist is illustrated to us by the law of the passover (Ex. 12); for the Old-Testament institutions, though they do not *bind us,* yet *instruct* us, by the help of a gospel-key to them. And these two ordinances lying here so near together, it may be good to compare them, and observe how much shorter and plainer the institution of the Lord's supper is, than that of the passover was. Christ's yoke is easy in comparison with that of the ceremonial law, and his ordinances are more spiritual.

2. It was instituted by the *example* of Christ himself; not with the ceremony and solemnity of a law, as the ordinance of baptism was, after Christ's resurrection (Mt. 28:19), with,

Be it enacted by the authority aforesaid, by a power given to Christ *in heaven and on earth* (*v.* 18); but by the practice of our Master himself, because intended for those who are already his disciples, and taken into covenant with him: but it has the obligation of the law, and was intended to remain in full force, power, and virtue, till his second coming.

3. It was instituted with *blessing* and *giving of thanks;* the gifts of common providence are to be so received (1 Tim. 4:4, 5), much more than the gifts of special grace. He *blessed* (*v.* 22), and *gave thanks, v.* 23. At his other meals, he was wont to *bless,* and *give thanks* (*ch.* 6:41; 8:7) so remarkably, that he was known by it, Lu. 24:30, 31. And he did the same at this meal.

4. It was instituted to be a *memorial* of his *death;* and therefore he *broke* the bread, to show how it pleased the Lord to *bruise him;* and he called the *wine,* which is the blood of the grape, the *blood of the New Testament.* The death Christ died was a *bloody death,* and frequent mention is made of the *blood,* the *precious* blood, as the pride of our redemption; for the blood is *the life,* and made *atonement for the soul,* Lev. 17:11–14. The pouring out of the blood was the most sensible indication of the *pouring out of his soul,* Isa. 53:12. Blood has a *voice* (Gen. 4:10); and *therefore* blood is so often mentioned, because it was to *speak,* Heb. 12:24. It is called the *blood of the New Testament;* for the covenant of grace became a *testament,* and of force by the death of Christ, the testator, Heb. 9:16. It is said to be *shed for many,* to justify *many* (Isa. 53:11), to bring *many* sons to glory, Heb. 2:10. It was sufficient for *many,* being of infinite value; it has been of use to *many;* we read of a great multitude which no man could number, that had all *washed their robes, and made them white in the blood of the Lamb* (Rev. 7:9–14); and still it is a *fountain opened.* How comfortable is this to poor repenting sinners, that the blood of Christ is *shed for many!* And if for *many,* why not for *me?* If for sinners, sinners of the Gentiles, the chief of sinners, then *why not for me?*

5. It was instituted to be a *ratification* of the covenant made with us in him, and a sign of the conveyance of those benefits to us, which were purchased for us by his death; and therefore he broke the bread *to them* (*v.* 22), and said, *Take, eat* of it: he gave the cup *to them,* and ordered them to *drink of it, v.* 23. Apply the doctrine of Christ crucified to yourselves, and let it be *meat* and *drink* to your souls, strengthening, nourishing, and refreshing, to you, and the support and comfort of your spiritual life.

6. It was instituted with an eye to the happiness of heaven, and to be an earnest and fore-taste of that, and thereby to put our mouths out of taste for all the pleasures and delights of sense (*v.* 25); *I will drink no more of the fruit of the vine,* as it is a bodily refreshment. I have done with it. *No one, having tasted spiritual* delights, *straightway desires* sensitive ones, for he saith, The *spiritual* is better (Lu. 5:39); but *every one* that hath tasted *spiritual* delights, straightway desires *eternal* ones, for he saith, Those are *better still;* and therefore let me *drink no more of the fruit of the vine,* it is dead and flat to those that have been made to *drink* of the *river* of God's pleasures; but, Lord, hasten the day, when I shall *drink* it new and fresh *in the kingdom of God,* where it shall be for ever new, and in perfection.

7. It was closed with a *hymn, v.* 26. Though Christ was in the midst of his enemies, yet he did not, for fear of them, omit this sweet duty of singing psalms. Paul and Silas sang, when the *prisoners heard them.* This was an *evangelical song,* and gospel times are often spoken of in the Old Testament, as times of rejoicing, and praise is expressed by *singing.* This was Christ's *swan-like* song, which he sung just before he entered upon his agony; probably, that which is usually sung, Ps. 113 to 118.

IV. Christ's discourse with his disciples, as they were returning to Bethany by moonlight. When the had *sung the hymn,* presently they *went out.* It was now near bedtime, but our Lord Jesus had his heart so much upon his suffering, that he would not *come into the tabernacle of his house,* norgo *up into his bed,* nor *give sleep to his eyes,* when that work was to be done, Ps. 132:3, 4. The Israelites were forbidden to go out of their houses the night that they ate the passover, for fear of the sword of the destroying angel, Ex. 12:22, 23. But because Christ, the *great shepherd,* was to be *smitten,* he *went out* purposely to expose himself to the sword, as a champion; they *evaded* the destroyer, but Christ *conquered* him, and brought *destructions to a perpetual end.*

1. Christ here foretels that in his sufferings he should be *deserted* by all his disciples; *"You will all be offended because of me, this night.* I know you will (*v.* 27), and what I tell you now, is no other than what the scripture has told you before; *I will smite the shepherd,* and then *the sheep will be scattered."* Christ knew this before, and yet welcomed them at his table; he sees the falls and miscarriages of his disciples, and yet doth not refuse them. Nor should we be discouraged from coming to the Lord's supper, by the fear of relapsing into sin afterward; but, the greater of our danger is, the more need we have to fortify ourselves by the diligent conscientious use of holy ordinances. Christ tells them that they would be *offended in him,* would begin to question whether he were the Messiah or no, when they saw him *overpowered* by his enemies. Hitherto, they had *continued with him in his temptations;* though they had sometimes offended him, yet they had not been *offended in him,* nor turned the back upon him; but now the storm would be so great, that they would all *slip their anchors,* and be in danger of *shipwreck.* Some trials are more particular (as Rev. 2:10, *The devil shall cast some of you into prison*); but others are more general, an *hour of temptation, which shall come upon all the world,* Rev. 3:10. The *smiting* of the shepherd is often the *scattering* of the sheep: magistrates, ministers, masters of families, if these are, as they should be, *shepherds* to those under their charge, when any thing comes amiss to them, the whole flock suffers for it, and is endangered by it.

But Christ encourages them with a promise that they shall rally again, shall return both to their duty and to their comfort (*v.* 28); *"After I am risen,* I will *gather you in* from all the places *wither you are scattered,* Eze. 34:12. I will *go before you into Galilee,* will see our friends, and enjoy one another there."

2. He foretels that he should be *denied* particularly by Peter. When they *went out* to go to the mount of Olives, we may suppose that they dropped Judas (he stole away from them), whereupon the rest began to think *highly* of themselves, that they *stuck* to their Master, when Judas quitted him. But Christ tells them, that though they should be kept by his grace from Judas's apostasy, yet they would have no reason to boast of their constancy. Note, Though God keeps us from being as bad as the worst, yet we may well be ashamed to think that we are not better than we are.

(1.) Peter is confident that he should not *do so ill* as the rest of his disciples (*v.* 29); *Though all should be offended,* all his brethren here present, *yet will not I.* He supposes himself not only stronger than others, but so much stronger, as to be able to receive the shock of a temptation, and bear up against it, *all alone;* to *stand,* though nobody stood *by him.* It is bred in the bone with us, to *think well* of ourselves, and *trust* to *our own hearts.*

(2.) Christ tells him that he will *do worse* than any of them. They will all *desert* him, but he will *deny* him; not once, but *thrice;* and that presently; *"This day, even this night before the cock crow twice,* thou wilt *deny* that ever thou hadst any knowledge of me, or acquaintance with me, as one ashamed and afraid to own me."

(3.) He stands to his promise; *"If I should die with thee, I will not deny thee;* I will adhere to thee, though it cost me my life:" and, no doubt, he thought as he said. Judas said nothing like this, when Christ told him he would betray him. He sinned by contrivance, Peter by surprise; he *devised the wickedness* (Mic. 2:1), Peter was *overtaken in this fault,* Gal. 6:1. It was ill done of Peter, to contradict his Master. If he had said, with fear and trembling, "Lord, give me grace to keep me from denying thee, lead me not into this temptation, deliver me from this evil," it might have been prevented: but they were all thus confident; they who said, *Lord, is it I?* now said, *It shall never be me.* Being acquitted from their fear of betraying Christ, they were now secure. But he that thinks he stands, must learn to take heed lest he fall; and he that *girdeth on the harness,* not boast *as though he had put it off.*

Verses 32–42

Christ is here entering upon his sufferings, and begins with those which were the sorest of all his sufferings, those in his *soul.* Here we have him in his *agony;* this melancholy story we had in Matthew; this *agony* in soul was the *wormwood and the gall* in the *affliction and misery;* and thereby it appeared that no sorrow was *forced upon him,* but that it was what he *freely* admitted.

I. He retired for prayer; *Sit ye here* (saith he to his disciples), while I go a little further, and *pray.* He had lately prayed *with them* (Jn. 17); and now he appoints them to withdraw while he goes to his Father upon an errand peculiar to himself. Note, Our praying with our families will not excuse our neglect of secret worship. When Jacob entered into his agony, he first *sent over all that he had,* and was *left alone,* and then *there wrestled a man with him* (Gen. 32:23, 24), though he had been at prayer before (*v.* 9), it is likely, with his family.

II. Even into that retirement he took with him *Peter, and James, and John* (*v.* 33), three competent witnesses of this part of his humiliation; and though great spirits care not how few know any thing of their agonies, he was not ashamed that they should see. These three had boasted most of their ability and willingness to suffer with him; Peter here, in this chapter, and James and John (*ch.* 10:39); and therefore Christ takes them to stand by, and see what a struggle he had with the *bloody baptism* and the *bitter cup,* to convince them that they knew not what they said. It is fit that they who are most confident, should be *first* tried, that they may be made sensible of their folly and weakness.

III. There he was in a tremendous agitation (*v.* 33); *He began to be sore amazed — ekthambeisthai,* a word not used in Matthew, but very significant; it bespeaks something like that *horror of great darkness,* which *fell upon Abraham* (Gen. 15:12), or, rather, something much worse, and more frightful. The *terrors of God set themselves in array against him,* and he allowed himself the actual and intense contemplation of them. Never was *sorrow* like unto *his* at that time; never any had such experience as he had from eternity of divine favours, and therefore never any had, or could have, such a sense as he had of divine favours. Yet there was not the least disorder or irregularity in this commotion of his spirits; his affections rose not tumultuously, but under direction, and as they were called up, for he had no corrupt nature to mix with them, as we have. If water have a sediment at the bottom, though it may be clear while it stands still, yet, when shaken, it grows muddy; so it is with our affections: but pure water in a clean glass, though ever so much stirred, continues clear; and so it was with Christ. Dr. Lightfoot thinks it very probable that the devil did now appear to our Saviour in a visible shape, in his *own shape* and *proper colour,* to terrify and affright him, and to drive him from his hope in God (which he aimed at in persecuting Job, a type of Christ, to make him *curse God, and die*), and to deter him from the further prosecution of his undertaking; whatever hindered him from that, he looked upon as coming from Satan, Mt. 16:23. When the devil had tempted him in the wilderness, it is said, He departed *from him for a season* (Lu. 4:13), intending another grapple with him, and in another way; finding that he could not by his flatteries *allure* him into sin, he would try by his terrors to *affright* him into it, and so *make void* his design.

IV. He made a sad complaint of this agitation. He said, *My soul is exceeding sorrowful.* 1. He was *made sin for us,* and therefore was thus *sorrowful;* he fully knew the *malignity* of the *sins* he was to *suffer for;* and having the highest degree of love to God, who was *offended* by them, and of love to *man,* who was damaged and endangered by them, now that those were set in order before him, no marvel that *his soul* was *exceeding sorrowful.* Now was he made to *serve with our sins,* and was thus *wearied with our iniquities.* 2. He *was made a curse* for us; the curses of the law were transferred to him as our surety and representative, not as originally *bound with us,* but a *bail to the action.* And when his soul was thus exceeding sorrowful, he did, as it were, yield to them, and lie down under the load, until by his death he had satisfied for sin, and so for ever abolished the curse. He now *tasted death* (as he is said to do, Heb. 2:9), which is not an extenuating expression, as if he did *but* taste it; no, he *drank up* even the dregs of the cup; but it is rather *aggravating;* it did not go down by wholesale, but he *tasted* all the bitterness of it. This was that *fear* which the apostle speaks of (Heb. 5:7), a natural fear of pain and death, which it is natural to human nature to startle at.

Now the consideration of Christ's sufferings in *his soul,* and his *sorrows* for us, should be of use to us,

(1.) To *embitter our sins.* Can we ever entertain a *favourable* or so much as a *slight* thought of sin, when we see what impression sin (though but imputed) made upon the Lord Jesus? Shall that *sit light* upon our souls, which sat *so heavy* upon his? Was Christ in such an agony for our sins, and shall we never be in an agony about them? How should we look upon him whom we have *pressed,* whom we have *pierced,* and *mourn,* and be *in bitterness!* It becomes us to be *exceeding sorrowful* for sin, because Christ was so, and never to *make a mock* at it. If Christ thus suffered for sin, let us *arm ourselves with the same mind.*

(2.) To *sweeten our sorrows;* if our souls be at any time *exceeding sorrowful,* through the afflictions of this present time, let us remember that our Master was so before us, and the *disciple is not greater than his Lord.* Why should we affect to *drive away* sorrow, when Christ for our sakes courted it, and submitted to it, and thereby not only took out the *sting* of it, and made it *tolerable,* but put *virtue* into it, and made it *profitable* (for *by the sadness of the countenance the heart is made better*), nay, and put *sweetness* into it, and made it comfortable. Blessed Paul was *sorrowful,* and yet *always rejoicing.* If we be *exceeding sorrowful,* it is but *unto death;* that will be the period of all our sorrows, if Christ be *ours;* when the *eyes* are closed, all tears are *wiped away* from them.

V. He ordered his disciples to keep with him, not because he needed their help, but because he would have them to *look upon him and receive instruction;* he said to them, *Tarry ye here and watch.* He had said to the other disciples nothing but, Sit ye here (*v.* 32); but these three he bids to tarry *and watch,* as expecting more from them than from the rest.

VI. He addressed himself to God by prayer (*v.* 35); He *fell on the ground, and prayed.* It was but a little before this, that in prayer he *lifted up his eyes* (Jn. 17:1); but here, being in an agony, he *fell upon his face,* accommodating himself to his present humiliation, and teaching us thus to abase ourselves before God; it becomes us to *be low,* when we come into the presence of the *Most High.* 1. As *Man,* he *deprecated* his sufferings, that, *if it were possible, the hour might pass from him* (*v.* 35); "This *short,* but *sharp* affliction, that which I am now *this hour* to enter upon, let man's salvation be, *if possible,* accomplished without it." We have his very words (*v.* 36), *Abba, Father.* The Syriac word is here retained, which Christ used, and which signifies *Father,* to intimate what an emphasis our Lord Jesus, in his *sorrows,* laid upon it, and would have us to lay. It is with an eye to this, that St. Paul retains this word, putting it into the mouths of all that have the *Spirit of adoption;* they are taught to cry, *Abba, Father,* Rom. 8:15; Gal. 4:6. Father, *all things are possible to thee.* Note, Even that which we cannot expect to be done for us, we ought yet to believe that God is *able to do:* and when we submit to his will, and refer ourselves to his wisdom and mercy, it must be with a believing acknowledgment of his power, that *all things are possible to him.* 2. As *Mediator,* he *acquiesced* in the will of God concerning them; *"Nevertheless, not what I will, but what thou wilt.* I know the matter is settled, and cannot be altered, *I must suffer* and die, and I bid it welcome."

VII. He roused his disciples, who were dropped asleep while he was at prayer, *v.* 37, 38. He comes to look after them, since they did not look after him; and he *finds them asleep,* so little affected were they with his sorrows, his complaints, and prayers. This carelessness of theirs was a presage of their further offence in deserting him; and it was an aggravation of it, that he had so lately commended them for *continuing with him in his temptations,* though they had not been without their faults. Was he so willing to make the best of them, and were they so indifferent in approving themselves to him? They had lately promised not to be *offended in him;* what! and yet mind him so little? He particularly upbraided Peter with his drowsiness; *Simon, sleepest thou? Kai sy teknon;* — *"What thou, my son?* Thou that didst so positively promise thou wouldest not deny me, dost thou slight me thus? From thee I expected better things. *Couldest thou not watch one hour?"* He did not require him to watch *all night* with him, only for *one hour.* It aggravates our faintness and short continuance in Christ's service, that he doth not over-task us, nor weary us with it, Isa. 43:23. He puts upon us *no other burthen* than to *hold fast till he comes* (Rev. 2:24, 25); and behold, *he comes quickly,* Rev. 3:11.

As those whom Christ *loves* he *rebukes* when they do amiss, so those whom he *rebukes* he counsels and comforts. 1. It was a very wise and faithful word of advice which Christ here gave to his disciples; *Watch and pray, lest ye enter into temptation, v.* 38. It was bad to *sleep* when Christ was in his agony, but they were entering into further temptation, and if they did not stir up themselves, and fetch in grace and strength from God by prayer, they would *do worse;* and so they did, when they all forsook him, and fled. 2. It was a very

kind and tender excuse that Christ made for them; *"The spirit truly is willing;* I know it is, it is *ready,* it is *forward;* you would willingly *keep awake,* but you cannot." This may be taken as a reason for that exhortation, *"Watch and pray;* because, though *the spirit is willing,* I grant it is (you have sincerely resolved never to be *offended in me*), yet *the flesh is weak,* and if you do not *watch* and *pray,* and use the means of perseverance, you may be overcome, notwithstanding." The consideration of the *weakness* and infirmity of *our flesh* should engage and quicken us to *prayer* and *watchfulness,* when we are entering into temptation.

VIII. He *repeated* his address to his Father (*v.* 39); *He went again, and prayed,* saying, *ton auton logon* — the *same word,* or matter, or business; he spoke to the same purport, and again *the third time.* This teaches us, that *men ought to pray, and not to faint,* Lu. 18:1. Though the answers to our prayers do not come quickly, yet we must renew our requests, and *continue instant in prayer;* for *the vision is for an appointed time, and at the end it shall speak, and not lie,* Hab. 2:3. Paul, when he was *buffeted by a messenger of Satan, besought the Lord thrice,* as Christ did here, before he obtained an answer of peace, 2 Co. 12:7, 8. A little before this, when Christ, in the *trouble of his soul,* prayed, *Father, glorify thy name,* he had an immediate answer by a voice from heaven, *I have both glorified it, and I will glorify it yet again;* but now he must come a second and third time, for the visits of God's grace, in answer to prayer, come sooner or later, according to the pleasure of his will, that we may be kept depending.

IX. He *repeated* his visits to his disciples. Thus he gave a specimen of his continued care for his church on earth, even when it is *half asleep,* and not duly concerned for itself, while he ever lives making intercession with his Father *in heaven.* See how, as became a *Mediator,* he passes and repasses between both. He came the *second time* to his disciples, and *found them asleep again, v.* 40. See how the infirmities of Christ's disciples *return* upon them, notwithstanding their resolutions, and *overpower* them, notwithstanding their resistance; and what clogs those bodies of ours are to our souls, which should make us long for that blessed state in which they shall be no more our encumbrance. This second time he spoke to them as before, but *they wist not what to answer him;* they were ashamed of their drowsiness, and had nothing to say in excuse for it. Or, They were so overpowered with it, that, like men between sleeping and waking, they knew not where they were, or what they said. But, the *third time,* they were bid to *sleep* if they would (*v.* 41); *"Sleep on now, and take your rest.* I have now no more occasion for your watching, you may sleep, if you will, for me." *It is enough;* we had not that word in Matthew. "You have had warning enough to keep awake, and would not take it; and now you shall see what little reason you have to be secure." *Apekei, I discharge you* from any *further attendance;* so some understand it; "Now *the hour is come,* in which I knew you would all forsake me, even take your course;" as he said to Judas, *What thou doest, do quickly.* The *Son of man* is now *betrayed into the hands of sinners,* the chief priests and elders; those *worst* of sinners, because they made a profession of sanctity. "Come, *rise up,* do not lie dozing there. *Let us go* and meet the enemy, for *lo, he that betrayeth me is at hand,* and I must not now think of making an escape." When we see trouble at the door, we are concerned to stir up ourselves to get ready for it.

Verses 43–52

We have here the *seizing* of our Lord Jesus by the officers of the chief priests. This was what his enemies had long aimed at, they had often sent to *take him;* but he had escaped out of their hands, because *his hour was not come,* nor could they now have taken him, had he not freely surrendered himself. He began first to suffer *in his soul,* but afterward suffered in his body, that he might satisfy for sin, which begins in the heart, but afterwards makes the members of the body *instruments of unrighteousness.*

I. Here is a band of rude miscreants employed to *take* our Lord Jesus and make him a prisoner; *a great multitude with swords and staves.* There is no wickedness so black, no villany so horrid, but there may be found among the children of men fit tools to be made use of, that will not scruple to be employed; so miserably depraved and vitiated is mankind. At the head of this rabble is Judas, *one of the twelve,* one of those that had been many years intimately conversant with our Lord Jesus, had prophesied in his name, and in his name

cast out devils, and yet *betrayed* him. It is no new thing for a very fair and plausible profession to end in a shameful and fatal apostasy. *How art thou fallen, O Lucifer!*

II. Men of no less figure than the *chief priests, and the scribes,* and *the elders,* sent them, and set them on work, who pretended to expect the Messiah, and to be ready to welcome him; and yet, when he *is come,* and has given undeniable proofs that it is he that *should come,* because he doth not make court to them, nor countenance and support their pomp and grandeur, because he appears not as a temporal prince, but sets up a spiritual kingdom, and preaches repentance, reformation, and a holy life, and directs men's thoughts, and affections, and aims, to another world, they set themselves against him, and, without giving the credentials he produces an impartial examination, resolve to run him down.

III. Judas betrayed him *with a kiss;* abusing the freedom Christ used to allow his disciples of kissing his cheek at their return when they had been any time absent. He called him, *Master, Master, and kissed him;* he said, *Rabbi, Rabbi,* as if he had been now more respectful to him than ever. It is enough to put one for ever out of conceit with being called of men *Rabbi, Rabbi* (Mt. 23:7), since it was with this compliment that Christ was betrayed. He bid them take him, and *lead him away safely.* Some think that he spoke this *ironically,* knowing that they could not secure him unless he pleased, that this Samson could break their bonds asunder as threads of tow, and make is escape, and then he should get the money, and Christ the honour, and no harm done; and I should think so too, but that Satan was *entered into him,* so that the worst and most malicious intention of this action is not too black to be supposed. Nay, he had often heard his Master say, that, being *betrayed,* he should be *crucified,* and had no reason to think otherwise.

IV. They arrested him, and made him their prisoner (*v.* 46); *They laid their hands on him,* rude and violent hands, and *took him* into custody; triumphing, it is likely, that they had done that which has been often before attempted in vain.

V. Peter laid about him in defence of his Master, and wounded one of the assailants, being for the present mindful of his promise, to venture his life with his Master. He was *one of them that stood by,* of them that *were with him* (so the word signifies), of *those three* disciples that were *with him* in the garden; he *drew a sword,* and aimed, it is likely, to cut off the head, but missed his blow, and only *cut off the ear,* of a servant of the high priest, *v.* 47. It is easier to *fight* for Christ, than to *die* for him; but Christ's good soldiers overcome, not by taking other people's lives, but by laying down their own, Rev. 12:11.

VI. Christ argues with them that had seized him, and shows them the absurdity of their proceedings against him. 1. That they came out *against him,* as against a *thief,* whereas he was *innocent* of any crime; he *taught daily in the temple,* and if he had any wicked design, there it would some time or other have been discovered; nay, these officers of the *chief priests,* being *retainers* to the temple, may be supposed to have heard his sermons there (I was *with you* in the temple); and had he not taught them excellent doctrine, even his enemies themselves being judges? Were not *all the words of his mouth in righteousness?* Was there any thing *froward or perverse* in them? Prov. 8:8. By his fruits he was known to be a good tree; why then did they come out against him *as a thief?* 2. That they came to take him thus *privately,* whereas he was neither *ashamed* nor *afraid* to appear *publicly* in the temple. He was none of those *evil-doers* that *hate the light,* neither come to the light, Jn. 3:20. If their masters had any thing to say to him, they might meet him any day in the temple, where he was ready to answer all challenges, all charges; and there they might do as they pleased with him, for the priests had the custody of the temple, and the command of the guards about it: but to come upon him thus at midnight, and in the place of his retirement, was base and cowardly. This was to do as David's enemy, that *sat in the lurking places of the villages, to murder the innocent,* Ps. 10:8. But this was not all. 3. They came *with swords and staves,* as if he had been in arms against the government, and must have the *posse comitatus* raised to reduce him. There was no occasion for those weapons; but they made this ado, (1.) To secure themselves from the rage of some; they came armed, because they *feared the people;* but thus *were they in great fear, where no fear was,* Ps. 53:5. (2.) To expose him to the rage of others. By coming *with swords and staves to take him,* they represented him to the people (who are apt to take impressions this way) as a dangerous turbulent man, and so endeavored to incense them against him, and make them cry out, *Crucify him, crucify him,* having no other way to gain their point.

VII. He reconciled himself to all this injurious, ignominious treatment, by referring himself to the Old-Testament predictions of the Messiah. I am hardly used, *but* I submit, for *the scriptures must be fulfilled, v.* 49. 1. See here what a regard Christ had to the *scriptures;* he would bear any thing rather than that the least jot or tittle of the word of God should fall to the ground; and as he had an eye to them in his sufferings, so he has in his glory; for what is Christ doing in the government of the world, but *fulfilling the scriptures?* 2. See what use we are to make of the Old Testament; we must search for Christ, the true *treasure hid in that field:* as the history of the New Testament expounds the prophecies of Old, so the prophecies of the Old Testament illustrate the history of the New.

VIII. All Christ's disciples, hereupon, deserted him (*v.* 50); *They all forsook him, and fled.* They were very confident that they should adhere to him; but even good men know not what they will do, till they are tried. If it was such a comfort to him as he had lately intimated, that they had hitherto *continued with him* in his lesser trials (Lu. 22:28), we may well imagine what a grief it was to him, that they deserted him now in the greatest, when they might have done him some service — when he was abused, to protect him, and when accused, to witness for him. Let not those that suffer for Christ, think it strange, if they be thus deserted, and if all the herd shun the wounded deer; they are not better than their Master, nor can expect to be better used either by their enemies or by their friends. When St. Paul was in peril, none *stood by him,* but *all men forsook him,* 2 Tim. 4:16.

IX. The noise disturbed the neighbourhood, and some of the neighbours were brought into danger by the riot, vi. 51, 52. This passage of story we have not in any other of the evangelists. Here is an account of a *certain young man,* who, as it should seem, was no disciple of Christ, nor, as some have imagined, a servant of the house wherein Christ had eaten the passover, who *followed him* to see what would become of him (as the *sons of the prophets,* when they understood that Elijah was to be *taken up,* went to *view afar off,* 2 Ki. 2:7), but some young man that lived near the garden, perhaps in the house to which the garden belonged. Now observe concerning him,

1. How he was *frightened out of his bed,* to be a *spectator* of Christ's sufferings. Such a *multitude,* so armed, and coming with so much fury, and in the dead of night, and in a quiet village, could not but produce a great stir; this alarmed our *young man,* who perhaps thought they was some tumult or rising in the city, some *uproar among the people,* and had the curiosity to go, and see what the matter was, and was in such haste to inform himself, that he could not stay to dress himself, but threw a sheet about him, as if he would appear like a walking ghost, in grave clothes, to frighten those who had frightened him, and ran among the thickest of them with this question, *What is to do here?* Being told, he had a mind to see the issue, having, no doubt, heard much of the fame of this Jesus; and therefore, when all his disciples had quitted him, he continued to *follow him,* desirous to *hear* what he would say, and *see* what he would do. Some think that his having no other garment than this *linen cloth* upon his naked body, intimates that he was one of those Jews who made a great profession of piety that their neighbours, in token of which, among other instances of austerity and mortification of the body, they used no clothes but one linen garment, which, though contrived to be modest enough, was thin and cold. But I rather think that this was not his constant wear.

2. See how he was *frightened into his bed* again, when he was in danger of being made a *sharer* in Christ's sufferings. His own disciples had run away from him; but this young man, having no concern for him, thought he might securely attend him, especially being so far from being armed, that he was not so much as clothed; but *the young men,* the Roman soldiers, who were called to assist, *laid hold of him,* for all was fish that came to their net. Perhaps they were now vexed at themselves, that they had suffered the disciples to *run away,* and they being got out of their reach they resolved to seize the first they could *lay their hands on;* though this young man was perhaps one of the *strictest sect* of the Jewish church, yet the Roman soldiers made no conscience of abusing him upon this occasion. Finding himself in danger, he *left the linen cloth* by which they had *caught hold of him,* and *fled away naked.* This passage is recorded to show what a barbarous crew this was, that was sent to seize Christ, and what a narrow escape the disciples had of falling into their hands, out of which nothing could have kept them but their Master's care of them; *If ye seek me, let these go their way,* Jn. 18:8. It also intimates that there is *no hold* of those who are led by curiosity only, and not by faith and conscience, to follow Christ.

Verses 53–65

We have here Christ's arraignment, trial, conviction, and condemnation, in the *ecclesiastical* court, before the great sanhedrim, of which the *high priest* was president, or judge of the court; the same Caiaphas that had lately adjudged it expedient he should be put to death, guilty or not guilty (Jn. 11:50), and who therefore might justly be excepted against as partial.

I. Christ is hurried away to his *house,* his *palace* it is called, such state did he live in. And there, though, in the dead of the night, *all the chief priests, and elders, and scribes,* that were in the secret, were *assembled,* ready to receive the prey; so sure were they of it.

II. *Peter followed* at a distance, such a degree of cowardice was his late courage dwindled into, *v.* 54. But when he came to the high priest's palace, he *sneakingly* went, and *sat with the servants,* that he might not be suspected to belong to Christ. The high priest's fire side was no proper place, nor his servants proper company, for Peter, but it was his *entrance into a temptation.*

III. Great diligence was used to procure, for love or money, false witnesses against Christ. They had seized him as a malefactor, and now they had him they had no indictment to prefer against him, no crime to lay to his charge, but they *sought for witnesses against him;* pumped some with ensnaring questions, offered bribes to others, if they *would accuse him,* and endeavored to frighten others, if they *would not, v.* 55, 56. The chief priests and elders were by the law entrusted with the prosecuting and punishing of *false witnesses* (Deu. 19:16, 17); yet those were now ringleaders in a crime that tends to overthrow of all justice. It is time to cry, *Help, Lord,* when the physicians of a land are its troublers, and those that should be the conservators of peace and equity, are the corrupters of both.

IV. He was at length charged with words spoken some years ago, which, as they were represented, seemed to threaten *the temple,* which they had made no better than an idol of (*v.* 57, 58); but the witnesses to this matter did not agree (*v.* 59), for one swore that he said, *I am able to destroy the temple of God, and to build it in three days* (so it is in Matthew); the other swore that he said, *I will destroy this temple, that is made with hands,* and *within three days, I will build* not it, but *another made without hands;* now these two differ much from each other; *oude isē ēn hē martyria — their testimony was not sufficient,* nor equal to the charge of a capital crime; so Dr. Hammond: they did not accuse him of that upon which a *sentence of death* might be founded, no not by the utmost stretch of their law.

V. He was urged to be his own accuser (*v.* 60); The *high priest stood up* in a heat, and said, *Answerest thou nothing?* This he said under pretence of justice and fair dealing, but really with a design to ensnare him, that they might *accuse him,* Lu. 11:53, 54; 20:20. We may well imagine with what an air of haughtiness and disdain this proud high priest brought our Lord Jesus to this question; "Come you, the prisoner at the bar, you hear what is sworn against you; what have you now to say for yourself?" Pleased to think that *he* seemed silent, who had so often silenced those that picked quarrels with him. Still Christ *answered nothing,* that he might set us an example, 1. Of *patience* under calumnies and false accusations; when we are *reviled,* let us not *revile again,* 1 Pt. 2:23. And, 2. Of *prudence,* when a man shall be made an *offender for a word* (Isa. 29:21), and our defence made our offence; it is an evil time indeed when the prudent shall *keep silence* (lest they make bad worse), *and commit their cause to him that judgeth righteously.* But,

VI. When he was asked *whether he was the Christ,* he confessed, and denied not, that *he was, v.* 61, 62. He asked, *Art thou the Son of the Blessed?* that is the Son of *God?* for, as Dr. Hammond observes, the Jews, when they named *God,* generally added, *blessed for ever;* and thence *the Blessed* is the title of *God,* a peculiar title, and applied to Christ, Rom. 9:5. And for the proof of his being the *Son of God,* he binds them over to his second coming; *"Ye shall see the Son of man sitting on the right hand of power;* that *Son of man* that now appears so mean and despicable, whom ye *see* and trample upon (Isa. 53:2, 3), you shall shortly see and *tremble before."* Now, one would think that such a word as this which our Lord Jesus seems to have spoken with a grandeur and majesty not agreeable to his present appearance (for through the thickest cloud of his humiliation some rays of glory were still darted forth), should have startled the court, and at least, in the opinion of some of them, should have amounted to a *demurrer,* or *arrest of judgment,* and that they should have stayed process till they had considered further of it; when Paul at the bar reasoned of the *judgment to come,* the judge *trembled,* and adjourned the trial, Acts 24:25. But these chief priests were so miserably blinded with malice and rage, that, like the horse rushing into the battle, they *mocked at fear, and were not affrighted,* neither *believed they that it was the sound of the trumpet,* Job 39:22, 24. And see Job 15:25, 26.

VII. The high priest, upon this confession of his, convicted him as a *blasphemer* (*v.* 63); He *rent his clothes — chitōnas autou.* Some think the word signifies his pontifical vestments, which, for the greater state, he had put on, though in the night, upon this occasion. As before, in his enmity to Christ, he said he knew not what (Jn. 11:51, 52), so now he did he knew not what. If Saul's rending Samuel's mantle was made to signify the rending of the kingdom from him (1 Sa. 15:27, 28), much more did Caiaphas's rending his own clothes signify the rending of the priesthood from him, as the rending of the veil, at Christ's death, signified the throwing of all open. Christ's clothes, even when he was crucified, were kept entire, and not rent: for when the Levitical priesthood was rent in pieces and done away, *This Man, because he continues ever, has an unchangeable priesthood.*

VIII. They agreed that he was a blasphemer, and, as such, was guilty of a capital crime, *v.* 64. The question *seemed* to be put fairly, *What think ye?* But it was really *prejudged,* for the high priest had said, *Ye have heard the blasphemy;* he gave judgment first, who, as president of the court, ought to have voted last. So they *all condemned him* to be *guilty of death;* what friends he had in the great sanhedrim, did not appear, it is probable that they had not notice.

IX. They set themselves to abuse him, and, as the Philistines with Samson, to make sport with him, *v.* 65. It should seem that some of the priests themselves that had condemned him, so far forgot the dignity, as well as duty, of their place, and the gravity which became them, that they helped their servants in playing the fool with a condemned prisoner. This they made their diversion, while they *waited for the morning,* to complete their villany. That *night of observations* (as the passover-night was called) they *made a merry night of.* If they did not think it below them to abuse Christ, shall we think any thing below us, by which we may do him honour?

Verses 66–72

We have here the story of Peter's denying Christ.

1. It began in *keeping at a distance* from him. Peter had followed *afar off* (*v.* 54), and now was *beneath in the palace,* at the lower end of the hall. Those that are *shy* of Christ, are in a fair way to *deny* him, that are shy of attending on holy ordinances, shy of the communion of the faithful, and loth to be seen on the side of despised godliness.

2. It was occasioned by his associating with the high priest's servants, and sitting among them. They that think it dangerous to be in company with Christ's disciples, because thence they may be drawn in to *suffer for him,* will find it much more dangerous to be in company with his enemies, because there they may be drawn in to *sin against him.*

3. The temptation was, his being charged as a disciple of Christ; *Thou also wert with Jesus of Nazareth, v.* 67. *This is one of them* (*v.* 69), *for thou art a Galilean,* one may know that by thy speaking broad, *v.* 70. It doth not appear that he was *challenged* upon it, or in danger of being *prosecuted* as a criminal for it, but only *bantered* upon it, and in danger of being ridiculed as a fool for it. While the chief priests were abusing the Master, the servants were abusing the disciples. Sometimes the cause of Christ seems to fall so much on the losing side, that every body has a stone to throw at it, and even the *abjects gather themselves together against* it. When Job was on the dunghill, he was had in derision of those that

were the *children of base men,* Job 30:8. Yet, all things considered, the temptation could not be called *formidable;* it was only a *maid* that casually cast her eye upon him, and, for aught that appears, without design of giving him any trouble, said, *Thou art one of them,* to which he needed not to have made any reply, or might have said, "And if I be, I hope that is no treason."

4. The sin was very great; he *denied Christ before men,* at a time when he ought to have confessed and owned him, and to have appeared in court a witness for him. Christ had often given notice to his disciples of his own sufferings; yet, when they came, they were to Peter as great a surprise and terror as if he had never heard of them before. He had often told them that they must *suffer* for him, must *take up their cross,* and follow him; and yet Peter is so terribly afraid of suffering, upon the very first alarm of it, that he will lie and swear, and do any thing, to avoid it. When Christ was admired and flocked after, he could readily own him; but now that he is deserted, and despised, and run down, he is ashamed of him, and will own no relation to him.

5. His repentance was very speedy. He repeated his denial thrice, and the third was worst of all, for then he *cursed* and *swore,* to confirm his denial; and that the third blow, which, one would think, should have *stunned him,* and knocked him down, *startled him,* and roused him up. Then the *cock crew* the second time, which put him in mind of his Master's words, the warning he had given him, with that particular circumstance of the *cock crowing twice;* by recollecting that, he was made sensible of his sin and the aggravations of it; and when he thought thereon, he wept. Some observe that this evangelist, who wrote, as some have thought, by St. Peter's direction, speaks as fully of Peter's sin as any of them, but more briefly of his *sorrow,* which Peter, in modesty, would not have to be magnified, and because he thought he could never sorrow enough for a great a sin. His repentance here is thus expressed, *epibalōv eklaie,* where something must be supplied. He *added to weep,* so some; making it a Hebraism; he wept, and the more he thought of it, the more he wept; he continued weeping; he *flung out,* and wept; *burst out* into tears; *threw himself down,* and wept; he *covered his face,* and wept, so some; cast his garment about his head, that he might not be seen to weep; he *cast his eyes* upon his Master, who turned, and looked upon him; so Dr. Hammond supplies it, and it is a probable conjecture. Or, as we understand it, *fixing his mind upon it,* he wept. It is not a transient thought of that which is humbling, that will suffice, but we must dwell upon it. Or, what if this word should mean his *laying a load* upon himself, throwing a confusion into his own face? he did as the *publican* that smote his breast, in sorrow for sin; and this amounts to his weeping bitterly.

CHAPTER 15

What we read of the sufferings of Christ, in the foregoing chapter, was but the prologue or introduction; here we have the completing of them. We left him condemned by the chief priests; but they could only show their teeth, they could not bite. Here we have him, I. Arraigned and accused before Pilate the Roman governor (*v.* 1–5). II. Cried out against by the common people, at the instigation of the priests (*v.* 6–14). III. Condemned to be crucified immediately (*v.* 15). IV. Bantered and abused, as a mock-king, by the Roman soldiers (*v.* 16–19). V. Led out to the place of execution with all possible ignominy and disgrace (*v.* 20–24). VI. Nailed to the cross between two thieves (*v.* 25–28). VII. Reviled and abused by all that passed by (*v.* 29–32). VIII. Forsaken for a time by his father (*v.* 33–36). IX. Dying, and rending the veil (*v.* 37, 38). X. Attested and witnessed to by the centurion and others (*v.* 39–41). XI. Buried in the sepulchre of Joseph of Arimathea (*v.* 42–47).

Verses 1–14

Here we have; I. A *consultation* held by the great Sanhedrim for the effectual prosecution of our Lord Jesus. They met *early in the morning* about it, and went into a grand committee, to find out *ways and means* to get him put to death; they lost no time, but followed their blow in good earnest, lest there should be an *uproar among the people.* The unwearied industry of wicked people in doing that which is evil, should shame us for our backwardness and slothfulness in that which is good. They that *war* against Christ and thy soul, are up early; *How long then wilt thou sleep, O sluggard?*

II. The delivering of him up a prisoner to Pilate; they *bound him.* He was to be the great sacrifice, and sacrifices must be bound with cords, Ps. 118:27. Christ was bound, to make bonds easy to us, and enable us, as Paul and Silas, to sing in bonds. It is good for us often to *remember the bonds* of the Lord Jesus, as bound with him who was *bound for us.* They led him through the streets of Jerusalem, to expose *him* to contempt, who, while he taught in the temple, but a day or two before, was had in veneration; and we may well imagine how miserably he looked after such a night's usage as he had had; so buffeted, spit upon, and abused. Their delivering him to the Roman power was a type of ruin of their church, which hereby they merited, and brought upon themselves; it signified that the promise, the covenant, and the oracles, of God, and the visible state church, which were the glory of Israel, and had been so long in their possession, should now be delivered up to the Gentiles. By delivering up the *king* they do, in effect, deliver up the *kingdom of God,* which is therefore, as it were, by their own consent, taken from them, and given to another nation. If they had delivered up Christ, to gratify the desires of the Romans, or to satisfy and jealousies of theirs concerning him, it had been another matter; but they voluntarily betrayed him that was *Israel's crown,* to them that were *Israel's yoke.*

III. The examining of him by Pilate upon interrogatories (*v.* 2); *"Art thou the king of the Jews?* Dost thou pretend to be so, to be that Messiah whom the Jews expect as a temporal prince?" — "Yea," saith Christ, "it is as *thou sayest,* I am that Messiah, but not such a one as they expect." He is the king that rules and protects his Israel according to the spirit, who are Jews inwardly by the circumcision of the spirit, and the king that will restrain and punish the carnal Jews, who continue in unbelief.

IV. The articles of impeachment exhibited against him, and his silence under the charge and accusation. The chief priests forgot the dignity of their place, when they turned informers, and did in person *accuse Christ of many things* (*v.* 3), and witness against him, *v.* 4. Many of the Old-Testament prophets charge the priests of their times with great wickedness, in which *well did they prophesy* of these priests; see Eze. 22:26; Hos. 5:1; 6:9; Mic. 3:11; Zep. 3:4; Mal. 1:6; 2:8. The destruction of Jerusalem by the Chaldeans is said to be for the *iniquity of the priests that shed the blood of the just,* Lam. 4:13. Note, Wicked priests are generally the worst of men. The better any thing is, the worse it is when it is corrupted. Lay persecutors have been generally found more compassionate than ecclesiastics. These priests were very eager and noisy in their accusation; but Christ *answered nothing, v.* 3. When Pilate urged him to clear himself, and was desirous he should (*v.* 4), yet still he stood mute (*v.* 5), he *answered nothing,* which Pilate thought very strange. He gave Pilate a direct answer (*v.* 2), but would not answer the prosecutors and witnesses, because the things they alleged, were notoriously false, and he knew Pilate himself was convinced they were so. Note, As Christ *spoke* to admiration, so he *kept silence* to admiration.

V. The proposal Pilate made to the people, to have Jesus released to them, since it was the custom of the feast to grace the solemnity with the release of one prisoner. The people expected and demanded that he should do *as he had ever done to them* (*v.* 8); it was not an ill usage, but they would have it kept up. Now Pilate perceived that the chief priests delivered up Jesus *for envy,* because he had got such a reputation among the people as eclipsed theirs, *v.* 10. It was easy to see, comparing the eagerness of the prosecutors with the slenderness of the proofs, that it was not his *guilt,* but his *goodness,* not any thing *mischievous* or *scandalous,* but something *meritorious* and *glorious,* that they were provoked at. And therefore, hearing how much he was the darling of the crowd, he thought that he might safely appeal from the priests to the people, and that they would be proud of rescuing him out of the priests' hands; and he proposed an expedient for their doing it without danger of an *uproar;* let them demand him to be *released,* and Pilate will be ready to do it, and stop the mouths of the priests with this — that the people insisted upon his release. There was indeed another prisoner, *one Barabbas,* that had an interest, and would have some votes; but he questioned not but Jesus would out-poll him.

VI. The unanimous outrageous clamours of the people have *Christ put to death,* and particularly to have him *crucified.* It was a great surprise to Pilate, when he found the people so much under the influence of the priests, that they all agreed to desire that Barabbas might be *released, v.* 11. Pilate opposed it all he could; *"What will ye that I shall do to him whom ye call the King of the Jews?* Would not ye then have him released too?" *v.* 12. No, say they, *Crucify him.* The priests having put that in their mouths, the insist upon it; when Pilate objected, *Why, what evil has he done?* (a very material question in such a case), they did not pretend to answer it, but *cried out more exceedingly,* as they were more and more instigated and irritated by the priests, *Crucify him, crucify him.* Now the priests, who were very busy dispersing themselves and their creatures among the mob, to keep up the cry, promised themselves that it would influence Pilate two ways to condemn him. 1. It might incline him to believe Christ *guilty,* when there was so general an out-cry against him. "Surely," might Pilate think, "he must needs be a bad man, whom all the world is weary of." He would now conclude that he had been *misinformed,* when he was told what an interest he had in the people, and that the matter was not so. But the priest had hurried on the prosecution with so much expedition, that we may suppose that they who were Christ's friends, and would have opposed this cry, were at the other end of the town, and knew nothing of the matter. Note, It has been the common artifice of Satan, to put Christ and his religion into an ill name, and so to run them down. When once this sect, as they called it, comes to be *every where spoken against,* though *without cause,* then that is looked upon as *cause enough* to condemn it. But let us *judge* of persons and things by their merits, and the standard of God's word, and not prejudge by common fame and the cry of the country. 2. It might induce him to condemn Christ, to *please* the people, and indeed for *fear of displeasing* them. Though he was not so *weak* as to be governed by their opinion, to believe him guilty, yet he was so *wicked* as to be swayed by their outrage, to condemn him, though he believed him innocent; induced thereunto by reasons of state, and the wisdom of the world. Our Lord Jesus dying as a *sacrifice* for the *sins of many,* he fell a sacrifice to the *rage of many.*

Verses 15–21

Here, I. Pilate, to gratify the Jews' malice, delivers Christ to be *crucified, v.* 15. *Willing to content the people,* to *do enough* for them (so the word is), and make them easy, that he might keep them quiet, he *released Barabbas unto them,* who was the scandal and plague of their nation, and *delivered Jesus* to be *crucified,* who was the glory and blessing of their nation. Though he *had scourged him* before, hoping that would *content* them, and then not designing to crucify him, yet he went on to that; for no wonder that he who could persuade himself to *chastise* one that was innocent (Lu. 23:16), could by degrees persuade himself to *crucify* him.

Christ was *crucified,* for that was, 1. A *bloody* death, and *without blood no remission,* Heb. 9:22. The blood is *the life* (Gen. 9:4); it is the *vehicle* of the *animal* spirits, which *connect* the soul and body, so that the exhausting of the blood is the exhausting of the life. Christ was to lay down *his life* for us, and therefore *shed his blood.* Blood *made atonement for the soul* (Lev. 17:11), and therefore in every sacrifice of propitiation special order was given for the *pouring out* of the blood, and the *sprinkling* of that before the Lord. Now, that Christ might answer all these types, he *shed his blood.* 2. It was a *painful* death; the pains were exquisite and acute, for death made its assaults upon the vitals by the exterior parts, which are *quickest of sense.* Christ died, so as that he might *feel himself die,* because he was to be both the priest and the sacrifice; so that he might be *active* in dying; because he was to *make his soul an offering* for sin. Tully calls crucifixion, *Teterrimum supplicium — A most tremendous punishment:* Christ would meet death in its greatest terror, and so conquer it. 3. It was a *shameful* death, the death of slaves, and the vilest malefactors; so it was accounted among the Romans. The *cross* and the *shame* are put together. God having been injured in his honour by the sin of man, it is *in his honour* that Christ makes him *satisfaction,* not only by denying himself in, and divesting himself of, the honours due to his divine nature, for a time, but by submitting the greatest reproach and ignominy the human nature was capable of being loaded with. Yet this was not the worst. 4. It was a *cursed* death; thus it was branded by the Jewish law (Deu. 21:23); *He that is hanged, is accursed of God,* is under a particular mark of God's displeasure. It was the death that Saul's sons were put to, when the guilt of their father' bloody house was to be expiated, 2 Sa. 21:6. Haman and his sons were *hanged,* Esth. 7:10; 9:13. We do not read any of the prophets of the Old Testament that were *hanged;* but now that Christ has submitted to be *hanged upon a tree,* the reproach and curse of that kind of death are quite rolled away, so that it ought to be any hindrance to the comfort of those who die either innocently or penitently, nor any diminution from, but rather an addition to, the glory of those who die martyrs for Christ, to be as he was, hanged upon a tree.

II. Pilate, to gratify the gay humour of the Roman soldiers, delivered him to them, to be abused and spitefully treated, while they were preparing for the execution. They called together *the whole regiment* that was then in waiting, and they went into an inner hall, where they ignominiously abused our Lord Jesus, as a king, just as in the high priest's hall his servants had ignominiously abused him as a Prophet and Saviour. 1. Do kings wear robes of purple or scarlet? They *clothed him with purple.* This abuse done to Christ in his apparel should be an intimation to Christians, not to make the putting on of apparel *their adorning,* 1 Pt. 3:4. Shall a purple or scarlet robe be matter of pride to a Christian, which was matter of reproach and shame to Christ. 2. Do kings wear *crowns?* They *platted a crown of thorns,* and *put it on his head.* A crown of straw, or rushes, would have been banter enough; but this was pain also. He wore the crown of thorns which we had deserved, that we might wear the crown of glory which he merited. Let us be *taught* by these *thorns,* as Gideon taught the men of Succoth, to hate sin, and be uneasy under it, and to be in love with Jesus Christ, who is here a lily among thorns. If we be at any time afflicted with a *thorn in the flesh,* let it be our comfort, that our high priest is touched with the feelings of our infirmities, having himself known what *thorns in the flesh* meant. 3. Are kings attended with the acclamations of their subjects, *O king, live for ever?* That also is mimicked; they saluted him with *"Hail, King of the Jews;* such a prince, and such a people, even good enough for one another." 4. Kings have *sceptres* put into their hand, marks of dominion, as the crown is of dignity; to imitate this, they put a *reed in his right hand.* Those that despise the authority of Jesus Christ, as not to be observed and obeyed, who regard not either the precepts of his word, or the threatenings of his wrath, do, in effect, *put a reed in his hand;* nay, and, as these here, *smite him on the head* with it, such is the indignity they do him. 5. Subjects, when they swear allegiance, were wont to *kiss* their sovereign; and this they offered to do, but, instead of that, *spit upon him.* 6. Kings used to be addressed upon the *knee;* and this also they brought into the jest, they *bowed the knee, and worshipped him;* this they did in scorn, to make themselves and one another laugh. We were by sin become liable to *everlasting shame and contempt,* to deliver us from which, our Lord Jesus submitted to this shame and contempt for us. He was thus mocked, not in *his own clothes,* but in another's, to signify that he suffered not for his own sin; the crime was ours, the shame his. Those who pretend subjection to Christ, but at the same time give themselves up to the service of the world and the flesh, do, in effect, the same that they did, who bowed the knee to him in mockery, and abused him with, *Hail, king of the Jews,* when they said, *We have no king but Caesar.* Those that bow the knee to Christ, but do not bow the soul, that *draw nigh to him with their mouths,* and *honour him with their lips,* but *their hearts are far from him,* put the same affront upon him that these here did.

III. The soldiers, at the hour appointed, led him away from Pilate's judgment-hall to the place of execution (*v.* 20), as a sheep to the slaughter; he was *led forth with the workers of iniquity,* though he did no sin. But lest his death, under the load of his cross, which he was to carry, should prevent the further cruelties they intended, they compelled one Simon of Cyrene to carry his cross for him. He *passed by, coming out of the country* or out of the *fields,* not thinking of any such matter. Note, We must not think it strange, if crosses come upon us suddenly, and we be surprised by them. The cross was a very troublesome unwieldy load: but he that carried it a few minutes, had the honour to have his name upon the record in the book of God, though otherwise an obscure person; so that, wherever this gospel is preached; so that, wherever this gospel is preached, there shall this be told for a memorial to him: in like manner, though *no affliction,* no cross, *for the present, be joyous, but grievous,* yet afterward it yields a crown of glory to them that are exercised thereby.

Verses 22–32

We have here the *crucifixion* of our Lord Jesus.

I. The *place where* he was crucified; it was called *Golgotha — the place of a scull:* some think, because of the heads of malefactors that were there cut off: it was the common place of execution, as Tyburn, for he was in all respects numbered with the transgressors. I know not how to give any credit to it, but divers of the ancients mention it as a current tradition, that in this place our first father Adam was buried, and they think it highly congruous that there Christ should be crucified; for as in Adam all die, so in Christ shall all be made alive. Tertullian, Origen, Chrysostom, and Epiphanius (great names), take notice of it; nay, Cyprian adds, *Creditur àpiis — Many good people believe* that the blood of Christ crucified did trickle down upon the scull of Adam, who was buried in the same place. Something more credible is the tradition, that this mount Calvary was *that mountain in the land of Moriah* (and in the land of Moriah it certainly was, for so the country about Jerusalem was called), on which Isaac was to be offered; and the ram was offered instead of him; and then Abraham had an eye to *this day* of Christ, when he called the place *Jehovah-jireh — The Lord will provide,* expecting that so it would be seen in the *mount of the Lord.*

II. The *time when* he was crucified; it was the *third hour, v.* 25. He was brought before Pilate about the sixth hour (Jn. 19:14), according to the Roman way of reckoning, which John uses, with which ours at this day agrees, that is at six o'clock in the morning; and then, at the *third hour,* according to the Jews' way of reckoning, that is, about nine of the clock in the morning, or soon after, they nailed him to the cross. Dr. Lightfoot thinks the *third hour* is here mentioned, to intimate an aggravation of the wickedness of the priests, they were here prosecuting Christ to the death, though it was after the *third hour,* when they ought to have been attending the service of the temple, and offering the peace-offerings; it being the first day of the *feast of unleavened bread,* when there was to be a *holy convocation.* At that very time, when they should have been, according to the duty of their place, presiding in the public devotions, were they here venting their malice against the Lord Jesus; yet these were the men that seemed so zealous for the temple, and condemned Christ for speaking against it. Note, There are many who pretend to be *for the church,* who yet care not how seldom they *go to church.*

III. The indignities that were done him, when he was nailed to the cross; as if that had not been ignominious enough, they added several things to the ignominy of it.

1. It being the custom to give *wine* to persons that were to be *put to death,* they *mingled* his with *myrrh,* which was *bitter,* and made it *nauseous;* he *tasted* it, but would not drink it; was willing to admit the bitterness of it, but not the benefit of it.

2. The garments of those that were crucified, being, as with us, the executioners' fee, the soldiers *cast lots* upon his garments (*v.* 24), threw dice (as our soldiers do upon a drum-head), for them: so making themselves merry with his misery, and sitting at their sport while he was hanging in pain.

3. They set up a superscription over his head, by which they intended to reproach him, but really did him both justice and honour, *The king of the Jews, v.* 26. Here was no crime alleged, but his sovereignty owned. Perhaps Pilate meant to cast disgrace upon Christ as a baffled king, or upon the Jews, who by their importunity had forced him, against his conscience, to condemn Christ, as a people that deserved no better a king than he seemed to be: however, God intended it to be the proclaiming even of Christ upon the cross, the *king of Israel;* though Pilate know not what he wrote, any more than Caiaphas what he said, Jn. 11:51. Christ crucified is king of his church, his spiritual Israel; and even then when he hung on the cross, he was like a king, *conquering* his and his people's enemies, and *triumphing* over them, Col. 2:15. Now he was writing his laws in his own blood, and preparing his favours for his subjects. Whenever we look unto Christ crucified, we must remember the inscription over his head, that he is a king, and we must give up ourselves to be his subjects, as Israelites indeed.

4. They crucified *two thieves* with him, *one on his right hand, the other on his left,* and him in the midst as the worst of the three (*v.* 27); so great a degree of dishonour did they hereby intend him. And, no doubt, it gave him *disturbance* too. Some that have been imprisoned in the common gaols, for the testimony of Jesus, have complained of the company of cursing, swearing prisoners, more than any other of the grievances of their prison. Now, in the midst of such our Lord Jesus was *crucified;* while he lived he had, and there was occasion, *associated* with sinners, to do them good; and now when he died, he was for the same purpose joined with them, for he *came into the world,* and went out of it, to *save sinners,* even the chief. But this evangelist takes particular notice of the fulfilling of the scriptures in it, *v.* 28. In that famous prediction of Christ's sufferings (Isa. 53:12), it was foretold that he should be numbered with the *transgressors,* because he was made *sin for us.*

5. The spectators, that is, the generality of them, instead of condoling with him in his misery, added to it by insulting over him. Surely never was such an instance of barbarous inhumanity toward the vilest malefactor: but thus the devil showed the utmost rage against him, and thus he submitted to the greatest dishonours that could be done him.

(1.) Even they that *passed by,* that were no way concerned, *railed on him, v.* 29. If their hearts were so hardened, that their compassions were not moved with such a spectacle, yet they should have thought it enough to have their curiosity gratified; but that will not serve: as if they were not only divested of all humanity, but were devils in human shape, they taunted him, and expressed themselves with the utmost detestation of him, and indignation at him, and shot thick at him their arrows, even *bitter words.* The chief priests, no doubt, put these sarcasms into their mouths, *Thou that destroyest the temple, and buildest it in three days, now,* if thou canst, *save thyself,* and *come down from the cross.* They triumph as if now that they had got him to the cross, there were no danger of his *destroying the temple;* whereas the *temple* of which *he* spoke, he was now *destroying,* and did within *three days build it up;* and the temple of which *they* spoke, he did by men, that were *his sword* and *his hand,* destroy not many years after. When secure sinners think the danger is over, it is then most ready to seize them: the day of the Lord *comes as a thief* upon those that *deny* his coming, and say, Where is the promise of it? much more upon those that *defy* his coming, and say, *Let him make speed, and hasten his work.*

(2.) Even the chief priests, who, being *taken from among men* and ordained for men, should have compassion even on those that are out of the way, should be tender of those that are suffering and dying (Heb. 5:1, 2), yet they poured vinegar instead of oil into his wounds, they *talked to the grief* of him *whom God had smitten* (Ps. 69:26), they *mocked him,* they said, *He saved others,* healed and helped them, but now it appears that it was not by his own power, for *himself he cannot save.* They challenged him to *come down from the cross,* if he could, *v.* 32. Let them but *see* that, and they would *believe;* whereas they would not believe, when he gave them a more convincing sign than that, when he came up from the grave. These chief priests, one would think, might now have found themselves *other work* to do: if they would not go to do their duty in *the temple,* yet they might have been employed in an office not foreign to their profession; though they would not offer any counsel or comfort to the Lord Jesus, yet they might have given some help to the thieves in their dying moments (the monks and priests in Popish countries are very officious about criminals broken upon the wheel, a death much like that of the cross); but they do not think that their business.

(3.) Even they that were crucified with him, reviled him (*v.* 32); one of them did, so wretchedly was his heart hardened even in the depth of misery, and at the door of eternity.

Verses 33–41

Here we have an account of Christ's dying, how his enemies abused him, and God honoured him at his death.

I. There was a thick *darkness* over *the whole land* (some think over the whole earth), for three hours, from noon till three of the clock. Now the scripture was fulfilled (Amos 8:9), *I will cause the sun to go down at noon,* and I will *darken the earth in the clear day;* and Jer. 15:9, *Her sun is gone down while it is yet day.* The Jews have often demanded of Christ a *sign from heaven;* and now they had one, but such a one as signified the blinding of their eyes. It was a sign of the darkness that was come, and coming, upon the Jewish church and nation. They were doing their utmost to extinguish the Sun of righteousness, which was now setting, and the rising again of which they would never own; and what then might be expected among them but a worse than Egyptian darkness? This intimated to them, that the things which belonged to their peace, were now *hid from their eyes,* and that the day of the Lord was at hand, which should be to them a *day of darkness and gloominess,* Joel 2:1, 2. It was the power of darkness that they were now under, the works of darkness that they were now doing; and such as this should their doom justly be, who *loved darkness rather than light.*

II. Toward the close of this darkness, our Lord Jesus, in the agony of his soul, cried out, *My God, my God, why hast thou forsaken me? v.* 34. The darkness signified the present cloud which the human soul of Christ was under, when he was making it an *offering for sin.* Mr. Fox, in his *Acts and Monuments* (vol. 3, p. 160), tells of one Dr. Hunter, a martyr in queen Mary's time, who, being fastened to the stake, to be burnt, put up this short prayer, *Son of God, shine upon me;* and immediately the sun in the firmament shone out of the dark cloud, so full in his face, that he was forced to look another way, which was very comfortable to him. But our Lord Jesus, on the contrary, was denied the light of the sun, when he was in his sufferings, to signifying the withdrawing of the light of God's countenance. And this he complained of more than any thing; he did not complain of his disciples' forsaking him, but of his Father's, 1. Because this *wounded his spirit;* and that is a thing *hard to bear* (Prov. 18:14); brought the waters into his soul, Ps. 69:1–3. 2. Because in this especially he was *made sin for us;* our iniquities had deserved *indignation and wrath* upon the soul (Rom. 2:8), and therefore, Christ, being made a *sacrifice,* underwent as much of it as he was capable of; and it could not but bear hard indeed upon him who had lain *in the bosom* of the Father from eternity, and was *always his light.* These symptoms of divine wrath, which Christ was under in his sufferings, were like that fire from heaven which had been sent sometimes, in extraordinary cases, to consume the sacrifices (as Lev. 9:24; 2 Chr. 7:1; 1 Ki. 18:38); and it was always a token of God's acceptance. The fire that should have fallen upon the *sinner,* if God had not been *pacified,* fell upon the *sacrifice,* as a token that he was so; therefore it now fell upon Christ, and extorted him from this *loud* and *bitter* cry. When Paul was to be *offered* as a sacrifice for the *service of saints,* he could *joy* and *rejoice* (Phil. 2:17); but it is another thing to be offered as a sacrifice for *the sin of sinners.* Now, at the *sixth hour,* and so to the *ninth,* the *sun* was *darkened* by an extraordinary eclipse; and if it be true, as some astronomers compute, that in the evening of this day on which Christ died there was an eclipse of the moon, that was natural and expected, in which seven digits of the moon were darkened, and it continued from five o'clock till seven, it is remarkable, and yet further significant of the darkness of the time that then was. When the *sun* shall be *darkened,* the *moon* also shall *not give her light.*

III. Christ's prayer was bantered by them that stood by (*v.* 35, 36); because he cried, *Eli, Eli,* or (as Mark has it, according to the Syriac dialect) *Eloi, Eloi,* they said, *He calls for Elias,* though they knew very well what he said, and what it signified, *My God, My God.* Thus did they represent him as *praying to saints,* either because he had abandoned God, or God had abandoned him; and hereby they would make him more and more odious to the people. One of them *filled a sponge with vinegar,* and reached it up to him upon a reed; "Let him cool his mouth with that, it is a drink good enough for him," *v.* 36. This was intended for a further affront and abuse to him; and whoever it was that checked him who did it, did but add to the reproach; *"Let him alone;* he has called for Elias: *let us see whether Elias will come take him down;* and if not, we may conclude that he also hath abandoned him."

IV. Christ did again *cry with a loud voice,* and so *gave up the ghost, v.* 37. He was now commending his soul into his Father's hand; and though God is not moved with any *bodily exercise,* yet this loud voice signified the great strength and ardency of affection wherewith he did it; to teach us, in every thing wherein we have to do with God, to put forth our utmost vigour, and to perform all the duties of religion, particularly that of *self-resignation,* with our whole heart and whole soul; and then, though speech fails, that we cannot *cry with a loud voice,* as Christ did, yet if God be the *strength of the heart,* that will not fail. Christ was really and truly *dead,* for he *gave up the ghost;* his human soul departed to the world of spirits, and left his body a breathless clod of clay.

V. Just at that instant that Christ died upon *mount Calvary,* the veil of the *temple* was *rent in twain from the top to the bottom, v.* 38. This bespoke a great deal, 1. Of the terror of the unbelieving Jews; for it was a presage of the utter destruction of their church and nation, which followed not long after; it was like the cutting asunder of the *staff of beauty* (for this veil was exceedingly splendid and glorious, Ex. 26:31), and that was done at the same time when they gave for his price *thirty pieces of silver* (Zec. 11:10, 12), to *break the covenant which he had made with that people.* Now it was time to cry, *Ichabod, The glory is departed from Israel.* Some think that the story which Josephus relates, of the temple door opening of its own accord, with that voice, *Let us depart hence,* some years before the destruction of Jerusalem, is the same with this; but that is not probable: however, this had the same signification, according to that (Hos. 5:14), *I will tear, and go away.* 2. It bespeaks a great deal of comfort to all believing Christians, for it signifies the consecrating and laying open to us of a *new and living way into the holiest* by the *blood of Jesus.*

VI. The centurion who commanded the detachment which had the oversight of the execution was convinced, and confessed that this Jesus was the *Son of God, v.* 39. One thing that satisfied him, was, that he *so cried out, and gave up the ghost:* that one who was ready to give up the ghost, should be able to cry out so, was very surprising. Of all the sad spectacles of this kind he never observed the like; and that one who had strength to cry so loud, should yet immediately give up the ghost, this also made him wonder; and he said, to the honour of Christ, and the shame of those that abused him, *Truly this man was the Son of God.* But what reason had he to say so? I answer, 1. He had reason to say that he suffered *unjustly,* and had a great deal of wrong done him. Note, He suffered for saying that he was *the Son of God;* and it was true, he did say so, so that if he suffered unjustly, as it was plain by all the circumstances of his suffering that he did, then what he said was true, and he was indeed the *Son of God.* 2. He had reason to say that he was a *favourite of heaven,* and one for whom the almighty power was particularly engaged, seeing how Heaven did him honour at his death, and frowned upon his persecutors. "Surely," thinks he, "this must be some divine person, highly beloved of God." This he expresses by such words as denote his eternal generation as God, and his special designation to the office of Mediator, though he meant not so. Our Lord Jesus, even in the depth of his sufferings and humiliation, was the Son of God, and was declared to be so *with power.*

VII. There were some of his friends, the good women especially, that attended him (*v.* 40, 41); *There were women looking on afar off:* the *men* durst not be seen at all, the mob was so very outrageous; *Currenti cede furori — Give way to the raging torrent,* they thought, was good counsel now. The women durst not come near, but stood at a distance, overwhelmed with grief. Some of these women are here named. *Mary Magdalene* was one; she had been his patient, and owed all her comfort to his power and goodness, which rescued her out of the possession of seven devils, in gratitude for which she thought she could never do enough for him. *Mary* also was there, *the mother of James the little, Jacobus parvus,* so the word is; probably, he was so called because he was, like Zaccheus, little of stature. This Mary was the wife of Cleophas or Alpheus, sister to the virgin Mary. These women had followed Christ *from Galilee,* though they were not required to attend the feast, as the males were; but it is probably that they came, in expectation that his temporal kingdom would now shortly be set up, and big with hopes of preferment for themselves, and their relations under him. It is plain that the mother of Zebedee's children was so (Mt. 20:21); and now to see *him* upon a cross, whom they thought to have seen upon a throne, could not but be a great disappointment to them. Note, Those that follow Christ, in expectation of great things in this world by him, and by the profession of his religion, may probably live to see themselves sadly disappointed.

Verses 42–47

We are here attending the funeral of our Lord Jesus, a solemn, mournful funeral. O that we may by grace be planted in the likeness of it! Observe,

I. How the body of Christ was *begged.* It was, as the dead bodies of malefactors are, at the disposal of the government. Those that hurried him to the cross, designed that he should make *his grave with the wicked;* but God designed he should make it *with the rich* (Isa. 53:9), and so he did. We are here told,

1. When the body of Christ was begged, in order to its being buried, and why such haste was made with the funeral; *The even was come,* and it was *the preparation,* that is, *the day before the sabbath, v.* 42. The Jews were more strict in the observation of the sabbath than of any other feast; and therefore, though this day was itself a *feast-day,* yet they observed it more religiously as the *eve* of the *sabbath;* when they prepared their houses and tables for the *splendid* and *joyful* solemnizing of the sabbath day. Note, The day before the sabbath should be a day of preparation for the sabbath, not of our houses and tables, but of our hearts, which, as much as possible, should be *freed* from the cares and business of the world, and *fixed,* and put in frame for the service and enjoyment of God. Such work is to be done, and such advantages are to be gained on the sabbath day, that it is requisite we should get ready for it a day before; nay, the whole week should be divided between the improvement of the foregoing sabbath and the preparation for the following sabbath.

2. Who was it that begged the body, and took care for the decent interment of it; it was *Joseph of Arimathea,* who is here called an *honourable counsellor* (*v.* 43), a person of character and distinction, and in an office of public trust; some think *in the state,* and that he was one of Pilate's privy council; his post rather seems to have been *in the church,* he was one of the *great Sanhedrim* of the Jews, or one of the high priest's council. He was *euschēmōn bouleutēs — a counsellor that conducted himself in his place as did become him.* Those are truly honourable, and those only, in place of power and trust, who make conscience of their duty, and whose deportment is agreeable to their preferment. But here is a more shining character put upon him; he was one that *waited for the kingdom of God,* the kingdom of grace on earth, and of glory in heaven, the kingdom of the Messiah. Note, Those who *wait for the kingdom of God,* and hope for an interest in the privileges of it, must show it by their forwardness to own Christ's cause and interest, even then when it seems to be crushed and run down. Observe, Even among the *honourable counsellors* there were some, there was *one* at least, that waited for the kingdom of God, whose faith will condemn the unbelief of all the rest. This man God raised up for this necessary service, when none of Christ's disciples could, or durst, undertake it, having neither purse, nor interest, nor courage, for it. *Joseph went in boldly to Pilate;* though he knew how much it would affront the chief priests, who had loaded him with so much reproach, to see any honour done him, yet he *put on courage;* perhaps at first he was a little afraid, but *tolmēsas — taking heart on it,* he determined to show this respect to the remains of the Lord Jesus, let the worst come to the worst.

3. What a surprise it was to Pilate, to hear that he was *dead* (Pilate, perhaps, expecting that he would have saved himself, and come down from the cross), especially that he was *already dead,* that one who seemed to have more than ordinary vigour, should so soon yield to death. Every circumstance of Christ's dying was marvellous; for from first to last his name was called *Wonderful.* Pilate doubted (so some understand it) whether he was yet dead or no, fearing lest he should be imposed upon, and the body should be *taken down alive,* and recovered, whereas the sentence was, as with us, to hang *till the body be dead.* He therefore called the centurion, his own officer, and asked him *whether he had been any while dead* (*v.* 44), whether it was so long since they perceived any sign of life in him, any breath or motion, that they might conclude he was dead past recall. The centurion could assure him of this, for he had particularly observed how *he gave up the ghost, v.* 39. There was a special providence in it, that Pilate should be so strict in examining this, that there might be no pretence to say that he was buried alive, and so to take away the truth of his resurrection; and so fully was this determined, that the objection was never started. Thus the truth of Christ gains confirmation, sometimes, even from its enemies.

II. How the body of Christ was *buried.* Pilate gave Joseph leave to take down the body, and do what he pleased with it. It was a wonder the chief priests were not too quick for him, and had not first begged the body of Pilate, to expose it and drag it about the streets, but that remainder of their wrath did God restrain, and gave that invaluable prize to Joseph, who knew how to value it; and the hearts of the priests were so influenced, that they did not oppose it. *Sit divus, modo non sit vivus — We care not for his being adored, provided he be not revived.*

1. Joseph bought *fine linen* to wrap the body in, though in such a case old linen that had been worn might have been thought sufficient. In paying respects to Christ it becomes us to be *generous,* and to serve him with the *best* that can be got, not with that which can be got at the best hand.

2. He *took down* the body, mangled and macerated as it was, and *wrapt it in the linen* as a treasure of great worth. Our Lord Jesus hath commanded himself to be delivered to us sacramentally in the ordinance of the Lord's supper, which we should receive in such a manner as may best express our love to him who loved us and died for us.

3. He *laid it in a sepulchre* of his own, in a private place. We sometimes find it spoken of in the story of the kings of Judah, as a slur upon the memory of the wicked kings, that they were not buried in the *sepulchres of the kings;* our Lord Jesus, though he did no evil but much good, and to him was given the throne of his father David, yet was buried in the graves of the common people, for it was not in this world, but in the other, that *his rest was glorious.* The sepulchre belonged to Joseph. Abraham when he had no other possession in the land of Canaan, yet had a burying-place, but Christ had not so much as that. This sepulchre was *hewn out of a rock,* for Christ died to make the grave a *refuge* and shelter to the saints, and being hewn out of a rock, it is a *strong* refuge. *O that thou wouldest hide me in the grave!* Christ himself is a *hiding place* to his people, that is, as *the shadow of a great rock.*

4. He *rolled a stone to the door of the sepulchre,* for so the manner of the Jews was to bury. When Daniel was put into the lion's den, a stone was laid to the mouth of it to keep him in, as here to the door of Christ's sepulchre, but neither of them could keep off the angels' visits to the prisoners.

5. Some of the good women attended the funeral, and *beheld where he was laid,* that they might come after the sabbath to anoint the dead body, because they had not time to do it now. When Moses, the mediator and lawgiver of the Jewish church, was buried, care was taken that no man should *know of his sepulchre* (Deu. 34:6), because the respect of the people towards his person were to die with him; but when our great Mediator and Lawgiver was buried, special notice was taken of his sepulchre, because he was to *rise again:* and the care taken of his body, bespeaks the care which he himself will take concerning his body the church. Even when it seems to be a dead body, and as a valley full of dry bones, it shall be preserved in order to a resurrection; as shall also the dead bodies of the saints, with whose dust there is a covenant in force which shall not be forgotten. Our mediations on Christ's burial should lead us to think of our own, and should help to make the grave familiar to us, and so to render that bed easy which we must shortly make in the darkness. Frequent thoughts of it would not only take off the dread and terror of it, but quicken us, since the *graves* are always ready for us, to get ready for the graves, Job 17:1.

CHAPTER 16

In this chapter, we have a short account of the resurrection and ascension of the Lord Jesus: and the joys and triumphs which it furnished all believers with, will be very acceptable to those who sympathised and suffered with Christ in the foregoing chapters. Here is, I. Christ's resurrection notified by an angel to the women that came to the sepulchre to anoint him (*v.* 1–8). II. His appearance to Mary Magdalene, and the account she gave of it to the disciples (*v.* 9–11). III. His appearance to the two disciples, going to Emmaus, and the report they made of it to their brethren (*v.* 12, 13). IV. His appearance to the eleven with the commission he gave them to set up his kingdom in the world, and full instructions and credentials in order thereunto, (*v.* 14–18). V. His ascension into heaven, the apostles' close application to their work, and God's owning of them in it (*v.* 19, 20).

Verses 1–8

Never was there such a *sabbath* since the sabbath was first instituted as this was, which the first words of this chapter tell us was *now past;* during all this sabbath our Lord Jesus lay in the grave. It was *to him* a sabbath of *rest,* but a *silent* sabbath, it was to his disciples a melancholy sabbath, spent in tears and fears. Never were the sabbath services in the temple such an *abomination to God,* though they had been often so, as they were now, when the chief priests, who presided in them, had their hands full of blood, the blood of Christ. Well, this sabbath is over, and the first day of the week is the first day of a new world. We have here,

I. The affectionate visit which the good women that had attended Christ, now made it to his sepulchre — not a *superstitious* one, but a *pious* one. They set out from their lodgings *very early in the morning,* at break of day, or sooner; but either they had a long walk, or they met with some hindrance, so that it was *sun-rising* by the time they got to the sepulchre. The had *bought sweet spices* too, and came not only to *bedew* the dead body with their tears (for nothing could more renew their grief than this), but to *perfume* it with their *spices, v.* 1. Nicodemus had bought a very large quantity of *dry spices, myrrh* and *aloes,* which served to dry the wounds, and dry up the blood, Jn. 19:39. But these good women did not think that enough; they bought spices, perhaps of another kind, some perfumed oils, to *anoint him.* Note, The respect which others have showed to Christ's name, should not hinder us from showing our respect to it.

II. The care they were in about the rolling away of the stone, and the superseding of that care (*v.* 3, 4); *They said among themselves,* as they were coming along, and now drew near the sepulchre, *Who shall roll us away the stone from the door of the sepulchre? For it was very great,* more than they with their united strength could move. They should have thought of this before they came out, and then discretion would have bid them not go, unless they had those to go with them, who could do it. And there was another difficulty much greater than this, to be got over, which they knew nothing of, to wit, a guard of soldiers set to *keep* the sepulchre; who, had they come before they were frightened away, would have frightened them away. But their gracious love to Christ carried them to the sepulchre; and see how by the time they came thither, both these difficulties were removed, both the *stone* which they *knew of,* and the *guard* which they *knew not of.* They *saw that the stone was rolled away,* which was the first thing that amazed them. Note, They who are carried by a holy zeal, to seek Christ diligently, will find the difficulties that lie in their way strangely to vanish, and themselves helped over them beyond their expectation.

III. The assurance that was given them by an angel, that the Lord Jesus was risen from the dead, and had taken leave of his sepulchre, and had left him there to tell those so who came thither to enquire after him.

1. They *entered into the sepulchre,* at least, a little way in, and saw that the body of Jesus was not there where they had left it the other night. He, who by his death undertook to pay our debt, in his resurrection took out our acquittance, for it was a fair and legal discharge, by which it appealed that his satisfaction was accepted for all the purposes for which it was intended, and the matter in dispute was determined by an incontestable evidence that he was the Son of God.

2. They saw a *young man sitting on the right side* of the sepulchre. The angel appeared in the likeness of *a man,* of a *young man;* for angels, though created in the beginning, grow not *old,* but are always the same perfection of beauty and strength; and so shall glorified saints be, when they are *as the angels.* This angel was *sitting* on *the right hand* as they went into the sepulchre, *clothed with a long white garment,* a garment down to the feet, such as great men were arrayed with. The sight of him might justly have encouraged them, but they were *affrighted.* Thus many times that which should be matter of comfort to us, through our own mistakes and misapprehensions proves a terror to us.

3. He silences their fears by assuring them that here was cause enough for triumph, but none for trembling (*v.* 6); *He saith to them, Be not affrighted.* Note, As angels rejoice in the conversation of sinners, so they do also in the consolation of sinners. Be not affrighted, for, (1.) "Ye are faithful lovers of Jesus Christ, and therefore, instead of being *confounded,* out to be *comforted. Ye seek Jesus of Nazareth, which was crucified."* Note, The enquiries of believing souls after Christ, have a particular regard to him as *crucified* (1 Co. 2:2), that they may know him, and the fellowship of his sufferings. His being *lifted up from the earth,* is that which *draws all men unto him.* Christ's cross is the ensign to which the Gentiles seek. Observe, He speaks of Jesus as one that *was crucified;* "The thing is *past,* that scene is over, ye must not dwell so much upon the sad circumstances of his crucifixion as to be unapt to believe the joyful news of his resurrection. He was *crucified in weakness,* yet that doth not hinder but that he may be raised in power, and therefore ye that seek him, be not *afraid of missing* of him." He *was* crucified, but he *is* glorified; and the shame of his sufferings is so far from lessening the glory of his exaltation, that that glory perfectly wipes away all the reproach of his sufferings. And therefore after his entrance upon his glory, he never drew any veil over his sufferings, nor was shy of having his cross spoken of. The angel here that proclaims his resurrection, calls him Jesus that *was crucified.* He himself owns (Rev. 1:18), *I am he that liveth, and was dead;* and he appears in the midst of the praises of the heavenly host as a *Lamb that had been slain,* Rev. 5:6. (2.) "It will therefore be good news to you, to hear that, instead of anointing him dead, you may rejoice in him living. *He is risen, he is not here,* not dead, but alive again. We cannot as yet show you *him,* but hereafter you will see him, and you may here see *the place where they laid him.* You see he is gone hence, not stolen either by his enemies or by his friends, but *risen."*

4. He orders them to give speedy notice of this to his disciples. Thus they were made the apostles of the apostles, which was a recompence of their affection and fidelity to him, in attending him on the cross, to the grave, and in the grave. They first came, and were first served; no other of the disciples durst come near his sepulchre, or enquire after him; so little danger was there of their coming by night to *steal him away,* that none came near him but a few women, who were not able so much as to *roll away the stone.*

(1.) They must tell the *disciples,* that *he is risen.* It is a dismal time with them, their dear Master is dead, and all their hopes and joys are buried in his grave; they look upon their cause as sunk, and themselves ready to fall an easy prey into the hands of their enemies, so that there remains no more spirit in them, they are perfectly at their wits' end, and every one is contriving how to shift for himself. "O, go quickly to them," said the angel, "tell them that *their Master is risen;* this will put some life and spirit into them, and keep them from sinking into despair." Note, [1.] Christ is not ashamed to own his poor disciples, no, not now that he is in his exalted state; his preferment doth not make him shy of them, for he took early care to have it *notified* to them. [2.] Christ is not extreme to mark what *they* do amiss, whose hearts are upright with him. The disciples had very unkindly deserted him, and yet he testified this concern for them. [3.] Seasonable comforts shall be sent to those that are lamenting after the Lord Jesus, and he will find a time to manifest himself to them.

(2.) They must be sure to tell Peter. This is particularly taken notice of by this evangelist, who is supposed to have written by Peter's direction. If it were told the disciples, it would be told Peter, for, as a token of his repentance for disowning his Master, he still associated with his disciples; yet he is particularly named: *Tell Peter,* for, [1.] It will be good news to him, more welcome to him than to any of them; for he is in sorrow for sin, and no tidings can be more welcome to true penitents than to hear of the resurrection of Christ, because he rose again for *their justification.* [2.] He will be afraid, lest the joy of this good news do not belong to him. Had the angel said only, *Go, tell his disciples,* poor Peter would have been ready to sigh, and say, "But I doubt I cannot look upon myself as one of them, for I disowned him, and deserve to be disowned by him;" to obviate that, "Go to Peter by name, and tell him, he shall be as welcome as any of the rest to *see* him in Galilee." Note, A sight of Christ will be very welcome to a true penitent, and a true penitent shall be very welcome to a sight of Christ, for there is joy in heaven concerning him.

(3.) They must appoint them all, and Peter by name, to give him the meeting in Galilee, as *he said unto you,* Mt. 26:32. In their journey down into Galilee they would have time to recollect themselves, and call to mind what he had often said to them there, that he should suffer and die, and *the third day be raised again;* whereas while they were at Jerusalem, among strangers and enemies, they could not recover themselves from the fright they had been in, nor compose themselves to the due entertainment of better tidings. Note, [1.] All the meetings between Christ and his disciples are of his own appointing. [2.] Christ never forgets his appointment, but will be sure to meet his people with the promised blessing in every place where he records his name. [3.] In all meetings between Christ and his disciples, he is the most forward. *He goes before you.*

IV. The account which the women did bring of this to the disciples (*v.* 8); They *went out quickly,* and *ran from the sepulchre,* to make all the haste they could to the disciples, *trembling* and *amazed.* See how much we are enemies to ourselves and our own comfort, in not considering and mixing faith with that Christ hath said to us. Christ had often told them, that *the third day he would rise again;* had they given that its due notice and credit, they would have come to the sepulchre, expecting to have found him risen, and would have received the news of it with a joyful assurance, and not with all this terror and amazement. But, being ordered to tell the disciples, because they were to tell it to all the world, they would not tell it to any one else, they showed not any thing of it to any man that they *met by the way,* for *they were afraid,* afraid it was too good news to be true. Note, Our disquieting fears often hinder us from doing that service to Christ and to the souls of men, which if faith and the *joy of faith* were strong, we might do.

Verses 9–13

We have here a very short account of two of Christ's appearances, and the little credit which the report of them gained with the disciples.

I. He appeared to Mary Magdalene, to her first in the garden, which we have a particular narrative of, Jn. 20:14. It was she *out of whom he had cast seven devils;* much was forgiven her, and much was given her, and done for her, and she *loved much;* and this honour Christ did her, that she was the first that saw him after his resurrection. The closer we cleave to Christ, the sooner we may expect to see him, and the more to see of him.

Now, 1. She brings notice of what she had seen, to the disciples; not only to the *eleven,* but to the rest that followed him, *as they mourned and wept, v.* 10. Now was the time of which Christ had told them, that they should *mourn and lament,* Jn. 16:20. And it was an evidence of their great love to Christ, and the deep sense they had of their loss of him. But when their *weeping* had *endured a night* or two, comfort returned, as Christ has promised; *I will see you again, and your heart shall rejoice.* Better news cannot be brought to disciples in tears, than to tell them of Christ's resurrection. And we should study to be comforters to disciples that are mourners, by communicating to them our experiences, and what we have *seen of Christ.*

2. They could not give credit to the report she brought them. They heard that *he was alive,* and had been seen of her. The story was plausible enough, and yet *they believed not.* They would not say that she made the story herself, or designed to deceive them; but they fear that she is *imposed upon,* and that it was but a fancy that she *saw him.* Had they believed the *frequent* predictions of it from his own mouth, they would not have been now so incredulous of the report of it.

II. He appeared to two of the disciples, *as they went into the country, v.* 12. This refers, no doubt, to that which is largely related (Lu. 24:13, etc.), of which passed between Christ and the two disciples *going to Emmaus.* He is here said to have appeared to them in *another form,* in another dress than what he usually wore, in the form of a *traveller,* as, in the garden, in such a dress, that Mary Magdalene took him for the gardener; but that he had really his own countenance, appears by this, that *their eyes were holden, that they should not know him;* and when that restrain on *their* eyes was taken off, immediately they *knew him,* Lu. 24:16–31. Now,

1. These *two* witnesses gave in their *testimony* to this proof of Christ's resurrection; *They went and told it to the residue, v.* 13. Being *satisfied* themselves, they were desirous to give their brethren the *satisfaction* they had, that they might be comforted as they were.

2. This did not gain credit with all; *Neither believed they them.* They suspected that their eyes also deceived them. Now there was a wise providence in it, the proofs of Christ's resurrection were given in thus *gradually,* and admitted thus *cautiously,* that so the assurance with which the apostles preached this doctrine afterward, when they ventured their all upon it, might be the more satisfying. We have the more reason to believe those who did themselves believe so slowly: had they swallowed it presently, they might have been thought *credulous,* and their testimony the less to be *regarded;* but their *disbelieving* at first, shows that they did not believe it afterward but upon a full conviction.

Verses 14–18

Here is, I. The *conviction* which Christ gave his apostles of the truth of his resurrection (*v.* 14); He *appeared to them* himself, when they were all together, *as they sat at meat,* which gave him an opportunity to *eat and drink with them,* for their full satisfaction; see Acts 10:41. And still, when he appeared to them, he *upbraided them with their unbelief and hardness of heart,* for even at the general meeting in *Galilee, some doubted,* as we find Mt. 28:17. Note, The evidences of the truth of the gospel are so full, that those who receive it not, may justly be *upbraided* with their unbelief; and it is owing not to any weakness or deficiency in the proofs, but to the *hardness of their heart,* its senselessness and stupidity. Though they had not till now seen him themselves, they are justly blamed *because they believed not them who had seen him after he was risen;* and perhaps it was owing in part to the *pride of their hearts,* that they did not; for they thought, "If indeed he be risen, to *whom should he delight to do* the *honour* of showing himself but to us?" And if he *pass them by,* and show himself to *others* first, they cannot believe it is he. Thus many disbelieve the doctrine of Christ, because they think it *below them* to give credit to such as he had chosen to be the witnesses and publishers of it. Observe, It will not suffice for an excuse of our infidelity in the great day, to say, "*We did not see him* after he was risen," for we ought to have believed the testimony of those who did see him.

II. The *commission* which he gave them to set up his kingdom among men by the preaching of his *gospel,* the glad tidings of reconciliation to God through a Mediator. Now observe,

1. *To whom* they were to preach *the gospel.* Hitherto they had been sent only to *the lost sheep of the house of Israel,* and were forbidden to go into the *way of the Gentiles,* or into any city of the Samaritans; but now their commission is enlarged, and they are authorized to *go into all the world,* into all parts of the world, the habitable world, and to *preach the gospel* of Christ to *every creature,* to the Gentiles as well as to the Jews; to every human creature that is capable of receiving it. "Inform them concerning Christ, the history of *his life,* and *death,* and *resurrection;* instruct them in the *meaning* and *intention* of these, and of the advantages which the children of men have, or may have, hereby; and invite them, without exception, to come and share in them. This is *gospel.* Let this be *preached* in all places, to all persons." These eleven men could not themselves preach it to all the world, much less to *every creature* in it; but they and the other disciples, seventy in number, with those who should afterward to be added to them, must *disperse* themselves several ways, and, wherever they went, carry the gospel along with them. They must send *others* to those places whither they could not *go themselves,* and, in short, make it the business of their lives to send those glad tidings *up and down the world* with all possible fidelity and care, not as an amusement or entertainment, but as a solemn message from God to men, and an appointed means of making men happy. "Tell as many as you can, and bid them tell others; it is a message of universal concern, and *therefore,* ought to *have* a universal welcome, because it *gives* a universal welcome."

2. What is the *summary of the gospel* they are to preach (*v.* 16); "Set before the world life and death, good and evil. Tell the children of men that they are all in a state of misery and danger, *condemned* by their prince, and *conquered* and *enslaved* by their enemies." This is supposed in their being *saved,* which they would not need to be if they were not *lost.* "Now go and tell them," (1.) "That if they *believe the gospel,* and give up themselves to be Christ's disciples; if they *renounce* the devil, the world, and the flesh, and be *devoted* to Christ as their prophet, priest, and king, and to God in Christ a their God in covenant, and evidence by their constant adherence to this covenant their sincerity herein, they *shall be saved* from the guilt and power of sin, it shall not *rule* them, it shall not *ruin* them. He that is a true Christian, shall be saved through Christ." *Baptism* was appointed to be the *inaugurating* rite, by which those that embraced Christ owned him; but it is here put rather for the *thing signified* than for the sign, for Simon Magus *believed* and was *baptized,* yet was not *saved,* Acts 8:13. *Believing with the heart, and confessing with the mouth the Lord Jesus* (Rom. 10:9), seems to be much the same with this here. Or thus, We must *assent* to gospel-truths, and *consent* to gospel-terms. (2.) "*If they believe not,* if they receive not the record God gives concerning his Son, they cannot expect any other way of salvation, but must inevitably perish; *they shall be damned,* by the sentence of a *despised* gospel, added to that of a broken law." And even this is *gospel,* it is good news, that nothing else but unbelief shall damn men, which is a sin against the remedy. Dr. Whitby here observes, that they who hence infer "that the infant seed of believers are not capable of baptism, because they cannot believe, must hence also infer that they cannot be saved; *faith* being here more expressly required to salvation than to baptism. And that in the latter clause baptism is omitted, because it is not simply the want of baptism, but the contemptuous neglect of it, which makes men guilty of damnation, otherwise infants might be damned for the mistakes or profaneness of their parents."

3. What power they should be endowed with, for the confirmation of the doctrine they were to preach (*v.* 17); *These signs shall follow them that believe.* Not that all who believe, shall be able to produce these signs, but some, even as many as were employed in propagating the faith, and bringing others to it; for signs are intended *for them that believe not;* see 1 Co. 14:22. It added much to the glory and evidence of the gospel, that the preachers not only wrought miracles themselves, but conferred upon others a power to work miracles, which power *followed* some of them that believed, wherever they went to preach. They shall do wonders *in Christ's name,* the same name into which they were baptized, in the virtue of power derived from him, and fetched in by prayer. Some particular signs are mentioned; (1.) They shall *cast out devils;* this power was more common among Christians than any other, and lasted longer, as appears by the testimonies of Justin Martyr, Origen, Irenaeus, Tertullian Minutius Felix, and others, cited by Grotius on this place. (2.) They shall *speak with new tongues,* which they had never learned, or been acquainted with; and this was both a *miracle* (a miracle *upon the mind*), for the confirming of the truth of the gospel, and a *means* of spreading the gospel among those nations that had not heard it. It saved the preachers a vast labour in learning the languages; and, no doubt, they who by *miracle* were made *masters of languages,* were *complete* masters of them and of all their native elegancies, which were proper both to *instruct* and *affect,* which would very much recommend them and their preaching. (3.) They shall *take up serpents.* This was fulfilled in Paul, who was not hurt by the *viper* that *fastened on his hand,* which was acknowledged a great miracle by the barbarous people, Acts 28:5, 6. They shall be kept unhurt by that *generation of vipers* among whom they live, and by the malice of the *old serpent.* (4.) If they be compelled by their persecutors to *drink any deadly* poisonous thing, *it shall not hurt them:* of which very thing some instances are found in ecclesiastical history. (5.) They shall not only be preserved from hurt themselves, but they shall be enabled to do good to others; *They shall lay hands on the sick, and they shall recover,* as multitudes had done by their master's *healing* touch. Many of the elders of the church had this power, as appears by Jam. 5:14, where, as an instituted sign of this miraculous healing, they are said to *anoint* the sick *with oil in the name of the Lord.* With what assurance of success might they go about executing their commission, when they had such credentials as these to produce!

Verses 19–20

Here is, 1. Christ *welcomed* into the *upper world* (*v.* 19): *After the Lord had spoken* what he had to say to his disciples, he *went up into heaven,* in a cloud; which we have a particular account of (Acts 1:9), and he had not only an admission, but an abundant *entrance,* into his kingdom there; he was *received up,* received in state, with loud acclamations of the heavenly hosts; and he *sat on the right hand of God:* sitting in a posture of *rest,* for now he had finished his work, and a posture of *rule,* for now he took possession of his kingdom; he sat *at the right hand of God,* which denotes the sovereign dignity he is advanced to, and the universal agency he is entrusted with. Whatever God does concerning us, gives to us, or accepts from us, it is *by his Son.* Now he is glorified with the glory he had before the world.

2. Christ *welcomed* in this *lower world;* his being *believed on in the world,* and *received up into glory,* are put together, 1 Tim. 3:16. (1.) We have here the apostles working diligently for him; they *went forth, and preached every where* far and near. Though the doctrine they preached, was *spiritual* and *heavenly,* and directly contrary to the *spirit* and *genius* of the world, though it met with abundance of opposition, and was utterly destitute of all secular supports and advantages, yet the preachers of it were neither *afraid* nor *ashamed;* they were so industrious in spreading the gospel, that within a few years the sound of it *went forth into the ends of the*

earth, Rom. 10:18. (2.) We have here God *working* effectually *with them,* to make their labours successful, by *confirming the word with signs following,* partly by the miracles that were wrought upon the *bodies* of the people, which were divine seals to the Christian doctrine, and partly by the influence it had upon the *minds* of the people, through the operation of the Spirit of God, see Heb. 2:4. These were properly *signs following* the word — the reformation of the world, the destruction of idolatry, the conversion of sinners, the comfort of saints; and these signs still follow it, and that they may do so more and more, for the honour of Christ and the good of mankind, the evangelist prays, and teaches us to say *Amen.* Father in heaven, thus let thy name be hallowed, and let thy kingdom come.

AN EXPOSITION, WITH PRACTICAL OBSERVATIONS, OF

THE GOSPEL ACCORDING TO ST. LUKE

We are now entering into the labours of another evangelist; his name *Luke,* which some take to be a contraction of *Lucilius;* born at Antioch, so St. Jerome. Some think that he was the only one of all the penmen of the scripture that was not of the seed of Israel. He was a Jewish proselyte, and, as some conjecture, converted to Christianity by the ministry of St. Paul at Antioch; and after his coming into Macedonia (Acts 16:10) he was his constant companion. He had employed himself in the study and practice of physic; hence, Paul calls him *Luke the beloved Physician,* Col. 4:14. Some of the pretended ancients tell you that he was a painter, and drew a picture of the virgin Mary. But Dr. Whitby thinks that there is nothing certain to the contrary, and that therefore it is probable that he was one of the seventy disciples, and a follower of Christ when he was here upon earth; and, if so, he was a native Israelite. I see not what can be objected against this, except some uncertain traditions of the ancients, which we can build nothing upon, and against which may be opposed the testimonies of Origen and Epiphanius, who both say that he was one of the seventy disciples. He is supposed to have written this gospel when he was associated with St. Paul in his travels, and by direction from him: and some think that this is *the brother* whom Paul speaks of (2 Co. 8:18), *whose praise is in the gospel throughout all the churches of Christ;* as if the meaning of it were, that he was celebrated *in all the churches* for writing *this gospel;* and that St. Paul means this when he speaks sometimes of *his* gospel, as Rom. 2:16. But there is no ground at all for this. Dr. Cave observes that his way and manner of writing are accurate and exact, his style polite and elegant, sublime and lofty, yet perspicuous; and that he expresses himself in a vein of purer Greek than is to be found in the other writers of the holy story. Thus he relates divers things more copiously than the other evangelists; and thus he especially treats of those things which relate to the priestly office of Christ. It is uncertain when, or about what time, this gospel was written. Some think that it was written in Achaia, during his travels with Paul, seventeen years (twenty-two years, say others) after Christ's ascension; others, that it was written at Rome, a little before he wrote his history of the *Acts of the Apostles* (which is a continuation of this), when he was there with Paul, while he was a prisoner, and preaching in his own hired house, with which the history of the Acts concludes; and then Paul saith that *only Luke was with him,* 2 Tim. 4:11. When he was under that voluntary confinement with Paul, he had leisure to compile these two histories (and many excellent writings the church has been indebted to a prison for): if so, it was written about twenty-seven years after Christ's ascension, and about the fourth year of Nero. Jerome says, He died when he was eighty-four years of age, and was never married. Some write that he suffered martyrdom; but, if he did, where and when is uncertain. Nor indeed is there much more credit to be given to the Christian traditions concerning the writers of the New Testament than to the Jewish traditions concerning those of the Old Testament.

CHAPTER 1

The narrative which this evangelist gives us (or rather God by him) of the life of Christ begins earlier than either Matthew or Mark. We have reason to thank God for them all, as we have for all the gifts and graces of Christ's ministers, which in one make up what is wanting in the other, while all put together make a harmony. In this chapter we have, I. Luke's preface to his gospel, or his epistle dedicatory to his friend Theophilus (*v.* 1–4). II. The prophecy and history of the conception of John Baptist, who was Christ's forerunner (*v.* 5–25). The annunciation of the virgin Mary, or the notice given to her that she should be the mother of the Messiah (*v.* 26–38). IV. The interview between Mary the mother of Jesus and Elisabeth the mother of John, when they were both with child of those pregnant births, and the prophecies they both uttered upon that occasion (*v.* 39–56). V. The birth and circumcision of John Baptist, six months before the birth of Christ (*v.* 57–66). VI. Zacharias's song of praise, in thankfulness for the birth of John, and in prospect of the birth of Jesus (*v.* 67–79). VII. A short account of John Baptist's infancy (*v.* 80). And these do more than give us an entertaining narrative; they will lead us into the understanding of the mystery of godliness, God manifest in the flesh.

Verses 1–4

Complimental prefaces and dedications, the language of flattery and the food and fuel of pride, are justly condemned by the wise and good; but it doth not therefore follow, that such as are useful and instructive are to be run down; such is this, in which St. Luke dedicates his gospel to his friend Theophilus, not as to his *patron,* though he was a man of honour, to protect it, but as to his *pupil,* to learn it, and hold it fast. It is not certain who this Theophilus was; the name signifies a *friend of God;* some think that it does not mean any particular person, but every one that is a *lover of God;* Dr. Hammond quotes some of the ancients understanding it so: and then it teaches us, that those who are truly lovers of God, will heartily welcome the gospel of Christ, the design and tendency of which are, to bring us to God. But it is rather to be understood of some particular person, probably a magistrate; because Luke gives him here the same title of respect which St. Paul gave to Festus the governor, *kratiste* (Acts 26:25), which we there translate *most noble Festus,* and here *most excellent Theophilus.* Note, Religion does not destroy civility and good manners, but teaches us, according to the usages of our country, to *give honour to them to whom honour is due.*

Now observe here, I. Why St. Luke wrote this gospel. It is certain that he was moved by the Holy Ghost, not only *to* the writing, but *in* the writing of it; but in both he was moved as a reasonable creature, and not as a mere machine; and he was made to consider,

1. That the things he wrote of were things that were *most surely believed among all Christians,* and therefore things which they ought to be instructed in, that they may know what they believe, and things which ought to be transmitted to posterity (who are as much concerned in them as we are); and, in order to that, to be committed to writing, which is the surest way of conveyance to the ages to come. He will not write about things of *doubtful disputation,* things about which Christians may safely differ from one another and hesitate within themselves; but the things which are, and ought to be, most *surely believed, pragmata peplērophorēmena — the things which were performed* (so some), which Christ and his apostles did, and did with such circumstances as gave a full assurance that they were really done, so that they have gained an established lasting credit. Note, Though it is not the foundation of our faith, yet it is a support to it, that the articles of our creed are things that have been long *most surely believed.* The doctrine of Christ is what thousands of the wisest and best of men have *ventured their souls upon* with the greatest assurance and satisfaction.

2. That it was requisite there should be a *declaration made in order* of those things; that the history of the life of Christ should be *methodized,* and committed to writing, for the greater certainty of the conveyance. When things are *put in order,* we know the better where to *find them* for *our own* use, and how to *keep* them for the benefit of *others.*

3. That there were *many who had undertaken* to *publish* narratives of the *life of Christ,* many well-meaning people, who *designed* well, and *did* well, and what they published had *done good,* though not done by divine inspiration, nor so well done as might be, nor intended for perpetuity. Note, (1.) The labours of others in the gospel of Christ, if faithful and honest, we ought to *commend* and *encourage,* and not to *despise,* though chargeable with many deficiencies. (2.) Others' services to Christ must not be reckoned to supersede ours, but rather to quicken them.

4. That the truth of the things he had to write was *confirmed* by the *concurring testimony* of those who were competent and unexceptionable witnesses of them; what had been published in writing already, and what he was now about to publish, agreed with that which had been delivered by word of mouth, over and over, by those who from the beginning were *eye-witnesses and ministers of the word, v.* 2. Note, (1.) The apostles were *ministers of the word* of Christ, who is *the Word* (so some understand it), or of the doctrine of Christ; they, having received it themselves, ministered it to others, 1 Jn. 1:1. They had not a gospel to make as masters, but a gospel to preach as ministers. (2.) The *ministers of the word* were *eye-witnesses* of the things which they preached, and, which is also included, *ear-witnesses.* They did themselves *hear* the doctrine of Christ, and *see* his miracles, and had them not by report, at second hand; and therefore they could not but speak, with the greatest assurance, the things which they had *seen and heard,* Acts 4:20. (3.) They were so *from the beginning* of Christ's ministry, *v.* 2. He had his disciples with him when he wrought his *first miracle,* Jn. 2:11. They *companied with him all the time he went in and out among them* (Acts 1:21), so that they not only heard and saw all that which was sufficient to confirm their faith, but, if there had been any thing to shock it, they had opportunity to discover it. (4.) The *written* gospel, which we have to *this day,* exactly agrees with the gospel which was *preached* in the *first days* of the church. (5.) That he himself had a *perfect understanding* of the *things* he wrote of, *from the first, v.* 3. Some think that here is a tacit reflection upon those who had written before him, that they had not a *perfect understanding* of what they wrote, and therefore, *Here am I, send me (— facit indignatio versum — my wrath impels my pen);* or rather, without reflecting on them, he asserts his own ability for this undertaking: "It seemed good to me, having attained to the exact knowledge of all things, *anōthen — from above;*" so I think it should be rendered; for if he meant the same with *from the beginning* (*v.* 2), as our translation intimates, he would have used the same word. [1.] He had diligently *searched* into these things, had *followed* after them (so the word is), as the Old-Testament prophets are said to have *enquired and searched diligently,* 1 Pt. 1:10. He had not taken things so easily and superficially as others who had written before him, but made it his business to inform himself concerning particulars. [2.] He had received his intelligence, not only by tradition, as others had done, but by revelation, confirming that tradition, and securing him from any error or mistake in the recording of it. He sought it *from above* (so the word intimates), and from thence he had it; thus, like Elihu, he *fetched his knowledge* from afar. He wrote his history as Moses wrote his, of things *reported* by tradition, but *ratified* by inspiration. [3.] He could therefore say that he had a *perfect understanding* of these things. He knew them, *akribōs — accurately,* exactly. "Now, having received this *from above,* it seemed good to me to communicate it;" for such a talent as this ought not to be buried.

II. Observe why he sent it to *Theophilus:* "I wrote unto thee these things *in order,* not that thou mayest give reputation to the work, but that thou mayest be edified by it (*v.* 4); *that thou mayest know the certainty of those things wherein thou has been instructed.*" 1. It is implied, that he had been *instructed* in these things either before his baptism, or since, or both, according to the rule, Mt. 28:19, 20. Probably, Luke had baptized him, and knew how well instructed he was; *peri hōn katēchēthēs — concerning which thou hast been catechized;* so the word is; the most knowing Christians began with being catechized. Theophilus was a person of quality, perhaps of noble birth; and so much the more pains should be taken with such when they are young, to teach them the principles of the oracles of God, that they may be fortified against temptations, and furnished for the opportunities, of a high condition in the world. 2. It was intended that he should *know the certainty of those things,* should understand them more clearly and believe more firmly. There is a *certainty* in the gospel of Christ, there is that therein which we may build upon; and those who have been well instructed in the things of God when they were young should afterwards give diligence to *know the certainty* of those things, to know not only what we believe, but why we believe it, that we may be able to give a *reason of the hope that is in us.*

Verses 5–25

The two preceding evangelists had agreed to begin the gospel with the baptism of John and his ministry, which commenced about six months before our Saviour's public ministry (and now, things being near a crisis, six months was *a deal* of time, which before was but *a little*), and therefore this evangelist, designing to give a more particular account than had been given of our Saviour's conception and birth, determines to do so of John Baptist, who in both was his harbinger and forerunner, the morning-star to the Sun of righteousness. The evangelist determines thus, not only because it is commonly reckoned a satisfaction and entertainment to know something of the original extraction and early days of those who afterwards prove great men, but because in the beginning of these there were many things miraculous, and presages of what they afterwards proved. In these verses our inspired historian begins as early as the conception of John Baptist. Now observe here,

I. The account given of *his parents* (*v.* 5): They lived *in the days of Herod the king,* who was a foreigner, and a deputy for the Romans, who had lately made Judea a province of the empire. This is taken notice of to show that the sceptre was quite departed from Judah, and therefore that now was the time for Shiloh to come, according to Jacob's prophecy, Gen. 49:10. The family of David was now sunk, when it was to rise, and flourish again, in the Messiah. Note, None ought to despair of the reviving and flourishing of religion, even when civil liberties are lost. Israel enslaved, yet then comes the glory of Israel.

Now the father of John Baptist was a priest, a son of Aaron; his name *Zacharias.* No families in the world were ever so honoured of God as those of Aaron and David; with one was made the covenant of priesthood, with the other that of royalty; they had both forfeited their honour, yet the gospel again puts honour upon both in their latter days, on that of Aaron in John Baptist, on that of David in Christ, and then they were both extinguished and lost. Christ was of David's house, his forerunner of Aaron's; for his priestly agency and influence opened the way to his kingly authority and dignity. This Zacharias was *of the course of Abia.* When in David's time the family of Aaron was multiplied, he divided them into twenty-four courses, for the more regular performances of their office, that it might never be either *neglected* for want of hands or *engrossed* by a few. The eighth of those was that of *Abia* (1 Chr. 24:10), who was descended from Eleazar, Aaron's eldest son; but Dr. Lightfoot suggests that many of the families of the priests were lost in the captivity, so that after their return they took in those of other families, retaining the names of the heads of the respective courses. The wife of this Zacharias was of the daughters of Aaron too, and her name was *Elisabeth,* the very same name with *Elisheba* the wife of Aaron, Ex. 6:23. The priests (Josephus saith) was very careful to marry within their own family, that they might maintain the dignity of the priesthood and keep it without mixture.

Now that which is observed concerning Zacharias and Elisabeth is,

1. That they were a very religious couple (*v.* 6): *They were both righteous before God;* they were so in his sight whose judgment, we are sure, is *according to truth;* they were sincerely and really so. They are righteous indeed that are so *before God,* as Noah in his generation, Gen. 7:1. They *approved* themselves *to him,* and he was graciously pleased to accept them. It is a happy thing when those who are joined to each other in marriage are both *joined to the Lord;* and it is especially requisite that the priests, the Lord's ministers, should with their yoke-fellows be *righteous before God,* that they may be *examples to the flock,* and rejoice their hearts. *They walked in all the commandments and ordinances of the Lord, blameless.* (1.) Their being *righteous before God* was evidenced by the course and tenour of their conversations; they showed it, not by their talk, but by their *works;* by the way they walked in and the rule they walked by. (2.) They were *of a piece* with themselves; for their devotions and their conversations agreed. They walked not only in the *ordinances* of the Lord, which related to divine worship, but in the *commandments* of the Lord, which have reference to all the instances of a good conversation, and must be regarded. (3.) They were universal in their obedience; not that they never did in any thing *come short* of their duty, but it was their constant care and endeavor to *come up* to it. (4.) Herein, though they were not *sinless,* yet they were *blameless;* nobody could charge them with any open scandalous sin; they lived *honestly* and *inoffensively,* as ministers and their families are in a special manner concerned to do, that the ministry be not blamed in *their* blame.

2. That they had been long *childless, v.* 7. Children are a *heritage of the Lord.* But there are many of his heirs in a married state, that yet are denied this *heritage;* they are valuable desirable blessings; yet many there are, who are *righteous before God,* and, if they had children, would bring them up in his fear, who yet are not thus blessed, while the *men of this world* are *full of children* (Ps. 17:14), *and send forth their little ones like a flock,* Job 21:11. Elisabeth was *barren,* and they began to despair of ever having children, for they were both now *well stricken in years,* when the women that have been most fruitful *leave off bearing.* Many eminent persons were born of mothers that had been long childless, as Isaac, Jacob, Joseph, Samson, Samuel, and so here John Baptist, to make their birth the more remarkable and the blessing of it the more valuable to their parents, and to show that when God keeps his people long waiting for mercy he sometimes is pleased to recompense them for their patience by *doubling* the worth of it when it comes.

II. The appearing of an angel to his father Zacharias, as he was ministering in the temple, *v.* 8–11. Zechariah the prophet was the last of the Old Testament that was conversant with angels, and Zacharias the priest the first in the New Testament. Observe,

1. How Zacharias was employed in the service of God (*v.* 8): He *executed the priest's office, before God, in the order of his course;* it was his *week of waiting,* and he was *upon duty.* Though his family was not built up, or made to grow, yet he made conscience of doing the work of his own place and day. Though we have not *desired mercies,* yet we must keep close to *enjoined services;* and, in our diligent and constant attendance on them, we may hope that mercy and comfort will come at last. Now it fell to Zacharias's lot to burn incense morning and evening for that week of his waiting, as other services fell to other priests *by lot* likewise. The services were directed by lot, that some might not decline them and others engross them, and that, the *disposal of the lot* being *from the Lord,* they might have the satisfaction of a divine call to the work. This was not the high priest burning incense on the day of atonement, as some have fondly imagined, who have thought by that to find out the time of our Saviour's birth; but it is plain that it was the burning of the daily incense at the *altar of incense* (*v.* 11), which was *in the temple* (*v.* 9), not in the most holy place, into which the high priest entered. The Jews say that one and the same priest burned not incense twice in all his days (there were such a multitude of them), at least never more than one week. It is very probable that this was *upon the sabbath day,* because there was a *multitude of people* attending (*v.* 10), which ordinarily was not on a week day; and thus God usually puts honour upon *his own day.* And then if Dr. Lightfoot reckon, with the help of the Jewish calender, that this course of Abia fell on the seventeenth day of the third month, the month Sivan, answering to part of May and part of June, it is worth observing that the portions of the law and the prophets which were read this day in synagogues were very agreeable to that which was doing in the temple; namely, the law of the Nazarites (Num. 6), and the conception of Samson, Jdg. 13.

While Zacharias was burning incense in the temple, *the whole multitude of the people were praying without, v.* 10. Dr. Lightfoot says that there were constantly in the temple, at the hour of prayer, the priests of the course that then served, and, if it were the sabbath day, those of that course also that had been in waiting the week before, and the Levites that served under the priests, and the *men of the station,* as the Rabbin call them, who were the representatives of the people, in putting their hands upon the head of the sacrifices, and many besides, who, moved by devotion, left their employments, for that time, to be present at the service of God; and those would make up *a great multitude,* especially on sabbaths and feast-days: now these all addressed themselves to their devotions (in mental prayer, for their voice was not heard), when by the tinkling of a bell they had notice that the priest was gone in to burn incense. Now observe here, (1.) That the true Israel of God always were a *praying* people; and prayer is the great and principal piece of service by which we give honour to God, fetch in favours from him, and keep up our communion with him. (2.) That *then,* when ritual and ceremonial appointments were in full force, as this of *burning incense,* yet moral and spiritual duties were required to go along with them, and were principally looked at. David knew that when he was at a distance from the altar his prayer might be heard *without incense,* for it might be directed before God *as incense,* Ps. 141:2. But, when he was *compassing the altar,* the incense could not be accepted *without prayer,* any more than the shell without the kernel. (3.) That is not enough for us to be where God is worshipped, if our hearts do not join in the worship, and go along with the minister, in all the parts of it. If he burn the incense ever so well, in the most pertinent, judicious, lively prayer, if we be not at the same time *praying* in concurrence with him, what will it avail us? (4.) All the prayers we offer up to God here in his courts are acceptable and successful only in virtue of the incense of Christ's intercession in the temple of God above. To this usage in the temple-service there seems to be an allusion (Rev. 8:1, 3, 4), where we find that *there was silence in heaven,* as there was in the temple, *for half an hour,* while the people were *silently* lifting up their hearts to God in prayer; and that there was an *angel,* the angel of the covenant, who offered up *much incense with the prayers of all saints before the throne.* We cannot expect an interest in Christ's intercession if we do not *pray,* and pray *with our spirits,* and continue instant in prayer. Nor can we expect that the best of our prayers should gain acceptance, and bring in an answer of peace, but through the mediation of Christ, who *ever lives, making intercession.*

2. How, when he was thus employed, he was *honoured* with a messenger, a special messenger sent from heaven to him (*v.* 11): *There appeared unto him an angel of the Lord.* Some observe, that we never read of an angel appearing in the temple, with a message from God, but only this one to Zacharias, because *there* God had other ways of making known his mind, as the Urim and Thummim, and by a still small voice from between the cherubim; but the ark and the oracle were wanting in the second temple, and therefore, when an express was to be sent to a priest in the temple, an angel was to be employed in it, and thereby the gospel was to be introduced, for *that,* as the *law,* was given at first very much by the *ministry of angels,* the appearance of which we often read of in the Gospels and the Acts, though the design both of the law and of the gospel, when brought to perfection, was to settle another way of correspondence, more spiritual, between God and man. This angel stood *on the right side of the altar of incense,* the north side of it, saith Dr. Lightfoot, on Zacharias's right hand; compare this with Zec. 3:1, where Satan stands at the *right hand* of Joshua the priest, to *resist him;* but Zacharias had a good angel standing *at his right hand,* to encourage him. Some think that this angel appeared coming *out of the most holy place,* which led him to stand at the right side of the altar.

3. What impression this made upon Zacharias (*v.* 12): *When Zacharias saw him,* it was a surprise upon him, even to a degree of terror, for he was *troubled,* and *fear fell upon him, v.* 12. Though he was *righteous before God,* and *blameless* in his conversation, yet he could not be without some apprehensions at the sight of one whose visage and surrounding lustre bespoke him more than *human.* Ever since man sinned, his mind has been unable to bear the glory of such revelations and his conscience afraid of evil tidings brought by them; even Daniel himself could not bear it, Dan. 10:8. And for this reason God chooses to speak to us by men like ourselves, whose *terror* shall *not make us afraid.*

III. The message which the angel had to deliver to him,

v. 13. He began his message, as angels generally did, with, *Fear not.* Perhaps it had never been Zacharias's lot to *burn incense* before; and, being a very serious conscientious man, we may suppose him full of care to do it *well,* and perhaps when he saw the angel he was afraid lest he came to rebuke him for some mistake or miscarriage; "No," saith the angel, "*fear not;* I have no ill tidings to bring thee from heaven. *Fear not,* but compose thyself, that thou mayest with a sedate and even spirit receive the message I have to deliver thee." Let us see what that is.

1. The *prayers* he has often made shall now receive an *answer of peace: Fear not, Zacharias, for thy prayer is heard.* (1.) If he means his particular prayer *for a son* to build up his family, it must be the prayers he had formerly made for that mercy, when he was likely to have children; but we may suppose, now that he and his wife were both *well stricken in years,* as they had done expecting it, so they had done praying for it: like Moses, it *sufficeth them,* and they *speak no more to God of that matter,* Deu. 3:26. But God will now, in giving this mercy, look a great way back to the prayers that he had made long since for and with his wife, as Isaac for and with his, Gen. 25:21. Note, Prayers of faith are *filed* in heaven, and are not *forgotten,* though the thing prayed for is not presently *given* in. Prayers made when we were young and coming into the world may be answered when we are old and going out of the world. But, (2.) If he means the prayers he was *now making,* and offering up with his incense, we may suppose that those were according to the duty of his place, for the Israel of God and their welfare, and the performance of the promises made to them concerning the Messiah and the coming of his kingdom: "This prayer of thine is now *heard:* for thy wife shall shortly conceive him that is to be the Messiah's forerunner." Some of the Jewish writers themselves say that the priest, when he burnt incense, prayed for the *salvation of the whole world;* and now that prayer shall be heard. Or, (3.) In general, "The prayers thou *now* makest, and all thy prayers, are accepted of God, and *come up for a memorial* before him" (as the angel said to Cornelius, when he visited him at prayer, Acts 10:30, 31); "and this shall be the sign that thou are accepted of God, Elisabeth shall *bear thee a son.*" Note, it is very comfortable to praying people to know that their *prayers* are *heard;* and those mercies are doubly sweet that are given in answer to prayer.

2. He shall have a son in his old age, by Elisabeth his wife, who had been long barren, that by his birth, which was *next* to miraculous, people might be prepared to receive and believe a virgin's bringing forth of a son, which was *perfectly* miraculous. He is directed what name to give his son: *Call him John,* in Hebrew *Johanan,* a name we often meet in the Old Testament: it signifies *gracious.* The priests must *beseech God that he will be gracious* (Mal. 1:9), and must so *bless the people,* Num. 6:25. Zacharias was now praying thus, and the angel tells him that his prayer is heard, and he shall have a son, whom, in token of an answer to his prayer, he shall call *Gracious,* or, *The Lord will be gracious,* Isa. 30:18, 19.

3. This son shall be the joy of his family and of all his relations, *v.* 14. He shall be another Isaac, thy laughter; and some think that is partly intended in his name, *John.* He shall be a *welcome child. Thou* for thy part *shall have joy and gladness.* Note, Mercies that have been long *waited for,* when they *come at last,* are the more acceptable. "He shall be such a son as thou shalt have reason to rejoice in; many parents, if they could foresee what their children will prove, instead of *rejoicing* at their birth, would wish they had *never been;* but I will tell thee what thy son will be, and then thou wilt not need to *rejoice with trembling* at his birth, as the best must do, but mayest rejoice with triumph at it." Nay, and *many shall rejoice at his birth;* all the relations of the family will rejoice in it, and all its well-wishers, because it is for the honour and comfort of the family, *v.* 58. All good people will rejoice that such a religious couple as Zacharias and Elisabeth have a son, because they will give him a good education, such as, it may be hoped, will make him a public blessing to his generation. Yea, and perhaps many shall rejoice by an *unaccountable instinct,* as a presage of the joyous days the gospel will introduce.

4. This son shall be a distinguished *favourite of Heaven,* and a distinguished *blessing to the earth.* The honour of having *a son* is nothing to the honour of having *such a son.*

(1.) He shall be *great in the sight of the Lord;* those are great indeed that are so in God's sight, not those that are so in the eye of a vain and carnal world. God will *set him before*

his face continually, will employ him in his work and send him on his errands; and that shall make him truly *great* and honourable. He shall be a *prophet,* yea *more than a prophet,* and upon that account as great as any that every were *born of women,* Mt. 11:11. He shall live very much *retired* from the world, out of men's sight, and, when he makes a public appearance, it will be very *mean;* but he shall be *much,* he shall be *great, in the sight of the Lord.*

(2.) He shall be a Nazarite, set apart to God from every thing that is *polluting;* in token of this, according to the law of Nazariteship, he *shall drink neither wine nor strong drink,* — or, rather, neither *old* wine *nor new;* for most think that the word here translated *strong drink* signifies some sort of wine, perhaps those that we call *made wines,* or any thing that is *intoxicating.* He shall be, as Samson was by the divine precept (Jdg. 13:7), and Samuel by his mother's vow (1 Sa. 1:11), a Nazarite for life. It is spoken of as a great instance of God's favour to his people that he *raised up* of *their sons for prophets,* and *their young men for Nazarites* (Amos 2:11), as if those that were designed for prophets were trained up under the discipline of the Nazarites; Samuel and John Baptist were; which intimates that those that would be *eminent* servants of God, and employed in *eminent* services, must learn to live a life of self-denial and mortification, must be dead to the pleasures of sense, and keep their minds from every thing that is darkening and disturbing to them.

(3.) He shall be abundantly fitted and qualified for those great and eminent services to which in due time he shall be called: *He shall be filled with the Holy Ghost, even from his mother's womb,* and as soon as it is possible he shall appear to have been so. Observe, [1.] Those that would be filled with the Holy Ghost must be sober and temperate, and very moderate in the use of wine and strong drink; for *that* is it that fits him for *this. Be not drunk with wine,* but *be filled with the Spirit,* with which that is not consistent, Eph. 5:18. [2.] It is possible that infants may be wrought upon by the *Holy Ghost, even from their mother's womb;* for John Baptist even then was *filled with the Holy Ghost,* who took possession of his heart betimes; and an early specimen was given of it, when he *leaped in his mother's womb for joy,* at the approach of the Saviour; and afterwards it appeared very early that he was *sanctified.* God had promised to *pour out his Spirit* upon the *seed* of believers (Isa. 44:3), and their first *springing up* in a dedication of themselves betimes to God is the fruit of it, *v.* 4, 5. Who then can forbid water, that they should not be baptized who for aught we know (and we can say no more of the adult, witness Simon Magus) have received the Holy Ghost as well as we, and have the *seeds of grace* sown in their hearts? Acts 10:47.

(4.) He shall be instrumental for the conversion of many souls to God, and the preparing of them to receive and entertain the gospel of Christ, *v.* 16, 17.

[1.] He shall be sent to the *children of Israel,* to the nation of the Jews, to whom the Messiah also was *first* sent, and not to the Gentiles; to the *whole* nation, and not the family of *the priests only,* with which, though he was himself of that family, we do not find he had any particular intimacy or influence.

[2.] He shall go before *the Lord their God,* that is, before the Messiah, whom they must expect to be, not *their king,* in the sense wherein they commonly take it, a *temporal prince* to their nation, but *their Lord* and *their God,* to rule and defend, and serve them in a *spiritual* way by his influence on their hearts. Thomas knew this, when he said to Christ, *My Lord* and *my God,* better than Nathanael did, when he said, *Rabbi, thou are the king of Israel.* John shall *go before him,* a little before him, to give notice of his approach, and to prepare people to receive him.

[3.] He shall go *in the spirit and power of Elias.* That is, *First,* He shall be such a man as Elias was, and do such work as Elias did, — shall, like him, preach the necessity of repentance and reformation to a very corrupt and degenerate age, — shall like him, be bold and zealous in reproving sin and witnessing against it even in the greatest, and be hated and persecuted for it by a Herod and his Herodias, as Elijah was by an Ahab and his Jezebel. He shall be carried on in his work, as Elijah was, by a divine *spirit* and *power,* which shall crown his ministry with wonderful success. As Elias went *before* the *writing* prophets of the Old Testament, and did as it were *usher* in that *signal* period of the Old-Testament dispensation by a little *writing* of his own (2 Chr. 21:12), so John Baptist went before Christ and his apostles, and intro-

duced the gospel dispensation by preaching the substance of the gospel doctrine and duty, *Repent, with an eye to the kingdom of heaven. Secondly,* He shall be that very person who was prophesied of by Malachi under the name of Elijah (Mal. 4:5), who should be sent *before the coming of the day of the Lord.* Behold, I *send you a prophet, even Elias,* not Elias the Tishbite (as the Septuagint has corruptly read it, to favour the Jews' traditions), but a prophet *in the spirit and power of Elias,* as the angel here expounds it.

[4.] He shall *turn many of the children of Israel to the Lord their God,* shall incline their hearts to receive the Messiah, and bid him welcome, by awakening them to a sense of sin and a desire of righteousness. Whatever has a tendency to *turn us from iniquity,* as John's preaching and baptism had, will turn us to Christ as *our Lord and our God;* for those who through grace are wrought upon to shake off the yoke of sin, that is, the dominion of the world and the flesh, will soon be persuaded to take upon them the yoke of the *Lord Jesus.*

[5.] Hereby he shall *turn the hearts of the fathers to the children,* that is, of the Jews to the Gentiles; shall help to conquer the rooted prejudices which the Jews have against the Gentiles, which was done by the gospel, as far as it prevailed, and was begun to be done by John Baptist, who came *for a witness, that all through him might believe,* who baptized and taught Roman soldiers as well as Jewish Pharisees, and who cured the pride and confidence of those Jews who gloried in their having Abraham to their father, and told them that God would *out of stones raise up children unto Abraham* (Mt. 3:9), which would tend to *cure* their enmity to the Gentiles. Dr. Lightfoot observes, It is the constant usage of the prophets to speak of the church of the Gentiles as children to the Jewish church, Isa. 54:5, 6, 13; 60:4, 9; 62:5; 66:12. When the Jews that embraced the faith of Christ were brought to join in communion with the Gentiles that did so too, then the heart of the fathers was turned to the children. And he shall *turn the disobedient to the wisdom of the just,* that is, he shall introduce the gospel, by which the Gentiles, who are now *disobedient,* shall be turned, no so much to their fathers the Jews, but to the faith of Christ, here called the *wisdom of the just,* in communion with the believing Jews; or thus, He shall *turn the hearts of the fathers with the children,* that is, the hearts of old and young, shall be instrumental to bring some of every age to be *religious,* to work a great reformation in the Jewish nation, to bring them *off from* a ritual traditional religion which that had rested in, and to bring them up to *substantial serious* godliness: and the effect of this will be, that enmities will be slain and discord made to cease; and they are at variance, being united in his baptism, will be better reconciled one to another. This agrees with the account Josephus gives of John Baptist, *Antiq.* 18.117–118. "That he was a good man, and taught the Jews the exercise of virtue, in piety towards God, and righteous towards one another, and that they should convene and knit together in baptism." And he saith, "The people flocked after him, and were exceedingly delighted in his doctrine." Thus he turned the hearts of fathers and children to God and to one another, by *turning the disobedient to the wisdom of the just.* Observe, *First,* True religion is *the wisdom of just men,* in distinction from the *wisdom of the world.* It is both our wisdom and our duty to be religious; there is both equity and prudence in it. *Secondly,* It is not possible but that those who have been unbelieving and *disobedient* may be turned to the *wisdom of the just;* divine grace can conquer the greatest ignorance and prejudice. *Thirdly,* The great design of the gospel is to bring people *home* to God, and to bring them nearer to *one another;* and on this errand John Baptist is sent. In the mention that is *twice* made of his *turning* people, there seems to be an allusion to the name of the Tishbite, which is given to Elijah, which, some think, does not denote the country or city he was of, but has an appellative signification, and therefore the render it Elijah the *converter,* one that was much employed, and very successful, in *conversion-work.* The Elias of the New Testament is therefore said to *turn* or *convert* many to the Lord their God.

[6.] Hereby he shall *make ready a people prepared for the Lord,* shall dispose the minds of people to receive the doctrine of Christ, that thereby they may be *prepared* for the comforts of his coming. Note, *First,* All that are to be *devoted* to the Lord, and *made happy* in him, must first be *prepared* and *made ready* for him. We must be prepared by grace in this world for the glory in the other, by the terrors of the law for the comforts of the gospel, by the spirit of bondage for the Spirit of adoption. *Secondly,* Nothing has a more direct tendency to prepare people for Christ than the doctrine of repentance received and submitted to. When sin is thereby made grievous, Christ will become very precious.

IV. Zacharias's unbelief of the angel's prediction, and the rebuke he was laid under for that unbelief. He heard all that the angel had to say, and should have bowed his head, and worshipped the Lord, saying, *Be it unto thy servant according to the word* which thou hast spoken; but it was not so. We are here told,

1. What his unbelief spoke, *v.* 18. He said to the angel, *Whereby shall I know this?* This was not a humble petition for the confirming of his faith, but a peevish objection against what was said to him as altogether incredible; as if he should say, "I can never be made to believe this." He could not but perceive that it was *an angel* that spoke to him; the message delivered, having reference to the Old-Testament prophecies, carried much of its own evidence along with it. There are many instances in the Old Testament of those that had children when they were old, yet he cannot believe that he shall have this child of promise: *"For I am an old man,* and my wife hath not only been all her days barren, but is now well *stricken in years,* and not likely ever to have children." Therefore he must have a *sign* given him, or he will not believe. Though the appearance of an angel, which had long been disused in the church, was sign enough, — though he had this notice given him in the temple, the place of God's oracles, where he had reason to think no evil angel would be permitted to come, — though it was given him when he was praying, and burning incense, — and though a firm belief of that great principle of religion that God has an almighty power, and with him *nothing is impossible,* which we ought not only to *know,* but to teach others, was enough to silence all objections, — yet, considering his own body and his wife's too much, unlike a son of Abraham, he *staggered at the promise,* Rom. 4:19, 20.

2. How his unbelief was *silenced,* and he *silenced* for it. (1.) The angel *stops his mouth,* by *asserting* his authority. Doth he ask, *Whereby shall I know this?* Let him know it by this, *I am Gabriel, v.* 19. He puts his name to his prophecy, doth as it were sign it with his own hand, *teste meipso — take my word for it.* Angels have sometimes refused to tell their names, as to Manoah and his wife; but his angel readily saith, *I am Gabriel,* which signifies *the power of God,* or the *mighty one of God,* intimating that the God who bade him say this was able to make it good. He also makes himself known by this name to put him in mind of the notices of the Messiah's coming sent to Daniel by the *man Gabriel,* Dan. 8:16; 9:21. *"I am the same* that was sent then, and am sent now in pursuance of the same intention." He is Gabriel, who *stands in the presence of God,* an immediate attendant upon the throne of God. The prime ministers of state in the Persian court are described by this, that they *saw the king's face,* Esth. 1:14. "Though I am now talking with thee here, yet *I stand in the presence of God.* I know his eye is upon me, and I dare not say any more than I have warrant to say. But I declare *I am sent to speak to thee,* sent on purpose to *show thee these glad tidings,* which, being so well worthy of all acceptation, thou oughtest to have received cheerfully."

(2.) The angel *stops his mouth* indeed, by *exerting his power:* "That thou mayest object no more, *behold thou shalt be dumb, v.* 20. If thou wilt have a sign for the support of thy faith, it shall be such a one as shall be also the punishment of thine unbelief; thou *shalt not be able to speak till the day that these things shall be performed," v.* 20. Thou shalt be both *dumb* and *deaf;* the same word signifies both, and it is plain that he lost his hearing as well as his speech, for his friends *made signs* to him (*v.* 62), as well as he to them, *v.* 22. Now, in striking him dumb, [1.] God dealt *justly* with him, because he had objected against God's word. Hence we may take occasion to admire the patience of God and his forbearance toward us, that we, who have often spoken to his dishonour, have not been struck dumb, as Zacharias was, and as we had been if God had dealt with us according to our sins. [2.] God dealt *kindly* with him, and very tenderly and graciously. For, *First,* Thus he prevented his speaking any more such distrustful unbelieving words. If he has *thought evil,* and will not himself *lay his hands upon his mouth,* nor keep it as with a bridle, God will. It is better not to speak at all than to *speak wickedly. Secondly,* Thus he *confirmed* his faith; and, by his being disabled to *speak,* he is enabled to *think* the better. If by the rebukes we are under for our sin we be brought to give more credit to the word of God, we have no reason to complain of them. *Thirdly,* Thus he was kept from divulging the vision, and boasting of it, which otherwise he would have been apt to do, whereas it was designed for the present to be lodged as a secret with him. *Fourthly,* It was a great mercy that God's words should be fulfilled in their season, notwithstanding his sinful distrust. The *unbelief of man* shall not *make the promises of God of no effect,* they shall be *fulfilled in their season,* and he shall not be for ever *dumb,* but only *till the day that these things shall be performed,* and then thy *lips* shall be *opened,* that thy *mouth* may *show forth God's praise.* Thus, though God *chastens* the *iniquity* of his people *with the rod,* yet his *loving kindness* he *will not take away.*

V. The return of Zacharias to the people, and at length to his family, and the conception of this child of promise, the son of his old age.

1. The people staid, expecting Zacharias to come out of the temple, because he was to pronounce the blessing upon them in the name of the Lord; and, though he staid beyond the usual time, yet they did not, as is too common in Christian congregations, hurry away without the blessing, but *waited* for him, marvelling that he *tarried so long in the temple,* and afraid let something was amiss, *v.* 21.

2. When he came out, he was *speechless, v.* 22. He was now to have dismissed the congregation with a blessing, but was dumb and not able to do it, that the people may be minded to expect the Messiah, who can *command* the blessing, who *blesseth indeed,* and in whom all *the nations of the earth are blessed.* Aaron's priesthood is now shortly to be *silenced* and *set aside,* to make way for the *bringing in* of a *better hope.*

3. He made a shift to give them to understand that he had *seen a vision,* by some awful signs he made, for he *beckoned to them,* and *remained speechless, v.* 22. This represents to us the weakness and deficiency of the Levitical priesthood, in comparison with Christ's priesthood and the dispensation of the gospel. The Old Testament speaks by signs, gives us some intimations of divine and heavenly things, but *imperfect* and uncertain; it *beckons to us,* but *remains speechless.* It is the gospel that speaks to us articulately, and gives us a clear view of that which the Old Testament was seen *through a glass darkly.*

4. He staid out the *days of his ministration;* for, his lot being to *burn incense,* he could do that, though he was *dumb* and *deaf.* When we cannot perform the service of God so well as we would, yet, if we perform it as well as we can, God will accept of us in it.

5. He then returned to his family, and his *wife conceived, v.* 23, 24. She conceived by virtue of the promise, and, being sensible of it, *she hid herself five months;* she kept house, and kept it private, and did not go abroad so much as she used to do, (1.) Lest she should do herself any prejudice, so as might occasion her miscarrying, or any hurt to the conception. (2.) Lest she should contract any ceremonial pollution which might intrench upon the Nazariteship of her child, remembering the command given to Samson's mother in a like case, and applying it to herself; she must not *touch any unclean thing* while she is with child of a Nazarite, Jdg. 13:14. And though *five months* are mentioned, because of what follows *in the sixth month,* yet we may suppose that she did in like manner take care of herself during the whole time of her being with child. (3.) Some think it was in an excess of modesty that she *hid herself,* ashamed it should be said that one of her age should be with child. *Shall she have pleasure, being old, her lord being old also?* Gen. 18:12. Or, it was in token of her humility, that she might not seem to boast of the honour God had put upon her. (4.) She *hid herself* for devotion, that she might spend her time in prayer and praise. The saints are God's *hidden ones;* she gives this reason for her retirement; *"For thus hath the Lord dealt with me;* not only thus *graciously* in giving me a child, but thus *honourably* in giving me such a child as is to be a Nazarite" (for so her husband might by writing signify to her); "he hath *taken away my reproach among men."* Fruitlessness was looked upon to be so great a blessing among the Jews, because of the promises of the increase of their nation, and the rising of the Messiah among them, that it was a great reproach to be barren; and those who were so, though ever so *blameless,* were concluded to be guilty of some great sin *unknown,* for which they were punished. Now Elisabeth triumphs, that not only this reproach is taken away, but great glory is put upon her instead of it: *Thus hath the Lord dealt with me,* beyond any thought or expectation of mine, *in the days wherein he looked on me.* Note, In God's gracious dealings with us we ought to observe his gracious regards to us. He has *looked upon us* with compassion and favour, and therefore has thus *dealt with us.*

Verses 26–38

We have here notice given us of all that it was fit we should know concerning the incarnation and conception of our blessed Saviour, six months after the conception of John. The same angel, Gabriel, that was employed in making known to Zacharias God's purpose concerning *his son,* is employed in this also; for in this, the same glorious work of redemption, which was *begun* in that, is *carried on.* As bad angels are none of the redeemed, so good angels are none of the redeemers; yet they are employed by the Redeemer as his messengers, and they go cheerfully on his errands, because they are his Father's humble servants, and his children's hearty friends and well-wishers.

I. We have here an account given of the mother of our Lord, of whom he was to be born, whom, though we are not to pray to, yet we ought to praise God for.

1. Her name was *Mary,* the same name with *Miriam,* the sister of Moses and Aaron; the name signifies *exalted,* and a great elevation it was to her indeed to be thus *favoured* above all the daughters of the house of David.

2. She was a daughter of the royal family, lineally descended from David, and she herself and all her friends knew it, for she went under the title and character of the *house of David,* though she was poor and low in the world; and she was enabled by God's providence, and the care of the Jews, to preserve their genealogies, to *make it out,* and as long as the promise of the Messiah was to be fulfilled it was *worth keeping;* but for those now, who are brought low in the world, to have descended from persons of honour, is not worth mentioning.

3. She was *a virgin,* a pure unspotted one, but *espoused* to one of the same royal stock, like her, however, of low estate; so that upon both accounts there was (as it was fit there should be) an equality between them; his name was Joseph; he also was *of the house of David,* Mt. 1:20. Christ's mother was a *virgin,* because he was not to be born by ordinary generation, but miraculously; it was necessary that he should be so, that, though he must partake of the nature of man, yet not of the corruption of that nature: but he was born of a *virgin espoused,* made up to be married, and contracted, to put honour upon the married state, that that might not be brought into contempt (which was an ordinance in innocency) by the Redeemer's being born of a virgin.

4. She lived in Nazareth, a *city of Galilee,* a remote corner of the country, and in no reputation for religion or learning, but which bordered upon the heathen, and therefore was called *Galilee of the Gentiles.* Christ's having his relations resident there intimates favour in reserve for the Gentile world. And Dr. Lightfoot observes that Jonah was by birth a Galilean, and Elijah and Elisha very much conversant in Galilee, who were all famous *prophets of the Gentiles.* The angel was sent to her from Nazareth. Note, No distance or disadvantage of place shall be a prejudice to those for whom God has favours in store. The angel Gabriel carries his message as cheerfully to Mary and Nazareth in Galilee as to Zacharias in the temple at Jerusalem.

II. The *address* of the angel to her, *v.* 28. We are not told what she was doing, or how employed, when the angel came *unto her;* but he surprised her with this salutation, *Hail, thou art highly favoured.* This was intended to raise in her, 1. A value for *herself;* and, though it is very rare that any need to have any sparks struck into their breast with such design, yet in some, who like Mary pore only on their *low estate,* there is occasion for it. 2. An expectation of great news, not from abroad, but from above. Heaven designs, no doubt, uncommon favours for one whom an angel makes court to with such respect, *Hail thou, chaire — rejoice thou;* it was the usual form of salutation; it expresses an esteem of her, and goodwill to her and her prosperity.

(1.) She is dignified: "Thou art *highly favoured.* God, in his choice of thee to be the mother of the Messiah, has put an honour upon thee peculiar to thyself, above that of Eve, who was the mother of *all living."* The vulgar Latin translates this *gratiâ plena — full of grace,* and thence gathers that she had more of the inherent graces of the Spirit than ever any had; whereas it is certain that this bespeaks no other than the singular favour done her in preferring her to conceive and bear our blessed Lord, an honour which, since he was to be the *seed of the woman,* some woman must have, not for *personal merit,* but purely for the sake of *free grace,* and she is pitched upon. *Even so, Father, because it seemed good unto thee.*

(2.) She has the presence of God with her: "*The Lord is with thee,* though poor and mean, and perhaps now forecasting how to get a livelihood and maintain a family in the married state." The angel with this word raised the faith of Gideon (Jdg. 6:12): *The Lord is with thee.* Nothing is to be despaired of, not the performance of any service, not the obtaining of any favour, though ever so great, if we have *God with us.* This word might put her in mind of the Immanuel, *God with us,* which a virgin shall *conceive* and *bear* (Isa. 7:14), and why not she?

(3.) She has the blessing of God upon her: "*Blessed art thou among women;* not only thou shalt be accounted so by men, but thou shalt be so. Thou that art so *highly favoured* in this instance mayest expect in other things to be *blessed.*" She explains this herself (*v.* 48), *All generations shall call me blessed.* Compare it with that which Deborah saith of Jael, another that was the glory of her sex (Jdg. 5:24), *Blessed shall she be above women in the tent.*

III. The consternation she was in, upon this address (*v.* 29). *When she saw him,* and the glories with which he was surrounded, she was *troubled* at the sight of him, and much more *at his saying.* Had she been a proud ambitious young woman, that aimed high, and flattered herself with the expectation of great things in the world, she would have been *pleased* at his saying, would have been puffed up with it, and (as we have reason to think she was a young woman of very good sense) would have had an answer ready, signifying so much: but, instead of that, she is *confounded* at it, as not conscious to herself of any thing that either *merited* or *promised* such great things; and she *cast in her mind what manner of salutation this should be.* Was it from heaven or of men? Was it to amuse her? was it to ensnare her? was it to banter her? or was there something substantial and weighty in it? But, of all the thoughts she had as to *what manner of salutation it should be,* I believe she had not the least idea of its being ever intended or used for a prayer, as it is, and has been, for many ages, by the corrupt, degenerate, and anti-christian ages of the church, and to be ten times repeated for the Lord's prayer once; so it is in the church of Rome. But her thoughtfulness upon this occasion gives a very useful intimation to young people of her sex, when addresses are made to them, to consider and *cast in their minds* what manner of *salutations* they are, whence they come, and what their tendency is, that they may receive them accordingly, and may always *stand on their guard.*

IV. The message itself which the angel had to deliver to her. Some time the angel gives her to *pause;* but, observing that this did but increase her perplexity, he went on with his errand, *v.* 30. To what he had said she made no reply; he therefore confirms it: "*Fear not, Mary,* I have no other design than to assure thee that *thou hast found favour with God* more than thou thinkest of, as there are many who think they are more favoured with God than they really are." Note, Those that have *found favour with God* should not give way to disquieting distrustful fears. Doth God favour thee? Fear not, though the world frown upon thee. Is he for thee? No matter who is against thee.

1. Though she is a *virgin,* she shall have the honour of being a *mother:* "*Thou shalt conceive in thy womb, and bring forth a son,* and thou shalt have the naming of him; thou shalt *call his name Jesus,*" *v.* 31. It was the sentence upon Eve, that, though she should have the honour to be the *mother of all living,* yet this mortification shall be an allay to that honour, that *her desire shall be to her husband,* and he *shall rule over her,* Gen. 3:16. But Mary has the honour without the allay.

2. Though she lives in *poverty* and *obscurity,* yet she shall have the honour to be the mother of the Messiah; her son shall be named *Jesus — a Saviour,* such a one as the world needs, rather than such one as the Jews *expect.*

(1.) He will be very *nearly allied to the upper world.* He *shall be great,* truly great, incontestably great; for he shall be called the *Son of the Highest,* the Son of God who is *the Highest;* of the same nature, as the son is of the same nature with the father; and very dear to him, as the son is to the father. He shall be *called,* and not *miscalled,* the *Son of the Highest;* for he is himself *God over all, blessed for evermore,* Rom. 9:5. Note, Those who are the children of God, though

but by adoption and regeneration, are *truly great,* and therefore are concerned to be *very good,* 1 Jn. 3:1, 2.

(2.) He will be very *highly preferred* in the *lower world;* for, though born under the most disadvantageous circumstances possible, and appearing in the form of a servant, yet the *Lord God shall give unto him the throne of his father David,* v. 32. He puts her in mind that she was *of the house of David;* and that therefore, since neither the *Salique law,* nor the right of primogeniture, took place in the entail of his throne, it was not impossible but that she might bring forth an heir to it, and therefore might the more easily *believe* it when she was told by an angel from heaven that she *should* do so, that after the sceptre had been long *departed* from that ancient and honourable family it should now at length return to it again, to remain in it, not by succession, but in the same hand to eternity. His people will not *give him that throne,* will not acknowledge his right to *rule them;* but the *Lord God* shall give him a right to *rule them,* and set him as *his king* upon the *holy hill of Zion.* He assures her, [1.] That his kingdom shall be *spiritual:* he shall *reign over the house of Jacob,* not *Israel according to the flesh,* for they neither came into his interests nor did they continue long a people; it must therefore be a *spiritual* kingdom, the house of Israel *according to the promise,* that he must *rule over.* [2.] That it shall be eternal: he shall reign *for ever,* and *of his kingdom there shall be no end,* as there had been long since of the temporal reign of David's house, and would shortly be of the state of Israel. Other crowns endure not *to every generation,* but Christ's doth, Prov. 27:24. The gospel is the *last* dispensation, we are to look for no other.

V. The further information given her, upon her enquiry concerning the birth of this prince.

1. It is a just enquiry which she makes: "*How shall this be? v.* 34. How can I now presently conceive a child" (for so the angel meant) "when I *know not a man;* must it therefore be otherwise than by ordinary generation? If so, let me now how?" She knew that the Messiah must be born of *a virgin;* and, if she must be his mother, she desires to know how. This was not the language of her distrust, or any doubt of what the angel said, but of a desire to be further instructed.

2. It is a satisfactory answer that is given to it, *v.* 35. (1.) She shall conceive by *the power of the Holy Ghost,* whose proper work and office is to *sanctify,* and therefore to sanctify the virgin for this purpose. The Holy Ghost is called the *power of the Highest.* Doth she ask how this shall be? This is enough to help her over all the difficulty there appears in it; a divine power will undertake it, not the power of an angel employed in it, as in other works of wonder, but the power of *the Holy Ghost* himself.

(2.) She must *ask no questions* concerning the way and manner how it shall be wrought; for the Holy Ghost, as the *power of the Highest,* shall *overshadow* her, as the *cloud* covered the tabernacle when the glory of God took possession of it, to conceal it from those that would too curiously observe the motions of it, and pry into the mystery of it. The formation of every babe in the womb, and the entrance of the spirit of life into it, is a mystery in nature; none knows *the way of the spirit, nor how the bones are formed in the womb of her that is with child,* Eccl. 11:5. We were *made in secret,* Ps. 139:15, 16. Much more was the formation of the child Jesus a *mystery;* without controversy, *great was the mystery of godliness, God manifest in the flesh,* 1 Tim. 3:16. It is a *new thing created in the earth* (Jer. 31:22), concerning which we must not covet to be *wise above what is written.*

(3.) The child she shall conceive is a *holy thing,* and therefore must not be conceived by *ordinary generation,* because he must not share in the common corruption and pollution of the human nature. He is spoken of emphatically, *That holy Thing,* such as never was; and he shall be called *the Son of God,* as the Son of the Father by eternal generation, as an indication of which he shall now be formed by the Holy Ghost in the present conception. His human nature must be so produced, as it was fit that should be which was to be taken into union with the divine nature.

3. It was a further encouragement to her faith to be told that *her cousin Elisabeth,* though stricken in years, was *with child, v.* 36. Here is an age of wonders beginning, and therefore be not surprised: here is one among thy own relations truly great, though not altogether so great as this; it is usual with God to advance in working wonders. *Greater works than these shall ye do.* Though Elisabeth was, on the father's side, of the *daughters of Aaron* (*v.* 5), yet on the mother's side she

might be of the house of David, for those two families often intermarried, as an earnest of the uniting of the royalty and the priesthood of the Messiah. *This is the sixth month with her that was called barren.* This intimates, as Dr. Lightfoot thinks, that all the instances in the Old Testament of those having children that had been long barren, which was above nature, were designed to prepare the world for the belief of a virgin's bearing a son, which was against nature. And therefore, even in the birth of Isaac, Abraham saw Christ's day, foresaw such a miracle in the birth of Christ. The angel assures Mary of this, to encourage her faith, and concludes with that great truth, of undoubted certainty and universal use, *For with God nothing shall be impossible* (*v.* 37), and, if nothing, then not this. Abraham therefore staggered not at the belief of the divine promise, because he was strong in his belief of the divine power, Rom. 4:20, 21. No *word* of God must be *incredible to us,* as long as no *work* of God is *impossible to him.*

VI. Her acquiescence in the will of God concerning her, *v.* 38. She owns herself, 1. A believing subject to the divine authority: "*Behold, the handmaid of the Lord.* Lord, I am at thy service, at thy disposal, to do what thou commandest me." She objects not the danger of spoiling her marriage, and blemishing her reputation, but leaves the issue with God, and submits entirely to his will. 2. A believing expectant of the divine favour. She is not only content that it should be so, but humbly desires that it may be so: *Be it unto me according to thy word.* Such a favour as this it was not for her to slight, or be indifferent to; and for what God has *promised* he will be *sought unto;* by prayer we must put our *amen,* or *so be it,* to the promise. *Remember,* and perform *thy word unto thy servant, upon which thou has caused me to hope.* We must, as Mary here, *guide* our desires by the word of God, and *ground* our hopes *upon* it. Be it unto me *according to thy word;* just so, and no otherwise.

Hereupon, *the angel departed from her;* having completed the errand he was sent upon, he returned, to give an account of it, and receive new instructions. Converse with angels was always a transient thing, and soon over; it will be constant and permanent in the future state. It is generally supposed that just at this instant the virgin *conceived,* by the *overshadowing power* of the Holy Ghost: but, the scripture being decently silent concerning it, it doth not become us to be *inquisitive,* much less *positive.*

Verses 39–56

We have here an interview between the two happy mothers, Elisabeth and Mary: the angel, by intimating to Mary the favour bestowed on her cousin Elisabeth (*v.* 36), gave occasion for it; and sometimes it may prove a better piece of service that we think to bring good people together, to compare notes. Here is,

I. The visit which Mary made to Elisabeth. Mary was the *younger,* and younger with child; and therefore, if they must come together, it was fittest that Mary should take the journey, not insisting on the preference which the greater dignity of her conception gave her, *v.* 39. She *arose,* and left her affairs, to attend this greater matter: *in those days, at that time* (as it is commonly explained, Jer. 33:15; 50:4), in a day or two after the angel had visited her, taking some time first, as it is supposed, for her devotion, or rather hastening away to her cousin's, where she would have more leisure, and better help, in the family of a priest. She went, *meta spoudēs* — with care, diligence, and expedition; not as young people commonly go abroad and visit their friends, to *divert* herself, but to *inform* herself: she went *to a city of Judah in the hill-country;* it is not named, but by comparing the description of it here with Jos. 21:10, 11, it appears to be *Hebron,* for that is there said to be *in the hill-country of Judah,* and to belong to the priests, the sons of Aaron; thither Mary hastened, though it was a long journey, some scores of miles.

1. Dr. Lightfoot offers a conjecture that she was to *conceive* our Saviour there at Hebron, and perhaps had so much intimated to her by the angel, or some other way; and therefore she made such haste thither. He thinks it probable that Shiloh, of the tribe of Judah, and the seed of David, should be *conceived* in a city of Judah and of David, as he was to be born in Bethlehem, another city which belonged to them both. In Hebron the promise was given to Isaac, circumcision was instituted. Here (saith he) Abraham had his first land, and David his first crown: here lay interred the three couples, Abraham and Sarah, Isaac and Rebecca, Jacob and Leah, and,

as antiquity has held, Adam and Eve. He therefore thinks that it suits singularly with the harmony and consent which God uses in his works that the promise should begin to take place by the conception of the Messias, even among those patriarchs to whom it was given. I see no improbability in the conjecture, but add this for the support of it, that Elisabeth said (*v.* 45), *There shall be a performance;* as if it were not performed yet, but was to be performed there.

2. It is generally supposed that she went thither for the confirming of her faith by the sign which the angel had given her, her cousin's being with child, and to rejoice with her sister-favourite. And, besides, she went thither, perhaps, that she might be more retired from company, or else might have more agreeable company than she could have in Nazareth. We may suppose that she did not acquaint any of her neighbours at Nazareth with the message she had received from heaven, yet longed to *talk over* a thing she had a thousand time *thought over,* and knew no person in the world with whom she could *freely* converse concerning it but her cousin Elisabeth, and therefore she hastened to her. Note, it is very beneficial and comfortable for those that have a good work of grace begun in their souls, and Christ in the *forming* there, to consult those who are in the same case, that they may communicate experiences one to another; and they will find that, as in water face answers to face, so doth the heart of man to man, of Christian to Christian.

II. The meeting between Mary and Elisabeth. Mary entered into the house of Zacharias; but he, being *dumb* and *deaf,* kept his chamber, it is probable, and saw no company; and therefore she *saluted Elisabeth* (*v.* 40), told her she was come to make her a visit, to know her state, and *rejoice with her* in her joy.

Now, at their first coming together, for the confirmation of the faith of both of them, there was something very extraordinary. Mary knew that Elisabeth was with child, but it does not appear that Elisabeth had been told any thing of her cousin Mary's being designed for the mother of the Messiah; and therefore what knowledge she appears to have had of it must have come by a *revelation,* which would be a great encouragement to Mary.

1. The babe *leaped in her womb, v.* 41. It is very probable that she had been several weeks *quick* (for she was six months gone), and that she had often felt the child stir; but this was a more than ordinary motion of the child, which alarmed her to expect something very extraordinary, *eskirtēse.* It is the same word that is used by the Septuagint (Gen. 25:22) for the *struggling* of Jacob and Esau in Rebecca's womb, and the mountains *skipping,* Ps. 114:4. The *babe leaped* as it were to give a signal to his mother that *he* was now at had whose forerunner he was to be, about six months in ministry, as he was in being; or, it was the effect of some strong impression made upon the mother. Now began to be fulfilled what the angel said to his father (*v.* 15), that he should be *filled with the Holy Ghost, even from his mother's womb;* and perhaps he himself had some reference to this, when he said (Jn. 3:29), *The friend of the Bridegroom rejoiceth greatly, because of the Bridegroom's voice,* heard, though not by him, yet by his mother.

2. Elisabeth was herself *filled with the Holy Ghost,* or a Spirit of prophecy, by which, as well as by the particular suggestions of the Holy Ghost she was filled with, she was given to understand that the Messiah was at hand, in whom prophecy should revive, and by whom the Holy Ghost should be more plentifully poured out than ever, according to the expectations of those who *waited for the consolation of Israel.* The uncommon motion of the babe in her womb was a token of extraordinary emotion of her spirit under a divine impulse. Note, Those whom Christ graciously visits may know it by their being *filled with the Holy Ghost;* for, *if any man have not the Spirit of Christ, he is none of his.*

III. The welcome which Elisabeth, by the Spirit of prophecy, gave to Mary, the mother of our Lord; not as to a common friend making a common visit, but as to one of whom the Messiah was to be born.

1. She congratulates her on her honour, and, though perhaps she knew not of it till *just now,* she acknowledges it with the greatest assurance and satisfaction. She *spoke with a loud voice,* which does not at all intimate (as some think) that there was a floor or a wall between them, but that she was in a transport or exultation of joy, and said what she cared not who knew. She said, *Blessed art thou among women,* the same word that the angels had said (*v.* 28); for thus this will of God, concerning honouring the Son, should be done *on earth* as it is *done in heaven.* But Elisabeth adds a reason, *Therefore blessed art thou* because *blessed is the fruit of thy womb;* thence it was that she derived this excelling dignity. Elisabeth was the wife of a priest, and in years, yet she *grudges* not that her kinswoman, who was many years younger than she, and every way her inferior, should have the honour of conceiving in her virginity, and being the mother of the Messiah, whereas the honour put upon her was *much less;* she *rejoices* in it, and is well pleased, as her son was afterwards, that she who *cometh after her is preferred before her,* Jn. 1:27. Note, While we cannot but own that we are more *favoured* of God than we deserve, let us by no means envy that others are *more highly* favoured than we are.

2. She acknowledges her condescension, in making her this visit (*v.* 43): *Whence is this to me, that the mother of my Lord should come to me?* Observe, (1.) She calls the virgin Mary the *mother of her Lord* (as David in spirit, called the Messiah Lord, *his Lord*), for she knew he was to be *Lord of all.* (2.) She not only bids her welcome to her house, though perhaps she came in mean circumstances, but reckons this visit a great favour, which she thought herself unworthy of. *Whence is this to me?* It is in reality, and not in compliment, that she saith, "This was a greater favour than I could have expected." Note, Those that are filled with the Holy Ghost have *low thoughts* of their own merits, and high thoughts of God's favours. Her son the Baptist spoke to the same purport with this, when he said, *Comest thou to me?* Mt. 3:14.

3. She acquaints her with the concurrence of the babe in her womb, in this welcome to her (*v.* 44): "Thou certainly bringest some extraordinary tidings, some extraordinary blessing, with thee; for *as soon as the voice of thy salutation sounded in my ears,* not only my heart *leaped for joy,* though I knew not immediately why or wherefore, but the *babe in my womb,* who was not capable of knowing, *did so* too." He *leaped* as it were *for joy* that the Messiah, whose harbinger he was to be, would himself come soon after him. This would serve very much to strengthen the faith of the virgin, that there were such assurances as these given to others; and it would be in part the accomplishment of what had been so often foretold, that there should be *universal joy before the Lord, when he cometh,* Ps. 98:8, 9.

4. She commends her faith, and encourages it (*v.* 45): *Blessed is she that believed.* Believing souls are blessed souls, and will be found so at last; this blessedness cometh *through faith,* even the blessedness of being related to Christ, and having him *formed in the soul.* They are *blessed* who *believe* the word of God, for that Word will not fail them; *there shall,* without doubt, *be a performance of those things which are told her from the Lord.* Note, The inviolable certainty of the promise is the undoubted felicity of those that build upon it and expect their all from it. The faithfulness of God is the blessedness of the faith of the saints. Those that have experienced the performance of God's promises themselves should encourage others to hope that he will be as good as his word to them also: *I will tell you what God has done for my soul.*

IV. Mary's song of praise, upon this occasion. Elisabeth's prophecy was an echo to the virgin Mary's salutation, and this song is yet a stronger *echo* to that prophecy, and shows her to be no less filled with the Holy Ghost than Elisabeth was. We may suppose the blessed virgin to come in, very much *fatigued* with her journey; yet she forgets that, and is inspired with new life, and vigour, and joy, upon the confirmation she here meets with of her faith; and since, by the sudden inspiration and transport, she finds that this was designed to be her errand hither, weary as she is, like Abraham's servant, she would *neither eat nor drink till she had told her errand.*

1. Here are the expressions of joy and praise, and God alone the object of the praise and centre of the joy. Some compare this song with that which her name-sake Miriam, the sister of Moses, sung, upon the triumphant departure of Israel out of Egypt, and their triumphant passage through the Red Sea; others think it better compared with the song of Hannah, upon the birth of Samuel, which, like this, passes from a family mercy to a public and general one. *This* begins, like *that, My heart rejoiceth in the Lord,* 1 Sa. 2:1. Observe how Mary here speaks of God.

(1.) With great reverence of him, as *the Lord: "My soul doth magnify the Lord;* I never saw him so *great* as now I find him so *good."* Note, Those, and those only, are *advanced* in mercy, who are thereby brought to think the more *highly* and *honourably* of God; whereas there are those whose prosperity and preferment make them say, *What is the Almighty, that we should serve him?* The more honour God has any way put upon us, the more honour we must study to give to him; and *then* only are we accepted in magnifying the Lord, when our *souls* magnify him, and *all that is within us.* Praising work must be soul work.

(2.) With great complacency in him as *her Saviour: My spirit rejoiceth in God my Saviour.* This seems to have reference to the Messiah, whom she was to be the mother of. She calls him *God her Saviour;* for the angel had told her that he should be the *Son of the Highest,* and that his name should be *Jesus, a Saviour;* this she fastened upon, with application to herself: *He is God my Saviour.* Even the mother of our Lord had need of an interest in him as her Saviour, and would have been undone without it: and she glories more in that happiness which she had in common with all believers than in being his mother, which was an honour peculiar to herself, and this agrees with the preference Christ have to obedient believers above his mother and brethren; see Mt. 12:50; Lu. 11:27, 28. Note, Those that have Christ for their God and Saviour have a great deal of reason to rejoice, to *rejoice in spirit,* that is rejoicing as Christ did (Lu. 10:21), with spiritual joy.

2. Here are just causes assigned for this joy and praise.

(1.) Upon *her own* account, *v.* 48, 49. [1.] Her *spirit rejoiced in the Lord,* because of the *kind* things he had done for her: his *condescension* and *compassion* to her. *He has regarded the low estate of his handmaiden;* that is, he has *looked* upon her *with pity,* for so the word is commonly used. "He has chosen me to this honour, notwithstanding my great meanness, poverty, and obscurity." Nay, the expression seems to intimate, not only (to allude to that of Gideon, Jdg. 6:15) that her *family* was poor in Judah, but that she was the *least in her father's house,* as if she were under some particular contempt and disgraced among her relations, was unjustly neglected, and the outcast of the family, and God put this honour upon her, to balance abundantly the contempt. I the rather suggest this, for we find something toward such honour as this put upon others, on the like consideration. Because God saw that Leah *was hated,* he *opened her womb,* Gen. 29:31. Because Hannah was provoked, and made to fret, and insulted over, by Peninnah, therefore God gave her a son, 1 Sa. 1:19. Whom men wrongfully depress and despise God doth sometimes, in compassion to them, especially if they have borne it patiently, prefer and advance; see Jdg. 11:7. So in Mary's case. And, if God *regards her low estate,* he not only thereby gives a specimen of his favour to the whole race of mankind, whom he *remembers in their low estate,* as the psalmist speaks (Ps. 136:23), but secures a lasting honour to her (for such the honour is that God bestows, honour that fades not away): *"From henceforth all generations shall call me blessed,* shall think me a happy woman and highly advanced." All that embrace Christ and his gospel will say, *Blessed was the womb that bore him and the paps which he sucked,* Lu. 11:27. Elizabeth had once and again called her *blessed:* "But that is not all," saith she, "all generations of Gentiles as well as Jews shall call me so." [2.] Her *soul magnifies* the Lord, because of the *wonderful* things he had done for her (*v.* 49): *He that is mighty has done to me great things.* A *great* thing indeed, that a *virgin* should *conceive.* A *great* thing indeed, that Messiah, who had been so long promised to the church, and so long expected by the church, should now at length be born. It is the *power of the Highest* that appears in this. She adds, *and holy is his name;* for so Hannah saith her song, *There is none holy as the Lord,* which she explains in the next words, *for there is none beside thee,* 1 Sa. 2:2. God is a Being *by himself,* and he manifests himself to be so, especially in the work of our redemption. He that is *mighty,* even he *whose name is holy,* has *done to me great things.* Glorious things may be expected from him that is both *mighty* and *holy;* who *can do every thing,* and *will* do every thing *well* and *for the best.*

(2.) Upon the account of *others.* The virgin Mary, as the mother of the Messiah, is become a kind of public person, wears a public character, and is therefore immediately endued with another spirit, a more public spirit than before she had, and therefore *looks abroad,* looks *about her,* looks *before her,* and takes notice of God's various dealings with the children of men (*v.* 50, etc.), as Hannah (1 Sa. 2:3, etc.). In this she has especially an eye to the coming of the Redeemer and God's manifesting himself therein.

[1.] It is a certain truth that God *has mercy in store,* mercy in reserve, *for all that have a reverence for his majesty,* and a due regard to his sovereignty and authority. But never did this appear so as in sending his Son into the world to save us (*v.* 50): *His mercy is on them that fear him;* it has always been so; he has ever looked upon *them* with an eye of *peculiar favour* who have looked up to him with and eye of *filial fear.* But he hath manifested this *mercy,* so as never before, in sending his Son to bring in an everlasting righteousness, and work out an everlasting salvation, for them that fear him, and this *from generation to generation;* for there are gospel privileges transmitted by entail, and intended for perpetuity. Those that *fear God,* as their Creator and Judge, are encouraged to hope for *mercy in him,* through their Mediator and Advocate; and in him *mercy* is settled upon all that *fear God,* pardoning mercy, healing mercy, accepting mercy, crowning mercy, *from generation to generation,* while the world stands. In Christ he *keepeth mercy for thousands.*

[2.] It has been a common observation that God in his providence puts *contempt* upon the *haughty* and *honour* upon the *humble;* and this he has done remarkably in the whole economy of the work of man's redemption. As God had, with his *mercy* to her, shown himself *mighty* also (*v.* 48, 49), so he had, with his *mercy on them that fear him, shown strength* likewise *with his arm. First,* In the course of his providence, it is his usual method to cross *the expectations of men,* and proceed quite otherwise than they promise themselves. *Proud men* expect to carry all before them, to have their way and their will; but he *scatters them in the imagination of their hearts,* breaks their measures, blasts their projects, nay, and brings them low, and brings them down, by those very counsels with which they thought to advance and establish themselves. The *mighty* think to secure themselves by might *in their seats,* but he *puts them down,* and overturns their seats; while, on the other hand, those of *low degree,* who despaired of ever advancing themselves, and thought of no other than of being *ever low,* are wonderfully *exalted.* This observation concerning *honour* holds likewise concerning *riches;* many who were so poor that they had not bread for themselves and their families, by some surprising turn of Providence in favour of them, come to be *filled with good things;* while, on the other hand, those who were rich, and thought no other than that to-morrow should be as this day, that their mountain stood strong and should never be moved, are strangely impoverished, and *sent away empty.* Now this is the same observation that Hannah had made, and enlarged upon, in her song, with application to the case of herself and her adversary (1 Sa. 2:4–7), which very much illustrates this here. And compare also Ps. 107:33–41; 113:7–9; and Eccl. 9:11. God takes a pleasure in *disappointing* their expectations who promise themselves *great things* in the world, and in *outdoing* the expectations of those who promise themselves but *a little;* as a *righteous* God, it is his glory to *abase* those who *exalt* themselves, and strike terror on the secure; and, as a *good* God, it is his glory to exalt those who humble themselves, and to speak comfort to those who fear before him. *Secondly,* This doth especially appear in the methods of gospel grace.

1. In the *spiritual honours* it dispenses. When the proud Pharisees were rejected, and Publicans and sinners went *into the kingdom of heaven* before them, — when the Jews, who *followed after the law of righteousness,* did not attain it, and the Gentiles, who never thought of it, attained to righteousness (Rom. 9:30, 31), — when God chose not the *wise men after the flesh,* not the *mighty,* or the *noble,* to preach the gospel, and plant Christianity in the world, but the *foolish* and *weak* things of the world, and things that were despised (1 Co. 1:26, 27) — then he *scattered the proud,* and *put down the mighty,* but *exalted them of low degree.* When the tyranny of the chief priests and elders was brought down, who had long *lorded it over God's heritage,* and hoped *always* to do so, and Christ's disciples, a company of poor despised fishermen, by the power they were clothed with, were made to *sit on thrones,* judging the twelve tribes of Israel, — when the power of the four monarchies was broken, and the kingdom of the Messiah, that *stone cut out of the mountain without hands,* is made to *fill the earth,* — then are the *proud scattered,* and those of low degree *exalted.*

2. In the *spiritual riches* it dispenses, *v.* 53. (1.) Those who see their need of Christ, and are importunately desirous of righteousness and life in him, he *fills* with *good things,* with the *best things;* he gives liberally to them, and they are *abundantly satisfied* with the blessings he gives. Those who are weary and heavy-laden shall find rest with Christ, and those who thirst are called to *come to him and drink;* for they only know how to value his gifts. *To the hungry soul every bitter thing is sweet,* manna is angels' food; and to the *thirsty* fair water is *honey out of the rock.* (2.) Those who are rich, who are not *hungry,* who, like Laodicea, think they have *need of nothing,* are full of themselves and their own righteousness, and think they have a sufficiency in themselves, those he *sends away* from his door, they are not welcome to him, he sends them *empty* away, they come *full of self,* and are sent away *empty of Christ.* He sends them to the *gods whom they served,* to their own righteousness and strength which they trusted to.

[3.] It was always expected that the Messiah should be, in a special manner, the strength and glory of his people Israel, and so he is in a peculiar manner (*v.* 54): *He hath helped his servant Israel, antelabeto.* He hath taken them by the hand, and *helped them up* that were fallen and could not help themselves. Those that were sunk under the burdens of a broken covenant of innocency are *helped up* by the blessings of a renewed covenant of grace. The sending of the Messiah, on whom *help* was *laid* for poor sinners, was the greatest kindness that could be done, the greatest help that could be provided for his people Israel, and that which magnifies it is,

First, That it is *in remembrance of his mercy,* the mercifulness of his nature, the mercy he has in store for *his servant Israel.* While this blessing was deferred, his people, who waited for it, were often ready to ask, *Has God forgotten to be gracious?* But now he made it appear that he had not forgotten, but *remembered, his mercy.* He remembered his former mercy, and repeated that to them in *spiritual* blessings which he had done formerly to them in *temporal* favours. *He remembered the days of old. Where is he that brought them up out of the sea,* out of Egypt? Isa. 63:11. He will do the like again, which that was a type of.

Secondly, That it is *in performance of his promise.* It is a mercy not only designed, but declared (*v.* 55); it was *what he spoke to our fathers,* that the Seed of the woman should break the head of the serpent; that God should dwell in the tents of Shem; and particularly to Abraham, that *in his seed all the families of the earth shall be blessed,* with the best of blessings, with the blessings that are *for ever,* and to the seed that shall be for ever; that is, his *spiritual* seed, for his carnal seed were *cut off* a little after this. Note, What God has spoken he will perform; what he hath spoken to the fathers will be performed to their seed; to their seed's seed, in blessings that shall last for ever.

Lastly, Mary's return to Nazareth (*v.* 56), after she had continued with Elisabeth about *three months,* so long as to be fully satisfied concerning herself that she was *with child,* and to be confirmed therein by her cousin Elisabeth. Some think, though her return is here mentioned before Elisabeth's being delivered, because the evangelist would finish this passage concerning Mary before he proceeded with the story of Elisabeth, yet that Mary staid till her cousin was (as we say) *down and up again;* that she might attend on her, and be with her in her lying-in, and have her own faith confirmed by the full accomplishment of the promise of God concerning Elisabeth. But most bind themselves to the order of the story as it lies, and think she returned again when Elisabeth was near her time; because she still affected retirement, and therefore would not be there when the birth of this child of promise would draw a great deal of company to the house. Those in whose hearts Christ is formed take more delight than they used to do in *sitting alone* and *keeping silence.*

Verses 57–66

In these verses, we have,

I. The birth of John Baptist, *v.* 57. Though he was conceived in the womb by miracle, he continued in the womb according to the ordinary course of nature (so did our Saviour): *Elisabeth's full time came, that she should be delivered,* and then *she brought forth a son.* Promised mercies are to be expected when the *full time* for them is come, and not before.

II. The great joy that was among all the relations of the family, upon this extraordinary occasion (*v.* 58): *Her neighbours and her cousins heard of it;* for it would be in every body's mouth, as next to miraculous. Dr. Lightfoot observes that Hebron was inhabited by priests of the family of Aaron, and that those were the cousins here spoken of; but the fields and villages about, by the children of Judah, and that those were the *neighbours.* Now these here discovered, 1. A *pious* regard to God. They acknowledged that *the Lord had magnified his mercy to her,* so the word is. It was a mercy to have her reproach taken away, a mercy to have her family built up, and the more being a family of *priests,* devoted to God, and employed for him. Many things concurred to make the mercy *great* — that she had been long barren, was now old, but especially that the child should be *great in the sight of the Lord.* 2. A *friendly* regard to Elisabeth. When she rejoiced, they *rejoiced with her.* We ought to take *pleasure* in the prosperity of our neighbours and friends, and to be thankful to God for *their* comforts as for our own.

III. The dispute that was among them concerning the naming him (*v.* 59): *On the eighth day,* as God has appointed, they *came together,* to *circumcise the child;* it was here, in Hebron, that *circumcision* was first instituted; and Isaac, who, like John Baptist, was born *by promise,* was one of the first that was submitted to it, at least the chief eyed in the institution of it. They that rejoiced in the birth of the child came together to the circumcising of him. Note, The greatest comfort we can take in our children is in *giving them up to God,* and recognizing their covenant-relation to him. The baptism of our children should be more our joy than their birth.

Now it was the custom, when they circumcised their children, to *name them,* because, when *Abram* was circumcised God gave him a new name, and called him *Abraham;* and it is not unfit that they should be left *nameless* till they are by name *given up to God.* Now,

1. *Some* proposed that he should be called by his father's name, *Zacharias.* We have not any instance in scripture that the child should bear the father's name; but perhaps it was of late come into use among the Jews, as it is with us, and they intended hereby to do honour to the father, who was not likely to have another child.

2. The *mother* opposed it, and would have called him *John;* having learned, either by inspiration of the Holy Ghost (as is most probable), or by information in writing from her husband, that God appointed this to be his name (*v.* 60); He shall be called *Johanan — Gracious,* because he shall introduce the gospel of Christ, wherein God's grace shines more brightly than ever.

3. The *relations* objected against that (*v.* 61): *"There is none of thy kindred,* none of the relations of thy family, *that is called by that name;* and therefore, if he may not have his father's name, yet let him have the name of some of his kindred, who will take it as a piece of respect to have such a *child of wonders* as this named from them." Note, As those that *have friends* must *show themselves friendly,* so those that have relations must be *obliging* to them in all the usual regards that are paid to *kindred.*

4. They appealed to the *father,* and would try if they could possibly get to know his mind; for it was his office to *name the child, v.* 62. They *made signs* to him, by which it appears that he was *deaf* as well as *dumb;* nay, it should seem, *mindless* of any thing, else one would think they should at first have desired him to write down his child's name, if he had ever communicated any thing by writing since he was *struck.* However, they would carry the matter as far as they could, and therefore gave him to understand what the dispute was which he only could determine; whereupon he made signs to them to give him a *table-book,* such as they then used, and with the pencil he wrote these words, *His name is John, v.* 63. Note, "It shall be so," or, "I would have it so," but "It is so." The matter is determined already; the *angel* had given him that name. Observe, When Zacharias could not *speak,* he *wrote.* When ministers have their mouths stopped, that they cannot preach, yet they may be doing good as long as they have not their hands tied, that they cannot write. Many of the martyrs in prison wrote letters to their friends, which were of great use; blessed Paul himself did so. Zacharias's pitching upon the same name that Elisabeth had chosen was a great surprise to the company: *They marvelled all;* for they knew not that, though by reason of his deafness and dumbness they could not *converse together,* yet they were both guided by *one and the same Spirit:* or perhaps they *marvelled* that he wrote so distinctly and intelligently, which (the stroke he was under being somewhat like that of a palsy) he had not done before.

5. He thereupon recovered the use of his speech (*v.* 64): *His mouth was opened immediately.* The time prefixed for his being silenced was *till the day that these blessed things*

shall be fulfilled (v. 20); not *all the things* going before concerning John's ministry, but those which relate to his birth and name (v. 13). That time was now expired, whereupon the restraint was taken off, and God gave him the *opening of the mouth again,* as he did to Ezekiel, *ch.* 3:27. Dr. Lightfoot compares this case of Zacharias with that of Moses, Ex. 4:24–26. Moses, for distrust, is in danger of his life, as Zacharias, for the same fault, is *struck dumb;* but, upon the circumcision of his child, and recovery of his faith, there, as here, the danger is removed. Infidelity closed his mouth, and now believing opens it again; *he believes, therefore he speaks.* David lay under guilt from the conception of his child till a few days after its birth; then *the Lord takes away his sin:* upon his repentance, he shall not die. So here he shall be no longer dumb; *his mouth was opened, and he spoke, and praised God.* Note, When God opens our lips, our mouths must *show forth his praise.* As good be without our speech as not use it in *praising God;* for then our tongue is most *our glory* when it is employed for *God's glory.*

6. These things were told all the country over, to the great amazement of all that heard them, v. 65, 66. The sentiments of the people are not to be slighted, but taken notice of. We are here told, (1.) That *these sayings were discoursed of,* and were the common talk all about the *hill-country of Judea.* It is a pity but a narrative of them had been drawn up, and published in the world, immediately. (2.) That most people who heard of these things were put into consternation by them: *Fear came on all them that dwell round about* there. If we have not a *good hope,* as we ought to have, built upon the gospel, we may expect that the tidings of it will fill us with *fear.* They believed and trembled, whereas they should have believed and triumphed. (3.) It raised the expectations of people concerning this child, and obliged them to have their eye upon him, to see what he would come to. They *laid up these presages in their hearts,* treasured them up in mind and memory, as foreseeing they should hereafter have occasion to *recollect* them. Note, What we hear, that may be of use to us, we should *treasure* up, that we may be able to bring forth, for the benefit of others, things new and old, and, when things come to perfection, may be able to look back upon the presages thereof, and to say, "It was what we might expect." They said *within* themselves, and said *among* themselves, *"What manner of child shall this be?* What will be the fruit when these are the buds, or rather when the *root* is out of such a *dry ground?"* Note, When children are born into the world, it is very uncertain what they will prove; yet sometimes there have been early indications of something great, as in the birth of Moses, Samson, Samuel, and here of John. And we have reason to think that there were some of those living at the time when John began his public ministry who could, and did, remember these things, and relate them to others, which contributed as much as any thing to the great flocking there was after him.

Lastly, It is said, *The hand of the Lord was with him;* that is, he was taken under the special protection of the Almighty, from his birth, as one designed for something great and considerable, and there were many instances of it. It appeared likewise that the Spirit was at work upon his soul very early. As soon as he began to speak or go, you might perceive something in him very extraordinary. Note, God has ways of operating upon children in their infancy, which we cannot account for. God never made a soul but he knew how to sanctify it.

Verses 67–80

We have here the song wherewith Zacharias *praised God* when his *mouth was opened; in* it he is said to *prophesy* (v. 67), and so he did in the strictest sense of *prophesying;* for he foretold things to come concerning the kingdom of the Messiah, to which all the prophets bear witness. Observe,

I. How he was qualified for this: *He was filled with the Holy Ghost,* was endued with more than ordinary measures and degrees of it, for this purpose; he was divinely inspired. God not only *forgave* him his unbelief and distrust (which was signified by discharging him from the punishment of it), but, as a *specimen* of the *abounding* of grace towards believers, he *filled him* with the *Holy Ghost,* and put this honour upon him, to employ him for his honour.

II. What the matter of his song was. Here is nothing said of the private concerns of his own family, the rolling away of the reproach from it and putting of a reputation upon it, by the birth of this child, though, no doubt, he found a time

to give thanks to God for this, with his family; but in this song he is wholly taken up with the kingdom of the Messiah, and the public blessings to be introduced by it. He could have little pleasure in this *fruitfulness* of his *vine,* and the *hopefulness* of his *olive-plant,* if herein he had not foreseen the *good of Jerusalem, peace upon Israel,* and *blessings* on both *out of Zion,* Ps. 128:3, 5, 6. The Old-Testament prophesies are often expressed in *praises* and *new songs,* so is the beginning of New-Testament prophecy: *Blessed be the Lord God of Israel. The God of the whole earth shall he be called;* yet Zacharias, speaking of the work of redemption, called him the *Lord God of Israel,* because to Israel the prophecies, promises, and types, of the redemption had hitherto been given, and to them the first proffers and proposals of it were now to be made. Israel, as a chosen people, was a type of the *elect of God* out of all nations, whom God had a particular eye to, in sending the Saviour; and therefore he is therein called the *Lord God of Israel.*

Now Zacharias here blesses God,

1. For the work of *salvation* that was to be wrought out by the Messiah himself, v. 68–75. This it is that *fills him,* when he is *filled with the Holy Ghost,* and it is that which all who have the *Spirit of Christ* are full of.

(1.) In sending the Messiah, God has *made a gracious visit* to his people, whom for many ages he had seemed to neglect, and to be estranged from; he hath *visited them* as a friend, to take cognizance of their case. God is said to have *visited* his people in bondage when he *delivered* them (Ex. 3:16; 4:31), to have *visited* his people in famine when he *gave them bread,* Ruth 1:6. He had often sent to them by his prophets, and had still kept up a correspondence with them; but now he himself made them a *visit.*

(2.) He has *wrought out* redemption for them: *He has redeemed his people.* This was the errand on which Christ *came into the world,* to redeem those that were sold *for* sin, and sold *under* sin; even God's own people, his Israel, his son, his *first-born,* his *free-born,* need to be *redeemed,* and are undone if they be not. Christ redeems them by *price* out of the hands of God's justice, and redeems them by *power* out of the hands of Satan's tyranny, as Israel out of Egypt.

(3.) He has fulfilled the *covenant of royalty* made with the most famous *Old-Testament prince,* that is, David. Glorious things had been said of his family, that on him, as a *mighty one,* help should be *laid,* that *his horn should be exalted,* and his *seed* perpetuated, Ps. 89:19, 20, 24, 29. But that family had been long in a manner *cast off* and *abhorred,* Ps. 89:38. Now here it is glorified in, that, according to the promise, the *horn* of David should again be *made to bud;* for, Ps. 132:17, he *hath raised up a horn of salvation for us in the house of his servant David* (v. 69), there, where it was promised and expected to arise. David is called God's *servant,* not only as a good man, but as a king that *ruled for God;* and he was an instrument of the *salvation* of Israel, by being employed in the *government* of Israel; so Christ is the *author of eternal redemption to those only that obey him.* There is in Christ, and in him only, *salvation for us,* and it is a *horn of salvation;* for, [1.] It is an *honourable* salvation. It is *raised up* above all other salvations, none of which are to be compared with it: in it the glory both of the Redeemer and of the redeemed are advanced, and their *horn exalted with honour.* [2.] It is a *plentiful* salvation. It is a *cornucopia — a horn of plenty,* a *salvation* in which we are blessed with *spiritual* blessings, in *heavenly things,* abundantly. [3.] It is a *powerful* salvation: the strength of the beast is in his *horn.* He has raised up such a salvation as shall *pull down* our spiritual enemies, and *protect* us from them. In the *chariots* of this *salvation* the Redeemer shall go forth, and go on, *conquering and to conquer.*

(4.) He has fulfilled all the precious promises made to the church by the most famous *Old-Testament prophets* (v. 70): *As he spoke by the mouth of his holy prophets.* His doctrine of salvation by the Messiah is confirmed by an appeal to the prophets, and the greatness and importance of that salvation thereby evidenced and magnified; it is the same that they spoke of, which therefore ought to be expected and welcomed; it is what they *enquired and searched diligently after* (1 Pt. 1:10, 11), which therefore ought not to be slighted or thought meanly of. God is now *doing* that which he has long ago *spoken of;* and therefore *be silent, O all flesh, before him,* and attend to him. See, [1.] How *sacred* the prophecies of this salvation were. The prophets who delivered them were *holy prophets,* who durst not deceive and who aimed at promoting holiness among men; and it was the *holy God* himself

that *spoke by* them. [2.] How *ancient* they were: ever *since the world began.* God having promised, when the world began, that the *Seed of the woman should break the serpent's head,* that promise was echoed to when Adam called his wife's name *Eve — Life,* for the sake of that Seed of hers; when Eve called her first son *Cain,* saying, *I have gotten a man from the Lord,* and another son, Seth, *settled;* when Noah was called *rest,* and foretold that God should dwell in the tents of Shem. And it was not long after the new world began in Noah that the promise was made to Abraham that in his Seed the *nations of the earth* should be *blessed.* [3.] What a wonderful *harmony* and *concert* we perceive among them. God spoke the same thing by them all, and therefore it is said to be *dia stomatos,* not by the *mouths,* but by the *mouth,* of the prophets, for they all speak of Christ as it were with one *mouth.*

Now what is this *salvation* which was prophesied of?

First, It is a *rescue* from the malice of *our enemies;* it is *sōtērian ex echthrōn hēmōn — a salvation out of our enemies,* from among them, and *out of the power of them that hate us* (v. 71); it is a salvation from sin, and the dominion of Satan over us, both by corruptions within and temptations without. The carnal Jews expected to be delivered from under the Roman yoke, but intimation was betimes given that it should be a redemption of another nature. He shall *save his people from their sins,* that they may not have dominion over them, Mt. 1:21.

Secondly, It is a *restoration* to the *favour of God;* it is to *perform the mercy promised to our forefathers,* v. 72. The Redeemer shall not only break the head of the serpent that was the author of our ruin, but he shall *re-instate* us in the *mercy of God* and re-establish us in *his covenant;* he shall bring us as it were into a paradise again, which was signified by the *promises* made to the patriarchs, and the *holy covenant* made with them, *the oath which he sware to our father Abraham,* v. 73. Observe, 1. That which was promised to the fathers, and is performed to us, is *mercy,* pure mercy; nothing in it is owing to our *merit* (we deserve wrath and the curse), but all to the *mercy* of God, which *designed* us grace and life: *ex mero motu — of his own good pleasure,* he loved us because he would love us. 2. God herein had an eye to *his covenant,* his *holy* covenant, that covenant with Abraham: *I will be a God to thee and thy seed.* This his seed had really forfeited by their transgressions; this he *seemed to have forgotten* in the calamities brought upon them; but he will now *remember* it, will make it appear that he remembers it, for upon that are grounded all his returns of mercy: Lev. 26:42, *Then will I remember my covenant.*

Thirdly, It is a *qualification* for, and an encouragement to, the service of God. Thus was *the oath he sware to our Father Abraham,* That he would *give* us power and grace to *serve him,* in an acceptable manner to him and a comfortable manner to ourselves, v. 74, 75. Here seems to be an allusion to the deliverance of Israel out of Egypt, which, God tells Moses, was in pursuance of the covenant he made with Abraham (Ex. 3:6–8), and that this was the design of his bringing them out of Egypt, *that they might serve God upon this mountain,* Ex. 3:12. Note, The great design of gospel grace is not to discharge us from, but to engage us to, and encourage us in, the service of God. Under this notion Christianity was always to be looked upon, as intended to make us truly religious, to admit us into the service of God, to bind us to it, and to quicken us in it. We are *therefore* delivered from the iron yoke of sin, that our necks may be put under the sweet and easy yoke of the Lord Jesus. The *very bonds which he has loosed* do bind us faster unto him, Ps. 116:16. We are hereby enabled, 1. To serve God *without fear — aphobōs.* We are *therefore* put into a state of *holy safety* that we might serve God with a *holy security* and *serenity of mind,* as those that are *quiet from the fears of evil.* God must be served with a *filial fear,* a reverent obedient fear, an awakening quickening fear, but not with a *slavish* fear, like that of the slothful servant, who represented him to himself as a *hard master,* and unreasonable; not with that fear that has *torment* and *amazement* in it; not with the fear of a legal spirit; a *spirit of bondage,* but with the boldness of an evangelical spirit, a *spirit of adoption.* 2. To serve him in *holiness and righteousness,* which includes the whole duty of man towards God and our neighbour. It is both the intention and the direct tendency of the gospel to renew upon us that image of God in which man was at first made, which consisted in *righteousness and true holiness,* Ps. 50:14. 3. To serve him, *before him,* in the duties of his *immediate* worship, wherein we present ourselves *before the Lord,* to serve him as those that have an eye always upon him, and see his eye always upon us, upon our inward man, that is serving him *before him.* 4. To serve him *all the days of our life.* The design of the gospel is to engage us in constancy and perseverance in the service of God, by showing us how much depends upon our not drawing back, and by showing us how Christ *loved us to the end,* and thereby engaged us to *love him to the end.*

2. He *blessed God* for the work of *preparation* for this salvation, which was to be done by John Baptist (*v.* 76): *Thou child,* though now but a child of eight days' old, shalt be called *the prophet of the Highest.* Jesus Christ is *the Highest,* for he is *God over all, blessed for evermore* (Rom. 9:5), equal with the Father. John Baptist was *his prophet,* as Aaron was Moses's prophet (Ex. 7:1); what he said was as his mouth, what he did was as his harbinger. Prophecy had now long ceased, but in John it *revived,* as it had done in Samuel, who was born of an aged mother, as John was, after a long cessation. John's business was,

(1.) To prepare people for the salvation, by preaching repentance and reformation as great gospel duties: *Thou shalt go before the face of the Lord,* and but a little before him, to *prepare his ways,* to call people to make room for him, and get ready for his entertainment. Let every thing that may obstruct his progress, or embarrass it, or hinder people from coming to him, be taken away: see Isa. 40:3, 4. Let *valleys be filled,* and *hills* be brought *low.*

(2.) To give people a general idea of the salvation, that they might know, not only what to do, but what to expect; for the doctrine he preached was that the *kingdom of heaven* is at hand. There are two things in which you must know that this salvation consists: —

[1.] The *forgiveness* of what we have *done amiss.* It is salvation *by the remission of sins,* those sins which stand in the way of the salvation, and by which we are all become liable to ruin and condemnation, *v.* 77. John Baptist gave people to understand that, though their case was sad, by reason of sin, it was not desperate, for pardon might be obtained *through the tender mercy of our God* (the *bowels of mercy,* so the word is): there was nothing in us but a *piteous case* to recommend us to the divine compassion.

[2.] *Direction* to *do better* for the time to come. The gospel salvation not only encourages us to hope that the works of darkness shall be forgiven us, but sets up a clear and true light, by which we may order our steps aright. In it *the day-spring hath visited us from on high* (*v.* 78); and this also is owing to the *tender mercy of our God.* Christ is *anatolē — the morning Light,* the *rising Sun,* Mal. 4:2. The gospel brings *light* with it (Jn. 3:19), leaves us not to wander in the darkness of Pagan ignorance, or in the moonlight of the Old-Testament types or figures, but in it the day dawns; in John Baptist it began to break, but increased apace, and *shone more and more to the perfect day.* We have as much reason to welcome the gospel day who enjoy it as those have to welcome the morning who had long waited for it. *First,* The gospel is *discovering;* it shows us that which before we were utterly in the dark about (*v.* 79); it is to *give light to them that sit in darkness,* the *light of the knowledge of the glory of God in the face of Jesus Christ;* the day-spring *visited* this dark world to *lighten the Gentiles,* Acts 26:18. *Secondly,* It is *reviving;* it brings light to them that sit *in the shadow of death,* as condemned prisoners in the dungeon, to bring them the tidings of a *pardon,* at least of a *reprieve* and opportunity of procuring a pardon; it proclaims the *opening of the prison* (Isa. 61:1), brings the *light of life.* How pleasant is that light! *Thirdly,* It is *directing;* it is to *guide our feet in the way of peace,* into that way which will bring us to peace at last. It is not only a light *to our eyes,* but a light *to our feet* (Ps. 119:105); it guides us into the way of making our peace with God, of keeping up a comfortable communion; that *way of peace* which as sinners we have wandered from and *have not known* (Rom. 3:17), nor could ever have known of ourselves.

In the last verse, we have short account of the younger years of John Baptist. Though he was the son of a priest, he did not, like Samuel, go up, when he was a child, to minister before the Lord; for he was to prepare the way for a better priesthood. But we are here told,

1. Of his *eminence* as to the *inward man:* The *child grew* in the capacities of his mind, much more than other children; so that he *waxed strong in the spirit;* had a strong judgment and strong resolution. Reason and conscience (both which are the candle of the Lord) were so strong in him that he had the inferior faculties of appetite and passion in complete subjection betimes. By this it appeared that he was betimes *filled with the Holy Ghost;* for those that are strong in the Lord are *strong in spirit.*

2. Of his *obscurity* as to the *outward man:* He *was in the deserts;* not that he lived a hermit; cut off from the society of men. No, we have reason to think that he went up to Jerusalem at the *feasts,* and frequented the synagogues on the sabbath day, but his constant residence was in some of those scattered houses that were in the wilderness of Zuph or Maon, which we read of in the story of David. There he spent most of his time, in contemplation and devotion, and had not his education in the schools, or at the feet of the rabbin. Note, Many a one is qualified for great usefulness, who yet is buried alive; and many are so long buried who are designed, and are thereby in the fitting, for so much greater usefulness at last; as John Baptist, who was *in the desert* only *till the day of his showing to Israel,* when he was in the thirtieth year of his age. Note, There is a time fixed for the *showing* of those favours to Israel which are reserved; *the vision* of them *is for an appointed time, and at the end it shall speak, and shall not lie.*

CHAPTER 2

In this chapter, we have an account of the birth and infancy of our Lord Jesus: having had notice of his conception, and of the birth and infancy of his forerunner, in the former chapter. The First-begotten is here brought into the world; let us go meet him with our hosannas, blessed is he that cometh. Here is, I. The place and other circumstances of his birth, which proved him to be the true Messiah, and such a one as we needed, but not such a one as the Jews expected (*v.* 1–7). II. The notifying of his birth to the shepherds in that neighbourhood by an angel, the song of praise which the angels sung upon that occasion, and the spreading of the report of it by the shepherds (*v.* 8–20). III. The circumcision of Christ, and the naming of him (*v.* 21). IV. The presenting of him in the temple (*v.* 22–24). V. The testimonies of Simeon, and Anna the prophetess, concerning him (*v.* 25–39). VI. Christ's growth and capacity (*v.* 40–52). VIII. His observing the passover at twelve years old, and his disputing with the doctors in the temple (*v.* 41–51). And this, with what we have met with (Mt. 1 and 2), is all we have concerning our Lord Jesus, till he entered upon his public work in the thirtieth year of his age.

Verses 1–7

The *fulness of time* was now come, when God would send forth his Son, *made of a woman,* and *made under the law;* and it was foretold that he should be born at Bethlehem. Now here we have an account of the time, place, and manner of it.

I. The time when our Lord Jesus was born. Several things may be gathered out of these verses which intimate to us that it was the *proper time.*

1. He was born at the time when the *fourth monarchy* was in its height, just when it was become, more than any of the three before it, a *universal monarchy.* He was born *in the days* of Augustus Caesar, when the Roman empire extended itself further than ever before or since, including Parthia one way, and Britain another way; so that it was then called *Terraram orbis imperium — The empire of the whole earth;* and here that empire is called *all the world* (*v.* 1), for there was scarcely any part of the civilized world, but what was dependent on it. Now this was the time when the Messiah was to be born, according to Daniel's prophecy (Dan. 2:44): *In the days of these kings,* the kings of the fourth monarchy, *shall the God of heaven set up a kingdom which shall never be destroyed.*

2. He was born when Judea was become a province of the empire, and tributary to it; as appears evidently by this, that when all the Roman empire was taxed, the Jews were taxed among the rest. Jerusalem was taken by Pompey the Roman general, about sixty years before this, who granted the government of the church to Hyrcanus, but not the government of the state; by degrees it was more and more reduced, till now at length it was quite subdued; for Judea was ruled by Cyrenius the Roman governor of Syria (*v.* 2): the Roman writers call him *Sulpitius Quirinus.* Now just at this juncture, the Messiah was to be born, for so was dying Jacob's prophecy, that Shiloh should come when the *sceptre was departed from Judah,* and the *lawgiver from between his feet,* Gen. 49:10. This was the *first taxing* that was made in Judea, the first badge of their servitude; therefore now Shiloh must come, to set up his kingdom.

3. There is another circumstance, as to the time, implied in this general enrolment of all the subjects of the empire, which is, that there was now universal peace in the empire. The temple of Janus was now shut, which it never used to be if any wars were on foot; and now it was fit for the Prince of peace to be born, in whose days *swords should be beaten into plough-shares.*

II. The place where our Lord Jesus was born is very observable. He was born at *Bethlehem;* so it was foretold (Mic. 5:2), the scribes so understood it (Mt. 2:5, 6), so did the common people, Jn. 7:42. The name of the place was significant. Bethlehem signifies *the house of bread;* a proper place for him to be born in who is the Bread of life, the Bread that *came down from heaven.* But that was not all; Bethlehem was the city of David, where he was born, and therefore there *he* must be born who was the *Son of David.* Zion was also called *the city of David* (2 Sa. 5:7), yet Christ was not born there; for Bethlehem was that city of David where he was born in meanness, to be a *shepherd;* and this our Saviour, when he humbled himself, chose for the place of his birth; not Zion, where he ruled in power and prosperity, that was to be a type of the church of Christ, *that mount Zion.* Now when the virgin Mary was with child, and near her time, Providence so ordered it that, by order from the emperor, all the subjects of the *Roman empire* were to be *taxed;* that is, they were to *give in their names* to the proper officers, and they were to be *registered* and *enrolled,* according to their families, which is the proper signification of the word here used; their being *taxed* was but secondary. It is supposed that they made profession of subjection to the Roman empire, either by some set form of words, or at least by payment of some small tribute, a penny suppose, in token of their allegiance, like a man's *atturning* tenant. Thus are they vassals upon record, and may thank themselves.

According to this *decree,* the Jews (who were now nice in distinguishing their tribes and families) provided that in their enrolments particular care should be had to preserve the memory of them. Thus foolishly are they solicitous to save the *shadow,* when they had lost the *substance.*

That which Augustus designed was either to gratify his *pride* in knowing the numbers of his people, and proclaiming it to the world, or he did it in *policy,* to strengthen his interest, and make his government appear the more formidable; but Providence had another reach in it. All the world shall be at the trouble of being *enrolled,* only that Joseph and Mary may. This brought them up from Nazareth in Galilee to Bethlehem in Judea, because they were *of the stock and lineage of David* (*v.* 4, 5); and perhaps, being poor and low, they thought the royalty of their extraction rather than a burden and expense to them than a matter of pride. Because it is difficult to suppose that every Jew (women as well as men) was obliged to repair to the city of which their ancestors were, and there be enrolled, now, at a time when they kept not to the bounds of their tribes, as formerly, it may be offered as a conjecture that this great exactness was used only with the *family of David,* concerning which, it is probable, the emperor gave particular orders, it having been the royal family, and still talked of as designed to be so, that he might know its number and strength. Divers ends of Providence were served by this.

1. Hereby the virgin Mary was brought, *great with child,* to Bethlehem, to be *delivered* there, according to the prediction; whereas she had designed to lie in at Nazareth. See how *man purposes and God disposes;* and how Providence orders all things for the fulfilling of the scripture, and makes use of the projects men have for serving their own purposes, quite beyond their intention, to serve his.

2. Hereby it appeared that Jesus Christ was of the *seed* of David; for what brings his mother to Bethlehem now, but because she *was of the stock and lineage of David?* This was a material thing to be proved, and required such an authentic proof as this. Justin Martyr and Tertullian, two of the earliest advocates for the Christian religion, appeal to these *rolls* or *records* of the *Roman empire,* for the proof of Christ's being born of the house of David.

3. Hereby it appeared that he was *made under the law;* for he became a subject of the Roman empire as soon as he was born, a *servant of rulers,* Isa. 49:7. Many suppose that, being born during the time of the taxing, he was enrolled as well as his father and mother, that it might appear how *he made himself of no reputation,* and *took upon him the form of a servant.* Instead of having kings tributaries to him, when he came into the world he was himself a tributary.

III. The circumstances of his birth, which were very mean, and under all possible marks of contempt. He was indeed a *first-born son;* but it was a poor honour to be the first-born of such a poor woman as Mary was, who had no inheritance to which he might be entitled as first-born, but what was *in nativity.*

1. He was under some abasements in common with other children; he was *wrapped in swaddling clothes,* as other children are when they are new-born, as if he could be bound, or needed to be kept straight. He that makes darkness a *swaddling band for the sea* was himself wrapped in *swaddling bands,* Job 38:9. The everlasting Father became a child of time, and men said to him whose out-goings were of old from everlasting, *We know this man, whence he is,* Jn. 7:27. The Ancient of days became an infant of a span long.

2. He was under some abasements peculiar to himself.

(1.) He was born *at an inn.* That son of David that was the glory of his father's house had no inheritance that he could command, no not in the city of David, no nor a friend that would accommodate his mother in distress with lodgings to be brought to bed in. Christ was born *in an inn,* to intimate that he came into the world but to sojourn here for awhile, as in an inn, and to teach us to do likewise. An inn receives all comers, and so does Christ. He hangs out the banner of love for his sign, and whoever comes to him, he will in no wise cast out; only, unlike other inns, he welcomes those that come *without money and without price.* All is on free cost.

(2.) He was born *in a stable;* so some think the word signifies which we translate *a manger,* a place for cattle to stand to be fed in. Because there was *no room in the inn,* and for want of conveniences, nay for want of necessaries, he was laid *in a manger,* instead of a cradle. The word which we render *swaddling clothes* some derive from a word that signifies to *rend,* or *tear,* and these infer that he was so far from having a good suit of child-bed linen, that his very swaddles were ragged and torn. His being born in a stable and laid in a manger was an instance, [1.] Of the poverty of his parents. Had they been rich, room would have been made for them; but, being poor, they must *shift* as they *could.* [2.] Of the corruption and degeneracy of manners in that age; that a woman in reputation for virtue and honour should be used so barbarously. If there had been any common humanity among them, they would not have turned a woman in travail into a stable. [3.] It was an instance of the humiliation of our Lord Jesus. We were become by sin like an out-cast infant, helpless and forlorn; and such a one Christ was. Thus he would answer the type of Moses, the great prophet and lawgiver of the Old Testament, who was in his infancy cast out in an ark of bulrushes, as Christ *in a manger.* Christ would hereby put a contempt upon all worldly glory, and teach us to slight it. Since *his own received him not,* let us not think it strange if they *receive us not.*

Verses 8–20

The meanest circumstances of Christ's humiliation were all along attended with some discoveries of his glory, to balance them, and take off the offence of them; for even when he humbled himself God did in some measure exalt him and give him earnests of his future exaltation. When we saw him *wrapped in swaddling clothes* and *laid in a manger,* we were tempted to say, "Surely this cannot be the *Son of God.*" But see his birth attended, as it is here, with a choir of angels, and we shall say, "Surely this cannot be the *Son of God.*" But see his birth attended, as it is here, with a choir of angels, and we shall say, "Surely it can be no other than the *Son of God,* concerning whom it was said, when he was *brought into the world, Let all the angels of God worship him,*" Heb. 1:6.

We had in Matthew an account of the notice given of the arrival of this ambassador, this prince from heaven, to the wise men, who were Gentiles, by a star; here we are told of the notice given of it to the shepherds, who were Jews, by an angel: to each God chose to speak in the language they were most conversant with.

I. See here how the shepherds were employed; they were *abiding in the fields* adjoining to Bethlehem, and *keeping watch over their flocks by night, v.* 8. The angel was not sent to the chief priests or the elders (they were not prepared to receive these tidings), but to a company of poor shepherds, who were like Jacob, *plain men dwelling in tents,* not like Esau, *cunning hunters.* The patriarchs were shepherds. Moses and David particularly were called from keeping sheep to rule God's people; and by this instance God would show that he had still a favour for those of that innocent employment. Tidings were brought to Moses of the deliverance of Israel out of Egypt, when he was keeping sheep, and to these shepherds, who, it is probable, were devout pious men, the tidings were brought of a *greater salvation.* Observe, 1. They were not *sleeping* in their beds, when this news was brought them (though many had very acceptable intelligence from heaven in *slumbering upon the bed*), but *abiding in the fields,* and *watching.* Those that would hear from God must *stir up themselves.* They were broad awake, and therefore could not be deceived in what they saw and heard, so as those may be who are half asleep. 2. They were employed now, not in acts of devotion, but in the business of their calling; they were *keeping watch over their flock,* to secure them from thieves and beasts of prey, it being probably in the summer time, when they kept their cattle out all night, as we do now, and did not house them. Note, We are not out of the way of divine visits when we are sensibly employed in an honest calling, and abide with God in it.

II. How they were surprised with the appearance of the angel (*v.* 9): *Behold, an angel of the Lord came upon them,* of a sudden, *epestē — stood over them;* most probably, in the air over their heads, as coming immediately from heaven. We read it, *the angel,* as if it were the same that appeared once and again in the chapter before, *the angel Gabriel,* that was caused to fly swiftly; but that is not certain. The angel's *coming upon them* intimates that they little thought of such a thing, or expected it; for it is in a *preventing* way that gracious visits are made us from heaven, *or ever we are aware.* That they might be sure it was an angel from heaven, they saw and heard the *glory of the Lord round about them;* such as made the night as bright as day, such a glory as used to attend God's appearance, a *heavenly* glory, or an *exceedingly great glory,* such as they could not bear the dazzling lustre of. This made them *sore afraid,* put them into great consternation, as fearing some evil tidings. While we are conscious to ourselves of so much guilt, we have reason to fear lest every express from heaven should be a messenger of wrath.

III. What the message was which the angel had to deliver to the shepherds, *v.* 10–12. 1. He gives a *supersedeas* to their *fears: "Fear not,* for we have nothing to say to you that needs be a terror to you; you *need not* fear your enemies, and *should not* fear your friends." 2. He furnishes them with abundant matter for joy: "Behold, I *evangelize to you great joy;* I solemnly declare it, and you have reason to bid it welcome, for it shall bring *joy to all people,* and not to the people of the Jews only; that *unto you is born this day,* at this time, *a Saviour,* the Saviour that has been so long expected, *which is Christ the Lord, in the city of David," v.* 11. Jesus is the Christ, the Messiah, the Anointed; he is *the Lord,* Lord of all; he is a sovereign prince; nay, he is God, for *the Lord,* in the Old Testament, answers to *Jehovah.* He is a Saviour, and he will be a Saviour to those only that accept him for their Lord. "The Saviour *is born,* he is born *this day;* and, since it is matter of *great joy to all people,* it is not to be kept secret, you may proclaim it, may tell it to whom you please. He is born in the place where it was foretold he should be born, in the *city of David;* and he is born *to you;* to you Jews he is sent in the first place, to *bless you,* to you *shepherds,* though poor and mean in the world." This refers to Isa. 9:6, *Unto us a child is born, unto us a son is given.* To *you* men, not to *us* angels; he took not on him the nature of angels. This is matter of *joy* indeed to all people, great joy. Long-looked for is come at last. Let heaven and earth rejoice before this Lord, *for he cometh.* 3. He gives them a sign for the confirming of their faith in this matter. "How shall we find out this child in Bethlehem, which is now full of the descendants from David?" "You will find him by this token: he is lying in a *manger,* where surely never any new-born infant was laid before." They expected to be told, "You shall find him, though a babe, dressed up in robes, and lying in the best house in the town, lying in state, with a numerous train of attendants in rich liveries." "No, you will find him wrapped in *swaddling clothes,* and *laid in a manger.*" When Christ was here upon earth, he *distinguished* himself, and made himself remarkable, by nothing so much as the instances of his *humiliation.*

IV. The angels' *doxology* to God, and *congratulations* of men, upon this solemn occasion, *v.* 13, 14. The message was no sooner delivered by one angel (that was sufficient to go express) than suddenly there was with that angel *a multitude of the heavenly hosts;* sufficient, we may be sure, to make a *chorus,* that were heard by the shepherds, *praising God;* and certainly their song was not like that (Rev. 14:3) which *no man could learn,* for it was designed that we should all learn it. 1. Let God have the honour of this work: *Glory to God in the highest.* God's good-will to men, manifested in sending the Messiah, redounds very much to his praise; and angels in the highest heavens, though not immediately interested in it themselves, will celebrate it to his honour, Rev. 5:11, 12. *Glory to God,* whose kindness and love designed this favour, and whose wisdom contrived it in such a way as that one divine attribute should not be glorified at the expense of another, but the honour of all effectually secured and advanced. Other works of God are for his glory, but the redemption of the world is for his *glory in the highest.* 2. Let men have the joy of it: *On earth peace, good-will toward men.* God's *good-will* in sending the Messiah introduced peace in this lower world, slew the enmity that sin had raised between God and man, and resettled a peaceable correspondence. If God be at peace with us, all peace results from it: peace of conscience, peace with angels, peace between Jew and Gentile. Peace is here put for *all good,* all that good which flows to us from the incarnation of Christ. All the *good* we have, or hope, is owing to God's *good-will;* and, if we have the comfort of it, he must have the glory of it. Nor must any *peace,* and *good,* be expected in a way inconsistent with the glory of God; therefore not in any way of sin, nor in any way but by *a Mediator.* Here was the *peace proclaimed* with great solemnity; whoever will, let them come and take the benefit of it. It is on earth peace, to *men of good-will* (so some copies read it), *en anthrōpois eudokias*; to men who have a *good-will to God,* and are willing to be reconciled; or to men whom God has a *good-will to,* though vessels of his mercy. See how well affected the angels are to man, and to his welfare and happiness; how well pleased they were in the incarnation of the Son of God, though he passed by their nature; and ought not we much more to be affected with it? This is a *faithful saying,* attested by an innumerable company of angels, and well *worthy of all acceptation, That the good-will of God toward men is glory to God in the highest, and peace on the earth.*

V. The visit which the shepherds made to the new-born Saviour. 1. They consulted about it, *v.* 15. While the angels were singing their hymn, they could attend to that only; but, *when they were gone away from them into heaven* (for angels, when they appeared, never made any long stay, but returned as soon as they had despatched their business), *the shepherds said one to another, Let us go to Bethlehem.* Note, When extraordinary messages from the upper world are no more to be expected, we must set ourselves to improve the advantages we have for the confirming of our faith, and the keeping up of our communion with God in this lower world. And it is no reflection upon the testimony of angels, no nor upon a divine testimony itself, to get it corroborated by observation and experience. But observe, These shepherds do not speak doubtfully, "Let us go see whether it be so or no;" but with assurance, *Let us go see this thing which is come to pass;* for what room was left to doubt of it, when *the Lord had* thus *made it known to them?* The *word spoken by angels was stedfast* and unquestionably true. 2. They immediately made the visit, *v.* 16. They lost no time, but *came with haste* to the place, which, probably, the angel directed them to more particularly than is recorded ("Go to the stable of such an inn"); and there *they found Mary and Joseph,* and *the babe lying in the manger.* The poverty and meanness in which they found *Christ the Lord* were no shock to their faith, who themselves knew what it was to live a life of comfortable communion with God in very poor and mean circumstances. We have reason to think that the shepherds told Joseph and Mary of the vision of the angels they had seen, and the song of the angels they had heard, which was a great encouragement to them, more than if a visit had been made them by the best ladies in the town. And it is probable that Joseph and Mary told the shepherds what visions they had had concerning the child; and so, by communicating their experiences to each other, they greatly strengthened one another's faith.

VI. The care which the shepherds took to spread the report of this (*v.* 17): *When they had seen it,* though they saw nothing in the child that should induce them to believe that he was *Christ the Lord,* yet the circumstances, how mean soever they were, agreeing with the sign that the angel had given them, they were abundantly satisfied; and as the lepers argued (2 Ki. 12:9, This being *a day of good tidings,* we dare not *hold our peace*), so they made *known abroad* the whole story of what was *told them,* both by the *angels,* and by Joseph and Mary, *concerning this child,* that he was the Saviour, even *Christ the Lord,* that in him there is *peace on earth,* and that he was *conceived by the power of the Holy Ghost,* and *born of a virgin.* This they told every body, and agreed in their testimony concerning it. And now if, when he *is in the world,* the world knows him not, it is *their own fault,* for they have sufficient notice given them. What impression did it make upon people? Why truly, *All they that heard it wondered at those things which were told them by the shepherds, v.* 18. The shepherds were plain, downright, *honest men,* and they could not suspect them guilty of any design to impose upon them; what they had said therefore was likely to be true, and, if true, they could not but wonder at it, that the Messiah should be born *in a stable* and not in a palace, that angels should bring news of it to *poor shepherds* and not to the chief priests. They wondered, but never *enquired any further* about the Saviour, their duty to him, or advantages by him, but let the thing drop as a *nine days' wonder.* O the amazing stupidity of the men of that generation! Justly were the things which belonged to their peace *hid from their eyes,* when they thus wilfully *shut their eyes* against them.

VII. The use which those made of these things, who did believe them. 1. The virgin Mary made them the matter of her *private meditation.* She said little, but *kept all these things,* and *pondered them in her heart, v.* 19. She laid the evidences together, and kept them in reserve, to be compared with the discoveries that should afterwards be made her. As she had silently left it to God to clear up her virtue, when that was suspected, so she silently leaves it to him to publish her honour, now when it was veiled; and it is satisfaction enough to find that, if no one else takes notice of the birth of her child, angels do. Note, The truths of Christ are worth keeping; and the way to keep them safe is to *ponder them.* Meditation is the best help to memory. 2. The shepherds made them the matter of their more *public praises.* If others were not affected with those things, yet they themselves were (*v.* 20): They *returned, glorifying and praising God,* in concurrence with the holy angels. If others would not regard the report they made to them, God would accept the thanksgivings they offered to him. They praised God for what *they had heard* from the angel, and for what *they had seen,* the babe *in the manger,* and just then *in the swaddling,* when they came in, as it had been spoken to them. They thanked God that they had seen Christ, though in the depth of his humiliation. As afterwards the cross of Christ, so now his *manger,* was to some *foolishness* and a *stumbling-block,* but others saw in it, and admired, and praised, the wisdom *of God* and the *power of God.*

Verses 21–24

Our Lord Jesus, being *made of a woman,* was *made under the law,* Gal. 4:4. He was not only, as the son of a daughter of Adam, made under the law of *nature,* but as the son of a daughter of Abraham was made under the law of *Moses;* he put his neck under that yoke, though it was a heavy yoke, and a *shadow of good things to come.* Though its institutions were *beggarly elements,* and *rudiments of this world,* as the apostle calls them, Christ submitted to it, that he might with the better grace cancel it, and set it aside for us.

Now here we have two instances of his being *made under* that *law,* and submitting to it.

I. He was *circumcised* on the very day that the law appointed (*v.* 21): *When eight days were accomplished,* that day seven-night that he was born, they *circumcised* him. 1. Though it was a *painful* operation *(Surely a bloody husband thou has been,* said Zipporah to Moses, *because of the circumcision,* Ex. 4:25), yet Christ would undergo it for us; nay, *therefore* he submitted to it, to give an instance of his early obedience, his obedience unto blood. Then he shed his blood by drops, which afterwards he poured out in purple streams. 2. Though it supposed him a *stranger,* that was by that ceremony to be admitted into covenant with God, whereas he had always been his *beloved Son;* nay, though it supposed him a *sinner,* that needed to have his filthiness taken away, whereas he had no impurity or superfluity of naughtiness to be cut off, *yet* he submitted to it; nay, *therefore* he submitted to it, because he would be made in the likeness, not only of *flesh,* but of *sinful flesh,* Rom. 8:3. 3. Though thereby he made himself a *debtor to the whole law* (Gal. 5:3), yet he submitted to it; nay, *therefore* he submitted to it, because he would take upon him the form of a servant, though he was free-born. Christ was circumcised, (1.) That he might own himself of the seed of Abraham, and of that nation *of whom, as concerning the flesh, Christ came,* and who was to *take on him the seed of Abraham,* Heb. 2:16. (2.) That he might own himself a surety for our sins, and an undertaker for our safety. Circumcision (saith Dr. Goodwin) was our *bond,* whereby we acknowledged ourselves *debtors to the law;* and Christ, by being circumcised, did as it were set his hand to it, being *made sin for us.* The ceremonial law consisted much in sacrifices; Christ hereby obliged himself to offer, not the blood of bulls or goats, but his own blood, which none that ever were circumcised before could oblige themselves to. (3.) That he might justify, and put an honour upon, the dedication of the infant seed of the church to God, by that ordinance which is the instituted seal of the covenant, and of the righteousness which is by faith, as circumcision was (Rom. 4:11), and baptism is. And certainly his being circumcised at eight days old doth make much more for the dedicating of the seed of the faithful by baptism in their infancy than his being baptized at thirty years old doth for the deferring of it till they are grown up. The change of the ceremony alters not the substance.

At his circumcision, according to the custom, he had his name given him; he was called *Jesus* or *Joshua,* for he was *so named of the angel* to his mother Mary *before he was conceived in the womb* (Lu. 1:31), and to his supposed father Joseph after, Mt. 1:21. [1.] It was a *common name* among the Jews, as John was (Col. 4:11), and in this he would be made *like unto his brethren.* [2.] It was the name of two eminent types of him in the Old Testament, Joshua, the successor of Moses, who was commander of Israel, and conqueror of Canaan; and Joshua, the high priest, who was therefore purposely crowned, that he might prefigure Christ as a *priest upon his throne,* Zec. 6:11, 13. [3.] It was very significant of his undertaking. Jesus signifies a *Saviour.* He would be denominated, not from the glories of his divine nature, but from his gracious designs as Mediator; he *brings salvation.*

II. He was *presented* in the temple. This was done with an eye to the law, and at the time appointed by the law, when he was forty days old, *when the days of her purification were accomplished, v.* 22. Many copies, and authentic ones, read *autōn* for *autēs,the days of their purification,* the purification both of the mother and of the child, for so it was intended to be by the law; and our Lord Jesus, though he had no impurity to be cleansed from, yet submitted to it, as he did to circumcision, because he was made *sin for us;* and that, as by the *circumcision of Christ* we might be *circumcised,* in the virtue of our union and communion with him, with a spiritual circumcision *made without hands* (Col. 2:11), so in the *purification* of Christ we might be *spiritually purified* from the filthiness and corruption which we brought into the world with us. Now, according to the law,

1. The child Jesus, being a first-born son, was *presented to the Lord,* in one of the courts of the temple. The law is here recited (*v.* 23): *Every male that opens the womb shall be called holy to the Lord,* because by a special writ of protection the first-born of the Egyptians were slain by the destroying angel; so that Christ, as first-born, was a priest by a title surer than that of Aaron's house. Christ was the *first-born* among many brethren, and was *called holy to the Lord,* so as never any other was; yet he was *presented to the Lord* as other first-born were, and no otherwise. Though he was newly come out of the bosom of the Father, yet he was *presented* to him by the hands of a priest, as if he had been a stranger, that needed one to introduce him. His being *presented to the Lord* now signified his *presenting himself* to the Lord as Mediator, when he was caused to *draw near* and *approach unto him,* Jer. 30:21. But, according to the law, he was *redeemed,* Num. 18:15. *The first-born of many shalt thou redeem,* and *five shekels* was the value, Lev. 27:6: Num. 18:16. But probably in case of poverty the priest was allowed to take less, or perhaps nothing; for no mention is made of it here. Christ was *presented to the Lord,* not to be *brought back,* for his *ear was bored* to God's *door-post* to serve him for ever; and though he is not left in the temple as Samuel was, to minister there, yet like him he is given to the Lord *as long as he lives,* and ministers to him in the true temple *not made with hands.*

2. The mother brought her offering, *v.* 24. When she had presented that son of hers unto the Lord who was to be the great sacrifice, she might have been excused from offering any other; but so *it is said in the law of the Lord,* that law which was yet in force, and therefore so it must be done, she must offer *a pair of turtle-doves, or two young pigeons;* had she been of ability, she must have brought a *lamb for a burnt-offering,* and a *dove for a sin-offering;* but, being poor, and not able to reach the price of a lamb, she brings *two doves,* one for *a burnt-offering and the other for a sin-offering* (see Lev. 12:6, 8), to teach us in every address to God, and particularly in those upon special occasions, both to give thanks to God for his mercies to us and to acknowledge with sorrow and shame our sins against him; in both we must give glory to him, nor do we ever want matter for both. Christ was not *conceived* and *born* in sin, as others are, so that there was not that occasion in his case which there is in others; yet, because he was made under the law, he complied with it. *Thus it became him to fulfil all righteousness.* Much more doth it become the best of men to join in confessions of sin; for *who can say, I have made my heart clean?*

Verses 25–40

Even when he humbles himself, still Christ has honour done him to balance the offence of it. That we might not be stumbled at the *meanness of his birth, angels* then did him honour; and now, that we may not be offended at his being presented in the temple, like other children born in sin, and without any manner of solemnity peculiar to him, but silently, and in the crowd of other children, Simeon and Anna now do him honour, by the inspiration of the Holy Ghost.

I. A very honourable testimony is borne to him by Simeon, which was both a reputation to the child and an encouragement to the parents, and might have been a happy introduction of the priests into an acquaintance with the Saviour, if those *watchmen* had not been *blind.* Now observe here,

1. The account that is given us concerning this Simeon, or Simon. He dwelt now in Jerusalem, and was eminent for his piety and communion with God. Some learned men, who have been conversant with the Jewish writers, find that there was at this time one Simeon, a man of great note in Jerusalem, the son of Hillel, and the first to whom they gave the title of *Rabban,* the highest title that they gave to their doctors, and which was never given but to seven of them. He succeeded his father Hillel, as president of the college which his father founded, and of the great Sanhedrim. The Jews say that he was endued with a *prophetical* spirit, and that he was turned out of his place because he witnessed against the common opinion of the Jews concerning the temporal kingdom of the Messiah; and they likewise observe that there is no mention of him in their Mishna, or book of traditions, which intimates that he was no patron of those fooleries. One thing objected against this conjecture is that at this time his father Hillel was living, and that he himself lived many years after this, as appears by the Jewish histories; but, as to that, he is not here said to be old; and his saying, *Now let thy servant depart* intimates that he was willing to die *now,* but does not conclude that therefore he did die quickly. St. Paul lived many years after he had spoken of his death as *near,* Acts 20:25. Another thing objected is that the son of Simeon was Gamaliel, a Pharisee, and an enemy to Christianity; but, as to that, it is no new thing for a faithful lover of Christ to have a son a bigoted Pharisee.

The account given of him here is, (1.) That he was *just* and *devout, just* towards men and *devout* towards God; these two must always go together, and each will befriend the other, but neither will atone for the defect of the other. (2.) That he *waited for the consolation of Israel,* that is, for the coming of the Messiah, in whom alone the nation of Israel, that was now miserably harassed and oppressed, would find *consolation.* Christ is not only the author of his people's comfort, but the matter and ground of it, the *consolation of Israel.* He was long a coming, and they who believed he would come continued *waiting, desiring* his coming, and *hoping* for it with *patience;* I had almost said, with some degree of *impatience* waiting till it came. He *understood by books,* as Daniel, that the time was at hand, and therefore was now more than ever big with expectation of it. The unbelieving Jews, who still expect that which is already come, use it as an oath, or solemn protestation, *As ever I hope to see the consolation of Israel,* so and so it is. Note, The consolation of Israel is to be waited for, and it is worth waiting for, and it will be very welcome to those who have *waited* for it, and continue waiting. (3.) The *Holy Ghost* was upon him, not only as a Spirit of holiness, but as a Spirit of prophecy; he was *filled with the Holy Ghost,* and enabled to speak things above himself. (4.) He had a gracious promise made him, that before he died he should have a sight of the Messiah, *v.* 26. He was searching *what manner of time* the Spirit of Christ in the Old-Testament prophets did signify, and whether it were not now at hand; and he received *this oracle* (for so the word signifies), *that he should not see death before he had seen* the Messiah, *the Lord's Anointed.* Note, Those, and those only, can with courage *see death,* and look it in the face without terror, that have had by faith a sight of Christ.

2. The seasonable coming of Simeon into the temple, at the time when Christ was presented there, *v.* 27. Just then, when Joseph and Mary brought in the child, to be registered as it were in the church-book, among the first-born, Simeon came, by direction of *the Spirit,* into the temple. The same Spirit that had provided for the support of his hope now provided for the transport of his joy. It was whispered in his ear, "Go to the temple now, and you shall see what you have longed to see." Note, Those that would see Christ must go to his temple; for there *The Lord, whom ye seek,* shall suddenly come to *meet you,* and there you must be ready to *meet him.*

3. The abundant satisfaction wherewith he welcomed this sight: *He took him up in his arms* (*v.* 28), he *embraced* him with the greatest affection imaginable, laid him in his bosom, as near his heart as he could, which was as full of joy as it could hold. He *took him up in his arms,* to present him to the Lord (so some think), to do either the parent's part or the priest's part; for divers of the ancients say that he was himself a priest. When we receive the record which the gospel gives us of Christ with a lively faith, and the offer it makes us of Christ with love and resignation, then we *take Christ in our arms.* It was promised him that he should have a sight of Christ; but more is *performed* than was *promised:* he has him in his arms.

4. The solemn declaration he made hereupon: *He blessed God,* and said, *Lord, now let thou thy servant depart in peace, v.* 29–32.

(1.) He has a pleasant prospect *concerning himself,* and (which is a great attainment) is got quite above the love of life and fear of death; nay, he is arrived at a holy contempt of life, and desire of death: *"Lord, now let thou thy servant depart,* for mine eyes have seen the salvation I was promised a sight of before I died." Here is, [1.] An acknowledgment that God had been *as good as his word;* there has not failed one tittle of his good promises, as Solomon owns, 1 Ki. 8:56. Note, Never any that hoped in God's word were made ashamed of their hope. [2.] A thanksgiving for it. He *blessed God* that he saw that salvation in his arms which many prophets and kings desired to see, and might not. [3.] A confession of his faith, that the child in his arms was the *saviour,* the *Salvation* itself; *thy salvation,* the salvation of thine appointing, the salvation *which thou has prepared* with a great deal of contrivance. And, while it has been thus long *in the coming,* it hath still been *in the preparing.* [4.] It is a farewell to this world: *"Now let thy servant depart;* now mine eyes have been blessed with this sight, let them be closed, and see no more in this world." The eye is not satisfied with seeing (Eccl. 1:8), till it hath *seen Christ,* and then it is. What a poor thing doth this world look to one that hath Christ in his arms and salvation in his eye! Now adieu to all my friends and relations, all my enjoyments and employments here, even the temple itself. [5.] It is a welcome to death: *Now let thy servant depart.* Note, Death is a departure, the soul's departure out of the body, from the world of sense to the world of spirits. We must not depart till God give us our discharge, for we are his *servants* and must not quit his service till we have accomplished our time. Moses was promised that he should see Canaan, and then *die;* but he prayed that this word might be altered, Deu. 3:24, 25. Simeon is promised that he should not *see death* till he had *seen Christ;* and he is willing to construe that beyond what was expressed, as an intimation that, when he had seen Christ, he should die: *Lord, be it so,* saith he, *now let me depart.* See here, *First,* How *comfortable* the death of a good man is; he departs *as God's servant* from the place of his toil to that of his rest. He departs *in peace,* peace with God, peace with his own conscience; in *peace* with death, well-reconciled to it, well-acquainted with it. He departs *according to God's word,* as Moses at the *word of the Lord* (Deu. 34:5): the word of precept, *Go up and die;* the word of promise, *I will come again and receive you to myself. Secondly,* What is the ground of this comfort? *For mine eyes have seen thy salvation.* This bespeaks more than a great complacency in the sight, like that of Jacob (Gen. 46:30), *Now let me die, since I have seen thy face.* It bespeaks a believing expectation of a happy state on the other side death, through this salvation he now had a sight of, which not only takes off the terror of death, but makes it *gain,* Phil. 1:21. Note, Those that have welcomed Christ may welcome death.

(2.) He has a pleasant prospect concerning the world, and concerning the church. This salvation shall be,

[1.] A blessing to the world. It is *prepared before the face of all people,* not to be hid in a corner, but to be made known; to be a *light to lighten the Gentiles* that now sit in darkness: they shall have the knowledge of him, and of God, and another world through him. This has reference to Isa. 49:6, *I will give thee for a light to the Gentiles;* for Christ came to be the light of the world, not a candle in the Jewish candlestick, but the *Sun of righteousness.*

[2.] A blessing to the church: *the glory of thy people Israel.* It was an honour to the Jewish nation that the Messiah sprang out of one of their tribes, and was born, and lived, and died, among them. And of those who were Israelites indeed of the spiritual Israel, he was indeed *the glory,* and will be so to eternity, Isa. 60:19. They shall *glory* in him. *In the Lord shall all the seed of Israel be justified and shall glory,* Isa. 45:25. When Christ ordered his apostles to preach the gospel to all nations, therein he made himself a *light to lighten the Gentiles;* and when he added, *beginning at Jerusalem,* he made himself *the glory of his* people Israel.

5. The prediction concerning this child, which he delivered, with his blessing, to Joseph and Mary. They *marvelled at those things* which were still more and more fully and plainly spoken concerning this child, *v.* 33. And because they were affected with, and had their faith strengthened by, that which was said to them, here is more said to them.

(1.) Simeon shows them what reason they had to *rejoice;* for he *blessed them* (*v.* 34), he pronounced them blessed who had the honour to be related to this child, and were entrusted with the bringing him up. He *prayed* for them, that God would *bless* them, and would have others do so too. They had reason to rejoice, for this child should be, not only a comfort and honour to them, but a public blessing. He is set *for the rising again of many in Israel,* that is, for the conversion of many to God that are dead and buried in sin, and for the consolation of many in God that are sunk and lost in sorrow and despair. Those whom he is set *for the fall of* may be the same with those whom he is set for the *rising again of.* He is set *eis ptōsin kai anastasin — for their fall, in order to their rising again;* to humble and abase them, and bring them off from all confidence in themselves, that they may be exalted by relying on Christ; he wounds and then heals, Paul *falls,* and rises again.

(2.) He shows them likewise what reason they had to *rejoice with trembling,* according to the advice given of old, with reference to the Messiah's kingdom, Ps. 2:11. Lest Joseph, and Mary especially, should be *lifted up* with the abundance of the revelations, here is a *thorn in the flesh* for them, an allay to their joy; and it is what we sometimes need.

[1.] It is true, Christ shall be a blessing to Israel; but there are those in Israel whom he is *set for the fall of,* whose corruptions will be provoked, who will be prejudiced and enraged against him, and offended, and whose sin and ruin will be aggravated by the revelation of Jesus Christ; many who will extract poison to themselves out of the balm of Gilead, and split their souls on the Rock of salvation, to whom this precious Foundation-stone will be a *stone of stumbling.* This refers to that prophecy (Isa. 8:14, 15), He shall be *for a sanctuary* to some, and yet for a *snare* to others, 1 Pt. 2:7, 8. Note, As it is pleasant to think how many there are to whom Christ and his gospel are a savour of life unto life, so it is sad to think how many there are to whom it is a savour of death unto death. He is set for *a sign,* to be admired by some, but by others, by many, spoken against. He had many *eyes upon him,* during the time of his public ministry, he was a *sign,* but he had many *tongues against* him, the contradiction and reproach of sinners, he was continually cavilled at and abused; and the effects of this will be that the *thoughts of many hearts will be revealed* (*v.* 35), that is, upon this occasion, men will *show themselves,* will discover, and so distinguish, themselves. The secret good affections and dispositions in the minds of some will be revealed by their embracing Christ, and closing with him; the secret corruptions and vicious dispositions of others, that otherwise would never have appeared so bad, will be revealed by their enmity to Christ and their rage against him. Men will be judged of by the thoughts of their hearts, their thoughts concerning Christ; are they for *him,* or are they for his *adversaries?* The *word of God* is a discerner of the *thoughts* and *intents of the heart,* and by it we are discovered to ourselves, and shall be judged hereafter.

[2.] It is true, Christ shall be a comfort to his mother; but be not thou too proud of it, for *a sword shall pass through thine own soul also.* He shall be a suffering Jesus; and, *First,* "Thou *shalt suffer with him,* by sympathy, more than any other of his friends, because of the nearness of thy relation, and strength of affection, to him." When he was abused, it was *a sword in her bones.* When she stood by his cross, and saw him dying, we may well think her inward grief was such that it might truly be said, *A sword pierced through her soul,* it cut her to the heart. *Secondly,* Thou shalt *suffer for him.* Many understand it as a prediction of her martyrdom; and some of the ancients say that it had its accomplishment in that. Note, In the midst of our greatest delights and advancements in this world, it is good for us to know that bonds and afflictions abide us.

II. He is taken notice of by one *Anna,* or *Ann, a prophetess,* that one of each sex might bear witness to him in whom both *men* and *women* are invited to believe, that they may be saved. Observe,

1. The account here given of this Anna, who she was. She was, (1.) *A prophetess;* the Spirit of prophecy now began to revive, which had ceased in Israel above three hundred years. Perhaps no more is meant than that she was one who had understanding in the scriptures above other women, and made it her business to instruct the *younger women* in the things of God. Though it was a very degenerate age of the church, yet God *left not himself without witness.* (2.) She was *the daughter of Phanuel;* her father's name (says Grotius) is mentioned, to put us in mind of Jacob's *Phanuel,* or *Penuel* (Gen. 32:30), that now the mystery of that should be unfolded, when in Christ we should as it were see God face to face, and our lives be preserved; and her name signifies *gracious.* (3.) She was of *the tribe of Asher,* which was in Galilee; this, some think, is taken notice of to refute those who said, *Out of Galilee ariseth no prophet,* when no sooner did prophecy revive but it appeared from Galilee. (4.) She was of *a great age,* a widow of about eighty-four years; some think she had now been eighty-four years a widow, and then she must be considerably above a hundred years old; others, rather than suppose that a woman so very old should be capable of fasting and praying as she did, suppose that she was only eighty-four years of age, and had been long a widow. Though she was a young widow, and had lived with her husband but seven years, yet she never married again, but continued a widow to her dying day, which is mentioned to her praise. (5.) She was a constant resident *in* or at least attendant *on* the temple. Some think she had lodgings in the courts of the temple, either in an alms-house, being maintained by the temple charities; or, as a prophetess, she was lodged there, as in a proper place to be consulted and advised with by those that desired to know the mind of God; others think her not *departing from the temple* means no more, than that she was constantly there at the time of divine service: when any good work was to be done, she was ready to join in it. It is most probable she had an apartment of her own among the outbuildings of the temple; and, besides her constant attendance on the public worship, abounded in private devotions, for she *served God with fastings and prayers night and day:* having no secular business to employ herself in, or being past it, she gave up herself wholly to her devotions, and not only *fasted twice in the week,* but always lived a mortified life, and spent that time in religious exercises which others spent in eating and drinking and sleeping; she not only observed the *hours of prayer,* but prayed *night and day;* was always in a praying frame, lived a life of prayer, gave herself to prayer, was frequent in ejaculations, large in solemn prayers, and very particular in her intercessions. And in these she *served* God; that was it that put a value upon them and an excellency into them. The Pharisees *fasted often,* and made *long prayers,* but they served themselves, and their own pride and covetousness, in their fastings and prayers; but this good woman not only did that which was good, but did it from a good principle, and with a good end; she *served God,* and aimed at

his honour, in *fasting and praying.* Note, [1.] Devotion is a thing we ought to be constant in; other duties are in season now and then, but we must *pray always.* [2.] It is a pleasant sight to see aged Christians abounding in acts of devotion, as those that are not *weary of well-doing,* that do not think themselves *above* these exercises, or *past* them, but that take more and more pleasure in them, and see more and more need of them, till they come to heaven. [3.] Those that are diligent and faithful in improving the light and means they have shall have further discoveries made them. Anna is now at length abundantly recompensed for her attendance so many years in the temple.

2. The testimony she bore to our Lord Jesus (*v.* 38): *She came in at that instant* when the child was presented, and Simeon discoursed concerning him; she, who was so *constant* to the temple, could not miss the opportunity.

Now, (1.) She *gave thanks likewise to the Lord,* just as Simeon, perhaps like him, wishing now to depart in peace. Note, Those to whom Christ is *made known* have reason enough to *give thanks to the Lord* for so great a favour; and we should be excited to that duty by the praises and thanksgivings of others; why should not we *give thanks likewise,* as well as they? Anna concurred with Simeon, and helped to make up the harmony. *She confessed unto the Lord* (so it may be read); she made an open profession of her faith concerning this child.

(2.) She, as a prophetess, instructed others concerning him: She *spoke of him to all them* that believed the Messiah would come, and with him *looked for redemption in Jerusalem.* Redemption was the thing wanted, waited for, and wished for; redemption *in Jerusalem,* for thence the *word of the Lord was to go forth,* Isa, 2:3. Some there were in Jerusalem that *looked for redemption;* yet but a few, for Anna, it should seem, had acquaintance with all them that were joint-expectants with her of the Messiah; she knew where to find them, or they where to find her, and she told them all the good news, that she had seen the Lord; and it was great news, this of his birth now, as afterwards that of his resurrection. Note, Those that have an acquaintance with Christ *themselves* should do all they can to bring *others* acquainted with him.

Lastly, Here is a short account of the infancy and childhood of our Lord Jesus.

1. *Where* he spent it, *v.* 39. When the ceremony of presenting the child, and purifying the mother, was all over, they *returned into Galilee.* Luke relates no more concerning them, till they were returned into Galilee; but it appears by St. Matthew's gospel (*ch.* 2) that from Jerusalem they returned to Bethlehem, where the wise men of the east found them, and there they continued till they were directed to flee into Egypt, to escape the malice and rage of Herod; and, returning thence when Herod was dead, they were directed to go to their old quarters in Nazareth, whence they had been perhaps some years absent. It is here called *their own city,* because there they had lived a great while, and their relations were there. He was ordered further from Jerusalem, because his kingdom and priesthood were to have no affinity with the present government of the Jewish church or state. He is sent into a place of obscurity and reproach; for in this, as in other things, he must humble himself and *make himself of no reputation.*

2. *How* he spent it, *v.* 40. In all things *it behoved him to be made like unto his brethren,* and therefore he passed through infancy and childhood as other children did, yet without sin; nay, with manifest indications of a divine nature in him. As other children, he *grew* in stature of body, and the improvement of understanding in his human soul, that his *natural* body might be a figure of his *mystical* body, which, though animated by a perfect spirit, yet *maketh increase of itself* till it comes to the *perfect man,* Eph. 4:13, 16. But, (1.) Whereas other children are weak in understanding and resolution, he was *strong in spirit.* By the Spirit of God his human soul was endued with extraordinary vigour, and all his faculties performed their offices in an extraordinary manner. He reasoned strongly, and his judgment was penetrating. (2.) Whereas other children have *foolishness bound in their hearts,* which appears in what they say or do, he was *filled with wisdom,* not by any advantages of instruction and education, but by the operation of the Holy Ghost; every thing he said and did was wisely said, and wisely done, above his years. (3.) Whereas other children show that the corruption of nature is in them, and *the tares of sin* grow up with the *wheat of reason,* he made it appear that nothing but *the grace*

of God was upon him (the wheat sprang up without tares), and that, whereas other children are by nature children of wrath, he was *greatly beloved,* and high in the favour of God; that God loved him, and cherished him, and took a particular care of him.

Verses 41–52

We have here the only passage of story recorded concerning our blessed Saviour, from his infancy to the day of his showing to Israel at twenty-nine years old, and therefore we are concerned to make much of this, for it is in vain to wish we had more. Here is,

I. Christ's *going up with his parents* to Jerusalem, at the feast of the passover, *v.* 41, 42. 1. It was their constant practice to attend there, according to the law, though it was a long journey, and they were poor, and perhaps not well able, without straitening themselves, to bear the expenses of it. Note, Public ordinances must be frequented, and we must *not forsake the assembling of ourselves together, as the manner of some is.* Worldly business must give way to spiritual concerns. Joseph and Mary had a son in the house with them, that was able to teach them better than all the rabbin at Jerusalem; yet they *went up* thither, *after the custom of the feast. The Lord loves the gates of Zion more than all the dwellings of Jacob,* and so should we. We have reason to suppose that Joseph went up likewise at the feasts of *pentecost* and *tabernacles;* for all the males were to appear there *thrice a year,* but Mary only at the *passover,* which was the greatest of the three feasts, and had most gospel in it. 2. The child Jesus, at *twelve years old,* went up with them. The Jewish doctors say that at twelve years old children must begin to fast from time to time, that they may learn to fast on the day of atonement; and that at thirteen years old a child begins to be *a son of the commandment,* that is, obliged to the duties of adult church-membership, having been from his infancy, by virtue of his circumcision, *a son of the covenant.* It is not said that this was the *first time* that Jesus went up to Jerusalem to worship at the feast: probably he had done it for some years before, having spirit and wisdom above his years; and all should attend on public worship that can *hear with understanding,* Neh. 8:2. Those children that are forward in other things should be put forward in religion. It is for the honour of Christ that children should attend on public worship, and he is pleased with their hosannas; and those children that were in their infancy dedicated to God should be called upon, when they are grown up, to come to the *gospel passover,* to the Lord's supper, that they make it their own act and deed to join themselves to the Lord.

II. Christ's *tarrying behind his parents at Jerusalem,* unknown to them, in which he designed to give an early specimen of what he was reserved for.

1. His parents did not return till they had *fulfilled the days;* they had staid there all the seven days at the feast, though it was not absolutely necessary that they should stay longer than the two first days, after which many went home. Note, It is good to stay to the conclusion of an ordinance, as becomes those who say, *It is good to be here,* and not to hasten away, as if we were like Doeg, *detained before the Lord.*

2. The child *tarried behind in Jerusalem,* not because he was loth to go home, or shy of his parents' company, but because he had business to do there, and would let his parents know that he had a *Father in heaven,* whom he was to be *observant* of more than of *them;* and respect to *him* must not be construed disrespect *to them.* Some conjecture that he tarried behind in the temple, for it was the custom of the pious Jews, on the morning that they were to go home, to go first to the temple, to worship God; there he *staid behind,* and found entertainment there till they found him again. Or, perhaps, he staid at the house where they lodged, or some other friend's house (and such a child as he was could not but be the darling of all that knew him, and every one would court his company), and went up to the temple only at church-time; but so it was that he staid behind. It is good to see young people willing to *dwell in the house of the Lord;* they are then like Christ.

3. His parents went the *first day's journey* without any suspicion that he was left behind, for they *supposed him to have been in the company, v.* 44. On these occasions, the crowd was very great, especially the first day's journey, and the roads full of people; and they concluded that he came along with some of their neighbours, and they *sought him among their kindred and acquaintance,* that were upon the road, going

down. Pray did *you* see our Son? or, Did *you* see him? Like the spouses's inquiry, *Saw ye him whom my soul loveth?* This was a jewel worth seeking after. They knew that every one would be desirous of his company, and that he would be willing to do good among *his kinsfolk and acquaintance,* but among them they *found him not, v.* 45. There are many, too many, who are our kinsfolk and acquaintance, that we cannot avoid conversing with, among whom we find little or nothing of Christ. When they could not hear of him in this and the other company upon the road, yet they hoped they should meet with him at the place where they lodged that night; but *there* they could learn no tidings of him. Compare this with Job 23:8, 9.

4. When they found him not at their quarters at night, they *turned back again,* next morning, *to Jerusalem, seeking him.* Note, Those that would find Christ must *seek till they find;* for he will at length be found of those that seek him, and will be found their bountiful rewarder. Those that have lost their comforts in Christ, and the evidences of their interest in him, must bethink themselves where, and when, and how, they lost them, and must *turn back again* to the place where they last had them; must *remember whence they are fallen, and repent, and do their first works,* and *return to their first love,* Rev. 2:4, 5. Those that would recover their lost acquaintance with Christ must go to Jerusalem, the *city of our solemnities,* the place which he has *chosen to put his name there;* must attend upon him in his ordinances, in the gospel-passover, there they may hope to meet him.

5. The *third day* they found him *in the temple,* in some of the apartments belonging to the temple, where the doctors of the law kept, not their courts, but their conferences rather, or their schools for disputation; and there they found him *sitting in the midst of them* (*v.* 46), not standing as a *catechumen* to be examined or instructed by them, for he had discovered such measures of knowledge and wisdom that they admitted him to sit among them as a fellow or member of their society. This is an instance, not only that he was *filled with wisdom* (*v.* 40), but that he had both a desire to increase it and a readiness to communicate it; and herein he is an example to children and young people, who should learn of Christ to delight in the company of those they may get good by, and choose to *sit in the midst of* the doctors rather than in the midst of the players. Let them begin at *twelve years old,* and sooner, to enquire after knowledge, and to associate with those that are able to instruct them; it is a hopeful and promising presage in youth to be desirous of instruction. Many a youth at Christ's age now would have been playing with the *children in the temple,* but he was sitting with the *doctors in the temple.* (1.) He *heard* them. Those that would learn must be *swift to hear.* (2.) He *asked them questions;* whether, as a teacher (he had authority so to ask) or as a learner (he had humility so to ask) I know not, or whether as an associate, or joint-searcher after truth, which must be found out by mutual amicable disquisitions. (3.) He returned *answers* to them, which were very surprising and satisfactory, *v.* 47. And his wisdom and *understanding* appeared as much in the questions he asked as in the answers he gave, so that all who heard him *were astonished:* they never heard one so young, no indeed any of their greatest doctors, talk sense at the rate that he did; like David, he had *more understanding than all his teachers,* yea, *than the ancients,* Ps. 119:99, 100. Now Christ showed forth some rays of his glory, which were presently drawn in again. He *gave them a taste* (says Calvin) of his divine wisdom and knowledge. Methinks this public appearance of Christ in the temple, as a teacher, was like Moses's early attempt to deliver Israel, which Stephen put this construction upon, that *he supposed his brethren would have understood,* by that, *how God by his hand would deliver them,* Acts 7:24, 25. They might have taken the hint, and been delivered then, but *they understood not;* so they here might have had Christ (for aught I know) to enter upon his work now, but they were only *astonished,* and *understood not* the indication; and therefore, like Moses, he retires into obscurity again, and they hear no more of him for many years after.

6. His mother talked with him privately about it. When the company broke up, she took him aside, and examined him about it with a deal of tenderness and affection, *v.* 48. Joseph and Mary were both *amazed* to find him there, and to find that he had so much respect showed him as to be admitted to *sit among the doctors,* and to be taken notice of. His father knew he had only the name of a father, and there-

fore said nothing. But, (1.) His mother told him how ill they took it: *"Son, why hast thou thus dealt with us?* Why didst thou put us into such a fright?" They were ready to say, as Jacob of Joseph, *"A wild beast has devoured him;* or, He is fallen into the hands of some more cruel enemy, who has at length found out that he was the young child whose life Herod had sought some years ago." A thousand imaginations, we may suppose, they had concerning him, each more frightful than another. "Now, why hast thou given us occasion for these fears? *Thy father and I have sought thee, sorrowing;* not only troubled that we lost thee, but vexed at ourselves that we did not take more care of thee, to bring thee along with us." Note, Those may have leave to complain of their losses that think they have lost Christ. But their *weeping* did not hinder *sowing;* they did not sorrow and sit down in despair, but sorrowed and *sought.* Note, If we would find Christ, we must seek him *sorrowing,* sorrowing that we have lost him, that we have provoked him to withdraw, and that we have sought him no sooner. They that thus seek him in sorrow shall find him, at length, with so much the greater joy. (2.) He gently reproved their inordinate solicitude about him (*v.* 49): *"How is it that you sought me?* You might have depended upon it, I would have followed you home when I had done the business I had to do here. I could not be lost in Jerusalem. Wist ye not that I *ought to be, en tois tou patros mou; — in my Father's house?"* so some read it; "where else should the Son be, who *abideth in the house for ever?* I ought to be," [1.] *"Under my Father's care* and protection; and therefore you should have cast the care of me upon him, and not have burdened yourselves with it." Christ is a shaft hid in his Father's quiver, Isa. 49:2. He takes care of his church likewise, and therefore let us never despair of its safety. [2.] *"At my Father's work"* (so we take it): "I must be *about my Father's business,* and therefore could not go home as soon as you might. *Wist ye not?* Have you not already perceived that concerning me, that I have devoted myself to the service of religion, and therefore must employ myself in the affairs of it?" Herein he hath left us an example; for it becomes the children of God, in conformity to Christ, to attend their heavenly Father's business, and to make all other business give way to it. This word of Christ we now think we understand very well, for he hath explained it in what he hath done and said. It was his errand into the world, and his meat and drink in the world, to do his Father's will, and finish his work: and yet at that time his parents *understood not this saying, v.* 50. They did not understand what business he had to do then in the temple for his Father. They believed him to be the Messiah, that should have the throne of his father David; but they thought that should rather bring him to the royal palace than to the temple. They *understood not* his prophetical office; and he was to do much of his work in that.

Lastly, Here is their return to Nazareth. This glimpse of his glory was to be short. It was now over, and he did not urge his parents either to come and settle at Jerusalem or to settle him there (though that was the place of improvement and preferment, and where he might have the best opportunities of showing his wisdom), but very willingly retired into his obscurity at Nazareth, where for many years he was, as it were, buried alive. Doubtless, he came up to Jerusalem, to worship at the feast, three times a year, but whether he ever went again into the temple, to dispute with the doctors there, we are not told; it is not improbable but he might. But here we are told,

1. That he was *subject to his parents.* Though once, to show that he was *more than a man,* he withdrew himself from his parents, to attend his heavenly Father's business, yet he did not, as yet, make that his constant practice, nor for many years after, but was *subject to them,* observed their order, and went and came as they directed, and, as it should seem, worked with his father at the trade of a carpenter. Herein he hath given an example to children to be dutiful and obedient to their parents in the Lord. Being *made of a woman,* he was made under the law of the fifth commandment, to teach the *seed* of the faithful thus to approve themselves to him a faithful seed. Though his parents were poor and mean, though his father was only his *supposed* father, yet he was *subject to them;* though he was *strong in spirit,* and *filled with wisdom* nay though he was the Son of God, yet he was subject to his parents; how then will *they* answer it who, though foolish and weak, yet are disobedient to their parents?

2. That his mother, though she did not perfectly understand her son's sayings, yet *kept them in her heart,* expecting that hereafter they would be explained to her, and she should fully understand them, and know how to make use of them. However we may neglect men's sayings because they are obscure *(Si non vis intelligi debes negligi — If it be not intelligible, it is not valuable),* yet we must not think so of God's sayings. That which at first is dark, so that we know not what to make of it, may afterwards become plain and easy; we should therefore *lay it up* for hereafter. See Jn. 2:22. We may find use for that another time which now we see not how to make useful to us. A *scholar* keeps those grammar rules in memory which at present he understands not the use of, because he is told that they will hereafter be of use to him; so we must do by Christ's sayings.

3. That he improved, and came on, to admiration (*v.* 52): *He increased in wisdom and stature.* In the perfections of his divine nature there could be no increase; but this is meant of his human nature, his body increased in *stature* and bulk, he grew in the growing age; and his soul increased *in wisdom,* and in all the endowments of a human soul. Though the Eternal Word was united to the human soul from his conception, yet the divinity that dwelt in him manifested itself to his humanity by degrees, *ad modum recipientis — in proportion to his capacity;* as the faculties of his human soul grew more and more capable, the gifts it received from the divine nature were more and more communicated. And he increased in *favour with God and man,* that is, in all those graces that rendered him acceptable to God and man. Herein Christ accommodated himself to his estate of humiliation, that, as he condescended to be an infant, a child, a youth, so the image of God shone brighter in him, when he grew up to be a youth, than it did, or could, while he was an *infant* and a *child.* Note, Young people, as they grow in stature, should grow in wisdom, and then, as they grow in wisdom, they will grow in favour *with God and man.*

CHAPTER 3

Nothing is related concerning our Lord Jesus from his twelfth year to his entrance on his thirtieth year. We often think it would have been a pleasure and advantage to us if we had journals, or at least annuls, of occurrences concerning him; but we have as much as Infinite Wisdom thought fit to communicate to us, and, if we improve not that, neither should we have improved more if we had had it. The great intention of the evangelists was to give us an account of the gospel of Christ, which we are to believe, and by which we hope for salvation: now that began in the ministry and baptism of John, and therefore they hasten to give us an account of that. We could wish, perhaps, that Luke had wholly passed by what was related by Matthew and Mark, and had written only what was new, as he has done in his two first chapters. But it was the will of the Spirit that some things should be established out of the mouth, not only of two, but of three witnesses; and we must not reckon it a needless repetition, nor shall we do so if we renew out meditations upon these things, with suitable affections. In this chapter we have, I. The beginning of John's baptism, and the scope and intention of it (*v.* 1–6). His exhortation to the multitude (*v.* 7–9), and the particular instructions he gave to those who desired to be told their duty (*v.* 10–14). II. The notice he gave them of the approach of the Messiah (*v.* 15–18), to which is added (though it happened after what follows) the mention of his imprisonment (*v.* 19–20). III. Christ coming to be baptized of John, and his entrance therein upon the execution of his prophetical office (*v.* 21, 22). IV. His pedigree and genealogy recorded up to Adam (*v.* 23–38).

Verses 1–14

John's baptism introducing a new dispensation, it was requisite that we should have a particular account of it. Glorious things were said of John, what a distinguished favourite of Heaven he should be, and what a great blessing to this earth (*ch.* 1:15, 17); but we lost him in the deserts, and there he remains until *the day of his showing unto Israel, ch.* 1:80. And now at last that day dawns, and a welcome day it was to them that waited for it more than they that waited for the morning. Observe here,

I. The date of the beginning of John's baptism, when it was that he appeared; this is here taken notice of, which was not by the other evangelists, that the truth of the thing might be confirmed by the exact fixing of the time. And it is dated,

1. By the government of the heathen, which the Jews were under, to show that they were a conquered people, and therefore it was time for the Messiah to come to set up a spiritual kingdom, and an eternal one, upon the ruins of all the temporal dignity and dominion of David and Judah.

(1.) It is dated by the reign of the Roman emperor; it was in the fifteenth year of Tiberius Caesar, the third of the twelve Caesars, a very bad man, given to covetousness, drunkenness, and cruelty; such a man is mentioned first (saith Dr. Lightfoot), as it were, to teach us what to look for from that cruel and abominable city wherein Satan reigned in all ages and successions. The people of the Jews, after a long struggle, were of late made a province of the empire, and were under the dominion of this Tiberius; and that country which once had made so great a figure, and had many nations tributaries to it, in the reigns of David and Solomon, is now itself an inconsiderable despicable part of the Roman empire, and rather trampled upon than triumphed in.

— *En quo discordia cives, Perduxit miseros*
— What dire effects from civil discord flow!

The lawgiver was now departed from between Judah's feet; and, as an evidence of that, their public acts are dated by the reign of the Roman emperor, and therefore now Shiloh must come.

(2.) It is dated by the governments of the viceroys that ruled in the several parts of the Holy Land under the Roman emperor, which was another badge of their servitude, for they were all foreigners, which bespeaks a sad change with that people whose *governors* used to be *of themselves* (Jer. 30:21), and it was their glory. *How is the gold become dim!* [1.] Pilate is here said to be the governor, president, or procurator, of Judea. This character is given of him by some other writers, that he was a wicked man, and one that made no conscience of a lie. He reigned ill, and at last was displaced by Vitellius, president of Syria, and sent to Rome, to answer for his mal-administrations. [2.] The other three are called *tetrarchs,* some think from the countries which they had the command of, each of them being over a *fourth part* of that which had been entirely under the government of Herod the Great. Others think that they are so called from the post of honour they held in the government; they had the *fourth* place, or were *fourth-rate* governors: the emperor was the *first,* the *pro-consul,* who governed a province, the *second,* a *king* the *third,* and a *tetrarch* the *fourth.* So Dr. Lightfoot.

2. By the government of the Jews among themselves, to show that they were a corrupt people, and that therefore it was time that the Messiah should come, to reform them, *v.* 2. Annas and Caiaphas were the high priests. God had appointed that there should be but one high priest at a time, but here were two, to serve some ill turn or other: one served one year and the other the other year; so some. One was the high priest, and the other the *sagan,* as the Jews called him, to officiate for him when he was disabled; or, as others say, one was high priest, and represented Aaron, and that was *Caiaphas;* Annas, the other, was *nasi,* or head of the sanhedrim, and represented Moses. But to us there is but one high priest, one Lord of all, to whom all judgment is committed.

II. The origin and tendency of John's baptism.

1. The origin of it was *from heaven: The word of God came unto John, v.* 2. He received full commission and full instructions from God to do what he did. It is the same expression that is used concerning the Old-Testament prophets (Jer. 1:2); for John was a prophet, yea, more than a prophet, and in him prophecy revived, which had been long suspended. We are not told how *the word of the Lord came* to John, whether by an angel, as to his father, or by dream, or vision, or voice, but it was to his satisfaction, and ought to be to ours. John is here called *the son of Zacharias,* to refer us to what the angel said to his father, when he assured him that he should have this son. The word of the Lord came to him *in the wilderness;* for those whom God *fits* he will find out, wherever they are. As the word of the Lord is not *bound* in a *prison,* so it is not *lost* in a *wilderness.* The *word of the Lord* made its way to Ezekiel among the captives by the river of Chebar, and to John in the isle of Patmos. John was the *son of a priest,* now entering upon the thirtieth year of his age; and therefore, according to the custom of the temple, he was now to be admitted into the temple-service, where he should have attended as a candidate five years before. But God had called him to a more honourable ministry, and therefore the Holy Ghost enrols him here, since he was not enrolled in the archives of the temple: *John the son of Zacharias began his ministration such a time.*

2. The scope and design of it were to bring all the people of his country off from their sins and home to their God, *v.* 3. *He came* first *into all the country about Jordan,* the neighbourhood wherein he resided, that part of the country which Israel took possession of first, when they entered the land of promise under Joshua's conduct; there was the banner of the gospel first displayed. John resided in the most solitary part of the country: but, when the word of the Lord came to him, he quitted his deserts, and came into the inhabited country. Those that are *best pleased* in their retirements must

cheerfully *exchange* them, when God calls them into places of concourse. *He came* out of the wilderness *into all the country,* with some marks of distinction, *preaching* a new *baptism;* not a sect, or party, but a *profession,* or distinguishing badge. The sign, or ceremony, was such as was ordinarily used among the Jews, *washing with water,* by which proselytes were sometimes admitted, or disciples to some great master; but the meaning of it was, *repentance for the remission of sins:* that is, all that submitted to his baptism,

(1.) Were thereby obliged to *repent of their sins,* to be *sorry* for what they had done amiss, and to *do so no more.* The former they *professed,* and were concerned to be *sincere* in their professions; the latter they *promised,* and were concerned to *make good* what they promised. He bound them, not to such ceremonious observances as were imposed by the tradition of the elders, but to change their mind, and change their way, to *cast away from them all their transgressions,* and to *make them new hearts* and to live new lives. The design of the gospel, which now began, was to make men devout and pious, holy and heavenly, humble and meek, sober and chaste, just and honest, charitable and kind, and good in every relation, who had been much otherwise; and this is to *repent.*

(2.) They were thereby assured of the pardon of their sins, upon their repentance. As the baptism he administered bound them not to submit to the power of sin, so it sealed to them a gracious and pleadable discharge from the guilt of sin. *Turn yourselves from all your transgressions, so iniquity shall not be your ruin;* agreeing with the word of the Lord, by the Old-Testament prophets, Eze. 18:30.

III. The fulfilling of the scriptures in the ministry of John. The other evangelists had referred us to the same text that is here referred to, that of Esaias, *ch.* 40:3. It is *written in the book of the words of Esaias the prophet,* which he heard from God, which he spoke for God, those words of his which were *written* for the generations to come. Among them it is found that there should be *the voice of one crying in the wilderness;* and John is that voice, a clear distinct voice, a loud voice, an articulate one; he cries, *Prepare ye the way of the Lord, and make his paths straight.* John's business is to *make way* for the entertainment of the gospel in the hearts of the people, to bring them into such a frame and temper as that Christ might be welcome to them, and they welcome to Christ. Luke goes further on with the quotation than Matthew and Mark had done, and applies the following words likewise to John's ministry (v. 5, 6), *Every valley shall be filled.* Dr. Hammond understands this as a prediction of the desolation coming upon the people of the Jews for their infidelity: the land should be made plain by the pioneers for the Roman army, and should be laid waste by it, and there should then be a visible distinction made between the impenitent on the one side and the receivers of the gospel on the other side. But it seems rather to be meant of the gospel of Christ, of which that was the introduction. 1. The humble shall by it be *enriched* with grace: *Every valley* that lies *low* and *moist* shall be *filled* and be *exalted.* 2. The proud shall by it be humbled; the *self-confident* that stand upon *their own bottom,* and the *self-conceited* that lift up *their own top,* shall have contempt put upon them: *Every mountain and hill shall be brought low.* If they repent, they are brought to the dust; if not, to the lowest hell. 3. Sinners shall be converted to God: *The crooked ways* and the *crooked* spirits shall be *made straight;* for, though *none can make that straight which God hath made crooked* (Eccl. 7:13), yet God by his grace can make that straight which sin hath made crooked. 4. Difficulties that were hindering and discouraging in the way to heaven shall be removed: *The rough ways shall be made smooth;* and they that love God's law shall have *great peace,* and *nothing shall offend them.* The gospel has made the way to heaven *plain* and easy to be *found, smooth* and easy to be *walked in.* 5. The great salvation shall be more fully discovered than ever, and the discovery of it shall spread further (v. 6): *All flesh shall see the salvation of God;* not the Jews only, but the Gentiles. All shall *see* it; they shall have it set before them and offered to them, and some of all sorts shall *see* it, enjoy it, and have the benefit of it. When way is made for the gospel into the heart, by the captivation of high thoughts and bringing them into obedience to Christ, by the leveling of the soul and the removing of all obstructions that stand in the way of Christ and his grace, then prepare to bid the salvation of God welcome.

IV. The general warnings and exhortations which he gave

to those who submitted to his baptism, v. 7–9. In Matthew he is said to have preached these same things to *many of the Pharisees and Sadducees,* that *came to his baptism* (Mt. 3:7–10); but here he is said to have spoken them *to the multitude, that came forth to be baptized of him,* v. 7. This was the purport of his preaching to all that came to him, and he did not alter it in compliment to the Pharisees and Sadducees, when they came, but dealt as plainly with them as with any other of his hearers. And as he did not flatter the *great,* so neither did he compliment the *many,* or make his court to them, but gave the same reproofs of sin and warnings of wrath to the *multitude* that he did to the Sadducees and Pharisees; for, if they had not the same faults, they had others as bad. Now observe here,

1. That the guilty corrupted race of mankind is become a *generation of vipers,* not only poisoned, but poisonous; hateful to God, hating one another. This magnifies the patience of God, in continuing the race of mankind upon the earth, and not destroying that *nest of vipers.* He did it once by water, and will again by fire.

2. This generation of vipers is fairly warned to *flee from the wrath to come,* which is certainly before them if they continue such; and their being a *multitude* will not be at all their security, for it will be neither *reproach* nor *loss* to God to cut them off. We are not only warned of this wrath, but are put into a way to escape it, if we look about us in time.

3. There is no way of *fleeing from the wrath to come,* but by repentance. They that submitted to the baptism of repentance thereby evidenced that they were *warned* to flee from the wrath to come and *took* the warning; and we by our baptism profess to have fled out of Sodom, for fear of what is coming upon it.

4. Those that profess repentance are highly concerned to live like penitents (v. 8): *"Bring forth therefore fruits meet for repentance,* else, notwithstanding your professions of repentance, you cannot escape *the wrath to come."* By the fruits of repentance it will be known whether it be sincere or no. By the change of our way must be evidenced the change of our mind.

5. If we be not really holy, both in heart and life, our profession of religion and relation to God and his church will stand us in no stead at all: *Begin not* now to frame excuses from this great duty of repentance, by *saying within yourselves, We have Abraham to our father.* What will it avail us to be the children of godly parents if we be not godly, to be within the pale of the Church if we be not brought into the bond of the covenant?

6. We have therefore no reason to depend upon our external privileges and professions of religion, because God has no need of us or of our services, but can effectually secure by his own honour and interest without us. If we were cut off and ruined, he could raise up to himself a church out of the most unlikely, — *children to Abraham* even *out of stones.*

7. The greater professions we make of repentance, and the greater assistances and encouragements are given us to repentance, the nearer and the sorer will our destruction be if we do not *bring forth fruits meet for repentance.* Now that the gospel begins to be preached, now that the kingdom of heaven is at hand, *now* that the *axe is laid to the root of the tree,* threatenings to the wicked and impenitent are now more terrible than before, as encouragements to the penitent are now more comfortable. "Now that you are upon your behaviour, look to yourselves."

8. Barren trees will be cast into the fire at length; it is the fittest place for them: *Every tree* that doth not bring forth fruit, *good fruit,* is *hewn down,* and *cast into the fire.* If it serve not for fruit, to the honour of God's grace, let it serve for fuel, to the honour of his justice.

V. The particular instructions he gave to several sorts of persons, that enquired of him concerning their duty: the *people,* the *publicans,* and the *soldiers.* Some of the Pharisees and Sadducees came to his baptism; but we do not find them asking, *What shall we do?* They thought they knew what they had to do as well as he could tell them, or were determined to do what they pleased, whatever he told them. But the *people,* the *publicans,* and the *soldiers,* who knew that they had done amiss, and that they ought to do better, and were conscious to themselves of great ignorance and unacquaintedness with the divine law, were particularly inquisitive: *What shall we do?* Note, 1. Those that are *baptized* must be *taught,* and those that have baptized them are concerned, as they have opportunity, to teach them, Mt. 28:19, 20. 2. Those that

profess and promise repentance in general must evidence it by particular instances of reformation, according as their place and condition are. 3. They that would do their duty must desire to know their duty, and enquire concerning it. The first good word Paul said, when he was converted, was, *Lord, what wilt thou have me to do?* These here enquire, not, *What shall this man do?* but, What shall *we* do? What *fruits meet for repentance* shall we *bring forth?* Now John gives answer to each, according to their place and station.

(1.) He tells the *people* their duty, and that is to be charitable (v. 11): He *that has two coats,* and, consequently, one to spare, let him *give,* or *lend* at least, *to him that has none,* to keep him warm. Perhaps he saw among his hearers some that were overloaded with clothes, while others were ready to perish in rags, and he puts those who had superfluities upon contributing to the relief of those that had not necessaries. The gospel requires *mercy,* and not sacrifice; and the design of it is to engage us to do all the good we can. *Food and raiment* are the two supports of life; he that hath *meat* to spare, let him give to him that is destitute of *daily food,* as well as he that hath clothes to spare: what we have we are but stewards of, and must use it, accordingly, as our Master directs.

(2.) He tells the *publicans* their duty, the collectors of the emperor's revenue (v. 13): *Exact no more than that which is appointed you.* They must do justice between the government and the merchant, and not oppress the people in levying the taxes, nor any way make them heavier or more burdensome than the law had made them. They must not think that because it was their office to take care that the people did not defraud the prince they might therefore, by the power they had, bear hard upon the people; as those that have ever so little a branch of power are apt to abuse it: "No, keep to your *book of rates,* and reckon it enough that you collect for Caesar the things that are Caesar's, and do not enrich yourselves by taking more." The public revenues must be applied to the public service, and not to gratify the avarice of private persons. Observe, He does not direct the publicans to quit their places, and to go no more to the receipt of custom; the employment is in itself lawful and necessary, but let them be just and honest in it.

(3.) He tells the *soldiers* their duty, v. 14. Some think that these soldiers were of the Jewish nation and religion: others think that they were Romans; for it was not likely either that the Jews would serve the Romans or that the Romans would trust the Jews in their garrisons in their own nation; and then it is an early instance of Gentiles embracing the gospel and submitting to it. Military men seldom seem inclined to religion; yet these submitted even to the Baptist's strict profession, and desired to receive the *word of command* from him: *What must we do?* Those who more than other men have their lives in their hands, and are in deaths often, are concerned to enquire what they shall do that they may be *found in peace.* In answer to this enquiry, John does not bid them lay down their arms, and desert the service, but cautions them against the sins that soldiers were commonly guilty of; for this is fruit meet for repentance, to *keep ourselves from our iniquity.* [1.] They must not be injurious to *the people* among whom they were quartered, and over whom indeed they were set: *"Do violence to no man.* Your business is to keep the peace, and prevent men's doing violence to one another; but do not you *do violence* to any. Shake no man" (so the word signifies); "do not put people into fear; for the sword of war, as well as that of justice, is to be a terror only to evil doers, but a protection to those that do well. Be not rude in your quarters; force not money from people by frightening them. Shed not the blood of war in peace; offer no incivility either to man or woman, nor have any hand in the barbarous devastations that armies sometimes make." Nor must they *accuse any falsely* to the government, thereby to make themselves formidable, and get bribes. [2.] They must not be injurious to their *fellow-soldiers;* for some think that caution, not to *accuse falsely,* has special reference to them: "Be not forward to complain one of another to your superior officers, that you may be revenged on those whom you have a pique against, or undermine those above you, and get into their places." *Do not oppress any;* so some think the word here signifies as used by the Septuagint in several passages of the Old Testament. [3.] They must not be given to mutiny, or contend with their generals about their pay: "Be *content with your wages.* While you have what you agreed for, do not murmur that it is not more." It is discontent with what they have that makes men oppressive and injurious; they that never think they have enough themselves will not scruple at any the most irregular practices to make it more, by defrauding others. It is a rule to all servants that they *be content with their wages;* for they that indulge themselves in discontents expose themselves to many temptations, and it is wisdom to make the best of that which is.

Verses 15–20

We are now drawing near to the appearance of our Lord Jesus publicly; the Sun will not be long after the morning-star. We are here told,

I. How the people took occasion, from the ministry and baptism of John, to think of the Messiah, and to think of him as at the door, as now come. Thus the way of the Lord was *prepared,* and people were prepared to bid Christ welcome; for, when men's expectations are raised, that which they are in expectation of becomes doubly acceptable. Now when they observed what an excellent doctrine John Baptist preached, what a divine power went along with it, and what a tendency it had to reform the world, 1. They began presently to consider that now was the time for the Messiah to appear. The sceptre was departed from Judah, for they had no king but Caesar; nay, and the law-giver too was gone from between his feet, for Herod had lately slain the sanhedrim. Daniel's seventy weeks were now expiring; and therefore it was but three or four years after this that they looked that the kingdom of heaven should appear immediately, Lu. 19:11. Never did the corrupt state of the Jews more need a reformation, nor their distressed state more need a deliverance, than now. 2. Their next thought was, "Is not his he that should come?" *All* thinking *men mused,* or reasoned, *in their hearts,* concerning John, *whether he were the Christ or not.* He had indeed none of the external pomp and grandeur in which they generally expected the Messiah to appear; but his life was holy and strict, his preaching powerful and with authority, and therefore "why may we not think that he is the Messiah, and that he will shortly throw off this disguise, and appear in more glory?" Note, That which puts people upon considering, reasoning with themselves, prepares the way for Christ.

II. How John disowned all pretensions to the honour of being himself the Messiah, but confirmed them in their expectations of him that really was the Messiah, *v.* 16, 17. John's office, as a crier or herald, was to give notice that the *kingdom of God* and the King of that kingdom were *at hand;* and therefore, when he had told all manner of people severally what they must do ("You must do this, and you must do that"), he tells them one thing more which they must all do: they must expect the Messiah now shortly to appear. And this serves as an *answer* to their *musings* and debates concerning himself. Though he knew not their thoughts, yet, in declaring this, he *answered* them.

1. He declares that the utmost he could do was to *baptize* them *with water.* He had no access to *the Spirit,* nor could command *that* or work upon *that;* he could only exhort them to *repent,* and assure them of forgiveness, upon repentance; he could not work repentance in them, nor confer remission on them.

2. He consigns them, and turns them over, as it were, to Jesus Christ, for whom he was sent to *prepare the way,* and to whom he was ready to transfer all the interest he had in the affections of the people, and would have them no longer to *debate* whether John was the Messiah or no, but to look for him that was really so.

(1.) John owns the Messiah to have a greater *excellency* than he had, and that he was in all things preferable to him; he is one the *latchet of whose shoe* he does not think himself *worthy to loose;* he does not think himself worthy to be the meanest of his servants, to help him on and off with his shoes. John was *a prophet,* yea *more than a prophet,* more so than any of the Old-Testament prophets; but Christ was a prophet more than John, for it was both *by the Spirit of Christ,* and *of the grace of Christ,* that all the prophets prophesied, and John among the rest, 1 Pt. 1:10, 11. This was a great truth which John came to preach; but the manner of his expressing it bespeaks his humility, and in it he not only *does justice* to the Lord Jesus, but *does him honour* too: "He is one whom I am not worthy to approach, or draw nigh to, no not as a servant." Thus highly does it become us to speak of Christ, and thus humbly of ourselves.

(2.) He owns him to have a greater *energy* than he had: "He is *mightier than I,* and does that which I cannot do, both for the comfort of the faithful and for the terror of hypocrites and dissemblers." They thought that a wonderful power went along with John; but what was that compared with the power which Jesus would come clothed with? [1.] John can do no more than *baptize with water,* in token of this, that they ought to purify and cleanse themselves; but Christ can, and will, *baptize with the Holy Ghost;* he can give the Spirit to cleanse and purify the heart, not only as *water* washes off the *dirt* on the outside, but as *fire* purges out the *dross* that is within, and *melts down* the metal, that it may be cast into a *new mould.* [2.] John can only preach a *distinguishing* doctrine, and by word and sign *separate between the precious and the vile;* but Christ hath his *fan in his hand,* with which he can, and will, perfectly separate between the wheat and the chaff. He *will thoroughly purge his floor;* it is *his own,* and therefore he will *purge* it, and will cast out of his church the unbelieving impenitent Jews, and confirm in his church all that faithfully follow him. [3.] John can only *speak comfort* to those that receive the gospel, and, like other prophets, *say to the righteous* that *it shall be well with them;* but Jesus Christ will *give them comfort.* John can only promise them that they shall be safe; but Christ will make them so: he will *gather the wheat into his garner;* good, serious, solid people he will gather now into his church on earth, which shall be made up of such, and he will shortly gather them into his church in heaven, where they shall be for ever sheltered. [4.] John can only *threaten* hypocrites, and tell the *barren trees* that they shall be *hewn down* and *cast into the fire;* but Christ can execute that threatening; those that are as *chaff,* light, and vain, and worthless, *he will burn with fire unquenchable.* John refers here to Mal. 3:18; 4:1, 2. *Then,* when the *floor is purged, ye shall return, and discern between the righteous and the wicked,* for *the day comes that shall burn as an oven.*

The evangelist concludes his account of John's preaching with an *et caetera* (*v.* 18): *Many other things in his exhortation preached he unto the people,* which are not recorded. *First,* John was an *affectionate* preacher. He was *parakalōn — exhorting,* beseeching; he pressed things home upon his hearers, followed his doctrine close, as one in earnest. *Secondly,* He was a *practical* preacher. Much of his preaching was *exhortation,* quickening them to their duty, directing them in it, and not amusing them with matters of nice speculation. *Thirdly,* He was a *popular* preacher. Though he had scribes and Pharisees, men of polite learning, attending his ministry, and Sadducees, men of *free thought,* as they pretended, yet he addressed himself *to the people, pros ton laon — to the laity,* and accommodated himself to their capacity, as promising himself best success among them. *Fourthly,* He was an *evangelical* preacher, for so the word here used signifies, *euēngelizeto — he preached the gospel* to the people; in all his *exhortations,* he directed people to Christ, and excited and encouraged their expectations of *him.* When we press duty upon people, we must direct them to Christ, both for righteousness and strength. *Fifthly,* He was a *copious* preacher: *Many other things he preached, polla men kai hetera — many things, and different.* He preached a great deal, shunned not to declare the whole counsel of God; and he *varied* in his preaching, that those who were not reached, and touched, and wrought upon, by one truth, might be by another.

III. How full a stop was put to John's preaching. When he was in the midst of his usefulness, going on thus successfully, he was imprisoned by the malice of Herod (*v.* 19, 20): *Herod the tetrarch being reproved by him,* not only for living in incest with his brother Philip's wife, but for the many other *evils which Herod had done* (for those that are wicked in one instance are commonly so in many others), he could not *bear it,* but contracted an antipathy to him for his plain dealing, and *added* this wickedness to all the rest, which was indeed *above all,* that he *shut up John in prison,* put that burning and shining light under a bushel. Because he could not bear his reproofs, others should be deprived of the benefit of his instructions and counsels. Some little good he might do to those who had access to him, when he was in prison; but nothing to what he might have done if he had had liberty to go about all the country, as he had done. We cannot think of Herod's doing this without the greatest compassion and lamentation, nor of God's permitting it without admiring the depth of the divine counsels, which we cannot account for. Must he be silenced who is the *voice of one crying in the wilderness?* Must such a preacher be shut up in prison who ought to have been set up in the courts of the temple? But thus the faith of his disciples must be tried; thus the unbelief of those who rejected him must be punished; thus he must be Christ's forerunner in suffering as well as preaching; and thus, having been for about a year and a half preparing people for Christ, he must now give way to him, and, the Sun being risen, the morning-star must of course disappear.

Verses 21–38

The evangelist mentioned John's imprisonment before Christ's being baptized, though it was nearly a year after it, because he would finish the story of John's ministry, and then introduce that of Christ. Now here we have,

I. A short account of Christ's baptism, which had been more fully related by St. Matthew. Jesus came, to be baptized of John, and he was so, *v.* 21, 22.

1. It is here said that, *when all the people were baptized,* then *Jesus was baptized:* all that were then present. Christ would be baptized last, among the common people, and in the rear of them; thus he humbled himself, and made himself of no reputation, as one of the least, nay, as less than the least. He saw what multitudes were hereby prepared to receive him, and then he appeared.

2. Notice is here taken of Christ's *praying* when he was *baptized,* which was not in Matthew: being baptized, and *praying.* He did not *confess sin,* as others did, for he had none to confess; but he *prayed,* as others did, for he would thus keep up communion with his Father. Note, The inward and spiritual grace of which sacraments are the outward and visible signs must be fetched in by prayer; and therefore prayer must always accompany them. We have reason to think that Christ now prayed for this manifestation of God's favour to him which immediately followed; he prayed for the discovery of his Father's favour to him, and the descent of the Spirit. What was promised to Christ, he must obtain by prayer: *Ask of me and I will give thee, etc.* Thus he would put an honour upon prayer, would tie us to it, and encourage us in it.

3. When he prayed, *the heaven was opened.* He that by his power parted the waters, to make a way through them to Canaan, now by his power parted the air, another fluid element, to open a correspondence with the heavenly Canaan. Thus was there opened to Christ, and by him to us, *a new and living way into the holiest;* sin had shut up heaven, but Christ's prayer opened it again. Prayer is an ordinance that *opens heaven: Knock, and it shall be opened unto you.*

4. *The Holy Ghost descended in a bodily shape like a dove upon him;* our Lord Jesus was now to receive greater measures of the Spirit than before, to qualify him for his prophetical office, Isa. 61:1. When he begins to preach, *the Spirit of the Lord is upon him.* Now this is here expressed by a sensible evidence for his encouragement in his work, and for the satisfaction of John the Baptist; for he was told before that by this sign it should be notified to him which was the Christ. Dr. Lightfoot suggests that the Holy Ghost descended in a bodily shape, that he might be revealed to be a personal substance, and not merely an operation of the Godhead: and thus (saith he) was made a full, clear, and sensible demonstration of the Trinity, at the beginning of the gospel; and very fitly is this done at Christ's baptism, who was to make the ordinance of baptism a badge of the profession of that faith in the doctrine of the Trinity, *Father, Son, and Holy Ghost.*

5. There came *a voice from heaven,* from God the Father, from the *excellent glory* (so it is expressed, 2 Pt. 1:17), *Thou art my beloved Son.* Here, and in Mark, it is expressed as spoken *to* Christ; in Matthew as spoken *of him: This is my beloved Son.* It comes all to one; it was intended to be a notification to John, and as such was properly expressed by, *This is my beloved Son;* and likewise an answer to his prayer, and so it is most fitly expressed by. *Thou art.* It was foretold concerning the Messiah, *I will be his Father, and he shall be my Son,* 2 Sa. 7:14. *I will make him my First-born,* Ps. 89:27. It was also foretold that he should be God's *elect, in whom his soul delighted* (Isa. 42:1); and, accordingly, it is here declared, *Thou art my beloved Son, in whom I am well pleased.*

II. A long account of Christ's pedigree, which had been more briefly related by St. Matthew. Here is,

1. His age: *He now began to be about thirty years of age.* So old Joseph was when he stood before Pharaoh (Gen. 41:46), David when he began to reign (2 Sa. 5:4), and at this age the priests were to enter upon the full execution of their office, Num. 4:3. Dr. Lightfoot thinks that it is plain, by the

manner of expression here, that he was just twenty-nine years old complete, and entering upon his thirtieth year, in the month *Tisri;* that, after this, he lived three years and a half, and died when he was thirty-two years and a half old. *Three years and a half,* the time of Christ's ministry, is a period of time very remarkable in scripture. *Three years and six months* the heavens were shut up in Elijah's time, Lu. 4:25; Jam. 5:17. This was the half week in which the Messiah was to confirm the covenant, Dan. 9:27. This period is expressed in the prophetical writings by a time, times, and half a time (Dan. 12:7; Rev. 12:14); and by forty-two months, and a thousand two hundred and threescore days, Rev. 11:2, 3. It is the time fixed for the witnesses' prophesying in sackcloth, in conformity to Christ's preaching in his humiliation just so long.

2. His pedigree, *v.* 23, etc. Matthew had given us somewhat of this. He goes no higher than Abraham, but Luke brings it as high as Adam. Matthew designed to show that Christ was the son of Abraham, in whom *all the families of the earth are blessed,* and that he was heir to the throne of David; and therefore he begins with Abraham, and brings the genealogy down to Jacob, who was the father of Joseph, and heir-male of the house of David: but Luke, designing to show that Christ was the *seed of the woman,* that should break the serpent's head, traces his pedigree upward as high as Adam, and begins it with Ei, or Heli, who was the father, not of Joseph, but of the virgin Mary. And some suggest that the supply which our translators all along insert here is not right, and that it should not be read *which,* that is, which *Joseph* was the son of Heli, but which *Jesus;* he was *the son of Joseph, of Eli, of Matthat,* etc., and he, that is, Jesus, was the son *of Seth, of Adam, of God, v.* 38. The difference between the two evangelists in the genealogy of Christ has been a stumbling-block to infidels that cavil at the word, but such a one as has been removed by the labours of learned men, both in the early ages of the church and in latter times, to which we refer ourselves. Matthew draws the pedigree from Solomon, whose natural line ending in Jechonias, the legal right was transferred to Salathiel, who was of the house of Nathan, another son of David, which line Luke here pursues, and so leaves out all the kings of Judah. It is well for us that our salvation doth not depend upon our being able to solve all these difficulties, nor is the divine authority of the gospels at all weakened by them; for the evangelists are not supposed to write these genealogies either of their own knowledge or by divine inspiration, but to have copied them out of the authentic records of the genealogies among the Jews, the heralds' books, which therefore they were obliged to follow; and in them they found the pedigree of Jacob, the father of Joseph, to be as it is set down in Matthew; and the pedigree of Heli, the father of Mary, to be as it is set down here in Luke. And this is the meaning of *hōs enomizeto* (*v.* 23), not, *as it was supposed,* referring only to Joseph, but *uti sancitum est lege — as it is entered into the books,* as we find it upon record; by which is appeared that Jesus was both by father and mother's side the Son of David, witness this extract out of their own records, which any one might at that time have liberty to compare with the original, and further the evangelists needed not to go; nay, had they varied from that, they had not gained their point. Its not being contradicted at that time is satisfaction enough to us now that it is a true copy, as it is further worthy of observation, that, when those records of the Jewish genealogies had continued thirty or forty years after these extracts out of them, long enough to justify the evangelists therein, they were all lost and destroyed with the Jewish state and nation; for now there was no more occasion for them.

One difficulty occurs between Abraham and Noah, which gives us some perplexity, *v.* 35, 36. Sala is said to be the *son of Cainan,* and he *the son of Arphaxad,* whereas Sala was the son of Arphaxad (Gen. 10:24; 11:12), and there is no such man as Cainan found there. But, as to that, it is sufficient to say that the Seventy Interpreters, who, before our Saviour's time, translated the Old Testament into Greek, for reasons best known to themselves inserted that Cainan; and St. Luke, writing among the *Hellenist Jews,* was obliged to make use of that translation, and therefore to take it as he found it.

The genealogy concludes with this, *who was the son of Adam, the son of God.* (1.) Some refer it to Adam; he was in a peculiar manner the *son of God,* being, more immediately than any of his offspring, the offspring of God by creation. (2.) Others refer it to Christ, and so make the last words of this genealogy to denote his divine and human nature. He

was both the *Son of Adam* and the *Son of God* that he might be a proper Mediator between God and the sons of Adam, and might bring the sons of Adam to be, through him, the *sons of God.*

CHAPTER 4

We left Christ newly baptized, and owned by a voice from heaven and the descent of the Holy Ghost upon him. Now, in this chapter, we have, I. A further preparation of him for his public ministry by his being tempted in the wilderness, of which we had the same account before in Matthew as we have here (*v.* 1–13). II. His entrance upon his public work in Galilee (*v.* 14, 15), particularly, 1. At Nazareth, the city where he had been bred up (*v.* 16–30), which we had no account of before in Matthew. 2. At Capernaum, where, having preached to admiration (*v.* 31–32), he cast the devil out of a man that was possessed (*v.* 33–37), cured Peter's mother-in-law of a fever (*v.* 38, 39), and many others that were sick and possessed (*v.* 40, 41), and then went and did the same in other cities of Galilee (*v.* 42–44).

Verses 1–13

The last words of the foregoing chapter, that Jesus was the *Son of Adam,* bespeak him to be the *seed of the woman;* being so, we have here, according to the promise, *breaking the serpent's head,* baffling and foiling the devil in all his temptations, who by one temptation had baffled and foiled our first parents. Thus, in the beginning of the war, he made reprisals upon him, and conquered the conqueror.

In this story of Christ's temptation, observe,

I. How he was *prepared* and *fitted* for it. He that designed him the trial furnished him accordingly; for though we know not what exercises may be before us, nor what encounters we may be reserved for, Christ did, and was provided accordingly; and God doth for us, and we hope will provide accordingly.

1. He was *full of the Holy Ghost,* who had *descended on him like a dove.* He had now greater measures of the gifts, graces, and comforts, of the Holy Ghost than ever before. Note, Those are well armed against the strongest temptations that are *full of the Holy Ghost.*

2. He was newly *returned from Jordan,* where he was baptized, and owned by a voice from heaven to be the beloved Son of God; and thus he was *prepared* for this combat. Note, When we have had the most comfortable communion with God, and the clearest discoveries of his favour to us, we may expect that Satan will set upon us (the richest ship is the pirate's prize), and that God will suffer him to do so, that the power of his grace may be manifested and magnified.

3. He was *led by the Spirit into the wilderness,* by the good Spirit, who led him as a champion into the field, to fight the enemy that he was sure to conquer. His being *led into the wilderness,* (1.) *Gave* some advantage to the tempter; for there he had him alone, no friend with him, by whose prayers and advice he might be assisted in the hour of temptation. Woe to him that is alone! He might give Satan advantage, who knew his own strength; *we may not,* who know our own weakness. (2.) He *gained* some advantage to himself, during his forty days' fasting in the wilderness. We may suppose that he was wholly taken up in proper meditation, and in consideration of his own undertaking, and the work he had before him; that he spent all his time in immediate, intimate, converse with his Father, as Moses in the mount, without any diversion, distraction, or interruption. Of all the days of Christ's life in the flesh, these seem to come nearest to the angelic perfection and the heavenly life, and this prepared him for Satan's assaults, and hereby he was fortified against them.

4. He continued fasting (*v.* 2): *In those days he did eat nothing.* This fast was altogether miraculous, like those of Moses and Elijah, and shows him to be, like them, a prophet *sent of God.* It is probable that it was in the wilderness of Horeb, the same wilderness in which Moses and Elijah fasted. As by retiring into the *wilderness* he showed himself perfectly indifferent to the *world,* so by his *fasting* he showed himself perfectly indifferent to the *body;* and Satan cannot easily take hold of those who are thus loosened from, and dead to, the *world* and the *flesh.* The more we *keep under the body,* and bring it into subjection, the less advantage Satan has against us.

II. How he was assaulted by one temptation after another, and how he defeated the design of the tempter in every assault, and became more than a conqueror. During the *forty days,* he was *tempted of the devil* (*v.* 2), not by an inward suggestion, for the prince of this world had nothing in Christ by which to inject any such; but by outward solicitations, per-

haps in the likeness of a serpent, as he tempted our first parents. But at the end of the forty days he came nearer to him, and did as it were close with him, when he perceived *that he was hungry, v.* 2. Probably, our Lord Jesus then began to look about among the trees, to see if he could find any thing that was eatable, whence the devil took occasion to make the following proposal to him.

1. He tempted him to *distrust his Father's* care of him, and to *set up for himself,* and shift for provision for himself in such a way as his Father had not appointed for him (*v.* 3): *If thou be the Son of God,* as the voice from heaven declared, *command this stone to be made bread.* (1.) "I counsel thee to do it; for God, if he be thy Father, has forgotten thee, and it will be long enough ere he sends either ravens or angels to feed thee." If we begin to think of being our own carvers, and of living by our own forecast, without depending upon divine providence, of getting wealth *by our might and the power of our hands,* we must look upon it as a temptation of Satan's, and reject it accordingly; it is Satan's counsel to think of an independence upon God. (2.) "I *challenge* thee to do it, if thou canst; if thou dost not do it, I will say thou art *not the Son of God;* for John Baptist said lately, *God is able of stones to raise up children to Abraham,* which is the greater; thou therefore hast not the power of the *Son of God,* if thou dost not of *stones make bread* for thyself, when thou needest it, which is the less." Thus was God himself tempted in the wilderness: *Can he furnish a table? Can he give bread?* Ps. 78:19, 20.

Now, [1.] Christ yielded not to the temptation; he would not *turn* that *stone* into *bread; no,* though he was hungry; *First,* Because he would not do what Satan bade him do, for that would have looked as if there had been indeed a compact between him and the prince of the devils. Note, We must not do any thing that looks like *giving place to the devil.* Miracles were wrought for the confirming of faith, and the devil had no faith to be confirmed, and therefore he would not do it *for him.* He did his signs *in the presence of his disciples* (Jn. 20:30), and particularly the *beginning of his miracles,* turning water into wine, which he did, that his disciples might believe on him (Jn. 2:11); but here in the wilderness he had no disciples with him. *Secondly,* He wrought miracles for the ratification of his doctrine, and therefore till he began to *preach* he would not begin to work miracles. *Thirdly,* He would not work miracles *for himself* and his own supply, lest he should seem impatient of *hunger,* whereas he came not to *please himself,* but to *suffer grief,* and that grief among others; and because he would show that he *pleased not himself,* he would rather turn *water into wine,* for the credit and convenience of his friends, than *stones into bread,* for his own *necessary supply. Fourthly,* He would reserve the proof of his being the Son of God for hereafter, and would rather be upbraided by Satan with being weak, and not able to do it, than be persuaded by Satan to do that which it was fit for him to do; thus he was upbraided by his enemies as if he could not *save himself,* and *come down from the cross,* when he could have come down, but would not, because it was not fit that he should. *Fifthly,* He would not do any thing that looked like distrust of his Father, or *acting separately* from him, or any thing disagreeable to his present state. Being in all things *made like unto his brethren,* he would, like the other children of God, live in a dependence upon the divine Providence and promise, and trust him either to send him a supply into the wilderness or to *lead him to a city of habitation* where there was a supply, as he used to do (Ps. 107:5–7), and in the mean time would *support* him, though he was hungry, as he had done these forty days past.

[2.] He returned a scripture-answer to it (*v.* 4): *It is written.* This is the first word recorded as spoken by Christ after his instalment in his prophetical office; and it is a quotation out of the Old Testament, to show that he came to assert and maintain the authority of the scripture as uncontrollable, even by Satan himself. And though he had the Spirit without measure, and had a doctrine of his own to preach and a religion to found, yet it agreed with Moses and the prophets, whose writings he therefore lays down as a rule to himself, and recommends to us as a reply to Satan and his temptations. The word of God is our *sword,* and faith in that word is our *shield;* we should therefore be *mighty in the scriptures,* and *go in that might,* go forth, and go on, in our spiritual warfare, know *what is written,* for it is *for our learning,* for *our use.* The text of scripture he makes use of is quoted from Deu. 8:3: "*Man shall not live by bread alone.* I need not turn the stone into bread, for God can send *manna* for my nourishment, as he did for Israel; man can live *by every word of God,* by whatever God will appoint that he shall live by." How had Christ lived, lived comfortably, these last forty days? Not *by bread,* but by the *word of God,* by meditation upon that word, and communion with it, and with God in and by it; and in like manner he could *live yet,* though now he began to be *hungry.* God has many ways of providing for his people, without the ordinary means of subsistence; and therefore he is not at any time to be distrusted, but at all times to be depended upon, in the way of duty. If meat be wanting, God can take away the appetite, or give such degrees of patience as will enable a man even to *laugh at destruction and famine* (Job 5:22), or make *pulse and water* more nourishing than *all the portion of the king's meat* (Dan. 1:12, 13), and enable his people to *rejoice in the Lord,* when the *fig-tree doth not blossom,* Hab. 3:17. She was an active believer who said that she had made many a meal's meat of the promises when she wanted bread.

2. He tempted him to *accept from him* the kingdom, which, as the *Son of God,* he expected to receive from *his Father,* and to *do him homage* for, *v.* 5–7. This evangelist puts this temptation second, which Matthew had put last, and which, it should seem, was really the last; but Luke was full of it, as the blackest and most violent, and therefore hastened to it. In the devil's tempting of our first parents, he presented to them the forbidden fruit, first as *good for food,* and then as *pleasant to the eyes;* and they were overpowered by both these charms. Satan here first tempted Christ to turn the stones into bread, which would be good for food, and then showed him the kingdoms of the world and the glory of them, which were *pleasant to the eyes;* but in both these he overpowered Satan, and perhaps with an eye to that, Luke changes the order. Now observe,

(1.) How Satan *managed* this temptation, to prevail with Christ to become a tributary to him, and to receive his kingdom by delegation from him.

[1.] He gave him a prospect of *all the kingdoms of the world in a moment of time,* an airy representation of them, such as he thought most likely to strike the fancy, and seem a *real* prospect. To succeed the better, he *took him up* for this purpose *into a high mountain;* and, because we next after the temptation find Christ on the other side Jordan, some think it probable that it was to the top of Pisgah that the devil took him, whence Moses has a sight of Canaan. That it was but a phantasm that the devil here presented our Saviour with, as the prince of the power of the air, is confirmed by that circumstance which Luke here takes notice of, that it was done *in a moment of time;* whereas, if a man take a prospect of but one country, he must do it successively, must turn himself round, and take a view first of one part and then of another. Thus the devil thought to impose upon our Saviour with a fallacy — *a deceptio visus;* and, by making him believe that he could *show him all the kingdoms of* the world, would draw him into an opinion that he could *give him* all those kingdoms.

[2.] He boldly alleged that these kingdoms were *all delivered to him* that he had power to dispose of them and all their *glory,* and to give them to *whomsoever he would, v.* 6. Some think that herein he pretended to be an angel of light, and that, as one of the angels that was set over the kingdoms, he had out-bought, or out-fought, all the rest, and so was *entrusted* with the disposal of them all, and, in God's name, would give them to him, knowing they were designed for him; but clogged with this condition, that he should *fall down and worship him,* which a good angel would have been so far from demanding that he would not have admitted it, no, not upon showing much greater things than these, as appears, Rev. 19:10; 22:9. But I rather take it that he claimed this power as Satan, and as *delivered to him* not by *the Lord,* but by the kings and people of these kingdoms, who gave their power and honour to the devil, Eph. 2:2. Hence he is called the *god of this world,* and the *prince of this world.* It was promised to the Son of God that he should have *the heathen for his inheritance,* Ps. 2:8. "Why," saith the devil, "the heathen are *mine,* are my subjects and votaries; but, however, they shall be thine, I will give them *thee,* upon condition that thou *worship me* for them, and say that they are the *rewards which I have given thee,* as others have done before *thee* (Hos. 2:12), and consent to have and *hold them by, from, and under, me.*"

[3.] He demanded of him homage and adoration: *If thou wilt worship me, all shall be thine, v.* 7. *First,* He would have him worship him himself. Perhaps he does not mean so as never to worship God, but let him worship him in conjunction with God; for the devil knows, if he can but once come in a partner, he shall soon be sole proprietor. *Secondly,* He would indent with him, that when, according to the promise made to him, he had got possession of the kingdoms of this world, he should make no alteration of religions in them, but permit and suffer the nations, as they had done hitherto, to *sacrifice to devils* (1 Co. 10:20); that he should still keep up *demon-worship* in the world, and then let him take all the power and glory of the kingdoms if he pleased. Let who will take the wealth and grandeur of this earth, Satan has all he would have if he can but have men's hearts, and affections, and adorations, can but *work in the children of* disobedience; for then he effectually *devours them.*

(2.) How our Lord Jesus *triumphed* over this temptation. He gave it a peremptory repulse, rejected it with abhorrence (*v.* 8): *"Get thee behind me, Satan,* I cannot bear the mention of it. What! worship the enemy of God whom I came to serve? and of man whom I came to save? No, I will never do it." Such a temptation as this was not to be *reasoned with,* but immediately refused; it was presently knocked on the head with one word, *It is written, Thou shalt worship the Lord thy God;* and not only so, but *him only,* him and *no other.* And therefore Christ will not worship Satan, nor, when he has the *kingdoms of the world delivered* to him by his Father, as he expects shortly to have, will he suffer any remains of the worship of the devil to continue in them. No, it shall be perfectly rooted out and abolished, wherever his gospel comes. He will make no composition with him. *Polytheism* and *idolatry* must go down, as Christ's kingdom gets up. Men must be *turned from the power of Satan unto God,* from the worship of devils to the worship of the only living and true God. This is the great divine law that Christ will re-establish among men, and by his holy religion reduce men to the obedience of, *That God only is to be served and worshipped;* and therefore whoever set up any creature as the object of religious worship, though it were a saint or an angel, or the virgin Mary herself, they directly thwart Christ's design, and relapse into heathenism.

3. He tempted him to be his own murderer, in a presumptuous confidence of his Father's protection, such as he had no warrant for. Observe,

(1.) What he designed in this temptation: *If thou be the Son of God, cast thyself down, v.* 9. [1.] He would have him seek for a new proof of his being the *Son of God,* as if that which his Father had given him by the voice from heaven, and the descent of the Spirit upon him, were not sufficient, which would have been a dishonour to God, as if he had not chosen the most proper way of giving him the assurance of it; and it would have argued a distrust of the Spirit's dwelling in him, which was the great and most convincing proof to himself of his being the *Son of God,* Heb. 1:8, 9. [2.] He would have him seek a new method of proclaiming and publishing this to the world. The devil, in effect, suggests that it was in an *obscure corner* that he was attested to be the Son of God, among a company of ordinary people, who attended John's baptism, that his honours were proclaimed; but if he would now declare from *the pinnacle of the temple,* among all the great people who attend the temple-service, that he was the Son of God, and then, for proof of it, throw himself down unhurt, he would presently be received by every body as a messenger sent from heaven. Thus Satan would have him seek honours of his devising (in contempt of those which God had put on him), and manifest himself in the temple at Jerusalem; whereas God designed he should be more manifest among John's penitents, to whom his doctrine would be more welcome than to the priests. [3.] It is probable he had some hopes that, though he could not throw him down, to do him the least mischief, yet, if he would but throw himself down, the fall might be his death, and then he should have got him finely out of the way.

(2.) How he backed and enforced this temptation. He suggested, *It is written, v.* 10. Christ had quoted scripture against him; and he thought he would be quits with him, and would show that he could quote scripture as well as he. It has been usual with heretics and seducers to pervert scripture, and to press the sacred writings into the service of the worst of wickednesses. *He shall give his angels charge over thee,* if thou be his Son, and *in their hands they shall bear thee up.* And now that he was upon the pinnacle of the temple he might especially expect this ministration of angels; for, if he was the Son of God, the *temple* was the proper place for him to be in (*ch.* 2:46); and, if any place under the sun had a guard of angels constantly, it must needs be that, Ps. 68:17. It is true, God has promised the protection of angels, to encourage us to trust him, not to tempt him; as far as the promise of God's presence with us, so far the promise of the angels' ministration goes, but no further: "They shall keep thee when thou goest on the ground, where thy way lies, but not if thou wilt presume to fly in the air."

(3.) How he was baffled and defeated in the temptation, *v.* 12. Christ quoted Deu. 6:16, where it is said, *Thou shalt not tempt the Lord thy God,* by desiring a sign for the proof of divine revelation, when he has already given that which is sufficient; for so Israel did, when they *tempted God in the wilderness,* saying, He *gave us water out of the rock; but can he give flesh also?* This Christ would be guilty of if he should say, "He did indeed prove me to be the Son of God, by sending the Spirit upon me, which is the *greater;* but can he also give his angels a charge concerning me, which is the *less?"*

III. What was the result and issue of this combat, *v.* 13. Our victorious Redeemer kept his ground, and came off a conqueror, not for himself only, but for us also.

1. The devil emptied his quiver: *He ended all the temptation.* Christ gave him opportunity to say and do all he could against him; he let him try all his force, and yet defeated him. Did Christ suffer, being tempted, till all the temptation was ended? And must not we expect also to pass all our trials, to go through the *hour of temptation* assigned us?

2. He then quitted the field: He *departed from him.* He saw it was to no purpose to attack him; he had *nothing in him* for his fiery darts to fasten upon; he had no blind side, no weak or unguarded part in his wall, and therefore Satan gave up the cause. Note, If we resist the devil, he will flee from us.

3. Yet he continued his malice against him, and departed with a resolution to attack him again; he departed but *for a season, achri kairou — till a season,* or till the season when he was again to be let loose upon him, not as a *tempter,* to draw him to *sin,* and so to strike at *his head,* which was what he now aimed at and was wholly defeated in; but as a *persecutor,* to bring him to *suffer* by Judas and the other wicked instruments whom he employed, and so to *bruise his heel,* which it was told him (Gen. 3:15) he should have to do, and would do, though it would be the breaking of *his own head.* He *departed now* till that season came which Christ calls the *power of darkness* (*ch.* 22:53), and when the prince of this world would again *come,* Jn. 14:30.

Verses 14–30

After Christ had vanquished the evil spirit, he made it appear how much he was under the influence of the good Spirit; and, having defended himself against the devil's assaults, he now begins to act *offensively,* and to make those attacks upon him, by his preaching and miracles, which he could not resist or repel. Observe,

I. What is here said in general of his preaching, and the entertainment it met with *in Galilee,* a remote part of the country, distant from Jerusalem; it was a part of Christ's humiliation that he began his ministry there.

But, 1. Thither he came *in the power of the Spirit.* The same Spirit that qualified him for the exercise of his prophetical office strongly inclined him to it. He was not to wait for a call from men, for he had light and life in himself. 2. There he *taught in their synagogues,* their places of public worship, where they met, not, as in the temple, for ceremonial services, but for the moral acts of devotion, to read, expound, and apply, the word, to pray and praise, and for church-discipline; these came to be more frequent since the captivity, when the ceremonial worship was near expiring. 3. This he did so as that he gained a great reputation. *A fame of him went through all that region* (*v.* 14), and it was a good fame; for (*v.* 15) he *was glorified of all.* Every body admired him, and cried him up; they never heard such preaching in all their lives. Now, at first, he met with no contempt or contradiction; all *glorified* him, and there were none as yet that vilified him.

II. Of his preaching at Nazareth, the city where he was brought up; and the entertainment it met with there. And here we are told how he *preached* there, and how he was *persecuted.*

1. How he preached there. In that observe,

(1.) The opportunity he had for it: *He came to Nazareth* when he had gained a reputation in other places, in hopes that thereby something at least of the contempt and prejudice with which his countrymen would look upon him might be worn off. There he took occasion to preach, [1.] In the *synagogue,* the proper place, where it had been *his custom* to attend when he was a private person, *v.* 16. We ought to attend on the public worship of God, as we have opportunity. But, now that he was entered upon his public ministry, there he preached. Where the multitudes of fish were, there this wise Fisherman would cast his net. [2.] On the sabbath day, the proper time which the pious Jews spent, not in a mere ceremonial rest from worldly labour, but in the duties of God's worship, as of old they frequented the schools of the prophets on the *new moons* and the *sabbaths.* Note, It is good to keep sabbaths in solemn assemblies.

(2.) The call he had to it. [1.] He *stood up to read.* They had in their synagogues seven readers every sabbath, the first a priest, the second a Levite, and the other five Israelites of that synagogue. We often find Christ *preaching* in other synagogues, but never *reading,* except in this synagogue at Nazareth, of which he had been many years a member. Now he offered his service as he had perhaps often done; he read one of the lessons out of the prophets, Acts 13:15. Note, The reading of the scripture is very proper work to be done in religious assemblies; and Christ himself did not think it any disparagement to him to be employed in it. [2.] The *book of the prophet Esaias* was *delivered to him,* either by the ruler of the synagogue or by the minister mentioned (*v.* 20), so that he was no intruder, but duly authorized *pro hac vice — on this occasion.* The second lesson for *that* day being in the prophecy of Esaias, they gave him that volume to read in.

(3.) The text he preached upon. He *stood up to read,* to teach us reverence in *reading* and *hearing* the word of God. When Ezra opened the book of the law, *all the people stood up* (Neh. 8:5); so did Christ here, when he read in the book of the prophets. Now the book being *delivered to him,* [1.] He *opened* it. The books of the Old Testament were in a manner *shut up* till Christ opened them, Isa. 29:11. Worthy *is the Lamb that was slain to take the book, and open the seals;* for he can open, not the book only, but the understanding. [2.] He *found* the place which was appointed to be read *that day* in course, which he needed not to be directed to; he soon found it, and read it, and took it for his text. Now his text was taken out of Isa. 61:1, 2, which is here quoted at large, *v.* 18, 19. There was a providence in it that that portion of scripture should be read that day, which speaks so very plainly of the Messiah, that they might be left inexcusable who *knew him not,* though they heard *the voices of the prophets* read *every sabbath day,* which bore witness of him, Acts 13:27. This text gives a full account of Christ's undertaking, and the work he came into the world to do. Observe,

First, How he was qualified for the work: *The Spirit of the Lord is upon me.* All the gifts and graces of the Spirit were conferred upon him, not by measure, as upon other prophets, but without measure, Jn. 3:34. He now came *in the power of the Spirit, v.* 14.

Secondly, How he was commissioned: *Because he had anointed me,* and *sent me.* His extraordinary qualification amounted to a commission; his being *anointed* signifies both his being fitted for the undertaking and called to it. Those whom God *appoints* to any service he *anoints* for it: "Because he hath sent me, he hath sent his Spirit along with me."

Thirdly, What his work was. He was qualified and commissioned,

1. To be a great *prophet.* He was *anointed to preach;* that is three times mentioned here, for that was the work he was now entering upon. Observe, (1.) To *whom* he was to preach: to the *poor;* to those that were *poor in the world,* whom the Jewish doctors disdained to undertake the teaching of and spoke of with contempt; to those that were *poor in spirit,* to the meek and humble, and to those that were truly sorrowful for sin: to them the gospel and the grace of it will be welcome, and they shall have it, Mt. 11:5. (2.) *What* he was to preach. In general, he must preach *the gospel.* He is sent *euangelizesthai — to evangelize* them; not only to preach to them, but to make that preaching effectual; to bring it, not only to their ears, but to their hearts, and deliver them into the mould of it. Three things he is to preach: —

[1.] *Deliverance to the captives,* The gospel is a proclamation of liberty, like that to Israel in Egypt and in Babylon.

By the merit of Christ sinners may be loosed from the bonds of guilt, and by his Spirit and grace from the bondage of corruption. It is a deliverance from the worst of thraldoms, which all those shall have the benefit of that are willing to make Christ their Head, and are willing to be ruled by him.

[2.] *Recovering of sight to the blind.* He came not only by the word of his gospel to bring *light* to them that sat *in the dark,* but by the power of his grace to give sight to them that were *blind;* not only the Gentile world, but every unregenerate soul, that is not only in *bondage,* but in *blindness,* like Samson and Zedekiah. Christ came to tell us that he has *eye-salve* for us, which we may have for the asking; that, if our prayer be, *Lord, that our eyes may be opened,* his answer shall be, *Receive your sight.*

[3.] *The acceptable year of the Lord, v.* 19. He came to let the world know that the God whom they had offended was willing to be reconciled to them, and to *accept* of them upon new terms; that there was yet a way of making their services acceptable to him; that there is now a time of *good will toward men.* It alludes to the year of *release,* or that of *jubilee,* which was an *acceptable year* to servants, who were then set at liberty; to debtors, against whom all actions then dropped; and to those who had mortgaged their lands, for then they returned to them again. Christ came to sound the *jubilee*-trumpet; and blessed were they that heard *the joyful sound,* Ps. 89:15. It was an acceptable time, for it was a day of salvation.

2. Christ came to be a great *Physician;* for he was sent to *heal the broken-hearted,* to comfort and cure afflicted consciences, to give peace to those that were troubled and humbled for sins, and under a dread of God's wrath against them for them, and to bring them to rest who were weary and heavy-laden, under the burden of guilt and corruption.

3. To be a great *Redeemer.* He not only proclaims liberty to the captives, as Cyrus did to the Jews in Babylon *(Whoever will, may go up),* but he sets at liberty them that are bruised; he doth by his Spirit *incline* and *enable* them to make use of the liberty granted, as then none did but those *whose spirit God stirred up,* Ezra 1:5. He came in God's name to discharge poor sinners that were debtors and prisoners to divine justice. The prophets could but *proclaim liberty,* but Christ, as one having authority, as one that had *power on earth to forgive sins,* came to *set at liberty;* and therefore this clause is added here. Dr. Lightfoot thinks that, according to a liberty the Jew allowed their readers, to compare scripture with scripture, in their reading, for the explication of the text, Christ added it from Isa. 58:6, where it is made the duty of the acceptable year to let *the oppressed go free,* where the phrase the Septuagint uses is the same with this here.

(4.) Here is Christ's *application* of this text to himself (*v.* 21): When he had read it, he *rolled up the book,* and gave it again *to the minister,* or *clerk,* that attended, and *sat down,* according to the custom of the Jewish teachers; he *sat daily in the temple, teaching,* Mt. 26:55. Now he *began* his discourse thus, "This day is this scripture fulfilled in your ears. This, which Isaiah wrote by way of prophecy, I have now read to you by way of history." It now began to be fulfilled in Christ's entrance upon his public ministry; *now,* in the report they heard of his preaching and miracles in other places; *now,* in his preaching to them in their own synagogue. It is most probable that Christ went on, and showed particularly how this scripture was fulfilled in the doctrine he preached concerning the *kingdom of heaven at hand;* that it was preaching liberty, and sight, and healing, and all the blessings of the *acceptable year of the Lord.* Many other gracious words proceeded out of his mouth, which these were but the *beginning* of; for Christ often preached long sermons, which we have but a short account of. This was enough to introduce a great deal: *This day is this scripture fulfilled.* Note, [1.] All the scriptures of the Old Testament that were to be fulfilled in the Messiah had their full accomplishment in the Lord Jesus, which abundantly proves that this was *he that should come.* [2.] In the providences of God, it is fit to observe the *fulfilling of the scriptures.* The works of God are the accomplishment not only of his secret word, but of his word revealed; and it will help us to understand both the scriptures and the providences of God to compare them one with another.

(5.) Here is the *attention* and *admiration* of the auditors.

[1.] Their *attention* (*v.* 20): *The eyes of all them that were in the synagogue* (and, probably, there were a great many) *were fastened on him,* big with expectation what he would

say, having heard so much of late concerning him. Note, It is good, in hearing the word, to keep the eye fixed upon the minister by whom God is speaking to us; for, as the eye effects the heart, so, usually, the heart follows the eye, and is wandering, or fixed, as that is. Or, rather, let us learn hence to keep the eye fixed upon Christ speaking to us in and by the minister. *What saith my Lord unto his servants?*

[2.] Their *admiration* (*v.* 22): *They all bore him witness* that he spoke admirably well, and to the purpose. They all commended him, and *wondered at the gracious words that proceeded out of his mouth;* and yet, as appears by what follows, they did not *believe in him.* Note, It is possible that those who are admirers of good ministers and good preaching may yet be themselves not true Christians. Observe, *First,* What it was they admired: The *gracious words which proceedeth out of his mouth.* The *words of grace;* good words, and spoken in a winning melting way. Note, Christ's words are *words of grace,* for, grace being *poured into his lips* (Ps. 45:2), words of grace poured from them. And these words of grace are to be *wondered at;* Christ's name was Wonderful, and in nothing was he more so than in his grace, in the words of his grace, and the power that went along with those words. We may well wonder that he should speak such *words of grace* to such graceless wretches as we are. *Secondly,* What it was that increased their wonder and that was the consideration of his original: *They said, Is not this Joseph's son,* and therefore his extraction mean and his education mean? Some from this suggestion took occasion perhaps so much the more to admire his *gracious words,* concluding he must needs be *taught of God,* for they knew no one else had taught him; while others perhaps with this consideration corrected their wonder at his gracious words, and concluded there could be nothing *really* admirable in them, whatever appeared, because he was the *Son of Joseph.* Can any thing great, or worthy our regard, come from one so mean?

(6.) Christ's anticipating an objection which he knew to be in the minds of many of his hearers. Observe,

[1.] What the objection was (*v.* 23): *"You will surely say to me, Physician, heal thyself.* Because you know that I am the Son of Joseph, your neighbour, you will expect that I should work miracles among you, as I have done in other places; as one would expect that a physician, if he be able, should heal, not only himself, but those of his own family and fraternity." Most of Christ's miracles were *cures;* — "Now why should not the sick in thine own city be *healed* as well as those in other cities?" They were designed to cure people of their unbelief; — "Now why should not the disease of unbelief, if it be indeed a disease, be cured in those of thine own city as well as in those of others? *Whatsoever we have heard done in Capernaum,* that has been so much talked of, *do here also in thine own country."* They were pleased with *Christ's gracious words,* only because they hoped they were but the introduction to some *wondrous works* of his. They wanted to have their lame, and blind, and sick, and lepers, healed and helped, that the charge of their town might be eased; and that was the chief thing they looked at. They thought their own town as worthy to be the stage of miracles as any other; and why should not he rather draw company to that than to any other? And why should not his neighbours and acquaintances have the benefit of his preaching and miracles, rather than any other?

[2.] How he answers this objection against the course he took.

First, By a plain and positive reason why he would not make Nazareth his headquarters (*v.* 24), because it generally holds true *that no prophet is accepted in his own country,* at least not so well, nor with such probability of doing good, as in some other country; experience seals this. When prophets have been sent with messages and miracles of mercy, few of their own country-men, that have known their extraction and education, have been fit to *receive them.* So Dr. Hammond. *Familiarity breeds contempt;* and we are apt to think meanly of those whose conversation we have been accustomed to; and they will scarcely be duly honoured as *prophets* who were well known when they were in the rank of *private men.* That is most esteemed that is *far-fetched* and *dear-bought,* above what is *home-bred,* though really more excellent. This arises likewise from the envy which neighbours commonly have towards one another, so that they cannot endure to see him their *superior* whom awhile ago they took to be every way their *inferior.* For this reason, Christ declined working miracles, or doing any thing extraordinary, at Nazareth, because of the rooted prejudices they had against him there.

Secondly, By pertinent examples of two of the most famous prophets of the Old Testament, who chose to dispense their favours among foreigners rather than among their own countrymen, and that, no doubt, by divine direction. 1. Elijah maintained a *widow of Sarepta,* a *city of Sidon,* one that was a stranger to the commonwealth of Israel, when there was a *famine in the land, v.* 25, 26. The story we have 1 Ki. 17:9, etc. It is said there that the heaven was shut up *three years and six months;* whereas it is said, 1 Ki. 18:1, that *in the third year Elijah* showed himself to Ahab, and there was *rain;* but that was not the third year of the drought, but the third year of Elijah's sojourning with the widow of Sarepta. As God would hereby show himself a *Father of the fatherless,* and a *Judge of the widows,* so he would show that he was rich in mercy to all, even to the Gentiles. 2. Elisha cleansed Naaman the Syrian of his leprosy, though he was a Syrian, and not only a foreigner, but an enemy to Israel (*v.* 27); *Many lepers were in Israel in the days of Eliseus,* four particularly, that brought the news of the Syrians' raising the siege of Samaria with precipitation, and leaving the plunder of their tents to enrich Samaria, when Elisha was himself in the besieged city, and this was the accomplishment of his prophecy too; see 2 Ki. 7:1, 3, etc. And yet we do not find that Elisha cleansed them, no not for a reward of their service, and the good tidings they brought, but only the Syrian; for none besides had faith to apply himself to the prophet for a cure. Christ himself often met with greater faith among Gentiles than in Israel. And here he mentions both these instances, to show that he did not dispense the favour of his miracles by private respect, but according to God's wise appointment. And the people of Israel might as justly have said to Elijah, or Elisha, as the Nazarenes to Christ, *Physician, heal thyself.* Nay, Christ wrought his miracles, though not among his townsmen, yet among Israelites, whereas these great prophets wrought theirs among Gentiles. The examples of the saints, though they will not make a bad action good, yet will help to free a good action from the blame of exceptious people.

2. How he was *persecuted* at Nazareth.

(1.) That which provoked them was his taking notice of the favour which God by Elijah and Elisha showed to the Gentiles: *When they heard these things, they were filled with wrath* (*v.* 28), they were *all so;* a great change since *v.* 22, when they *wondered at the gracious words that proceeded out of his mouth;* thus uncertain are the opinions and affections of the multitude, and so very fickle. If they had mixed faith with those gracious words of Christ which they wondered at, they would have been awakened by these latter words of his to take heed of sinning away their opportunities; but those only *pleased the ear,* and went no further, and therefore these - *grated on the ear,* and irritated their corruptions. They were angry that he should compare himself, whom they knew to be the son of Joseph, with those great prophets, and compare them with the men of that corrupt age, when all had bowed the knee to Baal. But that which especially exasperated them was that he intimated some kindness God had in reserve for the Gentiles, which the Jews could by no means bear the thoughts of, Acts 22:21. Their pious ancestors pleased themselves with the hopes of adding the Gentiles to the church (witness many of David's psalms and Isaiah's prophecies); but this degenerate race, when they had forfeited the covenant themselves, hated to think that any others should be taken in.

(2.) They were provoked to that degree that they made an attempt upon his life. This was a severe trial, now at his setting out, but a specimen of the usage he met with when he *came to his own,* and they *received him not.* [1.] They *rose up* in a tumultuous manner against him, interrupted him in his discourse, and themselves in their devotions, for they could not stay until their synagogue-worship was over. [2.] They *thrust him out of the city,* as one not worthy to have a residence among them, though there he had had a settlement so long. They thrust from them the Saviour and the salvation, as if he had been the offscouring of all things. How justly might he have called for fire from heaven upon them! But this was the day of his patience. [3.] They *led him to the brow of the hill,* with a purpose to *throw him down headlong,* as one not fit to live. Though they knew how inoffensively he had for so many years lived among them, how shining his conversation had been, — though they had heard such a fame of him and had but just now themselves *admired his gracious words,* — though in justice he ought to have been allowed a fair hearing and liberty to explain himself, yet they hurried him away in a popular fury, or frenzy rather, to put him to death in a most barbarous manner. Sometimes they were ready to stone him for the *good works* he did (Jn. 10:32), here for not doing the good works they expected from him. To such a height of wickedness was violence sprung up.

(3.) Yet he escaped, because his hour was not yet come: He *passed through the midst of them* unhurt. Either he blinded their eyes, as God did those of the Sodomites and Syrians, or he bound their hands, or filled them with confusion, so that they could not do what they designed; for his work was not done, it was but just begun; his hour was not yet come, when it was come, he freely surrendered himself. They *drove* him from them, and he *went his way.* He would have gathered Nazareth, but they *would not,* and therefore their house is *left to them desolate.* This added to the reproach of his being Jesus of Nazareth, that not only it was a place whence no good thing was expected, but that it was such a wicked, rude place, and so *unkind* to him. Yet there was a providence in it, that he should not be much respected by the men of Nazareth, for that would have looked like a collusion between him and his old acquaintance; but now, though they *received him not,* there were those that did.

Verses 31–44

When Christ was expelled Nazareth, he came to Capernaum, another city of Galilee. The account we have in these verses of his preaching and miracles there we had before, Mk. 1:21, etc. Observe,

I. His preaching: *He taught them on the sabbath days, v.* 31. In hearing the word preached, as an ordinance of God, we *worship God,* and it is a proper work for *sabbath days.* Christ's preaching much affected the people (*v.* 32); they were *astonished at his doctrine,* there was weight in every word he said, and admirable discoveries were made to them by it. The doctrine itself was astonishing, and not only as it came from one that had not had a liberal education. *His word was with power;* there was a commanding force in it, and a working power went along with it to the conscience of men. The doctrine Paul preached hereby proved itself to be of God, that it came *in demonstration of the Spirit and of power.*

II. His miracles. Of these we have here,

1. Two particularly specified, showing Christ to be,

(1.) A *controller* and *conqueror* of *Satan,* in the world of mankind, and in the souls of people, by his power to cast him out of the bodies of those he had taken possession of; for *for this purpose was he manifested, that he might destroy the works of the devil.*

Observe, [1.] The devil is an *unclean spirit,* his nature directly contrary to that of the pure and *holy* God, and degenerated from what it was at first. [2.] This unclean spirit works in the children of men; in the souls of many, as then in men's bodies. [3.] It is possible that those who are very much under the power and working of Satan may yet be found *in the synagogue,* among the worshippers of God. [4.] Even the devils *know and believe* that *Jesus Christ is the Holy One of God,* is sent of God, and is a *Holy One.* [5.] They believe and *tremble.* This unclean spirit *cried out with a loud voice,* under a *certain fearful looking for of judgment,* and apprehensive that Christ was now come to destroy him. Unclean spirits are subject to continual frights. [6.] The devils have *nothing to do with Jesus Christ,* nor desire to have any thing to do with him; for he took not on him the nature of angels. [7.] Christ has the devil under check: *He rebuked him,* saying, *Hold thy peace;* and this word he spoke *with power; phimōthēti — Be muzzled,* Christ did not only enjoin him silence, but stopped his mouth, and forced him to be silent against his will. [8.] In the breaking of Satan's power, both the enemy that is conquered shows his malice, and Christ, the conqueror, shows his over-ruling grace. Here, *First,* The devil showed what he would have done, when he *threw the man in the midst,* with force and fury, as if he would have dashed him to pieces. But, *Secondly,* Christ showed what a power he had over him, in that he not only forced him to leave him, but to leave him without so much as *hurting* him, without giving him a parting blow, a parting gripe. Whom Satan cannot *destroy,* he will do all the *hurt* he can to; but this is a comfort, he can harm them no further than Christ permits; nay, he shall not do them any real harm. He *came out,* and *hurt him not;* that is, the poor man was perfectly well in an instant, though the devil left him with so much rage that all that were present thought he had torn him to pieces. [9.] Christ's power over devils was universally acknowledged and adored, *v.* 36. No one doubted the truth of the miracle; it was evident beyond contradiction, nor was any thing suggested to diminish the glory of it, for they were *all amazed, saying, What a word is this!* They that pretended to cast out devils did it with abundance of charms and spells, to pacify the devil, and lull him asleep, as it were; but Christ commanded them *with authority and power,* which they could not gainsay or resist. Even the *prince of the power of the air* is his vassal, and trembles before him. [10.] This, as much as any thing, gained Christ a reputation, and spread his fame. This instance of his power, which many now-a-days make light of, was then, by them that were eye-witnesses of it (and those no fools either, but men of penetration), magnified, and was looked upon as greatly magnifying him (*v.* 37); upon the account of this, *the fame of him went out,* more than ever, *into every place of the country round about.* Our Lord Jesus, when he set out at first in his public ministry, was greatly talked of, more than afterwards, when people's admiration wore off with the novelty of the thing.

(2.) Christ showed himself to be *a healer of diseases.* In the former, he struck at the root of man's misery, which was Satan's enmity, the origin of all the mischief: in this, he strikes at one of the most spreading branches of it, one of the most common calamities of human life, and that is bodily diseases, which came in with sin, are the most common and sensible corrections for it in this life, and contribute as much as any thing towards the making of our few days *full of trouble.* These our Lord Jesus came to take away the sting of, and, as an indication of that intention, when he was on earth, chose to confirm his doctrine by such miracles, mostly, as took away the diseases themselves. Of all bodily diseases none are more common or fatal to grown people than *fevers;* these come suddenly, and suddenly cut off the number of men's months in the midst; they are sometimes *epidemical,* and *slay their thousands* in a little time. Now here we have Christ's curing a fever with a word's speaking; the place was in Simon's house, his patient was Simon's wife's mother, *v.* 38, 39. Observe, [1.] Christ is a guest that will pay well for his entertainment; those that bid him welcome into their hearts and houses shall be no losers by him; he comes with healing. [2.] Even families that Christ visits may be visited with sickness. Houses that are blessed with his *distinguishing favours* are liable to the *common calamities* of this life. Simon's wife's mother was *ill* of a *fever. Lord, behold, he whom thou lovest is sick.* [3.] Even good people may sometimes be exercised with the sharpest afflictions, more grievous than others: She was *taken with a great fever,* very acute, and high, and threatening; perhaps it seized her head, and made her delirious. The most gentle fevers may by degrees prove dangerous; but this was at first *a great fever.* [4.] No age can exempt from diseases. It is probable that Peter's mother-in-law was *in years,* and yet in a *fever.* [5.] When our relations are sick, we ought to apply ourselves to Christ, by faith and prayer, on their account: *They besought him for her;* and there is a particular promise that the prayer of faith shall benefit the sick. [6.] Christ has a tender concern for his people when they are in sickness and distress: *He stood over her,* as one concerned for her, and compassionating her case. [7.] Christ had, and still has, a sovereign power over bodily diseases: *He rebuked the fever,* and with a word's speaking commanded it away, and *it left her.* He saith to diseases, *Go,* and they go; *Come,* and they come; and can still *rebuke fevers,* even great fevers. [8.] This proves Christ's cures to be miraculous, that they were done in an instant: *Immediately she arose.* [9.] Where Christ gives a new life, in recovery from sickness, he designs and expects that it should be a new life indeed, spent more than ever in his service, to his glory. If distempers be rebuked, and we arise from a bed of sickness, we must set ourselves to minister to Jesus Christ. [10.] Those that minister to Christ must be ready to minister to all that are his for his sake: She *ministered to them,* not only to *him* that had cured her, but to them that had *besought him for her.* We must study to be grateful to those that have prayed for us.

2. A general account given by wholesale of many other miracles of the same kind, which Christ did.

(1.) He *cured many that were diseased,* even all without exception that made their application to him, and it was *when the sun was setting* (*v.* 40); in the evening of that sabbath day which he had spent in the synagogue. Note, It is good to do a full sabbath day's work, to abound in the work of the day, in some good work or other, even till sun-set; as those that call the sabbath, and the business of it, *a delight.* Observe, He cured *all that were sick,* poor as well as rich, and though they were sick of *divers diseases;* so that there was no room to suspect that he had only a specific for some one disease. He had a remedy for every malady. The sign he used in healing was *laying his hands* on the sick; not lifting up his hands for them, for he healed as having authority. He healed by his own power. And thus he would put honour upon that sign which was afterwards used in conferring the Holy Ghost.

(2.) He cast the devil out of many that were possessed, *v.* 41. Confessions were extorted from the demoniacs. They said, *Thou art Christ the Son of God,* but they said it *crying* with rage and indignation; it was a confession upon the rack, and therefore was not admitted in evidence. Christ *rebuked them,* and did not *suffer them to say that they knew him to be the Christ,* that it might appear, beyond all contradiction, that he had obtained a conquest over them, and not made a compact with them.

3. Here is his removal from Capernaum, *v.* 42, 43.

(1.) He *retired* for awhile into a place of *solitude.* It was but a little while that he allowed himself for sleep; not only because a *little served him,* but because he was *content with a little,* and never indulged himself in ease; but, *when it was day,* he *went into a desert place,* not to live constantly like a hermit, but to be sometimes *alone with God,* as even those should be, and contrive to be, that are most engaged in public work, or else their work will go on but poorly, and they will find themselves never *less alone* than when *thus alone.*

(2.) He *returned* again to the places of *concourse* and to the work he had to do there. Though a *desert place* may be a convenient *retreat,* yet it is not a *convenient residence,* because we were not sent into this world to *live to ourselves,* no, not to the *best part* of ourselves only, but to glorify God and do good in our generation. [1.] He was earnestly solicited to stay at Capernaum. *The people* were exceedingly fond of him; I doubt, more because he had healed their sick than because he had preached repentance to them. *They sought him,* enquired which way he went; and, though it was in a *desert place,* they *came unto him.* A desert is no desert if we be *with Christ* there. They *detained him that he should not depart from them,* so that if he would go it should not be for want of invitation. His old neighbours at Nazareth had driven him from them, but his new acquaintances at Capernaum were very importunate for his continuance with them. Note, It ought not to discourage the ministers of Christ that some reject them, for they will meet with others that will welcome them and their message. [2.] He chose rather to *diffuse* the light of his gospel to *many* places than to fix it to *one,* that no one might pretend to be a *mother-church* to the rest. Though he was welcome at Capernaum, and had done abundance of good there, yet he is *sent to preach the gospel to other cities also;* and Capernaum must not insist upon his stay there. They that enjoy the benefit of the gospel must be willing that others also should share in that benefit, and not covet the *monopoly* of it; and those ministers who are not *driven* from one place may yet be *drawn* to another by a prospect of greater usefulness. Christ, though he preached not in vain in the synagogue at Capernaum, yet would not be tied to that, but *preached in the synagogues of Galilee, v.* 44. *Bonum est sui diffusivum — What is good is self-diffusive.* It is well for us that our Lord Jesus has not tied himself to any one place or people, but, wherever two or three are gathered in his name, he will be in the midst of them: and even in *Galilee of the Gentiles* his special presence is in the Christian synagogues.

CHAPTER 5

In this chapter, we have, I. Christ preaching to the people out of Peter's ship, for want of a better pulpit (*v.* 1–3). II. The recompence he made to Peter for the loan of his boat, in a miraculous draught of fishes, by which he intimated to him and his partners his design to make them, as apostles, fishers of men (*v.* 4–11). III. His cleansing the leper (*v.* 12–15). IV. A short account of his private devotion and public ministry (*v.* 16, 17). V. His cure of the man sick of the palsy (*v.* 18–26). VI. His calling Levi the publican, and conversing with publicans on that occasion (*v.* 27–32). VII. His justifying his disciples in not fasting so frequently as the disciples of John and the Pharisees did (*v.* 33–39).

Verses 1–11

This passage of story fell, in order of time, before the two miracles we had in the close of the foregoing chapter, and is the same with that which was more briefly related by Matthew and Mark, of Christ's calling Peter and Andrew to be *fishers of men,* Mt. 4:18, and Mk. 1:16. They had not related this miraculous draught of fishes at that time, having only in view the calling of his disciples; but Luke gives us that story as one of the many signs which Jesus did in the presence of his disciples, which *had not been written* in the foregoing books, Jn. 20:30, 31. Observe here,

I. What vast *crowds* attended Christ's preaching: *The people pressed upon him to hear the word of God* (*v.* 1), insomuch that no house would contain them, but he was forced to draw them out to the *strand,* that they might be reminded of the promise made to Abraham, that his seed should be *as the sand upon the sea shore* (Gen. 22:17), and yet of them but *a remnant shall be saved,* Rom. 9:27. The people *flocked about him* (so the word signifies); they showed respect to his preaching, though not without some rudeness to his person, which was very excusable, for they *pressed upon him.* Some would reckon this a discredit to him, to be thus cried up by the vulgar, when none of the *rulers* or of *the Pharisees believed in him;* but he reckoned it an honour to him, for their souls were as precious as the souls of the grandees, and it is his aim to bring not so much the mighty as the *many sons* to God. It was foretold concerning him that *to him shall the gathering of the people be.* Christ was a popular preacher; and though he was able, at *twelve,* to *dispute* with the *doctors,* yet he chose, at *thirty,* to preach to the capacity of the *vulgar.* See how the people relished *good preaching,* though under all external disadvantages: they pressed to *hear the word of God;* they could perceive it to be the *word of God,* by the divine power and evidence that went along with it, and therefore they coveted to hear it.

II. What poor *conveniences* Christ had for preaching: *He stood by the lake of Gennesareth* (*v.* 1), upon a level with the crowd, so that they could neither see him nor hear him; he was lost among them, and, every one striving to get near him, he was crowded, and in danger of being crowded into the water: what must he do? It does not appear that his hearers had any contrivance to give him advantage, but *there were two ships,* or *fishing boats,* brought ashore, one belonging to Simon and Andrew, the other to Zebedee and *his sons, v.* 2. At first, Christ saw Peter and Andrew fishing at some distance (so Matthew tells us, *ch.* 4:18); but he waited till they came to land, and till the *fishermen,* that is, the servants, were *gone out of them* having washed their nets, and thrown them by for that time: so Christ *entered* into that *ship* that belonged to Simon, and begged of him that he would lend it him for a pulpit; and, though he might have commanded him, yet, for love's sake, he rather *prayed him* that he would *thrust out a little from the land,* which would be the worse for his being *heard,* but Christ would have it so, that he might the better be *seen;* and it is his being *lifted up* that *draws men to him.* Wisdom cries *in the top of high places,* Prov. 8:2. It intimates that Christ had a strong voice (strong indeed, for he made the *dead* to hear it), and that he did not desire to favour himself. There he *sat down,* and *taught the people* the good knowledge of the Lord.

III. What a particular acquaintance Christ, hereupon, fell into with these fishermen. They had had some conversation with him before, which began at John's baptism (Jn. 1:40, 41); they were with him at *Cana of Galilee* (Jn. 2:2), and in Judea (Jn. 4:3); but as yet they were not called to attend him constantly, and therefore here we have them at their calling, and now it was that they were called into a more intimate fellowship with Christ.

1. When Christ had done preaching, he ordered Peter to apply himself to the business of his calling again: *Launch out into the deep, and let down your nets, v.* 4. It was not the sabbath day, and therefore, as soon as the lecture was over, he set them to work. Time spent on week-days in the public exercises of religion may be but little hindrance to us *in time,* and a great furtherance to us in *temper of mind,* in our worldly business. With what cheerfulness may we go about the duties of our calling when we have been *in the mount* with God, and from thence fetch a double blessing into our worldly employments, and thus have them sanctified to us by the word and prayer! It is our wisdom and duty so to manage our religious exercises as that they may befriend our worldly business, and so to manage our worldly business as that it may be no enemy to our religious exercises.

2. Peter having *attended* upon Christ in his *preaching,* Christ will *accompany* him in his *fishing.* He staid with Christ at the shore, and now Christ will *launch out* with him *into the deep.* Note, Those that will be constant followers of Christ shall have him a constant guide to them.

3. Christ ordered Peter and his ship's crew to *cast their nets into the sea,* which they did, in obedience to him, though they had been hard at it all night, and had *caught nothing, v.* 4, 5. We may observe here,

(1.) How melancholy their business had now been: *"Master, we have toiled all the night,* when we should have been asleep in our beds, *and have taken nothing,* but have had our labour for our pains." One would have thought that this should have excused them from hearing the sermon; but such a love had they to the word of God that it was more refreshing and reviving to them, after a wearisome night, than the softest slumbers. But they mention it to Christ, when he bids them go a fishing again. Note, [1.] Some *callings* are much more *toilsome* than others are, and more perilous; yet Providence has so ordered it for the common good that there is no useful calling so discouraging but some or other have a genius for it. Those who follow their business, and get abundance by it with a great deal of ease, should think with compassion of those who cannot follow theirs but with a great fatigue, and hardly get a bare livelihood by it. When we have *rested all night,* let us not forget those who have *toiled all night,* as Jacob, when he kept Laban's sheep. [2.] Be the calling ever so laborious, it is good to see people diligent in it, and make the best of it; these fishermen, that were thus *industrious,* Christ singled out for his favourites. They were fit to be preferred as good soldiers of Jesus Christ who had thus learned to *endure hardness.* [3.] Even those who are most diligent in their business often meet with disappointments; they who *toiled all night* yet *caught nothing;* for the *race* is not always *to the swift.* God will have us to be diligent, purely in duty to his command and dependence upon his goodness, rather than with an assurance of worldly success. We must do our duty, and then leave the event to God. [4.] When we are tired with our worldly business, and crossed in our worldly affairs, we are welcome to come to Christ, and spread our case before him, who will take cognizance of it.

(2.) How ready their obedience was to the command of Christ: *Nevertheless, at thy word, I will let down the net.* [1.] Though they had *toiled all night,* yet, if Christ bid them, they will renew their toil, for they know that they who *wait on him shall renew their strength,* as work is renewed upon their hands; for every fresh service they shall have a fresh supply of *grace sufficient.* [2.] Though they have *taken nothing,* yet, if Christ bid them *let down for a draught,* they will hope to take *something.* Note, We must not abruptly quit the callings wherein we are called because we have not the success in them we promised ourselves. The ministers of the gospel must continue to *let down* that *net,* though they have perhaps *toiled long* and *caught nothing;* and this is thank-worthy, to continue unwearied in our labours, though we see not the success of them. [3.] In this they have an eye to the *word of Christ,* and a dependence upon that: *"At thy word, I will let down the net,* because thou dost enjoin it, and thou dost encourage it." We are *then* likely to speed well when we follow the guidance of Christ's word.

4. The draught of fish they caught was so much beyond what was ever known that it amounted to a miracle (*v.* 6): They *enclosed a great multitude of fishes,* so that *their net broke,* and yet, which is strange, they did not lose their draught. It was so great a *draught* that they had not hands sufficient to draw it up; but they were obliged to beckon to their partners, who were at a distance, out of call, to come and help them, *v.* 7. But the greatest evidence of the vastness of the draught was that they filled both the ships with fish, to such a degree that they overloaded them, and they *began to sink,* so that the fish had like to have been lost again with their own weight. Thus many an overgrown estate, raised out of the water, returns to the place whence it came. Suppose these ships were but five or six tons a piece, what a vast quantity of fish must there be to *load,* nay to *overload,* them both!

Now by this vast draught of fishes, (1.) Christ intended to show his *dominion* in the *seas* as well as on the *dry land,* over its *wealth* as over its *waves.* Thus he would show that he was that *Son of man* under whose feet all things were put, and particularly the *fish of the sea* and *whatsoever passeth through the paths of the sea,* Ps. 8:8. (2.) He intended hereby to confirm the doctrine he had just now preached out of Peter's ship. We may suppose that the people on shore, who heard the sermon, having a notion that the preacher was a prophet sent of God, carefully attended his motions afterward, and staid halting about there, to see what he would do next; and this miracle immediately following would be a confirmation to their faith, of his being at least *a teacher come from God.* (3.) He intended hereby to repay Peter for the loan of his boat; for Christ's gospel now, as his ark formerly in the house of Obed-edom, will be sure to make amends, rich amends, for its kind entertainment. None shall *shut a door or kindle a fire* in God's house *for nought,* Mal. 1:10. Christ's recompences for services done to his name are abundant, they are superabundant. (4.) He intended hereby to give a specimen, to those who were to be his ambassadors to the world, of the success of their embassy, that though they might for a time, and in one particular place, *toil* and *catch nothing,* yet they should be instrumental to bring in many to Christ, and enclose many in the gospel net.

5. The impression which this miraculous draught of fishes made upon Peter was very remarkable.

(1.) All *concerned* were *astonished,* and the more *astonished* for their being *concerned.* All the boat's crew were *astonished at the draught of fishes which they had taken* (*v.* 9); they were all surprised; and the more they considered it, and all the circumstances of it, the more they were *wonder-struck,* I had almost said *thunder-struck,* at the thought of it, *and so were also James and John, who were partners with Simon* (*v.* 10), and who, for aught that appears, were not so well acquainted with Christ, before this, as Peter and Andrew were. Now they were the more *affected* with it, [1.] Because they *understood* it better than others did. They that were well acquainted with this sea, and it is probable had plied upon it many years, had never seen such a draught of fishes fetched out of it, nor any thing like it, any thing near it; and therefore they could not be tempted to diminish it, as others might, by suggesting that it was accidental at this *time,* and what might as well have happened at *any time.* It greatly corroborates the evidence of Christ's miracles that those who were best *acquainted* with them most *admired* them. [2.] Because they were most *interested* in it, and *benefited* by it. Peter and his part-owners were gainers by this great draught of fishes; it was a rich booty for them and therefore it transported them, and their *joy* was a *helper* to their *faith.* Note, When Christ's works of wonder are to us, in particular, works of grace, then especially they command our faith in his doctrine.

(2.) Peter, above all the rest, was astonished to such a degree that he *fell down at Jesus's knees,* as he sat in the stern of his boat, and said, as one in an ecstasy or transport, that knew not where he was or what he said, *Depart from me, for I am a sinful man, O Lord, v.* 8. Not that he feared the weight of the fish would sink him because he was a sinful man, but that he thought himself unworthy of the favour of Christ's presence in his boat, and worthy that it should be to him a matter rather of terror than of comfort. This word of Peter's came from the same principle with theirs who, under the Old-Testament, so often said that they did *exceedingly fear and quake* at the extraordinary display of the divine glory and majesty. It was the language of Peter's humility and self-denial, and had not the least tincture of the devils' dialect, *What have we to do with thee, Jesus, thou Son of God?* [1.] His acknowledgment was very just, and what it becomes us all to make: *I am a sinful man, O Lord.* Note, Even the *best men* are *sinful men,* and should be ready upon all occasions to own it, and especially to own it to Jesus Christ; for to whom else, but to him who came into the world to *save sinners,* should *sinful men* apply themselves? [2.] His inference from it was what *might have been* just, though really it was not so. If I be a *sinful man,* as indeed I am, I ought to say, *"Come to me, O Lord,* or let me come to thee, or I am undone, *for ever undone."* But, considering what reason *sinful men* have to tremble before the holy Lord God and to dread his wrath, Peter may well be excused, if, in a sense of his own sinfulness and vileness, he cried out on a sudden, *Depart from me.* Note, Those whom Christ designs to admit to the most *intimate acquaintance* with him he first makes sensible that they deserve to be set at the *greatest distance* from him. We must all own ourselves *sinful men,* and that therefore Jesus Christ might justly *depart from us;* but we must *therefore fall down at his knees,* to pray him that he would not depart; for *woe unto us* if he *leave us,* if the Saviour depart from the sinful man.

6. The occasion which Christ took from this to intimate to Peter (*v.* 10), and soon after to James and John (Mt. 4:21), his purpose to make them his apostles, and instruments of planting his religion in the world. He *said unto Simon,* who was in the greatest surprise of any of them at this prodigious draught of fishes, "Thou shalt both see and do greater things than these; *fear not;* let not this astonish thee; be not afraid that, after having done thee this honour, it is so great that I shall never do thee more; no, *henceforth thou shalt catch men,* by enclosing them in the gospel net, and that shall be a greater instance of the Redeemer's power, and his favour to thee, than this is; that shall be a more *astonishing* miracle, and infinitely more *advantageous* than this." When by Peter's preaching *three thousand souls* were, *in one day,* added to the church, then the type of this great draught of fishes was abundantly answered.

Lastly, The fishermen's farewell to their calling, in order to their constant attendance on Christ (*v.* 11): *When they had brought their ships to land,* instead of going to seek for a market for their fish, that they might make the best hand they could of this miracle, they *forsook all and followed him,* being more solicitous to serve the interests of Christ than to advance any secular interests of their own. It is observable that they *left all to follow Christ,* when their calling prospered in their hands more than ever it had done and they had had uncommon success in it. When *riches increase,* and we are therefore most in temptation to *set our hearts* upon them, then to quit them for the service of Christ, this is *thank-worthy.*

Verses 12–16

Here is, I. The cleansing of a leper, *v.* 12–14. This narrative we had both in Matthew and Mark. It is here said to have been *in a certain city* (*v.* 12); it was in Capernaum, but the evangelist would not name it, perhaps because it was a reflection upon the government of the city that a leper was suffered to be *in it.* This man is said to be *full of leprosy;* he had that distemper in a high degree, which the more fitly represents our natural pollution by sin; we are *full of that leprosy, from the crown of the head to the sole of the foot there is no soundness in us.* Now let us learn here,

1. What we must do in the sense of our spiritual leprosy. (1.) We must *seek Jesus,* enquire after him, acquaint ourselves with him, and reckon the discoveries made to us of Christ by the gospel the most acceptable and welcome discoveries that could be made to us. (2.) We must humble ourselves before him, as this leper, seeing Jesus, *fell on his face.* We must be *ashamed* of our pollution, and, in the sense of it, blush to lift up our faces before the *holy Jesus.* (3.) We must earnestly desire to be *cleansed* from the defilement, and cured of the disease, of sin, which renders us unfit for communion with God. (4.) We must firmly believe Christ's ability and sufficiency to cleanse us: Lord, *thou canst make me clean,* though I be *full of leprosy.* No doubt is to be made of the merit and grace of Christ. (5.) We must be importunate in prayer for pardoning mercy and renewing grace: *He fell on his face and besought him;* they that would be cleansed must reckon it a favour worth wrestling for. (6.) We must refer ourselves to the good-will of Christ: *Lord, if thou wilt, thou canst.* This is not so much the language of his *diffidence,* or *distrust* of the good-will of Christ, as of his submission and reference of himself and his case to the will, to the good-will, of Jesus Christ.

2. What we may expect from Christ, if we thus apply ourselves to him. (1.) We shall find him very *condescending* and forward to take cognizance of our case (*v.* 13): *He put forth his hand and touched him.* When Christ visited this leprous world, unasked, unsought unto, he showed how low he could stoop, to do good. His *touching* the leper was wonderful condescension; but it is much greater to us when he is himself *touched with the feeling of our infirmities.* (2.) We shall find him very *compassionate,* and ready to relieve us; he said, *"I will,* never doubt of that; whosoever comes to me to be healed, *I will in no wise cast him out."* He is as willing to cleanse leprous souls as they can be to be cleansed. (3.) We shall find him all-sufficient, and able to heal and cleanse us, though we be ever so full of this loathsome leprosy. One word, one touch, from Christ, did the business: *Immediately the leprosy departed from him.* If Christ saith, "I will, be thou *justified,* be thou *sanctified,"* it is done; for he has power on earth to *forgive* sin, and power to give the Holy Spirit, 1 Co. 6:11.

3. What he requires from those that are cleansed, *v.* 14. Has Christ sent his word and healed us? (1.) We must be very *humble* (*v.* 14): *He charged him to tell no man.* This, it should seem, did not forbid him telling it to the honour of Christ, but he must not tell it to his own honour. Those whom Christ hath healed and cleansed must know that he hath done it in such a way as for ever excludes boasting. (2.) We must be very *thankful,* and make a grateful acknowledgment of the divine grace: *Go, and offer for thy cleansing.* Christ did not require him to give him a fee, but to bring the sacrifice of praise to God; so far was he from using his power to the prejudice of the law of Moses. (3.) We must *keep close to our duty;* go *to the priest,* and those that attend him. The man whom Christ had made whole he *found in the temple,* Jn. 5:14. Those who by any affliction have been detained from public ordinances should, when the affliction is removed, attend on them the more diligently, and adhere to them the more constantly.

4. Christ's *public serviceableness* to men and his *private communion* with God; these are put together here, to give lustre to each other.

(1.) Though never any had so much *pleasure* in his *retirements* as Christ had, yet he was *much in a crowd,* to do good, *v.* 15. Though the leper should altogether hold his peace, yet the thing could not be hid, *so much the more went there a fame abroad of him.* The more he sought to conceal himself under a veil of humility, the more notice did people take of him; for honour is like a shadow, which flees from those that pursue it *(for a man to seek his own glory is not glory),* but follows those that decline it, and draw from it. The less good men say of themselves, the more will others say of them. But Christ reckoned it a small honour to him that his *fame went abroad;* it was much more so that hereby multitudes were brought to receive benefit by him. [1.] By his preaching. They came together to *hear* him, and to receive instruction from him concerning the kingdom of God. [2.] By his miracles. They came *to be healed by him of their infirmities;* that invited them to come to hear him, confirmed his doctrine, and recommended it.

(2.) Though never any did so much *good in public,* yet he found time for *pious* and *devout retirements* (*v.* 16): *He withdrew himself into the wilderness, and prayed;* not that he needed to avoid either distraction or ostentation, but he would set us an example, who need to order the circumstances of our devotion so as to guard against both. It is likewise our wisdom so to order our affairs as that our public work and our secret work may not intrench upon, nor interfere with, one another. Note, Secret prayer must be performed secretly; and those that have ever so much to do of the best business in this world must keep up constant stated times for it.

Verses 17–26

Here is, I. A general account of Christ's preaching and miracles, *v.* 17. 1. He was *teaching on a certain day,* not on the sabbath day, then he would have said so, but on a *week-day; six days shalt thou labour,* not only for *the world,* but for *the soul,* and the welfare of that. Preaching and hearing the word of *God* are *good works,* if they be *done well,* any day in the *week,* as well as on sabbath days. It was not in the *synagogue,* but in a *private house;* for even there where we ordinarily converse with our friends it is not improper to give and receive good instruction. 2. There he *taught,* he *healed* (as before, *v.* 15): *And the power of the Lord was to heal them — ēn eis to iasthai autous.* It was *mighty* to heal them; it was *exerted* and *put forth* to heal them, to heal those whom he *taught* (we may understand it so), to heal their souls, to cure them of their spiritual diseases, and to give them a new life, a new nature. Note, Those who receive the word of Christ in faith will find a divine power going along with that word, to *heal them;* for Christ came with his comforts to *heal the broken-hearted, ch.* 4:18. The power of the Lord is *present* with the word, *present to those* that pray for it and submit to it, *present to heal them.* Or it may be meant (and so it is generally taken) of the healing of those who were *diseased in body,* who came to him for cures. Whenever there was occasion, Christ had not *to seek* for his power, it was *present to heal.* 3. There were some grandees present in this assembly, and, as it should seem, more than usual: *There were Pharisees, and doctors of the law, sitting by;* not sitting *at his feet,* to learn of him; then I should have been willing to take the following clause as referring to those who are spoken of immediately before (the *power of the Lord was present to heal them*); and why might not the word of Christ reach their hearts? But, by what follows (*v.* 21), it appears that they were *not healed,* but cavilled at Christ, which compels us to refer this to others, not to them; for they *sat by* as *persons unconcerned,* as if the word of Christ were nothing to them. They sat by as spectators, censors, and spies, to pick up something on which to ground a reproach or accusation. How many are there in the midst of our assemblies, where the gospel is preached, that do not *sit under* the word, but *sit by!* It is to them as a *tale* that is *told them,* not as a *message* that is *sent them;* they are willing that we should preach *before them,* not that we should preach *to them.* These Pharisees and scribes (or doctors of the law) *came out of every town of Galilee, and Judea, and Jerusalem;* they came from all parts of the nation. Probably, they appointed to meet at this time and place, to see what remarks they could make upon Christ and what he said and did. They were in a confederacy, as those that said, *Come, and let us devise devices against Jeremiah,* and agree to *smite him with the tongue,* Jer. 18:18. *Report, and we will report it,* Jer. 20:10. Observe, Christ went on with his work of *preaching* and *healing,* though he saw these Pharisees, and doctors of the Jewish church, *sitting by,* who, he knew, *despised* him, and watched to *ensnare him.*

II. A particular account of the cure of the man *sick of the palsy,* which was related much as it is here by both the foregoing evangelists: let us therefore only observe in short,

1. The doctrines that are taught us and confirmed to us by the story of this cure. (1.) That sin is the fountain of all sickness, and the forgiveness of sin is the only foundation upon which a recovery from sickness can comfortably be built. They presented the *sick man* to Christ, and he said, *"Man, thy sins are forgiven thee* (*v.* 20), that is the blessing thou art most to prize and seek; for if thy sins be forgiven thee, though the sickness be continued, it is in mercy; if they be not, though the sickness be removed, it is in wrath." The cords of our iniquity are the bands of our affliction. (2.) That Jesus Christ has power on earth to *forgive sins,* and his healing diseases was an *incontestable* proof of it. This was the thing intended to be proved (*v.* 24): *That ye may know* and believe *that the Son of man,* though now upon earth in his state of humiliation, *hath power to forgive sins,* and to release sinners, upon gospel terms, from the eternal punishment of sin, he *saith to the sick of the palsy, Arise, and walk;* and he is cured immediately. Christ claims one of the prerogatives of the King of kings when he undertakes to *forgive sin,* and it is justly expected that he should produce a good proof of it. "Well," saith he, "I will put it upon this issue: here is a man struck with a palsy, and *for his sin;* if I do not with a word's speaking cure his disease in an instant, which cannot be done by nature or art, but purely by the immediate power and efficacy of the God of nature, then say that I am not entitled to the prerogative of forgiving sin, am not the Messiah, am not the Son of God and King of Israel: but, if I do, you must own that *I have power to forgive sins."* Thus it was put upon a fair trial, and one word of Christ determined it. He did but say, *Arise, take up thy couch,* and that *chronical* disease had an *instantaneous* cure; *immediately he arose before them.* They must all own that there could be no cheat or fallacy in it. They that brought him could attest how perfectly *lame* he was before; they that saw him could attest how perfectly *well* he was now, insomuch that he had strength enough to take up and carry away the bed he lay upon. How well is it for us that this most comfortable doctrine of the gospel, that *Jesus Christ,* our *Redeemer and Saviour,* has *power to forgive sin,* has such a full attestation! (3.) That Jesus Christ is God. He appears to be so, [1.] By *knowing the thoughts* of the scribes and Pharisees (*v.* 22), which it is God's prerogative to do, though these scribes and Pharisees knew as well how to conceal their thoughts, and keep their countenances, as most men, and probably were industrious to do it at this time, for they *lay in wait secretly.* [2.] By doing that which their thoughts owned none could do but God only (*v.* 21): *Who can forgive sins,* say they, *but only God?* "I will prove," saith Christ, "that I can forgive sins;" and what follows then but that *he is God*? What horrid wickedness then were *they* guilty of who charged him with speaking the *worst* of *blasphemies,* even when he spoke the *best* of *blessings, Thy sins are forgiven thee!*

2. The duties that are taught us, and recommended to us, by this story. (1.) In our applications to Christ, we must be very *pressing* and *urgent:* that is an evidence of faith, and is very pleasing to Christ and prevailing with him. They that were the friends of this sick man *sought means to bring him in before Christ* (*v.* 18); and, when they were baffled in their endeavour, they did not give up their cause; but when they could not get in by *the door,* it was so crowded, they untiled the house, and let the poor patient down through the roof, *into the midst before Jesus, v.* 19. In this Jesus Christ *saw their faith, v.* 20. Now here he has taught us (and it were well if we could learn the lesson) to *put the best construction* upon words and actions that they *will bear.* When the centurion and the woman of Canaan were in no care at all to bring the patients they interceded for into Christ's presence, but believed that he could cure them *at a distance,* he commended *their faith.* But though in *these* there seemed to be a *different* notion of the thing, and an apprehension that it was requisite the *patient* should be *brought into his presence,* yet he did not *censure* and *condemn* their weakness, did not ask them, "Why do you give this disturbance to the assembly? Are you under such a degree of infidelity as to think I could not have cured him, though he had been out of doors?" But he made the best of it, and even in *this* he saw *their faith.* It is a comfort to us that we serve a Master that is willing to *make the best* of us. (2.) When we are sick, we should be more in care to get our sins pardoned than to get our sickness removed. Christ, in what he said to this man, taught us, when we seek to God for health, to begin with seeking to him for pardon. (3.) The mercies which we have the comfort of God must have the praise of. The man *departed to his own house, glorifying God, v.* 25. To him belong the escapes from death, and in them therefore he must be *glorified.* (4.) The miracles which Christ wrought were *amazing* to those that saw them, and we ought to *glorify* God in them, *v.* 26. They said, *"We have seen strange things to-day,* such as we never saw before, nor our fathers before us; they are altogether new." But they *glorified* God, who had sent into their country such a benefactor to it; and were *filled with fear,* with a reverence of God, with a jealous persuasion that this was the Messiah and that he was not treated by their nation as he ought to be, which might prove in the end the ruin of their state; perhaps they were some such thoughts as these that *filled them with fear,* and a concern likewise for themselves.

Verses 27–39

All this, except the last verse, we had before in Matthew and Mark; it is not the story of any *miracle in nature* wrought by our Lord Jesus, but it is an account of some of the *wonders of his grace,* which, to those who understand things aright, are no less cogent proofs of Christ's being sent of God than the other.

I. It was a wonder of his grace that he would call a *publican,* from the *receipt of custom,* to be his disciple and follower, *v.* 27. It was wonderful condescension that he should admit poor fishermen to that honour, men of the *lowest rank;* but much more wonderful that he should admit *publicans,* men of the *worst reputation,* men of *ill fame.* In this Christ *humbled himself,* and appeared *in the likeness of sinful flesh.* By this he *exposed himself,* and got the invidious character of a *friend of publicans and sinners.*

II. It was a wonder of his grace that the call was made *effectual,* became immediately so, *v.* 28. This publican, though those of that employment commonly had little inclination to religion, for his religion's sake left a good place in the customhouse (which, probably, was his livelihood, and where he stood fair for better preferment), and *rose up, and followed Christ.* There is no heart too hard for the Spirit and grace of Christ to work upon, nor any difficulties in the way of a sinner's conversion insuperable to his power.

III. It was a wonder of his grace that he would not only admit a converted publican into his family, but would keep company with unconverted publicans, that he might have an opportunity of doing their souls good; he justified himself in it, as agreeing with the great design of his coming into the world. Here is a wonder of grace indeed, that Christ undertakes to be the Physician of souls *distempered* by sin, and ready to *die* of the distemper (he is a Healer by office, *v.* 31) — that he has a particular regard to the sick, to sinners as his patients, convinced awakened sinners, that see their need of the Physician — that he came to call *sinners,* the worst of sinners, to repentance, and to assure them of pardon, upon repentance, *v.* 32. These are glad tidings of great joy indeed.

IV. It was a wonder of his grace that he did so patiently bear the *contradiction of sinners* against himself and his disciples, *v.* 30. He did not express his resentment of the cavils of the scribes and Pharisees, as he justly might have done, but answered them with reason and meekness; and, instead of taking that occasion to show his displeasure against the Pharisees, as afterwards he did, or of recriminating upon them, he took that occasion to show his compassion to poor publicans, another sort of sinners, and to encourage them.

V. It was a wonder of his grace that, in the discipline under which he trained up his disciples, he *considered their frame,* and proportioned their services to their strength and standing, and to the circumstances they were in. It was objected, as a blemish upon his conduct, that he did not make *his disciples* to *fast* so often as those of the *Pharisees* and John Baptist did, *v.* 33. He insisted most upon that which is the *soul* of fasting, the mortification of sin, the crucifying of the flesh, and the living of a life of self-denial, which is as much better than fasting and corporal penances as *mercy* is better than *sacrifice.*

VI. It was a wonder of his grace that Christ reserved the trials of his disciples for their latter times, when by his grace they were in some good measure better prepared and fitted for them than they were at first. Now they were as the *children of the bride-chamber,* when the *bridegroom is with them,* when they have plenty and joy, and every day is a festival. Christ was welcomed wherever he came, and they for his sake, and as yet they met with little or no opposition; but this will not last always. *The days will come* when the *bridegroom shall be taken away from them, v.* 35. When Christ shall leave them with their hearts full of sorrow, their hands full of work, and the world full of enmity and rage against them, *then shall they fast,* shall not be so well fed as they are now. *We both hunger and thirst and are naked,* 1 Co. 4:11. Then they shall keep many more *religious fasts* than they do now, for Providence will call them to it; they will then serve the Lord *with fastings,* Acts 13:2.

VII. It was a wonder of his grace that he proportioned their exercises to their strength. He would not put *new cloth upon an old garment* (*v.* 36), nor *new wine into old bottles* (*v.* 37, 38); he would not, as soon as ever he had called them out of the world, put them upon the strictnesses and austerities of discipleship, lest they should be tempted to *fly off.* When God brought Israel out of Egypt, he would not bring them *by the way of the Philistines,* lest they should *repent,* when they *saw war,* and *return to Egypt,* Ex. 13:17. So Christ would train up his followers gradually to the discipline of his family; for no man, having *drank old wine,* will *of a sudden,* straightway, *desire new,* or relish it, but will say, *The old is better,* because he has been *used to it, v.* 39. The disciples will be tempted to think their old way of living better, till they are by degrees trained up to this way whereunto they are called. Or, turn it the other way: "Let them be *accustomed* awhile to religious exercises, and then they will *abound* in them as much as you do: but we must not be too hasty with them." Calvin takes it as an admonition to the Pharisees not to boast of their fasting, and the noise and show they made with it, nor to despise his disciples because they did not in like manner *signalize* themselves; for the profession the Pharisees made was indeed *pompous* and *gay,* like *new wine* that is brisk and sparkling, whereas all wise men say, *The old is better;* for, though it does not give its colour so well in the cup, yet it is more warming in the stomach and more wholesome. Christ's disciples, though they had not so much of the *form of godliness,* had more of the *power of it.*

CHAPTER 6

In this chapter we have Christ's exposition of the moral law, which he came not to destroy, but to fulfil, and to fill up, by his gospel. I. Here is a proof of the lawfulness of works of necessity and mercy on the sabbath day, the former in vindication of his disciples' plucking the ears of corn, the latter in vindication of himself healing the withered hand on that day (*v.* 1–11). II. His retirement for secret prayer (*v.* 12). III. His calling his twelve apostles (*v.* 13–16). IV. His curing the multitudes of those under various diseases who made their application to him (*v.* 17–19). V. The sermon that he preached to his disciples and the multitude, instructing them in their duty both to God and man (*v.* 20–49).

Verses 1–11

These two passages of story we had both in Matthew and Mark, and they were there laid together (Mt. 12:1; Mk. 2:23; 3:1), because, though happening at some distance of time from each other, both were designed to rectify the mistakes of the scribes and Pharisees concerning the sabbath day, on the *bodily rest* of which they laid greater stress and required greater strictness than the Law-giver intended. Here,

I. Christ justifies his disciples in a *work of necessity* for themselves on that day, and that was *plucking the ears of corn,* when they were hungry on that day. This story here has a date, which we had not in the other evangelists; it was *on the second sabbath after the first* (*v.* 1), that is, as Dr. Whitby thinks is pretty clear, the *first sabbath after the second day of unleavened bread,* from which day they reckoned the *seven weeks* to the feast of pentecost; the first of which they called *Sabbaton deuteroprōton,* the second *deuterodeuteron,* and so on. Blessed be God we need not be critical in this matter. Whether this circumstance be mentioned to intimate that this sabbath was thought to have some peculiar honour upon it, which aggravated the offence of the disciples, or only to intimate that, being the first sabbath after the offering of the first fruits, it was the time of the year when the corn was nearly ripe, is not material. We may observe, 1. Christ's disciples ought not to be nice and curious in their diet, at any time, especially on sabbath days, but take up with what is easiest got, and be thankful. These disciples *plucked the ears of corn, and did eat* (*v.* 1); a little served them, and that which had no delicacy in it. 2. Many that are themselves guilty of the greatest crimes are forward to censure others for the most innocent and inoffensive actions, *v.* 2. The Pharisees quarrelled with them as doing that which it *was not lawful to do on the sabbath days,* when it was their own practice to feed deliciously on sabbath days, more than on all other days. 3. Jesus Christ will justify his disciples when they are unjustly censured, and will own and accept of them in many a thing which men tell them *it is not lawful for them to do.* How well is it for us that men are not to be our judges, and that Christ will be our Advocate! 4. Ceremonial appointments may be dispensed with, in cases of necessity; as the appropriating of the showbread to the priests was dispensed with, when David was by Providence brought into such a strait that he must have either that or none, *v.* 3, 4. And, if God's own appointments might be thus set aside for a greater good, much more may the traditions of men. 5. Works of necessity are particularly allowable on the sabbath day; but we must take heed that we turn not this liberty into licentiousness, and abuse God's favourable concessions and condescensions to the prejudice of the work of the day. 6. Jesus Christ, though he allowed works of necessity on the sabbath day, will notwithstanding have us to know and remember that it is his day, and therefore is to be spent in his service and to his honour (*v.* 5): *The Son of man is Lord also of the sabbath.* In the kingdom of the Redeemer, the sabbath day is to be turned into a *Lord's day;* the property of it is, in some respects, to be altered, and it is to be observed chiefly in honour of the Redeemer, as it had been before in honour of the Creator, Jer. 16:14, 15. In token of this, it shall not only have a new name, the *Lord's day* (yet not forgetting the old, for it is a sabbath of rest still) but shall be transferred to a new day, the first day of the week.

II. He justifies himself in doing *works of mercy* for others on the sabbath day. Observe in this, 1. Christ on the sabbath day *entered into the synagogue.* Note, It is our duty, as we have opportunity, to sanctify sabbaths in religious assemblies. On the sabbath there ought to be a *holy convocation;* and our place must not be empty without very good reason. 2. In the synagogue, on the sabbath day, *he taught.* Giving and receiving instruction from Christ is very proper work for a sabbath day, and for a *synagogue.* Christ took all opportunities to teach, not only his disciples, but the multitude. 3. Christ's patient was one of his hearers. *A man whose right hand was withered* came to learn from Christ. Whether he had any expectation to be healed by him does not appear. But those that would be *cured* by the grace of Christ must be willing to *learn* the doctrine of Christ. 4. Among those who were the hearers of Christ's excellent doctrine, and the eye-witnesses of his glorious miracles, there were some who came with no other design than to pick quarrels with him, *v.* 7. The scribes and Pharisees would not, as became *generous* adversaries, give him fair warning that, if he did *heal* on the sabbath day, they would construe it into a violation of the fourth commandment, which they ought in honour and justice to have done, because it was a case *without precedent* (none having ever cured as he did), but they basely *watched him,* as the lion does his prey, whether he would *heal on the sabbath day, that they might find an accusation against him,* and surprise him with a prosecution. 5. Jesus Christ was neither *ashamed* nor *afraid* to own the purposes of his grace, in the face of those who, he knew, confronted them, *v.* 8. *He knew their faults,* and what they designed, and he bade the man *rise, and stand forth,* hereby to try the patient's faith and boldness. 6. He appealed to his adversaries themselves, and to the convictions of natural conscience, whether it was the design of the fourth commandment to restrain men from doing good on the sabbath day, that good which their hand finds to do, which they have an opportunity for, and which cannot so well be put off to another time (*v.* 9): *Is it lawful to do good, or evil, on the sabbath days?* No wicked men are such *absurd* and *unreasonable* men as *persecutors* are, who study to *do evil* to men for *doing good.* 7. He healed the poor man, and restored him to the present use of his right hand, with a word's speaking, though he knew that his enemies would not only take offence at it, but take advantage against him for it, *v.* 10. Let not us be drawn off, either from our duty or usefulness, by the oppression we meet with in it. 8. His adversaries were hereby enraged so much the more against him, *v.* 11. Instead of being convinced by this miracle, as they ought to have been, that he was a teacher come from God, — instead of being brought to be in love with him as a benefactor to mankind, — they were *filled with madness,* vexed that they could not frighten him from doing good, or hinder the growth of his interest in the affections of the people. They were *mad* at Christ, *mad* at the people, *mad* at themselves. Anger is a *short madness,* malice is a *long* one; *impotent* malice, especially *disappointed* malice; such was theirs. When they could not prevent his working this miracle, they *communed one with another what they might do to Jesus,* what other way they might take to run him down. We may well stand amazed at it that the sons of men should be so wicked as to do thus, and that the Son of God should be so patient as to suffer it.

Verses 12–19

In these verses, we have our Lord Jesus in *secret,* in *his family,* and in *public;* and in all three acting like himself.

I. In *secret* we have him *praying to God, v.* 12. This evangelist takes frequent notice of Christ's retirements, to give us an example of secret prayer, by which we must keep up our communion with God daily, and without which it is impossible that the soul should prosper. *In those days,* when his enemies were filled with madness against him, and were contriving what to do to him, he went out to *pray;* that he might answer the type of David (Ps. 109:4), *For my love, they are my adversaries; but I give myself unto prayer.* Observe, 1. He was *alone* with God; he *went out into a mountain, to pray,* where he might have no disturbance or interruption given him; we are never less alone than when we are *thus* alone. Whether there was any convenient place built upon this mountain, for devout people to retire to for their private devotions, as some think, and that that *oratory,* or *place of prayer,* is meant here by *hē proseuchē tou theou,* to me seems very uncertain. He went into a mountain for privacy, and therefore, probably, would not go to a place frequented by others. 2. He was *long* alone with God: *He continued all night in prayer.* We think one half hour a great deal to spend in the *duties of the closet;* but Christ continued a *whole night* in meditation and secret prayer. We have a great deal of *business* at the throne of grace, and we should take a great *delight* in communion with God, and by both these we may be kept sometimes long at prayer.

II. In his *family* we have him nominating his immediate attendants, that should be the constant auditors of his doctrine and eye-witnesses of his miracles, that hereafter they might be sent forth as *apostles,* his *messengers* to the world, to preach his gospel to it, and plant his church in it, *v.* 13. After he had *continued all night in prayer,* one would have thought that, *when it was day,* he should have reposed himself, and got some sleep. No, as soon as any body was stirring, he *called unto him his disciples.* In serving God, our great care should be, not to *lose time,* but to make the end of one good duty the beginning of another. Ministers are to be ordained with *prayer* more than ordinarily *solemn.* The number of the apostles was *twelve.* Their names are here recorded; it is the *third time* that we have met with them, and in each of the *three* places the *order* of them differs, to teach both ministers and Christians not to be nice in precedency, not in *giving* it, much less in *taking* it, but to look upon it as a thing not worth taking notice of; let it be as it lights. He that in Mark was called *Thaddeus,* in Matthew *Lebbeus,* whose surname was *Thaddeus,* is here called *Judas the brother of James,* the same that wrote the epistle of Jude. Simon, who in Matthew and Mark was called the *Canaanite,* is here called *Simon Zelotes,* perhaps for his great zeal in religion. Concerning these twelve here named we have reason to say, as the queen of Sheba did of Solomon's servants, *Happy are thy men, and happy are these thy servants, that stand continually before thee, and hear thy wisdom;* never were men so privileged, and yet one of them had a devil, and proved a traitor (*v.* 16); yet Christ, when he chose him, was not deceived in him.

III. In *public* we have him *preaching* and *healing,* the two great works between which he divided his time, *v.* 17. He came down with the twelve from the mountain, and *stood in the plain,* ready to receive those that resorted to him; and there were presently gathered about him, not only the *company of his disciples,* who used to attend him, but also a great *multitude of people,* a mixed multitude *out of all Judea and Jerusalem.* Though it was some scores of miles from Jerusalem to that part of Galilee where Christ now was, — though at Jerusalem they had abundance of famous rabbin, that had great names, and bore a mighty sway, — yet they came to hear Christ. They came also from the *sea-coast of Tyre and Sidon.* Though they who lived there were generally men of business, and though they bordered upon Canaanites, yet there were some well affected to Christ; such there were dispersed in all parts, here and there one. 1. They *came to hear him* and he *preached* to them. Those that have not good preaching near them had better travel far for it than be without it. It is worth while to go a great way to hear the word of Christ, and to go out of the way of other business for it. 2. They came to be *cured* by him, and he *healed* them. Some were troubled *in body,* and some *in mind;* some had *diseases,* some had *devils;* but both the one and the other, upon their application to Christ, were *healed,* for he has power over *diseases* and *devils* (*v.* 17, 18), over the effects and over the causes. Nay, it should seem, those who had no *particular diseases* to complain of yet found it a great confirmation and renovation to their bodily *health* and *vigour* to partake of the *virtue that went out of him;* for (*v.* 19) *the whole multitude sought to touch him,* those that were in health as well as those that were sick, and they were all, one way or other, the better for him: he *healed them all;* and who is there that doth not need, upon some account or other, to be *healed?* There is a *fulness of grace* in Christ, and healing virtue in him, and ready to go out from him, that is enough for all, enough for each.

Verses 20–26

Here begins a practical discourse of Christ, which is continued to the end of the chapter, most of which is found in the *sermon upon the mount,* Mt. 5 and 7. Some think that this was preached at some other time and place, and there are other instances of Christ's preaching the same things, or to the same purport, at different times; but it is probable that this is only the evangelist's abridgment of that sermon, and perhaps that in Matthew too is but an abridgment; the beginning and the conclusion are much the same; and the story of the cure of the centurion's servant follows presently upon it, both there and here, but it is not material. In these verses, we have,

I. Blessings pronounced upon *suffering saints,* as *happy* people, though the world *pities them* (*v.* 20): He *lifted up his eyes upon his disciples,* not only the *twelve,* but the whole *company of them* (*v.* 17), and directed his discourse to them; for, when he had healed the sick in *the plain,* he went up again *to the mountain,* to preach. There he *sat,* as one having authority; thither *they come to him* (Mt. 5:1), and to them he directed his discourse, to them he applied it, and taught them to apply it to themselves. When he had laid it down for a truth, *Blessed are the poor in spirit,* he added, *Blessed are ye poor.* All believers, that take the precepts of the gospel to themselves, and *live by them* may take the promises of the gospel to themselves and *live upon them.* And the application, as it is here, seems especially designed to encourage the disciples, with reference to the hardships and difficulties they were likely to meet with, in following Christ.

1. "You are *poor,* you have *left all to follow me,* are content to live upon alms with me, are never to expect any worldly preferment in my service. You must work hard, and fare hard, as poor people do; but you are blessed in your poverty, it shall be no prejudice at all to your happiness; nay, you are blessed *for* it, all your losses shall be abundantly made up to you, for *yours is the kingdom of God,* all the comforts and graces of his kingdom here and all the glories and joys of his kingdom hereafter; yours it *shall be,* nay, yours *it is.*" Christ's *poor* are *rich in faith,* Jam. 2:5.

2. "You *hunger now* (*v.* 21), you are not *fed to the full* as

others are, you often rise hungry, your *commons* are so *short;* or you are so intent upon your work that you have not time to eat bread, you are glad of a few *ears of corn* for a meal's meat; thus you hunger now in this world, but in the other world *you shall be filled,* shall *hunger no more,* nor *thirst any more."*

3. "You *weep now,* are often in tears, tears of repentance, tears of sympathy; you are of them that mourn in Zion. But *blessed are you;* your present sorrows are no *prejudices* to your future joy, but *preparatories* for it: *You shall laugh.* You have triumphs in reserve; you are but *sowing in tears,* and shall shortly *reap in joy,"* Ps. 126:5, 6. They that now *sorrow after a godly sort* are treasuring up comforts for themselves, or, rather, God is treasuring up comforts for them; and the day is coming when their *mouth shall be filled with laughing and their lips with rejoicing,* Job 8:21.

4. "You now undergo *the world's ill will.* You must expect all the base treatment that a spiteful world can give you for Christ's sake, because you serve him and his interests; you must expect that wicked men will *hate you,* because your doctrine and life convict and condemn them; and those that have church-power in their hands will *separate you,* will force you to separate yourselves, and then excommunicate you for so doing, and lay you under the most ignominious censures. They will pronounce anathemas against you, as scandalous and incorrigible offenders. They will do this with all possible gravity and solemnity, and pomp and pageantry of appeals to Heaven, to make the world believe, and almost you yourselves too, that it is ratified in heaven. Thus will they endeavour to make you odious to others and a terror to yourselves." This is supposed to be the proper notion of *aphorisōsin hymas* — they shall cast you out of their synagogues. "And they that have not this power will not fail to show their malice, to the utmost of their power; for *they will reproach you,* will charge you with the blackest crimes, which you are perfectly innocent of, will fasten upon you the blackest characters, which you do not deserve; they will *cast out your name as evil,* your name as Christians, as apostles; they will do all they can to render these names odious." This is the application of the eighth beatitude, Mt. 5:10–12.

"Such usage as this seems hard; but *blessed are you* when you are so used. It is so far from depriving you of your happiness that it will greatly add to it. It is an honour to you, as it is to a brave hero to be employed in the wars, in the service of his prince; and therefore *rejoice you in that day, and leap for joy, v.* 23. Do not only *bear it,* but *triumph* in it. For," (1.) "You are hereby *highly dignified* in the *kingdom of grace,* for you are treated as the prophets were before you, and therefore not only need not be ashamed of it, but may justly rejoice in it, for it will be an evidence for you that you *walk in the same spirit,* and *in the same steps,* are engaged in the same cause, and employed in the same service, with them." (2.) "You will for this be abundantly *recompensed* in the *kingdom of glory;* not only your services for Christ, but your sufferings will come into the account: *Your reward is great in heaven.* Venture upon your sufferings, in a full belief that the glory of heaven will abundantly countervail all these hardships; so that, though you may be losers for Christ, you shall not be losers by him in the end."

II. *Woes* denounced against *prospering sinners as miserable people,* though the world *envies them.* These we had not in Matthew. It should seem, the best exposition of *these woes,* compared with the foregoing *blessings,* is the parable of the *rich man* and Lazarus. Lazarus had the blessedness of those that are *poor,* and *hunger,* and *weep,* now, for in Abraham's bosom all the promises made to them who did so were *made good* to him; but the rich man had the *woes* that follow here, as he had the character of those on whom these woes are entailed.

1. Here is a *woe* to them that are *rich,* that is, that *trust in riches,* that have abundance of this world's wealth, and, instead of serving God with it, serve their lusts with it; woe to them, for *they have received their consolation,* that which they placed their happiness in, and were willing to take up with for a portion, *v.* 24. They in their life-time received *their good things,* which, in their account, were the *best things,* and all the good things they are ever likely to receive from God. "You that are *rich* are in temptation to *set your hearts* upon a *smiling* world, and to say, Soul, *take thine ease* in the embraces of it, *This is my rest for ever, here will I dwell;* and *then woe unto you."* (1.) It is the *folly* of carnal worldlings that they make the things of this world *their consolation,*

which were intended only for their *convenience.* They please themselves with them, pride themselves in them, and make them their heaven upon earth; and to them the *consolations of God* are small, and of no account. (2.) It is their misery that they are *put off* with them as *their consolation.* Let them know it, to their terror, when they are parted from these things, there is an end of all their comfort, a final end of it, and nothing remains to them but everlasting misery and torment.

2. Here is a *woe* to them that are *full* (*v.* 25), that are *fed to the full,* and have *more than heart could wish* (Ps. 73:7), that have their *bellies filled with the hid treasures of this world* (Ps. 17:14), that, when they have abundance of these, are *full,* and think they have *enough,* they *need no more,* they *desire no more,* Rev. 3:17. *Now ye are full, now ye are rich,* 1 Co. 4:8. They are *full of themselves,* without God and Christ. Woe to such, for *they shall hunger,* they shall shortly be *stripped* and *emptied* of all the things they are so proud of; and, when they shall have *left behind them* in the world all those things which are their fulness, they shall *carry away with them* such appetites and desires as the world they remove to will afford them no gratifications of; for all the delights of sense, which they are now so full of, will in hell be *denied,* and in heaven *superseded.*

3. Here is a *woe* to them that *laugh now,* that have always a *disposition to be merry,* and always something to *make merry with;* that know no other joy than that which is carnal and sensual, and know no other use of this world's good than purely to indulge that carnal sensual joy that banishes sorrow, even godly sorrow, from their minds, and are always entertaining themselves with the laughter of the fool. *Woe unto such,* for it is but *now,* for a little time, that they *laugh;* they shall *mourn and weep* shortly, shall *mourn and weep* eternally, in a world where there is nothing but *weeping and wailing,* endless, easeless, and remediless sorrow.

4. Here is a *woe* to them *whom all men speak well of,* that is, who make it their great and only care to gain the praise and applause of men, who value themselves upon that more than upon the favour of God and his acceptance (*v.* 26): *"Woe unto you;* that is, it would be a bad sign that you were not faithful to your trust, and to the souls of men, if you preached so as that nobody would be disgusted; for your business is to tell people of their faults, and, if you do that as you ought, you will get that *ill will* which never *speaks well.* The false prophets indeed, that flattered your father in their wicked ways, that *prophesied smooth things* to them, were caressed and spoken well of; and, if you be in like manner cried up, you will be justly suspected to deal deceitfully as they did." We should desire to have the approbation of those that are wise and good, and not be indifferent to what people say of us; but, as we should despise the reproaches, so we should also despise the praises, of the fools in Israel.

Verses 27–36

These verses agree with Mt. 5:38, to the end of that chapter: *I say unto you that hear* (*v.* 27), to all you that hear, and not to disciples only, for these are lessons of universal concern. *He that has an ear, let him hear.* Those that diligently hearken to Christ shall find he has something to say to them well worth their hearing. Now the lessons Christ here teacheth us are,

I. That we must render to all their due, and be honest and just in all our dealings (*v.* 31): *As ye would that men should do to you, do ye also to them likewise;* for this is *loving your neighbour as yourselves.* What we should expect, in reason, to be done to us, either in justice or charity, by others, if they were in our condition and we in theirs, that, as the matter stands, we must do to them. We must *put our souls into their souls' stead,* and then pity and succour them, as we should desire and justly expect to be ourselves pitied and succoured.

II. That we must be free in *giving* to them that *need* (*v.* 30): *"Give to every man that asketh of thee,* to every one that is a proper object of charity, that wants necessaries, which thou hast wherewithal to supply out of thy superfluities. Give to those that are not able to help themselves, to those that have not relations in a capacity to help them." Christ would have his disciples ready to distribute, and willing to communicate, *to their power* in ordinary cases, and beyond their power in extraordinary.

III. That we must be generous in *forgiving* those that have been any way injurious to us.

1. We must not be *extreme* in *demanding* our right, when

it is denied us: *"Him that taketh away thy cloak,* either forcibly or fraudulently, *forbid him not* by any violent means to *take thy coat also, v.* 29. Let him have that too, rather than fight for it. And (*v.* 30) *of him that taketh thy goods"* (so Dr. Hammond thinks it should be read), "that borrows them, or that *takes them up* from thee upon trust, of such do not *exact them;* if Providence have made such insolvent, do not take the advantage of the law against them, but rather lose it than *take them by the throat,* Mt. 18:28. If a man run away in thy debt, and *take away thy goods* with him, do not perplex thyself, nor be incensed against him."

2. We must not be rigorous in revenging a wrong when it is done us: *"Unto him that smiteth thee on the one cheek,* instead of bringing an action against him, or sending for a writ for him, or bringing him before a justice, *offer also the other;"* that is, "pass it by, though thereby thou shouldest be in danger of bringing upon thyself another like in dignity, which is commonly pretended in excuse of taking the advantage of the law in such a case. If any one *smite thee on the cheek,* rather than give another blow to him, be ready to receive another from him;" that is, "leave it to God to plead thy cause, and do thou sit down silent under the affront." When we do thus, God will *smite our enemies,* as far as they are his, *upon the cheek bone,* so as to *break the teeth of the ungodly* (Ps. 3:7); for he hath said, *Vengeance is mine,* and he will make it appear that it is so when we leave it to him to take vengeance.

3. Nay, we must do good to them that do evil to us. This is that which our Saviour, in these verses, chiefly designs to teach us, as a law peculiar to his religion, and a branch of the perfection of it.

(1.) We must be kind to those from whom we have *received injuries.* We must not only *love our enemies,* and bear a good will to them, but we must *do good* to them, be as ready to do any good office to them as to any other person, if their case call for it, and it be in the power of our hands to do it. We must study to make it appear, by positive acts, if there be an opportunity for them, that we bear them no malice, nor see revenge. Do they *curse* us, speak ill of us, and wish ill to us? Do they *despitefully use* us, in word or deed? Do they endeavour to make us contemptible or odious? Let us *bless them,* and *pray for them,* speak well of them, the best we can, wish well to them, especially to their souls, and be intercessors with God for them. This is repeated, *v.* 35: *love your enemies,* and *do them good.* To recommend this difficult duty to us, it is represented as a generous thing, and an attainment few arrive at. *To love those that love us* has nothing *uncommon* in it, nothing peculiar to Christ's disciples, for *sinners* will *love those that love them.* There is nothing self-denying in that; it is but following nature, even in its corrupt state, and puts no force at all upon it (*v.* 32): it is no thanks to us to love those that say and do just as we would have them. "And (*v.* 33) *if you do good to them that do good to you,* and return their kindnesses, it is from a common principle of custom, honour, and gratitude; and therefore *what thanks have you?* What credit are you to the name of Christ, or what reputation do you bring to it? for *sinners also,* that know nothing of Christ and his doctrine, *do even the same.* But it becomes you to do something more excellent and eminent, herein to out-do your neighbours, to do that which sinners will not do, and which no principle of theirs can pretend to reach to: you must *render good for evil;"* not that any thanks are due to us, but *then* we are to our God *for a name and a praise* and he will have the thanks.

(2.) We must be kind to those from whom we expect no manner of advantage (*v.* 35): *Lend, hoping for nothing again.* It is meant of the rich lending to the poor a little money for their necessity, to buy daily bread for themselves and their families, or to keep them out of prison. In such a case, we must *lend,* with a resolution not to demand interest for what we lend, as we may most justly from those that borrow money to make purchases withal, or to trade with. But that is not all; we must *lend* though we have reason to suspect that what we *lend* we *lose,* lend to those who are so poor that it is not probable they will be able to pay us again. This precept will be best illustrated by that law of Moses (Deu. 15:7–10), which obliges them to lend to a *poor brother* as much as he *needed,* though the *year of release* was at hand. Here are two motives to this generous charity.

[1.] It will redound to our profit; for our *reward shall be great, v.* 35. What is given, or laid out, or lent and lost on earth, from a true principle of charity, will be made up to us in the other world, unspeakably to our advantage. "You shall not only be *repaid*, but *rewarded*, greatly rewarded; it will be said to you, *Come, ye blessed, inherit the kingdom*."

[2.] It will redound to our honour; for herein we shall resemble God in his goodness, which is the greatest glory: "*Ye shall be the children of the Highest*, shall be owned by him as his children, being like him." It is the glory of God that he is *kind to the unthankful and to the evil*, bestows the gifts of common providence even upon the worst of men, who are every day provoking him, and rebelling against him, and using those very gifts to his dishonour. Hence he infers (*v.* 36), *Be merciful, as your Father is merciful;* this explains Mt. 5:48, "*Be perfect, as our Father is perfect.* Imitate your Father in those things that are his brightest perfections." Those that are *merciful* as God is *merciful*, even *to the evil and the unthankful*, are *perfect* as God is *perfect;* so he is pleased graciously to accept it, though infinitely falling short. Charity is called the *bond of perfectness*, Col. 3:14. This should strongly engage us to be merciful to our brethren, even such as have been injurious to us, not only that God is so to others, but that he is so to us, though we have been, and are, evil and unthankful; it is of his mercies that *we* are not consumed.

Verses 37–49

All these sayings of Christ we had before in Matthew; some of them in *ch.* 7, others in other places. They were sayings that Christ often used; they needed only to be mentioned, it was easy to apply them. Grotius thinks that we need not be critical here in seeking for the coherence: they are golden sentences, like Solomon's proverbs or parables. Let us observe here,

I. We ought to be very candid in our censures of others, because we need grains of allowance ourselves: "Therefore *judge not* others, because then *you* yourselves *shall not be judged;* therefore *condemn not* others, because then *you* yourselves *shall not be condemned*, *v.* 37. Exercise towards others that charity which *thinks no evil*, which *bears all things, believes* and *hopes all things;* and then others will exercise that charity towards you. God will not *judge* and *condemn* you, men will not." They that are merciful to other people's names shall find others merciful to theirs.

II. If we are of a *giving* and a *forgiving* spirit, we shall ourselves reap the benefit of it: *Forgive and you shall be forgiven.* If we forgive the injuries done to us by others, others will forgive our inadvertencies. If we forgive others' trespasses against *us*, God will forgive our trespasses against *him.* And he will be no less mindful of the *liberal* that *devise liberal things* (*v.* 38): *Give, and it shall be given to you.* God, in his providence, will recompense it to you; it is *lent* to him, and *he is not unrighteous to forget* it (Heb. 6:10), but he will *pay it again. Men* shall *return it into your bosom;* for God often makes use of *men* as instruments, not only of his *avenging*, but of his *rewarding* justice. If we in a right manner give to others when they need, God will incline the hearts of others to give to us when we need, and to give liberally, *good measure pressed down and shaken together.* They that *sow plentifully* shall *reap plentifully.* Whom God recompenses he recompenses *abundantly.*

III. We must expect to be dealt with ourselves as we deal with others: *With the same measure that ye mete it shall be measured to you again.* Those that deal *hardly* with others must acknowledge, as Adoni-bezek did (Jdg. 1:7), that God is righteous, if others deal hardly with them, and they may expect to be paid in their own coin; but they that deal *kindly* with others have reason to hope that, when they have occasion, God will raise them up friends who will deal kindly with them. Though Providence does not always go by this rule, because the full and exact retributions are reserved for another world, yet, ordinarily, it observes a proportion sufficient to deter us from all acts of rigour and to encourage us in all acts of beneficence.

IV. Those who put themselves under the guidance of the ignorant and erroneous are likely to perish with them (*v.* 39): *Can the blind lead the blind?* Can the Pharisees, who are blinded with pride, prejudice, and bigotry, *lead the blind* people into the right way? *Shall not both fall* together *into the ditch?* How can they expect any other? Those that are led by the common opinion, course, and custom, of this world, are themselves blind, and are led by the blind, and will perish with the world that *sits in darkness.* Those that ignorantly, and at a venture, *follow the multitude to do evil*, follow the blind in the broad way that leads the many to *destruction.*

V. Christ's followers cannot expect better treatment in the world than their Master had, *v.* 40. Let them not promise themselves more honour or pleasure in the world than Christ had, nor aim at the worldly pomp and grandeur which he was never ambitious of, but always declined, nor affect that power in secular things which he would not assume; but every one that would show himself *perfect*, an established disciple, let him be *as his Master* — dead to the world, and every thing in it, as his Master is; let him live a life of labour and self-denial as his Master doth, and make himself a servant of all; let him stoop, and let him toil, and do all the good he can, and then he will be a complete disciple.

VI. Those who take upon them to rebuke and reform others are concerned to look to it that they be themselves blameless, and harmless, and without rebuke, *v.* 41, 42. 1. Those with a very ill grace censure the faults of others who are not aware of their own faults. It is very absurd for any to pretend to be so quick-sighted as to spy small faults in others, like a mote in the eye, when they are themselves so perfectly past feeling as not to perceive *a beam in their own eye.* 2. Those are altogether unfit to help to reform others whose reforming charity does not begin at home. How canst thou offer thy service to thy brother, to *pull out the mote from his eye*, which requires a good eye as well as a good hand, when thou thyself hast a *beam in thine own eye*, and makest no complaint of it? 3. Those therefore who would be serviceable to the souls of others must first make it appear that they are solicitous about their own souls. To help to pull the mote out of our brother's eye is a good work, but then we must qualify ourselves for it by beginning with ourselves; and our reforming our own lives may, by the influence of example, contribute to others reforming theirs.

VII. We may expect that men's words and actions will be according as *they* are, according as their hearts are, and according as their principles are.

1. The heart is the *tree*, and the words and actions are fruit according to the nature of the tree, *v.* 43, 44. If a man be really a *good man*, if he have a principle of grace in his heart, and the prevailing bent and bias of the soul be towards God and heaven, though perhaps he may not abound in fruit, though some of his fruits be blasted, and though he may be sometimes like a tree in winter, yet he does not *bring forth corrupt fruit;* though he may not do you all the good he should, yet he will not in any material instance do you hurt. If he cannot reform ill manners, he will not *corrupt good manners.* If the fruit that a man brings forth be *corrupt*, if a man's devotion tend to debauch the mind and conversation, if a man's conversation be vicious, if he be a drunkard or fornicator, if he be a swearer or liar, if he be in any instance unjust or unnatural, his *fruit is corrupt*, and you may be sure that he is not a *good tree.* On the other hand, a *corrupt tree doth not bring forth good fruit*, though it may bring forth green leaves; *for of thorns men do not gather figs, nor of a bramble do they gather grapes.* You may, if you please, stick figs upon thorns, and hang a bunch of grapes upon a bramble, but they neither are, nor can be, the natural product of the trees; so neither can you expect any *good conduct* from those who have justly a *bad character.* If the fruit be good, you may conclude that the tree is so; if the conversation be holy, heavenly, and regular, though you cannot infallibly know the heart, yet you may charitably hope that it is upright with God; for *every tree is known by its fruit.* But the *vile person will speak villany* (Isa. 32:6), and the experience of the moderns herein agrees with the *proverb of the ancients*, that *wickedness proceedeth from the wicked*, 1 Sa. 24:13.

2. The heart is the *treasure*, and the words and actions are the expenses or produce from that treasure, *v.* 45. This we had, Mt. 12:34, 35. The reigning love of God and Christ in the heart denominates a man *a good man;* and it is *a good treasure* a man may bring forth that which is good. But where the love of the world and the flesh reign there is an *evil treasure* in the heart, out of which an *evil man* is continually bringing forth *that which is evil;* and by what is brought forth you may know what is in the heart, as you may know what is in the vessel, water or wine, by what is *drawn out from it*, Jn. 2:8. *Of the abundance of the heart the mouth speaks;* what the mouth ordinarily speaks, speaks with relish and delight, generally agrees with what is innermost and uppermost in the heart: *He that speaks of the earth is earthly*, Jn. 3:31. Not but that a good man may possibly drop a bad word, and a wicked man make use of a good word to serve a bad turn; but, for the most part, the heart is as the words are, *vain* or *serious;* it therefore concerns us to get our hearts filled, not only with *good*, but with *abundance* of it.

VIII. It is not enough to *hear* the sayings of Christ, but we must *do* them; not enough to profess relation to him, as his servants, but we must make conscience of obeying him.

1. It is putting an *affront upon him* to call him *Lord, Lord*, as if we were wholly at his command, and had devoted ourselves to his service, if we do not make conscience of conforming to his will and serving the interests of his kingdom. We do but mock Christ, as they that in scorn said, *Hail, King of the Jews*, if we call him ever so often *Lord, Lord*, and yet walk in the way of our own hearts and in the sight of our own eyes. Why do we call him *Lord, Lord*, in prayer (compare Mt. 7:21, 22), if we do not obey his commands? He that *turns away his ear from hearing the law, his prayer shall be an abomination.*

2. It is *putting a cheat* upon ourselves if we think that a bare profession of religion will save us, that *hearing* the sayings of Christ will bring us to heaven, without *doing* them. This he illustrates by a similitude (*v.* 47–49), which shows,

(1.) That those only make sure work for their souls and eternity, and take the course that will stand them in stead in a trying time, who do not only *come* to Christ as his scholars, and *hear his sayings* but do them, who think, and speak, and act, in every thing according to the established rules of his holy religion. They are like a *house built on a rock.* These are they that *take pains* in religion, as they do, — that *dig deep*, that found their hope upon Christ, who is the Rock of ages (and other foundation can no man lay); these are they who *provide for hereafter*, who get ready for the worst, who lay up in store a good foundation for the *time to come*, for the *eternity to come*, 1 Tim. 6:19. They who do thus do well for themselves; for, [1.] They shall keep their integrity, in times of temptation and persecution; when others fall from their own stedfastness, as the seed on the stony ground, they shall *stand fast in the Lord.* [2.] They shall keep their comfort, and peace, and hope, and joy, in the midst of the greatest distresses. The *storms* and *streams* of affliction shall not shock them, for their feet are *set upon a rock*, a rock *higher than they.* [3.] Their everlasting welfare is secured. In death and judgment they are safe. Obedient believers are *kept by the power of Christ, through faith, unto salvation*, and shall never perish.

(2.) That those who rest in a bare hearing of the sayings of Christ, and do not live up to them, are but preparing for a fatal disappointment: *He that heareth and doeth not* (that knows his duty, but lives in the neglect of it), he is like a man that *built a house without a foundation.* He pleases himself with hopes that he has no ground for, and his hopes will fail him when he most needs the *comfort* of them, and when he expects the *crowning* of them; when the *stream beats vehemently* upon his house, it is gone, the sand it is built upon is washed away, and *immediately it falls*, Such is the *hope of the hypocrite, though he has gained, when God takes away his soul;* it is as the spider's web, and the giving up of the ghost.

CHAPTER 7

In this chapter we have, I. Christ confirming the doctrine he had preached in the former chapter, with two glorious miracles — the curing of one at a distance, and that was the centurion's servant (*v.* 1–10), and the raising of one to life that was dead, the widow's son at Nain (*v.* 11–18). II. Christ confirming the faith of John who was now in prison, and of some of his disciples, by sending him a short account of the miracles he wrought, in answer to a question he received from him (*v.* 19–23), to which he adds an honourable testimony concerning John, and a just reproof to the men of that generation for the contempt they put upon him and his doctrine (*v.* 24–35). III. Christ comforting a poor penitent that applied herself to him, all in tears of godly sorrow for sin, assuring her that her sins were pardoned, and justifying himself in the favour he showed her against the cavils of a proud Pharisee (*v.* 36–50).

Verses 1–10

Some difference there is between this story of the cure of the centurion's servant as it is related here and as we had it in Mt. 8:5, etc. There it was said that the centurion came to Christ; here it is said that he sent to him first some of the *elders of the Jews* (*v.* 3), and afterwards some other *friends*, *v.* 6. But it is a rule that *we are said to do that which we do by another — Quod facimus per alium, id ipsum facere judicamur.* The centurion might be said to do that which he did by his proxies; as a man takes possession by his attorney. But it is probable that the centurion himself came at last, when Christ said to him (Mt. 8:13), *As thou hast believed, so be it done unto thee.*

This miracle is here said to have been wrought by our Lord Jesus *when he had ended all his sayings in the audience of the people, v.* 1. What Christ said he said *publicly;* whoever would might come and hear him: *In secret have I said nothing,* Jn. 18:20. Now, to give an undeniable proof of the *authority* of his *preaching word,* he here gives an incontestable proof of the *power* and *efficacy* of his *healing word.* He that had such a commanding empire in the kingdom of nature as that he could command away diseases, no doubt has such a sovereignty in the kingdom of grace as to enjoin duties displeasing to flesh and blood, and bind, under the highest penalties, to the observance of them. This miracle was wrought in Capernaum, where most of Christ's mighty works were done, Mt. 11:23. Now observe,

I. The centurion's servant that was sick was *dear to his master, v.* 2. It was the praise of the servant that by his diligence and faithfulness, and a manifest concern for his master and his interest, as for himself and for his own, he recommended himself to his master's esteem and love. Servants should study to *endear* themselves to their masters. It was likewise the praise of the master that, when he had a good servant, he knew how to value him. Many masters, that are haughty and imperious, think it favour enough to the best servants they have not to rate them, and beat them, and be cruel to them, whereas they ought to be kind to them, and tender of them, and solicitous for their welfare and comfort.

II. The master, *when he heard of Jesus,* was for making application to him, *v.* 3. Masters ought to take particular care of their servants when they are *sick,* and not to neglect them then. This centurion begged that *Christ would come and heal his servant.* We may now, by faithful and fervent prayer, apply ourselves to Christ in heaven, and ought to do so, when sickness is in our families; for Christ is still the great Physician.

III. He sent some of the *elders of the Jews* to Christ, to represent the case, and solicit for him, thinking that a greater piece of respect to Christ than if he had come himself, because he was an uncircumcised Gentile, whom he thought Christ, being a prophet, would not care for conversing with. For that reason he sent Jews, whom he acknowledged to be favourites of Heaven, and not ordinary Jews neither, but *elders of the Jews,* persons in authority, that the dignity of the messengers might give honour to him to whom they were sent. Balak sent princes to Balaam.

IV. The elders of the Jews were hearty intercessors for the centurion: *They besought him instantly* (*v.* 4), were very urgent with him, pleading for the centurion that which he would never have pleaded for himself, *that he was worthy for whom he should do this.* If any Gentile was qualified to receive such a favour, surely he was. The centurion said, *I am not* so much as *worthy* of a visit (Mt. 8:8), but the elders of the Jews thought him worthy of the cure; thus *honour shall uphold the humble in spirit. Let another man praise thee, and not thy own mouth.* But that which they insisted upon in particular was, that, though he was a Gentile, yet he was a hearty well-wisher to the Jewish nation and religion, *v.* 5. They thought there needed as much with Christ as there did with them to remove the prejudices against him as a Gentile, a Roman, and an officer of the army, and therefore mention this, 1. That he was well-affected to the people of the Jews: *He loveth our nation* (which few of the Gentile did). Probably he had read the Old Testament, whence it was easy to advance to a very high esteem of the Jewish nation, as favoured by Heaven above all people. Note, Even conquerors, and those *in power,* ought to keep up an affection for the conquered, and those they have *power over.* 2. That he was well-affected to their worship: *He built them a* new *synagogue* at Capernaum, finding that what they had was either gone to decay or not large enough to contain the people, and that the inhabitants were not of ability to build one for themselves. Hereby he testified his veneration for the God of Israel, his belief of his being the one only living and true God, and his desire, like that of Darius, to have an interest in the prayers of God's Israel, Ezra 6:10. This centurion built a synagogue at his own proper costs and charges, and probably employed his soldiers that were in garrison there in the building, to keep them from idleness. Note, Building places of meeting for religious worship is a very *good work,* is an instance of love to God and his people; and those who do good works of that kind are *worthy of double honour.*

V. Jesus Christ was very ready to show kindness to the centurion. He presently *went with them* (*v.* 6), though he was a Gentile; for *is he the Saviour of the Jews only? Is he not also of the Gentiles? Yes, of the Gentiles also,* Rom. 3:29. The centurion did not think himself worthy to visit Christ (*v.* 7), yet Christ thought him worthy to be visited by him; for those that *humble themselves shall be exalted.*

VI. The centurion, when he heard that Christ was doing him the honour to come to his house, gave further proofs both of his humility and of his faith. Thus the graces of the saints are quickened by Christ's approaches towards them. *When he was now not far from the house,* and the centurion had notice of it, instead of setting his house in order for his reception, he *sends friends* to meet him with fresh expressions, 1. Of his *humility: "Lord, trouble not thyself,* for I am unworthy of such an honour, because I am a Gentile." This bespeaks not only his low thoughts of himself notwithstanding the greatness of his figure; but his high thoughts of Christ, notwithstanding the meanness of his figure in the world. He knew how to honour a prophet of God, though he was despised and rejected of men. 2. Of his *faith:* "Lord, *trouble not thyself,* for I know there is no occasion; thou canst *cure* my servant without coming *under my roof,* by that almighty power from which *no thought can be withholden. Say, in a word, and my servant shall be healed:"* so far was this centurion from Namaan's fancy, that he should come to him, and stand, and *strike his hand over the* patient, and so *recover* him, 2 Ki. 5:11. He illustrates this faith of his by a comparison taken from his own profession, and is confident that Christ can as easily command away the distemper as he can command any of his soldiers, can as easily send an angel with commission to cure this servant of his as he can send a soldier on an errand, *v.* 8. Christ has a sovereign power over all the creatures and all their actions, and can change the course of nature as he pleases, can rectify its disorders and repair its decays in human bodies; for *all power is given to him.*

VII. Our Lord Jesus was wonderfully well pleased with the faith of the centurion, and the more surprised at it because he was a Gentile; and, the centurion's faith having thus honoured Christ, see how he honoured it (*v.* 9): *He turned him about,* as one amazed, and *said to the people that followed him, I have not found so great faith, no not in Israel.* Note, Christ will have those that follow him to observe and take notice of the great examples of faith that are sometimes set before them — especially when any such are found among those that do not follow Christ so closely as they do in profession — that we may be shamed by the strength of their faith out of the weakness and waverings of ours.

VIII. The cure was *presently* and *perfectly* wrought (*v.* 10). *They that were sent* knew they had their errand, and therefore went back, and found the servant well, and under no remains at all of his distemper. Christ will take cognizance of the distressed case of poor servants, and be ready to relieve them; for there *is no respect of persons with him.* Nor are the Gentiles excluded from the benefit of his grace; nay, this was a specimen of that much greater faith which would be found among the Gentiles, when the gospel should be published, than among the Jews.

Verses 11–18

We have here the story of Christ's raising to life a widow's son at Nain, that was dead and in the carrying out to be buried, which Matthew and Mark had made no mention of; only, in the general, Matthew had recorded it, in Christ's answer to the disciples of John, that *the dead were raised* up, Mt. 11:5. Observe,

I. Where, and when, this miracle was wrought. It was the *next day after* he had cured the centurion's servant, *v.* 11. Christ was doing good *every day,* and never had cause to complain that he had *lost a day.* It was done at the gate of a small city, or town, called *Nain,* not far from Capernaum, probably the same with a city called *Nais,* which Jerome speaks of.

II. Who were the witnesses of it. It is as well attested as can be, for it was done in the sight of two crowds that met in or near the gate of the city. There was a crowd of *disciples* and other *people* attending Christ (*v.* 11), and a crowd of relations and neighbours attending the funeral of the young man, *v.* 12. Thus there was a sufficient number to attest the truth of this miracle, which furnished greater proof of Christ's divine authority than his healing diseases; for by no power of nature, or any means, can the dead be raised.

III. How it was wrought by our Lord Jesus.

1. The person raised to life was a *young man,* cut off by death in the beginning of his days — a common case; *man comes forth like a flower and is cut down.* That he was really dead was universally agreed. There could be no collusion in the case; for Christ was *entering into the town,* and had not seen him till now that he met him upon the bier. He was *carried out* of the city; for the Jews' burying-places were without their cities, and at some distance from them. This young man was the *only son of his mother,* and *she a widow.* She depended upon him to be the staff of her old age, but he proves a broken reed; every man at his best estate is so. How numerous, how various, how very calamitous, are the afflictions of the afflicted in this world! What a vale of tears is it! What a Bochim, a place of weepers! We may well think how deep the *sorrow* of this poor mother was for her *only son* (such sorrowing is referred to as expressive of the greatest grief, — Zec. 12:10), and it was the deeper in that she was a *widow,* broken with breach upon breach, and a *full end made of her comforts. Much people of the city was with her, condoling* with her loss, to *comfort* her.

2. Christ showed both his *pity* and his *power* in raising him to life, that he might give a specimen of both, which shine so brightly in man's redemption.

(1.) See how *tender* his *compassions* are towards the afflicted (*v.* 13): *When the Lord saw* the poor widow following her son to the grave, *he had compassion on her.* Here was not application made to him for her, not so much as that he would speak some words of comfort to her, but, *ex mero motu — purely from the goodness of his nature,* he was troubled for her. The case was piteous, and he looked upon it with pity. His eye affected his heart; and he *said unto her, Weep not.* Note, Christ has a concern for the mourners, for the miserable, and often *prevents them with the blessing of his goodness.* He undertook the work of our redemption and salvation, *in his love and in his pity,* Isa. 63:9. What a pleasing idea does this give us of the compassions of the Lord Jesus, and the multitude of his *tender mercies,* which may be very comfortable to us when at any time we are in sorrow! Let poor widows comfort themselves in their sorrows with this, that Christ *pities them* and knows their souls in adversity; and, if others despise their grief, he does not. Christ said, *Weep not;* and he could give her a reason for it which no one else could: "Weep not for a *dead son,* for he shall presently become a *living one."* This was a reason peculiar to her case; yet there is a reason common to all that sleep in Jesus, which is of equal force against inordinate and excessive grief for their death — that they shall rise again, shall rise in glory; and therefore we must *not sorrow as those that have no hope,* 1 Th. 4:13. Let Rachel, that *weeps for her children, refrain her eyes from tears,* for *there is hope in thine end, saith the Lord, that thy children shall come again to their own border,* Jer. 31:17. And let our *passion* at such a time be checked and claimed by the consideration of Christ's *compassion.*

(2.) See how *triumphant* his *commands* are over even death itself (*v.* 14): *He came, and touched the bier,* or coffin, in or upon which the dead body lay; for to him it would be no pollution. Hereby he intimated to the bearers that they should not proceed; he had something to say to the dead young man. *Deliver him from going down to the pit; I have found a ransom,* Job 33:24. Hereupon *they that bore him stood still,* and probably let down the bier from their shoulders to the ground, and opened the coffin, it if was closed up; and then with solemnity, as one that had authority, and to whom belonged the issues from death, he said, *Young man, I say unto thee, Arise.* The young man was *dead,* and could not arise by any power of his own (no more can those that are spiritually dead in trespasses and sins); yet it was no absurdity at all for Christ to bid him *arise,* when a power went along with that word to *put life* into him. The gospel call to all people, to young people particularly, is, *"Arise,* arise from the dead, and Christ shall give you light and life." Christ's dominion over death was evidenced by the immediate effect of his word (*v.* 15): *He that was dead sat up.* Have we grace from Christ? Let us show it. Another evidence of life was that he *began to speak;* for whenever Christ gives us spiritual life he *opens the lips* in prayer and praise. And, *lastly,* he would not oblige this young man, to whom he had given a new life, to go along with him as his disciple, to minister to him (though he owed him even his own self), much less as a trophy or show to get honour by him, but *delivered him to his mother,* to attend her as became a dutiful son; for Christ's miracles were miracles of mercy, and a great act of mercy this was to this widow; now she was *comforted,* according to the time in which she had been afflicted and much more, for she could now look upon this son as a particular favourite of Heaven, with more pleasure than if he had not died.

IV. What influence it had upon the people (*v.* 16): *There came a fear on all;* it frightened them all, to see a dead man start up alive out of his coffin in the open street, at the command of a man; they were all struck with wonder at his miracle, and *glorified God.* The Lord and his goodness, as well as the Lord and his greatness, are to be feared. The inference they drew from it was, *"A great prophet is risen up among us,* the great prophet that we have been long looking for; doubtless, he is one divinely inspired who can thus breathe life into the dead, and in him *God hath visited his people,* to redeem them, as was expected," Lu. 1:68. This would be *life from the dead* indeed to all them that waited for the consolation of Israel. When dead souls are thus raised to spiritual life, by a divine power going along with the gospel, we must glorify God, and look upon it as a gracious visit to his people. The report of this miracle was carried, 1. In general, all the country over (*v.* 17): *This rumour of him,* that he was the great prophet, *went forth* upon the wings of fame *through all Judea,* which lay a great way off, and throughout all Galilee, which was the *region round about.* Most had this notice of him, yet few believed in him, and gave up themselves to him. Many have the *rumour* of Christ's gospel in their ears that have not the *savour* and *relish* of it in their souls. 2. In particular, it was carefully brought to John Baptist, who was now in prison (*v.* 18): *His disciples came,* and gave him an account of all things, that he might know that though *he* was bound yet *the word of the Lord was not bound;* God's work was going on, though he was laid aside.

Verses 19–35

All this discourse concerning John Baptist, occasioned by his sending to ask whether he was the Messiah or no, we had, much as it is here related, Mt. 11:2–19.

I. We have here the message John Baptist sent to Christ, and the return he made to it. Observe,

1. The great thing we are to enquire concerning Christ is whether he be he that should come to redeem and save sinners, or whether we are to look for another, *v.* 19, 20. We are sure that God has promised that a Saviour shall come, an anointed Saviour; we are as sure that what he has promised he will perform in its season. If this Jesus be that promised Messiah, we will receive him, and will look for no other; but, if not, we will continue our expectations, and, though he tarry, will wait for him.

2. The faith of John Baptist himself, or at least of his disciples, wanted to be *confirmed* in this matter; for Christ had not yet publicly declared himself to be indeed the Christ, nay, he would not have his disciples, who knew him to be so, to speak of it, till the proofs of his being so were completed in his resurrection. The great men of the Jewish church had not owned him, nor had he gained any interest that was likely to set him upon the throne of his father David. Nothing of that power and grandeur was to be seen about him in which it was expected that the Messiah would appear; and therefore it is not strange that they should ask, *Art thou the Messiah?* not doubting but that, if he was not, he would direct them what *other* to *look for.*

3. Christ left it to his own works to praise him in the gates, to tell what he was and to prove it. While John's messengers were with him, he wrought many miraculous cures, *in that same hour,* which perhaps intimates that they staid but *an hour* with him; and what a deal of work did Christ do in a little time! *v.* 21. *He cured many of their infirmities and plagues* in body, and of *evil spirits* that affected the mind either with frenzy or melancholy, and *unto many that were blind he gave sight.* He multiplied the cures, that there might be no ground left to suspect a fraud; and then (*v.* 22) he bade them *go and tell John what they had seen.* And he and they might easily argue, as even the common people did (Jn. 7:31), *When Christ cometh, will he do more miracles than these which this man hath done?* These cures, which they saw him work, were not only confirmations of his commission, but explications of it. The Messiah must come to cure a diseased world, to give light and sight to them that sit in darkness, and to restrain and conquer evil spirits. You see that Jesus does this to the bodies of people, and therefore must conclude this is he that should come to do it to the souls of people, and you are to *look for no other.* To his miracles in the kingdom of nature he adds this in the kingdom of grace (*v.* 22), *To the poor the gospel is preached,* which they knew was to be done by the Messiah; for he was anointed to *preach the gospel to the meek* (Isa. 61:1), and to *save the souls of the poor and needy,* Ps. 72:13. Judge, therefore, whether you can look for any other that will more fully answer the characters of the Messiah and the great intentions of his coming.

4. He gave them an intimation of the danger people were in of being prejudiced against him, notwithstanding these evident proofs of his being the Messiah (*v.* 23): *Blessed is he whosoever shall not be offended in me,* or *scandalized* at me. We are here in a state of trial and probation; and it is agreeable to such a state that, as there are sufficient arguments to *confirm the truth* to those that are *honest* and *impartial* in searching after it, and have their minds prepared to receive it, so there should be also objections, to *cloud the truth* to those that are careless, worldly, and sensual. Christ's education at Nazareth, his residence at Galilee, the meanness of his family and relations, his poverty, and the despicableness of his followers – these and the like were stumbling-blocks to many, which all the miracles he wrought could not help them over. He is *blessed,* for he is wise, humble, and well disposed, that is not overcome by these prejudices. It is a sign that God has *blessed* him, for it is by his grace that he is helped over these stumbling-stones; *and he shall be blessed* indeed, blessed in Christ.

II. We have here the high encomium which Christ gave of John Baptist; not while his messengers were present (lest he should seem to flatter him), but *when they were departed* (*v.* 24), to make the people sensible of the advantages they had enjoyed in John's ministry, and were deprived of by his imprisonment. Let them now consider *what they went out into the wilderness to see,* who that was about whom there had been so much talk and such a great and general amazement. "Come," saith Christ, "I will tell you."

1. He was a man of unshaken *self-consistence,* a man of steadiness and constancy. He was not a *reed shaken with the wind,* first in one direction and then in another, shifting with every wind; he was *firm* as a *rock,* not *fickle* as a *reed.* If he could have bowed like a *reed* to Herod, and have complied with the court, he might have been a favourite there; but *none of these things moved him.*

2. He was a man of unparalleled *self-denial,* a great example of mortification and contempt of the world. He was not *a man clothed in soft raiment,* nor did he *live delicately* (*v.* 25); but, on the contrary, he lived in a wilderness and was clad and fed accordingly. Instead of adorning and pampering the body, he brought it under, and kept it in subjection.

3. He was *a prophet,* had his commission and instructions immediately from God, and not of man or by man. He was by birth a *priest,* but that is never taken notice of; for his glory, as a prophet, eclipsed the honour of his priesthood. Nay, he was *more,* he was *much more than a prophet* (*v.* 26), than any of the prophets of the Old Testament; for they spoke of Christ as at a distance, he spoke of him as at the door.

4. He was the harbinger and forerunner of the Messiah, and was himself prophesied of in the Old Testament (*v.* 27): *This is he of whom it is written* (Mal. 3:1), *Behold, I send my messenger before thy face.* Before he sent the Master himself, he sent a messenger, to give notice of his coming, and prepare people to receive him. Had the Messiah been to appear as a *temporal prince,* under which character the carnal Jews expected him, his *messenger* would have appeared either in the *pomp* of a *general* or the *gaiety* of a *herald at arms;* but it was a *previous* indication, plain enough, of the *spiritual* nature of Christ's kingdom, that the messenger he sent before him to *prepare his way* did it by preaching repentance and reformation of men's hearts and lives. Certainly that kingdom was not of this world which was thus ushered in.

5. He was, upon this account, so great, that really there was not a *greater prophet* than he. *Prophets* were the *greatest* that were *born of women,* more honourable than kings and princes, and John was the *greatest* of all the *prophets.* The country was not sensible what a *valuable,* what an *invaluable,* man it had in it, when John Baptist went about preaching and baptizing. And yet *he that is least in the kingdom of God is greater than he.* The least gospel minister, that has obtained mercy of the Lord to be *skilful* and *faithful* in his work, or the meanest of the *apostles* and first preachers of the gospel, being *employed* under a more *excellent* dispensation, are in a more honourable office than John Baptist. The meanest of those that *follow the Lamb* far excel the greatest of those that went before him. Those therefore who live under the gospel dispensation have so much the more to answer for.

III. We have here the just censure of the men of that generation, who were not wrought upon by the ministry either of John Baptist or of Jesus Christ himself.

1. Christ here shows what contempt was put upon John Baptist, while he was preaching and baptizing. (1.) Those who did show him any respect were but the common ordinary sort of people, who, in the eye of the gay part of mankind, were rather a disgrace to him than a credit, *v.* 29. *The people* indeed, the vulgar herd, of whom it was said, *This people, who know not the law, are cursed* (Jn. 7:49), and the publicans, men of ill fame, as being generally men of bad morals, or taken to be so, these were *baptized with his baptism,* and became his disciples; and these, though glorious monuments of divine grace, yet did not *magnify John* in the eye of the world; but by their repentance and reformation they *justified God,* justified his conduct and the wisdom of it in appointing such a one as John Baptist to be the forerunner of the Messiah: they hereby made it to appear that it was the best method that could be taken, for it was not in vain to *them* whatever it was to others. (2.) The great men of their church and nation, the *polite* and the *politicians,* that would have done him some credit in the eye of the world, did him all the dishonour they could; they heard him indeed, but they were not *baptized of him, v.* 30. The Pharisees, who were most in reputation for religion and devotion, and the lawyers, who were celebrated for their learning, especially their knowledge of the scriptures, *rejected the counsel of God against themselves;* they *frustrated it,* they *received the grace of God,* by the baptism of John, in *vain.* God in sending that *messenger* among them had a kind *purpose* of good to them, *designed* their salvation by it, and, if they had closed with the counsel of God, it had been *for themselves,* they had been made for ever; but they *rejected it,* would not comply with it, and it was *against themselves,* it was to their own ruin; they came short of the benefit intended them, and not only so, but forfeited the grace of God, put a bar in their own door, and, by refusing that discipline which was to fit them for the kingdom of the Messiah, shut themselves out of it, and they not only excluded themselves, but hindered others, and stood in their way.

2. He here shows the strange perverseness of the men of that generation, in their cavils both against John and Christ, and the prejudices they conceived against them.

(1.) They made but a jesting matter of the methods God took to do them good (*v.* 31): *"Whereunto shall I liken the men of this generation?* What can I think of absurd enough to represent them by? They are, then, *like children sitting in the market-place,* that mind nothing that is serious, but are as full of play as they can hold. As if God were but in jest with them, in all the methods he takes to do them good, as children are with one another in the market-place (*v.* 32), they turn it all off with a banter, and are not more affected with it than with a piece of pageantry." This is the ruin of multitudes, they can never persuade themselves to be *serious* in the concerns of their souls. Old men, sitting in the sanhedrim, were but as *children sitting in the market-place,* and no more affected with the things that belonged to their everlasting peace than people are with children's play. O the amazing stupidity and vanity of the blind and ungodly world! The Lord awaken them out of their security.

(2.) They still found something or other to carp at. [1.] John Baptist was a reserved austere man, lived much in solitude, and ought to have been admired for being such a humble, sober, self-denying man, and hearkened to as a man of thought and contemplation; but this, which was his praise, was turned to his reproach. Because he came *neither eating nor drinking,* so freely, plentifully, and cheerfully, as others did, *you say, "He has a devil;* he is a melancholy man, he is possessed, as the demoniac whose dwelling was *among the tombs,* though he be not quite so wild." [2.] Our Lord Jesus was of a more free and open conversation; he *came eating and drinking, v.* 34. He would go and dine with Pharisees, though he knew they did not care for him; and with publicans, though he knew they were no credit to him; yet, in hopes of doing good both to the one and the other, he conversed familiarly with them. By this it appears that the ministers of Christ may be of very different tempers and dispositions, very different ways of preaching and living, and yet all good and useful; *diversity of gifts*, but each given to *profit withal*. Therefore none must make themselves a standard to all others, nor judge hardly of those that do not do just as they do. John Baptist bore witness to Christ, and Christ applauded John Baptist, though they were the reverse of each other in their way of living. But the common enemies of them both reproached them both. The very same men that had represented John as *crazed in his intellects*, because he came *neither eating nor drinking*, represented our Lord Jesus as *corrupt in his morals*, because he came *eating and drinking; he is a gluttonous man, and a wine-bibber*. Ill-will never speaks well. See the malice of wicked people, and how they put the worst construction upon every thing they meet with in the gospel, and in the preachers and professors of it; and hereby they think to depreciate *them*, but really destroy *themselves*.

3. He shows that, notwithstanding this, God will be glorified in the salvation of a chosen remnant (*v.* 35): *Wisdom is justified of all her children*. There are those who are given to wisdom *as her children*, and they shall be brought by the grace of God to submit to wisdom's conduct and government, and thereby to justify wisdom in the ways she takes for bringing them to that submission; for to them they are effectual, and thereby appear well chosen. Wisdom's children are herein unanimous, one and all, they have all a complacency in the methods of grace which divine wisdom takes, and think never the worse of them for their being ridiculed by some.

Verses 36–50

When and where this passage of story happened does not appear; this evangelist does not observe order of time in his narrative so much as the other evangelists do; but it comes in here, upon occasion of Christ's being reproached as *a friend to publicans and sinners*, to show that it was only for their good, and to bring them to repentance, that he conversed with them; and that those whom he admitted hear him were reformed, or in a hopeful way to be so. Who this woman was that here testified so great an affection to Christ does not appear; it is commonly said to be Mary Magdalene, but I find no ground in scripture for it: she is described (*ch.* 8:2 and *Mk.* 16:9) to be one *out of whom Christ had cast seven devils;* but that is not mentioned here, and therefore it is probable that it was not she. Now observe here,

I. The civil entertainment which a Pharisee gave to Christ, and his gracious acceptance of that entertainment (*v.* 36): *One of the Pharisees desired him that he would eat with him*, either because he thought it would be a reputation to him to have such a guest at his table or because his company would be an entertainment to him and his family and friends. It appears that this Pharisee did not believe in Christ, for he will not own him to be a *prophet* (*v.* 39), and yet our Lord Jesus accepted his invitation, *went into his house, and sat down to meat*, that they might see he took the same liberty with Pharisees that he did with publicans, in hopes of *doing them good*. And those may venture further into the society of such as are prejudiced against Christ, and his religion, who have wisdom and grace sufficient to instruct and argue with them, than others may.

II. The great respect which a poor penitent sinner showed him, when he was at meat in the Pharisee's house. It was a woman in the city *that was a sinner*, a Gentile, a *harlot*, I doubt, known to be so, and infamous. She *knew that Jesus sat at meat in the Pharisee's house*, and, having been converted from her wicked course of life by his preaching, she came to acknowledge her obligations to him, having no opportunity of doing it in any other way than by *washing* his feet, and anointing them with some sweet ointment that she brought with her for that purpose. The way of sitting at table then was such that their feet were partly *behind them*. Now this woman did not look Christ in the face, but came *behind him*, and did the part of a *maid-servant*, whose office it was to *wash the feet* of the guests (1 Sa. 25:41) and to prepare the ointments.

Now in what this good woman did, we may observe,

1. Her *deep humiliation* for sin. She stood behind him *weeping;* her eyes had been the inlets and outlets of sin, and now she makes them fountains of tears. Her face is now foul with weeping, which perhaps used to be covered with paints. Her hair now made a towel of, which before had been plaited and adorned. We have reason to think that she had before sorrowed for sin; but, now that she had an opportunity of

coming into the presence of Christ, the wound bled afresh and her sorrow was renewed. Note, It well becomes penitents, upon all their approaches to Christ, to renew their godly sorrow and shame for sin, *when he is pacified*, Eze. 16:63.

2. Her *strong affection* to the Lord Jesus. This was what our Lord Jesus took special notice of, that she *loved much*, *v.* 42, 47. She *washed his feet*, in token of her ready submission to the meanest office in which she might *do him honour*. Nay, she washed them with *her tears*, tears of joy; she was in a transport, to find herself so near her Saviour, whom her soul loved. She *kissed his feet*, as one unworthy of the kisses of his mouth, which the spouse coveted, Cant. 1:2. It was a kiss of adoration as well as affection. *She wiped them with her hair*, as one entirely devoted to his honour. Her eyes shall yield water to wash them, and her hair be a towel to wipe them; and she *anointed* his feet *with the ointment*, owning him hereby to be the Messiah, the *Anointed*. She anointed his feet in token of her consent to God's design in anointing his head with the *oil of gladness*. Note, All true penitents have a dear love to the Lord Jesus.

III. The offence which the Pharisee took at Christ, for admitting the respect which this poor penitent paid him (*v.* 39): *He said within himself* (little thinking that Christ knew what he thought), *This man, if he were a prophet*, would then have so much *knowledge* as to perceive that *this woman is a sinner*, is a Gentile, is a woman of ill fame, and so much *sanctity* as *therefore* not to suffer her to come so near him; for can one of such a character approach a prophet, and his heart not rise at it? See how apt proud and narrow souls are to think that others should be as haughty and censorious as themselves. Simon, if she had touched him, would have said, *Stand by thyself, come not near me, for I am holier than thou* (Isa. 65:5); and he thought Christ should say so too.

IV. Christ's justification of the woman in what she did to him, and of himself in admitting it. Christ knew what the Pharisee spoke *within himself*, and made answer to it: *Simon, I have something to say unto thee, v.* 40. Though he was kindly entertained at his table, yet even there he reproved him for what he saw amiss in him, and would not *suffer sin upon him*. Those whom Christ hath *something against* he hath something to *say to*, for his Spirit shall *reprove*. Simon is willing to give him the hearing: He saith, Master, say on. Though he could not believe him to be a prophet (because he was not so nice and precise as he was), yet he can compliment him with the title of *Master*, among those that cry *Lord, Lord*, but *do not the things which he saith*. Now Christ, in his answer to the Pharisee, reasons thus: — It is true this woman has been a sinner: he knows it; but she is a *pardoned* sinner, which supposes her to be a *penitent* sinner. What she did to him was an expression of her *great love* to her Saviour, by whom her sins were forgiven. If she was pardoned, who had been *so great a sinner*, it might reasonably be expected that she should love her Saviour more than others, and should give greater proofs of it than others; and if this was the fruit of her love, and flowing from a sense of the pardon of her sin, it became him to accept of it, and it ill became the Pharisee to be offended at it. Now Christ has a further intention in this. The Pharisee doubted whether he was a *prophet* or no, nay, he did in effect deny it; but Christ shows that he was more than a prophet, for he is one that has *power on earth to forgive sins*, and to whom are due the affections and thankful acknowledgments of penitent pardoned sinners. Now, in his answer,

1. He by a parable forces Simon to acknowledge that the greater sinner this woman had been the greater love she ought to show to Jesus Christ when her *sins were pardoned*, *v.* 41–43. A man had *two debtors* that were both insolvent, but one of them owed him *ten times* more than the other. He very freely *forgave them both*, and did not take the advantage of the law against them, did not order them and their children to be sold, or *deliver them to the tormentors*. Now they were both sensible of the great kindness they had received; but *which of them will love him most?* Certainly, saith the Pharisee, he to *whom he forgave most;* and herein he rightly judged. Now we, being obliged to *forgive*, as we are and hope to be *forgiven*, may hence learn the duty between debtor and creditor.

(1.) The *debtor*, if he have *any thing to pay*, ought to make satisfaction to his *creditor*. No man can reckon any thing *his own* or have any comfortable enjoyment of it, but that which is so when *all his debts are paid*.

(2.) If God in his providence have disabled the debtor to

pay his debt, the creditor ought not to be severe with him, nor to go to the utmost rigour of the law with him, but *freely to forgive him. Summum jus est summa injuria — The law stretched into rigour becomes unjust*. Let the unmerciful creditor read that parable, Mt. 18:23, etc., and tremble; for *they shall have judgment without mercy that show no mercy*.

(3.) The debtor that has found his creditors merciful ought to be very grateful to them; and, if he cannot otherwise recompense them, ought to love them. Some insolvent debtors, instead of being *grateful*, are *spiteful*, to their creditors that lose by them, and cannot give them a good word, only because they complain, whereas losers may have leave to speak. But this parable speaks of God as the Creator (or rather of the Lord Jesus himself, for he it is that forgives, and is beloved by, the debtor) and sinners are the debtors: and so we may learn here, [1.] That *sin is a debt*, and *sinners are debtors* to God Almighty. As creatures, we owe a debt, a debt of obedience to the precept of the law, and, for non-payment of that, as sinners, we become liable to the penalty. We have not paid our rent; nay, we have wasted our Lord's goods, and so we become debtors. God has an action against us for the injury we have done him, and the omission of our duty to him. [2.] That some are deeper in debt to God, by reason of sin, than others are: *One owed five hundred pence and the other fifty*. The Pharisee was the less debtor, yet he a debtor too, which was more than he thought himself, but rather that God was his debtor, Lu. 18:10, 11. This woman, that had been a scandalous notorious sinner, was the *greater debtor*. Some sinners are in themselves greater debtors than others, and some sinners, by reason of divers aggravating circumstances, greater debtors; as those that have sinned most openly and scandalously, that have sinned against greater light and knowledge, more convictions and warnings, and more mercies and means. [3.] That, whether our debt be more or less, it is *more* than we are able to pay: *They had nothing to pay*, nothing at all to make a composition with; for the debt is great, and we have nothing at all to pay it with. Silver and gold will not pay our debt, nor will sacrifice and offering, no, not *thousands of rams*. No righteousness of our own will pay it, no, not our repentance and obedience for the future; for it is what we are already bound to, and it is God that works it within us. [4.] That the God of heaven is *ready* to forgive, *frankly* to *forgive*, poor sinners, upon gospel terms, though their debt be ever so great. If we repent, and believe in Christ, our iniquity shall not be our ruin, it shall not be laid to our charge. God has proclaimed his name gracious and merciful, and ready to forgive sin; and, his Son having purchased pardon for penitent believers, his gospel promises it to them, and his Spirit seals it and gives them the comfort of it. [5.] That those who have their sins *pardoned* are obliged to *love him* that pardoned them; and the more is forgiven them, the more they should love him. The *greater sinners* any have been before their conversion, the *greater saints* they should be after, the more they should study to do for God, and the more their hearts should be enlarged in obedience. When a *persecuting Saul* became a preaching Paul he *laboured more abundantly*.

2. He applies this parable to the different temper and conduct of the Pharisee and the sinner towards Christ. Though the Pharisee would not allow Christ to be a prophet, Christ seems ready to allow him to be in a justified state, and that he was one *forgiven*, though to him *less was forgiven*. He did indeed show some love to Christ, in inviting him to his house, but nothing to what this poor woman showed. "Observe," saith Christ to him, "she is one that has much forgiven her, and therefore, according to thine own judgment, it might be expected that she should love much more than thou dost, and so it appears. *Seest thou this woman? v.* 44. Thou lookest upon her with contempt, but consider how much kinder a friend she is to me than thou art; should I then accept thy kindness, and refuse hers?" (1.) "Thou didst not so much as order a basin of water to be brought, to wash my feet in, when I came in, wearied and dirtied with my walk, which would have been some refreshment to me; but she has done much more: *she has washed my feet with tears*, tears of affection to me, tears of affliction for sin, and has *wiped them with the hairs of her head*, in token of her great love to me." (2.) "Thou didst not so much as kiss my cheek" (which was a usual expression of a hearty and affectionate welcome to a friend); "but *this woman has not ceased to kiss my feet* (*v.* 45), thereby expressing both a humble and an affectionate love." (3.) "Thou didst not provide me a little common oil, as usual, to

anoint my head with; but she has bestowed a box of precious *ointment* upon *my feet* (*v.* 46), so far has she outdone thee." The reason why some people blame the pains and expense of zealous Christians, in religion, is because they are not willing themselves to come up to it, but resolve to rest in a *cheap* and *easy* religion.

3. He silenced the Pharisee's cavil: *I say unto thee,* Simon, *her sins, which are many, are forgiven, v.* 47. He owns that she had been guilty of *many sins:* "But they are *forgiven* her, and therefore it is no way unbecoming in me to accept her kindness. They *are forgiven, for she loved much.*" It should be rendered, *therefore she loved much;* for it is plain, by the tenour of Christ's discourse, that the loving much was not the *cause,* but the *effect,* of her pardon, and of her comfortable sense of it; for *we love God* because *he first loved us;* he did not forgive us because we first loved him. "But *to whom little is forgiven,* as is to thee, *the same loveth little,* as thou dost." Hereby he intimates to the Pharisee that his love to Christ was so little that he had reason to question whether he loved him at all in sincerity; and, consequently, whether indeed his sin, though comparatively *little,* were forgiven him. Instead of grudging greater sinners the mercy they find with Christ, upon their repentance, we should be stirred up by their example to examine ourselves whether we be indeed forgiven, and do love Christ.

4. He silenced her fears, who probably was discouraged by the Pharisee's conduct, and yet would not so far yield to the discouragement as to fly off. (1.) Christ said unto her, *Thy sins are forgiven, v.* 48. Note, The more we express our sorrow for sin, and our love to Christ, the clearer evidence we have of the forgiveness of our sins; for it is by the experience of a *work of grace* wrought *in us* that we obtain the assurance of an *act of grace* wrought *for us.* How well was she paid for her pains and cost, when she was dismissed with this word from Christ, *Thy sins are forgiven!* and what an effectual prevention would this be of her return to sin again! (2.) Though there were those present who quarrelled with Christ, in their own minds, for presuming to forgive sin, and to pronounce sinners absolved (*v.* 49), as those had done (Mt. 9:3), yet he *stood to what he had said;* for as he had there proved that he had *power to forgive sin,* by curing the man sick of the palsy, and therefore would not here take notice of the cavil, so he would now show that he had *pleasure in forgiving sin,* and it was his delight; he loves to speak pardon and peace to penitents: *He said to the woman, Thy faith hath saved thee, v.* 50. This would confirm and double her comfort in the forgiveness of her sin, that she was *justified by her faith.* All these expressions of sorrow for sin, and love to Christ, were the effects and products of faith; and therefore, as faith of all graces doth most honour God, so Christ doth of all graces put most honour upon faith. Note, They who know that their faith hath saved them may go in peace, may go on their way rejoicing.

CHAPTER 8

Most of this chapter is a repetition of divers passages of Christ's preaching and miracles which we had before in Matthew and Mark; they are all of such weight, that they are worth repeating, and therefore they are repeated, that out of the mouth not only of two, but of three, witnesses every word may be established. Here is, I. A general account of Christ's preaching, and how he had subsistence for himself and his numerous family by the charitable contributions of good people (*v.* 1–3). II. The parable of the sower, and the four sorts of ground, with the exposition of it, and some inferences from it (*v.* 4–18). III. The preference which Christ gave to his obedient disciples before his nearest relations according to the flesh (*v.* 19–21). IV. His stilling a storm at sea, with a word's speaking (*v.* 22–25). V. His casting a legion of devils out of a man that was possessed by them (*v.* 26–40). VI. His healing the woman that had the bloody issue, and raising Jairus's daughter to life (*v.* 41–56).

Verses 1–3

We are here told,

I. *What* Christ *made* the *constant business* of his *life* — it was *preaching;* in that work he was indefatigable, and went about doing good (*v.* 1), *afterward — en tō kathexēs — ordine,* in the proper *time* or *method.* Christ took his work before him and went about it regularly. He observed a *series* or order of business, so that the end of one good work was the beginning of another. Now observe here, 1. *Where* he preached: *He went about — diōdeue — peragrabat.* He was an *itinerant* preacher, did not confine himself to one place, but diffused the beams of his light. *Circumibat — He went his circuit,* as a judge, having found his preaching perhaps most *acceptable* where it was *new.* He went about *through every city,* that none might plead ignorance. Hereby he set an example to his disciples; they must traverse the nations of the earth, as he did the cities of Israel. Nor did he confine himself to the *cities,* but went into the *villages,* among the plain country-people, to preach *to the inhabitants of the villages,* Jdg. 5:11. 2. What he preached: *He showed the glad tidings of the kingdom of God,* that it was now to be set up among them. Tidings of the *kingdom of God* are *glad tidings,* and those Jesus Christ came to bring; to tell the children of men that God was willing to take all those *under his protection* that were willing to return *to their allegiance.* It was *glad tidings* to the world that there was hope of its being *reformed* and *reconciled.* 3. Who were his attendants: *The twelve were with him,* not to preach if he were present, but to learn from him what and how to preach hereafter, and, if occasion were, to be sent to places where he could not go. Happy were these his servants that heard his wisdom.

II. *Whence* he *had* the *necessary supports* of life: He lived upon the kindness of his friends. There were *certain women,* who frequently attended his ministry, that *ministered to him of their substance, v.* 2, 3. Some of them are named; but there were *many others,* who were zealously affected to the doctrine of Christ, and thought themselves bound *in justice* to *encourage* it, having themselves found benefit, and in *charity,* hoping that many others might find benefit by it too.

1. They were such, for the most part, as had been *Christ's patients,* and were the monuments of his power and mercy; they had been *healed by him of evil spirits and infirmities.* Some of them had been troubled in mind, had been melancholy, others of them afflicted in body, and he had been to them a powerful healer. He is the physician both of body and soul, and those who have been *healed by him* ought to study what they shall *render to him.* We are bound in *interest* to attend him, that we may be ready to apply ourselves to him for help in case of a relapse; and we are bound in *gratitude* to serve him and his gospel, who hath *saved* us, and saved us *by it.*

2. One of them was Mary Magdalene, out of whom had been *cast seven devils;* a certain number for an uncertain. Some think that she was one that had been *very wicked,* and then we may suppose her to be the woman that *was a sinner* mentioned just before, *ch.* 7:37. Dr. Lightfoot, finding in some of the Talmudists' writings that Mary Magdalene signified *Mary the plaiter of hair,* thinks it applicable to her, she having been noted, in the days of her iniquity and infamy, for that *plaiting of hair* which is opposed to *modest apparel,* 1 Tim. 2:9. But, though she had been an immodest woman, upon her repentance and reformation she found mercy, and became a zealous disciple of Christ. Note, The greatest of sinners must not despair of pardon; and the worse any have been before their conversion the more they should study to do for Christ after. Or, rather, she was one that had been *very melancholy,* and then, probably, it was Mary the sister of Lazarus, who was a woman of a *sorrowful spirit,* who might have been originally of Magdala, but removed to Bethany. This Mary Magdalene was attending on Christ's cross and his sepulchre, and, if she was not Mary the sister of Lazarus, either that particular friend and favourite of Christ's did not attend then, or the evangelists did not take notice of her, neither of which we can suppose; thus Dr. Lightfoot argues. Yet there is this to be objected against it that Mary Magdalene is reckoned *among the women that followed Jesus from Galilee* (Mt. 27:55, 56); whereas Mary the sister of Lazarus had her residence in Bethany.

3. Another of them was *Joanna the wife of Chuza, Herod's steward.* She had been his wife (so some), but was now a widow, and left in good circumstances. If she was now his wife, we have reason to think that her *husband,* though preferred in Herod's court, had received the gospel, and was very willing that his wife should be both a hearer of Christ and a contributor to him.

4. There were many of them that *ministered to Christ of their substance.* It was an instance of the meanness of that condition to which our Saviour humbled himself that he needed it, and of his great humility and condescension that he accepted it. Though he was rich, yet for our sakes *he became poor,* and lived upon alms. Let none say that they scorn to be beholden to the charity of their neighbours, when Providence has brought them into straits; but let them ask and be thankful for it as a favour. Christ would rather be beholden to his known friends for a maintenance for himself and his disciples than be burdensome to strangers in the cities and villages whither he came to preach. Note, It is the duty of those who are taught in the word to *communicate to them who teach them in all good things;* and those who are herein liberal and cheerful honour the Lord with their substance, and bring a blessing upon it.

Verses 4–21

The former paragraph began with an account of Christ's industry in *preaching* (*v.* 1); this begins with an account of the people's industry in hearing, *v.* 4. He *went into every city,* to preach; so they, one would think, should have contented themselves to hear him when he came to their own city (we know those that would); but there were those here that came *to him out of every city,* would not stay till he came to *them,* nor think that they had enough when he left *them,* but *met him* when he was coming towards them, and *followed him* when he was going from them. Nor did he excuse himself from going *to the cities* with this, that there were some *from* the cities that *came to him;* for, though there were, yet the most had not zeal enough to bring them to him, and therefore such is his wonderful condescension that he will go to them; for *he is found of those that sought him not,* Isa. 65:1.

Here was, it seems, a vast concourse, *much people were gathered together,* abundance of fish to cast their net among; and he was as ready and willing to *teach* as they were to be *taught.* Now in these verses we have,

I. Necessary and excellent rules and cautions for hearing the word, in the parable of *the sower* and the explanation and application of it, all which we had twice before more largely. When Christ had put forth this parable, 1. The disciples were *inquisitive* concerning the meaning of it, *v.* 9. They asked him, *What might this parable be?* Note, We should covet earnestly to know the true *in*tent, and full *ex*tent, of the word we hear, that we may be neither mistaken nor defective in our knowledge. 2. Christ made them sensible of what great advantage it was to them that they had opportunity of acquainting themselves with the mystery and meaning of his word, which others had not: *Unto you it is given, v.* 10. Note, Those who would receive instruction from Christ must know and consider what a privilege it is to be instructed by him, what a distinguishing privilege to be led into the light, such a light, when others are left in darkness, such a darkness. Happy are we, and for ever indebted to free grace, if the same thing that is a *parable* to others, with which they are only *amused,* is a *plain truth* to us, by which we are *enlightened* and *governed,* and into the mould of which we are *delivered.*

Now from the parable itself, and the explication of it, observe,

(1.) The *heart of man* is as *soil* to the *seed of God's word;* it is capable of receiving it, and bringing forth the fruits of it; but, unless that seed be sown in it, it will bring forth nothing valuable. Or care therefore must be to bring the *seed* and the *soil* together. To what purpose have we the *seed* in the scripture, if it be not *sown?* And to what purpose have we the soil in our own hearts, if it be not sown with that seed?

(2.) The *success* of the *seeding* is very much according to the nature and temper of the *soil,* and as that is, or is not, disposed to receive the seed. The word of God *is to us,* as *we are,* a *savour of life unto life,* or *of death unto death.*

(3.) The devil is a subtle and spiteful enemy, that makes it his business to hinder our profiting by the word of God. He takes the word out of the hearts of *careless* hearers, *lest they should believe and be saved, v.* 12. This is added here to teach us, [1.] That we cannot be *saved* unless we *believe.* The word of the gospel will not be a saving word to us, unless it be mixed with faith. [2.] That therefore the devil does all he can to keep us from *believing,* to make us not believe the word when we read and hear it; or, if we heed it for the present, to make us forget it again, and let it slip (Heb. 2:1); or, if we remember it, to create prejudices in our minds against it, or *divert* our minds from it to something else; and all is *lest we should believe and be saved,* lest we should believe and *rejoice,* while he believes and *trembles.*

(4.) Where the word of God is heard *carelessly* there is commonly a *contempt* put upon it too. It is added here in the parable that the seed which fell by the way-side was *trodden down, v.* 5. They that wilfully shut their ears against the word do in effect trample it under their feet; they *despise the commandment of the Lord.*

(5.) Those on whom the word makes *some* impressions, but they are not *deep* and *durable* ones, will show their hypocrisy in a time of trial; as the seed sown upon the rock, where it gains no root, v. 13. These *for awhile believe* a little while; their profession promises something, but in *time of temptation they fall away* from their good beginnings. Whether the temptation arises from the smiles or the frowns, of the world, they are easily overcome by it.

(6.) The *pleasures of this life* are as dangerous and mischievous thorns to choke the good seed of the word as any other. This is added here (v. 14), which was not in the other evangelists. Those that are *not entangled in the cares of this life*, nor inveigled with the *deceitfulness of riches*, but boast that they are dead to them, may yet be kept from heaven by an affected indolence, and the love of ease and pleasure. The delights of sense may ruin the soul, even lawful delights, indulged, and too much delighted in.

(7.) It is not enough that the fruit be brought forth, but it must be *brought to perfection*, it must be fully ripened. If it be not, it is as if there was no fruit at all brought forth; for that which in Matthew and Mark is said to be *unfruitful* is the same that here is said to *bring forth none to perfection*. For *factum non dicitur quod non perseverat — perseverance is necessary to the perfection of a work*.

(8.) The good ground, which brings forth *good fruit*, is an *honest* and *good heart*, well disposed to receive instruction and commandment (v. 15); a heart free from sinful pollutions, and firmly fixed for God and duty, an upright heart, a tender heart, and a heart that *trembles at the word*, is an honest and good heart, which, having heard the word, *understands* it (so it is in Matthew), *receives* it (so it is in Mark), and *keeps* it (so it is here), as the soil not only *receives*, but keeps, the seed; and the stomach not only receives, but keeps, the food or physic.

(9.) Where the word is well kept there is fruit brought forth *with patience*. This also is added here. There must be both *bearing* patience and *waiting* patience; patience to suffer the *tribulation* and *persecution* which may *arise because of the word;* patience to continue to the end in well-doing.

(10.) In consideration of all this, we ought to take *heed how we hear* (v. 18); take heed of those things that will hinder our profiting by the word we hear, watch over our hearts in hearing, and take heed lest they betray us; take heed *lest* we hear carelessly and slightly, lest, upon any account, we entertain prejudice against the word we hear; and take heed to the frame of our spirits after we have heard the word, lest we lose what we have gained.

II. Needful instructions given to those that are appointed to preach the word, and to those also that have heard it. 1. Those that have *received the gift* must *minister the same*. Ministers that have the dispensing of the gospel committed to them, people that have profited by the word and are thereby qualified to profit others, must look upon themselves as *lighted candles:* ministers must in solemn authoritative preaching, and people in brotherly familiar discourse, diffuse their light, for a *candle* must not be *covered with a vessel* nor *put under a bed*, v. 16. Ministers and Christians are to be lights in the world, *holding forth the word of life*. Their light must shine before men; they must not only *be good*, but *do good*. 2. We must expect that what is now done *in secret*, and from unseen springs, will shortly be *manifested* and *made known*, v. 17. What is committed to you *in secret* should be made manifest *by you;* for your Master did not give you talents to be buried, but to be traded with. Let that which is now hid be *made known;* for, if it be not manifested *by you*, it will be manifested *against you*, will be produced in evidence of your treachery. 3. The gifts we have will either be continued to us, or taken from us, according as we do, or do not, make use of them for the glory of God and the edification of our brethren: *Whosoever hath, to him shall be given*, v. 18. He that hath gifts, and does good with them, shall have more; he that *buries his talent* shall lose it. From him that hath not shall be taken away even *that which he hath*, so it is in Mark; that which he *seemeth to have*, so it is in Luke. Note, The grace that is lost was but *seeming* grace, was never *true*. Men do but *seem* to have what they do not *use*, and shows of religion will be lost and forfeited. They *went out from us, because they were not of us*, 1 Jn. 2:19. Let us see to it that we have grace in sincerity, the *root of the matter* found in us; that is a good part which shall never be taken away from those that have it.

III. Great encouragement given to those that prove themselves faithful *hearers of the word*, by being *doers of the work*, in a particular instance of Christ's respect to his disciples, in

---

preferring them even before his nearest relations (v. 19–21), which passage of story we had twice before. Observe, 1. What crowding there was after Christ. There was no coming near for the throng of people that attended him, who, though they were crowded very so much, would not be crowded out from his congregation. 2. Some of his nearest kindred were least solicitous to hear him preach. Instead of getting *within*, as they might easily have done if they had come in time, desiring to *hear him*, they stood *without*, desiring to *see him;* and, probably, out of a foolish fear, lest he should spend himself with too much speaking, designing nothing but to interrupt him, and oblige him to break off. 3. Jesus Christ would rather be busy at his work than conversing with his friends. He would not leave his preaching, to speak with his *mother* and his *brethren*, for it was his *meat and drink* to be so employed. 4. Christ is pleased to own those as his nearest and dearest relations that *hear the word of God and do it;* they are to him more than *his mother* and *brethren*.

Verses 22–39

We have here two illustrious proofs of the power of our Lord Jesus which we had before — his power over the *winds*, and his power over the *devils*. See Mk. 4 and 5.

I. His power over the winds, those *powers of the air* that are so much a terror to men, especially upon sea, and occasion the death of such multitudes. Observe,

1. Christ ordered his disciples to put to sea, that he might show his glory upon the water, in stilling the waves, and might do an act of kindness to a poor possessed man on the other side the water: *He went into a ship with his disciples*, v. 22. They that observe Christ's orders may assure themselves of his presence. If Christ sends his disciples, he goes *with them*. And those may safely and boldly venture any where that have Christ accompanying them. *He said, Let us go over unto the other side;* for he had a piece of good work to do there. He might have gone by land, a little way about; but he chose to go by *water*, that he might show his *wonders in the deep*.

2. Those that put to sea in a calm, yea, and at Christ's word, must yet *prepare for a storm*, and for the utmost peril in that storm; There *came down a storm of wind on the lake* (v. 23), as if it were there, and no where else; and presently their ship was so tossed that it was filled with water, and they were in jeopardy of their lives. Perhaps the devil, who is the *prince of the power of the air*, and who *raiseth winds* by the permission of God, had some suspicion, from some words which Christ might let fall, that he was coming over the lake now on purpose to cast that legion of devils out of the poor man on the other side, and therefore poured this storm upon the ship he was in, designing, if possible, to have sunk him and prevented that victory.

3. Christ was *asleep* in the storm, v. 23. Some bodily refreshment he must have, and he chose to take it when it would be least a hindrance to him in his work. The disciples of Christ may really have his gracious presence with them at sea, and in a storm, and yet he may seem as if he were *asleep;* he may not immediately appear for their relief, no, not when things seem to be brought even to the last extremity. Thus he will try their faith and patience, and quicken them by prayer to awake, and make their deliverance the more welcome when it comes at last.

4. A complaint to Christ of our danger, and the distress his church is in, is enough to engage him to awake, and appear for us, v. 24. They cried, *Master, master, we perish!* The way to have our fears silenced is to bring them to Christ, and lay them before him. Those that in sincerity call Christ *Master*, and with faith and fervency call upon him as *their Master*, may be sure that he will not let them *perish*. There is no relief for poor souls that are under a sense of guilt, and a fear of wrath, like this, to go to Christ, and call him *Master*, and say, "I am *undone*, if thou do not *help me*."

5. Christ's business is to *lay storms*, as it is Satan's business to *raise* them. He can do it; he has done it; he delights to do it: for he came to *proclaim peace on earth*. He *rebuked the wind and the raging of the water*, and immediately *they ceased* (v. 24); not, as at other times, by degrees, but all of a sudden, *there was a great calm*. Thus Christ showed that, though the devil pretends to be the prince of the power of the air, yet even there he has him in a chain.

6. When our dangers are over, it becomes us to take to ourselves the shame of our own fears and to give to Christ the glory of his power. When Christ had turned the *storm* into a *calm, then were they glad because they were quiet*, Ps.

107:30. And then, (1.) Christ gives them a rebuke for their inordinate fear: *Where is your faith? v.* 25. Note, Many that have *true faith* have it to seek when they have occasion to use it. They tremble, and are discouraged, if second causes frown upon them. A little thing disheartens them; and *where is their faith* then? (2.) They give him the glory of his power: *They, being afraid, wondered*. Those that had feared the storm, now that the danger was over with good reason feared him that had stilled it, and *said one to another, What manner of man is this!* They might as well have said, *Who is a God like unto thee?* For it is God's prerogative to *still the noise of the seas, the noise of their waves*, Ps. 65:7.

II. His power over the *devil, the prince of the power of the air*. In the next passage of story he comes into a closer grapple with him than he did when he commanded *the winds*. Presently after the winds were stilled they were brought to their desired haven, and *arrived at the country of the Gadarenes*, and there went ashore (v. 26, 27); and he soon met with that which was his business over, and which he thought it worth his while to go through a storm to accomplish.

We may learn a great deal out of this story concerning this world of infernal, malignant spirits, which, though not working now ordinarily in the same way as here, yet we are all concerned at all times to stand upon our guard against.

1. These *malignant* spirits are very *numerous*. They that had taken possession of this one man called themselves *Legion* (v. 30), because *many devils were entered into him:* he had *had devils a long time, v.* 27. But perhaps those that had been long in possession of him, upon some foresight of our Saviour's coming to make an attack upon them, and finding they could not prevent it by the storm they had raised, sent for recruits, intending this to be *a decisive* battle, and hoping now to be too hard for him that had cast out so many unclean spirits, and to give him a defeat. They either were, or at least would be thought to be, a *legion*, formidable as an *army with banners;* and now, at least, to be, what the *twentieth legion* of the Roman army, which was long quartered at Chester, was styled, *legio victrix* — a *victorious legion*.

2. They have an *inveterate enmity* to man, and all his conveniences and comforts. This man in whom the devils had got possession, and kept it long, being under their influence, *wore no clothes, neither abode in any house* (v. 27), though *clothing* and a *habitation* are two of the necessary supports of this life. Nay, and because man has a natural dread of the habitations of the dead, they forced this man to *abide in the tombs*, to make him so much the more a terror to himself and to all about him, so that his soul had as much cause as ever any man's had to be weary of his life, and to *choose strangling and death rather*.

3. They are very *strong, fierce*, and unruly, and hate and scorn to be restrained: *He was kept bound with chains and in fetters*, that he might not be mischievous either to others or to himself, but he *broke the bands, v.* 29. Note, Those that are *ungovernable* by any other thereby show that they are under Satan's government; and this is the language of those that are so, even concerning God and Christ, their best friends, that would not either bind them *from* or bind them *to* any thing but for their own good: *Let us break their bands in sunder. He was driven of the devil*. Those that are under Christ's government are *sweetly led* with the cords of a man and the bands of love; those that are under the devil's government are *furiously driven*.

4. They are much enraged against our Lord Jesus, and have a great dread and horror of him: *When the man* whom they had possession of, and who spoke as they would have him, *saw Jesus*, he roared out as one in an agony, and *fell down before him*, to deprecate his wrath, and owned him to be the *Son of God most high*, that was infinitely above him and too hard for him; but protested against having any league or confederacy with him (which might sufficiently have silenced the blasphemous cavils of the scribes and Pharisees): *What have I to do with thee?* The devils have neither inclination to do service to Christ nor expectation to receive benefit by him: *What have we to do with thee?* But they dreaded his power and wrath: *I beseech thee, torment me not*. They do not say, *I beseech thee, save me*, but only, *Torment me not*. See whose language *they* speak that have only a dread of hell as a place of torment, but no desire of heaven as a place of holiness and love.

5. They are perfectly *at the command*, and under *the power*, of our Lord Jesus; and they knew it, for they *besought him that he would not command them to go eis ton abys-*

son — into the deep, the place of their torment, which they acknowledge he could easily and justly do. O what a comfort is this to the Lord's people, that all the powers of darkness are under the check and control of the Lord Jesus! He has them all in a chain. He can send them to *their own place,* when he pleaseth.

6. They delight in *doing mischief.* When they found there was no remedy, but they must quit their hold of this poor man, they begged they might have leave to take possession of a *herd of swine, v.* 32. When the devil at first brought man into a miserable state he brought a curse likewise upon the whole creation, and that became subject to enmity. And here, as an instance of that extensive enmity of his, when he could not destroy the man, he would destroy the swine. If he could not hurt them in their bodies, he would hurt them in their goods, which sometimes prove a great temptation to men to draw them from Christ, as here. Christ *suffered them to enter into the swine,* to convince the country what mischief the devil could do in it, if he should suffer him. No sooner had the devils leave than they entered into the *swine;* and no sooner had they entered into them than the herd ran violently *down a steep place into the lake,* and were *drowned.* For it is a miracle of mercy if those whom Satan possesses are not brought to destruction and perdition. This, and other instances, show that that roaring lion and red dragon seeks *what* and whom he may devour.

7. When the devil's power is broken in any soul that soul recovers itself, and returns into a right frame, which supposes that those whom Satan gets possession of are put out of the possession of themselves: *The man out of whom the devils were departed sat at the feet of Jesus, v.* 35. While he was under the devil's power he was ready to *fly in the face* of Jesus; but now he *sits at his feet,* which is a sign that he is come to his *right mind.* If God has possession of us, he preserves to us the government and enjoyment of ourselves; but, if Satan has possession of us, he robs us of both. Let his power therefore in our souls be overturned, and let *him* come whose right our hearts are, and let us give them to him; for we are never more our own than when we are his.

Let us now see what was the effect of this miracle of casting the legion of devils out of this man.

(1.) What effect it had upon the people of that country who had lost their swine by it: *The swineherds went and told it* both *in city and country (v.* 34), perhaps with a design to incense people against Christ. They told *by what means he that was possessed of the devils was healed (v.* 36), that it was by sending the devils into the swine, which was capable of an invidious representation, as if Christ could not have delivered the man out of their hands, but by delivering the swine into them. *The people came out, to see what was done,* and to enquire into it; and *they were afraid (v.* 35); they were *taken with great fear (v.* 37); they were surprised and amazed at it, and knew not what to say to it. They thought more of the destruction of the swine than of the deliverance of their poor afflicted neighbour, and of the country from the terror of his frenzy, which was become a public nuisance; and therefore *the whole multitude besought Christ to depart from them* for fear he should bring some other judgment upon them; whereas indeed none need to be afraid of Christ that are willing to forsake their sins and give up themselves to him. But Christ took them at their word: *He went up into the ship, and returned back again.* Those lose their Saviour, and their hopes in him, that love their swine better.

(2.) What effect it had upon the poor man who had recovered himself by it. He *desired* Christ's company as much as others *dreaded* it: he besought Christ that *he might be with him* as others were *that had been healed by him of evil spirits and infirmities (v.* 2), that Christ might be to him a protector and teacher, and that he might be to Christ for a name and a praise. He was loth to stay among those rude and brutish Gadarenes that desired Christ to depart from them. *O gather not my soul with these sinners!* But Christ would not take him along with him, but sent him home, to publish among those that knew him the great things God had done for him, that so he might be a blessing to his country, as he had been a burden to it. We must sometimes deny ourselves the satisfaction even of spiritual benefits and comforts, to gain an opportunity of being serviceable to the souls of others. Perhaps Christ knew that, when the resentment of the loss of their swine was a little over, they would be better disposed to consider the miracle, and therefore left the man among them to be a standing monument, and a monitor to them of it.

Verses 40–56

Christ was driven away by the *Gadarenes;* they were weary of him, and willing to be rid of him. But when he had crossed the water, and returned to the *Galileans,* they gladly received him, *wished* and *waited* for his return, and *welcomed* him with all their hearts when he did return, v. 40. If some *will not* accept the favours Christ offers them, others *will.* If the Gadarenes be not gathered, yet there are many among whom *Christ shall be glorious.* When Christ had done his work on the other side of the water he returned, and found work to do in the place whence he came, fresh work. They that will lay out themselves to do good shall never want occasion for it. The needy you have always with you.

We have here two miracles interwoven, as they were in Matthew and Mark — the raising of Jairus's daughter to life, and the cure of the woman that had an issue of blood, as he was going in a crowd to Jairus's house. We have here,

I. A *public address* made to Christ by *a ruler of the synagogue,* whose name was *Jairus,* on the behalf of a little daughter of his, that was very ill, and, in the apprehension of all about here, *lay a dying.* This address was very humble and reverent. Jairus, though a *ruler, fell down at Jesus's feet,* as owning him to be a ruler *above* him. It was very importunate. He *besought him* that he would *come into his house;* not having the *faith,* at least not having the *thought,* of the centurion, who desired Christ only to *speak the* healing *word* at a distance. But Christ complied with his request; *he went along* with him. Strong faith shall be applauded, and yet weak faith shall not be rejected. In the houses where sickness and death are, it is very desirable to have the presence of Christ. When Christ was going, *the people thronged him,* some out of curiosity to see him, others out of an affection to him. Let us not complain of a crowd, and a throng, and a hurry, as long as we are in the way of our duty, and *doing good;* but otherwise it is what every wise man will keep himself out of as much as he can.

II. Here is a *secret application* made to Christ by a woman ill of a *bloody issue,* which had been the consumption of her body and the consumption of her purse too; for *she had spent all her living upon physicians,* and was never the better, v. 43. The nature of her disease was such that she did not care to make a public complaint of it (it was agreeable to the modesty of her sex to be very shy of speaking of it), and therefore she took this opportunity of coming to Christ *in a crowd;* and the more people were present the more likely she thought it was that she should be *concealed.* Her *faith* was very *strong;* for she doubted not but that by the *touch* of the *hem of his garment* she should derive from him healing virtue sufficient for her relief, looking upon him to be such a full fountain of mercies that she should *steal* a cure and he not *miss it.* Thus many a poor soul is *healed,* and *helped,* and *saved,* by Christ, that is *lost in a crowd,* and that nobody takes notice of. The woman found an immediate change for the better in herself, and that her disease was cured, v. 44. As believers have comfortable communion with Christ, so they have comfortable communications from him *incognito — secretly, meat to eat that the world knows not* of, and *joy* that *a stranger does not intermeddle with.*

III. Here is a *discovery* of this secret cure, to the glory both of the physician and the patient.

1. Christ takes notice that there is a cure wrought: *Virtue is gone out of me, v.* 46. Those that have been healed by virtue derived from Christ must *own* it, for he *knows it.* He speaks of it here, not in a way of *complaint,* as if he were hereby either *weakened* or *wronged,* but in a way of complacency. It was his delight that *virtue* was gone out of him to do any good, and he did not grudge it to the meanest; they were as welcome to it as to the light and heat of the sun. Nor had he the less virtue *in him* for the going out of the virtue *from him* for he is an *overflowing* fountain.

2. The poor patient owns her case, and the benefit she had received: *When she saw that she was not hid, she came, and fell down before him, v.* 47. Note, The consideration of this, that we cannot be *hid from Christ,* should engage us to *pour* out our hearts before him, and to show before him all our sin and all our trouble. *She came trembling,* and yet *her faith saved her, v.* 48. Note, There may be *trembling* where yet there is saving faith. She *declared before all the people for what cause she had touched him* because she believed that a touch would cure her, and it did so. Christ's patients should communicate their experiences to one another.

3. The great physician confirms her cure, and sends her

away with the comfort of it: *Be of good comfort; thy faith hath made thee whole, v.* 48. Jacob got the blessing from Isaac clandestinely, and by a wile; but, when the fraud was discovered, Isaac ratified it designedly. It was obtained *surreptitiously* and *under-hand,* but it was secured and seconded *above-board.* So was the cure here. He is *blessed,* and he *shall be blessed;* so here, She *is* healed, and she *shall be* healed.

IV. Here is an *encouragement* to Jairus not to distrust the power of Christ, *though his daughter was now dead,* and they that brought him the tidings advised him not to give *the Master any further trouble* about her: *Fear not,* saith Christ, *only believe.* Note, Our *faith in Christ* should be bold and daring, as well as our *zeal for him.* They that are willing to do any thing for him may depend upon his doing great things for them, above what they are able to ask or think. When the patient is dead there is no room for prayer, or the use of means; but here, though the child is dead, yet *believe,* and all shall be well. *Post mortem medicus — to call in the physician after death,* is an absurdity; but not *post mortem Christus — to call in Christ after death.*

V. The *preparatives* for the raising of her to life again. 1. The *choice* Christ made of witnesses that should see the miracle wrought. A *crowd* followed him, but perhaps they were rude and noisy; however, it was not fit to let such a multitude come into a gentleman's house, especially now that the family was all in sorrow; *therefore* he sent them back, and not because he was afraid to let the miracle pass their scrutiny; for he raised Lazarus and the widow's son *publicly.* He took none with him but Peter, and James, and John, that triumvirate of his disciples that he was most intimate with, designing these three, with the parents, to be the only spectators of the miracle, they being a competent number to attest the truth of it. 2. The *check* he gave to the mourners. *They all wept, and bewailed her;* for, it seems, she was a very agreeable hopeful child, and dear not only to the parents, but to all the neighbours. But Christ bid them *not weep; for she is not dead, but sleepeth.* He means, as to her peculiar case, that she was not dead for good and all, but that she should now shortly be raised to life, so that it would be to her friends as if she had been but a few hours asleep. But it is applicable to all that die in the Lord; therefore we should not sorrow for them as those that have *no hope,* because death is but a *sleep* to them, not only as it is a *rest* from all the *toils* of the *days of time,* but as there will be a *resurrection,* a waking and rising again to all the *glories* of the *days of eternity.* This was a comfortable word which Christ said to these mourners, yet they wickedly ridiculed it, and *laughed him to scorn* for it here was a *pearl cast before swine.* They were ignorant of the scriptures of the Old Testament who bantered it as an absurd thing to call death a *sleep;* yet *this* good came out of *that* evil that hereby the truth of the miracle was evinced; for they *knew that she was dead,* they were certain of it, and therefore nothing less than a *divine power* could restore her to life. We find not any answer that he made them; but he soon *explained himself,* I hope to their conviction, so that they would never again laugh at any word of his. But he *put them all out, v.* 54. They were unworthy to be the witnesses of this work of wonder; they who in the midst of their mourning were so merrily disposed as to laugh at him for what he *said* would, it may be, have found something to laugh at in what he *did,* and therefore are justly shut out.

VI. Her return to life, after a *short* visit to the *congregation of the dead: He took her by the hand* (as we do by one that we would awake out of sleep, and help up), and he called, saying, *Maid, arise, v.* 55. Thus the *hand of Christ's grace* goes along with the *calls of his word,* to make them effectual. Here that is expressed which was only implied in the other evangelists, that *her spirit came again;* her soul returned again to animate her body. This plainly proves that the soul exists and acts in a state of separation from the body, and therefore is immortal; that death does not extinguish this *candle of the Lord,* but takes it out of a *dark lantern.* It is not, as Grotius well observes, the *krasis* or *temperament* of the body, or anything that dies with it; but it is *anthypostaton ti — something that subsists by itself,* which, after death, is somewhere else than where the body is. Where the soul of this child was in this interval we are not told; it was in the hand of the *Father of spirits,* to whom all souls at death return. When *her spirit came again* she arose, and made it appear that she was alive by her motion, as she did also by her appetite; for Christ *commanded to give her meat.* As babes newly born, so those that are newly raised, desire spiritual food, that they may grow *thereby.* In the last verse, we need not wonder to find *her parents astonished;* but if that implies that *they only* were so, and not the other by-standers, who had laughed Christ to scorn, we may well wonder at their stupidity, which perhaps was the reason why Christ would not have it proclaimed, as well as to give an instance of his humility.

CHAPTER 9

In this chapter we have, I. The commission Christ gave to his twelve apostles to go out for some time to preach the gospel, and confirm it by miracles (*v.* 1–6). II. Herod's terror at the growing greatness of our Lord Jesus (*v.* 7–9). III. The apostles' return to Christ, his retirement with them into a place of solitude, the great resort of people to them notwithstanding, and his feeding five thousand men with five loaves and two fishes (*v.* 10–17). IV. His discourse with his disciples concerning himself and his own sufferings for them, and their for him (*v.* 18–27). V. Christ's transfiguration (*v.* 28–36). VI. The cure of a lunatic child (*v.* 37–42). VII. The repeated notice Christ gave his disciples of his approaching sufferings (*v.* 43–45). VIII. His check to the ambition of his disciples (*v.* 46–68), and to their monopolizing the power over devils to themselves (*v.* 49, 50). IX. The rebuke he gave them for an over-due resentment of an affront given him by a village of the Samaritans (*v.* 51–56). X. The answers he gave to several that were inclined to follow him, but not considerately, or not zealously and heartily, so inclined (*v.* 57–62).

Verses 1–9

We have here, I. The method Christ took to spread his gospel, to diffuse and enforce the light of it. He had *himself* travelled about, preaching and healing; but he could be only in one place at a time, and therefore now he *sent* his twelve disciples abroad, who by this time were pretty well instructed in the nature of the present dispensation, and able to instruct others and *deliver to them* what they had *received from the Lord.* Let them disperse themselves, some one way and some another, to *preach the kingdom of God,* as it was now about to be set up by the Messiah, to make people acquainted with the spiritual nature and tendency of it, and to persuade them to come into the interests and measures of it. For the confirming of their doctrine, because it was new and surprising, and very different from what they had been taught by the scribes and Pharisees, and because so much depended upon men's receiving, or not receiving it, he empowered them to work miracles (*v.* 1, 2): He *gave them authority over all devils,* to dispossess them, and cast them out, though ever so numerous, so subtle, so fierce, so obstinate. Christ designed a total rout and ruin to the kingdom of darkness, and therefore gave them power over *all* devils. He authorized and appointed them likewise to *cure disease,* and to *heal the sick,* which would make them welcome wherever they came, and not only convince people's judgments, but gain their affections. This was their commission. Now observe,

1. What Christ directed them to do, in prosecution of this commission at this time, when they were not to *go far* or be *out long.* (1.) They must not be solicitous to recommend themselves to people's esteem by their outward appearance. Now that they begin to set up for themselves, they must have no dress, nor study to make any other figure than what they made while they followed him: they must *go as they were,* and not change their clothes, or so much as put on a pair of new shoes. (2.) They must depend upon Providence, and the kindness of their friends, to furnish them with what was convenient for them. They must not take with them *either bread or money,* and yet believe they should not want. Christ would not have his disciples *shy* of receiving the kindnesses of their friends, but rather to *expect* them. Yet St. Paul saw cause not to go by this rule, when he *laboured with his hands* rather than be burdensome. (3.) They must not change their lodgings, as suspecting that those who entertained them were *weary* of them; they have no reason to be so, for the ark is a guest that always pays well for its entertainment: "*Whatsoever house ye enter into there abide* (*v.* 4), that people may know where to find you, that your friends may know you are not backward to *serve* them, and your enemies may know you are not ashamed nor afraid to *face* them; *there abide* till you *depart* out of that city; stay with those you are used to." (4.) They must put on authority, and speak *warning* to those who *refused* them as well as comfort to those that *received* them, *v.* 5. "If there be any place that will not entertain you, if the magistrates deny you admission and threaten to treat you as vagrants, leave them, do not force yourselves upon them, nor run yourselves into danger among them, but at the same time bind them over to the judgment of God for it; *shake off the dust of your feet* for a *testimony against them.*" This will, as it were, be produced in evidence against them, that the messengers of the gospel had been among them, to make them a fair offer of grace and peace, for this dust they left behind there; so that when they perish at last in their infidelity this will lay and leave their blood upon their own heads. *Shake off the dust of your feet,* as much as to say you abandon their city, and will have no more to do with them.

2. What they did, in prosecution of this commission (*v.* 6): *They departed* from their Master's presence; yet, having still his spiritual presence with them, his *eye* and his *arm* going along with them, and, thus borne up in their work, they *went through the towns,* some or other of them, all the towns within the circuit appointed them, *preaching the gospel, and healing every where.* Their work was the same with their Master's, doing good both to souls and bodies.

II. We have here Herod's perplexity and vexation at this. The communicating of Christ's power to those who were sent forth in his name, and acted by authority from him, was an *amazing* and *convincing* proof of his being the Messiah, above any thing else; that he could not only work miracles *himself,* but empower others to work miracles too, this spread his fame more than any thing, and made the rays of this *Sun of righteousness* the stronger by the *reflection* of them even from *the earth,* from such mean illiterate men as the apostles were, who had nothing else to recommend them, or to raise any expectations from them, but that *they had been with Jesus,* Acts 4:13. When the country sees such as these *healing the sick* in the name of Jesus it gives it an alarm. Now observe,

1. The *various speculations* it *raised* among the *people,* who, though they thought not *rightly,* yet could not but think *honourably,* of our Lord Jesus, and that he was an extraordinary person, one come from the other world; that either John Baptist, who was lately persecuted and slain for the cause of God, or *one of the old prophets,* that had been persecuted and slain long since in that cause, was *risen again,* to be recompensed for his sufferings by this honour put upon him; or that Elias, who was taken alive to heaven in a fiery chariot, *had appeared* as an express from heaven, *v.* 7, 8.

2. The *great perplexity* it *created* in the mind of Herod: *When he had heard of all that was done* by Christ, his guilty conscience flew in his face, and he was ready to conclude with them that *John was risen from the dead.* He thought he had got clear of John, and should never be troubled with him any more, but, it seems, he is mistaken; either John is come to life again or here is another in his spirit and power, for God will never *leave himself without witness.* "What shall I do now?" saith Herod. "John *have I beheaded, but who is this?* Is he carrying on John's work, or is he come to avenge John's death? John baptized, but he does not; *John did no miracle,* but he does, and therefore appears more formidable than John." Note, Those who oppose God will find themselves more and more *embarrassed.* However, he *desired to see him,* whether he resembled John or no; but he might soon have been put out of this pain if he would but have informed himself of that which thousands knew, that Jesus preached, and wrought miracles, a great while before John was beheaded, and therefore could not be John raised from the dead. He *desired to see him;* and why did he not go and see him? Probably, because he thought it *below him* either to go to him or to send for him; he had enough of John Baptist, and cared not for having to do with any more such reprovers of sin. He desired to see him, but we do not find that ever he did, till he saw him at his bar, and then *he and his men of war set him at nought,* Lu. 23:11. Had he prosecuted his convictions now, and gone to see him, who knows but a happy change might have ben wrought in him? But, delaying it now, his heart was hardened, and when he did see him he was as much prejudiced against him as any other.

Verses 10–17

We have here, I. The account which the twelve gave their Master of the success of their ministry. They were not long out; but, *when they returned, they told him all that they had done,* as became servants who were sent on an errand. They told him *what they had done,* that, if they had done any thing amiss, they might mend it next time.

II. Their *retirement,* for a little *breathing:* He *took them, and went aside privately into a desert place,* that they might have some relaxation from business and not be always upon the stretch. Note, He that hath appointed our man-servant and maid-servant to rest would have his servants to rest too. Those in the most public stations, and that are most publicly useful, must sometimes go aside privately, both for the repose of their bodies, to recruit them, and for the furnishing of their minds by meditation for further public work.

III. The *resort* of the people to him, and the kind *reception* he gave them. They *followed* him, though it was into a *desert place;* for that is no desert where Christ is. And, though they hereby disturbed the repose he designed here for himself and his disciples, yet he *welcomed* them, *v.* 11. Note, Pious zeal may excuse a little rudeness; it did with Christ, and should with us. Though they came unseasonably, yet Christ gave them what they came for. 1. He *spoke unto them of the kingdom of God,* the laws of that kingdom with which they must be bound, and the privileges of that kingdom with which they might be blessed. 2. He *healed them that had need of healing,* and, in a sense of their need, made their application to him. Though the disease was ever so inveterate, and incurable by the physicians, though the patients were ever so poor and mean, yet Christ *healed them.* There is healing in Christ for all that *need* it, whether for soul or body. Christ hath still a power over bodily diseases, and heals his people that *need healing.* Sometimes he sees that we need the *sickness* for the good of our souls, more than the *healing* for the ease of our bodies, and then we must be willing *for a season,* because *there is need,* to be in *heaviness;* but, when he sees that we *need healing,* we shall have it. Death is his servant, to heal the saints of *all diseases.* He heals spiritual maladies by his graces, by his comforts, and has for each what the case calls for; relief for every exigence.

IV. The plentiful provision Christ made for the multitude that attended him. With *five loaves* of bread, and *two fishes,* he fed *five thousand men.* This narrative we had twice before, and shall meet with it again; it is the only miracle of our Saviour's that is recorded by all the four evangelists. Let us only observe out of it, 1. Those who diligently attend upon Christ in the way of duty, and therein deny or expose themselves, or are made to forget themselves and their outward conveniences by their zeal for God's house, are taken under his particular care, and may depend upon *Jehovah-jireh — The Lord will provide.* He will not see those that fear him, and serve him faithfully, want any good thing. 2. Our Lord Jesus was of a free and generous spirit. His disciples said, *Send them away, that they may get victuals;* but Christ said, "No, *give ye them to eat;* let what we have go as far as it will reach, and they are welcome to it." Thus he has taught both ministers and Christians to *use hospitality without grudging,* 1 Pt. 4:9. Those that have but a little, let them do what they can with that little, and that is the way to make it more. *There is that scatters, and yet increases.* 3. Jesus Christ has not only physic, but food, for all those that by faith apply themselves to him; he not only *heals them that need healing,* cures the diseases of the soul, but feeds them too that need feeding, supports the spiritual life, relieves the necessities of it, and satisfies the desires of it. Christ has provided not only to save the soul from perishing by its diseases, but to nourish the soul unto life eternal, and strengthen it for all spiritual exercises. 4. All the gifts of Christ are to be received by the church in a regular orderly manner; *Make them sit down by fifties in a company, v.* 14. Notice is here taken of the number of each company which Christ appointed for the better distribution of the meat and the easier computation of the number of the guests. 5. When we are receiving our creature-comforts, we must *look up to heaven.* Christ did so, to teach us to do so. We must acknowledge that we receive them from God, and that we are unworthy to receive them, — that we owe them all, and all the comfort we have in them, to the mediation of Christ, by whom the curse is removed, and the covenant of peace settled, — that we depend upon God's blessing upon them to make them serviceable to us, and desire that blessing. 6. The blessing of Christ will make a little go a great way. The *little that the righteous man has is better than the riches of many wicked, a dinner of herbs better than a stalled ox.* 7. Those whom Christ *feeds* he *fills;* to whom he gives, he gives enough; as there is in him enough for *all,* so there is enough for *each.* He replenishes every hungry soul, abundantly satisfies it with the *goodness of his house.* Here were *fragments taken up,* to assure us that in our Father's house there is *bread enough, and to spare.* We are not straitened, or stinted, in him.

Verses 18–27

In these verses, we have Christ discoursing with his disciples about the great things that *pertained to the kingdom of God;* and one circumstance of this discourse is taken notice of here which we had not in the other evangelists — that Christ was *alone praying,* and his *disciples with him,* when he entered into this discourse, *v.* 18. Observe, 1. Though Christ had much public work to do, yet he found some time to be *alone* in private, for converse with himself, with his Father, and with his disciples. 2. When Christ was alone he was *praying.* It is good for us to improve our solitude for devotion, that, *when we are alone,* we may *not be alone,* but may have *the Father with us.* 3. When Christ was alone, praying, his *disciples were with him,* to join with him in his prayer; so that this was a family-prayer. Housekeepers ought to pray with their households, parents with their children, masters with their servants, teachers and tutors with their scholars and pupils. 4. Christ *prayed* with them before he *examined* them, that they might be directed and encouraged to answer him, by his prayers for them. Those we give instructions to we should put up prayers for and with. He discourses with them,

I. Concerning himself; and enquires,

1. What *the people* said of him: *Who say the people that I am?* Christ knew better than they did, but would have his disciples made sensible, by the mistakes of others concerning him, how happy they were that were led into the knowledge of him and of the truth concerning him. We should take notice of the ignorance and errors of others, that we may be the more thankful to him who has *manifested himself to us, and not unto the world,* and may *pity* them, and do what we can to help them and to teach them better. They tell him what conjectures concerning him they had heard in their converse with the common people. Ministers would know better how to suit their instructions, reproofs, and counsels, to the case of ordinary people, if they did but converse more frequently and familiarly with them; they would then be the better able to say what is proper to rectify their notions, correct their irregularities, and remove their prejudices. The more conversant the physician is with his patient, the better he knows what to do for him. Some said that he was John Baptist, who was beheaded but the other day; others Elias, or *one of the old prophets;* any thing but what he was.

2. What *they* said of him. "Now see what an advantage you have by your discipleship; you know better." "So we do," saith Peter, "thanks be to our Master for it; we know that thou art *the Christ of God,* the *Anointed* of God, the Messiah promised." It is matter of unspeakable comfort to us that our Lord Jesus is *God's anointed,* for then he has unquestionable authority and ability for his undertaking; for his being *anointed* signifies his being both appointed to it and qualified for it. Now one would have expected that Christ should have charged his disciples, who were so fully apprized and assured of this truth, to publish it to every one they met with; but no, he *strictly charged them to tell no man that thing* as yet, because there is a time for all things. After his resurrection, which completed the proof of it, Peter made the temple ring of it, that *God had made this same Jesus both Lord and Christ* (Acts 2:36); but as yet the evidence was not ready to be summed up, and therefore it must be concealed; while it was so, we may conclude that the belief of it was not necessary to salvation.

II. Concerning his own *sufferings* and *death,* of which he had yet said little. Now that his disciples were well established in the belief of his being the Christ, and able to bear it, he speaks of them expressly, and with great assurance, *v.* 22. It comes in as a reason why they must not yet preach that he was *the Christ,* because the wonders that would attend his death and resurrection would be the most convincing proof of his being *the Christ of God.* It was by his *exaltation* to the *right hand of the Father* that he was fully declared to be *the Christ,* and by the sending of the Spirit thereupon (Acts 2:33); and therefore wait till that is done.

III. Concerning their sufferings for him. So far must they be from thinking how to *prevent* his sufferings that they must rather prepare for their own.

1. We must *accustom* ourselves to all instances of *self-denial* and *patience, v.* 23. This is the best preparative for martyrdom. We must live a life of self-denial, mortification, and contempt of the world; we must not indulge our ease and appetite, for then it will be hard to bear toil, and weariness, and want, for Christ. We are *daily* subject to affliction, and we must *accommodate* ourselves to it, and *acquiesce* in the will of God in it, and must learn to endure hardship. We frequently meet with crosses in the way of duty; and, though we must not pull them upon our own heads, yet, when they are laid for us, we must *take them up,* carry them after Christ, and make the best of them.

2. We must *prefer the salvation and happiness of our souls* before any *secular concern* whatsoever. Reckon upon it, (1.) That he who to preserve his liberty or estate, his power or preferment, nay, or to save his life, denies Christ and his truths, wilfully wrongs his conscience, and sins against God, will be, not only not a *saver,* but an unspeakable *loser,* in the issue, when *profit* and *loss* come to be balanced: *He that will save his life upon these terms will lose it,* will lose that which is of infinitely more value, his precious soul. (2.) We must firmly believe also that, if we lose our life for cleaving to Christ and our religion, we shall *save* it to our unspeakable advantage; for we shall be abundantly recompensed in the resurrection of the just, when we shall have it again a new and an eternal life. (3.) That the gain of all the world, if we should forsake Christ, and fall in with the interests of the world, would be so far from countervailing the eternal loss and ruin of the soul that it would bear no manner of proportion to it, *v.* 25. If we could be supposed to gain all the wealth, honour, and pleasure, in the world, by denying Christ, yet when, by *so doing,* we *lose ourselves* to all eternity, and are *cast away* at last, what good will our worldly gain do us? Observe, In Matthew and Mark the dreadful issue is a man's *losing his own soul,* here it is *losing himself,* which plainly intimates that *our souls* are *ourselves. Animus cujusque is est quisque — The soul is the man;* and it is well or ill with us according as it is well or ill with our souls. If they perish for ever, under the weight of their own guilt and corruption, it is certain that *we* are undone. The body cannot be happy if the soul be miserable in the other world; but the soul may be happy though the body be greatly afflicted and oppressed in this world. If a man be himself *cast away, ē zēmiōtheis — if he be damaged,* — or if he be punished, *si mulctetur — if he have a mulct put upon his soul* by the righteous sentence of Christ, whose cause and interest he has treacherously deserted, — if it be adjudged a forfeiture of all his blessedness, and the forfeiture be taken, where is his gain? What is his hope?

3. We must therefore *never be ashamed* of Christ and his gospel, nor of any disgrace or reproach that we may undergo for our faithful adherence to him and it, *v.* 26. *For whosoever shall be ashamed of me and of my words, of him shall the Son of man be ashamed,* and justly. When the service and honour of Christ called for his testimony and agency, he denied them, because the interest *of Christ* was a *despised* interest, and *every where spoken against;* and therefore he can expect no other than that in the great day, when his case calls for Christ's appearance on his behalf, Christ will be ashamed to own such a cowardly, worldly, sneaking spirit, and will say, "He is none of mine; he belongs not to me." As Christ had a state of *humiliation* and of *exaltation,* so likewise has his cause. They, and they only, that are willing to suffer with it when it suffers, shall reign with it when it reigns; but those that cannot find in their hearts to share with it in its *disgrace,* and to say, *If this be to be vile, I will be yet more vile,* shall certainly have no share with it in its *triumphs.* Observe here, How Christ, to support himself and his followers under present disgraces, speaks *magnificently* of the lustre of his second coming, in prospect of which he *endured the cross, despising the shame.* (1.) He shall come *in his own glory.* This was not mentioned in Matthew and Mark. He shall come in the glory of the Mediator, *all the glory* which the Father *restored to him,* which he had with God before the worlds were, which he had *deposited* and *put in pledge,* as it were, for the accomplishing of his undertaking, and demanded again when he had gone through it. *Now, O Father, glorify thou me,* Jn. 17:4, 5. He shall come in *all that glory* which the Father *conferred upon him* when *he set him at his own right hand,* and *gave him to be head over all things to the church;* in all the glory that is due to him as the assertor of the glory of God, and the author of the glory of all the saints. This is *his own glory.* (2.) He shall come *in his Father's glory.* The Father will judge the world by him, having committed all judgment to him; and therefore will publicly own him in the judgment as the *brightness of his glory* and the *express image* of his person. (3.) He shall come in *the glory of the holy angels.* They shall all *attend* him, and *minister* to him, and add every thing they can to the lustre of his appearance. What a figure will the blessed Jesus make in that day! Did we believe it, we should never be ashamed of him or his words now.

Lastly, To encourage them in suffering for him, he assures them that *the kingdom of God* would now *shortly be set up,* notwithstanding the great opposition that was made to it, *v.* 27. "Though the second coming of the Son of man is at a great distance, the kingdom of God shall come in its power in the present age, while some here present are alive." They *saw the kingdom of God* when the Spirit was poured out, when the gospel was preached to all the world and nations were brought to Christ by it; they saw the kingdom of God triumph over the Gentile nations in their *conversion,* and over the Jewish nation in its *destruction.*

Verses 28–36

We have here the narrative of Christ's transfiguration, which was designed for a specimen of that glory of his in which he will come to judge the world, of which he had lately been speaking, and, consequently, an encouragement to his disciples to suffer for him, and never to be ashamed of him. We had this account before in Matthew and Mark, and it is well worthy to be repeated to us, and reconsidered by us, for the *confirmation of our faith* in the Lord Jesus, as *the brightness of his Father's glory* and the light of the world, for the *filling* of our minds with *high* and *honourable* thoughts of him, notwithstanding his being clothed with a body, and *giving* us *some idea* of the *glory* which he entered into at his *ascension,* and in which he now *appears* within the veil, and for the *raising* and *encouraging* of our *hopes* and *expectations* concerning the glory reserved for all believers in the future state.

I. Here is one circumstance of the narrative that seems to differ from the other two evangelists that related it. They said that it was *six days* after the foregoing sayings; Luke says that it was *about eight days after,* that is, it was that day sevennight, six whole days intervening, and it was the eighth day. Some think that it was *in the night* that Christ was transfigured, because the disciples were sleepy, as in his agony, and *in the night* his appearance in splendour would be the more illustrious; if in the night, the computation of the time would be the more doubtful and uncertain; probably, in the night, between the seventh and eighth day, and so about eight days.

II. Here are divers circumstances added and explained, which are very material.

1. We are *here* told that Christ had this honour put upon him when he was *praying:* He *went up into a mountain to pray,* as he frequently did (*v.* 28), and *as he prayed* he was *transfigured.* When Christ *humbled* himself to pray, he was thus *exalted.* He knew before that this was designed for him at this time, and therefore seeks it by prayer. Christ himself must *sue out* the favours that were purposed for him, and promised to him: *Ask of me, and I will give thee,* Ps. 2:8. And thus he intended to put an *honour* upon the duty of prayer, and to *recommend* it to us. It is a transfiguring, transforming duty; if our hearts be elevated and enlarged in it, so as in it to *behold the glory of the Lord,* we shall be *changed into the same image from glory to glory,* 2 Co. 3:18. By prayer we fetch in the wisdom, grace, and joy, which *make the face to shine.*

2. Luke does not use the word *transfigured — metamorphōthē* (which Matthew and Mark used), perhaps because it had been used so much in the Pagan theology, but makes use of a phrase equivalent, *to eidos tou prosōpou heteron — the fashion of his countenance was another thing from what it had been:* his face shone far beyond what Moses's did when he came down from the mount; and *his raiment* was *white and glistering:* it was *exastraptōn — bright like lightning* (a word used only here), so that he seemed to be arrayed all with light, to *cover himself with light as with a garment.*

3. It was said in Matthew and Mark that Moses and Elias *appeared to them;* here it is said that they *appeared in glory,* to teach us that saints departed are *in glory,* are in a *glorious* state; they shine in glory. He being in glory, they *appeared with him in glory,* as all the saints shall shortly do.

4. We are here told what was the subject of the discourse between Christ and the two great prophets of the Old Testament: *They spoke of his decease, which he should accomplish at Jerusalem. Elegon tēn exodon autou — his exodus, his departure;* that is, *his death.* (1.) The death of Christ is here called his *exit,* his *going out,* his *leaving the world.* Moses and Elias spoke of it to him under that notion, to reconcile him to it, and to make the foresight of it the more easy to his human nature. The death of the saints is their *exodus,* their departure out of the Egypt of this world, their release

out of a *house of bondage.* Some think that the ascension of Christ is included here in his departure; for the departure of Israel out of Egypt was a departure in *triumph,* so was *his* when he went from earth to heaven. (2.) This departure of his he *must accomplish;* for thus it was determined, the matter was immutably fixed in the counsel of God, and could not be altered. (3.) He must accomplish it at Jerusalem, though his residence was mostly in Galilee; for his most spiteful enemies were at Jerusalem, and there the sanhedrim sat, that took upon them to judge of prophets. (4.) Moses and Elias spoke of this, to intimate that the *sufferings* of Christ, and his *entrance into his glory,* were what Moses and *the prophets* had *spoken of;* see Lu. 24:26, 27; 1 Pt. 1:11. (5.) Our Lord Jesus, even in his transfiguration, was willing to enter into a discourse concerning his death and sufferings, to teach us that meditations on death, as it is our departure out of this world to another, are never unseasonable, but in a special manner seasonable when at any time we are *advanced,* lest we should be *lifted up above measure.* In our greatest glories on earth, let us remember that here *we have no continuing city.*

5. We are here told, which we were not before, that the disciples were *heavy with sleep, v.* 32. When the vision first began, Peter, and James, and John were drowsy, and inclined to sleep. Either it was late, or they were weary, or had been disturbed in their rest the night before; or perhaps a charming composing air, or some sweet and melodious sounds, which disposed them to soft and gentle slumbers, were a preface to the vision; or perhaps it was owing to a sinful carelessness: when Christ was at prayer with them, they did not regard his prayer as they should have done, and, to punish them for that, they were left to *sleep on now,* when he began to be *transfigured,* and so lost an opportunity of seeing how that work of wonder was wrought. These three were now asleep, when Christ was in *his glory,* as afterwards they were, when he was in *his agony;* see the *weakness* and *frailty* of human nature, even in the best, and what need they have of the grace of God. Nothing could be more affecting to these disciples, one would think, than the *glories* and the *agonies* of their Master, and both in the highest degree; and yet neither the one nor the other would serve to *keep them awake.* What need have we to pray to God for quickening grace, to make us not only *alive,* but *lively!* Yet that they might be competent witnesses of *this sign from heaven,* to those that demanded one, after awhile they *recovered themselves,* and became perfectly awake; and then they took an exact view of all those glories, so that they were able to give a particular account, as we find one of them does, of all that passed when they were with Christ *in the holy mount,* 2 Pt. 1:18.

6. It is here observed that it was when Moses and Elias were now about to *depart* that Peter said, *Lord, it is good to be here, let us make three tabernacles.* Thus we are often not sensible of the worth of our mercies till we are about to lose them; nor do we covet and court their continuance till they are upon the departure. Peter said this, *not knowing what he said.* Those know not what they say that talk of making tabernacles on earth for glorified saints in heaven, who have better mansions in the temple there, and long to return to them.

7. It is here added, concerning the *cloud* that *overshadowed them,* that they *feared as they entered into the cloud.* This cloud was a token of God's more peculiar presence. It was in a cloud that God of old took possession of the tabernacle and temple, and, when the cloud *covered the tabernacle, Moses was not able to enter* (Ex. 40:34, 35), and, when it filled the temple, the *priests could not stand to minister by reason of it,* 2 Chr. 5:14. Such a cloud was this, and then no wonder that the disciples were *afraid to enter into it.* But never let any be afraid to enter into a cloud with Jesus Christ; for he will be sure to bring them safely through it.

8. The *voice* which came from heaven is here, and in Mark, related not so fully as in Matthew: *This is my beloved Son, hear him:* though those words, *in whom I am well pleased,* which we have both in Matthew and Peter, are not expressed, they are implied in that, *This is my beloved Son;* for whom he *loves,* and in whom he is *well pleased,* come all to one; we are *accepted in the Beloved.*

Lastly, The apostles are here said to have kept this vision private. They *told no man in those days,* reserving the discovery of it for another opportunity, when the evidences of Christ's being the Son of God were completed in the pouring out of the Spirit, and that doctrine was to be published to all the world. As there is a time *to speak,* so there is a time to *keep silence.* Every thing is beautiful and useful in its season.

Verses 37–42

This passage of story in Matthew and Mark follows immediately upon that of Christ's transfiguration, and his discourse with his disciples after it; but here it is said to be *on the next day, as they were coming down from the hill,* which confirms the conjecture that Christ was transfigured *in the night,* and, it should seem, though they did not *make tabernacles* as Peter proposed, yet they found some shelter to repose themselves in all night, for it was not till next day that they *came down from the hill,* and then he found things in some disorder among his disciples, though not so bad as Moses did when he came down from the mount. When wise and good men are in their beloved retirements, they would do well to consider whether they are not wanted in their *public stations.*

In this narrative here, observe, 1. How forward the people were to receive Christ at his return to them. Though he had been but a little while absent, *much people met him,* as, at other times, much people *followed* him; for so it was foretold concerning him, that *to him should the gathering of the people be.* 2. How importunate the father of the lunatic child was with Christ for help for him (*v.* 38): *I beseech thee, look upon my son;* this is his request, and it is a very modest one; one compassionate look from Christ is enough to set every thing to rights. Let us bring ourselves and our children to Christ, to be *looked upon.* His plea is, *He is my only child.* They that have many children may balance their affliction in one with their comfort in the rest; yet, if it be an only child that is a grief, the affliction in that may be balanced with the love of God in giving his only-begotten Son for us. 3. How *deplorable* the case of the *child* was, *v.* 39. He was under the power of an evil spirit, that *took him;* and diseases of that nature are more frightful than such as arise merely from natural causes: when the fit seized him without any warning given, he suddenly *cried out,* and many a time his shrieks had pierced the heart of his tender father. This malicious spirit *tore him,* and *bruised* him, and *departed not from him* but with great difficulty, and a deadly gripe at parting. O the afflictions of the afflicted in this world! And what mischief doth Satan do where he gets possession! But happy they that have access to Christ! 4. How defective the disciples were in their faith. Though Christ had given them *power over unclean spirits,* yet they *could not* cast out this *evil spirit, v.* 40. Either they distrusted the power they were to fetch in strength from, or the commission given to them, or they did not exert themselves in prayer as they ought; for this Christ reproved them. O *faithless and perverse generation!* Dr. Clarke understands this as spoken to his disciples: "*Will ye be* yet so faithless and full of distrust that ye cannot execute the commission I have given you?" 5. How effectual the cure was, which Christ wrought upon this child, *v.* 42. Christ can do that for us which his disciples cannot: *Jesus rebuked the unclean spirit* then when he raged most. The devil *threw the child down,* and *tore him,* distorted him, as if he would have pulled him to pieces. But one word from Christ *healed the child,* and made good the damage the devil had done him. And it is here added that he *delivered him again to his father.* Note, When our children are recovered from sickness, we must receive them as delivered to us again, receive them as life from the dead, and as when we first received them. It is comfortable to receive them from the hand of Christ, to see him delivering them to us again: "Here, take this child, and be thankful; take it, and bring it up for me, for thou hast it again from me. Take it, and do not set thy heart too much upon it." With such cautions as these, parents should receive their children *from Christ's hands,* and then with comfort put them again *into his hands.*

Verses 43–50

We may observe here, I. The impression which Christ's miracles made upon all that beheld them (*v.* 43): *They were all amazed at the mighty power of God,* which they could not but see in all the miracles Christ wrought. Note, The works of God's almighty power are amazing, especially those that are wrought by the hand of the Lord Jesus; for he is *the power of God,* and his name is *Wonderful.* Their wonder was universal: they wondered *every one.* The causes of it were universal: they wondered at *all things which Jesus did;* all his actions had something uncommon and surprising in them.

II. The notice Christ gave to his disciples of his approaching sufferings: *The Son of man shall be delivered into the hands of men,* wicked men, men of the worst character; they shall be permitted to abuse him at their pleasure. That is here *implied* which is *expressed* by the other evangelists: *They shall kill him.* But that which is peculiar here is, 1. The connection of this with what goes next before, of the admiration with which the people were struck at beholding Christ's miracles (*v.* 43): *While they all wondered at all things which Jesus did, he said this to his disciples.* They had a fond conceit of his temporal kingdom, and that he should reign, and they with him, in secular pomp and power; and now they thought that this *mighty power* of his would easily effect the thing, and his interest gained by his miracles in the people would contribute to it; and therefore Christ, who knew what was in their hearts, takes this occasion to tell them again, what he had told them before, that he was so far from having men *delivered into his hands* that he must be *delivered into the hands of men,* so far from living in honour that he must die in disgrace; and all his miracles, and the interest he has by them gained in the hearts of the people, will not be able to prevent it. 2. The solemn preface with which it is introduced: "*Let these sayings sink down into your ears;* take special notice of what I say, and mix faith with it; let not the notions you have of the temporal kingdom of the Messiah stop your ears against it, nor make you unwilling to believe it. Admit what I say, and submit to it.*" Let it sink down into your hearts;* so the Syriac and Arabic read it. The word of Christ does us no good, unless we let it sink down into our heads and hearts. 3. The unaccountable stupidity of the disciples, with reference to this prediction of Christ's sufferings. It was said in Mark, *They understood not that saying.* It was plain enough, but they *would not* understand it in the literal sense, because it agreed not with their notions; and they *could not* understand it in any other, *and were afraid to ask him* lest they should be undeceived and awaked out of their pleasing dream. But it is here added that *it was hidden from them, that they perceived it not,* through the weakness of faith and the power of prejudice. We cannot think that it was *in mercy* hidden from them, lest they should be swallowed up with overmuch sorrow at the prospect of it; but that it was a paradox, because they *made it so* to themselves.

III. The rebuke Christ gave to his disciples for their disputing among themselves which should be greatest, *v.* 46–48. This passage we had before, and, the more is the pity, we shall meet with the like again. Observe here,

1. Ambition of honour, and strife for superiority and precedency, are sins that most easily beset the disciples of our Lord Jesus, for which they deserve to be severely rebuked; they flow from corruptions which they are highly concerned to subdue and mortify, *v.* 46. They that expect to be *great* in this world commonly aim high, and nothing will serve them short of being *greatest;* this exposes them to a great deal of temptation and trouble, which they are safe from that are content to be *little,* to be *least,* to be *less than the least.*

2. Jesus Christ is perfectly acquainted with the thoughts and intents of our hearts: He *perceived their thoughts, v.* 47. Thoughts are *words* to him, and *whispers* are loud cries. It is a good reason why we should keep up a strict government of our thoughts because Christ takes a strict cognizance of them.

3. Christ will have his disciples to aim at that honour which is to be obtained by a quiet and condescending humility, and not at that which is to be obtained by a restless and aspiring ambition. Christ *took a child, and set him by him, v.* 47 (for he always expressed a tenderness and kindness for little children), and he proposed *this child* to them for an example. (1.) Let them be of the *temper* of this child, *humble* and *quiet,* and *easy* to itself; let them not affect worldly pomp, or grandeur, or high titles, but be as dead to them as this child; let them bear no more malice to their rivals and competitors than this child did. Let them be willing to be *the least,* if that would contribute any thing to their usefulness, to stoop to the meanest office whereby they might *do good.* (2.) Let them assure themselves that this was the way to preferment; for this would recommend them to the esteem of their brethren: they that loved Christ would *therefore receive* them *in his name,* because they did most resemble him, and they would likewise recommend themselves to his favour, for

Christ would take the kindnesses done to them as done to himself: *Whosoever shall receive one such child,* a preacher of the gospel that is of such a disposition as this, he placeth his respect aright, and *receiveth me;* and *whosoever receiveth me,* in such a minister, *receiveth him that sent me;* and what greater honour can any man attain to in this world than to be received by men as a messenger of God and Christ, and to have God and Christ own themselves received and welcomed in him? This honour have all the humble disciples of Jesus Christ, and thus they shall be truly great that are least among them.

IV. The rebuke Christ gave to his disciples for discouraging one that honoured him and served him, but was not of their communion, not only not one of the twelve, nor one of the seventy, but not one of those that ever associated with them, or attended on them, but, upon occasional hearing of Christ, believed in him, and made use of his name with faith and prayer in a serious manner, for the casting out of devils. Now, 1. This man they *rebuked and restrained;* they would not let him pray and preach, though it was to the honour of Christ, though it did good to men and weakened Satan's kingdom, because he did not *follow Christ with them;* he separated from their church, was not ordained as they were, paid them no respect, nor gave them the right hand of fellowship. Now, if ever any society of Christians in this world had reason to silence those that were not of their communion, the twelve disciples at this time had; and yet, 2. Jesus Christ chid them for what they did, and warned them not to do the like again, nor any that profess to be successors of the apostles: "*Forbid him not* (*v.* 50), but rather encourage him, for he is carrying on the same design that you are, though, for reasons best known to himself, he does not follow *with you;* and he will meet you in *the same end,* though he does not accompany you in *the same way.* You *do well* to do as you do, but it does not therefore follow that he *does ill* to do as he does, and that you do well to put him under an interdict, for *he that is not against us is for us,* and therefore ought to be countenanced by us." We need not lose any of our friends, while we have so few, and so many enemies. Those may be found faithful followers of Christ, and, as such, may be accepted of him, though they do not follow *with us.* See Mk. 9:38, 39. O what a great deal of mischief to the church, even from those that boast of relation to Christ, and pretend to *envy for his sake,* would be prevented, if this passage of story were but duly considered!

Verses 51–56

This passage of story we have not in any other of the evangelists, and it seems to come in here for the sake of its affinity with that next before, for in this also Christ rebuked his disciples, because they envied for his sake. There, under colour of zeal for Christ, they were for silencing and restraining separatists: here, under the same colour, they were for putting infidels to death; and, as for *that,* so for *this* also, Christ reprimanded them, for a spirit of bigotry and persecution is directly contrary to the spirit of Christ and Christianity. Observe here,

I. The *readiness* and *resolution* of our Lord Jesus, in prosecuting his great undertaking for our redemption and salvation. Of this we have an instance, *v.* 51: *When the time was come that he should be received up, he stedfastly set his face to go to Jerusalem.* Observe 1. There was a time fixed for the sufferings and death of our Lord Jesus, and he knew well enough when it was, and had a clear and certain foresight of it, and yet was so far from keeping out of the way that then he appeared most publicly of all, and was most busy, knowing that his time was short. 2. When he saw his death and sufferings approaching, he looked through them and beyond them, to the glory that should follow; he looked upon it as the time when he should be *received up into glory* (1 Tim. 3:16), received up into the highest heavens, to be enthroned there. Moses and Elias spoke of his death as his departure out of this world, which made it not *formidable;* but he went further, and looked upon it as his translation to a better world, which made it very *desirable.* All good Christians may frame to themselves the same notion of death, and may call it their being *received up,* to be with Christ where he is; and, when the *time* of their being *received up* is at hand, let them lift up their heads, knowing that *their redemption draws nigh.* 3. On this prospect of the joy set before him, he *stedfastly set his face to go to Jerusalem* the place where he was to suffer and die. He was fully *determined* to go, and would not be dissuaded; he went *directly* to Jerusalem, because there now his business lay, and he did not go about to other towns, or fetch a compass, which if he had done, as commonly he did, he might have avoided going through Samaria. He went cheerfully and courageously thither, though he knew the things that should befal him there. He *did not fail nor was discouraged,* but *set his face as a flint, knowing* that he should be not only *justified,* but glorified (Isa. 50:7), not only not *run down,* but *received up.* How should this shame us *for,* and shame *us out of,* our backwardness to do and suffer for Christ! We draw back, and turn our faces another way from his service who stedfastly set his face against all opposition, to go through with the work of our salvation.

II. The *rudeness* of the Samaritans in a *certain village* (not named, nor deserving to be so) who would not *receive him,* nor suffer him to bait in their town, though his way lay through it. Observe here, 1. How *civil* he was to them: *He sent messengers before his face,* some of his disciples, that went to take up lodgings, and to know whether he might have leave to accommodate himself and his company among them; for he would not come to give *offence,* or if they took any umbrage at the number of his followers. He sent some to *make ready* for him, not for state, but convenience, and that his coming might be no surprise. 2. How *uncivil* they were to him, *v.* 53. They did not *receive him,* would not suffer him to come into their village, but ordered their watch to keep him out. He would have *paid* for all he *bespoke,* and been a generous guest among them, would have done them good, and preached the gospel to them, as he had done some time ago to another city of the Samaritans, Jn. 4:41. He would have been, if they pleased, the greatest blessing that ever came to their village, and yet they forbid him entrance. Such treatment his gospel and ministers have often met with. Now the reason was *because his face was as though he would go to Jerusalem;* they observed, by his motions, that he was steering his course that way. The great controversy between the Jews and the Samaritans was about the place of worship — whether Jerusalem or mount Gerizim near Sychar; see Jn. 4:20. And so hot was the controversy between them that the *Jews would have no dealings with the Samaritans,* nor they with them, Jn. 4:9. Yet we may suppose that they did not deny other Jews lodgings among them, no, not when they went up to the feast; for if that had been their constant practice Christ would not have attempted it, and it would have been a great way about for some of the Galileans to go to Jerusalem any other way than through Samaria. But they were particularly incensed against Christ, who was a celebrated teacher, for owning and adhering to the temple at Jerusalem, when the priests of that temple were such bitter enemies to him, which, they hoped, would have driven him to come and worship at *their* temple, and bring that into reputation; but when they saw that he would go forward to Jerusalem, notwithstanding this, they would not show him the common civility which probably they used formerly to show him in his journey thither.

III. The *resentment* which James and John expressed of this affront, *v.* 54. When these two heard this message brought, they were all in a flame presently, and nothing will serve them but Sodom's doom upon this village: "Lord," say they, "give us leave to command fire to come down from heaven, not to *frighten* them only, but to *consume* them."

1. Here indeed was something commendable, for they showed, (1.) A great confidence in the power they had received from Jesus Christ; though this had not been particularly mentioned in their commission, yet they could with a word's speaking fetch *fire from heaven. Theleis eipōmen — Wilt thou that we speak the word,* and the thing will be done. (2.) A great zeal for the honour of their Master. They took it very ill that he who did good wherever he came and found a hearty welcome should be denied the liberty of the road by a parcel of paltry Samaritans; they could not think of it without indignation that their Master should be thus slighted. (3.) A submission, notwithstanding, to their Master's good will and pleasure. They will not offer to do such a thing, unless Christ give leave: *Wilt thou* that we do it? (4.) A regard to the examples of the prophets that were before them. It is doing *as Elias did?* they would not have thought of such a thing if Elijah had not done it upon the soldiers that came to take him, once and again, 2 Ki. 1:10, 12. They thought that this *precedent* would be their *warrant;* so apt are we to misapply the examples of good men, and to think to justify ourselves by them in the irregular liberties we give ourselves, when the case is not parallel.

2. But though there was something right in what they said, yet there was much more amiss, for (1.) This was not the first time, by a great many, that our Lord Jesus had been thus affronted, witness the Nazarenes thrusting him out of their city, and the Gadarenes desiring him to depart out of their coast; and yet he never called for any judgment upon them, but patiently put up with the injury. (2.) These were Samaritans, from whom better was not to be expected, and perhaps they had heard that Christ had forbidden his disciples to *enter into any of the cities of the Samaritans* (Mt. 10:5), and therefore it was not so bad in them as in others who knew more of Christ, and had received so many favours from him. (3.) Perhaps it was only some few of the town that knew any thing of the matter, or that sent that rude message to him, while, for aught they knew, there were many in the town who, if they had heard of Christ's being so near them, would have gone to meet him and welcomed him; and must the whole town be laid in ashes for the wickedness of a few? Will they have the righteous destroyed with the wicked? (4.) Their Master had never yet upon any occasion called for *fire from heaven,* nay, he had refused to give the Pharisees any *sign from heaven* when they demanded it (Mt. 16:1, 2); and why should they think to introduce it? James and John were the two disciples whom Christ had called *Boanerges — sons of thunder* (Mk. 3:17); and will not that serve them, but they must be *sons of lightning* too? (5.) The example of Elias did not reach the case. Elijah was sent to display the terrors of the law, and to give proof of that, and to witness as a bold reprover against the idolatries and wickednesses of the court of Ahab, and it was agreeable enough to him to have his commission thus proved; but it is a dispensation of grace that is now to be introduced, to which such a terrible display of divine justice will not be at all agreeable. Archbishop Tillotson suggests that their being now near Samaria, where Elijah called for fire from heaven, might help to put it in their heads; perhaps at the very place; but, though the *place* was the same, the *times* were altered.

IV. The *reproof* he gave to James and John for their fiery, furious zeal (*v.* 55): He *turned* with a just displeasure, and *rebuked them;* for *as many as he loves he rebukes and chastens,* particularly for what they do, that is irregular and unbecoming them, under colour of zeal for him.

1. He shows them in particular their mistake: *Ye know not what manner of spirit ye are of;* that is, (1.) "You *are not aware* what an *evil spirit* and disposition you are of; how much there is of pride, and passion, and personal revenge, covered under this pretence of zeal for your Master." Note, There may be much corruption lurking, nay, and stirring too, in the hearts of good people, and they themselves not be sensible of it. (2.) "You *do not consider* what a *good spirit,* directly contrary to this, you *should be of.* Surely you have yet to learn, though you have been so long learning, what the spirit of Christ and Christianity is. Have you not been taught to *love your enemies,* and to *bless them that curse you,* and to call for grace from heaven, not fire from heaven, upon them? You know not how contrary your disposition herein is to that which it was the design of the gospel you should be *delivered* into. You are not now under the dispensation of bondage, and terror, and death, but under the dispensation of love, and liberty, and grace, which was ushered in with a proclamation of *peace on earth* and *good will toward men,* to which you ought to accommodate yourselves, and not by such imprecations as these oppose yourselves."

2. He shows them the general design and tendency of his religion (*v.* 56): *The Son of man* is not himself come, and therefore does not send you abroad *to destroy men's lives, but to save them.* He designed to propagate his holy religion by love and sweetness, and every thing that is inviting and endearing, not by fire and sword, and blood and slaughter; by miracles of healing, not by plagues and miracles of destruction, as Israel was brought out of Egypt. Christ came to *slay* all *enmities,* not to foster them. Those are certainly destitute of the spirit of the gospel that are for anathematizing and rooting out by violence and persecution all that are not of their mind and way, that cannot in conscience say as they say, and do as they do. Christ came, not only to save men's *souls,* but to save their *lives* too — witness the many miracles he wrought for the healing of diseases that would otherwise have been *mortal,* by which, and a thousand other instances of beneficence, it appears that Christ would have his disciples

do good to all, to the utmost of their power, but hurt to none, to draw men into his church with the *cords of a man and the bands of love,* but not think to drive men into it with a *rod of violence* or the *scourge of the tongue.*

V. His *retreat* from this village. Christ would not only not punish them for their rudeness, but would not insist upon his right of travelling the road (which was as free to him as to his neighbours), would not attempt to force his way, but quietly and peaceably *went to another village,* where they were not so stingy and bigoted, and there refreshed himself, and went on his way. Note, When a stream of opposition is strong, it is wisdom to get out of the way of it, rather than to contend with it. If some be very rude, instead of revenging it, we should try whether others will not be more civil.

Verses 57–62

We have here an account of three several persons that offered themselves to follow Christ, and the answers that Christ gave to each of them. The two former we had an account of in Mt. 19:21.

I. Here is one that is extremely forward to follow Christ immediately, but seems to have been too rash, hasty, and inconsiderate, and not to have set down and counted the cost.

1. He makes Christ a very large promise (*v.* 57): *As they went in the way,* going up to Jerusalem, where it was expected Christ would first appear in his glory, one said to him, *Lord, I will follow thee withersoever thou goest.* This must be the resolution of all that will be found Christ's disciples indeed; they *follow the Lamb whithersoever he goes* (Rev. 14:4), though it be through fire and water, to prisons and deaths.

2. Christ gives him a necessary caution, not to promise himself great things in the world, in following him, but, on the contrary, to count upon poverty and meanness; for *the Son of man has not where to lay his head.*

We may look upon this, (1.) As *setting forth* the *very low condition* that our Lord Jesus was in, in this world. He not only wanted the delights and ornaments that great princes usually have, but even such accommodations for mere necessity as the *foxes* have, and the *birds of the air.* See what a *depth of poverty* our Lord Jesus submitted to for us, to increase the worth and merit of his satisfaction, and to purchase for us a larger *allowance of grace, that we through his poverty might be rich,* 2 Co. 8:9. He that made all did not make a dwelling-place for himself, not a house of his own to put his head in, but what he was beholden to others for. He here calls himself the *Son of man,* a Son of Adam, partaker of flesh and blood. He glories in his condescension towards us, not only to the meanness of our nature, but to the meanest condition in that nature, to testify his love to us, and to teach us a holy contempt of the world and of great things in it, and a continual regard to another world. Christ was thus poor, to sanctify and sweeten poverty to his people; the apostles had not certain dwelling-place (1 Co. 4:11), which they might the better bear when they knew their Master had not; see 2 Sa. 11:11. We may well be content to fare as Christ did. (2.) As proposing this to the consideration of those who intend to be his disciples. If we mean to follow Christ, we must lay aside the thoughts of great things in the world, and not reckon upon making any thing *more than heaven* of our religion, as we must resolve not to take up with any thing *less.* Let us not go about to compound the profession of Christianity with secular advantages; Christ has *put them asunder,* let us not think of *joining them together;* on the contrary, we must expect to enter into the kingdom of heaven through many tribulations, must *deny ourselves,* and *take up our cross.* Christ tells this man what he must count upon if he followed him, to lie cold and uneasy, to fare hard, and live in contempt; if he could not submit to this, let him not pretend to follow Christ. This word sent him back, for aught that appears; but it will be no discouragement to any that know what there is in Christ and heaven to set in the scale against this.

II. Here is another, that seems *resolved* to follow Christ, but he *begs a day, v.* 59. To this man Christ first gave the call; he said to him, *Follow me.* He that proposed the thing of himself fled off when he heard of the difficulties that attended it; but this man to whom Christ gave a call, though he hesitated at first, yet, as it should seem, afterwards yielded; so true was that of Christ, *You have not chosen me, but I have chosen you,* Jn. 15:16. It is not of *him that willeth,* nor *of him that runneth* (as that forward spark in the foregoing verses), but of God that showeth mercy, that *gives* the call, and *makes* it *effectual,* as to this man here. Observe,

1. The excuse he made: *"Lord, suffer me first to go and bury my father.* I have an aged father at home, who cannot live long, and will need me while he does live; let me go and attend on him until he is dead, and I have performed my last office of love to him, and then I will do any thing." We may here see three temptations, by which we are in danger of being drawn and kept from following Christ, which therefore we should guard against: — (1.) We are tempted to *rest* in a *discipleship at large,* in which we may be *at a loose end,* and not to come *close,* and give up ourselves to be *strict* and *constant.* (2.) We are tempted to *defer* the doing of that which we know to be our duty, and to put if off to some other time. When we have got clear of such a care and difficulty, when we have despatched such a business, raised an estate to such a pitch, then we will begin to think of being religious; and so we are cozened out of all our time, by being cozened out of the present time. (3.) We are tempted to think that our duty to our relations will excuse us from our duty to Christ. It is a plausible excuse indeed: *"Let me go and bury my father,* — let me take care of my family, and provide for my children, and then I will think of serving Christ;" whereas the *kingdom of God and the righteousness thereof* must be sought ad minded *in the first place.*

2. Christ's answer to it (*v.* 60): *"Let the dead bury their dead.* Suppose (which is not likely) that there are none but the dead to bury their dead, or none but those who are themselves aged and dying, who are *as good as dead,* and fit for no other service, yet thou hast other work to do; *go thou, and preach the kingdom of God."* Not that Christ would have his followers or his ministers to be *unnatural;* our religion teaches us to be kind and good in every relation, to *show piety at home,* and to *requite our parents.* But we must not make these offices an excuse from our duty to God. If the nearest and dearest relation we have in the world stand in our way to keep us from Christ, it is necessary that we have a zeal that will make us forget *father and mother,* as Levi did, Deu. 33:9. This disciple was called to be a minister, and therefore must not *entangle himself* with the *affairs of this world,* 2 Tim. 2:4. And it is a rule that, whenever Christ calls to any duty, we must not *consult with flesh and blood,* Gal. 1:15, 16. No excuses must be admitted against a present obedience to the call of Christ.

III. Here is another that is willing to follow Christ, but he must have a *little time* to *talk with his friends* about it.

Observe, 1. His request for a dispensation, *v.* 61. He said, *"Lord, I will follow thee;* I design no other, I am determined to do it: but *let me first go bid them farewell that are at home."* This seemed reasonable; it was what Elisha desired when Elijah called him,*Let me kiss my father and my mother;* and it was allowed him: but the ministry of the gospel is *preferable,* and the service of it more urgent than that of the prophets; and therefore here it would not be allowed. Suffer me *apotaxasthai tois eis ton oikon mou — Let me go and set in order my household affairs,* and give direction concerning them; so some understand it. Now that which was amiss in this is, (1.) That he looked upon his following Christ as a melancholy, troublesome, dangerous thing; it was to him as if he were *going to die* and therefore he must take *leave* of all his friends, never to *see them again,* or never *with any comfort;* whereas, in following Christ, he might be more a comfort and blessing to them than if he had continued with them. (2.) That he seemed to have his worldly concerns more upon his heart than he ought to have, and than would consist with a close attendance to his duty as a follower of Christ. He seemed to hanker after his relations and family concerns, and he could not part easily and suitably from them, but they stuck to him. It may be he had bidden them *farewell* once, but *Loth to depart bids oft farewell,* and therefore he must bid them *farewell* once more, for they are *at home at his house.* (3.) That he was willing to enter into a temptation from his purpose of following Christ. To go and bid them *farewell* that were *at home at his house* would be to expose himself to the strongest solicitations imaginable to alter his resolution; for they would all be against it, and would *beg* and *pray* that he would not *leave them.* Now it was presumption in him to thrust himself into such a temptation. Those that resolve to walk with their Maker, and follow their Redeemer, must resolve that they will not so much as parley with their tempter.

2. The rebuke which Christ gave him for this request (*v.* 62): *"No man, having put his hand to the plough,* and designing to make good work of his ploughing, will *look back,* or look behind him, for then he makes balks with his plough, and the ground he ploughs is *not fit* to be sown; so thou, if thou hast a design to follow me and to reap the advantages of those that do so, yet if thou *lookest back* to a worldly life again and hankerest after that, if thou *lookest back* as Lot's wife did to Sodom, which seems to be alluded to here, *thou art not fit for the kingdom of God."* (1.) "Thou art not *soil* fit to receive the *good seed* of the kingdom of God if thou art thus *ploughed* by the *halves,* and not gone through with." (2.) "Thou art not a *sower* fit to *scatter* the good seed of the kingdom if thou canst *hold the plough* no better." Ploughing is in order to sowing. As those are not fit to be *sown* with divine comforts whose *fallow ground* is not first *broken up,* so those are not fit to be employed in sowing who know not how to break up the fallow ground, but, when they have *laid their hand to the plough,* upon every occasion look back and think of quitting it. Note, Those who begin with the work of God must resolve to *go on* with it, or they will make nothing of it. Looking back inclines to *drawing back,* and *drawing back* is to *perdition.* Those are not fit for heaven who, having set their faces heavenward, face about. But he, and he only, that *endures to the end, shall be saved.*

CHAPTER 10

In this chapter we have, I. The ample commission which Christ gave to the seventy disciples to preach the gospel, and to confirm it by miracles; and the full instructions he gave them how to manage themselves in the execution of their commissions, and great encouragements therein (*v.* 1–16). II. The report which the seventy disciples made to their Master of the success of their negotiation, and his discourse thereupon (*v.* 17–24). III. Christ's discourse with a lawyer concerning the way to heaven, and the instructions Christ gave him by a parable to look upon every one as his neighbour whom he had occasion to show kindness to, or receive kindness from (*v.* 25–37). IV. Christ's entertainment at Martha's house, the reproof he gave to her for her care about the world, and his commendation of Mary for her care about her soul (*v.* 38–42).

Verses 1–16

We have here the sending forth of seventy disciples, two and two, into divers parts of the country, to preach the gospel, and to work miracles in those places which Christ himself designed to visit, to make way for his entertainment. This is not taken notice of by the other evangelists: but the instructions here given them are much the same with those given to the twelve. Observe,

I. Their number: they were seventy. As in the choice of twelve apostles Christ had an eye to the twelve patriarchs, the twelve tribes, and the twelve princes of those tribes, so here he seems to have an eye to the *seventy* elders of Israel. So many went up with Moses and Aaron to the mount, and *saw the glory of the God of Israel* (Ex. 24:1, 9), and so many were afterwards chosen to assist Moses in the government, in order to which the Spirit of prophecy came unto them, Num. 11:24, 25. The *twelve wells of water* and the *seventy palm-trees* that were at Elim were a figure of the *twelve apostles* and the *seventy disciples,* Ex. 15:27. They were seventy elders of the Jews that were employed by Ptolemy king of Egypt in turning the Old Testament into Greek, whose translation is thence called the *Septuagint.* The great sanhedrim consisted of this number. Now,

1. We are glad to find that Christ had so many followers fit to be sent forth; his labour was not altogether in vain, though he met with much opposition. Note, Christ's interest is a *growing* interest, and his followers, like Israel in Egypt, though *afflicted* shall *multiply.* These *seventy,* though they did not attend him so closely and constantly as the *twelve* did, were nevertheless the constant hearers of his doctrine, and witnesses of his miracles, and believed in him. Those three mentioned in the close of the foregoing chapter might have been of these seventy, if they would have applied themselves in good earnest to their business. These seventy are those of whom Peter speaks as *"the men who companied with us all the time that the Lord Jesus went in and out among us,"* and were part of the one hundred and twenty there spoken of, Acts 1:15, 21. Many of those that were the companions of the apostles, whom we read of in the Acts and the Epistles, we may suppose, were of these seventy disciples.

2. We are glad to find there was work for so many ministers, hearers for so many preachers: thus the grain of mustard-seed began to *grow,* and the savour of the leaven to diffuse itself in the meal, in order to the leavening of the whole.

II. Their work and business: He sent them *two and two,* that they might strengthen and encourage one another. *If one fall, the other will help to raise him up.* He sent them, not to all the cities of Israel, as he did the *twelve,* but only *to every city and place whither he himself would come* (*v.* 1), as his harbingers; and we must suppose, though it is not recorded, that Christ soon after went to all those places whither he now sent them, though he could stay but a little while in a place. Two things they were ordered to do, the same that Christ did wherever he came: — 1. They must *heal the sick* (*v.* 9), heal them *in the name of Jesus,* which would make people long to see this Jesus, and ready to entertain him whose name was so powerful. 2. They must publish the approach of the kingdom of God, its approach *to them:* "Tell them this, *The kingdom of God is come nigh to you,* and you now stand fair for an admission into it, if you will but look about you. Now is the *day of your visitation,* know and understand it." It is good to be made sensible of our advantages and opportunities, that we may lay hold of them. When the *kingdom of God comes nigh us,* it concerns us to go forth to meet it.

III. The instructions he gives them.

1. They must set out with prayer (*v.* 2); and, in prayer, (1.) They must be duly affected with the necessities of the souls of men, which called for their help. They must *look about,* and see how *great the harvest was,* what abundance of people there were that wanted to have the gospel preached to them and were willing to receive it, nay, that had at this time their expectations raised of the coming of the Messiah and of his kingdom. There was corn ready to shed and be lost for want of hands to gather it in. Note, Ministers should apply themselves to their work under a deep concern for *precious souls,* looking upon them as the riches of this world, which ought to be secured for Christ. They must likewise be concerned that the *labourers were so few.* The Jewish teachers were indeed many, but they were not labourers; they did not gather in souls to God's kingdom, but to their own interest and party. Note, Those that are good ministers themselves wish that there were more good ministers, for there is work for more. It is common for tradesmen not to care how few there are of their own trade; but Christ would have the labourers in his vineyard reckon it a matter of complaint when the *labourers are few.* (2.) They must earnestly desire to receive their mission from God, that *he* would send them forth as *labourers into his harvest* who is the *Lord of the harvest,* and that he would send others forth; for, if God send them forth, they may hope he will go along with them and give them success. Let them therefore say, as the prophet (Isa. 6:8), *Here I am, send me.* It is desirable to receive our commission from God, and then we may go on boldly.

2. They must set out with an expectation of trouble and persecution: *"Behold, I send you forth as lambs among wolves;* but *go your ways,* and resolve to make the best of it. Your enemies will be as *wolves,* bloody and cruel, and ready to pull you to pieces; in their threatenings and revilings, they will be as *howling* wolves to *terrify* you; in their persecutions of you, they will be as *ravening* wolves to *tear* you. But you must be as *lambs,* peaceable and patient, though made an easy prey of." It would have been very hard thus to be sent forth as *sheep among wolves,* if he had not endued them with his spirit and courage.

3. They must not encumber themselves with a load of provisions, as if they were going a long voyage, but depend upon God and their friends to provide what was convenient for them: "Carry neither a *purse* for money, nor a *scrip* or knapsack for clothes or victuals, nor new *shoes* (as before to the twelve, *ch.* 9:3); and *salute no man by the way."* This command Elisha gave to his servant, when he sent him to see the Shunamite's dead child, 2 Ki. 4:29. Not that Christ would have his ministers to be rude, morose, and unmannerly; but, (1.) They must go as men *in haste,* that had their particular places assigned them, where they must deliver their message, and in their way directly to those places must not hinder or retard themselves with needless ceremonies or compliments. (2.) They must go as *men of business,* business that relates to another world, which they must be intent in, and intent upon, and therefore must not entangle themselves with conversation about secular affairs. *Minister verbi est; hoc age — You are a minister of the word; attend to your office.* (3.) They must go as *serious* men, and *men in sorrow.* It was the custom of mourners, during the first seven days of their mourning, not to *salute any,* Job 2:13. Christ was a man of sorrows and acquainted with grief; and it was fit that by this and other signs his messengers should resemble him, and likewise show themselves affected with the calamities of mankind which they came to relieve, and touched with a feeling of them.

4. They must show, not only *their goodwill,* but *God's good-will,* to all to whom they came, and leave the issue and success to him that knows the heart, *v.* 5, 6.

(1.) The charge given them was, Whatsoever *house* they *entered into,* they must say, *Peace be to this house.* Here, [1.] They are supposed to enter into *private houses;* for, being not admitted into the synagogues, they were forced to preach where they could have liberty. And, as their public preaching was driven into houses, so thither they carried it. Like their Master, wherever they *visited,* they *preached from house to house,* Acts 5:42; 20:20. Christ's church was at first very much *a church in the house.* [2.] They are instructed to say, *"Peace be to this house,* to all under this roof, to this family, and to all that belong to it." *Peace be to you* was the common form of salutation among the Jews. They must not use it in *formality,* according to custom, to those they met on the way, because they must use it with *solemnity* to those whose houses they entered into: *"Salute no man by the way* in compliment, but to those into whose house ye enter, say, *Peace be to you,* with seriousness and in reality; for this is intended to be more than a compliment." Christ's ministers go into all the world, to say, in Christ's name, *Peace be to you. First,* We are to *propose* peace to all, to *preach peace by Jesus Christ,* to proclaim the gospel of peace, the covenant of peace, *peace on earth,* and to invite the children of men to come and take the benefit of it. *Secondly,* We are to *pray* for peace to all. We must earnestly desire the salvation of the souls of those we preach to, and offer up those desires to God in prayer; and it may be well to let them know that we do thus pray for them, and bless them in the name of the Lord.

(2.) The success was to be different, according to the different dispositions of those whom they preached to and prayed for. According as the inhabitants were sons of peace or not, so their peace should or should not *rest upon the house. Recipitur ad modum recipientis — The quality of the receiver determines the nature of the reception.* [1.] "You will meet with some that are the *sons of peace,* that by the operations of divine grace, pursuant to the designations of the divine counsel, are ready to admit the word of the gospel in the light and love of it, and have their hearts made as soft wax to receive the impressions of it. Those are qualified to receive the comforts of the gospel in whom there is a good work of grace wrought. And, as to those, *your peace* shall find them out and *rest upon them;* your prayers for them shall be heard, the promises of the gospel shall be *confirmed* to them, the privileges of it *conferred* on them, and the fruit of both shall remain and continue with them — a good part that shall not be *taken away."* [2.] "You will meet with others that are no ways disposed to hear or heed your message, whole houses that have not one *son of peace* in them." Now it is certain that our peace shall *not come* upon *them,* they have no part nor lot in the matter; the blessing that rests upon the *sons of peace* shall never come upon the sons of Belial, nor can any expect the blessings of the covenant that will not come under the bonds of it. But it shall *return to us again;* that is, we shall have the comfort of having done our duty to God and discharged our trust. Our prayers like David's shall return *into our own bosom* (Ps. 35:13) and we shall have commission to go on in the work. Our peace shall return to us again, not only to be enjoyed by ourselves, but to be communicated to others, to the next we meet with, them that are *sons of peace.*

5. They must *receive* the kindnesses of those that should *entertain* them and *bid them welcome, v.* 7, 8. "Those that receive the gospel will receive you that preach it, and give you entertainment; you must not think to raise estates, but you may depend upon a subsistence; and," (1.) "Be not *shy;* do not suspect our welcome, nor be afraid of being troublesome, but *eat and drink* heartily *such things as they give;* for, whatever kindness they show you, it is but a small return for the kindness you do them in bringing the glad tidings of *peace.* You will deserve it, for *the labourer is worthy of his hire,* the labourer in the work of the ministry is so, if he be indeed a *labourer;* and it is not an act of charity, but of justice, in those who are *taught in the word to communicate to those that teach them"* (2.) "Be not *nice* and *curious* in your diet: *Eat and drink such things as they give* (*v.* 7), *such things as are set before you, v.* 8. Be thankful for plain food, and do not find fault, though it be not dressed according to art." It ill becomes Christ's disciples to be *desirous of dainties.* As he has not tied them up to the Pharisees' superstitious fasts, so he has not allowed the luxurious feasts of the Epicureans. Probably, Christ here refers to the traditions of the elders about their meat which were so many that those who observed them were extremely critical, you could hardly set a dish of meat before them, but there was some scruple or other concerning it; but Christ would not have them to regard those things, but eat what was given them, *asking no question for conscience' sake.*

6. They must *denounce* the judgments of God against those who should *reject* them and their *message:* "If you *enter into a city,* and they *do not receive you,* if there be none there disposed to hearken to your doctrine, leave them, *v.* 10. If they will not *give you welcome* into their houses, do you *give them warning* in their streets." He orders them to (*ch.* 9:5) do as he had ordered the apostles to do: "Say to them, not with rage, or scorn, or resentment, but with compassion to their poor perishing souls, and a holy dread of the ruin which they are bringing upon themselves, *Even the dust of your city, which cleaveth on us, we do wipe off against you, v.* 11. From them do not receive any kindnesses at all, be not beholden to them. It cost that prophet of the Lord dear who accepted a meal's meat with a prophet in Bethel, 1 Ki. 13:21, 22. Tell them that you will not carry with you the dust of their city; let them take it to themselves, for *dust they are."* It shall be a witness for Christ's messengers that they had been there according to their Master's order; *tender* and *refusal* were a discharge of their trust. But it shall be a witness against the recusants that they would not give Christ's messengers any entertainment, no, not so much as water to wash their feet with, but they were forced to wipe off the dust. "But tell them plainly, and bid them *be sure* of it, *The kingdom of God is come nigh to you.* Here is a fair offer made you; if you have not the benefit of it, it is your own fault. The gospel is brought to your doors; if you shut your doors against it, your blood is upon your own head. Now that the *kingdom of God is come nigh to you,* if you will not come up to it, and come into it, your sin will be inexcusable, and your condemnation intolerable." Note, The fairer offers we have of grace and life by Christ, the more we shall have to answer for another day, if we slight these offers: *It shall be more tolerable for Sodom than for that city, v.* 12. The Sodomites indeed rejected the warning given them by Lot; but rejecting the gospel is a more heinous crime, and will be punished accordingly *in that day.* He means the day of judgment (*v.* 14), but calls it, by way of emphasis, *that day,* because it is the last and great day, the day when we must account for all the *days of time,* and have our state determined for the *days of eternity.*

Upon this occasion, the evangelist repeats,

(1.) The particular doom of those cities wherein most of Christ's mighty works were done, which we had, Mt. 11:20, etc. Chorazin, Bethsaida, and Capernaum, all bordering upon the sea of Galilee, where Christ was most conversant, are the places here mentioned. [1.] They enjoyed greater privileges. Christ's *mighty works were done in them,* and they were all gracious works, works of mercy. They were hereby *exalted to heaven,* not only dignified and honoured, but put into a fair way of being happy; they were brought as near heaven as external means could bring them. [2.] God's design in favouring them thus was to bring them to *repentance* and *reformation* of life, *to sit in sackcloth and ashes,* both in humiliation for the sins they had committed, and in humility and a meek subjection to God's government. [3.] Their frustrating this design, and their receiving the grace of God therein in vain. It is implied that they *repented not;* they were not wrought upon by all the miracles of Christ to think the better of him, or the worse of sin; they did not bring forth fruits agreeable to the advantages they enjoyed. [4.] There was reason to think, morally speaking, that, if Christ had gone to Tyre and Sidon, Gentile cities, and had preached the same doctrine to them and wrought the same miracles among them that he did in these cities of Israel, they would have repented *long ago,* so speedy would their repentance have been, and that in *sackcloth and ashes,* so deep would it have been. Now to understand the wisdom of God, in *giving* the means of grace to those who would not improve them, and *denying* them to those that would, we must wait for the great day of discovery. [5.] The doom of those who thus receive the grace of God in vain will be very fearful. They that were *thus exalted,* not making use of their elevation, will be *thrust down to hell,* thrust down with disgrace and dishonour. They will thrust in to get into heaven, in the crowd of professors, but in vain; they shall be *thrust down,* to their everlasting grief and disappointment, into the lowest hell, and hell will be hell indeed to them. [6.] In the day of judgment Tyre and Sidon will fare better, and it will be more tolerable for them than for these cities.

(2.) The general rule which Christ would go by, as to those to whom he sent his ministers: He will reckon himself treated according as they treated his ministers, *v.* 16. What is done to the ambassador is done, as it were, to the prince that sends him. [1.] "*He that hearest you,* and regardeth what you say, *heareth me,* and herein doeth me honour. But," [2.] "He that *despiseth you* doth in effect *despise me,* and shall be reckoned with as having put an affront upon me; nay, he *despiseth him that sent me.*" Note, Those who contemn the Christian religion do in effect put a slight upon natural religion, which it is perfective of. And they who *despise* the faithful ministers of Christ, who, though they do not hate and persecute them, yet think meanly of them, look scornfully upon them, and turn their backs upon their ministry, will be reckoned with as despisers of God and Christ.

Verses 17–24

Christ sent forth the seventy disciples as he was going up to Jerusalem to the *feast of tabernacles,* when he *went up, not openly,* but *as it were in secret* (Jn. 7:10), having sent abroad so great a part of his ordinary retinue; and Dr. Lightfoot thinks it was before his return from that feast, and while he was yet at Jerusalem, or Bethany, which was hard by (for there he was, *v.* 38), that they, or at least some of them, returned to him. Now here we are told,

1. What account they gave him of the success of their expedition: *They returned again with joy* (*v.* 17); not complaining of the fatigue of their journeys, nor of the opposition and discouragement they met with, but rejoicing in their success, especially in casting out unclean spirits: *Lord, even the devils are subject unto us through thy name.* Though only the *healing of the sick* was mentioned in their commission (*v.* 19), yet no doubt the *casting out* of devils was included, and in this they had wonderful success. 1. They give Christ the glory of this: It is *through thy name.* Note, all our victories over Satan are obtained by power derived from Jesus Christ. We must *in his name* enter the lists with our spiritual enemies, and, whatever advantages we gain, he must have all the praise; if the work be done *in* his name, the honour is due *to* his name. 2. They entertain themselves with the comfort of it; they speak of it with an air of exultation: *Even the devils,* those potent enemies, are *subject to us.* Note, the saints have no greater joy or satisfaction in any of their triumphs than in those over Satan. If devils are *subject to us,* what can stand before us?

II. What acceptance they found with him, and how he received this account.

1. He confirmed what they said, as agreeing with his own observation (*v.* 18): "My heart and eye went along with you; I took notice of the success you had, and I *saw Satan fall as lightning from heaven.*" Note, Satan and his kingdom fell before the preaching of the gospel. "I see how it is," saith Christ, "as you get ground the devil loseth ground." He falls *as lightning falls from heaven,* so suddenly, so irrecoverably, so visibly, that all may perceive it, and say, "See how Satan's kingdom totters, see how it tumbles." They triumphed in casting devils out of the bodies of people; but Christ sees and rejoices in the fall of the devil from the interest he has in the souls of men, which is called his power *in high places,* Eph. 6:12. He foresees this to be but an earnest of what should now be shortly done and was already begun — the destroying of Satan's kingdom in the world by the extirpating of idolatry and the turning of the nations to the faith of Christ. Satan *falls from heaven* when he falls from the throne in men's hearts, Acts 26:18. And Christ foresaw that the preaching of the gospel, which would *fly like lightning* through the world, would wherever it went pull down Satan's kingdom. *Now is the prince of this world cast out.* Some have given another sense of this, as looking back to the fall of the angels, and designed for a caution to these disciples, lest their success should puff them up with pride: "I saw angels turned into devils by *pride:* that was the sin for which Satan was *cast down from heaven,* where he had been an angel of light I saw it, and give you an intimation of it lest you, being *lifted up with pride should fall*

into that condemnation of the devil, who fell by pride," 1 Tim. 3:6.

2. He repeated, ratified, and enlarged their commission: *Behold I give you power to tread on serpents, v.* 19. Note, To him that hath, and useth well what he hath, more shall be given. They had employed their power vigorously against Satan, and now Christ entrusts them with greater power. (1.) An *offensive* power, power to *tread on serpents and scorpions,* devils and malignant spirits, the old serpent: "You shall *bruise their heads* in my name," according to the first promise, Gen. 3:15. Come, *set your feet* on *the necks* of these enemies; you shall tread upon these *lions* and *adders* wherever you meet with them; you shall *trample them under foot,* Ps. 91:13. You shall *tread upon all the power of the enemy,* and the kingdom of the Messiah shall be every where set up upon the ruins of the devil's kingdom. As the devils have now been *subject to you,* so they shall still be. (2.) A *defensive* power: "*Nothing shall by any means hurt you;* not *serpents* nor *scorpions,* if you should be chastised with them or thrown into prisons and dungeons among them; you shall be unhurt by the most venomous creatures," as St. Paul was (Acts 28:5), and as is promised in Mk. 16:18. "If wicked men be as *serpents* to you, and you *dwell* among those *scorpions* (as Eze. 2:6), you may despise their rage, and *tread* upon it; *it* need not disturb you, for they have no power against you but what is *given them from above;* they may *hiss,* but they cannot *hurt.*" You may play upon the hole of the asp, for *death itself shall not hurt nor destroy,* Isa. 11:8, 19; 25:8.

3. He directed them to turn their joy into the right channel (*v.* 20): "*Notwithstanding in this rejoice not, that the spirits are subject unto you,* that they have been so, and shall be still so. Do not rejoice in this merely as it is your honour, and a confirmation of your mission, and as it sets you a degree above other good people; do not rejoice in this *only,* or in this *chiefly,* but *rather rejoice because your names are written in heaven,* because you are chosen of God to eternal life, and are the children of God through faith." Christ, who knew the counsels of God, could tell them that their *names were written in heaven,* for it is the *Lamb's book of life* that they are written in. All believers are through grace, entitled to the inheritance of sons, and have received the adoption of sons, and the Spirit of adoption, which is the earnest of that inheritance and so are enrolled among his family; now this is matter of joy, greater joy than casting out devils. Note, Power to become the children of God is to be valued more than a power to work miracles; for we read of those who did *in Christ's name cast out devils,* as Judas did, and yet will be disowned by Christ in the great day. But they whose *names are written in heaven* shall never perish; they are *Christ's sheep,* to whom he will give *eternal life.* Saving graces are more to be rejoiced in than spiritual gifts; holy love is *a more excellent way* than speaking with tongues.

4. He offered up a solemn thanksgiving to his Father, for employing such mean people as his disciples were in such high and honourable service, *v.* 21, 22. This we had before (Mt. 11:25–27), only here it is prefixed that *in that hour Jesus rejoiced.* It was fit that particular notice should be taken of *that* hour, because there were so few such, for he was a *man of sorrows.* In *that hour* in which he saw Satan fall, and heard of the good success of his ministers, *in that hour he rejoiced.* Note, Nothing rejoices the heart of the Lord Jesus so much as the progress of the gospel, and its getting ground of Satan, by the conversion of souls to Christ. Christ's joy was a solid substantial joy, an inward joy: *he rejoiced in spirit;* but his joy, like deep waters, made no noise; it was a joy that a stranger did not intermeddle with. Before he applied himself to *thank his Father,* he stirred up himself to *rejoice;* for, as *thankful praise* is the genuine language of *holy joy,* so *holy joy* is the root and spring of *thankful praise.* Two things he gives thanks for: —

(1.) For what was *revealed* by the *Father* through the *Son: I thank thee, O Father, Lord of heaven and earth, v.* 21. In all our adorations of God, we must have an eye to him, both as the Maker of heaven and earth and as the Father of our Lord Jesus Christ, and in him our Father. Now that which he gives thanks for is, [1.] That the counsels of God concerning man's reconciliation to himself were *revealed* to some of the children of men, who might be fit also to *teach others,* and it is God that *by his Son* has spoken these things *to us* and by his Spirit has revealed them *in us; he* has *revealed* that which had been *kept secret* from the beginning of the world. [2.] That they were revealed to *babes,* to those who were of

mean parts and capacities, whose extraction and education had nothing in them promising, who were but *children in understanding,* till God by his Spirit elevated their faculties, and furnished them with this knowledge, and an ability to communicate it. We have reason to thank God, not so much for the honour he has hereby put upon babes, as for the honour he has hereby done himself in perfecting strength *out of weakness.* [3.] That, at the same time when he revealed them unto babes, he *hid them from the wise and prudent,* the Gentile philosophers, the Jewish rabbin. He *did not reveal* the things of the gospel to them, nor employ them in preaching up his kingdom. Thanks be to God that the apostles were not fetched from their schools; for, *First,* they would have been apt to mingle their notions with the doctrine of Christ, which would have corrupted it, as afterwards it proved. For Christianity was much corrupted by the Platonic philosophy in the first ages of it, by the Peripatetic in its latter ages, and by the Judaizing teachers at the first planting of it. *Secondly,* If rabbin and philosophers had been made apostles, the success of the gospel would have been ascribed to their learning and wit and the force of their reasonings and eloquence; and therefore they must not be employed, lest they should have taken too much to themselves, and others should have attributed too much to them. They were passed by for the same reason that Gideon's army was reduced: *The people are yet too many,* Judges 7:4. Paul indeed was bred a scholar among the wise and prudent; but he became a *babe* when he became an apostle, and laid aside the *enticing words of man's wisdom,* forgot them all, and made neither show nor use of any other knowledge than that of *Christ and him crucified,* 1 Co. 2:2, 4. [4.] That God herein acted by way of sovereignty: *Even so, Father, for so it seemed good in thy sight.* If God gives his grace and the knowledge of his son to some that are less likely, and does not give it to others whom we should think better able to deliver it with advantage, this must satisfy: so it pleases God, whose thoughts are infinitely above ours. He chooses to entrust the dispensing of his gospel in the hands of those who with a *divine energy* will give it the *setting on,* rather than in theirs who with *human art* will give it the *setting off.*

(2.) For what was *secret* between the *Father* and the *Son, v.* 22. [1.] The vast *confidence* that the Father *puts* in the Son: *All things are delivered to me of my Father,* all wisdom and knowledge, all power and authority, all the grace and comfort which are intended for the chosen remnant; it is all delivered into the hands of the Lord Jesus; in him all fulness must *dwell,* and from him it must be *derived:* he is the great *trustee* that manages all the concerns of God's kingdom. [2.] The good understanding that there is between the Father and the Son, and their *mutual consciousness,* such as no creature can be admitted to: *No man knows who the Son is,* nor what his mind is, *but the Father,* who *possessed him in the beginning of his ways, before his works of old* (Prov. 8:22), nor *who the Father is,* and what his counsels are, *but the Son,* who lay in his bosom from eternity, was *by him as one brought up with him, and was daily his delight* (Prov. 8:30), *and he to whom the Son* by the Spirit *will reveal him.* The gospel is the revelation of Jesus Christ, to him we owe all the discoveries made to us of the will of God for our salvation; and here he speaks of being entrusted with it as that which was a great pleasure to himself and for which he was very thankful to his Father.

5. He told his disciples how well it was for them that they had these things revealed to them, *v.* 23, 24. Having addressed himself to his Father, he *turned to his disciples,* designing to make them sensible how much it was for their happiness, as well as for the glory and honour of God, that they knew the mysteries of the kingdom and were employed to lead others into the knowledge of them, considering, (1.) What a step it is *towards* something better. Though the bare knowledge of these things is not saving, yet it puts us in the way of salvation: *Blessed are the eyes which see the things which we see.* God therein blesseth them, and, if it be not their own fault it will be an eternal blessedness to them. (2.) What a step it is *above* those that went before them, even the greatest saints, and those that were most the favourites of Heaven: "*Many prophets and righteous men*" (so it is in Mt. 13:17), *many prophets and kings* (so it is here), "have *desired* to see and hear those things which you are daily and intimately conversant with, and *have not seen* and *heard* them." The honour and happiness of the New-Testament saints far exceed those even of the *prophets* and *kings* of the Old

Testament, though they also were *highly favoured.* The general ideas which the Old-Testament saints had, according to the intimations given them, of the graces and glories of the Messiah's kingdom, made them wish a thousand times that their lot had been reserved for those blessed days, and that they might see the substance of those things of which they had faint shadows. Note, The consideration of the great advantages which we have in the New-Testament light, above what they had who lived in Old-Testament times, should awaken our diligence in the improvement of it; for, if it do not, it will aggravate our condemnation for the non-improvement of it.

Verses 25–37

We have here Christ's discourse with a lawyer about some points of conscience, which we are all concerned to be rightly informed in and are so here from Christ though the questions were proposed with no good intention.

I. We are concerned to know what that good is which we should do in *this* life, in order to our attaining *eternal life.* A question to this purport was proposed to our Saviour by a *certain lawyer,* or *scribe,* only with a design to *try* him, not with a desire to be instructed by him, *v.* 25. The lawyer *stood up,* and *asked him, Master, what shall I do to inherit eternal life?* If Christ had any thing peculiar to prescribe, by this question he would get it out of him, and perhaps expose him for it; if not, he would expose his doctrine as needless, since it would give no other direction for obtaining happiness than what they had already received; or, perhaps, he had no malicious design against Christ, as some of the scribes had, only he was willing to have a little talk with him, just as people go to church to hear what the minister will say. This was a good question: *What shall I do to inherit eternal life?* But it lost all its goodness when it was proposed with an ill design, or a very mean one. Note, It is not enough to speak of the things of God, and to enquire about them, but we must do it with a suitable concern. If we speak of *eternal life,* and *the way* to it, in a careless manner, merely as matter of discourse, especially as matter of dispute, we do but take the name of God in vain, as the lawyer here did. Now this question being started, observe,

1. How Christ turned him over to the divine law, and bade him follow the direction of that. Though he knew the thoughts and intents of his heart, he did not answer him according to the folly of that, but according to the wisdom and goodness of the question he asked. He answered him with a question: *What is written in the law? How readest thou? v.* 26. He came to catechize Christ, and to know him; but Christ will catechize him, and make him know himself. He talks to him as a lawyer, as one conversant in the law: the studies of his profession would inform him; let him practise according to his knowledge, and he should not come short of *eternal life.* Note, It will be of great use to us, in our way to heaven, to consider *what is written in the law,* and *what we read* there. We must have recourse to our bibles, to the law, as it is now in the hand of Christ and walk in the way that is shown us there. It is a great mercy that we have the law *written,* that we have it thereby reduced to certainty, and that thereby it is capable of spreading the *further,* and lasting the *longer.* Having it *written,* it is our duty to read it, to read it with understanding, and to treasure up what we read, so that when there is occasion, we may be able to tell *what is written in the law,* and *how we read.* To this we must appeal; by this we must try doctrines and end disputes; this must be our oracle, our touchstone, our rule, our guide. What is written in the law? How do we read? if there be light in us, it will have regard to this light.

2. What a good account he gave of the law, of the principal commandments of the law, to the observance of which we must bind ourselves if we would inherit eternal life. He did not, like a Pharisee, refer himself to the tradition of the elders, but, like a good textuary, fastened upon the two first and great commandments of the law, as those which he thought must be most strictly observed in order to the obtaining of *eternal life,* and which included all the rest, *v.* 27. (1.) We must *love God with all our hearts,* must look upon him as the best of beings, in himself most amiable, and infinitely perfect and excellent; as one whom we lie under the greatest obligations to, both in gratitude and interest. We must prize him, and value ourselves by our elation to him; must please ourselves in him, and devote ourselves entirely to him. Our love to him must be sincere, hearty, and fervent; it must be a superlative love, a love that is as strong as death, but an intelligent love, and such as we can give a good account of the grounds and reasons of. It must be an *entire* love; he must have our *whole* souls, and must be served with *all that is within us.* We must love nothing *besides him,* but what we love *for him* and in subordination to him. (2.) We must love our neighbours as *ourselves,* which we shall easily do, if we, as we ought to do, love God *better than ourselves.* We must wish well to all and ill to none; must do all the good we can in the world and no hurt, and must fix it as a rule to ourselves to do to others as we would they should do to us; and this is to love our neighbour *as ourselves.*

3. Christ's approbation of what he said, *v.* 28. Though he came to tempt him, yet what he said that was good Christ commended: *Thou hast answered right.* Christ himself fastened upon these as the two great commandments of the law (Mt. 22:37): both sides agreed in this. Those who do well shall have praise of the same, and so should those have that speak well. So far is right; but he hardest part of this work yet remains: *"This do, and thou shalt live;* thou shalt *inherit eternal life."*

4. His care to avoid the conviction which was now ready to fasten upon him. When Christ said, *This do, and thou shalt live,* he began to be aware that Christ intended to draw from him an acknowledgment that he *had not done this,* and therefore an enquiry what he should do, which way he should look, to get his sins pardoned; an acknowledgment also that he *could not do this* perfectly for the future by any strength of his own, and therefore an enquiry which way he might fetch in strength to enable him to do it: but he was *willing to justify himself,* and therefore cared not for carrying on that discourse, but saith, in effect, as another did (Mt. 19:20), *All these things have I kept from my youth up.* Note, Many ask good questions with a design rather to *justify themselves* than to *inform themselves,* rather proudly to show what is good in them than humbly to see what is bad in them.

II. We are concerned to know who is our neighbour, whom by the second great commandment we are obliged to love. This is another of this lawyer's queries, which he started only that he might *drop* the former, lest Christ should have forced him, in the prosecution of it, to *condemn himself,* when he was resolved to *justify* himself. As to loving God, he was willing to say no more of it; but, as to his *neighbour,* he was sure that there he had come up to the rule, for he had always been very kind and respectful to all about him. Now observe,

1. What was the corrupt notion of the Jewish teachers in this matter. Dr. Lightfoot quotes their own words to this purport: "Where he saith, *Thou shalt love thy neighbour, he excepts all Gentiles,* for they are not *our neighbours,* but those only that are of our own nation and religion." They would not put an Israelite to death for killing a Gentile, for he was not his *neighbour:* they indeed say that they ought not to kill a Gentile whom they were not at war with; but, if they saw a Gentile in *danger of death,* they thought themselves under no obligation to help to *save his life.* Such wicked inferences did they draw from that holy covenant of peculiarity by which God had distinguished them, and by abusing it thus they had forfeited it; God justly took the forfeiture, and transferred covenant-favours to the Gentile world, to whom they brutishly denied common favours.

2. How Christ corrected this inhuman notion, and showed, by a parable, that whomsoever we *have need* to receive kindness *from,* and *find ready* to show us the kindness *we need,* we cannot but look upon as *our neighbour;* and therefore ought to look upon all those as such who need our kindness, and to show them kindness accordingly, though they be not of our own nation and religion. Now observe,

(1.) The parable itself, which represents to us a poor Jew in distressed circumstances, succoured and relieved by a good Samaritan. Let us see here,

[1.] How he was *abused* by his *enemies.* The honest man was traveling peaceably upon his lawful business in the road, and it was a great road that led from Jerusalem to Jericho, *v.* 30. The mentioning of those places intimates that it was matter of fact, and not a parable; probably it happened lately, just as it is here related. The occurrences of Providence would yield us many good instructions, if we would carefully observe and improve them, and would be equivalent to parables framed on purpose for instruction, and be more *affecting.* This poor man *fell among thieves.* Whether they were Arabians, plunderers, that lived by spoil, or some profligate wretches of his own nation, or some of the Roman soldiers, who, notwithstanding the strict discipline of their army, did this villany, does not appear; but they were very *barbarous;* they not only took his money, but stripped him of his clothes, and, that he might not be able to pursue them, or only to gratify a cruel disposition (for otherwise *what profit was there in his blood?*) they *wounded him,* and left him *half dead,* ready to die of his wounds. We may here conceive a just indignation at *highwaymen,* that have divested themselves of all humanity, and are as natural brute beasts, beasts of prey, made to be *taken and destroyed;* and at the same time we cannot but think with compassion on those that fall into the hands of such wicked and unreasonable men, and be ready, when it is in our power, to help them. What reason have we to thank God for our preservation from perils by robbers!

[2.] How he was *slighted* by those who should have been his friends, who were not only men of his own nation and religion, but one a priest and the other a Levite, men of a public character and station; nay, they were men of professed sanctity, whose offices obliged them to tenderness and compassion (Heb. 5:2), who ought to have taught others their duty in such a case as this, which was to *deliver them that were drawn unto death;* yet they would not themselves do it. Dr. Lightfoot tells us that many of the courses of the priests had their residence in Jericho, and thence came up to Jerusalem, when it was their turn to officiate there, and so back again, which occasioned abundance of *passing* and *repassing* of priests that way, and Levites their attendants. They came *this way,* and saw the poor wounded man. It is probable that they heard his groans, and could not but perceive that if he were not helped he must quickly perish. The Levite not only saw him, but *came and looked on him v.* 32. But they *passed by on the other side;* when they saw his case, they got as far off him as ever they could, as if they would have had a pretence to say, *Behold, we knew it not.* It is sad when those who should be examples of charity are prodigies of cruelty, and when those who should by displaying the mercies of God, open the bowels of compassion in others, shut up their own.

[3.] How he was *succoured* and *relieved* by a *stranger,* a *certain Samaritan,* of that nation which of all others the Jews most despised and detested and would have no dealings with. This man had some humanity in him, *v.* 33. The priest had his heart hardened against one of *his own people,* but the Samaritan had his opened towards one of *another* people. *When he saw him he had compassion on him,* and never took into consideration what country he was of. Though he was a Jew, he was a man, and a man in *misery,* and the Samaritan has learned to honour all men; he knows not how soon this poor man's case may be his own, and therefore pities him, as he himself would desire and expect to be pitied in the like case. That such great love should be found in a Samaritan was perhaps thought as wonderful as that great faith which Christ admired in a Roman, and in a woman of Canaan; but really it was not so, for pity is the work of a man, but faith is the work of divine *grace.* The *compassion* of this Samaritan was not an idle compassion; he did not think it enough to say, "Be healed, be helped" (Jam. 2:16); but, when he *drew out his soul,* he *reached forth his hand* also to this poor *needy* creature, Isa. 58:7, 10; Prov. 31:20. See how friendly this good Samaritan was. *First,* He *went to* the poor man, whom the priest and Levite kept at a distance from; he enquired, no doubt, how he came into this deplorable condition, and condoled with him. *Secondly,* He did the surgeon's part, for want of a better. He *bound up his wounds,* making use of his own linen, it is likely, for that purpose; and poured *in oil and wine,* which perhaps he had with him; wine to wash the wound, and oil to mollify it, and close it up. He did all he could to ease the pain, and prevent the peril, of his wounds, as one whose heart bled with him. *Thirdly,* He *set him on his own beast,* and went on foot himself, and *brought him to an inn.* A great mercy it is to have inns upon the road, where we may be furnished for our money with all the conveniences for food and rest. Perhaps the Samaritan, if he had not met with this hindrance, would have got that night to his journey's end; but, in compassion to that poor man, he takes up short at an inn. Some think that the priest and Levite pretended they could not stay to help the poor man, because they were in haste to go and attend the temple-service at Jerusalem. We suppose the Samaritan went upon business; but he understood that both his own business and God's sacrifice too must give place to such an act of mercy as this. *Fourthly,* He *took care of him* in the inn, got him to bed, had food for him that was proper, and due attendance, and, it may be, prayed with him. Nay, *Fifthly,* As if he had been his own child, or one he was obliged to look after, when he left him next morning, he left money with the landlord, to be laid out for his use, and passed his word for what he should spend more. *Twopence* of their money was about fifteen pence of ours, which, according to the rate of things then, would go a great way; however, here it was an earnest of satisfaction to the full of all demands. All this was kind and generous, and as much as one could have expected from a friend or a brother; and yet here it is done by a stranger and foreigner.

Now this parable is applicable to another purpose than that for which it was intended; and does excellently set forth the kindness and love of God our Saviour towards sinful miserable man. We were like this poor distressed traveller. Satan, our enemy, had *robbed* us, *stripped* us, *wounded* us; such is the mischief that sin had done us. We were by nature more than *half dead,* twice dead, in trespasses and sins; utterly unable to help ourselves, for we were without strength. The law of Moses, like the priest and Levite, the ministers of the law, *looks upon us,* but has no compassion on us, gives us no relief, *passes by on the other side,* as having neither pity nor power to help us; but then comes the blessed Jesus, that good Samaritan (and they said of him, by way of reproach, *he is a Samaritan*), he has compassion on us, he binds up our bleeding wounds (Ps. 147:3; Isa. 61:1), pours in, not *oil and wine,* but that which is infinitely more precious, *his own blood.* He takes care of us, and bids us put all the expenses of our cure upon his account; and all this though he was none of us, till he was pleased by his voluntary condescension to make himself so, but infinitely above us. This magnifies the riches of his love, and obliges us all to say, "How much are we indebted, and what shall we render?"

(2.) The application of the parable. [1.] The truth contained in it is extorted from the lawyer's own mouth. "Now tell me," saith Christ, *"which of these three was neighbour to him that fell among thieves* (*v.* 36), the priest, the Levite, or the Samaritan? Which of these did the neighbour's part?" To this the lawyer would not answer, as he ought to have done, "Doubtless, the Samaritan was;" but, *"He that showed mercy on him;* doubtless, he was a good neighbour to him, and very neighbourly, and I cannot but say that it was a good work thus to save an honest Jew from perishing." [2.] The duty inferred from it is pressed home upon the lawyer's own conscience: *Go, and do thou likewise.* The duty of relations is mutual and reciprocal; the titles of friends, brethren, neighbours, are, as Grotius here speaks *tōn pros ti — equally binding on both sides:* if one side be bound, the other cannot be loose, as is agreed in all contracts. If a Samaritan does well that helps a distressed Jew, certainly a Jew does not well if he refuses in like manner to help a distressed Samaritan. *Petimusque damusque vicissim — These kind offices are to be reciprocated.* "And therefore *go thou* and do as the Samaritan did, whenever occasion offers: show mercy to those that need thy help, and do it freely, and with concern and compassion, though they be not of thy own nation and thy own profession, or of thy own opinion and communion in religion. Let thy charity be thus extensive, before thou boastest of having conformed thyself to that great commandment of *loving thy neighbour.*" This lawyer valued himself much upon his learning and his knowledge of the laws, and in that he thought to have puzzled Christ himself; but Christ sends him to school to a Samaritan, to learn his duty: "Go, and do like him." Note, It is the duty of every one of us, in our places, and according to our ability, to succour, help, and relieve all that are in distress and necessity, and of lawyers particularly; and herein we must study to excel many that are proud of their being priests and Levites.

Verses 38–42

We may observe in this story,

I. The entertainment which Martha gave to Christ and his disciples at her house, *v.* 38. Observe,

1. Christ's coming to the village where Martha lived: *As they went* (Christ and his disciples together), he and they with him *entered into a certain village.* This village was *Bethany,* nigh to Jerusalem, whither Christ was now going up, and he took this in his way. Note (1.) Our Lord Jesus went about doing good (Acts 10:38), scattering his benign beams and influences as the true light of the world. (2.) Wherever Christ went his disciples went along with him. (3.) Christ honoured the country-villages with his presence and favour, and not the great and populous cities only; for, as he *chose privacy,* so he *countenanced poverty.*

2. His reception at Martha's house: *A certain woman, named Martha, received him into her house,* and made him welcome, for she was the housekeeper. Note, (1.) Our Lord Jesus, when he was here upon earth, was so poor that he was necessitated to be beholden to his friends for a subsistence. Though he was Zion's King, he had no house of his own either in Jerusalem or near it. (2.) There were some who were Christ's particular friends, whom he loved more than his other friends, and them he visited most frequently. He *loved* this family (Jn. 11:5), and often invited himself to them. Christ's visits are the tokens of his love, Jn. 14:23. (3.) There were those who kindly received Christ into their houses when he was here upon earth. It is called Martha's house, for, probably, she was a widow, and was the housekeeper. Though it was expensive to entertain Christ for he did not come alone, but brought his disciples with him, yet she would not regard the cost of it. (How can we spend what we have better than in Christ's service!) Nay, though at this time it was grown dangerous to entertain him especially so near Jerusalem, yet she cared not what hazard she ran for his name's sake. Though there were many that rejected him, and would not entertain him, yet there was one that would bid him welcome. Though Christ is every where spoken against, yet there is a remnant to whom he is dear, and who are dear to him.

II. The attendance which Mary, the sister of Martha, gave upon the word of Christ, *v.* 20. 1. She *heard his word.* It seems, our Lord Jesus, as soon as he came into Martha's house, even before entertainment was made for him, addressed himself to his great work of preaching the gospel. He presently took the chair with solemnity; for Mary sat to hear him, which intimates that it was a continued discourse. Note, A good sermon is never the worse for being preached in a house; and the visits of our friends should be so managed as to make them turn to a spiritual advantage. Mary, having this price put into her hands, sat herself to improve it, not knowing when she should have such another. Since Christ is forward to speak, we should be *swift to hear.* 2. She *sat* to hear, which denotes a close attention. Her mind was composed, and she resolved to abide by it: not to catch a word now and then, but to receive all that Christ delivered. She *sat at his feet,* as scholars at the feet of their tutors when they read their lectures; hence Paul is said to be *brought up at the feet of Gamaliel.* Our sitting at Christ's feet, when we hear his word, signifies a readiness to receive it, and a submission and entire resignation of ourselves to the guidance of it. We must either sit at Christ's feet or be made his footstool; but, if we sit with him at his feet now, we shall sit with him on his throne shortly.

III. The care of Martha about her domestic affairs: But Martha *was cumbered about much serving* (*v.* 40), and that was the reason why she was not where Mary was — sitting at Christ's feet, to hear his word. She was providing for the entertainment of Christ and those that came with him. Perhaps she had no notice before of his coming, and she was unprovided, but was in care to have every thing handsome upon this occasion; she had not such guests every day. Housekeepers know what care and bustle there must be when a great entertainment is to be made. Observe here,

1. Something *commendable,* which must not be overlooked. (1.) Here was a commendable *respect to our Lord Jesus;* for we have reason to think it was not for ostentation, but purely to testify her good-will to him, that she made this entertainment. Note, Those who truly love Christ will think that well bestowed that is laid out for his honour. (2.) Here was a commendable *care of her household affairs.* It appears, from the respect shown to this family among the Jews (Jn. 11:19), that they were persons of some quality and distinction; and yet Martha herself did not think it a disparagement to her to lay her hand even to the *service* of the family, when there was occasion for it. Note, It is the duty of those who have the charge of families to *look well to the ways of their household.* The affectation of state and the love of ease make many families neglected.

2. Here was something *culpable,* which we must take notice of too. (1.) She was for *much serving.* Her heart was upon it, to have a very sumptuous and splendid entertainment; great plenty, great variety, and great exactness, according to the fashion of the place. She was in care, *peri pollēn diakonian — concerning much attendance.* Note, It does not become the disciples of Christ to affect *much serving,* to affect varieties, dainties, and superfluities in eating and drinking; what need is there of *much serving,* when much less will serve? (2.) She was *cumbered* about it; *periespato* — she was just *distracted* with it. Note, Whatever cares the providence of God casts upon us we must not be *cumbered* with them, nor be disquieted and perplexed by them. *Care* is good and duty; but *cumber* is sin and folly. (2.) She was *then cumbered about much serving* when she should have been with her sister, sitting at Christ's feet to hear his word. Note, Worldly business is *then* a snare to us when it hinders us from serving God and getting good to our souls.

IV. The *complaint* which Martha made to Christ against her sister Mary, for not *assisting* her, upon this occasion, in the *business of the house* (*v.* 40): *"Lord, dost thou not care that my sister,* who is concerned as well as I in having things done well, *has left me to serve alone?* Therefore dismiss her from attending thee, and bid her come and help me." Now,

1. This complaint of Martha's may be considered as a *discovery* of her *worldliness:* it was the language of her inordinate care and cumber. She speaks as one in a mighty passion with her sister, else she would not have troubled Christ with the matter. Note, The inordinacy of worldly cares and pursuits is often the occasion of disturbance in families and of strife and contention among relations. Moreover, those that are eager upon the world themselves are apt to blame and censure those that are not so too; and while they justify themselves in their worldliness, and judge of others by their serviceableness to them in their worldly pursuits, they are ready to condemn those that addict themselves to the exercises of religion, as if they neglected the *main chance,* as they call it. Martha, being angry at her sister, appealed to Christ, and would have him say that she *did well to be angry. Lord, doest not thou care that my sister has let me to serve alone?* It should seem as if Christ had sometimes expressed himself tenderly concerned for her, and her ease and comfort, and would not have her go through so much toil and trouble, and she expected that he should now bid her sister take her share in it. When Martha was caring, she must have Mary, and Christ and all, to *care* too, or else she is not pleased. Note, Those are not always in the right that are most forward to appeal to God; we must therefore take heed, lest at any time we expect that Christ should espouse our unjust and groundless quarrels. The cares which he cast upon us we may cheerfully cast upon him, but not those which we foolishly draw upon ourselves. He will be the patron of the poor and injured, but not of the turbulent and injurious.

2. It may be considered as a discouragement of Mary's piety and devotion. Her sister should have *commended* her for it, should have told her that she was in the right; but, instead of this, she *condemns* her as wanting in her duty. Note, It is no strange thing for those that are zealous in religion to meet with hindrances and discouragements from those that are about them; not only with opposition from enemies, but with blame and censure from their friends. David's *fasting,* and his dancing *before the ark,* were turned *to his reproach.*

V. The reproof which Christ gave to Martha for her inordinate care, *v.* 41. She appealed to him, and he gives judgment against her: *Martha, Martha, thou art careful and troubled about many things,* whereas but *one thing is needful.*

1. He reproved her, though he was at this time her guest. Her fault was her over-solicitude to entertain him, and she expected he should justify her in it, yet he publicly checked her for it. Note, *As many as Christ loves he rebukes and chastens.* Even those that are dear to Christ, if any thing be amiss in them, shall be sure to hear of it. *Nevertheless I have something against thee.*

2. When he reproved her, he called her by her name, *Martha;* for reproofs are *then* most likely to do good when they are *particular,* applied to particular persons and cases, as Nathan's to David, *Thou art the man.* He repeated her name, *Martha, Martha;* he speaks as one in earnest, and deeply concerned for her welfare. Those that are *entangled* in the cares of this life are not easily *disentangled.* To them we must call again and again, *O earth, earth, earth, hear the word of the Lord.*

3. That which he reproved her for was her being *careful and troubled about many things.* He was not *pleased* that she should think to *please him* with a rich and splendid entertainment, and with perplexing herself to prepare it for him; whereas he would teach us, as not to be *sensual* in using such things, so not to be *selfish* in being willing that others should be *troubled,* no matter who or how many, so we may be grat-

ified. Christ reproves her, both for the *intenseness* of her care ("Thou art *careful and troubled, divided* and *disturbed* by thy care"), and for the *extensiveness of it,* "about *many things;* thou dost *grasp* at many *enjoyments,* and so art troubled at many *disappointments.* Poor Martha, thou hast many things to fret at, and this puts thee out of humour, whereas less ado would serve." Note, Inordinate care or trouble about many things in this world is a common fault among Christ's disciples; it is very displeasing to Christ, and that for which they often come under the rebukes of Providence. If they fret for no just cause, it is just with him to order them something to fret at.

4. That which aggravated the sin and folly of her care was that *but one thing is needful.* It is a *low* construction which some put upon this, that, whereas Martha was in care to provide *many* dishes of meat, there was occasion but for one, one would be enough. *There is need but of one thing — henos de esti chreia.* If we take it so, it furnishes us with a rule of *temperance,* not to affect varieties and dainties, but to be content to sit down to *one* dish of meat, to *half on one,* Prov. 23:1–3. It is a *forced* construction which some of the ancients put upon it: *But oneness is needful,* in opposition to distractions. There is need of *one heart* to attend upon the word, not divided and hurried to and fro, as Martha's was at this time. *The one thing needful* is certainly meant of that which Mary made her choice — *sitting at* Christ's feet, to hear his word. She was troubled about *many things,* when she should have applied herself to one; godliness *unites* the heart, which the world had *divided.* The *many things* she was troubled about were *needless,* while the *one thing* she neglected was *needful.* Martha's care and work were good in their proper season and place; but now she had something else to do, which was unspeakably more needful, and therefore should be done first, and most minded. She expected Christ to have blamed Mary for not doing as she did, but he blamed her for not doing as Mary did; and we are sure the *judgment of Christ* is *according to truth.* The day will come when Martha will wish she had set where Mary did.

VI. Christ's approbation and commendation of Mary for her serious piety: *Mary hath chosen the good part.* Mary said nothing in her own defence; but, since Martha has appealed to the Master, to him she is willing to refer it, and will abide by his award; and here we have it.

1. She had justly given the preference to that which best deserved it; for *one thing is needful,* this one thing that she has done, to give up herself to the guidance of Christ, and *receive the law* from his mouth. Note, Serious godliness is a *needful* thing, it is the *one thing needful;* for nothing without this will do us any real good in this world, and nothing but this will go with us into another world.

2. She had herein wisely done well for herself. Christ *justified Mary* against her sister's clamours. However we may be censured and condemned by men for our piety and zeal, our Lord Jesus will take our part: *But thou shalt answer, Lord, for me.* Let us not then condemn the pious zeal of any, lest we set Christ *against us;* and let us never be discouraged if we be censured for our pious zeal, for we have Christ for us. Note, Sooner or later, Mary's choice will be justified, and all those who make that choice, and abide by it. But this was not all; he *applauded* her for her wisdom: *She hath chosen the good part;* for she chose to be with Christ, to take her part with him; she chose the better business, and the better happiness, and took a better way of *honouring* Christ and of *pleasing* him, by receiving his word into her heart, than Martha did by providing for his entertainment in her house. Note, (1.) A *part with Christ* is a *good part;* it is a part for the soul and eternity, the part Christ gives to his favourites (Jn. 13:8), who are partakers *of Christ* (Heb. 3:14), and partakers *with Christ,* Rom. 8:17. (2.) It is a part that shall *never be taken away from those that have it.* A portion in this life will certainly be *taken away* from us, at the furthest, when we shall be taken away from it; but *nothing shall separate us from the love of Christ,* and our part in that love. Men and devils *cannot* take it away from us, and God and Christ *will not.* (3.) It is the wisdom and duty of every one of us to choose this *good part,* to choose the service of God for our business, and the favour of God for our happiness, and an interest in Christ, in order to both. In particular cases we must choose that which has a tendency to religion, and reckon that best for us that is best for our souls. Mary was at her choice whether she would partake with Martha in her care, and get the reputation of a fine *housekeeper,* or sit at the feet of Christ and approve herself a *zealous disciple;* and, by her choice in this particular, Christ judges of her general choice. (4.) Those who *choose this good part* shall not only have what they choose, but shall have their choice commended in the great day.

CHAPTER 11

In this chapter, I. Christ teaches his disciples to pray, and quickens and encourages them to be frequent, instant, and importunate in prayer (*v.* 1–13). II. He fully answers the blasphemous imputation of the Pharisees, who charged him with casting out devils by virtue of a compact and confederacy with Beelzebub, the prince of the devils, and shows the absurdity and wickedness of it (*v.* 14–26). III. He shows the honour of obedient disciples to be greater than that of his own mother (*v.* 27, 28). IV. He upbraids the men of that generation for their infidelity and obstinacy, notwithstanding all the means of conviction offered to them (*v.* 29–36). V. He severely reproves the Pharisees and consciences of those that submitted to them, and their hating and persecuting those that witnessed against their wickedness (*v.* 37–54).

Verses 1–13

Prayer is one of the great laws of natural religion. That man is a brute, is a monster, that never prays, that never gives glory to his Maker, nor feels his favour, nor owns his dependence upon him. One great design therefore of Christianity is to *assist us in prayer,* to enforce the duty upon us, to instruct us in it, and encourage us to expect advantage by it. Now here,

I. We find Christ himself *praying in a certain place,* probably where he used to pray, *v.* 1. As God, he was *prayed to;* as man, he *prayed;* and, though he was a Son, yet learned he this obedience. This evangelist has taken particular notice of Christ's *praying often,* more than any other of the evangelists: when he was baptized (*ch.* 3:21), he was *praying;* he *withdrew into the wilderness, and prayed* (*ch.* 5:16); he *went out into a mountain to pray, and continued all night in prayer* (*ch.* 6:12); he was *alone praying* (*ch.* 9:18); soon after, he *went up into a mountain to pray,* and *as he prayed he was transfigured* (*ch.* 9:28, 29); and here he was *praying in a certain place.* Thus, like a genuine son of David, he *gave himself unto prayer,* Ps. 109:4. Whether Christ was now *alone* praying, and the disciples only knew that he was so, or whether he prayed with them, is uncertain; it is most probable that they were joining with him.

II. His disciples applied themselves to him for direction in prayer. When he was praying, they asked, *Lord, teach us to pray.* Note, The gifts and graces of others should excite us to covet earnestly the same. Their zeal should provoke us to a holy imitation and emulation; why should not we do as well as they? Observe, They came to him with this request, *when he ceased;* for they would not disturb him when he was at prayer, no, not with this good motion. Every thing is beautiful in its season. *One of his disciples,* in the name of the rest, and perhaps by their appointment, said, *Lord, teach us.* Note, Though Christ is *apt to teach,* yet he will for this be enquired of, and his disciples must attend him for instruction.

Now, 1. Their request is, *"Lord, teach us to pray;* give us a rule or model by which to go in praying, and put words into our mouths." Note, It becomes the disciples of Christ to apply themselves to him for instruction in prayer. *Lord, teach us to pray,* is itself a good prayer, and a very needful one, for it is a hard thing to *pray well* and it is Jesus Christ only that can *teach us,* by his word and Spirit, *how to pray.* "Lord, teach me what it is to pray; Lord, excite and quicken me to the duty; Lord, direct me what to pray for; Lord, give me praying graces, that I may serve God acceptably in prayer; Lord, teach me to pray in proper words; give me a mouth and wisdom in prayer, that I may speak as I ought; *teach me what I shall say."*

2. Their plea is, *"As John also taught his disciples.* He took care to instruct his disciples in this necessary duty, and we would be taught as they were, for we have a better Master than they had." Dr. Lightfoot's notion of this is, That whereas the Jews' prayers were generally adorations, and praises of God, and doxologies, John taught his disciples such prayers as were more filled up with petitions and requests; for it is said of them that they did *deēseis poiountai — make prayers, ch.* 5:33. The word signifies such prayers as are properly petitionary. "Now, Lord, teach us this, to be added to those benedictions of the name of God which we have been accustomed to from our childhood." According to this sense, Christ did there teach them a prayer consisting wholly of petitions, and even omitting the doxology which had been affixed; and the *Amen,* which was usually said in the *giving of thanks* (1 Co. 14:16), and in the Psalms, is added to doxologies only. This disciple needed not to have urged John Baptist's example: Christ was more ready to teach than ever John Baptist was, and particularly taught to pray better than John did, or could, teach his disciples.

III. Christ gave them direction, much the same as he had given them before in his sermon upon the mount, Mt. 6:9, etc. We cannot think that they had forgotten it, but they ought to have had further and fuller instructions, and he did not, as yet, think fit to give them any; when the Spirit should be poured out upon them from on high, they would find all their requests couched in these few words, and would be able, in words of their own, to expatiate and enlarge upon them. In Matthew he had directed them to pray *after this manner;* here, *When ye pray, say;* which intimates that the Lord's prayer was intended to be used both as a form of prayer and a directory.

1. There are some differences between the Lord's prayer in Matthew and Luke, by which it appears that it was not the design of Christ that we should be *tied up* to these very words, for then there would have been no variation. Here is one difference in the translation only, which ought not to have been, when there is none in the original, and that is in the third petition: *As in heaven, so in earth;* whereas the words are the very same, and in the same order, as in Matthew. But there is a difference in the fourth petition. In Matthew we pray, "Give us daily bread *this* day:" here, "Give it us *day by day" — kath' hēmeran. Day by day;* that is, "Give us *each day* the bread which our bodies require, as they call for it:" not, "Give us *this day* bread for many days to come;" but as the Israelites had manna, "Let us have bread *to-day* for *today,* and to-*morrow* for to-*morrow;"* for thus we may be kept in a *continual dependence* upon God, as children upon their parents, and may have our mercies fresh from his hand daily, and may find ourselves under *fresh* obligations to do the work of every day in the day, according as the *duty of the day requires,* because we have from God the supplies of every day in the day, according as the *necessity of the day requires.* Here is likewise some difference in the fifth petition. In Matthew it is, *Forgive us our debts,* as we forgive: here it is, *Forgive us our sins;* which proves that our sins are our debts. *For we forgive;* not that our forgiving those that have offended us can *merit* pardon from God, or be an inducement to him to forgive us (he forgives for his own name's sake, and his Son's sake); but this is a very necessary qualification for forgiveness, and, if God have wrought it in us, we may plead that work of his grace for the enforcing of our petitions for the pardon of our sins: "Lord, forgive us, for thou hast thyself inclined us to forgive others." There is another addition here; we plead not only in general, We forgive *our debtors,* but in particular, "We profess *to forgive every one that is indebted to us,* without exception. We so *forgive our debtors* as not to bear malice or ill-will to any, but true love to all, without any exception whatsoever." Here also the doxology in the close is wholly omitted, and the *Amen;* for Christ would leave them at liberty to use that or any other doxology fetched out of David's psalms; or, rather, he left a vacuum here, to be filled up by a doxology more peculiar to the Christian institutes, ascribing glory to *Father, Son, and Holy Ghost.*

2. Yet it is, for substance, the same; and we shall therefore here only gather up some general lessons from it.

(1.) That in prayer we ought to come to God as children to *a Father,* a common Father to us and *all mankind,* but in a peculiar manner a Father to all the disciples of Jesus Christ. Let us therefore in our requests both for others and for ourselves, come to him with a humble boldness, confiding in his power and goodness.

(2.) That at the same time, and in the same petitions, which we address to God for *ourselves,* we should take in with us *all the children of men,* as God's creatures and our fellow-creatures. A rooted principle of *catholic charity,* and of *Christian sanctified humanity,* should go along with us, and dictate to us throughout this prayer, which is so worded as to be accommodated to that noble principle.

(3.) That in order to the confirming of the habit of heavenly-mindedness in us, which ought to actuate and govern us in the whole course of our conversation, we should, in all our devotions, with an eye of faith look *heavenward,* and view the God we pray to as our Father *in heaven,* that we may make the *upper world* more familiar to us, and may ourselves become better prepared for the future state.

(4.) That in prayer, as well as in the tenour of our lives,

we must *seek first the kingdom of God and the righteousness thereof,* by ascribing honour to his name, his *holy* name, and power to his government, both that of his providence in the world and that of his grace in the church. O that both the one and the other may be more manifested, and we and others more manifestly brought into subjection to both!

(5.) That the *principles* and *practices* of the *upper* world, the *unseen* world (which therefore by *faith* only we are *apprized of*), are the *great original — the archetypon,* to which we should desire that the principles and practices of this *lower* world, both in others and in ourselves, may be more conformable. Those words, *As in heaven, so on earth,* refer to all the first three petitions: "Father, let *thy name be sanctified* and *glorified,* and thy kingdom prevail, and thy will be done on this earth that is now alienated from thy service, as it is in yonder heaven that is entirely devoted to thy service."

(6.) That those who faithfully and sincerely mind the kingdom of God, and the righteousness thereof, may humbly hope that *all other things,* as far as to Infinite Wisdom seems good, *shall be added to them,* and they may in faith pray for them. If our first chief desire and care be that God's name may be sanctified, his kingdom come, and his will be done, we may then come boldly to the throne of grace for our *daily bread,* which will *then* be sanctified to us when we are sanctified to God, and God is sanctified by us.

(7.) That in our prayers for temporal blessings we must *moderate* our desires, and confine them to a *competency.* The expression here used of *day by day* is the very same with our *daily bread;* and therefore some think that we must look for another signification of the word *epiousios* than that of *daily,* which we give it, and that it means our *necessary* bread, that bread that is *suited* to the craving of our nature, the fruit that is brought out of the earth for our bodies that are made of the earth and are earthly, Ps. 104:14.

(8.) That sins are debts which we are daily contracting, and which therefore we should every day pray for the forgiveness of. We are not only going behind with our rent every day by *omissions* of duty and in duty, but are daily incurring the penalty of the law, as well as the forfeiture of our bond, by our *commissions.* Every day adds to the score of our guilt, and it is a miracle of mercy that we have so much encouragement given us to come every day to the throne of grace, to pray for the pardon of our sins of daily infirmity. God *multiplies to pardon* beyond seventy times seven.

(9.) That we have no reason to expect, nor can with any confidence pray, that God would forgive our sins against him, if we do not *sincerely,* and from a truly Christian principle of *charity,* forgive those that have at any time affronted us or been injurious to us. Though the *words of our mouth* be even *this* prayer to God, if the meditation of our heart at the same time be, as often it is, malice and revenge to our brethren, we are not accepted, nor can we expect an answer of peace.

(10.) That temptations to sin should be as much dreaded and deprecated by us as ruin by sin; and it should be as much our care and prayer to get the power of sin broken in us as to get the guilt of sin removed from us; and though temptation may be a charming, fawning, flattering thing, we must be as earnest with God that we may not be led into it as that we may not be led by that to sin, and by sin to ruin.

(11.) That God is to be depended upon, and sought unto, for our deliverance *from all evil;* and we should pray, not only that we may not be left to ourselves to run into evil, but that we may not be left to Satan to bring evil upon us. Dr. Lightfoot understands it of being delivered *from the evil one,* that is, the devil, and suggests that we should pray particularly against the apparitions of the devil and his possessions. The disciples were employed to *cast out devils,* and therefore were concerned to pray that they might be guarded against the particular spite he would always be sure to have against them.

IV. He stirs up and encourages importunity, fervency, and constancy, in prayer, by showing,

1. That importunity will go far in our dealings with men, *v.* 5–8. Suppose a man, upon a sudden emergency, goes to borrow a loaf or two of bread of a neighbour, at an unseasonable time of night, not for himself, but for his friend that came unexpectedly to him. His neighbour will be loth to accommodate him, for he has wakened him with his knocking, and put him out of humour, and he has a great deal to say in his excuse. The door is shut and locked, his children are asleep in bed, in the same room with him, and, if he make a noise, he shall disturb them. His servants are asleep, and he cannot make them hear; and, for his own part, he shall catch cold if he rise to give him. But his neighbour will have no nay, and therefore he continues *knocking* still, and tells him he will do so till he has what he comes for; so that he must give it to him, to be rid of him: *He will rise, and give him as many as he needs, because of his importunity.* He speaks this parable with the same intent that he speaks that in *ch.* 18:1: *That men ought always to pray, and not to faint.* Not that God can be wrought upon by importunity; we cannot be troublesome to him, nor by being so change his counsels. We prevail with men by importunity because they are *displeased* with it, but with God because he is *pleased* with it. Now this similitude may be of use to us,

(1.) To *direct* us in prayer. [1.] We must come to God with *boldness* and *confidence* for what we need, as a man does to the house of his neighbour or friend, who, he knows, loves him, and is inclined to be kind to him. [2.] We must come for *bread,* for that which is *needful,* and which we cannot be without. [3.] We must come to him by prayer *for others* as well as *for ourselves.* This man did not come for bread for himself, but for his friend. The Lord *accepted Job,* when he prayed for his friends, Job 42:10. We cannot come to God upon a more pleasing errand than when we come to him for grace to enable us to do good, to *feed many* with *our lips,* to entertain and edify those that come to us. [4.] We may come with the more boldness to God in a strait, if it be a strait that we have not brought ourselves into by our own folly and carelessness, but Providence has led us into it. This man would not have wanted bread if his friend had not come in *unexpectedly.* The care which Providence casts upon us, we may with cheerfulness cast back upon Providence. [5.] We ought to *continue instant* in prayer, and watch in the same with all perseverance.

(2.) To *encourage* us in prayer. If importunity could prevail thus with *a man* who was angry at it, much more with a God who is infinitely more kind and ready to do good *to us* than we are *to one another,* and is not angry at our importunity, but accepts it, especially when it is for spiritual mercies that we are importunate. If he do not answer our prayers presently, yet he will in due time, if we continue to pray.

2. That God has promised to give us what we ask of him. We have not only the goodness of nature to take comfort from, but the word which he has spoken (*v.* 9, 10): *"Ask, and it shall be given you;* either the thing itself you shall ask or that which is equivalent; either the thorn in the flesh removed, or grace sufficient given in." — We had this before, Mt. 7:7, 8. *I say unto you.* We have it from Christ's own mouth, who knows his Father's mind, and in whom all promises are yea and amen. We must not only *ask,* but we must *seek,* in the use of means, must second our prayers with our endeavours; and, in *asking* and *seeking,* we must continue *pressing,* still knocking at the same door, and we shall at length prevail, not only by our prayers in concert, but by our particular prayers: *Every one that asketh receiveth,* even the meanest saint that asks in faith. *This poor man cried, and the Lord heard him,* Ps. 34:6. When we ask of God those things which Christ has here directed us to ask, that his name may be sanctified, that his kingdom may come, and his will be done, in these requests we must be importunate, must *never hold our peace day or night;* we must not *keep silence,* nor *give God any rest, until he establish, until he make Jerusalem a praise in the earth,* Isa. 62:6, 7.

V. He gives us both instruction and encouragement in prayer from the consideration of our relation to God as a Father. Here is,

1. An *appeal* to the *bowels* of *earthly fathers:* "Let any of you that *is a father,* and knows the heart of a father, a father's affection to a child and care for a child, tell me, if his son *ask bread* for his breakfast, *will he give him a stone* to breakfast on? *If he ask a fish* for his dinner (when it may be a fish-day), *will he for a fish give him a serpent,* that will poison and sting him? Or, *if he shall ask an egg* for his supper (an egg and to bed), *will he offer him a scorpion?* You know you could not be so unnatural to your own children," *v.* 11, 12.

2. An *application* of this to the *blessings* of our *heavenly Father* (*v.* 13): *If ye then, being evil,* give, and know how to *give, good gifts to your children, much more shall God give you the Spirit.* He shall give *good things;* so it is in Matthew. Observe,

(1.) The direction he gives us what to *pray for.* We must ask for the *Holy Spirit,* not only a necessary in order to our *praying well,* but as inclusive of all the good things we are to pray for; we need no more to make us happy, for the Spirit is the worker of spiritual life, and the earnest of eternal life. Note, The gift of the Holy Ghost is a gift we are every one of us concerned earnestly and constantly to pray for.

(2.) The *encouragement* he gives us to hope that we shall speed in this prayer: *Your heavenly Father will give.* It is *in his power* to give the Spirit; he has all good things to bestow, wrapped up in that one; but that is not all, it is *in his promise,* the gift of *the Holy Ghost* is in the covenant, Acts 1:33, 38, and it is here inferred from parents' readiness to *supply* their children's *needs,* and *gratify* their *desires,* when they are natural and proper. If the child ask for a *serpent,* or a *scorpion,* the father, in kindness, will deny him, but not if he ask for what is *needful,* and will be *nourishing.* When God's children ask for the Spirit, they do, in effect, ask for *bread;* for the Spirit is the staff of life; nay, he is the Author of the soul's life. If our earthly parents, though *evil,* be yet so kind, if they, though *weak,* be yet so *knowing,* that they not only give, but give with discretion, give what is best, in the best manner and time, much more will our *heavenly Father,* who infinitely excels the fathers of our flesh both in wisdom and goodness, give us his *Holy Spirit.* If earthly parents be willing to lay out for the education of their children, to whom they design to leave their estates, much more will our heavenly Father give the spirit of sons to all those whom he has predestinated to the inheritance of sons.

Verses 14–26

The substance of these verses we had in Mt. 12:22, etc. Christ is here giving a general proof of his divine mission, by a particular proof of his power over Satan, his conquest of whom was an indication of his great design in coming into the world, which was, to *destroy the works of the devil.* Here too he gives an earnest of the success of that undertaking. He is here casting out *a devil* that made the poor possessed man *dumb:* in Matthew we are told that he was *blind* and *dumb.* When the devil was forced out by the word of Christ, the *dumb* spoke immediately, echoed to Christ's word, and the lips were opened to show forth his praise. Now,

I. Some were *affected* with this miracle. The people *wondered;* they admired the power of God, and especially that it should be exerted by the hand of one who made so small a figure, that one who did the work of the Messiah should have so little of that pomp of the Messiah which they expected.

II. Others were *offended* at it, and, to justify their infidelity, suggested that it was by virtue of a league with Beelzebub, the prince of the devils, that he did this, *v.* 15. It seems, in the devil's kingdom there are chiefs, which supposes that there are subalterns. Now they would have it *thought,* or *said* at least, that there was a correspondence settled between Christ and the devil, that the devil should have the advantage in the main and be victorious at last, but that in order hereto, in particular instances, he should yield Christ the advantage and retire by consent. Some, to *corroborate* this suggestion, and *confront* the evidence of Christ's miraculous power, challenged him to *give them a sign from heaven* (*v.* 16), to confirm his doctrine by some appearance in the *clouds,* such as was upon mount Sinai when the law was given; as if a *sign from heaven,* not disprovable by any sagacity of theirs, could not have been given them as well by a compact and collusion with *the prince of the power of the air, who works with power and lying wonders,* as the *casting out of a devil;* nay, that would not have been any present prejudice to his interest, which this manifestly was. Note, Obstinate infidelity will never be at a loss for something to say in its own excuse, though ever so frivolous and absurd. Now Christ here returns a full and direct answer to this cavil of theirs; in which he shows,

1. That it can by no means be imagined that such a subtle prince as Satan is should ever agree to measures that had such a direct tendency to his own overthrow, and the undermining of his own kingdom, *v.* 17, 18. What they objected they kept to themselves, afraid to speak it, lest it should be answered and baffled; but Jesus *knew their thoughts,* even when they industriously thought to conceal them, and he said, "You yourselves cannot but see the groundlessness, and consequently the spitefulness, of this charge; for it is an allowed maxim, confirmed by every day's experience, that no interest can stand that is divided against itself; not the more *pub-*

lic interest of a *kingdom,* nor the *private* interest of a house or family; if either the one or the other be *divided against itself,* it cannot stand. Satan would herein act against himself; not only by the miracle which turned him out of possession of the bodies of people, but much more in the doctrine for the explication and confirmation of which the miracle was wrought, which had a direct tendency to the ruin of Satan's interest in the minds of men, by mortifying sin, and turning men to the service of God. Now, if Satan should thus be *divided against himself,* he would hasten his own overthrow, which you cannot suppose an enemy to do that acts so subtlely for his own establishment, and is so solicitous to have his kingdom stand."

2. That was a very partial ill-natured thing for them to impute that in him to a compact with Satan which yet they applauded and admired in others that were of their own nation (*v.* 19): *"By whom do your sons cast them out?* Some of your own *kindred,* as Jews, nay, and some of your own *followers,* as Pharisees, have undertaken, in the name of the God of Israel, to cast out devils, and they were never charged with such a hellish combination as I am charged with." Note, It is gross hypocrisy to *condemn* that in those who *reprove* us which yet we *allow* in those that *flatter* us.

3. That, in opposing the conviction of this miracle, they were enemies to themselves, stood in their own light, and put a bar in their own door, for they thrust from them the kingdom of God (*v.* 20): *"If I with the finger of God cast out devils,* as you may assure yourselves I do, *no doubt the kingdom of God is come upon you,* the kingdom of the Messiah offers itself and all its advantages to you, and, if you receive it not, it is at your peril." In Matthew it is *by the Spirit of God,* here *by the finger of God;* the Spirit is the *arm of the Lord,* Isa. 53:1. His greatest and most mighty works were wrought by *his Spirit;* but, if the Spirit in this work is said to be the *finger of the Lord,* it perhaps may intimate how *easily* Christ did and could conquer Satan, even with the *finger of God,* the exerting of the divine power in a less and lower degree than in many other instances. He needed not make bare his *everlasting arm;* that roaring lion, when *he* pleases, is crushed, like a moth, with a touch of *a finger.* Perhaps here is an allusion to the acknowledgment of Pharaoh's magicians, when they were run aground (Ex. 8:19): This is *the finger of God.* "Now if the *kingdom of God* be herein *come to you,* and you be found by those cavils and blasphemies fighting against it, it will come *upon you* as a victorious force which you cannot stand before."

4. That his casting out devils was really the destroying of them and their power, for it confirmed a doctrine which had a direct tendency to the ruining of his kingdom, *v.* 21. 22. Perhaps there had been some who had cast out the inferior devils by compact with Beelzebub their chief, but that was without any real damage or prejudice to Satan and his kingdom, what he lost one way he gained another. The devil and such exorcists *played booty,* as we say, and, while the forlorn hope of his army *gave ground,* the main body thereby *gained ground;* the interest of Satan in the souls of men was not weakened by it in the least. But, when Christ cast out devils, he needed not do it by any compact with them, for he was *stronger than they,* and could do it *by force,* and did it so as to ruin Satan's power and blast his great design by that doctrine and that grace which break the power of sin, and so rout Satan's main body, take from him *all his armour,* and *divide his spoils,* which no one devil ever did to another or ever will. Now this is applicable to Christ's victories over Satan both in the world and in the hearts of particular persons, by that power which went along with the preaching of his gospel, and does still. And so we may observe here,

(1.) The miserable condition of an unconverted sinner. In his heart, which was fitted to be a habitation of God, the devil has his palace; and all the powers and the faculties of the soul, being employed by him in the service of sin, are *his goods.* Note, [1.] The heart of every unconverted sinner is the *devil's palace,* where he *resides* and where he *rules;* he *works* in the *children of disobedience.* The heart is a *palace,* a noble dwelling; but the unsanctified heart is the *devil's palace.* His will is obeyed, his interests are served, and the militia is in his hands; he *usurps* the throne in the soul. [2.] The devil, as a *strong man armed, keeps* this palace, does all he can to secure it to himself, and to fortify it against Christ. All the prejudices with which he hardens men's hearts against truth and holiness are the *strong-holds* which he erects for the *keeping of his palace;* this palace is his *garrison.* [3.] There is a kind of *peace* in the palace of an unconverted soul, while the devil, as a *strong man armed,* keeps it. The sinner has a good opinion of himself, is very secure and merry, has no doubt concerning the goodness of his state nor any dread of the judgment to come; he flatters himself in his own eyes, and cries peace to himself. Before Christ appeared, all was quiet, because all *went one way;* but the preaching of the gospel disturbed the peace of the devil's palace.

(2.) The wonderful change that is made in conversion, which is Christ's victory over this usurper. *Satan* is a *strong man armed;* but our Lord Jesus is *stronger than he,* as God, as Mediator. *If we speak of strength, he is strong:* more are *with* us than *against us.* Observe, [1.] The manner of this victory: *He comes upon him* by surprise, when his *goods are in peace* and the devil thinks it is all *his own* for ever, and *overcomes* him. Note, The conversion of a soul to God is Christ's victory over the devil and his power in that soul, restoring the soul to its liberty, and recovering his own interest in it and dominion over it. [2.] The evidences of this victory. *First,* He *takes from him all his armour wherein he trusted.* The devil is a *confident* adversary; he *trusts* to his *armour,* as Pharaoh to his rivers (Eze. 29:3): but Christ disarms him. When the power of sin and corruption in the soul is broken, when the mistakes are rectified, the eyes opened, the heart humbled and changed, and made serious and spiritual, then Satan's *armour* is *taken away. Secondly,* He *divides the spoils;* he *takes possession* of them for himself. All the endowments of mind and body, the estate, power, interest, which before were made use of in the service of sin and Satan, are now converted to Christ's service and employed for him; yet this is not all; he *makes a distribution* of them among his followers, and, and having conquered Satan, gives to all believers the benefit of that victory. Hence Christ infers that, since the whole drift of his doctrine and miracles was to break the power of the devil, that great enemy of mankind, it was the duty of all to join with him and to follow his guidance, to receive his gospel and come heartily into the interests of it; for otherwise they would justly be reckoned as siding with the enemy (*v.* 23): *He that is not with me is against me.* Those therefore who rejected the doctrine of Christ, and slighted his miracles, were looked upon as adversaries to him, and in the devil's interest.

5. That there was a vast difference between the devil's *going out* by compact and his being *cast out* by compulsion. Those out of whom Christ *cast him* he never entered into again, for so was Christ's charge (Mk. 9:25); whereas, if he had *gone out,* whenever he saw fit he would have made a re-entry, for that is the way of the unclean spirit, when he voluntarily and with design *goes out of a man, v.* 24–26. The prince of the devils may *give leave,* nay, may *give order,* to his forces to retreat, or make a feint, to draw the poor deluded soul into an *ambush;* but Christ, as he gives a *total,* so he gives a *final,* defeat to the enemy. In this part of the argument he has a further intention, which is to represent the state of those who have had fair offers made them, — among whom, and in whom, God has begun to break the devil's power and overthrow his kingdom, — but they reject his counsel against themselves, and relapse into a state of subjection to Satan. Here we have,

(1.) The condition of a *formal hypocrite,* his *bright side* and his *dark side.* His heart still remains the *devil's house;* he calls it his own, and he retains his interest in it; and yet, [1.] The *unclean spirit is gone out.* He was not *driven out* by the power of converting grace; there was none of that *violence* which the kingdom of heaven suffers; but he *went out,* withdrew for a time, so that the man seemed not to be under the power of Satan as formerly, nor so followed with his temptations. Satan is *gone,* or has *turned himself into an angel of light.* [2.] The *house is swept* from common pollutions, by a forced confession of sin, as Pharaoh's — a feigned contrition for it, as Ahab's, — and a partial reformation, as Herod's. There are those that have *escaped the pollutions of the world,* and yet are still under the power of the *god of this world,* 2 Pt. 2:20. The house is *swept,* but it is not *washed;* and Christ hath said, *If I wash thee not, thou hast no part with me;* the house must be *washed,* or it is *none of his.* Sweeping takes off only the loose dirt, while the sin that *besets* the sinner, the beloved sin, is untouched. It is swept from the filth that lies open to the eye of the world, but it is not searched and ransacked for secret filthiness, Mt. 23:25. It is *swept,* but the *leprosy is in the wall,* and will be till something more be done. [3.] The house is *garnished* with common gifts and graces. It is not *furnished* with any true grace, but *garnished* with the pictures of all graces. Simon Magus was *garnished* with faith, Balaam with good desires, Herod with a respect for John, the Pharisees with many external performances. It is garnished, but it is like a *potsherd covered with silver dross,* it is all paint and varnish, not real, not lasting. The house is *garnished,* but the property is not altered; it was never surrendered to Christ, nor inhabited by the Spirit. Let us therefore take heed of resting in that which a man may have and yet come short.

(2.) Here is the condition of a *final apostate,* into whom the devil returns after he had *gone out: Then goes he, and takes seven other spirits more wicked than himself* (*v.* 26); a certain number for an uncertain, as *seven devils* are said to be cast out of Mary Magdalene. *Seven wicked spirits* are opposed to the *seven spirits of God,* Rev. 3:1. These are said to be more wicked than himself. It seems, even devils are not all alike wicked; probably, the degrees of their wickedness, now that they are *fallen,* are as the degrees of their holiness were while they stood. When the devil would do mischief most effectually, he employs those that are more mischievous than himself. These *enter in* without any difficulty or opposition; they are welcomed, and they *dwell there;* there they *work,* there they *rule;* and the *last state of that man is worse than the first.* Note, [1.] Hypocrisy is the high road to apostasy. If the heart remains in the interest of sin and Satan, the shows and shadows will *come to nothing;* those that have not set that right will not long be stedfast. Where secret haunts of sin are kept up, under the cloak of a visible profession, conscience is debauched, God is provoked to withdraw his restraining grace, and the *close* hypocrite commonly proves an *open* apostate, [2.] The last state of such is *worse than the first,* in respect both of sin and punishment. Apostates are usually the worst of men, the most vain and profligate, the most bold and daring; their consciences are seared, and their sins of all others the most aggravated. God often sets marks of his displeasure upon them in *this* world, and in the other world they will *receive the greater damnation.* Let us therefore hear, and fear, and hold fast our integrity.

Verses 27–28

We had not this passage in the other evangelists, nor can we tack it, as Dr. Hammond does, to that of Christ's mother and brethren desiring to speak with him (for this evangelist also has related that in *ch.* 8:19), but it contains an interruption much like that, and, like that, occasion is taken from it for instruction.

1. The applause which an affectionate, honest, well-meaning woman gave to our Lord Jesus, upon hearing his excellent discourses. While the scribes and Pharisees despised and blasphemed them, this good woman (and probably she was a person of some quality) admired them, and the wisdom and power with which he spoke: *As he spoke these things* (*v.* 27), with a convincing force and evidence, a *certain woman of the company* was so pleased to hear how he had confounded the Pharisees, and conquered them, and put them to shame, and cleared himself from their vile insinuations, that she could not forbear crying out, *"Blessed is the womb that bore thee.* What an admirable, what an excellent man is this! Surely never was there a greater or better born of a woman: happy the woman that has him for her son. I should have thought myself very happy to have been the mother of one that *speaks as never man spoke,* that has so much of the grace of heaven in him, and is so great a blessing to this earth." This was *well said,* as it expressed her high esteem of Christ, and that for the sake of his doctrine; and it was not amiss that it reflected honour upon the virgin Mary his mother, for it agreed with what she herself had said (*ch.* 1:48), *All generations shall call me blessed;* some even of this generation, bad as it was. Note, To all that believe the word of Christ the person of Christ is precious, and he is *an honour,* 1 Pt. 2:7. Yet we must be careful, lest, as this good woman, we too much magnify the honour of his natural kindred, and so *know him after the flesh,* whereas we must now henceforth *know him so no more.*

2. The occasion which Christ took from this to pronounce *them* more happy who are his faithful and obedient followers than she was who bore and nursed him. He does not deny what this woman said, nor refuse her respect to him and his mother; but leads her from this to that which was of higher consideration, and which more concerned her: *Yea, rather,*

blessed are they that hear the word of God, and keep it, v. 28. He thinks them so; and his saying that they are so makes them so, and should make us of his mind. This is intended partly as a *check* to her, for doting so much upon his bodily presence and his human nature, partly as an *encouragement* to her to hope that she might be as happy as his own mother, whose happiness she was ready to envy, if she would *hear the word of God and keep it.* Note, Though it is a great privilege to hear the word of God, yet those only are truly blessed, that is, blessed of the Lord, that hear it and *keep* it, that keep it in memory, and keep to it as their way and rule.

Verses 29–36

Christ's discourse in these verses shows two things: —

I. What is the *sign* we may *expect* from God for the *confirmation* of our *faith.* The great and most convincing proof of Christ's being sent of God, and which they were yet to wait for, after the many signs that had been given them, was the resurrection of Christ from the dead. Here is,

1. A reproof to the people for demanding other signs than what had already been given them in great plenty: *The people were gathered thickly together* (*v.* 29), a vast crowd of them, expecting not so much to have their consciences informed by the doctrine of Christ as to have their curiosity gratified by his miracles. Christ knew what brought such a multitude together; they came *seeking a sign,* they came to gaze, to have something to talk of when they went home; and it is an *evil generation* which nothing will awaken and convince, no, not the most sensible demonstrations of divine power and goodness.

2. A promise that yet there should be *one sign* more given them, different from any that had yet been given them, even the *sign of Jonas the prophet,* which in Matthew is explained as meaning the *resurrection of Christ.* As Jonas being cast into the sea, and lying there three days, and then coming up alive and preaching repentance to the Ninevites, was a sign to them, upon which they turned from their evil way, so shall the death and resurrection of Christ, and the preaching of his gospel immediately after to the Gentile world, be the last warning to the Jewish nation. If they be provoked to a *holy jealousy* by this, well and good; but, if this do not work upon them, let them look for nothing but utter ruin: *The Son of Man shall be a sign to this generation* (*v.* 30), a sign speaking to them, though a sign spoken against by them.

3. A warning to them to improve this sign; for it was at their peril if they did not. (1.) The *queen of Sheba* would *rise up in judgment against them,* and condemn *their unbelief, v.* 31. She was a stranger to the commonwealth of Israel, and yet so readily gave credit to the report she heard of the glories of a king of Israel, that, notwithstanding the prejudices we are apt to conceive against foreigners, she came from the uttermost parts of the earth to *hear his wisdom,* not only to satisfy her curiosity, but to inform her mind, especially in the knowledge of the true God and his worship, which is upon record, to her honour; and, behold, a *greater than Solomon in here, pleion Solomōntos — more than a Solomon is here;* that is, says Dr. Hammond, more of wisdom and more heavenly divine doctrine than ever was in all Solomon's words or writings; and yet these wretched Jews will give no manner of regard to what Christ says to them, though he be in the midst of them. (2.) The Ninevites would rise up in judgment against them, and condemn their impenitency (*v.* 32): They *repented at the preaching of Jonas;* but here is preaching which far exceeds that of Jonas, is more powerful and awakening, and threatens a much sorer ruin than that of Nineveh, and yet none are startled by it, to turn *from their evil way,* as the Ninevites did.

II. What is the *sign* that God *expects* from us for the *evidencing* of our faith, and that is the serious practice of that religion which we profess to believe, and a readiness to entertain all divine truths, when brought to us in their proper evidence. Now observe,

1. They had *the light* with all the advantage they could desire. For God, having *lighted the candle* of the gospel, did not put it in a *secret place,* or *under a bushel;* Christ did not preach in corners. The apostles were ordered to preach the gospel to every creature; and both Christ and his ministers, Wisdom and her maidens, cry in the *chief places of concourse, v.* 33. It is a great privilege that the light of the gospel is put on a *candlestick,* so that all that come in may *see it,* and may *see by it* where they are and whither they are going, and what is the true, and sure, and only way to happiness.

2. Having the *light,* their concern was to have the *sight,* or else to what purpose had they the light? Be the *object* ever so *clear,* if the *organ* be not *right,* we are never the better: *The light of the body is the eye* (*v.* 34), which receives the light of the candle when it is brought into the room. So the light of the soul is the understanding and judgment, and its power of discerning between good and evil, truth and falsehood. Now, according as this is, so the light of divine revelation is to us, and our benefit by it; it is a savour of life unto life, or of death unto death. (1.) If this eye of the soul be *single,* if it see *clear,* see things as they are, and judge impartially concerning them, if it aim at *truth* only, and seek it for its own sake, and have not any sinister by-looks and intentions, the *whole body,* that is, the whole soul, is *full of light,* it receives and entertains the gospel, which will bring along with it into the soul both *knowledge* and *joy.* This denotes the same thing with that of the good ground, *receiving the word* and *understanding* it. If our understanding admits the gospel in its full light, it fills the soul, and it has enough to *fill* it. And if the soul be thus *filled* with the light of the gospel, *having no part dark,* — if all its powers and faculties be subjected to the government and influence of the gospel, and none left unsanctified, — then *the whole soul shall be full of light,* full of holiness and comfort. *It was darkness* itself, but now light in the Lord, *as when the bright shining of a candle doth give thee light, v.* 36. Note, The gospel will come into those souls whose doors and windows are thrown open to receive it; and where it comes it will bring light with it. But, (2.) If the *eye of the* soul be *evil,* — if the judgment be *bribed* and *biassed* by the corrupt and vicious dispositions of the mind, by pride and envy, by the love of the world and sensual pleasures, — if the understanding be *prejudiced* against divine truths, and resolved not to admit them, though brought with ever so convincing an evidence, — it is no wonder that the *whole body,* the whole soul, should be *full of darkness, v.* 34. How can they have instruction, information, direction, or comfort, from the gospel, that wilfully shut their eyes against it? and what hope is there of such? what remedy for them? The inference hence therefore is, *Take heed that the light which is in thee be not darkness, v.* 35. Take heed that the eye of the mind be not blinded by partiality, and prejudice, and sinful aims. Be sincere in your enquiries after truth, and ready to receive it in the light, and love, and power of it; and not as the men of *this generation* to whom Christ preached, who never sincerely *desired* to know God's will, nor *designed* to do it, and therefore no wonder that they *walked on in darkness,* wandered *endlessly,* and perished *eternally.*

Verses 37–54

Christ here says many of those things to a Pharisee and his guests, in a *private* conversation at table, which he afterwards said in a *public* discourse in the temple (Mt. 23); for what he said in public and private was *of a piece.* He would not say that in a corner which he durst not repeat and stand to in the great congregation; nor would he give those reproofs to any sort of sinners in general which he durst not apply to them in particular as he met with them; for he was, and is, the *faithful Witness.* Here is,

I. Christ's going to dine with a Pharisee that very civilly invited him to his house (*v.* 37); *As he spoke,* even while he was speaking, a *certain Pharisee* interrupted him with a request to him to come and *dine with him,* to come *forthwith,* for it was dinner-time. We are willing to hope that the Pharisee was so well pleased with his discourse that he was willing to show him respect, and desirous to have more of his company, and therefore gave him this invitation and bade him truly welcome; and yet we have some cause to suspect that it was with an *ill design,* to break off his discourse to the people, and to have an opportunity of ensnaring him and getting something out of him which might serve for matter of accusation or reproach, *v.* 53, 54. We know not the mind of this Pharisee; but, whatever it was, Christ knew it: if he meant ill, he shall know Christ does not fear him; if well, he shall know Christ is willing to do him good: so *he went in, and sat down to meat.* Note, Christ's disciples must learn of him to be *conversable,* and not *morose.* Though we have need to be *cautious* what company we keep, yet we need not be *rigid,* nor must we therefore *go out of the world.*

II. The offence which the Pharisee took at Christ, as those of that sort had sometimes done at the disciples of Christ, for not *washing before dinner, v.* 38. He wondered that a man of his sanctity, a prophet, a man of so much devotion, and such a strict conversation, should sit down to meat, and not first *wash his hands,* especially being newly come out of a mixed company, and there being in the Pharisee's dining-room, no doubt, all accommodations set ready for it, so that he need not fear being *troublesome;* and the Pharisee himself and all his guests, no doubt, *washing,* so that he could not be *singular;* what, and yet not wash? What harm had it been if he had washed? Was it not strictly commanded by the canons of their church? It was so, and *therefore* Christ would not do it, because he would witness against their assuming a power to impose that as a matter of religion which *God commanded them not.* The ceremonial law consisted in *divers washings,* but this was none of them, and therefore Christ would not practise it, no not in *complaisance* to the Pharisee who invited him, nor though he knew that offence would be taken at his omitting it.

III. The sharp reproof which Christ, upon this occasion, gave to the Pharisees, without begging pardon even of the Pharisee whose guest he now was; for we must not flatter our best friends in any evil thing.

1. He reproves them for placing religion so much in those instances of it which are only external, and fall under the eye of man, while those were not only *postponed,* but quite *expunged,* which respect the soul, and fall under the eye of God, *v.* 39, 40. Now observe here, (1.) The absurdity they were guilty of: *"You Pharisees make clean the outside* only, you wash your hands with water, but do not *wash your hearts from wickedness;* these are full of covetousness and malice, *covetousness* of men's goods, and malice against good men." Those can never be reckoned *cleanly* servants that wash only the *outside of the cup* out of which their master drinks, or *the platter* out of which he eats, and take no care to make clean the *inside,* the filth of which immediately *affects* the meat or drink. The frame or temper of the mind in every religious service is as the *inside* of the cup and platter; the impurity of this *infects* the services, and therefore to keep ourselves free from scandalous enormities, and yet to live under the dominion of spiritual wickedness, is as great an affront to God as it would be for a servant to give the cup into his master's hand, clean wiped from all the dust on the outside, but *within* full of cobwebs and spiders. *Ravening and wickedness,* that is, *reigning worldliness* and *reigning spitefulness,* which men think they can find some cloak and cover for, are the dangerous damning sins of many who have made the *outside of the cup* clean from the more gross, and scandalous, and inexcusable sins of whoredom and drunkenness. (2.) A particular instance of the absurdity of it: *"Ye fools, did not he that made that which is without make that which is within also? v.* 40. Did not that God who in the law of Moses appointed divers ceremonial washings, with which you justify yourselves in these practices and impositions, appoint also that you should cleanse and purify your hearts? He who made laws for that which is *without,* did not he even in those laws further intend something within, and by other laws show how little he regarded the *purifying of the flesh,* and the *putting away of the filth* of that, if the heart be not made clean?" Or, it may have regard to God not only as a *Lawgiver,* but (which the words seem rather to import) as a Creator. Did not God, who made us these bodies (and they *are fearfully and wonderfully made*), make us *these souls* also, which are more fearfully and wonderfully made? Now, if he made both, he justly expects we should take care of both; and therefore not only wash the *body,* which he is the *former* of, and make the hands clean in honour of his work, but wash the spirit, which he is the Father of, and get the leprosy in the heart cleansed.

To this he subjoins a rule for making our creature-comforts clean to us (*v.* 41): "Instead of *washing your hands* before you go to meat, *give alms of such things as you have*" (*ta enonta — of such things as are set before you, and present with you*); "let the poor have their share out of them, and then *all things are clean to you,* and you may use them comfortably." Here is a plain allusion to the law of Moses, by which it was provided that certain portions of the increase of their land should be given *to the Levite, the stranger, the fatherless, and the widow;* and, when that was done, what was reserved for their own use was *clean to them,* and they could in faith pray for a blessing upon it, Deu. 26:12–15. *Then* we can with comfort enjoy the gifts of God's bounty ourselves when we *send portions to them for whom nothing is prepared,* Neh. 8:10. *Job ate not his morsel alone,* but *the fatherless ate thereof,* and so it was *clean to him* (Job 31:17);

clean, that is, permitted and allowed to be used, and then only can it be used comfortably. Note, What we have is not our own, unless God have his dues out of it; and it is by *liberality to the poor* that we clear up to ourselves our *liberty* to make use of our creature-comforts.

2. He reproves them for laying stress upon trifles, and neglecting the weighty matters of the law, *v.* 42. (1.) Those laws which related only to the *means of religion* they were very exact in the observance of, as particularly those concerning the maintenance of the priests: *Ye pay tithe of mint and rue,* pay it in kind and to the full, and will not put off the priests with a *modus decimandi* or *compound* for it. By this they would gain reputation with the people as strict observers of the law, and would make an interest in the priests, in whose power it was many a time to do them a kindness; and no wonder if the priests and the Pharisees contrived how to strengthen one another's hands. Now Christ does not condemn them for being so exact in paying tithes *(these things ought ye to have done),* but to think that this would atone for the neglect of their greater duties; for, (2.) Those laws which relate to the *essentials of religion* they made nothing of: *You pass over judgment and the love of God,* you make no conscience of giving men their *dues* and God your *hearts.*

3. He reproves them for their pride and vanity, and affectations of precedency and praise of men (*v.* 43): *"Ye love the uppermost seats in the synagogues"* (or consistories where the elders met for government); "if you have not those seats, you are ambitious of them; if you have, you are proud of them; and *you love greetings in the markets,* to be complimented by the people and to have their cap and knee." It is not sitting uppermost, or being greeted, that is reproved, but *loving it.*

4. He reproves them for their hypocrisy, and their colouring over the wickedness of their hearts and lives with specious pretences (*v.* 44): *"You are as graves* overgrown with grass, which therefore *appear not,* and *the men that walk over them are not aware of them,* and so they contract the ceremonial pollution which by the law arose from the *touch of a grave."* These Pharisees were *within* full of *abominations,* as a grave of putrefaction; full of covetousness, envy, and malice; and yet they concealed it so artfully with a profession of devotion, that it did not appear, so that they who conversed with them, and followed their doctrine, were defiled with sin, infected with their corruptions and ill morals, and yet, they making a show of piety, suspected no danger by them. The contagion *insinuated* itself, and was *insensibly* caught, and those that caught it thought themselves never the worse.

IV. The testimony which he bore also against the lawyers or scribes, who made it their business to *expound* the law according to the tradition of the elders, as the Pharisees did to *observe* the law according to that tradition.

1. There was one of that profession who resented what he said against the Pharisees (*v.* 45): *"Master, thus saying thou reproachest us also,* for we are scribes; and we are therefore hypocrites?" Note, It is a common thing for unhumbled sinners to call and count reproofs reproaches. It is the wisdom of those who desire to have their sin mortified to make a *good use* of reproaches that come from *ill will,* and to turn them into reproofs. If we can in this way hear of our faults, and amend them, it is well: but it is the folly of those who are wedded to their sins, and resolved not to part with them, to make an *ill use* of the faithful and friendly admonitions given them, which come from love, and to have their passions provoked by them as if they were intended for *reproaches,* and therefore fly in the face of their reprovers, and justify themselves in rejecting the reproof. Thus the prophet complained (Jer. 6. 10): *The word of the Lord is to them a reproach; they have no delight in it.* This lawyer espoused the Pharisee's cause, and so made himself partaker of his sins.

2. Our Lord Jesus thereupon took them to task (*v.* 46): *Woe unto you also, ye lawyers;* and again (*v.* 52): *Woe unto you lawyers.* They blessed themselves in the reputation they had among the people, who thought them happy men, because they studied the law, and were always conversant with that, and had the honour of instructing the people in the knowledge of that; but Christ denounced *woes* against them, for he sees not as man sees. This was just upon him for taking the Pharisee's part, and quarrelling with Christ because he reproved them. Note, Those who quarrel with the reproofs of others, and suspect them to be reproaches to them, do but get *woes of their own* by so doing.

(1.) The lawyers are reproved for making the services of religion more *burdensome* to others, but more *easy* to themselves, than God had made them (*v.* 46): *"You lade men with burdens grievous to be borne,* by your traditions, which *bind them out from* many liberties God has allowed them, and *bind them up* to many slaveries which God never enjoined them, to show your authority, and to keep people in awe; *but you yourselves touch them not with one of your fingers;"* that is, [1.] "You will not *burden* yourselves with them, nor be yourselves bound by those restraints with which you hamper others." They would seem, by the hedges they pretended to make about the law, to be very strict for the observance of the law; but, if you could see their practices, you would find that they not only make nothing of those hedges themselves, but make nothing of the law itself neither: thus the confessors of the Romish church are said to do with their penitents. [2.] "You will not *lighten* them to those you have power over; *you will not touch them,* that is, either to repeal them or to dispense with them when you find them to be burdensome and grievous to the people." They would come in with *both hands* to dispense with a command of God, but not with a *finger* to mitigate the rigour of any of the traditions of the elders.

(2.) They are reproved for pretending a veneration for the memory of the prophets whom their fathers killed, when yet they hated and persecuted those in their own day who were sent to them on the same errand, to call them to repentance, and direct them to Christ, *v.* 47–49. [1.] These hypocrites, among other pretences of piety, *built the sepulchres of the prophets;* that is, they erected monuments over their graves, in honour of them, probably with large inscriptions containing high encomiums of them. They were not so superstitious as to enshrine their relics, or to think their devotions the more acceptable to God for being offered at the *tombs of the martyrs;* they did not burn incense or pray to them, or plead their merits with God; they did not add that iniquity to their hypocrisy; but, as if they owned themselves the *children of the prophets,* their heirs and executors, they *repaired* and *beautified* the monuments sacred to their *pious memory.* [2.] Notwithstanding this, they had an inveterate *enmity* to those in their *own day* that came to them in the *spirit* and *power* of those prophets; and, though they had not yet had an opportunity of carrying it far, yet they would soon do it, for the *Wisdom of God said,* that is, Christ himself would *so order* it, and did *now foretel* it, that they would *slay* and *persecute* the prophets and apostles that should be sent them. The *Wisdom of God* would thus make trial of them, and discover their odious hypocrisy, by sending them prophets, to reprove them for their sins and warn them of the judgments of God. Those prophets should prove themselves apostles, or messengers sent from heaven, by signs, and wonders, and gifts of the Holy Ghost. Or, *"I will send them prophets* under the style and title of apostles, who yet shall produce as good an authority as any of the old prophets did; and these they shall not only contradict and oppose, but *slay* and *persecute,* and put to death." Christ foresaw this, and yet did not otherwise than as became the *Wisdom of God* in sending them, for he knew how to bring glory to himself in the issue, by the recompences reserved both for the *persecutors* and the *persecuted* in the future state. [3.] That therefore God will justly put another construction upon their *building* the *tombs* of the prophets than what they would be thought to intend, and it shall be interpreted their *allowing the deeds of their fathers* (*v.* 45); for, since by their present actions it appeared that they had no true value for their prophets, the *building of their sepulchres* shall have this sense put upon it, that they resolved to keep them in their graves whom their fathers had hurried thither. Josiah, who had a real value for prophets, thought it enough not to disturb the grave of the *man of God at Beth-el: Let no man move his bones,* 2 Ki. 23:17, 18. If these lawyers will carry the matter further, and will build *their sepulchres,* it is such a piece of *over-doing* as gives cause to suspect an ill design in it, and that it is meant as a cover for some design against prophecy itself, like the kiss of a traitor, as *he that blesseth his friend with a loud voice, rising early in the morning, it shall be counted a curse to him,* Prov. 27:14.

[4.] That they must expect no other than to be reckoned with, as the *fillers up* of the *measure* of persecution, *v.* 50, 51. They keep up the trade as it were in succession, and therefore are responsible for the *debts of the company,* even those it has been *contracting* all along from *the blood of Abel,* when the world began, to that of Zacharias, and so forward to the end of the Jewish state; it shall all be *required of this generation,* this last generation of the Jews, whose sin in persecuting Christ's apostles would exceed any of the sins of that kind that their fathers were guilty of, and so would bring *wrath* upon them *to the uttermost,* 1 Th. 2:15, 16. Their destruction by the Romans was so terrible that it might well be reckoned the completing of God's vengeance upon that persecuting nation.

(3.) They are reproved for opposing the gospel of Christ, and doing all they could to obstruct the progress and success of it, *v.* 52. [1.] They had not, according to the duty of their place, faithfully expounded to the people those scriptures of the Old Testament which pointed at the Messiah, which if they had been led into the right understanding of by the lawyers, they would readily have embraced him and his doctrine: but, instead of that, they had perverted those texts, and had cast a mist before the eyes of the people, by their corrupt glosses upon them, and this is called *taking away the key of knowledge;* instead of *using* that key for the people, and helping them to use it aright, they *hid it* from them; this is called, in Matthew, *shutting up the kingdom of heaven against men,* Mt. 23:13. Note, those who take away the key of knowledge shut up the *kingdom of heaven.* [2.] They themselves did not embrace the gospel of Christ, though by their acquaintance with the Old Testament they could not but know that the *time was fulfilled,* and the *kingdom of God was at hand;* they saw the prophecies accomplished in that kingdom which our Lord Jesus was about to set up, and yet would not themselves *enter into it.* Nay, [3.] Them that without any guidance or assistance of theirs were *entering in* they did all they could to *hinder* and discourage, by threatening to *cast them out of the synagogue,* and otherwise terrifying them. It is bad for people to be averse to revelation, but much worse to be adverse to it.

Lastly, In the close of the chapter we are told how spitefully and maliciously the scribes and *Pharisees* contrived to draw him into a snare, *v.* 53, 54. They could not bear those cutting reproofs which they must own to be just; but what he had said against them in particular would not *bear an action,* nor could they ground upon it any *criminal* accusation, and therefore, as if, because his reproofs were warm, they hoped to stir him up to some intemperate heat and passion, so as to put him off his guard, they *began to urge him vehemently,* to be very fierce upon him, and to *provoke him to speak of many things,* to propose dangerous questions to him, *laying wait* for something which might serve the design they had of making him either *odious* to the people, or *obnoxious* to the government, or both. Thus did they seek occasion against him, like David's enemies that did *every day wrest his words,* Ps. 56:5. *Evil men dig up mischief.* Note, Faithful reprovers of sin must expect to have many enemies, and have need to set a watch before the door of their lips, because of *their observers* that watch for their halting. The prophet complains of those in his time who *make a man an offender for a word, and lay a snare for him that reproveth in the gate,* Isa. 29:21. That we may bear trials of this kind with patience, and get through them with prudence, let us *consider him who endured such contradiction of sinners against himself.*

CHAPTER 12

In this chapter we have divers excellent discourses of our Saviour's upon various occasions, many of which are to the same purport with what we had in Matthew upon other the like occasions; for we may suppose that our Lord Jesus preached the same doctrines, and pressed the same duties, at several times, in several companies, and that one of the evangelists took them as he delivered them at one time and another at another time; and we need thus to have precept upon precept, line upon line. Here, I. Christ warns his disciples to take heed of hypocrisy, and of cowardice in professing Christianity and preaching the gospel (*v.* 1–12). II. He gives a caution against covetousness, upon occasion of a covetous motion made to him, and illustrates that caution by a parable of a rich man suddenly cut off by death in the midst of his worldly projects and hopes (*v.* 13–21). III. He encourages his disciples to cast all their care upon God, and to live easy in a dependence upon his providence, and exhorts them to make religion their main business (*v.* 22–34). IV. He stirs them up to watchfulness for their Master's coming, from the consideration of the reward of those who are then found faithful, and the punishment of those who are found unfaithful (*v.* 35–48). V. He bids them expect trouble and persecution (*v.* 49–53). VI. He warns the people to observe and improve the day of their opportunities and to make their peace with God in time (*v.* 54–59).

Verses 1–12

We find here, I. A vast auditory that was got together to hear Christ preach. The *scribes* and *Pharisees* sought *to accuse him,* and do him mischief; but the people, who were not under the bias of their prejudices and jealousies, still *admired* him, attended on him, and did him honour. *In the mean time* (*v.* 1), while he was in the Pharisee's house, contending with them that sought to ensnare him, the people got together for an afternoon sermon, a sermon after *dinner,* after dinner with a Pharisee; and he would not disappoint them. Though in the morning sermon, when they were *gathered thickly together* (*ch.* 11:29), he had severely reproved them, as an *evil generation that seek a sign,* yet they renewed their attendance on him; so much better could the people bear *their* reproofs than the Pharisees *theirs.* The more the Pharisees strove to drive the people from Christ, the more flocking there was to him. Here was an *innumerable multitude of people gathered together, so that they trade one upon another,* in labouring to get foremost, and to come within hearing. It is a good sight to see people thus forward to hear the word, and venture upon inconvenience and danger rather than miss an opportunity for their souls. Who are these that thus *fly as the doves to their windows?* Isa. 60:8. When the net is cast where there is such a multitude of fish, it may be hoped that some will be enclosed.

II. The instructions which he gave his followers, in the hearing of this auditory.

1. He began with a caution against *hypocrisy.* This he said *to his disciples first of all;* either to the twelve, or to the seventy. These were his more peculiar charge, his family, his school, and therefore he particularly *warned them* as his *beloved sons;* they made more profession of religion than others and hypocrisy in *that* was the sin they were most in danger of. They were to preach to others; and, if they should *prevaricate,* corrupt the word, and deal deceitfully, hypocrisy would be worse in them than in others. Besides, there was a Judas among them, who was a hypocrite, and Christ knew it, and would hereby startle him, or leave him inexcusable. Christ's disciples were, for aught we know, the *best men* then in the world, yet they needed to be cautioned against hypocrisy. Christ said this to the disciples, *in the hearing* of this great multitude, rather than *privately* when he had them by themselves, to add the greater weight to the caution, and to let the world know that he would not countenance hypocrisy, no, not in *his own disciples.* Now observe,

(1.) The description of that sin which he warns them against: *It is the leaven of the Pharisees.* [1.] It is *leaven;* it is *spreading* as leaven, *insinuates* itself into the whole man, and all that he does; it is *swelling* and *souring* as leaven, for it puffs men up with pride, embitters them with malice, and makes their service unacceptable to God. [2.] It is the leaven of the Pharisees: "It is the sin they are most of them found in. Take heed of imitating them; be not you of their spirit; do not dissemble in Christianity as they do in Judaism; make not *your* religion a *cloak of maliciousness,* as they do theirs."

(2.) A good reason against it: *"For there is nothing covered that shall not be revealed, v.* 2, 3. It is to no purpose to dissemble, for, sooner or later, truth will come out; and a *lying tongue is but for a moment.* If you *speak in darkness* that which is unbecoming you, and is inconsistent with your public professions, *it shall be heard in the light;* some way or other it shall be discovered, *a bird of the air shall carry the voice* (Eccl. 10:20), and your folly and falsehood will be *made manifest."* The iniquity that is concealed with a show of piety will be discovered, perhaps in this world, as Judas's was, and Simon Magus's, at furthest in the great day, when the *secrets of all hearts* shall be made *manifest,* Eccl. 12:14; Rom. 2:16. If men's religion prevail not to conquer and cure the wickedness of their hearts, it shall not always serve for a cloak. The day is coming when hypocrites will be stripped of their fig-leaves.

2. To this he added a charge to them to be faithful to the trust reposed in them, and not to betray it, through cowardice or base fear. Some make *v.* 2, 3, to be a caution to them not to *conceal* those things which they had been *instructed* in, and were *employed* to publish to the world. "Whether men will *hear,* or whether they will *forbear,* tell them the *truth,* the *whole* truth, and *nothing but* the truth; what has been spoken to you, and you have talked of among yourselves, *privately,* and in corners, that do you preach *publicly,* whoever is offended; for, if you *please men,* you are not *Christ's servants,* nor can you please him," Gal. 1:10. But this was not the worst of it: it was likely to be a *suffering* cause, though never a *sinking* one: let them therefore arm themselves with courage; and divers arguments are furnished here to steel them with a holy resolution in their work. Consider,

(1.) "The power of your enemies is a limited power (*v.* 4): *I say unto you, my friends"* (Christ's disciples are his friends, he calls them *friends,* and gives them this *friendly* advice), *"be not afraid,* do not disquiet yourselves with tormenting fears of the power and rage of men." Note, Those whom Christ owns for *his friends* need not be afraid of any enemies. *"Be not afraid,* no, not of them that *kill the body,* let it not be in the power of *scoffers,* not even of *murderers,* to drive you off from your work, for you that have learned to triumph over death may say, even of them, Let them do their worst, *after that there is no more that they can do;* the immortal soul lives, and is happy, and enjoys itself and its God, and sets them all at defiance." Note, Those can do Christ's disciples no real harm, and therefore ought not to be dreaded, who can but *kill the body;* for they only send that to its rest, and the soul to its joy, the sooner.

(2.) God is to be feared more than the most powerful men: *"I will forewarn you whom you shall fear* (*v.* 5): that you may fear man less, fear God more. Moses conquers his fear of the *wrath of the king,* by having an eye to him *that is invisible.* By *owning Christ* you may incur the wrath of men, which can reach no further than to *put you to death* (and without God's permission they cannot do that); but by *denying* Christ, and disowning him, you will incur the wrath of God, which has power to send *you to hell,* and there is no resisting it. Now of two evils the less is to be chosen, and the greater is to be dreaded, and therefore *I say unto you, Fear him."* "It is true," said that blessed martyr, Bishop Hooper, "life is sweet, and death bitter; but eternal life is more sweet, and eternal death more bitter."

(3.) The lives of good Christians and good ministers are the particular care of divine Providence, *v.* 6, 7. To encourage us in times of difficulty and danger, we must have recourse to our first principles, and build upon them. Now a firm belief of the doctrine of God's universal providence, and the extent of it, will be satisfying to us when at any time we are in peril, and will encourage us to trust God in the way of duty. [1.] Providence takes cognizance of the *meanest creatures,* even of *the sparrows.* "Though they are of such small account that *five* of them are sold for *two farthings,* yet not one of them is *forgotten of God,* but is provided for, and notice is taken of its death. Now, *you are of more value than many sparrows,* and therefore you may be sure you *are not forgotten,* though imprisoned, though banished, though forgotten by your friends; much more *precious in the sight of the Lord is the death of saints* than the death of sparrows." [2.] Providence takes cognizance of the *meanest interest* of the disciples of Christ: *"Even the very hairs of your head are all numbered* (*v.* 7); much more are your sighs and tears numbered, and the drops of your blood, which you shed for Christ's name's sake. An account is kept of all your losses, that they *may be,* and without doubt they shall be, recompensed unspeakably to your advantage."

(4.) "You will be owned or disowned by Christ, in the great day, according as you now own or disown him," *v.* 8, 9. [1.] To engage us to *confess Christ before men,* whatever we may lose or suffer for our constancy to him, and how dear soever it may cost us, we are assured that they who *confess Christ* now shall be owned by him in the great day *before the angels of God,* to their everlasting comfort and honour. Jesus Christ will *confess,* not only that he suffered for them, and that they are to have the benefit of *his* sufferings, but that they suffered *for him,* and that his kingdom and interest on earth were advanced by *their* sufferings; and what greater honour can be done them? [2.] To deter us from *denying* Christ, and a cowardly *deserting* of his truths and ways, we are here assured that those who *deny Christ,* and treacherously depart from him, whatever they may save by it, though it were life itself, and whatever they may gain by it, though it were a kingdom, will be vast losers at last, for they shall be *denied before the angels of God;* Christ will not know them, will not own them, will not show them any favour, which will turn to their everlasting terror and contempt. By the stress here laid upon their being *confessed or denied before the angels of God,* it should seem to be a considerable part of the happiness of glorified saints that they will not only stand *right,* but stand *high,* in the esteem of the *holy angels;* they will love them, and honour them, and own them, if they be Christ's servants; they are their fellow-servants, and they will take them for their companions. On the contrary, a considerable part of the misery of damned sinners will be that the holy angels will abandon them, and will be the pleased witnesses, not only of their disgrace, as here, but of their misery, for they shall be *tormented in the presence of the holy angels* (Rev. 14:10), who will give them no relief.

(5.) The errand they were shortly to be sent out upon was of the highest and last importance to the children of men, to whom they were sent, *v.* 10. Let them be bold in preaching the gospel, for a sorer and heavier doom would attend those that rejected them (after the Spirit was poured upon them, which was to be the *last* method of conviction) than those that now rejected Christ himself, and opposed him: *"Greater works than those shall he do,* and, consequently, greater will be the punishment of those that blaspheme the gifts and operations of the Holy Ghost in you. *Whosoever shall speak a word against the Son of man,* shall stumble at the meanness of his appearance, and speak *slightly* and *spitefully* of him, it is capable of some excuse: *Father, forgive them, for they know not what they do.* But unto him that *blasphemes the Holy Ghost,* that blasphemes the Christian doctrine, and maliciously opposes it, after the pouring out of the Spirit and his attestation of Christ's *being glorified* (Acts 2:33; 5:32), the privilege of the *forgiveness of sins* shall be denied; he shall have no benefit by Christ and his gospel. You may shake off the dust of your feet against those that do so, and give them over as incurable; they have forfeited that *repentance* and that *remission* which Christ was *exalted to give,* and which you are *commissioned to preach."* The sin, no doubt, was the more daring, and consequently the case the more desperate, during the continuance of the *extraordinary* gifts and operations of the Spirit in the church, which were intended for a *sign to them who believed not,* 1 Co. 14:22. There were hopes of those who, though not convinced by them at first, yet admired them, but those who *blasphemed* them were given over.

(6.) Whatever trials they should be called out to, they should be sufficiently furnished for them, and honourably brought through them, *v.* 11, 12. The faithful martyr for Christ has not only *sufferings* to *undergo,* but a *testimony* to *bear,* a *good confession* to *witness,* and is concerned to do that *well,* so that the cause of Christ may not suffer, though he suffer for it; and, if this be his care, let him cast it upon God: "When they *bring you into the synagogues,* before church-rulers, before the Jewish courts, or before *magistrates and powers,* Gentile rulers, rulers in the state, to be examined about your doctrine, what it is, and what the proof of it, *take no thought what ye shall answer,"* [1.] "That you may *save yourselves.* Do not study by what art or rhetoric to mollify your judges, or by what tricks in law to bring yourselves off; if it be the will of God that you should come off, and your time is not yet come, he will bring it about effectually." [2.] "That you may *serve your Master;* aim at this, but do not perplex yourselves about what you ought to say, for *the Holy Ghost,* as a Spirit of wisdom, *shall teach you what you ought to say,* and how to say it, so that it may be for the honour of God and his cause."

Verses 13–21

We have in these verses,

I. The application that was made to Christ, very unseasonably, by one of his hearers, desiring him to interpose *between him and his brother* in a matter that concerned the estate of the family (*v.* 13): *"Master, speak to my brother;* speak as a prophet, speak as a king, speak with authority; he is one that will have regard to what thou sayest; speak to him, *that he divide the inheritance with me."* Now, 1. Some think that his brother *did him wrong,* and that he appealed to Christ to *right him,* because he knew the law was costly. His brother was such a one as the Jews called *Ben-hamesen — a son of violence,* that took not only his own part of the estate, but his brother's too, and forcibly detained it from him. Such brethren there are in the world, who have no sense at all either of *natural equity* or *natural affection,* who make a prey of those whom they ought to patronize and protect. They who are so wronged have God to go to, who will *execute* judgment and justice for *those that are oppressed.* 2. Others think that he had a mind to *do his brother wrong,* and would have Christ to *assist him;* that, whereas the law gave the elder brother a double portion of the estate, and the father himself could not dispose of what he had but by that rule (Deut. 21:16, 17), he would have Christ to *alter that law,* and oblige his brother, who perhaps was a follower of Christ at large, to *divide the inheritance* equally *with him,* in gavel-kind, share and share alike, and to allot him as much as his elder brother. I suspect that this was the case, because Christ takes occasion from it to warn against *covetousness, pleonexia desire of having more,* more than God in his providence has allotted us. It was not a lawful desire of getting his own, but a *sinful* desire of getting more than his own.

II. Christ's refusal to interpose in this matter (v. 14): *Man, who made me a judge or divider over you?* In matters of this nature, Christ will not assume either a *legislative* power to alter the settled rule of inheritances, or a *judicial* power to determine controversies concerning them. He could have done the judge's part, and the lawyer's, as well as he did the physician's, and have ended suits at law as happily as he did diseases; but he would not, for it was not in his commission: *Who made me a judge?* Probably he refers to the indignity done to Moses by his brethren in Egypt, with which Stephen upbraided the Jews, Acts 7:27, 35. "If I should offer to do this, you would taunt me as you did Moses, *Who made thee a judge or a divider?*" He corrects the man's mistake, will not admit his appeal (it was *coram non judice — not before the proper judge*), and so *dismisses* his bill. If he had come to him to desire him to assist his pursuit of the heavenly inheritance, Christ would have given him his best help; but as to this matter he has nothing to do: *Who made me a judge?* Note, Jesus Christ was no usurper; he took no honour, no power, to himself, but what was given him, Heb. 5:5. Whatever he did, he could tell by what authority he did it, and who gave him that authority. Now this shows us what is the nature and constitution of Christ's kingdom. It is a spiritual kingdom, and not of this world. 1. It does not interfere with civil powers, nor take the authority of princes out of their hands. Christianity leaves the matter as it found it, as to civil power. 2. It does not intermeddle with civil rights; it obliges all to do justly, according to the settled rules of equity, but dominion is not founded in grace. 3. It does not *encourage* our *expectations* of worldly advantages by our religion. If this man will be a disciple of Christ, and expects that in consideration of this Christ should give him his brother's estate, he is mistaken; the rewards of Christ's disciples are of another nature. 4. It does not *encourage* our *contests* with our brethren, and our being rigorous and high in our demands, but rather, for peace' sake, to recede from our right. 5. It does not allow ministers to *entangle* themselves in the affairs of this *life* (2 Tim. 2:4), to *leave the word of God to serve tables.* There are those whose business it is, let it be left to them, *Tractent fabrilia fabri — Each workman to his proper craft.*

III. The necessary caution which Christ took occasion from this to give to his hearers. Though he came not to be a *divider* of men's estates, he came to be a director of their consciences about them, and would have all take heed of harbouring that corrupt principle which they saw to be in others the *root* of *so much evil.* Here is,

1. The caution itself (v. 15): *Take heed and beware of covetousness; horate — "Observe yourselves,* keep a *jealous eye* upon your own hearts, lest covetous principles steal into them; and *phylassesthe — preserve yourselves,* keep a *strict band* upon your own hearts, lest covetous principles rule and give law in them." Covetousness is a sin which we have need constantly to *watch against,* and therefore frequently to be *warned against.*

2. The reason of it, or an argument to enforce this caution: *For a man's life consisteth not in the abundance of the things which he possesseth;* that is, "our happiness and comfort do not depend upon our having a great deal of the wealth of this world." (1.) The life of the *soul,* undoubtedly, does not depend upon it, and the soul is the man. The things of the world will not suit the nature of a soul, nor supply its needs, nor satisfy its desires, nor last so long as it will last. Nay, (2.) Even the life of the body and the happiness of that do not consist in an *abundance* of these things; for many live very contentedly and easily, and get through the world very comfortably, who have but a little of the wealth of it (a dinner of herbs with holy love is better than a *feast of fat things*); and, on the other hand, many live very miserably who have a great deal of the things of this world; they possess abundance, and yet have no comfort of it; they *bereave their souls of good,* Eccl. 4:8. Many who have abundance are discontented and fretful, as Ahab and Haman; and then what good does their abundance do them?

3. The illustration of this by a parable, the sum of which is to show the folly of carnal worldlings while they live, and their misery when they die, which is intended not only for a check to that man who came to Christ with an address about his estate, while he was in no care about his soul and another world, but for the enforcing of that necessary cau-

tion to us all, to *take heed of covetousness.* The parable gives us the life and death of a *rich man,* and leaves us to judge whether he was a *happy* man.

(1.) Here is an account of his worldly wealth and abundance (v. 16): *The ground of a certain rich man brought forth plentifully, chōra — regio — the country.* He had a whole country to himself, a lordship of his own; he was a little prince. Observe, His wealth lay much in the fruits of the earth, for *the king himself is served by the field,* Eccl. 5:9. He had a great deal of ground, and his ground was *fruitful; much* would have *more,* and he *had more.* Note, The fruitfulness of the earth is a great blessing, but it is a blessing which God often gives plentifully to wicked men, to whom it is a snare, that we may not think to judge of his love or hatred by what is before us.

(2.) Here are the workings of his heart, in the midst of this abundance. We are here told what *he thought within himself, v.* 17. Note, The God of heaven knows and observes whatever we think within ourselves, and we are accountable to him for it. He is both a discerner and judge of the thoughts and intents of the heart. We mistake if we imagine that thoughts are *hid* and thoughts are *free.* Let us here observe,

[1.] What his *cares* and *concerns* were. When he saw an extraordinary crop upon his ground, instead of *thanking God* for it, or rejoicing in the opportunity it would give him of doing the more good, he afflicts himself with this thought, *What shall I do, because I have no room where to bestow my fruits?* He speaks as one *at a loss,* and full of perplexity. *What shall I do now?* The poorest beggar in the country, that did not know where to get a meal's meat, could not have said a more anxious word. Disquieting care is the common fruit of an abundance of this world, and the common fault of those that have abundance. The more men have, the more perplexity they have with it, and the more solicitous they are to keep what they have and to add to it, how to spare and how to spend; so that even the *abundance* of the rich will not suffer them to *sleep,* for thinking what they shall do with what they have and how they shall dispose of it. The rich man seems to speak it with a sigh, *What shall I do?* And if you ask, Why, what is the matter? Truly he had *abundance* of wealth, and wants a place to *put it in,* that is all.

[2.] What his *projects* and *purposes* were, which were the result of his cares, and were indeed absurd and foolish like them (v. 18): "This will I do, and it is the wisest course I can take, *I will pull down my barns,* for they are too little, and I will build greater, and there will I bestow all my fruits and my goods,* and then I shall be at ease." Now here, *First,* It was folly for him to call the fruits of the ground *his* fruits and *his* goods. He seems to lay a pleasing emphasis upon that, *my* fruits and *my* goods; whereas what we have is but *lent* us for our use, the property is still in God; we are but stewards of our *Lord's goods,* tenants at will of our Lord's land. It is *my corn* (saith God) and *my wine,* Hos. 2:8, 9. *Secondly,* It was folly for him to *hoard up* what he had, and then to think it *well bestowed.* There will I bestow it *all;* as if none must be bestowed upon the poor, none upon his family, none upon the Levite and *the stranger,* the *fatherless and the widow,* but all in the great barn. *Thirdly,* It was folly for him to let his *mind* rise with his *condition;* when his ground brought forth more plentifully than usual, then to talk of bigger barns, as if the next year must needs be as fruitful as this, and much more abundant, whereas the barn might be as much too big the next year as it was too little this. Years of famine commonly follow years of plenty, as they did in Egypt; and therefore it were better to *stack* some of his corn for this once. *Fourthly,* It was folly for him to think to ease his care by building new barns, for the building of them would but increase his care; those know this who know any thing of the spirit of building. The way that God prescribes for the cure of inordinate care is certainly successful, but the way of the world does but increase it. Besides, when he had done this, there were other cares that would still attend him; the greater the barns, still the greater the cares, Eccl. 5:10. *Fifthly,* It was folly for him to contrive and resolve all this *absolutely* and *without reserve.* This *I will* do: *I will* pull down my barns and will build greater, yea, that *I will;* without so much as that necessary proviso, *If the Lord will, I shall live,* Jam. 4:13–15. Peremptory projects are foolish projects; for our times are in God's hand, and not in our own, and we do not so much as *know what shall be on the morrow.*

[3.] What his *pleasing hopes* and *expectations* were, when he should have made good these projects. "Then *I will say to my soul,* upon the credit of this security, whether God say

it or no, *Soul,* mark what I say, *thou hast much goods laid up for many years* in these barns; now *take thine ease,* enjoy thyself, *eat, drink, and be merry," v.* 19. Here also appears his folly, as much in the enjoyment of his wealth as in the pursuit of it. *First,* It was folly for him to put off his comfort in his abundance till he had compassed his projects concerning it. When he has built bigger barns, and filled them (which will be a work of time), then he will *take his ease;* and might he not as well have *done that now?* Grotius here quotes the story of Pyrrhus, who was projecting to make himself master of Sicily, Africa, and other places, in the prosecution of his victories. Well, says his friend Cyneas, and what must we do then? *Postea vivemus,* says he, *Then we will live; At hoc jam licet,* says Cyneas, *We may live now if we please. Secondly,* It was folly for him to be confident that his goods were *laid up for many years,* as if his bigger barns would be *safer* than those he had; whereas in an hour's time they might be burnt to the ground and all that was laid up in them, perhaps by lightning, against which there is no defence. A few years may make a great change; *moth and rust may corrupt, or thieves break through and steal. Thirdly,* It was folly for him to count upon certain *ease,* when he had laid up abundance of the wealth of this world, whereas there are many things that may make people uneasy in the midst of their greatest abundance. One dead fly may spoil a whole pot of precious ointment; and one thorn a whole bed of down. Pain and sickness of body, disagreeableness of relations, and especially a guilty conscience, may rob a man of his ease, who has ever so much of the wealth of this world. *Fourthly,* It was folly for him to think of making no other use of his plenty than to *eat* and *drink,* and to *be merry;* to indulge the flesh, and gratify the sensual appetite, without any thought of doing good to others, and being put thereby into a better capacity of serving God and his generation: as if we *lived* to *eat,* and did not *eat* to *live,* and the happiness of man consisted in nothing else but in having all the gratifications of sense wound up to the height of pleasurableness. *Fifthly,* It was the greatest folly of all to say all this to his *soul.* If he had said, *Body, take thine ease,* for *thou hast goods laid up for many years,* there had been sense in it; but the soul, considered as an immortal spirit, separable from the body, was no way interested in a barn full of corn or a bag full of gold. If he had had the *soul of a swine,* he might have *blessed it* with the satisfaction of *eating* and *drinking;* but what is this to the *soul of a man,* that has exigencies and desires which these things will be no ways suited to? It is the great absurdity which the children of this world are guilty of that they portion their souls in the wealth of the world and the pleasures of sense.

(3.) Here is God's sentence upon all this; and we are sure that his judgment is according to truth. He said to himself, said to his soul, *Take thine ease.* If God had said so too, the man had been happy, as his Spirit witnesses with the spirit of believers to make them easy. *But God said* quite otherwise; and by his judgment of us we must stand or fall, not by ours of ourselves, 1 Co. 4:3, 4. His neighbours blessed him (Ps. 10:3), praised him as *doing well for himself* (Ps. 49:18); but God said he did ill for himself: *Thou fool, this night thy soul shall be required of thee, v.* 20. *God said to him,* that is, decreed this concerning him, and let him know it, either by his conscience or by some awakening providence, or rather by both together. This was said when he was *in the fulness of his sufficiency* (Job 20:22), when his eyes were held waking upon his bed with his cares and contrivances about enlarging his barns, not by adding a bay or two more of building to them, which might serve to answer the end, but by pulling them down and building greater, which was requisite to please his fancy. When he was forecasting this, and had brought it to an issue, and then lulled himself asleep again with a pleasing dream of many years' enjoyment of his present improvements, *then* God said this to him. Thus Belshazzar was struck with terror by the hand-writing on the wall, in the midst of his jollity. Now observe what God said,

[1.] The character he gave him: *Thou fool,* thou *Nabal,* alluding to the story of Nabal, that *fool* (Nabal is his name, and folly is with him) whose heart was struck dead *as a stone* while he was regaling himself in the abundance of his provision for his sheep-shearers. Note, Carnal worldlings are fools, and the day is coming when God will call them by their own name, *Thou fool,* and they will call themselves so.

[2.] The sentence he passed upon him, a sentence of death: *This night thy soul shall be required of thee; they shall require thy soul* (so the words are), and then *whose shall those things be which thou hast provided?* He thought he had goods that should be his for many years, but he must part from them *this night;* he thought he should enjoy them himself, but he must leave them to he knows not who. Note, The death of carnal worldlings is miserable in itself and terrible to them.

First, It is a *force,* an *arrest;* it is the *requiring of the soul,* that soul that thou art making such a fool of; what hast thou to do with a soul, who canst use it no better? Thy soul shall be *required;* this intimates that he is loth to part with it. A good man, who has taken his heart off from this world, cheerfully resigns his soul at death, and gives it up; but a worldly man has it *torn* from him with violence; it is a terror to him to think of leaving this world. *They shall require thy soul.* God shall require it; he shall require an account of it. "Man, woman, what hast thou done with thy soul. Give an account of that stewardship." *They shall;* that is, evil angels as the messengers of God's justice. As good angels receive gracious souls to carry them to their joy, so evil angels receive wicked souls to carry them to the place of torment; they shall *require it* as a guilty soul to be punished. The devil requires thy soul as his own, for it did, in effect, give itself to him.

Secondly, It is a *surprize,* an *unexpected* force. It is in *the night,* and terrors in the night are most terrible. The time of death is day-time to a good man; it is his morning. But it is night to a worldling, a dark night; he *lies down in sorrow.* It is *this night,* this *present* night, without delay; there is no giving bail, or begging a day. This *pleasant* night, when thou art promising thyself many years to come, now thou must die, and go to judgment. Thou art entertaining thyself with the fancy of many a merry day, and merry night, and merry feast; but, in the midst of all, here is an end of all, Isa. 21:4.

Thirdly, It is the leaving of all *those things* behind *which they have provided,* which they have laboured for, and prepared for hereafter, with abundance of toil and care. All that which they have placed their happiness in, and built their hope upon, and raised their expectations from, they must leave behind. *Their pomp shall not descend after them* (Ps. 49:17), but they shall go as naked out of the world as they came into it, and they shall have no benefit at all by what they have hoarded up either in death, in judgment, or in their everlasting state.

Fourthly, It is leaving them to they *know not who:* "Then *whose shall those things be?* Not *thine* to be sure, and thou knowest not what *they* will prove for whom thou didst design them, thy children and relations, whether they will be *wise* or *fools* (Eccl. 2:18, 19), whether such as will bless thy memory or curse it, be a credit to thy family or a blemish, do good or hurt with what thou leavest them, keep it or spend it; nay, thou knowest not but those for whom thou dost design it may be prevented from the enjoyment of it, and it may be turned to somebody else thou little thinkest of; nay, though thou knowest to whom thou leavest it, thou knowest not to whom they will leave it, or into whose hand it will come at last." If many a man could have foreseen to whom his house would have come after his death, he would rather have burned it than beautified it.

Fifthly, It is a demonstration of his folly. Carnal worldlings are *fools* while they live: *this their way is their folly* (Ps. 49:13); but their folly is made most evident when they die: *at his end he shall be a fool* (Jer. 17:11); for then it will appear that he took pains to lay up treasure in a world he was hastening from, but took no care to lay it up in the world he was hastening to.

Lastly, Here is the application of this parable (*v.* 21): *So is he,* such a fool, a fool in God's judgment, a fool upon record, that *layeth up treasure for himself, and is not rich towards God.* This is the way and this is the end of such a man. Observe here,

1. The description of a worldly man: He *lays up treasure for himself,* for the body, for the world, for *himself* in opposition to God, for that *self* that is to be *denied.* (1.) It is his error that he counts his *flesh himself,* as if the *body* were the *man.* If *self* be rightly stated and understood, it is only the true Christian that lays up treasure for himself, and is *wise for himself,* Prov. 9:12. (2.) It is his error that he makes it his business to *lay up for the flesh,* which he calls laying up *for himself.* All his labour is *for his mouth* (Eccl. 6:7), *making provision for the flesh.* (3.) It is his error that he counts those things his *treasure* which are thus *laid up* for the world, and the body, and the life that now is; they are the wealth he trusts to, and spends upon, and lets out his affections toward. (4.) The greatest error of all is that he is in no care to be *rich towards God,* rich in the *account of God,* whose accounting us rich makes us so (Rev. 2:9), rich in the *things of God,* rich *in faith* (Jam. 2:5), rich in *good works,* in the *fruits of righteousness* (1 Tim. 6:18), rich in graces, and comforts, and spiritual gifts. Many who have abundance of this world are wholly destitute of that which will enrich their souls, which will make them rich towards God, rich for eternity.

2. The folly and misery of a worldly man: *So is he.* Our Lord Jesus Christ, who knows what the end of things will be, has here told us what his end will be. Note, It is the unspeakable folly of the most of men to mind and pursue the wealth of this world more than the wealth of the other world, that which is merely for the body and for time, more than that which is for the soul and eternity.

Verses 22–40

Our Lord Jesus is here inculcating some needful useful lessons upon his disciples, which he had before taught them, and had occasion afterwards to press upon them; for they need to have *precept upon precept, and line upon line: "Therefore,* because there are so many that are ruined by covetousness, and an inordinate affection to the wealth of this world, *I say unto you,* my disciples, take heed of it." *Thou, O man of God, flee these things,* as well as thou, O man of the world, 1 Tim. 6:11.

I. He charges them not to afflict themselves with disquieting perplexing cares about the necessary supports of life: *Take no thought for your life, v.* 22. In the foregoing parable he had given us warning against that branch of covetousness of which rich people are most in danger; and that is, a *sensual complacency* in the abundance of this world's goods. Now his disciples might think they were in no danger of this, for they had no plenty or variety to glory in; and therefore he here warns them against another branch of covetousness, which they are most in temptation to that have but a little of this world, which was the case of the disciples at best and much more now that they had left all to follow Christ, and that was, an *anxious solicitude* about the necessary supports of life: *"Take no thought for your life,* either for the preservation of it, if it be in danger, or for the provision that is to be made for it, either of food or clothing, *what ye shall eat* or *what ye shall put on."* This is the caution he had largely insisted upon, Mt. 6:25, etc.; and the arguments here used are much the same, designed for our encouragement to cast all our care upon God, which is the *right way* to *ease* ourselves of it. Consider then,

1. God, who has done the greater for us, may be depended upon to do the less. He has, without any care or forecast of our own, given us *life* and a *body,* and therefore we may cheerfully leave it to him to provide *meat* for the support of that life, and *raiment* for the defence of that body.

2. God, who provides for the inferior creatures, may be depended upon to provide for good Christians. "Trust God for *meat,* for he *feeds the ravens* (*v.* 24); they *neither sow nor reap,* they take neither care nor pains beforehand to provide for themselves, and yet they are *fed,* and never perish for want. Now consider *how much better ye are than the fowls,* than the ravens. Trust God for clothing, for he clothes the lilies (*v.* 27, 28); they make no preparation for their own clothing, they *toil not,* they *spin not,* the root in the ground is a naked thing, and without ornament, and yet, as the flower grows up, it appears wonderfully *beautified.* Now, if God has so clothed the flowers, which are fading perishing things, *shall he not much more clothe* you with such clothing as is fit for you, and with clothing suited to your nature, as theirs is?" When God fed Israel with *manna* in the wilderness, he also took care for their clothing; for though he did not furnish them with new clothes, yet (which came all to one) he provided that those they had should not *wax old upon them,* Deu. 8:4. Thus will he clothe his spiritual Israel; but then let them not be *of little faith.* Note, Our inordinate cares are owing to the weakness of our faith; for a powerful practical belief of the all-sufficiency of God, his covenant-relation to us as a Father, and especially his precious promises, relating both to this life and that to come, would be mighty, through God, to the pulling down of the strong holds of these disquieting perplexing imaginations.

3. Our cares are fruitless, vain, and insignificant, and therefore it is folly to indulge them. They will not gain us our wishes, and therefore ought not to hinder our repose (*v.* 25): *"Which of you by taking thought can add to his stature one cubit,* or one inch, can add to *his age* one year or one hour? Now if ye be *not able to do that which is least,* if it be not in your power to alter your statures, why should you perplex yourselves about other things, which are as much out of your power, and about which it is necessary that we refer ourselves to the providence of God?" Note, As in our *stature,* so in our *state,* it is our wisdom to take *it as it is,* and make the best of it; for fretting and vexing, carping and caring, will not mend it.

4. An inordinate anxious pursuit of the things of this world, even necessary things, very ill becomes the disciples of Christ (*v.* 29, 30): "Whatever others do, *seek not ye what ye shall eat, or what ye shall drink;* do not you afflict yourselves with perplexing cares, nor weary yourselves with constant toils; do not hurry hither and thither with enquiries *what you shall eat or drink,* as David's enemies, that *wandered up and down for meat* (Ps. 59:15), or as the eagle that *seeks the prey afar off,* Job 39:29. Let not the disciples of Christ thus *seek* their food, but ask it of God day by day; let them not be *of doubtful mind; mē meteōrizesthe — Be not as meteors in the air,* that are blown hither and thither with every wind; do not, like them, *rise* and *fall,* but maintain a consistency with yourselves; be even and steady, and have your hearts fixed; *live not in careful suspense;* let not your minds be continually perplexed between hope and fear, ever upon the rack." Let not the children of God make themselves uneasy; for,

(1.) This is to make themselves like the children of this world: *"All these things do the nations of the world seek after, v.* 30. They that take care for the body only, and not for the soul, for this world only, and not for the other, look no further than what they shall *eat* and *drink;* and, having no all-sufficient God to seek to and confide in, they burden themselves with anxious cares about those things. But it ill becomes you to do so. You, who are called out of the world, ought not to be thus conformed to the world, and to *walk in the way of this people,"* Isa. 8:11, 12. When inordinate cares prevail over us, we should think, "What am I, a Christian or a heathen? Baptized or not baptized? If a Christian, if baptized, shall I rank myself with Gentiles, and join with them in their pursuits?"

(2.) It is needless for them to disquiet themselves with care about the necessary supports of life; for they have a Father in heaven who does and will take care for them: *"Your Father knows that you have need of these things,* and considers it, and will supply your needs *according to his riches in glory;* for he is *your Father,* who *made* you subject to these necessities, and therefore will suit his compassions to them: *your Father,* who *maintains* you, educates you, and designs an inheritance for you, and therefore will take care that you *want no good thing."*

(3.) They have better things to mind and pursue (*v.* 31): *"But rather seek ye the kingdom of God,* and mind this, you, my disciples, who are to *preach the kingdom of God;* let your hearts be upon your work, and your great care how to do that well, and this will effectually divert your thoughts from inordinate care about things of the world. And let all that have souls to save *seek the kingdom of God,* in which only they can be *safe.* Seek admission into it, seek advancement in it; seek the *kingdom of grace,* to be subjects in that; the *kingdom of glory,* to be princes in that; and then *all these things shall be added to you.* Mind the affairs of your souls with diligence and care, and then trust God with all your other affairs."

(4.) They have better things to expect and hope for: *Fear not, little flock, v.* 32. For the banishing of inordinate cares, it is necessary that fears should be suppressed. When we frighten ourselves with an apprehension of evil to come, we put ourselves upon the stretch of care how to avoid it, when after all perhaps it is but the creature of our own imagination. Therefore *fear not, little flock,* but *hope to the end;* for *it is your Father's good pleasure to give you the kingdom.* This comfortable word we had not in Matthew. Note, [1.] Christ's flock in this world is a *little flock;* his sheep are but few and feeble. The church is a vineyard, a garden, a small spot, compared with the wilderness of this world; as Israel (1 Ki. 20:27), who were like two little flocks of kids, when *the Syrians filled the country.* [2.] Though it be a little flock, quite *overnumbered,* and therefore in danger of being *overpowered,* by its enemies, yet it is the will of Christ that they should not *be afraid: "Fear not, little flock,* but see yourselves safe under the protection and conduct of the great and good Shepherd, and lie easy." [3.] God has *a kingdom* in store for all that belong to Christ's *little flock,* a crown of glory (1 Pt. 5:4), a throne of power (Rev. 3:21), unsearchable riches, far exceeding the peculiar treasures of *kings and provinces.* The *sheep on the right hand* are called to *come* and *inherit the kingdom;* it is theirs for ever; a kingdom for each. [4.] The kingdom is given according to the *good pleasure* of the Father; *It is your Father's good pleasure;* it is given not of debt, but of grace, free grace, sovereign grace; *even so, Father, because it seemed good unto thee.* The kingdom is his; and may he not do what he will with his own? [5.] The believing hopes and prospects of *the kingdom* should silence and suppress the fears of Christ's little flock in this world. "Fear no trouble; for, though it should come, it shall not come between you and the kingdom, that is sure, it is near." (That is not an evil worth trembling at the thought of which cannot separate us from the love of God). *"Fear not the want of any* thing that is good for you; for, if it be *your Father's good pleasure to give you the kingdom,* you need not question but he will *bear your charges* thither."

II. He charged them to make sure work for their souls, by laying up their treasure in heaven, *v.* 33, 34. Those who have done this may be very easy as to all the events of time.

1. *"Sit loose to this world,* and to all your possessions in it: *Sell that ye have,* and *give alms,"* that is, "rather than want wherewith to relieve those that are truly *necessitous,* sell what you have that is *superfluous,* all that you can spare from the support of yourselves and families, and give it *to the poor. Sell what you have,* if you find it a hindrance from, or incumbrance in, the service of Christ. Do not think yourselves undone, if by being fined, imprisoned, or banished, for the testimony of Jesus, you be forced to sell your estates, thought they be *the inheritance of your fathers.* Do not sell to *hoard up* the money, or because you can make more of it by usury, but *sell and give alms;* what is given in alms, in a right manner, is put out to the *best* interest, upon the *best* security."

2. *"Set your hearts upon the other world,* and your expectations from that world. *Provide yourselves bags that wax not old,* that wax not empty, not of gold, but of grace in the heart and good works in the life; these are the bags that will last." Grace will *go with us* into another world, for it is *woven in* the soul; and our good works will *follow us,* for *God is not unrighteous to forget* them. These will be *treasures in heaven,* that will enrich us to eternity. (1.) It is treasure that will not be *exhausted;* we may spend upon it to eternity, and it will not be at all the less; there is no danger of seeing the bottom of it. (2.) It is treasure that we are in no danger of being robbed of, for *no thief approaches* near it; what is laid up in heaven is out of reach of enemies. (3.) It is treasure that will not *spoil* with *keeping,* any more than it will *waste* with *spending;* the *moth* does not *corrupt* it, as it does our garments which we now wear. Now by *this* it appears that we have laid up our treasure in heaven if our *hearts* be *there* while we are *here* (*v.* 34), if we think much of heaven and keep our eye upon it, if we quicken ourselves with the hopes of it and keep ourselves in awe with the fear of falling short of it. But, if your hearts be set upon the earth and the things of it, it is to be feared that you have your treasure and portion in it, and are undone when you leave it.

III. He charges them to get ready, and to keep in a readiness for Christ's coming, when all those who have laid up their treasure in heaven shall enter upon the enjoyment of it, *v.* 35, etc.

1. Christ is our *Master,* and we are his *servants,* not only *working* servants, but *waiting* servants, servants that are to do him honour, in *waiting* on him, and attending his motions: *If any man serve me, let him follow me. Follow the Lamb whithersoever he goes.* But that is not all: they must do him honour in *waiting for him,* and expecting his return. We must be as men that *wait for their Lord,* that sit up late while he stays out late, to be ready to receive him.

2. Christ our Master, though now *gone from us,* will *return again,* return *from the wedding,* from *solemnizing* the nuptials abroad, to *complete* them at home. Christ's servants are now in a state of expectation, *looking for their Master's glorious appearing,* and doing every thing with an eye to *that,* and in order to *that.* He *will come* to take cognizance of his servants, and, that being a *critical day,* they shall either stay with him or be turned out of doors, according as they are found in that day.

3. The time of our Master's return is uncertain; it will be *in the night,* it will be *far* in the night, when he has long *deferred* his coming, and when many have done looking for him; in the *second watch,* just before midnight, or in the *third watch,* next after midnight, *v.* 38. His coming to us, at our death, is uncertain, and to many it will be a great surprise; for *the Son of Man cometh at an hour that ye think not* (*v.* 40), without giving notice beforehand. This bespeaks not only the uncertainty of the time of his coming, but the prevailing security of the greatest part of men, who are *unthinking,* and altogether regardless of the notices given them, so that, whenever he comes, it is *in an hour that they think not.*

4. That which he expects and requires from his servants is that they be *ready to open to him immediately,* whenever he comes (*v.* 36), that is, that they be in a frame fit to receive him, or rather to be received by him; that they be found *as* his servants, in the posture that becomes them, with their *loins girded about,* alluding to the servants that are ready to go whither their master sends them, and do what their master bids them, having their long garments tucked up (which otherwise would hang about them, and hinder them), and *their lights burning,* with which to light their master into the house, and up to his chamber.

5. Those servants will be happy who shall be found ready, and in a good frame, when their Lord shall come (*v.* 37): *Blessed are those servants* who, after having waited long, continue in a waiting frame, until the hour that their Lord comes, and are then found awake and aware of his first approach, of his first knock; and again (*v.* 38): *Blessed are those servants,* for then will be the time of their preferment. Here is such an instance of honour done them as is scarcely to be found among men: He *will make them sit down to meat, and will serve them.* For the bridegroom to wait upon his bride at table is not uncommon, but to wait upon his servants is not *the manner of men;* yet Jesus Christ was among his disciples as *one that served,* and did once, to show his condescension, *gird himself,* and *serve them,* when he *washed their feet* (Jn. 13:4, 5); it signified the joy with which they shall be received into the other world by the Lord Jesus, who is gone before, to prepare for them, and has told them that his *Father* will *honour* them, Jn. 12:26.

6. We are *therefore* kept at uncertainty concerning the precise time of his coming that we may be always ready; for it is no thanks to a man to be ready for an attack, if he know beforehand just the time when it will be made: *The good man of the house, if he had known what hour the thief would have come,* though he were ever so careless a man, *would* yet *have watched,* and have frightened away the thieves, *v.* 39. But we do not know at what hour the alarm will be given us, and therefore are concerned to watch at all tines, and never to be off our guard. Or this may intimate the miserable case of those who are careless and unbelieving in this great matter. If the *good man of the house* had had notice of his danger of being robbed such a night, he would have sat up, and saved his house; but we have notice of the day of the Lord's coming, *as a thief in the night,* to the confusion and ruin of all secure sinners, and yet do not thus *watch.* If men will take such care of their houses, O let us be thus wise for our souls: *Be ye therefore ready also,* as ready as the good man of the house would be *if he knew what hour the thief would come.*

Verses 41–53

Here is, I. Peter's question, which he put to Christ upon occasion of the foregoing parable (*v.* 41): *"Lord, speakest thou this parable to us* that are thy constant followers, to us that are ministers, *or also to all* that come to be taught by thee, to all the hearers, and in them to all Christians?" Peter was now, as often, spokesman for the disciples. We have reason to bless God that there are some such forward men, that have a gift of utterance; let those that are such take heed of being proud. Now Peter desires Christ to explain himself, and to direct the arrow of the foregoing parable to the mark he intended. He calls it a *parable,* because it was not only figurative, but weighty, solid, and instructive. Lord, said Peter, was it intended for *us,* or for *all?* To this Christ gives a direct answer (Mk. 13:37): *What I say unto you, I say unto all.* Yet here he seems to show that the apostles were primarily concerned in it. Note, We are all concerned to take to ourselves what Christ in his word designs for us, and to enquire accordingly concerning it: *Speakest thou this to us?* To me? Speak, Lord, for thy servant hears. Doth this word belong to me? Speak it to *my heart.*

II. Christ's reply to this question, directed to Peter and the rest of the disciples. If what Christ had said before did not so peculiarly concern them, but in common with other Christians, who must all watch and pray for Christ's coming, *as his servants,* yet this that follows is peculiarly adapted to ministers, who are the *stewards* in Christ's house. Now our Lord Jesus here tells them,

1. What was their *duty as stewards,* and what the *trust* committed to them. (1.) They are made *rulers of God's household,* under Christ, whose own the house is; ministers derive an authority from Christ to preach the gospel, and to administer the ordinances of Christ, and apply the seals of the covenant of grace. (2.) Their business is to give God's children and servants *their portion of meat,* that which is proper for them and allotted to them; convictions and comfort to those to whom they respectively belong. *Suum cuique —to every one his own.* This is *rightly to divide the word of truth,* 2 Tim. 2:15. (3.) To give it to them *in due season,* at that time and in that way which are most suitable to the temper and condition of those that are to be fed; a word *in season* to him *that is weary.* (4.) Herein they must approve themselves *faithful* and *wise; faithful* to their Master, by whom this great trust is reposed in them, and faithful to their fellow-servants, for whose benefit they are put in trust; and *wise* to improve an opportunity of doing honour to their Master, and service in the family. Ministers must be both *skilful* and *faithful.*

2. What would be their happiness if they approved themselves faithful and wise (*v.* 43): *Blessed is that servant,* (1.) That is *doing,* and is not idle, nor indulgent of his ease; even the rulers of the household must be *doing,* and make themselves *servants of all.* (2.) That is *so* doing, doing as he should be, giving them their *portion of meat,* by public preaching and personal application. (3.) That is *found* so doing when his Lord comes; that perseveres to the end, notwithstanding the difficulties he may meet with in the way. Now his happiness is illustrated by the preferment of a steward that has approved himself within a lower and narrower degree of service; he shall be preferred to a larger and higher (*v.* 44): *He will make him ruler over all that he has,* which was Joseph's preferment in Pharaoh's court. Note, Ministers that obtain mercy of the Lord to be faithful shall obtain further mercy to be abundantly rewarded for their faithfulness in the day of the Lord.

3. What a dreadful reckoning there would be if they were treacherous and unfaithful, *v.* 45, 46. If that servant begin to be quarrelsome and profane, he shall be called to an account, and severely punished. We had all this before in Matthew, and therefore shall here only observe, (1.) Our looking upon Christ's second coming as a thing at a distance is the cause of all those irregularities which render the thought of it terrible to us: *He saith in his heart, My Lord delays his coming.* Christ's patience is very often misinterpreted his *delay,* to the *dis*couragement of his people, and the *en*couragement of his enemies. (2.) The persecutors of God's people are commonly abandoned to security and sensuality; *they beat their fellow-servants,* and then *eat and drink with the drunken,* altogether unconcerned either at their own sin or their brethren's sufferings, as the king and Haman, who *sat down to drink when the city Shushan was perplexed.* Thus they drink, to drown the clamours of their own consciences, and baffle them, which would otherwise fly in their faces. (3.) Death and judgment will be very terrible to all wicked people, but especially to wicked ministers. It will be a surprise to them: *At an hour when they are not aware.* It will be the determining of them to endless misery; they shall be cut in sunder, and have their portion assigned them with *the unbelievers.*

4. What an aggravation it would be of their sin and punishment that they knew their duty, and did not do it (*v.* 47, 48): *That servant that knew his lord's will, and did it not, shall be beaten with many stripes,* shall fall under a sorer punishment; and *he that knew not shall be beaten with few stripes,* his punishment shall, in consideration of this, be mitigated. Here seems to be an allusion to the law, which made a distinction between sins committed through ignorance, and presumptuous sins (Lev. 5:15, etc.; Num. 15:29, 30), as also to another law concerning the number of stripes given to a malefactor, to be according to the nature of the crime, Deu. 25:2, 3. Now, (1.) Ignorance of our duty is an extenuation of sin. He *that knew not his lord's will,* through carelessness and neglect, and his not having such opportunities as some others had of coming to the knowledge of it, and *did things worthy of stripes,* he shall *be beaten,* because he might have known his duty better, but *with few stripes;* his ignorance excuses in part, but not wholly. Thus *through ignorance* the Jews put Christ to death (Acts 3:17; 1 Co. 2:8), and Christ

pleaded that ignorance in their excuse: *They know not what they do.* (2.) The knowledge of our duty is an aggravation of our sin: *That servant that knew his lord's will, and yet did his own will, shall be beaten with many stripes.* God will justly inflict more upon him for abusing the means of knowledge he afforded him, which others would have made a better use of, because it argues a great degree of wilfulness and contempt to sin against knowledge; of how much sorer punishment then shall they be thought worthy, besides the many stripes that their own consciences will give them! Son, remember. Here is a good reason for this added: *To whomsoever much is given, of him shall be much required,* especially when it is *committed* as a trust he is to account for. Those have greater capacities of mind than others, more knowledge and learning, more acquaintance and converse with the scriptures, to them *much is given,* and their account will be accordingly.

III. A further discourse concerning his own sufferings, which he expected, and concerning the sufferings of his followers, which he would have them also to live in expectation of. In general (*v.* 49): *I am come to send fire on the earth.* By this some understand the preaching of the gospel, and the pouring out of the Spirit, holy fire; this Christ came to send with a commission to refine the world, to purge away its dross, to burn up its chaff, and it was *already kindled.* The gospel was begun to be preached; some prefaces there were to the pouring out of the Spirit. Christ baptized with the Holy Ghost and with fire; this Spirit descended in fiery tongues. But, by what follows, it seems rather to be understood of the fire of *persecution.* Christ is not the Author of it, as it is the sin of the incendiaries, the *persecutors;* but he *permits* it, nay, he *commissions* it, as a *refining* fire for the *trial* of the *persecuted.* This fire was *already kindled* in the enmity of the carnal Jews to Christ and his followers. *"What will I that it may presently be kindled? What thou doest, do quickly. If it be already kindled, what will I?* Shall I wait the *quenching* of it? No, for it must fasten upon myself, and upon all, and glory will redound to God from it."

1. He must himself suffer many things; he must pass through this fire that was already kindled (*v.* 50): *I have a baptism to be baptized with.* Afflictions are compared both to *fire* and *water,* Ps. 66:12; 69:1, 2. Christ's sufferings were both. He calls them a *baptism* (Mt. 20:22); for he was watered or sprinkled with them, as Israel was baptized *in the cloud,* and dipped into them, as Israel was baptized *in the sea,* 1 Co. 10:2. He must be sprinkled with his own blood, and with the blood of his enemies, Isa. 63:3. See here, (1.) Christ's *foresight* of his sufferings; he knew what he was to undergo, and the necessity of undergoing it: *I am to be baptized with a baptism.* He calls his sufferings by a name that *mitigates* them; it is a baptism, not a deluge; I must be *dipped* in them, not *drowned* in them; and by a name that *sanctifies* them, for baptism is a name that *sanctifies* them, for baptism is a sacred rite. Christ in his sufferings *devoted* himself to his Father's honour, and *consecrated* himself a priest for evermore, Heb. 7:27, 28. (2.) Christ's *forwardness* to his sufferings: *How am I straitened till it be accomplished!* He longed for the time when he should suffer and die, having an eye to the glorious issue of his sufferings. It is an allusion to a woman in travail, that is *pained to be delivered,* and welcomes her pains, because they hasten the birth of the child, and wishes them sharp and strong, that the *work* may be *cut short.* Christ's sufferings were the *travail of his soul,* which he cheerfully underwent, in hope that he should by them *see his seed,* Isa. 53:10, 11. So much was his heart set upon the redemption and salvation of man.

2. He tells those about him that they also must bear with hardships and difficulties (*v.* 51): *"Suppose ye that I came to give peace on earth,* to give you a peaceable possession of the earth, and outward prosperity on the earth?"* It is intimated that they were ready to entertain such a thought as this, nay, that they went upon this supposition, that the gospel would meet with a *universal* welcome, that people *unanimously* embrace it, and would therefore study to make the preachers of it *easy* and *great,* that Christ, if he did not give them *pomp* and *power,* would at least give them *peace;* and herein they were encouraged by divers passages of the Old Testament, which speak of the peace of the Messiah's kingdom, which they were willing to understand of external peace. "But," saith Christ, "you will be mistaken, the event will declare the contrary, and therefore do not flatter yourselves into a fool's paradise. You will find,"

(1.) "That the effect of the preaching of the gospel will be *division.*" Not but that the design of the gospel and its proper tendency are to unite the children of men to one another, to knit them together in holy love, and, if all would receive it, this would be the effect of it; but there being multitudes that not only will not receive it, but oppose it, and have their corruptions exasperated by it, and are enraged at those that do receive it, it proves, though not the *cause* yet the *occasion* of *division.* While the *strong man armed kept his palace,* in the Gentile world, *his goods were at peace;* all was quiet, for all went one way, the sects of philosophers agreed well enough, so did the worshippers of different deities; but when the gospel was preached, and many were enlightened by it, and turned from the power of Satan to God, then there was a disturbance, *a noise and a shaking,* Eze. 37:7. Some *distinguished* themselves by embracing the gospel, and others were angry that they did so. Yea, and among them that received the gospel there would be different sentiments in minor things, which would occasion *division;* and Christ permits it for holy ends (1 Co. 11:18), that Christians may learn and practise mutual forbearance, Rom. 14:1, 2.

(2.) "That this *division* will reach into private families, and the preaching of the gospel will give occasion for discord among the nearest relations" (*v.* 53): *The father shall be divided against the son, and the son against the father,* when the one turns Christian and the other does not; for the one that does turn Christian will be zealous by arguments and endearments to turn the other too, 1 Co. 7:16. As soon as ever Paul was converted, he *disputed,* Acts 9:29. The one that continues in unbelief will be provoked, and will hate and persecute the one that by his faith and obedience witnesses against, and condemns, his unbelief and disobedience. A spirit of bigotry and persecution will break through the strongest bonds of relation and natural affection; see Mt. 10:35; 24:7. Even *mothers* and *daughters* fall out about religion; and those that believe not are so violent and outrageous that they are ready to deliver up into the hands of the bloody persecutors those that believe, though otherwise very near and dear to them. We find in the *Acts* that, wherever the gospel came, *persecution* was *stirred up;* it was *every where spoken against,* and there was *no small stir about that way.* Therefore let not the disciples of Christ promise themselves *peace upon earth,* for they are sent forth *as sheep in the midst of wolves.*

Verses 54–59

Having given his disciples *their* lesson in the foregoing verses, here Christ turns to *the people,* and gives them *theirs,* *v.* 54. He *said also to the people:* he preached *ad populum — to the people,* as well as *ad clerum — to the clergy.* In general, he would have them be as wise in the affairs of their souls as they are in their outward affairs. Two things he specifies: —

I. Let them learn to *discern the way of God towards them,* that they may *prepare* accordingly. They were *weather-wise,* and by observing the winds and clouds could foresee when there would be *rain* and when there would be *hot weather* (*v.* 54, 55); and, according as they foresaw the weather would be, they either housed their hay and corn, or threw it abroad, and equipped themselves for a journey? Even in regard to changes of the weather God gives warning to us what is coming, and art has improved the notices of nature in weather-glasses. The prognostications here referred to had their origin in repeated observations upon the chain of causes: from what *has been* we conjecture what *will be.* See the benefit of experience; by *taking notice* we may come to *give notice.* Whose is wise will *observe* and *learn.* See now.

1. The particulars of the presages: *"When you see a cloud arising out of the west"* (the Hebrew would say, *out of the sea),* "perhaps it is at first *no bigger than a man's hand* (1 Ki. 18:44), but you say, There is a shower in the womb of it, and it proves so. When you *observe* the *south wind blow,* you say, *There will be heat"* (for the hot countries of Africa lay not far south from Judea), "and it usually *comes to pass;"* yet nature has not ties itself to such a track but that *sometimes* we are mistaken in our prognostics.

2. The inferences from them (*v.* 56): *"Ye hypocrites,* who pretend to be wise, but really are not so, who pretend to expect the Messiah and his kingdom" (for so the generality of the Jews did) "and yet are no way disposed to receive and entertain it, *how is it that you do not discern this time,* that you do not discern that now is the time, according to the indications given in the Old-Testament prophecies, for the Mes-

siah to appear, and that, according to the marks given of him, I am he? Why are you not aware that you have now an opportunity which you *will not have long,* and which you *may never have again,* of securing to yourselves an interest in the kingdom of God and the privileges of that kingdom?" *Now is the accepted time,* now or never. It is the folly and misery of man that he *knows not his time,* Eccl. 9:12. This was the ruin of the men of that generation, that they *knew not the day of their visitation, ch.* 19:44. But a *wise man's heart discerns time and judgment;* such was the wisdom of the men of Issachar, who *had understanding of the times,* 1 Chr. 12:32. He adds, *"Yea, and why even of yourselves,* though ye had not these loud alarms given you, *judge ye not what is right? v.* 57. You are not only stupid and regardless in matters that are purely of divine revelation, and take not the hints which that gives you, but you are so even in the dictates of the very light and law of nature." Christianity has reason and natural conscience on its side; and, if men would allow themselves the liberty of *judging what is right,* they would soon find that all Christ's precepts concerning all things are right, and that there is nothing more equitable in itself, nor better becoming us, than to submit to them and be ruled by them.

II. Let them hasten to *make their peace with God* in time, before it be too late, *v.* 58, 59. This we had upon another occasion, Mt. 5:25, 26. 1. We reckon it our wisdom in our temporal affairs to *compound* with those with whom we cannot *contend,* to *agree with our adversary* upon the best terms we can, before the equity be *foreclosed,* and we be left to the rigour of the law: *"When thou goest with thine adversary to the magistrate,* to whom the appeal is made, and knowest that he has an advantage against thee, and thou art in danger of being cast, thou knowest it is the most prudent course to make the matter up between yourselves; *as thou art in the way, give diligence to be delivered from him,* to get a discharge, lest judgment be given, and execution awarded according to law." Wise men will not let their quarrels go to an extremity, but accommodate them in time. 2. Let us do thus in the affairs of our souls. We have by sin made God our *adversary,* have provoked his displeasure against us, and he has both *right* and *might* on his side; so that it is to no purpose to think of carrying on the controversy with him either at *bar* or in *battle.* Christ, to whom all judgment is committed, is the magistrate before whom we are hastening to appear: if we stand a trial before him, and insist upon our own justification, the cause will certainly go against us, the *Judge* will *deliver* us to the *officer,* the ministers of his justice, and we shall be *cast into* the *prison* of hell, and the debt will be exacted to the utmost; though we cannot make a full satisfaction for it, it will be continually demanded, *till the last mite be paid,* which will not be to all eternity. Christ's sufferings were short, yet the *value* of them made them fully satisfactory. In the sufferings of damned sinners what is wanting in value must be made up in an endless duration. Now, in consideration of this, let us give diligence to be delivered *out of* the hands of God as an adversary, into his hands as a Father, and this *as we are in the way,* which has the chief stress laid upon it here. While we are alive, we are *in the way;* and *now* is our *time,* by repentance and faith through Christ (who is the Mediator as well as the magistrate), to get the quarrel made up, while it may be done, before it be too late. Thus was God in Christ *reconciling the world to himself, beseeching us to be reconciled.* Let us take hold on the arm of the Lord stretched out in this gracious offer, that we may make peace, and we *shall make peace* (Isa. 27:4, 5), for we cannot *walk together* till we be *agreed.*

CHAPTER 13

In this chapter we have, I. The good improvement Christ made of a piece of news that was brought him concerning some Galileans, that were lately massacred by Pilate, as they were sacrificing in the temple at Jerusalem (*v.* 1–5). II. The parable of the fruitless fig-tree, by which we are warned to bring forth fruits meet for that repentance to which he had in the foregoing passage called us (*v.* 6–9). III. Christ's healing a poor infirm woman on the sabbath day, and justifying himself in it (*v.* 11–17). IV. A repetition of the parables of the grain of mustard-seed and the leaven (*v.* 18–22). V. His answer to the question concerning the number of the saved (*v.* 23–30). VI. The slight he put upon Herod's malice and menaces, and the doom of Jerusalem read (*v.* 31–35).

Verses 1–5

We have here, I. Tidings brought to Christ of the death of some Galileans lately, whose blood *Pilate had mingled with their sacrifices, v.* 1. Let us consider,

1. What this tragical story was. It is briefly related here,

and is not met with in any of the historians of those times. Josephus indeed mentions Pilate's killing some Samaritans, who, under the conduct of a factious leader, were going in a tumultuous manner to mount Gerizim, where the Samaritans' temple was; but we can by no means allow that story to be the same with this. Some think that these Galileans were of the faction of Judas Gaulonita, called also *Judas of Galilee* (Acts 5:37), who disowned Caesar's authority and refused to pay tribute to him: or perhaps these, being Galileans, were only suspected by Pilate to be of that faction, and barbarously murdered, because those who were in league with that pretender were out of his reach. The Galileans being Herod's subjects, it is probable that this outrage committed upon them by Pilate occasioned the quarrel that was between Herod and Pilate, which we read of in *ch.* 23:12. We are not told what number they were, perhaps *but a few,* whom Pilate had some particular *pique* against (and therefore the story is overlooked by Josephus); but the circumstance remarked is that he *mingled their blood with their sacrifices* in the court of the temple. Though perhaps they had reason to fear Pilate's malice, yet they would not, under pretence of that fear, keep away from Jerusalem, whither the law obliged them to go up with their sacrifices. Dr Lightfoot thinks it probable that they were *themselves* killing their sacrifices (which was allowed, for the priest's work, they said, began with the *sprinkling of the blood*), and that Pilate's officers came upon them by surprise, just at the time when they were off their guard (for otherwise the Galileans were mettled men, and generally went well-armed), and mingled the blood of the sacrificers with the blood of the sacrifices, as if it had been equally acceptable to God. Neither the holiness of the place nor of the work would be a protection to them from the fury of an unjust judge, *who neither feared God nor regarded man.* The altar, which used to be a sanctuary and place of shelter, is now become a snare and a trap, a place of danger and slaughter.

2. Why it was related *at this season* to our Lord Jesus. (1.) Perhaps merely as a matter of news, which they supposed he had not heard before, and as a thing which they lamented, and believed he would do so too; for the Galileans were their countrymen. Note, Sad providences ought to be observed by us, and the knowledge of them communicated to others, that they and we may be suitably affected with them, and make a good use of them. (2.) Perhaps it was intended as a confirmation of what Christ had said in the close of the foregoing chapter, concerning the necessity of making our peace with God in time, before we be *delivered to the officer,* that is, to *death,* and so *cast into prison,* and then it will be too late to make agreements: "Now," say they, "Master, here is a fresh instance of some that were very suddenly *delivered to the officer,* that were taken away by death when they little expected it; and therefore we have all need to be ready." Note, It will be of good use to us both to explain the word of God and to enforce it upon ourselves by observing the providences of God. (3.) Perhaps they would stir him up, being himself of Galilee, and a prophet, and one that had a great interest in that country, to find out a way to revenge the death of these Galileans upon Herod. If they had any thoughts of this kind, they were quite mistaken; for Christ was now going up to Jerusalem, to be *delivered into the hands of Pilate,* and to have his blood, not mingled with his sacrifice, but itself made a sacrifice. (4.) Perhaps this was told Christ to *deter* him from going up to Jerusalem, to worship (*v.* 22), lest Pilate should serve him as he had served those Galileans, and should suggest against him, as probably he had insinuated against those Galileans, in vindication of his cruelty, that they came to sacrifice as Absalom did, with a *seditious* design, under colour of sacrificing, to raise rebellion. Now, lest Pilate, when his hand was in, should proceed further, they think it advisable that Christ should for the present keep out of the way. (5.) Christ's answer intimates that they told him this with a spiteful *innuendo,* that, though Pilate was unjust in killing them, yet without doubt they were secretly bad men, else God would not have permitted Pilate thus barbarously to cut them off. It was very invidious; rather than they would allow them to be martyrs, though they died sacrificing, and perhaps suffered for their devotion, they would, without any colour of proof, suppose them to be malefactors; and it may be for no other reason than because they were not of their party and denomination, differed from them, or had difference with them. This fate of theirs, which was capable not only of a favourable, but an honourable construction, shall be called a *just judgment* of God *upon them,* though they know not for what.

II. Christ's reply to this report, in which,

1. He seconded it with another story, which, like it, gave an instance of people's being taken away by sudden death. It is not long since *the tower of Siloam fell,* and there were eighteen persons killed and buried in the ruins of it. Dr Lightfoot's conjecture is that this tower adjoined to the *pool of Siloam,* which was the same with the pool of Bethesda, and that it belonged to those *porches* which were by the *pool,* in which the *impotent folks* lay, that *waited for the stirring* of the water (Jn. 5:3), and that they who were killed were some of them, or some of those who in this pool used to purify themselves for the temple-service, for it was near the temple. Whoever they were, it was a sad story; yet such melancholy accidents we often hear of: for *as the birds are caught in a snare, so are the sons of men snared in an evil time, when it falls suddenly upon them,* Eccl. 9:12. Towers, that were built for safety, often prove men's destruction.

2. He cautioned his hearers not to make an ill use of these and similar events, nor take occasion thence to censure *great sufferers,* as if they were *therefore* to be accounted *great sinners: Suppose ye that these Galileans,* who were slain as they were sacrificing, *were sinners above all the Galileans, because they suffered such things? I tell you nay, v.* 2, 3. Perhaps they that told him the story of the Galileans were Jews, and were glad of any thing that furnished them with matter of reflection upon the Galileans, and therefore Christ retorted upon them the story of the *men of Jerusalem,* that came to an untimely end; for, *with what measure* of that kind *we mete,* it *shall be measured to us again.* "Now suppose ye that *those eighteen* who met with their death from the tower of Siloam, while perhaps they were expecting their cure from the pool of Siloam, were *debtors* to divine justice *above all men that dwelt at Jerusalem? I tell you nay."* Whether it make for us or against us, we must abide by this rule, that we cannot judge of men's *sins* by their *sufferings* in this world; for many are thrown into the furnace as gold to be purified, not as dross and chaff to be consumed. We must therefore not be harsh in our censures of those that are afflicted more than their neighbours, as Job's friends were in their censures of him, lest we condemn *the generation of the righteous,* Ps. 72:14. If we will be judging, we have enough to do to judge ourselves; nor indeed can we *know love or hatred by all that is before us,* because *all things come alike to all,* Eccl. 9:1, 2. And we might as justly conclude that the *oppressors,* and Pilate among the rest, *on whose side are power* and success, are the greatest saints, as that the *oppressed,* and those Galileans among the rest, who are all in tears and have no comforter, no, not the priests and Levites that attended the altar, are the *greatest sinners.* Let us, in our censures of others, do as we would be done by; for as we do we shall be done by: *Judge not, that ye be not judged,* Mt. 7:1.

3. On these stories he founded a call to repentance, adding to each of them this awakening word, *Except ye repent, ye shall all likewise perish, v.* 3–5. (1.) This intimates that we all deserve to *perish* as much as *they did,* and had we been dealt with according to our sins, according to the *iniquity of our holy things,* our blood had been long ere this mingled with our sacrifices by the justice of God. It must moderate our censure, not only that we are *sinners,* but that we are as great sinners as they, have as much sin to repent of as they had to suffer for. (2.) That therefore we are all concerned to *repent,* to be sorry for what we have done amiss, and to do so no more. The judgments of God upon others are loud calls to us to *repent.* See how Christ improved every thing for the pressing of that great duty which he came not only to *gain room* for, and *give hopes* to, but to enjoin upon us — and that is, to *repent.* (3.) That repentance is the way to escape perishing, and it is a sure way: *so iniquity shall not be your ruin,* but upon no other terms. (4.) That, if we repent not, we shall certainly perish, as others have done before us. Some lay an emphasis upon the word *likewise,* and apply it to the destruction that was coming upon the people of the Jews, and particularly upon Jerusalem, who were destroyed by the Romans at the time of their passover, and so, like the Galileans, they had *their blood mingled with their sacrifices;* and many of them, both in Jerusalem and in other places, were destroyed by the fall of walls and buildings which were battered down about their ears, as those that died by the fall of the tower of Siloam. But certainly it looks further; except we repent, we shall perish eternally, as they perished out of this world. The same Jesus that calls us to *repent because the kingdom of heaven is at hand,* bids us *repent* because otherwise we shall perish; so that he has set before us life and death, good and evil, and put us to our choice. (5.) The perishing of *those* in their impenitency who have been most harsh and severe in judging others will be in a particular manner aggravated.

Verses 6–9

This parable is intended to enforce that word of warning immediately going before, *"Except ye repent, ye shall all likewise perish;* except you be reformed, you will be ruined, as the barren tree, except it bring forth fruit, will be cut down."

I. This parable primarily refers to the nation and people of the Jews. God chose them for his own, made them a people near to him, gave them advantages for knowing and serving him above any other people, and expected answerable returns of duty and obedience from them, which, turning to his praise and honour, he would have accounted *fruit;* but they disappointed his expectations: they did not do their duty; they were a reproach instead of being a credit to their profession. Upon this, he justly determined to abandon them, and cut them off, to deprive them of their privileges, to unchurch and unpeople them; but, upon Christ's intercession, as of old upon that of Moses, he graciously gave them further time and further mercy; tried them, as it were, another year, by sending his apostles among them, to call them to repentance, and in Christ's name to offer them pardon, upon repentance. Some of them were wrought upon to *repent,* and bring forth fruit, and with them all was well; but the body of the nation continued impenitent and unfruitful, and ruin without remedy came upon them; about forty years after they were cut down, and cast into the fire, as John Baptist had told them (Mt. 3:10), which saying of his this parable enlarges upon.

II. Yet it has, without doubt, a further reference, and is designed for the awakening of all that enjoy the means of grace, and the privileges of the visible church, to see to it that the temper of their minds and the tenour of their lives be answerable to their professions and opportunities, for that is the *fruit* required. Now observe here,

1. The advantages which this fig-tree had. It was *planted in a vineyard,* in better soil, and where it had more care taken of it and more pains taken with it, than other fig-trees had, that commonly grew, not in *vineyards* (Those are for vines), but by the *way-side,* Mt. 21:19. This fig-tree belonged to a *certain man,* that owned it, and was at expense upon it. Note, The church of God is *his vineyard,* distinguished from the common, and fenced about, Isa. 5:1, 2. We are *fig-trees planted* in this vineyard by our baptism; we have a place and a name in the visible church, and this is our privilege and happiness. It is a distinguishing favour: he has not *dealt so with other nations.*

2. The owner's expectation from it: *He came, and sought fruit thereon,* and he had reason to expect it. He did not *send,* but came himself, intimating his desire to find fruit. Christ came into this world, *came to his own,* to the Jews, seeking fruit. Note, The God of heaven requires and expects *fruit* from those that have a place in his vineyard. He has *his eye* upon those that *enjoy* the gospel, to see whether they *live* up to it; he seeks evidences of their getting good by the means of grace they enjoy. *Leaves* will not serve, crying, *Lord, Lord; blossoms* will not serve, beginning well and promising fair; there must be *fruit.* Our thoughts, words, and actions must be according to the gospel, light and love.

3. The disappointment of his expectation: *He found none,* none at all, not one fig. Note, It is sad to think how many enjoy the privileges of the gospel, and yet do nothing at all to the honour of God, nor to answer the end of his entrusting them with those privileges; and it is a disappointment to him and a grief to the Spirit of his grace.

(1.) He here complains of it to the dresser of the vineyard: I come, *seeking fruit,* but am disappointed — *I find none,* looking for grapes, but behold *wild grapes.* He is grieved with such a generation.

(2.) He aggravates it, with two considerations: — [1.] That he had waited long, and yet was disappointed. As he was not *high* in his expectations, he only expected fruit, not *much* fruit, so he was not *hasty, he came three years,* year after year: applying it to the Jews, he came one space of time before the captivity, another after that, and another in the preaching of John Baptist and of Christ himself; or it may allude to the three years of Christ's public ministry, which were now expiring. In general, it teaches us that the patience of God is stretched out to long-suffering with many that enjoy the gospel, and do not bring forth the fruits of it; and this patience is wretchedly abused, which provokes God to so much the greater severity. How many times three years has God come to many of us, *seeking fruit,* but has *found none,* or next to none, or worse than none! [2.] That this fig-tree did not only not bring forth fruit, but did hurt; it *cumbered the ground;* it took up the room of a fruitful tree, and was injurious to all about it. Note, Those who do not *do* good commonly *do hurt* by the influence of their bad example; they grieve and discourage those that are good; they harden and encourage those that are bad. And the mischief is the greater, and the ground the more cumbered, if it be a high, large, spreading tree, and if it be an old tree of long standing.

4. The doom passed upon it; *Cut it down.* He saith this to the *dresser of the vineyard,* to Christ, to whom all judgment is committed, to the ministers who are in his name to declare this doom. Note, No other can be expected concerning barren trees than that they should be *cut down.* As the unfruitful vineyard is dismantled, and thrown open to the common (Isa. 5:5, 6), so the unfruitful trees in the vineyard are cast out of it, and wither, Jn. 15:6. It is cut down by the judgments of God, especially spiritual judgments, such as those on the Jews that believed not, Isa. 6:9, 10. It is cut down by death, and cast into the fire of hell; and with good reason, for *why cumbers it the ground?* What reason is there why it should have a place in the vineyard to no purpose?

5. The dresser's intercession for it. Christ is the great Intercessor; he ever lives, interceding. Ministers are intercessors; they that *dress* the vineyard should *intercede* for it; those we *preach to* we should *pray for,* for we must give ourselves to the *word of God* and to *prayer.* Now observe,

(1.) What it is he prays for, and that is a reprieve: *Lord, let it alone this year also.* He doth not pray, "Lord, let it never be cut down," but, "Lord, not now. Lord, do not remove the dresser, do not withhold the dews, do not pluck up the tree." Note, [1.] It is desirable to have a barren tree reprieved. Some have not yet *grace to repent,* yet it is a mercy to them to have *space to repent,* as it was to the old world to have 120 years allowed them to make their peace with God. [2.] We owe it to Christ, the great Intercessor, that *barren* trees are not cut down immediately: had it not been for his interposition, the whole world had been cut down, upon the sin of Adam; but he said, *Lord, let it alone;* and it is he that upholds all things. [3.] We are encouraged to pray to God for the merciful reprieve of barren fig-trees: "Lord, *let them alone;* continue them yet awhile in their probation; bear with them a little longer, and wait to be gracious." Thus must we stand in the gap, to turn away wrath. [4.] Reprieves of mercy are but for a time; *Let it alone this year also,* a short time, but a sufficient time to make trial. When God has borne long, we may hope he will bear yet a little longer, but we cannot expect he should bear always. [5.] *Reprieves* may be obtained by the prayers of others for us, but not *pardons;* there must be our own faith, and repentance, and prayers, else no pardon.

(2.) How he promises to improve this reprieve, if it be obtained: *Till I shall dig about it, and dung it,* Note, [1.] In general, our prayers must always be seconded with our endeavours. The dresser seems to say, "Lord, it may be I have been wanting in that which is my part; but let it alone this year, and I will do more than I have done towards its fruitfulness." Thus in all our prayers we must request God's grace, with a humble resolution to do our duty, else we mock God, and show that we do not rightly value the mercies we pray for. [2.] In particular, when we pray to God for grace for ourselves or others, we must follow our prayers with diligence in the use of the means of grace. The dresser of the vineyard engages to do *his* part, and therein teaches ministers to do *theirs.* He will *dig about* the tree and will *dung* it. Unfruitful Christians must be *awakened* by the terrors of the law, which *break up the fallow ground,* and then encouraged by the promises of the gospel, which are warming and fattening, as manure to the tree. Both methods must be tried; the one prepares for the other, and all little enough.

(3.) Upon what foot he leaves the matter: "Let us try it, and try what we can do with it one year more, *and, if it bear fruit, well, v.* 9. It is possible, nay, there is hope, that yet it may be fruitful." In this hope the owner will have patience with it, and the dresser will take pains with it, and, if it should have the desired success, both will be pleased that it was not cut down. The word *well* is not in the original, but the expression is abrupt: *If it bear fruit!* — supply it how you please, so as to express how wonderfully well-pleased both the owner and dresser will be. If it bear fruit, there will be cause of rejoicing; we have what we would have. But it cannot be better expressed than as we do: *well.* Note, Unfruitful professors of religion, if after long unfruitfulness they will repent, and amend, and bring forth fruit, shall find *all is well.* God will be *pleased,* for he will be *praised;* ministers' hands will be strengthened, and such penitents will be their joy now and their crown shortly. Nay, there will be joy in heaven for it; the ground will be no longer cumbered, but bettered, the vineyard beautified, and the good trees in it made better. As for the tree itself, it is *well* for it; it shall not only not be cut down, but it shall *receive blessing from God* (Heb. 6:7); it shall be *purged,* and *shall bring forth more fruit,* for the Father is its husbandman (Jn. 15:2); and it shall at last be transplanted from the vineyard on earth to the paradise above.

But he adds, *If not, then after that thou shalt cut it down.* Observe here, [1.] That, though God bear long, he will not bear always with unfruitful professors; his patience will have an end, and, if it be abused, will give way to that wrath which will have no end. Barren trees will certainly be *cut down* at last, and *cast into the fire.* [2.] The longer God has *waited,* and the more cost he has been at upon them, the greater will their destruction be: to be cut down *after that,* after all these expectations from it, these debates concerning it, this concern for it, will be sad indeed, and will aggravate the condemnation. [3.] Cutting down, though it is work that shall be done, is work that God does not take pleasure in: for observe here, the owner said to the dresser, "Do thou *cut it down,* for it cumbereth the ground." "Nay," said the dresser, "if it must be done at last, *thou shalt cut it down;* let not my hand be upon it." [4.] Those that now intercede for barren trees, and take pains with them, if they persist in their unfruitfulness will be even content to see them cut down, and will not have one word more to say for them. Their best friends will acquiesce in, nay, they will approve and applaud, the righteous judgment of God, in the day of the manifestation of it, Rev. 15:3, 4.

Verses 10–17

Here is, I. The miraculous cure of a woman that had been long under a spirit of infirmity. Our Lord Jesus spent his *Sabbaths* in the *synagogues, v.* 10. We should make conscience of doing so, as we have opportunity, and not think we can spend the sabbath as well at home reading a good book; for religious assemblies are a divine institution, which we must bear our testimony to, though but of two or three. And, when he was in the synagogues on the sabbath day, *he was teaching there — ēn didaskōn.* It denotes a continued act; he *still taught the people knowledge.* He was in his element when he was teaching. Now to confirm the doctrine he preached, and recommend it as faithful, and well worthy of all acceptation, he wrought a miracle, a miracle of mercy.

1. The object of charity that presented itself was a woman in the synagogue that had *a spirit of infirmity eighteen years, v.* 11. She had an infirmity, which an evil spirit, by divine permission, had brought upon her, which was such that she was *bowed together* by strong convulsions, and could *in no wise lift up herself;* and, having been so long thus, the disease was incurable; she could not stand erect, which is reckoned man's honour above the beasts. Observe, Though she was under this infirmity, by which she was much *deformed,* and made to look mean, and not only so, but, as is supposed, motion was very painful to her, yet she went to the *synagogue on the sabbath day.* Note, Even bodily infirmities, unless they be very grievous indeed, should not keep us from public worship on the sabbath days; for God can help us, beyond our expectation.

2. The offer of this cure to one that sought it not bespeaks the preventing mercy and grace of Christ: *When Jesus saw her, he called her to him, v.* 12. It does not appear that she made any application to him, or had any expectation from him; but *before she called he answered.* She came to him to be *taught,* and to get good to her soul, and then Christ gave this relief to her bodily infirmity. Note, Those whose first and chief care is for their souls do best befriend the true interests of their bodies likewise, for *other things shall be added to them.* Christ in his gospel calls and invites those to come to him for healing that labour under *spiritual infirmities,* and, if he *calls us,* he will undoubtedly help us when we come to him.

3. The cure effectually and immediately wrought bespeaks his almighty power. He *laid his hands on her,* and said, "*Woman, thou art loosed from thine infirmity;* though thou hast been long labouring under it, thou art at length released from it." Let not those despair whose disease is *inveterate,* who have been long in affliction. God can at length relieve them, therefore though he tarry wait for him. Though it was a *spirit of infirmity,* an evil spirit, that she was under the power of, Christ has a power superior to that of Satan, is *stronger than he.* Though *she could in no wise lift up herself,* Christ could lift her up, and enable her to lift up herself. She that had been *crooked* was *immediately made straight,* and the scripture was fulfilled (Ps. 146:8): *The Lord raiseth them that are bowed down.* This cure represents the work of Christ's grace upon the souls of the people. (1.) In the *conversion* of sinners. Unsanctified hearts are under this *spirit of infirmity;* they are distorted, the faculties of the soul are quite out of place and order; they are *bowed down* towards things below. *O curvae in terram animae!* They can in no wise *lift up themselves* to God and heaven; the bent of the soul, in its natural state, is the quite contrary way. Such crooked souls seek not to Christ; but he calls them to him, lays the hand of his power and grace upon them, speaks a healing word to them, by which he *looses them from their infirmity,* makes the soul *straight,* reduces it to order, raises it above worldly regards, and directs its affections and aims heavenward. Though *man cannot make that straight which God has made crooked* (Eccl. 7:13), yet the grace of God can make that straight which the sin of man has made crooked. (2.) In the *consolation* of good people. Many of the children of God are long under a *spirit of infirmity,* a spirit of bondage; through prevailing grief and fear, their *souls* are *cast down* and *disquieted* within them, *they are troubled, they are bowed down greatly, they go mourning all the day long,* Ps. 38:6. But Christ, by his Spirit of adoption, looses them from this infirmity in due time, and raises them up.

4. The present effect of this cure upon the *soul* of the patient as well as upon her *body.* She *glorified God,* gave him the praise of her cure to whom all praise is due. When crooked souls are made straight, they will show it by their glorifying God.

II. The offence that was taken at this by the *ruler of the synagogue,* as if our Lord Jesus had committed some heinous crime, in healing this poor woman. He *had indignation* at it, because it was *on the sabbath day, v.* 14. One would think that the miracle should have convinced him, and that the circumstance of its being done on the sabbath day could not have served to counteract the conviction; but what light can shine so clear, so strong, that a spirit of bigotry and enmity to Christ and his gospel will not serve to shut men's eyes against it? Never was such honour done to the synagogue he was ruler of as Christ had now done it, and yet he had indignation at it. He had not indeed the impudence to quarrel with Christ; but he said *to the people,* reflecting upon Christ in what he said, *There are six days in which men ought to work, in them therefore come and be healed, and not on the sabbath day.* See here how light he made of the miracles Christ wrought, as if they were *things of course,* and no more than what quacks and mountebanks did every day: "You may *come* and be healed any day of the week." Christ's cures were become, in his eyes, cheap and common things. See also how he stretches the law beyond its intention, or any just construction that could be put upon it, in making either healing or being healed with a touch of the hand, or a word's speaking, to be that *work* which is *forbidden* on the sabbath day. This was evidently *the work of God;* and, when God tied us out from working that day, did he tie himself out? The same word in Hebrew signifies both *godly* and *merciful (chesed),* to intimate that works of *mercy* and *charity* are in a manner works of *piety* (1 Tim. 5:4) and therefore very proper on sabbath days.

III. Christ's justification of himself in what he had done (*v.* 15): *The Lord then answered him,* as he had answered others who in like manner cavilled at him, *Thou hypocrite.* Christ, who knows men's hearts, may call those *hypocrites* whom it would be presumption for us to call so. We *must* judge charitably, and *can* judge only according to the outward appearance. Christ knew that he had a real enmity to him and to his gospel, that he did but cloak this with a pretended zeal for the sabbath day, and that when he bade the people come on the *six days,* and be healed, he really would not have them be healed any day. Christ could have told him this, but he vouchsafes to reason the case with him; and,

1. He *appeals* to the common practice among the Jews, which was never disallowed, that of *watering* their cattle on the sabbath day. Those cattle that are kept up in the stable are constantly *loosed from the stall on the sabbath day, and led away to watering.* It would be a barbarous thing not to do it; for *a merciful man regards the life of his beast,* his own beast that serves him. Letting the cattle *rest* on the sabbath day, as the law directed, would be worse than working them, if they must be made to fast on that day, as the Ninevites' cattle on their fast-day, that were not permitted to *feed nor drink water,* Jon. 3:7.

2. He applies this to the present case (*v.* 16): "Must the *ox* and the *ass* have compassion shown them on the sabbath day, and have so much time and pains bestowed upon them *every* sabbath, to be loosed from the stall, led away perhaps a great way to the water, and then back again, and shall not this woman, only with a touch of the hand and a word's speaking, be *loosed* from a much *greater* grievance than that which the cattle undergo when they are kept a day without water? For consider," (1.) "She is *a daughter of Abraham,* in a relation to whom you all pride yourselves; she is *your sister,* and shall she be denied a favour that you grant to an ox or an ass, dispensing a little with the supposed strictness of the sabbath day? She is *a daughter of Abraham,* and therefore is entitled to the Messiah's blessings, to the *bread* which belongs to the *children.*" (2.) "She is one whom Satan *has bound.* He had a hand in the affliction, and therefore it was not only an act of charity to the poor woman, but of piety to God, to break the power of the devil, and baffle him." (3.) "She has been in this deplorable condition, *lo, these eighteen years,* and therefore, now that there is an opportunity of delivering her, it ought not to be deferred *a day* longer, as you would have it, for any of you would have thought eighteen years' affliction full long enough."

IV. The different effect that this had upon those that heard him. He had sufficiently made it out, not only that it was lawful, but that it was highly fit and proper, to heal this poor woman *on the sabbath day,* and thus publicly in the synagogue, that they might all be witnesses of the miracle. And now observe,

1. What a confusion this was to the malice of his persecutors: *When he had said these things, all his adversaries were ashamed* (*v.* 17); they were put to silence, and were vexed that they were so, that they had not a word to say for themselves. It was not a shame that worked repentance, but rather indignation. Note, Sooner or later, all the adversaries of Christ, and his doctrine and miracles, will be made *ashamed.*

2. What a confirmation this was to the faith of his friends: *All the people,* who had a better sense of things, and judged more impartially than their rulers, rejoiced *for all the glorious things that were done by him.* The shame of his foes was the joy of his followers; the increase of his interest was what the one fretted at, and the other triumphed in. The things Christ did were *glorious things;* they were all so, and, though now clouded, perhaps will appear to, and we ought to rejoice in them. Every thing that is the honour of Christ is the comfort of Christians.

Verses 18–22

Here is, I. The gospel's progress foretold in two parables, which we had before, Mt. 13:31–33. The *kingdom of the Messiah* is the *kingdom of God,* for it advances his glory; this kingdom was yet a mystery, and people were generally in the dark, and under mistakes, about it. Now, when we would describe a thing to those that are strangers to it, we choose to do it by similitudes. "Such a person you know not, but I will tell you whom he is like;" so Christ undertakes here to show *what the kingdom of God is like* (*v.* 18): *"Whereunto shall I liken the kingdom of God? v.* 20. It will be quite another thing from what you expect, and will operate, and gain its point, in quite another manner." 1. "You expect it will appear *great,* and will arrive at its perfection all of a sudden; but you are mistaken, *it is like a grain of mustard-seed,* a little thing, takes up but little room, makes but a little figure, and promises but little; yet, when sown in soil proper to receive it, it *waxes a great tree," v.* 19. Many perhaps were prejudiced against the gospel, and loth to come in *to the obedience* of it, because its beginning was so small; they were ready to say of Christ, *Can this man save us?* And of his gospel, *Is this likely ever to come to any thing?* Now Christ would remove this prejudice, by assuring them that though *its beginning was small its latter end should greatly increase;* so that many should come, should come upon the wing, should *fly like a cloud,* to lodge in the branches of it with more safety and satisfaction than in the branches of Nebuchadnezzar's tree, Dan. 4:21. 2. "You expect it will make its way by *external* means, by subduing nations and vanquishing armies, though it shall work *like leaven,* silently and insensibly, and without any force or violence, *v.* 21. A little leaven leaveneth the whole lump; so the doctrine of Christ will strangely *diffuse* its relish into the world of mankind: in this it triumphs, that *the savour of the knowledge of it* is unaccountably made manifest *in every place,* beyond what one could have expected, 2 Co. 2:14. But you must *give it time,* wait for the issue of the preaching of the gospel to the world, and you will find it does wonders, and alters the property of the souls of men. By degrees *the whole will be leavened,* even as many as are, like *the meal* to the *leaven,* prepared to receive the savour of it."

II. Christ's progress towards Jerusalem recorded: *He went through the cities and villages, teaching and journeying, v.* 22. Here we find Christ an itinerant, but an itinerant preacher, journeying towards Jerusalem, to the feast of dedication, which was *in the winter,* when travelling was uncomfortable, yet he would be about his Father's business; and therefore, whatever cities or villages he could make in his way, he gave them a sermon or two, not only in the cities, but in the country villages. Wherever Providence brings us, we should endeavour to be doing all the good we can.

Verses 23–30

We have here,

I. A question put to our Lord Jesus. Who it was that put it we are not told, whether a friend or a foe; for he both gave a great liberty of questioning him and returned answers to the thoughts and intents of the heart. The question was, *Are there few that are saved? v.* 23: *ei oligoi hoi sōzomenoi —"If the saved be few?* Master, I have heard thou shouldest say so; is it true?" 1. Perhaps it was a *captious* question. He put it to him, tempting him, with a design to ensnare him and lessen his reputation. If he should say that many would be saved, they would reproach him as too loose, and making salvation cheap; if few, they would reproach him as precise and strait-laced. The Jewish doctors said that *all Israel should have a place in the world to come;* and would he dare to contradict that? Those that have sucked in a corrupt nation are ready to make it the standard by which to measure all men's judgments; and in nothing do men more betray their ignorance, presumption, and partiality, than in judging of the salvation of others. 2. Perhaps it was a *curious* question, a nice speculation, which he had lately been disputing upon with his companions, and they all agreed to refer it to Christ. Note, Many are more inquisitive respecting who shall be saved, and who not, than respecting what they shall do to be saved. It is commonly asked, "May such and such be saved?" But it is well that we may be saved without knowing this. 3. Perhaps it was an *admiring* question. He had taken notice how strict the law of Christ was, and how bad the world was, and, comparing these together, cries out, "How few are there that will be saved!" Note, We have reason to wonder that of the many to whom the word of salvation is sent there are so few to whom it is indeed a saving word. 4. Perhaps it was an *enquiring* question: *"If there be few that be saved,* what then? What influence should this have upon me?" Note, It concerns us all seriously to improve the great truth of the fewness of those that are saved.

II. Christ's answer to this question, which directs us what use to make of this truth. Our Saviour did not give a direct answer to this enquiry, for he came to *guide* men's *consciences,* not to *gratify* their *curiosity.* Ask not, "How many shall be saved?" But, be they more or fewer, "Shall I be one of them?" Not, "What shall become of such and such, and *what shall this man do?"* But, "What shall I do, and what will become of me?" Now in Christ's answer observe,

1. A quickening exhortation and direction: *Strive to enter in at the strait gate.* This is directed not to him only that asked the question, but to all, to us, it is in the plural number: *Strive ye.* Note, (1.) All that will be saved must *enter in at the strait gate,* must undergo a change of the whole man, such as amounts to no less than being born again, and must submit to a strict discipline. (2.) Those that would enter in at the strait gate must *strive to enter.* It is a hard matter to get to heaven, and a point that will not be gained without a great deal of care and pains, of difficulty and diligence. We must strive with God in prayer, wrestle as Jacob, strive against sin and Satan. We must strive in every duty of religion; strive with our own hearts, *agōnizesthe — "Be in an agony;* strive as those that run for a prize; excite and exert ourselves to the utmost."

2. Divers awakening considerations, to enforce this exhortation. O that we may be all awakened and quickened by them! They are such considerations as will serve to answer the question, *Are there few that shall be saved?*

(1.) Think how many take *some pains* for salvation and yet perish because they do not take *enough,* and you will say that there are *few that will be saved* and that it highly concerns us to *strive: Many will seek to enter in, and shall not be able;* they *seek,* but they do not *strive.* Note, The reason why many come short of grace and glory is because they rest in a *lazy seeking* of that which will not be attained without a *laborious striving.* They have a *good mind to happiness,* and a *good opinion of holiness,* and take some *good steps* towards both. But their convictions are weak; they do not consider what they know and believe, and, consequently, their desires are cold, and their endeavours feeble, and there is no strength or steadiness in their resolutions; and thus they *come short,* and lose the prize, because they do not press forward. Christ avers this upon his own word: *I say unto you;* and we may take it upon his word, for he knows both the counsels of God and the hearts of the children of men.

(2.) Think of the *distinguishing* day that is coming and the *decisions* of that day, and you will say there are a *few that shall be saved* and that we are concerned to strive: The *Master of the house* will *rise up, and shut to the door, v.* 25. Christ is the *Master of the house,* that will take cognizance of all that frequent his house and are retainers to it, will examine comers and goers and those that pass and repass. Now he seems as if he left things at large; but the day is coming when he will *rise up, and shut to the door.* What door? [1.] A door of *distinction.* Now, within the temple of the church there are *carnal* professors who worship in the *outer-court,* and *spiritual* professors who worship *within the veil;* between these the door is now open, and they meet *promiscuously* in the same external performances. But, when the *Master of the house is risen up,* the door will be shut between them, that those who are in the *outer-court* may be kept out, and left to be *trodden underfoot by the Gentiles,* Rev. 11:2. As to those *that are filthy,* shut the door upon them, and let them be *filthy still;* that those who are within may be kept within, that those who are *holy may be holy still.* The door is shut to *separate* between the *precious* and the *vile,* that *sinners* may no longer *stand in the congregation of the righteous.* Then you shall return, and discern betwixt them. [2.] A door of *denial* and exclusion. The door of *mercy* and *grace* has long *stood open* to them, but they would *not come in by it,* would not be beholden to the *favour* of that door; they hoped to *climb up some other way,* and to get to heaven by their own merits, and therefore when the Master of the house is risen up he will justly *shut that door;* let them not expect to enter by it, but let them take their own measures. Thus, when Noah was safe in the ark, God *shut* the door, to *exclude* all those that depended upon shelters of their own in the approaching flood.

(3.) Think how many who were very *confident* that they should be *saved* will be rejected in the day of trial, and their confidences will deceive them, and you will say that there are *few* that *shall be saved* and that we are all concerned to *strive.* Consider,

[1.] What an *assurance* they had of *admission,* and how far their hope carried them, even to *heaven's gate.* There they *stand and knock,* knock as if they had authority, knock as those that belong to the house, *saying, "Lord, Lord, open to us,* for we think we have a right to enter; take us in among the *saved ones,* for we joined ourselves to them." Note, Many are ruined by an ill-grounded hope of heaven, which they never distrusted or called in question, and *therefore* conclude their state is good because they never doubted it. They call Christ, *Lord,* as if they were his servants; nay, in token of their importunity, they double it, *Lord, Lord;* they are desirous now to enter in by that door which they had formerly made light of, and would now gladly come in among those serious Christians whom they had secretly despised.

[2.] What *grounds* they had for this *confidence.* Let us see what their plea is, *v.* 26. *First,* They had been *Christ's guests,* had had an intimate converse with him, and had shared in his favours: *We have eaten and drunk in thy presence,* at thy table. Judas ate bread with Christ, dipped with him in the dish. Hypocrites, under the disguise of their external profession, receive the Lord's supper, and in it partake of the children's bread, as if they were children. *Secondly,* They had been *Christ's hearers,* had received instruction from him, and were well acquainted with his doctrine and law: *"Thou hast taught in our streets* — a distinguishing favour, which few had, and surely it might be taken as a pledge of distinguishing favour now; for wouldest thou teach us, and not save us?"

[3.] How their confidence will fail them, and all their pleas be rejected as frivolous. Christ will say to them, *I know you not whence you are, v.* 25. And again (*v.* 27), *I tell you, I know you not, depart from me.* He does not deny that what they pleaded was true; they had *eaten and drunk in his presence,* by the same token that they had no sooner eaten of his bread than they lifted up the heel against him. He had *taught in their streets,* by the same token that they had despised his instruction and would not submit to it. And therefore, *First,* He *disowns* them: *"I know you not;* you do not belong to my family." *The Lord knows them that are his,* but them that are not he does not know, he has nothing to do with them: *"I know you not whence you are.* You are not of me, you are not from above, you are not branches of my house, of my vine." *Secondly,* He *discards* them: *Depart from me.* It is the hell of hell to depart from Christ, the principal part of the misery of the damned. "Depart from my door, here is nothing for you, no, not a drop of water." *Thirdly,* He gives them such a character as is the reason of this doom: *You are workers of iniquity.* This is their ruin, that, under a pretence of piety, they kept up secret haunts of sin, and did the devil's drudgery in Christ's livery.

[4.] How terrible their punishment will be (*v.* 28): *There shall be weeping and gnashing of teeth,* the utmost degree of grief and indignation; and that which is the cause of it, and contributes to it, is a sight of the happiness of those that are saved: *You shall see the patriarchs and prophets in the kingdom of God, and yourselves thrust out.* Observe here, *First,* That the *Old-Testament saints* are in the kingdom of God; those had benefit by the Messiah who died before his coming, for they *saw his day* at a distance and it reflected comfort upon them. *Secondly,* That *New-Testament sinners* will be *thrust out* of the kingdom of God. It intimates that they will be *thrusting in,* and will presume upon admission, but in vain; they shall be *thrust out* with shame, as having no part or lot in the matter. *Thirdly,* That the sight of the saint's glory will be a great aggravation of sinner's misery; they shall thus far *see the kingdom of God* that they shall see the *prophets* in it, whom they hated and despised, and themselves, though they thought themselves sure of it, *thrust out.* This is that at which they will *gnash their teeth,* Ps. 112:10.

(4.) Think who are they that shall be saved, notwithstanding: *They shall come from the east and the west; and the last shall be first, v.* 29, 30. [1.] By what Christ said, it appears that but *few shall be saved* of those whom we think most likely, and who bid fairest for it. Yet do not say then that the gospel is preached in vain; for, though Israel be not *gathered,* Christ will be *glorious.* There shall come many from all parts of the Gentile world that shall be admitted into the kingdom of grace in this world, and of glory in the other. Plainly thus, when we come to heaven, we shall meet a great many there whom we little thought to have met there, and miss a great many thence whom we verily expected to have found there. [2.] Those who *sit down in the kingdom of God* are such as had taken pains to get thither, for they came from far — *from the east and from the west, from the north and from the south;* they had passed through different climates, had broken through many difficulties and discouragements. This shows that they who would enter into that kingdom must *strive,* as the queen of Sheba, who came from the *utmost parts of the earth to hear the wisdom of Solomon.* They who *travel* now in the service of God and religion shall shortly *sit down* to rest in the *kingdom of God.* [3.] Many who stood fair for heaven came short, and others who seemed cast behind, and thrown quite out of the way, will win and wear this prize, and therefore it concerns us to *strive to enter.* Let us be *provoked,* as Paul desires the Jews might be, to a holy emulation, by the zest an forwardness of the Gentiles, Rom. 11:14. Shall I be outstripped by my juniors? Shall I, who started first, and stood nearest, miss of heaven, when others, less likely, enter into it? If it be got by striving, why should not I strive?

Verses 31–35

Here is, I. A suggestion to Christ of his danger from Herod, now that he was in Galilee, within Herod's jurisdiction (*v.* 31): *Certain of the Pharisees* (for there were those of that sect dispersed all the nation over) *came* to Christ, pretending friendship and a concern for his safety, and said, *Get thee* out of this country, and *depart hence,* for otherwise *Herod will kill thee,* as he did John. Some think that these Pharisees had no ground at all for this, that Herod had not given out any words to this purport, but that they framed this lie, to drive him out of Galilee, where he had a great and growing interest, and to drive him into Judea, where they knew there were those that really sought his life. But, Christ's answer being directed to Herod himself, it should seem that the Pharisees had ground for what they said, and that Herod was enraged against Christ, and designed him a mischief, for the honourable testimony he had borne to John Baptist, and to the doctrine of repentance which John preached. Herod was willing to get rid of Christ out of his dominions; and, when he durst not put him to death, he hoped to *frighten him away* by sending him this threatening message.

II. His defiance of Herod's rage and the Pharisees' too; he fears neither the one nor the other: *Go you, and tell that fox so, v.* 32. In calling him a *fox,* he gives him his true character; for he was subtle as a fox, noted for his craft, and treachery, and baseness, and preying (as they say of a fox) furthest from his own den. And, though it is a black and ugly character, yet it did not ill become Christ to give it to him, nor was it in him a violation of that law, *Thou shalt not speak evil of the ruler of thy people.* For Christ was a prophet, and prophets always had a liberty of speech in reproving princes and great men. Nay, Christ was more than a prophet, he was a king, he was King of kings, and the greatest of men were accountable to him, and therefore it became him to call this proud king by his own name; but it is not to be drawn into an example by us. "Go, and tell *that* fox, yea, and *this* fox too" (for so it is in the original, *tē alōpeki tautē*); *"that Pharisee,* whoever he is, that whispers this in my ear, let him know that *I do not fear him,* nor regard his menaces. For," 1. "I know that I must die, and must die shortly; I expect it, and count upon it, *the third day,"* that is, "very shortly; my hour is at hand." Note, It will help us very much above the fear of death, and of them that have the power of death, to make death familiar to us, to expect it, think of it, and converse with it, and see it at the door. "If Herod should kill me, he will not surprise me." 2. "I know that death will be not only no prejudice to me, but that it will be my preferment; and therefore tell him I do not fear him; when I die, *I shall be perfected.* I shall then have *finished* the hardest part of my undertaking; I shall have completed my business;" *teleioumai — I shall be consecrated.* When Christ dies, he is said to have *sanctified himself;* he consecrated himself to his priestly office with his own blood. 3. "I know that neither he nor any one else can kill me *till I have done my work.* Go, and tell him that I value not his impotent rage. *I will cast out devils, and do cures, to-day and to-morrow,"* that is, "now and for some little space of time yet to come, in spite of him and all his threats. I *must walk,* I must *go on* in my intended journey, and it is not in his power to hinder me. I must *go about,* as I do, preaching and healing, *to-day, and to-morrow, and the day following."* Note, It is good for us to look upon the time we have before us as but a little, two or three days perhaps may be the utmost, that we may thereby be quickened to *do the work of the day in its day.* And it is a comfort to us, in reference to the power and malice of our enemies, that they can have no power to take us off as long as God has any work for us to do. The witnesses were not *slain* till they had *finished their testimony.* 4. "I know that Herod can do me no harm, not only because *my time* is not yet come, but because the place appointed for my death is Jerusalem, which is not within his jurisdiction: *It cannot be that a prophet perish out of Jerusalem,"* that is, "any where but at Jerusalem." If a *true prophet* was put to death, he was prosecuted as a *false prophet.* Now none undertook to try prophets, and to judge concerning them, but the great sanhedrim, which always sat at Jerusalem; it was a cause which the inferior courts did not take cognizance of, and therefore, if a *prophet* be *put to death,* it must be at Jerusalem.

III. His lamentation for Jerusalem, and his denunciation of wrath against that city, *v.* 34, 35. This we had Mt. 23:37–39. Perhaps this was not said now in Galilee, but the evangelist, not designing to bring it in in its proper place, inserts it here, upon occasion of Christ's mentioning his being put to death at Jerusalem.

Note, 1. The wickedness of persons and places that more eminently than others profess religion and relation to God is in a particular manner provoking and grieving to the Lord Jesus. How pathetically does he speak of the sin and ruin of that holy city! *O Jerusalem! Jerusalem!* 2. Those that enjoy great plenty of the means of grace, if they are not profited by them, are often prejudiced against them. They that would not hearken to the prophets, nor welcome those whom God had sent to them, *killed* them, and *stoned* them. If men's corruptions are not conquered, they are provoked. 3. Jesus Christ has shown himself willing, freely willing, to receive and entertain poor souls that come to him, and put themselves under his protection: *How often would I have gathered thy children together,* as a hen gathereth her brood under her wings, with such care and tenderness! 4. The reason why sinners are not protected and provided for by the Lord Jesus, as the chickens are by the hen, is because they will not: *I would,* I often would, and *ye would not.* Christ's willingness aggravates sinners' unwillingness, and leaves their blood upon their own heads. 5. The house that Christ leaves is *left desolate.* The temple, though richly adorned, though greatly frequented, is yet desolate if Christ has deserted it. He leaves it *to them;* they had made an idol of it, and let them take it to themselves, and make their best of it, Christ will trouble it no more. 6. Christ justly withdraws from those that drive him from them. They would not be *gathered* by him, and therefore, saith he, *"You shall not see me,* you shall not hear me, any more," as Moses said to Pharaoh, when he forbade him his presence, Ex. 10:28, 29. 7. The judgment of the great day will effectually convince unbelievers that would not now be convinced: "Then you will say, *Blessed is he that cometh,"* that is, "you will be glad to be among those that say so, and *will not see me* to be the Messiah till then when it is too late."

CHAPTER 14

In this chapter we have, I. The cure which our Lord Jesus wrought upon a man that had the dropsy, on the sabbath day, and his justifying himself therein against those who were offended at his doing it on that day (*v.* 1–6). II. A lesson of humility gives to those who were ambitious of the highest rooms (*v.* 7–11). III. A lesson of charity to those who feasted the rich, and did not feed the poor (*v.* 12–14). IV. The success of the gospel not foretold in the parable of the guests invited to a feast, signifying the rejection of the Jews and all others that set their hearts upon this world, and the entertainment of the Gentiles and all others that come to be filled with Christ (*v.* 15–24). V. The great law of discipleship laid down, with a caution to all that will be Christ's disciples to undertake it deliberately and with consideration, and particularly to ministers, to retain their savour (*v.* 25–35).

Verses 1–6

In this passage of story we find,

I. That *the Son of man came eating and drinking,* conversing familiarly with all sorts of people; not declining the society of publicans, though they were of *ill fame,* nor of Pharisees, though they bore him *ill will,* but accepting the friendly invitations both of the one and the other, that, if possible, he might do good to *both.* Here he *went into the house of one of the chief Pharisees,* a ruler, it may be, and a magistrate in his country, *to eat bread on the sabbath day, v.* 1. See how favourable God is to us, that he allows us time, even on his own day, for bodily refreshments; and how careful we should be not to abuse that liberty, or turn it into licentiousness. Christ went only to *eat bread,* to take such refreshment as was necessary on the sabbath day. Our sabbath meals must, with a particular care, be guarded against all manner of excess. On sabbath days we must do as Moses and Jethro did, *eat bread before God* (Ex. 18:12), and, as is said of the primitive Christians, on the Lord's day, must *eat and drink* as those that must *pray again before we go to rest,* that we may not be unfit for that.

II. That he *went about doing good.* Wherever he came he *sought* opportunities to *do good,* and not only improved those that *fell in his way.* Here was *a certain man before him who had the dropsy, v.* 2. We do not find that he offered himself, or that his friends offered him to be Christ's patient, but Christ *prevented him* with the blessings of his goodness, and *before he called* he answered him. Note, It is a happy thing to be where Christ is, to be present *before him,* though we be not presented *to him.* This man had the *dropsy,* it is probable, in a high degree, and appeared much swoln with it; probably he was some relation of the Pharisee's, that now *lodged* in his house, which is more likely than that he should be an *invited guest* at the table.

III. That he *endured the contradiction of sinners against himself: They watched him, v.* 1. The Pharisee that invited him, it should seem, did it with a design to pick some quarrel with him; if it were so, Christ *knew* it, and yet *went,* for he knew himself a match for the most *subtle* of them, and knew how to order his steps with an eye to *his observers.* Those that are *watched* had need to be *wary.* It is, as Dr. Hammond observes, contrary to all laws of hospitality to seek advantage against one that you invited to be your guest, for such a one you have taken under your protection. These lawyers and Pharisees, like the fowler that lies in wait to *ensnare* the birds, *held their peace,* and acted very *silently.* When Christ asked them *whether* they thought it *lawful to heal on the sabbath day* (and herein he is said to *answer* them, for it was an answer to *their thoughts,* and thoughts are *words* to Jesus Christ), they would say neither *yea* nor *nay,* for their design was to *inform against him,* not to be *informed by him.* They would not say *it was lawful to heal,* for then they would preclude themselves from imputing it to him as a crime; and yet the thing was so plain and self-evident that they could not for shame say it was *not lawful.* Note, Good men have often been persecuted for doing that which even their persecutors, if they would but give their consciences leave to speak out, could not but own to be lawful and good. Many a *good work* Christ did, for which they *cast stones* at him and his name.

IV. That Christ would not be hindered from *doing good* by the *opposition* and *contradiction* of sinners. He *took him, and healed him, and let him go, v.* 4. Perhaps he *took him aside* into another room, and healed him *there,* because he would neither *proclaim* himself, such was his humility, nor *provoke* his adversaries, such was his wisdom, his *meekness of wisdom.* Note, Though we must not be driven off from our duty by the malice of our enemies, yet we should order the circumstances of it so as to make it the least offensive. Or, He *took him,* that is, he *laid hands* on him, to cure him; *epilabomenos, complexus — he embraced him,* took him in his arms, big and unwieldy as he was (for so dropsical people generally are), and reduced him to shape. The cure of a dropsy, as much as any disease, one would think, should be gradual; yet Christ cured even *that* disease, perfectly cured it, in a moment. He then let him go, lest the Pharisees should fall upon him for *being healed,* though he was purely passive; for what absurdities would not such men as they were be guilty of?

V. That our Lord Jesus *did nothing but what he could justify,* to the conviction and confusion of those that quarrelled with him, *v.* 5, 6. He still answered their thoughts, and made them *hold their peace for shame* who before held their peace for *subtlety,* by an appeal to their own practice, as he had been used to do upon such occasions, that he might show them how in condemning him they condemned themselves: *which of you shall have an ass or an ox fallen into a pit,* by accident, *and will not pull him out on the sabbath day,* and that straightway, not deferring it till the sabbath be over, lest it perish? Observe, It is not so much out of *compassion to the poor creature* that they do it as a concern for their own interest. It is *their own ox,* and *their own ass,* that is worth money, and they will dispense with the law of the sabbath for the *saving of.* Now this was an evidence of their hypocrisy, and that it was not out of any real regard to the sabbath that they found fault with Christ for healing on the *sabbath day* (that was only the pretence), but really because they were angry at the *miraculous good works* which Christ wrought, and the *proof* he thereby gave of his divine mission, and the interest he thereby *gained* among the people. Many can easily dispense with that, for their own interest, which they cannot dispense with for God's glory and the good of their brethren. This question *silenced* them: *They could not answer him again to these things, v.* 6. Christ will be justified when he speaks, and every mouth must be stopped before him.

Verses 7–14

Our Lord Jesus here sets us an example of profitable edifying discourse at our tables, when we are in company with our friends. We find that when he had none but his disciples, who were his own family, with him at his table, his discourse with them was *good, and to the use of edifying;* and not only so, but when he was in company with strangers, nay, with enemies that *watched him,* he took occasion to reprove what he saw amiss in them, and to instruct them. Though the *wicked were before him,* he did not *keep silence from good* (as David did, Ps. 39:1, 2), for, notwithstanding the provocation given him, he had not his *heart hot within him,* nor was *his spirit stirred.* We must not only not allow any corrupt communication at our tables, such as that of the *hypocritical mockers at feasts,* but we must go beyond common harmless talk, and should take occasion from God's goodness to us at our tables to speak well of him, and learn to *spiritualize* common things. The lips of the righteous should then *feed many.* Our Lord Jesus was among persons of quality, yet, as one that had not respect of persons,

I. He takes occasion to reprove *the guests* for striving to *sit uppermost,* and thence gives us a lesson of *humility.*

1. He observed how these lawyers and Pharisees affected the *highest seats,* towards the head-end of the table, *v.* 7. He had charged that sort of men with this in general, *ch.* 11:43. Here he brings home the charge to particular persons; for Christ will give *every man his own.* He *marked* how they *chose out the chief rooms;* every man, as he came in, got as near the best seat as he could. Note, Even in the common actions of life, Christ's eye is upon us, and he *marks* what we do, not only in our religious assemblies, but at our tables, and *makes remarks* upon it.

2. He observed how those who were thus aspiring often exposed themselves, and came off *with a slur;* whereas, those who were modest, and seated themselves in the lowest seats, often *gained respect* by it. (1.) Those who, when they come in, assume the highest seats, may perhaps be *degraded,* and forced to *come down* to give place to one *more honourable, v.* 8, 9. Note, It ought to check our high thoughts of ourselves to think how many there are that are *more honourable* than we, not only in respect of worldly dignities, but of personal merits and accomplishments. Instead of being proud that so many give place to us, it should be humbling to us that there are so many that we must give place to. The master of the feast will marshal his guests, and will not see the *more honourable* kept out of the seat that is his due, and therefore will make bold to take him lower that usurped it; *Give this man place;* and this will be a disgrace before all the company to him that would be thought more deserving than he really was. Note, Pride will have *shame,* and will at last have a *fall.* (2.) Those who, when they come in, content themselves with the lowest seats, are likely to be preferred (*v.* 10): "Go, and *seat thyself in the lowest room,* as taking it for granted that thy friend, who invited thee, has guests to come that are of better rank and quality than thou are; but perhaps it may not prove so, and then it will be said to thee, *Friend, go up higher.* The master of the feast will be so just to thee as not to keep thee at the lower end of the table because thou wert so *modest* as to seat thyself there." Note, The way to *rise high* is to *begin low,* and this recommends a man to those about him: *"Thou shalt have honour and respect before those that sit with thee.* They will see thee to be an *honourable man,* beyond what at first they thought; and honour appears the brighter for shining *out of obscurity.* They will likewise see thee to be a *humble man,* which is the greatest honour of all. Our Saviour here refers to that advice of Solomon (Prov. 25:6, 7), *Stand not in the place of great men, for better it is that it be said unto thee, Come up hither, than that thou shouldest be put lower."* And Dr. Lightfoot quotes a parable out of one of the rabbin somewhat like this. "Three men," said he, "were bidden to a feast; one sat highest, For, said he, I am a prince; the other next, For, said he, I am a wise man; the other lowest, For, said he, I am a humble man. The king seated the humble man highest, and put the prince lowest."

3. He applied this generally, and would have us all learn not to *mind high things,* but to content ourselves with mean things, as for other reasons, so for this, because pride and ambition are disgraceful before men: for *whosoever exalteth himself shall be abased;* but humility and self-denial are really honourable: *he that humbleth himself shall be exalted, v.* 11. We see in other instances that *a man's pride will bring him low,* but *honour shall uphold the humble in spirit,* and *before honour is humility.*

II. He takes occasion to reprove the master of the feast for inviting so many *rich people,* who had wherewithal to dine very well at home, when he should rather have *invited the poor,* or, which was all one, have *sent portions to them for whom nothing was prepared,* and who could not afford themselves a good meal's meat. See Neh. 8:10. Our Saviour here teaches us that the using of what we have in works of charity is better, and will turn to a better account, than using it in works of generosity and in magnificent house-keeping.

1. "Covet not to *treat the rich;* invite not *thy friends, and brethren, and neighbours, that are rich," v.* 12. This does not *prohibit* the entertaining of such; there may be occasion for it, for the cultivating of friendship among relations and neighbours. But, (1.) "Do not make a common custom of it; spend as little as thou canst that way, that thou mayest not disable thyself to lay out in a much better way, in almsgiving. Thou wilt find it very expensive and troublesome; one feast for the rich will make a great many meals for the poor." Solomon saith, *He that giveth to the rich shall surely come to want,* Prov. 22:16. "Give" (saith Pliny, Epist.) "to thy friends, but let it be to thy *poor* friends, not to those that need thee not." (2.) "Be not *proud of it."* Many *make feasts* only to *make a show,* as Ahasuerus did (Esth. 1:3, 4), and it is no reputation to them, they think, if they have not persons of quality to dine with them, and thus rob their families, to please their fancies. (3.) "Aim not at being paid again in your own coin." This is that which our Saviour blames in making such entertainments: "You commonly do it in hopes that you will be invited by them, and *so a recompence will be made you;* you will be gratified with such dainties and varieties as you treat your friends with, and this will feed your sensuality and luxury, and you will be no real gainer at last."

2. "Be forward to *relieve the poor* (*v.* 13, 14): *When thou makest a feast,* instead of furnishing thyself with what is rare and nice, get thy table spread with a competency of plain and wholesome meat, which will not be so costly, and invite *the poor and maimed,* such as have nothing to live upon, nor are able to work for their living. These are objects of charity; they want necessaries; furnish them, and they will recompense thee with their prayers; they will commend thy provisions, which the rich, it may be, will despise. They will go away, and thank God for thee, when the rich will go away and reproach thee. Say not that thou art a *loser,* because *they cannot recompense thee,* thou art so much out of pocket; no, it is so much set out to the best interest, on the best security, for *thou shall be recompensed at the resurrection of the just."* There will be a *resurrection of the just, a future state* of the just. There is a state of happiness reserved for them in the other world; and we may be sure that the *charitable* will be remembered in the *resurrection of the just,* for alms are *righteousness.* Works of charity perhaps may not be rewarded *in this world,* for the things of this world are not the *best things,* and therefore God does not pay the best men in *those things;* but they shall *in no wise lose their reward;* they shall be recompensed in the *resurrection.* It will be found that the longest voyages make the richest returns, and that the charitable will be no losers, but unspeakable gainers, by having their recompense adjourned *till the resurrection.*

Verses 15–24

Here is another discourse of our Saviour's, in which he *spiritualizes* the feast he was invited to, which is another way of keeping up good discourse in the midst of common actions.

I. The occasion of the discourse was given by one of the guests, who, when Christ was giving rules about feasting, said to him, *Blessed is he that shall eat bread in the kingdom of God* (*v.* 15), which, some tell us, was a saying commonly used among the rabbin.

1. But with what design does this man bring it in here? (1.) Perhaps this man, observing that Christ reproved first the guests and then the master of the house, fearing he should put the company out of humour, started this, to *divert* the discourse to something else. Or, (2.) Admiring the good rules of humility and charity which Christ had now given, but despairing to see them lived up to in the present degenerate state of things, he longs for *the kingdom of God,* when these and other good laws shall prevail, and pronounces them *blessed* who shall have a place in that kingdom. Or, (3.) Christ having mentioned *the resurrection of the just,* as a recompence for acts of charity to the poor, he here confirms what he said, "Yea, Lord, they that shall be recompensed in the resurrection of the just, shall *eat bread in the kingdom,* and that is a greater recompence than being reinvited to the table of the greatest man on earth." Or, (4.) Observing Christ to be silent, after he had given the foregoing lessons, he was will-

ing to draw him in again to further discourse, so wonderfully well-pleased was he with what he said; and he knew nothing more likely to engage him than to mention the *kingdom of God.* Note, Even those that are not of ability to carry on good discourse themselves ought to put in a word now and then, to countenance it, and help it forward.

2. Now what this man said was a plain and acknowledged truth, and it was quoted very *appositely* now that they were *sitting at meat;* for we should take occasion from common things to think and speak of those heavenly and spiritual things which in scripture are *compared* to them, for that is one end of borrowing similitudes from them. And it will be good for us, when we are receiving the gifts of God's providence, to pass through them to the consideration of the gifts of his grace, those *better things.* This thought will be very seasonable when we are partaking of bodily refreshments: *Blessed are they that shall eat bread in the kingdom of God.* (1.) In the kingdom of grace, in the kingdom of the Messiah, which was expected now shortly to be set up. Christ promised his disciples that they should *eat and drink with him in his kingdom.* They that partake of the Lord's supper *eat bread in the kingdom of God.* (2.) In the kingdom of glory, at the resurrection. The happiness of heaven is an *everlasting feast;* blessed are they that shall sit down at that table, whence they shall rise no more.

II. The parable which our Lord Jesus put forth upon this occasion, *v.* 16, etc. Christ joins with the good man in what he said: "It is very true, *Blessed are they that shall partake* of the privileges of the Messiah's kingdom. But who are they that shall enjoy that privilege? You Jews, who think to have the monopoly of it, will generally reject it, and the Gentiles will be the greatest sharers in it." This he shows by a parable, for, if he had spoken it plainly, the Pharisees would not have borne it. Now in the parable we may observe,

1. The free grace and mercy of God, shining in the gospel of Christ; it appears,

(1.) In the rich provision he has made for poor souls, for their nourishment, refreshment, and entertainment (*v.* 16): *A certain man made a great supper.* There is that in Christ and the grace of the gospel which will be *food* and a *feast* for the soul of man that knows its own capacities, for the soul of a sinner that knows its own necessities and miseries. It is called a *supper,* because in those countries supper time was the chief feasting time, when the business of the day was over. The manifestation of gospel grace to the world was the evening of the world's day; and the fruition of the fulness of that grace in heaven is reserved for the evening of our day.

(2.) In gracious invitation given us to come and partake of this provision. Here is, [1.] A general invitation given: He *bade many.* Christ invited the whole nation and people of the Jews to partake of the benefits of his gospel. There is provision enough for as many as come; it was prophesied of as a *feast for all people,* Isa. 25:6. Christ in the gospel, as he keeps a *good* house, so he keeps an *open* house. [2.] A particular memorandum given, when the supper time was at hand; the servant was sent round to put them in mind of it: *Come, for all things are now ready.* When the Spirit was poured out, and the gospel church planted, those who before were invited were more closely pressed to come in *presently:* Now *all things are ready,* the full discovery of the gospel mystery is now made, all the ordinances of the gospel are now instituted, the society of Christians is now incorporated, and, which crowns all, the Holy Ghost is now given. This is the call now given to us: *"All things are now ready,* now is the *accepted time;* it is now, and *has not* been long; it is now, and *will not* be long; it is a season of grace that will be soon over, and therefore *come now;* do not delay; accept the invitation; believe yourselves welcome; *eat, O friends; drink, yea drink abundantly, O beloved."*

2. The cold entertainment which the grace of the gospel meets with. The invited guests declined coming. They did not say flatly and plainly that they *would not come,* but *they all with one consent began to make excuse, v.* 18. One would have expected that they should *all with one consent* have come to a good supper, when they were so kindly invited to it: who would have refused such an invitation? Yet, on the contrary, they all found out some pretence or other to shift off their attendance. This bespeaks the general neglect of the Jewish nation to close with Christ, and accept of the offers of his grace, and the contempt they put upon the invitation. It also intimates the backwardness there is in most people to close with the gospel call. They cannot for shame avow their refusal, but they desire to be *excused:* they all *ato mias,* some supply *hōras, all straightway,* they could give an answer *extempore,* and needed not to study for it, had *not to seek* for an excuse. Others supply *gnōmēs,* they were *unanimous* in it; *with one voice.* (1.) Here were *two* that were *purchasers,* who were in such haste to go and see their purchases that they could not find time to go to this supper. One had *purchased land;* he had *bought a piece of ground,* which was represented to him to be a good bargain, and he must needs *to and see* whether it was so or no; and therefore *I pray thee have me excused.* His heart was so much upon the enlarging of his estate that he could neither be civil to his friend nor kind to himself. Note, Those that have their hearts full of the world, and fond of *laying house to house* and *field to field,* have their ears deaf to the gospel invitation. But what a frivolous excuse was this! He might have deferred going to see his piece of ground till the next day, and have found it in the same place and plight it was now in, if he had so pleased. Another had purchased *stock* for his land. *"I have bought five yoke of oxen* for the plough, and I must just now go and *prove them,* must go and try whether they be fit for my purpose; and therefore excuse me for this time." The former intimates that inordinate *complacency* in the world, this the inordinate *care* and *concern* about the world, which keep people from Christ and his grace; both intimate a preference given to the body above the soul, and to the things of time above those of eternity. Note, It is very criminal, when we are called to any duty, to make excuses for our neglect of it: it is a sign that there are convictions that it is duty, but no inclination to it. These things here, that were the matter of the excuses, were, [1.] *Little things,* and of small concern. It had better become them to have said, "I am invited *to eat bread in the kingdom of God,* and therefore must be excused from going to see the *ground* or the *oxen."* [2.] *Lawful things.* Note, *Things lawful in themselves,* when the heart is too much set upon them, *prove fatal* hindrances in religion — *Licitus perimus omnes.* It is a hard matter so to manage our worldly affairs that they may not divert us from spiritual pursuits; and this ought to be our great care. (2.) Here was one that was *newly married,* and could not leave his wife to go out to supper, no, not for once (*v.* 30): *I have married a wife, and therefore,* in short, *I cannot come.* He pretends that he *cannot,* when the truth is he *will not.* Thus many pretend *inability* for the duties of religion when really they have an *aversion* to them. He has *married a wife.* It is true, he that married was excused by the law from going to war for the first year (Deu. 24:5), but would that excuse him from going up to the feasts of the Lord, which all the males were yearly to attend? Much less will it excuse from the gospel feast, of which the other were but types. Note, Our affection to our relations often proves a hindrance to us in our duty to God. Adam's excuse was, *The woman that thou gavest me persuaded me to eat;* this here was, *The woman persuaded me not to eat.* He might have gone and taken his wife along with him; they would both have been welcome.

3. The account which was brought to the master of the feast of the affront put upon him by his friends whom he had invited, who now showed how little they valued him (*v.* 21): *That servant came, and showed his lord these things,* told him with surprise that he was likely to sup alone, for the guests that were invited, though they had had timely notice a good while before, that they might order their affairs accordingly, yet were now engaged in some other business. He made the matter neither better nor worse, but related it just as it was. Note, Ministers must give account of the success of their ministry. They must do it now at the throne of grace. If they see of *the travail of their soul,* they must go to God with their *thanks;* if they *labour in vain,* they must go to God with their *complaints.* They will do it hereafter at the judgment-seat of Christ: they shall be produced as witnesses *against* those who persist and perish in their unbelief, to prove that they were fairly invited; and *for those* who accepted the call, *Behold, I and the children thou hast given me.* The apostle urges this as a reason why people should give ear to the word of God sent them by his ministers; for *they watch for your souls, as those that must give account,* Heb. 13:17.

4. The master's just resentment of this affront: *He was angry, v.* 21. Note, The ingratitude of those that slight gospel offers, and the contempt they put upon the God of heaven thereby, are a very great provocation to him, and justly so. Abused mercy turns into the greatest wrath. The doom he passed upon them was, *None of the men that were bidden shall taste of my supper.* This was like the doom passed upon the ungrateful Israel, when they despised the pleasant land: God *swore in his wrath that they should not enter into his rest.* Note, Grace despised is grace forfeited, like Esau's birthright. They that will not have Christ when they *may* shall not have him when they *would.* Even those that *were bidden,* if they slight the invitation, *shall be for*bidden; when the door is shut, the foolish virgins will be denied entrance.

5. The care that was taken to furnish the table with guests, as well as meat. "Go" (saith he to the servants), *"go first into the streets and lanes of the city,* and invite, not the merchants that are going from the custom-house, nor the tradesmen that are shutting up their shops; they will *desire to be excused* (one is going to his counting-house to cast up his books, another to the tavern to drink a bottle with his friend); but, that you may invite those that will be glad to come, bring in *hither the poor and the maimed, the halt and the blind;* pick up the common beggars." The servants object not that it will be a disparagement to the master and his house to have such guests at his table; for they know his mind, and they soon gather an abundance of such guests: *Lord, it is done as thou hast commanded.* Many of the Jews are brought in, not of the scribes and Pharisees, such as Christ was *now at dinner with,* who thought themselves most likely to be guests at the Messiah's table, but the publicans and sinners; these are *the poor and the maimed.* But *yet there is room* for more guests, and provision enough for them all. "Go, then, *secondly, into the highways and hedges.* Go out into the country, and pick up the vagrants, or those that are returning now in the evening from their work in the field, from hedging and ditching there, and *compel them to come in,* not by force of arms, but by force of arguments. Be earnest with them; for in this case it will be necessary to convince them that the invitation is *sincere* and not a *banter;* they will be shy and modest, and will hardly believe that they shall be welcome, and therefore be importunate with them and do not leave them till you have prevailed with them." This refers to the *calling of the Gentiles,* to whom the apostles were to *turn* when the Jews refused the offer, and with them the church was filled. Now observe here, (1.) The provision made for precious souls in the gospel of Christ shall appear not to have been made *in vain;* for, if some *reject it,* yet others will thankfully *accept* the offer of it. Christ comforts himself with this, that, *though Israel be not gathered,* yet he shall be *glorious, as a light to the Gentiles,* Isa. 49:5, 6. God will have a church in the world, though there are those that are unchurched; for *the unbelief of man shall not make the promise of God of no effect.* (2.) Those that are very poor and low in the world shall be as welcome to Christ as the rich and great; nay, and many times the gospel has greatest success among those that labour under worldly disadvantages, as the *poor,* and bodily infirmities, as *the maimed, and the halt,* and *the blind.* Christ here plainly refers to what he had said just before, in direction to us, to invite to our tables *the poor and maimed, the lame and blind, v.* 13. For consideration for the countenance which Christ's gospel gives to the poor should engage us to be charitable to them. His condescensions and compassions towards them should engage ours. (3.) Many times the gospel has the *greatest success* among those that are *least likely* to have the benefit of it, and whose submission to it was least expected. The publicans and harlots went into the kingdom of God before the scribes and Pharisees; *so the last shall be first, and the first last.* Let us not be *confident* concerning those that are most forward, nor despair of those that are least promising. (4.) Christ's ministers must be both very expeditious and very importunate in inviting to the gospel feast: *"Go out quickly* (*v.* 21); lose not time, because *all things are now ready.* Call to them to come *to-day, while it is called to-day;* and *compel them to come in,* by accosting them kindly, and *drawing* them *with the cords of a man and the bands of love."* Nothing can be more absurd than fetching an argument hence for compelling men's consciences, nay, for compelling men against their consciences, in matters of religion: "You shall receive the Lord's supper, or you shall be fined and imprisoned, and ruined in your estate." Certainly nothing like this was the compulsion here meant, but only that of reason and love; for *the weapons of our warfare are not carnal.* (5.) Though many have been brought in to partake of the benefits of the gospel, yet still *there is room for more;* for the riches of Christ are *unsearchable* and *inexhaustible;* there is in him enough for all, and enough for each; and the gospel excludes none that do not exclude themselves. (6.) Christ's

house, though it be *large,* shall at last be *filled;* it will be so when the number of the elect is completed, and as many as were *given him* are *brought to him.*

Verses 25–35

See how Christ in his doctrine suited himself to those to whom he spoke, and *gave every one his portion of meat.* To Pharisees he preached humility and charity. He is in these verses directing his discourse to the multitudes that crowded after him, and seemed zealous in following him; and his exhortation to them is to understand the terms of discipleship, before they undertook the profession of it, and to consider what they did. See here,

I. How zealous people were in their attendance on Christ (*v.* 25): *There went great multitudes with him,* many for love and more for company, for where there are *many* there will be *more.* Here was a *mixed multitude,* like that which went with Israel out of Egypt; such we must expect there will always be in the church, and it will therefore be necessary that ministers should carefully separate *between the precious and the vile.*

II. How *considerate* he would have them to be in their *zeal.* Those that undertake to follow Christ must count upon the worst, and prepare accordingly.

1. He tells them what the worst is that they must count upon, much the same with what he had gone through *before* them and *for* them. He takes it for granted that they had a mind to be *his disciples,* that they might be *qualified* for preferment in his kingdom. They expected that he should say, "If any man come to me, and be my disciple, he shall have wealth and honour in abundance; let me alone to make him a great man." But he tells them quite the contrary.

(1.) They must be willing to *quit* that which was *very dear,* and therefore must come to him thoroughly *weaned from* all their creature-comforts, and *dead* to them, so as cheerfully to part with them rather than quit their interest in Christ, *v.* 26. A man cannot be Christ's disciple but he must *hate father, and mother, and his own life.* He is not *sincere,* he will be *constant* and persevering, unless he love Christ better than any thing in this world, and be willing to part with that which he may and must leave, either as a *sacrifice,* when Christ may be glorified by our parting with it (so the martyrs, who *loved not their lives to death*), or as a *temptation,* when by our parting with it we are put into a better capacity of serving Christ. Thus Abraham parted with his own country, and Moses with Pharaoh's court. Mention is not made here of *houses* and *lands;* philosophy will teach a man to look upon these with contempt; but Christianity carries it higher. [1.] Every good man loves *his relations;* and yet, if he be a disciple of Christ, he must comparatively *hate them,* must love them *less than Christ,* as Leah is said to be *hated* when Rachel was better loved. Not that their persons must be in any degree hated, but our comfort and satisfaction in them must be lost and swallowed up in our love to Christ, as Levi's was, when he *said to his father, I have not seen him,* Deu. 33:9. When our duty to our parents comes in competition with our evident duty to Christ, we must give Christ the preference. If we must either *deny Christ* or be *banished* from our families and relations (as many of the primitive Christians were), we must rather lose their society than his favour. [2.] Every man loves *his own life,* no man ever yet *hated it;* and we cannot be Christ's disciples if we do not love him better than our own lives, so as rather to have our lives *embittered* by cruel *bondage,* nay, and *taken away* by cruel *deaths,* than to dishonour Christ, or depart from any of his truths and ways. The experience of the pleasures of the *spiritual life,* and the believing hopes and prospects of *eternal life,* will make this *hard saying* easy. When tribulation and persecution arise because of the word, then chiefly the trial is, whether we love better, Christ or our relations and lives; yet even in the *days of* peace this matter is sometimes brought to the trial. Those that decline the service of Christ, and opportunities of converse with him, and are ashamed to confess him, for fear of disobliging a relation or friend, or losing a customer, give cause to suspect that they love him better than Christ.

(2.) That they must be willing to *bear* that which was very *heavy* (*v.* 27): *Whosoever doth not bear his cross,* as those did that were condemned to be crucified, in *submission* to the sentence and in *expectation* of the execution of it, and so *come after me* whithersoever I shall lead him, he *cannot be my disciple;* that is (says Dr. Hammond), he is not *for my turn;* and my service, being so sure to bring persecution along with it, will not be *for his.* Though the disciples of Christ are not *all crucified,* yet they all *bear their cross,* as if they counted upon being crucified. They must be content to be put into an ill name, and to be loaded with infamy and disgrace; for no name is more ignominious than *Furcifer — the bearer of the gibbet.* He must bear his cross, and *come after Christ;* that is, he must bear it in the way of his duty, whenever it lies in that way. He must bear it when Christ calls him to it, and in bearing it he must have an eye to Christ, and fetch encouragements from him, and live in hope of a recompence with him.

2. He bids them count upon it, and then consider of it. Since he has been so *just to us* as to tell us plainly what difficulties we shall meet with in following him, let us be so *just to ourselves* as to weigh the matter seriously before we take upon us a profession of religion. Joshua obliged the people to consider what they did when they promised to *serve the Lord,* Jos. 24:19. It is better never to begin than not to proceed; and therefore before we begin we must consider what it is to proceed. This is to act rationally, and as becomes men, and as we do in other cases. The cause of Christ will bear a scrutiny. Satan shows the best, but hides the worst, because his best will not counter-vail his worst; but Christ's will abundantly. This considering of the case is necessary to perseverance, especially in suffering times. Our Saviour here illustrates the necessity of it by two similitudes, the former showing that we must consider the *expenses* of our religion, the latter that we must consider the *perils* of it.

(1.) When we take upon us a profession of religion we are like a man that undertakes to *build a tower,* and therefore must consider the *expense of it* (*v.* 28–30): *Which of you, intending to build a tower* or stately house for himself, *sitteth not down first, and counteth the cost?* and he must be sure to count upon a great deal more than his workmen will tell him it will cost. Let him compare the charge with his purse, lest he make himself to be laughed at, by *beginning to build* what he is *not able to finish.* Note, [1.] All that take upon them a profession of religion undertake to *build a tower,* not as the tower of Babel, in opposition to Heaven, which therefore was left unfinished, but in obedience to Heaven, which therefore shall have its *top-stone brought forth.* Begin low, and lay the foundation deep, lay it on the rock, and make sure work, and then aim as high as heaven. [2.] Those that intend to build this tower must *sit down and count the cost.* Let them consider that it *will cost them* the mortifying of their sins, even the most beloved lusts; it will cost them a life of self-denial and watchfulness, and a constant course of holy duties; it *may,* perhaps, *cost them* their reputation among men, their estates and liberties, and all that is dear to them in this world, even life itself. And if it should cost us all this, what is it in comparison with what it cost Christ to purchase the advantages of religion for us, which come to us without money and without price? [3.] Many that begin to *build this tower* do not *go on with it,* nor persevere in it, and it is their folly; they have not courage and resolution, have not a rooted fixed principle, and so bring nothing to pass. It is true, we have none of us in ourselves *sufficient to finish* this tower, but Christ hath said, *My grace is sufficient for thee,* and that grace shall not be wanting to any of us, if we seek for it and make use of it. [4.] Nothing is more *shameful* than for those that have begun well in religion to break off; every one will justly *mock him,* as having lost all his labour hitherto for want of perseverance. We *lose the things we have wrought* (2 Jn. 8), and all we have done and suffered is *in vain,* Gal. 3:4.

(2.) When we undertake to be Christ's disciples we are like a man that *goes to war,* and therefore must consider the *hazard* of it, and the difficulties that are to be encountered, *v.* 31, 32. A king that declares war against a neighbouring prince considers whether he has strength wherewith to make his part good, and, if not, he will lay aside his thoughts of war. Note, [1.] The state of a Christian in this world is a military state. *Is not* the Christian *life a warfare?* We have many passes in our way, that must be disputed with dint of sword; nay, we must fight every step we go, so restless are our spiritual enemies in their opposition. [2.] We ought to consider whether we can *endure the hardness* which a good soldier of Jesus Christ must expect and count upon, before we enlist ourselves under Christ's banner; *whether* we are able to encounter the forces of hell and earth, which come against us *twenty thousand* strong. [3.] Of the two it is better to make the best terms we can with the world than pretend to renounce it and afterwards, when tribulation and persecution arise because of the word, to *return to it.* That *young man* that could not find in his heart to part with his possessions for Christ did better to go away from Christ *sorrowing* than to have staid with him *dissembling.*

This parable is another way applicable, and may be taken as designed to teach us to begin *speedily* to be religious, rather than to begin *cautiously;* and may mean the same with Mt. 5:25, *Agree with thine adversary quickly.* Note, *First,* Those that persist in sin make war against God, the most unnatural, unjustifiable war; they rebel against their lawful sovereign, whose government is perfectly just and good. *Secondly,* The proudest and most daring sinner is no equal match for God; the disproportion of strength is much greater than that here supposed between *ten thousand* and *twenty thousand. Do we provoke the Lord to jealousy? Are we stronger than he?* No, surely; *who knows the power of his anger?* In consideration of this, it is our interest to make peace with him. We need not send to *desire conditions of peace;* they are offered to us, and are unexceptionable, and highly to our advantage. Let us acquaint ourselves with them, and be at peace; do this in time, *while the other is yet a great way off;* for delays in such a case are highly dangerous, and make after-applications difficult.

But the application of this parable here (*v.* 33) is to the consideration that ought to be exercised when we take upon us a profession of religion. Solomon saith, *With good advice make war* (Prov. 20:18); for he that *draws the sword throws away the scabbard;* so *with good advice* enter upon a profession of religion, as those that know that *except you forsake all you have you cannot be Christ's disciples;* that is, except you count upon forsaking all and consent to it, for all that will live godly in Christ Jesus must *suffer persecution,* and yet continue to *live godly.*

3. He warns them against apostasy and a degeneracy of mind from the truly Christian spirit and temper, for that would make them utterly useless, *v.* 34, 35. (1.) Good Christians are *the salt of the earth,* and good ministers especially (Mt. 5:13); and this *salt is good* and of great use; by their instructions and examples they season all they converse with, to keep them from putrefying, and to quicken them, and make them savoury. (2.) Degenerate Christians, who, rather than part with what they have in the world, will throw up their profession, and then of course become carnal, and worldly, and wholly destitute of a Christian spirit, are like *salt that has lost its savour,* like that which the chemists call the *caput mortuum,* that has all its salts drawn from it, that is the most useless worthless thing in the world; it has no manner of virtue or good property in it. [1.] It can never be recovered: *Wherewith shall it be seasoned?* You cannot salt it. This intimates that it is extremely difficult, and next to impossible, to recover an apostate, Heb. 6:4–6. If Christianity will not prevail to cure men of their worldliness and sensuality, if that remedy has been tried in vain, their ease must even be concluded desperate. [2.] It is of no use. It is *not fit,* as dung is, *for the land,* to manure that, nor will it be the better if it be laid in the dunghill to rot; there is nothing to be got out of it. A professor of religion whose mind and manners are depraved is the most *insipid* animal that can be. If he speaks of the things of God, of which he has had some knowledge, it is so *awkwardly* that none are the better for it: it is a *parable in the mouth of a fool.* [3.] It is abandoned: *Men cast it out,* as that which they will have no more to do with. Such scandalous professors ought to be cast out of the church, not only because they have forfeited all the honours and privileges of their church-membership, but because there is danger that others will be infected by them. Our Saviour concludes this with a call to all to take notice of it, and to take warning: *He that hath ears to hear, let him hear.* Now can the faculty of hearing be better employed than in attending to the word of Christ, and particularly to the alarms he has given us of the danger we are in *of* apostasy, and the danger we run ourselves into *by* apostasy?

CHAPTER 15

Evil manners, we say, beget good laws; so, in this chapter, the murmuring of the scribes and Pharisees at the grace of Christ, and the favour he showed to publicans and sinners, gave occasion for a more full discovery of that grace than perhaps otherwise we should have had in these three parables which we have in this chapter, the scope of all of which is the same, to show, not only what God had said and sworn in the Old Testament, that he had no pleasure in the death and ruin of sinners, but that he had great pleasure in their return and repentance, and rejoices in the gracious entertainment he gives them thereupon.

Here is, I. The offence which the Pharisees took at Christ for conversing with heathen men and publicans, and preaching his gospel to them (*v.* 1, 2). II. His justifying himself in it, by the design and proper tendency of it, with which many had been the effect of it, and that was, the bringing of them to repent and reform their lives, than which there could not be a more pleasing and acceptable service done to God, which he shows in the parables, 1. Of the lost sheep that was brought home with joy (*v.* 4–7). 2. Of the lost silver that was found with joy (*v.* 8–10). 3. Of the lost son that had been a prodigal, but returned to his father's house, and was received with great joy, though his elder brother, like these scribes and Pharisees, was offended at it (*v.* 11–32).

Verses 1–10

Here is, I. The diligent attendance of the publicans and sinners upon Christ's ministry. *Great multitudes* of Jews *went with him* (*ch.* 14:25), with such an assurance of admission into the kingdom of God that he found it requisite to say that to them which would shake their vain hopes. Here multitudes of *publicans* and *sinners* drew near to him, with a humble modest fear of being *rejected* by him, and to them he found it requisite to give encouragement, especially because there were some haughty supercilious people that frowned upon them. The *publicans,* who collected the tribute paid to the *Romans,* were perhaps some of them *bad men,* but they were all industriously put into an *ill name,* because of the prejudices of the Jewish nation against their office. They are sometimes ranked with *harlots* (Mt. 21:32); here and elsewhere with *sinners,* such as were openly vicious, that traded with *harlots,* known rakes. Some think that the *sinners* here meant were *heathen,* and that Christ was now on the other side Jordan, or in *Galilee of the Gentiles.* These *drew near,* when perhaps the multitude of the Jews that had followed him had (upon his discourse in the close of the foregoing chapter) *dropped off;* thus afterwards the Gentiles took their turn in hearing the apostles, when the Jews had rejected them. *They drew near to him,* being afraid of drawing nearer than just to come within *hearing.* They drew near to him, not, as some did, to solicit for cures, but to hear his excellent doctrine. Note, in all our approaches to Christ we must have this in our eye, to *hear him;* to hear the instructions he gives us, and his answers to our prayers.

II. The offence which the *scribes* and *Pharisees* took at this. They *murmured,* and turned it to the reproach of our Lord Jesus: *This man receiveth sinners, and eateth with them, v.* 2. 1. They were angry that *publicans* and *heathens* had the means of grace allowed them, were called to repent, and encouraged to hope for pardon upon repentance; for they looked upon their case as *desperate,* and thought that none but Jews had the privilege of repenting and being pardoned, though the prophets preached repentance to the nations, and Daniel particularly to Nebuchadnezzar. 2. They thought it a disparagement to Christ, and inconsistent with the dignity of his character, to make himself familiar with such sort of people, to *admit* them into his company and to *eat with them.* They could not, for shame, condemn him for *preaching to them,* though that was the thing they were most enraged at; and therefore they reproached him for *eating with them,* which was more expressly contrary to the tradition of the elders. Censure will fall, not only upon the most innocent and the most excellent *persons,* but upon the most innocent and most excellent *actions,* and we must not think it strange.

III. Christ's justifying himself in it, by showing that the worse these people were, to whom he preached, the more glory would redound to God, and the more joy there would be in heaven, if by his preaching they were brought to repentance. It would be a more pleasing sight in heaven to see Gentiles brought to the worship of the true God than to see Jews go on in it, and to see publicans and sinners live an orderly sort of life than to see *scribes* and *Pharisees* go on in living such a life. This he here illustrates by two parables, the explication of both of which is the same.

1. The parable of the *lost sheep.* Something like it we had in Mt. 18:12. There it was designed to show the care God takes for the preservation of saints, as a reason why we should not offend them; here it is designed to show the pleasure God takes in the conversion of sinners, as a reason why we should rejoice in it. We have here,

(1.) The case of a sinner that goes on in sinful ways. He is like a *lost sheep,* a sheep *gone astray;* he is *lost* to God, who has not the honour and service he should have from him; *lost* to the flock, which has not communion with him; *lost* to himself: he knows not where he is, wanders endlessly, is continually exposed to the beasts of prey, subject to frights and terrors, from under the shepherd's care, and wanting the green pastures; and he cannot of himself find the way back to the fold.

(2.) The care the God of heaven takes of poor wandering sinners. He *continues* his care of the sheep that did not go astray; they are *safe in the wilderness.* But there is a particular care to be taken of this lost sheep; and though he has a hundred sheep, a considerable flock, yet he will not *lose* that *one,* but he goes after it, and shows abundance of care, [1.] In *finding it out.* He follows it, enquiring after it, and looking about for it, until he *finds* it. God follows backsliding sinners with the calls of his word and the strivings of his Spirit, until at length they are wrought upon to think of returning. [2.] In *bringing it home.* Though he finds it *weary,* and perhaps *worried* and worn away with its wanderings, and not able to bear being driven home, yet he does not leave it to perish, and say, It is not wroth carrying home; but *lays it on his shoulders,* and, with a great deal of tenderness and labour, brings it to the fold. This is very applicable to the great work of our redemption. Mankind were gone astray, Isa. 53:6. The value of the whole race to God was not so much as that of one sheep to him that had a hundred; what loss would it have been to God if they had all been left to perish? There is a world of holy angels that are as the ninety-nine sheep, a noble flock; yet God sends his Son to *seek and save that which was lost, ch.* 19:10. Christ is said to *gather the lambs in his arms,* and carry *them in his bosom,* denoting his pity and tenderness towards poor sinners; here he is said to bear them *upon his shoulders,* denoting the power wherewith he supports and bears them up; those can never perish whom he carries upon his shoulders.

(3.) The pleasure that God takes in repenting returning sinners. He *lays it on his shoulders rejoicing* that he has not lost his labour in seeking; and the joy is the greater because he began to be out of hope of finding it; and he *calls his friends and neighbours,* the shepherds that keep their flocks about him, *saying, Rejoice with me.* Perhaps among the pastoral songs which the shepherds used to sing there was one for such an occasion as this, of which these words might be the burden, *Rejoice with me, for I have found my sheep which was lost;* whereas they never sung, *Rejoice with me, for I have lost none.* Observe, he calls it *his sheep,* though a *stray,* a wandering sheep. He has a right to it *(all souls are mine),* and he will claim his own, and recover his right; therefore he looks after it himself: *I have found it;* he did not send a servant, but his own Son, the great and good Shepherd, who will find what he seeks, and will be found of those that seek him not.

2. The parable of the *lost piece of silver.* (1.) The *loser* is here supposed to be *a woman,* who will more passionately grieve for her loss, and rejoice in finding what she had lost, than perhaps a man would do, and therefore it the better serves the purpose of the parable. She has *ten pieces of silver,* and out of them loses only one. Let this keep up in us high thoughts of the divine goodness, notwithstanding the sinfulness and misery of the world of mankind, that there are nine to one, nay, in the foregoing parable there are ninety-nine to one, of God's creation, that retain their integrity, in whom God *is* praised, and never *was* dishonoured. O the numberless beings, for aught we know numberless worlds of beings, that never were lost, nor stepped aside from the laws and ends of their creation! (2.) That which is lost is a piece of silver, *drachmēn — the fourth part of a shekel.* The soul is *silver,* of intrinsic worth and value; not base metal, as iron or lead, but *silver,* the mines of which are *royal mines.* The Hebrew word for *silver* is taken from the *desirableness* of it. It is *silver coin,* for so the *drachma* was; it is stamped with God's *image and superscription,* and therefore must be *rendered to him.* Yet it is comparatively but of small value; it was but seven pence half-penny; intimating that if sinful men be left to perish God would be no loser. This silver was lost *in the dirt;* a soul plunged in the world, and overwhelmed with the love of it and care about it, is like a piece of money in the dirt; any one would say, It is a thousand pities that it should *lie there.* (3.) Here is a great deal of care and pains taken in quest of it. The woman *lights a candle,* to look behind the door, under the table, and in every corner of the house, *sweeps the house,* and *seeks diligently till she finds it.* This represents the various means and methods God makes use of to bring lost souls home to himself: he has *lighted the candle* of the gospel, not to show himself the way to us, but to show us the way to him, to discover us to ourselves; he has *swept the house* by the convictions of the word; he *seeks diligently,* his heart is upon it, to bring lost souls to himself. (4.) Here is a great deal of joy for the finding of it: *Rejoice with me, for I have found the piece which I had lost, v.* 9. Those that rejoice desire that others should rejoice with them; those that are merry would have others merry with them. She was glad that she had found the piece of money, though she should spend it in entertaining those whom she called to *make merry with her.* The pleasing surprise of finding it put her, for the present, into a kind of transport, *heurēka, heurēka — I have found, I have found,* is the language of joy.

3. The explication of these two parables is to the same purport (*v.* 7, 10): *There is joy in heaven, joy in the presence of the angels of God, over one sinner that repenteth,* as those publicans and sinners did, some of them at least (and, if but *one of them* did repent, Christ would reckon it worth his while), more than *over* a great number of *just persons, who need no repentance.* Observe,

(1.) The *repentance* and *conversion of sinners* on earth are *matter of joy* and rejoicing *in heaven.* It is possible that the greatest sinners may be brought to repentance. While there is life there is hope, and the worst are not to be despaired of; and the worst of sinners, if they repent and turn, shall find mercy. Yet this is not all, [1.] God will *delight* to show them mercy, will reckon their conversion a return for all the expense he has been at upon them. There is always *joy in heaven.* God *rejoiceth in all his works,* but particularly in the works of his grace. He rejoiceth to do good to penitent sinners, with his *whole heart* and his *whole soul.* He rejoiceth not only in the conversion of churches and nations, but even over *one sinner that repenteth,* though but *one.* [2.] The good angels will be glad that mercy is shown them, so far are they from repining at it, though those of their nature that sinned be left to perish, and no mercy shown to them; though those sinners that repent, that are so mean, and have been so vile, are, upon their repentance, to be taken into communion with them, and shortly to be made like them, and equal to them. The conversion of sinners is the joy of angels, and they gladly become ministering spirits to them for their good, upon their conversion. The redemption of mankind was matter of joy in the presence of the angels; for they sung, *Glory to God in the highest, ch.* 2:14.

(2.) There is more joy over *one sinner that repenteth,* and turneth to be religious from a course of life that had been notoriously vile and vicious, than there is *over ninety-nine just persons, who need no repentance.* [1.] More joy for the redemption and salvation of fallen man than for the preservation and confirmation of the angels that stand, and did indeed need no repentance. [2.] More joy for the conversion of the sinners of the Gentiles, and of those publicans that now heard Christ preach, than for all the praises and devotions, and all the *God I thank thee,* of the Pharisees, and the other self-justifying Jews, who though that they *needed no repentance,* and that therefore God should abundantly rejoice in them, and *make his boast* of them, as those that were most *his honour;* but Christ tells them that it was quite otherwise, that God was more praised *in,* and pleased *with,* the penitent broken heart of one of those despised, envied sinners, than all the long prayers which the scribes and Pharisees made, who could not see any thing amiss in themselves. Nay, [3.] More joy for the conversion of one such great sinner, such a Pharisee as Paul had been in his time, than for the regular conversion of one that had always conducted himself decently and well, and comparatively *needs no repentance,* needs not such a universal change of the life as those great sinners need. Not but that it is best not to go astray; but the grace of God, both in the power and the pity of that grace, is more manifested in the *reducing* of great sinners than in the *conducting* of those that never went astray. And many times those that have been great sinners before their conversion prove more eminently and zealously good after, of which Paul is an instance, and therefore in him God was greatly *glorified,* Gal. 1:24. They to whom much is forgiven will love much. It is spoken after the manner of men. We are moved with a more sensible joy for the recovery of what we had lost than for the continuance of what we had always enjoyed, for health *out of* sickness than for health *without* sickness. It is as *life from the dead.* A constant course of religion may in itself be more valuable, and yet a sudden return from an evil course and way of sin may yield a more surprising pleasure. Now if there is such *joy in heaven,* for the conversion of sinners, then the Pharisees were very much strangers to a heavenly spirit, who did all they could to hinder it and were grieved at it, and who were exasperated at Christ when he was doing a piece of work that was of all others most grateful to Heaven.

Verses 11–32

We have here the parable of the prodigal son, the scope of which is the same with those before, to show how pleasing to God the conversion of sinners is, of great sinners, and how ready he is to receive and entertain such, upon their repentance; but the circumstances of the parable do much more largely and fully set forth the riches of gospel grace than those did, and it has been, and will be while the world stands, of unspeakable use to poor sinners, both to direct and to encourage them in repenting and returning to God. Now,

I. The parable represents God as a *common Father* to all mankind, to the whole family of Adam. We are all his *offspring,* have all *one Father,* and *one God created us,* Mal. 2:10. *From him* we *had* our being, *in him* we still *have it,* and from him we receive our *maintenance.* He is *our Father,* for he has the *educating* and *portioning* of us, and will *put us in* his testament, or *leave us out,* according as we are, or are not, dutiful children to him. Our Saviour hereby intimates to those proud Pharisees that these publicans and sinners, whom they thus despised, were their brethren, partakers of the same nature, and therefore they ought to be glad of any kindness shown them. God is the God, *not of the Jews only, but of the Gentiles,* (Rom. 3:29): the *same Lord over all, that is rich in mercy to all that call upon him.*

II. It represents the children of men as of *different* characters, though all related to God as their common Father. He had *two sons,* one of them a solid grave youth, *reserved* and *austere,* sober himself, but not at all *good-humoured* to those about him; such a one would adhere to his education, and not be easily drawn from it; but the other *volatile* and *mercurial,* and impatient of restraint, roving, and willing to try his fortune, and, if he fall into ill hands, likely to be a rake, notwithstanding his virtuous education. Now this latter represents the publicans and sinners, whom Christ is endeavouring to bring to repentance, and the Gentiles, to whom the apostles were to be sent forth to *preach repentance.* The former represents the Jews in general, and particularly the Pharisees, whom he was endeavouring to reconcile to that grace of God which was offered to, and bestowed upon, sinners.

The *younger son* is the prodigal, whose character and case are here designed to represent that of a sinner, that of every one of us in our natural state, but especially of some. Now we are to observe concerning him,

1. His *riot* and *ramble* when he was a prodigal, and the extravagances and miseries he fell into. We are told,

(1.) What his request to his father was (*v.* 12): *He said to his father,* proudly and pertly enough, *"Father, give me"* — he might have put a little more in his mouth, and have said, *Pray give me,* or, *Sir, if you please, give me,* but he makes an imperious demand — *"give me the portion of goods that falleth to me;* not so much as you *think fit* to allot to me, but that which falls to me as *my due."* Note, It is bad, and the beginning of worse, when men look upon God's gifts as debts. *"Give me the portion,* all *my child's part,* that falls to me;" not, *"Try me with a little,* and see how I can manage that, and accordingly trust me with more;" but, *"Give it me all* at present in possession, and I will never expect any thing in *reversion,* any thing *hereafter."* Note, The great folly of sinners, and that which ruins them, is being content to have *their portion in hand,* now in this lifetime to *receive their good things.* They look only at the things that are seen, that are temporal, and covet only a present gratification, but have no care for a future felicity, when that is spent and gone. And why did he desire to have his portion in his own hands? Was it that he might apply himself to business, and trade with it, and so make it more? No, he had no thought of that. But, [1.] He was *weary* of his *father's government,* of the good order and discipline of his father's family, and was fond of liberty falsely so called, but indeed the greatest slavery, for such a *liberty to sin* is. See the folly of many young men, who are religiously educated, but are impatient of the confinement of their education, and never think themselves their own masters, their own men, till they have broken all God's bands in sunder, and cast away his cords from them, and, instead of them, bound themselves with the cords of their own lust. Here is the original of the apostasy of sinners from God; they will not be tied up to the rules of *God's government;* they will themselves *be as gods,* knowing no other *good and evil* than what themselves please. [2.] He was willing to get *from under his father's eye,* for that was always a check upon him, and often gave a check to him. A shyness of God, and a willingness to disbelieve his omniscience, are at the bottom of the wickedness of the wicked. [3.] He was distrustful of his *father's management.* He would have his *portion of goods* himself, for he thought that his father would be laying up for hereafter for him, and, in order to that, would limit him in his present expenses, and that he did not like. [4.] He was *proud of himself,* and had a *great conceit of his own sufficiency.* He thought that if he had but his portion in his own hands he could manage it better than his father did, and make a better figure with it. There are more young people ruined by *pride* than by any one lust whatsoever. Our first parents ruined themselves and all theirs by a foolish ambition to be *independent,* and not to be beholden even to God himself; and this is at the bottom of sinners' persisting in their sin — they will be *for themselves.*

(2.) How kind his father was to him: *He divided unto them his living.* He computed what he had to dispose of between his sons, and gave the younger son *his share,* and offered the elder his, which ought to be a *double portion;* but, it should seem, he desired his father to keep it in his own hands still, and we may see what he got by it (*v.* 31): *All that I have is thine.* He got all by staying for something in reserve. He gave the younger son what he asked, and the son had no reason to complain that he did him any wrong in the dividend; he had as much as he expected, and perhaps more. [1.] Thus he might *now see his father's kindness,* how willing he was to please him and make him easy, and that he was not such an unkind father as he was willing to represent him when he wanted an excuse to be gone. [2.] Thus he would in a little time be made to see *his own folly,* and that he was not such a wise manager for himself as he would be thought to be. Note, God is a kind Father to all his children, and gives to them all *life, and breath, and all things,* even to the evil and unthankful, *dieilen autois ton bion — He divided to them life.* God's giving us life is putting us in a capacity to serve and glorify him.

(3.) How he managed himself when he had got his portion in his own hands. He set himself to spend it as fast as he could, and, as prodigals generally do, in a little time he made himself a beggar: *not many days after, v.* 13. Note, if God leave us ever so little to ourselves, it will not be long ere we depart from him. When the bridle of restraining grace is taken off we are soon gone. That which the younger son determined was to *be gone* presently, and, in order to that, he *gathered all together.* Sinners, that go astray from God, *venture their all.*

Now the condition of the prodigal in this ramble of his represents to us a *sinful state,* that *miserable* state into which man is *fallen.*

[1.] A sinful state is a state of *departure* and *distance* from God. *First,* It is the *sinfulness* of sin that it is an apostasy from God. He *took his journey* from his father's house. Sinners are fled from God; they *go a whoring from him;* they revolt from their allegiance to him, as a servant that runs from his service, or a wife that treacherously departs from her husband, and they say unto God, *Depart.* They get as far off him as they can. The world is the *far country* in which they take up their residence, and are as at home; and in the service and enjoyment of it they spend their all. *Secondly.* It is the misery of sinners that they are afar off from God, from him who is the Fountain of all good, and are going further and further from him. What is hell itself, but being *afar off* from God?

[2.] A sinful state is a *spending* state: There he *wasted his substance with riotous living* (*v.* 13), devoured it *with harlots* (*v.* 30), and in a little time *he had spent all, v.* 14. He bought fine clothes, spent a great deal in meat and drink, treated high, associated with those that helped him to make an end of what he had in a little time. As to this world, they that *live riotously waste* what they have, and will have a great deal to answer for, that they spend that upon their lusts which should be for the necessary substance of themselves and their families. But this is to be applied spiritually. Wilful sinners *waste* their patrimony; for they misemploy their thoughts and all the powers of their souls, misspend their time and all their opportunities, do not only bury, but embezzle, the talents they are entrusted to trade with for their Master's honour; and the gifts of Providence, which were intended to enable them to serve God and to do good with, are made the food and fuel of their lusts. The soul that is made a drudge, either to the world or to the flesh, *wastes its substance,* and *lives riotously. One sinner destroys much good,* Eccl. 9:18. The good he destroys is valuable, and it is none of his own; they are his *Lord's goods* that he *wastes,* which must be accounted for.

[3.] A sinful state is a *wanting* state: *When he had spent all* upon his harlots, they left him, to seek such another prey; and *there arose a mighty famine in that land,* every thing was scarce and dear, and he *began to be in want, v.* 14. Note, Wilful waste brings woeful want. Riotous living in time, perhaps in a little time, brings men to a *morsel of bread,* especially when *bad times* hasten on the consequences of *bad husbandry,* which good husbandry would have *provided for.* This represents the misery of *sinners,* who have thrown away *their own mercies,* the favour of God, their interest in Christ, the strivings of the Spirit, and admonitions of conscience; these they *gave away* for the pleasure of sense, and the wealth of the world, and then are ready to perish for want of them. Sinners want necessaries for their souls; they have neither food nor raiment for them, nor any provision for hereafter. A sinful state is like a land where *famine reigns,* a *mighty famine;* for the *heaven is as brass* (the dews of God's favour and blessing are withheld, and we must needs want good things if God deny them to us), and the *earth is as iron* (the sinner's heart, that should bring forth good things, is dry and barren, and has no good in it). Sinners are *wretchedly* and *miserably poor,* and, what aggravates it, they brought themselves into that condition, and keep themselves in it by refusing the supplies offered.

[4.] A sinful state is *a vile servile state.* When this young man's riot had brought him to want his want brought him to servitude. *He went, and joined himself to a citizen of that country, v.* 15. The same wicked life that before was represented by *riotous living* is here represented by *servile living;* for sinners are perfect slaves. The devil is the *citizen of that country;* for he is both in city and country. Sinners *join themselves* to him, hire themselves into his service, to do *his work,* to be at *his beck,* and to depend upon him for maintenance and a portion. They that commit sin are the *servants of sin,* Jn. 8:34. How did this young gentleman debase and disparage himself, when he hired himself into such a service and under such a master as this! He *sent him into the fields,* not to feed sheep (there had been some credit in that employment; Jacob, and Moses, and David, kept sheep), but to *feed swine.* The business of the devil's servants is to *make provision for the flesh, to fulfil the lusts thereof,* and that is no better than feeding greedy, dirty, noisy swine; and how can rational immortal souls more disgrace themselves?

[5.] A sinful state is a state of *perpetual dissatisfaction.* When the prodigal began to be in want, he thought to help himself by *going to service;* and he must be content with the provision which not the house, but the field, afforded; but it is poor provision: *He would fain have filled his belly,* satisfied his hunger, and nourished his body, *with the husks which the swine did eat, v.* 16. A fine pass my young master had brought himself to, to be fellow-commoner with the swine! Note, That which sinners, when they *depart from God,* promise themselves *satisfaction in,* will certainly disappoint them; they are *labouring for that which satisfieth not,* Isa. 55:2. That which is the *stumbling-block of their iniquity* will never *satisfy their souls, nor fill their bowels,* Eze. 7:19. Husks are food for swine, but not for men. The wealth of the world and the entertainments of sense will serve for bodies; but what are these to *precious souls?* They neither suit their nature, nor satisfy their desires, nor supply their needs. He that takes up with them *feeds on wind* (Hos. 12:1), *feeds on ashes,* Isa. 44:20.

[6.] A sinful state is a state which *cannot expect relief from any creature.* This prodigal, when he could not earn his bread by *working,* took to *begging;* but *no man gave unto him,* because they knew he had brought all this misery upon himself, and because he was rakish, and provoking to every body; such poor are *least pitied.* This, in the application of the parable, intimates that those who depart from God cannot be helped by any creature. In vain do we cry to the world and the flesh (those gods which we have served); they have that which will *poison* a soul, but have nothing to give it which will *feed* and *nourish* it. If thou refuse God's help, whence shall any creature help thee?

[7.] A sinful state is a *state of death: This my son was dead, v.* 24, 32. A sinner is not only dead in law, as he is under a sentence of death, but dead in state too, dead in trespasses and sins, destitute of spiritual life; no union with Christ, no spiritual senses exercised, no living to God, and therefore *dead.* The prodigal in the *far country* was *dead* to his father and his family, cut off from them, as a member from the body or a branch from the tree, and therefore *dead,* and it is his own doing.

[8.] A sinful state is a *lost state: This my son was lost —* lost to every thing that was good — lost to all virtue and honour — lost to his father's house; they had no joy of him. Souls that are separated from God are *lost* souls; lost as a *traveller* that is out of his way, and, if infinite mercy prevent not, will soon be lost as a ship that is sunk at sea, lost irrecoverably.

[9.] A sinful state is a state of *madness* and frenzy. This is intimated in that expression (v. 17), *when he came to himself,* which intimates that he had been *beside himself.* Surely he was so when he left his father's house, and much more so when he joined himself to the citizen of that country. *Madness* is said to be *in the heart* of sinners, Eccl. 9:3. Satan has got possession of the soul; and how raging mad was he that was possessed by Legion! Sinners, like those that are *mad,* destroy themselves with *foolish lusts,* and yet at the same time deceive themselves with foolish *hopes;* and they are, of all diseased persons, most enemies to their own cure.

2. We have here his *return* from this *ramble,* his penitent *return* to his father again. When he was brought to the last extremity, then he bethought himself how much it was his interest to go home. Note, We must not despair of the worst; for while there is life there is hope. The grace of God can soften the hardest heart, and give a happy turn to the strongest stream of corruption. Now observe here,

(1.) What was the *occasion* of his return and repentance. It was his *affliction;* when he was in *want,* then he *came to himself.* Note, Afflictions, when they are sanctified by divine grace, prove happy means of turning sinners from the error of their ways. By them the ear is opened to discipline and the heart disposed to receive instructions; and they are sensible proofs both of the vanity of the world and of the mischievousness of sin. Apply it spiritually. When we find the insufficiency of creatures to make us happy, and have tried all other ways of relief for our poor souls in vain, then it is time to think of returning to God. When we see what miserable comforters, what physicians of no value, all but Christ are, for a soul that groans under the guilt and power of sin, and no *man gives unto us* what we need, then surely we shall apply ourselves to Jesus Christ.

(2.) What was the *preparative* for it; it was *consideration.* He said within himself, he reasoned with himself, when he recovered his right mind, *How many hired servants of my father's have bread enough!* Note, Consideration is the first step towards conversion, Eze. 18:28. *He considers, and turns.* To consider is to retire into ourselves, to reflect upon ourselves, to compare one thing with another, and determine accordingly. Now observe what it was that he considered.

[1.] He considered how bad his condition was: *I perish with hunger.* Not only, "I am *hungry,*" but, *"I perish with hunger,* for I see not what way to expect relief." Note, Sinners will not come to the service of Christ till they are brought to see themselves just ready to perish in the service of sin; and the consideration of that should drive us to Christ. *Master, save us, we perish.* And though we be thus driven to Christ he will not therefore reject us, nor think himself dishonoured by our being forced to him, but rather honoured by his being applied to in a desperate case.

[2.] He considered how much better it might be made if he would but return: *How many hired servants of my father's,* the meanest in his family, the very day-labourers, *have bread enough, and to spare,* such a good house does he keep! Note, *First,* In our *Father's house* there is bread for all his family. This was taught by the twelve loaves of *showbread,* that were constantly upon the holy table in the sanctuary, a loaf for every tribe. *Secondly,* There is *enough* and to *spare,* enough for all, enough for each, enough to spare for such as will join themselves to his domestics, enough and *to spare* for *charity. Yet there is room;* there are *crumbs* that fall from his table, which many would be glad of, and thankful for. *Thirdly,* Even the *hired servants* in God's family are well provided for; the meanest that will but hire themselves into his family, to *do* his work, and *depend* upon his rewards, shall be well provided for. *Fourthly,* The consideration of this should encourage sinners, that have gone astray from God, to think of returning to him. Thus the adulteress reasons with herself, when she is disappointed in her new lovers: *I will go and re-*

turn to my first husband, for then was it better with me than now, Hos. 2:7.

(3.) What was the *purpose* of it. Since it is so, that his condition is so bad, and may be bettered by returning to his father, his consideration issues, at length, in this conclusion: *I will arise, and go to my father.* Note, Good purposes are good things, but still good performances are all in all.

[1.] He determined what to do: *I will arise and go to my father.* He will not take any longer time to consider of it, but will *forthwith* arise and go. Though he be in a *far country,* a great way off from his father's house, yet, far as it is, he will return; every step of backsliding from God must be a step back again in return to him. Though he be *joined to a citizen of this country,* he makes no difficulty of breaking his bargain with him. We *are not debtors to the flesh;* we are under no obligation at all to our Egyptian task-masters to give them warning, but are at liberty to quit the service when we will. Observe with what resolution he speaks: *"I will arise, and go to my father:* I am resolved I will, whatever the issue be, rather than *stay* here and *starve."*

[2.] He determined what to say. True repentance is a *rising,* and *coming to God: Behold, we come unto thee.* But what words shall we take with us? He here considers what to say. Note, In all our addresses to God, it is good to deliberate with ourselves beforehand what we shall say, that we may *order our cause before him,* and *fill our mouth with arguments.* We have *liberty of speech,* and we ought to consider seriously with ourselves, how we may use that liberty to the utmost, and yet not abuse it. Let us observe what he purposed to say.

First, He would confess his fault and folly: *I have sinned.* Note, Forasmuch as we have all sinned, it behoves us, and well becomes us, to own that we have sinned. The confession of sin is required and insisted upon, as a necessary condition of peace and pardon. If we plead *not guilty,* we put ourselves upon a trial by the covenant of innocency, which will certainly condemn us. If *guilty,* with a contrite, penitent, and obedient heart, we refer ourselves to the covenant of grace, which offers forgiveness to those that *confess their sins.*

Secondly, He would aggravate it, and would be so far from extenuating the matter that he would *lay a load* upon himself for it: I have sinned *against Heaven,* and *before thee.* Let those that are *undutiful* to their *earthly parents* think of this; they sin *against heaven, and before God.* Offences against them are offences against God. Let us all think of this, as that which renders our *sin exceedingly sinful,* and should render us exceedingly sorrowful for it. 1. Sin is committed in contempt of God's authority over us: *We have sinned against Heaven.* God is here called *Heaven,* to signify how highly he is exalted above us, and the dominion he has over us, for the *Heavens do rule.* The malignity of sin aims high; it is *against Heaven.* The daring sinner is said to have *set his mouth against the heavens,* Ps. 63:9. Yet it is *impotent* malice, for we cannot hurt the heavens. Nay, it is foolish malice; what is shot *against the heavens* will return upon the head of him that shoots it, Ps. 7:16. Sin is an affront to the *God of heaven,* it is a forfeiture of the glories and joys of heaven, and a contradiction to the designs of the kingdom of heaven. 2. It is committed in contempt of God's eye upon us: "I have sinned *against Heaven* and yet *before thee,* and under thine eye," than which there could not be a greater affront put upon him.

Thirdly, He would judge and condemn himself for it, and acknowledge himself to have forfeited all the privileges of the family: *I am no more worthy to be called thy son, v.* 19. He does not deny the relation (for that was all he had to trust to), but he owns that his father might justly deny the relation, and shut his doors against him. He had, at his own demand, the portion of goods that belonged to him, and had reason to expect no more. Note, It becomes sinners to acknowledge themselves unworthy to receive any favour from God, and to humble and abase themselves before him.

Fourthly, He would nevertheless sue for admission into the family, though it were into the meanest post there: "*Make me as one of thy hired servants:* that is good enough, and too good for me." Note, True penitents have a high value for God's house, and the privileges of it, and will be glad of any place, so they may but be in it, though it be but as *doorkeepers,* Ps. 84:10. If it be imposed on him as a mortification to sit with the servants, he will not only submit to it, but count it a preferment, in comparison with his present state. Those that return to God, from whom they have revolted, cannot but be desirous some way or other to be employed for him, and put into a capacity of serving and honouring him: "*Make*

me as a hired servant, that I may show I love my father's house as much as ever I slighted it."

Fifthly, In all this he would have an eye to his father as a father: *"I will arise, and go to my father, and will say unto him, Father."* Note, Eyeing God as a Father, and our Father, will be of great use in our repentance and return to him. It will make our sorrow for sin genuine, our resolutions against it strong, and encourage us to hope for pardon. God delights to be called *Father* both by penitents and petitioners. *Is not Ephraim a dear son?*

(4.) What was the performance of this purpose: *He arose, and came to his father.* His good resolve he put in execution without delay; he struck while the iron was hot, and did not adjourn the thought to some more convenient season. Note, It is our interest speedily to close with our convictions. Have we said that we will arise and go? Let us immediately arise and come. He did not come halfway, and then pretend that he was tired and could get no further, but, weak and weary as he was, he made a thorough business of it. *If thou wilt return, O Israel, return unto me,* and *do thy first works.*

3. We have here his reception and entertainment with his father: *He came to his father;* but was he welcome? Yes, heartily welcome. And, by the way, it is an example to parents whose children have been foolish and disobedient, if they repent, and submit themselves, not to be harsh and severe with them, but to be governed in such a case by the wisdom that is from above, which is *gentle and easy to be entreated;* herein let them be followers of God, and merciful, as he is. But it is chiefly designed to set forth the grace and mercy of God to poor sinners that repent and return to him, and his readiness to forgive them. Now here observe,

(1.) The great love and affection wherewith the father received the son: *When he was yet a great way off his father saw him, v.* 20. He expressed his kindness before the son expressed his repentance; for God prevents us with the blessings of his goodness. Even *before we call he answers;* for he knows what is in our hearts. *I said, I will confess, and thou forgavest.* How lively are the images presented here! [1.] Here were *eyes of mercy,* and those eyes quick-sighted: *When he was yet a great way off his father saw him,* before any other of the family were aware of him, as if from the top of some high tower he had been looking that way which his son was gone, with such a thought as this, "O that I could see yonder wretched son of mine coming home!" This intimates God's desire of the conversion of sinners, and his readiness to meet them that are coming towards him. *He looketh on men,* when they are gone astray from him, to see whether they will return to him, and he is aware of the first inclination towards him. [2.] Here were *bowels of mercy,* and those bowels turning within him, and yearning at the sight of his son: *He had compassion.* Misery is the object of pity, even the misery of a sinner; though he has brought it upon himself, yet God compassionates. *His soul was grieved for the misery of Israel,* Hos. 11:8; Jdg. 10:16. [3.] Here were *feet of mercy,* and those feet quick-paced: *He ran.* This denotes how swift God is to show mercy. The prodigal son came slowly, under a burden of shame and fear; but the tender father ran to meet him with his encouragements. [4.] Here were *arms of mercy,* and those arms stretched out to embrace him: *He fell on his neck.* Though guilty and deserving to be beaten, though dirty and newly come from feeding swine, so that any one who had not the strongest and tenderest compassions of a father would have loathed to touch him, yet he thus takes him in his arms, and lays him in his bosom. Thus dear are true penitents to God, thus welcome to the Lord Jesus. [5.] Here were *lips of mercy,* and those lips dropping as a honey-comb: *He kissed him.* This kiss not only *assured* him of his *welcome,* but *sealed his pardon;* his former follies shall be all forgiven, and not mentioned against him, nor is one word said by way of upbraiding. This was like David's kissing Absalom, 2 Sa. 14:33. And this intimates how ready, and free, and forward the Lord Jesus is to receive and entertain poor returning repenting sinners, according to his Father's will.

(2.) The penitent submission which the poor prodigal made to his father (v. 21): He *said unto him, Father, I have sinned.* As it commends the good father's kindness that he showed it before the prodigal expressed his repentance, so it commends the prodigal's repentance that he expressed it after his father had shown him so much kindness. When he had received the kiss which sealed his pardon, yet he said, *Father, I have sinned.* Note, Even those that have received the pardon of their sins, and the comfortable sense of their pardon, must have in their hearts a sincere contrition for it, and with their mouths must make a penitent confession of it, even of those sins which they have reason to hope are pardoned. David penned the fifty-first psalm after Nathan had said, *The Lord has taken away thy sin, thou shall not die.* Nay, the comfortable sense of the pardon of sin should increase our sorrow for it; and that is ingenuous evangelical sorrow which is increased by such a consideration. See Eze. 16:63, *Thou shalt be ashamed and confounded, when I am pacified towards thee.* The more we see of God's readiness to *forgive us,* the more difficult it should be to us to *forgive ourselves.*

(3.) The splendid provision which this kind father made for the returning prodigal. He was going on in his submission, but one word we find in his purpose to say (*v.* 19) which we do not find that he did say (*v.* 21), and that was, *Make me as one of thy hired servants.* We cannot think that he forgot it, much less that he changed his mind, and was now either less desirous to be in the family or less willing to be a hired servant there than when he made that purpose; but his father interrupted him, prevented his saying it: "Hold, son, talk no more of thy unworthiness, thou art heartily welcome, and, though not *worthy to be called a son,* shalt be treated as a *dear son,* as a *pleasant child.*" He who is thus entertained at first needs not ask to be made *as a hired servant.* Thus when *Ephraim bemoaned himself* God comforted him, Jer. 31:18–20. It is strange that here is not one word of rebuke: "Why did you not stay with your harlots and your swine? You could never find the way home till beaten hither with your own rod." No, here is nothing like this; which intimates that, when God forgives the sins of true penitents, he forgets them, he remembers them no more, they *shall not be mentioned against them,* Eze. 18:22. But this is not all; here is rich and royal provision made for him, according to his birth and quality, far beyond what he did or could expect. He would have thought it sufficient, and been very thankful, if his father had but taken notice of him, and bid him go to the kitchen, and get his dinner with his servants; but God does for those who return to their duty, and cast themselves upon his mercy, abundantly above what they are able to ask or think. The prodigal came home between hope and fear, fear of being rejected and hope of being received; but his father was not only better to him than his fears, but better to him than his hopes — not only *received* him, but received him with respect.

[1.] He came home *in rags,* and his father not only *clothed* him, but *adorned* him. He *said to the servants,* who all attended their master, upon notice that his son was come, *Bring forth the best robe, and put it on him.* The worst old clothes in the house might have served, and these had been good enough for him; but the father calls not for a *coat,* but for a *robe,* the garment of princes and great men, the *best robe — tēn stolēn tēn prōtēn.* There is a double emphasis: *"that robe, that principal robe,* you know which I mean;" the *first robe* (so it may be read); the robe he wore before he ran his ramble. When backsliders repent and do their *first works,* they shall be received and dressed in their *first robes.* "Bring hither that robe, and put it on him; he will be ashamed to wear it, and think that it ill becomes him who comes home in such a dirty pickle, but *put it on him,* and do not merely offer it to him: and *put a ring on his hand,* a signet-ring, with the arms of the family, in token of his being owned as a branch of the family." Rich people wore rings, and his father hereby signified that though he had spent one portion, yet, upon his repentance, he intended him another. He came home barefoot, his feet perhaps sore with travel, and therefore, "Put *shoes on his feet,* to make him easy." Thus does the grace of God provide for true penitents. *First,* The *righteousness of Christ* is the robe, that *principal robe,* with which they are clothed; they *put on the Lord Jesus Christ,* are *clothed* with that *Sun.* The *robe of righteousness* is the *garment of salvation,* Isa. 61:10. A *new nature* is this *best robe;* true penitents are clothed with this, being sanctified throughout. *Secondly,* The *earnest* of the Spirit, by whom we are sealed to the day of redemption, is the *ring on the hand.* After *you believed you were sealed.* They that are sanctified are adorned and dignified, are put in power, as Joseph was by Pharaoh's giving him a ring: *"Put a ring on his hand,* to be before him a constant memorial of his father's kindness, that he may never forget it." *Thirdly,* The *preparation of the gospel of peace* is as *shoes for our feet* (Eph. 6:15), so that, compared with this here, signifies (saith Grotius) that God, when he receives true penitents into his favour, makes use of them for the convincing and converting of others by their instructions, at least by their examples. David, when pardoned, will teach transgressors God's ways, and Peter, when converted, will strengthen his brethren. Or it intimates that they shall go on cheerfully, and with resolution, in the way of religion, as a man does when he has shoes on his feet, above what he does when he is barefoot.

[2.] He came home *hungry,* and his father not only *fed him,* but *feasted him* (*v.* 23): *"Bring hither the fatted calf,* that has been stall-fed, and long reserved for some special occasion, and *kill it,* that my son may be satisfied with the best we have." Cold meat might have served, or the leavings of the last meal; but he shall have fresh meat and hot meat, and the fatted calf can never be better bestowed. Note, There is excellent food provided by our heavenly Father for all those that *arise* and *come to him.* Christ himself is the Bread of Life; his flesh is meat indeed, and his blood drink indeed; in him there is a feast for souls, a feast for fat things. It was a great change with the prodigal, who just before *would fain have filled his belly with husks.* How sweet will the supplies of the new covenant be, and the relishes of its comforts, to those who have been *labouring in vain* for satisfaction in the creature! Now he found his own words made good, *In my father's house there is bread enough and to spare.*

(4.) The great joy and rejoicing occasioned by his return. The bringing of the fatted calf was designed to be not only a *feast* for him, but a *festival* for the family: *"Let us all eat, and be merry,* for it is a good day; for *this my son was dead,* when he was in his ramble, but his return is as *life from the dead,* he *is alive again;* we thought that he was dead, having heard nothing from him of a long time, but behold *he lives;* he *was lost,* we gave him up for lost, we despaired of hearing of him, but he *is found.*" Note, [1.] The conversion of a soul from sin to God is the raising of that soul from death to life, and the finding of that which seemed to be lost: it is a great, and wonderful, and happy change. What was in itself *dead* is made *alive,* what was *lost* to God and his church is *found,* and what was *unprofitable* becomes *profitable,* Philem. 11. It is such a change as that upon the face of the earth when the spring returns. [2.] The conversion of sinners is greatly pleasing to the God of heaven, and all that belong to his family ought to rejoice in it; those in heaven *do,* and those on earth *should.* Observe, It was *the father* that began the joy, and set all the rest on rejoicing. *Therefore* we should be glad of the repentance of sinners, because it accomplishes God's design; it is the bringing of those to Christ whom the Father had given him, and in whom he will be for ever glorified. *We joy for your sakes before our God,* with an eye to him (1 Th. 3:9), and *ye are our rejoicing in the presence of our Lord Jesus Christ,* who is the Master of the family, 1 Th. 2:19. The family complied with the master: *They began to be merry.* Note, God's children and servants ought to be affected with things as he is.

4. We have here the *repining and envying of the elder brother,* which is described by way of reproof to the scribes and Pharisees, to show them the folly and wickedness of their discontent at the repentance and conversion of the publicans and sinners, and the favour Christ showed them; and he represents it so as not to aggravate the matter, but as allowing them still the privileges of elder brethren: the Jews had those privileges (though the Gentiles were favoured), for the preaching of the gospel must begin at Jerusalem. Christ, when he reproved them for their faults, yet accosted them mildly, to smooth them into a good temper towards the poor publicans. But by the *elder brother* here we may understand those who are really good, and have been so from their youth up, and never went astray into any vicious course of living, who *comparatively* need no repentance; and to such these words in the close, *Son, thou art ever with me,* are applicable without any difficulty, but not to the scribes and Pharisees. Now concerning the elder brother, observe,

(1.) How *foolish* and *fretful* he was upon occasion of his brother's reception, and how he was disgusted at it. It seems he was abroad *in the field,* in the country, when his brother came, and by the time he had returned home the *mirth* was *begun; When he drew nigh to the house he heard music and dancing,* either while the dinner was getting ready, or rather after they had eaten and were full, *v.* 25. He enquired *what these things meant* (*v.* 26), and was informed that his brother was come, and his father had made him a feast for his *welcome home,* and great joy there was because he had received him *safe and sound, v.* 27. It is but one word in the original, he had *received* him *hygiainonta — in health,* well both in body and mind. He received him not only well in body, but a penitent, returned to his *right mind,* and well reconciled to his father's house, cured of his vices and his rakish disposition, else he had not been received *safe* and *sound.* Now this offended him to the highest degree: *He was angry, and would not go in* (*v.* 28), not only because he was resolved he would not himself join in the mirth, but because he would show his displeasure at it, and would intimate to his father that he should have kept out his younger brother. This shows what is a common fault,

[1.] In men's families. Those who have always been a comfort to their parents think they should have the monopoly of their parents' favours, and are apt to be *too sharp* upon those who have transgressed, and to grudge their parents' kindness to them.

[2.] In God's family. Those who are comparatively *innocents* seldom know how to be compassionate towards those who are manifestly *penitents.* The language of such we have here, in what the *elder brother* said (*v.* 29, 30), and it is written for warning to those who by the grace of God are kept from scandalous sin, and kept in the way of virtue and sobriety, that they sin not after the similitude of this transgression. Let us observe the particulars of it. *First,* He *boasted* of *himself* and *his own virtue* and *obedience.* He had not only not run from his father's house, as his brother did, but had made himself as a *servant* in it, and had long done so: *Lo, these many years do I serve thee, neither transgressed I at any time thy commandment.* Note, It is too common for those that are better than their neighbours to boast of it, yea, and to make their boast of it before God himself, as if he were indebted to them for it. I am apt to think that this elder brother said more than was true, when he gloried that he had never *transgressed his father's commands,* for them I believe he would not have been so obstinate as now he was to *his father's entreaties.* However, we will admit it comparatively; he had not been so disobedient as his brother had been. O what need have good men to take heed of pride, a corruption that arises out of the ashes of other corruptions! Those that have long served God, and been kept from gross sins, have a great deal to be humbly thankful for, but nothing proudly to boast of. *Secondly,* He *complained of his father,* as if he had not been so kind as he ought to have been to him, who had been so dutiful: *Thou never gavest me a kid, that I might make merry with my friends.* He was out of humour now, else he would not have made this complaint; for, no questions, if he had asked such a thing at any time, he might have had it at the first word; and we have reason to think that he did not desire it, but the *killing of the fatted calf* put him upon making this peevish reflection. When men are *in a passion* they are apt to reflect in a way they would not if they were in their right mind. He had been fed at his father's table, and had many a time been merry with him and the family; but his father had never given him so much as a kid, which was but a small token of love compared with the *fatted calf.* Note, Those that think *highly* of themselves and their services are apt to think *hardly* of their master and meanly of his favours. We ought to own ourselves utterly unworthy of those mercies which God has thought fit to give us, much more of those that he has not thought fit to give us, and therefore we must not *complain.* He would have had a kid, to *make merry with his friends* abroad, whereas the *fatted calf* he grudged so much was given to his brother, not to *make merry with his friends* abroad, but *with the family* at home: the mirth of God's children should be with their father and his family, in communion with God and his saints, and not with any *other friends. Thirdly,* He was very *ill-humoured* towards his younger brother, and harsh in what he thought and said concerning him. Some good people are apt to be overtaken in this fault, nay, and to indulge themselves too much in it, to look with disdain upon those who have not preserved their reputation so clean as they have done, and to be sour and morose towards them, yea, though they have given very good evidence of their repentance and reformation. This is not the Spirit of Christ, but of the Pharisees. Let us observe the instances of it. 1. He *would not go in,* except his brother were *turned out;* one house shall not hold him and his own brother, no, not his *father's house.* The language of this was that of the Pharisee (Isa. 65:5): *Stand by thyself, come not near to me, for I am holier than thou;* and (*ch.* 18:11) *I am not as other men are, nor even as this publican.* Note, Though we are to shun the society of those sinners by whom we are in danger of being infected, yet we must not be shy of the company of penitent sinners, by whom we may get good. He saw that his father had *taken him in,* and yet he would not *go in* to him. Note, We think too well of ourselves, if we cannot find in our hearts to *receive* those whom God *hath received,* and to admit those into favour, and friendship, and fellowship with us, whom we have reason to think God has a favour for, and who are taken into friendship and fellowship with him. 2. He would not call him *brother;* but *this thy son,* which sounds arrogantly, and not without reflection upon his father, as if his indulgence had made him a prodigal: "He is *thy son,* thy darling." Note, Forgetting the relation we stand in to our brethren, as brethren, and disowning that, are at the bottom of all our neglects of our duty to them and our contradictions to that duty. Let us give our relations, both in the flesh and in the Lord, the titles that belong to them. Let the rich call the poor *brethren,* and let the innocents call the penitents so. 3. He *aggravated his brother's faults,* and made the worst of them, endeavouring to incense his father against him: He *is thy son, who hath devoured thy living with harlots.* It is true, he had spent his own portion foolishly enough (whether *upon harlots* or no we are not told before, perhaps that was only the language of the elder brother's jealousy and ill will), but that he had devoured *all his father's living* was false; the father had still a good estate. Now this shows how apt we are, in censuring our brethren, to *make the worst* of every thing, and to set it out in the blackest colours, which is not doing as we would be done by, nor as our heavenly Father does by us, who is not extreme to mark iniquities. 4. He *grudged* him the *kindness* that his father *showed him: Thou hast killed for him the fatted calf,* as if he were such a son as he should be. Note, It is a wrong thing to *envy* penitents the grace of God, and to have our eye evil because he is good. As we must not envy those that *are* the worst of sinners the gifts of common providence *(Let not thine heart envy sinners),* so we must not envy those that *have been* the worst of sinners the gifts of covenant love upon their repentance; we must not envy them their pardon, and peace, and comfort, no, nor any extraordinary gift which God bestows upon them, which makes them eminently acceptable or useful. Paul, before his conversion, had been a prodigal, had *devoured* his heavenly Father's *living* by the *havoc* he made of the *church;* yet when after his conversion he had greater measures of grace given him, and more honour put upon him, than the other apostles, they who were the elder brethren, who had been *serving Christ* when he was persecuting him, and had not transgressed at any time his commandment, did not envy him his visions and revelations, nor his more extensive usefulness, but *glorified God in him,* which ought to be an example to us, as the reverse of this elder brother.

(2.) Let us now see how *favourable* and *friendly* his father was in *his carriage towards him* when he was thus sour and ill-humoured. This is as surprising as the former. Methinks the mercy and grace of our God in Christ shine almost as brightly in his tender and gentle bearing with *peevish saints,* represented by the elder brother here, as before in his reception of prodigal sinners upon their repentance, represented by the younger brother. The disciples of Christ themselves had many infirmities, and were men subject to like passions as others, yet Christ bore with them, as a nurse with her children. See 1 Th. 2:7.

[1.] When he would not come in, his *father came out, and entreated him,* accosted him mildly, gave him good words, and desired him to come in. He might justly have said, "If he will not come in, let him stay out, shut the doors against him, and send him to seek a lodging where he can find it. Is not the house my own? and may I not do what I please in it? Is not the fatted calf my own? and may I not do what I please with it?" No, as he to meet the younger son, so now he goes to court the elder, did not send a servant out with a kind message to him, but went himself. Now, *First,* This is designed to represent to us the goodness of God; how strangely gentle and winning he has been towards those that were strangely froward and provoking. He reasoned with Cain: *Why art thou wroth?* He *bore Israel's manners in the wilderness,* Acts 13:18. How mildly did God reason with Elijah, when he was upon the fret (1 Ki. 19:46), and especially with Jonah, whose case was very parallel with this here, for he was there disquieted at the repentance of Nineveh, and the mercy shown to it, as the elder brother here; and those questions, *Dost thou well to be angry?* and, *Should not I spare Nineveh?* are not unlike these expostulations of the father with the elder brother here. *Secondly,* It is to teach all superiors to be mild and gentle with their inferiors, even when they are in a fault and passionately justify themselves in it, than which nothing can be more provoking; and yet even in that case let fathers *not provoke their children to more wrath,* and let *masters forbear threatening,* and both show all *meekness.*

[2.] His father assured him that the kind entertainment he gave his younger brother was neither any reflection upon him nor should be any prejudice to him (*v.* 31): "Thou shalt fare never the worse for it, nor have ever the less for it. *Son, thou art ever with me;* the reception of him is no rejection of thee, nor what is laid out on him any sensible diminution of what I design for thee; thou shalt still remain entitled to the *pars enitia* (so our law calls it), the *double portion* (so the Jewish law called it); thou shalt be *haeres ex asse* (so the Roman law called it): *all that I have is thine,* by an indefeasible title." If he had not *given him a kid to make merry with his friends,* he had allowed him to eat bread at his table continually; and it is better to be *happy with our Father* in heaven than *merry* with any *friend* we have in this world. Note, *First,* It is the unspeakable happiness of all the children of God, who keep close to their Father's house, that they are, and shall be, ever with him. They are so in this world by faith; they shall be so in the other world by fruition; and all that he has is theirs; for, *if children, then heirs,* Rom. 8:17. *Secondly, Therefore* we ought not to envy others God's grace to them because we shall have never the less for their sharing in it. If we be true believers, all that God is, all that he has, is *ours;* and, if others come to be true believers, all that he is, and all that he has, is theirs too, and yet we have not the less, as they that walk in the light and warmth of the sun have all the benefit they can have by it, and yet not the less for others having as much; for Christ in his church is like what is said of the soul in the body: it is *tota in toto — the whole in the whole,* and yet *tota in qualibet parte — the whole in each part.*

[3.] His father gave him a good reason for this uncommon joy in the family: *It was meet that we should make merry and be glad, v.* 32. He might have insisted upon his own authority: "It was *my will* that the family should make merry and be glad." *Stat pro ratione voluntas — My reason is, I will it to be so.* But it does not become even those that have authority to be vouching and appealing to it upon every occasion, which does but make it cheap and common, it is better to give a convincing reason, as the father does here: *It was meet,* and very becoming, *that we should make merry* for the return of a prodigal son, more than for the perseverance of a dutiful son; for, though the latter is a greater blessing to a family, yet the former is a more sensible pleasure. Any family would be much more transported with joy at the raising of a dead child to life, yea, or at the recovery of a child from a sickness that was adjudged mortal, than for the continued life and health of many children. Note, God will be justified when he speaks, and all flesh shall, sooner or later, be silent before him. We do not find that the elder brother made any reply to what his father said, which intimates that he was entirely satisfied, and acquiesced in his father's will, and was well reconciled to his prodigal brother; and his father put him in mind that he was his brother: *This thy brother.* Note, A good man, though he have not such a command of himself at all times as to *keep his temper,* yet will, with the grace of God, *recover his temper;* though *he fall, yet shall he not be utterly cast down.* But as for the scribes and Pharisees, for whose conviction it was primarily intended, for aught that appears they continued the same disaffection to the sinners of the Gentiles, and to the gospel of Christ because it was preached to them.

CHAPTER 16

The scope of Christ's discourse in this chapter is to awaken and quicken us all so to use this world as not to abuse it, so to manage all our possessions and enjoyments here as that they may make for us, and may not make against us in the other world; for they will do either the one or the other, according as we use them now. I. If we do good with them, and lay out what we have in works of piety and charity, we shall reap the benefit of it in the world to come; and this he shows in the parable of the unjust steward, who made so good a hand of his lord's goods that, when he was turned out of his stewardship, he had a comfortable subsistence to betake himself to. The parable itself we have (*v.* 1–8); the explanation and application of it (*v.* 9–13); and the contempt which the Pharisees put upon the doctrine Christ preached to them, for which he sharply reproved them, adding some other weighty sayings (*v.* 14–18). II. It, instead of doing good with our worldly enjoyments, we make them the food and fuel of our lusts, of our luxury and sensuality, and deny relief to the poor, we shall certainly perish eternally, and the things of this world, which were thus abused, will but add to our misery and torment. This he shows in the other parable of the rich man and Lazarus, which has likewise a further intention, and that is, to awaken us all to take the warning given us by the written word, and not to expect immediate messages from the other world (*v.* 19–31).

Verses 1–18

We mistake if we imagine that the design of Christ's doctrine and holy religion was either to amuse us with notions of divine mysteries or to entertain us with notions of divine mercies. No, the divine revelation of both these in the gospel is intended to engage and quicken us to the practice of Christian duties, and, as much as any one thing, to the duty of beneficence and doing good to those who stand in need of any thing that either we have or can do for them. This our Saviour is here pressing us to, by reminding us that we are but *stewards of the manifold grace of God;* and since we have in divers instances been unfaithful, and have forfeited the favour of our Lord, it is our wisdom to think how we may, some other way, make what we have in the world turn to a good account. Parables must not be forced beyond their primary intention, and therefore we must not hence infer that any one can befriend us if we lie under the displeasure of our Lord, but that, in the general, we must so lay out what we have in works of piety and charity as that we may meet it again with comfort on the other side death and the grave. If we would act wisely, we must be diligent and industrious to employ our riches in the acts of piety and charity, in order to promote our future and eternal welfare, as worldly men are in laying them out to the greatest temporal profit, in making to themselves friends with them, and securing other secular interests. So *Dr. Clarke.* Now let us consider,

I. The parable itself, in which all the children of men are represented as *stewards* of what they have in this world, and we are but stewards. Whatever we have, the property of it is God's; we have only the use of it, and that according to the direction of our great Lord, and for his honour. Rabbi Kimchi, quoted by Dr. Lightfoot, says, "This world is a house; heaven the roof; the stars the lights; the earth, with its fruits, a table spread; the Master of the house is the holy and blessed God; man is the steward, into whose hands the goods of this house are delivered; if he behave himself well, he shall find favour in the eyes of his Lord; if not, he shall be turned out of his stewardship." Now,

1. Here is the *dishonesty* of this *steward.* He *wasted his lord's goods,* embezzled them, misapplied them, or through carelessness suffered them to be lost and damaged; and for this he was *accused to his lord, v.* 1. We are all *liable* to the same charge. We have not made a due improvement of what God has entrusted us with in this world, but have perverted his purpose; and, that we may not be for this *judged of our Lord,* it concerns us to *judge ourselves.*

2. His *discharge* out of his place. His lord *called for him,* and said, *"How is it that I hear this of thee?* I expected better things from thee." He speaks as one sorry to find himself disappointed in him, and under a necessity of dismissing him from his service: it troubles him to hear it; but the steward cannot deny it, and therefore there is no remedy, he must make up his accounts; and be gone in a little time, *v.* 2. Now this is designed to teach us, (1.) That we must all of us shortly be discharged from *our stewardship* in this world; we must not always enjoy those things which we now enjoy. Death will come, and *dismiss* us from our stewardship, will *deprive* us of the abilities and opportunities we now have of doing good, and others will come in our places and have the same. (2.) That our discharge from our stewardship at death is *just,* and what we have deserved, for we have wasted our Lord's goods, and thereby forfeited our trust, so that we cannot complain of any wrong done us. (3.) That when our stewardship is taken from us we must *give an account* of it to our Lord: *After death the judgment.* We are fairly warned both of our discharge and our account, and ought to be frequently thinking of them.

3. His *after-wisdom.* Now he began to consider, *What shall I do? v.* 3. He would have done well to have considered this before he had so foolishly thrown himself out of a good place by his unfaithfulness; but it is better to *consider* late than never. Note, Since we have all received notice that we must shortly be turned out of our stewardship, we are concerned to consider what we shall do then. He must live; which way

shall he have a livelihood? (1.) He knows that he has not such a degree of industry in him as to get his living by work: *"I cannot dig;* I cannot earn by bread by my labour." But why can he not dig? It does not appear that he is either old or lame; but the truth is, he is *lazy.* His *cannot* is a *will not;* it is not a natural but a moral disability that he labours under; if his master, when he turned him out of the stewardship, had continued him in his service as a labourer, and set a task-master over him, he would have made him dig. He *cannot dig,* for he was never used to it. Now this intimates that we cannot get a livelihood for our souls by any labour for this world, nor indeed do any thing to purpose for our souls by any ability of our own. (2.) He knows that he has not such a degree of *humility* as to get his bread by begging: To *beg I am ashamed.* This was the language of his pride, as the former of his slothfulness. Those whom God, in his providence, has disabled to help themselves, should not be *ashamed* to ask relief of others. This steward had more reason to be ashamed of cheating his master than of begging his bread. (3.) He therefore determines to make friends of his lord's debtors, or his tenants that were behind with their rent, and had given notes under their hands for it: *"I am resolved what to do, v.* 4. My lord turns me out of his house. I have none of my own to go to. I am acquainted with my lord's tenants, have done them many a good turn, and now I will do them one more, which will so oblige them that they will bid me welcome to their houses, and the best entertainment they afford; and so long as I live, at least till I can better dispose of myself, I will quarter upon them, and go from one good house to another." Now the way he would take to make them his friends was by striking off a considerable part of their debt to his lord, and giving it in his accounts so much less than it was. Accordingly, he sent for one, who owed his lord *a hundred measures of oil* (in that commodity he paid his rent): *Take thy bill,* said he, here it is, and *sit down quickly, and write fifty* (*v.* 6); so he reduced his debt to the one half. Observe, he was in haste to have it done: *"Sit down quickly,* and do it, lest we be taken treating, and suspected." He took another, who owed his lord *a hundred measures of wheat,* and from his bill he cut off a fifth part, and bade him write *fourscore* (*v.* 7); probably he did the like by others, abating more or less according as he expected kindness from them. See here what uncertain things our worldly possessions are; they are most so to those who have most of them, who devolve upon others all the care concerning them, and so put it into their power to *cheat them,* because they will not trouble themselves to see with their own eyes. See also what treachery is to be found even among those in whom trust is reposed. How hard is it to find one that confidence can be reposed in! *Let God be true, but every man a liar.* Though this steward is turned out for dealing dishonestly, yet still he does so. So rare is it for men to mend of a fault, though they smart for it.

4. The approbation of this: *The lord commended the unjust steward, because he had done wisely, v.* 8. It may be meant of *his lord,* the lord of that servant, who, though he could not but be angry at his knavery, yet was pleased with his ingenuity and policy for himself; but, taking it so, the latter part of the verse must be the words of *our Lord,* and therefore I think the whole is meant of him. Christ did, as it were, say, "Now commend me to such a man as this, that knows how to do well for himself, how to improve a present opportunity, and how to provide for a future necessity." He does not commend him because he had done *falsely* to his master, but because he had done *wisely* for himself. Yet perhaps herein he did well for his master too, and but justly with the tenants. He knew what *hard bargains* he had *set them,* so that they could not *pay their rent,* but, having been screwed up by his rigour, were thrown *behindhand,* and they and their families were likely to go to ruin; in consideration of this, he now, at going off, did as he ought to do both in justice and charity, not only easing them of part of their arrears, but abating their rent for the future. *How much owest thou?* may mean, "What rent dost thou sit upon? Come, I will set thee an easier bargain, and yet no easier than what thou oughtest to have." He had been *all for his lord,* but now he begins to consider the tenants, that he might have *their favour* when he had lost *his lord's.* The abating of their rent would be a lasting kindness, and more likely to engage them than abating their arrears only. Now this forecast of his, for a comfortable subsistence in this world, shames our improvidence for another world: *The children of this world,* who choose and have their portions in it, *are wiser for their generation,* act more considerately, and better consult their worldly interest and advantage, than the *children of light,* who enjoy the gospel, in *their generation,* that is, in the concerns of their souls and eternity. Note, (1.) The wisdom of worldly people in the concerns of this world is to be *imitated* by us in the concerns of our souls: it is their principle to improve their opportunities, to do that first which is most needful, in summer and harvest to lay up for winter, to take a good bargain when it is offered them, to trust the *faithful* and not the *false.* O that we were thus wise in our spiritual affairs! (2.) The children of light are commonly *outdone* by the children of this world. Not that the children of this world are *truly wise;* it is only *in their generation.* But in that they are *wiser than the children of light in theirs;* for, though we are told that we must shortly be *turned out of our stewardship,* yet we do not provide as we were to be *here always* and as if there were not *another life after this,* and are not so solicitous as this steward was to provide for *hereafter.* Though as *children of the light,* that light to which life and immortality are brought by the gospel, we cannot but see *another world* before us, yet we do not prepare for it, do not send our best effects and best affections thither, as we should.

II. The application of this parable, and the inferences drawn from it (*v.* 9): *"I say unto you,* you my disciples" (for to them this parable is directed, *v.* 1), "though you have but little in this world, consider how you may do good with that little." Observe,

1. What it is that our Lord Jesus here exhorts us to; to provide for our comfortable reception to the happiness of another world, by making good use of our possessions and enjoyments in this world: *"Make to yourselves friends of the mammon of unrighteousness,* as the steward with his lord's goods made his lord's tenants his friends." It is the wisdom of the men of this world so to manage their money as that they may have the benefit of it hereafter, and not for the present only; therefore they put it out to interest, buy land with it, put it into this or the other fund. Now we should learn of them to make use of our money so as that we may be the better for it hereafter in another world, as they do in hopes to be the better for it hereafter in this world; so *cast it upon the waters* as that we may *find it again after many days,* Eccl. 11:1. And in our case, though whatever we have *are our Lord's goods,* yet, as long as we dispose of them among *our Lord's tenants* and for their advantage, it is so far from being reckoned a wrong to our Lord, that it is a duty to him as well as policy for ourselves. Note, (1.) The things of this world are the *mammon of unrighteousness,* or the false *mammon,* not only because often got by fraud and unrighteousness, but because those who trust to it for satisfaction and happiness will certainly be deceived; for riches are perishing things, and will disappoint those that raise their expectations from them. (2.) Though this *mammon of unrighteousness* is not to be *trusted to* for a happiness, yet it may and must be *made use of* in subserviency to our pursuit of that which is our happiness. Though we cannot find true satisfaction in it, yet we may *make to ourselves friends* with it, not by way of *purchase or merit,* but *recommendation;* so we may make God and Christ our friends, the good angels and saints our friends, and the poor our friends; and it is a desirable thing to be *befriended* in the account and state to come. (3.) At death we must all *fail, hotan eklipēte — when ye suffer an eclipse.* Death eclipses us. A tradesman is said to *fail* when he becomes a *bankrupt.* We must all thus fail shortly; death shuts up the shop, seals up the hand. Our comforts and enjoyments on earth will *all fail* us; flesh and heart fail. (4.) It ought to be our great concern to make it sure to ourselves, that *when* we *fail* at death we may be *received into everlasting habitations* in heaven. The *habitations* in heaven are *everlasting,* not *made with hands,* but *eternal,* 2. Cor. 5:1. Christ is gone before, to prepare a place for those that are his, and is there ready to *receive them;* the bosom of Abraham is ready to receive them, and, when a *guard of angels* carries them thither, a *choir of angels* is ready to receive them there. The poor saints that are gone before to glory will receive those that in this world distributed to their necessities. (5.) This is a good reason why we should use what we have in the world for the honour of God and the good of our brethren, that thus we may with them *lay up in store a good bond,* a good security, a good foundation *for the time to come,* for an eternity to come. See 1 Tim. 6:17–19, which explains this here.

2. With what arguments he presses this exhortation to abound in works of piety and charity.

(1.) If we do not make a right use of the *gifts of God's providence,* how can we expect from him those present and future comforts which are the *gifts of his spiritual grace?* Our Saviour here compares these, and shows that though our faithful use of the things of this world cannot be thought to merit any favour at the hand of God, yet our unfaithfulness in the use of them may be justly reckoned a *forfeiture* of that grace which is necessary to bring us to glory, and that is it which our Saviour here shows, *v.* 10–14.

[1.] The riches of this world are the *less;* grace and glory are the *greater.* Now if we be unfaithful in the less, if we use the things of this world to other purposes than those for which they were given us, it may justly be feared that we should be so in the gifts of God's grace, that we should receive them also in vain, and therefore they will be denied us: *He that is faithful in that which is least is faithful also in much.* He that serves God, and does good, with his money, will serve God, and do good, with the more noble and valuable talents of wisdom and grace, and spiritual gifts, and the earnests of heaven; but he that buries the *one talent* of this world's wealth will never improve the *five talents* of spiritual riches. God withholds his grace from covetous worldly people more than we are aware of. [2.] The riches of this world are *deceitful* and *uncertain;* they are the *unrighteous mammon,* which is hastening from us apace, and, if we would make any advantage of it, we must bestir ourselves quickly; if we do not, how can we expect to be entrusted with spiritual riches, which are the only *true riches? v.* 11. Let us be convinced of this, that those are *truly* rich, and *very* rich, who are rich in *faith,* and rich *towards God,* rich in Christ, in the promises, and in the earnests of heaven; and therefore let us lay up our treasure in them, expect our portion from them, and mind them in the first place, the *kingdom of God and the righteousness thereof,* and then, if other things be added to us, use them *in ordine ad spiritualia — with a spiritual reference,* so that by using them well we may take the faster hold of the *true riches,* and may be qualified to receive yet *more grace* from God; *for God giveth to a man that is good in his sight,* that is, to a free-hearted charitable man, *wisdom, and knowledge, and joy* (Eccl. 2:26); that is, to a man that is *faithful in the unrighteous mammon,* he gives the *true riches.* [3.] The riches of this world are *another man's.* They are *ta allotria,* not *our own;* for they are foreign to the soul and its nature and interest. They are not *our own;* for they are God's; his title to them is prior and superior to ours; the property remains in him, we are but usufructuaries. They are *another man's;* we have them from others; we use them for others, and *what good has the owner* from his *goods* that *increase,* save *the beholding of them with his eyes,* while still *they are increased that eat them;* and we must shortly leave them to others, and we know not to whom? But spiritual and eternal riches are *our own* (they enter into the soul that becomes *possessed* of them) and *inseparably;* they are a good part that will never be taken away from us. If we make Christ our own, and the promises our own, and heaven our own, we have that which we may truly call *our own.* But how can we expect God should *enrich us* with these if we do not serve him with our worldly possessions, of which we are but stewards?

(2.) We have no other way to prove ourselves the servants of God than by giving up ourselves so entirely to his service as to make *mammon,* that is, all our worldly gain, serviceable to us in his service (*v.* 13): *No servant can serve two masters,* whose commands are so inconsistent as those of God and *mammon* are. If a man will *love* the world, and *hold to that,* it cannot be but he will *hate God* and *despise* him. He will make all his pretensions of religion truckle to his secular interests and designs, and the things of God shall be made to help him in serving and seeking the world. But, on the other hand, if a man will *love God,* and *adhere* to him, he will comparatively *hate* the world (whenever God and the world come in competition) and will *despise* it, and make all his business and success in the world some way or other conducive to his furtherance in the business of religion; and the things of the world shall be made to help him in serving God and working out his salvation. The matter is here laid plainly before us: *Ye cannot serve God and mammon.* So divided are their interests that their services can never be *compounded.* If therefore we be determined to *serve God,* we must disclaim and abjure the service of the world.

3. We are here told what entertainment this doctrine of

Christ met with among the Pharisees, and what rebuke he gave them.

(1.) They wickedly *ridiculed* him, *v.* 14. *The Pharisees, who were covetous, heard all these things,* and could not contradict him, but *they derided him.* Let us consider this, [1.] As their *sin,* and the fruit of their *covetousness,* which was their reigning sin, their own iniquity. Note, Many that make a great profession of religion, have much knowledge, and abound in the exercise of devotion, are yet ruined by the love of the world; nor does any thing harden the heart more against the word of Christ. These covetous Pharisees could not bear to have that *touched,* which was their *Delilah,* their darling lust; for this they derided him, ***exemyktērizon auton*** *— they snuffled up their noses at him,* or blew their noses on him. It is an expression of the utmost scorn and disdain imaginable; *the word of the Lord was to them a reproach,* Jer. 6:10. They laughed at him for going so contrary to the opinion and way of the world, for endeavouring to recover them from a sin which they were resolved to hold fast. Note, It is common for those to *make a jest* of the word of God who are resolved that they will not be ruled by it; but they will find at last that it cannot be turned off so. [2.] As *his suffering.* Our Lord Jesus endured not only the *contradiction* of sinners, but their *contempt;* they *had him in derision* all the day. He that spoke as never man spoke was bantered and ridiculed, that his faithful ministers, whose preaching is unjustly *derided,* may not be disheartened at it. It is no disgrace to a man to be laughed at, but to deserve to be laughed at. Christ's apostles were *mocked,* and no wonder; the *disciple is not greater than his Lord.*

(2.) He justly reproved them; not for *deriding* him (he knew how to *despise the shame*), but for *deceiving* themselves with the shows and colours of piety, when they were strangers to the power of it, *v.* 15. Here is,

[1.] Their *specious outside;* nay, it was a *splendid one. First,* They *justified themselves before men;* they denied whatever ill was laid to their charge, even by Christ himself. They claimed to be looked upon as men of singular sanctity and devotion, and justified themselves in that claim: "*You are they that* do that, so as none ever did, that make it your business to court the opinion of men, and, right or wrong, will justify yourselves before the world; you are *notorious* for this." *Secondly,* They were *highly esteemed among men.* Men did not only *acquit* them from any blame they were under, but *applauded* them, and had them in veneration, not only as *good men,* but as the *best of men.* Their sentiments were esteemed as oracles, their directions as laws, and their practices as inviolable prescriptions.

[2.] Their *odious inside,* which was under the eye of God: "He *knows your heart,* and it is in his sight an *abomination;* for it is full of all manner of wickedness." Note, *First,* It is folly to *justify ourselves before men,* and to think this enough to bear us out, and bring us off, in the judgment of the great day, that men *know no ill* of us; for God, who knows our hearts, knows that ill of us which no one else can know. This ought to check our value for ourselves, and our confidence in ourselves, that *God knows our hearts,* and how much deceit is there, for we have reason to abase and distrust ourselves. *Secondly,* It is folly to judge of persons and things by the opinion of men concerning them, and to go down with the stream of vulgar estimate; for that which is *highly esteemed among men,* who judge according to outward appearance, is perhaps *an abomination in the sight of God,* who sees things as they are, and whose judgment, we are sure, is according to truth. On the contrary, there are those whom men despise and condemn who yet are accepted and approved of God, 2 Co. 10:18.

(3.) He turned from them to the publicans and sinners, as more likely to be wrought upon by his gospel than those covetous conceited Pharisees (*v.* 16): "The *law and the prophets were* indeed *until John;* the Old-Testament dispensation, which was *confined* to you Jews, continued till John Baptist appeared, and you seemed to have the monopoly of righteousness and salvation; and you are puffed up with this, and this gains you esteem among men, that you are students in the law and the prophets; but since John Baptist appeared *the kingdom of God is preached,* a New-Testament dispensation, which does not value men at all for their being doctors of the law, but *every man presses* into the gospel kingdom, Gentiles as well as Jews, and no man thinks himself bound in good manners to let his betters go before him into it, or to stay till the *rulers* and the Pharisees have led him that way. It is not so much a political national constitution as the Jewish economy was, when *salvation was of the Jews;* but it is made a particular personal concern, and therefore *every man* that is convinced he has a soul to save, and an eternity to provide for, thrusts to get in, lest he should come short by trifling and complimenting." Some give this sense of it; they derided Christ or speaking in contempt of riches, for, thought they, were there not many promises of riches and other temporal good things in the *law and the prophets?* And were not many of the best of God's servants very rich, as Abraham and David? "It is true," saith Christ, "so it was, but now that the kingdom of God is begun to be preached things take a new turn; now blessed are the poor, and the mourners, and the persecuted." The Pharisees, to requite the people for their high opinion of them, allowed them in a cheap, easy, formal religion. "But," saith Christ, "now that the *gospel is preached* the eyes of the people are opened, and as they cannot now have a veneration for the Pharisees, as they have had, so they cannot content themselves with such an indifferency in religion as they have been trained up in, but they *press* with a holy violence into the kingdom of God." Note, Those that would go to heaven must take pains, must strive against the stream, must press against the crowd that are going the contrary way.

(4.) Yet still he protests against any design to invalidate the law (*v.* 17): *It is easier for heaven and earth to pass, parelthein — to pass by,* to pass away, though the foundations of the earth and the pillars of heaven are so firmly established, *than for one tittle of the law to fail.* The moral law is confirmed and ratified, and not one tittle of that fails; the duties enjoined by it are duties still; the sins forbidden by it are sins still. Nay, the precepts of it are explained and enforced by the gospel, and made to appear more spiritual. The ceremonial law is perfected in the gospel colours; not *one tittle* of that *fails,* for it is found printed off in the gospel, where, though the force of it is as a law taken off, yet the figure of it as a type shines very brightly, witness the epistle to the Hebrews. There were some things which were connived at by the law, for the preventing of greater mischiefs, the permission of which the gospel has indeed taken away, but without any detriment or disparagement to the law, for it has thereby reduced them to the primitive intention of the law, as in the case of divorce (*v.* 18), which we had before, Mt. 5:32; 19:9. Christ will not allow divorces, for his gospel is intended to strike at the bitter root of men's corrupt appetites and passions, to kill them, and pluck them up; and therefore they must not be so far *indulged* as that permission *did* indulge them, for the more they are indulged the more impetuous and headstrong they grow.

Verses 19–31

As the parable of the prodigal son set before us the grace of the gospel, which is encouraging to us all, so this sets before us the *wrath to come,* and is designed for our awakening; and very fast asleep those are in sin that will not be awakened by it. The Pharisees made a jest of Christ's sermon against worldliness; now this parable was intended to make those mockers serious. The tendency of the gospel of Christ is both to reconcile us to poverty and affliction and to arm us against temptations to worldliness and sensuality. Now this parable, by drawing the curtain, and letting us see what will be the end of both in the other world, goes very far in prosecuting those two great intentions. This parable is not like Christ's other parables, in which spiritual things are represented by similitudes borrowed from worldly things, as those of the sower and the seed (except that of the sheep and goats), the prodigal son, and indeed all the rest but this. But here the *spiritual things themselves* are represented in a narrative or description of the different state of good and bad in this world and the other. Yet we need not call it a history of a particular occurrence, but it is *matter of fact* that is true every day, that poor godly people, whom men neglect and trample upon, die away out of their miseries, and go to heavenly bliss and joy, which is made the more pleasant to them by their preceding sorrows; and that rich epicures, who live in luxury, and are unmerciful to the poor, die, and go into a state of insupportable torment, which is the more grievous and terrible to them because of the sensual lives they lived: and that there is no gaining any relief from their torments. Is this a parable? What similitude is there in this? The discourse indeed between Abraham and the rich man is only an illustration of the description, to make it the more affecting, like that between God and Satan in the story of Job. Our Saviour came to bring us acquainted with another world, and to show us the reference which *this* world has to *that;* and here is does it. In this description (for so I shall choose to call it) we may observe,

I. The different condition of a *wicked rich man,* and a *godly poor man,* in this world. We know that as some of late, so the Jews of old, were ready to make prosperity one of the marks of a true church, of a good man and a favourite of heaven, so that they could hardly have any favourable thoughts of a *poor man.* This mistake Christ, upon all occasions, set himself to correct, and here very fully, where we have,

1. A wicked man, and one that will be for ever miserable, in the height of prosperity (*v.* 19): *There was a certain rich man.* From the Latin we commonly call him *Dives — a rich man;* but, as Bishop Tillotson observes, he has no name given him, as the poor man has, because it had been invidious to have named any particular rich man in such a description as this, and apt to provoke and gain ill-will. But others observe that Christ would not do the rich man so much honour as to name him, though when perhaps he called his lands by his own name he thought it should long survive that of the beggar at his gate, which yet is here preserved, when that of the rich man is buried in oblivion. Now we are told concerning this rich man,

(1.) That he was *clothed in purple and fine linen,* and that was his *adorning.* He had *fine linen* for *pleasure,* and clean, no doubt, every day; night-linen, and day-linen. He had *purple* for *state,* for that was the wear of princes, which has made some conjecture that Christ had an eye to Herod in it. He never appeared abroad but in great magnificence.

(2.) He *fared* deliciously and *sumptuously every day.* His table was furnished with all the varieties and dainties that nature and art could supply; his side-table richly adorned with plate; his servants, who waited at table, in rich liveries; and the guests at his table, no doubt, such as he thought *graced* it. Well, and what harm was there in all this? It is no sin to be rich, no sin to wear purple and fine linen, nor to keep a plentiful table, if a man's estate will afford it. Not are we told that he got his estate by fraud, oppression, or extortion, no, nor that he was drunk, or made others drunk; but, [1.] Christ would hereby show that a man may have a great deal of the wealth, and pomp, and pleasure of this world, and yet lie and perish for ever under God's wrath and curse. We cannot infer from men's living great either that God loves them *in* giving them so much, or that they love God *for* giving them so much; happiness consists not in these things. [.2] That plenty and pleasure are a very *dangerous* and to many a *fatal* temptation to luxury, and sensuality, and forgetfulness of God and another world. This man might have been happy if he had not had great possessions and enjoyments. [3.] That the indulgence of the body, and the ease and pleasure of that, are the ruin of many a soul, and the interests of it. It is true, eating good meat and wearing good clothes are lawful; but it is true that they often become the food and fuel of pride and luxury, and so turn into sin to us. [4.] That feasting ourselves and our friends, and, at the same time, forgetting the distresses of the poor and afflicted, are very provoking to God and damning to the soul. The sin of this rich man was not so much his dress or his diet, but his providing only for himself.

2. Here is a godly man, and one that will be for ever happy, in the depth of adversity and distress (*v.* 20): *There was a certain beggar,* named *Lazarus.* A beggar of that name, eminently devout, and in great distress, was probably well known among good people at that time: a beggar, suppose such a one as Eleazar, or Lazarus. Some think Eleazar a proper name for any poor man, for it signifies the *help of God,* which they must fly to that are destitute of *other helps.* This poor man was reduced to the last extremity, as miserable, as to outward things, as you can lightly suppose a man to be in this world.

(1.) His body was *full of sores,* like Job. To be sick and weak in body is a great affliction; but sores are more *painful* to the patient, and more *loathsome* to those about him.

(2.) He was forced to beg his bread, and to take up with such scraps as he could get at rich people's doors. He was so sore and lame that he could not go himself, but was carried by some compassionate hand or other, and *laid at the rich man's gate.* Note, Those that are not able to help the poor with their *purses* should help them with their *pains;* those that cannot lend them *a penny* should lend them *a hand;* those that have not themselves wherewithal to give to them should either bring them, or go for them, to those that have. Lazarus, in his distress, had nothing of his own to subsist on, no relation to go to, nor did the parish take care of him. It is an instance of the degeneracy of the Jewish church at this time that such a godly man as Lazarus was should be suffered to perish for want of necessary food. Now observe,

[1.] His expectations from the rich man's table: *He desired to be fed with the crumbs, v.* 21. He did not look for a mess from off his table, though he ought to have had one, one of the best; but would be thankful for the crumbs from under the table, the broken meat which was the rich man's leavings; nay, the leavings of his dogs. *The poor use entreaties,* and must be content with such as they can get. Now this is taken notice of to show, *First,* What was the distress, and what the disposition, of the poor man. He was *poor,* but he was *poor in spirit,* contentedly poor. He did not lie at the rich man's gate complaining, and bawling, and making a noise, but silently and modestly desiring to be *fed with the crumbs.* This miserable man was a good man, and in favour with God. Note, It is often the lot of some of the dearest of God's saints and servants to be greatly afflicted in this world, while wicked people prosper, and have abundance; see Ps. 73:7, 10, 14. Here is a child of wrath and an heir of hell sitting in the house, faring sumptuously; and a child of love and an heir of heaven lying at the gate, perishing for hunger. And is men's spiritual state to be judged of then by their outward condition? *Secondly,* What was the temper of the rich man towards him. We are not told that he abused him, or forbade him his gate, or did him any harm, but it is intimated that he slighted him; he had no concern for him, took no care about him. Here was a *real* object of charity, and a very *moving* one, which spoke for itself; it was presented to him at *his own gate.* The poor man had a good character and good conduct, and every thing that could recommend him. A *little* thing would be a *great* kindness to him, and yet he took no cognizance of his case, did not order him to be taken in and lodged in the barn, or some of the out-buildings, but let him lie there. Note, It is not enough not to oppress and trample upon the poor; we shall be found unfaithful stewards of our Lord's goods, in the great day, if we do not succour and relieve them. The reason given for the most fearful doom is, *I was hungry, and you gave me no meat.* I wonder how those rich people who have read the gospel of Christ, and way that they believe it, can be so unconcerned as they often are in the necessities and miseries of the poor and afflicted.

[2.] The usage he had from the dogs; *The dogs came and licked his sores.* The rich man kept a kennel of hounds, it may be, or other dogs, for his diversion, and to please his fancy, and these were fed to the full, when poor Lazarus could not get enough to keep him alive. Note, Those will have a great deal to answer for hereafter that feed their dogs, but neglect the poor. And it is a great aggravation of the uncharitableness of many rich people that they bestow that upon their fancies and follies which would supply the necessity, and rejoice the heart, of many a good Christian in distress. Those offend God, nay, and they put a contempt upon human nature, that pamper their dogs and horses, and let the families of their poor neighbours starve. Now those dogs *came and licked the* sores of poor Lazarus, which may be taken, *First,* As an aggravation of his misery. His sores were *bloody,* which tempted the dogs to come, and lick them, as they did the blood of Naboth and Ahab, 1 Ki. 21:19. And we read of the *tongue of the dogs dipped* in the *blood of enemies,* Ps. 68:23. They attacked him while he was yet alive, as if he had been already dead, and he had not strength himself to keep them off, nor would any of the servants be so civil as to check them. The dogs were like their master, and thought they fared sumptuously when they regaled themselves with human gore. Or, it may be taken, *Secondly,* as some relief to him in his misery; *alla kai,* the master was *hard-hearted* towards him, *but* the dogs *came and licked his sores,* which mollified and eased them. It is not said, They *sucked* them, but *licked* them, which was good for them. The dogs were more kind to him than their master was.

II. Here is the *different condition* of this *godly poor man,* and this *wicked rich man, at* and *after death.* Hitherto the wicked man seems to have the advantage, but *Exitus acta probat — Let us wait awhile, to see the end hereof.*

1. They both died (*v.* 22): The *beggar died;* the *rich man also died.* Death is the common lot of rich and poor, godly and ungodly; there they meet together. One dieth *in his full strength,* and another in *the bitterness of his soul;* but they shall *lie down alike in the dust,* Job 21:26. Death favours not either the rich man for his riches or the poor man for his poverty. Saints die, that they may bring their sorrows to an end, and may enter upon their joys. Sinners die, that they may go to give up their account. It concerns both rich and poor to prepare for death, for it waits for them both. *Mors sceptra ligonibus aequat — Death blends the sceptre with the spade.*

— — aequo pulsat pede pauperum tabernas,
Regumque turres.

With equal pace, impartial fate
Knocks at the palace, as the cottage gate.

2. The beggar *died first.* God often takes godly people out of the world, when he leaves the wicked to flourish still. It was an advantage to the beggar that such a speedy end was put to his miseries; and, since he could find no other shelter or resting-place, he was *hid in the grave,* where the *weary are at rest.*

3. The rich man *died and was buried.* Nothing is said of the interment of the poor man. They dug a hole any where, and tumbled his body in, without any solemnity; he was *buried with the burial of an ass:* nay, it is well if they that let the dogs lick his sores did not let them gnaw his bones. But the rich man had a pompous funeral, lay in state, had a train of mourners to attend him to his grave, and a stately monument set up over it; probably he had a funeral oration in praise of him, and his generous way of living, and the good table he kept, which those would commend that had been feasted at it. It is said of the wicked man that he is *brought to the grave* with no small ado, and *laid in the tomb,* and *the clods of the valley,* were it possible, are made *sweet to him,* Job 21:32, 33. How foreign is the ceremony of a funeral to the happiness of the man!

4. The beggar died and was *carried by angels into Abraham's bosom.* How much did the honour done to his soul, by this convoy of it to its rest, exceed the honour done to the rich man, by the carrying of his body with so much magnificence to its grave! Observe, (1.) His soul *existed* in a state of separation from the body. It did not *die,* or *fall asleep,* with the body; his candle was not put out with him; but lives, and acted, and knew what it did, and what was done to it. (2.) His soul *removed* to another world, to the world of spirits; it returned to God who gave it, to its native country; this is implied in its being *carried.* The spirit of a man goes upward. (3.) Angels took care of it; it was *carried by angels.* They are ministering spirits to the heirs of salvation, not only while they live, but when they die, and have a charge concerning them, to *bear them up in their hands,* not only in their journeys to and fro on earth, but in their great journey to their long home in heaven, to be both their guide and their guard through regions unknown and unsafe. The soul of man, if not chained to this earth and clogged by it as unsanctified souls are, has in itself an elastic virtue, by which it *springs upward* as soon as it gets clear of the body; but Christ will not trust those that are his to that, and therefore will send special messengers to fetch them to himself. One angel one would think sufficient, but here are more, as many were sent for Elijah. Amasis king of Egypt had his chariot drawn by kings; but what was that honour to this? Saints ascend in the virtue of Christ's ascension; but this convoy of angels is added for state and decorum. Saints shall be brought home, not only safely, but honourably. What were the bearers at the rich man's funeral, though, probably, those of the first rank, compared with Lazarus's bearers? The angels were not shy of touching him, for his sores were on his *body,* not on his *soul; that* was presented to God *without spot, or wrinkle, or any such thing.* "Now, blessed angels," said a good man just expiring, "now come and do your office." (4.) It was carried *into Abraham's bosom.* The Jews expressed the happiness of the righteous at death three ways: — they to go *to the garden of Eden:* they go *to be under the throne of glory;* and they go *to the bosom of Abraham,* and it is this which our Saviour here makes use of. Abraham was the *father of the faithful;* and whither should the souls of the faithful be gathered but to him, who, as a tender father, lays them *in his bosom,* especially at their first coming, to bid them welcome, and to refresh them when newly come from the sorrows and fatigues of this world? He was carried *to his bosom,* that is, to feast with him, for at feasts the guests are said to lean on one another's breasts; and the saints in heaven *sit down with Abraham, and Isaac, and Jacob.* Abraham was a great and rich man, yet in heaven he does not disdain to lay poor Lazarus in his bosom. Rich saints and poor meet in heaven. This poor Lazarus, who might not be admitted within the rich man's gate, is conducted into the dining-room, into the bed-chamber, of the heavenly palace; and *he* is laid in the bosom of Abraham, whom the rich glutton scorned to *set with the dogs of his flock.*

5. The next news you hear of the *rich man,* after the account of his *death* and *burial,* is, that *in hell he lifted up his eyes, being in torment, v.* 23.

(1.) His state is very miserable. *He is in hell,* in *hades,* in the state of separate souls, and there he is in *the utmost misery* and *anguish* possible. As the souls of the faithful, immediately *after they are delivered from the burden of the flesh, are in joy and felicity,* so wicked and unsanctified souls, immediately after they are fetched from the pleasures of the flesh by death, are in misery and torment endless, useless, and remediless, and which will be much increased and completed at the resurrection. This *rich man* had entirely devoted himself to the pleasures of the *world of sense,* was wholly *taken up* with them, and *took up with them* for his portion, and therefore was wholly unfit for the pleasures of the *world of spirits;* to such a carnal mind as his they would indeed be no pleasure, nor could he have any relish of them, and therefore he is of course excluded from them. Yet this is not all; he was hard-hearted to God's poor, and therefore he is not only cut off from mercy, but he has *judgment without mercy,* and falls under a punishment of *sense* as well as a punishment of *loss.*

(2.) The misery of his state is aggravated by his knowledge of the happiness of Lazarus: He *lifts up his eyes,* and *sees Abraham afar off,* and *Lazarus in his bosom.* It is the soul that is *in torment,* and they are the eyes of the mind that are lifted up. He now began to consider what was become of Lazarus. He does not find him where he himself is, nay, he plainly sees him, and with as much assurance as if he had seen him with his bodily eyes, afar off in the bosom of Abraham. This same aggravation of the miseries of the damned we had before (*ch.* 13:28): *Ye shall see Abraham, and Isaac, and Jacob, and all the prophets, in the kingdom of God, and yourselves thrust out.* [1.] He saw *Abraham afar off.* To see Abraham we should think a pleasing sight; but to see him afar off was a tormenting sight. Near himself he saw devils and damned companions, frightful sights, and painful ones; afar off he saw Abraham. Note, Every sight in hell is aggravating. [2.] He saw *Lazarus in him bosom.* That same Lazarus whom he had looked upon with so much scorn and contempt, as not worthy his notice, he now sees preferred, and to be envied. The sight of him brought to his mind his own cruel and barbarous conduct towards him; and the sight of him in that happiness made his own misery the more grievous.

III. Here is an account of what passed between the rich man and Abraham in the separate state — a state of separation one from another, and of both from this world. Though it is probable that there will not be, nor are, any such dialogues or discourses between glorified saints and damned sinners, yet it is very proper, and what is usually done in descriptions, especially such as are designed to be pathetic and moving, by such dialogues to represent what will be the mind and sentiments both of the one and of the other. And since we find damned sinners tormented *in the presence of the Lamb* (Rev. 14:10), and the faithful servants of God looking upon them that have *transgressed the covenant,* there where their *worm dies not, and their fire is not quenched* (Isa. 66:23, 24), such a discourse as this is not incongruous to be supposed. Now in this discourse we have,

1. The request which the rich man made to Abraham for some mitigation of his present misery, *v.* 24. Seeing Abraham afar off, *he cried to him,* cried aloud, as one in earnest, and as one in pain and misery, mixing shrieks with his petitions, to enforce them by moving compassion. He that used to *command* aloud now *begs* aloud, louder than ever Lazarus did at his gate. The songs of his riot and revels are all turned into lamentations. Observe here,

(1.) The title he gives to Abraham: *Father Abraham.* Note, There are many in hell that can call Abraham *father,* that were Abraham's seed after the flesh, nay, and many that were, in name and profession, the children of the covenant made with Abraham. Perhaps this rich man, in his carnal mirth, had ridiculed Abraham and the story of Abraham, as the scoffers of the latter days do; but now he gives him a title of respect, *Father Abraham.* Note, The day is coming when wicked men will be glad to scrape acquaintance with the righteous, and to claim kindred to them, though now they slight them. Abraham in this description represents Christ, for to him all judgment is committed, and it is his mind that Abraham here speaks. Those that now slight Christ will shortly make their court to him, *Lord, Lord.*

(2.) The representation he makes to him of his present deplorable condition: *I am tormented in this flame.* It is the torment of his soul that he complains of, and therefore such a fire as will operate upon souls; and such a fire the *wrath of God* is, fastening upon a guilty conscience; such a fire horror of mind is, and the reproaches of a self-accusing self-condemning heart. Nothing is more painful and terrible to the body than to be tormented with fire; by this therefore the miseries and agonies of damned souls are represented.

(3.) His request to Abraham, in consideration of this misery: *Have mercy on me.* Note, The day is coming when those that make light of divine mercy will beg hard for it. O for *mercy, mercy,* when the day of mercy is over, and offers of mercy are no more made. He that had no mercy on Lazarus, yet expects Lazarus should have mercy on him; "for," thinks he, "Lazarus is better natured than ever I was." The particular favour he begs is, *Send Lazarus, that he may dip the tip of his finger in water, and cool my tongue.* [1.] Here he complains of the torment of his *tongue* particularly, as if he were more tormented there than in any other part, the punishment answering the sin. The *tongue* is one of the organs of speech, and by the torment of that he is put in mind of all the wicked words that he had spoken against God and man, his cursing, and swearing, and blasphemy, all his *hard speeches,* and *filthy speeches;* by his words *he is condemned,* and therefore in his tongue he is tormented. The tongue is also one of the organs of *tasting,* and therefore the torments of that will remind him of his inordinate relish of the delights of sense, which he had *rolled under his tongue.* [2.] He desires a *drop of water to cool his tongue.* He does not say, "Father Abraham, order me a release from this misery, help me out of this pit," for he utterly *despaired* of this; but he asks as small a thing as could be asked, *a drop of water* to cool his tongue for one moment. [3.] He sometimes suspected that he had herein an ill design upon Lazarus, and hoped, if he could get him within his reach, he should keep him from returning to the bosom of Abraham. The heart that is filled with rage against God is filled with rage against the people of God. But we will think more charitably even of a damned sinner, and suppose he intended here to show respect to Lazarus, as one to whom he would now gladly be beholden. He *names* him, because he *knows* him, and thinks Lazarus will not be unwilling to do him this good office for old acquaintance' sake. Grotius here quotes Plato describing the torments of wicked souls, and among other things he says, They are *continually raving* on those whom they have *murdered,* or been any way *injurious to,* calling upon them to *forgive them* the wrongs they did them. Note, There is a day coming when those that now hate and despise the people of God would gladly receive kindness from them.

2. The reply which Abraham gave to this request. In general, he did not grant it. He would not allow him one *drop of water, to cool* his tongue. Note, The damned in hell shall not have any the least abatement or mitigation of their torment. If we now improve the day of our opportunities, we may have a full and lasting satisfaction in the streams of mercy; but, if we now slight the offer, it will be in vain in hell to expect the least drop of mercy. See how justly this rich man is paid in his own coin. He that denied a crumb is denied a drop. Now it is said to us, *Ask, and it shall be given you;* but, if we let slip this accepted time, we may ask, and it shall not be given us. But this is not all; had Abraham only said, "You shall have nothing to abate your torment," it had been sad; but he says a great deal which would add to his torment, and make the flame the hotter, for every thing in hell will be tormenting.

(1.) He calls him *son,* a kind and civil title, but here it serves only to aggravate the denial of his request, which shut up the bowels of the compassion of a father from him. He had been a son, but a rebellious one, and now an abandoned disinherited one. See the folly of those who rely on that *plea, We have Abraham to our father,* when we find one in hell, and likely to be there for ever, whom Abraham calls *son.*

(2.) He puts him in mind of what had been both his own condition and the condition of Lazarus, in their *life-time: Son, remember;* this is a cutting word. The memories of damned souls will be their tormentors, and conscience will then be awakened and stirred up to do its office, which here they would not suffer it to do. Nothing will bring more oil to the flames of hell than *Son, remember.* Now sinners are called upon to *remember,* but they do not, they will not, they find ways to avoid it. "*Son, remember* thy Creator, thy Redeemer, remember thy latter end;" but they can turn a deaf ear to these *mementos,* and forget that for which they have their memories; justly therefore will their everlasting misery arise from a *Son, remember,* to which they will not be able to turn a deaf ear. What a dreadful peal will this ring in our ears, "*Son, remember* the many warnings that were given thee not to come to this place of torment, which thou wouldest not regard; remember the fair offers made thee of eternal life and glory, which thou wouldest not accept!" But that which he is here put in mind of is, [1.] That *thou in thy life-time receivedst thy good things.* He does not tell him that he had *abused* them, but that he had *received* them: "Remember what a bountiful benefactor God has been to thee, how ready he was to do thee good; thou canst not therefore say he owes thee any thing, no, not a *drop of water.* What he gave thee *thou receivedst,* and that was all; thou never gavest him a receipt for them, in a thankful acknowledgment of them, much less didst thou ever make any grateful return for them or improvement of them; thou hast been the grave of God's blessings, in which they were buried, not the field of them, in which they were sown. Thou receivedst *thy good things;* thou receivedst them, and usedst them, as if they had been *thine own,* and thou hadst not been at all accountable for them. Or, rather, they were the things which thou didst choose for *thy good things,* which were in thine eye the *best things,* which thou didst content thyself with, and portion thyself in. Thou hadst meat, and drink, and clothes of the richest and finest, and these were the things thou didst place thy happiness in; they were *thy reward, thy consolation,* the *penny* thou didst *agree for,* and thou hast had it. Thou wast for the *good things of thy life-time,* and hadst no thought of better things in another life, and therefore hast no reason to expect them. The day of thy *good things* is past and gone, and now is the day of thy *evil things,* of recompence for all thy evil deeds. Thou hast already had the last drop of the *vials of mercy* that thou couldest expect to fall to thy share; and there remains nothing but *vials of wrath* without mixture." [2.] "Remember too what *evil things Lazarus received.* Thou enviest him his happiness here; but think what a large share of miseries he had *in his life-time.* Thou hast *as much good* as could be thought to fall to the lot of so *bad a man,* and he *as much evil* as could be thought to fall to the lot of *so good a man.* He *received* his evil things; he bore them patiently, received them from the hand of God, as Job did (*ch.* 2:10, *Shall we receive good at the hand of the Lord, and shall we not receive evil also?*) — he *received* them as physic appointed for the cure of his spiritual distempers, and the cure was effected." As wicked people have *good things* in this life only, and at death they are for ever separated from all good, so godly people have evil things only *in this life,* and at death they are for ever put out of the reach of them. Now Abraham, by putting him in mind of both these together, awakens his conscience to remind him how he had behaved towards Lazarus, when he was reveling in his *good things* and Lazarus groaning under his *evil things;* he cannot forget that then he would not help Lazarus, and how then could he expect that Lazarus should now help him? Had Lazarus in his life-time afterwards grown rich, and he poor, Lazarus would have thought it his duty to relieve him, and not to have upbraided him with his former unkindness; but, in the future state of recompence and retribution, those that are now dealt with, both by God and man, better than they deserve, must expect to be rewarded *every man according to his works.*

(3.) He puts him in mind of Lazarus's present bliss, and his own misery: *But now* the tables are turned, and so they must abide for ever; *now he is comforted, and thou art tormented.* He did not need to be told that he was *tormented;* he felt it to his cost. He knew likewise that one who lay in the bosom of Abraham could not but be comforted there; yet Abraham puts him in mind of it, that he might, by comparing one thing with another, observe the *righteousness of God,* in recompensing *tribulation to them who trouble his people,* and *to those who are troubled rest,* 2 Th. 1:6, 7. Observe, [1.] Heaven is *comfort,* and hell is *torment:* heaven is *joy,* hell is *weeping, and wailing,* and pain in perfection. [2.] The soul, as soon as it leaves the body, goes either to heaven or hell, to comfort or torment, immediately, and does not sleep, or go into purgatory. [3.] Heaven will be heaven indeed to those that go thither through many and great calamities in this world; of those that had grace, but had little of the comfort of it here (perhaps their souls refused to be comforted), yet, when they are fallen asleep in Christ, you may truly say, "Now *they are comforted:* now *all their tears are wiped away,* and all their fears are vanished." In heaven there is everlasting consolation. And, on the other hand, hell will be hell indeed to those that go thither from the midst of the enjoyment of all the delights and pleasures of sense. To them the torture is the greater, as temporal calamities are described to be to the *tender and delicate woman, that would not set so much as the sole of her foot to the ground, for tenderness and delicacy.* Deu. 28:56.

(4.) He assures him that it was to no purpose to think of having any relief by the ministry of Lazarus; for (*v.* 26), *Besides all this,* worse yet, *between us and you there is a great gulf fixed,* an impassable one, *a great chasm,* that so there can be no communication between glorified saints and damned sinners. [1.] The kindest saint in heaven cannot make a visit to the congregation of the dead and damned, to comfort or relieve any there whom once were their friends. "*They that would pass hence to you cannot;* they cannot leave beholding the face of their Father, nor the work about his throne, to fetch water for you; that is no part of their business." [2.] The most daring sinner in hell cannot force his way out of that prison, cannot get over that great gulf. *They cannot pass to us that would come thence.* It is not to be expected, for the door of mercy is shut, the bridge is drawn; there is no coming out upon parole or bail, no, not for one hour. In this world, blessed be God, there is no gulf fixed between a state of nature and grace, but we may pass from the one to thee other, from sin to God; but if we die in our sins, if we throw ourselves into the pit of destruction, there is no coming out. It is a pit *in which there is no water,* and *out of which there is no redemption.* The decree and counsel of God have fixed this gulf, which all the world cannot unfix. This abandons this miserable creature to despair; it is now too late for any change of his condition, or any the least relief: it might have been prevented *in time,* but it cannot now be remedied *to eternity.* The state of damned sinners is fixed by an irreversible and unalterable sentence. A stone is rolled to the door of the pit, which cannot be rolled back.

3. The further request he had to make to his father Abraham, not for himself, his mouth is stopped, and he has not a word to say in answer to Abraham's denial of a drop of water. Damned sinners are made to know that the sentence they are under is just, and they cannot alleviate their own misery by making any objection against it. And, since he cannot obtain a drop of water to *cool his tongue,* we may suppose he *gnawed his tongue for pain,* as those are said to do on whom one of the *vials* of God's wrath is *poured out,* Rev. 16:10. The shrieks and outcries which we may suppose to be now uttered by him were hideous; but, having an opportunity of speaking to Abraham, he will improve it for his relations whom he has left behind, since he cannot improve it for his own advantage. Now as to this,

(1.) He begs that Lazarus might be *sent to his father's house,* upon an errand thither: *I pray thee therefore, father, v.* 27. Again he calls upon Abraham, and in this request he is importunate: "*I pray thee.* O deny me not this." When he was on earth he might have prayed and been heard, but now he prays in vain. "*Therefore,* because thou hast denied me the former request, surely thou wilt be so compassionate as not to deny this:" or, "*Therefore,* because *there is a great gulf fixed,* seeing there is no getting out hence when they are once here, O send to prevent their coming hither:" or, "Though there is a *great gulf fixed* between you and me, yet, since there is no such gulf fixed between you and them, send them hither. Send him back *to my father's house;* he knows well enough where it is, has been there many a time, having been denied the crumbs that fell from the table. He knows I have *five brethren* there; if he appear to them, they will *know him,* and will regard what he saith, for they knew him to be an honest man. Let him *testify to them;* let him tell them what condition I am in, and that I brought myself to it by my luxury and sensuality, and my unmercifulness to the poor. Let him warn them not to tread in my steps, nor to go on in the way wherein I led them, and left them, *lest they also come into this place of torment," v.* 28. Some observe that he speaks only of *five brethren,* whence they infer that he had *no children,* else he would have mentioned them, and then it was an aggravation of his uncharitableness that he had no children to provide for. Now he would have them stopped in their sinful course. He does not say, "Give me leave to go to them, that I may testify to them;" for he knew that there was a *gulf fixed,* and despaired of a permission so favourable to himself: his going would frighten them out of their *wits;* but, "Send Lazarus, whose address will be less terrible, and yet his testimony sufficient to frighten them out of their *sins.*" Now he desired the preventing of their ruin, partly in tenderness to *them,* for whom he could not but retain a *natural affection;* he knew their temper, their temptations, their ignorance, their infidelity, their inconsideration, and wished to prevent the destruction they were running into: but it was partly in tenderness *to himself,* for their coming to him, to that *place of torment,* would but aggravate the misery to him, who had helped to show them the way thither, as the sight of Lazarus helped to aggravate his misery. When partners in sin come to be sharers in woe, as tares bound in bundles for the fire, they will be a terror to one another.

(2.) Abraham denies him this favour too. There is no request granted in hell. Those who make the rich man's praying to Abraham a justification of their praying to saints departed, as they have far to seek for proofs, when the practice of a damned sinner must be valued for an example, so they have little encouragement to follow the example, when all his prayers were made *in vain.* Abraham leaves them to the testimony of Moses and the prophets, the ordinary means of conviction and conversion; they have the written word, which they may read and hear read. *"Let them* attend to that *sure word of prophecy,* for God will not go out of the common method of his grace for them." Here is their privilege: *They have Moses and the prophets;* and their duty: *"Let them hear them,* and mix faith with them, and that will be sufficient to keep them from this place of torment." By this it appears that there is sufficient evidence in the Old Testament, in Moses and *the prophets,* to convince those that will hear them impartially that there is another life after this, and a state of rewards and punishments for good and bad men; for that was the thing which the rich man would have his brethren assured of, and for that they are turned over to Moses and the prophets.

(3.) He urges his request yet further (*v.* 30): *"Nay, father Abraham,* give me leave to press this. It is true, they have Moses and the prophets, and, if they would but give a due regard to them, it would be sufficient; but they do not, they will not; yet it may be hoped, *if one went to them from the dead, they would repent,* that would be a more sensible conviction to them. They are used to Moses and the prophets, and therefore regard them the less; but this would be a *new thing,* and more startling; surely this would bring them to *repent,* and to change their wicked habit and course of life." Note, Foolish men are apt to think any method of conviction better than that which God has chosen and appointed.

(4.) Abraham insists upon the denial of it, with a conclusive reason (*v.* 31): *"If they hear not Moses and the prophets,* and will not believe the testimony nor take the warning they give, *neither will they be persuaded though one rose from the dead.* If they regard not the public revelation, which is confirmed by miracles, neither would they be wrought upon by a private testimony to themselves." [1.] The matter has been long since settled, upon trial, that God should speak by Moses and such prophets, and not by immediate messengers from heaven. Israel chose it in mount Sinai, because they could not bear the terrors of such expresses. [2.] A messenger from the dead could say no more than what is said in the scriptures, nor say it with more authority. [3.] There would be every jot as much reason to suspect that to be a cheat and a delusion as to suspect the scriptures to be so, and much more; and infidels in one case would certainly be so in another. [4.] The same strength of corruption that breaks through the convictions of the written word would certainly triumph over those by a witness *from the dead:* and, though a sinner might be frightened at first by such a testimony, when the fright was over he would soon return to his hardness. [5.] The scripture is now the ordinary way of God's making known his mind to us, and it is sufficient. It is presumption for us to prescribe any other way, nor have we any ground to expect or pray for the grace of God to work upon us in any other way abstracted from that and when that is rejected and set aside. What our Saviour here said was soon after verified in the unbelieving Jews, who would not hear Moses and the prophets, Christ and the apostles, and then would not be persuaded, though *Lazarus rose from the dead* (and perhaps it was with some eye to him that Christ named this poor man Lazarus), nay, they consulted to put him to death, and would not be persuaded by him neither, though he also *rose from the dead.* When Eutychus was raised to life, the people that were present continued to hear Paul preach, but did not turn to enquire of him, Acts 20:10, 11. Let us not therefore desire visions and apparitions, nor seek to the dead, but *to the law and to the testimony* (Isa. 8:19, 20), for that is *the sure word of prophecy,* upon which we may depend.

CHAPTER 17

In this chapter we have, I. Some particular discourses which Christ had with his disciples, in which he teaches them to take heed of giving offence, and to forgive the injuries done them (*v.* 1–4), encourages them to pray for the increase of their faith (*v.* 5, 6), and then teaches them humility, whatever service they had done for God (*v.* 7–10). II. His cleansing ten lepers, and the thanks he had from one of them only, and he a Samaritan (*v.* 11–19). III. His discourse with his disciples, upon occasion of an enquiry of the Pharisees, when the kingdom of God should appear (*v.* 20–37).

Verses 1–10

We are here taught,

I. That the *giving of offences* is a *great sin,* and that which we should every one of us avoid and carefully watch against, *v.* 1, 2. We can expect no other than that offences will come, considering the perverseness and frowardness that are in the nature of man, and the wise purpose and counsel of God, who will carry on his work even by those offences, and bring good out of evil. *It is* almost *impossible but that offences will come,* and therefore we are concerned to provide accordingly; but *woe to him through whom they come,* his doom will be heavy (*v.* 2), more terrible than that of the worst of the malefactors who are condemned to be thrown into the sea, for they perish under a load of guilt more *ponderous* than that of *millstones.* This includes a woe, 1. To persecutors, who offer any injury to the least of Christ's *little ones,* in word or deed, by which they are discouraged in serving Christ, and doing their duty, or in danger of being driven off from it. 2. To seducers, who corrupt the truths of Christ and his ordinances, and so *trouble the minds of the disciples;* for they are those by whom *offences come.* 3. To those who, under the profession of the Christian name, live scandalously, and thereby weaken the bands and sadden the hearts of God's people; for by them the offence comes, and it is no abatement of their guilt, nor will be any of their punishment, that it is impossible but offences will come.

II. That the *forgiving of offences* is a *great duty,* and that which we should every one of us make conscience of (*v.* 3): *Take heed to yourselves.* This may refer either to what goes before, or to what follows: *Take heed that you offend not one of these little ones.* Ministers must be very careful not to say or do any thing that may be a discouragement to weak Christians; there is need of great caution, and they ought to speak and act very considerately, for fear of this: or, "When *your brother trespasses against you,* does you any injury, puts any slight or affront upon you, if he be accessary to any damage done you in your property or reputation, *take heed to yourselves at such a time,* lest you be put into a passion; lest, when your spirits are provoked, you *speak unadvisedly,* and rashly vow to revenge (Prov. 24:29): *I will do so to him as he hath done to me.* Take heed what you say at such a time, lest you say amiss."

1. If you are permitted to *rebuke him,* you are advised to do so. Smother not the resentment, but give it vent. *Tell him his faults;* show him wherein he has not done well nor fairly by you, and, it may be, you will perceive (and you must be very willing to perceive it) that you mistook him, that it was not a *trespass against you,* or not designed, but an *oversight,* and then you will beg his pardon for misunderstanding him; as Jos. 22:30, 31.

2. You are commanded, upon his repentance, to forgive him, and to be perfectly reconciled to him: *If he repent, forgive him;* forget the injury, never think of it again, much less upbraid him with it. Though he do not repent, you must not therefore bear malice to him, nor meditate revenge; but, it he do not at least *say that he repents,* you are not bound to be so free and familiar with him as you have been. If he be guilty of gross sin, to the offence of the Christian community he is a member of, let him be gravely and mildly reproved for his sin, and, upon his repentance, received into friendship and communion again. This the apostle calls *forgiveness,* 2 Co. 2:7.

3. You are to repeat this every time he repeats his trespass, *v.* 4. "If he could be supposed to be either so negligent, or so impudent, as to *trespass against thee seven times in a day,* and as often profess himself sorry for his fault, and promise not again to offend in like manner, continue to *forgive him." Humanum est errare — To ere is human.* Note, Christians should be of a forgiving spirit, willing to make the best of every body, and to make all about them easy; forward to extenuate faults, and not to aggravate them; and they should contrive as much to show that they have forgiven an injury as others to show that they resent it.

III. That we have all need to get our *faith* strengthened, because, as that grace grows, all other graces grow. The more firmly we believe the doctrine of Christ, and the more confidently we rely upon the grace of Christ, the better it will be with us every way. Now observe here, 1. The address which the disciples made to Christ, for the strengthening of their faith, *v.* 5. *The apostles* themselves, so they are here called, though they were prime ministers of state in Christ's kingdom, yet acknowledged the weakness and deficiency of their faith, and saw their need of Christ's grace for the improvement of it; they *said unto the Lord, "Increase our faith,* and perfect what is lacking in it." Let the discoveries of faith be more clear, the desires of faith more strong, the dependences of faith more firm and fixed, the dedications of faith more entire and resolute, and the delights of faith more pleasing. Note, the increase of our faith is what we should earnestly desire, and we should offer up that desire to God in prayer. Some think that they put up this prayer to Christ upon occasion of his pressing upon them the duty of forgiving injuries: *"Lord, increase our faith,* or we shall never be able to practise such a difficult duty as this." Faith in God's pardoning mercy will enable us to get over the greatest difficulties that lie in the way of our forgiving our brother. Others think that it was upon some other occasion, when the apostles were run aground in working some miracle, and were reproved by Christ for the weakness of their faith, as Mt. 17:16, etc. To him that *blamed* them they must apply themselves for grace to *mend* them; to him they cry, *Lord, increase our faith.* 2. The assurance Christ gave them of the wonderful efficacy of true faith (*v.* 6): *"If ye had faith as a grain of mustard-seed,* so *small* as mustard-seed, but yours is yet less than the least; or so *sharp* as *mustard-seed,* so pungent, so exciting to all other graces, as mustard to the animal spirits," and therefore used in palsies, "you might do wonders much beyond what you now do; nothing would be too hard for you, that was fit to be done for the glory of God, and the confirmation of the doctrine you preach, yea, though it were the *transplanting of a tree* from the earth *to the sea."* See Mt. 17:20. As with God *nothing is impossible,* so are all *things possible to him that can believe.*

IV. That, whatever we do in the service of Christ, we must be very humble, and not imagine that we can merit any favour at his hand, or claim it as a debt; even the apostles themselves, who did so much more for Christ than others, must not think that they had thereby made him their debtor. 1. We are all *God's servants* (his *apostles* and *ministers* are in a special manner *so*), and, as servants, are bound to do all we can for his honour. Our whole strength and our whole time are to be employed for him; for *we are not our own,* nor at our own disposal, but at our Master's. 2. As God's servants, it becomes us to fill up our time with duty, and we have a variety of work appointed us to do; we ought to make the end of one service the beginning of another. The servant that has been *ploughing,* or *feeding cattle, in the field,* when he *comes home* at night has work to do still; he must *wait at table, v.* 7, 8. When we have been employed in the duties of a religious conversation, that will not excuse us from the exercises of devotion; when we have been *working for God,* still we must be *waiting on God,* waiting on him continually. 3. Our principal care here must be to do the duty of our relation, and leave it to our Master to give us the comfort of it, when and how he thinks fit. No servant expects that his master should say to him, *Go and sit down to meat;* it is time enough to do that when we have *done our day's work.* Let us be in care to finish our work, and to do that well, and then the reward will come in due time. 4. It is fit that Christ should be served before us: *Make ready wherewith I may sup, and afterwards thou shalt eat and drink.* Doubting Christians say that they cannot give to Christ the glory of his love as they should, because they have not yet obtained the comfort of it; but this is wrong. First let Christ have the glory of it, let us attend him with our praises, and then we shall *eat and drink* in the comfort of that love, and in this there is a feast. 5. Christ's servants, when they are to wait upon him, must *gird themselves,* must free themselves from every thing that is entangling and encumbering, and fit themselves with a close application of mind to go on, and go through, with their work; they must *gird up the loins of their mind.* When we have prepared for Christ's entertainment, have *made ready wherewith he may sup,* we must then *gird ourselves,* to attend him. This is expected from servants, and Christ might require it from us, but he does not insist upon it. He was *among his disciples as one that served,* and came not, as other masters, to take state, and *to be ministered unto, but to minister;* witness his washing his disciples' feet. 6. Christ's servants do not so much as merit his thanks for any service they do him: *"Does he thank that servant?* Does he reckon himself indebted to him for it? No, by no means." No good works of ours can merit any thing at the hand of God. We expect God's favour, not because we have by our services made him a debtor to us, but because he has by his promises made himself a debtor to his own honour, and this we may plead with him, but cannot sue for a *quantum meruit — according to merit.* 7. Whatever we do for Christ, though it should be more perhaps than some others do, yet it is no more than is our duty to do. Though we should *do all things that are commanded us,* and alas! in many things we come short of this, yet there is no work of *supererogation;* it is but what we are bound to by that first and great commandment of *loving God* with *all our heart and soul,* which includes the utmost. 8. The best servants of Christ, even when they do the best services, must humbly acknowledge that they are *unprofitable servants;* though they are not those unprofitable servants that bury their talents, and shall be cast into *utter darkness,* yet as to Christ, and any advantage that can accrue to him by their services, they are *unprofitable;* our *goodness extendeth not unto God,* nor *if we are righteous is he the better,* Ps. 16:2; Job 22:2; 35:7. God cannot be a *gainer* by our services, and therefore cannot be made a *debtor* by them. He has no need of us, nor can our services make any addition to his perfections. It becomes us therefore to call ourselves *unprofitable servants,* but to call his service a profitable service, for God is happy without us, but we are undone without him.

Verses 11–19

We have here an account of the cure of ten lepers, which we had not in any other of the evangelists. The leprosy was a disease which the Jews supposed to be inflicted for the punishment of some particular sin, and to be, more than other diseases, a mark of God's displeasure; and therefore Christ, who came to take away sin, and turn away wrath, took particular care to cleanse the lepers that fell in his way. Christ was now in his way to Jerusalem, about the mid-way, where he had little acquaintance in comparison with what he had either at Jerusalem or in Galilee. He was now in the frontier-country, the marches that lay between Samaria and Galilee. He went that road to find out these lepers, and to cure them; for he is *found of them that sought him not.* Observe,

I. The address of these lepers to Christ. They were ten in a company; for, though they were shut out from society with others, yet those that were infected were at liberty to converse with one another, which would be some comfort to them, as giving them an opportunity to compare notes, and to condole with one another. Now observe, 1. They *met* Christ *as he entered into a certain village.* They did not stay till he had refreshed himself for some time after the fatigue of his journey, but met him as he *entered* the town, weary as he was; and yet he did not put them off, nor adjourn their cause. 2. They *stood afar off,* knowing that by the law their disease obliged them to *keep their distance.* A sense of our spiritual leprosy should make us very humble in all our approaches to Christ. Who are we, that we should draw near to him that is infinitely pure? We are impure. 3. Their request was unanimous, and very importunate (*v.* 13): *They lifted up their voices,* being at a distance, and cried, *Jesus, Master, have mercy on us.* those that expect help from Christ must take him for their Master, and be at his command. If he be *Master,* he will be *Jesus, a Saviour,* and not otherwise. They ask not in particular to be cured of their leprosy, but, *Have mercy on us;* and it is enough to refer ourselves to the compassions of Christ, for they *fail not.* They heard the fame of this Jesus (though he had not been much conversant in that country), and that was such as encouraged them to make application to him; and, if but one of them began in so cheap and easy an address, they would all join.

II. Christ sent them to *the priest,* to be *inspected* by him, who was the judge of the leprosy. He did not tell them positively that they should be *cured,* but bade them *go show themselves to the priests, v.* 14. This was a trial of their obedience, and it was fit that it should be so tried, as Naaman's in a like case: *Go wash in Jordan.* Note, Those that expect Christ's favours must take them in his way and method. Some of these lepers perhaps would be ready to quarrel with the prescription: "Let him either cure or say that he will not, and not send us to the priests on a fool's errand;" but, over-ruled by the rest, they all *went to the priest.* As the ceremonial law was yet in force, Christ took care that it should be observed, and the reputation of it kept up, and due honour paid to the priests in things pertaining to their function; but, probably, he had here a further design, which was to have the priest's *judgment of,* and *testimony to,* the perfectness of the cure; and that the priest might be awakened, and others by him, to enquire after one that had such a commanding power over bodily diseases.

III. *As they went, they were cleansed,* and so became fit to be looked upon by the priest, and to have a certificate from him that they were clean. Observe, *Then* we may expect God to meet us with mercy when we are found in the way of duty. If we do what we can, God will not be wanting to do that for us which we cannot. Go, attend upon instituted ordinances; go and pray, and read the scriptures: *Go show thyself to the priests;* go and open thy case to a faithful minister, and, though the means will not heal thee of themselves, God will heal thee in the diligent use of those means.

IV. One of them, and but one, *returned, to give thanks, v.* 15. When he *saw that he was healed,* instead of going forward to the priest, to be by him declared clean, and so discharged from his confinement, which was all that the rest aimed at, he *turned back* towards him who was the Author of his cure, whom he wished to have the glory of it, before he received the benefit of it. He appears to have been very hearty and affectionate in his thanksgivings: *With a loud voice he glorified God,* acknowledging it to come originally from *him;* and he *lifted up his voice* in his praises, as he had done in his prayers, *v.* 13. Those that have received mercy from God should publish it to others, that they may praise God too, and may be encouraged by their experiences to trust in him. But he also made a particular address of thanks to Christ (*v.* 16): *He fell down at his feet,* put himself into the most humble reverent posture he could, and *gave him thanks.* Note, We ought to give thanks for the favours Christ bestows upon us, and particularly for recoveries from sickness; and we ought to be *speedy* in our returns of praise, and not defer them, lest time wear out the sense of the mercy. It becomes us also to be very humble in our thanksgivings, as well as in our prayers. It becomes the seed of Jacob, like him, to own themselves *less than the least of God's mercies,* when they have received them, as well as when they are in pursuit of them.

V. Christ took notice of this one that had thus distinguished himself; for, it seems, he was a Samaritan, whereas the rest were Jews, *v.* 16. The Samaritans were separatists from the Jewish church, and had not the pure knowledge and worship of God among them that the Jews had, and yet it was one of them that *glorified God,* when the Jews forgot, or, when it was moved to them, *refused,* to do it. Now observe here,

1. The particular notice Christ took of him, of the grateful return he made, and the ingratitude of those that were sharers with him in the mercy — that he who was a *stranger* to the commonwealth of Israel was the only one that *returned to give glory to God, v.* 17, 18. See here, (1.) How *rich* Christ is in *doing good: Were there not ten cleansed?* Here was a cure by *wholesale,* a whole *hospital* healed with *one* word's speaking. Note, There is an abundance of healing cleansing virtue in the blood of Christ, sufficient for all his patients, though ever so many. Here are *ten at a time* cleansed; we shall have never the less grace for others sharing it. (2.) How *poor* we are in our returns: *"Where are the nine?* Why did not they return to give thanks?" This intimates that ingratitude is a very common sin. Of the many that receive mercy from God, there are but few, very few, that *return to give thanks* in a right manner (scarcely *one in ten*), that render according to the benefit done to them. (3.) How those often prove most grateful from whom it was least expected. A Samaritan gives thanks, and a Jew does not. Thus many who profess revealed religion are out-done, and quite shamed, by some that are governed only by natural religion, not only in moral value, but in piety and devotion. This serves here to aggravate the ingratitude of those Jews of whom Christ speaks, as *taking it very ill* that his kindness was so slighted. And it intimates how justly he resents the ingratitude of the world of mankind, for whom he had *done so much,* and from whom he has *received so little.*

2. The great encouragement Christ gave him, *v.* 19. The rest had their *cure,* and had it not *revoked,* as justly it might have been, for their ingratitude, though they had such a good example of gratitude set before them; but he had his cure confirmed particularly with an encomium: *Thy faith hath made thee whole.* The rest were *made whole* by the power of Christ, in compassion to their distress, and in answer to their prayer; but he was made whole *by his faith,* by which Christ saw him distinguished from the rest. Note, Temporal mercies are *then* doubled and sweetened to us when they are *fetched* in by the prayers of faith, and *returned* by the praises of faith.

Verses 20–37

We have here a discourse of Christ's concerning the *kingdom of God,* that is, the kingdom of the Messiah, which was now shortly to be *set up,* and of which there was great expectation.

I. Here is the demand of the Pharisees concerning it, which occasioned this discourse. They asked *when the kingdom of God should come,* forming a notion of it as a *temporal kingdom,* which should advance the Jewish nation above the nations of the earth. They were impatient to hear some tidings of its approach; they understood, perhaps, that Christ had taught his disciples to pray for the coming of it, and they had long preached that it was *at hand.* "Now," say the Pharisees, "when will that glorious view open? When shall we see this *long-looked-for* kingdom?"

II. Christ's reply to this demand, directed to the Pharisees first, and afterwards to his own disciples, who knew better how to understand it (*v.* 22); what he said to both, he saith to us.

1. That the kingdom of the Messiah was to be a *spiritual kingdom,* and not temporal and external. They asked *when* it would come. "You know not what you ask," saith Christ; "it may come, and you not be aware of it." For it has not an *external show,* as other kingdoms have, the advancements and revolutions of which are taken notice of by the nations of the earth, and fill the newspapers; so they expected this kingdom of God would do. "No," saith Christ, (1.) "It will have a silent entrance, without pomp, without noise; it *cometh not with observation," meta paratērēseōs — with outward show.* They desired to have their curiosity satisfied concerning the *time* of it, to which Christ does not give them any answer, but will have their mistakes rectified concerning the nature of it: *"It is not for you to know the times* of this kingdom, these are *secret things,* which belong not to you; but the great intentions of this kingdom, these are *things revealed."* When Messiah the Prince comes to set up his kingdom, they shall not say, *Lo here,* or *Lo there,* as when a prince goes in progress to visit his territories it is in every body's mouth, he is here, or he is there; for *where the king is there is the court.* Christ will not come with all this talk; it will not be set up in this or that particular place; nor will the court of that kingdom be *here* or *there;* nor will it be *here* or *there* as it respects the country men are of, or the place they dwell in, as if that would place them nearer to, or further from, that kingdom. Those who confine Christianity and the church to this place or that party, cry, *Lo here,* or *Lo there,* than which nothing is more contrary to the designs of catholic Christianity; so do they who make prosperity and external pomp a mark of the true church. (2.) "It has a *spiritual* influence: *The kingdom of God is within you."* It is not of this world, Jn. 18:36. Its glory does not strike men's fancies, but affects their spirits, and its power is over their souls and consciences; from them it receives homage, and not from their bodies only. The *kingdom of God* will not change men's outward condition, but their hearts and lives. Then it *comes* when it makes those humble, and serious, and heavenly, that were proud, and vain,

and carnal, — when it *weans* those from the world that were *wedded* to the world; and therefore look for the kingdom of God in the revolutions of the heart, not of the civil government. The kingdom of God is *among you;* so some read it. "You enquire when it will come, and are not aware that it is already begun to be set up *in the midst of you.* The gospel is preached, it is *confirmed* by miracles, it is *embraced* by multitudes, so that it is *in your* nation, though not in your hearts." Note, It is the folly of many curious enquirers concerning the times to come that they look for that *before them* which is already *among them.*

2. That the setting up of this kingdom was a work that would meet with a great deal of *opposition* and *interruption, v.* 22. The *disciples* thought they should carry all before them, and expected a constant series of success in their work; but Christ tells them it would be otherwise: *"The days will come,* before you have finished your testimony and done your work, *when you shall desire to see one of the days of the Son of man"* (one such a day as we *now* have), "of the prosperity and progress of the gospel, and *shall not see it.* At first, indeed, you will have wonderful success" (so they had, when *thousands* were added to the church *in a day*); "but do not think it will be always so; no, you will be persecuted and scattered, silenced and imprisoned, so that you will not have opportunities of preaching the gospel without fear, as you now have; people will grow cool to it, when they have enjoyed it awhile, so that you will not see such harvests of souls gathered in to Christ afterwards as at first, nor such multitudes flocking to him *as doves to their windows."* This looks forward to his disciples in after-ages; they must expect much disappointment; the gospel will not be always preached with equal liberty and success. Ministers and churches will sometimes be under *outward restraints.* Teachers will be removed into corners, and solemn assemblies scattered. Then they will wish to see such days of opportunity as they have formerly enjoyed, sabbath days, sacrament days, preaching days, praying days; these are *days of the Son of man,* in which we hear from him, and converse with him. The time may come when we may in vain wish for such days. God teaches us to know the worth of such mercies by the want of them. It concerns us, while they are continued, to *improve* them, and in the years of plenty to lay up in store for the years of famine. Sometimes they will be under *inward restraints,* will not have such tokens of the *presence of the Son of man* with them as they have had. The Spirit is withdrawn from them; they *see not their signs;* the angel comes not down to stir the waters; there is a great stupidity among the children of men, and a great lukewarmness among the children of God; then they shall wish to see such *victorious triumphant* days of the *Son of man* as they have sometimes seen, when he has ridden forth with his bow and his crown, conquering and to conquer, but they will not see them. Note, We must not think that Christ's church and cause are lost because not always alike visible and prevailing.

3. That Christ and his kingdom are not to be looked for in this or that particular place, but his appearance will be general in all places at once (*v.* 23, 24): *"They will say to you, See here, or, See there;* here is one that will deliver the Jews out of the hands of the oppressing Romans, or there is one that will deliver the Christians out of the hands of the oppressing Jews; here is the Messiah, and there is his prophet; *here* in *this* mountain, or *there* at Jerusalem, you will find the true church. *Go not after them, nor follow them;* do not heed such suggestions. The kingdom of God was not designed to be the glory of one people only, but to *give light to the Gentiles;* for *as the lightning that lightens out of one part under heaven, and shines* all on a sudden irresistibly *to the other part under heaven, so shall also the Son of man be in his day."* (1.) "The *judgments* that are to destroy the Jewish nation, to lay them waste, and to deliver the Christians from them, shall *fly like lightning* through the land, shall lay all waste from one end of it to another; and those that are marked for this destruction can no more avoid it, nor oppose it, than they can a *flash of lightning."* (2.) "The gospel that is to set up Christ's kingdom in the world shall *fly like lightning* through the nations. The kingdom of the Messiah is not to be a *local* thing, but is to be dispersed far and wide over the face of the whole earth; it shall *shine* from Jerusalem to all parts about, and that *in a moment.* The kingdoms of the earth shall be leavened by the gospel ere they are aware of it." The trophies of Christ's victories shall be erected on the ruins of the devil's kingdom, even in those countries that could never be subdued to the Roman yoke. The design of the setting up of Christ's kingdom was not to make one *nation great,* but to make *all nations good* — some, at least, of all nations; and this point shall be gained, though the *nations rage,* and the *kings of the earth set themselves* with all their might against it.

4. That the Messiah must *suffer* before he must reign (*v.* 25): *"First must he suffer many things,* many hard things, and *be rejected of this generation;* and, if he be thus treated, his disciples must expect no other than to *suffer* and be *rejected* too for his sake." They thought of having the kingdom of the Messiah set up in external splendour: "No," saith Christ, "we must go by the cross to the crown. The *Son of man must suffer many things.* Pain, and shame, and death, are those *many things.* He must be *rejected by this generation* of unbelieving Jews, before he be embraced by another generation of believing Gentiles, that his gospel may have the honour of triumphing over the greatest opposition from those who ought to have given it the greatest assistance; and thus the excellency of the power will appear to be *of God, and not of man;* for, though Israel be not *gathered,* yet he will be *glorious* to the ends of the earth."

5. That the setting up of the kingdom of the Messiah would introduce the destruction of the Jewish nation, whom it would find in a deep sleep of *security,* and drowned in *sensuality,* as the old world was in the days of Noah, and Sodom in the days of Lot, *v.* 26, etc. Observe,

(1.) How it had been with sinners formerly, and in what posture the judgments of God, of which they had been fairly warned, did at length find them. Look as far back as the *old world,* when all flesh had *corrupted their way,* and the *earth was filled with violence.* Come a little lower, and think how it was with the men of Sodom, who were *wicked, and sinners before the Lord exceedingly.* Now observe concerning both these, [1.] That they had *fair warning given them* of the ruin that was coming upon them for their sins. Noah was a *preacher of righteousness* to the old world; so was Lot to the Sodomites. They gave them timely notice of what would be in the end of their wicked ways, and that it was not far off. [2.] That they did not regard the warning given them, and gave no credit, no heed to it. They were very secure, went on in their business as unconcerned as you could imagine; *they did eat, they drank,* indulged themselves in their pleasures, and took no care of any thing else, but to *make provision for the flesh,* counted upon the perpetuity of their present flourishing state, and therefore married wives, and *were given in marriage,* that their families might be built up. They were all very merry; so were the men of Sodom, and yet very busy too: *they bought, they sold, they planted, they builded.* These were lawful things, but the fault was that they minded these inordinately, and their hearts were entirely set upon them, as that they had no heart at all to prepare against the threatened judgments. When they should have been, as the men of Nineveh, *fasting and praying, repenting* and *reforming,* upon warning given them of an approaching judgment, they were going on securely, *eating flesh,* and *drinking wine,* when God called *to weeping and to mourning,* Isa. 22:12, 13. [3.] That they continued in their security and sensuality, till the threatened judgment came. Until the day *that Noah entered into the ark,* and *Lot went out of Sodom,* nothing said or done to them served to alarm or awaken them. Note, Though the stupidity of sinners in a sinful way is as strange as it is *without excuse,* yet we are not to think it strange, for it is not without example. It is the *old way that wicked men have trodden,* that have gone slumbering to hell, as if their damnation slumbered while they did. [4.] That God took care for the preservation of those that were his, who believed and feared, and took the warning themselves which they gave to others. Noah entered *into the ark,* and there he was safe; Lot went out of Sodom, and so went out of harm's way. If some run on *heedless* and *headlong* into destruction, that shall be no prejudice to the salvation of those that believe. [5.] That they were surprised with the ruin which they would not fear, and were swallowed up in it, to their unspeakable horror and amazement. The *flood came,* and destroyed all the sinners of the old world; *fire and brimstone* came, and *destroyed* all the sinners of Sodom. God has many arrows in his quiver, and uses which he will in making war upon his rebellious subjects, for he can make which he will effectual. But that which is especially intended here is to show what a dreadful surprise destruction will be to those who are secure and sensual.

(2.) How it will be with sinners still (*v.* 30): *Thus shall it be in the day when the Son of man is revealed.* When Christ comes to destroy the Jewish nation, by the Roman armies, the generality of that nation will be found under such a reigning security and stupidity as this. They have warning given by Christ now, and will have it repeated to them by the apostles after him, as they had by Noah and Lot; but it will be all *in vain.* They will continue secure, will go on in their neglect and opposition of Christ and his gospel, till all the Christians are withdrawn from among them and gone to the place of refuge. God will provide for them on the other side Jordan, and then a deluge of judgments shall flow in upon them, which will destroy all the unbelieving Jews. One would have thought that this discourse of our Saviour's, which was public, and not long after *published* to the world, should have awakened them; but it did not, for the hearts of that people were hardened, to their destruction. In like manner, when Jesus Christ shall come to judge the world, at the end of time, sinners will be found in the same secure and careless posture, altogether regardless of the judgment approaching, which will therefore come upon them as a snare; and in like manner the sinners of every age go on securely in their evil ways, and *remember not their latter end,* nor the account that they must give. *Woe to them that are thus at ease in Zion.*

6. That it ought to be the care of his disciples and followers to distinguish themselves from the unbelieving Jews in that day, and, leaving them, their city and country, to themselves, to flee at the signal given, according to the direction that should be given. Let them retire, as Noah to his ark, and Lot to his Zoar. You *would have healed Jerusalem,* as of old Babylon, *but she is not healed,* and therefore *forsake her, flee out of the midst of her,* and *deliver every man his soul,* Jer. 51:6, 9. This flight of theirs from Jerusalem must be *expeditious,* and must not be retarded by any concern about their worldly affairs (*v.* 31): *"He that shall be on the house-top,* when the alarm is given, *let him not come down, to take his stuff away,* both because he cannot spare so much time, and because the carrying away of his effects will but encumber him and retard his flight." Let him not *regard* his *stuff* at such a time, when it will be next to a miracle of mercy if he have his *life given him for a prey.* It will be better to leave his stuff behind him than to stay to look after it, and *perish with them that believe* not. It will be their concern to do as Lot and his family were charged to do: *Escape for thy life. Save yourselves from this untoward generation.* (2.) When they have made their escape, they must not think of returning (*v.* 32): *"Remember Lot's wife;* and take warning by her not only to flee from this Sodom (for so Jerusalem is become, Isa. 1:10), but to persevere in your flight, and do not *look back,* as she did; be not loth to leave a place marked for destruction, whomsoever or whatsoever you leave behind you, that is ever so dear to you." Those who have left the Sodom of a natural state, let them go forward, and not so much as look a kind look towards it again. Let them not *look back,* lest they should be tempted to *go back;* nay, lest that be construed a *going back in heart,* or an evidence that the heart was left behind. Lot's wife was *turned into a pillar of salt,* that she might remain a lasting monument of God's displeasure against apostates, who *begin in the spirit and end in the flesh.* (3.) There would be no other way of saving their lives than by quitting the Jews, and, if they thought to save themselves by a coalition with them, they would find themselves mistaken (*v.* 33): *"Whosoever shall seek to save his life,* by declining from his Christianity and complying with the Jews, he shall *lose it* with them and perish in the common calamity; but whosoever is willing to venture his life with the Christians, upon the same bottom on which they venture, to take his lot with them in life and in death, he shall *preserve* his life, for he shall make sure of *eternal life,* and is in a likelier way at that time to save his life than those who embark in a Jewish bottom, or *ensure* upon their securities." Note, Those do best themselves that trust God in the way of duty.

7. That all good Christians should certainly escape, but many of them very *narrowly,* from that destruction, *v.* 34–36. When God's judgments are laying all waste, he will take an effectual course to preserve those that are his, by remarkable providences distinguishing between them and others that were nearest to them: *two in a bed, one taken and the other left;* one snatched out of the burning and taken into a place of safety, while the other is left to perish in the common ruin. Note, Though the sword devours one as well as another, and *all things* seem to *come alike to all,* yet sooner or later it

shall be made to appear that the Lord knows them that are his and them that are not, and how to *take out the precious from the vile.* We are sure that *the Judge of all the earth will do right;* and therefore, when he sends a judgment on purpose to avenge the death of his Son upon those that crucified him, he will take care that none of those who glorified him, and gloried in his cross, shall be *taken away* by that judgment.

8. That this distinguishing, dividing, discriminating work shall be done in all places, as far as the kingdom of God shall extend, *v.* 37. *Where, Lord?* They had enquired concerning the time, and he would not gratify their curiosity with any information concerning that; they therefore tried him with another question: *"Where, Lord?* Where shall those be *safe* that are *taken?* Where shall those *perish* that are left?" The answer is proverbial, and may be explained so as to answer each side of the question: *Wheresoever the body is, thither will the eagles be gathered together.* (1.) Wherever the wicked are, who are marked for perdition, they shall *be found out* by the judgments of God; as wherever a dead carcase is, the birds of prey will smell it out, and make a prey of it. The Jews having made themselves a dead and putrefied carcase, *odious* to God's holiness and *obnoxious* to his justice, wherever any of that unbelieving generation is, the judgments of God shall fasten upon them, as the eagles do upon the prey: *Thine hand shall find out all thine enemies* (Ps. 21:8), though they *set their nests among the stars,* Obad. 4. The Roman soldiers will hunt the Jews out of all their recesses and fastnesses, and none shall escape. (2.) Wherever the godly are, who are marked for preservation, they *shall be found* happy in the enjoyment of Christ. As the dissolution of the Jewish church shall be extended to all parts, so shall the constitution of the Christian church. Wherever Christ is, believers will flock to him, and meet in him, as eagles about the prey, without being directed or shown the way, by the instinct of the new nature. Now Christ is where his gospel, and his ordinances, and his church are: *For where two or three are gathered in his name there is he in the midst of them,* and thither therefore others will be gathered to him. The kingdom of the Messiah is not to have one particular place for its *metropolis,* such as Jerusalem was to the Jewish church, to which all Jews were to resort; but, *wherever the body is,* wherever the gospel is preached and ordinances are ministered, thither will pious souls resort, there they will find Christ, and by faith feast upon him. Wherever Christ records his name he will meet his people, and bless them, Jn. 4:21, etc.; 1 Tim. 2:8. Many good interpreters understand it of the gathering of the saints together to Christ in the kingdom of glory: "Ask not where the carcase will be, and how they shall find the way to it, for they shall be under infallible direction; to him who is their living, quickening Head, and the centre of their unity, to him shall the gathering of the people be."

CHAPTER 18

In this chapter we have, I. The parable of the importunate widow, designed to teach us fervency in prayer (*v.* 1–8). II. The parable of the Pharisee and publican, designed to teach us humility, and humiliation for sin, in prayer (*v.* 9–14). III. Christ's favour to little children that were brought to him (*v.* 15–17). IV. The trial of a rich man that had a mind to follow Christ, whether he loved better Christ or his riches; his coming short upon that trial; and Christ's discourse with his disciples upon that occasion (*v.* 18–30). V. Christ's foretelling his own death and sufferings (*v.* 31–34). VI. His restoring sight to a blind man (*v.* 35–43). And these four passages we had before in Matthew and Mark.

Verses 1–8

This parable has its key hanging at the door; the drift and design of it are *prefixed.* Christ spoke it with this intent, to teach us that *men ought always to pray and not to faint, v.* 1. It supposes that all God's people are *praying* people; all God's children keep up both a *constant* and an *occasional* correspondence with him, send to him *statedly,* and upon *every emergency.* It is our privilege and honour that we *may* pray. It is our duty; we *ought to pray,* we sin if we neglect it. It is to be our constant work; we ought *always* to pray, it is that which *the duty of every day requires.* We must pray, and never grow weary of praying, nor think of leaving it off till it comes to be swallowed up in everlasting praise. But that which seems particularly designed here is to teach us constancy and perseverance in our requests for some spiritual mercies that we are in pursuit of, relating either to ourselves or to the church of God. When we are praying for strength against our spiritual enemies, our lusts and corruptions, which are our worst enemies, we must continue instant in prayer, must pray and *not faint,* for we shall not *seek God's face in vain.* So we must likewise in our prayers for the deliverance of the people of God out of the hands of their persecutors and oppressors.

I. Christ shows, by a parable, the *power of importunity* among men, who will be swayed by that, when nothing else will influence, to do what is just and right. He gives you an instance of an honest cause that succeeded before an unjust judge, not by the equity or compassionableness of it, but purely by *dint of importunity.* Observe here, 1. The bad character of the judge that was in a certain city. He *neither feared God nor regarded man;* he had no manner of concern either for his conscience or for his reputation; he stood in no awe either of the wrath of God against him or of the censures of men concerning him: or, he took no care to do his duty either to God or man; he was a perfect stranger both to godliness and honour, and had no notion of either. It is not strange if those that have cast off the fear of their Creator be altogether regardless of their fellow-creatures; where no *fear of God* is no good is to be expected. Such a prevalency of irreligion and inhumanity is bad in any, but very bad in a *judge,* who has power in his hand, in the use of which he ought to be guided by the principles of religion and justice, and, if he be not, instead of doing good with his power he will be in danger of doing hurt. *Wickedness in the place of judgment* was one of the sorest evils Solomon saw under the sun, Eccl. 3:16. 2. The distressed case of a poor widow that was necessitated to make her appeal to him, being wronged by some one that thought to bear her down with power and terror. She had manifestly right on her side; but, it should seem, in soliciting to have right done her, she tied not herself to the formalities of the law, but made personal application to the judge from day to day at his own house, still crying, *Avenge me of mine adversary;* that is, *Do me justice against mine adversary;* not that she desired to be revenged on him for any thing he had done against her, but that he might be obliged to restore what effects he had of hers in his hands, and might be disabled any more to oppress her. Note, Poor widows have often many adversaries, who barbarously take advantage of their weak and helpless state to invade their rights, and defraud them of what little they have; and magistrates are particularly charged, not only not to do *violence to the widow* (Jer. 21:3), but to *judge the fatherless,* and *plead for the widow* (Isa. 1:17), to be their patrons and protectors; then they are *as gods,* for God is so, Ps. 68:5. 3. The difficulty and discouragement she met with in her cause: *He would not for awhile.* According to his usual practice, he frowned upon her, took no notice of her cause, but connived at all the wrong her adversary did her; for she had no bribe to give him, no great man whom he stood in any awe of to speak for her, so that he did not at all incline to redress her grievances; and he himself was conscience of the reason of his dilatoriness, and could not but own within himself that he *neither feared God nor regarded man.* It is sad that a man should know so much amiss of himself, and be in no care to amend it. 4. The gaining of her point by continually *dunning* this unjust *judge* (*v.* 5): *"Because this widow troubleth me,* gives me a continual toil, I will hear her cause, and do her justice; not so much lest by her clamour against me she bring me into an ill name, as lest by her clamour to me she weary me; for she is resolved that she will give me no rest till it is done, and therefore I will do it, to save myself further trouble; as good at first as at last." Thus she got justice done her by continual craving; she begged it at his door, followed him in the streets, solicited him in open court, and still her cry was, *Avenge me of mine adversary,* which he was forced to do, to get rid of her; for his conscience, bad as he was, would not suffer him to send her to prison for an affront upon the court.

II. He applies this for the encouragement of God's praying people to pray with faith and fervency, and to persevere therein.

1. He assures them that God will at length be gracious to them (*v.* 6): *Hear what the unjust judge saith,* how he owns himself quite overcome by a constant importunity, *and shall not God avenge his own elect?* Observe,

(1.) What it is that they desire and expect: that God would *avenge his own elect.* Note, [1.] There are a people in the world that are God's people, his *elect,* his *own elect,* a choice people, a chosen people. And this he has an eye to in all he does for them; it is because they are his *chosen,* and in pursuance of the choice he has made of them. [2.] God's own elect meet with a great deal of trouble and opposition in this world; there are *many adversaries* that fight against them; Satan is their great adversary. [3.] That which is wanted and waited for is God's preserving and protecting them, and the work of his hands in them; his securing the interest of the church in the world and his grace in the heart.

(2.) What it is that is required of God's people in order to the obtaining of this: they must *cry day and night to him;* not that he needs their remonstrances, or can be moved by their pleadings, but this he has made their duty, and to this he has promised mercy. We ought to be particular in praying against our spiritual enemies, as St. Paul was: *For this thing I besought the Lord thrice, that it might depart from me;* like this importunate widow. Lord, mortify *this* corruption. Lord, arm me against *this* temptation. We ought to concern ourselves for the persecuted and oppressed churches, and to pray that God would do them justice, and set them in safety. And herein we must be very urgent; we must *cry* with earnestness: we must *cry day and night,* as those that believe prayer will be heard at last; we must *wrestle with God,* as those that know how to value the blessing, and will have no nay. God's praying people are told to *give him no rest,* Isa. 62:6, 7.

(3.) What discouragements they may perhaps meet with in their prayers and expectations. He may *bear long with them,* and may not presently appear for them, in answer to their prayers. He is *makrothymōn ep' autois* — he *exercises patience towards* the adversaries of his people, and does not take vengeance on them; and he *exercises the patience of his people,* and does not plead for them. He *bore long* with the *cry of the sin* of the Egyptians that oppressed Israel, and with the *cry of the sorrows* of those that were oppressed.

(4.) What assurance they have that mercy will come at last, though it be delayed, and how it is supported by what the unjust judge saith: If this widow prevail by being importunate, much more shall God's elect prevail. For, [1.] This widow was a *stranger,* nothing related to the judge; but God's praying people are his own elect, whom he knows, and loves, and delights in, and has always concerned himself for. [2.] She was but *one,* but the praying people of God are *many,* all of whom come to him on the same errand, and agree to ask what they need, Mt. 18:19. As the saints of heaven surround the throne of glory with their united praises, so saints on earth besiege the throne of grace with their united prayers. [3.] She came to a *judge* that bade her *keep her distance;* we come to a *Father* that bids us *come boldly to* him, and teaches us to cry, *Abba, Father.* [4.] She came to an *unjust judge;* we come to a *righteous Father* (Jn. 17:25), one that regards his own glory and the comforts of his poor creatures, especially those in distress, as *widows* and *fatherless.* [5.] She came to this judge purely upon her own account; but God is himself engaged in the cause which we are soliciting; and we can say, *Arise, O Lord, plead thine* own cause; and *what wilt thou do to thy great name?* [6.] She had no friend to speak for her, to add force to her petition, and to use interest for her more than her own; but we have an *Advocate with the Father,* his own Son, who *ever lives to make intercession* for us, and has a powerful prevailing interest in heaven. [7.] She had no promise off speeding, no, nor any encouragement given her to ask; but we have the golden sceptre held out to us, are told to ask, with a promise that it shall be given to us. [8.] She could have access to the judge only at some certain times; but we may cry to God *day and night,* at all hours, and therefore may the rather hope to prevail by importunity. [9.] Her importunity was provoking to the judge, and she might fear lest it should set him more against her; but our importunity is pleasing to God; the prayer of the upright is *his delight,* and therefore, we may hope, shall avail much, if it be an effectual fervent prayer.

2. He intimates to them that, notwithstanding this, they will begin to be weary of waiting for him (*v.* 8): *"Nevertheless,* though such assurances are given that God will avenge his own elect, yet, *when the Son of man cometh, shall he find faith on the earth?"* The Son of man will come to *avenge his own elect,* to plead the cause of persecuted Christians against the persecuting Jews; he will come in his providence to plead the cause of his injured people in every age, and at the great day he will come finally to determine the controversies of Zion. Now, when he comes, will he find faith on the earth? The question implies a strong negation: No, he will not; he himself foresees it.

(1.) This supposes that it is *on earth* only that there is occasion for *faith;* for sinners in hell are *feeling* that which they would not believe, and saints in heaven are *enjoying* that which they did believe.

(2.) It supposes that *faith* is the great thing that Jesus Christ *looks for.* He *looks down* upon the children of men, and does not ask, Is there innocency? but, *Is there faith?* He enquired concerning the faith of those who applied themselves to him for cures.

(3.) It supposes that if there were faith, though ever so little, he would discover it, and *find it out.* His eye is upon the weakest and most obscure believer.

(4.) It is foretold that, when Christ comes to plead his people's cause, he will find but *little faith* in comparison with what one might expect. That is, [1.] In general, he will find but *few good people,* few that are really and truly good. Many that have the form and fashion of godliness, but few that have faith, that are sincere and honest: nay, he will find little *fidelity* among men; the *faithful fail,* Ps. 12:1, 2. Even to the end of time there will still be occasion for the same complaint. The world will grow no better, no, not when it is drawing towards its period. Bad it is, and bad it will be, and worst of all just before Christ's coming; the last times will be the most perilous. [2.] In particular, he will find few that have *faith* concerning his coming. When he comes to *avenge his own elect* he looks if there be any faith *to help* and *to uphold,* and wonders that there is none, Isa. 59:16; 63:5. It intimates that Christ, both in his particular comings for the relief of his people, and in his general coming at the end of time, may, and will, delay his coming so long as that, *First,* Wicked people will begin to *defy it,* and to say, *Where is the promise of his coming?* 2 Pt. 3:4. They will challenge him to come (Isa. 5:10; Amos 5:19); and his delay will harden them in their wickedness, Mt. 24:48. *Secondly,* Even his own people will begin to *despair* of it, and to conclude he will never come, because he has passed their reckoning. God's time to appear for his people is when things are brought to the last extremity, and when Zion begins to say, *The Lord has forsaken me.* See Isa. 49:14; 40:27. But this is our comfort, that, when the time appointed comes, it will appear that the unbelief of man has not made the promise of God of no effect.

Verses 9–14

The scope of this parable likewise is prefixed to it, and we are told (*v.* 9) who they were whom it was levelled at, and for whom it was calculated. He designed it for the conviction of some who *trusted in themselves that they were righteous, and despised others.* They were such as had, 1. A great conceit of themselves, and of their own goodness; they thought themselves as holy as they needed to be, and holier than all their neighbours, and such as might serve for examples to them all. But that was not all; 2. They had a confidence in themselves before God, and not only had a high opinion of their own righteousness, but depended upon the merit of it, whenever they addressed God, as their plea: They *trusted in themselves as being righteous;* they thought they had made God their debtor, and might demand any thing from him; and, 3. They despised others, and looked upon them with contempt, as not worthy to be compared with them. Now Christ by this parable would show such their folly, and that thereby they shut themselves out from acceptance with God. This is called a *parable,* though there be nothing of similitude in it; but it is rather a description of the different temper and language of those that *proudly justify themselves,* and those that *humbly condemn themselves;* and their different standing before God. It is matter of fact every day.

I. Here are both these addressing themselves to the duty of prayer at the same place and time (*v.* 10): *Two men went up into the temple* (for the temple stood upon a hill) *to pray.* It was not the hour of public prayer, but they went thither to offer up their personal devotions, as was usual with good people at that time, when the temple was not only the *place,* but the *medium* of worship, and God had promised, in answer to Solomon's request, that, whatever prayer was made in a right manner *in* or *towards* that house, it should *therefore* the rather be accepted. Christ is our temple, and to him we must have an eye in all our approaches to God. The *Pharisees* and the *publican* both went to *the temple to pray.* Note, Among the worshippers of God, in the visible church, there is a mixture of good and bad, of some that are accepted of God, and some that are not; and so it has been ever since Cain and Abel brought their offering to the same altar. The Pharisee, proud as he was, could not think himself above prayer; nor could the publican, humble as he was, think himself shut out from the benefit of it; but we have reason to think that these went with different views. 1. The Pharisee went *to the temple* to pray because it was a *public* place, more public than the corners of the streets, and therefore he should have many eyes upon him, who would applaud his devotion, which perhaps was more than was expected. The character Christ gave of the Pharisees, that *all their works they did to be seen of men,* gives us occasion for this suspicion. Note, Hypocrites keep up the external performances of religion only to *save* or *gain* credit. There are many whom we see *every day* at the temple, whom, it is to be feared, we shall not see in the great day at Christ's right hand. 2. The publican went to the temple because it was appointed to be a *house of prayer for all people,* Isa. 56:7. The Pharisee came to the temple upon a *compliment,* the publican upon business; the Pharisee to make his appearance, the publican to make his request. Now God sees with what disposition and design we come to wait upon him in holy ordinances, and will judge of us accordingly.

II. Here is the Pharisee's address to God (for a prayer I cannot call it): He *stood* and *prayed thus with himself* (*v.* 11, 12): *standing by himself, he prayed thus,* so some read it; he was wholly intent upon himself, had nothing in his eye but *self,* his own praise, and not God's glory; or, standing in some conspicuous place, where he distinguished himself; or, *setting himself* with a great deal of state and formality, he prayed thus. Now that which he is here supposed to say is that which shows,

1. That he *trusted to himself that he was righteous.* A great many good things he said of himself, which we will suppose to be true. He was free from gross and scandalous sins; he was not an *extortioner,* not a usurer, not oppressive to debtors or tenants, but fair and kind to all that had dependence upon him. He was not *unjust* in any of his dealings; he did no man any wrong; he could say, as Samuel, *Whose ox or whose ass have I taken?* He was *no adulterer,* but had possessed his vessel in sanctification and honour. Yet this was not all; he *fasted twice in the week,* as an act partly of temperature, partly of devotion. The Pharisees and their disciples fasted twice a week, Monday and Thursday. Thus he glorified God with his body: yet that was not all; he *gave tithes of all that he possessed,* according to the law, and so glorified God with his worldly estate. Now all this was very well and commendable. Miserable is the condition of those who come short of the righteousness of this Pharisee: yet he was not accepted; and why was he not? (1.) His giving God thanks for this, though in itself a good thing, yet seems to be a mere formality. He does not say, *By the grace of God I am what I am,* as Paul did, but turns it off with a slight, *God, I thank thee,* which is intended but for a plausible introduction to a proud vainglorious ostentation of himself. (2.) He makes his boast of this, and dwells with delight upon this subject, as if all his business to the temple was to tell God Almighty how very good he was; and he is ready to say, with those hypocrites that we read of (Isa. 58:3), *Wherefore have we fasted, and thou seest not?* (3.) He *trusted* to it as a righteousness, and not only mentioned it, but pleaded it, as if hereby he had merited at the hands of God, and made him his debtor. (4.) Here is not one word of prayer in all he saith. He went *up to the temple to pray,* but forgot his errand, was so full of himself and his own goodness that he thought he had need of nothing, no, not of the favour and grace of God, which, it would seem, he did not think worth asking.

2. That he *despised others.* (1.) He thought meanly of all mankind but himself: *I thank thee that I am not as other men are.* He speaks indefinitely, as if he were better than any. We may have reason to thank God that we are not as *some men* are, that are notoriously wicked and vile; but to speak at random thus, as if *we* only were good, and all besides us were reprobates, is to judge by wholesale. (2.) He thought meanly in a particular manner of this publican, whom he had left behind, it is probable, in the court of the Gentiles, and whose company he had fallen into as he came to the temple. He knew that he was a publican, and therefore very uncharitably concluded that he was an *extortioner, unjust,* and all that is naught. Suppose it had been so, and he had known it, what business had he to take notice of it? Could not he *say his prayers* (and that was all that the Pharisees did) without reproaching his neighbours? Or was this a part of his *God, I thank thee?* And was he as much pleased with the publican's badness as with his own goodness? There could not be a plainer evidence, not only of the want of humility and charity, but of reigning pride and malice, than this was.

III. Here is the publican's address to God, which was the reverse of the Pharisee's, as full of *humility* and *humiliation* as his was of *pride* and *ostentation;* as full of *repentance* for sin, and *desire* towards God, as his was of *confidence* in *himself* and his own righteousness and sufficiency.

1. He expressed his repentance and humility in *what he did;* and his gesture, when he addressed himself to his devotions, was *expressive* of great seriousness and humility, and the proper clothing of a broken, penitent, and obedient heart. (1.) He *stood afar off.* The Pharisee *stood,* but crowded up as high as he could, to the upper end of the court; the publican *kept at a distance* under a sense of his unworthiness to draw near to God, and perhaps for fear of offending the Pharisee, whom he observed to look scornfully upon him, and of disturbing his devotions. Hereby he owned that God might justly *behold him afar off,* and send him into a state of eternal distance from him, and that it was a great favour that God was pleased to admit him *thus nigh.* (2.) He *would not lift up so much as his eyes to heaven,* much less his *hands,* as was usual in prayer. He did *lift up his heart* to God in the heavens, in *holy desires,* but, through prevailing shame and humiliation, he did not lift up his eyes in *holy confidence* and *courage.* His *iniquities* are *gone over his head, as a heavy burden,* so that he is *not able to look up,* Ps. 40:12. The dejection of his looks is an indication of the dejection of his mind at the thought of sin. (3.) He *smote upon his breast,* in a holy indignation at himself for sin: "Thus would I smite this wicked heart of mine, the poisoned fountain out of which flow all the streams of sin, if I could come at it." The sinner's heart first smites him in a penitent rebuke, 2 Sa. 24:10. *David's heart smote him.* Sinner, what hast thou done? And then he smites his heart with penitent remorse: *O wretched man that I am?* Ephraim is said to *smite upon his thigh,* Jer. 31:19. Great mourners are represented *tabouring upon their breasts,* Nah. 2:7.

2. He expressed it *in what he said.* His prayer was *short.* Fear and shame hindered him from saying much; sighs and groans swallowed up his words; but what he said was to the purpose: *God, be merciful to me a sinner.* And blessed be God that we have this prayer upon record as an answered prayer, and that we are sure that he who prayed it went to his house justified; and so shall we, if we pray it, as he did, through Jesus Christ: "*God, be merciful to me a sinner;* the God of infinite mercy be merciful to me, for, if he be not, I am for ever undone, for ever miserable. God be merciful to me, for I have been cruel to myself." (1.) He owns himself *a sinner* by nature, by practice, guilty before God. *Behold, I am vile, what shall I answer thee?* The Pharisee denies himself to be a *sinner;* none of his neighbours can charge him, and he sees no reason to charge himself, with any thing amiss; *he is clean, he is pure from sin.* But the publican gives himself no other character than that of a *sinner,* a convicted criminal at God's bar. (2.) He has no dependence but upon the *mercy of God,* that, and that only, he relies upon. The Pharisee had insisted upon the *merit* of his fastings and tithes; but the poor publican disclaims all thought of merit, and flies to mercy as his city of refuge, and takes hold of the horn of that altar. "Justice condemns me; nothing will save me but mercy, mercy." (3.) He earnestly prays for the benefit of that mercy: "*O God, be merciful,* be *propitious, to me;* forgive my sins; be reconciled to me; take me into thy favour; receive me graciously; love me freely." He comes as a beggar for an alms, when he is ready to perish for hunger. Probably he repeated this prayer with renewed affections, and perhaps said more to the same purport, made a particular confession of his sins, and mentioned the particular mercies he wanted, and waited upon God for; but still this was the burden of the song: *God, be merciful to me a sinner.*

IV. Here is the publican's *acceptance with God.* We have seen how differently these two addressed themselves to God; it is now worth while to enquire how they sped. There were those who would cry up the Pharisee, by whom he would go to his house applauded, and who would look with contempt upon this sneaking whining publican. But our Lord Jesus, to whom all hearts are open, all desires known, and from whom no secret is hid, who is perfectly acquainted with all proceedings in the court of heaven, assures us that this poor, penitent, broken-hearted publican *went to his house justified, rather than the other.* The Pharisee thought that if one of them must be justified, and not the other, certainly it must be he rather than the publican. "No," saith Christ, *"I tell you,* I affirm it with the utmost assurance, and declare it to you with the utmost concern, *I tell you,* it is the publican rather than the Pharisee." The proud Pharisee goes away, rejected of God; his thanksgivings are so far from being accepted that they are an *abomination;* he is *not justified,* his sins are not pardoned, nor is he delivered from condemnation: he is not accepted as righteous in God's sight, because he is so righteous in his own sight; but the publican, upon this humble address to Heaven, obtains the remission of his sins, and he whom the Pharisee would not set *with the dogs of his flock* God sets with the *children of his family.* The reason given for this is because God's glory is to *resist the proud, and give grace to the humble.* 1. Proud men, who *exalt themselves,* are *rivals with God,* and therefore *they shall* certainly be *abased.* God, in his discourse with Job, appeals to this proof that he is God, that he *looks upon every one that is proud, and brings him low,* Job 40:12. 2. Humble men, who *abase themselves,* are *subject to God,* and they shall be *exalted.* God has preferment in store for those that will take it as a favour, not for those that demand it as a debt. He shall be *exalted* into the love of God, and communion with him, shall be exalted into a satisfaction in himself, and exalted at last as high as heaven. See how the punishment answers the sin: *He that exalteth himself shall be abased.* See how the recompence answers the duty: *He that humbles himself shall be exalted.* See also the power of God's grace in bringing good out of evil; the publican had been a great sinner, and out of the greatness of his sin was brought the greatness of his repentance; *out of the eater came forth meat.* See, on the contrary, the power of Satan's malice in bringing evil out of good. It was good that the Pharisee was no extortioner, nor unjust; but the devil made him proud of this, to his ruin.

Verses 15–17

This passage of story we had both in Matthew and Mark; it very fitly follows here after the story of the publican, as a confirmation of the truth which was to be illustrated by that parable, that those shall be accepted with God, and honoured, who humble themselves, and for them Christ has *blessings in store,* the choicest and best of blessings. Observe here, 1. Those who are themselves blessed in Christ should desire to have their children also blessed in him, and should hereby testify the true honour they have for Christ, by their making use of him, and the true love they have for their children, by their concern about their souls. They brought to him *infants,* very young, not able to go, sucking children, as some think. None are too little, too young, to bring to Christ, who knows how to show kindness to them that are not capable of doing service to him. 2. One gracious touch of Christ's will make our children happy. They *brought infants to him, that he might touch them* in token of the application of his grace and Spirit to them, for that always makes way for his *blessing,* which likewise they expected: see Isa. 44:3. *I will first pour my Spirit upon thy seed, and then my blessing upon thine offspring.* 3. It is no strange thing for those who make their application to Jesus Christ, for themselves or for their children, to meet with discouragement, even from those who should countenance and encourage them: *When the disciples saw it,* they thought, if this were admitted, it would bring endless trouble upon their Master, and therefore they *rebuked them,* and frowned upon them. The spouse complained of *the watchmen,* Cant. 3:3; *v.* 7. 4. Many whom the disciples rebuke the Master invites: *Jesus called them unto him,* when, upon the disciples' check, they were retiring. They did not *appeal* from the disciples to the Master, but the Master took cognizance of their despised cause. 5. It is the mind of Christ that *little children* should be brought to him, and presented as living sacrifices to his honour: *"Suffer little children to come to me, and forbid them not;* let nothing be done to hinder them, for they shall be as welcome as any." *The promise is to us, and to our seed;* and therefore he that has the dispensing of promised blessings will bid them welcome to him with us. 6. The children of those who belong to the kingdom of God do likewise belong to that kingdom, as the children of freemen are freemen. If the parents be members of the visible church, the children are so too; for, if the root be holy, the branches are so. 7. So welcome are *children* to Christ that those grown people are most welcome to him who have in them most of the disposition of children (*v.* 17): *Whosoever shall not receive the kingdom of God as a little child,* that is, receive the benefits of it with humility and thankfulness,

not pretending to merit them as the Pharisee did, but gladly owning himself indebted to free grace for them, as the publican did; unless a man be brought to this self-denying frame he shall *in no wise enter* into that kingdom. They must receive the kingdom of God as *children,* receive their estates by descent and inheritance, not by purchase, and call it their Father's gift.

Verses 18–30

In these verses we have,

I. Christ's discourse with a ruler, that had a good mind to be directed by him in the way to heaven. In which we may observe,

1. It is a blessed sight to see persons of distinction in the world distinguish themselves from others of their rank by their concern about their souls and another life. Luke takes notice of it that he was a *ruler.* Few of the rulers had any esteem for Christ, but here was one that had; whether a church or state ruler does not appear, but he was one *in authority.*

2. The great thing we are every one of us concerned to enquire after is what we shall do to get to heaven, *what we shall do to inherit eternal life.* This implies such a belief of an eternal life after this as atheists and infidels have not, such a concern to make it sure as a careless unthinking world have not, and such a willingness to comply with any terms that it may be made sure as those have not who are resolvedly devoted to the world and the flesh.

3. Those who would inherit eternal life must apply themselves to Jesus Christ as their *Master,* their *teaching* Master, so it signifies here (*didaskale*), and their *ruling* Master, and so they shall certainly find him. There is no learning the way to heaven but in the school of Christ, by those that enter themselves into it, and continue in it.

4. Those who come to Christ as their Master must believe him to have not only a *divine mission,* but a *divine goodness.* Christ would have this ruler know that if he understood himself aright in calling him good he did, in effect, call him *God* and indeed he was so (*v.* 19): *"Why callest thou me good?* Thou knowest *there is none good but one, that is, God;* and dost thou then take me for God? If so, thou art in the right."

5. Our Master, Christ himself, has not altered the way to heaven from what it was before his coming, but has only made it more plain, and easy, and comfortable, and provided for our relief, in case we take any false step. *Thou knowest the commandments.* Christ came not to destroy the law and the prophets, but to establish them. Wouldest thou inherit eternal life? Govern thyself by the commandments.

6. The duties of the second table must be conscientiously observed, in order to our happiness, and we must not think that any acts of devotion, how plausible soever, will atone for the neglect of them. Nor is it enough to keep ourselves free from the gross violations of these commandments, but we must *know these commandments,* as Christ has *explained them* in his sermon upon the mount, in their extent and spiritual nature, and so observe them.

7. Men think themselves *innocent* because they are *ignorant;* so this ruler did. He said, *All these have I kept from my youth up, v.* 21. He knows no more evil of himself than the Pharisee did, *v.* 11. He boasts that he began *early* in a course of virtue, that he had continued in it to this day, and that he had not in any instance transgressed. Had he been acquainted with the extent and spiritual nature of the divine law, and with the workings of his own heart, — had he been but Christ's disciples awhile, and learned of him, he would have said quite the contrary: *"All these have* I broken from my youth up, in thought, word, and deed."

8. The great things by which we are to try our spiritual state are how we stand affected to Christ and to our brethren, to this world and to the other; by these this man was tried. For, (1.) If we have a true *affection to Christ,* he will *come and follow him,* will attend to his doctrine, and submit to his discipline, whatever it cost him. None shall inherit eternal life who are not willing to take their lot with the Lord Jesus, to follow the Lamb whithersoever he goes. (2.) If he have a true *affection to his brethren,* he will, as there is occasion, *distribute to the poor,* who are God's receivers of his dues out of our estates. (3.) If he think meanly of *this world,* as he ought, he will not stick at *selling what he has,* if there be a necessity for it, for the relief of God's poor. (4.) If he think highly of the other world, as he ought, he will desire no more than to have *treasure in heaven,* and will reckon that a suf-

ficient abundant recompence for all that he has left, or lost, or laid out for God in this world.

9. There are many that have a great deal in them that is very commendable, and yet they perish *for the lack of some one thing;* so this *ruler* here; he broke with Christ upon this, he liked all his terms very well but this which would part between him and his estate: "In this, I pray thee, have me excused." If this be the bargain, it is no bargain.

10. Many that are loth to leave Christ, yet do leave him. After a long struggle between their convictions and their corruptions, their corruptions carry the day at last; they are very sorry that they cannot serve God and mammon both; but, if one must be quitted, it shall be their God, not their worldly gain.

II. Christ's discourse with his disciples upon this occasion, in which we may observe, 1. Riches are a great hindrance to many in the way to heaven. Christ took notice of the reluctancy and regret with which the rich man broke off from him. He *saw that he was very sorrowful,* and was sorry for him; but thence he infers, *How hardly shall they that have riches enter into the kingdom of God! v.* 24. If this ruler had had but as little of the world as Peter, and James, and John had, in all probability he would have left it, to follow Christ, as they did; but, having a great estate, it had a great influence upon him, and he chose rather to take his leave of Christ than to lay himself under an obligation to dispose of his estate in charitable uses. Christ asserts the difficulty of the salvation of rich people very emphatically: *It is easier for a camel to go through a needle's eye than for a rich man to enter into the kingdom of God, v.* 25. It is a proverbial expression, that denotes the thing to be extremely difficult. 2. There is in the hearts of all people such a general affection to this world, and the things of it, that, since Christ has required it as necessary to salvation that we should sit loose to this world, it is really very hard for any to get to heaven. If we must *sell all,* or break with Christ, *who then can be saved? v.* 26. They do not find fault with what Christ required as hard and unreasonable. No, it is very fit that they who expect an eternal happiness in the other world should be willing to forego all that is dear to them in this world, in expectation of it. But they know how closely the hearts of most men cleave to this world, and are ready to despair of their being ever brought to this. 3. There are such difficulties in the way of our salvation: as could never be got over but by pure omnipotence, by that grace of God which is almighty, and to which that is *possible* which exceeds all created power and wisdom. The *things which are impossible with men* (and utterly impossible it is that men should work such a change upon their own spirits as to turn them from the world to God, it is like *dividing the sea,* and *driving Jordan back*), these things are *possible with God.* His grace can work upon the soul, so as to alter the bent and bias of it, and give it a contrary ply; and it is he that *works in us both to will and to do.* 4. There is an aptness in us to speak too much of what we have left and lost, of what we have done and suffered, for Christ. This appears in Peter: *Lo, we have left all, and followed thee, v.* 28. When it came in his way, he could not forbear magnifying his own and his brethren's affection to Christ, in *quitting* all to follow him. But this we should be so far from boasting of, that we should rather acknowledge it not worth taking notice of, and be ashamed of ourselves that there should have been any regret and difficulty in the doing of it, and any hankerings towards those things afterwards. 5. Whatever we have left, or laid out, for Christ, it shall without fail be abundantly made up to us in this world and that to come, notwithstanding our weaknesses and infirmities (*v.* 29, 30): *No man has left* the comfort of his estate or relations *for the kingdom of God's sake,* rather than they should hinder either his services to that kingdom or his enjoyments of it, *who shall not receive manifold more in this present time,* in the graces and comforts of God's Spirit, in the pleasures of communion with God and of a good conscience, advantages which, to those that know how to value and improve them, will abundantly countervail all their loses. Yet that is not all; in the world to come they *shall receive life everlasting,* which is the thing that the ruler seemed to have his eye and heart upon.

Verses 31–34

Here is, I. The notice Christ gave to his disciples of his sufferings and death approaching, and of the glorious issue of them, which he himself had a perfect sight and foreknowledge of, and thought it necessary to give them warning of, that it might be the less surprise and terror to them. Two things here are which we had not in the other evangelists: — 1. The *sufferings* of Christ are here spoken of as the *fulfilling of the scriptures,* with which consideration Christ reconciled himself to them, and would reconcile them: *All things that are written by the prophets concerning the Son of man,* especially the hardships he should undergo, *shall be accomplished.* Note, The Spirit of Christ, in the Old-Testament prophets, *testified beforehand his sufferings,* and *the glory that should follow,* 1 Pt. 1:11. This proves that the scriptures are the *word* of *God,* for they had their exact and full accomplishment; and that Jesus Christ was *sent of God,* for they had their accomplishment *in him;* this was *he that should come,* for whatever was *foretold* concerning the Messiah was verified in him; and he would submit to any thing for the fulfilling of scripture, that not one jot or tittle of that should fall to the ground. This makes the *offence of the cross to cease,* and puts an honour upon it. *Thus it was written, and thus it behoved Christ to suffer,* thus it became him. 2. The ignominy and disgrace done to Christ in his sufferings are here most insisted upon. The other evangelists had said that he should be *mocked;* but here it is added, *He shall be spitefully treated, hybristhēsetai — he shall be loaded with contumely and contempt,* shall have all possible reproach put upon him. This was that part of his sufferings by which in a spiritual manner he satisfied God's justice for the injury we had done him in his honour by sin. Here is one particular instance of disgrace done him, that *he was spit upon,* which had been particularly foretold, Isa. 50:6. But here, as always, when Christ spoke of his sufferings and death, he foretold his resurrection as that which took off both the terror and reproach of his sufferings: *The third day he shall rise again.*

II. The confusion that the disciples were hereby put into. This was so contrary to the notions they had had of the Messiah and his kingdom, such a balk to their expectations from their Master, and such a breaking of all their measures, that *they understood none of these things, v.* 34. Their prejudices were so strong that they *would not* understand them literally, and they *could not* understand them otherwise, so that they did not understand them at all. It was a mystery, it was a riddle to them, it must be so; but they think it impossible to be reconciled with the glory and honour of the Messiah, and the design of setting up his kingdom. This saying was *hidden from them, kekrymmenon ap' autōn,* it was apocrypha to them, they could not receive it: for their parts, they had read the Old Testament many a time, but they could never see any thing in it that would be *accomplished* in the disgrace and death of this Messiah. They were so intent upon those prophecies that spoke of his glory that they overlooked those that spoke of his *sufferings,* which the scribes and doctors of the law should have directed them to take notice of, and should have brought into their creeds and catechisms, as well as the other; but they did not suit their scheme, and therefore were laid aside. Note, *Therefore* it is that people run into mistakes, because they *read their Bibles by the halves,* and are as partial in the prophets as they are *in the law.* They are only for the *smooth things,* Isa. 30:10. Thus now we are too apt, in reading the prophecies that are yet to be fulfilled, to have our expectations raised of the glorious state of the church in the latter days. But we overlook its wilderness sackcloth state, and are willing to fancy that is over, and nothing is reserved for us but the halcyon days; and then, when tribulation and persecution arise, we do not *understand* it, neither *know we the things that are done,* though we are told as plainly as can be that *through many tribulations we must enter into the kingdom of God.*

Verses 35–43

Christ came not only to bring *light* to a *dark* world, and so to set before us the *objects* we are to have in view, but also to give *sight* to blind *souls,* and by healing the *organ* to enable them to view those objects. As a token of this, he cured many of their bodily blindness: we have now an account of one to whom he *gave sight* near Jericho. Mark gives us an account of one, and names him, whom he cured *as he went out of Jericho,* Mk. 10:46. Matthew speaks of two whom he cured *as they departed* from Jericho, Mt. 20:30. Luke says it was *en tō engizein auton — when he was near* to Jericho, which might be when he was going out of it as well as when he was coming into it. Observe,

I. This poor blind man *sat by the wayside, begging, v.* 35. It seems, he was not only *blind,* but *poor,* had nothing to subsist on, nor any relations to maintain him; the fitter emblem of the world of mankind which Christ came to heal and save; they are therefore *wretched* and *miserable,* for they are both *poor and blind,* Rev. 3:17. He sat begging, for he was blind, and could not work for his living. Note, Those ought to be relieved by charity whom the providence of God has any way disabled to get their own bread. Such objects of charity *by the way-side* ought not to be overlooked by us. Christ here cast a favourable eye upon a *common beggar,* and, though there are cheats among such, yet they must not therefore be all thought such.

II. Hearing the noise of a multitude passing by, he asked *what it meant, v.* 36. This we had not before. It teaches us that it is good to be *inquisitive,* and that those who are so some time or other find the benefit of it. Those who want their *sight* should make so much the better use of their *hearing,* and, when they cannot see with their own eyes, should, by *asking questions,* make use of other people's eyes. So this blind man did, and by that means came to understand that Jesus of Nazareth *passed by, v.* 37. It is good being in Christ's way; and, when we have an opportunity of applying ourselves to him, not to let it slip.

III. His prayer has in it a great deal both of faith and fervency: *Jesus, thou Son of David, have mercy on me, v.* 38. He owns Christ to be the *Son of David,* the Messiah promised; he believes him to be Jesus, a Saviour; he believes he is able to help and succour him, and earnestly begs his favour: *"Have mercy on me,* pardon my sin, pity my misery." Christ is a merciful king; those that apply themselves to him as the *Son of David* shall find him so, and ask enough for themselves when they pray, *Have mercy on us;* for Christ's mercy includes all.

IV. Those who are in good earnest for Christ's favours and blessings will not be put by from the pursuit of them, though they meet with opposition and rebuke. They who went along chid him as troublesome to the Master, noisy and impertinent, and bade him *hold his peace;* but he went on with his petition, nay, the check given him was but as a dam to a full stream, which makes it swell so much the more; he *cried the louder, Thou Son of David, have mercy on me.* Those who would speed in prayer must be importunate in prayer. This history, in the close of the chapter, intimates the same thing with the parable in the beginning of the chapter, that *men ought always to pray, and not to faint.*

V. Christ encourages poor beggars, whom men frown upon, and invites them to come to him, and is ready to entertain them, and bid them welcome: *He commanded him to be brought to him.* Note, Christ has more tenderness and compassion for distressed supplicants than any of his followers have. Though Christ was upon his journey, yet he stopped and *stood,* and *commanded him to be brought to him.* Those who had checked him must now lend him their hands to lead him to Christ.

VI. Though Christ knows all our wants, he will know them from us (*v.* 41): *What wilt thou that I shall do unto thee?* By spreading our case before God, with a particular representation of our wants and burdens, we teach ourselves to value the mercy we are in pursuit of; and it is necessary that we should, else we are not fit to receive it. This man poured out his soul before Christ, when he said, *Lord, that I may receive my sight.* Thus particular should we be in prayer, upon particular occasions.

VII. The prayer of faith, guided by Christ's encouraging promises, and grounded on them, shall not be in vain; nay, it shall not only receive an *answer of peace,* but of *honour* (*v.* 42); Christ said, *Receive thy sight, thy faith hath saved thee.* True faith will produce fervency in prayer, and both together will fetch in abundance of the fruits of Christ's favour; and they are then doubly comfortable when they come in that way, when we are *saved by faith.*

VIII. The *grace of Christ* ought to be thankfully acknowledged, to the *glory of God, v.* 43. 1. The poor beggar himself, that had his sight restored, *followed Christ, glorifying God.* Christ made it his business to glorify his Father; and those whom he healed *pleased him* best when they *praised God,* as those shall *please God* best who *praise Christ* and do him honour; for, in *confessing that he is Lord,* we *give glory to God the Father.* It is for the *glory of God* if we *follow Christ,* as those will do whose *eyes* are *opened.* 2. The *people that saw it* could not forbear *giving praise to God,* who had given such power to the *Son of Man,* and by him had conferred such favours on the *sons of men.* Note, We must give praise to God for his mercies to others as well as for mercies to ourselves.

CHAPTER 19

In this chapter we have, I. The conversion of Zaccheus the publican at Jericho (*v.* 1–10). II. The parable of the pounds which the king entrusted with his servants, and of his rebellious citizens (*v.* 11–27). III. Christ's riding in triumph (such triumph as it was) into Jerusalem; and his lamentation in prospect of the ruin of that city (*v.* 28–44). IV. His teaching in the temple, and casting the buyers and sellers out of it (*v.* 45–48).

Verses 1–10

Many, no doubt, were converted to the faith of Christ of whom no account is kept in the gospels; but the conversion of some, whose case had something in it extraordinary, is recorded, as this of Zaccheus. Christ passed through Jericho, *v.* 1. This city was build under a curse, yet Christ honoured it with his presence, for the gospel *takes away the curse.* Though it ought not to have been built, yet it was not therefore a sin to live in it when it was built. Christ was now going from the other side Jordan to Bethany near Jerusalem, to raise Lazarus to life; when he was going to do one good work he contrived to do many by the way. He did good both to the *souls* and to the *bodies* of people; we have here an instance of the former. Observe,

I. Who, and what, this Zaccheus was. His name bespeaks him a Jew. *Zaccai* was a common name among the Jews; they had a famous rabbi, much about this time, of that name. Observe, 1. His calling, and the post he was in: *He was the chief among the publicans,* receiver-general; other publicans were officers under him; he was, as some think, farmer of the customs. We often read of publicans coming to Christ; but here was one that was *chief* of the publicans, was in authority, that enquired after him. God has his remnant among all sorts. Christ came to save even the *chief of publicans.* 2. His circumstances in the world were very considerable: *He was rich.* The inferior publicans were commonly men of broken fortunes, and low in the world; but he that was *chief of the publicans* had raised a good estate. Christ had lately shown how *hard* it is for *rich people to enter into the kingdom of God,* yet presently produces an instance on one rich man that had been lost, and was found, and that not as the prodigal by being reduced to want.

II. How he came in Christ's way, and what was the occasion of his acquaintance with him. 1. He had a great *curiosity to see Jesus,* what kind of a man he was, having heard great talk of him, *v.* 3. It is natural to us to come in sight, if we can, of those whose fame has filled our ears, as being apt to imagine there is something extraordinary in their countenances; at least, we shall be able to say hereafter that we have seen such and such *great men.* But the eye is *not satisfied with seeing.* We should now *seek to see Jesus* with an eye of faith, to see *who he is;* we should address ourselves in holy ordinances with this in our eye, *We would see Jesus.* 2. He could not get his curiosity gratified in this matter because he was *little,* and the crowd was *great.* Christ did not study to *show himself,* was not carried on men's shoulders (as the pope is in procession), that all men might see him; neither he nor his kingdom *came with observation.* He did not ride in an open chariot, as princes do, but, as *one of us,* he was *lost in a crowd;* for that was the day of his humiliation. Zaccheus was *low of stature,* and over-topped by all about him, so that he could not get a sight of Jesus. Many that are little of stature have large souls, and are lively in spirit. Who would not rather be a Zaccheus than a Saul, though he was *higher by head and shoulders* than all about him? Let not those that are little of stature *take thought* of adding *cubits* to it. 3. Because he would not disappoint his curiosity he *forgot his gravity,* as chief of the publicans, and *ran before,* like a boy, and *climbed up into a sycamore-tree, to see him.* Note, Those that sincerely desire a sight of Christ will use the proper means for gaining a sight of him, and will break through a deal of difficulty and opposition, and be willing to take pains to see him. Those that find themselves *little* must take all the advantages they can get to *raise themselves* to a sight of Christ, and not be ashamed to own that they need them, and all little enough. Let not dwarfs despair, with good help, by aiming high to reach high.

III. The notice Christ took of him, the call he gave him to a further acquaintance (*v.* 5), and the efficacy of that call, *v.* 6. 1. Christ *invited himself* to Zaccheus's house, not doubting of his hearty welcome there; nay, wherever Christ comes, as he brings his own *entertainment* along with him, so he brings his own *welcome;* he opens the heart, and inclines it to receive him. Christ *looked* up into the tree, and *saw* Zaccheus. He came to look upon Christ, and resolved to take particular notice of him, but little thought of being taken notice of by Christ. That was an honour too great, and too far above his merit, for him to have any thought of. See how Christ *prevented* him with the blessings of his goodness, and *outdid* his expectations; and see how he *encouraged* very weak beginnings, and helped them forward. He that had a mind to know Christ shall be *known of him;* he that only courted to see him shall be admitted to converse with him. Note, Those that are faithful in a little shall be entrusted with more. And sometimes those that come to hear the word of Christ, as Zaccheus did, only for curiosity, beyond what they thought of, have their consciences awakened, and their hearts changed. Christ called him *by name, Zaccheus,* for he knows his chosen *by name; are they not in his book?* He might ask, as Nathanael did (Jn. 1:48), *Whence knowest thou me?* But before he climbed the sycamore-tree Christ saw him, and knew him. He bade him *make haste, and come down.* Those that Christ calls must *come down,* must humble themselves, and not think to climb to heaven by any righteousness of their own; and they must *make haste* and come down, for delays are dangerous. Zaccheus must not hesitate, but hasten; he knows it is not a matter that needs consideration whether he should welcome such a guest to his house. He must *come down,* for Christ intends this day to *bait at his house,* and stay an hour or two with him. *Behold, he stands at the door and knocks.* 2. Zaccheus was *overjoyed* to have such an honour put upon his house (*v.* 6): *He made haste, and came down, and received him joyfully;* and his receiving him *into his house* was an indication and token of his receiving him *into his heart.* Note, When Christ *calls* to us we must *make haste* to answer his calls; and when he *comes to us* we must *receive him joyfully. Lift up your heads, O ye gates.* We may well *receive him joyfully* who brings all good along with him, and, when he takes possession of the soul, opens springs of joy there which shall flow to eternity. How often has Christ said to us, *Open to me,* when we have, with the spouse, made excuses! Cant. 5:2, 3. Zaccheus's forwardness to receive Christ will shame us. We have not now Christ to entertain in our houses, but we have his disciples, and what is done to them he takes as done to himself.

IV. The offence which the people took at this *kind greeting* between Christ and Zaccheus. Those narrow-souled censorious Jews *murmured,* saying that he was *gone to be a guest with a man that is a sinner, para hamartōlō andri — with a sinful man;* and were not they themselves sinful men? Was it not Christ's errand into the world to seek and save *men* that are *sinners?* But Zaccheus they think to be a sinner above all men that dwelt in Jericho, such a sinner as was not fit to be conversed with. Now this was very unjust to blame Christ for going *to his house;* for, 1. Though he was a *publican,* and many of the publicans were *bad men,* it did not therefore follow that they were *all so.* We must take heed of condemning men in the lump, or by common fame, for at God's bar every man will be judged as he is. 2. Though he *had been a sinner,* it did not therefore follow that he was now as bad as he had been; though they knew his past life to be bad, Christ might know his present frame to be good. God allows room for repentance, and so must we. 3. Though he was *now a sinner,* they ought not to blame Christ for going to him, because he was in *no danger* of getting hurt by a sinner, but in *great hopes* of doing good to a sinner; whither should the physician go but to the sick? Yet see how that which is *well done* may be *ill construed.*

V. The proofs which Zaccheus gave publicly that, though he had been a *sinner,* he was now a *penitent,* and a true *convert, v.* 8. He does not expect to be justified by his works as the Pharisee who boasted of what he had done, but by his *good works* he will, through the grace of God, evidence the *sincerity* of his *faith* and *repentance;* and here he declares what his determination was. He made this declaration *standing,* that he might be seen and heard by those who murmured at Christ for coming to his house; *with the mouth confession is made* of repentance as well as faith. He *stood,* which denotes his saying it deliberately and with solemnity, in the nature of a vow to God. He addressed himself to Christ in it, not to the people (they were not to be his judges), but to the Lord, and he *stood* as it were at his bar. What we do that is good we must do *as unto him;* we must appeal to him, and approve ourselves to him, in our integrity, in all our good purposes and resolutions. He makes it appear that there is a change *in his heart* (and that is repentance), for there is a change in his way. His resolutions are of second-table duties; for Christ, upon all occasions, laid great stress on them: and they are such as are suited to his condition and character; for in them will best appear the truth of our repentance.

1. Zaccheus had a good estate, and, whereas he had been in it hitherto laying up treasure for himself, and doing hurt to himself, now he resolves that for the future he will be all towards God, and do good to others with it: *Behold, Lord, the half of my goods I give to the poor.* Not, "I *will* give it by my will when I die," but, "I *do* give it now." Probably he had heard of the command of trial which Christ gave to another rich man to sell what he had, and give to the poor (Mt. 19:21), and how he broke with Christ upon it. "But so will not I," saith Zaccheus; "I agree to it at the first word; though hitherto I have been uncharitable to the poor, now I will relieve them, and give so much the more for having neglected the duty so long, even the *half of my goods.*" This is a very large proportion to be set apart for works of piety and charity. The Jews used to say that a fifth part of a man's income yearly was very fair to be given to pious uses, and about that share the law directed; but Zaccheus would go much further, and give one moiety to the poor, which would oblige him to retrench all his extravagant expenses, as his retrenching these would enable him to relieve many with his superfluities. If we were but more temperate and self-denying, we should be more charitable; and, were we content with less ourselves, we should have the more to give to them that need. This he mentions here as a fruit of his repentance. Note, It well becomes converts to God to be charitable to the poor.

2. Zaccheus was conscious to himself that he had not gotten all he had honestly and fairly, but some by indirect and unlawful means, and of what he had gotten by such means he promises to make restitution: "If *I have taken any thing from any man by false accusation,* or if I have wronged any man in the way of my business as a *publican,* exacting more than was appointed, I promise to restore him *four-fold.*" This was the restitution that a thief was to make, Ex. 22:1. (1.) He seems plainly to own that he had *done wrong;* his office, as a publican, gave him opportunity to do wrong, imposing upon the merchants to curry favour with the government. True penitents will own themselves not only in general guilty before God, but will particularly reflect upon that which has been their own iniquity, and which, by reason of their business and employment in the world, has most easily beset them. (2.) That he had done wrong *by false accusation;* this was the temptation of the publicans, which John Baptist had warned them of particularly, *ch.* 3:14. They had the ear of the government, and every thing would be stretched in favour of the revenue, which gave them an opportunity of gratifying their revenge if they bore a man an ill will. (3.) He promises to restore *four-fold,* as far as he could recollect or find by his books that he had *wronged any man.* He does not say, "If I be sued, and compelled to it, I will make restitution" (some are *honest* when they cannot help it); but he will do it *voluntarily:* It shall be *my own act and deed.* Note, Those who are convinced of having done wrong cannot evidence the sincerity of their repentance but by *making restitution.* Observe, He does not think that his giving half his estate to the poor will atone for the wrong he has done. God *hates robbery for burnt-offerings,* and we must first *do justly* and then *love mercy.* It is no charity, but hypocrisy, to give that which is *none of our own;* and we are not to reckon that our own which we have not come honestly by, nor that our own which is not so when all our debts are paid, and restitution made for wrong done.

VI. Christ's *approbation* and *acceptance* of Zaccheus's conversion, by which also he cleared himself from any imputation in going to be a guest with him, *v.* 9, 10.

1. Zaccheus is declared to be now a *happy man.* Now he is turned from sin to God; now he has bidden Christ welcome to his house, and is become an honest, charitable, good man: *This day is salvation come to this house.* Now that he is *converted* he is in effect *saved,* saved from his sins, from the guilt of them, from the power of them; all the benefits of salvation are his. Christ is come *to his house,* and, where Christ comes, he brings salvation along with him. He is, and will be, the *Author of eternal salvation* to all that own him as Zaccheus did. Yet this is not all. Salvation this day *comes to his house.* (1.) When Zaccheus becomes a convert, he will be, more than he had been, a *blessing to his house.* He will bring the means of grace and salvation to his house, for he is a *son of Abraham* indeed now, and therefore, like Abraham, will teach his household to *keep the way of the Lord. He that is greedy of gain troubles his own house,* and brings a curse upon it (Hab. 2:9), but he that is charitable to the poor does a kindness to his own house, and brings a blessing upon it and salvation to it, temporal at least, Ps. 112:3. (2.) When Zaccheus is brought to Christ himself his *family* also become related to Christ, and his children are admitted members of his church, and so *salvation comes to his house,* for that he is *a son of Abraham,* and therefore interested in God's covenant with Abraham, that *blessing* of Abraham which comes upon the publicans, *upon the Gentiles,* through faith, that God will be a God *to them and to their children;* and therefore, when he believes, *salvation comes* to his house, as the gaoler's to whom it was said, Believe in the Lord Jesus Christ, *and thou shalt be saved, and thy house,* Acts 16:31. Zaccheus is by birth a son of Abraham, but, being a publican, he was deemed a heathen; they are put upon a level, Mt. 18:17. And as such the Jews were shy of conversing with him, and expected Christ should be so; but he shows that, being a true penitent, he is become *rectus in curia — upright in court,* as good a son of Abraham as if he had never been an publican, which therefore ought not to be mentioned against him.

2. What Christ had done to make him, in particular, a happy man, was consonant to the great design and intention of his coming into the world, *v.* 10. With the same argument he had before justified his conversing with publicans, Mt. 9:13. There he pleaded that he came to *call sinners to repentance;* now that he came to *seek and save that which was lost, to apolōlos — the lost thing.* Observe, (1.) The *deplorable case* of the *sons of men:* they were *lost;* and here the whole race of mankind is spoken of as *one body.* Note, The whole world of mankind, by the fall, is become a *lost world:* lost as a city is lost when it has revolted to the rebels, as a traveller is lost when he has missed his way in a wilderness, as a sick man is lost when his disease is incurable, or as a prisoner is lost when sentence is passed upon him. (2.) The *gracious design* of the *Son of God:* he came to *seek and save,* to seek in order to saving. He came from heaven to earth (a long journey), to *seek* that which was *lost* (which had *wandered and gone astray*), and to bring it back (Mt. 18:11, 12), and to *save* that which was lost, which was perishing, and in a manner destroyed and cut off. Christ undertook the cause when it was given up for *lost:* undertook to bring those to themselves that were *lost* to God and all goodness. Observe, Christ *came* into this lost world to seek and save it. His design was to *save,* when *there was not salvation in any other.* In prosecution of that design, he *sought,* took all probable means to effect that salvation. He seeks those that were not worth seeking to; he seeks those that sought him not, and asked not for him, as Zaccheus here.

Verses 11–27

Our Lord Jesus is now upon his way to Jerusalem, to his last passover, when he was to suffer and die; now here we are told,

I. How the expectations of his friends were *raised* upon this occasion: *They thought that the kingdom of God would immediately appear, v.* 11. The Pharisees expected it about this time (*ch.* 17:20), and, it seems, so did Christ's own disciples; but they both had a mistaken notion of it. The Pharisees thought that it must be introduced by some other temporal prince or potentate. The disciples thought that their Master would introduce it, but with temporal pomp and power, which, with the power he had to work miracles, they knew he could clothe himself with in a short time, whenever he pleased. Jerusalem, they concluded, must be the seat of his kingdom, and therefore, now that he is going directly thither, they doubt not but in a little time to see him upon the throne there. Note, Even good men are subject to mistakes concerning the kingdom of Christ, and to form wrong notions of it, and are ready to think that will *immediately* appear which is reserved for hereafter.

II. How their expectations were *checked,* and the mistakes *rectified* upon which they were founded; and this he does in three things: —

1. They expected that he should appear in his glory now *presently,* but he tells them that he must not be publicly installed in his kingdom for a great while yet. He is like *a certain nobleman anthrōpos tis eugenēs — a certain man of*

high birth (so Dr. Hammond), for he is the Lord from heaven, and is entitled by birth to the kingdom; but he *goes into a far country, to receive for himself a kingdom.* Christ must go to heaven, to sit down at the right hand of the Father there, and to receive from him *honour and glory,* before the Spirit was poured out by which his kingdom was to be set up on earth, and before a church was to be set up for him in the Gentile world. He must receive the kingdom, and then *return.* Christ returned when the Spirit was poured out, when Jerusalem was destroyed, by which time that generation, both of friends and enemies, which he had personally conversed with, was wholly worn off by death, and gone to give up their account. But his chief return here meant is that at the great day, of which we are yet in expectation. That which they thought would *immediately appear,* Christ tells them will not appear till this same Jesus who is taken into heaven shall *in like manner come again;* see Acts 1:11.

2. They expected that his apostles and immediate attendants should be advanced to dignity and honour, that they should all be made princes and peers, privy-counsellors and judges, and have all the pomp and preferments of the court and of the town. But Christ here tells them that, instead of this, he designed them to be *men of business;* they must expect no other preferment in this world than that of the trading end of the town; he would set them up with a stock under their hands, that they might employ it themselves, in serving him and the interest of his kingdom among men. That is the true honour of a Christian and a minister which, if we be as we ought to be truly ambitious of it, will enable us to look upon all temporal honours with a holy contempt. The apostles had dreamed of *sitting on his right hand and on his left in his kingdom,* enjoying ease after their present toil and honour after the present contempt put upon them, and were pleasing themselves with this dream; but Christ tells them that which, if they understood it aright, would fill them with care, and concern, and serious thoughts, instead of those *aspiring* ones with which they filled their heads.

(1.) They have a *great work* to do now. Their Master leaves them, to receive his kingdom, and, at parting, he gives each of them a *pound,* which the margin of our common bibles tells us amounts in our money to *three pounds* and *half a crown;* this signifies the same thing with the talents in the parable that is parallel to this (Mt. 25), all the gifts with which Christ's apostles were endued, and the advantages and capacities which they had of serving the interests of Christ in the world, and others, both ministers and Christians, like them in a lower degree. But perhaps it is in the parable thus represented to make them the more humble; their honour in this world is only that of *traders,* and that not of first-rate merchants, who have vast stocks to begin upon, but that of poor traders, who must take a great deal of care and pains to make any thing of what they have. He gave these pounds to his servants, not to buy rich liveries, much less robes, and a splendid equipage, for themselves to appear in, as they expected, but with this charge: *Occupy till I come.* Or, as it might much better be translated, *Trade till I come, Pragmateusasthe — Be busy.* So the word properly signifies. "You are sent forth to preach the gospel, to set up a church for Christ in the world, to bring the nations to the obedience of faith, and to build them up in it. *You shall receive power to do this,* for you shall be filled with the *Holy Ghost,*" Acts 1:8. When Christ *breathed on* the eleven disciples, saying, *Receive ye the Holy Ghost,* then he delivered them *ten pounds.* "Now," saith he, "mind your business, and make a business of it; set about it in good earnest, and stick to it. Lay out yourselves to do all the good you can to the souls of men, and to gather them in to Christ." Note, [1.] All Christians have *business* to do for Christ in this world, and ministers especially; the former were not *baptized,* nor the latter *ordained,* to be *idle.* [2.] Those that are called to business for Christ he furnishes with gifts necessary for their business; and, on the other hand, from those to whom he gives power he expects service. He delivers the *pounds* with this charge, Go work, go trade. *The manifestation of the Spirit is given to every man to profit withal,* 1 Co. 12:7. And *as every one has received the gift,* so let him *minister the same,* 1 Pt. 4:10. [3.] We must continue to mind our business *till our Master comes,* whatever difficulties or oppositions we may meet with in it; those only that *endure to the end* shall *be saved.*

(2.) They have a *great account* to make shortly. These servants are *called to him,* to show what use they made of the gifts they were dignified with, what service they had done

for Christ, and what good to the souls of men, *that he might know what every man had gained by trading.* Note,

[1.] They that trade diligently and faithfully in the service of Christ shall be *gainers.* We cannot say so of the business of the world; many a labouring tradesman has been a loser; but those that trade for Christ shall be *gainers;* though *Israel be not gathered,* yet they *will be glorious.*

[2.] The conversion of souls is the *winning* of them; every true convert is clear gain to Jesus Christ. Ministers are but factors for him, and to him they must give account what fish they have enclosed in the gospel-net, what guests they have prevailed with to come to the wedding-supper; that is, what they have *gained by trading.* Now observe,

First, The *good account* which was given by *some* of the servants, and the master's approbation of them. Two such are instanced, v. 16, 19. 1. They had both made considerable improvements, but not both *alike;* one had gained *ten pounds* by his trading, and another *five.* Those that are diligent and faithful in serving Christ are commonly blessed in being made blessings to the places where they live. They shall *see the travail of their soul,* and not *labour in vain.* And yet all that are alike *faithful* are not alike *successful.* And perhaps, though they were both faithful, it is intimated that one of them took more pains, and applied himself more closely to his business, than the other, and sped accordingly. Blessed Paul was surely this servant that gained *ten pounds,* double to what any of the rest did, for he *laboured more abundantly than they all,* and *fully preached the gospel of Christ.* 2. They both acknowledged their obligations to their Master for entrusting them with these abilities and opportunities to do him service: Lord, it is not *my* industry, but *thy* pound, that has gained *ten pounds.* Note, God must have all the glory of all our gains; *not unto us,* but unto him, must be *the praise,* Ps. 115:1. Paul, who gained the *ten pounds,* acknowledges, "*I laboured, yet not I. By the grace of God, I am what I am,* and do what I do; and *his grace was not in vain,*" 1 Co. 15:10. He will not speak of what he had done, but of what God *had done by him,* Rom. 15:18. 3. They were both commended for their fidelity and industry: *Well done, thou good servant,* v. 17. And to the other he *said likewise,* v. 19. Note, They who do that which is good shall have *praise of the same. Do well,* and Christ will say to thee, *Well done:* and, if he says *Well done,* the matter is not great who says otherwise. See Gen. 4:7. 4. They were *preferred* in proportion to the improvement they had made: "*Because thou hast been faithful in a very little,* and didst not say, 'As good sit still as go to trade with one pound, what can one do with so small a stock?' but didst humbly and honestly apply thyself to the improvement of that, *have thou authority over ten cities.*" Note, Those are in a fair way to rise who are content to begin low. *He that has used the office of a deacon well purchaseth to himself a good degree,* 1 Tim. 3:13. Two things are hereby promised the apostles: — (1.) That when they have taken pains to *plant* many churches they shall have the satisfaction and honour of presiding in them, and governing among them; they shall have great respect paid them, and have a great interest in the love and esteem of good Christians. *He that keepeth the fig-tree shall eat the fruit thereof;* and he that *laboureth in the word and doctrine* shall be *counted worthy of double honour.* (2.) That, when they have served their generation, according to the will of Christ, though they pass through this world despised and trampled upon, and perhaps pass out of it under disgrace and persecution as the apostles did, yet in the other world they shall reign as kings with Christ, shall sit with him on his throne, shall have *power over the nations,* Rev. 2:26. The happiness of heaven will be a much greater advancement to a good minister or Christian than it would be to a poor tradesman, that with much ado had cleared ten pounds, to be made governor of ten cities. He that had gained but *five pounds* had dominion over *five cities.* This intimates that there are *degrees of glory* in heaven; every vessel will be alike *full,* but not alike *large.* And the degrees of glory there will be according to the degrees of usefulness here.

Secondly, The *bad account* that was given by *one* of them, and the sentence passed upon him for his slothfulness and unfaithfulness, v. 20, etc. 1. He owned that he had not *traded* with the pound with which he had been entrusted (v. 20): "*Lord, behold, here is thy pound;* it is true, I have not made it *more,* but withal I have not made it *less;* I have kept it safely *laid up in a napkin.*" This represents the carelessness of those who have gifts, but never lay out themselves to do good with them. It is all one to them whether the interests of

Christ's kingdom sink or swim, go backward or forward; for their parts, they will take no care about it, no pains, be at no expenses, run no hazard. Those are the servants that lay up their pound *in a napkin* who think it enough to say that they have done no hurt in the world, but *did no good.* 2. He justified himself in his omission, with a plea that made the matter worse and not better (v. 21): *I feared thee, because thou art an austere man,* rigid and severe, *anthrōpos austēros ei. Austere* is the Greed word itself: a *sharp* man: *Thou takest up that which thou laidst not down.* He thought that his master put a hardship upon his servants when he required and expected the improvement of their pounds, and that it was *reaping where he did not sow;* whereas really it was reaping where he *had sown,* and, as the husbandman, expecting in proportion to what he had sown. He had no reason to *fear* his master's austerity, nor blame his expectations, but this was a mere sham, a frivolous groundless excuse for his idleness, which there was no manner of colour for. Note, The pleas of slothful professors, when they come to be examined, will be found more to their *shame* than in their *justification.* 3. His excuse is turned upon him: *Out of thine own mouth will I judge thee, thou wicked servant,* v. 22. He will be *condemned* by his crime, but *self-condemned* by his plea. "If thou didst look upon it as hard that I should expect the profit of thy trading, which would have been the greater profit, yet, if thou hadst had any regard to my interest, thou mightest have put my money *into the bank,* into some of the funds, that I might have had, not only *my own,* but my own *with usury,* which, though a *less* advantage, would have been *some.*" If he durst not *trade* for fear of *losing* the principal, and so being made accountable to his lord for it though it was lost, which he pretends, yet that would be no excuse for his not setting it out to interest, where it would be sure. Note, Whatever may be the pretences of slothful professors, in excuse of their slothfulness, the true reason of it is a reigning indifference to the interests of Christ and his kingdom, and their coldness therein. They care not whether religion gets around or loses ground, so they can but live at ease. 4. His pound is taken from him, v. 24. It is fit that those should *lose* their gifts who will not *use* them, and that those who have dealt falsely should be no longer trusted. Those who will not serve their Master with what he bestows upon them, why should they be suffered to serve themselves with it? *Take from him the pound.* 5. It is given to him that had the *ten pounds.* When this was objected against by the standers-by, because he had so much already *(Lord, he has ten pounds,* v. 25), it is answered (v. 26), *Unto every one that hath shall be given.* It is the rule of justice, (1.) That those should be most encouraged who have been most industrious, and that those who have laid out themselves most to do good should have their opportunities of doing good *enlarged,* and be put into a higher and more extensive sphere of usefulness. To him that hath gotten shall more be given, that he may be in a capacity to get more. (2.) That those who have their gifts, as if they had them not, who have them to no purpose, who do no good with them, should be deprived of them. To those who endeavour to increase the grace they have, God will impart more; those who neglect it, and suffer it to decline, can expect no other than that God should do so too. This needful warning Christ gives to his disciples, lest, while they were gaping for honours on earth, they should neglect their business, and so come short of their happiness in heaven.

3. Another thing they expected was, that, when the kingdom of God should appear, the body of the Jewish nation would immediately fall in with it, and submit to it, and all their aversions to Christ and his gospel would immediately vanish; but Christ tells them that, after his departure, the generality of them would persist in their obstinacy and rebellion, and it would be their ruin. This is shown here,

(1.) In the message which his citizens sent after him, v. 14. They not only opposed him, while he was in obscurity; but, when he was gone into glory, to be invested in his kingdom, then they continued their enmity to him, protested against his dominion, and said, *We will not have this man to reign over us.* [1.] This was fulfilled in the prevailing infidelity of the Jews after the ascension of Christ, and the setting up of the gospel kingdom. They would not submit their necks to his yoke, nor touch the top of his golden sceptre. They said, *Let us break his bands in sunder,* Ps. 2:1–3; Acts 4:26. [2.] It speaks the language of all unbelievers; they could be content that Christ should *save them,* but they will not have him to *reign over them;* whereas Christ is a Saviour to those only to whom he is a prince, and who are willing to obey him.

(2.) In the sentence passed upon them at his return: *Those mine enemies bring hither, v.* 27. When his faithful subjects are preferred and rewarded, then he will take vengeance on his enemies, and particularly on the Jewish nation, the doom of which is here read. When Christ had set up his gospel kingdom, and thereby put reputation upon the gospel ministry, then he comes to *reckon with* the Jews; then it is remembered against them that they had particularly disclaimed and protested against his kingly office, when they said, *We have no king but Caesar,* nor would own him for their king. They appealed to Caesar, and to Caesar they shall go; Caesar shall be their ruin. Then the *kingdom of God appeared* when vengeance was taken on those irreconcileable enemies to Christ and his government; they were *brought forth and slain before him.* Never was so much slaughter made in any war as in the wars of the Jews. That nation lived to see Christianity victorious in the Gentile world, in spite of their enmity and opposition to it, and then it was *taken away as dross.* The wrath of Christ came upon them to the uttermost (1 Th. 2:15, 16), and their destruction redounded very much to the honour of Christ and the peace of the church. But this is applicable to all others who *persist* in their infidelity, and will undoubtedly perish in it. Note, [1.] Utter ruin will certainly be the portion of all Christ's enemies; in the day of vengeance they shall all be brought *forth,* and *slain before him. Bring them hither,* to be made a spectacle to saints and angels; see Jos. 10:22, 24. *Bring them hither,* that they may see the glory and happiness of Christ and his followers, whom they hated and persecuted. *Bring them hither,* to have their frivolous pleas overruled, and to receive sentence according to their merits. Bring them, and *slay them before me,* as Agag before Samuel. The Saviour whom they have slighted will stand by and see them slain, and not interpose on their behalf. [2.] Those that *will not have Christ to reign over them* shall be reputed and dealt with as his enemies. We are ready to think that none are Christ's enemies but persecutors of Christianity, or scoffers at least; but you see that those will be accounted so that dislike the terms of salvation, will not submit to Christ's yoke, but will be their own masters. Note, Whoever will not be *ruled* by the grace of Christ will inevitably be ruined by the wrath of Christ.

Verses 28–40

We have here the same account of Christ's riding in some sort of triumph (such as it was) into Jerusalem which we had before in Matthew and Mark; let us therefore here only observe,

I. Jesus Christ was forward and willing to suffer and die for us. He went forward, *bound in the spirit, to Jerusalem,* knowing very well the *things* that should *befal him there,* and yet *he went before, ascending up to Jerusalem, v.* 28. He was the foremost of the company, as if he longed to be upon the spot, longed to engage, to take the field, and to enter upon action. Was he so forward to suffer and die for us, and shall we draw back from any service we are capable of doing for him?

II. It was no ways inconsistent either with Christ's humility or with his present state of humiliation to make a *public entry* into Jerusalem a little before he died. Thus he made himself to be the more taken notice of, that the ignominy of his death might appear the greater.

III. Christ is entitled to a dominion over all the creatures, and may use them when and as he pleases. No man has a property in his estate against Christ, but that *his* title is prior and superior. Christ sent to fetch an *ass* and her *colt* from their *owner's* and *master's crib,* when he had occasion for their service, and might do so, for all the *beasts of the forest are his,* and the tame beasts too.

IV. Christ has all men's hearts both under his eye and in his hand. He could influence those to whom the ass and the colt belonged to consent to their taking them away, as soon as they were told that the Lord had occasion for them.

V. Those that go on Christ's errands are sure to speed (*v.* 32): *They that were sent found* what he told them they should find, and the owners willing to part with them. It is a comfort to Christ's messengers that they shall bring what they are sent for, if indeed the Lord has occasion for it.

VI. The disciples of Christ, who fetch that for him from others which he has occasion for, and which they have not, should not think that enough, but, whatever they have themselves wherewith he may be served and honoured, they should be ready to serve him with it. Many can be willing to attend Christ at other people's expense who care not to be at any charge upon him themselves; but those disciples not only fetched the ass's colt for him, but *cast their* own *garments upon the colt,* and were willing that they should be used for his trappings.

VII. Christ's triumphs are the matter of his disciples' praises. When Christ came nigh to Jerusalem, God put it of a sudden into the hearts of the *whole multitude of the disciples,* not of the twelve only, but abundance more, that were disciples at large, *to rejoice and praise God* (*v.* 37), and the *spreading of their clothes in the way* (*v.* 36) was a common expression of joy, as at the feast of tabernacles. Observe, 1. What was the matter or occasion of their joy and praise. They praised God *for all the mighty works they had seen,* all the miracles Christ had wrought, especially the *raising of Lazarus,* which is particularly mentioned, Jn. 12:17, 18. That brought others to mind, for fresh miracles and mercies should revive the remembrance of the former. 2. How they expressed their joy and praise (*v.* 38): *Blessed be the king that cometh in the name of the Lord.* Christ is *the king;* he *comes in the name of the Lord,* clothed with a divine authority, commissioned from heaven to *give law* and treat of *peace. Blessed be he.* Let us *praise him,* let God *prosper him.* He is *blessed* for ever, and we will speak well of him. *Peace in heaven.* Let the God of heaven send peace and success to his undertaking, and then there will be *glory in the highest.* It will redound to the glory of the most high God; and the angels, the glorious inhabitants of the upper world, will give him the glory of it. Compare this song of the saints on earth with that of the angels, *ch.* 2:14. They both agree to give glory to God in the highest. There the praises of both centre; the angels say, *On earth peace,* rejoicing in the benefit which men on earth have by Christ; the saints say, *Peace in heaven,* rejoicing in the benefit which the angels have by Christ. Such is the communion we have with the holy angels that, as *they* rejoice in the *peace on earth,* so *we* rejoice in the *peace in heaven,* the *peace* God *makes in his high places* (Job 25:2), and both in Christ, who hath reconciled all things to himself, whether *things on earth or things in heaven.*

VIII. Christ's triumph's, and his disciples' joyful praises of them, are the vexation of proud Pharisees, that are enemies to him and his kingdom. There were some Pharisees among *the multitude* who were so far from joining with them that they were enraged at them, and, Christ being a famous example of humility, they thought that he would not admit such acclamations as these, and therefore expected that he should *rebuke his disciples, v.* 39. But it is the honour of Christ that, as he despises the contempt of the proud, so he accepts the praises of the humble.

IX. Whether men praise Christ or no he will, and shall, and must be praised (*v.* 40): *If these should hold their peace,* and not speak the praises of the Messiah's kingdom, *the stones would immediately cry out,* rather than that Christ should not be praised. This was, in effect, literally fulfilled, when, upon men's reviling Christ upon the cross, instead of praising him, and his own disciples' sinking into a profound silence, the *earth did quake and the rocks rent.* Pharisees would silence the praises of Christ, but they cannot gain their point; for as God can *out of stones raise up children unto Abraham,* so he can out of the mouths of those children perfect praise.

Verses 41–48

The great Ambassador from heaven is here making his public entry into Jerusalem, not to be *respected* there, but to be *rejected;* he knew what a nest of vipers he was throwing himself into, and yet see here two instances of his love to that place and his concern for it.

I. The *tears he shed* for the *approaching ruin* of the *city* (*v.* 41): *When he was come near, he beheld the city, and wept over it.* Probably, it was when he was coming down the descent of the hill from the *mount of Olives,* where he had a full view of the city, the large extent of it, and the many stately structures in it, and his eye affected his heart, and his heart his eye again. See here,

1. What a tender spirit Christ was of; we never read that he laughed, but we often find him in tears. In this very place his father David wept, and those that were with him, though he and they were *men of war.* There are cases in which it is no disparagement to the stoutest of men to melt into tears.

2. That Jesus Christ *wept* in the midst of his triumphs, *wept* when all about him were *rejoicing,* to show how little he was elevated with the applause and acclamation of the people. Thus he would teach us to *rejoice with trembling,* and *as though we rejoiced not.* If Providence do not stain the beauty of our triumphs, we may ourselves see cause to sully it with our sorrows.

3. That he *wept over Jerusalem.* Note, There are cities to be wept over, and none to be more lamented than Jerusalem, that had been the holy city, and the joy of the whole earth, if it be degenerated. But why did Christ weep at the sight of Jerusalem? Was it because "Yonder is the city in which I must be betrayed and bound, scourged and spit upon, condemned and crucified?" No, he himself gives us the reason of his tears.

(1.) Jerusalem has not improved the day of her opportunities. He wept, and said, *If thou hadst known, even thou at least in this thy day,* if thou wouldst but yet know, while the gospel is preached to thee, and salvation offered thee by it; if thou wouldest at length bethink thyself, and understand *the things that belong to thy peace,* the making of thy peace with God, and the securing of thine own spiritual and eternal welfare — but thou *dost not know the day of thy visitation, v.* 44. The manner of speaking is abrupt: *If thou hadst known! O that thou hadst,* so some take it; like that *O that my people had hearkened unto me,* Ps. 81:13; Isa. 48:18. Or, *If thou hadst known, well;* like that of the *fig-tree, ch.* 13:9. How happy had it been for thee! Or, "If thou hadst known, thou wouldest have wept for thyself, and I should have no occasion to weep for thee, but should have rejoiced rather." What he says lays all the blame of Jerusalem's impending ruin upon herself. Note, [1.] There are things which *belong to our peace,* which we are all concerned to *know* and *understand;* the way how peace is made, the offers made of peace, the terms on which we may have the benefit of peace. The things that belong to our peace are those things that relate to our present and future welfare; these we must know with application. [2.] There is a *time of visitation* when those things which *belong to our peace* may be *known by us,* and known to good purpose. When we enjoy the means of grace in great plenty, and have the word of God powerfully preached to us — when the Spirit strives with us, and our own consciences are startled and awakened — then is the *time of visitation,* which we are concerned to improve. [3.] With those that have long neglected the time of their visitation, if at length, if at last, in this their day, their eyes be opened, and they bethink themselves, all will be well yet. Those shall not be refused that come into the vineyard *at the eleventh hour.* [4.] It is the amazing folly of multitudes that enjoy the means of grace, and it will be of fatal consequence to them, that they do not improve the day of their opportunities. The *things of their peace* are revealed to them, but are not minded or regarded by them; they *hide their eyes* from them, as if they were not worth taking notice of. They are not aware of the *accepted time* and the *day of salvation,* and to let it slip and perish through mere carelessness. None are so *blind* as those that will not *see;* nor have any the things of their peace more certainly hidden from their eyes than those that turn their back upon them. [5.] The sin and folly of those that persist in a contempt of gospel grace are a great grief to the Lord Jesus, and should be so to us. He looks with weeping eyes upon lost souls, that continue impenitent, and run headlong upon their own ruin; he had rather that they would *turn and live* than *go on and die,* for he is not willing that any should perish.

(2.) Jerusalem cannot escape the day of her desolation. The *things of her peace* are now in a manner hidden from her eyes; they will be shortly. Not but that after this the gospel was preached to them by the apostles; *all the house of Israel* were called to *know assuredly* that Christ was their *peace* (Acts 2:36), and multitudes were convinced and converted. But as to the body of the nation, and the leading part of it, they were sealed up under unbelief; God had *given them the spirit of slumber,* Rom. 11:8. They were so prejudiced and enraged against the gospel, and those few that did embrace it then, that nothing less than a miracle of divine grace (like that which converted Paul) would work upon them; and it could not be expected that such a miracle should be wrought, and so they were justly given up to *judicial* blindness and hardness. The *peaceful things* are not *hidden from the eyes* of particular persons; but it is too late to think now of the nation of the Jews, *as such,* becoming a Christian nation, by embracing Christ. And therefore they are marked for ruin, which Christ here foresees and foretels, as the certain consequence of their rejecting Christ. Note, Neglecting the great salvation often brings temporal judgments upon a people; it did so upon Jerusalem in less than forty years after this, when all that Christ here foretold was exactly fulfilled. [1.] The Romans besieged the city, *cast a trench about it, compassed it round,* and *kept their* inhabitants in *on every side.* Josephus relates that Titus ran up a wall in a very short time, which surrounded the city, and cut off all hopes of escaping. [2.] They *laid it even with the ground.* Titus commanded his soldiers to *dig up the city,* and the whole compass of it was levelled, except three towers; see Josephus's history of the wars of the Jews, 5.356–360; 7.1. Not only the city, but the citizens were laid even with the ground *(thy children within thee),* by the cruel slaughters that were made of them: and there was scarcely one stone *left upon another.* This was for their crucifying Christ; this was because they *knew not the day of their visitation.* Let other cities and nations take warning.

II. The *zeal he showed* for the *present purification of the temple.* Though it must be destroyed ere long, it does not therefore follow that no care must be taken of it in the mean time.

1. Christ cleared it of those who profaned it. He went straight to the temple, and *began to cast out the buyers and sellers, v.* 45. Hereby (though he was represented as an enemy to the temple, and that was the crime laid to his charge before the high priest) he made it to appear that he had a truer love for the temple than they had who had such a veneration for its corban, its treasury, as a sacred thing; for its purity was more its glory than its wealth was. Christ gave reason for his dislodging the temple-merchants, *v.* 46. The temple is a *house of prayer,* set apart for communion with God: the *buyers* and *sellers* made it a *den of thieves* by the fraudulent bargains they made there, which was by no means to be suffered, for it would be a distraction to those who came there to pray.

2. He put it to the best use that ever it was put to, for he *taught daily in the temple, v.* 47. Note, It is not enough that the corruptions of a church be purged out, but the preaching of the gospel must be encouraged. Now, when Christ preached in the temple, observe here, (1.) How spiteful the church-rulers were against him; how industrious to seek an *opportunity, or pretence* rather, to do him a mischief (*v.* 47): *The chief priests and scribes, and the chief of the people,* the great sanhedrim, that should have attended him, and summoned the people too to attend him, *sought to destroy him,* and put him to death. (2.) How respectful the common people were to him. They were *very attentive to hear him.* He spent most of his time in the country, and did not then preach in the temple, but, when he did, the people paid him great respect, attended on his preaching with diligence, and let no opportunity slip of hearing him, attended to it with care, and would not lose a word. Some read it, *All the people as they heard him, took his part;* and so it comes in very properly as a reason why his enemies *could not find what they might* do against him; they saw the people ready to fly in their faces if they offered him any violence. Till his hour was come his interest in the common people protected him; but, when his hour was come, the chief priests' influence upon the common people delivered him up.

CHAPTER 20

In this chapter we have, I. Christ's answer to the chief priests' question concerning his authority (*v.* 1–8). II. The parable of the vineyard let out to the unjust and rebellious husbandmen (*v.* 9–19). III. Christ's answer to the question proposed to him concerning the lawfulness of paying tribute to Caesar (*v.* 20–26). IV. His vindication of that great fundamental doctrine of the Jewish and Christian institutes — the resurrection of the dead and the future state, from the foolish cavils of the Sadducees (*v.* 27–38). V. His puzzling the scribes with a question concerning the Messiah's being the Son of David (*v.* 39–44). VI. The caution he gave his disciples to take heed of the scribes (*v.* 45–47). All which passages we had before in Matthew and Mark, and therefore need not enlarge upon them here, unless on those particulars which we had not there.

Verses 1–8

In this passage of story nothing is added here to what we had in the other evangelists; but only in the first verse, where we are told,

I. That he was now *teaching the people in the temple,* and *preaching the gospel.* Note, Christ was a preacher of his own gospel. He not only *purchased* the salvation for us, but *published* it to us, which is a great confirmation of the truth of the gospel, and gives abundant encouragement to us to receive it, for it is a sign that the heart of Christ was much upon it, to have it received. This likewise puts an honour upon the preachers of the gospel, and upon their office and work, how much soever they are despised by a vain world. It puts an honour upon the *popular preachers* of the gospel; Christ condescended to the capacities of the *people* in preaching the gospel, and *taught them.* And observe, when he was *preaching the gospel to the people* he had this interruption given him. Note, Satan and his agents do all they can to hinder the *preaching of the gospel to the people,* for nothing weakens the interest of Satan's kingdom more.

II. That his enemies are here said to *come upon him — epestēsan.* The word is used only here, and it intimates,

1. That they thought to surprise him with this question; they *came upon him* suddenly, hoping to catch him unprovided with an answer, as if this were not a thing he had himself thought of.

2. That they thought to frighten him with this question. They *came upon him* in a body, with violence. But how could he be terrified with the *wrath of men,* when it was in his *own power to restrain it,* and make it turn to his praise? From this story itself we may learn, (1.) That it is not to be thought strange, if even that which is evident to a demonstration be disputed, and called in question, as a doubtful thing, by those that shut their eyes against the light. Christ's miracles plainly showed *by what authority he did these things,* and sealed his commission; and yet this is that which is here *arraigned.* (2.) Those that question Christ's authority, if they be but catechized themselves in the plainest and most evident principles of religion, will have their folly made manifest unto all men. Christ answered these priests and scribes with a question concerning the baptism of John, a plain question, which the meanest of the common people could answer: *Was it from heaven or of men?* They all knew it was *from heaven;* there was nothing in it that had an earthly relish or tendency, but it was all heavenly and divine. And this question gravelled them, and ran them aground, and served to shame them before the people. (3.) It is not strange if those that are governed by reputation and secular interest imprison the plainest truths, and smother and stifle the strongest convictions, as these priests and scribes did, who, to save their credit, would not own that John's baptism was *from heaven,* and had no other reason why they did not say it was *of men* but because they *feared the people.* What good can be expected from men of such a spirit? (4.) Those that bury the knowledge they have are justly denied further knowledge. It was just with Christ to refuse to give an account of his authority to them that knew the baptism of John to be from heaven and would not believe in him, nor own their knowledge, *v.* 7, 8.

Verses 9–19

Christ spoke this parable against those who were resolved not to own his authority, though the evidence of it was ever so full and convincing; and it comes very seasonably to show that by questioning his authority they forfeited their own. Their disowning the lord of their vineyard was a defeasance of their lease of the vineyard, and giving up of all their title.

I. The parable has nothing added here to what we had before in Matthew and Mark. The scope of it is to show that the Jewish nation, by persecuting the prophets, and at length Christ himself, had provoked God to take away from them all their church privileges, and to abandon them to ruin. It teaches us, 1. That those who enjoy the privileges of the visible church are as tenants and farmers that have a vineyard to look after, and rent to pay for it. God, by setting up revealed religion and instituted orders in the world, hath planted a vineyard, which he lets out to those people among whom his tabernacle is, *v.* 9. And they have *vineyard-work* to do, needful and constant work, but pleasant and profitable. Whereas man was, for sin, condemned to *till the ground,* they that have a place in the church are restored to that which was Adam's work in innocency, to *dress the garden,* and to keep it; for the church is a paradise, and Christ the tree of life in it. They have also *vineyard-fruits* to present to the Lord of the vineyard. There are rents to be paid and services to be done, which, though bearing no proportion to the value of the premises, yet must be *done* and must be *paid.* 2. That the work of God's ministers is to call upon those who enjoy the privileges of the church to *bring forth fruit* accordingly. They are God's rent-gatherers, to put the husbandmen in mind of their arrears, or rather to put them in mind that they have a landlord who expects to hear from them, and to receive some acknowledgment of their dependence on him, and obligations to him, *v.* 10. The Old-Testament prophets were sent on this errand to the Jewish church, to demand from them the duty and obedience they owed to God. 3. That it has often been the lot of God's faithful servants to be wretchedly abused by his own tenants; they have been *beaten* and *treated* shamefully by those that resolved to *send them empty* away. They that are resolved not to do their duty to God cannot bear to be called upon to do it. Some of the best men in the world have had the hardest usage from it, for their best services. 4. That God sent his Son into the world to carry on the same work that the prophets were employed in, to *gather the fruits of the vineyard* for God; and one would have thought that he would have been reverenced and received. The prophets spoke as *servants, Thus saith the Lord;* but Christ *as a Son,* among his own, *Verily, I say unto you.* Putting such an honour as this upon them, to send him, one would have thought, should have won upon them. 5. That those who reject Christ's ministers would reject Christ himself if he should come to them; for it has been tried, and found that the persecutors and murderers of his servants the prophets were the persecutors and murderers of himself. They said, *This is the heir, come let us kill him.* When they slew the servants, there were other servants sent. "But, if we can but be the death of the son, there is never another son to be sent, and then we shall be no longer molested with these demands; we may have a quiet possession of the vineyard for ourselves." The scribes and Pharisees promised themselves that, if they could but get Christ out of the way, they should for ever ride masters in the Jewish church; and therefore they took the bold step, they *cast him out of the vineyard, and killed him.* 6. That the putting of Christ to death filled up the measure of the Jewish iniquity, and brought upon them ruin without remedy. No other could be expected than that God should *destroy those wicked husbandmen.* They began in *not paying their rent,* but then proceeded to beat and kill the servants, and at length their young Master himself. Note, Those that live in the neglect of their duty to God know not what degrees of sin and destruction they are running themselves into.

II. To the application of the parable is added here, which we had not before, their deprecation of the doom included in it (*v.* 16): *When they heart it, they said, God forbid, Mē genoito — Let not this be done,* so it should be read. Though they could not but own that for such a sin such a punishment was just, and what might be expected, yet they could not bear to hear of it. Note, It is an instance of the folly and stupidity of sinners that they proceed and persevere in their sinful ways though at the same time they have a foresight and dread of the destruction that is at the end of those ways. And see what a cheat they put themselves, to think to avoid it by a cold *God forbid,* when they do nothing towards the preventing of it; but will this make the threatening of no effect? No, they shall know whose word shall stand, God's or theirs. Now observe what Christ said, in answer to this childish deprecation of their ruin. 1. He *beheld them.* This is taken notice of only by this evangelist, *v.* 17. He *looked upon* them with pity and compassion, grieved to see them cheat themselves thus to their own ruin. He *beheld them,* to see if they would blush at their own folly, or if he could discern in their countenances any indication of relenting. 2. He referred them to the scripture: *"What is this then that is written?* How can you escape the judgment of God, when you cannot prevent the exaltation of him whom you despise and reject? The word of God hath said it, that *the stone which the builders rejected is become the head of the corner."* The Lord Jesus will be exalted to the Father's right hand. He has all judgment and all power committed to him; he is the corner-stone and top-stone of the church, and, if so, his enemies can expect no other than to be destroyed. Even those that slight him, that stumble at him, and are offended in him, *shall be broken* — it will be their ruin; but as to those that not only reject him, but hate and persecute him, as the Jews did, he will fall upon them and crush them to pieces — will *grind them to powder.* The condemnation of spiteful persecutors will be much sorer than that of careless unbelievers.

Lastly, We are told how the chief priests and scribes were exasperated by this parable (*v.* 19): *They perceived that he had spoken this parable against them;* and so he had. A guilty conscience needs no accuser; but they, instead of yielding to the convictions of conscience, fell into a rage at him who awakened that sleeping lion in their bosoms, and *sought to lay hands on him.* Their corruptions rebelled against their convictions, and got the victory. And it was not because they had any fear of God or of his wrath before their eyes, but only because they *feared the people,* that they did not now fly in his face, and take him by the throat. They were just ready to make his words good: *This is the heir, come let us kill him.* Note, When the hearts of the sons of men are fully set in them to do evil, the fairest warnings both of the sin they are about to commit and of the consequences of it make no impression upon them. Christ tells them that instead of *kissing the Son* of God they would *kill him,* upon which they should have said, *What, is thy servant a dog?* But they do, in effect, say this: "And so we will; have at him now." And, though they deprecate the punishment of the sin, in the next breath they are projecting the commission of it.

Verses 20–26

We have here Christ's evading a snare which his enemies laid for him, by proposing a question to him about tribute. We had this passage before, both in Matthew and Mark. Here is,

I. The mischief designed him, and that is more fully related here than before. The plot was to *deliver him unto the power and authority of the governor, v.* 20. They could not themselves put him to death by course of law, nor otherwise than by a *popular tumult,* which they could not depend upon; and, since they could not be his judges, they would willingly condescend to be his prosecutors and accusers, and would themselves *inform* against him. They hoped to gain their point, if they could but incense the governor against him. Note, It has been the common artifice of persecuting church-rulers to make the secular powers the tools of their malice, and oblige the *kings of the earth to do* their drudgery, who, if they had not been instigated, would have let their neighbours live quietly by them, as Pilate did Christ till the chief priests and the scribes presented Christ to him. But thus Christ's word must be fulfilled by their cursed politics, that he should be *delivered into the hands of the Gentiles.*

II. The persons they employed. Matthew and Mark told us that they were disciples of the Pharisees, with some Herodians. Here it is added, They were *spies, who should feign themselves just men.* Note, It is no new thing for *bad men* to feign themselves *just men,* and to cover the most wicked projects with the most specious and plausible pretences. The devil can *transform himself into an angel of light,* and a Pharisee appear in the garb, and speak the language, of a disciple of Christ. A spy must go in disguise. These spies must take on them to have a value for Christ's judgment, and to depend upon it as an oracle, and therefore must desire his advice in a case of conscience. Note, Ministers are concerned to stand upon their guard against some that feign themselves to be *just men,* and to be *wise as serpents* when they are in the midst of a *generation of vipers* and *scorpions.*

III. The question they proposed, with which they hoped to ensnare him. 1. Their preface is very courtly: *Master, we know that thou sayest and teachest rightly, v.* 21. Thus they thought to flatter him into an incautious freedom and openness with them, and so to gain their point. They that are proud, and love to be commended, will be brought to do any thing for those that will but flatter them, and speak kindly to them; but they were much mistaken who thought thus to impose upon the humble Jesus. He was not pleased with the testimony of such hypocrites, nor thought himself honoured by it. It is true that he *accepts not the person of any,* but it is as true that he knows the hearts of all, and knew theirs, and the *seven abominations* that were there, though they *spoke fair.* It was certain that he *taught the way of God truly;* but he knew that they were unworthy to be taught by him, who came to *take hold of his words,* not to be *taken hold of* by them. 2. Their case is very nice: "Is it lawful *for us"* (this is added here in Luke) *"to give tribute to Caesar —* for us Jews, us the free-born seed of Abraham, us that pay the Lord's tribute, may give tribute to Caesar?" Their pride and covetousness made them loth to pay taxes, and then they would have it a question whether it was lawful or no. Now if Christ should say that *it was lawful* the people would take it ill, for they expected that he who set up to be the Messiah should in the first place free them from the Roman yoke, and stand by them in denying tribute to Caesar. But if he should say that *it was not lawful,* as they expected he would (for if he had not been of that mind they thought he could not have been so much the darling of the people as he was), then

they should have something to accuse him of to the governor, which was what they wanted.

IV. His evading the snare which they laid for him: *He perceived their craftiness, v.* 23. Note, Those that are most crafty in their designs against Christ and his gospel cannot with all their art conceal them from his cognizance. He can see through the most politic disguises, and so break through the most dangerous snare; for *surely in vain is the net spread in the sight of any bird.* He did not give them a direct answer, but reproved them for offering to impose upon him — *Why tempt ye me?* and called for a *piece of money,* current money with the merchants — *Show me a penny;* and asked them whose money it was, whose stamp it bore, who coined it. They owned, "It is Caesar's money." "Why them," saith Christ, "you should first have asked whether it was lawful to *pay* and *receive* Caesar's money among yourselves, and to admit that to be the instrument of your commerce. But, having granted this by a common consent, you are concluded by your own act, and, no doubt, you ought to give tribute to him who furnished you with this convenience for your trade, protects you in it, and lends you the sanction of his authority for the value of your money. You must therefore *render to Caesar the things that are Caesar's.* In civil things you ought to submit to the civil powers, and so, if Caesar protects you in your civil rights by laws and the administration of justice, you ought to *pay him tribute;* but in sacred things God only is your King. You are not bound to be of Caesar's religion; you must *render to God the things that are God's,* must worship and adore him only, and not any golden image that Caesar sets up;" and we must worship and adore him in such way as he had appointed, and not according to the inventions of Caesar. It is God only that has authority to say *My son, give me thy heart.*

V. The confusion they were hereby put into, *v.* 26. 1. The snare is broken; *They could not take hold of his words before the people.* They could not fasten upon any thing wherewith to incense either the governor or the people against him. 2. Christ is honoured; even the wrath of man is made to praise him. They *marvelled at his answer,* it was so discreet and unexceptionable, and such an evidence of that wisdom and sincerity which make the face to shine. 3. Their mouths are stopped; they *held their peace.* They had nothing to object, and durst ask him nothing else, lest he should shame and expose them.

Verses 27–38

This discourse with the Sadducees we had before, just as it is here, only that the description Christ gives of the future state is somewhat more full and large here. Observe here,

I. In every age there have been men of corrupt minds, that have endeavoured to subvert the fundamental principles of revealed religion. As there are deists now, who call themselves *free*-thinkers, but are really *false*-thinkers; so there were Sadducees in our Saviour's time, who bantered the doctrine of the resurrection of the dead and the life of the world to come, though they were plainly revealed in the Old Testament, and were articles of the Jewish faith. The Sadducees deny that *there is any resurrection,* any *future state,* so *anastasis* may signify; not only no return of the body *to life,* but no continuance of the soul *in life,* no world of spirits, no state of recompence and retribution for what was done in the body. Take away this, and all religion falls to the ground.

II. It is common for those that design to undermine any truth of God to perplex it, and load it with difficulties. So these Sadducees did; when they would weaken people's faith in the doctrine of the resurrection, they put a question upon the supposition of it, which they thought could not be answered either way to satisfaction. The case perhaps was matter of fact, at least it might be so, of a woman that had *seven husbands.* Now in the resurrection *whose wife shall she be?* whereas it was not at all material whose she was, for when death puts an end to that relation it is not to be resumed.

III. There is a great deal of difference between the state of the children of men on earth and that of the children of God in heaven, a vast unlikeness between *this world* and *that world;* and we wrong ourselves, and wrong the truth of Christ, when we form our notions of that world of spirits by our present enjoyments in this world of sense.

1. The children of men in this world *marry, and are given in marriage, hyioi tou aiōnos toutou — the children of this age,* this generation, both good and bad, marry themselves and give their children in marriage. Much of our business in

this world is to raise and build up families, and to provide for them. Much of our pleasure in this world is in our relations, our wives and children; nature inclines to it. Marriage is instituted for the comfort of human life, here in this state where we carry bodies about with us. It is likewise a remedy against fornication, that natural desires might not become brutal, but be under direction and control. The *children of this* world are dying and going off the stage, and *therefore* they marry and give their children in marriage, that they may furnish the world of mankind with needful recruits, that as one generation passeth away another may come, and that they may have some of their own offspring to leave the fruit of their labours to, especially that the chosen of God in future ages may be introduced, for it is a *godly seed* that is sought by *marriage* (Mal. 2:15), a seed to serve the Lord, that shall be a *generation to him.*

2. The world to come is quite another thing; it is called *that world,* by way of emphasis and eminency. Note, There are more worlds than one; a present visible world, and a future invisible world; and it is the concern of every one of us to compare worlds, *this world* and *that world,* and give the preference in our thoughts and cares to that which deserves them. Now observe,

(1.) Who shall be the inhabitants of *that world:* They that shall be *accounted worthy to obtain it,* that is, that are interested in *Christ's merit,* who *purchased it for us,* and have a holy *meetness* for it wrought in them by the Spirit, whose business it is to prepare us for it. They have not a *legal* worthiness, upon account of any thing in them or done by them, but an *evangelical* worthiness, upon account of the inestimable price which Christ paid for the *redemption of the purchased possession.* It is a worthiness imputed by which we are glorified, as well as righteousness imputed by which we are justified; *kataxiōthentes,* they are *made agreeable to that world.* The disagreeableness that there is in the corrupt nature is taken away, and the dispositions of the soul are by the grace of God conformed to that state. They are by grace made and *counted worthy to obtain that world;* it intimates some *difficulty* in reaching after it, and danger of coming short. We must *so run* as that we may obtain. They shall obtain the *resurrection from the dead,* that is, the blessed resurrection; for that of *condemnation* (as Christ calls it, Jn. 5:29), is rather a resurrection *to death,* a second death, an eternal death, than *from death.*

(2.) What shall be the happy state of the inhabitants of that world we cannot express or conceive, 1 Co. 2:9. See what Christ here says of it. [1.] They *neither marry nor are given in marriage.* Those that have entered into the joy of their Lord are entirely taken up with that, and need not the joy of the bridegroom in his bride. The love in that world of love is all seraphic, and such as eclipses and loses the purest and most pleasing loves we entertain ourselves with in this world of sense. Where the body itself shall be a spiritual body, the delights of sense will all be banished; and where there is a perfection of holiness there is no occasion for marriage as a preservative from sin. Into the *new Jerusalem* there enters nothing that defiles. [2.] They cannot *die any more;* and this comes in as a reason why they do not *marry.* In this dying world there must be marriage, in order to the filling up of the vacancies made by death; but, where there are no burials, there is no need of weddings. This crowns the comfort of that world that there is no more death there, which sullies all the beauty, and damps all the comforts, of this world. Here death reigns, but thence it is for ever excluded. [3.] They are *equal unto the angels.* In the other evangelists it was said, They are *as the angels — ōs angeloi,* but here they are said to be *equal to the angels, isangeloi —* angels' peers; they have a glory and bliss no way inferior to that of the holy angels. They shall see the same sight, be employed in the same work, and share in the same joys, with the holy angels. Saints, when they come to heaven, shall be *naturalized,* and, though by nature strangers, yet, having *obtained this freedom* with a *great sum,* which Christ paid for them, they have in all respects equal privileges with them that were free-born, the angels that are the natives and aborigines of that country. They shall be companions with the angels, and converse with those blessed spirits that love them dearly, and with an innumerable company, to whom they are now come in faith, hope, and love. [4.] They *are the children of God,* and so they are as the angels, who are called the *sons of God.* In the *inheritance of sons,* the *adoption of sons* will be completed. Hence believers are said to *wait for the adoption,* even *the redemption of the body,* Rom. 8:23. For till the body is redeemed from the grave the adoption is not completed. *Now are we the sons of God,* 1 Jn. 3:2. We have the nature and disposition of sons, but that will not be *perfected* till we come to heaven. [5.] They are the *children of the resurrection,* that is, they are made capable of the employments and enjoyments of the future state; they are *born to that world,* belong to that family, had their education for it here, and shall there have their inheritance in it. They are the *children of God,* being the *children of the resurrection.* Note, God owns those only for his children that are the children of the resurrection, that are born from above, are allied to the world of spirits, and prepared for that world, the children of that family.

IV. It is an undoubted truth that there is another life after this, and there were eminent discoveries made of this truth in the early ages of the church (*v.* 37, 38): *Moses showed this, as it was shown to Moses at the bush,* and he hath shown it to us, when *he calleth the Lord,* as the Lord calleth himself, the *God of Abraham, and the God of Isaac, and the God of Jacob. Abraham, Isaac, and Jacob,* were then *dead* as to our world; they had departed out of it many years before, and their bodies were turned into dust in the cave of Machpelah; how then could God say, not *I was,* but *I am* the *God or Abraham?* It is absurd that the living God and Fountain of life should continue related to them as their God, if there were no more of them in being than what lay in that cave, undistinguished from common dust. We must therefore conclude that they were then in being in another world; for *God is not the God of the dead, but of the living.* Luke here adds, *For all live unto him,* that is, all who, like them, are true believers; though they are dead, yet they *do live;* their souls, which *return to God who gave them* (Eccl. 12:7), live to him as the Father of spirits: and their bodies shall live again at the end of time by the power of God; for he calleth things that are not as though they were, because he is the God that *quickens the dead,* Rom. 4:17. But there is more in it yet; when God called himself *the God* of these patriarchs, he meant that he was their felicity and portion, a *God all-sufficient to them* (Gen. 17:1), their *exceeding great reward,* Gen. 15:1. Now it is plain by their history that he never did that for them in this world which would answer the *true intent* and *full extent* of that great undertaking, and therefore there must be another life after this, in which he will do that for them that will amount to a *discharge in full* of that promise — that he would be to them a God, which he is able to do, for *all live to him,* and he has wherewithal to make every soul happy that lives to him; enough for *all,* enough for *each.*

Verses 39–47

The scribes were *students* in the law, and *expositors* of it to the people, men in reputation for wisdom and honour, but the generality of them were enemies to Christ and his gospel. Now here we have some of them attending him, and four things we have in these verses concerning them, which we had before: —

I. We have them here commending the reply which Christ made to the Sadducees concerning the resurrection: *Certain of the scribes said, Master, thou hast well said, v.* 39. Christ had the testimony of his adversaries that he said well; and *therefore* the scribes were his enemies because he would not *conform* to the traditions of the elders, but yet when he vindicated the fundamental practices of religion, and appeared in the defence of them, even the scribes commended his performance, and owned that he said well. Many that call themselves Christians come short even of this spirit.

II. We have them here struck with an awe of Christ, and of his wisdom and authority (*v.* 40): *They durst not ask him any questions at all,* because they say that he was too hard for all that contended with him. His own disciples, though weak, yet, being willing to receive his doctrine, durst *ask him any question;* but the Sadducees, who contradicted and cavilled at his doctrine, durst ask him none.

III. We have them here *puzzled* and run aground with a question concerning the Messiah, *v.* 41. It was plain by many scriptures that Christ was to be the *Son of David;* even the blind man knew this (*ch.* 18:39); and yet it was plain that David called the Messiah *his Lord* (*v.* 42, 44), his owner, and ruler, and benefactor: *The Lord said to my Lord.* God said it to the Messiah, Ps. 110:1. Now if he be *his Son,* why doth he call him *his Lord?* If he be *his Lord,* why do *we* call him *his Son?* This he left them to consider of, but they could not rec-

oncile this seeming contradiction; thanks be to God, we can; that Christ, *as God,* was David's Lord, but Christ, *as man,* was David's Son. He was both the *root* and the *offspring of David,* Rev. 22:16. By his *human nature* he was the *offspring of David,* a branch of his family; by his *divine nature* he was the *root of David,* from whom he had his being and life, and all the supplies of grace.

IV. We have them here described in their black characters, and a public caution given to the disciples to take heed of them, *v.* 45–47. This we had, just as it is here, Mk. 12:38, and more largely Mt. 23. Christ bids his disciples *beware of the scribes,* that is,

1. "Take heed of being drawn *into sin* by them, of learning their way, and going into their measures; beware of such a spirit as they are governed by. Be not you such in the Christian church as they are in the Jewish church."

2. "Take heed of being *brought into trouble* by them," in the same sense that he had said (Mt. 10:17), "*Beware of men, for they will deliver you up to the councils;* beware of the scribes, for they will do so. Beware of them, for," (1.) "They are *proud* and *haughty.* They *desire* to walk about the streets in *long robes,* as those that are above business (for men of business went with their *loins girt up*), and as those that take state, and take place." *Cedant arma togae — Let arms yield to the gown.* They loved in their hearts to have people make their obeisance to them *in the markets,* that many might see what respect was paid them; and were very proud of the precedency that was given them in all places of concourse. They *loved the highest seats in the synagogues* and *the chief rooms at feasts,* and, when they were placed in them, looked upon themselves with great conceit and upon all about them with great contempt. *I sit as a queen.* (2.) "They are *covetous and oppressive,* and make their religion a cloak and cover for crime." They *devour widows' houses,* get their estates into their hands, and then by some trick or other make them their own, or they live upon them, and eat up what they have; and *widows* are an easy prey to them, because they are apt to be deluded by their specious pretences: *for a show they make long prayers,* perhaps long prayers with the widows when they are in sorrow, as if they had not only a *piteous* but a *pious* concern for them, and thus endeavour to ingratiate themselves with them, and get their money and effects into their hands. Such devout men may surely be trusted with *untold gold;* but they will give such an account of it as they think fit.

Christ reads them their doom in a few words: *These shall receive a more abundant judgment,* a double damnation, both for their abuse of the poor *widows,* whose houses they devoured, and for their abuse of religion, and particularly of prayer, which they had made use of as a pretence for the more plausible and effectual carrying on of their worldly and wicked projects; for *dissembled piety is double iniquity.*

CHAPTER 21

In this chapter we have, I. The notice Christ took, and the approbation he gave, of a poor widow that cast two mites into the treasury (*v.* 1–4). II. A prediction of future events, in answer to his disciples' enquiries concerning them (*v.* 5–7). 1. Of what should happen between that and the destruction of Jerusalem — false Christs arising, bloody wars and persecutions of Christ's followers (*v.* 8–19). 2. Of that destruction itself (*v.* 20–24). 3. Of the second coming of Jesus Christ to judge the world, under the type and figure of that (*v.* 25–33). III. A practical application of this, by way of caution and counsel (*v.* 34–36), and an account of Christ's preaching and the people's attendance on it (*v.* 37, 38).

Verses 1–4

This short passage of story we had before in Mark. It is thus recorded twice, to teach us, 1. That *charity* to the poor is a *main matter* in religion. Our Lord Jesus took all occasions to commend it and recommend it. He had just mentioned the barbarity of the scribes, who devoured *poor widows* (ch. 20); and perhaps this is designed as an aggravation of it, that the poor widows were the best benefactors to the public funds, of which the scribes had the disposal. 2. That Jesus Christ has his eye upon us, to observe what we give to the poor, and what we contribute to works of piety and charity. Christ, though intent upon his preaching, looked up, to see what *gifts were cast into the treasury, v.* 1. He observes whether we give largely and liberally, in proportion to what we have, or whether we be sneaking and paltry in it; nay, his eye goes further, he observes whether we give charitably and with a willing mind, or grudgingly and with reluctance. This should make us afraid of coming short of our duty in this matter; men may be deceived with excuses which

Christ knows to be frivolous. And this should encourage us to be abundant in it, without desiring that men should know it; it is enough that Christ does; he sees in secret, and will reward openly. 3. That Christ observes and accepts the charity of the poor in a particular manner. Those that have nothing *to give* may yet *do* a great deal in charity by ministering to the poor, and helping them, and begging for them, that cannot *help* themselves, or *beg* for themselves. But here was one that was herself poor and yet *gave* what little she had to the treasury. It was but *two mites,* which make a farthing; but Christ magnified it as a piece of charity exceeding all the rest: *She has cast in more than they all.* Christ does not blame her for indiscretion, in giving what she wanted herself, nor for vanity in giving among the rich to the treasury; but commended her liberality, and her willingness to part with what little she had for the glory of God, which proceeded from a belief of and dependence upon God's providence to take care of her. *Jehovah-jireh — the Lord will provide.* 4. That, whatever may be called *the offerings of God,* we ought to have a respect for, and to our power, yea, and beyond our power, to contribute cheerfully to. These have *cast in unto the offerings of God.* What is given to the support of the ministry and the gospel, to the spreading and propagating of religion, the education of youth, the release of prisoners, the relief of widows and strangers, and the maintenance of poor families, is given to the *offerings of God,* and it shall be so accepted and recompensed.

Verses 5–19

See here, I. With what admiration some spoke of the external pomp and magnificence of the temple, and they were some of Christ's own disciples too; and they took notice of it to him *how it was adorned with goodly stones and gifts, v.* 5. The outside was built up with goodly stones, and within it was beautified and enriched with the *presents* that were offered up for that purpose, and were *hung up* in it. They thought their Master should be as much affected with those things as they were, and should as much regret the destruction of them as they did. When we *speak of the temple,* it should be of the presence of God in it, and of the ordinances of God administered in it, and the communion which his people there have with him. It is a poor thing, when we speak of the church, to let our discourse dwell upon its pomps and revenues, and the dignities and powers of its officers and rulers; for the king's daughter is all *glorious within.*

II. With what contempt Christ spoke of them, and with what assurance of their being all made desolate very shortly (*v.* 6): "*As for those things which you behold,* those dear things which you are so much in love with, *behold, the days will come,* and some now living may live to see them, *in which there shall not be left one stone upon another.* This building, which seems so beautiful that one would think none could, for pity, pull it down, and which seems so strong that one would think none would be able to pull it down, shall yet be utterly ruined; and this shall be done as soon as ever the spiritual temple of the gospel church (the substance of that shadow) begins to flourish in the world." Did we by faith foresee the blasting and withering of all external glory, we should not set our hearts upon it as those do that cannot see, or will not look, so far before them.

III. With what curiosity those about him enquire concerning the time when this great desolation should be: *Master, when shall these things be? v.* 7. It is natural to us to covet to know future things and the time of them, which *it is not for us to know,* when we are more concerned to ask what is our duty in the prospect of these things, and how we may prepare for them, which it is for us to know. They enquire *what sign there shall be when these things shall come to pass.* They ask not for a *present* sign, to confirm the prediction itself, and to induce them to believe it (Christ's word was enough for that), but what the future signs will be of the approaching accomplishment of the prediction, by which they may be put in mind of it. These *signs of the times* Christ had taught them to observe.

IV. With what clearness and fulness Christ answers their enquiries, as far as was necessary to direct them in their duty; for all knowledge is desirable as far as it is in order to practice.

1. They must expect to hear of false Christs and false prophets appearing, and false prophecies given out (*v.* 8): *Many shall come in my name;* he does not mean *in the name of Jesus,* though there were some deceivers who pretended commissions from him (as Acts 19:13), but usurping the title

and character of the Messiah. Many pretended to be the deliverers of the Jewish church and nation from the Romans, and to fix the time when the deliverance should be wrought, by which multitudes were drawn into a snare, to their ruin. They shall say, *hoti egō eimi — I am he,* or *I am,* as if they would assume that incommunicable name of God, by which he made himself known when he came to deliver Israel out of Egypt, *I am;* and, to encourage people to follow them, they added, *"The time draws near* when the kingdom shall be restored to Israel, and all who will follow me shall share in it." Now as to this, he gives them a needful caution (1.) *"Take heed that you be not deceived;* do not imagine that I shall myself come again in external glory, to take possession of the throne of kingdoms. No, you must not expect any such thing, for my kingdom is not of this world." When they asked solicitously and eagerly, *Master, when shall these things be?* the first word Christ said was, *Take heed that you be not deceived.* Note, Those that are most *inquisitive* in the things of God (though it is very good to be so) are in most danger of being imposed upon, and have most need to be upon their guard. (2.) *"Go you not after them.* You know the Messiah is come, and you are not to look for any other; and therefore do not so much as hearken to them, nor have any thing to do with them." If we are sure that Jesus is the Christ, and his doctrine is the *gospel, of God,* we must be deaf to all intimations of another Christ and another gospel.

2. They must expect to hear of great commotions in the nations, and many terrible judgments inflicted upon the Jews and their neighbours. (1.) There shall be *bloody wars* (v. 10): *Nation shall rise against nation,* one part of the Jewish nation against another, or rather the whole against the Romans. Encouraged by the false Christs, they shall wickedly endeavour to throw off the Roman yoke, by taking up arms against the Roman powers; when they had rejected the liberty with which Christ would have made them free they were left to themselves, to grasp at their civil liberty in ways that were *sinful,* and therefore could not be *successful.* (2.) There shall be *earthquakes,* great earthquakes, *in divers places,* which shall not only frighten people, but destroy towns and houses, and bury many in the ruins of them. (3.) There shall be *famines* and *pestilences,* the common effects of war, which destroys the fruits of the earth, and, by exposing men to ill weather and reducing them to ill diet, occasions infectious diseases. God has various ways of punishing a provoking people. The four sorts of judgments which the Old-Testament prophets so often speak of are threatened by the New-Testament prophets too; for, though spiritual judgments are more commonly inflicted in gospel times, yet God makes use of temporal judgments also. (4.) There shall be *fearful sights* and *great signs from heaven,* uncommon appearances in the clouds, comets and blazing stars, which frighten the ordinary sort of beholders, and have always been looked upon as *ominous,* and *portending* something *bad.* Now, as to these, the caution he gives them is, *"Be not terrified.* Others will be frightened at them, but be not you frightened, v. 2. As to the *fearful sights,* let them not be fearful to you, who look above the visible heavens to the throne of God's government in the highest heavens. *Be not dismayed at the signs of heaven, for the heathen are dismayed at them,* Jer. 10:2. And, as to the *famines* and *pestilences,* you fall into the hands of God, who has promised to those who are his that *in the days of famine they shall be satisfied,* and that he will keep them from the *noisome pestilence;* trust therefore in him, and *be not afraid.* Nay, when you hear of wars, when without are fightings and within are fears, yet then *be not you terrified;* you know the worst that any of these judgments can do to you, and therefore be not afraid of them; for," [1.] "It is your interest to *make the best of that which is,* for all your fears cannot alter it: *these things must first come to pass;* there is no remedy; it will be your wisdom to make yourselves easy by accommodating yourselves to them." [2.] "There is *worse behind;* flatter not yourselves with a fancy that you will soon see an end of these troubles, no, not so soon as you think of: *the end is not by and by,* not *suddenly.* Be not *terrified,* for, if you begin so quickly to be discouraged, how will you bear up under what is yet before you?"

3. They must expect to be themselves for *signs and wonders* in Israel; their being *persecuted* would be a prognostic of the destruction of the city and temple, which he had now foretold. Nay, this would be the *first* sign of their ruin coming: *"Before all these, they shall lay their hands on you.* The judgment shall begin at the house of God; you must smart

first, for warning to them, that, if they have any consideration, they may consider, *If this be done to the green tree, what shall be done to the dry?* See 1 Pt. 4:17, 18. But this is not all; this must be considered not only as the *suffering* of the *persecuted,* but as the *sin* of the *persecutors. Before* God's judgments are brought upon them, they shall fill up the measure of their iniquity by *laying their* hands on you." Note, The ruin of a people is always introduced by their sin; and nothing introduces a surer or sorer ruin than the sin of persecution. This is a *sign* that God's wrath is coming upon a people to the uttermost when their *wrath* against the servants of God *comes to the uttermost.* Now as to this,

(1.) Christ tells them what hard things they should suffer for his name's sake, much to the same purport with what he had told them when he first called them to follow him, Mt. 10: They should know the wages of it, that they might *sit down and count the cost.* St. Paul, who was the greatest labourer and sufferer of them all, not being now among them, was told by Christ himself what *great things he should suffer for* his *name's sake* (Acts 9:16), so necessary is it that all who will live godly in Christ Jesus should count upon persecution. The Christians, having themselves been originally Jews, and still retaining an equal veneration with them for the Old Testament and all the essentials of their religion, and differing only in ceremony, might expect fair quarter with them; but Christ bids them not expect it: "No, they shall be the most forward to *persecute you.*" [1.] "They shall use their own church-power against you: *They shall deliver you up to the synagogues* to be scourged there, and stigmatized with their *anathemas.*" [2.] "They shall incense the magistrates against you: they shall *deliver you into prisons,* that you may be *brought before kings and rulers for my name's sake,* and be punished by them." [2.] "Your own relations will betray you (v. 16), *your parents, brethren, and kinsfolks, and friends;* so that you will not know whom to put a confidence in, or where to be safe." [4.] "Your religion will be made a capital crime, and you will be called to *resist unto blood. Some of you shall they cause to be put to death;* so far must you be from expecting honour and wealth that you must expect nothing but death in its most frightful shapes, death in all its dreadful pomp. Nay." [5.] *"You shall be hated of all men for my name's sake."* This is worse than death itself, and was fulfilled when the apostles were not only *appointed to death,* but made a *spectacle to the world,* and counted as the *filth of the world,* and the *offscouring of all things,* which every body loathes, 1 Co. 4:9, 13. They were hated of *all men,* that is, of all bad men, who could not bear the light of the gospel (because it discovered their evil deeds), and therefore hated those who brought in that light, flew in their faces, and would have pulled them to pieces. The wicked world, which hated to be reformed, hated Christ the great Reformer, and all that were his, for his sake. The rulers of the Jewish church, knowing very well that if the gospel obtained among the Jews their usurped abused power was at an end, raised all their forces against it, put it into an ill name, filled people's minds with prejudices against it, and so made the preachers and professors of it odious to the mob.

(2.) He encourages them to bear up under their trials, and to go on in their work, notwithstanding the opposition they would meet with.

[1.] God will bring glory both to himself and them out of their sufferings: *"It shall turn to you for a testimony, v.* 13. Your being set up thus for a mark, and publicly *persecuted,* will make you the more taken notice of and your doctrine and miracles the more enquired into; your being brought *before kings and rulers* will give you an opportunity of preaching the gospel to them, who otherwise would never have come within hearing of it; your suffering such severe things, and being so hated by the worst of men, men of the most vicious lives, will be a testimony that you are good, else you would not have such bad men for your enemies; your courage, and cheerfulness, and constancy under your sufferings will be a testimony for you, that you believe what you preach, that you are supported by a divine power, and that the Spirit of God and glory rests upon you."

[2.] "God will stand by you, and own you, and assist you, in your trials; you are his advocates, and you shall be well furnished with instructions, *v.* 14, 15. Instead of setting your hearts on work to contrive an answer to informations, indictments, articles, accusations, and interrogatories, that will be exhibited against you in the ecclesiastical and civil courts, on the contrary, *settle it in your hearts,* impress it upon them,

take pains with them to persuade them *not to meditate before what you shall answer;* do not *depend* upon your own wit and ingenuity, your own prudence and policy, and do not *distrust* or *despair* of the immediate and extraordinary aids of the divine grace. Think not to bring yourselves off in the cause of Christ as you would in a cause of your own, by your own parts and application, with the common assistance of divine Providence, but promise yourselves, for I promise you, the special assistance of divine grace: *I will give you a mouth and wisdom."* This proves Christ to be God; for it is God's prerogative to *give wisdom,* and he it is that *made man's mouth.* Note, *First,* A *mouth* and *wisdom* together completely fit a man both for services and sufferings; *wisdom* to know what to say, and a *mouth* wherewith to say it as it should be said. It is a great happiness to have both *matter* and *words* wherewith to honour God and do good; to have in the mind a *storehouse* well furnished with things *new and old,* and a *door of utterance* by which *to bring them forth. Secondly,* Those that plead Christ's cause may depend upon him to give them a *mouth and wisdom,* which way soever they are called to plead it, especially when they are brought before magistrates for his name's sake. It is not said that he will send an angel from heaven to answer for them, though he could do this, but that he will give them a *mouth* and *wisdom* to enable them to answer for themselves, which puts a greater honour upon them, which requires them to use the gifts and graces Christ furnishes them with, and redounds the more to the glory of God, who *stills the enemy and the avenger out of the mouths of babes and sucklings. Thirdly,* When Christ gives to his witnesses a *mouth and wisdom,* they are enabled to say that both for him and themselves which *all their adversaries are not able to gainsay or resist,* so that they are silenced, and put to confusion. This was remarkably fulfilled presently after the pouring out of the Spirit, by whom Christ gave his disciples this *mouth* and *wisdom,* when the apostles were brought before the priest sand rulers, and answered them so as to make them ashamed, Acts 4, 5, and 6.

[3.] "You shall suffer no real damage by all the hardships they shall put upon you (v. 18): *There shall not a hair of your head perish."* Shall some of them lose their heads, and yet not lose a hair? It is a proverbial expression, denoting the greatest indemnity and security imaginable; it is frequently used both in the Old Testament and New, in that sense. Some think that it refers to the preservation of the lives of all the Christians that were among the Jews when they were cut off by the Romans; historians tell us that not one Christian perished in that desolation. Others reconcile it with the deaths of multitudes in the cause of Christ, and take it figuratively in the same sense that Christ saith, *He that loseth his life for my sake shall find it.* "Not a hair of your head shall perish but," *First,* "I will take *cognizance* of it." To this end he had said (Mt. 10:30), *The hairs of your head are all numbered;* and an account is kept of them, so that none of them shall perish but he will miss it. *Secondly,* "It shall be upon a *valuable consideration."* We do not reckon that *lost* or *perishing* which is laid out for good purposes, and will turn to a good account. If we drop the body itself for Christ's name's sake, it does not perish, but is well bestowed. *Thirdly,* "It shall be abundantly recompensed; when you come to balance profit and loss, you will find that nothing has perished, but, on the contrary, that you have great gain in present comforts, especially in the joys of a life eternal;" so that though we may be losers for Christ we shall not, we cannot, be losers by him in the end.

[4.] "It is therefore your duty and interest, in the midst of your own sufferings and those of the nation, to maintain a holy sincerity and serenity of mind, which will keep you always easy (v. 19): *In your patience possess ye your souls;* get and keep possession of your souls." Some read it as a promise, "You *may* or *shall* possess your souls." It comes all to one. Note, *First,* It is our duty and interest at all times, especially in perilous trying times, to secure the possession of our own souls; not only that they be not destroyed and lost for ever, but that they be not distempered now, nor our possession of them disturbed and interrupted. *"Possess your souls,* be your own men, keep up the authority and dominion of reason, and keep under the tumults of passion, that neither grief nor fear may tyrannize over you, nor turn you out of the possession and enjoyment of yourselves." In difficult times, when we can keep possession of nothing else, then let us make that sure which may be made sure, and keep possession of our souls. *Secondly,* It is by patience, Christian patience, that we keep possession of our own souls. "In suffering times, set patience upon the guard for the preserving of your souls; by it keep your souls composed and in a good frame, and keep out all those impressions which would ruffle you and put you out of temper."

Verses 20–28

Having given them an idea of the times for about thirty-eight years next ensuing, he here comes to show them what all those things would issue in at last, namely, the destruction of Jerusalem, and the utter dispersion of the Jewish nation, which would be a little day of judgment, a type and figure of Christ's second coming, which was not so fully spoken of here as in the parallel place (Mt. 24), yet glanced at; for the destruction of Jerusalem would be as it were the destruction of the world to those whose hearts were bound up in it.

I. He tells them that they should see Jerusalem besieged, *compassed with armies* (*v.* 20), the Roman armies; and, when they saw this, they might conclude that *its desolation was nigh,* for in this the siege would infallibly *end,* though it might be a long siege. Note, As in mercy, so in judgment, when God begins, he will make an end.

II. He warns them, upon this signal given, to shift for their own safety (*v.* 21): *"Then let them that are in Judea* quit the country and *flee to the mountains; let them that are in the midst of it"* (Of Jerusalem) *"depart out,* before the city be closely shut up, and" (as we say now) "before the trenches be opened; and let not them that are in the countries and villages about enter into the city, thinking to be safe there. Do you abandon a city and country which you see God has abandoned and given up to ruin. *Come out of her, my people."*

III. He foretels the terrible havoc that should be made of the Jewish nation (*v.* 22): *Those are the days of vengeance* so often spoken of by the Old-Testament prophets, which would complete the ruin of that provoking people. All their predictions must now be fulfilled, and the blood of all the Old-Testament martyrs must now be required. *All things that are written must be fulfilled* at length. After days of patience long abused, there will come *days of vengeance;* for reprieves are not pardons. The greatness of that destruction is set forth, 1. By the inflicting cause of it. It is *wrath upon this people,* the wrath of God, that will kindle this devouring consuming fire. 2. By the particular terror it would be to women with child, and poor mothers that are nurses. *Woe to them,* not only because they are most subject to frights, and least able to shift for their own safety, but because it will be a very great torment to them to think of having borne and nursed children for the murderers. 3. By the general confusion that should be all the nation over. There shall be *great distress in the land,* for men will not know what course to take, nor how to help themselves.

IV. He describes the issue of the struggles between the Jews and the Romans, and what they will come to at last; in short, 1. Multitudes of them *shall fall by the edge of the sword.* It is computed that in those wars of the Jews there fell by the sword above eleven hundred thousand. And the siege of Jerusalem was, in effect, a military execution. 2. The rest shall be *led away captive;* not into *one* nations, as when they were conquered by the Chaldeans, which gave them an opportunity of keeping together, but *into all nations,* which made it impossible for them to *correspond* with each other, much less to *incorporate.* 3. Jerusalem itself was *trodden down of the Gentiles.* The Romans, when they had made themselves masters of it, laid it quite waste, as a *rebellious and bad city, hurtful to kings and provinces,* and therefore hateful to them.

V. He describes the great frights that people should generally be in. Many frightful *sights* shall be *in the sun, moon, and stars,* prodigies in the heavens, and here in this lower world, the *sea and the waves roaring,* with terrible storms and tempests, such as had not been known, and above the ordinary working of natural causes. The effect of this shall be universal confusion and consternation *upon the earth, distress of nations with perplexity, v.* 25. Dr. Hammond understands by the *nations* the several governments or tetrarchies of the Jewish nation, Judea, Samaria, and Galilee; these shall be brought to the last extremity. *Men's hearts shall fail them for fear* (*v.* 26), *apopsychontōn anthrōpōn — men being quite exanimated,* dispirited, *unsouled,* dying away for fear. Thus those are *killed all the day long* by whom Christ's apostles were so (Rom. 8:36), that is, they are all the day long in fear of being killed; sinking under that which lies upon them, and yet still trembling for fear of worse, and *looking after those things which are coming upon the world.* When *judgment begins at the house of God,* it will not end there; it shall be as if all the world were falling in pieces; and where can any be secure then? The *powers of heaven shall be shaken,*, and then the pillars of the earth cannot but tremble. Thus shall the present Jewish policy, religion, laws, and government, be all entirely dissolved by a series of unparalleled calamities, attended with the utmost confusion. So Dr. Clarke. But our Saviour makes use of these figurative expressions because at the end of time they shall be literally accomplished, when the *heavens shall be rolled together as a scroll,* and all their powers not only shaken, but broken, and the *earth* and *all the works that are therein* shall be burnt up, 2. Pet. 3:10, 12. As that day was all terror and destruction to the unbelieving Jews, so the great day will be to all unbelievers.

VI. He makes this to be a kind of *appearing of the Son of man: Then shall they see the Son of man coming in a cloud, with power and great glory, v.* 27. The destruction of Jerusalem was in a particular manner an act of Christ's judgment, the judgment committed to the Son of man; his religion could never be thoroughly established but by the destruction of the temple, and the abolishing of the Levitical priesthood and economy, after which even the converted Jews, and many of the Gentiles too, were still hankering, till they were destroyed; so that it might justly be looked upon as *a coming of the Son of man, in power and great glory,* yet not visibly, but *in the clouds;* for in executing such judgments as these *clouds and darkness are round about him.* Now this was, 1. An *evidence* of the first coming of the Messiah; so some understand it. Then the unbelieving Jews shall be confined, when it is too late, that Jesus was the Messiah; those that would not see him coming in the power of his grace to *save them* shall be made to see him coming in the power of his wrath to *destroy them;* those that would not have him to *reign over them* shall have him to *triumph over them.* 2. It was an *earnest* of his second coming. *Then* in the terrors of that day they shall *see the Son of man coming in a cloud,* and all the terrors of the last day. They shall see a *specimen* of it, a faint resemblance of it. If this be so terrible, what will that be?

VII. He encourages all the faithful disciples in reference to the terrors of that day (*v.* 28): *"When these things begin to come to pass,* when Jerusalem is besieged, and every thing is concurring to the destruction of the Jews, *then* do you look *up,* when others are looking down, look heavenward, in faith, hope, and prayer, and *lift up your heads* with cheerfulness and confidence, *for your redemption draws night."* 1. When Christ came to destroy the Jews, he came to redeem the Christians that were persecuted and oppressed by them; *then had the churches rest.* 2. When he comes to judge the world at the last day, he will *redeem* all that are his, from all their grievances. And the foresight of that day is as pleasant to all good Christians as it is terrible to the wicked and ungodly. Their death itself is so; when they see that day approaching, they can *lift up their heads with joy,* knowing that *their redemption draws nigh,* their removal to their Redeemer.

VIII. Here is one word of prediction that looks further than the destruction of the Jewish nation, which is not easily understood; we have it in *v.* 24: *Jerusalem shall be trodden down of the Gentiles, till the times of the Gentiles be fulfilled.* 1. Some understand it of what is past; so Dr. Hammond. The Gentiles, who have conquered Jerusalem, shall keep possession of it, and it shall be purely Gentile, till the times of the Gentiles be fulfilled, till a great part of the Gentile world shall have become Christian, and then after Jerusalem shall have been rebuilt by Adrian the emperor, with an exclusion of all the Jews from it, many of the Jews shall turn Christians, shall join with the Gentile Christians, to set up a church in Jerusalem, which shall flourish there for a long time. 2. Others understand it of what is yet to come; so Dr. Whitby. Jerusalem shall be possessed by the Gentiles, of one sort or other, for the most part, till the time come when the nations that yet remain infidels shall embrace the Christian faith, when the kingdoms of this world shall become Christ's kingdoms, and then all the Jews shall be converted. Jerusalem shall be inhabited by them, and neither they nor their city any longer trodden down by the Gentiles.

Verses 29–38

Here, in the close of this discourse,

I. Christ appoints his disciples to observe the signs of the times, which they might judge by, if they had an eye to the foregoing directions, with as much certainty and assurance as they could judge of the approach of summer by the budding forth of the trees, *v.* 29–31. As in the kingdom of nature there is a chain of causes, so in the kingdom of providence there is a consequence of one event upon another. When we see a nation filling up the measure of their iniquity, we may conclude that their ruin is nigh; when we see the ruin of persecuting powers hastening on, we may thence infer that *the kingdom of God is nigh at hand,* that when the opposition given to it is removed it shall gain ground. As we may lawfully prognosticate the change of the seasons when second causes have begun to work, so we may, in the disposal of events, expect something uncommon when God is already *raised up out of his holy habitation* (Zec. 2:13); then *stand still and see his salvation.*

II. He charges them to look upon those things as neither *doubtful* nor *distant* (for then they would not make a due impression on them), but as *sure* and very *near.* The destruction of the Jewish nation, 1. Was *near* (*v.* 32): *This generation shall not pass away till all be fulfilled.* There were some now alive that should see it; some that now heard the prediction of it. 2. It was *sure;* the sentence was irreversible; it was a *consumption determined;* the decree was gone forth (*v.* 33): *"Heaven and earth shall pass away* sooner than any word of mine: nay, they certainly shall pass away, but *my words shall not;* whether they *take hold* or no, they will *take effect,* and not one of them *fall to the ground,"* 1 Sa. 3:19.

III. He cautions them against security and sensuality, by which they would unfit themselves for the trying times that were coming on, and make them to be a great surprise and terror to them (*v.* 34, 35): *Take heed to yourselves.* This is the word of command given to all Christ's disciples: *"Take heed to yourselves,* that you be not overpowered by temptations, nor betrayed by your own corruptions." Note, We cannot be *safe* if we be *secure.* It concerns us at *all* times, but especially at *some* times, to be very cautious. See here, 1. What our *danger* is: that *the day* of death and judgment should *come upon us unawares,* when we do not *expect* it, and are not *prepared* for it, — lest, when we are called to meet our Lord, that be found the *furthest* thing from our thoughts which ought always to be laid *nearest* our hearts, lest it *come upon us as a snare;* for so *it will come upon* the most of men, who *dwell upon the earth,* and mind *earthly things only,* and have no converse with heaven; to them it will be *as a snare.* See Eccl. 9:12. It will be a *terror* and a *destruction* to them; it will put them into an inexpressible fright, and hold them fast for a doom yet more frightful. 2. What our *duty* is, in consideration of this danger: we must *take heed lest our hearts be overcharged,* lest they be burdened and overloaded, and so unfitted and disabled to do what must be done in preparation for death and judgment. Two things we must watch against, lest our hearts be overcharged with them: — (1.) The indulging of the appetites of the body, and allowing of ourselves in the gratifications of sense to an excess: *Take heed lest you be overcharged with surfeiting and drunkenness,* the immoderate use of meat and drink, which burden the heart, not only with the guilt thereby contracted, but by the ill influence which such disorders of the body have upon the mind; they make men dull and lifeless to their duty, dead and listless in their duty; they stupify the conscience, and cause the mind to be *unaffected* with those things that are most *affecting.* (2.) The inordinate pursuit of the good things of this world. The heart is overcharged with the *cares of this life.* The former is the snare of those that are given to their pleasures: this is the snare of the men of business, that *will be rich.* We have need to guard on both hands, not only lest at the time when death comes, but lest *at any time* our hearts should be thus overcharged. Our caution against sin, and our care of our own souls, must be *constant.*

IV. He counsels them to prepare and get ready for this great day, *v.* 36. Here see, 1. What should be *our aim:* that we may be *accounted worthy to escape all these things;* that, when the judgments of God are abroad, we may be preserved from the malignity of them; that either we may not be involved in the common calamity or it may not be that to us which it is to others; that in the day of death we may escape the sting of it, which is the wrath of God, and the damnation of hell. Yet we must aim not only to *escape that,* but to *stand before the Son of man;* not only to stand *acquitted* before him as our Judge (Ps. 1:5), to have boldness in the day of Christ (that is supposed in our *escaping* all those things), but to *stand before him,* to attend on him as our Master, to stand continually before his throne, and serve him day and night in his temple (Rev. 7:15), always to *behold his face,* as the angels, Mt. 18:10. The saints are here said to be *accounted worthy,* as before, *ch.* 20:35. God, by the good work of his grace in them, *makes them meet* for this happiness, and, by the good will of his grace towards them, *accounts them worthy* of it: but, as Grotius here says, a great part of our worthiness lies in an acknowledgment of our own unworthiness. 2. What should be our *actings* in these aims: *Watch therefore, and pray always.* Watching and praying must go together, Neh. 4:9. Those that would escape the wrath to come, and make sure of the joys to come, must *watch* and *pray,* and must do so always, must make it the constant business of their lives, (1.) To keep a guard upon themselves. "Watch against sin, watch to every duty, and to the improvement of every opportunity of doing good. Be awake, and keep awake, in expectation of your Lord's coming, that you may be in a right frame to receive him, and bid him welcome." (2.) To keep up their communion with God: *"Pray always;* be always in an habitual disposition to that duty; keep up stated times for it; abound in it; pray upon all occasions." Those shall be accounted worthy to live a life of praise in the other world that live a life of prayer in this world.

V. In the last two verses we have an account how Christ disposed of himself during those three or four days between his riding in triumph into Jerusalem and the night in which he was betrayed. 1. He was *all day teaching in the temple.* Christ preached on week-days as well as sabbath days. He was an indefatigable preacher; he preached in the face of opposition, and in the midst of those that he knew sought occasion against him. 2. At night he went out to lodge at a friend's house, in the mount of Olives, about a mile out of town. It is probable that he had some friends in the city that would gladly have lodged him, but he was willing to retire in the evening out of the noise of the town, that he might have more time for secret devotion, now that his hour was at hand. 3. Early in the morning he was in the temple again, where he had a morning lecture for those that were willing to attend it; and the people were forward to hear one that they saw forward to preach (*v.* 38): *They all came early in the morning,* flocking to the temple, like doves to their windows, *to hear him,* though the chief priests and scribes did all they could to prejudice them against him. Sometimes the taste and relish which serious, honest, plain people have of good preaching are more to be valued and judged by than the opinion of the witty and learned, and those in authority.

CHAPTER 22

All the evangelists, whatever they omit, give us a particular account of the death and resurrection of Christ, because he died for our sins and rose for our justification, this evangelist as fully as any, and with many circumstances and passages added which we had not before. In this chapter we have, I. The plot to take Jesus, and Judas's coming into it (*v.* 1–6). II. Christ's eating the passover with his disciples (*v.* 7–18). III. The instituting of the Lord's supper (*v.* 19, 20). IV. Christ's discourse with his disciples after supper, upon several heads (*v.* 21–38). V. His agony in the garden (*v.* 39–46). VI. The apprehending of him, by the assistance of Judas (*v.* 47–53). VII. Peter's denying him (*v.* 54–62). VIII. The indignities done to Christ by those that had him in custody, and his trial and condemnation in the ecclesiastical court (*v.* 63–71).

Verses 1–6

The *year of the redeemed* is now *come,* which had been from eternity fixed in the divine counsels, and long looked for by them that waited for the consolation of Israel. After the revolutions of many ages, it is at length *come,* Isa. 63:4. And, it is observable, it is in the very *first month* of that year that the redemption is wrought out, so much in haste was the Redeemer to perform his undertaking, so was he *straitened* till it was *accomplished.* It was in the same month, and at the same time of the month (in the *beginning of months,* Ex. 12:2), that God by Moses brought Israel out of Egypt, that the Antitype might answer the type. Christ is here delivered up, *when the feast of unleavened bread drew nigh, v.* 1. About as long before that feast as they began to make preparation for it, here was preparation making for our Passover's being offered for us. Here we have,

I. His sworn enemies contriving it (*v.* 2), *the chief priests,* men of sanctity, and the scribes, men of learning, *seeking how they might kill him,* either by force of fraud. Could they have had their will, it had been soon done, but they *feared the people,* and the more for what they now saw of their diligent attendance upon his preaching.

II. A treacherous disciple joining in with them, and coming to their assistance, Judas surnamed *Iscariot.* He is here said to be *of the number of the twelve,* that dignified distinguished number. One would wonder that Christ, who *knew* all men, should take a traitor into *that number,* and that one of *that number,* who could not but *know Christ,* should be so base as to betray him; but Christ had wise and holy ends in taking Judas to be a disciple, and how he who knew Christ so well yet came to betray him we are here told: *Satan entered into Judas, v.* 3. It was the devil's work, who thought hereby to ruin Christ's undertaking, to have broken his head; but it proved only the bruising of his heel. Whoever betrays Christ, or his truths or ways, it is Satan that puts them upon it. Judas knew how desirous the chief priests were to get Christ into their hands, and that they could not do it safely without the assistance of some that knew his retirements, as he did. He therefore went himself, and made the motion to them, *v.* 4. Note, It is hard to say whether more mischief is done to Christ's kingdom by the power and policy of its open enemies, or by the treachery and self-seeking of its pretended friends: nay, without the latter its enemies could not gain their point as they do. When you see Judas communing with the *chief priests,* be sure some mischief is hatching; it is for no good that they are laying their heads together.

III. The issue of the treaty between them. 1. Judas must *betray Christ to them,* must bring them to a place where they might seize him without danger of tumult, and this they would be *glad of.* 2. They must give him a sum of money for doing it, and this he would be glad of (*v.* 5): *They covenanted to give him money.* When the bargain was made, Judas sought *opportunity to betray him.* Probably, he slyly enquired of Peter and John, who were more intimate with their Master than he was, where he would be at such a time, and whither he would retire after the passover, and they were not sharp enough to suspect him. Somehow or other, in a little time he gained the advantage he sought, and fixed the time and place where it might be done, *in the absence of the multitude,* and *without tumult.*

Verses 7–20

What a hopeful prospect had we of Christ's doing a great deal of good by his preaching in the temple during the feast of unleavened bread, which continued seven days, when the people were *every* morning, and *early* in the morning, so attentive to hear him! But here is a stop put to it. He must enter upon work of another kind; in this, however, he shall do more good than in the other, for neither Christ's nor his church's suffering days are their idle empty days. Now here we have,

I. The preparation that was made for Christ's eating the passover with his disciples, upon the very *day of unleavened bread, when the passover must be killed* according to the law, *v.* 7. Christ was made under the law, and observed the ordinances of it, particularly that of the passover, to teach us in like manner to observe his gospel institutions, particularly that of the Lord's supper, and not to neglect them. It is probable that he went to the temple to preach in the morning, when he sent Peter and John another way into the city to *prepare the passover.* Those who have attendants about them, to do their secular business for them in a great measure, must not think that this *allows* them to be *idle;* it *engages* them to employ themselves more in *spiritual* business, or service to *the public.* He directed those whom he employed whither they should go (*v.* 9, 10): *they must follow a man bearing a pitcher of water,* and he must be their guide to the house. Christ could have described the house to them; probably it was a house they knew, and he might have said no more than, Go to such a one's house, or to a house in such a street, with such a sign, etc. But he directed them thus, to teach them to depend upon the conduct of Providence, and to follow that, *step by step.* They went, not knowing *whither they went,* nor *whom they followed.* Being come to the house, they must desire the master of the house to show them a room (*v.* 11), and he will readily do it, *v.* 12. Whether it was a friend's house or a public house does not appear; but the disciples found their guide, and the house, and the room, just as he had said to them (*v.* 13); for *they* need not fear a disappointment who go upon Christ's word; according to the orders given them, they got every thing in readiness for *the passover, v.* 11.

II. The solemnizing of the passover, according to the law. When *the hour was come* that they should go to supper *he sat down,* probably at the head-end of the table, and *the twelve apostles with him,* Judas not excepted; for it is possible that those whose hearts are filled with Satan, and all manner of wickedness, may yet continue a plausible profession of religion, and be found in the performance of its external services; and while it is in the heart, and does not break out into any thing scandalous, such cannot be denied the external privileges of their external profession. Though Judas has already been guilty of an *overt act* of treason, yet, it not being publicly known, Christ admits him to sit down with the rest at the passover. Now observe,

1. How Christ *bids this passover welcome,* to teach us in like manner to welcome his passover, the Lord's supper, and to come to it with an appetite (*v.* 15): *"With desire I have desired,* I have most earnestly desired, to *eat this passover with you before I suffer."* He knew it was to be the prologue to his sufferings, and *therefore* he desired it, because it was in order to his Father's glory and man's redemption. He *delighted* to do even this part of the *will of God* concerning him as Mediator. Shall we be *backward* to any service for him who was so *forward* in the work of our salvation? See the love he had to his disciples; he desired to eat it *with them,* that he and they might have a little time together, themselves, and none besides, for private conversation, which they could not have in Jerusalem but upon this occasion. He was now about to leave them, but was very desirous to *eat this passover with them before he suffered,* as if the comfort of that would carry him the more cheerfully through his sufferings, and make them the easier to him. Note, Our gospel passover, eaten by faith with Jesus Christ, will be an excellent preparation for sufferings, and trials, and death itself.

2. How Christ in it *takes his leave of all passovers,* thereby signifying his abrogating all the ordinances of the ceremonial law, of which that of the passover was one of the *earliest* and one of the most *eminent* (*v.* 16): *"I will not any more eat thereof,* nor shall it by any more celebrated by my disciples, *until it be fulfilled in the kingdom of God."* (1.) It was fulfilled when *Christ our Passover was sacrificed for us,* 1. Cor. 5:7. And *therefore* that type and shadow was laid aside, because now in the *kingdom of God* the substance was come, which superseded it. (2.) It was fulfilled in the *Lord's supper,* an ordinance of the gospel kingdom, in which the passover had its accomplishment, and which the disciples, after the pouring out of the Spirit, did frequently celebrate, as we find Acts 2:42, 46. They ate of it, and Christ might be said to eat with them, because of the spiritual communion they had with him in that ordinance. He is said to *sup with them* and *they with him,* Rev. 3:20. But, (3.) The complete accomplishment of that commemoration of liberty will be in the kingdom of glory, when all God's spiritual Israel shall be released from the bondage of death and sin, and be put in possession of the land of promise. What he had said of his eating of the paschal lamb, he repeats concerning his drinking of the *passover wine,* the cup of *blessing,* or of thanksgiving, in which all the company pledged the Master of the feast, at the close of the passover supper. This cup *he took,* according to the custom, and *gave thanks* for the deliverance of Israel out of Egypt, and the preservation of their first-born, and then said, *Take this, and divide it among yourselves, v.* 17. This is not said afterwards of the sacramental cup, which being probably of much more weight and value, being the *New Testament in his blood,* he might give into every one's hand, to teach them to make a particular application of it to their own souls; but, as for the paschal cup which is to be abolished, it is enough to say, *"Take* it, and *divide it among yourselves,* do what you will with it, for we shall have no more occasion for it, *v.* 18. *I will not drink of the fruit of the vine any more,* I will not have it any more drank of, *till the kingdom of God shall come,* till the Spirit be poured out, and then you shall in *the Lord's supper* commemorate a much more glorious redemption, of which both the deliverance out of Egypt and the passover commemoration of it were types and figures. The kingdom of God is now so near being set up that you will not need to eat or drink any more till it comes." Christ dying next day opened it. As Christ with a great deal of pleasure took leave of all the legal feasts (which fell of course with the passover) for the evangelical ones, both spiritual and sacramental; so may good Christians, when they are called to

remove from the church militant to that which is triumphant, cheerfully exchange even their spiritual repasts, much more their sacramental ones, for the eternal feast.

III. The institution of the Lord's supper, *v.* 19, 20. The *passover* and the *deliverance* out of Egypt were *typical* and *prophetic signs* of a Christ to come, who should by dying deliver us from sin and death, and the tyranny of Satan; but they shall no more say, *The Lord liveth, that brought us up out of the land of Egypt;* a much greater deliverance shall eclipse the lustre of that, and therefore the Lord's supper is instituted to be a commemorative sign or memorial of a Christ already come, that *has* by dying delivered us; and it is his death that is in a special manner set before us in that ordinance.

1. The *breaking of Christ's body* as a *sacrifice for us* is here commemorated by the *breaking of bread;* and the sacrifices under the law were called the *bread of our God* (Lev. 21:6, 8, 17): *This is my body which is given for you.* And there is a feast upon that sacrifice instituted, in which we are to apply it to ourselves, and to take the benefit and comfort of it. This bread that was given for us is given *to us* to be food for our souls, for nothing can be more *nourishing* and *satisfying* to our souls than the doctrine of Christ's making atonement for sin, and the assurance of our interest in that atonement; this bread that was *broken* and *given for us,* to satisfy for the guilt of our sins, is *broken* and *given to us,* to satisfy the desire of our souls. And this we do in *remembrance* of what he did for us, when he died for us, and for a *memorial* of what we *do,* in making ourselves *partakers of him,* and joining ourselves to him in an everlasting covenant; like the stone Joshua set up for a *witness,* Jos. 24:27.

2. The *shedding* of *Christ's blood,* by which the atonement was made (for *the blood made atonement for the soul,* Lev. 17:11), as represented by the wine in the cup; and that cup of wine is a sign and token of the New Testament, or new covenant, made with us. It *commemorates* the purchase of the covenant by the blood of Christ, and *confirms* the promises of the covenant, which are all *Yea* and *Amen* in him. This will be reviving and refreshing to our souls, as wine that *makes glad the heart.* In all our commemorations of the shedding of Christ's blood, we must have an eye to it as shed for us; we needed it, we take hold of it, we hope to have benefit by it; *who loved me, and gave himself for me.* And in all our regards to the New Testament we must have an eye to the *blood of Christ,* which gave life and being to it, and seals to us all the promises of it. Had it not been for the blood of Christ, we had never had the New Testament; and, had it not been for the New Testament, we had never know the meaning of Christ's blood shed.

Verses 21–38

We have here Christ's discourse with his disciples after supper, much of which is new here; and in St. John's gospel we shall find other additions. We should take example from him to entertain and edify our family and friends with such discourse at table as is good and to the use of edifying, which may minister grace to the hearers; but especially after we have been at the Lord's table, by Christian conference to keep one another in a suitable frame. The matters Christ here discoursed of were of weight, and to the present purpose.

I. He discoursed with them concerning him that should betray him, who was now present. 1. He signifies to them that the traitor was now among them, and one of them, *v.* 21. By placing this after the institution of the Lord's supper, though in Matthew and Mark it is placed before it, it seems plain that Judas did receive the Lord's supper, did *eat of that bread* and *drink of that cup;* for, after the solemnity was over, Christ said, *Behold, the hand of him that betrayeth me is with me on the table.* There have been those that have eaten bread with Christ and yet have betrayed him. 2. He foretels that the treason would take effect (*v.* 22): *Truly the Son of man goes as it was determined,* goes to the place where he will be betrayed; for he is delivered up by the counsel and foreknowledge of God, else Judas could not have delivered him up. Christ was not driven to his sufferings, but cheerfully *went to them.* He said, *Lo, I come.* 3. He threatens the traitor: *Woe to that man by whom he is betrayed.* Note, Neither the patience of the saints under their sufferings, nor the counsel of God concerning their sufferings, will be any excuse for those that have any hand in their sufferings, or that persecute them. Though God has *determined* that Christ shall be betrayed and he himself has cheerfully submitted to it, yet Judas's sin or punishment is not at all the less. 4. He frightens the rest of the disciples into a suspicion of themselves, by saying that it was one of them, and not naming which (*v.* 23): *They began to enquire among themselves,* to interrogate themselves, to put the question to themselves, *who it was that should do this thing,* that could be so base to so good a Master. The enquiry was not, *Is it you?* or, *Is it such a one?* but, *Is it I?*

II. Concerning the strife that was among them for precedency or supremacy.

1. See what the dispute was: *Which of them should be accounted the greatest.* Such and so many contests among the disciples for dignity and dominion, *before* the Spirit was poured upon them, were a sad presage of the like strifes for, and affections of, supremacy in the churches, after the Spirit should be provoked to depart from them. How inconsistent is this with that in the verse before! There they were enquiring which would be the traitor, and here which should be the prince. Could such an instance of humility, and such an instance of pride and vanity, be found in the same men, so near together? This is like *sweet* waters and *bitter* proceeding at the same time out of the same fountain. What a self-contradiction is the deceitful heart of man!

2. See what Christ said to this dispute. He was not sharp upon them, as might have been expected (he having so often reproved them for this very thing), but mildly showed them the sin and folly of it.

(1.) This was to make themselves like the *kings of the Gentiles,* who affect worldly pomp, and worldly power, *v.* 25. They *exercise lordship* over their subjects, and are ever and anon striving to exercise lordship too over the *princes* that are about them, though as *good* as themselves, if they think them not *so strong* as themselves. Note, The *exercising of lordship* better becomes the *kings of the Gentiles* than the ministers of Christ. But observe, *They that exercise authority,* and take upon themselves to bear sway, and give law, they are called *Benefactors — Euergetas,* they call themselves so, and so their flatterers call them, and those that set themselves to serve their interests. It is pretended that they have *been* benefactors, and upon *that* account they should be admitted to *have rule;* nay, that in exercising authority they are benefactors. However they may really serve themselves, they would be thought to *serve their country.* One of the Ptolemies was surnamed *Euergetes — The Benefactor.* Now our Saviour, by taking notice of this, intimates, [1.] That to *do good* is much more honourable than to *look great;* for these princes that were the *terror of the mighty* would not be called so, but rather the *benefactors of the needy;* so that, by their own confession, a benefactor to his country is much more valued than a ruler of his country. [2.] That to *do good* is the surest way to be great, else they that aimed to be *rulers* would not have been so solicitous to be called *Benefactors.* This therefore he would have his disciples believe, that their greats honour would be to do all the good they could in the world. They would indeed be *benefactors* to the world, by bringing the gospel to it. Let them value themselves upon that title, which they would indeed be *entitled* to, and then they need not strive which should be the greatest, for they would all be *greater* — treater blessings to mankind than the kings of the earth, that exercise lordship over them. If they have that which is confessedly the *greater* honour, of being benefactors, let them despise the less, of being rulers.

(2.) It was to make themselves unlike the disciples of Christ, and unlike Christ himself: *"You shall not be so," v.* 26, 27. "It was never intended that you should *rule* any otherwise than by the power of truth and grace, but that you should *serve."* When church-rulers affect external pomp and power, and bear up themselves by secular interests and influences, they debase their office, and it is an instance of degeneracy like that of Israel when they would have a king like the nations that were round about them, whereas the Lord was their King. See here, [1.] What is the rule Christ gave to his disciples: He that is *greater among you,* that is *senior,* to whom precedency is due upon the account of his age, let him be as the *younger,* both in point of *lowness of place* (let him condescend to sit with the younger, and be free and familiar with them) and in point of *labour* and *work.* We say, *Juniores ad labores, seniores ad honores — Let the young work, and the aged receive their honours.* But let the elder take pains as well as the younger; their age and honour, instead of warranting them to take their ease, bind them to double work. And he *that is chief, ho hēgoumenos — the president* of the college or assembly, let him be *as he that* serves, *hōs ho diakonōn — as the deacon;* let him stoop to the meanest and most toilsome services for the public good, if there be occasion. [2.] What was the example which he himself gave to this rule: *Whether is greater, he that sitteth at meat or he that serveth?* he that attendeth or he that is attended on? Now Christ was among his disciples just like one that waited at table. He was so far from *taking state,* or *taking his ease,* by commanding their attendance upon him, that he was ready to do any office of kindness and service for them; witness his *washing* their feet. Shall those take upon them the form of princes who call themselves followers of him that *took upon him the form of a servant?*

(3.) They ought not to strive for worldly honour and grandeur, because he had better honours in reserve for them, of another nature, a *kingdom,* a *feast,* a *throne,* for each of them, wherein they should all share alike, and should have no occasion to strive for precedency, *v.* 28–30. Where observe,

[1.] Christ's commendation of his disciples for their faithfulness to him; and this was honour enough for them, they needed not to strive for any greater. It is spoken with an air of encomium and applause: *"You are they who have continued with me in my temptations,* you are they who have stood by me and stuck to me when others have deserted me and turned their backs upon me." Christ had his temptations; he was despised and rejected of men, reproached and reviled, and *endured the contradiction of sinners.* But his disciples continued with him, and were afflicted in all his afflictions. It was but little help that they could give him, or service that they could do him; nevertheless, he took it kindly that they *continued with him,* and he here owns their kindness, though it was by the assistance of his own grace that they did continue. Christ's disciples had been very defective in their duty. We find them guilty of many mistakes and weaknesses: they were very dull and very forgetful, and often blundered, yet their Master passes all by and forgets it; he does not upbraid them with their infirmities, but gives them this memorable testimonial, *You are they who have continued with me.* Thus does he praise at parting, to show how willing he is to make the best of those whose hearts he knows to be upright with him.

[2.] The recompence he designed them for their fidelity: *I appoint, diatithemai, I bequeath, unto you a kingdom.* Or thus, *I appoint to you, as my Father has appointed a kingdom to me, that you may eat and drink at my table.* Understand it, *First,* Of what should be done for them in this world. God gave his Son a *kingdom among men,* the gospel church, of which he is the living, quickening, ruling, Head. This *kingdom* he *appointed* to his apostles and their successors in the ministry of the gospel, that they should enjoy the comforts and privileges of the gospel, help to communicate them to others by gospel ordinances, sit on thrones as officers of the church, not only declaratively, but exhortatively *judging the tribes of Israel* that persist in their infidelity, and denouncing the wrath of God against them, and ruling the gospel Israel, the spiritual Israel, by the instituted discipline of the church, administered with gentleness and love. This is the honour reserved for you. Or, *Secondly,* Of what should be done for them in the other world, which I take to be chiefly meant. Let them go on in their services in this world; their preferments shall be in the other world. God will give them *the kingdom,* in which they shall be sure to have, 1. The *richest dainties;* for they shall *eat and drink at Christ's table in his kingdom,* of which he had spoken, *v.* 16, 18. They shall partake of those joys and pleasures which were the recompence of his services and sufferings. They shall have a full satisfaction of soul in the vision and fruition of God; and herein they shall have the best society, as at a feast, in the perfection of love. 2. The *highest dignities:* "You shall not only be provided for at the royal table, as Mephibosheth at David's, but you shall be preferred to the royal throne; shall *sit down with me on my throne,* Rev. 3:21. In the great day you shall *sit on thrones,* as assessors with Christ, to approve of and applaud his judgment of the *twelve tribes of Israel."* If the *saints shall judge the world* (1 Co. 6:2), much more the church.

III. Concerning Peter's denying him. And in this part of the discourse we may observe,

1. The general notice Christ gives to Peter of the devil's design upon him and the rest of the apostles (*v.* 31): *The Lord said, Simon, Simon,* observe what I say; *Satan hath desired to have you,* to have you all in his hands, *that he may sift you as wheat.* Peter, who used to be the *mouth* of the rest

in speaking to Christ, is here made the *ear* of the rest; and what is designed for warning to them all *(all you shall be offended, because of me)* is directed to Peter, because he was principally concerned, being in particular manner struck at by the tempter: *Satan has desired to have you.* Probably Satan had *accused* the disciples to God as mercenary in following Christ, and aiming at nothing else therein but enriching and advancing themselves in this world, as he accused Job. "No," saith God, "they are honest men, and men of integrity." "Give me leave to try them," saith Satan, "and Peter particularly." He desired to have them, *that he might sift them,* that he might show them to be chaff, and not wheat. The troubles that were now coming upon them were *sifting,* would try what there was in them: but this was not all; Satan desired to sift them by his temptations, and endeavoured by those troubles to draw them into sin, to put them into a loss and hurry, as corn when it is sifted to bring the chaff uppermost, or rather to shake out the wheat and leave nothing but the chaff. Observe, Satan could not sift them unless God gave him leave: He *desired to have them,* as he begged of God a permission to try and tempt Job. *Exētēsato — "He has challenged you,* has undertaken to prove you a company of hypocrites, and Peter especially, the forwardest of you." Some suggest that Satan demanded leave to sift them as their punishment for striving who should be greatest, in which contest Peter perhaps was very warm: "Leave them to me, to sift them for it."

2. The particular encouragement he gave to Peter, in reference to this trial: *"I have prayed for thee,* because, though he desires to have them all, he is permitted to make his strongest onset upon thee only: thou wilt be most violently assaulted, *but I have prayed for thee, that thy faith fail not,* that it may not totally and finally fail." Note, (1.) If faith be kept up in an hour of temptation, though we may fall, yet we shall not be utterly cast down. Faith will quench Satan's fiery darts. (2.) Though there may be many failings in the faith of true believers, yet there shall not be a total and final failure of their faith. It is their seed, their root, remaining in them. (3.) It is owing to the mediation and intercession of Jesus Christ that the faith of his disciples, though sometimes sadly shaken, yet is not sunk. If they were left to themselves, they would fail; but they are *kept by the power of God* and the prayer of Christ. The intercession of Christ is not only general, for all that believe, but for *particular* believers (I have prayed for *thee*), which is an encouragement for us to pray for ourselves, and an engagement upon us to pray for others too.

3. The charge he gives to Peter to help others as he should himself be helped of God: *"When thou art converted, strengthen thy brethren;* when thou art recovered by the grace of God, and brought to repentance, do what thou canst to recover others; when thou hast found they faith kept from failing, labour to confirm the faith of others, and to establish them; when thou hast found mercy with God thyself, encourage others to hope that they also shall find mercy." Note, (1.) Those that have fallen into sin must be *converted from it;* those that have turned aside must *return;* those that have left their first love must do their first works. (2.) Those that through grace are converted from sin must do what they can to strengthen their brethren that stand, and to prevent *their falling;* see Ps. 51:11–13; 1 Tim. 1:13.

4. Peter's declared resolution to cleave to Christ, whatever it cost him (*v.* 33): *Lord, I am ready to go with thee, both into prison and to death.* This was a great word, and yet I believe no more than he meant at this time, and thought he should *make good* too. Judas never protested thus against denying Christ, though often warned of it; for his heart was as fully set in him to the evil as Peter's was against it. Note, All the true disciples of Christ sincerely desire and design to *follow him, whithersoever he goes,* and whithersoever he leads them, though into a prison, though out of the world.

5. Christ's express prediction of his denying him thrice (*v.* 34): *"I tell thee, Peter* (thou dost not know thine own heart, but must be left to thyself a little, that thou mayest know it, and mayest never trust to it again), *the cock shall not crow this day before thou even deny that thou knowest me."* Note, Christ knows us better than we know ourselves, and knows the evil that is in us, and will be done by us, which we ourselves do not suspect. It is well for us that Christ knows where we are weak better than we do, and therefore where to come in with grace sufficient; that he knows how far a temptation will prevail, and therefore when to say, *Hitherto shall it come, and no further.*

IV. Concerning the condition of all the disciples.

1. He appeals to them concerning what had been, *v.* 35. He had owned that they had been faithful servants to him, *v.* 28. Now he expects, at parting, that they should acknowledge that he had been a kind and careful Master to them ever since they left all to follow him: *When I sent you without purse, lacked you any thing?* (1.) He owns that he had sent them out in a very poor and bare condition, barefoot, and with no money in their purses, because they were not to go far, nor be out long; and he would thus teach them to depend upon the providence of God, and, under that, upon the kindness of their friends. If God thus send us out into the world, let us remember that better than we have thus begun low. (2.) Yet ye will have them own that, notwithstanding this, they had *lacked nothing;* they then lived as plentifully and comfortably as ever; and they readily acknowledged it: *"Nothing, Lord;* I have all, and abound." Note, [1.] It is good for us often to review the providences of God that have been concerning us all our days, and to observe how we have got through the straits and difficulties we have met with. [2.] Christ is a good Master, and his service a good service; for though his servants may sometimes be brought low, yet he will help them; and though he *try* them, yet will he not leave them. *Jehovah-jireh.* [3.] We must reckon ourselves well done by, and must not complain, but be thankful, if we have had the necessary supports of life, though we have had neither dainties nor superfluities, though we have lived from hand to mouth, and lived upon the kindness of our friends. The disciples lived upon contribution, and yet did not complain that their maintenance was precarious, but owned, to their Master's honour, that it was sufficient; they had wanted nothing.

2. He gives them notice of a very great change of their circumstances now approaching. For, (1.) He that was their Master was now entering upon his sufferings, which he had often foretold (*v.* 37): "Now *that which is written must be fulfilled in me,* and this among the rest, *He was numbered among the transgressors* — he must suffer and die as a malefactor, and in company with some of the vilest of malefactors. This is that which is *yet to be accomplished,* after all the rest, and then *the things concerning me,* the things written concerning me, will have an end; then I shall say, *It is finished."* Note, It may be the comfort of suffering Christians, as it was of a suffering Christ, that their sufferings were foretold, and *determined* in the counsels of heaven, and will shortly *determine* in the joys of heaven. They were *written* concerning them, and they *will have an end,* and will end well, everlastingly well. (2.) They must therefore expect troubles, and must not think now to have such an easy and comfortable life as they had had; no, the scene will alter. They must now in some degree suffer *with* their Master; and, when he is gone, they must expect to suffer *like* him. The servant is not better than his Lord. [1.] They must not now expect that their friends would be so kind and generous to them as they had been; and therefore, *He that has a purse, let him take it,* for he may have occasion for it, and for all the good husbandry he can use. [2.] They must now expect that their enemies would be more fierce upon them than they had been, and they would need magazines as well as stores: *He that has no sword* wherewith to defend himself against robbers and assassins (2 Co. 11:26) will find a great want of it, and will be ready to wish, some time or other, that he had sold his garment and bought one. This is intended only to show that the times would be very perilous, so that no man would think himself safe if he had not a sword by his side. But the *sword of the Spirit* is the sword which the disciples of Christ must furnish themselves with. *Christ having suffered for us,* we must *arm ourselves* with the same mind (1 Peter 4:1), arm ourselves with an expectation of trouble, that it may not be a surprise to us, and with a holy resignation to the will of God in it, that there may be no opposition in us to it: and then we are better prepared than if we had sold a coat to buy a sword. The disciples hereupon enquire what strength they had, and find they had among them *two swords* (*v.* 38), of which one was Peter's. The Galileans generally travelled with swords. Christ wore none himself, but he was not against his disciples' wearing them. But he intimates how little he would have them depend upon this when he saith, *It is enough,* which some think is spoken ironically: "Two swords among twelve men! you are bravely armed indeed when our enemies are now coming out against us in great multitudes, and every one with a sword!" Yet two swords are sufficient for those who need none, having God himself to be *the shield of their help and the sword of their excellency,* Deu. 33:29.

Verses 39–46

We have here the awful story of Christ's *agony in the garden,* just before he was betrayed, which was largely related by the other evangelists. In it Christ *accommodated himself* to that part of his undertaking which he was now entering upon — the making of *his soul an offering for sin.* He afflicted his own soul with grief for the sin he was to satisfy for, and an apprehension of the wrath of God to which man had by sin made himself obnoxious, which he was pleased as a sacrifice to admit the impressions of, the consuming of a sacrifice with fire from heaven being the surest token of its acceptance. In it Christ entered the lists with the powers of darkness, gave them all the advantages they could desire, and yet conquered them.

I. What we have in this passage which we had before is, 1. That when Christ went out, though it was in the night, and a long walk, *his disciples* (eleven of them, for Judas had given them the slip) *followed him.* Having continued with him hitherto in his temptations, they would not leave him now. 2. That he went to the place *where he was wont* to be private, which intimates that Christ accustomed himself to retirement, was often alone, to teach us to be so, for freedom of converse with God and our own hearts. Though Christ had no conveniency for retirement but a garden, yet he retired. This should particularly be our practice after we have been at the Lord's table; we have then work to do which requires us to be private. 3. That he exhorted his disciples to *pray* that, though the approaching trial could not be avoided, yet they might not in it *enter into temptation* to sin; that, when they were in the greatest fright and danger, yet they might not have any inclination to desert Christ, nor take a step towards it: "Pray that you may be *kept from sin."* 4. That he withdrew from them, and prayed himself; they had their errands at the throne of grace, and he had his, and therefore it was fit that they should pray separately, as sometimes, when they had joint errands, they prayed together. He withdrew about a *stone's cast* further into the garden, which some reckon about fifty of sixty paces, and there he *kneeled down* (so it is here) upon the bare ground; but the other evangelists say that afterwards he *fell on his face,* and there *prayed* that, if it were the will of God, this cup of suffering, this bitter cup, might be *removed from him.* This was the language of that innocent dread of suffering which, being really and truly man, he could not but have in his nature. 5. That he, knowing it to be his Father's will that he should suffer and die, and that, as the matter was now settled, it was necessary for our redemption and salvation, presently withdrew that petition, did not insist upon it, but resigned himself to his heavenly Father's will: *"Nevertheless not my will be done,* not the will of my human nature, but the will of God as it is written concerning me in the volume of the book, *which I delight to do,* let that be done," Ps. 40:7, 8. 6. That his disciples were *asleep* when he was at prayer, and when they should have been themselves praying, *v.* 45. When he *rose from prayer,* he *found them sleeping,* unconcerned in his sorrows; but see what a favourable construction is here put upon it, which we had not in the other evangelists — they were *sleeping for sorrow.* The great sorrow they were in upon the mournful farewells their Master had been this evening giving them had exhausted their spirits, and made them very dull and heavy, which (it being now late) disposed them to sleep. This teaches us to make the best of our brethren's infirmities, and, if there be one cause better than another, charitably impute them to that. 7. That when he awoke them, then he exhorted them to pray (*v.* 46): *"Why sleep ye?* Why do you allow yourselves to sleep? *Rise and pray. Shake off* your drowsiness, that you may be *fit to pray,* and *pray for grace,* that you may be able to *shake off* your drowsiness." This was like the ship-master's call to Jonah in a storm (Jon. 1:6): *Arise, call upon thy God.* When we find ourselves either by our outward circumstances or our inward dispositions entering into temptation, it concerns us to *rise and pray,* Lord, help me in this *time of need.* But,

II. There are three things in this passage which we had not in the other evangelists: —

1. That, when Christ was in his agony, *there appeared* to him *an angel from heaven, strengthening him, v.* 43. (1.) It

was an instance of the deep humiliation of our Lord Jesus that he *needed* the assistance of an angel, and would *admit* it. The influence of the divine nature withdrew for the present, and then, as to his human nature, he was for a little while *lower than the angels,* and was capable of receiving help from them. (2.) When he was not delivered from his sufferings, yet he was *strengthened* and supported under them, and that was *equivalent.* If God proportion the shoulders to the burden, we shall have no reason to complain, whatever he is pleased to lay upon us. David owns this a sufficient *answer to his prayer,* in the day of trouble, that God *strengthened him with strength in his soul,* and so does the son of David, Ps. 138:3. (3.) The angels ministered to the Lord Jesus in his sufferings. He could have had legions of them to rescue him; nay, this one could have done it, could have chased and conquered the whole band of men that came to take him; but he made use of his ministration only to *strengthen him;* and the very visit which this angel made him now in his grief, when his enemies were awake and his friends asleep, was such a seasonable token of the divine favour as would be a very great strengthening to him. Yet this was not all: he probably *said something* to him to strengthen him; put him in mind that his sufferings were in order to his Father's glory, to his own glory, and to the salvation of those that were given him, represented to him the joy set before him, the seed he should see; with these and the like suggestions he encouraged him to go on cheerfully; and what is comforting is strengthening. Perhaps he *did something* to strengthen him, wiped away his sweat and tears, perhaps ministered some cordial to him, as after his temptation, or, it may be, took him by the arm, and helped him off the ground, or bore him up when he was ready to faint away; and in these services of the angel the Holy Spirit was *enischyōn auton — putting strength into him;* for so the word signifies. *It pleased the Lord to bruise him* indeed; yet *did he plead against him with his great power?* No, but he *put strength in him* (Job 23:6), as he had promised, Ps. 89:21; Isa. 49:8; 50:7.

2. That, *being in an agony, he prayed more earnestly, v.* 44. As his sorrow and trouble grew upon him, he grew more importunate in prayer; not that there was before any coldness or indifferency in his prayers, but there was now a greater vehemency in them, which was expressed in his voice and gesture. Note, Prayer, though never out of season, is in a special manner seasonable when we are in an agony; and the stronger our agonies are the more lively and frequent our prayers should be. Now it was that Christ *offered up prayers and supplications with strong crying and tears, and was heard in that he feared* (Heb. 5:7), and in his fear *wrestled,* as Jacob with the angel.

3. That, in this agony, *his sweat was as it were great drops of blood falling down to the ground.* Sweat came in with sin, and was a branch of the curse, Gen. 3:19. And therefore, when Christ was made sin and a curse for us, he underwent a grievous sweat, that *in the sweat of his face* we might eat bread, and that he might sanctify and sweeten all our trials to us. There is some dispute among the critics whether this *sweat* is only *compared to* drops of *blood,* being much *thicker* than drops of sweat commonly are, the pores of the body being more than ordinarily opened, or whether *real* blood out of the capillary veins mingled with it, so that it was in colour like blood, and might truly be called a *bloody sweat;* the matter is not great. Some reckon this one of the times when Christ shed his blood for us, *for without the shedding of blood there is no remission.* Every pore was as it were a bleeding wound, and his blood stained all his raiment. This showed the *travail of his soul.* He was now abroad in the open air, in a cool season, upon the cold ground, far in the night, which, one would think, had been enough to strike in a sweat; yet now he breaks out into a sweat, which bespeaks the extremity of the agony he was in.

Verses 47–53

Satan, finding himself baffled in his attempts to terrify our Lord Jesus, and so to put him out of the possession of his own soul, betakes himself (according to his usual method) to force and arms, and brings a party into the field to seize him, and Satan was *in them.* Here is,

I. The marking of him by Judas. Here a numerous party appears, and Judas at the head of them, for he was *guide to them that took Jesus;* they knew not where to *find him,* but he brought them to the place: when they were there, they knew not which was he, but Judas told them that whomsoever he should kiss, that same was he; so he *drew near to him to kiss him,* according to the wonted freedom and familiarity to which our Lord Jesus admitted his disciples. Luke takes notice of the question Christ asked him, which we have not in the other evangelists: *Judas, betrayest thou the Son of man with a kiss?* What! Is this the signal? *v.* 48. Must the Son of man be *betrayed,* as if any thing could be concealed from him, and a plot carried on against him unknown to him? Must one of his own disciples betray him, as if he had been a hard Master to them, or deserved ill at their hands? Must he be betrayed with a kiss? Must the badge of friendship be the instrument of treachery? Was ever a love-token so desecrated and abused? Note, Nothing can be a greater affront or grief to the Lord Jesus than to be betrayed, and betrayed with a kiss, by those that profess relation to him and an affection for him. Those do so who, under pretence of zeal for his honour, persecute his servants, who, under the cloak of a seeming affection for the honour of free grace, give a blow to the root of holiness and strictness of conversation. Many instances there are of Christ's being betrayed with a kiss, by those who, under the form of godliness, fight against the power of it. It were well if their own consciences would put this question to them, which Christ here puts to Judas, *Betrayest thou the Son of man with a kiss?* And will he not resent it? Will he not revenge it?

II. The effort which his disciples made for his protection (*v.* 49): *When they saw what would follow,* that those armed men were come to seize him, they said, *"Lord, shall we smite with the sword?* Thou didst allow us to *have* two swords, shall we now make use of them? Never was there more occasion; and to what purpose should we have them if we do not use them?" They asked the question as if they would not have drawn the sword without commission from their Master, but they were in too much *haste* and too much *heat* to stay for an answer. But Peter, aiming at the head of one of the servants of the *high priest,* missed his blow, and *cut off his right ear.* As Christ, by throwing them to the ground that came to take him, showed what he could have done, so Peter, by this exploit, showed what he could have done too in so good a cause if he had had leave. The other evangelists tell us what was the check Christ gave to Peter for it. Luke here tells us, 1. How Christ excused the blow: *Suffer ye thus far, v.* 51. Dr. Whitby thinks he said this to his enemies who came to take him, to pacify them, that they might not be provoked by it to fall upon the disciples, whom he had undertaken the preservation of: *"Pass by* this injury and affront; it was without warrant from me, and there shall not be another blow struck." Though Christ had power to have struck them down, and struck them dead, yet he *speaks them fair,* and, as it were, *begs their pardon* for an assault made upon them by one of his followers, to teach us to give good words even to our enemies. 2. How he cured the wound, which was more than amends sufficient for the injury: *He touched his ear, and healed him;* fastened his ear on again, that he might not so much as go away *stigmatized,* though he well deserved it. Christ hereby gave them a proof, (1.) Of his power. He that could *heal* could *destroy* if he pleased, which should have obliged them in interest to submit to him. Had they returned the blow upon Peter, he would immediately have healed him; and what could not a small regiment do that had such a surgeon to it, immediately to help the *sick* and *wounded?* (2.) Of his mercy and goodness. Christ here gave an illustrious example to his own rule of *doing good to them that hate us,* as afterwards he did of *praying for them that despitefully use us.* Those who render good for evil do as Christ did. One would have thought that this generous piece of kindness should have overcome them, that such coals, heaped on their heads, should have *melted them,* that they could not have bound him as a malefactor who had approved himself such a benefactor; but their hearts were hardened.

III. Christ's expostulation with the officers of the detachment that came to apprehend him, to show what an absurd thing it was for them to make all this rout and noise, *v.* 52, 53. Matthew relates it as said to *the multitude.* Luke tells us that it was said to the *chief priests and captains of the temple* the latter commanded the several orders of the priests, and therefore are here put between the *chief priests* and *the elders,* so that they were all ecclesiastics, retainers to the temple, who were employed in this odious piece of service; and some of the first rank too disparaged themselves so far as to be seen in it. Now see here,

1. How Christ *reasons* with them concerning their proceedings. What occasion was there for them to come out in the dead of the night, and *with swords and staves?* (1.) They knew that he was one that would not *resist,* nor raise the mob against them; he never had done any thing like this. Why then *are ye come out as against a thief?* (2.) They knew he was one that would not *abscond,* for he was daily with them in the temple, in the midst of them, and never sought to conceal himself, nor did they offer to lay hands on him. Before his hour was come, it was folly for them to think to take him; and when his hour was come it was folly for them to make all this ado to take him.

2. How he reconciles himself to their proceedings; and this we had not before: *"But this is your hour, and the power of darkness.* How hard soever it may seem that I should be thus exposed, I submit, for so it is determined. This is the hour *allowed you* to have your will against me. There is an hour *appointed me* to reckon for it. Now the *power of darkness,* Satan, *the ruler of the darkness of this world,* is permitted to do his worst, to bruise the heel of the seed of the woman, and I resolve to acquiesce; let him do his worst. *The Lord shall laugh at him, for he sees that his day,* his hour, *is coming."* Ps. 37:13. Let this quiet us under the prevalency of the church's enemies; let it quiet us in a dying hour, that, (1.) It is but an *hour* that is permitted for the triumph of our adversary, a short time, a limited time. (2.) It is *their hour,* which is appointed them, and in which they are permitted to try their strength, that omnipotence may be the more glorified in their fall. (3.) It is *the power of darkness* that *rides master,* and darkness must give way to light, and the power of darkness be made to truckle to the prince of light. Christ was willing to wait for his triumphs till his warfare was accomplished, and we must be so too.

Verses 54–62

We have here the melancholy story of Peter's denying his Master, at the time when he was arraigned before the high priest, and those that were of the *cabal,* that were ready to receive the prey, and to prepare the evidence for his arraignment, *as soon as it was day,* before the *great* sanhedrim, *v.* 66. But notice is not taken here, as was in the other evangelists, of Christ's being now upon his examination before the high priest, only of his being brought into *the high priest's house, v.* 54. But the manner of expression is observable. They *took him, and led him, and brought him,* which methinks is like that concerning Saul (1 Sa. 15:12): *He is gone about, and passed on, and gone down;* and intimates that, even when they had seized their prey, they were in confusion, and, for fear of the people, or rather struck with inward terror upon what they had seen and heard, they took him the furthest way about, or, rather, knew not which way they hurried him, such a hurry were they in in their own bosoms. Now observe,

I. Peter's falling. 1. It began in *sneaking.* He *followed Christ* when he was had away prisoner; this was well, and showed a concern for his Master. But he followed *afar off,* that he might be out of danger. He thought to trim the matter, to *follow Christ,* and so to satisfy his conscience, but to follow *afar off,* and so to save his reputation, and sleep in a whole skin. 2. It proceeded in keeping his distance still, and associating himself with the high priest's servants, when he should have been at his master's elbow. The *servants kindled a fire in the midst of the hall* and *sat down together,* to talk over their night-expedition. Probably Malchus was among them, and *Peter sat down among them,* as if he had been one of them, at least would be thought to be so. His fall itself was disclaiming all acquaintance with Christ, and relation to him, disowning him because he was now in distress and danger. He was charged by a sorry simple maid, that belonged to the house, with being a retainer to this *Jesus,* about whom there was now so much noise. She *looked wistfully* upon him as he *at by the fire,* only because he was a stranger, and one whom she had not seen before; and concluding that at this time of night there were no neuters there, and knowing him not to be any of the retinue of the high priest, she concludes him to be one of the retinue of this Jesus, or perhaps she had been some time or other looking about her in the temple, and had seen Jesus there and Peter with him, officious about him, and remembered him; *and this man was with him,* saith she. And Peter, as he had not the courage to *own* the charge, so he had not the wit and presence of mind to *turn it off,* as he might have done many ways, and therefore flatly and plainly denies it: *Woman, I know him not.* 4. His fall was repeated a second time (*v.* 58): *After a little while,* before he had time to recollect himself, *another saw him,* and said, *"Even thou art one of them,* as slyly as thou sittest here among the high priest's servants." *Not I,* saith Peter; *Man, I am not.* And a *third* time, *about the space of an hour after* (for, saith the tempter, "When he is down, down with him; let us follow the blow, till we get him past recovery"), *another* confidently affirms, *strenuously* asserts it, *"Of a truth this fellow also was with him,* let him deny it if he can, for you may all perceive *he is a Galilean."* But he that has once told a lie is strongly tempted to persist in it; the *beginning of* that *sin is as the letting forth of water.* Peter now not only denies that he is a disciple of Christ, but that he knows any thing of him (*v.* 60): *"Man, I know not what thou sayest;* I never heard of this Jesus."

II. *Peter's getting up again.* See how happily he recovered himself, or, rather, the grace of God recovered him. See how it was brought about: —

1. The *cock crew* just as he was the third time denying that he knew Christ, and this startled him and put him upon thinking. Note, Small accidents may involve great consequences.

2. *The Lord turned and looked upon him.* This circumstance we had not in the other evangelists, but it is a very remarkable one. Christ is here called *the Lord,* for there was much of divine knowledge, power, and grace, appearing in this. Observe, Though Christ had now his back upon Peter, and was upon his trial (when, one would think, he had something else to mind), yet he knew all that Peter said. Note, Christ takes more notice of what we say and do than we think he does. When Peter disowned Christ, yet Christ did not disown him, though he might justly have cast him off, and never looked upon him more, but have denied him before his Father. It is well for us that Christ does not deal with us as we deal with him. Christ *looked upon Peter,* not doubting but that Peter would soon be aware of it; for he knew that, though he had denied him with his lips, yet his eye would still be towards him. Observe, Though Peter had now been guilty of a very great offence, and which was very provoking, yet Christ would not *call to him,* lest he should *shame* him or *expose* him; he only gave him *a look* which none but Peter would understand the meaning of, and it had a great deal in it. (1.) It was a *convincing* look. Peter said that he did not *know Christ.* Christ *turned, and looked upon him,* as if he should say, "Dost thou not know me, Peter? Look me in the face, and tell me so." (2.) It was a *chiding* look. We may suppose that he looked upon him and *frowned,* or some way signified his displeasure. Let us think with what an angry countenance Christ justly looks upon us when we have sinned. (3.) It was an *expostulating* upbraiding look: "What, Peter, art thou he that disownest me now, when thou shouldest come and witness for me? What thou a disciple? Thou that wast the most forward to confess me to be the Son of God, and didst solemnly promise thou wouldest never disown me?" (4.) It was a *compassionate* look; he looked upon him with tenderness. "Poor Peter, how weak is thine heart! How art thou fallen and undone if I do not help thee!" (5.) It was a *directing* look. Christ *guided him with his eye,* gave him a wink to go out from that sorry company, to *retire,* and bethink himself a little, and then he would soon see what he had to do. (6.) It was a *significant* look: it signified the conveying of grace to Peter's heart, to enable him to repent; the crowing of the cock would not have brought him to repentance without this look, nor will the external means without special efficacious grace. Power went along with this look, to change the heart of Peter, and to bring him to himself, to his *right mind.*

3. *Peter remembered the words of the Lord.* Note, The *grace of God* works in and by the *word of God,* brings that to mind, and sets that home upon the conscience, and so gives the soul a happy turn. *Tolle et lege — Take it up, and read.*

4. Then *Peter went out, and wept bitterly.* One look from Christ melted him into tears of godly sorrow for sin. The candle was newly put out, and then a little thing lighted it again. Christ looked upon the chief priests, and made no impression upon them as he did on Peter, who had the divine seed remaining in him to work upon. It was not the look from Christ, but the grace of God with it, that recovered Peter, and brought him to-rights.

Verses 63–71

We are here told, as before in the other gospels,

I. How our Lord Jesus was *abused* by the servants of the high priest. *The abjects,* the rude and barbarous servants, *gathered themselves together against him.* They that *held Jesus,* that had him in custody till the court sat, they *mocked him,* and *smote him* (*v.* 63), they would not allow him to *repose* himself one minute, though he had had no sleep all night, nor to *compose* himself, though he was hurried to his trial, and no time given him to prepare for it. They made sport with him: this sorrowful night to him shall be a merry night to them; and the blessed Jesus, like Samson, is made the fool in the play. They *hood-winked* him, and then, according to the common play that young people have among them, they *struck him on the face,* and continued to do so till he named the person that smote him (*v.* 64), intending hereby an affront to his prophetical office, and that knowledge of secret things which he was said to have. We are not told that he said *any thing,* but *bore every thing;* hell was let loose, and he suffered it to do its worst. A greater indignity could not be done to the blessed Jesus, yet this was but one instance of many; for *many other things blasphemously spoke they against him, v.* 65. They that condemned him for a blasphemer were themselves the vilest blasphemers that ever were.

II. How he was accused and condemned by the great sanhedrim, consisting of the *elders of the people, the chief priests, and the scribes,* who were all up betimes, and got together *as soon as it was day,* about five of the clock in the morning, to prosecute this matter. They were *working this evil upon their beds,* and, as soon as ever the *morning* was *light, practised* it, Mic. 2:1. They would not have been up so early for any good work. It is but a short account that we have here of his trial in the ecclesiastical court.

1. They ask him, *Art thou the Christ?* He was generally believed by his followers to be the Christ, but they could not prove it upon him that he had ever said so *totidem verbis — in so many words,* and therefore urge him to own it to them, *v.* 67. If they had asked him this question with a willingness to admit that he was the Christ, and to receive him accordingly if he could give sufficient proof of his being so, it had been *well,* and might have been for ever *well with them;* but they asked it with a resolution not to believe him, but a design to ensnare him.

2. He justly complained of their unfair and unjust usage of him, *v.* 67, 68. They all, as Jews, professed to expect the Messiah, and to expect him at *this time.* No other appeared, or had appeared, that pretended to be the Messiah. He had no competitor, nor was he likely to have any. He had given amazing proofs of a divine power going along with him, which made his claims very well worthy of a free and impartial enquiry. It had been but just for these leaders of the people to have taken him into their council, and examined him there as a *candidate* for the messiahship, not at the bar as a *criminal.* "But," saith he, (1.) *"If I tell you that I am the Christ,* and give you ever such convincing proofs of it, you are resolved that *you will not believe.* Why should the cause be brought on before you who have already prejudged it, and are resolved, right or wrong, to run it down, and to condemn it?" (2.) *"If I ask you* what you have to object against the proofs I produce, *you will not answer me."* Here he refers to their silence when he put a question to them, which would have led them to own his authority, *ch.* 20:5–7. They were neither fair judges, nor fair disputants; but, when they were pinched with an argument, would rather be silent than own their conviction: *"You will neither answer me nor let me go;* if I be *not* the Christ, you ought to *answer* the arguments with which I prove that I am; if I be, you ought to *let me go;* but you will do neither."

3. He referred them to his second coming, for the full proof of his being the Christ, to their confusion, since they would not now admit the proof of it, to their conviction (*v.* 69): *"Hereafter shall the Son of man sit,* and be seen to sit, *on the right hand of the power of God,* and then you will not need to ask whether he be the Christ or no."

4. Hence they inferred that he set up himself as the Son of God, and asked him *whether he were so* or *no* (*v.* 70): *Art thou then the Son of God?* He called himself the *Son of man,* referring to Daniel's vision of the *Son of man* that *came near before the Ancient of days,* Dan. 7:13, 14. But they understood so much as to know that if he was *that Son* of man, he was also *the Son of God.* And art thou so? By this it appears to have been the faith of the Jewish church that the Messiah should be both *Son of man* and *Son of God.*

5. He owns himself to be the Son of God: *Ye say that I am;* that is, "I am, as ye say." Compare Mk. 14:62. *Jesus said, I am.* This confirms Christ's testimony concerning himself, that he was the Son of God, that he stood to it, when he knew he should suffer for standing to it.

6. Upon this they ground his condemnation (*v.* 71): *What need we any further witness?* It was true, they needed not any further witness to prove that he said he was *the Son of God,* they had it from *his own mouth;* but did they not need proof that he was not so, before they condemned him as a blasphemer for saying that he was so? Had they no apprehension that it was possible he might be so, and then what horrid guilt they should bring upon themselves in putting him to death? No, *they know not, neither will they understand.* They cannot think it possible that he should be the Messiah, though ever so evidently clothed with divine power and grace, if he appear not, as they expect, in worldly pomp and grandeur. Their eyes being blinded with the admiration of that, they rush on in this dangerous prosecution, as the horse into the battle.

CHAPTER 23

This chapter carries on and concludes the history of Christ's sufferings and death. We have here, I. His arraignment before Pilate the Roman governor (*v.* 1–5). II. His examination before Herod, who was tetrarch of Galilee, under the Romans likewise (*v.* 6–12). III. Pilate's struggle with the people to release Jesus, his repeated testimonies concerning his innocency, but his yielding at length to their importunity and condemning him to be crucified (*v.* 13–25). IV. An account of what passed as they led him to be crucified, and his discourse to the people that followed (*v.* 26–31). V. An account of what passed at the place of execution, and the indignities done him there (*v.* 32–38). VI. The conversion of one of the thieves, as Christ was hanging on the cross (*v.* 39–43). VII. The death of Christ, and the prodigies that attended it (*v.* 44–49). VIII. His burial (*v.* 50–56).

Verses 1–12

Our Lord Jesus was condemned as a blasphemer in the spiritual court, but it was the most *impotent malice* that could be that this court was actuated by; for, when they had *condemned* him, they knew they could not *put him to death,* and therefore took another course.

I. They accused him before Pilate. The *whole multitude of them arose,* when they saw they could go no further with him in their court, and *led him unto Pilate,* though it was no judgment day, no assizes or sessions; and they demanded justice against him, not as a blasphemer (that was no crime that he took cognizance of), but as one disaffected to the Roman government, which they in their hearts did not look upon as any crime at all, or, if it was one, they themselves were much more chargeable with it than he was; only it would serve the turn and answer the purpose of their malice: and it is observable that that which was the *pretended crime,* for which they employed the Roman powers to destroy Christ, was the *real crime* for which the Roman powers not long after destroyed them.

1. Here is the indictment drawn up against him (*v.* 2), in which they pretended a zeal for Caesar, only to ingratiate themselves with Pilate, but it was all *malice* against Christ, and nothing else. They misrepresented him, (1.) As making the people *rebel against Caesar.* It was true, and Pilate knew it, that there was a general uneasiness in the people under the Roman yoke, and they wanted nothing but an opportunity to shake it off; now they would have Pilate believe that this Jesus was active to foment that general discontent, which, if the truth was known, they themselves were the aiders and abettors of: *We have found him perverting the nation;* as if converting them to God's government were *perverting them* from the civil government; whereas nothing tends more to make men good subjects than making them Christ's faithful followers. Christ had particularly taught that they *ought to give tribute to Caesar,* though he knew there were those that would be offended at him for it; and yet he is here falsely accused as *forbidding to give tribute to Caesar.* Innocency is no fence against calumny. (2.) As making himself a *rival with Caesar,* though the very reason why they rejected him, and would not own him to be the Messiah, was because he did not appear in worldly pomp and power, and did not set up for a temporal prince, nor offer to do any thing against Caesar; yet this is what they charged him with, that he said, *he himself is Christ a king.* He did say that he was *Christ,* and, if so, then *a king,* but not such a king as was ever likely to give disturbance to Caesar. When his followers would have made him a king (Jn. 6:15), he declined it, though by the many miracles he wrought he made it appear that if he would have

set up in competition with Caesar he would have been too hard for him.

2. His pleading to the indictment: *Pilate asked him, Art thou the king of the Jews? v.* 3. To which he answered, *Thou sayest it;* that is, "It is as thou sayest, that I am entitled to the government of the Jewish nation; but in rivalship with the scribes and Pharisees, who tyrannize over them in matters of religion, not in rivalship with Caesar, whose government relates only to their civil interests." Christ's kingdom is wholly spiritual, and will not interfere with Caesar's jurisdiction. Or, "*Thou sayest it;* but canst thou prove it? What evidence hast thou for it?" All that knew him knew the contrary, that he never pretended to be the *king of the Jews,* in opposition to Caesar as supreme, or to the governors that were sent by him, but the contrary.

3. Pilate's declaration of his innocency (*v.* 4): He *said to the chief priests, and the people* that seemed to join with them in the prosecution, "*I find no fault in this man.* What breaches of your law he may have been guilty of I am not concerned to enquire, but I find nothing proved upon him that makes him obnoxious to our court."

4. The continued fury and outrage of the prosecutors, *v.* 5. Instead of being moderated by Pilate's declaration of his innocency, and considering, as they ought to have done, whether they were not bringing the guilt of innocent blood upon themselves, they were the more exasperated, more exceedingly *fierce.* We do not find that they have any particular fact to produce, much less any evidence to prove it; but they resolve to carry it with noise and confidence, and say it, though they cannot prove it: *He stirs up the people* to rebel against Caesar, *teaching throughout all Judea, beginning from Galilee to this place.* He did *stir up the people,* but it was not to any thing factious or seditious, but to every thing that was virtuous and praiseworthy. He did *teach,* but they could not charge him with teaching any doctrine that tended to disturb the public peace, or make the government uneasy or jealous.

II. They accused him before Herod. 1. Pilate removed him and his cause to Herod's court. The accusers mentioned Galilee, the northern part of Canaan. "Why," saith Pilate, "is he of that country? Is he a Galilean?" *v.* 6. "Yes," said they, "that is his head-quarters; there he was spent most of his time." "Let us send him to Herod then," saith Pilate, "for Herod is now in town, and it is but fit he should have cognizance of his cause, since he belongs to Herod's jurisdiction." Pilate was already sick of the cause, and desirous to rid his hands of it, which seems to have been the true reason for sending him to Herod. But God ordered it so for the more evident fulfilling of the scripture, as appears Acts 4:26, 27, where that of David (Ps. 2:2), *The kings of the earth and the rulers set themselves against the Lord and his Anointed,* is expressly said to be fulfilled in Herod and Pontius Pilate. 2. Herod was very willing to have the examining of him (*v.* 8): *When he saw Jesus he was exceedingly glad,* and perhaps the more glad because he saw him a prisoner, saw him in bonds. He had *heard many things of him* in Galilee, where his miracles had for a great while been all the talk of the country; and he *longed to see him,* not for any affection he had for him or his doctrine, but purely out of curiosity; and it was only to gratify this that he *hoped to have seen some miracle done by him,* which would serve him to talk of as long as he lived. In order to this, he *questioned with him in many things,* that at length he might bring him to something in which he might show his power. Perhaps he pumped him concerning things *secret,* or things *to come,* or concerning his curing diseases. But Jesus *answered him nothing;* nor would he gratify him so much as with the performance of one miracle. The poorest beggar, that asked a miracle for the relief of his necessity, was *never denied;* but this proud prince, that asked a miracle merely for the gratifying of his curiosity, is denied. He might have seen Christ and his wondrous works many a time in Galilee, and *would not,* and therefore it is justly said, Now he would see them, and *shall not;* they are hidden from his eyes, because he knew not the day of his visitation. Herod thought, now that he had him in bonds, he might *command* a miracle, but miracles must not be made cheap, nor Omnipotence be at the beck of the greatest potentate. 3. His prosecutors appeared against him before Herod, for they were restless in the prosecution: *They stood, and vehemently accused him* (*v.* 10), *impudently* and *boldly,* so the word signifies. They would make Herod believe that he had poisoned Galilee too with his seditious notions. Note, It is no new thing for good

men and good ministers, that are real and useful friends to the civil government, to be falsely accused as factious and seditious, and enemies to government. 4. Herod was very *abusive* to him: He, with *his men of war,* his attendants, and officers, and great men, *set him at nought.* They *made nothing* of him; so the word is. Horrid wickedness! To *make nothing* of him who *made all things.* They laughed at him as *a fool;* for they knew he had wrought many miracles to befriend others, and why would he not now work one to befriend himself? Or, they laughed at him as one that had lost his power, and was become weak as other men. Herod, who had been acquainted with John Baptist, and had more knowledge of Christ too than Pilate had, was more *abusive* to Christ than Pilate was; for knowledge without grace does but make men the more *ingeniously* wicked. Herod arrayed Christ in a *gorgeous robe,* some gaudy painted clothes, as a mock-king; and so he taught Pilate's soldiers afterwards to do him the same indignity. He was ringleader in that abuse. 5. Herod sent him back to Pilate, and it proved an occasion of the making of them friends, they having been for some time before at variance. Herod could not get sight of a miracle, but would not condemn him neither as a malefactor, and therefore *sent him again to Pilate* (*v.* 11), and so returned Pilate's civility and respect in sending the prisoner to him; and this mutual obligation, with the messages that passed between them on this occasion, brought them to a better understanding one of another than there had been of late between them, *v.* 12. They had been *at enmity between themselves,* probably upon Pilate's killing of the Galileans, who were Herod's subjects (Lu. 13:1), or some other such matter of controversy as usually occurs among princes and great men. Observe how those that quarrelled with one another yet could unite against Christ; as Gebal, and Ammon, and Amalek, though divided among themselves, were confederate against the *Israel of God,* Ps. 83:7. Christ is the great peace-maker; both Pilate and Herod owned his innocency, and their agreeing in this cured their disagreeing in other things.

Verses 13–25

We have here the blessed Jesus run down by the mob, and hurried to the cross in the storm of a popular noise and tumult, raised by the malice and artifice of the *chief priests,* as agents for the prince of the power of the air.

I. Pilate solemnly protests that he believes he has done nothing worthy of death or of bonds. And, if he did believe so, he ought immediately to have *discharged* him, and not only so, but to have *protected* him from the fury of the priests and rabble, and to have bound his prosecutors to their good behaviour for their insolent conduct. But, being himself a bad man, he had no kindness for Christ, and, having made himself otherwise obnoxious, was afraid of displeasing either the emperor or the people; and therefore, for want of integrity, he *called together the chief priests, and rulers, and people* (whom he should have dispersed, as a *riotous and seditious assembly,* and forbid them to come near him), and will hear what they have to say, to whom he should have turned a deaf ear, for he plainly saw what spirit actuated them (*v.* 14): "*You have brought,*" saith he, "*this man to me,* and, because I have a respect for you, *I have examined him before you,* and have heard all you have to allege against him, and I can make nothing of it: *I find no fault in him;* you cannot prove the things whereof you accuse him."

II. He appeals to Herod concerning him (*v.* 15): "*I sent you to him,* who is supposed to have known more of him than I have done, and he has *sent him back,* not convicted of any thing, nor under any mark of his displeasure; in his opinion, his crimes are not capital. He has laughed at him as a weak man, but has not stigmatized him as a dangerous man." He thought Bedlam a fitter place for him than Tyburn.

III. He proposes to release him, if they will but consent to it. He ought to have done it without asking leave of them, *Fiat justitia, ruat coelum — Let justice have its course, though the heavens should be desolated.* But the fear of man brings many into this snare, that, whereas justice should take place, though heaven and earth come together, they will do an unjust thing, against their consciences, rather than pull an old house about their ears. Pilate declares him innocent, and therefore has a mind to release him; yet, to please the people, 1. He will release him under the notion of a malefactor, because *of necessity he must release one* (*v.* 17); so that whereas he ought to have been released by an *act of justice,* and thanks to nobody, he would have him released by an *act of*

grace, and not be beholden to the people for it. 2. He will *chastise* him, and release him. If *no fault be to be found in him,* why should he be chastised? There is as much injustice in scourging as in crucifying an innocent man; nor would it be justified by pretending that this would satisfy the clamours of the people, and make *him* the object of their pity who was not to be the object of their envy. We must not do evil that good may come.

IV. The people choose rather to have Barabbas released, a wretched fellow, that had nothing to recommend him to their favour but the daringness of his crimes. He was imprisoned for a *sedition made in the city,* and for *murder* (of all crimes among men the least pardonable), yet this was the criminal that was preferred before Christ: *Away with this man, and release unto us Barabbas, v.* 18, 19. And no wonder that such a man is the favourite and darling of such a *mob,* he that was really seditious, rather than he that was really loyal and falsely accused of sedition.

V. When Pilate urged the second time that Christ should be released, they cried out, *Crucify him, crucify him, v.* 20, 21. They not only will have him die, but will have him die so great a death; nothing less will serve but he must be crucified: *Crucify him, crucify him.*

VI. When Pilate the third time reasoned with them, to show them the unreasonableness and injustice of it, they were the more peremptory and outrageous (*v.* 22): "*Why? What evil hath he done?* Name his crime. *I have found no cause of death,* and you cannot say what cause of death you have found in him; and therefore, if you will but speak the word, *I will chastise him and let him go.*" But popular fury, the more it is complimented, the more furious it grows; they were *instant with loud voices,* with great noises or outcries, not requesting, but *requiring, that he might be crucified;* as if they had as much right, at the feast, to demand the crucifying of one that was innocent as the release of one that was guilty.

VII. Pilate's yielding, at length, to their importunity. The voice of the people and of the *chief priests prevailed,* and were too hard for Pilate, and overruled him to go contrary to his convictions and inclinations. He had not courage to go against so strong a stream, but *gave sentence that it should be as they required, v.* 24. Here is judgment *turned away backward,* and *justice standing afar off,* for fear of popular fury. *Truth is fallen in the street, and equity cannot enter,* Isa. 59:14. *Judgment* was looked for, *but behold oppression; righteousness, but behold a cry,* Isa. 5:7. This is repeated in *v.* 25, with the aggravating circumstance of the release of Barabbas: *He released unto them him that for sedition and murder was cast into prison,* who hereby would be hardened in his wickedness, and do the more mischief, because *him they had desired,* being altogether such a one as themselves; but he *delivered Jesus to their will,* and he could not deal more barbarously with him than to deliver him to *their will,* who hated him with a *perfect hatred,* and whose *tender mercies* were cruelty.

Verses 26–31

We have here the blessed Jesus, the Lamb of God, led as *a lamb to the slaughter,* to the sacrifice. It is strange with what expedition they went through his trial; how they could do so much work in such a little time, though they had so many great men to deal with, attendance on whom is usually a work of time. He was brought before the chief priests at break of day (ch. 22:66), after that to Pilate, then to Herod, then to Pilate again; and there seems to have been a long struggle between Pilate and the people about him. He was scourged, and crowned with thorns and contumeliously used, and all this was done in four or five hours' time, or six at most, for he was crucified between nine o'clock and twelve. Christ's persecutors resolve to lose no time, for fear lest his friends at the other end of the town should get notice of what they were doing, and should rise to rescue him. Never any one was so *chased out of the world* as Christ was, but so he himself said, *Yet a little while and ye shall not see me;* a very little while indeed. Now as they led him away to death we find,

I. One that was a *bearer,* that carried his cross, *Simon* by name, *a Cyrenian,* who probably was a friend of Christ, and was known to be so, and this was done to put a reproach upon him; they laid Christ's cross upon him, that he might *bear it after Jesus* (*v.* 26), lest Jesus should faint under it and die away, and so prevent the further instances of malice they designed. It was pity, but a *cruel pity,* that gave him this ease.

II. Many that were *mourners,* true mourners, who followed him, *bewailing* and *lamenting* him. These were not only his friends and well-wishers, but the common people, that were not his enemies, and were moved with compassion towards him, because they had heard the fame of him, and what an excellent useful man he was, and had reason to think he suffered unjustly. This drew a great crowd after him, as is usual at executions, especially of those that have been persons of distinction: *A great company of people followed him,* especially of women (*v.* 27), some led by pity, others by curiosity, but they *also* (as well as those that were his particular friends and acquaintance) *bewailed and lamented him.* Though there were many that reproached and reviled him, yet there were some that valued him, and pitied him, and were sorry for him, and were partakers with him in his sufferings. The dying of the Lord Jesus may perhaps move natural affections in many that are strangers to devout affections; many bewail Christ that do not believe in him, and lament him that do not love him above all. Now here we are told what Christ said to these mourners. Though one would think he should be wholly taken up with his own concern, yet he found time and heart to take cognizance of their tears. Christ *died lamented,* and has a bottle for the tears of those that lamented him. He *turned to them,* though they were strangers to him, and bade them *not weep for him, but for themselves.* He diverts their lamentation into another channel, *v.* 28.

1. He gives them a general direction concerning their lamentations: *Daughters of Jerusalem, weep not for me.* Not that they were to be blamed for weeping for him, but rather commended; those hearts were hard indeed that were not affected with such sufferings of such a person; but they must not weep for him only (those were profitless tears that they shed for him), but rather let them *weep for themselves and for their children,* with an eye to the destruction that was coming upon Jerusalem, which some of them might live to see and share in the calamities of, or, at least, their children would, for whom they ought to be solicitous. Note, When with an eye of faith we behold Christ crucified we ought to weep, not for him, but for ourselves. We must not be affected with the death of Christ as with the death of a common person whose calamity we pity, or of a common friend whom we are likely to part with. The death of Christ was a thing peculiar; it was his victory and triumph over his enemies; it was our deliverance, and the purchase of eternal life for us. And therefore let us weep, not for him, but for our own sins, and the sins of our children, that were the cause of his death; and weep for fear (such were the tears here prescribed) of the miseries we shall bring upon ourselves, if we slight his love, and reject his grace, as the Jewish nation did, which brought upon them the ruin here foretold. When our dear relations and friends die in Christ, we have no reason to weep for them, who have put off the burden of the flesh, are made perfect in holiness, and have entered into perfect rest and joy, but for ourselves and our children, who are left behind in a world of sins, and sorrows, and snares.

2. He gives them a particular reason why they should *weep for themselves and for their children: "Fore behold* sad times are coming upon your city; it will be destroyed, and you will be involved in the common destruction." When Christ's own disciples sorrowed after a *godly sort* for his leaving them, he wiped away their tears with the promise that he would *see them again,* and they should *rejoice,* Jn. 16:22. But, when these daughters of *Jerusalem bewailed him* only with a *worldly* sorrow, he turned their tears into another channel, and told them that they should have something given them to cry for. Let them *be afflicted, and mourn, and weep,* Jam. 4:9. He had lately wept over Jerusalem himself, and now he bids them weep over it. Christ's tears should set us a weeping. Let the daughters of Zion, that own Christ for their king, rejoice in him, for he comes to save them; but let the daughters of Jerusalem, that only weep for him, but do not take him for their king, weep and tremble to think of his coming to judge them. Now the destruction of Jerusalem is here foretold by two proverbial sayings, that might then fitly be used, which both bespeak it very terrible, that what people commonly dread they would then desire, to be *written childless* and to be *buried alive.* (1.) They would wish to be *written childless.* Whereas commonly those that have no children envy those that have, as Rachel envied Leah, then those that have children will find them such a burden in attempting to escape, and such a grief when they see them either *fainting* for famine or *falling* by the sword, that they will envy those that have none, and say, *Blessed are the barren, and the wombs that never bare,* that have no children to be *given up* to the murderer, or to be *snatched* out of his hands. It would not only go ill with those who at that time were *with child,* or *giving suck,* as Christ had said (Mt. 24:19), but it would be terrible to those who had had children, and suckled them, and had them now alive. See Hos. 9:11–14. See the vanity of the creature and the uncertainty of its comforts; for such may be the changes of Providence concerning us that those very things may become the greatest burdens, cares, and griefs to us, which we have delighted in as the greatest blessings. (2.) They would wish to be *buried alive: They shall begin to say to the mountains, Fall on us, and to the hills, Cover us, v.* 30. This also refers to a passage in the same prophecy with the former, Hos. 10:8. They shall wish to be hid in the darkest caves, that they may be out of the noise of these calamities. They will be willing to be sheltered upon any terms, though with the hazard of being crushed to pieces. This would be the language especially of the great and mighty men, Rev. 6:16. They that would not flee to Christ for refuge, and put themselves under his protection, will in vain call to *hills* and *mountains* to shelter them from his wrath.

2. He shows how natural it was for them to infer this desolation from his sufferings. *If they do these things in a green tree, what shall be done in the dry? v.* 31. Some think that this is borrowed from Eze. 20:47: *The fire shall devour every green tree in thee, and every dry tree.* These words may be applied, (1.) More particularly to the destruction of Jerusalem, which Christ here foretold, and which the Jews by putting him to death brought upon themselves: *"If they* (the Jews, and the inhabitants of Jerusalem) *do these things upon the green tree,* if they do thus abuse an innocent and excellent person for his *good works,* how may they expect God to deal with them *for their so doing,* who have made themselves a *dry tree,* a corrupt and wicked generation, and good for nothing? If this be their sin, what do you think will be their punishment?" Or take it thus: "If they (the Romans, their judges, and their soldiers) abuse me thus, who have given them no provocation, who am to them as a green tree, which you seem to be as much enraged at, *what will they do by Jerusalem* and the Jewish nation, who will be so very provoking to them, and make themselves as a *dry tree,* as fuel to the fire of their resentments? If God suffer those things to be done to me, what will he appoint to be done to those barren trees of whom it had been often said that they should be *hewn down and cast into the fire?"* Mt. 3:10; 7:19. (2.) They may be applied more generally to all the revelations of God's wrath against sin and sinners: "If God deliver me up to such sufferings as these because I am made a sacrifice for sin, what will he do with sinners themselves?" Christ was a *green tree,* fruitful and flourishing; now, if such things were done to him, we may thence infer what would have been done to the whole race of mankind if he had not *interposed,* and what shall be done to those that continue dry trees, notwithstanding all that is done to make them fruitful. If God did this to the Son of his love, when he found sin but imputed to him, what shall he do to the generation of his wrath, when he finds sin reigning in them? If the Father was pleased in doing these things to the green tree, why should he be loth to do it to the dry? Note, The consideration of the bitter sufferings of our Lord Jesus should engage us to stand in awe of the justice of God, and to tremble before him. The best saints, compared with Christ, are *dry tree;* if he suffer, why may not they expect so suffer? And what then shall the damnation of sinners be?

Verses 32–43

In these verses we have,

I. Divers passages which we had before in Matthew and Mark concerning Christ's sufferings. 1. That there were *two others, malefactors, led with him* to the place of execution, who, it is probable, had been for some time under sentence of death, and were designed to be executed on this day, which was probably the pretence for making such haste in the prosecution of Christ, that he and these two malefactors might be executed together, and one solemnity might serve. 2. That he was crucified at a place called *Calvary, Kranion,* the Greek name for *Golgotha — the place of a skull:* an ignominious place, to add to the reproach of his sufferings, but significant, for there he triumphed over death as it were upon his own dunghill. He was *crucified.* His hands and feet were nailed to the cross as it lay upon the ground, and it was then *lifted* up, and fastened into the earth, or into some socket made to receive it. This was a painful and shameful death above any other. 3. That he was crucified *in the midst between two thieves,* as if he had been the worst of the three. Thus he was not only treated as a transgressor, but *numbered with them,* the worst of them. 4. That the soldiers who were employed in the execution seized his garments as their fee, and divided them among themselves *by lot: They parted his raiment, and cast lots;* it was worth so little that, if divided, it would come to next to nothing, and therefore they cast lots for it. 5. That he was reviled and reproached, and treated with all the scorn and contempt imaginable, when he was *lifted up* upon the cross. It was strange that so much barbarity should be found in the human nature: *The people stood beholding,* not at all concerned, but rather pleasing themselves with the spectacle; and *the rulers,* whom from their office one would take to be men of sense and men of honour, stood among the rabble, *and derided him,* to set those on that were about them to do so too; and they said, *He saved others, let him save himself.* Thus was he upbraided for the good works he had done, as if it were indeed *for these* that they *crucified* him. They triumphed over him as if they had conquered him, whereas he was himself then more than a conqueror; they challenged him to save himself from the cross, when he was saving others by the cross: *If he be the Christ, the chosen of God,* let him save himself. They knew that *the Christ was the chosen of God,* designed by him, and dear to him. "If he, as the Christ, would deliver our nation from the Romans (and they could not form any other idea than that of the Messiah), let him deliver himself from the Romans that have him now in their hands." Thus the Jewish *rulers* jeered him as subdued by the Romans, instead of subduing them. The *Roman soldiers* jeered him as *the King of the Jews:* "A people good enough for such a prince, and a prince good enough for such a people." They *mocked him* (*v.* 36, 37); they made sport with him, and made a jest of his sufferings; and when they were drinking sharp sour wine themselves, such as was generally allotted them, they triumphantly asked him if he would pledge them, or drink with them. And they said, *If thou be the king of the Jews, save thyself;* for, as the Jews prosecuted him under the notion of a pretended Messiah, so the Romans under the notion of a pretended king. 6. That the superscription over his head, setting forth his crime, was, *This is the King of the Jews, v.* 38. He is put to death for pretending to be the king of the Jews; so they meant it; but God intended it to be a declaration of what he really was, notwithstanding his present disgrace: he is *the king of the Jews,* the king of the church, and his cross is the way to his crown. This was written in those that were called the three learned languages, *Greek, and Latin, and Hebrew,* for those are best learned that have learned Christ. It was written in these three languages that it might be known and read of all men; but God designed by it to signify that the gospel of Christ should be preached to all nations, *beginning at Jerusalem,* and be read in all languages. The Gentile philosophy made the Greek tongue famous, the Roman laws and government made the Latin tongue so, and the Hebrew excelled them all for the sake of the Old Testament. In these three languages is Jesus Christ *proclaimed king.* Young scholars, that are taking pains at school to make themselves masters of these three languages, should aim at this, that in the use of them they may increase their acquaintance with Christ.

II. Here are two passages which we had not before, and they are very remarkable ones.

1. Christ's prayer for his enemies (*v.* 34): *Father, forgive them.* Seven remarkable words Christ spoke after he was nailed to the cross, and before he died, and this is the first. One reason why he died the death of the cross was that he might have liberty of speech to the last, and so might glorify his Father and edify those about him. As soon as ever he was fastened to the cross, or while they were nailing him, he prayed this prayer, in which observe,

(1.) The petition: *Father, forgive them.* One would think that he should have prayed, "Father, consume them; the Lord look upon it, and requite it." The sin they were now guilty of might justly have been made unpardonable, and justly might they have been excepted by name out of the act of indemnity. No, these are particularly *prayed for.* Now he made intercession for transgressors, as was foretold (Isa. 53:12), and it is to be added to his prayer (Jn. 17), to complete the specimen he gave of his intercession within the veil: that for saints, this for sinners. Now the sayings of Christ upon the cross as well as his sufferings had a further intention than they seemed to have. This was a mediatorial word, and explicatory of the intent and meaning of his death: *"Father, forgive them,* not only these, but all that shall repent, and believe the gospel;" and he did not intend that these should be forgiven upon any other terms. "Father, that which I am now suffering and dying for is in order to this, that poor sinners may be pardoned." Note, [1.] The great thing which Christ died to purchase and procure for us is the forgiveness of sin. [2.] This is that for which Christ intercedes for all that repent and believe in the virtue of his satisfaction; his blood speaks this: *Father, forgive them.* [3.] The greatest sinners may, through Christ, upon their repentance, hope to find mercy. Though they were his persecutors and murderers, he prayed, Father, forgive *them.*

(2.) The plea: *For they know not what they do;* for, *if they had known,* they would not have crucified him, 1 Co. 2:8. There was a veil upon his glory and upon their understandings; and how could they see through two veils? They wished his blood on them and their children: but, had they known what they did, they would have unwished it again. Note, [1.] The crucifiers of Christ *know not what they do.* They that speak ill or religion speak ill of that which they know not, and it is because they will not know it. [2.] There is a kind of ignorance that does in part excuse sin: ignorance through want of the means of knowledge or of a capacity to receive instruction, through the infelicities of education, or inadvertency. The crucifiers of Christ were kept in ignorance by their rulers, and had prejudices against him instilled into them, so that in what they did against Christ and his doctrine they thought they did God service, Jn. 16:2. Such as to be pitied and prayed for. This prayer of Christ was answered not long after, when many of those that had a hand in his death were converted by Peter's preaching. This is written also for example to us. *First,* We must in prayer call God *Father,* and come to him with reverence and confidence, as children to a father. *Secondly,* The great thing we must beg of God, both for ourselves and others, is the forgiveness of sins. *Thirdly,* We must pray for *our enemies,* and those that hate and persecute us, must extenuate their offences, and not aggravate them as we must our own *(They know not what they do; peradventure it was an oversight);* and we must be earnest with God in prayer for the forgiveness of their sins, their sins against us. This is Christ's example to his own rule (Mt. 5:44, 45, *Love your enemies*); and it very much strengthens the rule, for, if Christ loved and prayed for such enemies, what enemies can we have that we are not obliged to *love* and *pray for?*

2. The conversion of the thief upon the cross, which is an illustrious instance of Christ's triumphing over principalities and powers even when he seemed to be triumphed over by them. Christ was crucified between two thieves, and in them were represented the different effects which the cross of Christ would have upon the children of men, to whom it would be *brought near* in the preaching of the gospel. They were all malefactors, all guilty before God. Now the cross of Christ is to some a *savour of life unto life,* to others of *death unto death.* To them that perish it is foolishness, but to them that are saved it is the wisdom of God and the power of God.

(1.) Here was one of these malefactors that was *hardened to the last.* Near to the cross of Christ, he *railed on him,* as others did (*v.* 39): he said, *If thou be the Christ,* as they say thou art, *save thyself and us.* Though he was now in pain and agony, and in the valley of the shadow of death, yet this did not humble his proud spirit, nor teach him to give good language, no, not to his fellow-sufferer. *Though thou bray a fool in a mortar, yet will not his foolishness depart from him.* No troubles will of themselves work a change in a wicked heart, but sometimes they *irritate* the corruption which one would think they should *mortify.* He challenges Christ to *save both himself and them.* Note, There are some that have the impudence to rail at Christ, and yet the confidence to expect to be saved by him; nay, and to conclude that, if he do not save them, he is not to be looked upon as the Saviour.

(2.) Here was the other of them that was *softened at the last.* It as said in Matthew and Mark that the *thieves,* even *they that were crucified with him, reviled him,* which some think is by a figure put for *one* of them, but others think that they both *reviled* him at first, till the heart of one of them was wonderfully changed, and with it his language on a sudden. This malefactor, when just ready to fall into the hands of Satan, was snatched as a brand out of the burning, and made a monument of divine mercy and grace, and Satan was left to roar as a lion disappointed of his prey. This gives no encouragement to any to put off their repentance to their death-bed, or to hope that then they shall find mercy; for, though it is certain that true repentance is never too late, it is as certain that late repentance is seldom true. None can be sure that they shall have time to repent at death, but every man may be sure that he cannot have the advantages that this penitent thief had, whose case was altogether extraordinary. He never had any offer of Christ, nor day of grace, before how: he was designed to be made a singular instance of the power of Christ's grace now at a time when he was *crucified in weakness.* Christ, having conquered Satan in the destruction of Judas and the preservation of Peter, erects this further trophy of his victory over him in the conversion of this malefactor, as a specimen of what he would do. We shall see the case to be extraordinary if we observe,

[1.] The extraordinary operations of God's grace upon him, which appeared in what he said. Here were so many evidences given in a short time of a blessed change wrought in him that more could not have been given in so little a compass.

First, See what he said to the other malefactor, *v.* 40, 41. 1. He reproved him for railing at Christ, as destitute of the *fear of God,* and having no sense at all of religion: *Dost not thou fear God?* This implies that it was the fear of God which restrained him from following the multitude to do this evil. "I fear God, and therefore dare not do it; and dost not thou?" All that have their eyes opened see this to be at the bottom of the wickedness of the wicked, that they have not the fear of God before their eyes. "If thou hadst any humanity in thee, thou wouldest not insult over one that is thy fellow-sufferer; *thou art in the same condition;* thou art a *dying man* too, and therefore, whatever these wicked people do, it ill becomes thee to abuse a dying man." 2. He owns that he deserves what was done to him: *We indeed justly.* It is probable that they both suffered for one and the same crime, and therefore he spoke with the more assurance, *We received the due reward of our deeds.* This magnifies divine grace, as acting in a distinguishing way. These two have been comrades in sin and suffering, and yet one is *saved* and the other *perishes;* two that had gone together all along hitherto, and yet now *one taken and the other left.* He does not say, *Thou* indeed justly, but *We.* Note, True penitents acknowledge the justice of God in all the punishments of their sin. God has *done right,* but *we have done wickedly.* 3. He believes Christ to have suffered *wrongfully.* Though he was condemned in two courts, and run upon as if he had been the worst of malefactors, yet this penitent thief is convinced, by his conduct in his sufferings, that *he has done nothing amiss, ouden atopon — nothing absurd, or unbecoming his character.* The chief priests would have him crucified *between* the malefactors, as *one of them;* but this thief has more sense than they, and owns he is *not one of them.* Whether he had before heard of Christ and of his wonderous works does not appear, but the Spirit of grace enlightened him with this knowledge, and enabled him to say, This man has *done nothing amiss.*

Secondly, See what he said to our Lord Jesus: *Lord, remember me when thou comest into thy kingdom, v.* 42. This is the prayer of a *dying sinner* to a *dying Saviour.* It was the honour of Christ to be *thus prayed to,* though he was upon the cross reproached and reviled. It was the happiness of the thief *thus to pray;* perhaps he never prayed before, and yet now was heard, and saved at the last gasp. While there is life there is hope, and while there is hope there is room for prayer. 1. Observe his *faith* in this prayer. In his confession of sin (*v.* 41) he discovered *repentance towards God.* In this petition he discovered *faith towards our Lord Jesus Christ.* He owns him to be *Lord,* and to have a *kingdom,* and that he was going to that kingdom, that he should have authority in that kingdom, and that those should be happy whom he favoured; and to *believe* and *confess* all this was a *great thing* at this time of day. Christ was now in the depth of disgrace, deserted by his own disciples, reviled by his own nation, suffering as a pretender, and not delivered by his Father He made this profession before those prodigies happened which put honour upon his sufferings, and which startled the centurion; yet *verily we have not found so great faith, no, not in Israel.* He believed *another life* after this, and desired to be happy in *that* life, not as the other thief, to be *saved from the cross,* but to be well provided for when the cross had done its worst. 2. Observe his humility in this prayer. All his request is, *Lord, remember me.* He does not pray, Lord, *prefer me* (as they did, Mt. 20:21), though, having the honour as none of the disciples had to drink of Christ's cup and to be baptized with his baptism either on his *right hand* or on *his left* in his sufferings when his own disciples had deserted him he might have had some colour to ask as they did to sit on his right hand and on his left in his kingdom. Acquaintance in sufferings has sometimes gained such a point, Jer. 52:31, 32. But he is far from the thought of it. All he begs is, *Lord, remember me,* referring himself to Christ in what way to remember him. It is a request like that of *Joseph to the chief butler, Think on me* (Gen. 40:14), and it sped better; the chief butler *forgot Joseph,* but Christ remembered this thief. 3. There is an air of importunity and fervency in this prayer. He does, as it were, breathe out his soul in it: *"Lord, remember me,* and I have enough; I desire no more; into thy hands I commit my case." Note, To be remembered by Christ, now that he is in his kingdom, is what we should earnestly desire and pray for, and it will be enough to secure our welfare living and dying. Christ is *in his kingdom,* interceding. *"Lord, remember me,* and intercede for me." He is there ruling. "Lord, remember me, and rule in me by thy Spirit." He is there preparing places for those that are his. "Lord, remember me, and prepare a place for me; remember me *at death,* remember me *in the resurrection."* See Job 14:13.

[2.] The extraordinary grants of Christ's favour to him: *Jesus said unto him,* in answer to his prayer, *"Verily I say unto thee,* I the *Amen,* the faithful Witness, I say *Amen* to this prayer, put my *fiat* to it: nay, thou shalt have more than thou didst ask, *This day thou shalt be with me in paradise," v.* 43. Observe,

First, To whom this was spoken: to the penitent thief, to him, and not to his companion. Christ upon the cross is like Christ upon the throne; for *now is the judgment of this world:* one departs with a curse, the other with a blessing. Though Christ himself was now in the greatest struggle and agony, yet he had a word of comfort to speak to a poor penitent that committed himself to him. Note, Even great sinners, if they be true penitents, shall, through Christ, obtain not only the pardon of their sins, but a place in the paradise of God, Heb. 9:15. This magnifies the riches of free grace, that rebels and traitors shall not only be pardoned, but preferred, thus preferred.

Secondly, By whom this was spoken. This was another mediatorial word which Christ spoke, though upon a particular occasion, yet with a general intention to explain the true intent and meaning of his sufferings; as he died to purchase the *forgiveness of sins* for us (*v.* 34), so also to purchase *eternal life* for us. By this word we are given to understand that Jesus Christ died to *open the kingdom of heaven to all penitent obedient believers.* 1. Christ here lets us know that he was going to paradise himself, to *hades — the invisible world.* His human soul was removing to the place of separate souls; not to the place of the damned, but to paradise, the place of the blessed. By this he assures us that his satisfaction was accepted, and the Father was well pleased in him, else he had not gone to paradise; that was the beginning of the joy set before him, with the prospect of which he comforted himself. He went by the cross to the crown, and we must not think of going any other way, or of being perfected but by sufferings. 2. He lets all penitent believers know that when they die they shall go to be with him there. He was now, as a priest, purchasing this happiness for them, and is ready, as a king, to confer it upon them when they are prepared and made ready for it. See here how the happiness of heaven is set forth to us. (1.) It is *paradise,* a garden of pleasure, the *paradise of God* (Rev. 2:7), alluding to the garden of Eden, in which our first parents were placed when they were innocent. In the second Adam we are restored to all we lost in the first Adam, and more, to a heavenly paradise instead of an earthly one. (2.) It is being *with Christ* there. That is the happiness of heaven, to see Christ, and sit with him, and share in his glory, Jn. 17:24. (3.) It is immediate upon death: *This day shalt thou be with me,* to-night, before to-morrow. *Thou souls of the faithful, after they are delivered from the burden of the flesh,* immediately *are in joy and felicity;* the spirits of just men are immediately *made perfect.* Lazarus departs, and is immediately *comforted;* Paul departs, and is immediately with Christ, Phil. 1:23.

Verses 44–49

In these verses we have three things: —

I. Christ's dying *magnified* by the *prodigies* that attended it: only two are here mentioned, which we had an account of before. 1. The *darkening of the sun at noon-day.* It was now about the *sixth hour,* that is, according to our computation, twelve o'clock at noon; and there was a *darkness over all the earth until the ninth hour.* The sun was eclipsed and the air exceedingly clouded at the same time, both which concurred to this thick darkness, which continued *three hours,* not *three days,* as that of Egypt did. 2. The *rending of the veil of the temple.* The former prodigy was in the *heavens,* this in the *temple;* for both these are the houses of God, and, when the Son of God was thus abused, they could not but feel the indignity, and thus signify their resentment of it. By this rending of the veil was signified the taking away of the ceremonial law, which was a wall of partition between Jews and Gentiles, and of all other difficulties and discouragements in our approaches to God, so that now we may *come boldly to the throne of grace.*

II. Christ's dying *explained* (*v.* 46) by the words with which he breathed out his soul. Jesus *had cried* with a loud voice when he said, *Why hast thou forsaken me?* So we are told in Matthew and Mark, and, it should seem, it was with a *loud voice* that he said this too, to show his earnestness, and that all the people might take notice of it: and this he said, *Father, into thy hands I commend my spirit.* 1. He borrowed these words from his father David (Ps. 31:5); not that he needed to have words put into his mouth, but he chose to make use of David's words to show that it was the Spirit of Christ that testified in the Old-Testament prophets, and that he came to fulfil the scripture. Christ died with scripture in his mouth. Thus he directs us to make use of scripture language in our addresses to God. 2. In this address to God he calls him *Father.* When he complained of being forsaken, he cried, *Eli, Eli, My God, my God;* but, to show that dreadful agony of his soul was now over, he here calls God *Father.* When he was giving up his life and soul for us, he did for us call God *Father,* that we through him might receive the adoption of sons. 3. Christ made use of these words in a sense peculiar to himself as Mediator. He was now to *make his soul an offering for our sin* (Isa. 53:10), to *give his life a ransom for many* (Mt. 20:28), *by the eternal Spirit to offer himself,* Heb. 9:14. He was himself both the priest and the sacrifice; our souls were forfeited, and his must go to redeem the forfeiture. The price must be paid *into the hands* of God, the party offended by sin; to him he had undertaken to make full satisfaction. Now by these words he *offered up the sacrifice,* did, as it were, lay his hand upon the head of it, and surrender it; *tithēmi* — "I *deposit* it, I pay it down into thy hands. Father, accept of my life and soul instead of the lives and souls of the sinners I die for." The *animus offerentis — the good will of the offerer,* was requisite to the acceptance of the offering. Now Christ here expresses his cheerful willingness to offer himself, as he had done when it was first proposed to him (Heb. 10:9, 10), *Lo, I come to do thy will, by which will we are sanctified.* 4. Christ hereby signifies his dependence upon his Father for his resurrection, by the re-union of his soul and body. He commends his spirit into his Father's hand, to be *received* into paradise, and *returned* the third day. By this it appears that our Lord Jesus, as he had a *true body,* so he had a reasonable soul, which existed in a state of separation from the body, and thus he was made like unto his brethren; this soul he lodged in his Father's hand, committed it to his custody, resting in hope that it should not be left in *hades,* in its *state of separation* from the body, no, not so long as that the body might see corruption. 5. Christ has hereby left us an example, has fitted those words of David to the purpose of dying saints, and hath, as it were, sanctified them for their use. In death our great care should be about our souls, and we cannot more effectually provide for their welfare than by committing them now into the hands of God, as a Father, to be sanctified and governed by his Spirit and grace, and at death committing them into his hands to be made perfect in holiness and happiness. We must show that we are freely willing to die, that we firmly believe in another life after this, and are desirous of it, by saying, *Father, into thy hands I commend my spirit.*

III. Christ's dying improved by the impressions it made upon those that attended him.

1. The centurion that had command of the guard was much affected with what he saw, *v.* 47. He was a Roman, a Gentile, a stranger to the consolations of Israel; and yet he *glorified God.* He never saw such amazing instances of divine power, and therefore took occasion thence to adore God as the *Almighty.* And he bore a testimony to the patient sufferer: *"Certainly this was a righteous man,* and was unjustly put to death." God's manifesting his power so much to do him honour was a plain evidence of his innocency. His testimony in Matthew and Mark goes further: *Truly this was the Son of God.* But in his case this amounts to the same; for, if he was *a righteous man,* he said very truly when he said that *he was the Son of God;* and therefore that testimony of his concerning himself must be admitted, for, if it were false, he was not a *righteous man.*

2. The disinterested spectators could not but be concerned. This is taken notice of only here, *v.* 48. *All the people that came together to that sight,* as is usual upon such occasions, *beholding the things which were done,* could not but go away very serious for the time, whatever they were when they came home: *They smote their breasts, and returned.* (1.) They laid the thing very much to heart for the present. They looked upon it as a wicked thing to put him to death, and could not but think that some judgment of God would come upon their nation for it. Probably these very people were of those that had cried, *Crucify him, crucify him,* and, when he was nailed to the cross, reviled and blasphemed him; but now they were so terrified with the darkness and the earthquake, and the uncommon manner of his expiring, that they had not only their mouths stopped, but their consciences startled, and in remorse for what they had done, as the publican, they *smote upon their breasts,* beat upon their own hearts, as those that had indignation at themselves. Some think that this was a happy step towards that good work which was afterwards wrought upon them, when they were pricked to the heart, Acts 2:37. (2.) Yet, it should seem, the impression soon wore off: *They smote their breasts, and returned.* They did not show any further token of respect to Christ, nor enquire more concerning him, but went home; and we have reason to fear that in a little time they quite forgot it. Thus many that see Christ evidently set forth crucified among them in the word and sacraments are a little affected for the present, but it does not continue; they smite their breasts, and return. They see Christ's face in the glass of the ordinances and admire him; but they *go away, and straightway forget what manner of man he is,* and what reason they have to love him.

3. His own friends and followers were obliged to keep their distance, and yet got as near as they could and durst, to see what was done (*v.* 49): *All his acquaintance,* that knew him and were known of him, *stood afar off,* for fear lest if they had been near him they should have been taken up as favourers of him; this was part of his sufferings, as of Job's (Job 19:13): *He hath put my brethren far from me, and mine acquaintance are verily estranged from me.* See Ps. 88:18. And *the women that followed him* together *from Galilee were beholding these things,* not knowing what to make of them, nor so ready as they should have been to take them for certain preludes of his resurrection. Now was Christ *set for a sign that should be spoken against,* as Simeon foretold, *that the thoughts of many hearts might be revealed, ch.* 2:34, 35.

Verses 50–56

We have here an account of Christ's burial; for he must be brought not only to death, but to the dust of death (Ps. 22:15), according to the sentence (Gen. 3:19), *To the dust thou shalt return.* Observe,

I. Who buried him. His acquaintance *stood afar off;* they had neither money to bear the *charge* nor courage to bear the *odium* of burying him decently; but God raised up one that had both, a *man named Joseph, v.* 50. His character is that he was *a good man and a just,* a man of unspotted reputation for virtue and piety, not only *just* to all, but good to all that needed him (and care to *bury the dead,* as becomes the hope of the resurrection of the dead, is one instance of goodness and beneficence); he was a person of quality, a counsellor, a senator, a member of the sanhedrim, one of the elders of the Jewish church. Having said this of him, it was necessary to add that, though he was of that body of men who had put Christ to death, yet he *had not consented to their counsel and deed* (*v.* 51), though it was carried by the majority, yet he entered his protest against it, and followed not the multitude to do evil. Note, That evil counsel or deed to which we have not consented shall not be reckoned our act. Nay, he not only *dissented* openly from those that were enemies to Christ, but be *consented* secretly with those that were his friends: *He himself waited for the kingdom of God;* he believed the Old-Testament prophecies of the Messiah and his kingdom, and expected the accomplishment of them. This was the man that appears upon this occasion to have had a true respect for the Lord Jesus. Note, There are many who are hearty in Christ's interests, how, though they do not make any show in their outward profession of it, yet will be more ready to do him a piece of real service, when there is occasion, than others who make a greater figure and noise.

II. What he did towards the burying of him. 1. He *went to Pilate,* the judge that condemned him, and *begged the body of Jesus,* for it was at his disposal; and, though he might have raised a party sufficient to have carried off the body by violence, yet he would take the regular course, and do it peaceably. 2. He *took it down,* it should seem, with his own hands, and *wrapped it in linen.* They tell us that it was the manner of the Jews to *roll* the bodies of the dead, as we do little children in their *swaddling-clothes,* and that the word here used signifies as much; so that the piece of fine linen, which he bought whole, he cut into many pieces for this purpose. It is said of Lazarus, *He was bound hand and foot,* Jn. 11:44. *Grave-clothes* are to the saints as *swaddling-clothes,* which they shall out-grow and put off, when they *come to the perfect man.*

III. Where he was buried. *In a sepulchre that was hewn in stone,* that the prison of the grave might be made strong, as the church, when she was brought into darkness, had her way *enclosed with hewn stone,* Lam. 3:2, 9. But it was *a sepulchre in which never man before was laid,* for he was buried on such an account as never any one before him was buried, only in order to his rising again the third day by his own power; and he was to triumph over the grave as never any man did.

IV. When he was buried. *On the day of the preparation, when the sabbath drew on, v.* 54. This is given as a reason why they made such haste with the funeral, because the *sabbath drew* on, which required their attendance to other work, preparing for the sabbath, and going forth to welcome it. Note, Weeping must not hinder sowing. Though they were in tears for the death of Christ, yet they must apply themselves to the sanctifying of the sabbath; and, when the sabbath draws on, there must be *preparation.* Our worldly affairs must be so ordered that they may not hinder us from our sabbath work, and our holy affections must be so excited that they may carry us on in it.

V. Who attended the funeral; not any of the disciples, but only *the women that came with him from Galilee* (*v.* 55), who, as they staid by him while he hung on the cross, so they *followed* him, all in tears no doubt, and *beheld the sepulchre* where it was, which was the way to it, and *how his body was laid in it.* They were led to this, not by their curiosity, but by their affection to the Lord Jesus, which was *strong as death* and which *many waters could not quench.* Here was a silent funeral, and not a solemn one, and yet *his rest was glorious.*

VI. What preparation was made for the embalming of his body after he was buried (*v.* 56): *They returned, and prepared spices and ointments,* which was more an evidence of their love than of their faith; for had they *remembered* and *believed* what he had so often told them, that he should *rise again the third day,* they would have spared their *cost* and *pains* herein, as knowing that in a short time there would be a greater honour put upon his body, by the glory of his resurrection, than they could put upon it with their most *precious ointments;* but, busy as they were in this preparation, they *rested on the sabbath day,* and did none of this servile work thereon, not only according to the custom of their nation, but *according to the commandments* of their God, which, though the day be altered, is still in full force: *Remember the sabbath day, to keep it holy.*

CHAPTER 24

Our Lord Jesus went gloriously down to death, in spite of the malice of his enemies, who did all they could to make his death ignominious; but he rose again more gloriously, of which we have an account in this chapter; and the proofs and evidences of Christ's resurrection are more fully related by this evangelist than they were by Matthew and Mark. Here is, I. Assurance given by two angels, to the woman who visited the sepulchre, that the Lord Jesus was risen from the dead, according to his own word, to which the angels refer them (*v.* 1–7), and the report of this to the apostles (*v.* 8–11). II. The visit which Peter made to the sepulchre, and his discoveries there (*v.* 12). III. Christ's conference with the two disciples that were going to Emmaus, and his making himself known to them (*v.* 13–35). IV. His appearing to the eleven disciples themselves, the same day at evening (*v.* 36–49). V. The farewell he gave them, his ascension into heaven, and the joy and praise of his disciples whom he left behind (*v.* 50–53).

Verses 1–12

The manner of the re-uniting of Christ's soul and body in his resurrection is a mystery, one of the *secret things* that *belong not to us;* but the *infallible proofs* of his resurrection, that he did indeed rise from the dead, and was thereby proved to be the Son of God, are *things revealed, which belong to us and to our children.* Some of them we have here in these verses, which relate the same story for substance that we had in Matthew and Mark.

I. We have here the affection and respect which the good women that had followed Christ showed to him, after he was dead and buried, *v.* 1. As soon as ever they could, after the sabbath was over, they *came to the sepulchre,* to embalm his body, not to take it out of the linen in which Joseph had wrapped it, but to anoint the head and face, and perhaps the wounded hands and feet, and to scatter sweet spices upon and about the body; as it is usual with us to strew flowers about the dead bodies and graves of our friends, only to show our good-will towards the taking off the deformity of death if we could, and to make them somewhat the less loathsome to those that are about them. The zeal of these good women for Christ did continue. The spices which they had prepared the evening before the sabbath, at a great expense, they did not, upon second thoughts, when they had slept upon it, dispose of otherwise, suggesting, *To what purpose is this waste?* but they brought them to the sepulchre on the morning after the sabbath, early, very early. It is a rule of charity, *Every man, according as he purposes in his heart, so let him give,* 2 Co. 9:7. What is prepared for Christ, let it be used for him. Notice is taken of the names of these women, *Mary Magdalene,* and *Joanna,* and *Mary* the mother of James; grave matronly women, it should seem, they were. Notice is also taken of certain others with them, *v.* 1, and again, *v.* 10. These, who had not joined in preparing the spices, would yet go along with them to the sepulchre; as if the number of Christ's friends increased when he was dead, Jn. 12:24, 32. The daughters of Jerusalem, when they saw how inquisitive the souse was after her Beloved, were desirous to seek him with her (Cant. 6:1), so were these *other women.* The zeal of some provokes others.

II. The surprise they were in, when they found the stone rolled away and the grave empty (*v.* 2, 3); they were *much perplexed* at that (*v.* 4) which they had much reason to rejoice in, that *the stone was rolled away from the sepulchre* (by which it appeared that he had a legal discharge, and leave to come out), and that they *found not the body of the Lord Jesus,* by which it appeared that he had made us of his discharge and was come out. Note, Good Christians often perplex themselves about that with which they should comfort and encourage themselves.

III. The plain account which they had of Christ's resurrection from two angels, who appeared to them *in shining garments,* not only white, but bright, and casting a lustre about them. They first saw *one* angel without the sepulchre, who presently *went in,* and sat with another angel in the sepulchre, *one at the head and the other at the feet, where the body of Jesus had lain;* so the evangelists may be reconciled. The women, when they saw the angels, *were afraid* lest they had some ill news for them; but, instead of enquiring of them, they *bowed down their faces to the earth,* to look for their dear Master in the grave. They would rather find him in his *grave-clothes* than angels themselves in their *shining garments.* A dying Jesus has more beauty in the eyes of a believer than angels themselves. These women, like the spouse, when found by the watchman (and angels are called *watchers*), enter not into any other conversation with them than this, *Saw ye him whom my soul loveth?* Now here, 1. They upbraid the women with the absurdity of the search they were making: *Why seek ye the living among the dead? v.* 5. Witness is hereby given to Christ that he is *living,* of him *it is witnessed that he liveth* (Heb. 7:8), and it is the comfort of all the saints, *I know that my Redeemer liveth;* for because he lives we shall live also. But a reproof is given to those that look for him *among the dead,* — that look for him among the dead heroes that the Gentiles worshipped, as if he were but like one of them, — that look for him in an image, or a crucifix, the work of men's hands, or among unwritten tradition and the inventions of men; and indeed all they that expect happiness and satisfaction in the creature, or perfection in this imperfect state, may be said to *seek the living among the dead.* 2. They assure them that he is risen from the dead (*v.* 6): *"He is not here, but is risen,* is risen by his own power; he has quitted his grace, to return no more to it." These angels were competent witnesses, for they had been sent express from heaven with orders for his discharge. And we are sure that their record is true; they durst not tell a lie. 3. They refer them to his own words: *Remember what he spoke to you, when he was yet in Galilee.* If they had duly believed and observed the prediction of it, they would easily have believed the thing itself when it came to pass; and therefore, that the tidings might not be such a surprise to them and they seemed to be, the angels repeat to them what Christ had often said in their hearing, *The Son of man must be delivered into the hands of sinful men,* and though it was done by the determinate counsel and foreknowledge of God, yet they that did it were not the less *sinful* for doing it. He told them that he *must be crucified.* Surely they could not forget that which they had with so much concern seen fulfilled; and would not this bring to their mind that which always followed, *The third day he shall rise again?* Observe, These angels from heaven bring not any *new gospel,* but put them in mind, as the angels of the churches do, of the sayings of Christ, and teach them how to improve and apply them.

IV. Their satisfaction in this account, *v.* 8. The women seemed to acquiesce; they *remembered his words,* when they were thus put in mind of them, and thence concluded that if he was risen it was not more than they had reason to expect; and now they were ashamed of the preparations they had made to embalm on the third day *him* who had often said that he would on the third day rise again. Note, A seasonable remembrance of the words of Christ will help us to a right understanding of his providence.

V. The report they brought of this to the apostles: *They returned from the sepulchre, and told all these things to the eleven, and to all the rest* of Christ's disciples, *v.* 9. It does not appear that they were together in a body; they were *scattered every one to his own,* perhaps scarcely two or three of them together in the same lodgings, but one went to some of them and another to others of them, so that in a little time, that morning, they all had notice of it. But we are told (*v.* 11) how the report was received: *Their words seemed to them as idle tales, and they believed them not.* They thought it was only the fancy of the women, and imputed it to the power of imagination; for they also had forgotten Christ's words, and wanted to be put in mind of them, not only what he had said to them in Galilee some time ago, but what he had said very lately, in the night wherein he was betrayed: *Again a little while, and ye shall see me. I will see you again.* One cannot but be amazed at the stupidity of these disciples, — who had themselves so often professed that they believed Christ to be the Son of God and the true Messiah, had been so often told that he must die and rise again, and then enter into his glory, had seen him more than once raise the dead, — that they should be so backward to believe in his raising himself. Surely it would seem the less strange to them, when hereafter this complaint would justly be taken up *by them,* to remember that there was a time when it might justly have been taken up against them, *Who hath believed our report?*

VI. The enquiry which Peter made hereupon, *v.* 12. It was Mary Magdalene that brought the report to him, as appears, Jn. 20:1, 2, where this story of his running to the sepulchre is more particularly related. 1. Peter hastened to the sepulchre upon the report, perhaps ashamed of himself, to think that Mary Magdalene should have been there before him; and yet, perhaps, he had not been so ready to go thither now if the women had not told him, among other things, that *the watch was fled.* Many that are *swift-footed* enough when there is no danger are but *cow-hearted* when there is. Peter now *ran to the sepulchre,* who but the other day *ran from his Master.* 2. He looked into the sepulchre, and took notice how orderly the linen clothes in which Christ was wrapped were taken off, and folded up, and laid by themselves, but the body gone. He was very particular in making his observations, as if he would rather credit his own eyes than the testimony of the angels. 3. He went away, as he thought, not much the wiser, *wondering in himself at that which was come to pass.* Had he remembered the words of Christ, even this was enough to satisfy him that he was risen from the dead; but, having forgotten them, he is only amazed with the thing, and knows not what to make of it. There is many a thing puzzling and perplexing to us which would be both plain and profitable if we did but rightly understand the words of Christ, and had them ready to us.

Verses 13–35

This appearance of Christ to the *two disciples* going to Emmaus was mentioned, and but just mentioned, before (Mk. 16:12); here it is largely related. It happened the same day that Christ rose, the first day of the new world that rose with him. One of these two disciples was *Cleopas* or *Alpheus,* said by the ancients to be the brother of Joseph, Christ's supposed father; who the other was is not certain. Some think it was Peter; it should seem indeed that Christ did appear particularly to Peter that day, which the eleven spoke of among themselves (*v.* 34), and Paul mentions, 1 Co. 15:5. But it could not be Peter that was one of the *two,* for he was one of the *eleven* to whom the *two* returned; and, besides, we know Peter so well as to think that if he had been one of the two he would have been the *chief speaker,* and not Cleopas. It was one of those that were associated with the eleven, mentioned *v.* 9. Now in this passage of story we may observe,

I. The *walk* and *talk* of these two disciples: *They went to a village called Emmaus,* which is reckoned to be about two hours' walk from Jerusalem; it is here said to be about sixty furlongs, seven measured miles, *v.* 13. Whether they went thither upon business, or to see some friend, does not appear. I suspect that they were going homewards to Galilee, with an intention not to enquire more after this Jesus; that they were meditating a retreat, and stole away from their company without asking leave or taking leave; for the accounts brought them that morning of their Master's resurrection seemed to them *as idle tales;* and, if so, no wonder that they began to think of making the best of their way home. But as they travelled they *talked together of all those things which had happened, v.* 14. They had not courage to *confer* of these things, and *consult* what was to be done in the present juncture at Jerusalem, for fear of the Jews; but, when they were got out of the hearing of the Jews, they could talk it over with more freedom. They *talked over these things,* reasoning with themselves concerning the probabilities of Christ's resurrection; for, according as these appeared, they would either go forward or return back to Jerusalem. Note, It well becomes the disciples of Christ, when they are together, to talk of his death and resurrection; thus they may improve one another's knowledge, refresh one another's memory, and stir up one another's devout affections.

II. The good company they met with upon the road, when Jesus himself came, and joined himself to them (*v.* 15): *They communed together, and reasoned,* and perhaps were warm at the argument, one hoping that their Master was risen, and would set up his kingdom, the other despairing. *Jesus himself drew near,* as a stranger who, seeing them travel the same way that he *went,* told them that he should be *glad of their company.* We may observe it, for our encouragement to keep up Christian conference and edifying discourse among us, that where but two together are well employed in work of that kind Christ will come to them, and make a third. When they that fear the Lord *speak one to another* the Lord *hearkens and hears,* and is with them of a truth; so that two thus twisted in faith and love become a *threefold cord, not easily broken,* Eccl. 4:12. They in their communings and reasonings together were searching for Christ, comparing notes concerning him, that they might come to more knowledge of him; and now Christ comes to them. Note, They who seek Christ shall find him: he will manifest himself to those that enquire after him, and give knowledge to those who use the helps for knowledge which they have. When the spouse enquired of the watchman concerning her beloved, *it was but a little that she passed from them, but she found him.* Cant. 3:4. But, though they had Christ with them, they were not at first aware of it (*v.* 16): *Their eyes were held, that they should not know him.* It should seem, there were both an alteration of the *object* (for it is said in Mark that now *he appeared in another form*) and a restraint upon the organ (for here it is said that *their eyes were held* by a divine power); or, as some think, there was a confusion in the *medium;* the air was so disposed that they could not discern who it was. No matter *how* it was, but *so* it was they did not *know him,* Christ so ordering it that they might the more freely discourse with him and he with them, and that it might appear that his word, and the influence of it, did not depend upon his bodily presence, which the disciples had too much doted upon, and must be weaned from; but he could teach them, and warm their hearts, by others, who should have his spiritual presence with them, and should have his grace going along with them unseen.

III. The conference that was between Christ and them, when he knew them, and they knew not him. Now Christ and his disciples, as is usual when friends meet incognito, or in a disguise, are here crossing questions.

1. Christ's first question to them is concerning *their* present *sadness*, which plainly appeared in their countenances: *What manner of communications are those that you have one with another as you walk, and are sad? v.* 17. It is a very kind and friendly enquiry. Observe,

(1.) They were *sad; it* appeared to a stranger that they were so. [1.] They had lost their dear Master, and were, in their own apprehensions, quite disappointed in their expectations from him. They had given up the cause, and knew not what course to take to retrieve it. Note, Christ's disciples have reason to be sad when he withdraws from them, to *fast* when the *Bridegroom* is taken from them. [2.] Though he was risen from the dead, yet either they did not know it or did not believe it, and so they were still in sorrow. Note, Christ's disciples are often sad and sorrowful even when they have reason to rejoice, but through the weakness of their faith they cannot take the comfort that is offered to them. [3.] Being sad, they had *communications one with another* concerning Christ. Note, *First*, It becomes Christians to talk of Christ. Were our hearts as full of him, and of what he has done and suffered for us, as they should be, *out of the abundance of the heart the mouth would speak*, not only of God and his providence, but of Christ and his grace and love. *Secondly*, Good company and good converse are an excellent antidote against prevailing melancholy. When Christ's disciples were sad they did not each one get by himself, but continued as he sent them out, two and two, for two are better than one, especially in times of sorrow. Giving *vent* to the grief may perhaps give *ease* to the grieved; and by talking it over we may talk ourselves or our friends may talk us into a better frame. Joint mourners should be mutual comforters; comforts sometimes come best from such.

(2.) Christ came up to them, and enquired into the matter of their talk, and the cause of their grief: *What manner of communications are these?* Though Christ had now entered into his state of exaltation, yet he continued tender of his disciples, and concerned for their comfort. He speaks as one troubled to see their melancholy: *Wherefore look ye so sadly to-day?* Gen. 40:7. Note, Our Lord Jesus takes notice of the sorrow and sadness of his disciples, and is afflicted in their afflictions. Christ has hereby taught us, [1.] To be *conversable*. Christ here fell into discourse with two grave serious persons, though he was a stranger to them and they knew him not, and they readily embraced him. It does not become Christians to be morose and shy, but to take pleasure in good society. [2.] We are hereby taught to be *compassionate*. When we see our friends in sorrow and sadness, we should, like Christ here, take cognizance of their grief, and give them the best counsel and comfort we can: *Weep with them that weep.*

2. In answer to this, they put a question to him concerning *his strangeness. Art thou only a stranger in Jerusalem, and hast not known the things that are come to pass there in these days?* Observe, (1.) Cleopas gave him a civil answer. He does not rudely ask him. "As for what we are talking of, what is that to you?" and bid him go about his business. Note, We ought to be civil to those who are civil to us, and to conduct ourselves obligingly to all, both in word and deed. It was a dangerous time now with Christ's disciples; yet he was not jealous of this stranger, that he had any design upon them, to inform against them, or bring them into trouble. Charity is not forward to *think evil*, no, not of strangers. (2.) He is full of Christ himself and of his death and sufferings, and wonders that every body else is not so too: "What! art thou such a stranger in Jerusalem as not to know what has been done to our Master there?" Note, Those are strangers indeed in Jerusalem that know not of the death and sufferings of Christ. What! are they *daughters of Jerusalem*, and yet so little acquainted with Christ as to ask, *What is thy beloved more than another beloved?* (3.) He is very willing to inform this stranger concerning Christ, and to draw on further discourse with him upon this subject. He would not have any one that had the face of a man to be ignorant of Christ. Note, Those who

have themselves the knowledge of Christ crucified should do what they can to spread that knowledge, and lead others into an acquaintance with him. And it is observable that these disciples, who were so forward to instruct the stranger, were instructed by him; for to him that has, and uses what he has, shall be given. (4.) It appears, by what Cleopas says, that the death of Christ made a great noise in Jerusalem, so that it could not be imagined that any man should be such a stranger in the city as not to know of it; it was all the talk of the town, and discoursed of in all companies. Thus the matter of fact came to be universally *known*, which, after the pouring out of the Spirit, was to be *explained*.

3. Christ, by way of reply, asked concerning *their knowledge* (v. 19): *He said unto them, What things?* thus making himself yet more a stranger. Observe, (1.) Jesus Christ made light of his own sufferings, in comparison with the joy set before him, which was the recompence of it. Now that he was entering upon his glory, see with what unconcernedness he looks back upon his sufferings: *What things?* He had reason to know what things; for to him they were bitter things, and heavy things, and yet he asks, *What things?* The sorrow was forgotten, for joy that the man-child of our salvation was born. He took pleasure in infirmities for our sakes, to teach us to do so for his sake. (2.) Those whom Christ will teach he will first examine how far they have learned; they must tell him *what things* they know, and then he will tell them what was the meaning of these things. and lead them into the mystery of them.

4. They, hereupon, gave him a particular account concerning Christ, and the present posture of his affairs. Observe the story they tell, v. 19, etc.

(1.) Here is a summary of Christ's *life* and *character*. The *things* they are full of are concerning *Jesus of Nazareth* (so he was commonly called), who *was a prophet*, a teacher come from God. He preached a true and excellent doctrine, which had manifestly its rise from heaven, and its tendency towards heaven. He confirmed it by many glorious miracles, miracles of mercy, so that he was *mighty in deed and word before God and all the people;* that is, he was both a great favourite of heaven and a great blessing to this earth. He was, and appeared to be, greatly beloved of God, and much the darling of his people. He had great acceptance with God, and a great reputation in the country. Many are *great before all the people*, and are caressed by them, who are not so *before God*, as the scribes and Pharisees; but Christ was mighty both in his *doctrine* and in his *doings, before God and all the people*. Those were strangers in Jerusalem that did not know this.

(2.) Here is a modest narrative of his sufferings and death, v. 20. "Though he was so dear both to God and man, yet the *chief priests and our rulers*, in contempt of both, *delivered him* to the Roman power, *to be condemned to death*, and *they have crucified him*." It is strange that they did not aggravate the matter more, and lay a greater load upon those that had been guilty of crucifying Christ; but perhaps because they spoke to one that was a stranger they thought it prudent to avoid all reflections upon the chief priests and their rulers, how just soever.

(3.) Here is an intimation of their disappointment in him, as the reason of their sadness: "*We trusted that it had been he who should have redeemed Israel, v.* 21. We are of those who not only looked upon him to be a prophet, like Moses, but, like him, a redeemer too." He was depended upon, and great things expected from him, by them that *looked for redemption*, and in it for the consolation of Israel. Now, if *hope deferred makes the heart sick*, hope disappointed, especially such a hope, kills the heart. But see how they made that the ground of their despair which if they had understood it aright was the surest ground of their hope, and that was the dying of the Lord Jesus: *We trusted* (say they) *that it had been he that should have redeemed Israel*. And is it not he that doth redeem Israel? Nay, is he not by his death paying the price of their redemption? Was it not necessary, in order to his saving Israel from their sins, that he should suffer? Sop that now, since that most difficult part of his undertaking was got over, they had more reason than ever to *trust* that *this was he that should deliver Israel;* yet now they are ready to give up the cause.

(4.) Here is an account of their present amazement with reference to his resurrection. [1.] "*This is the third day* since he was crucified and died, and that was the day when it was expected, if ever, that he should rise again, and rise in glory and outward pomp, and show himself as publicly in honour

as he had been shown three days before in disgrace; but we see no sign of it; nothing appears, as we expected, to the conviction and confusion of his prosecutors, and the consolation of his disciples, but all is silent." [2.] They own that there was a report among them that he was risen, but they seem to speak of it very slightly, and as what they gave no credit at all to (v. 22, 23): "*Certain women also of our company made us astonished* (and that was all), who were *early at the sepulchre*, and found the body gone, and they said that they had *seen a vision of angels, who said that he was alive;* but we are ready to think it was only their fancy, and no real thing, for angels would have been sent to the apostles, not to the women, and women are easily imposed upon." [3.] They acknowledge that some of the apostles had visited the sepulchre, and found it empty, v. 24. "But *him they saw not,* and therefore we have reason to fear that he *is not risen*, for, if he be, surely he would have *shown himself* to them; so that, upon the whole matter, we have no great reason to think that he is risen, and therefore have no expectations from him now; our hopes were all nailed to his cross, and buried in his grave."

(5.) Our Lord Jesus, though not known by face to them, makes himself known to them by his word.

[1.] He reproves them for their incogitancy, and the weakness of their faith in the scriptures of the Old Testament: *O fools, and slow of heart to believe, v.* 25. When Christ forbade us to say to our brother, *Thou fool*, it was intended to restrain us from giving unreasonable reproaches, not from giving just reproofs. Christ called them *fools*, not as it signifies *wicked men*, in which sense he forbade it to us, but as it signifies *weak men*. He might call them *fools*, for he *knows our foolishness*, the foolishness that is bound in our hearts. Those are fools that act against their own interest; so they did who would not admit the evidence given them that their Master was risen, but put away the comfort of it. That which is condemned in them as their *foolishness* is, *First*, Their *slowness to believe*. Believers are branded as fools by atheists, and infidels, and free-thinkers, and their most holy faith is censured as a fond credulity; but Christ tells us that those are *fools* who are *slow of heart to believe*, and are kept from it by prejudices never impartially examined. *Secondly*, Their slowness to believe *the writings of the prophets*. He does not so much blame them for their slowness to believe the testimony of the women and of the angels, but for that which was the cause thereof, their *slowness to believe* the prophets; for, if they had given the prophets of the Old Testament their due weight and consideration, they would have been as sure of Christ's *rising from the dead* that morning (being the third day after his death) as they were of the *rising of the sun;* for the *series* and *succession* of events as settled by *prophecy* are no less certain and inviolable than as settled by *providence*. Were we but more *conversant* with the scripture, and the divine counsels as far as they are made known in the scripture, we should not be subject to such perplexities as we often *entangle* ourselves in.

[2.] He shows them that the sufferings of Christ, which were such a stumbling-block to them, and made them unapt to believe his glory, were really the appointed way to his glory, and he could not go to it any other way (v. 26): "*Ought not the Christ* (the Messiah) to *have suffered these things, and to enter into his glory?* Was it not decreed, and was not that decree *declared*, that the promised Messiah must first suffer and then reign, that he must go by his cross to his crown?" Had they never read the fifty-third of Isaiah and the ninth of Daniel, where the prophets speak so very plainly of the *sufferings of Christ* and the *glory that should follow?* 1 Pt. 1:11. The cross of Christ was that to which they could not reconcile themselves; now here he shows them two things which take off the offence of the cross: — *First*, That the Messiah *ought to suffer* these things, and therefore his sufferings were not only no objection against his being the Messiah, but really a proof of it, as the afflictions of the saints are an evidence of their sonship; and they were so far from ruining their expectations that really they were the foundation of their hopes. He could not have been a *Saviour*, if he had not been a *sufferer*. Christ's undertaking our salvation was voluntary; but, having undertaken it, it was necessary that he should suffer and die. *Secondly*, That, when he had suffered these things, he should *enter into his glory*, which he did at his resurrection; that was his first step upward. Observe, It is called *his* glory, because he was *duly entitled* to it, and it was the glory he had before the world was; he *ought* to enter into it, for in that, as well as in his sufferings, the scripture must be fulfilled. He *ought* to suffer first, and then to enter into his glory; and thus the *reproach* of the cross is for ever *rolled away,* and we are directed to expect the crown of *thorns* and then that of *glory.*

[3.] He expounded to them the scriptures of the Old Testament, which spoke of the Messiah, and showed them how they were fulfilled in Jesus of Nazareth, and now can tell them more concerning him than they could before tell him (*v.* 27): *Beginning at Moses,* the first inspired writer of the Old Testament, he went in order through *all the prophets,* and *expounded to them the things concerning himself,* showing that the sufferings he had now gone through were so far from defeating the prophecies of the scripture concerning him that they were the accomplishment of them. He began at Moses, who recorded the first promise, in which it was plainly foretold that the Messiah should have his *heel bruised,* but that by it the serpent's head should be incurably broken. Note, *First,* There are things dispersed throughout *all the scriptures* concerning Christ, which it is of great advantage to have *collected* and *put together.* You cannot go far in any part of scripture but you meet with something that has reference to Christ, some prophecy, some promise, some prayer, some type or other; for he is the true *treasure his in the field* of the Old Testament. A golden thread of gospel grace runs through the whole web of the Old Testament. There is an *eye* of that *white* to be discerned in every place. *Secondly,* The things concerning Christ need to be *expounded.* The eunuch, though a scholar, would not pretend to understand them, *except some man should guide him* (Acts 8:31); for they were delivered darkly, according to that dispensation: but now that the veil is taken away the New Testament expounds the Old. *Thirdly,* Jesus Christ is himself the best expositor of scripture, particularly the scriptures concerning himself; and even after his resurrection it was in this way that he led people into the knowledge of the mystery concerning himself; not by advancing new notions independent upon the scripture, but by showing how the scripture was fulfilled, and turning them over to the study of it. Even the Apocalypse itself is but a second part of the Old-Testament prophecies, and has continually an eye to them. *If men believe not Moses and the prophets,* they are incurable. *Fourthly,* In *studying* the scriptures, it is good to be *methodical,* and to take them in order; for the Old-Testament light shone *gradually* to the *perfect day,* and it is good to observe how *at sundry times,* and in *divers manners* (subsequent predictions improving and giving light to the preceding ones), God spoke to the fathers *concerning* his Son, by whom he has now *spoken* to us. Some begin their bible at the wrong end, who study the Revelation first; but Christ has here taught us to *begin at Moses.* Thus far the conference between them.

IV. Here is the discovery which Christ at length made of himself to them. One would have given a great deal for a copy of the sermon Christ preached to them by the way, of that exposition of the bible which he gave them; but it is not thought fit that we should have it, we have the substance of it in other scriptures. The disciples are so charmed with it, that they think they are come too soon to their journey's end; but so it is: *They drew nigh to the village whither they went* (*v.* 28), where, it should seem, they determined to *take up* for that night. And now,

1. They courted his stay with them: *He made as though he would have gone further;* he did not *say* that he would, but he seemed to them to be going further, and did not readily turn into their friend's house, which it would not be decent for a stranger to do unless he were invited. He would have gone further if they had not courted his stay; so that here was nothing like dissimulation in the case. If a stranger be *shy,* every one knows the meaning of it; he will not thrust himself *rudely* upon your house or company; but, if you make it appear that you are freely desirous of him for your guest or companion, he knows not but he may accept your invitation, and this was all that Christ did when he *made as though he would have gone further.* Note, Those that would have Christ dwell with them must invite him, and be importunate with him; though he is often *found of those that seek him not,* yet those only that *seek* can be sure to *find;* and, if he seem to *draw off* from us, it is but to draw out our importunity; as here, *they constrained him;* both of them laid hold on him, with a kind and friendly violence, saying, *Abide with us.* Note, Those that have experienced the pleasure and profit of communion with Christ cannot but covet more of his company, and beg of him, not only to *walk with them* all day, but to *abide with them* at night. When *the day is far spent,* and it is *towards evening,* we begin to think of retiring for our repose, and then it is proper to have our eye to Christ, and to beg of him to *abide with us,* to manifest himself to us and to fill our minds with good thoughts of him and good affections to him. Christ yielded to their importunity: He *went in, to tarry with them.* Thus ready is Christ to give further instructions and comforts to those who improve what they have received. He has promised that *if any man open the door,* to bid him welcome, he will *come in to him,* Rev. 3:20.

2. He manifested himself to them, *v.* 30, 31. We may suppose that he continued his discourse with them, which he began upon the road; for thou must talk of the things of God *when thou sittest in the house as well as when thou walkest by the way.* While supper was getting ready (which perhaps was soon done, the provision was so small and mean), it is probable that he entertained them with such communications as were *good* and *to the use of edifying;* and so likewise as they *sat at meat* his *lips fed* them. But still they little thought that it was Jesus himself that was all this while talking with them, till at length he was pleased to throw off his disguise, and then to withdraw. (1.) They began to suspect it was he, when, as they *sat down to meat,* he undertook the office of the Master of the feast, which he performed so like himself, and like what he used to do among his disciples, that by it they discerned him: *He took bread, and blessed it,* and *brake, and gave to them.* This he did with his usual air both of authority and affection, with the same gestures and mien, with the same expressions perhaps in craving a blessing and in giving the bread to them. This was not a *miraculous* meal like that of the five loaves, nor a *sacramental* meal like that of the eucharist, but a *common* meal; yet Christ here did the same as he did in those, to teach us to keep up our communion with God through Christ in common providences as well as in special ordinances, and to crave a blessing and give thanks at every meal, and to see our daily bread provided for us and broken to us by the hand of Jesus Christ, the Master, not only of the great family, but of all our families. Wherever we *sit down to eat,* let us set Christ at the upper end of the table, take our meat as *blessed to us* by him, and *eat and drink* to his glory, and receive contentedly and thankfully what he is pleased to *carve* out to us, be the fare ever so coarse and mean. We may well receive it cheerfully, if we can by faith see it coming to us *from* Christ's hand, and with his blessing. (2.) Presently *their eyes were opened,* and then they saw who it was, and *knew him* well enough. Whatever it was which had hitherto concealed him from them, it was now taken out of the way; the mists were scattered, the veil was taken off, and then they made no question but it was their Master. He might, for wise and holy ends, put on the shape of another, but no other could put on his; and therefore it must be he. See how Christ by his Spirit and grace makes himself known to the souls of his people. [1.] He opens the scriptures to them, for they are they which testify of him to those who *search them,* and search for him in them. [2.] He meets them at his table, in the ordinance of the Lord's supper, and commonly there makes further discoveries of himself to them, is *known to them in the breaking of bread.* But, [3.] The work is completed by the opening of the eyes of their mind, and causing the scales to fall off from them, as from Paul's in his conversion. If he that gives the revelation do not give the understanding, we are in the dark still.

3. He immediately disappeared: *He vanished out of their sight. Aphantos egeneto* — He *withdrew himself* from them, slipped away of a sudden, and went *out of sight.* Or, he *became not visible by them,* was made inconspicuous by them. It should seem that though Christ's body, after his resurrection, was the very *same body* in which he suffered and died, as appeared by the marks in it, yet it was so far changed as to become either *visible* or *not visible* as he thought fit to make it, which was a step towards its being made a *glorious body.* As soon as he had given his disciples one glimpse of him he was gone presently. Such short and transient views have we of Christ in this world; we see him, but in a little while lose the sight of him again. When we come to heaven the vision of him will have no interruptions.

V. Here is the reflection which these disciples made upon this conference, and the report which they made of it to their brethren at Jerusalem.

1. The reflection they each of them made upon the influence which Christ's discourse had upon them (*v.* 32): *They said one to another, Did not our hearts burn within us?* "I am sure mine did," saith one; "And so did mine," saith the other, "I never was so affected with any discourse in all my life." Thus do they not so much compare *notes* as compare *hearts,* in the review of the sermon Christ had preached to them. They found the preaching powerful, even when they knew not the preacher. It made things very plain and clear to them; and, which was more, brought a *divine heat* with a *divine light* into their souls, such as put their hearts into a glow, and kindled a holy fire of pious and devout affections in them. Now this they take notice of, for the confirming of their belief, that it was indeed, as at last they saw, *Jesus himself* that had been talking with them all along. "What fools were we, that we were not sooner aware who it was! For none but he, no word but his, could *make our hearts burn within us* as they did; it must be he that has the key of the heart; it could be no other." See here, (1.) What *preaching* is likely to *do good* — such as Christ's was, *plain preaching,* and that which is familiar and level to our capacity — *he talked with us by the way;* and *scriptural* preaching — *he opened to us the scriptures,* the scriptures relating to himself. Ministers should show people their religion in their bibles, and that they preach no other doctrine to them than what is there; they must show that they make that the fountain of their knowledge and the foundation of their faith. Note, The expounding of those scriptures which speak of Christ has a direct tendency to warm the hearts of his disciples, both to quicken and to comfort them. (2.) What *hearing* is likely to *do good* — that which makes the *heart burn;* when we are much affected with the things of God, especially with the love of Christ in dying for us, and have our hearts thereby drawn out in love to him, and drawn up in holy desires and devotions, then our hearts *burn within us;* when our hearts are raised and elevated, and are as the sparks which *fly upwards* towards God, and when they are kindled and carried out with a holy zeal and indignation against sin, both in others and in ourselves, and we are in some measure refined and purified from it by the *spirit of judgment* and the *spirit of burning,* then we may say, "Through grace our hearts are thus inflamed."

2. The report they brought of this to their brethren at Jerusalem (*v.* 33): *They rose up the same hour,* so transported with joy at the discovery Christ had made of himself to them that they could not stay to make an end of their supper, but returned with all speed to Jerusalem, though it was towards evening. If they had had any thoughts of quitting their relation to Christ, this soon banished all such thoughts out of their mind, and there needed no more to send them back to his flock. It should seem that they intended at least to take up their quarters to-night at Emmaus; but now that they had seen Christ they could not rest till they had brought the good news to the disciples, both for the confirmation of their trembling faith and for the comfort of their sorrowful spirits, with the *same comforts wherewith they were comforted of God.* Note, It is the duty of those to whom Christ has manifested himself to let others know what he has done for their souls. When thou art converted, instructed, comforted, strengthen thy brethren. These disciples were *full* of this matter themselves, and must go to their brethren, to give vent to their joys, as well as to give them satisfaction that their Master was risen. Observe, (1.) How they found them, just when they came in among them, discoursing on the same subject, and relating another proof of the resurrection of Christ. They found the eleven, and those that were their usual companions, *gathered together* late in the night, to pray together, it may be, and to consider what was to be done in this juncture; and they found them *saying* among themselves (*legontas* it is the saying of the *eleven,* not of the *two,* as is plain by the original), and when these two came in, they repeated to them with joy and triumph, *The Lord is risen indeed, and hath appeared to Simon, v.* 34. That Peter had a sight of him before the rest of the disciples had appears 1 Co. 15:5, where it is said, *He was seen of Cephas, then of the twelve.* The angel having ordered the women to tell Peter of it particularly (Mk. 16:7), for his comfort, it is highly probable that our Lord Jesus did himself presently the same day appear to Peter, though we have no particular narrative of it, to *confirm the word of his messengers.* This he had related to his brethren; but, observe, Peter does not here proclaim it, and boast of it, himself (he thought this did not become a penitent), but the other disciples speak of it with exultation, *The Lord is risen indeed, ontōs — really;* it is now past

dispute, no room is left to doubt it, for he has appeared not only to the women, but to Simon. (2.) How they seconded their evidence with an account of what they had seen (*v.* 35): *They told what things were done in the way.* The words that were spoken by Christ to them in the way, having a wonderful effect and influence upon them, are here called the *things* that were *done in the way;* for the words that Christ speaks are not an empty sound, but *they are spirit and they are life,* and wondrous things are *done* by them, done *by the way,* by the by as it were, where it is not expected. They told also how he was at length *known to them in the breaking of bread;* then, when he was carving out blessings to them, God opened their eyes to discern who it was. Note, It would be of great use for the discovery and confirmation of truth if the disciples of Christ would compare their observations and experiences, and communicate to each other what they know and have felt in themselves.

Verses 36–49

Five times Christ was seen the same day that he rose: by Mary Magdalene alone in the garden (Jn. 20:14), by the women as they were going to tell the disciples (Mt. 28:9), by Peter alone, by the two disciples going to Emmaus, and now at night by the eleven, of which we have an account in these verses, as also Jn. 20:19. Observe,

1. The great *surprise* which his appearing gave them. He came in among them very *seasonably,* as they were comparing notes concerning the proofs of his resurrection: *As they thus spoke,* and were ready perhaps to *put it to the question* whether the proofs produced amounted to evidence sufficient of their Master's resurrection or no, and how they should proceed, *Jesus himself stood in the midst of them,* and *put it out of question.* Note, Those who make the best use they can of their evidences for their comfort may expect further assurances, and that the *Spirit of Christ* will *witness with their spirits* (as Christ here witnessed with the disciples, and confirmed their testimony) that they are the *children of God,* and risen with Christ. Observe, 1. The *comfort* Christ spoke to them: *Peace be unto you.* This intimates in general that it was a kind visit which Christ now paid them, a visit of love and friendship. Though they had very unkindly deserted him in his sufferings, yet he takes the first opportunity of seeing them together; for he deals not with us as we deserve. They did not *credit* those who had seen him; therefore he *comes himself,* that they might not continue in their disconsolate incredulity. He had promised that after his resurrection he *would see them in Galilee;* but so desirous was he to see them, and satisfy them, that he anticipated the appointment and *sees them at Jerusalem.* Note, Christ is often *better* than his word, but never *worse.* Now his first word to them was, *Peace be to you;* not in a way of compliment, but of consolation. This was a common form of salutation among the Jews, and Christ would thus express his usual familiarity with them, though he had now entered into his state of exaltation. Many, when they are advanced, forget their old friends and take state upon them; but we see Christ as free with them as ever. Thus Christ would at the first word intimate to them that he did not come to quarrel with Peter for *denying* him and the rest for *running away* from him; no, he *came peaceably,* to signify to them that he had forgiven them, and was reconciled to them. 2. The *fright* which they put themselves into upon it (*v.* 37): They were *terrified,* supposing that *they had seen a spirit,* because he came in among them without any noise, and was in the midst of them ere they were aware. The word used (Mt. 14:26), when they said *It is a spirit,* is *phantasma,* it is a *spectre,* an *apparition;* but the word here used is *pneuma,* the word that properly signifies *a spirit;* they supposed it to be a spirit not clothed with a real body. Though we have an alliance and correspondence with the world of spirits, and are hastening to it, yet while we are here in this world of sense and matter it is a terror to us to have a spirit so far change its own nature as to become visible to us, and conversable with us, for it is something, and bodes something, very extraordinary.

II. The great *satisfaction* which his discourse gave them, wherein we have,

1. The reproof he gave them for their causeless fears: *Why are you troubled, and why do* frightful *thoughts arise in your hearts? v.* 38. Observe here, (1.) That when at any time we are *troubled, thoughts* are apt to *rise in our hearts* that do us hurt. Sometimes the *trouble* is the effect of the *thoughts* that *arise in our hearts;* our griefs and fears take rise from those things that are the creatures of our own fancy. Sometimes the thoughts arising in the heart are the effect of the trouble, without are fightings and then within are fears. Those that are melancholy and troubled in mind have *thoughts arising in their hearts* which reflect dishonour upon God, and create disquiet to themselves. *I am cut off from thy sight. The Lord has forsaken and forgotten me.* (2.) That many of the troublesome thoughts with which our minds are disquieted arise from our mistakes concerning Christ. They here thought that they had *seen a spirit,* when they saw Christ, and that put them into this fright. We forget that Christ is our *elder brother,* and look upon him to be at as great a distance from us as the world of spirits is from this world, and therewith terrify ourselves. When Christ is by his Spirit convincing and humbling us, when he is by his providence trying and converting us, we *mistake him,* as if he designed our hurt, and this troubles us. (3.) That all the troublesome thoughts which rise in our hearts at any time are known to the Lord Jesus, even at the first rise of them, and they are displeasing to him. He chid his disciples for such *thoughts,* to teach us to chide ourselves for them. *Why art thou cast down, O my soul? Why art thou troubled?* Why do *thoughts arise* that are neither *true* nor *good,* that have neither *foundation* nor *fruit,* but hinder our joy in God, unfit us for our duty, give advantage to Satan, and deprive us of the comforts laid up for us?

2. The proof he gave them of his resurrection, both for the *silencing* of their *fears* by convincing them that he was *not a spirit,* and for the *strengthening* of their *faith* in that doctrine which they were to preach to the world by giving them full satisfaction concerning his resurrection. Two proofs he gives them: —

(1.) He shows them his body, particularly *his hands and his feet.* They saw that he had the shape, and features, and exact resemblance, of their Master; but is it not his ghost? "No," saith Christ, *"behold my hands and my feet;* you see I have *hands* and *feet,* and therefore have a *true* body; you see I can *move* these hands and feet, and therefore have a *living* body; and you see the marks of the nails in my hands and feet, and therefore it is *my own* body, the *same* that you saw crucified, and not a *borrowed* one." He lays down this principle — that a *spirit has not flesh and bones;* it is not compounded of gross matter, shaped into various members, and consisting of divers heterogeneous parts, as our bodies are. He does not tell us what a *spirit* is (it is time enough to know that when we go to the world of spirits), but what it is not: *It has not flesh and bones.* Now hence he infers, *"It is I myself,* whom you have been so intimately acquainted with, and have had such familiar conversation with; it is *I myself,* whom you have reason to rejoice in, and not to be afraid of." Those who *know Christ* aright, and know him as *theirs,* will have no reason to be terrified at his appearances, at his approaches. [1.] He appeals to their *sight, shows* them *his hands* and *his feet,* which were pierced with the nails. Christ retained the marks of them in his glorified body, that they might be proofs that it was he himself; and he was willing that they should be *seen.* He afterwards showed them to Thomas, for he is not ashamed of his sufferings for us; little reason then have we to be ashamed of them, or of ours for him. As he showed his wounds here to his disciples, for the enforcing of his instructions to them, so he showed them to his Father, for the enforcing of his intercessions with him. He appears in heaven *as a Lamb that had been slain* (Rev. 5:6); his *blood speaks,* Heb. 12:24. He makes intercession in the virtue of his satisfaction; he says to the Father, as here to the disciples, *Behold my hands and my feet,* Zec. 13:6, 7. [2.] He appeals to their *touch: Handle me, and see.* He would not let Mary Magdalene touch him at that time, Jn. 20:17. But the disciples here are entrusted to do it, that they who were to preach his resurrection, and to suffer for doing so, might be themselves abundantly satisfied concerning it. He bade them *handle him,* that they might be convinced that he was not a *spirit.* If there were really no spirits, or apparitions of spirits (as by this and other instances it is plain that the disciples did believe there were), this had been a proper time for Christ to have undeceived them, by telling them there were no such things; but he seems to take it for granted that there have been and may be apparitions of spirits, else what need was there of so much pains to prove that he was not one? There were many heretics in the primitive times, atheists I rather think they were, who said that Christ had never any substantial body, but that it was a mere phantasm, which was neither really born nor truly suffered. Such wild notions as these, we are told, the Valentinians and Manichees had, and the followers of Simon Magus; they were called *Dokētai* and *Phantysiastai.* Blessed be God, these heresies have long since been *buried;* and we know and are sure that Jesus Christ was no *spirit* or *apparition,* but had a true and real body, even after his resurrection.

(2.) He *eats* with them, to show that he had a real and true body, and that he was willing to converse freely and familiarly with his disciples, as one friend with another. Peter lays a great stress upon this (Acts 10:41): We *did eat and drink with him after he rose from the dead.*

[1.] When they *saw his hands and his feet,* yet they knew not what to say, *They believed not for joy, and wondered, v.* 41. It was their infirmity that they *believed not,* that *yet* they believed not, *eti apistountōn autōn — they as yet being unbelievers.* This very much corroborates the truth of Christ's resurrection that the disciples were so slow to believe it. Instead of stealing away his body, and saying, *He is risen,* when he is not, as the chief priests suggested they would do, they are ready to say again and again, *He is not risen,* when he is. Their being incredulous of it at first, and insisting upon the utmost proofs of it, show that when afterwards they did believe it, and venture their all upon it, it was not but upon the fullest demonstration of the thing that could be. But, though it was their infirmity, yet it was an excusable one; for it was not from any contempt of the evidence offered them that they believed not: but, *First,* They *believed not for joy,* as Jacob, when he was told that Joseph was alive; they thought it too good news to be true. When the faith and hope are therefore *weak* because the love and desires are *strong,* that weak faith shall be helped, and not rejected. *Secondly,* They *wondered;* they thought it not only *too good,* but *too great,* to be true, forgetting both the scriptures and the power of God.

[2.] For their further conviction and encouragement, he *called for some meat.* He sat down to meat with the two disciples at Emmaus, but it is not said that he did eat with *them;* now, lest that should be made an objection, he here did actually *eat* with *them* and *the rest,* to show that his body was really and truly *returned to life,* though he did not eat and drink, and converse constantly, with them, as he had done (and as Lazarus did after *his* resurrection, who not only returned to life, but to his former state of life, and to die again), because it was not agreeable to the economy of the state he was risen to. They gave him a *piece of a broiled fish, and of a honey-comb, v.* 42. The honey-comb, perhaps, was used as sauce to the broiled fish, for Canaan was a land *flowing with honey.* This was mean fare; yet, if it be the fare of the disciples, their Master will fare as they do, because in the kingdom of our Father they shall fare as he does, shall eat and drink with him in his kingdom.

3. The *insight* he gave them into the word of God, which they had *heard* and read, by which faith in the resurrection of Christ is wrought in them, and all the difficulties are cleared. (1.) He refers them to the *word* which they had *heard* from him when he was with them, and puts them in mind of that as the angel had done (*v.* 44): *These are the words which I said unto you* in private, many a time, *while I was yet with you.* We should better *understand* what Christ *does,* if we did but better *remember* what he hath *said,* and had but the art of comparing them together. (2.) He refers them to the *word* they had read in the Old Testament, to which the word they had heard from him directed them: *All things must be fulfilled which were written.* Christ had given them this general hint for the regulating of their expectations —that whatever they found written concerning the Messiah, in the Old Testament, must be fulfilled in him, what was written concerning his sufferings as well as what was written concerning his kingdom; these God had *joined together* in the prediction, and it could not be thought that they should be *put asunder* in the event. *All things* must be fulfilled, even the *hardest,* even the *heaviest,* even the *vinegar;* he could not die till he had that, because he could not till then say, *It is finished.* The several parts of the Old Testament are here mentioned, as containing each of them things concerning Christ: *The law of Moses,* that is, the Pentateuch, or the *five* books written by Moses, — the *prophets,* containing not only the books that are purely prophetical, but those historical books that were written by prophetical men, — the *Psalms,* containing the other writings, which they called the *Hagiographa.* See in what various ways of writing God did of old reveal his will; but all proceeded from one and the self-same

Spirit, who by them gave notice of the coming and kingdom of the Messiah; for *to him bore all the prophets witness.* (3.) By an immediate present work upon their minds, of which they themselves could not but be sensible, he gave them to apprehend the true intent and meaning of the Old-Testament prophecies of Christ, and to see them all fulfilled in him: *Then opened he their understanding, that they might understand the scriptures, v.* 45. In his discourse with the two disciples he took the veil from off the text, by *opening* the scriptures; here he took the veil from off the heart, *by opening the mind.* Observe here, [1.] That Jesus Christ by his Spirit operates on the minds of men, on the minds of all that are his. He has access to our spirits, and can immediately influence them. It is observable how he did now after his resurrection give a *specimen* of those two great operations of *his Spirit* upon the *spirits of* men, his enlightening the intellectual faculties with a divine light, when he opened the understandings of his disciples, and his invigorating the active powers with a divine heat, when he made their hearts burn within them. [2.] Even good men need to have their *understandings opened;* for though they are not *darkness,* as they were by nature, yet in many things they are *in the dark.* David prays, *Open mine eyes. Give me understanding.* And Paul, who knows so much of Christ, sees his need to learn more. [3.] Christ's way of working faith in the soul, and gaining the throne there, is by *opening the understanding* to discern the evidence of those things that are to be believed. Thus he comes into the soul by *the door,* while Satan, as a thief and a robber, climbs up some other way. [4.] The design of opening the understanding is *that we may understand the scriptures;* not that we may be *wise above what is written,* but that we may be *wiser in what is written,* and may be made *wise to salvation* by it. The Spirit in the word and the Spirit in the heart say the same thing. Christ's scholars never learn *above their bibles* in this world; but they need to be learning still more and more *out of their bibles,* and to grow more *ready* and *mighty* in the scriptures. That we may have right thoughts of Christ, and have our mistakes concerning him rectified, there needs no more than to be made to understand the scriptures.

4. The instructions he gave them as *apostles,* who were to be employed in setting up his kingdom in the world. They expected, while their Master was with them, that they should be preferred to posts of honour, of which they thought themselves quite disappointed when he was dead. "No," saith, he, "you are now to enter upon them; *you are* to be *witnesses of these things* (*v.* 48), to carry the notice of them to all the world; not only to *report* them as matter of news, but to *assert* them as evidence given upon the trial of the great cause that has been so long depending between God and Satan, the issue of which must be the casting down and casting out of the *prince of this world.* You are fully assured of these things yourselves, you are eye and ear-witnesses of them; go, and assure the world of them; and the same Spirit that has enlightened you shall go along with you for the enlightening of others." Now here they are told,

(1.) *What they must preach.* They must preach the gospel, must preach the *New Testament* as the full accomplishment of the *Old,* as the continuation and conclusion of divine revelation. They must take their bibles along with them (especially when they preached to the Jews; nay, and Peter, in his first sermon to the Gentiles, directed them to consult the prophets, Acts 10:43), and must show people how it was written of old concerning the Messiah, and the glories and graces of his kingdom, and then must tell them how, upon their certain knowledge, all this was fulfilled in the Lord Jesus.

[1.] The great *gospel truth* concerning the *death* and *resurrection* of Jesus Christ must be *published* to the children of men (*v.* 46): *Thus it was written* in the sealed book of the divine counsels from eternity, the volume of that book of the covenant of redemption; and thus it was written in the open book of the Old Testament, among the things revealed; and therefore *thus it behoved Christ to suffer,* for the divine counsels must be performed, and care taken that no word of God fall to the ground. "Go, and tell the world," *First,* "That Christ *suffered,* as it was written of him. Go, preach *Christ crucified;* be not ashamed of his cross, not ashamed of a suffering Jesus. Tell them what he suffered, and why he suffered, and how all the scriptures of the Old Testament were fulfilled in his sufferings. Tell them that it *behoved him to suffer,* that it was necessary to the taking away of the sin of the world, and the deliverance of mankind from death and ruin: nay, it *became him* to be perfected *through sufferings,"* Heb. 2:10. *Secondly,* "That he rose from the dead on *the third day,* by which not only all the offence of the cross was rolled away, but he was declared to be the Son of God with power, and in this also the *scriptures* were *fulfilled* (see 1 Co. 15:3, 4); go, tell the world how often you saw him after he rose from the dead, and how intimately you conversed with him. *Your eyes see"* (as Joseph said to his brethren, when his discovering himself to them was as life from the dead) *"that it is my mouth that speaketh unto you,* Gen. 45:12. Go, and tell them, then, that he that *was dead is alive,* and *lives for evermore,* and *has the keys of death and the grave,"*

[2.] The great *gospel duty* of *repentance* must be *pressed* upon the children of men. *Repentance for sin* must be preached in *Christ's name,* and by his authority, *v.* 47. *All men every where* must be called and *commanded to repent,* Acts 17:30. "Go, and tell all people that the God that made them, and the Lord that bought them, expects and requires that, immediately upon this notice given, they turn from the worship of the gods that they have made to the worship of the God that made them; and not only so, but from serving the interests of the world and the flesh; they must turn to the service of God in Christ, must mortify all sinful habits, and forsake all sinful practices. Their hearts and lives must be changed, and they must be universally renewed and reformed."

[3.] The great *gospel privilege* of the *remission of sins* must be *proposed* to all, and assured to all that *repent,* and *believe the gospel.* "Go, tell a guilty world, that stands convicted and condemned at God's bar, that an act of indemnity has passed the royal assent, which all that repent and believe shall have the benefit of, and not only be *pardoned,* but *preferred* by. Tell them that *there is hope* concerning them."

(2.) *To whom they must preach.* Whither must they carry these proposals, and how far does their commission extend? They are here told, [1.] That they must preach this *among all nations.* They must disperse themselves, like the sons of Noah after the flood, some one way and some another, and carry this light along with them wherever they go. The prophets had preached *repentance* and *remission* to the *Jews,* but the apostles must preach them to *all the world.* None are *exempted* from the obligations the gospel lays upon men to *repent,* nor are any *excluded* from those inestimable benefits which are included in the remission of sins, but those that by their unbelief and impenitency put a bar in their own door. [2.] That they must *begin at Jerusalem* There they must preach their first *gospel sermon;* there the *gospel church* must be first formed; there the gospel day must dawn, and thence that light shall go forth which must take hold on the ends of the earth. And why must they begin there? *First,* Because *thus it was written,* and therefore it *behoved them* to take this method. *The word of the* Lord must *go forth from Jerusalem,* Isa. 2:3. And see Joel 2:32; 3:16; Obad. 21; Zec. 14:8. *Secondly,* Because there the matters of fact on which the gospel was founded were transacted; and therefore there they were first attested, where, if there had been any just cause for it, they might be best contested and disproved. So strong, so bright, is the first shining forth of the glory of the risen Redeemer that it dares face those daring enemies of his that had put him to an ignominious death, and sets them at defiance. *"Begin at Jerusalem,* that the chief priests may try their strength to crush the gospel, and may rage to see themselves disappointed." *Thirdly,* Because he would give us a further example of forgiving enemies. Jerusalem had put the greatest affronts imaginable upon him (both the rulers and the multitude), for which that city might justly have been excepted by name out of the act of indemnity; but no, so far from that, the first offer of gospel grace is made to Jerusalem, and thousands there are in a little time brought to partake of that grace.

(3.) What *assistance they should have in preaching.* It is a vast undertaking that they are here called to, a very large and difficult province, especially considering the opposition this service would meet with, and the sufferings it would be attended with. If therefore they ask, *Who is sufficient for these things?* here is an answer ready: *Behold, I send the promise of my Father upon you,* and *you shall be endued with power from on high, v.* 49. He here assures them that in a little time the Spirit should be poured out upon them in greater measures than ever, and they should thereby be furnished with all those gifts and graces which were necessary to their discharge of this great trust; and therefore they must *tarry at Jerusalem,* and not enter upon it till this be done. Note, [1.] Those who *receive the Holy Ghost* are thereby *endued with a power from on high,* a supernatural power, a power above any of their own; it is *from on high,* and therefore draws the soul upward, and makes it to *aim high.* [2.] Christ's apostles could never have planted his gospel, and set up his kingdom in the world, as they did, if they had not been endued with such a power; and their admirable achievements prove that there was an excellency of power going along with them. [3.] *This power from on high* was the *promise of the Father,* the great promise of the New Testament, as the promise of the coming of Christ was of the Old Testament. And, if it be the *promise of the Father,* we may be sure that the promise is *inviolable* and the thing promised *invaluable.* [4.] Christ would not leave his disciples till the time was just at hand for the performing of this promise. It was but ten days after the *ascension* of Christ that there came the *descent* of the Spirit. [5.] Christ's ambassadors must stay till they have their powers, and not venture upon their embassy till they have received full instructions and credentials. Though, one would think, never was such haste as now for the preaching of the gospel, yet the preachers must tarry till they be endued with power from on high, and *tarry at Jerusalem,* though a place of danger, because there this promise of the Father was to find them, Joel 2:28.

Verses 50–53

This evangelist omits the solemn meeting between Christ and his disciples *in Galilee;* but what he said to them there, and at other interviews, he subjoins to what he said to them at the first visit he made them on the evening of the day he rose; and has now nothing more to account for but his ascension into heaven, of which we have a very brief narrative in these verses, in which we are told,

I. How solemnly Christ took leave of his disciples. Christ's design being to reconcile heaven and earth, and to continue a days-man between them, it was necessary that he should lay his hands on them both, and, in order thereunto, that he should *pass* and *repass.* He had business to do in both worlds, and accordingly came from heaven to earth in his incarnation, to despatch his business here, and, having finished this, he returned to heaven, to reside there, and negotiate our affairs with the Father. Observe, 1. Whence he ascended: from *Bethany,* near Jerusalem, adjoining to the *mount of Olives.* There he had done eminent services for his Father's glory, and there he entered upon his glory. There was the *garden* in which his sufferings began, there he was in his agony; and Bethany signifies *the house of sorrow.* Those that would go to heaven must ascend thither from the house of sufferings and sorrow, must go by agonies to their joys. The mount of Olives was pitched upon long since to be the place of Christ's ascension: *His feet shall stand in that day upon the mount of Olives,* Zec. 14:4. And here it was that awhile ago he began his triumphant entry into Jerusalem, *ch.* 19:29. 2. Who were the witnesses of his ascension: *He led out his disciples* to see him. Probably, it was very early in the morning that he ascended, before people were stirring; for he never showed himself openly to all the people after his resurrection, but only to *chosen witnesses.* The disciples did not see him rise out of the grace, because his resurrection was capable of being proved by their seeing him alive afterwards; but they saw him *ascend* into heaven, because they could not otherwise have an *ocular* demonstration of his ascension. They were *led out* on purpose to see him ascend, had their eye upon him when he ascended, and were not looking another way. 3. What was the farewell he gave them: *He lifted up his hands, and blessed them.* He did not go away in displeasure, but in love; he left a blessing behind him; *he lifted up his hands,* as the high priest did when he blessed the people; see Lev. 9:22. He blessed as one having authority, commanded the blessing which he had purchased; he *blessed them* as Jacob blessed his sons. The apostles were now as the representatives of the twelve tribes, so that in blessing them he blessed all his spiritual Israel, and put his Father's name upon them. He blessed them as Jacob blessed his sons, and Moses the tribes, at parting, to show that, having loved his own which were in the world, he loved them unto the end. 4. How he left them: *While he was blessing them, he was parted from them;* not as if he were taken away before he had said all he had to say, but to intimate that his being parted from them did not put an end to his blessing them, for the intercession which he went to heaven to make for all his is a continuation of the blessing. He *began* to bless them on earth, but he went to heaven to *go on* with it. Christ was now sending his apostles to preach his gospel to the world, and he gives them his blessing, not for *themselves* only, but to be conferred in his name upon *all* that should believe on him through their word; for in him *all the families of the earth were to be blessed.* 5. How his ascension is described. (1.) He was *parted from them,* was taken from their head, as Elijah from Elisha's. Note, The dearest friends must part. Those that love us, and pray for us, and instruct us, must be *parted form us.* The bodily presence of Christ himself was not to be expected always in this world; those that knew him after the flesh must now henceforth know him so no more. (2.) He was *carried up into heaven;* not by force, but by his own act and deed. As he arose, so he ascended, by his own power, yet attended by angels. There needed no chariot of fire, nor horses of fire; he knew the way, and, being the *Lord from heaven,* could go back himself. He ascended in a cloud, as the angel in the smoke of Manoah's sacrifice, Jdg. 13:20.

II. How cheerfully his disciples continued their attendance on him, and on God through him, even now that he was parted from them. 1. They paid their homage to him at his going away, to signify that though he was going into a far country, yet they would continue his loyal subjects, that they were willing to have him reign over them: *They worshipped him. v.* 52. Note, Christ expects *adoration* from those that receive blessings from him. He *blessed them,* in token of gratitude for which they *worshipped him.* This fresh display of Christ's glory drew from them fresh acknowledgments and adorations of it. They knew that though he was *parted form them,* yet he could, and did, take notice of their adorations of him; the cloud that received him out of their sight did not put them or their services out of his sight. 2. They *returned to Jerusalem with great joy.* There they were ordered to continue till the Spirit should be poured out upon them, and thither they went accordingly, though it was into the mouth of danger. Thither they went, and there they staid *with great joy.* This was a wonderful change, and an effect of the opening of their understandings. When Christ told them that he must leave them sorrow filled their hearts; yet now that they see him go they are *filled with joy,* being convinced at length that it was expedient for them and for the church that he should go away, to send the Comforter. Note, The glory of Christ is the joy, the exceeding joy, of all true believers, even while they are here in this world; much more will it be so when they go to the new Jerusalem, and find him there in his glory. 3. They abounded in acts of devotion while they were in expectation of the promise of the Father, *v.* 53. (1.) They attended the temple-service at the hours of prayer. God had not as yet quite forsaken it, and therefore they did not. *They were continually in the temple,* as their Master was when he was at Jerusalem. *The Lord loves the gates of Zion,* and so should we. Some think that they had their place of meeting, as disciples, in some of the chambers of the temple which belonged to some Levite that was *well affected* to them; but others think it is not likely that this either could be *concealed from,* or would be *connived at* by, the chief priests and *rulers of the temple.* (2.) Temple-sacrifices, they knew, were superseded by Christ's sacrifice, but the temple-songs they joined in. Note, While we are waiting for God's promises we must go forth to meet them with our praises. Praising and blessing God is work that is never out of season: and nothing better prepares the mind for the receiving of the Holy Ghost than holy joy and praise. Fears are silenced, sorrows sweetened and allayed, and hopes kept up.

The *amen* that concludes seems to be added by the church and every believer to the reading of the gospel, signifying an assent to the truths of the gospel, and a hearty concurrence with all the disciples of Christ in praising and blessing God. *Amen.* Let him be continually praised and blessed.

AN EXPOSITION, WITH PRACTICAL OBSERVATIONS, OF

THE GOSPEL ACCORDING TO ST. JOHN

It is not material to enquire when and where this gospel was written; we are sure that it was given by inspiration of God to John, the brother of James, one of the twelve apostles, distinguished by the honourable character of *that disciple whom Jesus loved,* one of the first three of the worthies of the Son of David, whom he took to be the witnesses of his retirements, particularly of his transfiguration and his agony. The ancients tell us that John lived longest of all the twelve apostles, and was the only one of them that died a natural death, all the rest suffering martyrdom; and some of them say that he wrote this gospel at Ephesus, at the request of the ministers of the several churches of Asia, in opposition to the heresy of Corinthus and the Ebionites, who held that our Lord was a *mere man.* It seems most probable that he wrote it before his banishment into the isle of Patmos, for there he wrote his *Apocalypse,* the close of which seems designed for the closing up of the canon of scripture; and, if so, this gospel was not written after. I cannot therefore give credit to those later fathers, who say that he wrote it in his banishment, or after his return from it, many years after the destruction of Jerusalem; when he was ninety years old, saith one of them; when he was a hundred, saith another of them. However, it is clear that he wrote last of the four evangelists, and, comparing his gospel with theirs, we may observe, 1. That he *relates* what they had *omitted;* he *brings up the rear,* and his gospel is as the *rearward* or *gathering host;* it gleans up what they has passed by. Thus there was a *later* collection of Solomon's wise sayings (Prov. 25:1), and yet far short of what he delivered, 1 Ki. 4:32. 2. That he gives us more of the *mystery* of that of which the other evangelists gave us only the *history.* It was necessary that the matters of fact should be first settled, which was done in their *declarations of those things which Jesus began both to do and teach,* Lu. 1:1; Acts 1:1. But, this being done out of the mouth of two or three witnesses, *John goes on to perfection* (Heb. 6:1), *not laying again the foundation,* but building upon it, leading us more within the veil. Some of the ancients observe that the other evangelists wrote more of the *ta sōmatika* — the *bodily* things of Christ; but John writes of the *ta pneumatika* — the *spiritual* things of the gospel, the life and soul of it; therefore some have called this gospel the *key of the evangelists.* Here is it that a *door* is *opened in heaven,* and the first voice we hear is, *Come up hither,* come up higher. Some of the ancients, that supposed the four living creatures in John's vision to represent the for evangelists, make John himself to be the *flying eagle,* so *high* does he *soar,* and *so clearly* does he *see* into divine and heavenly things.

CHAPTER 1

The scope and design of this chapter is to confirm our faith in Christ as the eternal Son of God, and the true Messiah and Saviour of the world, that we may be brought to receive him, and rely upon him, as our Prophet, Priest, and King, and to give up ourselves to be ruled, and taught, and saved by him. In order to this, we have here, I. An account given of him by the inspired penman himself, fairly laying down, in the beginning, what he designed his whole book should be the proof of (*v.* 1–5); and again (*v.* 10–14); and again, (*v.* 16–18). II. The testimony of John Baptist concerning him (*v.* 6–9, and *v.* 15); but most fully and particularly (*v.* 19–37). III. His own manifestation of himself to Andrew and Peter (*v.* 38–42), to Philip and Nathanael (*v.* 43–51).

Verses 1–5

Austin says (*de Civitate Dei,* lib. 10, cap. 29) that his friend Simplicius told him he had heard a Platonic philosopher say that these first verses of St. John's gospel were *worthy to be written in letters of gold.* The learned Francis Junius, in the account he gives of his own life, tells how he was in his youth infected with loose notions in religion, and by the grace of God was wonderfully recovered by reading accidentally these verses in a bible which his father had designedly laid in his way. He says that he observed such a divinity in the argument, such an authority and majesty in the style, that his flesh trembled, and he was struck with such amazement that for a whole day he scarcely knew where he was or what he did; and thence he dates the beginning of his being religious. Let us enquire what there is in those strong lines. The evangelist here lays down the great truth he is to prove, that Jesus Christ is God, one with the Father. Observe,

I. Of whom he speaks — *The Word — ho logos.* This is an idiom peculiar to John's writings. See 1 Jn. 1:1; 5:7; Rev. 19:13. Yet some think that Christ is meant by *the Word* in Acts 20:32; Heb. 4:12; Lu. 1:2. The Chaldee paraphrase very frequently calls the Messiah *Memra — the Word of Jehovah,* and speaks of many things in the Old Testament, said to be done by *the Lord,* as done by that *Word of the Lord.* Even the vulgar Jews were taught that the *Word of God* was the same with God. The evangelist, in the close of his discourse (*v.* 18), plainly tells us why he calls Christ *the Word — because he is the only begotten Son, who is in the bosom of the Father, and has declared him. Word* is two-fold: *logos endiathetos — word conceived;* and *logos prophorikos — word uttered.* The *logos ho esō* and *ho exō, ratio* and *oratio — intelligence* and *utterance.* 1. There is the *word conceived,* that is, *thought,* which is the first and only immediate product and conception of the soul (all the operations of which are performed by *thought*), and it is one with the soul. And thus the second person in the Trinity is fitly called *the Word;* for he is the *first-begotten of the Father,* that eternal essential Wisdom which *the Lord possessed,* as the soul does its thought, *in the beginning of his way,* Prov. 8:22. There is nothing we are more sure of than *that we think,* yet nothing we are more in the dark about than *how we think;* who can declare the generation of *thought* in the soul? Surely then the generations and births of the eternal mind may well be allowed to be great mysteries of godliness, the bottom of which we cannot fathom, while yet we adore the depth. 2. There is the *word uttered,* and this is *speech,* the chief and most natural indication of the mind. And thus Christ is *the Word,* for *by him* God has in *these last days spoken to us* (Heb. 1:2), and has directed us to *hear him,* Mt. 17:5. He has made known God's mind to us, as a man's word or speech makes known his thoughts, as far as he pleases, and no further. Christ is called that *wonderful speaker* (see notes on Dan. 8:13), the *speaker of things hidden* and *strange.* He is *the Word* speaking *from* God to us, and *to God* for us. John Baptist was *the voice,* but Christ *the Word:* being *the Word,* he is *the Truth,* the *Amen,* the *faithful Witness* of the mind of God.

II. What he saith of him, enough to prove beyond contradiction that *he is God.* He asserts,

1. His existence in the beginning: *In the beginning was the Word.* This bespeaks his existence, not only before his incarnation, but before all time. The beginning of time, in which all creatures were produced and brought into being, found this eternal Word in being. The world was *from* the beginning, but the Word was *in* the beginning. Eternity is usually expressed by being *before the foundation of the world.* The eternity of God is so described (Ps. 90:2), *Before the mountains were brought forth.* So Prov. 8:23. The Word had a being before the world had a beginning. He that *was* in the beginning *never* began, and therefore was *ever, achronos — without beginning of time.* So Nonnus.

2. His co-existence with the Father: *The Word was with God, and the Word was God.* Let none say that when we invite them to Christ we would draw them from God, for Christ is *with God* and *is God;* it is repeated in *v.* 2: *the same,* the very same that we believe in and preach, was *in the beginning with God,* that is, he was so from eternity. In the beginning the world was *from God,* as it was created by him; but the Word was *with God,* as ever with him. The Word was with God, (1.) In respect of *essence* and *substance;* for *the Word was God:* a distinct person or substance, for he was *with God;* and yet the same in substance, for he *was God,* Heb. 1:3. (2.) In respect of *complacency* and *felicity.* There was a

glory and happiness which Christ had *with God* before the world was (*ch.* 17:5), the Son infinitely happy in the enjoyment of his Father's bosom, and no less the Father's delight, the Son of his love, Prov. 8:30. (3.) In respect of *counsel* and *design.* The mystery of man's redemption by this Word incarnate was *hid in God* before all worlds, Eph. 3:9. He that undertook to *bring us to God* (1 Pt. 3:18) was himself from eternity *with God;* so that this grand affair of man's reconciliation to God was concerted between the Father and Son from eternity, and they understand one another perfectly well in it, Zec. 6:13; Mt. 11:27. He was *by him as one brought up with him* for this service, Prov. 8:30. He was *with God,* and therefore is said to *come forth from the Father.*

3. His agency in making the world, *v.* 3. This is here, (1.) Expressly asserted: *All things were made by him.* He was *with God,* not only so as to be *acquainted* with the divine counsels from eternity, but to be *active* in the divine operations in the beginning of time. *Then was I by him,* Prov. 8:30. God made the world *by a word* (Ps. 33:6) and Christ was *the Word.* By him, not as a subordinate instrument, but as a co-ordinate agent, God *made the world* (Heb. 1:2), not as the workman cuts by his axe, but as the body sees by the eye. (2.) The contrary is denied: *Without him was not any thing made that was made,* from the highest angel to the meanest worm. God the Father did nothing without him in that work. Now, [1.] This proves that *he is God;* for he that *built all things is God,* Heb. 3:4. The God of Israel often proved himself to be God with this, that he *made all things:* Isa. 40:12, 28; 41:4; and see Jer. 10:11, 12. [2.] This proves the excellency of the Christian religion, that the author and founder of it is the same that was the author and founder of the world. How excellent must that constitution needs be which derives its institution from him who is the fountain of all excellency! When we worship Christ, we worship him to whom the patriarchs gave honour as the Creator of the world, and on whom all creatures depend. [3.] This shows how well qualified he was for the work of our redemption and salvation. Help was laid upon one that was mighty indeed; for it was laid upon him that made all things; and he is appointed the author of our bliss who was the author of our being.

4. The original of life and light that is in him: *In him was life, v.* 4. This further proves that he is God, and every way qualified for his undertaking; for, (1.) He has *life in himself;* not only the *true God,* but the *living God.* God is life; he swears by himself when he saith, *As I live.* (2.) All living creatures have their life in him; not only all the *matter* of the creation was *made* by him, but all the *life* too that is in the creation is derived from him and supported by him. It was the Word of God that produced the *moving creatures that had life,* Gen. 1:20; Acts 17:25. He is that Word by which man lives more than by bread, Mt. 4:4. (3.) Reasonable creatures have their *light* from him; that *life* which is *the light of men* comes from him. Life in man is something greater and nobler than it is in other creatures; it is *rational,* and not merely *animal.* When man became a *living soul,* his life was *light,* his capacities such as distinguished him from, and dignified him above, the beasts that perish. The *spirit of a man is the candle of the Lord,* and it was the eternal Word that lighted this candle. The light of reason, as well as the life of sense, is derived from him, and depends upon him. This proves him fit to undertake our salvation; for life and light, spiritual and eternal life and light, are the two great things that fallen man, who lies so much under the power of *death* and *darkness,* has need of. From whom may we better expect the light of divine revelation than from him who gave us the light of human reason? And if, when God gave us natural life, that life was in his Son, how readily should we receive the gospel-record, that he hath given us *eternal* life, and *that life* too *is in his Son!*

5. The manifestation of him to the children of men. It might be objected, If this eternal Word was all in all thus in the creation of the world, whence is it that he has been so little taken notice of and regarded? To this he answers (*v.* 5), *The light shines, but the darkness comprehends it not.* Observe,

(1.) The discovery of the eternal Word to the lapsed world, even before he was manifested in the flesh: *The light shineth in darkness.* Light is self-evidencing, and will make itself known; this light, whence the light of men comes, hath shone, and doth shine. [1.] The eternal Word, *as God,* shines in *the darkness* of *natural conscience.* Though men by the fall are become *darkness,* yet that which may be known of God is manifested in them; see Rom. 1:19, 20. The light of nature is this light shining in darkness. Something of the power of the divine Word, both as *creating* and as *commanding,* all mankind have an innate sense of; were it not for this, earth would be a hell, a place of *utter darkness;* blessed be God, it is not so yet. [2.] The eternal Word, as Mediator, shone in the darkness of the Old-Testament types and figures, and the prophecies and promises which were of the Messiah from the beginning. He that had commanded the light of this world to shine out of darkness was himself long a light *shining in darkness;* there was a *veil* upon this *light,* 2 Co. 3:13.

(2.) The disability of the degenerate world to receive this discovery: *The darkness comprehended it not;* the most of men received the grace of God in these discoveries in vain. [1.] The world of mankind *comprehended not* the natural light that was in their understandings, but became *vain in their imaginations* concerning the eternal God and the eternal Word, Rom. 1:21, 28. The darkness of error and sin overpowered and quite eclipsed this light. God *spoke once, yea twice,* but *man perceived it not,* Job 33:14. [2.] The Jews, who had the light of the Old Testament, yet comprehended not Christ in it. As there was a veil upon Moses's face, so there was upon the people's hearts. In the *darkness* of the types and shadows the light shone; but such as the *darkness* of their understandings that they could not *see* it. It was therefore requisite that Christ should come, both to rectify the errors of the Gentile world and to improve the truths of the Jewish church.

Verses 6–14

The evangelist designs to bring in John Baptist bearing an honourable testimony to Jesus Christ, Now in these verses, before he does this,

I. He gives us some account of the witness he is about to produce. His name was *John,* which signifies *gracious;* his conversation was austere, but he was not the less *gracious.* Now,

1. We are here told concerning him, in general, that he was a *man sent of God.* The evangelist had said concerning Jesus Christ that he was *with God* and that he *was God;* but here concerning John that he was a *man,* a mere man. God is pleased to speak to us by men like ourselves. John was a *great man,* but he was a man, a son of man; he was *sent from God,* he was God's *messenger,* so he is called, Mal. 3:1. God gave him both his mission and his message, both his credentials and his instructions. John wrought no miracle, nor do we find that he had visions and revelations; but the strictness and purity of his life and doctrine, and the direct tendency of both to reform the world, and to revive the interests of God's kingdom among men, were plain indications that he was *sent of God.*

2. We are here told what his office and business were (*v.* 7): *The same came for a witness,* an eye-witness, a leading witness. He came *eis martyrian — for a testimony.* The legal institutions had been long a testimony for God in the Jewish church. By them revealed religion was kept up; hence we read of the *tabernacle of the testimony, the ark of the testimony, the law and the testimony:* but now divine revelation is to be turned into another channel; now the testimony of Christ is the testimony of God, 1 Co. 1:6; 2:1. Among the Gentiles, God indeed had not left himself without witness (Acts 14:17), but the Redeemer had no testimonies borne him among them. There was a profound silence concerning him, till John Baptist came for a witness to him. Now observe, (1.) The matter of his testimony: *He came to bear witness to the light.* Light is a thing which witnesses for itself, and carries its own evidence along with it; but to those who shut their eyes against the light it is necessary there should be those that bear witness to it. Christ's light needs not man's testimony, but the world's darkness does. John was like the night watchman that goes round the town, proclaiming the approach of the morning light to those that have closed their eyes, and are not willing themselves to observe it; or like that watchman that was set to tell those who asked him what of the night that *the morning comes,* and, *if you will enquire, enquire ye,* Isa. 21:11, 12. He was sent of God to tell the world that the long-looked-for Messiah was now come, who should be *a light to enlighten the Gentiles and the glory of his people Israel;* and to proclaim that dispensation at hand which would bring life and immortality to light. (2.) The design of his testimony: *That all men through him might believe;* not in him, but in Christ, whose way he was sent to prepare. He taught men to look through him, and pass through him, to Christ; through the doctrine of repentance for sin to that of faith in Christ. He prepared men for the reception and entertainment of Christ and his gospel, by awakening them to a sight and sense of sin; and that, their eyes being thereby opened, they might be ready to admit those beams of divine light which, in the person and doctrine of the Messiah, were now ready to shine in their faces. If they would but receive this witness of man, they would soon find that the witness of God was greater, 1 Jn. 5:9. See *ch.* 10:41. Observe, it was designed that all men through him might believe, excluding none from the kind and beneficial influences of his ministry that did not exclude themselves, as multitudes did, who rejected the counsel of God against themselves, and so received the grace of God in vain.

3. We are here cautioned not to mistake him for the light who only came to bear witness to it (*v.* 8): *He was not that light* that was expected and promised, but only was sent to bear witness of that great and ruling light. He was a star, like that which guided the wise men to Christ, a morning star; but he was not the Sun; not the Bridegroom, but a friend of the Bridegroom; not the Prince, but his harbinger. There were those who rested in John's baptism, and looked no further, as those Ephesians, Acts 19:3. To rectify this mistake, the evangelist here, when he speaks very honourably of him, yet shows that he must give place to Christ. He was great as the prophet of the Highest, but not the Highest himself. Note, We must take heed of over-valuing ministers, as well as of under-valuing them; they are not our lords, nor have they dominion over our faith, but ministers by whom we believe, stewards of our Lord's house. We must not give up ourselves by an implicit faith to their conduct, for they are not that light; but we must attend to, and receive, their testimony; for they are sent to bear witness of that light; so then let us esteem them, and not otherwise. Had John pretended to be that light he had not been so much as a faithful witness of that light. Those who usurp the honour of Christ forfeit the honour of being the servants of Christ; yet John was very serviceable as a witness to the light, though he was not that light. Those may be of great use to us who yet shine with a borrowed light.

II. Before he goes on with John's testimony, he returns to give us a further account of this Jesus to whom John bore record. Having shown in the beginning of the chapter the glories of his Godhead, he here comes to show the graces of his incarnation, and his favours to man as Mediator.

1. Christ was the *true Light* (*v.* 9); not as if John Baptist were a false light, but, in comparison with Christ, he was a very small light. Christ is the great light that deserves to be called so. Other lights are but figuratively and equivocally called so: Christ is the true light. The fountain of all knowledge and of all comfort must needs be the true light. He is the true light, for proof of which we are not referred to the emanations of his glory in the invisible world (the beams with which he enlightens that), but to those rays of his light which are darted downwards, and with which this dark world of ours is enlightened. But how does Christ enlighten every man that comes into the world? (1.) By his creating power he enlightens every man with the light of reason; that life which is the light of men is from him; all the discoveries and directions of reason, all the comfort it gives us, and all the beauty it puts upon us, are from Christ. (2.) By the publication of his gospel to all nations he does in effect enlighten every man. John Baptist was a light, but he enlightened only Jerusalem and Judea, and the region round about Jordan, like a candle that enlightens one room; but Christ is the true light, for he is a light to enlighten the Gentiles. His everlasting gospel is to be preached to every nation and language, Rev. 14:6. Like the sun which enlightens every man that will open his eyes, and receive its light (Ps. 19:6), to which the preaching of the gospel is compared. See Rom. 10:18. Divine revelation is not now to be confined, as it had been, to one people, but to be diffused to all people, Mt. 5:15. (3.) By the operation of his Spirit and grace he enlightens all those that are enlightened to salvation; and those that are not enlightened by him perish in darkness. *The light of the knowledge of the glory of God* is said to be *in the face of Jesus Christ,* and is compared with that light which was at the beginning commanded to shine out of darkness, and which enlightens every man that comes into the world. Whatever light any man has, he is indebted to Christ for it, whether it be natural or supernatural.

2. Christ *was in the world, v.* 10. He was in the world, as the essential Word, before his incarnation, upholding all

things; but this speaks of his being in the world when he took our nature upon him, and dwelt among us; see *ch.* 16:28. *I am come into the world.* The Son of the Highest was here in this *lower* world; that *light* in this *dark* world; that *holy thing* in this sinful polluted world. He left a world of bliss and glory, and was here in this melancholy miserable world. He undertook to reconcile the world to God, and therefore was *in the world,* to treat about it, and settle that affair; to satisfy God's justice for the world, and discover God's favour to the world. He was in the world, but not of it, and speaks with an air of triumph when he can say, *Now I am no more in it, ch.* 17:11. The greatest honour that ever was put upon this world, which is so mean and inconsiderable a part of the universe, was that the Son of God was once *in the world;* and, as it should engage our affections to things above that there Christ is, so it should reconcile us to our present abode in *this* world that once Christ was *here.* He *was* in the world for awhile, but it is spoken of as a thing past; and so it will be said of us shortly, We were in the world. O that when we are here no more we may be where Christ is! Now observe here, (1.) What reason Christ had to expect the most affectionate and respectful welcome possible in this world; for *the world was made by him. Therefore* he came to save a lost world because it was a world of his own making. Why should he not concern himself to revive the light that was of his own kindling, to restore a life of his own infusing, and to renew the image that was originally of his own impressing? The world was *made by him,* and therefore ought to do him homage. (2.) What cold entertainment he met with, notwithstanding: *The world knew him not.* The great Maker, Ruler, and Redeemer of the world was in it, and few or none of the inhabitants of the world were aware of it. The *ox knows his owner,* but the more brutish world did not. They did not own him, did not bid him welcome, because they did not *know him;* and they did not know him because he did not make himself known in the way that they expected — in external glory and majesty. His kingdom came not *with observation,* because it was to be a kingdom of trail and probation. When he shall come as a Judge the world shall *know* him.

3. He *came to his own* (*v.* 11); not only to the world, which was *his own,* but to the people of Israel, that were peculiarly *his own* above all people; of them he came, among them he lived, and to them he was *first sent.* The Jews were at this time a mean despicable people; *the crown was fallen from their head;* yet, in remembrance of the ancient covenant, bad as they were, and poor as they were, Christ was not ashamed to look upon them as his own. *Ta idia* — his own *things;* not *tous idious* — his own *persons,* as *true believers* are called, *ch.* 13:1. The Jews were *his,* as a man's house, and lands, and goods are *his,* which he uses and possesses; but believers are his as a man's wife and children are his own, which he loves and enjoys. He came to his own, to seek and save them, because they were *his own.* He was sent to the lost sheep of the house of Israel, for it was he whose own the sheep were. Now observe,

(1.) That the generality *rejected* him: *His own received him not.* He had reason to expect that those who were his own should have bidden him welcome, considering how great the *obligations* were which they *lay under* to him, and how fair the *opportunities* were which they had of coming to the knowledge of him. They had the oracles of God, which told them beforehand *when* and *where* to expect him, and of what tribe and family he should arise. He came among them himself, introduced with signs and wonders, and himself the greatest; and therefore it is not said of them, as it was of the world (*v.* 10), that they *knew him not;* but *his own,* though they could not but know him, yet *received him not;* did not receive his doctrine, did not welcome him as the Messiah, but fortified themselves against him. The *chief priests,* that were in a particular manner *his own* (for the Levites were God's tribe), were ring-leaders in this contempt put upon him. Now this was very *unjust,* because they were *his own,* and therefore he might *command* their respect; and it was very *unkind* and *ungrateful,* because he came to them, to seek and save them, and so to *court* their respect. Note, Many who in profession are *Christ's own,* yet do not *receive him,* because they will not part with their sins, nor have him to *reign over them.*

(2.) That yet there was a remnant who *owned* him, and were faithful to him. Though his own received him not, yet there were those that *received* him (*v.* 12): *But as many as received him. Though Israel were not gathered,* yet Christ was *glorious.* Though the body of that nation persisted and perished in unbelief, yet there were many of *them* that were wrought upon to submit to Christ, and many more that *were not of that fold.* Observe here,

[1.] The true Christian's *description* and *property;* and that is, that he *receives Christ,* and *believes on his name;* the latter explains the former. Note, *First,* To be a Christian indeed is to *believe on Christ's name;* it is to *assent* to the gospel discovery, and *consent* to the gospel proposal, concerning him. His name is *the Word of God; the King of kings, the Lord our righteousness; Jesus a Saviour.* Now to *believe* on his name is to *acknowledge* that he is what these great names bespeak him to be, and to *acquiesce* in it, that he may be so *to us. Secondly,* Believing in Christ's name is *receiving* him as a gift from God. We must receive his doctrine as true and good; receive his law as just and holy; receive his offers as kind and advantageous; and we must receive the image of his grace, and impressions of his love, as the governing principle of our affections and actions.

[2.] The true Christian's dignity and privilege are twofold:—

First, The *privilege of adoption,* which takes them into the number of God's children: *To them gave he power to become the sons of God.* Hitherto, the adoption pertained to the Jews only *(Israel is my son, my first-born);* but now, by faith in Christ, Gentiles are the *children of God,* Gal. 3:26. They have *power, exousian — authority;* for no man taketh this power to himself, but he who is *authorized* by the gospel charter. To them gave he a *right;* to them gave he this pre-eminence. *This power have all the saints.* Note, 1. It is the unspeakable privilege of all good Christians, that they are become the *children of God.* They were by nature children of wrath, children of this world. If they be the *children of God,* they *become* so, are *made* so *Fiunt, non nascuntur Christiani — Persons are not born Christians, but made such.* — Tertullian. *Behold what manner of love is this,* 1 Jn. 3:1. God calls them *his children,* they call him *Father,* and are entitled to all the privileges of children, those of their way and those of their home. 2. The privilege of adoption is entirely owing to *Jesus Christ;* he *gave* this power to them that believe on his name. God is his Father, and so ours; and it is by virtue of our espousals to him, and union with him, that we stand related to God as a Father. It was in Christ that we were *predestinated to the adoption;* from him we receive both the character and the Spirit of adoption, and he is the *first-born among many brethren.* The Son of God became a Son of man, that the sons and daughters of men might become the sons and daughters of God Almighty.

Secondly, The *privilege of regeneration* (*v.* 13): *Which were born.* Note, All the children of God are born again; all that are adopted are regenerated. This *real* change evermore attends that *relative* one. Wherever God confers the dignity of children, he creates the nature and disposition of children. Men cannot do so when they adopt. Now here we have an account of the original of this new birth. 1. Negatively. (1.) It is not *propagated* by natural generation from our parents. It is *not of blood, nor of the will of the flesh,* nor of *corruptible seed,* 1 Pt. 1:23. Man is called *flesh and blood,* because thence he has his original: but we do not become the children of God as we become the children of our natural parents. Note, Grace does not run in the blood, as corruption does. Man polluted *begat a son in his own likeness* (Gen. 5:3); but man sanctified and renewed does not beget a son in *that* likeness. The Jews gloried much in their parentage, and the noble blood that ran in their veins: *We are Abraham's seed;* and *therefore* to them *pertained the adoption* because they were born of that blood; but this New-Testament adoption is not founded in any such natural relation. (2.) It is not *produced* by the natural power of our own will. As it is not of *blood,* nor of *the will of the flesh,* so neither is it of the *will of man,* which labours under a moral impotency of determining itself to that which is good; so that the principles of the divine life are not of our own planting, it is the grace of God that makes us willing to be *his.* Nor can human laws or writings prevail to sanctify and regenerate a soul; if they could, the new birth would be by the will of man. But, 2. Positively: it is of *God.* This new birth is owing to the word of God as the means (1 Pt. 1:23), and to the Spirit of God as the great and sole author. True believers are *born of God,* 1 Jn. 3:9; 5:1. And this is necessary to their adoption; for we cannot expect the *love of God* if we have not something of his *likeness,* nor claim the privileges of adoption if we be not under the power of regeneration.

4. The *word was made flesh, v.* 14. This expresses Christ's incarnation more clearly than what went before. By his divine presence he always *was in the world,* and by his prophets he *came to his own.* But now that the fulness of time was come he was sent forth after another manner, *made of a woman* (Gal. 4:4); God manifested in the flesh, according to the faith and hope of holy Job; *Yet shall I see God in my flesh,* Job 19:26. Observe here,

(1.) The *human nature of Christ* with which he was veiled; and that expressed two ways.

[1.] *The word was made flesh. Forasmuch as the children,* who were to become the sons of God, *were partakers of flesh and blood, he also himself likewise took part of the same,* Heb. 2:14. The Socinians agree that Christ is both God and man, but they say that he *was man,* and was *made a God,* as Moses (Ex. 7:1), directly contrary to John here, who saith, *Theos ēn — He was God,* but *sarxegeneto — He was made flesh.* Compare *v.* 1 with this. This intimates not only that he was really and truly man, but that he subjected himself to the miseries and calamities of the human nature. He was made *flesh,* the meanest part of man. Flesh bespeaks man *weak,* and he was crucified through *weakness,* 2 Co. 13:4. *Flesh* bespeaks man *mortal* and *dying* (Ps. 78:39), and Christ was *put to death in the flesh* 1 Pt. 3:18. Nay, *flesh* bespeaks *man tainted with sin* (Gen. 6:3), and Christ, though he was perfectly holy and harmless, yet appeared *in the likeness of sinful flesh* (Rom. 8:3), and was made *sin for us,* 2 Co. 5:21. When Adam had sinned, God said to him, *Dust thou art;* not only because made out of the dust, but because by sin he was sunk into dust. His fall did, *sōmatoun tēn psychēn, turn him* as it were *all into body,* made him earthly; therefore he that was made a curse for us was made *flesh,* and *condemned sin in the flesh,* Rom. 8:3. Wonder at this, that the eternal Word should be made flesh, when flesh was come into such an ill name; that he who made *all things* should himself be made flesh, one of the meanest things, and submit to that from which he was at the greatest distance. The voice that ushered in the gospel cried, *All flesh is grass* (Isa. 40:6), to make the Redeemer's love the more wonderful, who, to *redeem* and *save* us, was made flesh, and withered as grass; but the *Word of the Lord,* who was made flesh, *endures for ever;* when made flesh, he ceased not to be the Word of God.

[2.] He *dwelt among us,* here in this lower world. Having taken upon him the nature of man, he put himself into the place and condition of other men. The Word might have been made flesh, and dwelt among the angels; but, having taken a *body* of the same mould with ours, in it he came, and resided in the same world with us. He *dwelt among us,* us worms of the earth, us that he had no need of, us that he got nothing by, us that were *corrupt* and *depraved,* and revolted from God. The Lord God came and dwelt even *among the rebellious,* Ps. 68:18. He that had dwelt among angels, those noble and excellent beings, came and dwelt *among us* that are a *generation of vipers,* us *sinners,* which was worse to him than David's swelling in Mesech and Kedar, or Ezekiel's dwelling *among scorpions,* or the church of Pergamus dwelling *where Satan's seat is.* When we look upon the upper world, the world of spirits, how mean and contemptible does this flesh, this body, appear, which we carry about with us, and this world in which our lot is cast, and how hard is it to a contemplative mind to be reconciled to them! But that the eternal Word was *made flesh,* was clothed with a body as we are, and dwelt in this world as we do, this has put an honour upon them both, and should make us willing to abide in the flesh while God has any work for us to do; for Christ dwelt in this lower world, bad as it is, till he had finished what he had to do here, *ch.* 17:4. He dwelt *among* the Jews, that the scripture might be fulfilled, *He shall dwell in the tents of Shem,* Gen. 9:27. And see Zec. 2:10. Though the Jews were unkind to him, yet he continued to dwell among them; though (as some of the ancient writers tell us) he was invited to better treatment by Abgarus king of Edessa, yet he removed not to any other nation. He *dwelt* among us. He was in the world, not as a wayfaring man that tarries but for a night, but he *dwelt* among us, made a long residence, the original word is observable, *eskēnōsen en hēmin — he dwelt among us,* he dwelt *as in a tabernacle,* which intimates, *First,* That he dwelt here in very *mean* circumstances, as shepherds that dwell in tents. He did not dwell among us *as in a palace,* but as in a *tent;* for he had not where to lay his head, and was always upon the remove. *Secondly,* That his state here was a *military* state. Soldiers *dwell in tents;* he had long since proclaimed war with the *seed of the serpent,* and now he takes *the field* in person, sets up his standard, and pitches his tent, to prosecute this war. *Thirdly,* That his stay among us was not to be perpetual. He dwelt here as *in a tent,* not as at *home.* The patriarchs, by dwelling in tabernacles, *confessed that they were strangers and pilgrims on earth,* and sought the better country, and so did Christ, leaving us an example, Heb. 13:13, 14. *Fourthly,* That as of old God dwelt in the tabernacle of Moses, by the shechinah between the cherubim, so now he dwells in the human nature of Christ; that is now the true shechinah, the symbol of God's peculiar presence. And we are to make all our addresses to God through Christ, and from him to receive divine oracles.

(2.) The *beams of his divine glory* that *darted* through this *veil of flesh: We beheld his glory, the glory as of the only begotten of the Father, full of grace and truth.* The sun is still the fountain of light, though eclipsed or clouded; so Christ was still the brightness of his Father's glory, even when he *dwelt among us* in this lower world. And how slightly soever the Jews thought of him there were those that saw through the veil. Observe,

[1.] Who were the witnesses of this glory: *we,* his disciples and followers, that conversed most freely and familiarly with him; we among whom he *dwelt.* Other men discover their weaknesses to those that are most familiar with them, but it was not so with Christ; those that were most intimate with him saw most of his glory. As it was with his *doctrine,* the disciples knew the mysteries of it, while others had it *under the veil of parables;* so it was with his *person,* they saw the glory of his divinity, while others saw only the veil of his human nature. He manifested himself *to them, and not unto the world.* These witnesses were a competent number, twelve of them, a whole jury of witnesses; men of plainness and integrity, and far from any thing of design or intrigue.

[2.] What evidence they had of it: *We saw it.* They had not their evidence by report, at second hand, but were themselves eye-witnesses of those proofs on which they built their testimony that he was the *Son of the living God: We saw it.* The word signifies a fixed abiding sight, such as gave them an opportunity of making their observations. This apostle himself explains this: *What we declare unto you* of the Word of life is what we have *seen with our eyes,* and what *we have looked upon,* 1 Jn. 1:1.

[3.] What the glory was: *The glory as of the only begotten of the Father.* The glory of the *Word made flesh* was such a glory as became the only *begotten Son of God,* and could not be the glory of any other. Note, *First,* Jesus Christ is the only begotten of the Father. Believers are the children of God by the special favour of adoption and the special grace of regeneration. They are in a sense ***homoiousioi*** *— of a like nature* (2 Pt. 1:4), and have the image of his perfections; but Christ is ***homousios*** *— of the same nature,* and is the express image of his person, and the Son of God by an eternal generation. Angels are sons of God, but he never said to any of them, *This day have I begotten thee,* Heb. 1:5. *Secondly,* He was evidently declared to be the only begotten of the Father, by that which was seen of his glory when he dwelt among us. Though he was in the *form of a servant,* in respect of outward circumstances, yet, in respect of graces, his form was as that of the *fourth* in the fiery furnace, *like the Son of God.* His divine glory appeared in the holiness and heavenliness of his doctrine; in his miracles, which extorted from many this acknowledgment, that he was the *Son of God;* it appeared in the purity, goodness, and beneficence, of his whole conversation. God's goodness is his glory, and he went about doing good; he spoke and acted in every thing as an incarnate Deity. Perhaps the evangelist had a particular regard to the glory of his *transfiguration,* of which he was an eye-witness; see 2 Pt. 1:16–18. God's calling him his *beloved Son, in whom he was well pleased,* intimated that he was the *only begotten of the Father;* but the full proof of this was at his resurrection.

[4.] What advantage those he dwelt among had from this. He dwelt among them, *full of grace and truth.* In the old tabernacle wherein God dwelt was the *law,* in *this* was grace; in that were *types,* in this was *truth.* The incarnate Word was every way qualified for his undertaking as Mediator; for he was *full of grace and truth,* the two great things that fallen man stands in need of; and this proved him to be the *Son of God* as much as the divine power and majesty that appeared in him. *First,* He has a fulness of grace and truth *for himself;* he had the Spirit without measure. He was full *of grace,* fully acceptable to his Father, and therefore qualified to intercede for us; and full *of truth,* fully apprized of the things he was to reveal, and therefore fit to instruct us. He had a fulness of knowledge and a fulness of compassion. *Secondly,* He has a fulness of grace and truth *for us.* He *received,* that he might *give,* and God was well pleased in him, that he might be well pleased with us in him; and this was the *truth* of the legal *types.*

Verses 15–18

In these verses,

I. The evangelist begins again to give us John Baptist's testimony concerning Christ, *v.* 15. He had said (*v.* 8) that he *came for a witness;* now here he tells us that he did accordingly *bear witness.* Here, Observe,

1. *How he expressed* his testimony: He *cried,* according to the prediction that he should be *the voice of one crying.* The Old-Testament prophets cried aloud, to show people their *sins;* this New-Testament prophet cried aloud, to show people their *Saviour.* This intimates, (1.) That it was an open *public* testimony, proclaimed, that all manner of persons might take notice of it, for all are concerned in it. False teachers *entice secretly,* but wisdom publishes her dictates in the chief places of concourse. (2.) That he was free and hearty in bearing this testimony. He *cried* as one that was both *well assured* of the truth to which he witnessed and *well affected* to it. He that had leaped in his *mother's womb for joy* of Christ's approach, when newly conceived, does now with a like exultation of spirit *welcome* his public appearance.

2. What his *testimony* was. He appeals to what he had said at the beginning of his ministry, when he had directed them to expect one that should *come after him,* whose forerunner he was, and never intended any other than to lead them to him, and to prepare his way. This he had given them notice of from the first. Note, It is very comfortable to a minister to have the testimony of his conscience for him that he set out in his ministry with honest principles and sincere intentions, with a single eye to the glory and honour of Christ. Now what he had then said he applies to this Jesus whom he had lately baptized, and who was so remarkably owned from heaven: *This was he of whom I spoke.* John did not tell them that there would shortly appear such a one among them, and then leave them to find him out; but in *this* he went beyond all the Old-Testament prophets that he particularly specified the person: "*This was he,* the very man I told you of, and to him all I said is to be accommodated." Now what was it he said?

(1.) He had given the preference to this Jesus: *He that comes after me,* in the time of his birth and public appearance, is preferred before me; he that *succeeds* me in preaching and making disciples is a more excellent person, upon all accounts; as the prince or peer that *comes after* is preferred before the harbinger or gentleman-usher that makes way for him. Note, Jesus Christ, who was to be called the *Son of the Highest* (Lu. 1:32), was preferred before John Baptist, who was to be called only the *prophet of the Highest,* Lu. 1:76. John was a minister of the New Testament, but Christ was the Mediator of the New Testament. And observe, though John was a great man, and had a great name and interest, yet he was forward to give the preference to him to whom it belonged. Note, All the ministers of Christ must prefer him and his interest before themselves and their own interests; they will make an ill account *that seek their own things, not the things of Christ,* Phil. 2:21. He comes *after me,* and yet is *preferred before me.* Note, God dispenses his gifts according to his good pleasure, and many times crosses hands, as Jacob did, preferring the *younger* before the *elder.* Paul far outstripped those that were in Christ before him.

(2.) He here gives a good reason for it: *For he was before me, prōtos mou ēn — He was my first,* or *first to me;* he was my first Cause, my original. The *First* is one of *God's names,* Isa. 44:6. He is *before me,* is *my first,* [1.] In respect of *seniority:* he was *before me,* for he was before Abraham, *ch.* 8:58. Nay, he was *before all things,* Col. 1:17. I am but of yesterday, he from eternity. It was but in *those days* that John Baptist came (Mt. 3:1), but the goings forth of our Lord Jesus *were of old, from everlasting,* Mic. 5:2. This proves two natures in Christ. Christ, as man, *came after* John as to his public appearance; Christ, as God, was *before him;* and how could he otherwise be before him but by an eternal existence? [2.] In respect of supremacy; for he was *my prince;* so some princes are called the *first; prōton,* "It is he for whose sake and service I am sent: he is my Master, I am his minister and messenger."

II. He presently returns again to speak of Jesus Christ, and cannot go on with John Baptist's testimony till *v.* 19. The 16th verse has a manifest connection with *v.* 14, where the incarnate Word was said to be *full of grace and truth.* Now here he makes this the matter, not only of our adoration, but of our thankfulness, because *from that fulness* of his *we all have received. He received gifts for men* (Ps. 68:18), that he might *give gifts to men,* Eph. 4:8. He was filled, that he might *fill all in all* (Eph. 1:23), might *fill our treasures,* Prov. 8:21. He has a fountain of fulness overflowing: *We all have received. All we* apostles; so some. We have received the favour of this apostleship, that is *grace;* and a fitness for it, that is *truth.* Or, rather, *All we* believers; as many as received him (*v.* 16), received from him. Note, All true believers receive from Christ's fulness; the best and greatest saints cannot live without him, the meanest and weakest may live by him. This excludes proud boasting, that we have nothing but *we have received it;* and silences perplexing fears, that we want nothing but *we may receive it.* Let us see what it is that we have received.

1. We have received *grace for grace.* Our receivings by Christ are all summed up in this one word, *grace;* we have received ***kai charin*** *— even grace,* so great a gift, so rich, so invaluable; we have received *no less* than grace; this is a gift to be spoken of with an emphasis. It is repeated, *grace for grace;* for to every stone in this building, as well as *to the top-stone,* we must cry, *Grace, grace.* Observe,

(1.) The blessing received. It is *grace;* the good will of God towards us, and the good work of God in us. God's good will works the good work, and then the good work qualifies us for further tokens of his good will. As the cistern receives water from the fulness of the fountain, the branches sap from the fulness of the root, and the air light from the fulness of the sun, so we receive grace from the fulness of Christ.

(2.) The manner of its reception: *Grace for grace — charin anti charitos.* The phrase is singular, and interpreters put different senses upon it, each of which will be of use to illustrate the unsearchable riches of the grace of Christ. *Grace for grace* bespeaks, [1.] The *freeness* of this grace. It is grace for grace' sake; so *Grotius.* We receive grace, not for *our sakes* (be it known to us), but even so, Father, *because it seemed good in thy sight.* It is a *gift according to grace,* Rom. 12:6. It is grace *to us* for the sake of grace to Jesus Christ. God was well pleased in him, and is therefore well pleased with us in him, Eph. 1:6. [2.] The *fulness* of this grace. *Grace for grace* is abundance of grace, grace upon grace (so *Camero*), one grace heaped upon another; as *skin for skin* is skin after skin, even all that a man has, Job 2:4. It is a blessing poured out, that there shall not be room to receive it, *plenteous redemption:* one grace a pledge of more grace. *Joseph — He will add.* It is such a fulness as is called *the fulness of God* which we are filled with. We are not straitened in the grace of Christ, if we be not straitened in our own bosoms. [3.] The *serviceableness* of this grace. *Grace for grace* is grace for the promoting and advancing of grace. Grace to be *exercised* by ourselves; gracious habits for gracious acts. Grace to be *ministered* to others; gracious vouchsafements for gracious performances: grace is a talent to be traded with. The apostles received grace (Rom. 1:5; Eph. 3:8), that they might communicate it, 1 Pt. 4:10. [4.] The *substitution* of New-Testament grace *in the room and stead* of Old-Testament grace: so *Beza.* And this sense is confirmed by what follows (*v.* 17); for the Old Testament had grace in type, the New Testament has grace in truth. There was a grace under the Old Testament, the gospel was preached then (Gal. 3:8); but that grace is superseded, and we have gospel grace instead of it, a *glory which excelleth,* 2 Co. 3:10. Discoveries of grace are now more clear, distributions of grace far more plentiful; this is grace instead of grace. [5.] It bespeaks the *augmentation* and *continuance of grace. Grace for grace* is one grace to improve, confirm, and perfect another grace. We are changed into the divine image, *from glory to glory,* from one degree of glorious grace to another, 2 Co. 3:18. Those that have *true* grace have that for *more grace,* Jam. 4:6. When God gives grace he saith, Take this *in part;* for he who hath promised will perform. [6.] It bespeaks the *agreeableness* and *conformity* of grace in the saints to the grace that is in Jesus Christ; so Mr. *Clark. Grace for grace* is grace in us answering to grace in him, as the impression upon the wax answers the seal line for line. The grace we receive from Christ *changes us into the same image* (2 Co. 3:18), the *image of the Son* (Rom. 8:29), the *image of the heavenly,* 1 Co. 15:49.

2. We have received *grace and truth, v.* 17. He had said (*v.* 14) that Christ was *full of grace and truth;* now here he says that by him *grace and truth* came to us. From Christ we *receive grace;* this is a string he delights to harp upon, he cannot go off from it. Two things he further observes in this verse concerning this grace: — (1.) Its *preference* above the law of Moses: *The law was given by Moses,* and it was a glorious discovery, both of God's *will concerning* man and his *good will to* man; but the gospel of Christ is a much clearer discovery both of duty and happiness. That which was given by Moses was purely terrifying and threatening, and bound with penalties, a law which could not *give life, which was* given with abundance of terror (Heb. 12:18); but that which is given by Jesus Christ is of another nature; it has all the beneficial uses of the law, but not the terror, for it is *grace:* grace *teaching* (Tit. 2:11), grace *reigning,* Rom. 5:21. It is a law, but a remedial law. The endearments of love are the genius of the gospel, not the affrightments of law and the curse. (2.) Its *connection* with truth: *grace and truth.* In the gospel we have the discovery of the greatest *truths* to be embraced by the understanding, as well as of the richest *grace* to be embraced by the will and affections. It is a *faithful saying,* and *worthy of all acceptation;* that is, it is *grace and truth.* The offers of *grace* are *sincere,* and what we may venture our souls upon; they are made *in earnest,* for it is *grace and truth.* It is *grace and truth* with reference to the *law* that was *given by Moses.* For it is, [1.] The performance of all the Old-Testament promises. In the Old Testament we often find *mercy* and *truth* put together, that is, mercy according to promise; so here *grace and truth* denote grace according to promise. See Lu. 1:72; 1 Ki. 8:56. [2.] It is the substance of all the Old-Testament types and shadows. Something of grace there was both in the ordinances that were instituted for Israel and the providences that occurred concerning Israel; but they were only shadows of good things to come, even of the grace that is to be *brought to us by the revelation of Jesus Christ.* He is the *true* paschal lamb, the *true* scape-goat, the true *manna.* They had grace in the picture; we have grace in the person, that is, *grace and truth. Grace and truth came, egeneto — was made;* the same word that was used (*v.* 3) concerning Christ's *making all things.* The law was only *made known* by Moses, but the *being* of this grace and truth, as well as the discovery of them, is owing to Jesus Christ; this was *made* by him, as the world at first was; and by him this *grace and truth* do *consist.*

3. Another thing we receive from Christ is a clear revelation of God to us (*v.* 18): He hath *declared* God to us, whom *no man hath seen at any time.* This was the grace and truth which came by Christ, the knowledge of God and an acquaintance with him. Observe,

(1.) The insufficiency of all other discoveries: *No man hath seen God at any time.* This intimates, [1.] That the nature of God being *spiritual,* he is invisible to bodily eyes, he is a being *whom no man hath seen, nor can see,* 1 Tim. 6:16. We have therefore need to *live by faith,* by which we *see him that is invisible,* Heb. 11:27. [2.] That the revelation which God made of himself in the Old Testament was very short and imperfect, in comparison with that which he has made by Christ: *No man hath seen God at any time;* that is, what was seen and known of God before the incarnation of Christ was nothing to that which is now seen and known; life and immortality are now brought to a much clearer light than they were then. [3.] That none of the Old-Testament prophets were so well qualified to make known the mind and will of God to the children of men as our Lord Jesus was, for none of them had *seen God at any time. Moses beheld the similitude of the Lord* (Num. 12:8), but was told that he could not *see his face,* Ex. 33:20. But *this* recommends Christ's holy religion to us that it was founded by one that had seen God, and knew more of his mind than any one else ever did.

(2.) The all-sufficiency of the gospel discovery proved from its author: *The only-begotten Son, who is in the bosom of the Father, he has declared him.* Observe here,

[1.] How *fit* he was to make this discovery, and every way qualified for it. He and he alone was *worthy to take the book, and to open the seals,* Rev. 5:9. For, *First,* He is *the only-begotten Son;* and who so likely to know the Father as the Son? or in whom is the Father better known than in the Son? Mt. 11:27. He is of the same nature with the Father, so that he who hath *seen him* hath seen *the Father, ch.* 14:9. The servant is not supposed to know so well *what his Lord does* as the Son, *ch.* 15:15. Moses was *faithful as a servant,* but Christ *as a Son. Secondly,* He is *in the bosom of the Father.* He had lain in his bosom from eternity. When he was here upon earth, yet still, as God, he was in the bosom of the Father, and thither he returned when he *ascended. In the bosom of the Father;* that is, 1. In the bosom of his *special love,* dear to him, in *whom he was well pleased,* always his delight. All God's saints are *in his hand,* but his Son was *in his bosom,* one in nature and essence, and therefore in the highest degree one *in love.* 2. In the bosom of his *secret counsels.* As there was a mutual *complacency,* so there was a mutual *consciousness,* between the Father and Son (Mt. 11:27); none so fit as he to make known God, for none knew his mind as he did. Our most secret counsels we are said to hide *in our bosom (in pectore);* Christ was privy to the *bosom-counsels* of the Father. The prophets *sat down at his feet* as scholars; Christ lay in his bosom as a friend. See Eph. 3:11.

[2.] How *free* he was in making this discovery: *He hath declared. Him* is not in the original. He has declared that of God which no man had at any time seen or known; not only that which was hid *of God,* but that which was hid *in* God (Eph. 3:9), *exēgēsato* — it signifies a plain, clear, and full discovery, not by general and doubtful hints, but by particular explications. He that runs may now read the will of God and the way of salvation. This is the *grace,* this the *truth,* that came by Jesus Christ.

Verses 19–28

We have here the testimony of John, which he delivered to the messengers who were sent from Jerusalem to examine him. Observe here,

I. Who they were that sent to him, and who they were that were sent. 1. They that sent to him were *the Jews at Jerusalem,* the great sanhedrim or high-commission court, which sat at Jerusalem, and was the representative of the Jewish church, who took cognizance of all matters relating to religion. One would think that they who were the fountains of learning, and the guides of the church, should have, by books, understood the times so well as to know that the Messiah was at hand, and therefore should presently have known him that was his forerunner, and readily embraced him; but, instead of this, they sent messengers to *cross questions* with him. Secular learning, honour, and power, seldom dispose men's minds to the reception of divine light. 2. They that were sent were, (1.) *Priests and Levites,* probably members of the council, men of learning, gravity, and authority. John Baptist was himself a priest of the seed of Aaron, and therefore it was not fit that he should be examined by any but priests. It was prophesied concerning John's ministry that it should *purify the Sons of Levi* (Mal. 3:3), and therefore they were jealous of him and his reformation. (2.) They were *of the Pharisees,* proud, self-justiciaries, that thought they needed no repentance, and therefore could not bear one that made it his business to preach repentance.

II. On what errand they were sent; it was to enquire concerning John and *his baptism.* They did not send for John to them, probably because they *feared the people,* lest the people where John was should be provoked to rise, or lest the people where they were should be brought acquainted with him; they thought it was good to keep him at a distance. They enquire concerning him, 1. To satisfy their curiosity; as the Athenians enquired concerning Paul's doctrine, for the novelty of it, Acts 17:19, 20. Such a proud conceit they had of themselves that the doctrine of repentance was to them strange doctrine. 2. It was to show their authority. They thought they *looked great* when they called him to account whom all men counted as a prophet, and arraigned him at their bar. 3. It was with a design to *suppress* him and silence him if they could find any colour for it; for they were jealous of his growing interest, and his ministry agreed neither with the Mosaic dispensation which they had been long under, nor with the notions they had formed of the Messiah's kingdom.

III. What was the answer he gave them, and his account, both concerning himself and concerning his baptism, in both which he witnessed to Christ.

1. Concerning himself, and what he professed himself to be. They asked him, *Sy tis ei — Thou, who art thou?* John's appearing in the world was surprising. He was in the wilderness till the day of his showing unto Israel. His spirit, his converse, he doctrine, had something in them which commanded and gained respect; but he did not, as seducers do, give out himself to be *some great one.* He was more industrious to *do good* than to *appear great;* and therefore waived saying any thing of himself till he was legally interrogated. Those speak best for Christ that say least of themselves, whose *own works* praise them, not *their own lips.* He answers their interrogatory,

(1.) *Negatively.* He was not that great one whom some took him to be. God's faithful witnesses stand more upon their guard *against undue respect* than against *unjust contempt.* Paul writes as warmly against those that overvalued him, and said, *I am of Paul,* as against those that undervalued him, and said that his bodily presence was weak; and he rent his clothes when he was called a god. [1.] John disowns himself to be *the Christ* (*v.* 20): *He said, I am not the Christ,* who was now expected and waited for. Note, The ministers of Christ must remember that *they are not Christ,* and therefore must not usurp his powers and prerogatives, nor assume the praises due to him only. They are not Christ, and therefore must not lord it over God's heritage, nor pretend to a dominion over the faith of Christians. They cannot created grace and peace; they cannot enlighten, convert, quicken, comfort; for they are not Christ. Observe how emphatically this is here expressed concerning John: He *confessed, and denied not, but confessed;* it denotes his vehemence and constancy in making this protestation. Note, Temptations to pride, and assuming that honour to ourselves which does not belong to us, ought to be resisted with a great deal of vigour and earnestness. When John was taken to be the Messiah, he did not connive at it with a *Si populus vult decipi, decipiatur — If the people will be deceived, let them;* but openly and solemnly, without any ambiguities, confessed, *I am not the Christ; hoti ouk eimi egō ho Christos — I am not the Christ, not I;* another is at hand, who is he, but I am not. His disowning himself to be the Christ is called his *confessing* and not *denying* Christ. Note, Those that humble and abase themselves thereby confess Christ, and give honour to him; but those that will not deny themselves do in effect deny Christ, [2.] He disowns himself to be Elias, *v.* 21. The Jews expected the person of Elias to return from heaven, and to live among them, and promised themselves great things from it. Hearing of John's character, doctrine, and baptism, and observing that he appeared as one dropped from heaven, in the same part of the country from which Elijah was carried to heaven, it is no wonder that they were ready to take him for this Elijah; but he disowned this honour too. He was indeed prophesied of under the name of Elijah (Mal. 4:5), and he came in the *spirit and power of Elias* (Lu. 1:17), and was the Elias that was to come (Mt. 11:14); but he was not the person of Elias, not that Elias that went to heaven in the fiery chariot, as he was that met Christ in his transfiguration. He was the Elias that God had promised, not the Elias that they foolishly dreamed of. Elias did come, and *they knew him not* (Mt. 17:12); nor did he make himself known to them as the Elias, because they had promised themselves such an Elias as God never promised them. [3.] He disowns himself to be that *prophet,* or the prophet. *First,* He was not *that* prophet which Moses said *the Lord* would *raise up to them of their brethren,* like unto him. If they meant this, they needed not ask that question, for that prophet was no other than the Messiah, and he had said already, *I am not the Christ. Secondly,* He was not such a prophet as they expected and wished for, who, like Samuel and Elijah, and some other of the prophets, would interpose in public affairs, and rescue them from under the Roman yoke. *Thirdly,* He was not one of the old prophets raised from the dead, as they expected one to come before Elias, as Elias before the Messiah. *Fourthly,* Though John was a prophet, yea, more than a prophet, yet he had his revelation, not by dreams and visions, as the Old-Testament prophets had theirs; his commission and work were of another nature, and belonged to another dispensation. If John had said that he was Elias, and was a prophet, he might have made his words good; but ministers must, upon all occasions, express themselves with the utmost caution, both that they may not confirm people in any mistakes, and particularly that they may not give occasion to any to think of them *above what is meet.*

(2.) *Affirmatively.* The committee that was sent to examine him pressed for a positive answer (*v.* 22), urging the authority of *those that sent them,* which they expected he should pay a deference to: "*Tell us, What art thou?* not that we may believe thee, and be baptized by three, but that we may *give an answer* to those that sent us, and that it may not be said we were sent on a fool's errand." John was looked upon as a man of sincerity, and therefore they believed he would not give an evasive ambiguous answer; but would be fair and above-board, and give a plain answer to a plain question: *What sayest thou of thyself?* And he did so, *I am the voice of one crying in the wilderness.* Observe,

[1.] He gives his answer in the words of scripture, to show that the scripture was fulfilled in him, and that his office was supported by a divine authority. What the scripture saith of the office of the ministry should be often thought of by those of that high calling, who must look upon themselves as that, and that only, which the word of God makes them.

[2.] He gives in his answer in very humble, modest, self-denying expressions. He chooses to apply that scripture to himself which denotes not his dignity, but his duty and dependence, which bespeaks him little: *I am the voice,* as if he were *vox et praeterea nihil* — mere voice.

[3.] He gives such an account of himself as might be profitable to them, and might excite and awaken them to hearken to him; for he *was the voice* (see Isa. 40:3), a voice to alarm, an articulate voice to instruct. Ministers are but the *voice,* the vehicle, by which God is pleased to communicate his mind. What are Paul and Apollos but messengers? Observe, *First,* He was a *human* voice. The people were prepared to receive the law by the voice of thunders, and a trumpet exceedingly loud, such as made them tremble; but they were prepared for the gospel by the voice of a man like ourselves, *a still small voice,* such as that in which God came to Elijah, 1 Ki. 19:12. *Secondly,* He was the voice of *one crying,* which denotes, 1. His *earnestness* and *importunity* in calling people to repentance; he *cried aloud, and did not spare.* Ministers must preach as those that are in earnest, and are themselves affected with those things with which they desire to affect others. Those words are not likely to *thaw* the hearers' hearts that *freeze* between the speaker's lips. 2. His *open publication* of the doctrine he preached; he was the voice of one *crying,* that all manner of persons might hear and take notice. *Doth not wisdom cry?* Prov. 8:1. *Thirdly,* It was in the *wilderness* that this voice was crying; in a place of silence and solitude, out of the noise of the world and the hurry of its business; the more retired we are from the tumult of secular affairs the better prepared we are to hear from God. *Fourthly,* That which he cried was, *Make straight the way of the Lord;* that is, 1. He came to *rectify* the mistakes of people concerning the ways of God; it is certain that they are right ways, but the scribes and Pharisees, with their corrupt glosses upon the law, had made them crooked. Now John Baptist calls people to return to the original rule. 2. He came to prepare and dispose people for the reception and entertainment of Christ and his gospel. It is an allusion to the harbingers of a prince or great man, that cry, *Make room.* Note, When God is coming towards us, we must prepare to meet him, and let the word of the Lord have *free course.* See Ps. 24:7.

2. Here is his testimony concerning *his baptism.*

(1.) The enquiry which the committee made about it: *Why baptizest thou, if thou be not the Christ, nor Elias, nor that prophet? v.* 25. [1.] They readily apprehended baptism to be fitly and properly used as a sacred rite or ceremony, for the Jewish church had used it with circumcision in the admission of proselytes, to signify the cleansing of them from the pollutions of their former state. That sign was made use of in the Christian church, that it might be the more passable. Christ did not affect novelty, nor should his ministers. [2.] They expected it would be used in the days of the Messiah, because it was promised that then there should be a *fountain opened* (Zec. 13:1), and *clean water sprinkled,* Eze. 36:25. It is taken for granted that Christ, and Elias, and *that prophet,* would baptize, when they came to *purify* a *polluted* world. Divine justice drowned the old world *in its filth,* but divine grace has provided for the cleansing of this new world *from its filth.* [3.] They would therefore know by what authority John baptized. His denying himself to be Elias, or *that prophet,* subjected him to this further question, *Why baptizest thou?* Note, It is no new thing for a man's modesty to be turned against him, and improved to his prejudice; but it is better that men should take advantage of our low thoughts of ourselves, to *trample upon us,* than the devil take advantage of our high thoughts of ourselves, to *tempt us* to pride and draw us into his condemnation.

(2.) The account he gave of it, *v.* 26, 27.

[1.] He owned himself to be only the minister of the outward sign: "*I baptize with water,* and that is all; I am no more,

and do no more, than what you see; I have no other title than *John the Baptist;* I cannot confer the spiritual grace signified by it." Paul was in care that none should think of him above what they saw him to be (2 Co. 12:6); so was John Baptist. Ministers must not set up for masters.

[2.] He directed them to one who was greater than himself, and would do that for them, if they pleased, which he could not do: "*I baptize with water,* and that is the utmost of my commission; I have nothing to do but by this to lead you to one that comes after me, and consign you to him." Note, The great business of Christ's ministers is to direct all people to him; we preach not ourselves, but *Christ Jesus the Lord.* John gave the same account to this committee that he had given to the people (*v.* 15): *This as he of whom I spoke.* John was constant and uniform in his testimony, not as a reed shaken with the wind. The sanhedrim were jealous of his interest in the people, but he is not afraid to tell them that there is one at the door that will go beyond him. *First,* He tells them of Christ's *presence among them* now at this time: *There stands one among you,* at this time, *whom you know not.* Christ stood among the common people, and was as one of them. Note, 1. Much true worth lies hid in this world; obscurity is often the lot of real excellency. Saints are God's *hidden ones,* therefore the *world knows them not.* 2. God himself is often nearer to us than we are aware of. *The Lord* is *in this place,* and *I knew it not.* They were gazing, in expectation of the messiah: *Lo he is here,* or he is there, when the kingdom of God was abroad and already *among them,* Lu. 17:21. *Secondly,* He tells them of Christ's *preference above himself:* He comes *after me,* and yet is *preferred before me.* This he had said before; he adds here, "Whose *shoe-latchet I am not worthy to loose;* I am not fit to be named the same day with him; it is an honour too great for me to pretend to be in the meanest office about him," 1 Sa. 25:41. Those to whom Christ is precious reckon his service, even the most despised instances of it, an honour to them. See Ps. 84:10. If so great a man as John accounted himself unworthy of the honour of being near Christ, how unworthy then should we account ourselves! Now, one would think, these chief priests and Pharisees, upon this intimation given concerning the approach of the Messiah, should presently have asked who, and where, this excellent person was; and who more likely to tell them than he who had given them this general notice? No, they did not think this any part of their business or concern; they came to molest John, not to receive any instructions from him: so that their ignorance was *wilful;* they might have known Christ, and would not.

Lastly, Notice is taken of the place where all this was done: *In Bethabara beyond Jordan, v.* 28. Bethabara signifies the *house of passage;* some think it was the very place where Israel passed over Jordan into the land of promise under the conduct of Joshua; there was opened the way into the gospel state by Jesus Christ. It was at a great *distance* from Jerusalem, beyond Jordan; probably because what he did *there* would be least offensive to the government. Amos must go prophesy in the country, not near the court; but it was sad that Jerusalem should put so far from her the things that belonged to *her peace.* He made this confession in the same place where he was *baptizing,* that all those who attended his baptism might be witnesses of it, and none might say that they knew not what to *make of him.*

Verses 29–36

We have in these verses an account of John's testimony concerning Jesus Christ, which he witnessed to his own disciples that followed him. As soon as ever Christ was *baptized* he was immediately hurried into the wilderness, to be *tempted;* and there he was forty days. During his absence John had continued to bear testimony to him, and to tell the people of him; but now at last he *sees Jesus coming to him,* returning from the wilderness of temptation. As soon as that conflict was over Christ immediately returned to John, who was *preaching* and *baptizing.* Now Christ was tempted for example and encouragement to us; and this teaches us, 1. That the *hardships* of a tempted state should engage us to keep close to ordinances; to go into the *sanctuary of God,* Ps. 73:17. Our combats with Satan should oblige us to keep close to the communion of saints: two are better than one. 2. That the *honours* of a victorious state must not set us *above ordinances.* Christ had triumphed over Satan, and been attended by angels, and yet, after all, he returns to the place where John was preaching and baptizing. As long as we are on this

side heaven, whatever extraordinary visits of divine grace we may have here at any time, we must still keep close to the ordinary means of grace and comfort, and walk with God in them. Now here are *two testimonies* borne by John to Christ, but those two *agree in one.*

I. Here is his testimony to Christ on the first day that he saw him coming from the wilderness; and here four things are witnessed by him concerning Christ, when he had him before his eyes: —

1. That he is *the Lamb of God which taketh away the sin of the world, v.* 29. Let us learn here,

(1.) That Jesus Christ is the *Lamb of God,* which bespeaks him the great sacrifice, by which atonement is made for sin, and man reconciled to God. Of all the legal sacrifices he chooses to allude to the *lambs* that were offered, not only because a lamb is an emblem of meekness, and Christ must be led as a *lamb to the slaughter* (Isa. 53:7), but with a special reference, [1.] To the *daily sacrifice,* which was offered every morning and evening continually, and that was always a *lamb* (Ex. 29:38), which was a type of Christ, as the everlasting propitiation, whose blood continually speaks. [2.] To the *paschal lamb,* the blood of which, being sprinkled upon the door-posts, secured the Israelites from the stroke of the destroying angel. Christ is *our passover,* 1 Co. 5:7. He is the Lamb *of God;* he is appointed by *him* (Rom. 3:25), he was devoted to him (*ch.* 17:19), and he was accepted with him; in him he was well pleased. The lot which fell on the goat that was to be offered for a sin-offering was called the *Lord's lot* (Lev. 16:8, 9); so Christ, who was to make atonement for sin, is called the *Lamb of God.*

(2.) That Jesus Christ, as the *Lamb of God, takes away the sin of the world.* This was his undertaking; he appeared, to *put away sin by the sacrifice of himself,* Heb. 9:26. John Baptist had called people to repent of their sins, in order to the remission of them. Now here he shows how and by whom that remission was to be expected, what ground of hope we have that our sins shall be pardoned upon our repentance, though our repentance makes no satisfaction for them. This ground of hope we have — Jesus Christ is *the Lamb of God.* [1.] He *takes away sin.* He, being Mediator between God and man, takes away that which is, above any thing, offensive to the *holiness* of God, and destructive to the *happiness* of man. He came, *First,* To take away the guilt of sin by the merit of his death, to vacate the judgment, and reverse the attainder, which mankind lay under, by an act of indemnity, of which all penitent obedient believers may claim the benefit. *Secondly,* To take away the power of sin by the Spirit of his grace, so that it shall not have dominion, Rom. 6:14. Christ, as the Lamb of God, washes us from our sins in his own blood; that is, he both *justifies* and *sanctifies* us: he *takes away sin.* He is *ho airōn* — *he is taking away* the sin of the world, which denotes it not a single but a continued act; it is his constant work and office to take *away sin,* which is such a *work of time* that it will never be completed till time shall be no more. He is always *taking away* sin, by the continual intercession of his blood in heaven, and the continual influence of his grace on earth. [2.] He takes away the *sin of the world;* purchases pardon for all those that repent, and believe the gospel, of what country, nation, or language, soever they be. The legal sacrifices had reference only to the sins of Israel, to make atonement for them; but the Lamb of God was offered to be a propitiation for the *sin of the whole world;* see 1 Jn. 2:2. This is encouraging to our faith; if Christ takes away the sin of the world, then why not my sin? Christ levelled his force at the main body of sin's army, struck at the root, and aimed at the overthrow, of that *wickedness* which the *whole world lay in.* God was in him reconciling the world to himself. [3.] He does this by *taking it upon himself.* He is the Lamb of God, that *bears the sin of the world;* so the margin reads it. He bore sin *for us,* and so bears it *from us;* he *bore the sin of many,* as the scape-goat had the sins of Israel put upon his head, Lev. 16:21. God could have taken away the sin by taking away the sinner, as he took away the sin of the old world; but he has found out a way of abolishing the sin, and yet sparing the sinner, by making his Son *sin for us.*

(3.) That it is our duty, with an eye of faith, to *behold* the Lamb of God thus taking away the *sin of the world.* See him taking away sin, and let that increase our hatred of sin, and resolutions against it. Let not us hold that fast which the Lamb of God came to take away: for Christ will either take our sins away or take us away. Let it increase our love to Christ, *who loved us, and washed us from our sins in his own blood,* Rev. 1:5. Whatever God is pleased to take away from us, if withal he take away our sins, we have reason to be thankful, and no reason to complain.

2. That this was he of whom he had spoken before (*v.* 30, 31): *This is he,* this person whom I now point at, you see where he stands, *this is he of whom I said, After me cometh a man.* Observe, (1.) This honour John had above all the prophets, that, whereas they spoke of him as one that should come, he saw him already come. *This is he.* He sees him *now,* he sees him *nigh,* Num. 24:17. Such a difference there is between present *faith* and future *vision.* Now we love one whom we have not seen; then we shall see him whom our souls love, shall see him, and say, This is he of whom I said, *my Christ,* and *my all, my beloved,* and *my friend.* (2.) John calls Christ *a man;* after me comes a man — *anēr,* a *strong man:* like *the man,* the branch, or the *man of God's right hand.* (3.) He refers to what he had himself said of him before: *This is he of whom I said.* Note, Those who have said the most honourable things of Christ will never see cause to unsay them; but the more they know him the more they are confirmed in their esteem of him. John still thinks as meanly of himself, and as highly of Christ, as ever. Though Christ appeared not in any external pomp or grandeur, yet John is not ashamed to own, *This is he whom I* meant, who is *preferred before me.* And it was necessary that John should thus show them the person, otherwise they could not have believed that one who made so mean a figure should be he of whom John had spoken such great things. (4.) He protests against any confederacy or combination with this Jesus: *And I knew him not.* Though there was some relation between them (Elisabeth was cousin to the virgin Mary), yet there was no acquaintance at all between them; John had no personal knowledge of Jesus till he saw him come to his baptism. Their manner of life had been different: John had spent his time in the wilderness, in solitude; Jesus at Nazareth, in conversation. There was no correspondence, no interview between them, that the matter might appear to be wholly carried on by the direction and disposal of Heaven, and not by any design or concert of the persons themselves. And as he hereby disowns all collusion, so also all partiality and sinister regard in it; he could not be supposed to favour him as a friend, for there was no friendship or familiarity between them. Nay, as he could not be biassed to speak honourably of him because he was a stranger to him, he was not able to say any thing of him but what he *received from above,* to which he appeals, *ch.* 3:27. Note, They who are taught believe and confess one whom they have not seen, and blessed are they who *yet have believed.* (5.) The great intention of John's ministry and baptism was to introduce Jesus Christ. That he should be *made manifest to Israel, therefore am I come baptizing with water.* Observe, [1.] Though John did not know Jesus by face, yet he knew that he should be made manifest. Note, We may know the certainty of that which yet we do not fully know the nature and intention of. We know that the happiness of heaven *shall be made manifest to Israel,* but cannot describe it. [2.] The general assurance John had that Christ *should be made manifest* served to carry him with diligence and resolution through his work, though he was kept in the dark concerning particulars: *Therefore am I come.* Our assurance of the reality of things, though they are unseen, is enough to quicken us to our duty. [3.] God reveals himself to his people by degrees. At first, John knew no more concerning Christ but that he should be made manifest; in confidence of that, he came baptizing, and now he is favoured with a sight of him. They who, upon God's word, believe what they do not see, shall shortly see what they now believe. [4.] The ministry of the word and sacraments is designed for no other end than to lead people to Christ, and to make him more and more manifest. [5.] Baptism with water made way for the manifesting of Christ, as it supposed our corruption and filthiness, and signified our cleansing by him who is the *fountain opened.*

3. That this was he *upon whom the Spirit descended from heaven like a dove.* For the confirming of his testimony concerning Christ, he here vouches the extraordinary appearance at his baptism, in which God himself bore witness to him. This was a considerable proof of Christ's mission. Now, to assure us of the truth of it, we are here told (*v.* 32–34),

(1.) That John Baptist saw it: He *bore record;* did not relate it as a story, but solemnly attested it, with all the seriousness and solemnity of *witness-bearing.* He made affidavit of it: *I saw the Spirit descending* from heaven. John could not see the *Spirit,* but he saw the dove which was a sign and representation of the Spirit. The Spirit came now upon Christ, both to *make him fir* for his *work* and to *make him known* to the *world.* Christ was notified, not by the descent of a crown upon him, or by a transfiguration, but by the descent of the Spirit as a dove upon him, to qualify him for his undertaking. Thus the first testimony given to the apostles was by the descent of the Spirit upon them. God's children are made manifest by their *graces;* their glories are reserved for their future state. Observe, [1.] The spirit descended *from heaven,* for every good and perfect gift is *from above.* [2.] He descended *like a dove* — an emblem of meekness, and mildness, and gentleness, which makes him *fit to teach.* The dove brought the olive-branch of peace, Gen. 8:11. [3.] The Spirit that descended upon Christ *abode upon him,* as was foretold, Isa. 11:2. The Spirit did not *move him at times,* as Samson (Jdg. 13:25), but *at all times.* The Spirit was given to him *without measure;* it was his prerogative to have the Spirit always upon him, so that he could at no time be found either *unqualified* for his work himself or *unfurnished* for the supply of those that seek to him for his grace.

(2.) That he was *told to expect it,* which very much corroborates the proof. It was not John's bare conjecture, that surely he on whom he saw the Spirit descending was the Son of God; but it was an *instituted* sign given him before, by which he might certainly know it (*v.* 33): *I knew him not.* He insists much upon this, that he knew no more of him than other people did, otherwise than by revelation. But *he that sent me to baptize* gave me this sign, *Upon whom thou shalt see the Spirit descending, the same is he.* [1.] See here what sure grounds John went upon in his ministry and baptism, that he might proceed with all imaginable satisfaction. *First,* He did not run *without sending:* God *sent him to baptize.* He had a warrant from heaven for what he did. When a minister's call is clear, his comfort is sure, though his success is not always so. *Secondly,* He did not run *without speeding;* for, when he was sent to *baptize with water,* he was directed to one that should *baptize with the Holy Ghost.* Under this notion John Baptist was taught to expect Christ, as one who would give that repentance and faith which he called people to, and would carry on and complete that blessed structure of which he was now laying the foundation. Note, It is a great comfort to Christ's ministers, in their administration of the outward signs, that he whose ministers they are can confer the grace signified thereby, and so put life, and soul, and power into their ministrations; can speak to the heart what they speak to the ear, and *breathe* upon the dry bones to which they *prophesy.* [2.] See what sure grounds he went upon in his designation of the person of the Messiah. God had before given him a sign, as he did to Samuel concerning Saul: "On whom thou shalt see the Spirit descend, *that same is he."* This not only prevented any mistakes, but gave him boldness in his testimony. When he had such assurance as this given him, he could speak with assurance. When John was told this before, his expectations could not but be very much raised; and, when the event exactly answered the prediction, his faith could not but be much confirmed: and these things are written that we may believe.

4. That he is *the Son of God.* This is the conclusion of John's testimony, that in which all the particulars centre, as the *quod erat demonstrandum — the fact to be demonstrated* (*v.* 34): *I saw, and bore record, that this is the Son of God.* (1.) The truth asserted is, *that this is the Son of God.* The voice from heaven proclaimed, and John subscribed to it, not only that he should baptize with the Holy Ghost by a divine authority, but that he has a divine nature. This was the peculiar Christian creed, that Jesus is the Son of God (Mt. 16:16), and here is the first framing of it. (2.) John's testimony to it: *"I saw, and bore record.* Not only I now bear record of it, but I did so as soon as I had seen it." Observe, [1.] What he *saw* he was forward to *bear record* of, as they, Acts 4:20: *We cannot but speak the things which we have seen.* [2.] What he *bore record* of was what he *saw.* Christ's witnesses were eye-witnesses, and therefore the more to be credited: they did not speak by hear-say and report, 2 Pt. 1:16.

II. Here is John's testimony to Christ, the next day after, *v.* 35, 36. Where observe, 1. He took every opportunity that offered itself to lead people to Christ: *John stood looking upon Jesus as he walked.* It should seem, John was now retired from the multitude, and was in close conversation with *two* of his disciples. Note, Ministers should not only in their public preaching, but in their private converse, witness to Christ, and serve his interests. He saw Jesus *walking* at some distance, yet did not go to him himself, because he would shun every thing that might give the least colour to suspect a combination. He was *looking upon Jesus — emblepsas;* he looked stedfastly, and fixed his eyes upon him. Those that would lead others to Christ must be diligent and frequent in the *contemplation* of him themselves. John had seen Christ before, but now looked upon him, 1 Jn. 1:1. 2. He repeated the same testimony which he had given to Christ the day before, though he could have delivered some other great truth concerning him; but thus he would show that he was uniform and constant in his testimony, and consistent with himself. His doctrine was the same in private that it was in public, as Paul's was, Acts 20:20, 21. It is good to have that repeated which we have heard, Phil. 3:1. The doctrine of Christ's sacrifice for the taking away of the sin of the world ought especially to be insisted upon by all good ministers: Christ, the Lamb of God, *Christ and him crucified.* 3. He intended this especially for his two disciples that stood with him; he was willing to turn them over to Christ, for to this end he bore witness to Christ in their hearing that they might leave all to follow him, even that they might leave *him.* He did not reckon that he lost those disciples who went over from him to Christ, any more than the schoolmaster reckons that scholar lost whom he sends to the university. John gathered disciples, not for himself, but for Christ to *prepare them for the Lord,* Lu. 1:17. So far was he from being jealous of Christ's growing interest, that there was nothing he was more desirous of. Humble generous souls will give others their due praise without fear of diminishing themselves by it. What we have of reputation, as well as of other things, will not be the less for our giving every body his own.

Verses 37–42

We have here the turning over of two disciples from John to Jesus, and one of them fetching in a third, and these are the first-fruits of Christ's disciples; see how small the church was in its beginnings, and what the dawning of the day of its great things was.

I. Andrew and another with him were the two that John Baptist had directed to Christ, *v.* 37. Who the other was we are not told; some think that it was Thomas, comparing *ch.* 21:2; others that it was John himself, the penman of this gospel, whose manner it is industriously to conceal his name, *ch.* 13:23, and 20:3.

1. Here is their readiness to go over to Christ: They *heard John speak* of Christ as the *Lamb of God,* and they *followed Jesus.* Probably they had heard John say the same thing the day before, and then it had not the effect upon them which now it had; see the benefit of repetition, and of private personal converse. They heard him speak of Christ as the *Lamb of God, that takes away the sin of the world,* and this made them *follow him.* The strongest and most prevailing argument with a sensible awakened soul to follow Christ is that it is he, and he only, that *takes away sin.*

2. The kind notice Christ took of them, *v.* 38. They came behind him; but, though he had his back towards them, he was soon aware of them, and *turned,* and *saw them following.* Note, Christ takes early cognizance of the first motions of a soul towards him, and the first step taken in the way to heaven; see Isa. 64:5; Lu. 15:20. He did not stay till they begged leave to speak with him, but spoke first. What communion there is between a soul and Christ, it is he that *begins the discourse.* He saith unto them, *What seek ye?* This was not a reprimand for their boldness in intruding into his company: he that came to *seek us* never checked any for *seeking* him; but, on the contrary, it is a kind invitation of them into his acquaintance whom he saw bashful and modest: "Come, what have you to say to me? What is your petition? What is your request." Note, Those whose business it is to instruct people in the affairs of their souls should be humble, and mild, and easy of access, and should encourage those that apply to them. The question Christ put to them is what we should all put to ourselves when we begin to follow Christ, and take upon us the profession of his holy religion: *"What seek ye?* What do we design and desire?" Those that *follow* Christ, and yet *seek* the world, or themselves, or the praise of men, deceive themselves. *"What seek we* in seeking Christ? Do we seek a teacher, ruler, and reconciler? In following Christ, do we seek the favour of God and eternal life?" If our *eye* be *single* in this, we are *full of light.*

3. Their modest enquiry concerning the place of his abode: *Rabbi, where dwellest thou?* (1.) In calling him *Rabbi,* they intimated that their design in coming to him was to be *taught by him; rabbi* signifies a *master,* a teaching master; the Jews called their doctors, or learned men, *rabbies.* The word comes from *rab, multus* or *magnus,* a *rabbi,* a *great man,* and one that, as we say, has *much in him.* Never was there such a rabbi as our Lord Jesus, such a *great one,* in whom were *hid all the treasures of wisdom and knowledge.* These came to Christ to be his scholars, so must all those that apply themselves to him. John had told them that he was the *Lamb of God;* now this *Lamb* is worthy to *take the book and open the seals* as a rabbi, Rev. 5:9. And, unless we give up ourselves to be ruled and taught by him, he will not *take away our sins.* (2.) In asking *where he dwelt,* they intimate a desire to be better acquainted with him. Christ was a stranger in this country, so that they meant where was his *inn* where he *lodged;* for there they would attend him at some seasonable time, when he should appoint, to receive instruction from him; they would not press rudely upon him, when it was not proper. Civility and good manners well become those who follow Christ. And, besides, they hoped to have more from him than they could have in a short conference now by the way. They resolved to make a business, not a by-business of conversing with Christ. Those that have had some communion with Christ cannot but desire, [1.] A *further communion* with him; they follow on to know more of him. [2.] A *fixed communion* with him; where they may sit down at his feet, and abide by his instructions. It is not enough to take a turn with Christ now and then, but we must *lodge with him.*

4. The courteous invitation Christ gave them to his lodgings: *He saith unto them, Come and see.* Thus should good desires towards Christ and communion with him be countenanced. (1.) He invites them to come to his lodgings: the nearer we approach to Christ, the more we see of his beauty and excellency. Deceivers maintain their interest in their followers by keeping them at a distance, but that which Christ desired to recommend him to the esteem and affections of his followers was that they would *come and see: "Come and see* what a mean lodging I have, what poor accommodations I take up with, that you may not expect any worldly advantage by following me, as they did who made their court to the scribes and Pharisees, and called them rabbin. *Come and see* what you must count upon if you follow me." See Mt. 8:20. (2.) He invites them to come *immediately* and without delay. They asked where he lodged, that they might wait upon him at a more convenient season; but Christ invites them immediately to *come and see;* never in better time than now. Hence learn, [1.] As to others, that it is best taking people when they are in a good mind; strike while the iron is hot. [2.] As to ourselves, that it is wisdom to embrace the present opportunities: *Now is the accepted time,* 2 Co. 6:2.

5. Their cheerful and (no doubt) thankful acceptance of his invitation: *They came and saw where he dwelt,* and *abode with him that day.* It had been greater modesty and manners than had done them good if they had refused this offer. (2.) They readily went along with him: *They came and saw where he dwelt.* Gracious souls cheerfully accept Christ's gracious invitations; as David, Ps. 27:8. They enquired not how they might be accommodated with him, but would put that to the venture, and make the best of what they found. It is good being where Christ is, wherever it be. (2.) They were so well pleased with what they found that they *abode with him that day* ("Master, it is good to be here"); and he bade them welcome. It was about the tenth hour. Some think that John reckons according to the Roman computation, and that it was about ten o'clock in the morning, and they staid with him till night; others think that John reckons as the other evangelists did, according to the Jewish computation, and that it was four o'clock in the afternoon, and they abode with him that night and the next day. Dr. Lightfoot conjectures that this next day that they spent with Christ was a sabbath-day, and, it being late, they could not get home before the sabbath. As it is our duty, wherever we are, to contrive to spend the sabbath as much as may be to our spiritual benefit and advantage, so they are blessed who, by the lively exercises of faith, love, and devotion, spend their sabbaths in communion with Christ. These are Lord's days indeed, *days of the Son of man.*

II. Andrew brought his brother Peter to Christ. If Peter had been the first-born of Christ's disciples, the papists would have made a noise with it: he did indeed afterwards come to be more eminent in gifts, but Andrew had the honour first to be acquainted with Christ, and to be the instrument of bringing Peter to him. Observe,

1. The *information* which Andrew gave to Peter, with an intimation to come to Christ.

(1.) He *found him: He first finds his own brother Simon;* his finding implies his seeking him. Simon came along with Andrew to attend John's ministry and baptism, and Andrew knew where to look for him. Perhaps the other disciple that was with him went out to seek some friend of his at the same time, but Andrew sped first: *He first findeth Simon,* who came only to attend on John, but has his expectations out-done; he meets with Jesus.

(2.) He told him whom they had found: *We have found the Messias.* Observe, [1.] he speaks *humbly;* not, "I have found," assuming the honour of the discovery to himself, but "*We* have," rejoicing that he had shared with others in it. [2.] He speaks *exultingly,* and with triumph: *We have found* that pearl of great price, that true treasure; and, having found it, he proclaims it as those lepers, 2 Ki. 7:9, for he knows that he shall have never the less in Christ for others sharing. [3.] He speaks *intelligently: We have found the Messias,* which was more than had yet been said. John had said, *He is the Lamb of God, and the Son of God,* which Andrew compares with the scriptures of the Old Testament, and, comparing them together, concludes that he is the Messiah promised to the fathers, for it is now that the fulness of time is come. Thus, by *making God's testimonies his meditation,* he speaks more clearly concerning Christ than ever *his teacher* had done, Ps. 119:99.

(3.) He *brought him to Jesus;* would not undertake to instruct him himself, but brought him to the fountain-head, persuaded him to come to Christ and introduced him. Now this was, [1.] An instance of true love to his brother, *his own* brother, so he is called here, because he was very dear to him. Note, We ought with a particular concern and application to seek the spiritual welfare of those that are related to us; for their relation to us adds both to the *obligation* and to the *opportunity* of doing good to their souls. [2.] It was an effect of his day's conversation with Christ. Note, the best evidence of our profiting by the means of grace is the piety and usefulness of our conversation afterwards. Hereby it appeared that Andrew had *been with Jesus* that he was so full of him, that he had been *in the mount,* for his face shone. He knew there was enough in Christ for all; and, having tasted that he is gracious, he could not rest till those he loved had tasted it too. Note, True grace hates monopolies, and loves not to eat its morsels alone.

2. The *entertainment* which Jesus Christ gave to Peter, who was never the less welcome for his being influenced by his brother to come, *v.* 42. Observe,

(1.) Christ called him by his name: *When Jesus beheld him, he said, Thou art Simon, the son of Jona.* It should seem that Peter was utterly a stranger to Christ, and if so, [1.] It was a proof of Christ's omniscience that upon the first sight, without any enquiry, he could tell the name both of him and of his father. *The Lord knows them that are his,* and their whole case. However, [2.] It was an instance of his condescending grace and favour, that he did thus freely and affably call him by his name, though he was of mean extraction, and *vir mullius nominis — a man of no name.* It was an instance of God's favour to Moses that he *knew him by name,* Ex. 33:17. Some observe the signification of these names: *Simon — obedient, Jona — a dove.* An obedient dove-like spirit qualifies us to be the disciples of Christ.

(2.) He gave him a new name: *Cephas.* [1.] His giving him a name intimates *Christ's favour* to him. A new name denotes some great dignity, Rev. 2:17; Isa. 62:2. By this Christ not only wiped off the reproach of his mean and obscure parentage, but adopted him into his family as one of his own. [2.] The name which he gave him bespeaks his *fidelity* to Christ: *Thou shalt be called Cephas* (that is Hebrew for *a stone), which is by interpretation Peter;* so it should be rendered, as Acts 9:36. *Tabitha, which by interpretation is called Dorcas;* the former Hebrew, the latter Greek, for a *young roe.* Peter's natural temper was stiff, and hardy, and resolute, which I take to be the principal reason why Christ called him *Cephas — a stone.* When Christ afterwards prayed for him, that his faith might not fail, that so he might be firm to Christ himself, and at the same time bade him *strengthen his brethren,* and lay out himself for the support of others, then he *made him* what he here called him, *Cephas — a stone.* Those that come to Christ must come with a fixed resolution to be firm and constant to him, *like a stone,* solid and stedfast; and it is by his grace that they are so. His saying, *Be thou steady,* makes them so. Now this does no more prove that Peter was the singular or only rock upon which the church is built than the calling of James and John *Boanerges* proves them the only *sons of thunder,* or the calling of Joses *Barnabas* proves him the only *son of consolation.*

Verses 43–51

We have here the call of Philip and Nathanael.

I. Philip was called immediately by Christ himself, not as Andrew, who was directed to Christ by John, or Peter, who was invited by his brother. God has various methods of bringing his chosen ones home to himself. But, whatever means he *uses,* he is not *tied* to any. 1. Philip was called in a *preventing* was: *Jesus findeth Philip.* Christ sought us, and found us, before we made any enquiries after him. The name *Philip* is of Greek origin, and much used among the Gentiles, which some make an instance of the degeneracy of the Jewish church at this time, and their conformity to the nations; yet Christ changed not his name. 2. He was called the *day following.* See how closely Christ applied himself to his business. When work is to be done for God, we must not *lose a day.* Yet observe, Christ now called one or two a day; but, after the Spirit was poured out, there were thousands a day effectually called, in which was fulfilled *ch.* 14:12. 3. Jesus *would go forth into Galilee* to call him. Christ will find out all those that are given to him, wherever they are, and none of them shall be lost. 4. Philip was brought to be a disciple by the power of Christ going along with that word, *Follow me.* See the nature of true Christianity; it is *following Christ,* devoting ourselves to his *converse* and *conduct,* attending his movements, and treading in his steps. See the efficacy of the grace of it is the *rod of his strength.* 5. We are told that Philip was of Bethsaida, and Andrew and Peter were so too, *v.* 44. These eminent disciples received not honour from the place of their nativity, but reflected honour upon it. *Bethsaida* signifies the *house of nets,* because inhabited mostly by fishermen; thence Christ chose disciples, who were to be furnished with extraordinary gifts, and therefore needed not the ordinary advantages of learning. Bethsaida was a wicked place (Mt. 11:21), yet even *there* was a remnant, according to the election of grace.

II. Nathanael was invited to Christ by Philip, and much is said concerning him. In which we may observe,

1. What passed between Philip and Nathanael, in which appears an observable mixture of pious zeal with weakness, such as is usually found in beginners, that are yet but *asking the way to Zion.* Here is,

(1.) The joyful news that Philip brought to Nathanael, *v.* 45. As Andrew before, so Philip here, having got some knowledge of Christ himself, rests not till he has *made manifest the savour of that knowledge.* Philip, though newly come to an acquaintance with Christ himself, yet steps aside to seek Nathanael. Note, When we have the fairest opportunities of getting good to our own souls, yet ever then we must seek opportunities of doing good to the souls of others, remembering the words of Christ, *It is more blessed to give than to receive,* Acts 20:35. O, saith Philip, *we have found him of whom Moses and the prophets did write,* Observe here, [1.] What a transport of joy Philip was in, upon this new acquaintance with Christ: "We have found him whom we have so often talked of, so long wished and waited for; at last, *he is come he is come,* and *we* have found him!" [2.] What an advantage it was to him that he was so well acquainted with the scriptures of the Old Testament, which prepared his mind for the reception of evangelical light, and made the entrance of it much the more easy: *Him of whom Moses and the prophets did write.* What was written entirely and from eternity in the *book of the divine counsels* was in part, at sundry times and in divers manners, copied out into the book of the *divine revelations.* Glorious things were written there concerning the Seed of the woman, the Seed of Abraham, Shiloh, the prophet like Moses, the Son of David, Emmanuel, the Man, the Branch, Messiah the Prince. Philip had studied these things, and was full of them, which made him readily welcome Christ. [3.] What mistakes and weaknesses he laboured under: he called Christ *Jesus of Nazareth,* whereas he was of *Bethlehem;* and the *Son of Joseph,* whereas he as but his *supposed* Son. Young beginners in religion are subject to mistakes, which time and the grace of God will rectify. It was his weakness to say, *We have found him,* for Christ found them before they found Christ. He did not yet *apprehend,* as Paul did, how he was *apprehended of Christ Jesus,* Phil. 3:12.

(2.) The objection which Nathanael made against this, *Can any good thing come out of Nazareth? v.* 46. Here, [1.] His *caution* was commendable, that he did not lightly assent to every thing that was said, but took it into examination; our rule is, *Prove all things.* But, [2.] His objection arose from Ignorance. If he meant that no good thing could come out of Nazareth it was owing to his ignorance of the divine grace, as if that were less affected to one place than another, or tied itself to men's foolish and ill-natured observations. If he meant that the Messiah, that great good thing, could not come out of Nazareth, so far he was right (Moses, in the law, said that he should come out of Judah, and the prophets had assigned Bethlehem for the place of his nativity); but then he was ignorant of the matter of *fact,* that this Jesus was born at Bethlehem; so that the blunder Philip made, in calling him *Jesus of Nazareth,* occasioned this objection. Note, The mistakes of preachers often give rise to the prejudices of hearers.

(3.) The short reply which Philip gave to this objection: *Come and see.* [1.] It was his *weakness* that he could not give a satisfactory answer to it; yet it is the common case of young beginners in religion. We may *know* enough to *satisfy* ourselves, and yet not be able to *say* enough to *silence* the cavils of a subtle adversary. [2.] It was his *wisdom* and zeal that, when he could not answer the objection himself, he would have him go to one that could: *Come and see.* Let us not stand arguing here, and raising difficulties to ourselves which we cannot get over; let us go and converse with Christ himself, and these difficulties will all vanish presently. Note, It is folly to spend that time in doubtful disputation which might be better spent, and to much better purpose, in the exercises of piety and devotion. *Come and see;* not, *Go and see,* but, "*Come,* and I will go along with thee;" as Isa. 2:3; Jer. 1. 5. From this parley between Philip and Nathanael, we may observe, *First,* That many people are kept from the ways of religion by the unreasonable prejudices they have conceived against religion, upon the account of some foreign circumstances which do not at all touch the merits of the case. *Secondly,* The best way to remove the prejudices they have entertained against religion is to prove themselves, and make trial of it. Let us not answer this matter before we hear it.

2. What passed between Nathanael and our Lord Jesus. He came and *saw,* not in vain.

(1.) Our Lord Jesus bore a very honourable testimony to Nathanael's integrity: *Jesus saw him* coming, and met him with favourable encouragement; he said of him to those about him, Nathanael himself being within hearing, *Behold an Israelite indeed.* Observe,

[1.] That he *commended* him; not to flatter him, or puff him up with a good conceit of himself, but perhaps because he knew him to be a *modest* man, if not a *melancholy* man, one that had hard and mean thoughts of himself, was ready to doubt his own sincerity; and Christ by this testimony put the matter out of doubt. Nathanael had, more than any of the candidates, objected against Christ; but Christ hereby showed that he excused it, and was not extreme to mark what he had said amiss, because he knew his heart was upright. He did not retort upon him, *Can any good thing come out of Cana* (*ch.* 21:2), an obscure town in Galilee? But kindly gives him this character, to encourage us to hope for acceptance with Christ, notwithstanding our weakness, and to teach us to speak honourably of those who without cause have spoken slightly of us, and to give them their due praise.

[2.] That he commended him for his *integrity. First, Behold an Israelite indeed.* It is Christ's prerogative to know what men are *indeed;* we can but *hope the best.* The whole nation were Israelites in name, but *all are not Israel that are of Israel* (Rom. 9:6); here, however, was *an Israelite indeed.* 1. A sincere follower of the good example of Israel, whose character it was that he was a *plain man,* in opposition to Esau's character of a *cunning man.* He was a genuine son of *honest Jacob,* not only of his *seed,* but of his *spirit.* 2. A sincere professor of the faith of Israel; he was true to the religion he professed, and lived up to it: he was really as good as he seemed, and his practice was *of a piece* with his profession. He is the Jew that is one *inwardly* (Rom. 2:29), so is he *the Christian. Secondly,* He is one in whom is *no guile* — that is the character of an Israelite indeed, a Christian indeed: *no guile* towards men; a man without trick or design; a man that one may trust; *no guile* towards God, that is, sincere in his repentance for sin; sincere in his covenanting with God; in whose spirit is *no guile,* Ps. 32:2. He does not say without *guilt,* but without *guile.* Though in many things he is foolish and forgetful, yet in nothing false, nor *wickedly departing from God:* there is no allowed approved guilt in him; not painted, though he have his spots: *"Behold* this Israelite *indeed."* 1. "Take notice of him, that you may learn his way, and do like him." 2. "Admire him; *behold,* and *wonder.*" The hypocrisy of the scribes and Pharisees had so leavened the Jewish church and nation, and their religion was so degenerated into formality or state-policy, that an Israelite indeed was a *man wondered at,* a miracle of divine grace, like Job, *ch.* 1:8.

(2.) Nathanael is much surprised at this, upon which Christ gives him a further proof of his omnisciency, and a kind memorial of his former devotion.

[1.] Here is Nathanael's modesty, in that he was soon put out of countenance at the kind notice Christ was pleased to take of him: *"Whence knowest thou me,* me that am unworthy of thy cognizance? *who am I, O Lord God?"* 2 Sa. 7:18. This was an evidence of his sincerity, that he did not catch at the praise he met with, but declined it. Christ knows us better than we know ourselves; we know not what is in a man's heart by looking in his face, but all things are naked and open before Christ, Heb. 4:12, 13. Doth Christ know us? Let us covet to know him.

[2.] Here is Christ's further *manifestation* of himself to him: *Before Philip called thee, I saw thee. First,* He gives him to understand that he *knew him,* and so manifests his divinity. It is God's prerogative infallibly to know all persons and all things; by this Christ proved himself to be God upon many occasions. It was prophesied concerning the Messiah that he should be of *quick understanding in the fear of the Lord,* that is, in judging the sincerity and degree of the fear of God in others, and that he should not *judge after the sight of his eyes,* Isa. 11:2, 3. Here he answers that prediction. See 2 Tim. 2:19. *Secondly,* That before Philip called him he saw him under the fig-tree; this manifests a particular kindness for him. 1. His eye was towards him before Philip called him, which was the first time that ever Nathanael was acquainted with Christ. Christ has knowledge of us before we have any knowledge of him; see Isa. 45:4; Gal. 4:9. 2. His eye was upon him when he as *under the fig-tree;* this was a private token which nobody understood but Nathanael: "When thou wast retired *under the fig-tree* in thy garden, and thoughtest that no eye saw thee, I have then my eye upon thee, and saw that which was very acceptable." It is most probable that Nathanael under the fig-tree was employed, as Isaac in the field, in meditation, and prayer, and communion with God. Perhaps then and there it was that he solemnly joined himself to the Lord in an inviolable covenant. Christ saw in secret, and by this public notice of it did in part reward him openly. *Sitting under the* fig-tree denotes quietness and composedness of spirit, which much befriend communion with God. See Mic. 4:4; Zec. 3:10. Nathanael herein was an Israelite indeed, that, like Israel, he *wrestled with God alone* (Gen. 32:24), prayed not like the hypocrites, in the corners of the streets, but under the fig-tree.

(3.) Nathanael hereby obtained a full assurance of faith in Jesus Christ, expressed in that noble acknowledgment (*v.* 49): *Rabbi, thou art the Son of God, thou art the king of Israel;* that is, in short, thou art the true Messiah. Observe here, [1.] How *firmly* he believed *with the heart.* Though he had lately laboured under some prejudices concerning Christ, they had now all vanished. Note, The grace of God, in working faith, casts down imaginations. Now he asks no more, *Can any good thing come out of Nazareth?* For he believes Jesus of Nazareth to be the chief good, and embraces him accordingly. [2.] How *freely* he confessed *with the mouth.* His confession is made in form of an adoration, directed to our Lord Jesus himself, which is a proper way of confessing our faith. *First,* He confesses Christ's prophetical office, in calling him *Rabbi,* a title which the Jews commonly gave to their teachers. Christ is the great rabbi, at whose feet we must all be *brought up. Secondly,* He confesses his divine nature and mission, in calling him the Son of God (that Son of God spoken of Ps. 2:7); though he had but a human *form* and *aspect,* yet having a divine knowledge, the knowledge of the heart, and of things distant and secret, Nathanael thence concludes him to be the *Son of God. Thirdly,* He confesses, *"Thou art the king of Israel;* that king of Israel whom we have been long waiting for." If he be the Son of God, he is king of the Israel of God. Nathanael hereby proves himself an Israelite indeed that he so readily owns and submits to the king of Israel.

(4.) Christ hereupon raises the hopes and expectations of Nathanael to something further and greater than all this, *v.* 50, 51. Christ is very tender of young converts, and will encourage good beginnings, though weak, Mt. 12:20.

[1.] He here signifies his acceptance, and (it should seem) his admiration, of the ready faith of Nathanael: *Because I said, I saw thee under the fig-tree, believest thou?* He wonders that such a small indication of Christ's divine knowledge should have such an effect; it was a sign that Nathanael's heart was prepared beforehand, else the work had not been done so suddenly. Note, It is much for the honour of Christ and his grace, when the heart is surrendered to him at the first summons.

[2.] He promises him much greater helps for the confirmation and increase of his faith than he had had for the first production of it.

First, In general: *"Thou shalt see greater things than these,* stronger proofs of my being the Messiah;" the miracles of Christ, and his resurrection. Note, 1. To him that hath, and maketh good use of what he hath, more shall be given. 2. Those who truly believe the gospel will find its evidences grow upon them, and will see more and more cause to believe it. 3. Whatever discoveries Christ is pleased to make of himself to his people while they are here in this world, he hath still greater things than these to make known to them; a glory yet further *to be revealed.*

Secondly, In particular: "Not thou only, but you, all you my disciples, whose faith this is intended for the confirmation of, you *shall see heaven opened;"* this is more than telling Nathanael of his being under the fig-tree. This is introduced with a solemn preface, *Verily, verily I say unto you,* which commands both a *fixed attention* to what is said as very weighty, and a *full assent* to it as undoubtedly true: "I say it, whose word you may rely upon, *amen, amen."* None used this word at the beginning of a sentence but Christ, though the Jews often used it at the close of a prayer, and sometimes doubled it. It is a solemn asseveration. Christ is called the *Amen* (Rev. 3:14), and so some take it here, *I the Amen, the Amen, say unto you.* I the faithful witness. Note, The assurances we have of the glory to be revealed are built upon the word of Christ. Now see what it is that Christ assures them of: *Hereafter,* or *within awhile,* or *ere long,* or henceforth, ye shall see heaven opened.

a. It is a mean title that Christ here takes to himself: *The Son of man;* a title frequently applied to him in the gospel, but always by himself. Nathanael had called him the *Son of God* and *king of Israel:* he calls himself *Son of man,* (1.) To express his *humility* in the midst of the honours done him. (*b.*) To teach his *humanity,* which is to be believed as well as his divinity. (*c.*) To intimate his present state of humiliation, that Nathanael might not expect this king of Israel to appear in external pomp.

b. Yet they are great things which he here foretels: *You shall see heaven opened,* and *the angels of God ascending and descending upon the Son of man.* (*a.*) Some understand it literally, as pointing at some particular event. Either, [*a.*] There was some vision of Christ's glory, in which this was exactly fulfilled, which Nathanael was an eye-witness of, as Peter, and James, and John were of his transfiguration. There were many things which Christ did, and those in the presence of his disciples, which were not written (*ch.* 20:30), and why not this? Or, [*b.*] It was fulfilled in the many ministrations of the angels to our Lord Jesus, especially that at his ascension, when heaven was opened to receive him, and the angels *ascended* and *descended,* to attend him and to do him honour, and this in the sight of the disciples. Christ's ascension was the great proof of his mission, and much confirmed the faith of his disciples, *ch.* 6:62. Or, [*c.*] It may refer to Christ's second coming, to judge the world, when the heavens shall be *open,* and every eye shall see him, and the angels of God shall ascend and descend about him, as attendants on him, every one employed; and a busy day it will be. See 2 Th. 1:10. (*b.*) Others take it figuratively, as speaking of a state or series of things to commence *from henceforth;* and so we may understand it, [*a.*] Of Christ's *miracles.* Nathanael believed, because Christ, as the prophets of old, could tell him things secret; but what is this? Christ is now beginning a dispensation of miracles, much more great and strange than this, as if heaven were opened; and such a power shall be exerted by the Son of man as if the angels, which excel in strength, were continually attending his orders. Immediately after this, Christ began to work miracles, *ch.* 2:11. Or, [*b.*] Of his *mediation,* and that blessed intercourse which he hath settled between heaven and earth, which his disciples should be degrees be let into the mystery of. *First,* By Christ, as Mediator, they shall see *heaven opened,* that we may *enter into the holiest* by his blood (Heb. 10:19, 20); heaven opened, that by faith we may *look in,* and at length may *go in;* may now behold the glory of the Lord, and hereafter enter into the joy of our Lord. And, *Secondly,* They shall *see angels ascending and descending upon the Son of man.* Through Christ we have communion with and benefit by the holy angels, and things in heaven and things on earth are *reconciled* and *gathered together.* Christ is to us as Jacob's ladder (Gen. 28:12), by whom angels continually ascend and descend for the good of the saints.

CHAPTER 2

In the close of the foregoing chapter we had an account of the first disciples whom Jesus called, Andrew and Peter, Philip and Nathanael. These were the first-fruits to God and to the Lamb, Rev. 14:4. Now, in this chapter, we have, I. The account of the first miracle which Jesus wrought — turning water into wine, at Cana of Galilee (*v.* 1–11), and his appearing at Capernaum (*v.* 12). II. The account of the first passover he kept at Jerusalem after he began his public ministry; his driving the buyers and sellers out of the temple (*v.* 13–17); and the sign he gave to those who quarrelled with him for it (*v.* 18–22), with an account of some almost believers, that followed him, thereupon, for some time (*v.* 23–25), but he knew them too well to put any confidence in them.

Verses 1–11

We have here the story of Christ's miraculous conversion of water into wine at a marriage in Cana of Galilee. There were some few so well disposed as to believe in Christ, and to follow him, when he *did no miracle;* yet it was not likely that many should be wrought upon till he had something wherewith to answer those that asked, *What sign showest thou?* He could have wrought miracles before, could have made them the common actions of his life and the common entertainments of his friends; but, miracles being designed for the sacred and solemn seals of his doctrine, he began not to work any till he began to preach his doctrine. Now observe,

I. The occasion of this miracle. Maimonides observes it to be to the honour of Moses that all the signs he did in the wilderness he did *upon necessity;* we needed food, he brought us manna, and so did Christ. Observe,

1. The time: the *third day* after he came into Galilee. The evangelist keeps a journal of occurrences, for no day passed without something extraordinary done or said. Our Master filled up his time better than his servants do, and never lay down at night complaining, as the Roman emperor did, that he had *lost a day.*

2. The place: it was at Cana in Galilee, in the tribe of Asher (Jos. 19:28), of which, before, it was said that *he shall yield royal dainties,* Gen. 49:20. Christ began to work miracles in an obscure corner of the country, remote from Jerusalem, which was the public scene of action, to show that he *sought not honour from men* (*ch.* 5:41), but would put honour *upon the lowly.* His doctrine and miracles would not be so much opposed by the plain and honest Galileans as they would be by the proud and prejudiced rabbies, politicians, and grandees, at Jerusalem.

3. The occasion itself was a *marriage;* probably one or both of the parties were akin to our Lord Jesus. The *mother of Jesus* is said to be *there,* and not to be *called,* as Jesus and his disciples were, which intimates that she was there as one at home. Observe the honour which Christ hereby put upon the ordinance of marriage, that he graced the solemnity of it, not only with his presence, but with his first miracle; because it was instituted and blessed in innocency, because by it he would still *seek a godly seed,* because it resembles the mystical union between him and his church, and because he foresaw that in the papal kingdom, while the marriage ceremony would be unduly *dignified* and advanced into a *sacrament,* the *married state* would be unduly *vilified,* as inconsistent with any sacred function. There was a *marriage — gamos,* a *marriage-feast,* to grace the solemnity. Marriages were usually celebrated with festivals (Gen. 29:22; Jdg. 14:10), in token of joy and friendly respect, and for the confirming of love.

4. Christ and his mother and disciples were principal guests at this entertainment. *The mother of Jesus* (that was her most honourable title) *was there;* no mention being made of Joseph, we conclude him dead before this. Jesus was *called,* and he came, accepted the invitation, and feasted with them, to teach us to be *respectful* to our relations, and *sociable* with them, though they be mean. Christ was to come in a way different from that of John Baptist, who came *neither eating nor drinking,* Mt. 11:18, 19. It is the wisdom of the prudent to study how to *improve* conversation rather than how to *decline* it.

(1.) *There was a marriage, and Jesus was called.* Note, [1.] It is very desirable, when there is a *marriage,* to have Jesus Christ *present* at it; to have his spiritual gracious presence, to have the marriage owned and blessed by him: the *marriage* is then *honourable* indeed; and they that *marry in* the Lord (1 Co. 7:39) do not marry *without him.* [2.] They that would have Christ with them at their marriage must invite him by prayer; that is the messenger that must be sent to heaven for him; and he will come: *Thou shalt call, and I will answer.* And he will turn the water into wine.

(2.) The disciples also were invited, those five whom he had called (*ch.* 1), for as yet he had no more; they were his family, and were invited with him. They had thrown themselves upon his care, and they soon found that, though he had no wealth, he had good friends. Note, [1.] Those that *follow* Christ shall *feast* with him, they shall *fare* as he *fares,* so he has *bespoken* for them (*ch.* 12:26): *Where I am, there shall my servant be also.* [2.] Love to Christ is testified by a love to those that are his, for his sake; *our goodness extendeth not to him,* but *to the saints.* Calvin observes how *generous* the maker of the feast was, though he seems to have been but of small substance, to invite four or five strangers more than he thought of, because they were followers of Christ, which shows, saith he, that there is more of freedom, and liberality, and true friendship, in the conversation of some meaner persons than among many of higher rank.

II. The miracle itself. In which observe,

1. They *wanted wine, v.* 3. (1.) There was *want* at a *feast;* though much was provided, yet all was spent. While we are in this world we sometimes find ourselves *in straits,* even then when we think ourselves in the *fulness of our sufficiency.* If always *spending,* perhaps all is spent ere we are aware. (2.) There was want at a *marriage feast.* Note, They who, being *married,* are come to *care for the things of the world* must expect *trouble in the flesh,* and count upon disappointment. (3.) It should seem, Christ and his disciples were the occasion of this want, because there was more company than was expected when the provision was made; but they who straiten themselves for Christ shall not lose by him.

2. The *mother of Jesus* solicited him to assist her friends in this strait. We are told (*v.* 3–5) what passed between Christ and his mother upon this occasion.

(1.) She acquaints him with the difficulty they were in (*v.* 3): *She saith unto him, They have no wine.* Some think that she did not expect from him any miraculous supply (he having as yet wrought no miracle), but that she would have him make some *decent* excuse to the company, and make the best of it, to save the bridegroom's reputation, and keep him in countenance; or (as Calvin suggests) would have him make up the want of wine with some holy profitable discourse. But, most probably, she looked for a miracle; for she knew he was now appearing as the great prophet, like unto Moses, who so often seasonably supplied the wants of Israel; and, though this was his first public miracle, perhaps he had sometimes relieved her and her husband in their low estate. The bridegroom might have sent out for more wine, but she was for going to the fountain-head. Note, [1.] We ought to be concerned for the wants and straits of our friends, and not *seek our own things* only. [2.] In our own and our friends' straits it is our wisdom and duty to apply ourselves to Christ by prayer. [3.] In our addresses to Christ, we must not prescribe to him, but humbly spread our case before him, and then *refer ourselves* to him to do as he pleases.

(2.) He gave her a reprimand for it, for he saw more amiss in it than we do, else he had not treated it thus. — Here is,

[1.] The rebuke itself: *Woman, what have I to do with thee?* As many as Christ loves, he rebukes and chastens. He calls her *woman,* not *mother.* When we begin to be assuming, we should be reminded what we are, *men* and *women,* frail, foolish, and corrupt. The question, *ti emoi kai soi,* might be read, *What is that to me and thee?* What is it to us if they do want? But it is always as we render it, *What have I to do with thee?* as Judges 11:12; 2 Sa. 16:10; Ezra 4:3; Mt. 8:29. It therefore bespeaks a resentment, yet not at all inconsistent with the reverence and subjection which he paid to his mother, according to the fifth commandment (Lu. 2:51); for there was a time when it was Levi's praise that he *said to his father, I have not known him,* Duet. 33:9. Now this was intended to be, *First,* A check to his mother for interposing in a matter which was the act of his Godhead, which had no dependence on her, and which she was not the mother of. Though, as man, he was David's Son and hers; yet, as God, he was David's Lord and hers, and he would have her know it. The greatest advancements must not make us forget ourselves and our place, nor the familiarity to which the covenant of grace admits us breed contempt. irreverence, or any kind or degree of presumption. *Secondly,* It was an instruction to others of his relations (many of whom were present here) that they must never expect him to have any regard to his kindred according to the flesh, in his working miracles, or that therein he should gratify them, who in this matter were no more to him than other people. In the things of God we must not *know faces. Thirdly,* It is a standing testimony against that idolatry which he foresaw his church would in after-ages sink into, in giving undue honours to the virgin Mary, a crime which the Roman catholics, as they call themselves, are notoriously guilty of, when they call her the *queen of heaven,* the *salvation of the world,* their *mediatrix,* their *life* and *hope;* not only depending upon her merit and intercession, but beseeching her to *command her Son* to do them good: *Monstra te esse matrem — Show that thou art his mother. Jussu matris impera salvatori — Lay thy maternal commands on the Saviour.* Does he not here expressly say, when a miracle was to be wrought, even in the days of his humiliation, and his mother did but tacitly hint an intercession, *Woman, what have I to do with thee?* This was plainly designed either to *prevent* or *aggravate* such gross idolatry, such horrid blasphemy. The Son of God is appointed our Advocate with the Father; but the mother of our Lord was never designed to be our advocate with the Son.

[2.] The reason of this rebuke: *Mine hour is not yet come.* For every thing Christ did, and that was done to him, he had *his hour,* the *fixed* time and the *fittest* time, which was punctually observed. *First,* "Mine hour for *working miracles* is not yet come." Yet afterwards he wrought this, before the hour, because he foresaw it would confirm the faith of his infant disciples (*v.* 11), which was the end of all his miracles: so that this was an earnest of the many miracles he would work when his *hour was come. Secondly,* "Mine hour of working miracles *openly* is *not yet come;* therefore do not talk of it thus *publicly.*" *Thirdly,* "It *not the hour* of my exemption from thy authority *yet come,* now that I have begun to act as a prophet?" So Gregory Nyssen. *Fourthly,* "Mine hour for working *this miracle* is not yet come." His mother moved him to help them *when the wine began to fail* (so it may be read, *v.* 3), but his hour was not yet come till it was quite spent, and there was a *total want;* not only to prevent any suspicion of mixing some of the wine that was left with the water, but to teach us that man's extremity is God's opportunity to appear for the help and relief of his people. Then *his hour is come* when we are reduced to the utmost strait, and know not what to do. This encouraged those that waited for him to believe that though his hour was not *yet come* it would come. Note, The delays of mercy are not to be construed the denials of prayer. *At the end it shall speak.*

(3.) Notwithstanding this, she encouraged herself with expectations that he would help her friends in this strait, for she bade the servants *observe his orders, v.* 5. [1.] She took the reproof very submissively, and did not reply to it. It is best not to deserve reproof from Christ, but next best to be meek and quiet under it, and to count it a kindness, Ps. 141:5. [2.] She kept her hope in Christ's mercy, that he would yet grant her desire. When we come to God in Christ for any mercy, two things discourage us: — *First,* Sense of *our own follies* and infirmities "Surely such imperfect prayers as ours cannot speed." *Secondly,* Sense of *our Lord's frowns and rebukes.* Afflictions are continued, deliverances delayed, and God seems angry at our prayers. This was the case of the mother of our Lord here, and yet she encourages herself with hope that he will at length give in an answer of peace, to teach us to wrestle with God by faith and fervency in prayer, even when he seems in his providence to walk contrary to us. We must *against hope believe in hope,* Rom. 4:18. [3.] She directed the servants to have an eye *to him* immediately, and not to make their applications to her, as it is probable *they had done.* She quits all pretensions to an *influence* upon him, or *intercession* with him; let their souls *wait only* on him, Ps.

62:5. [4.] She directed them punctually to observe his orders, without disputing, or asking questions. Being conscious to herself of a fault in *prescribing* to him, she cautions the servants to take heed of the same fault, and to attend both his time and his way for supply: *"Whatsoever he saith unto you, do it,* though you may think it ever so improper. If he saith, Give the guests water, when they call for wine, do it. If he saith, Pour out from the bottoms of the vessels that are spent, do it. He can make a few drops of wine multiply to so many draughts." Note, Those that expect Christ's *favours* must with an implicit obedience observe his *orders.* The way of duty is the way to mercy; and Christ's methods must not be objected against.

(4.) Christ did at length miraculously supply them; for he is often better than his word, but never worse.

[1.] The miracle itself was *turning water into wine;* the substance of water acquiring a new form, and having all the accidents and qualities of wine. Such a *transformation* is a *miracle;* but the popish *transubstantiation,* the substance changed, the accidents remaining the same, is a monster. By this Christ showed himself to be the God of nature, who maketh the earth to bring forth wine, Ps. 109:14, 15. The extracting of the blood of the grape every year from the moisture of the earth is no less a work of power, though, being according to the common law of nature, it is not such a work of wonder, as this. The beginning of Moses's miracles was turning water into blood (Ex. 4:9; 7:20), the beginning of Christ's miracles was turning water into wine; which intimates the difference between the law of Moses and the gospel of Christ. The curse of the law turns water into blood, common comforts into bitterness and terror; the blessing of the gospel turns water into wine. Christ hereby showed that his errand into the world was to heighten and improve creature-comforts to all believers, and make them comforts indeed. Shiloh is said to *wash his garments in wine* (Gen. 49:11), the water for washing being *turned into wine.* And the gospel call is, *Come ye to the waters, and buy wine,* Isa. 55:1.

[2.] The circumstances of it magnified it and freed it from all suspicion of cheat or collusion; for,

First, It was done in water-pots (*v.* 6): *There were set there six water-pots of stone.* Observe, 1. For what use these water-pots were intended: for the legal purifications from ceremonial pollutions enjoined by the law of God, and many more by the tradition of the elders. The *Jews eat not, except they wash often* (Mk. 7:3), and they used much water in their washing, for which reason here were six large water-pots provided. It was a saying among them, *Qui multâ utitur aquâ in lavando, multas consequetur in hoc mundo divitias — He who uses much water in washing will gain much wealth in this world.* 2. To what use Christ put them, quite different from what they were intended for; to be the receptacles of the miraculous wine. Thus Christ came to bring in the grace of the gospel, which is as *wine,* that cheereth God and man (Jdg. 9:13), instead of the shadows of the law, which were as water, *weak and beggarly elements.* These were *water-pots,* that had never been used to have wine in them; and of *stone,* which is not apt to retain the scent of former liquors, if ever they had had wine in them. They contained *two or three firkins apiece;* two or three *measures, baths,* or *ephahs;* the quantity is uncertain, but very considerable. We may be sure that it was not intended to be all drank at this feast, but for a further kindness to the new-married couple, as the multiplied oil was to the poor widow, out of which she might *pay her debt,* and *live of the rest,* 2 Ki. 4:7. Christ gives like himself, gives abundantly, according to his riches in glory. It is the penman's language to say, *They contained two or three firkins,* for the Holy Spirit could have ascertained just how much; thus (as *ch.* 6:19) teaching us to speak cautiously, and not confidently, of those things of which we have not good assurance.

Secondly, The water-pots were filled *up to the brim* by the servants at Christ's word, *v.* 7. As Moses, the servant of the Lord, when God bade him, went to the rock, to draw water; so these servants, when Christ bade them, went to the water, to fetch wine. Note, Since no difficulties can be opposed to the arm of God's power, no improbabilities are to be objected against the word of his command.

Thirdly, The miracle was wrought suddenly, and in such a manner as greatly magnified it.

a. As soon as they had filled the water-pots, presently he said, *Draw out now* (*v.* 8), and it was done, (*a.*) Without any ceremony, in the eye of the spectators. One would have thought, as Naaman, he should have come out, and *stood,* and *called on the name of God,* 2 Ki. 5:11. No, he sits still in his place, says not a word, but *wills* the thing, and so works it. Note, Christ does great things and marvellous *without noise,* works manifest changes in a hidden way. Sometimes Christ, in working miracles, used words and signs, but it was *for their sakes that stood by, ch.* 11:42. (*b.*) Without any hesitation or uncertainty in his own breast. He did not say, *Draw out now,* and let me *taste it,* questioning whether the thing were done as he willed it or no; but with the greatest assurance imaginable, though it was his *first miracle,* he recommends it to the master of the feast *first.* As he knew what he *would* do, so he knew what he *could* do, and made no essay in his work; but all was good, very good, even in the beginning.

b. Our Lord Jesus directed the servants, (*a.*) To *draw it out;* not to let it alone in the vessel, to be admired, but to *draw it out,* to be drank. Note, [*a.*] Christ's works are all *for use;* he gives no man a talent to be *buried,* but to be *traded with.* Has he turned thy water into wine, given thee knowledge and grace? It is to *profit withal;* and therefore *draw out now.* [*b.*] Those that would know Christ must make trial of him, must attend upon him in the use of ordinary means, and then may expect extraordinary influence. That which is *laid up* for all that *fear God* is *wrought for those that trust in him* (Ps. 31:19), that by the exercise of faith *draw out* what is *laid up.* (*b.*) To present it to *the governor of the feast.* Some think that this *governor of the feast* was only the chief guest, that sat at the upper end of the table; but, if so, surely our Lord Jesus should have had that place, for he was, upon all accounts, the principal guest; but it seems another had the uppermost room, probably one that *loved* it (Mt. 23:6), and *chose* it, Lu. 14:7. And Christ, according to his own rule, *sat down in the lowest room;* but, though he was not treated as the Master of the feast, he kindly approved himself a friend to the feast, and, if not its founder, yet its best benefactor. Others think that this *governor* was the inspector and monitor of the feast: the same with Plutarch's *symposiarcha,* whose office it was to see that each had enough, and none did exceed, and that there were no indecencies or disorders. Note, Feasts have need of governors, because too many, when they are at feasts, have not the government of themselves. Some think that this *governor* was the *chaplain,* some priest or Levite that craved a blessing and gave thanks, and Christ would have the cup brought to him, that he might bless it, and bless God for it; for the extraordinary tokens of Christ's presence and power were not to supersede, or jostle out, the ordinary rules and methods of piety and devotion.

Fourthly, The wine which was thus miraculously provided was of the best and richest kind, which was acknowledged by the governor of the feast; and that it was really so, and not his fancy, is certain, because he knew not whence it was, *v.* 9, 10. 1. It was certain that this was *wine.* The governor knew this when he drank it, though he knew not *whence it was;* the servants knew whence it was, but had not yet tasted it. if the taster had seen the drawing of it, or the drawers had had the tasting of it, something might have been imputed to fancy; but now no room is left for suspicion. 2. That it was the best wine. Note, Christ's works commend themselves even to those that know not their author. The products of miracles were always the best in their kind. This wine had a *stronger body,* and *better flavour,* than ordinary. This the governor of the feast takes notice of to the bridegroom, with an air of pleasantness, as *uncommon.* (1.) The common method was otherwise. Good wine is brought out to the best advantage at the beginning of a feast, when the guests have their heads clear and their appetites fresh, and can relish it, and will commend it; but *when they have well drank,* when their heads are confused, and their appetites palled, good wine is but thrown away upon them, worse will serve then. See the vanity of all the pleasures of sense; they soon surfeit, but never satisfy; the longer they are enjoyed, the less pleasant they grow. (2.) This bridegroom obliged his friends with a reserve of the best wine for the grace-cup: *Thou hast kept the good wine until now;* not knowing to whom they were indebted for this good wine, he returns the thanks of the table to the bridegroom. *She did not know that I gave her corn and wine,* Hos. 2:8. Now, [1.] Christ, in providing thus plentifully for the guests, though he hereby allows a sober cheerful use of wine, especially in times of rejoicing (Neh. 8:10), yet he does not invalidate his own caution, nor invade it, in the least, which is, that our hearts be not *at any time,* no not at a marriage feast, *overcharged with surfeiting and drunkenness,* Lu. 21:34. When Christ provided so much *good wine* for them that had *well drunk,* he intended to try their sobriety, and to teach them *how to abound,* as well as *how to want.* Temperance *per force* is a thankless virtue; but if divine providence gives us abundance of the delights of sense, and divine grace enables us to use them moderately, this is self-denial that is praiseworthy. He also intended that some should be left for the confirmation of the truth of the miracle to the faith of others. And we have reason to think that the guests at this table were so well *taught,* or at least were now so well awed by the presence of Christ, that none of them abused this wine to excess. Theses two considerations, drawn from this story, may be sufficient at any time to fortify us against temptations to intemperance: *First,* That our meat and drink are the *gifts of God's bounty* to us, and we owe our liberty to use them, and our comfort in the use of them, to the mediation of Christ; it is therefore ungrateful and impious to abuse them. *Secondly,* That, wherever we are, Christ has his eye upon us; we should *eat bread before God* (Ex. 18:12), and then we should not *feed ourselves without fear.* [2.] He has given us a specimen of the method he takes in dealing with those that deal with him, which is, to reserve the *best* for the *last,* and therefore they must *deal upon trust.* The recompence of their services and sufferings is reserved for the other world; it is a glory *to be revealed.* The pleasures of sin give their colour in the cup, but *at the last bite;* but the pleasures of religion will be *pleasures for evermore.*

III. In the conclusion of this story (*v.* 11) we are told, 1. That this was *the beginning of miracles* which Jesus did. Many miracles had been wrought *concerning* him at his birth and baptism, and he himself was the greatest miracle of all; but this was the first that was wrought *by* him. He could have wrought miracles when he disputed with the doctors, but his hour was not come. He had power, but there was a *time of the hiding of his power.* 2. That herein he *manifested his glory;* hereby he proved himself to be the Son of God, and his glory to be that of the only-begotten of the Father. He also discovered the nature and end of his office; the power of a God, and the grace of a Saviour, appearing in all his miracles, and particularly in this, manifested the glory of the long-expected Messiah. 3. That *his disciples believed on him.* Those whom he had called (*ch.* 1), who had seen no miracle, and yet followed him, now saw this, shared in it, and had their faith strengthened by it. Note, (1.) Even the faith that is true is at first but weak. The strongest men were once babes, so were the strongest Christians. (2.) The manifesting of the glory of Christ is the great confirmation of the faith of Christians.

Verses 12–22

Here we have,

I. The short visit Christ made to Capernaum, *v.* 12. It was a large and populous city, about a day's journey from Cana; it is called *his own city* (Mt. 9:1), because he made it his head-quarters in Galilee, and what little rest he had was there. It was a place of concourse, and *therefore* Christ chose it, that the fame of his doctrine and miracles might thence spread the further. Observe,

1. The company that attended him thither: *his mother, his brethren, and his disciples.* Wherever Christ went, (1.) He *would not* go alone, but would take those with him who had put themselves under his guidance, that he might instruct them, and that they might attest his miracles. (2.) He *could not* go alone, but they would follow him, because they liked the sweetness either of his doctrine or of his wine, *ch.* 6:26. His mother, though he had lately given her to understand that in the works of his ministry he should pay no more respect to her than to any other person, yet followed him; not to intercede with him, but to learn of him. His *brethren* also and relations, who were at the marriage and were wrought upon by the miracle there, and *his disciples,* who attended him wherever he went. It should seem, people were more affected with Christ's miracles at first than they were afterwards, when custom made them seem less strange.

2. His continuance there, which was at this time *not many days,* designing now only to *begin* the acquaintance he would afterwards *improve* there. Christ was still upon the remove, would not confine his usefulness to *one* place, because *many* needed him. And he would teach his followers to look upon themselves but as *sojourners* in this world, and his ministers to follow their opportunities, and go where their work led them. We do not now find Christ in the synagogues, but he

privately instructed his friends, and thus entered upon his work *by degrees.* It is good for young ministers to accustom themselves to pious and edifying discourse in private, that they may with the better preparation, and greater awe, approach their public work. He did not stay long at Capernaum, because the passover was at hand, and he must attend it at Jerusalem; for every thing is beautiful in its season. The less good must give way to the greater, and all the dwellings of Jacob must give place to the gates of Zion.

II. The passover he kept at Jerusalem; it is the *first* after his baptism, and the evangelist takes notice of all the passovers he kept henceforward, which were four in all, the *fourth* that at which he suffered (three years after this), and half a year was now past since his baptism. Christ, being *made under the law,* observed the passover at Jerusalem; see Ex. 23:17. Thus he taught us by his example a strict observance of divine institutions, and a diligent attendance on religious assemblies. He went up to Jerusalem when *the passover was at hand,* that he might be there *with the first.* It is called *the Jews' passover,* because it was peculiar to them (Christ is *our* Passover); now shortly God will no longer own it for his. Christ kept the passover at Jerusalem yearly, ever since he was twelve years old, in obedience to the law; but now that he has entered upon his public ministry we may expect something more from him than before; and two things we are here told he did there: —

1. He *purged the temple, v.* 14–17. Observe here,

(1.) The first place we find him in at Jerusalem was the *temple,* and, it should seem, he did not make any public appearance till he came thither; for his presence and preaching there were that glory of the latter house which was to *exceed the glory of the former,* Hag. 2:9. It was foretold (Mal. 3:1): *I will send my messenger,* John Baptist; he never preached in the temple, but *the Lord, whom ye seek,* he shall *suddenly come to his temple,* suddenly after the appearing of John Baptist; so that this was the time, and the temple the place, when, and where, the Messiah was to be expected.

(2.) The first work we find him at in the temple was the *purging* of it; for so it was foretold there (Mal. 3:2, 3): *He shall sit as a refiner and purify the sons of Levi.* Now was come the *time of reformation.* Christ came to be the great reformer; and, according to the method of the reforming kings of Judah, he first *purged out* what was amiss (and that used to be passover-work too, as in Hezekiah's time, 2 Chr. 30:14, 15, and Josiah's, 2 Ki. 23:4, etc.), and then taught them to do well. First *purge out the old leaven,* and then *keep the feast.* Christ's design in coming into the world was to reform the world; and he expects that all who come to him should reform their hearts and lives, Gen. 35:2. And this he has taught us by purging the temple. See here,

[1.] What were the corruptions that were to be purged out. He found a market in one of the courts of the temple, that which was called the *court of the Gentiles,* within the *mountain of that house.* There, *First,* They sold *oxen, and sheep, and doves,* for sacrifice; we will suppose, not for common use, but for the convenience of those who came out of the country, and could not bring their sacrifices *in kind* along with them; see Deu. 14:24–26. This *market* perhaps had been kept by the pool of Bethesda (*ch.* 5:2), but was admitted into the temple by the chief priests, for filthy lucre; for, no doubt, the rents for standing there, and fees for searching the beasts sold there, and certifying that they were *without blemish,* would be a considerable revenue to them. Great corruptions in the church owe their rise to the love of money, 1 Tim. 6:5, 10. *Secondly,* They *changed money,* for the convenience of those that were to pay a half-shekel *in specie* every year, by way of poll, for the service of the tabernacle (Ex. 30:12), and no doubt they got by it.

[2.] What course our Lord took to purge out those corruptions. He had seen these in the temple formerly, when he was in a private station; but never went about to drive them out till now, when he had taken upon him the public character of a prophet. He did not complain to the chief priests, for he knew they countenanced those corruptions. But he himself,

First, Drove out the sheep and oxen, and those that *sold them,* out of the temple. He never used *force* to drive any *into* the temple, but only to drive those out that profaned it. He did not seize the sheep and oxen for himself, did not *distrain* and impound them, though he found them *damage faissant — actual trespassers* upon his Father's ground; he only drove them out, and their owners with them. He made a scourge of *small cords,* which probably they had led their sheep and oxen with, and thrown them away upon the ground, whence Christ gathered them. Sinners prepare the scourges with which they themselves will be driven out from the temple of the Lord. He did not make a scourge to chastise the offenders (his punishments are of another nature), but only to drive out the cattle; he aimed no further than at reformation. See Rom. 13:3, 4; 2 Co. 10:8.

Secondly, He *poured out the changers' money, to kerma — the small money —* the *Nummorum Famulus.* In *pouring out* the money, he showed his contempt of it; he threw it to the ground, to the earth as it *was.* In *overthrowing* the tables, he showed his displeasure against those that make religion a matter of worldly gain. Money-changers in the temple are the scandal of it. Note, In reformation, it is good to make thorough work; he *drove them all out;* and not only threw out the money, but, in overturning the tables, threw out the trade too.

Thirdly, He said to them that sold doves (sacrifices for the poor), *Take these things hence.* The doves, though they took up less room, and were a less nuisance than the oxen and sheep, yet must not be allowed there. The sparrows and swallows were welcome, that were left to God's providence (Ps. 84:3), but not the doves, that were appropriated to man's profit. God's temple must not be made a pigeon-house. But see Christ's prudence in his zeal. When he drove out the sheep and oxen, the owners might follow them; when he poured out the money, they might gather it up again; but, if he had turned the doves flying, perhaps they could not have been retrieved; therefore to them that sold doves he said, *Take these things hence.* Note, Discretion must always guide and govern our zeal, that we do nothing unbecoming ourselves, or mischievous to others.

Fourthly, He gave them a good reason for what he did: *Make not my Father's house a house of merchandise.* Reason for conviction should accompany force for correction.

a. Here is a reason why they should not profane the temple, because it was the *house of God,* and not to be made a house of merchandise. Merchandise is a good thing in the exchange, but not in the temple. This was, (*a.*) to *alienate* that which was dedicated to the honour of God; it was *sacrilege;* it was robbing God. (*b.*) It was to debase that which was solemn and awful, and to make it mean. (*c.*) It was to disturb and distract those services in which men ought to be most solemn, serious, and intent. It was particularly an affront to the *sons of the stranger* in their worship to be forced to herd themselves with the sheep and oxen, and to be distracted in their worship by the noise of a market, for this market was kept in the court of the Gentiles. (*d.*) It was to make the business of religion subservient to a secular interest; for the holiness of the place must advance the market, and promote the sale of their commodities. Those make God's house a house of merchandise, [*a.*] Whose minds are filled with cares about worldly business when they are attending on religious exercises, as those, Amos 8:5; Eze. 33:31. [*b.*] Who perform divine offices for filthy lucre, and sell the gifts of the Holy Ghost, Acts 8:18.

b. Here is a reason why he was concerned to purge it, because it *was his Father's house.* And, (*a.*) Therefore he had authority to purge it, for he was faithful, as a Son *over his own house.* Heb. 3:5, 6. In calling God his Father, he intimates that he was the Messiah, of whom it was said, *He shall build a house for my name, and I will be his Father,* 2 Sa. 7:13, 14. (*b.*) Therefore he had a zeal for the purging of it: "It is *my Father's house,* and therefore I cannot bear to see it profaned, and *him* dishonoured." Note, If God be our Father in heaven, and it be therefore our desire that his name may be sanctified, it cannot but be our grief to see it polluted. Christ's purging the temple thus may justly be reckoned among his *wonderful works. Inter omnia signa quae fecit Dominus, hoc mihi videtur esse mirabilius — Of all Christ's wonderful works this appears to me the most wonderful. —* Hieron. Considering, [*a.*] That he did it without the *assistance* of any of his *friends;* probably it had been no hard matter to have raised the *mob,* who had a great veneration for the temple, against these profaners of it; but Christ never countenanced any thing that was tumultuous or disorderly. There was one to *uphold,* but his own arm did it. [*b.*] That he did it without the *resistance* of any of his *enemies,* either the market-people themselves, or the chief priests that gave them their licences, and had the *posse templi — temple force,* at their command. But the corruption was too plain to be justified; sinners' own consciences are reformers' best friends; yet that was not all, there was a divine power put forth herein, a power over the spirits of men; and in this non-resistance of theirs that scripture was fulfilled (Mal. 3:2, 3), *Who shall stand when he appeareth?*

Fifthly, Here is the remark which his disciples made upon it (*v.* 17): *They remembered that it was written, The Zeal of thine house hath eaten me up.* They were somewhat surprised at first to see him to whom they were directed as the *Lamb of God* in such a heat, and him whom they believed to be the *King of Israel* take so little state upon him as to do this himself; but one scripture came to their thoughts, which taught them to reconcile this action both with the meekness of the *Lamb of God* and with the majesty of the *King of Israel;* for David, speaking of the Messiah, takes notice of his *zeal for God's house,* as so great that it even *ate him up,* it made him forget himself, Ps. 69:9. Observe, 1. The disciples came to understand the meaning of what Christ did, by remembering the scriptures: *They remembered* now *that it was written.* Note, The word of God and the works of God do mutually explain and illustrate each other. Dark scriptures are expounded by their accomplishment in providence, and difficult providences are made easy by comparing them with the scriptures. See of what great use it is to the disciples of Christ to be *ready* and *mighty* in the scriptures, and to have their memories well stored with scripture truths, by which they will be *furnished for every good work,* 2. The scripture they remembered was very apposite: *The zeal of thine house hath eaten me up.* David was in this a type of Christ that he was *zealous for God's house,* Ps. 132:2, 3. What he did for it was *with all his might;* see 1 Chr. 29:2. The latter part of that verse (Ps. 69:9) is applied to Christ (Rom. 15:3), as the former part of it here. All the graces that were to be found among the Old-Testament saints were eminently in Christ, and particularly this of zeal for the house of God, and in them, as they were patterns to us, so they were types of him. Observe, (1.) Jesus Christ was zealously affected to the house of God, his church: he loved it, and was always jealous for its honour and welfare. (2.) This zeal did even *eat him up;* it made him *humble* himself, and *spend* himself, and *expose* himself. *My zeal has consumed me,* Ps. 119:139. Zeal for the house of God forbids us to consult our own credit, ease, and safety, when they come in competition with our duty and Christ's service, and sometimes carries on our souls in our duty so far and so fast that our bodies cannot keep pace with them, and makes us as deaf as our Master was to those who suggested, *Spare thyself.* The grievances here redressed might seem but small, and such as should have been connived at; but such was Christ's zeal that he could not bear even *those* that *sold and bought in the temple. Si ibi ebrios inveniret quid faceret Dominus!* (saith St. Austin.) *If he had found drunkards in the temple, how much more would he have been displeased!*

2. Christ, having thus purged the temple, gave a sign to those who demanded it to prove his authority for so doing. Observe here,

(1.) Their demand of a sign: *Then answered the Jews,* that is the multitude of the people, with their leaders. Being Jews, they should rather have stood by him, and assisted him to vindicate the honour of their temple; but, instead of this, they objected against it. note, Those who apply themselves in good earnest to the work of reformation must expect to meet with opposition. When they could object nothing against the thing itself, they questioned his authority to do it: "*What sign showest thou unto us,* to prove thyself authorized and commissioned to do these things?" It was indeed a good work to purge the temple; but what had he to do to undertake it, who was in no office there? They looked upon it as an act of jurisdiction, and that he must prove himself *a prophet, yea, more than a prophet.* But was not the thing itself sign enough? His ability to drive so many from their posts, without opposition, was a proof of his authority; he that was armed with such a divine power was surely armed with a divine commission. *What ailed these* buyers and sellers, *that they fled, that they were driven back?* Surely it was *at the presence of the Lord* (Ps. 114:5, 7), no less a presence.

(2.) Christ's answer to this demand, *v.* 19. He did not immediately work a miracle to convince them, but gave them a sign in something *to come,* the truth of which must appear by the event, according to Deu. 18:21, 22.

Now, [1.] The sign that he gives them is his own *death* and *resurrection.* He refers them to that which would be, *First,*

His *last* sign. If they would not be convinced by what they saw and heard, let them *wait*. Secondly, The *great sign* to prove him to be the Messiah; for concerning him it was foretold that he should be bruised (Isa. 53:5), *cut off* (Dan. 9:26), and yet that he should not see corruption, Ps. 16:10. These things were fulfilled in the blessed Jesus, and therefore *truly he was the Son of God,* and had authority in the temple, his Father's house.

[2.] He foretels his death and resurrection, not in plain terms, as he often did to his disciples, but in figurative expressions; as afterwards, when he gave this for a sign, he called it the *sign of the prophet Jonas,* so here, *Destroy this temple, and in three days I will raise it up.* Thus he spoke in parables to those who were willingly ignorant, that *they might not perceive,* Mt. 13:13, 14. Those that will not see shall not see. Nay, this figurative speech used here proved such a *stumbling-block* to them that it was produced in evidence against him at his trial to prove him a blasphemer. Mt. 26:60, 61. Had they humbly asked him the meaning of what he said, he would have told them, and it had been a savour of life unto life to them, but they were resolved to cavil, and it proved a savour of death unto death. They that would not be convinced were hardened, and the manner of expressing this prediction occasioned the accomplishment of the prediction itself. *First,* He foretels his death by the Jews' malice, in these words, *Destroy you this temple;* that is, "You will destroy it, I know you will. I will permit you to destroy it." Note, Christ, even at the beginning of his ministry, had a clear foresight of all his sufferings at the end of it, and yet went on cheerfully in it. It is good, at *setting out,* to expect the *worst.* Secondly, He foretels his resurrection by his own power: In *three days I will raise it up.* There were others that *were raised,* but Christ raised himself, resumed his own life.

[3.] He chose to express this by *destroying* and *re-edifying* the temple, *First,* Because he was now to justify himself in purging the temple, which they had profaned; as if he had said, "You that defile one temple will destroy another; and I will prove my authority to *purge* what you have *defiled* by *raising* what you will *destroy.*" The profaning of the temple is the *destroying* of it, and its reformation its *resurrection.* Secondly, Because the death of Christ was indeed the destruction of the Jewish temple, the procuring cause of it; and his resurrection was the raising up of another temple, the gospel church, Zec. 6:12. The ruins of their place and *nation* (ch. 11:48) were the riches of the world. See Amos 9:11; Acts 15:16.

(3.) Their cavil at this answer: *"Forty and six years was this temple in building, v.* 20. Temple work was always slow work, and canst thou make such quick work of it?" Now here, [1.] They show *some knowledge;* they could tell how long the temple was in building. Dr. Lightfoot computes that it was just forty-six years from the founding of Zerubbabel's temple, in the second year of Cyrus, to the complete settlement of the temple service, in the 32nd year of Artaxerxes; and the same from Herod's beginning to build this temple, in the 18th year of his reign, to this very time, when the Jews said that this as just forty-six years: *ōkodomēthē* — hath this temple been built. [2.] They show *more ignorance, First,* Of the *meaning of Christ's words.* Note, Men often run into gross mistakes by understanding that literally which the scripture speaks figuratively. What abundance of mischief has been done by interpreting, *This is my body,* after a corporal and carnal manner! Secondly, Of the *almighty power of Christ,* as if he could do no more than another man. Had they known that this was he who *built all things* in six days they would not have made it such an absurdity that he should build a temple in three days.

(4.) A vindication of Christ's answer from their cavil. The difficulty is soon solved by explaining the terms: *He spoke of the temple of his body, v.* 21. Though Christ had discovered a great respect for the temple, in *purging* it, yet he will have us know that the holiness of it, which he was so jealous for, was but *typical,* and leads us to the consideration of another temple of which that was but a shadow, the substance being Christ, Heb. 9:9; Col. 2:17. Some think that when he said, Destroy *this* temple, he pointed to his own body, or laid his hand upon it; however, it is certain that he *spoke of the temple of his body.* Note, The body of Christ is the true temple, of which that at Jerusalem was a type. [1.] Like the temple, it was built by immediate divine direction: *"A body hast thou prepared me,"* 1 Chr. 28:19. [2.] Like the temple, it was a *holy house;* it is called *that holy thing.* [3.] It was, like the temple, the habitation of God's glory; there the eternal Word

dwelt, the true shechinah. He is *Emmanuel* — *God with us.* [4.] The temple was the place and *medium* of intercourse between God and Israel: there God revealed himself to them; there they presented themselves and their services to him. Thus by Christ God speaks to us, and we speak to him. Worshippers looked *towards* that house, 1 Ki. 8:30, 35. So we must worship God with an eye to Christ.

(5.) A reflection which the disciples made upon this, long after, inserted here, to illustrate the story (v. 22): *When he was risen from the dead,* some years after, *his disciples remembered that he had said this.* We found them, 5:17, remembering what had been *written before of him,* and here we find them remembering what they had *heard from him.* Note, The memories of Christ's disciples should be like the treasure of the good house-holder, furnished with things both *new* and *old,* Mt. 13:52. Now observe,

[1.] *When they remembered* that saying: *When he was risen from the dead.* It seems, they did not at this time fully understand Christ's meaning, for they were as yet but babes in knowledge; but they laid up the saying in their hearts, and afterwards it became both intelligible and useful. Note, It is good to *hear for the time to come,* Isa. 42:23. The juniors in years and profession should treasure up those truths of which at present they do not well understand either the meaning or the use, for they will be serviceable to them hereafter, when they come to greater proficiency. It was said of the scholars of Pythagoras that his precepts seemed to freeze in them till they were forty years old, and then they began to thaw; so this saying of Christ revived in the memories of his disciples *when he was risen from the dead;* and why the? *First,* Because *then* the Spirit was poured out to bring things to their remembrance which Christ had said to them, and to make them both *easy* and *ready* to them, *ch.* 14:26. That very day that Christ rose form the dead he *opened their understandings,* Lu. 24:45. *Secondly,* Because then this saying of Christ was fulfilled. When the temple of his body had been *destroyed* and was *raised again,* and that upon the *third day,* then they remembered this among other words which Christ had said to this purport. Note, It contributes much to the understanding of the scripture to observe the fulfilling of the scripture. The event will expound the prophecy.

[2.] What use they made of it: *They believed the scripture, and the word that Jesus had said;* their belief of these was confirmed and received fresh support and vigour. They were slow of heart to believe (Lu. 24:25), but they were *sure.* The *scripture* and the *word of Christ* are here put together. not because they concur and exactly agree together, but because they mutually illustrate and strengthen each other. When the disciples saw both what they had read in the Old Testament, and what they had heard from Christ's own mouth, fulfilled in his death and resurrection, they were the more confirmed in their belief of both.

Verses 23–25

We have here an account of the success, the poor success, of Christ's preaching and miracles at Jerusalem, while he kept the passover there. Observe,

I. That our Lord Jesus, when he was at Jerusalem at the passover, did preach and work miracles. People's *believing on him* implied that he preached; and it is expressly said, *They saw the miracles he did.* He was now in Jerusalem, the holy city, whence the *word of the Lord* was to go *froth.* His residence was mostly in Galilee, and therefore when he was *in Jerusalem* he was very busy. The time was holy time, the *feast-day,* time appointed for the service of God; at the passover the *Levites taught the good knowledge of the Lord* (2 Chr. 30:22), and Christ took that opportunity of preaching, when the concourse of people was great, and thus he would own and honour the divine institution of the passover.

II. That hereby many were brought to *believe in his name,* to acknowledge him a *teacher come from God,* as Nicodemus did (ch. 3:2), a great prophet; and, probably, some of those who *looked for redemption in Jerusalem* believed him to be the Messiah promised, so ready were they to welcome the first appearance of that *bright and morning star.*

III. That yet *Jesus did not commit himself unto them* (v. 24): *ouk episteuen heauton autois* — *He did not trust himself with them.* It is the same word that is used for *believing* in him. So that to believe in Christ is to *commit ourselves* to him and to his guidance. Christ did not see cause to repose any confidence in these new converts at Jerusalem, where he had many enemies that sought to destroy him, either, 1. Because

they were *false,* at least some of them, and would betray him if they had an opportunity, or were strongly tempted to do so. He had more disciples that he could trust among the Galileans than among the dwellers at Jerusalem. In dangerous times and places, it is wisdom to take heed in whom you confide; *memnēso apistein* — *learn to distrust.* Or, 2. Because they were *weak,* and I would hope that this was the worst of it; not that they were *treacherous* and designed him a mischief, but, (1.) They were *timorous,* and wanted zeal and courage, and might perhaps be frightened to do a wrong thing. In times of difficulty and danger, cowards are not fit to be trusted. Or, (2.) They were *tumultuous,* and wanted discretion and management. These in Jerusalem perhaps had their expectations of the *temporal* reign of the Messiah more raised than others, and, in that expectation, would be ready to give some bold strokes at the government if Christ would have *committed himself to them* and put himself at the head of them; but he would not, for his kingdom is not of this world. We should be shy of turbulent unquiet people, as our Master here was, though they profess to *believe in Christ,* as these did.

IV. That the reason why he did not *commit himself* to them was because he *knew* them (v. 25), knew the wickedness of some and the weakness of others. The evangelist takes this occasion to assert Christ's omniscience. 1. He *knew all men,* not only their names and faces, as it is possible for us to know many, but their nature, dispositions, affections, designs, as we do not know *any man,* scarcely *ourselves.* He knows *all men,* for his powerful hand made them all, his piercing eye sees them all, sees into them. He knows his *subtle enemies,* and all their secret projects; his *false friends,* and their true characters; what they really are, whatever they pretend to be. He knows them that are truly his, knows their integrity, and knows their infirmity too. He *knows their frame.* 2. He *needed not that any should testify of man.* His knowledge was not by information from others, but by his own infallible intuition. It is the infelicity of earthly princes that they must see with other men's eyes, and hear with other men's ears, and take things as they are represented to them; but Christ goes purely upon his own knowledge. Angels are his messengers, but not his spies, for *his own eyes run to and fro through the earth,* 2 Chr. 16:9. This may comfort us in reference to Satan's accusations, that Christ will not take men's characters from him. 3. He *knew what was in man;* in particular persons, in the nature and race of man. We know what is done *by men;* Christ knows what is *in them, tries the heart and the reins.* This is the prerogative of that essential eternal Word, Heb. 4:12, 13. We invade his prerogative if we presume to judge men's hearts. How fit is Christ to be the *Saviour of men,* very fit to be the physician, who has such a perfect knowledge of the patient's state and case, temper and distemper; knows what is in him! How fit also to be the *Judge of all!* For the judgment of him who knows *all men,* all *in* men, must needs be *according to truth.*

Now this is all the success of Christ's preaching and miracles at Jerusalem, in this journey. The Lord comes to his temple, and none come to him but a parcel of weak simple people, that he can neither have *credit* from nor put *confidence* in; yet he shall at length *see of the travail of his soul.*

CHAPTER 3

In this chapter we have, I. Christ's discourse with Nicodemus, a Pharisee, concerning the great mysteries of the gospel, in which he here privately instructs him (v. 1–21). II. John Baptist's discourse with his disciples concerning Christ, upon occasion of his coming into the neighbourhood where John was (v. 22–36), in which he fairly and faithfully resigns all his honour and interest to him.

Verses 1–21

We found, in the close of the foregoing chapter, that few were brought to Christ at Jerusalem; yet here was *one,* a considerable one. It is worth while to go a great way for the salvation though but of *one soul.* Observe,

I. Who this Nicodemus was. Not many mighty and noble are called; yet some are, and here was one. *Not many* of the *rulers, or of the Pharisees;* yet. 1. This was a *man of the Pharisees,* bred to learning, a scholar. Let it not be said that all Christ's followers are *unlearned and ignorant men.* The principles of the Pharisees, and the peculiarities of their sect, were directly contrary to the spirit of Christianity; yet there were some in whom even those high thoughts were cast down and brought into obedience to Christ. The grace of Christ is able to subdue the greatest opposition. 2. He was a *ruler of the Jews,* a member of the great sanhedrim, a senator, a privy-counsellor, a man of authority in Jerusalem. Bad as things were, there were some rulers *well inclined,* who yet could do little good because the stream was so strong against them; they were over-ruled by the majority, and yoked with those that were corrupt, so that the good which they wished to do they could not do; yet Nicodemus continued in his place, and did what he *could,* when he could not do what he *would.*

II. His solemn address to our Lord Jesus Christ, *v.* 2. See here,

1. When he came: *He came to Jesus by night.* Observe, (1.) He made a private and particular address to Christ, and did not think it enough to hear his public discourses. He resolved to talk with him by himself, where he might be free with him. Personal converse with skilful faithful ministers about the affairs of our souls would be of great use to us, Mal. 2:7. (2.) He made this address *by night,* which may be considered, [1.] As an act of *prudence* and *discretion.* Christ was engaged all day in *public* work, and he would not interrupt him then, nor expect his attendance then, but observed *Christ's hour,* and waited on him when he was *at leisure.* Note, Private advantages to ourselves and our own families must give way to those that are public. The greater good must be preferred before the less. Christ had many enemies, and therefore Nicodemus came to him *incognito,* lest being known to the chief priests they should be the more enraged against Christ. [2.] As an act of *zeal* and *forwardness.* Nicodemus was a man of business, and could not spare time all day to make Christ a visit, and therefore he would rather take time from the diversions of the *evening,* or the rest of the *night,* than not converse with Christ. When others were sleeping, he was getting knowledge, as David by meditation, Ps. 63:6, and 119:148. Probably it was the very next night after he saw Christ's miracles, and he would not neglect the first opportunity of pursuing his convictions. He knew not how soon Christ might leave the town, nor what might happen betwixt that and another feast, and therefore would lose no time. In the night his converse with Christ would be more free, and less liable to disturbance. These were *Noctes Christianae — Christian nights,* much more instructive than the *Noctes Atticae — Attic nights.* Or, [3.] As an act of *fear* and *cowardice.* He was afraid, or ashamed, to be *seen* with Christ, and therefore came *in the night.* When religion is out of *fashion,* there are many Nicodemites, especially among the rulers, who have a better affection to Christ and his religion than they would be known to have. But observe, *First,* Though he came by night, Christ bade him welcome, accepted his integrity, and pardoned his infirmity; he considered his *temper,* which perhaps was *timorous,* and the *temptation* he was in from his place and office; and hereby taught his ministers to become all things to all men, and to encourage good beginnings, though weak. *Paul preached privately to those of reputation,* Gal. 2:2. *Secondly,* Though now he came *by night,* yet afterwards, when there was occasion, he owned Christ *publicly, ch.* 7:50; 19:39. The grace which is at first but a grain of mustard-seed may grow to be a great tree.

2. What he said. He did not come to talk with Christ about politics and state-affairs (though he was a ruler), but about the concerns of his own soul and its salvation, and, without circumlocution, comes immediately to the business; he calls Christ *Rabbi,* which signifies a *great man;* see Isa. 19:20. *He shall send them a Saviour, and a great one;* a *Saviour* and *a rabbi,* so the word is. There are hopes of those who have a respect for Christ, and think and speak honourably of him. He tells Christ how far *he had attained:* We *know that thou art a teacher.* Observe, (1.) His *assertion* concerning Christ: *Thou art a teacher come from God;* not educated nor ordained by men, as other teachers, but supported with divine inspiration and divine authority. He that was to be the sovereign Ruler came first to be a *teacher;* for he would rule with reason, not with rigour, by the power of truth, not of the sword. The world lay in ignorance and mistake; the Jewish teachers were corrupt, and caused them to err: *It is time for the Lord to work.* He came a *teacher from God,* from God as the *Father of mercies,* in pity to a dark deceived world; from God as the *Father of lights* and *fountain of truth,* all the light and truth upon which we may venture our souls. (2.) His *assurance* of it: *We know,* not only *I,* but *others;* so he took it for granted, the thing being so plain and self-evident. Perhaps he knew that there were divers of the Pharisees and rulers with whom he conversed that were under the same convictions, but had not the grace to own it. Or, we may suppose that he speaks in the plural number *(We know)* because he brought with him one or more of his friends and pupils, to receive instructions from Christ, knowing them to be of common concern. "Master," saith he, "we come with a desire to be taught, to be thy scholars, for we are fully satisfied thou art a divine teacher." (3.) The ground of this assurance: *No man can do those miracles that thou doest, except God be with him.* Here, [1.] We are assured of the truth of Christ's miracles, and that they were not counterfeit. Here was Nicodemus, a judicious, sensible, inquisitive man, one that had all the *reason* and *opportunity* imaginable to examine them, so fully satisfied that they were real miracles that he was wrought upon by them to go contrary to his interest, and to the stream of those of his own rank, who were prejudiced against Christ. [2.] We are directed what inference to draw from Christ's miracles: Therefore we are to receive him as a *teacher come from God.* His miracles were his credentials. The course of nature could not be altered but by the power of the God of nature, who, we are sure, is the God of truth and goodness, and would never set his seal to a lie or a cheat.

III. The discourse between Christ and Nicodemus hereupon, or, rather, the sermon Christ preached to him; the contents of it, and that perhaps an abstract of Christ's public preaching; see *v.* 11, 12. Four things our Saviour here discourses of: —

1. Concerning the *necessity and nature of regeneration* or the *new birth, v.* 3–8. Now we must consider this,

(1.) As *pertinently answered* to Nicodemus's address. Jesus *answered, v.* 3. This answer was wither, [1.] A *rebuke* of what he saw *defective* in the address of Nicodemus. It was not enough for him to admire Christ's miracles, and acknowledge his mission, but he must be *born again.* It is plain that he expected the *kingdom of heaven,* the kingdom of the Messiah now shortly to appear. He is betimes aware of the dawning of that day; and, according to the common notion of the Jews, he expects it to appear in external pomp and power. He doubts not but this Jesus, who works these miracles, is either the Messiah or his prophet, and therefore makes his court to him, compliments him, and so hopes to secure a share to himself of the advantages of that kingdom. But Christ tells him that he can have no benefit by that *change of the state,* unless there be a *change of the spirit,* of the principles and dispositions, equivalent to a new birth. Nicodemus came *by night:* "But this will not do," saith Christ. His religion must be owned before men; so Dr. Hammond. Or, [2.] A *reply* to what he saw *designed* in his address. When Nicodemus owned Christ a *teacher come from God,* one entrusted with an extraordinary revelation from heaven, he plainly intimated a desire to know what this revelation was and a readiness to receive it; and Christ declares it.

(2.) As *positively* and *vehemently* asserted by our Lord Jesus: *Verily, verily, I say unto thee. I the Amen, the Amen, say it;* so it may be read: "I the faithful and true witness." The matter is settled irreversibly that *except a man be born again he cannot see the kingdom of God.* "I say it to *thee,* though a Pharisee, though a master in Israel." Observe,

[1.] What it is that is required: to be *born again;* that is, *First,* We must *live a new life.* Birth is the beginning of life; to be *born again* is to begin anew, as those that have hitherto lived either much amiss or to little purpose. We must not think to patch up the old building, but begin from the foundation. *Secondly,* We must *have a new nature,* new principles, new affections, new aims. We must be born *anōthen,* which signifies both *denuo — again,* and *desuper — from above.* 1. We must be born *anew;* so the word is taken, Gal. 4:9, and *ab initio — from the beginning,* Lu. 1:3. By our *first birth* we are corrupt, shapen in sin and iniquity; we must therefore undergo a second birth; our souls must be *fashioned* and *enlivened* anew. 2. We must be born *from above,* so the word is used by the evangelist, *ch.* 3:31; 19:11, and I take this to be especially intended here, not excluding the other; for to be born *from above* supposes being *born again.* But this new birth has its rise *from* heaven (*ch.* 1:13) and its tendency *to* heaven: it is to be born to a *divine* and *heavenly* life, a life of communion with God and the upper world, and, in order to this, it is to partake of a *divine nature* and bear the *image of the heavenly.*

[2.] The indispensable necessity of this: "Except *a man* (Any one that partakes of the human nature, and consequently of its corruptions) *be born again, he cannot see the kingdom of God,* the kingdom of the Messiah begun in *grace* and perfected in *glory.*" Except we be *born from above,* we cannot *see* this. That is, *First,* We cannot *understand* the *nature* of it. Such is the nature of things pertaining to the kingdom of God (in which Nicodemus desired to be instructed) that the soul must be re-modelled and moulded, the natural man must become a spiritual man, before he is capable of receiving and understanding them, 1 Co. 2:14. *Secondly,* We cannot *receive the comfort* of it, cannot expect any benefit by Christ and his gospel, nor have any part or lot in the matter. Note, Regeneration is absolutely necessary to our happiness here and hereafter. Considering what we are by nature, how corrupt and sinful, — what *God* is, in whom alone we can be happy, — and *what heaven* is, to which the perfection of our happiness is reserved, — it will appear, in the nature of the thing, that we must be *born again,* because it is impossible that we should be *happy* if we be not *holy;* see 1 Co. 6:11, 12.

This great truth of the necessity of regeneration being thus solemnly laid down,

a. It is objected against by Nicodemus (*v.* 4): *How can a man be born when he is old,* old as I am: *gerōn ōn — being an old man? Can he enter the second time into his mother's womb, and be born?* Herein appears, (*a.*) His weakness in knowledge; what Christ spoke spiritually he seems to have understood after a corporal and carnal manner, as if there were no other way of regenerating and new-moulding an immortal soul than by new-framing the body, and bringing that back to the *rock out of which it was hewn,* as if there was such a connection between the soul and the body that there could be no fashioning the *heart anew* but by forming the *bones anew.* Nicodemus, as others of the Jews, valued himself, no doubt, very much on his *first birth* and its dignities and privileges, — the *place* of it, the Holy Land, perhaps the holy city, — his *parentage,* such as that which Paul could have gloried in, Phil. 3:5. And therefore it is a great surprise to him to hear of being *born again.* Could he be better bred and born than bred and born an Israelite, or by any other birth stand fairer for a place in the kingdom of the Messiah? Indeed they looked upon a proselyted Gentile to be as one *born again* or *born anew,* but could not imagine how a Jew, a Pharisee, could ever *better himself* by being *born again;* he therefore thinks, if he must be *born again,* it must be of *her* that *bore him first.* They that are proud of their *first birth* are hardly brought to a *new birth.* (*b.*) His willingness to be taught. He does not turn his back upon Christ because of his hard saying, but ingenuously acknowledges his ignorance, which implies a desire to be better informed; and so I take this, rather than that he had such gross notions of the new birth Christ spoke of: "Lord, make me to understand this, for it is a riddle to me; I am such a fool as to know no other way for a man to be born than of his mother." When we meet with that in the things of God which is *dark,* and *hard to be understood,* we must with humility and industry continue our attendance upon the means of knowledge, till God *shall reveal even that unto us.*

b. It is opened and further explained by our Lord Jesus, *v.* 5–8. From the objection he takes occasion,

(*a.*) To repeat and confirm what he had said (*v.* 5): *"Verily, verily, I say unto thee,* the very same that I said before." Note, The word of God is not yea and nay, but yea and amen; what he hath said he will abide by, whoever saith against it; nor will he retract any of his sayings for the ignorance and mistakes of men. Though Nicodemus understood not the mystery of regeneration, yet Christ asserts the necessity of it as positively as before. Note, It is folly to think of evading the obligation of evangelical precepts, by pleading that they are unintelligible, Rom. 3:3, 4.

(*b.*) To expound and clear what he had said concerning regeneration; for the explication of which he further shows,

[*a.*] The *author* of this blessed change, and who it is that works it. To be born again is to be *born of the Spirit, v.* 5–8. The change is not wrought by any wisdom or power of our own, but by the power and influence of the blessed Spirit of grace. It is the *sanctification of the Spirit* (1 Pt. 1:2) and *renewing of the Holy Ghost,* Tit. 3:5. The word he works by is his inspiration, and the heart to be wrought on he has access to.

[*b.*] The *nature* of this change, and what that is which is wrought; it is *spirit, v.* 6. Those that are regenerated are made *spiritual,* and refined from the dross and dregs of sensuality. The dictates and interests of the rational and immortal soul have retrieved the dominion they ought to have over the flesh. The Pharisees placed their religion in external purity and external performances; and it would be a mighty change indeed with them, no less than a new birth, to become *spiritual.*

[*c.*] The *necessity* of this change. *First,* Christ here shows that it is necessary in the *nature of the thing,* for we are not fit to enter into the kingdom of God till we are born again: *That which is born of the flesh if flesh, v.* 6. Here is our malady, with the causes of it, which are such that it is plain there is no remedy but we must be *born again.* 1. We are here told *what we are:* We are *flesh,* not only *corporeal* but *corrupt,* Gen. 6:3. The soul is still a spiritual substance, but so wedded to the flesh, so captivated by the will of the flesh, so in love with the delights of the flesh, so employed in making provision for the flesh, that it is mostly called *flesh;* it is carnal. And what communion can there be between God, who is a *spirit,* and a soul in this condition? 2. How we *came to be so;* by being *born of the flesh.* It is a corruption that is bred *in the bone* with us, and therefore we cannot have a new nature, but we must be *born again.* The corrupt nature, which is *flesh,* takes rise from our *first birth;* and therefore the new nature, which is *spirit,* must take rise from a second birth. Nicodemus spoke of entering again into his mother's womb, and being born; but, if he could do so, to what purpose? If he were born of his mother a hundred times, that would not mend the matter, for still that *which is born of the flesh if flesh;* a clean thing cannot be brought out of an unclean. He must seek for another original, must be born of the Spirit, or he cannot become spiritual. The case is, in short, this: though man is made to consist of body and soul, yet his spiritual part had then so much the dominion over his corporeal part that he was denominated a *living soul* (Gen. 2:7), but by indulging the appetite of the flesh, in eating forbidden fruit, he prostituted the just dominion of the soul to the tyranny of sensual lust, and became no longer a *living soul,* but flesh: *Dust thou art.* The living soul became dead and inactive; thus in *the day* he sinned he *surely died,* and so he became *earthly.* In this degenerate state, he begat a son *in his own likeness;* he transmitted the human nature, which had been entirely deposited in his hands, thus corrupted and depraved; and in the same plight it is still propagated. Corruption and sin are woven into our nature; we are *shapen in iniquity,* which makes it necessary that the nature be changed. It is not enough to put on a new coat or a new face, but we must put on the *new man,* we must be new creatures. *Secondly,* Christ makes it further necessary, by his own word: *Marvel not that I said unto thee, You must be born again, v.* 7. 1. Christ hath said it, and as he himself never did, nor ever will, unsay it, so all the world cannot gainsay it, that we *must be born* again. He who is the great *Lawgiver,* whose will is a law, — he who is the great Mediator of the new covenant, and has full power to settle the terms of our reconciliation to God and happiness in him, — he who is the great Physician of souls, knows their case, and what is necessary to their cure, — he hath said, *You must be born again.* "I said unto *thee* that which all are concerned in, You must, you all, one as well as another, *you must be born again:* not only the common people, but the rulers, the *masters in Israel."* 2. We are not to *marvel* at it; for when we consider the holiness of the God with whom we have to do, the great design of our redemption, the depravity of our nature, and the constitution of the happiness set before us, we shall not think it strange that so much stress is laid upon this as the one thing needful, that *we must be born again.*

[*d.*] This change is illustrated by two comparisons. *First,* The regenerating work of the Spirit is compared to *water, v.* 5. To be born again is to be *born of water* and of the Spirit, that is, of the Spirit working like water, as (Mt. 3:11) *with the Holy Ghost and with fire* means with the Holy Ghost *as* with fire. 1. That which is primarily intended here is to show that the Spirit, in sanctifying a soul, (1.) *Cleanses* and purifies it as water, takes away its filth, by which it was unfit for the kingdom of God. It is the *washing of regeneration,* Tit. 3:5. *You are washed,* 1 Co. 6:11. See Eze. 36:25. (2.) Cools and refreshes it, as water does the hunted hart and the weary traveller. The Spirit is compared to water, *ch.* 7:38, 39; Isa. 44:3. In the first creation, the fruits of heaven were *born of water* (Gen. 1:20), in allusion to which, perhaps, they that are born from above are said to be born of water. 2. It is probable that Christ had an eye to the ordinance of baptism, which John had used and he himself had begun to use, "You must be born again of the Spirit," which regeneration by the Spirit should be signified by washing with water, as the visible sign of that spiritual grace: not that all they, and they only, that are baptized, are saved; but without that new birth which is wrought by the Spirit, and signified by baptism, none shall be looked upon as the *protected privileged* subjects of the *kingdom of heaven.* The Jews cannot partake of the benefits of the Messiah's kingdom, they have so long looked for, unless they quit all expectations of being justified by the works of the law, and submit to the *baptism of repentance,* the great gospel duty, *for the remission of sins,* the great gospel privilege. *Secondly,* It is compared to *wind: The wind bloweth where it listeth, so is every one that is born of the Spirit, v.* 8. The same word (*pneuma*) signifies both the wind and the Spirit. The Spirit came upon the apostles in a *rushing mighty wind* (Acts 2:2), his *strong* influences on the hearts of sinners are compared to the *breathing of the wind* (Eze. 37:9), and his *sweet* influences on the souls of saints to the north and south wind, Cant. 4:16. This comparison is here used to show, 1. That the Spirit, in regeneration, works *arbitrarily,* and as a free agent. The *wind bloweth where it listeth* for us, and does not attend our order, nor is subject to our command. God *directs* it; it *fulfils his word,* Ps. 148:8. The Spirit dispenses his influences where, and when, on whom, and in what measure and degree, he pleases, *dividing to every man severally as he will,* 1 Co. 12:11. 2. That he works *powerfully,* and with evident effects: *Thou hearest the sound thereof;* though its causes are hidden, its effects are manifest. When the soul is brought to mourn for sin, to groan under the burden of corruption, to breathe after Christ, to cry *Abba — Father,* then we *hear the sound of the Spirit,* we find he is at work, as Acts 9:11, *Behold he prayeth.* 3. That he works *mysteriously,* and in secret hidden ways: *Thou canst not tell whence it comes, nor whither it goes.* How it gathers and how it spends its strength is a riddle to us; so the manner and methods of the Spirit's working are a mystery. *Which way went the Spirit?* 1 Ki. 22:24. See Eccl. 11:5, and compare it with Ps. 139:14.

2. Here is a discourse concerning the *certainty and sublimity of gospel truths,* which Christ takes occasion for from the weakness of Nicodemus. Here is,

(1.) The objection which Nicodemus still made (*v.* 9): *How can these things be?* Christ's explication of the doctrine of the necessity of regeneration, it should seem, made it never the clearer to him. The corruption of nature which makes it *necessary,* and the way of the Spirit which makes it *practicable,* are as much mysteries to him as the thing itself; though he had in general owned Christ a divine teacher, yet he was unwilling to receive his teachings when they did not agree with the notions he had imbibed. Thus many profess to admit the doctrine of Christ in general, and yet will neither believe the truths of Christianity nor submit to the laws of it further than *they please.* Christ shall be their teacher, provided they may choose their lesson. Now here, [1.] Nicodemus owns himself ignorant of Christ's meaning, after all: *"How can these things be?* They are things I do not understand, my capacity will not reach them." Thus the *things of the Spirit of God are foolishness to the natural man.* He is not only estranged from them, and therefore they are dark to him, but prejudiced against them, and therefore they are foolishness to him. [2.] Because this doctrine was *unintelligible* to him (so he was pleased to make it), he questions the truth of it; as if, because it was a *paradox* to him, it was a *chimera* in itself. Many have such an opinion of their own capacity as to think that that cannot be *proved* which they cannot *believe;* by *wisdom* they *knew not* Christ.

(2.) The reproof which Christ gave him for his dulness and ignorance: *"Art thou a master in Israel, Didaskalos — a teacher,* a tutor, one who sits in Moses's chair, and yet not only unacquainted with the doctrine of regeneration, but incapable of understanding it?" This word is a reproof, [1.] To those who undertake to teach others and yet are ignorant and unskilful in the word of righteousness themselves. [2.] To those that spend their time in learning and teaching notions and ceremonies in religion, niceties and criticisms in the scripture, and neglect that which is practical and tends to reform the heart and life. Two words in the reproof are very emphatic: — *First,* The place where his lot was cast: in *Israel,* where there was such great plenty of the means of knowledge, where divine revelation was. He might have learned this out of the Old Testament. *Secondly,* The things he was thus ignorant in: *these* things, these *necessary* things, there *great* things, these *divine* things; had he never read Ps. 50:5, 10; Eze. 18:31; 36:25, 26?

(3.) Christ's discourse, hereupon, of the certainty and sublimity of gospel truths (*v.* 11–13), to show the folly of those who make strange of these things, and to recommend them to our search. Observe here,

[1.] That the truths Christ taught were very *certain* and what we may venture upon (*v.* 11): *We speak that we do know. We;* whom does he mean besides himself? Some understand it of those that bore witness to him and with him on earth, the prophets and John Baptist; they *spoke* what they *knew,* and had seen, and were themselves abundantly satisfied in: divine revelation carries its own proof along with it. Others of those that bore witness from heaven, the Father and the Holy Ghost; the Father was with him, the Spirit of the Lord was upon him; therefore he speaks in the plural number, as *ch.* 14:23: *We will come unto him.* Observe, *First,* That the truths of Christ are of undoubted certainty. We have all the reason in the world to be assured that the sayings of Christ are *faithful sayings,* and such as we may venture our souls upon; for he is not only a *credible* witness, who would not go about to deceive us, but a *competent* witness, who could not himself be deceived: *We testify that we have seen.* He spoke not upon hear-say, but upon the clearest evidence, and therefore with the greatest assurance. What he spoke of God, of the invisible world, of heaven and hell, of the divine will concerning us, and the counsels of peace, was what he *knew,* and *had seen,* for he was *by him as one brought up with him,* Prov. 8:30. Whatever Christ spoke, he spoke *of his own knowledge. Secondly,* That the unbelief of sinners is greatly aggravated by the infallible certainty of the truths of Christ. The things are thus sure, thus clear; and yet *you receive not our witness.* Multitudes to be *unbelievers* of that which yet (so cogent are the motives of credibility) they cannot *disbelieve!*

[2.] The truths Christ taught, though communicated in language and expressions borrowed from common and earthly things, yet in their own nature were most sublime and heavenly; this is intimated, *v.* 12: *"If I have told them earthly things,* that is, have told them the great things of God in similitudes taken from earthly things, to make them the more easy and intelligible, as that of the *new birth* and the *wind,* — if I have thus accommodated myself to your capacities, and lisped to you in your own language, and cannot make you to understand my doctrine, — *what would you do* if I should accommodate myself to the nature of the things, and speak with the tongue of angels, that language which mortals cannot utter? If such *familiar expressions* be stumbling-blocks, what would *abstract ideas* be, and spiritual things painted *proper?"* Now we may learn hence, *First,* To admire the height and depth of the doctrine of Christ; it is a great mystery of godliness. The things of the gospel are *heavenly* things, out of the road of the enquiries of human reason, and much more out of the reach of its discoveries. *Secondly,* To acknowledge with thankfulness the condescension of Christ, that he is pleased to suit the manner of the gospel revelation to our capacities, *to speak to us as to children.* He considers our *frame,* that we are *of* the earth, and our *place,* that we are *on* the earth, and therefore speaks to us earthly things, and makes things sensible the vehicle of things spiritual, to make them the more easy and familiar to us. Thus he has done both in parables and in sacraments. *Thirdly,* To lament the corruption of our nature, and our great unaptness to receive and entertain the truths of Christ. Earthly things are despised because they are *vulgar,* and heavenly things because they are *abstruse;* and so, whatever method is taken, still some fault or other is found with it (Mt. 11:17), but Wisdom is, and will be, *justified of her children,* notwithstanding.

[3.] Our Lord Jesus, and he alone, was fit to reveal to us a doctrine thus certain, thus sublime: *No man hath ascended up into heaven but he, v.* 13.

First, None but Christ was able to reveal to us the will of God for our salvation. Nicodemus addressed Christ as a prophet; but he must know that he is greater than all the Old-Testament prophets, for none of them *had ascended into heaven.* They wrote by divine inspiration, and not of their own knowledge; see *ch.* 1:18. Moses ascended into the mount, but not into heaven. No man hath attained to the certain knowledge of God and heavenly things as Christ has; see Mt. 11:27. It is not for us to send to heaven for instructions; we must wait to receive what instructions Heaven will send to us; see Prov. 30:4; Deu. 30:12.

Secondly, Jesus Christ is able, and fit, and every way qualified, to reveal the will of God to us; for it is *he that came down from heaven* and *is in heaven.* He had said (*v.* 12), *How*

shall ye believe, if I tell you of heavenly things? Now here, 1. He gives them an instance of those *heavenly things* which he could tell them of, when he tells them of one that *came down from heaven,* and yet is the *Son of man;* is the *Son of man,* and yet is *in heaven.* If the regeneration of the *soul of man* is such a mystery, what then is the incarnation of the *Son of God?* These are divine and heavenly things indeed. We have here an intimation of Christ's two distinct natures in one person: his divine nature, in which he *came down from heaven;* his human nature, in which he is the *Son of man;* and that union of those two, in that while he is the Son of man yet he is *in heaven.* 2. He gives them a proof of his ability to speak to them *heavenly things,* and to lead them into the arcana of the kingdom of heaven, by telling them, (1.) That *he came down from heaven.* The intercourse settled between God and man began *above;* the first motion towards it did not arise from this earth, but *came down from heaven.* We love him, and send to him, because he first loved us, and sent to us. Now this intimates, [1.] Christ's divine nature. He that came down from heaven is certainly more than a mere man; he is the *Lord from heaven,* 1 Co. 15:47. [2.] His intimate acquaintance with the divine counsels; for, coming from the court of heaven, he had been from eternity conversant with them. [3.] The *manifestation of God.* Under the Old Testament God's favours to his people are expressed by his *hearing from heaven* (2 Chr. 7:14), *looking from heaven* (Ps. 80:14), *speaking from heaven* (Neh. 9:13), sending from heaven, Ps. 57:3. But the New Testament shows us God *coming down* from heaven, to teach and save us. That he thus *descended* is an admirable *mystery,* for the Godhead cannot change places, nor did he bring his body from heaven; but that he thus *condescended* for our redemption is a more admirable *mercy;* herein he commended his love. (2.) That *he is the Son of man, that* Son of man spoken of by Daniel (7:13), by which the Jews always understand to be meant the Messiah. Christ, in calling himself the *Son of man,* shows that he is the *second Adam,* for the first Adam was the *father of man.* And of all the Old-Testament titles of the Messiah he chose to make use of *this,* because it was most expressive of his *humility,* and most agreeable to his present state of *humiliation.* (3.) That he *is in heaven.* Now at this time, when he is talking with Nicodemus on earth, yet, as God, he is *in heaven.* The *Son of man,* as such, was not in heaven till his ascension; but he that was the Son of man was now, by his divine nature, every where present, and particularly in heaven. Thus the Lord of glory, as such, could not be crucified, nor could God, as such, shed his blood; yet that person who was the Lord of glory was crucified (1 Co. 2:8), and God purchased the church with *his own blood,* Acts 20:28. So close is the union of the two natures in one person that there is a communication of properties. He doth not say *hos esti.* GOD is the *ho ōn tō ouranō — he that is,* and heaven is the habitation of *his holiness.*

3. Christ here discourses of the *great design of his own coming into the world, and the happiness of those that believe in him, v.* 14–18. Here we have the very marrow and quintessence of the whole gospel, that *faithful saying* (1 Tim. 1:15), that Jesus Christ came to seek and to save the children of men from death, and recover them to life. Now sinners are *dead men* upon a twofold account: — (1.) As one that is mortally wounded, or sick of an incurable disease, is said to be a *dead man,* for he is dying; and so Christ came to save us, by *healing* us, as the brazen serpent healed the Israelites, *v.* 14, 15. (2.) As one that is justly condemned to die for an unpardonable crime is a *dead man,* he is *dead in law;* and, in reference to this part of our danger, Christ came to save as a prince or judge, publishing an act of indemnity, or general pardon, under certain provisos; this saving here is opposed to condemning, *v.* 16–18.

[1.] Jesus Christ came to save us by *healing* us, as the children of Israel that were stung with fiery serpents were cured and *lived* by looking up to the brazen serpent; we have the story of it, Num. 21:6–9. It was the *last* miracle that passed through the hand of Moses before his death. Now in this type of Christ we may observe,

First, The *deadly* and *destructive* nature of *sin,* which is implied here. The guilt of sin is like the *pain* of the biting of a fiery serpent; the power of corruption is like the *venom* diffused thereby. The devil is the old serpent, subtle at first (Gen. 3:1), but ever since *fiery,* and his temptations *fiery darts,* his assaults terrifying, his victories destroying. Ask awakened consciences, ask damned sinners, and they will tell you, how charming soever the allurements of sin are, *at the last it bites like a serpent,* Prov. 23:30–32. God's wrath against us for sin is as those fiery serpents which God sent among the people, to punish them for their murmurings. The curses of the law are as fiery serpents, so are all the tokens of divine wrath.

Secondly, The powerful remedy provided against this fatal malady. The case of poor sinners is deplorable; but is it desperate? Thanks be to God, it is not; there is balm in Gilead. The *Son of man is lifted up,* as the *serpent of brass* was by Moses, which cured the stung Israelites. 1. It was a *serpent of brass* that cured them. Brass is *bright;* we read of Christ's feet *shining like brass,* Rev. 1:15. It is *durable;* Christ is the same. It was made in the shape of a *fiery serpent,* and yet had no poison, no sting, fitly representing Christ, who was *made sin for us* and yet knew no sin; was *made in the likeness of sinful flesh* and yet not sinful; as harmless as a serpent of brass. The serpent was a cursed creature; Christ was made a *curse.* That which cured them reminded them of their plague; so in Christ sin is set before us most fiery and formidable. 2. It was lifted up upon a pole, and so *must* the Son of man be lifted up; thus it *behoved him,* Lu. 24:26, 46. No remedy now. Christ is lifted up, (1.) In his *crucifixion.* He was lifted up upon the cross. His death is called his being *lifted up, ch.* 12:32, 33. He was lifted up as a spectacle, as a mark, lifted up between heaven and earth, as if he had been unworthy of either and abandoned by both. (2.) In his *exaltation.* He was lifted up to the Father's right hand, to give repentance and remission; he was lifted up to the cross, to be further lifted up to the crown. (3.) In the *publishing* and *preaching* of his everlasting gospel, Rev. 14:6. The serpent was lifted up that all the thousands of Israel might see it. Christ in the gospel is exhibited to us, evidently set forth; Christ is *lifted up* as an *ensign,* Isa. 11:10. 3. It was lifted up by Moses. Christ was made under the law of Moses, and Moses testified of him. 4. Being thus lifted up, it was appointed for the cure of those that were bitten by fiery serpents. He that sent the plague provided the remedy. None could redeem and save us but he whose justice had condemned us. It was God himself that *found the ransom,* and the efficacy of it depends upon his appointment. The *fiery serpents* were sent to punish them for their *tempting Christ* (so the apostle saith, 1 Co. 10:9), and yet they were healed by virtue derived from him. He whom we have offended is *our peace.*

Thirdly, The way of *applying* this remedy, and that is by *believing,* which plainly alludes to the Israelites' *looking up* to the brazen serpent, in order to their being healed by it. If any stung Israelite was either so little sensible of his pain and peril, or had so little confidence in the word of Moses as not to look up to the brazen serpent, justly did he die of his wound; but every one that *looked up to it* did well, Num. 21:9. If any so far slight either their disease by sin or the method of cure by Christ as not to embrace Christ upon his own terms, their blood is upon their own head. He hath said, *Look, and be saved* (Isa. 45:22), look and live. We must take a complacency in and give consent to the methods which Infinite Wisdom has taken is saving a guilty world, by the mediation of Jesus Christ, as the great sacrifice and intercessor.

Fourthly, The great encouragements given us by faith to look up to him. 1. It was for this end that he was *lifted up,* that his followers might be saved; and he will pursue his end. 2. The offer that is made of salvation by him is general, that *whosoever believes* in him, without exception, might have benefit by him. 3. The salvation offered is complete. (1.) They *shall not perish,* shall not die of their wounds; though they may be pained and ill frightened, iniquity shall not be their ruin. But that is not all. (2.) They shall *have eternal life.* They shall not only not die of their wounds in the wilderness, but they shall reach Canaan (which they were then just ready to enter into); they shall enjoy the promised rest.

[2.] Jesus Christ came to save us by *pardoning us,* that we might not die by the sentence of the law, *v.* 16, 17. Here is *gospel* indeed, good *news,* the best that ever came from heaven to earth. Here is *much,* here is *all* in a little, the word of reconciliation in miniature.

First, Here is God's *love* in *giving his Son for the world* (*v.* 16), where we have three things: — 1. The great *gospel mystery* revealed: *God so loved the world that he gave his only-begotten Son.* The love of God the Father is the original of our regeneration by the Spirit and our reconciliation by the lifting up of the Son. Note, (1.) Jesus Christ is the *only-begotten Son of God.* This magnifies his love in giving him for us, in giving him to us; now know we that he loves us, when he has given his *only-begotten Son for us,* which expresses not only his dignity in himself, but his dearness to his Father; he was *always his delight.* (2.) In order to the redemption and salvation of man, it pleased God to *give his only-begotten Son.* He not only sent him into the world with full and ample power to negotiate a peace between heaven and earth, but he *gave him,* that is, he gave him up to suffer and die for us, as the great propitiation or expiatory sacrifice. It comes in here as a reason why he *must be lifted up;* for so it was determined and designed by the Father, who gave him for this purpose, and *prepared him a body* in order to it. His enemies could not have *taken him* if his Father had not *given* him. Though he was not yet crucified, yet in the determinate counsel of God he was *given* up, Acts 2:23. Nay, further, God has *given him,* that is, he has made an offer of him, to all, and given him to all true believers, to all the intents and purposes of the new covenant. He has given him to be our *prophet,* a *witness to the people,* the high priest of our profession, to be our peace, to be head of the church and head over all things to the church, to be to us all we need. (3.) Herein God has commended his *love to the world:* God so *loved the world,* so really, so richly. Now his creatures shall see that he loves them, and wishes them well. He so loved the world of fallen man as he did not love that of fallen angels; see Rom. 5:8; 1 Jn. 4:10. Behold, and wonder, that the *great God* should love such a *worthless* world! That the *holy God* should love such a *wicked* world with a love of good will, when he could not look upon it with any complacency. This was a *time of love indeed,* Eze. 16:6, 8. The Jews vainly conceited that the Messiah should be sent only in love to *their nation,* and to advance them upon the ruins of their neighbours; but Christ tells them that he came in love to the *whole world,* Gentiles as well as Jews, 1 Jn. 2:2. Though many of the world of mankind perish, yet God's giving his only-begotten Son was an instance of his love to the whole world, because through him there is a *general offer* of life and salvation made to all. It is love to the revolted rebellious province to issue out a proclamation of pardon and indemnity to all that will come in, plead it upon their knees, and return to their allegiance. So *far God loved the* apostate lapsed *world* that he sent his Son with this fair proposal, that *whosoever believes in him,* one or other, *shall not perish. Salvation* has been *of the Jews,* but now Christ is *known as salvation to the ends of the earth,* a *common salvation.* 2. Here is the great *gospel duty,* and that is to *believe in Jesus Christ* (Whom God has thus given, given *for us,* given *to us*), to accept the gift, and answer the intention of the giver. We must yield an unfeigned assent and consent to the record God hath given in his word concerning his Son. God having given him to us to be our prophet, priest, and king, we must give up ourselves to be ruled, and taught, and saved by him. 3. Here is the great gospel benefit: *That whosoever believes in Christ shall not perish.* This he had said before, and here repeats it. It is the unspeakable happiness of all true believers, for which they are eternally indebted to Christ, (1.) That they are saved from the miseries of hell, delivered from *going down to the pit;* they *shall not perish.* God has taken away their sin, they shall not die; a pardon is purchased, and so the attainder is reversed. (2.) They are entitled to the joys of heaven: they shall *have everlasting life.* The convicted traitor is not only pardoned, but preferred, and made a favourite, and treated as one whom the King of kings *delights to honour. Out of prison he comes to reign,* Eccl. 4:14. If believers, then children; and, if *children, then heirs.*

Secondly, Here is God's design in sending hi Son into the world: it was *that the world through him might be saved.* He came into the world with salvation in *his eye,* with salvation *in his hand.* Therefore the aforementioned offer of live and salvation is sincere, and shall be made good to all that by faith accept it (*v.* 17): *God sent his Son into the world,* this guilty, rebellious, apostate world; sent him as his agent or ambassador, not as sometimes he had sent angels into the world as visitants, but as resident. Ever since man sinned, he has dreaded the approach and appearance of any special messenger from heaven, as being conscious of guilt and looking for judgment: *We shall surely die, for we have seen God.* If therefore the Son of God himself come, we are concerned to enquire on what errand he comes: *Is it peace?* Or, as they asked Samuel trembling, *Comest thou peaceably?* And this scripture returns the answer, *Peaceably.* 1. He did not come to *condemn the world.* We had reason enough to expect that he should, for it is a guilty world; it is *convicted,* and what cause can be shown why judgment should not be given, and execution awarded, according to law? That *one blood* of which all *nations* of men are made (Acts 17:26) is not only *tainted* with an hereditary *disease,* like Gehazi's leprosy, but it is *tainted* with an hereditary *guilt,* like that of the Amalekites, with whom God had war *from generation to generation;* and justly may such a world as this be *condemned;* and if God would have sent to condemn it he had angels at command, to pour out the vials of his wrath, a cherub with a flaming sword ready to do execution. *If the Lord had been pleased to kill us,* he would not have sent his Son amongst us. He came with full powers indeed to *execute judgment* (*ch.* 5:22, 27), but did not begin with a judgment of condemnation, did not proceed upon the outlawry, nor take advantage against us for the breach of the *covenant of innocency,* but put us upon a new trial before a *throne of grace.* 2. He came *that the world through him might be saved,* that a door of salvation might be opened to the world, and whoever would might enter in by it. God was in Christ *reconciling the world to himself,* and so *saving* it. An act of indemnity is passed and published, through Christ a remedial law made, and the world of mankind dealt with, not according to the rigours of the first covenant, but according to the riches of the second; *that the world* through him might be saved, for it could never be saved but *through him; there is not salvation in any other.* This is good news to a convinced conscience, healing to broken bones and bleeding wounds, that Christ, our judge, came not to *condemn,* but to *save.*

[3.] From all this is inferred the happiness of true believers: *He that believeth on him is not condemned, v.* 18. Though he has been a sinner, a great sinner, and *stands convicted (habes confilentem reum — by his own confession),* yet, upon his believing, process is stayed, judgment is arrested, and he is *not condemned.* This denotes more than a reprieve; he *is not condemned,* that is, he is acquitted; he *stand upon his deliverance* (as we say), and if he be not condemned he is discharged; *ou krinetai — he is not judged,* not dealt with in strict justice, according to the desert of his sins. He is *accused,* and he cannot plead *not guilty* to the indictment, but he can plead *in bar,* can plead a *noli prosequi* upon the indictment, as blessed Paul does, *Who is he that condemns? It is Christ that died.* He is *afflicted,* chastened of God, persecuted by the world; but he is not *condemned.* The cross perhaps lies heavy upon him, but he is saved from the curse: condemned *by the world,* it may be, but not *condemned with the world,* Rom. 8:1; 1 Co. 11:32.

4. Christ, in the close, discourses concerning the *deplorable condition of those that persist in unbelief and wilful ignorance, v.* 18–21.

(1.) Read here the doom of those that will not *believe in Christ:* they *are condemned already.* Observe, [1.] How great the *sin* of unbelievers is; it is aggravated from the dignity of the person they slight; they *believe not in the name of the only-begotten Son of God,* who is infinitely *true,* and deserves to be believed, *infinitely good,* and deserves to be embraced. God sent one to save us that was *dearest* to himself; and shall not he be *dearest to us?* Shall we not believe on his name who has a name above every name? [2.] How great the *misery* of unbelievers is: they are *condemned already;* which bespeaks, *First,* A *certain* condemnation. They are as sure to be condemned in the judgment of the great day as if they were condemned already. *Secondly,* A *present* condemnation. The curse has already taken hold of them; the wrath of God now fastens upon them. They are condemned already, for their own hearts condemn them. *Thirdly,* A condemnation *grounded upon their former guilt:* He is condemned *already,* for he lies open to the law for all his sins; the obligation of the law is in full force, power, and virtue, against him, because he is not by faith interested in the gospel defeasance; *he is condemned already, because he has not believed.* Unbelief may truly be called *the great damning sin,* because it leaves us under the guilt of all our other sins; it is a sin against the *remedy,* against our *appeal.*

(2.) Read also the doom of those that would not so much as *know him, v.* 19. Many *inquisitive* people had knowledge of Christ and his doctrine and miracles, but they were prejudiced against him, and would not believe in him, while the generality were sottishly careless and stupid, and would not *know* him. And *this is the condemnation,* the sin that ruined them, *that light is come into the world, and they loved darkness rather.* Now here observe, [1.] That the gospel is light, and, when the gospel came, *light came into the world,* Light is *self-evidencing,* so is the gospel; it proves its own divine origin. Light is *discovering,* and *truly the light is sweet,* and rejoices the heart. It is a light shining in a dark place, and a dark place indeed the world would be without it. It is *come into all the world* (Col. 1:6), and not confined to one corner of it, as the Old-Testament light was. [2.] It is the unspeakable folly of the most of men that they loved darkness rather than light, rather than *this* light. The Jews loved the dark shadows of their law, and the instructions of their *blind guides,* rather than the doctrine of Christ. The Gentiles loved their superstitious services of *an unknown God,* whom they *ignorantly worshipped,* rather than the *reasonable service* which the gospel enjoins. Sinners that were wedded to their lusts loved their ignorance and mistakes, which supported them in their sins, rather than the truths of Christ, which would have parted them from their sins. Man's apostasy began in an affectation of forbidden knowledge, but is kept up by an affectation of forbidden ignorance. Wretched man is in love with his sickness, in love with his slavery, and will not be made *free,* will not be *made whole.* [3.] The true reason why men love darkness rather than light is *because their deeds are evil.* They love darkness because they think it is an excuse for their evil deeds, and they hate the light because it robs them of the good opinion they had of themselves, by showing them their sinfulness and misery. Their case is sad, and, because they are resolved that they will not *mend* it, they are resolved that they will not *see it.* [4.] Wilful ignorance is so far from excusing sin that it will be found, at the great day, to aggravate the condemnation: *This is the condemnation,* this is what ruins souls, that they shut their eyes against the light, and will not so much as admit a parley with Christ and his gospel; they set God so much at defiance that they desire not the knowledge of his ways, Job 21:14. We must account in the judgment, not only for the knowledge we *had,* and *used not,* but for the knowledge we *might have had,* and *would not;* not only for the knowledge we *sinned against,* but for the knowledge we *sinned away.* For the further illustration of this he shows (*v.* 20, 21) that according as men's hearts and lives are good or bad, so they stand affected to the light Christ has brought into the world.

First, It is not strange if those that do evil, and resolve to persist in it, hate the light of Christ's gospel; for it is a common observation that *every one that doeth evil hateth the light, v.* 20. Evil-doers seek concealment, out of a sense of shame and fear of punishment; see Job 24:13, etc. Sinful works are *works of darkness;* sin from the first affected concealment, Job 31:33. The *light shakes* the wicked, Job 38:12, 13. Thus the gospel is a terror to the wicked world: *They come not to this light,* but keep as far off it as they can, *lest their deeds should be reproved.* Note, 1. The light of the gospel is sent into the world to *reprove the evil deeds* of sinners; to make them manifest (Eph. 5:13), to *show* people *their transgressions,* to show that to be sin which was not thought to be so, and to show them the evil of their transgressions, *that sin by the* new *commandment* might appear *exceeding sinful.* The gospel has its convictions, to make way for its consolations. 2. It is for this reason that evil-doers *hate the light* of the gospel. There were those who *had done evil* and were sorry for it, who bade this light welcome, as the *publicans and harlots.* But he that *does evil,* that does it and resolves to go on in it, *hateth the light,* cannot bear to be told of his faults. All that opposition which the gospel of Christ has met with in the world comes from the *wicked heart,* influenced by the *wicked one.* Christ is hated because sin is loved. 3. They who do not *come to the light* thereby evidence a secret *hatred* of the light. If they had not an antipathy to *saving knowledge,* they would not sit down so contentedly in *damning ignorance.*

Secondly, On the other hand, upright hearts, that approve themselves to God in their integrity, bid this light welcome (*v.* 21): *He that doeth truth cometh to the light.* It seems, then, that though the gospel had many enemies it had some friends. It is a common observation that *truth seeks no corners.* Those who mean and act honestly dread not a scrutiny, but desire it rather. Now this is applicable to the gospel light; as it *convinces* and *terrifies* evil-doers, so it *confirms* and *comforts* those that walk in their integrity. Observe here, 1. The character of a *good man.* (1.) He is one that *doeth truth;* that is, he acts truly and sincerely in all he does. Though sometimes he comes short of *doing good,* the good he would do, yet he *doeth truth,* he aims honestly; he has his infirmities, but holds fast his integrity; as Gaius, that *did faithfully* (3 Jn. 5), as Paul (2 Co. 1:12), as Nathanael (*ch.* 1:47), as Asa, 1 Ki. 15:14. (2.) He is one that *cometh to the light.* He is ready to receive and entertain divine revelation as far as it appears to him to be so, what uneasiness soever it may create him. He that *doeth truth* is willing to know the *truth* by himself, and to *have his deeds made manifest.* A good man is much employed in trying himself, and is desirous that God would try him, Ps. 26:2. He is solicitous to *know* what the will of God is, and resolves to *do* it, though ever so contrary to his own will and interest. 2. Here is the character of a *good work:* it is *wrought in God,* in union with him by a covenanting faith, and in communion with him by devout affections. Our works are *then* good, and will bear the test, when the will of God is the rule of them and the glory of God the end of them; when they are done in his strength, and for his sake, to him, and not to men; and if, by the light of the gospel, it be manifest to us that our works are thus wrought, *then shall we have rejoicing,* Gal. 6:4; 2 Co. 1:12.

Thus far we have Christ's discourse with *Nicodemus;* it is probable that much more passed between them, and it had a good effect, for we find (*ch.* 19:39) that Nicodemus, though he was puzzled at first, yet afterwards became a faithful disciple of Christ.

Verses 22–36

In these verses we have,

I. Christ's removal into the land of Judea (*v.* 22), and there he tarried with his disciples. Observe, 1. Our Lord Jesus, after he entered upon his public work, travelled much, and removed often, as the patriarchs in their sojournings. As it was a good part of his humiliation that he had no certain dwelling-place, but was, as Paul, *in journeyings often,* so it was an instance of his unwearied industry, in the work for which he came into the world, that he went about in prosecution of it; many a weary step he took to do good to souls. The *Sun of righteousness* took a large circuit to diffuse his light and heat, Ps. 19:6. 2. He was not wont to stay long at Jerusalem. Though he went frequently thither, yet he soon returned into the country; as here. *After these things,* after he had had this discourse with Nicodemus, he came into the land of Judea; not so much for *greater privacy* (though mean and obscure places best suited the humble Jesus in his humble state) as for *greater usefulness.* His preaching and miracles, perhaps, made *most noise* at Jerusalem, the fountain-head of news, but did *least good* there, where the most considerable men of the Jewish church had so much the ascendant. 3. When he came into the land of Judea his *disciples came with him;* for these were *they that continued with him in his temptations.* Many that flocked to him at Jerusalem could not follow his motions into the country, they had no business there; but his disciples attended him. If the ark remove, it is better to *remove and go after it* (as those did, Jos. 3:3) than sit still without it, though it be in Jerusalem itself. 4. There he *tarried with them, dietribe — He conversed* with them, *discoursed* with them. He did not retire into the country for his ease and pleasure, but for more free conversation with his disciples and followers. See Cant. 7:11, 12. Note, Those that are ready to *go with Christ* shall find him as ready to *stay with them.* It is supposed that he now staid five or six months in this country. 5. There *he baptized;* he admitted disciples, such as believed in him, and had more honesty and courage than those had at Jerusalem, *ch.* 2:24. John began to baptize in the land of Judea (Mt. 3:1), therefore Christ began there, for John had said, *There comes one after me.* He himself *baptized* not, with his own hand, but his disciples by his orders and directions, as appears, *ch.* 4:2. But his disciples' baptizing was his baptizing. Holy ordinances are Christ's, though administered by weak men.

II. John's continuance in his work, as long as his opportunities laster, *v.* 23, 24. Here we are told,

1. That *John was baptizing.* Christ's baptism was, for substance, the same with John's, for John bore witness to Christ, and therefore they did not at all clash or interfere with one another. But, (1.) Christ began the work of preaching and baptizing before *John laid it down,* that he might be ready to receive John's disciples when he should be taken off, and so the wheels might be kept going. It is a comfort to useful men, when they are going off the stage, to see those rising up who are likely to fill up their place. (2.) John continued the work of preaching and baptizing though Christ had *taken it up;* for he would still, according to the *measure given to him,* advance the interests of God's kingdom. There was still work

for John to do, for Christ was not yet *generally known,* nor were the minds of people *thoroughly prepared* for him by repentance. From heaven John had received his *command,* and he would go on in his work till he thence received his *countermand,* and would have his dismission from the same hand that gave him his commission. He does not *come in* to Christ, lest what had formerly passed should look like a combination between them; but *he goes on* with his work, till Providence lays him aside. The greater gifts of some do not *render* the labours of others, that come short of them, *needless* and *useless;* there is work enough for all hands. They are sullen that will sit down and do nothing when they see themselves out-shone. Though we have but one talent, we must account for that: and, when we see ourselves *going off,* must yet *go on* to the last.

2. That he baptized in Enon near Salim, places we find nowhere else mentioned, and therefore the learned are altogether at a loss where to find them. Wherever it was, it seems that John removed from *place to place;* he did not think that there was any virtue in Jordan, because Jesus was baptized there, which should engage him to stay there, but as he saw cause he removed to other waters. Ministers must follow their opportunities. He chose a place where there was much water, *hydata polla — many waters,* that is, many *streams* of water; so that wherever he met with any that were willing to submit to his baptism water was at hand to baptize them with, *shallow* perhaps, as is usual where there are *many* brooks, but such as would serve his purpose. And in that country plenty of water was a valuable thing.

3. That thither people *came to him* and *were baptized.* Though they did not come in such vast crowds as they did when he first appeared, yet now he was not without encouragement, but there were still those that attended and owned him. Some refer this both to John and to Jesus: *They came and were baptized;* that is, some came to John, and were baptized by him, some to Jesus, and were baptized by him, and, as their baptism was one, so were their hearts.

4. It is noted (*v.* 24) that *John was not yet cast into prison,* to clear the order of the story, and to show that these passages are to come in before Mt. 6:12. John never desisted from his work as long as he had his liberty; nay, he seems to have been the more industrious, because he foresaw his time was short; he was not *yet cast into prison,* but he expected it ere long, *ch.* 9:4.

III. A contest between *John's disciples and the Jews about purifying, v.* 25. See how the gospel of Christ came not to *send peace upon earth,* but *division.* Observe, 1. Who were the disputants: *some of John's disciples, and the Jews* who had not submitted to his baptism of repentance. Penitents and impenitents divide this sinful world. In this contest, it should seem, John's disciples were the *aggressors,* and gave the *challenge;* and it is a sign that they were novices, who had more zeal than discretion. The truths of God have often suffered by the rashness of those that have undertaken to defend them before they were able to do it. 2. What was the matter in dispute: *about purifying,* about *religious washing.* (1.) We may suppose that John's disciples cried up his baptism, his purifying, as *instar omnium — superior to all others,* and gave the preference to that as perfecting and superseding all the purifications of the Jews, and they were in the right; but *young* converts are too apt to boast of their attainments, whereas he that finds the *treasure* should *hide it* till he is sure that he has it, and not talk of it too much at first. (2.) No doubt the Jews with as much assurance applauded the *purifyings* that were in use among them, both those that were instituted by the law of Moses and those that were imposed by the tradition of the elders; for the former they had a divine warrant, and for the latter the usage of the church. Now it is very likely that the Jews in this dispute, when they could not *deny* the excellent nature and design of John's baptism, raised an objection against it from Christ's baptism, which gave occasion for the complaint that follows here (*v.* 26): "Here is John baptizing in one place," say they, "and Jesus at the same time baptizing in another place; and therefore John's baptism, which his disciples so much applaud, is either," [1.] "*Dangerous,* and of *ill consequence* to the peace of the church and state, for you see it opens a door to endless parties. Now that John has begun, we shall have every little teacher set up for a baptist presently. Or," [2.] "At the best it is *defective* and *imperfect.* If John's baptism, which you cry up thus, have any good in it, yonder the baptism of Jesus goes beyond it, so that for your parts you are shaded already by a greater light, and your baptism is soon gone out of request." Thus objections are made against the gospel from the advancement and improvement of gospel light, as if childhood and manhood were contrary to each other, and the superstructure were against the foundation. There was no reason to object Christ's baptism against John's, for they consisted very well together.

IV. A complaint which John's disciples made to their master concerning Christ and his baptizing, *v.* 26. They, being *nonplussed* by the fore-mentioned objection, and probably *ruffled* and put into a heat by it, come to their master, and tell him, *"Rabbi, he that was with thee,* and was baptized of thee, is now set up for himself; he *baptizeth, and all men come to him;* and wilt thou suffer it?" Their itch for disputing occasioned this. It is common for men, when they find themselves run aground in the heat of disputation, to fall foul upon those that do them no harm. If these disciples of John had not undertaken to dispute about *purifying,* before they understood the *doctrine of baptism,* they might have answered the objection without being put into a passion. In their complaint, they speak respectfully to their own master, *Rabbit;* but speak very slightly of our Saviour, though they do not name him. 1. They suggest that Christ's setting up a baptism of his own was a piece of presumption, very unaccountable; as if John, having first set up this rite of baptizing, must have the monopoly of it, and, as it were, a patent for the invention: *"He that was with thee beyond Jordan,* as a disciple of thine, *behold,* and wonder, *the same,* the very same, *baptizes,* and takes thy work out of thy hand." Thus the voluntary condescensions of the Lord Jesus, as that of his being baptized by John, are often unjustly and very unkindly turned to his reproach. 2. They suggest that it was a piece of ingratitude to John. He *to whom thou barest witness* baptizes; as if Jesus owed all his reputation to the honourable character John gave of him, and yet had very unworthily improved it to the prejudice of John. But Christ needed not John's testimony, *ch.* 5:36. He reflected more honour upon John than he received from him, yet thus it is incident to us to think that others are more indebted to us than really they are. And besides, Christ's baptism was not in the least an *impeachment,* but indeed the greatest *improvement,* of John's baptism, which was but to lead the way to Christ's. John was *just* to Christ, in bearing witness to him; and Christ's answering his testimony did rather enrich than impoverish John's ministry. 3. They conclude that it would be a total eclipse to John's baptism: *"All men come to him;* they that used to follow with us now flock after him, it is therefore time for us to look about us." It was not indeed strange that *all men came to him.* As far as Christ is *manifested* he will be *magnified;* but why should John's disciples grieve at this? Note, Aiming at the monopoly of honour and respect has been in all ages the bane of the church, and the shame of its members and ministers; as also a vying of interests, and a jealousy of rivalship and competition. We mistake if we think that the excelling gifts and graces, and labours and usefulness, of one, are a diminution and disparagement to another that has obtained mercy to be faithful; for the Spirit is a free agent, *dispensing to every one severally as he will.* Paul rejoiced in the usefulness even of those that *opposed him,* Phil. 1:18. We must leave it to God to choose, employ, and honour his own instruments as he pleaseth, and not covet to be *placed alone.*

V. Here is John's answer to this complaint which his disciples made, *v.* 27, etc. His disciples expected that he would have resented this matter as they did; but Christ's *manifestation to Israel* was no *surprise* to John, but what he looked for; it was not *disturbance* to him, but what he wished for. He therefore checked the complaint, as Moses, *Enviest thou for my sake?* and took this occasion to confirm the testimonies he had formerly borne to Christ as superior to him, cheerfully consigning and turning over to him all the interest he had in Israel. In this discourse here, the first minister of the gospel (for so John was) is an excellent pattern to all ministers to *humble* themselves and to *exalt* the Lord Jesus.

1. John here *abases himself in comparison with Christ, v.* 27–30. The more others magnify us, the more we must humble ourselves, and fortify ourselves against the temptation of flattery and applause, and the jealousy of our friends for our honour, by remembering our place, and what we are, 1 Co. 3:5.

(1.) *John acquiesces* in the divine disposal, and satisfies himself with that (*v.* 27): *A man can receive nothing except it be given him from heaven,* whence *every good gift* comes (James 1:17), a general truth very applicable in this case. Different employments are according to the direction of divine Providence, different endowments according to the distribution of the divine grace. *No man can take* any true *honour* to himself, Heb. 5:4. We have as necessary and constant a dependence upon the grace of God in all the motions and actions of the spiritual life as we have upon the providence of God in all the motions and actions of the natural life: now this comes in here as a reason, [1.] Why we should not *envy* those that have a larger share of gifts than we have, or move in a larger sphere of usefulness. John reminds his disciples that Jesus would not have thus excelled him *except he had received it from heaven,* for, as *man* and *Mediator,* he *received gifts;* and, if God gave him *the Spirit without measure* (*v.* 34), shall they grudge at it? The same reason will hold as to others. If God is *pleased* to give to others more ability and success than to us, shall we be displeased at it, and reflect upon him as unjust, unwise, and partial? See Mt. 20:15. [2.] Why we should not be *discontented,* though we be inferior to others in gifts and usefulness, and be eclipsed by their excellencies. John was ready to own that it was the gift, the free gift, of heaven, that made him a preacher, a prophet, a baptist: it was God that gave him the interest he had in the love and esteem of the people; and, if now his interest decline, God's will be done! He that *gives* may *take.* What we *receive* from heaven we must take as it is *given.* Now John never received a commission for a standing *perpetual* office, but only for a *temporary* one, which must soon expire; and therefore, when he has fulfilled his ministry, he can contentedly see it go out of date. Some give quite another sense of these words: John had taken pains with his disciples, to teach them the reference which his baptism had to Christ, who should come after him, and yet be preferred before him, and do that for them which he could not do; and yet, after all, they dote upon John, and grudge this preference of Christ above him: Well saith John, I see *a man can receive* (that is, perceive) *nothing, except it be given him from heaven.* The labour of ministers if all lost labour, unless the grace of God make it effectual. Men do not understand that which is made most *plain,* nor believe that which is made most *evident,* unless it be given them from heaven to understand and believe it.

(2.) John appeals to the testimony he had formerly given concerning Christ (*v.* 28): You can bear me witness that I said, again and again, *I am not the Christ, but I am sent before him.* See how steady and constant John was in his testimony to Christ, and not as a *reed shaken with the wind;* neither the frowns of the chief priests, nor the flatteries of his own disciples, could make him change his note. Now this serves here, [1.] As a *conviction* to his disciples of the unreasonableness of their complaint. They had spoken of the witness which their master bore to Jesus (*v.* 26): "Now," saith John, "do you not remember what the testimony was that I did bear? Call that to mind, and you will see your own cavil answered. Did I not say, *I am not the Christ?* Why then do you set me up as a rival with him that is? Did I not say, *I am sent before him?* Why then does it seem strange to you that I should stand by and give way to him?" [2.] It is a *comfort* to himself that he had never *given* his disciples *any occasion* thus to set him up in competition with Christ; but, on the contrary, had particularly *cautioned* them against this mistake, though he might have made a hand of it for himself. It is a satisfaction to faithful ministers when they have done what they could in their places to prevent any extravagances that their people ran into. John had not only not encouraged them to hope that he was the Messiah, but had plainly told them the contrary, which was now a satisfaction to him. It is a common excuse for those who have undue honour paid them, *Si populus vult decipi, decipiatur — If the people will be deceived, let them;* but that is an ill maxim for those to go by whose business it is to *undeceive* people. *The lip of truth shall be established.*

(3.) John professes the great satisfaction he had in the advancement of Christ and his interest. He was so far from *regretting* it, as his disciples did, that he *rejoiced* in it. This he expresses (*v.* 29) by an elegant similitude. [1.] He compares our Saviour to the *bridegroom: "He that hath the bride is the bridegroom.* Do *all men come to him?* It is well, whither else should they go? Has he got the throne in men's affections? Who else should have it? It is his right; to whom should the bride be brought but to the bridegroom?" Christ was prophesied of in the Old Testament as a bridegroom, Ps. 45. *The Word was made flesh,* that the disparity of nature might not be a *bar to the match.* Provision is made for the purifying of the church, that the defilement of sin might be no bar. Christ espouses his church to himself; he *has* the bride, for he has her love, he has her promise; *the church is subject to Christ.* As far as particular souls are devoted to him in faith and love, so far the bridegroom has the bride. [2.] He compares himself to the *friend of the bridegroom,* who attends upon him, to do him honour and service, assists him in prosecuting the match, speaks a good word for him, uses his interest on his behalf, rejoices when the match goes on, and most of all when the point is gained, and he *has the bride.* All that John had done in preaching and baptizing was to introduce him; and, now that he was come, he had what he wished for: *The friend of the bridegroom stands, and hears him;* stands expecting him, and waiting for him; *rejoices with joy because of the bridegroom's voice,* because he is come to the marriage after he had been long expected. Note, *First,* Faithful ministers are friends of the bridegroom, to recommend him to the affections and choice of the children of men; to bring letters and messages from him, for he courts by proxy; and herein they must be faithful to him. *Secondly,* The friends of the bridegroom must *stand, and hear the bridegroom's voice;* must receive instructions from him, and attend his orders; must desire to have proofs of Christ speaking in them, and with them (2 Co. 13:3); that is the *bridegroom's voice. Thirdly,* The espousing of souls to Jesus Christ, in faith and love, is the fulfilling of the joy of every good minister. If the day of Christ's espousals be the day of the gladness of his heart (Cant. 3:11), it cannot but be of their too who love him and wish well to his honour and kingdom. Surely they have *no greater joy.*

(4.) He owns it highly fit and necessary that the reputation and interest of Christ should be advanced, and his own diminished (v. 30): *He must increase, but I must decrease.* If they grieve at the growing greatness of the Lord Jesus, they will have more and more occasion to grieve, as those have that indulge themselves in envy and emulation. John speaks of Christ's increase and his own decrease, not only as *necessary* and *unavoidable,* which could not be *helped* and therefore must be *borne,* but as highly *just* and *agreeable,* and affording him entire satisfaction. [1.] He was *well pleased* to see the kingdom of Christ getting ground: "*He must increase.* You think he has gained a great deal, but it is nothing to what he will gain." Note, The kingdom of Christ is, and will be, a growing kingdom, like the light of the morning, like the grain of mustard-seed. [2.] He was not at all *displeased* that the effect of this was the diminishing of his own interest: *I must decrease.* Created excellencies are under this law, they *must decrease. I have seen an end of all perfection.* Note, *First,* The shining forth of the glory of Christ eclipses the lustre of all other glory. The glory that stands in *competition* with Christ, that of the world and the flesh, decreases and loses ground in the soul as the knowledge and love of Christ increase and get ground; but it is here spoken of that which is *subservient* to him. As the light of the morning increases, that of the morning star decreases. *Secondly,* If our diminution or abasement may but in the least contribute to the advancement of Christ's name, we must cheerfully submit to it, and be content to be *any thing,* to be *nothing,* so that Christ may be *all.*

2. John Baptist here *advances* Christ, and instructs his disciples concerning him, that, instead of grieving that so many come to him, they might come to him themselves.

(1.) He instructs them concerning the *dignity of Christ's person* (v. 31): *He that cometh from above,* that *cometh from heaven, is above all.* Here, [1.] He supposes his divine origin, that he came *from above,* from *heaven,* which bespeaks not only his divine extraction, but his divine nature. He had a being before his conception, a heavenly being. None but he that came from heaven was fit to show us the will of heaven, or the way to heaven. When God would save man, he *sent from above.* [2.] Hence he infers his sovereign authority: he is *above all,* above all things and all persons, *God over all, blessed for evermore.* It is daring presumption to dispute precedency with him. When we come to speak of the honours of the Lord Jesus, we find they transcend all conception and expression, and we can say but this, *He is above all.* It was said of John Baptist, *There is not a greater among them that are born of women.* But the descent of Christ from heaven put such a dignity upon him as he was not divested of by his being made flesh; still he was *above all.* This he further illustrates by the meanness of those who stood in competition with him: *He that is of the earth, is earthly, ho ōn*

ek tēs gēs, ek tēs gēs esti — He that is of the earth is of the earth; he that has his origin of the earth has his food out of the earth, has his converse with earthly things, and his concern is for them. Note, *First,* Man has his rise out of the earth; not only Adam at first, but we also still are *formed out of the clay,* Job 33:6. Look to the rock whence we were hewn. *Secondly,* Man's constitution is therefore *earthly;* not only his body frail and mortal, but his soul corrupt and carnal, and its bent and bias strong towards earthly things. The prophets and apostles were of the same mould with other men; they were but *earthen vessels,* though they had a rich treasure lodged in them; and shall these be set up as rivals with Christ? *Let the potsherds strive with the potsherds of the earth;* but let them not cope with him that *came from heaven.*

(2.) Concerning the *excellency and certainty of his doctrine.* His disciples were displeased that Christ's preaching was admired, and attended upon, more than his; but he tells them that there was reason enough for it. For,

[1.] He, for his part, *spoke of the earth,* and so do all those that are *of the earth.* The prophets were men and spoke like men; *of themselves* they could not speak but *of the earth,* 2 Co. 3:5. The preaching of the prophets and of John was but low and flat compared with Christ's preaching; as heaven is high above the earth, so were his thoughts above theirs. By them God spoke *on earth,* but in Christ he speaketh *from heaven.*

[2.] But he that cometh from heaven is not only in his person, but in his doctrine, above all the prophets that ever lived on earth; none teacheth like him. The doctrine of Christ is here recommended to us,

First, As infallibly *sure* and *certain,* and to be entertained accordingly (v. 32): *What he hath seen and heard, that he testifieth.* See here, 1. Christ's divine knowledge; he testified nothing but *what he had seen and heard,* what he was perfectly apprized of and thoroughly acquainted with. What he discovered of the divine nature and of the invisible world was what he had *seen;* what he revealed of the mind of God was what he had *heard* immediately from him, and not at second hand. The prophets testified what was made known to them in creams and visions by the mediation of angels, but not what they had seen and heard. John was the crier's *voice,* that said, "*Make room for the witness,* and *keep silence* while the charge is given," but then leaves it to the witness to give in his testimony himself, and the judge to give the charge himself. The gospel of Christ is not a doubtful opinion, like an hypothesis or new notion in philosophy, which every one is at liberty to believe or not; but it is a revelation of the mind of God, which is of *eternal truth* in itself, and of *infinite concern* to us. 2. His divine grace and goodness: that which he had *seen* and *heard* he was pleased to make known to us, because he knew it nearly concerned us. What Paul had seen and heard in the third heavens he could not testify (2 Co. 12:4), but Christ knew how to utter what he had *seen* and *heard.* Christ's preaching is here called his *testifying,* to denote, (1.) The *convincing evidence* of it; it was not *reported* as news by hearsay, but it was *testified* as evidence given in court, with great caution and assurance. (2.) The affectionate earnestness of the delivery of it: it was testified with concern and importunity, as Acts 18:5.

From the *certainty* of Christ's doctrine, John takes occasion, [1.] To lament the infidelity of the most of men: though he testifies what is infallibly true, yet *no man* receiveth his testimony, that is, very few, next to none, none in comparison with those that refuse it. They receive it not, they will not hear it, they do not heed it, or give credit to it. This he speaks of not only as a matter of *wonder,* that such a testimony should not be received (Who hath believed our report? How stupid and foolish are the greatest part of mankind, what enemies to themselves!) but as matter of *grief;* John's disciples grieved that *all men came to Christ* (v. 26); they thought his followers too many. But John grieves that *no man came to him;* he thought them too few. Note, The unbelief of sinners is the grief of saints. It was for this that St. Paul had *great heaviness,* Rom. 9:2. [2.] He takes occasion to commend the faith of the chosen remnant (v. 33): *He that hath received his testimony* (and some such there were, though very few) hath *set to his seal that God is true.* God is true, though we do not *set our seal to it;* let God be true, and every man a liar; his truth needs not our faith to support it, but by faith we do ourselves the honour and justice to subscribe to his truth, and hereby God reckons himself honoured. God's promises are all *yea and amen;* by faith we put

our *amen* to them, as Rev. 22:20. Observe, He that receives the testimony of Christ subscribes not only to the truth of Christ, but to the truth of *God,* for his name is the *Word of God;* the commandments of God and the testimony of Christ are put together, Rev. 12:17. By believing in Christ we set to our seal, *First,* That God is true to all the promises which he has made *concerning Christ,* that which he spoke by the mouth of *all his holy prophets;* what he *swore to our fathers* is all accomplished, and not one iota or tittle of it fallen to the ground, Lu. 1:70, etc. Acts 13:32, 33. *Secondly,* That he is true to all the promises he has made *in Christ;* we venture our souls upon God's veracity, being satisfied that he is *true;* we are willing to deal with him *upon trust,* and to quit all in this world for a happiness in reversion and out of sight. By this we greatly honour God's faithfulness. Whom we *give credit* to we *give honour* to.

Secondly, It is recommended to us as a *divine* doctrine; not his own, but *his that sent* him (v. 34): *For he whom God hath sent speaketh the word of God,* which he was sent to speak, and enabled to speak; *for God giveth not the Spirit by measure unto him.* The prophets were as messengers that brought letters from heaven; but Christ came under the character of an *ambassador,* and treats with us as such; for, 1. He spoke the *words of God,* and nothing he said savoured of human infirmity; both substance and language were divine. He proved himself *sent of God* (ch. 3:2), and therefore his words are to be received as the words of God. By this rule we may try the spirits: those that speak *as the oracles of God,* and prophesy *according to the proportion of faith,* are to be received as *sent of God.* 2. He spoke as no other prophet did; for *God giveth not the Spirit by measure to him.* None can speak the *words of God* without the *Spirit of God,* 1 Co. 2:10, 11. The Old-Testament prophets had the Spirit, and in different degrees, 2 Ki. 2:9, 10. But, whereas God gave them the Spirit by *measure* (1 Co. 12:4), he gave him to Christ *without measure;* all fulness dwelt in him, the fulness of the Godhead, an immeasurable fulness. The Spirit was not in Christ as in a vessel, but as in a fountain, as in a bottomless ocean. "The prophets that had the Spirit in a limited manner, only with respect to some particular revelation, sometimes spoke of *themselves;* but he that had the Spirit always residing in him, without stint, always spoke *the words of God.*" So Dr. Whitby.

(3.) Concerning *the power and authority he is invested with,* which gives him the pre-eminence above all others, and a more excellent name than they.

[1.] He is the *beloved Son of the Father* (v. 35): *The Father loveth the Son.* The prophets were faithful as servants, but Christ as a Son; they were employed as servants, but Christ *beloved* as a son, always *his delight,* Prov. 8:30. The Father was well pleased in him; not only he *did* love him, but he *doth* love him; he continued his love to him even in his estate of humiliation, loved him never the less for his poverty and sufferings.

[2.] He is *Lord of all.* The Father, as an evidence of his love for him, *hath given all things into his hand.* Love is generous. The Father took such a complacency and had such a confidence in him that he constituted him the great *feoffee in trust* for mankind. Having given *him the Spirit without measure,* he gave him *all things;* for he was hereby qualified to be master and manager of all. Note, It is the honour of Christ, and the unspeakable comfort of all Christians, that the Father hath *given all things* into the hands of the Mediator. *First,* All *power;* so it is explained, Mt. 28:18. All the works of creation being put under his feet, all the affairs of redemption are put into his hand; he is Lord of all. Angels are his servants; devils are his captives. He has *power over all flesh,* the *heathen given him for his inheritance.* The kingdom of providence is committed to his administration. He has power to settle the terms of the covenant of peace as the great *plenipotentiary,* to govern his church as the great *lawgiver,* to dispense divine favours as the great *almoner,* and to call all to account as the great *Judge.* Both the golden sceptre and the iron rod are given into his hand. *Secondly,* All *grace* is given into his hand as the channel of conveyance; *all things,* all those good things which God intended to give to the children of men; *eternal life,* and all its preliminaries. We are unworthy that the Father should give those things *into our hands,* for we have made ourselves the *children of his wrath;* he hath therefore appointed the *Son of his love* to be trustee for us, and the things he intended for us he gives *into his hands,* who is worthy, and has merited both honours for himself and favours for us. They are given *into his hands,* by him to be given into ours. This is a great encouragement to faith, that the riches of the new covenant are deposited in so sure, so kind, so good a hand, the hand of him that purchased them for us, and us for himself, who is able to keep all that which both God and believers have agreed to *commit to him.*

[3.] He is the object of that faith which is made the great condition of eternal happiness, and herein he has the preeminence above all others: *He that believeth on the Son, hath life, v.* 36. We have here the application of what he had said concerning Christ and his doctrine; and it is the *conclusion of the whole matter.* If God has put this honour upon the Son, we must by faith give honour to him. As God offers and conveys good things to us by the *testimony* of Jesus Christ, whose word is the vehicle of divine favours, so we receive and partake of those favours by *believing* the testimony, and entertaining that word as *true* and *good;* this way of *receiving* fitly answers that way of *giving.* We have here the sum of that gospel which is to be preached to every creature, Mk. 16:16. Here is,

First, The blessed state of all true Christians: *He that believes on the Son hath everlasting life.* Note, 1. It is the character of every true Christian that he believes on *the Son of God;* not only *believes him,* that what he saith is true, but believes *on him,* consents to him, and confides in him. The benefit of true Christianity is no less than *everlasting life;* this is what Christ came to purchase for us and confer upon us; it can be no less than the happiness of an immortal soul *in* an immortal God. 2. True believers, even now, *have* everlasting life; not only they shall have it hereafter, but they have it now. For, (1.) They *have* very good security for it. The deed by which it passeth is sealed and delivered to them, and so they *have* it; it is put into the hands of their guardian for them, and so they have it, though the use be not yet transferred into possession. They have the Son of God, and in him *they have life;* and the Spirit of God, the earnest of this life. (2.) They have the comfortable *foretastes* of it, in present communion with God and the tokens of his love. Grace is glory begun.

Secondly, The wretched and miserable condition of unbelievers: *He that believeth not the Son* is undone, *ho apeithōn.* The word includes both *incredulity* and *disobedience.* An unbeliever is one that gives not credit to the doctrine of Christ, nor is in subjection to the government of Christ. Now those that will neither be *taught* nor *ruled* by Christ, 1. They *cannot be happy* in this world, nor that to come: *He shall not see life,* that life which Christ came to bestow. He shall not enjoy it, he shall not have any comfortable *prospect* of it, shall never come within ken of it, except to aggravate his loss of it. 2. They *cannot but be miserable: The wrath of God abides upon* an unbeliever. He is not only under the *wrath of God,* which is as surely *the soul's death* as his favour is *its life,* but it *abides upon him.* All the wrath he has made himself liable to by the violation of the law, if not removed by the grace of the gospel, is bound upon him. God's wrath for his daily actual transgressions lights and lies upon him. Old scores lie undischarged, and new ones are added: something is done every day to fill the measure, and nothing to empty it. Thus the wrath of God *abides,* for it is *treasured up against the day of wrath.*

CHAPTER 4

It was, more than any thing else, the glory of the land of Israel, that it was Emmanuel's land (Isa. 8:8), not only the place of his birth, but the scene of his preaching and miracles. This land in our Saviour's time was divided into three parts: Judea in the south, Galilee in the north, and Samaria lying between them. Now, in this chapter, we have Christ in each of these three parts of that land. I. Departing out of Judea (*v.* 1–3). II. Passing through Samaria, which, though a visit in transitu, here takes up most room. 1. His coming into Samaria (*v.* 4–6). 2. His discourse with the Samaritan woman at a well (*v.* 7–26). 3. The notice which the woman gave of him to the city (*v.* 27–30). 4. Christ's talk with his disciples in the meantime (*v.* 31–38). 5. The good effect of this among the Samaritans (*v.* 39–42). III. We find him residing for some time in Galilee (*v.* 43–46), and his curing a nobleman's son there, that was at death's door (*v.* 46–54).

Verses 1–3

We read of Christ's coming into Judea (*ch.* 3:22), after he had kept the feast at Jerusalem; and now he left Judea four months before harvest, as is said here (*v.* 35); so that it is computed that he staid in Judea about six months, to build upon the foundation John had laid there. We have no particular account of his sermons and miracles there, only in general, *v.* 1.

I. That he *made disciples;* he prevailed with many to embrace his doctrine, and to follow him as a teacher come from God. His ministry was successful, notwithstanding the opposition it met with (Ps. 110:2, 3); *mathētas poiei* — it signifies the same with *mathēteuō — to disciples.* Compare Gen. 12:5. *The souls which they had gotten,* which they had *made* (so the word is), which they had *made proselytes.* Note, It is Christ's prerogative to *make disciples,* first to bring them to his foot, and then to form and fashion them to his will. *Fit, non nascitur, Christianus — The Christian is made such, not born such.* Tertullian.

II. That he *baptized* those whom he *made disciples,* admitted them by *washing them with water;* not himself, but by the ministry of his disciples, *v.* 2. 1. Because he would put a difference between his baptism and that of John, who baptized all himself; for he baptized as a servant, Christ as a master. 2. He would apply himself more to preaching work, which was the more excellent, 1 Co. 1:17. 3. He would put honour upon his disciples, by empowering and employing them to do it; and so train them up to further services. 4. If he had baptized some himself, they would have been apt to value themselves upon that, and despise others, which he would prevent, as Paul, 1 Co. 1:13, 14. 5. He would reserve himself for the honour of baptizing with the Holy Ghost, Acts 1:5. 6. He would teach us that the efficacy of the sacraments depends not on any virtue in the hand that administers them, as also that what is done by his ministers, according to his direction, he owns as done by himself.

III. That he made and baptized *more disciples than John;* not only more than John did at this time, but more than he had done at any time. Christ's converse was more winning than John's. His miracles were convincing, and the cures he wrought *gratis* very inviting.

IV. That the Pharisees were informed of this; they heard what multitudes he baptized, for they had, from his first appearing, a jealous eye upon him, and wanted not spies to give them notice concerning him. Observe, 1. When the Pharisees thought they had got rid of John (for he was by this time imprisoned), and were pleasing themselves with that, Jesus appears, who was a greater vexation to them than ever John had been. The witnesses will rise again. 2. That which grieved them was that Christ made so many disciples. The success of the gospel exasperates its enemies, and it is a good sign that it is getting ground when the powers of darkness are enraged against it.

V. That our Lord Jesus knew very well what informations were given in against him to the Pharisees. It is probable the informers were willing to have their names concealed, and the Pharisees loth to have their designs known; but none can dig so keep as to *hide their counsels from the Lord* (Isa. 29:15), and Christ is here called *the Lord.* He knew what was told the Pharisees, and how much, it is likely, it exceeded the truth; for it is not likely that Jesus had yet baptized *more than John;* but so the thing was represented, to make him appear the more formidable; see 2 Ki. 6:12.

VI. That hereupon our Lord Jesus *left Judea* and *departed again* to go to Galilee.

1. He *left Judea,* because he was likely to be persecuted there even to the death; such was the rage of the Pharisees against him, and such their impious policy to devour the manchild in his infancy. To escape their designs, Christ quitted the country, and went where what he did would be less provoking than just under their eye. For, (1.) His hour was not yet come (*ch.* 7:30), the time fixed in the counsels of God, and the Old-Testament prophecies, for Messiah's being cut off. He had not finished his testimony, and therefore would not surrender or expose himself. (2.) The disciples he had gathered in Judea were not able to bear hardships, and therefore he would not expose them. (3.) Hereby he gave an example to his own rule: *When they persecute you in one city, flee to another.* We are not called to suffer, while we may avoid it without sin; and therefore, though we may not, for our own preservation, change our religion, yet we may change our place. Christ secured himself, not by a miracle, but in a way *common to men,* for the direction and encouragement of his suffering people.

2. He departed into Galilee, because he had work to do there, and many friends and fewer enemies. He went to Galilee now, (1.) Because John's ministry had now *made way* for him there; for Galilee, which was under Herod's jurisdiction, was the last scene of John's baptism. (2.) Because John's imprisonment had now *made room* for him there. That light being now put under a bushel, the minds of people would not be divided between him and Christ. Thus both the liberties and restraints of good ministers are for the furtherance of the gospel, Phil. 1:12. But to what purpose does he go into Galilee for safety? Herod, the persecutor of John, will never be the protector of Jesus. Chemnitius here notes, *Pii in hâc vitâ quos fugiant habent; ad quos vero fugiant ut in tuto sint non habent, nisi ad te, Deus, qui solus regugium nostrum es — The pious have those, in this life, to whom they can fly; but they have none to fly to, who can afford them refuge, except thee, O God.*

Verses 4–26

We have here an account of the good Christ did in Samaria, when he *passed through* that country in his way to Galilee. The Samaritans, both in *blood* and *religion,* were *mongrel Jews,* the posterity of those colonies which the king of Assyria planted there after the captivity of the ten tribes, with whom the poor of the land that were left behind, and many other Jews afterwards, incorporated themselves. They worshipped the God of Israel only, to whom they erected a temple on mount Gerizim, in competition with that at Jerusalem. There was great enmity between them and the Jews; the Samaritans would not admit Christ, when they saw he was going to Jerusalem (Lu. 9:53); the Jews thought they could not give him a worse name than to say, *He is a Samaritan.* When the Jews were in prosperity, the Samaritans claimed kindred to them (Ezra 4:2), but, when the Jews were in distress, they were Medes and Persians; see Joseph. *Antiq.* 11.340–341; 12.257. Now observe,

I. Christ's coming into Samaria. He charged his disciples not to *enter into any city of the Samaritans* (Mt. 10:5), that is, not to preach the gospel, or work miracles; nor did he here preach publicly, or work any miracle, his eye being to *the lost sheep of the house of Israel.* What kindness he here did them was *accidental;* it was only a *crumb* of the children's bread that casually *fell from the master's table.*

1. His *road* from Judea to Galilee lay through the *country* of Samaria (*v.* 4): *He must needs go through Samaria.* There was no other way, unless he would have fetched a compass on the other side *Jordan,* a great way about. The wicked and profane are at present so intermixed with God's Israel that, unless we will go *out of the world,* we cannot avoid *going through* the company of such, 1 Co. 5:10. We have therefore need of the armour of righteousness on the right hand and on the left, that we may neither give *provocation* to them nor contract *pollution* by them. We should not go into places of temptation but when we *needs must;* and then we should not reside in them, but *hasten through* them. Some think that Christ *must needs* go through Samaria because of the good work he had to do there; a poor woman to be converted, a lost sheep to be sought and saved. This was work his heart was upon, the *therefore* he *must needs* go this way. It was happy for Samaria that it lay *in Christ's way,* which gave him an opportunity of calling on them. *When I passed by thee, I said unto thee, Live,* Eze. 16:6.

2. His baiting place happened to be at a *city of Samaria.* Now observe,

(1.) The place described. It was called *Sychar;* probably the same with *Sichem,* or *Shechem,* a place which we read much of in the Old Testament. Thus are the names of places commonly corrupted by tract of time. Shechem yielded the first proselyte that ever came into the church of Israel (Gen. 34:24), and now it is the first place where the gospel is preached out of the commonwealth of Israel; so Dr. Lightfoot observes; as also that the *valley of Achor,* which was given for a *door of hope,* hope to the poor Gentiles, ran along by this city, Hos. 2:15. Abimelech was made king here; it was Jeroboam's royal seat; but the evangelist, when he would give us the antiquities of the place, takes notice of Jacob's interest there, which was more its honour than its crowned heads. [1.] Here lay Jacob's ground, the *parcel of ground which Jacob* gave to his son Joseph, whose bones were buried in it, Gen. 48:22; Jos. 24:32. Probably this is mentioned to intimate that Christ, when he reposed himself hard by here, took occasion from the ground which Jacob gave Joseph to meditate on the good report which the elders by faith obtained. Jerome chose to live in the land of Canaan, that the sight of the places might affect him the more with scripture stories. [2.] Here was Jacob's well which he digged, or at least used, for himself and his family. We find no mention of this well in the Old Testament; but the tradition was that it was Jacob's well.

(2.) The posture of our Lord Jesus at this place: *Being wearied with his journey, he sat thus on the well.* We have here our Lord Jesus,

[1.] Labouring under the common fatigue of travellers. He was *wearied with his journey.* Though it was yet but the sixth hour, and he had performed but half his day's journey, yet he was weary; or, *because* it was the sixth hour, the time of the heat of the day, therefore he was weary. Here we see, *First,* That he was a *true man,* and subject to the common infirmities of the human nature. Toil came in with sin (Gen. 3:19), and therefore Christ, having made himself a curse for us, submitted to it. *Secondly,* That he was a *poor man,* else he might have travelled on horseback or in a chariot. To this instance of meanness and mortification he humbled himself for us, that he went all his journeys on foot. When *servants* were on *horses, princes walked as servants on the earth,* Eccl. 10:7. When we are carried easily, let us think on the weariness of our Master. *Thirdly,* It should seem that he was but a *tender man,* and not of a robust constitution; it should seem, his disciples were not tired, for they went into the town without any difficulty, when their Master sat down, and could not go a step further. Bodies of the finest mould are most sensible of fatigue, and can worst bear it.

[2.] We have him here betaking himself to the common relief of travellers; *Being wearied, he sat thus on the well. First,* He sat *on the well,* an *uneasy place,* cold and hard; he had no couch, no easy chair to repose himself in, but took to that which was *next hand,* to teach us not to be nice and curious in the conveniences of this life, but content with *mean things. Secondly,* He sat *thus,* in an *uneasy posture;* sat *carelessly — incuriose et neglectim;* or he sat *so* as people that are wearied with travelling are accustomed to sit.

II. His discourse with a Samaritan woman, which is here recorded at large, while Christ's dispute with the doctors, and his discourse with Moses and Elias on the mount, are buried in silence. This discourse is reducible to four heads: —

1. They discourse *concerning the water, v.* 7–15.

(1.) Notice is taken of the *circumstances* that gave occasion to this discourse.

[1.] There comes a *woman* of Samaria to *draw water.* This intimates her poverty, she had no servant to be a *drawer of water;* and her industry, she would do it herself. See here, *First,* How God owns and approves of honest humble diligence in our places. Christ was made known to the shepherds when they were keeping their flock. *Secondly,* How the divine Providence brings about glorious purposes by events which seem to us fortuitous and accidental. This woman's meeting with Christ at the well may remind us of the stories of Rebekah, Rachel, and Jethro's daughter, who all met with husbands, good husbands, no worse than Isaac, Jacob, and Moses, when they came to the wells for water. *Thirdly,* How the preventing grace of God sometimes brings people unexpectedly under the means of conversion and salvation. He is found of them that sought him not.

[2.] His disciples were *gone away into the city to buy meat.* Hence learn a lesson, *First,* Of justice and honesty. The meat Christ ate, he bought and paid for, as Paul, 2 Th. 3:8. *Secondly,* Of daily dependence upon Providence: *Take no thought for the morrow.* Christ did not go into the city to eat, but sent his disciples to fetch his meat thither; not because he scrupled eating in a Samaritan city, but, 1. Because he had a good work to do at that well, which might be done while they were catering. It is wisdom to fill up our vacant minutes with that which is good, that the *fragments* of time may *not be lost.* Peter, while his dinner was getting ready, fell into a trance, Acts 10:10. 2. Because it was more private and retired, more cheap and homely, to have his dinner brought him hither, than to go into the town for it. Perhaps his purse was low, and he would teach us *good husbandry,* to *spend* according to what we *have* and not go beyond it. At least, he would teach us not to affect great things. Christ could eat his dinner as well upon a *draw well* as in the best inn in the town. Let us *comport* with our circumstances. Now this gave Christ an opportunity of discoursing with this woman about spiritual concerns, and he improved it; he often preached to multitudes that crowded after him for instruction, yet here he condescends to teach a single person, a woman, a poor woman, a stranger, a Samaritan, to teach his ministers to do likewise, as those that know what a glorious achievement it is to help to save, though but *one soul,* from death.

(2.) Let us observe the *particulars* of this discourse.

[1.] Jesus begins with a modest request for a draught of water: *Give me to drink.* He that *for our sakes became poor* here becomes a beggar, that those who are in want, and cannot dig, may not be ashamed to beg. Christ asked for it, not only because he needed it, and needed her help to come at it, but because he would draw on further discourse with her, and teach us to be willing to be beholden to the meanest when there is occasion. Christ is still begging in his poor members, and a *cup of cold water,* like this here, given to them in his name, shall not lose its reward.

[2.] The woman, though she does not deny his request, yet quarrels with him because he did not carry on the humour of his own nation (*v.* 9): *How is it?* Observe, *First,* What a mortal feud there was between the Jews and the Samaritans: *The Jews have no dealings with the Samaritans.* The Samaritans were the *adversaries of Judah* (Ezra 4:1), were upon all occasions mischievous to them. The Jews were extremely malicious against the Samaritans, "looked upon them as having no part in the resurrection, excommunicated and cursed them by the sacred name of God, by the glorious writing of the tables, and by the curse of the upper and lower house of judgment, with this law, That no Israelite eat of any thing that is a Samaritan's, for it is as if he should eat swine's flesh." So Dr. Lightfoot, out of *Rabbi Tanchum.* Note, Quarrels about religion are usually the most implacable of all quarrels. Men were made to *have dealing* one with another; but if men, because one worships at one temple and another at another, will deny the offices of humanity, and charity, and common civility, will be morose and unnatural, scornful and censorious, and this under colour of zeal for religion, they plainly show that however their religion may be *true* they are not *truly religious;* but, pretending to stickle for religion, subvert the design of it. *Secondly,* How ready the woman was to upbraid Christ with the haughtiness and ill nature of the Jewish nation: *How is it that thou, being a Jew, askest drink of me?* By his dress or dialect, or both, she knew him to be a Jew, and *thinks it strange* that he runs not to the same excess of riot against the Samaritans with other Jews. Note, Moderate men of all sides are, like Joshua and his fellows (Zec. 3:8), *men wondered at.* Two things this woman wonders at, 1. That he should *ask* this kindness; for it was the pride of the Jews that they would endure any hardship rather than be beholden to a Samaritan. It was part of Christ's humiliation that he was born of the Jewish nation, which was *now* not only in an *ill state,* subject to the Romans, but in an *ill name* among the nations. With what disdain did Pilate ask, *Am I a Jew?* Thus he *made himself* not only *of no reputation,* but of *ill reputation;* but herein he has set us an example of swimming against the stream of common corruptions. We must, like our master, put on *goodness* and *kindness,* though it should be ever so much the genius of our country, or the humour of our party, to be morose and ill-natured. This woman expected that Christ should be as other Jews were; but it is unjust to charge upon every individual person even the common faults of the community: no rule but has some exceptions. 2. She wonders that he should *expect to receive* this kindness from her that was a Samaritan: "You Jews could deny it to one of our nation, and why should we grant it to one of yours?" Thus quarrels are propagated endlessly by revenge and retaliation.

[3.] Christ takes this occasion to instruct her in divine things: *If thou knewest the gift of God, thou wouldst have asked, v.* 10. Observe,

First, He waives her objection of the feud between the Jews and Samaritans, and takes no notice of it. Some differences are best *healed* by being *slighted,* and by avoiding all occasions of *entering into dispute* about them. Christ will convert this woman, not by showing her that the Samaritan worship was *schismatical* (though really it was so), but by showing her her own ignorance and immoralities, and her need of a Saviour.

Secondly, He fills her with an apprehension that she had now an opportunity (a fairer opportunity than she was aware of) of gaining that which would be of unspeakable advantage to her. She had not the helps that the Jews had to discern the signs of the times, and therefore Christ tells her expressly that she had now a season of grace; this was *the day of her visitation.*

a. He hints to her what she *should know,* but was ignorant of: *If thou knewest the gift of God,* that is, as the next words explain it, *who it is that saith, Give me to drink.* If thou knewest *who I am.* She saw him to be a Jew, a poor weary traveller; but he would have her know something more concerning him that did yet appear. Note, (*a.*) Jesus Christ is the *gift of God,* the richest token of God's love to us, and the richest treasure of all good for us; *a gift,* not a debt which we could demand from God; not a *loan,* which he will demand from us again, but a gift, a free gift, *ch.* 3:16. (*b.*) It is an unspeakable privilege to have this gift of God proposed and offered to us; to have an opportunity of embracing it: "He who is the gift of God is now set before thee, and addresses himself to *thee;* it is he that saith, *Give me to drink;* this gift comes a begging to thee." (*c.*) Though Christ is set before us, and sues to us in and by his gospel, yet there are multitudes that *know him not.* They know not who it is that speaks to them in the gospel, that saith, *Give me to drink;* they perceive not that it is the Lord that calls them.

b. He hopes concerning her, what she would have done if she had known him; to be sure she would not have given him such a rude and uncivil answer; nay, she would have been so far from affronting him that she would have made her addresses to him: *Thou wouldest have asked.* Note, (*a.*) Those that would have any benefit by Christ must ask for it, must be earnest in prayer to God for it. (*b.*) Those that have a right knowledge of Christ will seek to him, and if we do not seek unto him it is a sign that we do not know him, Ps. 9:10. (*c.*) Christ knows what they that want the means of knowledge would have done if they had had them, Mt. 11:21.

c. He assures her what he would have done for her if she had applied to him: "He *would have given thee* (and not have upbraided thee as thou doest me) *living water.*" By this living water is meant the *Spirit,* who is not like the water in the bottom of the well, for some of which he asked, but like *living* or *running* water, which was much more valuable. Note, (*a.*) The Spirit of grace is as *living water;* see *ch.* 7:38. Under this similitude the blessings of the Messiah had been promised in the Old Testament, Isa. 12:3; 35:7; 44:3; 55:1; Zec. 14:8. The graces of the Spirit, and his comforts, satisfy the thirsting soul, that knows its own nature and necessity. (*b.*) Jesus Christ *can* and *will* give the Holy Spirit to them that ask him; for he *received* that he might *give.*

[4.] The woman objects against and cavils at the gracious intimation which Christ gave her (*v.* 11, 12): *Thou hast nothing to draw with;* and besides, *Art thou greater than our father Jacob?* What he spoke figuratively, she took literally; Nicodemus did so too. See what confused notions they have of spiritual things who are wholly taken up with the things that are sensible. Some respect she pays to this person, in calling him *Sir,* or *Lord;* but little respect to what he said, which she does but banter.

First, She does not think him capable of furnishing her with any water, no, not this in the well that is just at hand: *Thou has nothing to draw with,* and *the well is deep.* This she said, not knowing the power of Christ, for he who *causeth the vapours* to ascend from the ends of the earth needs *nothing to draw.* But there are those who will trust Christ no further than they can see him, and will not believe his promise, unless the means of the performance of it be *visible;* as if he were tied to our methods, and could not draw water without our buckets. She asks scornfully, "*Whence hast thou this living water?* I see not whence thou canst have it." Note, The springs of that living water which Christ has for those that come to him are secret and undiscovered. The fountain of life is hid with Christ. Christ has enough for us, though we see not whence he has it.

Secondly, She does not think it possible that he should furnish her with any better water than this which she could come at, but he could not: *Art thou greater than our father Jacob, who gave us the well?*

a. We will suppose the tradition true, that Jacob *himself, and his children, and cattle, did drink of this well.* And we may observe from it, (*a.*) The power and providence of God, in the continuance of the fountains of water from generation to generation, by the constant circulation of the rivers, like the blood in the body (Eccl. 1:7), to which circulation perhaps the flux and reflux of the sea, like the pulses of the heart, contribute. (*b.*) The plainness of the patriarch Jacob; his drink was water, and he and his children drank of the same well with his cattle.

b. Yet, allowing that to be true, she was out in several things; as, (*a.*) In calling Jacob *father.* What authority had the

Samaritans to reckon themselves of the seed of Jacob? They were descended from that mixed multitude which the king of Assyria had placed in the cities of Samaria; what have they to do then with Jacob? Because they were the *invaders* of Israel's rights, and the unjust possessors of Israel's lands, were they therefore the *inheritors* of Israel's blood and honour? How absurd were those pretensions! (*b.*) She is out in claiming this well as Jacob's gift, whereas he did no more give it than Moses gave the *manna, ch.* 6:32. But thus we are apt to call the *messengers* of God's gifts the *donors* of them, and to look so much at the hands they *pass through* as to forget the hand they *come from.* Jacob gave it to his sons, not to *them.* Yet thus the church's enemies not only *usurp,* but monopolize, the church's privileges. (*c.*) She was out in speaking of Christ as not worthy to be compared with our father Jacob. An over-fond veneration for antiquity makes God's graces, in the good people of our own day, to be slighted.

[5.] Christ answers this cavil, and makes it out that the *living water* he had to give was far better than that of Jacob's well, *v.* 13, 14. Though she spoke perversely, Christ did not cast her off, but instructed and encouraged her. He shows her,

First, That the water of Jacob's well yielded but a *transient* satisfaction and supply: "*Whoso drinketh of this water shall thirst again.*" It is no better than other water; it will quench the present thirst, but the thirst will return, and in a few hours a man will have as much *need,* and as much *desire,* of water as ever he had." This intimates, 1. The *infirmities* of our bodies in this present state; they are still *necessitous,* and ever *craving.* Life is a *fire,* a *lamp,* which will soon go out, without continual supplies of fuel and oil. The natural heat preys upon itself. 2. The *imperfections* of all our comforts in this world; they are not lasting, nor our satisfaction in them remaining. Whatever waters of comfort we drink of, we shall *thirst again.* Yesterday's meat and drink will not do to-day's work.

Secondly, That the living waters he would give should yield a lasting satisfaction and bliss, *v.* 14. Christ's gifts appear most valuable when they come to be compared with the things of this world; for there will appear no comparison between them. Whoever partakes of the Spirit of grace, and the comforts of the everlasting gospel,

a. He shall *never thirst,* he shall never want that which will abundantly satisfy his soul's desires; they are *longing,* but not *languishing.* A *desiring* thirst he has, nothing more *than* God, still more and more of God; but not a *despairing* thirst.

b. Therefore he shall never thirst, because this water that Christ gives *shall be in him a well of water. He* can never be reduced to extremity that has in himself a *fountain* of supply and satisfaction. (*a.*) *Ever ready,* for it shall be *in him.* The principle of grace planted *in him* is the spring of his comfort; see *ch.* 7:38. A good man is *satisfied from himself,* for Christ *dwells in his heart.* The anointing abides in him; he needs not sneak to the world for comfort; the *work* and the *witness* of the Spirit in the heart furnish him with a firm foundation of hope and an overflowing fountain of joy. (*b.*) *Never failing,* for it shall be in him a *well of water.* He that has at hand only a bucket of water needs not thirst as long as this lasts, but it will soon be *exhausted;* but believers have in them a *well of water,* overflowing, ever flowing. The *principles* and *affections* which Christ's holy religion *forms* in the souls of those that are brought under the power of it are this *well of water.* [*a.*] It is *springing up,* ever in motion, which bespeaks the actings of grace strong and vigorous. If good truths *stagnate* in our souls, like standing water, they do not answer the end of our receiving them. If there be a good treasure in the heart, we must thence bring forth good things. [*b.*] It is springing up *unto everlasting life;* which intimates, *First,* The *aims* of gracious actings. A sanctified soul has its eye upon heaven, means this, designs this, does all for this, will take up with nothing short of this. Spiritual life springs up towards its own perfection in eternal life. *Secondly,* The *constancy* of those actings; it will continue springing up till it come to perfection. *Thirdly,* The crown of them, eternal life at last. The living water rises *from* heaven, and therefore rises *towards* heaven; see Eccl. 1:7. And now is not this water better than that of Jacob's well?

[6.] The woman (whether in jest or earnest is hard to say) begs of him to give her some of this water (*v.* 15): *Give me this water, that I thirst not. First,* Some think that she speaks *tauntingly,* and ridicules what Christ had said as mere stuff; and, in derision of it, not *desires,* but *challenges* him to give

her some of this water: "A rare invention; it will save me a great deal of *pains* if I never *come hither to draw.*" But, *Secondly,* Others think that it was a *well-meant* but weak and ignorant desire. She apprehended that he meant something very good and useful, and therefore saith *Amen,* at a venture. *Whatever it be,* let me have it; *who will show me any good? Ease,* or saving of labour, is a valuable good to poor labouring people. Note, 1. Even those that are weak and ignorant may yet have some faint and fluctuating desires towards Christ and his gifts, and some good wishes of grace and glory. 2. Carnal hearts, in their best wishes, look no higher than carnal ends. "Give it to me," saith she, "not that I may have everlasting life" (which Christ proposed), "but that I *come not hither to draw.*"

2. The next subject of discourse with this woman in *concerning her husband, v.* 16–18. It was not to let fall the discourse of the water of life that Christ started this, as many who will bring in any *impertinence* in conversation that they may drop a serious subject; but it was with a gracious design that Christ mentioned it. What he had said concerning his grace and eternal life he found had made little impression upon her, because she had not been convinced of sin: therefore, waiving the discourse about the living water, he sets himself to awaken her conscience, to open the wound of guilt, and then she would more easily apprehend the remedy by grace. And this is the method of dealing with souls; they must first be made *weary* and *heavy-laden* under the burden of sin, and then brought to Christ for rest; first pricked to the heart, and then healed. This is the course of spiritual physic; and if we proceed not in this order we begin at the wrong end.

Observe, (1.) How discreetly and decently Christ introduces this discourse (*v.* 16): *Go, call thy husband, and come hither.* Now, [1.] The order Christ gave her had a *very good colour:* "*Call thy husband,* that he may teach thee, and help thee to understand these things, which thou art so ignorant of" The wives that will learn must *ask their husbands* (1 Co. 14:35), who must dwell with them *as men of knowledge,* 1 Pt. 3:7. "*Call thy husband,* that he may learn with thee; that then you may be *heirs together of the grace of life. Call thy husband,* that he may be witness to what passes between us." Christ would thus teach us to *provide things honest in the sight of all men,* and to study that which is of good report. [2.] As it had a good colour, so it had a *good design;* for hence he would take occasion to call her sin to remembrance. There is need of art and prudence in giving reproofs; to fetch a compass, as the woman of Tekoa, 2 Sa. 14:20.

(2.) How industriously the woman seeks to evade the conviction, and yet insensibly convicts herself, and, ere she is aware, owns her fault; she said, *I have no husband.* Her saying this intimated no more than that she did not care to have her husband spoken of, nor that matter mentioned any more. She would not have her husband come thither, lest, in further discourse, the truth of the matter should come out, to her shame; and therefore, "Pray go on to talk of something else, *I have no husband;*" she would be thought a *maid* or a *widow,* whereas, though she had no husband, she was neither. The carnal mind is very ingenious to *shift off* convictions, and to keep them from fastening, careful to *cover the sin.*

(3.) How closely our Lord Jesus brings home the conviction to her conscience. It is probable that he said more than is here recorded, for she thought that he told her all that ever she did (*v.* 29), but that which is here recorded is concerning her husbands. Here is, [1.] A *surprising narrative* of her *past* conversation: *Thou has had five husbands.* Doubtless, it was not her *affliction* (the burying of so many husbands), but her *sin,* that Christ intended to upbraid her with; either she had *eloped* (as the law speaks), had run away from her *husbands,* and married others, or by her undutiful, unclean, disloyal conduct, had provoked them to *divorce her,* or by indirect means had, contrary to law, *divorced them.* Those who make light of such scandalous practices as these, as no more than *nine days' wonder,* and as if the guilt were over as soon as the talk is over, should remember that Christ keeps account of all. [2.] A severe reproof of her present state of life: *He whom thou now hast is not thy husband.* Either she was never married to him at all, or he had some other wife, or, which is most probable, her former husband or husbands were living: so that, in short, *she lived in adultery.* Yet observe how mildly Christ tells her of it; he doth not call her *strumpet,* but tells her, *He with whom thou livest is not thy husband:*

and then leaves it to her own conscience to say the rest. Note, Reproofs are ordinarily *most profitable* when they are *least provoking.* [3.] Yet in this he puts a better construction than it would well bear upon what she said by way of shuffle and evasion: *Thou has well said I have no husband;* and again, *In that saidst thou truly.* What she intended as a *denial of the fact* (that she had none with whom she lived as a husband) he favourably interpreted, or at least turned upon her, as a *confession of the fault.* Note, Those who would win souls should *make the best* of them, whereby they may hope to *work* upon their *good-nature;* for, if they *make the worst* of them, they certainly *exasperate* their *ill-nature.*

3. The next subject of discourse with this woman is concerning *the place of worship, v.* 19–24. Observe,

(1.) A case of conscience proposed to Christ by the woman, concerning the place of worship, *v.* 19, 20.

[1.] The inducement she had to put this case: *Sir, I perceive that thou art a prophet.* She does not deny the truth of what he had charged her with, but by her silence owns the justice of the reproof; nor is she put into a passion by it, as many are when they are touched in a sore place, does not impute his censure to the general disgust the Jews had to the Samaritans, but (which is a rare thing) can bear to be told of a fault. But this is not all; she goes further: *First,* She speaks respectfully to him, calls him *Sir.* Thus should we *honour* those that deal faithfully with us. This was the effect of Christ's meekness in reproving her; he gave her no ill language, and then she gave him none. *Secondly,* She acknowledges him to be a *prophet,* one that had a correspondence with Heaven. Note, The power of the word of Christ in searching the heart, and convincing the conscience of secret sins, is a great proof of its divine authority, 1 Co. 14:24, 25. *Thirdly,* She desires some further instruction from him. Many that are not *angry* at their reprovers, nor fly in their faces, yet are *afraid* of them and keep out of their way; but this woman was willing to have some more discourse with him that told her of her faults.

[2.] The case itself that she propounded concerning the *place of religious worship in public.* Some think that she started this to shift off further discourse concerning her sin. Controversies in religion often prove great prejudices to serious godliness; but, it should seem, she proposed it with a good design; she knew she must worship God, and desired to do it aright; and therefore, meeting with a prophet, begs his direction. Note, It is our wisdom to improve all opportunities of getting knowledge in the things of God. When we are in company with those that are *fit to teach,* let us be *forward to learn,* and have a *good question* ready to put to those who are able to give a *good answer.* It was agreed between the Jews and the Samaritans that God is to be worshipped (even those who were such fools as to worship *false* gods were not such brutes as to worship none), and that religious worship is an affair of great importance: men would not *contend* about it if they were not *concerned* about it. But the matter in variance was *where* they should worship God. Observe how she states the case: —

First, As for the Samaritans: *Our fathers worshipped in this mountain,* near to this city and this well; there the Samaritan temple was built by Sanballat, in favour of which she insinuates, 1. That whatever the temple was the place was holy; it was mount *Gerizim,* the mount in which the blessings were pronounced; and some think the same on which Abraham built his altar (Gen. 12:6, 7), and Jacob his, Gen. 33:18–20. 2. That it might plead prescription: *Our fathers* worshipped here. She thinks they have antiquity, tradition, and succession, on their side. A *vain conversation* often supports itself with this, that it was *received by tradition from our fathers.* But she had little reason to boast of *their fathers;* for, when Antiochus persecuted the Jews, the Samaritans, for fear of sharing with them in their sufferings, not only renounced all relation to the Jews, but surrendered their temple to Antiochus, with a request that it might be dedicated to Jupiter Olympius, and called by his name. Joseph. *Antiq.* 12.257–264.

Secondly, As to the Jews: *You say* that in Jerusalem is the *place where men ought to worship.* The Samaritans governed themselves by the five books of Moses, and (some think) received *only them* as canonical. Now, though they found frequent mention there of the place God would choose, yet they did not find it named there; and they saw the temple at Jerusalem stripped of many of its ancient glories, and therefore thought themselves at liberty to set up another place, altar against altar.

(2.) Christ's answer to this case of conscience, *v.* 21, etc. Those that apply themselves to Christ for instruction shall find him *meek, to teach the meek his way.* Now here,

[1.] He puts *a slight* upon the question, as she had proposed it, concerning the place of worship (*v.* 21): *"Woman, believe me* as a prophet, and mark what I say. Thou art expecting the *hour to come* when either by some divine revelation, or some signal providence, this matter shall be decided in favour either of Jerusalem or of Mount Gerizim; but I tell thee the hour is at hand when it shall be no more a question; that which thou has been taught to lay so much weight on shall be set aside as a thing *indifferent."* Note, It should cool us in our contests to think that those things which now fill us, and which we make such a noise about, shall shortly *vanish,* and be *no more:* the very things we are striving about are passing away: *The hour comes when you shall neither in this mountain nor yet at Jerusalem worship the Father. First,* The object of worship is supposed to continue still the same — *God,* as a Father; under this notion the very heathen worshipped God, the Jews did so, and probably the Samaritans. *Secondly,* But a period shall be put to all niceness and all differences about the place of worship. The approaching dissolution of the Jewish economy, and the erecting of the evangelical state, shall set this matter *at large,* and lay all *in common,* so that it shall be a thing perfectly indifferent whether in either of these places or any other men worship God, for they shall not be tied to any place; neither *here* nor *there,* but *both,* and *any where,* and *every where.* Note, The worship of God is not now, under the gospel, appropriated to any place, as it was under the law, but it is God's will that men pray every where. 1 Tim. 2:8; Mal. 1:11. Our reason teaches us to consult *decency* and *convenience* in the places of our worship: but our religion gives no preference to one place above another, in respect to holiness and acceptableness to God. Those who prefer any worship merely for the sake of the house or building in which it is performed (though it were as magnificent and as *solemnly* consecrated as ever Solomon's temple was) forget that the *hour is come* when there shall be no difference put in God's account: no, not between Jerusalem, which *had been* so famous for sanctity, and the mountain of Samaria, which *had been* so infamous for impiety.

[2.] He *lays a stress* upon other things, in the matter of religious worship. When he made so light of the place of worship he did not intend to lessen our concern about the thing itself, of which therefore he takes occasion to discourse more fully.

First, As to the present state of the controversy, he *determines* against the Samaritan worship, and in favour of the Jews, *v.* 22. He tells here, 1. That the Samaritans were certainly *in the wrong;* not merely because they worshipped in this mountain, though, while Jerusalem's choice was in force, that was sinful, but because they were out in the object of their worship. If the worship itself had been as it should have been, its separation from Jerusalem might have been connived at, as the *high places* were in the best reigns: *But you worship you know not what,* or *that which you do not know.* They worshipped the God of Israel, the true God (Ezra 4:2; 2 Ki. 17:32); but they were sunk into gross ignorance; they worshipped him as the *God of that land* (2 Ki. 17:27, 33), as a local deity, like the gods of the nations, whereas God must be served *as God,* as the universal cause and Lord. Note, Ignorance is so far from being the *mother* of devotion that it is the *murderer* of it. Those that worship God *ignorantly* offer the *blind for sacrifice,* and it is the *sacrifice of fools.* 2. That the Jews were certainly *in the right.* For, (1.) *"We know what we worship.* We go upon sure grounds in our worship, for our people are catechised and trained up in the knowledge of God, as he has revealed himself in the scripture." Note, Those who by the scriptures have obtained some knowledge of God (a *certain* though not a *perfect* knowledge) may worship him *comfortably* to themselves, and *acceptably* to him, for they *know what they worship.* Christ elsewhere condemns the corruptions of the Jews' worship (Mt. 15:9), and yet here defends the worship itself; the worship may be *true* where yet it is not *pure* and *entire.* Observe, Our Lord Jesus was pleased to reckon himself among the *worshippers* of God: *We worship. Though he was a Son* (and then are the children free), *yet learned he this obedience,* in the days of his humiliation. Let not the greatest of men think the worship of God below them, when the Son of God himself did not. (2.) *Salvation is of the Jews;* and therefore they know what they worship, and what grounds they go upon in their worship. Not that all the Jews were saved, nor that it was not possible but that many of the Gentiles and Samaritans might be saved, for in *every nation* he that fears God and works righteousness is *accepted of him;* but, [1.] The author of eternal salvation comes of the Jews, appears among them (Rom. 9:5), and is sent first to *bless* them. [2.] The means of eternal salvation are afforded to them. The *word of salvation* (Acts 13:26) was *of the Jews.* It was delivered to them, and other nations derived it through them. This was a sure guide to them in their devotions, and they followed it, and therefore knew what they worshipped. To them were committed the *oracles of God* (Rom. 3:2), and the *service of God,* (Rom. 9:4). The Jews therefore being thus privileged and advanced, it was presumption for the Samaritans to vie with them.

Secondly, He describes the evangelical worship which alone God would accept and be well pleased with. Having shown that the place is *indifferent,* he comes to show what is *necessary* and *essential* — that we worship God *in spirit and in truth, v.* 23, 24. The stress is not to be laid upon the *place* where we worship God, but upon the state of *mind* in which we worship him. Note, The most effectual way to take up differences in the minor matters of religion is to be more zealous in the greater. Those who daily make it the matter of their care to worship *in the spirit,* one would think, should not make it the matter of their strife whether he should be worshipped here or there. Christ had justly preferred the Jewish worship before the Samaritan, yet here he intimates the imperfection of that. The worship was *ceremonial,* Heb. 9:1, 10. The worshippers were generally *carnal,* and strangers to the *inward part* of divine worship. Note, It is possible that we may be better than our neighbours, and yet not so good as we should be. It concerns us to be right, not only in the *object* of our worship, but in the *manner* of it; and it is this which Christ here instructs us in. Observe,

a. The great and glorious revolution which should introduce this change: *The hour cometh, and now is* — the fixed stated time, concerning which it was of old determined when it should come, and how long it should last. The time of its *appearance* if *fixed* to an hour, so punctual and exact are the divine counsels; the time of its *continuance* is *limited* to an hour, so close and pressing is the opportunity of divine grace, 2 Co. 6:2. This hour *cometh,* it is coming in its full strength, lustre, and perfection, it *now is* in the embryo and infancy. The *perfect day is coming,* and now it *dawns.*

b. The blessed change itself. In gospel times the *true worshippers shall worship the Father in spirit and in truth.* As creatures, we worship the Father of *all:* as Christians, we worship *the Father of our Lord Jesus.* Now the change shall be, (*a.*) In the *nature* of the worship. Christians shall worship God, not in the ceremonial observances of the Mosaic institution, but in *spiritual* ordinances, consisting less in *bodily exercise,* and animated and invigorated more with divine power and energy. The way of worship which Christ has instituted is rational and intellectual, and refined from those external rites and ceremonies with which the Old-Testament worship was both clouded and clogged. This is called true worship, in opposition to that which was typical. The legal services were *figures of the true,* Heb. 9:3, 24. Those that revolted from Christianity to Judaism are said to *begin in the spirit, and end in the flesh,* Gal. 3:3. Such was the difference between Old-Testament and New-Testament institutions. (*b.*) In the *temper* and *disposition* of the worshippers; and so the true worshippers are good Christians, distinguished from hypocrites; all *should,* and they will, worship God *in spirit and in truth.* It is spoken of (*v.* 23) as their character, and (*v.* 24) as their duty. Note, It is required of all that worship God that they worship him *in spirit and in truth.* We must worship God, [*a.*] *In spirit,* Phil. 3:3. We must depend upon *God's Spirit* for strength and assistance, laying our souls under his influences and operations; we must devote *our own spirits* to, and employ them in, the service of God (Rom. 1:9), must worship him with fixedness of thought and a flame of affection, with *all that is within us.* Spirit is sometimes put for the new nature, in opposition to the *flesh,* which is the corrupt nature; and so to worship God *with our spirits* is to worship him *with our graces,* Heb. 12:28. [*b.*] *In truth,* that is, in *sincerity.* God requires not only the *inward part* in our worship, but *truth in the inward part,* Ps. 51:6. We must mind the power more than the form, must aim at God's glory, and not to be *seen of men;* draw near with a *true heart,* Heb. 10:22.

Thirdly, He intimates the reasons why God must be thus worshipped.

a. Because in gospel times they, and they only, are accounted the *true* worshippers. The gospel erects a spiritual way of worship, so that the professors of the gospel are not true in their profession, do not live up to gospel light and laws, if they do not worship God *in spirit and in truth.*

b. Because *the Father seeketh such worshippers of him.* This intimates, (*a.*) That such worshippers are very rare, and seldom met with, Jer. 30:21. The gate of spiritual worshipping is strait. (*b.*) That such worship is necessary, and what the God of heaven insists upon. When God comes to *enquire* for worshippers, the question will not be, "Who worshipped at Jerusalem?" but, "Who worshipped in spirit?" That will be the touchstone. (*c.*) That God is greatly well pleased with and graciously accepts such worship and such worshippers. *I have desired it,* Ps. 132:13, 14; Cant. 2:14. (*d.*) That there has been, and will be to the end, a remnant of such worshippers; his *seeking* such worshippers implies his *making* them such. God is in all ages gathering in to himself a generation of spiritual worshippers.

c. Because *God is a spirit.* Christ came to *declare God* to us (*ch.* 1:18), and this he has declared concerning him; he declared it to this poor Samaritan woman, for the meanest are concerned to know God; and with this design, to rectify her mistakes concerning religious worship, to which nothing would contribute more than the right knowledge of God. Note, (*a.*) *God is a spirit,* for he is an infinite and eternal mind, an intelligent being, incorporeal, immaterial, invisible, and incorruptible. It is easier to say what God is not than what he is; a spirit *has not flesh and bones,* but *who knows the way of a spirit?* If God were not *a spirit,* he could not be *perfect,* nor infinite, nor eternal, nor independent, nor the Father of spirits. (*b.*) The spirituality of the divine nature is a very good reason for the spirituality of divine worship. If we do not worship God, who is *a spirit, in the spirit,* we neither *give him the glory due to his name,* and so do not perform the *act* of worship, nor can we hope to obtain his favour and acceptance, and so we miss of the *end* of worship, Mt. 15:8, 9.

4. The last subject of discourse with this woman is concerning the Messiah, *v.* 25, 26. Observe here,

(1.) The faith of the woman, by which she expected the Messiah: *I know that Messias cometh — and he will tell us all things.* She had nothing to object against what Christ had said; his discourse was, for aught she knew, what might become the Messiah then expected; but *from him* she would receive it, and in the mean time she thinks it best to suspend her belief. Thus many have no heart to the price *in their hand* (Prov. 17:16), because they think they have a better *in their eye,* and deceive themselves with a promise that they will learn that *hereafter* which they neglect *now.* Observe here,

[1.] Whom she expects: *I know that Messias cometh.* The Jews and Samaritans, though so much at variance, agreed in the expectation of the messiah and his kingdom. The Samaritans received the writings of Moses, and were no strangers to the prophets, nor to the hopes of the Jewish nation; those who knew least knew this, that Messias was to come; so general and uncontested was the expectation of him, and at this time more raised than ever (for the sceptre was departed from Judah, Daniel's weeks were near expiring), so that she concludes not only, *He will come,* but *erchetai — "He comes,* he is just at hand:" *Messias, who is called Christ.* The evangelist, though he retains the Hebrew word *Messias* (which the woman used) in honour to the holy language, and to the Jewish church, that used it familiarly, yet, writing for the use of the Gentiles, he takes care to render it by a Greek word of the same signification, *who is called Christ — Anointed,* giving an example to the apostle's rule, that whatever is spoken in an unknown or less vulgar tongue should be *interpreted,* 1 Co. 14:27, 28.

[2.] What she expects from him: *"He will tell us all things* relating to the service of God which it is needful for us to know, will tell us that which will supply our defects, rectify our mistakes, and put an end to all our disputes. He will tell us the mind of God fully and clearly, and keep back nothing." Now this implies an acknowledgement, *First,* Of the deficiency and imperfection of the discovery they now had of the divine will, and the rule they had of the divine worship; it *could not make the comers thereunto perfect,* and therefore they expected some great advance and improvement in matters of religion, a time of reformation. *Secondly,* Of the sufficiency of the Messiah to make this change: *"He will tell us all things* which we want to know, and about which we wrangle in the dark. He will introduce *peace,* by *leading us into all truth,* and dispelling the mists of error." It seems, this was the comfort of good people in those dark times that light would arise; if they found themselves at a loss, and run aground, it was a satisfaction to them to say, *When Messias comes, he will tell us all things;* as it may be to us now with reference to his second coming: now we see through a glass, but then *face to face.*

(2.) The favour of our Lord Jesus in making himself known to her: *I that speak to thee am he, v.* 26. Christ did never make himself known so expressly to any as he did here to this poor Samaritan, and to the blind man (*ch.* 9:37); no, not to John Baptist, when he sent to him (Mt. 11:4, 5); no, not to the Jews, when they challenged him to tell them whether he was the Christ, *ch.* 10:24. But, [1.] Christ would thus put an honour upon such as were poor and despised, Jam. 2:6. [2.] This woman, for aught we know, had never had any opportunity of seeing Christ's miracles, which were then the ordinary method of conviction. Note, To those who have not the advantage of the *external* means of knowledge and grace God hath *secret* ways of making up the want of them; we must therefore judge charitably concerning such. God can make the light of grace shine *into the heart* even where he doth not make the light of the gospel shine *in the face.* [3.] This woman was better prepared to receive such a discovery than others were; she was big with expectation of the Messiah, and ready to receive instruction from him. Christ will manifest himself to those who with an honest humble heart desire to be acquainted with him: *I that speak to thee am he.* See here, *First,* How near Jesus Christ was to her, when she knew not who he was, Gen. 28:16. Many are lamenting Christ's absence, and longing for his presence, when at the same time he is speaking to them. *Secondly,* How Christ makes himself known to us by *speaking* to us: *I that speak unto thee,* so closely, so convincingly, with such assurance, with such authority, *I am he.*

Verses 27–42

We have here the remainder of the story of what happened when Christ was in Samaria, after the long conference he had with the woman.

I. The *interruption given to this discourse* by the disciples' coming. It is probable that much more was said than is recorded; but just when the discourse was brought to a head, when Christ had made himself known to her as the true Messiah, *then came the disciples.* The *daughters of Jerusalem* shall not *stir up nor awake my love till he please.* 1. They wondered at Christ's converse with this woman, marvelled that he talked thus earnestly (as perhaps they observed at a distance) with a woman, a strange woman alone (he used to be more *reserved*), especially with a Samaritan woman, that was not of the lost sheep of the house of Israel; they thought their Master should be as shy of the Samaritans as the other Jews were, at least that he should not preach the gospel to them. They wondered he should condescend to talk with such a poor contemptible woman, forgetting what despicable men they themselves were when Christ first called them into fellowship with himself. 2. Yet they acquiesced in it; they knew it was for some good reason, and some good end, of which he was not bound to give them an account, and therefore none of them asked, *What seekest thou?* or, *Why talkest thou with her?* Thus, when particular difficulties occur in the word and providence of God, it is good to satisfy ourselves with this in general, that all is well which Jesus Christ saith and doeth. Perhaps there was something *amiss* in their *marveling* that *Christ talked with the woman:* it was something like the Pharisees being offended at his eating with publicans and sinners. But, whatever they *thought,* they said *nothing. If thou hast thought evil* at any time, *lay thy hand upon thy mouth,* to keep that evil thought from turning into an evil word, Prov. 30:32; Ps. 39:1–3.

The notice which the woman gave to her neighbours of the extraordinary person she had happily met with, *v.* 28, 29. Observe here,

1. How she *forgot her errand to the well, v.* 28. Therefore, because the disciples were come, and broke up the discourse, and perhaps she observed they were not pleased with it, she *went her way.* She withdrew, in civility to Christ, that he might have leisure to *eat his dinner.* She delighted in his discourse, but would not be *rude;* every thing is beautiful in its season. She supposed that Jesus, when he had dined, would go forward in his journey, and therefore hastened to tell her neighbours, that they might come quickly. *Yet a little while is the light with you.* See how she improved time; when one good work was done, she applied herself to another. When opportunities of *getting good* cease, or are interrupted, we should seek opportunities of *doing good;* when we have done *hearing* the word, then is a time to be *speaking* of it. Notice is taken of her *leaving her water-pot* or *pail.* (1.) She left it in kindness to Christ, that he might have water to drink; he turned water into wine for others, but not for himself. Compare this with Rebecca's civility to Abraham's servant (Gen. 24:18), and see that promise, Mt. 10:42. (2.) She left it that she might make the more haste into the city, to carry thither these good tidings. Those whose business it is to publish the name of Christ must not encumber or entangle themselves with any thing that will retard or hinder them therein. When the disciples are to be made fishers of men they must *forsake all.* (3.) She left her water-pot, as one *careless of it,* being wholly taken up with better things. Note, Those who are brought to the knowledge of Christ will show it by a holy contempt of this world and the things of it. And those who are *newly* acquainted with the things of God must be *excused,* if at first they be so taken up with the new world into which they are brought that the things of this world seem to be for a time wholly neglected. Mr. Hildersham, in one of his sermons on this verse, from this instance largely justifies those who leave their worldly business on week-days to go to hear sermons.

2. How she *minded her errand to the town,* for her heart was upon it. She *went into the city,* and said to *the men,* probably the aldermen, the men in authority, whom, it may be, she found met together upon some public business; or to *the men,* that is, to every man she met in the streets; she proclaimed it in the chief places of concourse: *Come, see a man who told me all things that ever I did. Is not this the Christ?* Observe,

(1.) How *solicitous* she was to *have her friends and neighbours* acquainted with Christ. When she had found that treasure, she *called together her friends and neighbours* (as Lu. 15:9), not only to *rejoice with her,* but to share with her, knowing there was enough to enrich herself and all that would partake with her. Note, They that have been themselves with Jesus, and have found comfort in him, should do all they can to bring others to him. Has he done us the honour to make himself known to us? Let us do him the honour to make him known to others; nor can we do ourselves a greater honour. This woman becomes an apostle. *Quae scortum fuerat egressa, regreditur magistra evangelica — She who went forth a specimen of impurity returns a teacher of evangelical truth,* saith *Aretius.* Christ had told her to *call her husband,* which she thought was warrant enough to *call every body.* She went into *the city,* the city where she dwelt, among her kinsfolks and acquaintance. Though every man is my neighbour that I have opportunity of doing good to, yet I have most *opportunity,* and therefore lie under the greatest *obligations,* to do good to those that live near me. *Where the tree falls,* there let it be made useful.

(2.) How fair and ingenuous she was in the notice she gave them concerning this stranger she had met with. [1.] She *tells them* plainly what induced her to admire him: *He has told me all things that ever I did.* No more is recorded than what he told her of her husbands; but it is not improbable that he had told her of more of her faults. Or, his telling her that which she knew he could not by any ordinary means come to the knowledge of convinced her that he could have told her all that she ever did. If he has a *divine* knowledge, it must be omniscience. He told her that which none knew but God and her own conscience. Two things affected her: — *First, the extent of his knowledge.* We ourselves cannot tell *all things that ever we did* (many things pass *unheeded,* and more pass away and are forgotten); but Jesus Christ knows all the thoughts, words, and actions, of all the children of men; see Heb. 4:13. He hath said, *I know thy works. Secondly, The power of his word.* This made a great impression upon her, that he told her her *secret sins* with such an unaccountable power and energy that, being told of one, she is *convinced of all, and judged of all.* She does not say, "Come, see a man that has told me strange things concerning religious worship, and the laws of it, that has decided the controversy between this mountain and Jerusalem, a man that calls himself the *Messias;*" but, *"Come see a man* that has told me of my sins." She fastens upon that part of Christ's discourse which one would think she would have been most shy of repeating; but experimental proofs of the power of Christ's word and Spirit are of all others the most cogent and convincing; and that *knowledge of Christ* into which we are led by the conviction of sin and humiliation is most likely to be *sound* and *saving.* [2.] She *invites them* to *come and see* him of whom she had conceived so high an opinion. Not barely, "Come and look upon him" (she does not invite them to him as a *show*), but, "Come and converse with him; come and *hear his wisdom,* as I have done, and you will be of my mind." She would not undertake to manage the arguments which had convinced her, in such a manner as to convince others; all that see the evidence of truth themselves are not able to make others see it; but, "Come, and talk with him, and you will find such a power in his word as far exceeds all other evidence." Note, Those who can do little else towards the conviction and conversion of others may and should bring them to those means of grace which they themselves have found effectual. Jesus was now at the town's end. "Now come see him." When opportunities of getting the knowledge of God are brought to our doors we are inexcusable if we neglect them; shall we not go over the threshold to see him whose day prophets and kings desired to see? [3.] She resolves to *appeal to themselves,* and their own sentiments upon the trial. *Is not this the Christ?* She does not peremptorily say, "He is the Messiah," how clear soever she was in her own mind, and yet she very prudently mentions the Messiah, of whom otherwise they would not have thought, and then refers it to themselves; she will not impose her faith upon them, but only propose it to them. By such fair but forcible appeals as these men's judgments and consciences are sometimes taken hold of ere they are aware.

(3.) What success she had in this invitation: *They went out of the city, and came to him, v.* 30. Though it might seem very improbable that a woman of so *small* a figure, and so *ill* a character, should have the honour of the first discovery of the Messiah among the Samaritans, yet it pleased God to incline their hearts to take notice of her report, and not to slight it as an idle tale. Time was when lepers were the first that brought tidings to Samaria of a great deliverance, 2 Ki. 7:3, etc. They *came unto him;* did not send for him into the city to them, but in token of their respect to him, and the earnestness of their desire to see him, they *went out to him.* Those that would know Christ must meet him where he records his name.

III. Christ's discourse with his disciples while the woman was absent, *v.* 31–38. See how industrious our Lord Jesus was to *redeem time,* to husband every minute of it, and to *fill up* the vacancies of it. When the disciples were gone into the town, his discourse with the woman was *edifying,* and suited to her case; when she was gone into the town, his discourse with them was no less edifying, and suited to their case; it were well if we could *thus* gather up the fragments of time, that none of it may be lost. Two things are observable in this discourse: —

1. How Christ *expresses the delight* which he himself had in his work. His work was to *seek and save* that which was lost, to go about doing good. Now with this work we here find him wholly taken up. For,

(1.) *He neglected his meat and drink for his work.* When he sat down upon the well, he was *weary,* and needed refreshment; but this opportunity of saving souls made him forget his weariness and hunger. And he minded *his food* so little that, [1.] His disciples were forced to invite him to it: *They prayed him,* they pressed him, saying, *Master, eat.* It was an instance of their *love to him* that they invited him, lest he should be faint and sick for want of some support; but it was a greater instance of his *love to souls* that he needed invitation. Let us learn hence a holy indifference even to the needful supports of life, in comparison with spiritual things. [2.] He minded it so little that they suspected he had had meat brought him in their absence (*v.* 33): *Has any man brought him aught to eat?* He had so little appetite for his dinner that they were ready to think he had dined already. Those that make religion their business will, when any of its affairs are to be attended, prefer them before their food; as Abraham's servant, that would not eat till he had told his errand (Gen. 24:33), and Samuel, that would not sit down till David was anointed, 1 Sa. 16:11.

(2.) He *made his work his meat and drink.* The work he *had to do* among the Samaritans, the prospect he now had of doing good to many, this was *meat and drink* to him; it was the greatest pleasure and satisfaction imaginable. Never did a hungry man, or an epicure, expect a plentiful feast with so much desire, nor feed upon its dainties with so much delight, as our Lord Jesus expected and improved an opportunity of doing good to souls. Concerning this he saith, [1.] That it was such *meat* as the disciples *knew not of.* They did not imagine that he had any design or prospect of planting his gospel among the Samaritans; this was a piece of usefulness they never thought of. Note, Christ by his gospel and Spirit does more good to the souls of men than his own disciples *know of* or *expect.* This may be said of good Christians too, who live by faith, that they have meat to eat which others know not of, joy with which a stranger does not intermeddle. Now this word made them ask, *Has any man brought him aught to eat?* so apt were even his own disciples to understand him after a corporal and carnal manner when he used similitudes. [2.] That the reason why his work was his meat and drink was because it was his Father's work, his Father's will: *My meat is to do the will of him that sent me, v.* 34. Note, *First,* The salvation of sinners is the *will of God,* and the instruction of them in order thereunto is *his work.* See 1 Tim. 2:4. There is a chosen remnant whose salvation is in a particular manner his will. *Secondly,* Christ was *sent into the world* on this errand, to bring people to God, to know him and to be happy in him. *Thirdly,* He made this work his business and delight. When his body needed food, his mind was so taken up with this that he forgot both hunger and thirst, both meat and drink. Nothing could be more grateful to him than doing good; when he was invited *to meat* he went, that he might *do good,* for that was his meat always. *Fourthly,* He was not only ready upon all occasions to go to his work, but he was *earnest* and in care to go *through* it, and to *finish his work* in all the parts of it. He resolved never to quit it, nor lay it down, till he could say, *It is finished.* Many have zeal to carry them *out* at first, but not zeal to carry them *on* to the last; but our Lord Jesus was intent upon *finishing his work.* Our Master has herein left us an example, that we may learn to do the will of God as he did; 1. With diligence and close application, as those that make a business of it. 2. With delight and pleasure in it, as in our element. 3. With constancy and perseverance; not only minding to *do,* but aiming to *finish,* our work.

2. See here how Christ, having expressed his delight in *his* work, excites his disciples to diligence in *their* work; they were workers *with him,* and therefore should be workers *like him,* and make their work their *meat,* as he did. The work they had to do was to *preach the gospel,* and to set up the kingdom of the Messiah. Now this work he here compares to *harvest work,* the gathering in of the fruits of the earth; and this similitude he prosecutes throughout the discourse, *v.* 35–38. Note, gospel time is harvest time, and gospel work harvest work. The harvest is *before appointed* and expected; so was the gospel. Harvest time is *busy* time; all hands must be then at work: every one must work for *himself,* that he may reap of the graces and comforts of the gospel: ministers must work *for God,* to gather in souls to him. Harvest time is *opportunity,* a short and limited time, which will not last always; and harvest work is work that must be done *then* or not at all; so the time of the enjoyment of the gospel is a particular season, which must be improved for its proper purposes; for, once past, it cannot be recalled. The disciples were to gather in a harvest of souls for Christ. Now he here suggests three things to them to quicken them to diligence: —

(1.) That it was *necessary work,* and the *occasion* for it very urgent and pressing (*v.* 35): *You say, It is four months to harvest;* but I say, *The fields are already white.* Here is, [1.] A saying of Christ's disciples concerning the *corn-harvest;* there *are yet four months, and then comes harvest,* which may be taken either *generally* — "You say, for the encouragement of the sower at seed-time, that it will be but four months to the harvest." With us it is but about four months between the barley-sowing and the barley-harvest, probably it was so with them as to other grain; or, "Particularly, now at this time you reckon it will be four months to next harvest, according to the ordinary course of providence." The Jews' harvest began at the Passover, about Easter, much earlier in the year than ours, by which it appears that this journey of Christ from Judea to Galilee was in the winter, about the end of November, for he travelled *all weathers* to do good. God has not only promised us a harvest every year, but has appointed the *weeks of harvest;* so that we know *when* to expect it, and take our measures accordingly.

[2.] A saying of Christ's concerning the *gospel harvest;* his heart was as much upon the fruits of his gospel as the hearts of others were upon the fruits of the earth; and to this he would lead the thoughts of his disciples: *Look, the fields are already white unto the harvest. First,* Here in *this* place, where they *now* were, there was harvest work for *him* to do. They would have him to *eat, v.* 31. "Eat!" saith he, "I have other work to do, that is more needful; *look* what crowds of Samaritans are coming out of the town over the fields that are ready to receive the gospel;" probably there were many now in view. People's forwardness to hear the word is a great excitement to ministers' diligence and liveliness in preaching it. *Secondly,* In *other places,* all the country over, there was harvest work enough for them all to do. "Consider the regions, think of the state of the country, and you will find there are multitudes as ready to receive the gospel as a field of corn that is fully ripe is ready to be reaped." The fields were now made *white to the harvest,* 1. By the *decree of God* revealed in the prophecies of the Old Testament. Now was the time when the gathering of the people should be to Christ (Gen. 49:10), when great accessions should be made to the church and the bounds of it should be enlarged, and therefore it was time for them to be busy. It is a great encouragement to us to engage in any work for God, if we understand by the signs of the times that this is the proper season for that work, for then it will prosper. 2. By the *disposition of men.* John Baptist had *made ready a people prepared for the Lord,* Lu. 1:17. Since he began to preach the kingdom of God *every man pressed into it,* Lu. 16:16. This, therefore, was a time for the preachers of the gospel to apply themselves to their work with the utmost vigour, to *thrust in their sickle,* when the harvest was ripe, Rev. 14:15. It was *necessary* to work now, pity that such a season should be let slip. If the corn that is *ripe* be not reaped, it will *shed* and be lost, and the fowls will pick it up. If souls that are under convictions, and have some good inclinations, be not helped now, their hopeful beginnings will come to nothing, and they will be a prey to pretenders. It was also *easy* to work now; when the people's hearts are *prepared* the work will be done *suddenly,* 2 Chr. 29:36. It cannot but quicken ministers to take *pains* in preaching the word when they observe that people *take pleasure* in hearing it.

(2.) That it was *profitable* and *advantageous* work, which they themselves would be gainers by (*v.* 36): "*He that reapeth receiveth wages,* and so shall you." Christ has undertaken to pay those well whom he employs in his work; for he will never do as Jehoiakim did, *who used his neighbour's service without wages* (Jer. 22:13), or those who by fraud kept back the hire of those particularly *who reaped their corn-fields,* Jam. 5:4. Christ's reapers, though they cry *to him* day and night, shall never have cause to cry *against him,* nor to say they served a hard Master. He that reapeth, not only *shall* but *does* receive wages. There is a present reward in the service of Christ, and his work is *its own wages.* [1.] Christ's reapers have *fruit: He gathereth fruit unto life eternal;* that is, he shall both save himself and those that hear him, 1 Tim. 4:16. If the faithful reaper save his own soul, that is fruit abounding to his account, it is fruit gathered to *life eternal;* and if, over and above this, he be instrumental to save the souls of others too, there is *fruit gathered.* Souls gathered to Christ are fruit, good fruit, the fruit that Christ seeks for (Rom. 1:13); it is gathered for Christ (Cant. 8:11, 12); it is gathered to *life eternal.* This is the comfort of faithful ministers, that their work has a tendency to the eternal salvation of precious souls. [2.] They have *joy: That he that sows and they that reap may rejoice together.* The minister who is the happy instrument of beginning a good work is *he that sows,* as John Baptist; he that is employed to carry it on and perfect it is *he that reaps:* and both shall rejoice together. Note, *First,* Though God is to have all the glory of the success of the gospel, yet faithful ministers may themselves take the comfort of it. The reapers share in the *joy of harvest,* though the profits belong to the master, 1 Th. 2:19. *Secondly,* Those ministers who are variously gifted and employed should be so far from envying one another that they should rather mutually rejoice in each other's success and usefulness. Though all Christ's ministers are not alike *serviceable,* nor alike *successful,* yet, if they have obtained mercy of the Lord to be *faithful,* they shall all enter *together* into the joy of their *Lord* at last.

(3.) That it was *easy work,* and work that was half done to their hands by those that were gone before them: *One soweth, and another reapeth, v.* 37, 38. This sometimes denotes

a grievous judgment upon him that sows, Mic. 6:15; Deu. 28:30, *Thou shalt sow, and another shall reap;* as Deu. 6:11, *Houses full of all good things, which thou filledst not.* So here. Moses, and the prophets, and John Baptist, had *paved* the way to the gospel, had sown the good seed which the New-Testament ministers did in effect but gather the fruit of. *I send you to reap that whereon you bestowed,* in comparison, no *labour.* Isa. 40:3–5. [1.] This intimates *two things* concerning the Old-Testament ministry: — *First,* That it was very much *short* of the New-Testament ministry. Moses and the prophets sowed, but they could not be said to *reap,* so little did they see of the fruit of their labours. Their writings have done much more good since they left us than ever their preaching did. *Secondly,* That it was very *serviceable* to the New-Testament ministry, and made way for it. The writings of the prophets, which were read in the synagogues every sabbath day, raised people's expectations of the Messiah, and so prepared them to bid him welcome. Had it not been for the seed sown by the prophets, this Samaritan woman could not have said, *We know that Messias cometh.* The writings of the Old Testament are in some respects more useful to us than they could be to those to whom they were first written, because better understood by the accomplishment of them. See 1 Pt. 1:12; Heb. 4:2; Rom. 16:25, 26. [2.] This also intimates *two things* concerning the ministry of the *apostles of Christ. First,* That it was a *fruitful* ministry: they were reapers that gathered in a great harvest of souls to Jesus Christ, and did more in seven years towards the setting up of the kingdom of God among men than the prophets of the Old Testament had done in twice so many ages. *Secondly,* That it was much *facilitated,* especially among the Jews, to whom they were first sent, by the writings of the prophets. The prophets *sowed in tears,* crying out, *We have laboured in vain;* the apostles *reaped in joy,* saying, *Thanks be to God, who always causeth us to triumph.* Note, From the labours of ministers that are dead and gone much good fruit may be reaped by the people that *survive* them and the ministers that *succeed* them. John Baptist, and those that assisted him, had *laboured,* and the disciples of Christ entered into their labours, built upon their foundation, and reaped the fruit of what they sowed. See what reason we have to bless God for those that are *gone before us,* for their preaching and their writing, for what they *did* and *suffered* in their day, for we are *entered into their labours;* their studies and services have made our work the easier. And when the ancient and modern labourers, those that came into the vineyard at the third hour and those that came in at the eleventh, meet in the day of account, they will be so far from envying one another the honour of their respective services that both *they that sowed* and *they that reaped* shall rejoice together; and the great Lord of the harvest shall have the glory of all.

IV. The *good effect* which this visit Christ made to the Samaritans *(en passant)* had upon them, and the fruit which was now presently gathered among them, *v.* 39–42. See what impressions were made on them,

1. By the *woman's testimony* concerning *Christ;* though a single testimony, and of one of no good report, and the testimony no more than this, *He told me all that ever I did,* yet it had a good influence upon many. One would have thought that his telling the woman of her secret sins would have made them afraid of coming to him, lest he should tell them also of their faults; but they will venture that rather than not be acquainted with one who they had reason to think was a prophet. And *two things* they were brought to: —

(1.) To *credit* Christ's *word* (*v.* 39): *Many of the Samaritans of that city believed on him for the saying of the woman.* So far they *believed on him* that they took him for a *prophet,* and were desirous to know the mind of God from him; this is favourably interpreted as believing on him. Now observe, [1.] Who they were that believed: *Many of the Samaritans,* who were not of the house of Israel. Their faith was not only an *aggravation* of the *unbelief* of the Jews, from whom better might have been expected, but an *earnest* of the *faith* of the Gentiles, who would welcome that which the Jews rejected. [2.] Upon what inducement they believed: *For the saying of the woman.* See here, *First,* How God is sometimes pleased to use very weak and unlikely instruments for the beginning and carrying on of a good work. A little maid directed a great prince to Elisha, 2 Ki. 5:2. *Secondly,* How great a matter a little fire kindles. Our Saviour, by instructing one poor woman, spread instruction to a whole town. Let not ministers be either *careless* in their preaching, or *discouraged* in it, because their hearers are *few* and *mean;* for, by doing good to *them,* good may be conveyed to *more,* and those that are more considerable. If they *teach every man his neighbour,* and *every man his brother,* a great number may learn at *second hand.* Philip preached the gospel to a single gentleman in his chariot upon the road, and he not only received it himself, but carried it into his country, and propagated it there. *Thirdly,* See how good it is to speak *experimentally* of Christ and the things of God. This woman could say little of Christ, but what she did say she spoke feelingly: *He told me all that ever I did.* Those are most likely to do good that can tell what God has done *for their souls,* Ps. 66:16.

(2.) They were brought to *court his stay* among them (*v.* 40): When they were come to him *they besought him that he would tarry with them.* Upon the woman's report, they believed him to be a prophet, and *came to him;* and, when they *saw* him, the meanness of his appearance and the manifest poverty of his outward condition did not lessen their esteem of him and expectations from him, but still they respected him as a prophet. Note, There is hope of those who are got over the vulgar prejudices that men have against *true worth* in a *low estate.* Blessed are they that are not offended in Christ at the *first sight.* So far were they from being offended in him that they begged he would tarry with them; [1.] That they might *testify their respect* to him, and treat him with the honour and kindness due to his character. God's prophets and ministers are welcome guests to all those who sincerely embrace the gospel; as to Lydia, Acts 16:15. [2.] That they might receive instruction from him. Those that are taught of God are truly desirous to learn more, and to be better acquainted with Christ. Many would have flocked to one that would tell them *their fortune,* but these flocked to one that would tell them *their faults,* tell them of their sin and duty. The historian seems to lay an emphasis upon their being Samaritans; as Lu. 10:33; 17:16. The Samaritans had not that reputation for religion which the Jews had; yet the Jews, who saw Christ's miracles, drove him from them: while the Samaritans, who saw not his miracles, nor shared in his favours, invited him to them. The *proof* of the gospel's success is not always according to the *probability,* nor what is *experienced* according to what is *expected* either way. The Samaritans were taught by the custom of their country to be shy of conversation with the Jews. There were Samaritans that refused to let Christ go through their town (Lu. 9:53), but these begged him to tarry with them. Note, It adds much to the praise of our love to Christ and his word if it conquers the prejudices of education and custom, and sets light by the censures of men. Now we are told that Christ granted their request.

First, He *abode there.* Though it was a city of the Samaritans nearly adjoining to their temple, yet, when he was *invited,* he *tarried* there; though he was upon a journey, and had further to go, yet, when he had an opportunity of doing good, he *abode there.* That is no real *hindrance* which will *further* our account. Yet he abode there but *two days,* because he had other places to visit and other work to do, and those *two* days were as many as came to the share of this city, out of the few days of our Saviour's sojourning upon earth.

Secondly, We are told what impressions were made upon them by Christ's own word, and his personal converse with them (*v.* 41, 42); what he *said* and *did* there is not related, whether he healed their sick or no; but it is intimated, in the effect, that he said and did that which convinced them that he was the Christ; and the labours of a minister are best told by the good fruit of them. Their hearing of *him* had a good effect, but *now their eyes saw him;* and the effect was, 1. That their number grew (*v.* 41): *Many more believed:* many that would not be persuaded to go out of the town to him were yet wrought upon, when he came among them, to believe in him. Note, It is comfortable to see the number of believers; and sometimes the zeal and forwardness of some may be a means to provoke many, and to stir them up to a holy emulation, Rom. 11:14. 2. That their faith grew. Those who had been wrought upon by the report of the woman now saw cause to say, *Now we believe, not because of thy saying, v.* 42. Here are three things in which their *faith grew:* — (1.) In the matter of it, or that which they did believe. Upon the testimony of the woman, they believed him to be *a prophet,* or some extraordinary messenger from heaven; but now that they have conversed with him they believe that he is *the Christ,* the *Anointed One,* the very same that was promised to the fathers and expected by them, and that, being the *Christ,* he is the *Saviour of the world;* for the work to which he was anointed was to *save his people from their sins.* They believed him to be the Saviour not only of the Jews, but of *the world,* which they hoped would take them in, though Samaritans, for it was promised that he should be *Salvation to the ends of the earth,* Isa. 49:6. (2.) In the *certainty* of it; their faith now grew up to a full assurance: *We know* that this is indeed the *Christ; alēthōs — truly;* not a pretended Christ, but a real one; not a *typical* Saviour, as many under the Old Testament, but *truly* one. Such an assurance as this of divine truths is what we should labour after; not only, We think it probable, and are willing to suppose that *Jesus* may be the *Christ,* but, We know that he is *indeed the Christ.* (3.) In the *ground* of it, which was a kind of spiritual sensation and experience: *Now we believe, not because of thy saying, for we have heard him ourselves.* They had before *believed for her saying,* and it was well, it was a good step; but now they find *further* and much *firmer* footing for their faith: *"Now we believe* because we have *heard him ourselves,* and have heard such excellent and divine truths, accompanied with such commanding power and evidence, that we are abundantly satisfied and assured that *this is the Christ."* This is like what the queen of Sheba said of Solomon (1 Ki. 10:6, 7): The *one half was not told me.* The Samaritans, who believed for the woman's saying, now gained further light; for *to him that hath shall be given;* he that is faithful in a little shall be trusted with more. In this instance we may see how *faith comes by hearing.* [1.] Faith comes *to the birth* by hearing the *report of men.* These Samaritans, for the sake of the woman's saying, believed so far as to *come and see,* to come and make trial. Thus the instructions of parents and preachers, and the testimony of the church and our experienced neighbours, *recommend* the doctrine of Christ *to our acquaintance,* and incline us to entertain it as highly probable. But, [2.] Faith *comes to its growth,* strength, and maturity, by hearing the testimony of Christ himself; and this goes further, and recommends his doctrine *to our acceptance,* and obliges us to believe it as undoubtedly certain. We were induced to look into the scriptures *by the saying* of those who told us that in them they had found eternal life; but when we ourselves have found it in them too, have experienced the enlightening, convincing, regenerating, sanctifying, comforting, power of the word, now we believe, *not for their saying,* but because we have searched them ourselves: and our faith *stands not in the wisdom of men, but in the power of God,* 1 Co. 2:5; 1 Jn. 5:9, 10.

Thus was the seed of the gospel sown in Samaria. What effect there was of this afterwards does not appear, but we find that four or five years after, when Philip preached the gospel in Samaria, he found such blessed remains of this good work now wrought that the *people with one accord gave heed to those things which Philip spoke,* Acts 8:5, 6, 8. But as some were pliable to good so were others to evil, whom Simon Magus bewitched with his sorceries, *v.* 9, 10.

Verses 43–54

In these verses we have,

I. Christ's *coming* into Galilee, *v.* 43. Though he was as welcome among the Samaritans as he could be any where, and had better success, yet *after two days* he left them, not so much because they were Samaritans, and he would not confirm those in their prejudices against him who said, *He is a Samaritan* (*ch.* 8:48), but because *he must preach to other cities,* Lu. 4:43. *He went into Galilee,* for there he spent much of his time. Now see here,

1. Whither Christ went; into Galilee, into the country of Galilee, but not to Nazareth, which was strictly *his own* country. He went among the villages, but declined going to Nazareth, the head city, for a reason here given, which *Jesus himself testified,* who knew the temper of his countrymen, the hearts of all men, and the experiences of all prophets, and it is this, That *a prophet has no honour in his own country.* Note, (1.) Prophets ought to have honour, because God has put honour upon them and we do or may receive benefit by them. (2.) The honour due to the Lord's prophets has very often been denied them, and contempt put upon them. (3.) This *due* honour is more frequently denied them *in their own country;* see Lu. 4:24; Mt. 13:57. Not that it is universally true (no rule but has some exceptions), but it holds for the most part. Joseph, when he began to be a prophet, was most hated by his brethren; David was disdained by his brother (1 Sa. 17:28); Jeremiah was maligned by the men of Anathoth (Jer. 11:21), Paul by his countrymen the Jews; and Christ's near kinsmen spoke most slightly of him, *ch.* 7:5. Men's pride and envy make them scorn to be instructed by those who once were their school-fellows and play-fellows. Desire of novelty, and of that which is far-fetched and dear-bought, and seems to drop out of the sky to them, makes them despise those persons and things which they have been long used to and know the rise of. (4.) It is a great discouragement to a minister to go among a people who have no value for him or his labours. Christ would not go to Nazareth, because he knew how little respect he should have there. (5.) It is just with God to deny his gospel to those that despise the ministers of it. They that mock the messengers forfeit the benefit of the message. Mt. 21:35, 41.

2. What entertainment he met with among the Galileans in the country (*v.* 45): They *received him,* bade him welcome, and cheerfully attended on his doctrine. Christ and his gospel are not sent in vain; if they have not honour with *some,* they shall have with *others.* Now the reason given why these Galileans were so ready to receive Christ is because they had seen *the miracles he did at Jerusalem, v.* 45. Observe, (1.) They went up to Jerusalem at the feast, the feast of the passover. The Galileans lay very remote from Jerusalem, and their way thither lay through the country of the Samaritans, which was troublesome for a Jew to pass through, worse than Baca's valley of old; yet, in obedience to God's command, they *went up to the feast,* and there they became acquainted with Christ. Note, They that are diligent and constant in attending on public ordinances some time or other meet with more spiritual benefit than they expect. (2.) At Jerusalem they *saw* Christ's miracles, which recommended him and his doctrine very much to their faith and affections. The miracles were wrought for the benefit of those at Jerusalem; yet the Galileans who were accidentally there got more advantage by them than they did for whom they were chiefly designed. Thus the word preached to a *mixed multitude* may perhaps edify *occasional* hearers more than the constant auditory.

3. What city he went to. When he would go to a city, he chose to go to Cana of Galilee, *where he had made the water wine* (*v.* 46); thither he went, to see if there were any good fruits of that miracle remaining; and, if there were, to confirm their faith, and water what he had planted. The evangelist mentions this miracle here to teach us to keep in remembrance what we *have seen* of the works of Christ.

II. His *curing* the *nobleman's son* that was sick of a fever. This story is not recorded by any other of the evangelists; it comes in Mt. 4:23.

Observe, 1. Who the *petitioner* was, and who the *patient:* the petitioner was a *nobleman;* the patient was his son: *There was a certain nobleman. Regulus* (so the Latin), a *little king;* so called, either for the largeness of his estate, or the extent of his power, or the royalties that belonged to his manor. Some understand it as denoting his *preferment* — he was a courtier in some office about the king; others as denoting his *party* — he was an Herodian, a royalist, a prerogative-man, one that espoused the interests of the Herods, father and son; perhaps it was Chuza, Herod's steward (Lu. 8:3), or Manaen, Herod's foster-brother, Acts 13:1. There were saints in Caesar's household. The father a nobleman, and yet the son sick; for dignities and titles of honour will be no security to persons and families from the assaults of sickness and death. It was fifteen miles from Capernaum where this nobleman lived to Cana, where Christ now was; yet this affliction in his family sent him so far to Christ.

2. How the petitioner made *his application* to the physician. Having heard that *Jesus was come out of* Judea to Galilee, and finding that he did not come towards Capernaum, but turned off towards the other side of the country, he *went to him* himself, and *besought him to come and heal his son, v.* 47. See here, (1.) His *tender affection* to his son, that when he was sick he would spare no pains to get help for him. (2.) His *great respect* to our Lord Jesus, that he would come himself to wait upon him, when he might have sent a servant; and that he *besought him,* when, as a man in authority, some would think he might have ordered his attendance. The greatest men, when they come to God, must become beggars, and sue *sub forma pauperis — as paupers.* As to the errand he came upon, we may observe a mixture in *his faith.* [1.] There was *sincerity* in it; he did believe that Christ could heal his son, though his disease was dangerous. It is probable he had physicians to him, who had given him over; but he believed that Christ could cure him when the case seemed deplorable. [2.] Yet there was *infirmity* in his faith; he believed that

Christ could heal his son, but, as it should seem, he thought he could not heal him at a distance, and therefore he besought him that he would *come down* and heal him, expecting, as Naaman did, that he would come and *strike his hand* over the patient, as if he could not cure him but by a *physical contact.* Thus we are apt to *limit the Holy One of Israel,* and to stint him to our forms. The centurion, a Gentile, a soldier, was so strong in faith as to say, *Lord, I am not worthy that thou shouldest come under my roof,* Mt. 8:8. This nobleman, a Jew, must have Christ to come down, though it was a good day's journey, and despairs of a cure unless he come down, as if he must teach Christ how to work. We are encouraged to *pray,* but we are not allowed to prescribe: Lord, heal me; but, whether with a word or a touch, *thy will be done.*

3. The gentle rebuke he met with in this address (*v.* 48): *Jesus said to him,* "I see how it is; *except you see signs and wonders, you will not believe,* as the Samaritans did, though they saw no signs and wonders, and therefore I must work miracles among you." Though he was a *nobleman,* and now in *grief* about his son, and had shown great respect to Christ in coming so far to him, yet Christ gives him a reproof. Men's dignity in the world shall not exempt them from the rebukes of the word or providence; for Christ reproves not *after the hearing of his ears,* but *with equity,* Isa. 11:3, 4. Observe, Christ first shows him his sin and weakness, to prepare him for mercy, and then grants his request. Those whom Christ intends to honour with his *favours* he first *humbles* with his *frowns.* The *Comforter* shall first *convince.* Herod longed to see some miracle (Lu. 23:8), and this courtier was of the same mind, and the generality of the people too. Now that which is blamed is, (1.) That, whereas they had heard by credible and incontestable report of the miracles he had wrought in other places, they would not believe except they saw them with their own eyes, Lu. 4:23. They must be *honoured,* and they must be *humoured,* or they will not be *convinced.* Their country must be graced, and their curiosity gratified, with signs and wonders, or else, though the doctrine of Christ be sufficiently proved by miracles wrought elsewhere, they *will not believe.* Like Thomas, they will yield to no method of conviction but what they shall prescribe. (2.) That, whereas they had seen divers miracles, the evidence of which they could not gainsay, but which sufficiently proved Christ to be a teacher come from God, and should now have applied themselves to him for instruction in his doctrine, which by its native excellency would have *gently led them on,* in believing, to a spiritual perfection, instead of this they would go no further in believing than they were *driven* by signs and wonders. The *spiritual* power of the word did not *affect them,* did not *attract* them, but only the *sensible* power of miracles, which were *for those* who believe not, while *prophesying* was *for those that believe,* 1 Co. 14:22. Those that admire *miracles* only, and *despise prophesying,* rank themselves with unbelievers.

4. His continued importunity in his address (*v.* 49): *Sir, come down ere my child die. Kyrie — Lord;* so it should be rendered. In this reply of his we have, (1.) Something that was commendable: he took the reproof patiently; he spoke to Christ respectfully. Though he was one of those that wore soft clothing, yet he could bear reproof. It is none of the privileges of peerage to be above the reproofs of the word of Christ; but it is a sign of a good temper and disposition in men, especially in great men, when they can be told of their faults and not be angry. And, as he did not take the reproof for an affront, so he did not take it for a denial, but still prosecuted his request, and continued to wrestle till he prevailed. Nay, he might argue thus: "If Christ heal *my soul,* surely he will heal *my son;* if he cure *my* unbelief, he will cure *his* fever." This is the method Christ takes, first to work *upon* us, and then to work *for* us; and there is hope if we find him entering upon this method. (2.) Something that was blameworthy, that was his infirmity; for, [1.] He seems to take no notice of the reproof Christ gave him, says nothing to it, by way either of confession or of excuse, for he is so wholly taken up with concern about his child that he can mind nothing else. Note, The sorrow of the world is a great prejudice to our profiting by the word of Christ. Inordinate care and grief are thorns that choke the good seed; see Ex. 6:9. [2.] He still discovered the weakness of his faith in the power of Christ. *First,* He must have Christ to come down, thinking that else he could do the child no kindness. It is hard to persuade ourselves that distance of time and place are no obstructions to the knowledge and power of our Lord Jesus; yet so it is: he sees afar off, for his word, the word of his power, *runs very swiftly. Secondly,* He believes that Christ could heal a *sick* child, but not that he could raise a *dead* child, and therefore, "O *come down, ere my child die,*" as if then it would be too late; whereas Christ has the same power over death that he has over bodily diseases. He forgot that Elijah and Elisha had raised dead children; and is Christ's power inferior to theirs? Observe what haste he is in: *Come down, ere my child die;* as if there were danger of Christ's slipping his time. *He that believeth does not make haste,* but refers himself to Christ. "Lord, what and when and how thou pleasest."

5. The answer of peace which Christ gave to his request at last (*v.* 50): *Go thy way, thy son liveth.* Christ here gives us an instance, (1.) Of his *power,* that he not only could heal, but could heal with so much ease, without the trouble of a visit. Here is nothing *said,* nothing *done,* nothing *ordered* to be done, and yet the cure wrought: *Thy son liveth.* The healing beams of the Sun of righteousness dispense benign influences from one end of heaven to another, and *there is nothing hid from the heat thereof.* Though Christ is now in heaven, and his church on earth, he can *send from above.* This nobleman would have Christ *come down and heal his son;* Christ will heal his son, and not *come down.* And thus the cure is the sooner wrought, the nobleman's mistake rectified, and his faith confirmed; so that the thing was better done in Christ's way. When he denies what we ask, he gives what is much more to our advantage; we ask for ease, he gives patience. Observe, His power was exerted by his word. In saying, *Thy son lives,* he showed that he has *life in himself,* and power to *quicken whom he will.* Christ's saying, *Thy soul lives,* makes it alive. (2.) Of his *pity;* he observed the nobleman to be *in pain* about his son, and his natural affection discovered itself in that word, *Ere my child,* my dear child, die; and therefore Christ dropped the reproof, and gave him assurance of the recovery of his child; for he knows how a father *pities his children.*

6. The nobleman's belief of the word of Christ: He *believed,* and *went away.* Though Christ did not gratify him so far as to go down with him, he is satisfied with the method Christ took, and reckons he has gained his point. How quickly, how easily, is that which is lacking in our faith perfected by the word and power of Christ. Now he *sees no sign or wonder,* and yet *believes* the wonder done. (1.) Christ said, *Thy son liveth,* and the man *believed* him; not only believed the omniscience of Christ, that he *knew* the child had recovered, but the omnipotence of Christ, that the cure was *effected* by his word. He left him *dying;* yet, when Christ said, *He lives,* like the father of the faithful, *against hope he believed in hope,* and *staggered not through unbelief.* (2.) Christ said, *Go thy way;* and, as an evidence of the sincerity of his faith, he *went his way,* and gave neither Christ nor himself any further disturbance. He did not press Christ to come down, did not say, "If he do recover, yet a visit will be acceptable;" no, he seems no further solicitous, but, like Hannah, he goes his way, and his countenance is *no more sad.* As one entirely satisfied, he made no great haste home; did not hurry home that night, but returned leisurely, as one that was perfectly easy in his own mind.

7. The further confirmation of his faith, by comparing notes with his servants at his return. (1.) His servants met him with the agreeable news of the child's recovery, *v.* 51. Probably they met him not far from his own house, and, knowing what their master's cares were, they were willing as soon as they could to make him easy. David's servants were loth to tell him when the child was dead. Christ said, *Thy son liveth;* and now the servants say the same. Good news will meet those that hope in God's word. (2.) He enquired what hour the child began to recover (*v.* 52); not as if he doubted the influence of Christ's word upon the child's recovery, but he was desirous to have his faith confirmed, that he might be able to satisfy any to whom he should mention the miracle; for it was a material circumstance. Note, [1.] It is good to furnish ourselves with all the corroborating proofs and evidences that may be, to strengthen our faith in the word of Christ, that it may grow up to *a full assurance. Show me a token for good.* [2.] The diligent comparison of the works of Christ with his word will be of great use to us for the confirming of our faith. This was the course the nobleman took: *He enquired of the servants the hour when he began to amend;* and they told him, *Yesterday at the seventh hour* (at one o'clock in the afternoon, or, as some think this evangelist reckons, at seven o'clock at night) the *fever left him;* not only he began to amend, but he was perfectly well on a sudden; so *the father knew that it was at the same hour* when Jesus said to him, *Thy son liveth.* As the word of God, well-studied, will help us to understand his providences, so the providence of God, well observed, will help us to understand his word; for God is every day *fulfilling the scripture.* Two things would help to confirm his faith: — *First,* That the child's recovery was *sudden* and not *gradual.* They name the precise time to an hour: *Yesterday,* not *about,* but *at* the seventh hour, *the fever left him;* not it *abated,* or began to *decrease,* but it *left him* in an instant. The word of Christ did not work like physic, which must have time to operate, and produce the effect, and perhaps *cures by expectation* only; no, with Christ it was *dictum factum — he spoke and it was done;* not, He spoke and it was *set a doing. Secondly,* That it was just at the same time that Christ spoke to him: *at that very hour.* The synchronisms and coincidents of events add very much to the beauty and harmony of Providence. Observe the *time,* and the *thing* itself will be more illustrious, for every thing is beautiful *in its time;* at the very time when it is *promised,* as Israel's deliverance (Ex. 12:41); at the very time when it is *prayed for,* as Peter's deliverance, Acts 12:12. In men's works, distance of place is the delay of time and the retarding of business; but it is not so in the works of Christ. The pardon, and peace, and comfort, and spiritual healing, which he speaks in heaven, are, if he pleases, at the same time effected and wrought in the souls of believers; and, when these two come to be *compared* in the great day, Christ will be *glorified in his saints, and admired in all them that believe.*

8. The *happy effect and issue of this.* The bringing of the cure to the family brought salvation to it. (1.) The nobleman *himself believed.* He had before *believed* the word of Christ, with reference to this particular occasion; but now he *believed in Christ* as the Messiah promised, and became one of his disciples. Thus the *particular* experience of the power and efficacy of *one* word of Christ may be a happy means to introduce and settle the whole authority of Christ's dominion in the soul. Christ has many ways of gaining the heart, and by the grant of a *temporal* mercy may make way for *better* things. (2.) His *whole house* believed likewise. [1.] Because of the *interest* they all had in the miracle, which preserved the *blossom* and *hopes* of the family; this affected them all, and endeared Christ to them, and recommended him to their best thoughts. [2.] Because of the *influence* the master of the family had upon them *all.* A master of a family cannot give faith to those under his charge, nor *force* them to believe, but he may be instrumental to remove *external prejudices,* which obstruct the operation of the evidence, and then the work is more than half done. *Abraham* was famous for this (Gen. 18:19), and Joshua, *ch.* 24:15. This was a *nobleman,* and probably he had a *great household;* but, when he comes into Christ's school, he brings them all along with him. What a blessed change was here in this house, occasioned by the sickness of the child! This should reconcile us to afflictions; we know not what good may follow from them. Probably, the conversion of this *nobleman* and his family at Capernaum might induce Christ to come afterwards, and settle at Capernaum, as his head-quarters in Galilee. When great men receive the gospel, they may be instrumental to bring it to the places where they live.

9. Here is the evangelist's remark upon this cure (*v.* 54); *This is the second miracle,* referring to *ch.* 2:11, where the turning of water into wine is said to be the first; that was soon after his first return out of Judea, this soon after his second. In Judea he had wrought many miracles, *ch.* 3:2; 4:45. They had the first offer; but, being driven thence, he wrought miracles in Galilee. Somewhere or other Christ will find a welcome. People may, if they please, shut the sun out of *their own houses,* but they cannot shut it *out of the world.* This is noted to be the *second* miracle, 1. To remind us of the first, wrought in the same place some months before. *Fresh* mercies should revive the remembrance of former mercies, as former mercies should encourage our hopes of further mercies. Christ keeps account of his favours, whether we do or no. 2. To let us know that *this* cure was *before* those many cures which the other evangelists mention to be wrought in Galilee, Mt. 4:23; Mk. 1:34; Lu. 4:40. Probably, the patient being a person of quality, the cure was the more talked of and sent him crowds of patients; when this nobleman applied himself to Christ, multitudes followed. What abundance of good may great men do, if they be good men!

CHAPTER 5

We have in the gospels a faithful record of all that Jesus began both to do and to teach, Acts 1:1. These two are interwoven, because what he taught explained what he did, and what he did confirmed what he taught. Accordingly, we have in this chapter a miracle and a sermon. I. The miracle was the cure of an impotent man that had been diseased thirty-eight years, with the circumstances of that cure (*v.* 1–16). II. The sermon was Christ's vindication of himself before the sanhedrim, when he was prosecuted as a criminal for healing the man on the sabbath day, in which, 1. He asserts his authority as Messiah, and Mediator between God and man (*v.* 17–29). 2. He proves it by the testimony of his Father, of John Baptist, of his miracles, and of the scriptures of the Old Testament, and condemns the Jews for their unbelief (*v.* 30–47).

Verses 1–16

This miraculous cure is not recorded by any other of the evangelists, who confine themselves mostly to the miracles wrought in Galilee, but John relates those wrought at Jerusalem. Concerning this observe,

I. *The time when* this cure was wrought: it was at a *feast of the Jews,* that is, the passover, for that was the most celebrated feast. Christ, though residing in Galilee, yet *went up to Jerusalem* at the feast, *v.* 1. 1. Because it was an *ordinance of God,* which, as a *subject,* he would observe, being made under the law; though as a *Son* he might have pleaded an exemption. Thus he would teach us to attend religious assemblies. Heb. 10:25. 2. Because it was an *opportunity of good;* for, (1.) there were great numbers gathered together there at that time; it was a general rendezvous, at least of all serious thinking people, from all parts of the country, besides proselytes from other nations: and Wisdom must *cry in the places of concourse,* Prov. 1:21. (2.) It was to be hoped that they were in a *good frame,* for they came together to *worship God* and to spend their time in religious exercises. Now a mind *inclined to devotion,* and sequestering itself to the exercises of piety, *lies very open* to the further discoveries of divine light and love, and to it Christ will be acceptable.

II. The *place where* this cure was wrought: at the *pool of Bethesda,* which had a miraculous healing virtue in it, and is here particularly described, *v.* 2–4.

1. Where it was situated: *At Jerusalem, by the sheep-market; epi tē probatikē.* It might as well be rendered the *sheep-cote,* where the sheep were kept, or the *sheep-gate,* which we read of, Neh. 3:1, through which the sheep were *brought,* as the *sheep-market,* where they were *sold.* Some think it was near the temple, and, if so, it yielded a melancholy but profitable spectacle to those that went up to the temple to pray.

2. How it was called: It was a *pool* (a pond or bath), *which is called in Hebrew, Bethesda — the house of mercy;* for therein appeared much of the *mercy of God* to the sick and diseased. In a world of so much misery as this is, it is well that there are some *Bethesdas — houses of mercy* (remedies against those maladies), that the scene is not all melancholy. An *alms-house,* so Dr. Hammond. Dr. Lightfoot's conjecture is that this was the *upper pool* (Isa. 7:3), and the *old pool,* Isa. 22:11; that it had been used for *washing* from ceremonial pollutions, for convenience of which the porches were built to dress and undress in, but it was lately become medicinal.

3. How it was fitted up: It had *five porches, cloisters, piazzas,* or *roofed walks,* in which the sick lay. Thus the charity of men concurred with the mercy of God for the relief of the distressed. Nature has provided *remedies,* but men must provide *hospitals.*

4. How it was frequented with sick and cripples (*v.* 3): *In these lay a great multitude of impotent folks.* How many are the afflictions of the afflicted in this world! How full of complaints are all places, and what multitudes of impotent folks! It may do us good to visit the hospitals sometimes, that we may take occasion, from the calamities of others, to thank God for our comforts. The evangelist specifies three sorts of diseased people that lay here, *blind, halt,* and *withered* or *sinew-shrunk,* either in one particular part, as the man with the *withered hand,* or all over paralytic. These are mentioned because, being least able to help themselves into the water, they lay longest waiting in the *porches.* Those that were sick of these bodily diseases took the pains to come *far* and had the patience to wait *long* for a cure; any of us would have done the same, and we ought to do so: but O that men were as wise for their souls, and as solicitous to get their spiritual diseases healed! We are all by nature *impotent folks* in spiritual things, *blind, halt,* and *withered;* but effectual provision is made for our cure if we will but observe orders.

5. What virtue it had for the cure of these impotent folks (*v.* 4). *An angel went down,* and *troubled the water;* and *whoso first stepped in was made whole.* That this strange virtue in the pool was *natural,* or *artificial* rather, and was the effect of the washing of the sacrifices, which impregnated the water with I know not what healing virtue even for *blind* people, and that the angel was a *messenger,* a common person, sent down to stir the water, is altogether groundless; there was a room in the temple on purpose to wash the sacrifices in. Expositors generally agree that the virtue this pool had was supernatural. It is true the Jewish writers, who are not sparing in recounting the praises of Jerusalem, do none of them make the least mention of this *healing pool,* of which silence in this matter perhaps this is the reason, that it was taken for a presage of the near approach of the Messiah, and therefore those who denied him to be come industriously concealed such an indication of his coming; so that this is all the account we have of it. Observe,

(1.) The *preparation* of the medicine by an angel, who *went down into the pool,* and *stirred the water.* Angels are God's servants, and friends to mankind; and perhaps are more active in the removing of diseases (as evil angels in the inflicting of them) than we are aware of. Raphael, the apocryphal name of an angel, signifies *medicina Dei — God's physic,* or *physician* rather. See what mean offices the holy angels condescend to, for the good of men. If we would do the will of God as the angels do it, we must think nothing below us but sin. The *troubling of the water* was the signal given of the descent of the angel, as the *going upon the tops of the mulberry trees* was to David, and then they must *bestir themselves.* The waters of the sanctuary are then *healing* when they are put in *motion.* Ministers must *stir up the gift* that is in them. When they are cold and dull in their ministrations, the waters *settle,* and are not apt to *heal.* The angel descended, to *stir the water,* not daily, perhaps not frequently, but *at a certain season;* some think, at the three solemn feasts, to grace those solemnities; or, *now and then,* as Infinite Wisdom saw fit. God is a free agent in dispensing his favours.

(2.) The *operation* of the medicine: *Whoever first stepped in was made whole.* here is, [1.] miraculous extent of the virtue as to the *diseases* cured; what disease soever it was, this water cured it. Natural and artificial baths are as *hurtful* in some cases as they are useful in others, but this was a remedy for every malady, even for those that came from contrary causes. The power of miracles *succeeds* where the power of nature *succumbs.* [2.] A miraculous limitation of the virtue as to the *persons* cured: He that first stepped in had the benefit; that is, he or they that stepped in immediately were cured, not those that lingered and came in afterwards. This teaches us to observe and improve our opportunities, and to *look about us,* that we slip not a season which may never return. The angel *stirred* the waters, but left the diseased to themselves to *get in.* God has put virtue into the scriptures and ordinances, for he would have healed us; but, if we do not make a due improvement of them, it is our own fault, we *would not be healed.*

Now this is all the account we have of this *standing* miracle; it is uncertain when it began and when it ceased. Some conjecture it began when Eliashib the high priest began the building of the wall about Jerusalem, and sanctified it with prayer; and that God testified his acceptance by putting this virtue into the adjoining pool. Some think it began now lately at Christ's birth; nay, others at his baptism. Dr. Lightfoot, finding in *Josephus, Antiq.* 15.121–122, mention of a great earthquake in the seventh year of Herod, thirty years before Christ's birth, supposed, since there used to be earthquakes at the descent of angels, that then the angel first descended to stir this water. Some think it ceased with this miracle, others at Christ's death; however, it is certain it had a gracious signification. *First,* it was a *token* of God's good will to that people, and an indication that, though they had been long without prophets and miracles, yet God had not *cast them off;* though they were now an oppressed despised people, and many were ready to say, *Where are all the wonders that our fathers told us of?* God did hereby let them know that he had still a kindness for the *city of their solemnities.* We may hence take occasion to acknowledge with thankfulness God's power and goodness in the mineral waters, that contribute so much to the health of mankind; for God *made the fountains of water,* Rev. 14:7. *Secondly,* It was a type of the Messiah, who is the *fountain opened;* and was intended to raise people's expectations of him who is the *Sun of righteousness,* that arises *with healing under his wings.* These waters had formerly been used for purifying, now for healing, to signify both the *cleansing* and *curing* virtue of the blood of Christ, that incomparable bath, which *heals all our diseases.* The waters of Siloam, which filled this pool, signified the kingdom of David, and of Christ the Son of David (Isa. 8:6); fitly therefore have they now this *sovereign* virtue put into them. The laver of regeneration is to us as Bethesda's pool, healing our spiritual diseases; not at certain seasons, but at all times. *Whoever will, let him come.*

III. The patient on whom this cure was wrought (*v.* 5): one that *had been infirm thirty-eight years.* 1. His *disease* was *grievous:* He had an *infirmity,* a weakness; he had lost the use of his limbs, at least on one side, as is usual in palsies. It is sad to have the body so disabled that, instead of being the soul's instrument, it is become, even in the affairs of this life, its burden. What reason have we to thank God for bodily strength, to use it for him, and to pity those who are *his prisoners!* 2. The duration of it was *tedious: Thirty-eight years.* He was lame longer than most live. Many are so long disabled for the offices of life that, as the psalmist complains, they seem to be *made in vain;* for suffering, not for service; born to be always dying. Shall we complain of one wearisome night, or one fit of illness, who perhaps for many years have scarcely known what it has been to be a day sick, when many others, better than we, have scarcely known what it has been to be a day well? Mr. Baxter's note on this passage is very affecting: "How great a mercy was it to live thirty-eight years under God's wholesome discipline! O my God," saith he, "I thank thee for the like discipline of fifty-eight years; how safe a life is this, in comparison of full prosperity and pleasure!"

IV. The cure and the circumstances of it briefly related, *v.* 6–9.

1. *Jesus saw him lie.* Observe, When Christ came up to Jerusalem he visited not the palaces, but the hospitals, which is an instance of his humility, and condescension, and tender compassion, and an *indication* of his great design in coming into the world, which was to seek and save the sick and wounded. There was a great multitude of poor cripples here at Bethesda, but Christ fastened his eye upon this one, and singled him out from the rest, because he was *senior* of the house, and in a more deplorable condition than any of the rest; and Christ delights to help the helpless, and hath mercy *on whom he will have mercy.* Perhaps his companions in tribulation insulted over him, because he had often been disappointed of a cure; therefore Christ took him for his patient: it is his honour to side with the weakest, and bear up those whom he sees *run down.*

2. He knew and considered *how long he had lain* in this condition. Those that have been long in affliction may comfort themselves with this, that God keeps account *how long,* and knows our frame.

3. He asked him, *Wilt thou be made whole?* A strange question to be asked one that had been so long ill. Some indeed would not be made whole, because their sores serve them to beg by and serve them for an excuse for idleness; but this poor man was as unable to *go a begging* as to *work,* yet Christ put it to him, (1.) To *express* his own pity and concern for him. Christ is tenderly inquisitive concerning the desires of those that are in affliction, and is willing to know *what is their petition:* "What shall I do for you?" (2.) To try him whether he would be beholden for a cure to him against whom the great people were so prejudiced and sought to prejudice others. (3.) To teach him to value the mercy, and to excite in him desires after it. In spiritual cases, people are not willing to be cured of their sins, are loth to part with them. If this point therefore were but gained, if people were willing to be *made whole,* the work were half done, for Christ is willing to heal, if we be but willing to be healed, Mt. 8:3.

4. The poor impotent man takes this opportunity to renew his complaint, and to set forth the misery of his case, which makes his cure the more illustrious: *Sir, I have no man to put me into the pool, v.* 7. He seems to take Christ's question as an imputation of carelessness and neglect: "If thou hadst had a mind to be healed, thou wouldest have looked better to thy hits, and have got into the healing waters long before now." "No, Master," saith the poor man, "It is not for want of a *good will,* but of a *good friend,* that I am unhealed. I

have done what I could to help myself, but in vain, for no one else will help me." (1.) He does not think of any other way of being cured than by these waters, and desires no other friendship than to be helped into *them;* therefore, when Christ cured him, his imagination or expectation could not contribute to it, for he thought of no such thing. (2.) He complains for want of friends to help him in: *"I have no man,* no friend to do me that kindness." One would think that some of those who had been themselves healed should have lent him a hand; but it is common for the poor to be destitute of friends; *no man careth for their soul.* To the sick and impotent it is as true a piece of charity to work for them as to relieve them; and thus the poor are capable of being charitable to one another, and ought to be so, though we seldom find that they are so; I speak it to their shame. (3.) He bewails his infelicity, that very often when *he* was coming *another stepped in before him.* But a step between him and a cure, and yet he continues impotent. None had the charity to say, "Your case is worse than mine, do you go in now, and I will stay till the next time;" for there is no getting over the old maxim, *Every one for himself.* Having been so often disappointed, he begins to despair, and now is Christ's time to come to his relief; he delights to help in desperate cases. Observe, How mildly this man speaks of the unkindness of those about him, without any peevish reflections. As we should be thankful for the least kindness, so we should be patient under the greatest contempts; and, let our resentments be ever so *just,* yet our expressions should ever be *calm.* And observe further, to his praise, that, though he had waited so long in vain, yet still he continued lying by the pool side, hoping that some time or other help would come, Hab. 2:3.

5. Our Lord Jesus hereupon cures him with a word speaking, though he neither asked it nor thought of it. Here is,

(1.) The word he said: *Rise, take up thy bed, v.* 8. [1.] He is bidden to *rise and walk;* a strange command to be given to an *impotent* man, that had been long disabled; but this divine word was to be the vehicle of a divine power; it was a command to the disease to *be gone,* to nature to *be strong,* but it is expressed as a command to him to *bestir himself.* He must *rise and walk,* that is, attempt to do it, and in the *essay* he should receive strength to do it. The conversion of a sinner is the cure of a chronic disease; this is ordinarily done by the word, a word of command: Arise, and walk; *turn, and live; make ye a new heart;* which no more supposes a power in us to do it, without the grace of God, *distinguishing* grace, than this supposed such a power in the impotent man. But, if he had not attempted to help himself, he had not been cured, and he must have *borne the blame;* yet it does not therefore follow that, when he did rise and walk, it was by his own strength; no, it was by the power of Christ, and he must have all the glory. Observe, Christ did not bid him rise and go into the waters, but *rise and walk.* Christ did that for us which the law could not do, and set that aside. [2.] He is bidden to *take up his bed. First,* To make it to appear that it was a *perfect cure,* and purely miraculous; for he did not recover strength by degrees, but from the extremity of weakness and impotency he suddenly stepped into the highest degree of bodily strength; so that he was able to carry as great a load as any porter that had been as long *used* to it as he had been *disused.* He, who this minute was not able to turn himself in his bed, the next minute was able to carry his bed. The man sick of the palsy (Mt. 9:6) was bidden to *go to his house,* but probably this man had no house to go to, the hospital was his home; therefore he is bidden to *rise and walk. Secondly,* It was to *proclaim* the cure, and make it public; for, being the sabbath day, whoever carried a burden through the streets made himself very remarkable, and every one would enquire what was the meaning of it; thereby notice of the miracle would spread, to the honour of God. *Thirdly,* Christ would thus witness against the tradition of the elders, which had stretched the law of the sabbath beyond its intention; and would likewise show that he was *Lord of the sabbath,* and had power to make what alterations he pleased about it, and to over-rule the law. Joshua, and the host of Israel, marched about Jericho on the sabbath day, when God commanded them, so did this man carry his bed, in obedience to a command. The case may be such that it may become a work of *necessity,* or *mercy,* to carry a bed on the sabbath day; but here it was more, it was a work of *piety,* being designed purely for the glory of God. *Fourthly,* He would hereby try the faith and obedience of his patient. By carrying his bed publicly, he exposed himself to the censure

of the ecclesiastical court, and was liable, at least, to be *scourged in the synagogue.* Now, will he run the hazard of this, in obedience to Christ? Yes, he will. Those that have been *healed by Christ's word* should be *ruled by his word,* whatever it cost them.

(2.) The efficacy of this word (*v.* 9): a divine power went alone with it, and immediately he was *made whole, took up his bed, and walked.* [1.] He felt the power of Christ's word healing him: *Immediately he was made whole.* What a joyful surprise was this to the poor cripple, to find himself all of a sudden so easy, so strong, so able to help himself! What a new world was he in, in an instant! Nothing is too hard for Christ to do. [2.] He obeyed the power of Christ's word commanding him. He *took up his bed and walked,* and did not care who blamed him or threatened him for it. The proof of our spiritual cure is our rising and walking. Hath Christ healed our spiritual diseases? Let us go whithersoever he sends us, and *take up* whatever he is pleased to lay upon us, and *walk before him.*

V. What became of the poor man after he was cured. We are here told,

1. What passed between him and the Jews who saw him carry his bed on the sabbath day; for on that day this cure was wrought, and it was the sabbath that fell within the passover week, and therefore a *high day, ch.* 19:31. Christ's work was such that he needed not make any difference between sabbath days and other days, for he was always about his Father's business; but he wrought many remarkable cures on that day, perhaps to encourage his church to expect those spiritual favours from him, in their observance of the Christian sabbath, which were typified by his miraculous cures. Now here,

(1.) The Jews quarrelled with the man for carrying his bed on the sabbath day, telling him that *it was not lawful, v.* 10. It does not appear whether they were magistrates, who had power to *punish* him, or common people, who could only *inform* against him; but thus far was commendable, that, while they knew not by *what authority* he did it, they were jealous for the honour of the sabbath, and could not unconcernedly see it *profaned;* like Nehemiah. Neh. 13:17.

(2.) The man justified himself in what he did by a warrant that would bear him out, *v.* 11. "I do not do it in contempt of the law and the sabbath, but in obedience to one who, by *making me whole,* has given me an undeniable proof that he is greater than either. He that could work such a miracle as to *make me whole* no doubt might give me such a command as to carry *my bed;* he that could overrule the powers of nature no doubt might overrule a positive law, especially in an instance not of the essence of the law. He that was so kind as to make me whole would not be so unkind as to bid me do what is sinful." Christ, by curing another paralytic, proved his power to *forgive sin,* here to *give law;* if his pardons are valid, his edicts are so, and his miracles prove both.

(3.) The Jews enquired further who it was that gave him this warrant (*v.* 12): *What man is that?* Observe, How industriously they *overlooked* that which might be a ground of their *faith in Christ.* They enquire not, no, not for curiosity, "Who is it that *made thee whole?"* While they industriously caught at that which might be a ground of reflection upon Christ (*What man is* it who said unto thee, *Take up thy bed?*) they would fain *subpoena* the patient to be witness against his physician, and to be his betrayer. In their question, observe, [1.] They resolve to look upon Christ as a *mere man: What man is that?* For, though he gave ever such convincing proofs of it, they were resolved that they would never own him to be the *Son of God.* [2.] They resolve to look upon him as a bad *man,* and take it for granted that he who bade this man carry his bed, whatever divine commission he might *produce,* was certainly a delinquent, and as such they resolve to prosecute him. *What man is that* who durst give such orders?

(4.) The poor man was unable to give them any account of him: *He wist not who he was, v.* 13.

[1.] Christ was *unknown* to him when he healed him. Probably he had heard of the name of Jesus, but had never seen him, and therefore could not tell that this was he. Note, Christ does many a good turn for those that know him not, Isa. 45:4, 5. He enlightens, strengthens, quickens, comforts us, and we *wist not who he is;* nor are aware how much we receive daily by his mediation. This man, being unacquainted with Christ, could not actually believe in him for a cure; but Christ

knew the dispositions of his soul, and suited his favours to them, as to the blind man in a like case, *ch.* 9:36. Our covenant and communion with God take rise, not so much from our knowledge of him, as from his knowledge of us. We *know God,* or, rather, are *known of him,* Gal. 4:9.

[2.] For the present he *kept himself unknown; for* as soon as he had wrought the cure he *conveyed himself away,* he *made himself unknown* (so some read it), *a multitude being in that place.* This is mentioned to show, either, *First,* How Christ conveyed himself away — by retiring into the crowd, so as not to be distinguished from a common person. He that was the chief of ten thousand often made himself one of the throng. It is sometimes the lot of those who have by their services signalized themselves to be levelled with the multitude, and overlooked. Or *Secondly, Why* he conveyed himself away, because there was *a multitude* there, and he industriously avoided both the *applause* of those who would admire the miracle and *cry that up,* and the censure of those who would censure him as a sabbath-breaker, and *run him down.* Those that are active for God in their generation must expect to pass through *evil report* and *good report;* and it is wisdom as much as may be to keep out of the hearing of both; lest by the one we be *exalted,* and by the other *depressed,* above measure. Christ left the miracle to commend itself, and the man on whom it was wrought to justify it.

2. What passed between him and our Lord Jesus at their next interview, *v.* 14. Observe here,

(1.) Where Christ found him: *in the temple,* the place of public worship. In our attendance on public worship we may expect to meet with Christ, and improve our acquaintance with him. Observe, [1.] Christ *went to the temple.* Though he had many enemies, yet he appeared in public, because there he bore his testimony to divine institutions, and had opportunity of doing good. [2.] The man that was cured *went to the temple.* There Christ found him the same day, as it should seem, that he was healed; thither he straightway went, *First,* Because he had, *by his infirmity,* been so long *detained* thence. Perhaps he had not been there for thirty-eight years, and therefore, as soon as ever the embargo is taken off, his first visit shall be to the temple, as Hezekiah intimates his shall be (Isa. 38:22): *What is the sign that I shall go up to the house of the Lord? Secondly,* Because he had *by his recovery* a good errand thither; he went up to the temple to return thanks to God for his recovery. When God has at any time restored us our health, we ought to attend him with solemn praises (Ps. 116:18, 19), and the sooner the better, while the sense of the mercy is fresh. *Thirdly,* Because he had, by *carrying his bed,* seemed to put a contempt on the sabbath, he would thus show that he had an honour for it, and made conscience of sabbath-sanctification, in that on which the chief stress of it is laid, which is the *public worship* of God. Works of necessity and mercy are allowed; but when they are over we must *go to the temple.*

(2.) What he said to him. When Christ has cured us, he has not done with us; he now applies himself to the healing of his soul, and this *by the word* too. [1.] He gives him a *memento* of his cure: *Behold thou art made whole.* He found himself made whole, yet Christ calls his attention to it. *Behold, consider* it seriously, how sudden, how strange, how cheap, how easy, the cure was: *admire it;* behold, and wonder: *Remember it;* let the impressions of it abide, and never be lost, Isa. 38:9. [2.] He gives him a caution against sin, in consideration hereof, *Being made whole, sin no more.* This implies that his disease was the punishment of sin; whether of some remarkably flagrant sin, or only of sin in general, we cannot tell, but we know that sin is the procuring cause of sickness, Ps. 107:17, 18. Some observe that Christ did not make mention of sin to any of his patients, except to this *impotent* man, and another who was in like manner diseased, Mk. 2:5. While those chronical diseases lasted, they prevented the outward acts of many sins, and therefore watchfulness was the more necessary when the disability was removed. Christ intimates that those who are *made whole,* who are eased of the present sensible punishment of sin, are in danger of *returning* to sin when the terror and restraint are over, unless divine grace dry up the fountain. When the trouble which only dammed up the current is over, the waters will return to their old course; and therefore there is great need of watchfulness, lest after healing mercy we return again to folly. The *misery* we were *made whole from* warns us to sin no more, having felt the smart of sin; the *mercy* we were *made whole by* is an engagement upon us not to offend him who healed us. This is the voice of every providence, *Go and sin no more.* This man began his new life very hopefully *in the temple,* yet Christ saw it necessary to give him this caution; for it is common for people, when they are sick, to *promise much,* when newly recovered to *perform something,* but after awhile to *forget all.* [3.] He gives him warning of his danger, in case he should return to his former sinful course: *Lest a worse thing come to thee.* Christ, who knows all men's hearts, knew that he was one of those that must be *frightened* from sin. Thirty-eight years' lameness, one would think, was a thing bad enough; yet there is something *worse* that will come to him if he relapse into sin after God has *given him such a deliverance* as this, Ezra 9:13, 14. The hospital where he lay was a melancholy place, but hell is much more so: the doom of apostates is a worse thing than thirty-eight years' lameness.

VI. Now, after this interview between Christ and his patient, observe in the two following verses, 1. The notice which the poor simple man gave to the Jews concerning Christ, *v.* 15. He told them it was Jesus that had *made him whole.* We have reason to think that he intended this for the honour of Christ and the benefit of the Jews, little thinking that he who had so much power and goodness could have *any* enemies; but those who wish well to Christ's kingdom must have the *wisdom of the serpent,* lest they do more hurt than good with their zeal, and must not cast pearls before swine. 2. The rage and enmity of the Jews against him: *Therefore did the* rulers of the Jews *persecute Jesus.* See, (1.) How absurd and unreasonable their enmity to Christ was. *Therefore,* because he had made a poor sick man well, and so eased the public charge, upon which, it is likely, he had subsisted; *therefore* they persecuted him, because he did good in Israel. (2.) How bloody and cruel it was: *They sought to slay him;* nothing less than his blood, his life, would satisfy them. (3.) How it was varnished over with a colour of zeal for the honour of the sabbath; for this was the pretended crime, *Because he had done these things on the sabbath day,* as if that circumstance were enough to vitiate the best and most divine actions, and to render *him* obnoxious whose deeds were otherwise most meritorious. Thus hypocrites often cover their real enmity against the *power* of godliness with a pretended zeal for the *form* of it.

Verses 17–30

We have here Christ's discourse upon occasion of his being accused as a sabbath-breaker, and it seems to be his vindication of himself before the sanhedrim, when he was arraigned before them: whether on the same day, or two or three days after, does not appear; probably the same day. Observe,

I. The doctrine laid down, by which he justified what he did on the sabbath day (*v.* 17): *He answered them.* This supposes that he had something laid to his charge: or what they suggested one to another, when they sought to slay him (*v.* 16), he *knew,* and gave this reply to, *My Father worketh hitherto, and I work.* At other times, in answer to the like charge, he had pleaded the example of David's eating the show-bread, of the priests' slaying the sacrifices, and of the people's watering their cattle on the sabbath day; but here he goes higher and alleges the example of his Father and his divine authority; waiving all other pleas, he insists upon that which was *instar omnium — equivalent to the whole,* and abides by it, which he had mentioned, Mt. 12:8. *The Son of man is Lord even of the sabbath day;* but he here enlarges on it. 1. He pleads that he was the Son of God, *plainly intimated in his calling God his Father;* and, if so, his holiness was *unquestionable* and his sovereignty *incontestable;* and he might make what alterations he pleased of the divine law. *Surely they will reverence the Son,* the heir of all things. 2. That he was a worker together with God. (1.) *My Father worketh hitherto.* The example of God's resting on the seventh day from all his work is, in the fourth commandment, made the ground of our observing it as a *sabbath* or *day of rest.* Now God rested only from such work as he had done the six days before; otherwise he *worketh hitherto,* he is every day working, sabbath days and week-days, upholding and governing all the creatures, and concurring by his common providence to all the motions and operations of nature, *to his own glory;* therefore, when we are appointed to rest on the sabbath day, yet we are not restrained from doing that which has a direct tendency *to the glory of God,* as the man's carrying his bed had. (2.) *I work;* not only therefore I *may* work, *like him,* in doing good on sabbath days as well as other days, but I also *work with him.* As God created all things by Christ, so he supports and governs all by him, Heb. 1:3. This sets what he does above all exception; he that is so great a worker must needs be an uncontrollable governor; he that does all is Lord of all, and therefore *Lord of the sabbath,* which particular branch of his authority he would now assert, because he was shortly to show it further, in the change of the day from the seventh to the first.

II. The offence that was taken at his doctrine (*v.* 18): *The Jews sought the more to kill him.* His defence was made his offence, as if by justifying himself he had made bad worse. Note, Those that will not be enlightened by the word of Christ will be enraged and exasperated by it, and nothing more vexes the enemies of Christ than his asserting his authority; see Ps. 2:3–5. They sought to kill him,

1. Because he had broken the sabbath; for, let him say what he would in his own justification, they are resolved, right or wrong, to *find him guilty* of sabbath breaking. When malice and envy sit upon the bench, reason and justice may even be silent at the bar, for whatever they can say will undoubtedly be over-ruled.

2. Not only so, but he had said also *that God was his Father.* Now they pretend a jealousy for *God's honour,* as before for the sabbath day, and charge Christ with it as a heinous crime that he made himself equal with God; and a heinous crime it had been if he had not really been so. It was the sin of Lucifer, *I will be like the Most High.* Now, (1.) This was justly inferred from what he said, that he was the *Son of God,* and that God was *his Father, patera idion — his own Father;* his, so as he was no one's else. He had said that he worked with his Father, by the same authority and power, and hereby he made himself equal with God. *Ecee intelligunt Judaei, quod non intelligunt Ariani — Behold, the Jews understand what the Arians do not.* (2.) Yet it was unjustly imputed to him as an offence that he equalled himself with God, for he was and is God, equal with the Father (Phil. 2:6); and therefore Christ, in answer to this charge, does not except against the innuendo as strained or forced, makes out his claim and proves that he is equal with God in power and glory.

III. Christ's discourse upon this occasion, which continues without interruption to the end of the chapter. In these verses he explains, and afterwards confirms, his commission, as Mediator and plenipotentiary in the treaty between God and man. And, as the honours he is hereby *entitled to* are such as it is not fit for any creature to receive, so the work he is hereby entrusted with is such as it is not possible for any creature to go through with, and therefore he is God, equal with the Father.

1. *In general.* He is one with the Father in all he does as Mediator, and there was a perfectly good understanding between them in the whole matter. It is ushered in with a solemn preface (*v.* 19): *Verily, verily, I say unto you;* I the Amen, the Amen, say it. This intimates that the things declared are, (1.) Very awful and great, and such as should command the most serious attention. (2.) Very sure, and such as should command an unfeigned assent. (3.) That they are matters purely of divine revelation; things which Christ has told us, and which we could not otherwise have come to the knowledge of. Two things he saith in general concerning the Son's oneness with the Father in working: —

[1.] That the Son *conforms to the Father* (*v.* 19): *The Son can do nothing of himself but what he sees the Father do; for these things does the Son.* The Lord Jesus, as Mediator, is *First, Obedient to his Father's will;* so entirely obedient that he *can do nothing of himself,* in the same sense as it is said, *God cannot* lie, *cannot deny* himself, which expresses the perfection of his truth, not any imperfection in his strength; so here, Christ was so entirely devoted to his Father's will that it was impossible for him in any thing to act separately. *Secondly,* He is *observant of his Father's counsel;* he can, he will, do nothing *but what he sees the Father do.* No man can *find out the work of God,* but the only-begotten Son, who lay in his bosom, sees what he does, is intimately acquainted with his purposes, and has the plan of them ever before him. What he did as Mediator, throughout his whole undertaking, was the exact transcript or counterpart of what the Father did; that is, what he designed, when he formed the plan of our redemption in his eternal counsels, and settled those measures in every thing which never could be *broken,* nor ever needed to be *altered.* It was the copy of that *great original;* it was Christ's faithfulness, as it was Moses's, that he did all *according to the pattern shown him in the mount.* This is expressed in the present tense, what he *sees the Father do,* for the same reason that, when he was here upon earth, it was said, He *is* in heaven (*ch.* 3:13), and *is* in the bosom of the Father (*ch.* 1:18); as he was even then by his divine nature present in heaven, so the things done in heaven were *present* to his knowledge. What the Father did in his counsels, the Son had ever in his view, and still he had his eye upon it, as David in spirit spoke of him, *I have set the Lord always before me,* Ps. 16:8. *Thirdly,* Yet he is *equal* with the Father in *working;* for *what things soever* the Father does *these also does the Son likewise;* he did the *same* things, not *such* things, but *tauta,* the *same* things; and he did them in the *same manner, homoiōs, likewise,* with the same authority, and liberty, and wisdom, the same energy and efficacy. Does the Father enact, repeal, and alter, positive laws? Does he over-rule the course of nature, know men's hearts? So does the Son. The power of the Mediator is a divine power.

[2.] That the Father *communicates* to the Son, *v.* 20. Observe,

First, The inducement to it: *The Father loveth the Son;* he declared, *This is my beloved Son.* He had not only a good will to the undertaking, but an infinite complacency in the undertaker. Christ was now hated of men, one whom the nation abhorred (Isa. 49:7); but he comforted himself with this, that his Father loved him.

Secondly, The instances of it. He shows it, 1. In what he *does* communicate to him: *He shows him all things that himself doth.* The Father's measures in making and ruling the world are shown to the Son, that he may take the same measures in framing and governing the church, which work was to be a duplicate of the work of creation and providence, and it is therefore called *the world to come.* He shows him all things *ha autos poiei — which he does,* that is, which the *Son* does, so it might be construed; all that the Son does is by direction from the Father; he *shows* him. 2. In what he *will* communicate; he will *show him,* that is, will appoint and direct him to do *greater works than these.* (1.) Works of greater *power* than the *curing of the impotent man;* for he should raise the dead, and should himself rise from the dead. By the power of nature, with the use of means, a disease may possibly in time be cured; but nature can never, by the use of any means, in any time raise the dead. (2.) Works of greater *authority* than warranting the man to *carry his bed on the sabbath day.* They thought this a daring attempt; but what was this to his abrogating the whole ceremonial law, and instituting new ordinances, which he would shortly do, *"that you may marvel!"* Now they looked upon his works with contempt and indignation, but he will shortly do that which they will look upon with amazement, Lu. 7:16. Many are brought to marvel at Christ's works, whereby he has the honour of them, who are not brought to believe, by which they would have the benefit of them.

2. *In particular.* He proves his equality with the Father, by specifying some of those works which he does that are the peculiar works of God. This is enlarged upon, *v.* 21–30. He does, and shall do, that which is the peculiar work of God's sovereign dominion and jurisdiction — *judging* and *executing judgment, v.* 22–24, 27. These two are interwoven, as being nearly connected; and what is said once is repeated and inculcated; put both together, and they will prove that Christ said not amiss when he made himself *equal with God.*

(1.) Observe what is here said concerning the Mediator's power to *raise the dead* and *give life.* See [1.] His *authority* to do it (*v.* 21): *As the Father raiseth up the dead,* so *the Son quickeneth whom he will. First,* It is God's prerogative to raise the dead, and give life, even his who first *breathed* into man the *breath of life,* and so made him a *living soul;* see Deu. 32:30; 1 Sa. 2:6; Ps. 68:20; Rom. 4:17. This God had done by the prophets Elijah and Elisha, and it was a confirmation of their mission. A *resurrection from the dead* never lay in the common road of nature, nor ever fell within the thought of those that studied only the compass of nature's power, one of whose received axioms was point blank against it: *A privatione ad habitum non datur regressus — Existence, when once extinguished, cannot be rekindled.* It was therefore ridiculed at Athens as an *absurd* thing, Acts 17:32. It is purely the work of a divine power, and the knowledge of it purely by divine revelation. This the Jews would own. *Secondly,* The Mediator is invested with this prerogative: *He quickens whom he will;* raises to life whom he pleases, and when he pleases.

He does not enliven things by natural necessity, as the sun does, whose beams revive of course; but he acts as a free agent, has the dispensing of his power in his own hand, and is never either *con*strained, or *re*strained, in the use of it. As he has the power, so he has the wisdom and sovereignty, of a God; has the *key of the grave and of death* (Rev. 1:18), not as a servant, to open and shut as he is bidden, for he has it as the *key of David,* which he is master of, Rev. 3:7. An absolute prince is described by this (Dan. 5:19): *Whom he would he slew or kept alive;* it is true of Christ without hyperbole.

[2.] His *ability* to do it. *Therefore* he has power to quicken whom he will as the Father does, because *he has life in himself, as the Father has, v.* 26. *First,* It is certain that the Father *has life in himself.* Not only he is a *self-existent* Being, who does not derive from, or depend upon, any other (Ex. 3:14), but he is a sovereign giver of life; he has the disposal of life in himself; and of all good (for so *life* sometimes signifies); it is all derived from him, and dependent on him. He is to his creatures the fountain of life, and all good; author of their being and well-being; the living God, and the God of all living. *Secondly,* It is as certain that he has *given to the Son to have life in himself.* As the Father is the original of all natural life and good, being the great Creator, so the Son, as Redeemer, is the original of all spiritual life and good; is that to the church which the Father is to the world; see 1 Co. 8:6; Col. 1:19. The kingdom of grace, and all the life in that kingdom, are as fully and absolutely in the hand of the Redeemer as the kingdom of providence is in the hand of the Creator; and as God, who gives being to all things, has his being of himself, so Christ, who gives life, raised himself to life by his own power, *ch.* 10:18.

[3.] His *acting* according to this authority and ability. Having *life in himself,* and being authorized to *quicken whom he will,* by virtue hereof there are, accordingly, two resurrections performed by his powerful word, both which are here spoken of: —

First, A resurrection that *now is* (*v.* 29), a resurrection from the death of sin to the life of righteousness, by the power of Christ's grace. *The hour is coming, and now is.* It is a resurrection begun already, and further to be carried on, *when the dead shall hear the voice of the Son of God.* This is plainly distinguished from that in *v.* 28, which speaks of the resurrection at the end of time. This says nothing, as that does, of the dead in their graces, and of all of them, and their coming forth. Now, 1. Some think this was fulfilled in those whom he miraculously raised to life, Jairus's daughter, the widow's son, and Lazarus; and it is observable that all whom Christ raised were *spoken to,* as, *Damsel, arise; Young man, arise; Lazarus, come forth;* whereas those raised under the Old Testament were raised, not by a word, but other applications, 1 Ki. 17:21; 2 Ki. 4:34; 13:21. Some understand it of those saints that rose with Christ; but we do not read of the *voice of the Son of God* calling them. But, 2. I rather understand it of the power of the doctrine of Christ, for the recovering and quickening of those that were *dead in trespasses and sins,* Eph. 2:1. The *hour* was *coming* when dead souls should be made alive by the *preaching* of the gospel, and a spirit of life from God accompanying it: nay, it *then was,* while Christ was upon earth. It may refer especially to the *calling of the Gentiles,* which is said to be as life from the dead, and, some think, was prefigured by Ezekiel's vision (*ch.* 37:1), and foretold, Isa. 26:19. *Thy dead men shall live.* But it is to be applied to all the wonderful success of the gospel, among both Jews and Gentiles; an hour which still *is,* and is still *coming,* till all the elect be effectually called. Note, (1.) Sinners are spiritually *dead,* destitute of spiritual life, sense, strength, and motion, dead to God, miserable, but neither sensible of their misery nor able to help themselves out of it. (2.) The conversion of a soul to God is its resurrection from death to life; then it begins to live when it begins to *live to God,* to breathe after him, and move towards him. (3.) It is by the *voice of the Son of God* that souls are raised to spiritual life; it is wrought by his power, and that power conveyed and communicated by his word: *The dead shall hear,* shall be made to hear, to understand, receive, and believe, the *voice of the Son of God,* to hear it as his voice; then the Spirit by it gives life, otherwise the *letter kills.* (4.) The voice of Christ must be heard by us, that we may live by it. They that hear, and attend to what they hear, shall live. *Hear and your soul shall live,* Isa. 55:3.

Secondly, A resurrection yet *to come;* this is spoken of, *v.* 28, 29, introduced with, *"Marvel not at this,* which I have said of the *first* resurrection, do not reject it as incredible and absurd, for at the end of time you shall all see a more sensible and amazing proof of the power and authority of the Son of man." As *his own* resurrection was reserved to be the final and concluding proof of his personal commission, so the resurrection of *all men* is reserved to be a like proof of his commission to be executed by his spirit. Now observe here,

a. When this resurrection shall be: *The hour is coming;* it is *fixed* to an hour, so very punctual is this great appointment. The judgment is not adjourned *sine die — to some time not yet pitched upon;* no, *he hath appointed a day. The hour is coming.* (*a.*) It is *not yet* come, it is not the hour spoken of at *v.* 25, that is coming, and *now is.* Those erred dangerously who said that the *resurrection was past already,* 2 Tim. 2:18, But, (*b.*) It *will certainly* come, it is coming on, nearer every day than other; it is at the door. How far off it is we know not; but we know that it is infallibly designed and unalterably determined.

b. Who shall be raised: *All that are in the graves,* all that have died from the beginning of time, and all that shall die to the end of time. It was said (Dan. 12:2), *Many* shall arise; Christ here tells us that those *many* shall be *all; all* must appear before the Judge, and therefore *all* must be raised; every person, and the whole of every person; every soul shall return to its body, and every *bone to its bone.* The grave is the prison of dead bodies, where they are *detained;* their furnace, where they are *consumed* (Job 24:19); yet, in prospect of their resurrection, we may call it their *bed,* where they sleep to be *awaked* again; their treasury, where they are laid up to be used again. Even those that are not *put into graves* shall arise; but, because most are put into graves, Christ uses this expression, *all that are in the graves.* The Jews used the word *sheol* for the *grave,* which signifies *the state of the dead;* all that are in that state *shall hear.*

c. How they shall be raised. Two things are here told us: — (*a.*) The efficient of this resurrection: *They shall hear his voice;* that is, he shall cause them to hear it, as Lazarus was made to hear that word, *Come forth;* a divine power shall go along with the voice, to put life into them, and enable them to obey it. When Christ rose, there was no voice heard, not a word spoken, because he rose by his own power; but at the resurrection of the children of men we find three voices spoken of, 1 Th. 4:16. The Lord shall descend with a *shout,* the shout of a king, with *the voice of the archangel;* either Christ himself, the prince of the angels, or the commander-in-chief, under him, of the heavenly hosts; and with *the trumpet of God:* the soldier's trumpet sounding the alarm of war, the judge's trumpet publishing the summons to the court. (*b.*) The effect of it: *They shall come forth* out of their graves, as prisoners out of their prison-house; they shall *arise out* of the dust, and shake themselves from it; see Isa. 52:1, 2, 11. But this is not all; they shall *appear* before Christ's tribunal, shall *come forth* as those that are to be tried, *come forth* to the bar, publicly to receive their doom.

d. To what they shall be raised; to a different state of happiness or misery, according to their different character; to a state of retribution, according to what they did in the state of probation.

(*a.*) *They that have done good shall come forth to the resurrection of life;* they shall live again, to live for ever. Note, [*a.*] Whatever name men are called by, or whatever plausible profession they make, it will be well in the great day with those only that have *done good,* have done that which is pleasing to God and profitable to others. [*b.*] The resurrection of the body will be a resurrection of life to all those, and those only, that have been sincere and constant in *doing good.* They shall not only be publicly *acquitted,* as a pardoned criminal, we say, has *his life,* but they shall be *admitted* into the presence of God, and that is life, it is better than life; they shall be *attended* with comforts in perfection. To live is to be *happy,* and they shall be *advanced* above the fear of death; that is *life* indeed in which *mortality* is for ever *swallowed* up.

(*b.*) *They that have done evil to the resurrection of damnation;* they shall live again, to be for ever dying. The Pharisees thought that the resurrection pertained only to the just, but Christ here rectifies that mistake. Note, [*a.*] *Evil doers,* whatever they pretend, will be treated in the day of judgment as *evil men.* [*b.*] The resurrection will be to evil doers, who did not by repentance undo what they had done amiss, a *resurrection* of damnation. They shall come forth to be publicly convicted of rebellion against God, and publicly *condemned* to everlasting punishment; to be *sentenced* to it, and immediately *sent* to it without reprieve. Such will the resurrection be.

(2.) Observe what is here said concerning the Mediator's *authority to execute judgment, v.* 22–24, 27. As he has an almighty power, so he has a sovereign jurisdiction; and who so fit to preside in the great affairs of the other life as he who is the Father and fountain of life? Here is,

[1.] Christ's commission or delegation to the office of a judge, which is twice spoken of here (*v.* 22): *He hath committed all judgment to the Son;* and again (*v.* 27): *he hath given him authority.*

First, The *Father judges no man;* not that the Father hath resigned the government, but he is pleased to govern by Jesus Christ; so that man is not under the terror of dealing with God immediately, but has the comfort of access to him by a Mediator. Having made us, he *may* do what he *pleases* with us, as the potter with the clay; yet he does not take advantage of this, but draws us *with the cords of a man.* 2. He does not determine our everlasting condition by the *covenant of innocency,* nor take the advantage he has against us for the violation of that covenant. The Mediator having undertaken to make a *vicarious* satisfaction, the matter is referred to him, and God is willing to enter upon a new treaty; *not under the law* of the Creator, *but the grace* of the Redeemer.

Secondly, He has committed all judgment to the Son, has constituted him *Lord of all* (Acts 10:36; Rom. 14:9), as Joseph in Egypt, Gen. 41:40. This was prophesied of, Ps. 72:1; Isa. 11:3, 4; Jer. 23:5; Mic. 5:1–4; Ps. 67:4; 96:13; 98:9. All judgment is committed to our Lord Jesus; for 1. He is *entrusted* with the administration of the *providential kingdom,* is *head over all things* (Eph. 1:11), head of every man, 1 Co. 11:3. All things consist by him, Col. 1:17. 2. He is empowered to make laws immediately to bind conscience. *I say unto you* is now the form in which the statues of the kingdom of heaven run. *Be it enacted* by the Lord Jesus, and by *his* authority. All the acts now in force are touched with his sceptre. 3. He is authorized to appoint and settle the terms of the new covenant, and to draw up the articles of peace between God and man; it is God in Christ that reconciles the world, and to him he has given power to confer eternal life. The book of life is the Lamb's book; by his award we must stand or fall. 4. He is commissioned to carry on and complete the war with the powers of darkness; to cast out and *give judgment against the prince of this world, ch.* 12:31. He is commissioned not only to *judge,* but to *make war,* Rev. 19:11. All that will fight *for God against Satan* must enlist themselves under *his* banner. 5. He is constituted sole manager of the judgment of the great day. The ancients generally understood these words of that *crowning act* of his judicial power. The final and universal judgment is committed to the Son of man; the tribunal is *his,* it is the judgment-seat of Christ; the retinue is his, *his* mighty angels; he will try the causes, and pass the sentence. Acts 17:31.

Thirdly, He has *given him authority to execute judgment also, v.* 27. Observe, 1. What the authority is which our Redeemer is invested with: *An authority to execute judgment;* he has not only a legislative and judicial power, but an *executive* power too. The phrase here is used particularly for the judgment of condemnation, Jude 15. *poiēsai krisin — to execute judgment* upon all; the same with his *taking vengeance,* 2 Th. 1:8. The ruin of impenitent sinners comes from the hand of Christ; he that *executes judgment* upon them is the same that would have *wrought salvation* for them, which makes the sentence unexceptionable; and there is no relief against the sentence of the Redeemer; salvation itself cannot save those whom the Saviour *condemns,* which makes the ruin *remediless.* 2. Whence he has that authority: the Father *gave it to him.* Christ's authority as Mediator is delegated and derived; he acts as the Father's Viceregent, as the Lord's Anointed, the Lord's Christ. Now all this redounds very much to the honour of Christ, acquitting him from the guilt of blasphemy, in making himself *equal with God;* and very much to the comfort of all believers, who may with the greatest assurance venture their all in such hands.

[2.] Here are the reasons (reasons of state) for which this commission was given him. He has all judgment committed to him for two reasons: —

First, Because he is the *Son of man;* which denotes these three things: — 1. His humiliation and gracious condescension. Man is a worm, the son of man a worm; yet this was the nature, this the character, which the Redeemer assumed, in pursuance of the counsels of love; to this low estate he stooped, and submitted to all the mortifications attending it, because it was *his Father's will;* in recompence therefore of this wonderful obedience, God did thus dignify him. Because he condescended to be the *Son of man,* his Father made him *Lord of all,* Phil. 2:8, 9. 2. His affinity and alliance to us. The Father has committed the government of the children of men to him, because, being the *Son of man,* he is of the same nature with those whom he is *set over,* and therefore the more unexceptionable, and the more acceptable, as a Judge. *Their governor shall proceed from the midst of them,* Jer. 30:21. Of this that law was typical; *One of thy brethren shalt thou set king over thee,* Deu. 17:15. 3. His being the Messiah promised. In that famous vision of his kingdom and glory, Dan. 7:13, 14, he is called the *Son of man;* and Ps. 8:4–6. Thou has made the Son of man have *dominion over the works of thy hands.* He is the Messiah, and therefore is invested with all this power. The Jews usually called the Christ the *Son of David;* but Christ usually called himself the *Son of man,* which was the more humble title, and bespeaks him a prince and Saviour, not the Jewish nation only, but to the whole race of mankind.

Secondly, That all men should honour the Son, v. 23. The honouring of Jesus Christ is here spoken of as God's great design (the Son intended to glorify the Father, and therefore the Father intended to glorify the Son, *ch.* 12:32); and as man's great duty, in compliance with that design. If God will have the Son honoured, it is the duty of all to whom he is made known to honour him. Observe here, 1. The *respect* that is to be paid to our Lord Jesus: We must *honour the Son,* must look upon him as one that is to be *honoured,* both on account of his transcendent excellences and perfections in himself, and of the relations he stands in to us, and must study to give him honour accordingly; must *confess that he is Lord,* and worship him; must honour him who was dishonoured for us. 2. The degree of it: *Even as they honour the Father.* This *supposes* it to be our duty to *honour the Father;* for revealed religion is founded on natural religion, and *directs* us to *honour the Son,* to honour him with *divine* honour; we must honour the Redeemer with the same honour with which we honour the Creator. So far was it from blasphemy for him to make himself *equal with God* that it is the highest injury that can be for us to make him otherwise. The truths and laws of the Christian religion, so far as they are revealed, are as sacred and honourable as those of natural religion, and to be equally had in estimation; for we lie under the same obligations to Christ, the Author of our being; and have as necessary a dependence upon the Redeemer's grace as upon the Creator's providence, which is a sufficient ground for this law — *to honour the Son as we honour the Father.* To enforce this law, it is added, *He that honours not the Son honours not the Father* who has sent him. Some pretend a reverence for the Creator, and speak *honourably* of him, who make light of the Redeemer, and speak *contemptibly* of him; but let such know that the honours and interests of the Father and Son are so inseparably twisted and interwoven that the Father never reckons himself *honoured* by any that *dishonour* the Son. Note, (1.) Indignities done to the Lord Jesus reflect upon God himself, and will so be construed and reckoned for in the court of heaven. The Son having so far espoused the Father's honour as to take *to himself* the *reproaches cast on him* (Rom. 15:3), the Father does no less espouse the Son's honour, and counts himself struck at through him. (2.) The reason of this is because the Son is sent and commissioned by the Father; it is the *Father who hath sent him.* Affronts to an ambassador are justly resented by the prince that sends him. And by this rule those who truly *honour the Son honour the Father also;* see Phil. 2:11.

[3.] Here is the rule by which the Son goes in executing this commission, so those words seem to come in (*v.* 24): *He that heareth and believeth* hath *everlasting life.* Here we have the substance of the whole gospel; the preface commands *attention* to a thing most weighty, and *assent* to a thing most certain: *"Verily, verily, I say unto you, I,* to whom you hear *all judgment is committed,* I, in whose lips is a divine sentence; take from *me* the Christian's *character* and *charter."*

First, The *character* of a Christian: *He that heareth my word, and believeth on him that sent me.* To be a Christian indeed is, 1. To *hear the word of Christ.* It is not enough to be within hearing of it, but we must *attend on* it, as scholars on the instructions of their teachers; and *attend to* it, as servants to the commands of their masters; we must hear and obey it, must abide by the gospel of Christ as the fixed rule of our faith and practice. 2. To *believe on him that sent him;* for Christ's design is to *bring us to God;* and, as he is the first original of all grace, so is he the last object of all faith. Christ is our *way;* God is our rest. We must believe on God as *having sent* Jesus Christ, and recommended himself to our faith and love, by manifesting his glory in *the face of Jesus Christ* (2 Co. 4:6), as *his* Father and *our Father.*

Secondly, The *charter* of a Christian, in which all that are Christians indeed are interested. See what we get by Christ. 1. A charter of pardon: *He shall not come into condemnation.* The grace of the gospel is a full discharge from the curse of the law. A believer shall not only not *lie under* condemnation eternally, but shall not *come into condemnation* now, not come into the danger of it (Rom. 8:1), not *come into judgment,* not be so much as arraigned. 2. A charter of privileges: He is *passed out of death to life,* is invested in a present happiness in spiritual life and entitled to a future happiness in eternal life. The tenour of the first covenant was, *Do this and live;* the man that doeth them shall live in them. Now this proves Christ equal with the Father that he has power to propose the *same* benefit to the *hearers of his word* that had been proposed to the *keepers of the old law,* that is, life: *Hear and live, believe and live,* is what we may venture our souls upon, when we are disabled to *do and live;* see *ch.* 17:2.

[4.] Here is the righteousness of his proceedings pursuant to this commission, *v.* 30. All judgment being committed to him, we cannot but ask *how he manages it.* And here he answers, *My judgment is just.* All Christ's acts of government, both *legislative* and *judicial,* are exactly agreeable to the rules of equity; see Prov. 8:8. There can lie no exceptions against any of the determinations of the Redeemer; and therefore, as there shall be no repeal of any of his statutes, so there shall be no appeal from any of his sentences. His judgments are certainly just, for they are directed,

First, By the Father's *wisdom: I can of my ownself* do nothing, nothing without the Father, but *as I hear I judge,* as he had said before (*v.* 19), The Son *can do nothing but what he sees the Father do;* so here, nothing but what he hears the Father *say: As I hear,* 1. From the secret eternal counsels of the Father, *so I judge.* Would we know what we may depend upon in our dealing with God? *Hear the word* of Christ. We need not dive into the divine counsels, those *secret things* which belong not to us, but attend to the revealed dictates of Christ's government and judgment, which will furnish us with an unerring guide; for what Christ has adjudged is an exact copy or counterpart of what the Father has decreed. 2. From the published records of the Old Testament. Christ, in all the execution of his undertaking, had an eye to the scripture, and made it his business to conform to this, and *fulfil* it: *As it was written in the volume of the book.* Thus he taught us to do *nothing of ourselves,* but, *as we hear* from the word of God, *so to judge* of things, and act accordingly.

Secondly, By the Father's *will: My judgment is just,* and cannot be otherwise, *because I seek not my own will,* but *his who sent me.* Not as if the will of Christ were contrary to the will of the Father, as the flesh is contrary to the spirit in us; but, 1. Christ had, as man, the natural and innocent affections of the human nature, *sense of pain* and *pleasure,* an inclination to life, an aversion to death: yet he *pleased not himself,* did not confer with these, nor consult these, when he was to go on his undertaking, but acquiesced entirely in the will of his Father. 2. What he did as Mediator was not the result of any *peculiar* or *particular* purpose and design of his own; what he did *seek* to do was not for his own mind's sake, but he was therein guided by his Father's will, and the purpose which he had *purposed to himself.* This our Saviour did upon all occasions *refer himself to* and govern himself by.

Thus our Lord Jesus has opened his commission (whether to the conviction of his enemies or no) to his own honour and the everlasting comfort of all his friends, who here see him *able to save to the uttermost.*

Verses 31–47

In these verses our Lord Jesus proves and confirms the commission he had produced, and makes it out that he was sent of God to be the Messiah.

I. He *sets aside* his own testimony of himself (*v.* 31): *"If I bear witness of myself,* though it is infallibly true (*ch.* 8:14), yet, according to the common rule of judgment among men, you will not admit it as *legal proof,* nor allow it to be *given in evidence."* Now, 1. This reflects reproach upon the sons of men, and their veracity and integrity. Surely we may say deliberately, what David said in haste, *All men are liars,* else it would never have been such a received maxim that a man's testimony of himself is suspicious, and not to be relied on; it is a sign that self-love is stronger than the love of truth. And yet, 2. It reflects honour on the Son of God, and bespeaks his wonderful condescension, that, though he is the *faithful witness,* the truth itself, who may challenge to be credited *upon his honour,* and his own single testimony, yet he is pleased to *waive his privilege,* and, for the confirmation of our faith, refers himself to his *vouchers,* that we may have full satisfaction.

II. He produces other witnesses that bear testimony to him that he was sent of God.

1. The Father himself bore testimony to him (*v.* 32): *There is another that beareth witness.* I take this to be meant of God the Father, for Christ mentions *his* testimony with his own (*ch.* 8:18): *I bear witness of myself, and the Father beareth witness of me.* Observe,

(1.) The seal which the Father put to his commission: He *beareth witness of me,* not only has done so by a voice from heaven, but still does so by the tokens of his presence with me. See who they are to whom God will bear witness. [1.] Those whom he *sends* and *employs;* where he gives commissions he give credentials. [2.] Those who *bear witness* to him; so Christ did. God will own and honour those that own and honour him. [3.] Those who decline *bearing witness of themselves;* so Christ did. God will take care that those who humble and abase themselves, and seek not their own glory, shall not *lose by it.*

(2.) The satisfaction Christ had in this testimony: *"I know that the witness which he witnesseth of me is true.* I am very well assured that I have a divine mission, and do not in the least hesitate concerning it; thus he had the *witness in himself."* The devil tempted him to question his being the Son of God, but he never yielded.

2. John Baptist witnessed to Christ, *v.* 33, etc. John came to *bear witness of the light* (*ch.* 1:7); his business was to prepare his way, and direct people to him: *Behold the Lamb of God.*

(1.) Now the testimony of John was, [1.] A *solemn* and public testimony: "You sent an embassy of priests and Levites to John, which gave him an opportunity of publishing what he had to say; it was not a popular, but a judicial testimony." [2.] It was a *true* testimony: *He bore witness to the truth,* as a witness ought to do, the *whole truth,* and *nothing but the truth.* Christ does not say, *He bore witness to me* (though every one knew he did), but, like an honest man, *He bore witness to the truth.* Now John was confessedly such a holy, good man, so mortified to the world, and so conversant with divine things, that it could not be imagined he should be guilty of such a forgery and imposture as to say what he did concerning Christ if it had not been so, and if he had not been sure of it.

(2.) Two things are added concerning John's testimony: —

[1.] That it was a testimony *ex abundanti — more than he needed to vouch* (*v.* 34): *I receive not testimony from man.* Though Christ saw fit to quote John's testimony, it was with a protestation that it shall not be deemed or construed so as to prejudice the prerogative of his self-sufficiency. Christ needs no letters or commendation, no testimonials or certificates, but what his own worth and excellency bring with him; why then did Christ here urge the testimony of John? Why, *these things I say, that you may be saved.* This he aimed at in all this discourse, to save not his own life, but the souls of others; he produced John's testimony because, being one *of themselves,* it was to be hoped that they would hearken to it. Note, *First,* Christ desires and designs the salvation even of his enemies and persecutors. *Secondly,* The word of Christ is the ordinary means of salvation. *Thirdly,* Christ in his word considers our infirmities and condescends to our capacities, consulting not so much what it befits so great a prince to say as what we can bear, and what will be most likely to do us good.

[2.] That it was a testimony *ad hominem — to the man,* because John Baptist was one whom *they* had a respect for (*v.* 35): *He was a light* among you.

First, The character of John Baptist: *He was a burning and a shining light.* Christ often spoke honourably of John; he was now in prison under a cloud, yet Christ gives him his *due praise,* which we must be ready to do to all that faithfully serve God. 1. He was a *light,* not *phōs — lux, light* (so

Christ was *the* light), but *lyknos — lucerna, a luminary,* a derived subordinate light. His office was to enlighten a dark world with notices of the Messiah's approach, to whom he was as the *morning star.* 2. He was a *burning* light, which denotes *sincerity;* painted fire may be made to shine, but that which burns is true fire. It denotes also his *activity,* zeal, and fervency, burning in love to God and the souls of men; fire is always working on itself or something else, so is a good minister. 3. He was a *shining* light, which denotes either his *exemplary conversation,* in which our light should shine (Mt. 5:16), or an *eminent* diffusive influence. He was illustrious in the sight of others; though he affected obscurity and retirement, and was *in the deserts,* yet such were his doctrine, his baptism, his life, that he became very *remarkable,* and attracted the eyes of the nation.

Secondly, The affections of the people to him: *you were willing for a season to rejoice in his light.* 1. It was a *transport* that they were *in,* upon the appearing of John: *"You were willing — ēthelēsate, you delighted to rejoice in his light;* you were very proud that you had such a man among you, who was the honour of your country; you were willing *agalliasthēnai* — willing to *dance,* and make a noise about this light, as boys about a bonfire." 2. It was but *transient,* and soon over: "You were fond of him, *pros hōran — for an hour,* for *a season,* as little children are fond of a new thing, you were pleased with John awhile, but soon grew weary of him and his ministry, and said that *he had a devil,* and now you have him in prison." Note, Many, that seem to be affected and pleased with the gospel at first, afterwards despise and reject it; it is common for forward and noisy professors to cool and fall off. These here rejoiced in John's light, but never walked in it, and therefore did not keep to it; they were like the stony ground. While Herod was a friend to John Baptist, the people caressed him; but when he fell under Herod's frowns he lost their favours: *"You were willing* to countenance John, *pros hōran* that is, for *temporal ends"* (so some take it); "you were glad of him, in hopes to make a tool of him, by his interest and under the shelter of his name to have shaken off the Roman yoke, and recovered the civil liberty and honour of your country." Now, (1.) Christ mentions their respect to John, to *condemn* them for their present opposition to himself, to whom John bore witness. If they had continued their veneration for John, as they ought to have done, they would have embraced Christ. (2.) He mentions the passing away of their respect, to justify God in depriving them, as he had now done, of John's ministry, and putting that light under a bushel.

3. Christ's own works witnessed to him (*v.* 36): *I have a testimony greater than that of John;* for *if we believe the witness of men* sent of God, as John was, the *witness of God* immediately, and not by the ministry of men, *is greater,* 1 Jn. 5:9. Observe, Though the witness of John was a less *cogent* and less *considerable* witness, yet our Lord was pleased to make use of it. We must be glad of all the supports that offer themselves for the confirmation of our faith, though they may not amount to a demonstration, and we must not *invalidate* any, under pretence that there are others more *conclusive;* we have occasion for them all. Now this greater testimony was that of the *works* which *his Father had given him to finish.* That is, (1.) In general the whole course of his life and ministry — his revealing God and his will to us, setting up his kingdom among men, reforming the world, destroying Satan's kingdom, restoring fallen man to his primitive purity and felicity, and shedding abroad in men's hearts the love of God and of one another — all that work of which he said when he died, *It is finished,* it was all, from first to last, *opus Deo dignum — a work worthy of God;* all he said and did was *holy* and *heavenly,* and a divine purity, power, and grace shone in it, proving abundantly that he was *sent of God.* (2.) In particular. The miracles he wrought for the proof of his divine mission witnessed of him. Now it is here said, [1.] That these works were *given him by the Father,* that is, he was both *appointed* and *empowered* to work them; for, as Mediator, he *derived* both commission and strength from his Father. [2.] They were given to him to *finish;* he must do all those works of wonder which the counsel and foreknowledge of God had before determined to be done; and his finishing them proves a divine power; for as *for God his work is perfect.* [3.] These works did *bear witness of him,* did prove that he was sent of God, and that what he said concerning himself was true; see Heb. 2:4; Acts 2:22. That the Father had sent him as *a Father,* not as a master sends his servant on an errand, but as a father sends his son to take possession for himself; if God had not sent him, he would not have *seconded* him, would not have *sealed* him, as he did by the works he gave him to do; for the world's Creator will never be its deceiver.

4. He produces, more fully than before, his Father's testimony concerning him (*v.* 37): *The Father that sent me hath borne witness of me.* The prince is not accustomed to follow his ambassador himself, to confirm his commission *viva voce — by speaking;* but God was pleased to bear witness of his Son himself by a voice from heaven at his baptism (Mt. 3:17): This is my ambassador, *This is my beloved Son.* The Jews reckoned *Bath-kol; — the daughter of a voice,* a voice from heaven, one of the ways by which God made known his mind; and in that way he had owned Christ publicly and solemnly, and repeated it, Mt. 17:5. Note, (1.) Those whom God *sends* he will *bear witness* of; where he gives a commission, he will not fail to seal it; he that never *left himself without witness* (Acts 14:17) will never leave any of his servants so, who go upon his errand. (2.) Where God demands belief, he will not fail to give sufficient *evidence,* as he has done concerning Christ. That which was to be witnessed concerning Christ was chiefly this, that the God we had offended was willing to accept of him as a Mediator. Now concerning this he has *himself* given us full satisfaction (and he was fittest to do it), declaring himself well-pleased in him; if we be so, the work is done. Now, it might be suggested, if God himself thus bore witness of Christ, how came it to pass that he was not universally received by the Jewish nation and their rulers? To this Christ here answers that it was not to be thought strange, nor could their infidelity weaken his credibility, for two reasons: — [1.] Because they were not acquainted with such extraordinary revelations of God and his will: *You have neither heard his voice at any time, nor seen his shape,* or *appearance.* They showed themselves to be as ignorant of God, though they professed relation to him, as we are of a man we never either saw or heard. "But why do I talk to you of God's bearing witness of me? He is one you know nothing of, nor have any acquaintance or communion with." Note, Ignorance of God is the true reason of men's rejecting the record he has given concerning his Son. A right understanding of *natural religion* would discover to us such admirable congruities in the *Christian* religion as would greatly dispose our minds to the entertainment of it. Some give this sense of it: "The Father bore witness of me by a *voice,* and the *descent of a dove,* which is such an extraordinary thing that you never saw or heard the like; and yet for my sake there was such a voice and appearance; yea, and you might have *heard that voice,* you might have *seen that appearance,* as others did, if you had closely attended the ministry of John, but by slighting it you missed of that testimony." [2.] Because they were not affected, no, not with the ordinary ways by which God had revealed himself to them: *You have not his word abiding in you, v.* 38. They had the scriptures of the Old Testament; might they not by them be disposed to receive Christ? Yes, if they had had their due influence upon them. But, *First,* The word of God was not in them; it was *among them,* in their country, in their hands, but not *in them,* in their hearts; not ruling in their souls, but only shining in their eyes and sounding in their ears. What did it avail them that they had the oracles of God *committed* to them (Rom. 3:2), when they had not these oracles *commanding* in them? If they had, they would readily have embraced Christ. *Secondly,* It did not *abide.* Many have the word of God coming into them, and making some impressions for awhile, but it does not *abide* with them; it is not constantly in them, as a man at home, but only now and then, as a *wayfaring man.* If the word *abide in* us, if we converse with it by frequent meditation, consult with it upon every occasion, and conform to it in our conversation, we shall then readily receive the witness of the Father concerning Christ; see *ch.* 7:17. But how did it appear that they *had not the word of God abiding in them?* It appeared by this, *Whom he hath sent, him ye believe not.* There was so much said in the Old Testament concerning Christ, to direct people when and where to look for him, and so to facilitate the discovery of him, that, if they had duly considered these things, they could not have avoided the conviction of Christ's being sent of God; so that their not believing in Christ was a certain sign that the word of God did not abide in them. Note, The in-dwelling of the word, and Spirit, and grace of God in us, is best tried by its effects, particularly by our *receiving what he sends,* the commands, the messengers, the providences he sends, especially Christ whom he hath sent.

5. The last witness he calls is the Old Testament, which witnessed of him, and to it he appeals (*v.* 39, etc.): *Search the scriptures, ereunate.*

(1.) This may be read, either, [1.] *"You search the scriptures,* and you do well to do so; you read them daily in your synagogues, you have rabbies, and doctors, and scribes, that make it their business to study them, and criticize upon them." The Jews boasted of the flourishing of scripture-learning in the days of Hillel, who died about twelve years after Christ's birth, and reckoned some of those who were then members of the sanhedrim the *beauties of their wisdom* and the *glories of their law;* and Christ owns that they did indeed search the scriptures, but it was in search of their *own glory: "You search the scriptures,* and therefore, if you were not *wilfully blind,* you would *believe in me."* Note, It is possible for men to be very studious in the letter of the scripture, and yet to be strangers to the power and influence of it. Or, [2.] As we read it: *Search the scriptures;* and so, *First,* It was spoken to *them* in the nature of an *appeal:* "You profess to receive and believe the scripture; here I will *join issue* with you, let this be the judge, provided you will not *rest in the letter" (haerere in cortice),* "but will *search* into it." Note, when appeals are made to the scriptures, they must be searched. Search the whole book of scripture *throughout,* compare one passage with another, and explain one by another. We must likewise search particular passages *to the bottom,* and see not what they *seem* to say *prima facie — at the first appearance,* but what they say *indeed. Secondly,* It is spoken to *us* in the nature of an *advice,* or a command to all Christians to search the scriptures. Note, All those who would *find Christ* must *search the scriptures;* not only read them, and hear them, but search them, which denotes, 1. *Diligence* in seeking, labour, and study, and close application of mind. 2. *Desire* and *design* of finding. We must aim at some spiritual benefit and advantage in reading and studying the scripture, and often ask, "What am I now searching for?" We must search as for *hidden treasures* (Prov. 2:4), as those that *sink* for gold or silver, or that *dive* for pearl, Job 28:1–11. This ennobled the Bereans, Acts 17:11.

(2.) Now there are two things which we are here directed to have in our eye, in our searching the scripture: *heaven* our end, and *Christ* our way. [1.] We must search the scriptures for *heaven* as our *great end: For in them you think you have eternal life.* The scripture assures us of an eternal state set before us, and offers to us an eternal life in that state: it contains the *chart* that *describes* it, the *charter* that *conveys* it, the *direction* in the way that leads to it, and the *foundation* upon which the hope of it is built; and this is worth searching for where we are sure to find it. But to the Jews Christ saith only, *You think* you have *eternal life* in the scriptures, because, though they did retain the belief and hope of eternal life, and grounded their expectations of it upon the scriptures, yet herein they missed it, that they looked for it by the bare reading and studying of the scripture. It was a common but corrupt saying among them, *He that has the words of the law has eternal life;* they thought they were sure of heaven if they could say by *heart,* or rather by *rote,* such and such passages of scripture as they were directed to by the tradition of the elders; as they thought all the *vulgar* cursed because they did not thus know the law (*ch.* 7:49), so they concluded all the *learned* undoubtedly *blessed.* [2.] We must *search the scriptures* for *Christ,* as the new and living *way* that leads to this *end.* These are *they,* the great and principal witnesses, *that testify of me.* Note, *First,* The scriptures, even those of the Old Testament, *testify* of Christ, and by them God *bears witness* to him. The Spirit of Christ in the prophets testified beforehand of him (1 Pt. 1:11), the purposes and promises of God concerning him, and the previous notices of him. The Jews knew very well that the Old Testament testified of the Messiah, and were critical in their remarks upon the passages that looked that way; and yet were careless, and wretchedly overseen, in the application of them. *Secondly, Therefore* we must *search the scriptures,* and may hope to find eternal life in that search, because they testify of Christ; for this is *life eternal, to know him;* see 1 Jn. 5:11. Christ is the treasure hid in the field of the scriptures, the water in those wells, the milk in those breasts.

(3.) To this testimony he annexes a reproof of their infidelity and wickedness in four instances; particularly,

[1.] Their *neglect of him* and his doctrine: *"You will not come tome, that you might have life, v.* 40. You search the scriptures, you believe the prophets, who you cannot but see testify of me; and yet you will not *come to me,* to whom they direct you." Their estrangement from Christ was the fault not so much of their *understandings* as of their *wills.* This is expressed as a complaint; Christ offered life, and it was not accepted. Note, *First,* There is *life* to be had with Jesus Christ for poor souls; we may have life, the life of *pardon* and *grace,* and *comfort* and *glory:* life is the perfection of our being, and inclusive of all happiness; and Christ is our life. *Secondly,* Those that would have this life must *come* to Jesus Christ for it; we may have it for the coming for. It *supposes* an assent of the understanding to the doctrine of Christ and the record given concerning him; it *lies in* the consent of the will to his government and grace, and it *produces* an answerable compliance in the affections and actions. *Thirdly,* The only reason why sinners die is because they *will not come* to Christ for life and happiness; it is not because they *cannot,* but because they *will not.* They will neither *accept* the life offered, because *spiritual* and *divine,* nor will they *agree* to the terms on which it is offered, nor *apply* themselves to the use of the appointed means: they will not be cured, for they will not observe the methods of cure. *Fourthly,* The wilfulness and obstinacy of sinners in rejecting the tenders of grace are a great grief to the Lord Jesus, and what he complains of. Those words (*v.* 41), *I receive not honour from men,* come in a parenthesis, to obviate an objection against him, as if he sought his own glory, and made himself the head of a party, in obliging all to come to *him,* and applaud him. Note, 1. He did not *covet* nor *court* the applause of men, did not in the least affect that worldly pomp and splendour in which the carnal Jews expected their Messiah to appear. He charged those whom he cured not to make him known, and withdrew from those that would have made him king. 2. He *had not* the applause of men. Instead of *receiving honour* from men, he received a great deal of *dishonour* and disgrace from men, for he made himself of no reputation. 3. He *needed* not the applause of men; it was no addition to his glory whom all the angels of God worship, nor was he any otherwise pleased with it than as it was according to his Father's will, and for the happiness of those who, in giving honour *to him,* received much greater honour *from him.*

[2.] Their *want of the love of God* (*v.* 42): "*I know you* very well, *that you have not the love of God in you.* Why should I wonder that you do not come to me, when you want even the first principle of *natural religion,* which is the *love of God?*" Note, The reason why people *slight Christ* is because they do not *love God;* for, if we did indeed love God, we should love him who is his express image, and hasten to him by whom only we may be restored to the favour of God. He charged them (*v.* 37) with *ignorance* of God, and here with want of love to him; *therefore* men have not the love of God because they desire not the knowledge of him. Observe, *First,* The crime charged upon them: *You have not the love of God in you.* They pretended a great love to God, and thought they proved it by their zeal for the law, the temple, and the sabbath; and yet they were really without the love of God. Note, There are many who make a great profession of religion who yet show they want the love of God by their neglect of Christ and their contempt of his commandments; they hate his holiness and undervalue his goodness. Observe, It is the love of God *in us,* that love seated *in the heart,* a living active principle there, that God will *accept;* the love *shed abroad* there, Rom. 5:5. *Secondly,* The proof of this charge, by the personal knowledge of Christ, who *searches the heart* (Rev. 2:23) and knows what is *in man: I know you.* Christ sees through all our disguises, and can say to each of us, *I know thee.* 1. Christ knows men better than *their neighbours know them.* The people thought that the scribes and Pharisees were very devout and good men, but Christ knew that they had not the love of God in them. 2. Christ knows men better than *they know themselves.* These Jews had a very good opinion of themselves, but Christ knew how corrupt their inside was, notwithstanding the speciousness of their outside; we may deceive ourselves, but we cannot deceive him. 3. Christ knows men who do not, and will not, know him; he looks *on* those who industriously look *off* from him, and calls by their own name, their true name, those who have not known him.

[3.] Another crime charged upon them is their readiness to entertain false Christs and false prophets, while they obstinately opposed him who was the true Messias (*v.* 43): *I am come in my Father's name, and you receive me not. If an-*

other shall come in his own name, him you will receive. Be astonished, O heavens, at this (Jer. 2:12, 13); *for my people have committed two evils,* great evils indeed. *First,* They have *forsaken the fountain of living waters,* for they would not receive Christ, who came in his Father's name, had his commission from his Father, and did all for his glory. *Secondly,* They have *hewn out broken cisterns,* they hearken to every one that will set up in his own name. They forsake their own mercies, which is bad enough; and it is for *lying vanities,* which is worse. observe here, 1. Those are false prophets who come in their own name, who run without being sent, and set up for themselves only. 2. It is just with God to suffer those to be deceived with false prophets who receive not the truth in the love of it. 2 Th. 2:10, 11. The errors of antichrist are the just punishment of those who obey not the doctrine of Christ. They that shut their eyes against the true light are by the judgment of God given up to wander endlessly after *false lights,* and to be led aside after every *ignis fatuus.* 3. It is the gross folly of many that, while they *nauseate* ancient truths, they are *fond* of upstart errors; they loathe manna, and at the same time *feed upon ashes.* After the Jews had rejected Christ and his gospel, they were continually haunted with spectres, with *false Christs* and *false prophets* (Mt. 24:24), and their proneness to follow such occasioned those distractions and seditions that hastened their ruin.

[4.] They are here charged with pride and vain-glory, and unbelief, the effect of them, *v.* 44. Having sharply reproved their unbelief, like a wise physician, he here searches into the cause, lays the axe to the root. They *therefore* slighted and undervalued Christ because they *admired* and *overvalued* themselves. Here is,

First, Their ambition of worldly honour. Christ despised it, *v.* 41. They set their hearts upon it: *You receive honour one of another;* that is, "You look for a Messiah in outward pomp, and promise yourselves worldly honour by him." *You receive honour:* — 1. "You desire to receive it, and aim at this in all you do." 2. "You give honour to others, and applaud them, only that they may return it, and may applaud you." *Petimus dabimusque vicissim — We ask and we bestow.* It is the proud man's art to throw honour upon others only that it may rebound upon himself. 3. "You are very careful to keep all the honours to yourselves, and confine them to your own party, as if you had the monopoly of that which is honourable." 4. "What respect is shown to you you *receive* yourselves, and do not transmit to God, as Herod." Idolizing men and their sentiments, and affecting to be idolized by them and their applauses, are pieces of idolatry as directly contrary to Christianity as any other.

Secondly, Their neglect of spiritual honour, called here *the honour that comes from God only;* this they sought not, nor minded. Note, 1. True honour is that which *comes from God only,* that is real and lasting honour; those are honourable indeed whom he takes into covenant and communion with himself. 2. *This honour have all the saints.* All that believe in Christ, through him receive the honour that comes from God. he is not partial, but will give glory wherever he gives grace. 3. This honour that comes from God we must *seek,* must aim at it, and act for it, and take up with nothing short of it (Rom. 2:29); we must account it *our reward,* as the Pharisees accounted the praise of men. 4. Those that will not come to Christ, and those that are ambitious of worldly honour, make it appear that they seek not the honour that comes from God, and it is their folly and ruin.

Thirdly, The influence this had upon their infidelity. *How can you believe* who are thus affected? Observe here, 1. The difficulty of believing arises from ourselves and our own corruption; we make our work hard to ourselves, and then complain it is impracticable. 2. The ambition and affectation of worldly honour are a great hindrance to faith in Christ. How can they believe who make the praise and applause of men their idol? When the profession and practice of serious godliness are unfashionable, are *every where spoken against,* — when Christ and his followers are men wondered at, and to be a Christian is to be like a *speckled bird* (and this is the common case), — how can they believe the summit of whose ambition is to *make a fair show in the flesh?*

6. The last witness here called is Moses, *v.* 45, etc. The Jews had a great veneration for Moses, and valued themselves upon their being the *disciples* of Moses, and pretended to adhere to Moses, in their opposition to Christ; but Christ here shows them,

(1.) That Moses was a witness against the unbelieving Jews, *and accused them to the Father: There is one that accuses you, even Moses.* This may be understood either, [1.] As showing the difference between the law and the gospel. Moses, that is, the law, *accuses you,* for by the law is the knowledge of sin; it *condemns* you, it is to those that trust to it a ministration of death and condemnation. But it is not the design of Christ's gospel to *accuse* us: *Think not that I will accuse you.* Christ did not come into the world as a *Momus,* to find fault and pick quarrels with every body, or as a *spy* upon the actions of men, or a *promoter,* to fish for crimes; no, he came to be an advocate, not an accuser; to reconcile God and man, and not to set them more at variance. What fools were they then that adhered to Moses against Christ, and *desired to be under the law!* Gal. 4:21. Or, [2.] As showing the manifest unreasonableness of their infidelity: "Think not that I will appeal from your bar to God's and challenge you to answer there for what you do against me, as injured innocency usually does; no, I do not need; you are already accused, and cast, in the court of heaven; Moses himself says enough to convict you of, and condemn you for, your unbelief." Let them not mistake *concerning Christ;* though he was a prophet, he did not improve his interest in heaven against those that persecuted him, did not, as Elias, *make intercession against Israel* (Rom. 6:2), nor as Jeremiah desire to *see God's vengeance on them.* Nor let them mistake concerning Moses, as if he would stand by them in rejecting Christ; no, *There is one that accuses you, even Moses in whom you trust.* Note, *First,* External privileges and advantages are commonly the vain confidence of those who reject Christ and his grace. The Jews *trusted* in Moses, and thought their having his laws and ordinances would save them. *Secondly,* Those that confide in their privileges, and do not improve them, will find not only that their confidence is disappointed, but that those very privileges will be witnesses against them.

(2.) That Moses was a witness for Christ and to his doctrine (*v.* 46, 47): *He wrote of me.* Moses did particularly prophesy of Christ, as the Seed of the woman, the Seed of Abraham, the Shiloh, the great Prophet; the ceremonies of the law of Moses were *figures of him that was to come.* The Jews made Moses the patron of their opposition to Christ; but Christ here shows them their error, that Moses was so far from writing against Christ that he wrote *for him,* and of *him.* But, [1.] Christ here charges it on the Jews that they *did not believe Moses.* He had said (*v.* 45) that they *trusted* in Moses, and yet here he undertakes to make out that they did not believe Moses; they trusted to his name, but they did not receive his doctrine in its true sense and meaning; they did not rightly understand, nor give credit to, what there was in the writings of Moses concerning the Messiah. [2.] He proves this charge from their disbelief of him: *Had you believed Moses, you would have believed me.* Note, *First,* The surest trial of faith is by the effects it produces. Many say that they believe whose actions give their words the lie; for had they believed the scriptures they would have done otherwise than they did. *Secondly,* Those who rightly believe one part of scripture will receive every part. The prophecies of the old Testament were so fully accomplished in Christ that those who rejected Christ did in effect deny those prophecies, and set them aside. [3.] From their disbelief of Moses he infers that it was not strange that they rejected him: *If you believe not his writings, how shall you believe my words?* How can it be thought that you should? *First,* "If you do not believe sacred *writings,* those oracles which are in black and white, which is the most certain way of conveyance, *how shall you believe my words,* words being usually less regarded?" *Secondly,* "If you do not believe Moses, for whom you have such a profound veneration, how is it likely that you should believe me, whom you look upon with so much contempt?" See Ex. 6:12. *Thirdly,* "If you believe not what Moses spoke and wrote of me, which is a strong and cogent testimony for me, how shall you believe me and my mission?" If we admit not the premises, how shall we admit the conclusion? The truth of the Christian religion, it being a matter purely of divine revelation, depends upon the divine authority of the scripture; if therefore we believe not the divine inspiration of those writings, how shall be receive the doctrine of Christ?

Thus ends Christ's plea for himself, in answer to the charge exhibited against him. What effect it had we know not; it would seem to have had this, their *mouths* were *stopped* for the present, and they could not for shame but drop the prosecution, and yet their *hearts* were *hardened.*

CHAPTER 6

In this chapter we have, I. The miracle of the loaves (*v.* 1–14). II. Christ's walking upon the water (*v.* 15–21). III. The people's flocking after him to Capernaum (*v.* 22–25). IV. His conference with them, occasioned by the miracle of the loaves, in which he reproves them for seeking carnal food, and directs them to spiritual food (*v.* 26, 27), showing them how they must labour for spiritual food (*v.* 28, 29), and what that spiritual food is (*v.* 30–59). V. Their discontent at what he said, and the reproof he gave them for it (*v.* 60–65). VI. The apostasy of many from him, and his discourse with his disciples that adhered to him upon that occasion (*v.* 66–71).

Verses 1–14

We have here an account of Christ's feeding five thousand men with five loaves and two fishes, which miracle is in *this* respect remarkable, that it is the only passage of the actions of *Christ's life* that is recorded by all the four evangelists. John, who does not usually relate what had been recorded by those who wrote before him, yet relates this, because of the reference the following discourse has to it. Observe,

I. The *place* and *time* where and when this miracle was wrought, which are noted for the greater evidence of the truth of the story; it is not said that it was done once upon a time, nobody knows where, but the circumstances are specified, that the fact might be enquired into.

1. The country that Christ was in (*v.* 1): *He went over the sea of Galilee,* called elsewhere *the lake of Gennesareth,* here *the sea of Tiberias,* from a city adjoining, which Herod had lately enlarged and beautified, and called so in honour of Tiberius the emperor, and probably had made his metropolis. Christ did not go directly over cross this inland sea, but made a *coasting* voyage to another place on the same side. It is not tempting God to choose to go *by water,* when there is convenience for it, even to those places whither we might go *by land;* for Christ never *tempted the Lord his God,* Mt. 4:7.

2. The company that he was attended with: *A great multitude followed him, because they saw his miracles, v.* 2. Note, (1.) Our Lord Jesus, while he went about *doing good,* lived continually in *a crowd,* which gave him more trouble than honour. Good and useful men must not complain of a *hurry* of business, when they are serving God and their generation; it will be time enough to *enjoy ourselves* when we come to that world where we shall *enjoy God.* (2.) Christ's miracles drew many *after him* that were not effectually drawn *to him.* They had their curiosity gratified by the strangeness of them, who had not their consciences convinced by the power of them.

3. Christ's posting himself advantageously to entertain them (*v.* 3): *He went up into a mountain,* and there he *sat with his disciples,* that he might the more conveniently be seen and heard by the multitude that crowded after him; this was a *natural* pulpit, and not, like Ezra's, made *for the purpose.* Christ was now driven to be a *field preacher;* but his word was never the worse, nor the less acceptable, for that, to those who knew how to value it, who followed him still, not only when he *went out* to a desert place, but when he *went up* to a mountain, though *up-hill* be *against heart.* He *sat* there, as teachers do *in cathedra — in the chair of instruction.* He did not sit at ease, not sit in state, yet he sat as one having authority, sat ready to receive addresses that were made to him; whoever would might come, and find him there. He sat *with his disciples;* he condescended to take them to *sit with him,* to put a reputation upon them before the people, and give them an earnest of the glory in which they should shortly sit with him. We are said to *sit with him,* Eph. 2:6.

4. The time when it was. The first words, *After those things,* do not signify that this immediately followed what was related in the foregoing chapter, for it was a considerable time after, and they signify no more than in process of time; but we are told (*v.* 4) that it was *when the passover was nigh,* which is here noted, (1.) Because, perhaps, that had brought in all the apostles from their respective expeditions, whither they were sent as itinerant preachers, that they might attend their Master to Jerusalem, to keep the feast. (2.) Because it was a custom with the Jews religiously to observe the approach of the passover *thirty days* before, with some sort of solemnity; so long before they had it in their eye, repaired the roads, mended bridges, if there was occasion, and discoursed of the passover and the institution of it. (3.) Because, perhaps, the approach of the passover, when every one knew Christ would go up to Jerusalem, and be absent for some time, made the multitude flock the more after him and attend the more diligently on him. Note, The prospect of losing our opportunities should quicken us to improve them with double diligence; and, when solemn ordinances are approaching, it is good to prepare for them by conversing with the word of Christ.

II. The miracle itself. And here observe,

1. The notice Christ took of the crowd that attended him (*v.* 5): He *lifted up his eyes,* and *saw a great company come to him,* poor, mean, ordinary people, no doubt, for such make up the multitudes, especially in such remote corners of the country; yet Christ showed himself pleased with their attendance, and concerned for their welfare, to teach us to *condescend to those of low estate,* and not to *set* those *with the dogs of our flock* whom Christ hath set with the lambs of his. The souls of the poor are as precious to Christ, and should be so to us, as those of the rich.

2. The enquiry he made concerning the way of providing for them. He directed himself to Philip, who had been his disciple from the first, and had seen all his miracles, and particularly that of his turning water into wine, and therefore it might be expected that he should have said, "Lord, if thou wilt, it is easy to thee to feed them all." Those that, like Israel, have been witnesses of Christ's works, and have shared in the benefit of them, are inexcusable if they say, *Can he furnish a table in the wilderness?* Philip was of Bethsaida, in the neighbourhood of which town Christ now was, and therefore he was most likely to help them to provision at the best hand; and probably much of the company was known to him, and he was concerned for them. Now Christ asked, *Whence shall we buy bread, that these* may eat? (1.) He takes it for granted that they must all *eat with him.* One would think that when he had taught and healed them he had done his part; and that now they should rather have been contriving how to treat him and his disciples, for some of the people were probably *rich,* and we are sure that Christ and his disciples were *poor;* yet he is solicitous to entertain them. Those that will accept Christ's spiritual gifts, instead of *paying* for them, shall be *paid* for their acceptance of them. Christ, having fed their souls with the bread of life, feeds their bodies also with *food convenient,* to show that the Lord is for the body, and to encourage us to pray for our daily bread, and to set us an example of compassion to the poor, James 2:15, 16. (2.) His enquiry is, *Whence shall we buy bread?* One would think, considering his poverty, that he should rather have asked, *Where shall we have money to buy for them?* But he will rather lay out all he has than they shall want. He will buy to give, and we must *labour,* that we may give, Eph. 4:28.

3. The design of this enquiry; it was only to try the faith of Philip, *for he himself knew what he would do, v.* 6. Note, (1.) Our Lord Jesus is never at a loss in his counsels; but, how difficult soever the case is, he knows what he has to do and what course he will take, Acts 15:18. *He knows the thoughts he has towards his people* (Jer. 29:11) and is never at uncertainty; when we know not, he *himself knows what he will do.* (2.) When Christ is pleased to *puzzle* his people, it is only with a design to *prove* them. The question put Philip to a nonplus, yet Christ proposed it, to try whether he would say, "Lord, if thou wilt exert thy power for them, we need not buy bread."

4. Philip's answer to this question: *"Two hundred pennyworth of bread is not sufficient, v.* 7. Master, it is to no purpose to talk of buying bread for them, for neither will the country afford so much bread, nor can we afford to lay out so much money; ask Judas, who carries the bag." Two hundred pence of *their* money amount to about six pounds of *ours,* and, if they lay out all that at once, it will exhaust their fund, and break them, and they must starve themselves. Grotius computes that *two hundred pennyworth of bread* would scarcely reach to *two thousand,* but Philip would go as near hand as he could, would have *every one to take a little;* and nature, we say, is content with a little. See the weakness of Philip's faith, that in this strait, as if the Master of the family had been an *ordinary person,* he looked for supply only in an *ordinary way.* Christ might now have said to him, as he did afterwards, Have I *been so long time with you, and yet hast thou not known me, Philip?* Or, as God to Moses in a like case, *Is the Lord's hand waxen short?* We are apt thus to distrust God's power when visible and ordinary means fail, that is, to trust him no further than we can see him.

5. The information which Christ received from another of his disciples concerning the provision they had. It was Andrew, here said to be *Simon Peter's brother;* though he was senior to Peter in discipleship, and instrumental to bring Peter to Christ, yet Peter afterwards so far outshone him that he is described by his relation to Peter: he acquainted Christ with what they had at hand; and in this we may see,

(1.) The *strength* of his *love* to those for whom he saw his Master concerned, in that he was willing to bring out all they had, though he knew not but they might want themselves, and any one would have said, *Charity begins at home.* He did not go about to conceal it, under pretence of being a better husband of their provision than the master was, but honestly gives in an account of all they had. There is a lad here, *paidarion — a little lad,* probably one that used to follow this company, as settlers do the camp, with provisions to sell, and the disciples had bespoken what he had for themselves; and it was *five barley-loaves,* and two small fishes. Here, [1.] The provision was *coarse* and *ordinary;* they were *barley loaves.* Canaan was a *land of wheat* (Deu. 8:8); its inhabitants were commonly fed with the finest wheat (Ps. 81:16), the kidneys of wheat (Deu. 32:14); yet Christ and his disciples were glad of *barley-bread.* It does not follow hence that we should tie ourselves to such coarse fare, and place religion in it (when God brings that which is finer to our hands, let us receive it, and be thankful); but it does follow that therefore we must not be *desirous of dainties* (Ps. 23:3); nor murmur if we be reduced to coarse fare, but be content and thankful, and well reconciled to it; barley-bread is what Christ *had,* and better than we *deserve.* Nor let us despise the mean provision of the poor, nor look upon it with contempt, remembering how Christ was provided for. [2.] It was but *short* and *scanty;* there were but *five loaves,* and those so small that one little lad carried them all; and we find (2 Ki. 4:42, 43) that *twenty barley-loaves,* with some other provision to help out, would not dine a hundred men without a miracle. There were but two fishes, and those *small* ones (*dyo opsaria*), so small that one of them was but a morsel, *pisciculi assati.* I take the fish to have been *pickled,* or *soused,* for they had not fire to dress them with. The provision of *bread* was *little,* but that of *fish* was *less* in proportion to it, so that many a bit of dry bread they must eat before they could make a meal of this provision; but they were content with it. *Bread* is meat for our hunger; but of those that murmured for flesh it is said, *They asked meat for their lust,* Ps. 78:18. Well, Andrew was willing that the people should have this, as far as it would go. Note, A distrustful fear of wanting ourselves should not hinder us from needful charity to others.

(2.) See here the *weakness* of his *faith* in that word, *"But what are they among so many?* To offer this to such a multitude is but to mock them." Philip and he had not that actual consideration of the power of Christ (of which they had had such large experience) which they should have had. Who fed the camp of Israel in the wilderness? He that could make *one man chase a thousand* could make one loaf feed a thousand.

6. The directions Christ gave the disciples to seat the guests (*v.* 10): *"Make the men sit down,* though you have nothing to set before them, and trust me for that." This was like *sending providence* to *market,* and going to buy without money: Christ would thus try their obedience. Observe, (1.) The furniture of the dining-room: *there was much grass in that place,* though a desert place; see how bountiful nature is, it *makes grass to grow upon the mountains,* Ps. 147:8. This grass was uneaten; God gives not only enough, but more then enough. Here was this plenty of grass where Christ was preaching; the gospel brings other blessings along with it: *Then shall the earth yield her increase,* Ps. 67:6. This plenty of grass made the place the more commodious for those that must sit on the ground, and served them for cushions, or *beds* (as they called what they sat on at meat, Esth. 1:6), and, considering what Christ says of the grass of the field (Mt. 6:29, 30), these beds excelled those of Ahasuerus: nature's pomp is the most glorious. (2.) The number of the guests: *About five thousand:* a great entertainment, representing that of the gospel, which is a *feast for all nations* (Isa. 25:6), a feast for all *comers.*

7. The distribution of the provision, *v.* 11. Observe,

(1.) It was done with thanksgiving: *He gave thanks.* Note, [1.] We ought to give thanks to God for our food, for it is a mercy to have it, and we have it from the hand of God, and must *receive it with thanksgiving,* 1 Tim. 4:4, 5. And this is the sweetness of our creature-comforts, that they will furnish us with *matter,* and give us occasion, for that excellent duty of thanksgiving. [2.] Though our provision be coarse and scanty, though we have neither plenty nor dainty, yet we must give thanks to God for what we have.

(2.) It was distributed from the hand of Christ by the hands of his disciples, *v.* 11. Note, [1.] All our comforts come to us *originally* from the hand of Christ; whoever *brings* them, it is he that *sends* them, he distributes to those who distribute to us. [2.] In distributing the bread of life to those that follow him, he is pleased to make use of the ministration of his disciples; they are the servitors at Christ's table, or rather rulers in his household, to give to *every one his portion of meat in due season.*

(3.) It was done to universal satisfaction. They did not every one take a little, but all had *as much as they would;* not a short allowance, but a full meal; and considering how long they had fasted, with what an appetite they sat down, how agreeable this miraculous food may be supposed to have been, above common food, it was not a little that served them when they ate as much as they would and on free cost. Those whom Christ feeds with the bread of life he does not stint, Ps. 81:10. There were but *two small fishes,* and yet they had *of them* too *as much as they would.* He did not reserve them for the better sort of the guests, and put off the poor with dry bread, but treated them all alike, for they were all alike welcome. Those who call feeding upon fish *fasting* reproach the entertainment Christ here made, which was a *full feast.*

8. The care that was taken of the broken meat. (1.) The orders Christ gave concerning it (*v.* 12): *When they were filled,* and every man had within him a sensible witness to the truth of the miracle, Christ *said to the disciples,* the servants he employed, *Gather up the fragments.* Note, We must always take care that we make no waste of any of God's good creatures; for the grant we have of them, though large and full, is with this proviso, *wilful waste only excepted.* It is just with God to bring us to the want of that which we make waste of. The Jews were very careful not to lose any bread, nor let it fall to the ground, to be trodden upon. *Qui panem contemnit in gravem incidit paupertatem — He who despises bread falls into the depths of poverty,* was a saying among them. Though Christ could command supplies whenever he pleased, yet he would have the fragments gathered up. When we are filled we must remember that others want, and we may want. Those that would have wherewith to be *charitable* must be *provident.* Had this broken meat been left upon the grass, the beasts and fowls would have gathered it up; but that which is fit to be meat for men is wasted and lost if it be thrown to the brute-creatures. Christ did not order the broken meat to be gathered up till all were filled; we must not begin to hoard and lay up till all is laid out that ought to be, for that is withholding more than is meet. Mr. Baxter notes here, "How much less should we lose God's word, or helps, or our time, or such greater mercies!" (2.) The observance of these orders (*v.* 13): *They filled twelve baskets with the fragments,* which was an evidence not only of the *truth* of the miracle, that they were fed, not with fancy, but with real food (witness those remains), but of the *greatness* of it; they were not only filled, but there was all this over and above. See how large the divine bounty is; it not only *fills* the cup, but makes it *run over;* bread enough, and to spare, in our Father's house. The fragments filled twelve baskets, one for each disciple; they were thus repaid with interest for their willingness to part with what they had for public service; see 2 Chr. 31:10. The Jews lay it as a law upon themselves, when they have eaten a meal, to be sure to leave a piece of bread upon the table, upon which the blessing after meat may rest; for it is a curse upon the wicked man (Job 20:21) that *there shall none of his meat be left.*

III. Here is the influence which this miracle had upon the people who tasted of the benefit of it (*v.* 14): *They said, This is of a truth that prophet.* Note, 1. Even the vulgar Jews with great assurance expected the Messiah to come into the world, and to be a *great prophet,* They speak here with assurance of his coming. The Pharisees despised them as *not knowing the law;* but, it should seem, they knew more of him that is the *end of the law* than the Pharisees did. 2. The miracles which Christ wrought did clearly demonstrate that he was the Messiah promised, a teacher come from God, the great prophet, and could not but convince the amazed spectators that this was he that should come. There were many who were convinced he was that prophet that should come into the world who yet did not cordially receive his doctrine, for they did not continue in it. Such a wretched incoherence and inconsistency there is between the faculties of the corrupt unsanctified soul, that it is possible for men to acknowledge that Christ is that prophet, and yet to turn a deaf ear to him.

Verses 15–21

Here is, I. Christ's retirement from the multitude.

1. Observe what induced him to retire; because he perceived that those who acknowledged him to be that prophet that should come into the world would come, and *take him by force, to make him a king, v.* 15. Now here we have an instance,

(1.) Of the irregular zeal of some of Christ's followers; nothing would serve but they would make him *a king.* Now, [1.] This was *an act of zeal* for the honour of Christ, and against the contempt which the ruling part of the Jewish church put upon him. They were concerned to see so great a benefactor to the world so little esteemed in it; and therefore, since royal titles are counted the most illustrious, they would make him a king, knowing that the Messiah was to be a king; and if a prophet, like Moses, then a sovereign prince and lawgiver, like him; and, if they cannot set him up *upon the holy hill of Zion,* a *mountain* in Galilee shall serve for the present. Those whom Christ has feasted with the royal dainties of heaven should, in return for his favour, make him *their* king, and set him upon the throne in their souls: let him that has *fed* us *rule us.* But, [2.] It was an *irregular* zeal; for *First,* It was grounded upon a mistake concerning the nature of Christ's kingdom, as if it were to be *of this world,* and he must appear with outward pomp, a crown on his head, and an army at his foot; such a king as this they would make him, which was as great a disparagement to his glory as it would be to lacquer gold or paint a ruby. Right notions of Christ's kingdom would keep us to right methods for advancing it. *Secondly,* It was excited by the love of the flesh; they would make *him* their king who could feed them so plentifully without their toil, and save them from the curse of *eating their bread in the sweat of their face. Thirdly,* It was intended to carry on a *secular* design; they hoped this might be a fair opportunity of shaking off the Roman yoke, of which they were weary. If they had one to head them who could victual an army cheaper than another could provide for a family, they were sure of the sinews of the war, and could not fail of success, and the recovery of their ancient liberties. Thus is religion often prostituted to a secular interest, and Christ is served only to *serve a turn,* Rom. 16:18. *Vix quaritur* Jesus *propter* Jesusm, *sed propter aliud — Jesus is usually sought after for something else, not for his own sake.* — Augustine. Nay, *Fourthly,* It was a tumultuous, seditious attempt, and a disturbance of the public peace; it would make the country a seat of war, and expose it to the resentments of the Roman power. *Fifthly,* It was contrary to the mind of our Lord Jesus himself; for they would take him *by force,* whether he would or no. Note, Those who force honours upon Christ which he has not required at their hands displease him, and do him the greatest dishonour. Those that say *I am of Christ,* in opposition to those that are of Apollos and Cephas (so making Christ the head of a party), take him by force, to make him a king, contrary to his own mind.

(2.) Here is an instance of the humility and self-denial of the Lord Jesus, that, when they would have made him a king, he *departed;* so far was he from countenancing the design that he effectually quashed it. Herein he has left a testimony, [1.] Against ambition and affectation of worldly honour, to which he was perfectly mortified, and has taught us to be so. Had they come to take him by force and make him a prisoner, he could not have been more industrious to abscond than he was when they would make him a king. Let us not then covet to be the *idols of the crowd,* nor be *desirous of vainglory.* [2.] Against faction and sedition, treason and rebellion, and whatever tends to disturb the peace of kings and provinces. By this it appears that he was no enemy to Caesar, nor would have his followers be so, but the *quiet in the land;* that he would have his ministers decline every thing that looks *like* sedition, or looks *towards* it, and improve their interest only for their work's sake.

2. Observe *whither* he retired: *He departed again into a mountain, eis to oros — into the* mountain, the mountain where he had preached (*v.* 3), whence he came down into the plain, to feed the people, and then returned to it alone, to be private. Christ, though so useful in the places of concourse, yet chose sometimes to be alone, to teach us to sequester ourselves from the world now and then, for the more free converse with God and our own souls; and *never less alone,* says the serious Christian, *than when alone.* Public services must not jostle out private devotions.

II. Here is the disciples' distress at sea. *They that go down to the sea in ships, these see the works of the Lord, for he raiseth the stormy wind,* Ps. 17:23, 24. Apply this to these disciples.

1. Here is their *going down to the sea* in a ship (*v.* 16, 17): *When even was come,* and they had done their day's work, it was time to look homeward, and therefore they went aboard, and set sail for Capernaum. This they did by particular direction from their Master, with design (as it should seem) to get them out of the way of the temptation of countenancing those that would have made him a king.

2. Here is the *stormy wind* arising and *fulfilling the word of God.* They were Christ's disciples, and were now in the way of their duty, and Christ was now in the mount praying for them; and yet they were in this distress. The perils and afflictions of this present time may very well consist with our interest in Christ and his intercession. They had lately been feasted at Christ's table; but after the sun-shine of comfort expect a storm. (1.) *It was now dark;* this made the storm the more dangerous and uncomfortable. Sometimes the people of God are in trouble, and cannot see their way out; in the dark concerning the cause of their trouble, concerning the design and tendency of it, and what the issue will be. (2.) Jesus *was not come to them.* When they were in that storm (Mt. 8:23, etc.) *Jesus was with them;* but now their beloved had withdrawn himself, and was gone. The absence of Christ is the great aggravation of the troubles of Christians. (3.) The *sea arose by reason of a great wind.* It was calm and fair when they put to sea (they were not so presumptuous as to launch out in a storm), but it arose when they were *at sea.* In times of tranquillity we must prepare for trouble, for it may arise when we little think of it. Let it comfort good people, when they happen to be in storms at sea, that the disciples of Christ were so; and let the promises of a gracious God balance the threats of an angry sea. Though in a storm, and *in the dark,* they are no worse off than Christ's disciples were. Clouds and darkness sometimes surround the children of the light, and of the day.

3. Here is Christ's seasonable approach to them when they were in this peril, *v.* 19. *They had rowed* (being forced by the contrary winds to betake themselves to their oars) *about twenty-five or thirty furlongs.* The Holy Spirit that indicted this could have ascertained the number of furlongs precisely, but this, being only circumstantial, is left to be expressed according to the conjecture of the penman. And, when they were got off a good way at sea, they *see Jesus walking on the sea.* See here, (1.) The power Christ has over the laws and customs of nature, to control and dispense with them at his pleasure. It is natural for heavy bodies to sink in water, but Christ walked *upon* the water as upon dry land, which was more than Moses's dividing the water and walking *through* the water. (2.) The concern Christ has for his disciples in distress: *He drew nigh to the ship;* for *therefore* he walked upon the water, as he *rides upon the heavens, for the help of his people,* Deu. 33:26. He will not leave them comfortless when they seem to be *tossed with tempests* and *not comforted.* When they are banished (as John) into remote places, or shut up (as Paul and Silas) in close places, he will find access to them, and will be nigh them. (3.) The relief Christ gives to his disciples in their fears. They *were afraid,* more afraid of an apparition (for so they supposed him to be) than of the winds and waves. It is more terrible to wrestle with the rulers of the darkness of this world than with a tempestuous sea. When they thought a demon haunted them, and perhaps was instrumental to raise the storm, they were more terrified than they had been while they saw nothing in it but what was natural. Note, [1.] Our real distresses are often much increased by our imaginary ones, the creatures of our own fancy. [2.] Even the approaches of comfort and deliverance are often so misconstrued as to become the occasions of fear and perplexity. We are often not only *worse frightened than hurt,* but *then* most *frightened* when we are ready to be *helped.* But, when they were in this fright, how affectionately did Christ silence their fears with that compassionate word (*v.* 20), *It is I, be not afraid!* Nothing is more powerful to convince sinners than that word, *I am Jesus whom thou persecutest;* nothing more powerful to comfort saints than this, *"I am Jesus whom thou lovest;* it is I that love thee, and seek thy good; be not afraid of me, nor of the storm." When trouble is nigh Christ is nigh.

4. Here is their speedy arrival at the port they were bound for, *v.* 17. (1.) They *welcomed* Christ into the ship; they *willingly received him*. Note, Christ's absenting himself for a time is but so much the more to *endear himself*, at his return, to his disciples, who value his presence above any thing; see Cant. 3:4. (2.) Christ brought them safely to the shore: *Immediately the ship was at the land whither they went*. Note, [1.] The ship of the church, in which the disciples of Christ have *embarked* themselves and their all, may be much shattered and distressed, yet it shall come safe to the harbour at last; *tossed* at sea, but not *lost;* cast down, but not destroyed; the bush burning, but not consumed. [2.] The power and presence of the church's King shall expedite and facilitate her deliverance, and conquer the difficulties which have baffled the skill and industry of all her other friends. The disciples had rowed hard, but could not make their point till they had got Christ in the ship, and then the work was *done suddenly*. If we have received Christ Jesus the Lord, have received him willingly, though the night be dark and the wind high, yet we may comfort ourselves with this, that we shall be at shore shortly, and are nearer to it than we think we are. Many a doubting soul is fetched to heaven by a pleasing surprise, or ever it is aware.

Verses 22–27

In these verses we have,

I. The careful enquiry which the people made after Christ, *v.* 23, 24. They saw the disciples go to sea; they saw Christ retire to the mountain, probably with an intimation that he desired to be private for some time; but, their hearts being set upon *making him a king*, they way-laid his return, and *the day following*, the hot fit of their zeal still continuing,

1. They were *much at a loss* for him. He was gone, and they knew not what was become of him. They saw there was *no boat there* but that in which the disciples went off, Providence so ordering it for the confirming of the miracle of his walking on the sea, for there was no boat for him to go in. They observed also that *Jesus did not go with his disciples*, but that they went off alone, and left him among them on *their* side of the water. Note, Those that would find Christ must diligently observe all his motions, and learn to understand the tokens of his presence and absence, that they may steer accordingly.

2. They were very *industrious in seeking* him. They searched the places thereabouts, and when *they saw that Jesus was not there, nor his disciples* (neither he nor any one that could give tidings of him), they resolved to search elsewhere. Note, Those that would find Christ must accomplish a diligent search, must seek till they find, must go from sea to sea, to seek the word of God, rather than live without it; and those whom Christ has feasted with the bread of life should have their souls carried out in earnest desires towards him. Much would have more, in communion with Christ. Now, (1.) They resolved to go to Capernaum in quest of him. There were his head-quarters, where he usually resided. Thither his disciples were gone; and they knew he would not be long absent from *them*. Those that would find Christ must go forth by the footsteps of the flock. (2.) Providence favoured them with an opportunity of going thither by sea, which was the speediest way; for there *came other boats from Tiberias*, which lay further off upon the same shore, *nigh*, though not so nigh to the place where they did *eat bread*, in which they might soon make a trip to Capernaum, and probably the boats were bound for that port. Note, Those that in sincerity seek Christ, and seek opportunities of converse with him, are commonly owned and assisted by Providence in those pursuits. The evangelist, having occasion to mention their eating the *multiplied* bread, adds, *After that the Lord had given thanks, v.* 11. So much were the disciples affected with their Master's giving thanks that they could never forget the impressions made upon them by it, but took a pleasure in remembering the gracious words that then proceeded out of his mouth. This was the grace and beauty of that meal, and made it remarkable; their hearts burned within them.

3. They laid hold of the opportunity that offered itself, and *they also took shipping, and came to Capernaum, seeking for Jesus*. They did not defer, in hopes to see him again on *this side the water;* but their convictions being strong, and their desires warm, they followed him presently. Good motions are often crushed, and come to nothing, for want of being *prosecuted* in *time*. They came to Capernaum, and, for

aught that appears, these unsound hypocritical followers of Christ had a *calm* and *pleasant* passage, while his sincere disciples had a *rough* and *stormy* one. It is not strange if it fare worst with the best men in this evil world. They came, *seeking Jesus*. Note, Those that would find Christ, and find comfort in him, must be willing to take pains, and, as here, to *compass* sea and land to seek and serve him who came from heaven to earth to seek and save us.

II. The success of this enquiry: *They found him on the other side of the sea, v.* 25. Note, Christ will be found of those that seek him, first or last; and it is worth while to cross a sea, nay, to go *from sea to sea, and from the river to the ends of the earth*, to seek Christ, if we may but find him at last. These people appeared afterwards to be unsound, and not actuated by any good principle, and yet were thus zealous. Note, Hypocrites may be very forward in their attendance on God's ordinances. If men have *no more* to show for their love to Christ than their running after sermons and prayers, and their pangs of affection to good preaching, they have reason to suspect themselves no better than this *eager crowd*. But though these people were no better principled, and Christ knew it, yet he was willing to be found of them, and admitted them into fellowship with him. If we could know the hearts of hypocrites, yet, while their profession is plausible, we must not exclude them from our communion, much less when we do not know their hearts.

III. The question they put to him when they found him: *Rabbi, when camest thou hither?* It should seem by *v.* 59 that they found him *in the synagogue*. They knew this was the likeliest place to seek Christ in, for it was *his custom* to attend public assemblies for religious worship, Lu. 4:16. Note, Christ must be sought, and will be found, in the congregations of his people and in the administration of his ordinances; public worship is what Christ chooses to own and grace with his presence and the manifestations of himself. There they found him, and all they had to say to him was, *Rabbi, when camest thou hither?* They saw he would not be made a king, and therefore say no more of this, but call him Rabbi, their teacher. Their enquiry refers not only to the *time*, but to the *manner*, of his conveying himself thither; not only *When*, but, *"How*, camest thou thither?" for there was no boat for him to come in. They were curious in asking concerning Christ's motions, but not solicitous to observe their own.

IV. The answer Christ gave them, not direct to their question (what was it to them *when* and *how* he came thither?) but such an answer as their case required.

1. He discovers the *corrupt principle* they *acted from* in following him (*v.* 26): *"Verily, verily, I say unto you,* I that search the heart, and know what is in man, I the Amen, the faithful witness, Rev. 3:14, 15. *You seek me;* that is well, but it is not from a good principle." Christ knows not only *what* we do, but *why* we do it. These followed Christ, (1.) Not for his doctrine's sake: *Not because you saw the miracles*. The miracles were the great confirmation of his doctrine; Nicodemus sought for him for the sake of them (*ch.* 3:2), and argued from the power of his works to the truth of his word; but these were so stupid and mindless that they never considered this. But, (2.) It was for their own bellies' sake: *Because you did eat of the loaves, and were filled;* not because he taught them, but because he fed them. He had given them, [1.] A *full* meal's meat: *They did eat, and were filled;* and some of them perhaps were so poor that they had not known of a long time before now what it was to have enough, to eat and leave. [2.] A *dainty* meal's meat; it is probable that, as the miraculous wine was the best wine, so was the miraculous food more than usually pleasant. [3.] A *cheap* meal's meat, that cost them nothing; no reckoning was brought in. Note, Many follow Christ for *loaves*, and not for *love*. Thus those do who aim at secular advantage in their profession of religion, and follow it because by this craft they get their preferments. *Quantis profuit nobis haec fabula de Christo — This fable respecting Christ, what a gainful concern we have made of it!* said one of the popes. These people *complimented* Christ with Rabbi, and showed him great respect, yet he told them thus faithfully of their hypocrisy; his ministers must hence learn not to flatter those that flatter them, nor to be bribed by fair words to cry *peace* to all that cry *rabbi* to them, but to give faithful reproofs where there is cause for them.

2. He directs them to better principles (*v.* 27): *Labour for that meat which endures to everlasting life*. With the woman of Samaria he had discoursed of spiritual things under the similitude of *water;* here he speaks of them under the si-

militude of *meat*, taking occasion from the loaves they had eaten. His design is,

(1.) To moderate our worldly pursuits: *Labour not for the meat that perishes*. This does not forbid honest labour for food convenient, 2 Th. 3:12. But we must not make the things of this world our chief care and concern. Note, [1.] The things of the world are *meat that perishes*. Worldly wealth, honour, and pleasure, are *meat;* they *feed the fancy* (and many times this is all) and *fill the belly*. These are things which mean *hunger* after as *meat*, and glut themselves with, and which a carnal heart, as long as they last, may make a shift to live upon; but they *perish*, are of a perishing nature, wither of themselves, and are exposed to a thousand accidents; those that have the largest share of them are not sure to have them while they live, but are sure to leave them and lose them when they die. [2.] It is therefore folly for us inordinately to labour after them. *First*, We must not labour in religion, nor work the works thereof, *for this perishing meat*, with an eye to this; we must not make our religion subservient to a worldly interest, nor aim at *secular advantages* in *sacred exercises*. *Secondly*, We must not at all *labour* for this meat; that is, we must not make these perishing things our *chief good*, nor make our care and pains about them our *chief business;* not seek those things *first* and *most*, Prov. 23:4, 5.

(2.) To quicken and excite our gracious pursuits: "Bestow your pains to better purpose, and *labour for that meat* which belongs to the soul," of which he shows,

[1.] That it is *unspeakably desirable:* It is meat which *endures to everlasting life;* it is a happiness which will last as long as we must, which not only itself endures eternally, but will nourish us up to everlasting life. The blessings of the new covenant are our preparative for eternal life, our preservative to it, and the pledge and earnest of it.

[2.] It is *undoubtedly attainable*. Shall all the treasures of the world be ransacked, and all the fruits of the earth gathered together, to furnish us with provisions that will last to eternity? No, *The sea saith, It is not in me*, among all the treasures hidden in the sand. *It cannot be gotten for gold;* but it is that *which the Son of man shall give; hēn dōsei*, either which *meat*, or which *life*, the Son of man shall give. Observe here, *First*, Who gives this meat: the *Son of man*, the great householder and master of the stores, who is entrusted with the administration of the kingdom of God among men, and the dispensation of the gifts, graces, and comforts of that kingdom, and has power to give eternal life, with all the means of it and preparatives for it. We are told to *labour for it*, as if it were to be got by our own industry, and sold upon that valuable consideration, as the heathen said, *Dii laboribus omnia vendunt — The gods sell all advantages to the industrious*. But when we have laboured ever so much for it, we have not merited it as our *hire*, but the Son of man *gives it*. And what more free than gift? It is an encouragement that he who has the giving of it is the *Son of man*, for then we may hope the *sons of men* that seek it, and labour for it, shall not fail to have it. *Secondly*, What authority he has to give it; for *him has God the Father sealed, touton gar ho Patēr esphragisen, ho Theos — for him the Father has sealed* (proved and evidenced) *to be God;* so some read it: he has declared him to be the Son of God with power. He has *sealed him*, that is, has given him full authority to deal between God and man, as God's *ambassador* to man and man's *intercessor* with God, and has proved his commission by miracles. Having given him *authority*, he has given us *assurance* of it; having entrusted him with *unlimited powers*, he has satisfied us with *undoubted proofs* of them; so that as he might go on with confidence in his undertaking for us, so may we in our resignations to him. *God the Father* scaled him with the Spirit that rested on him, by the voice from heaven, by the testimony he bore to him in signs and wonders. Divine revelation is perfected in him, in him the *vision* and *prophecy* is *sealed up* (Dan. 9:24), to him all believers *seal* that he is true (*ch.* 3:33), and in him they are all *sealed*, 2 Co. 1:22.

Verses 28–59

Whether this conference was with the Capernaites, in whose synagogue Christ now was, or with those who came from the other side of the sea, is not certain nor material; however, it is an instance of Christ's condescension that he gave them leave to ask him questions, and did not resent the interruption as an affront, no, not from his common hearers, though not his immediate followers. Those that would be apt to teach must be swift to hear, and study to answer. It is the wisdom of teachers, when they are asked even impertinent unprofitable questions, thence to take occasion to answer in that which is profitable, that the question may be rejected, but not the request. Now,

I. Christ having told them that *they* must *work for the meat* he spoke of, must *labour* for it, they enquire what work they must do, and he answers them, *v.* 28, 29. 1. Their *enquiry* was *pertinent* enough (*v.* 28): *What shall we do, that we may work the works of God?* Some understand it as a pert question: "What works of God can we do more and better than those we do in obedience to the law of Moses?" But I rather take it as a humble serious question, showing them to be, at least for the present, in a good mind, and willing to know and do their duty; and I imagine that those who asked this question, How and What (*v.* 30), and made the request (*v.* 34), were not the same persons with those that murmured (*v.* 41, 42), and strove (*v.* 52), for those are expressly called *the Jews,* who came out of Judea (for those were strictly called Jews) to cavil, whereas these were of Galilee, and came to be taught. This question here intimates that they were convinced that those who would obtain this everlasting meat, (1.) Must aim to do something great. Those who *look high* in their expectations, and hope to enjoy the *glory of God,* must *aim high* in those endeavours, and study to *do the works of God,* works which he requires and will accept, *works of God,* distinguished from the works of worldly men in their worldly pursuits. It is not enough to speak the words of God, but we must do the works of God. (2.) Must be willing to do any thing: *What shall we do?* Lord, I am ready to do whatever thou shalt appoint, though ever so displeasing to flesh and blood, Acts 9:6. 2. Christ's answer was plain enough (*v.* 29): *This is the work of God that ye believe.* Note, (1.) The work of faith is the work of God. They enquire after the *works* of God (in the plural number), being careful about *many things;* but Christ directs them to one work, which includes all, the one thing needful: that *you believe,* which supersedes all the works of the ceremonial law; the work which is necessary to the acceptance of all the other works, and which produces them, for without faith you cannot please God. It is *God's work,* for it is of his *working in us,* it subjects the soul to his working on us, and quickens the soul in working *for him,* (2.) That faith is the work of God which closes with Christ, and relies upon him. It is to *believe on him* as one whom God *hath sent,* as God's commissioner in the great affair of peace between God and man, and as such to *rest* upon him, and *resign ourselves* to him. See *ch.* 14:1.

II. Christ having told them that the *Son of man* would *give them this meat,* they enquire concerning him, and he answers their enquiry.

1. Their enquiry is after *a sign* (*v.* 30): *What sign showest thou?* Thus far they were right, that, since he required them to give him *credit,* he should produce his *credentials,* and make it out by miracle that he was *sent of God.* Moses having confirmed his mission by *signs,* it was requisite that Christ, who came to set aside the ceremonial law, should in like manner confirm his: "*What dost thou work?* What doest thou drive at? What lasting characters of a divine power does thou design to leave upon thy doctrine?" But *herein* they missed it,

(1.) That they overlooked the many miracles which they had seen wrought by him, and which amounted to an abundant proof of his divine mission. Is this a time of day to ask, "What sign showest thou?" especially at Capernaum, the *staple* of miracles, where he had done so *many mighty works, signs* so significant of his office and undertaking? Were not these very persons but the other day miraculously fed by him? None so blind as they that will not see; for they may be so blind as to question whether it be day or no, when the sun shines in their faces.

(2.) That they preferred the miraculous feeding of Israel in the wilderness before all the miracles Christ wrought (*v.* 31): *Our fathers did eat manna in the desert;* and, to strengthen the objection, they quote a scripture for it: *He gave them bread from heaven* (taken from Ps. 78:24), *he gave them of the corn of heaven.* What a good use might be made of this story to which they here refer! It was a memorable instance of God's power and goodness, often mentioned to the glory of God (Neh. 19:20, 21), yet see how these people perverted it, and made an ill use of it. [1.] Christ reproved them for their fondness of the miraculous bread, and bade them not set their hearts upon *meat which perisheth;* "Why," say they, "*meat for the belly* was the great good thing that God gave to our

fathers in the desert; and why should not we then labour for that meat? If God made much of them, why should not we be for those that will make much of us?" [2.] Christ had fed five thousand men with five loaves, and had given them that as one sign to prove him *sent of God;* but, under colour of *magnifying* the miracles of Moses, they tacitly *undervalue* this miracle of Christ, and *evade* the evidence of it. "Christ fed his thousands; but Moses his hundreds of thousands; Christ fed them but once, and then reproved those who followed him in hope to be still fed, and put them off with a discourse of spiritual food; but Moses fed his followers forty years, and miracles were not their rarities, but their daily bread: Christ fed them with bread out of *the earth,* barley-bread, and fishes out of *the sea;* but Moses fed Israel with bread *from heaven,* angel's food." Thus big did these Jews talk of the *manna* which *their fathers did eat;* but their fathers had slighted it as much as they did now the barley-loaves, and called *light bread,* Num. 21:5. Thus apt are we to slight and overlook the appearances of God's power and grace in our own times, while we pretend to admire the wonders of which *our fathers told us.* Suppose *this* miracle of Christ was outdone by that of Moses, yet there were other instances in which Christ's miracles outshone his; and, besides, all true miracles prove a divine doctrine, though not equally illustrious in the circumstances, which were ever *diversified* according as the occasion did require. As much as the manna excelled the barley-loaves, so much, and much more, did the doctrine of Christ excel the law of Moses, and his heavenly institutions the carnal ordinances of that dispensation.

2. Here is Christ's reply to this enquiry, wherein,

(1.) He *rectifies* their *mistake* concerning the *typical* manna. It was true that their fathers did eat *manna* in the desert. But, [1.] It was not Moses that gave it to them, nor were they obliged to him for it; he was but the instrument, and therefore they must look beyond him to God. We do not find that Moses did so much as pray to God for the *manna;* and he spoke unadvisedly when he said, *Must we fetch water out of the rock?* Moses gave them not either *that* bread or *that water.* [2.] It was not given them, as they imagined, *from heaven,* from the highest heavens, but only from *the clouds,* and therefore not so much superior to that which had its rise from the earth as they thought. Because the scripture saith, *He gave them bread from heaven,* it does not follow that it was *heavenly* bread, or was intended to be the nourishment of souls. Misunderstanding scripture language occasions many mistakes in the things of God.

(2.) He *informs* them concerning the *true* manna, of which that was a type: *But my Father giveth you the true bread from heaven;* that which is truly and properly the *bread from heaven,* of which the manna was but a shadow and figure, is *now given,* not to *your fathers,* who are dead and gone, but *to you* of this present age, for whom the *better things were reserved:* he is *now giving* you that *bread from heaven,* which is *truly* so called. As much as the throne of God's glory is above the clouds of the air, so much does the *spiritual bread* of the everlasting gospel excel the *manna.* In calling God *his Father,* he proclaims himself greater than Moses; for Moses was faithful but as a servant, Christ as a *Son,* Heb. 3:5, 6.

III. Christ, having replied to their enquiries, takes further occasion from their objection concerning the *manna* to discourse of *himself* under the similitude of *bread,* and of *believing* under the similitude of *eating and drinking;* to which, together with his putting both together in the *eating* of his flesh and *drinking* of his blood, and with the remarks made upon it by the hearers, the rest of this conference may be reduced.

1. Christ having spoken of *himself* as the great *gift of God,* and the *true bread* (*v.* 32), largely *explains* and *confirms* this, that we may rightly know him.

(1.) He here shows that he is the *true bread;* this he repeats again and again, *v.* 33, 35, 48–51. Observe, [1.] That Christ is *bread* is that to the soul which bread is to the body, nourishes and supports the spiritual life (is the staff of it) as bread does the bodily life; *it is the staff of life.* The doctrines of the gospel concerning Christ — that he is the mediator between God and man, that he is our peace, our righteousness, our Redeemer; *by these things do men live.* Our bodies could better live without food than our souls without Christ. *Bread-corn is bruised* (Isa. 28:28), so was Christ; he was born at Bethlehem, the *house of bread,* and typified by the *show-bread.* [2.] That he is the *bread of God* (*v.* 33), divine bread; it is he that is *of God* (*v.* 46), bread which my Father gives

(*v.* 32), which he has made to be the food of our souls; the bread of God's family, his *children's bread.* The Levitical sacrifices are called the *bread of God* (Lev. 21:21, 22), and Christ is the great sacrifice; Christ, in his word and ordinances, the *feast* upon the sacrifice. [3.] That he is the *bread of life* (*v.* 35, and again, *v.* 48), *that* bread of life, alluding to the tree of life in the midst of the garden of Eden, which was to Adam the seal of that part of the covenant, *Do this and live,* of which he might *eat and live.* Christ is the bread of life, for he is the fruit of the *tree of life. First,* He is the *living bread* (so he explains himself, *v.* 51): *I am the living bread.* Bread is itself a dead thing, and nourishes not but by the help of the faculties of a living body; but Christ is himself *living bread,* and nourishes by his own power. Manna was a dead thing; if kept but one night, it putrefied and bred worms; but Christ is ever living, everlasting bread, that never moulds, nor waxes old. The doctrine of Christ crucified is now as strengthening and comforting to a believer as ever it was, and his mediation still of as much value and efficacy as ever. *Secondly,* He gives *life unto the world* (*v.* 33), spiritual and eternal life; the life of the soul in union and communion with God here, and in the vision and fruition of him hereafter; a life that includes in it all happiness. The *manna* did only reserve and support life, did not preserve and perpetuate life, much less restore it; but Christ *gives* life to those that were dead in sin. The manna was ordained only for the life of the Israelites, but Christ is given for the *life of the world;* none are excluded from the benefit of this bread, but such as exclude themselves. Christ came to *put life* into the minds of men, principles productive of acceptable performances. [4.] That he is the *bread which came down from heaven;* this is often repeated here, *v.* 33, 50, 51, 58. This denotes, *First,* The divinity of Christ's person. As God, he had a being in heaven, whence he came to take our nature upon him: *I came down from heaven,* whence we may infer his *antiquity,* he was in the beginning with God; his *ability,* for heaven is the firmament of power; and his *authority,* he came with a divine commission. *Secondly,* The divine original of all that good which flows to us through him. He *comes,* not only *katabas — that came down* (*v.* 51), but *katabainōi — that comes down;* he is descending, denoting a constant communication of light, life, and love, from God to believers through Christ, as the *manna* descended daily; see Eph. 1:3. *Omnia desuper — All things from above.* [5.] That he is *that bread* of which the *manna* was a type and figure (*v.* 58), *that* bread, the true bread, *v.* 32. As the rock that they drank of was Christ, so was the manna they ate of *spiritual bread,* 1 Co. 10:3, 4. *Manna* was given to Israel; so Christ to the spiritual Israel. There was manna enough for them all; so in Christ a fulness of grace for all believers; he that *gathers much* of this *manna* will have none to spare when he comes to use it; and he that gathers little, when his grace comes to be perfected in glory, shall find that *he has no lack. Manna* was to be gathered in the morning; and those that would find Christ must *seek him early.* Manna was sweet, and, as the author of the *Wisdom of Solomon* tells us (Wisd. 16:20), was agreeable to every palate; and to those that believe Christ is *precious.* Israel lived upon *manna* till they came to Canaan; and Christ is our life. There was a memorial of the *manna* preserved in the ark; so of Christ in the Lord's supper, as the food of souls.

(2.) He here shows what his undertaking was, and what his errand into the world. Laying aside the metaphor, he speaks plainly, and speaks no proverb, giving us an account of his business among men, *v.* 38–40.

[1.] He assures us, in general, that he came from heaven upon his Father's business (*v.* 38), not *do his own will, but the will of him that sent him.* He *came from heaven,* which bespeaks him an intelligent active being, who voluntarily descended to this lower world, a long journey, and a great step downward, considering the glories of the world he came from and the calamities of the world he came to; we may well ask with wonder, "What moved him to such an expedition?" Here he tells that he came to do, not *his own will,* but the will of his Father; not that he had any will that stood in competition with the will of his Father, but those to whom he spoke suspected he might. "No," saith he, "my own will is not the spring I act from, nor the rule I go by, but I am come to *do the will of him that sent me.*" That is, *First,* Christ did not come into the world as a *private* person, that acts for himself only, but under a *public character,* to act for others as an ambassador, or plenipotentiary, authorized by a public commission; he came into the world as God's great agent and the world's great physician. It was not any private business that brought him hither, but he came to settle affairs between parties no less considerable than the great Creator and the whole creation. *Secondly,* Christ, when he was in the world, did not carry on any *private* design, nor had any *separate interest* at all, distinct from theirs for whom he acted. The scope of his whole life was to glorify God and do good to men. He therefore never consulted his own ease, safety, or quiet; but, when he was to lay down his life, though he had a human nature which startled at it, he set aside the consideration of that, and resolved his will as man into the will of God: *Not as I will, but as thou wilt.*

[2.] He acquaints us, in particular, with that will of the Father which he came to do; he here *declares the decree,* the instructions he was to pursue.

First, The *private instructions* given to Christ, that he should be sure to save all the chosen remnant; and this is the *covenant of redemption* between the Father and the Son (*v.* 38): *"This is the Father's will, who hath sent me;* this is the charge I am entrusted with, that *of all whom he hath given me I should lose none."* Note, 1. There is a certain number of the children of men *given* by the Father to Jesus Christ, to be his care, and so to be to him for a name and a praise; given him for *an inheritance,* for a possession. Let him do all that for them which their case requires; teach them, and heal them, pay their debt, and plead their cause, prepare them for, and preserve them to, eternal life, and then let him make his best of them. The Father might dispose of them as he pleased: as creatures, their lives and beings were *derived from* him; as sinners, their lives and beings were *forfeited to him.* He might have sold them for the satisfaction of his justice, and delivered them *to the tormentors;* but he pitched upon them to be the monuments of his mercy, and delivered them to the Saviour. Those whom God chose to be the objects of his special love he lodged as a trust in the hands of Christ. 2. Jesus Christ has undertaken that he will *lose none* of those that were thus *given him* of the Father. The *many sons* whom he was to *bring to glory* shall all be forth-coming, and none of them missing, Mt. 18:14. None of them shall be lost, for want of a sufficient grace to sanctify them. *If I bring him not unto thee, and set him before thee, then let me bear the blame for ever,* Gen. 43:9. 3. Christ's undertaking for those that are given him extends to the resurrection of their bodies. *I will raise it up again at the last day,* which supposes all that goes before, but this is to crown and complete the undertaking. The body is a part of the man, and therefore a part of Christ's purchase and charge; it pertains to the promises, and therefore it shall not be *lost.* The undertaking is not only that he shall *lose none,* no *person,* but that he shall *lose nothing,* no part of the person, and therefore not the body. Christ's undertaking will never be accomplished till the resurrection, when the souls and bodies of the saints shall be re-united and gathered to Christ, that he may present them to the Father: *Behold I, and the children that thou has given me,* Heb. 2:13; 2 Tim. 1:12. 4. The spring and original of all this is the *sovereign will of God,* the counsels of his will, according to which he works all this. This was the commandment he gave to his Son, when he sent him into the world, and to which the Son always had an eye.

Secondly, The *public instructions* which were to be given to the children of men, in what way, and upon what terms, they might obtain salvation by Christ; and this is the *covenant of grace* between God and man. Who the particular persons were that were given to Christ is a *secret: The Lord knows them that are his,* we do not, nor is it fit we should; but, though their names are concealed, their characters are published. An offer is made of life and happiness upon gospel terms, that by it those that were given to Christ might be brought to him, and others left inexcusable (*v.* 40): *"This is the will,* the revealed will, *of him that sent me,* the method agreed upon, upon which to proceed with the children of men, that *every one,* Jew or Gentile, that *sees the Son, and believes on him,* may have *everlasting life,* and *I will raise him up."* This is *gospel* indeed, good news. Is it now reviving to hear this? 1. That *eternal life* may be had, if it be not our own fault; that whereas, upon the sin of the first Adam, the *way of the tree of life* was blocked up, by the grace of the second Adam it is laid upon again. The crown of glory is set before us as the prize of our high calling, which we may run for and obtain. 2. Every one may have it. This gospel is to be preached, this offer made, to all, and none can say, "It belongs not to me," Rev. 22:17. 3. This everlasting life is sure to all those who believe in Christ, and to them only. He that *sees the Son,* and *believes on him,* shall be saved. Some understand this *seeing* as a *limitation* of this condition of salvation to those only that have the revelation of Christ and his grace made to them. Every one that has the opportunity of being acquainted with Christ, and improves this so well as to *believe* in him, shall have everlasting life, so that none shall be condemned for unbelief (however they maybe for other sins) but those who have had the gospel preached to them, who, like these Jews here (*v.* 36), have *seen,* and yet have *not* believed; have known Christ, and yet not trusted in him. But I rather understand *seeing* here to mean the same thing with *believing,* for it is *theōrōn,* which signifies not so much the sight of the eye (as *v.* 36, *heōrakate me — ye have seen me*) as the *contemplation of the mind.* Every one that *sees the Son,* that is, *believes on him,* sees him with an eye of faith, by which we come to be duly acquainted and affected with the doctrine of the gospel concerning him. It is to look upon him, as the stung Israelites upon the brazen serpent. It is not a *blind* faith that Christ requires, that we should be willing to have our *eyes put out,* and then follow him, but that we should *see him,* and see what ground we go upon in our faith. It is *then* right when it is not taken up upon *hearsay* (believing as the church believes), but is the result of a due consideration of, and insight into, the motives of credibility: *Now mine eye sees thee. We have heard him ourselves.* 4. Those who believe in Jesus Christ, in order to their having everlasting life, shall be raised up by his power at the last day. He had it in charge as his Father's will (*v.* 39), and here he solemnly makes it his own undertaking: I *will raise him up,* which signifies not only the return of the body to life, but the putting of the *whole man* into a full possession of the eternal life promised.

2. Now Christ discoursing thus concerning himself, as the *bread of life* that came down from heaven, let us see what remarks his hearers made upon it.

(1.) When they heard of such a thing as the *bread of God,* which *gives life,* they heartily prayed for it (*v.* 34): *Lord, evermore give us this bread.* I cannot think that this is spoken scoffingly, and in a way of derision, as most interpreters understand it: "Give us such bread as this, if thou canst; let us be fed with it, not for one meal, as with the five loaves, but *evermore;*" as if this were no better a prayer than that of the impenitent thief: *If thou be the Christ, save thyself and us.* But I take this request to be made, though ignorantly, yet honestly, and to be well meant; for they call him *Lord,* and desire a share in what he *gives,* whatever he means by it. General and confused notions of divine things produce in carnal hearts some kind of desires towards them, and wishes of them; like Balaam's wish, to die the *death of the righteous.* Those who have an indistinct knowledge of the things of God, who see men as trees walking, make, as I may call them, *inarticulate* prayers for spiritual blessings. They think the favour of God a *good thing,* and heaven a *fine place,* and cannot but wish them their own, while they have no value nor desire at all for that holiness which is necessary both to the one and to the other. Let this be the desire of our souls; have we tasted that the Lord is gracious, been feasted with the word of God, and Christ in the word? Let us say, *"Lord, evermore give us this bread;* let the bread of life be our daily bread, the heavenly manna our continual feast, and let us never know the want of it."

(2.) But, when they understood that by this *bread of life* Jesus meant *himself,* then they *despised* it. Whether they were the same persons that had prayed for it (*v.* 34), or some others of the company, does not appear; it seems to be some others, for they are called *Jews.* Now it is said (*v.* 41), *They murmured at him.* This comes in immediately after that solemn declaration which Christ had made of God's will and his own undertaking concerning man's salvation (*v.* 39, 40), which certainly were some of the most weighty and gracious words that ever proceeded out of the mouth of our Lord Jesus, the most faithful, and best worthy of all acceptation. One would think that, like Israel in Egypt, when they heard that God had thus *visited* them, they should have *bowed their heads and worshipped;* but on the contrary, instead of closing with the offer made them, they *murmured,* quarrelled with what Christ said, and, though they did not openly oppose and contradict it, yet they privately whispered among themselves in contempt of it, and instilled into one another's minds prejudices against it. Many that will not professedly contradict the doctrine of Christ (their cavils are so weak and groundless that they are either ashamed to own them or afraid to have them silenced), yet say in their hearts that they *do not like it.* Now, [1.] That which offended them was Christ's asserting his origin to be *from heaven, v.* 41, 42. How is it that he saith, *I came down from heaven?* They had heard of angels coming down *from heaven,* but never of a man, overlooking the proofs he had given them of his being more than a man. [2.] That which they thought justified them herein was that they knew his extraction on earth: *Is not this Jesus the son of Joseph, whose father and mother we know?* They took it amiss that he should say that he came down from heaven, when he was *one of them.* They speak slightly of his blessed name, *Jesus: Is not this Jesus.* They take it for granted that Joseph was really his father, though he was only *reputed* to be so. Note, Mistakes concerning the person of Christ, as if he were a mere man, conceived and born by ordinary generation, occasion the offence that is taken at his doctrine and offices. Those who set him on a level with the other sons of men, whose father and mother we know, no wonder if they derogate from the honour of his satisfaction and the mysteries of his undertaking, and, like the Jews here, murmur at his promise to *raise us up at the last day.*

3. Christ, having spoken of faith as the great *work of God* (*v.* 29), discourses largely concerning this work, instructing and encouraging us in it.

(1.) He shows what it is to *believe in Christ.* [1.] To believe in Christ is to *come to Christ.* He that *comes to* me is the same with him that *believes in me* (*v.* 35), and again (*v.* 37): *He that comes unto me;* so *v.* 44, 45. Repentance towards God is *coming to him* (Jer. 3:22) as our chief good and highest end; and so faith towards our Lord Jesus Christ is coming to him as our prince and Saviour, and our way to the Father. It denotes the out-goings of our affection towards him, for these are the motions of the soul, and actions agreeable; it is to *come off* from all those things that stand in opposition to him or competition with him, and to *come up* to those terms upon which life and salvation are offered to us through him. When he was here on earth it was more that barely coming where he was; so it is now more than coming to his word and ordinances. [2.] It is to *feed upon Christ* (*v.* 51): *If any man eat of this bread.* The former denotes applying ourselves to Christ; this denotes applying Christ to ourselves, with appetite and delight, that we may receive life, and strength, and comfort from him. To feed on him as the Israelites on the manna, having quitted the *fleshpots* of Egypt, and not depending on the *labour of their hands* (to eat of that), but living purely on the bread given them from heaven.

(2.) He shows what is to be got by believing in Christ. What will he give us if we *come to him?* What shall we be the better of we *feed upon him? Want* and *death* are the chief things we dread; may we but be assured of the comforts of our being, and the continuance of it in the midst of these comforts, we have enough; now these two are here secured to true believers.

[1.] They shall never want, *never hunger, never thirst, v.* 35. Desires they have, earnest desires, but these so suitably, so seasonably, so abundantly satisfied, that they cannot be called hunger and thirst, which are uneasy and painful. Those that did eat manna, and drink of the rock, hungered and thirsted afterwards. Manna surfeited them; water out of the rock failed them. But there is such an *over-flowing fulness* in Christ as can never be *exhausted,* and there are such *ever-flowing communications* from him as can never be interrupted.

[2.] They shall *never die,* not die eternally; for, *First,* He that believes on Christ *has everlasting life* (*v.* 47); he has the assurance of it, the grant of it, the earnest of it; he has it in the promise and first-fruits. Union with Christ and communion with God in Christ are *everlasting life* begun. *Secondly,* Whereas they that did *eat manna* died, Christ is such bread as a man may eat of and never die, *v.* 49, 50. Observe here, 1. The insufficiency of the typical manna: *Your fathers did eat manna in the wilderness, and are dead.* There may be much good use made of the death of our fathers; their graves speak to us, and their monuments are our memorials, particularly of this, that the greatest *plenty* of the most *dainty* food will neither prolong the thread of life nor avert the stroke of death. Those that did eat manna, angel's food, died like other men. There could be nothing amiss in their diet, to shorten their days, nor could their deaths be hastened by the toils and fatigues of life (for they neither sowed nor reaped), and *yet they died.* (1.) Many of them died by the immediate strokes of God's vengeance for their unbelief and murmurings; for, *though they did eat that spiritual meat,* yet with many of them God *was not well-pleased, but they were overthrown in the wilderness,* 1 Co. 10:3–5. Their eating manna was no security to *them* from the *wrath of God,* as believing in Christ is to *us.* (2.) The rest of them died in a course of nature, and their carcases fell, under a divine sentence, in that wilderness where they did *eat manna.* In that very age when miracles were *daily bread* was the life of man reduced to the stint it now stands at, as appears, Ps. 90:10. Let them not then boast so much of *manna.* 2. The all-sufficiency of the true *manna,* of which the other was a type: *This is the bread that cometh down from heaven,* that truly divine and heavenly food, *that a man may eat thereof and not die;* that is, not fall under the wrath of God, which is killing to the soul; *not die* the second death; no, nor the first death finally and irrecoverably. *Not die,* that is, not perish, not come short of the heavenly Canaan, as the Israelites did of the earthly, for want of *faith,* though they had *manna.* This is further explained by that promise in the next words: *If any man eat of this bread, he shall live for ever, v.* 51. This is the meaning of this *never dying:* though he go down *to death,* he shall pass through it to that world where there shall be *no more death.* To *live for ever* is not to *be* for ever (the damned in hell shall *be* for ever, the soul of man was made for an endless state), but to be *happy* for ever. And because the body must needs die, and be as water spilt upon the ground, Christ here undertakes for the gathering of that up too (as before, *v.* 44, *I will raise him up at the last day*); and even that shall live for ever.

(3.) He shows what encouragements we have to believe in Christ. Christ here speaks of some who *had seen him and yet believed not, v.* 36. They saw his person and miracles, and heard him preach, and yet were not wrought upon to believe in him. Faith is not always the effect of sight; the soldiers were eye-witnesses of his resurrection, and yet, instead of *believing* in him, they *belied* him; so that it is a difficult thing to bring people to believe in Christ: and, by the operation of the Spirit of grace, those that *have not seen have yet believed.* Two things we are here assured of, to encourage our faith: —

[1.] That the Son will bid all those welcome that come to him (*v.* 37): *Him that cometh to me I will in no wise cast out.* How welcome should this word be to our souls which bids us welcome to Christ! *Him* that cometh; it is in the singular number, denoting favour, not only to the body of believers in general, but to every particular soul that applies itself to Christ. Here, *First,* The duty required is a pure gospel duty: to *come to Christ,* that we may come to God by him. His beauty and love, those great attractives, must *draw* us to him; sense of need and fear of danger must *drive* us to him; any thing to bring us to Christ. *Secondly,* The promise is a pure gospel promise: *I will in no wise cast out — ou mē ekbagō exō.* There are two negatives: *I will not, no, I will not.* 1. Much favour is expressed here. We have reason to fear that he should *cast us out.* Considering our meanness, our vileness, our unworthiness to come, our weakness in coming, we may justly expect that he should frown upon us, and shut his doors against us; but he obviates these fears with this assurance, he *will not* do it; will not disdain us though we are mean, will not reject us though we are sinful. Do poor scholars come to him to be taught? Though they be dull and slow, he will not *cast them out.* Do poor *patients* come to him to be *cured,* poor *clients* come to him to be *advised?* Though their case be bad, and though they come empty-handed, he will *in no wise cast them out.* But, 2. More favour is implied than is expressed; when it is said that he will no cast them out the meaning is, He will receive them, and entertain them, and give them all that which they come to him for. As he will not refuse them at their first coming, so he will not afterwards, upon every displeasure, cast them out. *His gifts and callings are without repentance.*

[2.] That the Father will, without fail, bring all those to him in due time that were given him. In the federal transactions between the Father and the Son, relating to man's redemption, as the Son undertook for the justification, sanctification, and salvation, of all that should come to him ("Let me have them put into my hands, and then leave the management of them to me"), so the Father, the fountain and original of being, life, and grace, undertook to put into his hand all that were given him, and bring them to him. Now,

First, He here *assures* us *that* this shall be done: *All that the Father giveth me shall come to me, v.* 37. Christ had complained (*v.* 36) of those who, though they had *seen* him, yet would not believe on him; and then he adds this,

a. For *their* conviction and awakening, plainly intimating that their not coming to him, and believing on him, if they persisted in it, would be a certain sign that they did not belong to the election of grace; for how can we think that God gave us to Christ if we give ourselves to the world and the flesh? 2 Pt. 1:10.

b. For *his own* comfort and encouragement: *Though Israel be not gathered, yet shall I be glorious.* The election *has obtained,* and shall though multitudes be *blinded,* Rom. 11:7. Though he lose many of his *creatures,* yet none of his *charge: All that the Father gives him shall come to him* notwithstanding. Here we have, (*a.*) The election described: *All that the father giveth me, pan ho didōsi — every thing* which the Father *giveth to me;* the persons of the elect, and all that belongs to them; all their services, all their interests. As all that he has is *theirs,* so all that they have is *his,* and he speaks of them as his all: they were given him in full recompense of his undertaking. Not only all persons, but all things, are gathered together in Christ (Eph. 1:10) and reconciled, Col. 1:20. The giving of the chosen remnant to Christ is spoken of (*v.* 39) as a thing *done;* he *hath given* them. Here it is spoken of as a thing *in the doing;* he *giveth them;* because, *when the first begotten was brought into the world,* it should seem, there was a renewal of the grant; see Heb. 10:5, etc. God was now about to *give him the heathen for his inheritance* (Ps. 2:8), to put him in possession of *the desolate heritages* (Isa. 49:8), to *divide him a portion with the great,* Isa. 53:12. And though the Jews, who *saw* him, *believed not* on him, yet these (saith he) shall *come to me;* the other sheep, which are not of this fold, shall be *brought, ch.* 10:15, 16. See Acts 13:45–48. (*b.*) The effect of it secured: *They shall come to me.* This is not in the nature of a *promise,* but a *prediction,* that as many as were in the counsel of God ordained to life shall be brought to life by being brought to Christ. They are *scattered,* are mingled among the nations, yet none of them shall be forgotten; not a grain of God's corn shall be lost, as is promised, Amos 9:9. They are by nature *alienated* from Christ, and averse to him, and yet *they shall come.* As God's omniscience is engaged for the finding of them all out, so is his omnipotence for the bringing of them all in. Not, They shall be *driven,* to me, but, They shall come freely, shall be made *willing.*

Secondly, He here *acquaints* us *how* it shall be done. How shall those who are given to Christ be brought to him? Two things are to be done in order to it: —

a. Their *understandings* shall be *enlightened;* this is promised, *v.* 45, 46. It is written in the prophets, who spoke of these things before, *And they shall be all taught of God;* this we find, Isa. 54:13, and Jer. 31:34. *They shall all know me.* Note,

(*a.*) In order to our *believing in Jesus Christ,* it is necessary that we be *taught of God;* that is, [*a.*] That there be a *divine revelation made to us,* discovering to us both what we are to believe concerning Christ and why we are to believe it. There are some things which *even nature teaches,* but to bring us to Christ there is need of a higher light. [*b.*] That there be a *divine work wrought in us,* enabling us to understand and receive these revealed truths and the evidence of them. God, in giving us reason, teaches us more than the *beasts of the earth;* but in giving us faith he teaches more than the *natural man.* Thus all the church's children, all that are *genuine,* are *taught of God;* he hath undertaken their education.

(*b.*) It follows then, by way of inference from this, that *every man* that has *heard and learned of the Father comes to Christ, v.* 45. [*a.*] It is here implied that none will come to Christ but those that have *heard* and *learned of the Father.* We shall never be brought to Christ but under a divine conduct; except God by his grace enlighten our minds, inform our judgments, and rectify our mistakes, and not only *tell* us that we may *hear,* but teach us, that we may *learn* the truth as it is in Jesus, we shall never be brought to believe in Christ. [*b.*] That this *divine teaching* does so necessarily produce the *faith of God's elect* that we may conclude that those who do not *come to Christ* have never *heard* nor *learned* of the Father; for, if they had, doubtless they would have come to Christ. In vain do men pretend to be *taught of God* if they believe not in Christ, for he teaches no other lesson, Gal. 1:8, 9. See how God deals with men as reasonable creatures, draws them with the *cords of a man,* opens the understanding first, and then by that, in a regular way, influences the inferior faculties; thus he comes in by the door, but Satan, as a robber, climbs up another way. But lest any should dream of a visible appearance of God the Father to the children of men (to teach them these things), and entertain any gross conceptions about hearing and learning of the Father, he adds (*v.* 46): *Not that any man hath seen the Father;* it is implied, nor *can* see him, with bodily eyes, or may expect to learn of him as Moses did, to whom he spoke *face to face;* but God, in enlightening men's eyes and teaching them, works in a spiritual way. The Father of spirits hath access to, and influence upon, men's spirits, undiscerned. The Father of spirits hath access to, and influence upon, men's spirits, undiscerned. Those that have not seen his face have felt his power. And yet there is one intimately acquainted with the Father, he *who is of God,* Christ himself, he hath *seen the Father, ch.* 1:18. Note, *First,* Jesus Christ is of God in a peculiar manner, God of God, light of light; not only sent of God, but begotten of God before all worlds. *Secondly,* It is the prerogative of Christ to have *seen the Father,* perfectly to know him and his counsels. *Thirdly,* Even that illumination which is preparative to faith is conveyed to us through Christ. Those that *learn of the Father,* forasmuch as they cannot see him themselves, must learn of Christ, who alone hath seen him. As all divine discoveries are made through Christ, so through him all divine powers are exerted.

b. Their *wills* shall be *bowed.* If the soul of man had now its original rectitude there needed no more to influence the will than the illumination of the understanding; but in the depraved soul of fallen man there is a rebellion of the will against the right dictates of the understanding; a *carnal mind,* which is *enmity* itself to the divine light and law. It is therefore requisite that there be a work of grace wrought upon the will, which is here called *drawing,* (*v.* 44): *No man can come to me except the Father, who hath sent me, draw him.* The Jews murmured at the doctrine of Christ; not only would not receive it themselves, but were angry that others did. Christ overheard their secret whisperings, and said (*v.* 43), *"Murmur not among yourselves;* lay not the fault of your dislike of my doctrine one upon another, as if it were because you find it generally distasted; no, it is owing to yourselves, and your own corrupt dispositions, which are such as amount to a *moral impotency;* your antipathies to the truths of God, and prejudices against them, are so strong that nothing less than a divine power can conquer them." And this is the case of all mankind: *"No man can come to me,* can persuade himself to come up to the terms of the gospel, *except the Father, who hath sent me, draw him," v.* 44. Observe, (*a.*) The nature of the work: It is *drawing,* which denotes not a *force* put upon the will, whereby of unwilling we are made willing, and a new bias is given to the soul, by which it inclines to God. This seems to be more than a *moral suasion,* for by that it is in the power to *draw;* yet it is not to be called a *physical impulse,* for it lies out of the road of *nature;* but he that *formed the spirit of man within him* by his creating power, and *fashions the hearts of men* by his providential influence, knows how to new-mould the soul, and to alter its bent and temper, and make it conformable to himself and his own will, without doing any wrong to its natural liberty. It is such a drawing as works not only a *compliance,* but a cheerful compliance, a complacency: *Draw us, and we will run after thee.* (*b.*) The necessity of it: *No man,* in this weak and helpless state, can come to Christ without it. As we *cannot* do any natural action without the concurrence of *common providence,* so we cannot do any action morally good without the influence of *special grace,* in which the *new man* lives, and moves, and has its being, as much as the *mere man* has in the divine providence. (*c.*) The author of it: The *Father who hath sent me.* The Father, having sent Christ, will succeed him, for he would not send him on a fruitless errand. Christ having undertaken to bring souls to glory, God promised him, in order thereunto, to bring them to him, and so to give him possession of those to whom he had given him a right. God, having by promise given the kingdom of Israel to David, did at length *draw the hearts* of the people to him; so, having sent Christ to save souls, he sends souls to him to be saved by him. (*d.*) The crown and perfection of this work: And *I will raise him up at the last day.* This is four times mentioned in this discourse, and doubtless it includes all the intermediate and preparatory workings of divine grace. When he *raises them up at the last day,* he will put the *last hand* to his undertaking, will *bring forth the topstone.* If he undertakes this, surely he *can* do any thing, and will do every thing that is necessary in order to do it. Let our expectations be carried out towards a happiness reserved for the *last day,* when all the years of time shall be fully complete and ended.

4. Christ, having thus spoken of himself as the *bread of life,* and of faith as *the work of God,* comes more particularly to show *what of himself* is this bread, namely, his flesh, and that to believe is to eat of that, *v.* 51–58, where he still prosecutes the metaphor of food. Observe, here, the *preparation* of this food: *The bread that I will give is my flesh* (*v.* 51), *the flesh of the Son of man and his blood, v.* 53. *His flesh is meat indeed, and his blood is drink indeed, v.* 55. observe, also, the *participation* of this food: We must *eat the flesh of the Son of man and drink his blood* (*v.* 53); and again (*v.* 54), *Whoso eateth my flesh and drinketh my blood;* and the same words (*v.* 56, 57), he that *eateth me.* This is certainly a parable or figurative discourse, wherein the actings of the soul upon things spiritual and divine are represented by bodily actions about things sensible, which made the truths of Christ more intelligible to some, and less so to others, Mk. 4:11–12. Now,

(1.) Let us see how this discourse of Christ was liable to mistake and misconstruction, that *men might see, and not perceive.* [1.] It was misconstrued by the carnal *Jews,* to whom it was first delivered (*v.* 52): *They strove among themselves;* they whispered in each other's ears their dissatisfaction: *How can this man give us his flesh to eat?* Christ spoke (*v.* 51) of giving his flesh *for us,* to suffer and die; but they, without due consideration, understood it of his giving it *to us,* to be eaten, which gave occasion to Christ to tell them that, however what he said was otherwise intended, yet even that also of *eating of his flesh* was no such absurd thing (if rightly understood) as *prima facie — in the first instance,* they took it to be. [2.] It has been wretchedly misconstrued by the church of Rome for the support of their monstrous doctrine of transubstantiation, which gives the lie to our senses, contradicts the nature of a sacrament, and overthrows all convincing evidence. They, like these Jews here, understand it of a corporal and carnal eating of Christ's body, like Nicodemus, *ch.* 3, 4. The Lord's supper was not yet instituted, and therefore it could have no reference to that; it is a *spiritual* eating and drinking that is here spoken of, not a *sacramental.* [3.] It is misunderstood by many ignorant carnal people, who hence infer that, if they take the sacrament when they die, they shall certainly go to heaven, which, as it makes many that are weak causelessly uneasy if they want it, so it makes many that are wicked causelessly easy if they have it. Therefore,

(2.) Let us see how this discourse of Christ is to be understood.

[1.] What is meant by the *flesh and blood of Christ.* It is called (*v.* 53), *The flesh of the Son of man, and his blood, his* as Messiah and Mediator: the *flesh and blood* which he *assumed* in his incarnation (Heb. 2:14), and which he *gave up* in his *death* and *suffering: my flesh which I will give* to be crucified and slain. It is said to be *given for the life of the world,* that is, *First, Instead* of the *life of the world,* which was *forfeited* by sin, Christ gives his own flesh as a ransom or counterprice. Christ was our bail, bound *body for body* (as we say), and therefore *his* life must go for *ours,* that ours may be spared. *Here am I, let these go their way. Secondly, In order to* the *life of the world,* to purchase a *general* offer of eternal life to all the world, and the *special* assurances of it to all believers. So that the *flesh and blood* of the Son of man denote the Redeemer *incarnate* and *dying;* Christ and *him crucified,* and the redemption wrought out by him, with all the precious benefits of redemption: pardon of sin, acceptance with God, the adoption of sons, access to the throne of grace, the promises of the covenant, and eternal life; these are called *the flesh and blood* of Christ, 1. Because they are purchased by his flesh and blood, by the breaking of his body, and shedding of his blood. Well may the purchased privileges be denominated from the price that was paid for them, for it puts a value upon them; write upon them *pretium sanguinis — the price of blood.* 2. Because they are meat and drink to our souls. *Flesh with the blood* was prohibited (Gen. 9:4), but the privileges of the gospel are as flesh and blood to us, prepared for the nourishment of our souls. He had before compared himself to *bread,* which is necessary food; here to *flesh,* which is delicious. It is a *feast of fat things,* Isa. 25:6. The soul is satisfied with Christ as *with marrow and fatness,* Ps. 63:5. It is *meat indeed,* and *drink indeed; truly so,* that is spiritually; so Dr. Whitby; as Christ is called the *true vine;* or *truly meat,* in opposition to the shows and shadows with which the world shams off those that feed upon it. In Christ and his gospel there is real supply, solid satisfaction; that is *meat indeed,* and *drink indeed,* which satiates and replenishes, Jer. 31:25, 26.

[2.] What is meant by *eating this flesh* and *drinking* this *blood,* which is so necessary and beneficial; it is certain that is means neither more nor less than believing in Christ. As we partake of meat and drink by eating and drinking, so we partake of Christ and his benefits by faith: and *believing in Christ* includes these four things, which *eating and drinking* do: — *First,* It implies an *appetite* to Christ. This spiritual eating and drinking begins with *hungering* and *thirsting* (Mt. 5:6), earnest and importunate desires after Christ, not willing to take up with any thing short of an interest in him: "Give me Christ or else I die." *Secondly,* An *application* of Christ to ourselves. Meat *looked upon* will not nourish us, but meat *fed upon,* and so made *our own,* and as it were *one with us.* We must so accept of Christ as to appropriate him to ourselves: *my Lord, and my God, ch.* 20:28. *Thirdly,* A *delight* in Christ and his salvation. The doctrine of Christ crucified must be *meat and drink* to us, most pleasant and delightful. We must feast upon the dainties of the *New Testament in the blood of Christ,* taking as great a complacency in the methods which Infinite Wisdom has taken to redeem and save us as ever we did in the most needful supplies or grateful delights of nature. *Fourthly,* A *derivation of nourishment* from him and a dependence upon him for the support and comfort of our spiritual life, and the strength, growth, and vigour of the new man. To *feed upon Christ* is to do all *in his name,* in union with him, and by virtue drawn from him; it is to live upon him as we do upon our meat. How our bodies are nourished by our food we cannot describe, but that they are so we know and find; so it is with this spiritual nourishment. Our Saviour was so well pleased with this metaphor (as very significant and expressive) that, when afterwards he would institute some outward sensible signs, by which to represent our *communicating* of the benefits of his death, he chose those of *eating* and *drinking,* and made them *sacramental* actions.

(3.) Having thus explained the general meaning of this part of Christ's discourse, the particulars are reducible to two heads: —

[1.] The *necessity* of our *feeding upon Christ* (*v.* 53): *Except you eat the flesh of the Son of man, and drink his blood, you have no life in you.* That is, *First,* "It is a certain sign that you *have no* spiritual *life* in you if you have no *desire* towards Christ, nor *delight* in him." If the soul does not *hunger* and *thirst,* certainly it does not *live:* it is a sign that we are dead indeed if we are dead to such meat and drink as this. When *artificial* bees, that by curious springs were made to move to and fro, were to be *distinguished* from *natural* ones (they say), it was done by putting honey among them, which the natural bees only flocked to, but the artificial ones minded not, for *they had no life in them. Secondly,* "It is certain that you *can have* no spiritual life, unless you derive it from Christ by faith; separated from him you can do nothing." Faith in Christ is the *primum vivens — the first living principle* of grace; without it we have not the *truth* of *spiritual* life, nor any title to eternal life: our bodies may as well live without meat as our souls without Christ.

[2.] The *benefit* and *advantage* of it, in two things: —

First, We shall be *one with Christ,* as our bodies are with our food when it is digested (*v.* 56): *He that eats my flesh, and drinks my blood,* that lives by faith in Christ crucified (it is spoken of as a continued act), he *dwelleth in me, and I in him.* By faith we have a close and intimate union with Christ; he is *in us,* and we *in him, ch.* 17:21–23; 1 Jn. 3:24. Believers dwell in Christ as their stronghold or city of refuge; Christ dwells in them as the master of the house, to rule it and provide for it. Such is the union between Christ and believers that he shares in their griefs, and they share in his graces and joys; he *sups* with them upon their bitter herbs, and *they with him* upon his *rich dainties.* It is an inseparable union, like that between the body and digested food, Rom. 8:35; 1 Jn. 4:13.

Secondly, We shall *live,* shall live eternally, *by him,* as our bodies live by our food.

a. We shall *live by him* (*v.* 57): *As the living Father hath sent me, and I live by the Father, so he that eateth me, even he shall live by me.* We have here the series and order of the divine life. (*a.*) God is the *living Father,* hath life in and of himself. *I am that I am* is his name for ever. (*b.*) Jesus Christ, as Mediator, lives *by the Father;* he has life *in himself* (*ch.* 5:26), but he has it of the Father. He that sent him, not only qualified him with that life which was necessary to so great an undertaking, but constituted him the treasury of divine life to us; he breathed into the second Adam the breath of spiritual lives, as into the first Adam the breath of natural lives. (*c.*) True believers receive this divine life by virtue of their union with Christ, which is inferred from the union between the Father and the Son, as it is compared to it, *ch.* 17:21. For therefore *he that eateth me,* or feeds on me, *even he shall live by me:* those that live *upon* Christ shall live *by* him. The life of believers is *had from Christ* (*ch.* 1:16); it is *hid with Christ* (Col. 3:4), we live by *him* as the members by the head, the branches by the root; because he lives, we shall live also.

b. We shall live *eternally* by him (*v.* 54): *Whoso eateth my flesh, and drinketh my blood,* as prepared in the gospel to be the food of souls, he *hath eternal life,* he hath it now, as *v.* 40. He has that in him which is eternal life begun; he has the earnest and foretaste of it, and the hope of it; he shall live *for ever, v.* 58. His happiness shall run parallel with the longest line of eternity itself.

Lastly, The historian concludes with an account *where* Christ had this discourse with the Jews (*v.* 59): *In the synagogue as he taught,* implying that he taught them many other things besides these, but this was that in his discourse which was new. He adds this, that he said these things *in the synagogue,* to show, 1. The credit of Christ's doctrine. His truths sought no corners, but were publicly preached in mixed assemblies, as able to abide the most severe and impartial test. Christ pleaded this upon his trial (*ch.* 18:20): *I ever taught in the synagogue.* 2. The credibility of this narrative of it. To assure you that the discourse was fairly represented, he appeals to the synagogue at Capernaum, where it might be examined.

Verses 60–71

We have here an account of the effects of Christ's discourse. Some were offended and others edified by it; some driven *from him* and others brought nearer *to him.*

I. To some it was a *savour of death unto death;* not only to the Jews, who were professed enemies to him and his doctrine, but even to many of *his disciples,* such as were disciples *at large,* who were his frequent hearers, and followed him *in public;* a mixed multitude, like those among Israel, that began all the discontents. Now here we have,

1. Their murmurings at the doctrine they heard (*v.* 60): *This is a hard saying, who can hear it?* (1.) They do not like it themselves: "What stuff is this? *Eat the flesh, and drink the blood, of the Son of man!* If it is to be understood figuratively, it is not intelligible; if literally, not practicable. What! must we turn cannibals? Can we not be religious, but we must be barbarous?" *Si Christiani adorant quod comedunt* (said Averroes), *sit anima mea cum philosophis — If Christians adore what they eat, my mind shall continue with the philosophers.* Now, when they found it a hard saying, if they had humbly begged of Christ to have *declared unto them this parable,* he would have opened it, and their understandings too; for *the meek will he teach his way.* But they were not willing to have Christ's sayings explained to them, because they would not lose *this* pretence for rejecting them — that they were *hard sayings.* (2.) They think it impossible that any one else should like it: "*Who can hear it?* Surely none can." Thus the scoffers at religion are ready to undertake that all the intelligent part of mankind concur with them. They conclude with great assurance that no *man of sense* will admit the doctrine of Christ, nor any *man of spirit* submit to his laws. Because they cannot bear to be so *tutored,* so *tied up,* themselves, they think none else can: *Who can hear it?* Thanks be to God, thousands have *heard* these sayings of Christ, and have found them not only easy, but pleasant, as their *necessary food.*

2. Christ's animadversions upon their murmurings.

(1.) He well enough knew their murmurings, *v.* 61. Their cavils were secret in their own breasts, or whispered among themselves in a corner. But, [1.] Christ *knew* them; he saw them, he heard them. Note, Christ takes notice not only of the bold and open *defiances* that are done to his name and glory by *daring sinners,* but of the secret slights that are put upon his doctrine by carnal professors; he knows that which the *fool saith in his heart,* and cannot for shame *speak out;* he observes how his doctrine is *resented* by those to whom it is *preached;* who *rejoice* in it, and who *murmur* at it; who are reconciled to it, and bow before it, and who quarrel with it, and rebel against it, though ever so secretly. [2.] He knew it *in himself,* not by any information given him, nor any external indication of the thing, but by his own divine omniscience. He knew it not as the prophets, by a *divine revelation* made to him (that which the prophets desired to know was sometimes hid from them, as 2 Ki. 4:27), but by a *divine knowledge* in him. He is that essential Word that *discerns the thoughts of the heart,* Heb. 4:12, 13. Thoughts are words to Christ; we should therefore take heed not only what we say and do, but what we think.

(2.) He well enough knew how to answer them: *"Doth this offend you?* Is this a stumbling-block to you?" See how people by their own wilful mistakes create offences to themselves: they take offence where there is none given, and even make it where there is nothing to make it of. Note, We may justly wonder that so much offence should be taken at the doctrine of Christ for so little cause. Christ speaks of it here with wonder: *"Doth this offend you?"* Now, in answer to those who condemned his doctrine as intricate and obscure *(Si non vis intelligi, debes negligi — If you are unwilling to be understood, you ought to be neglected),*

[1.] He gives them a hint of his ascension into heaven, as that which would give an irresistible evidence of the truth of his doctrine (*v.* 62): *What and if you shall see the Son of man ascend up where he was before?* And what then? *First,* "If I should tell you of that, surely it would much more offend you, and you would think my pretensions too high indeed. If this be so hard a saying that you cannot hear it, how will you digest it when I tell you of my returning *to* heaven, whence I came down?" See *ch.* 3:12. Those who stumble at smaller difficulties should consider how they will get over greater. *Secondly,* "When you see the Son of man ascend, this will much more offend you, for then my body will be less capable of being eaten by you in that gross sense wherein you now understand it;" so Dr. Whitby. Or, *Thirdly,* "When you see that, or hear it from those that shall see it, surely then you will be satisfied. You think I take too much upon me when I say, *I came down from heaven,* for it was with this that you quarrelled (*v.* 42); but will you think so when you see me return to heaven?" If he *ascended,* certainly he *descended,* Eph. 4:9, 10. Christ did often refer himself thus to *subsequent* proofs, as *ch.* 1:50, 51; 2:14; Mt. 12:40; 26:64. Let us wait awhile, till the mystery of God shall be finished, and then we shall see that there was no reason to be offended at any of Christ's sayings.

[2.] He gives them a general key to this and all such parabolical discourses, teaching them that they are to be understood spiritually, and not after a corporal and carnal manner: *It is the spirit that quickeneth, the flesh profiteth nothing, v.* 63. As it is in the natural body, the animal spirits quicken and enliven it, and without these the most nourishing food would profit nothing (what would the body be the better for bread, if it were not quickened and animated by the spirit), so it is with the soul. *First,* The bare participation of ordinances, unless the Spirit of God work with them, and quicken the soul by them, *profits nothing;* the word and ordinances, if the Spirit works with them, are as food to a living man, if not, they are as food to a dead man. Even the flesh of Christ, the sacrifice for sin, will avail us nothing unless the blessed Spirit quicken our souls thereby, and enforce the powerful influences of his death upon us, till we by his grace are planted together in the likeness of it. *Secondly,* The doctrine of eating Christ's flesh and drinking his blood, if it be understood literally, *profits nothing,* but rather leads us into mistakes and prejudices; but the spiritual sense or meaning of it quickens the soul, makes it *alive* and *lively;* for so it follows: *The words that I speak unto you, they are spirit, and they are life. To eat the flesh of Christ!* this is a hard saying, but to believe that Christ died for me, to derive from that doctrine strength and comfort in my approaches to God, my oppositions to sin and preparations for a future state, this is the *spirit and life* of that saying, and, construing it thus, it is an excellent saying. The reason why men *dislike* Christ's sayings if because they *mistake* them. The literal sense of a parable does us no good, we are never the wiser for it, but the spiritual meaning is instructive. *Thirdly,* The flesh profits nothing — those that *are in the flesh* (so some understand it), that are under the power of a carnal mind, *profit not* by Christ's discourses; but *the Spirit quickeneth* — those that have the Spirit, that are spiritual, are quickened and enlivened by them; for they are received *ad modum recipientis — so as to correspond with the state of the receiver's mind.* They found fault with Christ's sayings, whereas the fault was in themselves; it is only to *sensual* minds that spiritual things are *senseless* and *sapless,* spiritual minds *relish* them; see 1 Co. 2:14, 15.

[3.] He gives them an intimation of his *knowledge of them,* and that he had expected no better from them, though they called themselves his disciples, *v.* 64, 65. Now was fulfilled that of the prophet, speaking of Christ and his doctrine (Isa. 53:1), *Who hath believed our report? and to whom is the arm of the Lord revealed?* Both these Christ here takes notice of.

First, They did not *believe his report:* "There are *some of you* who said you would leave all to follow me who yet *believe not;"* and this was the reason why the *word preached did not profit them,* because it was *not mixed with faith,* Heb. 4:2. They did not believe him to be the Messiah, else they would have acquiesced in the doctrine he preached, and not have quarrelled with it, though there were some things in it *dark, and hard to be understood. Oportet discentum credere — Young beginners in learning must take things upon their teacher's word.* Note, 1. Among those who are *nominal Christians,* there are many who are *real infidels.* 2. The unbelief of hypocrites, before it discovers itself to the world, is naked and open before the eyes of Christ. He *knew from the beginning* who they were of the multitudes that followed him that *believed,* and who of the twelve should betray him; he knew *from the beginning* of their acquaintance with him, and attendance on him, when they were in the hottest pang of their zeal, who were sincere, as Nathanael (*ch.* 1:47), and who were not. Before they distinguished themselves by an overt act, he could infallibly distinguish *who believed* and who did not, whose love was *counterfeit* and whose *cordial.* We may gather hence, (1.) That the apostasy of those who have long made a plausible profession of religion is a certain proof of their constant hypocrisy, and that *from the beginning they believed not,* but is not a proof of the possibility of the total and final apostasy of any true believers: such revolts are not to be called the fall of real saints, but the discovery of pretended ones; see 1 Jn. 2:19. *Stella cadens non stella fuit —The star that falls never was a star.* (2.) That it is Christ's prerogative to *know the heart;* he knows who they are that *believe not,* but dissemble in their profession, and yet continues them room in his church, the use of his ordinances, and the credit of his name, and does not discover them in this world, unless they by their own wickedness discover themselves; because such is the constitution of his visible church, and the discovering day is yet to come. But, if we pretend to judge men's hearts, we step into Christ's throne, and anticipate his judgment. We are often deceived in men, and see cause to change our sentiments of them; but this we are sure of, that Christ knows all men, and *his judgment is according to truth.*

Secondly, The reason why they did not believe his report was because the *arm of the Lord* was not *revealed* to them (*v.* 65): *Therefore said I unto you that no man can come to me, except it be given unto him of my Father;* referring to *v.* 44. Christ therefore could not but know who believed and who did not, because faith is the gift and work of God, and all his Father's gifts and works could not but be known to him, for they all passed through his hands. There he had said that none could *come to him, except the Father draw him;* here he saith, *except it be given him of my Father,* which shows that God *draws* souls by giving them grace and strength, and a heart to come, without which, such is the moral impotency of man, in his fallen state, that he *cannot come.*

3. We have here their final apostasy from Christ hereupon: *From that time many of his disciples went back, and walked no more with him, v.* 66. When we admit into our minds hard thoughts of the word and works of Christ, and conceive a secret dislike, and are willing to hear insinuations tending to their reproach, we are then *entering into temptation;* it is as the letting forth of water; it is *looking back,* which, if infinite mercy prevent not, will end in *drawing back;* therefore *Obsta principiis — Take heed of the beginnings* of apostasy. (1.) See here the *backsliding* of these *disciples. Many of them went back* to their houses, and families, and callings, which they had left for a time to follow him; *went back,* one to his farm and another to his merchandise; *went back,* as Orpah did, to their people, and to their gods, Ruth 1:15. They had entered themselves in Christ's school, but they *went back,* did not only play truant for once, but took leave of him and his doctrine for ever. Note, The apostasy of Christ's disciples from him, though really a strange thing, yet has been such a common thing that we need not be surprised at it. Here were *many* that *went back.* It is often so; when some backslide many backslide with them; the disease is infectious. (2.) The occasion of this backsliding: *From that time,* from the time that Christ preached this comfortable doctrine, that he is the *bread of life,* and that those who by faith feed *upon him* shall live *by him* (which, one would think, should have engaged them to cleave more closely to him) — from *that* time they withdrew. Note, The corrupt and wicked heart of man often makes that an occasion of offence which is indeed matter of the greatest comfort. Christ foresaw that they would thus take offence at what he said, and yet he said it. That which is the undoubted word and truth of Christ must be faithfully delivered, whoever may be offended at it. Men's humours must be captivated to God's word, and not God's word accommodated to men's humours. (3.) The degree of their apostasy: *They walked no more with him,* returned no more to him and attended no more upon his ministry. It is hard for those who have been *once enlightened,* and have *tasted the good word of God, if they fall away, to renew them again to repentance,* Heb. 6:4–6.

II. This discourse was to others a *savour of life unto life. Many went back,* but, thanks be to God, all did not; even then the *twelve* stuck to him. Though the *faith of some be overthrown,* yet the *foundation of God stands sure.* Observe here,

1. The affectionate question which Christ put to the twelve (*v.* 67): *Will you also go away?* He saith nothing to those who went back. *If the unbelieving depart, let them depart;* it was no great *loss* of those whom he never *had;* lightly come, lightly go; but he takes this occasion to speak to the twelve, to confirm them, and by trying their stedfastness the more to fix them: *Will you also go away?* (1.) "It is *at your choice* whether you will or no; if you will forsake me, now is the time, when so many do: it is an hour of temptation; if you will go back, go now." Note, Christ will detain none with him against their wills; his soldiers are volunteers, not pressed men. The twelve had now had time enough to try how they liked Christ and his doctrine, and that none of them might afterwards say that they were trepanned into discipleship, and if it were to do again they would not do it, he here allows them a power of revocation, and leaves them at their liberty; as Jos. 24:15; Ruth 1:15. (2.) "It is *at your peril* if you do go away." If there was any secret inclination in the heart of any of them to depart from him, he stops it with this awakening question, *"Wilt you also go away?* Think not that you hang at as loose an end as they did, and may go away as easily as they could. They have not been so intimate with me as you have been, nor received so many favours from me; they are gone, but will *you* also go? Remember your character, and say, Whatever others do, we will never go away. *Should such a man as I flee?"* Neh. 6:11. Note, The nearer we have been to Christ and the longer we have been with him, the more engagements we have laid ourselves under to him, the greater will be our sin if we desert him. (3.) "I have reason *to think you will not.* Will you go away? No, I have faster hold of you than so; *I hope better things of you* (Heb. 6:9), for *you are they that have continued with me,"* Lu. 22:28. When the apostasy of some is a grief to the Lord Jesus, the constancy of others is so much the more his honour, and he is pleased with it accordingly. Christ and believers know one another too well to part upon every displeasure.

2. The believing reply which Peter, in the name of the rest, made to this question, *v.* 68, 69. Christ put the question to them, as Joshua put Israel to their choice whom they would serve, with design to draw out from them a promise to adhere to him, and it had the like effect. *Nay, but we will serve the Lord,* Peter was upon all occasions the *mouth of the rest,* not so much because he had more of his Master's ear than they, but because he had more tongue of his own; and what he said was sometimes approved and sometimes reprimanded (Mt. 16:17, 23) — the common lot of those who are swift to speak. This here was well said, admirably well; and probably he said it by the direction, and with the express assent, of his fellow-disciples; at least he knew their mind, and spoke the sense of them all, and did not except Judas, for we must hope the best.

(1.) Here is a good resolution to adhere to Christ, and so expressed as to intimate that they would not entertain the least thought of leaving him: *"Lord, to whom shall we go?* It were folly to go from thee, unless we knew where to better ourselves; no, Lord, we like our choice too well to change." Note, Those who leave Christ would do well to consider to whom they will go, and whether they can expect to find rest and peace any where but in him. See Ps. 73:27, 28; Hos. 2:9.

"*Whither shall we go?* Shall we make our court to the world? It will certainly *deceive* us. Shall we return to sin? It will certainly *destroy* us. Shall we leave the *fountain of living waters* for *broken cisterns?"* The disciples resolve to continue their pursuit of life and happiness, and will have a guide to it, and will adhere to Christ as their guide, for they can never have a better. "Shall we go to the heathen philosophers, and become their disciples? They are become vain in their imaginations, and, professing themselves to be wise in other things, are become fools in religion. Shall we go to the scribes and Pharisees, and sit at their feet? What good can they do us who have made void the commandments of God by their traditions? Shall we go to Moses? He will send us back again to thee. Therefore, if ever we find the way to happiness, it must be in following thee." Note, Christ's holy religion appears to great advantage when it is compared with other institutions, for then it will be seen how far it excels them all. Let those who find fault with this religion find a better before they quit it. A divine teacher we must have; can we find a better than Christ? A divine revelation we cannot be without; if the scripture be not such a one, where else may we look for it?

(2.) Here is a good reason for this resolution. It was not the inconsiderate resolve of a blind affection, but the result of mature deliberation. The disciples were resolved never to go away from Christ,

[1.] Because of the *advantage* they promised themselves by him: *Thou hast the words of eternal life.* They themselves did not fully understand Christ's discourse, for as yet the doctrine of the cross was a riddle to them; but in the general they were satisfied that *he had the words of eternal life,* that is, *First,* That the word of his doctrine showed the way to *eternal life,* set it before us, and directed us what to do, that we might inherit it. *Secondly,* That the word of his *determination* must confer eternal life. His *having the words of eternal life* is the same with his having *power to give eternal life to as many as were given him, ch.* 17:2. He had in the foregoing discourse assured *eternal life* to his followers; these disciples fastened upon this plain saying, and therefore resolved to stick to him, when the others overlooked this, and fastened upon the *hard sayings,* and therefore forsook him. Though we cannot account for every mystery, every obscurity, in Christ's doctrine, yet we know, in the general, that it is the word of eternal life, and therefore must live and die by it; for if we forsake Christ *we forsake our own mercies.*

[2.] Because of the assurance they had concerning him (*v.* 69): *We believe, and are sure, that thou art that Christ.* if he be the promised Messiah, he must *bring in an everlasting righteousness* (Dan. 9:24), and therefore has the *words of eternal life,* for *righteousness reigns to eternal life,* Rom. 5:21. observe, *First,* The *doctrine* they believed: that this Jesus was the Messiah promised to the fathers and expected by them, and that he was not a mere man, but the Son of the living God, the same to whom God had said, *Thou art my Son,* Ps. 2:7. In times of temptation to apostasy it is good to have recourse to our first principles, and stick to them; and, if we faithfully abide by that which is *past dispute,* we shall be the better able both to *find* and to *keep* the truth in matters of doubtful disputation. *Secondly,* The *degree* of their faith: it rose up to a full assurance: *We are sure.* We have known it *by experience;* this is the best knowledge. We should take occasion from others' wavering to be so much the more established, especially in that which is the present truth. When we have so strong a faith in the gospel of Christ as boldly to venture our souls *upon it,* knowing *whom we have believed,* then, and not till then, we shall be willing to venture every thing else for it.

3. The melancholy remark which our Lord Jesus made upon this reply of Peter's (*v.* 70, 71): *Have not I chosen you twelve, and one of you is a devil?* And the evangelist tells us whom he meant: *he spoke of Judas Iscariot.* Peter had undertaken for them all that they would be faithful to their Master. Now Christ does not condemn his charity (it is always good to hope the best), but he tacitly corrects his confidence. We must not be too sure concerning any. God knows those that are his; we do not. Observe here, (1.) Hypocrites and betrayers of Christ are no better than devils. Judas not only *had* a devil, but he *was* a devil. One of you is a *false accuser;* so **diabolos** sometimes signifies (2 Tim. 3:3); and it is probable that Judas, when he sold his Master to the chief priests, represented him to them as a bad man, to justify himself in what he did. But I rather take it as we read it: *He is a devil,* a devil incarnate, a fallen apostle, as the devil a fallen angel. He is Satan, an adversary, an enemy to Christ. He is Abaddon, and Apollyon, a son of perdition. He was of his father the devil, did his lusts, was in his interests, as Cain, 1 Jn. 3:12. Those whose bodies were possessed by the devil are never called *devils* (*demoniacs,* but not *devils*); but Judas, into whose *heart* Satan entered, and filled it, is called a *devil.* (2.) Many that are *seeming* saints are *real* devils. Judas had as fair an outside as many of the apostles; his venom was, like that of the serpent, covered with a fine skin. He *cast out devils,* and appeared an enemy to the devil's kingdom, and yet was himself a devil all the while. Not only he *will be* one shortly, but he *is one* now. It is *strange,* and to be wondered at; Christ speaks of it with wonder: *Have not I?* It is *sad,* and to be lamented, that ever Christianity should be made a cloak to diabolism. (3.) The disguises of hypocrites, however they may deceive men, and put a cheat upon them, cannot deceive Christ, for his piercing eye sees through them. He can call those *devils* that call themselves *Christians,* like the prophet's greeting to Jeroboam's wife, when she came to him in masquerade (1 Ki. 14:6): *Come in, thou wife of Jeroboam.* Christ's *divine sight,* far better than any *double sight,* can see spirits. (4.) There are those who are chosen by Christ to special services who yet prove false to him: *I have chosen you* to the *apostleship,* for it is expressly said that Judas was not chosen to eternal life (*ch.* 13:18), and yet one of *you* is a devil. Note, Advancement to places of honour and trust in the church is no certain evidence of saving grace. *We have prophesied in thy name.* (5.) In the most *select* societies on this side heaven it is no new thing to meet with those that are corrupt. Of the twelve that were chosen to an intimate conversation with an *incarnate Deity,* as great an honour and privilege as ever men were chosen to, one was an *incarnate devil.* The historian lays an emphasis upon this, that Judas was *one of the twelve* that were so dignified and distinguished. Let us not reject and unchurch the twelve because *one of them is a devil,* nor say that they are all cheats and hypocrites because one of them was so; let those that are so bear the blame, and not those who, while they are undiscovered, incorporate with them. There is a society within the veil into which no unclean thing shall enter, a church of first-born, in which are no *false brethren.*

CHAPTER 7

In this chapter we have, I. Christ's declining for some time to appear publicly in Judea (*v.* 1). II. His design to go up to Jerusalem at the feast of tabernacles, and his discourse with his kindred in Galilee concerning his going up to this feast (*v.* 2–13). III. His preaching publicly in the temple at that feast. 1. In the midst of the feast (*v.* 14, 15). We have his discourse with the Jews, (1.) Concerning his doctrine (*v.* 16–18). (2.) Concerning the crime of sabbath-breaking laid to his charge (*v.* 19–24). (3.) Concerning himself, both whence he came and whither he was going (*v.* 25–36). 2. On the last day of he feast. (1.) His gracious invitation to poor souls to come to him (*v.* 37–39). (2.) The reception that it met with. [1.] Many of the people disputed about it (*v.* 40–44). [2.] The chief priests would have brought him into trouble for it, but were first disappointed by their officers (*v.* 45–49) and then silenced by one of their own court (*v.* 50–53).

Verses 1–13

We have here, I. The reason given why Christ spent more of his time in Galilee than in Judea (*v.* 1): *because the Jews,* the people in Judea and Jerusalem, sought to *kill him,* for curing the impotent man on the sabbath day, *ch.* 5:16. They thought to be the death of him, either by a popular tumult or by a legal prosecution, in consideration of which he kept at a distance in another part of the country, very much out of the lines of Jerusalem's communication. It is not said, He *durst not,* but, He *would not,* walk in Jewry; it was not through fear and cowardice that he declined it, but in *prudence,* because his hour was not yet come. Note, 1. Gospel light is justly *taken away* from those that endeavour to extinguish it. Christ will withdraw from those that drive him from them, will hide his face from those that spit in it, and justly shut up his bowels from those who spurn at them. 2. In times of imminent peril it is not only *allowable,* but *advisable,* to *withdraw* and *abscond* for our own safety and preservation, and to choose the service of those places which are least perilous, Mt. 10:23. *Then,* and not till *then,* we are called to expose and lay down our lives, when we cannot save them without sin. 3. If the providence of God casts persons of *merit* into places of obscurity and little note, it must not be thought strange; it was the lot of our Master himself. He who was fit to have sat in the highest of Moses's seats willingly walked in Galilee among the ordinary sort of people. Observe, He did not sit still in Galilee, nor bury himself alive there, but *walked;* he went about doing good. When we cannot do *what* and *where* we *would,* we must do *what* and *where* we *can.*

II. The approach of the *feast of tabernacles* (*v.* 2), one of the three solemnities which called for the personal attendance of all the males at Jerusalem; see the institution of it, Lev. 23:34, etc., and the revival of it after a long disuse, Neh. 8:14. It was intended to be both a *memorial* of the tabernacle state of Israel in the wilderness, and a *figure* of the tabernacle state of God's spiritual Israel in this world. This feast, which was instituted so many hundred years before, was still religiously observed. Note, Divine institutions are never antiquated, nor go out of date, by length of time: nor must wilderness mercies ever be forgotten. But it is called the *Jews' feast,* because it was now shortly to be *abolished,* as a mere Jewish thing, and left to them that *served the tabernacle.*

III. Christ's discourse with his *brethren,* some of his kindred, whether by his mother or his supposed father is not certain; but they were such as pretended to have an interest in him, and therefore interposed to advise him in his conduct. And observe,

1. Their ambition and vain-glory in urging him to make a more public appearance than he did: *"Depart hence,"* said they, *"and go into Judea* (*v.* 3), where thou wilt make a better figure than thou canst here."

(1.) They give two reasons for this advice: [1.] That it would be an encouragement to those in and about Jerusalem who had a respect for him; for, expecting his temporal kingdom, the royal seat of which they concluded must be at Jerusalem, they would have had the disciples *there* particularly countenanced, and thought the time he spent among his Galilean disciples wasted and thrown away, and his miracles turning to no account unless those at Jerusalem saw them. Or, "That *thy disciples,* all of them in general, who will be gathered at Jerusalem to keep the feast, may *see thy works,* and not, as here, a few at one time and a few at another." [2.] That it would be for the advancement of his name and honour: *There is no man that does any thing in secret* if he himself *seeks to be known* openly. They took it for granted that Christ sought to make himself known, and therefore thought it absurd for him to conceal his miracles: *"If thou do these things,* if thou be so well able to gain the applause of the people and the approbation of the rulers by thy miracles, venture abroad, and *show thyself to the world.* Supported with these credentials, thou canst not fail of acceptance, and therefore it is high time to set up for an interest, and to think of being *great."*

(2.) One would not think there was any harm in this advice, and yet the evangelist noted it is an evidence of their infidelity: *For neither did his brethren believe in him* (*v.* 5), if they had, they would not have said this. Observe, [1.] It was an honour to be of the kindred of Christ, but no *saving* honour; they that hear his word and keep it are the kindred he values. Surely grace runs in no blood in the world, when not in that of Christ's family. [2.] It was a sign that Christ did not aim at any secular interest, for then his kindred would have struck in with him, and he would have secured them first. [3.] There were those who were akin to Christ according to the flesh who did believe in him (three of the twelve were *his brethren*), and yet others, as nearly allied to him as they, did not believe in him. Many that have the same external privileges and advantages do not make the same use of them. But,

(3.) What was there amiss in the advice which they gave him? I answer, [1.] It was a piece of presumption for them to prescribe to Christ, and to teach him what measures to take; it was a sign that they *did not believe him* able to guide them, when they did not think him sufficient to guide himself. [2.] They discovered a great carelessness about his safety, when they would have him go to Judea, where they knew the Jews sought to kill him. Those that believed in him, and loved him, dissuaded him from Judea, *ch.* 11:8. [3.] Some think they hoped that if his miracles were wrought at Jerusalem the Pharisees and rulers would try them, and discover some cheat in them, which would justify their unbelief. So. Dr. Whitby. [4.] Perhaps they were weary of his company in Galilee (for *are not all these that speak Galileans?*) and this was, in effect, a desire that he would *depart out of their coasts.* [5.] They causelessly insinuate that he neglected his disciples, and denied them such a *sight of his works* as was necessary to the support of their faith. [6.] They tacitly reproach him as *mean-spirited,* that he durst not enter the lists with the great men, nor trust himself upon the stage of public action, which, if he had any courage and *greatness of soul,* he would do, and not sneak thus and skulk in a corner; thus Christ's humility, and his humiliation, and the small figure which his religion has usually made in the world, have been often turned to the reproach of both *him* and *it.* [7.] They seem to question the truth of the miracles he wrought, in saying, *"If thou do these things,* if they will bear the test of a public scrutiny in the courts above, produce them there." [8.] They think Christ altogether such a one as themselves, as subject as they to worldly policy, and as desirous as they to *make a fair show in the flesh;* whereas he sought not honour from men. [9.] Self was at the bottom of all; they hoped, if he would make himself as great as he might, they, being his kinsmen, should share in his honour, and have respect paid them for his sake. Note, *First,* Many carnal people go to public ordinances, to worship at the feast, only to *show themselves,* and all their care is to make a *good appearance,* to present themselves handsomely to the world. *Secondly,* Many that seem to seek Christ's honour do really therein seek their own, and make it serve a turn for themselves.

2. The prudence and humility of our Lord Jesus, which appeared in his answer to the advice his brethren gave him, *v.* 6–8. Though there were so many base insinuations in it, he answered them mildly. Note, Even that which is said without *reason* should be answered without *passion;* we should learn of our Master to reply with meekness even to that which is most *impertinent* and *imperious,* and, where it is easy to find much amiss, to seem not to see it, and wink at the affront. They expected Christ's company with them to the feast, perhaps hoping he would bear their charges: but here,

(1.) He shows the difference between himself and them, in two things: — [1.] His *time* was *set,* so was not *theirs: My time is not yet come, but your time is always ready.* Understand it of the time of his going up to the feast. It was an indifferent thing to them when they went, for they had nothing of moment to do either where they were, to *detain* them *there,* or where they were going, to *hasten* them *thither;* but every minute of Christ's time was precious, and had its own particular business allotted to it. He had some work yet to do in Galilee before he left the country: in the harmony of the gospels betwixt this *motion* made by his kindred and his *going up* to this feast comes in the story of his sending forth the seventy disciples (Lu. 10:1, etc.), which was an affair of very great consequence; his time is *not yet,* for that must be done first. Those who live useless lives have *their time always ready;* they can go and come when they please. But those whose *time* is filled up with *duty* will often find themselves *straitened,* and they have *not yet time* for that which others can do *at any time.* Those who are made the servants of God, as all men are, and who have made themselves the servants of all, as all useful men have, must not expect not covet to be *masters of their own time.* The confinement of business is a thousand times better than the liberty of idleness. or, it may be meant of the *time* of his appearing publicly at Jerusalem; Christ, who knows all men and all things, knew that the best and most proper time for it would be about the *middle of the feast.* We, who are ignorant and short-sighted, are apt to prescribe to him, and to think he should deliver his people, and so show himself now. The present time is *our* time, but he is fittest to judge, and, it may be, *his time is not yet come;* his people are not yet ready for deliverance, nor his enemies ripe for ruin; let us therefore wait with patience for *his time,* for all he does will be most glorious in its season. [2.] His *life* was *sought,* so was not *theirs, v.* 7. They, in *showing themselves* to the world, did not expose themselves: *"The world cannot hate you,* for you are *of the world,* its children, its servants, and in with its interests; and no doubt the world will *love its own;"* see *ch.* 15:19. Unholy souls, whom the holy God *cannot love,* the world that lies in wickedness *cannot hate;* but Christ, in showing himself to the world, laid himself open to the greatest danger; for *me it hateth.* Christ was not only *slighted,* as inconsiderable in the world *(the world knew him not),* but *hated,* as if he had been hurtful to the world; thus ill was he requited for his love to the world: reigning sin is a rooted antipathy and enmity to Christ. But why did the world hate Christ? What evil had he done to it? Had he, like Alexander, under colour of conquering it, laid it waste? "No, but because" (saith he) *"I testify of it, that the works of it are evil."* Note, *First,* The works of an evil world are *evil works;* as the tree is, so are the fruits: it is a dark world, and an apostate world, and its works are works of darkness and rebellion. *Secondly,* Our Lord Jesus, both by himself and by his ministers, did and will both discover and testify against the evil works of this wicked world. *Thirdly,* It is a great uneasiness and provocation to the world to be convicted of the evil of its works. It is for the honour of virtue and piety that those who are impious and vicious do not care for hearing of it, for their own consciences make them *ashamed* of the turpitude there is *in* sin and *afraid* of the punishment that follows *after* sin. *Fourthly,* Whatever is *pretended,* the *real* cause of the world's enmity to the gospel is the testimony it bears against sin and sinners. Christ's witnesses by their doctrine and conversation *torment* those that dwell on the earth, and therefore are treated so barbarously, Rev. 11:10. But it is better to incur the world's hatred, by testifying against its wickedness, than gain its good-will by going down the stream with it.

(2.) He dismisses them, with a design to stay behind for some time in Galilee (*v.* 8): *Go you up to this feast, I go not up yet.* [1.] He allows their going to the feast, though they were carnal and hypocritical in it. Note, Even those who go not to holy ordinances with right affections and sincere intentions must not be hindered nor discouraged from going; who knows but they may be wrought upon there? [2.] He denies them his company when they went to the feast, because they were carnal and hypocritical. Those who go to ordinances for ostentation, or to serve some secular purpose, go without Christ, and will speed accordingly. How sad is the condition of that man, though he reckon himself akin to Christ, to whom he saith, *"Go up* to such an ordinance, Go pray, Go hear the word, Go receive the sacrament, but *I go not up* with thee? *Go thou* and appear before God, but I will not appear *for thee,"* as Ex. 33:1–3. But, if the presence of Christ go not with us, to what purpose should we go up? *Go you up, I go not up.* When we are going to, or coming from, solemn ordinances, it becomes us to be careful what company we *have* and *choose,* and to avoid that which is vain and carnal, lest the coal of good affections be quenched by corrupt communication. *I go not up yet to this feast;* he does not say, I will not go up at all, but not yet. There may be reasons for deferring a particular duty, which yet must not be wholly omitted or laid aside; see Num. 9:6–11. The reason he gives is, *My time is not yet fully come.* Note, Our Lord Jesus is very exact and punctual in knowing and keeping his time, and, as it was the time *fixed,* so it was the *best* time.

3. Christ's continuance in Galilee till his *full time* was come, *v.* 9. He, saying these things to them (*tauta de eipōn*) *abode still in Galilee;* because of this discourse he continued there; for, (1.) He would not be influenced by those who advised him to seek honour from men, nor go along with those who put him upon making a figure; he would not seem to countenance the temptation. (2.) He would not depart from his own purpose. He had said, upon a clear foresight and mature deliberation, that he would not go up yet to this feast, and therefore he abode still in Galilee. It becomes the followers of Christ thus to be *steady,* and not to *use lightness.*

4. His going up to the feast when his time was come. Observe, (1.) *When* he went: *When his brethren were gone up.* He would not go up *with them,* lest they should make a noise and disturbance, under pretence of *showing him to the world;* whereas it agreed both with the prediction and with his spirit not to *strive nor cry,* nor let his *voice be heard in the streets,* Isa. 42:2. But he went up *after them.* We may lawfully join in the same religious worship with those with whom we should yet decline an intimate acquaintance and converse; for the blessing of ordinances depends upon the grace of God, and not upon the grace of our fellow-worshippers. His carnal brethren went up *first,* and then he went. Note, In the external performances of religion it is possible that formal hypocrites may *get the start* of those that are sincere. Many come *first to the temple* who are brought thither by vain-glory, and go thence unjustified, as he, Lu. 18:11. It is not, Who comes *first?* that will be the question, but, Who comes *fittest?* If we bring our hearts *with us,* it is no matter who gets *before us.* (2.) *How* he went, *ōs en kryptō — as if he were hiding himself: not openly, but as it were in secret,* rather for fear of *giving offence* than of *receiving injury.* He went up to the feast, because it was an opportunity of honouring God and doing good; but he went up as it were in secret, because he would not provoke the government. Note, Provided the work of God be done effectually, it is best done when done with *least noise.* The kingdom of God need not come *with observation,* Lu. 17:20. We may do the work of God *privately,* and yet not do it *deceitfully.*

5. The great expectation that there was of him among the Jews at Jerusalem, *v.* 11–14. Having formerly come up to the feasts, and signalized himself by the miracles he wrought, he had made himself the subject of much discourse and observation.

(1.) They could not but think of him (*v.* 11): *The Jews sought him at the feast, and said, Where is he?* [1.] The common people longed to see him there, that they might have their curiosity gratified with the sight of his person and miracles. They did not think it worth while to go to him into Galilee, though if they had they would not have lost their labour, but they hoped the feast would bring him to Jerusalem, and then they should see him. If an opportunity of acquaintance with Christ come to their door, they can like it well enough. They *sought him at the feast.* When we attend upon God in his holy ordinances, we should seek Christ in them, seek him at the gospel feasts. Those who would *see* Christ at a feast must *seek* him there. Or, [2.] Perhaps it was his enemies that were thus waiting an opportunity to seize him, and, if possible, to put an effectual stop to his progress. They said, *Where is he? pou esin ekeinos — where is that fellow?* Thus scornfully and contemptibly do they speak of him. When they should have welcomed the feast as an opportunity of serving God, they were glad of it as an opportunity of persecuting Christ. Thus Saul hoped to slay David at the new moon, 1 Sa. 20:27. Those who seek *opportunity to sin* in solemn assemblies for religious worship profane God's ordinances to the last degree, and defy him upon his own ground; it is like striking *within the verge of the court.*

(2.) The people differed much in their sentiments concerning him (*v.* 12): *There was much murmuring,* or *muttering* rather, *among the people concerning him.* The enmity of the rulers against Christ, and their enquiries after him, caused him to be so much the more talked of and observed among the people. This ground the gospel of Christ has got by the opposition made to it, that it has been the more enquired into, and, by being *every where spoken against,* it has come to be every where *spoken of,* and by this means has been spread the further, and the merits of his cause have been the more *searched into.* This murmuring was not *against* Christ, but *concerning* him; some murmured at the rulers, because they did not countenance and encourage him: others murmured at them, because they did not silence and restrain him. Some murmured that he had so great an interest in Galilee; others, that he had so little interest in Jerusalem. Note, Christ and his religion have been, and will be, the subject of much controversy and debate, Lu. 12:51. 52. If all would agree to entertain Christ as they ought, there would be perfect peace; but, when some receive the light and others resolve against it, there will be murmuring. The *bones in the valley,* while they were *dead* and *dry,* lay quiet; but when it was said unto them, *Live,* there was *a noise* and *a shaking,* Eze. 37:7. But the noise and rencounter of liberty and business are preferable, surely, to the silence and agreement of a prison. Now what were the sentiments of the people concerning him? [1.] Some said, *he is a good man.* This was a truth, but it was far short of being the *whole truth.* He was not only a *good man,* but more than a man, he was the *Son of God.* Many who have no *ill* thoughts of Christ have yet *low* thoughts of him, and scarcely honour him, even when they speak well of him, because they do not *say enough;* yet indeed it was his honour, and the reproach of those who persecuted him, that even those who would not believe him to be the Messiah could not but own he was a *good man.* [2.] Others said, *Nay, but he deceiveth the people;* if this had been true, he had been a very bad man. The doctrine he preached was sound, and could not be contested; his miracles were real, and could not be disproved; his conversation was manifestly holy and good; and yet it must be taken for granted, notwithstanding, that there was some undiscovered cheat at the bottom, because it was the interest of the chief priests to oppose him and run him down. Such murmuring as there was among the Jews concerning Christ there is still among us: the Socinians say, *He is a good man,* and further they say not; the *deists* will not allow this, but say, *He deceived the people.* Thus some depreciate him, others abuse him, but *great is the truth.* [3.] They were frightened by their superiors from speaking much of him (*v.* 13): *No man spoke openly of him, for fear of the Jews.* Either, *First,* They durst not openly speak *well* of him. While any one was at liberty to censure and reproach him, none durst vindicate him. Or, *Secondly,* They durst not speak *at all* of him openly. Because nothing could justly be said *against* him, they would not suffer any thing to be said *of* him. It was a crime to name him. Thus many have aimed to suppress truth, under colour of silencing disputes about it, and would have all talk of religion hushed, in hopes thereby to bury in oblivion religion itself.

Verses 14–36

Here is, I. Christ's public preaching in the temple (*v.* 14): He *went up into the temple, and taught,* according to his custom when he was at Jerusalem. His business was to preach the gospel of the kingdom, and he did it in every place of concourse. His sermon is not recorded, because, probably, it was to the same purport with the sermons he had preached in Galilee, which were recorded by the other evangelists. For the gospel is the same to the *plain* and to the *polite.* But that which is observable here is that it was *about the midst of the feast;* the fourth or fifth day of the eight. Whether he did not come up to Jerusalem till the middle of the feast, or whether he came up at the beginning, but kept private till now, is not certain. But, *Query,* Why did he not go to the temple *sooner,* to preach? *Answer,* 1. Because the people would have more leisure to hear him, and, it might be hoped, would be better disposed to hear him, when they had spent some days in their booths, as they did at the feast of tabernacles. 2. Because he would choose to appear when both his friends and his enemies had done looking for him; and so give a specimen of the method he would observe in his appearances, which is to come at midnight, Mt. 25:6. But why did he appear thus publicly now? Surely it was to *shame* his persecutors, the chief priests and elders. (1.) By showing that, though they were very bitter against him, yet he did not fear them, nor their power. See Isa. 50:7, 8. (2.) By taking their work out of their hands. Their office was to teach the people in the temple, and particularly at the *feast of tabernacles,* Neh. 8:17, 18. But they either did not teach them at all or taught for doctrines the commandments of men, and therefore he goes up to the temple and teaches the people. When the shepherds of Israel made a prey of the flock it was time for the chief Shepherd to appear, as was promised. Eze. 34:22, 23; Mal. 3:1.

II. His discourse with the Jews hereupon; and the conference is reducible to four heads:

1. Concerning *his doctrine.* See here,

(1.) How the Jews *admired* it (*v.* 15): They marvelled, saying, *How knoweth this man letters, having never learned?* Observe here, [1.] That our Lord Jesus was not educated in the schools of the prophets, or at the feet of the rabbin; not only did not travel for learning, as the philosophers did, but did not make any use of the schools and academies in his own country. Moses was taught the learning of the Egyptians, but Christ was not taught so much as the learning of the Jews; having received the Spirit *without measure,* he needed not receive any knowledge *from man, or by man.* At the time of Christ's appearing, learning flourished both in the Roman empire and in the Jewish church more than in any age before or since, and in such a time of enquiry Christ chose to establish his religion, not in an illiterate age, lest it should look like a design to impose upon the world; yet he himself studied not the learning then in vogue. [2.] That Christ *had letters,* though he had never *learned* them; was mighty in the scriptures, though he never had any doctor of the law for his tutor. It is necessary that Christ's ministers should have *learning,* as he had; and since they cannot expect to have it as he had it, by inspiration, they must take pains to get it in an ordinary way. [3.] That Christ's having learning, though he had not been taught it, made him truly great and wonderful; the Jews speak of it here with wonder. *First,* Some, it is likely, took notice of it to his honour: He that had no human learning, and yet so far excelled all that had, certainly must be endued with a divine knowledge. *Secondly,* Others, probably, mentioned it in disparagement and contempt of him: Whatever he *seems* to have, he cannot really have any true learning, for he was never at the university, nor took his degree. *Thirdly,* Some perhaps suggested that he had got his learning by magic arts, or some unlawful means or other. Since they know not how he could be a scholar, they will think him a conjurer.

(2.) What he *asserted* concerning it; three things: —

[1.] That his *doctrine* is divine (*v.* 16): My doctrine is not *mine, but his that sent me.* They were offended because he undertook to *teach* though he had never learned, in answer to which he tells them that his doctrine was such as was not to be *learned,* for it was not the product of *human thought* and natural powers enlarged and elevated by reading and conversation, but it was a *divine revelation.* As God, equal with the Father, he might truly have said, *My doctrine is mine, and his that sent me;* but being now in his estate of humiliation, and being, as Mediator, God's servant, it was more congruous to say, "*My doctrine is not mine,* not mine only, nor mine originally, as man and mediator, but *his that sent me;* it does not centre in myself, nor lead ultimately to myself, but to him that sent me." God had promised concerning the great prophet that he would *put his words into his mouth* (Deu. 18:18), to which Christ seems here to refer. Note, It is the comfort of those who embrace Christ's doctrine, and the condemnation of those who reject it, that it is a divine doctrine: it is *of God and not of man.*

[2.] That the most competent judges of the truth and divine authority of Christ's doctrine are those that with a sincere and upright heart desire and endeavour to do the will of God (*v.* 17): *If any man be willing to do the will of God,* have his will melted into the *will of God, he shall know of the doctrine whether it be of God or whether I speak of myself.* Observe here, *First,* What the question is, concerning the doctrine of Christ, *whether it be of God* or no; whether the gospel be a divine revelation or an imposture. Christ himself was willing to have his doctrine enquired into, whether it were of God or no, much more should his ministers; and we are concerned to examine what grounds we go upon, for, if we be deceived, we are miserably deceived. *Secondly,* Who are likely to succeed in this search: those that *do the will of God,* at least are desirous to do it. Now see, 1. Who they are that *will do the will of God.* They are such as are *impartial* in their enquiries concerning the will of God, and are not biassed by any lust or interest, and such as are resolved by the grace of God, when they find out what the will of God is, to conform to it. They are such as have an honest principle of regard to God, and are truly desirous to glorify and please him. 2. Whence it is that such a one shall know of the truth of Christ's doctrine. (1.) Christ has promised to *give knowledge* to such; he hath said, *He shall know,* and he can give an understanding. Those who improve the light they have, and carefully live up to it, shall be secured by divine grace from destructive mistakes. (2.) They are disposed and prepared to *receive* that knowledge. He that is inclined to submit to the rules of the divine law is disposed to admit the rays of divine light. *To him that has shall be given;* those have a *good understanding* that *do his commandments,* Ps. 111:10. Those who *resemble* God are most likely to *understand* him.

[3.] That hereby it appeared that Christ, as a teacher, did not speak of *himself,* because he did not seek himself, *v.* 18. *First,* See here the character of a deceiver: he *seeketh his own glory,* which is a sign that he *speaks of himself,* as the false Christs and false prophets did. Here is the description of the *cheat:* they *speak of themselves,* and have no commission nor instructions from God; no warrant but their own will, no inspiration but their own imagination, their own policy and artifice. Ambassadors *speak not of themselves;* those ministers disclaim that character who glory in this that they *speak of themselves.* But see the discovery of the cheat; by this their pretensions are disproved, they consult purely *their own glory;* self-seekers are self-speakers. Those who speak from God will speak *for God,* and for his glory; those who aim at their own preferment and interest make it to appear that they had no commission form God. *Secondly,* See the contrary character Christ gives of himself and his doctrine: He *that seeks his glory that sent him,* as I do, makes it to appear that *he is true.* 1. He was *sent of God.* Those teachers, and those only, who are sent of God, are to be received and entertained by us. Those who bring a divine message must prove a divine mission, either by special revelation or by regular institution. 2. He *sought the glory of God.* It was both the tendency of his doctrine and the tenour of his whole conversation to *glorify God.* 3. This was a proof that he was *true,* and there was *no unrighteousness in him.* False teachers are most *unrighteous;* they are unjust to God whose name they abuse, and unjust to the souls of men whom they impose upon. There cannot be a greater piece of unrighteousness than this. But Christ made it appear that he was *true,* that he was really what he said he was, that there was *no un-*

righteousness in him, no falsehood in his doctrine, no fallacy nor fraud in his dealings with us.

2. They discourse concerning the *crime* that was laid to his charge for curing the impotent man, and bidding him carry his bed on the sabbath day, for which they had formerly prosecuted him, and which was still the pretence of their enmity to him.

(1.) He argues against them by way of *recrimination,* convicting them of far worse practices, *v.* 19. How could they for shame censure him for a breach of the law of Moses, when they themselves were such notorious breakers of it? *Did not Moses give you the law?* And it was their privilege that they had the law, no nation had such a law; but it was their wickedness that *none of them kept the law,* that they rebelled against it, and lived contrary to it. Many that have the law given them, when they have it do not keep it. Their neglect of the law was universal: *None of you keepeth* it: neither those of them that were in *posts of honour,* who should have been most *knowing,* nor those who were in *posts of subjection,* who should have been most *obedient.* They boasted of the law, and pretended a zeal for it, and were enraged at Christ for seeming to transgress it, and yet none of them kept it; like those who say that they are for the church, and yet never go to church. It was an aggravation of their wickedness, in persecuting Christ for breaking the law, that they themselves did not keep it: "*None of you keepeth the law,* why then go ye about to kill me for not keeping it?" Note, Those are commonly most censorious of others who are most faulty themselves. Thus hypocrites, who are forward to pull a mote out of their brother's eye, are not aware of a beam in their own. *Why go ye about to kill me?* Some take this as the evidence of their not keeping the law: "*You keep not the law;* if you did, you would understand yourselves better than to go about to kill me for doing a good work." Those that support themselves and their interest by persecution and violence, whatever they pretend (though they may call themselves *custodes utriusque tabulae — the guardians of both tables),* are not keepers of the law of God. Chemnitius understands this as a reason why it was time to supersede the law of Moses by the gospel, because the law was found insufficient to *restrain sin:* "Moses gave you the law, but you do not keep it, nor are kept by it from the greatest wickedness; there is therefore need of a clearer light and better law to be brought in; why then do you aim to kill me for introducing it?"

Here the *people* rudely interrupted him in his discourse, and contradicted what he said (*v.* 20): *Thou has a devil; who goes about to kill thee?* This intimates, [1.] The good opinion they had of their rulers, who, they think, would never attempt so atrocious a thing as to kill him; no, such a veneration they had for their elders and chief priests that they would swear for them they would do no harm to an innocent man. Probably the rulers had their little emissaries among the people who suggested this to them; many deny that wickedness which at the same time they are contriving. [2.] The *ill opinion* they had of our Lord Jesus: "*Thou hast a devil,* thou art possessed with a lying spirit, and art a *bad man* for saying so;" so some: or rather, "Thou art melancholy, and art a *weak man;* thou frightenest thyself with causeless fears, as hypochondriacal people are apt to do." Not only open frenzies, but silent melancholies, were then commonly imputed to the power of Satan. "Thou art crazed, has a distempered brain." Let us not think it strange if the best of men are put under the worst of characters. To this vile calumny our Saviour returns no direct answer, but seems as if he took no notice of it. Note, Those who would be like Christ must put up with affronts, and pass by the indignities and injuries done them; must not *regard* them, much less *resent* them, and least of all *revenge* them. *I, as a deaf man, heard not.* When Christ was *reviled,* he *reviled not again,*

(2.) He argues by way of appeal and vindication.

[1.] He appeals to *their own sentiments* of this miracle: "*I have done one work,* and you all marvel, *v.* 21. You cannot choose but marvel at it as truly great, and altogether supernatural; you must all own it to be marvellous." Or, "Though I have done but *one work* that you have any colour to find fault with, yet you marvel, you are offended and displeased as if I had been guilty of some heinous or enormous crime."

[2.] He appeals to their own practice in other instances: "*I have done one work* on the sabbath, and it was done easily, with a word's speaking, and you all marvel, you make a mighty strange thing of it, that a religious man should dare do such a thing, whereas you yourselves *many a time* do that which is a much more servile work on the sabbath day, in the case of circumcision; if it be lawful for you, nay, and your duty, to circumcise a child on the sabbath day, when it happens to be the eighth day, as no doubt it is, much more was it lawful and good for me to heal a diseased man on that day." Observe,

First, The rise and origin of circumcision: *Moses gave you circumcision,* gave you the law concerning it. Here, 1. Circumcision is said to *be given,* and (*v.* 23) they are said to *receive* it; it was not imposed upon them as a yoke, but conferred upon them as a favour. Note, The ordinances of God, and particularly those which are seals of the covenant, are *gifts given to men,* and are to be received as such. 2. Moses is said to give it, because it was a part of that law which was *given by Moses;* yet, as Christ said of the manna (*ch.* 6:32), Moses did not give it them, but God; nay, and it was not of Moses first, but *of the fathers, v.* 22. Though it was incorporated into the Mosaic institution, yet it was ordained long before, for it was a seal of the righteousness of faith, and therefore commenced with the promise four hundred and thirty years before, Gal. 3:17. The church membership of believers and their seed was not of Moses or his law, and therefore did not fall with it; but was *of the fathers,* belonged to the patriarchal church, and was part of that blessing of Abraham which was to come upon the Gentiles, Gal. 3:14.

Secondly, The respect paid to the law of circumcision above that of the sabbath, in the constant practice of the Jewish church. The Jewish casuists frequently take notice of it, *Circumcisio et ejus sanatio pellit sabbbatum — Circumcision and its cure drive away the sabbath;* so that if a child was born one sabbath day it was without fail circumcised the next. If then, when the *sabbath rest* was more strictly insisted on, yet those works were allowed which were *in ordine ad spiritualia — for the keeping up of religion,* much more are they allowed now under the gospel, when the stress is laid more upon the *sabbath work.*

Thirdly, The inference Christ draws hence in justification of himself, and of what he had done (*v.* 23): *A man-child on the sabbath day receives circumcision, that the law of circumcision might not be broken;* or, as the margin reads it, *without breaking the law,* namely, of the sabbath. Divine commands must be construed so as to agree with each other. "Now, if this be allowed by yourselves, how unreasonable are you, who are *angry with me because I have made a man every whit whole on the sabbath day!" emoi cholate.* The word is used only here, from *chogē — fel, gall.* They were angry at him with the greatest indignation; it was a spiteful anger, anger with gall in it. Note, It is very absurd and unreasonable for us to condemn others for that in which we justify ourselves. Observe the comparison Christ here makes between their *circumcising a child* and his *healing a man* on the sabbath day. 1. Circumcision was but a ceremonial institution; it was *of the fathers* indeed, but not from the beginning; but what Christ did was a good work by the law of nature, a more excellent law than that which made circumcision a good work. 2. Circumcision was a *bloody* ordinance, and *made sore;* but what Christ did was healing, and made whole. The law works pain, and, if that work may be done on the sabbath day, much more a gospel work, which produces peace. 3. Especially considering that whereas, when they had circumcised a child, their care was only to heal up that part which was circumcised, which might be done and yet the child remain under other illnesses, Christ had made this man *every whit whole, holon anthrōpon hygiē — I have made the whole man healthful* and sound. The *whole body* was *healed,* for the disease affected the whole body; and it was a perfect cure, such as left no relics of the disease behind; nay, Christ not only healed his body, but his soul too, by that admonition, *Go, and sin no more,* and so indeed made the *whole man* sound, for the soul is the man. Circumcision indeed was intended for the good of the soul, and to make the *whole man* as it should be; but they had perverted it, and turned it into a mere carnal ordinance; but Christ accompanied his outward cures with inward grace, and so made them sacramental, and healed the *whole man.*

He concludes this argument with that rule (*v.* 24): *Judge not according to the appearance, but judge righteous judgment.* This may be applied, either, *First,* In particular, to this work which they quarrelled with as a violation of the law. Be not partial in your judgment; judge not, *kat' opsin — with respect of persons;* knowing faces, as the Hebrew phrase is, Deu. 1:17. It is contrary to the law of justice, as well as charity, to censure those who differ in opinion from us as transgressors, in taking that liberty which yet in those of our own party, and way, and opinion, we allow of; as it is also to commend that in some as necessary strictness and severity which in others we condemn as imposition and persecution. Or, *Secondly,* In general, to Christ's person and preaching, which they were offended at and prejudiced against. Those things that are false, and designed to impose upon men, commonly appear best when they are judged of *according to the outward appearance,* they appear most plausible *prima facie — at the first glance.* It was this that gained the Pharisees such an interest and reputation, that they *appeared right* unto men (Mt. 23:27, 28), and men judged of them by that appearance, and so were sadly mistaken in them. "But," saith Christ, "be not too confident that all are real saints who are seeming ones." With reference to himself, his *outward appearance* was far short of his real dignity and excellency, for he took upon him the *form of a servant* (Phil. 2:7), was in the *likeness of sinful flesh* (Rom. 8:3), had *no form nor comeliness,* Isa. 53:2. So that those who undertook to judge whether he was the Son of God or no by his *outward appearance* were not likely to *judge righteous judgment.* The Jews expected the outward appearance of the Messiah to be pompous and magnificent, and attended with all the ceremonies of secular grandeur; and, judging of Christ by that rule, their judgment was from first to last a *continual* mistake, for the kingdom of Christ was not to be *of this world,* nor to *come with observation.* If a divine power accompanied him, and God bore him witness, and the scriptures were fulfilled in him, though his appearance was ever so mean, they ought to receive him, and to judge by faith, and not by the sight of the eye. See Isa. 11:3, and 1 Sa. 16:7. Christ and his doctrine and doings desire nothing but *righteous judgment;* if truth and justice may but pass the sentence, Christ and his cause will carry the day. We must not judge concerning any by their *outward appearance,* not by their titles, the figure they make in the world, and their fluttering show, but by their intrinsic worth, and the gifts and graces of God's Spirit in them.

3. Christ discourses with them here concerning *himself,* whence he came, and whither he was going, *v.* 25–36.

(1.) *Whence he came, v.* 25–31. In the account of this observe,

[1.] The objection concerning this stated by some of the inhabitants of Jerusalem, who seem to have been of all others most prejudiced against him, *v.* 25. One would think that those who lived at the fountain-head of knowledge and religion should have been most ready to receive the Messiah: but it proved quite contrary. Those that have plenty of the means of knowledge and grace, if they are not *made better* by them, are commonly *made worse;* and our Lord Jesus has often met with the least welcome from those that one would expect the best from. But it was not without some just cause that it came into a proverb, *The nearer the church the further from God.* These people of Jerusalem showed their ill-will to Christ,

First, By their reflecting on the rulers, because they let him alone: *Is not this he whom they seek to kill?* The multitude of the people that came up out of the country to the feast did not suspect there was any design on foot against him, and therefore they said, *Who goes about to kill thee? v.* 20. But those of Jerusalem knew the plot, and irritated their rulers to put it into execution: *"Is not this he whom they seek to kill?* Why do they not do it then? Who hinders them? They say that they have a mind to get him out of the way, and yet, lo, *he speaketh boldly,* and *they say nothing to him;* do *the rulers know indeed that this is the very Christ?" v.* 26. Here they slyly and maliciously insinuate two things, to exasperate the rulers against Christ, when indeed they needed to spur. 1. That by conniving at his preaching they *brought their authority into contempt.* "Must a man that is condemned by the *sanhedrim* as a deceiver be permitted to *speak boldly,* without any check or contradiction? This makes their sentence to be but *brutem fulmen — a vain menace;* if our rulers will suffer themselves to be thus trampled upon, they may thank themselves if none stand in awe of them and their laws." Note, The worst of persecutions have often been carried on under colour of the necessary support of authority and government. 2. That hereby they brought *their judgment* into *suspicion. Do they know that this is the Christ?* It is spoken ironically, "How came they to change their mind? What new discovery have they lighted on? They give people occasion to think that they believe him to be the Christ, and it behoves them to act vigorously against him to clear themselves from the suspicion." Thus the rulers, who had made the people enemies to Christ, made them *seven times more the children of hell than themselves,* Mt. 23:15. When religion and the profession of Christ's name are *out of fashion,* and consequently *out of repute,* many are strongly tempted to persecute and oppose them, only that they may not be thought to favour them and incline to them. And for this reason apostates, and the degenerate offspring of good parents, have been sometimes worse than others, as it were to wipe off the stain of their profession. It was strange that the rulers, thus irritated, did not seize Christ; but his hour was not yet come; and God can tie men's hands to admiration, though he should not turn their hearts.

Secondly, By their exception against his being the Christ, in which appeared more malice than matter, *v.* 27. "If the rulers think him to be the Christ, we neither can nor will believe him to be so, for we have this argument against it, that *we know this man, whence he is; but when Christ comes no man knows whence he is."* Here is a fallacy in the argument, for the propositions are not body *ad idem — adapted to the same view of the subject.* 1. If they speak of his *divine nature,* it is true that when Christ comes *no man knows whence he is,* for he is a priest after the order of Melchizedek, who was *without descent,* and *his goings forth have been from of old, from everlasting,* Mic. 5:2. But then it is not true that as for this man they knew whence he was, for they knew not his divine nature, nor how *the Word* was *made flesh.* 2. If they speak of his *human nature,* it is true that they knew whence he was, who was his mother, and where he was bred up; but then it is false that ever it was said of the Messiah that none should know whence he was, for it was known before *where he should be born,* Mt. 2:4, 5. Observe, (1.) How they *despised him,* because they knew *whence he was.* Familiarity breeds contempt, and we are apt to disdain the *use* of those whom we know the *rise of.* Christ's own received him not, because he was *their own,* for which very reason they should the rather have loved him, and been thankful that their nation and their age were honoured with his appearance. (2.) How they endeavoured unjustly to fasten the ground of their prejudice upon the scriptures, as if they countenanced them, when there was no such thing. *Therefore* people err concerning Christ, because they *know not the scripture.*

[2.] Christ's answer to this objection, *v.* 28, 29.

First, He spoke freely and boldly, he *cried in the temple, as he taught,* he spoke this louder than the rest of his discourse, 1. To express his earnestness, being *grieved for the hardness of their hearts.* There may be a vehemency in contending for the truth where yet there is no intemperate heat nor passion. We may instruct gainsayers with warmth, and yet with *meekness.* 2. The priests and those that were prejudiced against him, did not come near enough to hear his preaching, and therefore he must speak louder than ordinary what he will have them to hear. Whoever has ears to hear, let him hear this.

Secondly, His answer to their cavil is, 1. By way of *concession,* granting that they did or might know his origin as to the flesh: *"You both know me, and you know whence I am.* You know I am of your own nation, and one of yourselves." It is no disparagement to the doctrine of Christ that there is that in it which is level to the capacities of the meanest, plain truths, discovered even by nature's light, of which we may say, We know whence they are. *"You know me,* you think you know me; but you are mistaken; you take me to be the carpenter's son, and born at Nazareth, but it is not so." 2. By way of *negation,* denying that that which they did see in him, and know of him, was all that was to be known; and therefore, if they looked no further, they judged by the outward appearance only. They knew *whence* he came perhaps, and *where* he had his birth, but he will tell them what they knew not, *from whom* he came. (1.) That he did not *come of himself;* that he did not run without sending, nor come as a private person, but with a public character. (2.) That he was sent of his Father; this is twice mentioned: *He hath sent me.* And again, *"He hath sent me,* to say what I say, and do what I do." This he was himself well assured of, and therefore knew that his Father would bear him out; and it is well for us that we are assured of it too, that we may with holy confidence go to God by him. (3.) That he was *from his Father, par' autou eimi — I am from him;* not only sent from him as a servant from his master, but from him by eternal generation, as a son from his father, by essential emanation, as the beams from the sun. (4.) *That the Father who sent him is true;* he had promised to give the Messiah, and, though the Jews had forfeited the promise, yet he that made the promise is *true,* and has performed it. He had promised that the Messiah should see his seed, and be successful in his undertaking; and, though the generality of the Jews reject him and his gospel, yet he *is true,* and will fulfil the promise in the calling of the Gentiles. (5.) That these unbelieving Jews did *not know the Father: He that sent me, whom you know not.* There is much ignorance of God even with many that have a *form of knowledge;* and the true reason why people reject Christ is because they do not *know God;* for there is such a harmony of the divine attributes in the work of redemption, and such an admirable agreement between natural and revealed religion, that the right knowledge of the former would not only admit, but introduce, the latter. (6.) Our Lord Jesus was intimately acquainted with the Father that *sent him: but I know him.* He knew him so well that he was not at all *in doubt* concerning his mission from him, but perfectly *assured* of it; nor at all *in the dark* concerning the work he had to do, but perfectly *apprized* of it, Mt. 11:27.

[3.] The provocation which this gave to his enemies, who hated him because he *told them the truth, v.* 30. *They sought therefore to take him,* to lay violent hands on him, not only to do him a mischief, but some way or other to be the death of him; but by the restraint of an invisible power it was prevented; nobody touched him, *because his hour was not yet come;* this was not their reason why they did it not, but God's reason why he hindered them from doing it. Note, *First,* The faithful preachers of the truths of God, though they behave themselves with ever so much prudence and meekness, must expect to be hated and persecuted by those who think themselves tormented by their testimony, Rev. 11:10. *Secondly,* God has wicked men in a chain, and, whatever mischief they *would do,* they *can do* no more than God will suffer them to do. The malice of persecutors is *impotent* even when it is most *impetuous,* and, when Satan *fills their hearts,* yet God *ties their hands. Thirdly,* God's servants are sometimes wonderfully protected by indiscernible unaccountable means. Their enemies do not do the mischief they designed, and yet neither they themselves nor any one else can tell why they do not. *Fourthly,* Christ had *his hour* set, which was to put a period to his day and work on earth; so have all his people and all his ministers, and, till that hour comes, the attempts of their enemies against them are ineffectual, and their day shall be lengthened as long as their Master has any work for them to do; nor can all the powers of hell and earth prevail against them, until they have *finished their testimony.*

[4.] The good effect which Christ's discourse had, notwithstanding this, upon some of his hearers (*v.* 31): *Many of the people believed on him.* As he was set for the fall of some, so for the rising again of others. Even where the gospel meets with opposition there may yet be a great deal of good done, 1 Th. 2:2. Observe here, *First, Who* they were that believed; not a few, but many, more than one would have expected when the stream ran so strongly the other way. But these *many* were *of the people, ek tou ochlou — of the multitude,* the crowd, the inferior sort, the mob, the rabble, some would have called them. We must not measure the prosperity of the gospel by its success among the great ones; nor much ministers say that they labour in vain, though none but the *poor,* and those of no *figure,* receive the gospel, 1 Co. 1:26. *Secondly,* What *induced* them to believe: the *miracles which he did,* which were not only the accomplishment of the Old-Testament prophecies (Isa. 35:5, 6), but an argument of a divine power. He that had an ability to do that which none but God *can do,* to control and overrule the powers of nature, no doubt had authority to enact that which none but God can *enact,* a law that shall *bind conscience,* and a covenant that shall *give life. Thirdly,* How *weak* their faith was: they do not positively assert, as the Samaritans did, *This is indeed the Christ,* but they only argue, *When Christ comes will he do more miracles than these?* They take it for granted that Christ will come, and, when he comes, will do many miracles. "Is not this he then? In him we see, though not all the worldly pomp we have fancied, yet all the divine power we have *believed* the Messiah should appear in; and therefore why may not this be he?" They *believe* it, but have not courage to own it. Note, Even weak faith may be true faith, and so *accounted,* so *accepted,* by the Lord Jesus, who *despises not the day of small things.*

(2.) *Whither he was going, v.* 32–36. Here observe,

[1.] The design of the Pharisees and chief priests against him, *v.* 32. *First,* The provocation given them was that they had information brought them by their spies, who insinuated themselves into the conversation of the people, and gathered stories to carry to their jealous masters, that *the people murmured such things concerning him,* that there were many who had a respect and value for him, notwithstanding all they had done to render him odious. Though the people did but whisper these things, and had not courage to speak out, yet the Pharisees were enraged at it. The equity of that government is justly *suspected* by others which is so *suspicious* of itself as to take notice of, or be influenced by, the secret, various, uncertain *mutterings* of the common people. The Pharisees valued themselves very much upon the respect of the people, and were sensible that if Christ did thus *increase* they must *decrease. Secondly,* The project they laid hereupon was to seize Jesus, and take him into custody: *They sent officers to take him,* not to take up those who murmured concerning him and frighten them; no, the most effectual way to disperse the flock is to *smite the shepherd.* The Pharisees seem to have been the ringleaders in this prosecution, but they, *as such,* had no power, and therefore they god the *chief priests,* the judges of the ecclesiastical court, to join with them, who were ready enough to do so. The Pharisees were the great pretenders to *learning,* and the *chief priests* to *sanctify.* As *the world by wisdom knew not God,* but the greatest philosophers were guilty of the greatest blunders in natural religion, so the Jewish church by their wisdom knew not Christ, but their greatest rabbin were the greatest fools concerning him, nay, they were the most inveterate enemies to him. Those wicked rulers had their officers, officers of their court, church-officers, whom they employed to take Christ, and who were ready to go on their errand, though it was an ill errand. If Saul's footmen will not *turn and fall upon the priests of the Lord,* he has a herdsman that will, 1 Sa. 22:17, 18.

[2.] The discourse of our Lord Jesus hereupon (*v.* 33, 34): *Yet a little while I am with you, and then I go to him that sent me; you shall seek me, and shall not find me; and where I am, thither you cannot come.* These words, like the pillar of cloud and fire, have a *bright* side and a *dark* side.

First, They have a *bright side* towards our Lord Jesus himself, and speak abundance of comfort to him and all his faithful followers that are exposed to difficulties and dangers for his sake. Three things Christ here comforted himself with: — 1. That he had but *a little time* to continue here in this troublesome world. He sees that he is never likely to have a quiet day among them; but the best of it is his warfare will shortly be accomplished, and then he shall be *no more in this world, ch.* 17:11. Whomsoever we are *with* in this world, friends or foes, it is but a *little while* that we shall be with them; and it is a matter of comfort to those who are *in* the world, but not *of* it, and therefore are hated by it and sick of it, that they shall not be *in it always,* they shall not be *in it long.* We must be *awhile* with those that are pricking briars and grieving thorns; but thanks be to God, it is but a little while, and we shall be out of their reach. Our days being *evil,* it is well they are *few.* 2. That, when he should quit this troublesome world, he should *go to him that sent him; I go.* Not, "I am driven away by force," but, "I voluntarily *go;* having finished my embassy, I return to him on whose errand I came. When I have done my work with you, then, and not till then, I go to him *that sent me,* and will *receive me,* will prefer me, as ambassadors are preferred when they return." Their rage against him would not only not hinder him from, but would hasten him to the glory and joy that were set before him. Let those who suffer for Christ comfort themselves with this, that they have a God to go to, and are going to him, going apace, to be for ever with him. 3. That, though they persecuted him here, wherever he went, yet none of their persecutions could follow him to heaven: *You shall seek me, and shall not find me.* It appears, by their enmity to his followers when he was gone, that if they could have reached him they would have persecuted him: "But you cannot enter into that temple as you do into this." *Where I am,* that is, where I then *shall be;* but he expressed it thus because, even when he was on earth, by his divine nature and divine affections he was in heaven, *ch.* 3:13. Or it denotes that he should be *so soon* there that he was as good as there already. Note, It adds to the happiness of glorified saints that they are out of the reach of the devil and all his wicked instruments.

Secondly, These words have a *black and dark side* towards those wicked Jews that hated and persecuted Christ. They now longed to be rid of him, *Away with him from the earth;* but let them know, 1. That according to their choice so shall their doom be. They were industrious to *drive him* from them, and their sin shall be their punishment; he will not trouble them long, yet a little while and he will *depart* from them. It is just with God to forsake those that think his presence a burden. They that are weary of Christ need no more to make them miserable than to have *their wish.* 2. That they would certainly repent their choice when it was too late. (1.) They should in vain seek the presence of the Messiah: "*You shall seek me, and shall not find me.* You shall expect the *Christ to come,* but your eyes shall fail with looking for him, and you shall never find him." Those who rejected the true Messiah when he did come were justly abandoned to a miserable and endless expectation of one that should never come. Or, it may refer to the final rejection of sinners from the favours and grace of Christ at the great day: those who now seek Christ shall find him, but the day is coming when those who now refuse him *shall seek him, and shall not find him.* See Prov. 1:28. They will in vain cry, *Lord, Lord, open to us.* Or, perhaps, these words might be fulfilled in the despair of some of the Jews, who possibly might be convinced and not converted, who would wish in vain to see Christ, and to hear him preach again; but the day of grace is over (Lu. 17:22); yet this is not all. (2.) They should in vain expect a place in heaven: *Where I am,* and where all believers shall be with me, *thither ye cannot come.* Not only because they are *excluded* by the just and irreversible sentence of the judge, and the sword of the angel at every gate of the new Jerusalem, to keep *the way of the tree of life* against those who have *no right to enter,* but because they are disabled by their own iniquity and infidelity: *You cannot come,* because you *will not.* Those who hate to be where Christ is, in his word and ordinances on earth, are very unfit to be where he is in his glory in heaven; for indeed heaven would be no heaven to them, such are the antipathies of an unsanctified soul to the felicities of that state.

[3.] Their descant upon this discourse (*v.* 35, 36): *They said among themselves, Whither will he go?* See here, *First,* Their wilful ignorance and blindness. He had expressly said whither he would go — to him that sent him, to his Father in heaven, and yet they ask, *Whither will he go?* and *What manner of saying is this?* None so blind as those that will not see, that will not heed. Christ's sayings are *plain to him that understandeth,* and difficult only to those that are disposed to quarrel. *Secondly,* Their daring contempt of Christ's threatenings. Instead of trembling at that terrible word, *You shall seek me, and not find me,* which denotes the utmost degree of misery, they banter it and make a jest of it, as those sinners that *mock at fear, and are not affrighted* (Isa. 5:19); Amos 5:18. *Let him make speed. But be ye not mockers, lest your bands be made strong. Thirdly,* Their inveterate malice and rage against Christ. All they dreaded in his *departure* was that he would be out of the reach of their power: "*Whither will he go, that we shall not find him?* If he be above ground, we will have him; we will leave no place unsearched," as Ahab in quest of Elijah, 1 Ki. 18:10. *Fourthly,* Their proud disdain of the Gentiles, whom they here call the *dispersed of the Gentiles;* meaning either the Jews that were *scattered* abroad among the Greeks (James 1:1; 1 Pt. 1:1.); will he go and make an interest among those silly people? or, the Gentiles *dispersed* over the world, in distinction from the Jews, who were *incorporated* into one church and nation; will he make his court to them? *Fifthly,* Their jealousy of the least intimation of favour to the Gentiles: "Will he go and *teach the Gentiles?* Will he carry his doctrine to them?" Perhaps they had heard of some items of respect shown by him to the Gentiles, as in his sermon at Nazareth, and in the case of the centurion and the woman of Canaan, and there was nothing they dreaded more than the *comprehension* of the Gentiles. So common is it for those who have lost the power of religion to be very jealous for the monopoly of the name. They now made a *jest* of his going *to teach the Gentiles;* but not long after he did it *in good earnest* by his apostles and ministers, and gathered those *dispersed* people, sorely to the grief of the Jews, Rom. 10:19. So true is that of Solomon, *The fear of the wicked, it shall come upon him.*

Verses 37–44

In these verses we have,

I. Christ's discourse, with the explication of it, *v.* 37–39.

It is probable that these are only short hints of what he enlarged upon, but they have in them the substance of the whole gospel; here is a *gospel invitation to come to Christ,* and a *gospel promise* of comfort and happiness in him. Now observe,

1. *When* he gave this invitation: *On the last day* of the feast of tabernacles, *that great day.* The *eighth day,* which concluded that solemnity, was to be a *holy convocation,* Lev. 23:36. Now on this day Christ published this gospel-call, because (1.) Much people were gathered together, and, if the invitation were given to *many,* it might be hoped that *some* would accept of it, Prov. 1:20. Numerous assemblies give opportunity of doing the more good. (2.) The people were now returning to their homes, and he would give them this to carry away with them as his parting word. When a great congregation is to be dismissed, and is about to scatter, as here, it is affecting to think that in all probability they will never come all together again in this world, and therefore, if we can say or do any thing to help them to heaven, that must be the time. It is good to be lively at the close of an ordinance. Christ made this offer *on the last day of the feast.* [1.] To those who had turned a deaf ear to his preaching on the foregoing days of this sacred week; he will try them once more, and, if they will yet hear his voice, they shall live. [2.] To those who perhaps might never have such another offer made them, and therefore were concerned to accept of this; it would be half a year before there would be another feast, and in that time they would many of them be in their graves. *Behold now is the accepted time.*

2. *How* he gave this invitation: *Jesus stood and cried,* which denotes, (1.) His great earnestness and importunity. His heart was upon it, to bring poor souls in to himself. The erection of his body and the elevation of his voice were indications of the intenseness of his mind. Love to souls will make preachers lively. (2.) His desire that all might take notice, and take hold of this invitation. He *stood, and cried,* that he might the better be heard; for this is what every one that hath ears is concerned to hear. Gospel truth seeks no corners, because it fears no trials. The heathen oracles were delivered privately by them that *peeped and muttered;* but the oracles of the gospel were proclaimed by one that *stood, and cried.* How sad is the case of man, that he must be *importuned* to be happy, and how wonderful the grace of Christ, that he will *importune* him! *Ho, every one,* Isa. 55:1.

3. The invitation itself is very general: *If any man* thirst, whoever he be, he is invited to Christ, be he high or low, rich or poor, young or old, bond or free, Jew or Gentile. It is also very *gracious: "If any man thirst, let him come to me and drink.* If any man desires to be truly and eternally happy, let him apply himself to me, and be ruled by me, and I will undertake to make him so."

(1.) The persons invited are such as *thirst,* which may be understood, either, [1.] Of the *indigence* of their cases; either as to their *outward* condition (if any man be destitute of the comforts of this life, or fatigued with the crosses of it, let his poverty and afflictions draw him to Christ for that peace which the world can neither give nor take away), or as to their *inward* state: "If any man want spiritual blessings, he may be supplied by me." Or, [2.] Of the *inclination* of their souls and their desires towards a spiritual happiness. If any man hunger and thirst after righteousness, that is, truly desire the good will of God towards him, and the good work of God in him.

(2.) The invitation itself: *Let him come to me.* Let him not go to the ceremonial law, which would neither *pacify* the conscience nor *purify it,* and therefore could not make the *comers thereunto perfect,* Heb. 10:1. Nor let him go to the heathen philosophy, which does but beguile men, lead them into a wood, and leave them there; but let him *go to Christ,* admit his doctrine, submit to his discipline, believe in him; come to him as the fountain of living waters, the giver of all comfort.

(3.) The satisfaction promised: "Let him come *and drink,* he shall have what he comes for, and abundantly more, shall have that which will not only *refresh,* but *replenish,* a soul that desires to be happy."

4. A gracious promise annexed to this gracious call (*v.* 38): *He that believeth on me, out of his belly shall flow* — (1.) See here what it is to come to Christ: It is *to believe on him, as the scripture hath said;* it is to receive and entertain him as he is offered to us in the gospel. We must not frame a Christ according to our fancy, but believe in a Christ according to the scripture. (2.) See how thirsty souls, that come to Christ, shall be made *to drink.* Israel, that believed Moses, drank of the *rock that followed them,* the streams followed; but believers drink of a rock *in them, Christ in them;* he is in them a *well of living water, ch.* 4:14. Provision is made not only for their *present* satisfaction, but for their *continual perpetual* comfort. Here is, [1.] *Living water, running* water, which the Hebrew language calls *living,* because still in motion. The graces and comforts of the Spirit are compared to *living* (meaning *running*) *water,* because they are the active quickening principles of spiritual life, and the earnests and beginnings of eternal life. See Jer. 2:13. [2.] *Rivers* of living water, denoting both plenty and constancy. The comfort flows in both *plentifully* and *constantly* as a river; strong as a stream to bear down the oppositions of doubts and fears. There is a fulness in Christ of grace for grace. [3.] These flow out *of his belly,* that is, out of his heart or soul, which is the subject of the Spirit's working and the seat of his government. There *gracious principles* are planted; and out of the heart, in which the Spirit dwells, flow the *issues of life,* Prov. 4:23. There divine comforts are lodged, and the *joy* that a *stranger doth not intermeddle with. He that believes has the witness in himself,* 1 Jn. 5:10. *Sat lucis intus — Light abounds within.* Observe, further, where there are *springs* of grace and comfort in the soul that will *send forth streams: Out of his belly shall flow rivers. First,* Grace and comfort will produce good actions, and a holy heart will be seen in a holy life; the tree is known by its fruits, and the fountain by its streams. *Secondly,* They will *communicate themselves* for the benefit of others; a good man is a common good. His *mouth* is a *well of life,* Prov. 10:11. It is not enough that we *drink waters out of our own cistern,* that we ourselves take the comfort of the grace given us, but we must let our *fountains* be *dispersed abroad,* Prov. 5:15, 16.

Those words, *as the scripture hath said,* seem to refer to some promise in the Old Testament to this purport, and there are many; as that God would *pour out* his Spirit, which is a metaphor borrowed from waters (Prov. 1:23; Joel 2:28; Isa. 44:3; Zec. 12:10); that the *dry land* should become *springs of water* (Isa. 41:18); that there should be *rivers in the desert* (Isa. 43:19); that gracious souls should be like a *spring of water* (Isa. 58:11); and the church a *well of living water,* Cant. 4:15. And here may be an allusion to the waters issuing out of Ezekiel's temple, Eze. 47:1. Compare Rev. 22:1, and see Zec. 14:8. Dr. Lightfoot and others tell us it was a custom of the Jews, which they received by tradition, *the last day of the feast* of tabernacles to have a solemnity, which they called *Libatio aquae — The pouring out of water.* They fetched a golden vessel of water from the pool of Siloam, brought it into the temple with sound of trumpet and other ceremonies, and, upon the ascent to the altar, poured it out before the Lord with all possible expressions of joy. Some of their writers make the water to signify *the law,* and refer to Isa. 12:3; 55:1. Others, *the Holy Spirit.* And it is thought that our Saviour might here allude to this custom. Believers shall have the comfort, not of a vessel of water fetched from a pool, but of a river flowing from themselves. The joy of the law, and the pouring out of the water, which signified this, are not to be compared with the joy of the gospel in the wells of salvation.

5. Here is the evangelist's exposition of this promise (*v.* 39): *This spoke he of the Spirit:* not of any outward advantages accruing to believers (as perhaps some misunderstood him), but of the gifts, graces, and comforts of the Spirit. See how scripture is the best interpreter of scripture. Observe,

(1.) It is promised to *all that believe* on Christ that they shall *receive the Holy Ghost.* Some received his miraculous gifts (Mk. 16:17, 18); all receive his sanctifying graces. The gift of the Holy Ghost is one of the great blessings promised in the new covenant (Acts 2:39), and, if *promised,* no doubt *performed* to all that have an interest in that covenant.

(2.) The Spirit dwelling and working in believers is as a *fountain of living* running *water,* out of which plentiful streams flow, cooling and cleansing as water, mollifying and moistening as water, making them fruitful, and others joyful; see *ch.* 3:5. When the apostles spoke so *fluently* of the things of God, as the Spirit gave them utterance (Acts 2:4), and afterwards preached and wrote the gospel of Christ with such a *flood* of divine eloquence, then this was fulfilled, *Out of his belly shall flow rivers.*

(3.) This plentiful effusion of the Spirit was yet the matter of a promise; for *the Holy Ghost was not yet given, because Jesus was not yet glorified.* See here [1.] That *Jesus was not yet glorified.* It was certain that he should be glorified, and he was ever worthy of all honour; but he was as yet in a state of humiliation and contempt. He had never forfeited the glory he had before all worlds, nay, he had *merited* a further glory, and, besides his *hereditary* honours, might claim the *achievement* of a *mediatorial* crown; and yet all this is in reversion. Jesus is now *upheld* (Isa. 42:1), is now *satisfied* (Isa. 53:11), is now *justified* (1 Tim. 3:16), but he is *not yet glorified.* And, if Christ must wait for his glory, let not us think it much to wait for ours. [2.] That *the Holy Ghost was not yet given. oupō gar hēn pneuma — for the Holy Ghost was not yet.* The Spirit of God was from eternity, for in the beginning he *moved upon the face of the waters.* He was in the Old-Testament prophets and saints, and Zacharias and Elisabeth were both *filled with the Holy Ghost.* This therefore must be understood of the eminent, plentiful, and general effusion of the Spirit which was promised, Joel 2:28, and accomplished, Acts 2:1, etc. *The Holy Ghost was not yet given* in that visible manner that was intended. if we compare the clear knowledge and strong grace of the disciples of Christ themselves, after the day of Pentecost, with their darkness and weakness before, we shall understand in what sense *the Holy Ghost was not yet given;* the earnests and first-fruits of the Spirit were given, but the full harvest was not yet come. That which is most properly called the *dispensation of the Spirit* did not yet commence. The *Holy Ghost* was *not yet given* in such rivers of living water as should issue forth to water the whole earth, even the Gentile world, not in the *gifts of tongues,* to which perhaps this promise principally refers. [3.] That the reason why *the Holy Ghost was not given* was because *Jesus was not yet glorified. First,* The death of Christ is sometimes called his glorification (*ch.* 13:31); for in his cross he conquered and triumphed. Now the gift of the Holy Ghost was purchased by the blood of Christ: this was the *valuable consideration* upon which the *grant* was grounded, and therefore till this *price was paid* (though many other gifts were bestowed upon its being *secured* to be paid) the Holy Ghost was not given. *Secondly,* There was not so much need of the Spirit, while Christ himself was here upon earth, as there was when he was gone, to supply the want of him. *Thirdly,* The giving of the Holy Ghost was to be both an *answer* to Christ's *intercession* (*ch.* 14:16), and an *act* of his *dominion;* and therefore till he is glorified, and enters upon both these, the Holy Ghost is not given. *Fourthly,* The conversion of the Gentiles was the glorifying of Jesus. When certain Greeks began to enquire after Christ, he said, *Now is the Son of man glorified, ch.* 12:23. Now the time when the gospel should be propagated in the nations was not yet come, and therefore there was as yet no occasion for the *gift of tongues,* that *river of living water.* But observe, though the Holy Ghost was not yet given, yet he was *promised;* it was now the great *promise of the Father,* Acts 1:4. Though the gifts of Christ's grace are *long deferred,* yet they are *well secured:* and, while we are waiting for the good promise, we have the promise to live upon, which *shall speak and shall not lie.*

II. The consequents of this discourse, what entertainment it met with; in general, it occasioned differences: *There was a division among the people because of him, v.* 43. There was a *schism,* so the word is; there were diversities of opinions, and those managed with heat and contention; various sentiments, and those such as set them at *variance.* Think we that Christ came to send peace, that all would unanimously embrace his gospel? No, the effect of the preaching of his gospel would be *division,* for, while some are *gathered to it,* others will be *gathered against it;* and this will put things into a *ferment,* as here; but this is no more the fault of the gospel than it is the fault of a wholesome medicine that it stirs up the *peccant* humours in the body, in order to the discharge of them. Observe what the debate was: —

1. Some were *taken with him,* and well affected to him: *Many of the people, when they heard this saying,* heard him with such compassion and kindness invite poor sinners to him, and with such authority engage to make them happy, that they could not but think highly of him. (1.) Some of them said, *O, a truth this is the prophet,* that prophet whom Moses spoke of to the fathers, who should be *like unto him;* or, This is *the prophet* who, according to the received notions of the Jewish church, is to be the harbinger and forerunner of the Messiah; or, *This is truly a prophet,* one divinely inspired and sent of God. (2.) Others went further, and said, *This is the Christ* (*v.* 41), not the *prophet* of the Messiah, but the Messiah himself. The Jews had at this time a more than ordi-

nary expectation of the Messiah, which made them ready to say upon every occasion, *Lo, here is Christ,* or *Lo, he is there;* and this seems to be only the effect of some such confused and floating notions which caught at the first appearance, for we do not find that these people became his disciples and followers; a good opinion of Christ is far short of a lively faith in Christ; many give Christ a good word that give him no more. These here said, *This is the prophet,* and *this is the Christ,* but could not persuade themselves to leave all and follow him; and so this their testimony to Christ was but a testimony *against themselves.*

2. Others were *prejudiced against him.* No sooner was this great truth started, that *Jesus is the Christ,* than immediately it was contradicted and argued against: and this one thing, that his rise and origin were (as they took it for granted) out of Galilee, was thought enough to answer all the arguments for his being the Christ. For, *shall Christ come out of Galilee?* Has not *the scripture said that Christ comes of the seed of David?* See here, (1.) A laudable knowledge of the scripture. They were so far in the right, that the Messiah was to be a *rod out of the stem of Jesse* (Isa. 11:1), that out of Bethlehem should *arise the Governor,* Mic. 5:2. This even the common people knew by the traditional expositions which their scribes gave them. Perhaps the people who had these scriptures so ready to object against Christ were not alike knowing in other parts of holy writ, but had had these put into their mouths by their leaders, to fortify their prejudices against Christ. Many that espouse some corrupt notions, and spend their zeal in defence of them, seem to be very ready in the scriptures, when indeed they know little more than those scriptures which they have been taught to *pervert.* (2.) A culpable ignorance of our Lord Jesus. They speak of it as certain and past dispute that *Jesus was of Galilee,* whereas by enquiring of himself, or his mother, or his disciples, or by consulting the genealogies of the family of David, or the register at Bethlehem, they might have known that he was the Son of David, and a native of Bethlehem; but *this they willingly are ignorant of.* Thus gross falsehoods in matters of fact, concerning persons and things, are often taken up by prejudiced and partial men, and great resolves founded upon them, even in the same place and the same age wherein the persons live and the things are done, while the truth might easily be found out.

3. Others were *enraged against him,* and they *would have taken him, v.* 44. Though what he said was most sweet and gracious, yet they were exasperated against him for it. Thus did our Master suffer ill for saying and doing well. *They would have taken him;* they hoped somebody or other would seize him, and, if they had thought no one else would, they would have done it themselves. They *would have taken him;* but no man *laid hands on him,* being restrained by an invisible power, because his hour was not come. As the malice of Christ's enemies is always *unreasonable,* so sometimes the suspension of it is *unaccountable.*

Verses 45–53

The chief priests and Pharisees are here in a close cabal, contriving how to suppress Christ; though this was the *great day of the feast,* they attended not the religious services of the day, but left them to the vulgar, to whom it was common for those great ecclesiastics to consign and turn over the business of devotion, while they thought themselves better employed in the affairs of church-policy. They sat in the council-chamber, expecting Christ to be brought a prisoner to them, as they had issued out warrants for apprehending him, *v.* 32. Now here we are told,

I. What passed between them and their own officers, who returned without him, *re infecta — having done nothing.* Observe,

1. The reproof they gave the officers for not executing the warrant they gave them: *Why have you not brought him?* He appeared publicly; the people were many of them disgusted, and would have assisted them in taking him; this was *the last day of the feast,* and they would not have such another opportunity; "why then did you neglect your duty?" It vexed them that those who were their own creatures, who depended on them, and on whom they depended, into whose minds they had instilled prejudices against Christ, should thus disappoint them. Note, Mischievous men fret that they cannot do the mischief they would, Ps. 112:10; Neh. 6:16.

2. The reason which the officers gave for the non-execution of their warrant: *Never man spoke like this man, v.* 46. Now, (1.) This was a very great truth, that *never any man spoke with* that wisdom, and power, and grace, that convincing clearness, and that charming sweetness, wherewith Christ spoke; none of the prophets, no, not Moses himself. (2.) The very officers that were sent to take him were taken with him, and acknowledged this. Though they were probably men who had no quick sense of reason or eloquence, and certainly had no inclination to think well of Jesus, yet so much *self-evidence* was there in what Christ said that they could not but prefer him before all those that sat in Moses's seat. Thus Christ was preserved by the power God has upon the consciences even of bad men. (3.) They said this to their lords and masters, who could not endure to hear any thing that tended to the honour of Christ and yet could not avoid hearing this. Providence ordered it so that this should be said to them, that it might be a vexation in their sin and an aggravation of their sin. Their own officers, who could not be suspected to be biassed in favour of Christ, are witnesses against them. This testimony of theirs should have made them reflect upon themselves, with this thought, "Do we know what we are doing, when we are hating and persecuting one that speaks so admirably well?"

3. The Pharisees endeavour to secure their officers to their interest, and to beget in them prejudices against Christ, to whom they saw them begin to be well affected. They suggest two things: —

(1.) That if they embrace the gospel of Christ they will *deceive themselves* (*v.* 47): *Are you also deceived?* Christianity has, from its first rise, been represented to the world as a great cheat upon it, and they that embraced it as men *deceived,* then when they began to be *undeceived.* Those that looked for a Messiah in external pomp thought those deceived who believed in a Messiah that appeared in poverty and disgrace; but the event declares that none were ever more shamefully deceived, nor put a greater cheat upon themselves, than those who promised themselves worldly wealth and secular dominion with the Messiah. Observe what a *compliment* the Pharisees paid to these officers: *"Are you also deceived?* What! men of your sense, and thought, and figure; men that know better than to be imposed upon by every pretender and upstart teacher?" They endeavour to prejudice them against Christ by persuading them to think well of themselves.

(2.) That they will *disparage themselves.* Most men, even in their religion, are willing to be governed by the example of those of the *first rank;* these officers therefore, whose preferments, such as they were, gave them a *sense of honour,* are desired to consider,

[1.] That, if they become disciples of Christ, they go contrary to those who were persons of quality and reputation: *"Have any of the rulers, or of the Pharisees, believed on him?* You know they have not, and you ought to be bound up by their judgment, and to *believe* and *do* in religion according to the will of your superiors; will you be wiser than they?" Some of the rulers did embrace Christ (Mt. 9:18; *ch.* 4:53), and more believed in him, but wanted courage to confess him (*ch.* 12:42); but, when the interest of Christ runs low in the world, it is common for its adversaries to represent it as lower than really it is. But it was too true that few, very few, of them did. Note, *First,* The cause of Christ has seldom had rulers and Pharisees on its side. It needs not secular supports, nor proposes secular advantages, and therefore neither courts nor is courted by the great men of this world. *Self-denial* and the *cross* are hard lessons to *rulers* and Pharisees. *Secondly,* This has confirmed many in their prejudices against Christ and his gospel, that the rulers and Pharisees have been no friends to them. Shall *secular* men pretend to be more concerned about *spiritual* things than spiritual men themselves, or to see further into religion than those who make its study their profession? If *rulers* and *Pharisees* do not believe in Christ, they that do believe in him will be the most singular, unfashionable, ungenteel people in the world, and quite out of the way of preferment; thus are people foolishly swayed by *external motives* in matters of *eternal moment,* are willing to be damned for fashion-sake, and to go to hell in compliment to the *rulers* and *Pharisees.*

[2.] That they will link themselves with the despicable vulgar sort of people (*v.* 43): *But this people, who know not the law, are cursed,* meaning especially those that were well-affected to the doctrine of Christ. Observe, *First,* How scornfully and disdainfully they speak of them: *This people.* It is not *laos,* this *lay-people,* distinguished from them that were the clergy, but *ochlos outos,* this *rabble-people,* this pitiful, scandalous, scoundrel people, whom they disdained to *set with the dogs of their flock* though God had set them with the lambs of his. If they meant the *commonalty of the Jewish nation,* they were the seed of Abraham, and in covenant with God, and not to be spoken of with such contempt. The church's common interests are betrayed when any one part of it studies to render the other mean and despicable. If they meant the *followers of Christ,* though they were generally persons of small figure and fortune, yet by owning Christ they discovered such a sagacity, integrity, and interest in the favours of Heaven, as made them truly great and considerable. Note, As the wisdom of God has often chosen base things, and things which are despised, so the folly of men has commonly debased and despised those whom God has chosen. *Secondly,* How unjustly they reproach them as ignorant of the word of God: *They know not the law;* as if none knew the law but those that knew it *from them,* and no scripture-knowledge were current but what came out of their mint; and as if none knew the law but such as were observant of their canons and traditions. Perhaps many of those whom they thus despised *knew the law,* and the prophets too, better than they did. Many a plain, honest, unlearned disciple of Christ, by meditation, experience, prayers, and especially obedience, attains to a more clear, sound, and useful knowledge of the word of God, than some great scholars with all their wit and learning. Thus David came to understand *more than the ancients* and *all his teachers,* Ps. 119:99, 100. If the common people did not *know the law,* yet the chief priests and Pharisees, of all men, should not have upbraided them with this; for whose fault was it but theirs, who should have *taught them better,* but, instead of that, *took away the key of knowledge?* Lu. 11:52. *Thirdly,* How magisterially they pronounce sentence upon them: they are *cursed,* hateful to God, and all wise men; *epikatartoi — an execrable* people. It is well that their saying they were cursed did not make them so, for the *curse causeless shall not come.* It is a usurpation of God's prerogative, as well as great uncharitableness, to say of any particular persons, much more of any body of people, that they are reprobates. We are unable to *try,* and therefore unfit to *condemn,* and our rule is, *Bless, and curse not.* Some think they meant no more than that the people were *apt to be deceived* and *made fools of;* but they use this odious word, They are *cursed,* to express their own indignation, and to frighten their officers from having any thing to do with them; thus the language of hell, in our profane age, calls every thing that is displeasing *cursed,* and *damned,* and *confounded.* Now, for aught that appears, these officers had their convictions baffled and stifled by these suggestions, and they never enquire further after Christ; one word from a *ruler* or *Pharisee* will sway more with many than the true reason of things, and the great interests of their souls.

II. What passed between them and Nicodemus, a member of their own body, *v.* 50, etc. Observe,

1. The just and rational objection which Nicodemus made against their proceedings. Even in their corrupt and wicked sanhedrim God left not himself quite *without* witness against their enmity; nor was the vote against Christ carried *nemine contradicente — unanimously.* Observe,

(1.) Who it was that appeared against them; it was Nicodemus, *he that came to Jesus by night, being one of them, v.* 50. Observe, concerning him, [1.] That, though he had been with Jesus, and taken him for his teacher, yet he retained his place in the council, and his vote among them. Some impute this to his *weakness* and cowardice, and think it was his fault that he did not quit his place, but Christ had never said to him, *Follow me,* else he would have done as others that left all to follow him; therefore it seems rather to have been his *wisdom* not immediately to throw up his place, because there he might have opportunity of serving Christ and his interest, and stemming the tide of the Jewish rage, which perhaps he did more than we are aware of. He might there be as Hushai among Absalom's counsellors, instrumental to *turn their counsels into foolishness.* Though we must in no case deny our Master, yet we may wait for an opportunity of confessing him to the best advantage. God has his remnant among all sorts, and many times finds, or puts, or makes, some good in the worst places and societies. There was Daniel in Nebuchadnezzar's court, and Nehemiah in Artaxerxes's. [2.] That though at first he came to Jesus *by night,* for fear of being known, and still continued in his post; yet, when there was occasion, he boldly appeared in defence of Christ, and opposed the whole council that were set against him.

Thus many believers who at first were timorous, and ready to *flee at the shaking of a leaf,* have at length, by divine grace, grown courageous, and able to *laugh at the shaking of a spear.* Let none justify the disguising of their faith by the example of Nicodemus, unless, like him, they be ready upon the first occasion openly to appear in the cause of Christ, though they stand alone in it; for so Nicodemus did here, and *ch.* 19:39.

(2.) What he alleged against their proceedings (*v.* 51): *Doth our law judge any man before it hear him* (*akousē par' autou — hear from himself*) and *know what he doeth?* By no means, nor doth the law of any civilized nation allow it. Observe, [1.] He prudently argues from the principles of their own law, and an incontestable rule of justice, that no man is to be condemned *unheard.* Had he urged the excellency of Christ's doctrine or the evidence of his miracles, or repeated to them his divine discourse with him (*ch.* 3), it had been but to *cast pearls before swine,* who would *trample them under their feet,* and would *turn again and rend him;* therefore he waives them. [2.] Whereas they had reproached the people, especially the followers of Christ, as *ignorant of the law,* he here tacitly retorts the charge upon themselves, and shows how ignorant they were of some of the first principles of the law, so unfit were they to give law to others. [3.] The law is here said to *judge,* and *hear,* and *know,* when magistrates that govern and are governed by it *judge,* and *hear,* and *know;* for they are the *mouth of the law,* and whatsoever they bind and loose according to the law is justly said to be bound and loosed by the law. [4.] It is highly fit that none should come under the *sentence* of the law, till they have first by a fair trial undergone the *scrutiny* of it. Judges, when they receive the complaints of the accuser, must always reserve in their minds room for the defence of the accused, for they have two ears, to remind them to hear both sides; this is said to be the manner of the Romans, Acts 25:18. The method of our law is *Oyer* and *Terminer,* first to *hear* and then to *determine.* [5.] Persons are to be judged, not by what is *said* of them, but by what they *do. Our law* will not ask what men's opinions are of them, or out-cries against them, but, What have they done? What *overt-acts* can they be convicted of? Sentence must be given, *secundum allegata et probata — according to what is alleged and proved.* Facts, and not faces, must be known in judgment; and the *scale* of justice must be used before the *sword* of justice.

Now we may suppose that the motion Nicodemus made in the house upon this was, That Jesus should be desired to come and give them an account of himself and his doctrine, and that they should favour him with an impartial and unprejudiced hearing; but, though none of them could gainsay his maxim, none of them would second his motion.

2. What was said to this objection. Here is no direct reply given to it; but, when they could not resist the force of his argument, they fell foul upon him, and what was to seek in *reason* they made up in railing and reproach. Note, It is a sign of a bad cause when men cannot bear to *hear reason,* and take it as an affront to be reminded of its maxims. Whoever are *against reason* give cause to suspect that *reason* is *against them.* See how they taunt him: *Art thou also of Galilee? v.* 52. Some think he was well enough served for continuing among those whom he knew to be enemies to Christ, and for his speaking no more on the behalf of Christ than what he might have said on behalf of the greatest criminal — that he should not be condemned unheard. Had he said, "As for this Jesus, I have heard him myself, and know he is a *teacher come from God,* and you in opposing him fight against God," as he ought to have said, he could not have been more abused than he was for this feeble effort of his tenderness for Christ. As to what they said to Nicodemus, we may observe,

(1.) How *false* the grounds of their arguing were, for, [1.] They suppose that Christ was of Galilee, and this was false, and if they would have been at the pains of an impartial enquiry they would have found it so. [2.] They suppose that because most of his disciples were Galileans they were all such, whereas he had abundance of disciples in Judea. [3.] They suppose that out of Galilee no prophet had *risen,* and for this appeal to Nicodemus's search; yet this was false too: Jonah was of Gath-hepher, Nahum an Elkoshite, both of Galilee. Thus do they *make lies their refuge.*

(2.) How *absurd* their arguings were upon these grounds, such as were a shame to *rulers* and *Pharisees.* [1.] Is any man of worth and virtue ever the worse for the poverty and obscurity of his country? The Galileans were the seed of Abraham; barbarians and Scythians are the seed of Adam; and *have we not all one Father?* [2.] Supposing no prophet had risen out of Galilee, yet it is not impossible that any should arise thence. If Elijah was the first prophet of Gilead (as perhaps he was), and if the Gileadites were called *fugitives,* must it therefore be questioned whether he was a prophet or no?

3. The hasty adjournment of the court hereupon. They broke up the assembly in confusion, and with precipitation, and *every man went to his own house.* They met to take *counsel together against the Lord and his Anointed,* but they *imagined a vain think;* and not only he that sits in heaven laughed at them, but we may sit on earth and laugh at them too, to see all the policy of the close cabal broken to pieces with one plain honest word. They were not willing to hear Nicodemus, because they could not answer him. As soon as they perceived they had one such among them, they saw it was to no purpose to go on with their design, and therefore put off the debate to a more convenient season, when he was absent. Thus the counsel of the Lord is made to stand, in spite of the devices in the hearts of men.

CHAPTER 8

In this chapter we have, I. Christ's evading the snare which the Jews laid for him, in bringing to him a woman taken in adultery (*v.* 1–11). II. Divers discourses or conferences of his with the Jews that cavilled at him, and sought occasion against him, and made every thing he said a matter of controversy. 1. Concerning his being the light of the world (*v.* 12–20). 2. Concerning the ruin of the unbelieving Jews (*v.* 21–30). 3. Concerning liberty and bondage (*v.* 31–37). 4. Concerning his Father and their father (*v.* 38–47). 5. Here is his discourse in answer to their blasphemous reproaches (*v.* 48–50). 6. Concerning the immortality of believers (*v.* 51–59). And in all this he endured the contradiction of sinners against himself.

Verses 1–11

Though Christ was basely abused in the foregoing chapter, both by the rulers and by the people, yet here we have him still at Jerusalem, still in the temple. *How often would he have gathered them!* Observe,

I. His retirement in the evening out of the town (*v.* 1): *He went unto the mount of olives;* whether to some friend's house, or to some booth pitched there, now at the feast of tabernacles, is not certain; whether he rested there, or, as some think, continued all night in prayer to God, we are not told. But he went out of Jerusalem, perhaps because he had no friend there that had either kindness or courage enough to give him a night's lodging; while his persecutors had *houses* of their own to go to (*ch.* 7:53), he could not so much as borrow a place to lay his head on, but what he must go a mile or two out of town for. He retired (as some think) because he would not expose himself to the peril of a popular tumult in the night. It is prudent to go out of the way of danger whenever we can do it without going out of the way of duty. In the day-time, when he had work to do in the temple, he willingly exposed himself, and was under special protection, Isa. 49:2. But in the night, when he had not work to do, he withdrew into the country, and sheltered himself there.

II. His return in the morning to the temple, and to his work there, *v.* 2. Observe,

1. What a diligent preacher Christ was: *Early in the morning he came again, and taught.* Though he had been teaching the day before, he taught again to-day. Christ was a constant preacher, in season and out of season. Three things were taken notice of here concerning Christ's preaching. (1.) The time: *Early in the morning.* Though he lodged out of town, and perhaps had spent much of the night in secret prayer, yet he came *early.* When a day's work is to be done for God and souls it is good to begin betimes, and take the day before us. (2.) The place: *In the temple;* not so much because it was a *consecrated* place (for then he would have chosen it at other times) as because it was now a *place of concourse;* and he would hereby countenance solemn assemblies for religious worship, and encourage people to come up to the temple, for he had not yet left it desolate. (3.) His posture: *He sat down,* and taught, as one having authority, and as one that intended to abide by it for some time.

2. How diligently his preaching was attended upon: *All the people came unto him;* and perhaps many of them were the country-people, who were this day to return home from the feast, and were desirous to hear one sermon more from the mouth of Christ before they returned. They came to him, though he came early. They that *seek him early shall find him.* Though the rulers were displeased at those that came to hear him, yet they would come; and *he taught them,* though they were angry at *him* too. Though there were few or none among them that were persons of any figure, yet Christ bade them welcome, and taught them.

III. His dealing with those that brought to him the *woman taken in adultery, tempting* him. The scribes and Pharisees would not only not hear Christ patiently themselves, but they disturbed him when the people were attending on him. Observe here,

1. The case proposed to him by the scribes and Pharisees, who herein contrived to pick a quarrel with him, and bring him into a snare, *v.* 3–6.

(1.) They set the prisoner to the bar (*v.* 3): they brought him *a woman taken in adultery,* perhaps now lately taken, during the time of the feast of tabernacles, when, it may be, their dwelling in booths, and their feasting and joy, might, by wicked minds, which corrupt the best things, be made occasions of sin. Those that were *taken in adultery* were by the Jewish law to be put to death, which the Roman powers allowed them the execution of, and therefore she was brought before the ecclesiastical court. Observe, She *was taken in her adultery.* Though adultery is a work of darkness, which the criminals commonly take all the care they can to conceal, yet sometimes it is strangely brought to light. Those that promise themselves secrecy in sin deceive themselves. The scribes and Pharisees bring her to Christ, and set her in the midst of the assembly, as if they would leave her wholly to the judgment of Christ, he having *sat down,* as a judge upon the bench.

(2.) They prefer an indictment against her: *Master, this woman was taken in adultery, v.* 4. Here they call him *Master* whom but the day before they had called a *deceiver,* in hopes with their flatteries to have ensnared him, as those, Lu. 20:20. But, though men may be imposed upon with compliments, he that searches the heart cannot.

[1.] The crime for which the prisoner stands indicted is no less than adultery, which even in the patriarchal age, before the law of Moses, was looked upon as *an iniquity to be punished by the judges,* Job 31:9–11; Gen. 38:24. The Pharisees, by their vigorous prosecution of this offender, seemed to have a great zeal against the sin, when it appeared afterwards that they themselves were not free from it; nay, they were within *full of all uncleanness,* Mt. 23:27, 28. Note, It is common for those that are indulgent to their own sin to be severe against the sins of others.

[2.] The proof of the crime was from the notorious evidence of the fact, an incontestable proof; she was *taken in the act,* so that there was no room left to plead not guilty. Had she not been taken in this act, she might have gone on to another, till her heart had been perfectly hardened; but sometimes it proves a mercy to sinners to have their sin brought to light, that they may *do no more presumptuously.* Better our sin should *shame* us than *damn* us, and be set in order before us for our conviction than for our condemnation.

(3.) They produce the statute in this case made and provided, and upon which she was indicted, *v.* 5. Moses in the law commanded *that such should be stoned.* Moses commanded that they should be *put to death* (Lev. 20:10; Deu. 22:22), but not that they should be stoned, unless the adulteress was espoused, not married, or was a priest's daughter, Deu. 22:21. Note, Adultery is an exceedingly sinful sin, for it is the rebellion of a vile lust, not only against the command, but against the covenant, of our God. It is the violation of a divine institution in innocency, by the indulgence of one of the basest lusts of man in his degeneracy.

(4.) They pray his judgment in the case: *"But what sayest thou,* who pretendest to be a teacher come from God to repeal old laws and enact new ones? What hast thou to say in this case?" If they had asked this question in sincerity, with a humble desire to know his mind, it had been very commendable. Those that are entrusted with the administration of justice should look up to Christ for direction; but *this they said tempting him, that they might have to accuse him, v.* 6. [1.] If he should confirm the sentence of the law, and let it take its course, they would censure him as inconsistent with himself (he having received publicans and harlots) and with the character of the Messiah, who should be meek, and have salvation, and proclaim a year of release; and perhaps they would accuse him to the Roman governor, for countenancing the Jews in the exercise of a judicial power. But, [2.] If he should acquit her, and give his opinion that the sentence should not be executed (as they expected he would), they would represent him, *First,* As an enemy to the law of Moses, and as one that usurped an authority to correct and control it, and would confirm that prejudice against him which his enemies were so industrious to propagate, that he came to *destroy the law and the prophets. Secondly,* As a friend to sinners, and, consequently, a favourer of sin; if he should seem to connive at such wickedness, and let it go unpunished, they would represent him as countenancing it, and being a patron of offences, if he was a protector of offenders, than which no reflection could be more invidious upon one that professed the strictness, purity, and business of a prophet.

2. The method he took to resolve this case, and so to break this snare.

(1.) He seemed to slight it, and turned a deaf ear to it: He *stooped down, and wrote on the ground.* It is impossible to tell, and therefore needless to ask, what he wrote; but this is the only mention made in the gospels of Christ's writing. Eusebius indeed speaks of his writing to Abgarus, king of Edessa. Some think they have a liberty of conjecture as to what he wrote here. Grotius says, It was some grave weighty saying, and that it was usual for wise men, when they were very thoughtful concerning any thing, to do so. Jerome and Ambrose suppose he wrote, *Let the names of these wicked men be written in the dust.* Others this, *The earth accuses the earth, but the judgment is mine.* Christ by this teaches us to be slow to speak when difficult cases are proposed to us, not quickly to shoot our bolt; and when provocations are given us, or we are bantered, to pause and consider before we reply; think twice before we speak once: *The heart of the wise studies to answer.* Our translation from some Greek copies, which add, *mē prospoioumenos* (though most copies have it not), give this account of the reason of his writing on the ground, *as though he heard them not.* He did as it were look another way, to show that he was not willing to take notice of their address, saying, in effect, *Who made me a judge or a divider?* It is safe in many cases to be deaf to that which it is not safe to answer, Ps. 38:13. Christ would not have his ministers to be entangled in secular affairs. Let them rather employ themselves in any lawful studies, and fill up their time in writing on the ground (which nobody will heed), than busy themselves in that which does not belong to them. But, when Christ seemed as though he heard them not, he made it appear that he not only heard their words, but knew their thoughts.

(2.) When they importunately, or rather impertinently, pressed him for an answer, he turned the conviction of the prisoner upon the prosecutors, *v.* 7.

[1.] They *continued asking him,* and his seeming not to take notice of them made them the more vehement; for now they thought sure enough that they had run him aground, and that he could not avoid the imputation of contradicting either the law of Moses, if he should acquit the prisoner, or his own doctrine of mercy and pardon, if he should condemn her; and therefore they pushed on their appeal to him with vigour; whereas they should have construed his disregard of them as a check to their design, and an intimation to them to desist, as they tendered their own reputation.

[2.] At last he put them all to shame and silence with one word: *He lifted up himself,* awaking as one out of sleep (Ps. 78:65), and *said unto them, He that is without sin among you, let him first cast a stone at her.*

First, Here Christ avoided the snare which they had laid for him, and effectually saved his own reputation. He neither reflected upon the law nor excused the prisoner's guilt, nor did he on the other hand encourage the prosecution or countenance their heat; see the good effect of consideration. When we cannot make our point by steering a direct course, it is good to fetch a compass.

Secondly, In the net which they spread is their own foot taken. They came with design to accuse him, but they were forced to accuse themselves. Christ owns it was fit the prisoner should be prosecuted, but appeals to their consciences whether they were fit to be the prosecutors.

a. He here refers to that rule which the law of Moses prescribed in the execution of criminals, that the *hand of the witnesses must be first upon them* (Deu. 17:7), as in the stoning of Stephen, Acts 7:58. The scribes and Pharisees were the witnesses against this woman. Now Christ puts it to them whether, according to their own law, they would dare to be the executioners. Durst they take away that life with their hands which they were now taking away with their tongues? would not their own consciences fly in their faces if they did?

b. He builds upon an uncontested maxim in morality, that it is very absurd for men to be zealous in punishing the offences of others, while they are every whit as guilty themselves, and they are not better than self-condemned who judge others, and yet themselves do the same thing: "If there be any of you who is *without sin,* without sin of this nature, that has not some time or other been guilty of fornication or adultery, let him cast the first stone at her." Not that magistrates, who are conscious of guilt themselves, should therefore connive at others' guilt. But therefore, (*a.*) Whenever we find fault with others, we ought to reflect upon ourselves, and to be more severe against sin in ourselves than in others. (*b.*) We ought to be favourable, though not to the sins, yet to the persons, of those that offend, and to restore them with a *spirit of meekness,* considering ourselves and our own corrupt nature. *Aut sumus, aut fuimus, vel possumus esse quod hic est — We either are, or have been, or may be, what he is.* Let this restrain us from *throwing stones* at our brethren, and proclaiming their faults. *Let him that is without sin* begin such discourse as this, and then those that are truly humbled for their own sins will blush at it, and be glad to *let it drop.* (*c.*) Those that are any way obliged to animadvert upon the faults of others are concerned to look well to themselves, and keep themselves pure (Mt. 7:5), *Qui alterum incusat probri, ipsum se intueri oportet.* The snuffers of the tabernacle were of *pure gold.*

c. Perhaps he refers to the trial of the suspected wife by the jealous husband with the waters of jealousy. The man was to bring her to the priest (Num. 5:15), as the scribes and Pharisees brought this woman to Christ. Now it was a received opinion among the Jews, and confirmed by experience, that if the husband who brought his wife to that trial had himself been at any time guilty of adultery, *Aquae non explorant ejus uxorem — The bitter water had no effect upon the wife.* "Come then," saith Christ, "according to your own tradition will I judge you; if you are without sin, stand to the charge, and let the adulteress be executed; but if not, though she be guilty, while you that present her are equally so, according to your own rule she shall be free."

d. In this he attended to the great work which he came into the world about, and that was to bring sinners to repentance; not to destroy, but to save. He aimed to bring, not only the prisoner to repentance, by showing her his mercy, but the prosecutors too, by showing them their sins. They sought to ensnare him; he sought to convince and convert them. Thus *the blood-thirsty hate the upright, but the just seek his soul.*

[3.] Having given them this startling word, he left them to consider of it, *and again stooped down, and wrote on the ground, v.* 8. As when they made their address he seemed to slight their question, so now that he had given them an answer he slighted their resentment of it, not caring what they said to it; nay, they needed not to make any reply; the matter was lodged in their own breasts, let them make the best of it there. Or, he would not seem to wait for an answer, lest they should on a sudden justify themselves, and then think themselves bound in honour to persist in it; but gives them time to pause, and to commune with their own hearts. God saith, *I hearkened and heard,* Jer. 8:6. Some Greek copies here read, He *wrote on the ground, enos hekastou autōn tas hamartias — the sins of every one of them;* this he could do, for he *sets our iniquities before him;* and this he will do, for he will *set them in order* before us too; he *seals up our transgressions,* Job 14:17. But he does not write men's sins *in the sand;* no, they are written as with a *pen of iron* and the *point of a diamond* (Jer. 17:1), never to be forgotten till they are forgiven.

[4.] The scribes and Pharisees were so strangely thunderstruck with the words of Christ that they let fall their persecution of Christ, whom they durst no further tempt, and their prosecution of the woman, whom they durst no longer accuse (*v.* 9): *They went out one by one.*

First, Perhaps his writing on the ground frightened them, as the hand-writing on the wall frightened Belshazzar. They concluded he was writing bitter things against them, writing their doom. Happy they who have no reason to be afraid of Christ's writing!

Secondly, What he said frightened them by sending them to their own consciences; he had *shown them to themselves,* and they were afraid if they should stay till he lifted up himself again his next word would show them to the world, and shame them before men, and therefore they thought it best to withdraw. They went out *one by one,* that they might go out *softly,* and not by a noisy flight disturb Christ; they went away by *stealth,* as *people being ashamed steal away when they flee in battle,* 2 Sa. 19:3. The order of their departure is taken notice of, *beginning at the eldest,* either because they were most guilty, or first aware of the danger they were in of being put to the blush; and if the eldest quit the field, and retreat ingloriously, no marvel if the younger follow them. Now see here, 1. The *force* of the word of Christ for the conviction of sinners: *They who heard it were convicted by their own consciences.* Conscience is God's deputy in the soul, and one word from him will set it on work, Heb. 4:12. Those that had been old in adulteries, and long fixed in a proud opinion of themselves, were here, even the oldest of them, startled by the word of Christ; even scribes and Pharisees, who were most conceited of themselves, are by the power of Christ's word made to retire with shame. 2. The *folly* of sinners under these convictions, which appears in these scribes and Pharisees. (1.) It is folly for those that are under convictions to make it their principal care to *avoid shame,* as Judah (Gen. 38:23), *lest we be shamed.* Our care should be more to save our souls than to save our credit. Saul evidenced his hypocrisy when he said, *I have sinned, yet now honour me, I pray thee.* There is no way to get the honour and comfort of penitents, but by taking the shame of penitents. (2.) It is folly for those that are under convictions to contrive how to *shift off* their convictions, and to get rid of them. The scribes and Pharisees had the wound *opened,* and now they should have been desirous to have it *searched,* and then it might have been *healed,* but this was the thing they *dreaded* and *declined.* (3.) It is folly for those that are under convictions to *get away from Jesus Christ,* as these here did, for he is the only one that can heal the wounds of conscience, and speak peace to us. Those that are convicted by their consciences will be condemned by their Judge, if they be not justified by their Redeemer; and will they then go from him? To whom will they go?

[5.] When the *self-conceited* prosecutors quitted the field, and *fled for the same,* the *self-condemned* prisoner stood her ground, with a resolution to abide by the judgment of our Lord Jesus: *Jesus was left alone* from the company of the scribes and Pharisees, free from their molestations, *and the woman standing in the midst* of the assembly that were attending on Christ's preaching, where they set her, *v.* 3. She did not seek to make her escape, though she had opportunity for it; but her prosecutors had appealed unto Jesus, and to him she would go, on him she would wait for her doom. Note, Those whose cause is brought before our Lord Jesus will never have occasion to remove it into any other court, for he is the refuge of penitents. The law which accuses us, and calls for judgment against us, is by the gospel of Christ made to withdraw; its demands are answered, and its clamours silenced, by the blood of Jesus. Our cause is lodged in the gospel court; we are *left with Jesus alone,* it is with him only that we have now to deal, for to him all judgment is committed; let us therefore secure our interest in him, and we are made for ever. Let his gospel *rule us,* and it will infallibly *save us.*

[6.] Here is the conclusion of the trial, and the issue it was brought to: *Jesus lifted up himself, and he saw none but the woman, v.* 10, 11. Though Christ may seem to take no notice of what is said and done, but leave it to the *contending* sons of men to *deal it out among themselves,* yet, when the hour of his judgment is come, he will no longer keep silence. When David had appealed to God, he prayed, *Lift up thyself,* Ps. 7:6, and 94:2. The woman, it is likely, stood trembling at the bar, as one doubtful of the issue. Christ was *without sin,* and might cast the first stone; but though none more severe than he against sin, for he is infinitely just and holy, none more compassionate than he to sinners, for he is infinitely gracious and merciful, and this poor malefactor finds him so, now that she *stands upon her deliverance.* Here is the method of courts of judicature observed.

First, The prosecutors are called: *Where are those thine accusers? Hath no man condemned thee?* Not but that Christ knew where they were; but he asked, that he might shame them, who declined his judgment, and encourage her who resolved to abide by it. St. Paul's challenge is like this, *Who shall lay any thing to the charge of God's elect?* Where are those their accusers? The *accuser of the brethren shall* be fairly *cast out,* and all indictments legally and regularly quashed.

Secondly, They do not appear when the question is asked: *Hath no man condemned thee?* She said, *No man, Lord.* She speaks respectfully to Christ, calls him *Lord,* but is silent concerning her prosecutors, says nothing in answer to that question which concerned them, *Where are those thine accusers?* She does not triumph in their retreat nor insult over them as witnesses against themselves, not against her. If we hope to be forgiven by our Judge, we must forgive our accusers; and if their accusations, how invidious soever, were the happy occasion of awakening our consciences, we may easily *forgive them this wrong.* But she answered the question which concerned herself, *Has no man condemned thee?* True penitents find it enough to give an account of themselves to God, and will not undertake to give an account of other people.

Thirdly, The prisoner is therefore discharged: *Neither do I condemn thee; go, and sin no more.* Consider this,

(*a.*) As her discharge from the temporal punishment: "If they do not condemn thee to be *stoned to death,* neither *do I.*" Not that Christ came to disarm the magistrate of his sword of justice, nor that it is his will that capital punishments should not be inflicted on malefactors; so far from this, the administration of public justice is established by the gospel, and made subservient to Christ's kingdom: *By me kings reign.* But Christ would not condemn this woman, (*a.*) Because it was *none of his business;* he was no judge nor divider, and therefore would not intermeddle in secular affairs. His *kingdom* was *not of this world. Tractent fabrilia fabri — Let every one act in his own province.* (*b.*) Because she was prosecuted by those that were more guilty than she and could not for shame insist upon their demand of justice against her. The law appointed the hands of the witnesses to be first upon the criminal, and afterwards the hands of all the people, so that if they fly off, and do not condemn her, the prosecution drops. The justice of God, in inflicting temporal judgments, sometimes takes notice of a *comparative righteousness,* and spares those who are otherwise obnoxious when the punishing of them would gratify those that are worse than they, Deu. 32:26, 27. But, when Christ dismissed her, it was with this caution, *Go, and sin no more.* Impunity emboldens malefactors, and therefore those who are guilty, and yet have found means to escape the edge of the law, need to double their watch, *lest Satan get advantage;* for the fairer the escape was, the fairer the warning was to go and sin no more. Those who help to save the life of a criminal should, as Christ here, help to save the soul with this caution.

(*b.*) As her discharge from the eternal punishment. For Christ to say, *I do not condemn thee* is, in effect, to say, *I do forgive thee;* and the *Son of man had power on earth to forgive sins,* and could upon good grounds give this absolution; for as he knew the hardness and impenitent hearts of the prosecutors, and therefore said that which would confound them, so he knew the tenderness and sincere repentance of the prisoner, and therefore said that which would comfort her, as he did to that woman who was a sinner, such a sinner as this, who was likewise looked upon with disdain by a Pharisee (Lu. 7:48, 50): *Thy sins are forgiven thee, go in peace.* So here, *Neither do I condemn thee.* Note, (*a.*) Those are truly happy whom Christ *doth not condemn,* for his discharge is a sufficient answer to all other challenges; they are all *coram non judice — before an unauthorized judge.* (*b.*) Christ will not condemn those who, though they have sinned, will *go and sin no more,* Ps. 85:8; Isa. 55:7. he will not take the advantage he has against us for our former rebellions, if we will but lay down our arms and return to our allegiance. (*c.*) Christ's favour to us in the remission of the sins that are past should be a prevailing argument with us to *go and sin no more,* Rom. 6:1, 2. Will not Christ condemn thee? Go then and sin no more.

Verses 12–20

The rest of the chapter is taken up with debates between Christ and contradicting sinners, who cavilled at the most gracious words that proceeded out of his mouth. It is not certain whether these disputes were the same day that the adulteress was discharged; it is probable they were, for the evangelist mentions no other day, and takes notice (*v.* 2) how early Christ began that day's work. Though those Pharisees that accused the woman had absconded, yet there were other Pharisees (*v.* 13) to confront Christ, who had brass enough in their foreheads to keep them in countenance, though some of their party were put to such a shameful retreat; nay perhaps that made them the more industrious to pick quarrels with him, to retrieve, if possible, the reputation of their baffled party. In these verses we have,

I. A great doctrine laid down, with the application of it.

1. The doctrine is, *That Christ is the light of the world* (*v.* 12): *Then spoke Jesus again unto them;* though he had spoken a great deal to them to little purpose, and what he had said was opposed, yet he *spoke again,* for he *speaketh once, yea, twice.* They had turned a deaf ear to what he said, and yet he *spoke again to them,* saying, *I am the light of the world.* Note, Jesus Christ is the light of the world. One of the rabbies saith, *Light* is the name of the Messiah, as it is written, Dan. 2:22, *And light dwelleth with him.* God is light, and Christ is *the image of the invisible God;* God of gods, Light of lights. He was expected to be a *light to enlighten the Gentiles* (Lu. 2:32), and so the *light of the world,* and not of the Jewish church only. The visible light of the world is the sun, and Christ is the *Sun of righteousness.* One sun enlightens the whole world, so does one Christ, and there needs no more. Christ in calling himself the light expresses, (1.) What he is in himself — most excellent and glorious. (2.) What he is to the world — the fountain of light, enlightening every man. What a dungeon would the world be without the sun! So would it be without Christ by whom *light came into the world, ch.* 3:19.

2. The inference from this doctrine is, *He that followeth me,* as a traveller follows the light in a dark night, *shall not walk in darkness,* but *shall have the light of life.* If Christ be the light, then, (1.) It is our duty to *follow him,* to submit ourselves to his guidance, and in every thing take directions from him, in the way that leads to happiness. Many follow *false lights — ignes fatui,* that lead them to destruction; but Christ is the *true light.* It is not enough to *look at* this light, and to *gaze* upon it, but we must follow it, believe in it, and walk in it, for it is a light to *our feet,* not *our eyes* only. (2.) It is the happiness of those who follow Christ that they *shall not walk in darkness.* They shall not be left destitute of those instructions in the way of truth which are necessary to keep them from destroying error, and those directions in the way of duty which are necessary to keep them from damning sin. They shall have the *light of life,* that knowledge and enjoyment of God which will be to them the light of spiritual life in this world and of everlasting life in the other world, where there will be no death nor darkness. Follow Christ, and we shall undoubtedly be happy in both worlds. Follow Christ, and we shall follow him to heaven.

II. The objection which the Pharisees made against this doctrine, and it was very trifling and frivolous: *Thou bearest record of thyself; thy record is not true, v.* 13. In this objection they went upon the suspicion which we commonly have of men's self-condemnation, which is concluded to be the native language of self-love, such as we are all ready to condemn in others, but few are willing to own in themselves. But in this case the objection was very unjust, for, 1. They made that his crime, and a diminution to the credibility of his doctrine, which in the case of one who introduced a divine revelation was necessary and unavoidable. Did not Moses and all the prophets bear witness of themselves when they avouched themselves to be God's messengers? Did not the Pharisees ask John Baptist, *What sayest thou of thyself?* 2. They overlooked the testimony of all the other witnesses, which corroborated the testimony he bore of himself. Had he only borne record of himself, his testimony had indeed been *suspicious,* and the belief of it might have been *suspended;* but his doctrine was attested by more than *two or three* credible *witnesses,* enough to *establish every word* of it.

III. Christ's reply to this objection, *v.* 14. He does not retort upon them as he might ("You profess yourselves to be devout and good men, but your witness is not *true*"), but plainly vindicates himself; and, though he had waived his own testimony (*ch.* 5:31), yet here he abides by it, that it did not derogate from the credibility of his other proofs, but was necessary to show the force of them. He is the light of the world, and it is the property of light to be self-evidencing. First principles prove themselves. He urges three things to prove that his testimony, though of himself, was true and cogent.

1. That he was conscious to himself of his own authority, and abundantly satisfied in himself concerning it. He did not speak as one at uncertainty, nor propose a disputable notion, about which he himself hesitated, but *declared a decree,* and gave such an account of himself as he would *abide by: I know whence I came, and whither I go.* He was fully apprised of his own undertaking from first to last; knew whose errand he went upon, and what his success would be. He knew what he *was* before his manifestation to the world, and what he *should be* after; that he came *from the Father,* and was going *to him* (*ch.* 16:28), came *from glory,* and was going *to glory,* (*ch.* 17:5). This is the satisfaction of all good Christians, that though the world know them not, as it knew him not, yet they know whence their spiritual life comes, and whither it tends, and go upon sure grounds.

2. That they are very incompetent judges of him, and of his doctrine, and not to be regarded. (1.) Because they were *ignorant,* willingly and resolvedly *ignorant: You cannot tell whence I came, and whither I go.* To what purpose is it to talk with those who know nothing of the matter, nor desire to know? He had told them of his coming from heaven and returning to heaven, but it was *foolishness to them,* they *received it not;* it was what the *brutish man knows not,* Ps. 92:6. They took upon them to judge of that which they did not understand, which lay quite out of the road of their acquaintance. Those that despise Christ's dominions and dignities speak evil of what they *know not,* Jude, *v.* 8, 10. (2.) Because they were *partial* (*v.* 15): *You judge after the flesh.* When fleshly wisdom gives the rule of judgment, and outward appearances only are given in evidence, and the case decided according to them, then men *judge after the flesh;* and when the consideration of a secular interest turns the scale in judging of spiritual matters, when we judge in favour of that which pleases the carnal mind, and recommends us to a carnal world, we judge after the flesh; and the judgment cannot be right when the rule is wrong. The Jews judged of Christ and his gospel by outward appearances, and, because he appeared so mean, thought it impossible he should be the light of the world; as if the sun under a cloud were no sun. (3.) Because they were *unjust* and *unfair* towards him, intimated in this: *"I judge no man;* I neither make nor meddle with your political affairs, nor does my doctrine or practice at all intrench upon, or interfere with, your civil rights or secular powers." He thus *judged no man.* Now, if he did not *war after the flesh,* it was very unreasonable for them to *judge him after the flesh,* and to treat him as an offender against the civil government. Or, *"I judge no man,"* that is, "not now in my first coming, that is deferred till I come again," *ch.* 3:17. *Prima dispensatio Christi medicinalis est, non judicialis — The first coming of Christ was for the purpose of administering, not justice, but medicine.*

3. That his testimony of himself was sufficiently supported and corroborated by the testimony of his Father *with him and for him* (*v.* 16): *And yet, if I judge, my judgment is true.* He did in his doctrine judge (*ch.* 9:39), though not *politically.* Consider him then,

(1.) As a judge, and his own judgment was valid: *"If I judge,* I who have authority to execute judgments, I to whom all things are delivered, I who am the Son of God, and have the Spirit of God, if I judge, *my judgment is true,* of incontestable rectitude and uncontrollable authority, Rom. 2:2. *If* I *should judge,* my judgment must be true, and then you would be condemned; but the judgment-day is not yet come, you are not yet to be condemned, but spared, and therefore now *I judge no man;"* so Chrysostom. Now that which makes his judgment unexceptionable is, [1.] His Father's concurrence with him: *I am not alone, but I and the Father.* He has the Father's concurring *counsels* to *direct;* as he was with the Father before the world in forming the counsels, so the Father was with him in the world in prosecuting and executing those counsels, and never left him *inops consilii — without advice,* Isa. 11:2. All the *counsels of peace* (and of war too) *were between them both,* Zec. 6:13. He had also the Father's concurring power to authorize and confirm what he did; see Ps. 89:21, etc.; Isa. 42:1. He did not act *separately,* but in his own name and his Father's, and *by the authority aforesaid, ch.* 5:17, and 14:9, 10. [2.] His Father's commission to him: "It is the Father that *sent me."* Note, God will go along with those that he sends; see Ex. 3:10, 12: *Come, and I will send thee,* and *certainly I will be with thee.* Now, if Christ had a *commission* from the Father, and the Father's *presence* with him in all his administrations, no doubt his *judgment* was *true* and valid; no exception lay *against* it, no appeal lay *from* it.

(2.) Look upon him as *a witness,* and now he appeared no otherwise (having not as yet taken the throne of judgment), and as such his testimony was true and unexceptionable; this he shows, *v.* 17, 18, where,

[1.] He quotes a maxim of the Jewish law, *v.* 17. That *the testimony of two men is true.* Not as if it were always true *in itself,* for many a time hand has been joined in hand to bear a *false* testimony, 1 Ki. 21:10. But it is allowed as sufficient evidence upon which to ground a verdict *(verum dictum),* and if nothing appear to the contrary it is taken for granted to be *true.* Reference is here had to that law (Deu. 17:6), *At the mouth of two witnesses shall he that is worthy of death be put to death.* And see Deu. 9:15; Num. 35:30. It was in *favour of life* that in capital cases two witnesses wee required, as with us in case of treason. See Heb. 6:18.

[2.] He applies this to the case in hand (*v.* 18): *I am one that bear witness of myself, and the Father that sent me bears witness of me.* Behold two witnesses! Though in human courts, where two witnesses are required, the criminal or candidate is not admitted to be a witness for himself; yet in a matter purely divine, which can be proved only by a divine testimony, and God himself must be the witness, if the formality of two or three witnesses be insisted on, there can be no other than the eternal Father, the eternal Son of the Father, and the eternal Spirit. Now if the testimony of two distinct persons, that are *men,* and therefore may deceive or be deceived, is conclusive, much more ought the testimony of the Son of God concerning himself, backed with the testimony of his Father concerning him, to command assent; see 1 Jn. 5:7, 9–11. Now this proves not only that the Father and the Son are two distinct persons (for their respective testimonies are here spoken of as the testimonies of two several persons), but that these two are one, not only one in their testimony, but equal in power and glory, and therefore the same in substance. St. Austin here takes occasion to caution his hearers against Sabellianism on the one hand, which confounded the persons in the Godhead, and Arianism on the other, which denied the Godhead of the Son and Spirit. *Alius est filius, et alius pater, non tamed aliud, sed hoc ipsum est et pater, et filius, scilicet unus Deus est — The Son is one Person, and the Father is another; they do not, however, constitute two Beings, but the Father is the same Being that the Son is, that is, the only true God.* Tract. 36, *in* Joann. Christ here speaks of himself and the Father as witnesses to the world, giving in evidence to the reason and conscience of the children of men, whom he deals with as men. And these witnesses *to* the world now will in the great day be witnesses *against* those that persist in unbelief, and *their* word will judge men.

This was the sum of the first conference between Christ and these carnal Jews, in the conclusion of which we are told how their tongues were let loose, and their hands tied.

First, How their tongues were let loose (such was the malice of hell) to cavil at his discourse, *v.* 19. Though in what he said there appeared nothing of human policy or artifice, but a divine security, yet they set themselves to *cross questions* with him. None so incurably *blind* as those that resolve they *will not see.* Observe,

a. How they evaded the *conviction* with a *cavil: Then said they unto him, Where is thy Father?* They might easily have understood, by the tenour of this and his other discourses, that when he spoke of his *Father* he meant no other than God himself; yet they pretend to understand him of a common person, and, since he appeals to his testimony, they bid him *call his witness,* and challenge him, if he can, to produce him: *Where is thy Father?* Thus, as Christ said of them (*v.* 15), they *judge after the flesh.* Perhaps they hereby intend a reflection upon the meanness and obscurity of his family: *Where is thy Father,* that he should be fit to give evidence in such a case as this? Thus they turned it off with a taunt, when they *could not resist the wisdom and spirit with which he spoke.*

b. How he evaded the *cavil* with a further *conviction;* he did not tell them where his Father was, but charged them with wilful ignorance: *"You neither know me nor my Father.* It is to no purpose to discourse to you about divine things, who talk of them as blind men do of colours. Poor creatures! you know nothing of the matter." (*a.*) He charges them with ignorance of God: *"You know not my Father."* In Judah was God known (Ps. 76:1); they had some knowledge of him as the God that made the world, but their eyes were darkened that they could not see the light of his glory shining *in the face of Jesus Christ.* The *little children* of the Christian church *know the Father,* know him as a Father (1 Jn. 2:13); but these rulers of the Jews did not, because they would not so know him. (*b.*) He shows them the true cause of their ignorance of God: *If you had known me, you would have known my Father also.* The reason why men are ignorant of God is because they are unacquainted with Jesus Christ. Did we know Christ, [*a.*] In knowing him we should know the Father, of whose person he is the express image, *ch.* 14:9. Chrysostom proves hence the Godhead of Christ, and his equality with his Father. We cannot say, "He that knows a man knows an angel," or, "He that knows a creature knows the Creator;" but he that knows Christ knows the Father. [*b.*] By him we should be instructed in the knowledge of God, and introduced into an acquaintance with him. If we *knew Christ* better, we should *know the Father* better; but, where the Christian religion is slighted and opposed, natural religion will soon be lost and laid aside. Deism makes way for atheism. Those become vain in their imaginations concerning God that will not learn of Christ.

Secondly, See how their hands were tied, though their tongues were thus let loose; such was the power of Heaven to restrain the malice of hell. *These words spoke Jesus,* these bold words, these words of conviction and reproof, *in the treasury,* an apartment of the temple, where, to be sure, the chief priests, whose gain was their godliness, were mostly resident, attending the business of the revenue. Christ *taught in the temple,* sometimes in one part, sometimes in another, as he saw occasion. Now the priests who had so great a concern in the temple, and looked upon it as their *demesne,* might easily, with the assistance of the janizaries that were at their beck, either have seized him and exposed him to the rage of the mob, and that punishment which they called the *beating of the rebels;* or, at least, have *silenced* him, and stopped his mouth there, as Amos, though tolerated in the land of Judah, was forbidden to prophesy in the king's chapel, Amos, 7:12, 13. Yet even *in the temple,* where they had him in their reach, *no man laid hands on him,* for *his hour was not yet come.* See here, 1. The restraint laid upon his persecutors by an invisible power; none of them durst meddle with him. God can set bounds to the wrath of men, as he does to the waves of the sea. Let us not therefore fear danger in the way of duty; for God hath Satan and all his instruments in a chain. 2. The reason of this restraint: *His hour was not yet come.* The frequent mention of this intimates how much the time of our departure out of the world depends upon the fixed counsel and decree of God. It *will* come, it is coming; not yet come, but it is at hand. Our enemies cannot hasten it any sooner, nor our friends delay it any longer, than the time appointed of the Father, which is very comfortable to every good man, who can look up and say with pleasure, *My times are in thy hands;* and better there than in our own. His hour was not yet come, because his work was not done, nor his testimony finished. To all God's purposes *there is a time.*

Verses 21–30

Christ here gives fair warning to the careless unbelieving Jews to consider what would be the consequence of their infidelity, that they might prevent it before it was too late; for he spoke words of terror as well as words of grace. Observe here,

I. The wrath threatened (*v.* 21): *Jesus said again unto them* that which might be likely to do them good. He continued to teach, in kindness to those few who received his doctrine, though there were many that resisted it, which is an example to ministers to go on with their work, notwithstanding opposition, because a remnant shall be saved. Here Christ changes his voice; he had *piped to them* in the offers of his grace, and they *had not danced;* now he mourns to them in the denunciations of his wrath, to try if they would lament. He said, *I go my way, and you shall seek me, and shall die in your sins. Whither I go you cannot come.* Every word is terrible, and bespeaks spiritual judgments, which are the sorest of all judgments; worse than war, pestilence, and captivity, which the Old-Testament prophets denounced. Four things are here threatened against the Jews.

1. Christ's departure from them: *I go my way,* that is, "It shall not be long before I go; you need not take so much pains to drive me from you, I shall go of myself." They said to him, *Depart from us, we desire not the knowledge of thy ways;* and he takes them at their word; but woe to those from whom Christ departs. Ichabod, the glory is gone, our defence is departed, when Christ goes. Christ frequently warned them of his departure before he left them: he *bade often farewell,* as one *loth to depart,* and willing to be invited, and that would have them *stir up themselves to take hold on him.*

2. Their enmity to the true Messiah, and their fruitless and infatuated enquiries after another Messiah when he was gone away, which were both their sin and their punishment: *You shall seek me,* which intimates either, (1.) Their *enmity* to the *true Christ:* "You shall seek to ruin my interest, by persecuting my doctrine and followers, with a fruitless design to root them out." This was a continual vexation and torment to themselves, made them incurably *ill-natured,* and brought *wrath upon them* (God's and their own) *to the uttermost.* Or, (2.) Their *enquiries* after *false Christs:* "You shall continue your expectations of the Messiah, and be the self-perplexing seekers of a Christ to come, when he is already come;" like the Sodomites, who, being struck with blindness, wearied themselves to find the door. See Rom. 9:31, 32.

3. Their final impenitency: *You shall die in your sins.* Here is an error in all our English Bibles, even the old bishops' translation, and that of Geneva (the Rhemists only excepted), for all the Greek copies have it in the singular number, *en tē hamartia hymōn — in your sin,* so all the Latin versions; and Calvin has a note upon the difference between this and *v.* 24, where it is plural, *tais hamartiais,* that here it is meant especially of the sin of unbelief, *in hoc peccato vestro — in this sin of yours.* Note, Those that live in unbelief are for ever undone if they die in unbelief. Or, it may be understood in general, *You shall die in your iniquity,* as Eze. 3:19, and 33:9. Many that have long lived in sin are, through grace, saved by a timely repentance from *dying in sin;* but for those who go out of this world of probation into that of retribution under the guilt of sin unpardoned, and the power of sin unbroken, there remaineth no relief: salvation itself cannot save them, Job 20:11; Eze. 32:27.

4. Their eternal separation from Christ and all happiness in him: *Whither I go you cannot come.* When Christ left the world, he went to a state of perfect happiness; he went to paradise. Thither he took the penitent thief with him, that did not die in his sins; but the impenitent not only *shall not* come to him, but they *cannot;* it is morally impossible, for heaven would not be heaven to those that die unsanctified and unmeet for it. You cannot come, because you have *no right* to enter into that Jerusalem, Rev. 22:14. *Whither I go you cannot come,* to fetch me thence, so Dr. Whitby; and the same is the comfort of all good Christians, that, when they get to heaven, they will be out of the reach of their enemies' malice.

II. The jest they made of this threatening. Instead of trembling at this word, they bantered it, and turned it into ridicule (*v.* 22): *Will he kill himself?* See here, 1. What slight thoughts they had of Christ's threatenings; they could make themselves and one another merry with them, as those that mocked the messengers of the Lord, and turned the *burden of the word of the Lord* into a *by-word,* and *precept upon precept, line upon line,* into a merry song, Isa. 28:13. But *be ye not mockers, lest your bands be made strong.* 2. What ill thoughts they had of Christ's meaning, as if he had an inhuman design upon his own life, to avoid the indignities done him, like Saul. This is indeed (say they) to go whither we cannot follow him, for we will never *kill ourselves.* Thus they make him not only such a one as themselves, but worse; yet in the calamities brought by the Romans upon the Jews many of them in discontent and despair did kill themselves. They had put a much more favourable construction upon this word of his (*ch.* 7:34, 35): *Will he go to the dispersed among the Gentiles?* But see how indulged malice grows more and more malicious.

III. The confirmation of what he had said.

1. He had said, *Whither I go you cannot come,* and here he gives the reason for this (*v.* 23): *You are from beneath, I am from above; you are of this world, I am not of this world.* You are *ek tōn katō — of those things which are beneath;* noting, not so much their rise from beneath as their affection to these lower things: "You are *in with these things,* as those that belong to them; how can you come where I go, when your spirit and disposition are so directly contrary to mine?" See here, (1.) What the *spirit of the Lord Jesus* was — not of *this world,* but from *above.* He was perfectly dead to the wealth of the world, the ease of the body, and the praise of men, and was wholly taken up with divine and heavenly things; and none shall be with him but those who are *born from above* and have their *conversation in heaven.* (2.) How contrary to this *their* spirit was: *"You are from beneath,* and of this world." The Pharisees were of a carnal worldly spirit; and what communion could Christ have with them?

2. He had said, *You shall die in your sins,* and here he

stand to it: "Therefore I said, You shall die in your sins, because *you are from beneath;*" and he gives this further reason for it, *If you believe not that I am he, you shall die in your sins, v.* 24. See here, (1.) What we are required to believe: *that I am he, hoti egō eimi — that I am,* which is one of God's names, Ex. 3:14. It was the Son of God that there said, *Ehejeh asher Ehejeh — I will be what I will be;* for the deliverance of Israel was but a figure of good things to come, but now he saith, *"I am he;* he that should come, he that you expect the Messias to be, that you would have me to be to you. I am more than the bare name of the Messiah; I do not only call myself so, but I *am he."* True faith does not *amuse* the soul with an empty sound of words, but *affects* it with the doctrine of Christ's mediation, as a real thing that has real effects. (2.) How necessary it is that we believe this. If we have not this faith, *we shall die in our sins;* for the matter is so settled that without this faith, [1.] We cannot be saved from the power of sin while we live, and therefore shall certainly continue in it to the last. Nothing but the *doctrine* of Christ's grace will be an argument powerful enough, and none but the *Spirit* of Christ's grace will be an agent powerful enough, to turn us from sin to God; and that Spirit is given, and that doctrine given, to be effectual to those only who believe in Christ: so that, if Satan be not by faith dispossessed, he has a lease of the soul for its life; if Christ do not cure us, our case is desperate, and we shall *die in our sins.* [2.] Without faith we cannot be saved from the punishment of sin when we die, for the *wrath of God remains* upon them that believe not, Mk. 16:16. Unbelief is the damning sin; it is a sin against the remedy. Now this implies the great gospel promise: *If we believe that Christ is he,* and receive him accordingly, *we shall not die in our sins.* The law saith absolutely to all, as Christ said (*v.* 21), *You shall die in your sins,* for we are all guilty before God; but the gospel is a defeasance of the obligation upon condition of believing. The curse of the law is vacated and annulled to all that submit to the grace of the gospel. Believers die in Christ, in his love, in his arms, and so are saved from dying *in their sins.*

IV. Here is a further discourse concerning *himself,* occasioned by his requiring faith in himself as the condition of salvation, *v.* 25–29. Observe,

1. The question which the Jews put to him (*v.* 25): *Who art thou?* This they asked tauntingly, and not with any desire to be instructed. he had said, You must believe that *I am he.* By his not saying expressly who he was, he plainly intimated that in his person he was such a one as could not be *described* by any, and in his office such a one as was *expected* by all that looked for redemption in Israel; yet this awful manner of speaking, which had so much significancy in it, they turned to his reproach, as if he knew not what to say of himself: *"Who art thou,* that we must with an implicit faith believe in thee, that thou art some mighty HE, we know not *who* or *what,* nor are *worthy to know?"*

2. His answer to this question, wherein he directs them three ways for information: —

(1.) He refers them to *what he had said* all along: "Do you ask who I am? *Even the same that I said unto you from the beginning."* The original here is a little intricate, *tēn archēn ho ti kai lalō hymin* which some read thus: *I am the beginning, which also I speak unto you.* So Austin takes it. Christ is called *Archē — the beginning* (Col. 1:18; Rev. 1:8; 21:6; 3:14), and so it agrees with *v.* 24, *I am he.* Compare Isa. 41:4: *I am the first, I am he.* Those who object that it is the accusative case, and therefore not properly answering to *tis ei,* must undertake to construe by grammar rules that parallel expression, Rev. 1:8, *ho ēn.* But most interpreters agree with our version, Do you ask *who I am?* [1.] I am *the same that I said to you from the beginning* of time in the scriptures of the Old-Testament, the same that from the beginning was said to be *the Seed of the woman, that should break the serpent's head,* the same that in all the ages of the church was the Mediator of the covenant, and the faith of the patriarchs. [2.] *From the beginning* of my public ministry. The account he had already given of himself he resolved to *abide by;* he had declared himself to be the *Son of God* (*ch.* 5:17), to be the Christ (*ch.* 4:26), and the bread of life, and had proposed himself as the object of that faith which is necessary to salvation, and to this he refers them for an answer to their question. Christ is *one with himself;* what he had said from the beginning, he saith still. His is an *everlasting gospel.*

(2.) He refers them to his Father's judgment, and the instructions he had from him (*v.* 26): *"I have many things,* more than you think of, *to say, and* in them *to judge of you.* But why should I trouble myself any further with you? I know very well that *he who sent me is true,* and will stand by me, and bear me out, for *I speak to the world* (to which I am sent as an ambassador) *those things,* all those and those only, *which I have heard of him."* Here,

[1.] He suppresses his accusation of them. He had *many things* to charge them with, and many evidences to produce against them; but for the present he had said enough. Note, Whatever discoveries of sin are made to us, he that searches the heart has still more to judge of us, 1 Jn. 3:20. How much soever God reckons with sinners in this world there is still a further reckoning yet behind, Deu. 32:34. Let us learn hence not to be forward to say all we can say, even against the worst of men; we may have many things to say, by way of censure, which yet it is better to leave *unsaid,* for what is it to us?

[2.] He enters his appeal against them to his Father: *He that sent me.* Here two things comfort him: — *First,* That he had been *true to his Father,* and to the trust reposed in him: *I speak to the world* (for his gospel was to be preached to every creature) *those things which I have heard of him.* Being given for a *witness to the people* (Isa. 55:4), he was *Amen,* a *faithful witness,* Rev. 3:14. He did not *conceal* his doctrine, but spoke it *to the world* (being of common concern, it was to be of common notice); nor did he change or alter it, nor vary from the instructions he received from him that sent him. *Secondly,* That his Father would be *true to him;* true to the promise that he would *make his mouth like a sharp sword;* true to his purpose concerning him, which was a *decree* (Ps. 2:7); true to the threatenings of his wrath against those that should reject him. Though he should not *accuse* them to his Father, yet the Father, who sent him, would undoubtedly reckon with them, and would be *true* to what he had said (Deu. 18:19), that whosoever would not hearken to that prophet whom God would raise up *he would require it of him.* Christ would not accuse them; "for," saith he, "he that sent me is true, and will pass judgment on them, though I should not demand judgment against them." Thus, when he *lets fall* the present prosecution, he *binds them over* to the judgment-day, when it will be too late to dispute what they will not now be persuaded to believe. *I, as a deaf man, heard not; for thou wilt hear,* Ps. 38:13, 15. Upon this part of our Saviour's discourse the evangelist has a melancholy remark (*v.* 27): *They understood not that he spoke to them of the Father.* See here, 1. The power of Satan to blind the minds of those who believe not. Though Christ spoke so plainly of God as his Father in heaven, yet they did not understand whom he meant, but thought he spoke of some father he had in Galilee. Thus the plainest things are riddles and parables to those who are resolved to hold fast their prejudices; day and night are alike to the blind. 2. The reason why the threatenings of the word make so little impression upon the minds of sinners; it is because they understand not whose the wrath is that is revealed in them. When Christ told them of the truth of him that sent him, as a warning to them to prepare for his judgment, which is *according to truth,* they slighted the warning, because they understood not to whose judgment it was that they made themselves obnoxious.

(3.) He refers them to *their own convictions* hereafter, *v.* 28, 29. He finds they will not understand him, and therefore adjourns the trial till further evidence should come in; they that *will not see shall see,* Isa. 26:11. Now observe here,

[1.] *What* they should ere long be *convinced of: "You shall know that I am he,* that Jesus is the true Messiah. Whether you will own it or no before men, you shall be made to know it in your own consciences, the convictions of which, though you may *stifle,* yet you cannot *baffle: that I am he,* not that you represent me to be, but he that I preach myself to be, he that should come!" Two things they should be convinced of, in order to this: — *First,* That he did nothing *of himself,* not of himself as man, of himself alone, of himself without the Father, with whom he was *one.* He does not hereby derogate from his own inherent power, but only denies their charge against him as a *false prophet;* for of false prophets it is said that they prophesied *out of their own hearts,* and followed *their own spirits. Secondly,* That as *his Father taught him* so he *spoke these things,* that he was not *autodidaktos — selftaught,* but *Theodidaktos — taught of God.* The doctrine he preached was the counterpart of the counsels of God, with which he was intimately acquainted; *kathōs edidaxe, tauta lalō* — I speak those things, not only *which* he taught me, but *as* he taught me, with the same divine power and authority.

[2.] *When* they should be convinced of this: *When you have lifted up the Son of man,* lifted him up upon the cross, as the brazen serpent upon the pole (*ch.* 3:14), as the sacrifices under the law (for Christ is the great sacrifice), which, when they were offered, were said to be *elevated,* or *lifted up;* hence the burnt-offerings, the most ancient and honourable of all, were called *elevations* (*Gnoloth* from *Gnolah, asendit — he ascended*), and in many other offerings they used the significant ceremony of *heaving* the sacrifice up, and *moving* it before the Lord; thus was Christ *lifted up.* Or the expression denotes that his death was his exaltation. They that put him to death thought thereby for ever to have *sunk* him and his interest, but it proved to be the advancement of both, *ch.* 12:24. When the Son of man was *crucified,* the Son of man was *glorified.* Christ had called his dying his *going away;* here he calls it his being lifted *up;* thus the death of the saints, as it is their departure out of this world, so it is their advancement to a better. Observe, He speaks of those he is now talking with as the *instruments* of his death: when *you have lifted up the Son of man;* not that they were to be the *priests* to offer him up (no, that was his own act, he *offered up himself*), but they would be his betrayers and murderers; see Acts 2:23. They *lifted him up* to the cross, but then he lifted up himself to his Father. Observe with what tenderness and mildness Christ here speaks to those who he certainly knew would put him to death, to teach us not to hate or seek the hurt of any, though we may have reason to think they hate us and seek our hurt. Now, Christ speaks of his death as that which would be a powerful conviction of the infidelity of the Jews. *When you have lifted up the Son of man, then shall you know* this. And why then? *First,* Because careless and unthinking people are often taught the worth of mercies by the want of them, Lu. 17:22. *Secondly,* The guilt of their sin in putting Christ to death would so awaken their consciences that they would be put upon serious enquiries after a Saviour, and then would know that Jesus was he who alone could save them. And so it proved, when, being told that with wicked hands they had *crucified and slain* the Son of God, they cried out, *What shall we do?* and were made to know assuredly that this Jesus was *Lord and Christ,* Acts 2:36. *Thirdly,* There would be such signs and wonders attending his death, and the *lifting of him up* from death in his resurrection, as would give a stronger proof of his being the Messiah than any that had been yet given: and multitudes were hereby brought to believe that Jesus is the Christ, who had before contradicted and opposed him. *Fourthly,* By the death of Christ the pouring out of the Spirit was purchased, who would convince the world that *Jesus is he, ch.* 16:7, 8. *Fifthly,* The judgments which the Jews brought upon themselves, by putting Christ to death, which filled up the measure of their iniquity, were a sensible conviction to the most hardened among them that *Jesus was he.* Christ had often foretold that desolation as the just punishment of their invincible unbelief, and *when it came to pass (lo, it did come)* they could not but know that the great *prophet had been among them,* Eze. 33:33.

[3.] What supported our Lord Jesus in the mean time (*v.* 29): *He that sent me is with me,* in my whole undertaking; *for the Father* (the fountain and first spring of this affair, from whom as its great cause and author it is derived) *hath not left me alone,* to manage it myself, hath not deserted the business nor me in the prosecution of it, for *do I always those things that please him.* Here is,

First, The assurance which Christ had of his Father's *presence* with him, which includes both a divine *power* going along with him to *enable* him for his work, and a divine *favour* manifested to him to *encourage* him in it. *He that sent me is with me,* Isa. 42:1; Ps. 89:21. This greatly *emboldens* our faith in Christ and our reliance upon his word that he had, and knew he had, his Father with him, to *confirm the word of his servant,* Isa. 44:26. The King of kings accompanied his own ambassador, to attest his mission and assist his management, and *never left him alone,* either solitary or weak; it also *aggravated* the wickedness of those that opposed him, and was an intimation to them of the *premunire* they ran themselves into by resisting him, for thereby they were found *fighters against God.* How easily soever they might think to crush him and run him down, let them know he had one to back him with whom it is the greatest madness that can be to *contend.*

Secondly, The ground of this assurance: *For I do always*

those things that please him. That is, 1. That great affair in which our Lord Jesus was *continually* engaged was an affair which the *Father that sent him* was highly *well pleased with.* His whole undertaking is called the *pleasure of the Lord* (Isa. 53:10), because of the counsels of the eternal mind about it, and the complacency of the eternal mind in it. 2. His management of that affair was in nothing *displeasing* to his Father; in executing his commission he punctually observed all his instructions, and did in nothing vary from them. No mere man since the fall could say such a word as this (for *in many things we offend all*) but our Lord Jesus never offended his Father in any thing, but, as became him, he *fulfilled all righteousness.* This was necessary to the validity and value of the sacrifice he was to offer up; for if he had in any thing *displeased* the Father himself, and so had had any sin of his own to answer for, the Father could not have been pleased with him as a propitiation for our sins; but such a priest and such a sacrifice became us as was perfectly pure and spotless. We may likewise learn hence that God's servants may *then* expect God's presence with them when they *choose* and do *those things that please him,* Isa. 66:4, 5.

V. Here is the good effect which this discourse of Christ's had upon some of his hearers (v. 30): *As he spoke these words many believed on him.* Note, 1. Though multitudes perish in their unbelief, yet there is a remnant according to the election of grace, who *believe to the saving of the soul.* If Israel, the whole body of the people, *be not gathered,* yet there are those of them in whom Christ will be *glorious,* Isa. 49:5. This the apostle insists upon, to reconcile the Jews' rejection with the *promises made unto their fathers.* There is a remnant, Rom. 11:5. 2. The words of Christ, and particularly his *threatening* words, are made effectual by the grace of God to bring in poor souls to believe in him. When Christ told them that if they *believed not* they should *die in their sins,* and never get to heaven, they thought it was time to look about them, Rom, 1:16, 18. 3. Sometimes there is a *wide door opened,* and an *effectual* one, even where they are *many adversaries.* Christ will carry on his work, though *the heathen rage.* The gospel sometimes gains great victories where it meets with great opposition. Let this encourage God's ministers to preach the gospel, though it be with *much contention,* for they shall not *labour in vain.* Many may be *secretly* brought home to God by those endeavours which are openly contradicted and cavilled at by men of corrupt minds. Austin has an affectionate ejaculation in his lecture upon these words: *Utinam et, me loquenti, multi credant; non in me, sed mecum in eo — I wish that when I speak, many may believe, not on me, but with me on him.*

Verses 31–37

We have in these verses,

I. A comfortable doctrine laid down concerning the *spiritual liberty* of Christ's disciples, intended for the encouragement of *those* Jews *that believed.* Christ, knowing that his doctrine began to work upon some of his hearers, and perceiving that virtue had gone out of him, turned his discourse from the proud Pharisees, and addressed himself to those *weak* believers. When he had denounced wrath against those that were hardened in unbelief, then he spoke comfort to those few feeble *Jews that believed in him.* See here,

1. How graciously the Lord Jesus looks to those that *tremble at his word,* and are ready to receive it; he has something to say to those who have hearing ears, and will not pass by those who set themselves in his way, without speaking to them.

2. How carefully he cherishes the beginnings of grace, and meets those that are coming towards him. These *Jews that believed* were yet but *weak;* but Christ did not therefore cast them off, for he *gathers the lambs in his arms.* When faith is in its infancy, he has *knees* to *prevent it, breasts* for it to *suck,* that it may not *die from the womb.* In what he said to them, we have two things, which he saith to all that should at any time believe: —

(1.) The character of a true disciple of Christ: *If you continue in my word, then are you my disciples indeed.* When they *believed on him,* as the great prophet, they gave up themselves to be *his disciples.* Now, at their entrance into his school, he lays down this for a settled rule, that he would own none for his disciples but those that *continued in his word.* [1.] It is implied that there are many who profess themselves Christ's disciples who are not his *disciples indeed,* but only in show and name. [2.] It highly concerns those that are

not *strong in faith* to see to it that they be *sound in the faith,* that, though not disciples of the highest form, they are nevertheless *disciples indeed.* [3.] Those who seem willing to be Christ's disciples ought to be told that they had as good never come to him, unless they come with a resolution by his grace to abide by him. Let those who have thoughts of covenanting with Christ have no thoughts of reserving a power of revocation. Children are sent to school, and bound apprentices, only for a *few years;* but those only are Christ's who are willing to be bound to him *for the term of life.* [4.] Those only that *continue in Christ's word* shall be accepted as his *disciples indeed,* that adhere to his word in every instance without partiality, and abide by it to the end without apostasy. It is *menein* — *to dwell* in Christ's word, as a man does at home, which is his centre, and rest, and refuge. Our converse with the word and conformity to it must be constant. If we continue disciples to the last, then, and not otherwise, we approve ourselves *disciples indeed.*

(2.) The privilege of a true disciple of Christ. Here are two precious promises made to those who thus approve themselves disciples indeed, *v.* 32.

[1.] *"You shall know the truth,* shall know all that truth which it is needful and profitable for you to know, and shall be more confirmed in the belief of it, shall know the certainty of it." Note, *First,* Even those who are true believers, and disciples indeed, yet may be, and are, much in the dark concerning many things which they should know. God's children are but children, and understand and speak as children. Did we not need to be taught, we should not need to be disciples. *Secondly,* It is a very great privilege to *know the truth,* to know the particular truths which we are to believe, in their mutual dependences and connections, and the grounds and reasons of our belief, — to know what is truth and what proves it to be so. *Thirdly,* It is a gracious promise of Christ, to all who continue in his word, that they shall know the truth as far as is needful and profitable for them. Christ's scholars are sure to be well taught.

[2.] *The truth shall make you free;* that is, *First,* The truth which Christ teaches tends to make men free, Isa. 61:1. Justification makes us free from the guilt of sin, by which we were *bound over* to the judgment of God, and *bound under* amazing fears; sanctification makes us free from the bondage of corruption, by which we were *restrained* from that service which is perfect freedom, and *constrained* to that which is perfect slavery. Gospel truth frees us from the yoke of the ceremonial law, and the more grievous burdens of the traditions of the elders. It makes us *free from* our spiritual enemies, free *in* the service of God, free *to* the privileges of sons, and free *of* the Jerusalem which is from above, which is free. *Secondly,* The knowing, entertaining, and believing, of this truth does actually *make us free,* free from prejudices, mistakes, and false notions, than which nothing more *enslaves* and *entangles* the soul, free from the dominion of lust and passion; and restores the soul to the government of itself, by reducing it into obedience to its Creator. The mind, by admitting the truth of Christ in the light and power, is vastly enlarged, and has scope and compass given it, is greatly elevated and raised above things of sense, and never acts with so true a liberty as when it acts under a divine command, 2 Co. 3:17. The enemies of Christianity pretend to *free thinking,* whereas really those are the freest reasonings that are guided by faith, and those are men of *free thought* whose thoughts are captivated and brought into obedience to Christ.

II. The offence which the carnal Jews took at this doctrine, and their objection against it. Though it was a doctrine that brought glad tidings of liberty to the captives, yet they cavilled at it, *v.* 33. The Pharisees grudged this comfortable word to those that believed, the standers by, who had *no part nor lot in this matter;* they thought themselves reflected upon and affronted by the gracious charter of liberty granted to those that believed, and therefore with a great deal of pride and envy they answered him, *"We Jews are Abraham's seed,* and therefore are *free-born,* and have not lost our birthright-freedom; *we were never in bondage to any man; how sayest thou then,* to us Jews, *You shall be made free?"* See here,

1. What it was that they were grieved at; it was an *innuendo* in those words, *You shall be made free,* as if the Jewish church and nation were in some sort of bondage, which reflected on the Jews in general, and as if all that did not believe in Christ continued in that bondage, which reflected on the Pharisees in particular. Note, The privileges of the faithful are the envy and vexation of unbelievers, Ps. 112:10.

2. What it was that they alleged against it; whereas Christ intimated that they needed to be made free, they urge, (1.) *"We are Abraham's seed,* and Abraham was a *prince and a great man;* though we live in Canaan, we are not descended from Canaan, nor under his doom, *a servant of servants shall he be;* we hold in *frank-almoign* — *free alms,* and not in *villenage* — *by a servile tenure."* It is common for a sinking decaying family to boast of the glory and dignity of its ancestors, and to borrow honour from that name to which they repay disgrace; so the Jews here did. But this was not all. Abraham was in covenant with God, and his children by his right, Rom. 11:28. Now that covenant, no doubt, was a free charter, and invested them with privileges not consistent with a state of slavery, Rom. 9:4. And therefore they thought they had no occasion with so *great a sum* as they reckoned faith in Christ to be *to obtain this freedom,* when they were thus free-born. Note, It is the common fault and folly of those that have pious parentage and education to trust to their privilege and boast of it, as if it would atone for the want of real holiness. They were Abraham's seed, but what would this avail them, when we find one in hell that could call Abraham father? Saving benefits are not, like common privileges, conveyed by *entail* to us and our issue, nor can a title to heaven be made by *descent,* nor may we claim as *heirs at law,* by making out our pedigree; our title is purely by purchase, not our own but our Redeemer's for us, under certain provisos and limitations, which if we do not observe it will not avail us to be Abraham's seed. Thus many, when they are pressed with the necessity of regeneration, turn it off with this, *We are the church's children;* but they are not all Israel that are of Israel. (2.) *We were never in bondage to any man.* Now observe, [1.] How false this allegation was. I wonder how they could have the assurance to say a thing in the face of a congregation which was so notoriously *untrue.* Were not the seed of Abraham in bondage to the Egyptians? Were they not often in bondage to the neighbouring nations in the time of the judges? Were they not seventy years captives in Babylon? Nay, were they not at this time tributaries to the Romans, and, though not in a *personal,* yet in a *national* bondage to them, and groaning to be made free? And yet, to confront Christ, they have the impudence to say, *We were never in bondage.* Thus they would expose Christ to the ill-will both of the Jews, who were very jealous for the honour of their liberty, and of the Romans, who would not be thought to enslave the nations they conquered. [2.] How foolish the application was. Christ had spoken of a liberty wherewith the *truth* would make them free, which must be meant of a *spiritual* liberty, for truth as it is the *enriching,* so it is the *enfranchising* of the mind, and the *enlarging* of that from the captivity of error and prejudice; and yet they plead against the offer of *spiritual* liberty that they were never in *corporal* thraldom, as if, because they were never in bondage to any *man,* they were never in bondage to any *lust.* Note, Carnal hearts are sensible of no other grievances than those that molest the body and injure their secular affairs. Talk to them of encroachments upon their civil liberty and property, — tell them of waste committed upon their lands, or damage done to their houses, — and they understand you very well, and can give you a sensible answer; the thing touches them and affects them. But discourse to them of the bondage of sin, a captivity to Satan, and a liberty by Christ, — tell them of wrong done to their precious souls, and the hazard of their eternal welfare, — and *you bring certain strange things to their ears;* they say of it (as those did, Eze. 20:49), *Doth he not speak parables?* This was much like the blunder Nicodemus made about being *born again.*

III. Our Saviour's vindication of his doctrine from these objections, and the further explication of it, *v.* 34–37, where he does these four things: —

1. He shows that, notwithstanding their civil liberties and their visible church-membership, yet it was possible that they might be in a state of bondage (v. 34): *Whosoever commits sin,* though he be of Abraham's seed, and was never in bondage to any man, is the servant of sin. Observe, Christ does not upbraid them with the falsehood of their plea, or their present bondage, but further explains what he had said for their edification. Thus ministers should with meekness instruct those that oppose them, that they may *recover themselves,* not with passion provoke them to entangle themselves yet more. Now here,

(1.) The preface is very solemn: *Verily, verily, I say unto you;* an awful asseveration, which our Saviour often used, to command a reverent attention and a ready assent. The style of the prophets was, *Thus saith the Lord,* for they were *faithful as servants;* but Christ, being a Son, speaks in his own name: *I say unto you,* I the *Amen,* the faithful witness; he pawns his veracity upon it. "I say it to you, who boast of your relation to Abraham, as if that would save you."

(2.) The truth is of universal concern, though here delivered upon a particular occasion: *Whosoever commits sin is the servant of sin,* and sadly needs to be made free. A state of sin is a state of bondage. [1.] See who it is on whom this brand is fastened — on him that *commits sin, pas ho poiōn hamartian — every one that makes sin.* There is not a *just man* upon earth, that *lives, and sins not;* yet every one that sins is not a servant of sin, for then God would have no servants; but he that *makes sin,* that *makes choice* of sin, prefers the way of wickedness before the way of holiness (Jer. 44:16, 17), — that *makes a covenant* with sin, enters into league with it, and *makes a marriage* with it, — that *makes contrivances* of sin, *makes provision* for the flesh, and devises iniquity, — and that *makes a custom* of sin, who walks after the flesh, and *makes a trade* of sin. [2.] See what the brand is which Christ fastens upon those that thus *commit sin.* He stigmatizes them, gives them a mark of servitude. They are *servants of sin,* imprisoned under the guilt of sin, under an arrest, in hold for it, *concluded under sin,* and they are subject to the power of sin. He is a *servant of sin,* that is, he makes himself so, and is so accounted; he has *sold himself to work wickedness;* his lusts give law to him, he is at their beck, and is not his own master. He does the work of sin, supports its interest, and accepts its wages, Rom. 6:16.

2. He shows them that, being in a state of bondage, their having a place in the house of God would not entitle them to the inheritance of sons; for (*v.* 35) *the servant,* though he be in the house for awhile, yet, being but a *servant, abideth not in the house for ever.* Services (we say) are no inheritances, they are but *temporary,* and not for a *perpetuity; but the son* of the family abideth ever. Now, (1.) This points primarily at the rejection of the Jewish church and nation. Israel had been *God's son,* his *first-born;* but they wretchedly degenerated into a *servile* disposition, were enslaved to the world and the flesh, and therefore, though by virtue of their birthright they thought themselves secure of their church membership, Christ tells them that having thus made themselves servants they should not *abide in the house for ever.* Jerusalem, by opposing the gospel of Christ, which proclaimed liberty, and adhering to the Sinai-covenant, which gendered to bondage, after its term was *expired* came to be *in bondage with her children* (Gal. 4:24, 25), and therefore was unchurched and disfranchised, her charter seized and taken away, and she was cast out as the son of the bond-woman, Gen. 21:14. Chrysostom gives this sense of this place: "Think not to be made free from sin by the rites and ceremonies of the law of Moses, for Moses was but a servant, and had not that perpetual authority in the church which the Son had; but, if the Son make you free, it is well," *v.* 36. But, (2.) It looks further, to the rejection of all that are the *servants of sin,* and receive not the *adoption* of the *sons of God;* though those unprofitable servants may be in God's house awhile, as retainers to his family, yet there is a day coming when the children of the *bondwoman* and of the *free* shall be distinguished. True believers only, who are the children of the promise and of the covenant, are accounted free, and shall abide for ever in the house, as Isaac: they shall have a *nail* in the holy place on earth (Ezra 9:8) and *mansions* in the holy place in heaven, *ch.* 14:2.

3. He shows them the way of deliverance out of the state of bondage into the *glorious liberty of the children of God,* Rom. 8:21. The case of those that are the servants of sin is sad, but thanks be to God it is not helpless, it is not hopeless. As it is the privilege of all the sons of the family, and their dignity above the servants, that they abide in the house for ever; so he who is *the Son,* the first-born among many brethren, and the heir of all things, has a power both of manumission and of adoption (*v.* 36): *If the Son shall make you free, you shall be free indeed.* Note,

(1.) Jesus Christ in the gospel offers us *our freedom;* he has authority and power to *make free.* [1.] To *discharge prisoners;* this he does *in justification,* by making satisfaction for *our guilt* (on which the gospel offer is grounded, which is to all a conditional *act of indemnity,* and to all true believers, upon their believing, an absolute *charter of pardon*), and for *our debts,* for which we were by the law arrested and in execution. Christ, as our surety, or rather our *bail* (for he was not originally bound *with us,* but upon our insolvency bound *for us*), compounds with the creditor, answers the demands of injured justice with more than an *equivalent,* takes the *bond* and *judgment* into his own hands, and gives them up *cancelled* to all that by faith and repentance give him (if I may so say) a *counter-security* to save his honour harmless, and so they are *made free;* and from the debt, and every part thereof, they are for ever acquitted, exonerated, and discharged, and a general release is sealed of all actions and claims; while against those who refuse to come up to these terms the securities lie still in the Redeemer's hands, in full force. [2.] He has a power to rescue *bond-slaves,* and this he does in *sanctification;* by the powerful arguments of his gospel, and the powerful operations of his Spirit, he breaks the power of corruption in the soul, rallies the scattered forces of reason and virtue, and fortifies God's interest against sin and Satan, and so the soul is made free. [3.] He has a power to *naturalize strangers and foreigners,* and this he does in *adoption.* This is a further act of grace; we are not only forgiven and healed, but *preferred;* there is a charter of privileges as well as pardon; and thus the Son makes us free *denizens* of the kingdom of priests, the holy nation, the new Jerusalem.

(2.) Those whom Christ makes free are *free indeed.* It is not *alēthōs,* the word used (*v.* 31) for disciples *indeed, but ontōs — really.* It denotes, [1.] The truth and certainty of the promise, the liberty which the Jews boasted of was an *imaginary* liberty; they boasted of a *false gift;* but the liberty which Christ gives is a certain thing, it is real, and has real effects. The servants of sin promise themselves liberty, and fancy themselves free, when they have broken religion's bands asunder; but they cheat themselves. None are *free indeed* but those whom Christ *makes free.* [2.] It denotes the singular excellency of the freedom promised; it is a freedom that deserves the name, in comparison with which all other liberties are no better than slaveries, so much does it turn to the honour and advantage of those that are *made free* by it. It is a *glorious* liberty. It is that which *is* (so *ontōs* signifies); it is *substance* (Prov. 8:21); while the things of the world are shadows, things that *are not.*

4. He applies this to these unbelieving cavilling Jews, in answer to their boasts of relation to Abraham (*v.* 37): *"I know* very well *that you are Abraham's seed, but now you seek to kill me,* and therefore have forfeited the honour of your relation to Abraham, *because my word hath no place in you."* Observe here,

(1.) The dignity of their extraction admitted: *"I know that you are Abraham's seed,* every one knows it, and it is your honour." He grants them what was true, and in what they said that was false (that they were *never* in bondage to any) he does not *contradict* them, for he studied to *profit* them, and not to *provoke* them, and therefore said that which would please them: *I know that you are Abraham's seed.* They boasted of their descent from *Abraham,* as that which *aggrandized* their names, and made them exceedingly honourable; whereas really it did but *aggravate* their crimes, and make them exceedingly sinful. Out of their own mouths will he judge vain-glorious hypocrites, who boast of their parentage and education: "Are you Abraham's seed? Why then did you not tread in the steps of his faith and obedience?"

(2.) The inconsistency of their practice with this dignity: *But you seek to kill me.* They had attempted it several times, and were now designing it, which quickly appeared (*v.* 59), when they *took up stones to cast at him.* Christ knows all the wickedness, not only which men do, but which they seek, and design, and endeavour to do. To seek to kill any innocent man is a crime black enough, but to *compass and imagine* the death of him that was King of kings was a crime the heinousness of which we want words to express.

(3.) The reason of this inconsistency. Why were they that were Abraham's seed so very inveterate against Abraham's promised seed, in whom they and *all the families of the earth* should be *blessed?* Our Saviour here tells them, It is because *my word hath no place in you, ou chōrei en hymin, Non capit in vobis,* so the Vulgate. "My word *does not take with you,* you have no inclination to it, no relish of it, other things are more taking, more pleasing." Or, "It does not *take hold of you,* it has no power over you, makes no impression upon you." Some of the critics read it, *My word does not penetrate into you;* it descended as the rain, but it came upon them as the rain upon the rock, which it runs off, and did not soak into their hearts, as the rain upon the ploughed ground. The Syriac reads it, *"Because you do not acquiesce in my word;* you are not persuaded of the truth of it, nor pleased with the goodness of it." Our translation is very significant: *It has no place in you.* They *sought to kill him,* and so effectually to *silence* him, not because he had done they any harm, but because they could not bear the convincing, commanding power of his word. Note, [1.] The words of Christ ought to have a place in us, the innermost and uppermost place, — a *dwelling* place, as a man at home, and not as a stranger or sojourner, — a *working* place; it must have room to operate, to work sin out of us, and to work grace in us; it must have a *ruling* place, its place must be *upon the throne,* it must dwell in us richly. [2.] There are many that make a profession of religion in whom *the word of* Christ has no place; they will not *allow* it a place, for they do not like it; Satan does all he can to *displace* it; and other things possess the place it should have in us. [3.] Where the word of God has no place no good is to be expected, for room is left there for all wickedness. If the unclean spirit find the heart empty of Christ's word, he *enters in, and dwells there.*

Verses 38–47

Here Christ and the Jews are still at issue; he sets himself to convince and convert them, while they still set themselves to contradict and oppose him.

I. He here traces the difference between his sentiments and theirs to a different rise and origin (*v.* 38): *I speak that which I have seen with my Father,* and *you* do *what you have seen with your father.* Here are two fathers spoken of, according to the two families into which the sons of men are divided — God and the devil, and without controversy these are contrary the one to the other.

1. Christ's *doctrine* was from *heaven;* it was *copied* out of the *counsels* of infinite wisdom, and the kind intentions of eternal love. (1.) *I speak that which I have seen.* The discoveries Christ has made to us of God and another world are not grounded upon guess and hearsay, but upon ocular inspection; so that he was thoroughly *apprized* of the nature, and *assured* of the truth, of all he said. He that is given to be a witness to the people is an eye-witness, and therefore unexceptionable. (2.) It is what I have seen *with my Father.* The doctrine of Christ is not a plausible hypothesis, supported by probable arguments, but it is an exact counterpart of the incontestable truths lodged in the eternal mind. It was not only what he had *heard from* his Father, but what he had *seen with him* when *the counsel of peace was between them both.* Moses spoke what he heard from God, but he might not see the face of God; Paul had been in the third heaven, but what he had seen there he could not, he must not, utter; for it was Christ's prerogative to have *seen* what he *spoke,* and to *speak* what he had *seen.*

2. Their *doings* were from hell: *"You do that which you have seen with your father.* You do, by your own works, father yourselves, for it is evident whom you resemble, and therefore easy to find out your origin." As a child that is trained up with his father learns his father's words and fashions, and grows like him by an affected imitation as well as by a natural image, so these Jews, by their malicious opposition to Christ and the gospel, made themselves as like the devil as if they had industriously set him before them for their pattern.

II. He takes off and answers their vain-glorious boasts of relation to Abraham and to God as their fathers, and shows the vanity and falsehood of their pretensions.

1. They pleaded relation to Abraham, and he replies to this plea. *They said, Abraham is our father, v.* 39. In this they intended, (1.) To do honour to themselves, and to make themselves look great. They had forgotten the mortification given them by that acknowledgement prescribed them (Deu. 26:5), *A Syrian ready to perish was my father;* and the charge exhibited against their degenerate ancestors (whose steps they trod in, and not those of the first founder of the family), *Thy father was an Amorite, and thy mother a Hittite,* Eze. 16:3. As it is common for those families that are sinking and going to decay to boast most of their pedigree, so it is common for those churches that are corrupt and depraved to value themselves upon their antiquity and the eminence of their first planters. *Fuimus Troes, fuit Ilium — We have been Trojans, and there once was Troy.* (2.) They designed to cast an odium upon Christ as if he reflected upon the patriarch Abraham, in speaking of their father as one they had learned evil from. See how they sought an occasion to quarrel with him.

Now Christ overthrows this plea, and exposes the vanity of it by a plain and cogent argument: "Abraham's children will do the works of Abraham, but you do not do Abraham's works, therefore you are not Abraham's children."

[1.] The proposition is plain: *"If you were Abraham's children,* such children of Abraham as could claim an interest in the covenant made with him and his seed, which would indeed put an honour upon you, then you would *do the works of Abraham,* for to those only of Abraham's house who *kept the way of the Lord,* as Abraham did, would God *perform what he had spoken,"* Gen. 18:19. Those only are reckoned the seed of Abraham, to whom the promise belongs, who *tread in the steps* of his faith and obedience, Rom. 4:12. Though the Jews had their genealogies, and kept them exact, yet they could not by them make out their relation to Abraham, so as to take the benefit of the old entail *(performam doni — according to the form of the gift),* unless they walked in the same spirit; good women's relation to Sarah is proved only by this — *whose daughters you are as long as you do well,* and no longer, 1 Pt. 3:6. Note, Those who would approve themselves Abraham's seed must not only be of Abraham's faith, but do Abraham's works (James 2:21, 22), — must come at God's call, as he did, — must resign their dearest comforts to him, — must be strangers and sojourners in this world, — must keep up the worship of God in their families, and always walk before God in their uprightness; for these were the works of Abraham.

[2.] The assumption is evident likewise: *But you do not do* the works of Abraham, for *you seek to kill me, a man that has told you the truth, which I have heard of God; this did not Abraham, v.* 40.

First, He shows them what their work was, their present work, which they were now about; they *sought to kill him;* and three things are intimated as an aggravation of their intention: — 1. They were so *unnatural* as to seek the life of *a man,* a man like themselves, bone of their bone, and flesh of their flesh, who had done them no harm, nor given them any provocation. You *imagine mischief against a man,* Ps. 62:3. 2. They were so *ungrateful* as to seek the life of one who had *told them the truth,* had not only done them no injury, but had done them the greatest kindness that could be; had not only not imposed upon them with a lie, but had instructed them in the most necessary and important truths; *was he therefore become their enemy?* 3. They were so *ungodly* as to seek the life of one who told them the truth *which he had heard from God,* who was a messenger sent from God to them, so that their attempt against him was *quasi deicidium — an act of malice against God.* This was their work, and they persisted in it.

Secondly, He shows them that this did not become the children of Abraham; for *this did not Abraham.* 1. "He did nothing like this." He was famous for his humanity, witness his rescue of the captives; and for his piety, witness his obedience to the heavenly vision in many instances, and some tender ones. Abraham believed God; they were obstinate in unbelief: Abraham followed God; they fought against him; so that he would be *ignorant of them, and would not acknowledge them,* they were so unlike him, Isa. 63:16. See Jer. 22:15–17. 2. "He would not have done thus if he had lived now, or I had lived then." *Hoc Abraham non fecisset — He would not have done this;* so some read it. We should thus reason ourselves out of any way of wickedness; would Abraham, and Isaac, and Jacob have done so? We cannot expect to be *ever with them,* if we be *never like them.*

[3.] The conclusion follows of course (*v.* 41): "Whatever your boasts and pretensions be, you are not Abraham's children, but father yourselves upon another family (*v.* 41); there is *a father whose deeds you do,* whose spirit you are of, and whom you resemble." He does not *yet* say plainly that he means the devil, till they by their continued cavils forced him so to explain himself, which teaches us to treat even bad men with civility and respect, and not to be forward to say that *of* them, or *to* them, which, though *true,* sounds *harsh.* He tried whether they would suffer their own consciences to infer from what he said that they were the devil's children; and it is better to hear it from them now that we are called to *repent,* that is, to change our father and change our family, by changing our spirit and way, than to hear it from Christ in the great day.

2. So far were they from owning their unworthiness of relation to Abraham that they pleaded relation to God himself as their Father: "We are *not born of fornication,* we are not bastards, but legitimate sons; *we have one Father, even God."*

(1.) Some understand this literally. They were not the sons of the bondwoman, as the Ishmaelites were; nor begotten in incest, as the Moabites and Ammonites were (Deu. 23:3); nor were they a spurious brood in Abraham's family, but Hebrews of the Hebrews; and, being born in *lawful* wedlock, they might call God *Father,* who instituted that honourable estate in innocency; for a legitimate seed, not tainted with divorces nor the plurality of wives, is called a *seed of God,* Mal. 2:15.

(2.) Others take it figuratively. They begin to be aware now that Christ spoke of a *spiritual* not a *carnal* father, of the father of their religion; and so,

[1.] They deny themselves to be a generation of idolaters: "We are *not born of fornication,* are not the children of idolatrous parents, nor have been bred up in idolatrous worships." Idolatry is often spoken of as spiritual *whoredom,* and idolaters as *children of whoredoms,* Hosea 2:4; Isa. 57:3. Now, if they meant that they were not the posterity of idolaters, the allegation was false, for no nation was more addicted to idolatry than the Jews before the captivity; if they meant no more than that they themselves were not idolaters, what then? A man may be free from idolatry, and yet perish in another iniquity, and be shut out of Abraham's covenant. *If thou commit no idolatry* (apply it to this spiritual fornication), yet if thou kill thou art become a *transgressor* of the covenant. A rebellious prodigal son will be disinherited, though he be not *born of fornication.*

[2.] They boast themselves to be true worshippers of the true God. We have not many fathers, as the heathens had, *gods many and lords many,* and yet were without God, as *filius populi — a son of the people,* has many fathers and yet none certain; no, *the Lord our God is one Lord* and *one Father,* and therefore it is well with us. Note, Those flatter themselves, and put a damning cheat upon their own souls, who imagine that their professing the true religion and worshipping the true God will save them, though they worship not God in spirit and in truth, nor are true to their profession. Now our Saviour gives a full answer to this fallacious plea (*v.* 42, 43), and proves, by two arguments, that they had no right to call God Father.

First, They did not love Christ: *If God were your Father, you would love me.* He had disproved their relation to Abraham by their going about to kill him (*v.* 40), but here he disproves their relation to God by their not loving and owning him. A man may pass for a *child* of Abraham if he do not appear an enemy to Christ by gross sin; but he cannot approve himself a child of God unless he be a faithful friend and follower of Christ. Note, All that have God for their Father have a true love to Jesus Christ, and esteem of his person, a grateful sense of his love, a sincere affection to his cause and kingdom, a complacency in the salvation wrought out by him and in the method and terms of it, and a care to keep his commandments, which is the surest evidence of our love to him. We are here in a state of probation, upon our trial how we will conduct ourselves towards our Maker, and accordingly it will be with us in the state of retribution. God has taken various methods to prove us, and this was one: he sent his Son into the world, with sufficient proofs of his sonship and mission, concluding that all that called him Father would *kiss his Son,* and bid *him* welcome who was the first-born among many brethren; see 1 Jn. 5:1. By this our adoption will be proved or disproved — Did we love Christ, or no? *If any man do not,* he is so far from being a child of God that he is *anathema,* accursed, 1 Co. 16:22. Now our Saviour proves that if they were God's children they would *love him;* for, saith he, I proceeded *forth and came from God.* They will love him; for, 1. He was the *Son of God: I proceeded forth from God. Exēlthon* this means his divine *exeleusis,* or origin from the Father, by the communication of the divine essence, and also the union of the divine *logos* to his human nature; so Dr. Whitby. Now this could not but recommend him to the affections of all that were *born of God.* Christ is called the *beloved,* because, being the beloved of the Father, he is certainly the beloved of all the saints, Eph. 1:6. 2. He was *sent of God,* came from him as an ambassador to the world of mankind. He did not *come of himself,* as the false prophets, who had not either their *mission* or their *message* from God, Jer. 23:21. Observe the emphasis he lays upon this: *I came from God; neither came I of myself, but he sent me.* He had both his credentials and his instructions from God; he came to *gather together in one the children of God* (*ch.* 11:51), to bring *many sons to glory,* Heb. 2:10. And would not all God's children embrace with both arms a messenger sent from their Father on *such* errands? But these Jews made it appear that they were nothing akin to God, by their want of affection to Jesus Christ.

Secondly, They did not understand him. It was a sign they did not belong to God's family that they did not understand the language and dialect of the family: *You do not understand my speech* (*v.* 43), *tēn lalian tēn emēn.* Christ's speech was divine and heavenly, but intelligible enough to those that were acquainted with the voice of Christ in the Old Testament. Those that had made the word of the Creator familiar to them needed no other key to the dialect of the Redeemer; and yet these Jews make strange of the doctrine of Christ, and find knots in it, and I know not what stumbling stones. Could a Galilean be known by his speech? An Ephraimite by his *sibboleth?* And would any have the confidence to call God Father to whom the Son of God was a barbarian, even when he spoke the will of God in the words of the Spirit of God? Note, Those who are not acquainted with the divine speech have reason to fear that they are strangers to the divine nature. Christ spoke the words of God (*ch.* 3:34) in the dialect of the kingdom of God; and yet they, who pretended to belong to the kingdom, understood not the idioms and properties of it, but like strangers, and rude ones too, ridiculed it. And the reason why they did not understand Christ's speech made the matter much worse: *Even because you cannot hear my word,* that is, "You cannot persuade yourselves to hear it attentively, impartially, and without prejudice, as it should be heard." The meaning of this *cannot* is an obstinate *will not;* as the Jews could not hear Stephen (Acts 7:57) nor Paul, Acts 23:22. Note, The rooted antipathy of men's corrupt hearts to the doctrine of Christ is the true reason of their ignorance of it, and of their errors and mistakes about it. They do not like it nor love it, and therefore they will not understand it; like Peter, who pretended he *knew not what the damsel said* (Mt. 26:70), when in truth he knew not what to say to it. *You cannot hear my words,* for you have *stopped your ears* (Ps. 58:4, 5), and God, in a way of righteous judgment, *has made your ears heavy,* Isa. 6:10.

III. Having thus disproved their relation both to Abraham and to God, he comes next to tell them plainly whose children they were: *You are of your father the devil, v.* 44. If they were not God's children, they were the devil's, for God and Satan divide the world of mankind; the devil is *therefore* said to *work in the children of disobedience,* Eph. 2:2. All wicked people are the devil's children, *children of Belial* (2 Co. 6:15), the serpent's seed (Gen. 3:15), children of the wicked one, Mt. 13:38. They partake of his nature, bear his image, obey his commands, and follow his example. Idolaters *said to a stock, Thou art our father,* Jer. 2:27.

This is a high charge, and sounds very harsh and horrid, that any of the children of men, especially the church's children, should be called *children of the devil,* and therefore our Saviour fully proves it.

1. By a general argument: *The lusts of your father you will do, thelete poiein.* (1.) "You *do* the devil's lusts, the lusts which he would have you to fulfil; you gratify and please him, and comply with his temptation, and are *led captive by him at his will:* nay, you do those lusts which the devil himself fulfils." Fleshly lusts and worldly lusts the devil tempts men to; but, being a spirit, he cannot fulfil them himself. The peculiar lusts of the devil are *spiritual wickedness;* the lusts of the intellectual powers, and their corrupt reasonings; pride and envy, and wrath and malice; enmity to that which is good, and enticing others to that which is evil; these are lusts which the devil fulfils, and those who are under the dominion of these lusts resemble the devil, as the child does the parent. The more there is of contemplation, and contrivance, and secret complacency, in sin, the more it resembles the *lusts of the devil.* (2.) You *will do* the devil's lusts. The more there is of the *will* in these lusts, the more there is of the devil in them. When sin is committed *of choice* and not by surprise, with *pleasure* and not with reluctancy, when it is persisted in with a daring presumption and a desperate resolution, like theirs that said, *We have loved strangers and after them we will go,* then the sinner *will* do the devil's lusts. "The lusts of your father you *delight to do;"* so Dr. Hammond; they are rolled under the tongue as a sweet morsel.

2. By two particular instances, wherein they manifestly resembled the devil — *murder* and *lying.* The devil is an

enemy to life, because God is the God of life and life is the happiness of man; and an enemy to truth, because God is the God of truth and truth is the bond of human society.

(1.) He was *a murderer from the beginning,* not from his own beginning, for he was created an angel of light, and had a first estate which was pure and good, but from the beginning of his apostasy, which was soon after the creation of man. He was *anthrōpoktonos — homicida, a man-slayer.* [1.] He was a *hater of man,* and so in affection an disposition a murderer of him. He has his name, *Satan,* from *sitnah — hatred.* He maligned God's image upon man, envied his happiness, and earnestly desired his ruin, was an avowed enemy to the whole race. [2.] He was man's tempter to *that* sin which brought death into the world, and so he was effectually the murderer of all mankind, which in Adam had but *one neck.* He was a murderer of souls, *deceived* them into sin, and by it *slew them* (Rom. 7:11), poisoned man with the forbidden fruit, and, to aggravate the matter, made him his own murderer. Thus he was not only *at* the beginning, but *from* the beginning, which intimates that thus he *has been* ever since; as he began, so he continues, the murderer of men by his temptations. The great tempter is the great destroyer. The Jews called the devil *the angel of death.* [3.] He was the first wheel in the first murder that ever was committed by Cain, who was of that wicked one, and slew his brother, 1 Jn. 3:12. If the devil had not been very strong in Cain, he could not have done such an unnatural thing as to kill his own brother. Cain killing his brother by the instigation of the devil, the devil is called the *murderer,* which does not speak Cain's personal guilt the less, but the devil's the more, whose torments, we have reason to think, will be the greater, when the time comes, for all that wickedness into which he has drawn men. See what reason we have to *stand* upon our guard *against the wiles of the devil,* and never to hearken to him (for he is a murderer, and certainly aims to do us mischief, even when he *speaks fair*), and to wonder that he who is the murderer of the children of men should yet be, by their own consent, so much their master. Now herein these Jews were followers of him, and were murderers, like him; murderers of souls, which they led blindfold into the ditch, and made the *children of hell;* sworn enemies of Christ, and now ready to be his betrayers and murderers, for the same reason that Cain killed Abel. These Jews were that *seed of the serpent* that were to *bruise the heel* of the *seed of the woman; Now you seek to kill me.*

(2.) He was *a liar.* A lie is opposed to truth (1 Jn. 2:21), and accordingly the devil is here described to be,

[1.] An enemy to truth, and therefore to Christ. *First,* He is a *deserter,* from the truth; he *abode not in the truth,* did not continue in the purity and rectitude of his nature wherein he was created, but left his first state; when he degenerated from goodness, he departed from truth, for his apostasy was founded in a lie. The angels were the *hosts of the Lord;* those that fell were not *true* to their commander and sovereign, they were not to be *trusted,* being charged with folly and defection, Job 4:18. By *the truth* here we may understand the revealed will of God concerning the salvation of man by Jesus Christ, the truth which Christ was now preaching, and which the Jews opposed; herein they did *like their father the devil,* who, *seeing* the honour put upon the human nature in the *first Adam,* and *foreseeing* the much greater honour intended in the *second Adam,* would not be reconciled to that counsel of God, nor *stand in the truth* concerning it, but, from a spirit of pride and envy, set himself to resist it, and to thwart the designs of it; and so did these Jews here, as his children and agents. *Secondly,* He is *destitute* of the truth: *There is no truth in him.* His interest in the world is supported by lies and falsehoods, and there is no truth, nothing you can confide in, in him, nor in any thing he says or does. The notions he propagates concerning good and evil are false and erroneous, his proofs are lying wonders, his temptations are all cheats; he has great knowledge of the truth, but having no affection to it, but on the contrary being a sworn enemy to it, he is said to have *no truth in him.*

[2.] He is a friend and patron of lying: *When he speaketh a lie he speaketh of his own.* Three things are here said of the devil with reference to the sin of lying: — *First,* That he is *a liar;* his oracles were lying oracles, his prophets lying prophets, and the images in which he was worshipped *teachers of lies.* He tempted our first parents with a downright lie. All his temptations are carried on by lies, calling *evil good and good evil,* and promising impunity in sin; he knows them to be lies, and suggests them with an intention to deceive, and so to destroy. When he now *contradicted* the gospel, in the scribes and Pharisees, it was by lies; and when afterwards he *corrupted it,* in the *man of sin,* it was by strong delusions, and a great complicated lie. *Secondly,* That when he *speaks a lie* he *speaks of his own, ek tōn idiōn.* It is the proper *idiom* of his language; of *his own,* not of God; his Creator never put it into him. When men speak a lie they borrow it from the devil, *Satan fills their hearts to lie* (Acts 5:3); but when the devil speaks a lie the *model* of it is of his own framing, the motives to it are from himself, which bespeaks the desperate depth of wickedness into which those apostate spirits are sunk; as in their first defection they had no tempter, so their sinfulness is still their own. *Thirdly,* That he is the *father of it, autou.* 1. He is the father of every *lie;* not only of the lies which he himself suggests, but of those which others speak; he is the author and founder of all lies. When men speak lies, they speak from him, and as his mouth; they come originally from him, and bear his image. 2. He is the father of *every liar;* so it may be understood. God made men with a disposition to truth. It is congruous to reason and natural light, to the order of our faculties and the laws of society, that we should speak truth; but the devil, the author of sin, the spirit that works in the children of disobedience, has so corrupted the nature of man that the wicked are said to be *estranged from the womb, speaking lies* (Ps. 58:3); he has taught them *with their tongues to use deceit,* Rom. 3:13. He is the father of liars, who begat them, who trained them up in the *way of lying,* whom they resemble and obey, and with whom all *liars* shall have their portion for ever.

IV. Christ, having thus proved all murderers and all liars to be the devil's children, leaves it to the consciences of his hearers to say, *Thou art the man.* But he comes in the following verses to assist them in the application of it to themselves; he does not call them *liars,* but shows them that they were *no friends to truth,* and therein resembled him who *abode not in the truth, because there is no truth in him.* Two things he charges upon them: —

1. That they would not *believe the word of truth* (*v.* 45), *hoti tēn alētheian legō, ou pisteuete moi.*

(1.) Two ways it may be taken; — [1.] "Though I tell you the truth, yet you will not believe me (*hoti*), *that I do so.*" Though he gave abundant proof of his commission from God, and his affection to the children of men, yet they would not believe that he told them the truth. Now was *truth fallen in the street,* Isa. 59:14, 15. The greatest truths with some gained not the least credit; for they *rebelled against the light,* Job 24:13. Or, [2.] *Because I tell you the truth* (so we read it) therefore *you believe me not.* They would not receive him, nor entertain him as a prophet, because he told them some unpleasing truths which they did not care to hear, told them the truth concerning themselves and their own case, showed them their faces in a glass that would not flatter them; therefore they would not believe a word he said. Miserable is the case of those to whom the light of divine truth is become a torment.

(2.) Now, to show them the unreasonableness of their infidelity, he condescends to put the matter to this fair issue, *v.* 46. He and they being contrary, either he was in an error or they were. Now take it either way.

[1.] If *he* were in an error, why did they not convince him? The falsehood of *pretended* prophets was discovered either by the *ill tendency* of their doctrines (Deu. 13:2), or by the *ill tenour* of their conversation: *You shall know them by their fruits;* but (saith Christ) *which of you,* you of the sanhedrim, that take upon you to judge of prophets, *which of you convinceth me of sin?* They accused him of some of the worst of crimes — gluttony, drunkenness, blasphemy, sabbath-breaking, confederacy with Satan, and what not. But their accusations were malicious groundless calumnies, and such as every one that knew him knew to be *utterly false.* When they had done their utmost by trick and artifice, subornation and perjury, to prove some crime upon him, the very judge that condemned him owned he *found no fault in him.* The *sin* he here challenges them to convict him of is, *First,* An inconsistent doctrine. They had heard his testimony; could they show any thing in it absurd or unworthy to be believed, any contradiction either of himself or of the scriptures, or any corruption of truth or manners insinuated by his doctrine? *ch.* 18:20. Or, *Secondly,* An incongruous conversation: "Which of you can justly charge me with any thing, in word or deed, unbecoming a prophet?" See the wonderful condescension of our Lord Jesus, that he demanded not credit any further than the allowed motives of credibility supported his demands. See Jer. 2:5, 31; Mic. 6:3. Ministers may hence learn, 1. To *walk* so *circumspectly* as that it may not be in the power of their most strict observers to convince them of sin, *that the ministry be not blamed.* The only way not to be convicted of sin is not to sin. 2. To be willing to *admit a scrutiny;* though we are confident in many things that we are in the right, yet we should be willing to have it tried whether we be not in the wrong. See Job 6:24.

[2.] If *they* were in an error, why were they not convinced by him? *"If I say the truth, why do you not believe me?* If you cannot convince me of error, you must own that I *say the truth,* and why do you not then *give me credit?* Why will you not deal with me upon trust?" Note, If men would but enquire into the reason of their infidelity, and examine why they do not believe that which they cannot gainsay, they would find themselves reduced to such absurdities as they could not but be ashamed of; for it will be found that the reason why we believe not in Jesus Christ is because we are not willing to part with our sins, and deny ourselves, and serve God faithfully; that we are not of the Christian religion, because we would not indeed be of any, and unbelief of our Redeemer resolves itself into a downright rebellion against our Creator.

2. Another thing charged upon them is that they would not hear the words of God (*v.* 47), which further shows how groundless their claim of relation to God was. Here is,

(1.) A doctrine laid down: *He that is of God heareth God's words;* that is, [1.] He is *willing* and *ready* to hear them, is sincerely desirous to know what the mind of God is, and cheerfully embraces whatever he knows to be so. God's words have such an authority over, and such an agreeableness with all that are born of God, that they meet them, as the child Samuel did, with, *Speak, Lord, for thy servant heareth.* Let the word of the Lord come. [2.] He *apprehends* and *discerns* them, he so hears them as to perceive the *voice of God* in them, which the natural man does not, 1 Co. 2:14. He that is of God is *soon aware* of the discoveries he makes of himself of the *nearness of his name* (Ps. 75:1), as they of the family know the master's tread, and the master's knock, and *open to him immediately* (Lu. 12:36), as the sheep know the voice of their shepherd from that of a stranger, *ch.* 10:4, 5; Cant. 2:8.

(2.) The application of this doctrine, for the conviction of these unbelieving Jews: *You therefore hear them not;* that is, "You heed not, you understand not, you believe not, the words of God, nor care to hear them, *because you are not of God.* Your being thus deaf and dead to the words of God is a plain evidence that you are *not of God."* It is in his word that God manifests himself and is present among us; we are therefore reckoned to be well or ill affected to his word; see 2 Co. 4:4; 1 Jn. 4:6. Or, their not being of God was the reason why they did not profitably *hear the words of God,* which Christ spoke; they did not understand and believe him, not because the things themselves were obscure or wanted evidence, but because the hearers were *not of God,* were not born again. If the word of the kingdom do not bring forth fruit, the blame is to be laid upon the soil, not upon the seed, as appears by the parable of the sower, Mt. 13:3.

Verses 48–50

Here is, I. The malice of hell breaking out in the base language which the unbelieving Jews gave to our Lord Jesus. Hitherto they had cavilled at his doctrine, and had made invidious remarks upon it; but, having shown themselves uneasy when he complained (*v.* 43, 47) that they would not hear him, now at length they fall to downright railing, *v.* 48. They were not the common people, but, as it should seem, the scribes and Pharisees, the men of consequence, who, when they saw themselves convicted of an obstinate infidelity, scornfully turned off the conviction with this: *Say we not well that thou art a Samaritan, and hast a devil?* See here, see it and wonder, see it and tremble,

1. What was the blasphemous character commonly given of our Lord Jesus among the wicked Jews, to which they refer. (1.) That he was a Samaritan, that is, that he was an enemy to their church and nation, one that they hated and could not endure. Thus they exposed him to the ill will of the people, with whom you could not put a man into a worse name than to call him *a Samaritan.* If he had been a Samaritan, he had been punishable, by the *beating of the rebels* (as they called it), for coming into the temple. They had often enough called him *a Galilean — a mean man;* but as if that were not

enough, though it contradicted the other, they will have him a *Samaritan — a bad man.* The Jews to this day call the Christians, in reproach, *Cuthaei — Samaritans.* Note, Great endeavours have in all ages been used to make good people odious by putting them under black characters, and it is easy to run that down with a crowd and a cry which is once put into an ill name. Perhaps because Christ justly inveighed against the pride and tyranny of the priests and elders, they hereby suggest that he aimed at the ruin of their church, in aiming at its reformation, and was *falling away* to the Samaritans. (2.) That *he had a devil.* Either, [1.] That he was *in league with the devil.* Having reproached his doctrine as tending to Samaritanism, here they reflect upon his miracles as done in combination with Beelzebub. Or, rather [2.] That he was possessed with a devil, that he was a melancholy man, whose brain was *clouded,* or a mad man, whose brain was *heated,* and that which he said was no more to be believed than the extravagant rambles of a distracted man, or one in a delirium. Thus the divine revelation of those things which are above the discovery of reason have been often branded with the charge of enthusiasm, and the prophet was called a *mad fellow,* 2 Ki. 9:11; Hosea 9:7. The inspiration of the Pagan oracles and prophets was indeed a frenzy, and those that had it were for the time beside themselves; but that which was truly *divine* was not so. *Wisdom is justified of her children,* as wisdom indeed.

2. How they undertook to justify this character, and applied it to the present occasion: *Say we not well that thou art so?* One would think that his excellent discourses should have altered their opinion of him, and have made them recant; but, instead of this, their hearts were more hardened and their prejudices confirmed. They value themselves on their enmity to Christ, as if they had never spoken *better* than when they spoke the worst they could of Jesus Christ. Those have arrived at the highest pitch of wickedness who avow their impiety, repeat what they should retract, and justify themselves in that for which they ought to condemn themselves. It is bad to say and do ill, but it is worse to *stand to it;* I do *well to be angry.* When Christ spoke with so much boldness against the sins of the great men, and thereby incensed them against him, those who were sensible of no interest but what is secular and sensual concluded him *beside himself,* for they thought none but a madman would lose his preferment, and hazard his life, for his religion and conscience.

II. The meekness and mercifulness of Heaven shining in Christ's reply to this vile calumny, *v.* 49, 50.

1. He denies their charge against him: *I have not a devil;* as Paul (Acts 26:25), *I am not mad.* The imputation is unjust; "I am neither actuated by a devil, nor in compact with one;" and this he evidenced by what he did against the devil's kingdom. He takes no notice of their calling him a *Samaritan,* because it was a calumny that disproved itself, it was a personal reflection, and not worth taking notice of: but saying he had a devil reflected on his commission, and therefore he answered that. St. Augustine gives this gloss upon his not saying any thing to their calling him a Samaritan — that he was indeed that good Samaritan spoken of in the parable, Lu. 10:33.

2. He asserts the sincerity of his own intentions: But *I honour my Father.* They suggested that he took undue honours to himself, and derogated from the honour due to God only, both which he *denies* here, in saying that he made it his business to honour his Father, and him only. It also proves that he *had not a devil;* for, if he had, he would not honour God. Note, Those who can truly way that they make it their constant care to honour God are sufficiently armed against the censures and reproaches of men.

3. He complains of the wrong they did him by their calumnies: *You do dishonour me.* By this it appears that, as man, he had a tender sense of the disgrace and indignity done him; reproach was a sword in his bones, and yet he underwent it for our salvation. It is the will of God that *all men should honour the Son,* yet there are many that *dishonour him;* such a contradiction is there in the carnal mind to the will of God. Christ honoured his Father so as never man did, and yet was himself dishonoured so as never man was; for, though God has promised that those who honour him he will honour, he never promised that men should honour them.

4. He clears himself from the imputation of vain glory, in saying this concerning himself, *v.* 50. See here, (1.) His *contempt* of worldly honour: *I seek not mine own glory.* He did not aim at this in what he had said of himself or against his persecutors; he did not court the applause of men, nor covet preferment in the world, but industriously declined both. He did not *seek his own glory* distinct from his Father's, nor had any separate interest of his own. For men to *search their own glory* is *not glory* indeed (Prov. 25:27), but rather their shame to be so much *out in their aim.* This comes in here as a reason why Christ made so light of their reproaches: *"You do dishonour me,* but cannot disturb me, shall not disquiet me, for I *seek not my own glory."* Note, Those who are dead to men's praise can safely bear their contempt. (2.) His *comfort* under worldly dishonour: *There is one that seeketh and judgeth.* In two things Christ made it appear that he *sought not his own glory;* and here he tells us what satisfied him as to both. [1.] He did not *court* men's respect, but was indifferent to it, and in reference to this he saith, *"There is one that seeketh,* that will secure and advance, my interest in the esteem and affections of the people, while I am in no care about it." Note, God will seek *their* honour that do not seek *their own;* for before honour is humility. [2.] He did not *revenge* men's affronts, but was unconcerned at them, and in reference to this he saith, *"There is one that judgeth,* that will vindicate my honour, and severely reckon with those that trample upon it." Probably he refers here to the judgments that were coming upon the nation of the Jews for the indignities they did to the Lord Jesus. See Ps. 37:13–15. *I heard not, for thou wilt hear.* If we undertake to judge for ourselves, whatever damage we sustain, our recompence is in our own hands; but if we be, as we ought to be, humble appellants and patient expectants, we shall find, to our comfort, *there is one that judgeth.*

Verses 51–59

In these verses we have,

I. The doctrine of the immortality of believers laid down, *v.* 51. It is ushered in with the usual solemn preface, *Verily, verily, I say unto you,* which commands both attention and assent, and this is what he says, *If a man keep my sayings, he shall never see death.* Here we have, 1. The *character* of a believer: he is one that *keeps the sayings* of the Lord Jesus, *ton logon ton emon — my word;* that *word of mine* which I have delivered to you; this we must not only *receive,* but *keep;* not only *have,* but *hold.* We must keep it in mind and memory, keep it in love and affection, so keep it as in nothing to violate it or go contrary to it, keep it *without spot* (1 Tim. 6:14), keep it as a trust committed to us, keep in it as our way, keep to it as our rule. 2. The *privilege* of a believer: *He shall by no means see death for ever;* so it is in the original. Not as if the bodies of believers were secured from the stroke of death. No, even the *children of the Most High* must *die like men,* and the followers of Christ have been, more than other men, in deaths often, and *killed all the day long;* how then is this promise made good that they *shall not see death?* Answer, (1.) The property of death is so altered to them that they do not see it as death, they do not see the terror of death, it is quite taken off; their sight does not *terminate* in death, as theirs does who *live by sense;* no, they look so clearly, so comfortably, through death, and beyond death, and are so taken up with their state on the other side death, that they overlook death, and *see it not.* (2.) The power of death is so broken that though there is no remedy, but they must see *death,* yet they shall not see death *for ever,* shall not be always shut up under its arrests, the day will come when *death shall be swallowed up in victory.* (3.) They are perfectly delivered from *eternal death,* shall not be *hurt of the second death.* That is the death especially meant here, that death which is *for ever,* which is opposed to everlasting life; this they shall never see, for they shall *never come into condemnation;* they shall have their everlasting lot where there will be *no more death,* where they *cannot die any more,* Lu. 20:36. Though now they cannot avoid seeing death, and tasting it too, yet they shall shortly be there where it will be *seen no more for ever,* Ex. 14:13.

II. The Jews cavil at this doctrine. Instead of laying hold of this precious promise of immortality, which the nature of man has an ambition of (who is there that does not love life, and dread the sight of death?) they lay hold of this occasion to reproach him that makes them so kind an offer: *Now we know that thou hast a devil.* Abraham *is dead.* Observe here,

1. Their *railing: "Now we know that thou hast a devil,* that thou art a madman; thou ravest, and sayest thou knowest not what." See how these swine trample underfoot the precious pearls of gospel promises. If now at last they had evidence to prove him *mad,* why did they say (*v.* 48), before they had that proof, *Thou hast a devil?* But this is the method of malice, first to *fasten* an invidious charge, and then to *fish* for evidence of it: *Now we know that thou hast a devil.* If he had not abundantly proved himself a *teacher come from God,* his promises of immortality to his credulous followers might justly have been ridiculed, and charity itself would have imputed them to a crazed fancy; but his doctrine was evidently divine, his miracles confirmed it, and the Jews' religion taught them to expect such a prophet, and to believe in him; for them therefore thus to reject him was to abandon that promise to which their *twelve tribes hoped to come,* Acts 26:7.

2. Their *reasoning,* and the colour they had to *run him down* thus. In short, they look upon him as guilty of an insufferable piece of arrogance, in making himself greater than *Abraham and the prophets: Abraham is dead,* and *the prophets,* they are dead too; very true, by the same token that these Jews were the genuine offspring of those that killed them. Now, (1.) It is true that Abraham and the prophets were great men, great in the favour of God, and great in the esteem of all good men. (2.) It is true that they *kept God's sayings,* and were obedient to them; and yet, (3.) It is true that they *died;* they never pretended to *have,* much less to *give,* immortality, but every one in his own order was *gathered to his people.* It was their honour that they *died in faith,* but die they must. Why should a good man be afraid to die, when Abraham is dead, and the prophets are dead? They have *tracked* the way through that darksome valley, which should reconcile us to death and help to take off the terror of it. Now they think Christ talks madly, when he saith, *If a man keep my sayings, he shall never taste death. Tasting* death means the same thing with *seeing* it; and well may death be represented as grievous to *several* of the senses, which is the destruction of them *all.* Now their arguing goes upon two mistakes: — [1.] They understood Christ of an immortality in this world, and this was a mistake. In the sense that Christ spoke, it was not true that *Abraham and the prophets were dead,* for God is still the *God of Abraham* and the *God of the holy prophets* (Rev. 22:6); now God is not the God of the dead, but of the living; therefore Abraham and the prophets are still alive, and, as Christ meant it, they had not *seen* nor *tasted* death. [2.] They thought none could be greater than Abraham and the prophets, whereas they could not but know that the Messiah would be greater than Abraham or any of the prophets; they did virtuously, but he excelled them all; nay, they borrowed their greatness from him. It was the honour of Abraham that he was the Father of the Messiah, and the honour of the prophets that they testified beforehand concerning him: so that he certainly *obtained a* far *more excellent name than they.* Therefore, instead of inferring from Christ's making himself greater than Abraham that he had a *devil,* they should have inferred from his proving himself so (by doing the works which neither Abraham nor the prophets ever did) that he was the Christ; but their eyes were blinded. They scornfully asked, *Whom makest thou thyself?* As if he had been guilty of pride and vain-glory; whereas he was so far from making himself greater than he was that he now drew a veil over his own glory, emptied himself, and made himself less than he was, and was the greatest example of humility that ever was.

III. Christ's reply to this cavil; still he vouchsafes to reason with them, that every mouth may be stopped. No doubt he could have struck them dumb or dead upon the spot, but this was the *day of his patience.*

1. In his answer he insists not upon his own testimony concerning himself, but waives it as not sufficient nor conclusive (*v.* 54): *If I honour myself, my honour is nothing, ean egō doxazō — if I glorify myself.* Note, Self-honour is no honour; and the affectation of glory is both the forfeiture and the defeasance of it: it is *not glory* (Prov. 25:27), but so great a reproach that there is no sin which men are more industrious to hide than this; even he that most affects praise would not be thought to do it. Honour of our own creating is a mere chimera, has nothing in it, and therefore is called *vain-glory.* Self-admirers are self-*deceivers.* Our Lord Jesus was not one that *honoured himself,* as they represented him; he was *crowned* by him who is the fountain of honour, and glorified not himself to be made a high priest, Heb. 5:4, 5.

2. He refers himself to *his* Father, God; and to *their* father, Abraham.

(1.) To his Father, *God: It is my Father that honoureth me.* By this he means, [1.] That he *derived* from his Father all the honour he now claimed; he had commanded them to believe in him, to follow him, and to keep his word, all which put an honour upon him; but it was the Father that *laid help* upon him, that *lodged* all *fulness* in him, that sanctified him, and sealed him, and sent him into the world to receive all the honours due to the Messiah, and this justified him in all these demands of respect. [2.] That he *depended* upon his Father for all the honour he further *looked for.* He courted not the applauses of the age, but despised them; for his eye and heart were upon the glory which the Father had promised him, and *which he had with the Father before the world was.* He aimed at an advancement with which the Father was to *exalt him, a name* he was to *give him,* Phil. 2:8, 9. Note, Christ and all that are his depend upon God for their honour; and he that is sure of honour where he is known cares not though he be slighted where he is in disguise. Appealing thus often to his Father, and his Father's testimony of him, which yet the Jews did not admit nor give credit to,

First, He here takes occasion to show the reason of *their* incredulity, notwithstanding *this* testimony — and this was their *unacquaintedness* with God; as if he had said, "But why should I talk to you of my Father's honouring me, when he is one you know nothing of? You *say of him that he is your God, yet you have not known him.*" Here observe,

a. The profession they made of relation to God: *"You say that he is your God,* the God you have chosen, and are in covenant with; you say that you are Israel; but all are not so indeed that are of Israel," Rom. 9:6. Note, Many pretend to have an interest in God, and say that he is *theirs,* who yet have no just cause to say so. Those who called themselves the *temple of the Lord,* having *profaned the excellency of Jacob,* did but trust in lying words. What will it avail us to say, He is *our God,* if we be not in sincerity *his people,* nor such as he will own? Christ mentions here their profession of relation to God, as that which was an aggravation of their unbelief. All people will honour those whom their God honours; but these Jews, who said that the Lord was their God, studied how to put the utmost disgrace upon one upon whom their God put honour. Note, The Profession we make of a covenant relation to God, and an interest in him, if it be not improved *by us* will be improved *against us.*

b. Their ignorance of him, and estrangement from him, notwithstanding this profession: *Yet you have not known him.* (*a.*) *You know him not at all.* These Pharisees were so taken up with the study of their traditions concerning things foreign and trifling that they never minded the most needful and useful knowledge; like the false prophets of old, who *caused people to forget God's name by their dreams,* Jer. 23:27. Or, (*b.*) *You know him not aright,* but mistake concerning him; and this is as bad as not knowing him at all, or worse. Men may be able to dispute subtly concerning God, and yet may think him such a one as themselves, and *not know him.* You say that he is *yours,* and it is natural to us to desire to know *our own,* yet you *know him not.* Note, There are many who *claim-kindred* to God who yet have no acquaintance with him. It is only the name of God which they have learned to talk of, and to hector with; but for the nature of God, his attributes and perfections, and relations to his creatures, they know nothing of the matter; we *speak this to their shame,* 1 Co. 15:34. Multitudes satisfy themselves, but deceive themselves, with a titular relation to an *unknown God.* This Christ charges upon the Jews here, [*a.*] To show how vain and groundless their pretensions of relation to God were. "You say that he is yours, but you give yourselves the lie, for it is plain that you do not know him;" and we reckon that a cheat is effectually convicted if it be found that he is ignorant of the persons he pretends alliance to. [*b.*] To show the true reason why they were not wrought upon by Christ's doctrine and miracles. They knew not God; and therefore perceived not the image of God, nor the voice of God in Christ. Note, The reason why men receive not the *gospel of Christ* is because they have not the *knowledge of God.* Men *submit not to the righteousness of Christ* because they are *ignorant of God's righteousness,* Rom. 10:3. They that know not God, and obey not the gospel of Christ, are put together, 2 Th. 1:8.

Secondly, He gives them the reason of *his* assurance that his Father would *honour* him and *own him: But I know him;* and again, *I know him;* which bespeaks, not only his *acquaintance* with him, having lain in his bosom, but his *confidence* in him, to stand by him, and bear him out in his whole undertaking; as was prophesied concerning him (Isa. 50:7, 8), *I know* that I shall not be ashamed, for he is near that justifies; and as Paul, *"I know whom I have believed* (2 Tim. 1:12), I know him to be faithful, and powerful, and heartily engaged in the cause which I know to be his *own."* Observe, 1. How he *professes* his knowledge of his Father, with the greatest certainty, as one that was neither afraid nor ashamed to own it: *If I should say I know him not, I should be a liar like unto you.* He would not deny his relation to God, to humour the Jews, and to avoid their reproaches, and prevent further trouble; nor would he retract what he had said, nor confess himself either deceived or a deceiver; if he should, he would be found a false witness against God and himself. Note, Those who disown their religion and relation to God, as Peter, are liars, as much as hypocrites are, who pretend to know him, when they do not. See 1 Tim. 6:13, 14. Mr Clark observes well, upon this, that it is a great sin to deny God's grace in us. 2. How he *proves* his knowledge of his Father: *I know him and keep his sayings,* or *his word.* Christ, as man, was obedient to the moral law, and, as Redeemer, to the mediatorial law; and in both he kept *his Father's* word, and *his own word* with the Father. Christ requires of us (*v.* 51) that we *keep his sayings;* and he has set before us a copy of obedience, a copy without a blot: he *kept his Father's sayings;* well might he who *learned obedience* teach it; see Heb. 5:8, 9. Christ by this evinced that he knew the Father. Note, The best proof of our acquaintance with God is our obedience to him. Those only know God aright that keep his word; it is a ruled case, 1 Jn. 2:3. *Hereby we know that we know him* (and do not only fancy it), *if we keep his commandments.*

(2.) Christ refers them to *their* father, whom they boasted so much of a relation to, and that was Abraham, and this closes the discourse.

[1.] Christ asserts Abraham's prospect of him, and respect to him: *Your father Abraham rejoiced to see my day, and he saw it, and was glad, v.* 56. And by this he proves that he was not at all out of the way when he *made himself greater than Abraham.* Two things he here speaks of as instances of that patriarch's respect to the promised Messiah: —

First, The ambition he had to *see his day: He rejoiced, ēgalliasto — he leaped at it.* The word, though it commonly signifies *rejoicing,* must here signify a transport of *desire* rather than of *joy,* for otherwise the latter part of the verse would be a tautology; he *saw it, and was glad.* He *reached out,* or *stretched himself forth,* that he might *see my day;* as Zaccheus, that ran before, and climbed the tree, *to see Jesus.* The notices he had received of the Messiah to come had raised in him an expectation of something *great,* which he earnestly longed to know more of. The dark intimation of that which is considerable puts men upon enquiry, and makes them earnestly ask *Who?* and *What?* and *Where?* and *When?* and *How?* And thus the prophets of the Old Testament, having a general idea of a grace that should *come, searched diligently* (1 Pt. 1:10), and Abraham was as industrious herein as any of them. God told him of a land that he would give his posterity, and of the wealth and honour he designed them (Gen. 15:14); but he never *leaped* thus to see that day, as he did to see the day of the Son of man. He could not look with so much indifferency upon the promised *seed* as he did upon the promised land; *in that* he was, but *to the other* he could not be, contentedly a stranger. Note, Those who rightly know any thing of Christ cannot but be earnestly desirous to know more of him. Those who discern the dawning of the light of the Sun of righteousness cannot but wish to see his rising. The mystery of redemption is that which *angels desire to look into,* much more should we, who are more immediately concerned in it. Abraham desired to see Christ's day, though it was at a great distance; but this degenerate seed of his discerned not his day, nor bade it welcome when it came. The appearing of Christ, which gracious souls love and long for, carnal hearts dread and loathe.

Secondly, The satisfaction he had in what he did see of it: *He saw it, and was glad.* Observe here,

a. How God gratified the pious desire of Abraham; he longed to see Christ's day, and he *saw it.* Though he saw it not so plainly, and fully, and distinctly as we now see it under the gospel, yet he saw something of it, more *afterwards* than he did at first. Note, To him that has, and to him that asks, shall be given; to him that uses and improves what he has, and that desires and prays for more of the knowledge of Christ, God will give more. But how did Abraham see Christ's day? (*a.*) Some understand it of the sight he had of it in the other world. The separate soul of Abraham, when the veil of flesh was rent, saw the mysteries of the kingdom of God in heaven. Calvin mentions this sense of it, and does not much disallow it. Note, The longings of gracious souls after Jesus Christ will be fully satisfied when they come to heaven, and not till then. But, (*b.*) It is more commonly understood of some sight he had of *Christ's day* in this world. They that *received not the promises,* yet *saw them afar off,* Heb. 11:13. Balaam saw Christ, but not *now,* not *nigh.* There is room to conjecture that Abraham had some vision of Christ and his day, for his own private satisfaction, which is not, nor must be, recorded in his story, like that of Daniel's, which must be *shut up, and sealed unto the time of the end,* Dan. 12:4. Christ knew what Abraham saw better than Moses did. But there are divers things recorded in which Abraham saw more of that which he longed to see than he did when the promise was first made to him. He saw in Melchizedek one *made like unto the Son of God,* and a priest for ever; he saw an appearance of Jehovah, attended with two angels, in the plains of Mamre. In the prevalency of his intercession for Sodom he saw a specimen of Christ's intercession; in the casting out of Ishmael, and the establishment of the covenant with Isaac, he saw a figure of the gospel day, which is Christ's day; for these things were an allegory. In offering Isaac, and the ram instead of Isaac, he saw a double type of the great sacrifice; and his calling the place *Jehovah-jireh — It shall be seen,* intimates that he saw something more in it than others did, which time would produce; and in making his servant *put his hand under his thigh,* when he swore, he had a regard to the Messiah.

b. How *Abraham* entertained these discoveries of Christ's day, and bade them welcome: *He saw, and was glad.* He was glad of what he *saw* of God's favour to himself, and glad of what he *foresaw* of the mercy God had in store for the world. Perhaps this refers to Abraham's laughing when God assured him of a son by Sarah (Gen. 17:16, 17), for that was not a laughter of distrust as Sarah's but of joy; in that promise he saw Christ's day, and it *filled him with joy unspeakable.* Thus he embraced the promises. Note, A believing sight of Christ and his day will put gladness into the heart. No joy like the joy of faith; we are never acquainted with true pleasure till we are acquainted with Christ.

[2.] The Jews cavil at this, and reproach him for it (*v.* 57): *Thou art not yet fifty years old, and hast thou seen Abraham?* Here, *First,* They suppose that if Abraham saw him and his day he also had seen Abraham, which yet was not a necessary *innuendo,* but this turn of his words would best serve to expose him; yet it was true that Christ had seen Abraham, and had talked with him as a man talks with his friend. *Secondly,* They suppose it a very absurd thing for him to pretend to have seen Abraham, who was *dead* so many ages before he was born. The state of the dead is an *invisible* state; but here they ran upon the old mistake, understanding that corporally which Christ spoke spiritually. Now this gave them occasion to *despise his youth,* and to upbraid him with it, as if he were *but of yesterday, and knew* nothing: *Thou art not yet fifty years old.* They might as well have said, *Thou art not forty;* for he was now but thirty-two or thirty-three years old. As to this, Irenaeus, one of the first fathers, with this passage supports the tradition which he says he had from some that had conversed with St. John, that our Saviour lived to be fifty years old, which he contends for, *Advers. Haeres.* lib. 2, cap. 39, 40. See what little credit is to be given to tradition; and, as to this here, the Jews spoke *at random;* some year they would mention, and therefore pitched upon one that they thought he was far enough short of; he did not look to be forty, but they were sure he could not be fifty, much less contemporary with Abraham. Old age is reckoned to begin at fifty (Num. 4:47), so that they meant no more than this, "Thou art not to be reckoned an old man; many of us are much thy seniors, and yet pretend not to have seen Abraham." Some think that his countenance was so altered, with grief and watching, that, together with the gravity of his aspect, it made him look like a man of fifty years old: *his visage was so marred,* Isa. 52:14.

[3.] Our Saviour gives an effectual answer to this cavil, by a solemn assertion of his own seniority even to Abraham himself (*v.* 58): *"Verily, verily, I say unto you;* I do not only say it in private to my own disciples, who will be sure to say as I say, but *to you* my enemies and persecutors; I say it to your faces, take it how you will: *Before Abraham was, I am;" prin Abraam genesthai, egō eimi, Before Abraham was made or born, I am.* The change of the word is observable, and bespeaks Abraham a creature, and himself the Creator; well therefore might he make himself *greater* than Abraham. *Before Abraham he was, First,* As God. *I am,* is the name of God (Ex. 3:14); it denotes his self-existence; he does not say, *I was,* but *I am,* for he is the first and the last, immutably the same (Rev. 1:8); thus he was not only before Abraham, but before *all worlds, ch.* 1:1; Prov. 8:23. *Secondly,* As Mediator. He was the appointed Messiah, long before Abraham; the *Lamb slain from the foundation of the world* (Rev. 13:8), the channel of conveyance of light, life, and love from God to man. This supposes his divine nature, that he is the same in himself from eternity (Heb. 13:8), and that he is the same to man ever since the fall; he was made of God wisdom, righteousness, sanctification, and redemption, to Adam, and Abel, and Enoch, and Noah, and Shem, and all the patriarchs that lived and died by faith in him before Abraham was born. Abraham was the root of the Jewish nation, the rock out of which they were hewn. If Christ was before Abraham, his doctrine and religion were no novelty, but were, in the substance of them, prior to Judaism, and ought to take place of it.

[4.] This great word ended the dispute *abruptly,* and put a period to it: they could bear to hear no more from him, and he needed to say no more to them, having witnessed this good confession, which was sufficient to support all his claims. One would think that Christ's discourse, in which shone so much both of grace and glory, should have captivated them all; but their inveterate prejudice against the holy spiritual doctrine and law of Christ, which were so contrary to their pride and worldliness, baffled all the methods of conviction. Now was fulfilled that prophecy (Mal. 3:1, 2), that when the messenger of the covenant should *come to his temple they would not abide the day of his coming,* because he would be *like a refiner's fire.* Observe here,

First, How they were *enraged* at Christ for what he said: *They took up stones to cast at him, v.* 59. Perhaps they looked upon him as a blasphemer, and such were indeed to be stoned (Lev. 24:16); but they must be first legally tried and convicted. Farewell justice and order if every man pretend to execute a law at his pleasure. Besides, they had said but just now that he was a distracted crack-brained man, and if so it was against all reason and equity to punish him as a malefactor for what he said. *They took up stones.* Dr. Lightfoot will tell you how they came to have stones so ready in the temple; they had workmen at this time repairing the temple, or making some additions, and the pieces of stone which they hewed off served for this purpose. See here the desperate power of sin and Satan in and over the children of disobedience. Who would think that ever there should be such wickedness as this in men, such an open and daring rebellion against one that undeniably proved himself to be the Son of God? Thus every one has a stone to throw at his holy religion, Acts 28:22.

Secondly, How he made his *escape* out of their hands. 1. He *absconded;* Jesus *hid himself; ekrybē — he was hid,* either by the crowd of those that wished well to him, to shelter him (he that ought to have been upon a throne, high and lifted up, is content to be *lost in a crowd*); or perhaps he concealed himself behind some of the walls or pillars of the temple *(in the secret of his tabernacle he shall hide me,* Ps. 27:5); or by a divine power, casting a mist before their eyes, he made himself invisible to them. *When the wicked rise a man is hidden,* a wise and good man, Prov. 28:12, 28. Not that Christ was afraid or ashamed to stand by what he had said, but his *hour was not yet come,* and he would countenance the flight of his ministers and people in times of persecution, when they are called to it. The Lord hid Jeremiah and Baruch, Jer. 36:26. 2. He *departed,* he *went out of the temple,* going *through the midst of them,* undiscovered, and *so passed by.* This was not a cowardly inglorious flight, nor such as argued either guilt or fear. It was foretold concerning him that he should not fail nor be discouraged, Isa. 42:4. But, (1.) It was an instance of his power over his enemies, and that they could do no more against him than he gave them leave to do; by which it appears that when afterwards he was taken in their pits he *offered himself, ch.* 10:18. They now thought they had made sure of him and yet he *passed through the midst* of them, either their eyes being blinded or their hands tied, and thus he left them to fume, like a lion *disappointed of his prey.* (2.) It was an instance of his prudent provision for his own safety, when he knew that his work was not done, nor his testimony finished; thus he gave an example to his own rule, *When they persecute you in one city flee to another;* nay, if occasion be, to a *wilderness,* for so Elijah did (1 Ki. 19:3, 4), and the woman, the church, Rev. 12:6. When they took up loose stones to throw at Christ, he could have commanded the fixed stones, which did *cry out of the wall* against them, to avenge his cause, or the earth to open and swallow them up; but he chose to accommodate himself to the state he was in, to make the example imitable by the prudence of his followers, without a miracle. (3.) It was a righteous deserting of those who (worse than the Gadarenes, who *prayed him to depart)* stoned him from among them. Christ will not long stay with those who bid him be gone. Christ did again visit the temple after this; as one *loth to depart,* he *bade oft farewell;* but at last he abandoned it for ever, and left it *desolate.* Christ now *went through* the midst of the Jews, and none of them courted his stay, nor stirred up himself to take hold of him, but were even content to let him go. Note, God never forsakes any till they have first provoked him to withdraw, and will have none of him. Calvin observes that these chief priests, when they had driven Christ out of the temple, valued themselves on the possession they kept of it: "But," says he, "those deceive themselves who are proud of a church or temple which Christ has forsaken." *Longe falluntur, cum templum se habere putant Deo vacuum.* When Christ left them it is said that he passed by silently and unobserved; *parēgen houtōs,* so that they were not aware of him. Note, Christ's departures from a church, or a particular soul, are often *secret,* and not soon taken notice of. As *the kingdom of God comes not,* so it *goes not, with observation.* See Jdg. 16:20. *Samson wist not that the Lord was departed from him.* Thus it was with these forsaken Jews, God left them, and they never missed him.

CHAPTER 9

After Christ's departure out of the temple, in the close of the foregoing chapter, and before this happened which is recorded in this chapter, he had been for some time abroad in the country, it is supposed about two or three months; in which interval of time Dr. Lightfoot and other harmonists place all the passages that occur from Lu. 10:17 to 13:17. What is recorded in *ch.* 7 and 8 was at the feast of tabernacles, in September; what is recorded in this and the following chapter was at the feast of dedication in December, *ch.* 10:22. Mr. Clark and others place this immediately after the foregoing chapter. In this chapter we have, I. The miraculous cure of a man that was born blind (*v.* 1–7). II. The discourses which were occasioned by it. 1. A discourse of the neighbours among themselves, and with the man (*v.* 8–12). 2. Between the Pharisees and the man (*v.* 13–34). 3. Between Christ and the poor man (*v.* 35–38). 4. Between Christ and the Pharisees (*v.* 39 to the end).

Verses 1–7

We have here sight given to a poor beggar that had been blind from his birth. Observe,

I. The notice which our Lord Jesus took of the piteous case of this poor blind man (*v.* 1): *As Jesus passed by he saw a man which was blind from his birth.* The first words seem to refer to the last of the foregoing chapter, and countenance the opinion of those who in the harmony place this story immediately after that. There it was said, *parēgen — he passed by,* and here, without so much as repeating him name (though our translators supply it) *kai paragō — and as he passed by.* 1. Though the Jews had so basely abused him, both by word and deed gave him the highest provocation imaginable, yet he did not miss any opportunity of doing good among them, nor take up a resolution, as justly he might have done, never to have favoured them with any good offices. The cure of this blind man was a kindness to *the public,* enabling him to work for his living who before was a charge and burden to the neighbourhood. It is noble, and generous, and Christ-like, to be willing to *serve the public,* even when we are slighted and disobliged by them, or think ourselves so. Though he was in his flight from a threatening danger, and escaping for his life, yet he willingly halted and staid awhile to show mercy to this poor man. We make more haste than good speed when we out-run opportunities of doing good. 3. When the Pharisees drove Christ from them, he went to this poor blind beggar. Some of the ancients make this a figure of the bringing of the gospel to the Gentiles, *who sat in darkness,* when the Jews had rejected it, and driven it from them. 4. Christ took this poor blind man in his way, and cured him *in transitu — as he passed by.* Thus should we take occasions of doing good, even as we *pass by,* wherever we are.

Now, (1.) The condition of this poor man was very sad. He was *blind,* and had been so *from his birth.* If the light is sweet, how melancholy must it needs be for a man, all his days, *to eat in darkness!* He that is *blind* has no *enjoyment* of the light, but he that is *born blind* has no *idea* of it. Methinks such a one would give a great deal to have his curiosity satisfied with but one day's sight of light and colours, shapes and figures, though he were never to see them more. *Why is* the *light* of life *given to one that is in this misery,* that is deprived of the light of the sun, *whose way is* thus *hid, and whom God hath* thus *hedged in?* Job 3:20–23. Let us bless God that it was not our case. The eye is one of the most curious parts of the body, its structure exceedingly nice and fine. In the formation of animals, it is said to be the first part that appears distinctly discernible. What a mercy is it that there was no miscarriage in the making of ours! Christ cured many that were blind by disease or accident, but here he cured one that was *born blind.* [1.] That he might give an instance of his power to help in the most desperate cases, and to relieve when none else can. [2.] That he might give a *specimen* of the work of his grace upon the souls of sinners, which gives sight to those that were by nature blind.

(2.) The compassions of our Lord Jesus towards him were very tender. He *saw him;* that is, he took cognizance of his case, and looked upon him with concern. When God is about to work deliverance, he is said to see *the affliction;* so Christ saw this poor man. Others saw him, but not as he did. This poor man could not see Christ, but Christ saw him, and anticipated both his prayers and expectations with a surprising cure. Christ is often found of those that seek him not, nor see him, Isa. 65:1. And, if we know or apprehend any thing of Christ, it is because we were first *known of him* (Gal. 4:9) and *apprehended* by him, Phil. 3:12.

II. The discourse between Christ and his disciples concerning this man. When he *departed out of the temple* they went along with him: for these were they that *continued with him in his temptations,* and followed him whithersoever he went; and they lost nothing by their adherence to him, but gained experience abundantly. Observe,

1. The question which the disciples put to their Master upon this blind man's case, *v.* 2. When Christ looked upon him, they had an eye to him too; Christ's compassion should kindle ours. It is probable that Christ told them this poor man was born blind, or they knew it by common fame; but they did not move Christ to heal him. Instead of this, they started a very odd question concerning him: *Rabbi, who sinned, this man or his parents, that he was born blind?* Now this question of theirs was,

(1.) *Uncharitably censorious.* They take it for granted that this extraordinary calamity was the punishment of some uncommon wickedness, and that this man was a sinner above all men that dwelt at Jerusalem, Lu. 13:4. For the *barbarous people* to infer, *Surely this man is a murderer,* was not so strange; but it was *inexcusable* in them, who knew the scriptures, who had read that *all things come alike to all,* and knew that it was adjudged in Job's case that the greatest sufferers are not *therefore* to be looked upon as the greatest sinners. The grace of repentance calls our own afflictions *punishments,* but the grace of charity calls the afflictions of others *trials,* unless the contrary is very evident.

(2.) It was *unnecessarily curious.* Concluding this calamity to be inflicted for some very heinous crime, they ask, *Who were the criminals, this man or his parents?* And what was this to them? Or what good would it do them to know it? We are apt to be more inquisitive concerning other people's sins than concerning our own; whereas, it is more our concern to know wherefore God contends with us than wherefore he contends with others; for to judge ourselves is our sin. They enquire, [1.] Whether this man was punished thus for some sin of his own, either committed or foreseen before his birth. Some think that the disciples were tainted with the Pythagorean notion of the *pre-existence* of souls, and their *transmigration* from one body to another. Was this man's soul condemned to the dungeon of this blind body to punish it for some great sin committed in another body which it had before animated? The Pharisees seem to have had the same opinion of his case when they said, *Thou wast altogether born in sin* (*v.* 34), as if all those, and those only, were born in sin whom nature had *stigmatized.* Or, [2.] Whether he was punished for the wickedness of his parents, which God sometimes *visits upon the children.* It is a good reason why parents should take heed of sin, lest their children smart for it when they are gone. Let not us thus be cruel to our own, as the *ostrich in the wilderness.* Perhaps the disciples asked this, not as believing that this was the punishment of some actual sin of his own or his parents, but Christ having intimated to another patient that his sin was the cause of this impotency (*ch.* 5:14), "Master," say they, "whose sin is the cause of this impotency?" Being at a loss what construction to put upon this providence, they desire to be informed. The equity of God's dispensations is always certain, for *his righteousness is as the great mountains,* but not always to be accounted for, for his *judgments are a great deep.*

2. Christ's answer to this question. He was always *apt to teach,* and to rectify his disciples' mistakes.

(1.) He gives the reason of this poor man's blindness: "*Neither has this man sinned nor his parents,* but he was born blind, and has continued so to this day, that now at last *the works of God should be made manifest in him,*" *v.* 3. Here Christ, who perfectly knew the secret springs of the divine counsels, told them two things concerning such uncommon calamities: — [1.] That they are not always inflicted as punishments of sin. The sinfulness of the whole race of mankind does indeed justify God in all the miseries of human life; so that those who have the least share of them must say that God is *kind,* and those who have the largest share must not say that he is *unjust;* but many are made much more *miserable* than others in this life who are not at all more *sinful.* Not but that this man was a sinner, and his parents sinners, but is was not any uncommon guilt that God had an eye to in inflicting this upon him. Note, We must take heed of judging any to be great sinners merely because they are great sufferers, lest we be found, not only *persecuting those whom God has smitten* (Ps. 69:26), but accusing those whom he has justified, and *condemning* those for whom *Christ died,* which is daring and dangerous, Rom. 8:33, 34. [2.] That they are sometimes intended purely *for the glory of God,* and the *manifesting of his works.* God has a sovereignty over all his creatures and an exclusive right in them, and may make them serviceable to his glory in such a way as he thinks fit, in doing or suffering; and if God be glorified, either by us or in us, we were not made *in vain.* This man was *born blind,* and it was worth while for him to be so, and to continue thus long dark, *that the works of God might be manifest in him.* That is, *First,* That the *attributes of God* might be made manifest in him: his justice in making sinful man liable to such grievous calamities; his ordinary power and goodness in supporting a poor man under such a grievous and tedious affliction, especially that his extraordinary power and goodness might be manifested in curing him. Note, The difficulties of providence, otherwise unaccountable, may be resolved into this — God intends in them to *show himself,* to declare his glory, to make himself to be taken notice of. Those who regard him not in the ordinary course of things are sometimes alarmed by things extraordinary. How contentedly then may a good man be a *loser in his comforts,* while he is sure that thereby God will be one way or other a *gainer in his glory! Secondly,* That the counsels of God concerning the Redeemer might be manifested in him. He was *born blind* that our Lord Jesus might have the honour of *curing him,* and might therein prove himself sent of God to be the true light to the world. Thus the fall of man was permitted, and the *blindness* that followed it, that the works of God might be manifest in *opening the eyes of the blind.* It was now a great while since this man was born blind, and yet it never appeared till now *why* he was so. Note, The intentions of Providence commonly do not appear till a great while after the event, perhaps *many years* after. The sentences in the book of providence are sometimes *long,* and you must read a great way before you can apprehend the sense of them.

(2.) He gives the reason of his own forwardness and readiness to help and heal him, *v.* 4, 5. It was not for ostentation, but in pursuance of his undertaking: *I must work the works of him that sent me* (of which this is one), *while it is day,* and working time; *the night cometh,* the period of that day, *when no man can work.* This is not only a reason shy Christ was constant in doing good to the souls and bodies of men, but why particularly he did this, though it was the sabbath day, on which works of necessity might be done, and he proves this to be a work of necessity.

[1.] It was his Father's will: *I must work the works of him that sent me.* Note, *First,* The Father, when he sent his Son into the world, gave him *work to do;* he did not come into the world to take state, but to do business; whom God sends he employs, for he sends none to be idle. *Secondly,* The works Christ had to do were the *works of him that sent him,* not only appointed *by him,* but done *for him;* he was a worker together with God. *Thirdly,* He was pleased to lay himself under the strongest obligations to do the business he was sent about: I *must work.* He *engaged his heart,* in the covenant of redemption, to *draw near,* and *approach* to God as Mediator, Jer. 30:21. Shall we be willing to be *loose,* when Christ was willing to be *bound? Fourthly,* Christ, having laid himself under obligations to do his work, laid out himself with the utmost vigour and industry in his work. He *worked the works* he had to do; did *ergazesthai ta erga — made a business of that which was his business.* It is not enough to look at our work, and talk over it, but we must work it.

[2.] Now was his opportunity: I must work *while it is day,* while the time lasts which is appointed to work in, and while the light lasts which is given to work by. Christ himself had *his day. First,* All the business of the *mediatorial kingdom* was to be done within the limits of time, and in this world; for at the end of the world, when time shall be no more, the *kingdom shall be delivered up to God, even the Father,* and the *mystery of God finished. Secondly,* all the work he had to do *in his own person* here on earth was to be done *before his death;* the time of his living in this world is *the day* here spoken of. Note, The time of our life is our day, in which it concerns us to do the *work of the day.* Day-time is the proper season for work (Ps. 104:22, 23); during the day of life we must be busy, not waste *day-time,* nor play by *day-light;* it will be time enough to rest when our day is done, for it is *but a day.*

[3.] The period of his opportunity was at hand, and therefore he would be busy; *The night comes when no man can work.* Note, The consideration of our death approaching should quicken us to improve all the opportunities of life, both for doing and getting good. *The night comes,* it will come certainly, may come suddenly, is coming nearer and nearer. We cannot compute how nigh our sun is, it may go down at noon; nor can we promise ourselves a twilight between the day of life and the night of death. When the night comes we *cannot work,* because the light afforded us to work by is *extinguished;* the grave is a land of darkness, and our work cannot be done *in the dark.* And, besides, our time allotted us for our work will then have *expired;* when our Master tied us to duty he tied us to time too; when night comes, *call the labourers;* we must then *show our work,* and receive according to the things done. In the world of retribution we are no longer probationers; it is too late to *bid* when the inch of candle is *dropped.* Christ uses this as an argument with himself to be diligent, though he had no opposition from within to struggle with; much more need have we to work upon our hearts these and the like considerations to quicken us.

[4.] His business in the world was to enlighten it (*v.* 5): *As long as I am in the world,* and that will not be long, *I am the light of the world.* He had said this before, *ch.* 8:12. He is the *Sun of righteousness,* that has not only light in his wings for those that can see, but healing in his wings, or beams, for those that are blind and cannot see, therein far exceeding in virtue that great light which rules *by day.* Christ would cure this blind man, the representative of a blind world, because he came to be *the light of the world,* not only to give *light,* but to give *sight.* Now this gives us, *First,* A great *encouragement* to come to him, as a guiding, quickening, refreshing light. To whom should we look but to him? Which way should we turn our eyes, but to the light? We partake of the sun's light, and so we may of Christ's grace, without money and without price. *Secondly,* A good *example* of usefulness in the world. What Christ saith of himself, he saith of his disciples: *You are lights in the world,* and, if so, *Let your light shine.* What were candles made for but to burn?

III. The manner of the cure of the blind man, *v.* 6, 7. The circumstances of the miracle are singular, and no doubt significant. *When he had thus spoken* for the instruction of his disciples, and the opening of their understandings, he addressed himself to the opening of the blind man's eyes. He did not defer it till he could do it either more privately, for his greater safety, or more publicly, for his greater honour, or till the sabbath was past, when it would give less offence. What good we have opportunity of doing we should do quickly; he that will never do a good work till there is nothing to be objected against it will leave many a good work for ever undone, Eccl. 11:4. In the cure observe,

1. The preparation of the eye-salve. Christ *spat on the ground, and made clay of the spittle.* He could have cured him with a word, as he did others, but he chose to do it in this way to show that he is not *tied* to any method. He made clay of his own spittle, because there was no water near; and he would teach us not to be nice or curious, but, when we have at any time occasion, to be willing to take up with that which is *next hand,* if it will but serve the turn. Why should we *go about* for that which may as well be had and done a *nearer way?* Christ's making use of his own spittle intimates that there is healing virtue in every thing that belongs to Christ; clay made of Christ's spittle was much more precious than the balm of Gilead.

2. The application of it to the place: *He anointed the eyes of the blind man with the clay.* Or, as the margin reads it, *He spread* (*epechrise*), *he daubed the clay upon the eyes of the blind man,* like a tender physician; he did it himself with his own hand, though the patient was a beggar. Now Christ did this, (1.) To magnify his power in making a blind man to see by that method which one would think more likely to make a seeing man blind. Daubing clay on the eyes would *close them* up, but never *open them.* Note, The power of God often works by contraries; and he makes men feel their own blindness before he gives them sight. (2.) To give an intimation that it was his mighty hand, the very same that at first made man out of *the clay;* for by him God *made the worlds,* both the great world, and man the little world. Man was *formed out of the clay,* and moulded like the clay, and here Christ used the same materials to give sight to the body that at first he used to give being to it. (3.) To represent and typify the healing and opening of the eyes of the mind by the grace of Jesus Christ. The design of the gospel is to *open men's eyes,* Acts 26:18. Now the eye-salve that does the work is of Christ's preparing; it is made up, not as this, of his spittle, but of his blood, the blood and water that came out of his pierced side; we must come to Christ for *the eye-salve,* Rev. 3:18. He only is *able,* and he only is *appointed,* to make it up, Lu. 4:18. The means used in this work are very weak and unlikely, and are made effectual only by the power of Christ; when a dark world was to be enlightened, and nations of blind souls were to have their eyes opened, God chose the *foolish things, and weak, and despised,* for the doing of it. And the method Christ takes is first to make men feel themselves blind, as this poor man did whose eyes were daubed with clay, and then to give them sight. Paul in his conversion was *struck blind* for three days, and then the *scales fell from his eyes.* The way prescribed for getting spiritual wisdom is, *Let a man become a fool, that he may be wise,* 1 Co. 3:18. We must be made uneasy with our blindness, as this man here, and then healed.

3. The directions given to the patient, *v.* 7. His physician said to him, *Go, wash in the pool of Siloam.* Not that this washing was needful to effect the cure; but, (1.) Christ would hereby try his obedience, and whether he would with an implicit faith obey the orders of one he was so much a stranger to. (2.) He would likewise try how he stood affected to the tradition of the elders, which taught, and perhaps had taught him (for many that are *blind* are very knowing), that it was not lawful to wash the eyes, no not with spittle medicinally, on the sabbath day, much less to go to a pool of water to wash them. (3.) He would hereby represent the method of spiritual healing, in which, though the effect is owing purely to his power and grace, there is duty to be done by us. Go, search the scriptures, attend upon the ministry, converse with the wise; this is like washing in the pool of Siloam. Promised graces must be expected in the way of instituted ordinances. The waters of baptism were to those who had been trained up in darkness like the pool of Siloam, in which they might not only wash and be clean, but *wash, and have their eyes opened.* Hence they that were baptized are said to be *phōtisthentes — enlightened;* and the ancients called baptism *phōtismos — illumination.* Concerning the pool of Siloam observe, [1.] That it was supplied with water from mount Zion, so that these were the *waters of the sanctuary* (Ps. 46:4), living waters, which were *healing,* Eze. 47:9. [2.] That the waters of Siloam had of old signified the throne and kingdom of the house of David, pointing at the Messiah (Isa. 8:6), and the Jews who *refused the waters of Shiloa,* Christ's doctrine and law, and rejoiced in the tradition of the elders. Christ would try this man, whether he would cleave to the waters of Siloam or no. [3.] The evangelist takes notice of the signification of the name, its being interpreted *sent.* Christ is often called the *sent of God,* the Messenger of the covenant (Mal. 3:1); so that when Christ sent him to the pool of Siloam he did in effect send him to himself; for Christ is *all in all* to the healing of souls. Christ as a prophet directs us to him-

self as a priest. *Go, wash in the fountain opened,* a fountain of life, not a *pool.*

4. The patient's obedience to these directions: *He went his way therefore,* probably led by some friend or other; or perhaps he was so well acquainted with Jerusalem that he could find the way himself. Nature often supplies the want of sight with an uncommon sagacity; and *he washed his eyes;* probably the disciples, or some stander by, informed him that he who bade him do it was that Jesus whom he had heard so much of, else he would not have gone, at his bidding, on that which looked so much like a fool's errand; in confidence of Christ's power, as well as in obedience to his command, he went, and washed.

5. The cure effected: *He came seeing.* There is more glory in this concise narrative, *He went* and *washed,* and *came seeing,* than in Caesar's *Veni, vidi, vici — I came, I saw, I conquered.* When the clay was *washed off* from his eyes, all the other impediments were removed with it; so when the pangs and struggles of the new birth are over, and the pains and terrors of conviction past, the bands of sin fly off with them, and a glorious light and liberty succeed. See here an instance, (1.) Of the power of Christ. What cannot *he* do who could not only do *this,* but do it *thus?* With a lump of clay laid on either eye, and washed off again, he couched those cataracts immediately which the most skilful oculist, with the finest instrument and the most curious hand, could not remove. No doubt this is *he that should come,* for by him the blind receive their sight. (2.) It is an instance of the virtue of faith and obedience. This man let Christ do what *he* pleased, and did what he appointed him to do, and so was cured. Those that would be healed by Christ must be ruled by him. He *came back* from the pool to his neighbours and acquaintance, wondering and wondered at; he came *seeing.* This represents the benefit gracious souls find in attending on instituted ordinances, according to Christ's appointment; they have gone to the pool of Siloam weak, and have come away strengthened; have gone doubting, and come away satisfied; have gone mourning, and come away rejoicing; have gone trembling, and come away triumphing; have gone *blind,* and come away *seeing,* come away singing, Isa. 52:8.

Verses 8–12

Such a wonderful event as the giving of sight to a man born blind could not but be the talk of the town, and many heeded it no more than they do other town-talk, that is but nine days' wonder; but here we are told what the neighbours said of it, for the confirmation of the matter of fact. That which at first was not believed without *scrutiny* may afterwards be admitted without *scruple.* Two things are debated in this conference about it: —

I. Whether this was the same man that had before been blind, *v.* 8.

1. The neighbours that lived near the place where he was born and bred, and knew that he had been blind, could not but be amazed when they saw that he had his eye-sight, had it on a sudden, and perfectly; and they said, *Is not this he that sat and begged?* It seems, this blind man was a common beggar, being disabled to work for his living; and so discharged from the obligation of the law, that if *any would not work, neither should he eat.* When he could not go about, he *sat;* if we cannot *work* for God, we must *sit still* quietly for him. When he could not labour, his parents not being able to maintain him, he *begged.* Note, Those who cannot otherwise subsist must not, like the unjust steward, be *ashamed to beg;* let no man be ashamed of anything but sin. There are some common beggars that are objects of charity, that should be distinguished; and we must not let the bees starve for the sake of the drones or wasps that are among them. As to this man, (1.) It was well ordered by Providence that he on whom this miracle was wrought should be a common beggar, and so generally known and remarkable, by which means the truth of the miracle was better attested, and there were more to witness against those infidel Jews who would not believe *that he had been blind* than if he had been maintained in his father's house. (2.) It was the greater instance of Christ's condescension that he seemed (as I may say) to take more pains about the cure of a common beggar than of others. When it was for the advantage of his miracles that they should be wrought on those that were remarkable, he pitched upon those that were made so by their poverty and misery; not by their dignity.

2. In answer to this inquiry, (1.) Some said, *This is he,* the very same man; and these are witnesses to the truth of the miracle, for they had long known him stone-blind. (2.) Others, who could not think it possible that a man born blind should thus on a sudden receive his sight, for that reason, and no other, said, *He is not he, but is like him,* and so, by their confession, if it be he, it is a great miracle that is wrought upon him. Hence we may take occasion to think, [1.] Of the wisdom and power of Providence in ordering such a universal variety of the faces of men and women, so that no two are so alike but that they may be distinguished, which is necessary to society, and commerce, and the administration of justice. And, [2.] Of the wonderful change which the converting grace of God makes upon some who before were very wicked and vile, but are thereby so universally and visibly altered that one would not take them to be the same persons.

3. This controversy was soon decided by the man himself: *He said, I am he,* the very man that so lately sat and begged; "I am he that was blind, and was an object of the charity of men, but now see, and am a monument of the mercy and grace of God." We do not find that the neighbours appealed to him in this matter, but he, hearing the debate, interposed, and put an end to it. It is a piece of justice we owe to our neighbours to rectify their mistakes, and to set things before them, as far as we are able, in a true light. Applying it spiritually, it teaches us that those who are savingly enlightened by the grace of God should be ready to own what they were before that blessed change was wrought, 1 Tim. 1:13, 14.

II. How he came to have his eyes opened, *v.* 10–12. They will now turn aside, and *see this great sight,* and enquire further concerning it. He did not *sound a trumpet* when he did these alms, nor perform his cures *upon a stage;* and yet, like a city upon a hill, they could not be hid. Two things these neighbours enquire after: —

1. The manner of the cure: *How were thine eyes opened?* The works of the Lord being great, they ought to be *sought out,* Ps. 111:2. It is good to observe the way and method of God's works, and they will appear the more wonderful. We may apply it spiritually; it is strange that blind eyes should be opened, but more strange when we consider how they are opened; how weak the means are that are used, and how strong the opposition that is conquered. In answer to this enquiry the poor man gives them a plain and full account of the matter: *A man that is called Jesus made clay, — and I received sight. v.* 11. Note, Those who have experienced special instances of God's power and goodness, in temporal or spiritual things, should be ready upon all occasions to communicate their experiences, for the glory of God and the instruction and encouragement of others. See David's collection of his experiences, his own and others', Ps. 34:4–6. It is a debt we owe to our benefactor, and to our brethren. God's favours are lost *upon* us, when they are lost *with us,* and go no further.

2. The author of it (*v.* 12): *Where is he?* Some perhaps asked this question out of curiosity. "Where is he, that we may see him?" A man that did such cures as these might well be a show, which one would go a good way for the sight of. Others, perhaps, asked out of ill-will. "Where is he, that we may *seize* him?" There was a proclamation out for the discovering and apprehending of him (*ch.* 11:57); and the unthinking crowd, in spite of all reason and equity, will have ill thoughts of those that are put into an ill name. Some, we hope, asked this question out of *good-will.* "Where is he, that we may be acquainted with him? Where is he, that we may come to him, and share in the favours he is so free of?" In answer to this, he could say nothing: *I know not.* As soon as Christ had sent him to the pool of Siloam, it should seem, he withdrew immediately (as he did, *ch.* 5:13), and did not stay till the man returned, as if he either doubted of the effect or waited for the man's thanks. Humble souls take more pleasure in *doing good* than in hearing of it again; it will be time enough to hear of it in the *resurrection of the just.* The man had never seen Jesus, for by the time that he had gained his sight he had lost his Physician; and he asked, it is probable, *Where is he?* None of all the new and surprising objects that presented themselves could be so grateful to him as one sight of Christ, but as yet he knew no more of him than that he was called, and rightly called, *Jesus — a Saviour.* Thus in the work of grace wrought upon the soul we see the change, but see not the hand that makes it; for the way of the Spirit is like that of the wind, which thou hearest the sound of, but canst not tell *whence it comes nor whither it goes.*

Verses 13–34

One would have expected that such a miracle as Christ wrought upon the blind man would have settled his reputation, and silenced and shamed all opposition, but it had the contrary effect; instead of being embraced as a prophet for it, he is prosecuted as a criminal.

I. Here is the information that was given in to the Pharisees concerning this matter: *They brought to the Pharisees him that aforetime was blind, v.* 13. They brought him to the great sanhedrim, which consisted chiefly of Pharisees, at least the Pharisees in the sanhedrim were most active against Christ. 1. Some think that those who brought this man to the Pharisees did it with a *good design,* to show them that this Jesus, whom they persecuted, was not what they represented him, but really a great man, and one that gave considerable proofs of a divine mission. What hath convinced us of the truth and excellency of religion, and hath removed our prejudices against it, we should be forward, as we have opportunity, to offer to others for their conviction. 2. It should seem, rather, that they did it with an *ill design,* to exasperate the Pharisees the more against Christ, and there was no need of this, for they were bitter enough of themselves. They brought him with such a suggestion as that in *ch.* 11:47, 48, *If we let him thus alone, all men will believe on him.* Note, Those rulers that are of a persecuting spirit shall never want ill instruments about them, that will blow the coals, and make them worse.

II. The ground which was pretended for this information, and the colour given to it. That which is good was never maligned but under the imputation of something evil. And the crime objected here (*v.* 14) was that *it was the sabbath day when Jesus made the clay, and opened his eyes.* The profanation of the sabbath day is certainly wicked, and gives a man a very ill character; but the traditions of the Jews had made that to be a violation of the law of the sabbath which was far from being so. Many a time this matter was contested between Christ and the Jews, that it might be settled for the benefit of the church in all ages. But it may be asked, "Why would Christ not only work miracles on the sabbath day, but work them in such a manner as he knew would give offence to the Jews? When he had healed the impotent man, why should he bid him carry his bed? Could he not have cured this blind man without making clay?" I answer, 1. He would not seem to yield to the usurped power of the scribes and Pharisees. Their government was illegal, their impositions were arbitrary, and their zeal for the rituals consumed the substantials of religion; and therefore Christ would not *give place* to them, *by subjection, no not for an hour.* Christ was made under the law of God, but not under their law. 2. He did it that he might, both by word and action, expound the law of the fourth commandment, and vindicate it from their corrupt glosses, and so teach us that a weekly sabbath is to be *perpetually* observed in the church, one day in seven (for what need was there to explain that law, if it must be presently abrogated?) and that it is not to be so *ceremonially* observed by us as it was by the Jews? Works of necessity and mercy are allowed, and the sabbath-rest to be kept, not so much for its own sake as in order to the sabbath-work. 3. Christ chose to work his cures on the sabbath day to dignify and sanctify the day, and to intimate that spiritual cures should be wrought mostly on the Christian sabbath day. How many blind eyes have been opened by the preaching of the gospel, that blessed eye-salve, on the Lord's day! How many impotent souls cured on that day!

III. The trial and examination of this matter by the Pharisees, *v.* 15. So much passion, prejudice, and ill-humour, and so little reason, appear here, that the discourse is nothing but crossing questions. One would think, when a man in these circumstances was brought before them, they would have been so taken up in admiring the miracle, and congratulating the happiness of the poor man, that they could not have been peevish with him. But their enmity to Christ had divested them of all manner of humanity, and divinity too. Let us see how they teased this man.

1. They interrogated him concerning the cure itself.

(1.) They doubted whether he had indeed been *born blind,* and demanded proof of that which even the prosecutors had acknowledged (*v.* 18): They *did not believe,* that is, they would not, that he was *born blind.* Men that seek occasion to quarrel with the clearest truths may find it if they please; and they that resolve to *hold fast deceit* will never want a handle to hold it by. This was not a prudent caution, but a prejudiced infidelity. However, it was a good way that they took for the clearing of this: *They called the parents of the man who had received his sight.* This they did in hopes to disprove the miracle. These parents were poor and timorous, and if they had said that they could not be sure that this was their son, or that it was only some weakness or dimness in his sight that he had been born with, which if they had been able to get help for him might have been cured long since, or had otherwise prevaricated, for fear of the court, the Pharisees had gained their point, had robbed Christ of the honour of this miracle, which would have lessened the reputation of all the rest. But God so ordered and overruled this counsel of theirs that it turned to the more effectual proof of the miracle, and left them under a necessity of being either convinced or confounded. Now in this part of the examination we have,

[1.] The questions that were put to them (*v.* 19): They *asked them* in an imperious threatening way, *"Is this your son?* Dare you swear to it? *Do you say he was born blind?* Are you sure of it? Or did he but pretend to be so, to have an excuse for his begging? *How then doth he now see?* That is impossible, and therefore you had better unsay it." Those who cannot bear the light of truth do all they can to *eclipse* it, and hinder the discovery of it. Thus the *managers of evidence,* or mismanagers rather, lead witnesses out of the way, and teach them how to conceal or disguise the truth, and so involve themselves in a double guilt, like that of Jeroboam, who sinned, and made Israel to sin.

[2.] Their answers to these interrogatories, in which,

First, They fully attest that which they could safely say in this matter; *safely,* that is, upon their own knowledge, and *safely,* that is, without running themselves into a *premunire* (*v.* 20): *We know that this is our son* (for they were daily conversant with him, and had such a natural affection to him as the true mother had, 1 Ki. 3:26, which made them know it was *their own*); and we know that he was *born blind.* They had reason to know it, inasmuch as it had cost them many a sad thought, and many a careful troublesome hour, about him. How often had they looked upon him with grief, and lamented their child's blindness more than all the burdens and inconveniences of their poverty, and wished he had never been born, rather than be born to such an uncomfortable life! Those who are ashamed of their children, or any of their relations, because of their bodily infirmities, may take a reproof from *these* parents, who freely owned, This is *our son,* though he was *born blind,* and lived upon alms.

Secondly, They cautiously decline giving any evidence concerning his cure; partly because they were not themselves eye-witnesses of it, and could say nothing to it *of their own knowledge;* and partly because they found it was a *tender point,* and would not bear to be meddled with. And therefore, having owned that he was *their son* and was *born blind,* further these deponents say not.

a. Observe how warily they express themselves (*v.* 21): *"By what means he now seeth we know not,* or *who has opened his eyes we know not,* otherwise than by *hearsay;* we can give no account either by what means or by whose hand it was done." See how the wisdom of this world teaches men to *trim* the matter in critical junctures. Christ was accused as a sabbath-breaker, and as an imposter. Now these parents of the blind man, though they were not eye-witnesses of the cure, were yet fully assured of it, and were bound in gratitude to have borne their testimony to the honour of the Lord Jesus, who had done their son so great a kindness; but they had not courage to do it, and then thought it might serve to atone for their not appearing in favour of him that they said nothing to his prejudice; whereas, in the day of trial, he that is not *apparently* for Christ is justly looked upon as *really against* him, Lu. 11:23; Mk. 8:38. That they might not be further urged in this matter, they refer themselves and the court to him: *He is of age, ask him, he shall speak for himself.* This implies that while children are not of age (while they are *infants,* such as cannot speak) it is incumbent upon their parents to *speak for them,* speak to God for them in prayer, speak to the church for them in baptism; but, when they are of age, it is fit that they should be asked whether they be willing to stand to that which their parents did for them, and let them speak for themselves. This man, though he was *born blind,* seems to have been of quick understanding above many, which enabled him to speak for himself better than his friends could speak for him. Thus God often by a kind providence makes up in the mind what is wanting in the body, 1 Co. 12:23, 24. His parents turning them over to him was only to save themselves from trouble, and expose him; whereas they that had so great an interest in his *mercies* had reason to embark with him in his *hazards* for the honour of that Jesus who had done so much for them.

b. See the reason why they were so cautious (*v.* 22, 23): *Because they feared the Jews.* It was not because they would put an honour upon their son, by making him his own advocate, or because they would have the matter cleared by the *best hand,* but because they would shift trouble off from themselves, as most people are in care to do, no matter on whom they throw it. Near is my friend, and near is my child, and perhaps near is my religion, but *nearer is myself — Proximus egomet mihi.* But Christianity teaches another lesson, 1 Co. 10:24; Esth. 8:6. Here is,

(*a.*) The *late law* which the sanhedrim had made. It was agreed and enacted by their authority that, if any man within their jurisdiction did *confess* that Jesus *was Christ, he should be put out of the synagogue.* Observe,

[*a.*] The crime designed to be punished, and so prevented, by this statute, and that was embracing Jesus of Nazareth as the promised Messiah, and manifesting this by any overt-act, which amounted to a confessing of him. They themselves did expect a Messiah, but they could by no means bear to think that this Jesus should be he, nor admit the question whether he were or no, for two reasons: — *First,* Because his precepts were all so contrary to their traditional *laws.* The spiritual worship he prescribed overthrew their formalities; nor did any thing more effectually destroy their singularity and narrow-spiritedness than that universal charity which he taught; humility and mortification, repentance and self-denial, were lessons new to them, and sounded harsh and strange in their ears. *Secondly,* Because him promises and appearances were so contrary to their traditional hopes. They expected a Messiah in outward pomp and splendour, that should not only free the nation from the Roman yoke, but advance the grandeur of the sanhedrim, and make all the members of it princes and peers: and now to hear of a Messiah whose outward circumstances were all mean and poor, whose first appearance and principal residence were in Galilee, a despised province, who never made his court to them, nor sought their favour, whose followers were neither swordmen nor gown-men, nor any men of honour, but contemptible fishermen, who proposed and promised no redemption but from sin, no consolation of Israel but what is spiritual and divine, and at the same time bade his followers expect the cross, and count upon persecution; this was such a reproach to all the ideas they had formed and filled the minds of their people with, such a blow to their power and interest, and such a disappointment to all their hopes, that they could never be reconciled to it, nor so much as give it a fair or patient hearing, but, right or wrong, it must be *crushed.*

[*b.*] The penalty to be inflicted for this crime. If any should own himself a disciple of Jesus, he should be deemed and taken as an apostate from the faith of the Jewish church, and a rebel and traitor against the government of it, and should therefore be *put out of the synagogue,* as one that had rendered himself unworthy of the honours, and incapable of the privileges, of their church; he should be excommunicated, and expelled the commonwealth of Israel. Nor was this merely an ecclesiastical censure, which a man that made no conscience of their authority might slight, but it was, in effect, an *outlawry,* which excluded a man from civil commerce and deprived him of his liberty and property. Note, *First,* Christ's holy religion, from its first rise, has been opposed by penal laws made against the professors of it; as if men's consciences would otherwise *naturally* embrace it, this unnatural force has been put upon them. *Secondly,* The church's artillery, when the command of it has fallen into ill hands, has often been turned against itself, and ecclesiastical censures have been made to serve a carnal secular interest. It is no new thing to see those cast out of the synagogue that were the greatest ornaments and blessings of it, and to hear those that expelled them say, *The Lord be glorified,* Isa. 66:5. Now of this edict it is said, 1. That the Jews had agreed it, or *conspired* it. Their consultation and communion herein were a perfect conspiracy against the crown and dignity of the Redeemer, against the Lord and his Anointed. 2. That they had already agreed it. Though he had been but a few months in any public character among them, and, one would think, in so short a time could not have made them jealous of him, yet thus early were they aware of his growing interest, and already agreed to do their utmost to suppress it. He had lately made his escape out of the temple, and, when they saw themselves baffled in their attempts to take him, they presently took this course, to make it penal for any body to own him. Thus unanimous and thus expeditious are the enemies of the church, and their counsels; but he that *sits in heaven laughs at them,* and *has them in derision,* and so may we.

(*b.*) The influence which this law had upon the parents of the blind man. They declined saying any thing of Christ, and shuffled it off to their son, *because they feared the Jews.* Christ had incurred the frowns of the government to do their son a kindness, but they would not incur them to do him any honour. Note, *The fear of man brings a snare* (Prov. 29:25), and often makes people deny and disown Christ, and his truths and ways, and act against their consciences. Well, the parents have thus disentangled themselves, and are discharged from any further attendance; let us now go on with the examination of the man himself; the doubt of the Pharisees, whether he was *born blind,* was put out of doubt *by them;* and therefore,

(2.) They enquired of *him* concerning the *manner of the cure,* and made their remarks upon it, *v.* 15, 16.

[1.] The same question which his neighbours had put to him *now again the Pharisees asked him, how he had received his sight.* This they enquired not with any sincere desire to find out the truth, by tracing the report to the original, but with a desire to find an occasion against Christ; for, if the man should relate the matter fully, they would prove Christ a sabbath-breaker; if he should vary from his former story, they would have some colour to suspect the whole to be a collusion.

[2.] The same answer, in effect, which he had before given to his neighbours, he here repeats to the Pharisees: *He put clay upon mine eyes, and I washed, and do see.* He does not here speak of the making of the clay, for indeed he had not seen it made. That circumstance was not essential, and might give the Pharisees most occasion against him, and therefore he waives it. In the former account he said, *I washed, and received sight;* but lest they should think it was only a glimpse for the present, which a heated imagination might fancy itself to have, he now says, *"I do see:* it is a complete and lasting cure."

[3.] The remarks made upon this story were very different, and occasioned a debate in the court, *v.* 16.

First, Some took this occasion to censure and condemn Christ for what he had done. Some of the Pharisees said, *This man is not of God,* as he pretends, *because he keepeth not the sabbath day.* 1. The doctrine upon which this censure is grounded is very true — that those *are not of God* — those pretenders to prophecy not *sent of God,* those pretenders to saintship not *born of God* — who do not *keep the sabbath day.* Those that are of God will *keep the commandments of God;* and this is his commandment, that we sanctify the sabbath. Those that are of God keep up communion with God, and delight to hear from him, and speak to him, and therefore will observe the sabbath, which is a day appointed for intercourse with heaven. The sabbath is called a *sign,* for the sanctifying of it is a sign of a sanctified heart, and the profaning of it a sign of a profane heart. But, 2. The application of it to our Saviour is very unjust, for he did religiously observe the sabbath day, and never in any instance violated it, never did otherwise than *well* on the sabbath day. He did not keep the sabbath according to the tradition of the elders and the superstitious observances of the Pharisees, but he kept it according to the command of God, and therefore, no doubt, he was of God, and his miracles proved him to be *Lord also of the sabbath day.* Note, much unrighteous and uncharitable judging is occasioned by men's making the rules of religion more strict than God has made them, and adding their own fancies to God's appointments, as the Jews here, in the case of sabbath-sanctification. We ourselves may forbear such and such things, on the sabbath day, as we find a distraction to us, and we do well, but we must not therefore tie up others to the same strictness. Every thing that we take for a rule of practice must not presently be made a rule of judgment.

Secondly, Others spoke in his favour, and very pertinently urged, *How can a man that is a sinner do such miracles?* It seems that even in this *council of the ungodly* there were some that were capable of a *free thought,* and were witnesses for Christ, even in the midst of his enemies. The matter of fact was plain, that this was a true miracle, the more it was searched into the more it was cleared; and this brought his former similar works to mind, and gave occasion to speak magnificently of them, *toiauta sēmeia — such great signs,* so many, so evident. And the inference from it is very natural: Such things as these could never be done by a *man that is a sinner,* that is, not by any mere man, in his own name, and by his own power; or, rather, not by one that is a cheat or an imposter, and in that sense a a sinner; such a one may indeed show some *signs and lying wonders,* but not such signs and true wonders as Christ wrought. How could a man produce such divine credentials, if he had not a divine commission? Thus there was a *division among them, a schism,* so the word is; they clashed in their opinion, a warm debate arose, and the *house divided* upon it. Thus God defeats the counsels of his enemies by dividing them; and by such testimonies as these given against the malice of persecutors, and the rubs they meet with, their designs against the church are sometimes rendered ineffectual and always inexcusable.

2. After their enquiry concerning the cure, we must observe their enquiry concerning the *author* of it. And here observe,

(1.) What the man said of him, in answer to their enquiry. They ask him (*v.* 17), "*What sayest thou of him, seeing that he has opened thine eyes?* What dost thou think of his doing this? And what idea hast thou of him that did it?" If he should speak *slightly* of Christ, in answer to this, as he might be tempted to do, to please them, now that he was in their hands, as his parents had done — if he should say, "I know not what to make of him; he may be a conjuror for aught I know, or some mountebank" — they would have triumphed in it. Nothing confirms Christ's enemies in their enmity to him so much as the slights put upon him by those that have passed for his friends. But, if he should speak honourably of Christ, they would prosecute him upon their new law, which did not except, no, not his own patient; they would make him an example, and so deter others from applying to Christ for cures, for which, though they came cheap from Christ, yet they would make them pay dearly. Or perhaps Christ's friends proposed to have the man's own sentiments concerning his physician, and were willing to know, since he appeared to be a sensible man, what he thought of him. Note, Those whose eyes Christ has opened know best what to say of him, and have great reason, upon all occasions, to say well of him. What think we of Christ? To this question the poor man makes a short, plain, and direct answer: "*He is a prophet,* he is one inspired and sent of God to preach, and work miracles, and deliver to the world a divine message." There had been no prophets among the Jews for three hundred years; yet they did not conclude that they should have no more, for they knew that he was yet to come who should *seal up vision and prophecy,* Dan. 9:24. It should seem, this man had not any thoughts that Christ was the Messiah, the great prophet, but one of the same rank with the other prophets. The woman of Samaria concluded he was *a prophet* before she had any thought of his being the Messiah (*ch.* 4:19); so this blind man thought well of Christ according to the light he had, though he did not think well enough of him; but, being faithful in what he had already attained to, God revealed even *that* unto him. This poor blind beggar had a clearer judgment of the things pertaining to the kingdom of God, and saw further into the proofs of a divine mission, than the *masters in Israel,* that assumed an authority to judge of prophets.

(2.) What they said of him, in reply to the man's testimony. Having in vain attempted to invalidate the evidence of the fact, and finding that indeed a *notable miracle was wrought,* and they *could not deny it,* they renew their attempt to banter it, and run it down, and do all they can to shake the good opinion the man had of him that opened his eyes, and to convince him that Christ was a bad man (*v.* 24): *Give God the praise, we know that this man is a sinner.* Two ways this is understood: [1.] By way of *advice,* to take heed of ascribing the praise of his cure to a sinful man, but to give it all to God, to whom it was due. Thus, under colour of zeal for the honour of God, they rob Christ of his honour, as those do who will not worship Christ as God, under pretence of zeal for this great truth, that there is but one God to be worshipped; whereas this is his declared will, that all men should *honour the Son even as they honour the Father;* and in confessing that Christ is Lord we *give glory to God the Father.* When God makes use of men that are sinners as instruments of good to us, we must *give God the glory,* for every creature

is that to us which he makes it to be; and yet there is gratitude owing to the instruments. It was a good word, *Give God the praise,* but here it was ill used; and there seems to be this further in it, "This man is a *sinner,* a *bad man,* and therefore give the praise so much the more to God, who could work by such an instrument." [2.] By way of *adjuration;* so some take it. "We know (though thou dost not, who hast but lately come, as it were, into a new world) that this man is a *sinner,* a great impostor, and cheats the country; this we are sure of, therefore *give God praise*" (as Joshua said to Achan) "by making an ingenuous confession of the fraud and collusion which we are confident there is in this matter; in God's name, man, tell the truth." Thus is God's name abused in papal inquisitions, when by oaths, *ex officio,* they extort accusations of *themselves* from the *innocent,* and of *others* from the *ignorant.* See how basely they speak of the Lord Jesus: *We know that this man is a sinner,* is a man of sin. In which we may observe, *First,* Their insolence and pride. They would not have it thought, when they asked the man what he thought of him, that they needed information; nay, they know very well that he is a sinner, and nobody can convince them of the contrary. He had challenged them to their faces (*ch.* 8:46) to *convince him of sin,* and they had nothing to say; but now behind his back they speak of him as a malefactor, convicted upon the notorious evidence of the fact. Thus false accusers make up in confidence what is wanting in proof. *Secondly,* The injury and indignity hereby done to the Lord Jesus. When he became man, he took upon him the form not only of a *servant,* but of a *sinner* (Rom. 8:3), and passed for a sinner in common with the rest of mankind. Nay, he was represented as a sinner of the first magnitude, a sinner above all men; and, being *made sin for us,* he despised even this shame.

3. The debate that arose between the Pharisees and this poor man concerning Christ. They say, *He is a sinner;* he says, *He is a prophet.* As it is an encouragement to those who are concerned for the cause of Christ to hope that it shall never be lost for want of witnesses, when they find a poor blind beggar picked up from the way-side, and made a witness for Christ, to the faces of his most impudent enemies; so it is an encouragement to those who are called out to witness for Christ to find with what prudence and courage this man managed his defence, according to the promise, *It shall be given you in that same hour what you shall speak.* Though he had never seen Jesus, he had felt his grace. Now in the parley between the Pharisees and this poor man we may observe three steps: —

(1.) He sticks to the certain matter of fact the evidence of which they endeavour to shake. That which is doubtful is best resolved into that which is plain, and therefore, [1.] He adheres to that which to himself at least, and to his own satisfaction, was past dispute (*v.* 25): *"Whether he be a sinner or no I know not,* I will not now stand to dispute, nor need I, the matter is plain, and though I should altogether hold my peace would speak for itself;" or, as it might better be rendered, "*If he be a sinner, I know it not,* I see no reason to say so, but the contrary; for this *one thing I know,* and can be more sure of than you can be of that of which you are so confident, *that whereas I was blind, now I see,* and therefore must not only say that he has been a good friend to me, but that he is a *prophet;* I am both able and bound to speak well of him." Now here, *First,* He tacitly reproves their great assurance of the ill character they gave of the blessed Jesus: "You say that you *know* him to be a *sinner;* I, who know him as well as you do, cannot give any such character." *Secondly,* He boldly relies upon his own experience of the power and goodness of the holy Jesus, and resolves to abide by it. There is no disputing against experience, nor arguing a man out of his senses; here is one that is properly an eyewitness of the power and grace of Christ, though he had never seen him. Note, As Christ's mercies are most valued by those that have felt the want of them, that have been blind and now see, so the most powerful and durable affections to Christ are those that arise from an experimental knowledge of him, 1 Jn. 1:1; Acts 4:20. The poor man does not here give a nice account of the method of the cure, nor pretend to describe it *philosophically,* but in short, *Whereas I was blind, now I see.* Thus in the work of grace in the soul, though we cannot tell when and how, by what instruments and by what steps and advances, the blessed change was wrought, yet we may take the comfort of it if we can say, through grace, "*Whereas I was blind, now I see.* I did live a carnal, worldly, sensual life,

but, thanks be to God, it is now otherwise with me," Eph. 5:8. [2.] They endeavour to baffle and stifle the evidence by a needless repetition of their enquiries into it (*v.* 26): *What did he to thee? How opened he thine eyes?* They asked these questions, *First,* Because they wanted something to say, and would rather speak *impertinently* than seem to be silenced or run a-ground. Thus eager disputants, that resolve they will have the last word, by such vain repetitions, to avoid the shame of being silenced, make themselves accountable for many idle words. *Secondly,* Because they hoped, by putting the man upon repeating his evidence, to catch him tripping in it, or wavering, and then they would think they had gained a good point.

(2.) He upbraids them with their obstinate infidelity and invincible prejudices, and they revile him as a disciple of Jesus, *v.* 27–29, where the man is more bold with them and they are more sharp upon him than before.

[1.] The man boldly upbraids them with their wilful and unreasonable opposition to the evidence of this miracle, *v.* 27. He would not gratify them with a repetition of the story, but bravely replied, *I have told you already, and you did not hear, wherefore would you hear it again, will you also be his disciples?* Some think that he spoke *seriously,* and really expecting that they would be convinced. "He had many disciples, I will be one, will you also come in among them?" Some zealous young Christians see so much reason for religion that they are ready to think every one will presently be on their mind. But it rather seems to be spoken *ironically:* "*Will you be his disciples?* No, I know you abhor the thoughts of it; why then should you desire to hear that which will either make you his disciples or leave you inexcusable if you be not?" Those that wilfully shut their eyes against the light, as these Pharisees here did, *First,* Make themselves contemptible and base, as these here did, who were justly exposed by this poor man for denying the conclusion, when they had nothing to object against either of the premises. *Secondly,* They forfeit all the benefit of further instructions and means of knowledge and conviction: they that have been told once, and *would not hear,* why should they be told it again? Jer. 51:9. See Mt. 10:14. *Thirdly,* They hereby *receive the grace of God in vain.* This implied in that, *"Will you be his disciples?* No, you resolve you will not; why then would you hear it again, only that you may be his accusers and persecutors?" Those who will not see cause to embrace Christ, and join with his followers, yet, one would think, should see cause enough not to hate and persecute him and them.

[2.] For this they scorn and revile him, *v.* 28. When they could not resist the wisdom and spirit by which he spoke, they broke out into a passion, and scolded him, began to call names, and give him ill language. See what Christ's faithful witnesses must expect from the adversaries of his truth and cause; let them count upon *all manner of evil* to be said of them, Mt. 5:11. The method commonly taken by unreasonable man is to make out with railing what is wanting in truth and reason.

First, They taunted this man for his affection to Christ; they said, *Thou art his disciple,* as if that were reproach enough, and they could not say worse of him. "We scorn to be his disciples, and will leave that preferment to thee, and such scoundrels as thou art." They do what they can to put Christ's religion in an ill name, and to represent the profession of it as a contemptible scandalous thing. They *reviled him.* The Vulgate reads it, *maledixerunt eum — they cursed him;* and what was their curse? It was this, *Be thou his disciple.* "May such a curse" (saith St. Augustine here) "ever be on us and on our children!" If we take our measures of credit and disgrace from the sentiment or rather clamours of a blind deluded world, we shall *glory in our shame,* and be *ashamed of our glory.* They had no reason to call this man a *disciple* of Christ, he had neither seen him nor heard him preach, only he had spoken favourably of a kindness Christ had done him, and this they could not bear.

Secondly, They gloried in their relation to Moses as their Master: *"We are Moses's disciples,* and do not either need or desire any other teacher." Note, 1. Carnal professors of religion are very apt to trust to, and be proud of, the dignities and privileges of their profession, while they are strangers to the principles and powers of their religion. These Pharisees had before boasted of their good parentage: *We are Abraham's seed;* here they boast of their good education, *We are Moses's disciples;* as if these would save them. 2. It is sad to see how much one part of religion is opposed, under colour of zeal for another part. There was a perfect harmony between Christ and Moses; Moses prepared for Christ, and Christ perfected Moses, so that they might be disciples of Moses, and become the disciples of Christ too; and yet they here put them in opposition, nor could they have persecuted Christ but under the shelter of the abused name of Moses. Thus those who gainsay the doctrine of free grace value themselves as promoters of man's duty, *We are Moses's disciples;* while, on the other hand, those that cancel the obligation of the law value themselves as the assertors of free grace, and as if none were the disciples of Jesus but they; whereas, if we rightly understand the matter, we shall see God's grace and man's duty meet together and kiss and befriend each other.

Thirdly, They gave some sort of reason for their adhering to Moses against Christ (*v.* 29): *We know that God spoke unto Moses; as for this fellow, we know not whence he is.* But did they not know that among other things which God spoke unto Moses this was one, that they must expect another prophet, and further revelation of the mind of God? yet, when our Lord Jesus, pursuant to what God said to Moses, did appear, and gave sufficient proofs of his being that prophet, under pretence of sticking to the old religion, and the established church, they not only forfeited, but forsook, their own mercies. In this argument of their observe, 1. How impertinently they allege, in defence of their enmity to Christ, that which none of his followers ever denied: *We know that God spoke unto Moses,* and, thanks be to God, we know it too, more plainly to Moses than to any other of the prophets; but what then? God spoke to Moses, and does it therefore follow that Jesus is an impostor? Moses was a prophet also? Moses spoke honourably of Jesus (*ch.* 5:46), and Jesus spoke honourably of Moses (Lu. 16:29); they were both faithful in the same house of God, Moses as a servant, Christ as a Son; therefore their pleading Moses' divine warrant in opposition to Christ's was an artifice, to make unthinking people believe it was as certain that Jesus was a false prophet as that Moses was a true one; whereas they were both true. 2. How absurdly they urge their ignorance of Christ as a reason to justify their contempt of him: *As for this fellow.* Thus scornfully do they speak of the blessed Jesus, as if they did not think it worth while to charge their memories with a name so inconsiderable; they express themselves with as much disdain of the Shepherd of Israel as if he had not been worthy to be *set with the dogs of their flock: As for this fellow,* this sorry fellow, *we know not whence he is.* They looked upon themselves to have the key of knowledge, that none must preach without a license first had and obtained from them, under the seal of their court. They expected that all who set up for teachers should apply to them, and give them satisfaction, which this Jesus had never done, never so far owned their power as to ask their leave, and therefore they concluded him an intruder, and one that came not in by the door: *They knew not whence* nor what *he was,* and therefore concluded him a *sinner;* whereas those we know little of we should judge charitably of; but proud and narrow souls will think none good but themselves, and those that are in their interest. It was not long ago that the Jews had made the contrary to this an objection against Christ (*ch.* 7:27): *We know this man whence he is, but when Christ comes no man knows whence he is.* Thus they could with the greatest assurance either affirm or deny the same thing, according as they saw it would serve their turn. They *knew not whence he was;* and whose fault was that? (1.) It is certain that they ought to have enquired. The Messiah was to appear about this time, and it concerned them to look about them, and examine every indication; but these priests, like those, Jer. 2:6, *said not, Where is the Lord?* (2.) It is certain that they might have known whence he was, might not only have known, by searching the register, that he was born in Bethlehem; but by enquiring into his doctrine, miracles, and conversation, they might have known that he was sent of God, and had better orders, a better commission, and far better instructions, than any they could give him. See the absurdity of infidelity. Men will not know the doctrine of Christ because they are resolved they will not believe it, and then pretend they do not believe it because they do not know it. Such ignorance and unbelief, which support one another, aggravate one another.

(3.) He reasons with them concerning this matter, and they excommunicate him.

[1.] The poor man, finding that he had reason on his side, which they could not answer, grows more bold, and, in prosecution of his argument, is very close upon them.

First, He wonders at their obstinate infidelity (*v.* 30); not at all daunted by their frowns, nor shaken by their confidence, he bravely answered, *"Why, herein is a marvelous thing,* the strangest instance of wilful ignorance that ever was heard of among men that pretend to sense, that *you know not whence he is,* and yet he has opened mine eyes." Two things he wonders at: — 1. That they should be strangers to a man so *famous.* He that could open the eyes of the blind must certainly be a considerable man, and worth taking notice of. The Pharisees were inquisitive men, had a large correspondence and acquaintance, thought themselves the eyes of the church and its watchmen, and yet that they should talk as if they thought it below them to take cognizance of such a man as this, and have conversation with him, this is a strange thing indeed. There are many who pass for learned and knowing men, who understand business, and can talk sensibly in other things, who yet are ignorant, to a wonder, of the doctrine of Christ, who have no concern, no, not so much as a curiosity, to acquaint themselves with that which the *angels desire to look into.* 2. That they should question the divine mission of one that had undoubtedly wrought a divine miracle. When they said, *We know not whence he is,* they meant, "We know not any proof that his doctrine and ministry are from heaven." "Now this is strange," saith the poor man, "that the miracle wrought upon me has not convinced you, and put the matter out of doubt, — that you, whose education and studies give you advantages above others of discerning the things of God, should thus shut your eyes against the light." It is a *marvelous work and wonder, when the wisdom of the wise thus perisheth* (Isa. 29:14), that they deny the truth of that of which they cannot gainsay the evidence. Note, (1.) The unbelief of those who enjoy the means of knowledge and conviction is indeed a marvelous thing, Mk. 6:6. (2.) Those who have themselves experienced the power and grace of the Lord Jesus do especially wonder at the wilfulness of those who reject him, and, having such good thoughts of him themselves, are amazed that others have not. Had Christ opened the eyes of the Pharisees, they would not have doubted his being a prophet.

Secondly, He argues strongly against them, *v.* 31–33. They had determined concerning Jesus that he was not of God (*v.* 16), but was a *sinner* (*v.* 24), in answer to which the man here proves not only that he was *not a sinner* (*v.* 31), but that he was *of God, v.* 33.

a. He argues here, (*a.*) With great knowledge. Though he could not read a letter of the book, he was well acquainted with the scripture and the things of God; he had wanted the sense of seeing, yet had well improved that of hearing, by which faith cometh; yet this would not have served him if he had not had an extraordinary presence of God with him, and special aids of his Spirit, upon this occasion. (*b.*) With great zeal for the honour of Christ, whom he could not endure to hear run down, and evil spoken of. (*c.*) With great boldness, and courage, and undauntedness, not terrified by the proudest of his adversaries. Those that are ambitious of the favours of God must not be afraid of the frowns of men. "See here," saith Dr. Whitby, "a blind man and unlearned judging more rightly of divine things than the whole learned council of the Pharisees, whence we learn that we are not always to be led by the authority of councils, popes, or bishops; and that it is not absurd for laymen sometimes to vary from their opinions, these overseers being sometimes guilty of great oversights."

b. His argument may be reduced into form, somewhat like that of David, Ps. 66:18–20. The proposition in David's argument is, *If I regard iniquity in my heart, God will not hear me;* here it is to the same purport, *God heareth not sinners:* the assumption there is, *But verily God hath heard me;* here it is, Verily God hath heard Jesus, he hath been honoured with the doing of that which was never done before: the conclusion there is to the honour, *Blessed be God;* here to the honour of the Lord Jesus, He is *of God.*

(*a.*) He lays it down for an undoubted truth that none but good men are the favourites of heaven (*v.* 31): *Now we know,* you know it as well as I, *that God heareth not sinners;* but *if any man be a worshipper of God, and does his will, him he heareth.* Here,

[*a.*] The assertions, rightly understood, are true. *First,* Be it spoken to the terror of the wicked, *God heareth not sinners,* that is, such sinners as the Pharisees meant when they said of Christ, *He is a sinner,* one that, under the shelter of God's name, advanced the devil's interest. This bespeaks no discouragement to repenting returning sinners, but to those that go on still in their trespasses, that make their prayers not only consistent with, but subservient to, their sins, as the hypocrites do; God will not *hear* them, he will not own them, nor give an answer of peace to their prayers. *Secondly,* Be it spoken to the comfort of the righteous, *If any man be a worshipper of God, and does his will, him he heareth.* Here is, 1. The complete character of a good man: he is one that *worships God,* and *does his will;* he is constant in his devotions at set times, and regular in his conversation at all times. He is one that makes it his business to glorify his Creator by the solemn adoration of his name and a sincere obedience to his will and law; both must go together. 2. The unspeakable comfort of such a man: him *God hears;* hears his complaints, and relieves him; hears his appeals, and rights him; hears his praises, and accepts them; hears his prayers, and answers them, Ps. 34:15.

[*b.*] The application of these truths is very pertinent to prove that he, at whose word such a divine power was put forth as cured one born blind, was not a bad man, but, having manifestly such an interest in the holy God as that he *heard him always* (*ch.* 9:41, 42), was certainly a holy one.

(*b.*) He magnifies the miracles which Christ had wrought, to strengthen the argument the more (*v.* 32): *Since the world began was it not heard that any man opened the eyes of one that was born blind.* This is to show either, [*a.*] That it was a true miracle, and above the power of nature; it was never heard that any man, by the use of natural means, had cured one that was *born blind;* no doubt, this man and his parents had been very inquisitive into cases of this nature, whether any such had been helped, and could hear of none, which enabled him to speak this with the more assurance. Or, [*b.*] That it was an extraordinary miracle, and beyond the precedents of former miracles; neither Moses nor any of the prophets, though they did great things, ever did such things as this, wherein divine power and divine goodness seem to strive which should outshine. Moses wrought miraculous plagues, but Christ wrought miraculous cures. Note, *First,* The wondrous works of the Lord Jesus were such as the like had never been done before. *Secondly,* It becomes those who have received mercy from God to magnify the mercies they have received, and to speak honourably of them; not that thereby glory may redound to themselves, and they may seem to be extraordinary favourites of Heaven, but that God may have so much the more glory.

(*c.*) He therefore concludes, *If this man were not of God, he could no nothing,* that is, nothing extraordinary, no such thing as *this;* and therefore, no doubt, he is *of God,* notwithstanding his nonconformity to your traditions in the business of the sabbath day. Note, What Christ did on earth sufficiently demonstrated what he was in heaven; for, if he had not been sent of God, he could not have wrought such miracles. It is true the man of sin comes with *lying wonders,* but not with real miracles; it is likewise supposed that a false prophet might, by divine permission, give a *sign or a wonder* (Deu. 13:1, 2), yet the case is so put as that it would carry with it its own confutation, for it is to enforce a temptation to serve other gods, which was to set God *against himself.* It is true, likewise, that many wicked people have in Christ's name done many wonderful works, which did not prove those that wrought them to be of God, but him in whose name they were wrought. We may each of us know by this whether we are of God or no: *What do we?* What do we for God, for our souls, in working out our salvation? What do we more than others?

[2.] The Pharisees, finding themselves unable either to answer his reasonings or to bear them, fell foul upon him, and with a great deal of pride and passion broke off the discourse, *v.* 34. Here we are told,

First, What they *said.* Having nothing to reply to his argument, they reflected upon his person: *Thou wast altogether born in sin, and dost thou teach us?* They take that amiss which they had reason to take kindly, and are cut to the heart with rage by that which should have pricked them to the heart with penitence. Observe, 1. How they despised him, and what a severe censure they passed upon him: *"Thou wast not only born in sin,* as every man is, but altogether so, wholly corrupt, and bearing about with thee in thy body as well as in thy soul the marks of that corruption; thou wast one whom nature *stigmatized."* Had he still continued blind, it had been barbarous to upbraid him with it, and thence to gather that he was more deeply tainted with sin than other people; but it was most unjust to take notice of it now that the cure had not only rolled away the reproach of his blindness, but had *signalized* him as a favourite of Heaven. Some take it thus: "Thou hast been a common beggar, and such are too often common sinners, and thou hast, no doubt, been as bad as any of them;" whereas by his discourse he had proved the contrary, and had evinced a deep tincture of piety. But when proud imperious Pharisees resolve to run a man down, any thing shall serve for a pretence. 2. How they *disdain* to learn of him, or to receive instruction from him: *Dost thou teach us?* A mighty emphasis must be laid here upon *thou* and *us.* "What! wilt *thou,* a silly sorry fellow, ignorant and illiterate, that hast not seen the light of the sun a day to an end, a beggar by the way-side, of the very dregs and refuse of the town, wilt thou pretend to teach *us,* that are the sages of the law and grandees of the church, that sit in Moses's chair and are masters in Israel?" Note, Proud men scorn to be taught, especially by their inferiors, whereas we should never think ourselves too old, nor too wise, nor too good, to learn. Those that have much wealth would have more; and why not those that have much knowledge? And those are to be valued by whom we may improve in learning. What a poor excuse was this for the Pharisees' infidelity, that it would be a disparagement to them to be instructed, and informed, and convinced, by such a silly fellow as this!

Secondly, What they did: They *cast him out.* Some understand it only of a rude and scornful dismission of him from their council-board; they turned him out of the room by head and shoulders, and perhaps ordered their servants to kick him; they thought it was time to send *him* far enough who came so near their consciences. But it seems rather to be a judicial act; they excommunicated him, probably with the highest degree of excommunication; they cut him off from being a member of the church of Israel. "This poor man," says Dr. Lightfoot, "was the first confessor, as John Baptist was the first martyr, of the Christian church." There was a law made that if any confessed Jesus to be the Christ he should be *cast out of the synagogue, v.* 22. But this man had only said of Jesus that he was a prophet, was *of God:* and yet they stretch the law to bring him under the lash of it, as if he had confessed him to be the Christ. To be justly excommunicated and cast out of a pure church, *clave non errante — when the key commits no error,* it is a very dreadful thing; for what is so bound on earth is bound in heaven; but to be cast out of a corrupt church (which it is our duty to go out of) and that unjustly, though cast out with an *anathema,* and all the bug-bear ceremonies of bell, book, and candle, is what we have no reason at all to dread or be aggrieved at. *The curse causeless shall not come.* If they cast Christ's followers out of their synagogues, as he foretels (*ch.* 16:2), there is no harm done, when they are become *synagogues of Satan.*

Verses 35–38

In these verses we may observe,

I. The tender care which our Lord Jesus took of this poor man (*v.* 35): *When Jesus heard that they had cast him out* (for it is likely the town rang of it, and everybody cried out shame upon them for it), then he *found him,* which implies his seeking him and looking after him, that he might encourage and comfort him, 1. Because he had, to the best of his knowledge, spoken so very well, so bravely, so boldly, in defence of the Lord Jesus. Note, Jesus Christ will be sure to stand by his witnesses, and own those that own him and his truth and ways. Earthly princes neither do, nor can, take cognizance of all that vindicate them and their government and administration; but our Lord Jesus knows and observes all the faithful testimonies we bear to him at any time, and a book of remembrance is written, and it shall redound not only to our credit hereafter, but our comfort now. 2. Because the Pharisees had cast him out and abused him. Besides the common regard which the righteous Judge of the world has to those who suffer wrongfully (Ps. 103:6), there is a particular notice taken of those that suffer in the cause of Christ and for the testimony of a good conscience. Here was one poor man suffering for Christ, and he took care that as his afflictions abounded his consolations should *much more abound.* Note, (1.) Though persecutors may exclude good men from their communion, yet they cannot exclude them from communion with Christ, nor put them out of the way of his visits. Happy are they who have a friend from whom men can-

not debar them. (2.) Jesus Christ will graciously find and receive those who for his sake are unjustly rejected and cast out by men. He will be a hiding place to his outcasts, and appear, to the joy of those whom their brethren hated and cast out.

II. The comfortable converse Christ had with him, wherein he brings him acquainted with the consolation of Israel. He had well improved the knowledge he had, and now Christ gives him further instruction; for he that is faithful in a little shall be entrusted with more, Mt. 13:12.

1. Our Lord Jesus examines his faith: *"Dost thou believe on the Son of God?* Dost thou give credit to the promises of the Messiah? Dost thou expect his coming, and art thou ready to receive and embrace him when he is manifested to thee?" This was that faith of the Son of God by which the saints lived before his manifestation. Observe, (1.) The Messiah is here called the *Son of God,* and so the Jews had learned to call him from the prophecies, Ps. 2:7; 89:27. See *ch.* 1:49, *Thou art the Son of God,* that is, the true Messiah. Those that expected the temporal kingdom of the Messiah delighted rather in calling him the *Son of David,* which gave more countenance to that expectation, Mt. 22:42. But Christ, that he might give us an idea of his kingdom, as purely spiritual and divine, calls himself the *Son of God,* and rather *Son of man* in general than of David in particular. (2.) The desires and expectations of the Messiah, which the Old-Testament saints had, guided by and grounded upon the promise, were graciously interpreted and accepted as their believing on the *Son of God.* This faith Christ here enquires after: *Dost thou believe?* Note, The great thing which is now required of us (1 Jn. 3:23), and which will shortly be enquired after concerning us, is our *believing on the Son of God,* and by this we must stand or fall for ever.

2. The poor man solicitously enquires concerning the Messiah he was to believe in, professing his readiness to embrace him and close with him (*v.* 36): *Who is he, Lord, that I may believe on him?* (1.) Some think he did know that Jesus, who cured him, was the Son of God, but did not know which was Jesus, and therefore, supposing this person that talked with him to be a follower of Jesus, desired him to do him the favour to direct him to his master; not that he might satisfy his curiosity with the sight of him, but that he might the more firmly believe in him, and profess his faith, and *know whom he had believed.* See Cant. 5:6, 7; 3:2, 3. It is Christ only that can direct us to himself. (2.) Others think he did know that this person who talked with him was Jesus, the same that cured him, whom he believed a great and good man and a prophet, but did not yet know that he was the Son of God and the true Messiah. "Lord, I believe there is a Christ to come; thou who hast given me bodily sight, tell me, O tell me, who and where this Son of God is." Christ's question intimated that the Messiah was come, and was now among them, which he presently takes the hint of, and asks, *Where is he, Lord?* The question was rational and just: *Who is he, Lord, that I may believe on him?* For how could he believe in one of whom he had not heard; the work of ministers is to tell us *who the Son of God is,* that we may believe on him, *ch.* 20:31.

3. Our Lord Jesus graciously reveals himself to him as that Son of God on whom he must believe: *Thou hast both seen him, and it is he that talketh with thee, v.* 37. Thou needest not go far to find out the Son of God, *Behold the Word is nigh thee.* We do not find that Christ did thus expressly, and in so many words, reveal himself to any other as to this man here and to the woman of *Samaria: I that speak unto thee am he.* He left others to find out by arguments who he was, but to these weak and foolish things of the world he chose to manifest himself, so as not to the *wise and prudent.* Christ here describes himself to this man by two things, which express his great favour to him: — (1.) *Thou hast seen him;* and he was much indebted to the Lord Jesus for opening his eyes, that he might see him. Now he was made sensible, more than ever, what an unspeakable mercy it was to be cured of his blindness, that he might see the Son of God, a sight which rejoiced his heart more than that of the *light of this world.* Note, The Greatest comfort of bodily eyesight is its serviceableness to our faith and the interests of our souls. How contentedly might this man have returned to his former blindness, like old Simeon, now that his eyes had *seen God's salvation!* If we apply this to the opening of the eyes of the mind, it intimates that spiritual sight is given principally for this end, that we may see Christ, 2 Co. 4:6. Can we say that by faith

we have seen Christ, seen him in his beauty and glory, in his ability and willingness to save, so seen him as to be satisfied concerning him, to be satisfied in him? Let us give him the praise, who opened our eyes. (2.) *It is he that talketh with thee;* and he was indebted to Christ for condescending to do this. He was not only favoured with a sight of Christ, but was admitted into fellowship and communion with him. Great princes are willing to be *seen* by those whom yet they will not vouchsafe to *talk with.* But Christ, by his word and Spirit, talks with those whose desires are towards him, and in talking with them manifests himself to them, as he did to the two disciples, when he talked their hearts warm, Lu. 24:32. Observe, This poor man was solicitously enquiring after the Saviour, when at the same time he saw him, and was talking with him. Note, Jesus Christ is often nearer the souls that seek him than they themselves are aware of. Doubting Christians are sometimes saying, *Where is the Lord?* and fearing that they are cast out from his sight when at the same time it is he that *talks with them,* and *puts strength into them.*

4. The poor man readily entertains this surprising revelation, and, in a transport of joy and wonder, he said, Lord, *I believe, and he worshipped him.* (1.) He professed his faith in Christ: *Lord, I believe thee to be the Son of God.* He would not dispute any thing that *he* said who had shown such mercy to him, and wrought such a miracle for him, nor doubt of the truth of a doctrine which was confirmed by such signs. Believing with the heart, he thus confesses with the mouth; and now the bruised reed was become a cedar. (2.) He paid his homage to him: *He worshipped him,* not only gave him the civil respect due to a great man, and the acknowledgments owing to a kind benefactor, but herein gave him divine honour, and worshipped him as the *Son of God* manifested in the flesh. None but God is to be worshipped; so that in worshipping Jesus he owned him to be God. Note, True faith will show itself in a humble adoration of the Lord Jesus. Those who believe in him will see all the reason in the world to worship him. We never read any more of this man; but, it is very likely, from henceforth he became a constant follower of Christ.

Verses 39–41

Christ, having spoken comfort to the poor man that was persecuted, here speaks conviction to his persecutors, a specimen of the distributions of trouble and rest at the great day, 2 Th. 1:6, 7. Probably this was not immediately after his discourse with the man, but he took the next opportunity that offered itself to address the Pharisees. Here is,

I. The account Christ gives of his design in coming into the world (*v.* 39): *"For judgment I am* come to order and administer the great affairs of the *kingdom of God among men,* and am invested with a judicial power in order thereunto, to be executed in conformity to the wise counsels of God, and in pursuance of them." What Christ spoke, he spoke not as a preacher in the pulpit, but as a king upon the throne, and a judge upon the bench.

1. His business into the world was *great;* he came to keep the assizes and general goal-delivery. He came *for judgment,* that is, (1.) To preach a doctrine and a law which would try men, and effectually discover and distinguish them, and would be completely fitted, in all respects, to be the rule of government now and of judgment shortly. (2.) To put a difference between men, by revealing the thoughts of many hearts, and laying open men's true characters, by this one test, whether they were well or ill affected to him. (3.) To change the face of government in his church, to abolish the Jewish economy, to take down that fabric, which, though erected for the time by the hand of God himself, yet by lapse of time was antiquated, and by the incurable corruptions of the managers of it was become rotten and dangerous, and to erect a new building by another model, to institute new ordinances and offices, to abrogate Judaism and enact Christianity; *for this judgment he came into the world,* and it was a great revolution.

2. This great truth he explains by a metaphor borrowed from the miracle which he had lately wrought. That *those who see not might see, and that those who see might be made blind.* Such a difference of Christ's coming is often spoken of; to some his gospel is a *savour of life unto life,* to others of *death unto death.* (1.) This is applicable to nations and people, that the Gentiles, who had long been destitute of the light of divine revelation, might see it; and the Jews, who had long enjoyed it, might have the things of their peace hid from their

eyes, Hos. 1:10; 2:23. The Gentiles see a great light, while blindness is *happened unto Israel,* and their *eyes are darkened.* (2.) To particular sons. Christ came into the world, [1.] Intentionally and designedly to give sight to those that were spiritually blind; by his word to reveal the object, and by his Spirit to heal the organ, that many precious souls might be turned *from darkness to light.* He came *for judgment,* that is, to set those at liberty from their dark prison that were willing to be released, Isa. 61:1. [2.] Eventually, and in the issue, *that those who see might be made blind;* that those who have a high conceit of their own wisdom, and set up that in contradiction to divine revelation, might be sealed up in ignorance and infidelity. The preaching of the cross was foolishness, and an infatuating think, to those who by wisdom *knew not God.* Christ *came into the world for* this *judgment,* to administer the affairs of a spiritual kingdom, seated in men's minds. Whereas, in the Jewish church, the blessings and judgments of God's government were mostly temporal, now the method of administration should be changed; and as the good subjects of his kingdom should be blessed with spiritual blessings in heavenly things, such as arise from a due illumination of the mind, so the rebels should be punished with spiritual plagues, not war, famine, and pestilence, as formerly, but such as arise from a *judicial infatuation,* hardness of heart, terror of conscience, strong delusions, vile affections. In this way Christ will *judge between cattle and cattle,* Eze. 34:17, 22.

II. The Pharisees' cavil at this. They were *with him,* not desirous to learn any good from him, but to form evil against him; and they said, *Are we blind also?* When Christ said that *those who saw* should by his coming be made blind, they apprehended that he meant them, who were the *seers* of the people, and valued themselves on their *insight* and *foresight.* "Now," say they, "we know that the common people are blind; but *are we blind also?* What we? The rabbin, the doctors, the learned in the laws, the graduates in the schools, *are we blind too?"* This is *scandalum magnatum — a libel on the great.* Note, Frequently those that need reproof most, and deserve it best, though they have wit enough to discern a *tacit* one, have not grace enough to bear a *just* one. These Pharisees took this reproof for a reproach, as those lawyers (Lu. 11:45): *"Are we blind also?* Darest thou say that we are blind, whose judgment every one has such a veneration for, values, and yields to?" Note, Nothing fortifies men's corrupt hearts more against the convictions of the word, nor more effectually repels them, than the good opinion, especially if it be a high opinion, which others have of them; as if all that had gained applause with men must needs obtain acceptance with God, than which nothing is more false and deceitful, for God sees not as man sees.

III. Christ's answer to this cavil, which, if it did not convince them, yet silenced them: *If you were blind you should have no sin; but now you say, We see, therefore your sin remaineth.* They gloried that they were not blind, as the common people, were not so credulous and manageable as they, but would *see with their own eyes,* having abilities, as they thought, sufficient for their own guidance, so that they needed not any body to lead them. This very thing which they gloried in, Christ here tells them, was their shame and ruin. For,

1. *If you were blind, you would have no sin.* (1.) "If you had been really ignorant, your sin had not been so deeply aggravated, nor would you have had so much sin to answer for as now you have. If you were blind, as the poor Gentiles are, and many of your own poor subjects, from whom you have taken the key of knowledge, you would have had comparatively *no sin."* The times of ignorance God *winked at;* invincible ignorance, though it does not justify sin, excuses it, and lessens the guilt. It will be more tolerable with those that perish for lack of vision than with those that *rebel against the light.* (2.) "If you had been sensible of your own blindness, if when you would see nothing else you could have seen the need of one to lead you, you would soon have accepted Christ as your guide, and then you would *have had no sin,* you would have submitted to an evangelical righteousness, and have been put into a justified state." Note, Those that are convinced of their disease are in a fair way to be cured, for there is not a greater hindrance to the salvation of souls than self-sufficiency.

2. *"But now you say, We see;* now that you have knowledge, and are instructed out of the law, your sin is highly aggravated; and now that you have a conceit of that knowledge, and think you see your way better than any body can show it you, *therefore your sin remains,* your case is desperate, and your disease incurable." And as those are most blind who *will not see,* so their blindness is most dangerous who fancy they do see. No patients are so hardly managed as those in a frenzy who say that they are *well,* and nothing ails them. The sin of those who are self-conceited and self-confident *remains,* for they reject the gospel of grace, and therefore the guilt of their sin remains unpardoned; and they forfeit the Spirit of grace, and therefore the power of their sin remains unbroken. *Seest thou a wise man in his own conceit?* Hearest thou the Pharisees say, *We see? There is more hope of a fool,* of a publican and a harlot, than of such.

CHAPTER 10

In this chapter we have, I. Christ's parabolical discourse concerning himself as the door of the sheepfold, and the shepherd of the sheep (*v.* 1–18). II. The various sentiments of people upon it (*v.* 19–21). III. The dispute Christ had with the Jews in the temple at the feast of dedication (*v.* 22–39). IV. His departure into the country thereupon (*v.* 40–42).

Verses 1–18

It is not certain whether this discourse was at the *feast of dedication* in the winter (spoken of *v.* 22), which may be taken as the date, not only of what follows, but of what goes before (that which countenances this is, that Christ, in his discourse there, carries on the metaphor of the sheep, *v.* 26, 27, whence it seems that that discourse and this were at the same time); or whether this was a continuation of his parley with the Pharisees, in the close of the foregoing chapter. The Pharisees supported themselves in their opposition to Christ with this principle, that they were the *pastors of the church,* and that Jesus, having no commission from them, was an intruder and an impostor, and therefore the people were bound in duty to stick to *then,* against *him.* In opposition to this, Christ here describes who were the false shepherds, and who the true, leaving them to infer what they were.

I. Here is the parable or similitude proposed (*v.* 1–5); it is borrowed from the custom of that country, in the management of their sheep. Similitudes, used for the illustration of divine truths, should be taken from those things that are most familiar and common, that the things of God be not clouded by that which should clear them. The preface to this discourse is solemn: *Verily, verily, I say unto you, — Amen, amen.* This vehement asseveration intimates the certainty and weight of what he said; we find *amen* doubled in the church's praises and prayers, Ps. 41:13; 72:19; 89:52. If we would have our *amens* accepted in heaven, let Christ's *amens* be prevailing on earth; his repeated *amens.*

1. In the parable we have, (1.) The evidence of a thief and robber, that comes to do mischief to the flock, and damage to the owner, *v.* 1. *He enters not by the door,* as having no lawful cause of entry, but *climbs up some other way,* at a window, or some breach in the wall. How industrious are wicked people to do mischief! What plots will they lay, what pains will they take, what hazards will they run, in their wicked pursuits! This should shame us out of our slothfulness and cowardice in the service of God. (2.) The character that distinguishes the rightful owner, who has a property in the sheep, and a care for them: *He enters in by the door,* as one having authority (*v.* 2), and he comes to do them some good office or other, to *bind up that which is broken,* and *strengthen that which is sick,* Eze. 34:16. Sheep need man's care, and, in return for it, are serviceable to man (1 Co. 9:7); they clothe and feed those by whom they are coted and fed. (3.) The ready entrance that the shepherd finds: *To him the porter openeth, v.* 3. Anciently they had their sheepfolds within the outer gates of their houses, for the greater safety of their flocks, so that none could come to them the right way, but such as the porter opened to or the master of the house gave the keys to. (4.) The care he takes and the provision he makes for his sheep. The *sheep hear his voice,* when he speaks familiarly to them, when they come into the fold, as men now do to their dogs and horses; and, which is more, he *calls his own sheep by name,* so exact is the notice he takes of them, the account he keeps of them; and he leads them our from the fold to the green pastures; and (*v.* 4, 5) when he *turns them out* to graze he does not drive them, but (such was the custom in those times) he goes before them, to prevent any mischief or danger that might meet them, and they, being used to it, *follow him,* and are safe. (5.) The strange attendance of the sheep upon the shepherd: *They know his voice,* so as to discern his mind by it, and to distinguish it from that of a stranger (for *the ox knows his owner,* Isa. 1:3), and *a stranger will they not follow,* but, as suspecting some ill design, will flee from him, not *knowing his voice,* but that it is not the voice of their own shepherd. This is the parable; we have the key to it, Eze. 34:31: *You my flock are men, and I am your God.*

2. Let us observe from this parable, (1.) That good men are fitly compared to sheep. Men, as creatures depending on their Creator, are called the *sheep of his pasture.* Good men, as new creatures, have the good qualities of sheep, *harmless* and inoffensive as sheep; *meek* and quiet, without noise; *patient* as sheep under the hand both of the shearer and of the butcher; *useful* and profitable, tame and tractable, to the shepherd, and *sociable* one with another, and much used in sacrifices. (2.) The church of God in the world is a *sheepfold,* into which the *children of God* that were scattered abroad are *gathered together* (*ch.* 11:52), and in which they are united and incorporated; it is a good fold, Eze. 34:14. See Mic. 2:12. This fold is well fortified, for God himself is as a *wall of fire about it,* Zec. 2:5. (3.) This sheepfold lies much exposed to thieves and robbers; crafty seducers that debauch and deceive, and cruel persecutors that destroy and devour; *grievous wolves* (Acts 20:29); thieves that would steal Christ's sheep from him, to sacrifice them to devils, or steal their food from them, that they might perish for lack of it; *wolves* in sheep's clothing, Mt. 7:15. (4.) The great Shepherd of the sheep takes wonderful care of the flock and of all that belong to it. God is the great Shepherd, Ps. 23:1. He knows those that are his calls them by name, marks them for himself, leads them out to fat pastures, makes them both feed and rest there, speaks comfortably to them, guards them by his providence, guides them by his Spirit and word, and goes before them, *to set them in the way of his steps.* (5.) The under-shepherds, who are entrusted to feed the flock of God, ought to be careful and faithful in the discharge of that trust; magistrates must defend them, and protect and advance all their secular interests; ministers must serve them in their spiritual interests, must *feed their souls* with the word of God faithfully opened and applied, and with gospel ordinances duly administered, *taking the oversight of them.* They must *enter by the door* of a regular ordination, and to such *the porter will open;* the Spirit of Christ will *set before them an open door,* give them authority in the church, and assurance in their own bosoms. They must know the members of their flocks by name, and watch over them; must lead them into the pastures of public ordinances, preside among them, be their mouth to God and God's to them; and in their conversation must be examples to the believers. (6.) Those who are truly the sheep of Christ will be very observant of their Shepherd, and very cautious and shy of strangers. [1.] *They follow their Shepherd,* for they *know his voice,* having both a discerning ear, and an obedient heart. [2.] *They flee from a stranger,* and dread following him, because they know not his voice. It is dangerous following those in whom we discern not the *voice of Christ,* and who would draw us from *faith in him* to *fancies concerning him.* And those who have experienced the power and efficacy of divine truths upon their souls, and have the savour and relish of them, have a wonderful sagacity to discover Satan's wiles, and to discern between good and evil.

II. The Jew's ignorance of the drift and meaning of this discourse (*v.* 6): *Jesus spoke this parable* to them, this figurative, but wise, elegant, and instructive discourse, *but they understood not what the things were which he spoke unto them,* were not aware whom he meant by the *thieves and robbers* and whom by the *good Shepherd.* It is the sin and shame of many who hear the word of Christ that they do not understand it, and they do not because they will not, and because they will *mis-understand it.* They have no acquaintance with, nor taste of, the things themselves, and therefore do not understand the parables and comparisons with which they are illustrated. The Pharisees had a great conceit of their own knowledge, and could not bear that it should be questioned, and yet they had not sense enough to *understand the things that Jesus spoke of;* they were above their capacity. Frequently the greatest pretenders to knowledge are most ignorant in the things of God.

III. Christ's explication of this parable, opening the particulars of it fully. Whatever difficulties there may be in the sayings of the Lord Jesus, we shall find him ready to explain himself, if we be but willing to understand him. We shall find one scripture expounding another, and the *blessed Spirit* interpreter to the *blessed Jesus.* Christ, in the parable, had distinguished the shepherd from the robber by this, that he *enters in by the door.* Now, in the explication of the parable, he makes himself to be both *the door* by which the shepherd enters and the shepherd that enters in by the door. Though it may be a solecism in rhetoric to make the same person to be both the *door* and the *shepherd,* it is no solecism in divinity to make Christ to have his authority from himself, as he has life in himself; and *himself* to *enter by his own blood,* as the door, *into the holy place.*

1. Christ is *the door.* This he saith to those who pretended to *seek for righteousness,* but, like the Sodomites, *wearied themselves to find the door,* where it was not to be found. He saith it to the Jews, who would be thought God's only sheep, and to the Pharisees, who would be thought their only shepherds: *I am the door* of the sheepfold; the door of the church.

(1.) In general, [1.] He is as a *door shut,* to keep out thieves and robbers, and such as are not fit to be admitted. The shutting of the door is the securing of the house; and what greater security has the church of God than the interposal of the Lord Jesus, and his wisdom, power, and goodness, betwixt it and all its enemies? [2.] He is as a *door open* for passage and communication. *First,* By Christ, as the door, we have our first admission into the flock of God, *ch.* 14:6. *Secondly,* We go in and out in a religious conversation, assisted by him, accepted in him; waling up and down in his name, Zec. 10:12. *Thirdly,* By him God comes to his church, visits it, and communicates himself to it. *Fourthly,* By him, as the door, the sheep are at last admitted into the heavenly kingdom, Mt. 25:34.

(2.) More particularly,

[1.] Christ is the door of *the shepherds,* so that none who come not in by him are to be accounted *pastors,* but (according to the rule laid down, *v.* 1) *thieves and robbers* (though they pretended to be *shepherds*); but the *sheep did not hear them.* This refers to all those that had the character of shepherds in *Israel,* whether magistrates or ministers, that exercised their office without any regard to the Messiah, or any other expectations of him than what were suggested by their own carnal interest. Observe, *First,* The character given of them: they are *thieves and robbers* (*v.* 8); all that *went before him,* not in time, many of them were faithful shepherds, but all that *anticipated* his commission, and went before he sent them (Jer. 23:21), that assumed a precedency and superiority above him, as the antichrist is said to *exalt himself,* 2 Th. 2:4. "The scribes, and Pharisees, and chief priests, *all, even as many as have come before me,* that have endeavoured to forestal my interest, and to prevent my gaining any room in the minds of people, by prepossessing them with prejudices against me, they are *thieves and robbers,* and steal those hearts which they have no title to, defrauding the right owner of his property." They condemned our Saviour as a thief and a robber, because he did not come in by them as the door, nor take out a license from them; but he shows that they ought to have received their commission from him, to have been admitted by him, and to have come after him, and because they did not, but stepped *before him,* they were *thieves and robbers.* They would not come in as his disciples, and therefore were condemned as usurpers, and their pretended commissions vacated and superseded. Note, Rivals with Christ are robbers of his church, however they pretend to be *shepherds,* nay, *shepherds of shepherds. Secondly,* The care taken to preserve the sheep from them: *But the sheep did not hear them.* Those that had a true savour of piety, that were spiritual and heavenly, and sincerely devoted to God and godliness, could by no means approve of the traditions of the elders, nor relish their formalities. Christ's disciples, without any particular instructions from their Master, made no conscience of eating with unwashen hands, or plucking the ears of corn on the sabbath day; for nothing is more opposite to true Christianity than Pharisaism is, nor any thing more disrelishing to a soul truly devout than their hypocritical devotions.

[2.] Christ is the door of *the sheep* (*v.* 9): *By me* (*di emou — through me* as the door) *if any man enter into the sheepfold,* as one of the flock, he *shall be saved;* shall not only by safe from thieves and robbers, but he shall be happy, he *shall go in and out.* Here are, *First,* Plain directions how to come into the fold: we must come in *by Jesus Christ* as the door. By faith in him, as the great Mediator between God and man, we come into covenant and communion with God. There is no entering into God's church but by coming into Christ's church; nor are any looked upon as members of the kingdom of God among men but those that are willing to submit to the grace and government of the Redeemer. We must now enter by the *door of faith* (Acts 14:27), since the door of *innocency* is shut against us, and that *pass* become unpassable, Gen. 3:24. *Secondly,* Precious promises to those who observe this direction. 1. They *shall be saved hereafter;* this is the privilege of *their home.* These sheep shall be saved from being distrained and impounded by divine justice for trespass done, satisfaction being made for the damage by their great Shepherd, saved from being a prey to the roaring lion; they shall be *for ever happy.* 2. In the mean time they shall *go in and out and find pasture;* this is the privilege of *their way.* They shall have their conversation in the world by the grace of Christ, shall be in his fold as a man at his own house, where he has *free ingress, egress,* and *regress.* True believers are *at home* in Christ; when they go out, they are not *shut out* as strangers, but have liberty to come in again; when they come in, they are not *shut in* as trespassers, but have liberty to go out. They go out to the field in the morning, they come into the fold at night; and in both the Shepherd leads and keeps them, and they *find pasture* in both: grass in the field, fodder in the fold. In public, in private, they have the word of God to converse with, by which their spiritual life is supported and nourished, and out of which their gracious desires are satisfied; they are replenished with the goodness of God's house.

2. Christ is the *shepherd, v.* 11, etc. He was prophesied of under the Old Testament as a *shepherd,* Isa. 40:11; Eze. 34:23; 37:24; Zec. 13:7. In the New Testament he is spoken of as the *great Shepherd* (Heb. 13:20), the *chief Shepherd* (1 Pt. 5:4), the *Shepherd and bishop of our souls,* 1 Pt. 2:25. God, our great owner, the sheep of whose pasture we are by creation, has constituted his Son Jesus to be our *shepherd;* and here again and again he owns the relation. He has all that care of his church, and every believer, that a good shepherd has of his flock; and expects all that attendance and observance from the church, and every believer, which the shepherds in those countries had from their flocks.

(1.) Christ is *a shepherd,* and not as the thief, not as those that *came not in by the door.* Observe,

[1.] The mischievous design of the thief (*v.* 10): *The thief cometh not* with any good intent, but to *steal, and to kill, and to destroy. First,* Those whom they *steal,* whose hearts and affections they steal from Christ and his pastures, they *kill and destroy* spiritually; for the *heresies* they *privily bring in* are *damnable.* Deceivers of souls are murderers of souls. Those that steal away the scripture by keeping it in an unknown tongue, that steal away the sacraments by maiming them and altering the property of them, that steal away Christ's ordinances to put their own inventions in the room of them, they *kill and destroy;* ignorance and idolatry are destructive things. *Secondly,* Those whom they cannot *steal,* whom they can neither lead, drive, nor carry away, from the flock of Christ, they aim by persecutions and massacres to *kill and destroy* corporally. He that will not suffer himself to be robbed is in danger of being slain.

[2.] The gracious design of the shepherd; he is come,

First, To *give life to the sheep.* In opposition to the design of the thief, which is to *kill and destroy* (which was the design of the *scribes* and *Pharisees*) Christ saith, *I am come among men,* 1. That *they might have life.* He came to put life into the flock, the church in general, which had seemed rather like a valley full of dry bones than like a pasture covered over with flocks. Christ came to vindicate divine truths, to purify divine ordinances, to redress grievances, and to revive dying zeal, to *seek* those of his flock that were *lost,* to *bind up that which was broken* (Eze. 34:16), and this to his church is *as life from the dead.* He came to *give life* to particular believers. Life is inclusive of all good, and stands in opposition to the death threatened (Gen. 2:17); that *we might have life,* as a criminal has when he is pardoned, as a sick man when he is cured, a dead man when he is raised; that we might be justified, sanctified, and at last glorified. 2. That they might have it *more abundantly, kai perisson echōsin.* As we read it, it is *comparative,* that they might have a life *more abundant* than that which was lost and forfeited by sin, more abundant than that which was promised by the law of Moses, length of days in Canaan, more abundant than could have been expected or than we are *able to ask or think.* But it may be construed without a note of comparison, *that they might have abundance,* or might *have it abundantly.* Christ came to give life and *perisson ti — something more,* something *better,* life with advantage; that in Christ we might not only live, but live comfortably, live plentifully, live and rejoice. Life in abundance is *eternal life,* life without death or fear of death, life and *much more.*

Secondly, To *give his life for the sheep,* and this that he might give life *to them* (*v.* 11): *The good shepherd giveth his life for the sheep.* 1. It is the property of every good shepherd to hazard and expose his life for the sheep. Jacob did so, when he would go through such a fatigue to attend them, Gen. 31:40. So did David, when he *slew the lion and the bear.* Such a shepherd of souls was St. Paul, who would gladly *spend, and be spent,* for their service, and *counted not his life dear to him,* in comparison with their salvation. But, 2. It was the prerogative of the great Shepherd to give his life to purchase his flock (Acts 20:28), to satisfy for their trespass, and to shed his blood to wash and cleanse them.

(2.) Christ is *a good shepherd,* and not as a hireling. There were many that were not thieves, aiming to kill and destroy the sheep, but passed for shepherds, yet were very careless in the discharge of their duty, and through their neglect the flock was greatly damaged; *foolish shepherds, idle shepherds,* Zec. 11:15, 17. In opposition to these,

[1.] Christ here *calls himself the good shepherd* (*v.* 11), and again (*v.* 14) *ho poimēn ho kalos — that shepherd, that good Shepherd,* whom God had promised. Note, Jesus Christ is the best of shepherds, the best in the world to take the oversight of souls, none so skilful, so faithful, so tender, as he, no such feeder and leader, no such protector and healer of souls as he.

[2.] He *proves himself* so, in opposition to all hirelings, *v.* 12–14. Where observe,

First, The carelessness of the unfaithful shepherd described (*v.* 12, 13); he that is a hireling, that is employed as a servant and is paid for his pains, *whose own the sheep are not,* who has neither profit nor loss by them, *sees the wolf coming,* or some other danger threatening, and *leaves the sheep* to the wolf, for in truth he *careth not for them.* Here is plain reference to that of the idol-shepherd, Zec. 11:17. Evil shepherds, magistrates and ministers, are here described both by their bad principles and their bad practices.

a. Their *bad principles,* the root of their bad practices. What makes those that have the charge of souls in trying times to betray their trust, and in quiet times not to mind it? What makes them false, and trifling, and self-seeking? It is because they are *hirelings,* and *care not for the sheep.* That is, (*a.*) The wealth of the world is the chief of their good; it is because they are *hirelings.* They undertook the shepherds' office, as a trade to live and grow rich by, not as an opportunity of serving Christ and doing good. It is the love of money, and of their own bellies, that carries them on in it. Not that those are hirelings who, while they *serve at the altar, live,* and live comfortably, *upon the altar.* The labourer is worthy of his meat; and a scandalous maintenance will soon make a scandalous ministry. But those are *hirelings* that love the wages more than the work, and *set their hearts* upon that, as the hireling is said to do, Deu. 24:15. See 1 Sa. 2:29; Isa. 56:11; Mic. 3:5, 11. (*b.*) The work of their place is the least of their care. They *value not the sheep,* are unconcerned in the souls of others; their business is to be their brothers' lords, not their brothers' keepers or helpers; they *seek their own things,* and do not, like Timothy, *naturally care for the state of souls.* What can be expected but that they will flee when the *wolf comes.* He *careth not for the sheep,* for he is one *whose own the sheep are not.* In one respect we may say of the best of the under-shepherds that the sheep are *not their own,* they have not dominion over them not property in them *(feed my sheep* and *my lambs,* saith Christ); but in respect of dearness and affection they should be *their own.* Paul looked upon those as *his own* whom he called his *dearly beloved and longed for.* Those who do not cordially espouse the church's interests, and make them their own, will not long be faithful to them.

b. Their *bad practices,* the effect of these bad principles, *v.* 12. See here, (*a.*) How basely the hireling deserts his post; when he sees *the wolf coming,* though then there is most need of him, he *leaves the sheep and flees.* Note, Those who mind their safety more than their duty are an easy prey to Satan's temptations. (*b.*) How fatal the consequences are! the hireling fancies the sheep may look to themselves, but it does not prove so: *the wolf catches them,* and *scatters the sheep,* and woeful havoc is made of the flock, which will all be charged upon the treacherous shepherd. The blood of perishing souls is required at the hand of the careless watchmen.

Secondly, See here the grace and tenderness of the good Shepherd set over against the former, as it was in the prophecy (Eze. 34:21, 22, etc.): *I am the good Shepherd.* It is matter of comfort to the church, and all her friends, that, however she may be damaged and endangered by the treachery and mismanagement of her under-officers, the Lord Jesus is, and will be, as he ever has been, *the good Shepherd.* Here are two great instances of the shepherd's goodness.

a. His *acquainting* himself with his flock, with all that belong or in any wise appertain to his flock, which are of two sorts, both known to him: —

(*a.*) He is acquainted with all that *are now of his flock* (*v.* 14, 15), as the good Shepherd (*v.* 3, 4): *I know my sheep and am known of mine.* Note, There is a mutual acquaintance between Christ and true believers; they know one another very well, and knowledge notes affection.

[*a.*] Christ *knows his sheep.* He knows with a *distinguishing* eye who are his sheep, and who are not; he knows the sheep under their many infirmities, and the goats under their most plausible disguises. He knows with a *favourable* eye those that in truth are his own sheep; he takes cognizance of their state, concerns himself for them, has a tender and affectionate regard to them, and is continually mindful of them in the intercession he ever lives to make within the veil; he visits them graciously by his Spirit, and has communion with them; he *knows* them, that is, he approves and accepts of them, as Ps. 1:6; 37:18; Ex. 33:17.

[*b.*] He is *known of them.* He observes them with an eye of favour, and they observe him with an eye of faith. Christ's knowing his sheep is put before their knowing him, for he knew and loved us first (1 Jn. 4:19), and it is not so much our knowing him as our being known of him that is our happiness, Gal. 4:9. Yet it is the character of Christ's sheep that *they know him;* know him from all pretenders and intruders; they know his mind, know his voice, know by experience the power of his death. Christ speaks here as if he gloried in being known by his sheep, and thought their respect an honour to him. Upon this occasion Christ mentions (*v.* 15) the mutual acquaintance between his Father and himself: *As the Father knoweth me, even so know I the Father.* Now this may be considered, either, *First,* As the *ground* of that intimate acquaintance and relation which subsist between Christ and believers. The covenant of grace, which is the bond of this relation, is founded in the covenant of redemption between the Father and the Son, which, we may be sure, stands firm; for the Father and the Son understood one another perfectly well in that matter, and there could be no mistake, which might leave the matter at any uncertainty, or bring it into any hazard. The Lord Jesus *knows whom he hath chosen,* and is sure of them (*ch.* 13:18), and they also *know whom they have trusted,* and are sure of him (2 Tim. 1:12), and the ground of both is the perfect knowledge which the Father and the Son had of one another's mind, when *the counsel of peace was between them both.* Or, *Secondly,* As an apt similitude, illustrating the intimacy that is between Christ and believers. It may be connected with the foregoing words, thus: *I know my sheep, and am known of mine, even as the Father knows me, and I know the Father;* compare *ch.* 17:21. 1. As the Father knew the Son, and loved him, and owned him in his sufferings, when he was *led as a sheep to the slaughter,* so Christ knows his sheep, and has a watchful tender eye upon them, will be with them when they are *left alone,* as his Father was with him. 2. As the Son knew the Father, loved and obeyed him, and always did those things that pleased him, confiding in him as his God even when he seemed to forsake him, so believers know Christ with an obediential fiducial regard.

(*b.*) He is acquainted with those that are *hereafter to be of this flock* (*v.* 16): *Other sheep I have,* have a right to and an interest in, *which are not of this fold,* of the Jewish church; *them also I must bring.* Observe,

[*a.*] The eye that Christ had to the poor Gentiles. He had sometimes intimated his special concern for *the lost sheep of the house of Israel;* to them indeed his personal ministry was confined; but, saith he, *I have other sheep.* Those who in process of time should believe in Christ, and be brought into obedience to him from among the Gentiles, are here called *sheep,* and he is said to have them, though as yet they were *uncalled,* and many of them *unborn,* because they were chosen of God, and given to Christ in the counsels of divine love from eternity. Christ has a right, by virtue of the Father's donation and his own purchase, to many a soul of which he has not yet the possession; thus he had *much people* in Corinth, when as yet it lay in wickedness, Acts 18:10. "Those other sheep *I have,*" saith Christ, "I have them on my heart, have them in my eye, am as sure to have them as if I had them already." Now Christ speaks of those *other sheep, First,* To take off the contempt that was put upon him, as having *few followers,* as having but a *little flock,* and therefore, if a *good* shepherd, yet a *poor* shepherd: "But," saith he, "I have more sheep than you see." *Secondly,* To take down the pride and vain-glory of the Jews, who thought the Messiah must gather all his sheep from among them. "No," saith Christ, "I have others whom I will set with the lambs of my flock, though you disdain to set them with the dogs of your flock."

[*b.*] The purposes and resolves of his grace concerning them: *"Them also I must bring,* bring home to God, bring into the church, and, in order to this, bring off from their vain conversation, bring them back from their wanderings, as that *lost sheep,"* Lu. 15:5. But why *must* he bring them? What was the necessity? *First,* The *necessity of their case* required it: "I *must* bring, or they must be left to wander endlessly, for, like sheep, they will never come back of themselves, and no other can or will bring them." *Secondly,* The *necessity of his own engagements* required it; he must bring them, or he would not be faithful to his trust, and true to his undertaking. "They are *my own,* bought and paid for, and therefore I *must not* neglect them nor leave them to perish." He *must* in honour *bring* those with whom he was entrusted.

[*c.*] The happy effect and consequence of this, in two things: — *First,* "They shall hear my voice. Not only my voice shall be heard *among them* (whereas they have not heard, and therefore could not believe, now the *sound* of the gospel shall *go to the ends of the earth*), but it shall be heard *by them;* I will speak, and give to them to hear." Faith comes by hearing, and our diligent observance of the voice of Christ is both a means and an evidence of our being brought to Christ, and to God by him. *Secondly, There shall be one fold and one shepherd.* As there is one shepherd, so there shall be one fold. Both Jews and Gentiles, upon their turning to the faith of Christ, shall be incorporated in one church, be joint and equal sharers in the privileges of it, without distinction. Being united to Christ, they shall unite in him; two sticks shall become one in the hand of the Lord. Note, One shepherd makes one fold; one Christ makes one church. As the church is one in its constitution, subject to one head, animated by one Spirit, and guided by one rule, so the members of it ought to be one in love and affection, Eph. 4:3–6.

b. Christ's *offering up himself for his sheep* is another proof of his being a *good shepherd,* and in this he yet more *commended his love, v.* 15, 17, 18.

(*a.*) He declares his purpose of *dying for his flock* (*v.* 15): *I lay down my life for the sheep.* He not only ventured his life for them (in such a case, the hope of *saving* it might balance the fear of *losing it*), but he actually *deposited* it, and submitted to a necessity of dying for our redemption; *tithēmi — I put it* as a pawn or pledge; as purchase-money paid down. Sheep appointed for the slaughter, ready to be sacrificed, were ransomed with the blood of the shepherd. He laid down his life, *hyper tōn probatōn,* not only for the good of the sheep, but *in their stead.* Thousands of sheep had been offered in sacrifice for their shepherds, as sin-offerings, but here, by a surprising reverse, the shepherd is sacrificed for the sheep. When David, the shepherd of Israel, was himself guilty, and the destroying angel drew his sword against the flock for his sake, with good reason did he plead, *These sheep, what evil have they done? Let thy hand be against me,* 2 Sa. 24:17. But the Son of David was sinless and spotless; and his sheep, what evil have they not done? Yet he saith, *Let thine hand be against me.* Christ here seems to refer to that prophecy, Zec. 13:7, *Awake, O sword, against my shepherd;* and, though the smiting of the shepherd be for the present the *scattering* of the flock, it is in order to the gathering of them in.

(*b.*) He takes off the offence of the cross, which to many is a stone of stumbling, by four considerations: —

[*a.*] That his *laying down his life for the sheep* was the condition, the performance of which entitled him to the honours and powers of his exalted state (*v.* 17): *"Therefore doth my Father love me, because I lay down my life.* Upon these terms I am, as Mediator, to expect my Father's acceptance and approbation, and the glory designed me — that I become a sacrifice for the chosen remnant." Not but that, as the Son of God, he was beloved of his Father from eternity, but as *God-man,* as *Immanuel,* he was *therefore* beloved of the Father because he undertook to *die for the sheep; therefore* God's soul delighted in him as his elect because herein he was his *faithful servant* (Isa. 42:1); therefore he said, *This is my beloved Son.* What an instance is this of God's love to man, that he loved his Son the more for loving us! See what a value Christ puts upon his Father's love, that, to recommend himself to that, he would lay down his life for the sheep. Did he think God's love recompence sufficient for all his services and sufferings, and shall we think it too little for ours, and court the smiles of the world to make it up? *Therefore doth my Father love me,* that is, me, and all that by faith become one with me; me, and the mystical body, *because I lay down my life.*

[*b.*] That his laying down his life was in order to his resuming it: *I lay down my life, that I may receive it again. First,* This was the effect of his Father's love, and the first step of his exaltation, the fruit of that love. Because he was God's *holy one,* he must not *see corruption,* Ps. 16:10. God loved him too well to leave him in the grave. *Secondly,* This he had in his eye, in laying down his life, that he might have an opportunity of declaring himself to be the Son of God with power by his resurrection, Rom. 1:4. By a divine stratagem (like that before Ai, Jos. 8:15) he yielded to death, as if he were smitten before it, that he might the more gloriously conquer death, and triumph over the grave. He laid down a *vilified* body, that he might assume a *glorified* one, fit to ascend to the world of spirits; laid down a life adapted to this world, but assumed one adapted to the other, like a corn of wheat, *ch.* 12:24.

[*c.*] That he was perfectly voluntary in his sufferings and death (*v.* 18): "No one doth or can force my life from me against my will, but I freely *lay it down of myself,* I deliver it as my own act and deed, for I *have* (which no man has) *power to lay it down, and to take it again."*

First, See here the power of Christ, as the Lord of life, particularly of his own life, which he had *in himself.* 1. He had power to *keep his life* against all the world, so that it could not be wrested from him without his own consent. Though Christ's life seemed to be taken by storm, yet really it was surrendered, otherwise it had been impregnable, and never taken. The Lord Jesus did not fall into the hands of his persecutors because he could not avoid it, but threw himself into their hands because his hour was come. *No man taketh my life from me.* This was such a challenge as was never given by the most daring hero. 2. He had power to *lay down his life.* (1.) He had ability to do it. He could, when he pleased, slip the knot of union between soul and body, and, without any act of violence done to himself, could disengage them from each other: having voluntarily *taken up* a body, he could voluntarily lay it down again, which appeared when he cried with a loud voice, and gave up the ghost. (2.) He had authority to do it, *exousian.* Though we could find instruments of cruelty, wherewith to make an end of our own lives, yet *Id possumus quod jure possumus — we can do that, and that only, which we can do lawfully.* We are not at liberty to do it; but Christ had a sovereign authority to dispose of his own life as he pleased. He was no debtor (as we are) either to life or death, but perfectly *sui juris.* 3. He had power to *take it again;* we have not. Our life, once laid down, is *as water spilt upon the ground;* but Christ, when he laid down his life, still had it within reach, within call, and could resume it. Parting with it by a voluntary conveyance, he might limit the surrender at pleasure, and he did it with a power of revocation, which was necessary to preserve the intentions of the surrender.

Secondly, See here the grace of Christ; since none could demand his life of him by law, or extort it by force, he *laid it down of himself,* for our redemption. He offered himself to be the Saviour: *Lo, I come;* and then, the necessity of our case calling for it, he offered himself to be a sacrifice: *Here am I, let these go their way; by which will we are sanctified,* Heb. 10:10. He was both the offerer and the offering, so that *his laying down his life* was his offering up himself.

[*d.*] That he did all this by the express order and appointment of his Father, into which he ultimately resolves the whole affair: *This commandment have I received of my Father;* not such a commandment as made what he did necessary, prior to his own voluntary undertaking; but this was the *law of mediation,* which he was willing to have *written in his heart,* so as to *delight* in doing *the will of God* according to it, Ps. 40:8.

Verses 19–21

We have here an account of the people's different sentiments concerning Christ, on occasion of the foregoing discourse; there was a division, a *schism,* among them; they differed in their opinions, which threw them into heats and parties. Such a ferment as this they had been in before (*ch.* 7:43; 9:16); and where there has once been a division again. Rents are sooner made than made up or mended. This division was occasioned by the sayings of Christ, which, one would think, should rather have united them all in him as their centre; but they set them at variance, as Christ foresaw, Lu. 12:51. But it is better that men should be *divided* about the doctrine of Christ than *united* in the service of sin, Lu. 11:21. See what the debate was in particular.

I. Some upon this occasion spoke ill of Christ and of his sayings, either openly in the face of the assembly, for his enemies were very impudent, or privately among themselves. They said, *He has a devil, and is mad, why do you hear him?* 1. They reproach him as a demoniac. The worst of characters is put upon the best of men. He is a distracted man, he raves and is delirious, and no more to be heard than the rambles of a man in bedlam. Thus still, if a man preaches seriously and pressingly of another world, he shall be said to talk like an enthusiast; and his conduct shall be imputed to fancy, a heated brain, and a crazed imagination. 2. They ridicule his hearers: *"Why hear you him?* Why do you so far encourage him as to take notice of what he says?" Note, Satan ruins many by putting them out of conceit with the word and ordinances, and representing it as a weak and silly thing to attend upon them. Men would not thus be laughed out of their necessary food, and yet suffer themselves to be laughed out of what is more necessary. Those that hear Christ, and mix faith with what they hear, will soon be able to give a good account *why they hear him.*

II. Others stood up in defence of him and his discourse, and, though the stream ran strong, dared to swim against it; and, though perhaps they did not believe on him as the Messiah, they could not bear to hear him thus abused. If they could say no more of him, this they would maintain, that he was a man in his wits, that he had not a devil, that he was neither senseless nor graceless. The absurd and most unreasonable reproaches, that have sometimes been cast upon Christ and his gospel, have excited those to appear for him and it who otherwise had no great affection to either. Two things they plead: — 1. The excellency of his doctrine: *"These are not the words of him that hath a devil;* they are not idle words; distracted men are not used to talk at this rate. These are not the words of one that is either violently possessed with a devil or voluntarily in league with the devil." Christianity, if it be not the true religion, is certainly the greatest cheat that ever was put upon the world; and, if so, it must be of the devil, who is the father of all lies: but it is certain that the doctrine of Christ is no doctrine of devils, for it is levelled directly against the devil's kingdom, and Satan is too subtle to be divided against himself. So much of holiness there is in the words of Christ that we may conclude they are *not the words of one that has a devil,* and therefore are the words of one that was sent of God; are not from hell, and therefore must be from heaven. 2. The power of his miracles: *Can a devil,* that is, a man that has a devil, *open the eyes of the blind?* Neither mad men nor bad men can work miracles. Devils are not such lords of the power of nature as to be able to work such miracles; nor are they such friends to mankind as to be willing to work them if they were able. The devil will sooner put out men's eyes than open them. Therefore Jesus *had not a devil.*

Verses 22–38

We have here another rencounter between Christ and the Jews in the temple, in which it is hard to say which is more strange, the gracious words that came out of his mouth or the spiteful ones that came out of theirs.

I. We have here the time when this conference was: *It was at the feast of dedication, and it was winter,* a feast that was annually observed by consent, in remembrance of the dedication of a new altar and the purging of the temple, by Judas Maccabaeus, after the temple had been profaned and the altar defiled; we have the story of it at large in the history of the Maccabees (lib. 1, cap. 4); we have the prophecy of it, Dan.

8:13, 14. See more of the feast, 2 Mac. 1:18. The return of their liberty was to them as life from the dead, and, in remembrance of it, they kept an annual feast on the twenty-fifth day of the month *Cisleu,* about the beginning of *December,* and seven days after. The celebrating of it was not confined to Jerusalem, as that of the divine feasts was, but every one observed it in his own place, not as a *holy time* (it is only a divine institution that can sanctify a day), but as a *good time,* as the days of Purim, Esth. 9:19. Christ forecasted to be now at Jerusalem, not in honour of the feast, which did not require his attendance there, but that he might improve those eight days of vacation for good purposes.

II. The place where it was (*v.* 23): *Jesus walked in the temple in Solomon's porch;* so called (Acts 3:11), not because built by Solomon, but because built in the same place with that which had borne his name in the first temple, and the name was kept up for the greater reputation of it. Here Christ walked, to observe the proceedings of the great sanhedrim that sat here (Ps. 82:1); *he walked,* ready to give audience to any that should apply to him, and to offer them his services. He walked, as it should seem, for some time *alone,* as one neglected; walked pensive, in the foresight of the ruin of the temple. Those that have any thing to say to Christ may find him in the temple and walk with him there.

III. The conference itself, in which observe,

1. A weighty question put to him by the Jews, *v.* 24. They *came round about him,* to tease him; he was waiting for an opportunity to do them a kindness, and they took the opportunity to do him a mischief. Ill-will for good-will is no rare and uncommon return. He could not enjoy himself, no, not in the temple, his Father's house, without disturbance. They came about him, as it were, to lay siege to him: *encompassed him about like bees.* They came about him as if they had a joint and unanimous desire to be satisfied; came as one man, pretending an impartial and importunate enquiry after truth, but intending a general assault upon our Lord Jesus; and they seemed to speak the sense of their nation, as if they were the mouth of all the Jews: *How long dost thou make us to doubt? If thou be the Christ tell us.*

(1.) They quarrel with him, as if he had unfairly held them in suspense hitherto. *Tēn psychēn hēmōn aireis* — *How long dost thou steal away our hearts?* Or, *take away our souls?* So some read it; basely intimating that what share he had of the people's love and respect he did not obtain fairly, but by indirect methods, as Absalom stole the hearts of the men of Israel; and as seducers deceive the *hearts of the simple,* and so *draw away disciples after them,* Rom. 16:18; Acts 20:30. But most interpreters understand it as we do: *"How long dost thou keep us in suspense?* How long are we kept debating whether thou be the Christ or no, and not able to determine the question?" Now, [1.] It was the effect of their infidelity, and powerful prejudices, that after our Lord Jesus had so fully proved himself to be the Christ they were still in doubt concerning it; this they willingly hesitated about, when they might easily have been satisfied. The struggle was between their convictions, which told them he was Christ, and their corruptions, which said, No, because he was not such a Christ as they expected. Those who choose to be sceptics may, if they please, hold the balance so that the most cogent arguments may not weigh down the most trifling objections, but scales may still hang even. [2.] It was an instance of their impudence and presumption that they laid the blame of their doubting upon Christ himself, as if he *made them to* doubt by inconsistency with himself, whereas in truth they made themselves doubt by indulging their prejudices. If Wisdom's sayings appear doubtful, the fault is not in the object, but in the eye; they are all *plain to him that understands.* Christ would make us to believe; we make ourselves to *doubt.*

(2.) They challenge him to give a direct and categorical answer whether he was the Messiah or no: *"If thou be the Christ,* as many believe thou art, *tell us plainly,* not by parables, as, *I am the light of the world,* and *the good Shepherd,* and the like, but *totidem verbis — in so many words,* either that thou art the Christ, or, as John Baptist, that thou art not," *ch.* 1:20. Now this pressing query of theirs was *seemingly good;* they pretended to be desirous to know the truth, as if they were ready to embrace it; but it was *really bad,* and put with an ill design; for, if he should tell them plainly that he was the Christ, there needed no more to make him obnoxious to the jealousy and severity of the Roman government. Every one knew the Messiah was to be a king, and therefore whoever pretended to be the Messiah would be

prosecuted as a traitor, which was the thing they would have been at; for, let him tell them ever so plainly that he was the Christ, they would have this to say presently, *Thou bearest witness of thyself,* as they had said, *ch.* 8:13.

2. Christ's answer to this question, in which,

(1.) He justifies himself as not at all accessary to their infidelity and skepticism, referring them, [1.] To what he had said: *I have told you.* He had told them that he was the Son of God, the Son of man, that he had life in himself, that he had *authority to execute judgment,* etc. And is not this the Christ then? These things he had told them, and they believed not; why then should they be told them again, merely to gratify their curiosity? *You believed not.* They pretended that they only doubted, but Christ tells them that they did not believe. Skepticism in religion is no better than downright infidelity. It is now for us to teach God how he should teach us, nor prescribe to him how plainly he should tell us his mind, but to be thankful for divine revelation as we have it. If we do not believe this, neither should we be persuaded if it were ever so much adapted to our humour. [2.] He refers them to his works, to the example of his life, which was not only perfectly pure, but highly beneficent, and of a piece with his doctrine; and especially to his miracles, which he wrought for the confirmation of his doctrine. It was certain that no man could do those miracles except God were with him, and God would not be with him to attest a forgery.

(2.) He condemns them for their obstinate unbelief, notwithstanding all the most plain and powerful arguments used to convince them: *"You believed not;* and again, *You believed not.* You still are what you always were, obstinate in your unbelief." But the reason he gives is very surprising: *"You believed not, because you are not of my sheep:* you believe not in me, because you belong not to me." [1.] "You are not disposed to be my followers, are not of a tractable teachable temper, have no inclination to receive the doctrine and law of the Messiah; you will not herd yourselves with my sheep, will not come and see, come and hear my voice." Rooted antipathies to the gospel of Christ are the bonds of iniquity and infidelity. [2.] "You are not *designed* to be my followers; you are not of those that were given me by my Father, to be brought to grace and glory. You are not of the number of the elect; and your unbelief, if you persist in it, will be a certain evidence that you are not." Note, Those to whom God never gives the grace of faith were never designed for heaven and happiness. What Solomon saith of immorality is true of infidelity, It is *a deep ditch, and he that is abhorred of the Lord shall fall therein,* Prov. 22:14. *Non esse electum, non est causa incredulitatis propriè dicta, sed causa per accidens. Fides autem est donum Dei et effectus praedestinationis — The not being included among the elect is not the* proper *cause of infidelity, but merely the* accidental *cause. But faith is the gift of God, and the effect of predestination.* So Jansenius distinguishes well here.

(3.) He takes this occasion to describe both the gracious disposition and the happy state of those that are his sheep; for such there are, though *they* be not.

[1.] To convince them that they were not his sheep, he tells them what were the characters of his sheep. *First,* They *hear his voice* (*v.* 27), for they know it to be his (*v.* 4), and he has undertaken that they shall hear it, *v.* 16. They discern it, *It is the voice of my beloved,* Cant. 2:8. They delight in it, are in their element when they are sitting at his feet to hear his word. They do according to it, and make his word their rule. Christ will not account those his sheep that are deaf to his calls, deaf to his charms, Ps. 58:5. *Secondly,* They *follow him;* they submit to his guidance by a willing obedience to all his commands, and a cheerful conformity to his spirit and pattern. The word of command has always been, *Follow me.* We must eye him as our leader and captain, and *tread in his steps,* and walk as he walked — follow the prescriptions of his word, the intimations of his providence, and the directions of his Spirit — *follow the Lamb* (the *dux gregis — the leader of the flock) whithersoever he goes.* In vain do we *hear his voice* if we do not *follow him.*

[2.] To convince them that it was their great unhappiness and misery not to be of Christ's sheep, he here describes the blessed state and case of those that are, which would likewise serve for the support and comfort of his poor despised followers, and keep them from envying the power and grandeur of those that were not of his sheep.

First, Our Lord Jesus *takes cognizance* of his sheep: They *hear my voice,* and *I know them.* He distinguishes them from others (2 Tim. 2:19), has a particular regard to every individual (Ps. 34:6); he knows their wants and desires, knows their souls in adversity, where to find them, and what to do for them. He knows others afar off, but knows them near at hand.

Secondly, He has provided a happiness for them, suited to them: *I give unto them eternal life, v.* 28. 1. The estate settled upon them is rich and valuable; it is life, eternal life. Man has a living soul; therefore the happiness provided is life, suited to his nature. Man has an immortal soul: therefore the happiness provided is eternal life, running parallel with his duration. *Life eternal* is the felicity and chief good of a *soul immortal.* 2. The manner of conveyance is *free: I give it* to them; it is not bargained and sold upon a valuable consideration, but given by the free grace of Jesus Christ. The donor has power to give it. He who is the fountain of life, and Father of eternity, has authorized Christ to give eternal life, *ch.* 17:2. Not *I will* give it, but *I do* give it; it is a present gift. He gives the assurance of it, the pledge and earnest of it, the first-fruits and foretastes of it, that *spiritual* life which is *eternal* life begun, heaven in the seed, in the bud, in the embryo.

Thirdly, He has undertaken for their security and preservation to this happiness.

a. They shall be *saved from everlasting perdition. They shall by no means perish for ever;* so the words are. As there is an eternal life, so there is an eternal destruction; the soul not *annihilated,* but *ruined;* its being continued, but its comfort and happiness irrecoverably lost. All believers are saved from this; whatever cross they may come under, they shall not *come into condemnation.* A man is never undone till he is in hell, and they shall not go down to that. Shepherds that have large flocks often lose some of the sheep and suffer them to perish; but Christ has engaged that none of his sheep shall perish, not one.

b. They cannot be kept from their *everlasting happiness;* it is in reserve, but he that gives it to them will preserve them to it. (*a.*) His own power is engaged for them: *Neither shall any man pluck them out of my hand.* A mighty contest is here supposed about these sheep. The Shepherd is so careful of their welfare that he has them not only within his fold, and under his eye, but *in his hand,* interested in his special love and taken under his special protection *(all his saints are in thy hand,* Deu. 33:3); yet their enemies are so daring that they attempt to pluck them out of his hand — *his* whose *own* they are, whose *care* they are; but they cannot, they shall not, do it. Note, Those are safe who are in the hands of the Lord Jesus. The saints are *preserved in Christ Jesus:* and their salvation is not in their own keeping, but in the keeping of a Mediator. The Pharisees and rulers did all they could to frighten the disciples of Christ from following him, reproving and threatening them, but Christ saith that they shall not prevail. (*b.*) His Father's power is likewise engaged for their preservation, *v.* 29. He now appeared in weakness, and, lest his security should therefore be thought *insufficient,* he brings in his Father as a further security. Observe, [*a.*] The power of the Father: *My Father is greater than all;* greater than all the other *friends* of the church, all the other shepherds, magistrates or ministers, and able to do that for them which they cannot do. Those shepherds slumber and sleep, and it will be easy to pluck the sheep out of their hands; but he keeps his flock day and night. He is greater than all the enemies of the church, all the opposition given to her interests, and able to secure his own against all their insults; he is *greater than all* the combined force of hell and earth. He is greater in wisdom than the *old serpent,* though noted for subtlety; greater in strength than the great red dragon, though his name be *legion,* and his title *principalities and powers.* The devil and his angels have had many a push, many a pluck for the mastery, but have never yet prevailed, Rev. 12:7, 8. *The Lord on high is mightier.* [*b.*] The interest of the Father in the sheep, for the sake of which this power is engaged for them: "It is my Father *that gave them to me,* and he is concerned in honour to uphold his gift." They were given to the Son as a trust to be managed by him, and therefore God will still look after them. All the divine power is engaged for the accomplishment of all the divine counsels. [*c.*] The safety of the saints inferred from these two. If this be so, then *none* (neither man nor devil) is *able to pluck them out of the Father's hand,* not able to deprive them of the grace they have, nor to hinder them from the glory that is designed them; not able to put them out of God's protection, nor get them into their own power. Christ had himself experienced

the power of his Father *upholding* and *strengthening* him, and therefore puts all his followers into his hand too. He that secured the glory of the Redeemer will secure the glory of the redeemed. Further to corroborate the security, that the sheep of Christ may have strong consolation, he asserts the union of these two undertakers: "*I and my Father are one,* and have jointly and severally undertaken for the protection of the saints and their perfection." This denotes more than the harmony, and consent, and good understanding, that were between the Father and the Son in the work of man's redemption. Every good man is so far one with God as to concur with him; therefore it must be meant of the *oneness of the nature* of Father and Son, that they are the same in substance, and equal in power and glory. The fathers urged this both against the Sabellians, to prove the distinction and plurality of the persons, that the Father and the Son are two, and against the Arians, to prove the unity of the nature, that these two are *one.* If we should altogether hold our peace concerning this sense of the words, even the stones which the Jews took up to cast at him would speak it out, for the Jews understood him as hereby making himself God (*v.* 33) and he did not deny it. He proves that none could pluck them out *of his hand* because they could not pluck them out *of the Father's hand,* which had not been a conclusive argument if the Son had not had the same almighty power with the Father, and consequently been one with him in essence and operation.

IV. The rage, the outrage, of the Jews against him for this discourse: *The Jews took up stones again, v.* 31. It is not the word that is used before (*ch.* 8:59), but *ebastasan lithous* — *they carried stones* — great stones, stones that were a *load,* such as they used in stoning malefactors. They *brought* them from some place at a distance, as it were preparing things for his execution without any judicial process; as if he were convicted of blasphemy upon the notorious evidence of the fact, which needed no further trial. The absurdity of this insult which the Jews offered to Christ will appear if we consider, 1. That they had *imperiously,* not to say *impudently,* challenged him to tell them plainly whether he was the Christ or no; and yet now that he not only said he was the Christ, but proved himself so, they condemned him as a malefactor. If the preachers of the truth propose it *modestly,* they are branded as cowards; if *boldly,* as insolent; but *Wisdom is justified of her children.* 2. That when they had before made a similar attempt it was in vain; he *escaped through the midst of them* (*ch.* 8:59); yet they repeat their baffled attempt. Daring sinners will throw stones at heaven, though they return upon their own heads; and will strengthen themselves against the Almighty, though none ever hardened themselves against him and prospered.

V. Christ's tender expostulation with them upon occasion of this outrage (*v.* 32): *Jesus answered* what they *did,* for we do not find that they *said any thing,* unless perhaps they stirred up the crown that they had gathered about him to join with them, crying, *Stone him, stone him,* as afterwards, *Crucify him, crucify him.* When he could have answered them with fire from heaven, he mildly replied, *Many good works have I shown you from my Father: for which of those works do you stone me?* Words so very tender that one would think they should have melted a heart of stone. In dealing with his enemies he still argued from his works (men evidence what they *are* by what they *do*), his *good works* — *kala erga* excellent, eminent works. *Opera eximia vel praeclara;* the expression signifies both *great works* and *good works.*

1. The divine power of his works convicted them of the most obstinate infidelity. They were works *from his Father,* so far above the reach and course of nature as to prove him who did them *sent of God,* and acting by commission from him. These works he *showed* them; he did them openly before the people, and not in a corner. His works would bear the test, and refer themselves to the testimony of the most inquisitive and impartial spectators. He did not show his works by candle-light, as those that are concerned only for *show,* but he showed them at noon-day before the world, *ch.* 18:20. See Ps. 111:6. His works so undeniably *demonstrated* that they were an incontestable *demonstration* of the validity of his commission.

2. The divine grace of his works convicted them of the most base ingratitude. The works he did among them were not only miracles, but mercies; not only works of wonder to amaze them, but works of love and kindness to do them good, and so make them good, and endear himself to them. He healed the sick, cleansed the lepers, cast out devils, which

were favours, not only to the persons concerned, but to the public; these he had repeated, and multiplied: "*Now for which of these do you stone me?* You cannot say that I have done you any harm, or given you any just provocation; if therefore you will pick a quarrel with me, it must be for some good work, some good turn done you; tell me for which." Note, (1.) The horrid ingratitude that there is in our sins against God and Jesus Christ is a great aggravation of them, and makes them appear exceedingly sinful. See how God argues to this purpose, Deu. 32:6, Jer. 2:5; Mic. 6:3. (2.) We must not think it strange if we meet with those who not only hate us without cause, but are our adversaries for our love, Ps. 35:12; 41:9. When he asks, *For which of these do you stone me?* as he intimates the abundant satisfaction he had in his own innocency, which gives a man courage in a suffering day, so he puts his persecutors upon considering what was the true reason of their enmity, and asking, as all those should do that create trouble to their neighbour, *Why persecute we him?* As Job advises his friends to do, Job 19:28.

VI. Their vindication of the attempt they made upon Christ, and the cause upon which they grounded their prosecution, *v.* 33. What sin will want fig-leaves with which to cover itself, when even the bloody persecutors of the Son of God could find something to say for themselves?

1. They would not be thought such enemies to their country as to persecute him for a good work: *For a good work we stone thee not.* For indeed they would scarcely allow any of his works to be so. His curing the impotent man (*ch.* 5) and the blind man (*ch.* 9) were so far from being acknowledged good services to the town, and meritorious, that they were put upon the score of his crimes, because done on the sabbath day. But, if he had done any good works, they would not own that they stoned him *for them,* though these were really the things that did most exasperate them, *ch.* 11:47. Thus, though most absurd, they could not be brought to own their absurdities.

2. They would be thought such friends to God and his glory as to prosecute him for blasphemy: *Because that thou, being a man, makest thyself God.* Here is,

(1.) A pretended zeal for the law. They seem mightily concerned for the honour of the divine majesty, and to be seized with a religious horror at that which they imagined to be a reproach to it. A blasphemer was to be *stoned,* Lev. 24:16. This law, they thought, did not only justify, but sanctify, what they attempted, as Acts 26:9. Note, The vilest practices are often varnished with plausible pretences. As nothing is more *courageous* than a well-informed conscience, so nothing is more *outrageous* than a mistaken one. See Isa. 66:5; *ch.* 16:2.

(2.) A real enmity to the gospel, on which they could not put a greater affront than by representing Christ as a blasphemer. It is no new thing for the worst of characters to be put upon the best of men, by those that resolve to give them the worst of treatment. [1.] The crime laid to his charge is *blasphemy,* speaking reproachfully and despitefully of God. God himself is out of the sinner's reach, and not capable of receiving any real injury; and therefore enmity to God spits its venom at his name, and so shows its ill-will. [2.] The proof of the crime: *Thou, being a man, makest thyself God.* As it is God's glory that *he is God,* which we rob him of when we make him altogether such a one as ourselves, so it is his glory that *besides him there is no other,* which we rob him of when we make ourselves, or any creature, altogether like him. Now, *First,* Thus far they were in the right, that what Christ said of himself amounted to this — that he was God, for he had said that he was *one with the Father* and that he would *give eternal life;* and Christ does not deny it, which he would have done if it had been a mistaken inference from his words. But, *secondly,* They were much mistaken when they looked upon him as a *mere man,* and that the Godhead he claimed was a usurpation, and of his own making. They thought it absurd and impious that such a one as he, who appeared in the fashion of a poor, mean, despicable man, should profess himself the Messiah, and entitle himself to the honours confessedly due to the Son of God. Note, 1. Those who say that Jesus is a *mere man,* and only a *made God,* as the Socinians say, do in effect charge *him* with blasphemy, but do effectually prove it upon themselves. 2. He who, being a man, a sinful man, makes himself a god as the Pope does, who claims divine powers and prerogatives, is unquestionably a *blasphemer,* and *that* antichrist.

VII. Christ's reply to their accusation of him (for such their vindication of themselves was), and his making good those claims which they imputed to him as blasphemous (*v.* 34, etc.), where he proves himself to be no blasphemer, by two arguments: —

1. By an argument taken from *God's word.* He appeals to what was *written in their law,* that is, in the Old Testament; whoever opposes Christ, he is sure to have the scripture *on his side.* It is written (Ps. 82:6), *I have said, You are gods.* It is an argument *a minore ad majus — from the less to the greater.* If they were gods, much more am I. Observe,

(1.) How he explains the text (*v.* 35): *He called them gods to whom the word of God came, and the scripture cannot be broken.* The word of God's commission came to them, appointing them to their offices, as judges, and therefore they are called *gods,* Ex. 22:28. To some the word of God came immediately, as to Moses; to others in the way of an instituted ordinance. Magistracy is a divine institution; and magistrates are God's delegates, and therefore the scripture calleth them gods; and we are sure that the scripture *cannot be broken,* or broken in upon, or found fault with. Every word of God is *right;* the very style and language of scripture are unexceptionable, and not to be corrected, Mt. 5:18.

(2.) How he applies it. Thus much in general is easily inferred, that those were very rash and unreasonable who condemned Christ as a blasphemer, only for calling himself the Son of God, when yet they themselves called their rulers so, and therein the scripture warranted them. But the argument goes further (*v.* 36): If magistrates were called Gods, because they were commissioned to administer justice in the nation, *say you of him whom the Father hath sanctified, Thou blasphemest?* We have here two things concerning the Lord Jesus: — [1.] The honour done him by the *Father,* which he justly glories in: He *sanctified him,* and *sent him into the world.* Magistrates were called *the sons of God,* though the word of God only came to them, and the spirit of government came upon them by measure, as upon Saul; but our Lord Jesus was himself the *Word,* and had the *Spirit without measure.* They were constituted for a particular country, city, or nation; but he was sent *into the world,* vested with a universal authority, as Lord of all. They were *sent to,* as persons at a distance; he was *sent forth,* as having been from eternity with God. The Father *sanctified him,* that is, designed him and set him apart to the office of Mediator, and qualified and fitted him for that office. *Sanctifying* him is the same with *sealing* him, *ch.* 6:27. Note, Whom the Father sends he sanctifies; whom he designs for holy purposes he prepares with holy principles and dispositions. The holy God will reward, and therefore will employ, none but such as he finds or makes holy. The Father's sanctifying and sending him is here vouched as a sufficient warrant for his calling himself the *Son of God;* for because he was a *holy thing* he was *called the Son of God,* Lu. 1:35. See Rom. 1:4. [2.] The dishonour done him by the Jews, which he justly complains of — that they impiously said of him, whom the Father had thus dignified, that he was a *blasphemer,* because he called himself the *Son of God: "Say you of him* so and so? Dare you say so? Dare you thus set your mouths against the heavens? Have you brow and brass enough to tell the God of truth that he lies, or *to condemn him that is most just?* Look me in the face, and say it if you can. What! say you of the Son of God that *he is a blasphemer?"* If devils, whom he came to condemn, had said so of him, it had not been so strange; but that *men,* whom he came to teach and save, should say so of him, *be astonished, O heavens! at this.* See what is the language of an obstinate unbelief; it does, in effect, call the holy Jesus a blasphemer. It is hard to say which is more to be wondered at, that men who breathe in God's air should yet speak such things, or that men who have spoken such things should still be suffered to breathe in God's air. The wickedness of man, and the patience of God, as it were, contend which shall be most *wonderful.*

2. By an argument taken from *his own works, v.* 37, 38. In the former he only answered the charge of blasphemy by an argument *ad hominem — turning a man's own argument against himself;* but he here makes out his own claims, and proves that he and the Father are one (*v.* 37, 38): *If I do not the works of my Father, believe me not.* Though he might justly have abandoned such blasphemous wretches as incurable, yet he vouchsafes to reason with them. Observe,

(1.) *From what* he argues — from his works, which he had often vouched as his credentials, and the proofs of his mission. As he proved himself sent of God by the *divinity* of his works, so we must prove ourselves allied to Christ by the *Christianity* of ours. [1.] The argument is very cogent; for the works he did were the *works of his Father,* which the Father only could do, and which could not be done in the ordinary course of nature, but only by the sovereign over-ruling power of the God of nature. *Opera Deo propria — works peculiar to God,* and *Opera Deo Digna — works worthy of God* — the works of a divine power. He that can dispense with the laws of nature, repeal, altar, and overrule them at his pleasure, by his own power, is certainly the sovereign prince who first instituted and enacted those laws. The miracles which the apostles wrought in his name, by his power, and for the confirmation of his doctrine, corroborated this argument, and continued the evidence of it when he was gone. [2.] It is proposed as fairly as can be desired, and put to a short issue. *First, If I do not the works of my Father, believe me not.* He does not demand a blind and implicit faith, nor an assent to his divine mission further than he gave proof of it. He did not wind himself into the affections of the people, nor wheedle them by sly insinuations, nor impose upon their credulity by bold assertions, but with the greatest fairness imaginable quitted all demands of their faith, further than he produced warrants for these demands. Christ is no hard master, who expects to reap in assents where he has not sown in arguments. None shall perish for the disbelief of that which was not proposed to them with sufficient motives of credibility, Infinite Wisdom itself being judge. *Secondly,* "But if I do *the works of my Father, if I work* undeniable miracles for the confirmation of a holy doctrine, *though you believe not me,* though you are so scrupulous as not to take my word, yet *believe the works:* believe your own eyes, your own reason; the thing speaks itself plainly enough." As the invisible things of the Creator are clearly seen by his works of creation and common providence (Rom. 1:20), so the invisible things of the Redeemer were seen by his miracles, and by all his works both of power and mercy; so that those who were not convinced by these works were *without excuse.*

(2.) *For what* he argues — *that you may know and believe,* may believe it intelligently, and with an entire satisfaction, that *the Father is in me and I in him;* which is the same with what he had said (*v.* 30): *I and my Father are one.* The Father was so in the Son as that in him *dwelt all the fulness of the Godhead,* and it was by a divine power that he wrought his miracles; the Son was so in the Father as that he was perfectly acquainted with the whole of his mind, not by communication, but by consciousness, having lain in his bosom. This we must *know;* not know and *explain* (for we cannot by searching find it out to perfection), but know and *believe* it; acknowledging and adoring the depth, when we cannot find the bottom.

Verses 39–42

We have here the issue of the conference with the Jews. One would have thought it would have convinced and melted them, but their hearts were hardened. Here we are told,

I. How they attacked him by force. Therefore *they sought again to take him, v.* 39. Therefore, 1. Because he had fully answered their charge of blasphemy, and wiped off that imputation, so that they could not for shame go on with their attempts to stone him, therefore they contrived to seize him, and prosecute him as an offender against the state. When they were constrained to drop their attempt by a popular tumult, they would try what they could do under colour of a legal process. See Rev. 12:13. Or, 2. Because he persevered in the same testimony concerning himself, they persisted in their malice against him. What he had said before he did in effect say again, for the *faithful witness* never departs from what he has once said; and therefore, having the same provocation, they express the same resentment, and justify their attempt to stone him by another attempt to take him. Such is the temper of a persecuting spirit, and such its policy, *malè facta malè factis tegere ne perpluant — to cover one set of bad deeds with another, lest the former should fall through.*

II. How he avoided them by flight; not an inglorious retreat, in which there was any thing of human infirmity, but a glorious retirement, in which there was much of a divine power. He *escaped out of their hands,* not by the interposal of any friend that helped him, but by his own wisdom he *got clear* of them; he drew a veil over himself, or cast a mist before their eyes, or tied the hands of those whose hearts he did not turn. Note, No weapon formed against our Lord Jesus shall prosper, Ps. 2:4. He *escaped,* not because he was afraid to suffer, but because *his hour was not come.* And he who knew how to *deliver himself* no doubt knows how to *deliver the godly out of temptation,* and to make *a way for them to escape.*

III. How he disposed of himself in his retirement: He *went away again beyond Jordan, v.* 40. The bishop of our souls came not to be fixed in one see, but to go about from place to place, doing good. This great benefactor was never out of his way, for wherever he came there was work to be done. Though Jerusalem was the royal city, yet he made many a kind visit to the country, not only to his own country Galilee, but to other parts, even those that lay most remote beyond Jordan. Now observe,

1. What *shelter* he found there. He went into a private part of the country, and *there he abode;* there he found some rest and quietness, when in Jerusalem he could find none. Note, Though persecutors may drive Christ and his gospel out of their own city or country, they cannot drive him or it out of the world. Though Jerusalem was not gathered, nor would be, yet Christ was glorious, and would be. Christ's going now beyond Jordan was a figure of the taking of the kingdom of God from the Jews, and bringing it to the Gentiles. Christ and his gospel have often found better entertainment among the plain country-people than among *the wise, the mighty, the noble,* 1 Co. 1:26, 27.

2. What *success* he found there. He did not go thither merely for his own security, but to do good there; and he chose to go thither, where John at first baptized (*ch.* 1:28), because there could not but remain some impressions of John's ministry and baptism thereabouts, which would dispose them to receive Christ and his doctrine; for it was not three years since John was baptizing, and Christ was himself baptized here at Bethabara. Christ came hither now to see what fruit there was of all the pains John Baptist had taken among them, and what they retained of the things they then heard and received. The event in some measure answered expectation; for we are told,

(1.) That they flocked after him (*v.* 41): *Many resorted to him.* The return of the means of grace to a place, after they have been for some time intermitted, commonly occasions a great stirring of affections. Some think Christ chose to *abide* at *Bethabara,* the *house of passage,* where the ferry-boats lay by which they crossed the river Jordan, that the confluence of people thither might give an opportunity of teaching many who would come to hear him when it *lay in their way,* but who would scarcely go a step out of the road for an opportunity of attending on his word.

(2.) That they reasoned in his favour, and sought arguments to induce them to close with him as much as those at Jerusalem sought objections against him. They said very judiciously, *John did no miracle, but all things that John spoke of this man were true.* Two things they considered, upon recollecting what they had seen and heard from John, and comparing it with Christ's ministry. [1.] That Christ far exceeded John Baptist's power, for *John did no miracle,* but Jesus does many; whence it is easy to infer that Jesus is greater than John. And, if John was so great a prophet, how great then is this Jesus! Christ is best known and acknowledged by such a comparison with others as sets him superlatively above others. Though John came in the spirit and power of Elias, yet he did not work miracles, as Elias did, lest the minds of people should be made to hesitate between him and Jesus; therefore the honour of working miracles was reserved for Jesus as a flower of his crown, that there might be a sensible demonstration, and *undeniable* one, that though he came after John, yet he was *preferred far before him.* [2.] That Christ exactly answered John Baptist's testimony. John not only *did no miracle* to *divert* people from Christ, but he said a great deal to direct them to Christ, and to turn them over as apprentices to him, and this came to their minds *now:* all things that *John said of this man were true,* that he should be the *Lamb of God,* should *baptize with Holy Ghost and with fire.* Great things John had said of him, which raised their expectations; so that though they had not zeal enough to carry them into his country to enquire after him, yet, when he came into theirs, and brought his gospel to their doors, they acknowledged him as great as John had said he would be. When we get acquainted with Christ, and come to know him experimentally, we find all things that the scripture saith of him to be true; nay, and that the reality exceeds the report, 1 Ki. 10:6, 7. John Baptist was now dead and gone, and yet his hearers profited by what they had heard formerly, and, by comparing what they heard then with what they saw now, they gained a double advantage; for, *First,* They were confirmed in their belief that *John was a prophet,* who foretold such things, and spoke of the eminency to which this Jesus would arrive, though his beginning was so small. *Secondly,* They were prepared to believe that *Jesus was the Christ,* in whom they saw those things accomplished which John foretold. By this we see that the success and efficacy of the word preached are not confined to the life of the preacher, nor do they expire with his breath, but that which seemed as *water spilt upon the ground* may afterwards be *gathered up again.* See Zec. 1:5, 6.

(3.) That many believed on him there. Believing that he who wrought such miracles, and in whom John's predictions were fulfilled, was what he declared himself to be, the Son of God, they gave up themselves to him as his disciples, *v.* 42. An emphasis is here to be laid, [1.] Upon the persons that believed on him; they were *many.* While those that received and embraced his doctrine at Jerusalem were but as the grape-gleanings of the vintage, those that believed on him in the country, beyond the Jordan, were a full harvest gathered in to him. [2.] Upon the place where this was; it was where John had been preaching and baptizing and had had great success; *there* many believed on the Lord Jesus. Where the preaching of the doctrine of repentance has had success, as desired, there the preaching of the doctrine of reconciliation and gospel grace is most likely to be prosperous. Where John has been acceptable, Jesus will not be unacceptable. The jubilee-trumpet sounds sweetest in the ears of those who in the day of atonement have afflicted their souls for sin.

CHAPTER 11

In this chapter we have the history of that illustrious miracle which Christ wrought a little before his death — the raising of Lazarus to life, which is recorded only by this evangelist; for the other three confine themselves to what Christ did in Galilee, where he resided most, and scarcely ever carried their history into Jerusalem till the passion-week: whereas John's memoirs relate chiefly to what passed at Jerusalem; this passage therefore was reserved for his pen. Some suggest that, when the other evangelists wrote, Lazarus was alive, and it would not well agree either with his safety or with his humility to have it recorded till now, when it is supposed he was dead. It is more largely recorded than any other of Christ's miracles, not only because there are many circumstances of it so very instructive and the miracle of itself so great a proof of Christ's mission, but because it was an earnest of that which was to be the crowning proof of all — Christ's own resurrection. Here is, I. The tidings sent to our Lord Jesus of the sickness of Lazarus, and his entertainment of those tidings (*v.* 1–16). II. The visit he made to Lazarus's relations when he had heard of his death, and their entertainment of the visit (*v.* 17–32). III. The miracle wrought in the raising of Lazarus from the dead (*v.* 33–44). IV. The effect wrought by this miracle upon others (*v.* 45–57).

Verses 1–16

We have in these verses,

I. A particular account of the parties principally concerned in this story, *v.* 1, 2. 1. They lived at *Bethany,* a village nor far from Jerusalem, where Christ usually lodged when he came up to the feasts. It is here called the *town of Mary and Martha,* that is, the town where they dwelt, as Bethsaida is called the *city of Andrew and Peter, ch.* 1:44. For I see no reason to think, as some do, that Martha and Mary were owners of the town, and the rest were *their* tenants. 2. Here was a brother named *Lazarus;* his *Hebrew* name probably was *Eleazar,* which being contracted, and a Greek termination put to it, is made *Lazarus.* Perhaps in prospect of this history our Saviour made use of the name of *Lazarus* in that parable wherein he designed to set forth the blessedness of the righteous in the bosom of Abraham immediately after death, Lu. 16:22. 3. Here were two sisters, *Martha* and *Mary,* who seem to have been the housekeepers, and to have managed the affairs of the family, while perhaps Lazarus lived a retired life, and gave himself to study and contemplation. Here was a decent, happy, well-ordered family, and a family that Christ was very much conversant with, where yet there was neither husband nor wife (for aught that appears), but the house kept by a brother, and his sisters dwelling together in unity. 4. One of the sisters is particularly described to be *that Mary which anointed the Lord with ointment, v.* 2. Some think she was that woman that we read of, Lu. 7:37, 38, who had been a *sinner,* a bad woman. I rather think it refers to that anointing of Christ which this evangelist relates (*ch.* 12:3); for the evangelists do never refer one to another, but John frequently refers in one place of his gospel to another. Extraordinary acts of piety and devotion, that come from an honest principle of love to Christ, will not only find acceptance with him, but gain reputation in the church, Mt. 26:13. This was she *whose brother Lazarus was sick;* and the sickness of those we love is our affliction. The more friends we have the more frequently we are thus afflicted by sympathy; and the dearer they are the more grievous it is. The multiplying of our comforts is but the multiplying of our cares and crosses.

II. The tidings that were sent to our Lord Jesus of the sickness of Lazarus, *v.* 3. *His sisters* knew where Jesus was, a great way off beyond Jordan, and they sent a special messenger to him, to acquaint him with the affliction of their family, in which they manifest, 1. The affection and concern they had for their brother. Though, it is likely, his estate would come to them after his death, yet they earnestly desired his life, as they ought to do. They showed their love to him now that he was sick, for a *brother is born for adversity,* and so is a sister too. We must weep with our friends when they weep, as well as rejoice with them when they rejoice. 2. The regard they had to the Lord Jesus, whom they were willing to make acquainted with all their concerns, and, like Jephthah, to utter all their words before him. Though God knows all our wants, and griefs, and cares, he will know them from us, and is honoured by our laying them before him. The message they sent was very short, not *petitioning,* much less *prescribing* or *pressing,* but barely relating the case with the tender insinuation of a powerful plea, *Lord, behold, he whom thou lovest is sick.* They do not say, He whom *we* love, but *he whom thou lovest.* Our greatest encouragements in prayer are fetched from God himself and from his grace. They do not say, Lord, behold, he *who loveth thee,* but *he whom thou lovest;* for *herein is love, not that we loved God, but that he loved us.* Our love to him is not worth speaking of, but his to us can never be enough spoken of. Note, (1.) There are some of the friends and followers of the Lord Jesus for whom he has a special kindness above others. Among the twelve there was one whom Jesus loved. (2.) It is no new thing for those whom Christ loves to be sick: all things come alike to all. Bodily distempers correct the corruption, and try the graces, of God's people. (3.) It is a great comfort to us, when we are sick, to have those about us that will pray for us. (4.) We have great encouragement in our prayers for those who are sick, if we have ground to hope that they are such as Christ loves; and we have reason to love and pray for those whom we have reason to think Christ loves and cares for.

III. An account how Christ entertained the tidings brought him of the illness of his friend.

1. He prognosticated the event and issue of the sickness, and probably sent it as a message to the sisters of Lazarus by the express, to support them while he delayed to come to them. Two things he prognosticates: —

(1.) *This sickness is not unto death.* It was mortal, proved *fatal,* and no doubt but Lazarus was truly dead for four days. But, [1.] That was not the errand upon which this sickness was sent; it came not, as in a common case, to be a summons to the grave, but there was a further intention in it. Had it been sent on that errand, his *rising from the dead would have defeated it.* [2.] That was not the final effect of this sickness. He *died,* and yet it might be said he did not *die,* for *factum non dicitur quod non perseverat — That is not said to be done which is not done for a perpetuity.* Death is an everlasting farewell to this world; it is the way whence we shall not return; and in this sense it was *not unto death.* The grave was his *long home,* his *house of eternity.* Thus Christ said of the maid whom he proposed to restore to life, *She is not dead.* The sickness of good people, how threatening soever, is *nor unto death,* for it is not unto *eternal* death. The body's death to this world is the soul's birth into another world; when we or our friends are sick, we make it our principal support that there is hope of a recovery, but in that we may be disappointed; therefore it is our wisdom to build upon that in which we cannot be disappointed; if they belong to Christ, let the worst come to the worst, they cannot be *hurt of the second death,* and then not much hurt of the first.

(2.) *But it is for the glory of God,* that an opportunity may be given for the manifesting of God's glorious power. The afflictions of the saints are designed for the glory of God, that he may have opportunity of showing them favour; for the sweetest mercies, and the most effecting, are those which are occasioned by trouble. Let this reconcile us to the darkest dispensations of Providence, they are all for the glory of God, this sickness, this loss, or this disappointment, is so; and, if God be glorified, we ought to be satisfied, Lev. 10:3. It was for the glory of God, for it was *that the Son of God might be glorified thereby,* as it gave him occasion to work that glorious miracle, the *raising of him from the dead.* As, before, the man was *born blind* that Christ might have the honour of curing him (*ch.* 9:3), so Lazarus must be sick and die, that Christ may be glorified as the Lord of life. Let this comfort those whom Christ loves under all their grievances that the design of them all is that *the Son of God may be glorified thereby,* his wisdom, power, and goodness, glorified in supporting and relieving them; see 2 Co. 12:9, 10.

2. He deferred visiting his patient, *v.* 5, 6. They had pleaded, *Lord, it is he whom thou lovest,* and the plea is allowed (*v.* 5): *Jesus loved Martha, and her sister, and Lazarus.* Thus the claims of faith are ratified in the court of heaven. Now one would think it should follow, *When he heard therefore that he was sick* he made all the haste that he could to him; if he loved them, now was a time to show it by hastening to them, for he knew they impatiently expected him. But he took the contrary way to show his love: it is not said, He loved them and *yet* he lingered; but he loved them and *therefore* he lingered; when he heard that his friend was sick, instead of coming post to him, he abode *two days still in the same place where he was.* (1.) He *loved them,* that is, had a great opinion of Martha and Mary, of their wisdom and grace, of their faith and patience, above others of his disciples, and therefore he deferred coming to them, that he might try them, that their trial might at last *be found to praise and honour.* (2.) He *loved them,* that is, he designed to do something great and extraordinary for them, to work such a miracle for their relief as he had not wrought for any of his friends; and therefore he delayed coming to them, that Lazarus might be *dead* and *buried* before he came. If Christ had come presently, and cured the sickness of Lazarus, he had done no more than he did for *many;* if he had raised him to life when newly dead, no more than he had done for *some:* but, deferring his relief so long, he had an opportunity of doing more for him than for *any.* Note, God hath gracious intentions even in seeming delays, Isa. 54:7, 8; 49:14, etc. Christ's friends at Bethany were not out of his thoughts, though, when he heard of their distress, he made no haste to them. When the work of deliverance, temporal or spiritual, public or personal, stands at a stay, it does but stay the time, and *every thing is beautiful in its season.*

IV. The discourse he had with his disciples when he was about to visit his friends at Bethany, *v.* 7–16. The conference is so very free and familiar as to make out what Christ saith, *I have called you friends.* Two things he discourses about — his own *danger* and Lazarus's *death.*

1. His own danger in going into Judea, *v.* 7–10.

(1.) Here is the notice which Christ gave his disciples of his purpose to go into Judea towards Jerusalem. His disciples were the men of his counsel, and to them he saith (*v.* 7), "*Let us go into Judea again,* though those of Judea are unworthy of such a favour." Thus Christ repeats the tenders of his mercy to those who have often rejected them. Now this may be considered, [1.] As a purpose of his kindness to his friends at Bethany, whose affliction, and all the aggravating circumstances of it, he knew very well, though no more expresses were sent to him; for he was present in spirit, though absent in body. When he knew they were brought to the last extremity, when the brother and sisters had given and taken a final farewell, "Now," saith he, "let us go to Judea." Christ will arise in favour of his people when *the time to favour them, yea, the set time, is come;* and the worst time is commonly the set time — when *our hope is lost, and we are cut off for our parts;* then they shall *know that I am the Lord* when *I have opened the graves,* Eze. 37:11, 13. In the depths of affliction, let this therefore keep us out of the depths of despair, that man's extremity is God's opportunity, *Jehovah-jireh.* Or, [2.] As a trial of the courage of the disciples, whether they would venture to follow him thither, where they had so lately been frightened by an attempt upon their Master's life, which they looked upon as an attempt upon theirs too. To go to Judea, which was so lately made *too hot* for them, was a saying that *proved them.* But Christ did not say, "*Go you into Judea,* and I will stay and take shelter here;" no, *Let us go.* Note, Christ never brings his people into any peril but he accompanies them in it, and is with them even when they *walk through the valley of the shadow of death.*

(2.) Their objection against this journey (*v.* 8): *Master, the Jews of late sought to stone thee, and goest thou thither again?* Here, [1.] They remind him of the danger he had been in there not long since. Christ's disciples are apt to make a greater matter of sufferings than their Master does, and to remember injuries longer. He had put up with the affront, it was over and gone, and forgotten, but his disciples could not forget it; *of late, nyn — now,* as if it were this very day, they *sought to stone thee.* Though it was at least two months ago, the remembrance of the fright was fresh in their minds. [2.] They marvel that he will *go thither again.* "Wilt thou favour those with thy presence that have expelled thee out of their coasts?" Christ's ways in passing by offences are *above our ways.* "Wilt thou expose thyself among a people that are so desperately enraged against thee? *Goest thou thither again,* where thou hast been so ill used?" Here they showed great care for their Master's safety, as Peter did, when he said, *Master, spare thyself;* had Christ been inclined to shift off suffering, he did not want friends to persuade him to it, but he had *opened his mouth to the Lord,* and he would not, he could not, go back. Yet, while the disciples show a concern for his safety, they discover at the same time, *First,* A distrust of his power; as if he could not secure both himself and them now in Judea as well as he had done formerly. Is his arm shortened? When we are solicitous for the interests of Christ's church and kingdom in the world, we must yet rest satisfied in the wisdom and power of the Lord Jesus, who knows how to secure a flock of sheep in the midst of a herd of wolves. *Secondly,* A secret fear of suffering themselves; for they count upon this if he suffer. When our own private interests happen to run in the same channel with those of the public, we are apt to think ourselves zealous for the Lord of hosts, when really we are only zealous for our own wealth, credit, ease, and safety, and *seek our own things,* under colour of seeking the things of Christ; we have therefore need to distinguish upon our principles.

(3.) Christ's answer to this objection (v. 9, 10): *Are there not twelve hours in the day?* The Jews divided every day into twelve hours, and made their hours longer or shorter according as the days were, so that an hour with them was the twelfth part of the time between sun and sun; so some. Or, lying much more south than we, their days were nearer twelve hours long than ours. The divine Providence has given us day-light to work by, and lengthens it out to a competent time; and, reckoning the year round, *every country* has just as much *daylight as night,* and so much more as the *twilights* amount to. Man's life is a *day;* this day is divided into divers ages, states, and opportunities, as into hours shorter or longer, as God has appointed; the consideration of this should make us not only *very busy,* as to the *work* of life (if there were *twelve hours in the day,* each of them ought to be filled up with duty, and none of *them* trifled away), but also *very easy,* as to the perils of life; our day shall be lengthened out till our work be done, and our testimony finished. This Christ applies to his case, and shows why he must go to Judea, because he had a *clear call to go.* For the opening of this, [1.] He shows the comfort and satisfaction which a man has in his own mind while he keeps in the way of his duty, as it is in general prescribed by the word of God, and particularly determined by the providence of God: *If any man walk in the day, he stumbles not;* that is, If a man keep close to his duty, and mind that, and set the will of God before him as his rule, with an impartial respect to all God's commandments, he does not *hesitate* in his own mind, but, *walking uprightly, walks surely,* and with a holy confidence. As he that walks in the day stumbles not, but goes on steadily and cheerfully in his way, *because he sees the light of this world,* and by it sees his way before him; so a good man, without any collateral security or sinister aims, relies upon the word of God as his rule, and regards the glory of God as his end, *because he sees* those two great lights, and keeps his eye upon them; thus he is furnished with a faithful guide in all his doubts, and a powerful guard in all his dangers, Gal. 6:4; Ps. 119:6. Christ, wherever he went, walked *in the day,* and so shall we, if we follow his steps. [2.] He shows the pain and peril a man is in who walks not according to this rule (v. 10): *If a man walk in the night, he stumbles;* that is, If a man walk in the way of his heart, and the sight of his eyes, and according to the course of this world, — if he consult his own carnal reasonings more than the will and glory of God, — he falls into temptations and snares, is liable to great uneasiness and frightful apprehensions, trembles at the *shaking of a leaf,* and *flees* when none *pursues;* while an upright man *laughs at the shaking of the spear,* and stands undaunted when ten thousand invade. See Isa. 33:14–16, he stumbles, *because there is no light in him,* for light in us is that to our

moral actions which light about us is to our natural actions. He has not a good principle within; he is not sincere; his eye is evil. Thus Christ not only justifies his purpose of going into Judea, but encourages his disciples to go along with him, and fear no evil.

2. The death of Lazarus is here discoursed of between Christ and his disciples, v. 11–16, where we have,

(1.) The notice Christ gave his disciples of death of Lazarus, and an intimation that his business into Judea was to look after him, v. 11. After he had prepared his disciples for this dangerous march into an enemy's country, he then gives them,

[1.] Plain intelligence of the death of Lazarus, though he had received no advice of it: *Our friend Lazarus sleepeth.* See here how Christ calls a believer and a believer's death.

First, He calls a believer his friend: *Our friend Lazarus.* Note, 1. There is a covenant of friendship between Christ and believers, and a friendly affection and communion pursuant to it, which our Lord Jesus will own and not be ashamed of. *His secret is with the righteous.* 2. Those whom Christ is pleased to own as his friends all his disciples should take for *theirs.* Christ speaks of Lazarus as their common friend: *Our friend.* 3. Death itself does not break the bond of friendship between Christ and a believer. Lazarus is dead, and yet he is still *our friend.*

Secondly, He calls the death of a believer a *sleep: he sleepeth.* It is good to call death by such names and titles as will help to make it more *familiar* and less *formidable* to us. The death of Lazarus was in a peculiar sense a sleep, as that of Jairus's daughter, because he was to be raised again speedily; and, since we are sure to *rise again at last,* why should that make any great difference? And why should not the believing hope of that resurrection to eternal life make it as easy to us to put off the body and die as it is to put off our clothes and go to sleep? A good Christian, when he dies, does but sleep: he rests from the labours of the day past, and is refreshing himself for the next morning. Nay, herein death has the advantage of sleep, that sleep is only the *parenthesis,* but death is the *period,* of our cares and toils. The soul does not sleep, but becomes more active; but the body sleeps without any toss, without any terror; not distempered nor disturbed. The grave to the wicked is a prison, and its grave-clothes as the shackles of a criminal reserved for execution; but to the godly it is a bed, and all its bands as the soft and downy fetters of an easy quiet sleep. Though the body *corrupt,* it will rise in the morning as if it had never seen corruption; it is but putting off our clothes to be mended and trimmed up for the marriage day, the coronation day, to which we must rise. See Isa. 57:2; 1 Th. 4:14. The Greeks called their burying–places *dormitories — koimētēria.*

[2.] Particular intimations of his favourable intentions concerning Lazarus: *but I go, that I may awake him out of sleep.* He could have done it, and yet have staid where he was: he that restored at a distance one that was *dying* (ch. 4:50) could have raised at a distance one that was *dead;* but he would put this honour upon the miracle, to work it by the grave side: *I go, to awake him.* As sleep is a resemblance of death, so a man's awaking out of sleep when he is called, especially when he is called by his own name, is an emblem of the resurrection (Job 14:15): *Then shalt thou call.* Christ had no sooner said, *Our friend sleeps,* but presently he adds, *I go, that I may awake him.* When Christ tells his people at any time how bad the case is he lets them know in the same breath how easily, how quickly, he can mend it. Christ's telling his disciples that this was his business to Judea might help to take off their fear of going with him thither; he did not go upon a public errand to the temple, but a private visit, which would not so much expose him and them; and, besides, it was to do a kindness to a family to which they were all obliged.

(2.) Their mistake of the meaning of this notice, and the blunder they made about it (v. 12, 13): They said, *Lord, if he sleep, he shall do well.* This intimates, [1.] *Some concern* they had for their friend Lazarus; they hoped he would recover; *sōthēsetai — he shall be saved* from dying at this time. Probably they had understood, by the messenger who brought news of his illness, that one of the most threatening symptoms he was under was that he was restless, and could get no sleep; and now that they heard he slept they concluded the fever was going off, and the worst was past. Sleep is often nature's physic, and reviving to its weak and weary powers. This is true of the sleep of death; if a good Christian so

sleep, he shall do well, better than he did here. [2.] A *greater concern* for themselves; for hereby they insinuate that it was now needless for Christ to go to him, and expose himself and them. "If he sleep, he will be quickly well, and we may stay where we are." Thus we are willing to hope that the good work which we are called to do will do itself, or will be done by some other hand, if there be peril in the doing of it.

(3.) This mistake of theirs rectified (v. 13): *Jesus spoke of his death.* See here, [1.] How dull of understanding Christ's disciples as yet were. Let us not therefore condemn all those as heretics who mistake the sense of some of Christ's sayings. It is not good to aggravate our brethren's mistakes; yet this was a *gross* one, for it had easily been prevented if they had remembered how frequently death is called a sleep in the Old Testament. They should have understood Christ when he spoke scripture language. Besides, it would sound oddly for their Master to undertake a journey of two or three days only to awake a friend out of a natural sleep, which any one else might do. What Christ undertakes to do, we may be sure, is something great and uncommon, and a work *worthy of himself.* [2.] How carefully the evangelist corrects this error: *Jesus spoke of his death.* Those that speak in an unknown tongue, or use similitudes, should learn hence to *explain themselves,* and pray that they may interpret, to prevent mistakes.

(4.) The plain and express declaration which Jesus made to them of the death of Lazarus, and his resolution to go to Bethany, v. 14, 15. [1.] He gives them notice of the death of Lazarus; what he had before said darkly he now says plainly, and without a figure: *Lazarus is dead,* v. 14. Christ takes cognizance of the death of his saints, for it is precious in his sight (Ps. 116:15), and he is not pleased if we do not consider it, and lay it to heart. See what a compassionate teacher Christ is, and how he condescends to those that are out of the way, and by his subsequent sayings and doings explains the difficulties of what went before. [2.] He gives them the reason why he had delayed so long to go and see him: *I am glad for your sakes that I was not there.* If he had been there time enough, he would have healed his disease and prevented his death, which would have been much for the comfort of Lazarus's friends, but then his disciples would have seen no further proof of his power than what they had often seen, and, consequently, their faith had received no improvement; but now that he went and raised him from the dead, as there were many brought to *believe on him* who before did no (v. 45), so there was much done towards the perfecting of what was lacking in the faith of those that did, which Christ aimed at: *To the intent that you may believe.* [3.] He resolves now to go to Bethany, and take his disciples along with him: *Let us go unto him.* Not, "Let us go to his sisters, to comfort them" (which is the utmost we can do), but, Let us go *to him;* for Christ can *show wonders to the dead.* Death, which will separate us from all our other friends, and cut us off from correspondence with them, cannot separate us from the love of Christ, nor put us out of the reach of his calls; as he will maintain his *covenant with the dust,* so he can make visits to the dust. *Lazarus is dead,* but *let us go to him;* though perhaps those who said, If he sleep there is *no need* to go, were ready to say, If he be dead it is to *no purpose* to go.

(5.) Thomas exciting his fellow-disciples cheerfully to attend their Master's motions (v. 16): *Thomas, who is called Didymus.* Thomas in Hebrew and Didymus in Greek signify a *twin;* it is said of Rebekah (Gen. 25:24) that there were *twins in her womb;* the word is *Thomim.* Probably Thomas was a *twin.* He said to *his fellow-disciples* (who probably looked with fear and concern upon one another when Christ had said so positively, *Let us go to him*), very courageously, *Let us also go that we may die with him;* with him, that is,

[1.] With Lazarus, who was now dead; so some take it. Lazarus was a dear and loving friend both to Christ and his disciples, and perhaps Thomas had a particular intimacy with him. Now if he be dead, saith he, *let us* even *go and die with him.* For, *First,* "If we *survive,* we know not how to *live without him.*" Probably Lazarus had done them many good offices, sheltered them, and provided for them, and been to them *instead of eyes;* and now that he was gone they had *no man like-minded,* and "Therefore," saith he, "we had as good die with him." Thus we are sometimes ready to think our lives bound up in the lives of some that were dear to us: but God will teach us to live, and to live comfortably, up himself, when those are gone without whom we thought we could not live. But this is not all. *Secondly,* "If we die, we hope to be *happy with him.*" Such a firm belief he has of a happiness on the other side death, and such good hope through grace of their own and Lazarus's interest in it, that he is willing they should all go and *die with him.* It is better to die, and go along with our Christian friends to that world which is enriched by their removal to it, than stay behind in a world that is impoverished by their departure out of it. The more of our friends are translated hence, the fewer cords we have to bind us to this earth, and the more to draw our hearts heavenwards. How pleasantly does the good man speak of dying, as if it were but undressing and going to bed!

[2.] "Let us go and die *with our Master,* who is now exposing himself to death by venturing into Judea;" and so I rather think it is meant. "If he will go into danger, let us also go and take our lot with him, according to the command we received, *Follow me.*" Thomas knew so much of the malice of the Jews against Christ, and the counsels of God concerning him, which he had often told them of, that it was no foreign supposition that he was now going to die. And now Thomas manifests, *First,* A gracious readiness to die with Christ himself, flowing from strong affections to him, though his faith was weak, as appeared afterwards, *ch.* 14:5; 20:25. *Where thou diest I will die,* Ruth 1:17. *Secondly,* A zealous desire to help his fellow-disciples into the same frame: *"Let us go,* one and all, and *die with him;* if they stone him, let them stone us; who would desire to survive such a Master?" Thus, in difficult times, Christians should animate one another. We may each of us say, *Let us die with him.* Note, The consideration of the dying of the Lord Jesus should make us willing to die whenever God calls for us.

Verses 17–32

The matter being determined, that Christ will go to Judea, and his disciples with him, they address themselves to their journey; in this journey some circumstances happened which the other evangelists record, as the healing of the blind man at Jericho, and the conversion of Zaccheus. We must not reckon ourselves out of our way, while we are in the way of doing good; nor be so intent upon one good office as to neglect another.

At length, he comes near to Bethany, which is said to be about *fifteen furlongs* from Jerusalem, about two measured miles, *v.* 18. Notice is taken of this, that this miracle was in effect wrought *in Jerusalem,* and so was put to her score. Christ's miracles in Galilee were more *numerous,* but those in or near Jerusalem were more *illustrious;* there he healed one that had been diseased *thirty-eight years,* another that had been blind *from his birth,* and raised one that had been dead *four days.* To Bethany Christ came, and observe,

I. What posture he found his friends there in. When he had been last with them it is probable that he left them well, in health and joy; but when we part from our friends (though Christ knew) we know not what changes may affect us or them before we meet again.

1. He found his friend Lazarus *in the grave, v.* 17. When he came near the town, probably by the burying-place belonging to the town, he was told by the neighbours, or some persons whom he met, that Lazarus had been *four days buried.* Some think that Lazarus died the same day that the messenger came to Jesus with the tidings of his sickness, and so reckon two days for his abode in the same place and two days for his journey. I rather think that Lazarus died at the very instant that Jesus, *"Our friend sleepeth,* he is now newly fallen asleep;" and that the time between his death and burial (which among the Jews was but short), with the four days of his lying in the grave, was taken up in this journey; for Christ travelled publicly, as appears by his passing through Jericho, and his abode at Zaccheus's house took up some time. Promised salvations, though they always come surely, yet often come slowly.

2. He found his friends that survived *in grief.* Martha and Mary were almost swallowed up with sorrow for the death of their brother, which is intimated where it is said that *many of the Jews came to Martha and Mary to comfort them.* Note, (1.) Ordinarily, where death is there are *mourners,* especially when those that were agreeable and amiable to their relations, and serviceable to their generation, are taken away. The house where death is called *the house of mourning,* Eccl. 7:2. When man goes to his long home the *mourners go about the streets* (Eccl. 12:5), or rather sit alone, and *keep silence.* Here was Martha's house, a house where the fear of God was, and on which his blessing rested, yet made a *house of mourning.* Grace will keep sorrow from the heart (*ch.* 14:1), not from the house. (2.) Where there are mourners there ought to be comforters. It is a duty we owe to those that are in sorrow to mourn with them, and to comfort them; and our mourning with them will be some comfort to them. When we are under the present impressions of grief, we are apt to forget those things which would minister comfort to us, and therefore have need of remembrancers. It is a mercy to have remembrancers when we are in sorrow, and our duty to be remembrancers to those who are in sorrow. The Jewish doctors laid great stress upon this, obliging their disciples to make conscience of comforting the mourners after the burial of the dead. They comforted them *concerning their brother,* that is, by speaking to them of him, not only of the good name he left behind, but of the happy state he was gone to. When godly relations and friends are taken from us, whatever occasion we have to be afflicted concerning ourselves, who are left behind and miss them, we have reason to be comforted concerning those who are gone before us to a happiness where they have no need of us. This visit which the Jews made to Martha and Mary is an evidence that they were persons of distinction, and made a figure; as also that they behaved obligingly to all; so that though they were followers of Christ, yet those who had no respect for him were civil to them. There was also a providence in it, that so many Jews, Jewish ladies it is probable, should come together, just at this time, to comfort the mourners, that they might be unexceptionable witnesses of the miracle, and see what miserable comforters they were, in comparison with Christ. Christ did not usually send for witnesses to his miracles, and yet had none been by but relations this would have been excepted against; therefore God's counsel so ordered it that these should come together accidentally, to bear their testimony to it, that infidelity might stop her mouth.

II. What passed between him and his surviving friends at this interview. When Christ defers his visits for a time they are thereby made the more acceptable, much the more welcome; so it was here. His departures endear his returns, and his absence teaches us how to value his presence. We have here,

1. The interview between Christ and Martha.

(1.) We are told that she *went and met him, v.* 20. [1.] It should seem that Martha was earnestly expecting Christ's arrival, and enquiring for it. Either she had sent out messengers, to bring her tidings of his first approach, or she had often asked, *Saw you him whom my soul loveth?* so that the first who discovered him ran to her with the welcome news. However it was, she heard of his coming before he arrived. She had waited long, and often asked, *Is he come?* and could hear no tidings of him; but long-looked-for came at last. *At the end the vision will speak, and not lie.* [2.] Martha, when the good news was brought that Jesus was coming, threw all aside, and *went and met him,* in token of a most affectionate welcome. She waived all ceremony and compliment to the Jews who came to visit her, and hastened to go and meet Jesus. Note, When God by his grace or providence is coming towards us in ways of mercy and comfort, we should go forth by faith, hope, and prayer to meet him. Some suggest that Martha went out of the town to meet Jesus, to let him know that there were several Jews in the house, who were no friends to him, that if he pleased he might keep out of the way of them. [3.] When Martha went to meet Jesus, Mary *sat still in the house.* Some think she did *not* hear the tidings, being in her drawing-room, receiving visits of condolence, while Martha who was busied in the household-affairs had early notice of it. Perhaps Martha would not tell her sister that Christ was coming, being ambitious of the honour of receiving him first. *Sancta est prudentia clam fratribus clam parentibus ad Christum esse conferre — Holy prudence conducts us to Christ, while brethren and parents know not what we are doing.* — Maldonat. in locum. Others think she *did* hear that Christ was come, but was so overwhelmed with sorrow that she did not care to stir, choosing rather to indulge her sorrow, and to sit poring upon her affliction, and saying, *I do well to* mourn. Comparing this story with that in Lu. 10:38, etc., we may observe the different tempers of these two sisters, and the temptations and advantages of each. Martha's natural temper was active and busy; she loved to be here and there, and at the end of every thing; and this had been a snare to her when by it she was not only careful and cumbered about many things, but hindered from the exercises of devotion: but now in a day of affliction this active temper did her a kindness, kept the grief from her heart, and made her forward to meet Christ, and so she received comfort from him the sooner. On the other hand, Mary's natural temper was contemplative and reserved. This had been formerly an advantage to her, when it placed her Christ's feet, to hear his word, and enabled her there to attend upon him without those distractions with which Martha was cumbered; but now in the day of affliction that same temper proved a snare to her, made her less able to grapple with her grief, and disposed her to melancholy: *But Mary sat still in the house.* See here how much it will be our wisdom carefully to watch against the temptations, and improve the advantages, of our natural temper.

(2.) Here is fully related the discourse between Christ and Martha.

[1.] Martha's address to Christ, *v.* 21, 22.

First, She complains of Christ's long absence and delay. She said it, not only with grief for the death of her brother, but with some resentment of the seeming unkindness of the Master: *Lord if you hadst been here, my brother had not died.* Here is, 1. Some evidence of faith. She believed Christ's *power,* that, though her brother's sickness was very grievous, yet he could have cured it, and so have prevented his death. She believed his *pity,* that if he had but seen Lazarus in his extreme illness, and his dear relations all in tears about him, he would have had compassion, and have prevented so sad a breach, for his compassions fail not. But, 2. Here are sad instances of unbelief. Her faith was true, but weak as a bruised reed, for she limits the power of Christ, in saying, *If thou hadst been here;* whereas she ought to have known that Christ could cure at a distance, and that his gracious operations were not limited to his bodily presence. She reflects likewise upon the wisdom and kindness of Christ, that he did not hasten to them when they sent for him, as if he had not *timed his business* well, and now might as well have staid away, and not have come at all, as to come too late; and, as for any help now, she can scarcely entertain the thought of it.

Secondly, Yet she corrects and comforts herself with the thoughts of the prevailing interest Christ had in heaven; at least, she blames herself for blaming her Master, and for suggesting that he comes too late: *for I know that even now,* desperate as the case is, *whatsoever thou wilt ask of God, God will give it to thee.* Observe, 1. How *willing* her hope was. Though she had not courage to ask of Jesus that he should raise him to life again, there having been no precedent as yet of any one raised to life that had been so long dead, yet, like a modest petitioner, she humbly recommends the case to the wise and compassionate consideration of the Lord Jesus. When we know not what in particular to ask or expect, let us in general refer ourselves to God, let him do as seemeth him good. *Judicii tui est, non praesumptionis meae — I leave it to thy judgment, not to my presumption.* — Aug. in locum. When we know not what to pray for, it is our comfort that the great Intercessor knows what to ask for us, and is always heard. 2. How *weak* her faith was. She should have said, "Lord, thou canst do whatsoever thou wilt;" but she only says, "Thou canst obtain whatsoever thou prayest for." She had forgotten that the Son had *life in himself,* that he wrought miracles by his own power. Yet both these considerations must be taken in for the encouragement of our faith and hope, and neither excluded: the dominion Christ has on earth and his interest and intercession in heaven. He has in the one hand the golden sceptre, and in the other the golden censer; his power is always predominant, his intercession always prevalent.

[2.] The comfortable word which Christ gave to Martha, in an answer to her pathetic address (*v.* 23): *Jesus saith unto her, Thy brother shall rise again.* Martha, in her complaint, looked back, reflecting with regret *that Christ was not there,* for then, thinks she, my brother had been now alive. We are apt, in such cases, to add to our own trouble, by fancying what *might have been.* "If such a method had been taken, such a physician employed, my friend had not died;" which is more than we know: but what good does this do? When God's will is done, our business is to submit to him. Christ directs Martha, and us in her, to look forward, and to think what *shall be,* for that is a certainty, and yields sure comfort: *Thy brother shall rise again. First,* This was true of Lazarus in a sense peculiar to him: he was now presently to be raised; but Christ speaks of it in general as a thing to be done, not which he himself would do, so humbly did our Lord Jesus speak of what he did. He also expresses it *ambiguously,* leaving her uncertain at first whether he would raise him presently or not till the last day, that he might try her faith and patience. *Secondly,* It is applicable to all the saints, and their resurrection at the last day. Note, It is a matter of comfort to us, when we have buried our godly friends and relations, to think that they shall *rise again.* As the soul at death is not lost, but gone before, so the body is not lost, but laid up. Think you hear Christ saying, "Thy parent, thy child, thy yoke-fellow, shall rise again; *these dry bones shall live.*"

[3.] The faith which Martha mixed with this word, and the unbelief mixed with this faith, *v.* 24.

First, She accounts it a *faithful saying* that *he shall rise again at the last day.* Though the doctrine of the resurrection was to have its full proof from Christ's resurrection, yet, as it was already revealed, she firmly believed it, Acts 24:15. 1. That there shall be a *last day,* with which all the days of time shall be numbered and finished. 2. That there shall be a *general* resurrection at that day, when the earth and sea shall give up their dead. 3. That there shall be a *particular* resurrection of each one: "I know that I shall rise again, and this and the other relation that was dear to me." As bone shall return to his bone in that day, so friend to his friend.

Secondly, Yet she seems to think this saying not so well worthy of all acceptation as really it was: *"I know he shall rise again at the last day;* but what are we the better for that now?" As if the comforts of the resurrection to eternal life were not worth speaking of, or yielded not satisfaction sufficient to balance her affliction. See our weakness and folly, that we suffer present sensible things to make a deeper impression upon us, both of grief and joy, than those things which are the objects of faith. *I know that he shall rise again at the last day;* and is not this enough? She seems to think it is not. Thus, by our discontent under present crosses, we greatly undervalue our future hopes, and put a slight upon them, as if not worth regarding.

[4.] The further instruction and encouragement which Jesus Christ gave her; for he will not quench the smoking flax nor break the bruised reed. He said to her, *I am the resurrection and the life, v.* 25, 26. Two things Christ possesses her with the belief of, in reference to the present distress; and they are the things which our faith should fasten upon in the like cases.

First, The power of Christ, his sovereign power: *I am the resurrection and the life,* the fountain of life, and the head and author of the resurrection. Martha believed that at his prayer God would give any thing, but he would have her know that by his word he could work anything. Martha believed a resurrection at the *last day;* Christ tells her that he had that power lodged in his own hand, that the dead were to *hear his voice* (*ch.* 5:25), whence it was easy to infer, He that could raise a world of men that had been dead many ages could doubtless raise one man that had been dead but *four days.* Note, It is an unspeakable comfort to all good Christians that Jesus Christ is the resurrection and the life, and will be so to them. *Resurrection* is a return to life; Christ is the author of that return, and of that life to which it is a return. We look for the *resurrection of the dead* and the *life of the world to come,* and Christ is both; the author and principle of both, and the ground of our hope of both.

Secondly, The promises of the new covenant, which give us further ground of hope that *we shall live.* Observe,

a. To whom these promises are made — to those that believe in Jesus Christ, to those that consent to, and confide in, Jesus Christ as the only Mediator of reconciliation and communion between God and man, that receive the record God has given in his word concerning his Son, sincerely comply with it, and answer all the great intentions of it. The condition of the latter promise is thus expressed: *Whosoever liveth and believeth in me,* which may be understood, either, (*a.*) Of *natural* life: *Whosoever lives in this world,* whether he be Jew or Gentile, wherever he lives, if he believe in Christ, he shall live by him. Yet it limits the time: Whoever during *life,* while he is here in this state of probation, *believes in me,* shall be happy in me, but after death it will be too late. Whoever *lives* and *believes,* that is, lives by faith (Gal. 2:20), has a faith that influences his conversation. Or, (*b.*) Of *spiritual* life: He that *lives* and *believes* is he that by faith is born again to a heavenly and divine life, to whom *to live is Christ* — that makes Christ the life of his soul.

b. What the promises are (*v.* 25): *Though he die, yet shall he live,* nay, *he shall never die, v.* 26. Man consists of body and soul, and provision is made for the happiness of both.

(*a.*) For the *body;* here is the promise of a *blessed resurrection.* Though the body be dead because of sin (there is no remedy but it will die), yet it *shall live again.* All the difficulties that attend the state of the dead are here overlooked, and made nothing of. Though the sentence of death was just, though the effects of death be dismal, though the bands of death be strong, though he be dead and buried, dead and putrefied, though the scattered dust be so mixed with common dust that no art of man can distinguish, much less separate them, put the case as strongly as you will on that side, yet we are sure that *he shall live* again: the body shall be raised a glorious body.

(*b.*) For the *soul;* here is the promise of a *blessed immortality.* He that *liveth and believeth,* who, being united to Christ by faith, lives spiritually by virtue of that union, he shall *never die.* That spiritual life shall never be extinguished, but perfected in eternal life. As the soul, being in its nature spiritual, is therefore immortal; so if by faith it live a spiritual life, consonant to its nature, its felicity shall be immortal too. It *shall never die,* shall never be otherwise than easy and happy, and there is not any intermission or interruption of its life, as there is of the life of the body. The *mortality* of the body shall at length be *swallowed up of life;* but the life of the soul, the believing soul, shall be immediately at death swallowed up of immortality. *He shall not die, eis ton aiōna, for ever — Non morietur in aeternum;* so Cyprian quotes it. The body shall not be *for ever* dead in the grave; it dies (like the two witnesses) but for a *time, times, and the dividing of time;* and when time shall be no more, and all the divisions of it shall be numbered and finished, a *spirit of life from God shall enter into it.* But this is not all; the souls shall not die that death which is *for ever,* shall *not die eternally, Blessed and holy,* that is, blessed and happy, is he that by faith *has part in the first resurrection,* has part in Christ, who is that resurrection; for on such the *second death,* which is a death for ever, *shall have no power;* see *ch.* 6:40. Christ asks her, *"Believest thou this?* Canst thou *assent* to it with application? Canst thou take my word for it?" Note, When we have read or heard the word of Christ, concerning the great things of the other world, we should seriously put it to ourselves, *"Do we believe this, this* truth in particular, *this* which is attended with so many difficulties, *this* which is suited to my case? Does my belief of it realize it to me, and give my soul an assurance of it, so that I can say not only *this* I believe, but *thus* I believe it?" Martha was doting upon her brother's being raised in this world; before Christ gave her hopes of this, he directed her thoughts to another life, another world: "No matter for *that,* but *believest thou this* that I tell thee concerning the *future* state?" The crosses and comforts of this present time would not make such an impression upon us as they do if we did but believe the things of eternity as we ought.

[5.] Martha's unfeigned assent yielded to what Christ said, *v.* 27. We have here Martha's creed, the good confession she witnessed, the same with that for which Peter was commended (Mt. 16:16, 17), and it is the *conclusion of the whole matter.*

First, Here is the *guide of her faith,* and that is the word of Christ; without any alteration, exception, or proviso, she takes it entire as Christ had said it: *Yea, Lord,* whereby she subscribes to the truth of all and every part of that which Christ had promised, in his own sense: *Even so.* Faith is an echo to divine revelation, returns the same words, and resolves to abide by them: *Yea, Lord, As the word did make it so I believe and take it,* said queen Elizabeth.

Secondly, The *ground of her faith,* and that is the authority of Christ; she believes *this* because she believes that he who saith it is Christ. She has recourse to the foundation for the support of the superstructure. *I believe, pepisteuka, "I have believed* that thou art Christ, and therefore *I do believe this."* Observe here,

a. What she believed and confessed concerning Jesus; three things, all to the same effect: — (*a.*) That he was the Christ, or Messiah, promised and expected under this name and notion, the *anointed one.* (*b.*) That he was the *Son of God;* so the Messiah was called (Ps. 2:7), not by office only, but by nature. (*c.*) That it was *he who should come* into the world, the *ho erchomenos.* That blessing of blessings which the church had for so many ages waited for as *future,* she embraced as *present.*

b. What she inferred hence, and what she alleged this for. If she admits this, that Jesus is the Christ, there is no difficulty in believing that he is the resurrection and the life; for if he be the Christ, then, (*a.*) He is the fountain of light and truth, and we may take all his sayings for faithful and divine, upon his own word. If he be the Christ, he is that prophet whom we are to hear *in all things.* (*b.*) He is the fountain of life and blessedness, and we may therefore depend upon his ability as well as upon his veracity. How shall bodies, turned to dust, *live again?* How shall souls, clogged and clouded as ours are, *live for ever?* We could not believe this, but that we believe him that undertakes it to be *the Son of God,* who has life *in himself,* and has it for us.

2. The interview between Christ and Mary the other sister. And here observe,

(1.) The notice which Martha gave her of Christ's coming (*v.* 28): *When she had so said,* as one that needed to say no more, *she went her way,* easy in her mind, and *called Mary her sister.* [1.] Martha, having received instruction and comfort from Christ herself, called her sister to share with her. Time was when Martha would have drawn Mary from Christ, to come and help her in *much serving* (Lu. 10:40); but, to make her amends for this, here she is industrious to draw her to Christ. [2.] She called her *secretly,* and whispered it in her ear, because there was company by, Jews, who were no friends to Christ. The saints are called *into the fellowship of Jesus Christ* by an invitation that is secret and distinguishing, given to them and not to others; they have meat to eat that the world knows not of, joy that a stranger does not intermeddle with. [3.] She called her by order from Christ; he bade her *go call her sister.* This call that is *effectual,* whoever brings it, is sent by Christ. *The Master is come, and calleth for thee. First,* She calls Christ *the Master, didaskalos,* a *teaching master;* by that title he was commonly called and known among them. Mr. George Herbert took pleasure in calling Christ, *my Master. Secondly,* She triumphs in his arrival: *The Master is come.* He whom we have long wished and waited for, *he is come, he is come;* this was the best cordial in the present distress. "Lazarus is gone, and our comfort in him is gone; but the *Master is come,* who is better than the dearest friend, and has that in him which will abundantly make up all our losses. He is come who is our *teacher,* who will teach us how to get good by our sorrow (Ps. 94:12), who will *teach,* and so comfort." *Thirdly,* She invites her sister to go and meet him: *"He calls for thee,* enquires what is become of thee, and would have thee sent for." Note, When Christ our Master comes, he *calls for us.* He comes in his word and ordinances, calls us to them, calls us by them, calls us to himself. He calls for thee in particular, for thee *by name* (Ps. 27:8); and, if he call thee, he will cure thee, he will comfort thee.

(2.) The haste which Mary made to Christ upon this notice given her (*v.* 29): *As soon as she heard* this good news, that the *Master was come,* she *arose quickly,* and came to him. She little thought how near he was to her, for he is often nearer to them that mourn in Zion than they are aware of; but, when she knew how near he was, she started up, and in a transport of joy ran to meet him. The least intimation of Christ's gracious approaches is enough to a lively faith, which stands ready to take the hint, and answer the first call. When Christ was come, [1.] She did not consult the decorum of her mourning, but, forgetting ceremony, and the common usage in such cases, she ran through the town, to meet Christ. Let no nice punctilios of decency and honour deprive us at any time of opportunities of conversing with Christ. [2.] She did not consult her neighbours, the Jews that were *with her, comforting her;* she left them all, to come to him, and did not only not ask their advice, but not so much as ask their leave, or beg their pardon for her rudeness.

(3.) We are told (*v.* 30) where she found the Master; he was not yet come into Bethany, but was at the town's end, *in that place where Martha met him.* See here, [1.] Christ's love to his work. He staid near the place where the grave was, that he might be ready to go to it. He would not go into the town, to *refresh himself* after the fatigue of his journey, till he had done the work he came to do; nor would he go into the town, lest it should look like ostentation, and a design to levy a crowd to be spectators of the miracle. [2.] Mary's love to Christ; still she *loved much.* Though Christ had seemed unkind in his delays, yet she could take nothing amiss from him. Let us go thus to Christ *without the camp,* Heb. 13:13.

(4.) The misconstruction which the Jews that were with Mary made of her going away so hastily (*v.* 31): They said, *She goes to the grave, to weep there.* Martha bore up better under this affliction than Mary did, who was a woman of a tender and sorrowful spirit; such was her natural temper. Those that are so have need to watch against melancholy, and ought to be pitied and helped. These comforters found that their formalities did her no service, but that she hardened herself in sorrow: and therefore concluded when she went out, and turned that way, it was to go *to the grave* and *weep there.* See, [1.] What often is the folly and fault of mourners; they contrive how to aggravate their own grief, and to make bad worse. We are apt in such cases to take a strange pleasure in our own pain, and to say, *We do well* to be passionate in our grief, even unto death; we are apt to fasten upon those things that aggravate the affliction, and what good does this do us, when it is our duty to reconcile ourselves to the will of God in it? Why should mourners go to the grave to weep there, when they sorrow not as those that have no hope? Affliction of itself is grievous; why should we make it more so? [2.] What is the wisdom and duty of comforters; and that is, to prevent as much as may be, in those who grieve inordinately, the revival of the sorrow, and to divert it. Those Jews that followed Mary were thereby led to Christ, and became the witnesses of one of his most glorious miracles. It is good cleaving to Christ's friends in their sorrows, for thereby we may come to know him better.

(5.) Mary's address to our Lord Jesus (*v.* 32): She came, attended with her train of comforters, and *fell down at his feet,* as one overwhelmed with a passionate sorrow, and said with many tears (as appears *v.* 33), *Lord, if thou hadst been here, my brother had not died,* as Martha said before, for they had often said it to one another. Now here, [1.] Her posture is very humble and submissive: *She fell down at his feet,* which was more than Martha did, who had a greater command of her passions. She fell down not as a sinking mourner, but fell down at his feet as a humble petitioner. This Mary had sat *at Christ's feet to hear his word* (Lu. 10:39), and here we find her there on another errand. Note, Those that in a day of peace place themselves at Christ's feet, to receive instructions from him, may with comfort and confidence in a day of trouble cast themselves at his feet with hope to find favour with him. She *fell at his feet,* as one submitting to his will in what was done, and referring herself to his good-will in what was now to be done. When we are in affliction we must cast ourselves at Christ's feet in a penitent sorrow and self-abasement for sin, and a patient resignation of ourselves to the divine disposal. Mary's casting herself at Christ's feet was in token of the profound respect and veneration she had for him. Thus subjects were wont to give honour to their kings and princes; but, our Lord Jesus not appearing in secular glory as an earthly prince, those who by this posture of adoration gave honour to him certainly looked upon him as more than man, and intended hereby to give him divine honour. Mary hereby made profession of the Christian faith as truly as Martha did, and in effect said, *I believe that thou art the Christ; bowing the knee to* Christ, and *confessing him with the tongue,* are put together as equivalent, Rom. 14:11; Phil. 2:10, 11. This she did in presence of *the Jews* that attended her, who, though friends to her and her family, yet were bitter enemies to Christ; yet in their sight she fell at Christ's feet, as one that was neither ashamed to own the veneration she had for Christ nor afraid of disobliging her friends and neighbours by it. Let them resent it as they pleased, she falls at his feet; and, if this be to be vile, she will be yet more vile; see Cant. 8:1. We serve a Master of whom we have no reason to be ashamed, and whose acceptance of our services is sufficient to balance the reproach of men and all their revilings. [2.] Her address is very pathetic: *Lord, if thou hadst been here, my brother had not died.* Christ's delay was designed for the best, and proved so; yet both the sisters very indecently *cast the same in his teeth,* and in effect charge him with the death of their brother. This repeated challenge he might justly have resented, might have told them he had something else to do than to be at their beck and to attend them; he must come when his business would permit him: but not a word of this; he considered the circumstances of their affliction, and that losers think they may have leave to speak, and therefore overlooked the rudeness of this welcome, and gave us an example of mildness and meekness in such cases. Mary added no more, as Martha did; but it appears, by what follows, that what she fell short in words she made up in tears; she said less than Martha, but wept more; and tears of devout affection have a voice, a loud prevailing voice, in the ears of Christ; no rhetoric like this.

Verses 33–44

Here we have, I. Christ's tender *sympathy* with his afflicted friends, and the share he took to himself in their sorrows, which appeared three ways: —

1. By the inward groans and troubles of his spirit (*v.* 33): *Jesus saw Mary weeping* for the loss of a loving brother, and the *Jews that came with her weeping* for the loss of a good neighbour and friend; when he saw what a *place of weepers, a bochim,* this was, *he groaned in the spirit, and was troubled.* See here,

(1.) The griefs of the sons of men represented in the tears of Mary and her friends. What an emblem was here of this world, this vale of tears! Nature itself teaches us to weep over our dear relations, when they are removed by death; Providence thereby calls to *weeping and mourning.* It is probable that Lazarus's estate devolved upon his sisters, and was a considerable addition to their fortunes; and in such a case people say, now-a-days, though they cannot wish their relations dead (that is, they do not say they do), yet, if they were dead, they would not wish them alive again; but these sisters, whatever they got by their brother's death, heartily wished him alive again. Religion teaches us likewise to *weep with them that weep,* as these Jews wept with Mary, considering that we ourselves also *are in the body.* Those that truly love their friends will share with them in their joys and griefs; for what is friendship but a communication of affections? Job 16:5.

(2.) The grace of the Son of God and his compassion towards those that are in misery. *In all their afflictions he is afflicted,* Isa. 63:9; Jdg. 10:16. When Christ saw them all in tears,

[1.] He *groaned in the spirit.* He suffered himself to be tempted (as we are when we are disturbed by some great affliction), *yet without sin.* This was an expression, either, *First,* Of his displeasure at the inordinate grief of those about him, as Mk. 5:39: *"Why make ye this ado and weep?* What a hurry is here! does this become those that believe in a God, a heaven, and another world?" Or, *Secondly,* Of his feeling sense of the calamitous state of human lie, and the power of death, to which fallen man is subject. Having now to make a vigorous attack upon death and the grave, he thus stirred up himself to the encounter, *put on the garments of vengeance,* and *his fury it upheld him;* and that he might the more resolutely undertake the redress of our grievances, and the cure of our griefs, he was pleased to make himself sensible of the weight of them, and under the burden of them he now *groaned in spirit.* Or, *Thirdly,* It was an expression of his kind sympathy with his friends that were in sorrow. Here was the sounding of the bowels, the mercies which the afflicted church so earnestly solicits, Is. 63:15. Christ not only seemed concerned, but he *groaned in the spirit;* he was inwardly and sincerely affected with the case. David's pretended friends counterfeited sympathy, to disguise their enmity (Ps. 41:6); but we must learn of Christ to have our love and sympathy *without dissimulation.* Christ's was a deep and hearty sigh.

[2.] He was *troubled.* He *troubled himself;* so the phrase is, very significantly. He had all the passions and affections of the human nature, for in all things he must *be like to his brethren;* but he had a perfect command of them, so that they were never *up,* but *when* and *as* they were called; he was never troubled, but when he *troubled himself,* as he saw cause. He often *composed* himself to trouble, but was never discomposed or disordered by it. He was voluntary both in his passion and in his compassion. He had power to lay down his grief, and power to take it again.

2. His concern for them appeared by his *kind enquiry* after the poor remains of his deceased friend (*v.* 34): Where *have you laid him?* He knew where he was laid, and yet asks, because, (1.) He would thus express himself as *a man,* even when he was going to exert the power of a God. Being found in fashion as a man, he accommodates himself to the way and manner of the sons of men: *Non nescit, sed quasi nescit — He is not ignorant, but he makes as if he were,* saith Austin here. (2.) He enquired where the grave was, lest, if he had gone straight to it of his own knowledge, the unbelieving Jews should have thence taken occasion to suspect a collusion between him and Lazarus, and a trick in the case. Many expositors observe this from Chrysostom. (3.) He would thus divert the grief of his mourning friends, by raising their expectations of something great; as if he had said, "I did not come hither with an address of condolence, to mingle a few fruitless insignificant tears with yours; no, I have other work to do; come, let us adjourn to the grave, and go about our business there." Note, A serious address to our work is the best remedy against inordinate grief. (4.) He would hereby intimate to us the special care he takes of the bodies of the saints while they lie in the grave; he takes notice *where they are laid,* and will look after them. There is not only a covenant with the dust, but a guard upon it.

3. It appeared by *his tears.* Those about him did not tell him where the body was buried, but desired him to *come and see,* and led him directly to the grave, that his eye might yet more affect his heart with the calamity.

(1.) As he was going to the grave, as if he had been following the corpse thither, *Jesus wept, v.* 35. A very short verse, but it affords many useful instructions. [1.] That Jesus Christ was really and truly man, and partook with the children, not only of flesh and blood, but of a human soul, susceptible of the impressions of joy, and grief, and other affections. Christ gave this proof of his humanity, in both senses of the word; that, as a man, he could weep, and, as a merciful man, he *would weep,* before he gave this proof of his divinity. [2.] That he was *a man of sorrows,* and *acquainted with grief,* as was foretold, Isa. 53:3. We never read that he laughed, but more than once we have him in tears. Thus he shows not only that a mournful state will consist with the love of God, but that those who sow to the Spirit must sow in tears. [3.] Tears of compassion well become Christians, and make them most to resemble Christ. It is a relief to those who are in sorrow to have their friends sympathize with them, especially such a friend as their Lord Jesus.

(2.) Different constructions were put upon Christ's weeping. [1.] Some made a kind and candid interpretation of it, and what was very natural (*v.* 36): *Then said the Jews, Behold how he loved him!* They seem to wonder that he should have so strong an affection for one to whom he was not related, and with whom he had not had any long acquaintance, for Christ spent most of his time in Galilee, a great way from Bethany. It becomes us, according to this example of Christ, to show our love to our friends, both living and dying. We must sorrow for our brethren that sleep in Jesus as those that are full of love, though not void of hope; as the *devout men* that buried Stephen, Acts 8:2. Though our tears profit not the dead, they embalm their memory. These tears were indications of his particular love to Lazarus, but he has given proofs no less evident of his love to all the saints, in that he died for them. When he only dropped a tear over Lazarus, they said, *See how he loved him!* Much more reason have we to say so, for whom he hath laid down his life: *See how he loved us! Greater love has no man than this* [2.] Others made a peevish unfair reflection upon it, as if these tears bespoke his inability to help his friend (*v.* 37): *Could not this man, who opened the eyes of the blind,* have prevented the death of Lazarus? Here it is slyly insinuated, *First,* That the death of Lazarus being (as it seemed by his tears) a great grief to him, if he could have prevented it he would, and therefore because he *did not* they incline to think that he *could not;* as, when he was dying, they concluded that he could not, because he did not, save himself, and *come down from the cross;* not considering that divine power is always directed in its operations by divine wisdom, not merely according to his will, but according to the counsel of his will, wherein it becomes us to acquiesce. If Christ's friends, whom he loves, die, — if his church, whom he loves, be persecuted and afflicted, — we must not impute it to any defect either in his power or love, but conclude that it is because he sees it for the best. *Secondly,* That therefore it might justly be questioned whether he did indeed *open the eyes of the blind,* that is, whether it was not a sham. His not working this miracle they thought enough to invalidate the former; at least, it should seem that he had limited power, and therefore not a divine one. Christ soon convinced these *whisperers,* by raising Lazarus from the dead, which was the greater work, that he could have prevented his death, but therefore did not because he would glorify himself the more.

II. Christ's approach to the grave, and the preparation that was made for working this miracle.

1. Christ repeats his groans upon his coming near the grave (*v.* 38): *Again groaning in himself, he comes to the grave:* he groaned, (1.) Being displeased at the unbelief of those who spoke doubtingly of his power, and blamed him for not preventing the death of Lazarus; he was *grieved for the hardness of their hearts.* He never groaned so much for his own pains and sufferings as for the sins and follies of men, particularly Jerusalem's, Mt. 23:37. (2.) Being affected with the fresh lamentations which, it is likely, the mourning sisters

made when they came near the grave, more passionately and pathetically than before, his tender spirit was sensibly touched with their wailings. (3.) Some think that he *groaned in spirit* because, to gratify the desire of his friends, he was to bring Lazarus again into this sinful troublesome world, from that rest into which he was newly entered; it would be a kindness to Martha and Mary, but it would be to him like thrusting one out to a stormy sea again who was newly got into a safe and quiet harbour. If Lazarus had been let alone, Christ would quickly have gone to him into the other world; but, being restored to life, Christ quickly left him behind in this world. (4.) Christ groaned as one that would affect himself with the calamitous state of the human nature, as subject to death, from which he was now about to redeem Lazarus. Thus he stirred up himself to take hold on God in the prayer he was to make, that he might *offer it up with strong crying,* Heb. 5:7. Ministers, when they are sent by the preaching of the gospel to raise dead souls, should be much affected with the deplorable condition of those they preach to and pray for, and groan in themselves to think of it.

2. The grave wherein Lazarus lay is here described: *It was a cave, and a stone lay upon it.* The graves of the common people, probably, were dug as ours are; but persons of distinction were, as with us, interred in vaults, so Lazarus was, and such was the sepulchre in which Christ was buried. Probably this fashion was kept up among the Jews, in imitation of the patriarchs, who buried their dead in the cave of Machpelah, Gen. 23:19. This care taken of the dead bodies of their friends intimates their expectation of their resurrection; they reckoned the solemnity of the funeral ended when the stone was rolled to the grave, or, as here, *laid upon it,* like that on the mouth of the den into which Daniel was cast (Dan. 6:17), that the *purpose might not be changed;* intimating that the dead are separated from the living, and gone the *way whence they shall not return.* This stone was probably a *gravestone,* with an inscription upon it, which the Greeks called *mnēmeion — a memorandum,* because it is both a *memorial* of the dead and a *memento* to the living, putting them in remembrance of that which we are all concerned to remember. It is called by the Latins, *Monumentum, à monendo,* because it gives *warning.*

3. Orders are given to remove the stone (*v.* 39): *Take away the stone.* He would have this stone removed that all the standersby might see the body lie dead in the sepulchre, and that way might be made for its coming out, and it might appear to be a true body, and not a *ghost* or *spectre.* He would have some of the servants to remove it, that they might be witnesses, by the smell of the putrefaction of the body, and that therefore it was truly dead. It is a good step towards the raising of a soul to spiritual life when the stone is taken away, when prejudices are removed and got over, and way made for the word to the heart, that it may do its work there, and say what it has to say.

4. An objection made by Martha against the opening of the grave: *Lord, by this time he stinketh,* or *is become noisome, for he has been dead four days, tetartaios gar esti quatriduanus est;* he is *four days old* in the other world; a citizen and inhabitant of the grave of four days' standing. Probably Martha perceived the body to smell, as they were removing the stone, and therefore cried out thus.

(1.) It is easy to observe hence the nature of human bodies: four days are but a little while, yet what a great change will this time make with the body of man, if it be but so long *without food,* much more if so long *without life!* Dead bodies (saith Dr. Hammond) after a revolution of the humours, which is completed in seventy-two hours, naturally tend to putrefaction; and the Jews say that by the fourth day after death the body is so altered that one cannot be sure it is such a person; so Maimonides in Lightfoot. Christ rose the third day because he was not to *see corruption.*

(2.) It is not so easy to say what was Martha's design in saying this. [1.] Some think she said it in a due tenderness, and such as decency teaches to the dead body; now that it began to putrefy, she did not care it should be thus publicly shown and made a spectacle of. [2.] Others think she said it out of a concern for Christ, lest the smell of the dead body should be *offensive* to him. That which is very noisome is compared to an open sepulchre, Ps. 5:9. If there were any thing noisome she would not have her Master near it; but he was none of those tender and delicate ones that cannot bear as ill smell; if he had, he would not have visited the world of mankind, which sin had made a perfect dunghill, altogether noisome, Ps. 14:3. [3.] It should seem, by Christ's answer, that it was the language of her unbelief and distrust: "Lord, it is too late now to attempt any kindness to him; his body begins to rot, and it is impossible that this putrid carcase should *live.*" She gives up his case as helpless and hopeless, there having been no instances, either of late or formerly, of any raised to life after they had begun to see corruption. When *our bones are dried,* we are ready to say, *Our hope is lost.* Yet this distrustful word of hers served to make the miracle both the more evident and the more illustrious; by this it appeared that he was truly dead, and not in a trance; for, though the posture of a dead body might be counterfeited, the smell could not. Her suggesting that it *could not be done* puts the more honour upon him that *did it.*

5. The gentle reproof Christ gave to Martha for the weakness of her faith (*v.* 40): *Said I not unto thee that if thou wouldest believe thou shouldest see the glory of God?* This word of his to her was not before recorded; it is probable that he said it to her when she had said (*v.* 27), *Lord, I believe:* and it is enough that it is recorded here, where it is repeated. Note, (1.) Our Lord Jesus has given us all the assurances imaginable that a sincere faith shall at length be crowned with a blessed vision: "If thou believe, thou shalt see God's glorious appearances for thee in this world, and to thee in the other world." If we will take Christ's word, and rely on his power and faithfulness, we shall see the glory of God, and be happy in the sight. (2.) We have need to be often reminded of these *sure mercies* with which our Lord Jesus hath encouraged us. Christ does not give a direct answer to what Martha had said, nor any particular promise of what he would do, but orders her to keep hold of the general assurances he had already given: *Only believe.* We are apt to forget what Christ has spoken, and need him to put us in mind of it by his Spirit: "*Said I not unto thee* so and so? And dost thou think that he will ever unsay it?"

6. The opening of the grave, in obedience to Christ's order, notwithstanding Martha's objection (*v.* 41): *Then they took away the stone.* When Martha was satisfied, and had waived her objection, *then* they proceeded. If we will see the glory of God, we must let Christ take his own way, and not *prescribe* but *subscribe* to him. *They took away the stone,* and this was all they could do; Christ only could *give life.* What man can do is but to *prepare the way of the Lord,* to fill the valleys, and level the hills, and, as here, to *take away the stone.*

III. The miracle itself wrought. The spectators, invited by the rolling away of the stone, gathered about the grave, not to commit *dust to dust, earth to earth,* but to receive dust from the dust, and earth from the earth again; and, their expectations being raised, our Lord Jesus addresses himself to his work.

1. He applies himself to his *living Father in heaven,* so he had called him (*ch.* 6:17), and so eyes him here.

(1.) The gesture he used was very significant: *He lifted up his eyes,* an outward expression of the elevation of his mind, and to show those who stood by whence he derived his power; also to set us an example; this outward sign is hereby recommended to our practice; see *ch.* 17:1. Look how those will answer it who profanely ridicule it; but that which is especially charged upon us hereby is to *lift up our hearts* to God in the heavens; what is prayer, but the ascent of the soul to God, and the directing of its affections and motions heavenward? He *lifted up* his eyes, as looking above, looking beyond the grave where Lazarus lay, and overlooking all the difficulties that arose thence, that he might have his eyes fixed upon the divine omnipotence; to teach us to do as Abraham, who considered not *his own body now dead, nor the deadness of Sarah's womb,* never took these into his thoughts, and so gained such a degree of faith as not to *stagger at the promise,* Rom. 4:20.

(2.) His address to God was with great assurance, and such a confidence as became him: *Father, I thank thee that thou hast heard me.*

[1.] He has here taught us, by his own example, *First,* In prayer to call God Father, and to draw nigh to him as children to a father, with a humble reverence, and yet with a holy boldness. *Secondly,* In our *prayers* to *praise him,* and, when we come to beg for further mercy, thankfully to acknowledge former favours. Thanksgivings, which bespeak *God's glory* (not *our own,* like the Pharisee's God, *I thank thee*), are decent forms into which to put our supplications.

[2.] But our Saviour's thanksgiving here was intended to express the unshaken assurance he had of the effecting of this miracle, which he had in his own power to do in concurrence with his Father: *"Father, I thank thee* that my will and thine are in this matter, as always, the same." Elijah and Elisha raised the dead, as servants, by *entreaty;* but Christ, as a Son, by *authority,* having life in himself, and power to quicken whom he would; and he speaks of this as his own act (*v.* 11): *I go, that I may awake him;* yet he speaks of it as what he had obtained by prayer, for his Father *heard him:* probably he put up the prayer for it when he *groaned in spirit* once and again (*v.* 33, 38), in a *mental* prayer, with groanings which could not be *uttered.*

First, Christ speaks of this miracle as an answer to prayer, 1. Because he would thus *humble himself;* though he was a Son, yet *learned he this obedience,* to ask and receive. His mediatorial crown was granted him upon request, though it is *of right,* Ps. 2:8, and *ch.* 17:5. He prays for the glory he had before the world was, though, having never forfeited it, he might have demanded it. 2. Because he was pleased thus to *honour prayer,* making it the key wherewith even he unlocked the treasures of divine power and grace. Thus he would teach us in prayer, by the lively exercise of faith, to *enter into the holiest.*

Secondly, Christ, being assured that his prayer was answered, professes,

a. His thankful acceptance of this answer: *I thank thee that thou hast heard me.* Though the miracle was not yet wrought, yet the prayer was answered, and he triumphs before the victory. No other can pretend to such an assurance as Christ had; yet we may by faith in the promise have a prospect of mercy before it be actually given in, and may rejoice in that prospect, and give God thanks for it. In David's devotions, the same psalm which begins with prayer for a mercy closes with thanksgivings for it. Note, (*a.*) Mercies in answer to prayer ought in a special manner to be acknowledged with thankfulness. Besides the grant of the mercy itself, we are to value it as a great favour to have our poor prayers taken notice of. (*b.*) We ought to *meet* the first appearances of the return of prayer with early thanksgivings. As God *answers* us with mercy, even *before we call,* and *hears while we are yet speaking,* so we should answer him with praise even before he grants, and give him thanks while he is yet speaking good words and comfortable words.

b. His cheerful assurance of a ready answer at any time (*v.* 42): *And I know that thou hearest me always.* Let none think that this was some uncommon favour granted him now, such as he never had before, nor should ever have again; no, he had the same divine power going along with him in his whole undertaking, and undertook nothing but what he knew to be agreeable to the counsel of God's will. "I *gave thanks"* (saith he) "for being heard in this, because I am sure to be heard in every thing." See here, (*a.*) The interest our Lord Jesus had in heaven; the Father *heard him always,* he had access to the Father upon every occasion, and success with him in every errand. And we may be sure that his interest is not the less for his going to heaven, which may encourage us to depend upon his intercession, and put all our petitions into his hand, for we are sure that him the Father *hears always.* (*b.*) The confidence he had of that interest: *I knew it.* He did not in the least hesitate or doubt concerning it, but had an entire satisfaction in his own mind of the Father's complacency in him and concurrence with him in every thing. We cannot have such a particular assurance as he had; but this we know, that *whatsoever we ask according to his will he heareth us,* 1 Jn. 5:14, 15.

Thirdly, But why should Christ give this public intimation of his obtaining this miracle by prayer? He adds, It is *because of the people who stand by, that they may believe that thou hast sent me;* for *prayer may preach.* 1. It was to obviate the objections of his enemies, and their reflections. It was blasphemously suggested by the Pharisees, and their creatures, that he wrought his miracles by compact with the devil; now, to evidence the contrary, he openly made his address to God, using *prayers,* and not *charms,* not *peeping and muttering* as those did that used *familiar spirits* (Isa. 8:19), but, with elevated eyes and voice professing his communication with Heaven, and dependence on Heaven. 2. It was to corroborate the faith of those that were well inclined to him: *That they may believe that thou hast sent me,* not to destroy men's lives, but to save them. Moses, to show that God sent him, made the earth open and swallow men up (Num. 16:31); Elijah, to show that God sent him, made fire come from heaven and devour men; for the law was a dispensation of terror and death but Christ proves his mission by raising to life one that was dead. Some give this sense: had Christ declared his doing it freely by his own power, some of his weak disciples, who as yet understood not his divine nature, would have thought he took too much upon him, and have been stumbled at it. These *babes* could not bear that *strong meat*, therefore he chooses to speak of his power as received and derived he speaks self-denyingly of himself, that he might speak the more plainly to us. *Non ita respexit ad swam dignitatem atque ad nostram salutem — In what he said, he consulted not so much his dignity as our salvation.* — Jansenius.

2. He now applies himself to his *dead friend in the earth.* He *cried with a loud voice, Lazarus come forth.*

(1.) He could have raised Lazarus by a silent exertion of his power and will, and the indiscernible operations of the Spirit of life; but he did it by a call, a loud call,

[1.] To be significant of the power then put forth for the raising of Lazarus, how he *created this new thing; he spoke, and it was done.* He cried aloud, to signify the greatness of the work, and of the power employed in it, and to excite himself as it were to this attack upon the gates of death, as soldiers engage with a shout. Speaking to Lazarus, it was proper to *cry with a loud voice;* for, *First,* The soul of Lazarus, which was to be called back, was at a distance, not hovering about the grave, as the Jews fancied, but removed to Hades, the world of spirits; now it is natural to speak loud when we call to those at a distance. *Secondly,* The body of Lazarus, which was to be called up, was *asleep,* and we usually speak loud when we would awake any out of sleep. He cried with a loud voice that the scripture might be fulfilled (Isa. 45:19), *I have not spoken in secret, in a dark place of the earth.*

[2.] To be typical of other works of wonder, and particularly other resurrections, which the power of Christ was to effect. This loud call was a figure, *First,* Of the gospel call, by which dead souls were to be brought out of the grave of sin, which resurrection Christ had formerly spoken of (ch. 5:25), and of his word as the means of it (ch. 6:63), and now he gives a specimen of it. By his word, he saith to souls, *Live, yea, he* saith to them, *Live,* Eze. 16:6. *Arise from the dead,* Eph. 5:14. The spirit of life from God entered into those that had been dead and dry bones, when Ezekiel prophesied over them, Eze. 37:10. Those who infer from the commands of the word to *turn and live* that man has a power of his own to convert and regenerate himself might as well infer from this call to Lazarus that he had a power to raise himself to life. *Secondly,* Of the sound of the archangel's trumpet at the last day, with which they that sleep in the dust shall be awakened and summoned before the great tribunal, when Christ shall *descend with a shout, a call, or command,* like this here, *Come forth,* Ps. 50:4. *He shall call* both *to the heavens* for their souls, *and to the earth* for their bodies, *that he may judge his people.*

(2.) This *loud call* was but *short,* yet *mighty through God* to the battering down of the strongholds of the grave. [1.] He calls him by name, Lazarus, as we call those by their names whom we would awake out of a fast sleep. God said to Moses, as a mark of his favour, *I know thee by name.* The naming of him intimates that the same individual person that died shall rise again at the last day. He that *calls the stars by their names* can distinguish by name his stars that are in the dust of the earth, and will lose none of them. [2.] He calls him *out of the grave,* speaking to him as if he were already alive, and had nothing to do but to come out of his grave. He does not say unto him, *Live;* for he himself must give life; but he saith to him, *Move,* for when by the grace of Christ we live spiritually we must stir up ourselves to *move;* the grave of sin and this world is no place for those whom Christ has quickened, and therefore they must *come forth.* [3.] The event was according to the intention: *He that was dead came forth, v. 44.* Power went along with the word of Christ to re-unite the soul and the body of Lazarus, and then he came forth. The miracle is described, not by its invisible springs, to satisfy our curiosity, but by its visible effects, to conform our faith. Do any ask where the soul of Lazarus was during the four days of its separation? We are not told, but have reason to think it was in paradise; *in joy and felicity;* but you will say, "Was it not then really an unkindness to it to cause it to return into the prison of the body?" And if it were, yet, being for the honour of Christ and the serving of the interests of his kingdom, it was no more an injury to him than

it was to St. Paul to continue in the flesh when he knew that to depart to Christ was so much better. If any ask whether Lazarus, after he was raised, could give an account or description of his soul's removal out of the body or return to it, or what he saw in the other world, I suppose both those changes were so unaccountable to himself that he must say with Paul, *Whether in the body or out of the body, I cannot tell;* and of what he saw and heard, that it was not lawful nor possible to express it. In a world of sense we cannot frame to ourselves, much less communicate to others, any adequate ideas of the world of spirits and the affairs of that world. Let us not covet to be wise above what is written, and this is all that is written concerning the resurrection of that Lazarus, that *he that was dead came forth.* Some have observed that though we read of many who were raised from the dead, who no doubt conversed familiarly with men afterwards, yet the scripture has not recorded one word spoken by any of them, except by our Lord Jesus only.

(3.) This miracle was wrought, [1.] *Speedily.* Nothing intervenes between the command, *Come forth,* and the effect, *He came forth; dictum factum — no sooner said than done;* let there be life, and there was life. Thus the change in the resurrection will be *in a moment, in the twinkling of an eye,* 1 Co. 15:52. The almighty power that can do it can do it in an instant: *Then shalt thou call and I will answer;* will come at the call, as Lazarus, *Here am I.* [2.] *Perfectly.* He was so thoroughly revived that he got up out of his grave as strongly as ever he got up out of his bed, and returned not only to life, but health. He was not raised to serve a present turn, but to live as other men. [3.] With this additional miracle, as some reckon it, that he came out of his grave, though he was fettered with his grave-clothes, with which he was *bound hand and foot,* and *his face bound about with a napkin* (for so the manner of the Jews was to bury); and he came forth in the same dress wherein he was buried, that it might appear that it was he himself and not another, and that he was not only alive, but strong, and able to walk, after a sort, even in his grave-clothes. The *binding of his face with a napkin* proved that he had been really dead, for otherwise, in less than so many days' time, that would have smothered him. And the standers-by, in unbinding him, would *handle him, and see him, that it was he himself,* and so be witnesses of the miracle. Now see here, *First,* How little we carry away with us, when we leave the world — only a winding-sheet and a coffin; there is no change of raiment in the grave, nothing but a single suit of grave-clothes. *Secondly,* What condition we shall be in in the grave. What *wisdom or device* can there be where the eyes are hoodwinked, or what working where the hands and feet are fettered? And so it will be in the grave, whither we are going. Lazarus being *come forth,* hampered and embarrassed with his grave-clothes, we may well imagine that those about the grave were exceedingly surprised and frightened at it; we should be so if we should see a dead body rise; but Christ, to make the thing familiar, sets them to work: *"Loose him,* slacken his grave-clothes, that they may serve for day-clothes till he comes to his house, and then he will go himself, so clad, without guide or supporter to his own house." As, in the Old Testament, the translations of Enoch and Elias were sensible demonstrations of an invisible and future state, the one about the middle of the patriarchal age, the other of the Mosaic economy, so the resurrection of Lazarus, in the New Testament, was designed for the confirmation of the doctrine of the resurrection.

Verses 45–57

We have here an account of the consequences of this glorious miracle, which were as usual; to some it was a savour of life unto life, to others of death unto death.

I. Some were invited by it, and induced to believe. Many of the Jews, when they *saw the things that Jesus did, believed on him,* and well they might, for it was an incontestable proof of his divine mission. They had often heard of his miracles, and yet evaded the conviction of them, by calling in question the matter of fact; but now that they had themselves seen this done their unbelief was conquered, and they yielded at last. But *blessed are those who have not seen and yet have believed.* The more we see of Christ the more cause we shall see to love him and confide in him. These were some of those Jews that came to Mary, to comfort her. When we are doing good offices to others we put ourselves in the way of receiving favours from God, and have opportunities of getting good when we are doing good.

II. Others were irritated by it, and hardened in their unbelief.

1. The *informers* were so (v. 46): *Some of them,* who were eye-witnesses of the miracle, were so far from being convinced that they *went to the Pharisees,* whom they knew to be his implacable enemies, and *told them what things Jesus had done;* not merely as a matter of news worthy their notice, much less as an inducement to them to think more favourably of Christ, but with a spiteful design to excite those who needed no spur the more vigorously to prosecute him. Here is a strange instance, (1.) Of a most *obstinate infidelity,* refusing to yield to the most powerful means of conviction; and it is hard to imagine how they could evade the force of this evidence, but that the *god of this world* had *blinded their minds.* (2.) Of a most *inveterate enmity.* If they would not be satisfied that he was to be believed in as the Christ, yet one would think they should have been mollified, and persuaded not to persecute him; but, if the water be not sufficient to *quench* the fire, it will *inflame* it. They told *what Jesus had done,* and told no more than what was true; but their malice gave a tincture of diabolism to their information equal to that of *lying;* perverting what is true is as bad as forging what is false. *Doeg* is called a *false, lying,* and *deceitful tongue* (Ps. 52:2–4; 120:2, 3), though what he said was *true.*

2. The judges, the leaders, the *blind leaders,* of the people were no less exasperated by the report made to them, and here we are told what they did.

(1.) A special council is called and held (v. 47): *Then gathered the chief priests and Pharisees a council,* as was foretold, Ps. 2:2, *The rulers take counsel together against the Lord.* Consultations of the sanhedrim were intended for the public good; but here, under colour of this, the greatest injury and mischief are done to the people. The things that belong to the nation's peace were hid from the eyes of those that were entrusted with its counsels. This council was called, not only for joint advice, but for mutual irritation; that as iron sharpens iron, and as coals are to burning coals and wood to fire, so they might exasperate and inflame one another with enmity and rage against Christ and his doctrine.

(2.) The case is proposed, and shown to be weighty and of great consequence.

[1.] The matter to be debated was what course they should take with this Jesus, to stop the growth of his interest; they said *What do we? For this man doeth many miracles.* The information given about the raising of Lazarus was produced, and the *men, brethren, and fathers* were called in to help as solicitously as if a formidable enemy had been with an army in the heart of their country. *First,* They own the truth of Christ's miracles, and that he had wrought many of them; they are therefore witnesses against themselves, for they acknowledge his credentials and yet deny his commission. *Secondly,* They consider what is to be done, and chide themselves that they have not done something sooner effectually to crush him. They do not take it at all into their consideration whether they shall not receive him and own him as the Messiah, though they profess to expect him, and Jesus gave pregnant proofs of his being so; but they take it for granted that he is an enemy, and as such is to be run down: "*What do we?* Have we no care to support our church? Is it nothing to us that a doctrine so destructive to our interest spreads thus? Shall we tamely yield up the ground we have got in the affections of the people? Shall we see our authority brought into contempt, and the craft by which we get our living ruined, and not bestir ourselves? What have we been doing all this while? And what are we now thinking of? Shall we be always talking, and bring nothing to pass?"

[2.] That which made this matter weighty was the peril they apprehended their church and nation to be in from the Romans (v. 48): "If we do not silence him, and take him off, *all men will believe on him;* and, this being the setting up of a new king, the Romans will take umbrage at it, *and will come* with an army, and *take away our place and nation,* and therefore it is no time to trifle." See what an opinion they have,

First, Of their own *power.* They speak as if they thought Christ's progress and success in his work depended upon their connivance; as if he could not go on to work miracles, and make disciples, unless they *let him alone;* as if it were in their power to conquer him who had conquered death, or as if they could *fight against God,* and prosper. But he that sits in heaven laughs at the fond conceit which impotent malice has of its own omnipotence.

Secondly, Of their own *policy.* They fancy themselves to

be men of mighty insight and foresight, and great sagacity in their moral prognostications.

a. They take on them to prophecy that, in a little time, if he have liberty to go on, *all men will believe on him,* hereby owning, when it was to serve their purpose, that his doctrine and miracles had a very convincing power in them, such as could not be resisted, but that all men would become his proselytes and votaries. Thus do they now make his interest formidable, though, to serve another turn, these same men strove to make it contemptible, *ch.* 7:48, *Have any of the rulers believed on him?* This was the thing they were afraid of, that men would *believe on him,* and then all their measures were broken. Note, The success of the gospel is the dread of its adversaries; if souls be saved, they are undone.

b. They foretel that if the generality of the nation be *drawn after him,* the rage of the Romans will be *drawn upon them.* They *will come and take away our place;* the country in general, especially Jerusalem, or the temple, the *holy place,* and *their* place, their darling, their idol; or, their *preferments* in the temple, their *places* of power and trust. Now it was true that the Romans had a very jealous eye upon them, and knew they wanted nothing but power and opportunity to shake off their yoke. It was likewise true that if the Romans should pour an army in upon them it would be very hard for them to make any head against it; yet here appeared a cowardice which one would not have found in the priests of the Lord if they had not by their wickedness forfeited their interest in God and all good men. Had they kept their integrity, they needed not to have feared the Romans; but they speak like a dispirited people, as the men of Judah when they basely said to Samson, *Knowest thou not that the Philistines rule over us?* Jdg. 15:11. When men lose their piety they lose their courage. But, (*a.*) It was false that there was any danger of the Romans' being irritated against their nation by the progress of Christ's gospel, for it was no way *hurtful to kings nor provinces,* but highly beneficial. The Romans had no jealousy at all of his growing interest; for he taught men to give tribute to Caesar, and not to *resist evil,* but to take up the cross. The Roman governor, at his trial, could *find no fault in him.* There was more danger of the Romans' being incensed against the Jewish nation by the priests than by Christ. Note, Pretended fears are often the colour of malicious designs. (*b.*) Had there really been some danger of displeasing the Romans by tolerating Christ's preaching, yet this would not justify their hating and persecuting a good man. Note, [*a.*] The enemies of Christ and his gospel have often coloured their enmity with a seeming care for the *public good* and the *common safety,* and, in order to this, have branded his prophets and ministers as troublers of Israel, and men that *turn the world upside down.* [*b.*] Carnal policy commonly sets up *reasons of state,* in opposition to *rules of justice.* When men are concerned for their own wealth and safety more than for truth and duty, it is wisdom from beneath, which is *earthly, sensual, and devilish.* But see what was the issue; they pretended to be afraid that their tolerating Christ's gospel would bring desolation upon them by the Romans, and therefore, *right or wrong,* set themselves against it; but it proved that their persecuting the gospel brought upon them that which they feared, filled up the measure of their iniquity, and the Romans came and *took away their place and nation,* and their place *knows them no more.* Note, That calamity, which we seek to escape by sin we take the most effectual course to bring upon our own heads; and those who think by opposing Christ's kingdom to secure or advance their own secular interest will find Jerusalem a more *burdensome stone* than they think it is, Zec. 12:3. The *fear of the wicked it shall come upon them,* Prov. 10:24.

(3.) Caiaphas makes a malicious but mystical speech in the council on this occasion.

[1.] The *malice* of it appears evident at first view, *v.* 49, 50. He, being the high priest, and so president of the council, took upon him to decide the matter before it was debated: *"You know nothing at all,* your hesitating betrays your ignorance, for it is not a thing that will bear a dispute, it is soon determined, if you consider that received maxim, *That it is expedient for us that one man should die for the people."* Here,

First, The counsellor was Caiaphas, who was *high priest that same year.* The high priesthood was by divine appointment settled upon the heir male of the house of Aaron, for and during the term of his natural life, and then to his heir male; but in those degenerate times it was become, though not an annual office, like a consulship, yet frequently changed, as they could make an interest with the Roman powers. Now it happened that *this year* Caiaphas wore the mitre.

Secondly, The drift of the advice was, in short, this, That some way or other must be found out to put Jesus to death. We have reason to think that they strongly suspected him to be indeed the Messiah; but his doctrine was so contrary to their darling traditions and secular interest, and his design did so thwart their notions of the Messiah's kingdom, that they resolve, be he who he will, he must be put to death. Caiaphas does not say, Let him be silenced, imprisoned, banished, though amply sufficient for the *restraint* of one they thought dangerous; but *die he must.* Note, Those that have set themselves against Christianity have commonly divested themselves of humanity, and been infamous for cruelty.

Thirdly, This is plausibly insinuated, with all the subtlety as well as malice of the old serpent. 1. He suggests his own sagacity, which we must suppose him as high priest to excel in, though the *Urim* and *Thummim* were long since lost. How scornfully does he say, *"You know nothing,* who are but common priests; but you must give me leave to see further into things than you do!" Thus it is common for those in authority to impose their corrupt dictates by virtue of that; and, because they *should be* the wisest and best, to expect that every body should believe they *are so.* 2. He takes it for granted that the case is plain and past dispute, and that those are very ignorant who do not see it to be so. Note, Reason and justice are often run down with a high hand. *Truth is fallen in the streets,* and, when it is down, down with it; and *equity cannot enter,* and, when it is out, out with it, Isa. 59:14. 3. He insists upon a maxim in politics, That the welfare of communities is to be preferred before that of particular persons. *It is expedient for us* as priests, whose all lies at stake, that *one man die for the people.* Thus far it holds true, that it is *expedient,* and more than so, it is truly *honourable,* for a man to hazard his life in the service of his country (Phil. 2:17; 1 Jn. 3:16); but to put an innocent man to death under colour of consulting the public safety is the devil's policy. Caiaphas craftily insinuates that the greatest and best man, though *major singulis — greater than any one individual,* is *minor universis — less than the collected mass,* and ought to think his life well spent, nay well lost, to save his country from ruin. But what is this to the murdering of one that was evidently a great blessing under pretence of preventing an imaginary mischief to the country? The case ought to have been put thus: Was it expedient for them to bring upon themselves and upon their nation the guilt of blood, a prophet's blood, for the securing of their civil interests from a danger which they had no just reason to be afraid of? Was it expedient for them to drive God and their glory from them, rather than venture the Romans' displeasure, who could do them no harm if they had God on their side? Note, Carnal policy, which steers only by secular considerations, while it thinks to *save all* by sin, *ruins all* at last.

[2.] The *mystery* that was in this counsel of Caiaphas does not appear at first view, but the evangelist leads us into it (*v.* 51, 52): *This spoke he not of himself,* it was not only the language of his own enmity and policy, but in these words he prophesied, though he himself was not aware of it, *that Jesus should die for that nation.* Here is a precious comment upon a pernicious text; the counsel of cursed Caiaphas so construed as to fall in with the counsels of the blessed God. Charity teaches us to put the most favourable construction upon men's words and actions that they will fear; but piety teaches us to make a good improvement of them, even contrary to that for which they were intended. If wicked men, in what they *do* against us, *are God's hand* to humble and reform us, why may they not in what they say against us be God's mouth to instruct and convince us? But in this of Caiaphas there was an extraordinary direction of Heaven prompting him to say that which was capable of a very sublime sense. As the hearts of all men are in God's hand, so are their tongues. Those are deceived who say, *"Our tongues are our own,* so that either we *may* say what we will, and are not accountable to God's judgment, or we *can* say what we will, and are not restrainable by his providence and power." Balaam could not say what he would, when he came to curse Israel, nor Laban when he pursued Jacob.

(4.) The evangelist explains and enlarges upon Caiaphas's words.

[1.] He explains what he said, and shows how it not only was, but was intended to be, accommodated to an excellent purpose. He did not *speak it of himself.* As it was an artifice to stir up the council against Christ, he spoke it of himself, or of the devil rather; but as it was an *oracle,* declaring it the purpose and design of God by the death of Christ to save God's spiritual Israel from sin and wrath, he did not speak it of himself, for he knew nothing of the matter, he *meant not so, neither did his heart think so,* for nothing was in his heart but to destroy and cut off, Isa. 10:7.

First, He *prophesied,* and those that prophesied did not, in their prophesying, *speak of themselves.* But is Caiaphas also among the prophets? He is so, *pro hâc vice — this once,* though a bad man, and an implacable enemy to Christ and his gospel. Note, 1. God can and often does make wicked men instruments to serve his own purposes, even contrary to their own intentions; for he has them not only *in a chain,* to restrain them from doing the mischief they would, but *in a bridle,* to lead them to do the service they would not. 2. Words of prophecy in the mouth are no infallible evidence of a principle of grace in the heart. *Lord, Lord, have we not prophesied in thy name?* will be rejected as a frivolous plea.

Secondly, He prophesied, *being high priest that year;* not that his being high priest did at all dispose or qualify him to be a prophet; we cannot suppose the pontifical mitre to have first inspired with prophecy the basest head that ever wore it; but, 1. Being high priest, and therefore of note and eminence in the conclave, God was pleased to put this significant word into his mouth rather than into the mouth of any other, that it might be the more observed or the nonobservance of it the more aggravated. The apophthegms of great men have been thought worthy of special regard: *A divine sentence is in the lips of the king;* therefore this divine sentence was put into the lips of the high priest, that even out of his mouth this word might be established, That Christ died for *the good of the nation,* and not *for any iniquity in his hands.* He happened to be high priest that year which was fixed to be the *year of the redeemed,* when Messiah the prince *must be cut off, but not for himself* (Dan. 9:26), and he must own it. 2. Being high priest *that year,* that famous year, in which there was to be such a plentiful effusion of the Spirit, more than had ever been yet, according to the prophecy (Joel 2:28, 29, compared with Acts 2:17), some drops of the blessed shower light upon Caiaphas, as the crumbs (says Dr. Lightfoot) of the children's bread, which fall from the table among the dogs. This year was the year of the expiration of the Levitical priesthood; and out of the mouth of him who was that year high priest was extorted an implicit resignation of it to him who should not (as they had done for many ages) offer beasts for that nation, but offer himself, and so make an end of the *sin-offering.* This resignation he made *inwittingly,* as Isaac gave the blessing to Jacob.

Thirdly, The matter of his prophecy was *that Jesus should die for that nation,* the very thing to which all the prophets bore witness, who *testified beforehand the sufferings of Christ* (1 Pt. 1:11), that the death of Christ must be the life and salvation of Israel; he meant by *that nation* those in it that obstinately adhered to Judaism, but God meant those in it that would receive the doctrine of Christ, and become followers of him, all believers, the spiritual seed of Abraham. The death of Christ, which Caiaphas was now projecting, proved the ruin of that interest in the nation of which he intended it should be the security and establishment, for it brought wrath upon them to the uttermost; but it proved the advancement of that interest of which he hoped it would have been the ruin, for Christ, being lifted up from the earth, drew all men unto him. It is a great thing that is here prophesied: That Jesus should *die,* die for others, not only *for their good,* but *in their stead, dies for that nation,* for they had the first offer made them of salvation by his death. If the whole nation of the Jews had unanimously believed in Christ, and received his gospel, they had been not only saved eternally, but saved as a nation from their grievances. The fountain was first *opened to the house of David,* Zec. 13:1. He so died for *that nation* as that *the whole nation should not perish,* but that *a remnant should be saved,* Rom. 11:5.

[2.] The evangelist enlarges upon this word of Caiaphas (*v.* 52), *not for that nation only,* how much soever it thought itself the darling of Heaven, but *that also he should gather together in one the children of God that were scattered abroad.* Observe here,

First, The persons Christ died for: *Not for the nation* of the Jews *only* (it would have been comparatively but *a light thing* for the Son of God to go through so vast an undertaking only to restore the *preserved of Jacob,* and *the outcasts of Israel*); no, he must be *salvation to the ends of the earth,* Isa. 49:6. He must die for *the children of God that were scattered abroad.* 1. Some understand it of the children of God that were then *in being,* scattered abroad in the Gentile world, *devout men* of every nation (Acts 2:5), that *feared God* (Acts 10:2), and worshipped him (Acts 17:4), proselytes of the gate, who served the God of Abraham, but submitted not to the ceremonial law of Moses, persons that had a savour of natural religion, but were *dispersed* in the nations, had no solemn assemblies of their own, nor any peculiar profession to unite in or distinguish themselves by. Now Christ died to incorporate these in one great society, to be denominated from him and governed by him; and this was the setting up of a standard, to which all that had a regard to God and a concern for their souls might have recourse, and under which they might enlist themselves. 2. Others take in with these all that belong to the election of grace, who are called the children of God, though not yet born, because they are *predestinated to the adoption of children,* Eph. 1:5. Now these are *scattered abroad* in several *places of the earth,* out of all kindreds and tongues (Rev. 7:9), and in several *ages of the world,* to the end of time; there are those that *fear him throughout all generations,* to all these he had an eye in the atonement he made by his blood; as he prayed, so he died, for *all that should believe on him.*

Secondly, The purpose and intention of his death concerning those persons; he died to *gather in* those who wandered, and to *gather together in one* those who were scattered; to invite those to him who were at a distance from him, and to unite those in him who were at a distance from each other. Christ's dying is, 1. The great *attractive of our hearts;* for this end he is lifted up, to draw men to him. The conversion of souls is the gathering to them in to Christ as their ruler and refuge, as the doves to their windows; and he died to effect this. By dying he purchased them to himself, and the gift of the Holy Ghost for them; his love in dying for us is the great loadstone of our love. 2. The great *centre of our unity.* He gathers them together *in one,* Eph. 1:10. They are one with him, one body, one spirit, and one with each other in him. All the saints in all places and ages meet in Christ, as all the members in the head, and all the branches in the root. Christ by the merit of his death recommended all the saints in *one* to the grace and favour *of God* (Heb. 2:11–13), and by the motive of his death recommends them all severally to the love and affection one of another, *ch.* 13:34.

(5.) The result of this debate is a resolve of the council to put Jesus to death (*v.* 53): *From that day they took counsel together, to put him to death.* They now understood one another's minds, and so each was fixed in his own, that Jesus must die; and, it should seem, a committee was appointed to sit, *de die in diem — daily,* to consider of it, to consult about it, and to receive proposals for effecting it. Note, The wickedness of the wicked ripens by degrees, James 1:15; Eze. 7:10. Two considerable advances were now made in their accursed design against Christ. [1.] What before they had thought of *severally* now they *jointly* concurred in, and so strengthened the hands one of another in this wickedness, and proceeded with the greater assurance. Evil men confirm and encourage themselves and one another in evil practices, by comparing notes; men of corrupt minds bless themselves when they find others of *the same mind:* then the wickedness which before seemed impracticable appears not only possible, but easy to be effected, *vis unita fortior — energies, when united, become more efficient.* [2.] What before they wished done, but *wanted a colour for,* now they are furnished with a plausible pretence to justify themselves in, which will serve, if not to take off the guilt (that is the least of their care), yet to take off the odium, and so satisfy, if not the personal, yet the political conscience, as some subtly distinguish. Many will go on very securely in doing an evil thing as long as they have but something to say in excuse for it. Now this resolution of theirs to put him to death, right or wrong, proves that all the formality of a trial, which he afterwards underwent, was but show and pretence; they were before determined what to do.

(6.) Christ hereupon absconded, knowing very well what was the vote of their close cabal, *v.* 54.

[1.] He suspended his public appearances: *He walked no more openly among the Jews,* among the inhabitants of Judea, who were properly called Jews, especially those at Jerusalem; *ou periepatei — he did not walk up and down*

among them, did not go from place to place, preaching and working miracles with the freedom and openness that he had done, but while he staid in Judea, he was there *incognito.* Thus the chief priests put the light of Israel *under a bushel.*

[2.] He withdrew into an obscure part of the country, so obscure that the name of the town he retired to is scarcely met with any where else. He went to a country *near the wilderness,* as if he were driven out from among men, or rather wishing, with Jeremiah, that he might have in the wilderness a *lodging place of way-faring men,* Jer. 9:2. He entered into a city called Ephraim, some think Ephratah, that is, Bethlehem, where he was born, and which bordered upon the wilderness of Judah; others think Ephron, or Ephraim, mentioned 2 Chr. 13:19. Thither his disciples went with him; neither would they leave him in solitude, nor would he leave them in danger. There he continued, *dietribe,* there he *conversed,* he knew how to improve this time of retirement in private conversation, when he had not an opportunity of preaching publicly. He *conversed with his disciples,* who were his family, when he was forced from the temple, and his *diatribai,* or *discourses* there, no doubt, were very edifying. We must do the good we can, when we cannot do the good we would. But why would Christ abscond now? It was not because he either feared the power of his enemies or distrusted his own power; he had many ways to save himself, and was neither averse to suffering nor unprepared for it; but he retired, *First,* To put a mark of his displeasure upon Jerusalem and the people of the Jews. They rejected him and his gospel; justly therefore did he remove himself and his gospel from them. The prince of *teachers* was now *removed into a corner* (Isa. 30:20); there was *no open vision* of him; and it was a sad presage of that thick darkness which was shortly to come upon Jerusalem, because she knew not the day of her visitation. *Secondly,* To render the cruelty of his enemies against him the more inexcusable. If that which was grievous to them, and thought dangerous to the public, was his *public appearance,* he would try whether their anger would be turned away by his retirement into privacy; when David had fled to Gath, Saul was satisfied, and sought no more for him, 1 Sa. 27:4. But it was the *life,* the precious life, that these wicked men hunted after. *Thirdly,* His hour was not *yet come,* and therefore he declined danger, and did it in a way common to men, both to warrant and encourage the flight of his servants in time of persecution and to comfort those who are forced from their usefulness, and buried alive in privacy and obscurity; *the disciple is not better than his Lord. Fourthly,* His retirement, for awhile, was to make his return into Jerusalem, when his hour was come, the more remarkable and illustrious. This swelled the acclamations of joy with which his well-wishers welcomed him at his next public appearance, when he rode triumphantly into the city.

(7.) The strict enquiry made for him during his recess, *v.* 55–57.

[1.] The occasion of it was the approach of the passover, at which they expected his presence, according to custom (*v.* 55): *The Jews' passover was nigh at hand;* a festival which shone bright in their calendar, and which there was great expectation of for some time before. This was Christ's fourth and last passover, since he entered upon his public ministry, and it might truly be said (as, 2 Chr. 35:18), *There never was such a passover in Israel,* for in it *Christ our passover was sacrificed for us.* Now the passover being at hand, *many went out* of all parts of *the country to Jerusalem, to purify themselves.* This was either, *First,* A *necessary purification* of those who had contracted any ceremonial pollution; they came to be sprinkled with the *water of purification,* and to perform the other rites of cleansing according to the law, for they might not eat the passover in their uncleanness, Num. 9:6. Thus before our gospel passover we must renew our repentance, and by faith wash in the blood of Christ, and so *compass God's altar.* Or, *Secondly,* A *voluntary purification,* or self-sequestration, by fasting and prayer, and other religious exercises, which many that were more devout than their neighbours spent some time in before the passover, and chose to do it at Jerusalem, because of the advantage of the temple-service. Thus must we by solemn preparation set bounds about the mount on which we expect to meet with God.

[2.] The enquiry was very solicitous: *They said, What think you, that he will not come to the feast? v.* 56.

First, Some think this was said by those who wished well to him, and expected his coming, that they might hear his doctrine and see his miracles. Those who came early out of

the country, that they might purify themselves, were very desirous to meet with Christ, and perhaps came up the sooner with that expectation, and therefore *as they stood in the temple,* the place of their purification, they enquired what news of Christ? Could any body give them hopes of seeing him? If there were those, and those of the most devout people, and best affected to religion, who showed this respect to Christ, it was a check to the enmity of the chief priests, and a witness against them.

Secondly, It should rather seem that they were his enemies who made this enquiry after him, who wished for an opportunity to lay hands on him. They, seeing the town begin to fill with devout people out of the country, wondered they did not find him among them. When they should have been assisting those that came to purify themselves, according to the duty of their place, they were plotting against Christ. How miserably degenerate was the Jewish church, when the priests of the Lord were become like the priests of the calves, a *snare upon Mizpeh, and a net spread upon Tabor,* and were *profound to make slaughter* (Hos. 5:1, 2), — when, instead of keeping the feast with unleavened bread, they were themselves soured with the leaven of the worst malice! Their asking, *What think you? Will he not come up to the feast?* implies, 1. An invidious reflection upon Christ, as if he would omit his attendance on the feast of the Lord for fear of exposing himself. If others, through irreligion, be absent, they are not animadverted upon; but if Christ be absent, for his own preservation (for God will have mercy, and not sacrifice), it is turned to his reproach, as it was to David's that his seat was empty at the feast, though Saul wanted him only that he might have an opportunity of nailing him to the wall with his javelin, 1 Sa. 20:25–27, etc. It is sad to see holy ordinances prostituted to such unholy purposes. 2. A fearful apprehension that they had of missing their game: "*Will he not come up to the feast?* If he do not, our measures are broken, and we are all undone; for there is no sending a pursuivant into the country, to fetch him up."

[3.] The orders issued out by the government for the apprehending of him were very strict, *v.* 57. The great sanhedrim issued out a proclamation, strictly charging and requiring that if any person in city or country *knew where he was* (pretending that he was a criminal, and had fled from justice) they should show it, that he might be taken, probably promising a reward to any that would discover him, and imposing a penalty on such as harboured him; so that hereby he was represented to the people as an obnoxious dangerous man, an outlaw, whom any one might have a blow at. Saul issued out such a proclamation for the apprehending of David, and Ahab of Elijah. See, *First,* How intent they were upon this prosecution, and how indefatigably they laboured in it, now at a time when, if they had had any sense of religion and the duty of their function, they would have found something else to do. *Secondly,* How willing they were to involve others in the guilt with them; if any man were capable of betraying Christ, they would have him think himself bound to do it. Thus was the interest they had in the people abused to the worst purposes. Note, It is an aggravation of the sins of wicked rulers that they commonly make those that are under them instruments of their unrighteousness. But notwithstanding this proclamation, though doubtless many knew where he was, yet such was his interest in the affections of some, and such God's hold of the consciences of others, that he continued undiscovered, for the *Lord hid him.*

CHAPTER 12

It was a melancholy account which we had in the close of the foregoing chapter of the dishonour done to our Lord Jesus, when the scribes and Pharisees proclaimed him a traitor to their church, and put upon him all the marks of ignominy they could: but the story of this chapter balances that, by giving us an account of the honour done to the Redeemer, notwithstanding all that reproach thrown upon him. Thus the one was set over against the other. Let us see what honours were heaped on the head of the Lord Jesus, even in the depths of his humiliation. I. Mary did him honour, by anointing his feet at the supper in Bethany (*v.* 1–11). II. The common people did him honour, with their acclamations of joy, when he rode in triumph into Jerusalem (*v.* 12–19). III. The Greeks did him honour, by enquiring after him with a longing desire to see him (*v.* 20–26). IV. God the Father did him honour, by a voice from heaven, bearing testimony to him (*v.* 27–36). V. He had honour done him by the Old Testament prophets, who foretold the infidelity of those that heard the report of him (*v.* 37–41). VI. He had honour done him by some of the chief rulers, whose consciences witnessed for him, though they had not courage to own it (*v.* 42, 43). VII. He claimed honour to himself, by asserting his divine mission, and the account he gave of his errand into the world (*v.* 44–50).

Verses 1–11

In these verses we have,

I. The *kind visit* our Lord Jesus paid to his friends at Bethany, *v.* 1. He came up out of the country, *six days before the passover,* and took up at Bethany, a town which, according to the computation of our metropolis, lay so near Jerusalem as to be within the bills of mortality. He lodged here with his friend Lazarus, whom he had lately *raised from the dead.* His coming to Bethany now may be considered,

1. As a preface to the passover he intended to celebrate, to which reference is made in assigning the date of his coming: *Six days before the passover.* Devout men set time apart before, to prepare themselves for that solemnity, and thus it became our Lord Jesus to *fulfil all righteousness.* Thus he has set us an example of solemn self-sequestration, before the solemnities of the gospel passover; let us hear the voice crying, *Prepare ye the way of the Lord.*

2. As a voluntary exposing of himself to the fury of his enemies; now that his hour was at hand he came within their reach, and freely offered himself to them, though he had shown them how easily he could evade all their snares. Note, (1.) Our Lord Jesus was voluntary in his sufferings; his life was not *forced* from him, but *resigned: Lo, I come.* As the strength of his persecutors could not overpower him, so their subtlety could not surprise him, but he died because he would. (2.) As there is a time when we are allowed to shift for our own preservation, so there is a time when we are called to hazard our lives in the cause of God, as St. Paul, when he *went bound in the Spirit to Jerusalem.*

3. As an instance of his kindness to his friends at Bethany, whom he loved, and from whom he was shortly to be taken away. This was a farewell visit; he came to take leave of them, and to leave with them words of comfort against the day of trial that was approaching. Note, Though Christ depart for a time from his people, he will give them intimations that he departs in love, and not in anger. Bethany is here described to be the town *where Lazarus was, whom he raised from the dead.* The miracle wrought here put a new honour upon the place, and made it remarkable. Christ came hither to observe what improvement was made of this miracle; for where Christ works wonders, and shows signal favours, he looks after them, to see whether the intention of them be answered. Where he has sown plentifully, he observes whether it comes up again.

II. The *kind entertainment* which his friends there gave him: They *made him a supper* (*v.* 2), a great supper, a feast. It is queried whether this was the same with that which is recorded, Mt. 24:6, etc., in the house of Simon. Most commentators think it was; for the substance of the story and many of the circumstances agree; but that comes in after what was said *two days* before the passover, whereas this was done *six days* before; nor is it likely that Martha should serve in any house but her own; and therefore I incline with Dr. Lightfoot to think them different: that in Matthew on the third day of the passover week, but this the seventh day of the week before, being the Jewish sabbath, the night before he rode in triumph into Jerusalem; that in the house of Simon; this of Lazarus. These two being the most public and solemn entertainments given him in Bethany, Mary probably graced them *both* with this token of her respect; and what she *left* of her ointment this first time, when she spent but a *pound* of it (*v.* 3), she used that second time, when she *poured it all out,* Mk. 14:3. Let us see the account of this entertainment. 1. They *made him a supper;* for with them, ordinarily, supper was the best meal. This they did in token of their respect and gratitude, for a feast is made for *friendship;* and that they might have an opportunity of free and pleasant conversation with him, for a feast is made for *fellowship.* Perhaps it is in allusion to this and the like entertainments given to Christ in the days of his flesh that he promises, to such as open the door of their hearts to him, that he will *sup with them,* Rev. 3:20. 2. Martha *served;* she herself waited at table, in token of her great respect to the Master. Though a person of some quality, she did not think it below her to *serve,* when Christ sat at meat; nor should we think it a dishonour or disparagement to us to stoop to any service whereby Christ may be honoured. Christ had formerly reproved Martha for being *troubled with much serving.* But she did not therefore leave off serving, as some, who, when they are reproved for one extreme, peevishly run into another; no, still she *served;* not as then at a distance, but *within hearing* of Christ's gracious words, reckoning those happy who, as the queen of Sheba said concerning Solomon's servants, stood continually before him, to hear his wisdom; better be a *waiter* at Christ's table than a *guest* at the table of a prince. 3. Lazarus was *one of those that sat at meat.* It proved the truth of his resurrection, as it did of Christ's, that there were those who did *eat and drink with him,* Acts 10:41. Lazarus did not retire into a *wilderness* after his resurrection, as if, when he had made a visit to the other world, he must ever after be a hermit in this; no, he conversed familiarly with people, as others did. He *sat at meat,* as a monument of the miracle Christ had wrought. Those whom Christ has *raised up* to a spiritual life are made to *sit together with him.* See Eph. 2:5, 6.

III. The particular respect which Mary showed him, above the rest, in anointing his feet with sweet ointment, *v.* 3. She had a *pound of ointment of spikenard, very costly,* which probably she had by her for her own use; but the death and resurrection of her brother had quite weaned her from the use of all such things, and with this she *anointed the feet of Jesus,* and, as a further token of her reverence for him and negligence of herself, she *wiped them with her hair,* and this was taken notice of by all that were present, for *the house was filled with the odour of the ointment.* See Prov. 27:16.

1. Doubtless she intended this as a token of her love to Christ, who had given real tokens of his love to her and her family; and thus she studies what she shall render. Now by this her love to Christ appears to have been, (1.) A *generous* love; so far from sparing necessary charges in his service, she is as ingenious to *create* an occasion of expense in religion as most are to avoid it. If she had any thing more valuable than another, that must be brought out for the honour of Christ. Note, Those who love Christ truly love him so much better than this world as to be willing to lay out the best they have for him. (2.) A *condescending* love; she not only bestowed her ointment upon Christ, but with her own hands poured it upon him, which she might have ordered one of her servants to have done; nay, she did not, as usual, anoint his *head* with it, but his *feet.* True love, as it does not spare charges, so it does not spare pains, in honouring Christ. Considering what Christ has done and suffered for us, we are very ungrateful if we think any service too hard to do, or too mean to stoop to, whereby he may *really* be glorified. (3.) A *believing* love; there was faith working by this love, faith in Jesus as the Messiah, the Christ, the Anointed, who, being both priest and king, was anointed as Aaron and David were. Note, *God's Anointed* should be *our Anointed.* Has God poured on him the oil of gladness above his fellows? Let us pour on him the ointment of our best affections above all competitors. By consenting to Christ as *our* king, we must comply with God's designs, appointing him *our head* whom he has appointed, Hos. 1:11.

2. The *filling of the house* with the pleasant *odour of the ointment* may intimate to us, (1.) That those who entertain Christ in their hearts and houses bring a sweet odour into them; Christ's presence brings with it an ointment and *perfume which rejoice the heart.* (2.) Honours done to Christ are comforts to all his friends and followers; they are to God and good men an offering of a *sweet-smelling savour.*

IV. Judas's dislike of Mary's compliment, or token of her respect to Christ, *v.* 4, 5, where observe,

1. The person that carped at it was Judas, *one of his disciples;* not one of their nature, but only one of their number. It is possible for the worst of men to lurk under the disguise of the best profession; and there are many who pretend to stand in relation to Christ who really have no kindness for him. Judas was an apostle, a preacher of the gospel, and yet one that discouraged and checked this instance of pious affection and devotion. Note, It is sad to see the life of religion and holy zeal frowned upon and discountenanced by such as are bound by their office to assist and encourage it. But this was he that should *betray Christ.* Note, Coldness of love to Christ, and a secret contempt of serious piety, when they appear in professors of religion, are sad presages of a final apostasy. Hypocrites, by less instances of worldliness, discover themselves to be ready for a compliance with greater temptations.

2. The pretence with which he covered his dislike (*v.* 5): *"Why was not this ointment,* since it was designed for a pious use, sold for three hundred pence" (*8l. 10s.* of our money), "and *given to the poor?"* (1.) Here is a foul iniquity gilded over with a specious and plausible pretence, for Satan transforms himself into an angel of light. (2.) Here is worldly wisdom passing a censure upon pious zeal, as guilty of imprudence and mismanagement. Those who value themselves upon their *secular policy,* and undervalue others for their *serious piety,* have more in them of the spirit of Judas than they would be thought to have. (3.) Here is charity to the poor made a colour for opposing a piece of piety to Christ, and secretly made a cloak for covetousness. Many excuse themselves from *laying out* in charity under pretence of *laying up* for charity: whereas, if the clouds be full of rain, they will *empty themselves.* Judas asked, *Why was it not given to the poor?* To which it is easy to answer, Because it was better bestowed upon the Lord Jesus. Note, We must not conclude that those do no acceptable piece of service who do not do it in our way, and just as we would have them; as if every thing must be adjudged imprudent and unfit which does not take its measures from us and our sentiments. Proud men think all ill-advised who do not advise with them.

3. The detection and discovery of Judas's hypocrisy herein, *v.* 6. Here is the evangelist's remark upon it, by the direction of him who *searches the heart: This he said, not that he cared for the poor,* as he pretended, *but because he was a thief, and had the bag.*

(1.) It did not come from a principle of charity: *Not that he cared for the poor.* He had no compassion towards them, no concern for them: what were the poor to him any further than he might serve his own ends by being overseer of the poor? Thus some warmly contend for the *power* of the church, as others for its *purity,* when perhaps it may be said, Not that they care for the church; it is all one to them whether its *true interest* sink or swim, but under the pretence of this they are advancing themselves. Simeon and Levi pretended zeal for circumcision, *not that they cared* for the seal of the covenant, any more than Jehu for the Lord of hosts, when he said, *Come see my zeal.*

(2.) It did come from a principle of covetousness. The truth of the matter was, this ointment being designed for his Master, he would rather have had it in money, to be put in the common stock with which he was entrusted, and then he knew what to do with it. Observe,

[1.] Judas was treasurer of Christ's household, whence some think he was called *Iscariot,* the *bag-bearer. First,* See what *estate* Jesus and his disciples had to live upon. It was but *little;* they had neither farms nor merchandise, neither barns nor storehouses, only a *bag;* or, as some think the word signifies, a *box,* or *coffer,* wherein they kept just enough for their subsistence, giving the overplus, if any were, to the poor; this they carried about with them, wherever they went. *Omnia mea mecum porto — I carry all my property about me.* This bag was supplied by the contributions of good people, and the Master and his disciples had all *in common;* let this lessen our esteem of worldly wealth, and deaden us to the punctilios of state and ceremony, and reconcile us to a mean and despicable way of living, if this be our lot, that it was our Master's lot; for our sakes he *became poor. Secondly,* See who was the *steward* of the little they had; it was Judas, he was purse-bearer. It was his office to receive and pay, and we do not find that he gave any account what markets he made. He was appointed to this office, either, 1. Because he was the least and lowest of all the disciples; it was not Peter nor John that was made steward (though it was a place of trust and profit), but Judas, the meanest of them. Note, Secular employments, as they are a digression, so they are a degradation to a minister of the gospel; see 1 Co. 6:4. The prime-ministers of state in Christ's kingdom refused to be concerned in the revenue, Acts 6:2. 2. Because he was desirous of the place. He loved in his heart to be fingering money, and therefore had the moneybag committed to him, either, (1.) As a kindness, to please him, and thereby oblige him to be true to his Master. Subjects are sometimes disaffected to the government because disappointed of their preferment; but Judas had no cause to complain of this; the bag he chose, and the bag he had. Or, (2.) In judgment upon him, to punish him for his secret wickedness; that was put into his hands which would be a snare and trap to him. Note, Strong inclinations to sin within are often justly punished with strong temptations to sin without. We have little reason to be fond of the bag, or proud of it, for at the best we are but stewards of it; and it was Judas, one of an ill character, and born to be hanged (pardon the expression), that was steward of the bag. *The prosperity of fools destroys them.*

[2.] Being trusted with the bag, he was *a thief,* that is, he had a thievish disposition. The reigning love of money is *heart-theft* as much as anger and revenge are *heart-murder.*

Or perhaps he had been really guilty of embezzling his Master's stores, and converting to his own use what was given to the public stock. And some conjecture that he was now contriving to fill his pockets, and then run away and leave his Master, having heard him speak so much of troubles approaching, to which he could by no means reconcile himself. Note, Those to whom the management and disposal of public money is committed have need to be governed by steady principles of justice and honesty, that no blot cleave to their hands; for though some make a jest of cheating the government, or the church, or the country, if cheating be *thieving,* and, communities being more considerable than particular persons, if robbing them be the greater sin, the guilt of theft and the portion of thieves will be found no jesting matter. Judas, who had betrayed his trust, soon after betrayed his Master.

V. Christ's justification of what Mary did (*v.* 7, 8): *Let her alone.* Hereby he intimated his acceptance of her kindness (though he was perfectly mortified to all the delights of sense, yet, as it was a token of her goodwill, he signified himself well-pleased with it), and his care that she should not be molested in it: *Pardon her,* so it may be read; "excuse her this once, if it be an error it is an error of her love." Note, Christ would not have those censured nor discouraged who sincerely design to please him, though in their honest endeavours there be not all the discretion that may be, Rom. 14:3. Though we would not do as they do, yet *let them alone.* For Mary's justification,

1. Christ puts a favourable construction upon what she did, which those that condemned it were not aware of: *Against the day of my burying she has kept this.* Or, *She has reserved this for the day of my embalming;* so Dr. Hammond. "You do not grudge the ointment used for the embalming of your dead friends, nor say that it should be sold, and given to the poor. Now this anointing either was so *intended,* or at least may be so *interpreted;* for the day of my burying is now at hand, and she has anointed a body that is already *as good as dead.*" Note, (1.) Our Lord Jesus thought much and often of his own death and burial; it would be good for us to do so too. (2.) Providence does often so open a door of opportunity to good Christians, and the Spirit of grace does so open their hearts, that the expressions of their pious zeal prove to be more *seasonable,* and more *beautiful,* than any foresight of their own could make them. (3.) The grace of Christ puts kind comments upon the pious words and actions of good people, and not only makes the best of what is amiss, but makes the most of what is good.

2. He gives a sufficient answer to Judas's objection, *v.* 8. (1.) It is so ordered in the kingdom of Providence that *the poor we have always with us,* some or other that are proper objects of charity (Deu. 15:11); such there will be as long as there are in this lapsed state of mankind so much folly and so much affliction. (2.) It is so ordered in the kingdom of grace that the church should not always have the bodily presence of Jesus Christ: *"Me you have not always,"* but only nor for a little time." Note, We need wisdom, when two duties come in competition, to know which to give the preference to, which must be determined by the circumstances. Opportunities are to be improved, and those opportunities first and most vigorously which are likely to be of the shortest continuance, and which we see most speedily hastening away. That good duty which may be done *at any time* ought to give way to that which cannot be done but *just now.*

VI. The public notice which was taken of our Lord Jesus here at this supper in Bethany (*v.* 9): *Much people of the Jews knew that he was there,* for he was the talk of the town, and *they came* flocking thither; the more because he had lately absconded, and now broke out as the sun from behind a dark cloud. 1. They came to see Jesus, whose name was very much magnified, and made considerable by the late miracle he had wrought in raising Lazarus. They came, not to hear him, but to gratify their curiosity with a sight of him here at Bethany, fearing he would not appear publicly, as he used to do, this passover. They came, not to seize him, or inform against him, though the government had prosecuted him to an outlawry, but to see him and show him respect. Note, There are some in whose affections Christ will have an interest, in spite of all the attempts of his enemies to misrepresent him. It being known where Christ was, multitudes came to him. Note, Where the king is there is the court; where Christ is there will the *gathering of the people be,* Lu. 17:37. 2. They came

to see Lazarus and Christ together, which was a very inviting sight. Some came for the confirmation of their faith in Christ, to have the story perhaps from Lazarus's own mouth. Others came only for the gratifying of their curiosity, that they might say they had seen a man who had been dead and buried, and yet lived again; so that Lazarus served for a *show,* these holy-days, to those who, like the Athenians, spent their time in telling and hearing new things. Perhaps some came to put curious questions to Lazarus about the state of the dead, to ask what news from the other world; we ourselves have sometimes said, it may be, We would have gone a great way for one hour's discourse with Lazarus. But if any came on this errand it is probable that Lazarus was silent, and gave them no account of his voyage; at least, the scripture is silent, and gives us no account of it; and we must not covet to be wise above what is written. But our Lord Jesus was present, who was a much fitter person for them to apply to than Lazarus;; for if we hear not Moses and the prophets, Christ and the apostles, if we heed not what they tell us concerning another world, neither should we be persuaded though Lazarus rose from the dead. We have a more sure word of prophecy.

VII. The indignation of the chief priests at the growing interest of our Lord Jesus, and their plot to crush it (*v.* 10, 11): They *consulted* (or decreed) *how they might put Lazarus also to death,* because that *by reason of him* (of what was done to him, not of any thing he said or did) *many of the Jews went away, and believed on Jesus.* Here observe,

1. How vain and unsuccessful their attempts against Christ had hitherto been. They had done all they could to alienate the people from him, and exasperate them against him, and yet many of the Jews, their neighbours, their creatures, their admirers, were so overcome by the convincing evidence of Christ's miracles that they *went away* from the interest and party of the priests, went off from obedience to their tyranny, *and believed on Jesus;* and it was by reason of Lazarus; his resurrection put life into their faith, and convinced them that this Jesus was undoubtedly the Messiah, and had life in himself, and power to give life. This miracle confirmed them in the belief of his other miracles, which they had heard he wrought in Galilee: what was impossible to him that could raise the dead?

2. How absurd and unreasonable this day's vote was — that Lazarus must be put to death. This is an instance of the most brutish rage that could be; they were like a *wild bull in a net,* full of fury, and laying about them without any consideration. It was a sign that they *neither feared God nor regarded man.* For, (1.) If they had feared God, they would not have done such an act of defiance to him. God will have Lazarus to live by miracle, and they will have him to die by malice. They cry, *Away with such a fellow, it is not fit he should live,* when God had so lately sent him back to the earth, declaring it highly fit he should live; what was this but *walking contrary to God?* They would put Lazarus to death, and challenge almighty power to raise him again, as if they could contend with God, and try titles with the King of kings. Who has the keys of death and the grave, he or they? *O caeca malitia! Christus qui suscitare potuit mortuum, non possit occisum.* — Blind malice, to suppose that Christ, who could raise one that had died a natural death, could not raise one that had been slain! — Augustine in loc. Lazarus is singled out to be the object of their special hatred, because God has distinguished him by the tokens of his peculiar love, as if they had made a league offensive and defensive with death and hell, and resolved to be severe upon all deserters. One would think that they should rather have consulted how they might have joined in friendship with Lazarus and his family, and by their mediation have reconciled themselves to this Jesus whom they had persecuted; but the god of this world had *blinded their minds.* (2.) If they had regarded man, they would not have done such an act of injustice to Lazarus, an innocent man, to whose charge they could not pretend to lay any crime. What bands are strong enough to hold those who can so easily break through the most sacred ties of common justice, and violate the maxims which even nature itself teaches? But the support of their own tyranny and superstition was thought sufficient, as in the church of Rome, not only to justify, but to consecrate the greatest villanies, and make them meritorious.

Verses 12–19

This story of Christ's riding in triumph to Jerusalem is re-

corded by all the evangelists, as worthy of special remark; and in it we may observe,

I. The respect that was paid to our Lord Jesus by the common people, *v.* 12, 13, where we are told,

1. Who they were that paid him this respect: *much people, ochlos polys — a great crowd* of those that came up to the feast; not the inhabitants of Jerusalem, but the country people that came from remote parts to worship at the feast; the nearer the temple of the Lord, the further from the Lord of the temple. They were such as *came up to the feast.* (1.) Perhaps they had been Christ's hearers in the country, and great admirers of him there, and therefore were forward to testify their respect to him at Jerusalem, where they knew he had many enemies. Note, Those that have a true value and veneration for Christ will neither be ashamed nor afraid to own him before men in any instance whereby they may do him honour. (2.) Perhaps they were those more *devout Jews* that came up to the feast some time before, to purify themselves, that were more inclined to religion than their neighbours, and these were they that were so forward to honour Christ. Note, The more regard men have to God and religion in general, the better disposed they will be to entertain Christ and his religion, which is not destructive but perfective of all previous discoveries and institutions. They were not the rulers, nor the great men, that went out to meet Christ, but the commonalty; some would have called them a mob, a rabble: but Christ has chosen the weak and foolish things (1 Co. 1:27), and is honoured more by the multitude than by the magnificence of his followers; for he values men by their souls, not their names and titles of honour.

2. On what occasion they did it: *They heard that Jesus was coming to Jerusalem.* They had enquired for him (*ch.* 11:55, 56): *Will he not come up to the feast?* And now they hear he is coming; for none that seek Christ seek in vain. Now when they heard he was coming, they bestirred themselves, to give him an agreeable reception. Note, Tidings of the approach of Christ and his kingdom should awaken us to consider what is the work of the day, that it may be done in the day. Israel must prepare to meet *their God* (Amos 4:12), and the virgins to *meet the bridegroom.*

3. In what way they expressed their respect; they had not the keys of the city to present to him, nor the sword nor mace to carry before him, none of the city music to compliment him with, but such as they had they gave him; and even this despicable crowd was a faint resemblance of that glorious company which John saw *before the throne, and before the Lamb,* Rev. 7:9, 10. Though these were not before the throne, they were before the Lamb, the paschal Lamb, who now, according to the usual ceremony, four days before the feast, was set apart to be sacrificed for us. There it is said of that celestial choir,

(1.) That they had palms in their hands, and so had these *branches of palm-trees.* The palm-tree has ever been an emblem of victory and triumph; Cicero calls one that had won many prizes *plurimarum palmarum homo — a man of many palms.* Christ was now by his death to conquer principalities and powers, and therefore it was fit that he should have the victor's palm borne before him; though he was but girding on the harness, yet he could boast as though he had put it off. But this was not all; the carrying of palm-branches was part of the ceremony of the feast of tabernacles (Lev. 23:40; Neh. 8:15), and their using this expression of joy in the welcome given to our Lord Jesus intimates that all the feasts pointed at his gospel, had their accomplishment in it, and particularly that of the feast of tabernacles, Zec. 14:16.

(2.) That they *cried with a loud voice, saying, Salvation to our God* (Rev. 7:10); so did these here, they shouted before him, as is usual in popular welcomes, *Hosanna, blessed is the king of Israel, that comes in the name of the Lord;* and *hosanna* signifies *salvation.* It is quoted from Ps. 118:25, 26. See how well acquainted these common people were with the scripture, and how pertinently they apply it to the Messiah. High thoughts of Christ will be best expressed in scripture-words. Now in their acclamations, [1.] They acknowledge our Lord Jesus to be the king of Israel, that comes *in the name of the Lord.* Though he went now in poverty and disgrace, yet, contrary to the notions their scribes had given them of the Messiah, they own him to be a king, which bespeaks both his dignity and honour, which we must adore; and his dominion and power, to which we must submit. They own him to be, *First,* A rightful king, coming in *the name of the Lord* (Ps. 2:6), sent of God, not only as a prophet, but as a king.

Secondly, The promised and long-expected king, Messiah the prince, for he is *king of Israel.* According to the light they had, they proclaimed him king of Israel in the streets of Jerusalem; and, they themselves being Israelites, hereby they avouched him for their king. [2.] They heartily wish well to his kingdom, which is the meaning of hosanna; let the king of Israel prosper, as when Solomon was crowned they cried, *God save king Solomon,* 1 Ki. 1:39. In crying hosanna they prayed for three things: — *First,* That his kingdom might come, in the light and knowledge of it, and in the power and efficacy of it. God speed the gospel plough. *Secondly,* That it might conquer, and be victorious over all opposition, Rev. 6:2. *Thirdly,* That it might continue. Hosanna is, *Let the king live for ever;* though his kingdom may be disturbed, let it never be destroyed, Ps. 72:17. [3.] They bid him welcome into Jerusalem: "*Welcome is he that cometh;* we are heartily glad to see him; *come in thou blessed of the Lord;* and well may we attend with our blessings him who meets us with his." This welcome is like that (Ps. 24:7–9), *Lift up your heads, O ye gates.* Thus we must every one of us bid Christ welcome into our hearts, that is, we must praise him, and be well pleased in him. As we should be highly pleased with the being and attributes of God, and his relation to us, so we should be with the person and offices of the Lord Jesus, and his meditation between us and God. Faith saith, *Blessed is he that cometh.*

II. The posture Christ puts himself into for receiving the respect that was paid him (*v.* 14): *When he had found,* or procured, *a young ass,* he *sat thereon.* It was but a poor sort of figure he made, he alone upon an ass, and a crowd of people about him shouting *Hosanna.* 1. This was much more of state than he used to take; he used to travel on foot, but now was mounted. Though his followers should be willing to take up with mean things, and not affect any thing that looks like grandeur, yet they are allowed to use the service of the inferior creatures, according as God in his providence gives particular possession of those things over which, by his covenant with Noah and his sons, he has given to man a general dominion. 2. Yet it was much less of state than the great ones of the world usually take. If he would have made a public entry, according to the state of a man of high degree, he should have rode in a chariot like that of Solomon's (Cant. 3:9, 10), with *pillars of silver,* the *bottom of gold,* and the *covering of purple;* but, if we judge according to the fashion of this world, to be introduced thus was rather a disparagement than any honour to the king of Israel, for it seemed as if he would look great, and knew not how. His kingdom was not of this world, and therefore came not with outward pomp. He was now humbling himself, but in his exalted state John sees him in a vision *on a white horse, with a bow and a crown.*

III. The fulfilling of the scripture in this: *As it is written, Fear not, daughter of Sion, v.* 15. This is quoted from Zec. 9:19. To him bore all the prophets witness, and particularly to this concerning him.

1. It was foretold that Zion's king should come, should come *thus, sitting on an ass's colt;* even this minute circumstance was foretold, and Christ took care it should be punctually fulfilled. Note, (1.) Christ is Zion's king; the holy hill of Zion was of old destined to be the metropolis or royal city of the Messiah. (2.) Zion's king does and will look after her, and come to her; though for a short time he retires, in due time he returns. (3.) Though he comes but slowly (an ass is slow-paced), yet he comes surely, and with such expressions of humility and condescension as greatly encourage the addresses and expectations of his loyal subjects. Humble supplicants may reach to speak with him. If this be a discouragement to Zion, that her king appears in no greater state or strength, let her know that though he comes to her riding on an ass's colt, yet he goes forth against her enemies riding *on the heavens for her help,* Deu. 33:26.

2. The daughter of Zion is therefore called upon to *behold her king,* to take notice of him and his approaches; behold and wonder, for he comes with observation, though not with outward show, Cant. 3:11. *Fear not.* In the prophecy, Zion is told to rejoice greatly, and to shout, but here it is rendered, *Fear not.* Unbelieving fears are enemies to spiritual joys; if they be cured, if they be conquered, joy will come of course; Christ comes to his people to *silence* their fears. If the case be so that we cannot reach to the exultations of joy, yet we should labour to get from under the oppressions of fear. *Rejoice greatly;* at least, *fear not.*

IV. The remark made by the evangelist respecting the disciples (*v.* 16): *They understood not at first* why Christ did this, and how the scripture was fulfilled; but when *Jesus was glorified,* and thereupon the Spirit poured out, then they remembered that *these things were written of him* in the Old Testament, and that they and others had, in pursuance thereof, *done these things to him.*

1. See here the imperfection of the disciples in their infant state; even *they understood not these things at first.* They did not consider, when they fetched the ass and set him thereon, that they were performing the ceremony of the inauguration of Zion's king. Now observe, (1.) The scripture is often fulfilled by the agency of those who have not themselves an eye to the scripture in what they do, Isa. 45:4. (2.) There are many excellent things, both in the word and providence of God, which the disciples themselves do not at first understand: not at their first acquaintance with the things of God, while they *see men as trees walking;* not at the first proposal of the things to their view and consideration. That which afterwards is clear was at first dark and doubtful. (3.) It well becomes the disciples of Christ, when they are grown up to maturity in knowledge, frequently to reflect upon the follies and weaknesses of their first beginning, that free grace may have the glory of their proficiency, and they may have compassion on the ignorant. *When I was a child, I spoke as a child.*

2. See here the improvement of the disciples in their adult state. Though they had been children, they were not always so, but went on to perfection. Observe,

(1.) When they understood it: *When Jesus was glorified;* for, [1.] Till then they did not rightly apprehend the nature of his kingdom, but expected it to appear in external pomp and power, and therefore knew not how to apply the scriptures which spoke of it to so mean an appearance. Note, The right understanding of the spiritual nature of Christ's kingdom, of its powers, glories, and victories, would prevent our misinterpreting and misapplying the scriptures that speak of it. [2.] Till then the Spirit was not poured out, who was to lead them into all truth. Note, The disciples of Christ are enabled to understand the scriptures by the same Spirit that indited the scriptures. *The spirit of revelation is* to all the saints a *spirit of wisdom,* Eph. 1:17, 18.

(2.) How they understood it; they compared the prophecy with the event, and put them together, that they might mutually receive light from each other, and so they came to understand both: *Then remembered they that these things were written of him* by the prophets, consonant to which they were done to him. Note, Such an admirable harmony there is between the word and works of God that the remembrance of what is written will enable us to understand what is done, and the observation of what is done will help us to understand what is written. *As we have heard, so have we seen.* The scripture is every day fulfilling.

V. The reason which induced the people to pay this respect to our Lord Jesus upon his coming into Jerusalem, though the government was so much set against him. It was because of the illustrious miracle he had lately wrought in raising Lazarus.

1. See here what account and what assurance they had of this miracle; no doubt, the city rang of it, the report of it was in all people's mouths. But those who considered it as a proof of Christ's mission, and a ground of their faith in him, that they might be well satisfied of the matter of fact, traced the report to those who were eye-witnesses of it, that they might *know the certainty* of it by the utmost evidence the thing was capable of: *The people therefore that* stood by *when he called Lazarus* out of his grave, being found out and examined, *bore record, v.* 17. They unanimously averred the thing to be true, beyond dispute or contradiction, and were ready, if called to it, to depose it upon oath, for so much is implied in the word *Emartyrei.* Note, The truth of Christ's miracles was evidenced by incontestable proofs. It is probable that those who had seen this miracle did not only assert it to those who asked them, but published it unasked, that this might add to the triumphs of this solemn day; and Christ's coming in now from Bethany, where it was done, would put them in mind of it. Note, Those who wish well to Christ's kingdom should be forward to proclaim what they know that may redound to his honour.

2. What improvement they made of it, and what influence it had upon them (*v.* 18): *For this cause,* as much as any other, *the people met him.* (1.) Some, out of curiosity, were desirous to see one that had done such a wonderful work. Many a good sermon he had preached in Jerusalem, which drew not such crowds after him as this one miracle did. But, (2.) Others, out of conscience, studied to do him honour, as one sent of God. This miracle was reserved for one of the last, that it might confirm those which went before, and might gain him this honour just before his sufferings; Christ's works were all not only *well done* (Mk. 7:7) but *well timed.*

VI. The indignation of the Pharisees at all this; some of them, probably, saw, and they all soon heard of, Christ's public entry. The committee appointed to find out expedients to crush him thought they had gained their point when he had retired unto privacy, and that he would soon be forgotten in Jerusalem, but they now rage and fret when they see they imagined but a *vain thing.* 1. They own that they had got no ground against him; it was plainly to be perceived that they *prevailed nothing.* They could not, with all their insinuations, alienate the people's affections from him, nor with their menaces restrain them from showing their affection to him. Note, Those who oppose Christ, and fight against his kingdom, will be made to perceive that they prevail nothing. God will accomplish his own purposes in spite of them, and the little efforts of their impotent malice. *You prevail nothing, ouk ōpheleite — you profit nothing.* Note, There is nothing got by opposing Christ. 2. They own that he had got ground: *The world is gone after him;* there is a vast crowd attending him, a *world of people:* an hyperbole common in most languages. Yet here, like Caiaphas, ere they were aware, they prophesied that *the world would go after him;* some of all sorts, some from all parts; nations shall be discipled. But to what intent was this said? (1.) Thus they *express* their own vexation at the growth of his interest; their envy makes them fret. If the *horn of the righteous be exalted with honour, the wicked see it, and are grieved* (Ps. 112:9, 10); considering how great these Pharisees were, and what abundance of respect was paid them, one would think they needed not grudge Christ so inconsiderable a piece of honour as was now done him; but proud men would monopolize honour, and have none share with them, like Haman. (2.) Thus they excite themselves and one another, to a more vigorous carrying on of the war against Christ. As if they should say, "Dallying and delaying thus will never do. We must take some other and more effectual course, to put a stop to this infection; it is time to try our utmost skill and force, before the grievance grows past redress." Thus the enemies of religion are made more resolute and active by being baffled; and shall its friends be disheartened with every disappointment, who know its cause is righteous and will at last be victorious?

Verses 20–26

Honour is here paid to Christ by certain Greeks that enquired or him with respect. We are not told what day of Christ's last week this was, probably not the same day he rode into Jerusalem (for that day was taken up in public work), but a day or two after.

I. We are told who they were that paid this honour to our Lord Jesus: *Certain Greeks among* the people who *came up to worship at the feast, v.* 20. Some think they were *Jews of the dispersion,* some of the twelve tribes that were scattered among the Gentiles, and were called *Greeks,* Hellenist Jews; but others think they were Gentiles, those whom they called *proselytes of the gate,* such as the eunuch and Cornelius. Pure natural religion met with the best assistance among the Jews, and therefore those among the Gentiles who were piously inclined joined with them in their solemn meetings, as far as was allowed them. There were devout worshippers of the true God even among those that were strangers to the commonwealth of Israel. It was in the latter ages of the Jewish church that there was this flocking of the Gentiles to the temple at Jerusalem, — a happy presage of the taking down of the partition-wall between Jews and Gentiles. The forbidding of the priests to accept of any oblation or sacrifice from a Gentile (which was done by Eleazar the son of Ananias, the high priest), Josephus says, was one of those things that brought the Romans upon them, *War* 2.409–410. Though these Greeks, if uncircumcised, were not admitted to eat the passover, yet they came to *worship at the feast.* We must thankfully use the privileges we have, though there may be others from which we are shut out.

II. What was the honour they paid him: they desired to be acquainted with him, *v.* 21. Having come to worship at the feast, they desired to make the best use they could of their time, and therefore applied to Philip, desiring that he would put them in a way to get some personal converse with the Lord Jesus. 1. Having a desire to see Christ, they were industrious in the use of proper means. They did not conclude it impossible, because he was so much crowded, to get to speak with him, nor rest in bare wishes, but resolved to try what could be done. Note, Those that would have the knowledge of Christ must seek it. 2. They made their application to Philip, one of his disciples. Some think that they had acquaintance with him formerly, and that they lived near Bethsaida in Galilee of the Gentiles; and then it teaches us that we should improve our acquaintance with good people, for our increase in the knowledge of Christ. It is good to know those who know the Lord. But if these Greeks had been near Galilee it is probable that they would have attended Christ there, where he mostly resided; therefore I think that they applied to him only because they saw him a close follower of Christ, and he was the first they could get to speak with. It was an instance of the veneration they had for Christ that they made an interest with one of his disciples for an opportunity to converse with him, a sign that they looked upon him as some great one, though he appeared mean. Those that would see Jesus by faith now that he is in heaven must apply to his ministers, whom he had appointed for this purpose, to guide poor souls in their enquiries after him. Paul must send for Ananias, and Cornelius for Peter. The bringing of these Greeks to the knowledge of Christ by the means of Philip signified the agency of the apostles, and the use made of their ministry in the conversion of the Gentiles to the faith and the discipling of the nations. 3. Their address to Philip was in short this: *Sir, we would see Jesus.* They gave him a title of respect, as one worthy of honour, because he was in relation to Christ. Their business is, they would *see Jesus;* not only see his face, that they might be able to say, when they came home, they had seen one that was so much talked of (it is probable they had seen him when he appeared publicly); but they would have some free conversation with him, and be taught by him, for which it was no easy thing to find him at leisure, his hands were so full of public work. Now that they were come to worship at the feast, they would see Jesus. Note, In our attendance upon holy ordinances, and particularly the gospel passover, the great desire of our souls should be to see Jesus; to have our acquaintance with him increased, our dependence on him encouraged, our conformity to him carried on; to see him as ours, to keep up communion with him, and derive communications of grace from him: we miss of our end in coming if we do not see Jesus. 4. Here is the report which Philip made of this to his Master, *v.* 22. He tells Andrew, who was of Bethsaida likewise, and was a *senior fellow* in the college of the apostles, contemporary with Peter, and consults him what was to be done, whether he thought the motion would be acceptable or no, because Christ had sometimes said that he was *not sent but to the house of Israel.* They agree that it must be made; but then he would have Andrew go along with him, remembering the favourable acceptance Christ had promised them, in case *two of them should agree touching any thing they should ask,* Mt. 18:19. Note, Christ's ministers should be helpful to one another and concur in helping souls to Christ: *Two are better than one.* It should seem that Andrew and Philip brought this message to Christ when he was teaching in public, for we read (*v.* 29) of the *people that stood by;* but he was seldom alone.

III. Christ's acceptance of this honour paid him, signified by what he said to the people hereupon, *v.* 23, etc., where he foretels both the honour which he himself should have in being followed (*v.* 23, 24) and the honour which those should have that followed him, *v.* 25, 26. This was intended for the direction and encouragement of these Greeks, and all others that desired acquaintance with him.

1. He foresees that plentiful harvest, in the conversion of the Gentiles, of which this was as it were the first-fruits, *v.* 23. Christ said to the two disciples who spoke a good word for these Greeks, but doubted whether they should speed or no, *The hour is come when the Son of Man shall be glorified,* by the accession of the Gentiles to the church, and in order to that he must be rejected of the Jews. Observe,

(1.) The end designed hereby, and that is the glorifying of the Redeemer: "And is it so? Do the Gentiles begin to enquire after me? Does the morning-star appear to them? and that blessed *say-spring,* which knows its place and time too, does that begin to *take hold of the ends of the earth?* Then the hour is come for the *glorifying of the Son of man.*" This was no surprise to Christ, but a paradox to those about him. Note, [1.] The calling, the effectual calling, of the Gentiles into the church of God greatly redounded to the glory of the Son of man. The multiplying of the redeemed was the magnifying of the Redeemer. [2.] there was a time, a set time, an hour, a certain hour, for the glorifying of the Son of man, which did come at last, when the days of his humiliation were numbered and finished, and he speaks of the approach of it with exultation and triumph: *The hour is come.*

(2.) The strange way in which this end was to be attained, and that was by the death of Christ, intimated in that similitude (*v.* 24): "*Verily, verily, I say unto you,* you to whom I have spoken of my death and sufferings, *except a corn of wheat* fall not only *to,* but *into, the ground,* and *die,* and be buried and lost, it *abideth alone,* and you never see any more of it; but *if it die* according to the course of nature (otherwise it would be a miracle) it *bringeth forth much fruit,* God giving to every seed its own body." Christ is the corn of wheat, the most valuable and useful grain. Now here is,

[1.] The necessity of Christ's humiliation intimated. He would never have been the living quickening head and root of the church if he had not descended from heaven to this accursed earth and ascended from earth to the accursed tree, and so accomplished our redemption. He must *pour out his soul unto death,* else he cannot *divide a portion with the great,* Isa. 53:12. He shall have a seed given him, but he must shed his blood to purchase them and purify, must win them and wear them. It was necessary likewise as a qualification for that glory which he was to have by the accession of multitudes to his church; for if he had not by his sufferings made satisfaction for sin, and so brought in an everlasting righteousness, he would not have been sufficiently provided for the entertainment of those that should come to him, and therefore must *abide alone.*

[2.] The advantage of Christ's humiliation illustrated. He *fell to the ground* in his incarnation, seemed to be buried alive in this earth, so much was his glory veiled; but this was not all: *he died.* This immortal seed submitted to the laws of mortality, he lay in the grave like seed under the clods; but as the seed comes up again green, and fresh, and flourishing, and with a great increase, so one dying Christ gathered to himself thousands of living Christians, and he became their root. The salvation of souls hitherto, and henceforward to the end of time, is all owing to the dying of this *corn of wheat.* Hereby the Father and the Son are glorified, the church is replenished, the mystical body is kept up, and will at length be completed; and, when time shall be no more, the Captain of our salvation, *bringing many sons to glory* by the virtue of his death, and being so made perfect by sufferings, shall be celebrated for ever with the admiring praises of saints and angels, Heb. 2:10, 13.

2. He foretels and promises an abundant recompence to those who should cordially embrace him and his gospel and interest, and should make it appear that they do so by their faithfulness in suffering for him or in serving him.

(1.) In suffering for him (*v.* 25): *He that loves his life* better than Christ *shall lose it;* but he that hates *his life in this world,* and prefers the favour of God and an interest in Christ before it, shall *keep it unto life eternal.* This doctrine Christ much insisted on, it being the great design of his religion to wean us from this world, by setting before us another world.

[1.] See here the fatal consequences of an inordinate love of life; many a man hugs himself to death, and loses his life by over-loving it. He that so loves his animal life as to indulge his appetite, and make *provision for the flesh, to fulfil the lusts thereof,* shall thereby shorten his days, shall lose the life he is so fond of, and another infinitely better. He that is so much in love with the life of the body, and the ornaments and delights of it, as, for fear of exposing it or them, to deny Christ, he shall lose it, that is, lose a real happiness in the other world, while he thinks to secure an imaginary one in this. *Skin for skin* a man may give for his life, and make a good bargain, but he that gives his soul, his God, his heaven, for it, buys life too dear, and is guilty of the folly of him who sold a birth-right for a mess of pottage.

[2.] See also the blessed recompence of a holy contempt of life. He that so hates the life of the body as to venture it for the preserving of the life of his soul shall find both, with unspeakable advantage, in eternal life. Note, *First,* It is required of the disciples of Christ that they hate *their life in this world;* a life in this world supposes a life in the other world, and this is hated when it is loved less than that. Our life in this world includes all the enjoyments of our present state, riches, honours, pleasures, and long life in the possession of them; these we must hate, that is, despise them as vain and insufficient to make us happy, dread the temptations that are in them, and cheerfully part with them whenever they come in competition with the service of Christ, Acts 20:24; 21:13; Rev. 12:11. See here much of the *power of godliness* — that it conquers the strongest natural affections; and much of the *mystery of godliness* — that it is the greatest wisdom, and yet makes men hate their own lives. *Secondly,* Those who, in love to Christ, hate their own lives in this world, shall be abundantly recompensed in the resurrection of the just. *He that hateth his life shall keep it;* he puts it into the hands of one that will *keep it to life eternal,* and restore it with as great an improvement as the heavenly life can make of the earthly one.

(2.) In serving him (*v.* 26): *If any man* profess *to serve me,* let him *follow me,* as a servant follows his master; and *where I am, ekei kai ho diakonos ho emos estai* — there *let my servant be;* so some read it, as part of the duty, there let him be, to attend upon me; we read it as part of the promise, *there shall he be* in happiness with me. And, lest this should seem a small matter, he adds, *If any man serve me, him will my Father honour;* and that is enough, more than enough. The Greeks desired to see Jesus (*v.* 21), but Christ lets them know that it was not enough to see him, they must *serve him.* He did not come into the world, to be a show for us to gaze at, but a king to be ruled by. And he says this for the encouragement of those who enquired after him to become his servants. In taking servants it is usual to fix both the work and the wages; Christ does both here.

[1.] Here is the work which Christ expects from his servants; and it is very easy and reasonable, and such as becomes them.

First, Let them attend their Master's movements: *If any man serve me, let him follow me.* Christians must follow Christ, follow his methods and prescriptions, *do the things that he says,* follow his example and pattern, *walk as he also walked,* follow his conduct by his providence and Spirit. We must go whither he leads us, and in the way he leads us; must follow the Lamb whithersoever he goes before us. "If any man serve me, if he put himself into that relation to me, let him apply himself to the business of my service, and be always ready at my call." Or, "If any man do indeed serve me, let him make an open and public profession of his relation to me, by following me, as the servant owns his Master by following him in the streets."

Secondly, Let them attend their Master's repose: *Where I am, there let my servant be,* to wait upon me. Christ is where his church is, in the assemblies of his saints, where his ordinances are administered; and *there let his servants be,* to present themselves before him, and receive instructions from him. Or, "Where I am to be in heaven, whither I am now going, there let the thoughts and affections of my servants be, there let their conversation be, *where Christ sitteth.*" Col. 3:1, 2.

[2.] Here are the wages which Christ promises to his servants; and they are very rich and noble.

First, They shall be happy with him: *Where I am, there shall also my servant be.* To be with him, when he was here in poverty and disgrace, would seem but poor preferment, and therefore, doubtless, he means being with him in paradise, sitting with him at his table above, on his throne there; it is the happiness of heaven to be with Christ there, *ch.* 17:24. Christ speaks of heaven's happiness as if he were already in it: Where *I am;* because he was sure of it, and near to it, and it was still *upon his heart,* and *in his eye.* And the same joy and glory which he thought recompence enough for all his services and sufferings are proposed to his servants as the recompence of theirs. Those that follow him in the way shall be with him in the end.

Secondly, They shall be honoured by his Father; he will make them amends for all their pains and loss, by conferring an honour upon them, such as becomes a great God to give, but far beyond what such worthless worms of the earth could expect to receive. The rewarder is God himself, who takes the services done to the Lord Jesus as done to himself. The reward is honour, true lasting honour, the highest honour; it is the honour that comes from God. It is said (Prov. 27:18), *He that waits on his Master* (humbly and diligently) *shall be honoured.* Those that wait on Christ God will put honour upon, such as will be taken notice of another day, though now under a veil. Those that serve Christ must humble themselves, and are commonly vilified by the world, in recompence of both which they shall be exalted in due time.

Thus far Christ's discourse has reference to those Greeks who desired to *see him,* encouraging them to serve him. What became of those Greeks we are not told, but are willing to hope that those who thus asked the way to heaven with their faces thitherward, found it, and walked in it.

Verses 27–36

Honour is here done to Christ by his Father in a voice from heaven, occasioned by the following part of his discourse, and which gave occasion to a further conference with the people. In these verses we have,

I. Christ's address to his Father, upon occasion of the trouble which seized his spirit at this time: *Now is my soul troubled, v.* 27. A strange word to come from Christ's mouth, and at this time surprising, for it comes in the midst of divers pleasing prospects, in which, one would think, he should have said, Now is my soul *pleased.* Note, Trouble of soul sometimes follows after great enlargements of spirit. In this world of mixture and change we must expect damps upon our joy, and the highest degree of comfort to be the next degree to trouble. When Paul had been in the third heavens, he had a *thorn in the flesh.* Observe,

1. Christ's dread of his approaching sufferings: *Now is my soul troubled.* Now the black and dismal scene began, now were the first throes of the travail of his soul, now his agony began, his soul *began to be exceedingly sorrowful.* Note, (1.) The sin of our soul was the trouble of Christ's soul, when he undertook to redeem and save us, and to make his soul an offering for our sin. (2.) The trouble of his soul was designed to ease the trouble of our souls; for, after this, he said to his disciples (*ch.* 14:1), *"Let not your hearts be troubled;* why should yours be troubled and mine too?" Our Lord Jesus went on cheerfully in his work, in prospect of the joy set before him, and yet submitted to a trouble of soul. Holy mourning is consistent with spiritual joy, and the way to eternal joy. Christ was *now* troubled, now in sorrow, now in fear, now for a season; but it would not be so always, it would not be so long. The same is the comfort of Christians in their troubles; they are but *for a moment,* and will be turned into joy.

2. The strait he seems to be in hereupon, intimated in those words, *And what shall I say?* This does not imply his consulting with any other, as if he needed advice, but considering with himself what was fit to be said now. When our souls are troubled we must take heed of speaking unadvisedly, but debate with ourselves what we shall say. Christ speaks like one at a loss, as if what he should choose he wot not. There was a struggle between the work he had taken upon him, which required sufferings, and the nature he had taken upon him, which dreaded them; between these two he here pauses with, *What shall I say?* He looked, and there was *none to help,* which put him to a stand. Calvin observes this as a great instance of Christ's humiliation, that he should speak thus like one at a loss. *Quo se magis exinanivit gloriae Dominus, eo luculentius habemus erga nos amoris specimen — The more entirely the Lord of glory emptied himself, the brighter is the proof of the love he bore us.* Thus he was *in all points tempted like as we are,* to encourage us, when we know not what to do, to direct our eyes to him.

3. His prayer to God in this strait: *Father, save me from this hour, ek tēs ōras tautēs — out of this hour,* praying, not so much that it might not come as that he might be brought through it. *Save me from this hour;* this was the language of innocent nature, and its feelings poured forth in prayer. Note, It is the duty and interest of troubled souls to have recourse to God by faithful and fervent prayer, and in prayer to eye him as a Father. Christ was voluntary in his sufferings, and yet prayed to be saved from them. Note, Prayer against a trouble may very well consist with patience under it and submission to the will of God in it. Observe, He calls his suffering *this hour,* meaning the expected events of the time now at hand. Hereby he intimates that the time of his suffering was, (1.) A set time, set to an hour, and he knew it. It was said twice before that his hour was not yet come, but it was now so near that he might say it was come. (2.) A short time. An hour is soon over, so were Christ's sufferings; he could see through them to the *joy set before him.*

4. His acquiescence in his Father's will, notwithstanding. He presently corrects himself, and, as it were, recals what he had said: *But for this cause came I to this hour.* Innocent nature got the first word, but divine wisdom and love got the last. Note, those who would proceed regularly must go upon second thoughts. The complainant speaks first; but, if we would judge righteously, we must hear the other side. With the second thought he checked himself: *For this cause came I to this hour;* he does not silence himself with this, that he could not avoid it, there was no remedy; but satisfies himself with this, that he would not avoid it, for it was pursuant to his own voluntary engagement, and was to be the crown of his whole undertaking; should he now fly off, this would frustrate all that had been done hitherto. Reference is here had to the divine counsels concerning his sufferings, by virtue of which it behoved him thus to submit and suffer. Note, This should reconcile us to the darkest hours of our lives, that we were all along designed for them; see 1 Th. 3:3.

5. His regard to his Father's honour herein. Upon the withdrawing of his former petition, he presents another, which he will abide by: *Father, glorify thy name,* to the same purport with *Father, thy will be done;* for God's will is for his own glory. This expresses more than barely a submission to the will of God; it is a consecration of his sufferings to the glory of God. It was a mediatorial word, and was spoken by him as our surety, who had undertaken to satisfy divine justice for our sin. The wrong which by sin we have done to God is in his glory, his declarative glory; for in nothing else are we capable of doing him injury. We were never able to make him satisfaction for this wrong done him, nor any creature for us; nothing therefore remained but that God should get him honour upon us in our utter ruin. Here therefore our Lord Jesus interposed, undertook to satisfy God's injured honour, and he did it by his humiliation; he denied himself in, and divested himself of, the honours due to the Son of God incarnate, and submitted to the greatest reproach. Now here he makes a tender of this satisfaction as an equivalent: *"Father, glorify thy name;* let thy justice be honoured upon the sacrifice, not upon the sinner; let the debt be levied upon me, I am solvent, the principal is not." Thus he *restored that which he took not away.*

II. The Father's answer to this address; for he heard him always, and does still. Observe, 1. How this answer was given. By a voice from heaven. The Jews speak much of a *Bath-kól — the daughter of a voice,* as one of those divers manners by which God in time past spoke to the prophets; but we do not find any instance of his speaking thus to any but to our Lord Jesus; it was an honour reserved for him (Mt. 3:17; 17:5), and here, probably, this audible voice was introduced by some visible appearance, either of light or darkness, for both have been used as vehicles of the divine glory. 2. What the answer was. It was an express return to that petition, *Father, glorify thy name: I have glorified it* already, and *I will glorify it yet again.* When we pray as we are taught, *Our Father, hallowed be thy name,* this is a comfort to us, that is it an answered prayer; answered to Christ here, and in him to all true believers. (1.) The name of God had been glorified in the life of Christ, in his doctrine and miracles, and all the examples he gave of holiness and goodness. (2.) It should be further glorified in the death and sufferings of Christ. His wisdom and power, his justice and holiness, his truth and goodness, were greatly glorified; the demands of a broken law were fully answered; the affront done to God's government satisfied for; and God accepted the satisfaction, and declared himself well pleased. What God has done for the glorifying of his own name is an encouragement to us to expect what he will yet further do. He that has secured the interests of his own glory will still secure them.

III. The opinion of the standers-by concerning this voice, *v.* 29. We may hope there were some among them whose minds were so well prepared to receive a divine revelation that they understood what was said and bore record of it. But notice is here taken of the perverse suggestion of the multitude: some of them said that *it thundered:* others, who took notice that there was plainly an articulate intelligible voice, said that certainly *an angel spoke to him.* Now this shows, 1. That it was a real thing, even in the judgment of those that were not at all well affected to him. 2. That they were loth to admit so plain a proof of Christ's divine mission. They would rather say that it was this, or that, or any thing, than that God spoke to him in answer to his prayer; and yet, if it thundered with articulate sounds (as Rev. 10:3, 4), was not that God's voice? Or, if angels spoke to him, are not they God's messengers? But thus *God speaks once, yea twice, and man perceives it not.*

IV. The account which our Saviour himself gives of this voice.

1. Why it was sent (*v.* 30): "It came *not because of me,* not merely for my encouragement and satisfaction" (then it might have been whispered in his ear privately), *"but for your sakes."* (1.) "That all you who heard it may *believe that the Father hath sent me."* What is said from heaven concerning our Lord Jesus, and the glorifying of the Father in him, is said for our sakes, that we may be brought to submit to him and rest upon him. (2.) "That you my disciples, who are to follow me in sufferings, may therein be comforted with the same comforts that carry me on." Let this encourage them to part with life itself for his sake, if they be called to it, that it will redound to the honour of God. Note, The promises and supports granted to our Lord Jesus in his sufferings were intended for our sakes. *For our sakes* he *sanctified himself,* and *comforted himself.*

2. What was the meaning of it. He that lay in the Father's bosom knew his voice, and what was the meaning of it; and two things God intended when he said that he would *glorify his own name: —*

(1.) That by the death of Christ Satan should be conquered (*v.* 31): *Now is the judgment.* He speaks with a divine exultation and triumph. "Now the year of my redeemed is come, and the time prefixed for breaking the serpent's head, and giving a total rent to the powers of darkness; now for that glorious achievement: *now, now,* that great work is to be done which has been so long thought of in the divine counsels, so long talked of in the written word, which has been so much the hope of saints and the dread of devils." The matter of the triumph is, [1.] That *now is the judgment of the world; krisis,* take it as a medical term: "Now is the *crisis* of this world." The sick and diseased world is now upon the turning point; this is the critical day upon which the trembling scale will turn for life or death, to all mankind; all that are not recovered by this will be left helpless and hopeless. Or, rather, it is a law term, as we take it: "Now, judgment is entered, in order to the taking out of execution against the prince of this world." Note, The death of Christ was the *judgment of this world. First,* It is a judgment of discovery and distinction — *judicium discretionis;* so Austin. Now is the trial of this world, for men shall have their character according as the cross of Christ is to them; to some it is foolishness and a stumbling-block, to others it is the wisdom and power of God; of which there was a figure in the two thieves that were crucified with him. By this men are judged, what they think of the death of Christ. *Secondly,* It is a judgment of favour and absolution to the chosen ones that are in the world. Christ upon the cross interposed between a righteous God and a guilty world as a sacrifice for sin and a surety for sinners, so that when he was judged, and *iniquity laid upon him,* and he was wounded for our transgressions, it was as it were the judgment of this world, for an everlasting righteousness was thereby brought in, not for Jews only, but the whole world, 1 Jn. 2:1, 2; Dan. 9:24. *Thirdly,* It is a judgment of condemnation given against the powers of darkness; see *ch.* 16:11. Judgment is put for vindication and deliverance, the asserting of an invaded right. At the death of Christ there was a famous trial between Christ and Satan, the serpent and the promised seed; the trial was for the world, and the lordship of it; the devil had long borne sway among the children of men, time out of mind; he now pleads prescription, grounding his claim also upon the forfeiture incurred by sin. We find him willing to have come to a composition (Lu. 4:6, 7); he would have given the kingdoms of this world to Christ, provided he would hold them by, from, and under him. But Christ would try it out with; by dying he takes off the forfeiture to divine justice, and then fairly disputes the title, and recovers it in the court of heaven. Satan's dominion is declared to be a usurpation, and the world adjudged to the Lord Jesus as his right, Ps. 2:6, 8. The judgment of this world is, that it belongs to Christ, and not to Satan; to Christ therefore let us all *atturn* tenants. [2.] That *now is the prince of this world cast out. First,* It is the devil that is here called the *prince of this world,* because he rules over the men of the world by the things of the world; he is the *ruler of the darkness of this world,* that is, of this dark world, of those in it that *walk in darkness,* 2 Co. 4:4; Eph. 4:12. *Secondly,* He is said to be *cast out,* to be *now* cast out; for, whatever had been done hitherto towards the weakening of the devil's kingdom was done in the virtue of a Christ to come, and therefore is said to be done *now.* Christ, reconciling the world to God by the merit of his death, broke the power of death, and cast out Satan as a destroyer; Christ, reducing the world to God by the doctrine of his cross, broke the power of sin, and cast out Satan as a deceiver. The bruising of his heel was the breaking of the serpent's head, Gen. 3:15. When his oracles were silenced, his temples forsaken, his idols famished, and the kingdoms of the world became Christ's kingdoms, then was the *prince of the world cast out,* as appears by comparing this with John's vision (Rev. 12:8–11), where it is said to be done by the *blood of the Lamb.* Christ's frequent casting of devils out of the bodies of people was an indication of the great design of his whole undertaking. Observe, With what assurance Christ here speaks of the victory over Satan; it is as good as done, and even when he yields to death he triumphs over it.

(2.) That by the death of Christ souls should be converted, and this would be the casting out of Satan (*v.* 32): *If I be lifted up from the earth, I will draw all men unto me.* Here observe two things: —

[1.] The great design of our Lord Jesus, which was to *draw all men to him,* not the Jews only, who had been long in a profession a people *near to God,* but the Gentiles also, who had been *afar off;* for he was to be the *desire of all nations* (Hag. 2:7), and *to him must the gathering of the people be.* That which his enemies dreaded was that the world would go after him; and he would draw them to him, notwithstanding their opposition. Observe here how Christ himself is all in all in the conversion of a soul. *First,* It is Christ that draws: I *will draw.* It is sometimes ascribed to the Father (*ch.* 6:44), but here to the Son, who is the *arm of the Lord.* He does not drive by force, but draws with the *cords of a man* (Hos. 11:4; Jer. 31:3), draws as the loadstone; the soul is *made willing,* but it is in a *day of power. Secondly,* It is to Christ that we are drawn: "I will draw them to me as the centre of their unity." The soul that was at a distance from Christ is brought into an acquaintance with him, he that was shy and distrustful of him is brought to love him and trust in him, — drawn up to his terms, into his arms. Christ was now going to heaven, and he would draw men's hearts to him thither.

[2.] The strange method he took to accomplish his design by *being lifted up from the earth.* What he meant by this, to prevent mistake, we are told (*v.* 33): *This he spoke signifying by what death he should die,* the death of the cross, though they had designed and attempted to stone him to death. He that was crucified was first nailed to the cross, and then lifted up upon it. He was *lifted up as a spectacle to the world;* lifted up between heaven and earth, as unworthy of either; yet the word here used signifies an honourable advancement, *ean hypsōthō — If I be exalted;* he reckoned his sufferings his honour. Whatever death we die, if we die in Christ we shall be lifted up out of this dungeon, this den of lions, into the regions of light and love. We should learn of our Master to speak of dying with a holy pleasantness, and to say, "We shall then be lifted up." Now Christ's drawing all men to him followed his being *lifted up from the earth. First,* It followed after it in time. The great increase of the church was after the death of Christ; while Christ lived, we read of thousands at a sermon miraculously fed, but after his death we read of thousands at a sermon added to the church. Israel began to multiply in Egypt after the death of Joseph. *Secondly,* It followed upon it as a blessed consequence of it. Note, There is a powerful virtue and efficacy in the death of Christ to draw souls to him. The cross of Christ, though to some a *stumbling-stone,* is to others a *loadstone.* Some make it an allusion to the drawing of fish into a net; the lifting up of Christ was as the spreading of the net (Mt. 13:47, 48); or to the setting up of a standard, which draws soldiers together; or, rather, it refers to the lifting up of the brazen serpent in the wilderness, which drew all those to it who were stung with fiery serpents, as soon as ever it was known that it was lifted up, and there was healing virtue in it. O what flocking was there to it! So there was to Christ, when salvation through him was preached to all nations; see *ch.* 3:14, 15. Perhaps it has some reference to the posture in which Christ was crucified, with his arms stretched out, to invite all to him, and embrace all that come. Those that put Christ to that ignominious death thought thereby to drive all men from him; but the devil was outshot in his own bow. *Out of the eater came forth meat.*

V. The people's exception against what he said, and their cavil at it, *v.* 34. Though they had heard the voice from heaven, and the gracious words that proceeded out of his mouth, yet they object, and pick quarrels with him. Christ had called himself the *Son of man* (*v.* 23), which they knew to be one of the titles of the Messiah, Dan. 7:13. He had also said that the *Son of man must be lifted up,* which they understood of his dying, and probably he explained himself so, and some think he repeated what he said to Nicodemus (*ch.* 3:14), *So must the Son of man be lifted up.* Now against this,

1. They alleged those scriptures of the Old Testament which speak of the perpetuity of the Messiah, that he should be so far from being cut off in the midst of his days that he should be a *priest for ever* (Ps. 110:4), and a king *for ever* (Ps. 89:29, etc.), that he should have *length of days for ever and ever,* and *his years as many generations* (Ps. 21:4; 61:6), from all which they inferred that the Messiah should not die. Thus great knowledge in the letter of the scripture, if the heart be unsanctified, is capable of being abused to serve the cause of infidelity, and to fight against Christianity with its own weapons. Their perverseness in opposing this to what Jesus had said will appear if we consider, (1.) That, when they vouched the scripture to prove that the Messiah *abideth for ever,* they took no notice of those texts which speak of the Messiah's death and sufferings: they had heard out of the law that *Messiah abideth for ever;* and had they never heard out of the law that Messiah should *be cut off* (Dan. 9:26), and that he should *pour out his soul unto death* (Isa. 53:12), and particularly that his *hands and feet* should be pierced? Why then do they make so strange of the *lifting up of the Son of man?* Note, We often run into great mistakes, and then defend them with scripture arguments, by putting those things asunder which God in his word has put together, and opposing one truth under pretence of supporting another. We have heard out of the gospel that which exalts free grace, we have heard also that which enjoins duty, and we just cordially embrace both, and not separate them, nor set them at variance. (2.) That, when they opposed what Christ said concerning the sufferings of the Son of man, they took no notice of what he had said concerning his glory and exaltation. They had heard out of the law that *Christ abideth for ever;* and had they not heard our Lord Jesus say that he should be glorified, that he should bring forth much fruit, and draw all men to him? Had he not just now promised immortal honours to his followers, which supposed his abiding for ever? But this they overlooked. Thus unfair disputants oppose some parts of the opinion of an adversary, to which, if they would but take it entire, they could not but subscribe; and in the doctrine of Christ there are paradoxes, which to men of corrupt minds are stones of stumbling — as Christ *crucified,* and yet *glorified; lifted up from the earth,* and yet *drawing all men to him.*

2. They asked hereupon, *Who is the Son of man?* This they asked, not with a desire to be instructed, but tauntingly and insultingly, as if now they had baffled him, and run him down. "Thou sayest, *The Son of man must die;* we have proved the Messiah must not, and where is then thy Messiahship? This Son of man, as thou callest thyself, cannot be the Messiah, thou must therefore think of something else to pretend to." Now that which prejudiced them against Christ was his meanness and poverty; they would rather have no Christ than a suffering one.

VI. What Christ said to this exception, or rather what he said *upon it.* The objection was a perfect cavil; they might, if they pleased, answer it themselves: man dies, and yet is immortal, and abideth for ever, so the *Son of man.* Therefore, instead of answering these fools according to their folly, he gives them a serious caution to take heed of trifling away the day of their opportunities in such vain and fruitless cavils as these (*v.* 35, 36): *"Yet a little while,* and but a little while, *is the light with you;* therefore be wise for yourselves, and *walk while you have the light."*

1. In general, we may observe here, (1.) The concern Christ has for the souls of men, and his desire of their welfare. With what tenderness does he here admonish those to look well to themselves who were contriving ill against him! Even when he *endured the contradiction of sinners,* he sought their conversion. See Prov. 29:10. (2.) The method he takes with these objectors, *with meekness instructing those that opposed themselves,* 2 Tim. 2:25. Were but men's consciences awakened with a due concern about their everlasting state, and did they consider how little time they have to spend, and none to spare, they would not waste precious thoughts and time in trifling cavils.

2. Particularly we have here,

(1.) The advantage they enjoyed in having Christ and his gospel among them, with the shortness and uncertainty of their enjoyment of it: *Yet a little while is the light with you.* Christ is this light; and some of the ancients suggest that, in calling himself the light, he gives a tacit answer to their objection. His dying upon the cross was as consistent with his *abiding for ever* as the setting of the sun every night is with his perpetuity. The duration of Christ's kingdom is compared to that of the sun and moon, Ps. 72:17; 89:36, 37. The ordinances of heaven are unchangeably fixed, and yet the sun and moon set and are eclipsed; so Christ the Sun of righteousness abides for ever, and yet was eclipsed by his sufferings, and was but a little while within our horizon. Now, [1.] The Jews at this time had the *light with them;* they had Christ's bodily presence, heard his preaching, saw his miracles. The scripture is to us a light shining in a dark place. [2.] It was to be but a little while with them; Christ would shortly leave them, their visible church state would soon after be dissolved and the kingdom of God taken from them, and blindness and hardness would happen unto Israel. Note, It is good for us all to consider what a little while we are to have the light with us. Time is short, and perhaps opportunity not so long. The candlestick may be removed; at least, we must be removed shortly. Yet a little while is the light of life with us; yet a little while is the light of the gospel with us, the day of grace, the means of grace, the Spirit of grace, yet a very little while.

(2.) The warning given them to make the best of this privilege while they enjoyed it, because of the danger they were in of losing it: *Walk while you have the light;* as travellers who make the best of their way forward, that they may not be benighted in their journey, because travelling in the night is uncomfortable and unsafe. "Come," say they, "let us mend our pace, and get forward, while we have day-light." Thus wise should we be for our souls who are journeying towards eternity. Note, [1.] It is our business to walk, to press forward towards heaven, and to get nearer to it by being made fitter for it. Our life is but a day, and we have a day's journey to go. [2.] The best time of walking is while we have the light. The day is the proper season for work, as the night is for rest. The proper time for getting grace is when we have the word of grace preached to us, and the Spirit of grace striving with us, and therefore then is the time to be busy. [3.] We are highly concerned thus to improve our opportunities, for fear lest our day be finished before we have finished our day's work and our day's journey: *"Lest darkness come upon you,* lest you lose your opportunities, and can neither recover them nor despatch the business you have to do without them." Then *darkness* comes, that is, such an utter incapacity to make sure the great salvation as renders the state of the careless sinner quite deplorable; so that, if his work be undone then, it is likely to be undone for ever.

(3.) The sad condition of those who have sinned away the gospel, and are come to the period of their day of grace. *They walk in darkness,* and know neither *where* they go, nor *whither* they go; neither the way they are walking in, nor the end they are walking towards. He that is destitute of the light of the gospel, and is not acquainted with its discoveries and directions, wanders endlessly in mistakes and errors, and a thousand crooked paths, and is not aware of it. Set aside the instructions of the Christian doctrine, and we know little of the difference between good and evil. He is going to destruction, and knows not his danger, for he is either sleeping or dancing at the pit's brink.

(4.) The great duty and interest of every one of us inferred from all this (*v.* 36): *While you have light, believe in the light.* The Jews had now Christ's presence with them, let them improve it; afterwards they had the first offers of the gospel made to them by the apostles wherever they came; now this is an admonition to them not to out-stand their market, but to accept the offer when it was made to them: the same Christ saith to all who enjoy the gospel. Note, [1.] It is the duty of every one of us *to believe in the gospel light,* to receive it as a divine light, to subscribe to the truths it discovers, for it is a light to our eyes, and to follow its guidance, for it is a light to our feet. Christ is the light, and we must believe in him as he is revealed to us; as a true light that will not deceive us, a sure light that will not misguide us. [2.] We are concerned to do this while we have the light, to lay hold on

Christ while we have the gospel to show us the way to him and direct us in that way. [3.] Those that believe in the light *shall be the children of light;* they shall be owned as *Christians,* who are called *children of light* (Lu. 16:8; Eph. 5:8) and of the day, 1 Th. 5:5. Those that have God for their Father are children of light, for God is light; they are born from above, and heirs of heaven, and children of light, for heaven is light.

VII. Christ's retiring from them, hereupon: *These things spoke Jesus,* and said no more at this time, but left this to their consideration, *and departed, and did hide himself from them.* And this he did, 1. For their conviction and awakening. If they will not regard what he hath said, he will have nothing more to say to them. They are joined to their infidelity, as Ephraim to idols; *let them alone.* Note, Christ justly removes the means of grace from those that quarrel with him, and *hides his face* from *a froward generation,* Deu. 32:20. 2. For his own preservation. He hid himself from their rage and fury, retreating, it is probable, to Bethany, where he lodged. By this it appears that what he said irritated and exasperated them, and they were made worse by that which should have made them better.

Verses 37–41

We have here the honour done to our Lord Jesus by the Old-Testament prophets, who foretold and lamented the infidelity of the many that believed not on him. It was indeed a dishonour and grief to Christ that his doctrine met with so little acceptance and so much opposition; but *this* takes off the wonder and reproach, makes the offence of it to cease, and made it no disappointment to Christ, that herein the scriptures were fulfilled. Two things are here said concerning this untractable people, and both were foretold by the evangelical prophet Isaiah, that they *did not* believe, and that they *could not* believe.

I. They did not believe (*v.* 37): *Though he had done so many miracles before them,* which, one would think, should have convinced them, yet they believed not, but opposed him. Observe,

1. The abundance of the means of conviction which Christ afforded them: He *did miracles, so many miracles; tosauta sēmeia* signifying both so many and so great. This refers to all the miracles he had wrought formerly; nay, the blind and lame now came to him into the temple, and he healed them, Mt. 21:14. His miracles were the great proof of his mission, and on the evidence of them he relied. Two things concerning them he here insists upon: — (1.) The number of them; they were *many,* — various and of divers kinds; numerous and often repeated; and every new miracle confirmed the reality of all that went before. The multitude of his miracles was not only a proof of his unexhausted power, but gave the greater opportunity to examine them; and, if there had been a cheat in them, it was morally impossible but that in some or other of them it would have been discovered; and, being all *miracles of mercy,* the more there were the more good was done. (2.) The notoriety of them. He wrought these miracles *before them,* not at a distance, not in a corner, but before many witnesses, appearing to their own eyes.

2. The inefficacy of these means: *Yet they believed not on him.* They could not gainsay the premises, and yet would not grant the conclusion. Note, The most plentiful and powerful means of conviction will not of themselves work faith in the depraved prejudiced hearts of men. These *saw,* and yet *believed not.*

3. The fulfilling of the scripture in this (*v.* 38): *That the saying of Esaias might be fulfilled.* Not that these infidel Jews designed the fulfilling of the scripture (they rather fancied those scriptures which speak of the church's best sons to be fulfilled in themselves), but the event exactly answered the prediction, *so that (ut for ita ut)* this saying of Esaias was fulfilled. The more improbable any event is, the more does a divine foresight appear in the prediction of it. One could not have imagined that the kingdom of the Messiah, supported with such pregnant proofs, should have met with so much opposition among the Jews, and therefore their unbelief is called a *marvellous work, and a wonder,* Isa. 29:14. Christ himself *marvelled at it,* but it was what Isaiah foretold (Isa. 53:1), and now it is accomplished. Observe, (1.) The gospel is here called *their report: Who has believed, tē akon hēmōn — our hearing,* which we have heard from God, and which you have heard from us. Our report is the report that we bring, like the report of a matter of fact, or the report of a solemn resolution in the senate. (2.) It is foretold that a few comparatively of those to whom this report is brought will be persuaded to give credit to it. Many hear it, but few heed it and embrace it: *Who hath believed it?* Here and there one, but none to speak of; not the wise, not the noble; it is to them but a report which wants confirmation. (3.) It is spoken of as a thing to be greatly lamented that so few believe the report of the gospel. *Lord* is here prefixed from the Septuagint, but is not in the Hebrew, and intimates a sorrowful account brought to God by the messengers of the cold entertainment which they and their report had; as *the servant came, and showed his lord all these things,* Lu. 14:21. (4.) The reason why men believe not the report of the gospel is because *the arm of the Lord* is not *revealed* to them, that is, because they do not acquaint themselves with, and submit themselves to, the grace of God; they do not experimentally know the virtue and fellowship of Christ's death and resurrection, in which the arm of the Lord is revealed. They saw Christ's miracles, but did not see the *arm of the Lord revealed in them.*

II. They could not believe, and *therefore* they could not *because Esaias said, He hath blinded their eyes.* This is a hard saying, who can explain it? We are sure that God is infinitely just and merciful, and therefore we cannot think there is in any such an impotency to good, resulting from the counsels of God, as lays them under a fatal necessity of being evil. God dams none by mere sovereignty; yet it is said, *They could not believe.* St. Austin, coming in course to the exposition of these words, expresses himself with a holy fear of entering upon an enquiry into this mystery. *Justa sunt judicia ejus, sed occulta — His judgments are just, but hidden.*

1. They *could not* believe, that is, they *would not;* they were obstinately resolved in their infidelity; thus Chrysostom and Austin incline to understand it; and the former gives divers instances of scripture of the putting of an impotency to signify the invincible refusal of the will, as Gen. 37:4, *They could not speak peaceably to him.* And *ch.* 7:7. This is a *moral* impotency, like that of one that is accustomed to do evil, Jer. 13:23. But,

2. They could not because Esaias had said, *He hath blinded their eyes.* Here the difficulty increases; it is certain that God is not the author of sin, and yet,

(1.) There is a righteous hand of God sometimes to be acknowledged in the blindness and obstinacy of those who persist in impenitency and unbelief, by which they are justly punished for their former resistance of the divine light and rebellion against the divine law. If God withhold abused grace, and give men over to indulged lusts, — if he permit the evil spirit to do his work on those that resisted the good Spirit, — and if in his providence he lay stumbling-blocks in the way of sinners, which confirm their prejudices, then he *blinds their eyes,* and *hardens their hearts,* and these are spiritual judgments, like the giving up of idolatrous Gentiles to *vile affections,* and degenerate Christians to *strong delusions.* Observe the method of conversion implied here, and the steps taken in it. [1.] Sinners are brought to *see with their eyes,* to discern the reality of divine things and to have some knowledge of them. [2.] To *understand with their heart,* to apply these things to themselves; not only to assent and approve, but to consent and accept. [3.] To *be converted,* and effectually turned from sin to Christ, from the world and the flesh to God, as their felicity and portion. [4.] Then God will *heal* them, will justify and sanctify them; will *pardon* their sins, which are as bleeding wounds, and mortify their corruptions, which are as lurking diseases. Now when God denies his grace nothing of this is done; the alienation of the mind from, and its aversion to, God and the divine life, grow into a rooted and invincible antipathy, and so the case becomes desperate.

(2.) Judicial blindness and hardness are in the word of God threatened against those who wilfully persist in wickedness, and were particularly foretold concerning the Jewish church and nation. Known unto God are all his works, and all ours too. Christ knew before who would betray him, and spoke of it, *ch.* 6:70. This is a confirmation of the truth of scripture prophecies, and thus even the unbelief of the Jews may help to strengthen our faith. It is also intended for caution to particular persons, to *beware lest that come upon them which was spoken of in the prophets,* Acts 13:40.

(3.) What God has foretold will certainly come to pass, and so, by a necessary consequence, in order of arguing, it might be said that *therefore* they *could not believe,* because God by the prophets had foretold they would not; for such is the knowledge of God that he cannot be deceived in what he foresees, and such his truth that he cannot deceive in what he foretels, so that the scripture cannot be broken. Yet be it observed that the prophecy did not name particular persons; so that it might not be said, "Therefore such a one and such a one could not believe, because Esaias had said so and so;" but it pointed at the body of the Jewish nation, which would persist in their infidelity till their cities were wasted without inhabitants, as it follows (Isa. 6:11, 12); yet still reserving a remnant (*v.* 13, *in it shall be a tenth*), which reserve was sufficient to keep a door of hope open to particular persons; for each one might say, Why may not I be of that remnant?

Lastly, The evangelist, having quoted the prophecy, shows (*v.* 41) that it was intended to look further than the prophet's own days, and that its principal reference was to the days of the Messiah: *These things said Esaias when he saw his glory, and spoke of him.* 1. We read in the prophecy that this was said to Esaias, Isa. 6:8, 9. But here we are told that it was said *by him* to the purpose. For nothing was said by him as a prophet which was not first said to him; nor was any thing said to him which was not afterwards said by him to those to whom he was sent. See Isa. 21:10. 2. The vision which the prophet there had of the *glory of God* is here said to be his *seeing the glory* of Jesus Christ: He *saw his glory.* Jesus Christ therefore is equal in power and glory with the Father, and his praises are equally celebrated. Christ had a glory *before the foundation of the world,* and Esaias saw this. 3. It is said that the prophet there *spoke of him.* It seems to have been spoken of the prophet himself (for to him the commission and instructions were there given), and yet it is here said to be spoken of Christ, for as all the prophets testified of him so they all typified him. This they spoke of him, that as to many his coming would be not only fruitless, but fatal, a savour of death unto death. It might be objected against his doctrine, If it was from heaven, why did not the Jews believe it? But this is an answer to it; it was not for want of evidence, but because their *heart was made fat,* and their *ears were heavy.* It was spoken of Christ, that he should be glorified in the ruin of an unbelieving multitude, as well as in the salvation of a distinguished remnant.

Verses 42–43

Some honour was done to Christ by these rulers: for they *believed on him,* were convinced that he was sent of God, and received his doctrine as divine; but they did not do him honour enough, for they had not courage to own their faith in him. Many professed more kindness for Christ than really they had; these had more kindness for him than they were willing to profess. See here what a struggle was in these rulers between their convictions and their corruptions.

I. See the power of the word in the convictions that many of them were under, who did not wilfully shut their eyes against the light. They *believed on him* as Nicodemus, received him as a teacher come from God. Note, The truth of the gospel has perhaps a better interest in the consciences of men than we are aware of. Many cannot but approve of that in their hearts which yet outwardly they are shy of. Perhaps these chief rulers were *true* believers, though very weak, and their faith like smoking flax. Note, It may be, there are more good people than we think there are. Elijah thought he was left alone, when God had seven thousand faithful worshippers in Israel. Some are really better than they seem to be. Their faults are known, but their repentance is not; a man's goodness may be concealed by a *culpable* yet pardonable weakness, which he himself truly repents of. The *kingdom of God comes not* in all *with* a like *observation;* nor have all who are good the same faculty of appearing to be so.

II. See the power of the world in the smothering of these convictions. They believed in Christ, but because of the Pharisees, who had it in their power to do them a diskindness, they durst not confess him for fear of being excommunicated. Observe here, 1. Wherein they failed and were defective; They did not *confess* Christ. Note, There is cause to question the sincerity of that faith which is either afraid or ashamed to show itself; for those who believe with the heart ought to *confess with the mouth,* Rom. 10:9. 2. What they feared: being *put out of the synagogue,* which they thought would be a disgrace and damage to them; as if it would do them any harm to be expelled from a synagogue that had made itself a synagogue of Satan, and from which God was departing. 3. What was at the bottom of this fear: *They loved the praise of men,* chose it as a more valuable good, and pursued it as a more desirable end, than the *praise of God;* which was an implicit idolatry, like that (Rom. 1:25) of *worshipping and serving the creature more than the Creator.* They set these two in the scale one against the other, and, having weighed them, they proceeded accordingly. (1.) They set the praise of men in one scale, and considered how good it was to give praise to men, and to pay a deference to the opinion of the Pharisees, and receive praise from men, to be commended by the chief priests and applauded by the people as good sons of the church, the Jewish church; and they would not confess Christ, lest they should thereby derogate from the reputation of the Pharisees, and forfeit their own, and thus hinder their own preferment. And, besides, the followers of Christ were put into an *ill name,* and were looked upon with contempt, which those who had been used to honour could not bear. Yet perhaps if they had known one another's minds they would have had more courage; but each one thought that if he should declare himself in favour of Christ he should stand alone, and have nobody to back him; whereas, if any one had had resolution to *break the ice,* he would have had more *seconds* than he thought of. (2.) They put the praise of God in the other scale. They were sensible that by confessing Christ they should both give praise to God, and have praise from God, that he would be pleased with them, and say, *Well done;* but, (3.) They gave the preference to the praise of men, and this turned the scale; sense prevailed above faith, and represented it as more desirable to stand right in the opinion of the Pharisees than to be accepted of God. Note, Love of the praise of men is a very great prejudice to the power and practice of religion and godliness. Many come short of the glory of God by having a regard to the applause of men, and a value for that. Love of the praise of men, as a by-end in that which is good, will make a man a hypocrite when religion is in fashion and credit is to be got by it; and love of the praise of men, as a base principle in that which is evil, will make a man an apostate when religion is in disgrace, and credit is to be lost for it, as here. See Rom. 2:29.

Verses 44–50

We have here the honour Christ not assumed, but asserted, to himself, in the account he gave of his mission and his errand into the world. Probably this discourse was not at the same time with that before (for them *he departed, v.* 36), but some time after, when he made another public appearance; and, as this evangelist records it, it was Christ's farewell sermon to the Jews, and his last public discourse; all that follows was private with his disciples. Now observe how our Lord Jesus delivered this parting word: he *cried and said. Doth not wisdom cry* (Prov. 8:1), cry *without?* Prov. 1:20. The raising of his voice and crying intimate, 1. His boldness in speaking. Though they had not courage openly to profess faith in his doctrine, he had courage openly to publish it; if they were ashamed of it, he was not, but set his face as a flint, Isa. 50:7. 2. His earnestness in speaking. He cried as one that was serious and importunate, and in good earnest in what he said, and was willing to impart to them, not only the gospel of God, but *even his own soul.* 3. It denotes his desire that all might take notice of it. This being the last time of the publication of his gospel by himself in person, he makes proclamation, "Whoever will hear me, let them come now." Now what is the conclusion of the whole matter, this closing summary of all Christ's discourses? It is much like that of Moses (Deu. 30:15): *See, I have set before you life and death.* So Christ here takes leave of the temple, with a solemn declaration of three things: —

I. The privileges and dignities of those that believe; this gives great encouragement to us to believe in Christ and to profess that faith. It is a thing of such a nature that we need not be shy either of doing it or of owning it; for,

1. By believing in Christ we are brought into an *honourable acquaintance with God* (*v.* 44, 45): *He that believes on me,* and so *sees me, believes on him that sent me,* and so *sees him.* He that believes on Christ, (1.) He does not believe in a mere man, such a one as he seemed to be, and was generally taken to be, but he believes in one that is the Son of God and equal in power and glory with the Father. Or rather, (2.) His faith does not terminate in Christ, but through him it is carried out to the Father, that sent him, to whom, as our end, we come by Christ as our way. The doctrine of Christ is believed and received as the truth of God. The rest of a believing soul is in God through Christ as Mediator; for its resignation to Christ is in order to being presented to God. Christianity is made up, not of philosophy nor politics, but pure divinity. This is illustrated, *v.* 45. He that *sees me* (which is the same with *believing* in him, for faith is the eye of the soul) *sees him that sent me;* in getting an acquaintance with Christ, we come to the knowledge of God. For, [1.] God makes himself known in the face of Christ (2 Co. 4:6), who is the express image of his person, Heb. 1:3. [2.] All that have a believing sight of Christ are led by him to the knowledge of God, whom Christ has revealed to us by his word and Spirit. Christ, as God, was the image of his Father's person; but Christ, as Mediator, was his Father's representative in his relation to man, the divine light, law, and love, being communicated to us in and through him; so that in seeing him (that is, in eying him as our Saviour, Prince, and Lord, in the right of redemption), we see and eye the Father as our owner, ruler, and benefactor, in the right of creation: for God is pleased to deal with fallen man by proxy.

2. We are hereby brought into a comfortable enjoyment of ourselves (*v.* 46): *I am come a light into the world, that whoever believes in me,* Jew or Gentile, *should not abide in darkness.* Observe, (1.) The character of Christ: *I am come a light into the world,* to be a light to it. This implies that he had a being, and a being as light, before he came into the world, as the sun is before it rises; the prophets and apostles were made lights to the world, but it was Christ only that came a light into this world, having before been a glorious light in the upper world, *ch.* 3:19. (2.) The comfort of Christians: They *do not abide in darkness.* [1.] They do not continue in that dark condition in which they were by nature; they are *light in the Lord.* They are without any true comfort, or joy, or hope, but do not continue in that condition; light is sown for them. [2.] Whatever darkness of affliction, disquietment, or fear, they may afterwards be in, provision is made that they may not long abide in it. [3.] They are delivered from that darkness which is perpetual, and which *abideth for ever,* that utter darkness where there is not the least gleam of light nor hope of it.

II. The peril and danger of those that believe not, which gives fair warning to take heed of persisting in unbelief (*v.* 47, 48): *"If any man hear my words, and believe not, I judge him not,* not I only, or not now, lest I should be looked upon as unfair in being judge in my own cause; yet let not infidelity think therefore to go unpunished, *though I judge him not, there is one that judgeth him."* So that we have here the doom of unbelief. Observe,

1. Who they are whose unbelief is here condemned: those who *hear Christ's words* and yet *believe them not.* Those shall not be condemned for their infidelity that never had, nor could have, the gospel; every man shall be judged according to the dispensation of light he was under: *Those that have sinned without law shall be judged without law.* But those that have heard, or might have heard, and would not, lie open to this doom.

2. What is the constructive malignity of their unbelief: not receiving Christ's word; it is interpreted (*v.* 48) a *rejecting* of Christ, *ho athetōn eme.* It denotes a rejection with scorn and contempt. Where the banner of the gospel is displayed, no neutrality is admitted; every man is either a subject or an enemy.

3. The wonderful patience and forbearance of our Lord Jesus, exercised towards those who slighted him when he was come here upon earth: *I judge him not,* not now. Note, Christ was not quick or hasty to take advantage against those who refused the first offers of his grace, but continued waiting to be gracious. He did not strike those dumb or dead who contradicted him, never made intercession against Israel, as Elias did; though he had authority to judge, he suspended the execution of it, because he had work of another nature to do first, and that was to *save the world.* (1.) To save effectually those that were given him before he came to judge the degenerate body of mankind. (2.) To offer salvation to all the world, and thus far to save them that it is their own fault if they be not saved. He was to put away sin by the sacrifice of himself. Now the executing of the power of a judge was not congruous with that undertaking, Acts 8:33. *In his humiliation his judgment was taken away,* it was suspended for a time.

4. The certain and unavoidable judgment of unbelievers at the great day, the day of the revelation of the righteous judgment of God: unbelief will certainly be a damning sin. Some think when Christ saith, *I judge no man,* he means that they are *condemned already.* There needs no process, they are *self-judged;* no execution, they are *self-ruined;* judgment goes against them of course, Heb. 2:3. Christ needs not appear against them as their accuser, they are miserable if he do not appear for them as their advocate; however, he tells them plainly when and where they will be reckoned with. (1.) There is *one that judgeth them.* Nothing is more dreadful than abused patience, and grace trampled on; though for awhile *mercy rejoiceth against judgment,* yet there will be *judgment without mercy.* (2.) Their final judgment is reserved to the *last day;* to that day of judgment Christ here binds over all unbelievers, to answer then for all the contempts they have put upon him. Divine justice has *appointed a day,* and adjourns the sentence to that day, as Mt. 26:64. (3.) The word of Christ will judge them then: *The words that I have spoken,* how light soever you have made of them, *the same shall judge* the unbeliever *in the last day;* as the apostles, the preachers of Christ's word, are said to judge, Lu. 22:30. Christ's words will judge unbelievers two ways: — [1.] As the evidence of their crime, they will convict them. Every word Christ spoke, every sermon, every argument, every kind offer, will be produced as a testimony against those who slighted all he said. [2.] As the rule of their doom, they will condemn them; they shall be judged according to the tenour of that covenant which Christ procured and published. That word of Christ, *He that believes not shall be damned,* will judge all unbelievers to eternal ruin; and there are *many such like words.*

III. A solemn declaration of the authority Christ had to demand our faith, and require us to receive his doctrine upon pain of damnation, *v.* 49, 50, where observe,

1. The commission which our Lord Jesus received from the Father to deliver his doctrine to the world (*v.* 49): *I have not spoken myself,* as a mere man, much less as a common man; *but the Father gave me a commandment what I should say.* This is the same with what he said *ch.* 7:16. *My doctrine is,* (1.) *Not mine,* for *I have not spoken of myself.* Christ, as *Son of man,* did not speak that which was of human contrivance or composure; as Son of God, he did not act separately, or by himself alone, but what he said was the result of the counsels of peace; as Mediator, his coming into the world was voluntary, and with his full consent, but not arbitrary, and of his own head. But, (2.) It was his that sent him. God the Father gave him, [1.] His commission. God sent him as his agent and plenipotentiary, to concert matters between him and man, to set a treaty of peace on foot, and to settle the articles. [2.] His instructions, here called a *commandment,* for they were like those given to an ambassador, directing him not only what he may say, but what he must say. The messenger of the covenant was entrusted with an errand which he must deliver. Note, Our Lord Jesus learned obedience himself, before he taught it to us, though he was a Son. *The Lord God commanded* the first Adam, and he by his disobedience ruined us; he commanded the second Adam, and he by his obedience saved us. God commanded him what he should *say* and what he should *speak,* two words signifying the same thing, to denote that every word was divine. The Old-Testament prophets sometimes spoke of themselves; but Christ spoke by the Spirit at all times. Some make this distinction: He was directed what he should say in his set sermons, and what he should speak in his familiar discourses. Others this: He was directed what he should say in his preaching now, and what he should speak in his judging at the last day; for he had commission and instruction for both.

2. The scope, design, and tendency of this commission: *I know that his commandment is life everlasting, v.* 50. The commission given to Christ had a reference to the everlasting state of the children of men, and was in order to their everlasting life and happiness in that state: the instructions given to Christ as a prophet were to reveal eternal life (1 Jn. 5:11); the power, given to Christ as a king was to give eternal life, *ch.* 17:2. Thus the command given him was life everlasting. This Christ says he knew: "I know it is so," which intimates how cheerfully and with what assurance Christ pursued his undertaking, knowing very well that he went upon a good errand, and that which would bring forth fruit unto life eternal. It intimates likewise how justly those will perish who reject Christ and his word. Those who disobey Christ despise everlasting life, and renounce it; so that not only Christ's words will judge them, but even their own; so shall their doom be, themselves have decided it; and who can except against it?

3. Christ's exact observance of the commission and instructions given him, and his steady acting in pursuance of them: *Whatsoever I speak,* it is *as the Father said unto me.* Christ was intimately acquainted with the counsels of God, and was faithful in discovering so much of them to the children of men as it was agreed should be discovered, and *kept back nothing that was profitable.* As the faithful witness delivers souls, so did he, and spoke the truth, the whole truth, and nothing but the truth. Note, (1.) This is a great encouragement to faith; the sayings of Christ, rightly understood, are what we may venture our souls upon. (2.) It is a great example of obedience. Christ said as he was bidden, and so must we, communicated what the Father had said to him, and so must we. See Acts 4:20. In the midst of all the respect paid to him, this is the honour he values himself upon, that what the Father had said to him that he spoke, and in the manner as he was directed so he spoke. This was his glory, that, as a Son, he was faithful to him that appointed him; and, by an unfeigned belief of every word of Christ, and an entire subjection of soul to it, we must give him the glory due to his name.

CHAPTER 13

Our Saviour having finished his public discourses, in which he "endured the contradiction of sinners," now applies himself to a private conversation with his friends, in which he designed the consolation of saints. Henceforward we have an account of what passed between him and his disciples, who were to be entrusted with the affairs of his household, when he was gone into a far country; the necessary instructions and comforts he furnished them with. His hour being at hand, he applies himself to set his house in order. In this chapter I. He washes his disciples' feet (*v.* 1–17). II. He foretels who should betray him (*v.* 18–30). III. He instructs them in the great doctrine of his own death, and the great duty of brotherly love (*v.* 31–35). IV. He foretels Peter's denying him (*v.* 36–38).

Verses 1–17

It has generally been taken for granted by commentators that Christ's washing his disciples' feet, and the discourse that followed it, were the same night in which he was betrayed, and at the same sitting wherein he ate the passover and instituted the Lord's supper; but whether before the solemnity began, or after it was all over, or between the eating of the passover and the institution of the Lord's supper, they are not agreed. This evangelist, making it his business to gather up those passages which the others had omitted, industriously omits those which the others had recorded, which occasions some difficulty in putting them together. If it was then, we suppose that *Judas went out* (*v.* 30) to get his men ready that were to apprehend the Lord Jesus in the garden. But Dr. Lightfoot is clearly of opinion that this was done and said, even all that is recorded to the end of *ch.* 14, not at the passover supper, for it is here said (*v.* 1) to be *before the feast of the passover,* but at the supper in Bethany, two days before the passover (of which we read Mt. 26:2–6), at which Mary the second time anointed Christ's head with the remainder of her box of ointment. Or, it might be at some other supper the night before the passover, not as that was in the house of Simon the leper, but in his own lodgings, where he had none but his disciples about him, and could be more free with them.

In these verses we have the story of Christ's washing his disciples' feet; it was an action of a singular nature; no miracle, unless we call it a miracle of humility. Mary had just anointed his head; now, lest his acceptance of this should look like taking state, he presently balances it with this act of abasement. But why would Christ do this? If the disciples' feet needed washing, they could wash them themselves; a wise man will not do a thing that looks odd and unusual, but for very good causes and considerations. We are sure that it was not in a humour or a frolic that this was done; no, the transaction was very solemn, and carried on with a great deal of seriousness; and four reasons are here intimated why Christ did this: — 1. That he might testify his love to his disciples, *v.* 1, 2. 2. That he might give an instance of his own voluntary humility and condescension, *v.* 3–5. 3. That he might signify to them spiritual washing, which is referred to in his discourse with Peter, *v.* 6–11. 4. That he might set them an example, *v.* 12–17. And the opening of these four reasons will take in the exposition of the whole story.

I. Christ washed his disciples' feet that he might give a proof of that great love wherewith he loved them; loved them to the end, *v.* 1, 2.

1. It is here laid down as an undoubted truth that our Lord Jesus, *having loved his own that were in the world, loved them to the end, v.* 1.

(1.) This is true of the disciples that were his immediate followers, in particular the twelve. These were his own in the world, his family, his school, his bosom-friends. Children he had none to call his own, but he adopted them, and took them as his own. He had those that were his own in the other world, but he left them for a time, to look after his own in this world. These he loved, he called them into fellowship with himself, conversed familiarly with them, was always tender of them, and of their comfort and reputation. He allowed them to be very free with him, and bore with their infirmities. He loved them to the end, continued his love to them as long as he lived, and after his resurrection; he never took away his loving kindness. Though there were some persons of quality that espoused his cause, he did not lay aside his old friends, to make room for new ones, but still stuck to his poor fishermen. They were weak and defective in knowledge and grace, dull and forgetful; and yet, though he reproved them often, he never ceased to love them and take care of them.

(2.) It is true of all believers, for these twelve patriarchs were the representatives of all the tribes of God's spiritual Israel. Note, [1.] Our Lord Jesus has a people in the world that are his own, — his own, for they were given him by the Father, he has purchased them, and paid dearly for them, and he has set them apart for himself, — his own, for they have devoted themselves to him as a peculiar people. *His own;* where *his own* were spoken of that *received him not,* it is *tous idious* — *his own persons,* as a man's wife and children are his own, to whom he stands in a constant relation. [2.] Christ has a cordial love for his own that are in the world. He *did* love them with a love of goodwill when he gave himself for their redemption. He *does* love them with a love of complacency when he admits them into communion with himself. Though they are *in this world,* a world of darkness and distance, of sin and corruption, yet he loves them. He was now going to his own in heaven, the spirits of just men made perfect there; but he seems most concerned for his own on earth, because they most needed his care: the sickly child is most indulged. [3.] Those whom Christ loves *he loves to the end;* he is constant in his love to his people; he *rests in his love.* He loves with an everlasting love (Jer. 31:3), from everlasting in the counsels of it to everlasting in the consequences of it. Nothing can separate a believer *from the love of Christ;* he loves his own, *eis telos* — *unto perfection,* for he will perfect what concerns them, will bring them to that world where love is perfect.

2. Christ manifested his love to them by washing their feet, as that good woman (Lu. 7:38) showed her love to Christ by washing his feet and wiping them. Thus he would show that as his love to them was constant so it was condescending, — that in prosecution of the designs of it he was willing to humble himself, — and that the glories of his exalted state, which he was now entering upon, should be no obstruction at all to the favour he bore to his chosen; and thus he would confirm the promise he had made to all the saints that he would *make them sit down to meat, and would come forth and serve them* (Lu. 12:37), would put honour upon them as great and surprising as for a lord to serve his servants. The disciples had just now betrayed the weakness of their love to him, in grudging the ointment that was poured upon his head (Mt. 26:8), yet he presently gives this proof of his love to them. Our infirmities are foils to Christ's kindnesses, and set them off.

3. He chose this time to do it, a little before his last passover, for two reasons: —

(1.) Because now *he knew that his hour was come,* which he had long expected, *when he should depart out of this world to the Father.* Observe here, [1.] The change that was to pass over our Lord Jesus; he must *depart.* This began at his death, but was completed at his ascension. As Christ himself, so all believers, by virtue of their union with him, when they depart out of the world, are absent from the body, *go to the Father,* are present with the Lord. It is a departure *out of the world,* this unkind, injurious world, this faithless, treacherous world — this world of labour, toil, and temptation — this vale of tears; and it is a going *to the Father,* to the vision of the Father of spirits, and the fruition of him as ours. [2.] The time of this change: *His hour was come.* It is sometimes called his enemies' hour (Lu. 22:53), the hour of their triumph; sometimes his hour, the hour of his triumph, the hour he had

had in his eye all along. The time of his sufferings was fixed to an hour, and the continuance of them but for an hour. [3.] His foresight of it: He *knew that his hour was come;* he knew from the beginning that it would come, and when, but now he knew that it *was come.* We know not when our hour will come, and therefore what we have to do in habitual preparation for it ought never to be undone; but, when we know by the harbingers that our hour is come, we must vigorously apply ourselves to an actual preparation, as our Master did, 2 Pt. 3:14. Now it was in the immediate foresight of his departure that he *washed his disciples' feet;* that, as his own head was anointed just now *against the day of his burial,* so their feet might be washed against the day of their consecration by the descent of the Holy Ghost fifty days after, as the priests were washed, Lev. 8:6. When we see our day approaching, we should do what good we can to those we leave behind.

(2.) Because the *devil had now put it into the heart of Judas to betray him, v.* 2. These words in a parenthesis may be considered, [1.] As tracing Judas's treason to its origin; it was a sin of such a nature that it evidently bore the devil's image and superscription. What way of access the devil has to men's hearts, and by what methods he darts in his suggestions, and mingles them undiscerned with those thoughts which are the natives of the heart, we cannot tell. But there are some sins in their own nature so exceedingly sinful, and to which there is so little temptation from the world and the flesh, that it is plain Satan lays the egg of them in a heart disposed to be the nest to hatch them in. For Judas to betray such a master, to betray him so cheaply and upon no provocation, was such downright enmity to God as could not be forged but by Satan himself, who thereby thought to ruin the Redeemer's kingdom, but did in fact ruin his own. [2.] As intimating a reason why Christ now washed his disciples' feet. *First,* Judas being now resolved to betray him, the time of his departure could not be far off; if this matter be determined, it is easy to infer with St. Paul, *I am now ready to be offered.* Note, The more malicious we perceive our enemies to be against us, the more industrious we should be to prepare for the worst that may come. *Secondly,* Judas being now got into the snare, and the devil aiming at Peter and the rest of them (Lu. 22:31), Christ would fortify his own against him. If the wolf has seized one of the flock, it is time for the shepherd to look well to the rest. Antidotes must be stirring, when the infection is begun. Dr. Lightfoot observes that the disciples had learned of Judas to murmur at the anointing of Christ; compare *ch.* 12:4, etc. with Mt. 26:8. Now, lest those that had learned that of him should learn worse, he fortifies them by a lesson of humility against his most dangerous assaults. *Thirdly,* Judas, who was now plotting to betray him, was *one of the twelve.* Now Christ would hereby show that he did not design to cast them all off for the faults of one. Though one of their college had a devil, and was a traitor, yet they should fare never the worse for that. Christ loves his church though there are hypocrites in it, and had still a kindness for his disciples though there was a Judas among them and he knew it.

II. Christ washed his disciples' feet that he might give an instance of his own wonderful humility, and show how lowly and condescending he was, and let all the world know how low he could stoop in love to his own. This is intimated, *v.* 3–5. *Jesus knowing,* and now actually considering, and, perhaps discoursing of, his honours as Mediator, and telling his friends that *the Father had given all things into his hand, rises from supper,* and, to the great surprise of the company, who wondered what he was going to do, *washed his disciples' feet.*

1. Here is the rightful advancement of the Lord Jesus. Glorious things are here said of Christ as Mediator.

(1.) *The Father had given all things into his hands;* had given him a propriety in all, and a power over all, as possessor of heaven and earth, in pursuance of the great designs of his undertaking; see Mt. 11:27. The accommodation and arbitration of all matters in variance between God and man were committed into his hands as the great umpire and referee; and the administration of the kingdom of God among men, in all the branches of it, was committed to him; so that all acts, both of government and judgment, were to pass through his hands; he is *heir of all things.*

(2.) He *came from God.* This implies that he was in the beginning with God, and had a being and glory, not only before he was born into this world, but before the world itself was born; and that when he came into the world he came as God's ambassador, with a commission from him. He came from God as the son of God, and the sent of God. The Old-Testament prophets were raised up and employed for God, but Christ came directly from him.

(3.) He *went to God,* to be glorified with him with the same glory which he had with God from eternity. That which comes from God shall go to God; those that are born from heaven are bound for heaven. As Christ came from God to be an agent for him on earth, so he went to God to be an agent for us in heaven; and it is a comfort to us to think how welcome he was there: he was brought near to the *Ancient of days,* Dan. 7:13. And it was said to him, *Sit thou at my right hand,* Ps. 110:1.

(4.) He *knew* all this; was not like a prince in the cradle, that knows nothing of the honour he is born to, or like Moses, who *wist not that his face shone;* no, he had a full view of all the honours of his exalted state, and yet stooped thus low. But how does this come in here? [1.] As an inducement to him now quickly to leave what lessons and legacies he had to leave to his disciples, because his hour was now come when he must take his leave of them, and be exalted above that familiar converse which he now had with them, *v.* 1. [2.] It may come in as that which supported him under his sufferings, and carried him cheerfully through this sharp encounter. Judas was now betraying him, and he knew it, and knew what would be the consequence of it; yet, knowing also *that he came from God and went to God,* he did not draw back, but went on cheerfully. [3.] It seems to come in as a foil to his condescension, to make it the more admirable. The reasons of divine grace are sometimes represented in scripture as strange and surprising (as Isa. 57:17, 18; Hos. 2:13, 14); so here, that is given as an inducement to Christ to stoop which should rather have been a reason for his taking state; for God's thoughts are not as ours. Compare with this those passages which preface the most signal instances of condescending grace with the displays of divine glory, as Ps. 68:4, 5; Isa. 57:15; 66:1, 2.

2. Here is the voluntary abasement of our Lord Jesus notwithstanding this. *Jesus knowing* his own glory as God, and his own authority and power as Mediator, one would think it should follow, *He rises from supper,* lays aside his ordinary garments, calls for robes, bids them keep their distance, and do him homage; but no, quite the contrary, when he considered this he gave the greatest instance of humility. Note, A well-grounded assurance of heaven and happiness, instead of puffing a man up with pride, will make and keep him very humble. Those that would be found conformable to Christ, and partakers of his Spirit, must study to keep their minds low in the midst of the greatest advancements. Now that which Christ humbled himself to was to *wash his disciples' feet.*

(1.) The action itself was mean and servile, and that which servants of the lowest rank were employed in. *Let thine handmaid* (saith Abigail) *be a servant to wash the feet of the servants of my lord;* let me be in the meanest employment, 1 Sa. 25:41. If he had washed their hands or faces, it had been great condescension (Elisha poured water on the hands of Elijah, 2 Ki. 3:11); but for Christ to stoop to such a piece of drudgery as this may well excite our admiration. Thus he would teach us to think nothing below us wherein we may be serviceable to God's glory and the good of our brethren.

(2.) The condescension was so much the greater that he did this for his own disciples, who in themselves were of a low and despicable condition, not curious about their bodies; their feet, it is likely, were seldom washed, and therefore very dirty. In relation to him, they were his scholars, his servants, and such as should have washed his feet, whose dependence was upon him, and their expectations from him. Many of great spirits otherwise will do a mean thing to curry favour with their superiors; they rise by stooping, and climb by cringing; but for Christ to do this to *his disciples* could be no act of policy nor complaisance, but pure humility.

(3.) He *rose from supper* to do it. Though we translate it (*v.* 2) *supper being ended,* it might be better read, *there being a supper made,* or *he being at supper,* for he sat down again (*v.* 12), and we find him dipping a sop (*v.* 26), so that he did it in the midst of his meal, and thereby taught us, [1.] Not to reckon it a disturbance, nor any just cause of uneasiness, to be called from our meal to do God or our brother any real service, esteeming the discharge of our duty *more than our necessary food, ch.* 4:34. Christ would not leave his preaching to oblige his nearest relations (Mk. 3:33), but would leave his supper to show his love to his disciples. [2.] Not to be over nice about our meat. It would have turned many a squeamish stomach to wash dirty feet at supper-time; but Christ did it, not that we might learn to be rude and slovenly (cleanliness and godliness will do well together), but to teach us not to be curious, not to indulge, but mortify, the delicacy of the appetite, giving good manners their due place, and no more.

(4.) He put himself into the garb of a servant, to do it: he *laid aside* his loose and upper *garments,* that he might apply himself to this service the more expeditely. We must address ourselves to duty as those that are resolved not to take state, but to take pains; we must divest ourselves of every thing that would either feed our pride or hang in our way and hinder us in what we have to do, must *gird up the loins of our mind,* as those that in earnest buckle to business.

(5.) He did it with all the humble ceremony that could be, went through all the parts of the service distinctly, and passed by none of them; he did it as if he had been used thus to serve; did it himself alone, and had none to minister to him in it. He *girded himself with the towel,* as servants throw a napkin on their arm, or put an apron before them; he *poured water into the basin* out of the water-pots that stood by (*ch.* 2:6), and then *washed their feet;* and, to complete the service, *wiped them.* Some think that he did not wash the feet of them all, but only four or five of them, that being thought sufficient to answer the end; but I see nothing to countenance this conjecture, for in other places where he did make a difference it is taken notice of; and his washing the feet of them *all,* without exception, teaches us a catholic and extensive charity to all Christ's disciples, even the least.

(6.) Nothing appears to the contrary but that he washed the feet of Judas among the rest, for he was present, *v.* 26. It is the character of a *widow indeed* that she had washed the saints' feet (1 Tim. 5:10), and there is some comfort in this; but the blessed Jesus here washed the feet of a sinner, the worst of sinners, the worst to him, who was at this time contriving to betray him.

Many interpreters consider Christ's washing his disciples' feet as a representation of *his whole undertaking.* He knew that he was equal with God, and all things were his; and yet he rose from his table in glory, laid aside his robes of light, girded himself with our nature, took upon him the form of a servant, *came not to be ministered to, but to minister,* poured out his blood, poured out his soul unto death, and thereby prepared a laver to wash us from our sins, Rev. 1:5.

III. Christ washed his disciples' feet that he might signify to them spiritual washing, and the cleansing of the soul from the pollutions of sin. This is plainly intimated in his discourse with Peter upon it, *v.* 6–11, in which we may observe,

1. The surprise Peter was in when he saw his Master go about this mean service (*v.* 6): *Then cometh he to Simon Peter,* with his towel and basin, and bids him put out his feet to be washed. Chrysostom conjectures that he first washed the feet of Judas, who readily admitted the honour, and was pleased to see his Master so disparage himself. It is most probable that when he *went about* this service (which is all that is meant by his *beginning* to wash, *v.* 5) he took Peter first, and that the rest would not have suffered it, if they had not first heard it explained in what passed between Christ and Peter. Whether Christ came first to Peter or no, when he did come to him, Peter was startled at the proposal: *Lord* (saith he) *dost thou wash my feet?* Here is an emphasis to be laid upon the persons, *thou* and *me;* and the placing of the words is observable, *sy mou — what, thou mine? Tu mihi lavas pedes? Quid est tu? Quid est mihi? Cogitanda sunt potius quam dicenda — Dost thou wash my feet? What is it thou? What to me? These things are rather to be contemplated than uttered.* — Aug. in loc. What *thou,* our Lord and Master, whom we know and believe to be the Son of God, and Saviour and ruler of the world, do this for *me,* a worthless worm of the earth, *a sinful man, O Lord?* Shall those hands wash my feet which with a touch have cleansed lepers, given sight to the blind, and raised the dead? So Theophylact, and from him Dr. Taylor. Very willingly would Peter have taken the basin and towel, and washed his Master's feet, and been proud of the honour, Lu. 17:7, 8. "This had been natural and regular; for *my Master* to wash my feet is such a solecism as never was; such a paradox as I cannot understand. *Is this the manner of men?*" Note, Christ's condescensions, especially his condescensions to *us,* wherein we find ourselves taken notice of by his grace, are justly the matter of our admiration, *ch.* 14:22. *Who am I, Lord God? And what is my father's house?*

2. The immediate satisfaction Christ gave to this question of surprise. This was at least sufficient to silence his objections (*v.* 7): *What I do, thou knowest not now, but thou shalt know hereafter.* Here are two reasons why Peter must submit to what Christ was doing: —

(1.) Because he was at present in the dark concerning it, and ought not to oppose what he did not understand, but acquiesce in the will and wisdom of one who could give a good reason for all he said and did. Christ would teach Peter an *implicit obedience: "What I do thou knowest not now,* and therefore art no competent judge of it, but must believe it is well done because I do it." Note, Consciousness to ourselves of the darkness we labour under, and our inability to judge of what God does, should make us sparing and modest in our censures of his proceedings; see Heb. 11:8.

(2.) Because there was something considerable in it, of which he should hereafter know the meaning: *"Thou shalt know hereafter* what need thou hast of being washed, when thou shalt be guilty of the heinous sin of denying me;" so some. "Thou shalt know, when, in the discharge of the office of an apostle, thou wilt be employed in washing off from those under thy charge the sins and defilements of their earthly affections;" so Dr. Hammond. Note, [1.] Our Lord Jesus does many things the meaning of which even his own disciples do not for the present know, but they *shall know afterwards.* What he did when he became man for us and what he did when he became a worm and no man for us, what he did when he lived our life and what he did when he laid it down, could not be understood till afterwards, and then it appeared that *it behoved him,* Heb. 2:17. Subsequent providences explain preceding ones; and we see afterwards what was the kind tendency of events that seemed most cross; and the way which we thought was *about* proved the *right way.* [2.] Christ's washing his disciples' feet had a significancy in it, which they themselves did not understand till afterwards, when Christ explained it to be a specimen of the laver of regeneration, and till the Spirit was poured out upon them from on high. We must let Christ take his own way, both in ordinances and providences, and we shall find in the issue it was the best way.

3. Peter's peremptory refusal, notwithstanding this, to let Christ wash his feet (*v.* 8): *Thou shalt by no means wash my feet; no, never.* So it is in the original. It is the language of a fixed resolution. Now, (1.) Here was a show of humility and modesty. Peter herein seemed to have, and no doubt he really had, a great respect for his Master, as he had, Lu. 5:8. Thus many are beguiled of their reward in a *voluntary humility* (Col. 2:18, 23), such a self-denial as Christ neither appoints nor accepts; for, (2.) Under this show of humility there was a real contradiction to the will of the Lord Jesus: "I *will wash thy feet,"* saith Christ; "But thou never shalt," saith Peter, "it is not a fitting thing;" so making himself wiser than Christ. It is not humility, but infidelity, to put away the offers of the gospel, as if too rich to be made to us or too good news to be true.

4. Christ's insisting upon his offer, and a good reason given to Peter why he should accept it: *If I wash thee not, thou hast no part with me.* This may be taken, (1.) As a severe caution against disobedience: *"If I wash thee not,* if thou continue refractory, and wilt not comply with thy Master's will in so small a matter, thou shalt not be owned as one of my disciples, but be justly discarded and cashiered for not observing orders." Thus several of the ancients understand it; if Peter will make himself wiser than his Master, and dispute the commands he ought to obey, he does in effect renounce his allegiance, and say, as they did, *What portion have we in David,* in the Son of David? And so shall his doom be, he shall have no part in him. Let him use no more manners than will do him good, for *to obey is better than sacrifice,* 1 Sa. 15:22. Or, (2.) As a declaration of the necessity of spiritual washing; and so I think it is to be understood: *"If I wash not* thy soul from the pollution of sin, *thou hast no part with me,* no interest in me, no communion with me, no benefit by me." Note, All those, and those only, that are spiritually washed by Christ, have a part in Christ. [1.] To have a part in Christ, or with Christ, has all the happiness of a Christian bound up in it, to be *partakers of Christ* (Heb. 3:14), to share in those inestimable privileges which result from a union with him and relation to him. It is that *good part* the having of which is the *one thing needful.* [2.] It is necessary to our having a part in Christ that he wash us. All those whom Christ owns

and saves he justifies and sanctifies, and both are included in his washing them. We cannot partake of his glory if we partake not of his merit and righteousness, and of his Spirit and grace.

5. Peter's more than submission, his earnest request, to be washed by Christ, *v.* 9. If this be the meaning of it, *Lord, wash not my feet only, but also my hands and my head.* How soon is Peter's mind changed! When the mistake of his understanding was rectified, the corrupt resolution of his will was soon altered. Let us therefore not be peremptory in any resolve (except in our resolve to follow Christ), because we may soon see cause to retract it, but cautious in taking up a purpose we will be tenacious of. Observe,

(1.) How ready Peter is to recede from what he had said: "Lord, what a fool was I to speak such a hasty word!" Now that the washing of him appeared to be an act of Christ's authority and grace he admits it; but disliked when it seemed only an act of humiliation. Note, [1.] Good men, when they see their error, will not be loth to recant it. [2.] Sooner or later, Christ will bring all to be of his mind.

(2.) How importunate he is for the purifying grace of the Lord Jesus, and the universal influence of it, even upon his hands and head. Note, A divorce from Christ, and an exclusion from having a part in him, is the most formidable evil in the eyes of all that are enlightened, for the fear of which they will be persuaded to any thing. And for fear of this we should be earnest with God in prayer, that he will wash us, will justify and sanctify us. "Lord, that I may not be cut off from thee, make me fit for thee, by the washing of regeneration. *Lord, wash not my feet only* from the gross pollutions that cleave to them, *but also my hands and my head* from the spots which they have contracted, and the undiscerned filth which proceeds by perspiration from the body itself." Note, Those who truly desire to be sanctified desire to be sanctified throughout, and to have the whole man, with all its parts and powers, purified, 1 Th. 5:23.

6. Christ's further explication of this sign, as it represented spiritual washing.

(1.) With reference to his disciples that were faithful to him (*v.* 10): *He that is washed* all over in the bath (as was frequently practised in those countries), when he returns to his house, *needeth not save to wash his feet,* his hands and head having been washed, and he having only dirtied his feet in walking home. Peter had gone from one extreme to the other. At first he would not let Christ wash his feet; and now he overlooks what Christ had done for him in his baptism, and what was signified thereby, and cries out to have his hands and head washed. Now Christ directs him into the meaning; he must have his feet washed, but not his hands and head. [1.] See here what is the comfort and privilege of such as are in a justified state; they are washed by Christ, and are *clean every whit,* that is, they are graciously accepted of God, as if they were so; and, though they offend, yet they need not, upon their repentance, be again put into a justified state, for then should they often be baptized. The evidence of a justified state may be clouded, and the comfort of it suspended, when yet the charter of it is not vacated or taken away. Though we have occasion to repent daily, God's gifts and callings are without repentance. The heart may be swept and garnished, and yet still remain the devil's palace; but, if it be washed, it belongs to Christ, and he will not lose it. [2.] See what ought to be the daily care of those who through grace are in a justified state, and that is to wash their feet; to cleanse themselves from the guilt they contract daily through infirmity and inadvertence, by the renewed exercise of repentance, with a believing application of the virtue of Christ's blood. We must also wash our feet by constant watchfulness against every thing that is defiling, for we must cleanse our way, and cleanse our feet *by taking heed thereto,* Ps. 119:9. The priests, when they were consecrated, were washed with water; and, though they did not need afterwards to be so washed all over, yet, whenever they went in to minister, they must wash their feet and hands at the laver, on pain of death, Ex. 30:19, 20. The provision made for our cleansing should not make us presumptuous, but the more cautious. *I have washed my feet, how shall I defile them?* From yesterday's pardon, we should fetch an argument against this day's temptation.

(2.) With reflection upon Judas: *And you are clean, but not all, v.* 10, 11. He pronounces his disciples clean, clean *through the word he had spoken to them, ch.* 15:3. He washed them himself, and then said, *You are clean;* but he excepts Judas: *not all;* they were all baptized, even Judas, yet not all clean; many have the sign that have not the thing signified. Note, [1.] Even among those who are called disciples of Christ, and profess relation to him, there are some who are not clean, Prov. 30:12. [2.] The Lord knows those that are his, and those that are not, 2 Tim. 2:19. The eye of Christ can separate between the precious and the vile, the clean and the unclean. [3.] When those that have called themselves disciples afterwards prove traitors, their apostasy at last is a certain evidence of their hypocrisy all along. [4.] Christ sees it necessary to let his disciples know that they are not all clean; that we may all be jealous over ourselves *(Is it I? Lord, is it I* that am among the clean, yet not clean?) and that, when hypocrites are discovered, it may be no surprise nor stumbling to us.

IV. Christ washed his disciples' feet to set before us an example. This explication he gave of what he had done, when he had done it, *v.* 12–17. Observe,

1. With what solemnity he gave an account of the meaning of what he had done (*v.* 12): *After he had washed their feet,* he said, *Know you what I have done?*

(1.) He adjourned the explication till he had finished the transaction, [1.] To try their submission and implicit obedience. What he did they should not know till afterwards, that they might learn to acquiesce in his will when they could not give a reason for it. [2.] Because it was proper to finish the riddle before he unriddled it. Thus, as to his whole undertaking, when his sufferings were finished, when he had resumed the garments of his exalted state and was ready to sit down again, then he *opened the understandings of his disciples,* and poured out his Spirit, Lu. 24:45, 46.

(2.) Before he explained it, he asked them if they could construe it: *Know you what I have done to you?* He put this question to them, not only to make them sensible of their ignorance, and the need they had to be instructed (as Zec. 4:5, 13, *Knowest thou not what these be? and I said, No, my Lord*), but to raise their desires and expectations of instruction: "I *would have you know,* and, if you will give attention, I will tell you." Note, It is the will of Christ that sacramental signs should be explained, and that his people should be acquainted with the meaning of them; otherwise, though ever so significant, to those who know not the thing signified they are insignificant. Hence they are directed to ask, *What mean you by this service?* Ex. 12:26.

2. Upon what he grounds that which he had to say (*v.* 13): *"You call me Master and Lord,* you give me those titles, in speaking of me, in speaking to me, and *you say well,* for *so I am;* you are in the relation of scholars to me, and I do the part of a master to you." Note, (1.) Jesus Christ is our Master and Lord; he that is our Redeemer and Saviour is, in order to that, our Lord and Master. He is our Master, *didaskalos* — our teacher and instructor in all necessary truths and rules, as a prophet revealing to us the will of God. He is our Lord, ***kyrios*** — our ruler and owner, that has authority over us and propriety in us. (2.) It becomes the disciples of Christ to call him Master and Lord, not in compliment, but in reality; not by constraint, but with delight. Devout Mr. Herbert, when he mentioned the name of Christ, used to add, my Master; and thus expresses himself concerning it in one of his poems:

> How sweetly doth my Master sound, my Master!
> As ambergris leaves a rich scent unto the taster,
> So do these words a sweet content,
> an oriental fragrancy, my Master.

(3.) Our calling Christ Master and Lord is an obligation upon us to receive and observe the instruction he gives us. Christ would thus pre-engage their obedience to a command that was displeasing to flesh and blood. If Christ be our Master and Lord, be so by our own consent, and we have often called him so, we are bound in honour and honesty to be observant of him.

3. The lesson which he hereby taught: *You also ought to wash one another's feet, v.* 14.

(1.) Some have understood this literally, and have thought these words amount to the institution of a standing ordinance in the church; that Christians should, in a solemn religious manner, *wash one another's feet,* in token of their condescending love to one another. St. Ambrose took it so, and practised it in the church of Milan. St. Austin saith that those Christians who did not do it with their hands, yet (he hoped) did it with their hearts in humility; but he saith, It is much better to do it with the hands also, when there is occasion, as 1 Tim. 5:10. What Christ has done Christians should not disdain to do. Calvin saith that the pope, in the annual observance of this ceremony on Thursday in the passion week, is rather Christ's ape than his follower, for the duty enjoined, in conformity to Christ, was *mutual: Wash one another's feet.* And Jansenius saith, It is done, *Frigidè et dissimiliter — Frigidly, and unlike the primitive model.*

(2.) But doubtless it is to be understood figuratively; it is an instructive sign, but not sacramental, as the eucharist. This was a parable to the eye; and three things our Master hereby designed to teach us: — [1.] A humble condescension. We must learn of our Master to be *lowly in heart* (Mt. 11:29), and walk with all lowliness; we must think meanly of ourselves and respectfully of our brethren, and deem nothing below us but sin; we must say of that which seems mean, but has a tendency to the glory of God and our brethren's good, as David (2 Sa. 6:22), *If this be to be vile, I will be yet more vile.* Christ had often taught his disciples humility, and they had forgotten the lesson; but now he teaches them in such a way as surely they could never forget. [2.] A condescension to be serviceable. To wash one another's feet is to stoop to the meanest offices of love, for the real good and benefit one of another, as blessed Paul, who, though free from all, made himself *servant of all;* and the blessed Jesus, who *came not to be ministered unto, but to minister.* We must not grudge to take care and pains, and to spend time, and to diminish ourselves for the good of those to whom we are not under any particular obligations, even of our inferiors, and such as are not in a capacity of making us any requital. Washing the feet after travelling contributes both to the decency of the person and to his ease, so that to wash one another's feet is to consult both the credit and the comfort one of another, to do what we can both to advance our brethren's reputation and to make their minds easy. See 1 Co. 10:24; Heb. 6:10. The duty is *mutual;* we must both accept help from our brethren and afford help to our brethren. [3.] A serviceableness to the sanctification one of another: *You ought to wash one another's feet,* from the pollutions of sin. Austin takes it in this sense, and many others. We cannot satisfy for one another's sins, this is peculiar to Christ, but we may help to purify one another from sin. We must in the first place wash ourselves; this charity must begin at home (Mt. 7:5), but it must not end there; we must sorrow for the failings and follies of our brethren, much more for their gross pollutions (1 Co. 5:2), must wash our brethren's polluted feet in tears. We must faithfully reprove them, and do what we can to bring them to repentance (Gal. 6:1), and we must admonish them, to prevent their falling into the mire; this is washing their feet.

4. Here is the ratifying and enforcing of this command from the example of what Christ had now done: *If I your Lord and Master have* done it to you, you ought to do it *to one another.* He shows the cogency of this argument in two things: —

(1.) I am *your Master,* and you are my disciples, and therefore you ought to *learn of me* (*v.* 15); for in this, as in other things, *I have given you an example,* that *you should do* to others *as I have done* to you. Observe, [1.] What a good teacher Christ is. He teaches by example as well as doctrine, and for this end came into this world, and dwelt among us, that he might set us a copy of all those graces and duties which his holy religion teaches; and it is a copy without one false stroke. Hereby he made his own laws more intelligible and honourable. Christ is a commander like Gideon, who said to his soldiers, *Look on me, and do likewise* (Jdg. 7:17); like Abimelech, who said, *What you have seen me do, make haste and do as I have done* (Jdg. 9:48); and like Caesar, who called his soldiers, not *milites — soldiers,* but, *commilitones — fellow-soldiers,* and whose usual word was, not *Ite illue,* but *Venite huc;* not *Go,* but *Come.* [2.] What good scholars we must be. We must *do as he hath done;* for therefore he gave us a copy, that we should write after it, that we might be as he was in this world (1 Jn. 4:17), and walk *as he walked,* 1 Jn. 2:6. Christ's example herein is to be followed by ministers in particular, in whom the graces of humility and holy love should especially appear, and by the exercise thereof they effectually serve the interests of their Master and the ends of their ministry. When Christ sent his apostles abroad as his agents, it was with this charge, that they should not take state upon them, nor carry things with a high hand, but *become all things to all men,* 1 Co. 9:22. What I have done to your dirty feet that do you to the polluted souls of sinners; *wash them.* Some who suppose this to have been done at the passover supper think it intimates a rule in admitting communicants to the Lord's-supper, to see that they be first washed and cleansed by reformation and a blameless conversation, and then take them in to *compass God's altar.* But all Christians likewise are here taught to condescend to each other in love, and to do it as Christ did it, unasked, unpaid; we must not be mercenary in the services of love, nor do them with reluctancy.

(2.) I am *your Master,* and you are my disciples, and therefore you cannot think it below you to do that, how mean soever it may seem, which you have seen me do, for (*v.* 16) *the servant is not greater than his Lord, neither he that is sent,* though sent with all the pomp and power of an ambassador, *greater than he that sent him.* Christ had urged this (Mt. 10:24, 25) as a reason why they should not think it strange if they suffered as he did; here he urges it as a reason why they should not think it much to humble themselves as he did. What he did not think a disparagement to him, they must not think a disparagement to them. Perhaps the disciples were inwardly disgusted at this precept of washing one another's feet, as inconsistent with the dignity they expected shortly to be preferred to. To obviate such thoughts, Christ reminds them of their place as his servants; they were not better men than their Master, and what was consistent with his dignity was much more consistent with theirs. If he was humble and condescending, it ill became them to be proud and assuming. Note, [1.] We must take good heed to ourselves, lest Christ's gracious condescensions to us, and advancements of us, through the corruption of nature occasion us to entertain high thoughts of ourselves or low thoughts of him. We need to be put in mind of this, that we are not *greater than our Lord.* [2.] Whatever our Master was pleased to condescend to in favour to us, we should much more condescend to in conformity to him. Christ, by humbling himself, has dignified humility, and put an honour upon it, and obliged his followers to think nothing below them but sin. We commonly say to those who disdain to do such or such a thing, As good as you have done it, and been never the worse thought of; and true indeed it is, if our Master has done it. When we see our Master serving, we cannot but see how ill it becomes us to be domineering.

5. Our Saviour closes this part of his discourse with an intimation of the necessity of their obedience to these instructions: *If you know these things:* or, seeing you know them, *happy are you if you do them.* Most people think, Happy are those that rise and rule. Washing one another's feet will never get estates and preferments; but Christ saith, notwithstanding this, Happy are those that stoop and obey, *If you know these things.* This may be understood either as intimating a doubt whether thy knew them or no; so strong was their conceit of a temporal kingdom that it was a question whether they could entertain the notion of a duty so contrary to that conceit. Or, as taking it for granted that they did know these things; since they had such excellent precepts given them, recommended by such an excellent pattern, it will be necessary to the completing of their happiness that they practise accordingly. (1.) This is applicable to the commands of Christ in general. Note, Though it is a great advantage to know our duty, yet we shall come short of happiness if we do not do our duty. Knowing is in order to doing; that knowledge therefore is vain and fruitless which is not reduced to practice; nay, it will aggravate the sin and ruin, Lu. 12:47, 48; James 4:17. It is knowing and doing that will demonstrate us of *Christ's kingdom,* and wise builders. See Ps. 103:17, 18. (2.) It is to be applied especially to this command of humility and serviceableness. Nothing is better known, nor more readily acknowledged, than this, that we should be humble; and therefore, though many will own themselves to be passionate and intemperate, few will own themselves to be proud, for it is as inexcusable a sin, and as hateful, as any other; and yet how little is to be seen of true humility, and that mutual subjection and condescension upon which the law of Christ so much insists! Most know these things so well as to expect that others should do accordingly to them, yield to them, and serve them, but not so well as to do so themselves.

Verses 18–30

We have here the discovery of Judas's plot to betray his Master. Christ knew it from the beginning; but now first he discovered it to his disciples, who did not expect Christ should be betrayed, though he had often told them so, much less did they suspect that one of them should do it. Now here,

I. Christ gives them a general intimation of it (*v.* 18): *I speak not of you all,* I cannot expect you will all do these things, for *I know whom I have chosen,* and whom I have passed by; but the scripture will be fulfilled (Ps. 41:9), *He that eateth bread with me hath lifted up his heel against me.* He does not yet speak out, either of the crime or the criminal, but raises their expectations of a further discovery.

1. He intimates to them that they were not all right. He had said (*v.* 10), *You are clean, but not all.* So here, *I speak not of you all.* Note, What is said of the excellencies of Christ's disciples cannot be said of all that are called so. The word of Christ is a distinguishing word, which separates *between cattle and cattle,* and will distinguish thousands into hell who flattered themselves with hopes that they were going to heaven. *I speak not of you all;* you my disciples and followers. Note, There is a mixture of bad with good in the best societies, a Judas among the apostles; it will be so till we come to the blessed society into which shall enter nothing unclean or disguised.

2. That he himself knew who were right, and who were not: *I know whom I have chosen,* who the few are that are chosen among the many that are called with the common call. Note, (1.) Those that are chosen, Christ himself had the choosing of them; he nominated the persons he undertook for. (2.) Those that are chosen are known to Christ, for he never forgets any whom he has once had in his thoughts of love, 2 Tim. 2:19.

3. That in the treachery of him that proved false to him the scripture was fulfilled, which takes off very much both the surprise and offence of the thing. Christ took one into his family whom he foresaw to be a traitor, and did not by effectual grace prevent his being so, *that the scripture might be fulfilled.* Let it not therefore be a stumbling-block to any; for, though it do not at all lessen Judas's offence, it may lessen our offence at it. The scripture referred to is David's complaint of the treachery of some of his enemies; the Jewish expositors, and ours from them generally understand it of Ahithophel: Grotius thinks it intimates that the death of Judas would be like that of Ahithophel. But because that psalm speaks of David's sickness, of which we read nothing at the time of Ahithophel's deserting him, it may better be understood of some other friend of his, that proved false to him. This our Saviour applies to Judas. (1.) Judas, as an apostle, was admitted to the highest privilege: he did *eat bread with Christ.* He was familiar with him, and favoured by him, was one of his family, one of those with whom he was intimately conversant. David saith of his treacherous friend, He did eat *of my bread;* but Christ, being poor, had no bread he could properly call his own. He saith, He did *eat bread with me;* such as he had by the kindness of his friends, that ministered to him, his disciples had their share of, Judas among the rest. Wherever he went, Judas was welcome with him, did not dine among servants, but sat at table with his Master, ate of the same dish, drank of the same cup, and in all respects fared as he fared. He ate miraculous bread with him, when the loaves were multiplied, ate the passover with him. Note, All that eat bread with Christ are not his disciples indeed. See 1 Co. 10:3–5. (2.) Judas, as an apostate, was guilty of the basest treachery: he *lifted up the heel* against Christ. [1.] He forsook him, turned his back upon him, went out from the society of his disciples, *v.* 30. [2.] He despised him, shook off the dust of his feet against him, in contempt of him and his gospel. Nay, [3.] He became an enemy to him; spurned at him, as wrestlers do at their adversaries, whom they would overthrow. Note, It is no new thing for those that were Christ's seeming friends to prove his real enemies. Those who pretended to magnify him magnify themselves against him, and thereby prove themselves guilty, not only of the basest ingratitude, but the basest treachery and perfidiousness.

II. He gives them a reason why he told them beforehand of the treachery of Judas (*v.* 19): *"Now I tell you before it come,* before Judas has begun to put his wicked plot in execution, *that when it is come to pass you may,* instead of stumbling at it, be confirmed in your *belief that I am he,* he that should come." 1. By his clear and certain foresight of things to come, of which in this, as in other instances, he gave incontestable proof, he proved himself to be the true God, before whom all things are naked and open. Christ foretold that Judas would betray him when there was no ground to suspect such a thing, and so proved himself the eternal Word, which is a *discerner of the thoughts and intents of the heart.* The prophecies of the New Testament concerning the apostasy of the latter times (which we have, 2 Th. 2; 1 Tim. 4, and in the Apocalypse) being evidently accomplished is a proof that those writings were divinely inspired, and confirms our faith in the whole canon of scripture. 2. By this application of the types and prophecies of the Old Testament to himself, he proved himself to be the true Messiah, to whom *all the prophets bore witness.* Thus *it was written, and thus it behoved Christ to suffer,* and he suffered just as it was written, Lu. 24:25, 26; *ch.* 8:28.

III. He gives a word of encouragement to his apostles, and all his ministers whom he employs in his service (*v.* 20): *He that receiveth whomsoever I send receiveth me.* The purport of these words is the same with what we have in other scriptures, but it is not easy to make out their coherence here. Christ had told his disciples that they must humble and abase themselves. "Now," saith he, "though there may be those that will despise you for your condescension, yet there will be those that will do you honour, and shall be honoured for so doing." Those who know themselves dignified by Christ's commission may be content to be vilified in the world's opinion. Or, he intended to silence the scruples of those who, because there was a traitor among the apostles, would be shy of receiving any of them; for, if one of them was false to his Master, to whom would any of them be true? *Ex uno disce omnes — They are all alike.* No, as Christ will think never the worse of them for Judas's crime, so he will stand by them, and own them, and will raise up such as shall receive them. Those that had received Judas when he was a preacher, and perhaps were converted and edified by his preaching, were never the worse, nor should reflect upon it with any regret, though he afterwards proved a traitor; for he was one whom Christ sent. We cannot know what men are, much less what they will be, but those who appear to be sent of Christ we must receive, till the contrary appear. Though some, by entertaining strangers, have entertained robbers unawares, yet we must still be hospitable, for thereby some have entertained angels. The abuses put upon our charity, though ordered with ever so much discretion, will neither justify our uncharitableness, nor lose us the reward of our charity. 1. We are here encouraged to receive ministers as *sent of Christ: "He that receiveth whomsoever I send,* though weak and poor, and subject to like passions as others (for as the law, so the gospel, *makes men priests that have infirmity*), yet if he deliver my message, and be regularly called and appointed to do so, and as an officer give himself to the word and prayer, he that entertains him shall be owned as a friend of mine." Christ was now leaving the world, but he would leave an order of men to be his agents, to deliver his word, and those who receive *this,* in the light and love of it, receive *him.* To believe the doctrine of Christ, and obey his law, and accept the salvation offered upon the terms proposed; this is receiving those whom Christ sends, and it is *receiving Christ Jesus the Lord* himself. 2. We are here encouraged to receive Christ as sent of God: *He that* thus *receiveth me,* that receiveth Christ in his ministers, receiveth the Father also, for they come upon his errand likewise, baptizing in the name of the Father, as well as of the Son. Or, in general, *He that receiveth me* as his prince and Saviour receiveth *him that sent me* as his portion and felicity. Christ was sent of God, and in embracing his religion we embrace the *only true* religion.

IV. Christ more particularly notifies to them the plot which one of their number was now hatching against him (*v.* 21): *When Jesus had thus said* in general, to prepare them for a more particular discovery, he was *troubled in spirit,* and showed it by some gesture or sign, and *he testified,* he solemnly declared it *(cum animo testandi — with the solemnity of a witness on oath), "One of you shall betray me;* one of you my apostles and constant followers." None indeed could be said to *betray* him but those in whom he reposed a confidence, and who were the witnesses of his retirements. This did not determine Judas to the sin by any fatal necessity; for, though the event did follow according to the prediction, yet not from the prediction. Christ is not the author of sin; yet as to this heinous sin of Judas, 1. Christ foresaw it; for even that which is secret and future, and hidden from the eyes of all living, naked and open before the eyes of Christ. He *knows what is in men* better than they do themselves (2 Ki. 8:12), and therefore sees what will be done by them. *I knew that thou wouldest deal very treacherously,* Isa. 48:8. 2. He foretold it, not only for the sake of the rest of the disciples, but for the sake of Judas himself, that he might take warning, and recover himself out of the snare of the devil. Traitors proceed not in their plots when they find they are discovered; surely Judas, when he finds that his Master knows his design, will retreat in time; if not, it will aggravate his condemnation. 3. He spoke of it with a manifest concern; he was *troubled in spirit* when he mentioned it. He had often spoken of his own sufferings and death, without any such trouble of spirit as he here manifested when he spoke of the ingratitude and treachery of Judas. This touched him in a tender part. Note, The falls and miscarriages of the disciples of Christ are a great trouble of spirit to their Master; the sins of Christians are the grief of Christ. "What! *One of you betray me?* You that have received from me such distinguishing favours; you that I had reason to think would be firm to me, that have professed such a respect for me; what iniquity have you found in me that one of you should betray me?" This went to his heart, as the undutifulness of children grieves those who have *nourished and brought them up,* Isa. 1:2. See Ps. 95:10; Isa. 63:10.

V. The disciples quickly take the alarm. They knew their Master would neither deceive them nor jest with them; and therefore *looked one upon another,* with a manifest concern, *doubting of whom he spake.* 1. By looking one upon another they evinced the trouble they were in upon this notice given them; it struck such a horror upon them that they knew not well which way to look, nor what to say. They saw their Master troubled, and therefore they were troubled. This was at a feast where they were cheerfully entertained; but hence we must be taught to rejoice with trembling, and as though we rejoiced not. When David wept for his son's rebellion, all his followers wept with him (2 Sa. 15:30); so Christ's disciples here. Note, That which grieves Christ is, and should be, a grief to all that are his, particularly the scandalous miscarriages of those that are called by his name: *Who is offended, and I burn not?* 2. Hereby they endeavoured to *discover* the traitor. They looked wistfully in one another's face, to see who blushed, or, by some disorder in the countenance, manifested guilt in the heart, upon this notice; but, while those who were faithful had their consciences so clear that they could *lift up their faces without spot,* he that was false had his conscience so seared that he was not ashamed, neither could he blush, and so no discovery could be made in this way. Christ thus perplexed his disciples for a time, and put them into confusion, that he might *humble them, and prove them,* might excite in them a jealousy of themselves, and an indignation at the baseness of Judas. It is good for us sometimes to be put to a gaze, to be put to a pause.

VI. The disciples were solicitous to get their Master to explain himself, and to tell them particularly whom he meant; for nothing but this can put them out of their present pain, for each of them thought he had as much reason to suspect himself as any of his brethren; now,

1. Of all the disciples John was most fit to ask, because he was the favourite, and sat next his Master (*v.* 23): *There was leaning on Jesus's bosom one of the disciples whom Jesus loved.* It appears that this was John, by comparing *ch.* 21:20, 24. Observe, (1.) The particular kindness which Jesus had for him; he was known by this periphrasis, that he was *the disciple whom Jesus loved.* He loved them all (*v.* 1), but John was particularly dear to him. His name signifies *gracious.* Daniel, who was honoured with the revelations of the Old Testament, as John of the New, was *a man greatly beloved,* Dan. 9:23. Note, Among the disciples of Christ some are dearer to him than others. (2.) His place and posture at this time: He was *leaning on Jesus's bosom.* Some say that it was the fashion in those countries to sit at meat in a leaning posture, so that the second lay in the bosom of the first, and so on, which does not seem probable to me, for in such a posture as this they could neither eat nor drink conveniently; but, whether this was the case or not, John now *leaned on Christ's bosom,* and it seems to be an extraordinary expression of endearment used at this time. Note, There are some of Christ's disciples whom he lays in his bosom, who have more free and intimate communion with him than others. The Father loved the Son, and laid him *in his bosom* (*ch.* 1:18), and believers are in like manner one with Christ, *ch.* 17:21. This honour all the saints shall have shortly in the bosom of Abraham. Those who lay themselves at Christ's feet, he will lay in his bosom. (3.) Yet he conceals his name, because he himself was the penman of the story. He put this instead of his name, to show that he was pleased with it; it is his title of honour, that he was *the disciple whom Jesus loved,* as in David's and Solomon's court there was one that was the *king's friend;* yet he does not put his name down, to show that he was not proud of it, nor would seem to boast of it. Paul in a like case saith, *I knew a man in Christ.*

2. Of all the disciples Peter was most forward to know, *v.* 24. Peter, sitting at some distance, beckoned to John, by some sign or other, to ask. Peter was generally the leading man, most apt to put himself forth; and, where men's natural tempers lead them to be thus bold in answering and asking, if kept under the laws of humility and wisdom, they make men very serviceable. God gives his gifts variously; but that the forward men in the church may not think too well of themselves, nor the modest be discouraged, it must be noted that it was not Peter, but John, that was the beloved disciple. Peter was desirous to know, not only that he might be sure it was not he, but that, knowing who it was, they might withdraw from him, and guard against him, and, if possible, prevent his design. It were a desirable thing, we should think, to know who in the church will deceive us; yet let this suffice — Christ knows, though we do not. The reason why Peter did not himself ask was because John had a much fairer opportunity, by the advantage of his seat at table, to whisper the question into the ear of Christ, and to receive a like private answer. It is good to improve our interest in those that are near to Christ, and to engage their prayers for us. Do we know any that we have reason to think lie in Christ's bosom? Let us beg of them to speak a good word for us.

3. The question was asked accordingly (*v.* 25): *He then, lying at the breast of Jesus,* and so having the convenience of whispering with him, *saith unto him, Lord, who is it?* Now here John shows, (1.) A regard to his fellow-disciple, and to the motion he made. Though Peter had not the honour he had at this time, yet he did not therefore disdain to take the hint and intimation he gave him. Note, Those who lie in Christ's bosom may often learn from those who lie at his feet something that will be profitable for them, and be reminded of that which they did not of themselves think of. John was willing to gratify Peter herein, having so fair an opportunity for it. As every one hath received the gift, so let him minister the same for a common good, Rom. 12:6. (2.) A reverence of his Master. Though he whispered this in Christ's ear, yet he called him Lord; the familiarity he was admitted to did not at all lessen his respect for his Master. It becomes us to use a reverence in expression, and to observe a decorum even in our secret devotions, which no eye is a witness to, as well as in public assemblies. The more intimate communion gracious souls have with Christ, the more sensible they are of his worthiness and their own unworthiness, as Gen. 18:27.

4. Christ gave a speedy answer to this question, but whispered it in John's ear; for it appears (*v.* 29) that the rest were still ignorant of the matter. *He it is to whom I shall give a sop, psōmion — a morsel, a crust, when I have dipped it* in the sauce. And *when he had dipped the sop,* John strictly observing his motion, *he gave it to Judas;* and Judas took it readily enough, not suspecting the design of it, but glad of a savoury bit, to make up his mouth with. (1.) Christ notified the traitor by a sign. He could have told John by name who he was (The adversary and enemy is that wicked Judas, he is the traitor, and none but he); but thus he would exercise the observation of John, and intimate what need his ministers have of a spirit of discerning; for the false brethren we are to stand upon our guard against are not made known to us by words, but by signs; they are to be known to us by *their fruits,* by *their spirits;* it requires great diligence and care to form a right judgment upon them. (2.) That sign was a sop which Christ gave him, a very proper sign, because it was the fulfilling of the scripture (*v.* 18) that the traitor should be one that *ate bread with him,* that was at this time a fellow-commoner with him. It had likewise a significancy in it, and teaches us, [1.] That Christ sometimes gives sops to traitors; worldly riches, honours, and pleasures are sops (if I may so speak), which Providence sometimes gives into the hands of wicked men. Judas perhaps thought himself a favourite because he had the sop, like Benjamin at Joseph's table, a mess by himself; thus the prosperity of fools, like a stupifying sop, helps to *destroy them.* [2.] That we must not be outrageous against those whom we know to be very malicious against us. Christ carved to Judas as kindly as to any at the table, though he knew he was then plotting his death. *If thine enemy hunger, feed him;* this is to do as Christ does.

VII. Judas himself, instead of being convinced hereby of his wickedness, was the more confirmed in it, and the warning given him was to him a *savour of death unto death;* for it follows,

1. The devil hereupon took possession of him (*v.* 27): *After the sop, Satan entered into him:* not to make him melancholy, nor drive him distracted, which was the effect of his possessing some; not to hurry him into the fire, nor into the water; happy had it been for him if that had been the worst of it, or if with the swine he had been choked in the sea; but Satan entered into him to possess him with a prevailing prejudice against Christ and his doctrine, and a contempt of him, as one whose life was of small value, to excite in him a covetous desire of the wages of unrighteousness and a resolution to stick at nothing for the obtaining of them. But,

(1.) Was not Satan in him before? How then is it said that now *Satan entered into him?* Judas was all along a devil (*ch.* 6:70), a son of perdition, but now Satan gained a more full possession of him, had a *more abundant entrance* into him. His purpose to betray his Master was now ripened into a fixed resolution; now he returned with seven other spirits more wicked than himself, Lu. 11:26. Note, [1.] Though the devil is in every wicked man that does his works (Eph. 2:2), yet sometimes he enters more manifestly and more powerfully than at other times, when he puts them upon some enormous wickedness, which humanity and natural conscience startle at. [2.] Betrayers of Christ have much of the devil in them. Christ speaks of the sin of Judas as greater than that of any of his persecutors.

(2.) How came Satan to enter into him *after the sop?* Perhaps he was presently aware that it was the discovery of him, and it made him desperate in his resolutions. Many are made worse by the gifts of Christ's bounty, and are confirmed in their impenitency by that which should have led them to repentance. The *coals of fire heaped upon their heads,* instead of melting them, harden them.

2. Christ hereupon dismissed him, and delivered him up to his own heart's lusts: *Then said Jesus unto him, What thou doest, do quickly.* This is not to be understood as either advising him to his wickedness or warranting him in it; but either, (1.) As abandoning him to the conduct and power of Satan. Christ knew that Satan had entered into him, and had peaceable possession; and now he gives him up as hopeless. The various methods Christ had used for his conviction were ineffectual; and therefore, "What thou doest thou wilt do quickly; if thou art resolved to ruin thyself, go on, and take what comes." Note, When the evil spirit is willingly admitted, the good Spirit justly withdraws. Or, (2.) As challenging him to do his worst: "Thou art plotting against me, put thy plot in execution and welcome, the sooner the better, I do not fear thee, I am ready for thee." Note, our Lord Jesus was very forward to suffer and die for us, and was impatient of delay in the perfecting of his undertaking. Christ speaks of Judas's betraying him as a thing he was now doing, though he was only purposing it. Those who are contriving and designing mischief are, in God's account, doing mischief.

3. Those that were at table understood not what he meant, because they did not hear what he whispered to John (*v.* 28, 29): *No man at table,* neither the disciples nor any other of the guests, except John, *knew for what intent* he spoke this to him. (1.) They did not suspect that Christ said it to Judas as a traitor, because it did not enter into their heads that Judas was such a one, or would prove so. Note, It is an excusable dulness in the disciples of Christ not to be quick-sighted in their censures. Most are ready enough to say, when they hear harsh things spoken in general, Now such a one is meant, and now such a one; but Christ's disciples were so well taught to love one another that they could not easily learn to suspect one another; *charity thinks no evil.* (2.) They therefore took it for granted that he said it to him as a trustee, or treasurer of the household, giving him order for the laying out of some money. Their surmises in this case discover to us for what uses and purposes our Lord Jesus commonly directed payments out of that little stock he had, and so teach us how to honour the Lord with our substance. They concluded something was to be laid out, either, [1.] In works of piety: *Buy those things that we have need of against the feast.* Though he borrowed a room to eat the passover in, yet he bought in provision for it. That is to be reckoned well bestowed which is laid out upon *those things we have need of* for the maintenance of God's ordinances among us; and we have the less reason to grudge that expense now because our gospel-worship is far from being so chargeable as the legal worship was. [2.] Or in works of charity: *That he should give*

something to the poor. By this it appears, *First,* That our Lord Jesus, though he lived upon alms himself (Lu. 8:3), yet gave alms to the poor, a little out of a little. Though he might very well be excused, not only because he was poor himself, but because he did so much good in other ways, curing so many *gratis;* yet, to set us an example, he gave, for the relief of the poor, out of that which he had for the subsistence of his family; see Eph. 4:28. *Secondly,* That the time of a religious feast was thought a proper time for works of charity. When he celebrated the passover he ordered something for the poor. When we experience God's bounty to us, this should make us bountiful to the poor.

4. Judas hereupon sets himself vigorously to pursue his design against him: He *went away.* Notice is taken,

(1.) Of his speedy departure: *He went out presently,* and quitted the house, [1.] For fear of being more plainly discovered to the company, for, if he were, he expected they would all fall upon him, and be the death of him, or at least of his project. [2.] He went out as one weary of Christ's company and the society of his apostles. Christ needed not to expel him, he expelled himself. Note, Withdrawing from the communion of the faithful is commonly the first overt-act of a backslider, and the beginning of an apostasy. [3.] *He went out* to prosecute his design, to look for those with whom he was to make his bargain, and to settle the agreement with them. Now that Satan had got into him he hurried him on with precipitation, lest he should see his error and repent of it.

(2.) Of the time of his departure: *It was night.* [1.] Though it was night, an unseasonable time for business, yet, Satan having entered into him, he made no difficulty of the coldness and darkness of the night. This should shame us out of our slothfulness and cowardice in the service of Christ, that the devil's servants are so earnest and venturous in his service. [2.] Because it was night, and this gave him advantage of privacy and concealment. He was not willing to be *seen* treating with the chief priests, and therefore chose the dark night as the fittest time for such works of darkness. Those whose deeds are evil love darkness rather than light. See Job 24:13, etc.

Verses 31–35

This and what follows, to the end of *ch.* 14, was Christ's table-talk with his disciples. When supper was done, Judas went out; but what did the Master and his disciples do, whom he left sitting at table? They applied themselves to profitable discourse, to teach us as much as we can to make conversation with our friends at table serviceable to religion. Christ begins this discourse. The more forward we are humbly to promote that communication which is good, and to the use of edifying, the more like we are to Jesus Christ. Those especially that by their place, reputation, and gifts, *command the company,* to whom *men give ear,* ought to use the interest they have in other respects as an opportunity of doing them good. Now our Lord Jesus discourses with them (and probably discourses much more largely than is here recorded),

I. Concerning the great mystery of his own death and sufferings, about which they were as yet so much in the dark that they could not persuade themselves to expect the thing itself, much less did they understand the meaning of it; and therefore Christ gives them such instructions concerning it as made the offence of the cross to cease. Christ did not begin this discourse till Judas was gone out, for he was a false brother. The presence of wicked people is often a hindrance to good discourse. When Judas *was gone out,* Christ said, *now is the Son of man glorified;* now that Judas is discovered and discarded, who was a spot in their love-feast and a scandal to their family, *now is the Son of man glorified.* Note, Christ is glorified by the purifying of Christian societies: corruptions in his church are a reproach to him; the purging out of those corruptions rolls away the reproach. Or, rather, now Judas was gone to set the wheels a-going, in order to his being put to death, and the thing was likely to be effected shortly: *Now is the Son of man glorified,* meaning, *Now he is crucified.*

1. Here is something which Christ instructs them in, concerning his sufferings, that was very *comforting.*

(1.) That he should himself be glorified in them. Now the Son of man is to be exposed to the greatest ignominy and disgrace, to be despitefully used to the last degree, and dishonoured both by the cowardice of his friends and the insolence of his enemies; yet *now he is glorified;* For, [1.] Now he is to obtain a glorious victory over Satan and all the pow-

ers of darkness, to spoil them, and triumph over them. He is now *girding on the harness,* to take the field against these adversaries of God and man, with as great an assurance as if he had *put it off.* [2.] Now he is to work out a glorious deliverance for his people, by his death to reconcile them to God, and bring in an everlasting righteousness and happiness for them; to shed that blood which is to be an inexhaustible fountain of joys and blessings to all believers. [3.] Now he is to give a glorious example of self-denial and patience under the cross, courage and contempt of the world, zeal for the glory of God, and love to the souls of men, such as will make him to be for ever admired and had in honour. Christ had been glorified in many miracles he had wrought, and yet he speaks of his being glorified *now* in his sufferings, as if that were more than all his other glories in his humble state.

(2.) That God the Father should be glorified in them. The sufferings of Christ were, [1.] The satisfaction of God's justice, and so God was glorified in them. Reparation was thereby made with great advantage for the wrong done him in his honour by the sin of man. The ends of the law were abundantly answered, and the glory of his government effectually asserted and maintained. [2.] They were the manifestation of his holiness and mercy. The attributes of God shine brightly in creation and providence, but much more in the work of redemption; see 1 Co. 1:24; 2 Co. 4:6. God is love, and herein he hath commended his love.

(3.) That he should himself be greatly glorified after them, in consideration of God's being greatly glorified by them, *v.* 32. Observe how he enlarges upon it. [1.] He is sure that God will glorify him; and those whom God glorifies are glorious indeed. Hell and earth set themselves to vilify Christ, but God resolved to glorify him, and he did it. He glorified him in his sufferings by the amazing signs and wonders, both in heaven and earth, which attended them, and extorted even from his crucifiers an acknowledgment that he was the Son of God. But especially after his sufferings he glorified him, when he set him *at his own right hand,* gave him a *name above every name.* [2.] That he will glorify him *in himself* — *en heautō.* Either, *First,* In Christ himself. He will glorify him in his own person, and not only in his kingdom among men. This supposes his speedy resurrection. A common person may be honoured after his death, in his memory or posterity, but Christ was honoured in *himself.* Or, *secondly,* in God himself. God will glorify him *with himself,* as it is explained, *ch.* 17:5. *He shall sit down with the Father upon his throne,* Rev. 3:21. This is true glory. [3.] That he will glorify him straightway. He looked upon the joy and glory set before him, not only as great, but as near; and his sorrows and sufferings short and soon over. Good services done to earthly princes often remain long unrewarded; but Christ had his preferments presently. It was but forty hours (or not so much) from his death to his resurrection, and forty days thence to his ascension, so that it might well be said that he was *straightway glorified,* Ps. 16:10. [4.] All this in consideration of God's being glorified in and by his sufferings: *Seeing God is glorified in him,* and receives honour from his sufferings, God shall in like manner glorify him in himself, and give honour to him. Note, *first,* In the exaltation of Christ there was a regard had to his humiliation, and a reward given for it. *Because he humbled himself, therefore God highly exalted him.* If the Father be so great a gainer in his glory by the death of Christ, we may be sure that the Son shall be no loser in his. See the covenant between them, Isa. 53:12. *Secondly,* Those who mind the business of glorifying God no doubt shall have the happiness of being glorified with him.

2. Here is something that Christ instructs them in, concerning his sufferings, which was *awakening,* for as yet they were slow of heart to understand it (v. 33): *Little children, yet a little while I am with you,* etc. Two things Christ here suggests, to quicken his disciples to improve their present opportunities; two serious words: —

(1.) That his stay in this world, to be with them here, they would find to be very short. *Little children.* This compellation does not bespeak so much their weakness as his tenderness and compassion; he speaks to them with the affection of a father, now that he is about to leaven them, and to leave blessings with them. Know this, then, that *yet a little while I am with you.* Whether we understand this as referring to his death or his ascension it comes much to one; he had but a little time to spend with them, and therefore, [1.] Let them improve the advantage they now had. If they

had any good question to ask, if they would have any advice, instruction, or comfort, let them speak quickly; for *yet a little while I am with you.* We must make the best of the helps we have for our souls while we have them, because we shall not have them long; they will be taken from us, or we from them. [2.] Let them not doat upon his bodily presence, as if their happiness and comfort were bound up in that; no, they must think of living without it; not be always little children, but go alone, without their nurses. Ways and means are appointed but for a *little while,* and are not to be rested in, but pressed through to our rest, to which they have a reference.

(2.) That their following him to the other world, to be with him there, they would find to be very difficult. What he had said to the Jews (*ch.* 7:34) he saith to his disciples; for they have need to be quickened by the same considerations that are propounded for the convincing and awakening of sinners. Christ tells them here, [1.] That when he was gone they would feel the want of him; *You shall seek me,* that is "you shall wish you had me again with you." We are often taught the worth of mercies by the want of them. Though the presence of the Comforter yielded them real and effectual relief in straits and difficulties, yet it was not such a *sensible* satisfaction as his bodily presence would have been to those who had been used to it. But observe, Christ said to the Jews, You shall seek me and *not find me;* but to the disciples he only saith, *You shall seek me,* intimating that though they should not find his bodily presence any more than the Jews, yet they should find that which was tantamount, and should not seek in vain. When they sought his body in the sepulchre, though they did not find it, yet they sought to good purpose. [2.] That whither he went they *could not come,* which suggests to them high thoughts of him, who was going to an invisible inaccessible world, to dwell in that *light which none can approach unto;* and also low thoughts of themselves, and serious thoughts of their future state. Christ tells them that they could not follow him (as Joshua told the people that they could not serve the Lord) only to quicken them to so much the more diligence and care. They could not follow him to his cross, for they had not courage and resolution; it appeared that they could not when they all forsook him and fled. Nor could they follow him to his crown, for they had not a sufficiency of their own, nor were their work and warfare yet finished.

II. He discourses with them concerning the great duty of brotherly love (v. 34, 35): *You shall love one another.* Judas was now gone out, and had proved himself a false brother; but they must not therefore harbour such jealousies and suspicions one of another as would be the bane of love: though there was one Judas among them, yet they were not all Judases. Now that the enmity of the Jews against Christ and his followers was swelling to the height, and they must expect such treatment as their Master had, it concerned them by brotherly love to strengthen one another's hands. Three arguments for mutual love are here urged: —

1. The command of their Master (v. 34): *A new commandment I give unto you.* He not only commends it as amiable and pleasant, not only counsels it as excellent and profitable, but commands it, and makes it one of the fundamental laws of his kingdom; it goes a-breast with the command of believing in Christ, 1 Jn. 3:23; 1 Pt. 1:22. It is the command of our ruler, who has a right to give law to us; it is the command of our Redeemer, who gives us this law in order to the curing of our spiritual diseases and the preparing of us for our eternal bliss. It is *a new commandment;* that is, (1.) It is a renewed commandment; it was a commandment *from the beginning* (1 Jn. 2:7), as old as the law of nature, it was the second great commandment of the law of Moses; yet, because it is also one of the great commandments of the New Testament, of Christ the new Lawgiver, it is called a new commandment; it is like an old book in a new edition corrected and enlarged. This commandment has been so corrupted by the traditions of the Jewish church that when Christ revived it, and set it in a true light, it might well be called a *new commandment.* Laws of revenge and retaliation were so much in vogue, and self-love had so much the ascendant, that the law of brotherly love was forgotten as obsolete and out of date; so that as it came from Christ new, it was new to the people. (2.) It is an excellent command, as a *new song* is an excellent song, that has an uncommon gratefulness in it. (3.) It is an everlasting command; so strangely new as to be always so; as the *new covenant,* which shall never decay (Heb.

8:13); it shall be new to eternity, when faith and hope are antiquated. (4.) As Christ gives it, it is *new.* Before it was, *Thou shalt love thy neighbour;* now it is, You shall love *one another;* it is pressed in a more winning way when it is thus pressed as mutual duty owing to one another.

2. The example of their Saviour is another argument for brotherly love: *As I have loved you.* It is this that makes it a *new commandment* — that this rule and reason of *love (as I have loved you)* is perfectly new, and such as had been hidden from ages and generations. Understand this, (1.) Of all the instances of Christ's love to his disciples, which they had already experienced during the time he went in and out among them. He spoke kindly to them, concerned himself heartily for them, and for their welfare, instructed, counselled, and comforted them, prayed with them and for them, vindicated them when they were accused, took their part when they were run down, and publicly owned them to be dearer to him that his *mother, or sister, or brother.* He reproved them for what was amiss, and yet compassionately bore with their failings, excused them, made the best of them, and passed by many an oversight. Thus he *had* loved them, and just now washed their feet; and thus they *must* love one another, and love *to the end.* Or, (2.) It may be understood of the special instance of love to all his disciples which he was now about to give, in laying down his life for them. *Greater love hath no man than this, ch.* 15:13. Has he thus loved us all? Justly may he expect that we should be loving to one another. Not that we are capable of doing any thing of the *same nature* for each other (Ps. 49:7), but we must love one another in some respects after the *same manner;* we must set this before us as our copy, and take directions from it. Our love to one another must be free and ready, laborious and expensive, constant and persevering; it must be love *to the souls* one of another. We must also love one another from *this motive,* and upon this consideration — because Christ has loved us. See Rom. 15:1, 3; Eph. 5:2, 25; Phil. 2:1–5.

3. The reputation of their profession (*v.* 35): *By this shall all men know that you are my disciples, if you have love one to another.* Observe, We must have love, not only show love, but have it in the root and habit of it, and have it when there is not any present occasion to show it; have it *ready.* "Hereby it will appear that you are indeed my followers by following me in this." Note, Brotherly love is the badge of Christ's disciples. By this he knows them, by this they may know themselves (1 Jn. 2:14), and by this others may know them. This is the livery of his family, the distinguishing character of his disciples; this he would have them *noted for,* as that wherein they excelled all others — their loving one another. This was what their Master was famous for; all that ever heard of him have heard of his love, his great love; and therefore, if you see any people more affectionate one to another than what is common, say, "Certainly these are the followers of Christ, they have been with Jesus." Now by this it appears, (1.) That the heart of Christ was very much upon it, that his disciples *should love one another.* In this they must be *singular;* whereas the way of the world is to be *every one for himself,* they should be hearty for one another. He does not say, *By this shall men know* that you are my disciples — if you *work miracles,* for a worker of miracles is but a cypher without charity (1 Co. 13:1, 2); but *if you love one another* from a principle of self-denial and gratitude to Christ. This Christ would have to be the *proprium* of his religion, the principal note of the true church. (2.) That it is the true honour of Christ's disciples to excel in brotherly love. Nothing will be more effectual than this to recommend them to the esteem and respect of others. See what a powerful attractive it was, Acts 2:46, 47. Tertullian speaks of it as the glory of the primitive church that the Christians were known by their affection to one another. Their adversaries took notice of it, and said, *See how these Christians love one another,* Apol. cap. 39. (3.) That, if the followers of Christ do not love one another, they not only cast an unjust reproach upon their profession, but give just cause to suspect their own sincerity. *O Jesus! are these thy Christians,* these passionate, malicious, spiteful, ill-natured people? *Is this thy son's coat?* When our brethren stand in need of help from us, and we have an opportunity of being serviceable to them, when they differ in opinion and practice from us, or are any ways rivals with or provoking to us, and so we have an occasion to condescend and forgive, in such cases as this it will be known whether we have this badge of Christ's disciples.

Verses 36–38

In these verses we have,

I. Peter's curiosity, and the check given to that.

1. Peter's question was bold and blunt (*v.* 36): *Lord, whither goest thou?* referring to what Christ had said (*v.* 33), *Whither I go, you cannot come.* The practical instructions Christ had given them concerning brotherly love he overlooks, and asks no questions upon them, but fastens upon that concerning which Christ purposely kept them in the dark. Note, It is a common fault among us to be more inquisitive concerning things secret, which belong to God only, than concerning things *revealed, which belong to us and our children,* more desirous to have our curiosity gratified than our consciences directed, to know what is done in heaven than what we may do to get thither. It is easy to observe it in the converse of Christians, how soon a discourse of that which is plain and edifying is dropped, and no more said to it, the subject is exhausted; which in a matter of doubtful disputation runs into an endless strife of words.

2. Christ's answer was instructive. He did not gratify him with any particular account of the world he was going to, nor ever foretold his glories and joys so distinctly as he did his sufferings, but said what he had said before (*v.* 36): Let this suffice, *thou canst not follow me now, but shalt follow me hereafter,* (1.) We may understand it of his following him to the cross: "Thou hast not yet strength enough of faith and resolution to drink of my cup;" and it appeared so by his cowardice when Christ was suffering. For this reason, when Christ was seized, he provided for the safety of his disciples. *Let these go their way,* because they could not *follow him now.* Christ considers the frame of his disciples, and will not cut out for them that work and hardship which they are not as yet fit for; the day shall be as the strength is. Peter, though designed for martyrdom, cannot follow Christ now, not being come to his full growth, but he *shall follow* him *hereafter;* he shall be crucified at last, like his Master. Let him not think that because he escapes suffering now he shall never suffer. From our missing the cross once, we must not infer that we shall never meet it; we may be reserved for greater trials than we have yet known. (2.) We may understand it of his following him to the crown. Christ was now going to his glory, and Peter was very desirous to go with him: "No," saith Christ, *"thou canst not follow me now,* thou art not yet ripe for heaven, nor hast thou finished thy work on earth. The forerunner must *first enter to prepare a place* for thee, but *thou shalt follow me afterwards,* after thou hast fought the good fight, and at the time appointed." Note, Believers must not expect to be glorified as soon as they are effectually called, for there is a wilderness between the Red Sea and Canaan.

II. Peter's confidence, and the check given to that.

1. Peter makes a daring protestation of his constancy. He is not content to be left behind, but asks, *"Lord why cannot I follow thee now?* Dost thou question my sincerity and resolution? I promise thee, if there be occasion, *I will lay down my life for thy sake."* Some think Peter had a conceit, as the Jews had in a like case (*ch.* 7:35), that Christ was designing a journey or voyage into some remote country, and that he declared his resolution to go along with him wherever he went; but, having heard his Master so often speak of his own sufferings, surely he could not understand him any otherwise than of his going away by death; and he resolves as Thomas did that he will *go and die with him;* and better die with him than live without him. See here, (1.) What an affectionate love Peter had to our Lord Jesus: *"I will lay down my life for thy sake,* and I can do no more." I believe Peter spoke as he thought, and though he was inconsiderate he was not insincere, in his resolution. Note, Christ should be dearer to us than our own lives, which therefore, when we are called to it, we should be willing to lay down for his sake, Acts 20:24. (2.) How ill he took it to have it questioned, intimated in that expostulation, *"Lord, why cannot I follow thee now?* Dost thou suspect my fidelity to thee?" 1 Sa. 29:8. Note, It is with regret that true love hears its own sincerity arraigned, as *ch.* 21:17. Christ had indeed said that one of them was a devil, but he was discovered, and gone out, and therefore Peter thinks he may speak with the more assurance of his own sincerity; "Lord, I am resolved I will never leave thee, and therefore *why cannot I follow thee?"* We are apt to think that we can do any thing, and take it amiss to be told that this and the other we cannot do, whereas without Christ we can do nothing.

2. Christ gives him a surprising prediction of his inconstancy, *v.* 38. Jesus Christ knows us better than we know ourselves, and has many ways of discovering those to themselves whom he loves, and will hide pride from. (1.) He upbraids Peter with his confidence: *Wilt thou lay down thy life for my sake?* Me thinks, he seems to have said this with a smile: "Peter, thy promises are too large, too lavish to be relied on; thou dost not consider with what reluctancy and struggle a life is laid down, and what a hard task it is to die; not so soon done as said." Christ hereby puts Peter upon second thoughts, not that he might retract his resolution, or recede from it, but that he might insert into it that necessary proviso, "Lord, *thy grace enabling me,* I will lay down my life for thy sake." "Wilt thou undertake to die for me? What! thou that trembledst to walk upon the water to me? What! thou that, when sufferings were spoken of, criedst out, *Be it far from thee, Lord?* It was an easy thing to leave thy boats and nets to follow me, but not so easy to lay down thy life." His Master himself struggled when it came to his, and *the disciple is not greater than his Lord.* Note, It is good for us to shame ourselves out of our presumptuous confidence in ourselves. Shall a bruised reed set up for a pillar, or a sickly child undertake to be a champion? What a fool am I to talk so big. (2.) He plainly foretels his cowardice in the critical hour. To stop the mouth of his boasting, lest Peter should say it again, Yea Master, that I will, Christ solemnly asserts it with, *Verily, verily, I say unto thee, the cock shall not crow till thou hast denied me thrice.* He does not say as afterwards, *This night,* for it seems to have been two nights before the passover; but, "Shortly thou wilt have denied me thrice within the space of one night; nay, within so short a space as between the first and last crowing of the cock: *The cock shall not crow,* shall not have crowed his crowing out, till thou has again and again denied me, and that for fear of suffering." The crowing of the cock is mentioned, [1.] To intimate that the trial in which he would miscarry thus should be in the night, which was an improbable circumstance, but Christ's foretelling it was an instance of his infallible foresight. [2.] Because the crowing of the cock was to be the occasion of his repentance, which of itself would not have been if Christ had not put this into the prediction. Christ not only foresaw that Judas would betray him though he only in heart designed it, but he foresaw that Peter would deny him though he did not design it, but the contrary. He knows not only the wickedness of sinners, but the weakness of saints. Christ told Peter, *First,* That he would deny him, would renounce and abjure him: "Thou wilt not only not follow me still, but wilt be ashamed to own that ever thou didst follow me." *Secondly,* That he would do this not once only by a hasty slip of the tongue, but after he had paused would repeat it a second and third time; and it proved too true. We commonly give it as a reason why the prophecies of scripture are expressed darkly and figuratively, because, if they did *plainly* describe the event, the accomplishment would thereby either be defeated or necessitated by a fatality inconsistent with human liberty; and yet this plain and express prophecy of Peter's denying Christ did neither, nor did in the least make Christ accessary to Peter's sin. But we may well imagine what a mortification it was to Peter's confidence of his own courage to be told this, and to be told it in such a manner that he durst not contradict it, else he would have said as Hazael, *What! is thy servant a dog?* This could not but fill him with confusion. Note, The most secure are commonly the least safe; and those most shamefully betray their own weakness that most confidently presume upon their own strength, 1 Co. 10:12.

CHAPTER 14

This chapter is a continuation of Christ's discourse with his disciples after supper. When he had convicted and discarded Judas, he set himself to comfort the rest, who were full of sorrow upon what he had said of leaving them, and a great many good words and comfortable words he here speaks to them. The discourse in interlocutory; as Peter in the foregoing chapter, so Thomas, and Philip, and Jude, in this interposed their thoughts upon what he said, according to the liberty he was pleased to allow them. Free conferences are as instructive as solemn speeches, and more so. The general scope of this chapter is in the first verse; it is designed to keep trouble from their hearts; now in order to this they must believe: and let them consider, I. Heaven as their everlasting rest (*v.* 2, 3). II. Christ himself as their way (*v.* 4–11). III. The great power they shall be clothed with by the prevalency of their prayers (*v.* 12–14). IV. The coming of another comforter (*v.* 15–17). V. The fellowship and communion that should be between him and them after his departure (*v.* 18–24). VI. The instructions which the Holy Ghost should give them (*v.* 25, 26). VII. The peace Christ bequeathed to them (*v.* 27). VII. Christ's own cheerfulness in his departure (*v.* 28–31). And this which he said to them is designed for the comfort of all his faithful followers.

Verses 1–3

In these verses we have,

I. A general caution which Christ gives to his disciples against *trouble of heart* (v. 1): *Let not your heart be troubled.* They now began to be troubled, were entering into this temptation. Now here see,

1. How Christ took notice of it. Perhaps it was apparent in their looks; it was said (*ch.* 13:22), *They looked one upon another* with anxiety and concern, and Christ looked upon them all, and observed it; at least, it was intelligible to the Lord Jesus, who is acquainted with all our secret undiscovered sorrows, with the wound that bleeds inwardly; he knows not only how we are afflicted, but how we stand affected under our afflictions, and how near they lie to our hearts; he takes cognizance of all the trouble which his people are at any time in danger of being overwhelmed with; *he knows our souls in adversity.* Many things concurred to trouble the disciples now.

(1.) Christ had just told them of the unkindness he should receive from some of them, and this troubled them all. Peter, no doubt, looked very sorrowful upon what Christ said to him, and all the rest were sorry for him and for themselves too, not knowing whose turn it should be to be told next of some ill thing or other they should do. As to this, Christ comforts them; though a godly jealousy over ourselves is of great use to keep us humble and watchful, yet it must not prevail to the disquieting of our spirits and the damping of our holy joy.

(2.) He had just told them of his own departure from them, that he should not only go away, but go away in a cloud of sufferings. They must shortly hear him loaded with reproaches, and these will be *as a sword in their bones;* they must see him barbarously abused and put to death, and this also will be a sword piercing *through their own souls,* for they had loved him, and chosen him, and left all to follow him. When we now look upon Christ pierced, we cannot but *mourn and be in bitterness,* though we see the glorious issue and fruit of it; much more grievous must the sight be to them, who could then look no further. If Christ depart from them [1.] They will think themselves shamefully disappointed; for they looked that this had been he that should have delivered Israel, and should have set upon his kingdom in secular power and glory, and, in expectation of this, had lost all to follow him. Now, if he leave the world in the same circumstances of meanness and poverty in which he had lived, and worse, they are quite defeated. [2.] They will think themselves sadly deserted and exposed. They knew by experience what little presence of mind they had in difficult emergencies, that they could count upon nothing but being ruined and run down if they part with their Master. Now, in reference to all these, *Let not your heart be troubled.* Here are three words, upon any of which the emphasis may significantly be laid. *First,* Upon the word *troubled,* mē tarassesthō. Be not so troubled as to be put into a hurry and confusion, *like the troubled sea when* it cannot rest. He does not say, "Let not your hearts be sensible of the griefs, or sad because of them" but, "Be not ruffled and discomposed, be not cast down and disquieted," Ps. 42:5. *Secondly,* Upon the word *heart:* "Though the nation and city be troubled, though your little family and flock be troubled, yet *let not your heart be troubled.* Keep possession of your own souls when you can keep possession of nothing else." The heart is the main fort; whatever you do, keep trouble from this, keep this with *all diligence.* The spirit must *sustain the infirmity,* therefore, see that this be not *wounded. Thirdly,* Upon the word *your:* "You that are my disciples and followers, my redeemed, chosen, sanctified ones, however others are overwhelmed with the sorrows of this present time, be not you so, for you know better; let *the sinners in Zion* tremble, but let the *sons of Zion be joyful in their king."* Herein Christ's disciples should do *more than others,* should keep their minds quiet, when every thing else is unquiet.

2. The remedy he prescribes against this trouble of mind, which he saw ready to prevail over them; in general, *believe — pisteuete.* (1.) Some read it in both parts imperatively, *"Believe in God,* and his perfections and providence, *believe also in me,* and my mediation. Build with confidence upon the great acknowledged principles of natural religion: that there is a God, that he is most holy, wise, powerful, and good; that he is the governor of the world, and has the sovereign disposal of all events; and comfort yourselves likewise with the peculiar doctrines of that holy religion which I have taught you." But, (2.) We read the former as an acknowledg-

ment that they did believe in God, for which he commends them: "But, if you would effectually provide against a stormy day, *believe also in me."* Through Christ we are brought into covenant with God, and become interested in his favour and promise, which otherwise as sinners we must despair of, and the remembrance of God would have been our trouble; but, by believing in Christ as the Mediator between God and man, our belief in God becomes comfortable; and this is the will of God, that *all men should honour the Son as they honour the Father,* by believing in the Son as they believe in the Father. Those that rightly believe in God will believe in Jesus Christ, whom he has made known to them; and believing in God through Jesus Christ is an excellent means of keeping trouble from the heart. The joy of faith is the best remedy against the griefs of sense; it is a remedy with a promise annexed to it; *the just shall live by faith;* a remedy with a *probatum est* annexed to it. *I had fainted unless I had believed.*

II. Here is a particular direction to act faith upon the promise of eternal life, v. 2, 3. He had directed them to trust to God, and to trust in him; but what must they trust God and Christ for? Trust them for a happiness to come when this body and this world shall be no more, and for a happiness to last as long as the immortal soul and the eternal world shall last. Now this is proposed as a sovereign cordial under all the troubles of this present time, to which there is that in the happiness of heaven which is admirably adapted and accommodated. The saints have encouraged themselves with this in their greatest extremities, *That heaven would make amends for all.* Let us see how this is suggested here.

1. Believe and consider that really there is such a happiness: *In my Father's house there are many mansions; if it were not so, I would have told you,* v. 2.

(1.) See under what notion the happiness of heaven is here represented: as *mansions,* many mansions in Christ's Father's house. [1.] Heaven is a house, not a tent or tabernacle; it is *a house not made with hands, eternal in the heavens.* [2.] It is a Father's house: *my Father's house;* and his Father is our Father, to whom he was now ascending; so that in right of their elder brother all true believers shall be welcome to that happiness as to their home. It is his house who is King of kings and Lord of lords, dwells in light, and inhabits eternity. [3.] There are *mansions* there; that is, *First,* Distinct dwellings, an apartment for each. Perhaps there is an allusion to the priests' chambers that were about the temple. In heaven there are accommodations for particular saints; though all shall be swallowed up in God, yet our individuality shall not be lost there; every Israelite had his lot in Canaan, and every elder *a seat,* Rev. 4:4. *Secondly,* Durable dwellings. *Monai,* from *mneiō, maneo, abiding places.* The house itself is lasting; our estate in it is not for a term of years, but a perpetuity. Here we are as in an inn; in heaven we shall gain a settlement. The disciples had quitted their houses to attend Christ, who had not where to lay his head, but the mansions in heaven will make them amends. [4.] There are *many* mansions, for there are many sons to be brought to glory, and Christ exactly knows their number, nor will be straitened for room by the coming of more company than he expects. He had told Peter that he should follow him (*ch.* 13:36), but let not the rest be discouraged, in heaven there are mansions for them *all. Rehoboth,* Gen. 26:22.

(2.) See what assurance we have of the reality of the happiness itself, and the sincerity of the proposal of it to us: *"If it were not so, I would have told you.* If you had deceived yourselves, when you quitted your livelihoods, and ventured your lives for me, in prospect of a happiness future and unseen, I would soon have undeceived you." The assurance is built, [1.] Upon the veracity of his word. It is implied, "If there were not such a happiness, valuable and attainable, I would not have told you that there was." [2.] Upon the sincerity of his affection to them. As he is true, and would not impose upon them himself, so he is kind, and would not suffer them to be imposed upon. If either there were no such mansions, or none designed for them, who had left all to follow him, he would have given them timely notice of the mistake, that they might have made an honourable retreat to the world again, and have made the best they could of it. Note, Christ's good-will to us is a great encouragement to our hope in him. He loves us too well, and means us too well, to disappoint the expectations of his own raising, or to leave those to be of all men most miserable who have been of him most observant.

2. Believe and consider that the design of Christ's going away was to prepare a place in heaven for his disciples. "You are grieved to think of my going away, whereas I go on your errand, *as the forerunner; I am to enter for you."* He went to prepare a place for us; that is, (1.) To take possession for us, as our advocate or attorney, and so to secure our title as indefeasible. Livery of seisin was given to Christ, for the use and behoof of all that should believe on him. (2.) To make provision for us as our friend and father. The happiness of heaven, though prepared *before the foundation of the world,* yet must be further fitted up for man in his fallen state. It consisting much in the presence of Christ there, it was therefore necessary that he should *go before,* to enter into that glory which his disciples were to share in. Heaven would be an *unready* place for a Christian if Christ were not there. He went to prepare a table for them, to prepare thrones for them, Lu. 22:30. Thus Christ declares the fitness of heaven's happiness for the saints, for whom it is prepared.

3. Believe and consider that *therefore* he would certainly come again in due time, to fetch them to that blessed place which he was now going to possess for himself and prepare for them (v. 3): *"If I go and prepare a place for you,* if this be the errand of my journey, you may be sure, when every thing is ready, *I will come again, and receive you to myself,* so that you shall follow me hereafter, *that where I am there you may be also."* Now these are comfortable words indeed. (1.) That Jesus Christ will come again; *erchomai — I do come,* intimating the certainty of it, that he will come and that he is daily coming. We say, We are coming, when we are busy in preparing for our coming, and so he is; all he does has a reference and tendency to his second coming. Note, The belief of Christ's second coming, of which he has given us the assurance, is an excellent preservative against trouble of heart, Phil. 4:5; James 5:8. (2.) That he will come again to receive all his faithful followers to himself. He sends for them privately at death, and gathers them one by one; but they are to make their public entry in solemn state all together at the last day, and then Christ himself will come to receive them, to conduct them in the abundance of his grace, and to welcome them in the abundance of his love. He will hereby testify the utmost respect and endearment imaginable. The coming of Christ is in order to our *gathering together unto him,* 2 Th. 2:1. (3.) *That where he is there they shall be also.* This intimates, what many other scriptures declare, that the quintessence of heaven's happiness is being with Christ *there, ch.* 17:24; Phil. 1:23; 1 Th. 4:17. Christ speaks of his being there as now present, *that where I am;* where I am to be shortly, where I am to be eternally; there you shall be shortly, there you shall be eternally: not only *there,* in the same place; but *here,* in the same state: not only spectators of his glory, as the three disciples on the mount, but sharers in it. (4.) That this may be inferred from his *going to prepare a place* for us, for his preparations shall not be in vain. He will not build and furnish lodgings, and let them stand empty. He will be the finisher of that of which he is the author. If he has prepared the place for us, he will prepare us for it, and in due time put us in possession of it. As the resurrection of Christ is the assurance of our resurrection, so his ascension, victory, and glory, are an assurance of ours.

Verses 4–11

Christ, having set the happiness of heaven before them as the end, here shows them himself as the way to it, and tells them that they were better acquainted both with the end they were to aim at and with the way they were to walk in than they thought they were: *You know,* that is, 1. "You may know; it is none of the *secret things* which belong not to you, but one of the *things revealed;* you *need not ascend into heaven, nor go down into the deep,* for *the word is nigh you* (Rom. 10:6–8), level to you." 2. "You do know; you know that which is the home and which is the way, though perhaps not as the home and as the way. You have been told it, and cannot but know, if you would recollect and consider it." Note, Jesus Christ is willing to make the best of his people's knowledge, though they are weak and defective in it. He knows the good that is in them better than they do themselves, and is certain that they have that knowledge, and faith, and love, of which they themselves are not sensible, or not certain.

This word of Christ gave occasion to two of his disciples to address themselves to him, and he answers them both.

I. Thomas enquired concerning the way (v. 5), without any apology for contradicting his Master.

1. He said, "*Lord, we know not whither thou goest,* to what place or what state, *and how can we know the way* in which we must follow thee? We can neither guess at it, nor enquire it out, but must still be at a loss." Christ's testimony concerning their knowledge made them more sensible of their ignorance, and more inquisitive after further light. Thomas here shows more modesty than Peter, who thought he could follow Christ now. Peter was the more solicitous to know *whither Christ went.* Thomas here, though he complains that he did not know this, yet seems more solicitous to know *the way.* Now, (1.) His confession of his ignorance was commendable enough. If good men be in the dark, and know but in part, yet they are willing to own their defects. But, (2.) The cause of his ignorance was culpable. They knew not whither Christ went, because they dreamed of a temporal kingdom in external pomp and power, and doted upon this, notwithstanding what he had said again and again to the contrary. Hence it was that, when Christ spoke of going away and their following him, their fancy ran upon his going to some remarkable city or other, Bethlehem, or Nazareth, or Capernaum, or some of the cities of the Gentiles, as David to Hebron, there to be anointed king, and *to restore the kingdom to Israel;* and which way this place lay, where these castles in the air were to be built, east, west, north, or south, they could not tell, and therefore knew not the way. Thus still we think ourselves more in the dark than we need be concerning the future state of the church, because we expect its worldly prosperity, whereas it is spiritual advancement that the promise points at. Had Thomas understood, as he might have done, that Christ was going to the invisible world, the world of spirits, to which spiritual things only have a reference, he would not have said, *Lord, we do not know the way.*

II. Now to this complaint of their ignorance, which included a desire to be taught, Christ gives a full answer, *v.* 6, 7. Thomas had enquired both whither he went and what was the way, and Christ answers both these enquiries and makes good what he had said, that they would have needed no answer if they had understood themselves aright; for they knew him, and he was the way; they knew the Father, and he was the end; and therefore, *whither I go you know, and the way you know.* Believe in God as the end, and in me as the way (*v.* 1), and you do all you should do.

(1.) He speaks of himself as the way, *v.* 6. Dost thou *not know the way? I am the way,* and I only, for *no man comes to the Father but by me.* Great things Christ here saith of himself, showing us,

[1.] The nature of his mediation: He is *the way, the truth, and the life.*

First, Let us consider these first distinctly. 1. Christ is *the way, the highway* spoken of, Isa. 35:8. Christ was his own way, for by *his own blood he entered into the holy place* (Heb. 9:12), and he is our way, for we enter by him. By his doctrine and example he teaches us our duty, by his merit and intercession he procures our happiness, and so he is the way. In him God and man meet, and are brought together. We could not get to the tree of life in the way of innocency; but Christ is another way to it. By Christ, as the way an intercourse is settled and kept up between heaven and earth; the angels of God ascend and descend; our prayers go to God, and his blessings come to us by him; this is *the way that leads to rest, the good old way.* The disciples followed him, and Christ tells them that they followed the road, and, while they continued following him, they would never be out of their way. 2. He is *the truth.* (1.) As truth is opposed to figure and shadow. Christ is the substance of all the Old-Testament types, which are therefore said to be *figures of the true,* Heb. 9:24. Christ is *the true manna* (ch. 6:32), *the true tabernacle,* Heb. 8:2. (2.) As truth is opposed to falsehood and error; the doctrine of Christ is true doctrine. When we enquire for truth, we need learn no more than *the truth as it is in Jesus.* (3.) As truth is opposed to fallacy and deceit; he is true to all that trust in him, as true as truth itself, 2 Co. 1:20. 3. He is *the life;* for we are *alive unto God* only in and *through Jesus Christ,* Rom. 6:11. Christ formed in us is that to our souls which our souls are to our bodies. Christ is *the resurrection and the life.*

Secondly, Let us consider these jointly, and with reference to each other. Christ is *the way, the truth, and the life; that is,* 1. He is the beginning, the middle, and the end. In him we must set out, go on, and finish. As *the truth,* he is the guide of our way; as *the life,* he is the end of it. 2. He is the *true and living way* (Heb. 10:20); there are *truth* and *life* in the way, as well as at the end of it. 3. He is *the true way to*

life, the only true way; other ways may seem right, but the end of them is *the way of death.*

[2.] The necessity of his mediation: *No man cometh to the Father but by me.* Fallen man must come to God as a Judge, but cannot come to him as a Father, otherwise than by Christ as Mediator. We cannot perform the duty of coming to God, by repentance and the acts of worship, without the Spirit and grace of Christ, nor obtain the happiness of coming to God as our Father without his merit and righteousness; he is the *high priest of our profession,* our advocate.

(2.) He speaks of his Father as the end (*v.* 7): *"If you had known me* aright, *you would have known my Father also; and henceforth,* by the glory you have seen in me and the doctrine you have heard from me, *you know him and have seen him."* Here is, [1.] A tacit rebuke to them for their dulness and carelessness in not acquainting themselves with Jesus Christ, though they had been his constant followers and associates: *If you had known me — .* They knew him, and yet did not know him so well as they might and should have known him. They knew him to be the Christ, but did not follow on to know God in him. Christ had said to the Jews (ch. 8:19): *If you had known me, you would have known my Father also;* and here the same to his disciples; for it is hard to say which is more strange, the wilful ignorance of those that are enemies to the light, or the defects and mistakes of *the children of light,* that have had such opportunities of knowledge. If they had known Christ aright, they would have known that his kingdom is spiritual, and *not of this world;* that *he came down from heaven,* and therefore must return *to heaven;* and then they would have known his Father also, would have known whither he designed to go, when he said, *I go to the Father,* to a glory in the other world, not in this. If we knew Christianity better, we should better know natural religion. [2.] A favourable intimation that he was well satisfied concerning their sincerity, notwithstanding the weakness of their understanding: *"And henceforth,* from my giving you this hint, which will serve as a key to all the instructions I have given you hitherto, let me tell you, *you know him, and have seen him,* inasmuch as you know me, and have seen me;" for in the face of Christ we see the glory of God, as we see a father in his son that resembles him. Christ tells his disciples that they were not so ignorant as they seemed to be; for, though *little children,* yet they had known the Father, 1 Jn. 2:13. Note, Many of the disciples of Christ have more knowledge and more grace than they think they have, and Christ takes notice of, and is well pleased with, that good in them which they themselves are not aware of; for those that know God do not all at once know that they know him, 1 Jn. 2:3.

II. Philip enquired concerning the Father (*v.* 8), and Christ answered him, *v.* 9–11, where observe,

1. Philip's request for some extraordinary discovery of the Father. He was not so forward to speak as some others of them were, and yet, from an earnest desire of further light, he cries out, *Show us the Father.* Philip listened to what Christ said to Thomas, and fastened upon the last words, *You have seen him.* "Nay," says Philip, "that is what we want, that is what we would have: *Show us the Father and it sufficeth us."* (1.) This supposes an earnest desire of acquaintance with God as a Father. The petition is, *"Show us the Father;* give us to know him in that relation to us;" and this he begs, not for himself only, but for the rest of the disciples. The plea is, *It sufficeth us.* He not only professes it himself, but will pass his word for his fellow-disciples. Grant us but one sight of the Father, and we have enough. Jansenius saith, "Though Philip did not mean it, yet the Holy Ghost, by his mouth, designed here to teach us that the satisfaction and happiness of a soul consist in the vision and fruition of God," Ps. 16:11; 17:15. In the knowledge of God the understanding rests, and is at the summit of its ambition; in the knowledge of God as our Father the soul is satisfied; a sight of the Father is a heaven upon earth, fills us *with joy unspeakable.* (2.) As Philip speaks it here, it intimates that he was not satisfied with such a discovery of the Father as Christ thought fit to give them, but he would prescribe to him, and press upon him, something further and no less than some visible appearance of *the glory of God,* like that to Moses (Ex. 33:22), and to *the elders of Israel,* Ex. 24:9–11. "Let us see the Father with our bodily eyes, as we see thee, *and it sufficeth us;* we will trouble thee with no more questions, *Whither goest thou?"* And so it manifests not only the weakness of his faith, but his ignorance of the gospel way of manifesting *the Father,* which

is spiritual, and not sensible. Such a sight of God, he thinks, would *suffice* them, and yet those who did thus see him were not *sufficed,* but soon *corrupted themselves, and made a graven image.* Christ's institutions have provided better for the confirmation of our faith than our own inventions would.

2. Christ's reply, referring him to the discoveries already made of the Father, *v.* 9–11.

(1.) He refers him to what he had seen, *v.* 9. He upbraids him with his ignorance and inadvertency: *"Have I been so long time with you,* now above three years intimately conversant with you, *and yet hast thou not known me, Philip?* Now, *he that hath seen me hath seen the Father; and how sayest thou then, Show us the Father?* Wilt thou ask for that which thou hast already?" Now here,

[1.] He reproves him for two things: *First,* For not improving his acquaintance with Christ, as he might have done, to a clear and distinct knowledge of him: *"Hast thou not known me, Philip,* whom thou hast followed so long, and conversed with so much?" Philip, the first day he came to him, declared that he knew him to be the Messiah (ch. 1:45), and yet to this day did *not know the Father* in him. Many that have good knowledge in the scripture and divine things fall short of the attainments justly expected from them, for want of compounding the ideas they have, and going on to perfection. Many know Christ, who yet do not know what they might know of him, nor see what they should see in him. That which aggravated Philip's dulness was that he had so long an opportunity of improvement: *I have been so long time with thee.* Note, The longer we enjoy the means of knowledge and grace, the more inexcusable we are if we be found defective in grace and knowledge. Christ expects that our proficiency should be in some measure according to our standing, that we should not be always babes. Let us thus reason with ourselves: "Have I been so long a hearer of sermons, a student in the scripture, a scholar in the school of Christ, and yet so weak in *the knowledge of Christ,* and so unskilful in *the word of righteousness?"* *Secondly,* He reproves him for his infirmity in the prayer made, *Show us the Father.* Note, Herein appears much of the weakness of Christ's disciples that they *know not what to pray for as they ought* (Rom. 8:26), but often *ask amiss* (Jam. 4:3), for that which either is not promised or is already bestowed in the sense of the promise, as here.

[2.] He instructs him, and gives him a maxim which not only in general magnifies Christ and leads us to the knowledge of God in him, but justifies what Christ had said (*v.* 7): *You know the Father, and have seen him;* and answered what Philip had asked, *Show us the Father.* Why, saith Christ, the difficulty is soon over, for *he that hath seen me hath seen the Father. First,* All that saw *Christ in the flesh* might *have seen the Father* in him, if Satan had not *blinded their minds,* and kept them from a sight of Christ, as *the image of God,* 2 Co. 4:4. *Secondly,* All that saw Christ by faith did *see the Father* in him, though they were not suddenly aware that they did so. In the light of Christ's doctrine they saw God as the *father of lights;* in the miracles they saw God *as the God of power, the finger of God.* The holiness of God shone in the spotless purity of Christ's life, and his grace in all the acts of grace he did.

(2.) He refers him to what he had reason to believe (*v.* 10, 11): *"Believest thou not that I am in the Father, and the Father in me,* and therefore that in *seeing me* thou hast *seen the Father?* Hast thou not believed this? If not, take my word for it, and believe it now."

[1.] See here what it is which we are to believe: *That I am in the Father, and the Father in me;* that is, as he had said (ch. 10:30), *I and my Father are one.* He speaks of the Father and himself as two persons, and yet so one as never any two were or can be. In knowing Christ as *God of God, light of light, very God of very God, begotten, not made,* and as *being of one substance with the Father, by whom all things were made,* we know the Father; and in seeing him thus we see the Father. In Christ we behold more of *the glory of God* than Moses did at Mount Horeb.

[2.] See here what inducements we have to believe this; and they are two: — We must believe it, *First,* For his word's sake: *The words that I speak to you, I speak not of myself.* See ch. 7:16, *My doctrine is not mine.* What he said seemed to them careless as *the word of man,* speaking his own thought at his own pleasure; but really it was the wisdom of God that indited it and the will of God that enforced it. *He spoke not of himself* only, but the mind of God according to the eternal counsels. *Secondly,* For his works' sake: *The Father that dwelleth in me, he doeth them;* and therefore *believe me for their sake.* Observe, 1. The Father is said to *dwell* in him *ho en emoi menōn — he abideth in me,* by the inseparable union of the divine and human nature: never had God such a temple to dwell in on earth as *the body of the Lord Jesus, ch.* 2:21. Here was the true Shechinah, of which that in the tabernacle was but a type. *The fulness of the Godhead dwelt in him bodily,* Col. 2:9. The Father so dwells in Christ that in him he may *be found,* as a man where he dwells. *Seek ye the Lord, seek* him in Christ, and *he will be found,* for in him he dwells. 2. *He doeth the works.* Many words of power, and works of mercy, Christ did, and the Father did them in him; and the work of redemption in general was God's own work. 3. We are bound to believe this, *for the very works' sake.* As we are to believe the being and perfections of God for the sake of the works of creation, which declare his glory; so we are to believe the revelation of God to man in Jesus Christ for the sake of the works of the Redeemer, those mighty works which, by showing forth themselves (Mt. 14:2), *Show forth him, and God in him.* Note, Christ's miracles are proofs of his divine mission, not only for the conviction of infidels, but for the confirmation of the faith of his own disciples, *ch.* 2:11; 5:36; 10:37.

Verses 12–14

The disciples, as they were full of grief to think of parting with their Master, so they were full of care what would become of themselves when he was gone; while he was with them, he was a support to them, kept them in countenance, kept them in heart; but, if he leave them, they will be *as sheep having no shepherd,* an easy prey to those who seek to run them down. Now, to silence these fears, Christ here assures them that they should be clothed with powers sufficient to bear them out. As Christ has *all power,* they, in his name, should have great *power, both in heaven and in earth.*

I. Great power on earth (*v.* 12): *He that believeth on me* (as I know you do), *the works that I do shall he do also.* This does not weaken the argument Christ had taken from his works, to prove himself one with the Father (that others should do as *great works*), but rather strengthens it; for the miracles which the apostles wrought were *wrought in his name,* and *by faith in him;* and this magnifies his power more than any thing, that he not only wrought miracles himself, but gave power to others to do so too.

1. Two things he assures them of: —

(1.) That they should be enabled to do such works as he had done, and that they should have a more ample power for the doing of them than they had had when he first sent them forth, Mt. 10:8. Did Christ *heal the sick, cleanse the leper, raise the dead?* So should they. Did he convince and convert sinners, and draw multitudes to him? So should they. Though he should depart, the work should not cease, nor fall to the ground, but should be carried on as vigorously and successfully as ever; and it is still in the doing.

(2.) That they should do *greater works than these.* [1.] In the kingdom of nature they should work greater miracles. No miracle is little, but some to our apprehension seem greater than others. Christ had healed with the hem of his garment, but Peter with his shadow (Acts 5:15), Paul by the handkerchief that had touched him, Acts 19:12. Christ wrought miracles for two or three years in one country, but his followers wrought miracles in his name for many ages in divers countries. *You shall do greater works,* if there be occasion, for the glory of God. *The prayer of faith,* if at any time it had been necessary, would have *removed mountains.* [2.] In the kingdom of grace. They should obtain greater victories by the gospel than had been obtained while Christ was upon earth. The truth is, the captivating of so great a part of the world to Christ, under such outward disadvantages, was the miracle of all. I think this refers especially to *the gift of tongues;* this was the immediate effect of the *pouring out of the Spirit,* which was a constant miracle upon the mind, in which words are framed, and which was made to serve so glorious an intention as that of spreading the gospel to all nations *in their own language.* This was a greater *sign to them that believed not* (1 Co. 14:22), and more powerful for their conviction, than any other miracle whatever.

2. The reason Christ gives for this is, *Because I go unto my Father,* (1.) "*Because I go,* it will be requisite that you should have such a power, lest the work suffer damage by my absence." (2.) "*Because I go to the Father,* I shall be in

a capacity to furnish you with such a power, for *I go to the Father, to send the Comforter,* from whom *you shall receive power,*" Acts 1:8. The wonderful works which they did in Christ's name were part of the glories of his exalted state, *when he ascended on high,* Eph. 4:8.

II. Great *power in heaven: "Whatsoever you shall ask, that will I do* (*v.* 13, 14), as Israel, who was a prince with God. Therefore you shall do such mighty works, because you have such an interest in me, and I in *my Father.*" Observe,

1. In what way they were to keep up communion with him, and derive power from him, when he was gone to the Father — by prayer. When dear friends are to be removed to a distance from each other, they provide for the settling of a correspondence; thus, when Christ was going to his Father, he tells his disciples how they might write to him upon every occasion, and send their epistles by a safe and ready way of conveyance, without danger of miscarrying, or lying by the way: "Let me hear from you by prayer, *the prayer of faith,* and you shall hear from me by the Spirit." This was the old way of intercourse with Heaven, ever since *men began to call upon the name of the Lord;* but Christ by his death has laid it more open, and it is still open to us. Here is, (1.) Humility prescribed: *You shall ask.* Though they had quitted all for Christ, they could demand nothing of him as a debt, but must be humble supplicants, beg or starve, beg or perish. (2.) Liberty allowed: "Ask any thing, any thing that is good and proper for you; any thing, provided you know what you ask, you may ask; you may ask for assistance in your work, for a mouth and wisdom, for preservation out of the hands of your enemies, for power to work miracles when there is occasion, for the success of the ministry in the conversion of souls; ask to be informed, directed, vindicated." Occasions vary, but they shall be welcome to the throne of grace upon every occasion.

2. In what name they were to present their petitions: *Ask in my name.* To ask in Christ's name is, (1.) To plead his merit and intercession, and to depend upon that plea. The Old-Testament saints had an eye to this when they prayed *for the Lord's sake* (Dan. 9:17), and *for the sake of the anointed* (Ps. 84:9), but Christ's mediation is brought to a clearer light by the gospel, and so we are enabled more expressly to *ask in his name.* When Christ dictated the Lord's prayer, this was not inserted, because they did not then so fully understand this matter as they did afterwards, when the Spirit was poured out. If we ask in *our own name,* we cannot expect to speed, for, being strangers, we have *no name* in heaven; being sinners, we have an *ill name* there; but Christ's is a good name, well known in heaven, and very precious. (2.) It is to aim at his glory and to seek this as our highest end in all our prayers.

3. What success they should have in their prayers: "What you ask, *that will I do,*" *v.* 13. And again (*v.* 14), "*I will do it.* You may be sure I will: not only it shall be done, I will see it done, or give orders for the doing of it, but *I will do it;*" for he has not only the interest of an intercessor, but the power of a sovereign prince, who *sits at the right hand of God,* the hand of action, and has the doing of all in the kingdom of God. By faith in his name we may have what we will for the asking.

4. For what reason their prayers should speed so well: *That the Father may be glorified in the Son.* That is, (1.) This they ought to aim at, and have their eye upon, in asking. In this all our desires and prayers should meet as in their centre; to this they must all be directed, that God in Christ may be honoured by our services, and in our salvation. *Hallowed be thy name* is an answered prayer, and is put first, because, if the heart be sincere in this, it does in a manner *consecrate* all the other petitions. (2.) This Christ will aim at in granting, and for the sake of this will do what they ask, that hereby the glory of the Father in the Son may be manifested. The wisdom, power, and goodness of God were magnified in the Redeemer when by a power derived from him, and exerted in his name and for his service, his apostles and ministers were enabled to do such great things, both in the proofs of their doctrine and in the successes of it.

Verses 15–17

Christ not only proposes such things to them as were the matter of their comfort, but here promises to send the Spirit, whose office it should be to be their Comforter, to *impress* these things upon them.

I. He premises to this a memento of duty (*v.* 15): *If you love me, keep my commandments.* Keeping the command-

ments of Christ is here put for the practice of godliness in general, and for the faithful and diligent discharge of their office as apostles in particular. Now observe, 1. When Christ is comforting them, he bids them *keep his commandments;* for we must not expect comfort but in the way of duty. The same word (*parakaleō*) signifies both to exhort and to comfort. 2. When they were in care what they should do, now that their Master was leaving them, and what would become of them now, he bids them *keep his commandments,* and then nothing could come amiss to them. In difficult times our care concerning the events of the day should be swallowed up in a care concerning the duty of the day. 3. When they were showing their love to Christ by their grieving to think of his departure, and the sorrow which filled their hearts upon the foresight of that, he bids them, if they would show their love to him, do it, not by these weak and feminine passions, but by their conscientious care to perform their trust, and by a universal obedience to his commands; this is better than sacrifice, better than tears. *Lovest thou me? Feed my lambs.* 4. When Christ has given them precious promises, of the answer of their prayers and the coming of the Comforter, he lays down this as a limitation of the promises, "Provided you keep my commandments, from a principle of love to me." Christ will not be an advocate for any but those that will be ruled and advised by him as their counsel. Follow the conduct of the Spirit, and you shall have the comfort of the Spirit.

II. He promises this great and unspeakable blessing to them, *v.* 16, 17.

1. It is promised that they shall have *another comforter.* This is the great New-Testament promise (Acts 1:4), as that of the Messiah was of the Old Testament; a promise adapted to the present distress of the disciples, who were in sorrow, and needed a comforter. Observe here,

(1.) The blessing promised: *allon paraklēton.* The word is used only here in these discourses of Christ's, and 1 Jn. 2:1, where we translate it an *advocate.* The Rhemists, and Dr. Hammond, are for retaining the *Greek* word *Paraclete;* we read, Acts 9:31, of the *paraklēsis tou hagiou pneumatos,* the *comfort of the Holy Ghost,* including his whole office as a paraclete. [1.] You shall have another *advocate.* The office of the Spirit was to be Christ's advocate with them and others, to plead his cause, and take care of his concerns, on earth; to be *vicarius Christi — Christ's Vicar,* as one of the ancients call him; and to be their advocate with their opposers. When Christ was with them he spoke for them as there was occasion; but now that he is leaving them they shall not be run down, the Spirit of the Father shall speak in them, Mt. 10:19, 20. And the cause cannot miscarry that is pleaded by such an advocate. [2.] You shall have another *master* or *teacher,* another *exhorter.* While they had Christ with them he excited and exhorted them to their duty; but now that he is going he leaves one with them that shall do this as effectually, though silently. Jansenius thinks the most proper word to render it by is a *patron,* one that shall both instruct and protect you. [3.] Another *comforter.* Christ was expected as the consolation of Israel. One of the names of the Messiah among the Jews was *Menahem — the Comforter.* The Targum calls the days of the Messiah *the years of consolation.* Christ comforted his disciples when he was with them, and now that he was leaving them in their greatest need he promises them *another.*

(2.) The giver of this blessing: *The Father* shall give him, *my Father* and *your Father;* it includes both. The same that gave the Son to be our Saviour will give his Spirit to be our comforter, pursuant to the same design. The Son is said to send the Comforter (*ch.* 15:26), but the Father is the prime agent.

(3.) How this blessing is procured — by the intercession of the Lord Jesus: *I will pray the Father.* He said (*v.* 14) *I will do it;* here he saith, *I will pray for it,* to show not only that he is both God and man, but that he is both king and priest. As priest he is ordained for men to make intercession, as king he is authorized by the Father to execute judgment. When Christ saith, *I will pray the Father,* it does not suppose that the Father is unwilling, or must be importuned to it, but only that the gift of the Spirit is a fruit of Christ's mediation, purchased by his merit, and taken out by his intercession.

(4.) The continuance of this blessing: *That he may abide with you for ever.* That is, [1.] "*With you,* as long as you live. You shall never know the want of a comforter, nor lament his departure, as you are now lamenting mine." Note, It should support us under the loss of those comforts which were designed us for a time that there are everlasting consolations provided for us. It was not expedient that Christ should be with them for ever, for they who were designed for public service, must not always live a college-life; they must disperse, and therefore a comforter that would be with them all, in all places alike, wheresoever dispersed and howsoever distressed, was alone fit to be with them for ever. [2.] "With your successors, when you are gone, to the end of time; your successors in Christianity, in the ministry." [3.] If we take *for ever* in its utmost extent, the promise will be accomplished in those consolations of God which will be the eternal joy of all the saints, *pleasures for ever.*

2. This comforter is the *Spirit of truth, whom you know, v.* 16, 17. They might think it impossible to have a comforter equivalent to him who is the Son of God: "Yea," saith Christ, "you shall have the Spirit of God, who is equal in power and glory with the Son."

(1.) The comforter promised is *the Spirit,* one who should do his work in a spiritual way and manner, inwardly and invisibly, by working on men's spirits.

(2.) "He is the *Spirit of truth."* He will be true to you, and to his undertaking for you, which he will perform to the utmost. He will *teach you the truth,* will enlighten your minds with the knowledge of it, will strengthen and confirm your belief of it, and will increase your love to it. The Gentiles by their idolatries, and the Jews by their traditions, were led into gross errors and mistakes; but the Spirit of truth shall not only *lead you into all truth,* but others by your ministry. Christ is the truth, and he is the Spirit of Christ, the Spirit that he was anointed with.

(3.) He is one *whom the world cannot receive;* but *you know him. Therefore he abideth with you.* [1.] The disciples of Christ are here distinguished from the world, for they are chosen and called out of the world that lies in wickedness; they are the children and heirs of another world, not of this. [2.] It is the misery of those that are invincibly devoted to the world that they *cannot receive* the Spirit of truth. The spirit *of the world* and *of God* are spoken of as directly contrary the one to the other (1 Co. 2:12); for where the spirit of the world has the ascendant, the Spirit of God is excluded. Even the *princes of this world,* though, as princes, they had advantages of knowledge, yet, as princes of this world, they laboured under invincible prejudices, so that they knew not *the things of the Spirit of God,* 1 Co. 2:8. [3.] Therefore men *cannot receive the Spirit of truth* because they *see him not, neither know him.* The comforts of the Spirit are *foolishness to them,* as much as ever the cross of Christ was, and the great things of the gospel, like those of the law, are counted as a strange thing. These are judgments far above out of their sight. Speak to the children of this world of the operations of the Spirit, and you are as a barbarian to them. [4.] The best knowledge of the Spirit of truth is that which is got by experience: *You know him, for he dwelleth with you.* Christ had dwelt with them, and by their acquaintance with him they could not but know *the Spirit of truth.* They had themselves been endued with the Spirit in some measure. What enabled them to leave all to follow Christ, and to continue with him in his temptations? What enabled them to preach the gospel, and work miracles, but the Spirit dwelling in them? The experiences of the saints are the explications of the promises; paradoxes to others are axioms to them. [5.] Those that have an experimental acquaintance with the Spirit have a comfortable assurance of his continuance: He *dwelleth with you, and shall be in you,* for the blessed Spirit doth not use to shift his lodging. Those that know him know how to value him, invite him and bid him welcome; and therefore he shall be in them, as the light in the air, as the sap in the tree, as the soul in the body. Their communion with him shall be intimate, and their union with him inseparable. [6.] The gift of the Holy Ghost is a peculiar gift, bestowed upon the disciples of Christ in a distinguishing way — them, and not the world; it is to them *hidden manna,* and the *white stone.* No comforts comparable to those which make no show, make no noise. This is the favour God bears to his chosen; it is the *heritage of those that fear his name.*

Verses 18–24

When friends are parting, it is a common request they make to each other, "Pray let us hear from you as often as you can:" this Christ engaged to his disciples, that out of sight they should not be out of mind.

I. He promises that he would continue his care of them (*v.* 18): *"I will not leave you orphans,* or *fatherless;* for, though I leave you, yet I leave you this comfort, *I will come to you."* His departure from them was that which grieved them; but it was not so bad as they apprehended, for it was neither total nor final. 1. Not total. "Though I leave you without my bodily presence, yet I do not leave you without comfort." Though children, and left *little,* yet they had received the adoption of sons, and his Father would be their Father, with whom those who otherwise would be fatherless find mercy. Note, The case of true believers, though sometimes it may be sorrowful, is never comfortless, because they are never orphans: for God is their Father, who is an *everlasting Father.* 2. Not final: *I will come to you, erchomai — I do come;* that is, (1.) "I will come speedily to you at my resurrection, I will not be long away, but will be with you again in a little time." He had often said, *The third day I will rise again.* (2.) "I will be coming daily to you in my Spirit;" in the tokens of his love, and visits of his grace, he is still coming. (3.) "I will come certainly at the end of time; surely I will come quickly to introduce you into the joy of your Lord." Note, The consideration of Christ's coming to us saves us from being comfortless in his removals from us; for, if he *depart for a season,* it is *that we may receive him for ever.* Let this moderate our grief, *The Lord is at hand.*

II. He promises that they should continue their acquaintance with him and interest in him (*v.* 19, 20): *Yet a little while, and the world sees me no more,* that is, Now I am no more in the world. After his death, *the world saw him no more,* for, though he rose to life, he never *showed himself to all the people,* Acts 10:41. The malignant world thought they had seen enough of him, and *cried, Away with him; crucify him;* and so shall their doom be; they shall see him no more. Those only that see Christ with an eye of faith shall see him for ever. The world sees him no more till his second coming; but his disciples have communion with him in his absence.

1. *You see me,* and shall continue to see me, when *the world sees me no more.* They saw him with their bodily eyes after his resurrection, for he showed himself to them *by many infallible proofs,* Acts 1:8. And *then were the disciples glad when they saw the Lord.* They saw him with an eye of faith after his ascension, sitting at God's right hand, as Lord of all; saw that in him which the world saw not.

2. *Because I live, you shall live also.* That which grieved them was, that their Master was dying, and they counted upon nothing else but to die with him. No, saith Christ, (1.) *I live;* this the great God glories in, *I live,* saith the Lord, and Christ saith the same; not only, I shall live, as he saith of them, but, I do live; for he has *life in himself,* and *lives for evermore.* We are not comfortless, while *we know that our Redeemer lives.* (2.) Therefore *you shall live also.* Note, The life of Christians is bound up in the life of Christ; as sure and as long as he lives, those that by faith are united to him shall live also; they shall live spiritually, a divine life in communion with God. This life is hid with Christ; if the head and root live, the members and branches live also. They shall *live eternally;* their bodies shall rise in the virtue of Christ's resurrection; it will be well with them in the world to come. It cannot but be well with all that are his, Isa. 26:19.

3. You shall have the assurance of this (*v.* 20): *At that day,* when I am glorified, when the Spirit is poured out, *you shall know* more clearly and certainly than you do now that *I am in my Father, and you in me, and I in you.* (1.) These glorious mysteries will be fully known in heaven; *At that day,* when I shall receive you to myself, you shall know perfectly that which now you *see through a glass darkly.* Now it appears not *what we shall be,* but then it will appear what we were. (2.) They were more fully known after the pouring out of the Spirit upon the apostles; at that day divine light should shine, and their eyes should see more clearly, their knowledge should greatly advance and increase then, would become more extensive and more distinct, and like the blind man's at the second touch of Christ's hand, who at first only *saw men as trees walking.* (3.) They are known by all that receive the Spirit of truth, to their abundant satisfaction, for in the knowledge of this is founded their *fellowship with the Father* and *his Son Jesus Christ.* They know, [1.] That *Christ is in the Father,* is one with the Father, by their experience of what he has wrought for them and in them; they find what an admirable consent and harmony there is between Christianity and natural religion, that that is grafted into this, and so they know that Christ *is in the Father.* [2.] That Christ is in them; experienced Christians know by the Spirit that Christ abides in them, 1 Jn. 3:24. [3.] That they are in Christ, for the relation is mutual, and equally near on both sides, Christ in them and they in Christ, which speaks an intimate and inseparable union; in the virtue of which it is that *because he lives they shall live also.* Note, *First,* Union with Christ is the life of believers; and their relation to him, and to God through him, is their felicity. *Secondly,* The knowledge of this union is their unspeakable joy and satisfaction; they were now in Christ, and he in them, but he speaks of it as a further act of grace that they should know it, and have the comfort of it. An interest in Christ and the knowledge of it are sometimes separated.

III. He promises that he would love them, and manifest himself to them, *v.* 21–24. Here observe,

1. Who they are whom Christ will look upon, and accept, as lovers of him; those that *have his commandments, and keep them.* By this Christ shows that the kind things he here said to his disciples were intended not for those only that were *now* his *followers,* but for all that should *believe in him through their word.* Here is, (1.) The duty of those who claim the dignity of being disciples. Having Christ's commandments, we must keep them; as Christians in name and profession we have Christ's commandments, we have them sounding in our ears, written before our eyes, we have the knowledge of them; but this is not enough; would we approve ourselves Christians indeed, we must keep them. Having them in our heads, we must keep them in our hearts and lives. (2.) The dignity of those that do the duty of disciples. They are looked upon by Christ to be such as love him. Not those that have the greatest wit and know how to talk for him, but those that *keep his commandments.* Note, The surest evidence of our love to Christ is obedience to the laws of Christ. Such is the love of a subject to his sovereign, a dutiful, respectful, obediential love, a conformity to his will, and satisfaction in his wisdom.

2. What returns he will make to them for their love; rich returns; there is no love lost upon Christ. (1.) They shall have the Father's love: *He that loveth me shall be loved of my Father.* We could not love God if he did not first, out of his goodwill to us, give us his grace to love him; but there is a love of complacency promised to those that do love God, Prov. 8:17. He loves them, and lets them know that he loves them, smiles upon them, and embraces them. God so loves the Son as to love all those that love him. (2.) They shall have Christ's love: *And I will love him,* as God-man, as Mediator. God will love him as a Father, and I will love him as a brother, an elder brother. The Creator will love him, and be the felicity of his being; the Redeemer will love him, and be the protector of his well-being. In the nature of God, nothing shines more brightly than this, that *God is love.* And in the undertaking of Christ nothing appears more glorious than this, that *he loved us.* Now both these loves are the crown and comfort, the *grace and glory,* which shall be to all those that *love the Lord Jesus Christ in sincerity.* Christ was now leaving his disciples, but promises to continue his love to them; for he not only retains a kindness for believers, though absent, but is doing them kindness while absent, for he bears them on his heart, and ever lives interceding for them. (3.) They shall have the comfort of that love: *I will manifest myself to him.* Some understand it of Christ's showing himself alive to his disciples after his resurrection; but, being promised to all that *love him and keep his commandments,* it must be construed so as to extend to them. There is a spiritual manifestation of Christ and his love made to all believers. When he enlightens their minds to know his love, and the dimensions of it (Eph. 3:18, 19), enlivens their graces, and draws them into exercise, and thus enlarges their comforts in himself — when he clears up the evidences of their interest in him, and gives them tokens of his love, experience of his tenderness, and earnests of his kingdom and glory, — then he manifests himself to them; and Christ is manifested to none but those to whom he is pleased to manifest himself.

3. What occurred upon Christ's making this promise.

(1.) One of the disciples expresses his wonder and surprise at it, *v.* 22. Observe, [1.] Who it was that said this — *Judas, not Iscariot.* Judah, or Judas, was a famous name; the most famous tribe in Israel was that of Judah; two of Christ's disciples were of that name: one of them was the traitor, the other was the brother of James (Lu. 6:16), one of those that were akin to Christ, Mt. 13:55. He is called *Lebbeus* and *Thaddeus,* was the penman of the last of the epistles, which in our translation, for distinction's sake, we call *the epistle of*

Jude. This was he that spoke here. Observe, *First,* There was a very good man, and a very bad man, called by the same name; for names commend us not to God, nor do they make men worse. Judas the apostle was never the worse, nor Judas the apostate ever the better, for being namesakes. But, *Secondly,* The evangelist carefully distinguishes between them; when he speaks of this pious Judas, he adds, *not Iscariot.* Take heed of mistaking; let us not confound the precious and the vile. [2.] What he said — *Lord how is it?* which intimates either, *First,* the weakness of his understanding. So some take it. He expected the temporal kingdom of the Messiah, that it should appear in external pomp and power, such as all the world would wonder after. "How, then," thinks he, "should it be confined to us only?" *ti gegonen — "what is the matter* now, that thou wilt not show thyself openly as is expected, that *the Gentiles may come to thy light, and kings to the brightness of thy rising?"* Note, We create difficulties to ourselves by mistaking the nature of Christ's kingdom, as if it were of this world. Or, *Secondly,* as expressing the strength of his affections, and the humble and thankful sense he had of Christ's distinguishing favours to them: *Lord, how is it?* He is amazed at the condescensions of divine grace, as David, 2 Sa. 7:18. What is there in us to deserve so great a favour? Note, 1. Christ's manifesting himself to his disciples is done in a distinguishing way — to them, and *not to the world* that *sits in darkness;* to the *base,* and not to the *mighty* and *noble;* to *babes,* and not to the *wise* and *prudent.* Distinguishing favours are very obliging; considering who are passed by, and who are pitched upon. 2. It is justly *marvellous in our eyes;* for it is unaccountable, and must be resolved into free and sovereign grace. *Even so, Father, because it seemed good unto thee.*

(2.) Christ, in answer hereto, explains and confirms what he had said, *v.* 23, 24. He overlooks what infirmity there was in what Judas spoke, and goes on with his comforts.

[1.] He further explains the condition of the promise, which was loving him, and keeping his commandments. And, as to this, he shows what an inseparable connection there is between love and obedience; love is the root, obedience is the fruit. *First,* Where a sincere love to Christ is in the heart, there will be obedience: *"If a man love me* indeed, that love will be such a commanding constraining principle in him, that, no question, he will *keep my words."* Where there is true love to Christ there is a value for his favour, a veneration for his authority, and an entire surrender of the whole man to his direction and government. Where love is, duty follows of course, is easy and natural, and flows from a principle of gratitude. *Secondly,* On the other hand, where there is no true love to Christ there will be no care to obey him: *He that loveth me not keepeth not my sayings, v.* 24. This comes in here as a discovery of those that *do not love Christ;* whatever they pretend, certainly those do not love him that believe not his truths, and obey not his laws, to whom Christ's sayings are but as idle tales, which he heeds not, or hard sayings, which he likes not. It is also a reason why Christ will not manifest himself to the world that doth not *love him,* because they put this affront upon him, not to *keep his sayings;* why should Christ be familiar with those that will be strange to him?

[2.] He further explains the promise (*v.* 23): *If a man thus love me, I will manifest myself to him. First, My Father will love him;* this he had said before (*v.* 21), and here repeats it for the confirming of our faith; because it is hard to imagine that the great god should make those the objects of his love that had made themselves *vessels of his wrath.* Jude wondered that Christ should *manifest himself to them;* but this answers it, "If my Father love you, why should not I be free with you?" *Secondly, We will come unto him, and make our abode with him.* This explains the meaning of Christ's manifesting himself to him, and magnifies the favour. 1. Not only,*I will,* but, *We will, I and the Father,* who, in this, *are one.* See *v.* 9. The light and love of God are communicated to man in the light and love of the Redeemer, so that wherever Christ is formed the image of God is stamped. 2. Not only, *"I will show myself to him* at a distance," but, *"We will come to him,* to be near him, to be with him," such are the powerful influences of divine graces and comforts upon the souls of those that love Christ in sincerity. 3. Not only, "I will give him a transient view of me, or make him a short and running visit," but, *We will take up our abode with him* which denotes complacency in him and constancy to him. God will not only love obedient believers, but he will take a pleasure in loving them,

will rest in love to them, Zep. 3:17. He will be with them as at his home.

[3.] He gives a good reason both to bind us to observe the condition and encourage us to depend upon the promise. *The word which you hear is not mine, but his that sent me, v.* 24. To this purport he had often spoken (*ch.* 7:16; 8:28; 12:44), and here it comes in very pertinently. *First,* the stress of duty is laid upon the precept of Christ as our rule, and justly, for that word of Christ which we are to keep is the Father's word, and his will the Father's will. *Secondly,* The stress of our comfort is laid upon the promise of Christ. But forasmuch as, in dependence upon that promise, we must deny ourselves, and take up our cross, and quit all, it concerns us to enquire whether the security be sufficient for us to venture our all upon; and this satisfies us that it is, that the promise is not Christ's bare word, but the Father's which sent him, which therefore we may rely upon.

Verses 25–27

Two things Christ here comforts his disciples with: —

I. That they should be under the tuition of his Spirit, *v.* 25, 26, where we may observe,

1. The reflection Christ would have them make upon the instructions he had given them: *These things have I spoken unto you* (referring to all the good lessons he had taught them, since they entered themselves into his school), *being yet present with you.* This intimates, (1.) That what he had said he did not retract nor unsay, but ratify it, or stand to it. What he had spoken he had spoken, and would abide by it. (2.) That he had improved the opportunity of his bodily presence with them to the utmost: "As long as I have been yet present with them, you know I have lost no time." Note, When our teachers are about to be removed from us we should call to mind what they have spoken, *being yet present with us.*

2. The encouragement given them to expect another teacher, and that Christ would find out a way of speaking to them after his departure from them, *v.* 26. He had told them before that the Father would give them this other comforter (*v.* 16), and here he returns to speak of it again; for as the promise of the Messiah had been, so the promise of the Spirit now was, the consolation of Israel. Two things he here tells them further concerning the sending of the Holy Ghost: —

(1.) On whose account he should be sent: "The Father will send him *in my name;* that is, for *my sake,* at my special instance and request:" or, "as my agent and representative." He came in his Father's name, as his ambassador: the Spirit comes in his name, as resident in his absence, to carry on his undertaking, and to ripen things for his second coming. Hence he is called *the Spirit of Christ,* for he pleads his cause, and does his work.

(2.) On what errand he should be sent; two things he shall do: — [1.] *He shall teach you all things,* as a Spirit of wisdom and revelation Christ was a teacher to his disciples; if he leave them now that they have made so little proficiency, what will become of them? Why, the Spirit shall teach them, shall be their standing tutor. He shall teach them all things necessary for them either to learn themselves, or to teach others. For those that would teach the things of God must first themselves be taught of God; this is the Spirit's work. See Isa. 59:21. [2.] *He shall bring all things to your remembrance whatsoever I have said unto you.* Many a good lesson Christ had taught them, which they had forgotten, and which would be to seek when they had occasion for it. Many things they did not retain the remembrance of, because they did not rightly understand the meaning of them. The Spirit shall not teach them a new gospel, but bring to their minds that which they had been taught, by leading them into the understanding of it. The apostles were all of them to preach, and some of them to write, the things that Jesus did and taught, to transmit them to distant nations and future ages; now, if they had been left to themselves herein, some needful things might have been forgotten, others misrepresented, through the treachery of their memories; therefore the Spirit is promised to enable them truly to relate and record what Christ said unto them. And to all the saints the Spirit of grace is given to be a remembrancer, and to him by faith and prayer we should commit the keeping of what we hear and know.

II. That they should be under the influence of his peace (*v.* 27): *Peace I leave with you.* When Christ was about to leave the world he *made his will.* His soul he committed to his Father; his body he bequeathed to Joseph, to be decently inter-

red; his clothes fell to the soldiers; his mother he left to the care of John: but what should he leave to his poor disciples, that had left all for him? Silver and gold he had none; but he left them that which was infinitely better, *his peace.* "I *leave you,* but I leave *my peace* with you. I not only give you a title to it, but put you in possession of it." He did not part in anger, but in love; for this was his farewell, *Peace I leave with you,* as a dying father leaves portions to his children; and this is a *worthy portion.* Observe,

1. The legacy that is here bequeathed *Peace, my peace.* Peace is put for all good, and Christ has left us all needful good, all that is really and truly good, as all the purchased promised good. Peace is put for reconciliation and love; the peace bequeathed is peace with God, peace with one another; peace *in our own bosoms* seems to be especially meant; a tranquillity of mind arising from a sense of our justification before God. It is the counterpart of our pardons, and the composure of our minds. This Christ calls *his* peace, for he is himself our peace, Eph. 2:14. It is the peace he purchased for us and preached to us, and on which the angels congratulated men at his birth, Lu. 2:14.

2. To whom this legacy is bequeathed: "To you, my disciples and followers, that will be exposed to trouble, and have need of peace; to you that are the sons of peace, and are qualified to receive it." This legacy was left to them as the representatives of the church, to them and their successors, to them and all true Christians in all ages.

3. In what manner it is left: *Not as the world giveth, give I unto you.* That is, (1.) "I do not compliment you with *Peace be unto you;* no, it is not a mere formality, but a real blessing." (2.) "The peace I give is of such a nature that the smiles of the world cannot give it, nor the frowns of the world take it away." Or, (3.) "The gifts I give to you are not such as this world gives to its children and votaries, to whom it is kind." The world's gifts concern only the body and time; Christ's gifts enrich the soul for eternity: the world gives lying vanities, and that which will cheat us; Christ gives substantial blessings, which will never fail us: the world gives and takes; Christ gives a good part that shall *never be taken away.* (4.) The peace which Christ gives is infinitely more valuable than that which the world gives. The world's peace begins in ignorance, consists with sin, and ends in endless troubles; Christ's peace begins in grace, consists with no allowed sin, and ends at length in everlasting peace. As is the difference between a killing lethargy and a reviving refreshing sleep, such is the difference between Christ's peace and the world's.

4. What use they should make of it: *Let not your heart be troubled, for any evils past or present, neither let it be afraid* of any evil to come. Note, Those that are interested in the covenant of grace, and entitled to the peace which Christ gives, ought not to yield to overwhelming griefs and fears. This comes in here as the conclusion of the whole matter; he had said (*v.* 1), *Let not your heart be troubled,* and here he repeats it as that for which he had now given sufficient reason.

Verses 28–31

Christ here gives his disciples another reason why their hearts should not be troubled for his going away; and that is, because his heart was not. And here he tells them what it was that enabled him to endure the cross and despise the shame, that they might *look unto him,* and *run with patience.* He comforted himself,

I. That, though he went away, he should *come again:* "You have heard how I have said, and now I say it again, *I go away, and come again."* Note, What we have heard of the doctrine of Christ, especially concerning his second coming, we have need to be told again and again. When we are under the power of any transport of passion, grief, or fear, or care, we forget that Christ will come again. See Phil. 4:5. Christ encouraged himself with *this,* in his sufferings and death, that he should *come again,* and the same should comfort us in our departure at death; we go away to come again; the leave we take of our friends at that parting is only a good night, not a final farewell. See 1 Th. 4:13, 14.

II. That he *went to his Father:* "If you loved me, as by your sorrow you say you do, *you would rejoice* instead of mourning, because, though I leave you, yet I said, *I go unto the Father,* not only mine, but yours, which will be my advancement and your advantage; for *my Father is greater than I."* Observe here, 1. It is matter of joy to Christ's disciples that he is gone to the Father, to take possession for orphans, and make intercession for transgressors. His departure had a bright side as well as a dark side. Therefore he sent this message after his resurrection (*ch.* 20:17), *I ascend to my Father and your Father,* as most comfortable. 2. The reason of this is, because *the Father is greater than he,* which, if it be a proper proof of that for which it is alleged (as no doubt it is), must be understood thus, that his state with his Father would be much more excellent and glorious than his present state; his returning to his Father (so Dr. Hammond) would be the advancing of him to a much higher condition than that which he was now in. Or thus, His going to the Father himself, and bringing all his followers to him there, was the ultimate end of his undertaking, and therefore greater than the means. Thus Christ raises the thoughts and expectations of his disciples to something greater than that in which now they thought all their happiness bound up. The kingdom of the Father, wherein he shall be all in all, will be greater than the mediatorial kingdom. 3. The disciples of Christ should show that they love him by their rejoicing in the glories of his exaltation, rather than by lamenting the sorrows of his humiliation, and rejoicing that he is gone to his Father, where he would be, and where we shall be shortly with him. Many that love Christ, let their love run out in a wrong channel; they think if they love him they must be continually in pain because of him; whereas those that love him should *dwell at ease* in him, should *rejoice in Christ Jesus.*

III. That his going away, compared with the prophecies which went before of it, would be a means of confirming the faith of his disciples (*v.* 29): *"I have told you before it come to pass* that I must die and rise again, and ascend to the Father, and send the Comforter, *that, when it is come to pass, you might believe."* See this reason, *ch.* 13:19; 16:4. Christ told his disciples of his death, though he knew it would both puzzle them and grieve them, because it would afterwards redound to the confirmation of their faith in two things: — 1. That he who foretold these things had a divine prescience, and knew beforehand what day would bring forth. When St. Paul was going to Jerusalem, he *knew not the things that did abide him there,* but Christ did. 2. That the things foretold were according to the divine purpose and designation, not sudden resolves, but the counterparts of an eternal counsel. Let them therefore not be troubled at that which would be for the confirmation of their faith, and so would redound to their real benefit; for the *trial of our faith* is very precious, though it cost us present *heaviness, through manifold temptations,* 1 Pt. 1:6.

IV. That he was sure of a victory over Satan, with whom he knew he was to have a struggle in his departure (*v.* 30): *"Henceforth I will not talk much with you,* having not much to say, but what may be adjourned to the pouring out of the Spirit." He had a great deal of good talk with them after this (*ch.* 15 and 16), but, in comparison with what he had said, it was not much. His time was now short, and he therefore spoke largely to them now, because the opportunity would soon be over. Note, We should always endeavour to talk to the purpose, because perhaps we may not have time to talk much. We know not how soon our breath may be stopped, and therefore should be always breathing something that is good. When we come to be sick and die, perhaps we may not be capable of talking much to those about us; and therefore what good counsel we have to give them, let us give it while we are in health. One reason why he would not talk much with them was because he had now other work to apply himself to: *The prince of this world comes.* He called the devil the *prince of this world, ch.* 12:31. The disciples dreamed of their Master being the prince of this world, and they worldly princes under him. But Christ tells them that the *prince of this world* was his enemy, and so were the *princes of this world,* that were actuated and ruled by him, 1 Co. 2:8. But *he has nothing in me.* Observe here, 1. The prospect Christ had of an approaching conflict, not only with men, but with the powers of darkness. The devil had set upon him with his temptations (Mt. 4), had offered him the *kingdoms of this world,* if he would hold them as tributary to him, with an eye to which Christ calls him, in disdain, *the prince of this world. Then the devil departed from him for a season;* "But now," says Christ, "I see him rallying again, preparing to make a furious onset, and so to gain by terrors that which he could not gain by allurements;" to frighten from his undertaking, when he could not entice from it. Note, The foresight of a temptation gives us great advantage in our resistance of it; for, being fore-warned, we should be fore-armed.

While we are here, we may see Satan continually coming against us, and ought therefore to be always upon our guard. 2. The assurance he had of good success in the conflict: *He hath nothing in me, ouk echei ouden — He hath nothing at all.* (1.) There was no guilt in Christ to give authority to *the prince of this world* in his terrors. The devil is said to have *the power of death* (Heb. 2:14); the Jews called him the *angel of death,* as an executioner. Now Christ having done no evil, Satan had no legal power against him, and therefore, though he prevailed to crucify him, he could not prevail to terrify him; though he hurried him to death, yet not to despair. When Satan comes to disquiet us, he has something in us to perplex us with, for we have all sinned; but, when he would disturb Christ, he found no occasion against him. (2.) There was no corruption in Christ, to give advantage to *the prince of this world* in his temptations. He could not crush his undertaking by drawing him to sin, because there was nothing sinful in him, nothing irregular for his temptations to fasten upon, no tinder for him to strike fire into; such was the spotless purity of his nature that he was above the possibility of sinning. The more Satan's interest in us is crushed and decays, the more comfortably may we expect sufferings and death.

V. That his departure was in compliance with, and obedience to, his Father. Satan could not force his life from him, and yet he would die: *that the world may know that I love the Father, v.* 31. We may take this,

1. As confirming what he had often said, that his undertaking, as Mediator, was a demonstration to the world, (1.) Of his compliance with the Father; hereby it appeared that he loved the Father. As it was an evidence of his love to man that he died for his salvation, so it was of his love to God that he died for his glory and the accomplishing of his purposes. Let the world know that between the Father and the Son there is not love lost. *As the Father loved the Son, and gave all things into his hands;* so *the Son loved the Father, and gave his spirit into his hand.* (2.) Of his obedience to his Father: *"As the Father gave me commandment, even so I did* — did the thing commanded me in the manner commanded." Note, The best evidence of our love to the Father is our doing as he hath given us commandment. As Christ loved the Father, and obeyed him, *even to the death,* so we must love Christ, and obey him. Christ's eye to the Father's commandment, obliging him to suffer and die, bore him up with cheerfulness, and overcame the reluctancies of nature; this took off the offence of the cross, that what he did was by order from the Father. The command of God is sufficient to bear us out in that which is most disputed by others, and therefore should be sufficient to bear us up in that which is most difficult to ourselves: *This is the will of him* that made me, *that sent me.*

2. As concluding what he had now said; having brought it to this, here he leaves it: *that the world may know that I love the Father.* You shall see how cheerfully I can meet the appointed cross: *"Arise, let us go hence* to the garden;" so some; or, to *Jerusalem.* When we talk of troubles at a distance, it is easy to say, *Lord, I will follow thee whithersoever thou goest;* but when it comes to the pinch, when an unavoidable cross lies in the way of duty, then to say, *"Arise, let us go* to meet it," instead of going out of our way to miss it, this lets *the world know that we love the Father.* If this discourse was at the close of the passover-supper, it should seem that at these words he arose from the table, and retired into the drawing-room, where he might the more freely carry on the discourse with his disciples in the following chapters, and pray with them. Dr. Goodwin's remark upon this is, that Christ mentioning the great motive of his sufferings, his Father's commandment, was in all haste to go forth to suffer and die, was afraid of slipping the time of Judas's meeting him: *Arise,* says he, *let us go hence* but he looks upon the glass, as it were, sees it not quite out, and therefore sits down again, and preaches another sermon. Now, (1.) In these words he gives his disciples an encouragement to follow him. He does not say, *I must go;* but, *Let us go.* He calls them out to no hardships but what he himself goes before them in as their leader. They had promised they would not desert him: "Come," says he, *"let us go* then; let us see how you will make the words good." (2.) He gives them an example, teaching them at all times, especially in suffering times, to sit loose to all things here below, and often to think and speak of leaving them. Though we sit easy, and in the midst of the delights of an agreeable conversation, yet we must not think

of being here always: *Arise, let us go hence.* If it was at the close of the paschal and eucharistical supper, it teaches us that the solemnities of our communion with God are not to be constant in this world. When we sit down under Christ's shadow with delight, and say, *It is good to be here;* yet we must think of rising and going hence; going down from the mount.

CHAPTER 15

It is generally agreed that Christ's discourse in this and the next chapter was at the close of the last supper, the night in which he was betrayed, and it is a continued discourse, not interrupted as that in the foregoing chapter was; and what he chooses to discourse of is very pertinent to the present sad occasion of a farewell sermon. Now that he was about to leave them, I. They would be tempted to leave him, and return to Moses again; and therefore he tells them how necessary it was that they should by faith adhere to him and abide in him. II. They would be tempted to grow strange one to another; and therefore he presses it upon them to love one another, and to keep up that communion when he was gone which had hitherto been their comfort. III. They would be tempted to shrink from their apostleship when they met with hardships; and therefore he prepared them to bear the shock of the world's ill will. There are four words to which his discourse in this chapter may be reduced; 1. Fruit (*v.* 1–8). 2. Love (*v.* 9–17). 3. Hatred (*v.* 18–25). The Comforter (*v.* 26, 27).

Verses 1–8

Here Christ discourses concerning the fruit, *the fruits of the Spirit,* which his disciples were to bring forth, under the similitude of a vine. Observe here,

I. The doctrine of this similitude; what notion we ought to have of it.

1. That Jesus Christ is *the vine, the true vine.* It is an instance of the humility of Christ that he is pleased to speak of himself under low and humble comparisons. He that is *the Sun of righteousness,* and *the bright and morning Star,* compares himself to a *vine.* The church, which is Christ mystical, is a vine (Ps. 80:8), so is Christ, who is the church seminal. Christ and his church are thus set forth. (1.) He is *the vine,* planted in the vineyard, and not a spontaneous product; planted in the earth, for his is the *Word made flesh.* The vine has an unsightly unpromising outside; and Christ had *no form nor comeliness,* Isa. 53:2. The vine is a spreading plant, and Christ will be known as *salvation to the ends of the earth.* The fruit of the vine honours God and cheers man (Jdg. 9:13), so does the fruit of Christ's mediation; it is *better than gold,* Prov. 8:19. (2.) He is *the true vine,* as truth is opposed to pretence and counterfeit; he is really a fruitful plant, a plant of renown. He is not like that wild vine which deceived those who gathered of it (2 Ki. 4:39), but a true vine. Unfruitful trees are said to *lie* (Hab. 3:17. *marg.*), but Christ is a vine that will not deceive. Whatever excellency there is in any creature, serviceable to man, it is but a shadow of that grace which is in Christ for his people's good. He is that true vine typified by Judah's vine, which enriched him with the blood of the grape (Gen. 49:11), by Joseph's vine, the branches of which *ran over the wall* (Gen. 49:22), by Israel's vine, under which he *dwelt safely,* 1 Ki. 4:25.

2. That believers are branches of this vine, which supposes that Christ is the root of the vine. The root is unseen, and our *life is hid with Christ;* the root bears the tree (Rom. 11:18), diffuses sap to it, and is all in all to its flourishing and fruitfulness; and in Christ are all supports and supplies. The branches of the vine are many, some on one side of the house or wall, others on the other side; yet, meeting in the root, are all but one vine; thus all good Christians, though in place and opinion distant from each other, yet meet in Christ, the centre of their unity. Believers, like the branches of the vine, are weak, and insufficient to stand of themselves, but as they are borne up. See Eze. 15:2.

3. That *the Father is the husbandman, geōrgos — the land-worker.* Though *the earth is the Lord's,* it yields him no fruit unless he work it. God has not only a propriety in, but a care of, the vine and all the branches. He *hath planted, and watered, and gives the increase;* for *we are God's husbandry,* 1 Co. 3:9. See Isa. 5:1, 2; 27:2, 3. He had an eye upon Christ, the root, and upheld him, and made him to flourish *out of a dry ground.* He has an eye upon all the branches, and prunes them, and watches over them, that nothing hurt them. Never was any husbandman so wise, so watchful, about his vineyard, as God is about his church, which therefore must needs prosper.

II. The duty taught us by this similitude, which is to *bring forth fruit,* and, in order to this, to *abide* in Christ.

1. We must be fruitful. From a vine we look for grapes

(Isa. 5:2), and from a Christian we look for Christianity; this is the *fruit,* a Christian temper and disposition, a Christian life and conversation, Christian devotions and Christian designs. We must honour God, and do good, and exemplify the purity and power of the religion we profess; and this is bearing fruit. The disciples here must be fruitful, as Christians, in all *the fruits of righteousness,* and as apostles, in diffusing the savour of the knowledge of Christ. To persuade them to this, he urges,

(1.) The doom of the unfruitful (*v.* 2): They are *taken away.* [1.] It is here intimated that there are many who pass for *branches* in Christ who yet do *not bear fruit.* Were they really united to Christ by faith, they would bear fruit; but being only tied to him by the thread of an outward profession, though they seem to be branches, they will soon be seen to be dry ones. Unfruitful professors are unfaithful professors; professors, and no more. It might be read, *Every branch that beareth not fruit in me,* and it comes much to one; for those that do not bear fruit in Christ, and in his Spirit and grace, are as if they bore no fruit at all, Hos. 10:1. [2.] It is here threatened that they shall be *taken away,* in justice to them and in kindness to the rest of the branches. From him that has not real union with Christ, and fruit produced thereby, *shall be taken away even that which he seemed to have,* Lu. 8:18. Some think this refers primarily to Judas.

(2.) The promise made to the fruitful: *He purgeth them, that they may bring forth more fruit.* Note, [1.] Further fruitfulness is the blessed reward of forward fruitfulness. The first blessing was, *Be fruitful;* and it is still a great blessing. [2.] Even fruitful branches, in order to their further fruitfulness, have need of purging or pruning; *kathairei — he taketh away that which is superfluous* and luxuriant, which hinders its growth and fruitfulness. The best have that in them which is peccant, *aliquid amputandum — something which should be taken away;* some notions, passions, or humours, that want to be purged away, which Christ has promised to do by his word, and Spirit, and providence; and these shall be taken off by degrees in the proper season. [3.] The purging of fruitful branches, in order to their greater fruitfulness, is the care and work of the great husbandman, for his own glory.

(3.) The benefits which believers have by the doctrine of Christ, the power of which they should labour to exemplify in a fruitful conversation: *Now you are clean, v.* 3. [1.] Their society was clean, now that Judas was expelled by that word of Christ, *What thou doest, do quickly;* and till they were got clear of him *they were not all clean.* The word of Christ is a distinguishing word, and separates *between the precious and the vile;* it will purify *the church of the first-born* in the great dividing day. [2.] They were each of them clean, that is, sanctified, by the truth of Christ (*ch.* 17:17); that faith by which they received the word of Christ *purified their hearts,* Acts 15:9. The Spirit of grace by the word refined them from the dross of the world and the flesh, and purged out of them *the leaven of the scribes and Pharisees,* from which, when they saw their inveterate rage and enmity against their Master, they were now pretty well cleansed. Apply it to all believers. The word of Christ is spoken to them; there is a cleansing virtue in that word, as it works grace, and works out corruption. It cleanses as fire cleanses the gold from its dross, and as physic cleanses the body from its disease. We then evidence that we are cleansed by the word when we *bring forth fruit unto holiness.* Perhaps here is an allusion to the law concerning vineyards in Canaan; the fruit of them was as unclean, and uncircumcised, the first three years after it was planted, and *the fourth year it* was to *be holiness of praise unto the Lord;* and then it was clean, Lev. 19:23, 24. The disciples had now been three years under Christ's instruction; and *now you are clean.*

(4.) The glory that will redound to God by our fruitfulness, with the comfort and honour that will come to ourselves by it, *v.* 8. If we *bear much fruit,* [1.] Herein our Father will be glorified. The fruitfulness of the apostles, as such, in the diligent discharge of their office, would be to the glory of God in the conversion of souls, and the offering of them up to him, Rom. 15:9, 16. The fruitfulness of all Christians, in a lower or narrower sphere, is to the glory of God. By the eminent good works of Christians many are brought to *glorify our Father who is in heaven.* [2.] So shall we be Christ's disciples indeed, approving ourselves so, and making it to appear that we are really what we call ourselves. So shall we both evidence our discipleship and adorn it, and be to our Master *for a name and a praise,* and a glory, that is, disciples indeed, Jer. 13:11. So shall we be owned by our Master in the great day, and have the reward of disciples, a share *in the joy of our Lord.* And the more fruit we bring forth, the more we abound in that which is good, the more he is glorified.

2. In order to our fruitfulness, we must abide in Christ, must keep up our union with him by faith, and do all we do in religion in the virtue of that union. Here is,

(1.) The duty enjoined (*v.* 4): *Abide in me, and I in you.* Note, It is the great concern of all Christ's disciples constantly to keep up a dependence upon Christ and communion with him, habitually to adhere to him, and actually to derive supplies from him. Those that are come to Christ must abide in him: *"Abide in me,* by faith; *and I in you,* by my Spirit; *abide in me,* and then fear not but I will *abide in you;"* for the communion between Christ and believers never fails on his side. We must abide in Christ's word by a regard to it, and it in us as a *light to our feet.* We must abide in Christ's merit as our righteousness and plea, and it in us as our support and comfort. The knot of the branch abides in the vine, and the sap of the vine abides in the branch, and so there is a constant communication between them.

(2.) The necessity of our abiding in Christ, in order to our fruitfulness (*v.* 4, 5): *"You cannot bring forth fruit, except you abide in me;* but, if you do, you *bring forth much fruit; for,* in short, *without me,* or separate from me, *you can do nothing."* So necessary is it to our comfort and happiness that we be fruitful, that the best argument to engage us to abide in Christ is, that otherwise we cannot be fruitful. [1.] Abiding in Christ is necessary in order to our doing much good. He that is constant in the exercise of faith in Christ and love to him, that lives upon his promises and is led by his Spirit, *bringeth forth much fruit,* he is very serviceable to God's glory, and his own account in the great day. Note, Union with Christ is a noble principle, productive of all good. A life of faith in the Son of God is incomparably the most excellent life a man can live in this world; it is regular and even, pure and heavenly; it is useful and comfortable, and all that answers the end of life. [2.] It is necessary to our doing any good. It is not only a means of cultivating ad increasing what good there is already in us, but it is the root and spring of all good: *"Without me you can do nothing:* not only no great thing, *heal the sick, or raise the dead,* but nothing." Note, We have as necessary and constant a dependence upon the grace of the Mediator for all the actions of the spiritual and divine life as we have upon the providence of the Creator for all the actions of the natural life; for, as to both, it is in the divine power *that we live, move, and have our being.* Abstracted from the merit of Christ, we can do nothing towards our justification; and from the Spirit of Christ nothing towards our sanctification. *Without Christ we can do nothing* aright, nothing that will be fruit pleasing to God or profitable to ourselves, 2 Co. 3:5. We depend upon Christ, not only as the vine upon the wall, for support; but, as the branch on the root, for sap.

(3.) The fatal consequences of forsaking Christ (*v.* 6): *If any man abide not in me, he is cast forth as a branch.* This is a description of the fearful state of hypocrites that are *not in Christ,* and of apostates that *abide not in Christ.* [1.] They are cast forth as dry and withered branches, which are plucked off because they cumber the tree. It is just that those should have no benefit by Christ who think they have no need of him; and that those who reject him should be rejected by him. Those that abide not in Christ shall be abandoned by him; they are left to themselves, to fall into scandalous sin, and then are justly cast out of the communion of the faithful. [2.] They are withered, as a branch broken off from the tree. Those that abide not in Christ, though they may flourish awhile in a plausible, at least a passable profession, yet in a little time wither and come to nothing. Their parts and gifts wither; their zeal and devotion wither; their credit and reputation wither; their hopes and comforts wither, Job 8:11–13. Note, Those that bear no fruit, after while will bear no leaves. *How soon is that fig-tree withered away* which Christ has cursed! [3.] *Men gather them.* Satan's agents and emissaries pick them up, and make an easy prey of them. Those that fall off from Christ presently fall in with sinners; and the sheep that wander from Christ's fold, the devil stands ready to seize them for himself. When the Spirit of the Lord had departed from Saul, an evil spirit possessed him. [4.] They *cast them into the fire,* that is, they are cast into the fire; and those who seduce them and draw them to sin do in effect cast them there; for they *make them children of hell.* Fire is the fittest place for withered branches, for they are good for nothing else, Eze. 15:2–4. [5.] *They are burned;* this follows of course, but it is here added very emphatically, and makes the threatening very terrible. They will not be consumed in a moment, like *thorns under a pot* (Eccl. 7:6), but *kaietai,* they are burning for ever in a fire, which not only cannot be quenched, but will never spend itself. This comes of quitting Christ, this is the end of barren trees. Apostates are *twice dead* (Jude 12), and when it is said, *They are cast into the fire and are burned,* it speaks as if they were twice damned. Some apply men's gathering them to the ministry of the angels in the great day, when they shall gather out of Christ's kingdom all things that offend, and shall *bundle the tares for the fire.*

(4.) The blessed privilege which those have that *abide in Christ* (*v.* 7): *If my words abide in you, you shall ask what you will* of my Father in my name, *and it shall be done.* See here, [1.] How our union with Christ is maintained — by the word: *If you abide in me;* he had said before, *and I in you;* here he explains himself, *and my words abide in you;* for it is in the word that Christ is set before us, and offered to us, Rom. 10:6–8. It is in the word that we receive and embrace him; and so where the *word of Christ dwells richly* there Christ dwells. If the word be our constant guide and monitor, if it be in us as at home, then we abide in Christ, and he in us. [2.] How our communion with Christ is maintained — by prayer: *You shall ask what you will, and it shall be done to you.* And what can we desire more than to have what we will for the asking? Note, Those that abide in Christ as their heart's delight shall have, through Christ, their heart's desire. If we have Christ, we shall want nothing that is good for us. Two things are implied in this promise: — *First,* That if we abide in Christ, and his word in us, we shall not ask any thing but what is proper to be done for us. The promises abiding in us lie ready to be turned into prayers; and the prayers so regulated cannot but speed. *Secondly,* That if we *abide in Christ and his word* we shall have such an interest in God's favour and Christ's mediation that we shall have an answer of peace to all our prayers.

Verses 9–17

Christ, who is love itself, is here discoursing concerning love, a fourfold love.

I. Concerning the Father's love to him; and concerning this he here tells us, 1. That the Father did love him (*v.* 9): *As the Father hath loved me.* He loved him as Mediator: *This is my beloved Son.* He was the Son of his love. He loved him, and gave *all things into his hand;* and yet so *loved the world* as to deliver him up for us all. When Christ was entering upon his sufferings he comforted himself with this, that his Father loved him. Those whom God loves as a Father may despise the hatred of all the world. 2. That he abode in his Father's love, *v.* 10. He continually loved his Father, and was beloved of him. Even when he was made sin and a curse for us, and *it pleased the Lord to bruise him,* yet he abode in his Father's love. See Ps. 89:33. Because he continued to love his Father, he went cheerfully through his sufferings, and therefore his Father continued to love him. 3. That therefore he abode in his Father's love because he kept his Father's law: *I have kept my Father's commandments,* as Mediator, and so *abide in his love.* Hereby he showed that he continued to love his Father, that he went on, and went through, with his undertaking, and therefore the Father continued to love him. His soul *delighted in him,* because he *did not fail, nor was discouraged,* Isa. 42:1–4. We having broken the law of creation, and thereby thrown ourselves out of the love of God; Christ satisfied for us by obeying the law of redemption, and so he abode in his love, and restored us to it.

II. Concerning his own love to his disciples. Though he leaves them, he loves them. And observe here,

1. The pattern of this love: *As the Father has loved me, so have I loved you.* A strange expression of the condescending grace of Christ! As the Father loved him, who was most worthy, he loved them, who were most unworthy. The Father loved him as his Son, and he loves them as his children. *The Father gave all things into his hand;* so, with himself, *he freely giveth us all things.* The Father loved him as Mediator, as head of the church, and the great trustee of divine grace and favour, which he had not for himself only, but for the benefit of those for whom he was entrusted; and, says he,

"I have been a faithful trustee. As the Father has committed his love to me, so I transmit it to you." Therefore the Father was well pleased with him, that he might be well pleased with us in him; and loved him, that in him, as beloved, he might *make us accepted,* Eph. 1:6.

2. The proofs and products of this love, which are four: —

(1.) Christ loved his disciples, for he laid down his life for them (*v.* 13): *Greater* proof of *love hath no man* to show *than this,* to *lay down his life for his friend.* And this is the love wherewith *Christ hath loved us,* he is our *antipsychos — bail for us,* body for body, life for life, though he knew our insolvency, and foresaw how much the engagement would cost him. Observe here, [1.] The extent of the love of the children of men to one another. The highest proof of it is laying down one's life for a friend, to save his life, and perhaps there have been some such heroic achievements of love, more than *plucking out one's own eyes,* Gal. 4:15. If *all that a man has he will give for his life,* he that gives this for his friend gives all, and can give no more; this may sometimes be our duty, 1 Jn. 3:16. Paul was ambitious of the honour (Phil. 2:17); and *for a good man some will even dare to die,* Rom. 5:7. It is love in the highest degree, which is *strong as death.* [2.] The excellency of the love of Christ beyond all other love. He has not only equaled, but exceeded, the most illustrious lovers. Others have laid down their lives, content that they should be taken from them; but Christ gave up his, was not merely passive, but made it his own act and deed. The life which others have laid down has been but of equal value with the life for which it was laid down, and perhaps less valuable; but Christ is infinitely more worth than ten thousand of us. Others have thus laid down their lives for their friends, but Christ laid down his for us *when we were enemies,* Rom. 5:8, 10. *Plusquam ferrea aut lapidea corda esse oportet, quae non emolliet tam incomparabilis divini amoris suavitas — Those hearts must be harder than iron or stone which are not softened by such incomparable sweetness of divine love.* — Calvin

(2.) Christ loved his disciples, for he took them into a covenant of friendship with himself, *v.* 14, 15. "If you approve yourselves by your obedience my disciples indeed, *you are my friends,* and shall be treated as friends." Note, The followers of Christ are the friends of Christ, and he is graciously pleased to call and account them so. Those that do the duty of his servants are admitted and advanced to the dignity of his friends. David had one servant in his court, and Solomon one in his, that was in a particular manner *the king's friend* (2 Sa. 15:37; 1 Ki. 4:5); but this honour have all Christ's servants. We may in some particular instance befriend a stranger; but we espouse all the interests of a friend, and concern ourselves in all his cares: thus Christ takes believers to be his friends. He visits them and converses with them as his friends, bears with them and makes the best of them, is afflicted in their afflictions, and takes pleasure in their prosperity; he pleads for them in heaven and takes care of all their interests there. Have friends but one soul? He that is joined to the Lord is *one spirit,* 1 Co. 6:17. Though they often show themselves unfriendly, he is a friend that loves at all times. Observe how endearingly this is expressed here. [1.] He will not *call them servants,* though they call him *Master* and *Lord.* Those that would be like Christ in humility must not take a pride in insisting upon all occasions on their authority and superiority, but remember that their servants are their fellow-servants. But, [2.] He will *call them his friends;* he will not only love them, but will let them know it; for *in his tongue is the law of kindness.* After his resurrection he seems to speak with more affectionate tenderness of and to his disciples than before. *Go to my brethren, ch.* 20:17. *Children, have you any meat? ch.* 21:5. But observe, though Christ called *them his friends,* they called themselves *his servants:* Peter, *a servant of Christ* (1 Pt. 1:1), and so James, *ch.* 1:1. The more honour Christ puts upon us, the more honour we should study to do him; the higher in his eyes, the lower in our own.

(3.) Christ loved his disciples, for he was very free in communicating his mind to them (*v.* 15): "Henceforth you shall not be kept so much in the dark as you have been, like *servants* that are only told their present work; but, when the Spirit is poured out, you shall know your Master's designs as *friends. All things that I have heard of my Father I have declared unto you.*" As to the secret will of God, there are many things which we must be content not to know; but, as to the revealed will of God, Jesus Christ has faithfully handed to us what he received of the Father, *ch.* 1:18; Mt. 11:27. The great things relating to man's redemption Christ declared to his disciples, that they might declare them to others; they were the men of his counsel, Mt. 13:11.

(4.) Christ loved his disciples, for he chose and ordained them to be the prime instruments of his glory and honour in the world (*v.* 16): *I have chosen you, and ordained you,* His love to them appeared,

[1.] In their election, their election to their apostleship (*ch.* 6:70): *I have chosen you twelve.* It did not begin on their side: *You have not chosen me,* but I first *chose you.* Why were they admitted to such an intimacy with him, employed in such an embassy for him, and endued with such power from on high? It was not owing to their wisdom and goodness in choosing him for their Master, but to his favour and grace in choosing them for his disciples. It is fit that Christ should have the choosing of his own ministers; still he does it by his providence and Spirit. Though ministers make that holy calling their own choice, Christ's choice is prior to theirs and directs and determines it. Of all that are chosen to grace and glory it may be said, They have not chosen Christ, but he had chosen them, Deu. 7:7, 8.

[2.] In their ordination: *I have ordained you; hethēka hymas — "I have put you* into the ministry (1 Tim. 1:12), put you into commission." By this it appeared that he took them for his friends when he crowned their heads with such an honour, and filled their hands with such a trust. It was a mighty confidence he reposed in them, when he made them his ambassadors to negotiate the affairs of his kingdom in this lower world, and the prime ministers of state in the administration of it. The treasure of the gospel was committed to them, *First,* That it might be propagated: that you should go, *hina hymeis hypagēte — "that you should go as under a yoke* or burden, for the ministry is a work, and you that go about it must resolve to undergo a great deal; *that you may go* from place to place all the world over, and *bring forth fruit.*" They were ordained, not to sit still, but to go about, to be diligent in their work, and to lay out themselves unweariedly in doing good. They were ordained, not to beat the air, but to be instrumental in God's hand for the bringing of nations into obedience to Christ, Rom. 1:13. Note, Those whom Christ ordains should and shall be fruitful; should labour, and shall not labour in vain. *Secondly,* That it might be perpetuated; that the fruit may remain, that the good effect of their labours may continue in the world from generation to generation, to the end of time. The church of Christ was not to be a short-lived thing, as many of the sects of the philosophers, that were a nine days' wonder; it did not *come up in a night,* nor should it *perish in a night,* but be as the days of heaven. The sermons and writings of the apostles are transmitted to us, and we at this day are built upon that foundation, ever since the Christian church was first founded by the ministry of the apostles and seventy disciples; as one generation of ministers and Christians has passed away, still another has come. By virtue of that great charter (Mt. 28:19), Christ has a church in the world, which, as our lawyers say of bodies corporate, does *not die,* but lives in a succession; and thus *their fruit remains* to this day, and shall do while the earth remains.

[3.] His love to them appeared in the interest they had at the throne of grace: *Whatsoever you shall ask of my Father, in my name, he will give it you.* Probably this refers in the first place to the power of working miracles which the apostles were clothed with, which was to be drawn out by prayer. "Whatever gifts are necessary to the furtherance of your labours, whatever help from heaven you have occasion for at any time, it is but ask and have." Three things are here hinted to us for our encouragement in prayer, and very encouraging they are. *First,* That we have a God to go to who is a Father; Christ here calls him *the Father,* both mine and yours; and the Spirit in the word and in the heart teaches us to cry, *Abba, Father. Secondly,* That we come in a good name. Whatever errand we come upon to the throne of grace according to God's will, we may with a humble boldness mention Christ's name in it, and plead that we are related to him, and he is concerned for us. *Thirdly,* That an answer of peace is promised us. What you come for shall be given you. This great promise made to that great duty keeps up a comfortable and gainful intercourse between heaven and earth.

III. Concerning the disciples' love to Christ, enjoined in consideration of the great love wherewith he had loved them. Three things he exhorts them to: —

1. To continue in his love, *v.* 9. "Continue in your love to me, and in mine to you." Both may be taken in. We must place our happiness in the continuance of Christ's love to us, and make it our business to give continued proofs of our love to Christ, that nothing may tempt us to withdraw from him, or provoke him to withdraw from us. Note, All that love Christ should continue in their love to him, that is, be always loving him, and taking all occasions to show it, and love to the end. The disciples were to go out upon service for Christ, in which they would meet with many troubles; but, says Christ, *"Continue in my love.* Keep up your love to me, and then all the troubles you meet with will be easy; love made seven years' hard service easy to Jacob. Let not the troubles you meet with for Christ's sake quench your love to Christ, but rather quicken it.

2. To let his joy remain in them, and fill them, *v.* 11. This he designed in those precepts and promises given them.

(1.) That his joy might remain in them. The words are so placed, in the original, that they may be read either, [1.] That *my joy in you may remain.* If they bring forth much fruit, and continue in his love, he will continue to rejoice in them as he had done. Note, Fruitful and faithful disciples are the joy of the Lord Jesus; he *rests in his love* to them, Zep. 3:17. As there is a transport of joy in heaven in the conversion of sinners, so there is a remaining joy in the perseverance of saints. Or, [2.] That *my joy,* that is, your joy in me, *may remain.* It is the will of Christ that his disciples should constantly and continually rejoice in him, Phil. 4:4. The joy of the hypocrite is but for a moment, but the joy of those who abide in Christ's love is a continual feast. The word of the Lord enduring for ever, the joys that flow from it, and are founded on it, do so too.

(2.) *That your joy might be full;* not only that you might be full of joy, but that your joy in me and in my love may rise higher and higher, till it come to perfection, when you *enter into the joy of your Lord.*" Note, [1.] Those and those only that have Christ's joy remaining in them have their joy full; worldly joys are empty, soon surfeit but never satisfy. It is only wisdom's joy that will fill the soul, Ps. 36:8. [2.] The design of Christ in his world is to *fill the joy* of his people; see 1 Jn. 1:4. This and the other he hath said, that our joy might be fuller and fuller, and perfect at last.

3. To evidence their love to him by keeping his commandments: *"If you keep my commandments, you shall abide in my love, v.* 10. This will be an evidence of the fidelity and constancy of your love to me, and then you may be sure of the continuance of my love to you." Observe here, (1.) The promise *"You shall abide in my love* as in a dwelling place, at home in Christ's love; as in a resting place, at ease in Christ's love; as in a stronghold, safe in it. *You shall abide in my love,* you shall have grace and strength to persevere in loving me." If the same hand that first shed abroad the love of Christ in our hearts did not keep us in that love, we should not long abide in it, but, through the love of the world, should go *out of love* with Christ himself. (2.) The condition of the promise: *If you keep my commandments.* The disciples were to keep Christ's commandments, not only by a constant conformity to them themselves, but by a faithful delivery of them to others; they were to keep them as trustees, in whose hands that great *depositum* was lodged, for they were to *teach all things that Christ had commanded,* Mt. 28:20. *This commandment* they must *keep without spot* (1 Tim. 6:14), and thus they must show that they abide in his love.

To induce them to keep his commandments, he urges, [1.] His own example: *As I have kept my Father's commandments, and abide in his love.* Christ submitted to the law of mediation, and so preserved the honour and comfort of it, to teach us to submit to the laws of the Mediator, for we cannot otherwise preserve the honour and comfort of our relation to him. [2.] The necessity of it to their interest in him (*v.* 14): *"You are my friends if you do whatsoever I command you* and not otherwise." Note, *First,* Those only will be accounted Christ's faithful friends that approve themselves his obedient servants; for those that will not have him to reign over them shall be treated as his enemies. *Idem velle et idem nolle ea demum vera est amicitia — Friendship involves a fellowship of aversions and attachments.* — Sallust. *Secondly,* It is universal obedience to Christ that is the only acceptable obedience; to obey him in every thing that he commands us, not *excepting,* much less *excepting against,* any command.

IV. Concerning the *disciples' love one to another,* enjoined as an evidence of their love to Christ, and a grateful return for his love to them. We must keep his commandments, and this is his commandment, that we *love one another, v.* 12, and again, *v.* 17. No one duty of religion is more frequently inculcated, nor more pathetically urged upon us, by our Lord Jesus, than that of mutual love, and for good reason. 1. It is here recommended by Christ's pattern (*v.* 12): *as I have loved you.* Christ's love to us should direct and engage our love to each other; in this manner, and from this motive, we should love one another, as, and because, Christ has loved us. He here specifies some of the expressions of his love to them; he called them friends, communicated his mind to them, was ready to give them what they asked. *Go you and do likewise.* 2. It is required by his precept. He interposes his authority, has made it one of the statute-laws of his kingdom. Observe how differently it is expressed in these two verses, and both very emphatic. (1.) *This is my commandment* (*v.* 12), as if this were the most necessary of all the commandments. As under the law the prohibition of idolatry was the commandment more insisted on than any other, foreseeing the people's addictedness to that sin, so Christ, foreseeing the addictedness of the Christian church to uncharitableness, has laid most stress upon this precept. (2.) *These things I command you, v.* 17. He speaks as if he were about to give them many things in charge, and yet names this only, *that you love one another;* not only because this includes many duties, but because it will have a good influence upon all.

Verses 18–25

Here Christ discourses concerning *hatred,* which is the character and genius of the devil's kingdom, as love is of the kingdom of Christ. Observe here,

I. Who they are in whom this hatred is found — the world, the children of this world, as distinguished from the children of God; those who are in the interests of the god of this world, whose image they bear, and whose power they are subject to; all those, whether Jews or Gentiles, who would not come into the church of Christ, which he audibly called, and visibly separates from this evil world. The calling of these *the world* intimates, 1. Their number; there were a world of people that opposed Christ and Christianity. Lord, how were they increased that troubled the Son of David! I fear, if we should put it to the vote between Christ and Satan, Satan would outpoll us quite. 2. Their confederacy and combination; these numerous hosts are embodied, and are as one, Ps. 83:5. Jews and Gentiles, that could agree in nothing else, agreed to persecute Christ's minister. 3. Their spirit and disposition; they are *men of the world* (Ps. 16:13, 14), wholly devoted to this world and the things of it, and never thinking of another world. The people of God, though they are taught to hate the sins of sinners, yet not their persons, but to love and do good to all men. A malicious, spiteful, envious spirit, is not the spirit of Christ, but of the world.

II. Who are they against whom this hatred is levelled — against the disciples of Christ, against Christ himself, and against the Father.

1. The world hates the disciples of Christ: *The world hateth you* (*v.* 19); and he speaks of it as that which they must expect and count upon, *v.* 18, as 1 Jn. 3:13.

(1.) Observe how this comes in here. [1.] Christ had expressed the great kindness he had for them as friends; but, lest they should be puffed up with this, there was given them, as there was to Paul, a *thorn in the flesh,* that is, as it is explained there, reproaches and persecutions for Christ's sake, 2 Co. 12:7, 10. [2.] He had appointed them their work, but tells them what hardships they should meet with in it, that it might not be a surprise to them, and that they might prepare accordingly. [3.] He had charged them to *love one another,* and need enough they had to love one another, for the world would hate them; to be kind to one another, for they would have a great deal of unkindness and ill-will from those that were without. "Keep peace among yourselves, and this will fortify you against the world's quarrels with you." Those that are in the midst of enemies are concerned to hold together.

(2.) Observe what is here included.

[1.] The world's enmity against the followers of Christ: it *hateth them.* Note, Whom Christ blesseth the world curseth. The favourites and heirs of heaven have never been the darlings of this world, since the old enmity was put between the seed of the woman and of the serpent. Why did Cain hate Abel, but *because his works were righteous?* Esau hated Jacob because of the blessing; Joseph's brethren hated him because his father loved him; Saul hated David because *the Lord was with him;* Ahab hated Micaiah because of his prophecies; such are the causeless causes of the world's hatred.

[2.] The fruits of that enmity, two of which we have here, *v.* 20. *First,* They will persecute you, because they hate you, for hatred is a restless passion. It is the common lot of those who will live godly in Christ Jesus to *suffer persecution,* 2 Tim. 3:12. Christ foresaw what ill usage his ambassadors would meet with in the world, and yet, for the sake of those few that by their ministry were to be called out of the world, he sent them forth as sheep in the midst of wolves. *Secondly,* Another fruit of their enmity is implied, that they would reject their doctrine. When Christ says, *If they have kept my sayings, they will keep yours,* he means, They will keep yours, and regard yours, no more than they have regarded and kept mine. Note, The preachers of the gospel cannot but take the despising of their message to be the greatest injury that can be done to themselves; as it was a great affront to Jeremiah to say, *Let us not give heed to any of his words,* Jer. 18:18.

[3.] The causes of that enmity. The world will hate them, *First,* Because they do not belong to it (*v.* 19): *"If you were of the world,* of its spirit, and in its interests, if you were carnal and worldly, *the world would love you* as its own; but, because you are called out of the world, it hates you, and ever will." Note, 1. We are not to wonder if those that are devoted to the world are caressed by it as its friends; most men *bless the covetous,* Ps. 10:3; 49:18. 2. Nor are we to wonder if those that are delivered from the world are maligned by it as its enemies; when Israel is rescued out of Egypt, the Egyptians will pursue them. Observe, The reason why Christ's disciples are not of the world is not because they have by their own wisdom and virtue distinguished themselves from the world, but because Christ hath chosen them out of it, to set them apart for himself; and this is the reason why the world hates them; for, (1.) The glory which by virtue of this choice they are designed for sets them above the world, and so makes them the objects of its envy. The saints shall judge the world, and the upright have dominion, and therefore they are hated. (2.) The grace which by virtue of this choice they are endued with sets them against the world; they swim against the stream of the world, and are not conformed to it; they witness against it, and are not conformed to it. This would support them under all the calamities which the world's hatred would bring upon them, that they were hated because they were the choice and the chosen ones of the Lord Jesus, and were not of the world. Now, [1.] This was no just cause for the world's hatred of them. If we do any thing to make ourselves hateful, we have reason to lament it; but, if men hate us for that for which they should love and value us, we have reason to pity them, but no reason to perplex ourselves. Nay, [2.] This was just cause for their own joy. He that is hated because he is rich and prospers cares not who has the vexation of it, while he has the satisfaction of it.

> — *Populus me sibilat, at mihi plaudo ipse domi —*
> — — Let them hiss on, he cries,
> While in my own opinion fully blessed. — *Timon in Hor.*

Much more may those hug themselves whom the world hates, but whom Christ loves.

Secondly, "Another cause of the world's hating you will be because you do belong to Christ (*v.* 21): *For my name's sake."* Here is the core of the controversy; whatever is pretended, this is the ground of the quarrel, they hate Christ's disciples because they *bear his name,* and *bear up his name* in the world. Note, 1. It is the character of Christ's disciples that they stand up for his name. The name into which they were baptized is that which they will live and die by. 2. It has commonly been the lot of those that appear for Christ's name to suffer for so doing, to suffer many things, and hard things, *all these things.* It is matter of comfort to the greatest sufferers if they suffer for Christ's name's sake. *If you be reproached for the name of Christ, happy are you* (1 Pt. 4:14), happy indeed, considering not only the honour that is imprinted upon those sufferings (Acts 5:41), but the comfort that is infused into them, and especially the crown of glory which those sufferings lead to. *If we suffer with Christ,* and for Christ, *we shall reign with him.*

Thirdly, After all, it is the world's ignorance that is the true cause of its enmity to the disciples of Christ (*v.* 21): *Because they know not him that sent me.* 1. They know not God. If men had but a due acquaintance with the very first principles of natural religion, and did but know God, though they did not embrace Christianity, yet they could not hate and persecute it. Those have no knowledge who eat up God's people, Ps. 14:4. 2. They know not God as he that sent our Lord Jesus, and authorized him to be the great Mediator of the peace. We do not rightly know God if we do not know him in Christ, and those who persecute those whom he sends make it to appear that they know not that he was sent of God. See 1 Co. 2:8.

2. The world hates Christ himself. And this is spoken of here for two ends: —

(1.) To mitigate the trouble of his followers, arising from the world's hatred, and to make it the less strange, and the less grievous (*v.* 18): *You know that it hated me before you, prōton hymōn.* We read it as signifying priority of time; he began in the bitter cup of suffering, and then left us to pledge him; but it may be read as expressing his superiority over them: *"You know* that it hated me, *your first,* your chief and captain, your leader and commander." [1.] If Christ, who excelled in goodness, and was perfectly innocent and universally beneficent, was hated, can we expect that any virtue or merit of ours should screen us from malice? [2.] If our Master, the founder of our religion, met with so much opposition in the planting of it, his servants and followers can look for no other in propagating and professing it. For this he refers them (*v.* 20) to his own word, at their admission into discipleship: *Remember the word that I said unto you.* It would help us to understand Christ's latter sayings to compare them with his former sayings. Nor would any thing contribute more to the making of us easy than remembering the words of Christ, which will expound his providences. Now in this word there is, *First,* A plain truth: *The servant is not greater than his Lord.* This he had said to them. Mt. 10:24. Christ is our Lord, and therefore we must diligently attend all his motions, and patiently acquiesce in all his disposals, for the servant is inferior to his lord. The plainest truths are sometimes the strongest arguments for the hardest duties; Elihu answers a multitude of Job's murmurings with this one self-evident truth, that God is greater than man, Job 33:12. So here is, *Secondly,* A proper inference drawn from it: *"If they have persecuted men,* as you have seen, and are likely to see much more, *they will also persecute you;* you may expect it and count upon it: for," 1. "You will do the same that I have done to provoke them; you will reprove them for their sins, and call them to repentance, and give them strict rules of holy living, which they will not bear." 2. "You cannot do more than I have done to oblige them; after so great an instance, let none wonder if they suffer ill for doing well." He adds, *"If they have kept my sayings, they will keep yours also;* as there have been a few, and but a few, that have been wrought upon by my preaching, so there will be by yours a few, and but a few." Some give another sense of this, making *etērēsan* to be put for *paretērēsan.* "If they have lain in wait for my sayings, with a design to ensnare me, they will in like manner lie in wait to entangle you in your talk."

(2.) To aggravate the wickedness of this unbelieving world, and to discover its exceeding sinfulness; to hate and persecute the apostles was bad enough, but in them to hate and persecute Christ himself was much worse. The world is generally in an ill name in scripture, and nothing can put it into a worse name than this, that it hated Jesus Christ. There is a world of people that are haters of Christ. Two things he insists upon to aggravate the wickedness of those that hated him: —

[1.] That there was the greatest reason imaginable why they should love him; men's good words and good works usually recommend them; now as to Christ,

First, His words were such as merited their love (*v.* 22): *"If I had not spoken unto them,* to court their love, *they had not had sin,* their opposition had not amounted to a hatred of me, their sin had been comparatively no sin. But now that I have said so much to them to recommend myself to their best affections they have no pretence, no excuse for their sin." Observe here, 1. The advantage which those have that enjoy the gospel; Christ in it comes and speaks to them; he spoke in person to the men of that generation, and is still speaking to us by our Bibles and ministers, and as one that has the most unquestionable authority over us, and affection for us. Every word of his is pure, carries with it a commanding majesty, and yet a condescending tenderness, able, one would think, to charm the deafest adder. 2. The excuse which those have that enjoy not the gospel: *"If I had not spoken to them,* if they had ever heard of Christ and of salvation by him, *they had not had sin."* (1.) Not this kind of sin. They had not been chargeable with a contempt of Christ if he had not come and made a tender of his grace to them. As *sin is not imputed where there is no law,* so unbelief is not imputed where there is no gospel; and, where it is imputed, it is thus far the only damning sin, that, being a sin against the remedy, other sin would not damn if the guilt of them were not bound on with this. (2.) Not such a degree of sin. If they had not had the gospel among them, their other sins had not been so bad; for the *times of ignorance God winked at,* Lu. 12:47, 48. 3. The aggravated guilt which those lie under to whom Christ has *come and spoken in vain,* whom he has called and invited in vain, with whom he has reasoned and pleaded in vain; *They have no cloak for their sin;* they are altogether inexcusable, and in the judgment day will be speechless, and will not have a word to say for themselves. Note, The clearer and fuller the discoveries are which are made to us of the grace and truth of Jesus Christ, the more is said to us that is convincing and endearing, the greater is our sin if we do not love him and believe in him. The word of Christ strips sin of its cloak, that it may appear sin.

Secondly, His works were such as merited their love, as well as his words (*v.* 24): *"If I had not done among them, in their country, and before their eyes, such works as no other man ever did, they had not had sin;* their unbelief and enmity had been excusable, and they might have had some colour to say that my word was not to be credited, if not otherwise confirmed;" but he produced satisfactory proofs of his divine mission, *works which no other man did.* Note, 1. As the Creator demonstrates his power and Godhead by his works (Rom. 1:20), so doth the Redeemer. His miracles, his mercies, works of wonder and works of grace, prove him sent of God, and sent on a kind errand. 2. Christ's works were such as *no man ever did.* No common person that had not a commission from heaven, and God with him, could work miracles, *ch.* 3:2. And no prophet ever wrought such miracles, so many, so illustrious. Moses and Elias wrought miracles as servants, by a derived power; but Christ, as a Son, by his own power. This was it that amazed the people, that with authority he commanded diseases and devils (Mk. 1:27); they owned they never saw the like, Mk. 2:12. They were all good works, works of mercy; and this seems especially intended here, for he is upbraiding them with this, that they hated him. One that was so universally useful, more than ever any man was, one would think, should have been universally beloved, and yet even he is hated. 3. The works of Christ enhance the guilt of sinners' infidelity and enmity to him, to the last degree of wickedness and absurdity. If they had only heard his words, and not seen his works, — if we had only his sermons upon record, and not his miracles, unbelief might have pleaded want of proof; but now it has no excuse. Nay, the rejecting of Christ, both by them and us, has in it the sin, not only of obstinate unbelief, but of base ingratitude. They saw Christ to be most amiable, and studious to do them a kindness; yet they hated him, and studied to do him mischief. And we see in his word that great love wherewith he loved us, and yet are not wrought upon by it.

[2.] That there was no reason at all why they should hate him. Some that at one time will say and do that which is recommending, yet at another time will say and do that which is provoking and disobliging; but our Lord Jesus not only did much to merit men's esteem and good-will, but never did any thing justly to incur their displeasure; this he pleads by quoting a scripture for it (*v.* 25): *"This comes to pass,* this unreasonable hatred of me, and of my disciples for my sake, *that the word might be fulfilled which is written in their law"* (that is, in the Old Testament, which is a law, and was received by them as a law), *"They hated me without a cause;"* this David speaks of himself as a type of Christ, Ps. 35:19; 69:4. Not, *First,* Those that hate Christ hate him without any just cause; enmity to Christ is unreasonable enmity. We think those deserve to be hated that are haughty and froward, but Christ is meek and lowly, compassionate and tender; those also that under colour of complaisance are malicious, envious, and revengeful, but Christ devoted himself to the service of those that used him, nay, and of those that abused him; toiled for others' ease, and impoverished himself to enrich us. Those we think hateful that are *hurtful to kings and provinces,* and disturbers of the public peace; but Christ, on the contrary, was the greatest blessing imaginable to his country, and yet was hated. He testified indeed that *their works were evil,* with a design to make them good, but to hate him for this cause was to hate him without cause. *Secondly,* Here-

in the scripture was fulfilled, and the antitype answered the type. Saul and his courtiers hated David without cause, for he had been serviceable to him with his harp, and with his sword; Absalom and his party hated him, though to him he had been an indulgent father, and to them a great benefactor. Thus was the Son of David hated, and hunted most unjustly. Those that hated Christ did not design there in to fulfil the scripture; but God, in permitting it, had that in his eye; and it confirms our faith in Christ as the Messiah that even this was foretold concerning him, and, being foretold, was accomplished in him. And we must not think it strange or hard if it have a further accomplishment in us. We are apt to justify our complaints of injuries done us with this, that they are causeless, whereas the more they are so the more they are like the sufferings of Christ, and may be the more easily borne.

3. In Christ the world hates God himself; this is twice said here (*v.* 23): *He that hateth me,* though he thinks his hatred goes no further, yet really he *hates my Father also.* And again, *v.* 24, They have *seen and hated both me and my Father.* Note, (1.) There are those that hate God, notwithstanding the beauty of his nature and the bounty of his providence; they are enraged at his justice, as the devils that believe it and tremble, are vexed at his dominion, and would gladly *break his bands asunder.* Those who cannot bring themselves to deny that there is a God, and yet wish there were none, they see and hate him. (2.) Hatred of Christ will be construed and adjudged hatred of God, for he is in his person his Father's express image, and in his office his great agent and ambassador. God will have all men to honour the Son as they honour the Father, and therefore what entertainment the Son has, that the Father has. Hence it is easy to infer that those who are enemies to the Christian religion, however they may cry up natural religion, are really enemies to all religion. Deists are in effect atheists, and those that ridicule the light of the gospel would, if they could, extinguish even natural light, and shake off all obligations of conscience and the fear of God. Let an unbelieving malignant world know that their enmity to the gospel of Christ will be looked upon in the great day as an enmity to the blessed God himself; and let all that suffer for righteousness' sake, according to the will of God, take comfort from this; if God himself be hated in them, and struck at through him, they need not be either ashamed of their cause or afraid of the issue.

Verses 26–27

Christ having spoken of the great opposition which his gospel was likely to meet with in the world, and the hardships that would be put upon the preachers of it, lest any should fear that they and it would be run down by that violent torrent, he here intimates to all those that were well-wishers to his cause and interest what effectual provision was made for supporting it, both by the principal testimony of the Spirit (*v.* 26), and the subordinate testimony of the apostles (*v.* 27), and testimonies are the proper supports of truth.

I. It is here promised that the blessed Spirit shall maintain the cause of Christ in the world, notwithstanding the opposition it should meet with. Christ, when he was reviled, committed his injured cause to his Father, and did not lose by his silence, for the Comforter came, pleaded it powerfully, and carried it triumphantly. *"When the Comforter* or Advocate *is come, who proceedeth from the Father,* and *whom I will send* to supply the want of my bodily presence, *he shall testify of me* against those that *hate me without cause."* We have more in this verse concerning the Holy Ghost than in any one verse besides in the Bible; and, being baptized into his name, we are concerned to acquaint ourselves with him as far as he is revealed.

1. Here is an account of him in his essence, or subsistence rather. He is *the Spirit of truth, who proceedeth from the Father.* Here, (1.) He is spoken of as a distinct person; not a quality or property, but a person under the proper name of a *Spirit,* and proper title of the *Spirit of truth,* a title fitly given him where he is brought in testifying. (2.) As a divine person, that *proceedeth from the Father,* by out-goings that were of old, *from everlasting.* The spirit or breath of man, called the *breath of life,* proceeds from the man, and by it modified he delivers his mind, by it invigorated he sometimes exerts his strength to *blow out* what he would extinguish, and *blow up* what he would excite. Thus the blessed Spirit is the emanation of divine light, and the energy of divine power. The rays of the sun, by which it dispenses and dif-

fuses its light, heat, and influence, proceed from the sun, and yet are one with it. The *Nicene* Creed says, The Spirit *proceedeth from the Father and the Son,* for he is called the *Spirit of the Son,* Gal. 4:6. And the Son is here said to *send him.* The Greek church chose rather to say, *from the Father by the Son.*

2. In his mission. (1.) He will come in a more plentiful effusion of his gifts, graces, and powers, than had ever yet been. Christ had been long the *ho erchomenos — he that should come;* now the blessed Spirit is so. (2.) *I will send him to you from the Father.* He had said (*ch.* 14:16), *I will pray the Father, and he shall send you the Comforter,* which bespeaks the Spirit to be the fruit of the intercession Christ makes within the veil: here he says, *I will send him,* which bespeaks him to be the fruit of his dominion within the veil. The Spirit was sent, [1.] By Christ as Mediator, now *ascended on high to give gifts unto men,* and all power being given to him. [2.] From the Father: "Not only from heaven, my Father's house" (the Spirit was given in a *sound from heaven,* Acts 2:2), "but according to my Father's will and appointment, and with his concurring power and authority." [3.] To the apostles to instruct them in their preaching, enable them for working, and carry them through their sufferings. He was given to them and their successors, both in Christianity and in the ministry; to them and their seed, and their seed's seed, according to that promise, Isa. 59:21.

3. In his office and operations, which are two: — (1.) One implied in the title given to him; he is the *Comforter,* or *Advocate.* An advocate for Christ, to maintain his cause against the world's infidelity, a comforter to the saints against the world's hatred. (2.) Another expressed: *He shall testify of me.* He is not only an advocate, but a witness for Jesus Christ; he is one of the three that *bear record in heaven,* and the first of the three that *bear witness on earth.* 1 Jn. 5:7, 8. He instructed the apostles, and enabled them to work miracles; he indited the scriptures, which are the standing witnesses that *testify of Christ, ch.* 5:39. The power of the ministry is derived from the Spirit, for he qualifies ministers; and the power of Christianity too, for he sanctifies Christians, and in both testifies of Christ.

II. It is here promised that the apostles also, by the Spirit's assistance, should have the honour of being Christ's witnesses (*v.* 27): *And you also shall bear witness* of me, being competent witnesses, for *you have been with* me from the beginning of my ministry. Observe here,

1. That the apostles were appointed to be witnesses for Christ in the world. When he had said, *The Spirit shall testify,* he adds, *And you also shall bear witness.* Note, The Spirit's working is not to supersede, but to engage and encourage ours. Though the Spirit testify, ministers also must bear their testimony, and people attend to it; for the Spirit of grace witnesses and works by the means of grace. The apostles were the first witnesses that were called in the famous trial between Christ and the prince of this world, which issued in the ejectment of the intruder. This intimates, (1.) The work cut out for them; they were to attest the truth, the whole truth, and nothing but the truth, concerning Christ, for the recovering of his just right, and the maintaining of his crown and dignity. Though Christ's disciples fled when they should have been witnesses for him upon his trial before the high priest and Pilate, yet after the Spirit was poured out upon them they appeared courageous in vindication of the cause of Christ against the accusations it was loaded with. The truth of the Christian religion was to be proved very much by the evidence of matter of fact, especially Christ's resurrection, of which the apostles were in a particular manner chosen witnesses (Act. 10:41), and they bore their testimony accordingly, Acts 3:15; 5:32. Christ's ministers are his witnesses. (2.) The honour put upon them hereby — that they should be *workers together with God.* "The *Spirit shall testify of me,* and you also, under the conduct of the Spirit, and in concurrence with the Spirit (who will preserve you from mistaking in that which you relate on your own knowledge, and will inform you of that which you cannot know but by revelation), *shall bear witness."* This might encourage them against the hatred and contempt of the world, that Christ had honoured them, and would own them.

2. That they were qualified to be so: *You have been with me from the beginning.* They not only heard his public sermons, but had constant private converse with him. He *went about doing good,* and, while others saw the wonderful and merciful works that he did in their own town and country

only, those that went about with him were witnesses of them all. They had likewise opportunity of observing the unspotted purity of his conversation, and could witness for him that they never saw in him, nor heard from him, any thing that had the least tincture of human frailty. Note. (1.) We have great reason to receive the record which the apostles gave of Christ, for they did not speak by hearsay, but what they had the greatest assurance of imaginable, 2 Pt. 1:16; 1 Jn. 1:1, 3. (2.) Those are best able to bear witness for Christ that have themselves been with him, by faith, hope, and love, and by living a life of communion with God in him. Ministers must first learn Christ, and then preach him. Those speak best of the things of God that speak experimentally. It is particularly a great advantage to have been acquainted with Christ *from the beginning,* to understand all things from the *very first,* Lu. 1:3. To have been with him from the beginning of our days. An early acquaintance and constant converse with the gospel of Christ will make a man like a good householder.

CHAPTER 16

Among other glorious things God hath spoken of himself this is one, I wound, and I heal, Deu. 32, 39. Christ's discourse in this chapter, which continues and concludes his farewell sermon to his disciples, does so. I. Here are wounding words in the notice he gives them of the troubles that were before them (*v.* 1–6). II. Here are healing words in the comforts he administers to them for their support under those troubles, which are five: — 1. That he would send them the Comforter (*v.* 7–15). 2. That he would visit them again at his resurrection (*v.* 16–22). 3. That he would secure to them an answer of peace to all their prayers (*v.* 23–27). 4. That he was now but returning to his Father (*v.* 28–32). 5. That, whatever troubles they might meet with in this world, by virtue of his victory over it they should be sure of peace in him (*v.* 33).

Verses 1–6

Christ dealt faithfully with his disciples when he sent them forth on his errands, for he told them the worst of it, that they might sit down and count the cost. He had told them in the chapter before to expect the world's hatred; now here in these verses,

I. He gives them a reason why he alarmed them thus with the expectation of trouble: *These things have I spoken unto you, that you should not be offended,* or *scandalized, v.* 1. 1. The disciples of Christ are apt to be offended at the cross; and the offence of the cross is a dangerous temptation, even to good men, to turn back from the ways of God, or turn aside out of them, or drive on heavily in them; to quit either their integrity or their comfort. It is not for nothing that a suffering time is called *an hour of temptation.* 2. Our Lord Jesus, by giving us notice of trouble, designed to take off the terror of it, that it might not be a surprise to us. Of all the adversaries of our peace, in this world of troubles, none insult us more violently, nor put our troops more into disorder, than disappointment does; but we can easily welcome a guest we expect, and *being fore-warned are fore-armed — Praemoniti, praemuniti.*

II. He foretels particularly what they should suffer (*v.* 2): "Those that have power to do it shall *put you out of their synagogues;* and this is not the worst, *they shall kill you." Ecce duo-gladii — Behold two swords* drawn against the followers of the Lord Jesus.

1. The sword of ecclesiastical censure; this is drawn against them by the Jews, for they were the only pretenders to church-power. They shall *cast you out of their synagogues; aposynagōgous poiēsousin hymas — they shall make you excommunicates.* (1.) "They shall cast you out of the particular synagogues you were members of." At first, they scourged them in their synagogues as contemners of the law (Mt. 10:17), and at length cast them out as incorrigible. (2.) "They shall cast you out of the congregation of Israel in general, the national church of the Jews; shall debar you from the privileges of that, put you into the condition of an outlaw," *qui caput gerit lupinum — to be knocked on the head, like another wolf;* "they will look upon you as Samaritans, as heathen men and publicans." *Interdico tibi aqua et igne — I forbid you the use of water and fire.* And were it not for the penalties, forfeitures, and incapacities, incurred hereby, it would be no injury to be thus driven out of a house infected and falling. Note, It has often been the lot of Christ's disciples to be unjustly excommunicated. Many a good truth has been branded with an anathema, and many a child of God *delivered to Satan.*

2. The sword of civil power: "The time cometh, *the hour is come;* now things are likely to be worse with you than hitherto they have been; when you are expelled as heretics, they will *kill you, and think they do God service,* and others will think so too." (1.) You will find them really cruel: They will *kill you.* Christ's sheep have been accounted as sheep for the slaughter; the twelve apostles (we are told) were all put to death, except John. Christ had said (*ch.* 15, 27), You shall *bear witness, martyreite — you shall be martyrs,* shall seal the truth with your blood, your heart's blood. (2.) You will find them *seemingly conscientious;* they will think they do God service; they will seem *latreian prospherein — to offer a good sacrifice* to God; as those that cast out God's servants of old, and said, *Let the Lord be glorified,* Isa. 66:5. Note, [1.] It is possible for those that are real enemies to God's service to pretend a mighty zeal for it. The devil's work has many a time been done in God's livery, and one of the most mischievous enemies Christianity ever had sits *in the temple of God.* Nay, [2.] It is common to patronise an enmity to religion with a color of duty to God, and service to his church. God's people have suffered the greatest hardships from conscientious persecutors. Paul verily thought he *ought to do* what he did *against the name of Jesus.* This does not at all lessen the sin of the persecutors, for villanies will never be consecrated by putting the name of God to them; but it does enhance the sufferings of the persecuted, to die under the character of being enemies to God; but there will be a resurrection of names as well as of bodies at the great day.

III. He gives them the true reason of the world's enmity and rage against them (*v.* 3): *"These things will they do unto you,* not because you have done them any harm, but *because they have not known the Father, nor me.* Let this comfort you, that none will be your enemies but the worst of men." Note, 1. Many that pretend to know God are wretchedly ignorant of him. Those that pretend to *do him service* thought they knew him, but it was a wrong notion they had of him. Israel transgressed the covenant, and yet cried, *My God, we know thee.* Hos. 8:1, 2. 2. Those that are ignorant of Christ cannot have any right knowledge of God. In vain do men pretend to know God and religion, while they slight Christ and Christianity. 3. Those are very ignorant indeed of God and Christ that think it an acceptable piece of service to persecute good people. Those that know Christ know that he *came not into the world to destroy men's lives, but to save them;* that he rules by the power of truth and love, not of fire and sword. Never was such a persecuting church as that which makes *ignorance the mother of devotion.*

IV. He tells them why he gave them notice of this now, and why not sooner.

1. Why he told them of it now (*v.* 4), not to discourage them, or add to their present sorrow; nor did he tell them of their danger that they might contrive how to avoid it, but that "when *the time shall come* (and you may be sure it will come), you may *remember that I told you."* Note, When suffering times come it will be of use to us to remember what Christ has told us of sufferings. (1.) That our belief of Christ's foresight and faithfulness may be confirmed; and, (2.) That the trouble may be the less grievous, for we were told of it before, and we took up our profession in expectation of it, so that it ought not to be a surprise to us, nor looked upon as a wrong to us. As Christ in his sufferings, so his followers in theirs, should have an eye to the *fulfilling of the scripture.*

2. Why he did not tell them of it sooner: *"I spoke not this to you from the beginning* when you and I came to be first acquainted, because *I was with you."* (1.) While he was with them, he bore the shock of the world's malice, and stood in the front of the battle; against him the powers of darkness levelled all their force, not against *small or great,* but only against the *king of Israel,* and therefore he did not need to say so much to them of suffering, because it did not fall much to their share; but we do find that from the beginning he bade them prepare for sufferings; and therefore, (2.) It seems rather to be meant of the promise of *another comforter.* This he had said little of to them *at the beginning,* because he was himself with them to instruct, guide, and comfort them, and then they needed not the promise of the Spirit's extraordinary presence. The children of the bride-chamber would not have so much need of a comforter till the bridegroom should be *taken away.*

V. He expresses a very affectionate concern for the present sadness of his disciples, upon occasion of what he had said to them (*v.* 5, 6): *"Now* I am to be no longer with you, but *go my way to him that sent me,* to repose there, after this fatigue; and *none of you asketh me,* with any courage, *Whither goest thou?* But, instead of enquiring after that which would comfort you, you pore upon that which looks melancholy, and *sorrow has filled your heart."*

1. He had told them that he was about to leave them: *Now I go my way.* He was not driven away by force, but voluntarily departed; his life was not extorted from him, but deposited by him. He went *to him that sent him,* to give an account of his negotiation. Thus, when we depart out of this world, we *go to him that sent us* into it, which should make us all solicitous to live to good purposes, remembering we have a commission to execute, which must be returned at a certain day.

2. He had told them what hard times they must suffer when he was gone, and that they must not expect such an easy quiet life as they had had. Now, if these were the legacies he had to leave to them, who had *left all* for him, they would be tempted to think they had made a sorry bargain of it, and were, for the present, in a consternation about it, in which their master sympathizes with them, yet blames them, (1.) That they were careless of the means of comfort, and did not stir up themselves to seek it: *None of you asks me, Whither goest thou?* Peter had started this question (*ch.* 13:36), and Thomas had seconded it (*ch.* 14:5), but they did not pursue it, they did not take the answer; they were in the dark concerning it, and did not enquire further, nor seek for fuller satisfaction; they did not continue seeking, continue knocking. See what a compassionate teacher Christ is, and how condescending to the weak and ignorant. Many a teacher will not endure that the learner should ask the same question twice; if he cannot take a thing quickly, let him go without it; but our Lord Jesus knows how to deal with babes, that must be taught with *precept upon precept.* If the disciples here would have found that his going away was for his advancement, and therefore his departure from them should not inordinately trouble them (for why should they be against his preferment?) and for their advantage, and therefore their sufferings for him should not inordinately trouble them; for a sight of *Jesus at the right hand of God* would be an effectual support to them, as it was to Stephen. Note, A humble believing enquiry into the design and tendency of the darkest dispensations of Providence would help to reconcile us to them, and to grieve the less, and fear the less, because of them; it will silence us to ask, Whence came they? but will abundantly satisfy us to ask, Whither go they? for we know they *work for good,* Rom. 8:28.

(2.) That they were too intent, and pored too much, upon the occasions of their grief: *Sorrow has filled their hearts.* Christ had said enough to fill them with joy (*ch.* 15:11); but by looking at that only which made against them, and overlooking that which made for them, they were so full of sorrow that there was no room left for joy. Note, It is the common fault and folly of melancholy Christians to dwell upon the dark side of the cloud, to meditate nothing but terror, and turn a deaf ear to *the voice of joy and gladness.* That which filled the disciples' hearts with sorrow, and hindered the operation of the cordials Christ administered, was too great an affection to this present life. They were big with hopes of their Master's external kingdom and glory, and that they should shine and reign with him: and now, instead of that, to hear of nothing but bonds and afflictions, this filled them with sorrow. Nothing is a greater prejudice to our joy in God than *the love of the world;* and *the sorrow of the world,* the consequence of it.

Verses 7–15

As it was usual with the Old Testament prophets to comfort the church in its calamities with the promise of the Messiah (Isa. 9:6; Mic. 5:6; Zec. 3:8); so, the Messiah being come, the promise of the Spirit was the great cordial, and is still.

Three things we have here concerning *the Comforter's coming: —*

I. That Christ's departure was absolutely necessary to the Comforter's coming, *v.* 7. The disciples were so loth to believe this that Christ saw cause to assert it with a more than ordinary solemnity: *I tell you the truth.* We may be confident of *the truth* of everything that Christ told us; he has no design to impose upon us. Now, to make them easy, he here tells them,

1. In general, *It was expedient for them that he should go away.* This was strange doctrine, but if it was true it was comfortable enough, and showed them how absurd their sorrow was. *It is expedient,* not only for me, but *for you* also, *that I go away;* though they did not see it, and are loth to

believe it, so it is. Note, (1.) Those things often seem grievous to us that are really expedient for us; and particularly our going away when we have finished our course. (2.) Our Lord Jesus is always for that which is most expedient for us, whether we think so or no. He deals not with us according to the folly of our own choice, but graciously over-rules it, and gives us the physic we are loth to take, because he knows it is good for us.

2. *It was therefore expedient* because it was in order to the sending of the Spirit. Now observe,

(1.) That Christ's going was in order to the Comforter's coming.

[1.] This is expressed negatively: *If I go not away, the Comforter will not come.* And why not? *First,* So it was settled in the divine counsels concerning this affair, and the measure must not be altered; *shall the earth be forsaken for them?* He that gives freely may recall one gift before he bestows another, while we would fondly hold all. *Secondly,* It is congruous enough that the ambassador extraordinary should be recalled, before the envoy come, that is constantly to reside. *Thirdly,* The sending of the Spirit was to be the fruit of Christ's purchase, and that purchase was to be made by his death, which was his going away. *Fourthly,* It was to be an answer to his intercession within the veil. See *ch.* 14:16. Thus must this gift be both paid for, and prayed for, by our Lord Jesus, that we might learn to put the greater value upon it. *Fifthly,* The great argument the Spirit was to use in convincing the world must be Christ's ascension into heaven, and his welcome here. See *v.* 10, and *ch.* 7:39. *Lastly,* The disciples must be weaned from his bodily presence, which they were too apt to dote upon, before they were duly prepared to receive the spiritual aids and comforts of a new dispensation.

[2.] It is expressed positively: *If I depart I will send him to you;* as though he had said, "Trust me to provide effectually that you shall be no loser by my departure." The glorified Redeemer is not unmindful of his church on earth, nor will ever leave it without its necessary supports. Though he *departs, he sends the Comforter,* nay, he departs on purpose to send him. Thus still, though one generation of ministers and Christians depart, another is raised up in their room, for Christ will maintain his own cause.

(2.) That the presence of Christ's Spirit in his church is so much better, and more desirable, than his bodily presence, that it was really expedient for us that he should go away, to send the Comforter. His corporal presence could be put in one place at one time, but his Spirit is every where, in all places, at all times, wherever *two or three are gathered in his name.* Christ's bodily presence draws men's eyes, his Spirit draws their hearts; that was *the letter* which *kills,* his *Spirit gives life.*

II. That the coming of *the Spirit* was absolutely necessary to the carrying on of Christ's interests on earth (*v.* 8): *And when he is come, elthōn ekeinos.* He that is sent is willing of himself to come, and at his first coming he will do this, *he will reprove,* or, as the margin reads it, *he will convince the world,* by your ministry, concerning *sin, righteousness, and judgment.*

1. See here what the office of the Spirit is, and on what errand he is sent. (1.) To *reprove.* The Spirit, by the word and conscience, is a reprover; ministers are reprovers by office, and by them the Spirit reproves. (2.) To *convince.* It is a lawterm, and speaks the office of the judge in summing up the evidence, and setting a matter that has been long canvassed in a clear and true light. He shall *convince,* that is, "He shall put to silence the adversaries of Christ and his cause, by discovering and demonstrating the falsehood and fallacy of that which they have maintained, and the truth and certainty of that which they have opposed." Note, Convincing work is the Spirit's work; he can do it effectually, and none but he; man may open the cause, but it is the Spirit only that can open the heart. The Spirit is called the *Comforter* (*v.* 7), and here it is said, *He shall convince.* One would think this were cold comfort, but it is the method the Spirit takes, first to convince, and then to comfort; first to lay open the wound, and then to apply healing medicines. Or, taking conviction more generally, for a demonstration of what is right, it intimates that the Spirit's comforts are solid, and grounded upon truth.

2. See who they are whom he is to reprove and convince: *The world,* both Jew and Gentile. (1.) He shall give the world the most powerful means of conviction, for the apostles shall go into all the world, backed by the Spirit, to preach the gospel, fully proved. (2.) He shall sufficiently provide for the taking off and silencing of the objections and prejudices of the world against the gospel. Many an infidel was *convinced of all and judged of all,* 1 Co. 14:24. (3.) He shall effectually and savingly convince many in the world, some in every age, in every place, in order to their conversion to the faith of Christ. Now this was an encouragement to the disciples, in reference to the difficulties they were likely to meet with, [1.] That they should see good done, Satan's kingdom *fall like lightning,* which would be their joy, as it was his. Even this malignant world the Spirit shall work upon; and the conviction of sinners is the comfort of faithful ministers. [2.] That this would be the fruit of their services and sufferings, these should contribute very much to this good work.

3. See what the Spirit shall convince the world of.

(1.) *Of sin* (*v.* 9), *because they believe not on me.* [1.] The Spirit is sent to convince sinners of sin, not barely to tell them of it; in conviction there is more than this; it is to prove it upon them, and force them to own it, as they (*ch.* 8:9) that were *convicted of their own consciences. Make them to know their abominations.* The Spirit convinces of the fact of sin, that we have done so and so; of the fault of sin, that we have done ill in doing so; of the folly of sin, that we have acted against right reason, and our true interest; of the filth of sin, that by it we are become odious to God; of the fountain of sin, the corrupt nature; and lastly, of the fruit of sin, that the end thereof is death. The Spirit demonstrates the depravity and degeneracy of the whole world, that all the world is guilty before God. [2.] The Spirit, in conviction, fastens especially upon the sin of unbelief, their not believing in Christ, *First,* As the great reigning sin. There was, and is, a world of people, that believe not in Jesus Christ, and they are not sensible that it is their sin. Natural conscience tells them that murder and theft are sin; but it is a supernatural work of the spirit to convince them that it is a sin to suspend their belief of the gospel, and to reject the salvation offered by it. Natural religion, after it has given us its best discoveries and directions, lays and leaves us under this further obligation, that whatever divine revelation shall be made to us at any time, with sufficient evidence to prove it divine, we accept it, and submit to it. This law those transgress who, when *God speaketh to us by his Son, refuse him that speaketh;* and therefore it is sin. *Secondly,* As the great ruining sin. Every sin is so in its own nature; no sin is so to them that believe in Christ; so that it is unbelief that damns sinners. It is because of this that they cannot *enter into rest,* that they cannot *escape the wrath of God;* it is a sin against the remedy. *Thirdly,* As that which is at the bottom of all sin; so Calvin takes it. The Spirit shall convince the world that the true reason why sin reigns among them is because they are not by faith united to Christ. *Ne putimus vel guttam unam rectitudinis sine Christo nobis inesse — Let us not suppose that, apart from Christ, we have a drop of rectitude.* — Calvin.

(2.) *Of righteousness, because I go to my Father, and you see me no more,* v. 10. We may understand this, [1.] Of Christ's personal righteousness. He shall convince the world that Jesus of Nazareth was Christ the righteous (1 Jn. 2:1), as the centurion owned (Lu. 23:47), *Certainly this was a righteous man.* His enemies put him under the worst of characters, and multitudes were not or would not be convinced but that he was a bad man, which strengthened their prejudices against his doctrine; but he is *justified by the spirit* (1 Tim. 3:16), he is proved to be a *righteous man,* and not, a deceiver; and then the point is in effect gained; for he is either the great Redeemer or a great cheat; but a cheat we are sure he is not. Now by what medium or argument will the Spirit convince men of the sincerity of the Lord Jesus? Why, *First,* Their *seeing him no more* will contribute something towards the removal of their prejudices; they shall see him no more *in the likeness of sinful flesh, in the form of a servant,* which made them slight him. Moses was more respected after his removal than before. But, *Secondly,* His *going to the Father* would be a full conviction of it. The coming of the Spirit, according to the promise, was a proof of Christ's exaltation to God's *right hand* (Acts 2:33), and this was a demonstration of his righteousness; for the holy God would never set a deceiver at his right hand. [2.] Of Christ's righteousness communicated to us for our justification and salvation; that everlasting righteousness which Messiah was to bring in, Dan. 9:24. Now, *First,* The Spirit shall convince men of this righteousness. Having by convictions of sin shown them their need of a righteousness, lest this should drive them to despair he will show them where it is to be had, and how they may, upon

their believing, be acquitted from guilt, and accepted as righteous in God's sight. It was hard to convince those of this righteousness that *went about to establish their own* (Rom. 10:3), but the Spirit will do it. *Secondly,* Christ's ascension is the great argument proper to convince men of this righteousness: *I go to the Father, and,* as an evidence of my welcome with him, *you shall see me no more.* If Christ had left any part of his undertaking unfinished, he had been sent back again; but now that we are sure he is *at the right hand of God,* we are sure of being justified through him.

(3.) *Of judgment, because the prince of this world is judged,* v. 11. Observe here, [1.] The devil, *the prince of this world,* was judged, was discovered to be a great deceiver and destroyer, and as such judgment was entered against him, and execution in part done. He was cast out of the Gentile world when his oracles were silenced and his altars deserted, cast out of the bodies of many in Christ's name, which miraculous power continued long in the church; he was cast out of the souls of people by the grace of God working with the gospel of Christ; he *fell as lightning from heaven.* [2.] This is a good argument wherewith the Spirit convinces the world of judgment, that is, *First,* Of inherent holiness and sanctification, Mt. 12:18. By *the judgment of the prince of this world,* it appears that Christ is stronger than Satan, and can disarm and dispossess him, and set up his throne upon the ruin of his. *Secondly,* Of a new and better dispensation of things. He shall show that Christ's errand into the world was to set things to right in it, and to introduce times of reformation and regeneration; and he proves it by this, that *the prince of this world,* the great master of misrule, is judged and expelled. All will be well when his power is broken who made the mischief. *Thirdly,* Of the power and dominion of the Lord Jesus. He shall convince the world that *all judgment is committed to him,* and that he is the *Lord of all,* which is evident by this, that he has judged the prince of this world, has broken *the serpent's head, destroyed him that had the power of death, and spoiled principalities,* if Satan be thus subdued by Christ, we may be sure no other power can stand before him. *Fourthly,* Of the final day of judgment: all the obstinate enemies of Christ's gospel and kingdom shall certainly be reckoned with at last, for the devil, their ringleader, is judged.

III. That the coming of the Spirit would be of unspeakable advantage to the disciples themselves. The Spirit has work to do, not only on the enemies of Christ, to convince and humble them, but upon his servants and agents, to instruct and comfort them; and therefore it was *expedient for them that he should go away.*

1. He intimates to them the tender sense he had of their present weakness (*v.* 12): *I have yet many things to say unto you* (not which should have been said, but which he could and would have said), *but you cannot bear them now.* See what a teacher Christ is. (1.) None like him for copiousness; when he has said much, he has still many things more to say; treasures of wisdom and knowledge are hid in him, if we be not straitened in ourselves. (2.) None like him for compassion; he would have told them more of *the things pertaining to the kingdom of God,* particularly of the rejection of the Jews and the calling of the Gentiles, but they could not bear it, it would have confounded and stumbled them, rather than have given them any satisfaction. When, after his resurrection, they spoke to him of *restoring the kingdom to Israel,* he referred them to *the coming of the Holy Ghost,* by which they should receive power to bear those discoveries which were so contrary to the notions they had received that they could not *bear them now.*

2. He assures them of sufficient assistances, by the pouring out of the Spirit. They were now conscious to themselves of great dulness, and many mistakes; and what shall they do now their master is leaving them? *"But when he, the Spirit of Truth, is come,* you will be easy, and all will be well." Well indeed; for he shall undertake to guide the apostles, and glorify Christ.

(1.) To guide the apostles. He will take care,

[1.] That they do not miss their way: *He will guide you;* as the camp of Israel was guided through the wilderness by *the pillar of cloud and fire.* The Spirit guided their tongues in speaking, and their pens in writing, to secure them from mistakes. The Spirit is given us to be our guide (Rom. 8:14), not only to show us the way, but to go along with us, by his continued aids and influences.

[2.] That they do not come short of their end: *He will guide them into all truth,* as the skilful pilot guides the ship into the port it is bound for. To be led *into a truth* is more than barely to know it; it is to be intimately and experimentally acquainted with it; to be piously and strongly affected with it; not only to have the notion of it in our heads, but the relish and savour and power of it in our hearts; it denotes a gradual discovery of truth shining more and more: "He shall lead you by those truths that are plain and easy to those that are more difficult." But how into *all truth?* The meaning is,

First, Into the whole truth relating to their embassy; whatever was needful or useful for them to know, in order to the due discharge of their office, they should be fully instructed in it; what truths they were to teach others the Spirit would teach them, would give them the understanding of, and enable them both to explain and to defend.

Secondly, Into nothing but the truth. All that *he shall guide you into* shall be *truth* (1 Jn. 2:27); *the anointing is truth.* In the following words he proves both these: — 1. "The Spirit shall teach nothing but the truth, *for he shall not speak of himself* any doctrine distinct from mine, *but whatsoever he shall hear,* and knows to be the mind of the Father, *that,* and that only, *shall he speak.*" This intimates, (1.) That the testimony of the Spirit, in the word and by the apostles, is what we may rely upon. The *Spirit* knows *and searches all things, even the deep things of God,* and the apostles received that Spirit (1 Co. 2:10, 11), so that we may venture our souls upon the Spirit's word. (2.) That the testimony of the Spirit always concurs with the word of Christ, *for he does not speak of himself,* has no separate interest or intention of his own, but, as in essence so in records, he *is one with the Father and the Son,* 1 Jn. 5:7. Men's word and spirit often disagree, but the eternal Word and the eternal Spirit never do. 2. "He shall teach you all truth, and keep back nothing that is profitable for you, for *he will show you things to come.*" The Spirit was in the apostles a Spirit of prophecy; it was foretold that he should be so (Joel 2:28), and he was so. *The Spirit showed them things to come,* as Acts 11:28; 20:23; 21:11. The Spirit spoke of the apostasy of the *latter times,* 1 Tim. 4:1. John, when he was in the Spirit had *things to come* shown him in vision. Now this was a great satisfaction to their own minds, and of use to them in their conduct, and was also a great confirmation of their mission. Jansenius has a pious note upon this: We should not grudge that the Spirit does not *show us things to come* in this world, as he did to the apostles; let it suffice that the Spirit in the word hath *shown us things to come* in the other world, which are our chief concern.

(2.) The Spirit undertook to glorify Christ, *v.* 14, 15. [1.] Even the sending of the Spirit was the glorifying of Christ. God the Father glorified him in heaven, and the Spirit glorified him on earth. It was the honour of the Redeemer that the Spirit was both sent in his name and sent on his errand, to carry on and perfect his undertaking. All the gifts and graces of the Spirit, all the preaching and all the writing of the apostles, under the influence of the Spirit, the tongues, and miracles, were to glorify Christ. [2.] The Spirit glorified Christ by leading his followers into *the truth as it is in Jesus,* Eph. 4:21. He assures them, *First,* that the Spirit should communicate the things of Christ to them: *He shall receive of mine, and shall show it unto you.* As in essence *he proceeded from the Son,* so in influence and operation he derived from him. *He shall take ek tou emou — of that which is mine.* All that the Spirit shows us, that is, applies to us, for our instruction and comfort, all that he gives us for our strength and quickening, and all that he secures and seals to us, did all belong to Christ, and was had and received from him. All was his, for he bought it, and paid dearly for it, and therefore he had reason to call it his own; his, for he first received it; it was given him as the head of the church, to be communicated by him to all his members. The Spirit came not to erect a new kingdom, but to advance and establish the same kingdom that Christ had erected, to maintain the same interest and pursue the same design; those therefore that pretend to the Spirit, and vilify Christ, give themselves the lie, for he came to glorify Christ. *Secondly,* That herein the things of God should be communicated to us. Lest any should think that the receiving of this would not make them much the richer, he adds, *All things that the Father hath are mine.* As God, all that self-existent light and self-sufficient happiness which *the Father has,* he has; as Mediator, *all things are delivered to him of the Father* (Mt. 11:27); all that *grace and truth* which God designed to show us he lodged in the hands of the Lord Jesus, Col. 1:19. Spiritual blessings in heavenly things are given by the Father to the Son for us, and the Son entrusts the Spirit to convey them to us. Some apply it to that which goes just before: *He shall show you things to come,* and so it is explained by Rev. 1:1. God gave *it to Christ, and he signified it to John, who wrote what the Spirit said,* Rev. 1:1.

Verses 16–22

Our Lord Jesus, for the comfort of his sorrowful disciples, here promises that he would visit them again.

I. Observe the intimation he gave them of the comfort he designed them, *v.* 16. Here he tells them,

1. That they should now shortly lose the sight of him: *A little while, and you* that have seen me so long, and still desire to *see me, shall not see me;* and therefore, if they had any good question to ask him, they must ask quickly, for he was now taking his leave of them. Note, It is good to consider how near to a period our seasons of grace are, that we may be quickened to improve them while they are continued. Now our eyes see our teachers, see the days *of the Son of man;* but, perhaps, yet a *little while, and we shall not see them.* They lost the sight of Christ, (1.) At his death, when he withdrew from this world, and never after showed himself openly in it. The most that death does to our Christian friends is to take them out of our sight, not out of being, not out of bliss, but out of all relation to us, only out of sight, and then not out of mind. (2.) At his ascension, when he withdrew from them (from those who, after his resurrection, had for some time conversed with him), *out of their sight; a cloud received* him, and, though they looked up steadfastly after him, *they saw him no more,* Acts 1:9, 10; 2 Ki. 2:12. See 2 Co. 5:16.

2. That yet they should speedily recover the sight of him; *Again a little while, and you shall see me,* and therefore you ought not to *sorrow as those that have no hope.* His farewell was not a final farewell; they should see him again, (1.) At his resurrection, soon after his death, when *he showed himself alive,* by many infallible proofs, and this in a very little while, not forty hours. See Hos. 6:2. (2.) By the pouring out of the Spirit, soon after his ascension, which scattered the mists of ignorance and mistake they were almost lost in, and gave them a much clearer insight into the mysteries of Christ's gospel than they had yet had. The Spirit's coming was Christ's visit to his disciples, not a transient but a permanent one, and such a visit as abundantly retrieved the sight of him. (3.) At his second coming. They saw him again as they removed one by one to him at death, and they shall see him together at the end of time, when *he shall come in the clouds, and every eye shall see him.* It might be truly said of this that it was but *a little while, and they should see him;* for what are the days of time, to the days of eternity? 2 Pt. 3:8, 9.

3. He assigns the reason: *"Because I go to the Father;* and therefore," (1.) "I must leave you for a time, because my business calls me to the upper world, and you must be content to spare me, for really my business is yours." (2.) "Therefore you shall see me again shortly, for the Father will not detain me to your prejudice. If I go upon your errand, you shall see me again as soon as my business is done, as soon as is convenient."

It should seem, all this refers rather to his going away at death, and return at his resurrection, than his going away at the ascension, and his return at the end of time; for it was his death that was their grief, not his ascension (Lu. 24:52), and between his death and resurrection it was indeed a *little while.* And it may be read, not, *yet a little while* (it is not *eti mikron,* as it is *ch.* 12:35), but *mikron — for a little while you shall not see me,* namely, the three days of his lying in the grave; and again, *for a little while you shall see me,* namely, the forty days between his resurrection and ascension. Thus we may say of our ministers and Christian friends, *Yet a little while, and we shall not see them,* either they must leave us or we must leave them, but it is certain that we must part shortly, and yet not part for ever. It is but a good night to those whom we hope to see with *joy in the morning.*

II. The perplexity of the disciples upon the intimation given them; they were at a loss what to make of it (*v.* 17, 18); *Some of them said,* softly, *among themselves,* either some of the weakest, that were least able, or some of the most inquisitive, that were most desirous, to understand him, *What is this that he saith to us?* Though Christ had often spoken to this purport before, yet still they were in the dark; though *precept be upon precept,* it is in vain, unless God gave the understanding. Now see here, 1. The disciples' weakness, in that they could not understand so plain a saying, to which Christ had already given them a key, having told them so often in plain terms that he should *be killed, and the third day rise again;* yet, say they, *We cannot tell what he saith;* for, (1.) *Sorrow had filled their heart,* and made them unapt to receive the impressions of comfort. The darkness of ignorance and the darkness of melancholy commonly increase and thicken one another; mistakes cause griefs, and then griefs confirm mistakes. (2.) The notion of Christ's secular kingdom was so deeply rooted in them that they could make no sense at all of those sayings of his which they knew not how to reconcile with that notion. When we think the scripture must be made to agree with the false ideas we have imbibed, no wonder that we complain of difficulty; but when our reasonings are captivated to revelation, the matter becomes easy. (3.) It should seem, that which puzzled them was the *little while.* If he must go at least, yet they could not conceive how he should leave them quickly, when his stay hitherto had been so short, and so little while, comparatively. Thus it is hard for us to represent to ourselves that change as near which yet we know will come certainly, and may come suddenly. When we are told, *Yet a little while* and we must go hence, *yet a little while* and we must *give up our account,* we know not how to digest it; for we always took the vision to be *for a great while to come,* Eze. 12:27. 2. Their willingness to be instructed. When they were at a loss about the meaning of Christ's words, they conferred together upon it, and asked help of one another. By mutual converse about divine things we both borrow the light of others and improve our own. Observe how exactly they repeat Christ's words. Though we cannot fully solve every difficulty we meet with in scripture, yet we must not therefore throw it by, but revolve what we cannot explain, and wait *till God shall reveal even this unto us.*

III. The further explication of what Christ had said.

1. See here *why* Christ explained it (*v.* 19); because he *knew they were desirous to ask him,* and designed it. Note, The knots we cannot untie we must bring to him who alone can give an understanding. Christ *knew they were desirous to ask him,* but were bashful and ashamed to ask. Note, Christ takes cognizance of pious desires, though they be not as yet offered up, the *groanings that cannot be uttered,* and even *anticipates them with the blessings of his goodness.* Christ instructed those who he *knew were desirous to ask him,* though they did not ask. *Before we call, he answers.* Another reason why Christ explained it was because he observed them canvassing this matter among themselves: *"Do you enquire this among yourselves?* Well, I will make it easy to you." This intimates to us who they are that Christ will teach: (1.) The humble, that confess their ignorance, for so much their enquiry implied. (2.) The diligent, that use the means they have: *"Do you enquire?* You shall be taught. *To him that hath shall be given."*

2. See here *how* he explained it; not by a nice and critical descant upon the words, but by bringing the thing more closely to them; he had told them of *not seeing him, and seeing him,* and they did not apprehend the meaning, and therefore he explains it by their sorrowing and rejoicing, because we commonly measure things according as they affect us (*v.* 20): *You shall weep and lament,* for my departure, *but the world shall rejoice* in it; *and you shall be sorrowful,* while I am absent, *but,* upon my return to you, *your sorrow will be turned into joy.* But he says nothing of the *little while,* because he saw that this perplexed them more than any thing; and it is of no consequence to us to know *the times and the seasons.* Note, Believers have joy or sorrow according as they have or have not a sight of Christ, and the tokens of his presence with them.

(1.) What Christ says here, and in *v.* 21, 22, of their sorrow and joy, is primarily to be understood of the present state and circumstances of the disciples, and so we have,

[1.] Their grief foretold: *You shall weep and lament, and you shall be sorrowful.* The sufferings of Christ could not but be the sorrow of his disciples. They wept for him because they loved him; the pain of our friend is a pain to ourselves; when they slept, it was for sorrow, Lu. 22:45. They wept for themselves, and their own loss, and the sad apprehensions they had of what would become of them when he was gone. It could not but be a grief to lose him for whom they had left their all, and from whom they had expected so much. Christ has given notice to his disciples beforehand to expect sorrow, that they may treasure up comforts accordingly.

[2.] The world's rejoicing at the same time: *But the world shall rejoice.* That which is the grief of saints is the joy of sinners. *First,* Those that are *strangers to Christ* will continue in their carnal mirth, and not at all interest themselves in their sorrows. *It is nothing to them that pass by,* Lam. 1:12. Nay, *Secondly,* Those that are *enemies to Christ* will rejoice because they hope they have conquered him, and ruined his interest. When the chief priests had Christ upon the cross, we may suppose they made merry over him, as those that dwell on earth over the slain witnesses, Rev. 11:10. Let it be no surprise to us if we see others triumphing, when we are *trembling for the ark.*

[3.] The return of joy to them in due time: *But your sorrow shall be turned into joy.* As *the joy of the hypocrite,* so the sorrow of the true Christian, is *but for a moment. The disciples were glad when they saw the Lord.* His resurrection was *life from the dead* to them, and their sorrow for Christ's sufferings was turned into a joy of such a nature as could not be damped and embittered by any sufferings of their own. They were *sorrowful, and yet always rejoicing* (2 Co. 6:10), had sorrowful lives and yet joyful hearts.

(2.) It is applicable to all the faithful followers of the Lamb, and describes the common case of Christians.

[1.] Their condition and disposition are both mournful; sorrows are their lot, and seriousness is their temper: those that are acquainted with Christ must, as he was, be *acquainted with grief;* they *weep and lament* for that which others make light of, their own sins, and the sins of those about them; they mourn with sufferers that mourn, and mourn for sinners that mourn not for themselves.

[2.] The world, at the same time, goes away with all the mirth; they laugh now, and spend their days so jovially that one would think they neither knew sorrow nor feared it. Carnal mirth and pleasures are surely none of the best things, for then the worst men would not have so large a share of them, and the favourites of heaven be such strangers to them.

[3.] Spiritual mourning will shortly be turned into eternal rejoicing. *Gladness is sown for the upright in heart, that sow tears,* and without doubt *they will* shortly *reap in joy.* Their sorrow will not only be followed with joy, but turned into it; for the most precious comforts take rise from pious griefs. Thus he illustrates by a similitude taken from a woman in travail, to whose sorrows he compares those of his disciples, for their encouragement; for it is the will of Christ that his people should be a comforted people.

First, Here is the similitude or parable itself (*v.* 21): *A woman,* we know, *when she is in travail, hath sorrow,* she is in exquisite pain, *because her hour is come,* the hour which nature and providence have fixed, which she has expected, and cannot escape; *but as soon as she is delivered of the child,* provided she be safely delivered, and the child be, though a *Jabez* (1 Chr. 4:9), yet not a *Benoni* (Gen. 35:18), then *she remembers no more the anguish,* her groans and complaints are over, and the after-pains are more easily borne, *for joy that a man is born into the world, anthrōpos,* one of the human race, a child, be it son or daughter, for the word signifies either. Observe,

a. The fruit of the curse, in the sorrow and pain of a woman in travail, according to the sentence (Gen. 3:16), *In sorrow shalt thou bring forth.* These pains are extreme, the greatest griefs and pains are compared to them (Ps. 48:6; Isa. 13:3; Jer. 4:31; 6:24), and they are inevitable, 1 Th. 5:3. See what this world is; all its roses are surrounded with thorns, all the children of men are upon this account foolish children, that they are *the heaviness of her that bore them* from the very first. This comes of sin.

b. The fruit of the blessing, in *the joy there is for a child born into the world.* If God had not preserved the blessing in force after the fall, *Be fruitful and multiply,* parents could never have looked upon their children with any comfort; but what is the fruit of a blessing is matter of joy; the birth of a living child is, (*a.*) The parents' joy; it makes them very glad, Jer. 20:15. Though children are certain cares, uncertain comforts, and often prove the greatest crosses, yet it is natural to us to rejoice at their birth. Could we be sure that our children, like John, would *be filled with the Holy Ghost,* we might, indeed, like his parents, have *joy and gladness* in their birth, Lu. 1:14, 15. But when we consider, not only that they are born in sin, but, as it is expressed, that *they are born into the world,* a world of snares and a vale of tears, we shall see reason to rejoice with trembling, lest it should prove *better for them that they had never been born.* (*b.*) It is such joy as makes the anguish not to be remembered, or *remembered as waters that pass away,* Job 11:16. *Haec olim meminisse juvabit.* Gen. 41:51. Now this is very proper to set forth, [*a.*] The sorrows of Christ's disciples in this world; they are like travailing pains, sure and sharp, but not to last long, and in order to a joyful product; they are in *pain to be delivered,* as the church is described (Rev. 12:2), and *the whole creation,* Rom. 8:22. And, [*b.*] Their joys after these sorrows, which will *wipe away all tears,* for *the former things are passed away,* Rev. 21:4. When they are born into that blessed world, and reap the fruit of all their services and sorrows, the toil and anguish of this world will be no more remembered, as Christ's were not, when *he saw of the travail of his soul* abundantly to his satisfaction, Isa. 53:11.

Secondly, The application of the similitude (*v.* 22): *"You now have sorrow,* and are likely to have more, *but I will see you again,* and you me, and then all will be well."

a. Here again he tells them of their *sorrow: "You now therefore have sorrow; therefore,* because I am leaving you," as is intimated in the antithesis, *I will see you again.* Note, Christ's withdrawings are just cause of grief to his disciples. *If he hide his face,* they cannot be *troubled.* When the sun sets, the sun-flower will hang the head. And Christ takes notice of these griefs, has a bottle for the tears, and a book for the sighs, of all gracious mourners.

b. He, more largely than before, assures them of a return of joy, Ps. 30:5, 11. He himself went through his own griefs, and bore ours, *for the joy that was set before him;* and he would have us encourage ourselves with the same prospect. Three things recommend the joy: — (*a.*) The cause of it: *"I will see you again.* I will make you a kind and friendly visit, to enquire after you, and minister comfort to you." Note, [*a.*] Christ will graciously return to those that wait for him, though *for a small moment* he has seemed *to forsake them,* Isa. 54:7. Men, when they are exalted, will scarcely look upon their inferiors; but the exalted Jesus will visit his disciples. They shall not only see him in his glory, but he will see them in their meanness. [*b.*] Christ's returns are returns of joy to all his disciples. When clouded evidences are cleared up and interrupted communion is revived, *then is the mouth filled with laughter.* (*b.*) The cordiality of it: *Your heart shall rejoice.* Divine consolation *put gladness into the heart.* Joy in the heart is solid, and not flashy; it is secret, and that which a *stranger does not intermeddle with;* it is sweet, and gives a good man satisfaction in himself; it is sure, and not easily broken in upon. Christ's disciples should heartily rejoice in his returns, sincerely and greatly. (*c.*) The continuance of it: *Your joy no man taketh from you.* Men will attempt to take their joy from them; they would if they could; but they shall not prevail. Some understand it of the eternal joy of those that are glorified; those that have *entered into the joy of the Lord shall go no more out.* Our joys on earth we are liable to be robbed of by a thousand accidents, but heavenly joys are everlasting. I rather understand it of the spiritual joys of those that are sanctified, particularly the apostles' joy in their apostleship. *Thanks be to God,* says Paul, in the name of the rest, *who always causes us to triumph,* 2 Co. 2:14. A malicious world would have taken it from them, they would have lost it; but, when they took everything else from them, they could not take this; *as sorrowful, yet always rejoicing.* They could not rob them of their joy, because they could not *separate them from the love of Christ,* could not rob them of their God, nor of their *treasure in heaven.*

Verses 23–27

An answer to their askings is here promised, for their further comfort. Now there are two ways of asking: asking by way of enquiry, which is the asking of the ignorant; and asking by way of request, which is the asking of the indigent. Christ here speaks of both.

I. By way of enquiry, they should not need to ask (*v.* 23): *"In that day you shall ask me nothing;" ouk erōtēsete ouden — you shall ask no questions;* "you shall have such a clear knowledge of gospel mysteries, by the opening of your understandings, that you shall not need to enquire" (as Heb. 8:11, *they shall not teach*); "you shall have more knowledge on a sudden than hitherto you have had by diligent attendance." They had asked some ignorant questions (as *ch.* 9:2), some ambitious questions (as Mt. 18:1), some distrustful ones (as Mt. 19:27), some impertinent ones, (as *ch.* 21:21), some curious ones (as Acts 1:6); but after the Spirit was poured out, nothing of all this. In the story *of the apostles' Acts* we seldom find them asking questions, as David, *Shall I do this?* Or, *Shall I go thither?* For they were constantly under a divine guidance. In that weighty case of preaching *the gospel to the Gentiles,* Peter went, *nothing doubting,* Acts 10:20. Asking questions supposes us at a loss, or at least at a stand, and the best of us have need to ask questions; but we should aim at such a full assurance of understanding that we may not hesitate, but be constantly led in a plain path both of truth and duty.

Now for this he gives a reason (*v.* 25), which plainly refers to this promise, that they should not need to ask questions: *"These things have I spoken unto you in proverbs,* in such a way as you have thought not so plain and intelligible as you could have wished, *but the time cometh when I shall show you plainly,* as plainly as you can desire, *of the Father,* so that you shall not need to ask questions."

1. The great thing Christ would lead them into was the knowledge of God: *"I will show you the Father,* and bring you acquainted with him." This is that which Christ designs to give and which all true Christians desire to have. When Christ would express the greatest favour intended for his disciples, he tells them that it would, *show them plainly of the Father;* for what is the happiness of heaven, but immediately and everlastingly to see God? *To know God as the Father of our Lord Jesus Christ* is the greatest mystery for the understanding to please itself with the contemplation of; and to know him as our Father is the greatest happiness for the will and affections to please themselves with the choice and enjoyment of.

2. Of this he had hitherto spoken to them in proverbs, which are wise and instructive sayings, but figurative, and resting in generals. Christ had spoken many things very plainly to them, and expounded his parables privately to the disciples, but, (1.) Considering their dulness, and unaptness to receive what he said to them, he might be said to speak in proverbs; what he said to them was as a book sealed, Isa. 29:11. (2.) Comparing the discoveries he had made to them, in what he had spoken to their ears, with what he would make to them when he would *put his Spirit into their heart,* all hitherto had been proverbs. It would be a pleasing surprise to themselves, and they would think themselves in a new world, when they would reflect upon all their former notions as confused and enigmatical, compared with their present clear and distinct knowledge of divine things. *The ministration of the letter* was nothing to *that of the Spirit,* 2 Co. 3:8–11. (3.) Confining it to what he had said of *the Father,* and the counsels of *the Father.* what he had said was very dark, compared with what was shortly to be revealed, Col. 2:2.

3. He would speak to them *plainly, parrēsia — with freedom,* of the Father. When the Spirit was poured out, the apostles attained to a much greater knowledge of divine things than they had before, as appears by the utterance the Spirit gave them, Acts 2:4. They were led into the mystery of those things of which they had previously a very confused idea; and what the Spirit showed them Christ is here said to show them, for, as the Father speaks by the Son, so the Son by the Spirit. But this promise will have its full accomplishment in heaven, where we shall see the Father as he is, *face to face,* not as we do now, *through a glass darkly* (1 Co. 13:12), which is matter of comfort to us under the cloud of present darkness, by reason of which we cannot *order our speech,* but often disorder it. While we are here, we have many questions to ask concerning the invisible God and the invisible world; but in that day we shall see all things clearly, and *ask no more questions.*

II. He promises that by way of request they should ask nothing in vain. it is taken for granted that all Christ's disciples give themselves to prayer. He has taught them by his precept and pattern to be much in prayer; this must be their support and comfort when he had left them; their instruction, direction, strength, and success, must be fetched in by prayer. Now,

1. Here is an express promise of a grant, *v.* 23. The preface to this promise is such as makes it inviolably sure, and leaves no room to question it: *"Verily, verily, I say unto you,* I pledge my veracity upon it." The promise itself is incomparably rich and sweet; the golden sceptre is here held out to us, with the word, *What is thy petition, and it shall be granted?* For he says, *Whatsoever you shall ask the Father in my name, he will give it to you.* We had it before, *ch.* 14:13. What would we more? The promise is as express as we can desire. (1.) We are here taught how to seek; we must *ask the Father*

in Christ's name; we must have an eye to God as a Father, and come as children to him; and to Christ as Mediator, and come as clients. Asking of the Father includes a sense of spiritual blessings, with a conviction that they are to be had from God only. It included also humility of address to him, with a believing confidence in him, as a Father able and ready to help us. Asking in Christ's name includes an acknowledgment of our own unworthiness to receive any favour from God, a complacency in the method God has taken of keeping up a correspondence with us by his Son, and an entire dependence upon Christ as *the Lord our Righteousness.* (2.) We are here told how we shall speed: *He will give it to you.* What more can we wish for than to have what we want, nay, to have what we will, in conformity to God's will, for the asking? He *will give it to you* from whom *proceedeth every good and perfect gift.* What Christ purchased by the merit of his death, he needed not for himself, but intended it for, and consigned it to, his faithful followers; and having given a valuable consideration for it, which was accepted in full, by this promise he draws a bill as it were upon the treasury in heaven, which we are to present by prayer, and *in his name* to ask for that which is purchased and promised, according to the true intent of the new covenant. Christ had promised them great illumination by the Spirit, but they must pray for it, and did so, Acts 1:14. God will for this be enquired of. He had promised them perfection hereafter, but what shall they do in the mean time? They must continue praying. Perfect fruition is reserved for the land of our rest; asking and receiving are the comfort of the land of our pilgrimage.

2. Here is an invitation for them to petition. It is thought sufficient if great men permit addresses, but Christ calls upon us to petition, *v.* 24.

(1.) He looks back upon their practice hitherto: *Hitherto have you asked nothing in my name.* This refers either [1.] To the matter of their prayers: "You have asked nothing comparatively, nothing to what you might have asked, and will ask when the Spirit is poured out." See what a generous benefactor our Lord Jesus is, above all benefactors; he gives liberally, and is so far from upbraiding us with the frequency and largeness of his gifts that he rather upbraids us with the seldomness and straitness of our requests: *"You have asked nothing* in comparison of what you want, and what I have to give, and have promised to give." We are told to *open our mouth wide.* Or, [2.] To the name in which they prayed. They prayed many a prayer, but never so expressly in the name of Christ as now he was directing them to do; for he had not as yet offered up that great sacrifice in the virtue of which our prayers were to be accepted, nor entered upon his intercession for us, the incense whereof was to perfume all our devotions, and so enable us to pray in his name. Hitherto they had cast out devils, and healed diseases, in the name of Christ, as a king and a prophet, but they could not as yet distinctly pray in his name as a priest.

(2.) He looks forward to their practice for the future: *Ask and you shall receive, that your joy may be full.* Here, [1.] He directs them to ask for all that they needed and he had promised. [2.] He assures them that they shall *receive.* What we ask from a principle of grace God will graciously give: *You shall receive it.* There is something more in this than the promise that he will give it. He will not only give it, but give you to receive it, give you the comfort and benefit of it, *a heart to eat of it,* Eccl. 6:2. [3.] That hereby *their joy shall be full.* This denotes, *First.* The blessed effect of the *prayer of faith;* it helps to fill up the *joy of faith.* Would we have our joy full, as full as it is capable of being in this world, we must be *much in prayer.* When we are told to *rejoice evermore,* it follows immediately, *Pray without ceasing.* See how high we are to aim in prayer — not only at peace, but joy, a *fulness of joy.* Or, *Secondly,* The blessed effects of the *answer of peace:* "Ask, and you shall receive that which will *fill your joy."* God's gifts, through Christ, fill the treasures of the soul, they fill its joy, Prov. 8:21. "Ask for the gift of the Holy Ghost, and you shall receive it; and whereas other knowledge *increaseth sorrow* (Eccl. 1:18), the knowledge he gives will increase, will fill, *your joy."*

3. Here are the grounds upon which they might hope to speed (*v.* 26, 27), which are summed up in short by the apostle (1 Jn. 2:1): *"We have an advocate with the Father."*

(1.) We have an advocate; as to this, Christ saw cause at present not to insist upon it, only to make the following encouragement shine the brighter: *"I say not unto you that I will pray the Father for you.* Suppose I should not tell you that I will intercede for you, should not undertake to solicit every particular cause you have depending there, yet it may be a general ground of comfort that I have settled a correspondence between you and God, have erected a throne of grace, and consecrated for you a *new and living way into the holiest."* He speaks as if they needed not any favours, when he had prevailed for the gift of the Holy Ghost to *make intercession within them,* as Spirit of adoption, crying *Abba, Father;* as if they had no further need of him to pray for them now, but we shall find that he does more for us than he says he will. Men's performances often come short of their promises, but Christ's go beyond them.

(2.) We have to do with a Father, which is so great an encouragement that it does in a manner supersede the other: *"For the Father himself loveth you, philei hymas,* he is a friend to you, and you cannot be better befriended." Note, The disciples of Christ are the beloved of God himself. Christ not only turned away God's wrath from us, and brought us into a covenant of peace and reconciliation, but purchased his favour for us, and brought us into a covenant of friendship. Observe what an emphasis is laid upon this *"The Father himself loveth you,* who is perfectly happy in the enjoyment of himself, whose self-love is both his infinite rectitude and his infinite blessedness; yet he is pleased to love you." The Father himself, whose favour you have forfeited, and whose wrath you have incurred, and with whom you need an advocate, he himself now loves you. Observe, [1.] Why the Father loved the disciples of Christ: *Because you have loved me, and have believed that I am come from God,* that is, because you are my disciples indeed: not as if the love began on their side, but when by his grace he has wrought in us a love to him he is well pleased with the work of his own hands. See here, *First,* What is the character of Christ's disciples; they love him, because they *believe he came out from God,* is the only-begotten of the Father, and his high-commissioner to the world. Note, Faith in Christ works by love to him, Gal. 5:6. If we believe him to be the Son of God, we cannot but love him as infinitely lovely in himself; and if we believe him to be our Saviour, we cannot but love him as the most kind to us. Observe with what respect Christ is pleased to speak of his disciples' love to him, and how kindly he took it; he speaks of it as that which recommended them to his Father's favour: "You have loved me and believed in me when the world has hated and rejected me; and you shall be distinguished yourselves." *Secondly,* See what advantage Christ's faithful disciples have, the Father loves them, and that because they love Christ; so well pleased is he in him that he is well pleased with all his friends. [2.] What encouragement this gave them in prayer. They need not fear speeding when they came to one that loved them, and wished them well. *First,* This cautions us against hard thoughts of God. When we are taught in prayer to plead Christ's merit and intercession, it is not as if all the kindness were in Christ only, and in God nothing but wrath and fury; no, the matter is not so, the Father's love and good-will appointed Christ to be the Mediator; so that we owe Christ's merit to God's mercy in giving him for us. *Secondly,* Let it cherish and confirm in us good thoughts of God. Believers, that love Christ, ought to know that God loves them, and therefore to come boldly to him as children to a loving Father.

Verses 28–33

Two things Christ here comforts his disciples with: —

I. With an assurance that, though he was leaving the world, he was returning to his Father, from whom he came forth *v.* 28–32, where we have,

1. A plain declaration of Christ's mission from the Father, and his return to him (*v.* 28): *I came forth from the Father, and am come,* as you see, *into the world. Again, I leave the world,* as you will see shortly, *and go to the Father.* This is the conclusion of the whole matter. There was nothing he had more inculcated upon them than these two things — whence he came, and whither he went, the *Alpha* and *Omega* of the *mystery of godliness* (1 Tim. 3:16), that the Redeemer, in his entrance, was *God manifest in the flesh,* and in his exit was *received up into glory.*

(1.) These two great truths are here, [1.] Contracted, and put into a few words. Brief summaries of Christian doctrine are of great use to young beginners. The principles of the oracles of God brought into a little compass in creeds and catechisms have, like the beams of the sun contracted in a burning glass, conveyed divine light and heat with a wonderful power. Such we have, Job 28:28; Eccl. 12:13; 1 Tim. 1:15; Tit. 2:11, 12; 1 Jn. 5:11; much in a little. [2.] Compared, and set the one over against the other. There is an admirable harmony in divine truths; they both corroborate and illustrate one another; Christ's coming and his going do so. Christ had commended his disciples for believing that he came forth from God (*v.* 27), and thence infers the necessity and equity of his returning to God again, which therefore should not seem to them either strange or sad. Note, The due improvement of what we know and own would help us into the understanding of that which seems difficult and doubtful.

(2.) If we ask concerning the Redeemer *whence he came,* and *whither he went,* we are told, [1.] That he *came from the Father,* who sanctified and sealed him; and he came into this world, this lower world, this world of mankind, among whom by his incarnation he was pleased to incorporate himself. Here his business lay, and hither he came to attend it. He left his home for this strange country; his palace for this cottage; wonderful condescension! [2. That, when he had done his work on earth, he left the world, and went back to his Father at his ascension. He was not forced away, but made it his own act and deed to leave the world, to return to it no more till he comes to put an end to it; yet still he is spiritually present with his church, and will be to the end.

2. The disciples' satisfaction in this declaration (*v.* 29, 30): *Lo, now speakest though plainly.* It should seem, this one word of Christ did them more good than all the rest, though he had said many things likely enough to fasten upon them. The Spirit, as the wind, blows when and where, and by what word he pleases; perhaps a word that has been *spoken once, yea twice,* and not perceived, yet, being often repeated, takes hold at last. Two things they improved in by this saying: —

(1.) In knowledge: *Lo, now speakest thou plainly.* When they were in the dark concerning what he said, they did not say, *Lo, now speakest thou obscurely,* as blaming him; but now that they apprehend his meaning they give him glory for condescending to their capacity: *Lo, now speakest thou plainly.* Divine truths are most likely to do good when they are spoken plainly, 1 Co. 2:4. Observe how they triumphed, as the mathematician did with his ***heurēka, heurēka,*** when he had hit upon a demonstration he had long been in quest of: *I have found it, I have found it.* Note, When Christ is pleased to speak plainly to our souls, and to bring us with open face to behold his glory, we have reason to rejoice in it.

(2.) In faith: *Now are we sure.* Observe,

[1.] What was the matter of their faith: *We believe that thou camest forth from God.* He had said (*v.* 27) that they did believe this; "Lord" (say they) "we do believe it, and we have cause to believe it, and we know that we believe it, and have the comfort of it."

[2.] What was the motive of their faith — his omniscience. This proved him a teacher come from God, and more than a prophet, that he knew all things, which they were convinced of by this that he resolved those doubts which were hid in their hearts, and answered the scruples they had not confessed. Note, Those know Christ best that know him by experience, that can say of his power, It works in me; of his love, He loved me. And this proves Christ not only to have a divine mission, but to be a divine person, that he is a discerner of the thoughts and intents of the heart, therefore the essential, eternal Word, Heb. 4:12, 13. He has made all the churches to know that he searches the reins and the heart, Rev. 2:23. This confirmed the faith of the disciples here, as it made the first impression upon the woman of Samaria that Christ *told her all the things that ever she did (ch.* 4:29), and upon Nathanael that Christ *saw him under the fig-tree, ch.* 1:48, 49.

These words, *and needest not that any man should ask thee,* may bespeak either, *First,* Christ's aptness to teach. He prevents us with his instructions, and is communicative of the *treasures of wisdom and knowledge* that are hid in him, and needs not to be importuned. Or, *Secondly,* His ability to teach: "Thou needest not, as other teachers, to have the learners' doubts told thee, for thou knowest, without being told, what they stumble at." The best of teachers can only answer what is spoken, but Christ can answer what is thought, what we are afraid to ask, as the disciples were, Mk. 9:32. Thus he *can have compassion,* Heb. 5:2.

3. The gentle rebuke Christ gave the disciples for their confidence that they now understood him, *v.* 31, 32. Observing how they triumphed in their attainments, he said, *"Do*

you now believe? Do you now look upon yourselves as advanced and confirmed disciples? Do you now think you shall make no more blunders? Alas! you know not your own weakness; you will very shortly *be scattered every man to his own,"* etc. Here we have,

(1.) A question, designed to put them upon consideration: *Do you now believe?* [1.] "If now, why not sooner? Have you not heard the same things many a time before?" Those who after many instructions and invitations are at last persuaded to believe have reason to be ashamed that they stood it out so long. [2.] "If now, why not ever? When an hour of temptation comes, where will your faith be then?" As far as there is inconstancy in our faith there is cause to question the sincerity of it, and to ask, "Do we indeed believe?"

(2.) A prediction of their fall, that, how confident soever they were now of their own stability, in a little time they would all desert him, which was fulfilled that very night, when, upon his being seized by a party of the guards, *all his disciples forsook him and fled,* Mt. 26:56. They were scattered, [1.] From one another; they shifted every one for his own safety, without any care or concern for each other. Troublous times are times of scattering to Christian societies; in the cloudy and dark day the flock of Christ is dispersed, Eze. 34:12. So Christ, as a society, is not visible. [2.] Scattered for him: *You shall leave me alone.* They should have been witnesses for him upon his trial, should have ministered to him in his sufferings; if they could have given him no comfort they might have done him some credit; but they were ashamed of his chain, and afraid of sharing with him in his sufferings, and left him alone. Note, Many a good cause, when it is distressed by its enemies, is deserted by its friends. The disciples had *continued with Christ* in his other temptations and yet turned their back upon him now; those that are tried, do not always prove trusty. If we at any time find our friends unkind to us, let us remember that Christ's were so to him. When they left him alone, they were scattered *every man to his own;* not to their own possessions or habitations, these were in Galilee; but to their own friends and acquaintance in Jerusalem; every one went his own way, where he fancied he should be most safe. Every man to secure his own; himself and his own life. Note, Those will not dare to suffer for their religion that *seek their own things* more than the *things of Christ,* and that look upon the things of this world as their *ta idia — their own property,* and in which their happiness is bound up. Now observe here, *First,* Christ knew before that his disciples would thus desert him in the critical moment, and yet he was still tender of them, and in nothing unkind. We are ready to say of some, "If we could have foreseen their ingratitude, we would not have been so prodigal of our favours to them;" Christ did foresee theirs, and yet was kind to them. *Secondly,* He told them of it, to be a rebuke to their exultation in their present attainments: *"Do you now believe?* Be not high-minded, but fear; for you will find your faith so sorely shaken as to make it questionable whether it be sincere or no, in a little time." Note, even when we are taking the comfort of our graces, it is good to be reminded of our dangers from our corruptions. When our faith is strong, our love flaming, and our evidences are clear, yet we cannot infer thence that *to-morrow shall be as this day.* Even when we have most reason to think we stand, yet we have reason enough to take heed lest we fall. *Thirdly,* He spoke of it as a thing very near. *The hour was* already *come,* in a manner, when they would be as shy of him as ever they had been fond of him. Note, A little time may produce great changes, both concerning us and in us.

(3.) An assurance of his own comfort notwithstanding: *Yet I am not alone.* He would not be thought to complain of their deserting him, as if it were any real damage to him; for in their absence he should be sure of his Father's presence, which was *instar omnium — every thing: The Father is with me.* We may consider this, [1.] As a privilege peculiar to the Lord Jesus; the Father was so with him in his sufferings as he never was with any, for still he was *in the bosom of the Father.* The divine nature did not desert the human nature, but supported it, and put an invincible comfort and an inestimable value into his sufferings. The Father had engaged to be with him in his whole undertaking (Ps. 89:21 etc.), and to preserve him (Isa. 49:8); this emboldened him, Isa. 50:7. Even when he complained of his Father's forsaking him, yet he called him *My God,* and presently after was so well assured of his favourable presence with him as to commit his Spirit into his hand. This he had comforted himself with all along (*ch.* 8:29), *He that sent me is with me, the Father hath not left me alone,* and especially now at last. This assists our faith in the acceptableness of Christ's satisfaction; no doubt, the Father was well pleased in him, for he went along with him in his undertaking from first to last. [2.] As a privilege common to all believers, by virtue of their union with Christ; when they are alone, they are *not alone,* but *the Father is with them. First,* When solitude is their choice, when they are alone, as Isaac in the field, Nathanael under the fig-tree, Peter upon the house-top, meditating and praying, the Father is with them. Those that converse with God in solitude are never less alone than when alone. A good God and a good heart are good company at any time. *Secondly,* When solitude is their affliction, their enemies lay them alone, and their friends leave them so, their company, like Job's, is made desolate; yet they are not so much alone as they are thought to be, *the Father is with them,* as he was with Joseph in his bonds and with John in his banishment. In their greatest troubles they are as one whom his father pities, as one whom his mother comforts. And, while we have God's favourable presence with us, we are happy, and ought to be easy, though all the world forsake us. *Non deo tribuimus justum honorem nisi solus ipse nobis sufficiat — We do not render due honour to God, unless we deem him alone all-sufficient.* — Calvin.

II. He comforts them with a promise of peace in him, by virtue of his victory over the world, whatever troubles they might meet with in it (*v.* 33): *"These things have I spoken, that in me you might have peace;* and if you have it not in me you will not have it at all, for *in the world you shall have tribulation;* you must expect no other, and yet may cheer up yourselves, for *I have overcome the world."* Observe,

1. The end Christ aimed at in preaching this farewell sermon to his disciples: *That in him they might have peace.* He did not hereby intend to give them a full view of that doctrine which they were shortly to be made masters of by the pouring out of the Spirit, but only to satisfy them for the present that his departure from them was really for the best. Or, we may take it more generally: Christ had said all this to them that by enjoying him they might have the best enjoyment of themselves. Note, (1.) It is the will of Christ that his disciples should have peace within, whatever their troubles may be without. (2.) Peace in Christ is the only true peace, and in him alone believers have it, for *this man shall be the peace,* Mic. 5:5. Through him we have peace with God, and so in him we have peace in our own minds. (3.) The word of Christ aims at this, *that in him we may have peace.* Peace is the *fruit of the lips, and of his lips,* Isa. 57:19.

2. The entertainment they were likely to meet with in the world: "You shall not have outward peace, never expect it." Though they were sent to proclaim *peace on earth,* and *goodwill towards men,* they must expect trouble on earth, and ill-will from men. Note, It has been the lot of Christ's disciples to have more or less tribulation in this world. Men persecute them because they are so good, and God corrects them because they are no better. Men design to cut them off from the earth, and God designs by affliction to make them meet for heaven; and so between both *they shall have tribulation.*

3. The encouragement Christ gives them with reference hereto: *But be of good cheer, tharseite.* "Not only be of good comfort, but be of good courage; have a good heart on it, all shall be well." Note, In the midst of the tribulations of this world it is the duty and interest of Christ's disciples to be of good cheer, to keep up their delight in God whatever is pressing, and their hope in God whatever is threatening; as sorrowful indeed, in compliance with the temper of the climate, and yet always rejoicing, always cheerful (2 Co. 6:10), even *in tribulation,* Rom. 5:3.

4. The ground of that encouragement: *I have overcome the world.* Christ's victory is a Christian triumph. Christ overcame the prince of this world, disarmed him, and cast him out; and still treads Satan under our feet. He overcame the children of this world, by the conversion of many to the faith and obedience of his gospel, making them the children of his kingdom. When he sends his disciples to preach the gospel to all the world, *"Be of good cheer,"* says he, *"I have overcome the world* as far as I have gone, and so shall you; though you have tribulation in the world, yet you shall gain your point, and captivate the world," Rev. 6:2. He overcame the wicked of the world, for many a time he put his enemies to silence, to shame; "And be you of good cheer, for the Spirit will enable you to do so too." He overcame the evil things of the world by submitting to them; he endured the cross, despising it and the shame of it; and he overcame the good things of it by being wholly dead to them; its honours had no beauty in his eye, its pleasures no charms. Never was there such a conqueror of the world as Christ was, and we ought to be encouraged by it, (1.) Because Christ has overcome the world before us; so that we may look upon it as a conquered enemy, that has many a time been baffled. Nay, (2.) He has conquered it for us, as the captain of our salvation. We are interested in his victory; by his cross the world is *crucified to us,* which bespeaks it completely conquered and put into our possession; all is yours, even *the world.* Christ having overcome the world, believers have nothing to do but to pursue their victory, and divide the spoil; and this we do by faith, 1 Jn. 5:4. *We are more than conquerors through him that loved us.*

CHAPTER 17

This chapter is a prayer, it is the Lord's prayer, the Lord Christ's prayer. There was one Lord's prayer which he taught us to pray, and did not pray himself, for he needed not to pray for the forgiveness of sin; but this was properly and peculiarly his, and suited him only as a Mediator, and is a sample of his intercession, and yet is of use to us both for instruction and encouragement in prayer. Observe, I. The circumstances of the prayer (*v.* 1). II. The prayer itself. 1. He prays for himself (*v.* 1–5). 2. He prays for those that are his. And in this see, (1.) The general pleas with which he introduces his petitions for them (*v.* 6–10). (2.) The particular petitions he puts up for them [1.] That they might be kept (*v.* 11–16). [2.] That they might be sanctified (*v.* 17–19). [3.] That they might be united (*v.* 11 and 20–23). [4.] That they might be glorified (*v.* 24–26).

Verses 1–5

Here we have, I. The circumstances of this prayer, *v.* 1. Many a solemn prayer Christ made in the days of his flesh (sometimes he continued all night in prayer), but none of his prayers are recorded so fully as this. Observe,

1. The time when he prayed this prayer; when he had *spoken these words,* had given the foregoing farewell to his disciples, he prayed this prayer in their hearing; so that, (1.) It was a prayer after a sermon; when he had spoken from God to them, he turned to speak to God for them. Note, Those we preach to we must pray for. He that was to prophesy upon the dry bones was also to pray, *Come, O breath, and breathe* upon them. And the word preached should be prayed over, for God *gives the increase.* (2.) It was a prayer after sacrament; after Christ and his disciples had eaten the passover and the Lord's supper together, and he had given them a suitable exhortation, he closed the solemnity with this prayer, that God would preserve the good impressions of the ordinance upon them. (3.) It was a family-prayer. Christ's disciples were his family, and, to set a good example before the masters of families, he not only, as the son of Abraham, taught his household (Gen. 18:19), but, as a son of David, blessed his household (2 Sa. 6:20), prayed for them and with them. (4.) It was a parting prayer. When we and our friends are parting, it is good to part with prayer, Acts 20:36. Christ was parting by death, and that parting should be sanctified and sweetened by prayer. Dying Jacob blessed the twelve patriarchs, dying Moses the twelve tribes, and so, here, dying Jesus the twelve apostles. (5.) It was a prayer that was a preface to his sacrifice, which he was now about to offer on earth, specifying the favours and blessings designed to be purchased by the merit of his death for those that were his; like a deed *leading the uses of a fine,* and directing to what intents and purposes it shall be levied. Christ prayed then as a priest now offering sacrifice, in the virtue of which all prayers were to be made. (6.) It was a prayer that was a specimen of his intercession, which he ever lives to make for us within the veil. Not that in his exalted state he addresses himself to his Father by way of humble petition, as when he was on earth. No, his intercession in heaven is a presenting of his merit to his Father, with a suing out of the benefit of it for all his chosen ones.

2. The outward expression of fervent desire which he used in this prayer: He *lifted up his eyes to heaven,* as before (*ch.* 11:41); not that Christ needed thus to engage his own attention, but he was pleased thus to sanctify this gesture to those that use it, and justify it against those that ridicule it. It is significant of the lifting up of the soul to God in prayer, Ps. 25:1. *Sursum corda* was anciently used as a call to prayer, *Up with your hearts,* up to heaven; thither we must direct our desires in prayer, and thence we must expect to receive the good things we pray for.

II. The first part of the prayer itself, in which Christ prays for himself. Observe here,

1. He prays to God as a Father: He *lifted up his eyes, and*

said, Father. Note, As prayer is to be made to God only, so it is our duty in prayer to eye him as a Father, and to call him *our Father.* All that have the Spirit of adoption are taught to cry *Abba, Father, v.* 25. For it will be of great use to us in prayer, both for direction and for encouragement, to call God as we hope to find him.

2. He prayed for himself first. Though Christ, as God, was prayed to, Christ, as man, prayed; thus *it became him to fulfill all righteousness.* It was said to him, as it is said to us, *Ask, and I will give thee,* Ps. 2:8. What he had purchased he must ask for; and shall we expect to have what we never merited, but have a thousand times forfeited, unless we pray for it? This puts an honour upon prayer, that it was the messenger Christ sent on his errands, the way in which even he corresponded with Heaven. It likewise gives great encouragement to praying people, and cause to hope that even the *prayer of the destitute* shall not be despised; time was when he that is advocate for us had a cause of his own to solicit, a great cause, on the success of which depended all his honour as Mediator; and this he was to solicit in the same method that is prescribed to us, *by prayers and supplications* (Heb. 5:7), so that he knows the heart of a petitioner (Ex. 23:9), he knows the way. Now observe, Christ began with prayer for himself, and afterwards prayed for his disciples; this charity must begin at home, though it must not end there. We must love and pray for our neighbor as ourselves, and therefore must in a right manner love and pray for ourselves first. Christ was much shorter in his prayer for himself than in his prayer for his disciples. Our prayers for the church must not be crowded into a corner of our prayers; in making *supplication for all saints,* we have room enough to enlarge, and should not straiten ourselves. Now here are two petitions which Christ puts up for himself, and these two are one — that he might be glorified. But this one petition, *Glorify thou me,* is twice put up, because it has a double reference. To the prosecution of his undertaking further: *Glorify me, that I may glorify thee,* in doing what is agreed upon to be yet done, *v.* 1–3. And to the performance of his undertaking hitherto: "*Glorify me, for I have glorified thee.* I have done my part, and now, Lord, do thine," *v.* 4, 5.

(1.) Christ here prays to be *glorified,* in order to his *glorifying God (v.* 1): *Glorify thy Son* according to thy promise, *that thy Son may glorify thee* according to his understanding. Here observe,

[1.] What he prays for — that he might be glorified in this world: *"The hour is come* when all the powers of darkness will combine to vilify thy Son; now, Father, glorify him." The Father glorified the *Son* upon earth, *First,* Even in his sufferings, by the signs and wonders which attended them. When they that came to take him were thunder-struck with a word, — when Judas confessed him innocent, and sealed that confession with his own guilty blood, — when the judge's wife asleep, and the judge himself awake, pronounced him righteous, — when the sun was darkened, and the veil of the temple rent, then the Father not only justified, but glorified the Son. Nay, *Secondly,* Even by his sufferings; when he was crucified, he was magnified, he was glorified, *ch.* 13:31. It was in his cross that he conquered Satan and death; his thorns were a crown, and Pilate in the inscription over his head wrote more than he thought. But, *Thirdly,* Much more after his sufferings. The Father glorified the Son when he *raised him from the dead,* showed him openly to chosen witnesses, and poured out the Spirit to support and plead his cause, and to set up his kingdom among men, then he *glorified him.* This he here prays for, and insists upon.

[2.] What he pleads to enforce this request.

First, He pleads relation: *Glorify thy Son;* thy Son as God, as Mediator. It is in consideration of this that the heathen are *given him for his inheritance;* for *thou art my Son,* Ps. 2:7, 8. The devil had tempted him to renounce his sonship with an offer of the kingdoms of this world; but he rejected the offer with disdain, and depended upon his Father for his preferment, and here applies himself to him for it. Note, Those that have received the adoption of sons may in faith pray for the inheritance of sons; if sanctified, then glorified: *Father, glorify thy Son.*

Secondly, He pleads the time: *The hour is come;* the season prefixed to an hour. The hour of Christ's passion was determined in the counsel of God. He had often said his hour was not yet come; but now it was come, and he knew it. *Man knows not his time* (Eccl. 9:12), but the Son of man did. He calls it *this hour (ch.* 12:27), and here, *the hour;* compare Mk.

14:35; *ch.* 16:21. For the hour of the Redeemer's death, which was also the hour of the Redeemer's birth, was the most signal and remarkable hour, and, without doubt, the most critical, that ever was since the clock of time was first set a going. Never was there such an hour as that, nor did ever any hour challenge such expectations of it before, nor such reflections upon it after. 1. *"The hour is come* in the midst of which I need to be owned." Now is the hour when this grand affair is come to a crisis; after many a skirmish the decisive battle between heaven and hell is now to be fought, and that great cause in which God's honour and man's happiness are together embarked must now be either won or lost for ever. The two champions David and Goliath, Michael and the dragon, are now entering the lists; the trumpet sounds for an engagement that will be irretrievably fatal either to the one or to the other: "*Now glorify thy Son,* now give him victory over *principalities and powers,* now let *the bruising of his heel* be *the breaking of the serpent's head,* now let thy Son be so upheld as not to fail nor be discouraged." When Joshua went *forth conquering and to conquer,* it is said, *The Lord magnified Joshua;* so he *glorified his Son* when he made the cross his triumphant chariot. 2. *"The hour is come* in the close of which I expect to be crowned; *the hour is come* when I am *to be glorified,* and, *set at thy right hand."* Betwixt him and that glory there intervened a bloody scene of suffering; but, being short, he speaks as if he made little of it: *The hour is come that I must be glorified;* and he did not expect it till then. Good Christians in a trying hour, particularly a dying hour, may thus plead: *"Now the hour is come,* stand by me, appear for me, now or never: now *the earthly tabernacle is to be dissolved, the hour is come that I should be glorified."* 2 Co. 5:1.

Thirdly, He pleads the Father's own interest and concern herein: *That thy Son may also glorify thee;* for he had consecrated his whole undertaking to his Father's honour. He desired to be carried triumphantly through his sufferings to his glory, that he might glorify the Father two ways: — 1. By *the death of the cross,* which he was now to suffer. *Father, glorify thy name,* expressed the great intention of his sufferings, which was to retrieve his Father's injured honour among men, and, by his satisfaction, to come up to the glory of God, which man, by his sin, came short of: "Father, own me in my sufferings, that I may honour thee by them." 2. By the doctrine of the cross, which was now shortly to be published to the world, by which God's kingdom was to be re-established among men. He prays that his Father would so grace his sufferings, and crown them, as not only to take off *the offence of the cross,* but to make it, *to those that are saved, the wisdom of God and the power of God.* If God had not glorified Christ crucified, *by raising him from the dead,* his whole undertaking had been crushed; therefore *glorify me, that I may glorify thee.* Now thereby he hath taught us, (1.) What to eye and aim at in our prayers, in all our designs and desires — and that is, the honour of God. It being our chief end to glorify God, other things must be sought and attended to in subordination and subserviency to the Lord. "Do this and the other for thy servant, that thy servant may glorify thee. Give me health, that I may glorify thee with my body; success, that I may glorify thee with my estate," etc. *Hallowed be thy name* must be our first petition, which must fix our end in all our other petitions, 1 Peter 4:11. (2.) He hath taught us what to expect and hope for. If we sincerely set ourselves to glorify our Father, he will not be wanting to do that for us which is requisite to put us into a capacity of glorifying him, to give us the grace he knows sufficient, and the opportunity he sees convenient. But, if we secretly honour ourselves more than him, it is just with him to leave us in the hand of our own counsels, and then, instead of honouring ourselves, we shall shame ourselves.

Fourthly, He pleads his commission (*v.* 2, 3); he desires to glorify his Father, in conformity to, and in pursuance of, the commission given him: "*Glorify thy Son, as thou hast given him power, glorify him in the execution of the powers thou hast given him,"* so it is connected with the petition; or, *that thy Son may glorify thee* according to *the power given him,* so it is connected with the plea. Now see here the power of the Mediator.

a. The origin of his power: *Thou hast given him power;* he has it from God, *to whom all power belongs.* Man, in his fallen state, must, in order to his recovery, be taken under a new model of government, which could not be erected but by a special commission under the broad seal of heaven, di-

rected to the undertaker of that glorious work, and constituting him sole arbitrator of the grand difference that was, and sole guarantee of the grand alliance that was to be, between God and man; so as to this office, he received his power, which was to be executed in a way distinct from his power and government as Creator. Note, The church's king is no usurper, as the prince of this world is; Christ's right to rule is incontestable.

b. The extent of his power: He has *power over all flesh.* (*a.*) Over all mankind. He has power in and over the world of spirits, the powers of the upper and unseen world are subject to him (1 Peter 3:22); but, being now mediating between God and man, he here *pleads his power over all flesh.* They were men whom he was to subdue and save; out of that race he had a remnant given him, and therefore all that rank of beings was *put under his feet.* (*b.*) Over mankind considered as corrupt and fallen, for so he is called *flesh,* Gen. 6:3. If he had not in this sense been flesh, he had not needed a Redeemer. Over this sinful race the Lord Jesus has all power; and *all judgment,* concerning them, *is committed to him;* power to bind or loose, acquit or condemn; *power on earth to forgive sins* or not. Christ, as Mediator, has the government of the whole world put into his hand; he is king of nations, has power even over those *that know him not, nor obey his gospel;* whom he does not rule, he over-rules, Ps. 22:28; 72:8; Mt. 28:18; *ch.* 3:35.

c. The grand intention and design of this power: *That he should give eternal life to as many as thou hast given him.* Here is the mystery of our salvation laid open.

(*a.*) Here is the Father making over the elect to the Redeemer, and giving them to him as his charge and trust; as the crown and recompence of his undertaking. He has a sovereign power over all the fallen race, but a peculiar interest in the chosen remnant; *all things were put under his feet,* but they were *delivered into his hand.*

(*b.*) Here is the Son undertaking to secure the happiness of those that were given him, that he would *give eternal life to them.* See how great the authority of the Redeemer is. He has lives and crowns to give, eternal lives that never die, immortal crowns that never fade. Now consider how great the Lord Jesus is, who has such preferments in his gift; and how gracious he is in giving eternal life to those whom he undertakes to save. [*a.*] He sanctifies them in this world, gives them the spiritual life which is eternal life in the bud and embryo, *ch.* 4:14. Grace in the soul is heaven in that soul. [*b.*] He will glorify them in the other world; their happiness shall be completed in the vision and fruition of God. This only is mentioned, because it supposes all the other parts of his undertaking, teaching them, satisfying for them, sanctifying them, and preparing them for that eternal life; and indeed all the other were in order to this; we are *called to his kingdom and glory,* and *begotten to the inheritance.* What is last in execution was first in intention, and *that is eternal life.*

(*c.*) Here is the subserviency of the Redeemer's universal dominion to this: He has *power over all flesh,* on purpose that he might give eternal life to the select number. Note, Christ's dominion over the children of men is in order to the salvation of the children of God. *All things are for their sakes,* 2 Co. 4:15. All Christ's laws, ordinances, and promises, which are given to all, are designed effectually to convey spiritual life, and secure eternal life, to all that were given to Christ; he is *head over all things to the church.* The administration of the kingdoms of providence and grace are put into the same hand, that all things may be made to concur for good to the called.

d. Here is a further explication of this grand design (*v.* 3): *"This is life eternal,* which I am empowered and have undertaken to give, this is the nature of it, and this the way leading to it, *to know thee the only true God,* and all the discoveries and principles of natural religion, and Jesus Christ whom, thou has sent, as Mediator, and the doctrines and laws of that holy religion which he instituted for the recovery of man out of his lapsed state." Here is,

(*a.*) The great end which the Christian religion sets before us, and that is, eternal life, the happiness of an immortal soul in the vision and fruition of an eternal God. This he was to reveal to all, and secure to all that were given him. By the gospel *life and immortality are brought to light,* are brought to hand, a life which transcends this as much in excellency as it does in duration.

(*b.*) The sure way of attaining this blessed end, which is, by the right knowledge of God and Jesus Christ: *"This is life eternal, to know thee,"* which may be taken two ways — [*a.*] *Life eternal* lies in the knowledge of God and Jesus Christ; the present principle of this life is the believing knowledge of God and Christ; the future perfection of that life will be the intuitive knowledge of God and Christ. Those that are brought into union with Christ, and live a life of communion with God in Christ, know, in some measure, by experience, what eternal life is, and will say, "If this be heaven, heaven is sweet." See Ps. 17:15. [*b.*] The knowledge of God and Christ leads to life eternal; this is the way in which Christ gives eternal life, by the knowledge of him that has called us (2 Peter 1:3), and this is the way in which we come to receive it. The Christian religion shows us the way to heaven, *First,* By directing us to God, as the author and felicity of our being; for Christ died to *bring us to God.* To know him as our Creator, and to love him, obey him, submit to him, and trust in him, as our owner ruler, and benefactor, — to devote ourselves to him as our sovereign Lord, depend upon him as our chief good, and direct all to his praise as our highest end, — *this is life eternal.* God is here called the *only true God,* to distinguish him from the false gods of the heathen, which were counterfeits and pretenders, not from the person of the Son, of whom it is expressly said that he is *the true God and eternal life* (1 Jn. 5:20), and who in this text is proposed as the object of the same religious regard with the Father. It is certain there is but one only living and true God and the God we adore is he. He is the true God, and not a mere name or notion; the only true God, and all that ever set up as rivals with him are vanity and a lie; the service of him is the only true religion. *Secondly,* By directing us to Jesus Christ, as the Mediator between God and man: *Jesus Christ, whom thou hast sent.* If man had continued innocent, the knowledge of the only true God would have been life eternal to him; but now that he is fallen there must be something more; now that we are under guilt, to know God is to know him as a righteous Judge, whose curse we are under; and nothing is more killing than to know this. We are therefore concerned to know Christ as our Redeemer, by whom alone we can now have access to God; it is life eternal to believe in Christ; and this he has undertaken to give to as many as were given him. See *ch.* 6:39 40. Those that are acquainted with God and Christ are already in the suburbs of life eternal.

(2.) Christ here prays to be glorified in consideration of his having glorified the Father hitherto, *v.* 4, 5. The meaning of the former petition was, Glorify me in this world; the meaning of the latter is, Glorify me in the other world. *I have glorified thee on the earth, and now glorify thou me.* Observe here,

[1.] With what comfort Christ reflects on the life he had lived on earth: *I have glorified thee, and finished my work;* it is as good as finished. He does not complain of the poverty and disgrace he had lived in, what a weary life he had upon earth, as ever any man of sorrows had. He overlooks this, and pleases himself in reviewing the service he had done his Father, and the progress he had made in his undertaking. This is here recorded, *First,* For the honour of Christ, that his life upon earth did in all respects fully answer the end of his coming into the world. Note, 1. Our Lord Jesus had work given him to do by him that sent him; he came not into the world to live at ease, but to go *about doing good,* and to *fulfill all righteousness.* His Father gave him his work, his work in the vineyard, both appointed him to it and assisted him in it. 2. *The work that was given him to do* he finished. Though he had not, as yet, gone through the last part of his undertaking, yet he was so near being *made perfect through sufferings* that he might say, I have finished it; it was as good as done, he was giving it its finishing stroke *eteleiōsa — I have finished.* The word signifies his performing every part of his undertaking in the most complete and perfect manner. 3. Herein he glorified his Father; he pleased him, he praised him. It is the glory of God that *his work is perfect,* and the same is the glory of the Redeemer; what he is the author of he will be the finisher of. It was a strange way for the Son to glorify the Father by abasing himself (this looked more likely to disparage him), yet it was contrived that so he should glorify him: *"I have glorified thee on the earth,* in such a way as men on earth could bear the manifestation of thy glory." *Secondly,* It is recorded for example to all, *that we may follow his example.* 1. We must make it our business to do the work God has appointed us to do, according to our capacity and the sphere of our activity; we must each of us do all the good we can in this world. 2. We must aim at the glory of God in all. We must glorify him on the earth, which he has given *unto the children of men,* demanding only this quit-rent; on the earth, where we are in a state of probation and preparation for eternity. 3. We must persevere herein to the end of our days; we must not sit down till we have finished our work, and *accomplished as a hireling our day. Thirdly,* It is recorded for encouragement to all those that rest upon him. If he has *finished the work that was given him to do,* then he is a complete Saviour, and did not do his work by the halves. And he that finished his work for us will finish it in us *to the day of Christ.*

[2.] See with what confidence he expects *the joy set before him* (*v.* 5): *Now, O Father, glorify thou me.* It is what he depends upon, and cannot be denied him.

First, See here what he prayed for: *Glorify thou me,* as before, *v.* 1. All repetitions in prayer are not to be counted *vain repetitions;* Christ *prayed, saying the same words* (Mt. 26:44), and yet *prayed more earnestly.* What his Father had promised him, and he was assured of, yet he must pray for; promises are not designed to supercede prayers, but to be the guide of our desires and the ground of our hopes. Christ's being glorified includes all the honours, powers, and joys, of his exalted state. See how it is described. 1. It is a glory with God; not only, *Glorify my name on earth,* but, *Glorify me with thine own self.* It was paradise, it was heaven, to be with his Father, as Prov. 8:30; Dan. 7:13; Heb. 8:1. Note, The brightest glories of the exalted Redeemer were to be displayed within the veil, where the Father manifests his glory. The praises of the upper world are offered up *to him that sits upon the throne and to the lamb* in conjunction (Rev. 5:13), and the prayers of the lower world draw out grace and peace *from God our Father and our Lord Jesus Christ* in conjunction; and thus the Father has glorified him with himself. 2. It is *the glory he had with God before the world was.* By this it appears, (1.) That Jesus Christ, as God, had a being *before the world was,* co-eternal with the Father; our religion acquaints us with one that *was before all things, and by whom all things consist.* (2.) That his glory with the Father is from everlasting, as well as his existence with the Father; for he was from eternity *the brightness of his Father's glory,* Heb. 1:3. As God's making the world only declared his glory, but made no real additions to it; so Christ undertook the work of redemption, not because he needed glory, for he had a glory *with the Father before the world,* but because we needed glory. (3.) That Jesus Christ in his state of humiliation divested himself of this glory, and drew a veil over it; though he was still God, yet he was *God manifested in the flesh,* not in his glory. He laid down this glory for a time, as a pledge that he would go through with his undertaking, according to the appointment of his Father. (4.) That in his exalted state he resumed this glory, and clad himself again with his former robes of light. Having performed his undertaking, he did, as it were, *reposcere pignus — take up his pledge,* by this demand, *Glorify thou me.* He prays that even his human nature might be advanced to the highest honour it was capable of, his body a glorious body; and that the glory of the Godhead might now be manifested in the person of the Mediator, Emmanuel, Godman. He does not pray to be glorified with the princes and great men of the earth: no; he that knew both worlds, and might choose which he would have his preferment in, chose it in the glory of the other world, as far exceeding all the glory of this. He had despised *the kingdoms of this world and the glory of them,* when Satan offered them to him, and therefore might the more boldly claim the glories of the other world. *Let the same mind be in us.* "Lord, give the glories of this world to whom thou wilt give them, but let me have my portion of glory in the world to come. It is no matter, though I be vilified with men; but, *Father, glorify thou me with thine own self."*

Secondly, See here what he pleaded: *I have glorified thee;* and now, in consideration thereof, *glorify thou me.* For, 1. There was an equity in it, and an admirable becomingness, *that if God was glorified in him, he should glorify him in himself,* as he had observed, *ch.* 13:32. Such an infinite value there was in what Christ did to glorify his Father that he properly merited all the glories of his exalted state. If the Father was a gainer in his glory by the Son's humiliation, it was fit the Son should be no loser by it at long run, in his glory. 2. It was according to the covenant between them, that if the Son would *make his soul an offering for sin* he should *divide the spoil with the strong* (Isa. 53:10, 12), and *the kingdom should be his;* and this he had an eye to, and depended upon, in his sufferings; it was *for the joy set before him* that *he endured the cross:* and now in his exalted state he still expects the completing of his exaltation, because he perfected his undertaking, Heb. 10:13. 3. It was the most proper evidence of his Father's accepting and approving the work he had finished. By the glorifying of Christ we are satisfied that God was satisfied, and therein a real demonstration was given that the Father was well pleased in him as his beloved Son. 4. Thus we must be taught that those, and only those, who glorify God on earth, and persevere in the work God hath given them to do, shall be glorified with the Father, when they must be no more in this world. Not that we can merit the glory, as Christ did, but our glorifying God is required as an evidence of our interest in Christ, through whom eternal life is God's free gift.

Verses 6–10

Christ, having prayed for himself, comes next to pray for those that are his, and he knew them by name, though he did not here name them. Now observe here,

I. Whom he did not pray for (*v.* 9): *I pray not for the world.* Note, There is a world of people that Jesus Christ did not pray for. It is not meant of the world of mankind general (he prays for that here, *v.* 21, *That the world may believe that thou hast sent me*); nor is it meant of the Gentiles, in distinction from the Jews; but the world is here opposed to the elect, who are given to Christ out of the world. Take the world for a heap of unwinnowed corn in the floor, and God loves it, Christ prays for it, and dies for it, *for a blessing is in it;* but, *the Lord perfectly knowing those that are his,* he eyes particularly those *that were given him out of the world,* extracts them; and then take the world for the remaining heap of rejected, worthless chaff, and Christ neither prays for it, nor dies for it, but abandons it, and *the wind drives it away.* These are called *the world,* because they are governed by the spirit of this world, and have their portion in it; for these Christ does not pray; not but that there are some things which he intercedes with God for on their behalf, as the dresser for the reprieve of the barren tree; but he does not pray for them in this prayer, that *have not part nor lot* in the blessings here prayed for. He does not say, I pray against the world, as Elias made intercession against Israel; but, *I pray not for them,* I pass them by, and leave them to themselves; they are *not written in the Lamb's book of life,* and therefore not in the breast-plate of the great high-priest. And miserable is the condition of such, as it was of those whom the prophet was forbidden to pray for, and more so, Jer. 7:16. We that know not who are chosen, and who are passed by, must *pray for all men,* 1 Tim. 2:1, 4. While there is life, there is hope, and room for prayer. See 1 Sa. 12:23.

II. Whom he did pray for; not for angels, but for the children of men. 1. He prays *for those that were given him,* meaning primarily the disciples that had attended *him in this regeneration;* but it is doubtless to be extended further, to all who come under the same character, who receive and believe the words of Christ, *v.* 6, 8. 2. He prays *for all that should believe on him* (*v.* 20), and it is not only the petitions that follow, but those also which went before, that must be construed to extend to all believers, in every place and every age; for he has a concern for them all, and calls *things that are not as though they were.*

III. What encouragement he had to pray for them, and what are the general pleas with which he introduces his petitions for them, and recommends them to his Father's favour; they are five: —

1. The charge he had received concerning them: *Thine they were, and thou gavest them me* (*v.* 6), and again (*v.* 9), *Thou whom thou hast given me.* "Father, those I am now praying for are such as thou hast entrusted me with, and what I have to say for them is in pursuance of the charge I have received concerning them." Now,

(1.) This is meant primarily of the disciples that then were, who were given to Christ as his pupils to be educated by him while he was on earth, and his agents to be employed for him when he went to heaven. They were given him to be the learners of his doctrine, the witnesses of his life and miracles, and the monuments of his grace and favour, in order to their being the publishers of his gospel and the planters of his church. When they left all to follow him, this was the secret spring of that strange resolution: they were given to him, else they had not given themselves to him. Note, The apostleship and ministry, which are Christ's gift to the church, were first the Father's gift to Jesus Christ. As under the law the Levites were given to Aaron (Num. 3:9), to him (the *great high priest of our profession*) the Father gave the apostles first, and ministers in every age, *to keep his charge, and the charge of the whole congregation, and to do the service of the tabernacle.* See Eph. 4:8, 11; Ps. 68:18. Christ received this gift for men, that he might give it to men. As this puts a great honour upon the ministry of the gospel, and magnifies that office, which is so much vilified; so it lays a mighty obligation upon the ministers of the gospel to devote themselves entirely to Christ's service, as being *given to him,*

(2.) But it is designed to extend to all the elect, for they are elsewhere said to be given to Christ (*ch.* 6:37, 39), and he often laid a stress upon this, that those he was to save were given to him as his charge; to his care they were committed, from his hand they were expected, and concerning them he received commandments. He here shows,

[1.] That the Father had authority to give them: *Thine they were.* He did not give that which was none of his own, but covenanted that he had a good title. The elect, whom the Father gave to Christ, were his own in three ways: — *First,* they were creatures, and their lives and beings were derived from him. When they were given to Christ to be *vessels of honour,* they were *in his hand, as clay in the hand of the potter,* to be disposed of as God's wisdom saw most for God's glory. *Secondly,* They were criminals, and their lives and beings were forfeited to him. It was a remnant of fallen mankind that was given to Christ to be redeemed, that might have been made sacrifices to justice when they were pitched upon to be the *monuments of mercy;* might justly have been *delivered to the tormentors* when they were delivered to the Saviour. *Thirdly,* They were chosen, and their lives and beings were designed, for him; they were set apart for God, and were consigned to Christ as his agent. This he insists upon again (*v.* 7): *All things whatsoever thou hast given me are of thee,* which, though it may take in all that appertained to his office as Mediator, yet seems especially to be meant of those that were given him. "They *are of thee,* their being is of thee as the God of nature, their well-being is of thee as the God of grace; they *are all of thee,* and therefore, Father, I bring them all to thee, that they may be all for thee."

[2.] That he did accordingly give them to the Son. *Thou gavest them to me,* as sheep to the shepherd, to be kept; as patients to the physician, to be cured; children to a tutor, to be educated; thus he will deliver up his charge (Heb. 2:13), *The children thou hast given me.* They were delivered to Christ, *First,* That the election of grace might not be frustrated, *that not one,* no not *of the little ones, might perish.* That great concern must be lodged in some one good hand, able to give sufficient security, *that the purpose of God according to election might stand. Secondly,* That the undertaking of Christ might not be fruitless; they were *given to him as his seed,* in whom he should *see of the travail of his soul and be satisfied* (Isa. 53:10, 11), and might not *spend his strength,* and shed his blood, *for nought, and in vain,* Isa. 49:4. We may plead, as Christ does, "Lord, keep my graces, keep my comforts, for *thine they were, and thou gavest them to me.*"

2. The care he had taken of them to teach them (*v.* 6): *I have manifested thy name to them. I have given to them the words which thou gavest to me, v.* 8. Observe here,

(1.) The great design of Christ's doctrine, which was to manifest God's name, to declare him (*ch.* 1:18), to instruct the ignorant, and rectify the mistakes of a dark and foolish world concerning God, that he might be better loved and worshipped.

(2.) His faithful discharge of this undertaking: *I have* done it. His fidelity appears, [1.] In the truth of the doctrine. It agreed exactly with the instructions he received from his Father. He gave not only the things, but the very *words, that were given him.* Ministers, in wording their message, must have an eye to *the words which the Holy Ghost teaches.* [2.] In the tendency of his doctrine, which was to manifest God's name. He did not seek himself, but, in all he did and said, aimed to magnify his Father. Note, *First,* It is Christ's prerogative to manifest God's name to the souls of the children of men. *No man knows the Father, but he to whom the Son will reveal him,* Mt. 11:27. He only has acquaintance with the Father, and so is able to open the truth; and he only has access to the spirits of men, and so is able to open the understanding. Ministers may *publish the name of the Lord* (as Moses, Deu. 32:3), but Christ only can manifest that name. By the word of Christ God is revealed to us; by the Spirit of Christ God is revealed in us. Ministers may speak the words of God to us, but Christ can give us his words, can put them in us, as food, as treasure. *Secondly,* Sooner or later, Christ will manifest God's name to all that were given him, and will give them his word, to be the seed of their new birth, the support of their spiritual life, and the earnest of their everlasting bliss.

3. The good effect of the care he had taken of them, and the pains he had taken with them, (*v.* 6): *They have kept thy word* (*v.* 7), *they have known that all things are of thee* (*v.* 8); *they have received thy words,* and embraced them, have given their assent and consent to them, *and have known surely that I came out from thee, and have believed that thou didst send me.* Observe here,

(1.) What success the doctrine of Christ had among those *that were given to him,* in several particulars: —

[1.] "They have received the words which I gave them, as the ground receives the seed, and the earth drinks in the rain." They attended to the words of Christ, apprehended in some measure the meaning of them, and were affected with them: they received the impression of them. The word was to them an *ingrafted word.*

[2.] "*They have kept thy word,* have continued in it; they have conformed to it." Christ's commandment is then only kept when it is obeyed. Those that have to teach others the commands of Christ ought to be themselves observant of them. It was requisite that these should *keep what was committed to them,* for it was to be transmitted by them to every place for every age.

[3.] "They have understood the word, and have been sensible on what ground they went in receiving and keeping it. They have been aware that thou art the original author of that holy religion which I am come to institute, *that all things whatsoever thou hast given me are of thee.*" All Christ's offices and powers, all the gifts of the Spirit, all his graces and comforts, which God *gave without measure to him,* were all from God, contrived by his wisdom, appointed by his will, and designed by his grace, for his own glory in man's salvation. Note, It is a great satisfaction to us, in our reliance upon Christ, that he, and all he is and has, all he said and did, all he is doing and will do, are of God, 1 Co. 1:30. We may therefore venture our souls upon Christ's mediation, for it has a good bottom. If the righteousness be of God's appointing, we shall be justified; if the grace be of his dispensing, we shall be sanctified.

[4.] They have set their seal to it: *They have known surely that I came out from God, v.* 8. See here, *First,* What it is to believe; it is to *know surely,* to know *that it is so of a truth.* The disciples were very weak and defective in knowledge; yet Christ, who knew them better than they knew themselves, passes his word for them that they did believe. Note, We may know surely that which we neither do nor can know fully; *may know the certainty of the things which are not seen,* though we cannot particularly describe the nature of them. *We walk by faith,* which knows surely, *not yet by sight,* which knows clearly. *Secondly,* What it is we are to believe: *that Jesus Christ came out from God,* as he is the Son of God, in his person *the image of the invisible God,* and that God did not send him; that in his undertaking he is the ambassador of the eternal king: so that the Christian religion stands upon the same footing, and is of equal authority, with natural religion; and therefore all the doctrines of Christ are to be received as divine truths, all his commands obeyed as divine laws, and all his promises depended upon as divine securities.

(2.) How Jesus Christ here speaks of this: he enlarges upon it, [1.] As pleased with it himself. Though the many instances of his disciples' dulness and weakness had grieved him, yet their constant adherence to him, their gradual improvements, and their great attainments at last, were his joy. Christ is a Master that delights in the proficiency of his scholars. He accepts the sincerity of their faith, and graciously passes by the infirmity of it. See how willing he is to make the best of us, and to say the best of us, thereby encouraging our faith in him, and teaching us charity to one another, [2.] As pleading it with the Father. He is praying for *those that were given to him;* and he pleads that they had given themselves to him. Note, The due improvement of grace received is a good plea, according to the tenour of the new covenant, for further grace; for so runs the promise. *To him that hath shall be given.* Those that keep Christ's word, and believe on him, let Christ alone to commend them, and, which is more, to recommend them to his Father.

4. He pleads the Father's own interest in them (*v.* 9): *I pray for them, for they are thine;* and this by virtue of a joint and mutual interest, which he and the Father have in what pertained to each: *All mine are thine, and thine are mine.* Between the Father and Son there can be no dispute (as there is among the children of men) about *meum* and *tuum — mine and thine,* for the matter was settled from eternity; *all mine are thine, and thine are mine.* Here is,

(1.) The plea particularly urged for his disciples: *They are thine.* The consigning of the elect to Christ was so far from making them less the Father's that it was in order to making them the more so. Note, [1.] All that receive Christ's word, and believe in him, are taken into covenant-relation to the Father, and are looked upon as his; Christ presents them to him, and they, through Christ, present themselves to him. Christ has *redeemed us,* not to himself only, but *to God, by his blood,* Rev. 5:9, 10. They are *first-fruits unto God,* Rev. 14:4. [2.] This is a good plea in prayer, Christ here pleads it, *They are thine;* we may plead it for ourselves, *I am thine, save me;* and for others (as Moses, Ex. 32:11), "*They are thy people. They are thine;* wilt thou not provide for thine own? Wilt thou not secure them, that they may not be run down by the devil and the world? Wilt thou not secure thy interest in them, that they may not depart from thee? *They are thine,* own them as thine."

(2.) The foundation on which this plea is grounded: *All mine are thine, and thine are mine.* This bespeaks the Father and Son to be, [1.] One in essence. Every creature must say to God, *All mine are thine;* but none can say to him, *All thine are mine,* but he that is the same in substance with him and equal in power and glory. [2.] One in interest; no separate or divided interests between them. *First,* What the Father has as Creator is delivered over to the Son, to be used and disposed of in subserviency to his great undertaking. *All things are delivered to him* (Mt. 11:27); the grant is so general that nothing is excepted but *he that did put all things under him. Secondly,* What the Son has as Redeemer is designed for the Father, and his kingdom shall shortly be delivered up to him. All the benefits of redemption, purchased by the Son, are intended for the Father's praise, and in his glory all the lines of his undertaking centre: *All mine are thine.* The Son owns none for his that are not devoted to the service of the Father; nor will any thing be accepted as a piece of service to the Christian religion which clashes with the dictates and laws of natural religion. In a limited sense, every true believer may say, *All thine are mine;* if God be ours in covenant, all he is and has is so far ours that it shall be engaged for our good; and in an unlimited sense every true believer does say, Lord, *all mine are thine;* all laid at his feet, to be serviceable to him. And what we have may be comfortably committed to God's care and blessing when it is cheerfully submitted to his government and disposal: "Lord, take care of what I have, for it is *all thine.*"

5. He pleads his own concern in them: *I am glorified in them — dedoxasmai.* (1.) *I have been glorified in them.* What little honour Christ had in this world was among his disciples; he had been glorified by their attendance on him and obedience to him, their preaching and working miracles in his name; and therefore *I pray for them.* Note, Those shall have an interest in Christ's intercession in and by whom he is glorified. (2.) "*I am to be glorified in them* when I am gone to heaven; they are to bear up my name." The apostles preached and wrought miracles *in Christ's name; the Spirit in them glorified Christ* (*ch.* 16:14): "*I am glorified in them,* and therefore," [1.] "I concern myself for them." What little interest Christ has in this degenerate world lies in his church; and therefore it and all its affairs lie near his heart, within the veil. [2.] "Therefore I commit them to the Father, who has engaged to glorify the Son, and, upon this account, will have a gracious eye to those in whom he is glorified." That in which God and Christ are glorified may, with humble confidence, be committed to God's special care.

Verses 11–16

After the general pleas with which Christ recommended his disciples to his Father's care follow the particular petitions he puts up for them; and, 1. They all relate to spiritual blessings in heavenly things. He does not pray that they might be rich and great in the world, that they might raise estates and get preferments, but that they might be kept from sin, and furnished for their duty, and brought safely to heaven. Note, The prosperity of the soul is the best prosperity; for what relates to this Christ came to purchase and bestow, and so teaches us to seek, in the first place, both for others and for ourselves. 2. They are such blessings as were suited to their present state and case, and their various exigencies and occasions. Note, Christ's intercession is always pertinent. Our *advocate with the Father* is acquainted with all the particulars of our wants and burdens, our dangers and difficulties, and knows how to accommodate his intercession to each, as to Peter's peril, which he himself was not aware of (Lu. 22:32), *I have prayed for thee.* 3. He is large and full in the petitions, orders them before his Father, and *fills his mouth with arguments,* to teach us fervency and importunity in prayer, to be large in prayer, and dwell upon our errands at the throne of grace, wrestling as Jacob, *I will not let thee go, except thou bless me.*

Now the first thing Christ prays for, for his disciples, is their preservation, in these verses, in order to which he commits them all to his Father's custody. Keeping supposes danger, and their danger arose *from the world,* the world wherein they were, *the evil* of this he begs they might be kept from. Now observe,

I. The request itself: *Keep them from the world.* There were two ways of their being delivered from the world: —

1. By taking them out of it; and he does not pray that they might be so delivered: *I pray not that thou shouldest take them out of the world;* that is,

(1.) "I pray not that they may be speedily removed by death." If the world will be vexatious to them, the readiest way to secure them would be to hasten them out of it to a better world, that will give them better treatment. Send chariots and horses of fire for them, to fetch them to heaven; Job, Elijah, Jonah, Moses, when that occurred which fretted them, prayed that they might be *taken out of the world;* but Christ would not pray so for his disciples, for two reasons: — [1.] Because he came to conquer, not to countenance, those intemperate heats and passions which make men impatient of life, and importunate for death. It is his will that we should take up our cross, and not outrun it. [2.] Because he had work for them to do in the world; the world, though sick of them (Acts 22:22), and therefore not worthy of them (Heb. 11:38), yet could ill spare them. In pity therefore to this dark world, Christ would not have these lights removed out of it, but continued in it, especially for the sake of those in the world that were to *believe in him through their word.* Let not them be taken out of the world when their Master is; they must each in his own order die a martyr, but not till they have finished their testimony. Note, *First,* The taking of good people out of the world is a thing by no means to be desired, but rather dreaded and laid to heart, Isa. 57:1. *Secondly,* Though Christ loves his disciples, he does not presently send for them to heaven, as soon as they are effectually called, but leaves them for some time in this world, that they may do good and glorify God upon earth, and be ripened for heaven. Many good people are spared to live, because they can ill be spared to die.

(2.) "I pray not that they may be totally freed and exempted from the troubles of this world, and taken out of the toil and terror of it into some place of ease and safety, there to live undisturbed; this is not the preservation I desire for them." *Non ut omni molestia liberati otium et delicias colant, sed ut inter media pericula salvi tamen maneant Dei auxilio — Not that, being freed from all trouble, they may bask in luxurious ease, but that by the help of God they may be preserved in a scene of danger;* so Calvin. Not that they may be kept from all conflict with the world, but that they may not be overcome by it; not that, as Jeremiah wished, they might *leave their people, and go from them* (Jer. 9:2), but that, like Ezekiel, *their faces may be strong against the faces of wicked men,* Eze. 3:8. It is more the honour of a Christian soldier by faith to *overcome the world* than by a monastical vow to retreat from it; and more for the honour of Christ to serve him in a city than to serve him in a cell.

2. Another way is by keeping them from the corruption that is in the world; and he prays they may be thus kept, *v.* 11, 15. Here are three branches of this petition: —

(1.) *Holy Father, keep those whom thou hast given me.* [1.] Christ was now leaving them; but let them not think that their defence was departed from them; no, he does here, in their hearing, commit them to the custody of his Father and their Father. Note, It is the unspeakable comfort of all believers that Christ himself has committed them to the care of God. Those cannot but be safe whom the almighty God keeps, and he cannot but keep those whom the Son of his love commits to him, in the virtue of which we may by faith

commit the keeping of our souls to God, 1 Pt. 4:19; 2 Tim. 1:12. *First,* He here puts them under the divine protection, that they may not be run down by the malice of their enemies; that they and all their concerns may be the particular care of the divine Providence: "*Keep* their lives, till they have done their work; keep their comforts, and let them not be broken in upon by the hardships they meet with; keep up their interest in the world, and let it not sink." To this prayer is owing the wonderful preservation of the gospel ministry and gospel church in the world unto this day; if God had not graciously kept both, and kept up both, they had been extinguished and lost long ago. *Secondly,* He puts them under the divine tuition, that they may not themselves run away from their duty, nor be led aside by the treachery of their own hearts: "*Keep them* in their integrity, keep them disciples, keep them close to their duty." We need God's power not only to put us into a state of grace, but to keep us in it. See, *ch.* 10:28, 29; 1 Pt. 1:5.

[2.] The titles he gives to him he prays to, and them he prays for, enforce the petition. *First,* He speaks to God as a *holy Father.* In committing ourselves and others to the divine care, we may take encouragement, 1. From the attribute of his holiness, for this is engaged for the preservation of his holy ones; he hath *sworn by his holiness,* Ps. 89:35. If he be a holy God and hate sin, he will make those holy that are his, and keep them from sin, which they also hate and dread as the greatest evil. 2. From this relation of a Father, wherein he stands to us through Christ. If he be a Father, he will take care of his own children, will teach them and keep them; who else should? *Secondly,* He speaks of them as those whom the Father had *given him.* What we receive as our Father's gifts, we may comfortably remit to our Father's care. "Father, keep the graces and comforts thou hast given me; the children thou hast given me; the ministry *I have received.*"

(2.) *Keep them through thine own name.* That is, [1.] Keep them for thy name's sake; so some. "Thy name and honour are concerned in their preservation as well as mine, for both will suffer by it if they either revolt or sink." The Old Testament saints often pleaded, for *thy name's sake;* and those may with comfort plead it that are indeed more concerned for the honour of God's name than for any interest of their own. [2.] Keep them in thy name; so others; the original is so, *en tō onomati.* "Keep them in the knowledge and fear of thy name; keep them in the profession and service of thy name, whatever it cost them. Keep them in the interest of thy name, and let them ever be faithful to this; keep them in thy truths, in thine ordinances, in the way of thy commandments." [3.] Keep them by or through thy name; so others. "Keep them by thine own power, in thine own hand; keep them thyself, undertake for them, let them be thine own immediate care. Keep them by those means of preservation which thou hast thyself appointed, and by which thou hast made thyself known. Keep them by thy word and ordinances; let thy name be their strong tower, thy tabernacle their pavilion."

(3.) *Keep them from the evil,* or out of the evil. He had taught them to pray daily, *Deliver us from evil,* and this would encourage them to pray. [1.] "Keep them from the evil one, the devil and all his instruments; that wicked one and all his children. Keep them from Satan as a tempter, that either he may not have leave to sift them, or that their faith may not fail. Keep them from him as a destroyer, that he may not drive them to despair." [2.] "Keep them from the evil thing, that is sin; from every thing that looks like it, or leads to it. Keep them, that they do no evil," 2 Co. 13:7. Sin is that evil which, above any other, we should dread and deprecate. [3.] "Keep them from the evil of the world, and of their tribulation in it, so that it may have no sting in it, no malignity;" not that they might be kept from affliction, but kept through it, that the property of their afflictions might be so altered as that there might be no evil in them, nothing to them any harm.

II. The reasons with which he enforces these requests for their preservation, which are five: —

1. He pleads that hitherto he had kept them (*v.* 12): "*While I was with them in the world, I have kept them in thy name,* in the true faith of the gospel and the service of God; those that thou gavest me for my constant attendants I have kept, they are all safe, and none of them missing, none of them revolted nor ruined, *but the son of perdition;* he is lost, that the scripture might be fulfilled." Observe,

(1.) Christ's faithful discharge of his undertaking concern-

ing his disciples: *While he was with them, he kept them,* and his care concerning them was not in vain. He kept them in God's name, preserved them from falling into any dangerous errors or sins, from striking in with the Pharisees, who would have *compassed sea and land to make proselytes* of them; he kept them from deserting him, and returning to the little all they had left for him; he had them still under his eye and care when he sent them to peach; *went not his heart with them?* Many that followed him awhile took offence at something or other, and went off; but he kept the twelve that they should not go away. He kept them from falling into the hands of persecuting enemies that sought their lives; kept them when he surrendered himself, *ch.* 18:9. *While he was with them* he kept them in a visible manner by instructions till sounding in their ears, miracles still done before their eyes; when he was gone from them, they must be kept in a more spiritual manner. Sensible comforts and supports are sometimes given and sometimes withheld; but, when they are withdrawn, yet they are not left comfortless. What Christ here says of his immediate followers is true of all the saints while they are here in this world; Christ keeps them *in God's name.* It is implied, [1.] That they are weak, and cannot keep themselves; their own hands are not sufficient for them. [2.] That they are, in God's account, valuable and worth the keeping; precious in his sight and honourable; his treasure, his jewels. [3.] That their salvation is designed, for to this it is that they are kept, 1 Pt. 1:5. As the wicked are reserved for the day of evil, so the righteous are preserved for the day of bliss. [4.] That they are the charge of the Lord Jesus; for as his charge he keeps them, and exposed himself like the good shepherd for the preservation of the sheep.

(2.) The comfortable account he gives of his undertaking: *None of them is lost.* Note, Jesus Christ will certainly keep all that were given to him, so that none of them shall be totally and finally lost; they may think themselves lost, and may be nearly lost (in imminent peril); but it is the Father's will that he should *lose none,* and none he will lose (*ch.* 6:39); so it will appear when they come all together, and none of them shall be wanting.

(3.) A brand put upon Judas, as none of those whom he had undertaken to keep. He was among those that were given to Christ, but not of them. He speaks of Judas as already lost, for he had abandoned the society of his Master and his fellow-disciples, and abandoned himself to the devil's guidance, and in a little time would *go to his own place;* he is as good as lost. But the apostasy and ruin of Judas were no reproach at all to his Master, or his family; for, [1.] He was *the son of perdition,* and therefore not one of those that were given to Christ to be kept. He deserved perdition, and God left him to throw himself headlong into it. He was *the son of the destroyer,* as Cain, *who was of that wicked one.* That great enemy whom the Lord *will consume* is called a *son of perdition,* because he is a *man of sin,* 2 Th. 2:3. It is an awful consideration that one of the apostles proved a son of perdition. No man's place or name in the church, no man's privileges or opportunities of getting grace, no man's profession or external performances, will secure him from ruin, if his heart be not right with God; nor are any more likely to prove sons of perdition at last, after a plausible course of profession, than those that like Judas love the bag; but Christ's distinguishing Judas from those that were given him (for *ei mē* is adversative, not exceptive) intimates that the truth and true religion ought not to suffer for the treachery of those that are false to it, 1 Jn. 2:19. [2.] The scripture was fulfilled; the sin of Judas was foreseen of God's counsel and foretold in his word, and the event would certainly follow after the prediction as a consequent, though it cannot be said necessarily to follow from it as an effect. See Ps. 41:9; 69:25; 109:8. We should be amazed at the treachery of apostates, were we not *told of it before.*

2. He pleads that he was now under a necessity of leaving them, and could no longer watch over them in the way that he had hitherto done (*v.* 11): "Keep them now, that I may not lose the labour I bestowed upon them while I was with them. Keep them, *that they may be one* with us *as we are* with each other." We shall have occasion to speak of this, *v.* 21. But see here,

(1.) With what pleasure he speaks of his own departure. He expresses himself concerning it with an air of triumph and exultation, with reference both to the world he left and the world he removed to. [1.] "*Now I am no more in the world.* Now farewell to this provoking troublesome world. I have had enough of it, and now the welcome hour is at hand when I shall be *no more in it.* Now that I have finished the work I had to do in it, I have done with it; nothing remains now but to hasten out of it as fast as I can." Note, It should be a pleasure to those that have their home in the other world to think of being *no more in this world;* for when we have done what we have to do in this world, and are made meet for that, what is there here that should court our stay? When we receive a sentence of death within ourselves, with what a holy triumph should we say, *"Now I am no more in this world,* this dark deceitful world, this poor empty world, this tempting defiling world; no more vexed with its thorns and briars, no more endangered by its nets and snares; now I shall wander no more in this howling wilderness, be tossed no more on this stormy sea; *now I am no more in this world,* but can cheerfully quit it, and give it a final farewell." [2.] *Now I come to thee.* To get clear of the world is but the one half of the comfort of a dying Christ, of a dying Christian; the far better half is to think of going to the Father, to sit down in the immediate, uninterrupted, and everlasting enjoyment of him. Note, Those who love God cannot but be pleased to think of coming to him, though it be through the valley of the shadow of death. When we go, to be *absent from the body,* it is to be *present with the Lord,* like children fetched home from school to their father's house. "Now come I to thee whom I have chosen and served, and whom my soul thirsteth after; to thee the fountain of light and life, the crown and centre of bliss and joy; now my longings shall be satisfied, my hopes accomplished, my happiness completed, for *now come I to thee."*

(2.) With what a tender concern he speaks of those whom he left behind: *"But these are in the world.* I have found what an evil world it is, what will become of these dear little ones that must stay in it? *Holy Father, keep them;* they will want my presence, let them have thine. They have now more need than ever to be kept, for I am sending them out further into the world than they have yet ventured; they must *launch forth into the deep,* and have business to do in these great waters, and will be lost if thou do not keep them." Observe here, [1.] That, when our Lord Jesus was going to the Father, he carried with him a tender concern for *his own that are in the world;* and continued to compassionate them. He bears their names upon his breast-plate, nay, upon his heart, and has *graven them* with the nails of his cross *upon the palms of his hands;* and when he is out of their sight they are not out of his, much less out of his mind. We should have such a pity for those that are launching out into the world when we are got almost through it, and for those that are left behind in it when we are leaving it. [2.] That, when Christ would express the utmost need his disciples had of divine preservation, he only says, *They are in the world;* this bespeaks danger enough to those who are bound for heaven, whom a flattering world would divert and seduce, and a malignant world would hate and persecute.

3. He pleads what a satisfaction it would be to them to know themselves safe, and what a satisfaction it would be to him to see them easy: *I speak this, that they may have my joy fulfilled in themselves, v.* 13. Observe,

(1.) Christ earnestly desired the fulness of the joy of his disciples, for it is his will that they should rejoice evermore. He was leaving them in tears and troubles, and yet took effectual care to *fulfil their joy.* When they thought their joy in him was brought to an end, then was it advanced nearer to perfection than ever it had been, and they were fuller of it. We are here taught, [1.] To found our joy in Christ: "It is *my joy,* joy of my giving, or rather joy that I am the matter of." Christ is a Christian's joy, his chief joy. Joy in the world is withering with it; joy in Christ is everlasting, like him. [2.] To build up our joy with diligence; for it is the duty as well as privilege of all true believers; no part of the Christian life is pressed upon us more earnestly, Phil. 3:1; 4:4. [3.] To aim at the perfection of this joy, that we may have it fulfilled in us, for this Christ would have.

(2.) In order hereunto, he did thus solemnly commit them to his Father's care and keeping and took them for witnesses that he did so: *These things I speak in the world,* while I am yet with them in the world. His intercession in heaven for their preservation would have been as effectual in itself; but saying this in the world would be a greater satisfaction and encouragement to them, and would enable them to *rejoice in tribulation.* Note, [1.] Christ has not only treasured up comforts for his people, in providing for their future welfare, but has given out comforts to them, and said that which will be for their present satisfaction. He here condescended in the presence of his disciples to publish his last will and testament, and (which many a testator is shy of) lets them know what legacies he had left them, and how well they were secured, that they might have strong consolation. [2.] Christ's intercession for us is enough to fulfil or joy in him; nothing more effectual to silence all our fears and mistrusts, and to furnish us with strong consolation, than this, that he always appears in the presence of God for us; therefore the apostle puts a *yea rather* upon this, Rom. 8:34. And see Heb. 7:25.

4. He pleads the ill usage they were likely to meet with in the world, for his sake (*v.* 14): *"I have given them thy word* to be published to the world, *and they have received it,* have believed it themselves, and accepted the trust of transmitting it to the world; and therefore *the world hath hated them,* as also because they are *not of the world,* any more than I." Here we have,

(1.) The world's enmity to Christ's followers. While Christ was with them, though as yet they had given but little opposition to the world, yet it hates them, much more would it do so when by their more extensive preaching of the gospel they would *turn the world upside down.* "Father, stand their friend," says Christ, "for they are likely to have many enemies; let them have thy love, for the world's hatred is entailed upon them. In the midst of those fiery darts, let them be *compassed with thy favour as with a shield."* It is God's honour to take part with the weaker side, and to help the helpless. *Lord, be merciful to them, for men would swallow* them up.

(2.) The reasons of this enmity, which strengthen the plea. [1.] It is implied that one reason is because they had received the word of God as it was sent them by the hand of Christ, when the greatest part of the world rejected it, and set themselves against those who were the preachers and professors of it. Note, Those that receive Christ's good will and good word must expect the world's ill will and ill word. Gospel ministers have been in a particular manner hated by the world, because they call men out of the world, and separate them from it, and teach them not to conform to it, and so condemn the world. *"Father, keep them* for it is for thy sake that they are exposed; they are sufferers for thee." Thus the psalmist pleads, *For thy sake I have borne reproach,* Ps. 69:7. Note, Those that keep the word of Christ's patience are entitled to special protection in the hour of temptation, Rev. 3:10. That cause which makes a martyr may well make a joyful sufferer. [2.] Another reason is more express; the world hates them, because they *are not of the world.* Those to whom the word of Christ comes in power are not of the world, for it has this effect upon all that receive it in the love of it that it weans them from the wealth of the world, and turns them against the wickedness of the world, and therefore the world bears them a grudge.

5. He pleads their conformity to himself in a holy nonconformity to the world (*v.* 16): "Father, keep them, for they are of my spirit and mind, *they are not of the world, even as I am not of the world."* Those may in faith commit themselves to God's custody, (1.) Who are *as Christ was in this world,* and tread in his steps. God will love those that are like Christ. (2.) Who do not engage themselves in the world's interest, nor devote themselves to its service. Observe, [1.] That Jesus Christ was not of this world; he never had been of it, and least of all now that he was upon the point of leaving it. This intimates, *First,* His state; he was none of the world's favourites nor darlings, none of its princes nor grandees; worldly possessions he had none, not even *where to lay his head;* nor worldly power, he was no judge nor divider. *Secondly,* His Spirit; he was perfectly dead to the world, the prince of this world had nothing in him, the things of this world were nothing to him; not honour, for he *made himself of no reputation;* not riches, for *for our sakes he became poor;* not pleasures, for he *acquainted himself with grief.* See *ch.* 8:23. [2.] That therefore true Christians are not of this world. The Spirit of Christ in them is opposite to the spirit of the world. *First,* It is their lot to be despised by the world; they are not in favour with the world any more than their Master before them was. *Secondly,* It is their privilege to be delivered from the world; as Abraham out of the land of his nativity. *Thirdly,* It is their duty and character to be dead to the world. Their most pleasing converse is, and should be, with another world, and their prevailing concern about the business of that world, not of this. Christ's disciples were weak, and had many infirmities; yet this he could say for them, They were not of the world, not of the earth, and therefore he recommends them to the care of Heaven.

Verses 17–19

The next thing he prayed for for them was that they might be sanctified; not only kept from evil, but made good.

I. Here is the petition (*v.* 17): *Sanctify them through thy truth,* through thy word, for *thy word is truth;* it is true — it is truth itself. He desires they may be sanctified,

1. As Christians. Father, make them holy, and this will be their preservation, 1 Th. 5:23. Observe here,

(1.) The grace desired — sanctification. The disciples were sanctified, for they were not of the world; yet he prays, *Father sanctify them,* that is, [1.] "Confirm the work of sanctification in them, strengthen their faith, inflame their good affections, rivet their good resolutions." [2.] "Carry on that good work in them, and continue it; let the *light shine more and more."* [3.] "Complete it, crown it with the perfection of holiness; sanctify them throughout and to the end." Note, *First,* It is the prayer of Christ for all that are his that they may be sanctified; because he cannot for shame own them as his, either here or hereafter, either employ them in his work or present them to his Father, if they be not sanctified. *Secondly,* Those that through grace are sanctified have need to be sanctified more and more. Even disciples must pray for sanctifying grace; for, if he that was the author of the good work be not the finisher of it, we are undone. Not to go forward is to go backward; *he that is holy must be holy still,* more holy still, pressing forward, soaring upward, as those that have not attained. *Thirdly,* It is God that sanctifies as well as God that justified, 2 Co. 5:5. *Fourthly,* It is an encouragement to us, in our prayers for sanctifying grace, that it is what Christ intercedes for for us.

(2.) The means of conferring this grace — *through thy truth, thy word is truth.* Not that the Holy One of Israel is hereby limited to means, but in the *counsel of peace* among other things it was settled and agreed, [1.] That all needful truth should be comprised and summed up in the word of God. Divine revelation, as it now stands in the written word, is not only pure truth without mixture, but entire truth without deficiency. [2.] That this word of truth should be the outward and ordinary means of our sanctification; not of itself, for then it would always sanctify, but as the instrument which the Spirit commonly uses in beginning and carrying on that good work; it is the seed of the new birth (1 Pt. 1:23), and the food of the new life, 1 Pt. 2:1–2.

2. As ministers. *"Sanctify them,* set them apart for thyself and service; let their call to the apostleship be ratified in heaven." Prophets were said to be sanctified, Jer. 1:5. Priests and Levites were so. *Sanctify them;* that is, (1.) "Qualify them for the office, with Christian graces and ministerial gifts, to make them able ministers of the New Testament." (2.) "Separate them to the office, Rom. 1:1. I have called them, they have consented; Father, say *Amen* to it." (3.) "Own them in the office; let thy hand go along with them; sanctify them by or in thy truth, as truth is opposed to figure and shadow; sanctify them really, not ritually and ceremonially, as the Levitical priests were, by anointing and sacrifice. Sanctify them to thy truth, the word of thy truth, to be the preachers of thy truth to the world; as the priests were sanctified to serve at the altar, so let them be to preach the gospel." 1 Co. 9:13, 14. Note, [1.] Jesus Christ intercedes for his ministers with a particular concern, and recommends to his Father's grace those stars he carries in his right hand. [2.] The great thing to be asked of God for gospel ministers is that they may be sanctified, effectually separated from the world, entirely devoted to God, and experimentally acquainted with the influence of that word upon their own hearts which they preach to others. Let them have the *Urim* and *Thummim, light* and *integrity.*

II. We have here two pleas or arguments to enforce the petition for the disciples' sanctification: —

1. The mission they had from him (*v.* 18): *"As thou hast sent me into the world,* to be thine ambassador to the children of men, so now that I am recalled *have I sent them into the world,* as my delegates." Now here,

(1.) Christ speaks with great assurance of his own mission: *Thou hast sent me into the world.* The great author of the Christian religion had his commission and instructions from him who is the origin and object of all religion. He was sent of God to say what he said, and do what he did, and be what he is to those that believe on him; which was his comfort in his undertaking, and may be ours abundantly in our dependence upon him; his record was on high, for thence his mission was.

(2.) He speaks with great satisfaction of the commission he had given his disciples "*So have I sent them* on the same errand, and to carry on the same design;" to preach the same doctrine that he preached, and to confirm it with the same proofs, with a charge likewise to commit to other faithful men that which was committed to them. He gave them their commission (*ch.* 20:21) with a reference to his own, and it magnifies their office that it comes from Christ, and that there is some affinity between the commission given to the ministers of reconciliation and that given to the Mediator; he is called an *apostle* (Heb. 3:1), a *minister* (Rom. 15:8), a *messenger,* Mal. 3:1. Only they are sent as servants, he as a Son. Now this comes in here as a reason, [1.] Why Christ was concerned so much for them, and laid their case so near his heart; because he had himself put them into a difficult office, which required great abilities for the due discharge of it. Note, Whom Christ sends he will stand by, and interest himself in those that are employed for him; what he calls us out to he will fit us out for, and bear us up in. [2.] Why he committed them to his Father; because he was concerned in their cause, their mission being in prosecution of his, and as it were an assignment out of it. Christ *received gifts for men* (Ps. 68:18), and then gave them to men (Eph. 4:8), and therefore *prays aid* of his Father to warrant and uphold those gifts, and confirm his grant of them. The Father *sanctified him* when *he sent him into the world, ch.* 10:36. Now, they being sent as he was, let them also be sanctified.

2. The merit he had for them is another thing here pleaded (*v.* 19): *For their sakes I sanctify myself.* Here is, (1.) Christ's designation of himself to the work and office of Mediator: *I sanctified myself.* He entirely devoted himself to the undertaking, and all the parts of it, especially that which he was now going about — the *offering up of himself without spot unto God, by the eternal Spirit.* He, as the priest and altar, sanctified himself as the sacrifice. When he said, Father, *glorify thy name* — Father, *thy will be done* — Father, I *commit my spirit into thy hands,* he paid down the satisfaction he had engaged to make, and so sanctified himself. This he pleads with his Father, for his intercession is made in the virtue of his satisfaction; *by his own blood he entered into the holy place* (Heb. 9:12), as the high priest, on the day of atonement, sprinkled the blood of the sacrifice at the same time that he burnt incense within the veil, Lev. 16:12, 14. (2.) Christ's design of kindness to his disciples herein; it is *for their sakes,* that *they may be sanctified,* that is, that they may be martyrs; so some. "I sacrifice myself, that they may be sacrificed to the glory of God and the church's good." Paul speaks of his being offered, Phil. 2:17; 2 Tim. 4:6. Whatever there is in the *death of the saints* that is *precious in the sight of the Lord,* it is owing to the death of the Lord Jesus. But I rather take it more generally, that they may be saints and ministers, duly qualified and accepted of God. [1.] The office of the ministry is the purchase of Christ's blood, and one of the blessed fruits of his satisfaction, and owes its virtue and value to Christ's merit. The priests under the law were consecrated with the blood of bulls and goats, but gospel ministers with the blood of Jesus. [2.] The real holiness of all good Christians is the fruit of Christ's death, by which the gift of the Holy Ghost was purchased; he *gave himself for his church,* to *sanctify it,* Eph. 5:25, 26. And he that designed the end designed also the means, that they might be sanctified *by the truth,* the truth which Christ came into the world to bear witness to and died to confirm. The word of truth receives its sanctifying virtue and power from the death of Christ. Some read it, that they may be sanctified *in truth,* that is, truly; for as God must be served, so, in order to this, we must be sanctified, *in the spirit, and in truth.* And this Christ has prayed for, for all that are his; for *this is his will, even their sanctification,* which encourages them to pray for it,

Verses 20–23

Next to their purity he prays for their unity; for the wisdom from above is *first pure, then peaceable;* and amity is amiable indeed when it is like the ointment on Aaron's holy head, and the dew on Zion's holy hill. Observe,

I. Who are included in this prayer (*v.* 20): "*Not these only,* not these only that are now my disciples" (the eleven, the seventy, with others, men and women that followed him when he was here on earth), "but *for those also who shall believe on me through their word,* either preached by them in their own day or written by them for the generations to come; I pray *for them all,* that they all may be one in their interest in this prayer, and may all receive benefit by it." Note, here, 1. Those, and those only, are interested in the mediation of Christ, that do, or shall, believe in him. This is that by which they are described, and it comprehends all the character and duty of a Christian. They that lived then, *saw and believed,* but they in after ages *have not seen,* and yet *have believed.* 2. It is *through the word* that souls are brought to believe on Christ, and it is for this end that Christ appointed the scriptures to be written, and a standing ministry to continue in the church, while the church stands, that is, while the world stands, for the raising up of a seed. 3. It is certainly and infallibly known to Christ who shall believe on him. He does not here pray at a venture, upon a contingency depending on the treacherous will of man, which pretends to be free, but by reason of sin is *in bondage with its children;* no, Christ knew very well whom he prayed for, the matter was reduced to a certainty by the divine prescience and purpose; he knew who were given him, who being ordained to eternal life, were *entered in the Lamb's book,* and should undoubtedly believe, Acts 13:48. 4. Jesus Christ intercedes not only for great and eminent believers, but for the meanest and weakest; not for those only that are to be employed in the highest post of trust and honour in his kingdom, but for all, even those that in the eye of the world are inconsiderable. As the divine providence extends itself to the meanest creature, so does the divine grace to the meanest Christian. The good Shepherd has an eye even to *the poor of the flock.* 5. Jesus Christ in his mediation had an actual regard to those of the chosen remnant that were yet unborn, the people that *should be created* (Ps. 22:31), the *other sheep* which he *must yet bring.* Before they are *formed in the womb he knows them* (Jer. 1:5), and prayers are filed in heaven for them beforehand, by him who *declareth the end from the beginning, and calleth things that are not as though they were.*

II. What is intended in this prayer (*v.* 21): *That they all may be one.* The same was said before (*v.* 11), *that they may be one as we are,* and again, *v.* 22. The heart of Christ was much upon this. Some think that the oneness prayed for in *v.* 11 has special reference to the disciples as ministers and apostles, that they might be one in their testimony to Christ; and that the harmony of the evangelists, and concurrence of the first preachers of the gospel, are owing to this prayer. Let them be not only of *one heart,* but of *one mouth,* speaking the same thing. The unity of the gospel ministers is both the beauty and strength of the gospel interest. But it is certain that the oneness prayed for in *v.* 21 respects all believers. It is the prayer of Christ for all that are his, and we may be sure it is an answered prayer — *that they all may be one,* one in us (*v.* 21), one *as e are one* (*v.* 22), made *perfect in one, v.* 23. It includes three things: —

1. That they might all be *incorporated in one body.* "Father, look upon them all as one, and ratify that great charter by which they are embodied as one church. Though they live in distant places, from one end of heaven to the other, and in several ages, from the beginning to the close of time, and so cannot have any personal acquaintance or correspondence with each other, yet let them be united in me their common head." As Christ died, so he prayed, to *gather them all in one, ch.* 11:52; Eph. 1:10.

2. That they might all be animated by one Spirit. This is plainly implied in this — *that they may be one in us.* Union with the Father and Son is obtained and kept up only by the Holy Ghost. *He that is joined to the Lord in one spirit,* 1 Co. 6:17. Let them all be stamped with the same image and superscription, and influenced by the same power.

3. That they might all be *knit together* in the bond of love and charity, all of one heart. *That they all may be one,* (1.) In judgment and sentiment; not in every little thing — this is neither possible nor needful, but in the great things of God, and in them, by the virtue of this prayer, they are all agreed — that God's favour is better than life — that sin is the worst of evils, Christ the best of friends — that there is another life after this, and the like. (2.) In disposition and inclination. All that are sanctified have the same divine nature and image; they have all a new heart, and it is *one heart.* (3.) They are all one in their designs and aims. Every true Christian, *as far as he is so,* eyes the glory of God as his highest end, and the glory of heaven as his chief good. (4.) They are all one in their desires and prayers; though they differ in words and the manner of expressions, yet, having received the same *spirit of adoption,* and observing the same rule, they pray for the same things in effect. (5.) All one in love and affection. Every true Christian has that in him which inclines him to love all true Christians as such. That which Christ here prays for is that *communion of saints* which we profess to believe; the fellowship which all believers have with God, and their intimate union with all the saints in heaven and earth, 1 Jn. 1:3. But this prayer of Christ will not have its complete answer till all the saints come to heaven, for then, and not till then, they shall be *perfect in one, v.* 23; Eph. 4:13.

III. What is intimated by way of plea or argument to enforce this petition; three things: —

1. The oneness that is between the Father and the Son, which is mentioned again and again, *v.* 11, 21–23. (1.) It is taken for granted that the Father and Son are one, one in nature and essence, equal in power and glory, one in mutual endearments. The *Father loveth the Son,* and the Son always pleased the Father. They are one in design, and one in operation. The intimacy of this oneness is expressed in these words, *thou in me, and I in thee.* This he often mentions for his support under his present sufferings, when his enemies were ready to fall upon him, and his friends to fall off from him; yet he was in the Father, and the Father in him. (2.) This is insisted on in Christ's prayer for his disciples' oneness, [1.] As the pattern of that oneness, showing how he desired they might be one. Believers are one in some measure as God and Christ are one; for, *First,* The union of believers is a strict and close union; they are united by a divine nature, by the power of divine grace, in pursuance of the divine counsels. *Secondly,* It is a holy union, in the Holy Spirit, for holy ends; not a body politic for any secular purpose. *Thirdly,* It is, and will be at last, a complete union. Father and Son have the same attributes, properties, and perfections; so have believers now, as far as they are sanctified, and when grace shall be perfected in glory they will be exactly consonant to each other, all changed into the same image. [2.] As the centre of that oneness; that they may be *one in us,* all meeting here. There is *one God* and *one Mediator;* and herein believers are one, that they all agree to depend upon the favour of this one God as their felicity and the merit of this one Mediator as their righteousness. That is a conspiracy, not a union, which doth not centre in God as the end, and Christ as the way. All who are truly united to God and Christ, who *are one,* will soon be *united one to another.* [3.] As a plea for that oneness. The Creator and Redeemer are one in interest and design; but to what purpose are they so, if all believers be not one body with Christ, and do not jointly receive grace for grace from him, as he has received it for them? Christ's design was to reduce revolted mankind to God: "Father," says he, "let all that believe be one, that *in one body* they may be reconciled" (Eph. 2:15, 16), which speaks of the uniting of Jews and Gentiles in the church; that great mystery, that the Gentiles should be *fellow-heirs, and of the same body* (Eph. 3:6), to which I think this prayer of Christ principally refers, it being one great thing he aimed at in his dying; and I wonder none of the expositors I have met with should so apply it. "Father, let the Gentiles that believe be incorporated with the believing Jews, and *make of twain one new man.*" Those words, *I in them, and thou in me,* show what that union is which is so necessary, not only to the beauty, but to the very being, of his church. *First,* Union with Christ: *I in them.* Christ dwelling in the hearts of believers is the life and soul of the new man. *Secondly,* Union with God through him: *Thou in me,* so as by me to be in them. *Thirdly,* Union with each other, resulting from these: *that they* hereby *may be made perfect in one.* We are complete in him.

2. The design of Christ in all his communications of light and grace to them (*v.* 22): "*The glory which thou gavest me,* as the trustee or channel of conveyance, *I have* accordingly *given them,* to this intent, *that they may be one, as we are one;* so that those gifts will be in vain, if they be not one." Now these gifts are either, (1.) Those that were conferred upon the apostles, and first planters of the church. The glory of being God's ambassadors to the world — the glory of working miracles — the glory of gathering a church out of the world, and erecting the throne of God's kingdom among men — this glory was given to Christ, and some of the honour he put upon them when he sent them to *disciple all nations.* Or, (2.) Those that are given in common to all believers. The glory of being in covenant with the Father, and accepted of

him, of being laid in his bosom, and designed for a place at his right hand, was the glory which the Father gave to the Redeemer, and he has confirmed it to the redeemed. [1.] This honour he says he *hath given them,* because he hath intended it for them, settled it upon them, and secured it to them upon their believing Christ's promises to be real gifts. [2.] This was given to him to give to them; it was conveyed to him in trust for them, and he was faithful to him that appointed him. [3.] He gave it to them, that they *might be one. First,* to entitle them to the privilege of unity, that by virtue of their common relation to *one God the Father,* and *one Lord Jesus Christ,* they might be truly denominated one. The gift of the Spirit, that great glory which the Father gave to the Son, by him to be given to all believers, makes them one, for he works *all in all,* 1 Co. 12:4, etc. *Secondly,* To engage them to the duty of unity. That in consideration of their agreement and communion in one creed and one covenant, one Spirit and one Bible — in consideration of what they have in one God and one Christ, and of what they hope for in one heaven, they may be of one mind and one mouth. Worldly glory sets men at variance; for if some be advanced others are eclipsed, and therefore, while the disciples dreamed of a temporal kingdom, they were ever and anon quarrelling; but spiritual honours being conferred alike upon all Christ's subjects, they being all *made to our God kings and priests,* there is no occasion for contest nor emulation. The more Christians are taken up with the glory Christ has given them, the less desirous they will be of vain-glory, and, consequently, the less disposed to quarrel.

3. He pleads the happy influence their oneness would have upon others, and the furtherance it would give to the public good. This is twice urged (*v.* 21): *That the world may believe that thou hast sent me.* And again (*v.* 23): *That the world may know it,* for without knowledge there can be no true faith. Believers must know what they believe, and why and wherefore they believe it. Those who believe *at a venture,* venture too far. Now Christ here shows,

(1.) His good-will to the world of mankind in general. Herein he is of his Father's mind, as we are sure he is in every thing, that he would have all men to be saved, and to *come to the knowledge of the truth,* 1 Tim. 2:4; 2 Pt. 3:9. Therefore it is his will that all means possible should be used, and no stone left unturned, for the conviction and conversion of the world. We know not who are chosen, but we must in our places do our utmost to further men's salvation, and take heed of doing any thing to hinder it.

(2.) The good fruit of the church's oneness; it will be an evidence of the truth of Christianity, and a means of bringing many to embrace it.

[1.] In general, it will recommend Christianity to the world, and to the good opinion of those that are without. *First,* The embodying of Christians in one society by the gospel charter will greatly promote Christianity. When the world shall see so many of those that were its children called out of its family, distinguished from others, and changed from what they themselves sometimes were, — when they shall see this society raised by the foolishness of preaching, and kept up by miracles of divine providence and grace, and how admirably well it is modelled and constituted, they will be ready to say, *We will go with you, for we see that God is with you. Secondly,* The uniting of Christians in love and charity is the beauty of their profession, and invites others to join with them, as the love that was among those primo-primitive Christians, Acts 2:42, 43; 4:32, 33. When Christianity, instead of causing quarrels about itself, makes all other strifes to cease, — when it cools the fiery, smooths the rugged, and disposes men to be kind and loving, courteous and beneficent, to all men, studious to preserve and promote peace in all relations and societies, this will recommend it to all that have any thing either of natural religion or natural affection in them.

[2.] In particular, it will beget in men good thoughts, *First,* Of Christ: They will know and believe that *thou hast sent me,* By this it will appear that Christ was sent of God, and that his doctrine was divine, in that his religion prevails to join so many of different capacities, tempers, and interests in other things, in one body by faith, with one heart by love. Certainly he was sent by the God of power, who fashions men's hearts alike, and the God of love and peace; when the worshippers of God are one, he is one, and his name one. *Secondly,* Of Christians: They will *know that thou hast loved them as thou hast loved me.* Here is, 1. The privilege of believers: *the Father* himself loveth them with a love resembling his love to his Son, for they are loved in him with an everlasting love. 2. The evidence of their interest in this privilege, and that is their being one. By this it will appear that God loves us, if we *love one another with a pure heart;* for wherever *the love of God is shed abroad in the heart* it will change it into the same image. See how much good it would do to the world to know better how dear to God all good Christians are. The Jews had a saying, *If the world did but know the worth of good men, they would hedge them about with pearls.* Those that have so much of God's love should have more of ours.

Verses 24–26

Here is, I. A petition for the glorifying of all those that were given to Christ (*v.* 24), not only these apostles, but all believers: *Father, I will that they may be with me.* Observe,

1. The connection of this request with those foregoing. He had prayed that God would preserve, sanctify, and unite them; and now he prays that he would crown all his gifts with their glorification. In this method we must pray, first for grace, and then for glory (Ps. 84:11); for in this method God gives. Far be it from the only wise God to come under the imputation either of that *foolish builder who without a foundation built upon the sand,* as he would if he should glorify any whom he has not first sanctified; or of that *foolish builder who began to build and was not able to finish,* as he would if he should sanctify any, and not glorify them.

2. The manner of the request: *Father, I will.* Here, as before, he addresses himself to God as a Father, and therein we must do likewise; but when he says, *thelō — I will,* he speaks a language peculiar to himself, and such as does not become ordinary petitioners, but very well became him who paid for what he prayed for. (1.) This intimates the authority of his intercession in general; his word was with power in heaven, as well as on earth. He entering *with his own blood into the holy place,* his intercession there has an uncontrollable efficacy. He intercedes as a king, for he is a priest upon his throne (like Melchizedek), a king-priest. (2.) It intimates his particular authority in this matter; he had a power to *give eternal life* (*v.* 2), and, pursuant to that power, he says, *Father, I will.* Though now he *took upon him the form of a servant,* yet that power being to be most illustriously exerted when he shall come the second time in the glory of a judge, to say, *Come ye blessed,* having that in his eye, he might well say, *Father, I will.*

3. The request itself — that all the elect might come to be with him in heaven at last, to see his glory, and to share in it. Now observe here,

(1.) Under what notion we are to hope for heaven? wherein does that happiness consist? three things make heaven: — [1.] It is to be where Christ is: *Where I am;* in the paradise whither Christ's soul went at death; in the third heavens whither his soul and body went at his ascension: — *Where I am,* am to be shortly, am to be eternally. In this world we are but *in transitu — on our passage;* there we truly are where we are to be for ever; so Christ reckoned, and so must we. [2.] It is to be with him where he is; this is not tautology, but intimates that we shall not only be in the same happy place where Christ is, but that the happiness of the place will consist in his presence; this is *the fulness of its joy.* The very heaven of heaven is to be with Christ, there in company with him, and communion with him, Phil. 1:23. [3.] It is to *behold his glory, which the Father* has given him. Observe, *First,* The glory of the Redeemer is the brightness of heaven. That glory before which angels cover their faces was his glory, *ch.* 12:41. The Lamb is the light of the new Jerusalem, Rev. 21:23. Christ will *come in the glory of his Father,* for *he is the brightness of his glory.* God shows his glory there, as he does his grace here, through Christ. *"The Father has given me this glory,"* though he was as yet in his low estate; but it was very true, and very near. *Secondly,* The felicity of the redeemed consists very much in the beholding of this glory; they will have the immediate view of his glorious person. *I shall see God in my flesh,* Job 19:26, 27. They will have a clear insight into his glorious undertaking, as it will be then accomplished; they will see into those springs of love from which flow all the streams of grace; they shall have an appropriating sight of Christ's glory *(Uxor fulget radiis mariti — The wife shines with the radiance of her husband),* and an assimilating sight: they shall *be changed into the same image, from glory to glory.*

(2.) Upon what ground we are to hope for heaven; no other than purely the mediation and intercession of Christ, because he hath said, *Father, I will.* Our sanctification is our evidence, for *he that has this hope in him purifies himself;* but it is the will of Christ that is our title, *by which will we are sanctified,* Heb. 10:10. Christ speaks here as if he did not count his own happiness complete unless he had his elect to share with him in it, for it is *the bringing of many sons to glory that makes the captain of our salvation perfect,* Heb. 2:10.

4. The argument to back this request: *for thou lovedst me before the foundation of the world.* This is a reason, (1.) Why he expected this glory himself. Thou wilt *give it to me, for thou lovedst me.* The honour and power given to the Son as Mediator were founded in the Father's love to him (*ch.* 5:20): *the Father loves the Son,* is infinitely well pleased in his undertaking, and *therefore has given all things into his hands;* and, the matter being concerted in the divine counsels from eternity, he is said to love him as Mediator *before the foundation of the world.* Or, (2.) Why he expected that those who *were given to him* should be with him to share in his glory: *"Thou lovedst me,* and them in me, and canst deny me nothing I ask for them."

II. The conclusion of the prayer, which is designed to enforce all the petitions for the disciples, especially the last, that they may be glorified. Two things he insists upon, and pleads: —

1. The respect he had to his Father, *v.* 25. Observe,

(1.) The title he gives to God: *O righteous Father.* When he prayed that they might be sanctified, he called him *holy Father;* when he prays that they may be glorified, he calls him *righteous Father;* for it is a *crown of righteousness which the righteous Judge shall give.* God's righteousness was engaged for the giving out of all that good which the Father had promised and the Son had purchased.

(2.) The character he gives of the world that lay in wickedness: *The world has not known thee.* Note, Ignorance of God overspreads the world of mankind; this is the darkness they sit in. Now this is urged here, [1.] To show that these disciples need the aids of special grace, both because of the necessity of their work — they were to bring a world that knew not God to the knowledge of him; and also, because of the difficulty of their work — they must bring light to those that rebelled against the light; therefore keep them. [2.] To show that they were qualified for further peculiar favours, for they had that knowledge of God which the world had not.

(3.) The plea he insists upon for himself: *But I have known thee.* Christ knew the Father as no one else ever did; knew upon what grounds he went in his undertaking, knew his Father's mind in every thing, and therefore, in this prayer, came to him with confidence, as we do to one we know. Christ is here suing out blessings for those that were his; pursuing this petition, when he had said, *The world has not known thee,* one would expect it should follow, *but they have known thee;* no, their knowledge was not to be boasted of, *but I have known thee,* which intimates that there is nothing in us to recommend us to God's favour, but all our interest in him, and intercourse with him, result from, and depend upon, Christ's interest and intercourse. We are unworthy, but he is worthy.

(4.) The plea he insists upon for his disciples: *And they have known that thou hast sent me;* and, [1.] Hereby they are distinguished from the unbelieving world. When multitudes to whom Christ was sent, and his grace offered, would not *believe that God had sent him,* these knew it, and believed it, and were not ashamed to own it. Note, To know and believe in Jesus Christ, in the midst of a world that persists in ignorance and infidelity, is highly pleasing to God, and shall certainly be crowned with distinguishing glory. Singular faith qualifies for singular favours. [2.] Hereby they are interested in the mediation of Christ, and partake of the benefit of his acquaintance with the Father: *"I have known thee,* immediately and perfectly; and these, though they have not so known thee, nor were capable of knowing thee so, yet *have known that thou hast sent me,* have known that which was required of them to know, have known the Creator in the Redeemer." Knowing Christ as sent of God, they have, in him, known the Father, and are introduced to an acquaintance with him; therefore, "Father, look after them for my sake."

2. The respect he had to his disciples (*v.* 26): "I have led them into the knowledge of thee, and will do it yet more and more; with this great and kind intention, *that the love wherewith thou hast loved me may be in them, and I in them."* Observe here,

(1.) What Christ had done for them: *I have declared unto*

them thy name. [1.] This he had done for those that were his immediate followers. *All the time that he went in and out among them,* he made it his business to declare his Father's name to them, and to beget in them a veneration for it. The tendency of all his sermons and miracles was to advance his Father's honours, and to spread the knowledge of him, *ch.* 1:18. [2.] This he had done for all that believe on him; for they had not been brought to believe if Christ had not made known to them his Father's name. Note, *First,* We are indebted to Christ for all the knowledge we have of the Father's name; he declares it, and he opens the understanding to receive that revelation. *Secondly,* Those whom Christ recommends to the favour of God he first leads into an acquaintance with God.

(2.) What he intended to do yet further for them: *I will declare it.* To the disciples he designed to give further instructions after his resurrection (Acts 1:3), and to bring them into a much more intimate acquaintance with divine things by the pouring out of the Spirit after his ascension; and to all believers, into whose hearts he hath shined, he shines more and more. Where Christ has *declared his Father's name, he will declare it;* for *to him that hath shall be given;* and those that know God both need and desire to know more of him. This is fitly pleaded for them: "Father, own and favour them, for they will own and honour thee."

(3.) What he aimed at in all this; not to fill their heads with curious speculations, and furnish them with something to talk of among the learned, but to secure and advance their real happiness in two things: —

[1.] Communion with God: "Therefore I have given them the knowledge of thy name, of all that whereby thou hast made thyself known, *that thy love,* even that *wherewith thou hast loved me, may be,* not only towards them, but *in them;*" that is, *First,* "Let them have the fruits of that love for their sanctification; let *the Spirit of love,* with which thou hast filled me, *be in them.*" Christ declares his Father's name to believers, that with that divine light darted into their minds a divine love may be shed abroad in their hearts, to be in them a commanding constraining principle of holiness, that they may partake of a divine nature. When God's love to us comes to be in us, it is like the virtue which the loadstone gives the needle, inclining it to move towards the pole; it draws out the soul towards God in pious and devout affections, which are as the spirits of the divine life in the soul. *Secondly,* "Let them have the taste and relish of that love for their consolation; let them not only be interested in the love of God, by having God's name declared to them, but, by a further declaration of it, let them have the comfort of that interest; that they may not only know God, but *know that they know him,*" 1 Jn. 2:3. It is *the love of God* thus *shed abroad in the heart* that fills it with joy, Rom. 5:3, 5. This God has provided for, that we may not only be satisfied with his loving kindness, but be satisfied of it; and so may live a life of complacency in God and communion with him; this we must pray for, this we must press after; if we have it, we must thank Christ for it; if we want it, we may thank ourselves.

[2.] Union with Christ in order hereunto: *And I in them.* There is no getting into the love of God but through Christ, nor can we keep ourselves in that love but by abiding in Christ, that is, having him to abide in us; nor can we have the sense and apprehension of that love but by our experience of the indwelling of Christ, that is, the Spirit of Christ in our hearts. It is *Christ in us that* is the only *hope of glory* that will *not make us ashamed,* Col. 1:27. All our communion with God, the reception of his love to us with our return of love to him again, passes through the hands of the Lord Jesus, and the comfort of it is owing purely to him. Christ had said but a little before, *I in them* (*v.* 23), and here it is repeated (though the sense was complete without it), and the prayer closed with it, to show how much the heart of Christ was sent upon it; all his petitions centre in this, and with this *the prayers of Jesus, the Son of David, are ended: "I in them;* let me have this, and I desire no more." It is the glory of the Redeemer to dwell in the redeemed: it is his *rest for ever,* and he has desired it. Let us therefore make sure our union with Christ, and then take the comfort of his intercession. *This* prayer had an end, but *that* he ever lives to make.

CHAPTER 18

Hitherto this evangelist has recorded little of the history of Christ, only so far as was requisite to introduce his discourses; but now that the time drew nigh that Jesus must die he is very particular in relating the circumstances of his sufferings, and some which the others had omitted, especially his sayings. So far were his followers from being ashamed of his cross, or endeavouring to conceal it, that this was what, both by word and writing, they were most industrious to proclaim, and gloried in it. This chapter relates, I. How Christ was arrested in the garden and surrendered himself a prisoner (*v.* 1–12). II. How he was abused in the high priest's court, and how Peter, in the meantime, denied him (*v.* 13–27). III. How he was prosecuted before Pilate, and examined by him, and put in election with Barabbas for the favour of the people, and lost it (*v.* 28–40).

Verses 1–12

The hour was now come that *the captain of our salvation,* who was to be *made perfect by sufferings,* should engage the enemy. We have here his entrance upon the encounter. The day of recompence is in his heart, and *the year of his redeemed is come, and his own arm works the salvation,* for he has no second. *Let us turn aside now, and see this great sight.*

I. Our Lord Jesus, like a bold champion, takes the field first (*v.* 1, 2): *When he had spoken these words,* preached the sermon, prayed his prayer, and so finished his testimony, he would lose no time, but *went forth* immediately out of the house, out of the city, by moon-light, for the passover was observed at the full moon, *with his disciples* (the eleven, for Judas was otherwise employed), and *he went over the brook Cedron,* which runs between Jerusalem and the mount of Olives, *where was a garden,* not his own, but some friend's, who allowed him the liberty of it. Observe,

1. That our Lord Jesus entered upon his sufferings *when he had spoken these words,* as Mt. 26:1, *When he had finished all these sayings.* Here it is intimated, (1.) That our Lord Jesus took his work before him. The office of the priest was to teach, and pray, and offer sacrifice. Christ, after teaching and praying, applies himself to make atonement. Christ had said all he had to say as a prophet, and now he addresses himself to the discharge of his office as a priest, to *make his soul an offering for sin;* and, when he had gone through this, he entered upon his kingly office. (2.) That having by his sermon prepared his disciples for this hour of trial, and by his prayer prepared himself for it, he then courageously went out to meet it. When he had put on his armour, he entered the lists, and not till then. Let those that suffer according to the will of God, in a good cause, with a good conscience, and having a clear call to it, comfort themselves with this, that Christ will not engage those that are his in any conflict, but he will first do that for them which is necessary to prepare them for it; and if we receive Christ's instructions and comforts, and be interested in his intercession, we may, with an unshaken resolution, venture through the greatest hardships in the way of duty.

2. That *he went forth with his disciples.* Judas knew what house he was in in the city, and he could have staid and met his sufferings there; but, (1.) He would do as he was wont to do, and not alter his method, either to meet the cross or to miss it, when his hour was come. It was his custom when he was at Jerusalem, after he had spent the day in public work, to retire at night *to the mount of Olives;* there his quarters were, in the skirts of the city, for they would not make room for him in the palaces, in the heart of the town. This being his custom, he could not be put out of his method by the foresight of his sufferings, but, as Daniel, did then just *as he did aforetime,* Dan. 6:10. (2.) He was as unwilling that there should be *an uproar among the people* as his enemies were, for it was not his way *to strive or cry.* If he had been seized in the city, and a tumult raised thereby, mischief might have been done, and a great deal of blood shed, and therefore he withdrew. Note, When we find ourselves involved in trouble, we should be afraid of involving others with us. It is no disgrace to the followers of Christ to fall tamely. Those who aim at honour from men value themselves upon a resolution to sell their lives as dearly as they can; but those who know that their blood is precious to Christ, and that not a drop of it shall be shed but upon a valuable consideration, need not stand upon such terms. (3.) He would set us an example in the beginning of his passion, as he did at the end of it, of retirement from the world. *Let us go forth to him, without the camp, bearing his reproach,* Heb. 13:13. We must lay aside, and leave behind, the crowds, and cares, and comforts, of cities, even holy cities, if we would cheerfully take up our cross, and keep up our communion with God therein.

3. That he went *over the brook Cedron.* He must go over this to go to *the mount of Olives,* but the notice taken of it intimates that there was something in it significant; and it points, (1.) At David's prophecy concerning the Messiah (Ps. 110:7), that *he shall drink of the brook in the way;* the brook of suffering in the way to his glory and our salvation, signified by *the brook Cedron, the black brook,* so called either from the darkness of the valley it ran through or the colour of the water, tainted with the dirt of the city; such a brook Christ drank of, when it lay in the way of our redemption, and *therefore shall he lift up the head,* his own and ours. (2.) At David's pattern, as a type of the Messiah. In his flight from Absalom, particular notice is taken of his *passing over the brook Cedron, and going up by the ascent of mount Olivet, weeping,* and all that were with him in tears too, 2 Sa. 15:23, 30. *The Son of David,* being driven out by the rebellious Jews, who would *not have him to reign over them* (and Judas, like Ahithophel, being in the plot against him), passed over the brook in meanness and humiliation, attended by a company of true mourners. The godly kings of Judah had burnt and destroyed the idols they found at *the brook Cedron;* Asa, 2 Chr. 15:16; Hezekiah, 2 Chr. 30:14; Josiah, 2 Ki. 23:4, 6. Into that brook the abominable things were cast. Christ, *being now made sin for us,* that he might abolish it and take it away, began his passion by the same brook. Mount Olivet, where Christ began his sufferings, lay on the east side of Jerusalem; mount Calvary, where he finished them, on the west; for in them he had an eye to such as should *come from the east and the west.*

4. That he entered into a garden. This circumstance is taken notice of only by this evangelist, that Christ's sufferings began in a garden. In the garden of Eden sin began; there the curse was pronounced, there the Redeemer was promised, and therefore in a garden that promised seed entered the lists with the old serpent. Christ was buried also in a garden. (1.) Let us, when we walk in our gardens, take occasion thence to meditate on Christ's sufferings in a garden, to which we owe all the pleasure we have in our gardens, for by them the curse upon the ground for man's sake was removed. (2.) When we are in the midst of our possessions and enjoyments, we must keep up an expectation of troubles, for our gardens of delight are in a vale of tears.

5. That he had his disciples with him, (1.) Because he used to take them with him when he retired for prayer. (2.) They must be witnesses of his sufferings, and his patience under them, that they might with the more assurance and affection preach them to the world (Lu. 24:48), and be themselves prepared to suffer. (3.) He would take them into the danger to show them their weakness, notwithstanding the promises they had made of fidelity. Christ sometimes brings his people into difficulties, that he may magnify himself in their deliverance.

6. That Judas the traitor *knew the place,* knew it to be the place of his usual retirement, and probably, by some word Christ had dropped, knew that he intended to be there that night, for want of a better closet. A solitary garden is a proper place for meditation and prayer, and after a passover is a proper time to retire for private devotion, that we may pray over the impressions made and the vows renewed, and clench the nail. Mention is made of Judas's knowing the place, (1.) To aggravate the sin of Judas, that he would betray his Master, notwithstanding the intimate acquaintance he had with him; nay, and that he would make use of his familiarity with Christ, as giving him an opportunity of betraying him; a generous mind would have scorned to do so base a thing. Thus has Christ's holy religion been *wounded in the house of its friends,* as it could not have been wounded any where else. Many an apostate could not have been so profane, if he had not been a professor; could not have ridiculed scriptures and ordinances, if he had not known them. (2.) To magnify the love of Christ, that, though he knew where the traitor would seek him, thither he went to be found of him, now that he knew his *hour was come.* Thus he showed himself willing to suffer and die for us. What he did was not by constraint, but by consent; though as man he said, *Let this cup pass away,* as Mediator he said, *"Lo, I come,* I come with a good will." It was late in the night (we may suppose eight or nine o'clock) when Christ went out to the garden; for it was not only his *meat and drink,* but his rest and sleep, *to do the will of him that sent him.* When others were going to bed, he was going to prayer, going to suffer.

II. *The captain of our salvation* having taken the field, the enemy presently comes upon the spot, and attacks him (*v.* 3): Judas with his men comes thither, commissioned by the chief priests, especially those among them that were Pharisees, who were the most bitter enemies to Christ. This evangelist passes over Christ's agony, because the other three had fully related it, and presently introduces Judas and his company that came to seize him. Observe,

1. The persons employed in this action — *a band of men and officers from the chief priests, with Judas.* (1.) Here is a multitude engaged against Christ — *a band of men, speira — cohors, a regiment,* a Roman band, which some think was five hundred men, others a thousand. Christ's friends were few, his enemies many. Let us therefore *not follow a multitude to do evil,* nor fear a multitude designing evil to us, *if God be for us.* (2.) Here is a mixed multitude; the band of men were Gentiles, Roman soldiers, a detachment out of the guards that were posted in the tower of Antonia, to be a curb upon the city; the *officers of the chief priests, hypēretas.* Either their domestic servants, or the officers of their courts, were Jews; these had an enmity to each other, but were united against Christ, who came to *reconcile both to God in one body.* (3.) It is a commissioned multitude, not a popular tumult; no, they have received orders *from the chief priests,* upon whose suggestion to the governor that this Jesus was a dangerous man, it is likely they had a warrant from him too to take him up, *for they feared the people.* See what enemies Christ and his gospel have had, and are likely to have, numerous and potent, and therefore formidable: ecclesiastical and civil powers combined against them, Ps. 2:1, 2. Christ said it would be so (Mt. 10:18), and found it so. (4.) All under the direction of Judas. He *received* this *band of men;* it is probable that he requested it, alleging that it was necessary to send a good force, being as ambitious of the honour of commanding in chief in this expedition as he was covetous of *the wages of* this *unrighteousness.* He thought himself wonderfully preferred from coming in the rear of the contemptible twelve to be placed at the head of these formidable hundreds; he never made such a figure before, and promised himself, perhaps, that this should not be the last time, but he should be rewarded with a captain's commission, or better, if he succeeded well in this enterprise.

2. The preparation they had made for an attack: They came *with lanterns, and torches, and weapons.* (1.) If Christ should abscond, though they had moonlight, they would have occasion for their lights; but they might have spared these; the second Adam was not driven, as the first was, to hide himself, either for fear or shame, *among the trees of the garden.* It was folly to light a candle to seek the Sun by. (2.) If he should resist, they would have occasion for their arms. *The weapons of his warfare were spiritual,* and at these *weapons* he had often beaten them, and *put them to silence,* and therefore they have now recourse to other *weapons, swords and staves.*

III. Our Lord Jesus gloriously repulsed the first onset of the enemy, *v.* 4–6, where observe,

1. How he received them, with all the mildness imaginable towards them, and all the calmness imaginable in himself.

(1.) He met them with a very soft and mild question (*v.* 4): *Knowing all things that should come upon him,* and therefore not at all surprised with this alarm, with a wonderful intrepidity and presence of mind, undisturbed and undaunted, he *went forth* to meet them, and, as if he had been unconcerned, softly asked, "*Whom seek you?* What is the matter? What means this bustle at this time of night?" See here, [1.] Christ's foresight of his sufferings; He *knew all those things that should come upon him,* for he had bound himself to suffer them. Unless we had strength, as Christ had, to bear the discovery, we should not covet to know what shall come upon us; it would but anticipate our pain; *sufficient unto the day is the evil thereof:* yet it will do us good to expect sufferings in general, so that when they come we may say, "It is but what we looked for, the cost we sat down and counted upon." [2.] Christ's forwardness to his sufferings; he did not run away from them, but went out to meet them, and reached forth his hand to take the bitter cup. When the people would have forced him to a crown, and offered to make him a king in Galilee, but he withdrew, and hid himself (*ch.* 6:15); but, when they came to force him to a cross, he offered himself; for he came to this world to suffer and went to the other world to reign. This will not warrant us needlessly to expose ourselves to trouble, for we know not when our hour is come; but we are called to suffering when we have no way to avoid it but by sin; and, when it comes to this, let *none of these things move* us, for they cannot hurt us.

(2.) He met them with a very calm and mild answer when they told him whom they were in quest of, *v.* 5. They said, *Jesus of Nazareth;* and he said, *I am he.* [1.] It should seem, *their eyes were held, that they could not know him.* It is highly probable that many of the Roman band, at least the officers of the temple, had often seen him, if only to satisfy their curiosity; Judas, however, to be sure, knew him well enough, and yet none of them could pretend to say, *Thou art the man* we seek. Thus he showed them the folly of bringing lights to see for him, for he could make them not to know him when they saw him; and he has herein shown us how easily he can infatuate the counsels of his enemies, and make them lose themselves, when they are seeking mischief. [2.] In their enquiries for him they called him *Jesus of Nazareth,* which was the only title they knew him by, and probably he was so called in their warrant. It was a name of reproach given him, to darken the evidence of his being the Messiah. By this it appears that they knew him not, whence he was; for, if they had known him, surely they would not have persecuted him. [3.] He fairly answers them: *I am he.* He did not improve the advantage he had against them by their blindness, as Elisha did against the Syrians, telling them, *This is not the way, neither is this the city;* but improves it as an opportunity of showing his willingness to suffer. Though they called him Jesus of Nazareth, he answered to the name, for he despised the reproach; he might have said, *I am not he,* for he was *Jesus of Bethlehem;* but he would by no means allow equivocations. He has hereby taught us to own him, whatever it cost us; not to be *ashamed of him or his words;* but even in difficult times *to confess Christ crucified, and manfully to fight under his banner. I am he, Egō eimi — I am he,* is the glorious name of the blessed God (Ex. 3:14), and the honour of that name is justly challenged by the blessed Jesus. [4.] Particular notice is taken, in a parenthesis, *that Judas stood with them.* He that used to stand with those that followed Christ now stood with those that fought against him. This describes an apostate; he is one that changes sides. He herds himself with those with whom his heart always was, and with whom he shall have his lot in the judgment-day. This is mentioned, *First,* To show the impudence of Judas. One would wonder where he got the confidence with which he now faced his Master, and *was not ashamed, neither could he blush;* Satan in his heart gave him a whore's forehead. *Secondly,* To show that Judas was particularly aimed at in the power which went along with that word, *I am he,* to foil the aggressors. It was an arrow levelled at the traitor's conscience, and pierced him to the quick; for Christ's coming and his voice will be more terrible to apostates and betrayers than to sinners of any other class.

2. See how he terrified them, and obliged them to retire (*v.* 6): *They went backward, and,* like men thunder-struck, *fell to the ground.* It should seem, they did not fall forward, as humbling themselves before him, and yielding to him, but backward, as standing it out to the utmost. Thus Christ was declared to be more than a man, even when he was trampled upon as *a worm, and no man.* This word, *I am he,* had revived his disciples, and raised them up (Mt. 14:27); but the same word strikes his enemies down. Hereby he showed plainly,

(1.) What he could have done with them. When he struck them down, he could have struck them dead; when he spoke them *to the ground,* he could have spoken them to hell, and have sent them, like Korah's company, the next way thither; but he would not do so, [1.] Because the hour of his suffering was come, and he would not put it by; he would only show that his life was not forced from him, but *he laid it down of himself,* as he had said. [2.] Because he would give an instance of his patience and forbearance with the worst of men, and his compassionate love to his very enemies. In striking them down, and no more, he gave them both a call to repent and space to repent; but *their hearts were hardened,* and all was in vain.

(2.) What he will do at last with all his implacable enemies, *that will not repent to give him glory; they shall flee, they shall fall, before him.* Now the scripture was accomplished (Ps. 21:12), *Thou shalt make them turn their back,* and Ps. 20:8. And it will be accomplished more and more; *with the breath of his mouth he will slay the wicked,* 2 Th. 2:8; Rev. 19:21. *Quid judicaturus faciet, qui judicandus hoc facit? — What will he do when he shall come to judge, seeing he did this when he came to be judged?* — Augustine.

IV. Having given his enemies a repulse, he gives his friends a protection, and that by his word too, *v.* 7–9, where we may observe,

1. How he continued to expose himself to their rage, *v.* 7. They did not lie long where they fell, but, by divine permission, got up again; it is only in the other world that God's judgments are everlasting. When they were down, one would have thought Christ should have made his escape; when they were up again, one would have thought they should have let fall their pursuit; but still we find, (1.) They are as eager as ever to seize him. It is in some confusion and disorder that they recover themselves; they cannot imagine what ailed them, that they could not keep their ground, but will impute it to any thing rather than Christ's power. Note, There are hearts so very hard in sin that nothing will work upon them to reduce and reclaim them. (2.) He is as willing as ever to be seized. When they were fallen before him, he did not insult over them, but seeing them at a loss, asked them the same question, *Whom seek you?* And they gave him the same answer, *Jesus of Nazareth.* In his repeating the question, he seems to come yet closer to their consciences: "Do you not know *whom you seek?* Are you not aware that you are in error, and will you meddle with your match? Have you not had enough of it, but will you try the other struggle? *Did ever any harden his heart against God and prosper?*" In their repeating the same answer, they showed an obstinacy in their wicked way; they still call him *Jesus of Nazareth,* with as much disdain as ever, and Judas is as unrelenting as any of them. *Let us therefore fear lest,* by a few bold steps at first in a sinful way, *our hearts be hardened.*

2. How he contrived to secure his disciples from their rage. He improved this advantage against them for the protection of his followers. When he shows his courage with reference to himself, *I have told you that I am he,* he shows his care for his disciples, *Let these go their way.* He speaks this as a command to them, rather than a contract with them; for they lay at his mercy, not he at theirs. He charges them therefore as *one having authority: "Let these go their way;* it is at your peril if you meddle with them" This aggravated the sin of the disciples in forsaking him, and particularly Peter's in denying him, that Christ had given them this pass, or warrant of protection, and yet they had not faith and courage enough to rely upon it, but betook themselves to such base and sorry shifts for their security. When Christ said, *Let these go their way,* he intended,

(1.) To manifest his affectionate concern for his disciples. When he exposed himself, he excused them, because they were not as yet fit to suffer; their faith was weak, and their spirits were low, and it would have been as much as their souls, and the lives of their souls, were worth, to bring them into sufferings now. *New wine* must not be *put into old bottles.* And, besides, they had other work to do; they must go their way, for they are to go into all the world, to preach the gospel. *Destroy them not, for a blessing is in them.* Now herein, [1.] Christ gives us a great encouragement to follow him; for, though he has allotted us sufferings, yet he considers our frame, will wisely time the cross, and proportion it to our strength, and will *deliver the godly out of temptation,* either from it, or through it. [2.] He gives us a good example of love to our brethren and concern for their welfare. We must not consult our own ease and safety only, but others, as well as our own, and in some cases more than our own. There is a generous and heroic love, which will enable us to *lay down our lives for the brethren,* 1 Jn. 3:16.

(2.) He intended to give a specimen of his undertaking as Mediator. When he offered himself to suffer and die, it was that we might escape. He was our *antipsychos — a sufferer in our stead;* when he said, *Lo, I come,* he said also, *Let these go their way;* like the ram offered instead of Isaac.

3. Now herein he confirmed the word which he had spoken a little before (*ch.* 17:12), *Of those whom thou gavest me, I have lost none.* Christ, by fulfilling that word in this particular, gave an assurance that it should be accomplished in the full extent of it, not only for those that were now with him, but for all that should believe on him through their word. Though Christ's keeping them was meant especially of the preservation of their souls from sin and apostasy, yet it is here applied to the preservation of their natural lives, and very fitly, for even the body was a part of Christ's charge and care; he is to *raise it up at the last day,* and therefore to preserve it as well as *the spirit and soul,* 1 Th. 5:23; 2 Tim. 4:17, 18. Christ will preserve the natural life for the service to which it is designed; it is given to him to be used for him, and he

will not lose the service of it, but will be magnified in it, *whether by life or death;* it shall be held in life as long as any use is to be made of it. Christ's witnesses shall not die till they have given in their evidence. But this is not all; this preservation of the disciples was, in the tendency of it, a spiritual preservation. They were now so weak in faith and resolution that in all probability, if they had been called out to suffer at this time, they would have shamed themselves and their Master, and some of them, at least the weaker of them, would have been lost; and therefore, that he might *lose none,* he would not expose them. The safety and preservation of the saints are owing, not only to the divine grace in proportioning the strength to the trial, but to the divine providence in proportioning the trial to the strength.

V. Having provided for the safety of his disciples, he rebukes the rashness of one of them, and represses the violence of his followers, as he had repulsed the violence of his persecutors, *v.* 10, 11, where we have,

1. Peter's rashness. He had a sword; it is not likely that he wore one constantly as a gentleman, but they had two swords among them all (Lu. 22:38), and Peter, being entrusted with one, drew it; for now, if ever, he thought it was his time to use it; and *he smote one of the high priest's servants,* who was probably one of the forwardest, and aiming, it is likely, to cleave him down the head, missed his blow, and only *cut off his right ear. The servant's name,* for the greater certainty of the narrative, is recorded; it *was Malchus,* or *Malluch,* Neh. 10:4.

(1.) We must here acknowledge Peter's good-will; he had an honest zeal for his Master, though now misguided. He had lately promised to venture his life for him, and would now make his words good. Probably it exasperated Peter to see Judas at the head of this gang; his baseness excited Peter's boldness, and I wonder that when he did draw his sword he did not aim at the traitor's head.

(2.) Yet we must acknowledge Peter's ill conduct; and, though his good intention did excuse, yet it would not justify him. [1.] He had no warrant from his Master for what he did. Christ's soldiers must wait the word of command, and not outrun it; before they expose themselves to sufferings, they must see to it, not only that their cause be good, but their call clear. [2.] He transgressed the duty of his place, and resisted the powers that were, which Christ had never countenanced, but forbidden (Mt. 5:39): *that you resist not evil* [3.] He opposed his Master's sufferings, and, notwithstanding the rebuke he had for it once, is ready to repeat, *Master, spare thyself;* suffering be *far from thee;* though Christ had told him that he must and would suffer, and that his hour was now come. Thus, while he seemed to fight for Christ, he fought against him. [4.] He broke the capitulation his Master had lately made with the enemy. When he said, *Let these go their way,* he not only indented for their safety, but in effect passed his word for their good behaviour, that they should go away peaceably; this Peter heard, and yet would not be bound by it. As we may be guilty of a sinful cowardice when we are called to appear, so we may be of a sinful forwardness when we are called to retire. [5.] He foolishly exposed himself and his fellow disciples to the fury of this enraged multitude. If he had cut off Malchus's head when he cut off his ear, we may suppose the soldiers would have fallen upon all the disciples, and have hewn them to pieces, and would have represented Christ as not better than Barabbas. Thus many have been guilty of self-destruction, in their zeal for self-preservation. [6.] Peter played the coward so soon after this (denying his Master) that we have reason to think he would not have done this but that he saw his Master cause them to fall on the ground, and then he could deal with them; but, when he saw him surrender himself notwithstanding, his courage failed him; whereas the true Christian hero will appear in the cause of Christ, not only when it is prevailing, but when it seems to be declining; will be on the right side, though it be not the rising side.

(3.) We must acknowledge God's over-ruling providence in directing the stroke (so that it should do no more execution, but only cut off his ear, which was rather marking him than maiming him), as also in giving Christ an opportunity to manifest his power and goodness in healing the hurt, Lu. 22:51. Thus what was in danger of turning to Christ's reproach proved an occasion of that which redounded much to his honour, even among his adversaries.

2. The rebuke his Master gave him (*v.* 11): *Put up thy sword into the sheath,* or scabbard; it is a gentle reproof, because

it was his zeal that carried him beyond the bounds of discretion. Christ did not aggravate the matter, only bade him *do so no more.* Many think their being in grief and distress will excuse them if they be hot and hasty with those about them; but Christ has here set us an example of meekness in sufferings. Peter must put up his sword, for it was the *sword of the Spirit* that was to be committed to him — *weapons of warfare not carnal,* yet *mighty.* When Christ with a word felled the aggressors, he showed Peter how he should be armed with a *word, quick and powerful, and sharper than any two-edged sword,* and with that, not long after this, he laid Ananias and Sapphira dead at his feet.

3. The reason for this rebuke: *The cup which my Father has given me, shall I not drink it?* Matthew relates another reason which Christ gave for this rebuke, but John preserves this, which he had omitted; in which Christ gives us, (1.) A full proof of his own submission to his Father's will. Of all that was amiss in what Peter did, he seems to resent nothing so much as that he would have hindered his sufferings now that his *hour was come:* "What, *Peter,* wilt thou step in between the cup and the lip? *Get thee hence, Satan.*" If Christ be determined to suffer and die, it is presumption for Peter in word or deed to oppose it: *Shall I not drink it?* The manner of expression bespeaks a settled resolution, and that he would not entertain a thought to the contrary. He was willing to drink of this cup, though it was a bitter cup, an infusion of the wormwood and the gall, the cup of trembling, a bloody cup, the *dregs of the cup of the Lord's wrath,* Isa. 51:22. He drank it, that he might put into our hands the cup of salvation, the cup of consolation, the cup of blessing; and *therefore* he is willing to drink it, because *his Father put it into his hand.* If his Father will have it so, it is for the best, and be it so. (2.) A fair pattern to us of submission to God's will in every thing that concerns us. We must *pledge* Christ in the cup that he drank of (Mt. 20:23), and must argue ourselves into a compliance. [1.] It is but a *cup;* a small matter comparatively, be it what it will. It is not a sea, a red sea, a dead sea, for it is not hell; it is light, and but for a moment. [2.] It is a cup that is given us; sufferings are gifts. [3.] It is given us by a Father, who has a Father's authority, and does us no wrong; a Father's affection, and means us no hurt.

VI. Having entirely reconciled himself to the dispensation, he calmly surrendered, and yielded himself a prisoner, not because he could not have made his escape, but because he would not. One would have thought the cure of Malchus's ear should have made them relent, but nothing would win upon them. *Maledictus furor, quem nec majestast miraculi nec pietas beneficii confringere potuit* — *Accursed rage, which the grandeur of the miracle could not appease, nor the tenderness of the favour conciliate.* — Anselm. Observe here,

1. How they seized him: *They took Jesus.* Only some few of them could lay hands on him, but it is charged upon them all, for they were all aiding and abetting. In treason there are not accessaries; all are principals. Now the scripture was fulfilled, *Bulls have compassed me* (Ps. 22:12), *compassed me like bees,* Ps. 118:12. The *breath of our nostrils is taken in their pit,* Lam. 4:20. They had so often been frustrated in their attempts to seize him that now, having got him into their hands, we may suppose they flew upon him with so much the more violence.

2. How they secured him: *They bound him.* This particular of his sufferings is taken notice of only by this evangelist, that, as soon as ever he was taken, he was bound, pinioned, handcuffed; tradition says, "They bound him with such cruelty that the blood started out at his fingers' ends; and, having bound his hands behind him, they clapped an iron chain about his neck, and with that dragged him along." See *Gerhard. Harm.* cap. 5.

(1.) This shows the spite of his persecutors. They bound him, [1.] That they might torment him, and put him in pain, as they bound Samson to afflict him. [2.] That they might disgrace him, and put him to shame; slaves were bound, so was Christ, though free-born. [3.] That they might prevent his escape, Judas having told them to hold him fast. See their folly, that they should think to fetter that power which had but just now proved itself omnipotent. [4.] They bound him as one already condemned, for they were resolved to prosecute him to the death, and that he should die as a fool dieth, that is, as a malefactor, with his hands bound, 2 Sa. 3:33, 34. Christ had bound the consciences of his persecutors with the power of his word, which galled them; and, to be revenged on him, they laid these bonds on him.

(2.) Christ's being bound was very significant; in this as in other things there was a mystery. [1.] Before they bound him, he had bound himself by his own undertaking to the work and office of a Mediator. He was already bound to the horns of the altar with the cords of his own love to man, and duty to his Father, else their cords would not have held him. [2.] We were *bound with the cords of our iniquities* (Prov. 5:22), with the *yoke of our transgressions,* Lam. 1:14. Guilt is a bond on the soul, by which we are bound over to the judgment of God; corruption is a bond on the soul, by which we are bound under the power of Satan. Christ, being made sin for us, to free us from those bonds, himself submitted to be bound for us, else we had been bound hand and foot, and reserved in chains of darkness. To his bonds we owe our liberty; his confinement was our enlargement; thus the Son maketh us free. [3.] The types and prophecies of the Old Testament were herein accomplished. Isaac was bound, that he might be sacrificed; Joseph was bound, and the *irons entered into his soul,* in order to his being brought from prison to reign, Ps. 105:18, etc. Samson was bound in order to his slaying more of the Philistines at his death than he had done in his life. And the Messiah was prophesied of as a prisoner, Isa. 53:8. [4.] Christ was bound, that he might bind us to duty and obedience. His bonds for us are bonds upon us, by which we are for ever obliged to love him and serve him. Paul's salutation to his friends is Christ's to us all: *"Remember my bonds* (Col. 4:18), remember them as bound with him from all sin, and to all duty." [5.] Christ's bonds for us were designed to make our bonds for him easy to us, if at any time we be so called out to suffer for him, to sanctify and sweeten them, and put honour upon them; these enabled Paul and Silas to sing in the stocks, and Ignatius to call his bonds for Christ spiritual pearls. — *Epist. ad Ephes.*

Verses 13–27

We have here an account of Christ's arraignment before the high priest, and some circumstances that occurred therein which were omitted by the other evangelists; and Peter's denying him, which the other evangelists had given the story of entire by itself, is interwoven with the other passages. The crime laid to his charge having relation to religion, the judges of the spiritual court took it to fall directly under their cognizance. Both Jews and Gentiles seized him, and so both Jews and Gentiles tried and condemned him, for he died for the sins of both. Let us go over the story in order.

I. Having seized him, they *led him away to Annas first,* before they brought him to the court that was sat, expecting him, in the house of Caiaphas, *v.* 13. 1. They *led him away,* led him in triumph, as a trophy of their victory; led him *as a lamb to the slaughter,* and they led him through the sheep-gate spoken of Neh. 3:1. For through that they went from the mount of Olives into Jerusalem. They hurried him away with violence, as if he had been the worst and vilest of malefactors. We had been led away of our own impetuous lusts, and led captive by Satan at his will, and, that we might be rescued, Christ was led away, led captive by Satan's agents and instruments. 2. They led him away to their masters that sent them. It was now about midnight, and one would think they should have put him in ward (Lev. 24:12), should have led him to some prison, till it was a proper time to call a court; but he is hurried away immediately, not to the justices of peace, to be committed, but to the judges to be condemned; so extremely violent was the prosecution, partly because they feared a rescue, which they would thus not only leave no time for, but give a terror to; partly because they greedily thirsted after Christ's blood, as *the eagle that hasteth to the prey.* 3. They led him to Annas first. Probably his house lay in the way, and was convenient for them to call at to refresh themselves, and, as some think, to be paid for their service. I suppose Annas was old and infirm, and could not be present in council with the rest at that time of night, and yet earnestly desired to see the prey. To gratify him therefore with the assurance of their success, that the old man might sleep the better, and to receive his blessing for it, they produce their prisoner before him. It is sad to see those that are old and sickly, when they cannot commit sin as formerly, taking pleasure in those that do. Dr. Lightfoot thinks Annas was not present, because he had to attend early that morning in the temple, to examine the sacrifices which were that day to be offered, whether they were without blemish; if so, there was a significancy in it, that Christ, the great sacrifice, was presented to him, and sent away bound, as approved and ready for the altar. 4. This Annas was father-in-law to Caiaphas the high priest; this kindred by marriage between them comes in as a reason either why Caiaphas ordered that this piece of respect should be done to Annas, to favour him with the first sight of the prisoner, or why Annas was willing to countenance Caiaphas in a matter his heart was so much upon. Note, Acquaintance and alliance with wicked people are a great confirmation to many in their wicked ways.

II. Annas did not long detain them, being as willing as any of them to have the prosecution pushed on, and therefore sent him bound to Caiaphas, to his house, which was appointed for the rendezvous of the sanhedrim upon this occasion, or to the usual place in the temple where the high priest kept his court; this is mentioned, *v.* 24. But our translators intimate in the margin that it should come in here, and, accordingly, read it there, *Annas had sent him.* Observe here,

1. The power of Caiaphas intimated (*v.* 13). He was *high priest that same year.* The high priest's commission was during life; but there were now such frequent changes, by the Simoniacal artifices of aspiring men with the government, that it was become almost an annual office, a presage of its final period approaching; while they were undermining one another. God was overturning them all, that he might come whose right it was. Caiaphas was high priest that same year when Messiah was to be cut off, which intimates, (1.) That when a bad thing was to be done by a high priest, according to the foreknowledge of God, Providence so ordered it that a bad man should be in the chair to do it. (2.) That, when God would make it to appear what corruption there was in the heart of a bad man, he put him into a place of power, where he had temptation and opportunity to exert it. It was the ruin of Caiaphas that he was high priest that year, and so became a ringleader in the putting of Christ to death. Many a man's advancement has lost him his reputation, and he had not been dishonoured if he had not been preferred.

2. The malice of Caiaphas, which is intimated (*v.* 14) by the repeating of what he had said some time before, that, right or wrong, guilty or innocent, *it was expedient that one man should die for the people,* which refers to the story *ch.* 11:50. This comes in here to show, (1.) What a bad man he was; this was that Caiaphas that governed himself and the church by rules of policy, in defiance of the rules of equity. (2.) What ill usage Christ was likely to meet with in his court, when his case was adjudged before it was heard, and they were already resolved what to do with him; *he must die;* so that his trial was a jest. Thus the enemies of Christ's gospel are resolved, true or false, to run it down. (3.) It is a testimony to the innocency of our Lord Jesus, from the mouth of one of his worst enemies, who owned that he fell a sacrifice to the public good, and that it was not just he should die, but *expedient* only.

3. The concurrence of Annas in the prosecution of Christ. He made himself a partaker in guilt, (1.) With the captain and officers, that without law or mercy had bound him; for he approved it by continuing him bound when he should have loosed him, he not being convicted of any crime, nor having attempted an escape. If we do not what we can to undo what others have ill done, we are accessaries *ex post facto — after the fact.* It was more excusable in the rude soldiers to bind him than in Annas, who should have known better, to continue him bound. (2.) With the chief priest and council that condemned him, and prosecuted him to death. This Annas was not present with them, yet thus he wished them *good speed,* and became a *partaker of their evil deeds.*

III. In the house of Caiaphas, Simon Peter began to deny his Master, *v.* 15–18.

1. It was with much ado that Peter got into the hall where the court was sitting, an account of which we have *v.* 15, 16. Here we may observe,

(1.) Peter's kindness to Christ, which (though it proved no kindness) appeared in two things: — [1.] That he *followed Jesus* when he was *led away;* though at first he fled with the rest, yet afterwards he took heart a little, and followed at some distance, calling to mind the promises he had made to adhere to him, whatever it should cost him. Those that had followed Christ in the midst of his honours, and shared with him in those honours, when the people cried Hosanna to him, ought to have followed him now in the midst of his reproaches, and to have shared with him in these. Those that truly love and value Christ will follow him all weathers and all ways. [2.] When he could not get in where Jesus was in the midst of his enemies, he *stood at the door without,* will-

ing to be as near him as he could, and waiting for an opportunity to get nearer. Thus when we meet with opposition in following Christ we must show our good-will. But yet this kindness of Peter's was no kindness, because he had not strength and courage enough to persevere in it, and so, as it proved, he did but run himself into a snare: and even his following Christ, considering all things, was to be blamed, because Christ, who knew him better than he knew himself, had expressly told him (*ch.* 13:36), *Whither I go thou canst not follow me now,* and had told him again and again that he would deny him; and he had lately had experience of his own weakness in forsaking him. Note, We must take heed of tempting God by running upon difficulties beyond our strength, and venturing too far in a way of suffering. If our call be clear to expose ourselves, we may hope that God will enable us to honour him; but, if it be not, we may fear that God will leave us to shame ourselves.

(2.) The other disciple's kindness to Peter, which yet, as it proved, was no kindness neither. St. John several times in this gospel speaking of himself as another disciple, many interpreters have been led by this to fancy that this other disciple here was John; and many conjectures they have how he should come to be known to the high-priest; *propter generis nobilitatem — being of superior birth,* saith *Jerome, Epitaph. Marcel.,* as if he were a better gentleman born than his brother James, when they were both the sons of Zebedee the fisherman; some will tell you that he had sold his estate to the high priest, others that he supplied his family with fish, both which are very improbable. But I see no reason to think that this other disciple was John, or one of the twelve; other sheep Christ had, which were not of the fold; and this might be, as the Syriac read it, *unus ex discipulis aliis — one of those other disciples* that believe in Christ, but resided at Jerusalem, and kept their places there; perhaps Joseph of Arimathea, or Nicodemus, known to the high priest, but not known to him to be disciples of Christ. Note, As there are many who seem disciples and are not so, so there are many who are disciples and seem not so. There are good people hid in courts, even in Nero's, as well as hid in crowds. We must not conclude a man to be no friend to Christ merely because he has acquaintance and conversation with those that were his known enemies. Now, [1.] This other disciple, whoever he was, showed a respect to Peter, in introducing him, not only to gratify his curiosity and affection, but to give him an opportunity of being serviceable to his Master upon his trial, if there were occasion. Those that have a real kindness for Christ and his ways, though their temper may be reserved and their circumstances may lead them to be cautious and retired, yet, if their faith be sincere, they will discover, when they are called to it, which way their inclination lies, by being ready to do a professed disciple a good turn. Peter perhaps had formerly introduced this disciple into conversation with Christ, and now he requites his kindness, and is not ashamed to own him, though, it should seem, he had at this time but a poor downcast appearance. [2.] But this kindness proved no kindness, nay a great diskindness; by letting him into the high priest's hall, he let him into temptation, and the consequence was bad. Note, The courtesies of our friends often prove a snare to us, through a misguided affection.

2. Peter, having got in, was immediately assaulted with the temptation, and foiled by it, *v.* 17. Observe here,

(1.) How slight the attack was. It was but a silly maid, of so small account that she was set to keep the door, that challenged him, and she only asked him carelessly, *Art not thou one of this man's disciples?* probably suspecting it by his sheepish look, and coming in timorously. We should many a time better maintain a good cause if we had a *good heart on it,* and could put a *good face on it.* Peter would have had some reason to take the alarm if Malchus had set upon him, and had said, "This is he that cut off my ear, and I will have his head for it;" but when a maid only asked him, *Art not thou one of them?* he might without danger have answered, *And what if I am?* Suppose the servants had ridiculed him, and insulted over him, upon it, those can bear but little for Christ that cannot *bear this;* this is but *running with the footmen.*

(2.) How speedy the surrender was. Without taking time to recollect himself, he suddenly answered, *I am not.* If he had had the boldness of the lion, he would have said, "It is my honour that I am so;" or, if he had had the wisdom of the serpent, he would have kept silence at this time, for it

was an evil time. But, all his care being for his own safety, he thought he could not secure this but by a peremptory denial: *I am not;* he not only denies it, but even disdains it, and scorns her words.

(3.) Yet he goes further into the temptation: *And the servants and officers stood there, and Peter with them v.* 18.

[1.] See how the servants made much of themselves; the night being cold, they made a fire in the hall, not for their masters (they were so eager in persecuting Christ that they forgot cold), but for themselves to refresh themselves. They cared not what became of Christ; all their care was to sit and warm themselves, Amos 6:6.

[2.] See how Peter herded himself with them, and made one among them. *He sat and warmed himself. First,* It was a fault bad enough that he did not attend his Master, and appear for him at the upper end of the hall, where he was now under examination. He might have been a witness for him, and have confronted the false witnesses that swore against him, if his Master had called him; at least, he might have been a witness to him, might have taken an exact notice of what passed, that he might relate it to the other disciples, who could none of them get in to hear the trial; he might have learned by his Master's example how to carry himself when it should come to his turn to suffer thus; yet neither his conscience nor his curiosity could bring him into the court, but he sits by, as if, like Gallio, he cared for none of these things. And yet at the same time we have reason to think his heart was as full of grief and concern as it could hold, but he had not the courage to own it. *Lord, lead us not into temptation. Secondly,* It was much worse that he joined himself with those that were his Master's enemies: *He stood with them, and warmed himself;* this was a poor excuse for joining with them. A little thing will draw those into bad company that will be drawn to it by the love of a good fire. If Peter's zeal for his Master had not frozen, but had continued in the heat it seemed to be of but a few hours before, he had not had occasion to warm himself now. Peter was much to be blamed, 1. Because he associated with these wicked men, and kept company with them. Doubtless they were diverting themselves with this night's expedition, scoffing at Christ, at what he had said, at what he had done, and triumphing in their victory over him; and what sort of entertainment would this give to Peter? If he said as they said, or by silence gave consent, he involved himself in sin; if not, he exposed himself to danger. If Peter had not so much courage as to appear publicly for his Master, yet he might have had so much devotion as to retire into a corner, and weep in secret for his Master's sufferings, and his own sin in forsaking him; if he could not have done good, he might have kept out of the way of doing hurt. It is better to abscond than appear to no purpose, or bad purpose. 2. Because he desired to be thought *one of them,* that he might not be suspected to be a disciple of Christ. Is this Peter? What a contradiction is this to the prayer of every good man, *Gather not my soul with sinners! Saul among the prophets* is not so absurd as David among the Philistines. Those that deprecate the lot of the scornful hereafter should dread the *seat of the scornful* now. It is ill warming ourselves with those with whom we are in danger of burning ourselves, Ps. 141:4.

IV. Peter, Christ's friend, having begun to deny him, the high priest, his enemy, begins to accuse him, or rather urges him to accuse himself, *v.* 19–21. It should seem, the first attempt was to prove him a seducer, and a teacher of false doctrine, which this evangelist relates; and, when they failed in the proof of this, then they charged him with blasphemy, which is related by the other evangelists, and therefore omitted here. Observe,

1. The articles or heads upon which Christ was examined (*v.* 19): concerning *his disciples and his doctrine.* Observe,

(1.) The irregularity of the process; it was against all law and equity. They seize him as a criminal, and now that he is their prisoner they have nothing to *lay to his charge;* no libel, no prosecutor; but the judge himself must be the prosecutor, and the prisoner himself the witness, and, against all reason and justice, he is put on to be his own accuser.

(2.) The intention. The *high priest then* (oun — *therefore,* which seems to refer to *v.* 14), because he had resolved that Christ must be sacrificed to their private malice under colour of the public good, examined him upon those interrogatories which would touch his life. He examined him, [1.] Concerning his disciples, that he might charge him with sedition, and represent him as dangerous to the Roman government, as well as to the Jewish church. He asked him who were his disciples — what number they were — of what country — what were their names and characters, insinuating that his scholars were designed for soldiers, and would in time become a formidable body. Some think his question concerning his disciples was, "What is now become of them all? Where are they? Why do they not appear?" upbraiding him with their cowardice in deserting him, and thus adding to the affliction of it. There was something significant in this, that Christ's calling and owning his disciples was the first thing laid to his charge, for it was *for their sakes* that he *sanctified himself* and suffered. [2.] Concerning his doctrine, that they might charge him with heresy, and bring him under the penalty of the law against false prophets, Deu. 13:9, 10. This was a matter properly cognizable in that court (Deu. 17:12), therefore a prophet could not perish but at Jerusalem, where that court sat. They could not prove any false doctrine upon him; but they hoped to extort something from him which they might distort to his prejudice, and to make him an offender for some word or other, Isa. 29:21. They said nothing to him concerning his miracles, by which he had done so much good, and proved his doctrine beyond contradiction, because of these they were sure they could take no hold. Thus the adversaries of Christ while they are industriously quarrelling with his truth, willfully shut their eyes against the evidences of it, and take no notice of them.

2. The appeal Christ made, in answer to these interrogatories. (1.) As to his disciples, he said nothing, because it was an impertinent question; if his doctrine was sound and good, his having disciples to whom to communicate it was no more than what was practised and allowed by their own doctors. If Caiaphas, in asking him concerning his disciples, designed to ensnare them, and bring them into trouble, it was in kindness to them that Christ said nothing of them, for he had said, *Let these go their way.* If he meant to upbraid him with their cowardice, no wonder that he said nothing, for

> *Rudet haec opprobria nobis,*
> *Et dici potuisse, et non potuisse refelli —*
>
> Shame attaches when charges are exhibited that cannot be refuted:

he would say nothing to condemn them, and could say nothing to justify them. (2.) As to his doctrine, he said nothing in particular, but in general referred himself to those that heard him, being not only made manifest to God, but made manifest also in their consciences, *v.* 20, 21.

[1.] He tacitly charges his judges with illegal proceedings. He does not indeed speak evil of the rulers of the people, nor say now to these princes, *You are wicked;* but he appeals to the settled rules of their own court, whether they dealt fairly by him. *Do you indeed judge righteously?* Ps. 58:1. So here, *Why ask you me?* Which implies two absurdities in judgment: *First, "Why ask you me now* concerning my doctrine, when you have already condemned it?" They had made an order of court for excommunicating all that owned him (ch. 9:22), had issued out a proclamation for apprehending him; and now they come to ask what his doctrine is! Thus was he condemned, as his doctrine and cause commonly are, unheard. *Secondly, "Why ask you me?* Must I accuse myself, when you have no evidence against me?"

[2.] He insists upon his fair and open dealing with them in the publication of his doctrine, and justifies himself with this. The crime which the sanhedrim by the law was to enquire after was the clandestine spreading of dangerous doctrines, enticing secretly, Deu. 13:6. As to this, therefore, Christ clears himself very fully. *First,* As to the manner of his preaching. He spoke openly, *parrēsia — with freedom and plainness of speech;* he did not deliver things ambiguously, as Apollo did his oracles. Those that would undermine the truth, and spread corrupt notions, seek to accomplish their purpose by sly insinuation, putting queries, starting difficulties, and asserting nothing; but Christ explained himself fully, with, *Verily, verily, I say unto you;* his reproofs were free and bold, and his testimonies express against the corruptions of the age. *Secondly,* As to the persons he preached to: *He spoke to the world,* to all that had *ears to hear,* and were willing to hear him, high or low, learned or unlearned, Jew or Gentile, friend or foe. His doctrine feared not the censure of a mixed multitude; nor did he grudge the knowledge of it to any (as the masters of some rare invention commonly do), but freely communicated it, as the sun does his beams. *Thirdly,* As to the places he preached in. When he was in the country, he preached ordinarily in the synagogues — the places

of meeting for worship, and on the sabbath-day — the time of meeting; when he came up to Jerusalem, he preached the same doctrine in the temple at the time of the solemn feasts, when the Jews from all parts assembled there; and though he often preached in private houses, and on mountains, and by the sea-side, to show that his word and worship were not to be confined to temples and synagogues, yet what he preached in private was the very same with what he delivered publicly. Note, The doctrine of Christ, purely and plainly preached, needs not be ashamed to appear in the most numerous assembly, for it carries its own strength and beauty along with it. What Christ's faithful ministers say they would be willing all the world should hear. Wisdom cries in the places of concourse, Prov. 1:21; 8:3; 9:3. *Fourthly,* As to the doctrine itself. He *said nothing in secret* contrary to what he said in public, but only by way of repetition and explication: *In secret have I said nothing;* as if he had been either suspicious of the truth of it, or conscious of any ill design in it. He sought no corners, for he feared no colours, nor said any thing that he needed to be ashamed of; what he did speak in private to his disciples he ordered them to proclaim on the house-tops, Mt. 10:27. God saith of himself (Isa. 45:19), *I have not spoken in secret;* his commandment is not hidden, Deu. 30:11. And the righteousness of faith speaks in like manner, Rom. 10:6. *Veritas nihil metuit nisi abscondi — truth fears nothing but concealment. —* Tertullian.

[3.] He appeals to those that had heard him, and desires that they might be examined what doctrine he had preached, and whether it had that dangerous tendency that was surmised: *"Ask those that heard me what I said unto them;* some of them may be in court, or may be sent for out of their beds." He means not his friends and followers, who might be presumed to speak in his favour, but, Ask any impartial hearer; ask your own officers. Some think he pointed to them, when he said, *Behold, they know what I said,* referring to the report which they had made of his preaching (ch. 7:46), *Never man spoke like this man.* Nay, you may ask some upon the bench; for it is probable that some of them had heard him, and had been put to silence by him. Note, The doctrine of Christ may safely appeal to all that know it, and has so much right and reason on its side that those who will judge impartially cannot but witness to it.

V. While the judges were examining him, the servants that stood by were abusing him, *v.* 22, 23.

1. It was a base affront which one of the officers gave him; though he spoke with so much calmness and convincing evidence, this insolent fellow *struck him with the palm of his hand,* probably on the side of his head or face, saying, *Answerest thou the high priest so?* as if he had behaved himself rudely to the court.

(1.) He *struck him, edōke rhapisma — he gave him a blow.* Some think it signifies a blow with a rod or wand, from *rhabdos,* or with the staff which was the badge of his office. Now the scripture was fulfilled (Isa. 50:6), *I gave my cheeks, eis rhapismata* (so the Septuagint) *to blows,* the word here used. And Mic. 5:1, *They shall smite the judge of Israel with a rod upon the cheek;* and the type answered (Job 16:10), *They have smitten me upon the cheek reproachfully.* It was unjust to strike one that neither said nor did amiss; it was insolent for a mean servant to strike one that was confessedly a person of account; it was cowardly to strike one that had his hands tied; and barbarous to strike a prisoner at the bar. Here was a breach of the peace in the face of the court, and yet the judges countenanced it. Confusion of face was our due; but Christ here took it to himself: "Upon me be the curse, the shame."

(2.) He checked him in a haughty imperious manner: *Answerest thou the high priest so?* As if the blessed Jesus were not good enough to speak to his master, or not wise enough to know how to speak to him, but, like a rude and ignorant prisoner, must be controlled by the jailor, and taught how to behave. Some of the ancients suggest that this officer was Malchus, who owed to Christ the healing of his ear, and the saving of his head, and yet made him this ill return. But, whoever it was, it was done to please the high priest, and to curry favour with him; for what he said implied a jealousy for the dignity of the high priest. Wicked rulers will not want wicked servants, who will *help forward the affliction* of those whom their masters persecute. There was a successor of this high priest that commanded the bystanders to smite Paul thus *on the mouth,* Acts 23:2. Some think this officer took himself to be affronted by Christ's appeal to those about him con-

cerning his doctrine, as if he would have vouched him to be a witness; and perhaps he was one of those officers that had spoken honourably of him (ch. 7:46), and, lest he should now be thought a secret friend to him, he thus appears a bitter enemy.

2. Christ bore this affront with wonderful meekness and patience (*v.* 23): *"If I have spoken evil,* in what I have now said, *bear witness of the evil.* Observe it to the court, and let them judge of it, who are the proper judges; but if well, and as it did become me, *why smitest thou me?"* Christ could have answered him with a miracle of wrath, could have struck him dumb or dead, or have withered the hand that was lifted up against him. But this was the day of his patience and suffering, and he answered him with the *meekness of wisdom,* to teach us not to avenge ourselves, not to render *railing for railing,* but with the *innocency of the dove* to bear injuries, even when with the *wisdom of the serpent,* as our Saviour, we show the injustice of them, and appeal to the magistrate concerning them. Christ did not here *turn the other cheek,* by which it appears that that rule, Mt. 5:39, is not to be understood literally; a man may possibly *turn the other cheek,* and yet have his heart full of malice; but, comparing Christ's precept with his pattern, we learn, (1.) That in such cases we must not be our own avengers, nor judges in our own cause. We must rather receive than give the second blow, which makes the quarrel; we are allowed to defend ourselves, but not to avenge ourselves: the magistrate (if it be necessary for the preserving of the public peace, and the restraining and terrifying of evil-doers) is to be the avenger, Rom. 13:4. (2.) Our resentment of injuries done us must always be rational, and never passionate; such Christ's here was; *when he suffered,* he reasoned, but *threatened not.* He fairly expostulated with him that did him the injury, and so may we. (3.) When we are called out to suffering, we must *accommodate ourselves* to the inconveniences of a suffering state, with patience, and by one indignity done us be prepared to receive another, and to make the best of it.

VI. While the servants were thus abusing him, Peter was proceeding to deny him, *v.* 25–27. It is a sad story, and none of the least of Christ's sufferings.

1. He repeated the sin the second time, *v.* 25. While he was warming himself with the servants, as one of them, they asked him, *Art not thou one of his disciples?* What dost thou here among us? He, perhaps, hearing that Christ was examined about his disciples, and fearing he should be seized, or at least smitten, as his Master was, if he should own it, flatly denied it, and said, *I am not.*

(1.) It was his great folly to thrust himself into the temptation, by continuing in the company of those that were unsuitable for him, and that he had nothing to do with. He staid to warm himself; but those that warm themselves with evil doers grow cold towards good people and good things, and those that are fond of the devil's fire-side are in danger of the devil's fire. Peter might have stood by his Master at the bar, and have warmed himself better than here, at the fire of his Master's love, which *many waters could not quench,* Cant. 8:6, 7. He might there have warmed himself with zeal for his Master, and indignation at his persecutors; but he chose rather to warm with them than to warm against them. But how could one (one disciple) be warm alone? Eccl. 4:11.

(2.) It was his great unhappiness that he was again assaulted by the temptation; and no other could be expected, for this was a place, this an hour, of temptation. When the judge asked Christ about his disciples, probably the servants took the hint, and challenged Peter for one of them, "Answer to thy name." See here, [1.] The subtlety of the tempter in running down one whom he saw falling, and mustering a greater force against him; not a maid now, but all the servants. Note, Yielding to one temptation invites another, and perhaps a stronger. Satan redoubles his attacks when we give ground. [2.] The danger of bad company. We commonly study to approve ourselves to those with whom we choose to associate; we value ourselves upon their good word and covet to stand right in their opinion. As we choose our people we choose our praise, and govern ourselves accordingly; we are therefore concerned to make the first choice well, and not to mingle with those whom we cannot please without displeasing God.

(3.) It was his great weakness, nay, it was his great wickedness, to yield to the temptation, and to say, *I am not one* of his disciples, as one ashamed of that which was his honour, and afraid of suffering for it, which would have been yet more his honour. See how the *fear of man brings a snare.* When Christ was admired, and caressed, and treated with respect, Peter pleased himself, and perhaps prided himself, in this, that he was a disciple of Christ, and so put in for a share in the honours done to his Master. Thus many who seem fond of the reputation of religion when it is in fashion are ashamed of the reproach of it; but we must take it *for better and worse.*

2. He repeated the sin the third time, *v.* 26, 27. Here he was attacked by one of the servants, who was kinsman to Malchus, who, when he heard Peter deny himself to be a disciple of Christ, gave him the lie with great assurance: *"Did not I see thee in the garden with him?* Witness my kinsman's ear." Peter then denied again, as if he knew nothing of Christ, nothing of the garden, nothing of all this matter.

(1.) This third assault of the temptation was more close than the former: before his relation to Christ was only suspected, here it is proved upon him by one that saw him with Jesus, and saw him draw his sword in his defence. Note, Those who by sin think to help themselves out of trouble do but entangle and embarrass themselves the more. Dare to be brave, for truth will out. *A bird of the air* may perhaps *tell the matter* which we seek to conceal with a lie. Notice is taken of this servant's being akin to Malchus, because this circumstance would make it the more a terror to Peter. "Now," thinks he, "I am gone, my business is done, there needs no other witness nor prosecutor." We should not make any man in particular our enemy if we can help it, because the time may come when either he or some of his relations may have us at their mercy. He that may need a friend should not make a foe. But observe, though here was sufficient evidence against Peter, and sufficient provocation given by his denial to have prosecuted him, yet he escapes, has no harm done him nor attempted to be done. Note, We are often drawn into sin by groundless causeless fears, which there is no occasion for, and which a small degree of wisdom and resolution would make nothing of.

(2.) His yielding to it was no less base than the former: *He denied again.* See here, [1.] The nature of sin in general: *the heart is hardened by the deceitfulness of it,* Heb. 3:13. It was a strange degree of effrontery that Peter had arrived to on a sudden, that he could with such assurance stand in a lie against so clear a disproof; but *the beginning of sin is as the letting forth of water,* when once the fence is broken men easily go from bad to worse. [2.] Of the sin of lying in particular; it is a fruitful sin, and upon this account *exceedingly sinful:* one lie needs another to support it, and that another. It is a rule in the devil's politics *Male facta male factis tegere, ne perpluant — To cover sin with sin, in order to escape detection.*

(3.) The hint given him for the awakening of his conscience was seasonable and happy: *Immediately the cock crew;* and this is all that is here said of his repentance, it being recorded by the other evangelists. This brought him to himself, by bringing to his mind the words of Christ. See here, [1.] The care Christ has of those that are his, notwithstanding their follies; though *they fall, they are not utterly cast down,* not utterly cast off. [2.] The advantage of having faithful remembrancers near us, who, though they cannot tell us more than we know already, yet may remind us of that which we know, but have forgotten. The crowing of the cock to others was an accidental thing, and had not significancy; but to Peter it was the voice of God, and had a blessed tendency to awaken his conscience, by putting him in mind of the word of Christ.

Verses 28–40

We have here an account of Christ's arraignment before Pilate, the Roman governor, in the *praetorium* (a Latin word made Greek), the praetor's house, or *hall of judgment;* thither they hurried him, to get him condemned in the Roman court, and executed by the Roman power. Being resolved on his death, they took this course, 1. That he might be put to death the more legally and regularly, according to the present constitution of their government, since they became a province of the empire; not stoned in a popular tumult, as Stephen, but put to death with the present formalities of justice. Thus he was treated as a malefactor, *being made sin for us.* 2. That he might be put to death the more safely. If they could engage the Roman government in the matter, which the people stood in awe of, there would be little danger of an uproar. 3. That he might be put to death with more reproach to himself. *The death of the cross,* which the Romans commonly used, being of all deaths the most ignominious, they were desirous by it to put an indelible mark of infamy upon him, and so to sink his reputation for ever. This therefore they harped upon, *Crucify him.* 4. That he might be put to death with less reproach to them. It was an invidious thing to put one to death that had done so much good in the world, and therefore they were willing to throw the odium upon the Roman government, to make that the less acceptable to the people, and save themselves from the reproach. Thus many are more afraid of the scandal of a bad action than of the sin of it. See Acts 5:28. Two things are here observed concerning the prosecution: — (1.) Their policy and industry in the prosecution: *It was early;* some think about two or three in the morning, others about five or six, when most people were in their beds; and so there would be the less danger of opposition from the people that were for Christ; while, at the same time, they had their agents about, to call those together whom they could influence to cry out against him. See how much their heart was upon it, and how violent they were in the prosecution. Now that they had him in their hands, they would lose no time till they had him upon the cross, but denied themselves their natural rest, to push on this matter. See Mic. 2:1. (2.) Their superstition and vile hypocrisy: *The chief priests and elders,* though they came along with the prisoner, that the thing might be done effectually, *went not into the judgment-hall,* because it was the house of an uncircumcised Gentile, *lest they should be defiled,* but kept out of doors, *that they might eat the passover,* not the paschal lamb (that was eaten the night before) but the passover-feast, upon the sacrifices which were offered on the fifteenth day, *the Chagigah,* as they called it, the passover-bullocks spoken of Deu. 16:2; 2 Chr. 30:24; 35:8, 9. These they were to eat of, and therefore would not go into the court, for fear of touching a Gentile, and thereby contracting, not a legal, but only a traditional pollution. This they scrupled, but made no scruple of breaking through all the laws of equity to persecute Christ to the death. *They strained at a gnat, and swallowed a camel.* Let us now see what passed at *the judgment-hall.* Here is,

I. Pilate's conference with the prosecutors. They were called first, and stated what they had to say against the prisoner, as was very fit, *v.* 29–32.

1. The judge calls for the indictment. Because they would not come into the hall, *he went out to them* into the court before the house, to talk with them. Looking upon Pilate as a magistrate, that we may give every one his due, here are three things commendable in him: — (1.) His diligent and close application to business. If it had been upon a good occasion, it had been very well that he was willing to be called up early to the judgment-seat. Men in public trusts must not love their ease. (2.) His condescending to the humour of the people, and receding from the honour of his place to gratify their scruples. He might have said, "If they be so nice as not to come in to me, let them go home as they came;" by the same rule as we might say, "If the complainant scruple to take off his hat to the magistrate, let not his complaint be heard;" but Pilate insists not upon it, bears with them, and goes out to them; for, when it is for good, we should *become all things to all men.* (3.) His adherence to the rule of justice, in demanding the accusation, suspecting the prosecution to be malicious: *"What accusation bring you against this man?"* What is the crime you charge him with, and what proof have you of it? It was a law of nature, before Valerius Publicola made it a Roman law, *Ne quis indicta causa condemnetur — No man should be condemned unheard.* See Acts 25:16, 17. It is unreasonable to commit a man, without alleging some cause in the warrant, and much more to arraign a man when there is no bill of indictment found against him.

2. The prosecutors demand judgment against him upon a general surmise that he was a criminal, not alleging, much less proving, any thing in particular *worthy of death or of bonds* (*v.* 30): *If he were not a malefactor,* or evildoer, *we would not have delivered him to thee* to be condemned. This bespeaks them, (1.) Very rude and uncivil to Pilate, a company of ill-natured men, that affected to despise dominion. When Pilate was so complaisant to them as to come out to treat with them, yet they were to the highest degree out of humour with him. He put the most reasonable question to them that could be; but, if it had been the most absurd, they could not have answered him with more disdain. (2.) Very spiteful and malicious towards our Lord Jesus: right or wrong, they will have him to be a malefactor, and treated as one. We are to presume a man innocent till he is proved guilty, but they will presume him guilty who could prove himself innocent. They cannot say, "He is a traitor, a murderer, a felon, a breaker of the peace," but they say, "He is an evil-doer." He an evil-doer who *went about doing good!* Let those be called whom he had cured, and fed, and taught; whom he has rescued from devils, and raised from death; and let them be asked whether he be an evil-doer or no. Note, It is no new thing for the best of benefactors to be branded and run down as the worst of malefactors. (3.) Very proud and conceited of themselves, and their own judgment and justice, as if their delivering a man up, under the general character of a malefactor, were sufficient for the civil magistrate to ground a judicial sentence upon, than which what could be more haughty?

3. The judge remands him to their own court (*v.* 31): *"Take you him, and judge him according to your* own *law,* and do not trouble me with him." Now, (1.) Some think Pilate herein complimented them, acknowledging the remains of their power, and allowing them to exert it. Corporal punishment they might inflict, as *scourging in their synagogues;* whether capital or no is uncertain. "But," saith Pilate, "go as far as your law will allow you, and, if you go further, it shall be connived at." This he said, willing to do the Jews a pleasure, but unwilling to do them the service they required. (2.) Others think he bantered them, and upbraided them with their present state of weakness and subjection. They would be the sole judges of the guilt. "Pray," saith Pilate, "if you will be so, go on as you have begun; you have found him guilty by your own law, condemn him, if you dare, by your own law, to carry on the humour." Nothing is more absurd, nor more deserves to be exposed, than for those to pretend to dictate, and boast of their wisdom, who are weak and in subordinate stations, and whose lot it is to be dictated to. Some think Pilate here reflects upon the law of Moses, as if it allowed them what the Roman law would by no means allow — the judging of a man unheard. "It may be your law will suffer such a thing, but ours will not." Thus, through their corruptions, the law of God was blasphemed; and so is his gospel too.

4. They disown any authority as judges, and (since it must be so) are content to be prosecutors. They now grow less insolent and more submissive, and own, *"It is not lawful for us to put any man to death,* whatever less punishment we may inflict, and this is a malefactor whom we would have the blood of."

(1.) Some think they had lost their power to give judgment in matters of life and death only by their own carelessness, and cowardly yielding to the darling iniquities of the age; so Dr. Lightfoot *ouk exesti — It is not* in our power to pass sentence of death upon *any,* if we do, we shall have the mob about us immediately.

(2.) Others think their power was taken from them by the Romans, because they had not used it well, or because it was thought too great a trust to be lodged in the hands of a conquered and yet an unsubdued people. Their acknowledgement of this they designed for a compliment to Pilate, and to atone for their rudeness (*v.* 30), but it amounts to a full evidence that *the sceptre was departed from Judah,* and therefore that now the Messiah was come, Gen. 49:10. If the Jews have no power *to put any man to death,* where is the sceptre? Yet they ask not, *Where is the Shiloh?*

(3.) However, there was a providence in it, that either they should have not power to put any man to death, or should decline the exercise of it upon this occasion, *That the saying of Jesus might be fulfilled, which he spoke, signifying what death he should die, v.* 32. Observe, [1.] In general, that even those who designed the defeating of Christ's sayings were, beyond their intention, made serviceable to the fulfilling of them by an overruling hand of God. *No word of Christ shall fall to the ground;* he can never either deceive or be deceived. Even *the chief priests,* while they persecuted him as *a deceiver,* had their spirit so directed as to help to prove him true, when we should think that by taking other measures they might have defeated his predictions. *Howbeit, they meant not so,* Isa. 10:7. [2.] Those sayings of Christ in particular were fulfilled which he had spoken concerning his own death. Two sayings of Christ concerning his death were fulfilled, by the Jews declining to *judge him according to their law. First,* He had said that he should be *delivered to the Gentiles,* and that *they should put him to death* (Mt. 20:19; Mk. 10:33; Lu. 18:32, 33), and hereby that saying was fulfilled. *Secondly,* He had said that he should be crucified (Mt. 20:19; 26:2), *lifted up, ch.* 3:14; 12:32. Now, if they had *judged him by their law,* he had been stoned; burning, strangling, and beheading, were in some cases used among the Jews, but never crucifying. It was therefore necessary that Christ should be put to death by the Romans, that, being *hanged upon a tree,* he might be *made a curse for us* (Gal. 3:13), and *his hands and feet* might be *pierced.* As the Roman power had brought him to be born at Bethlehem, so now to die upon a cross, and both according to the scriptures. It is likewise determined concerning us, though not discovered to us, *what death we shall die,* which should free us from all disquieting cares about that matter. "Lord, what, and when, and how thou hast appointed."

II. Here is Pilate's conference with the prisoner, *v.* 33, etc., where we have,

1. The prisoner set to the bar. Pilate, after he had conferred with the chief priests at his door, entered into the hall, and called for Jesus to be brought in. He would not examine him in the crowd, where he might be disturbed by the noise, but ordered him to be brought *into the hall;* for he made no difficulty of going in among the Gentiles. We by sin were become liable to the judgment of God, and were to be brought before his bar; therefore *Christ, being made sin and a curse for us,* was arraigned as a criminal. Pilate entered into judgment with him, that God might not enter into judgment with us.

2. His examination. The other evangelists tell us that his accusers had laid it to his charge that *he perverted the nation, forbidding to give tribute to Caesar,* and upon this he is examined.

(1.) Here is a question put to him, with a design to ensnare him and to find out something upon which to ground an accusation: *"Art thou the king of the Jews? ho basileus — that king of the Jews* who has been so much talked of and so long expected — Messiah the prince, art thou he? Dost thou pretend to be he? Dost thou call thyself, and wouldest thou be thought so?" For he was far from imagining that really he was so, or making a question of that. Some think Pilate asked this with an air of scorn and contempt: "What! *art thou a king,* who makest so mean a figure? *Art thou the king of the Jews,* by whom thou art thus hated and persecuted? *Art thou king de jure — of right,* while the emperor is only king *de facto — in fact?"* Since it could not be proved he ever said it, he would constrain him to say it now, that he might proceed upon his own confession.

(2.) Christ answers this question with another; not for evasion, but as an intimation to Pilate to consider what he did, and upon what grounds he went (*v.* 34): *"Sayest thou this thing of thyself,* from a suspicion arising in thy own breast, *or did others tell it thee of me,* and dost thou ask it only to oblige them?" [1.] "It is plain that thou hast no reason to *say this of thyself."* Pilate was bound by his office to take care of the interests of the Roman government, but he could not say that this was in any danger, or suffered any damage, from any thing our Lord Jesus had ever said or done. He never appeared in worldly pomp, never assumed any secular power, never acted as a judge or divider; never were any traitorous principles or practices objected to him, nor any thing that might give the least shadow of suspicion. [2.] "If others *tell it thee of me,* to incense thee against me, thou oughtest to consider who they are, and upon what principles they go, and whether those who represent me as an *enemy to Caesar* are not really such themselves, and therefore use this only as a pretence to cover their malice, for, if so, the matter ought to be well weighed by a judge that would do justice." Nay, if Pilate had been as inquisitive as he ought to have been in this matter, he would have found that the true reason why the chief priests were outrageous against Jesus was because he did not set up a temporal kingdom in opposition to the Roman power; if he would have done this, and would have wrought miracles to bring the Jews out of the Roman bondage, as Moses did to bring them out of the Egyptian, they would have been so far from siding with the Romans against him that they would have made him their king, and have fought under him against the Romans; but, not answering this expectation of theirs, they charged that upon him of which they were themselves most notoriously guilty — disaffection to and design against the present government; and was such an information as this fit to be countenanced?

(3.) Pilate resents Christ's answer, and takes it very ill, *v.* 35. This is a direct answer to Christ's question, *v.* 34. [1.] Christ had asked him whether he spoke of himself. "No," says he; *"am I a Jew,* that thou suspectest me to be in the plot against thee? I know nothing of the Messiah, nor desire to know, and therefore interest not myself in the dispute who is the Messiah and who not; the dispute who is the Messiah and who not; it is all alike to me." Observe with what disdain Pilate asks, *Am I a Jew?* The Jews were, upon many accounts, an honourable people; but, having corrupted the covenant of their God, *he made them contemptible and base before all the people* (Mal. 2:8, 9), so that a man of sense and honour reckoned it a scandal to be counted a Jew. Thus good names often suffer for the sake of the bad men that wear them. It is sad that when a Turk is suspected of dishonesty he should ask, "What! do you take me for a Christian?" [2.] Christ had asked him whether others told him. "Yes," says he, "and those *thine own people,* who, one would think would be biased in favour of thee, and *the priests,* whose testimony, *in verbum sacerdotis — on the word of a priest,* ought to be regarded; and therefore I have nothing to do but to proceed upon their information." Thus Christ, in his religion, still suffers by those that are of his own nation, even the priests, that profess relation to him, but do not live up to their profession. [3.] Christ had declined answering that question, *Art thou the king of the Jews?* And therefore Pilate puts another question to him more general, *"What hast thou done?* What provocation hast thou given to thy own nation, and particularly the priests, to be so violent against thee? Surely there cannot be all this smoke without some fire, what is it?"

(4.) Christ, in his next reply, gives a more full and direct answer to Pilate's former question, *Art thou a king?* explaining in what sense he was a king, but not such a king as was any ways dangerous to the Roman government, not a secular king, for his interest was not supported by secular methods, *v.* 36. Observe,

[1.] An account of the nature and constitution of Christ's kingdom: It *is not of this world.* It is expressed negatively to rectify the present mistakes concerning it; but the positive is implied, it is *the kingdom of heaven,* and belongs to another world. Christ is a king, and has a kingdom, but *not of this world. First* Its rise is not from this world; the kingdoms of men arise *out of the sea and the earth* (Dan. 7:3; Rev. 13:1, 11); but *the holy city comes from God out of heaven,* Rev. 22:2. His kingdom is not by succession, election, or conquest, but by the immediate and special designation of the divine will and counsel. *Secondly,* Its nature is not worldly; it is a kingdom within men (Lu. 16:21), set up in their hearts and consciences (Rom. 14:17), its riches spiritual, its powers spiritual, and *all its glory within.* The ministers of state in Christ's kingdom have not *the spirit of the world,* 1 Co. 2:12. *Thirdly,* Its guards and supports are not worldly; its weapons are spiritual. It neither needed nor used secular force to maintain and advance it, nor was it carried on in a way *hurtful to kings or provinces;* it did not in the least interfere with the prerogatives of princes nor the property of their subjects; it tended not to alter any national establishment in secular things, nor opposed any kingdom but that of sin and Satan. *Fourthly,* Its tendency and design are not worldly. Christ neither aimed nor would allow his disciples to aim at the pomp and power of *the great men of the earth. Fifthly,* Its subjects, though they are in the world, yet *are not of the world;* they *are called and chosen out of the world,* are born from, and bound for, another world; they are neither the world's pupils nor its darlings, neither governed by its wisdom nor enriched with its wealth.

[2.] An evidence of the spiritual nature of Christ's kingdom produced. If he had designed an opposition to the government, he would have fought them at their own weapons, and would have repelled force with force of the same nature; but he did not take this course: *If my kingdom were of this world, then would my servants fight, that I should not be delivered to the Jews,* and my kingdom be ruined by them. But, *First,* His followers did not offer to fight; there was no uproar, no attempt to rescue him, though the town was now full of Galileans, his friends and countrymen, and they were generally armed; but the peaceable behaviour of his disciples on this occasion was enough *to put to silence the ignorance of foolish men. Secondly,* He did not order them to fight; nay, he forbade them, which was an evidence both that he did not depend upon worldly aids (for he could have summoned *legions of angels* into his service, which showed that his *kingdom was from above*), and also that he did not dread worldly opposition, for he was very willing to be *delivered to the Jews,* as knowing that what would have been the destruction of any worldly kingdom would be the advancement and establishment of his; justly therefore does he conclude, *Now* you may see *my kingdom is not from hence;* in the world but not of it.

(5.) In answer to Pilate's further query, he replies yet more directly, *v.* 37, where we have, [1.] Pilate's plain question: *"Art thou a king then?* Thou speakest of a kingdom thou hast; art thou then, in any sense, a king? And what colour hast thou for such a claim? Explain thyself." [2.] The good confession which our Lord Jesus witnessed before Pontius Pilate, in answer to this (1 Tim. 6:13): *Thou sayest that I am a king,* that is, It is as thou sayest, I am a king; for *I came to bear witness of the truth. First,* He grants himself to be a king, though not in the sense that Pilate meant. The Messiah was expected under the character of a king, *Messiah the prince;* and therefore, having owned to Caiaphas that he was the Christ, he would not disown to Pilate that he was king, lest he should seem inconsistent with himself. Note, Though Christ *took upon him the form of a servant,* yet even then he justly claimed the honour and authority of a king. *Secondly,* He explains himself, and shows how he is a king, as *he came to bear witness of the truth;* he rules in the minds of men by the power of truth. If he had meant to declare himself a temporal prince, he would have said, *For this end was I born, and for this cause came I into the world,* to rule the nations, to conquer kings, and to take possession of kingdoms; no, *he came to be a witness,* a witness for the God that made the world, and against sin that ruins the world, and by this *word of his testimony* he sets up, and keeps up, his kingdom. It was foretold that he should be *a witness to the people,* and, as such, *a leader and commander to the people,* Isa. 55:4. Christ's kingdom was not of this world, in which *truth faileth* (Isa. 59:15, *Qui nescit dissimulare, nescit regnare — He that cannot dissemble knows not how to reign*), but of that world in which truth reigns eternally. Christ's errand into the world, and his business in the world, were *to bear witness to the truth.* 1. To reveal it, to discover to the world that which otherwise could not have been known concerning God and his will and *good-will to men, ch.* 1:18; 17:26. 2. To confirm it, Rom. 15:8. By his miracles *he bore witness to the truth* of religion, the truth of divine revelation, and of God's perfections and providence, and the truth of his promise and covenant, *that all men through him might believe.* Now by doing this he is a king, and sets up a kingdom. (1.) The foundation and power, the spirit and genius, of Christ's kingdom, is truth, divine truth. When he said, *I am the truth,* he said, in effect, I am a king. He conquers by the convincing evidence of truth; he rules by the commanding power of truth, and *in his majesty rides prosperously, because of truth,* Ps. 45:4. It is with his truth that he shall judge the people, Ps. 96:13. It is the sceptre of his kingdom; he *draws with the cords of a man,* with truth revealed to us, and received by us in *the love of it;* and thus he *brings thoughts into obedience.* He came *a light into the world,* and rules as the sun by day. (2.) The subjects of this kingdom are those that are *of the truth.* All that by the grace of God are rescued from under the power of *the father of lies,* and are disposed to receive the truth and submit to the power and influence of it, will hear Christ's voice, will become his subjects, and will bear faith and true allegiance to him. Every one that has any real sense of true religion will entertain the Christian religion, and they belong to his kingdom; by the power of truth he makes them willing, Ps. 90:3. All that are in love with truth will hear the voice of Christ, for greater, better, surer, sweeter truths can nowhere be found than are found in Christ, by whom *grace and truth came;* so that, by *hearing Christ's voice,* we know that we are *of the truth,* 1 Jn. 3:19.

(6.) Pilate, hereupon, puts a good question to him, but does not stay for an answer, *v.* 38. He said, *What is truth?* and *immediately went out again.*

[1.] It is certain that this was a good question, and could not be put to one that was better able to answer it. Truth is that *pearl of great price* which the human understanding has a desire for and is in quest of; for it cannot rest but in that which is, or at least is apprehended to be, truth. When we *search the scriptures,* and attend the ministry of the word, it must be with this enquiry, *What is truth?* and with this prayer, *Lead me in thy truth, into all truth.* But many put this question that have not patience and constancy enough to persevere in their search after truth, or not humility and sincerity enough to receive it when they have found it, 2 Tim. 3:7. Thus many deal with their own consciences; they ask them those needful questions, "What am I?" "What have I done?" but will not take time for an answer.

[2.] It is uncertain with what design Pilate asked this question. *First,* Perhaps he spoke it as a learner, as one that began to think well of Christ, and to look upon him with some respect, and desired to be informed what new notions he advanced and what improvements he pretended to in religion and learning. But while he desired to hear some new truth from him, as Herod to see some miracle, the clamour and outrage of the priests' mob at his gate obliged him abruptly to let fall the discourse. *Secondly,* Some think he spoke it as a judge, enquiring further into the cause now brought before him: "Let me into this mystery, and tell me what the truth of it is, the true state of this matter." *Thirdly,* Others think he spoke it as a scoffer, in a jeering way: "Thou talkest of truth; canst thou tell what truth is, or give me a definition of it?" Thus he makes a jest of the everlasting gospel, that great truth which the chief priests hated and persecuted, and which Christ was now witnessing to and suffering for; and like men of no religion, who take a pleasure in bantering all religions, he ridicules both sides; and therefore Christ made him no reply. *Answer not a fool according to his folly; cast not pearls before swine.* But, though Christ would not tell Pilate what is truth, he has told his disciples, and by them has told us, *ch.* 14:6.

III. The result of both these conferences with the prosecutors and the prisoner (*v.* 38–40), in two things: —

1. The judge appeared his friend, and favourable to him, for,

(1.) He publicly declared him innocent, *v.* 38. Upon the whole matter, *I find in him no fault at all.* He supposes there might be some controversy in religion between him and them, wherein he was as likely to be in the right as they; but nothing criminal appears against him. This solemn declaration of Christ's innocency was, [1.] For the justification and honour of the Lord Jesus. By this it appears that though he was treated as the worst of malefactors he had never merited such treatment. [2.] For explaining the design and intention of his death, that he did not die for any sin of his own, even in the judgement of the judge himself, and therefore he died as a sacrifice for our sins, and that, even in the judgment of the prosecutors themselves, *one man should die for the people, ch.* 11:50. This is he that *did no violence, neither was any deceit in his mouth* (Isa. 53:9), who was to *be cut off, but not for himself,* Dan. 9:26. [3.] For aggravating the sin of the Jews that prosecuted him with so much violence. If a prisoner has had a fair trial, and has been acquitted by those that are proper judges of the crime, especially if there be no cause to suspect them partial in his favour, he must be believed innocent, and his accusers are bound to acquiesce. But our Lord Jesus, though brought in not guilty, is still run down as a malefactor, and his blood thirsted for.

(2.) He proposed an expedient for his discharge (*v.* 39): *You have a custom, that I should release to you a prisoner at the passover;* shall it be this king of the Jews? He proposed this, not to the chief priests (he knew they would never agree to it), but to the multitude; it was an appeal to the people, as appears, Mt. 27:15. Probably he had heard how this Jesus had been attended but the other day with the hosannas of the common people; he therefore looked upon him to be the darling of the multitude, and the envy only of the rulers, and therefore he made no doubt but they would demand the release of Jesus, and this would stop the mouth of the prosecutors, and all would be well. [1.] He allows their custom, for which, perhaps, they had had a long prescription, in honour of the passover, which was a memorial of their release. But it was adding to God's words, as if he had not instituted enough for the due commemoration of that deliverance, and, though an act of mercy, might be injustice to the public, Prov. 17:15. [2.] He offers to release Jesus to them, according to the custom. If Pilate had had the honesty and courage that became a judge, he would not have named an innocent person to be competitor with a notorious criminal for this favour; if he *found no fault in him,* he was bound in conscience to discharge him. But he was willing to trim the matter, and please all sides, being governed more by worldly wisdom than by the rules of equity.

2. The people appeared his enemies, and implacable against him (*v.* 40): *They cried all again* and again, *Not this man,* let not him be released, *but Barabbas.* Observe, (1.) How fierce and outrageous they were. Pilate proposed the thing to them calmly, as worthy their mature consideration, but they resolved it in a heat, and gave in their resolution with clamour and noise, and in the utmost confusion. Note, The enemies of Christ's holy religion cry it down, and so hope to run it down; witness the outcry at Ephesus, Acts 19:34. But those who think the worse of things or persons merely for their being thus exclaimed against have a very small share of constancy and consideration. Nay, there is cause to suspect a deficiency of reason and justice on that side which calls in the assistance of popular tumult. (2.) How foolish and absurd they were, as is intimated in the short account here given of the other candidate: *Now Barabbas was a robber,* and therefore, [1.] A breaker of the law of God; and yet he shall be spared, rather than one who reproved the pride, avarice, and tyranny of the priests and elders. Though Barabbas be a robber, he will not rob them of Moses's seat, nor of their traditions, and then no matter. [2.] He was an enemy to the public safety and personal property. The clamour of the town is wont to be against robbers (Job 30:5, *Men cried after them as after a thief*), yet here it is for one. Thus those do who prefer their sins before Christ. Sin is a robber, every base lust is a robber, and yet foolishly chosen rather than Christ, who would truly enrich us.

CHAPTER 19

Though in the history hitherto this evangelist seems industriously to have declined the recording of such passages as had been related by the other evangelists, yet, when he comes to the sufferings and death of Christ, instead of passing them over, as one ashamed of his Master's chain and cross, and looking upon them as the blemishes of his story, he repeats what had been before related, with considerable enlargements, as one that desired to know nothing but Christ and him crucified, to glory in nothing save in the cross of Christ. In the story of this chapter we have, I. he remainder of Christ's trial before Pilate, which was tumultuous and confused (*v.* 1–15). II. Sentence given, and execution done upon it (*v.* 16–18). III. The title over his head (*v.* 19–22). IV. The parting of his garment (*v.* 23, 24). V. The care he took of his mother (*v.* 25–27). VI. The giving him vinegar to drink (*v.* 28, 29). VII. His dying word (*v.* 30). VIII. The piercing of his side (*v.* 31–37). IX. The burial of his body (*v.* 38–42). O that in meditating on these things we may experimentally know the power of Christ's death, and the fellowship of his sufferings!

Verses 1–15

Here is a further account of the unfair trial which they gave to our Lord Jesus. The prosecutors carrying it on with great confusion among the people, and the judge with great confusion in his own breast, between both the narrative is such as is not easily reduced to method; we must therefore take the parts of it as they lie.

I. The judge abuses the prisoner, though he declares him innocent, and hopes therewith to pacify the prosecutors; wherein his intention, if indeed it was good, will by no means justify his proceedings, which were palpably unjust.

1. He ordered him to be whipped as a criminal, *v.* 1. *Pilate,* seeing the people so outrageous, and being disappointed in his project of releasing him upon the people's choice, *took Jesus, and scourged him,* that is, appointed the lictors that attended him to do it. Bede is of opinion that Pilate scourged Jesus himself with his own hands, because it is said, *He took him and scourged him,* that it might be done favourably. Matthew and Mark mention his scourging after his condemnation, but here it appears to have been before. Luke speaks of Pilate's offering to *chastise him, and let him go,* which must be before sentence. This scourging of him was designed only to pacify the Jews, and in it Pilate put a compliment upon them, that he would take their word against his own sentiments so far. The Roman scourgings were ordinarily very severe, not limited, as among the Jews, to *forty stripes;* yet this pain and shame Christ submitted to for our sakes. (1.) *That the scripture might be fulfilled,* which spoke of his being *stricken, smitten, and afflicted,* and *the chastisement of our peace* being *upon him* (Isa. 53:5), of his giving his back to the smiters (Isa. 50:6), of the ploughers ploughing upon his back, Ps. 129:3. He himself likewise had foretold it, Mt. 20:19; Mk. 10:34; Lu. 18:33. (2.) *That by his stripes we might be healed,* 1 Pt. 2:4. We deserved to have been chastised *with whips and scorpions,* and *beaten with many stripes,* having known our Lord's will and not done it; but Christ underwent the stripes for us, bearing the rod of his Father's wrath, Lam. 3:1. Pilate's design in scourging him was that he might not be condemned, which did not take effect, but intimated what was God's design, that his being scourged might prevent our being condemned, we having fellowship in his sufferings, and this did take effect: the physician scourged, and so the patient healed. (3.) That stripes, for his sake, might be sanctified and made easy to his followers; and they might, as they did, rejoice in that shame (Acts 5:41; 16:22, 25), as Paul did, who was *in stripes above measure,* 2 Co. 11:23. Christ's stripes take out the sting of theirs, and alter the property of them. *We are chastened of the Lord, that we may not be condemned with the world,* 1 Co. 11:32.

2. He turned him over to his soldiers, to be ridiculed and made sport with as a fool (*v.* 2, 3): *The soldiers,* who were the governor's life-guard, *put a crown of thorns upon his head;* such a crown they thought fittest for such a king; *they put on him a purple robe,* some old threadbare coat of that colour, which they thought good enough to be the badge of his royalty; and they complemented him with, *Hail, king of the Jews* (like people like king), and then *smote him with their hands.*

(1.) See here the baseness and injustice of Pilate, that he would suffer one whom he believed an innocent person, and if so an excellent person, to be thus abused and trampled on by his own servants. Those who are under the arrest of the law ought to be under the protection of it; and their being secured is to be their security. But Pilate did this, [1.] To oblige his soldiers' merry humour, and perhaps his own too, notwithstanding the gravity one might have expected in a judge. *Herod,* as well as *his men of war,* had just before done the same, Lu. 23:11. It was as good as a stage-play to them, now that it was a festival time; as the Philistines made sport with Samson. [2.] To oblige the Jews' malicious humour, and to gratify them, who desired that all possible disgrace might be done to Christ, and the utmost indignities put upon him.

(2.) See here the rudeness and insolence of the soldiers, how perfectly lost they were to all justice and humanity, who could thus triumph over a man in misery, and one that had been in reputation for wisdom and honour, and never did any thing to forfeit it. But thus hath Christ's holy religion been basely misrepresented, dressed up by bad men at their pleasure, and so exposed to contempt and ridicule, as Christ was here. [1.] They clothe him with a mock-robe, as if it were a sham and a jest, and nothing but the product of a heated fancy and a crazed imagination. And as Christ is here represented as a king in conceit only, so is his religion as a concern in conceit only, and God and the soul, sin and duty, heaven and hell, are with many all chimeras. [2.] They crown him with thorns; as if the religion of Christ were a perfect penance, and the greatest pain and hardship in the world; as if to submit to the control of God and conscience were to thrust one's head into a thicket of thorns; but this is an unjust imputation; *thorns and snares are in the way of the froward,* but roses and laurels in religion's ways.

(3.) See here the wonderful condescension of our Lord Jesus in his sufferings for us. Great and generous minds can bear any thing better than ignominy, any toil, any pain, any loss, rather than reproach; yet this the great and holy Jesus submitted to for us. See and admire, [1.] The invincible patience of a sufferer, leaving us an example of contentment and courage, evenness, and easiness of spirit, under the greatest hardships we may meet with in the way of duty. [2.] The invincible love and kindness of a Saviour, who not only cheerfuly and resolutely went through all this, but voluntarily undertook it for us and for our salvation. Herein he commended his love, that he would not only die for us, but die as a fool dies. *First,* He *endured the pain;* not the pangs of death only, though in the death of the cross these were most exquisite; but, as if these were too little, he submitted to those previous pains. Shall we complain of a thorn in the flesh, and of being buffeted by affliction, because we need it to hide pride from us, when Christ humbled himself to bear those thorns in the head, and those buffetings, to save and teach us? 2 Co. 12:7. *Secondly,* He *despised the shame,* the shame of a fool's coat, and the mock-respect paid him, with, *Hail, king of the Jews.* If we be at any time ridiculed for well-doing, let us not be ashamed, but glorify God, for thus we are partakers of Christ's sufferings. He that bore these sham honours was recompensed with real honours, and so shall we, if we patiently suffer shame for him.

II. Pilate, having thus abused the prisoner, presents him to the prosecutors, in hope that they would now be satisfied, and drop the prosecution, *v.* 4, 5. Here he proposes two things to their consideration: —

1. That he had not found any thing in him which made him obnoxious to the Roman government (*v.* 4): *I find no fault in him; oudemian aitian heuriskō — I do not find in him the least fault,* or *cause of accusation.* Upon further enquiry,

he repeats the declaration he had made, *ch.* 18:38. Hereby he condemns himself; if he found no fault in him, why did he scourge him, why did he suffer him to be abused? None ought to suffer ill but those that do ill; yet thus many banter and abuse religion, who yet, if they be serious, cannot but own they find no fault in it. If he found no fault in him, why did he bring him out to his prosecutors, and not immediately release him, as he ought to have done? If Pilate had consulted his own conscience only, he would neither have scourged Christ nor crucified him; but, thinking to trim the matter, to please the people by scourging Christ, and save his conscience by not crucifying him, behold he does both; whereas, if he had at first resolved to crucify him, he need not have scourged him. It is common for those who think to keep themselves from greater sins by venturing upon less sins to run into both.

2. That he had done that to him which would make him the less dangerous to them and to their government, *v.* 5. He brought him out to them, wearing the crown of thorns, his head and face all bloody, and said, *"Behold the man* whom you are so jealous of," intimating that though his having been so popular might have given them some cause to fear that his interest in the country would lessen theirs, yet he had taken an effectual course to prevent it, by treating him as a slave, and exposing him to contempt, after which he supposed the people would never look upon him with any respect, nor could he ever retrieve his reputation again. Little did Pilate think with what veneration even these sufferings of Christ would in after ages be commemorated by the best and greatest of men, who would glory in that cross and those stripes which he thought would have been to him and his followers a perpetual and indelible reproach. (1.) Observe here our Lord Jesus shows himself dressed up in all the marks of ignominy. He came forth, willing to be made a spectacle, and to be hooted at, as no doubt he was when he came forth in this garb, knowing that he was set for a *sign that should be spoken against,* Lu. 2:34. Did he go forth thus bearing our reproach? Let us go forth to him *bearing his reproach,* Heb. 13:13. (2.) How Pilate shows him: *Pilate saith unto them, Behold the man. He saith unto them:* so the original is; and, the immediate antecedent being *Jesus,* I see no inconvenience in supposing these to be Christ's own words; he said, *"Behold the man* against whom you are so exasperated." But some of the Greek copies, and the generality of the translators, supply it as we do, Pilate saith unto them, with a design to appease them, *Behold the man;* not so much to move their pity, Behold a man worthy your compassion, as to silence their jealousies, Behold a man not worthy your suspicion, a man from whom you can henceforth fear no danger; his crown is *profaned, and cast to the ground,* and now all mankind will make a jest of him. The word however is very affecting: *Behold the man.* It is good for every one of us, with an eye of faith, to behold the man Christ Jesus in his sufferings. *Behold this king with the crown wherewith his mother crowned him,* the crown of thorns, Cant. 3:11. "Behold him, and be suitably affected with the sight. Behold him, and mourn because of him. Behold him, and love him; be still *looking unto Jesus.*"

III. The prosecutors, instead of being pacified, were but the more exasperated, *v.* 6, 7.

1. Observe here their clamour and outrage. *The chief priests,* who headed the mob, *cried out* with fury and indignation, and their officers, or servants, who must say as they said, joined with them in crying, *Crucify him, crucify him.* The common people perhaps would have acquiesced in Pilate's declaration of his innocency, but their leaders, the priests, *caused them to err.* Now by this it appears that their malice against Christ was, (1.) Unreasonable and most absurd, in that they offer not to make good their charges against him, nor to object against the judgment of Pilate concerning him; but, though he be innocent, he must be crucified. (2.) It was insatiable and very cruel. Neither the extremity of his scourging, nor his patience under it, nor the tender expostulations of the judge, could mollify them in the least; no, nor could the jest into which Pilate had turned the cause, put them into a pleasant humour. (3.) It was violent and exceedingly resolute; they will have it their own way, and hazard the governor's favour, the peace of the city, and their own safety, rather than abate of the utmost of their demands. Were they so violent in running down our Lord Jesus, and in crying, *Crucify him, crucify him?* and shall not we be vigorous and zealous in advancing his name, and in crying, *Crown him, Crown him?* Did their hatred of him sharpen their endeavours against him? and shall not our love to him quicken our endeavours for him and his kingdom?

2. The check Pilate gave to their fury, still insisting upon the prisoner's innocency: *"Take you him and crucify him,* if he must be crucified." This is spoken ironically; he knew they could not, they durst not, crucify him; but it is as if he should say, "You shall not make me a drudge to your malice; I cannot with a safe conscience crucify him." A good resolve, if he would but have stuck to it. He found no fault in him, and therefore should not have continued to parley with the prosecutors. Those that would be safe from sin should be deaf to temptation. Nay, he should have secured the prisoner from their insults. What was he armed with power for, but to protect the injured? The guards of governors ought to be the guards of justice. But Pilate had not courage enough to act according to his conscience; and his cowardice betrayed him into a snare.

3. The further colour which the prosecutors gave to their demand (*v.* 7): *We have a law, and by our law,* if it were but in our power to execute it, *he ought to die, because he made himself the Son of God.* Now here observe, (1.) They *made their boast of the law,* even when *through breaking the law they dishonoured God,* as is charged upon the Jews, Rom. 2:23. They had indeed an excellent law, far exceeding the statutes and judgments of other nations; but in vain did they boast of their law, when they abused it to such bad purposes. (2.) They discover a restless and inveterate malice against our Lord Jesus. When they could not incense Pilate against him by alleging that he pretended himself a king, they urged this, that he pretended himself a God. Thus they turn every stone to take him off. (3.) They pervert the law, and make that the instrument of their malice. Some think they refer to a law made particularly against Christ, as if, being a law, it must be executed, right or wrong; whereas there is a woe to them that *decree unrighteous decrees,* and that *write the grievousness which they have prescribed,* Isa. 10:1. See Mic. 6:16. But it should seem they rather refer to the law of Moses; and if so, [1.] It was true that blasphemers, idolaters, and false prophets, were to be put to death by that law. Whoever falsely pretended to be the Son of God was guilty of blasphemy, Lev. 24:16. But then, [2.] It was false that Christ pretended to be the Son of God, for he really was so; and they ought to have enquired into the proofs he produced of his being so. If he said that he was the Son of God, and the scope and tendency of his doctrine were not to draw people from God, but to bring them to him, and if he confirmed his mission and doctrine by miracles, as undoubtedly he did, beyond contradiction, by their law they ought to *hearken to him* (Deu. 18:18, 19), and, if they did not, they were to be *cut off.* That which was his honour, and might have been their happiness, if they had not stood in their own light, they impute to him as a crime, for which he ought not to be crucified, for this was no death inflicted by their law.

IV. The judge brings the prisoner again to his trial, upon this new suggestion. Observe,

1. The concern Pilate was in, when he heard this alleged (*v.* 8): When he heard that his prisoner pretended not to royalty only, but to deity, he was *the more afraid.* This embarrassed him more than ever, and made the case more difficult both ways; for, (1.) There was the more danger of offending the people if he should acquit him, for he knew how jealous that people were for the unity of the Godhead, and what aversion they now had to other gods; and therefore, though he might hope to pacify their rage against a pretended king, he could never reconcile them to a pretended God. "If this be at the bottom of the tumult," thinks Pilate, "it will not be turned off with a jest." (2.) There was the more danger of offending his own conscience if he should condemn him. "Is he one" (thinks Pilate) "that makes himself *the Son of God?* and what if it should prove that he is so? What will become of me then?" Even natural conscience makes men afraid of being found *fighting against God.* The heathen had some fabulous traditions of incarnate deities appearing sometimes in mean circumstances, and treated ill by some that paid dearly for their so doing. Pilate fears lest he should thus run himself into a premunire.

2. His further examination of our Lord Jesus thereupon, *v.* 9. That he might give the prosecutors all the fair play they could desire, he resumed the debate, went into the judgment-hall, and asked Christ, *Whence art thou?* Observe,

(1.) The place he chose for this examination: He *went into the judgment-hall* for privacy, that he might be out of the noise and clamour of the crowd, and might examine the thing the more closely. Those that would find out the truth as it is in Jesus must get out of the noise of prejudice, and retire as it were into the judgment-hall, to converse with Christ alone.

(2.) The question he put to him: *Whence art thou?* Art thou from men or from heaven? From beneath or from above? He had before asked directly, *Art thou a King?* But here he does not directly ask, *Art thou the Son of God?* lest he should seem to meddle with divine things too boldly. But in general, *"Whence art thou?* Where wast thou, and in what world hadst thou a being, before thy coming into this world?"

(3.) The silence of our Lord Jesus when he was examined upon this head; but *Jesus gave him no answer.* This was not a sullen silence, in contempt of the court, nor was it because he knew not what to say; but, [1.] It was a patient silence, that the scripture might be fulfilled, *as a sheep before the shearers is dumb, so he opened not his mouth,* Isa. 53:7. This silence loudly bespoke his submission to his Father's will in his present sufferings, which he thus accommodated himself to, and composed himself to bear. He was silent, because he would say nothing to hinder his sufferings. If Christ had avowed himself a God as plainly as he avowed himself a king, it is probable that Pilate would not have condemned him (for he was afraid at the mention of it by the prosecutors); and the Romans, though they triumphed over the *kings of the nations* they conquered, yet stood in awe of their gods. See 1 Co. 2:8. *If they had known* him to be the *Lord of glory,* they would *not have crucified him;* and how then could we have been saved? [2.] It was a prudent silence. When the chief priests asked him, *Art thou the Son of the Blessed?* he answered, *I am,* for he knew they went upon the scriptures of the Old Testament which spoke of the Messiah; but when Pilate asked him he knew he did not understand his own question, having no notion of the Messiah, and of his being the *Son of God,* and therefore to what purpose should he reply to him whose head was filled with the pagan theology, to which he would have turned his answer?

(4.) The haughty check which Pilate gave him for his silence (*v.* 10): *"Speakest thou not unto me?* Dost thou put such an affront upon me as to stand mute? What *knowest thou not* that, as president of the province, *I have power,* if I think fit, *to crucify thee, and have power,* if I think fit, to *release thee?"* Observe here, [1.] How Pilate magnified himself, and boasts of his own authority, as not inferior to that of Nebuchadnezzar, of whom it is said that *whom he would he slew, and whom he would he kept alive.* Dan. 5:19. Men in power are apt to be puffed up with their power, and the more absolute and arbitrary it is the more it gratifies and humours their pride. But he magnifies his power to an exorbitant degree when he boasts that he has power to crucify one whom he had declared innocent, for no prince or potentate has authority to do wrong. *Id possumus, quod jure possumus — We can do that only which we can do justly.* [2.] How he tramples upon our blessed Saviour: *Speakest thou not unto me?* He reflects upon him, *First,* As if he were undutiful and disrespectful to those in authority, not speaking when he was spoken to. *Secondly,* As if he were ungrateful to one that had been tender of him: "Speakest thou not to me who have laboured to secure thy release?" *Thirdly,* As if he were unwise for himself: "Wilt thou not speak to clear thyself to one that is willing to clear thee?" If Christ had indeed sought to save his life, now had been his time to have spoken; but that which he had to do was to lay down his life.

(5.) Christ's pertinent answer to this check, *v.* 11, where,

[1.] He boldly rebukes his arrogance, and rectifies his mistake: "Big as thou lookest and talkest, *thou couldest have no power at all against me,* no power to scourge, no power to crucify, *except it were given thee from above."* Though Christ did not think fit to answer him when he was impertinent (then *answer not a fool according to his folly, lest thou also be like him*), yet he did think fit to answer him when he was imperious; then *answer a fool according to his folly, lest he be wise in his own conceit,* Prov. 26:4, 5. When Pilate used his power, Christ silently submitted to it; but, when he grew proud of it, he made him know himself: "All the power thou hast is given thee from above," which may be taken two ways: — *First,* As reminding him that his power in general, as a magistrate, was a limited power, and he could do no more than God would suffer him to do. God is the fountain of power; and the *powers that are,* as they are ordained by him and derived from him, so they are subject to him. They ought to go no further than his law directs them; they can go no further than his providence permits them. They are God's hand and his sword, Ps. 17:13, 14. Though the axe may *boast itself against him that heweth therewith,* yet still it is but a tool, Isa. 10:5, 15. Let the proud oppressors know that there is *a higher than they,* to whom they are accountable, Eccl. 5:8. And let this silence the murmurings of the oppressed, *It is the Lord.* God has bidden Shimei curse David; and let it comfort them that their persecutors can do no more than God will let them. See Isa. 51:12, 13. *Secondly,* As informing him that his power against him in particular, and all the efforts of that power, were *by the determinate counsel and foreknowledge of God,* Acts 2:23. Pilate never fancied himself to look so great as now, when he sat in judgment upon such a prisoner as this, who was looked upon by many as the *Son of God* and king of Israel, and had the fate of so great a man at his disposal; but Christ lets him know that he was herein but an instrument in God's hand, and could no nothing against him, but by the appointment of Heaven, Acts 4:27, 28.

[2.] He mildly excuses and extenuates his sin, in comparison with the sin of the ringleaders: *"Therefore he that delivered me unto thee* lies under greater guilt; for thou as a magistrate hast *power from above,* and art in thy place, thy sin is less than theirs who, from envy and malice, urge thee to abuse thy power."

First, It is plainly intimated that what Pilate did was sin, a great sin, and that the force which the Jews put upon him, and which he put upon himself in it, would not justify him. Christ hereby intended a hint for the awakening of his conscience and the increase of the fear he was now under. The guilt of others will not acquit us, nor will it avail in the great day to say that others were worse than we, for we are not to be judged by comparison, but must *bear our own burden.*

Secondly, Yet theirs that delivered him to Pilate was the greater sin. By this it appears that all sins are not equal, but some more heinous than others; some comparatively as gnats, others as camels; some as motes in the eyes, others as beams; some as pence, others as pounds. *He that delivered Christ to Pilate* was either, 1. The people of the Jews, who cried out, *Crucify him, crucify him.* They had seen Christ's miracles, which Pilate had not; to them the Messiah was first sent; they were his own; and to them, who were now enslaved, a Redeemer should have been most welcome, and therefore it was much worse in them to appear against him than in Pilate. 2. Or rather he means Caiaphas in particular, who was at the head of the conspiracy against Christ, and first advised his death, *ch.* 11:49, 50. The sin of Caiaphas was abundantly greater than the sin of Pilate. Caiaphas prosecuted Christ from pure enmity to him and his doctrine, deliberately and of malice prepense. Pilate condemned him purely for fear of the people, and it was a hasty resolution which he had not time to cool upon. 3. Some think Christ means Judas; for, though he did not immediately deliver him into the hands of Pilate, yet he betrayed him to those that did. The sin of Judas was, upon many accounts, greater than the sin of Pilate. Pilate was a stranger to Christ; Judas was his friend and follower. Pilate found no fault in him, but Judas knew a great deal of good of him. Pilate, though biassed, was not bribed, but Judas took a *reward against the innocent;* the sin of Judas was a leading sin, and let in all that followed. He was a *guide to them that took Jesus.* So great was the sin of Judas that *vengeance suffered him not to live;* but when Christ said this, or soon after, he was gone *to his own place.*

V. Pilate struggles with the Jews to deliver Jesus out of their hands, but in vain. We hear no more after this of any thing that passed between Pilate and the prisoner; what remains lay between him and the prosecutors.

1. Pilate seems more zealous than before to get Jesus discharged (*v.* 12): *Thenceforth,* from this time, and for this reason, because Christ had given him that answer (*v.* 11), which, though it had a rebuke in it, yet he took kindly; and, though Christ found fault with him, he still continued to find no fault in Christ, but *sought to release him,* desired it, endeavoured it. *He sought to release him;* he contrived how to do it handsomely and safely, and so as not to disoblige the priests. It never does well when our resolutions to do our duty are swallowed up in projects how to do it plausibly and conveniently. If Pilate's policy had not prevailed above his justice, he would not have been long seeking to release him, but would have done it. *Fiat justitia, ruat coelum — Let justice be done, though heaven itself should fall.*

2. The Jews were more furious than ever, and more violent to get Jesus crucified. Still they carry on their design with noise and clamour as before; so now they cried out. They would have it thought that the commonalty was against him, and therefore laboured to get him cried down by a multitude, and it is no hard matter to pack a mob; whereas, if a fair poll had been granted, I doubt not but it would have been carried by a great majority for the releasing of him. A few madmen may out-shout many wise men, and then fancy themselves to speak the sense (when it is but the nonsense) of a nation, or of all mankind; but it is not so easy a thing to change the sense of the people as it is to misrepresent it, and to change their cry. Now that Christ was in the hands of his enemies his friends were shy and silent, and disappeared, and those that were against him were forward to show themselves so; and this gave the chief priests an opportunity to represent it as the concurring vote of all the Jews that he should be crucified. In this outcry they sought two things: — (1.) To blacken the prisoner as an enemy to Caesar. He had refused the kingdoms of this world and the glory of them, had declared his kingdom not to be of this world, and yet they will have it that he *speaks against Caesar; antilegei — he opposed Caesar,* invades his dignity and sovereignty. It has always been the artifice of the enemies of religion to represent it as hurtful to kings and provinces, when it would be highly beneficial to both. (2.) To frighten the judge, as no friend to Caesar: "If thou *let this man go* unpunished, and let him go on, *thou art not Caesar's friend,* and therefore false to thy trust and the duty of thy place, obnoxious to the emperor's displeasure, and liable to be turned out." They intimate a threatening that they would inform against him, and get him displaced; and here they touched him in a sensible and very tender part. But, of all people, these Jews should not have pretended a concern for Caesar, who were themselves so ill affected to him and his government. They should not talk of being friends to Caesar, who were themselves such back friends to him; yet thus a pretended zeal for that which is good often serves to cover a real malice against that which is better.

3. When other expedients had been tried in vain, Pilate slightly endeavoured to banter them out of their fury, and yet, in doing this, betrayed himself to them, and yielded to the rapid stream, *v.* 13–15. After he had stood it out a great while, and seemed now as if he would have made a vigorous resistance upon this attack (*v.* 12), he basely surrendered. Observe here,

(1.) What it was that shocked Pilate (*v.* 13): *When he heard that saying,* that he could not be true to Caesar's honour, nor sure of Caesar's favour, if he did not put Jesus to death, then he thought it was time to look about him. All they had said to prove Christ a malefactor, and that therefore it was Pilate's duty to condemn him, did not move him, but he still kept to his conviction of Christ's innocency; but, when they urged that it was his interest to condemn him, then he began to yield. Note, Those that bind up their happiness in the favour of men make themselves an easy prey to the temptations of Satan.

(2.) What preparation was made for a definitive sentence upon this matter: *Pilate brought Jesus forth,* and he himself in great state took the chair. We may suppose that he called for his robes, that he might look big, and then *sat down in the judgment-seat.*

[1.] Christ was condemned with all the ceremony that could be. *First,* To bring us off at God's bar, and that all believers through Christ, being judged here, might be acquitted in the court of heaven. *Secondly,* To take off the terror of pompous trials, which his followers would be brought to for his sake. Paul might the better stand at Caesar's judgment-seat when his Master had stood there before him.

[2.] Notice is here taken of the place and time.

First, The place where Christ was condemned: in a *place called the Pavement, but in Hebrew, Gabbatha,* probably the place where he used to sit to try causes or criminals. Some make *Gabbatha* to signify an *enclosed place,* fenced against the insults of the people, whom therefore he did the less need to fear; others an *elevated place,* raised that all might see him.

Secondly, The time, *v.* 14. It was the preparation of the passover, and *about the sixth hour.* Observe, 1. The day: It was the preparation of the passover, that is, for the passover-sabbath, and the solemnities of that and the rest of the days of the feast of unleavened bread. This is plain from Lu. 23:54, *It was the preparation, and the sabbath drew on.* So that this preparation was for the sabbath. Note, Before the passover there ought to be preparation. This is mentioned as an aggravation of their sin, in persecuting Christ with so much malice and fury, that it was when they should have been purging out the old leaven, to get ready for the passover; but the better the day the worse the deed. 2. The hour: *It was about the sixth hour.* Some ancient Greek and Latin manuscripts read it about the third hour, which agrees with Mk. 15:25. And it appears by Mt. 27:45 that he was upon the cross before the sixth hour. But it should seem to come in here, not as a precise determination of the time, but as an additional aggravation of the sin of his prosecutors, that they were pushing on the prosecution, not only on a solemn day, the *day of the preparation,* but, from the third to the sixth hour (which was, as we call it, church-time) on that day, they were employed in this wickedness; so that for this day, though they were priests, they dropped the temple-service, for they did not leave Christ till the sixth hour, when the darkness began, which frightened them away. Some think that the sixth hour, with this evangelist, is, according to the Roman reckoning and ours, six of the clock in the morning, answering to the Jews' first hour of the day; this is very probable, that Christ's trial before Pilate was at the height about six in the morning, which was then a little after sun-rising.

(3.) The rencounter Pilate had with the Jews, both priests and people, before he proceeded to give judgment, endeavouring in vain to stem the tide of their rage.

[1.] He saith unto the Jews, *Behold your king.* This is a reproof to them for the absurdity and malice of their insinuating that this Jesus made himself a king: *"Behold your king,* that is, him whom you accuse as a pretender to the crown. Is this a man likely to be dangerous to the government? I am satisfied he is not, and you may be so too, and let him alone." Some think he hereby upbraids them with their secret disaffection to Caesar: "You would have this man to be your king, if he would but have headed a rebellion against Caesar." But Pilate, though he was far from meaning so, seems as if he were the voice of God to them. Christ, now crowned with thorns, is, as a king at his coronation, offered to the people: *"Behold your king,* the king whom God hath set upon his holy hill of Zion;" but they, instead of entering into it with acclamations of joyful consent, protest against him; they will not have a king of God's choosing.

[2.] They cried out with the greatest indignation, *Away with him, away with him,* which speaks disdain as well as malice, *aron, aron — "Take him,* he is none of ours; we disown him for our kinsman, much more for our king; we have not only no veneration for him, but no compassion; *away with him* out of our sight:" for so it was written of him, he is one *whom the nation abhors* (Isa. 49:7), and they *hid as it were their faces from him* Isa. 53:2, 3. *Away with him from the earth,* Acts 22:22. This shows, *First,* How we deserved to have been treated at God's tribunal. We were by sin become odious to God's holiness, which cried, *Away with them, away with them,* for God is *of purer eyes than to behold iniquity.* We were also become obnoxious to God's justice, which cried against us, *"Crucify them, crucify them,* let the sentence of the law be executed." Had not Christ interposed, and been thus rejected of men, we had been for ever rejected of God. *Secondly,* It shows how we ought to treat our sins. We are often in scripture said to crucify sin, in conformity to Christ's death. Now they that crucified Christ did it with detestation. With a pious indignation we should run down sin in us, as they with an impious indignation ran him down who was made sin for us. The true penitent casts away from him his transgressions, *Away with them, away with them* (Isa. 2:20; 30:22), *crucify them, crucify them;* it is not fit that they should live in my soul, Hos. 14:8.

[3.] Pilate, willing to have Jesus released, and yet that it should be their doing, asks them, *Shall I crucify your king?* In saying this, he designed either, *First,* To stop their mouths, by showing them how absurd it was for them to reject one who offered himself to them to be their king at a time when they needed one more than ever. Have they no sense of slavery? No desire of liberty? No value for a deliverer? Though he saw no cause to fear him, they might see cause to hope for something from him; since crushed and sinking interests are ready to catch at any thing. Or, *Secondly,* To stop the mouth of his own conscience. "If this Jesus be a king" (thinks Pilate), "he is only kin of the Jews, and therefore I have nothing to do but to make a fair tender of him to them; if they refuse him, and will have their king crucified, what is that to me?" He banters them for their folly in expecting a Messiah, and yet running down one that bade so fair to be he.

[4.] The chief priests, that they might effectually renounce Christ, and engage Pilate to crucify him, but otherwise sorely against their will, cried out, *We have no king but Caesar.* This they knew would please Pilate, and so they hoped to carry their point, though at the same time they hated Caesar and his government. But observe here, *First,* What a plain indication this is that the time for the Messiah to appear, even the set time, was now come; for, if the Jews have no king but Caesar, then is the *sceptre departed from Judas, and the lawgiver from between his feet,* which should never be till Shiloh come to set up a spiritual kingdom. And, *Secondly,* What a righteous thing it was with God to bring upon them that ruin by the Romans which followed not long after. 1. They adhere to Caesar, and to Caesar they shall go. God soon gave them enough of their Caesars, and, according to Jotham's parable, since the trees choose the bramble for their king, rather than the vine and the olive, an evil spirit is sent among them, for they could not do it truly and sincerely, Jdg. 9:12, 19. Henceforward they were rebels to the Caesars, and the Caesars tyrants to them, and their disaffection ended in the overthrow of their place and nation. It is just with God to make that a scourge and plague to us which we prefer before Christ. 2. They would have no other king than Caesar, and never have they had any other to this day, but have now *abode many days without a king, and without a prince* (Hos. 3:4), without any of their own, but the kings of the nations have ruled over them; since they will have no king but Caesar, so shall their doom be, themselves have decided it.

Verses 16–18

We have here sentence of death passed upon our Lord Jesus, and execution done soon after. A mighty struggle Pilate had had within him between his convictions and his corruptions; but at length his convictions yielded, and his corruptions prevailed, the fear of man having a greater power over him than the fear of God.

I. *Pilate gave judgment* against Christ, and signed the warrant for his execution, *v.* 16. We may see here, 1. How Pilate sinned against his conscience: he had again and again pronounced him innocent, and yet at last condemned him as guilty. Pilate, since he came to be governor, had in many instances disobliged and exasperated the Jewish nation; for he was a man of a haughty and implacable spirit, and extremely wedded to his humour. He had seized upon the Corban, and spent it upon a water-work; he had brought into Jerusalem shields stamped with Caesar's image, which was very provoking to the Jews; he had sacrificed the lives of many to his resolutions herein. Fearing therefore that he should be complained of for these and other insolences, he was willing to gratify the Jews. Now this makes the matter much worse. If he had been of an easy, soft, and pliable disposition, his yielding to so strong a stream had been the more excusable; but for a man that was so wilful in other things, and of so fierce a resolution, to be overcome in a thing of this nature, shows him to be a bad man indeed, that could better bear the wronging of his conscience than the crossing of his humour. 2. How he endeavoured to transfer the guilt upon the Jews. He *delivered him* not to his own officers (as usual), but to the prosecutors, the chief priests and elders; so excusing the wrong to his own conscience with this, that it was but a permissive condemnation, and that he did not put Christ to death, but only connived at those that did it. 3. How Christ was *made sin for us.* We deserved to have been condemned, but Christ was condemned for us, that to us there might be *no condemnation.* God was now entering into judgment with his Son, that he might not enter into judgment with his servants.

II. Judgment was no sooner given than with all possible expedition the prosecutors, having gained their point, resolved to lose not time lest Pilate should change his mind, and order a reprieve (those are enemies to our souls, the worst of enemies, that hurry us to sin, and then leave us no room to undo what we have done amiss), and also lest there should be *an uproar among the people,* and they should find a greater number against them than they had with so much artifice got to be for them. It were well if we would be thus expeditious in that which is good, and not stay for more difficulties.

1. They immediately hurried away the prisoner. The chief priests greedily flew upon the prey which they had been long waiting for; now it is drawn into their net. Or *they,* that is, the soldiers who were to attend the execution, they took him and led him away, not to the place whence he came, and thence to the place of execution, as is usual with us, but directly to the place of execution. Both the priests and the soldiers joined in leading him away. Now was the *Son of man delivered into the hands of men,* wicked and unreasonable men. By the law of Moses (and in appeals by our law) the prosecutors were to be the executioners, Deu. 17:7. And the priests here were proud of the office. His being *led away* does not suppose him to have made any opposition, but *the scripture must be fulfilled,* he was *led as a sheep to the slaughter,* Acts 8:32. We deserved to have been *led forth with the workers of iniquity* as criminals to execution, Ps. 125:5. But he was led forth for us, that we might escape.

2. To add to his misery, they obliged him as long as he was able, to carry his cross (*v.* 17), according to the custom among the Romans; hence *Furcifer* was among them a name of reproach. Their crosses did not stand up constantly, as our gibbets do in the places of execution, because the malefactor was nailed to the cross as it lay along upon the ground, and then it was lifted up, and fastened in the earth, and removed when the execution was over, and commonly buried with the body; so that every one that was crucified had a cross of his own. Now Christ's carrying his cross may be considered, (1.) As a part of his sufferings; he endured the cross literally. It was a long and thick piece of timber that was necessary for such a use, and some think it was neither seasoned nor hewn. The blessed body of the Lord Jesus was tender, and unaccustomed to such burdens; it had now lately been harassed and tired out; his shoulders were sore with the stripes they had given him; every jog of the cross would renew his smart, and be apt to strike the thorns he was crowned with into his head; yet all this he patiently underwent, and it was but the *beginning of sorrows.* (2.) As answering the type which went before him; Isaac, when he was to be offered, carried the wood on which he was to be bound and with which he was to be burned. (3.) As very significant of his undertaking, the Father having *laid upon him the iniquity of us all* (Isa. 53:6), and he having to *take away sin* by *bearing it in his own body upon the tree,* 1 Pt. 2:24. He had said in effect, *On me be the curse;* for he was made a curse for us, and therefore on him was the cross. (4.) As very instructive to us. Our Master hereby taught all his disciples to take up their cross, and follow him. Whatever cross he calls us out to bear at any time, we must remember that he bore the cross first, and, by bearing it for us, bears it off from us in great measure, for thus he hath made *his yoke easy, and his burden light.* He bore that end of the cross that had the curse upon it; this was the heavy end; and hence all that are his are enabled to call their afflictions for him *light,* and *but for a moment.*

3. They brought him to the place of execution: He *went forth,* not dragged against his will, but voluntary in his sufferings. He went forth out of the city, for he was *crucified without the gate,* Heb. 13:12. And, to put the greater infamy upon his sufferings, he was brought to the common place of execution, as one in all points *numbered among the transgressors,* a place called *Golgotha, the place of a skull,* where they threw dead men's skulls and bones, or where the heads of beheaded malefactors were left, — a place *ceremonially unclean;* there Christ suffered, because he was *made sin for us,* that he might *purge our consciences from dead works,* and the pollution of them. If one would take notice of the traditions of the elders, there are two which are mentioned by many of the ancient writers concerning this place: — (1.) That Adam was buried here, and that this was the place of his skull, and they observe that where death triumphed over the first Adam there the second Adam triumphed over him. Gerhard quotes for this tradition Origen, Cyprian, Epiphanius, Austin, Jerome, and others. (2.) That this was that mountain in the land of Moriah on which Abraham offered up Isaac, and the ram was a ransom for Isaac.

4. There they crucified him, and the other malefactors with him (*v.* 18): *There they crucified him.* Observe (1.) What death Christ died; the death of the cross, a bloody, painful, shameful death, a cursed death. He was nailed to the cross, as a sacrifice bound to the altar, as a Saviour fixed for his undertaking; his ear nailed to God's door-post, to serve him for ever. He was lifted up as the brazen serpent, hung between heaven and earth because we were unworthy of either, and abandoned by both. His hands were stretched out to invite and embrace us; he hung upon the tree some hours, dying gradually in the full use of reason and speech, that he might actually resign himself a sacrifice. (2.) In what company he died: *Two others with him.* Probably these would not have been executed at that time, but at the request of the chief priests, to add to the disgrace of our Lord Jesus, which might be the reason why one of them reviled him, because their death was hastened for his sake. Had they taken two of his disciples, and crucified them with him, it had been an honour to him; but, if such as they had been partakers with him in suffering, it would have looked as if they had been undertakers with him in satisfaction. Therefore it was ordered that his fellow-sufferers should be the worst of sinners, that he might *bear our reproach,* and that the merit might appear to be his only. This exposed him much to the people's contempt and hatred, who are apt to judge of persons by the lump, and are not curious in distinguishing, and would conclude him not only malefactor because he was yoked with malefactors, but the worst of the three because put in the midst. But thus the scripture was fulfilled, *He was numbered among the transgressors.* He did not die at the altar among the sacrifices, nor mingle his blood with that of bulls and goats; but he died among the criminals, and mingled his blood with theirs who were sacrificed to public justice.

And now let us pause awhile, and with an eye of faith look upon Jesus. Was ever sorrow like unto his sorrow? See him who was clothed with glory stripped of it all, and clothed with shame — him who was the *praise of angels* made a *reproach of men* — him who had been with eternal delight and joy in the bosom of his Father now in the extremities of pain and agony. See him bleeding, see him struggling, see him dying, see him and love him, love him and live to him, and study what we shall render.

Verses 19–30

Here are some remarkable circumstances of Christ's dying more fully related than before, which those will take special notice of who covet to know Christ and him crucified.

I. The title set up over his head. Observe,

1. The inscription itself which Pilate wrote, and ordered to be fixed to the top of the cross, declaring the cause for which he was crucified, *v.* 19. Matthew called it, ***aitia*** *— the accusation;* Mark and Luke called it *epigraphē — the inscription;* John calls it by the proper Latin name, ***titlos*** *— the title:* and it was this, *Jesus of Nazareth, the King of the Jews,* Pilate intended this for his reproach, that he, being *Jesus of Nazareth,* should pretend to be king of the Jews, and set up in competition with Caesar, to whom Pilate would thus recommend himself, as very jealous for his honour and interest, when he would treat but a titular king, a king in metaphor, as the worst of malefactors; but God overruled this matter, (1.) That it might be a further testimony to the innocency of our Lord Jesus; for here was an accusation which, as it was worded, contained no crime. If this be all they have to lay to his charge, surely he has done nothing worthy of death or of bonds. (2.) That it might show forth his dignity and honour. This is Jesus a Saviour, *Nazōraios,* the blessed Nazarite, sanctified to God; this is the *king of the Jews, Messiah the prince,* the *sceptre* that *should rise out of Israel,* as Balaam had foretold; dying for the good of his people, as Caiaphas had foretold. Thus all these three bad men witnessed to Christ, though they meant not so.

2. The notice taken of this inscription (*v.* 20): *Many of the Jews read it,* not only those of Jerusalem, but those out of the country, and from other countries, strangers and proselytes, that came up to worship at the feast. Multitudes read it, and it occasioned a great variety of reflections and speculations, as men stood affected. Christ himself was set for a sign, a title. Here are two reasons why the title was so much read: — (1.) Because the place where Jesus was crucified, though without the gate, was yet *nigh the city,* which intimates that if it had been any great distance off they would not have been led, no not by their curiosity, to go and see it, and read it. It is an advantage to have the means of knowing Christ brought to our doors. (2.) Because it was written in Hebrew, and Greek, and Latin, which made it legible by all; they all understood one or other of these languages, and none were more careful to bring up their children to read than the Jews generally were. It likewise made it the more considerable; everyone would be curious to enquire what it was which was so industriously published in the three most known languages. In the Hebrew the oracles of God were

recorded; in Greek the learning of the philosophers; and in Latin the laws of the empire. In each of these Christ is proclaimed king, in whom are hid all the treasures of revelation, wisdom, and power. God so ordering it that this should be written in the three then most known tongues, it was intimated thereby that Jesus Christ should be a Saviour to all nations, and not to the Jews only; and also that every nation should hear *in their own tongue the wonderful works* of the Redeemer. Hebrew, Greek, and Latin, were the vulgar languages at that time in this part of the world; so that this is so far from intimating (as the Papists would have it) that the scripture is still to be retained in these three languages, that on the contrary it teaches us that the knowledge of Christ ought to be diffused throughout every nation in their own tongue, as the proper vehicle of it, that people may converse as freely with the scriptures as they do with their neighbours.

3. The offence which the prosecutors took at it, *v.* 21. They would not have it written, *the king of the Jews;* but that he said of himself, *I am the king of the Jews.* Here they show themselves, (1.) Very spiteful and malicious against Christ. It was not enough to have him crucified, but they must have his name crucified too. To justify themselves in giving him such bad treatment, they thought themselves concerned to give him a bad character, and to represent him as a usurper of honours and powers that he was not entitled to. (2.) Foolishly jealous of the honour of their nation. Though they were a conquered and enslaved people, yet they stood so much upon the punctilio of their reputation that they scorned to have it said that this was their king. (3.) Very impertinent and troublesome to Pilate. They could not but be sensible that they had forced him, against his mind, to condemn Christ, and yet, in such a trivial thing as this, they continue to tease him; and it was so much the worse in that, though they had charged him with pretending to be the king of the Jews, yet they had not proved it, nor had he ever said so.

4. The judge's resolution to adhere to it: *"What I have written I have written,* and will not alter it to humour them."

(1.) Hereby an affront was put upon the chief priests, who would still be dictating. It seems, by Pilate's manner of speaking, that he was uneasy in himself for yielding to them, and vexed at them for forcing him to it, and therefore he was resolved to be cross with them; and by this inscription he insinuates, [1.] That, notwithstanding their pretences, they were not sincere in their affections to Caesar and his government; they were willing enough to have a king of the Jews, if they could have one to their mind. [2.] That such a king as this, so mean and despicable, was good enough to be the king of the Jews; and this would be the fate of all that should dare to oppose the Roman power. [3.] That they had been very unjust and unreasonable in prosecuting this Jesus, when there was no fault to be found in him.

(2.) Hereby honour was done to the Lord Jesus. Pilate stuck to it with resolution, that he was the king of the Jews. What he had written was what God had first written, and therefore he could not alter it; for thus it was written, that Messiah the prince should be *cut off,* Dan. 9:26. This therefore is the true cause of his death; he dies because the king of Israel must die, must thus die. When the Jews reject Christ, and will not have him for their king, Pilate, a Gentile, sticks to it that he is a king, which was an earnest of what came to pass soon after, when the Gentiles submitted to the kingdom of the Messiah, which the unbelieving Jews had rebelled against.

II. The dividing of his garments among the executioners, *v.* 23, 24. Four soldiers were employed, who, *when they had crucified Jesus,* had nailed him to the cross, and lifted it up, and him upon it, and nothing more was to be done than to wait his expiring through the extremity of pain, as, with us, when the prisoner is turned off, then they went to make a dividend of his clothes, each claiming an equal share, and so they *made four parts,* as nearly of the same value as they could, *to every soldier a part;* but *his coat,* or upper garment whether cloak or gown, being a pretty piece of curiosity, *without seam, woven from the top throughout,* they agreed to *cast lots for it.* Here observe, 1. The shame they put upon our Lord Jesus, in stripping him of his garments before they crucified him. The shame of nakedness came in with sin. He therefore who was made sin for us bore that shame, to roll away our reproach. He was stripped, that we might be clothed with *white raiment* (Rev. 3:18), and that when we are unclothed *we may not be found naked.* 2. The wages with which these soldiers paid themselves for crucifying Christ. They were willing to do it for his old clothes. Nothing is to be done so bad, but there will be found men bad enough to do it for a trifle. Probably they hoped to make more than ordinary advantage of his clothes, having heard of cures wrought by the touch of the hem of his garment, or expecting that his admirers would give any money for them. 3. The sport they made about his seamless coat. We read not of any thing about him valuable or remarkable but this, and this not for the richness, but only the variety of it, for it was *woven from the top throughout;* there was no curiosity therefore in the shape, but a designed plainness. Tradition says, his mother wove it for him, and adds this further, that it was made for him when he was a child, and, like the Israelites' clothes in the wilderness, *waxed not old;* but this is a groundless fancy. The soldiers thought it a pity to rend it, for then it would unravel, and a piece of it would be good for nothing; they would *therefore cast lots for it.* While Christ was in his dying agonies, they were merrily dividing his spoils. The preserving of Christ's seamless coat is commonly alluded to to show the care all Christians ought to take that they rend not the church of Christ with strifes and divisions; yet some have observed that the reason why the soldiers would not rend Christ's coat was not out of any respect to Christ, but because each of them hoped to have it entire for himself. And so many cry out against schism, only that they may engross all the wealth and power to themselves. Those who opposed Luther's separation from the church of Rome urged much the *tunica inconsutilis — the seamless coat;* and some of them laid so much stress upon it that they were called the *Inconsutilistae — The seamless.* 4. The fulfilling of the scripture in this. David, in spirit, foretold this very circumstance of Christ's sufferings, in that passage, Ps. 22:18. The event so exactly answering the prediction proves, (1.) That *the scripture* is the word of God, which foretold contingent events concerning Christ so long before, and they came to pass according to the prediction. (2.) That Jesus is the true Messiah; for in him all the Old-Testament prophecies concerning the Messiah had, and have, their full accomplishment. *These things therefore the soldiers did.*

III. The care that he took of his poor mother.

1. His mother attends him to his death (*v.* 25): *There stood by the cross,* as near as they could get, *his mother,* and some of his relations and friends with her. At first, they stood near, as it is said here; but afterwards, it is probable, the soldiers forced them to stand afar off, as it is said in Matthew and Mark: or they themselves removed out of the ground. (1.) See here the tender affection of these pious women to our Lord Jesus in his sufferings. When all his disciples, except John, has forsaken him, they continued their attendance on him. Thus *the feeble were as David* (Zec. 12:8): they were not deterred by the fury of the enemy nor the horror of the sight; they could not rescue him nor relieve him, yet they attended him, to show their good-will. It is an impious and blasphemous construction which some of the popish writers put upon the virgin Mary standing by the cross, that thereby she contributed to the satisfaction he made for sin no less than he did, and so became a joint-mediatrix and co-adjutrix in our salvation. (2.) We may easily suppose what an affliction it was to these poor women to see him thus abused, especially to the blessed virgin. Now was fulfilled Simeon's word, *A sword shall pierce through thy own soul,* Lu. 2:35. His torments were her tortures; she was upon the rack, while he was upon the cross; and her heart bled with his wounds; and *the reproaches wherewith they reproached* him fell on those that attended him. (3.) We may justly admire the power of divine grace in supporting these women, especially the virgin Mary, under this heavy trial. We do not find his mother wringing her hands, or tearing her hair, or rending her clothes, or making an outcry; but, with a wonderful composure, *standing by the cross,* and her friends with her. Surely she and they were strengthened by a divine power to this degree of patience; and surely the virgin Mary had a fuller expectation of his resurrection than the rest had, which supported her thus. We know not what we can bear till we are tried, and then we know who has said, *My grace is sufficient for thee.*

2. He tenderly provides for his mother at his death. It is probable that Joseph, her husband, was long since dead, and that her son Jesus had supported her, and her relation to him had been her maintenance; and now that he was dying what would become of her? He saw her standing by, and knew her cares and griefs; and he saw John standing not far off, and so he settled a new relation between his beloved mother and his beloved disciple; for he said to her, *"Woman, behold thy son,* for whom henceforward thou must have a motherly affection;" and to him, *"Behold thy mother,* to whom thou must pay a filial duty." And so *from that hour,* that hour never to be forgotten, *that disciple took her to his own home.* See here,

(1.) The care Christ took of his dear mother. He was not so much taken up with a sense of his sufferings as to forget his friends, all whose concerns he bore upon his heart. His mother, perhaps, was so taken up with his sufferings that she thought not of what would become of her; but he admitted that thought. *Silver and gold he had none* to leave, no estate, real or personal; his clothes the soldiers had seized, and we hear no more of the bag since Judas, who had carried it, hanged himself. He had therefore no other way to provide for his mother than by his interest in a friend, which he does here. [1.] He calls her *woman,* not mother, not out of any disrespect to her, but because mother would have been a cutting word to her that was already wounded to the heart with grief; like Isaac saying to Abraham, *My father.* He speaks as one that was *now no more in this world,* but was already dead to those in it that were dearest to him. His speaking in this seemingly slight manner to his mother, as he had done formerly, was designed to obviate and give a check to the undue honours which he foresaw would be given to her in the Romish church, as if she were a joint purchaser with him in the honours of the Redeemer. [2.] He directs her to look upon John as her son: "Behold him as thy son, who stands there by thee, and be as a mother to him." See here, *First,* An instance of divine goodness, to be observed for our encouragement. Sometimes, when God removes one comfort from us, he raises up another for us, perhaps where we looked not for it. We read of children which the church shall have after she has lost the other, Isa. 49:21. Let none therefore reckon all gone with one cistern dried up, for from the same fountain another may be filled. *Secondly,* An instance of filial duty, to be observed for our imitation. Christ has here taught children to provide, to the utmost of their power, for the comfort of their aged parents. When David was in distress, he took care of his parents, and found out a shelter for them (1 Sa. 22:3); so the Son of David here. Children at their death, according to their ability, should provide for their parents, if they survive them, and need their kindness.

(2.) The confidence he reposed in the beloved disciple. It is to him he says, *Behold thy mother,* that is, I recommend her to thy care, be thou as a son to her to guide her (Isa. 51:18); and *forsake her not when she is old,* Prov. 23:22. Now, [1.] This was an honour put upon John, and a testimony both to his prudence and to his fidelity. If he who knows all things had not known that John loved him, he would not have made him his mother's guardian. It is a great honour to be employed for Christ, and to be entrusted with any of his interest in the world. But, [2.] It would be a care and some charge to John; but he cheerfully accepted it, *and took her to his own home,* not objecting the trouble nor expense, nor his obligations to his own family, nor the ill-will he might contract by it. Note, Those that truly love Christ, and are beloved of him, will be glad of an opportunity to do any service to him or his. *Nicephoras's Eccl. Hist. lib. 2 cap. 3,* saith that the virgin Mary lived with John at Jerusalem eleven years, and then died. Others, that she lived to remove with him to Ephesus.

IV. The fulfilling of the scripture, in the giving of him vinegar to drink, *v.* 28, 29. Observe,

1. How much respect Christ showed to the scripture (*v.* 28): *Knowing that all things* hitherto *were accomplished, that the scripture might be fulfilled,* which spoke of his drinking in his sufferings, *he saith, I thirst,* that is, he called for drink.

(1.) It was not at all strange that he was thirsty; we find him *thirsty* in a journey (*ch.* 4:6, 7), and now thirsty when he was just at his journey's end. Well might he thirst after all the toil and hurry which he had undergone, and being now in the agonies of death, ready to expire purely by the loss of blood and extremity of pain. The torments of hell are represented by a violent thirst in the complaint of the rich man that begged for a *drop of water to cool his tongue.* To that everlasting thirst we had been condemned, had not Christ suffered for us.

(2.) But the reason of his complaining of it is somewhat surprising; it is the only word he spoke that looked like complaint of his outward sufferings. When they scourged him, and crowned him with thorns, he did not cry, O my head! or, My back! But now he cried, *I thirst.* For, [1.] He would thus express *the travail of his soul,* Isa. 53:11. He thirsted after the glorifying of God, and the accomplishment of the work of our redemption, and the happy issue of his undertaking. [2.] He would thus take care to see the scripture fulfilled. Hitherto, all had been accomplished, and he knew it, for this was the thing he had carefully observed all along; and now he called to mind one thing more, which this was the proper season for the performance of. By this it appears that he was the Messiah, in that not only the scripture was punctually fulfilled in him, but it was strictly eyed by him. By this it appears *that God was with him of a truth* — that in all he did he went exactly according to the word of God, taking care *not to destroy, but to fulfil, the law and the prophets.* Now, *First,* The scripture had foretold his thirst, and therefore he himself related it, because it could not otherwise be known, saying, *I thirst;* it was foretold that his tongue should cleave to his jaws, Ps. 22:15. Samson, an eminent type of Christ, when he was laying *the Philistines heaps upon heaps,* was himself *sore athirst* (Jdg. 15:18); so was Christ, when he was upon the cross, *spoiling principalities and powers. Secondly,* The scripture had foretold that in his thirst he should have vinegar given him to drink, Ps. 69:21. They had given him vinegar to drink before they crucified him (Mt. 27:34), but the prophecy was not exactly fulfilled in that, because that was not in his thirst; therefore now he said, *I thirst,* and called for it again: then he would not drink, but now he received it Christ would rather court an affront than see any prophecy unfulfilled. This should satisfy us under all our trials, that the will of God is done, and the word of God accomplished.

2. See how little respect his persecutors showed to him (*v.* 29): *There was set a vessel full of vinegar,* probably according to the custom at all executions of this nature; or, as others think, it was now set designedly for an abuse to Christ, instead of the cup of wine which they used to give *to those that were ready to perish;* with this *they filled a sponge,* for they would not allow him a cup, *and they put it upon hyssop,* a hyssop-stalk, and with this heaved it to his mouth; *hyssōpō perithentes — they stuck it round with hyssop;* so it may be taken; or, as others, they mingled it with hyssop-water, and this they gave him to drink when he was thirsty; a drop of water would have cooled his tongue better than a draught of vinegar: yet this he submitted to for us. *We had taken the sour grapes,* and *thus his teeth were set on edge;* we had forfeited all comforts and refreshments, and therefore they were withheld from him. When heaven denied him a beam of light earth denied him a drop of water, and put vinegar in the room of it.

V. The dying word wherewith he breathed out his soul (*v.* 30): *When he had received the vinegar,* as much of it as he thought fit, *he said, It is finished;* and, with that, *bowed his head, and gave up the ghost.* Observe,

1. What he said, and we may suppose him to say it with triumph and exultation, *Tetelestai — It is finished,* a comprehensive word, and a comfortable one. (1.) *It is finished,* that is, the malice and enmity of his persecutors had now done their worst; *when he had received* that last indignity in *the vinegar they gave him, he said,* "This is the last; I am now going out of their reach, *where the wicked cease from troubling.*" (2.) *It is finished,* that is, the counsel and commandment of his Father concerning his sufferings were now fulfilled; it was a *determinate counsel,* and he took care to see every iota and tittle of it exactly answered, Acts 2:23. He had said, when he entered upon his sufferings, *Father, thy will be done;* and now he saith with pleasure, *It is done.* It was *his meat and drink to finish his work* (*ch.* 4:34), and the meat and drink refreshed him, when they gave him gall and vinegar. (3.) *It is finished,* that is, all the types and prophecies of the Old Testament, which pointed at the sufferings of the Messiah, were accomplished and answered. He speaks as if, now that *they had given him the vinegar,* he could not bethink himself of any word in the Old Testament that was to be fulfilled between him and his death but it had its accomplishment; such as, his being *sold for thirty pieces of silver, his hands and feet being pierced, his garments divided, etc.;* and now that this is done. *It is finished.* (4.) *It is finished,* that is, the ceremonial law is abolished, and a period put to the obligation of it. The substance is now come, and all the shadows are done away. Just now *the veil is rent, the wall of partition is taken down,* even *the law of commandments contained in ordinances,* Eph. 2:14, 15. The Mosaic economy is dissolved, *to make way for a better hope.* (5.) *It is finished,* that is, sin is finished, and an end made of transgression, by *the bringing in of an everlasting righteousness.* It seems to refer to Dan. 9:24. *The Lamb of God was sacrificed to take away the sin of the world,* and it is done, Heb. 9:26. (6.) *It is finished,* that is, his sufferings were now finished, both those of his soul and those of his body. The storm is over, the worst is past; all his pains and agonies are at an end, and he is just going to paradise, entering upon *the joy set before him.* Let all that *suffer for Christ,* and with Christ, comfort themselves with this, *that yet a little while* and they also shall say, *It is finished.* (7.) *It is finished,* that is, his life was now finished, he was just ready to breathe his last, and *now he is no more in this world, ch.* 17:11. This is like that of blessed Paul (2 Tim. 4:7), *I have finished my course,* my race is run, my glass is out, *mene, mene — numbered* and *finished.* This we must all come to shortly. (8.) *It is finished,* that is, the work of man's redemption and salvation is now completed, at least the hardest part of the undertaking is over; a full satisfaction is made to the justice of God, a fatal blow given to the power of Satan, a fountain of grace opened that shall ever flow, a foundation of peace and happiness laid that shall never fail. Christ had now gone through with his work, and *finished it, ch.* 17:4. For, *as for God, his work is perfect; when I begin,* saith he, *I will also make an end.* And, as in the purchase, so in the application of the redemption, *he that has begun a good work will perform it;* the mystery of God shall be finished.

2. What he did: *He bowed his head, and gave up the ghost.* He was voluntary in dying; for he was not only the sacrifice, but the priest and the offerer; and the *animus offerentis — the mind of the offerer,* was all in all in the sacrifice. Christ showed his will in his sufferings, *by which will we are sanctified.* (1.) *He gave up the ghost.* His life was not forcibly extorted from him, but freely resigned. He had said, *Father, into thy hands I commit my spirit,* thereby expressing the intention of this act. I give up myself as a *ransom for many;* and, accordingly, he did give up his spirit, paid down the price of pardon and life at his Father's hands. *Father, glorify thy name.* (2.) *He bowed his head.* Those that were crucified, in dying stretched up their heads to gasp for breath, and did not drop their heads till they had breathed their last; but Christ, to show himself active in dying, *bowed his head* first, composing himself, as it were, to fall asleep. God *had laid upon him the iniquity of us all,* putting it upon the head of this great sacrifice; and some think that by this bowing of his head he would intimate his sense of the weight upon him. See Ps. 38:4; 40:12. The bowing of his head shows his submission to his Father's will, and his obedience to death. He accommodated himself to his dying work, as Jacob, *who gathered up his feet into the bed, and then yielded up the ghost.*

Verses 31–37

This passage concerning the piercing of Christ's side after his death is recorded only by this evangelist.

I. Observe the superstition of the Jews, which occasioned it (*v.* 31): *Because it was the preparation for the sabbath, and that sabbath day,* because it fell in the passover-week, *was a high day,* that they might show a veneration for the sabbath, they would *not have the dead bodies to remain on the crosses on the sabbath-day,* but *besought Pilate that their legs might be broken,* which would be a certain, but cruel dispatch, and that then they might be buried out of sight. Note here, 1. The esteem they would be thought to have for the approaching sabbath, because it was one of the days of unleavened bread, and (some reckon) the day of the offering of the first-fruits. Every sabbath day is a holy day, and a good day, but this was a high day, *megalē hēmera — a great day.* Passover sabbaths are high days; sacrament-days, supper-days, communion-days are high days, and there ought to be more than ordinary preparation for them, that these may be high days indeed to us, *as the days of heaven.* 2. The reproach which they reckoned it would be to that day if the dead bodies should be left hanging on the crosses. Dead bodies were not to be left at any time (Deu. 21:23); yet, in this case, the Jews would have left the Roman custom to take place, had it not been an extraordinary day; and, many strangers from all parts being then at Jerusalem, it would have been an offence to them; nor could they well bear the sight of Christ's crucified body, for, unless their consciences were quite seared, when the heat of their rage was a little over, they would upbraid them. 3. Their petition to Pilate, that their bodies, now as good as dead, might be dispatched; not by strangling or beheading them, which would have been a compassionate hastening of them out of their misery, like the *coup de grace* (as the French call it) to those that are broken upon the wheel, *the stroke of mercy,* but by the breaking of their legs, which would carry them off in the most exquisite pain. Note, (1.) *The tender mercies of the wicked are cruel.* (2.) The pretended sanctity of hypocrites is abominable. These Jews would be thought to bear a great regard for the sabbath, and yet had not regard to justice and righteousness; they made no conscience of bringing an innocent and excellent person to the cross, and yet scrupled letting a dead body hang upon the cross.

II. The dispatching of *the two thieves that were crucified with him, v.* 32. Pilate was still gratifying the Jews, and gave orders as they desired; *and the soldiers came,* hardened against all impressions of pity, *and broke the legs of the two thieves,* which, no doubt, extorted from them hideous outcries, and made them die according to the bloody disposition of Nero, so as to feel themselves die. One of these thieves was a penitent, and had received from Christ an assurance that he should shortly be with him in paradise, and yet died in the same pain and misery that the other thief did; for *all things come alike to all.* Many go to heaven that *have bands in their death,* and *die in the bitterness of their soul.* The extremity of dying agonies is no obstruction to the living comforts that wait for holy souls on the other side death. Christ died, and went to paradise, but appointed a guard to convey him thither. This is the order of going to heaven — *Christ, the first-fruits* and forerunner, *afterwards those that are Christ's.*

III. The trial that was made whether Christ was dead or no, and the putting of it out of doubt.

1. They supposed him to be dead, and therefore *did not break his legs, v.* 33. Observe here, (1.) That Jesus died in less time than persons crucified ordinarily did. The structure of his body, perhaps, being extraordinarily fine and tender, was the sooner broken by pain; or, rather, it was to show that he laid down his life of himself, and could die when he pleased, though his hands were nailed. Though he yielded to death, yet he was not conquered. (2.) That his enemies were satisfied he was really dead. The Jews, who stood by to see the execution effectually done, would not have omitted this piece of cruelty, if they had not been sure he was got out of the reach of it. (3.) *Whatever devices are in men's hearts, the counsel of the Lord shall stand.* It was fully designed to break his legs, but, God's counsel being otherwise, see how it was prevented.

2. Because they would be sure he was dead they made such an experiment as would put it past dispute. *One of the soldiers with a spear pierced his side,* aiming at his heart, *and forthwith came thereout blood and water, v.* 34.

(1.) The soldier hereby designed to decide the question whether he was dead or no, and by this honourable wound in his side to supersede the ignominious method of dispatch they took with the other two. Tradition says that this soldier's name was *Longinus,* and that, having some distemper in his eyes, he was immediately cured of it, by some drops of blood that flowed out of Christ's side falling on them: significant enough, if we had any good authority for the story.

(2.) But God had a further design herein, which was,

[1.] To give an evidence of the truth of his death, in order to the proof of his resurrection. If he was only in a trance or swoon, his resurrection was a sham; but, by this experiment, he was certainly dead, for this spear broke up the very fountains of life, and, according to all the law and course of nature, it was impossible a human body should survive such a wound as this in the vitals, and such an evacuation thence.

[2.] To give an illustration of the design of his death. There was much of mystery in it, and its being solemnly attested (*v.* 35) intimates there was something miraculous in it, that *the blood and water* should come out distinct and separate from the same wound; at least it was very significant; this same apostle refers to it as a very considerable thing, 1 Jn. 5:6, 8.

First, the opening of his side was significant. When we would protest our sincerity, we wish there were a window in our hearts, that the thoughts and intents of them might be visible to all. Through this window, opened in Christ's side, you may look into his heart, and see love flaming there, love strong as death; see our names written there. Some make it an allusion to the opening of Adam's side in innocency. When Christ, the second Adam, was fallen into a deep sleep upon the cross, then was his side opened, and out of it was his church taken, which he espoused to himself. See Eph. 5:30, 32. Our devout poet, Mr. George Herbert, in his poem called *The Bag,* very affectingly brings in our Saviour, when his side was pierced, thus speaking to his disciples: —

If ye have any thing to send, or write
(I have no bag, but here is room),
Unto my Father's hands and sight
(Believe me) it shall safely come.
That I shall mind what you impart,
Look, you may put it very near my heart;
Or, if hereafter any of my friends
Will use me in this kind, the door
Shall still be open; what he sends
I will present, and somewhat more,
Not to his hurt. Sighs will convey
Any thing to me. Hark, Despair, away.

Secondly, The blood and water that flowed out of it were significant. 1. They signified the two great benefits which all believers partake of through Christ — justification and sanctification; blood for remission, water for regeneration; blood for atonement, water for purification. Blood and water were used very much under the law. Guilt contracted must be expiated by blood; stains contracted must be done away by *the water of purification.* These two must always go together. *You are sanctified, you are justified,* 1 Co. 6:11. Christ has joined them together, and we must not think to put them asunder. They both flowed from the pierced side of our Redeemer. To Christ crucified we owe both merit for our justification, and Spirit and grace for our sanctification; and we have as much need of the latter as of the former, 1 Co. 1:30. 2. They signified the two great ordinances of baptism and the Lord's supper, by which those benefits are represented, sealed, and applied, to believers; they both owe their institution and efficacy to Christ. It is not the water in the font that will be to us *the washing of regeneration,* but the water out of the side of Christ; not the blood of the grape that will pacify the conscience and refresh the soul, but the blood out of the side of Christ. Now was the rock smitten (1 Co. 10:4), now was the fountain opened (Zec. 13:1), now were the wells of salvation digged, Isa. 12:3. Here *is the river, the streams whereof make glad the city of our God.*

IV. The attestation of the truth of this by an eye-witness (*v.* 35), the evangelist himself. Observe,

1. What a competent witness he was of the matters of fact. (1.) What he bore record of he saw; he had it not by hearsay, nor was it only his own conjecture, but he was an eyewitness of it; it is *what we have seen and looked upon* (1 Jn. 1:1; 2 Pt. 1:16), and *had perfect understanding of,* Lu. 1:3. (2.) What he saw he faithfully bore record of; as a faithful witness, he told not only the truth, but the whole truth; and did not only attest it by word of mouth, but left it upon record in writing, *in perpetuam rei memoriam — for a perpetual memorial.* (3.) *His record is* undoubtedly *true;* for he wrote not only from his own personal knowledge and observation, but from the dictates of the Spirit of truth, that leads into all truth. (4.) He had himself a full assurance of the truth of what he wrote, and did not persuade others to believe that which he did not believe himself: *He knows that he saith true.* (5.) He *therefore* witnessed these things, *that we might believe;* he did not record them merely for his own satisfaction or the private use of his friends, but made them public to the world; not to please the curious nor entertain the ingenious, but to draw men to believe the gospel in order to their eternal welfare.

2. What care he showed in this particular instance. That we may be well assured of the truth of Christ's death, he saw his heart's blood, his life's blood, let out; and also of the benefits that flow to us from his death, signified by the blood and water which came out of his side. Let this silence the fears of weak Christians, and encourage their hopes, *iniquity shall not be their ruin,* for there came both water and blood out of Christ's pierced side, both to justify and sanctify them; and if you ask, How can we be sure of this? You may be sure, for *he that saw it bore record.*

V. The accomplishment of the scripture in all this (*v.* 36): *That the scripture might be fulfilled,* and so both the honour of the Old Testament preserved and the truth of the New Testament confirmed. Here are two instances of it together: —

1. The scripture was fulfilled in the preserving of his legs from being broken; therein that word was fulfilled, *A bone of him shall not be broken.* (1.) There was a promise of this made indeed to all *the righteous,* but principally pointing at *Jesus Christ the righteous* (Ps. 34:20): *He keepeth all his bones, not one of them is broken.* And David, in spirit, says, *All my bones shall say, Lord, who is like unto thee?* Ps. 35:10. (2.) There was a type of this in the paschal lamb, which seems to be specially referred to here (Ex. 12:46): *Neither shall you break a bone thereof;* and it is repeated (Num. 9:12), *You shall not break any bone of it;* for which law the will of the lawmaker is the reason, but the antitype must answer the type. *Christ our Passover is sacrificed for us,* 1 Co. 5:7. He is *the Lamb of God* (*ch.* 1:29), and, as the true passover, his bones were kept unbroken. This commandment was given concerning his bones, when dead, as of Joseph's, Heb. 11:22. (3.) There was a significancy in it; the strength of the body is in the bones. The Hebrew word for the bones signifies the strength, and therefore *not a bone of Christ must be broken,* to show that though *he be crucified in weakness* his strength to save is not at all broken. Sin breaks our bones, as it broke David's (Ps. 51:8); but it did not break Christ's bones; he stood firm under the burden, mighty to save.

2. *The scripture was fulfilled in the piercing of his side* (*v.* 37): *They shall look on me whom they had pierced;* so it is written, Zec. 12:10. And there the same that pours out the Spirit of grace, and can be no less than the God of the holy prophets, says, *They shall look upon me,* which is here applied to Christ, *They shall look upon him.* (1.) It is here implied that the Messiah shall be pierced; and here it had a more full accomplishment than in *the piercing of his hands and feet;* he was pierced by *the house of David* and *the inhabitants of Jerusalem, wounded in the house of his friends,* as it follows, Zec. 13:6. (2.) It is promised that *when the Spirit is poured out they shall look on him and mourn.* This was in part fulfilled when many of those that were his betrayers and murderers *were pricked to the heart,* and brought to believe in him; it will be further fulfilled, in mercy, *when all Israel shall be saved;* and, in wrath, when those who persisted in their infidelity shall *see him whom they have pierced, and wail because of him,* Rev. 1:7. But it is applicable to us all. We have all been guilty of piercing the Lord Jesus, and are all concerned with suitable affections to look on him.

Verses 38–42

We have here an account of the burial of the blessed body of our Lord Jesus. The solemn funerals of great men are usually looked at with curiosity; the mournful funerals of dear friends are attended with concern. Come and see an extraordinary funeral; never was the like! Come and see a burial that conquered the grave, and buried it, a burial that beautified the grave and softened it for all believers. *Let us turn aside now, and see this great sight.* Here is,

I. The body begged, *v.* 38. This was done by the interest of *Joseph of Ramah,* or *Arimathea,* of whom no mention is made in all the New-Testament story, but only in the narrative which each of the evangelists gives us of Christ's burial, wherein he was chiefly concerned. Observe, 1. The character of this Joseph. He was a disciple of Christ *incognito — in secret,* a better friend to Christ than he would willingly be known to be. It was his honour that he was a disciple of Christ; and some such there are, that are themselves great men, and unavoidably linked with bad men. But it was his weakness that he was so secretly, when he should have confessed Christ before men, yea, though he had lost his preferment by it. Disciples should openly own themselves, yet Christ may have many that are his disciples sincerely, though secretly; better secretly than not at all, especially if, like Joseph here, they grow stronger and stronger. Some who in less trials have been timorous, yet in greater have been very courageous; so Joseph here. He concealed his affection to Christ *for fear of the Jews,* lest they should put him out of the synagogue, at least out of the sanhedrim, which was all they could do. To Pilate the governor he *went boldly,* and yet *feared the Jews.* The impotent malice of those that can but censure, and revile, and clamour, is sometimes more formidable even to wise and good men than one would think. 2. The part he bore in this affair. He, having by his place access to Pilate, desired leave of him to dispose of the body. His mother and dear relations had neither spirit nor interest to attempt such a thing. His disciples were gone; if nobody appeared, the Jews or soldiers would bury him with the thieves; therefore God raised up this gentleman to interpose in it, that the scripture might be fulfilled, and the decorum owing to his approaching resurrection maintained. Note, When God has work to do he can find out such as are proper to do it, and embolden them for it. Observe it as an instance of the humiliation of Christ, that his dead body lay at the mercy of a heathen judge, and must be begged before it could be buried, and also that Joseph would not take the body of Christ till he had asked and obtained leave of the governor; for in those things wherein the power of the magistrate is concerned we must ever pay a deference to that power, and peaceably submit to it.

II. The embalming prepared, *v.* 39. This was done by Nicodemus, another person of quality, and in a public post. He brought a *mixture of myrrh and aloes,* which some think were bitter ingredients, to preserve the body, others fragrant ones, to perfume it. Here is. 1. The character of Nicodemus, which is much the same with that of Joseph; he was a secret friend to Christ, though not his constant follower. He at first *came to Jesus by night,* but now owned him publicly, as before, *ch.* 7:50, 51. That grace which at first is like a bruised reed may afterwards become like a strong cedar, and the trembling lamb *bold as a lion.* See Rom. 14:4. It is a wonder that Joseph and Nicodemus, men of such interest, did not appear sooner, and solicit Pilate not to condemn Christ, especially seeing him so loth to do it. Begging his life would have been a nobler piece of service than begging his body. But Christ would have none of his friends to endeavour to prevent his death when his hour was come. While his persecutors were forwarding the accomplishment of the scriptures, his followers must not obstruct it. 2. The kindness of Nicodemus, which was considerable, though of a different nature. Joseph served Christ with his interest, Nicodemus with his purse. Probably, they agreed it between them, that, while one was procuring the grant, the other should be preparing the spices; and this for expedition, because they were straitened in time. But why did they make this ado about Christ's dead body? (1.) Some think we may see in it the weakness of their faith. A firm belief of the resurrection of Christ on the third day would have saved them this care and cost, and have been more acceptable than all spices. Those bodies indeed to whom the grave is a long home need to be clad accordingly; but what need of such furniture of the grave for one that, like a wayfaring man, did but turn aside into it, to *tarry for a night or two?* (2.) However, we may plainly see in it the strength of their love. Hereby they showed the value they had for his person and doctrine, and that it was not lessened by the reproach of the cross. Those that had been so industrious to profane his crown, and lay his honour in the dust, might already see that they had imagined a vain thing; for, as God had done him honour in his sufferings, so did men too, even great men. They showed not only the charitable respect of committing his body to the earth, but the honourable respect shown to great men. This they might do, and yet believe and look for his resurrection; nay, this they might do in the belief and expectation of it. Since God designed honour for this body, they would put honour upon it. However, we must do our duty according as the present day and opportunity are, and leave it to God to fulfil his promises in his own way and time.

III. The body got ready, *v.* 40. They *took it* into some house adjoining, and, having washed it from blood and dust, *wound it in linen clothes* very decently, with the spices melted down, it is likely, into an ointment, as *the manner of the Jews is to bury,* or to *embalm* (so Dr. Hammond), as we sear dead bodies. 1. Here was care taken of Christ's body: It was *wound in linen clothes.* Among clothing that belongs to us, Christ put on even the grave-clothes, to make them easy to us, and to enable us to call them our wedding-clothes. They wound the body *with the spices,* for *all his garments,* his grave-clothes not excepted, *smell of myrrh and aloes* (the spices here mentioned) *out of the ivory palaces* (Ps. 45:8), and an ivory palace the sepulchre hewn out of a rock was to Christ. Dead bodies and graves are noisome and offensive; hence sin is compared to a *body of death* and an *open sepulchre;* but Christ's sacrifice, being to God as a sweet-smelling savour, hath taken away our pollution. No ointment or perfume can rejoice the heart so as the grave of our Redeemer does, where there is faith to perceive the fragrant odours of it. 2. In conformity to this example, we ought to have regard to the dead bodies of Christians; not to enshrine and adore their relics, no, not those of the most eminent saints and martyrs (nothing like that was done to the dead body of Christ himself), but carefully to deposit them, the dust in the dust, as those who believe that the dead bodies of the saints are still united to Christ and designed for glory and immortality at the last day. The resurrection of the saints will be in virtue of Christ's resurrection, and therefore in burying them we should have an eye to Christ's burial, for he, being dead, thus speaketh. *Thy dead men shall live,* Isa. 26:19. In burying our dead it is not necessary that in all circumstances we imitate the burial of Christ, as if we must be buried in linen, and in a garden, and be embalmed as he was; but his being buried after *the manner of the Jews* teaches us that in things of this nature we should conform to the usages of the country where we live, except in those that are superstitious.

IV. The grave pitched upon, in a garden which belonged to Joseph of Arimathea, very near the place where he was crucified. There was a sepulchre, or vault, prepared for the first occasion, but not yet used. Observe,

1. That Christ was buried without the city, for thus the manner of the Jews was to bury, not in their cities, much less in their synagogues, which some have thought better than our way of burying: yet there was then a peculiar reason for it, which does not hold now, because the touching of a grave contracted a ceremonial pollution: but now that the resurrection of Christ has altered the property of the grave, and done away its pollution for all believers, we need not keep at such a distance from it; nor is it incapable of a good improvement, to have the congregation of the dead in the church-yard, encompassing the congregation of the living in the church, since they also are dying, and in *the midst of life we are in death.* Those that would not superstitiously, but by faith, visit the holy sepulchre, must go forth out of the noise of this world.

2. That Christ was buried in a garden. Observe, (1.) That Joseph had his sepulchre in his garden; so he contrived it, that it might be a memento, [1.] To himself while living; when he was taking the pleasure of his garden, and reaping the products of it, let him think of dying, and be quickened to prepare for it. The garden is a proper place for meditation, and a sepulchre there may furnish us with a proper subject for meditation, and such a one as we are loth to admit in the midst of our pleasures. [2.] To his heirs and successors when he was gone. It is good to acquaint ourselves with the *place of our fathers' sepulchres;* and perhaps we might make our own less formidable if we made theirs more familiar. (2.) That in a sepulchre in a garden Christ's body was laid. In the garden of Eden death and the grave first received their power, and now in a garden they are conquered, disarmed, and triumphed over. In a garden Christ began his passion, and from a garden he would rise, and begin his exaltation. Christ fell to the ground *as a corn of wheat* (*ch.* 12:24), and therefore was sown in a garden among the seeds, for *his dew is as the dew of herbs,* Isa. 26:19. He is the *fountain of gardens,* Cant. 4:15.

3. That he was buried in a new sepulchre. This was so ordered (1.) For the honour of Christ; he was not a common person, and therefore must not mix with common dust He that was born from a virgin-womb must rise from a virgin-tomb. (2.) For the confirming of the truth of his resurrection, that it might not be suggested that it was not he, but some other that rose now, when many bodies of saints arose; or, that he rose by the power of some other, as the man that was raised by the touch of Elisha's bones, and not by his own power. He that has *made all things new* has new-made the grave for us.

V. The funeral solemnized (*v.* 42): *There laid they Jesus,* that is, the dead body of Jesus. Some think the calling of this *Jesus* intimates the inseparable union between the divine and human nature. Even this dead body was *Jesus — a Saviour,* for his death is our life; Jesus is still the same, Heb. 13:8. There they laid him because it was the preparation day.

1. Observe here the deference which the Jews paid to the sabbath, and to the day of preparation. Before the passover-sabbath they had a solemn day of preparation. This day had been ill kept by the chief priests, who called themselves the church, but was well kept by the disciples of Christ, who were branded as dangerous to the church; and it is often so. (1.) They would not put off the funeral till the sabbath day, because the sabbath is to be a day of holy rest and joy, with which the business and sorrow of a funeral do not well agree. (2.) They would not drive it too late on the day of preparation for the sabbath. What is to be done the evening before the sabbath should be so contrived that it may neither intrench upon sabbath time, nor indispose us for sabbath work.

2. Observe the convenience they took of an adjoining sepulchre; the sepulchre they made use of was *nigh at hand.* Perhaps, if they had had time, they would have carried him to Bethany, and buried him among his friends there. And I am sure he had more right to have been buried in the chief of the sepulchres of the sons of David than any of the kings of Judah had; but it was so ordered that he should be laid in a sepulchre nigh at hand, (1.) Because he was to lie there but awhile, as in an inn, and therefore he took the first that offered itself. (2.) Because this was a new sepulchre. Those that prepared it little thought who should handsel it; but the wisdom of God has reaches infinitely beyond ours, and he makes what use he pleases of us and all we have. (3.) We are hereby taught not to be over-curious in the place of our burial. Where the tree falls, why should it not lie? For Christ was buried in the sepulchre that was next at hand. It was faith in the promise of Canaan that directed the Patriarch's desires to be carried thither for a burying-place; but now, since that promise is superseded by a better, that care is over.

Thus without pomp or solemnity is the body of Jesus laid in the cold and silent grave. Here lies our surety under arrest for our debts, so that if he be released his discharge will be ours. Here is the Sun of righteousness set for awhile, to rise again in greater glory, and set no more. Here lies a seeming captive to death, but a real conqueror over death; for here lies death itself slain, and the grave conquered. *Thanks be to God, who giveth us the victory.*

CHAPTER 20

This evangelist, though he began not his gospel as the rest did, yet concludes it as they did, with the history of Christ' resurrection; not of the thing itself, for none of them describe how he rose, but of the proofs and evidences of it, which demonstrated that he was risen. The proofs of Christ's resurrection, which we have in this chapter, are I. Such as occurred immediately at the sepulchre. 1. The sepulchre found empty, and the graveclothes in good order (*v.* 1–10). 2. Two angels appearing to Mary Magdalene at the sepulchre (*v.* 11–13). 3. Christ himself appearing to her (*v.* 14–18). II. Such as occurred afterwards at the meetings of the apostles. 1. At one, the same day at evening that Christ rose, when Thomas was absent (*v.* 19–25). 2. At another, that day seven-night, when Thomas was with them (*v.* 26–31). What is related here is mostly what was omitted by the other evangelists.

Verses 1–10

There was no one thing of which the apostles were more concerned to produce substantial proof than the resurrection of their Master, 1. Because it was that which he himself appealed to as the last and most cogent proof of his being the Messiah. Those that would not believe other signs were referred to this sign of the prophet Jonas. And therefore enemies were most solicitous to stifle the notice of this, because it was put on this issue, and, if he be risen, they are not only murderers, but murderers of the Messiah. 2. Because it was upon this the performance of his undertaking for our redemption and salvation did depend. If he give his life a ransom, and do not resume it, it does not appear that his giving it was accepted as a satisfaction. If he be imprisoned for our debt, and lie by it, we are undone, 1 Co. 15:17. 3. Because he never showed himself alive after his resurrection to all the people, Acts 10:40, 41. We should have said, "Let his ignominious death be private, and his glorious resurrection public." But God's thoughts are not as ours; and he ordered it that his death should be public before the sun, by the same token that the sun blushed and hid his face upon it. But the demonstrations of his resurrection should be reserved as a favour for his particular friends, and by them be published to the world, that those might be blessed who have not seen, and yet have believed. The method of proof is such as gives abundant satisfaction to those who are piously disposed to receive the doctrine and law of Christ, and yet leaves room for those to object who are willingly ignorant and obstinate in their unbelief. And this is a fair trial, suited to the case of those who are probationers.

In these verses we have the first step towards the proof of Christ's resurrection, which is, that the sepulchre was found empty. *He is not here,* and, if so, they must tell us where he is or we conclude him risen.

I. Mary Magdalene, coming to the sepulchre, finds the *stone taken away.* This evangelist does not mention the other women that went with Mary Magdalene, but here only, because she was the most active and forward in this visit to the sepulchre, and in her appeared the most affection; and it was an affection kindled by a good cause, in consideration of the great things Christ had done for her. Much was forgiven her, therefore she loved much. She had shown her affection to him while he lived, attended his doctrine, ministered to him of her substance, Lu. 8:2, 3. It does not appear that she had any business now at Jerusalem, but to wait upon him for the women were not bound to go up to the feast, and probably she and others followed him the closer, as Elisha did Elijah, now that they knew their Master would shortly be *taken from their head,* 2 Ki. 2:1–6. The continued instances of her respect to him at and after his death prove the sincerity of her love. Note, Love to Christ, if it be cordial, will be constant. Her love to Christ was *strong as death,* the death of the cross, for it stood by that; *cruel as the grave,* for it made a visit to that, and was not deterred by its terrors.

1. She *came to the sepulchre,* to wash the dead body with her tears, for she *went to the grave, to weep there,* and to *anoint it with the ointment* she had prepared. The grave is a house that people do not care for making visits to. They that are *free among the dead* are *separated from the living;* and it must be an extraordinary affection to the person which will endear his grave to us. It is especially frightful to the weak and timourous sex. Could she, that had not strength enough to *roll away the stone,* pretend to such a presence of mind as to enter the grave? The Jews' religion forbade them to meddle any more than needs must with graves and dead bodies. In visiting Christ's sepulchre she exposed herself, and perhaps the disciples, to the suspicion of a design to *steal him away;* and what real service could she do him by it? But her love answers these, and a thousand such objections. Note, (1.) We must study to do honour to Christ in those things wherein yet we cannot be profitable to him. (2.) Love to Christ will take off the terror of death and the grave. If we cannot come to Christ but through that darksome valley, even in that, if we love him, we shall *fear no evil.*

2. She came as soon as she could, for she came, (1.) Upon the *first day of the week,* as soon as ever the sabbath was gone, longing, not to *sell corn* and to *set forth wheat* (as Amos 8:5), but to be at the sepulchre. Those that love Christ will take the first opportunity of testifying their respect to him. This was the first Christian sabbath, and she begins it accordingly with enquiries after Christ. She had spent the day before in commemorating the work of creation, and therefore rested; but now she is upon search into the work of redemption, and therefore makes a visit to Christ and him crucified. (2.) She came *early, while it was yet dark;* so early did she set out. Note, Those who would seek Christ so as to find him must seek him early; that is, [1.] Seek him solicitously, with such a care as even breaks the sleep; be up early for fear of missing him. [2.] Seek him industriously; we must deny ourselves and our own repose in pursuit of Christ. [3.] Seek him betimes, early in our days, early every day. *My voice shalt thou hear in the morning.* That day is in a fair way to be well ended that is thus begun. Those that diligently enquire after Christ *while it is yet dark* shall have such light given them concerning him as shall shine *more and more.*

3. She found the stone taken away, which she had seen *rolled to the door of the sepulchre.* Now this was, (1.) A surprise to her, for she little expected it. Christ crucified is the fountain of life. His grave is one of the wells of salvation; if we come to it in faith; though to a carnal heart it be a spring shut up, we shall find the stone rolled away (as Gen. 29:10) and free access to the comforts of it. Surprising comforts are the frequent encouragements of early seekers. (2.) It was the beginning of a glorious discovery; the Lord was risen, though she did not at first apprehend it so. Note, [1.] Those that are most constant in their adherence to Christ, and most diligent in their enquiries after him, have commonly the first and sweetest notices of the divine grace. Mary Magdalene, who followed Christ to the last in his humiliation, met him with the first in his exaltation. [2.] God ordinarily reveals himself and his comforts to us by degrees; to raise our expectations and quicken our enquiries.

II. Finding the stone taken away, she hastens back to Peter and John, who probably lodged together at that end of the town, not far off, and acquaints them with it: *"They have taken the Lord out of the sepulchre,* envying him the honour of such a decent burying-place, *and we know not where they have laid him,* nor where to find him, that we may pay him the remainder of our last respects." Observe here, 1. What a notion Mary had of the thing as it now appeared; she found the stone gone, looked into the grave, and saw it empty. Now one would expect that the first thought that offered itself would have been, Surely the Lord is risen; for whenever he had told them that he should be crucified, which she had now lately seen accomplished, he still subjoined in the same breath that *the third day he should rise again.* Could she feel the great earthquake that happened as she was coming to the sepulchre, or getting ready to come, and now see the grave empty, and yet have no thought of the resurrection enter into her mind? what, no conjecture, no suspicion of it? So it seems by the odd construction she puts upon the removing of the stone, which was very far fetched. Note, When we come to reflect upon our own conduct in a *cloudy and dark day,* we shall stand amazed at our dulness and forgetfulness, that we could miss of such thoughts as afterwards appear obvious, and how they could be so far out of the way when we had occasion for them. She suggested, *They have taken away the Lord;* either the chief priests have taken him away, to put him in a worse place, or Joseph and Nicodemus have, upon second thoughts, taken him away, to avoid the ill-will of the Jews. Whatever was her suspicion, it seems it was a great vexation and disturbance to her that the body was gone; whereas, if she had understood it rightly, nothing could be more happy. Note, Weak believers often make that the matter of their complaint which is really just ground of hope, and matter of joy. We cry out that this and the other creature-comfort are taken away, and we know not how to retrieve them, when indeed the removal of our temporal comforts, which we lament, is in order to the resurrection of our spiritual comforts, which we should rejoice in too. 2. What a narrative she made of it to Peter and John. She did not stand poring upon the grief herself, but acquaints her friends with it. Note, The communication of sorrows is one good improvement of the communion of saints. Observe, Peter, though he had denied his Master, had not deserted his Master's friends; by this appears the sincerity of his repentance, that he associated with the disciple whom Jesus loved. And the disciples' keeping up their intimacy with him as formerly, notwithstanding his fall, teaches us to restore those with a spirit of meekness that have been faulty. If God has received them upon their repentance, why should not we?

III. Peter and John go with all speed to the sepulchre, to satisfy themselves of the truth of what was told them, and to see if they could make any further discoveries, *v.* 3, 4. Some think that the other disciples were with Peter and John when the news came; for they *told these things to the eleven,* Lu. 24:9. Others think that Mary Magdalene told her story only to Peter and John, and that the other women told theirs to the other disciples; yet none of them went to the sepulchre but Peter and John, who were two of the first three of Christ's disciples, often distinguished from the rest by special favours. Note, It is well when those that are more honoured than others with the privileges of disciples are more active than others in the duty of disciples, more willing to take pains and run hazards in a good work. 1. See here what use we should make of the experience and observations of others. When Mary told them what she had seen, they would not in this sense take her word, but would go and see with their own eyes. Do others tell us of the comfort and benefit of ordinances? Let us be engaged thereby to make trial of them. Come and see how good it is to draw near to God. 2. See how ready we should be to share with our friends in their cares and fears. Peter and John hastened to the sepulchre, that they might be able to give Mary a satisfactory answer to her jealousies. We should not grudge any pains we take for the succouring and comforting of the weak and timorous followers of Christ. 3. See what haste we should make in a good work, and when we are going on a good errand. Peter and John consulted neither their ease nor their gravity, but ran to the sepulchre, that they might show the strength of their zeal and affection, and might lose no time. If we are in the way of God's commandments, we should run in that way. 4. See what a good thing it is to have good company in a good work. Perhaps neither of these disciples would have ventured to the sepulchre alone, but, being both together, they made no difficulty of it. See Eccl. 4:9. 5. See what a laudable emulation it is among disciples to strive which shall excel, which shall exceed, in that which is good. It was no breach of ill manners for John, though the younger, to out-run Peter, and get before him. We must do our best, and neither envy those that can do better, nor despise those that do as they can, though they come behind. (1.) He that got foremost in this race as *the disciple whom Jesus loved* in a special manner, and who therefore in a special manner loved Jesus. Note, Sense of Christ's love to us, kindling love in us to him again, will make us to excel in virtue. The love of Christ will constrain us more than any thing to abound in duty. (2.) He that was cast behind was Peter, who had denied his Master, and was in sorrow and shame for it, and this clogged

him as a weight; sense of guilt cramps us, and hinders our enlargement in the service of God. When conscience is offended we lose ground.

IV. Peter and John, having come to the sepulchre, prosecute the enquiry, yet improve little in the discovery.

1. John went no further than Mary Magdalene had done. (1.) He had the curiosity to look into the sepulchre, and saw it was empty. He *stooped down,* and *looked in.* Those that would find the knowledge of Christ must stoop down, and look in, must with a humble heart submit to the authority of divine revelation, and must *look wistly.* (2.) Yet he had not courage to go into the sepulchre. The warmest affections are not always accompanied with the boldest resolutions; many are swift to run religion's race that are not stout to fight her battles.

2. Peter, though he came last, went in first, and made a more exact discovery than John had done, *v.* 6, 7. Though John outran him, he did not therefore turn back, nor stand still, but made after him as fast as he could; and, while John was with much caution looking in, he came, and with great courage *went into the sepulchre.*

(1.) Observe here the boldness of Peter, and how God dispenses his gifts variously. John could out-run Peter, but Peter could out-dare John. It is seldom true of the same persons, what David says poetically of Saul and Jonathan, that they were *swifter than eagles,* and yet *stronger than lions,* 2 Sa. 1:23. Some disciples are quick, and they are useful to quicken those that are slow; others are bold, and they are useful to embolden those that are timorous; *diversity of gifts, but one Spirit.* Peter's venturing into the sepulchre may teach us, [1.] That those who in good earnest seek after Christ must not frighten themselves with bugbears and foolish fancies: "There is a lion in the way, a ghost in the grave." [2.] That good Christians need not be afraid of the grave, since Christ has lain in it; for to them there is nothing in it frightful; it is not the pit of destruction, nor are the worms in it never-dying worms. Let us therefore not indulge, but conquer, the fear we are apt to conceive upon the sight of a dead body, or being alone among the graves; and, since we must be dead and in the grave shortly, let us make death and the grave familiar to us, as our near kindred, Job 17:14. [3.] We must be willing to go through the grave to Christ; that way he went to his glory, and so must we. If we cannot see God's face and live, better die than never see it. See Job 19:25, etc.

(2.) Observe the posture in which he found things in the sepulchre. [1.] Christ had left his grave-clothes behind him there; what clothes he appeared in to his disciples we are not told, but he never appeared in his grave-clothes, as ghosts are supposed to do; no, he laid them aside, *First,* Because he arose to die no more; death was to have no more dominion over him, Rom. 6:9. Lazarus came out with his grave-clothes on, for he was to use them again; but Christ, rising to an immortal life, came out free from those incumbrances. *Secondly,* because he was going to be clothed with the robes of glory, therefore he lays aside these rags; in the heavenly paradise there will be no more occasion for clothes than there was in the earthly. The ascending prophet dropped his mantle. *Thirdly,* When we arise from the death of sin to the life of righteousness, we must leave our grave-clothes behind us, must put off all our corruptions. *Fourthly,* Christ left those in the grave, as it were, for our use if the grave be a bed to the saints, thus he hath sheeted that bed, and made it ready for them; and the napkin by itself is of use for the mourning survivors to *wipe away their tears.* [2.] The grave-clothes were found in very good order, which serves for an evidence that his body was not stolen away while men slept. Robbers of tombs have been known to take away the clothes and leave the body; but none [prior to the practices of modern resurrectionists] ever took away the body and left the clothes, especially when it was fine linen and new, Mk. 15:46. Any one would rather choose to carry a dead body in its clothes than naked. Or, if those that were supposed to have stolen it would have left the grave-clothes behind, yet it cannot be supposed they should find leisure to fold up the linen.

(3.) See how Peter's boldness encouraged John; now he took heart and ventured in (*v.* 8), and *he saw and believed;* not barely believed what Mary said, that the body was gone (no thanks to him to believe what *he* saw), but he began to believe that Jesus was risen to life again, though his faith, as yet, was weak and wavering.

[1.] John followed Peter in venturing. It should seem, he durst not have gone into the sepulchre if Peter had not gone

in first. Note, It is good to be emboldened in a good work by the boldness of others. The dread of difficulty and danger will be taken off by observing the resolution and courage of others. Perhaps John's quickness had made Peter run faster, and now Peter's boldness makes John venture further, than otherwise either the one or the other would have done; though Peter had lately fallen under the disgrace of being a deserter, and John had been advanced to the honour of a confidant (Christ having committed his mother to him), yet John not only associated with Peter, but thought it no disparagement to follow him.

[2.] Yet, it should seem, John got the start of Peter in believing. Peter saw and wondered (Lu. 24:12), but John saw and believed. A mind disposed to contemplation may perhaps sooner receive the evidence of divine truth than a mind disposed to action. But what was the reason that they were so slow of heart to believe? The evangelist tells us (*v.* 9), as yet they *knew not the scripture,* that is, they did not consider, and apply, and duly improve, what they knew of the scripture, that he must *rise again from the dead.* The Old Testament spoke of the resurrection of the Messiah; they believed him to be the Messiah; he himself had often told them that, according to the scriptures of the Old Testament, he should rise again; but they had not presence of mind sufficient by these to explain the present appearances. Observe here, *First,* How unapt the disciples themselves were, at first, to believe the resurrection of Christ, which confirms the testimony they afterwards gave with so much assurance concerning it; for, by their backwardness to believe it, it appears that they were not credulous concerning it, nor of those simple ones that believe every word. If they had had any design to advance their own interest by it, they would greedily have caught at the first spark of its evidence, would have raised and supported one another's expectations of it, and have prepared the minds of those that followed them to receive the notices of it; but we find, on the contrary, that their hopes were frustrated, it was to them as a strange thing, and one of the furthest things from their thoughts. Peter and John were so shy of believing it at first that nothing less than the most convincing proof the thing was capable of could bring them to testify it afterwards with so much assurance. Hereby it appears that they were not only honest men, who would not deceive others, but cautious men, who would not themselves be imposed upon. *Secondly,* What was the reason of their slowness to believe; because as yet they *knew not the scripture.* This seems to be the evangelist's acknowledgment of his own fault among the rest; he does not say, "For as yet Jesus had not appeared to them, had not shown them his hands and his side," but, "As yet he had not *opened their understandings to understand the scripture"* (Lu. 24:44, 45), for that is the *most sure word of prophecy.*

3. Peter and John pursued their enquiry no further, but desisted, hovering between faith and unbelief (*v.* 10): *The disciples went away,* not much the wiser, *to their own home, pros heautous — to their own friends and companions,* the rest of the disciples to their own lodgings, for homes they had none at Jerusalem. They went away, (1.) For fear of being taken up upon suspicion of a design to steal away the body, or of being charged with it now that it was gone Instead of improving their faith, their care is to secure themselves, to shift for their own safety. In difficult dangerous times it is hard even for good men to go on in their work with the resolution that becomes them. (2.) Because they were at a loss, and knew not what to do next, nor what to make of what they had seen; and, therefore, not having courage to stay at the grave, they resolve to go home, and wait till God shall *reveal even this unto them,* which is an instance of their weakness as yet. (3.) It is probable that the rest of the disciples were together; to them they return, to make report of what they had discovered and to consult with them what was to be done; and, probably, now they appointed their meeting in the evening, when Christ came to them. It is observable that before Peter and John came to the sepulchre an angel had appeared there, rolled away the stone, frightened the guard, and comforted the women; as soon as they were gone from the sepulchre, Mary Magdalene here sees two angels in the sepulchre (*v.* 12), and yet Peter and John come to the sepulchre, and go into it, and see none. What shall we make of this? Where were the angels when Peter and John were at the sepulchre, who appeared there before and after? [1.] Angels appear and disappear at pleasure, according to the orders and instructions given them. They may be, and

are really, where they are not visibly; nay, it should seem, may be visible to one and not to another, at the same time, Num. 22:23; 2 Ki. 6:17. How they make themselves visible, then invisible, and then visible again, it is presumption for us to enquire; but that they do so is plain from this story. [2.] This favour was shown to those who were early and constant in their enquiries after Christ, and was the reward of those that came first and staid last, but denied to those that made a transient visit. [3.] The apostles were not to receive their instructions from the angels, but from the Spirit of grace. See Heb. 2:5.

Verses 11–18

St. Mark tells us that Christ appeared first to Mary Magdalene (Mk. 16:9); that appearance is here largely related; and we may observe,

I. The constancy and fervency of Mary Magdalene's affection to the Lord Jesus, v. 11.

1. She staid at the sepulchre, when Peter and John were gone, because there her Master had lain, and there she was likeliest to hear some tidings of him. Note, (1.) Where there is a true love to Christ there will be a constant adherence to him, and a resolution with purpose of heart to cleave to him. This good woman, though she has lost him, yet, rather than seem to desert him, will abide by his grave for his sake, and continue in his love even when she wants the comfort of it. (2.) Where there is a true desire of acquaintance with Christ there will be a constant attendance on the means of knowledge. See Hos. 6:2, 3, *The third day he will raise us up;* and then shall we know the meaning of that resurrection, if we follow on to know, as Mary here.

2. She staid there weeping, and these tears loudly bespoke her affection to her Master. Those that have lost Christ have cause to weep; she wept at the remembrance of his bitter sufferings; wept for his death, and the loss which she and her friends and the country sustained by it; wept to think of returning home without him; wept because she did not now find his body. Those that seek Christ must *seek him sorrowing* (Lu. 2:48), must weep, not for him, but for themselves.

3. *As she wept, she looked into the sepulchre,* that her eye might affect her heart. When we are in search of something that we have lost we look again and again in the place where we last left it, and expected to have found it. She will look *yet seven times,* not knowing but that at length she may see some encouragement. Note, (1.) Weeping must not hinder seeking. Though she wept, she *stooped down and looked in.* (2.) Those are likely to seek and find that seek with affection, that seek in tears.

II. The vision she had of two angels in the sepulchre, v. 12. Observe here,

1. The description of the persons she saw. They were *two angels in white, sitting* (probably on some benches or ledges hewn out in the rock) one at *the head,* and the other at the *feet,* of the grave. Here we have,

(1.) Their nature. They were angels, messengers from heaven, sent on purpose, on this great occasion, [1.] To honour the Son and to grace the solemnity of his resurrection. Now that the Son of God was again to be brought into the world, the angels have a charge to attend him, as they did at his birth, Heb. 1:6. [2.] To comfort the saints; to speak good words to those that were in sorrow, and, by giving them notice that the Lord was risen, to prepare them for the sight of him.

(2.) Their number: *two,* not a *multitude of the heavenly host,* to sing praise, only two, to bear witness; for out of the mouth of two witnesses this word would be established.

(3.) Their array: They were *in white,* denoting, [1.] Their purity and holiness. The best of men *standing before the angels,* and compared with them, *are clothed in filthy garments* (Zec. 3:3), but angels are spotless; and glorified saints, when they come to be as the angels, shall *walk with Christ in white.* [2.] Their glory, and glorying, upon this occasion. The white in which they appeared represented the brightness of that state into which Christ was now risen.

(4.) Their posture and place: They sat, as it were, reposing themselves in Christ's grave; for angels, though they needed not a restoration, were obliged to Christ for their establishment. These angels went into the grave, to teach us not to be afraid of it, nor to think that our resting in it awhile will be any prejudice to our immortality; no, matters are so ordered that the grave is not much out of our way to heaven. It intimates likewise that angels are to be employed about

the saints, not only at their death, to carry their souls into Abraham's bosom, but at the great day, *to raise their bodies,* Mt. 24:31. These angelic guards (and angels are called *watchers* Dan. 4:23), keeping possession of the sepulchre, when they had frightened away the guards which the enemies had set, represents Christ's victory over the powers of darkness, routing and defeating them. Thus Michael and his angels are more than conquerors. Their sitting to face one another, one at his bed's head, the other at his bed's feet, denotes their care of the entire body of Christ, his mystical as well as his natural body, from head to foot; it may also remind us of the two cherubim, placed one at either end of the mercy-seat, looking one at another, Ex. 25:18. Christ crucified was the great propitiatory, at the head and feet of which were these two cherubim, not with flaming swords, to keep us from, but welcome messengers, to direct us to, the way of life.

2. Their compassionate enquiry into the cause of Mary Magdalene's grief (v. 13): *Woman, why weepest thou?* This question was, (1.) A rebuke to her weeping: "*Why weepest thou,* when thou has cause to rejoice?" Many of the floods of our tears would *dry away* before such a search as this into the fountain of them. *Why are thou cast down?* (2.) It was designed to show how much angels are concerned at the griefs of the saints, having a charge to minister to them for their comfort. Christians should thus sympathize with one another. (3.) It was only to make an occasion of informing her of that which would turn her mourning into rejoicing, would *put off her sackcloth, and gird her with gladness.*

3. The melancholy account she gives them of her present distress: *Because they have taken away* the blessed body I came to embalm, *and I know not where they have laid it.* The same story she had told, v. 2. In it we may see, (1.) The weakness of her faith. If she had had faith *as a grain of mustard-seed,* this mountain would have been removed; but we often perplex ourselves needlessly with imaginary difficulties, which faith would discover to us as real advantages. Many good people complain of the clouds and darkness they are under, which are the necessary methods of grace for the humbling of their souls, the mortifying of their sins, and the endearing of Christ to them. (2.) The strength of her love. Those that have a true affection for Christ cannot but be in great affliction when they have lost either the comfortable tokens of his love in their souls or the comfortable opportunities of conversing with him, and doing him honour, in his ordinances. Mary Magdalene is not diverted from her enquiries by the surprise of the vision, nor satisfied with the honour of it; but still she harps upon the same string: *They have taken away my Lord.* A sight of angels and their smiles will not suffice without a sight of Christ and God's smiles in him. Nay, the sight of angels is but an opportunity of pursuing her enquiries after Christ. All creatures, the most excellent, the most dear, should be used as means, and but as means, to bring us into acquaintance with God in Christ. The angels asked her, *Why weepest thou?* I have cause enough to weep, says she, for *they have taken away my Lord,* and, like Micah, *What have I more?* Do you ask, Why I weep? *My beloved has withdrawn himself, and is gone.* Note, None know, but those who have experienced it, the sorrow of a deserted soul, that has had comfortable evidences of the love of God in Christ, and hopes of heaven, but has now lost them, and walks in darkness; such a *wounded spirit who can bear?*

III. Christ's appearing to her while she was talking with the angels, and telling them her case. Before they had given her any answer, Christ himself steps in, to satisfy her enquiries, for God now speaketh to us by his Son; none but he himself can direct us to himself. Mary would fain know where her Lord is, and behold he is at her right hand. Note, 1. Those that will be content with nothing short of a sight of Christ shall be put off with nothing less. He never said to the soul that sought him, *Seek in vain.* "Is it Christ that thou wouldest have? Christ thou shalt have." 2. Christ, in manifesting himself to those that seek him, often outdoes their expectations. Mary longs to see the dead body of Christ, and complains of the loss of that, and behold she sees him alive. Thus he does for his praying people more than they are able to ask or think. In this appearance of Christ to Mary observe,

(1.) How he did at first conceal himself from her.

[1.] He stood as a common person, and she looked upon him accordingly, v. 14. She stood expecting an answer to her complaint from the angels; and either seeing the shadow, or hearing the tread, of some person behind her, she *turned herself back* from talking with the angels, and *sees Jesus himself standing,* the very person she was looking for, and yet she *knew not that it was Jesus.* Note, *First, The Lord is nigh unto them that are of a broken heart* (Ps. 34:18), nearer than they are aware. Those that seek Christ, though they do not see him, may yet be sure he is not far from them. *Secondly,* Those that diligently seek the Lord will turn every way in their enquiry after him. *Mary turned herself back,* in hopes of some discoveries. Several of the ancients suggest that Mary was directed to look behind her by the angels' rising up, and doing their obeisance to the Lord Jesus, whom they saw before Mary did; and that she looked back to see to whom it was they paid such a profound reverence. But, if so, it is not likely that she would have taken him for the gardener; rather, therefore, it was her earnest desire in seeking that made her turn every way. *Thirdly,* Christ is often near his people, and they are not aware of him. She *knew not that it was Jesus;* not that he appeared in any other likeness, but either it was a careless transient look she cast upon him, and, her eyes being full of care, she could not so well distinguish, or *they were holden, that she should not know him,* as those of the two disciples, Lu. 24:16.

[2.] He asked her a common question, and she answered him accordingly, v. 15.

First, The question he asked her was natural enough, and what any one would have asked her: "*Woman, why weepest thou? Whom seekest thou?* What business hast thou here in the garden so early? And what is all this noise and ado for?" Perhaps it was spoken with some roughness, as Joseph spoke to his brethren when he made himself strange, before he made himself known to them. It should seem, this was the first word Christ spoke after his resurrection: "*Why weepest thou? I am risen.*" The resurrection of Christ has enough in it to ally all our sorrows, to check the streams, and dry up the fountains, of our tears. Observe here, Christ takes cognizance, 1. Of his people's griefs, and enquires, *Why weep you?* He bottles their tears, and records them in his book. 2. Of his people's cares and enquires, *Whom seek you, and what would you have?* When he knows they are seeking him, yet he will know it from them; they must tell him whom they seek.

Secondly, The reply she made him is natural enough; she does not give him a direct answer, but, as if she should say, "Why do you banter me, and upbraid me with my tears? You know why I weep, and whom I seek;" and therefore, *supposing him to be the gardener,* the person employed by Joseph to dress and keep his garden, who, she thought, was come thither thus early to his work, she said, *Sir, if thou hast carried him hence, pray tell me where thou hast laid him, and I will take him away.* See here, 1. The error of her understanding. She supposed our Lord Jesus to be the gardener, perhaps because he asked what authority she had to be there. Note, Troubled spirits, in a cloudy and dark day, are apt to misrepresent Christ to themselves, and to put wrong constructions upon the methods of his providence and grace. 2. The truth of her affection. See how her heart was set upon finding Christ. She puts the question to every one she meets, like the careful spouse, *Saw you him whom my soul loveth?* She speaks respectfully to a gardener, and calls him *Sir,* in hopes to gain some intelligence from him concerning her beloved. When she speaks of Christ, she does not name him; but, *If thou have borne him hence,* taking it for granted that this gardener was full of thoughts concerning this Jesus as well as she, and therefore could not but know whom she meant. Another evidence of the strength of her affection was that, wherever he was laid, she would undertake to remove him. Such a body, with such a weight of spices about it, was much more than she could pretend to carry; but true love thinks it can do more than it can, and makes nothing of difficulties. She supposed this gardener grudged that the body of one that was ignominiously crucified should have the honour to be laid in his master's new tomb, and that therefore he had removed it to some sorry place, which he thought fitter for it. Yet Mary does not threaten to tell his master, and get him turned out of his place for it; but undertakes to find out some other sepulchre, to which he might be welcome. Christ needs not to stay where he is thought a burden.

(2.) How Christ at length made himself known to her, and, by a pleasing surprise, gave her infallible assurances of his resurrection. Joseph at length said to his brethren, *I am Joseph.* So Christ here to Mary Magdalene, now that he is entered upon his exalted state. Observe,

[1.] How Christ discovered himself to this good woman

that was seeking him in tears (*v.* 16): *Jesus saith unto her, Mary.* It was said with an emphasis, and the air of kindness and freedom with which he was wont to speak to her. Now he changed his voice, and spoke like himself, not like the gardener. Christ's way of making himself known to his people is by his word, his word applied to their souls, speaking to them in particular. When those whom God *knew by name* in the counsels of his love (Ex. 33:12) *are called by name* in the efficacy of his grace, then *he reveals his Son in them* as in Paul (Gal. 1:16), when Christ called to him by name, *Saul, Saul.* Christ's *sheep know his voice, ch.* 10:4. This one word, *Mary,* was like that to the disciples in the storm, *It is I.* Then the word of Christ does us good when we put our names into the precepts and promises. "In this Christ calls to me, and speaks to me."

[2.] How readily she received this discovery. When Christ said, "Mary, dost thou not know me? are you and I grown such strangers?" she was presently aware who it was, as the spouse (Cant. 2:8), *It is the voice of my beloved.* She turned herself, and said, *Rabboni, My Master.* It might properly be read with an interrogation, *"Rabboni? Is it my master?* Nay, but is it indeed?" Observe, *First,* The title of respect she gives Him: *My Master; didaskale — a teaching master.* The Jews called their doctors *Rabbies,* great men. Their critics tell us that *Rabbon* was with them a more honourable title than *Rabbi;* and therefore Mary chooses that, and adds a note of appropriation, *My great Master.* Note, Notwithstanding the freedom of communion which Christ is pleased to admit us to with himself, we must remember that he is our *Master,* and to be approached with a *godly fear. Secondly,* With what liveliness of affection she gives this title to Christ. *She turned* from the angels, whom she had in her eye, to look unto Jesus. We must take off our regards from all creatures, even the brightest and best, to fix them upon Christ, from whom nothing must divert us, and with whom nothing must interfere. When *she thought it had been the gardener,* she looked another way while speaking to him; but now that she knew the voice of Christ *she turned herself.* The soul that hears Christ's voice, and is turned to him, calls him, with joy and triumph, *My Master.* See with what pleasure those who love Christ speak of his authority over them. *My Master, my great Master.*

[3.] The further instructions that Christ gave her (*v.* 17): *"Touch me not,* but go and carry the news to the disciples."

First, He diverts her from the expectation of familiar society and conversation with him at this time: *Touch me not, for I am not yet ascended.* Mary was so transported with the sight of her dear Master that she forgot herself, and that state of glory into which he was now entering, and was ready to express her joy by affectionate embraces of him, which Christ here forbids at this time. 1. *Touch me not* thus at all, for I am to ascend to heaven. He bade the disciples touch him, for the confirmation of their faith; he allowed the women to take hold of his feet, and worship him (Mt. 28:9); but Mary, supposing that he was risen, as Lazarus was, to live among them constantly, and converse with them freely as he had done, upon that presumption was about to take hold of his hand with her usual freedom. This mistake Christ rectified; she must believe him, and adore him, as exalted, but must not expect to be familiar with him as formerly. See 2 Co. 5:16. He forbids her to dote upon his bodily presence, to set her heart on this, or expect its continuance, and leads her to the spiritual converse and communion which she should have with him after he was ascended to his Father; for the greatest joy of his resurrection was that it was a step towards his ascension. Mary thought, now that her Master was risen, he would presently set up a temporal kingdom, such as they had long promised themselves. "No," says Christ, "touch me not, with any such thought; think not to lay hold on me, so as to detain me here; for, though *I am not yet ascended, go to my brethren, and tell them, I am to ascend."* As before his death, so now after his resurrection, he still harps upon this, that he was going away, was *no more in the world;* and therefore they must look higher than his bodily presence, and look further than the present state of things. 2. *"Touch me not,* do not stay to touch me now, stay not now to make any further enquiries, or give any further expressions of joy, for *I am not yet ascended,* I shall not depart immediately, it may as well be done another time; the best service thou canst do now is to carry the tidings to the disciples; lose no time therefore, but go away with all speed." Note, Public service ought to be preferred before private satisfaction. *It is more blessed to give than to receive.* Jacob must let an angel go, when the day breaks, and it is time for him to look after his family. Mary must not stay to talk with her Master, but must carry his message; for it is a day of good tidings, which she must not engross the comfort of, but hand it to others. See that story, 2 Ki. 7:9.

Secondly, He directs her what message to carry to his disciples: *But go to my brethren, and tell them,* not only that I am risen (she could have told them that of herself, for she had seen him), but that *I ascend.* Observe,

a. To whom this message is sent: *Go to my brethren* with it; for he is not ashamed to call them so. (1.) He was now entering upon his glory, and was *declared to be the Son of God with* greater *power* than ever, yet he owns his disciples as his brethren, and expresses himself with more tender affection to them than before; he had called them friends, but never brethren till now. Though Christ be high, yet he is not haughty. Notwithstanding his elevation, he disdains not to own his poor relations. (*b.*) His disciples had lately carried themselves very disingenuously towards him; he had never seen them together since *they all forsook him and fled,* when he was apprehended; justly might he now have sent them an angry message: "Go to yonder treacherous deserters, and tell them, I will never trust them any more, or have any thing more to do with them." No, he forgives, he forgets, and does not upbraid.

b. By whom it is sent: by *Mary Magdalene, out of whom had been cast seven devils,* yet now thus favoured. This was her reward for her constancy in adhering to Christ, and enquiring after him; and a tacit rebuke to the apostles, who had not been so close as she was in attending on the dying Jesus, nor so early as she was in meeting the rising Jesus; she becomes an apostle to the apostles.

c. What the message itself is: *I ascend to my Father.* Two full breasts of consolation are here in these words: —

(*a.*) Our joint-relation to God, resulting from our union with Christ, is an unspeakable comfort. Speaking of that inexhaustible spring of light, life, and bliss, he says, He is *my Father, and our Father; my God, and your God.* This is very expressive of the near relation that subsists between Christ and believers: *he that sanctifieth, and those that are sanctified, are both one; for they agree in one,* Heb. 2:11. Here we have such an advancement of Christians, and such a condescension of Christ, as bring them very near together, so admirably well is the matter contrived, in order to their union. [*a.*] It is the great dignity of believers that *the Father of our Lord Jesus Christ* is, in him, *their Father.* A vast difference indeed there is between the respective foundations of the relation; he is Christ's Father by eternal generation, ours by a gracious adoption; yet even this warrants us to call him, as Christ did, *Abba, Father.* This gives a reason why Christ called them brethren, because his Father was their Father. Christ was now ascending to appear as an *advocate with the Father* — with *his Father,* and therefore we may hope he will prevail for any thing — with *our Father,* and therefore we may hope he will prevail for us. [*b.*] It is the great condescension of Christ that he is pleased to own the believer's God for his God: *My God, and your God;* mine, that he may be yours; the God of the Redeemer, to support him (Ps. 89:26), that he might be the God of the redeemed, to save them. The summary of the new covenant is that God *will be to us a God;* and therefore Christ being the surety and head of the covenant, who is primarily dealt with, and believers only through him as his spiritual seed, this covenant-relation fastens first upon him, God becomes his God, and so ours; we partaking of a divine nature, Christ's Father is our Father; and, he partaking of the human nature, our God is his God.

(*b.*) Christ's ascension into heaven, in further prosecution of his undertaking for us, is likewise an unspeakable comfort: "Tell them I must shortly ascend; that is the next step I am to take." Now this was intended to be, [*a.*] A word of caution to these disciples, not to expect the continuance of his bodily presence on earth, nor the setting up of his temporal kingdom among men, which they dreamed of. "No, tell them, I am risen, not to stay with them, but to go on their errand to heaven." Thus those who are raised to a spiritual life, in conformity to Christ's resurrection, must reckon that they rise to ascend; *they are quickened with Christ that they may sit with him in heavenly places,* Eph. 2:5, 6. Let them not think that this earth is to be their home and rest; no, being born from heaven, they are bound for heaven; their eye and aim must be upon another world, and this must be ever upon their hearts, I ascend, therefore must I seek things above. [*b.*] A word of comfort to them, and to all *that shall believe in him through their word;* he was then ascending, he is now *ascended to his Father, and our Father.* This was his advancement; he ascended to receive those honours and powers which were to be the recompence of his humiliation; he says it with triumph, that those who love him may rejoice. This is our advantage; for he ascended as a conqueror, *leading captivity captive* for us (Ps. 68:18), he ascended as our forerunner, *to prepare a place for us,* and to be ready to receive us. This message was like that which Joseph's brethren brought to Jacob concerning him (Gen. 45:26), *Joseph is yet alive,* and not only so, *vivit imo, et in senatum venit — he lives, and comes into the senate too; he is governor over all the land of Egypt;* all power is his.

Some make those words, *I ascend to my God and your God,* to include a promise of our resurrection, in the virtue of Christ's resurrection; for Christ had proved the resurrection of the dead from these words, *I am the God of Abraham,* Mt. 22:32. So that Christ here insinuates, "As he is my God, and hath therefore raised me, so he is your God, and will therefore raise you, and be your God, Rev. 21:3. *Because I live, you shall live also.* I now ascend, to honour my God, and you shall ascend to him as your God.

IV. Here is Mary Magdalene's faithful report of what she had seen and heard to the disciples (*v.* 18): *She came and told the disciples,* whom she found together, *that she had seen the Lord.* Peter and John had left her seeking him carefully with tears, and would not stay to seek him with her; and now she comes to tell them that she had found him, and to rectify the mistake she had led them into by enquiring after the dead body, for now she found it was a living body and a glorified one; so that she found what she sought, and, what was infinitely better, she had joy in her sight of the Master herself, and was willing to communicate of her joy, for she knew it would be good news to them. When God comforts us, it is with this design, that we may comfort others. And as she told them what she had seen, so also what she had heard; she had seen the Lord alive, of which this was a token (and a good token it was) *that he had spoken these things unto her* as a message to be delivered to them, and she delivered it faithfully. Those that are acquainted with the word of Christ themselves should communicate their knowledge for the good of others, and not grudge that others should know as much as they do.

Verses 19–25

The infallible proof of Christ's resurrection was his *showing himself alive,* Acts 1:3. In these verses, we have an account of his first appearance to the college of the disciples, on the day on which he rose. He had sent them the tidings of his resurrection by trusty and credible messengers; but to show his love to them, and confirm their faith in him, he came himself, and gave them all the assurances they could desire of the truth of it, that they might not have it by hearsay only, and at second hand, but might themselves be eye-witnesses of his being alive, because they must attest it to the world, and build the church upon that testimony. Now observe here,

I. When and where this appearance was, *v.* 19. It was *the same day* that he rose, *being the first day of the week,* the day after the Jewish sabbath, at a private meeting of the disciples, ten of them, and some more of their friends with them, Lu. 24:33.

There are three secondary ordinances (as I may call them) instituted by our Lord Jesus, to continue in his church, for the support of it, and for the due administration of the principal ordinances — the word, sacraments, and prayer; these are, the Lord's day, solemn assemblies, and standing ministry. The mind of Christ concerning each of these is plainly intimated to us in these verses; of the first two, here, in the circumstances of this appearance, the other *v.* 21. Christ's kingdom was to be set up among men, immediately upon his resurrection; and accordingly we find the very day he arose, though but a day of small things, yet graced with those solemnities which should help to keep up a face of religion throughout all the ages of the church.

1. Here is a Christian sabbath observed by the disciples, and owned by our Lord Jesus. The visit Christ made to his disciples was on *the first day of the week.* And the first day of the week is (I think) the only day of the week, or month, or year, that is ever mentioned by number in all the New Testament; and this is several times spoken of as a day religiously observed. Though it was said here expressly (*v.* 1) that

Christ arose on *the first day of the week,* and it might have been sufficient to say here (*v.* 19), he appeared the same day at evening; yet, to put an honour upon the day, it is repeated, *being the first day of the week;* not that the apostles designed to put honour upon the day (they were yet in doubt concerning the occasion of it), but God designed to put honour upon it, by ordering it that they should be altogether, to receive Christ's first visit on that day. Thus, in effect, he blessed and sanctified that day, because in it the Redeemer rested.

2. Here is a Christian assembly solemnized by the disciples, and also owned by the Lord Jesus. Probably the disciples met here for some religious exercise, to pray together; or, perhaps, they met to compare notes, and consider whether they had sufficient evidence of their Master's resurrection, and to consult what was now to be done, whether they should keep together or scatter; they met to know one another's minds, strengthen one another's hands, and concert proper measures to be taken in the present critical juncture. This meeting was private, because they durst not appear publicly, especially in a body. They met in a house, but they kept the door shut, that they might not be seen together, and that no one might come among them but such as they knew; for they feared the Jews, who would prosecute the disciples as criminals, that they might seem to believe the lie they would deceive the world with, that his *disciples came by night, and stole him away.* Note, (1.) The disciples of Christ, even in difficult times, must not *forsake the assembling of themselves together,* Heb. 10:25. Those *sheep of the flock were scattered* in the storm; but sheep are sociable, and will come together again. It is no new thing for the assemblies of Christ's disciples to be driven into corners, and forced into the wilderness, Rev. 12:14; Prov. 28:12. (2.) God's people have been often obliged to *enter into their chambers, and shut their doors,* as here, *for fear of the Jews.* Persecution is allotted them, and retirement from persecution is allowed them; and then where shall we look for them but in *dens and caves of the earth.* It is a real grief, but no real reproach, to Christ's disciples, thus to abscond.

II. What was said and done in this visit Christ made to his disciples, and his interview between them. When they were assembled, Jesus came among them, in his own likeness, yet drawing a veil over the brightness of his body, now begun to be glorified, else it would have dazzled their eyes, as in his transfiguration. Christ came among them, to give them a specimen of the performance of his promise, that, *where two or three are gathered together in his name, he will be in the midst of them.* He came, though *the doors were shut.* This does not at all weaken the evidence of his having a real human body after his resurrection; though the doors were shut, he knew how to open them without any noise, and come in so that they might not hear him, as formerly he had walked on the water, and yet had a true body. It is a comfort to Christ's disciples, when their solemn assemblies are reduced to privacy, that no doors can shut out Christ's presence from them. We have five things in this appearance of Christ: —

(1.) His kind and familiar salutation of his disciples: *He said, Peace be unto you.* This was not a word of course, though commonly used so at the meeting of friends, but a solemn, uncommon benediction, conferring upon them all the blessed fruits and effects of his death and resurrection. The phrase was common, but the sense was now peculiar. *Peace be unto you* is as much as, All good be to you, all peace always by all means. Christ had left them his peace for their legacy, *ch.* 14:27. By the death of the testator the testament was become of force, and he was now risen from the dead, to prove the will, and to be himself the executor of it. Accordingly, he here makes prompt payment of the legacy: *Peace be unto you.* His speaking peace makes peace, *creates the fruit of the lips, peace;* peace with God, peace in your own consciences, peace with one another; all this peace be with you; not peace with the world, but peace in Christ. His sudden appearing in *the midst of them* when they were full of doubts concerning him, full of fears concerning themselves, could not but put them into some disorder and consternation, the noise of which waves he stills with this word, *Peace be unto you.*

(2.) His clear and undeniable manifestation of himself to them, *v.* 20. And here observe,

[1.] The method he took to convince them of the truth of his resurrection, They now saw him alive whom multitudes had seen dead two or three days before. Now the only doubt was whether this that they saw alive was the same individual body that had been seen dead; and none could desire a further proof that it was so than the scars or marks of the wounds in the body. Now, *First,* The marks of the wounds, and very deep marks (though without any pain or soreness), remained in the body of the Lord Jesus even after his resurrection, that they might be demonstrations of the truth of it. Conquerors glory in the marks of their wounds. Christ's wounds were to speak on earth that it was he himself, and therefore he arose with them; they were to speak in heaven, in the intercession he must ever live to make, and therefore he ascended with them, and appeared in the midst of *the throne, a Lamb as it had been slain, and bleeding afresh,* Rev. 5:6. Nay, it should seem, he will come again with his scars, that *they may look on him whom they pierced. Secondly,* These marks he showed to his disciples, for their conviction. They had not only the satisfaction of seeing him look with the same countenance, and hearing him speak with the same voice they had been so long accustomed to, *Sic oculos, sic ille manus, sic ora, ferebat — Such were his gestures, such his eyes and hands!* but they had the further evidence of these peculiar marks: he opened his hands to them, that they might see the marks of the wounds on them; he opened his breast, as the nurse hers to the child, to show them the wound there. Note, The exalted Redeemer will ever show himself openhanded and open-hearted to all his faithful friends and followers. When Christ manifests his love to believers by the comforts of his Spirit, assures them that *because he lives they shall live also,* then *he shows them his hands and his side.*

[2.] The impression it made upon them, and the good it did them. *First,* They were convinced that they saw the Lord: so was their faith confirmed. At first, they thought they saw an apparition only, a phantasm; but now they knew it was the Lord himself. Thus many true believers, who, while they were weak, feared their comforts were but imaginary, afterwards find them, through grace, real and substantial. They ask not, Is it the Lord? but are assured, it is he. *Secondly, Then they were glad;* that which strengthened their faith raised their joy; *believing they rejoice.* The evangelist seems to write it with somewhat of transport and triumph. *Then! then! were the disciples glad, when they saw the Lord,* If it *revived the spirit of Jacob* to hear that *Joseph was yet alive,* how would it revive the heart of these disciples to hear that Jesus is again alive? It is life from the dead to them. Now that word of Christ was fulfilled (*ch.* 16:22), *I will see you again, and your heart shall rejoice.* This wiped away all tears from their eyes. Note, A sight of Christ will gladden the heart of a disciple at any time; the more we see of Christ, the more we shall rejoice in him; and our joy will never be perfect till we come *where we shall see him as he is.*

(3.) The honourable and ample commission he gave them to be his agents in the planting of his church, *v.* 21. Here is,

[1.] The preface to their commission, which was the solemn repetition of the salutation before: *Peace be unto you.* This was intended, either, *First,* To raise their attention to the commission he was about to give them. The former salutation was to still the tumult of their fear, that they might calmly attend to the proofs of his resurrection; this was to reduce the transport of their joy, that they might sedately hear what he had further to say to them; or, *Secondly,* To encourage them to accept of the commission he was giving them. Though it would involve them in a great deal of trouble, yet he designed their honour and comfort in it, and, in the issue, it would be peace to them. Gideon received his commission with this word, *Peace be unto thee,* Jdg. 6:22, 23. Christ is our Peace; if he is with us, peace is to us. Christ was now sending the disciples to publish peace to the world (Isa. 52:7), and he here not only confers it upon them for their own satisfaction, but commits it to them as a trust to be by them transmitted to all the sons of peace, Lu. 10:5, 6.

[2.] The commission itself, which sounds very great: *As my Father hath sent me, even so send I you.*

First, It is easy to understand how Christ sent them; he appointed them to go on with his work upon earth, and to lay out themselves for the spreading of his gospel, and the setting up of his kingdom, among men. He sent them authorized with a divine warrant, armed with a divine power, — sent them as ambassadors to treat of peace, and as heralds to proclaim it, — sent them as servants to bid to the marriage. Hence they were called *apostles — men sent.*

Secondly, But how Christ sent them as the Father sent him is not so easily understood; certainly their commissions and powers were infinitely inferior to his; but, 1. Their work was of the same kind with his, and they were to go on where he left off. They were not sent to be priests and kings, like him, but only prophets. As he was sent to bear witness to the truth, so were they; not to be mediators of the reconciliation, but only preachers and publishers of it. Was he sent, *not to be ministered to, but to minister? not to do his own will, but the will of him that sent him? not to destroy the law and the prophets, but to fill them up?* So were they. As the Father sent him *to the lost sheep of the house of Israel,* so he sent them into all the world. 2. He had a power to send them equal to that which the Father had to send him. Here the force of the comparison seems to lie. By the same authority that the Father sent me do I send you. This proves the Godhead of Christ; the commissions he gave were of equal authority with those which the Father gave, and as valid and effectual to all intents and purposes, equal with those he gave to the Old-Testament prophets in visions. The commissions of Peter and John, by the plain word of Christ, are as good as those of Isaiah and Ezekiel, by *the Lord sitting on his throne;* nay, equal with that which was given to the Mediator himself for his work. Had he an incontestable authority, and an irresistible ability, for his work? so had they for theirs. Or thus, *As the Father hath sent me* is, as it were, the recital of his power; by virtue of the authority given him as a Mediator, he gave authority to them, as his ministers, to act for him, and in his name, with the children of men; so that those who received them, or rejected them, received or rejected him, and him that sent him, *ch.* 13:20.

(4.) The qualifying of them for the discharge of the trust reposed in them by their commission (*v.* 22): *He breathed on them, and said, Receive ye the Holy Ghost.* Observe,

[1.] The sign he used to assure them of, and affect them with, the gift he was now about to bestow upon them: *He breathed on them;* not only to show them, by this breath of life, that he himself was really alive, but to signify to them the spiritual life and power which they should receive from him for all the services that lay before them. Probably he breathed upon them all together, not upon each severally and, though Thomas was not with them, yet the Spirit of the Lord knew where to find him, as he did Eldad and Medad, Num. 11:26. Christ here seems to refer to the creation of man at first, by the breathing of the breath of life into him (Gen. 2:7), and to intimate that he himself was the author of that work, and that the spiritual life and strength of ministers and Christians are derived from him, and depend upon him, as much as the natural life of Adam and his seed. As *the breath of the Almighty* gave life to man and began the old world, so the breath of the mighty Saviour gave life to his ministers, and began a new world, Job 33:4. Now this intimates to us, *First,* That the Spirit is the breath of Christ, *proceeding from the Son.* The Spirit, in the Old Testament, is compared to breath (Eze. 37:9), *Come, O breath;* but the New Testament tells us it is Christ's breath. *The breath of God* is put for the power of his wrath (Isa. 11:4; 30:33); but the breath of Christ signifies the power of his grace; the breathing of threatenings is changed into the breathings of love by the mediation of Christ. Our words are uttered by our breath, so the word of Christ *is spirit and life.* The word comes from the Spirit, and the Spirit comes along with the word. *Secondly,* That the Spirit is the gift of Christ. The apostles communicated the Holy Ghost by the laying on of hands, those hands being first lifted up in prayer, for they could only beg this blessing, and carry it as messengers; but Christ conferred the Holy Ghost by breathing, for he is the author of the gift, and from him it comes originally. Moses could not give his Spirit, God did it (Num. 11:17); but Christ did it himself.

[2.] The solemn grant he made, signified by this sign, *Receive ye the Holy Ghost,* in part now, as an earnest of what you shall further receive *not many days hence."* They now received more of the Holy Ghost than they had yet received. Thus spiritual blessings are given gradually; to him that has shall be given. Now that Jesus began to be glorified more of the Spirit began to be given: see *ch.* 7:39. Let us see what is contained in this grant. *First,* Christ hereby gives them assurance of the Spirit's aid in their future work, in the execution of the commission now given them: *"I send you,* and you shall have the Spirit to go along with you." Now the *Spirit of the Lord rested upon them* to qualify them for all the services that lay before them. Whom Christ employs he will clothe with his Spirit, and furnish with all needful powers. *Secondly,* He hereby gives them experience of the Spirit's influences in their present case. He had shown them his hands and his side, to convince them of the truth of his resurrection; but the plainest evidences will not of themselves work faith, witness the infidelity of the soldiers, who were the only eye-witnesses of the resurrection. "Therefore *receive ye the Holy Ghost,* to work faith in you, and to open your understandings." They were now in danger of the Jews: "Therefore receive ye the Holy Ghost, to work courage in you." What Christ said to them he says to all true believers, *Receive ye the Holy Ghost,* Eph. 1:13. What Christ gives we must receive, must submit ourselves and our whole souls to the quickening, sanctifying, influences of the blessed Spirit — receive his motions, and comply with them — receive his powers and make use of them: and those who thus obey this word as a precept shall have the benefit of it as a promise; they shall receive the Holy Ghost as the guide of their way and the earnest of their inheritance.

(5.) One particular branch of the power given them by their commission particularized (*v.* 23): "*Whosesoever sins you remit,* in the due execution of the powers you are entrusted with, they are remitted to them, and they may take the comfort of it; *and whosesoever sins you retain,* that is, pronounce unpardoned and the guilt of them bound on, *they are retained,* and the sinner may be sure of it, to his sorrow." Now this follows upon their receiving the Holy Ghost; for, if they had not had an extraordinary spirit of discerning, they had not been fit to be entrusted with such an authority; for, in the strictest sense, this is a special commission to the apostles themselves and the first preachers of the gospel, who could distinguish who were in the *gall of bitterness and bond of iniquity,* and who were not. By virtue of this power, Peter struck Ananias and Sapphira dead, and Paul struck Elymas blind. Yet it must be understood as a general charter to the church and her ministers, not securing an infallibility of judgment to any man or company of men in the world, but encouraging the faithful stewards of the mysteries of God to stand to the gospel they were sent to preach, for that God himself will stand to it. The apostles, in preaching remission, must begin at Jerusalem, though she had lately brought upon herself the guilt of Christ's blood: "Yet you may declare their sins remitted upon gospel terms." And Peter did so, Acts 2:38; 3:19. Christ, being risen for our justification, sends his gospel heralds to proclaim the jubilee begun, the act of indemnity now passed; and by this rule men shall be judged, *ch.* 12:48; Rom. 2:16; Jam. 2:12. God will never alter this rule of judgment, nor vary from it; those whom the gospel acquits shall be acquitted, and those whom the gospel condemns shall be condemned, which puts immense honour upon the ministry, and should put immense courage into ministers. Two ways the apostles and ministers of Christ remit and retain sin, and both as having authority: — [1.] By sound doctrine. They are commissioned to tell the world that salvation is to be had upon gospel terms, and no other, and they shall find God will say *Amen* to it; so shall their doom be. [2.] By a strict discipline, applying the general rule of the gospel to particular persons. "Whom you admit into communion with you, according to the rules of the gospel, God will admit into communion with himself; and whom you cast out of communion as impenitent, and obstinate in scandalous and infectious sins, shall be bound over to the righteous judgment of God."

III. The incredulity of Thomas, when the report of this was made to him, which introduced Christ's second appearance.

1. Here is Thomas's absence from this meeting, *v.* 24. He is said to be *one of the twelve,* one of the college of the apostles, who, though now eleven, had been twelve, and were to be so again. They were but eleven, and one of them was missing: Christ's disciples will never be all together till the general assembly at the great day. Perhaps it was Thomas's unhappiness that he was absent — either he was not well, or had not notice; or perhaps it was his sin and folly — either he was diverted by business or company, which he preferred before this opportunity, or he durst not come for *fear of the Jews;* and he called that his prudence and caution which was his cowardice. However, by his absence he missed the satisfaction of seeing his Master risen, and of sharing with the disciples in their joy upon that occasion. Note, Those know not what they lose who carelessly absent themselves from the stated solemn assemblies of Christians.

2. The account which the other disciples gave him of the visit their Master had made them, *v.* 25. The next time they saw him they *said unto him,* with joy enough, *We have seen the Lord;* and no doubt they related to him all that had passed, particularly the satisfaction he had given them by showing them his hands and his side. It seems, though Thomas was then from them, he was not long from them; absentees for a time must not be condemned as apostates for ever: Thomas is not Judas. Observe with what exultation and triumph they speak it: "*We have seen the Lord,* the most comfortable sight we ever saw." This they said to Thomas, (1.) To upbraid him with his absence: "*We have seen the Lord,* but thou hast not." Or rather, (2.) To inform him: "*We have seen the Lord,* and we wish thou hadst been here, to see him too, for thou wouldest have seen enough to satisfy thee." Note, The disciples of Christ should endeavour to *build up one another in their most holy faith,* both by repeating what they have heard to those that were absent, that they may hear it at second hand, and also by communicating what they have experienced. Those that by faith have seen the Lord, and tasted that he is gracious, should tell others what God has done for their souls; only let boasting be excluded.

3. The objections Thomas raised against the evidence, to justify himself in his unwillingness to admit it. "Tell me not that you have seen the Lord alive; you are too credulous; somebody has made fools of you. For my part, *except I shall* not only *see in his hands the print of the nails,* but put my finger into it, *and thrust my hand* into the wound *in his side,* I am resolved *I will not believe.*" Some, by comparing this with what he said (*ch.* 11:16; 14:5), conjecture him to have been a man of a rough, morose temper, apt to speak peevishly; for all good people are not alike happy in their temper. However, there was certainly much amiss in his conduct at this time. (1.) He had either not heeded, or not duly regarded, what Christ had so often said, and that too according to the Old Testament, that he would *rise again the third day;* so that he ought to have said, *He is risen,* though he had not seen him, nor spoken with any that had. (2.) He did not pay a just deference to the testimony of his fellow-disciples, who were men of wisdom and integrity, and ought to have been credited. He knew them to be honest men; they all ten of them concurred in the testimony with great assurance; and yet he could not persuade himself to say that *their record was true.* Christ had chosen them to be his witnesses of this very thing to all nations; and yet Thomas, one of their own fraternity, would not allow them to be competent witnesses, nor trust them further than he could see them. It was not, however, their veracity that he questioned, but their prudence; he feared they were too credulous. (3.) He tempted Christ, and *limited the Holy One of Israel,* when he would be convinced by his own method, or not at all. He could not be sure that the print of the nails, which the apostles told him they had seen, would admit the putting of his finger into it, or the wound in his side the thrusting in of his hand; nor was it fit to deal so roughly with a living body; yet Thomas ties up his faith to this evidence. Either he will be humoured, and have his fancy gratified, or he will not believe; see Mt. 16:1; 27:42. (4.) The open avowal of this in the presence of the disciples was an offence and discouragement to them. It was not only a sin, but a scandal. As one coward makes many, so does one believer, one sceptic, *making his brethren's heart to faint like his heart,* Deu. 20:8. Had he only thought this evil, and then laid his hand upon his mouth, to suppress it, his error had remained with himself; but his proclaiming his infidelity, and that so peremptorily, might be of ill consequence to the rest, who were as yet but weak and wavering.

Verses 26–31

We have here an account of another appearance of Christ to his disciples, after his resurrection, when Thomas was now with them. And concerning this we may observe,

I. When it was that Christ repeated his visit to his disciples: *After eight days,* that day seven-night after he rose, which must therefore be, as that was, *the first day of the week.*

1. He deferred his next appearance for some time, to show his disciples that he was not risen to such a life as he had formerly lived, to converse constantly with them but was as one that belonged to another world, and visited this only as angels do, now and then, when there was occasion. Where Christ was during these eight days, and the rest of the time of his abode on earth, it is folly to enquire, and presumption to determine. Wherever he was, no doubt *angels ministered unto him.* In the beginning of his ministry he had been forty days unseen, tempted by the evil spirit, Mt. 4:1, 2. And now in the beginning of his glory he was forty days, for the most part unseen, attended by good spirits.

2. He deferred it so long as seven days. And why so? (1.) That he might put a rebuke upon Thomas for his incredulity. He had neglected the former meeting of the disciples; and, to teach him to prize those seasons of grace better for the future, he cannot have such another opportunity for several days. He that slips one tide must stay a good while for another. A very melancholy week, we have reason to think Thomas had of it, drooping, and in suspense, while the other disciples were full of joy; and it was owing to himself and his own folly. (2.) That he might try the faith and patience of the rest of the disciples. They had gained a great point when they were satisfied that they had seen the Lord. *Then were the disciples glad;* but he would try whether they could keep the ground they had got, when they saw no more of him for some days. And thus he would gradually wean them from his bodily presence, which they had doted and depended too much upon. (3.) That he might put an honour upon the first day of the week, and give a plain intimation of his will, that it should be observed in his church as the Christian sabbath, the weekly day of holy rest and holy convocations. That one day in seven should be religiously observed was an appointment from the beginning, as old as innocency; and that in the kingdom of the Messiah the first day of the week should be that solemn day this was indication enough, that Christ on that day once and again met his disciples in a religious assembly. It is highly probable that in his former appearance to them he appointed them that day seven-night to be together again, and promised to meet them; and also that he appeared to them every first day of the week, besides other times, during the forty days. The religious observance of that day has been thence transmitted down to us through every age of the church. This therefore is *the day which the Lord has made.*

II. Where, and how, Christ made them this visit. It was at Jerusalem, for the doors were shut now, as before, for fear of the Jews. There they staid, to keep the feast of unleavened bread seven days, which expired the day before this; yet they would not set out on their journey to Galilee on the first day of the week, because it was the Christian sabbath, but staid till the day after. Now observe, 1. That Thomas was with them; though he had withdrawn himself once, yet not a second time. When we have lost one opportunity, we should give the more earnest heed to lay hold on the next, that we may recover our losses. It is a good sign if such a loss whet our desires, and a bad sign if it cool them. The disciples admitted him among them, and did not insist upon his believing the resurrection of Christ, as they did, because as yet it was but darkly revealed; they did not receive him to doubtful disputation, but bade him welcome to come and see. But observe, Christ did not appear to Thomas, for his satisfaction, till he found him in society with the rest of his disciples, because he would countenance the meetings of Christians and ministers, for there will he be *in the midst of them.* And, besides, he would have all the disciples witnesses of the rebuke he gave to Thomas, and yet withal of the tender care he had of him. 2. That Christ *came* in among them, and *stood in the midst,* and they all knew him, for he showed himself now, just as he had shown himself before (*v.* 19), still the same, and no changeling. See the condescension of our Lord Jesus. The gates of heaven were ready to be opened to him, and there he might have been in the midst of the adorations of a world of angels; yet, for the benefit of his church, he lingered on earth, and visited the little private meetings of his poor disciples, and is in the midst of them. 3. He saluted them all in a friendly manner, as he had done before; he said, *Peace be unto you.* This was no vain repetition, but significant of the abundant and assured peace which Christ gives, and of the continuance of his blessings upon his people, for they *fail not,* but are *new every morning,* new every meeting.

III. What passed between Christ and Thomas at this meeting; and that only is recorded, though we may suppose he said a great deal to the rest of them. Here is,

1. Christ's gracious condescension to Thomas, *v.* 27. He singled him out from the rest, and applied himself particularly to him: "*Reach hither thy finger,* and, since thou wilt have it so, *behold my hands,* and satisfy thy curiosity to the utmost about the *print of the nails; reach hither thy hand,* and, if nothing less will convince thee, *thrust it into my side.*" Here we have, (1.) An implicit rebuke of Thomas's incredulity, in the plain reference which is here had to what Thomas had said, answering it word for word, for he had heard it, though unseen; and one would think that his telling him of it should put him to the blush. Note, There is not an unbe-

lieving word on our tongues, no, nor thought in our minds, at any time, but it is known to the Lord Jesus. Ps. 78:21. (2.) An express condescension to this weakness, which appears in two things: — [1.] That he suffers his wisdom to be prescribed to. Great spirits will not be dictated to by their inferiors, especially in their acts of grace; yet Christ is pleased here to accommodate himself even to Thomas's fancy in a needless thing, rather than break with him, and leave him in his unbelief. He will not *break the bruised reed,* but, as a good shepherd, *gathers that which was driven away,* Eze. 34:16. We ought thus to *bear the infirmities of the weak,* Rom. 15:1, 2. [2.] He suffers his wounds to be raked into, allows Thomas even to thrust his hand into his side, if then at last he would believe. Thus, for the confirmation of our faith, he has instituted an ordinance on purpose to keep his death in remembrance, though it was an ignominious, shameful death, and one would think should rather have been forgotten, and no more said of it; yet, because it was such an evidence of his love as would be an encouragement to our faith, he appoints the memorial of it to be celebrated. And in that ordinance where in we *show the Lord's death* we are called, as it were, to put our finger *into the print of the nails. Reach hither thy hand* to him, who reacheth forth his helping, inviting, giving hand to thee.

It is an affecting word with which Christ closes up what he had to say to Thomas: *Be not faithless but believing; mē ginou apistos — do not thou become an unbeliever;* as if he would have been sealed up under unbelief, had he not yielded now. This warning is given to us all: *Be not faithless;* for, if we are faithless, we are Christless and graceless, hopeless and joyless; let us therefore say, *Lord, I believe, help thou my unbelief.*

2. Thomas's believing consent to Jesus Christ. He is now ashamed of his incredulity, and cries out, *My Lord and my God, v.* 28. We are not told whether he did put his finger into the print of the nails; it should seem, he did not, for Christ says (*v.* 29), *Thou hast seem, and believed;* seeing sufficed. And now faith comes off a conqueror, after a struggle with unbelief.

(1.) Thomas is now fully satisfied of the truth of Christ's resurrection — that the same Jesus that was crucified is now alive, and this is he. His slowness and backwardness to believe may help to strengthen our faith; for hereby it appears that the witnesses of Christ's resurrection, who attested it to the world, and pawned their lives upon it, were not easy credulous men, but cautious enough, and suspended their belief of it till they saw the utmost evidence of it they could desire. Thus *out of the eater came forth meat.*

(2.) He therefore believed him to be Lord and God, and we are to believe him so. [1.] We must believe his deity — that he is God; not a man made God, but God made man, as this evangelist had laid down his thesis at first, *ch.* 1:1. The author and head of our holy religion has the wisdom, power, sovereignty, and unchangeableness of God, which was necessary, because he was to be not only the founder of it, but the foundation of it for its constant support, and the fountain of life for its supply. [2.] His mediation — that he is Lord, the one Lord, 1 Co. 8:6; 1 Tim. 2:5. He is sufficiently authorized, as pleni-potentiary, to settle the great concerns that lie between God and man, to take up the controversy which would inevitably have been our ruin, and to establish the correspondence that was necessary to our happiness; see Acts 2:36; Rom. 14:9.

(3.) He consented to him as his Lord and his God. In faith there must be the consent of the will to gospel terms, as well as the assent of the understanding to gospel truths. We must accept of Christ to be that to us which the Father hath appointed him. *My Lord* refers to *Adonai* — my foundation and stay; *my God to Elohim* — my prince and judge. God having constituted him the umpire and referee, we must approve the choice, and entirely refer ourselves to him. This is the vital act of faith, He is mine, Cant. 2:16.

(4.) He made an open profession of this, before those that had been the witnesses of his unbelieving doubts. He says it to Christ, and, to complete the sense, we must read it, *Thou art* my Lord and my God; or, speaking to his brethren, *This is* my Lord and my God. Do we accept of Christ as our *Lord God?* We must go to him, and tell him so, as David (Ps. 16:2), deliver the surrender to him as *our act and deed,* tell others so, as those that triumph in our relation to Christ: *This is my beloved.* Thomas speaks with an ardency of affection, as one that took hold of Christ with all his might, *My Lord* and *my God.*

3. The judgment of Christ upon the whole (*v.* 29): "*Thomas because thou hast seen me, thou hast believed,* and it is well thou art brought to it at last upon any terms; but *blessed are those that have not seen, and yet have believed.*" Here,

(1.) Christ owns Thomas a believer. Sound and sincere believers, though they be slow and weak, shall be graciously accepted of the Lord Jesus. Those who have long stood it out, if at last they yield, shall find him ready to forgive. No sooner did Thomas consent to Christ than Christ gives him the comfort of it, and lets him know that he believes.

(2.) He upbraids him with his former incredulity. He might well be ashamed to think, [1.] That he had been so backward to believe, and came so slowly to his own comforts. Those that in sincerity have closed with Christ see a great deal of reason to lament that they did not do it sooner. [2.] That it was not without much ado that he was brought to believe at last: "If thou hadst not seen me alive, thou wouldst not have believed;" but if no evidence must be admitted but that of our own senses, and we must believe nothing but what we ourselves are eye-witnesses of, farewell all commerce and conversation. If this must be the only method of proof, how must the world be converted to the faith of Christ? He is therefore justly blamed for laying so much stress upon this.

(3.) He commends the faith of those who believe upon easier terms. Thomas, as a believer, was truly blessed; but rather *blessed are those that have not seen.* It is not meant of not seeing the objects of faith (for these are invisible, Heb. 11:1; 2 Co. 4:18), but the motives of faith — Christ's miracles, and especially his resurrection; blessed are those that see not these, and yet believe in Christ. This may look, either backward, upon the Old-Testament saints, who had not seen the things which they saw, and yet believed the promise made unto the father, and lived by that faith; or forward, upon those who should afterwards believe, the Gentiles, who had never seen Christ in the flesh, as the Jews had. This faith is more laudable and praise-worthy than theirs who saw and believed; for, [1.] It evidences a better temper of mind in those that do believe. Not to see and yet to believe argues greater industry in searching after truth, and greater ingenuousness of mind in embracing it. He that believes upon that sight has his resistance conquered by a sort of violence; but he that believes without it, like the Bereans, is more noble. [2.] It is a greater instance of the power of divine grace. The less sensible the evidence is the more does the work of faith appear to be the Lord's doing. Peter is blessed in his faith, because flesh and blood have not revealed it to him, Mt. 16:17. Flesh and blood contribute more to their faith that see and believe, than to theirs who see not and yet believe. Dr. Lightfoot quotes a saying of one of the rabbin, "That one proselyte is more acceptable to God than all the thousands of Israel that stood before mount Sinai; for they saw and received the law, but a proselyte sees not, and yet receives it."

IV. The remark which the evangelist makes upon his narrative, like an historian drawing towards a conclusion, *v.* 30, 31. And here,

1. He assures us that many other things occurred, which were all worthy to be recorded, but are *not written in the book: many signs.* Some refer this to all the signs that Jesus did during his whole life, all the wondrous words he spoke, and all the wondrous works he did. But it seems rather to be confined to the signs he did after his resurrection, for these were in the presence of the disciples only, who are here spoken of, Acts 10:41. Divers of his appearances are not recorded, as appears, 1 Co. 15:5–7. See Acts 1:3. Now, (1.) We may here improve this general attestation, that there were other signs, many others, for the confirmation of our faith; and, being added to the particular narratives, they very much strengthen the evidence. Those that recorded the resurrection of Christ were not put to fish for evidence, to take up such short and scanty proofs as they could find, and make up the rest with conjecture. No, they had evidence enough and to spare, and more witnesses to produce than they had occasion for. The disciples, in whose presence these other signs were done, were to be preachers of Christ's resurrection to others, and therefore it was requisite they should have proofs of it *ex abundanti — in abundance,* that they might have a strong consolation, who ventured life and all upon it. (2.) We need not ask why they were not all written, or why not more than these, or others than these; for it is enough for us that so it seemed good to the Holy Spirit, by whose inspiration this was given. Had this history been a mere human composition, it had been swelled with a multitude of depositions and affidavits, to prove the contested truth of Christ's resurrection and long argument drawn up for the demonstration of it; but, being a divine history, the penmen write with a noble security, relating what amounted to a competent proof, sufficient to convince those that were willing to be taught and to condemn those that were obstinate in their unbelief; and, if this satisfy not, more would not. Men produce all they have to say, that they may gain credit; but God does not, for he can give faith. Had this history been written for the entertainment of the curious, it would have been more copious, or every circumstance would have brightened and embellished the story; but it was written to bring men to believe, and enough is said to answer that intention, whether men will hear or whether they will forbear.

2. He instructs us in the design of recording what we do find here (*v.* 31): "These accounts are given in this and the following chapter, *that you might believe* upon these evidences; that you might believe that Jesus is the Christ, the Son of God, declared with power to be so by his resurrection."

(1.) Here is the design of those that wrote the gospel. Some write books for their diversion, and publish them for their profit or applause, others to oblige the Athenian humour, others to instruct the world in arts and sciences for their secular advantage; but the evangelists wrote without any view of temporal benefit to themselves or others, but to bring men to Christ and heaven, and, in order to this, to persuade men to believe; and for this they took the most fitting methods, they brought to the world a divine revelation, supported with its due evidences.

(2.) The duty of those that read and hear the gospel. It is their duty to believe, to embrace, the doctrine of Christ, and that record given concerning him 1 Jn. 5:11. [1.] We are here told what the great gospel truth is which we are to believe — that *Jesus is that Christ,* that *Son of God. First,* That he is the Christ, the person who, under the title of the Messiah, was promised to, and expected by, the Old-Testament saints, and who, according to the signification of the name, is *anointed* of God to be a prince and a Saviour. *Secondly,* That he is the Son of God; not only as Mediator (for then he had not been greater than Moses, who was a prophet, intercessor, and lawgiver), but antecedent to his being the Mediator; for if he had not been a divine person, endued with the power of God and entitled to the glory of God, he had not been qualified for the undertaking — not fit either to do the Redeemer's work or to wear the Redeemer's crown. [2.] What the great gospel blessedness is which we are to hope for — *That believing we shall have life through his name.* This is, *First,* To direct our faith; it must have an eye to the life, the crown of life, the tree of life set before us. Life through Christ's name, the life proposed in the covenant which is made with us in Christ, is what we must propose to ourselves as the fulness of our joy and the abundant recompence of all our services and sufferings. *Secondly,* To encourage our faith, and invite us to believe. Upon the prospect of some great advantage, men will venture far; and greater advantage there cannot be than that which is offered by the *words of this life,* as the gospel is called, Acts 5:20. It includes both spiritual life, in conformity to God and communion with him, and eternal life, in the vision and fruition of him. Both are through Christ's name, by his merit and power, and both indefeasibly sure to all true believers.

CHAPTER 21

The evangelist seemed to have concluded his history with the foregoing chapter; but (as St. Paul sometimes in his epistles), new matter occurring, he begins again. He had said that there were many other signs which Jesus did for the proof of his resurrection. And in this chapter he mentions one of these many, which was Christ's appearance to some of his disciples at the sea of Tiberias, in which we have an account, I. How he discovered himself to them as they were fishing, filled their net, and then very familiarly came and dined with them upon what they had caught (*v.* 1–14). II. What discourse he had with Peter after dinner, 1. Concerning himself (*v.* 15–19). 2. Concerning John (*v.* 20–23). III. The solemn conclusion of this gospel (*v.* 24, 25). It is strange that any should suppose that this chapter was added by some other hand, when it is expressly said (*v.* 24) that the disciple whom Jesus loved is he which testifieth of these things.

Verses 1–14

We have here an account of Christ's appearance to his disciples at the sea of Tiberias. Now, 1. Let us compare this appearance with those that *went before,* In those Christ showed himself to his disciples when they were met in a solemn assembly (it should seem, for religious worship) upon a Lord's day, and when they were all together, perhaps expecting his appearing; but in this he showed himself to some of them occasionally, upon a week-day, when they were fishing, and little thought of it. Christ has many ways of making himself known to his people usually in his ordinances, but sometimes by his Spirit he visits them when they are employed in common business, as the *shepherds* who were *keeping their flocks by night* (Lu. 2:8), even so *here also,* Gen. 16:13. 2. Let us compare it with that which followed at the mountain in Galilee, where Christ had appointed them to meet him, Mat. 28:16. Thitherward they moved as soon as the days of unleavened bread were over, and disposed of themselves as they saw fit, till the time fixed for this interview, or general rendezvous. Now this appearance was while they were waiting for that, that they might not be weary of waiting. Christ is often better than his word, but never worse, often anticipates and outdoes the believing expectations of his people, but never disappoints them. As to the particulars of the story, we may observe,

I. Who they were to whom Christ now showed himself (*v.* 2): not to all the twelve, but to seven of them only. Nathanael is mentioned as one of them, whom we have not met with since, *ch.* 1. But some think he was the same with Bartholomew, one of the twelve. The two not named are supposed to be Philip of Bethsaida and Andrew of Capernaum. Observe here, 1. It is good for the disciples of Christ to be much together; not only in solemn religious assemblies, but in common conversation, and about common business. Good Christians should by this means both testify and increase their affection to, and delight in, each other, and edify one another both by discourse and example. 2. Christ chose to manifest himself to them when they were together; not only to countenance Christian society, but that they might be joint witnesses of the same matter of fact, and so might corroborate one another's testimony. Here were seven together to attest this, on which some observe that the Roman law required seven witnesses to a testament. 3. Thomas was one of them, and is named next to Peter, as if he now kept closer to the meetings of the apostles than ever. It is well if losses by our neglects make us more careful afterwards not to let opportunities slip.

II. How they were employed, *v.* 3. Observe,

1. Their agreement to go a fishing. They knew not well what to do with themselves. For my part, says Peter, *I will go a fishing; We will go with thee* then, say they, for we will keep together. Though commonly two of a trade cannot agree, yet they could. Some think they did amiss in returning to their boats and nets, which they had left; but then Christ would not have countenanced them in it with a visit. It was rather commendable in them; for they did it, (1.) To redeem time, and not be idle. They were not yet appointed to preach the resurrection of Christ. Their commission was in the drawing, but not perfected. The hour for entering upon action was to come. It is probable that their Master had directed them to say nothing of his resurrection till after his ascension, nay, not till after the pouring out of the Spirit, and then they were to begin at Jerusalem. Now, in the mean time, rather than do nothing, they would go a fishing; not for recreation, but for business. It is an instance of their humility. Though they were advanced to be sent of Christ, as he was of the Father, yet they did not take state upon them, but remembered *the rock out of which they were hewn.* It is an instance likewise of their industry, and bespeaks them good husbands of their time. While they were waiting, they would not be idling. Those who would give an account of their time with joy should contrive to fill up the vacancies of it, to gather up the fragments of it. (2.) That they might help to maintain themselves and not be burdensome to any. While their Master was with them those who ministered to him were kind to them; but now that the *bridegroom was taken from them* they must *fast* in those days, and therefore their own hands, as Paul's, must *minister to their necessities* and for this reason Christ asked them, *Have you any meat?* This teaches us with quietness *to work and eat our own bread.*

2. Their disappointment in their fishing. That night they caught nothing, though, it is probable, they *toiled all night,* as Lu. 5:5. See the vanity of this world; the hand of the diligent often returns empty. Even good men may come short of desired success in their honest undertakings. We may be in the way of our duty, and yet not prosper. Providence so ordered it that all that night they should catch nothing, that the miraculous draught of fishes in the morning might be the more wonderful and the more acceptable. In those disappointments which to us are very grievous God has often designs that are very gracious. Man has indeed *a dominion over the fish of the sea,* but they are not always at his beck; God only knows the *paths of the sea,* and commands that which passeth through them.

III. After what manner Christ made himself known to them. It is said (*v.* 1), *He showed himself.* His body, though a true and real body, was raised, as ours will be, a spiritual body, and so was visible only when he himself was pleased to make it so; or, rather, came and removed so quickly that it was here or there in an instant, *in a moment, in the twinkling of an eye.* Four things are observable in the appearance of Christ to them: —

1. He showed himself to them seasonably (*v.* 4): *When the morning was now come,* after a fruitless night's toil, Jesus *stood on the shore.* Christ's time of making himself known to his people is when they are most at a loss. When they think they have lost themselves, he will let them know that they have not lost him. Weeping may *endure for a night; but joy comes,* if Christ comes, *in the morning.* Christ appeared to them, not *walking upon the water,* because, being *risen from the dead,* he was not to be with them as he had been; but *standing upon the shore,* because now they were to make towards him. Some of the ancients put this significancy upon it, that Christ, having finished his work, was got through a stormy sea, a sea of blood, to a safe and quiet shore, where he stood in triumph; but the disciples, having their work before them, were yet at sea, in toil and peril. It is a comfort to us, when our passage is rough and stormy, that our Master is at shore, and we are hastening to him.

2. He showed himself to them gradually. The disciples, though they had been intimately acquainted with him, *knew not,* all at once, *that it was Jesus.* Little expecting to see him there, and not looking intently upon him, they took him for some common person waiting the arrival of their boat, to buy their fish. Note, Christ is often nearer to us than we think he is, and so we shall find afterwards, to our comfort.

3. He showed himself to them by an instance of his pity, *v.* 5. He called to them, *Children, paidia — "Lads, have you any meat?* Have you caught any fish?" Here, (1.) The compellation is very familiar; he speaks unto them as unto his sons, with the care and tenderness of a father: *Children.* Though he had now entered upon his exalted state, he spoke to his disciples with as much kindness and affection as ever. They were not children in age, but they were his children, the children which God had given him. (2.) The question is very kind: *Have you any meat?* He asks as a tender father concerning his children whether they be provided with that which is fit for them, that if they be not, he may take care for their supply. Note, *The Lord is for the body,* 1 Co. 6:13. Christ takes cognizance of the temporal wants of his people, and has promised them not only grace sufficient, but food convenient. *Verily they shall be fed,* Ps. 27:3. Christ looks into the cottages of the poor, and asks, *Children, have you any meat?* thereby inviting them to open their case before him, and by the prayer of faith to *make their requests known* to him: and then let them *be careful for nothing;* for Christ takes care of them, takes care for them. Christ has herein set us an example of compassionate concern for our brethren. There are many poor householders disabled for labour, or disappointed in it, that are reduced to straits, whom the rich should enquire after thus, *Have you any meat?* For the most necessitous are commonly the least clamorous. To this question the disciples gave a short answer, and, some think, with an air of discontent and peevishness. They said, *No;* not giving him any such friendly and respectful title as he had given them. So short do the best come in their returns of love to the Lord Jesus. Christ put the question to them, not because he did not know their wants, but because he would know them *from them.* Those that would have supplies from Christ must own themselves empty and needy.

4. He showed himself to them by an instance of his power; and this perfected the discovery (*v.* 6): he ordered them to *cast the net on the right side of the ship,* the contrary side to what they had been casting it on; and then they, who were going home empty-handed, were enriched with a great draught of fishes. Here we have, (1.) The orders Christ gave them, and the promise annexed to those orders: *Cast the net* there in such a place, and *you shall find.* He from whom nothing is hid, no, not the *inhabitants under the waters* (Job 26:5), knew on what side of the ship the shoal of fishes was, and to that side he directs them. Note, Divine providence extends itself to things most minute and contingent; and they are happy that know how to take hints thence in the conduct of their affairs, and acknowledge it in all their ways. (2.) Their obedience of these orders, and the good success of it. As yet *they knew not that it was Jesus;* however, they were willing to be advised by any body, and did not bid this supposed stranger mind his own business and not meddle with theirs, but took his counsel; in being thus observant of strangers, they were obedient to their Master unawares. And it sped wonderfully well; now they had a draught that paid them for all their pains. Note, Those that are humble, diligent, and patient (though their labours may be crossed) shall be crowned; they sometimes live to see their affairs take a happy turn, after many struggles and fruitless attempts. There is nothing lost by observing Christ's orders. Those are likely to speed well that follow the rule of the word, the guidances of the Spirit, and the intimations of Providence; for this is *casting the net on the right side of the ship.* Now the draught of fishes may be considered, [1.] As a miracle in itself: and so it was designed to prove that Jesus Christ was *raised in power,* though *sown in weakness,* and that all things were *put under his feet, the fishes of the sea* not excepted. Christ manifests himself to his people by doing that for them which none else can do, and things which *they looked not for.* [2.] As a mercy to them; for the seasonable and abundant supply of their necessities. When their ingenuity and industry failed them, the power of Christ came in opportunely for their relief; for he would take care that those who had left all for him should not want any good thing. When we are most at a loss, *Jehovah-jireh.* [3.] As the memorial of a former mercy, with which Christ had formerly recompensed Peter for the loan of his boat, Lu. 5:4, etc. This miracle nearly resembled that, and could not but put Peter in mind of it, which helped him to improve this; for both that and this affected him much, as meeting him in his own element, in his own employment. Latter favours are designed to bring to mind former favours, that eaten bread may not be forgotten. [4.] As a mystery, and very significant of that work to which Christ was now with an enlarged commission sending them forth. The prophets had been fishing for souls, and caught nothing, or very little; but the apostles, who let down the net at Christ's word, had wonderful success. *Many were the children of the desolate,* Gal. 4:27. They themselves, in pursuance of their former mission, when they were first made *fishers of men,* had had small success in comparison with what they should now have. When, soon after this, three thousand were converted in one day, then the net was *cast on the right side of the ship.* It is an encouragement to Christ's ministers to continue their diligence in their work. One happy draught, at length, may be sufficient to repay many years of toil at the gospel net.

IV. How the disciples received this discovery which Christ made of himself, *v.* 7, 8, where we find,

1. That John was the most intelligent and quick-sighted disciple. He whom Jesus loved was the first that said, *It is the Lord;* for those whom Christ loves he will in a special manner manifest himself to: his secret is with his favourites. John had adhered more closely to his Master in his sufferings than any of them: and therefore he has a clearer eye and a more discerning judgment than any of them, in recompence for his constancy. When John was himself aware that it was the Lord, he communicated his knowledge to those with him; for this *dispensation of the Spirit is given to every one to profit withal.* Those that know Christ themselves should endeavor to bring others acquainted with him; we need not engross him, there is enough in him for us all. John tells Peter particularly his thoughts, that it was the Lord, knowing he would be glad to see him above any of them. Though Peter had denied his Master, yet, having repented, and being taken into the communion of the disciples again, they were as free and familiar with him as ever.

2. That Peter was the most zealous and warm-hearted disciple; for as soon as he heard it was the Lord (for which he took John's word) the ship could not hold him, nor could he stay till the bringing of it to shore, but into the sea he throws himself presently, that he might come first to Christ. (1.) He showed his respect to Christ by *girding his fisher's coat* about him that he might appear before his Master in the best clothes he had, and to rudely rush into his presence, stripped as he was to his waistcoat and drawers, because the work he was

about was toilsome, and he was resolved to take pains in it. Perhaps the fisher's coat was made of leather, or oil-cloth, and would keep out wet; and he girt it to him that he might make the best of his way through the water to Christ, as he used to do after his nets, when he was intent upon his fishing. (2.) He showed the strength of his affection to Christ, and his earnest desire to be with him, by casting himself into the sea; and either wading or swimming to shore, to come to him. When he walked upon the water to Christ (Mt. 14:28, 29), it was said, *He came down out of the ship* deliberately; but here it is said, *He cast himself into the sea* with precipitation; sink or swim, he would show his good-will and aim to be with Jesus. "If Christ suffer me," thinks he, "to drown, and come short of him, it is but what I deserve for denying him." Peter had had much forgiven, and made it appear he loved much by his willingness to run hazards, and undergo hardships, to come to him. Those that have been with Jesus will be willing to swim through a stormy sea, a sea of blood, to come to him. And it is a laudable contention amongst Christ's disciples to strive who shall be first with him.

3. That the rest of the disciples were careful and honest hearted. Though they were not in such a transport of zeal as to throw themselves into the sea, like Peter, yet they hastened in the boat to the shore, and made the best of their way (*v.* 8): *The other disciples,* and John with them, who had first discovered that it was Christ, came slowly, yet they came to Christ. Now here we may observe, (1.) How variously God dispenses his gifts. Some excel, as Peter and John; are very eminent in gifts and graces, and are thereby distinguished from their brethren; others are but ordinary disciples, that mind their duty, and are faithful to him, but do nothing to make themselves remarkable; and yet both the one and the other, the eminent and the obscure, shall sit down together with Christ in glory; nay, and perhaps *the last shall be first.* Of those that do excel, some, like John, are eminently contemplative, have great gifts of knowledge, and serve the church with them; others, like Peter, are eminently active and courageous, are strong, and do exploits, and are thus very serviceable to their generation. Some are useful as the church's eyes, others as the church's hands, and all for the good of the body. (2.) What a great deal of difference there may be between some good people and others in the way of their honouring Christ, and yet both *accepted of him.* Some serve Christ more in acts of devotion, and extraordinary expressions of a religious zeal; and they do well, *to the Lord they do it.* Peter ought not to be censured for casting himself into the sea, but commended for his zeal and the strength of his affection; and so must those be who, in love to Christ, quit the world, with Mary, to *sit at his feet.* But others serve Christ more in the affairs of the world. They continue in that ship, drag the net, and bring the fish to shore, as the other disciples here; and such ought not to be censured as worldly, for they, in their place, are as truly serving Christ as the other, even in serving tables. If all the disciples had done as Peter did, what had become of their fish and their nets? And yet if Peter had done as they did we had wanted this instance of holy zeal. Christ was well pleased with both, and so must we be. (3.) That there are several ways of bringing Christ's disciples to shore to him from off the sea of this world. Some are brought to him by a violent death, as the martyrs, who threw themselves into the sea, in their zeal for Christ; others are brought to him by a natural death, dragging the net, which is less terrible; but both meet at length on the safe and quiet shore with Christ.

V. What entertainment the Lord Jesus gave them when they came ashore.

1. He had provision ready for them. When they came to land, wet and cold, weary and hungry, they found a good fire there to warm them and dry them, and fish and bread, competent provision for a good meal. (1.) We need not be curious in enquiring whence this fire, and fish, and bread, came, any more than whence the meat came which the ravens brought to Elijah. He that could multiply the loaves and fishes that were could make new ones if he pleased, or turn stones into bread, or send his angels to fetch it, where he knew it was to be had. It is uncertain whether this provision was made ready in the open air, or in some fisher's cabin or hut upon the shore; but here was nothing stately or delicate. We should be content with mean things, for Christ was. (2.) We may be comforted in this instance of Christ's care of his disciples; he has wherewith to supply all our wants, and *knows what things we have need of.* He kindly provided for those fishermen, when they came weary from their work; for *verily those shall be fed who trust in the Lord and do good.* It is encouraging to Christ's ministers, whom he hath made fishers of men, that they may depend upon him who employs them to provide for them; and if they should miss of encouragement in this world, should be reduced as Paul was to *hunger, and thirst,* and *fastings often,* let them content themselves with what they have here; they have better things in reserve, and shall *eat and drink with Christ at his table in his kingdom,* Lu. 22:30. Awhile ago, *the disciples* had entertained Christ with a *broiled fish* (Lu. 24:42), and now, as a friend, he returned their kindness, and entertained them with one; nay, in the draught of fishes, he repaid them more than a hundred fold.

2. He called for some of that which they had caught, and they produced it, *v.* 10, 11. Observe here,

(1.) The command Christ gave them to bring their draught of fish to shore: "Bring of the fish hither, which you have now caught, and let us have some of them;" not as if he needed it; and could not make up a dinner for them without it; but, [1.] He would have them eat the labour of their hands, Ps. 128:2. What is got by God's blessing on our own industry and honest labour, if withal *God give us power to eat of it, and enjoy good in our labour,* hath a peculiar sweetness in it. It is said of the slothful man that *he roasteth not that which he took in hunting;* he cannot find in his heart to dress what he has been at the pains to take, Prov. 12:27. But Christ would hereby teach us to use what we have. [2.] He would have them taste the gifts of his miraculous bounty, that they might be witnesses both of his power and of his goodness. The benefits Christ bestows upon us are not to be buried and laid up, but to be used and laid out. [3.] He would give a specimen of the spiritual entertainment he has for all believers, which, in this respect, is most free and familiar — that *he sups with them, and they with him;* their graces are pleasing to him, and his comforts are so to them; what he works in them he accepts from them. [4.] Ministers, who are fishers of men, must bring all they catch to their Master, for on him their success depends.

(2.) Their obedience to this command, *v.* 11. It was said (*v.* 6), *They were not able to draw the net to shore, for the multitude of fishes;* that is, they found it difficult, it was more than they could well do; but he that bade them bring it to shore made it easy. Thus the fishers of men, when they have enclosed souls in the gospel net, cannot bring them to shore, cannot carry on and complete the good work begun, without the continued influence of the divine grace. If he that helped us to catch them, when without his help we should have caught nothing, do not help us to keep them, and draw them to land, by *building them up in their most holy faith,* we shall lose them at last, 1 Co. 3:7. Observe, [1.] Who it was that was most active in landing the fishes: it was Peter, who, as in the former instance (*v.* 7), had shown a more zealous affection to his Master's person than any of them, so in this he showed a more ready obedience to his Master's command; but all that are faithful are not alike forward. [2.] The number of the fishes that were caught. They had the curiosity to count them, and perhaps it was in order to the making of a dividend; they were in all *a hundred and fifty three,* and all *great fishes.* These were many more than they needed for their present supply, but they might sell them, and the money would serve to bear their charges back to Jerusalem, whither they were shortly to return. [3.] A further instance of Christ's care of them, to increase both the miracle and the mercy: *For all there were so many,* and *great fishes* too, *yet was not the net broken;* so that they lost none of their fish, nor damaged their net. It was said (Lu. 5:6), *Their net broke.* Perhaps this was a borrowed net, for they had long since left their own; and, if so, Christ would teach us to take care of what we have borrowed, as much as if it were our own. It was well that their net did not break, for they had not now the leisure they had formerly had to mend their nets. The net of the gospel has enclosed multitudes, three thousand in one day, and yet is not broken; it is still as mighty as ever to bring souls to God.

3. He invited them to dinner. Observing them to keep their distance and that *they were afraid to ask him, Who art thou?* because they *knew it was their Lord,* he called to them very familiarly, *Come, and dine.*

(1.) See here how free Christ was with his disciples; he treated them as friends; he did not say, Come, and wait, Come, and attend me, but *Come, and dine;* not, Go dine by yourselves, as servants are appointed to do, but *Come, and dine* with me. This kind invitation may be alluded to, to illustrate, [1.] The call Christ gives his disciples into communion with him in grace here. *All things are now ready; Come, and dine.* Christ is a feast; come, dine upon him; his flesh is meat indeed, his blood drink indeed. Christ is a friend; come, dine with him, he will bid you welcome, Cant. 5:1. [2.] The call he will give into the fruition of him in glory hereafter: *Come, ye blessed of my Father; come, and sit down with Abraham, and Isaac, and Jacob.* Christ has wherewithal to dine all his friends and followers; there is room and provision enough for them all.

(2.) See how reverent the disciples were before Christ. They were somewhat shy of using the freedom he invited them to, and, by his courting them to their meat, it should seem that they stood pausing. Being *to eat with a ruler,* such a ruler, *they consider diligently what is before them. None of them durst ask him, Who art thou?* Either, [1.] Because they would not be so bold with him. Though perhaps he appeared now in something of a disguise at first, as to the two disciples when *their eyes were holden that they should not know him,* yet they had very good reason to think it was he, and could be no other. Or, [2.] Because they would not so far betray their own folly. When he had given them this instance of his power and goodness, they must be stupid indeed if they questioned whether it was he or no. When God, in his providence, has given us sensible proofs of his care for our bodies, and has given us, in his grace, manifest proofs of his good-will to our souls, and good work upon them, we should be ashamed of our distrusts, and not dare to question that which he has left us no room to question. Groundless doubts must be stifled, and not started.

4. He carved for them, as the master of the feast, *v.* 13. Observing them to be still shy and timorous, *he comes, and takes bread himself,* and *gives them,* some to each of them, *and fish likewise.* No doubt he craved a blessing and gave thanks (as Lu. 24:30), but, it being his known and constant practice, it did not need to be mentioned. (1.) The entertainment here was but ordinary; it was only a fish-dinner, and coarsely dressed; here was nothing pompous, nothing curious; plentiful indeed, but plain and homely. Hunger is the best sauce. Christ, though he entered upon his exalted state, *showed himself alive by eating,* not showed himself a prince by feasting. Those that could not content themselves with bread and fish, unless they had sauce and wine, would scarcely have found in their hearts to dine with Christ himself here. (2.) Christ himself began. Though, perhaps, having a glorified body, he needed not eat, yet he would show that he had a true body, which was capable of eating. The apostles produced this as one proof of his resurrection, that *they had eaten and drank with him,* Acts 10:41. (3.) He gave the meat about to all his guests. He not only provided it for them, and invited them to it, but he himself divided it among them, and put it into their hands. Thus to him we owe the application, as well as the purchase, of the benefits of redemption. He gives us power to eat of them.

The evangelist leaves them at dinner, and makes this remark (*v.* 14): *This is now the third time that Jesus showed himself alive to his disciples,* or the greater part of them. *This is the third day;* so some. On the day he rose he appeared five times; the second day was that day seven-night; and this was the third. Or this was his third appearance to any considerable number of his disciples together; though he had appeared to Mary, to the women, to the two disciples, and to Cephas, yet he had but twice before this appeared to any company of them together. This is taken notice of, [1.] For confirming the truth of his resurrection; the vision was doubled, was trebled, for the thing was certain. Those who believed not the first sign would be brought to believe the voice of the latter signs. [2.] As an instance of Christ's continued kindness to his disciples; once, and again, and a third time, he visited them. It is good to keep account of Christ's gracious visits; for he keeps account of them, and they will be remembered against us if we walk unworthily of them, as they were against Solomon, when he was reminded that the Lord God of Israel had appeared unto him twice. *This is now the third;* have we made a due improvement of *the first and second?* See 2 Co. 12:14. *This is the third,* perhaps it may be the last.

Verses 15–19

We have here Christ's discourse with Peter after dinner, so much of it as relates to himself, in which,

I. He examines his love to him, and gives him a charge concerning his flock, *v.* 15–17. Observe,

1. When Christ entered into this discourse with Peter. — It was after they had dined: they had all eaten, and were filled, and, it is probable, were entertained with such edifying discourse as our Lord Jesus used to make his table-talk. Christ foresaw that what he had to say to Peter would give him some uneasiness, and therefore would not say it till they had dined, because he would not spoil his dinner. Peter was conscious to himself that he had incurred his Master's displeasure, and could expect no other than to be upbraided with his treachery and ingratitude. "Was this thy kindness to thy friend? Did not I tell thee what a coward thou wouldest prove?" Nay, he might justly expect to be struck out of the roll of the disciples, and to be expelled the sacred college. Twice, if not thrice, he had seen his Master since his resurrection, and he said not a word to him of it. We may suppose Peter full of doubts upon what terms he stood with his Master; sometimes hoping the best, because he had received favour from him in common with the rest; yet not without some fears, lest the chiding would come at last that would pay for all. But now, at length, his Master put him out of his pain, said what he had to say to him, and confirmed him in his place as an apostle. He did not tell him of his fault hastily, but deferred it for some time; did not tell him of it unseasonably, to disturb the company at dinner, but *when they had dined* together, in token of reconciliation, then discoursed he with him about it, not as with a criminal, but as with a friend. Peter had reproached himself for it, and therefore Christ did not reproach him for it, nor tell him of it directly, but only by a tacit intimation; and, being satisfied in his sincerity, the offence was not only forgiven, but forgotten; and Christ let him know that he was as dear to him as ever. Herein he has given us an encouraging instance of his tenderness towards penitents, and has taught us, in like manner, to restore such as are fallen with a spirit of meekness.

2. What was the discourse itself. Here was the same question three times asked, the same answer three times returned, and the same reply three times given, with very little variation, and yet no *vain repetition.* The same thing was repeated by our Saviour, in speaking it, the more to affect Peter, and the other disciples that were present; it is repeated by the evangelist, in writing it, the more to affect us, and all that read it.

(1.) Three times Christ asks Peter whether he loves him or no. The first time the question is, *Simon, son of Jonas, lovest thou me more than these?* Observe,

[1.] How he calls him: *Simon, son of Jonas.* He speaks to him by name, the more to affect him, as Lu. 22:31. *Simon, Simon.* He does not call him *Cephas,* nor *Peter,* the name he had given him (for he had lost the credit of his strength and stability, which those names signified), but his original name, *Simon.* Yet he gives him no hard language, does not call him out of his name, though he deserved it; but as he had called him when he pronounced him blessed, *Simon Bar-jona,* Mt. 16:17. He calls him *son of Jonas* (or *John* or *Johanan*), to remind him of his extraction, how mean it was, and unworthy the honour to which he was advanced.

[2.] How he catechises him: *Lovest thou me more than these?*

First, Lovest thou me? If we would try whether we are Christ's disciples indeed, this must be the enquiry, Do we love him? But there was a special reason why Christ put in now to Peter. 1. His fall had given occasion to doubt of his love: "Peter, I have cause to suspect thy love; for if thou hadst loved me thou wouldst not have been ashamed and afraid to own me in my sufferings. How canst thou say thou lovest me, when thy heart was not with me?" Note, We must not reckon it an affront to have our sincerity questioned, when we ourselves have done that which makes it questionable; after a shaking fall, we must take heed of settling too soon, lest we settle upon a wrong bottom. The question is affecting; he does not ask, "Dost thou fear me? Dost thou honour me? Dost thou admire me?" but, "Dost thou love me? Give but proof of this, and the affront shall be passed by, and no more said of it." Peter had professed himself a penitent, witness his tears, and his return to the society of the disciples; he was now upon his probation as a penitent; but the question is not, "Simon, how much hast thou wept? how often hast thou fasted, and afflicted thy soul?" but, Dost thou love me? It is this that will make the other expressions of repentance acceptable. The great thing Christ eyes in penitents is their eyeing him in their repentance. *Much is forgiven her,* not because *she wept much,* but because *she loved much.* 2. His function would give occasion for the exercise of his *love.* Before Christ would commit his *sheep* to his care, he asked him, *Lovest thou me?* Christ has such a tender regard to his flock that he will not trust it with any but those that love him, and therefore will love all that are his for his sake. Those that do not truly love Christ will never truly love the souls of men, or will naturally care for their state as they should; nor will that minister love his work that does not love his Master. Nothing but the love of Christ will constrain ministers to go cheerfully through the difficulties and discouragements they meet with in their work, 2 Co. 5:13, 14. But this love will make their work easy, and them in good earnest in it.

Secondly, Lovest thou me more than these? pleion toutōn. 1. *"Lovest thou me more than thou lovest these,* more than thou lovest these persons?" Dost thou love me more than thou dost James or John, thy intimate friends, or Andrew, thy own brother and companion: Those do not love Christ aright that do not love him better than the best friend they have in the world, and make it to appear whenever they stand in comparison or in competition. Or, *"more than thou lovest these things,* these boats and nets — more than all the pleasure of fishing, which some make a recreation of — more than the gain of fishing, which others make a calling of." Those only love Christ indeed that love him better than all the delights of sense and all the profits of this world. *"Lovest thou me more than thou lovest these* occupations thou art now employed in? If so, leave them, to employ thyself wholly in feeding my flock." So Dr. Whitby. 2. *"Lovest thou me more than these love me,* more than any of the rest of the disciples love me?" And then the question is intended to upbraid him with his vain-glorious boast, *Though all men should deny thee, yet will not I.* "Art thou still of the same mind?" Or, to intimate to him that he had now more reason to love him than any of them had, for more had been forgiven to him than to any of them, as much as his sin in denying Christ was greater than theirs in forsaking him. *Tell me therefore which of them will love him most?* Lu. 7:42. Note, We should all study to excel in our love to Christ. It is no breach of the peace to strive which shall love Christ best; nor any breach of good manners to go before others in this love.

Thirdly, The second and third time that Christ put this question, 1. He left out the comparison *more than these,* because Peter, in his answer, modestly left it out, not willing to compare himself with his brethren, much less to prefer himself before them. Though we cannot say, *We* love Christ more than others do, yet we shall be accepted if we can say, We love him indeed. 2. In the last he altered the word, as it is in the original. In the first two enquiries, the original word is *Agapas me — Dost thou retain a kindness for me?* In answer to which Peter uses another word, more emphatic, *Philō se — I love thee dearly.* In putting the question the last time, Christ uses that word: And dost thou indeed love me dearly?

(2.) Three times Peter returns the same answer to Christ: *Yea, Lord, thou knowest that I love thee.* Observe, [1.] Peter does not pretend to love Christ more than the rest of the disciples did. He is now ashamed of that rash word of his, *Though all men deny thee, yet will not I;* and he had reason to be ashamed of it. Note, Though we must aim to be better than others, yet we must, *in lowliness of mind, esteem others better than ourselves;* for we know more evil of ourselves than we do of any of our brethren. [2.] Yet he professes again and again that he loves Christ: *"Yea, Lord,* surely *I love thee;* I were unworthy to live if I did not." He had a high esteem and value for him, a grateful sense of his kindness, and was entirely devoted to his honour and interest; his desire was towards him, as one he was undone without; and his delight in him, as one he should be unspeakably happy in. This amounts to a profession of repentance for his sin, for it grieves us to have affronted one we love; and to a promise of adherence to him for the future *Lord, I love thee,* and *will never leave thee.* Christ *prayed that his faith might not fail* (Lu. 22:32), and, because his faith did not fail, his love did not; for faith will work by love. Peter had forfeited his claim of relation to Christ. He was now to be re-admitted, upon his repentance. Christ puts his trial upon this issue: *Dost thou love me?* And Peter joins issue upon it: *Lord, I love thee.* Note, Those who can truly say, through grace, that they love Jesus Christ, may take the comfort of their interest in him, notwithstanding their daily infirmities. [3.] He appeals to Christ himself for the proof of it: *Thou knowest that I love thee;* and *the third time* yet more emphatically: *Thou knowest all things, thou knowest that I love thee.* He does not vouch his fellow-disciples to witness for him — they might be deceived in him; nor does he think his own word might be taken — the credit of that was destroyed already; but he calls Christ himself to witness, *First,* Peter was sure that Christ knew all things, and particularly that he knew the heart, and was a *discerner of the thoughts and intents of it, ch.* 16:30. *Secondly,* Peter was satisfied of this, that Christ, who knew all things, knew the sincerity of his love to him, and would be ready to attest it in his favour. It is a terror to a hypocrite to think that Christ knows all things; for the divine omniscience will be a witness against him. But it is a comfort to a sincere Christian that he has that to appeal to: *My witness is in heaven, my record is on high.* Christ knows us better than we know ourselves. Though we know not our own uprightness, he knows it. [4.] *He was grieved* when Christ asked him the *third time, Lovest thou me? v.* 17. *First,* Because it put him in mind of his threefold denial of Christ, and was plainly designed to do so; *and when he thought thereon he wept.* Every remembrance of past sins, even pardoned sins, renews the sorrow of a true penitent. *Thou shalt be ashamed, when I am pacified towards thee. Secondly,* Because it put him in fear lest his Master foresaw some further miscarriage of his, which would be as great a contradiction to this profession of love to him as the former was. "Surely," thinks Peter, "my Master would not thus put me upon the rack if he did not see some cause for it. What would become of me if I should be again tempted?" Godly sorrow works carefulness and fear, 2 Co. 7:11.

(3.) Three times Christ committed the care of his flock to Peter: *Feed my lambs; feed my sheep; feed my sheep.* [1.] Those whom Christ committed to Peter's care were his lambs and his sheep. The church of Christ is his flock, *which he hath purchased with his own blood* (Acts 20:28), and he is *the chief shepherd* of it. In this flock some are lambs, young and tender and weak, others are sheep, grown to some strength and maturity. The Shepherd here takes care of both, and of the lambs first, for upon all occasions he showed a particular tenderness for them. *He gathers the lambs in his arms, and carries them in his bosom.* Isa. 40:11. [2.] The charge he gives him concerning them is to feed them. The word used in *v.* 15, 17, is *boske,* which strictly signifies to *give them food;* but the word used in *v.* 16 is *poimaine,* which signifies more largely to do all the offices of a shepherd to them: *"Feed the lambs* with that which is proper for them, and *the sheep* likewise with *food convenient. The lost sheep of the house of Israel,* seek and feed them, and *the other sheep* also *which are not of this fold."* Note, It is the duty of all Christ's ministers to feed his lambs and sheep. *Feed them,* that is, teach them; for the doctrine of the gospel is spiritual food. *Feed them,* that is, "Lead them to the green pastures, presiding in their religious assemblies, and ministering all the ordinances to them. Feed them by personal application to their respective state and case; not only lay meat before them, but feed those with it that are wilful and will not, or weak and cannot feed themselves." *When Christ ascended on high, he gave pastors,* left his flock with those that loved him, and would take care of them for his sake. [3.] But why did he give this charge particularly to Peter? Ask the advocates for the pope's supremacy, and they will tell you that Christ hereby designed to give to Peter, and therefore to his successors, and therefore to the bishops of Rome, an absolute dominion and headship over the whole Christian church as if a charge to serve the sheep gave a power to lord it over all the shepherds; whereas, it is plain, Peter himself never claimed such a power, nor did the other disciples ever own it in him. This charge given to Peter to preach the gospel is by a strange artifice made to support the usurpation of his pretended successors, that fleece the sheep, and, instead of feeding them, feed upon them. But the particular application to Peter here was designed, *First,* To restore him to his apostleship, now that he repented of his abjuration of it, and to renew his commission, both for his own satisfaction, and for the satisfaction of his brethren. A commission given to one convicted of a crime is supposed to amount to a pardon; no doubt, this commission given to Peter was an evidence that Christ was reconciled to him else he would never have reposed such a confidence in him. Of some that have deceived us we say, "Though we forgive them, we will never trust them;" but Christ, when he forgave Peter, trusted him with the most valuable treasure he had on earth. Secondly, It was designed to quicken him to a diligent discharge of his office as an apostle. Peter was a man of a bold and zealous spirit, always forward to speak and act, and, lest he should be tempted to take upon him the directing of the shepherds, he is charged to feed the sheep, as he himself charges all the presbyters to do, and not *to lord it over God's heritage*, 1 Pt. 5:2, 3. If he will be doing, let him do this, and pretend no further. *Thirdly*, What Christ said to him he said to all his disciples; he charged them all, not only to be fishers of men (though that was said to Peter, Lu. 5:10), by the conversion of sinners, but feeders of the flock, by the edification of saints.

II. Christ, having thus appointed Peter his doing work, next appoints him his suffering work. Having confirmed to him the honour of an apostle, he now tells him of further preferment designed him — the honour of a martyr. Observe,

1. How his martyrdom is foretold (v. 18): *Thou shalt stretch forth thy hands*, being compelled to it, and *another shall gird thee* (as a prisoner that is pinioned) *and carry thee whither* naturally *thou wouldest not*.

(1.) He prefaces the notice he gives to Peter of his sufferings with a solemn asseveration, *Verily, verily, I say unto thee*. It was not spoken of as a thing probable, which perhaps might happen, but as a thing certain, *I say it to thee*. "Others, perhaps, will say to thee, as thou didst to me, *This shall not be unto thee*; but I say it shall." As Christ foresaw all his own sufferings, so he foresaw the sufferings of all his followers, and foretold them, though not in particular, as to Peter, yet in general, that they must take up their cross. Having charged him to feed his sheep, he bids him not to expect ease and honour in it, but trouble and persecution, and to suffer ill for doing well.

(2.) He foretels particularly that he should die a violent death, by the hands of an executioner. The stretching out of his hands, some think, points at the manner of his death by crucifying; and the tradition of the ancients, if we may rely upon that, informs us that Peter was crucified at Rome under Nero, A.D. 68, or, as others say, 79. Others think it points at the bonds and imprisonments which those are hampered with that are sentenced to death. The pomp and solemnity of an execution add much to the terror of death, and to any eye of sense make it look doubly formidable. Death, in these horrid shapes, has often been the lot of Christ's faithful ones, who yet have *overcome it by the blood of the Lamb*. This prediction, though pointing chiefly at his death, was to have its accomplishment in his previous sufferings. It began to be fulfilled presently, when he was imprisoned, Acts 6:3; 5:18; 12:4. No more is implied here in his being carried whither he would not than that it was a violent death that he should be carried to, such a death as even innocent nature could not think of without dread, nor approach without some reluctance. He that puts on the Christian does not put off the man. Christ himself prayed against the bitter cup. A natural aversion to pain and death is well reconcileable with a holy submission to the will of God in both. Blessed Paul, though longing to be unloaded, owns he cannot desire *to be unclothed*, 2 Co. 5:4.

(3.) He compares this with his former liberty. "Time was when thou knewest not any of these hardships, *thou girdest thyself, and walkedst whither thou wouldest*." Where trouble comes we are apt to aggravate it with this, that it has been otherwise; and to fret the more at the grievances of restraint, sickness, and poverty, because we have known the sweets of liberty, health, and plenty, Job 29:2; Ps. 42:4. But we may turn it the other way, and reason thus with ourselves: "How many years of prosperity have I enjoyed more than I deserved and improved? And, having received good, shall I not receive evil also?" See here, [1.] What a change may possibly be made with us, as to our condition in this world! Those that have *girded themselves with strength and honour*, and indulged themselves in the greatest liberties, perhaps levities, may be reduced to such circumstances as are the reverse of all this. See 1 Sa. 2:5. [2.] What a change is presently made with those that leave all to follow Christ! They must no longer gird themselves, but he must gird them! and must no longer walk whither they will, but whither he will. [3.] What a change will certainly be made with us if we should live to be old! Those who, when they were young, had strength of body and vigour of mind, and could easily go through business and hardship, and take the pleasures they had a mind to, when they shall be old, will find their strength gone, like Samson, when his hair was cut and he could *not shake himself as at other times*.

(4.) Christ tells Peter he should suffer thus in his old age. [1.] Though he should be old, and in the course of nature not likely to live long, yet his enemies would hasten him out of the world violently when he was about to retire out of it peaceably, and would put out his candle when it was almost burned down to the socket. See 2 Chr. 36:17. [2.] God would shelter him from the rage of his enemies till he should come to be old, that he might be made the fitter for sufferings, and the church might the longer enjoy his services.

2. The explication of this prediction (v. 19), *This spoke he* to Peter, *signifying by what death he should glorify God*, when he had finished his course. Observe, (1.) That it is not only *appointed to all once to die*, but it is appointed to each what death he shall die, whether natural or violent, slow or sudden, easy or painful. When Paul speaks of so *great a death*, he intimates that there are degrees of death; there is one way into the world, but many ways out, and God has determined which way we should go. (2.) That it is the great concern of every good man, whatever death he dies, to glorify God in it; for what is our chief end but this, *to die to the Lord, at the word of the Lord?* When we die patiently, submitting to the will of God, — die cheerfully, rejoicing in hope of the glory of God, — and die usefully, witnessing to the truth and goodness of religion and encouraging others, we glorify God in dying: and this is *the earnest expectation and hope* of all good Christians, as it was Paul's, *that Christ may be magnified in them living and dying*, Phil. 1:20. (3.) That the death of the martyrs was in a special manner for the glorifying of God. The truths of God, which they died in the defence of, are hereby confirmed. The grace of God, which carried them with so much constancy through their sufferings, is hereby magnified. And the consolations of God, which have abounded towards them in their sufferings, and his promises, the springs of their consolations, have hereby been recommended to the faith and joy of all the saints. The blood of the martyrs has been the seed of the church, and the conversion and establishment of thousands. *Precious* therefore *in the sight of the Lord is the death of his saints*, as that which honours him; and those who thereby at such an expense honour him he will honour.

3. The word of command he gives him hereupon: *When he had spoken thus*, observing Peter perhaps to look blank upon it, *he saith unto him, Follow me*. Probably he rose from the place where he had sat at dinner, walked off a little, and bade Peter attend him. This word, *Follow me*, was (1.) A further confirmation of his restoration to his Master's favour, and to his apostleship; for *Follow me* was the first call. (2.) It was an explication of the prediction of his sufferings, which perhaps Peter at first did not fully understand, till Christ gave him that key to it, *Follow me*: "Expect to be treated as I have been, and to tread the same bloody path that I have trodden before thee; *for the disciple is not greater than his Lord*." (3.) It was to excite him to, and encourage him in, faithfulness and diligence in his work as an apostle. He had told him to *feed his sheep*, and let him set his Master before him as an example of pastoral care: "Do as I have done." Let the undershepherds study to imitate the Chief Shepherd. They had followed Christ while he was here upon earth, and now that he was leaving them he till preached the same duty to them though to be performed in another way, *Follow me*; still they must follow the rules he had given them and the example he had set them. And what greater encouragement could they have than this, both in services and in sufferings? [1.] That herein they did follow him, and it was their present honour; who would be ashamed to follow such a leader? [2.] That hereafter they should follow him, and that would be their future happiness; and so it is a repetition of the promise Christ had given Peter (ch. 13:36), *Thou shalt follow me afterwards*. Those that faithfully follow Christ in grace shall certainly follow him to glory.

Verses 20–25

In these verses, we have,

I. The conference Christ had with Peter concerning John, the beloved disciple, in which we have,

1. The eye Peter cast upon him (v. 20): Peter, in obedience to his Master's orders, followed him, and *turning about*, pleased with the honours his Master now did him, *he sees the disciple whom Jesus loved following* likewise. Observe here, (1.) How John is described. He does not name himself, as thinking his own name not worthy to be preserved in these records; but gives such a description of himself as sufficient-

ly informs us whom he meant, and withal gives us a reason why he followed Christ so closely. *He was the disciple whom Jesus loved*, for whom he had a particular kindness above the rest; and therefore you cannot blame him for coveting to be as much as possible within hearing of Christ's gracious words during those few precious minutes with which Christ favoured his disciples. It is probable that mention in here made of John's having *leaned on Jesus's breast* and his enquiring concerning the traitor, which he did at the instigation of Peter (ch. 13:24), as a reason why Peter made the following enquiry concerning him, to repay him for the former kindness. Then John was in the favourite's place, lying in Christ's bosom, and he improved the opportunity to oblige Peter. And now that Peter was in the favourite's place, called to take a walk with Christ, he thought himself bound in gratitude to put such a question for John as he thought would oblige him, we all being desirous to know things to come. Note, As we have interest at the throne of grace, we should improve it for the benefit of one another. Those that help us by their prayers at one time should be helped by us with ours at another time. This is the *communion of saints*. (2.) What he did: he also followed Jesus, which shows how well he loved his company; where he was there also would this servant of his be. When Christ called Peter to follow him, it looked as if he designed to have some private talk with him; but such an affection John had to his Master that he would rather do a thing that seemed rude than lose the benefit of any of Christ's discourse. What Christ said to Peter he took as said to himself; for that word of command, *Follow me*, was given to all the disciples. At least he desired to have fellowship with those that had fellowship with Christ, and to accompany those that attended him. The bringing of one to follow Christ should engage others. *Draw me and we will run after thee*, Cant. 1:4. (3.) The notice Peter took of it: *He, turning about, seeth him*. This may be looked upon either, [1.] As a culpable diversion from following his Master; he should have been wholly intent upon that, and have waited to hear what Christ had further to say to him, and then was he looking about him to see who followed. Note, The best men find it hard to *attend upon the Lord without distraction*, hard to keep their minds so closely fixed as they should be in following Christ: and a needless and unseasonable regard to our brethren often diverts us from communion with God. Or, [2.] As a laudable concern for his fellow-disciples. He was not so elevated with the honour his Master did him, in singling him out from the rest, as to deny a kind look to one that followed. Acts of love to our brethren must go along with actings of faith in Christ.

2. The enquiry Peter made concerning him (v. 21): "*Lord, and what shall this man do?* Thou hast told me my work — to feed the sheep; and my lot — to be *carried whither I would not*. What shall be his work, and his lot?" Now this may be taken as the language, (1.) Of concern for John, and kindness to him: "Lord, thou showest me a great deal of favour. Here comes thy beloved disciple, who never forfeited thy favour, as I have done; he expects to be taken notice of; hast thou nothing to say to him? Wilt thou not tell how he must be employed, and how he must be honoured?" (2.) Or of uneasiness at what Christ had said to him concerning his sufferings: "Lord, must I alone be *carried whither I would not?* Must I be marked out to be run down, and must this man have no share of the cross?" It is hard to reconcile ourselves to distinguishing sufferings, and the troubles in which we think we stand alone. (3.) Or of curiosity, and a fond desire of knowing things to come, concerning others, as well as himself. It seems, by Christ's answer, there was something amiss in the question. When Christ had given him the charge of such a treasure, and the notice of such a trial, it had well become him to have said, "Lord, and what shall I do then to approve myself faithful to such a trust, in such a trial? *Lord, increase my faith.* As my day is, let my strength be." But instead of this, [1.] He seems more concerned for another than for himself. So apt are we to be busy in other men's matters, but negligent in the concerns of our own souls — quicksighted abroad, but dim-sighted at home — judging others, and prognosticating what they will do, when we have enough to do to *prove our own work*, and *understand our own way*. [2.] He seems more concerned about events than about duty. John was younger than Peter, and, in the course of nature, likely to survive him: "Lord," says he, "what times shall he be reserved for?" Whereas, if God by his grace enable us to persevere to the end, and finish well, and get safely to heav-

en, we need not ask, "What shall be the lot of those that shall come after us?" Is it not well if peace and truth be in my days? Scripture-predictions must be eyed for the directing of our consciences, not the satisfying of our curiosity.

3. Christ's reply to this enquiry (*v.* 22), *"If I will that he tarry till I come,* and do not suffer as thou must, *what is that to thee.* Mind thou thy own duty, the present duty, *follow thou me."*

(1.) There seems to be here an intimation of Christ's purpose concerning John, in two things: — [1.] That he should not die a violent death, like Peter, but should tarry till Christ himself came by a natural death to fetch him to himself. The most credible of the ancient historians tell us that John was the only one of all the twelve that did not actually die a martyr. He was often in jeopardy, in bonds and banishments; but at length died in his bed in a good old age. Note, *First,* At death Christ comes to us to call us to account; and it concerns us to be ready for his coming. *Secondly,* Though Christ calls out some of his disciples to resist unto blood, yet not all. Though the crown of martyrdom is bright and glorious, yet the beloved disciple comes short of it. [2.] That he should not die till after Christ's coming to destroy Jerusalem: so some understand his tarrying till Christ comes. All the other apostles died before that destruction; but John survived it many years. God wisely so ordered it that one of the apostles should live so long as to close up the canon of the New Testament, which John did solemnly (Rev. 22:18), and to obviate the design of the enemy that sowed tares even before the servants fell asleep. John lived to confront Ebion, and Cerinthus, and other heretics, who rose betimes, *speaking perverse things.*

(2.) Others think that it is only a rebuke to Peter's curiosity, and that his tarrying till Christ's second coming is only the supposition of an absurdity: "Wherefore askest thou after that which is foreign and secret? Suppose I should design that John should never die, what does that concern thee? It is nothing to thee, when or where, or how, John must die. I have told thee how thou must die for thy part; it is enough for thee to know that, *Follow thou me."* Note, It is the will of Christ that his disciples should mind their own present duty, and not be curious in their enquiries about future events, concerning either themselves or others. [1.] There are many things we are apt to be solicitous about that are nothing to us. Other people's characters are nothing to us; it is out of our line to judge them, Rom. 14:4. Whatsoever they are, saith Paul, it makes no matter to me. Other people's affairs are nothing to us to intermeddle in; we must quietly work, and mind our own business. Many nice and curious questions are put by the *scribes* and *disputers of this world* concerning the counsels of God, and the state of the invisible world, concerning which we may say, *What is this to us?* What do you think will become of such and such? is a common question, which may easily be answered with another: *What is that to me?* To his own Master he stands or falls. What is it to us to *know the times and the seasons?* Secret things belong not to us. [2.] The great thing that is all in all to us is duty, and not event; for duty is ours, events are God's — our own duty, and not another's; for every one shall bear his own burden — our present duty, and not the duty of the time to come; for sufficient to the day shall be the directions thereof: a *good man's steps are ordered by the Lord,* (Ps. 37:23); he is guided step by step. Now all our duty is summed up in this one of following Christ. We must attend his motions, and accommodate ourselves to them, follow him to do him honour, as the servant his master; we must walk in the way in which he walked, and aim to be where he is. And, if we will closely attend to the duty of following Christ, we shall find neither heart nor time to meddle with at which does not belong to us.

4. The mistake which arose from this saying of Christ, that *that disciple should not die,* but abide with the church to the end of time; together with the suppressing of this motion by a repetition of Christ's words, *v.* 23. Observe here,

(1.) The easy rise of a mistake in the church by misconstruing the sayings of Christ, and turning a supposition to a position. Because John must not die a martyr, they conclude he must not die at all.

[1.] They were inclined to expect it because they could not choose but desire it. *Quod volumus facile crediumus — We easily believe what we wish to be true.* For John to abide in the flesh when the rest were gone, and to continue in the world till Christ's second coming, they think, will be a great blessing to the church, which in every age might have recourse to him as an oracle. When they must lose Christ's bodily presence, they hope they shall have that of his beloved disciple; as if that must supply the want of his, forgetting that the blessed Spirit, the Comforter, was to do that. Note, We are apt to dote too much on men and means, instruments and external helps, and to think we are happy if we may but have them always with us; whereas God will change his workmen, and yet carry on his work, that the *excellency of the power may be of God, and not of men.* There is no need of immortal ministers to be the guides of the church, while it is under the conduct of an eternal Spirit.

[2.] Perhaps they were confirmed in their expectations when they now found that John survived all the rest of the apostles. Because he lived long, they were ready to think he should live always; whereas *that which waxeth old is ready to vanish away,* Heb. 8:13.

[3.] However, it took rise from a saying of Christ's, misunderstood, and then made a saying of the church. Hence learn, *First,* The uncertainty of human tradition, and the folly of building our faith upon it. Here was a tradition, an apostolical tradition, a saying that *went abroad among the brethren.* It was early; it was common; it was public; and yet it was false. How little then are those unwritten traditions to be relied upon which the council of Trent hath decreed to be received with a *veneration and pious affection equal to that which is owing to the holy scripture.* Here was a traditional exposition of scripture. No new saying of Christ's advanced, but only a construction put by the brethren upon what he did really say, and yet it was a misconstruction. Let the scripture be its own interpreter and explain itself, as it is in a great measure its own evidence and proves itself, for it is light. *Secondly,* The aptness of men to misinterpret the sayings of Christ. The grossest errors have sometimes shrouded themselves under the umbrage of incontestable truths; and the scriptures themselves have ben wrested by the unlearned and unstable. We must not think it strange if we hear the sayings of Christ misinterpreted, quoted to patronise the errors of antichrist, and the impudent doctrine of transubstantiation — for instance, pretending to build upon that blessed word of Christ, *This is my body.*

(2.) The easy rectifying of such mistakes, by adhering to the word of Christ, and abiding by that. So the evangelist here corrects and controls that saying among the brethren, by repeating the very words of Christ. He did not say that the disciple should not die. Let us not say so then; but he said, *If I will that he tarry till I come, what is that to thee?* He said so, and no more. *Add thou not unto his words.* Let the words of Christ speak for themselves, and let no sense be put upon them but what is genuine and natural; and in that let us agree. Note, The best end of men's controversies would be to keep to the express words of scripture, and speak, as well as think, according to that word, Isa. 8:20. Scripture language is the safest and most proper vehicle of scripture truth: the *words which the Holy Ghost teacheth,* 1 Co. 2:13. As the scripture itself, duly attended to, is the best weapon wherewith to wound all dangerous errors (and therefore deists, Socinians, papists, and enthusiasts do all they can to derogate the authority of scripture), so the scripture itself, humbly subscribed to, is the best weapon-salve to heal the wounds that are made by different modes of expression concerning the same truths. Those that cannot agree in the same logic and metaphysics, and the propriety of the same terms of air, and the application of them, may yet agree in the same scripture terms, and then may agree to love one another.

II. We have here the conclusion of this gospel, and with it of the evangelical story, *v.* 24, 25. This evangelist ends not so abruptly as the other three did, but with a sort of cadency.

1. This gospel concludes with an account of the author or penman of it, connected by a decent transition to that which went before (*v.* 24): *This is the disciple which testifies of these things* to the present age, and wrote these things for the benefit of posterity, even this same that Peter and his Master had that conference about in the foregoing verses — John the apostle. Observe here, (1.) Those who wrote the history of Christ were not ashamed to put their names to it. John here does in effect subscribe his name. As we are sure who was the author of the first five books of the Old Testament, which were the foundation of that revelation, so we are sure who were the penmen of the four gospels and the Acts, the pentateuch of the New Testament. The record of Christ's life and death is not the report of we know not who, but was drawn up by men of known integrity, who were ready not only to depose it upon oath, but, which was more, to *seal it with their blood.* (2.) Those who wrote the history of Christ wrote upon their own knowledge, not by hearsay, but what they themselves were eye and ear witnesses of. The penman of this history was a disciple, a beloved disciple, one that had leaned on Christ's breast, that had himself heard his sermons and conferences, had seen his miracles, and the proofs of his resurrection. This is he who testifies what he was well assured of. (3.) Those who wrote the history of Christ, as they testified what they had seen, so they wrote what they had first testified. It was published by word of mouth, with the greatest assurance, before it was committed to writing. They testified it in the pulpit, testified it at the bar, solemnly averred it, stedfastly avowed it, not as travellers give an account of their travels, to entertain the company, but as witnesses upon oath give account of what they know in a matter of consequence, with the utmost caution and exactness, to found a verdict upon. What they wrote they wrote as an affidavit, which they would abide by. Their writings are standing testimonies to the world of the truth of Christ's doctrine, and will be testimonies either for us or against us according as we do or do not receive it. (4.) It was graciously appointed, for the support and benefit of the church, that the history of Christ should be put into writing, that it might with the greater fulness and certainty spread to every place, and last through every age.

2. It concludes with an attestation of the truth of what had been here related: *We know that his testimony is true.* This may be taken either, (1.) As expressing the common sense of mankind in matters of this nature, which is, that the testimony of one who is an eye-witness, is of unspotted reputation, solemnly deposes what he has seen, and puts it into writing for the greater certainty, is an unexceptionable evidence. *We know,* that is, All the world knows, that the testimony of such a one is valid, and the common faith of mankind requires us to give credit to it, unless we can disprove it; and in other cases verdict and judgment are given upon such testimonies. The truth of the gospel comes confirmed by all the evidence we can rationally desire or expect in a thing of this nature. The matter of fact, that Jesus did preach such doctrines, and work such miracles, and rise from the dead, is proved, beyond contradiction, by such evidence as is always admitted in other cases, and therefore to the satisfaction of all that are impartial; and then let the doctrine recommend itself, and let the miracles prove it to be of God. Or, (2.) As expressing the satisfaction of the churches *at that time* concerning the truth of what is here related. Some take it for the subscription of the church of Ephesus, others of the angels or ministers of the churches of Asia to this narrative. Not as if an inspired writing needed any attestation from men, or could thence receive any addition to its credibility; but hereby they recommended it to the notice of the churches, as an inspired writing, and declared the satisfaction they received by it. Or, (3.) As expressing the evangelist's own assurance of the truth of what he wrote, like that (*ch.* 19:35), *He knows that he saith true.* He speaks of himself in the plural number, *We know,* not for majesty-sake, but for modesty-sake, as 1 Jn. 1:1, *That which we have seen;* and 2 Pt. 1:16. Note, The evangelists themselves were entirely satisfied of the truth of what they have testified and transmitted to us. They do not require us to believe what they did not believe themselves; no, they knew that their testimony was true, for they ventured both this life and the other upon it; threw away this life, and depended upon another, on the credit of what they spoke and wrote.

3. It concludes with an *et cetera,* with a reference to *many other things,* very memorable, said and done by our Lord Jesus, which were well known by many then living, but not thought fit to be recorded for posterity, *v.* 25. There were many things very remarkable and improvable, which, if they should be written at large, with the several circumstances of them, even the world itself, that is, all the libraries in it, could not contain the books that might be written. Thus he concludes like an orator, as Paul (Heb. 11:32), *What shall I more say? For the time would fail me.* If it be asked why the gospels are not larger, why they did not make the New Testament history as copious and as long as the Old, it may be answered,

(1.) It was not because they had exhausted their subject, and had nothing more to write that was worth writing; no, there were many of Christ's sayings and doings not recorded by any of the evangelists, which yet were worthy to be written in letter of gold. For, [1.] Every thing that Christ said and did was worth our notice, and capable of being improved. He never spoke an idle word, nor did an idle thing; nay, he never spoke nor did any thing mean, or little, or trifling, which is more than can be said of the wisest or best of men. [2.] His miracles were many, very many, of many kinds, and the same often repeated, as occasion offered. Though one true miracle might perhaps suffice to prove a divine commission, yet the repetition of the miracles upon a great variety of persons, in a great variety of cases, and before a great variety of witnesses, helped very much to prove them true miracles. Every new miracle rendered the report of the former the more credible; and the multitude of them renders the whole report incontestable. [3.] The evangelists upon several occasions give general accounts of Christ's preaching and miracles, inclusive of many particulars, as Mt. 4:23, 24; 9:35; 11:1; 14:14, 36; 15:30; 19:2; and many others. When we speak of Christ, we have a copious subject before us; the reality exceeds the report, and, after all, *the one half is not told us.* St. Paul quotes one of Christ's sayings, which is not recorded by any of the evangelists (Acts 20:35), and doubtless there were many more. All his sayings were apophthegms.

(2.) But it was for these three reasons: — [1.] Because it was not needful to write more. This is implied here. There were many other things, which were not written because there was no occasion for writing them. What is written is a sufficient revelation of the doctrine of Christ and the proof of it, and the rest was but to the same purport. Those that argue from this against the sufficiency of the scripture as the rule of our faith and practice, and for the necessity of unwritten traditions, ought to show what there is in the traditions they pretend to be perfective of the written word; we are sure there is that which is contrary to it, and therefore reject them. By these therefore *let us be admonished, for of making many books there is no end,* Eccl. 12:12. If we do not believe and improve what is written, neither should we if there had been much more. [2.] It was not possible to write all. It was possible for the Spirit to indite all, but morally impossible for the penmen to pen all. *The world could not contain the books.* It is a hyperbole common enough and justifiable, when no more is intended than this, that it would fill a vast and incredible number of volumes. It would be such a large and overgrown history as never was; such as would jostle out all other writings, and leave us no room for them. What volumes would be filled with Christ's prayers, had we the record of all those he made, when he *continued all night in prayer to God,* without any vain repetitions? Much more if all his sermons and conferences were particularly related, his miracles, his cures, all his labours, all his sufferings; it would have been an endless thing. [3.] It was not advisable to write much; for *the world,* in a moral sense, *could not contain the books that should be written.* Christ said not what he might have said to his disciples, *because they were not able to bear it;* and for the same reason the evangelists wrote not what they might have written. *The world could not contain, chōrēsai.* It is the word that is used, *ch.* 8:37, "My word *has no place* in you." They would have been so many that they would have found no room. All people's time would have been spent in reading, and other duties would thereby have been crowded out. Much is overlooked of what is written, much forgotten, and much made the matter of doubtful disputation; this would have been the case much more if there had been such a world of books of equal authority and necessity as the whole history would have swelled to; especially since it was requisite that what was written should be meditated upon and expounded, which God wisely thought fit to leave room for. Parents and ministers, in giving instruction, must consider the capacities of those they teach, and, like Jacob, must take heed of over-driving. Let us be thankful for the books that are written, and not prize them the less for their plainness and brevity, but diligently improve what God has thought fit to reveal, and long to be above, where our capacities shall be so elevated and enlarged that there will be no danger of their being over-loaded.

The evangelist, concluding with *Amen,* thereby sets to his seal, and let us set to ours, an *Amen* of faith, subscribing to the gospel, that it is true, all true; and an *Amen* of satisfaction in what is written, as able to make us wise to salvation. *Amen;* so be it.

AN EXPOSITION, WITH PRACTICAL OBSERVATIONS, OF

THE ACTS OF THE APOSTLES

We have with an abundant satisfaction seen the foundation of our holy religion laid in the history of our blessed Saviour, its great author, which was related and left upon record by four several inspired writers, who all agree in this sacred truth, and the incontestable proofs of it, that *Jesus is the Christ, the Son of the living God.* Upon this rock the Christian church is built. How it began to be built upon this rock comes next to be related in this book which we have now before us, and of this we have the testimony only of *one witness;* for the matters of fact concerning Christ were much more necessary to be fully related and attested than those concerning the apostles. Had Infinite Wisdom seen fit, we might have had as many books of the Acts of the Apostles as we have gospels, nay, as we might have had gospels: but, for fear of over-burdening the world (Jn. 21:25), we have sufficient to answer the end, if we will but make use of it. The history of this book (which was always received as a part of the sacred canon) may be considered.

I. As looking back to the preceding gospels, giving light to them, and greatly assisting our faith in them. The promises there made we here find made good, particularly the great promises of the descent of the Holy Ghost, and his wonderful operations, both *on* the apostles (whom here in a few days we find quite other men than what the gospels left them; no longer weak-headed and weak-hearted, but able to say that which then they were not able to bear (Jn. 16:12) as bold as lions to face those hardships at the thought of which they then trembled as lambs), and also with the apostles, making the word mighty to the *pulling down of* Satan's *strong holds,* which had been before comparatively preached in vain. The commission there granted to the apostles we here find executed, and the powers there lodged in them we here find exerted in miracles wrought on the bodies of people — miracles of mercy, restoring sick bodies to health and dead bodies to life — miracles of judgment, striking rebels blind or dead; and much greater miracles wrought on the minds of people, in conferring spiritual gifts upon them, both of understanding and utterance; and this in pursuance of Christ's purposes, and in performance of his promises, which we had in the gospels. The proofs of Christ's resurrection with which the gospels closed are here abundantly corroborated, not only by the constant and undaunted testimony of those that conversed with him after he arose (who had all deserted him, and one of them denied him, and would not otherwise have been rallied again but by his resurrection, but must have been irretrievably dispersed, and yet by that were enabled to own him more resolutely than ever, in defiance of bonds and deaths), but by the working of the Spirit with that testimony for the conversion of multitudes to the faith of Christ, according to the word of Christ, that his resurrection, the sign of the prophet Jonas, which was reserved to the last, should be the most convincing proof of his divine mission. Christ had told his disciples that they should be his witnesses, and this book brings them in witnessing for him, — that they should be *fishers of men,* and here we have them enclosing multitudes in the gospel-net, — that they should be the *lights of the world,* and here we have the world enlightened by them; but that day-spring from on high the first appearing of which we there discerned we here find shining more and more. The *corn of wheat,* which there fell to the ground, here springs up and bears much fruit; the *grain of mustard-seed* there is here a *great tree;* and *the kingdom of heaven,* which was then *at hand,* is here set up. Christ's predictions of the virulent persecutions which the preachers of the gospel should be afflicted with (though one could not have imagined that a doctrine so well worthy of all acceptation should meet with so much opposition) we here find abundantly fulfilled, and also the assurances he gave them of extraordinary supports and comforts under their sufferings. Thus, as the latter part of the history of the Old Testament verifies the promises made to the fathers of the former part (as appears by that famous and solemn acknowledgment of Solomon's, which runs like a receipt in full, 1 Ki. 8:56, *There has not failed one word of all his good promises which he promised by the hand of Moses his servant),* so this latter part of the history of the New Testament exactly answers to the world of Christ in the former part of it: and thus they mutually confirm and illustrate each other.

II. As looking forward to the following epistles, which are an explication of the gospels, which open the mysteries of Christ's death and resurrection, the history of which we had in the gospels. This book introduces them and is a key to them, as the history of David is to David's psalms. We are members of the Christian church, that *tabernacle of God among men,* and it is our honour and privilege that we are so. Now this book gives us an account of the framing and rearing of that tabernacle. The four gospels showed us how the foundation of that house was laid; this shows us how the superstructure began to be raised, 1. Among the Jews and Samaritans, which we have an account of in the former part of this book. 2. Among the Gentiles, which we have an account of in the latter part: from thence, and downward to our own day, we find the Christian church subsisting in a visible profession of faith in Christ, as the Son of God and Saviour of the world, made by his baptized disciples, incorporated into religious societies, statedly meeting in religious assemblies, attending on the apostles' doctrine, and joining in prayers and the breaking of bread, under the guidance and presidency of men that gave themselves to prayer and the ministry of the word, and in a spiritual communion with all in every place that do likewise. Such a body as this thee is now in the world, which we belong to: and, to our great satisfaction and honour, in this book we find the rise and origin of it, vastly different from the Jewish church, and erected upon its ruins; but undeniably appearing to be of God, and not of man. With what confidence and comfort may we proceed in, and adhere to, our Christian profession, as far as we find it agrees with this *pattern in the mount,* to which we ought religiously to conform and confine ourselves!

Two things more are to be observed concerning this book: — (1.) The penman of it. It was written by Luke, who wrote the third of the four gospels, which bears his name; and who (as the learned Dr. Whitby shows) was, very probably, one of the seventy disciples, whose commission (Lu. 10:1, etc.) was little inferior to that of the twelve apostles. This Luke was very much a companion of Paul in his services and sufferings. *Only Luke is with me,* 2 Tim. 4:11. We may know by his style in the latter part of this book when and where he was with him, for then he writes, We did so and so, as *ch.* 16:10; 20:6; and thenceforward to the end of the book. He was with Paul in his dangerous voyage to Rome, when he was carried thither a prisoner, was with him when from his prison there he wrote his epistles to the Colossians and Philemon, in both which he is named. And it should seem that St. Luke wrote this history when he was with St. Paul at Rome, during his imprisonment there, and was assistant to him; for the history concludes with St. Paul's preaching there in his *own hired house.* (2.) The title of it: *The Acts of the Apostles; of the holy Apostles,* so the Greek copies generally read it, and so they are called, Rev. 18:20, *Rejoice over her you holy apostles.* One copy inscribes it, *The Acts of the Apostles by Luke the Evangelist.* [1.] It is the history of the apostles; yet there is in it the history of Stephen, Barnabas, and some other apostolical men, who, though not of the twelve, were endued with the same Spirit, and employed in the same work; and, of those that were apostles, it is the history of Peter and Paul only that is here recorded (and Paul was now of the twelve), Peter the apostle of the circumcision, and Paul the apostles of the Gentiles, Gal. 2:7. But this suffices as a specimen of what the rest did in other places, pursuant to their commission, for there were none of them idle; and as we are to think what is related in the gospels concerning Christ sufficient, because Infinite Wisdom thought so, the same we are to think here concerning what is related of the apostles and their labours; for what more is told us from tradition of the labours and sufferings of the apostles, and the churches they planted, is altogether doubtful and uncertain, and what I think we cannot build upon with any satisfaction at all. This is *gold, silver,* and *precious stones,* built upon the *foundation:* that is *wood, hay, and stubble.* [2.] It is called their *acts,* or *doings; Gesta apostolorum;* so some. *Praxeis* — their practices of the lessons their Master had taught them. The apostles where active men; and though the wonders they did were by the word, yet they are fitly called *their acts;* they spoke, or rather the Spirit by them *spoke, and it was done.* The history is filled with their sermons and their sufferings; yet so much did they labour in their preaching, and so voluntarily did they expose themselves to sufferings, and such were their achievements by both, that they may very well be called their *acts.*

CHAPTER 1

The inspired historian begins his narrative of the Acts of the Apostles, I. With a reference to, and a brief recapitulation of, his gospel, or history of the life of Christ, inscribing this, as he had done that, to his friend Theophilus (*v.* 1, 2). II. With a summary of the proofs of Christ's resurrection, his conference with his disciples, and the instructions he gave them during the forty days, of his continuance on earth (*v.* 3–5). III. With a particular narrative of Christ's ascension into heaven, his disciples' discourse with him before he ascended, and the angels' discourse with them after he ascended (*v.* 6–11). IV. With a general idea of the embryo of the Christian church, and its state from Christ's ascension to the pouring out of the Spirit (*v.* 12–14). V. With a particular account of the filling up of the vacancy that was made in the sacred college by the death of Judas, by the electing of Matthias in his room (*v.* 15–26).

Verses 1–5

In these verses, I. Theophilus is put in mind, and we in him, of St. Luke's gospel, which it will be of use for us to cast an eye upon before we enter upon the study of this book, that we may not only see how this begins where that breaks off, but that, *as in water face answers to face,* so do the acts of the apostles to the acts of their Master, the acts of his grace.

1. His patron, to whom he dedicates this book (I should rather say his *pupil,* for he designs, in dedicating it to him, to instruct and direct him, and not to crave his countenance or protection), is Theophilus, *v.* 1. In the epistle dedicatory before his gospel, he had called him *most excellent Theophilus;* here he calls him no more than *O Theophilus;* not that he had lost his excellency, nor that it was diminished and become less illustrious; but perhaps he had now quitted his place, whatever it was, for the sake of which that title was given him, — or he was now grown into years, and despised such titles of respect more than he had done, — or Luke was grown more intimate with him, and therefore could address him with the more freedom. It was usual with the ancients, both Christian and heathen writers, thus to inscribe their writings to some particular persons. But the directing some of the books of the scripture so is an intimation to each of us to receive them as if directed to us in particular, to us by name; for *whatsoever things were written aforetime were written for our learning.*

2. His gospel is here called *the former treatise which he had made,* which he had an eye to in writing this, intending this for a continuation and confirmation of that, *ton prōton logon — the former word.* What is written of the gospel is the word as truly as what was spoken; nay, we now know no unwritten word that we are to give credit to, but as it agrees with that which is written. He made the former treatise, and now is divinely inspired to make this, for Christ's scholars must *go on towards perfection,* Heb. 6:1. And therefore their guides must help them on, must *still teach the people knowledge* (Eccl. 12:9), and not think that their former labours, though ever so good, will excuse them from further labours; but they should rather be quickened and encouraged by them, as St. Luke here, who, because he had laid the foundation in a former treatise, will build upon it in this. Let not this therefore drive out that; let not new sermons and new books make us forget old ones, but put us in mind of them, and help us to improve them.

3. The contents of his gospel were *that, all that, which Jesus began both to do and teach;* and the same is the subject of the writings of the other three evangelists. Observe, (1.) Christ both did and taught. The doctrine he taught was confirmed by the miraculous works he did, which proved him *a teacher come from God* (Jn. 3:2); and the duties he taught were copied out in the holy gracious works he did, for he hath *left us an example,* and that such as proves him *a teacher come from God* too, for *by their fruits you shall know them.* Those are the best ministers that both do and teach, whose lives are a constant sermon. (2.) *He began both to do and teach;* he laid the foundation of all that was to be taught and done in the Christian church. His apostles were to carry on and continue what he began, and to do and teach the same things. Christ set them in, and then left them to go on, but sent his Spirit to empower them both to do and teach. It is a comfort to those who are endeavouring to carry on the work of the gospel that Christ himself began it. The great salvation *at the first began to be spoken by the Lord,* Heb. 2:3. (3.) The four evangelists, and Luke particularly, have handed down to us *all that Jesus began both to do and to teach;* not all the particulars — the world could not have contained them; but all the heads, samples of all, so many, and in such variety, that by them we may judge of the rest. We have the beginnings of his doctrine (Mt. 4:17), and the beginnings of his miracles, Jn. 2:11. Luke had spoken, had treated, of all Christ's sayings and doings, had given us a general idea of them, though he had not recorded each in particular.

4. The period of the evangelical story is fixed *to the day in which he was taken up, v.* 2. Then it was that he left this world, and his bodily presence was no more in it. St. Mark's gospel concludes with *the Lord's being received up into heaven* (Mk. 16:19), and so does St. Luke's, Lu. 24:51. Christ continued doing and teaching to the last, *till he was taken up* to the other work he had to do within the veil.

II. The truth of Christ's resurrection is maintained and evidenced, *v.* 3. That part of what was related in *the former treatise* was so material that it was necessary to be upon all occasions repeated. The great evidence of his resurrection was that *he showed himself alive to his apostles;* being alive, he showed himself so, and *he was seen of them.* They were honest men, and one may depend upon their testimony; but the question is whether they were not imposed upon, as many a well-meaning man is. No, they were not; for, 1. The proofs were infallible, *tekmēria — plain indications,* both that he was *alive* (he walked and talked with them, he ate and drank with them) and that *it was he himself, and not another;* for he showed them again and again the marks of *the wounds in his hands, and feet, and side,* which was the utmost proof the thing was capable of or required. 2. They were many, and often repeated: *He was seen by them forty days,* not constantly residing with them, but frequently appearing to them, and bringing them by degrees to be fully satisfied concerning it, so that all their sorrow for his departure was done away by it. Christ's staying upon earth so long after he had entered upon his state of exaltation and glory, to confirm the faith of his disciples and comfort their hearts, was such an instance of condescension and compassion to believers as may fully assure us *that we have a high priest that is touched with the feeling of our infirmities.*

III. A general hint given of the instructions he furnished his disciples with, now that he was about to leave them, and they, since *he breathed on them* and *opened their understandings,* were better able to receive them. 1. He instructed them concerning the work they were to do: *He gave commandments to the apostles whom he had chosen.* Note, Christ's choice is always attended with his charge. Those whom he elected into the apostleship expected he should give them preferments, instead of which *he gave them commandments.* When *he took his journey, and gave authority to his servants, and to every one his work* (Mk. 13:34), *he gave them commandments through the Holy Ghost,* which he was himself filled with as Mediator, and which he had breathed into them. In giving them the Holy Ghost, he gave them his commandments; for the Comforter will be a commander; and his office was *to bring to their remembrance what Christ had said. He charged those that were apostles by the Holy Ghost;* so the words are placed. It was their receiving the Holy Ghost that sealed their commission, Jn. 20:22. He was not taken up till after he had given them their charge, and so finished his work. 2. He instructed them concerning the doctrine they were to preach: *He spoke to them of the things pertaining to the kingdom of God.* He had given them a general idea of that kingdom, and the certain time it should be set up in the world (in his parable, Mk. 13), but here he instructed them more in the nature of it, as a kingdom of grace in this world and of glory in the other, and opened to them that covenant which is the great charter by which it is incorporated. Now this was intended, (1.) To prepare them to receive the Holy Ghost, and to go through that which they were designed for. He tells them in secret what they must tell the world; and they shall find that the Spirit of truth, when he comes, will say the same. (2.) To be one of the proofs of Christ's resurrection; so it comes in here; the disciples, to whom *he showed himself alive,* knew that it was he, not only by what he showed them, but by what he said to them. None but he could speak thus clearly, thus fully, *of the things pertaining to the kingdom of God.* He did not entertain them with discourses of politics or the kingdoms of men, of philosophy or the kingdom of nature, but pure divinity and the kingdom of grace, the things which most nearly concerned them, and those to whom they were sent.

IV. A particular assurance given them that they should now shortly receive the Holy Ghost, with orders given them to expect it (*v.* 4, 5), he *being assembled together with them,* probably in the interview at the mountain in Galilee which he had appointed before his death; for there is mention of their *coming together again* (*v.* 6), to attend his ascension. Though he had now ordered them to Galilee, yet they must not think to continue there; no, they must return to Jerusalem, and not depart thence. Observe,

1. The command he gives them to wait. This was to raise their expectations of something great; and something very great they had reason to expect from their exalted Redeemer. (1.) They must wait till the time appointed, which is now *not many days hence.* Those that by faith hope promised mercies will come must with patience wait till they do come, according *to the time, the set time.* And when *the time draws nigh,* as now it did, we must, as Daniel, look earnestly for it, Dan. 9:3. (2.) They must wait in the place appointed, *in Jerusalem,* for there the Spirit must be first poured out, because Christ was to be as *king upon the holy hill of Zion;* and because *the word of the Lord must go forth from Jerusalem;* this must be the mother-church. There Christ was put to shame, and therefore there he will have this honour done him, and this favour is done to Jerusalem to teach us to forgive our enemies and persecutors. The apostles were more exposed to danger at Jerusalem than they would have been in Galilee; but we may cheerfully trust God with our safety, when we keep in the way of our duty. The apostles were now to put on a public character, and therefore must venture in a public station. Jerusalem was the fittest candlestick for those lights to be set up in.

2. The assurance he gives them that they shall not wait in vain.

(1.) The blessing designed them shall come, and they shall find it was worth waiting for; *You shall be baptized with the Holy Ghost;* that is, [1.] "The Holy Ghost shall be poured out upon you more plentifully than ever." They had already been breathed upon with the Holy Ghost (Jn. 20:22), and they had found the benefit of it; but now they shall have larger measures of his gifts, graces, and comforts, and *be baptized with them,* in which there seems to be an allusion to those Old-Testament promises of the pouring out of the Spirit, Joel 2:28; Isa. 44:3; 32:15. [2.] "You shall be cleansed and purified by the Holy Ghost," as the priests were baptized and washed with water, when they were consecrated to the sacred function: "They had the sign; you shall have the thing signified. You shall be sanctified by the truth, as the Spirit shall lead you more and more into it, and have your consciences purged by the witness of the Spirit, that you may serve the living God in the apostleship." [3.] "You shall hereby be more effectually than ever engaged to your Master, and to his guidance, as Israel was *baptized unto Moses in the cloud, and in the sea;* you shall be tied so fast to Christ that you shall never, for fear of any sufferings, forsake him again, as once you did."

(2.) Now this gift of the Holy Ghost he speaks of,

[1.] As *the promise of the Father, which they had heard of him,* and might therefore depend upon. *First,* The Spirit was given by promise, and it was at this time the great promise, as that of the Messiah was before (Lu. 1:72), and that of eternal life is now, 1 Jn. 2:25. Temporal good things are given by Providence, but the Spirit and spiritual blessings are given by promise, Gal. 3:18. The Spirit of God is not given as the spirit of men is given us, and formed within us, by a course of nature (Zec. 12:1), but by the word of God. 1. That the gift may be the more valuable, Christ thought the promise of the Spirit a legacy worth leaving to his church. 2. That it may be the more sure, and that the heirs of promise may be confident of the immutability of God's counsel herein. 3. That it may be of grace, peculiar grace, and may be received by faith, laying hold on the promise, and depending upon it. As Christ, so the Spirit, is received by faith. *Secondly,* It was *the promise of the Father,* 1. Of Christ's Father. Christ, as Mediator, had an eye to God as his Father, fathering his design, and owning it all along. 2. Of our Father, who, if he give us *the adoption of sons,* will certainly give us *the Spirit of adoption,* Gal. 4:5, 6. He will give the Spirit, as *the Father of lights,* as *the Father of spirits,* and as *the Father of mercies;* it is *the promise of the Father. Thirdly,* This promise of the Father they had heard from Christ many a time, especially in the farewell sermon he preached to them a little before he died, wherein he assured them, again and again, that *the Comforter* should come. This confirms the promise of God, and encourages us to depend upon it, that we have heard it from Jesus Christ; *for in him all the promises of God are yea, and amen.* "You have heard it from me; and I will make it good."

[2.] As the prediction of John Baptist; for so far back Christ here directs them to look (*v.* 5): "You have not only heard it from me, but you had it from John; when he turned you over to me, he said (Mt. 3:11), *I indeed baptize you with water, but he that comes after me shall baptize you with the Holy Ghost.*" It is a great honour that Christ now does to John, not only to quote his words, but to make this great gift of the Spirit, now at hand, to be the accomplishment of them. Thus *he confirmeth the word of his servants, his messengers,* Isa. 44:26. But Christ can do more than any of his ministers. It is an honour to them to be employed in dispensing the means of grace, but it his prerogative to give *the Spirit of grace. He shall baptize you with the Holy Ghost,* shall teach you by his Spirit, and give his Spirit to make intercession in you, which is more than the best ministers preaching with us.

(3.) Now this gift of the Holy Ghost thus promised, thus prophesied of, thus waited for, is that which we find the apostles received in the next chapter, for in that this promise had its full accomplishment; this was it *that should come,* and *we look for no other;* for it is here promised to be given *not many days hence.* He does not tell them how many, because they must keep every day in a frame fit to receive it. Other scriptures speak of *the gift of the Holy Ghost* to ordinary believers; this speaks of that particular power which, by the Holy Ghost, the first preachers of the gospel, and planters of the church, were endued with, enabling them infallibly to relate to that age, and record to posterity, the doctrine of Christ, and the proofs of it; so that by virtue of this promise, and the performance of it, we receive the New Testament as of divine inspiration, and venture our souls upon it.

Verses 6–11

In Jerusalem Christ, by his angel, had appointed his disciples to meet him in Galilee; there he appointed them to meet him in Jerusalem again, such a day. Thus he would try their obedience, and it was found ready and cheerful; *they came together,* as he appointed them, to be *the witnesses* of his ascension, of which we have here an account. Observe,

I. The question they asked him at this interview. *They came together* to him, as those that had consulted one another about it, and concurred in the question *nemine contradicente — unanimously;* they came in a body, and put it to him as the sense of the house, *Lord, wilt thou at this time restore again the kingdom to Israel?* Two ways this may be taken: —

1. "Surely thou wilt not at all restore it to the present rulers of Israel, the chief priests and the elders, that put thee to death, and, to compass that design, tamely gave up the kingdom to Caesar, and owned themselves his subjects. What! Shall those that hate and persecute thee and us be trusted with power? *This be far from thee.*" Or rather,

2. "Surely thou wilt now restore it to the Jewish nation, as far as it will submit to thee as their king." Now two things were amiss in this question: —

(1.) Their expectation of the thing itself. They thought Christ would *restore the kingdom to Israel,* that is, that he would make the nation of the Jews as great and considerable among the nations as it was *in the days of David and Solomon, of Asa and Jehoshaphat;* that, as Shiloh, he would *restore the sceptre to Judah, and the lawgiver;* whereas Christ came to set up his own kingdom, and that a kingdom of heaven, not to *restore the kingdom to Israel,* an earthly kingdom. See here, [1.] How apt even good men are to place the happiness of the church too much in external pomp and power; as if Israel could not be glorious unless the kingdom were restored to it, nor Christ's disciples honoured unless they were peers of the realm; whereas we are told to expect the cross in this world, and to wait for the kingdom in the other world. [2.] How apt we are to retain what we have imbibed, and how hard it is to get over the prejudices of education. The disciples, having sucked in this notion with their milk that the Messiah was to be a temporal prince, were long before they could be brought to have any idea of his kingdom as spiritual. [3.] How naturally we are biassed in favour of our own people. They thought God would have no kingdom in the world unless it were *restored to Israel;* whereas the kingdoms of this world were to become his, in whom he would be glorified, whether Israel should sink or swim. [4.] How apt we are to misunderstand scripture — to understand that literally which is spoken figuratively, and to expound scripture by our schemes, whereas we ought to form our schemes by the scriptures. But, *when the Spirit shall be poured out from on high,* our mistakes will be rectified, as the apostles' soon after were.

(2.) Their enquiry concerning the time of it: *"Lord, wilt thou* do it *at this time?* Now that thou hast called us together is it for this purpose, that proper measures may be concerted for the restoring of the kingdom to Israel? Surely there cannot be a more favourable juncture than this." Now herein they missed their mark, [1.] That they were inquisitive into that which their Master had never directed nor encouraged them to enquire into. [2.] That they were impatient for the setting up of that kingdom in which they promised themselves so great a share, and would anticipate the divine counsels. Christ had told them that they should *sit on thrones* (Lu. 22:30), and now nothing will serve them but they must be in the throne immediately, and cannot stay the time; whereas *he that believeth doth not make haste,* but is satisfied that God's time is the best time.

II. The check which Christ gave to this question, like that which he had a little before given to Peter's enquiry concerning John, *What is that to thee? v.* 7, *It is not for you to know the times and seasons.* He does not contradict their expectation that the kingdom would be restored to Israel, because that mistake would soon be rectified by the pouring out of the Spirit, after which they never had any more thoughts of the temporal kingdom; and also because there is a sense of the expectation which is true, the setting up of the gospel kingdom in the world; and their mistake of the promise shall not make it of no effect; but he checks their enquiry after the time.

1. The knowledge of this is not allowed to them: *It is not for you to know,* and therefore it is not for you to ask. (1.) Christ is now parting from them, and parts in love; and yet he gives them this rebuke, which is intended for a caution to his church in all ages, to take heed of splitting upon the rock which was fatal to our first parents — an inordinate desire of forbidden knowledge, and intruding into things which we have not seen because God has not shown them. *Nescire velle quae magister maximus docere non vult, erudita inscitia est — It is folly to covet to be wise above what is written, and wisdom to be content to be no wiser.* (2.) Christ had given his disciples a great deal of knowledge above others *(to you it is given to know the mysteries of the kingdom of God),* and had promised them his Spirit, to teach them more; now, lest they should be puffed up with the abundance of the revelations, he here lets them understand that there were some things which it was not for them to know. We shall see how little reason we have to be proud of our knowledge when we consider how many things we are ignorant of. (3.) Christ had given his disciples instructions sufficient for the discharge of their duty, both before his death and since his resurrection, and in this knowledge he will have them to be satisfied; for it is enough for a Christian, in whom vain curiosity is a corrupt humour, to be mortified, and not gratified. (4.) Christ had himself told his disciples *the things pertaining to the kingdom of God,* and had promised that the Spirit should *show them things to come* concerning it, Jn. 16:13. He had likewise given them *signs of the times,* which it was their duty to observe, and a sin to overlook, Mt. 24:33; 16:3. But they must not expect nor desire to know either all the particulars of future events or the exact times of them. It is good for us to be kept in the dark, and left at uncertainty concerning *the times and moments* (as Dr. Hammond reads it) of future events concerning the church, as well as concerning ourselves, — concerning all the periods of time and the final period of it, as well as concerning the period of our own time.

Prudens futuri temporis exitum
Caliginosa nocte premit Deus —

But Jove, in goodness ever wise,
Hath hid, in clouds of thickest night,
All that in future prospect lies
Beyond the ken of mortal sight. — Hor.

As to the times and seasons of the year, we know, in general, there will be summer and winter counterchanged, but we know not particularly which day will be fair or which foul, either in summer or in winter; so, as to our affairs in this world, when it is a summer-time of prosperity, that we may not be secure, we are told there will come a wintertime of trouble; and in that winter, that we may not despond and despair, we are assured that summer will return; but what this or that particular *day will bring forth* we cannot tell, but must accommodate ourselves to it, whatever it is, and make the best of it.

2. The knowledge of it is reserved to God as his prerogative; it is what *the Father hath put in his own power;* it is hid with him. None besides can reveal the times and seasons to come. *Known unto God are all his works,* but not to us, *ch.* 15:18. It is in his power, and in his only, *to declare the end from the beginning;* and by this he proves himself to be God, Isa. 46:10. "And though he did think fit sometimes to let the Old-Testament prophets know the times and the seasons (as of the Israelites' bondage in Egypt four hundred years, and in Babylon seventy years), yet he has not fit to let you know the times and seasons, no not just how long it shall be before Jerusalem be destroyed, though you be so well assured of the thing itself. He hath not said that he will not give you to know something more than you do of the times and seasons;" he did so afterwards *to his servant John;* "but he has put it in his own power to do it or not, as he thinks fit;" and what is in that New-Testament prophecy discovered concerning the times and the seasons is so dark, and hard to be understood, that, when we come to apply it, it concerns us to remember this work, that it is not for us to be positive in determining the times and the seasons. Buxtorf mentions a saying of the rabbin concerning the coming of the Messiah: *Rumpatur spiritus eorum qui supputant tempora — Perish the men who calculate the time.*

III. He appoints them their work, and with authority assures them of an ability to go on with it, and of success in it. *"It is not for you to know the times and the seasons —* this would do you no good; but know this (*v.* 8) that you shall receive a spiritual *power,* by the *descent of the Holy Ghost upon you,* and shall not receive it in vain, for *you shall be witnesses unto me* and my glory; and your testimony shall not be in vain, for it shall be received here in Jerusalem, in the country about, and all the world over," *v.* 8. If Christ make us serviceable to his honour in our own day and generation, let this be enough for us, and let not us perplex ourselves about times and seasons to come. Christ here tells them,

1. That their work should be honourable and glorious: *You shall be witnesses unto me.* (1.) They shall proclaim him king, and publish those truths to the world by which his kingdom should be set up, and he would rule. They must openly and solemnly preach his gospel to the world. (2.) They shall prove this, shall confirm their testimony, not as witnesses do, with an oath, but with the divine seal of miracles and supernatural gifts: *You shall be martyrs to me,* or *my martyrs,* as some copies read it; for they attested the truth of the gospel with their sufferings, even unto death.

2. That their power for this work should be sufficient. They had not strength of their own for it, nor wisdom nor courage enough; they were naturally of *the weak and foolish things of the world;* they durst not appear as witnesses for Christ upon his trial, neither as yet were they able. *"But you shall receive the power of the Holy Ghost coming upon you"* (so it may be read), "shall be animated and actuated by a better spirit than your own; you shall have power to preach the gospel, and to prove it out of the scriptures of the Old Testament" (which, when they were *filled with the Holy Ghost,* they did to admiration, *ch.* 18:28), "and to confirm it both by miracles and by sufferings." Note, Christ's witnesses shall receive power for that work to which he calls them; those

whom he employs in his service he will qualify for it, and will bear them out in it.

3. That their influence should be great and very extensive: *"You shall be witnesses* for Christ, and shall carry his cause,"* (1.) *"In Jerusalem;* there you must begin, and many there will receive your testimony; and those that do not will be left inexcusable." (2.) "Your light shall thence shine throughout all Judea, where before you have laboured in vain." (3.) "Thence you shall proceed *to Samaria,* though at your first mission you were forbidden to preach in *any of the cities of the Samaritans."* (4.) "Your usefulness shall reach *to the uttermost part of the earth,* and you shall be blessings to the whole world."

IV. Having left these instructions with them, he leaves them (*v.* 9): *When he had spoken these things,* and had said all that he had to say, *he blessed them* (so we were told, Lu. 24:50); and *while they beheld him,* and had their eye fixed upon him, receiving his blessing, *he was* gradually *taken up, and a cloud received him out of their sight.* We have here Christ's ascending on high; not fetched away, as Elijah was, with *a chariot of fire and horses of fire,* but rising to heaven, as he rose from the grave, purely by his own power, his body being now, as the bodies of the saints will be at the resurrection, a spiritual body, and raised in power and incorruption. Observe, 1. He began his ascension in the sight of his disciples, even *while they beheld.* They did not see him come up out of the grave, because they might see him after he had risen, which would be satisfaction enough; but they saw him go up towards heaven, and had actually their eye upon him with so much care and earnestness of mind that they could not be deceived. It is probable that he did not fly swiftly up, but moved upwards gently, for the further satisfaction of his disciples. 2. He *vanished out of their sight, in a cloud,* either a thick cloud, for God said that he would *dwell in the thick darkness;* or a bright cloud, to signify the splendour of his glorious body. It was a bright cloud that overshadowed him in his transfiguration, and most probably this was so, Mt. 17:5. This *cloud received him,* it is probable, when he had gone about as far from the earth as the clouds generally are; yet it was not such a spreading cloud as we commonly see, but such as just served to enclose him. Now he *made the clouds his chariot,* Ps. 104:3. God had often come down in a cloud; now he went up in one. Dr. Hammond thinks that the clouds receiving him here were the angels receiving him; for the appearance of angels is ordinarily described by a cloud, comparing Ex. 25:22 with Lev. 16:2. By the clouds there is a sort of communication kept up between the upper and lower world; in them the vapours are sent up from the earth, and the dews sent down from heaven. Fitly therefore does he ascend in a cloud who is *the Mediator between God and man,* by whom God's mercies come down upon us and our prayers come up to him. This was the last that was seen of him. The eyes of a great many witnesses followed him into the cloud; and, if we would know what became of him then, we may find (Dan. 7:13), *That one like the Son of man came with the clouds of heaven, and came to the Ancient of days, and they brought him* in the clouds as he came *near before him.*

V. The disciples, when he had gone out of their sight, yet still continued *looking up stedfastly to heaven* (*v.* 10), and this longer than it was fit they should; and why so? 1. Perhaps they hoped that Christ would presently come back to them again, to restore the kingdom to Israel, and were loth to believe they should now part with him for good and all; so much did they still dote upon his bodily presence, though he had told them that *it was expedient for them that he should go away.* or, they looked after him, as doubting whether he might not be dropped, as *the sons of the prophets* thought concerning Elijah (2 Ki. 2:16), and so they might have him again. 2. Perhaps they expected to see some change in the visible heavens now upon Christ's ascension, that either *the sun should be ashamed or the moon confounded* (Isa. 24:23), as being out-shone by his lustre; or, rather, that they should show some sign of joy and triumph; or perhaps they promised themselves a sight of the glory of the invisible heavens, upon their opening to receive him. Christ had told them that hereafter they should *see heaven opened* (Jn. 1:51), and why should not they expect it now?

VI. Two angels appeared to them, and delivered them a seasonable message from God. There was a world of angels ready to receive our Redeemer, now that he made his public entry into *the Jerusalem above:* we may suppose these two

loth to be absent then; yet, to show how much Christ had at heart the concerns of his church on earth, he sent back to his disciples two of those that came to meet him, who appear as *two men in white apparel,* bright and glittering; for they know, according to the duty of their place, that they are really serving Christ when they are ministering to his servants on earth. Now we are told what the angels said to them, 1. To check their curiosity: *You men of Galilee, why stand you gazing up into heaven?* He calls them *men of Galilee,* to put them in mind of *the rock out of which they were hewn.* Christ had put a great honour upon them, in making them his ambassadors; but they must remember that they are men, earthen vessels, and men of Galilee, illiterate men, looked upon with disdain. Now, say they, *"Why stand you here,* like Galileans, rude and unpolished men, *gazing up into heaven?* What would you see? You have seen all that you were called together to see, and why do you look any further? *Why stand you gazing,* as men frightened and perplexed, as men astonished and at their wits' end?" Christ's disciples should never stand at a gaze, because they have a sure rule to go by, and a sure foundation to build upon. 2. To confirm their faith concerning Christ's second coming. Their Master had often told them of this, and the angels are sent at this time seasonably to put them in mind of it: *"This same Jesus, who is taken up from you into heaven,* and whom you are looking thus long after, wishing you had him with you again, is not gone for ever; for there is a day appointed in which he *will come in like manner thence, as you have seen him go thither,* and you must not expect him back till that appointed day." (1.) *"This same Jesus* shall come again in his own person, clothed with a glorious body; *this same Jesus,* who came once *to put away sin by the sacrifice of himself, will appear a second time without sin* (Heb. 9:26, 28), who came once in disgrace to be judged, will come again in glory to judge. *The same Jesus* who has given you your charge will come again to call you to an account how you have performed your trust; *he, and not another,"* Job 19:27. (2.) "He *shall come in like manner.* He is gone away in a *cloud,* and *attended with angels;* and, *behold, he comes in the clouds, and with him an innumerable company of angels!* He is gone up with a shout and with the sound of a trumpet (Ps. 47:5), and he will *descend from heaven with a shout and with the trump of God,* 1 Th. 4:16. You have now lost the sight of him in the clouds and in the air; and *whither he is gone you cannot follow him now,* but shall then, when you shall *be caught up in the clouds, to meet the Lord in the air."* When we stand gazing and trifling, the consideration of our Master's second coming should quicken and awaken us; and, when we stand gazing and trembling, the consideration of it should comfort and encourage us.

Verses 12–14

We are here told, I. Whence Christ ascended — *from the mount of Olives* (*v.* 12), from that part of it where the town of Bethany stood, Lu. 24:50. There he began his sufferings (Lu. 22:39), and therefore there he rolled away the reproach of them by his glorious ascension, and thus showed that his passion and his ascension had the same reference and tendency. Thus would he enter upon his kingdom in the sight of Jerusalem, and of those undutiful ungrateful citizens of his that would not have him to reign over them. It was prophesied of him (Zec. 14:4), *That his feet should stand upon the mount of Olives, which is before Jerusalem,* should stand last there; and presently it follows, *The mount of Olives shall cleave in two. From the mount of Olives he* ascended who is *the good olive-tree,* whence we receive *the unction,* Zec. 4:12; Rom. 11:24. This mount is here said to be near Jerusalem, *a sabbath day's journey* from it, that is, a little way; no further than devout people used to walk out on a sabbath evening, after the public worship was over, for meditation. Some reckon it a thousand paces, others two thousand cubits; some seven furlongs, others eight. Bethany indeed was *fifteen furlongs from Jerusalem* (Jn. 11:18), but that part of the mount of Olives which was next to Jerusalem, whence Christ began to ride in triumph, was but seven or eight furlongs off. The Chaldee paraphrast on Ruth 1 says, *We are commanded to keep the sabbaths and the holy days, so as not to go above two thousand cubits,* which they build upon Jos. 3:4, where, in their march through Jordan, the space between them and the ark was to be *two thousand cubits.* God had not then thus limited them, but they limited themselves; and thus far it is a rule to us, not to journey on

the sabbath any more than in order to the sabbath work; and as far as is necessary to this we are not only allowed, but enjoined, 2 Ki. 4:23.

II. Whither the disciples returned: They came to Jerusalem, according to their Master's appointment, though there they were in the midst of enemies; but it should seem that though immediately after Christ's resurrection they were watched, and were *in fear of the Jews,* yet after it was known that they were gone into Galilee no notice was taken of their return to Jerusalem, nor any further search made for them. God can find out hiding-places for his people in the midst of their enemies, and so influence Saul that he shall not seek for David any more. At Jerusalem they *went up into an upper room, and there abode;* not that they all lodged and dieted together in one room, but there they assembled every day, and spent time together in religious exercises, in expectation of the descent of the Spirit. Divers conjectures the learned have about this upper room. Some think it was one of the upper rooms in the temple; but it cannot be thought that the chief priests, who had the letting of these rooms, would suffer Christ's disciples constantly to reside in any of them. It was said indeed, by the same historian, that *they were continually in the temple* (Lu. 24:53), but that was *in the courts of the temple, at the hours of prayer,* where they could not be hindered from attending; but, it should seem, this upper room was in a private house. Mr. Gregory, of Oxford, is of this opinion, and quotes a Syriac scholiast upon this place, who says that it was *the same upper room in which they had eaten the passover;* and though that was called *anōgeon,* this *hyperōon,* both may signify the same. "Whether," says he, "it was in the house of St. John the evangelist, as Euodius delivered, or that of Mary the mother of John Mark, as others have collected, cannot be certain." Notes, *ch.* 13.

III. Who the disciples were, that kept together. The eleven apostles are here named (*v.* 13), so is Mary the mother of our Lord (*v.* 14), and it is the last time that ever any mention is made of her in the scriptures. There were others that are here said to be the brethren of our Lord, *his kinsmen according to the flesh;* and, to make up *the hundred and twenty* spoken of (*v.* 15), we may suppose that all or most of *the seventy disciples* were with them, that were associates with the apostles, and were employed as evangelists.

IV. How they spent their time: *They all continued with one accord in prayer and supplication.* Observe, 1. *They prayed, and made supplication.* All God's people are praying people, and *give themselves to prayer.* It was now a time of trouble and danger with the disciples of Christ; they were as sheep in the midst of wolves; and, *Is any afflicted? Let him pray;* this will silence cares and fears. They had new work before them, great work, and, before they entered upon it, *they were instant in prayer to God* for his presence with them in it. Before they were first sent forth Christ spent time in prayer for them, and now they spent time in prayer for themselves. They were waiting for the descent of the Spirit upon them, and therefore abounded thus in prayer. The Spirit descended upon our Saviour when he was praying, Lu. 3:21. Those are in the best frame to receive spiritual blessings that are in a praying frame. Christ had promised now shortly to send the Holy Ghost; now this promise was not to supersede prayer, but to quicken and encourage it. God will be enquired of for promised mercies, and the nearer the performance seems to be the more earnest we should be in prayer for it. 2. *They continued in prayer,* spent much time in it, more than ordinary, prayed frequently, and were long in prayer. They never missed an hour of prayer; they resolved to persevere herein till the Holy Ghost came, according to the promise, *to pray, and not to faint.* It is said (Lu. 24:53), *They were praising and blessing God;* here, *They continued in prayer and supplication;* for as praise for the promise is a decent way of begging for the performance, and praise for former mercy of begging further mercy, so, in seeking to God, we give him the glory of the mercy and grace which we have found in him. 3. They did this *with one accord.* This intimates that they were together in holy love, and that there was no quarrel nor discord among them; and those who so keep *the unity of the Spirit in the bond of peace* are best prepared to receive the *comforts of the Holy Ghost.* It also intimates their worthy concurrence in the supplications that were made; though but one spoke, they all prayed, and if, when *two agree to ask, it shall be done for them,* much more when many agree in the same petition. See Mt. 18:19.

Verses 15–26

The sin of Judas was not only his shame and ruin, but it made a vacancy in the college of the apostles. They were ordained twelve, with an eye *to the twelve tribes of Israel,* descended from the twelve patriarchs; they were *the twelve stars* that make up the church's crown (Rev. 12:1), and for them *twelve thrones* were designated, Mt. 19:28. Now being twelve when they were learners, if they were but eleven when they were to be teachers, it would occasion every one to enquire what had become of the twelfth, and so revive the remembrance of the scandal of their society; and therefore care was taken, before the descent of the Spirit, to fill up the vacancy, of the doing of which we now have an account, our Lord Jesus, probably, having given directions about it, among other things which he spoke *pertaining to the kingdom of God.* Observe,

I. The persons concerned in this affair. 1. The house consisted of *about a hundred and twenty.* This was *the number of the names,* that is, the persons; some think the men only, distinguished from the women. Dr. Lightfoot reckons that *the eleven apostles, the seventy disciples,* and about thirty-nine more, all of Christ's own kindred, country, and concourse, made up this *one hundred and twenty,* and that these were a sort of synod, or congregation of ministers, a standing presbytery (*ch.* 4:23), *to whom none of the rest durst join themselves* (*ch.* 5:13), and that they continued together till the persecution at Stephen's death dispersed them all but the apostles (*ch.* 8:1); but he thinks that besides these there were many hundreds in Jerusalem, if not thousands, at this time, that believed; and we have indeed read of many that *believed on him there, but durst not confess him,* and therefore I cannot think, as he does, that they were now formed into distinct congregations, for the preaching of the word and other acts of worship; nor that there was any thing of this till after the pouring out of the Spirit, and the conversions recorded in the following chapter. Here was the beginning of the Christian church: this hundred and twenty was the grain of mustard-seed that grew into a tree, the leaven that leavened the whole lump. 2. The speaker was Peter, who had been, and still was, the most forward man; and therefore notice is taken of his forwardness and zeal, to show that he had perfectly recovered the ground he lost by his denying his Master, and, Peter being designed to be the apostle of the circumcision, while the sacred story stays among the Jews, he is still brought in, as afterwards, when it comes to speak of the Gentiles, it keeps to the story of Paul.

II. The proposal which Peter made for the choice of another apostle. He *stood up in the midst of the disciples, v.* 15. He did not sit down, as one that gave laws, or had any supremacy over the rest, but stood up, as one that had only a motion to make, in which he paid a deference to his brethren, standing up when he spoke to them. Now in his speech we may observe,

1. The account he gives of the vacancy made by the death of Judas, in which he is very particular, and, as became one that Christ had breathed upon, takes notice of the fulfilling of the scriptures in it. Here is,

(1.) The power to which Judas had been advanced (*v.* 17): *He was numbered with us, and had obtained part of this ministry* which we are invested with. Note, Many are numbered with the saints in this world that will not be found among them in the day of separation between the precious and the vile. What will it avail us to be added to the number of Christians, if we partake not of the spirit and nature of Christians? Judas's having obtained part of this ministry was but an aggravation of his sin and ruin, as it will be of theirs who *prophesied in Christ's name,* and yet were *workers of iniquity.*

(2.) The sin of Judas, notwithstanding his advancement to this honour. He was *guide to those that took Jesus,* not only informed Christ's persecutors where they might find him (which they might have done effectually though he had kept out of sight), but he had the impudence to appear openly at the head of the party that seized him. He went before them to the place, and, as if he had been proud of the honour, gave the word of command: *That same is he, hold him fast.* Note, Ringleaders in sin are the worst of sinners, especially if those that by their office should have been guides to the friends of Christ are guides to his enemies.

(3.) The ruin of Judas by this sin. Perceiving the chief priests to seek the life of Christ and his disciples, he thought to save his by going over to them, and not only so, but to get an estate under them, of which his wages for his service, he hoped, would be but an earnest; but see what came of it. [1.] He lost his money shamefully enough (*v.* 18): *He purchased a field* with the *thirty pieces of silver,* which were the *reward of his iniquity.* He did not purchase the field, but the wages of his unrighteousness did, and it is very elegantly expressed thus, in derision of his projects to enrich himself by this bargain. He thought to have purchased a field for himself, as Gehazi did with what he got from Naaman by a lie (see 2 Ki. 5:26), but it proved the purchase of a field to bury strangers in; and what was he or any of his the better for this? It was to him an unrighteous mammon, it deceived him; and the reward of his iniquity was the *stumbling-block of his iniquity.* [2.] He lost his life m ore shamefully. We were told (Mt. 27:5) that he *went away* in despair, and was suffocated (so the word signifies there, and no more); here it is added (as latter historians add to those who went before) that, being strangled, or choked with grief and horror, he *fell headlong,* fell *on his face* (so Dr. Hammond), and partly with the swelling of his own breast, and partly with the violence of the fall, he *burst asunder in the midst,* so that *all his bowels tumbled out.* If, when the devil was cast out of a child, he *tore him, threw him down,* and *rent him,* and almost killed him (as we find Mk. 9:26; Lu. 9:42), no wonder if, when he had full possession of Judas, he threw him headlong, and burst him. The suffocation of him, which Matthew relates, would make him swell till he burst, which Peter relates. he burst asunder *with a great noise* (so Dr. Edwards), which was heard by the neighbours, and so, as it follows, it came *to be known* (*v.* 19): *His bowels gushed out;* Luke writes like a physician, understanding all the entrails of the middle and lower ventricle. Bowelling is part of the punishment of traitors. Justly do those bowels gush out that were shut up against the Lord Jesus. And perhaps Christ had an eye to the fate of Judas, when he said of the wicked servant that he would *cut him in sunder,* Mt. 24:51.

(4.) The public notice that was taken of this: *It was known to all the dwellers in Jerusalem.* It was, as it were, put into the newspapers, and was all the talk of the town, as a remarkable judgment of God upon him that betrayed his Master, *v.* 19. It was not only discoursed of among the disciples, but it was in every body's mouth, and nobody disputed the truth of the fact. *It was known,* that is, it was known to be true, incontestably so. Now one would think this should have awakened those to repentance that had had any hand in the death of Christ when they saw him that had the first hand thus made an example. But their hearts were hardened, and, as to those of them that were to be softened, it must be done by the word, and the Spirit working with it. Here is one proof of the notoriety of the thing mentioned, that the field which was purchased with Judas's money was called *Aceldama — the field of blood,* because it was bought with the *price of blood,* which perpetuated the infamy not only of him that sold that innocent precious blood, but of those that bought it too. Look how they will answer it, when God shall make inquisition for blood.

(5.) The fulfilling of the scriptures in this, which had spoken so plainly of it, *that it must needs be fulfilled, v.* 16. Let none be surprised nor stumble at it, that this should be the exit of one of the twelve, for David had not only foretold his sin (which Christ had taken notice of, Jn. 13:18, from Ps. 41:9, He that *eateth bread with me* hath *lifted up the heel against me*), but had also foretold, [1.] His punishment (Ps. 69:25): *Let his habitation be desolate.* This Psalm refers to the Messiah. Mention is made but two or three verses before of their giving him gall and vinegar, and therefore the following predictions of the destruction of David's enemies must be applied to the enemies of Christ, and particularly to Judas. Perhaps he had some habitation of his own at Jerusalem, which, upon this, every body was afraid to live in, and so it became desolate. This prediction signifies the same with that of Bildad concerning the wicked man, that his *confidence shall be rooted out of his tabernacle, and shall bring him to the king of terrors: it shall dwell in his tabernacle, because it is none of his; brimstone shall be scattered upon his habitation,* Job 18:14, 15. [2.] The substitution of another in his room. His *bishopric,* or *his office* (for so the word signifies in general) *shall another take,* which is quoted from Ps. 109:8. With this quotation Peter very aptly introduces the following proposal. Note, We are not to think the worse of any office that God has instituted (whether magistracy or ministry) either for the wickedness of any that are in that office or for the ignominious punishment of that wickedness; nor will God suffer any purpose of his to be frustrated, any commission of his to be vacated, or any work of his to be undone, for the miscarriages of those that are entrusted therewith. *The unbelief of man shall not make the promise of God of no effect.* Judas is hanged, but his bishopric is not lost. It is said of *his habitation,* that *no man shall dwell therein,* there he shall have no heir; but it is not said so of his bishopric, there he shall not want a successor. It is with the officers of the church as with the members of it, if the *natural branches* be *broken off,* others shall be *grafted in,* Rom. 11:17. Christ's cause shall never be lost for want of witnesses.

2. The motion he makes for the choice of another apostle, *v.* 21, 22. Here observe, (1.) How the person must be qualified that must fill the vacancy. It must be one of *these men,* these seventy disciples, *that have companied with us,* that have constantly attended us, *all the time that the Lord Jesus went in and out among us,* preaching and working miracles for three years and a half, *beginning from the baptism of John,* from which the gospel of Christ commenced, *unto that same day that he was taken up from us.* Those that have been diligent, faithful, and constant, in the discharge of their duty in a lower station, are fittest to be preferred to a higher; those that have been faithful in a little shall be entrusted with more. And none should be employed as ministers of Christ, preachers of his gospel, and rulers in his church, but those that are well acquainted with his doctrine and doings, from first to last. None shall be an apostle but one that has companied with the apostles, and that continually; not that has visited them now and then, but been intimately conversant with them. (2.) To what work he is called that must fill up the vacancy: He must be *a witness with us of his resurrection.* By this it appears that others of the disciples were with the eleven when Christ appeared to them, else they could not have been *witnesses with them,* as competent witnesses as they, of his resurrection. The great thing which the apostles were to attest to the world was Christ's resurrection, for this was the great proof of his being the Messiah, and the foundation of our hope in him. See what the apostles were ordained to, not to a secular dignity and dominion, but to preach Christ, and the power of his resurrection.

III. The nomination of the person that was to succeed Judas in his office as an apostle.

1. Two, who were known to have been Christ's constant attendants, and men of great integrity, were set up as candidates for the place (*v.* 23): *They appointed two;* not the *eleven,* they did not take upon them to determine who should be put up, but the *hundred and twenty,* for to them Peter spoke, and not to the eleven. The two they nominated were *Joseph* and *Matthias,* of neither of whom do we read elsewhere, except this Joseph be the same with that *Jesus who is called Justus,* of whom Paul speaks (Col. 4:11), and who is said to be *of the circumcision,* a native Jew, as this was, and who was a *fellow-worker with Paul in the kingdom of God* and a comfort to him; and then it is observable that, though he came short of being an apostle, he did not therefore quit the ministry, but was very useful in a lower station; for, *Are all apostles? Are all prophets?* Some think this Joseph is he that is called *Joses* (Mk. 6:3), the *brother of James the less* (Mk. 15:40), and was called *Joses the just,* as he was called *James the just.* Some confound this with that Joses mentioned Acts 4:36. But that was of Cyprus, this of Galilee; and, it should seem, to distinguish them, that was called *Barnabas — a son of consolation;* this *Barsabas — a son of the oath.* These two were both of them such worthy men, and so well qualified for the office, that they could not tell which of them was the fitter, but all agreed it must be one of these two. They did not propose themselves nor strive for the place, but humbly sat still, and were appointed to it.

2. They applied to God by prayer for direction, not which of the seventy, for none of the rest could stand in competition with these in the opinion of all present, but *which of these two? v.* 24, 25. (1.) They appeal to God as the searcher of hearts: *"Thou, Lord, who knowest the hearts of all men,* which we do not, and better than they know their own." Observe, When an apostle was to be chosen, he must be chosen by his heart, and the temper and disposition of that. Yet Jesus, who knew all men's hearts, for wise and holy ends chose Judas to be one of the twelve. It is comfortable to us, in our prayers for the welfare of the church and its ministers, that the God to whom we pray *knows the hearts of all men,* and has them not only under his eye, but in his hand, and turns them which way soever he will, can make them fit for

his purpose, if he do not find them so, by giving them another spirit. (2.) They desire to know which of these God had chosen: *Lord, show us this,* and we are satisfied. It is fit that God should choose his own servants; and so far as he in any way by the disposals of his providence or the gifts of his Spirit, shows whom he hath chosen, or what he hath chosen, for us, we ought to comply with him. (3.) They are ready to receive him as a brother whom God hath chosen; for they are not contriving to have so much the more dignity themselves, by keeping out another, but desire to have one to *take part of this ministry and apostleship,* to join with them in the work and share with them in the honour, *from which Judas by transgression fell,* threw himself, by deserting and betraying his Master, *from the place* of an apostle, of which he was unworthy, that he might go *to his own place,* the place of a traitor, the fittest place for him, not only to the gibbet, but to hell — this was his own place. Note, Those that betray Christ, as they fall from the dignity of relation to him, so they fall into all misery. It is said of Balaam (Num. 24:25) that he *went to his own place,* that is, says one of the rabbin, *he went to hell.* Dr. Whitby quotes Ignatius saying, There is appointed to every man *idios topos — a proper place,* which imports the same with that of God's rendering to every man according to his works. And our Saviour had said that Judas's own place should be such that *it had been better for him that he had never been born* (Mt. 26:24) — his misery such as to be worse than not being. Judas had been a hypocrite, and hell is the proper place of such; other sinners, as inmates, have their portion with them, Mt. 24:51. (4.) The doubt was determined by lot (*v.* 26), which is an appeal to God, and lawful to be used for determining matters not otherwise determinable, provided it be done in a solemn religious manner, and with prayer, the prayer of faith; for *the lot is cast into the lap, but the whole disposal thereof is of the Lord,* Prov. 16:33. Matthias was not ordained by the imposition of hands, as presbyters were, for he was chosen by lot, which was the act of God; and therefore, as he must be baptized, so he must be ordained, by the Holy Ghost, as they all were not many days after. Thus the number of the apostles was made up, as afterwards, when James, another of the twelve, was martyred, Paul was made an apostle.

CHAPTER 2

Between the promise of the Messiah (even the latest of those promises) and his coming many ages intervened; but between the promise of the Spirit and his coming there were but a few days; and during those days the apostles, though they had received orders to preach the gospel to every creature, and to begin at Jerusalem, yet lay perfectly wind-bound, incognito — concealed, and not offering to preach. But in this chapter the north wind and the south wind awake, and then they awake, and we have them in the pulpit presently. Here is, I. The descent of the Spirit upon the apostles, and those that were with them, on the day of pentecost (*v.* 1–4). II. The various speculations which this occasioned among the people that were now met in Jerusalem from all parts (*v.* 5–13) III. The sermon which Peter preached to them hereupon, wherein he shows that this pouring out of the Spirit was the accomplishment of an Old-Testament promise (*v.* 14–21), that it was a confirmation of Christ's being the Messiah, which was already proved by his resurrection (*v.* 22–32), and that is was a fruit and evidence of his ascension into heaven (*v.* 33–36). IV. The good effect of this sermon in the conversion of many to the faith of Christ, and their addition to the church (*v.* 37–41). V. The eminent piety and charity of those primitive Christians, and the manifest tokens of God's presence with them, and power in them (*v.* 42–47).

Verses 1–4

We have here an account of the descent of the Holy Ghost upon the disciples of Christ. Observe,

I. When, and where, this was done, which are particularly noted, for the greater certainty of the thing.

1. It was *when the day of pentecost was fully come,* in which there seems to be a reference to the manner of the expression in the institution of this feast, where it is said (Lev. 23:15), *You shall count unto you seven sabbaths complete,* from the day of the offering of the first-fruits, which was the next day but one after the passover, the sixteenth day of the month Abib, which was the day that Christ arose. This day was *fully come,* that is, the night preceding, with a part of the day, was fully past. (1.) The Holy Ghost came down at the time of a solemn feast, because there was then a great concourse of people to Jerusalem from all parts of the country, and the proselytes from other countries, which would make it the more public, and the fame of it to be spread the sooner and further, which would contribute much to the propagating of the gospel into all nations. Thus now, as before at the passover, the Jewish feasts served to toll the bell for gospel services and entertainments. (2.) This feast of pentecost was kept in remembrance of the giving of the law upon mount Sinai, whence the incorporating of the Jewish church was to be dated, which Dr. Lightfoot reckons to be just one thousand four hundred and forty-seven years before this. Fitly, therefore, is the Holy Ghost given at that feast, in fire and in tongues, for the promulgation of the evangelical law, not as that to one nation, but to every creature. (3.) This feast of pentecost happened on the *first day of the week,* which was an additional honour put on that day, and a confirmation of it to be the Christian sabbath, *the day which the Lord hath made,* to be a standing memorial in his church of those two great blessings — the resurrection of Christ, and the pouring out of the Spirit, both on that day of the week. This serves not only to justify us in observing that day under the style and title of *the Lord's day,* but to direct us in the sanctifying of it to give God praise particularly for those two great blessings; every Lord's day in the year, I think, there should be a full and particular notice taken in our prayers and praises of these two, as there is by some churches of the one once a year, upon Easter-day, and of the other once a year, upon Whit-sunday. Oh! that we may do it with suitable affections!

2. It was when *they were all with one accord in one place.* What place it was we are not told particularly, whether in the temple, where they attended at public times (Lu. 24:53), or whether in their own upper room, where they met at other times. But it was at Jerusalem, because this had been the place which God chose, to put his name there, and the prophecy was that thence the word of the Lord should go forth to all nations, Isa. 2:3. It was now the place of the general rendezvous of all devout people: here God had promised to meet them and bless them; here therefore he meets them with this blessing of blessings. Though Jerusalem had done the utmost dishonour imaginable to Christ, yet he did this honour to Jerusalem, to teach his remnant in all places; he had this in Jerusalem. Here the disciples were in one place, and they were not as yet so many but that one place, and no large one, would hold them all. And here they were *with one accord.* We cannot forget how often, while their Master was with them, there were *strifes among them, who should be the greatest;* but now all these strifes were at an end, we hear no more of them. What they had received already of the Holy Ghost, when Christ breathed on them, had in a good measure rectified the mistakes upon which those contests were grounded, and had disposed them to holy love. They had prayed more together of late than usual (*ch.* 1:14), and this made them love one another better. By his grace he thus prepared them for the gift of the Holy Ghost; for that blessed dove comes not where there is noise and clamour, but moves upon the face of the still waters, not the rugged ones. Would we have the Spirit *poured out upon us from on high?* Let us be all of one accord, and, notwithstanding variety of sentiments and interests, as no doubt there was among those disciples, let us agree to love one another; for, where *brethren dwell together in unity,* there it is that *the Lord commands his blessing.*

II. How, and in what manner, the Holy Ghost came upon them. We often read in the old Testament of God's coming down in a cloud; as when he took possession first of the tabernacle, and afterwards of the temple, which intimates the darkness of that dispensation. And Christ went up to heaven in a cloud, to intimate how much we are kept in the dark concerning the upper world. But the Holy Ghost did not descend in a cloud; for he was to dispel and scatter the clouds that overspread men's minds, and to bring light into the world.

1. Here is an audible summons given them to awaken their expectations of something great, *v.* 2. It is here said, (1.) That it came *suddenly,* did not rise gradually, as common winds do, but was at the height immediately. It came sooner than they expected, and startled even those that were now together waiting, and probably employed in some religious exercises. (2.) It was *a sound from heaven,* like a thunder-clap, Rev. 6:1. God is said to *bring the winds out of his treasuries* (Ps. 135:7), and *to gather them in his hands,* Prov. 30:4. From him this sound came, like the voice of one crying, *Prepare ye the way of the Lord.* (3.) It was the sound of a wind, for the way of the Spirit is like that of the wind (Jn. 3:3), *thou hearest the sound thereof, but canst not tell whence it comes nor whither it goes.* When the Spirit of life is to enter into the dry bones, the prophet is told to *prophecy unto the wind: Come from the four winds, O breath,* Eze. 37:9. And though it was not *in the wind* that the Lord came to Elijah, yet this prepared him to receive his discovery of himself in the *still small voice,* 1 Ki. 19:11, 12. *God's way is in the whirlwind and the storm* (Nah. 1:3), and out of the whirlwind he spoke to Job. (4.) It was a *rushing mighty wind;* it was strong and violent, and came not only with a great noise, but with great force, as if it would bear down all before it. This was to signify the powerful influences and operations of the Spirit of God upon the minds of men, and thereby upon the world, that they should be *mighty through God, to the casting down of imaginations.* (5.) *It filled* not only the room, but *all the house where they were sitting.* Probably it alarmed the whole city, but, to show that it was supernatural, presently fixed upon that particular house: as some think the wind that was sent to arrest Jonah affected only the ship that he was in (Jon. 1:4), and as the wise men's star stood over the house where the child was. This would direct the people who observed it whither to go to enquire the meaning of it. This wind filling the house would strike an awe upon the disciples, and help to put them into a very serious, reverent, and composed frame, for the receiving of the Holy Ghost. Thus the convictions of the Spirit make way for his comforts; and the rough blasts of that blessed wind prepare the soul for its soft and gentle gales.

2. Here is a visible sign of the gift they were to receive. They saw *cloven tongues, like as of fire* (*v.* 3), and *it sat — ekathise,* not *they* sat, those cloven tongues, but he, that is the Spirit (signified thereby), rested upon each of them, as he is said to rest upon the prophets of old. Or, as Dr. Hammond describes it, "There was an appearance of something like flaming fire lighting on every one of them, which divided asunder, and so formed the resemblance of tongues, with that part of them that was next their heads divided or cloven." The flame of a candle is somewhat like a tongue; and there is a meteor which naturalists call *ignis lambens — a gentle flame,* not a devouring fire; such was this. Observe,

(1.) There was an outward sensible sign, for the confirming of the faith of the disciples themselves, and for the convincing of others. Thus the prophets of old had frequently their first mission confirmed by signs, that all Israel might know them to be established prophets.

(2.) The sign given was fire, that John Baptist's saying concerning Christ might be fulfilled, *He shall baptize you with the Holy Ghost and with fire;* with the Holy Ghost as with fire. They were now, in the feast of pentecost, celebrating the memorial of the giving of the law upon mount Sinai; and as that was given in fire, and therefore is called a fiery law, so is the gospel. Ezekiel's mission was confirmed by a vision of *burning coals of fire* (*ch.* 1:13), and Isaiah's by *a coal of fire* touching his lips, *ch.* 6:7. The Spirit, like fire, melts the heart, separates and burns up the dross, and kindles pious and devout affections in the soul, in which, as in the fire upon the altar, the spiritual sacrifices are offered up. This is that fire which Christ came to send upon the earth. Lu. 12:49.

(3.) This fire appeared in cloven tongues. The operations of the Spirit were many; that of speaking with divers tongues was one, and was singled out to be the first indication of the gift of the Holy Ghost, and to that this sign had a reference. [1.] They were tongues; for from the Spirit we have the word of God, and by him Christ would speak to the world, and he gave the Spirit to the disciples, not only to endue them with knowledge, but to endue them with a power to publish and proclaim to the world what they knew; for *the dispensation of the Spirit is given to every man to profit withal.* [2.] These tongues were cloven, to signify that God would hereby divide unto all nations the knowledge of his grace, as he is said to have divided to them by his providence the light of the heavenly bodies, Deu. 4:19. The tongues were divided, and yet they still continued all of one accord; for there may be a sincere unity of affections where yet there is a diversity of expression. Dr. Lightfoot observes that the dividing of tongues at Babel was the casting off of the heathen; for when they had lost the language in which alone God was spoken of and preached, they utterly lost the knowledge of God and religion, and fell into idolatry. But now, after above two thousand years, God, by another dividing of tongues, restores the knowledge of himself to the nations.

(4.) This fire sat upon them for some time, to denote the constant residence of the Holy Ghost with them. The prophetic gifts of old were conferred sparingly and but at some times, but the disciples of Christ had the gifts of the Spirit always with them, though the sign, we may suppose, soon disappeared. Whether these flames of fire passed from one to another, or whether there were as many flames as there were persons, is not certain. But they must be strong and bright flames that would be visible in the day-light, as it now was, for the day was fully come.

III. What was the immediate effect of this? 1. *They were all filled with the Holy Ghost,* more plentifully and powerfully than they were before. They were filled with the graces of the Spirit, and were more than ever under his sanctifying influences — were now holy, and heavenly, and spiritual, more weaned from this world and better acquainted with the other. They were more filled with the comforts of the Spirit, rejoiced more than ever in the love of Christ and the hope of heaven, and in it all their griefs and fears were swallowed up. They were also, for the proof of this, filled with the gifts of the Holy Ghost, which are especially meant here; they were endued with miraculous powers for the furtherance of the gospel. It seems evident to me that not only the twelve apostles, but all the hundred and twenty disciples were *filled with the Holy Ghost* alike at this time — all the seventy disciples, who were apostolic men, and employed in the same work, and all the rest too that were to preach the gospel; for it is said expressly (Eph. 4:8, 11), *When Christ ascended on high* (which refers to this, *v.* 33), *he gave gifts unto men,* not only *some apostles* (such were the twelve), but *some prophets* and *some evangelists* (such were many of the seventy disciples, itinerant preachers), and some *pastors and teachers* settled in particular churches, as we may suppose some of these afterwards were. The *all* here must refer to the *all* that were together, *v.* 1; *ch.* 1:14, 15. 2. *They began to speak with other tongues,* besides their native language, though they had never learned any other. They spoke not matters of common conversation, but the word of God, and the praises of his name, *as the Spirit gave them utterance,* or gave them to speak *apophthengesthai — apophthegms,* substantial and weighty sayings, worthy to be had in remembrance. It is probable that it was not only one that was enabled to speak one language, and another another (as it was with the several families that were dispersed from Babel), but that every one was enabled to speak divers languages, as he should have occasion to use them. And we may suppose that they understood not only themselves but one another too, which the builders of Babel did not, Gen. 11:7. They did not speak here and there a word of another tongue, or stammer out some broken sentences, but spoke it as readily, properly, and elegantly, as if it had been their mother-tongue; for whatever was produced by miracle was the best of the kind. They spoke not from any previous thought or meditation, but *as the Spirit gave them utterance;* he furnished them with the matter as well as the language. Now this was, (1.) A very great miracle; it was a miracle upon the mind (and so had most of the nature of a gospel miracle), for in the mind words are framed. They had not only never learned these languages, but had never learned any foreign tongue, which might have facilitated these; nay, for aught that appears, they had never so much as heard these languages spoken, nor had any idea of them. They were neither scholars nor travellers, nor had had any opportunity of learning languages either by books or conversation. Peter indeed was forward enough to speak in his own tongue, but the rest of them were no spokesmen, nor were they quick of apprehension; yet now not only *the heart of the rash understands knowledge, but the tongue of the stammerers is ready to speak eloquently,* Isa. 32:4. When Moses complained, *I am slow of speech,* God said, *I will be with thy mouth,* and *Aaron shall be thy spokesman.* But he did more for these messengers of his: he that made man's mouth new-made theirs. (2.) A very proper, needful, and serviceable miracle. The language the disciples spoke was Syriac, a dialect of the Hebrew; so that it was necessary that they should be endued with the gift, for the understanding both of the original Hebrew of the Old Testament, in which it was written, and of the original Greek of the New Testament, in which it was to be written. But this was not all; they were commissioned to *preach the gospel to every creature, to disciple all nations.* But here is an insuperable difficulty at the threshold. How shall they master the several languages so as to speak intelligibly to all nations? It will be the work of a man's life to learn their languages. And therefore, to prove that Christ could give authority to preach to the nations, he gives ability to preach to them in their own language. And it should seem that this was the accomplishment of that promise which Christ made to his disciples (Jn. 14:12), *Greater works than these shall you do.* For this may well be reckoned, all things considered, a greater work than the miraculous cures Christ wrought. Christ himself did not speak with other tongues, nor did he enable his disciples to do so while he was with them: but it was the first effect of the *pouring out of the Spirit* upon them. And archbishop Tillotson thinks it probable that if the conversion of infidels to Christianity were now sincerely and vigorously attempted, by men of honest minds, God would extraordinarily countenance such an attempt with all fitting assistance, as he did the first publication of the gospel.

Verses 5–13

We have here an account of the public notice that was taken of this extraordinary gift with which the disciples were all on a sudden endued. Observe,

I. The great concourse of people that there was now at Jerusalem, it should seem more than was usual at the feast of pentecost. *There were dwelling* or abiding *at Jerusalem* Jews that were *devout men,* disposed to religion, and that had the fear of God before their eyes (so the word properly signifies), some of them *proselytes of righteousness,* that were circumcised, and admitted members of the Jewish church, others only *proselytes of the gate,* that forsook idolatry, and gave up themselves to the worship of the true God, but not to the ceremonial law; some of those that were at Jerusalem now, *out of every nation under heaven,* whither the Jews were dispersed, or whence proselytes were come. The expression is hyperbolical, denoting that there were some from most of the then known parts of the world; as much as ever Tyre was, or London is, the rendezvous of trading people from all parts, Jerusalem at that time was of religious people from all parts. Now, 1. We may here see what were some of those countries whence those strangers came (*v.* 9–11), some from the eastern countries, as the *Parthians, Medes, Elamites, and dwellers in Mesopotamia,* the posterity of Shem; thence we come in order to Judea, which ought to be mentioned, because, though the language of those in Judea was the same with that which the disciples spoke, yet, before, they spoke it with the north-country tone and dialect *(Thou art a Galilean, and thy speech betrays thee),* but now they spoke it as correctly as the inhabitants of Judea themselves did. Next come the inhabitants of Cappadocia, Pontus, and that country about Propontis which was particularly called *Asia,* and these were the countries in which those strangers were scattered to whom St. Peter writes. 1 Pt. 1:1. Next come the dwellers in *Phrygia and Pamphylia,* which lay westward, the posterity of Japhet, as were also the *strangers of Rome;* there were some also that dwelt in the southern parts of *Egypt, in the parts of Libya about Cyrene;* there were also some from the island of Crete, and some from the deserts of Arabia; but they were all either Jews originally, dispersed into those countries; or *proselytes* to the Jewish religion, but natives of those countries. Dr. Whitby observes that the Jewish writers about this time, as Philo and Josephus, speak of the Jews as *dwelling every where through the whole earth;* and that *there is not a people upon earth among whom some Jews do not inhabit.* 2. We may enquire what brought all those Jews and proselytes together to Jerusalem at this time: not to make a transient visit thither to the feast of pentecost, for they are said to dwell there. They took lodgings there, because there was at this time a general expectation of the appearing of the Messiah; for Daniel's weeks had just now expired, the sceptre had departed from Judah, and it was then generally thought that *the kingdom of God would immediately appear,* Lu. 19:11. This brought those who were most zealous and devout to Jerusalem, to sojourn there, that they might have an early share in the kingdom of the Messiah and the blessings of that kingdom.

II. The amazement with which these strangers were seized when they heard the disciples speak in their own tongues. It should seem, the disciples spoke in various languages before the people of those languages came to them; for it is intimated (*v.* 6) that the spreading of the report of this abroad was that which *brought the multitude together,* especially those of different countries, who seem to have been more affected with this work of wonder than the inhabitants of Jerusalem themselves.

1. They observe that the speakers are all Galileans, that know no other than their mother tongue (*v.* 7); they are despicable men, from whom nothing learned nor polite is to be expected. God chose the weak and foolish things of the world to confound the wise and mighty. Christ was thought to be a Galilean, and his disciples really were so, unlearned and ignorant men.

2. They acknowledge that they spoke intelligibly and readily their own language (which they were the most competent judges of), so correctly and fluently that none of their own countrymen could speak it better: *We hear every man in our own tongue wherein we were born* (*v.* 8), that is, we hear one or other of them speak our native language. The Parthians hear one of them speak their language, the Medes hear another of them speak theirs; and so of the rest; *v.* 11, *We do hear them speak in our tongues the wonderful works of God.* Their respective languages were not only unknown at Jerusalem, but probably despised and undervalued, and therefore it was not only a surprise, but a pleasing surprise, to them to hear the language of their own country spoken, as it naturally is to those that are strangers in a strange land. (1.) The things they heard the apostles discourse of were the *wonderful works of God, megaleia tou Theou — Magnalia Dei, the great things of God.* It is probable that the apostles spoke of Christ, and redemption by him, and the grace of the gospel; and these are indeed the *great things of God,* which will be for ever *marvellous in our eyes.* (2.) They heard them both praise God for these great things and instruct the people concerning these things, *in their own tongue,* according as they perceived the language of their hearers, or those that enquired of them, to be. Now though, perhaps, by dwelling some time at Jerusalem, they were got to be so much masters of the Jewish language that they could have understood the meaning of the disciples if they had spoken that language, yet, [1.] This was more strange, and helped to convince their judgment, that this doctrine was of God; for *tongues were for a sign* to those that believed not, 1 Co. 14:22. [2.] It was more kind, and helped to engage their affections, as it was a plain indication of the favour intended to the Gentiles, and that the knowledge and worship of God should no longer be confined to the Jews, but the partition-wall should be broken down; and this is to us a plain intimation of the mind and will of God, that the sacred records of God's wonderful works should be preserved by all nations *in their own tongue;* that the scriptures should be read, and public worship performed, in the vulgar languages of the nations.

3. They wonder at it, and look upon it as an astonishing thing (*v.* 12): *They were all amazed,* they were in an *ecstacy,* so the word is; and they were in doubt what the meaning of it was, and whether it was to introduce the kingdom of the Messiah, which they were big with the expectation of; they asked themselves and one another *ti an theloi touto einai; — Quid hoc sibi vult? — What is the tendency of this?* Surely it is to dignify, and so to distinguish, these men as messengers from heaven; and therefore, like Moses at the bush, they will *turn aside, and see this great sight.*

III. The scorn which some made of it who were natives of Judea and Jerusalem, probably the scribes and Pharisees, and chief priests, who always resisted the Holy Ghost; they said, *These men are full of new wine,* or *sweet wine;* they have drunk too much this festival-time, *v.* 13. Not that they were so absurd as to think that wine in the head would enable men to speak languages which they never learned; but these, being native Jews, knew not, as the others did, that what was spoken was really the languages of other nations, and therefore took it to be gibberish and nonsense, such as drunkards, those *fools in Israel,* sometimes talk. As when they resolved not to believe the finger of the Spirit in Christ's miracles, they turned it off with this, "He casteth out devils by compact with the prince of the devils;" so, when they resolved not to believe the voice of the Spirit in the apostles' preaching, they turned it off with this, *These men are full of new wine.* And, if they called the Master of the house a wine-bibber, no marvel if they so call those of his household.

Verses 14–36

We have here the first-fruits of the Spirit in the sermon which Peter preached immediately, directed, not to those of other nations in a strange language (we are not told what answer he gave to those that were amazed, and said, *What meaneth this?*) but to the Jews in the vulgar language, even to those that mocked; for he begins with the notice of that (*v.* 15), and addresses his discourse (*v.* 14) *to the men of Judea and the inhabitants of Jerusalem;* but we have reason enough to think that the other disciples continued to speak to those who understood them (and therefore flocked about them), in the languages of their respective countries, *the wonderful works of God.* And it was not by Peter's preaching only, but that of all, or most, of the rest of the hundred and twenty, *that three thousand souls were* that day converted, and added to the church; but Peter's sermon only is recorded, to be an evidence for him that he was thoroughly recovered from his fall, and thoroughly restored to the divine favour. He that had sneakingly denied Christ now as courageously confesses him. Observe,

I. His introduction or preface, wherein he craves the attention of the auditory, or demands it rather: *Peter stood up* (*v.* 14), to show that he was not drunk, *with the eleven,* who concurred with him in what he said, and probably in their turns spoke likewise to the same purport; those that were of greatest authority stood up to speak to the scoffing Jews, and to confront those who contradicted and blasphemed, but left the seventy disciples to speak to the willing proselytes from other nations, who were not so prejudiced, in their own language. Thus among Christ's ministers, some of greater gifts are called out to instruct those that oppose themselves, to take hold of sword and spear; others of meaner abilities are employed in instructing those that resign themselves, and to be vine-dressers and husband-men. *Peter lifted up his voice,* as one that was both well assured of and much affected with what he said, and was neither afraid nor ashamed to own it. He applied himself to *the men of Judea, andres Ioudaioi — the men that were Jews;* so it should be read; "and you especially *that dwell at Jerusalem,* who were accessory to the death of Jesus, *be this known unto you,* which you did not know before, and which you are concerned to know now, *and hearken to my words,* who would draw you to Christ, and not to the words of the scribes and Pharisees, that would draw you from him. My Master is gone, whose words you have often heard in vain, and shall hear no more as you have done, but he speaks to you by us; hearken now to our words."

II. His answer to their blasphemous calumny (*v.* 15): "*These men are not drunken, as you suppose.* These disciples of Christ, that now *speak with other tongues,* speak good sense, and know what they say, and so do those they speak to, who are led by their discourses into the knowledge of *the wonderful works of God.* You cannot think they are drunk, for *it is but the third hour of the day,*" nine of the clock in the morning; and before this time, on the sabbaths and solemn feasts, the Jews did not eat nor drink: nay, ordinarily, *those that are drunk are drunk in the night,* and not in the morning; those are besotted drunkards indeed who, *when they awake,* immediately *seek it yet again,* Prov. 23:35.

III. His account of the miraculous effusion of the Spirit, which is designed to awaken them all to embrace the faith of Christ, and to join themselves to his church. Two things he resolves it into: — that it was the fulfilling of the scripture, and the fruit of Christ's resurrection and ascension, and consequently the proof of both.

1. That it was the accomplishment of the prophecies of the Old Testament which related to the kingdom of the Messiah, and therefore an evidence that this kingdom is come, and the other predictions of it are fulfilled. He specifies one, that of *the prophet Joel, ch.* 2:28. It is observable that though Peter *was filled with the Holy Ghost, and spoke with tongues as the Spirit gave him utterance,* yet he did not set aside the scriptures, nor think himself above them; nay, much of his discourse is quotation out of the Old Testament, to which he appeals, and with which he proves what he says. Christ's scholars never learn above their Bible; and the Spirit is given not to supersede the scriptures, but to enable us to understand and improve the scriptures. Observe,

(1.) The text itself that Peter quotes, *v.* 17–21. It refers to *the last days,* the times of the gospel, which are called *the last days* because the dispensation of God's kingdom among men, which the gospel sets up, is the last dispensation of divine grace, and we are to look for no other than the continuation of this to the end of time. Or, *in the last days,* that is, a great while after the ceasing of prophecy in the Old-Testament church. Or, in the days immediately preceding the destruction of the Jewish nation, in the last days of that people, just before *that great and notable day of the Lord* spoken of, *v.* 20. "It was prophesied of and promised, and therefore you ought to expect it, and not to be surprised at it; to desire it, and bid it welcome, and not to dispute it, as not worth taking notice of." The apostle quotes the whole paragraph, for it is good to take scripture entire; now it was foretold,

[1.] That there should be a more plentiful and extensive effusion of the Spirit of grace from on high than had ever yet been. The prophets of the Old Testament had been *filled with the Holy Ghost,* and it was said of the people of Israel *that God gave them his good Spirit to instruct them,* Neh. 9:20. But now *the Spirit shall be poured out,* not only upon the Jews, but *upon all flesh,* Gentiles as well as Jews, though yet Peter himself did not understand it so, as appears, *ch.* 11:17. Or, *upon all flesh,* that is, upon some of all ranks and conditions of men. The Jewish doctors taught that the Spirit came only upon wise and rich men, and such as were of the seed of Israel; but God will not tie himself to their rules.

[2.] That the Spirit should be in them a Spirit of prophecy; by the Spirit they should be enabled to foretel things to come, and to *preach the gospel to every creature.* This power shall be given without distinction of sex — now only *your sons,* but *your daughters shall prophesy;* without distinction of age — both *your young men and your old men shall see visions, and dream dreams,* and in them receive divine revelations, to be communicated to the church; and without distinction of outward condition — even the *servants and handmaids* shall receive of *the Spirit, and shall prophesy* (*v.* 18); or, in general, men and women, whom God calls his servants and his handmaids. In the beginning of the age of prophecy in the Old Testament there were *schools of the prophets,* and, before that, *the Spirit of prophecy* came upon *the elders of Israel* that were appointed to the government; but now the Spirit shall be poured out upon persons of inferior rank, and such as were not brought up in the schools of the prophets, for the kingdom of the Messiah is to be purely spiritual. The mention of *the daughters* (*v.* 17) and *the handmaidens* (*v.* 18) would make one think that *the women* who were taken notice of (*ch.* 1:14) received the extraordinary gifts of the Holy Ghost, as well as the men. Philip, the evangelist, had *four daughters who did prophesy* (*ch.* 21:9), and St. Paul, finding abundance of the gifts both of tongues and prophecy in the church of Corinth, saw it needful to prohibit women's use of those gifts in public, 1 Co. 14:26, 34.

[3.] That one great thing which they should prophesy of should be the judgment that was coming upon the Jewish nation, for this was the chief thing that Christ himself had foretold (Mt. 24) at his entrance into Jerusalem (Lu. 19:41); and when he was going to die (Lu. 23:29); and these judgments were to be brought upon them to punish for their contempt of the gospel, and their opposition to it, though it came to them thus proved. Those that would not submit to the power of God's grace, in this wonderful effusion of his Spirit, should fall and lie under the pourings out of the vials of his wrath. Those shall break that will not bend. *First,* The destruction of Jerusalem, which was about forty years after Christ's death, is here called *that great and notable day of the Lord,* because it put a final period to the Mosaic economy; the Levitical priesthood and the ceremonial law were thereby for ever abolished and done away. The desolation itself was such as was never brought upon any place or nation, either before or since. It was *the day of the Lord,* for it was the day of his vengeance upon that people for crucifying Christ, and persecuting his ministers; it was *the year of recompences for that controversy;* yea, and for all the blood of the saints and martyrs, *from the blood of righteous Abel,* Mt. 23:35. It was a little day of judgment; it was a *notable day:* in Joel it is called a *terrible day,* for so it was to men on earth; but here *epiphanē* (after the Septuagint), *a glorious, illustrious* day, for so it was to Christ in heaven; it was the epiphany, his appearing, so he himself spoke of it, Mt. 24:30. The destruction of the Jews was the deliverance of the Christians, who were hated and persecuted by them; and therefore that day was often spoken of by the prophets of that time, for the encouragement of suffering Christians, *that the Lord was at hand, the coming of the Lord drew nigh, the Judge stood before the door,* James 5:8, 9. *Secondly,* The terrible presages of that destruction are here foretold: *There shall be wonders in heaven above, the sun turned into darkness and the moon into blood; and signs* too *in the earth beneath, blood and fire.* Josephus, in his preface to his history of the wars of the Jews, speaks of the signs and prodigies that preceded them, terrible thunders, lightnings, and earthquakes; there was a fiery comet that hung over the city for a year, and a flaming sword was seen pointing down upon it; a light shone upon the temple and the altar at midnight, as if it had been noon-day. Dr. Lightfoot gives another sense of these presages: *The blood of the Son of God, the fire of the Holy Ghost* now appearing, the vapour of the smoke in which Christ ascended, *the sun darkened, and the moon made blood,* at the time of Christ's passion, were all loud warnings given to that unbelieving people to prepare for the judgments coming upon them. Or, it may be applied, and very fitly, to the previous judgments themselves by which that desolation was brought on. *The blood* points at the wars of the Jews with the neighbouring nations, with the Samaritans, Syrians, and Greeks, in which abundance of blood was shed, as there was also in their civil wars, and the struggles of the *seditious* (as they called them), which were very bloody; there was no peace to him that went out nor to him that came in. *The fire and vapour of smoke,* here foretold, literally came to pass in the burning of their cities, and towns, and synagogues, and temple at last. And this turning of *the sun into darkness, and the moon into blood,* bespeaks the dissolution of their government, civil and sacred, and the extinguishing of all their lights. *Thirdly,* The signal preservation of the Lord's people is here promised (*v.* 21): *Whosoever shall call upon the name of the Lord Jesus* (which is the description of a true Christian, 1 Co. 1:2) *shall be saved,* shall escape that judgment which shall be a type and earnest of everlasting salvation. In the destruction of Jerusalem by the Chaldeans, there was a remnant sealed to be hid in *the day of the Lord's anger;* and in the destruction by the Romans not one Christian perished. Those that distinguish themselves by singular piety shall be distinguished by special preservation. And observe, the saved remnant are described by this, that they are a praying people: *they call on the name of the Lord,* which intimates that they are not saved by any merit or righteousness of their own, but purely by the favour of God, which must be sued out by prayer. It is *the name of the Lord* which *they call upon* that is *their strong tower.*

(2.) The application of this prophecy to the present event (*v.* 16): *This is that which was spoken by the prophet Joel;* it is the accomplishment of that, it is the full accomplishment of it. This is that effusion of the Spirit upon all flesh which should come, and we are to look for no other, no more than we are to look for another Messiah; for as our Messiah ever lives in heaven, reigning and interceding for his church on earth, so this Spirit of grace, the Advocate, or Comforter, that was given now, according to the promise, will, according to the same promise, continue with the church on earth to the end, and will work all its works in it and for it, and every member of it, ordinary and extraordinary, by means of the scriptures and the ministry.

2. That it was the gift of Christ, and the product and proof of his resurrection and ascension. From this *gift of the Holy Ghost,* he takes occasion to preach unto them Jesus; and this part of his sermon he introduces with another solemn preface (*v.* 22): "*You men of Israel, hear these words.* It is a mercy that you are within hearing of them, and it is your duty to give heed to them." Words concerning Christ should be acceptable words to the men of Israel. Here is,

(1.) An abstract of the history of the life of Christ, *v.* 22. He calls him *Jesus of Nazareth,* because by that name he was generally known, but (which was sufficient to roll away that reproach) he was *a man approved of God among you,* censured and condemned by men, but approved of God: God testified his approbation of his doctrine by the power he gave him to work miracles: *a man marked out by God,* so Dr. Hammond reads it; "signalized and made remarkable among you that now hear me. He was sent to you, set up, a glorious light in your land; you yourselves are witnesses how he became famous by *miracles, wonders, and signs,* works above the power of nature, out of its ordinary course, and contrary to it, *which God did by him;* that is, which he did by that divine power with which he was clothed, and in which God plainly went along with him; *for no man could do such works unless God were with him.*" See what a stress Peter lays upon Christ's miracles. [1.] The matter of fact was not to be denied: "They were done *in the midst of you,* in the midst of your country, your city, your solemn assemblies, *as you yourselves also know.* You have been eyewitnesses of his miracles; I appeal to yourselves whether you have any thing to object against them or can offer any thing to disprove them." [2.] The inference from them cannot be disputed; the reasoning is as strong as the evidence; if he did those miracles, certainly God approved him, *declared him to be,* what he declared himself to be, *the Son of God* and *the Saviour of the world;* for the God of truth would never set his seal to a lie.

(2.) An account of his death and sufferings which they were witness of also but a few weeks ago; and this was the greatest miracle of all, that a man approved of God should thus seem to be abandoned of him; and a man thus approved among the people, and in the midst of them, should be thus abandoned by them too. But both these mysteries are here explained (v. 23), and his death considered, [1.] As God's act; and in him it was an act of wonderful grace and wisdom. He *delivered him to death;* not only permitted him to be put to death, but gave him up, devoted him: this is explained Rom. 8:32, *He delivered him up for us all.* And yet he was approved of God, and there was nothing in this that signified the disapproving of him; for it was done by *the determinate counsel and foreknowledge of God,* in infinite wisdom, and for holy ends, which Christ himself concurred in, and in the means leading to them. Thus divine justice must be satisfied, sinners saved, God and man brought together again, and Christ himself glorified. It was not only according to the will of God, but according *to the counsel of his will,* that he suffered and died; according to an eternal counsel, which could not be altered. This reconciled him to the cross: *Father, thy will be done;* and *Father, glorify thy name;* let thy purpose take effect, and let the great end of it be attained. [2.] As the people's act; and in them it was an act of prodigious sin and folly; it was fighting against God to persecute one whom he approved as the darling of heaven; and fighting against their own mercies to persecute one that was the greatest blessing of this earth. Neither God's designing it from eternity, nor his bringing good out of it to eternity, would in the least excuse their sin; for it was their voluntary act and deed, from a principle morally evil, and therefore "they were *wicked hands with which you have crucified and slain* him." It is probable that some of those were here present who had cried, *Crucify him, crucify him,* or had been otherwise aiding and abetting in the murder; and Peter knew it. However, it was justly looked upon as a national act, because done both by the vote of the great council and by the voice of the great crowd. It is a rule, *Refertur ad universos quod publice fit per majorem partem — That which is done publicly by the greater part we attribute to all.* He charges it particularly on them as parts of the nation on which it would be visited, the more effectually to bring them to faith and repentance, because that was the only way to distinguish themselves from the guilty and discharge themselves from the guilt.

(3.) An attestation of his resurrection, which effectually wiped away the reproach of his death (v. 24): *Whom God raised up;* the same that delivered him *to death* delivers him *from death,* and thereby gave a higher approbation of him than he had done by any other of *the signs and wonders wrought by him,* or by all put together. This therefore he insists most largely upon.

[1.] He describes his resurrection: God *loosed the pains of death,* because it was impossible that he should be *holden of it;* *ōdinas — the sorrows of death;* the word is used for *travailing pains,* and some think it signifies the *trouble and agony* of his soul, in which *it was exceedingly sorrowful, even to the death;* from *these pains and sorrows of soul,* this *travail of soul,* the Father *loosed him* when at his death he said, *It is finished.* Thus Dr. Godwin understands it: "Those terrors which made Heman's soul lie like *the slain* (Ps. 88:5, 15) had hold of Christ; but he was too strong for them, and broke through them; this was *the resurrection of his soul* (and it is a great thing to bring a soul *out of the depths* of spiritual agonies); this was not leaving his soul in hell; as that which follows, *that he should not see corruption,* speaks of the resurrection of his body; and both together make up the great resurrection." Dr. Lightfoot gives another sense of this: "Having *dissolved the pains of death,* in reference to all that believe in him, God raised up Christ, and by his resurrection *broke all the power of death,* and destroyed its pangs upon his own people. He *has abolished death,* has altered the property of it, and, because *it was not possible that he should be long holden of it, it is not possible that they should be* for ever holden." But most refer this to the resurrection of Christ's body. And death (says Mr. Baxter) is by privation a penal state, though not dolorous by positive evil. But Dr. Hammond shows that the Septuagint, and from them the apostle here, uses the word for *cords and bands* (as Ps. 18:4), to which the metaphor of loosing and being held best agrees. Christ was imprisoned for our debt, was thrown into the bands of death; but, divine justice being satisfied, it was not possible he should be detained there, either by right or by force; for he had life in himself, and in his own power, and had conquered the prince of death.

[2.] He attests the truth of his resurrection (v. 32): *God hath raised him up, whereof we all are witnesses* — we apostles, and others our companions, that were intimately acquainted with him before his death, were intimately conversant with him after his resurrection, *did eat and drink with him.* They *received power,* by *the descent of the Holy Ghost upon them,* on purpose that they might be skilful, faithful, and courageous witnesses of this thing, notwithstanding their being charged by his enemies as having stolen him away.

[3.] He showed it to be the fulfilling of the scripture, and, because the scripture had said that he must rise again before he saw corruption, therefore *it was impossible that he should be holden by death* and *the grave; for David speaks* of his being raised, so it comes in, v. 25. The scripture he refers to is that of David (Ps. 16:8–11), which, though in part applicable to David as a saint, yet refers chiefly to Jesus Christ, of whom David was a type. Here is,

First, The text quoted at large (v. 25–28), for it was all fulfilled in him, and shows us, 1. The constant regard that our Lord Jesus had to his Father in his whole undertaking: *I foresaw the Lord before me continually.* He set before him his Father's glory as his end in all — *for he saw* that his sufferings would redound abundantly to the honour of God, and would issue in his own joy; these were *set before him,* and these he had an eye to, in all he did and suffered; and with the prospect of these he was borne up and carried on, Jn. 13:31, 32; 17:4, 5. 2. The assurance he had of his Father's presence and power going along with him: *"He is on my right hand,* the hand of action, strengthening, guiding, and upholding that, *that I should not be moved,* nor driven off from my undertaking, notwithstanding the hardships I must undergo." This was an article of the covenant of redemption (Ps. 89:21), *With him my hand shall be established, my arm also shall strengthen him;* and therefore he is confident the work shall not miscarry in his hand. If God be at our right hand we shall not be moved. 3. The cheerfulness with which our Lord Jesus went on in his work, notwithstanding the sorrows he was to pass through: "Being satisfied *that I shall not be moved,* but the good pleasure of the Lord shall prosper in my hand, therefore *doth my heart rejoice, and my tongue is glad,* and the thought of my sorrow is as nothing to me." Note, It was a constant pleasure to our Lord Jesus to look *to the end of his work,* and to be sure that the issue would be glorious; so well pleased is he with his undertaking that it does his heart good to think how the issue would answer the design. *He rejoiced in spirit,* Lu. 10:21. *My tongue was glad.* In the psalm it is, *My glory rejoiceth;* which intimates that our tongue is our glory, the faculty of speaking is an honour to us, and never more so than when it is employed in praising God. Christ's *tongue was glad,* for when he was just entering upon his sufferings, in the close of his last supper, he *sang a hymn.* 4. The pleasing prospect he had of the happy issue of his death and sufferings; it was this that carried him, not only with courage, but with cheerfulness, through them; he was putting off the body, but *my flesh shall rest;* the grave shall be to the body, while it lies there, a bed of repose, and hope shall give it a sweet repose; *it shall rest in hope, hoti, that thou wilt no leave my soul in hell;* what follows is the matter of his hope, or assurance rather, (1.) That the soul shall not continue in a state of separation from the body; for, besides that this is some uneasiness to a human soul made for its body, it would be the continuance of death's triumph over him who was in truth a conqueror over death: *"Thou wilt not leave my soul in hell"* (in *hades,* in *the invisible state,* so *hades* properly signifies); "but, though thou suffer it for a time to remove thither, and to remain there, yet thou wilt remand it; *thou wilt not leave it* there, as thou dost the souls of other men." (2.) That the body shall lie but a little while in the grave: *Thou wilt not suffer thy Holy One to see corruption;* the body shall not continue dead so long as to begin to putrefy or become noisome; and therefore it must return to life on or before the third day after its death. Christ was God's *Holy One,* sanctified and set apart to his service in the work of redemption; he must die, for he must be *consecrated by his own blood;* but he must *not see corruption,* for his death was to be unto God of *a sweet smelling savour.* This was typified by the law concerning the sacrifice, *that no part of the flesh of the sacrifice which was to be eaten should be kept till the third day,* for fear it should see corruption and begin to putrefy, Lev. 7:15–18. (3.) That his death and sufferings should be, not to him only, but to all his, an inlet to a blessed immortality: *"Thou has made known to me the ways of life, and*

by me made them known to the world, and laid them open." When *the Father gave to the Son to have life in himself, a power to lay down his life and to take it again,* then he showed him *the way of life,* both to and fro; *the gates of death were open to him and the doors of the shadow of death* (Job 38:17), to pass and repass through them, as his occasion led him, for man's redemption. (4.) That all his sorrows and sufferings should end in perfect and perpetual felicity: *Thou shalt make me full of joy with thy countenance.* The reward set before him was *joy, a fulness of joy,* and that in God's *countenance,* in the countenance he gave to his undertaking, and to all those, for his sake, that should believe in him. The smiles with which the Father received him, when, at his ascension, he was *brought to the Ancient of days,* filled him *with joy unspeakable,* and that is *the joy of our Lord,* into which all his shall enter, and in which they shall be for ever happy.

Secondly, The comment upon this text, especially so much of it as relates to the resurrection of Christ. He addresses himself to them with a title of respect, *Men and brethren,* v. 29. "You are men, and therefore should be ruled by reason; you are brethren, and therefore should take kindly what is said to you by one who, being nearly related to you, is heartily concerned for you, and wishes you well. Now, give me leave *freely to speak to you concerning the patriarch David,* and let it be no offence to you if I tell you that David cannot be understood here as speaking of himself, but of the Christ to come." David is here called a patriarch, because he was the father of the royal family, and a man of great note and eminency in his generation, and whose name and memory were justly very precious. Now when we read that psalm of his, we must consider, 1. That he could not say *that of himself,* for *he died, and was buried, and his sepulchre remained in Jerusalem till now,* when Peter spoke this, and his bones and ashes in it. Nobody ever pretended that he had risen, and therefore he could never say of himself that he *should not see corruption;* for it was plain he did see corruption. St. Paul urges this, *ch.* 13:35–37. Though he *was a man after God's own heart,* yet he went the way of all the earth, as he saith himself (1 Ki. 2:2), both in death and burial. 2. Therefore certainly he spoke *it as a prophet,* with an eye to the Messiah, whose sufferings the prophets testified beforehand, and with them *the glory that should follow;* so did David in that psalm, as Peter here plainly shows. (1.) David knew that the Messiah should descend from his loins (v. 30), *that God had sworn to him, that of the fruit of his loins, according to the flesh, he would raise up Christ to sit on his throne.* He promised him a Son, *the throne of whose kingdom should be established for ever,* 2 Sa. 7:12. And it is said (Ps. 132:11), *God swore it in truth unto David.* When our Lord Jesus was born, it was promised *that the Lord God would give him the throne of his father David,* Lu. 1:32. And all Israel knew that the Messiah was to be the Son of David, that is, that, *according to the flesh,* he should be so by his human nature; for otherwise, *according to the spirit,* and by his divine nature, he was *to be David's Lord,* not his son. God having sworn to David that the Messiah, promised to his fathers, should be his son and successor, the fruit of his loins, and heir to his throne, he kept this in view, in penning his psalms. (2.) Christ being the *fruit of his loins,* and consequently in his loins when he penned that psalm (as Levi is said to be in Abraham's loins when he paid *tithes to Melchizedek*), if what he says, as in his own person, be not applicable to himself (as it is plain that it is not), we must conclude it points to that son of his that was then in his loins, in whom his family and kingdom were to have their perfection and perpetuity; and therefore, when he says that *his soul should not be left in its separate state, nor his flesh see corruption,* without doubt he must be understood to speak of the resurrection of Christ, v. 31. And as *Christ died,* so *he rose again, according to the scriptures;* and *that he did so we are witnesses.* (3.) Here is a glance at his ascension too. As David did not rise from the dead, so neither did he *ascend into the heavens,* bodily, as Christ did, v. 34. And further, to prove that when he spoke of the resurrection he meant it of Christ, he observes that when in another psalm he speaks of the next step of his exaltation he plainly shows that he spoke of another person, and such another as was his Lord (Ps. 110:1): *"The Lord said unto my Lord,* when he had raised him from the dead, *Sit thou at my right hand,* in the highest dignity and dominion there; be thou entrusted with the administration of the kingdom both of providence and grace; *sit there* as king, *until I make thy foes* either thy friends or thy footstool," v. 35. Christ rose from the grave to rise higher, and therefore it must be of his resurrection that David spoke, and not his own, in the 16th Psalm; for there was no occasion for him to rise out of his grave who was not to ascend to heaven.

(4.) The application of this discourse concerning the death, resurrection, and ascension of Christ.

[1.] This explains the meaning of the present wonderful effusion of the Spirit in those extraordinary gifts. Some of the people had asked (*v.* 12), *What meaneth this?* I will tell you the meaning of it, says Peter. *This Jesus being exalted to the right hand of God,* so some read it, to sit there; *exalted by the right hand of God,* so we read it, by his power and authority — it comes all to one; and *having received of the Father,* to whom he has ascended, *the promise of the Holy Ghost,* he hath given what he received (Ps. 68:18), and *hath shed forth this which you now see and hear;* for the Holy Ghost was to be given when Jesus was glorified, and not before, Jn. 7:39. You see and hear us speak with tongues that we never learned; probably there was an observable change in the air of their countenances, which they saw, as well as heard the change of their voice and language; now this is from the Holy Ghost, whose coming is an evidence that Jesus is exalted, and he has *received this gift from the Father,* to confer it upon the church, which plainly bespeaks him to be the Mediator, or middle person between God and the church. *The gift of the Holy Ghost* was, *First,* A performance of divine promises already made; here it is called *the promise of the Holy Ghost;* many *exceedingly great and precious promises* the divine power has given us, but this is *the promise,* by way of eminency, as that of the Messiah had been, and this is the promise that includes all the rest; hence God's giving *the Holy Spirit to those that ask him* (Lu. 11:13) is his giving them all *good things,* Mt. 7:11. Christ received *the promise of the Holy Ghost,* that is, the promised gift of the Holy Ghost, and has given it to us; for all *the promises are yea and amen in him. Secondly,* It was a pledge of all divine favours further intended; what you now see and hear is but an earnest of greater things.

[2.] This proves what you are all bound to believe, that Christ Jesus is the true Messiah and Saviour of the world; this he closes his sermon with, as *the conclusion of the whole matter,* the *quod erat demonstrandum — the truth to be demonstrated* (*v.* 36): *Therefore let all the house of Israel know assuredly* that this truth has now received its full confirmation, and we our full commission to publish it, *That God has made that same Jesus whom you have crucified both Lord and Christ.* They were charged to *tell no man that he was Jesus the Christ* till after his resurrection (Mt. 16:20; 17:9); but now it must be *proclaimed on the housetops, to all the house of Israel; he that hath ears to hear, let him hear it.* It is not proposed as probable, but deposed as certain: *Let them know it assuredly,* and know that it is their duty to receive it as *a faithful saying, First,* That God has glorified him *whom they have crucified.* This aggravates their wickedness, that they crucified one whom God designed to glorify, and put him to death as a deceiver who had given such pregnant proofs of his divine mission; and it magnifies the wisdom and power of God that though they crucified him, and thought thereby to have put him under an indelible mark of infamy, yet God had glorified him, and the indignities they had done him served as a foil to his lustre. *Secondly,* That he has glorified him to such a degree as to make him *both Lord and Christ:* these signify the same; he is *Lord of all,* and he is not a usurper, but is *Christ, anointed* to be so. He is *one Lord to the Gentiles,* who had had lords many; and *to the Jews he is Messiah,* which includes all his offices. He is *the king Messiah,* as the Chaldee paraphrast calls him; or, as the angel to Daniel, *Messiah the prince,* Dan. 9:25. This is the great truth of the gospel which we are to believe, *that that same Jesus,* the very same *that was crucified at Jerusalem,* is he to whom we owe allegiance, and from whom we are to expect protection, as *Lord and Christ.*

Verses 37–41

We have seen the wonderful effect of the pouring out of the Spirit, in its influence upon the preachers of the gospel. Peter, in all his life, never spoke at the rate that he had done now, with such fulness, perspicuity, and power. We are now to see another blessed fruit of the pouring out of the Spirit in its influence upon the hearers of the gospel. From the first delivery of that divine message, it appeared that there was a divine power going along with it, and *it was mighty, through God,* to do wonders: thousands were immediately brought by it to the *obedience of faith;* it was *the rod of God's strength sent out of Zion,* Ps. 110:2, 3. We have here the first-fruits of that vast harvest of souls which by it were gathered in to Jesus Christ. Come and see, in these verses, the exalted Redeemer riding forth, in these chariots of salvation, *conquering and to conquer,* Rev. 6:2.

In these verses we find the word of God the means of beginning and carrying on a good work of grace in the hearts of many, *the Spirit of the Lord working by it.* Let us see the method of it.

I. They were startled, and convinced, and put upon a serious enquiry, *v.* 37. *When they heard,* or *having heard,* having patiently heard Peter out, and not given him the interruption they had been used to give to Christ in his discourses (this was one good point gained, that they were become attentive to the word), *they were pricked to the heart,* or *in the heart,* and, under a deep concern and perplexity, applied themselves to the preachers with this question, *What shall we do?* It was very strange that such impressions should be made upon such hard hearts all of a sudden. They were Jews, bred up in the opinion of the sufficiency of their religion to save them, had lately seen this Jesus crucified in weakness and disgrace, and were told by their rulers that he was a deceiver. Peter had charged them with having a hand, a *wicked hand,* in his death, which was likely to have exasperated them against him; yet, when they heard this plain scriptural sermon, they were much affected with it.

1. It put them in pain: *They were pricked in their hearts.* We read of those that were *cut to the heart* with indignation at the preacher (*ch.* 7:54), but these were *pricked to the heart* with indignation at themselves for having been accessory to the death of Christ. Peter, charging it upon them, awakened their consciences, touched them to the quick, and the reflection they now made upon it was as *a sword in their bones,* it pierced them as they had pierced Christ. Note, Sinners, when their eyes are opened, cannot but be *pricked to the heart* for sin, cannot but experience an inward uneasiness; this is having the *heart rent* (Joel 2:13), *a broken and contrite heart,* Ps. 51:17. Those that are truly sorry for their sins, and ashamed of them, and afraid of the consequences of them, are *pricked to the heart.* A prick in the heart is mortal, and under those commotions (says Paul) I died, Rom. 7:9. "All my good opinion of myself and confidence in myself failed me."

2. It put them upon enquiry. *Our of the abundance of the heart,* thus pricked, *the mouth spoke.* Observe,

(1.) To whom they thus addressed themselves: *To Peter and to the rest of the apostles,* some to one and some to another; to them they opened their case; by them they had been convinced, and therefore by them they expect to be counselled and comforted. They do not appeal from them to the scribes and Pharisees, to justify them against the apostles' charge, but apply to them, as owning the charge, and referring the case to them. They call them *men* and *brethren,* as Peter had called them (*v.* 29): it is a style of friendship and love, rather than a title of honour: "You are men, look upon us with humanity; you are brethren, look upon us with brotherly love." Note, Ministers are spiritual physicians; they should be advised with by those whose consciences are wounded; and it is good for people to be free and familiar with those ministers, as men and their brethren, who deal for their souls as for their own.

(2.) What the address is: *What shall we do?* [1.] They speak as men at a stand, that did not know what to do; in a perfect surprise: *"Is that Jesus* whom we have crucified both *Lord and Christ?* Then what will become of us who crucified him? We are all undone!" Note, No way of being happy but by seeing ourselves miserable. When we find ourselves in danger of being lost for ever, there is hope of our being made for ever, and not till then. [2.] They speak as men at a point, that were resolved to do any thing they should be directed to immediately; they are not for taking time to consider, nor for adjourning the prosecution of their convictions to a more convenient season, but desire now to be told what they must do to escape the misery they were liable to. Note, Those that are convinced of sin would gladly know the way to peace and pardon, *ch.* 9:6; 16:30.

II. Peter and the other apostles direct them in short what they must do, and what in so doing they might expect, *v.* 38, 39. Sinners convinced must be encouraged; and that which is broken must be bound up (Eze. 34:16); they must be told that though their case is sad it is not desperate, there is hope for them.

1. He here shows them the course they must take. (1.) *Repent;* this is a plank after shipwreck. "Let the sense of this horrid guilt which you have brought upon yourselves by putting Christ to death awaken you to a penitent reflection upon all your other sins (as the demand of some one great debt brings to light all the debts of a poor bankrupt) and to bitter remorse and sorrow for them" This was the same duty that John the Baptist and Christ had preached, and now that the Spirit is poured out is it still insisted on: *"Repent, repent;* change your mind, change your way; admit an after-thought." (2.) *Be baptized every one of you in the name of Jesus Christ;* that is, "firmly believe the doctrine of Christ, and submit to his grace and government; and make an open solemn profession of this, and come under an engagement to abide by it, by submitting to the ordinance of baptism; be proselyted to Christ and to his holy religion, and renounce your infidelity." They must be baptized *in the name of Jesus Christ.* They did believe in the Father and the Holy Ghost speaking by the prophets; but they must also believe in the name of Jesus, that he is the Christ, the Messias promised to the fathers. "Take Jesus for your king, and by baptism swear allegiance to him; take him for your prophet, and hear him; take him for your priest, to make atonement for you," which seems peculiarly intended here; for they must be baptized *in his name* for the *remission of sins* upon the score of his righteousness. (3.) This is pressed upon each particular person: *Every one of you.* "Even those of you that have been the greatest sinners, if they repent and believe, are welcome to be baptized; and those who think they have been the greatest saints have yet need to repent, and believe, and be baptized. There is grace enough in Christ for every one of you, be you ever so many, and grace suited to the case of every one. Israel of old were baptized unto Moses in the camp, the whole body of the Israelites together, when they passed *through the cloud* and *the sea* (1 Co. 10:1, 2), for the covenant of peculiarity was national; but now *every one of you* distinctly must be *baptized in the name of the Lord Jesus,* and transact for himself in this great affair." See Col. 1:28.

2. He gives them encouragement to take this course: — (1.) "It shall be for *the remission of sins.* Repent of your sin, and it shall not be your ruin; be baptized into the faith of Christ, and in truth you shall be justified, which you could never be by the law of Moses. Aim at this, and depend upon Christ for it, and this you shall have. As the cup in the Lord's supper is the New Testament in the blood of Christ for the remission of sins, so baptism is in the name of Christ for the remission of sins. Be washed, and you shall be washed." (2.) "You shall *receive the gift of the Holy Ghost* as well as we; for it is designed for a general blessing: some of you shall receive these external gifts, and each of you, if you be sincere in your faith and repentance, shall receive his internal graces and comforts, shall be *sealed with the Holy Spirit of promise."* Note, All that receive the remission of sins *receive the gift of the Holy Ghost.* All that are justified are sanctified. (3.) "Your children shall still have, as they have had, an interest in the covenant, and a title to the external seal of it. Come over to Christ, to receive those inestimable benefits; for the promise of the remission of sins, and the gift of the Holy Ghost, is *to you and to your children," v.* 39. It was very express (Isa. 44:3): *I will pour my Spirit upon thy seed.* And (Isa. 59:21), *My Spirit and my word shall not depart from thy seed, and thy seed's seed.* When God took Abraham into covenant, he said, *I will be a God to thee, and to thy seed* (Gen. 17:7); and, accordingly, every Israelite had his son circumcised at eight days old. Now it is proper for an Israelite, when he is by baptism to come into a new dispensation of this covenant, to ask, "What must be done with my children? Must they be thrown out, or taken in with me?" "Taken in" (says Peter) "by all means; for the promise, that great promise of God's being to you a God, is as much to you and to your children now as ever it was." (4.) "Though the promise is still extended to your children as it has been, yet it is not, as it has been, confined to you and them, but the benefit of it is *designed* for *all that are afar off;"* we may add, *and their children,* for the blessing of Abraham comes upon the Gentiles, through Jesus Christ, Gal. 3:14. The promise had long pertained to the Israelites (Rom. 9:4); but now it is sent to *those that are afar off,* the remotest nations of the Gentiles, and *every one* of them too, *all that are afar off.* To this general the following limitation must refer, *even as many of them,*

as many particular persons in each nation, *as the Lord our God shall call* effectually into the fellowship of Jesus Christ. Note, God can make his call to reach those that are ever so far off, and none come but those whom he calls.

III. These directions are followed with a needful caution (*v.* 40): *With many other words,* to the same purport, *did he testify* gospel truths, and exhort to gospel duties; now that the word began to work he followed it; he had said much in a little (*v.* 38, 39), and that which, one would think, included all, and yet he had more to say. When we have heard those words which have done our souls good, we cannot but wish to hear more, to hear many more such words. Among other things he said (and it should seem inculcated it), *Save yourselves from this untoward generation. Be you free* from them. The unbelieving Jews were an untoward generation, perverse and obstinate; they walked contrary to God and man (1 Th. 2:15), wedded to sin and marked for ruin. Now as to them, 1. "Give diligence to save yourselves from their ruin, that you may not be involved in that, and may *escape all those things"* (as the Christians did): *"Repent, and be baptized;* and then you shall not be sharers in destruction with those with whom you have been sharers in sin." *O gather not my soul with sinners.* 2. "In order to this continue not with them in their sin, persist not with them in infidelity. *Save yourselves,* that is, separate yourselves, distinguish yourselves, from this *untoward generation. Be not rebellious like this rebellious house;* partake not with them in their sins, that you share not with them in their plagues." Note, To separate ourselves from wicked people is the only way to save ourselves from them; though we hereby expose ourselves to their rage and enmity, we really save ourselves from them; for, if we consider whither they are hastening, we shall see it is better to have the trouble of swimming against their stream than the danger of being carried down their stream. Those that repent of their sins, and give up themselves to Jesus Christ, must evidence their sincerity by breaking off all intimate society with wicked people. *Depart from me, ye evil doers,* is the language of one that determines to keep *the commandments of his God,* Ps. 119:115. We must *save ourselves* from them, which denotes avoiding them with dread and holy fear, as we would save ourselves from an enemy that seeks to destroy us, or from a house infected with the plague.

IV. Here is the happy success and issue of this, *v.* 41. The Spirit wrought with the word, and wrought wonders by it. These same persons that had many of them been eyewitnesses of the death of Christ, and the prodigies that attended it, and were not wrought upon by them, were yet wrought upon by the preaching of the word, for it is this that is the *power of God unto salvation.* 1. They received the word; and *then* only the word does us good, when we do receive it, embrace it, and bid it welcome. They admitted the conviction of it, and accepted the offers of it. 2. They gladly received it. Herod *heard* the word gladly, but these gladly *received* it, were not only glad that they had it to receive, but glad that by the grace of God they were enabled to receive it, though it would be a humbling changing word to them, and would expose them to the enmity of their countrymen. 3. They were baptized; believing with the heart, they made confession with the mouth, and enrolled themselves among the disciples of Christ by that sacred rite and ceremony which he had instituted. And though Peter had said, "Be baptized in the name of *the Lord Jesus"* (because the doctrine of Christ was the present truth), yet we have reason to think that, in baptizing them, the whole form Christ prescribed was used, *in the name of the Father, the Son, and the Holy Ghost.* Note, Those that receive the Christian covenant ought to receive the Christian baptism. 4. Hereby there were added to the disciples to the number of about *three thousand souls that same day.* All those that had received the Holy Ghost had their tongues at work to preach, and their hands at work to baptize; for it was time to be busy, when such a harvest was to be gathered in. The conversion of these three thousand with these words was a *greater work* than the feeding of four or five thousand with a few loaves. Now Israel began to multiply after the death of our Joseph. They are said to be *three thousand souls* (which word is generally used for persons when women and children are included with men, as Gen. 14:21, *margin, Give me the souls;* Gen. 46:27, *seventy souls*), which intimates that those that were here baptized were not so many men, but so many heads of families as, with their children and servants baptized, might make up *three thousand souls.* These were *added to them.* Note, Those who are joined to Christ are added to the disciples of Christ, and join with them. When we take God for our God, we must take his people to be our people.

Verses 42–47

We often speak of the primitive church, and appeal to it, and to the history of it; in these verses we have the history of the *truly primitive church,* of the *first days* of it, its state of infancy indeed, but, like that, the state of its greatest *innocence.*

I. They kept close to holy ordinances, and abounded in all instances of piety and devotion, for Christianity, admitted in the power of it, will dispose the soul to communion with God in all those ways wherein he has appointed us to meet him and promised to meet us.

1. They were diligent and constant inn their attendance upon the *preaching of the word.* They *continued in the apostles' doctrine,* and never disowned nor deserted it; or, as it may be read, *they continued constant to the apostles' teaching* or *instruction;* by *baptism* they were discipled to be taught, and they were willing to be taught. Note, Those who have given up their names to Christ must make conscience of hearing his word; for thereby we give honour to him, and build up ourselves in our most holy faith.

2. They kept up the *communion of saints.* They continued *in fellowship* (*v.* 42), and *continued daily with one accord in the temple, v.* 46. They not only had a mutual affection to each other, but a great deal of mutual conversation with each other; they were much together. When they withdrew from *the untoward* generation, they did not turn hermits, but were very intimate with one another, and took all occasions to meet; wherever you saw one disciple, you would see more, like *birds of a feather.* See how these Christians love one another. They were concerned for one another, sympathized with one another, and heartily espoused one another's interests. They had fellowship with one another in religious worship. They met *in the temple:* there was their rendezvous; for joint-fellowship with God is the best fellowship we can have with one another, 1 Jn. 1:3. Observe, (1.) They were daily in the temple, not only on the days of the sabbaths and solemn feasts, but on other days, every day. Worshiping God is to be our daily work, and, where there is opportunity, the oftener it is done publicly the better. God loves the gates of Zion, and so must we. (2.) They were *with one accord;* not only no discord nor strife, but a great deal of holy love among them; and they heartily joined in their public services. Though they met with the Jews in the courts of the temple, yet the Christians kept together by themselves, and were unanimous in their separate devotions.

3. They frequently joined in the ordinance of the Lord's supper. They continued *in the breaking of bread,* in celebrating that memorial of their Master's death, as those that were not ashamed to own their relation to, and their dependence upon, Christ and him crucified. They could not forget the death of Christ, yet they kept up this memorial of it, and made it their constant practice, because it was an institution of Christ, to be transmitted to the succeeding ages of the church. They broke bread *from house to house; kat' oikon — house by house;* they did not think fit to celebrate the eucharist in the temple, for that was peculiar to the Christian institutes, and therefore they administered that ordinance in private houses, choosing such houses of the converted Christians as were convenient, to which the neighbours resorted; and they went from one to another of these little synagogues or domestic chapels, houses that had churches in them, and there celebrated the eucharist with those that usually met there to worship God.

4. They continued *in prayers. After* the Spirit was poured out, as well as before, while they were waiting for him, they continued instant in prayer; for prayer will never be superseded till it comes to be swallowed up in everlasting praise. *Breaking of bread* comes in between the *work* and *prayer,* for it has reference to both, and is a help to both. The Lord's supper is a sermon to the eye, and a confirmation of God's word to us; and it is an encouragement to our prayers, and a solemn expression of the ascent of our souls to God.

5. They abounded in thanksgiving; were continually *praising God, v.* 47. This should have a part in every prayer, and not be crowded into a corner. Those that have received the gift of the Holy Ghost will be much in praise.

II. They were loving one to another, and very kind; their charity was as eminent as their piety, and their joining together in holy ordinances knit their hearts to each other, and very much endeared them to one another.

1. They had frequent meetings for Christian converse (*v.* 44): *All that believed were together;* not all those thousands in one place (this was impracticable); but, as Dr. Lightfoot explains it, they kept together in several companies or congregations, according as their languages, nations, or other associations, brought them and kept them together. And thus joining together, because it was apart from those that believed not, and because it was in the same profession and practice of the duties of religion, they are said to be together, *epi to auto.* They associated together, and so both expressed and increased their mutual love.

2. They had *all things common;* perhaps they had common tables (as the Spartans of old), for familiarity, temperance and freedom of conversation; they *ate together,* that those who had much might have the less, and so be kept from the temptations of abundance; and they who had little might have the more, and so be kept from the temptations of want and poverty. Or, There was such a concern for one another, and such a readiness to help one another as there was occasion, that it might be said, They had *all things common,* according to the law of friendship; one wanted not what another had; for he might have it for the asking.

3. They were very cheerful, and very generous in the use of what they had. Besides the religion that was in their sacred feasts (their *breaking bread from house to house*) a great deal of it appeared in their common meals; they did *eat their meat with gladness and singleness of heart.* They brought the comforts of *God's table* along with them to *their own,* which had two good effects upon them: — (1.) It made them very pleasant, and enlarged their hearts with holy joy; they did eat their bread with joy, and *drank their wine with a merry heart,* as knowing that *God now accepted their works.* None have such cause to be cheerful as good Christians have; it is a pity but that they should always have hearts to be so. (2.) It made them very liberal to their poor brethren, and enlarged their hearts in charity. They did *eat their meat with singleness of heart, en aphelotēti kardias — with liberality of heart;* so some: they did not eat their morsels alone, but bade the poor welcome to their table, not grudgingly, but with all the hearty freedom imaginable. Note, It becomes Christians to be open-hearted and open-handed, and in every good work to sow plentifully, as those on whom God hath sown plentifully, and who hope to reap so.

4. They raised a fund for charity (*v.* 45): They *sold their possessions and goods;* some sold their lands and houses, others their stocks and the furniture of their houses, and *parted* the money to their brethren, *as every man had need.* This was to destroy, not property (as Mr. Baxter says), but selfishness. Herein, probably, they had an eye to the command which Christ gave to the rich man, as a test of his sincerity, *Sell that thou hast, and give to the poor.* Not that this was intended for an example to be a constant binding rule, as if all Christians in all places and ages were bound to sell their estates, and give away the money in charity. For St. Paul's epistles, after this, often speak of the distinction of rich and poor, and Christ hath said that *the poor we always have with us,* and shall have, and the rich must be always doing them good out of the rents, issues, and profits, of their estates, which they disable themselves to do, if they sell them, and give all away at once. But here the case was extraordinary (1.) They were under no obligation of a divine command to do this, as appears by what Peter said to Ananias (*ch.* 5:4): *Was it not in thine own power?* But it was a very commendable instance of their raisedness above the world, their contempt of it, their assurance of another world, their love to their brethren, their compassion to the poor, and their great zeal for the encouraging of Christianity, and the nursing of it in its infancy. The apostles left all to follow Christ, and were to give themselves wholly to the word and prayer, and something must be done for their maintenance; so that this extraordinary liberality was like that of Israel in the wilderness towards the building of the tabernacle, which needed to be restrained, Ex. 36:5, 6. Our rule is, to give according as God has blessed us; yet, in such an extraordinary case as this, those are to be praised who give *beyond their power,* 2 Co. 8:3. (2.) They were Jews that did this, and those who believed Christ must believe that the Jewish nation would shortly be destroyed, and an end put to the possession of estates and goods in it, and, in the belief of this, they sold them for the present service of Christ and his church.

III. God owned them, and gave them signal tokens of his presence with them (*v.* 43): *Many wonders and signs were done by the apostles* of divers sorts, which confirmed their doctrine, and incontestably proved that it was from God. Those that could work miracles could have maintained themselves and the poor that were among them miraculously, as Christ fed thousands with a little food; but it was as much for the glory of God that it should be done by a miracle of grace (inclining people to sell their estates, to do it) as if it had been done by a miracle in nature.

But the Lord's giving them power to work miracles was not all he did for them; he *added to the church daily.* The word in their mouths *did wonders,* and God blessed their endeavours for the increase of the number of believers. Note, It is God's work to add souls to the church; and it is a great comfort both to ministers and Christians to see it.

IV. The people were influenced by it; those that were without, the standers by, that were spectators. 1. They *feared them,* and had a veneration for them (*v.* 43): *Fear came upon every soul,* that is, upon very many who saw the *wonders* and *signs* done by the apostles, and were afraid lest their not being respected as they should be would bring desolation upon their nation. The common people stood in awe of them, as Herod feared John. Though they had nothing of external pomp to command external respect, as the *scribes' long robes* gained them the *greetings in the market-places,* yet they had abundance of spiritual gifts that were truly honourable, which possessed men with an inward reverence for them. Fear came upon *every soul;* the *souls* of people were strangely influenced by their awful preaching and living. 2. They *favoured them.* Though we have reason to think there were those that despised them and hated them (we are sure the Pharisees and chief priests did), yet far the greater part of the common people had a kindness for them — they *had favour with all the people.* Christ was so violently run upon and run down by a *packed mob,* which cried, *Crucify him, crucify him,* that one would think his doctrine and followers were never likely to have an interest in the common people any more. And yet here we find them *in favour with them all,* by which it appears that their prosecuting Christ was a sort of force put upon them by the artifices of the priests; now they returned to their wits, to their right mind. Note, Undissembled piety and charity will command respect; and cheerfulness in serving God will recommend religion to those that are without. Some read it, *They had charity to all the people — charin echontes pros holon ton laon*; they did not confine their charity to those of their own community, but it was *catholic* and *extensive;* and this recommended them very much. 3. They *fell over* to them. Some or other were daily coming in, though not so many as the first day; and they were such as *should be saved.* Note, Those that God has designed for eternal salvation shall one time or other be effectually brought to Christ: and those that are brought to Christ are *added to the church* in a holy covenant by baptism, and in holy communion by other ordinances.

CHAPTER 3

In this chapter we have a miracle and a sermon: the miracle wrought to make way for the sermon, to confirm the doctrine that was to be preached, and to make way for it into the minds of the people; and then the sermon to explain the miracle, and to sow the ground which by it was broken up. I. The miracle was the healing of a man that was lame from his birth, with a word speaking (*v.* 1–8), and the impression which this made upon the people (*v.* 9–11). II. The scope of the sermon which was preached hereupon was to bring people to Christ, to repent of their sin in crucifying him (*v.* 12–19), to believe in him now that he was glorified, and to comply with the Father's design in glorifying him (*v.* 20–26). The former part of the discourse opens the wound, the latter applies the remedy.

Verses 1–11

We were told in general (*ch.* 2:43) that *many signs and wonders were done by the apostles,* which are not written in this book; but here we have one given us for an instance. As they wrought miracles, not upon every body as every body had occasion for them, but as the Holy Spirit gave direction, so as to answer the end of their commission; so all the miracles they did work are not written in this book, but such only are recorded as the Holy Ghost thought fit, to serve the end of this sacred history.

I. The persons by whose ministry this miracle was wrought were Peter and John, two principal men among the apostles; they were so in Christ's time, one speaker of the house for the most part, the other favourite of the Master; and they continue so. When, upon the conversion of thousands, the church was divided into several societies, perhaps Peter and John presided in that which Luke associated with, and therefore he is more particular in recording what they said and did, as afterwards what Paul said and did when he attended him, both the one and the other being designed for specimens of what the other apostles did.

Peter and John had each of them a brother among the twelve, with whom they were coupled when they were sent out; yet now they seem to be knit together more closely than either of them to his brother, for the bond of friendship is sometimes stronger than that of relation: *there is a friend that sticks closer than a brother.* Peter and John seem to have had a peculiar intimacy after Christ's resurrection more than before, Jn. 20:2. The reason of which (if I may have liberty to conjecture) might be this, that John, a disciple made up of love, was more compassionate to Peter upon his fall and repentance, and more tender of him in his *bitter weeping* for his sin, than any other of the apostles were, and more solicitous to restore him in the *spirit of meekness,* which made him very dear to Peter ever after; and it was good evidence of Peter's acceptance with God, upon his repentance, that Christ's favourite was made his bosom friend. David prayed, after his fall, *Let those that fear thee turn unto me,* Ps. 119:79.

II. The time and place are here set down. 1. It was in *the temple,* whither *Peter and John went up together,* because it was the place of concourse; there were the shoals of fish among which the net of the gospel was to be cast, especially during the days of pentecost, within the compass of which we may suppose this to have happened. Note, It is good to go up to the temple, to attend on public ordinances; and it is comfortable to go up together to the temple: *I was glad when they said unto me, Let us go.* The best society is society in worshipping God. 2. It was *at the hour of prayer,* one of the hours of public worship commonly appointed and observed among the Jews. Time and place are two necessary circumstances of every action, which must be determined by consent, as is most convenient for edification. With reference to public worship, there must be a house of prayer and an hour of prayer: the ninth hour, that is, three o'clock in the afternoon, was one of the hours of prayer among the Jews; nine in the morning and twelve at noon were the other two. See Ps. 55:17; Dan. 6:10. It is of use for private Christians so far to have their hours of prayer as may serve, though not to bind, yet to remind conscience: *every thing is beautiful in its season.*

III. The patient on whom this miraculous cure was wrought is here described, *v.* 2. He was a poor lame beggar at the temple gate. 1. he was a cripple, not by accident, but born so; he was *lame from his mother's womb,* as it should seem, by a paralytic distemper, which weakened his limbs; for it is said in the description of his cure (*v.* 7), *His feet and ankle bones received strength.* Some such piteous cases now and then there are, which we ought to be affected with and look upon with compassion, and which are designed to show us what we all are by nature spiritually: *without strength,* lame from our birth, unable to work or walk in God's service. 2. He was a beggar. Being unable to work for his living, he must live upon alms; such are God's poor. He was *laid daily* by his friends at *one of the gates of the temple,* a miserable spectacle, unable to do any thing for himself but to *ask alms of those that entered into the temple* or came out. There was a concourse, — a concourse of devout good people, from whom charity might be expected, and a concourse of such people when it might be hoped they were in the best frame; and there he was laid. Those that need, and cannot work, must not be ashamed to beg. He would not have been laid there, and laid there daily, if he had not been used to meet with supplies, daily supplies there. Note, Our prayers and our alms should go together; Cornelius's did, *ch.* 10:4. Objects of charity should be in a particular manner welcome to us when we go up to the temple to pray; it is a pity that common beggars at church doors should any of them be of such a character as to discourage charity; but they ought not always to be overlooked: some there are surely that merit regard, and better feed ten drones, yea, and some wasps, than let one bee starve. The gate of the temple at which he was laid is here named: it was called *Beautiful,* for the extraordinary splendour and magnificence of it. Dr. Lightfoot observes that this was the gate that led out of the court of the Gentiles into that of the Jews, and he supposes that the cripple would beg only of the Jews, as disdaining to ask any thing of the Gentiles. But Dr. Whitby takes it to be at the first entrance into the temple, and beautified sumptuously, as became the frontispiece of that place where the divine Majesty vouchsafed to dwell; and it was no diminution to the beauty of this gate that a poor man lay there begging. 3. He begged of Peter and John (*v.* 3), begged an alms; this was the utmost he expected from them, who had the reputation of being charitable men, and who, though they had not much, yet did good with what they had. It was not many weeks ago that the blind and the lame came to Christ in the temple, and were healed there, Mt. 21:14. And why might not he have asked more than an alms, if he knew that Peter and John were Christ's messengers, and preached and wrought miracles in his name? But he had that done for him which he looked not for; he *asked an alms,* and had a cure.

IV. We have here the method of the cure.

1. His expectations were raised. Peter, instead of turning his eyes form him, as many do from objects of charity, turned his eyes to him, nay, he *fastened his eyes upon him,* that his eye might affect his heart with compassion towards him, *v.* 4. John did so too, for they were both guided by one and the same Spirit, and concurred in this miracle; they said, *Look on us.* Our eye must be ever towards the Lord (the eye of our mind), and, in token of this, the eye of the body may properly be fixed on those whom he employs as the ministers of his grace. This man needed not to be bidden twice to look on the apostles; for he justly thought this gave him cause to expect that he should *receive something form them,* and therefore he *gave heed to them, v.* 5. Note, We must come to God both to attend on his word and to apply ourselves to him in prayer, with hearts fixed and expectations raised. We must look up to heaven and expect to receive benefit by that which God speaks thence, and an answer of peace to the prayers sent up thither. *I will direct my prayer unto thee, and will look up.*

2. His expectation of an alms was disappointed. *Peter said, "Silver and gold have I none,* and therefore none to give thee;" yet he intimated that if he had had any he would have given him an alms, not brass, but silver or gold. Note, (1.) It is not often that Christ's friends and favourites have abundance of the wealth of this world. The apostles were very poor, had but just enough for themselves, and no overplus. Peter and John had abundance of money laid at their feet, but this was appropriated to the maintenance of the poor of the church, and they would not convert any of it to their own use, nor dispose of it otherwise than according tot he intention of the donors. Public trusts ought to be strictly and faithfully observed. (2.) Many who are well inclined to works of charity are yet not in a capacity of doing any thing considerable, while others, who have wherewithal to do much, have not a heart to do any thing.

3. His expectations, notwithstanding, were quite outdone. Peter had not money to give him; but, (1.) He had that which was better, such an interest in heaven, such a power from heaven, as to be able to cure his disease. Note, Those who are poor in the world may yet be rich, very rich, in spiritual gifts, graces, and comforts; certainly there is that which we are capable of possessing which is infinitely better than silver and gold; the merchandise and gain of it are better, Job 28:12, etc.; Prov. 3:14, etc. (2.) He gave him that which was better — the cure of his disease, which he would gladly have given a great deal of silver and gold for, if he had had it, and the cure could have been so obtained. This would enable him to work for his living, so that he would not need to beg any more; nay, he would *have to give to those that needed,* and it *is more blessed to give than to receive.* A miraculous cure would be a greater instance of God's favour, and would put a greater honour upon him, than thousands of gold and silver could. observe, When Peter had no silver and gold to give, yet (says he) *such as I have I give thee.* Note, Those may be, and ought to be, otherwise charitable and helpful to the poor, who have not wherewithal to give in charity; those who have not silver and gold have their limbs and senses, and with these may be serviceable to the blind, and lame, and sick, and if they be not, as there is occasion, neither would they give to them if they had silver and gold. *As every one hath received the gift, so let him minister it.* Let us now see how the cure was wrought. [1.] Christ *sent his word, and healed him* (Ps. 107:20); for healing grace is given by the word of Christ; this is the vehicle of the healing virtue derived from Christ. Christ spoke cures by himself; the apostles spoke them in his name. Peter bids a lame man *rise up and walk,* which

would have been a banter upon him if he had not premised *in the name of Jesus Christ of Nazareth:* "I say it by warrant from him, and it shall be done by power from him, and all the glory and praise of it shall be ascribed to him." He calls Christ *Jesus of Nazareth,* which was a name of reproach, to intimate that the indignities done him on earth served but as a foil to his glories now that he was in heaven. "Give him what name you will, call him if you will in scorn Jesus of Nazareth, in that name you shall see wonders done; for, because he humbled himself, thus highly was he exalted." He bids the cripple *rise up and walk,* which does not prove that he had power in himself to do it, but that if he attempt to rise and walk, and, in a sense of his own impotency, depend upon a divine power to enable him to do it, he shall be enabled; and by rising and walking he must evidence what that power has wrought upon him; and then let him take the comfort, and let God have the praise. Thus it is in the healing of our souls, which are spiritually impotent. [2.] Peter lent his hand, and helped him (*v.* 7): *He took him by the right hand,* in the same name in which he had spoken to him to arise and walk, *and lifted him up.* Not that this could contribute any thing to his cure; but it was a sign, plainly intimating the help he should receive from God, if he exerted himself as he was bidden. When God by his word commands us to rise, and walk in the way of his commandments, if we mix faith with that word, and lay our souls under the power of it, he will give his Spirit to take us by the hand, and lift us up. If we set ourselves to do what we can, God has promised his grace to enable us to do what we cannot; and by that promise we partake of a new nature, and that grace shall not be in vain; it was not here: *His feet and ankle-bones received strength,* which they had not done if he had not attempted to rise, and been helped up; he does his part, and Peter does his, and yet it is Christ that does all: it is he that puts strength into him. As the bread was multiplied in the breaking, and the water turned into wine in the pouring out, so strength was given to the cripple's feet in his stirring them and using them.

V. Here is the impression which this cure made upon the patient himself, which we may best conceive of if we put our soul into his soul's stead. 1. He leaped up, in obedience to the command, *Arise.* He found in himself such a degree of strength in his feet and ankle-bones that he did not steal up gently, with fear and trembling, as weak people do when they begin to recover strength; but he started up, as one refreshed with sleep, boldly, and with great agility, and as one that questioned not his own strength. The incomes of strength were sudden, and he was no less sudden in showing them. He leaped, as one glad to quit the bed or pad of straw on which he had lain so long lame. 2. He stood, and walked. He stood without either leaning or trembling, stood straight up, and walked without a staff. He trod strongly, and moved steadily; and this was to manifest the cure, and that it was a thorough cure. Note, Those who have had experience of the working of divine grace upon them should evidence what they have experienced. Has God put strength into us? Let us stand before him in the exercises of devotion; let us walk before him in all the instances of a religious conversation. Let us stand up resolutely for him, and walk cheerfully with him, and both in strength derived and received form him. 3. He *held Peter and John, v.* 11. We need not ask why he held them. I believe he scarcely knew himself: but it was in a transport of joy that he embraced them as the best benefactors he had ever met with, and hung upon them to a degree of rudeness; he would not let them go forward, but would have them stay with him, while he published to all about him what God had done for him by them. Thus he testified his affection to them; he held them, and would not let them go. Some suggest that he clung to them for fear lest, if they should leave him, his lameness should return. Those whom God hath healed love those whom he made instruments of their healing, and see the need of their further help. 4. He *entered with them into the temple.* His strong affection to them held them; but it could not hold them so fast as to keep them out of the temple, whither they were going to preach Christ. We should never suffer ourselves to be diverted by the utmost affectionate kindnesses of our friends from going in the way of our duty. But, if they will not stay with him, he is resolved to go with them, and the rather because they are going into the temple, whence he had been so long kept by his weakness and his begging: like the impotent man whom Christ cured, he was presently found in the temple, Jn. 5:14. He went into the temple, not only to offer up his praises and thanksgivings to God, but to hear more from the apostles of that Jesus in whose name he had been healed. Those that have experienced the power of Christ should earnestly desire to grow in their acquaintance with Christ. 5. He was there *walking, and leaping, and praising God.* Note, The strength God has given us, both in mind and body, should be made us of to his praise, and we should study how to honour him with it. Those that are healed in his name must walk up and down in his name and in his strength, Zec. 10:12. This man, as soon as he could leap, leaped for joy in God, and praised him. Here was that scripture fulfilled (Isa. 35:6): *Then shall the lame man leap as a hart.* Now that this man was newly cured he was in this excess of joy and thankfulness. All true converts walk and praise God; but perhaps young converts leap more in his praises.

VI. How the people that were eye-witnesses of this miracle were influenced by it we are next told. 1. They were entirely satisfied in the truth of the miracle, and had nothing to object against it. *They knew it was he that sat begging at the beautiful gate of the temple, v.* 10. He had sat there so long that they all knew him; and for this reason he was chosen to be the vessel of this mercy. Now they were not so perverse as to make any doubt whether he was the same man, as the Pharisees had questioned concerning the blind man that Christ cured, Jn. 9:9, 18. They now saw him *walking, and praising God* (*v.* 9), and perhaps took notice of a change in his mind; for he was now as loud in praising God as he had before been in begging relief. The best evidence that it was a complete cure was that he now praised God for it. Mercies are then perfected, when they are sanctified. 2. They were astonished at it: They were *filled with wonder and amazement* (*v.* 10); *greatly wondering, v.* 11. They were in an *ecstasy.* There seems to have been this effect of the pouring out of the Spirit, that the people, at least those in Jerusalem, were much more affected with the miracles the apostles wrought than they had been with those of the same kind that had been wrought by Christ himself; and this was in order to the miracles answering their end. 3. They gathered about Peter and John: *All the people ran together unto them in Solomon's porch:* some only to gratify their curiosity with the sight of men that had such power; others with a desire to hear them preach, concluding that their doctrine must needs be of divine origin, which thus had a divine ratification. They flocked to them in Solomon's porch, a part of the court of the Gentiles, where Solomon had built the outer porch of the temple; or, some cloisters or piazzas which Herod had erected upon the same foundation upon which Solomon had built the stately porch that bore his name, Herod being ambitious herein to be a second Solomon. Here the people met, to see this great sight.

Verses 12–26

We have here the sermon which Peter preached after he had cured the lame man. *When Peter saw it.* 1. When he saw the people got together in a crowd, he took that opportunity to preach Christ to them, especially the temple being the place of their concourse, and Solomon's porch there: let them come and hear a more excellent wisdom than Solomon's, for, behold, a greater than Solomon is here preached. 2. When he saw the people affected with the miracle, and filed with admiration, then he sowed the gospel seed in the ground which was thus broken up, and prepared to receive it. 3. When he saw the people ready to adore him and John, he stepped in immediately, and diverted their respect from them, that it might be directed to Christ only; to this *he answered* presently, as Paul and Barnabas at Lystra. See *ch.* 14:14, 15. In the sermon,

I. He humbly disclaims the honour of the miracle as not due to them, who were only the ministers of Christ, or instruments in his hand for the doing of it. The doctrines they preached were not of their own invention, nor were the seals of it their own, but his whose the doctrines were. He addresses himself to them as *men of Israel,* men to whom pertained, not only the law and the promises, but the gospel and the performances, and who were nearly interested in the present dispensation. Two things he asks them: — 1. Why they were so surprised at the miracle itself: *Why marvel you at this?* It was indeed marvellous, and they justly wondered at it, but it was not more than what Christ had done many a time, and they had not duly regarded it, nor been affected with it. It was but a little before that Christ had *raised Lazarus from the dead;* and why should this then seem so strange? Note, Stupid people think that strange now which might have been familiar to them if it had not been their own fault. Christ had lately risen from the dead himself; why did they not marvel at this? why were they not convinced by this? 2. Why they gave so much of the praise of it to them, who were only the instruments of it: *Why look you so earnestly on us?* (1.) It was certain that they *had made this man to walk,* by which it appeared that the apostles not only were sent of God, but were sent to be blessings to the world, benefactors to mankind, and were sent to heal sick and distempered souls, that were spiritually lame and impotent, to set broken bones, and make them rejoice. (2.) Yet they did not do it by any *power or holiness of their own.* It was not done by any might of their own, any skill they had in physic or surgery, nor any virtue in their word: the power they did it by was wholly derived from Christ. Nor was it done by any merit of their own; the power which Christ gave them to do it they had not deserved: it was not by their own holiness; for, as they were weak things, so they were foolish things, that Christ chose to employ; Peter was a sinful man. What holiness had Judas? Yet he wrought miracles in Christ's name. What holiness any of them had it was wrought in them, and they could not pretend to merit by it. (3.) It was the people's fault that they attributed it to their power and holiness, and accordingly looked at them. Note, The instruments of God's favour to us, though they must be respected, must not be idolized; we must take heed of reckoning that to be done by the instrument which God is the author of. (4.) It was the praise of Peter and John that they would not take the honour of this miracle to themselves, but carefully transmitted it to Christ. Useful men must see to it that they be very humble. *Not unto us, O Lord, not unto us, but to thy name give glory.* Every crown must be cast at the feet of Christ; *not I, but the grace of God with me.*

II. He preaches Christ to them; this was his business, that he might lead them into obedience to Christ.

1. He preaches Christ, as the true Messiah promised to the fathers (*v.* 13); for, (1.) He is Jesus the Son of God; though they had lately condemned Christ as a blasphemer for saying that he was the Son of God, yet Peter avows it: he is *his Son Jesus;* to him dear as a Son; to us, *Jesus,* a Saviour. (2.) God hath glorified him, in raising him up to be king, priest, and prophet, of his church; he glorified him in his life and in his death, as well as in his resurrection and ascension. (3.) He hath glorified him as *the God of our fathers,* whom he names with respect (for they were great names with the men of Israel, and justly), *the God of Abraham, of Isaac, and of Jacob.* God sent him into the world, pursuant to the promises made to those patriarchs, *that in their seed the families of the earth should be blessed,* and the covenant made with them, *that God would be a God to them, and their seed.* The apostles call the patriarchs their fathers, and God the God of those patriarchs from whom the Jews were descended, to intimate to them that they had no evil design upon the Jewish nation (that they should look upon them with a jealous eye), but had a value and concern for it, and were hereby well-wishers to it; and the gospel they preached was the revelation of the mind and will of the God of Abraham. See *ch.* 26:7, 22; Lu. 1:72, 73.

2. He charges them flatly and plainly with the murder of this Jesus, as he had done before. (1.) "*You delivered him up* to your chief priests and elders, the representative body of the nation; and you of the common people were influenced by them to clamour against him, as if he had been a public grievance." (2.) "*You denied him,* and you disowned him, would not have him then to be your king, could not look upon him as the Messiah, because he came not in external pomp and power; *you denied him in the presence of Pilate,* renounced all the expectations of your church, in the presence of the Roman governor, who justly laughed at you for it; *you denied him against the face of Pilate*" (so Dr. Hammond), "in defiance of his reasonings with you" (*Pilate had determined to let him go,* but the people opposed it, and overruled him). "You were worse than Pilate, for he would have released him, if you had let him follow his own judgment. *You denied the Holy One and the Just,* who had approved himself so, and all the malice of his persecutors could not disprove it." The holiness and justice of the Lord Jesus, which are something more than his innocency, were a great aggravation of the sin of those that put him to death. (3.) "*You desired a murderer to be released,* and Christ crucified; as if Barabbas had deserved better at your hands than the Lord Jesus, than which

a greater affront could not be put upon him." (4.) You *killed the prince of life.* Observe the antithesis: "You preserved *a murderer,* a destroyer of life; and destroyed the Saviour, *the author of life. You killed* him who was sent to be to you *the prince of life,* and so not only forsook, but rebelled against your own mercies. You did an ungrateful thing, in taking away his life who would have been your life. You did a foolish thing to think you could conquer *the prince of life,* who has life in himself, and would soon resume the life he resigned."

3. He attests his resurrection as before, *ch.* 11. 32. "You thought *the prince of life* might be deprived of his life, as any other prince might be deprived of his dignity and dominion, but you found yourselves mistaken, for *God raised him from the dead;* so that in putting him to death you fought against God, and were baffled. *God raised him from the dead,* and thereby ratified his demands, and confirmed his doctrine, and rolled away all the reproach of his sufferings, and *for the truth of his resurrection we are all witnesses."*

4. He ascribes the cure of this impotent man to the power of Christ, (*v.* 16): *His name, through faith in his name,* in that discovery which he hath made of himself, *has made this man strong.* He repeats it again, *The faith which is by him hath given him this soundness.* Here, (1.) He appeals to themselves concerning the truth of the miracle; the man on whom it was wrought is one *whom you see, and know, and have known;* he was not acquainted with Peter and John before, so that there was no room to suspect a compact between them: "You know him to have been a cripple from a child. The miracle was wrought publicly, *in the presence of you all;* not in a corner, but in the gate of the temple; you saw in what manner it was done, so that there could be no juggle in it; you had liberty to examine it immediately, and may yet. The cure is complete; it is a *perfect soundness;* you see the man walks and leaps, as one that has no remainder either of weakness or pain." (2.) He acquaints them with the power by which it was wrought. [1.] It is done by the name of Christ, not merely by naming it as a spell or charm, but it is done by us as professors and teachers of his name, by virtue of a commission and instructions we have received from him, and a power which he has invested us with, that name which Christ has above every name; his authority, his command has done it; as writs run in the king's name, though it is an inferior officer that executes them. [2.] The power of Christ is fetched in *through faith in his name,* a confidence in him, a dependence on him, a believing application to him, and expectation from him, even *that faith which is, di' autou — by him,* which is of his working; *it is not of ourselves, it is the gift of Christ;* and it is for his sake, that he may have the glory of it; for he is both *the author and finisher of our faith.* Dr. Lightfoot suggests that faith is twice named in this verse, because of the apostles' faith in doing this miracle and the cripple's faith in receiving it; but I suppose it relates chiefly, if not only, to the former. Those that wrought this miracle by faith derived power from Christ to work it, and therefore returned all the glory to him. By this true and just account of the miracle, Peter both confirmed the great gospel truth they were to preach to the world — that Jesus Christ is the fountain of all power and grace, and the great healer and Saviour — and recommended the great gospel duty of faith in him as the only way of receiving benefit by him. It explains likewise the great gospel mystery of our salvation by Christ; it is his name that justifies us, that glorious name of his, *The Lord our righteousness;* but we, in particular, are justified by that name, through faith in it, applying it to ourselves. Thus does Peter preach unto them Jesus, and him crucified, as a faithful friend of the bridegroom, to whose service and honour he devoted all his interest.

III. He encourages them to hope that, though they had been guilty of putting Christ to death, yet they might find mercy; he does all he can to convince them, yet is careful not to drive them to despair. The guilt was very great, but, 1. He mollifies their crime by a candid imputation of it to their ignorance. Perhaps he perceived by the countenance of his hearers that they were struck with great horror when he told them that they had *killed the prince of life,* and were ready either to sink down or to fly off, and therefore he saw it needful to mitigate the rigour of the charge by calling them *brethren;* and well might he call them so, for he had been himself a brother with them in this iniquity: he had *denied the holy One and the Just,* and sworn that he did not know him; he did it by surprise; "and, for your parts, *I know that through ignorance you did it, as did also your rulers," v.* 17. This was the language of Peter's charity, and teaches us to make the best of those whom we desire to make better. Peter had searched the wound to the bottom, and now he begins to think of healing it up, in order to which it is necessary to beget in them a good opinion of their physician; and could any thing be more winning than this? That which bears him out in it is that he has the example of his Master's praying for his crucifiers, and pleading in their behalf that they knew not what they did. And it is said of the rulers that *if they had known they would not have crucified the Lord of glory.* See 1 Co. 2:8. Perhaps some of the rulers, and of the people, did therein rebel against the light and the convictions of their own consciences, and did it through malice; but the generality went down the stream, and did it through ignorance; as Paul persecuted the church, *ignorantly, and in unbelief,* 1 Tim. 1:13. 2. He mollifies the effects of their crime — the death of *the prince of life;* this sounds very dreadful, but it was *according to the scriptures* (*v.* 18), the predictions of which, though they did not necessitate their sin, yet did necessitate his sufferings; so he himself saith: *Thus it is written, and thus it behoved Christ to suffer. You did it through ignorance* may be taken in this sense: "You fulfilled the scripture, and did not know it; *God,* by your hands, *hath fulfilled what he showed by the mouth of all his prophets, that Christ should suffer;* this was his design in delivering him up to you, but you had views of your own, and were altogether ignorant of this design; *you meant not so, neither did your heart think so.* God was fulfilling the scripture when you were gratifying your own passions." Observe, It was not only determined in the secret counsel of God, but declared to the world many ages before, *by the mouth* and pen *of the prophets, that Christ should suffer,* in order to the accomplishment of his undertaking; and it was God himself that *showed* it by them, who will see that his words be made good; what he showed he fulfilled, he so fulfilled as he had shown, punctually and exactly, without any variation. Now, though this is no extenuation at all of their sin in hating and persecuting Christ *to the death* (this still appears exceedingly sinful), yet it was an encouragement to them to repent, and hope for mercy upon their repentance; not only because in general God's gracious designs were carried on by it (ant thus it agrees with the encouragement Joseph gave to his brethren, when they thought their offence against him almost unpardonable: *Fear not,* saith he, *you thought evil against me, but God meant it unto good,* Gen. 50:15, 20), but because in particular the death and sufferings of Christ were for *the remission of sins,* and the ground of that display of mercy for which he now encouraged them to hope.

IV. He exhorts them all to turn Christians, and assures them it would be unspeakably for their advantage to do so; it would be the making of them for ever. This is the application of his sermon.

1. He tells them what they must believe. (1.) They must believe that Jesus Christ is the promised see, that seed in which God had told Abraham *all the kindreds of the earth should be blessed, v.* 25. This refers to that promise made to Abraham (Gen. 12:3), which promise was long ere it was fulfilled, but now at length had its accomplishment in this *Jesus,* who was of *the seed of Abraham, according to the flesh,* and *in him all the families of the earth are blessed,* and not the families of Israel only; all have some benefits by him, and some have all benefits. (2.) They must believe that Jesus Christ is a prophet, *that prophet like unto Moses* whom God had promised to *raise up to them from among their brethren, v.* 22. This refers to that promise, Deu. 18:18. Christ is a prophet, for by him God speaks unto us; in him all divine revelation centres, and by him it is handed to us; he is a *prophet like unto Moses,* a favourite of Heaven; more intimately acquainted with the divine counsel, and more familiarly conversed with, than any other prophet. He was a deliverer of his people out of bondage, and their guide through the wilderness, like Moses; a prince and a lawgiver, like Moses; the builder of the true tabernacle, as Moses was of the typical one. Moses was *faithful as a servant,* Christ *as a Son.* Moses was murmured against by Israel, defied by Pharaoh, yet God owned him, and ratified his commission. Moses was a pattern of meekness and patience, so is Christ. Moses died by *the word of the Lord,* so did Christ. *There was no prophet like unto Moses* (Num. 12:6, 7; Deu. 34:10), but a greater than Moses is here where Christ is. He is a prophet of God's raising up, for he took not this honour of himself, but was called of God to it. He was raised up unto Israel in the first place. He executed this office in his own person among them only. They had the first offer of divine grace made to them; and therefore he was *raised up from among them — of them, as concerning the flesh, Christ came,* which, as it was a great honour done to them, so it was both an obligation upon them and an encouragement to them to embrace him. If he come to his own, one would think, they should receive him. The Old-Testament church was blessed with many prophets, with schools of prophets, for many ages with a constant succession of prophets (which is here taken notice of, from *Samuel, and those that follow after, v.* 24, for from Samuel the prophetic era commenced); but, these servants being abused, last of all God sent them his Son, who had been in his bosom. (3.) They must believe *that times of refreshing will come from the presence of the Lord* (*v.* 19), and that they will be *the times of the restitution of all things, v.* 21. There is a future state, another life after this; those times will come from the presence of the Lord, from his glorious appearance at that day, his coming at the end of time. The absence of the Lord occasions many of the securities of sinners and the distrusts of saints; but his presence is hastening on, which will for ever silence both. *Behold, the Judge standeth before the door.* The presence of the Lord will introduce, [1.] *The restitution of all things* (*v.* 21); *the new heavens, and the new earth,* which will be the product of the dissolution of all things (Rev. 21:1), the renovation of the whole creation, which is that which it grieves after, as its present burden under the sin of man is that which it groans under. Some understand this of a state on this side the end of time; but it is rather to be understood of that *end of all things which God hath spoken of by the mouth of all his holy prophets since the world began;* for this is that which *Enoch, the seventh from Adam, prophesied of* (Jude 14), and the temporal judgments which the other prophets foretold were typical of that which the apostle calls *the eternal judgment.* This is more clearly and plainly revealed in the New Testament than it had been before, and all that receive the gospel have an expectation of it. [2.] With this will come *the times of refreshing* (*v.* 19), of consolation to the Lord's people, like a cool shade to those *that have borne the burden and heat of the day.* All Christians look for *a rest that remains for the people of God,* after the travails and toils of their present state, and, with the prospect of this, they are borne up under their present sufferings and carried on in their present services. The refreshing that then *comes from the presence of the Lord* will continue eternally in the presence of the Lord.

2. He tells them what they must do. (1.) They must *repent,* must bethink themselves of what they have done amiss, must return to their right mind, admit a second thought, and submit to the convictions of it; they must begin anew. Peter, who had himself denied Christ, repented, and he would have them to do so too. (2.) They must *be converted,* must face about, and direct both their faces and steps the contrary way to what they had been; they must *return to the Lord their God,* from whom they had revolted. It is not enough to repent of sin, but we must be converted from it, and not return to it again. They must not only exchange the profession of Judaism for that of Christianity, but the power and dominion of a carnal, worldly, sensual mind, for that of holy, heavenly, and divine principles and affections. (3.) They must hear Christ, the great prophet: *"Him shall you hear in all things whatsoever he shall say unto you.* Attend his dictates, receive his doctrine, submit to his government. Hear him with a divine faith, as prophets should be heard, that come with a divine commission. *Him shall you hear,* and to him shall you subscribe with an implicit faith and obedience. *Hear him in all things;* let his laws govern all your actions, and his counsels determine all your submissions. Whenever he has a mouth to speak, you must have an ear to hear. Whatever he saith to you, though ever so displeasing to flesh and blood, bid it welcome." *Speak, Lord, for thy servant hears.* A good reason is here given why we should be observant of, and obedient to, the word of Christ; for it is at our peril if we turn a deaf ear to his call and a stiff neck to his yoke (*v.* 23): *Every soul that will not hear that prophet,* and be directed by what he saith, *shall be destroyed from among the people.* The destruction of the city and nation, by war and famine, was threatened for slighting the prophets of the Old Testament; but the destruction of the soul, a spiritual and eternal destruction, is threatened for slighting Christ, *this great prophet.* Those that will not be advised by the Saviour can expect no other than to fall into the hands of the destroyer.

3. He tells them what they might expect.

(1.) That they should have the pardon of their sins; this is always spoken of as the great privilege of all those that embrace the gospel (*v.* 19): *Repent, and be converted, that your sins may be blotted out.* This implies, [1.] That the remission of sin is the blotting of it out, as a cloud is blotted out by the beams of the sun (Isa. 44:22), as a debt is crossed and blotted out when it is remitted. It intimates that when God forgives sin he remembers it no more against the sinner; it is forgotten, as that which is blotted out; all the bitter things written against the sinner (Job 13:26) are wiped out as it were with a sponge; it is the cancelling of a bond, the vacating of a judgment. [2.] That we cannot expect our sins should be pardoned unless we repent of them, and turn from them to God. Though Christ has died to purchase the remission of sin, yet, that we may have the benefit of that purchase in the forgiveness of our sins, we must repent, and be converted: if no repentance, no remission. [3.] Hopes of the pardon of sin upon repentance should be a powerful inducement to us to repent. *Repent, that your sins may be blotted out:* and that repentance is evangelical which flows from an apprehension of the mercy of God in Christ, and the hopes of pardon. This was the first and great argument, *Repent, for the kingdom of heaven is at hand.* [4.] The most comfortable fruit of the forgiveness of our sins will be *when the times of refreshing shall come;* if our sins be forgiven us, we have now reason to be of good cheer; but the comfort will be complete when the pardon shall be allowed in open court, and our justification published *before angels and men* — when *whom he has justified, them he glorifies,* Rom. 8:30. As *now we are the sons of God* (1 Jn. 3:2), so now we have our sins blotted out; *but it doth not yet appear what* are the blessed fruits of it, till *the times of refreshing shall come.* During these times of toil and conflict (doubts and fears within, troubles and dangers without) we cannot have that full satisfaction of our pardon, and in it, that we shall have when the refreshing times come, which shall wipe away all tears.

(2.) That they should have the comfort of Christ's coming (*v.* 20, 21): *"He shall send Jesus Christ,* the same Jesus, the very same *that before was preached unto you;* for you must not expect another dispensation, another gospel, but the continuance and completion of this; you must not expect another prophet like unto Jesus, as Moses bade you expect another like unto him; for, though *the heavens must receive him till the times of the restitution of all things;* yet, if you *repent and be converted,* you shall find no want of him; some way or other he shall be seen of you." [1.] We must not expect Christ's personal presence with us in this world; for the heavens, which received him out of the sight of the disciples, must retain him till the end of time. To that seat of the blessed his bodily presence is confined, and will be to the end of time, the accomplishment of all things (so it may be read); and therefore those dishonour him, and deceive themselves, who dream of his corporal presence in the eucharist. It is agreeable to a state of trial and probation that the glorified Redeemer should be out of sight, because we must live by that faith in him which is *the evidence of things not seen;* because he must be *believed on in the world,* he must be *received up into glory.* Dr. Hammond reads it, *Who must receive the heavens,* that is, who must *receive the glory and power of the upper world; he must reign till all be made subject to him,* 1 Co. 15:25; Ps. 75:2. [2.] Yet it is promised that he shall be sent to all that repent and are converted (*v.* 20): *"He shall send Jesus Christ, who was preached to you* by his disciples, both before and since his resurrection, and is, and will be, all in all to them." *First,* "You shall have his spiritual presence. He that is sent into the world shall be sent to you; you shall have the comfort of his being sent; he shall be sent among you in his gospel, which shall be his tabernacle, his chariot of war." *Secondly, "He shall send Jesus Christ* to destroy Jerusalem, and the nation of unbelieving Jews, that are enemies to Christ and Christianity, and to deliver his ministers and people from them, and give them peace in the profession of the gospel, and that shall be a time of refreshing, in which you shall share." *Then had the churches rest;* so Dr. Hammond. *Thirdly,* "The sending of Christ to judge the world, at the end of time, will be a blessing to you; you shall then *lift up your heads with joy, knowing that your redemption draws nigh."* It seems to refer to this, for till then *the heavens must receive him, v.* 21. As God's counsels from eternity, so his predictions from the beginning of time, had a reference to the transactions of the last day, when *the mystery of God shall be finished, as he had declared to his servants the prophets,* Rev. 10:7. The institution of all things in the church had an eye to the restitution of all things at the end of time.

4. He tells them what ground they had to expect these things, if they were converted to Christ. Though they had denied him, and put him to death, yet they might hope to find favour through him, upon the account of their being Israelites. For,

(1.) As Israelites, they had the monopoly of the grace of the Old Testament; they were, above any other, God's favourite nation, and the favours God bestowed upon them were such as had a reference to the Messiah, and his kingdom: *You are the children of the prophets, and of the covenant.* A double privilege. [1.] They were *the children,* that is, the disciples, *of the prophets,* as children at school; *not sons of the prophets,* in the sense that we read of such in the Old Testament, from Samuel and downward, who were, or are, trained up to be *endued with the spirit of prophecy;* but you are of that people from among whom prophets were raised up, and to whom prophets were sent. It is spoken of as a great favour to Israel *that God raised up of their sons for prophets,* Amos 2:11. All the inspired writers, both of the Old and New Testament, were of *the seed of Abraham;* and it was their honour and advantage *that unto them were committed the oracles of God,* Rom. 3:2. Their government was constituted by prophecy, that is, by divine revelation; and by it their affairs were for many ages very much managed. See Hos. 12:13. *By a prophet the Lord brought Israel out of Egypt, and by a prophet was he preserved.* Those of the latter ages of the church, when prophecy had ceased, might yet be fitly called *the children of the prophets,* because they heard, though they did not know, *the voices of the prophets, which were read in their synagogues every sabbath day, ch.* 13:27. Now this should quicken them to embrace Christ, and they might hope to be accepted of him; for their own prophets had foretold *that this grace should be brought unto them at the revelation of Jesus Christ* (1 Pt. 1:13), and therefore ought not to be neglected by them, nor should be denied to them. Those that are blessed with prophets and prophecy (as all are that have the scriptures) are concerned not to receive the grace of God therein in vain. We may apply it particularly to ministers' children, who, if they plead their parentage effectually with themselves, as an inducement to be faithful and forward in religion, may comfortably plead it with God, and hope *that the children of God's servants shall continue.* [2.] They were *the children,* that is, the heirs, *of the covenant which God made with our Fathers,* as children in the family. God's covenant was made *with Abraham and his seed,* and they were *that seed* with whom the *covenant was made,* and on whom *the blessings of the covenant were entailed:* "The promise of the Messiah was made to you, and therefore if you forsake not your own mercies, and do not by an obstinate infidelity put a bar in your own door, you may hope it shall be made good to you." That promise here mentioned, as the principal article of the covenant, *In thy seed shall all the kindreds of the earth be blessed,* though referring principally to Christ (Gal. 3:16), yet may include the church also, which is his body, all believers, that are the spiritual seed of Abraham. *All the kindreds of the earth were blessed* in having a church for Christ among them; and those that were *the seed of Abraham according to the flesh* stood fairest for this privilege. If all the kindreds of the earth were to be blessed in Christ, much more that kindred, *his kinsmen according to the flesh.*

(2.) As Israelites, they had the first offer of the grace of the New Testament. Because *they were the children of the prophets and the covenant,* therefore to them the Redeemer was first sent, which was an encouragement to them to hope that if they did repent, and were converted, he should be yet further sent for their comfort (*v.* 20): *He shall send Jesus Christ,* for to you first he hath sent him, *v.* 26. *Unto you first,* you Jews, though not to you only, *God, having raised up his Son Jesus,* appointed and authorized him *to be a prince and a Saviour,* and, in confirmation of this, *raised him from the dead, sent him to bless you,* to make a tender of his blessing to you, especially that great blessing of *turning every one of you from his iniquities;* and therefore it concerns you to receive this blessing, and turn from your iniquities, and you may be encouraged to hope that you shall. [1.] We are here told whence Christ had his mission: *God raised up his Son Jesus, and sent him.* God raised him up when he constituted him a prophet, owned his by a voice from heaven, and filled him with his Spirit without measure, and then sent him; for to this end he raised him up, that he might be his commissioner to treat of peace. He sent him to bear witness of the truth, sent him to seek and save lost souls, sent him against his enemies, to conquer them. Some refer *the raising of him up to the resurrection,* which was the first step towards his exaltation; this was, as it were, the renewing of his commission; and though, having raised him up, he seemed presently to take him from us, yet he did really send him afresh to us in his gospel and Spirit. [2.] To whom he was sent: *"Unto you first.* You of the seed of Abraham, you that are *the children of the prophets, and of the covenant,* to you is the tender made of gospel grace." The personal ministry of Christ, as that of the prophets, was confined to the Jews; he was not then *sent but to the lost sheep of the house of Israel,* and he forbade the disciples he then sent forth to go any further. After his resurrection, he was to be preached indeed to all nations, but they must *begin at Jerusalem,* Lu. 24:47. And, when they went to other nations, they first preached to the Jews they found therein. They were the first-born, and, as such, had the privilege of the first offer. So far were they from being excluded for their putting Christ to death, that, when he is risen, he is first sent to them, and they are primarily intended to have benefit by his death. [3.] On what errand he was sent: *"He is sent to you first, to bless you;* this is his primary errand, not to condemn you, as you deserve, but to justify you, if you will accept of the justification offered you, in the way wherein it is offered; but he that sends him first to bless you, if you refuse and reject that blessing, will send him to curse you with a curse," Mal. 4:6. Note, *First,* Christ's errand into the world was to bless us, to bring a blessing with him, for *the Sun of righteousness rose with healing under his wings;* and, when he left the world, he left a blessing behind him for he was *parted from the disciples as he blessed them,* Lu. 24:51. He sent his Spirit to be the great blessing, the blessing of blessings, Isa. 44:3. It is by Christ that God sends blessings to us, and through him only we can expect to receive them. *Secondly,* The great blessing wherewith Christ came to bless us was the turning of us away from our iniquities, the saving of us from our sins (Mt. 1:21), to turn us from sin, that we may be qualified to receive all other blessings. Sin is that to which naturally we cleave; the design of divine grace is to turn us from it, nay, to turn us against it, that we may not only forsake it, but hate it. The gospel has a direct tendency to do this, not only as it requires us, every one of us, to turn from our iniquities, but as it promises us grace to enable us to do so. "Therefore, do your part; *repent, and be converted,* because Christ is ready to do his, *in turning you from your iniquities,* and so blessing you."

CHAPTER 4

In going over the last two chapters, where we met with so many good things that the apostles did, I wondered what was become of the scribes and Pharisees, and chief priests, that they did not appear to contradict and oppose them, as they had used to treat Christ himself; surely they were so confounded at first with the pouring out of the Spirit that they were for a time struck dumb! But I find we have not lost them; their forces rally again, and here we have an encounter between them and the apostles; for from the beginning the gospel met with opposition. Here, I. Peter and John are taken up, upon a warrant from the priests, and committed to jail (*v.* 1–4). II. They are examined by a committee of the great sanhedrim (*v.* 5–7). III. They bravely avow what they have done, and preach Christ to their persecutors (*v.* 8–12). IV. Their persecutors, being unable to answer them, enjoin them silence, threatening them if they go on to preach the gospel, and so dismiss them (*v.* 13–22). V. They apply to God by prayer, for the further operations of that grace which they had already experienced (*v.* 23–30). VI. God owns them, both outwardly and inwardly, by manifest tokens of his presence with them (*v.* 31–33). VII. The believers had their hearts knit together in holy love, and enlarged their charity to the poor, and the church flourished more than ever, to the glory of Christ (*v.* 33–37).

Verses 1–4

We have here the interests of the kingdom of heaven successfully carried on, and the powers of darkness appearing against them to put a stop to them. let Christ's servants be ever so resolute, Satan's agents will be spiteful; and therefore, let Satan's agents be ever so spiteful, Christ's servants ought to be resolute.

I. The apostles, Peter and John, went on in their work, and did not labour in vain. The Spirit enabled the ministers to do their part, and the people theirs.

1. The preachers faithfully deliver the doctrine of Christ: *They spoke unto the people,* to all that were within hearing, *v.* 1. What they said concerned them all, and they spoke it

openly and publicly. *They taught the people,* still *taught the people knowledge;* taught those that as yet did not believe, for their conviction and conversion; and taught those that did believe, for their comfort and establishment. *They preached through Jesus the resurrection from the dead.* The doctrine of the resurrection of the dead, (1.) Was verified in Jesus; this they proved, that Jesus Christ had risen from the dead, as the first, the chief, that should rise from the dead, *ch.* 26:23. They preached the resurrection of Christ as their warrant for what they did. Or, (2.) It is secured by him to all believers. The resurrection of the dead includes all the happiness of the future state. This *they preached through Jesus Christ,* attainable through him (Phil. 3:10, 11), and through him only. They meddled not with matters of state, but kept to their business, and preached to the people heaven as their end and Christ as their way. See *ch.* 17:18.

2. The hearers cheerfully receive it (*v.* 4): *Many of those who heard the word believed;* not all — perhaps not the most, yet many, *to the number of about five thousand,* over and above the three thousand we read of before. See how the gospel got ground, and it was the effect of the pouring out of the Spirit. Though the preachers were persecuted, the word prevailed; for sometimes the church's suffering days have been her growing days: the days of her infancy were so.

II. The chief priests and their party now made head against them, and did what they could to crush them; their hands were tied awhile, but their hearts were not in the least changed. Now here observe, 1. Who they were that appeared against the apostles. They were *the priests;* you may be sure, in the first place, they were always sworn enemies to Christ and his gospel; they were as jealous for their priesthood as Caesar for his monarchy, and would not bear one they thought their rival now, when he was preached as a priest, as much as when he himself preached as a prophet. With them was joined *the captain of the temple,* who, it is supposed, was a Roman officer, governor of the garrison placed in the tower of Antonia, for the guard of the temple: so that still here were both Jews and Gentiles confederate against Christ. *The Sadducees* also, who denied the *being of spirits* and *the future state,* were zealous against them. "One would wonder" (saith Mr. Baxter) "what should make such brutists as the Sadducees were to be such furious silencers and persecutors. If there is no life to come, what harm can other men's hopes of it do them? But in depraved souls all faculties are vitiated. A blind man has a malignant heart and a cruel hand, to this day." 2. How they stood affected to the apostles' preaching: *They were grieved that they taught the people, v.* 2. It grieved them, both that the gospel doctrine was preached (was so preached, so publicly, so boldly), and that the people were so ready to hear it. They thought, when they had put Christ to such an ignominious death, his disciples would ever after be ashamed and afraid to own him, and the people would have invincible prejudices against his doctrine; and now it vexed them to see themselves disappointed, and that his gospel got ground, instead of losing it. *The wicked shall see it, and be grieved,* Ps. 112:10. They were grieved at that which they should have rejoiced in, at that which angels rejoice in. Miserable is their case to whom the glory of Christ's kingdom is a grief; for, since the glory of that kingdom is everlasting, it follows of course that their grief will be everlasting too. It grieved them that the apostles *preached through Jesus the resurrection from the dead.* The Sadducees were grieved that the resurrection from the dead was preached; for they opposed that doctrine, and could not bear to hear of a future state, to hear it so well attested. The chief priests were grieved that they preached the resurrection of the dead through Jesus, that he should have the honour of it; and, though they professed to believe the resurrection of the dead against the Sadducees, yet they would rather give up that important article than have it preached and proved to be through Jesus. 3. How far they proceeded against the apostles (*v.* 3): *They laid hands on them* (that is, their servants and officers did at their command), and *put them in hold,* committed them to the custody of the proper officer until the next day; they could not examine them now, for it was even-tide, and yet would defer it no longer than *till next day.* See how God trains up his servants for sufferings by degrees, and by less trials prepares them for greater; now they resist unto bonds only, but afterwards to blood.

Verses 5–14

We have here the trial of Peter and John before the judges

of the ecclesiastical court, for preaching a sermon concerning Jesus Christ, and working a miracle in his name. This is charged upon them as a crime, which was the best service they could do to God or men.

I. Here is the court set. An extraordinary court, it should seem, was called on purpose upon this occasion. Observe, 1. The time when the court sat (*v.* 5) — *on the morrow;* not in the night, as when Christ was to be tried before them, for they seem not to have been so hot upon this prosecution as they were upon that; it was well if they began to relent. But they adjourned it to the morrow, and no longer; for they were impatient to get them silenced, and would lose no time. 2. The place where — in Jerusalem (*v.* 6); there it was that he told his disciples they must expect to suffer hard things, as he had done before them in that place. This seems to come in here as an aggravation of their sin, that in Jerusalem, where there were so many that looked for redemption before it came, yet there were more that would not look upon it when it did come. How is that faithful city become a harlot! See Mt. 23:37. It was in the foresight of Jerusalem's standing in her own light that Christ beheld the city, and wept over it. 3. The judges of the court. (1.) Their general character: they were *rulers, elders,* and *scribes, v.* 5. The scribes were men of learning, who came to dispute with the apostles, and hoped to confute them. The rulers and elders were men in power, who, if they could not answer them, thought they could find some cause or other to silence them. If the gospel of Christ had not been of God, it could not have made its way, for it had both the learning and power of the world against it, both the colleges of the scribes and the courts of the elders. (2.) The names of some of them, who were most considerable. Here were Annas and Caiaphas, ringleaders in this persecution; Annas the president of the sanhedrim, and Caiaphas the high priest (though Annas is here called so) and *father of the house of judgment.* It should seem that Annas and Caiaphas executed the high priest's office alternately, year for year. These two were most active against Christ; then Caiaphas was high priest, now Annas was; however they were both equally malignant against Christ and his gospel. John is supposed to be the son of Annas; and Alexander is mentioned by Josephus as a man that made a figure at that time. There were others likewise that were *of the kindred of the high priest,* who having dependence on him, and expectations from him, would be sure to say as he said, and vote with him against the apostles. Great relations, and not good, have been a snare to many.

II. The prisoners are arraigned, *v.* 7. 1. They are brought to the bar; they *set them in the midst,* for the sanhedrim sat in a circle, and those who had any thing to do in the court stood or sat in the midst of them (Lu. 2:46), so Dr. Lightfoot. Thus the scripture was fulfilled, *The assembly of the wicked has enclosed me,* Ps. 22:16. *They compassed me about like bees,* Ps. 118:12. They were seated on every side. 2. The question they asked them was, *"By what power, or by what name, have you done this?* By what authority do you these things?" (the same question that they had asked their Master, Mt. 21:23): "Who commissioned you to preach such a doctrine as this, and empowered you to work such a miracle as this? You have no warrant nor license from us, and therefore are accountable to us whence you have your warrant." Some think this question was grounded upon a fond conceit that the very naming of some names might do wonders, as *ch.* 19:13. The Jewish exorcists made use of the name of Jesus. Now they would know what name they made use of in their cure, and consequently what name they set themselves to advance in their preaching. They knew very well that they preached Jesus, and the resurrection of the dead, and the healing of the sick, through Jesus (*v.* 2), yet they asked them, to tease them, and try if they could get any thing out of them that looked criminal.

III. The plea they put in, the design of which was not so much to clear and secure themselves as to advance the name and honour of their Master, who had told them that their being brought before governors and kings would give them an opportunity of preaching the gospel to those to whom otherwise they could not have had access, and it should be *a testimony against them.* Mk. 13:19. Observe,

1. By whom this plea was drawn up: it was dictated by the Holy Ghost, who fitted Peter more than before for this occasion. The apostles, with a holy negligence of their own preservation, set themselves to preach Christ as he had directed them to do in such a case, and then Christ made good

to them his promise, that the Holy Ghost should *give them in that same hour what they should speak.* Christ's faithful advocates shall never want instructions, Mk. 13:11.

2. To whom it was given in: Peter, who is still the chief speaker, addresses himself to the judges of the court, as the *rulers of the people, and elders of* Israel; for the wickedness of those in power does not divest them of their power, but the consideration of the power they are entrusted with should prevail to divest them of their wickedness. "You are rulers and elders, and should know more than others of the signs of the times, and not oppose that which you are bound by the duty of your place to embrace and advance, that is, the kingdom of the Messiah; you are rulers and elders of Israel, God's people, and if you mislead them, and cause them to err, you will have a great deal to answer for."

3. What the plea is: it is a solemn declaration,

(1.) That what they did was in the name of Jesus Christ, which was a direct answer to the question the court asked them (*v.* 9, 10): *"If we this day be examined,* be called to an account as criminals, so the word signifies, for *a good deed* (as any one will own it to be) *done to the impotent man,* — if this be the ground of the commitment, this the matter of the indictment, — if we are put to the question, *by what means,* or by whom, *he is made whole,* we have an answer ready, and it is the same we gave to the people (*ch.* 3:16), we will repeat it to you, as that which we will stand by. *Be it known to you all* who pretend to be ignorant of this matter, and not to you only, but *to all the people of Israel,* for they are all concerned to know it, *that by the name of Jesus Christ,* that precious, powerful, prevailing name, that name above every name, even by him whom you in contempt called Jesus of Nazareth, *whom you crucified,* both rulers and people, and *whom God hath raised from the dead* and advanced to the highest dignity and dominion, *even by him doth this man stand here before you whole,* a monument of the power of the Lord Jesus." Here, [1.] He justifies what he and his colleague had done in curing the lame man. It was a *good deed;* it was a kindness to the man that had begged, but could not work for his living; a kindness to the temple, and to those that went in to worship, who were now freed from the noise and clamour of this common beggar. "Now, if we be reckoned with for this good deed, we have no reason to be ashamed, 1 Pt. 2:20; *ch.* 4:14, 16. Let those be ashamed who bring us into trouble for it." Note, It is no new thing for good men to suffer ill for doing well. *Bene agere et male pati vere Christianum est — To do well and to suffer punishment is the Christian's lot.* [2.] He transfers all the praise and glory of this good deed to Jesus Christ. "It is by him, and not by any power of ours, that this man is cured." The apostles seek not to raise an interest for themselves, nor to recommend themselves by this miracle to the good opinion of the court; but, "Let the Lord alone be exalted, no matter what becomes of us." [3.] He charges it upon the judges themselves, that they had been the murderers of this Jesus: "It is he *whom you crucified,* look how you will answer it;" in order to the bringing of them to believe in Christ (for he aims at no less than this) he endeavours to convince them of sin, of that sin which, one would think, of all others, was most likely to startle conscience — their putting Christ to death. Let them take it how they will, Peter will miss no occasion to tell them of it. [4.] He attests the resurrection of Christ as the strongest testimony for him, and against his persecutors: *"They crucified him,* but God *raised him from the dead;* they took away his life, but God gave it to him again, and your further opposition to his interest will speed no better." He tells them that God raised him from the dead, and they could not for shame answer him with that foolish suggestion which they palmed upon the people, that *his disciples came by night and stole him away.* [5.] He preaches this to all the bystanders, to be by them repeated to all their neighbours, and commands all manner of persons, from the highest to the lowest, to take notice of it at their peril: *"Be it known to you all* that are here present, and it shall be made known to *all the people of Israel,* wherever they are dispersed, in spite of all your endeavours to stifle and suppress the notice of it: as the Lord God of gods knows, so Israel shall know, all Israel shall know, that wonders are wrought in the name of Jesus, not by repeating it as a charm, but believing in it as a divine revelation of grace and goodwill to men."

(2.) That the name of this Jesus, by the authority of which they acted, is that name alone by which we can be saved. He passes from this particular instance to show that it is not a particular sect or party that is designed to be set up by the doctrine they preached, and the miracle they wrought, which people might either join with or keep off from at their pleasure, as it was with the sects of the philosophers and those among the Jews; but that it is a sacred and divine institution that is hereby ratified and confirmed, and which all people are highly concerned to submit to and come into the measures of. It is not an indifferent thing, but of absolute necessity, that people believe in this name, and call upon it. [1.] We are obliged to it in duty to God, and in compliance with his designs (*v.* 11): "*This is the stone which was set at nought of your builders,* you that are *the rulers of the people, and the elders of Israel,* that should be the builders of the church, that pretend to be so, for the church is God's building. Here was a stone offered you, to be put in the chief place of the building, to be the main pillar on which the fabric might entirely rest; but you set it at nought, rejected it, would not make use of it, but threw it by as good for nothing but to make a stepping-stone of; but this stone is *now become the head of the corner;* God has raised up this Jesus whom you rejected, and, by setting him at his right hand, has made him both the corner stone and the head stone, the centre of unity and the fountain of power." Probably St. Peter here chose to make use of this quotation because Christ had himself made use of it, in answer to the demand of the chief priests and the elders concerning his authority, not long before this, Mt. 21:42. Scripture is a tried weapon in our spiritual conflicts: let us therefore stick to it. [2.] We are obliged to it for our own interest. We are undone if we do not take shelter in this name, and make it our refuge and strong tower; for we cannot be saved but by Jesus Christ, and, if we be not eternally saved, we are eternally undone (*v.* 12): *Neither is there salvation in any other.* As there is no other name by which diseased bodies can be cured, so there is no other by which sinful souls can be saved. "By him, and him only, by receiving and embracing his doctrine, salvation must now be hoped for by all. For there is no other religion in the world, no, not that delivered by Moses, by which salvation can be had for those that do not now come into this, at the preaching of it." So. Dr. Hammond. Observe here, *First,* Our salvation is our chief concern, and that which ought to lie nearest to our hearts — our rescue from wrath and the curse, and our restoration to God's favour and blessing. *Secondly,* Our salvation is not in ourselves, nor can be obtained by any merit or strength of our own; we can destroy ourselves, but we cannot save ourselves. *Thirdly,* There are among men many names that pretend to be saving names, but really are not so; many institutions in religion that pretend to settle a reconciliation and correspondence between God and man, but cannot do it. *Fourthly,* It is only by Christ and his name that those favours can be expected from God which are necessary to our salvation, and that our services can be accepted with God. This is the honour of Christ's name, that it is the only name whereby we must be saved, the only name we have to plead in all our addresses to God. This name is *given.* God has appointed it, and it is an inestimable benefit freely conferred upon us. It is given *under heaven.* Christ has not only a great name in heaven, but a great name under heaven; for he has all power both in the upper and in the lower world. It is given *among men,* who need salvation, men who are ready to perish. We may be saved by his name, that name of his, *The Lord our righteousness;* and we cannot be saved by any other. How far those may find favour with God who have not the knowledge of Christ, nor any actual faith in him, yet live up to the light they have, it is not our business to determine. But this we know, that whatever saving favour such may receive it is upon the account of Christ, and for his sake only; so that still *there is no salvation in any other. I have surnamed thee, though thou hast not known me,* Isa. 45:4.

IV. The stand that the court was put to in the prosecution, by this plea, *v.* 13, 14. Now was fulfilled that promise Christ made, that he would give them *a mouth and wisdom, such as all their adversaries should not be able to gainsay nor resist.*

1. They could not deny the cure of the lame man to be both a good deed and a miracle. He was there standing with Peter and John, ready to attest the cure, if there were occasion, and they had *nothing to say against it* (*v.* 14), either to disprove it or to disparage it. It was well that it was not the sabbath day, else they would have had that to say against it.

2. They could not, with all their pomp and power, face down Peter and John. This was a miracle not inferior to the cure of the lame man, considering both what cruel bloody enemies these priests had been to the name of Christ (enough to make any one tremble that appeared for him), and considering what cowardly faint-hearted advocates those disciples had lately been for him, Peter particularly, who denied him for fear of a silly maid; yet now they see *the boldness of Peter and John, v.* 13. Probably there was something extraordinary and very surprising in their looks; they appeared not only undaunted by the rulers, but daring and daunting to them; they had something majestic in their foreheads, sparkling in their eyes, and commanding, if not terrifying, in their voice. They *set their faces like a flint,* as the prophet, Isa. 50:7; Eze. 3:9. The courage of Christ's faithful confessors has often been the confusion of their cruel persecutors. Now, (1.) We are here told what increased their wonder: They *perceived that they were unlearned and ignorant men.* They enquired either of the apostles or themselves or of others, and found that they were of mean extraction, born in Galilee, that they were bred fishermen, and had no learned education, had never been at any university, were not brought up at the feet of any of the rabbin, had never been conversant in courts, camps, or colleges; nay, perhaps, talk to them at this time upon any point in natural philosophy, mathematics, or politics, and you will find they know nothing of the matter; and yet speak to them of the Messiah and his kingdom, and they speak with so much clearness, evidence, and assurance, so pertinently and so fluently, and are so ready in the scriptures of the Old Testament relating to it, that the most learned judge upon the bench is not able to answer them, nor to enter the lists with them. They were *ignorant men — idiōtai, private men,* men that had not any public character nor employment; and therefore they wondered they should have such high pretensions. They were *idiots* (so the word signifies): they looked upon them with as much contempt as if they had been *mere naturals,* and expected no more from them, which made them wonder to see what freedom they took. (2.) We are told what made their wonder in a great measure to cease: they *took knowledge of them that they had been with Jesus;* they, themselves, it is probable, had seen them with him in the temple, and now recollected that they had seen them; or some of their servants or those about them informed them of it, for they would not be thought themselves to have taken notice of such inferior people. But when they understood that *they had been with Jesus,* had been conversant with him, attendant on him, and trained up under him, they knew what to impute their boldness to; nay, their boldness in divine things was enough to show with whom they had had their education. Note, Those that *have been with Jesus,* in converse and communion with him, have been attending on his word, praying in his name, and celebrating the memorials of his death and resurrection, should conduct themselves, in every thing, so that those who converse with them may *take knowledge of them that they have been with Jesus;* and this makes them so holy, and heavenly, and spiritual, and cheerful; this has raised them so much above this world, and filled them with another. One may know that they have been in the mount by the shining of their faces.

Verses 15–22

We have here the issue of the trial of Peter and John before the council. They came off now with flying colours, because they must be trained up to sufferings by degrees, and by less trials be prepared for greater. They now but *run with the footmen;* hereafter we shall have them *contending with horses,* Jer. 12:5.

I. Here is the consultation and resolution of the court about this matter, and their proceeding thereupon.

1. The prisoners were ordered to withdraw (*v.* 15): They *commanded them to go aside out of the council,* willing enough to get clear of them (they spoke so home to their consciences), and not willing they should hear the acknowledgements that were extorted from them; but, though they might not hear from them, we have them here upon record. The designs of Christ's enemies are carried on in close cabals, and they dig deep, as if they would hide their counsels from the Lord.

2. A debate arose upon this matter: *They conferred among themselves;* every one is desired to speak his mind freely, and to give advice upon this important affair. *Now the scripture was fulfilled* that the rulers would *take counsel together against the Lord, and against his anointed,* Ps. 2:2. The question proposed was, *What shall we do to these men? v.* 16. If they would have yielded to the convincing commanding power of truth, it had been easy to say what they should do to these men. They should have placed them at the head of their council, and received their doctrine, and been baptized by them in the name of the Lord Jesus, and joined in fellowship with them. But, when men will not be persuaded to do what they should do, it is no marvel that they are ever and anon at a loss what to do. The truths of Christ, if men would but entertain them as they should, would give them no manner of trouble or uneasiness; but, if they *hold them* or imprison them *in unrighteousness* (Rom. 1:18), they will find them a burdensome stone that they will not know what to do with, Zec. 12:3.

3. They came at last to a resolution, in two things: —

(1.) That it was not safe to punish the apostles for what they had done. Very willingly would they have done it, but they had not courage to do it, because the people espoused their cause, and cried up the miracle; and they stood now in as much awe of them as they had done formerly, when they durst not lay hands of Christ *for fear of the people.* By this it appears that the outcry of the mob against our Saviour was a forced or managed thing, the stream soon returned to its former channel. Now they could not find how they might punish Peter and John, what colour they might have for it, *because of the people.* They knew it would be an unrighteous thing to punish them, and therefore should have been restrained from it by the fear of God; but they considered it only as a dangerous thing, and therefore were held in from it only by the fear of *the people.* For, [1.] The people were convinced of the truth of the miracle; it was a *notable miracle, gnōston sēmeion — a known miracle;* it was known that they did it in Christ's name, and that Christ himself had often the like before. This was a known instance of the power of Christ, and a proof of his doctrine. That it was a great miracle, and wrought for the confirmation of the doctrine they preached (for it was a sign), was *manifest to all that dwelt in Jerusalem:* it was an opinion universally received, and, the miracle being wrought at the gate of the temple, universal notice was taken of it; and they themselves, with all the craftiness and all the effrontery they had, *could not deny it* to be a true miracle; every body would have hooted at them if they had. They could easily deny it to their own consciences, but not to the world. The proofs of the gospel were undeniable. [2.] They went further, and were not only convinced of the truth of the miracle, but all men *glorified God for that which was done.* Even those that were not persuaded by it to believe in Christ were yet so affected with it, as a mercy to a poor man and an honour to their country, that they could not but give praise to God for it; even natural religion taught them to do this. And, if the priests had punished Peter and John for that for which all men glorified God, they would have lost all their interest in the people, and been abandoned as enemies both to God and man. Thus therefore their wrath shall be made to praise God, and the remainder thereof shall be restrained.

(2.) That it was nevertheless necessary to silence them for the future, *v.* 17, 18. They could not prove that they had said or done any thing amiss, and yet they must no more say nor do what they have done. All their care is that the doctrine of Christ *spread no further among the people;* as if that healing institution were a plague begun, the contagion of which must be stopped. See how the malice of hell fights against the counsels of heaven; God will have the knowledge of Christ to spread all the world over, but the chief priests would have it spread no further, which he that sits in heaven laughs at. Now, to prevent the further spreading of this doctrine, [1.] They charge the apostles never to preach it any more. Be it enacted by their authority (which they think every Israelite is bound in conscience to submit to) that *no man speak at all nor teach in the name of Jesus, v.* 18. We do not find that they give them any reason why the doctrine of Christ must be suppressed; they cannot say it is false or dangerous, or of any ill tendency, and they are ashamed to own the true reason, that it testifies against their hypocrisy and wickedness, and shocks their tyranny. But, *Stat pro ratione voluntas — They can assign no reason but their will.* "We strictly charge and command you, not only that you do not preach this doctrine publicly, but that you *speak henceforth to no man,* not to any particular person privately, *in this name,*" *v.* 17. There is not a greater service done to the devil's kingdom than the silencing of faithful ministers; and putting those under a bushel that are the lights of the world. [2.] They threaten them if they do, strictly threaten them: it is at their peril. This court will reckon itself highly affronted if they do, and they shall fall under its displeasure. Christ had not only charged them to preach the gospel to every creature, but had promised to bear them out in it, and reward them for it. Now these priests not only forbid the preaching of the gospel, but threaten to punish it as a heinous crime; but those who know how to put a just value upon the world's threatenings, though they be threatenings of slaughter that it breathes out, *ch.* 9:1.

II. Here is the courageous resolution of the prisoners to go on in their work, notwithstanding the resolutions of this court, and their declaration of this resolution, *v.* 19, 20. Peter and John needed not confer together to know one another's minds (for they were both actuated by one and the same Spirit), but agree presently in the same sentiments, and jointly put in the answer: *"Whether it be right in the sight of God,* to whom both you and we are accountable, *to hearken unto you more than unto God,* we appeal to yourselves, *judge you; for we cannot forbear speaking* to every body *the things which we have seen and heard,* and are ourselves full of, and are charged to publish." The prudence of the serpent would have directed them to be silent, and, though they could not with a good conscience promise that they would not preach the gospel any more, yet they needed not tell the rulers that they would. But the boldness of the lion directed them thus to set both the authority and the malignity of their persecutors at defiance. They do, in effect, tell them that they are resolved to go on in preaching, and justify themselves in it with two things: — 1. The command of God: "You charge us not to preach the gospel; he has charged us to preach it, has committed it to us as a trust, requiring us upon our allegiance faithfully to dispense it; now whom must we obey, God or you?" Here they appeal to one of the *communes notitiae — to a settled and acknowledged maxim* in the law of nature, that if men's commands and God's interfere God's commands must take place. It is a rule in the common law of England that if any statute be made contrary to the law of God it is null and void. Nothing can be more absurd than to hearken unto weak and fallible men, that are fellow-creatures and fellow-subjects, more than unto a God that is infinitely wise and holy, our Creator and sovereign Lord, and the Judge to whom we are all accountable. The case is so plain, so uncontroverted and self-evident, that we will venture to leave it to yourselves to judge of it, though you are biassed and prejudiced. Can you think it *right in the sight of God* to break a divine command in obedience to a human injunction? That is right indeed which is *right in the sight of God;* for his judgment, we are sure, is according to truth, and therefore by that we ought to govern ourselves. 2. The convictions of their consciences. Even if they had not had such an express command from heaven to preach the doctrine of Christ, yet they *could not but speak,* and speak publicly, *those things which they had seen and heard.* Like Elihu, they were *full of this matter,* and *the Spirit within them constrained them,* they must speak, that they might be refreshed, Job 32:18. 20. (1.) They felt the influence of it upon themselves, what a blessed change it had wrought upon them, had brought them into a new world, and therefore they could not but speak of it: and those speak the doctrine of Christ best that have felt the power of it, and tasted the sweetness of it, and have themselves been deeply affected with it; it is as a *fire in their bones,* Jer. 20:9. (2.) They knew the importance of it to others. They look with concern upon perishing souls, and know that they cannot escape eternal ruin but by Jesus Christ, and therefore will be faithful to them in giving them warning, and showing them the right way. They are things *which we have seen and heard,* and therefore will be faithful to them in giving them warning, and showing them the right way. They are things which we only have seen and heard, and therefore, if we do not publish them, who will? Who can? *Knowing the* favour, as well as the *terror of the Lord, we persuade men; for the love of Christ* and the love of souls constrain us, 2 Co. 5:11, 14.

III. Here is the discharge of the prisoners (*v.* 21): *They further threatened them,* and thought they frightened them, and then *let them go.* There were many whom they terrified into an obedience to their unrighteous decrees; they knew how to keep men in awe with their excommunication (Jn. 9:22), and thought they could have the same influence upon the apostles that they had upon other men; but they were deceived, for they had been with Jesus. They threatened them, and that was all they did now: when they had done this they *let them go,* 1. Because they durst not contradict the people, who *glorified God for that which was done,* and would have been ready (at least they thought so) to pull them out of their seats, if they had punished the apostles for doing it. As rulers by the ordinance of God are made a terror and restraint to wicked people, so people are sometimes by the providence of God made a terror and restrain to wicked rulers. 2. Because they could not contradict the miracle: *For* (*v.* 22) *the man was above forty years old on whom this miracle of healing was shown.* And therefore, (1.) The miracle was so much the greater, he having been lame *from his mother's womb, ch.* 3:2. The older he grew the more inveterate the disease was, and the more hardly cured. If those that are grown into years, and have been long accustomed to evil, are cured of their spiritual impotency to good, and thereby of their evil customs, the power of divine grace is therein so much the more magnified. (2.) The truth of it was so much the better attested; for *the man being above forty years old,* he was able, like the blind man whom Christ healed, when he was asked, to *speak for himself,* Jn. 9:21.

Verses 23–31

We hear no more at present of the chief priests, what they did when they had dismissed Peter and John, but are to attend those *two witnesses.* And here we have,

I. Their return to their brethren, the apostles and ministers, and perhaps some private Christians (*v.* 23): *Being let go, they went to their own company,* who perhaps at this time were met together in pain for them, and praying for them; as *ch.* 12:12. As soon as ever they were at liberty, they went to their old friends, and returned to their church-fellowship. 1. Though God had highly honoured them, in calling them out to be his witnesses, and enabling them to acquit themselves so well, yet they were not puffed up with the honour done them, nor thought themselves thereby exalted above their brethren, but *went to their own company.* No advancement in gifts or usefulness should make us think ourselves above either the duties or the privileges of the communion of saints. 2. Though their enemies had severely threatened them, and endeavoured to break their knot, and frighten them from the work they were jointly engaged in, yet they *went to their own company,* and feared not the wrath of their rulers. They might have had comfort, if, being let go, they had retired to their closets, and spent some time in devotion there. But they were men in a public station, and must seek not so much their own personal satisfaction as the public good. Christ's followers do best in company, provided it be in their own company.

II. The account they gave them of what had passed: They *reported all that the chief priests and elders had said to them,* adding, no doubt, what they were enabled by the grace of God to reply to them, and how their trial issued. They related it to them, 1. That they might know what to expect both from men and from God in the progress of their work. From men they might expect every thing that was terrifying, but from God every thing that was encouraging; men would do their utmost to run them down, but God would take effectual care to bear them up. Thus the brethren in the Lord would wax confident through their bonds, and their experiences, as Phil. 1:14. 2. That they might have it recorded in the history of the church, for the benefit of posterity, particularly for the confirmation of our faith touching the resurrection of Christ. The silence of an adversary, in some cases, is next door to the consent and testimony of an adversary. These apostles told the chief priests to their faces that God had *raised up Jesus from the dead,* and, though they were a body of them together, they had not the confidence to deny it, but, in the silliest and most sneaking manner imaginable, bade the apostles not to tell any body of it. 3. That they might now join with them in prayers and praises; and by such a concert as this God would be the more glorified, and the church the more edified. We should therefore communicate to our brethren the providences of God that relate to us, and our experience of his presence with us, that they may assist us in our acknowledgment of God therein.

III. Their address to God upon this occasion: *When they heard* of the impotent malice of the priests, and the potent courage of the sufferers, they called their company together and went to prayer: *They lifted up their voice to God with one accord, v.* 24. Not that it can be supposed that they all said the same words at the same time (though it was possible they might, being all inspired by one and the same Spirit), but one in the name of the rest *lifted up his voice to God* and the rest joined with him, *hymothymadon — with one mind* (so the word signifies); their hearts went along with him, and so, though but one spoke, they all prayed; one lifted up his voice, and, in concurrence with him, they all lifted up their hearts, which was, in effect, lifting up their voice to God; for thoughts are as words to God. *Moses cried unto God,* when we find not a word said. Now in this solemn address to God we have,

1. Their adoration of God as the Creator of the world (*v.* 24): With *one mind,* and so, in effect, with *one mouth,* they *glorified God,* Rom. 15:6. They *said, "O Lord, thou art God,* God alone; *Despota,* thou art *our Master and sovereign Ruler"* (so the word signifies), "thou art God; God, and not man; God, and not the work of men's hands; the Creator of all, and not the creature of men's fancies. Thou art the God *who hast made heaven, and earth, and the sea,* the upper and lower world, and all the creatures that are in both." Thus we Christians distinguish ourselves from the heathen, that, while they worship gods which they have made, we are worshipping the God that made us and all the world. And it is very proper to begin our prayers, as well as our creed, with the acknowledgement of this, that God is the *Father almighty, Maker of heaven and earth, and of all things visible and invisible.* Though the apostles were at this time full of the mystery of the world's redemption, yet they did not forget nor overlook the history of the world's creation; for the Christian religion was intended to confirm and improve, not to eclipse nor jostle out, the truths and dictates of natural religion. It is a great encouragement to God's servants, both in doing work and suffering work, that they serve the God that made all things, and therefore has the disposal of their times, and all events concerning them, and is able to strengthen them under all their difficulties. And, if we give him the glory of this, we may take the comfort of it.

2. Their reconciling themselves to the present dispensations of Providence, by reflecting upon those scriptures in the Old Testament which foretold that the kingdom of the Messiah would meet with such opposition as this at the first setting of it up in the world, *v.* 25, 26. God, who *made heaven and earth,* cannot meet with any [effectual] opposition to his designs, since none dare [at least, can prevailingly] dispute or contest with him. Yea, thus it was written, *thus he spoke by the mouth,* thus he wrote by the pen, *of his servant David,* who, as appears by this, was the penman of the second psalm, and therefore, most probably, of the first, and other psalms that are not ascribed to any other, though they have not his name in the title. Let it not therefore be a surprise to them, nor any discouragement to any in embracing their doctrine, for the *scripture must be fulfilled.* It was foretold, Ps. 2:1, 2, (1.) That the heathen would rage at Christ and his kingdom, and be angry at the attempts to set it up, because that would be the pulling down of the gods of the heathen, and giving a check to the wickedness of the heathen. (2.) That the people would imagine all the things that could be against it, to silence the teachers of it, to discountenance the subjects of it, and to crush all the interests of it. If they prove vain things in the issue, no thanks to those who imagined them. (3.) That the kings of the earth, particularly, would stand up in opposition to the kingdom of Christ, as if they were jealous (though there is no occasion for their being so) that it would interfere with their powers, and intrench upon their prerogatives. The kings of the earth that are most favoured and honoured by divine Providence, and should do most for God, are strangers and enemies to divine grace, and do most against God. (4.) That the rulers would gather together against God and Christ; not only monarchs, that have the power in their single persons, but where the power is in many rulers, councils, and senates, they *gather together,* to consult and decree *against the Lord and against his Christ* — against both natural and revealed religion. What is done against Christ, God takes as done against himself. Christianity was not only destitute of the advantage of the countenance and support of kings and rulers (it had neither their power nor their purses), but it was opposed and fought against by them, and they combined to run it down and yet it made its way.

3. Their representation of the present accomplishment of those predictions in the enmity and malice of the rulers against Christ. What was foretold we see fulfilled, *v.* 27, 28. It is *of a truth* — it is certainly so, it is too plain to be denied, and in it appears the truth of the prediction that Herod and

Pilate, the two Roman governors, with the Gentiles (the Roman soldiers under their command), and with the *people of Israel* (the rulers of the Jews and the mob that is under their influence), were *gathered together* in a confederacy *against thy holy child Jesus whom thou has anointed.* Some copies add another circumstance, *en tē polei sou tautē — in this thy holy city,* where, above any place, he should have been welcomed. But herein they do *that which thy hand and thy counsel determined before to be done.* See here (1.) The wise and holy designs God had concerning Christ. He is here called the *child Jesus,* as he was called (Lu. 2:27, 43) in his infancy, to intimate that even in his exalted state he is not ashamed of his condescensions for us, and that he continues meek and lowly in heart. In the height of his glory he is the *Lamb of God,* and the *child Jesus.* But he is the *holy child Jesus* (so he was called, Lu. 1:35, *that holy thing*), and *thy* holy child; the word signifies both a son and a servant, *paida sou.* He was the Son of God; and yet in the work of redemption he acted as his Father's servant (Isa. 42:1), *My servant whom I uphold.* It was he whom God anointed, both qualified for the undertaking and called to it; and thence he was called the Lord's Christ, *v.* 26. And this comes in as a reason why they set themselves with so much rage and violence against him, because God had anointed him, and they were resolved not to resign, much less to submit to him. David was envied by Saul, because he was the Lord's anointed. And the Philistines came up to seek David when they heard he was anointed, 2 Sa. 5:17. Now the God that anointed Christ determined what should be done to him, pursuant to that anointing. He was anointed to be a Saviour, and therefore it was determined he should be a sacrifice to make atonement for sin. He must die — therefore he must be slain; yet not by his own hands — therefore God wisely determined before by what hands it should be done. It must be by the hands of those who will treat him as a criminal and malefactor, and therefore it cannot be done by the hands either of angels or of good men; he must therefore be *delivered into the hands of sinners* as Job was, *ch.* 16:11. And as David was delivered to Shimei to be *made a curse* (2 Sa. 16:11): *The Lord has bidden him. God's hand and his counsel determined it* — his will, and his wisdom. God's *hand,* which properly denotes his executive power, is here put for his purpose and decree, because with him saying and doing are not two things, as they are with us. His hand and his counsel always agree; for *whatsoever the Lord pleased that did he.* Dr. Hammon makes this phrase of *God's hand determining it* to be an allusion to the high priest's casting lots upon the two goats on the day of atonement (Lev. 16:8), in which he lifted up the hand that he happened to have the lot for the Lord in, and that goat on which it fell was immediately sacrificed; and the disposal of this lot was from the Lord, Prov. 16:33. Thus God's hand determined what should be done, that Christ should be the sacrifice slain. Or, if I may offer a conjecture, when God's hand is here said to determine, it may be meant, not of God's acting hand, but his writing hand, as Job 13:26, *Thou writest bitter things against us;* and God's decree is said to be *that which is written in the scriptures of truth* (Dan. 10:21), and *in the volume of the book it was written of Christ,* Ps. 40:7. It was *God's hand* that wrote it, his hand according to his counsel. The commission was given under his hand. (2.) The wicked and unholy instruments that were employed in the executing of this design, though they *meant not so, neither did their hearts think so.* Herod and Pilate, Gentiles and Jews, who had been at variance with each other, united against Christ. And God's serving his own purposes by what they did was no excuse at all for their malice and wickedness in the doing of it, any more than God's making the blood of the martyrs the seed of the church extenuated the guilt of their bloody persecutors. Sin is not the less evil for God's bringing good out of it, but he is by this the more glorified, and will appear to be so when the mystery of God shall be finished.

4. Their petition with reference to the case at this time. The enemies *were gathered together against Christ,* and then no wonder that they were so against his ministers: *the disciple is not better than his Master,* nor must expect better treatment; but, being thus insulted, they pray,

(1.) That God would take cognizance of the malice of their enemies: *Now, Lord, behold their threatenings, v.* 29. Behold them, as thou art said to behold them in the psalm before quoted (Ps. 2:4), when they thought *to break his bands asunder, and cast away his cords from them; he that sits in heav-*

en laughs at them, and has them in derision; and *then the virgin, the daughter of Zion, may despise* the impotent menaces even of *the great king, the king of Assyria,* Isa. 37:22. And *now, Lord; ta nyn* there is an emphasis upon the *now,* to intimate that then is God's time to appear for his people, when the power of their enemies is most daring and threatening. They do not dictate to God what he shall do, but refer themselves to and him, like *Hezekiah* (Isa. 37:17): "Open thine eyes, O Lord, and see; thou knowest what they say, *thou beholdest mischief and spite* (Ps. 10:14); to thee we appeal, *behold their threatenings,* and either tie their hands or turn their hearts; make their wrath, as far as it is let loose, to praise thee, and the remainder thereof do thou restrain," Ps. 76:10. It is a comfort to us that if we be unjustly threatened, and bear it patiently, we may make ourselves easy by spreading the case before the Lord, and leaving it with him.

(2.) That God, by his grace, would keep up their spirits, and animate them to go on cheerfully with their work: *Grant unto thy servants that with all boldness they may speak thy word,* though the priests and rulers have enjoined them silence. Note, In threatening times, our care should not be so much that troubles may be prevented as that we may be enabled to go on with cheerfulness and resolution in our work and duty, whatever troubles we may meet with. Their prayer is not, "Lord, behold their threatenings, and frighten them, and stop their mouths, and fill their faces with shame;" but, "Behold their threatenings, and animate us, open our mouths and fill our hearts with courage." They do not pray, "Lord, give us a fair opportunity to retire from our work, now that it is become dangerous;" but, "Lord, give us grace to go on in our work and not to be afraid of the face of man." Observe, [1.] Those that are sent on God's errands ought to deliver their message with boldness, with all boldness, with all liberty of speech, *not shunning to declare the whole counsel of God,* whoever is offended; not doubting of what they say, nor of being borne out in saying it. [2.] God is to be sought unto for an ability to speak his word with boldness, and those that desire divine aids and encouragements may depend upon them, and ought to go forth and go on *in the strength of the Lord God.* [3.] The threatenings of our enemies, that are designed to weaken our hands and drive us off from our work, should rather stir us up to so much the more courage and resolution in our work. Are they daring that fight against Christ? For shame, let not us be sneaking that are for him.

(3.) That God would still give them power to work miracles for the confirmation of the doctrine they preached, which, by *the cure of the lame man,* they found to contribute very much to their success, and would contribute abundantly to their further progress: *Lord, grant us boldness, by stretching forth thy hand to heal.* Note, Nothing emboldens faithful ministers more in their work than the tokens of God's presence with them, and a divine power going along with them. They pray, [1.] That God would *stretch forth his hand to heal* both the bodies and souls of men; else in vain do *they stretch forth their hands,* either in preaching (Isa. 65:2), or in curing, *ch.* 9:17. [2.] *That signs and wonders might be done by the name of the holy child Jesus,* which would be convincing to the people, and confounding to the enemies. Christ had promised them a power to work miracles, for the proof of their commission (Mk. 16:17, 18); yet they must pray for it; and, though they had it, must pray for the continuance of it. Christ himself must ask, and it shall be given him. Observe, It is the honour of Christ that they aim at in this request, that the wonders might be done by the name of Jesus, the holy child Jesus, and his name shall have all the glory.

IV. The gracious answer God gave to this address, not in word, but in power. 1. God gave them a sign of the acceptance of their prayers (v. 31): *When they had prayed* (perhaps many of them prayed successively), one by one, according to the rule (1 Co. 14:31), and when they had concluded the work of the day, *the place was shaken where they were assembled together;* there was a *strong mighty wind,* such as that when the Spirit was poured out upon them (*ch.* 2:1, 2), *which shook the house,* which was now their house of prayer. This shaking of the place was designed to strike an awe upon them, to awaken and raise their expectations, and to give them a sensible token that God was with them of a truth: and perhaps it was to put them in mind of that prophecy (Hag. 2:7), *I will shake all nations, and will fill this house with glory.* This was to show them what reason they had to fear God more, and then they would fear man less. He that shook this place could make the hearts of those who threatened his ser-

vants thus to tremble, for he *cuts off the spirit of princes, and is terrible to the kings of the earth.* The place was shaken, that their faith might be established and unshaken. 2. God gave them greater degrees of his Spirit, which was what they prayed for. Their prayer, without doubt, was accepted, for it was answered: *They were all filled with the Holy Ghost,* more than ever; by which they were not only encouraged, but enabled to speak the word of God with boldness, and not to be afraid of the proud and haughty looks of men. The Holy Ghost taught them not only *what* to speak, but *how* to speak. Those that were endued habitually with the powers of the Holy Ghost had yet occasion for fresh supplies of the Spirit, according as the various occurrences of their service were. They were *filled with the Holy Ghost* at the bar (*v.* 8), and now *filled with the Holy Ghost* in the pulpit, which teaches us to live in an actual dependence upon the grace of God, according as the duty of every day requires; we need to be *anointed with fresh oil* upon every fresh occasion. As in the providence of God, so in the grace of God, we not only in general *live, and have our being,* but *move* in every particular action, *ch.* 17:28. We have here an instance of the performance of that promise, *that God will give the Holy Spirit to those that ask him* (Lu. 11:13), for it was in answer to prayer that *they were filled with the Holy Ghost:* and we have also an example of the improvement of that gift, which is required of all on whom it is bestowed; have it and use it, use it and have more of it. When *they were filled with the Holy Ghost, they spoke the word with all boldness;* for *the ministration of the Spirit is given to every man, to profit withal.* Talents must be traded with, not buried. When they find *the Lord God help them* by his Spirit, they know they shall *not be confounded,* Isa. 50:7.

Verses 32–37

We have a general idea given us in these verses, and it is a very beautiful one, of the spirit and state of this truly primitive church; it is *conspectus saeculi — a view of that age of infancy and innocence.*

I. The disciples loved one another dearly. Behold, how good and how pleasant it was to see how *the multitude of those that believed were of one heart, and of one soul* (v. 32), and there was no such thing as discord nor division among them. Observe here, 1. There were multitudes that believed; even in Jerusalem, where the malignant influence of the chief priests was most strong, *there were three thousand* converted on one day, and *five thousand* on another, and, besides these, *there were added to the church daily;* and no doubt they were all baptized, and made profession of the faith; for the same Spirit that endued the apostles with courage to preach the faith of Christ endued them with courage to confess it. Note, The increase of the church is the glory of it, and the multitude of those that believe, more than their quality. Now the church shines, and her light is come, when souls thus fly like a cloud into her bosom, and *like doves to their windows,* Isa. 60:1, 8. 2. They *were all of one heart, and of one soul.* Though there were many, very many, of different ages, tempers, and conditions, in the world, who perhaps, before they believed, were perfect strangers to one another, yet, when they met in Christ, they were as intimately acquainted as if they had known one another many years. Perhaps they had been of different sects among the Jews, before their conversion, or had had discords upon civil accounts; but now these were all forgotten and laid aside, and they were unanimous in the faith of Christ, and, being all *joined to the Lord, they were joined to one another in holy love.* This was the blessed fruit of Christ's dying precept to his disciples, to *love one another,* and his dying prayer for them, *that they all might be one.* We have reason to think they divided themselves into several congregations, or worshipping assemblies, according as their dwellings were, under their respective ministers; and yet this occasioned no jealousy or uneasiness; for *they were all of one heart, and one soul,* notwithstanding; and loved those of other congregations as truly as those of their own. Thus it was then, and we may not despair of seeing it so again, *when the Spirit shall be poured out upon us from on high.*

II. The ministers went on in their work with great vigour and success (v. 33): *With great power gave the apostles witness of the resurrection of the Lord Jesus.* The doctrine they preached was, the resurrection of Christ: a matter of fact, which served not only for the confirmation of the truth of Christ's holy religion, but being duly explained and illustrated, with the proper inferences from it, served for a summary of all the duties, privileges, and comforts of Christians. The resurrection of Christ, rightly understood and improved, will let us into the great mysteries of religion. By the great power wherewith the apostles attested the resurrection may be meant, 1. The great vigour, spirit, and courage, with which they published and avowed this doctrine; they did it not softly and diffidently, but with liveliness and resolution, as those that were themselves abundantly satisfied of the truth of it, and earnestly desired that others should be so too. Or, 2. The miracles which they wrought to confirm their doctrine. With works of great power, they *gave witness to the resurrection of Christ,* God himself, in them, *bearing witness* too.

III. The beauty of the Lord our God shone upon them, and all their performances: *Great grace was upon them all,* not only all the apostles, but all the believers, *charis megalē* — *grace* that had something *great* in it (magnificent and very extraordinary) *was upon them all.* 1. Christ poured out abundance of *grace upon them,* such as qualified them for great services, by enduing them with *great power;* it came *upon them* from on high, from above. 2. There were evident fruits of this grace in all they said and did, such as put an honour upon them, and recommended them to the favour of God, as being in his sight *of great price.* 3. Some think it includes the favour they were in with the people. Every one saw a beauty and excellency in them, and respected them.

IV. They were very liberal to the poor, and dead to this world. This was as great an evidence of the grace of God in them as any other, and recommended them as much to the esteem of the people.

1. They insisted not upon property, which even children seem to have a sense of and a jealousy for, and which worldly people triumph in, as Laban (Gen. 31:43): *All that thou seest is mine;* and Nabal (1 Sa. 25:11): *My bread and my water.* These believers were so taken up with the hopes of an inheritance in the other world that this was as nothing to them. *No man said that aught of the things which he possessed was his own, v.* 32. They did not take away property, but they were indifferent to it. They did not call what they had their own, in a way of pride and vainglory, boasting of it, or trusting in it. They did not call it their own, because they had, in affection, forsaken all for Christ, and were continually expecting to be stripped of all for their adherence to him. They did not say that aught was their own; for we can call nothing our own but sin. What we have in the world is more God's than our own; we have it from him, must use it for him, and are accountable for it to him. *No man said that what he had was his own, idion* — *his peculiar;* for he was *ready to distribute, willing to communicate,* and desired not to eat his morsel alone, but what he had to spare from himself and family his poor neighbours were welcome to. Those that had estates were not solicitous to lay up, but very willing to lay out, and would straiten themselves to help their brethren. No marvel that *they were of one heart and soul,* when they sat so loose to the wealth of this world; for *meum — mine,* and *tuum — thine,* are the great makebates. Men's holding their own, and grasping at more than their own, are the rise of wars and fightings.

2. They abounded in charity, so that, in effect, *they had all things common;* for (*v.* 34) *there was not any among them that lacked,* but care was taken for their supply. Those that had been maintained upon the public charity were probably excluded when they turned Christians, and therefore it was fit that the church should take care of them. As there were many poor that received the gospel, so there were some rich that were able to maintain them, and the grace of God made them willing. Those *that gather much have nothing over,* because what they have over they have for those who gather little, that they may have no lack, 2 Co. 8:14, 15. The gospel hath laid *all things common,* not so that the poor are allowed to rob the rich, but so that the rich are appointed to relieve the poor.

3. They did many of them sell their estates, to raise a fund for charity: *As many as had possession of lands or houses sold them, v.* 34. Dr. Lightfoot computes that this was the year of jubilee in the Jewish nation, the fiftieth year (the twenty-eighth since they settled in Canaan fourteen hundred years ago), so that, what was sold that year being not to return till the next jubilee, lands then took a good price, and so the sale of those lands would raise the more money. Now,

(1.) We are here told what they did with the money that was so raised: They *laid it at the apostles' feet* — the left it

to them to be disposed of as they thought fit; probably they had their support from it; for whence else could they have it? Observe, The apostles would have it laid at their feet, in token of their holy contempt of the wealth of the world; they thought it fitter it should be laid at their feet than lodged in their hands or in their bosoms. Being laid there, it was not hoarded up, but *distribution was made,* by proper persons, *unto every man according as he had need.* Great care ought to be taken in the distribution of public charity, [1.] That it be given to such as have need; such as are not able to procure a competent maintenance of themselves, through age, infancy, sickness, or bodily disability, or incapacity of mind, want either of ingenuity or activity, cross providences, losses, oppressions, or a numerous charge. Those who upon any of these accounts, or any other, have real need, and have not relations of their own to help them — but, above all, those that are reduced to want for well doing, and for the *testimony of a good conscience,* ought to be taken care of, and provided for, and, with such a prudent application of what is given, as may be most for their benefit. [2.] That it be given to *every man* for whom it is intended, *according as he has need,* without partiality or respect of persons. It is a rule in dispensing charity, as well as in administering justice, *ut parium par sit ratio — that those who are equally needy and equally deserving should be equally helped,* and that the charity should be suited and adapted to the necessity, as the word is.

(2.) Here is one particular person mentioned that was remarkable for this generous charity: it was *Barnabas,* afterwards Paul's colleague. Observe, [1.] The account here given concerning him, *v.* 36. His name was *Joses;* he was of *the tribe of Levi,* for there were Levites among the Jews of the dispersion, who, it is probable, presided in their synagogue-worship, and, according to the duty of that tribe, *taught them the good knowledge of the Lord.* He was born in Cyprus, a great way off from Jerusalem, his parents, though Jews, having a settlement there. Notice is taken of the apostles' changing his name after he associated with them. It is probable that he was one of the seventy disciples, and, as he increased in gifts and graces, grew eminent, and was respected by the apostles, who, in token of their value for him, gave him a name, *Barnabas — the son of prophecy* (so it properly signifies), he being endued with extraordinary gifts of prophecy. But the Hellenist Jews (saith Grotius) called *praying paraklēsis,* and therefore by that word it is rendered here: *A son of exhortation* (so some), one that had an excellent faculty of healing and persuading; we have an instance of it, *ch.* 11:22–24. *A son of consolation* (so we read it); one that did himself walk very much in *the comforts of the Holy Ghost* — a cheerful Christian, and this enlarged his heart in charity to the poor; or one that was eminent for comforting the Lord's people, and speaking peace to wounded troubled consciences; he had an admirable facility that way. There were two among the apostles that were called *Boanerges — sons of thunder* (Mk. 3:17); but here was a *son of consolation* with them. Each had his several gift. Neither must censure the other, but both case one another; let the one search the wound, and then let the other heal it and bind it up. [2.] Here is an account of his charity, and great generosity to the public fund. This is particularly taken notice of, because of the eminency of his services afterwards in the church of God, especially in carrying the gospel to the Gentiles; and, that this might not appear to come from any ill-will to his own nation, we have here his benevolence to the Jewish converts. Or perhaps this is mentioned because it was a leading card, and an example to others: *He having land,* whether in Cyprus, where he was born, or in Judea, where he now lived, or elsewhere, is not certain, but he *sold it,* not to buy elsewhere to advantage, but, as a Levite indeed, who knew he had the Lord God of Israel for his inheritance, he despised earthly inheritances, would be encumbered no more with them, but *brought the money, and laid it at the apostles' feet,* to be given in charity. Thus, as one that was designed to be a preacher of the gospel, he disentangled himself from the affairs of this life: and he lost nothing upon the balance of the account, by laying the purchase-money at the apostles' feet, when he himself was, in effect, numbered among the apostles, by that word of the Holy Ghost, *Separate me Barnabas and Saul for the work whereunto I have called them, ch.* 13:2. Thus, for the respect he showed to the apostles as apostles, he had an apostle's reward.

CHAPTER 5

In this chapter we have, I. The sin and punishment of Ananias and Sapphira, who, for lying to the Holy Ghost, were struck dead at the word of Peter (*v.* 1–11). II. The flourishing state of the church, in the power that went along with the preaching of the gospel (*v.* 12–16). III. The imprisonment of the apostles, and their miraculous discharge out of prison, with fresh orders to go on to preach the gospel, which they did, to the great vexation of their persecutors (*v.* 17–26). IV. Their arraignment before the great sanhedrim, and their justification of themselves in what they did (*v.* 27–33). V. Gamaliel's counsel concerning them, that they should not persecute them, but let them alone, and see what would come of it, and their concurrence, for the present, with this advice, in the dismission of the apostles' cheerful progress in their work notwithstanding the prohibition laid upon them and the indignity done them (*v.* 41, 42).

Verses 1–11

The chapter begins with a melancholy *but,* which puts a stop to the pleasant and agreeable prospect of things which we had in the foregoing chapters; as every man, so every church, in its best state has its *but.* 1. The disciples were very holy, and heavenly, and seemed to be all exceedingly good; *but* there were hypocrites among them, whose *hearts were not right in the sight of God,* who, when they were baptized, and took upon them *the form of godliness, denied the power of godliness,* and stopped short of that. There is a mixture of bad with good in the best societies on this side heaven; tares will grow among the wheat until the harvest. 2. It was the praise of the disciples that they came up to that perfection which Christ recommended to the rich young man — they *sold what they had, and gave to the poor; but* even that proved a cloak and cover of hypocrisy which was thought the greatest proof and evidence of sincerity. 3. The signs and wonders which the apostles wrought were hitherto miracles of mercy; *but* now comes in a miracle of judgment, and here is an instance of severity following the instances of goodness, that God may be both loved and feared. Observe here,

I. The sin of Ananias and Sapphira his wife. It is good to see husband and wife joining together in that which is good, but to be confederate in evil is to be like Adam and Eve, when they agreed to eat the forbidden fruit, and were one in their disobedience. Now their sin was, 1. That they were ambitious of being thought eminent disciples, and of the first rank, when really they were not true disciples; they would pass for some of the most fruitful trees in Christ's vineyard, when really the root of the matter was not found in them. They *sold a possession, and brought the money* (as Barnabas did) *to the apostles' feet,* that they might not seem to be behind the very chief of believers, but might be applauded and cried up, and stand so much the fairer for preferment in the church, which perhaps they thought would shortly shine in secular pomp and grandeur. Note, It is possible that hypocrites may deny themselves in one thing, but then it is to serve themselves in another; they may forego their secular advantage in one instance, with a prospect of finding their account in something else. Ananias and Sapphira would take upon them a profession of Christianity, *and make a fair show in the flesh* with it, and so would mock God, and deceive others, when they knew they could not go through with the Christian profession. It was commendable, and so far it was right, in that rich young man, that he would not pretend to follow Christ, when, if it should come to a pinch, he knew he could not come up to his terms, *but he went away sorrowful.* Ananias and Sapphira pretended they could come up to the terms, that they might have the credit of being disciples, when really they could not, and so were a discredit to discipleship. Note, It is often of fatal consequence for people to go a greater length in profession than their inward principle will admit of. 2. That they were covetous of the wealth of the world, and distrustful of God and his providence: *They sold their land,* and perhaps then, in a pang of zeal, designed no other than to dedicate the whole of the purchase-money to pious uses, and made a vow, or at least conceived a full purpose, to do so; but, when the money was received, their heart failed them, and *they kept back part of the price,* (*v.* 2), because they loved the money, and thought it was too much to part with at once, and to trust in the apostles' hands, and because they knew not but they might want it themselves; though now all things were common, yet it would not be so long, and what should they do in a time of need, if they should leave themselves nothing to take to? They could not take God's word that they should be provided for, but thought they would play a wiser part than the rest had done, and lay up for a rainy day. Thus they thought to serve both God and mammon — God, by bringing part of the money to the apostles' feet, and mammon, by keeping the other part in their own pockets; as if there were not an all-sufficiency in God to make up the whole to them, except they retained some in their own hands by way of caution-money. Their hearts were divided, so *they were found faulty,* Hos. 10:2. They *halted between two;* if they had been thorough-paced worldlings, they would not have sold their possession; and, if they had been thorough-paced Christians, they would not have detained part of the price. 3. That they thought to deceive the apostles, and make them believe they brought the whole purchase-money, when really it was but a part. They came with as good an assurance, and as great a show of piety and devotion, as any of them, and *laid the money at the apostles' feet,* as if it were their all. They dissembled with God and his Spirit, with Christ and his church and ministers; and this was their sin.

II. The indictment of Ananias, which proved both his condemnation and execution for this sin. When he brought the money, and expected to be commended and encouraged, as others were, Peter took him to task about it, He, without any enquiry or examination of witnesses concerning it, charges him peremptorily with the crime, and aggravates it, and lays a load upon him for it, showing it to him in its own colour, *v.* 3, 4. The Spirit of God in Peter not only discovered the fact without any information (when perhaps no man in the world knew it but the man and his wife themselves), but likewise discerned the principle of reigning infidelity in the heart of Ananias, which was at the bottom of it, and therefore proceeded against him so suddenly. Had it been a sin of infirmity, through the surprise of a temptation, Peter would have taken Ananias aside, and have bidden him go home, and fetch the rest of the money, and repent of his folly in attempting to put this cheat upon them; but he knew *that his heart was fully set in him to do this evil,* and therefore allowed him not space to repent. He here showed him,

1. The origin of his sin: *Satan filled his heart;* he not only suggested it to him, and put it into his head, but hurried him on with resolution to do it. Whatever is contrary to the good Spirit proceeds from the evil spirit, and those hearts are filled by Satan in which worldliness reigns, and has the ascendant. Some think that Ananias was one of those that had received the Holy Ghost, and was filled with his gifts, but, having provoked the Spirit to withdraw from him, now *Satan filled his heart;* as, *when the Spirit of the Lord departed from Saul, an evil spirit from God troubled him.* Satan is a lying spirit; he was so in the mouth of Ahab's prophets, and so he was in the mouth of Ananias, and by this made it appear that he filled his heart.

2. The sin itself: *He lied to the Holy Ghost;* a sin of such a heinous nature that he could not have been guilty of it if Satan had not filled his heart.

(1.) The phrase which we render *lying to the Holy Ghost, pseusasthai se to pneuma to hagion,* some read, *to belie the Holy Ghost,* which may be taken two ways: [1.] That he belied the Holy Ghost in himself; so Dr. Lightfoot takes it, and supposes that Ananias was not an ordinary believer, but a minister, and one that had received the gift of the Holy Ghost with the hundred and twenty (for mention is made of him immediately after Barnabas); yet he durst thus, by dissembling, belie and shame that gift. Or thus; Those who had sold their estates, and laid the money at the apostles' feet, did it by the special impulse of the Holy Ghost, enabling them to do an act so very great and generous; and Ananias pretended that he was moved by the Holy Ghost to do what he did, as others were; whereas it appeared by his baseness that he was not under the influence of the good Spirit at all; for, had it been his work, it would have been perfect. [2.] That he belied the Holy Ghost in the apostles, to whom he brought the money; he misrepresented the Spirit they were actuated by, either by a suspicion that they would not faithfully distribute what they were entrusted with (which was a base suggestion, as if they were false to the trust reposed in them), or by an assurance that they could not discover the fraud. He belied the Holy Ghost when by what he did he would have it thought that those who are endued with the gifts of the Holy Ghost might as easily be imposed upon as other men; like Gehazi, whom his master convicted of his error by that word, *Went not my heart with thee?* 2 Ki. 5:26. It is charged upon the house of Israel and Judah, when, like Ananias here, they dealt very treacherously, that they belied the Lord, *saying, It is not he,* Jer. 5:11, 12. Thus Ananias thought the apostles were altogether such as himself, and this was belying the Holy Ghost in them, as if he were not in them a discerner of spirits, whereas they had all the gifts of the Spirit in them, which to others were divided severally. See 1 Co. 12:8–11. Those that pretend to an inspiration of the Spirit, in imposing upon the church their own fancies, either in opinion or practice — that say they are moved from above when they are carried on by their pride, covetousness, or affectation of dominion, belie the Holy Ghost.

(2.) But we read it, *to lie unto the Holy Ghost,* which reading is countenanced by *v.* 4, *Thou hast not lied unto men, but unto God.* [1.] Ananias told a lie, a deliberate lie, and with a purpose to deceive; he told Peter that he had sold a possession (house or lands) and this was the purchase-money. Perhaps he expressed himself in words that were capable of a double meaning, used some equivocations about it, which he thought might palliate the matter a little, and save him from the guilt of a downright lie: or perhaps he said nothing; but it was all one, he did as the rest did who brought the whole price, and would be thought to do so, and expected the praise those had that did so, and the same privilege and access to the common stock as they had; and therefore it was an implicit protestation that he brought the whole price, as they did; and this was a lie, for he kept back part. Note, Many are brought to gross lying by reigning pride, and affectation of the applause of men, particularly in works of charity to the poor. That therefore we may not be found boasting of a false gift given to us, or given by us (Prov. 25:14), we must not boast even of a true gift, which is the meaning of our Saviour's caution in works of charity, *Let not thy left hand know what thy right hand doeth.* Those that boast of good works they never did, or promise good works they never do, or make the good works they do more or better than really they are, come under the guilt of Ananias's lie, which it concerns us all to dread the thought of. [2.] He told this lie *to the Holy Ghost.* It was not so much to the apostles as to the Holy Ghost in them that the money was brought, and that was said which was said, *v.* 4, *Thou hast not lied unto men* (not to men only, not to men chiefly, though the apostles be but men), *but thou hast lied unto God.* Hence it is justly inferred that the Holy Ghost is God; for he that lieth to the Holy Ghost lieth to God. "Those that lied to the apostles, actuated and acting by the Spirit of God, are said to lie to God, because the apostles acted by the power and authority of God, whence it follows (as Dr. Whitby well observes) that the power and authority of the Spirit must be the power and authority of God." And, as he further argues, "Ananias is said to lie to God, because he lied to that Spirit in the apostles which enabled them to discern the secrets of men's hearts and actions, which being the property of God alone, he that lies to him must therefore lie to God, because he lies to one who has the incommunicable property of God, and consequently the divine essence."

3. The aggravations of the sin (*v.* 4): *While it remained, was it not thine own? And, after it was sold, was it not in thine own power?* Which may be understood two ways: — (1.) "Thou wast under no temptation *to keep back part of the price;* before it was sold it was thy own, and not mortgaged nor encumbered, nor any way engaged for debt; and when it was sold it was in thy own power to dispose of the money at thy pleasure; so that thou mightest as well have brought the whole as a part. Thou hadst no debts to pay, perhaps no children to provide for; so that thou wast not under the influence of any particular inducement to keep back part of the price. Thou was a transgressor without a cause." Or, (2.) "Thou wast under no necessity of selling thy land at all, nor bringing any of the money to the apostles' feet. Thou mightest have kept the money, if thou hadst pleased, and the land too, and never have pretended to this piece of perfection." This rule of charity the apostle gives, that people be not pressed, and that it be not urged as of necessity, because God loves a cheerful giver (2 Co. 9:7), and Philemon must do a good work, *not as it were of necessity, but willingly,* Philem. 14. As it is better not to vow than to vow and not to pay, so better had it been for him not to have sold his land at all than thus to keep back part of the price; not to have pretended to do the good work than thus to do it by the halves. *"When it was sold, it was in thine own power;* but it was not so when it was vowed: thou hadst then opened thy mouth to the Lord, and couldst not go back." Thus, in giving our hearts to God, we are not admitted to divide them. Satan, like the mother whose own the child was not, would take up with a half; but God will have all or none.

4. All this guilt, thus aggravated, is charged upon him: *Why hast thou conceived this thing in thine heart?* Observe, Though Satan filled his heart to do it, yet he is said to have conceived it in his own heart, which shows that we cannot extenuate our sins by laying the fault of them upon the devil; he tempts, but he cannot force; it is of *our own lusts that we are drawn away and enticed.* The evil thing, whatever it is, that is said or done, the sinner has conceived it in his own heart; and therefore, *if thou scornest, thou alone shalt bear it.* The close of the charge is very high, but very just: *Thou hast not lied unto men, but unto God.* What emphasis does the prophet lay upon that of Ahaz, *not wearying men only, but wearying my God also!* Isa. 7:13. And Moses upon that of Israel, *Your murmurings are not against us, but against the Lord!* Ex. 16:8. So here, Thou mightest have imposed upon us, who are men like thyself; but, *be not deceived, God is not mocked.* If we think to put a cheat upon God, we shall prove in the end to have put a fatal cheat upon our own souls.

III. The death and burial of Ananias, *v.* 5, 6.

1. He died upon the spot: *Ananias, hearing these words, was speechless,* in the same sense that he was who was charged with intruding into the wedding feast without a wedding garment: he had nothing to say for himself; but this was not all: he was struck speechless with a witness, for he was struck dead: *He fell down, and gave up the ghost.* It does not appear whether Peter designed and expected that this would follow upon what he said to him; it is probable that he did, for to Sapphira his wife Peter particularly spoke death, *v.* 9. Some think that an angel struck him, that he died, as Herod, *ch.* 12:23. Or, his own conscience smote him with such horror and amazement at the sense of his guilt, that he sunk and died away under the load of it. And perhaps, when he was convicted of lying to the Holy Ghost, he remembered the unpardonableness of *the blasphemy against the Holy Ghost,* which struck him like a dagger to the heart. See the power of the word of God in the mouth of the apostles. As it was to some *a savour of life unto life,* so it was to others *a savour of death unto death.* As there are those whom the gospel justifies, so there are those whom it condemns. This punishment of Ananias may seem severe, but we are sure it was just. (1.) It was designed to maintain the honour of the Holy Ghost as now lately poured out upon the apostles, in order to the setting up of the gospel kingdom. It was a great affront which Ananias put upon the Holy Ghost, as if he could be imposed upon: and it had a direct tendency to invalidate the apostles' testimony; for, if they could not by the Spirit discover this fraud, how could they by this Spirit discover the deep things of God, which they were to reveal to the children of men? It was therefore necessary that the credit of the apostles' gifts and powers should be supported, though it was at this expense. (2.) It was designed to deter others from the like presumptions, now at the beginning of this dispensation. Simon Magus afterwards was not thus punished, nor Elymas; but Ananias was made an example now at first, that, with the sensible proofs given what a comfortable thing it is to receive the Spirit, there might be also sensible proofs given what a dangerous thing it is to resist the Spirit, and do despite to him. How severely was the worshipping of the golden calf punished, and the gathering of sticks on the sabbath-day, when the laws of the second and fourth commandments were now newly given! So was the offering of strange fire by Nadab and Abihu, and the mutiny of Korah and his company, when the fire from heaven was now newly given, and the authority of Moses and Aaron now newly established. The doing of this by the ministry of Peter, who himself with a lie denied his Master but a little while ago, intimates that it was not the resentment of a wrong done to himself; for then he, who had himself been faulty, would have had charity for those that offended; and he, who himself had repented and been forgiven, would have forgiven this affront, and endeavoured to bring this offender to repentance; but it was the act of the Spirit of God in Peter: to him the indignity was done, and by him the punishment was inflicted.

2. He was buried immediately, for this was the manner of the Jews (*v.* 6): *The young men,* who it is probable were appointed to that office in the church of burying the dead, as among the Romans the *libitinarii* and *polinctores;* or the young men that attended the apostles, and waited on them, they *wound up* the dead body in grave-clothes, *carried it out*

of the city, and *buried it* decently, though he died in sin, and by an immediate stroke of divine vengeance.

IV. The reckoning with Sapphira, the wife of Ananias, who perhaps was first in the transgression, and tempted her husband to eat this forbidden fruit. *She came in* to the place where the apostles were, which, as it should seem, was Solomon's porch, for there we find them (*v.* 12), a part of the temple where Christ used to walk, Jn. 10:23. *She came in about three hours after,* expecting to share in the thanks of the house for her coming in, and consenting to the sale of the land, of which perhaps she was entitled to her dower or thirds; for *she knew not what had been done.* It was strange that nobody ran to tell her of the sudden death of her husband, that she might keep away; perhaps some one did, and she was not at home; and so when she came to present herself before the apostles, as a benefactor to the fund she met with a breach instead of a blessing.

1. She was found guilty of sharing with her husband in his sin, by a question that Peter asked her (*v.* 8): *Tell me whether you sold the land for so much?* naming the sum which Ananias had brought and laid at the apostles' feet. "Was this all you received for the sale of the land, and had you no more for it?" "No," saith she, "we had no more, but that was every farthing we received." Ananias and his wife agreed to tell the same story, and the bargain being private, and by consent kept to themselves, nobody could disprove them, and therefore they thought they might safely stand in the lie, and should gain credit to it. It is sad to see those relations who should quicken one another to that which is good harden one another in that which is evil.

2. Sentence was passed upon her, that she should partake in her husband's doom, *v.* 9.

(1.) Her sin is opened: *How is it that you have agreed together to tempt the Spirit of the Lord?* Before he passes sentence, he makes her to know her abominations, and shows her the evil of her sin. Observe, [1.] That they tempted the Spirit of the Lord; as Israel tempted God in the desert, when they said, *Is the Lord among us, or is he not?* after they had seen so many miraculous proofs of his power; and not only his presence, but his presidency, when they said, *Can God furnish a table?* So here, "Can the Spirit in the apostles discover this fraud? Can they discern that this is but a part of the price, when we tell them it is the whole?" *Can he judge through this dark cloud?* Job 22:13. They saw that the apostles had the gift of tongues; but had they the gift of discerning spirits? Those that presume upon security and impunity in sin tempt the Spirit of God; they tempt God as if he were altogether such a one as themselves. [2.] That they agreed together to do it, making the bond of their relation to each other (which by the divine institution is a sacred tie) to become a bond of iniquity. It is hard to say which is worse between yoke-fellows and other relations — a discord in good or concord in evil. It seems to intimate that their agreeing together to do it was a further tempting of the Spirit; as if, when they had engaged to keep one another's counsel in this matter, even the Spirit of the Lord himself could not discover them. Thus they *digged deep to hide their counsel from the Lord,* but were made to know it is in vain. "How is it that you are thus infatuated? What strange stupidity has seized you, that you would venture to make trial of that which is past dispute? How is it that you, who are baptized Christians, do not understand yourselves better? How durst you run so great a risk?"

(2.) Her doom is read: *Behold, the feet of those who have buried thy husband are at the door* (perhaps he heard them coming, or knew that they could not be long): *and* they *shall carry thee out.* As Adam and Eve, who agreed to eat the forbidden fruit, were turned together out of paradise, so Ananias and Sapphira, who agreed to tempt the Spirit of the Lord, were together chased out of the world.

3. The sentence executed itself. There needed no executioner, a killing power went along with Peter's word, as sometimes a healing power did; for the God in whose name he spoke *kills and makes alive;* and *out of his mouth* (and Peter was now his mouth) *both evil and good proceed* (*v.* 10): *Then fell she down straightway at his feet.* Some sinners God makes quick work with, while others he bears long with; for which difference, doubtless, there are good reasons; but he is not accountable to us for them. She heard not till now that her husband was dead, the notice of which, with the discovery of her sin, and the sentence of death passed upon her, struck her as a thunderbolt and took her away as with a whirlwind. And many instances there are of sudden deaths which are not to be looked upon as the punishment of some gross sin, like this. We must not think that all who die suddenly are sinners above others; perhaps it is in favour to them, that they have a quick passage: however, it is forewarning to all to be always ready. But here it is plain that it was in judgment. Some put the question concerning the eternal state of Ananias and Sapphira, and incline to think that the destruction of the flesh was that *the spirit might be saved in the day of the Lord Jesus.* And I should go in with that charitable opinion if there had been any space given them to repent, as there was to the incestuous Corinthian. But secret things belong not to us. It is said, *She fell down at Peter's feet;* there, where she should have laid the whole price and did not, she was herself laid, as it were to make up the deficiency. The *young men* that had the care of funerals coming in *found her dead;* and it is not said, *They wound her up,* as they did Ananias, but, *They carried her out* as she was, *and buried her by her husband;* and probably an inscription was set over their graves, intimating that they were joint-monuments of divine wrath against those that lie to the Holy Ghost. Some ask whether the apostles kept the money which they did bring, and concerning which they lied? I am apt to think they did; they had not the superstition of those who said, *It is not lawful for us to put it into the treasury:* for unto the pure all things are pure. What they brought was not polluted to those to whom they brought it; but what they kept back was polluted to those that kept it back. Use was made of the censers of Korah's mutineers.

V. The impression that this made upon the people. Notice is taken of this in the midst of the story (*v.* 5): *Great fear came upon all that heard these things,* that heard what Peter said, and saw what followed; or upon all that heard the story of it; for, no doubt, it was all the talk of the city. And again (*v.* 11), *Great fear came upon all the church, and upon as many as heard these things.* 1. Those that had joined themselves to the church were thereby struck with an awe of God and of his judgments, and with a greater veneration for this dispensation of the Spirit which they were now under. It was not a damp or check to their holy joy, but it taught them to be serious in it, and to rejoice with trembling. All that laid their money at the apostles' feet after this were afraid of keeping back any part of the price. 2. All that heard it were put into a consternation by it, and were ready to say, *Who is able to stand before this holy Lord God* and his Spirit in the apostles? As 1 Sa. 6:20.

Verses 12–16

We have here an account of the progress of the gospel, notwithstanding this terrible judgment inflicted upon two hypocrites.

I. Here is a general account of the miracles which the apostles wrought (*v.* 12): *By the hands of the apostles were many signs and wonders wrought among the people,* many miracles of mercy for one of judgment. Now the gospel power returned to its proper channel, which is that of mercy and grace. God had come out of his place to punish, but now returns to his place, to his mercy-seat again. The miracles they wrought proved their divine mission. They were not a few, but many, of divers kinds and often repeated; they were signs and wonders, such wonders as were confessedly signs of a divine presence and power. They were not done in a corner, but among the people, who were at liberty to enquire into them, and, if there had been any fraud or collusion in them, would have discovered it.

II. We are here told what were the effects of these miracles which the apostles wrought.

1. The church was hereby kept together, and confirmed in its adherence both to the apostles and to one another: *They* of the church *were all with one accord in Solomon's porch.* (1.) They met in the temple, in the open place that was called Solomon's porch. It was strange that the rulers of the temple suffered them to keep their meeting there. But God inclined their hearts to tolerate them there awhile, for the more convenient spreading of the gospel; and those who permitted buyers and sellers could not for shame prohibit such preachers and healers there. They all met in public worship; so early was the institution of religious assemblies observed in the church, which must by no means be forsaken or let fall, for in them a profession of religion is kept up. (2.) They were there with one accord, unanimous in their doctrine, worship, and discipline; and there was no discontent nor murmuring about the death of Ananias and Sapphira, as there was against Moses and Aaron about the death of Korah and his company: *You have killed the people of the Lord,* Num. 16:41. The separation of hypocrites, by distinguishing judgments, should make the sincere cleave so much the closer to each other and to the gospel ministry.

2. It gained the apostles, who were the prime ministers in Christ's kingdom, very great respect. (1.) The other ministers kept their distance: *Of the rest* of their company *durst no man join himself to them,* as their equal or an associate with them; though others of them were endued with the Holy Ghost, and spoke with tongues, yet none of them at this time did such signs and wonders as the apostles did: and therefore they acknowledged their superiority, and in every thing yielded to them. (2.) All *the people magnified them,* and had them in great veneration, spoke of them with respect, and represented them as the favourites of Heaven, and unspeakable blessings to this earth. Though the chief priests vilified them, and did all they could to make them contemptible, this did not hinder the people from magnifying them, who saw the thing in a true light. Observe, The apostles were far from magnifying themselves; they transmitted the glory of all they did very carefully and faithfully to Christ, and yet the people magnified them; for those that humble themselves shall be exalted, and those honoured that honour God only.

3. The church increased in number (*v.* 14): *Believers were the more added to the Lord,* and no doubt joined themselves to the church, when they saw that God was in it of a truth, even *multitudes both of men and women.* They were so far from being deterred by the example that was made of Ananias and Sapphira that they were rather invited by it into a society that kept such a strict discipline. Observe, (1.) Believers are added to the Lord Jesus, joined to him, and so joined to his mystical body, from which nothing can separate us and cut us off, but that which separates us and cuts us off from Christ. Many have been brought to the Lord, and yet there is room for others to be added to him, added to the number of those that are united to him; and additions will still be making till the mystery of God shall be finished, and the number of the elect accomplished. (2.) Notice is taken of the conversion of *women* as well as *men;* more notice than generally was in the Jewish church, in which they neither received the sign of circumcision nor were obliged to attend the solemn feasts; and the *court of the women* was one of the outer courts of the temple. But, as among those that followed Christ while he was upon earth, so among those that believed on him after he went to heaven, great notice was taken of the good women.

4. The apostles had abundance of patients, and gained abundance of reputation both to themselves and their doctrine by the cure of them all, *v.* 15, 16. So many *signs and wonders were wrought by the apostles* that all manner of people put in for the benefit of them, both in city and country, and had it. (1.) In the city: They *brought forth their sick into the streets;* for it is probable that the priests would not suffer them to bring them into the temple to Solomon's porch, and the apostles had not leisure to go to the houses of them all. And they *laid them on beds and couches* (because they were so weak that they could neither go nor stand), *that at the least the shadow of Peter, passing by, might overshadow some of them,* though it could not reach them all; and, it should seem, it had the desired effect, as the woman's touch of the hem of Christ's garment had; and in this, among other things, that word of Christ was fulfilled, *Greater works than these shall you do.* God expresses his care of his people, by his being their *shade on their right hand;* and the benign influences of Christ as a king are compared to the *shadow of a great rock.* Peter comes between them and the sun, and so heals them, cuts them off from a dependence upon creature sufficiency as insufficient, that they may expect help only from that Spirit of grace with whom he was filled. And, if such miracles were wrought by Peter's shadow, we have reason to think they were so by the other apostles, as by the handkerchiefs from Paul's body (*ch.* 19:12), no doubt both being with an actual intention in the minds of the apostles thus to heal; so that it is absurd to infer hence a healing virtue in the relics of saints that are dead and gone; we read not of any cured by the relics of Christ himself, after he was gone, as certainly we should if there had been any such thing. (2.) In the country towns: Multitudes came to Jerusalem from *the cities round about, bringing sick folks* that were afflicted in body, and *those that were vexed with unclean spirits,* that

were troubled in mind, and they were *healed every one;* distempered bodies and distempered minds were set to rights. Thus opportunity was given to the apostles, both to convince people's judgments by these miracles of the heavenly origin of the doctrine they preached, and also to engage people's affections both to them and it, by giving them a specimen of its beneficial tendency to the welfare of this lower world.

Verses 17–25

Never did any good work go on with any hope of success, but it met with opposition; those that are bent to do mischief cannot be reconciled to those who make it their business to do good. Satan, the destroyer of mankind, ever was, and will be, an adversary to those who are the benefactors of mankind; and it would have been strange if the apostles had gone on thus teaching and healing and had had no check. In these verses we have the malice of hell and the grace of heaven struggling about them, the one to drive them off from this good work, the other to animate them in it,

I. The priests were enraged at them, and shut them up in prison, *v.* 17, 18. Observe, 1. Who their enemies and persecutors were. The high priest was the ringleader, Annas or Caiaphas, who saw their wealth and dignity, their power and tyranny, that is, their all, at stake, and inevitably lost, if the spiritual and heavenly doctrine of Christ should get ground and prevail among the people. Those that were most forward to join with the high priest herein were the *sect of the Sadducees,* who had a particularly enmity to the gospel of Christ, because it confirmed and established the doctrine of the invisible world, the resurrection of the dead, and the future state, which they denied. It is not strange if men of no religion be bigoted in their opposition to true and pure religion. 2. How they were affected towards them, ill affected, and exasperated to the last degree. When they heard and saw what flocking there was to the apostles, and how considerable they were become, they *rose up* in a passion, as men that could no longer bear it, and were resolved to make head against it, being *filled with indignation* at the apostles for preaching the doctrine of Christ, and curing the sick, — at the people for hearing them, and bringing the sick to them to be cured, — and at themselves and their own party for suffering this matter to go so far, and not knocking it on the head at first. Thus are the enemies of Christ and his gospel a torment to themselves. *Envy slays the silly one.* 3. How they proceeded against them (*v.* 18): *They laid their hands on them,* perhaps their own hands (so low did their malice make them stoop), or, rather, the hands of their officers, and *put them in the common prison,* among the worst of malefactors. Hereby they designed, (1.) To put a restraint upon them; though they could not lay any thing criminal to their charge worthy of death or of bonds, yet while they had them in prison they kept them from going on in their work, and this they reckoned a good point gained. Thus early were the ambassadors of Christ in bonds. (2.) To put a terror upon them, and so to drive them off from their work. The last time they had them before them, they only threatened them (*ch.* 4:21); but now, finding that this did not do, they imprisoned them, to make them afraid of them. (3.) To put a disgrace upon them, and therefore they chose to clap them up in the common prison, that, being thus vilified, the people might not, as they had done, magnify them. Satan has carried on his design against the gospel very much by making the preachers and professors of it appear despicable.

II. God sent his angel to release them out of prison, and to renew their commission to preach the gospel. The powers of darkness fight against them, but the Father of lights fights for them, and sends an angel of light to plead their cause. The Lord will never desert his witnesses, his advocates, but will certainly stand by them, and bear them out.

1. The apostles are discharged, legally discharged, from their imprisonment (*v.* 19): *The angel of the Lord by night,* in spite of all the locks and bars that were upon them, *opened the prison doors,* and, in spite of all the vigilance and resolution of the keepers that *stood without before the doors, brought forth* the prisoners (see *v.* 23), gave them authority to go out without crime, and led them through all opposition. This deliverance is not so particularly related as that of Peter (*ch.* 12:7, etc.); but the miracle here was the very same. Note, There is no prison so dark, so strong, but God can both visit his people in it, and, if he pleased, fetch them out of it. This discharge of the apostles out of prison by an angel was a resemblance of Christ's resurrection, and his discharge out of the prison of the grave, and would help to confirm the apostles' preaching of it.

2. They are charged, and legally charged, to go on with their work, so as thereby to be discharged from the prohibition which the high priest laid them under; the angel bade them, *Go, stand, and speak in the temple to the people all the words of this life, v.* 20. When they were miraculously set at liberty, they must not think it was that they might save their lives by making their escape out of the hands of their enemies. No; it was that they might to on with their work with so much the more boldness. Recoveries from sickness, releases out of trouble, are granted us, and are to be looked upon by us as granted, not that we may enjoy the comforts of our life, but that God may be honoured with the services of our life. *Let my soul live, and it shall praise thee,* Ps. 119:175. *Bring my soul out of prison* (as the apostles here), *that I may praise thy name,* Ps. 143:7. See Isa. 38:22. Now in this charge given them, observe, (1.) Where they must preach: *Speak in the temple.* One would think, though they might not quit their work, yet it had been prudent to go on with it in a more private place, where it would give less offence to the priests than in the temple, and so would the less expose them. No; "Speak in the temple, for this is the place of concourse, this is your Father's house, and it is not to be as yet quite left desolate." It is not for the preachers of Christ's gospel to retire into corners, as long as they can have any opportunity of preaching in the great congregation. (2.) To whom they must preach: "*Speak to the people;* not to the princes and rulers, for they will not hearken; but to the people, who are willing and desirous to be taught, and whose souls are as precious to Christ, and ought to be so to you, as the souls of the greatest. Speak to the people, to all in general, for all are concerned." (3.) How they must preach: *Go, stand, and speak,* which intimates, not only they must speak publicly, stand up and speak, that all may hear; but that they must speak boldly and resolutely: *Stand and speak;* that is, "Speak it as those that resolve to stand to it, to live and die by it." (4.) What they must speak: *All the words of this life. This life* which you have been speaking of among yourselves, referring perhaps to the conferences concerning heaven which they had among themselves for their own and one another's encouragement in prison: "Go, and preach the same to the world, that others may be comforted with the same comforts with which you yourselves are comforted of God." Or, "of this life which the Sadducees deny, and therefore persecute you; preach this, though you know it is this that they have indignation at." Or, "of this life emphatically; this heavenly, divine life, in comparison with which the present earthly life does not deserve the name." Or, "*these words of life,* the very same you have preached, these words which the Holy Ghost puts into your mouth." Note, The words of the gospel are the words of life, quickening words; they are spirit, and they are life; *words whereby we may be saved* — that is the same with this here, *ch.* 11:14. The gospel is the word of this life, for it secures to us the privileges of our way as well as those of our home, and the promises of the life that now is as well as of that to come. And yet even spiritual and eternal life are brought so much to light in the gospel that they may be called *this life;* for the word is nigh thee. Note, The gospel is concerning matters of life and death, and ministers must preach it and people hear it accordingly. They must speak *all the words of this life,* and not conceal any for fear of offending, or in hope of ingratiating themselves with their rulers. Christ's witnesses are sworn to speak the whole truth.

III. They went on with their work (*v.* 21): *When they heard this,* when they heard that it was the will of God that they should continue to preach in the temple, they *returned to Solomon's porch, v.* 12. 1. It was a great satisfaction to them to have these fresh orders. Perhaps they began to question whether, if they had their liberty, they should preach as publicly in the temple as they had done, because they had been told, when they were *persecuted in one city, to flee to another.* But, now that the angel ordered them to go preach in the temple, their way was plain, and they ventured without any difficulty, entered into the temple, and feared not the face of man. Note, If we may but be satisfied concerning our duty, our business is to keep close to this, and then we may cheerfully trust God with our safety. (2.) They set themselves immediately to execute them, without dispute or delay. They *entered into the temples early in the morning* (as soon as the gates were opened, and people began to come together there), and taught them the gospel of the kingdom: and did not at all fear what man could do unto them. The case here was extraordinary: the whole treasure of the gospel is lodged in their hands; if they be silent now the springs are shut up, and the whole work falls to the ground and is made to cease, which is not the case of ordinary ministers, who therefore are not by this example bound to throw themselves into the mouth of danger; and yet when God gives opportunity of doing good, though we be under the restraint and terror of human powers, we should venture far rather than let go such an opportunity.

IV. The high priest and his party went on with their prosecution, *v.* 21. They, supposing they had the apostles sure enough, *called the council together,* a great and extraordinary council, for they summoned *all the senate of the children of Israel.* See here,

1. How they were prepared, and how big with expectation, to crush the gospel of Christ and the preachers of it, for they raised the whole posse. The last time they had the apostles in custody they convened them only before a committee of those that were of the kindred of the high priest, who were obliged to act cautiously; but now, that they might proceed further and with more assurance, they called together, *pasan tēn gerousian — all the eldership,* that is (says Dr. Lightfoot), all the three courts or benches of judges in Jerusalem, not only the great sanhedrim, consisting of seventy elders, but the other two judicatories that were erected one in the outer-court gate of the temple, the other in the inner or beautiful gate, consisting of twenty-three judges each; so that, if there was a full appearance, here were one hundred and sixteen judges. Thus God ordered it, that the confusion of the enemies, and the apostles' testimony against them, might be more public, and that those might hear the gospel who would not hear it otherwise than from the bar. Howbeit, the high priest *meant not so, neither did his heart think so;* but it was in his heart to rally all his forces against the apostles, and by a universal consent to cut them all off at once.

2. How they were disappointed, and had their faces filled with shame: *He that sits in heaven laughs at them,* and so may we too, to see how gravely the court is set; and we may suppose the high priest makes a solemn speech to them, setting forth the occasion of their coming together — that a very dangerous faction was now lately raised at Jerusalem, by the preaching of the doctrine of Jesus, which it was needful, for the preservation of their church (which never was in such danger as now), speedily and effectually to suppress — that it was now in the power of their hands to do it, for he had the ringleaders of the faction now in the common prison, to be proceeded against, if they would but agree to it, with the utmost severity. An officer is, in order hereunto, despatched immediately to fetch the prisoners to the bar. But see how they are baffled. (1.) The officers come, and tell them that they are not to be found in the prison, *v.* 22, 23. They last time they were forthcoming when they were called for, *ch.* 4:7. But now they were gone, and the report which the officers make is, *"The prison-doors truly found we shut with all safety"* (nothing had been done to weaken them); *"the keepers* had not been wanting to their duty; we found them *standing without before the doors,* and knowing nothing to the contrary but that the prisoners were all safe: but when we went in *we found no man* therein, that is, none of the men we were sent to fetch." It is probable that they found the common prisoners there. Which way the angel fetched them, whether by some back way, or opening the door and fastening it closely again (the keepers all the while asleep), we are not told; however it was, they were gone. The Lord knows, though we do not, how to deliver the godly out of temptation, and how to loose those that are in bonds for his name's sake, and he will do it, as here, when he has occasion for them. Now think how confused the court looked, when the officers made this return upon their order (*v.* 24): *When the high priest, and the captain of the temple,* and the *chief priests, heard these things,* they were all at a plunge, and looked one upon another, *doubting what this thing should be.* They were extremely perplexed, were at their wits' end, having never been so disappointed in all their lives of any thing they were so sure of. It occasioned various speculations, some suggesting that they were conjured out of the prison, and made their escape by magic arts; others that the keepers had played tricks with them, knowing how many friends these prisoners had, that were so much the darlings of the people. Some feared that, having made such a wonderful

escape, they would be the more followed; others that, though perhaps they had frightened them from Jerusalem, they should hear of them again in some part or other of the country, where they would do yet more mischief, and it would be yet more out of their power to stop the spreading of the infection; and now they begin to fear that instead of curing the ill they have made it worse. Note, Those often distress and embarrass themselves that think to distress and embarrass the cause of Christ. (2.) Their doubt is, in part, determined; and yet their vexation is increased by another messenger, who brings them word that their prisoners are preaching in the temple (*v.* 25): *"Behold, the men whom you put in prison,* and have sent for to your bar, *are now* hard by you here, *standing in the temple,* under your nose and in defiance of you, *teaching the people."* Prisoners, that have broken prison, usually abscond, for fear of being retaken; but these prisoners, that here made their escape, dare to show their faces even where their persecutors have the greatest influence. Now this confounded them more than any thing. Common malefactors may have art enough to break prison; but those are uncommon ones that have courage enough to avow it when they have so done.

Verses 26–42

We are not told what it was that the apostles preached to the people; no doubt it was according to the direction of the angel — *the words of this life;* but what passed between them and the council we have here an account of; for in their sufferings there appeared more of a divine power and energy than even in their preaching. Now here we have,

I. The seizing of the apostles a second time. We may think, if God designed this, "Why were they rescued from their first imprisonment?" But this was designed to humble the pride, and check the fury, of their persecutors; and now he would show that they were discharged, not because they feared a trial, for they were ready to surrender themselves and make their appearance before the greatest of their enemies. 1. They brought them without violence, with all the respect and tenderness that could be: did not pull them out of the pulpit, nor bind them, nor drag them along, but accosted them respectfully; and one would think they had reason to do so, in reverence to the temple, that holy place, and for fear of the apostles, lest they should strike them, as they did Ananias, or call for fire from heaven upon them, as Elias did; but all that restrained their violence was their fear of the people, who had such a veneration for the apostles that they would have stoned the officers if they had offered them any abuse. 2. Yet they brought them to those who, they knew, were violent against them, and were resolved to take violent courses with them (*v.* 27): They *brought them, to set them before the council,* as delinquents. Thus the powers that should have been a terror to evil works and workers became so to the good.

II. Their examination. Being brought before this august assembly, the high priest, as the mouth of the court, told them what it was they had to lay to their charge, *v.* 28. 1. That they had disobeyed the commands of authority, and would not submit to the injunctions and prohibitions given them (*v.* 28), *"Did not we,* by virtue of our authority, strictly charge and command you, upon pain of our highest displeasure, *that you should not teach in this name?* But you have disobeyed our commands, and gone on to preach not only without our licence, but against our express order." Thus those who make void the commandments of God are commonly very strict in binding on their own commandments, and insisting upon their own power: *Did not we command you?* Yes, they did; but did not Peter at the same time tell them that God's authority was superior to theirs, and his commands must take place of theirs? And they had forgotten this. 2. That they had spread false doctrine among the people, or at least a singular doctrine, which was not allowed by the Jewish church, nor agreed with what was delivered form Moses's chair. *"You have filled Jerusalem with your doctrine,* and thereby have disturbed the public peace, and drawn people from the public establishment." Some take this for a haughty scornful word: "This silly senseless doctrine of yours, that is not worth taking notice of, you have made such a noise with, that even Jerusalem, the great and holy city, is become full of it, and it is all the talk of the town." They are angry that men, whom they look upon as despicable, should make themselves thus considerable. 3. That they had a malicious design against the government, and aimed to stir up the people against it, by representing it as wicked and tyrannical, and as having made itself justly odious both to God and man: *"You intend to bring this man's blood,* the guilt of it before God, the shame of it before men, *upon us."* Thus they charge them not only with contumacy and contempt of the court, but with sedition and faction, and a plot both to set the people against them, for having persecuted even to death not only so innocent but so good and great a man as this Jesus, and also the Romans, for having drawn them into it. See here how those who with a great del of presumption will do an evil thing yet cannot bear to hear of it afterwards, nor to have it charged upon them. When they were in the heat of the persecution they could cry daringly enough, *"His blood be upon us and upon our children;* let us bear the blame for ever." But now that they have time for a cooler thought they take it as a great affront to have his blood laid at their door. Thus are they convicted and condemned by their own consciences, and dread lying under that guilt in which they were not afraid to involve themselves.

III. Their answer to the charge exhibited against them: *Peter and the other apostles* all spoke to the same purport; whether severally examined, or answering jointly, they spoke as one and the same Spirit gave them utterance, depending upon the promise their Master had made them, that, when they were brought before councils, it should be *given them in that same hour what they should speak,* and courage to speak it.

1. They justified themselves in their disobedience to the commands of the great sanhedrim, great as it was (*v.* 29): *We ought to obey God rather than men.* They do not plead the power they had to work miracles (this spoke sufficiently for them, and therefore they humbly decline mentioning it themselves), but they appeal to a maxim universally owned, which even natural conscience subscribes to, and which comes home to their case. God had commanded them to teach in the name of Christ, and therefore they ought to do it, though the chief priests forbade them. Note, Those rulers set up in opposition to God, and have a great deal to answer for, who punish men for disobedience to them in that which is their duty to God.

2. They justified themselves in doing what they could to fill Jerusalem with the doctrine of Christ, though, in preaching him up, they did indeed reflect upon those that maliciously ran him down, and if they thereby bring his blood upon them they may thank themselves. It is charged upon them as a crime that they preached Christ and his gospel. "Now," say they, "we will tell you who this Christ is, and what his gospel is, and then do you judge whether we ought not to preach it; nay, and we shall take this opportunity to preach it to you, *whether you will hear, or whether you will forbear."*

(1.) The chief priests are told to their faces the indignities they did to this Jesus: *"You slew him and hanged him on a tree,* you cannot deny it." The apostles, instead of making an excuse, or begging their pardon, for bringing the guilt of this man's blood upon them, repeat the charge, and stand to it: "It was you that slew him; it was your act and deed." Note, People's being unwilling to hear of their faults is no good reason why they should not be faithfully told of them. It is a common excuse made for not reproving sin that the times will not bear it. But those whose office it is to reprove must not be awed by this; the times must bear it, and shall bear it. *Cry aloud and spare not;* cry aloud and fear not.

(2.) They are told also what honours God put upon this Jesus, and then let them judge who was in the right, the persecutors of his doctrine or the preachers of it. He calls God the *God of our fathers,* not only *ours,* but *yours,* to show that in preaching Christ they did not preach a new god, nor entice people to come and worship other gods; not did they set up an institution contrary to that of Moses and the prophets, but they adhered to the God of the Jewish fathers; and that name of Christ which they preached answered the promises made to the fathers, and the covenant God entered into with them, and the types and figures of the law he gave them. The God of *Abraham, Isaac,* and *Jacob,* is the *God and Father of our Lord Jesus Christ;* see what honour he did him. [1.] He *raised him up;* he qualified him for, and called him to, his great undertaking. It seems to refer to the promise God made by Moses, *A prophet shall the Lord your God raise up unto you.* God raised him up out of obscurity, and made him great. Or, it may be meant of his raising him up from the grave: "You put him to death, but God has restored him to life, so that God and you are manifestly contesting about this Jesus; and which must we side with?" [2.] He *exalted him with his right hand, hypsōse — hath lifted him up.* "You loaded him with disgrace, but God has crowned him with honour; and ought we not to honour him whom God honours?" God has *exalted him, tē dexia autou — with his right hand,* that is, by his power put forth; Christ is said to *live by the power of God.* Or, to his right hand, to sit there, to rest there, to rule there. "He has invested him with the highest authority, and therefore we must teach in his name, for God has *given him a name above every name."* [3.] "He has appointed him to be *a prince and a Saviour,* and therefore we ought to preach in his name, and to publish the laws of his government as he is a prince, and the offers of his grace as he is a Saviour." Observe, There is no having Christ to be our Saviour, unless we be willing to take him for our prince. We cannot expect to be redeemed and healed by him, unless we give up ourselves to be ruled by him. The judges of old were saviours. Christ's ruling is in order to his saving, and faith takes an entire Christ, that came, not to save us in our sins, but to save us from our sins. [4.] He is appointed, as a prince and a Saviour, to *give repentance to Israel and remission of sins.* Therefore they must preach in his name to the people of Israel, for his favours were designed primarily and principally for them; and none that truly loved their country could be against this. Why should the rulers and elders of Israel oppose one who came with no less a blessing to Israel than repentance and pardon? Had he been exalted to give deliverance to Israel from the Roman yoke, and dominion over the neighbouring nations, the chief priests would have welcomed him with all their hearts. But repentance and remission of sins are blessings they neither value nor see their need of, and therefore they can by no means admit his doctrine. Observe here, *First,* Repentance and remission go together; wherever repentance is wrought, remission is without fail granted, and the favour is given to all those to whom is given the qualification for it. On the other hand, no remission without repentance; none are freed from the guilt and punishment of sin but those that are freed from the power and dominion of sin, that are turned from it and turned against it. *Secondly,* It is Jesus Christ that gives, and is authorized to give, both repentance and remission. Whatsoever is required in the gospel-covenant is promised. Are we appointed to repent? Christ is appointed to give repentance, by his Spirit working with the word, to awaken the conscience, to work contrition for sin, and an effectual change in the heart and life. The new heart is his work, and the broken spirit a sacrifice of his providing; and, when he has given repentance, if he should not give remission he would *forsake the work of his own hands.* See how necessary it is that we repent, and that we apply ourselves to Christ by faith for his grace to work repentance in us. [5.] All this is well attested, *First,* by the apostles themselves; they are ready to testify upon oath, if required, that they saw him alive after his resurrection, and saw him ascend into heaven; and also that they experienced the power of his grace upon their hearts, raising them up to that which was far above their natural capacities: *"We are his witnesses,* appointed by him to publish this to the world; and if we should be silent, as you would have us, we should betray a trust, and be false to it." When a cause is trying, witnesses, of all men, ought not to be silenced, for the issue of the cause depends on their testimony. *Secondly,* By the Spirit of God: "We are witnesses, competent ones, and whose testimony is sufficient before any human judicature." But this is not all: *The Holy Ghost is witness,* a witness from heaven; for God hath given his gifts and graces to those that obey Christ. Therefore we must preach in this name, because for this end the Holy Ghost is given us, whose operations we cannot stifle. Note, The giving of the Holy Ghost to obedient believers, not only to bring them to the obedience of faith, but to make them eminently useful therein, is a very strong proof of the truth of Christianity. God gave the Holy Ghost by his Son and in his name (Jn. 14:26), and in answer to his prayer (Jn. 14:16), nay, it was Christ that sent him from the Father (Jn. 15:26; 16:7), and this proves the glory to which the Father has exalted him. The great work of the Spirit being not only to justify Christ (1 Tim. 3:16), but to glorify him, and all his gifts having a direct tendency to exalt his name, prove that his doctrine is divine, else it would not be carried on thus by divine power. And, *Lastly,* The giving of the Holy Ghost to those that obey Christ, both for their assistance in their obedience and as a present recompence for their obedience, is a plain evidence that it is the will of God that Christ should be obeyed; "judge then whether we ought to obey you in opposition to him."

IV. The impression which the apostles' defence of themselves made upon the court. It was contrary to what one would have expected from men that pretended to reason, learning, and sanctity. Surely such fair reasoning could not but clear the prisoners, and convert the judges. No, instead of yielding to it, they raged against it, and were filled, 1. With indignation at what the apostles said: They were *cut to the heart,* angry to see their own sin set in order before them; stark mad to find that the gospel of Christ had so much to say for itself, and consequently was likely to get ground. When a sermon was preached to the people to this purport, they were *pricked to the heart,* in remorse and godly sorrow, *ch.* 2:37. These here were *cut to the heart* with rage and indignation. Thus the same gospel is to some a savour of life unto life, to others of death unto death. The enemies of the gospel not only deprive themselves of its comforts, but fill themselves with terrors, and are their own tormentors. 2. With malice against the apostles themselves. Since they see they cannot stop their mouths any other way than by stopping their breath, they *take counsel to slay them,* hoping that so they shall *cause the work to cease.* While the apostles went on in the service of Christ, with a holy security and serenity of mind, perfectly composed, and in a sweet enjoyment of themselves, their persecutors went on in their opposition to Christ, with a constant perplexity and perturbation of mind, and vexation to themselves.

V. The grave advice which Gamaliel, a leading man in the council, gave upon this occasion, the scope of which was to moderate the fury of these bigots, and check the violence of the prosecution. This Gamaliel is here said to be a *Pharisee* by his profession and sect, and by office a *doctor of the law,* one that studied the scriptures of the Old Testament, read lectures upon the sacred authors, and trained up pupils in the knowledge of them. Paul was brought up at his feet (*ch.* 22:3), and tradition says that so were Stephen and Barnabas. Some say he was the son of that Simeon that took up Christ in his arms, when he was presented in the temple, and grandson of the famous Hillel. He is here said to be *in reputation among all the people* for his wisdom and conduct, it appearing by this passage that he was a moderate man, and not apt to go in with furious measures. Men of temper and charity are justly had in reputation, for checking the incendiaries that otherwise would set the world on fire. Now observe here,

1. The necessary caution he gives to the council, with reference to the case before them: *He commanded to put the apostles forth a little while,* that he might speak the more freely, and be the more freely answered (it was fit that the prisoners should withdraw when their case was to be debated); and then put the house in mind of the importance of this matter, which in their heat they were not capable of considering as they ought: *You men of Israel,* saith he, *take heed to yourselves,* consider what you do, or *intend to do, as touching these men,* v. 35. It is not a common case, and therefore should not be hastily determined. He calls them *men of Israel,* to enforce this caution: "You are men, that should be governed by reason, be not then as *the horse and the mule that have no understanding;* you are men of Israel, that should be governed by revelation, be not then as strangers and heathens, that have no regard to God and his word. *Take heed to yourselves* now that you are angry with these men, lest you *meddle to your own hurt.*" Note, The persecutors of God's people had best look to themselves, lest they fall into the pit which they dig. We have need to be cautious whom we give trouble to, lest we be found making the hearts of the righteous sad. 2. The cases he cites, to pave the way to his opinion. Two instances he gives of factious seditious men (such as they would have the apostles thought to be), whose attempts came to nothing of themselves; whence he infers that if these men were indeed such as they represented them the cause would sink with its own weight, and Providence would infatuate and defeat them, and then they needed not persecute them. (1.) There was one *Theudas,* that made a mighty noise for awhile, as one sent of God, *boasting himself to be somebody, some great one* (so the word is), either a teacher or a prince, with a divine commission to effect some great revolution in the church or in the state; and he observes here (*v.* 36) concerning him, [1.] How far he prevailed: *"A number of men, about four hundred* in all, joined themselves to him, that knew not what to do with themselves, or hoped to better themselves; and they seemed then a for-

midable body." [2.] How soon his pretensions were all dashed: "When *he was slain*" (probably in war) "there needed no more ado, *all, as many as obeyed him, were scattered,* and melted away like snow before the sun. Now compare that case with this. You have slain Jesus, the ringleader of this faction; you have taken him off. Now if he was, as you say he was, an impostor and pretender, his death, like that of Theudas, will be the death of his cause, and the final dispersion of his followers." From what has been we may infer what will be in a like case; the smiting of the shepherd will be the scattering of the sheep: and, if the God of peace had not *brought again from the dead that great Shepherd,* the dispersion of the sheep, at his death, had been total and final. (2.) The case was the same with *Judas of Galilee, v.* 37. Observe, [1.] The attempt he made. It is said to be *after this,* which some read, *besides this,* or, Let me mention, *after this,* — supposing that Judas's insurrection was long before that of Theudas; for it was *in the time of the taxation,* namely, that at our Saviour's birth (Lu. 2:1), and that of Theudas, whom Josephus speaks of, that mutinied, in the time of *Cuspius Fadus;* but this was in the days of Claudius Caesar, some years after Gamaliel spoke this, and therefore could not be the same. It is not easy to determine particularly when these events happened, nor whether this taxing was the same with that at our Saviour's birth or one of a later date. Some think this Judas of Galilee was the same with Judas Gaulonites, whom Josephus speaks of, others not. It is probable that they were cases which lately happened, and were fresh in memory. This *Judas drew away much people after him,* who gave credit to his pretensions. But, [2.] Here is the defeat of his attempt, and that without any interposal of the great sanhedrim, or any decree of theirs against him (it did not need it); *he also perished, and all, even as many as obeyed him,* or were persuaded by him, were dispersed. Many have foolishly thrown away their lives, and brought others into the same snares, by a jealousy for their liberties, *in the days of the taxing,* who had better have been content, when Providence had so determined, *to serve the king of Babylon.*

3. His opinion upon the whole matter.

(1.) That they should not persecute the apostles (*v.* 38): *Now I say unto you, ta nyn — for the present,* as the matter now stands, my advice is, *"Refrain from these men;* neither punish them for what they have done nor restrain them for the future. Connive at them; let them take their course; *let not our hand be upon them."* It is uncertain whether he spoke this out of policy, for fear of offending either the people or the Romans and making further mischief. The apostles did not attempt any thing by outward force. The weapons of their warfare were not carnal; and therefore why should any outward force be used against them? Or, whether he was under any present convictions, at least of the probability of the truth of the Christian doctrine, and thought it deserved better treatment, at least a fair trial. Or, whether it was only the language of a mild quiet spirit, that was against persecution for conscience' sake. Or, whether God put this word into his mouth beyond his own intention, for the deliverance of the apostles at this time. We are sure there was an overruling Providence in it, that the servants of Christ might not only come off, but come off honourably.

(2.) That they should refer this matter to Providence: "Wait the issue, and see what it will come to. *If it be of men, it will come to nought* of itself; *if of God, it will stand,* in spite of all your powers and policies." That which is apparently wicked and immoral must be suppressed, else the magistrate bears the sword in vain; but that which has a show of good, and it is doubtful whether it be of God or men, it is best to let it alone, and let it take its fate, not to use any external force for the suppressing of it. Christ rules by the power of truth, not of the sword. What Christ asked concerning John's baptism, *Was it from heaven or of men?* was a question proper to be asked concerning the apostles' doctrine and baptism, which followed Christ, as John Baptist's went before him. Now they, having owned, concerning the former, that they could not tell whether it was from heaven or of men, ought not to be too confident concerning the latter. But, take it which way you will, it is a reason why they should not be persecuted. [1.] "If this *counsel, and this work,* this forming of a society, and incorporating it in the name of Jesus, *be of men, it will come to nothing.* If it be the counsel and work of foolish crack-brained men that know not what they do, let them alone awhile, and they will run themselves out of breath, and *their folly will be manifest before all men,* and they will make

themselves ridiculous. If it be the counsel and work of politic and designing men, who under colour of religion are setting up a secular interest, let them alone awhile, and they will throw off the mask, and their knavery will be manifest to all men, and they will make themselves odious; Providence will never countenance it. *It will come to nothing* in a little time; and, if so, your persecuting and opposing it is very needless; there is no occasion for giving yourselves so much trouble, and bringing such an odium upon yourselves, to kill that which, if you give it a little time, will die of itself. The unnecessary use of power is an abuse of it. But," [2.] "If it should prove (and as wise men as you have been mistaken) *that this counsel and this work is of God,* that these preachers have their commissions and instructions from him, that they are as truly his messengers to the world as the Old-Testament prophets were, then what do you think of persecuting them, of this attempt of yours (*v.* 33) *to slay them?* You must conclude it to be," *First,* "A fruitless attempt against them: *If it be of God, you cannot overthrow it;* for *there is no wisdom nor counsel against the Lord; he that sits in heaven laughs at you."* It may be the comfort of all who are sincerely on God's side, who have a single eye to his will as their rule and his glory as their end, that whatsoever is of God cannot be overthrown totally and finally, though it may be very vigorously opposed; it may be run upon, but cannot be run down. *Secondly,* "A dangerous attempt to yourselves. Pray let it alone, *lest haply you be found even to fight against God;* and I need not tell you who will come off by the worse in that contest." *Woe unto him that strives with his Maker;* for he will not only be overcome as an impotent enemy, but severely reckoned with as a rebel and traitor against his rightful prince. Those that hate and abuse God's faithful people, that restrain and silence his faithful ministers, fight against God, for he takes what is done against them as done against himself. *Whoso touches them, touches the apple of his eye.* Well, this was the advice of Gamaliel: we wish it were duly considered by those that persecute for conscience' sake, for it was a good thought, and natural enough, though we are uncertain what the man was. The tradition of the Jewish writers is that, for all this, he lived and died an inveterate enemy to Christ and his gospel; and though (now at least) he was not for persecuting the followers of Christ, yet he was the man who composed that prayer which the Jews use to this day for the extirpating of Christians and Christianity. On the contrary, the tradition of the Papists is that he turned Christian, and became an eminent patron of Christianity and a follower of Paul, who had formerly sat at his feet. If it had been so, it is very probable that we should have heard of him somewhere in the *Acts* or *Epistles.*

VI. The determination of the council upon the whole matter, *v.* 40. 1. Thus far they agreed with Gamaliel that they let fall the design of putting the apostles to death. They saw a great deal of reason in what Gamaliel said, and, for the present, it gave some check to their fury, and a reminder of their wrath was restrained by it. 2. Yet they could not forbear giving some vent to their rage (so outrageous was it) contrary to the convictions of their judgments and consciences; for, though they were advised to let them alone, yet, (1.) *They beat them,* scourged them as malefactors, stripped them, and whipped them, as they used to do in the synagogues, and notice is taken (*v.* 41) of the ignominy of it. Thus they thought to make them ashamed of preaching, and the people ashamed of hearing them; as Pilate scourged our Saviour to expose him, when yet he declared he found no fault in him. (2.) *They commanded them that they should not speak* any more *in the name of Jesus,* that, if they could find no other fault with their preaching, they might have this ground to reproach it, that it was against law, and not only without the permissions, but against the express order of their superiors.

VII. The wonderful courage and constancy of the apostles in the midst of all these injuries and indignities done them. When they were dismissed *they departed from the council,* and we do not find one word they said by way of reflection upon the court and the unjust treatment given them. *When they were reviled they reviled not again; and when they suffered they threatened not; but committed their cause to him* to whom Gamaliel had referred it, even *to a God who judgeth righteously.* All their business was to preserve the possession of their own souls, and to make full proof of their ministry, notwithstanding the opposition given them; and both these they did to admiration.

1. They bore their sufferings with an invincible cheerfulness (*v.* 41): When *they went out,* perhaps with the marks of the lashes given them on their arms and hands appearing, hissed at by the servants and rabble, it may be, or public notice given of the infamous punishment they had undergone, instead of being ashamed of Christ, and their relation to him, *they rejoiced that they were counted worthy to suffer shame for his name.* They were men, and men in reputation, that had never done any thing to make themselves vile, and therefore could not but have a sense of the shame they suffered, which, it should seem, was more grievous to them than the smart, as it usually is to ingenuous minds; but they considered that it was for the name of Christ that they were thus abused, because they belonged to him and served his interest, and their sufferings should be made to contribute to the further advancement of his name; and therefore, (1.) They reckoned it an honour, looked upon it *that they were counted worthy to suffer shame, katēxiōthēsan atimasthēnai — that they were honoured to be dishonoured for Christ.* Reproach for Christ is true preferment, as it makes us conformable to his pattern and serviceable to his interest. (2.) They rejoiced in it, remembering what their Master had said to them at their first setting out (Mt. 5:11, 12): *When men shall revile you, and persecute you, rejoice and be exceedingly glad.* They rejoiced, not only though they suffered shame (their troubles did not diminish their joy), but *that they suffered shame;* their troubles increased their joy, and added to it. If we suffer ill for doing well, provided we suffer it well, and as we should, we ought to rejoice in that grace which enables us so to do.

2. They went on in their work with indefatigable diligence (*v.* 41): They were punished for preaching, and were commanded *not to preach,* and *yet they ceased not to teach and preach;* they omitted no opportunity, nor abated any thing of their zeal or forwardness. Observe, (1.) When they preached — *daily;* not only on sabbath days, or on Lord's days, but every day, as duly as the day came, without intermitting any day, as their Master did (Mt. 26:55, Lu. 19:47), not fearing that they should either kill themselves or cloy their hearers. (2.) Where they preached — both publicly *in the temple,* and privately *in every house;* in promiscuous assemblies, to which all resorted, and in the select assemblies of Christians for special ordinances. They did not think that either one would excuse them from the other, for the word must be *preached in season and out of season.* Though in the temple they were more exposed, and under the eye of their enemies, yet they did not confine themselves to their little oratories in their own houses, but ventured into the post of danger; and though they had the liberty of the temple, a consecrated place, yet they made no difficulty of preaching in houses, in every house, even the poorest cottage. They visited the families of those that were under their charge, and gave particular instructions to them according as their case required, even to the children and servants. (3.) What was the subject matter of their preaching: *They preached Jesus Christ;* they preached concerning him; and this was not all, they preached him up, they proposed him to those who heard them, *to be their prince and Saviour.* They did *not preach themselves, but Christ,* as faithful friends to the bridegroom, making it their business to advance his interest. This was the preaching that gave most offence to the priests, who were willing they should preach any thing but Christ; but they would not alter their subject to please them. It ought to be the constant business of gospel ministers to preach Christ; *Christ, and him crucified; Christ, and him glorified;* nothing besides this but what is reducible to it.

CHAPTER 6

In this chapter we have, I. The discontent that was among the disciples about the distribution of the public charity (*v.* 1). II. The election and ordination of seven men, who should take care of that matter, and ease the apostles of the burden (*v.* 2–6). III. The increase of the church, by the addition of many to it (*v.* 7). IV. A particular account of Stephen, one of the seven. 1. His great activity for Christ (*v.* 8). 2. The opposition he met with from the enemies of Christianity, and his disputes with them (*v.* 9, 10). 3. The convening of him before the great sanhedrim, and the crimes laid to his charge (*v.* 11–14). 4. God's owning him upon his trial (*v.* 15).

Verses 1–7

Having seen the church's struggles with her enemies, and triumphed with her in her victories, we now come to take a view of the administration of her affairs at home; and here we have,

I. An unhappy disagreement among some of the church-members, which might have been of ill consequence, but was prudently accommodated and taken up in time (*v.* 1): *When the number of the disciples* (for so Christians were at first called, learners of Christ) *was multiplied* to many thousands in Jerusalem, *there arose a murmuring.*

1. It does our hearts good to find *that the number of the disciples is multiplied,* as, no doubt, it vexed *the priests and Sadducees* to the heart to see it. The opposition that the preaching of the gospel met with, instead of checking its progress, contributed to the success of it; and this infant Christian church, like the infant Jewish church in Egypt, *the more it was afflicted, the more it multiplied.* The preachers were beaten, threatened, and abused, and yet the people received their doctrine, invited, no doubt, thereto by their wonderful patience and cheerfulness under their trials, which convinced men that they were borne up and carried on by a better spirit than their own.

2. Yet it casts a damp upon us to find that the multiplying of the disciples proves an occasion of discord. Hitherto *they were all with one accord.* This had been often taken notice of to their honour; but now that they were multiplied, they began to murmur; as in the old world, *when men began to multiply, they corrupted themselves. Thou hast multiplied the nation, and not increased their joy,* Isa. 9:3. When Abraham and Lot increased their families, *there was a strife between their herdsmen;* so it was here: *There arose a murmuring,* not an open falling out, but a secret heart-burning.

(1.) The complainants were *the Grecians,* or Hellenists, *against the Hebrews* — the Jews that were scattered in Greece, and other parts, who ordinarily spoke the Greek tongue, and read the Old Testament in the Greek version, and not the original Hebrew, many of whom being at Jerusalem at the feast embraced the faith of Christ, and were added to the church, and so continued there. These complained against the Hebrews, the native Jews, that used the original Hebrew of the Old Testament. Some of each of these became Christians, and, it seems, their joint-embracing of the faith of Christ did not prevail, as it ought to have done, to extinguish the little jealousies they had one of another before their conversion, but they retained somewhat of that old leaven; not understanding, or not remembering, *that in Christ Jesus there is neither Greek nor Jew,* no distinction of Hebrew and Hellenist, but all are alike welcome to Christ, and should be, for his sake, dear to one another.

(2.) The complaint of these Grecians was *that their widows were neglected in the daily administration,* that is in the distribution of the public charity, and the Hebrew widows had more care taken of them. Observe, The first contention in the Christian church was about a money-matter; but it is a pity *that the little things of this world* should be makebates among those that profess to be taken up with *the great things of another world.* A great deal of money was gathered for the relief of the poor, but, as often happens in such cases, it was impossible to please every body in the laying of it out. *The apostles, at whose feet it was laid,* did their best to dispose of it so as to answer the intentions of the donors, and no doubt designed to do it with the utmost impartiality, and were far from respecting the Hebrews more than the Grecians; and yet here they are complained to, and tacitly complained of, *that the Grecian widows were neglected;* though they were as real objects of charity, yet they had not so much allowed them, or not to so many, or not so duly paid them, as the Hebrews. Now, [1.] Perhaps this complaint was groundless and unjust, and there was no cause for it; but those who, upon any account, lie under disadvantages (as the Grecian Jews did, in comparison with those that were Hebrews of the Hebrews) are apt to be jealous that they are slighted when really they are not so; and it is the common fault of poor people that, instead of being thankful for what is given them, they are querulous and clamorous, and apt to find fault that more is not given them, or that more is given to others than to them; and there are envy and covetousness, those roots of bitterness, to be found among the poor as well as among the rich, notwithstanding the humbling providences they are under, and should accommodate themselves to. But, [2.] We will suppose there might be some occasion for their complaint. *First,* Some suggest that though their other poor were well provided for, yet their widows were neglected, because the managers governed themselves by an ancient rule which the Hebrews observed, *that a widow was to be maintained by her husband's children.* See 1 Tim. 5:4. But, *Secondly,* I take it that the widows are here put for all the poor, because many of those that were in the church-book, and received alms, were widows, who were well provided for by the industry of their husbands while they lived, but were reduced to straits when they were gone. As those that have the administration of public justice ought in a particular manner to protect widows from injury (Isa. 1:17; Lu. 18:3); so those that have the administration of public charity ought in a particular manner to provide for widows what is necessary. See 1 Tim. 5:3. And observe, The widows here, and the other poor, had a daily ministration; perhaps they wanted forecast, and could not save for hereafter, and therefore the managers of the fund, in kindness to them, gave them day by day their daily bread; they lived from hand to mouth. Now, it seems, the Grecian widows were, comparatively, neglected. Perhaps those that disposed of the money considered that there was more brought into the fund by the rich Hebrews than by the rich Grecians, who had not estates to sell, as the Hebrews had, and therefore the poor Grecians should have less out of the fund; this, though there was some tolerant reason for it, they thought hard and unfair. Note, In the best-ordered church in the world there will be something amiss, some mal-administration or other, some grievances, or at least some complaints; those are the best that have the least and the fewest.

II. The happy accommodating of this matter, and the expedient pitched upon for the taking away of the cause of this murmuring. The apostles had hitherto the directing of the matter. Applications were made to them, and appeals in cases of grievances. They were obliged to employ persons under them, who did not take all the care they might have taken, nor were so well fortified as they should have been against temptations to partiality; and therefore some persons must be chosen to manage this matter who have more leisure to attend to it than the apostles had, and were better qualified for the trust than those whom the apostles employed were. Now observe,

1. How the method was proposed by the apostles: They *called the multitude of the disciples unto them,* the heads of the congregations of Christians in Jerusalem, the principal leading men. The twelve themselves would not determine any thing without them, for *in multitude of counsellors there is safety;* and in an affair of this nature those might be best able to advise who were more conversant in the affairs of this life than the apostles were.

(1.) The apostles urge that they could by no means admit so great a diversion, as this would be, from their great work (*v.* 2): *It is not reasonable that we should leave the word of God and serve tables.* The receiving and paying of money was serving tables, too like *the tables of the money-changers in the temple.* This was foreign to the business which the apostles were called to. They were *to preach the word of God;* and though they had not such occasion to study for what they preached as we have (it being *given in that same hour what they should speak*), yet they thought that was work enough for a whole man, and to employ all their thoughts, and cares, and time, though one man of them was more than ten of us, *than ten thousand.* If they serve tables, they must, in some measure, *leave the word of God;* they could not attend their preaching work so closely as they ought. *Pectora nostra duas non admittentia curas — These minds of ours admit not of two distinct anxious employments.* Though this serving of tables was for pious uses, and serving the charity of rich Christians and the necessity of poor Christians, and in both serving Christ, yet the apostles would not take so much time from their preaching as this would require. They will no more be drawn from their preaching by the money laid at their feet than they will be driven from it by the stripes laid on their backs. While the number of the disciples was small, the apostles might manage this matter without making it any considerable interruption to their main business; but, now that their number was increased, they could not do it. *It is not reason, ouk areston estin — it is not fit,* or commendable, that we should neglect the business of feeding souls with the bread of life, to attend the business of relieving the bodies of the poor. Note, Preaching the gospel is the best work, and the most proper and needful that a minister can be employed in, and that which he must give himself wholly to (1 Tim. 4:15), which that he may do, he must not entangle himself in the affairs of this life (2 Tim. 2:4), no, not in the outward business of the house of God, Neh. 11:16.

(2.) They therefore desire *that seven men* might be chosen, well qualified for the purpose, whose business it should be *to serve tables, diakonein trapezais — to be deacons to the tables, v.* 2. The business must be minded, must be better minded than it had been, and than the apostles could mind it; and therefore proper persons must be occasionally employed in the word, and prayer, were not so entirely devoted to it as the apostles were; and these must take care of the church's stock — must review, and pay, and keep accounts — must *buy those things which they had need of against the feast* (Jn. 13:29), and attend to all those things which are necessary *in ordine ad spiritualia — in order to spiritual exercises,* that every thing might be done decently and in order, and no person nor thing neglected. Now,

[1.] The persons must be duly qualified. The people are to choose, and the apostles to ordain; but the people have no authority to choose, nor the apostles to ordain, men utterly unfit for the office: *Look out seven men;* so many they thought might suffice for the present, more might be added afterwards if there were occasion. These must be, *First, Of honest report,* men free from scandal, that were looked upon by their neighbours as men of integrity, and faithful men, well attested, as men that might be trusted, not under a blemish for any vice, but, on the contrary, well spoken of for every thing that is virtuous and praiseworthy; *martyroumenous — men that can produce good testimonials* concerning their conversation. Note, Those that are employed in any office in the church ought to be men of honest report, of a blameless, nay, of an admirable character, which is requisite not only to the credit of their office, but to the due discharge of it. *Secondly,* They must be *full of the Holy Ghost,* must be filled with those gifts and graces of the Holy Ghost which were necessary to the right management of this trust. They must not only be honest men, but they must be men of ability and men of courage; such as were to be made judges in Israel (Ex. 18:21), *able men, fearing God; men of truth, and hating covetousness;* and hereby appearing to be *full of the Holy Ghost. Thirdly,* They must be *full of wisdom.* It was not enough that they were honest, good men, but they must be discreet, judicious men, that could not be imposed upon, and would order things for the best, and with consideration: *full of the Holy Ghost, and wisdom,* that is, of the Holy Ghost as a Spirit of wisdom. We find the word of wisdom given by the Spirit, as distinct form the word of knowledge by the same Spirit, 1 Co. 12:8. Those must be full of wisdom who are entrusted with public money, that it may be disposed of, not only with fidelity, but with frugality.

[2.] The people must nominate the persons: *"Look you out among yourselves seven men;* consider among yourselves who are the fittest for such a trust, and whom you can with the most satisfaction confide in." They might be presumed to know better, or at least were fitter to enquire, what character men had, than the apostles; and therefore they are entrusted with the choice.

[3.] They apostles will ordain them to the service, will give them their charge, that they may know what they have to do and make conscience of doing it, and give them their authority, that the persons concerned may know whom they are to apply to, and submit to, in affairs of that nature: *Men, whom we may appoint.* In many editions of our English Bibles there has been an error of the press here; for they have read it, *whom ye may appoint,* as if the power were in the people; whereas it was certainly in the apostles: *whom we may appoint over this business,* to take care of it, and to see that there be neither waste nor want.

(3.) The apostles engage to addict themselves wholly to their work as ministers, and the more closely if they can but get fairly quit of this troublesome office (*v.* 4): *We will give ourselves continually to prayer, and to the ministry of the word.* See here, [1.] What are the two great gospel ordinances — *the word, and prayer;* by these two communion between God and his people is kept up and maintained; by the word he speaks to them, and by prayer they speak to him; and these have a mutual reference to each other. By these two the kingdom of Christ must be advanced, and additions made to it; we must *prophesy upon the dry bones,* and *then pray for a spirit of life* from God *to enter into them.* By the word and prayer other ordinances are sanctified to us, and sacraments have their efficacy. [2.] What is the great business of gospel ministers — to give themselves continually to prayer, and to the ministry of the word; they must still be either fitting and furnishing themselves for those services, or employing themselves in them; either publicly or privately; in the stated times, or out of them. They must be God's mouth to the people in the ministry of the word, and the people's mouth to God in prayer. In order to the conviction and conversion of sinners, and the edification and consolation of saints, we must not only offer up our prayers for them, but we must minister the word to them, seconding our prayers with our endeavours, in the use of appointed means. Nor must we only minister the word to them, but we must pray for them, that it may be effectual; for God's grace can do all without our preaching, but our preaching can do nothing without God's grace. The apostles were endued with extraordinary gifts of the Holy Ghost, tongues and miracles; and yet that to which they gave themselves continually was preaching and praying, by which they might edify the church: and those ministers, without doubt, are the successors of the apostles (not in the plenitude of the apostolical power — those are daring usurpers who pretend to this, but in the best and most excellent of the apostolical works) who give themselves continually to prayer, and to the ministry of the word; and such Christ will always be with, *even to the end of the world.*

2. How this proposal was agreed to, and presently put in execution, by the disciples. It was not imposed upon them by an absolute power, though they might have been bold in Christ to do this (Philem. 8), but proposed, as that which was highly convenient, and *then the saying pleased the whole multitude, v.* 5. It pleased them to see the apostles so willing to have themselves discharged from intermeddling in secular affairs, and to transmit them to others; it pleased them to hear that they would give themselves to the word and prayer; and therefore they neither disputed the matter nor deferred the execution of it.

(1.) They pitched upon the persons. It is not probable that they all cast their eye upon the same men. Everyone had his friend, whom he thought well of. But the majority of votes fell upon the persons here named; and the rest both of the candidates and the electors acquiesced, and made no disturbance, as the members of societies in such cases ought to do. An apostle, who was an extraordinary officer, was chosen by lot, which is more immediately the act of God; but the overseers of the poor were chosen by the suffrage of the people, in which yet a regard is to be had to the providence of God, who has all men's hearts and tongues in his hand. We have a list of the persons chosen. Some think they were such as were before of the seventy disciples; but this is not likely, for they were ordained by Christ himself, long since, *to preach the gospel;* and there was not more reason that they should leave the word of God to serve tables than that the apostles should. It is therefore more probable that they were of those that were converted since the pouring out of the Spirit; for it was promised to all that would be baptized that they should *receive the gift of the Holy Ghost;* and the gift, according to that promise, is that fulness of the Holy Ghost which was required in those that were to be chosen to this service. We may further conjecture, concerning these seven, [1.] That they were such as had sold their estates, and brought the money into the common stock; for *caeteris paribus — other things being equal,* those were fittest to be entrusted with the distribution of it who had been most generous in the contribution to it. [2.] That these seven were all of the Grecian or Hellenist Jews, for they have all Greek names, and this would be most likely *to silence the murmurings of the Grecians* (which occasioned this institution), to have the trust lodged in those that were foreigners, like themselves, who would be sure not to neglect them. *Nicolas,* it is plain, was one of them, for he was *a proselyte of Antioch;* and some think the manner of expression intimates that they were all proselytes of Jerusalem, as he was of Antioch. The first named is *Stephen,* the glory of these *septemviri, a man full of faith and of the Holy Ghost;* he had a strong faith in the doctrine of Christ, and was full of it above most; *full of fidelity, full of courage* (so some), for he was *full of the Holy Ghost,* of his gifts and graces. He was an extraordinary man, and excelled in every thing that was good; his name signifies *a crown. Phillip* is put next, because he, having *used this office of a deacon well, thereby obtained a good degree,* and was afterwards ordained to the office of an evangelist, a companion and assistant to the apostles, for so he is expressly called, *ch.* 21:8. Compare Eph. 4:11. And his preaching and baptizing (which we read of *ch.* 8:12) were certainly not as a deacon (for it is plain that that office was *serving tables,* in opposition *to the ministry of the word*), but as an evangelist; and, when he was preferred to that office, we have reason to think he quitted this office, as incompatible with that. As for *Stephen,* nothing we find done by him proves him to be a preacher of the gospel; for he only disputes in the schools, and pleads for his life at the bar, *v.* 9, and *ch.* 7:2. The last named is *Nicolas,* who, some say, afterwards degenerated (as the Judas among these seven) and was the founder of *the sect of the Nicolaitans* which we read of (Rev. 2:6, 15), and which Christ there says, once and again, was a thing he hated. But some of the ancients clear him from this charge, and tell us that, though that vile impure sect denominated themselves from him, yet it was unjustly, and because he only insisted much upon it *that those that had wives should be as though they had none,* thence they wickedly inferred *that those that had wives should have them in common,* which therefore Tertullian, when he speaks of the community of goods, particularly excepts: *Omnia indiscreta apud nos, praeter uxores — All things are common among us, except our wives.* — Apol. cap, 39.

(2.) The apostles appointed them to this work of serving tables for the present, *v.* 6. The people presented them to the apostles, who approved their choice, and ordained them. [1.] They prayed with them, and for them, that God would give them more and more of the Holy Ghost and of wisdom — that he would qualify them for the service to which they were called, and own them in it, and make them thereby a blessing to the church, and particularly to the poor of the flock. All that are employed in the service of the church ought to be committed to the conduct of the divine grace by the prayers of the church. [2.] *They laid their hands on them,* that is, *they blessed them in the name of the Lord,* for laying on hands was used in blessing; so *Jacob blessed both the sons of Joseph;* and, without controversy, *the less is blessed of the greater* (Heb. 7:7); the deacons are blessed by the apostles, and the overseers of the poor by the pastors of the congregation. Having by prayer implored a blessing upon them, they did by the laying on of hands assure them that the blessing was conferred in answer to the prayer; and this was giving them authority to execute that office, and laying an obligation upon the people to be observant of them therein.

III. The advancement of the church hereupon. When things were thus put into good order in the church (grievances were redressed and discontents silenced) then religion got ground, *v.* 7. 1. *The word of God increased.* Now that the apostles resolved to stick more closely than ever to their preaching, it spread the gospel further, and brought it home with the more power. Ministers disentangling themselves from secular employments, and addicting themselves entirely and vigorously to their work, will contribute very much, as a means, to the success of the gospel. The word of God is said to increase as the seed sown increases when it comes up again thirty, sixty, a hundred fold. 2. Christians became numerous: *The number of the disciples multiplied in Jerusalem greatly.* When Christ was upon earth, his ministry had least success in Jerusalem; yet now that city affords most converts. God has his remnant even in the worst of places. 3. *A great company of the priests were obedient to the faith. Then* is the word and grace of God greatly magnified when those are wrought upon by it that were least likely, as the priests here, who either had opposed it, or at least were linked in with those that had. The priests, whose preferments arose from the law of Moses, were yet willing to let them go for the gospel of Christ; and, it should seem, they came *in a body;* many of them agreed together, for the keeping up of one another's credit, and the strengthening of one another's hands, to join at once in giving up their names to Christ: *polis ochlos — a great crowd of priests* were, by the grace of God helped over their prejudices, and *were obedient to the faith,* so their conversion is described. (1.) They embraced the doctrine of the gospel; their understandings were captivated to the power of the truths of Christ, and every opposing objecting thought brought into obedience to him, 2 Co. 10:4, 5. The gospel is said to be *made known for the obedience of faith,* Rom. 16:26. Faith is an act of obedience, for this is God's commandment, *that we believe,* 1 Jn. 3:23. (2.) They envinced the sincerity of their believing the gospel of Christ by a cheerful compliance with all the rules and precepts of the gospel. The design of the gospel is to refine and reform our hearts and lives; faith gives law to us, and we must be obedient to it.

Verses 8–15

Stephen, no doubt was diligent and faithful in the discharge of his office as distributor of the church's charity, and laid out himself to put that affair in a good method, which he did to universal satisfaction; and though it appears here that he was a man of uncommon gifts, and fitted for a higher station, yet, being called to that office, he did not think it below him to do the duty of it. And, being faithful in a little, he was entrusted with more; and, though we do not find him propagating the gospel by preaching and baptizing, yet we find him here called out to very honourable services, and owned in them.

I. He proved the truth of the gospel, by working miracles in Christ's name, v. 8. 1. He was *full of faith and power,* that is, of a strong faith, by which he was enabled to do great things. Those that are full of faith are full of power, because by faith the power of God is engaged for us. His faith did so fill him that it left no room for unbelief and made room for the influences of divine grace, so that, as the prophet speaks, he was *full of power by the Spirit of the Lord of hosts,* Mic. 3:8. By faith we are emptied of self, and so are filled with Christ, who is the *wisdom of God and the power of God.* 2. Being so *he did great wonders and miracles among the people,* openly, and in the sight of all; for Christ's miracles feared not the strictest scrutiny. It is not strange that Stephen, though he was not a preacher by office, did these great wonders, for we find that these were distinct gifts of the Spirit, and divided severally, for *to one was given the working of miracles, and to another prophecy,* 1 Co. 12:10, 11. And *these signs followed* not only those that preached, but those that believed. Mk. 16:17

II. He pleaded the cause of Christianity against those that opposed it, and argued against it (v. 9, 10); he served the interests of religion as a disputant, in the high places of the field, while others were serving them as vinedressers and husbandmen.

1. We are here told who were his opponents, v. 9. They were Jews, but Hellenist Jews, Jews of the dispersion, who seem to have been more zealous for their religion than the native Jews; it was with difficulty that they retained the practice and profession of it in the country where they lived, where they were as speckled birds, and not without great expense and toil that they kept up their attendance at Jerusalem, and this made them more active sticklers for Judaism than those were whose profession of their religion was cheap and easy. They were *of the synagogue which is called the synagogue of the Libertines;* the Romans called those *Liberti,* or *Libertini,* who either, being foreigners, were naturalized, or, being slaves by birth, were manumitted, or made freemen. Some think that these Libertines were such of the Jews as had obtained the Roman freedom, as Paul had (*ch.* 22:27, 28); and it is probable that he was the most forward man of this synagogue of the Libertines in disputing with Stephen, and engaged others in the dispute, for we find him busy in the stoning of Stephen, and consenting to his death. There were others that belonged to the synagogue of the Cyrenians and Alexandrians, of which synagogue the Jewish writers speak; and others that belonged to their synagogue who were of Cilicia and Asia; and if Paul, as a freeman of Rome, did not belong to the synagogue of the Libertines, he belonged to this, as a native of Tarsus, a city of Cilicia: it is probable that he might be a member of both. The Jews that were born in other countries, and had concerns in them, had frequent occasion, not only to resort to, but to reside in, Jerusalem. Each nation had its synagogue, as in London there are French, and Dutch, and Danish churches: and those synagogues were the schools to which the Jews of those nations sent their youth to be educated in the Jewish learning. Now those that were tutors and professors in these synagogues, seeing the gospel grow, and the rulers conniving at the growth of it, and fearing what would be the consequence of it to the Jewish religion, which they were jealous for, being confident of the goodness of their cause, and their own sufficiency to manage it, would undertake to run down Christianity by force of argument. It was a fair and rational way of dealing with it, and what religion is always ready to admit. *Produce your cause, saith the Lord, bring forth your strong reasons,* Isa. 41:21. But why did they dispute with Stephen? And why not with the apostles themselves? (1.) Some think because they despised the apostles as *unlearned and ignorant men,* whom they thought it below them to engage with; but Stephen was bred a scholar, and they thought it their honour to meddle with their match. (2.) Others think it was because they stood in awe of the apostles, and could not be so free and familiar with them as they could be with Stephen, who was in an in-

ferior office. (3.) Perhaps, they having given a public challenge, Stephen was chosen and appointed by the disciples to be their champion; for it was not meet that the apostles should leave the preaching of the word of God to engage in controversy. Stephen, who was only a deacon in the church, and a very sharp young man, of bright parts, and better qualified to deal with wrangling disputants than the apostles themselves, was appointed to this service. Some historians say that Stephen had been bred up at the feet of Gamaliel, and that Saul and the rest of them set upon him as a deserter, and with a particular fury made him their mark. (4.) It is probable that they disputed with Stephen because he was zealous to argue with them and convince them, and this was the service to which God had called him.

2. We are here told how he carried the point in this dispute (v. 10): *They were not able to resist the wisdom and the Spirit by which he spoke.* They could neither support their own arguments nor answer his. He proved by such irresistible arguments that Jesus is the Christ, and delivered himself with so much clearness and fulness that they had nothing to object against what he said; though they were not convinced, yet they were confounded. It is not said, They were not able to resist him, but, They were not able to resist the *wisdom and the Spirit by which he spoke,* that Spirit of wisdom which spoke by him. Now was fulfilled that promise, *I will give you a mouth and wisdom which all your adversaries shall not be able to gainsay nor resist,* Lu. 21:15. They thought they had only disputed with Stephen, and could make their part good with him; but they were disputing with the Spirit of God in him, for whom they were an unequal match.

III. At length, he sealed it with his blood; so we shall find he did in the next chapter; here we have some steps taken by his enemies towards it. When they could not answer his arguments as a disputant, they prosecuted him as a criminal, and suborned witnesses against him, to swear blasphemy upon him. "On such terms (saith Mr. Baxter here) do we dispute with malignant men. And it is next to a miracle of providence that no greater number of religious persons have been murdered in the world, by the way of perjury and pretence of law, when so many thousands hate them who make no conscience of false oaths." They suborned men, that is, instructed them what to say, and then hired them to swear it. They were the more enraged against him because he had proved them to be in the wrong, and shown them the right way; for which they ought to have given him their best thanks. *Was he therefore become their enemy, because he told them the truth,* and proved it to be so? Now let us observe here,

1. How with all possible art and industry they incensed both the government and the mob against him, that, if they could not prevail by the one, they might by the other (v. 12): *They stirred up the people* against him, that, if the sanhedrim should still think fit (according to Gamaliel's advice) to let him alone, yet they might run him down by a popular rage and tumult; they also found means to stir up the elders and scribes against him, that, if the people should countenance and protect him, they might prevail by authority. Thus they doubted not but to gain their point, when then had two strings to their bow.

2. How they got him to the bar: *They came upon him,* when he little thought of it, *and caught him and brought him to the council.* They came upon him in a body, and flew upon him as a lion upon his prey; so the word signifies. By their rude and violent treatment of him, they would represent him, both to the people, and to the government, as a dangerous man, that would either flee from justice if he were not watched, or fight with it if he were not put under a force. Having caught him, they brought him triumphantly into the council, and, as it should seem, so hastily that he had none of his friends with him. They had found, when they brought many together, that they emboldened one another, and strengthened one another's hands; and therefore they will try how to deal with them singly.

3. How they were prepared with evidence ready to produce against him. They were resolved that they would not be run a-ground, as they were when they brought our Saviour upon his trial, and then had to seek for witnesses. These were got ready beforehand, and were instructed to make oath that they had *heard him speak blasphemous words against Moses and against God* (v. 11) – against this *holy place and the law* (v. 13); for they heard him say what Jesus would do to their place and their customs, v. 14. It is probable that he

had said something to that purport; and yet those who swore it against him are called *false witnesses,* because, though there was something of truth in their testimony, yet they put a wrong and malicious construction upon what he had said, and perverted it. Observe,

(1.) What was the general charge exhibited against him – that he *spoke blasphemous words;* and, to aggravate the matter, "He *ceases not to speak blasphemous words;* it is his common talk, his discourse in all companies; wheresoever he comes, he makes it his business to instil his notions into all he converses with." It intimates likewise something of contumacy and contempt of admonition. "He has been warned against it, and yet ceases not to talk at this rate." Blasphemy is justly reckoned a heinous crime (to speak contemptibly and reproachfully of God our Maker), and therefore Stephen's persecutors would be thought to have a deep concern upon them for the honour of God's name, and to do this in a jealousy for that. As it was with the confessors and martyrs of the Old Testament, so it was with those of the New — their brethren that hated them, and cast them out, said, *Let the Lord be glorified;* and pretended they did him service in it. He is said to have spoken blasphemous words *against Moses and against God.* Thus far they were right, that those who blaspheme Moses (if they meant the writings of Moses, which were given by inspiration of God) blaspheme God himself. Those that speak reproachfully of the scriptures, and ridicule them, reflect upon God himself, and do despite to him. His great intention is to *magnify the law and make it honourable;* those therefore that vilify the law, and make it contemptible, blaspheme his name; for he has *magnified his word above all his name.* But did Stephen blaspheme Moses? By no means, he was far from it. Christ, and the preachers of his gospel, never said any thing that looked like blaspheming Moses; they always quoted his writings with respect, appealed to them, and said no other things than what Moses said should come; very unjustly therefore is Stephen indicted for blaspheming Moses. But,

(2.) Let us see how this charge is supported and made out; why, truly, when the thing was to be proved, all they can charge him with is that he *hath spoken blasphemous words against this holy place and the law;* and this must be deemed and taken as blasphemy against Moses and against God himself. Thus does the charge dwindle when it comes to the evidence. [1.] He is charged with blaspheming *this holy place.* Some understand this of the city of Jerusalem, which was the holy city, and which they had a mighty jealousy for. But it is rather meant of the temple, that holy house. Christ was condemned as a blasphemer for words which were thought to reflect upon the temple, which they seemed concerned for the honour of, even when they by their wickedness had profaned it. [2.] He is charged with blaspheming *the law,* of which they *made their boast,* and in which they put their trust, when through *breaking the law they dishonoured God,* Rom. 2:23. Well, but how can they make this out? Why, here the charge dwindles again; for all they can accuse him of is that *they had* themselves *heard him say* (but how it came in, or what explication he gave to if, they think not themselves bound to give account) that this *Jesus of Nazareth,* who was so much talked of, *shall destroy this place, and change the customs which Moses delivered to us.* He could not be charged with having said any thing to the disparagement either of the temple or of the law. The priests had themselves profaned the temple, by making it not only a house of merchandise, but a den of thieves; yet they would be thought zealous for the honour of it, against one that had never said any thing amiss of it, but had attended it more as a house of prayer, according to the true intention of it, than they had. Nor had he ever reproached the law as they had. But, *First,* He had said, *Jesus of Nazareth shall destroy this place,* destroy the temple, destroy Jerusalem. It is probable that he might say so; and what blasphemy was it against the holy place to say that it should not be perpetual any more than Shiloh was, and that the just and holy God would not continue the privileges of his sanctuary to those that abused them? Had not the prophets given the same warning to their fathers of the destruction of that holy place by the Chaldeans? Nay, when the temple was first built, had not God himself given the same warning: *This house, which is high, shall be an astonishment,* 2 Chr. 7:21. And is he a blasphemer, then, who tells them that Jesus of Nazareth, if they continue their opposition to him, will bring a just destruction upon their place and nation, and they may thank themselves? Those wickedly abuse their profession of religion who, under colour of that, call the reproofs given them for their disagreeable conversations blasphemous reflections upon their religion. *Secondly,* He had said, *This Jesus shall change the customs which Moses delivered to us.* And it was expected that in the days of the Messiah they should be changed, and that the shadows should be done away when the substance was come; yet this was no essential change of the law, but the perfecting of it. *Christ came, not to destroy,* but to fulfil, the law; and, if he changed some customs that Moses delivered, it was to introduce and establish those that were much better; and if the Jewish church had not obstinately refused to come into this new establishment, and adhered to the ceremonial law, for aught I know *their place* had not been destroyed; so that for putting them into a certain way to prevent their destruction, and for giving them certain notice of their destruction if they did not take that way, he is accused as a blasphemer.

IV. We are here told how God owned him when he was brought before the council, and made it to appear that he stood by him (*v.* 15): *All that sat in the council,* the priests, scribes, and elders, *looking stedfastly on him,* being a stranger, and one they had not yet had before them, *saw his face as it had been the face of an angel.* It is usual for judges to observe the countenance of the prisoner, which sometimes is an indication either of guilt or innocence. Now Stephen appeared at the bar with the countenance *as of an angel.* 1. Perhaps it intimates no more than that he had an extraordinarily pleasant, cheerful countenance, and there was not in it the least sign either of fear for himself or anger at his persecutors. He looked as if he had never been better pleased in his life than he was now when he was called out to bear his testimony to the gospel of Christ, thus publicly, and stood fair for the crown of martyrdom. Such an undisturbed serenity, such an undaunted courage, and such an unaccountable mixture of mildness and majesty, there was in his countenance, that every one said he looked like an angel; enough surely to convince the Sadducees that there are angels, when they saw before their eyes an incarnate angel. 2. It should rather seem that there was a miraculous splendour and brightness upon his countenance, like that of our Saviour when he was transfigured — or, at least, that of Moses when he came down from the mount — God designing thereby to put honour upon his faithful witness and confusion upon his persecutors and judges, whose sin would be highly aggravated, and would be indeed a rebellion against the light, if, notwithstanding this, they proceeded against him. Whether he himself knew that the skin of his face shone or no we are not told; but *all that sat in the council saw it,* and probably took notice of it to one another, and an arrant shame it was that when they saw, and could not but see by it that he was owned of God, they did not call him from standing at the bar to sit in the chief seat upon the bench. Wisdom and holiness make a man's face to shine, and yet these will not secure men from the greatest indignities; and no wonder, when the shining of Stephen's face could not be his protection; though it had been easy to prove that if he had been guilty of putting any dishonour upon Moses God would not thus have put Moses's honour upon him.

CHAPTER 7

When our Lord Jesus called his apostles out to be employed in services and sufferings for him, he told them that yet the last should be first, and the first last, which was remarkably fulfilled in St. Stephen and St. Paul, who were both of them late converts, in comparison of the apostles, and yet got the start of them both in services and sufferings; for God, in conferring honours and favours, often crosses hands. In this chapter we have the martyrdom of Stephen, the first martyr of the Christian church, who led the van in the noble army. And therefore his sufferings and death are more largely related than those of any other, for direction and encouragement to all those who are called out to resist unto blood, as he did. Here is, I. His defence of himself before the council, in answer to the matters and things he stood charged with, the scope of which is to show that it was no blasphemy against God, nor any injury at all to the glory of his name, to say that the temple should be destroyed and the customs of the ceremonial law changed. And, 1. He shows this by going over the history of the Old Testament, and observing that God never intended to confine his favours to that place, or that ceremonial law; and that they had no reason to expect he should, for the people of the Jews had always been a provoking people, and had forfeited the privileges of their peculiarity: nay, that that holy place and that law were but figures of good things to come, and it was no disparagement at all to them to say that they must give place to better things (*v.* 1–50). And then, 2. He applies this to those that prosecuted him, and sat in judgment upon him, sharply reproving them for their wickedness, by which they had brought upon themselves the ruin of their place and nation, and then could not bear to hear of it (*v.* 51–53). II. The putting of him to death by stoning him, and his patient, cheerful, pious submission to it (*v.* 54–60).

Verses 1–16

Stephen is now at the bar before the great council of the nation, indicted for blasphemy: what the witnesses swore against him we had an account of in the foregoing chapter, that he spoke blasphemous words against Moses and God; for he spoke against this holy place and the law. Now here,

I. The high priest calls upon him to answer for himself, *v.* 1. He was president, and, as such, the mouth of the court, and therefore he saith, "You, the prisoner at the bar, you hear what is sworn against you; what do you say to it? *Are these things so?* Have you ever spoken any words to this purport? If you have, will you recant them, or will you stand to them? *Guilty or not guilty?*" This carried a show of fairness, and yet seems to have been spoken with an air of haughtiness; and thus far he seems to have prejudged the cause, that, if it were so, that he had spoken such and such words, he shall certainly be adjudged a blasphemer, whatever he may offer in justification or explanation of them.

II. He begins his defence, and it is long; but it should seem by his breaking off abruptly, just when he came to the main point (*v.* 50), that it would have been much longer if his enemies would have given him leave to say all he had to say. In general we may observe,

1. That in this discourse he appears to be a man ready and mighty in the scriptures, and thereby thoroughly furnished for every good word and work. He can relate scripture stories, and such as were very pertinent to his purpose, off-hand without looking in his Bible. He was *filled with the Holy Ghost,* not so much to reveal to him new things, or open to him the secret counsels and decrees of God concerning the Jewish nation, with them to convict these gainsayers; no, but to bring to his remembrance the scriptures of the Old Testament, and to teach him how to make use of them for their conviction. Those that are full of the Holy Ghost will be full of the scripture, as Stephen was.

2. That he quotes the scriptures according to the Septuagint translation, by which it appears he was one of the Hellenist Jews, who used that version in their synagogues. His following this, occasions divers variations from the Hebrew original in this discourse, which the judges of the court did not correct, because they knew how he was led into them; nor is it any derogation to the authority of that Spirit by which he spoke, for the variations are not material. We have a maxim, *Apices juris non sunt jura — Mere points of law are not law itself.* These verses carry on this his compendium of church history to the end of the book of Genesis. Observe,

(1.) His preface: *Men, brethren, and fathers, hearken.* He gives them, though not flattering titles, yet civil and respectful ones, signifying his expectation of fair treatment with them; from men he hopes to be treated with humanity, and he hopes that brethren and fathers will use him in a fatherly brotherly way. They are ready to look upon him as an apostate from the Jewish church, and an enemy to them. But, to make way for their conviction to the contrary, he addresses himself to them as *men, brethren, and fathers,* resolving to look on himself as one of them, though they would not so look on him. He craves their attention: *Hearken;* though he was about to tell them what they already knew, yet he begs them to hearken to it, because, though they knew it all, yet they would not without a very close application of mind know how to apply it to the case before them.

(2.) His entrance upon the discourse, which (whatever it may seem to those that read it carelessly) is far from being a long ramble only to amuse the hearers, and give them a diversion by telling them an old story. No; it is all pertinent and *ad rem — to the purpose,* to show them that God had no this heart so much upon that holy place and the law as they had; but, as he had a church in the world many ages before that holy place was founded and the ceremonial law given, so he would have when they should both have had their period.

[1.] He begins with the call of Abraham out of Ur of the Chaldees, by which he was set apart for God to be the trustee of the promise, and the father of the Old-Testament church. This we had an account of (Gen. 12:1, etc.), and it is referred to, Neh. 9:7, 8. His native country was an idolatrous country, it was Mesopotamia, (*v.* 2), *the land of the Chaldeans* (*v.* 4); thence God brought him at two removes, not too far at once, dealing tenderly with him; he first brought him out of the land of the Chaldeans to Charran, or Haran, a place midway between that and Canaan (Gen. 11:31), and thence five years after, when his father was dead, he *removed him into* the land of *Canaan, wherein you now dwell.* It should seem, the first time that God spoke to Abraham, he appeared in some visible display of the divine presence, as the *God of glory* (*v.* 2), to settle a correspondence with him: and then afterwards he kept up that correspondence, and spoke to him from time to time as there was occasion, without repeating his visible appearances as the God of glory.

First, From this call of Abraham we may observe, 1. That in all our ways we must acknowledge God, and attend the directions of his providence, as of the pillar of cloud and fire. It is not said, Abraham removed, but, *God removed him into this land wherein you now dwell,* and he did but follow his Leader. 2. Those whom God takes into covenant with himself he distinguishes from the children of this world; they are effectually called out of the state, out of the land, of their nativity; they must sit loose to the world, and live above it and every thing in it, even that in it which is most dear to them, and must trust God to make it up to them in another and better country, that is, the heavenly, which he will show them. God's chosen must follow him with an implicit faith and obedience.

Secondly, But let us see what this is to Stephen's case. 1. They had charged him as a blasphemer of God, and an apostate from the church; therefore he shows that he is a son of Abraham, and values himself upon his being able to say, *Our father Abraham,* and that he is a faithful worshipper of the God of Abraham, whom therefore he here calls *the God of glory.* He also shows that he owns divine revelation, and that particularly by which the Jewish church was founded and incorporated. 2. They were proud of their being circumcised; and therefore he shows that Abraham was taken under God's guidance, and into communion with him, before he was circumcised, for that was not till *v.* 8. With this argument Paul proves that Abraham was justified by faith, because he was justified when he was in uncircumcision: and so here. 3. They had a mighty jealousy for this holy place, which may be meant of the whole land of Canaan; for it was called the *holy land, Immanuel's land;* and the destruction of the holy house inferred that of the holy land. "Now," says Stephen, "you need not be so proud of it; for," (1.) "You came originally out of *Ur of the Chaldees,* where *your fathers served other gods* (Jos. 24:2), and you were not the first planters of this country. Look therefore *unto the rock whence you were hewn, and the holy of the pit out of which you were digged;*" that is, as it follows there, *"look unto Abraham your father,* for *I called him alone* (Isa. 51:1, 2) — think of the meanness of your beginnings, and how you are entirely indebted to divine grace, and then you will see boasting to be for ever excluded. It was God that *raised up the righteous man from the east, and called him to his foot.* Isa. 41:2. But, if his seed degenerate, let them know that God can destroy this holy place, and raise up to himself another people, for he is not a debtor to them." (2.) "God appeared in his glory to Abraham a great way off in Mesopotamia, before he came near Canaan, nay, before he dwelt in Charran; so that you must not think God's visits are confined to *this land;* no; he that brought the seed of the church from a country so far east can, if he pleases, carry the fruit of it to another country as far west." (3.) "God made no haste to bring him into this land, but let him linger some years by the way, which shows that God has not his heart so much upon this land as you have yours, neither is his honour, nor the happiness of his people, bound up in it. It is therefore neither blasphemy nor treason to say, It shall be destroyed,"

[2.] The unsettled state of Abraham and his seed for many ages after he was called out of Ur of the Chaldees. God did indeed promise that he would *give it to him for a possession, and to his seed after him, v.* 5. But, *First, As yet he had no child,* nor any by Sarah for many years after. *Secondly,* He himself was but a stranger and a sojourner in that land, and God *gave him no inheritance in it, no, not so much as to set his foot on;* but there he was as in a strange country, where he was always upon the remove, and could call nothing his own. *Thirdly,* His posterity did not come to the possession of it for a long time: *After four hundred years* they shall come *and serve me in this place,* and not till then, *v.* 7. Nay, *Fourthly,* They must undergo a great deal of hardship and difficulty before they shall be put into the possession of that land: they shall be brought into bondage, and ill treated in a strange land: and this, not as the punishment of any particular sin, as their wandering in the wilderness was, for we never find any such account given of their bondage in Egypt; but so God had appointed, and it must be. And *at the end of four hundred years,* reckoning from the birth of Isaac, *that nation to whom they shall be in bondage will I judge, saith God.* Now this teaches us, 1. That *known unto God are all his works* beforehand. When Abraham had neither inheritance nor heir, yet he was told he should have both, the one a land of promise, and the other a child of promise; and therefore both had, and received, by faith. 2. That God's promises, though they are slow, are sure in the operation of them; they will be fulfilled in the season of them, though perhaps not so soon as we expect. 3. That though the people of God may be in distress and trouble for a time, yet God will at length both rescue them and reckon with those that do oppress them; for, *verily there is a God that judgeth in the earth.*

But let us see how this serves Stephen's purpose. 1. The Jewish nation, for the honour of which they were so jealous, was very inconsiderable in its beginnings; as their common father Abraham was fetched out of obscurity in Ur of the Chaldees, so their tribes, and the heads of them, were fetched out of servitude in Egypt, when they were the *fewest of all people,* Deu. 7:7. And what need is there of so much ado, as if their ruin, when they bring it upon themselves by sin, must be the ruin of the world, and of all God's interests in it? No; he that brought them out of Egypt can bring them into it again, as he threatened (Deu. 28:68), and yet be no loser, while he can out of stones raise up children unto Abraham. 2. The slow steps by which the promise made to Abraham advanced towards the performance, and the many seeming contradictions here taken notice of, plainly show that it had a spiritual meaning, and that the land principally intended to be conveyed and secured by it was the *better country, that is, the heavenly;* as the apostle shows from this very argument that the patriarchs *sojourned in the land of promise, as in a strange country,* thence inferring that *they looked for a city that had foundations,* Heb. 11:9, 10. It was therefore no blasphemy to say, *Jesus shall destroy this place,* when at the same time we say, "He shall lead us to the heavenly Canaan, and put us in possession of that, of which the earthly Canaan was but a type and figure."

[3.] The building up of the family of Abraham, with the entail of divine grace upon it, and the disposals of divine Providence concerning it, which take up the rest of the book of Genesis.

First, God engaged to be a God to Abraham and his seed; and, in token of this, appointed that he and his male seed should be circumcised, Gen. 17:9, 10. He *gave him the covenant of circumcision,* that is, the covenant of which circumcision was the seal; and accordingly, when Abraham had a son born, he *circumcised him the eighth day* (*v.* 8), by which he was both bound by the divine law and interested in the divine promise; for circumcision had reference to both, being a seal of the covenant both on God's part — I will be to thee *a God all-sufficient,* and on man's part — *Walk before me, and be thou perfect.* And then when effectual care was thus taken for the securing of Abraham's seed, to be a *seed to serve the Lord,* they began to multiply: *Isaac begat Jacob, and Jacob the twelve patriarchs,* or roots of the respective tribes.

Secondly, Joseph, the darling and blessing of his father's house, was abused by his brethren; they *envied him* because of his dreams, and *sold him into Egypt.* Thus early did the children of Israel begin to grudge those among them that were eminent and outshone others, of which their enmity to Christ, who, like Joseph, was a *Nazarite among his brethren,* was a great instance.

Thirdly, God owned Joseph in his troubles, and was with him (Gen. 39:2, 21), by the influence of his Spirit, both on his mind, giving him comfort, and on the minds of those he was concerned with, giving him favour in their eyes. And thus at length he *delivered him out of his afflictions,* and Pharaoh made him the second man in the kingdom, Ps. 105:20–22. And thus he not only arrived at great preferment among the Egyptians, but became the *shepherd and stone of Israel,* Gen. 49:24.

Fourthly, Jacob was compelled to go down into Egypt, by a famine which forced him out of Canaan, *a dearth* (which was a *great affliction*), to that degree that *our fathers found no sustenance* in Canaan, *v.* 11. That *fruitful land was turned into barrenness.* But, hearing that there was *corn in Egypt* (treasured up by the wisdom of his own son), he *sent out our fathers first* to fetch corn, *v.* 12. And the *second time* that they went, Joseph, who at first made himself strange to them, made himself known to them, and it was notified to Pharaoh that they were Joseph's kindred and had a dependence upon him (*v.* 13), whereupon, with Pharaoh's leave, *Joseph sent for his father Jacob to him into Egypt,* with *all his kindred and family,* to the number of *seventy-five souls,* to be subsisted there, *v.* 13. In Genesis they are said to be *seventy souls,* Gen. 46:27. But the Septuagint there makes them seventy-five, and Stephen or Luke follows that version, as Lu. 3:36, where Cainan is inserted, which is not in the Hebrew text, but in the Septuagint. Some, by excluding Joseph and his sons, who were in Egypt before (which reduces the number to sixty-four), and adding the sons of the eleven patriarch, make the number seventy-five.

Fifthly, Jacob and his sons died in Egypt (*v.* 15), but were carried over to be buried in Canaan, *v.* 16. A very considerable difficulty occurs here: it is said, *They were carried over into Sychem,* whereas Jacob was buried not in Sychem, but near Hebron, in the cave of Machpelah, where Abraham and Isaac were buried, Gen. 50:13. Joseph's bones indeed were buried in Sychem (Jos. 24:32), and it seems by this (though it is not mentioned in the story) that the bones of all the other patriarchs were carried with his, each of them giving the same commandment concerning them that he had done; and of them this must be understood, not of Jacob himself. But then the sepulchre in Sychem was bought by Jacob (Gen. 33:19), and by this it is described, Jos. 24:32. How then is it here said to be bought by Abraham? Dr. Whitby's solution of this is very sufficient. He supplies it thus: *Jacob went down into Egypt and died, he and our fathers;* and (*our fathers*) *were carried over into Sychem; and he,* that is, *Jacob,* was laid *in the sepulchre that Abraham brought for a sum of money,* Gen. 23:16. (Or, they were laid there, that is, Abraham, Isaac, and Jacob.) *And they,* namely, the other patriarchs, were *buried in the sepulchre bought of the sons of Emmor, the father of Sychem.*

Let us now see what this is to Stephen's purpose. 1. He still reminds them of the mean beginning of the Jewish nation, as a check to their priding themselves in the glories of that nation; and that it was by a miracle of mercy that they were raised up out of nothing to what they were, from so small a number to be so great a nation; but, if they answer not the intention of their being so raised, they can expect no other than to be destroyed. The prophets frequently put them in mind of the bringing of them out of Egypt, as a aggravation of their contempt of the law of God, and here it is urged upon them as an aggravation of their contempt of the gospel of Christ. 2. He reminds them likewise of the wickedness of those that were the patriarchs of their tribes, in envying their brother Joseph, and selling him into Egypt; and the same spirit was still working in them towards Christ and his ministers. 3. Their holy land, which they doted so much upon, their fathers were long kept out of the possession of, and met with dearth and great affliction in it; and therefore let them not think it strange if, after it has been so long polluted with sin, it be at length destroyed. 4. The faith of the patriarchs in desiring to be buried in the land of Canaan plainly showed that they had an eye to the heavenly country, to which it was the design of this Jesus to lead them.

Verses 17–29

Stephen here goes on to relate,

I. The wonderful increase of the people of Israel in Egypt; it was by a wonder of providence that in a little time they advanced from a family into a nation. 1. It was *when the time of the promise drew nigh* — the time when they were to be formed into a people. During the first two hundred and fifteen years after the promise made to Abraham, the children of the covenant were increased but to seventy; but in the latter two hundred and fifteen years they increased to six hundred thousand fighting men. The motion of providence is sometimes quickest when it comes nearest the centre. Let us not be discouraged at the slowness of the proceedings towards the accomplishment of God's promises; God knows how to redeem the time that seems to have been lost, and, *when the year of the redeemed is at hand,* can do a double work in a single day. 2. It was *in Egypt,* where they were oppressed, and ruled with rigour; when their lives were made so bitter to them that, one would think, they should have wished to be written childless, yet they married, in faith that God in due time would visit them; and God *blessed them,* who thus honoured him, saying, *Be fruitful, and multiply.* Suffering times have often been growing times with the church.

II. The extreme hardships which they underwent there, *v.* 18, 19. When the Egyptians observed them to increase in number they increased their burdens, in which Stephen observes three things: — 1. Their base ingratitude: They were oppressed by *another king that knew not Joseph,* that is, did not consider the good service that Joseph had done to that nation; for, if he had, he would not have made so ill a requital to his relations and family. Those that injure good people are very ungrateful, for they are the blessings of the age and place they live in. 2. Their hellish craft and policy: *They dealt subtly with our kindred. Come on,* said they, *let us deal wisely,* thinking thereby to secure themselves, but it proved dealing foolishly, for they did but treasure up wrath by it. Those are in a great mistake who think they deal wisely for themselves when they deal deceitfully or unmercifully with their brethren. 3. Their barbarous and inhuman cruelty. That they might effectually extirpate them, *they cast out their young children, to the end they might not live.* The killing of their infant seed seemed a very likely way to crush an infant nation. Now Stephen seems to observe this to them, not only that they might further see how mean their beginnings were, fitly represented (perhaps with an eye to the exposing of the young children in Egypt) by the forlorn state of a helpless, out-cast infant (Eze. 16:4), and how much they were indebted to God for his care of them, which they had forfeited, and made themselves unworthy of: but also that they might consider that what they were now doing against the Christian church in its infancy was as impious and unjust, and would be in the issue as fruitless and ineffectual, as that was which the Egyptians did against the Jewish church in its infancy. "You think you deal subtly in your ill treatment of us, and, in persecuting young converts, you do as they did in casting out the young children; but you will find it is to no purpose, in spite of your malice Christ's disciples will *increase and multiply.*"

III. The raising up of *Moses to be their deliverer.* Stephen was charged with having spoken blasphemous words against Moses, in answer to which charge he here speaks very honourably of him. 1. Moses was born when the persecution of Israel was at the hottest, especially in that most cruel instance of it, the murdering of the new-born children: *At that time, Moses was born* (*v.* 20), and was himself in danger, as soon as he came into the world (as our Saviour also was at Bethlehem) of falling a sacrifice to that bloody edict. God is preparing for his people's deliverance, when their way is darkest, and their distress deepest. 2. *He was exceedingly fair;* his face began to shine as soon as he was born, as a happy presage of the honour God designed to put upon him; he was *asteios tō Theō — fair towards God;* he was sanctified from the womb, and this made him beautiful in God's eyes; for it is the beauty of holiness that is in God's sight of great price. 3. He was wonderfully preserved in his infancy, first, by the care of his tender parents, who *nourished him three months in their own house,* as long as they durst; and then by a favourable providence that threw him *into the arms of Pharaoh's daughter, who took him up, and nourished him as her own son* (*v.* 21); for those whom God designs to make special use of he will take special care of. And did he thus protect the child Moses? Much more will he secure the interests of his holy child Jesus (as he is called *ch.* 4:27) from *the enemies that are gathered together against him.* 4. He became a great scholar (*v.* 22): *He was learned in all the wisdom of the Egyptians,* who were then famed for all manner of polite literature, particularly philosophy, astronomy, and (which perhaps helped to lead them to idolatry) hieroglyphics. Moses, having his education at court, had opportunity of improving himself by the best books, tutors, and conversation, in all the arts and sciences, and had a genius for them. Only we have reason to think that he had not so far forgotten the God of his fathers as to acquaint himself with the unlawful studies and practices of the magicians of Egypt, any further than was necessary to the confuting of them. 5. He became a prime minister of state in Egypt. This seems to be meant by his being *mighty in words and deeds.* Though he had not a ready way of expressing himself, but stammered, yet he spoke admirably good sense, and every thing he said commanded assent, and carried its own evidence and force of reason along with it; and, in business, none went on with such courage, and conduct, and success. Thus was he prepared, by human helps, for those services, which, after all, he could not be thoroughly furnished for without divine illumination. Now, by all this, Stephen will make it appear that, notwithstanding the malicious insinuations of his persecutors, he had as high and honourable thoughts of Moses as they had.

IV. The attempts which Moses made to deliver Israel, which they spurned, and would not close in with. This Stephen insists much upon, and it serves for a key to this story (Ex. 2:11–15), as does also that other construction which is put upon it by the apostle, Heb. 11:24–26. There it is represented as an act of holy self-denial, here as a designed prelude to, or entrance upon, the public service he was to be called out to (v. 23): *When he was full forty years old,* in the prime of his time for preferment in the court of Egypt, *it came into his heart* (for God put it there) *to visit his brethren the children of Israel,* and to see which way he might do them any service; and he showed himself as a public person, with a public character. 1. As Israel's saviour. This he gave a specimen of in avenging an oppressed Israelite, and killing the Egyptian that abused him (v. 24). *Seeing one of his brethren suffer wrong,* he was moved with compassion towards the sufferer, and a just indignation at the wrong-doer, as men in public stations should be, and *he avenged him that was oppressed, and smote the Egyptian,* which, if he had been only a private person, he could not lawfully have done; but he knew that his commission from heaven would bear him out, and *he supposed that his brethren* (who could not but have some knowledge of the promise made to Abraham, *that the nation that should oppress them God would judge) would have understood that God by his hand would deliver them;* for he could not have had either presence of mind or strength of body to do what he did, if he had not been clothed with such a divine power as evinced a divine authority. If they had but understood the signs of the times, they might have taken this for the dawning of the day of their deliverance; *but they understood not,* they did not take this, as it was designed, for the setting up of a standard, and sounding of a trumpet, to proclaim Moses *their deliverer.* 2. As Israel's judge. This he gave a specimen of, *the* very *next day,* in offering to accommodate matters between two contending Hebrews, wherein he plainly assumed a public character (v. 26): *He showed himself to them as they strove,* and, putting on an air of majesty and authority, *he would have set them at one again,* and as their prince have determined the controversy between them, *saying, Sirs, you are brethren,* by birth and profession of religion; *why do you wrong one to another?* For he observed that (as in most strifes) there was a fault on both sides; and therefore, in order to peace and friendship, there must be a mutual remission and condescension. When Moses was to be Israel's deliverer out of Egypt, he slew the Egyptians, and so delivered Israel out of their hands; but, when he was to be Israel's judge and lawgiver, he ruled them with the golden sceptre, not the iron rod; he did not kill and slay them when they strove, but gave them excellent laws and statutes, and decided upon their complaints and appeals made to him, Ex. 18:16. *But* the contending Israelite that was most in *the wrong thrust him away* (v. 27), would not bear the reproof, though a just and gentle one, but was ready to fly in his face, with, *Who made thee a ruler and a judge over us?* Proud and litigious spirits are impatient of check and control. Rather would these Israelites have their bodies ruled with rigour by their task-masters than be delivered, and have their minds ruled with reason, by their deliverer. The wrong-doer was so enraged at the reproof given him that he upbraided Moses with the service he had done to their nation in killing the Egyptian, which, if they had pleased, would have been the earnest of further and greater service: *Wilt thou kill me, as thou didst the Egyptian yesterday? v.* 28, charging that upon him as his crime, and threatening to accuse him for it, which was the hanging out of the flag of defiance to the Egyptians, and the banner of love and deliverance to Israel. Hereupon *Moses fled into the land of Midian,* and made no further attempt to deliver Israel till forty years after; he settled as a stranger in Midian, married, and had two sons, by Jethro's daughter, *v.* 29.

Now let us see how this serves Stephen's purpose. 1. They charged him with blaspheming Moses, in answer to which he retorts upon them the indignities which their fathers did to Moses, which they ought to be ashamed of, and humbled for, instead of picking quarrels thus, under pretence of zeal for the honour of Moses, with one that had as great a veneration for him as any of them had. 2. They persecuted him

for disputing in defence of Christ and his gospel, in opposition to which they set up Moses and his law: "But," saith he, "you had best take heed," (1.) "Lest you hereby do as your fathers did, refuse and reject one *whom God has raised up to be to you a prince and a Saviour;* you may understand, if you will not wilfully shut your eyes against the light, that God will, by this Jesus, deliver you out of a worse slavery than that in Egypt; take heed then of thrusting him away, but receive him as a ruler and a judge over you." (2.) "Lest you hereby fare as your fathers fared, who for this were very justly left to die in their slavery, for the deliverance came not till forty years after. This will be the issue of it, you put away the gospel from you, and it will be *sent to the Gentiles;* you will not have Christ, and you shall not have him, so shall your doom be." Mt. 23:38, 39.

Verses 30–41

Stephen here proceeds in his story of Moses; and let any one judge whether these are the words of one that was a blasphemer of Moses or no; nothing could be spoken more honourably of him. Here is,

I. The vision which he saw of the glory of God at the bush (v. 30): *When forty years had expired* (during all which time Moses was buried alive in Midian, and was now grown old, and one would think past service), that it might appear that all his performances were products of a divine power and promise (as it appeared that Isaac was a child of promise by his being born of parents stricken in years), now, at eighty years old, he enters upon that post of honour to which he was born, in recompence for his self-denial at forty years old. Observe, 1. Where God appeared to him: *In the wilderness of Mount Sinai, v.* 30. And, when he appeared to him there, that was holy ground (v. 33), which Stephen takes notice of, as a check to those who prided themselves in the temple, that holy place, as if there were no communion to be had with God but there; whereas God met Moses, and manifested himself to him, in a remote obscure place in the wilderness of Sinai. They deceive themselves if they think God is confined to places; he can bring his people into a wilderness, and there speak comfortably to them. 2. How he appeared to him: *In a flame of fire* (for our God is a consuming fire), and yet *the bush,* in which this fire was, though combustible matter, *was not consumed,* which, as it represented the state of Israel in Egypt (where, though they were in the fire of affliction, yet they were not consumed), so perhaps it may be looked upon as a type of Christ's incarnation, and the union between the divine and human nature: God, manifested in the flesh, was as the flame of fire manifested in the bush. 3. How Moses was affected with this: (1.) *He wondered at the sight, v.* 31. It was a phenomenon with the solution of which all his Egyptian learning could not furnish him. He had the curiosity at first to pry into it: *I will turn aside now, and see this great sight;* but the nearer he drew the more he was struck with amazement; and, (2.) *He trembled, and durst not behold,* durst not look stedfastly upon it; for he was soon aware that it was not a fiery meteor, but *the angel of the Lord;* and no other than *the Angel of the covenant,* the Son of God himself. This set him a trembling. Stephen was accused for blaspheming Moses and God (ch. 6:11), as if Moses had been a little god; but by this it appears that he was a *man, subject to like passions as we are,* and particularly that of fear, upon any appearance of the divine majesty and glory.

II. The declaration which he heard of the covenant of God (v. 32): *The voice of the Lord came to him;* for faith comes by hearing; and this was it: *I am the God of Isaac, and the God of Jacob;* and therefore, 1. "I am the same that I was." The covenant God made with Abraham some ages ago was, *I will be to thee a God,* a God all-sufficient. "Now," saith God, "that covenant is still in full force; it is not cancelled nor forgotten, but I am, as I was, the God of Abraham, and now I will make it to appear so;" for all the favours, all the honours God put upon Israel, were founded upon this covenant with Abraham, and flowed from it. 2. "I will be the same that I am." For if the death of Abraham, Isaac, and Jacob, cannot break the covenant-relation between God and them (as by this it appears it cannot), then nothing else can: and then he will be a God, (1.) To their souls, which are now separated from their bodies. Our Saviour by this proves the future state, Mt. 22:31, 32. Abraham is dead, and yet God is still his God, therefore Abraham is still alive. God never did that for him in this world which would answer the true intent and full extent of that promise, that he would be the God of Abraham;

and therefore it must be done for him in the other world. Now this is that life and immortality which are brought to light by the gospel, for the full conviction of the Sadducees, who denied it. Those therefore who stood up in defence of the gospel, and endeavoured to propagate it, were so far from blaspheming Moses that they did the greatest honour imaginable to Moses, and that glorious discovery which God made of himself to him at the bush. (2.) To their seed. God, in declaring himself thus the God of their fathers, intimated his kindness to their seed, that they should be *beloved for the fathers' sakes,* Rom. 11:28; Deu. 7:8. Now the preachers of the gospel preached up this covenant, *the promise made of God unto the fathers; unto which promise* those of *the twelve tribes* that did continue *serving God hoped to come,* ch. 26:6, 7. And shall they, under colour of supporting the holy place and the law, oppose the covenant which was made with Abraham and his seed, his spiritual seed, before the law was given, and long before the holy place was built? Since God's glory must be for ever advanced, and our glorying for ever silenced, God will have our salvation to be by promise, and not by the law;; the Jews therefore who persecuted the Christians, under pretence that they blasphemed the law, did themselves blaspheme the promise, and forsook all their own mercies that were contained in it.

III. The commission which God gave him to deliver Israel out of Egypt. The Jews set up Moses in competition with Christ, and accused Stephen as a blasphemer because he did not do so too. But Stephen here shows that Moses was an eminent type of Christ, as he was Israel's deliverer. When God had declared himself the God of Abraham he proceeded, 1. To order Moses into a reverent posture: "*Put off thy shoes from thy feet.* Enter not upon sacred things with low, and cold, and common thoughts. *Keep thy foot,* Eccl. 5:1. Be not hasty and rash in thy approaches to God; tread softly." 2. To order Moses into a very eminent service. When he is ready to receive commands, he shall have commission. He is commissioned to demand leave from Pharaoh for Israel to go out of his land, and to enforce that demand, *v.* 34. Observe, (1.) The notice God took both of their sufferings and of their sense of their sufferings: *I have seen, I have seen their affliction, and have heard their groaning.* God has a compassionate regard to the troubles of his church, and the groans of his persecuted people; and their deliverance takes rise from his pity. (2.) The determination he fixed to redeem them by the hand of Moses: *I am come down to deliver them.* It should seem, though God is present in all places, yet he uses that expression here of coming down to deliver them because that deliverance was typical of what Christ did, when, *for us men, and for our salvation, he came down from heaven; he that ascended first descended.* Moses is the man that must be employed: *Come, and I will send thee into Egypt:* and, if God send him, he will own him and give him success.

IV. His acting in pursuance of this commission, wherein he was a figure of the Messiah. And Stephen takes notice here again of the slights they had put upon him, the affronts they had given him, and their refusal to have him to reign over them, as tending very much to magnify his agency in their deliverance. 1. God put honour upon him whom they put contempt upon (v. 35): *This Moses whom they refused* (whose kind offers and good offices they rejected with scorn, *saying, Who made thee a ruler and a judge? Thou takest too much upon thee, thou son of Levi,* Num. 16:3), this same Moses *did God send to be a ruler, and a deliverer, by the hand of the angel which appeared to him in the bush.* It may be understood either that God sent to him by the hand of the angel going along with him he became a complete deliverer. Now, by this example, Stephen would intimate to the council *that this Jesus whom they now refused,* as their fathers did Moses, *saying, Who made thee a prophet and a king? Who gave thee this authority?* even this same has God advanced *to be a prince and a Saviour, a ruler and a deliverer;* as the apostles had told them awhile ago (ch. 5:30, 31), *that the stone which the builders refused was become the head-stone in the corner,* ch. 4:11. 2. God showed favour to them by him, and he was very forward to serve them, though they had thrust him away. God might justly have refused them his service, and he might justly have declined it; but it is all forgotten: they are not so much as upbraided with it, *v.* 36. *He brought them out,* notwithstanding, *after he had shown wonders and signs in the land of Egypt* (which were afterwards continued for the completing of their deliverance, according as the case called for them) *in the Red Sea and in the wilderness forty years.* So far is he from blaspheming Moses that he admires him as a glorious instrument in the hand of God for the forming of the Old-Testament church. But it does not at all derogate from his just honour to say that he was but an instrument, and that he is outshone by this Jesus, whom he encourages these Jews yet to close with, and to come into his interest, not fearing but that then they should be received into his favour, and receive benefit by him, as the people of Israel were delivered by Moses, though they had once refused him.

V. His prophecy of Christ and his grace, *v.* 37. He not only was a type of Christ (many were so that perhaps had not an actual foresight of his day), but Moses spoke of him (*v.* 37): *This is that Moses who said unto the children of Israel, A prophet shall the Lord your God raise up unto you of your brethren.* This is spoken of as one of the greatest honours God put upon him (nay, as that which exceeded all the rest), that by him he gave notice to the children of Israel of the great prophet that should come into the world, raised their expectation of him, and required them to receive him. When his bringing them out of Egypt is spoken of it is with an emphasis of honour, *This is that Moses,* Ex. 6:26. And so it is here, *This is that Moses.* Now this is very full to Stephen's purpose; in asserting that Jesus should change the customs of the ceremonial law, he was so far from blaspheming Moses that really he did him the greatest honour imaginable, by showing how the prophecy of Moses was accomplished, which was so clear, that, as Christ told them himself, *If they had believed Moses, they would have believed him,* Jn. 5:46. 1. Moses, in God's name, told them that, in the fulness of time, they should have a prophet raised up among them, one of their own nation, that should be like unto him (Deu. 18:15, 18), — a ruler and a deliverer, a judge and a lawgiver, like him, — who should therefore have authority to change the customs that he had delivered, and to bring in a better hope, as *the Mediator of a better testament.* 2. He charged them to hear that prophet, to receive his dictates, to admit the change he would make in their customs, and to submit to him in every thing; "and this will be the greatest honour you can do to Moses and to his law, who said, *Hear you him;* and came to be a witness to the repetition of this charge by *a voice from heaven,* at the transfiguration of Christ, and by his silence gave consent to it," Mt. 17:5.

VI. The eminent services which Moses continued to do to the people of Israel, after he had been instrumental to bring them out of Egypt, *v.* 38. And herein also he was a type of Christ, who yet so far exceeds him that it is no blasphemy to say, "He has authority to change the customs that Moses delivered." It was the honour of Moses, 1. That *he was in the church in the wilderness;* he presided in all the affairs of it for forty years, was king in Jeshurun, Deu. 33:5. The camp of Israel is here called *the church in the wilderness;* for it was a sacred society, incorporated by a divine charter under a divine government, and blessed with divine revelation. The church in the wilderness was a church, though it was not yet perfectly formed, as it was to be when they came to Canaan, *but every man did that which was right in his own eyes,* Deu. 12:8, 9. It was the honour of Moses that he was in that church, and many a time it had been destroyed if Moses had not been in it to intercede for it. But Christ is the president and guide of a more excellent and glorious church than that in the wilderness was, and is more in it, as the life and soul of it, than Moses could be in that. 2. That *he was with the angel that spoke to him in the mount Sinai, and with our fathers* — was with him in the holy mount twice forty days, with the angel of the covenant, Michael, our prince. Moses was immediately conversant with God, but never lay in his bosom as Christ did from eternity. Or these words may be taken thus: *Moses was in the church in the wilderness,* but it was *with the angel that spoke to him in mount Sinai,* that is, at the burning bush; for that was said to be at mount Sinai (*v.* 30); that angel went before him, and was guide to him, else he could not have been a guide to Israel; of this God speaks (Ex. 23:20), *I send an angel before thee,* and Ex. 33:2. And see Num. 20:16. He was in the church with the angel, without whom he could have done no service to the church; but Christ is himself that angel which was with the church in the wilderness, and therefore has an authority above Moses. 3. That *he received the lively oracles to give unto them;* not only the ten commandments, but the other instructions which *the Lord spoke unto Moses, saying, Speak them to the children of Israel.* (1.) The words of God are *oracles,* certain and infallible, and of unquestionable authority and obligation; they are to be consulted as oracles, and by them all controversies must be determined. (2.) They are *lively oracles,* for they are the oracles of the living God, not of the dumb and dead idols of the heathens: the word that God speaks is spirit and life; not that the law of Moses could give life, but it showed the way to life: *If thou wilt enter into life, keep the commandments.* (3.) Moses received them from God, and delivered nothing as an oracle to the people but what *he had first received from God.* (4.) The lively oracles which he received from God he faithfully gave to the people, to be observed and preserved. It was the principal privilege of the Jews that *to them were committed the oracles of God;* and it was by the hand of Moses that they were committed. As Moses gave them not that bread, so neither did he give them that law from heaven (Jn. 6:32), but God gave it to them; and he that gave them those customs by his servant Moses might, no doubt, when he pleased, change the customs by his Son Jesus, who received more lively oracles to give unto us than Moses did.

VII. The contempt that was, after this, and notwithstanding this, put upon him by the people. Those that charged Stephen with speaking against Moses would do well to answer what their own ancestors had done, and they tread in their ancestors' steps. 1. *They would not obey him, but thrust him from them, v.* 39. They murmured at him, mutinied against him, refused to obey his orders, and sometimes were ready to stone him. Moses did indeed give them an excellent law, but by this it appeared that *it could not make the comers there unto perfect* (Heb. 10:1), for *in their hearts they turned back again into Egypt,* and preferred their garlic and onions there before the manna they had under the guidance of Moses, or the milk and honey they hoped for in Canaan. Observe, Their secret disaffection to Moses, with their inclination to Egyptianism, if I may so call it. This was, in effect, turning back to Egypt; it was doing it in heart. Many that pretend to be going forward towards Canaan, by keeping up a show and profession of religion, are, at the same time, in their hearts turning back to Egypt, like Lot's wife to Sodom, and will be dealt with as deserters, for it is the heart that God looks at. Now, if the customs that Moses delivered to them could not prevail to change them, wonder not that Christ comes to change the customs, and to introduce a more spiritual way of worship. 2. *They made a golden calf* instead of him, which besides the affront that was thereby offered to God, was a great indignity to Moses: for it was upon this consideration that they made the calf, because *"as for this Moses, who brought us out of the land of Egypt, we know not what is become of him;* therefore make us gods of gold;" as if a calf were sufficient to supply the want of Moses, and as capable of going before them into the promised land. *So they made a calf in those days* when the law was given them, *and offered sacrifices unto the idol, and rejoiced in the work of their own hands.* So proud were they of their new god that when they had *sat down to eat and drink, they rose up to play!* By all this it appears that there was a great deal which the law could not do, *in that it was weak through the flesh;* it was therefore necessary that this law should be perfected by a better hand, and he was no blasphemer against Moses who said that Christ had done it.

Verses 42–50

Two things we have in these verses: —

I. Stephen upbraids them with the idolatry of their fathers, which God gave them up to, as a punishment for their early forsaking him in worshipping the golden calf; and this was the saddest punishment of all for that sin, as it was of the idolatry of the Gentile world *that God gave them up to a reprobate mind.* When *Israel was joined to idols,* joined to the golden calf, and not long after to Baal-peor, God said, *Let them alone;* let them go on (*v.* 42): *Then God turned, and gave them up to worship the host of heaven.* He particularly cautioned them not to do it, at their peril, and gave them reasons why they should not; but, when they were bent upon it, *he gave them up to their own hearts; lust,* withdrew his restraining grace, and then they walked in their own counsels, and were so scandalously mad upon their idols as never any people were. Compare Deu. 4:19 with Jer. 8:2. For this he quotes a passage out of Amos 5:25. For it would be less invidious to tell them their own [character and doom] from an Old-Testament prophet, who upbraids them,

1. For not sacrificing to their own God in the wilderness (*v.* 42): *Have you offered to me slain beasts, and sacrifices, by the space of forty years in the wilderness?* No; during all that time sacrifices to God were intermitted; they did not so much as keep the passover after the second year. It was God's condescension to them that he did not insist upon it during their unsettled state; but then let them consider how ill they requited him in offering sacrifices to idols, when God dispensed with their offering them to him. This is also a check to their zeal for the customs that Moses delivered to them, and their fear of having them changed by *this Jesus,* that immediately after they were delivered these customs were for forty years together disused as needless things.

2. For sacrificing to other gods after they came to Canaan (*v.* 43): *You took up the tabernacle of Moloch.* Moloch was the idol of the children of Ammon, to which they barbarously offered their own children in sacrifice, which they could not do without great terror and grief to themselves and their families; yet this unnatural idolatry they arrived at, when *God gave them up to worship the host of heaven.* See 2 Chr. 28:3. It was surely the strongest delusion that ever people were given up to, and the greatest instance of the power of Satan in the children of disobedience, and therefore it is here spoken of emphatically: *Yea, you took up the tabernacle of Moloch,* you submitted even to that, and to the worship of *the star of your god Remphan.* Some think Remphan signifies *the moon,* as Moloch does *the sun;* others take it for *Saturn,* for that planet is called *Remphan* in the Syriac and Persian languages. The Septuagint puts it for *Chiun,* as being a name more commonly known. They had images representing the star, like the silver shrines for Diana, here called *the figures which they made to worship.* Dr. Lightfoot thinks they had figures representing the whole starry firmament, with all the constellations, and the planets, and these are called *Remphan* — "the high representation," like the celestial globe: a poor thing to make an idol of, and yet better than a golden calf! Now for this it is threatened, *I will carry you away beyond Babylon.* In Amos it is *beyond Damascus,* meaning *to Babylon, the land of the north.* But Stephen changes it, with an eye to the captivity of the ten tribes, who were *carried away beyond Babylon, by the river of Gozan, and in the cities of the Medes,* 2 Ki. 17:6. Let it not therefore seem strange to them to hear of the destruction of this place, for they had heard of it many a time from the prophets of the Old Testament, who were not therefore accused as blasphemers by any but the wicked rulers. It was observed, in the debate on Jeremiah's case, that Micah was not called to an account though he prophesied, saying, *Zion shall be ploughed as a field,* Jer. 26:18, 19.

II. He gives an answer particularly to the charge exhibited against him relating to the temple, *that he spoke blasphemous words against that holy place, v.* 44–50. He was accused for saying that Jesus would destroy this holy place: "And what if I did say so?" (saith Stephen) "the glory of the holy God is not bound up in the glory of this holy place, but that may be preserved untouched, though this be laid in the dust;" for, 1. "It was not till our fathers came into the wilderness, in their way to Canaan, that they had any fixed place of worship; and yet the patriarchs, many ages before, worshipped God acceptably at the altars they had adjoining to their own tents *in the open air — sub dio;* and he that was worshipped without a holy place in the first, and best, and purest ages of the Old-Testament church, may and will be so when this holy place is destroyed, without any diminution to his glory." 2. The holy place was at first but a tabernacle, mean and movable, showing itself to be short-lived, and not designed to continue always. Why might not this holy place, though built of stones, be decently brought to its end, and give place to its betters, as well as that though framed of curtains? As it was no dishonour, but an honour to God, that the tabernacle gave way to the temple, so it is now that the material temple gives way to the spiritual one, and so it will be when, at last, the spiritual temple shall give way to the eternal one. 3. That tabernacle was *a tabernacle of witness,* or of testimony, *a figure of good things to come, of the true tabernacle which the Lord pitched, and not men,* Heb. 8:2. This was the glory both of the tabernacle and temple, that they were erected for a testimony of that temple of God which in the latter days should be opened in heaven (Rev. 11:19), and of Christ's tabernacling on earth (as the word is, Jn. 1:14), and of the temple of his body. 4. That tabernacle was framed just as God appointed, and *according to the fashion which Moses saw in the mount,* which plainly intimates that it had reference to good things to come. Its rise being heavenly, its meaning and tendency were so; and therefore it was no diminution at all to its glory to say that this temple made with hands should be destroyed, in order to the building of *another made without hands,* which was Christ's crime (Mk. 14:58), and Stephen's. 5. That tabernacle was pitched first in the wilderness; it was not a native of this land of yours (to which you think it must for ever be confined), but was brought in in the next age, by our fathers, who came after those who first erected it, into the possession of the Gentiles, into the land of Canaan, which had long been in the possession of the devoted nations *whom God drove out before the face of our fathers.* And why may not God set up his spiritual temple, as he had done the material tabernacle, in those countries that were now the possession of the Gentiles? That tabernacle was brought in by those who came *with Jesus,* that is, *Joshua.* And I think, for distinction sake, and to prevent mistakes, it ought to be so read, both here and Heb. 4:8. Yet in naming *Joshua* here, which in Greek is *Jesus,* there may be a tacit intimation that as the Old-Testament Joshua brought in that typical tabernacle, so the New-Testament Joshua should bring in the true tabernacle into the possession of the Gentiles. 6. That tabernacle continued for many ages, *even to the days of David,* above four hundred years, before there was any thought of building a temple, *v.* 45. David, having *found favour before God,* did indeed desire this further favour, to have leave to build God a house, to be a constant settled tabernacle, or dwelling-place, for the Shechinah, or the tokens of the presence of the God of Jacob, *v.* 46. Those who have found favour with God should show themselves forward to advance the interests of his kingdom among men. 7. God had his heart so little upon a temple, or such a holy place as they were so jealous for, that, when David desired to build one, he was forbidden to do it; God was in no haste for one, as he told David (2 Sa. 7:7), and therefore it was not he, but his son Solomon, some years after, that built him a house. David had all that sweet communion with God in public worship which we read of in his Psalms before there was any temple built. 8. God often declared that temples made with hands were not his delight, nor could add any thing to the perfection of his rest and joy. Solomon, when he dedicated the temple, acknowledged that God *dwelleth not in temples made with hands;* he has not need of them, is not benefited by them, cannot be confined to them. The whole world is his temple, in which he is every where present, and fills it with his glory; and what occasion has he for a temple then to manifest himself in? Indeed the pretended deities of the heathen needed temples made with hands, for they were gods made with hands (*v.* 41), and had no other place to manifest themselves in than in their own temples; but the one only true and living God needs no temple, for *the heaven is his throne,* in which he rests, *and the earth is his footstool,* over which he rules (*v.* 49, 50), and therefore, *What house will you build me,* comparable to this which I have already? *Or, what is the place of my rest?* What need have I of a house, either to repose myself in or to show myself? *Hath not my hand made all these things?* And *these show his eternal power and Godhead* (Rom. 1:20); they so show themselves to all mankind that those who worship other gods are without excuse. And as the world is thus God's temple, wherein he is manifested, so it is God's temple in which he will be worshipped. As the earth is full of his glory, and is therefore his temple (Isa. 6:3), so the earth is, or shall be, full of his praise (Hab. 3:3), *and all the ends of the earth shall fear him* (Ps. 67:7), and upon this account it is his temple. It was therefore no reflection at all upon this holy place, however they might take it, to say *that Jesus should destroy this temple,* and set up another, into which all nations should be admitted, *ch.* 15:16, 17. And it would not seem strange to those who considered that scripture which Stephen here quotes (Isa. 66:1–3), which, as it expressed God's comparative contempt of the external part of his service, so it plainly foretold the rejection of the unbelieving Jews, and the welcome of the Gentiles that were of a contrite spirit into the church.

Verses 51–53

Stephen was going on in his discourse (as it should seem by the thread of it) to show that, as the temple, so the temple-service must come to an end, and it would be the glory of both to give way to that worship of the Father in spirit and in truth which was to be established in the kingdom of the Messiah, stripped of the pompous ceremonies of the old law, and so he was going to apply all this which he had said more closely to his present purpose; but he perceived they could not bear it. They could patiently hear the history of the Old Testament told (it was a piece of learning which they themselves dealt much in); but if Stephen go about to tell them that their power and tyranny must come down, and that the church must be governed by a spirit of holiness and love, and heavenly-mindedness, they will not so much as give him the hearing. It is probable that he perceived this, and that they were going to silence him; and therefore he breaks off abruptly in the midst of his discourse, and by that spirit of wisdom, courage, and power, wherewith he was filled, he sharply rebuked his persecutors, and exposed their true character; for, if they will not admit the testimony of the gospel to them, it shall become a testimony against them.

I. They, like their fathers, were stubborn and wilful, and would not be wrought upon by the various methods God took to reclaim and reform them; they were like their fathers, inflexible both to the word of God and to his providences. 1. They, like their fathers, were stubborn and wilful, and would not be wrought upon by the various methods God took to reclaim and reform them; they were like their fathers, inflexible both to the word of God and to his providences. 1. They were *stiff-necked* (*v.* 51), and would not submit their necks to the sweet and easy yoke of God's government, nor draw in it, but were *like a bullock unaccustomed to the yoke;* or they would not bow their heads, no, not to God himself, would not do obeisance to him, would not humble themselves before him. The stiff neck is the same with the hard heart, obstinate and contumacious, and that will not yield — the general character of the Jewish nation, Ex. 32:9; 33:33, 5; 34:9; Deu. 9:6, 13; 31:27; Eze. 2:4. 2. They were *uncircumcised in heart and ears* their hearts and ears were not devoted and given up to God, as the body of the people were in profession by the sign of circumcision: "In name and show you are circumcised Jews, but in heart and ears you are still uncircumcised heathens, and pay no more deference to the authority of your God than they do, Jer. 9:26. You are under the power of unmortified lusts and corruptions, which stop your ears to the voice of God, and harden your hearts to that which is both most commanding and most affecting." They had not that *circumcision made without hands, in putting off the body of the sins of the flesh,* Col. 2:11.

II. They, like their fathers, were not only not influenced by the methods God took to reform them, but they were enraged and incensed against them: *You do always resist the Holy Ghost.* 1. They resisted the Holy Ghost speaking to them by the prophets, whom they opposed and contradicted, hated and ridiculed; this seems especially meant here, by the following explication, *Which of the prophets have not your fathers persecuted?* In persecuting and silencing those that spoke by the inspiration of the Holy Ghost they resisted the Holy Ghost. Their fathers resisted the Holy Ghost in the prophets that God raised up to them, and so did they in Christ's apostles and ministers, who spoke by the same Spirit, and had greater measures of his gifts than the prophets of the Old Testament had, and yet were more resisted. 2. They resisted the Holy Ghost striving with them by their own consciences, and would not comply with the convictions and dictates of them. God's Spirit strove with them as with the old world, but in vain; they resisted him, took part with their corruptions against their convictions, and rebelled against the light. There is that in our sinful hearts that always resists the Holy Ghost, a flesh that lusts against the Spirit, and wars against his motions; but in the hearts of God's elect, when the fulness of time comes, this resistance is overcomer and overpowered, and after a struggle the throne of Christ is set up in the soul, and every thought that had exalted itself against it is brought into captivity to it, 2 Co. 10:4, 5. That grace therefore which effects this change might more fitly be called *victorious* grace than *irresistible.*

III. They, like their fathers, persecuted and slew those whom God sent unto them to call them to duty, and make them offers of mercy. 1. Their fathers had been the cruel and constant persecutors of the Old-Testament prophets (*v.* 51): *Which of the prophets have not your fathers persecuted?* More or less, one time or other, they had a blow at them all. With regard even to those that lived in the best reigns, when the princes did not persecute them, there was a malignant party in the nation that mocked at them and abused them, and most of them were at last, either by colour of law or popular fury, put to death; and that which aggravated the sin of persecuting the prophets was, that the business of the prophets they were so spiteful at was to *show before of the coming of the just One,* to give notice of God's kind intentions towards that people, to send the Messiah among them in the fulness of time. Those that were the messengers of such glad tidings should have been courted and caressed, and have had the preferments of the best of benefactors; but, instead of this, they had the treatment of the worst of malefactors. 2. They had been the *betrayers and murderers of the just One* himself, as Peter had told them, *ch.* 3:14, 15; 5:30. They had hired Judas to betray him, and had in a manner forced Pilate to condemn him; and therefore it is charged upon them that they were his betrayers and murders. Thus they were the genuine seed of those who slew the prophets that foretold his coming, which, by slaying him, they showed they would have done if they had lived then; and thus, as our Saviour had told them, they brought upon themselves the guilt of the blood of all the prophets. To which of the prophets would those have shown any respect who had no regard to the Son of God himself?

IV. They, like their fathers, put contempt upon divine revelation, and would not be guided and governed by it; and this was the aggravation of their sin, that God had given, as to their fathers his law, so to them his gospel, in vain. 1. Their fathers received the law, and did not observe it, *v.* 53. God wrote to them the great things of his law, after he had first spoken them to them; and yet they were counted by them as a strange or foreign thing, which they were no way concerned in. The law is said to be *received by the disposition of angels,* because angels were employed in the solemnity of giving the law, in the thunderings and lightnings, and the sound of the trumpet. It is said to be *ordained by angels* (Gal. 3:19), God is said to come *with ten thousand* of his saints to give the law (Deu. 33:2), and it was a *word spoken by angels,* Heb. 2:2. This put an honour both upon the law and the Lawgiver, and should increase our veneration for both. But those that thus received the law yet kept it not, but by making the golden calf broke it immediately in a capital instance. 2. They received the gospel now, by the disposition, not of angels, but of the Holy Ghost, — not with the sound of a trumpet, but, which was more strange, in the gift of tongues, and yet they did not embrace it. They would not yield to the plainest demonstrations, any more than their fathers before them did, for they were resolved not to comply with God either in his law or in his gospel.

We have reason to think Stephen had a great deal more to say, and would have said it if they would have suffered him; but they were wicked and unreasonable men with whom he had to do, that could no more hear reason than they could speak it.

Verses 54–60

We have here the death of the first martyr of the Christian church, and there is in this story a lively instance of the outrage and fury of the persecutors (such as we may expect to meet with if we are called out to suffer for Christ), and of the courage and comfort of the persecuted, that are thus called out. Here is hell in its fire and darkness, and heaven in its light and brightness; and these serve as foils to set off each other. It is not here said that the votes of the council were taken upon his case, and that by the majority he was found guilty, and then condemned and ordered to be stoned to death, according to the law, as a blasphemer; but, it is likely, so it was, and that it was not by the violence of the people, without order of the council, that he was put to death; for here is the usual ceremony of regular executions — he was cast out of the city, and the hands of the witnesses were first upon him.

Let us observe here the wonderful discomposure of the spirits of his enemies and persecutors, and the wonderful composure of his spirit.

I. See the strength of corruption in the persecutors of Stephen — malice in perfection, hell itself broken loose, men become incarnate devils, and the serpent's seed spitting their venom.

1. *When they heard these things they were cut to the heart* (*v.* 54), *dieprionto,* the same word that is used Heb. 11:37, and translated *they were sawn asunder.* They were put to as much torture in their minds as ever the martyrs were put to in their bodies. They were filled with indignation at the unanswerable arguments that Stephen urged for their conviction, and that they could find nothing to say against them. They were not pricked to the heart with sorrow, as those were *ch.* 2:37, but cut to the heart with rage and fury, as they them-

selves were, *ch.* 5:33. Stephen rebuked them sharply, as Paul expresses it (Tit. 1:13), *apotomōs — cuttingly,* for they were cut to the heart by the reproof. Note, Rejecters of the gospel and opposers of it are really tormentors to themselves. Enmity to God is a heart-cutting thing; faith and love are heart-healing. When they heard how he that *looked like an angel* before he began his discourse talked like an angel, like a messenger from heaven, before he concluded it, they were *like a wild bull in a net, full of the fury of the Lord,* (Isa. 51:20), despairing to run down a cause so bravely pleaded, and yet resolved not to yield to it.

2. They *gnashed upon him with their teeth.* This denotes, (1.) Great malice and rage against him. Job complained of his enemy that he *gnashed upon him with his teeth,* Job 16:9. The language of this was, *Oh that we had of his flesh to eat!* Job 31:31. They *grinned at him,* as dogs at those they are enraged at; and therefore Paul, cautioning against those of the circumcision, says, *Beware of dogs,* Phil. 3:2. Enmity at the saints turns men into brute beasts. (2.) Great vexation within themselves; they fretted to see in him such manifest tokens of a divine power and presence, and it vexed them to the heart. The *wicked shall see it and be grieved, he shall gnash with his teeth and melt away,* Ps. 112:10. Gnashing with the teeth is often used to express the horror and torments of the damned. Those that have the malice of hell cannot but have with it some of the pains of hell.

3. *They cried out with a loud voice* (*v.* 57), to irritate and excite one another, and to drown the noise of the clamours of their own and one another's consciences; when he said, *I see heaven opened,* they cried with a loud voice, that he might not be heard to speak. Note, It is very common for a righteous cause, particularly the righteous cause of Christ's religion, to be attempted to be run down by noise and clamour; what is wanting in reason is made up in tumult, and *the cry of him that ruleth among fools, while the words of the wise are heard in quiet.* They cried with a loud voice, as soldiers when they are going to engage in battle, mustering up all their spirit and vigour for this desperate encounter.

4. They *stopped their ears,* that they might not hear their own noisiness; or perhaps under pretence that they could not bear to hear his blasphemies. As Caiaphas rent his clothes when Christ said, *Hereafter you shall see the Son of man coming in glory* (Mt. 26:64, 65), so here these *stopped their ears* when Stephen said, *I now see the Son of man standing in glory,* both pretending that what was spoken was not to be heard with patience. Their stopping their ears was, (1.) A manifest specimen of their wilful obstinacy; they were resolved they would not hear what had a tendency to convince them, which was what the prophets often complained of: they were *like the deaf adder, that will not hear the voice of the charmer,* Ps. 58:4, 5. (2.) It was a fatal omen of that judicial hardness to which God would give them up. They stopped their ears, and then God, in a way of righteous judgment, stopped them. This was the work that was now in doing with the unbelieving Jews: *Make the heart of this people fat, and their ears heavy;* thus was Stephen's character of them answered, *You uncircumcised in heart and ears.*

5. They *ran upon him with one accord* — the people and the elders of the people, judges, prosecutors, witnesses, and spectators, they all flew upon him, as beasts upon their prey. See how violent they were, and in what haste — they ran upon him, though there was no danger of his outrunning them; and see how unanimous they were in this evil thing — they ran upon him *with one accord,* one and all, hoping thereby to terrify him, and put him into confusion, envying him his composure and comfort in soul, with which he wonderfully enjoyed himself in the midst of this hurry; they did all they could to ruffle him.

6. They *cast him out of the city, and stoned him,* as if he were not worthy to live in Jerusalem; nay, not worthy to live in this world, pretending herein to execute the law of Moses (Lev. 24:16), *He that blasphemeth the name of the Lord shall surely be put to death, all the congregation shall certainly stone him.* And thus they had put Christ to death, when this same court had found him guilty of blasphemy, but that, for his greater ignominy, they were desirous he should be crucified, and God overruled it for the fulfilling of the scripture. The fury with which they managed the execution is intimated in this: they cast him out of the city, as if they could not bear the sight of him; they treated him as an anathema, as the offscouring of all things. The witnesses against him were the leaders in the execution, according to the law (Deu. 17:7), *The hands of the witnesses shall be first upon him, to put him to death,* and particularly in the case of blasphemy, Lev. 24:14; Deu. 13:9. Thus they were to confirm their testimony. Now, the stoning of a man being a laborious piece of work, the witnesses took off their upper garments, that they might not hang in their way, *and they laid them down at a young man's feet, whose name was Saul,* now a pleased spectator of this tragedy. It is the first time we find mention of his name; we shall know it and love it better when we find it changed to *Paul,* and him changed from a persecutor into a preacher. This little instance of his agency in Stephen's death he afterwards reflected upon with regret (*ch.* 22:20): *I kept the raiment of those that slew him.*

II. See the strength of grace in Stephen, and the wonderful instances of God's favour to him, and working in him. As his persecutors were full of Satan, so was he *full of the Holy Ghost,* fuller than ordinary, anointed with fresh oil for the combat, that, as the day, so might the strength be. Upon this account those are *blessed who are persecuted for righteousness' sake,* that *the Spirit of God and of glory rests upon them,* 1 Pt. 4:14. When he was chosen to public service, he was described to be a man *full of the Holy Ghost* (*ch.* 6:5), and now he is called out to martyrdom he has still the same character. Note, Those that are full of the Holy Ghost are fit for any thing, either to act for Christ or to suffer for him. And those whom God calls out to difficult services for his name he will qualify for those services, and carry comfortably through them, by filling them with the Holy Ghost, that, as their afflictions for Christ abound, their consolation in him may yet more abound, and then *none of these things move them.* Now here we have a remarkable communion between this blessed martyr and the blessed Jesus in this critical moment. When the followers of Christ are for his sake *killed all the day long, and accounted as sheep for the slaughter,* does this separate them from the love of Christ? Does he love them the less? Do they love him the less? No, by no means; and so it appears by this narrative, in which we may observe.

1. Christ's gracious manifestation of himself to Stephen, both for his comfort and for his honour, in the midst of his sufferings. When they were cut to the heart, and gnashed upon him with their teeth, ready to eat him up, then he had a view of the glory of Christ sufficient to fill him with joy unspeakable, which was intended not only for his encouragement, but for the support and comfort of all God's suffering servants in all ages.

(1.) He, *being full of the Holy Ghost, looked up stedfastly into heaven, v.* 55. [1.] Thus he looked above the power and fury of his persecutors, and did as it were despise them, and laugh them to scorn, as the daughter of Zion, Isa. 37:22. They had their eyes fixed upon him, full of malice and cruelty; but he looked up to heaven, and never minded them, was so taken up with the eternal life now in prospect that he seemed to have no manner of concern for the natural life now at state. Instead of looking about him, to see either which way he was in danger or which way he might make his escape, he looks up to heaven; thence only comes his help, and thitherward his way is still open; though they compass him about on every side, they cannot interrupt his intercourse with heaven. Note, A believing regard to God and the upper world will be of great use to us, to set us above the fear of man; for as far as we are under the influence of that fear we *forget the Lord our Maker,* Isa. 51:13. [2.] Thus he directed his sufferings to the glory of God, to the honour of Christ, and did as it were appeal to heaven concerning them (Lord, for thy sake I suffer this) and express his earnest expectation that Christ should be magnified in his body. Now that he was ready to be offered he looks up stedfastly to heaven, as one willing to offer himself. [3.] Thus he lifted up his soul with his eyes to God in the heavens, in pious ejaculations, calling upon God for wisdom and grace to carry him through this trial in a right manner. God has promised that he will be with his servants whom he calls out to suffer for him; but he will for this be sought unto. He is nigh unto them, but it is *in that for which they call upon him. Is any afflicted? Let him pray.* [4.] Thus he breathed after the heavenly country, to which he saw the fury of his persecutors would presently send him. It is good for dying saints to look up stedfastly to heaven: "Yonder is the place whither death will carry my better part, and then, *O death! where is thy sting?"* [5.] Thus he made it to appear that he was full of the Holy Ghost; for, wherever the Spirit of grace dwells, and works, and reigns, he directs the eye of the soul upward. Those that are full of the Holy Ghost will look up stedfastly to heaven, for there their heart is. [6.] Thus he put himself into a posture to receive the following manifestation of the divine glory and grace. If we expect to hear from heaven, we must look up stedfastly to heaven.

(2.) He saw the glory of God (*v.* 55); *for he saw,* in order to this, *the heavens opened, v.* 56. Some think his eyes were strengthened, and the sight of them so raised above its natural pitch, by a supernatural power, that he saw into the third heavens, though at so vast a distance, as Moses's sight was enlarged to see the whole land of Canaan. Others think it was a representation of the glory of God set before his eyes, as, before, Isaiah and Ezekiel; heaven did as it were come down to him, as Rev. 21:2. The heavens were opened, to give him a view of the happiness he was going to, that he might, in prospect of it, go cheerfully through death, so great a death. Would we by faith look up stedfastly, we might see the heavens opened by the mediation of Christ, the veil being rent, and a new and living way laid open for us into the holiest. The heaven is opened for the settling of a correspondence between God and men, that his favours and blessings may come down to us, and our prayers and praises may go up to him. We may also see the glory of God, as far as he has revealed it in his word, and the sight of this will carry us through all the terrors of sufferings and death.

(3.) He *saw Jesus standing on the right hand of God* (*v.* 55), *the Son of man,* so it is *v.* 546. Jesus, being the Son of man, having taken our nature with him to heaven, and being there clothed with a body, might be seen with bodily eyes, and so Stephen saw him. When the Old-Testament prophets saw the glory of God it was attended with angels. The Shechinah or divine presence in Isaiah's vision was attended with seraphim, in Ezekiel's vision with cherubim, both signifying the angels, the ministers of God's providence. But here no mention is made of the angels, though they surround the throne and the Lamb; instead of them Stephen sees Jesus at the right hand of God, the great Mediator of God's grace, from whom more glory redounds to God than from all the ministration of the holy angels. The glory of God shines brightest in the face of Jesus Christ; for there shines the glory of his grace, which is the most illustrious instance of his glory. God appears more glorious with Jesus standing at his right hand than with millions of angels about him. Now, [1.] Here is a proof of the exaltation of Christ to the Father's right hand; the apostles saw him ascend, but they did not see him sit down, *A cloud received him out of their sight.* We are told that he sat down on the right hand of God; but was he ever seen there? Yes, Stephen saw him there, and was abundantly satisfied with the sight. He saw Jesus at the right hand of God, denoting both his transcendent dignity and his sovereign dominion, his uncontrollable ability and his universal agency; whatever God's right hand gives to us, or receives from us, or does concerning us, it is by him; for he is his right hand. [2.] He is usually said to *sit* there; but Stephen sees him *standing* there, as one more than ordinarily concerned at present for his suffering servant; he stood up as a judge to plead his cause against his persecutors; he is *raised up out of his holy habitation* (Zec. 2:13), *comes out of his place to punish,* Isa. 26:21. He stands ready to receive him and crown him, and in the mean time to give him a prospect of the joy set before him. [3.] This was intended for the encouragement of Stephen. He sees Christ is for him, and then no matter who is against him. When our Lord Jesus was in his agony an angel appeared to him, strengthening him; but Stephen had Christ himself appearing to him. Note, Nothing so comfortable to dying saints, nor so animating to suffering saints, as to see Jesus at the right hand of God; and, blessed be God, by faith we may see him there.

(4.) He told those about him what he saw (*v.* 56): *Behold, I see the heavens opened.* That which was a cordial to him ought to have been a conviction to them, and a caution to them to take heed of proceeding against one upon whom heaven thus smiled; and therefore what he saw he declared, let them make what use they pleased of it. If some were exasperated by it, others perhaps might be wrought upon to consider this Jesus whom they persecuted, and to believe in him.

2. Stephen's pious addresses to Jesus Christ. The manifestation of God's glory to him did not set him above praying, but rather set him upon it: *They stoned Stephen, calling upon God, v.* 59. Though he called upon God, and by that showed himself to be a true-born Israelite, yet they proceeded to stone him, not considering how dangerous it is to fight

against those who have an interest in heaven. Though they stoned him, yet he called upon God; nay, therefore he called upon him. Note, It is the comfort of those who are unjustly hated and persecuted by men that they have a God to go to, a God all-sufficient to call upon. Men stop their ears, as they did here (*v.* 57), but God does not. Stephen was now cast out of the city, but he was not cast out from his God. He was now taking his leave of the world, and therefore calls upon God; for we must do this as long as we live. Note, It is good to die praying; then we need help — strength we never had, to do a work we never did — and how can we fetch in that help and strength but by prayer? Two short prayers Stephen offered up to God in his dying moments, and in them as it were breathed out his soul: —

(1.) Here is a prayer for himself: *Lord Jesus, receive my spirit.* Thus Christ had himself resigned his spirit immediately into the hands of the Father. We are here taught to resign ours into the hands of Christ as Mediator, by him to be recommended to the Father. Stephen saw Jesus standing at the Father's right hand, and he thus calls to him: "Blessed Jesus, do that for me now which thou standest there to do for all thine, receive my departing spirit into thy hand." Observe, [1.] The soul is the man, and our great concern, living and dying, must be about our souls. Stephen's body was to be miserably broken and shattered, and overwhelmed with a shower of stones, the earthly house of this tabernacle violently beaten down and abused; but, however it goes with that, "Lord," saith he, "'let my spirit be safe; let it go well with my poor soul." Thus, while we live, our care should be that though the body be starved or stripped the soul may be fed and clothed, though the body lie in pain the soul may dwell at ease; and, when we die, that though the body be thrown by as a despised broken vessel, and a vessel in which there is no pleasure, yet the soul may be presented a vessel of honour, that God may be the strength of the heart and its portion, though the flesh fail. [2.] Our Lord Jesus is God, to whom we are to seek, and in whom we are to confide and comfort ourselves living and dying. Stephen here prays to Christ, and so must we; for it is the will of God that all men should thus *honour the Son, even as they honour the Father.* It is Christ we are to commit ourselves to, who alone is able to keep what we commit to him against that day; it is necessary that we have an eye to Christ when we come to die, for there is no venturing into another world but under his conduct, no living comforts in dying moments but what are fetched from him. [3.] Christ's receiving our spirits at death is the great thing we are to be careful about, and to comfort ourselves with. We ought to be in care about this while we live, that Christ may receive our spirits when we die; for, if he reject and disown them, whither will they betake themselves? How can they escape being a prey to the roaring lion? To him therefore we must commit them daily, to be ruled and sanctified, and made meet for heaven, and then, and not otherwise, he will receive them. And, if this has been our care while we live, it may be our comfort when we come to die, that we shall be received into everlasting habitations.

(2.) Here is a prayer for his persecutors, *v.* 60.

[1.] The circumstances of this prayer are observable; for it seems to have been offered up with something more of solemnity than the former. *First,* He *knelt down,* which was an expression of his humility in prayer. *Secondly,* He *cried with a loud voice,* which was an expression of his importunity. But why should he thus show more humility and importunity in this request than in the former? Why, none could doubt of his being in good earnest in his prayers for himself, and therefore there he needed not to use such outward expressions of it; but in his prayer for his enemies, because that is so much against the grain of corrupt nature, it was requisite he should give proofs of his being in earnest.

[2.] The prayer itself: *Lord, lay not this sin to their charge.* Herein he followed the example of his dying Master, who prayed thus for his persecutors, *Father, forgive them;* and set an example to all following sufferers in the cause of Christ thus to pray for those that persecute them. Prayer may preach. This did so to those who stoned Stephen, and he knelt down that they might take notice he was going to pray, and cried with a loud voice that they might take notice of what he said, and might learn, *First,* That what they did was a sin, a great sin, which, if divine mercy and grace did not prevent, would be laid to their charge, to their everlasting confusion. *Secondly,* That, notwithstanding their malice and fury against him, he was in charity with them, and was so far from desiring that God would avenge his death upon them that it was his hearty prayer to God that it might not in any degree be laid to their charge. A sad reckoning there would be for it. If they did not repent, it would certainly be laid to their charge; but he, for his part, did not desire the woeful day. Let them take notice of this, and, when their thoughts were cool, surely they would not easily forgive themselves for putting him to death who could so easily forgive them. *The blood-thirsty hate the upright, but the just seek his soul,* Prov. 29:10. *Thirdly,* That, though the sin was very heinous, yet they must not despair of the pardon of it upon their repentance. If they would lay it to their hearts, God would not lay it to their charge. "Do you think," saith St. Austin, "that Paul heard Stephen pray this prayer? It is likely he did and ridiculed it then *(audivit subsannans, sed irrisit — he heard with scorn),* but afterwards he had the benefit of it, and fared the better for it."

3. His expiring with this: *When he had said this, he fell asleep;* or, as he was saying this, the blow came that was mortal. Note, Death is but a sleep to good people; not the sleep of the soul (Stephen had given that up into Christ's hand), but the sleep of the body; it is its rest from all its griefs and toils; it is perfect ease from toil and pain. Stephen died as much in a hurry as ever any man did, and yet, when he died, he fell asleep. He applied himself to his dying work with as much composure of mind as if he had been going to sleep; it was but closing his eyes, and dying. Observe, He fell asleep when he was praying for his persecutors; it is expressed as if he thought he could not die in peace till he had done this. It contributes very much to our dying comfortably to die in charity with all men; we are then found of Christ in peace; let not the sun of life go down upon our wrath. He fell asleep; the vulgar Latin adds, *in the Lord,* in the embraces of his love. If he thus sleep, he shall do well; he shall awake again in the morning of the resurrection.

CHAPTER 8

In this chapter we have an account of the persecutions of the Christians, and the propagating of Christianity thereby. It was strange, but very true, that the disciples of Christ the more they were afflicted the more they multiplied. I. Here is the church suffering; upon the occasion of putting Stephen to death a very sharp storm arose, which forced many from Jerusalem (*v.* 1–3). II. Here is the church spreading by the ministry of Philip and others that were dispersed upon that occasion. We have here, 1. The gospel brought to Samaria, preached there (*v.* 4, 5), embraced there (*v.* 6–8), even by Simon Magus (*v.* 9–13); the gift of the Holy Ghost conferred upon some of the believing Samaritans by the imposition of the hands of Peter and John (*v.* 14–17); and the severe rebuke given by Peter to Simon Magus for offering money for a power to bestow that gift (*v.* 18–25). 2. The gospel sent to Ethiopia, by the eunuch, a person of quality of that country. He is returning home in his chariot from Jerusalem (*v.* 26–28). Philip is sent to him, and in his chariot preaches Christ to him (*v.* 29–35), baptizes him upon his profession of the Christian faith (*v.* 36–38), and the leaves him (*v.* 39–40). Thus in different ways and methods the gospel was dispersed among the nations, and, one way or other, "Have they not all heard?"

Verses 1–3

In these verses we have,

I. Something more concerning Stephen and his death; how people stood affected to it — variously, as generally in such cases, according to men's different sentiments of things. Christ had said to his disciples, when he was parting with them (Jn. 16:20), *You shall weep and lament, but the world shall rejoice.* Accordingly here is, 1. Stephen's death rejoiced in by one — by many, no doubt, but by one in particular, and that was Saul, who was afterwards called Paul; he was *consenting to his death, syneudokōn — he consented to it with delight* (so the word signifies); he was pleased with it. He fed his eyes with this bloody spectacle, in hopes it would put a stop to the growth of Christianity. We have reason to think that Paul ordered Luke to insert this, for shame to himself, and glory to free grace. Thus he owns himself guilty of the blood of Stephen, and aggravates it with this, that he did not do it with regret and reluctancy, but with delight and a full satisfaction, like those who not only *do such things, but have pleasure in those that do them.* 2. Stephen's death bewailed by others (*v.* 2) — *devout men,* which some understand of those that were properly so called, *proselytes,* one of whom Stephen himself probably was. Or, it may be taken more largely; some of the church that were more devout and zealous than the rest went and gathered up the poor crushed and broken remains, to which they gave a decent interment, probably in the *field of blood,* which was bought some time ago to bury strangers in. They buried him solemnly, and made great lamentation over him. Though his death was of great advantage to himself, and great service to the church, yet they bewailed it as a general loss, so well qualified was he for the service, and so likely to be useful both as a deacon and as a disputant. It is a bad symptom if, when such men are taken away, it is not laid to heart. Those devout men paid these their last respects to Stephen, (1.) To show that they were not ashamed of the cause for which he suffered, nor afraid of the wrath of those that were enemies to it; for, though they now triumph, the cause is a righteous cause, and will be at last a victorious one. (2.) To show the great value and esteem they had for this faithful servant of Jesus Christ, this first martyr for the gospel, whose memory shall always be precious to them, notwithstanding the ignominy of his death. They study to do honour to him upon whom God put honour. (3.) To testify their belief and hope of the *resurrection of the dead, and the life of the world to come.*

II. An account of this persecution of the church, which begins upon the martyrdom of Stephen. When the fury of the Jews ran with such violence, and to such a height, against Stephen, it could not quickly either stop itself or spend itself. The bloody are often in scripture called *blood-thirsty;* for when they have tasted blood they thirst for more. One would have thought Stephen's dying prayers and dying comforts should have overcome them, and melted them into a better opinion of Christians and Christianity; but it seems they did not: the persecution goes on; for they were more exasperated when they saw they could prevail nothing, and, as if they hoped to be too hard for God himself, they resolve to follow their blow; and perhaps, because they were none of them struck dead upon the place for stoning Stephen, their hearts were the more fully set in them to do evil. Perhaps the disciples were also the more emboldened to dispute against them as Stephen did, seeing how triumphantly he finished his course, which would provoke them so much the more. Observe,

1. Against whom this persecution was raised: It was *against the church in Jerusalem,* which is no sooner planted than it is persecuted, as Christ often intimated that tribulation and persecution would arise *because of the word.* And Christ had particularly foretold that Jerusalem would soon be made too hot for his followers, for that city had been famous for killing the prophets and stoning those that were sent to it, Mt. 23:37. It should seem that in this persecution many were put to death, for Paul owns that at this time he persecuted this way *unto the death* (*ch.* 21:4), and (*ch.* 26:10) that *when they were put to death he gave his voice against them.*

2. Who was an active man in it; none so zealous, so busy, as Saul, a young Pharisee, *v.* 3. As for Saul (who had been twice mentioned before, and now again for a notorious persecutor) *he made havoc of the church;* he did all he could to lay it waste and ruin it; he cared not what mischief he did to the disciples of Christ, nor knew when to stop. He aimed at no less than the cutting off of the gospel Israel, that the name of it should be no more in remembrance, Ps. 83:4. He was the fittest tool the chief priests could find out to serve their purposes; he was informer-general against the disciples, a messenger of the great council to be employed in searching for meetings, and seizing all that were suspected to favour that way. Saul was bred a scholar, a gentleman, and yet did not think it below him to be employed in the vilest work of that kind. (1.) He *entered into every house,* making no difficulty of breaking open doors, night or day, and having a force attending him for that purpose. He entered into every house where they used to hold their meetings, or every house that had any Christians in it, or was thought to have. No man could be secure in his own house, though it was his castle. (2.) He haled, with the utmost contempt and cruelty, both men and women, dragged them along the streets, without any regard to the tenderness of the weaker sex; he stooped so low as to take cognizance of the meanest that were leavened with the gospel, so extremely bigoted was he. (3.) He committed them to prison, in order to their being tried and put to death, unless they would renounce Christ; and some, we find, were compelled by him to blaspheme, *ch.* 26:11.

3. What was the effect of this persecution: *They were all scattered abroad* (*v.* 1), not all the believers, but all the preachers, who were principally struck at, and against whom warrants were issued out to take them up. They, remembering our Master's rule *(when they persecute you in one city, flee*

to another), dispersed themselves by agreement *throughout the regions of Judea* and of Samaria; not so much for fear of sufferings (for Judea and Samaria were not so far off from Jerusalem but that, if they made a public appearance there, as they determined to do, their persecutors' power would soon reach them there), but because they looked upon this as an intimation of Providence to them to scatter. Their work was pretty well done in Jerusalem, and now it was time to think of the necessities of other places; for their Master had told them that they must be his witnesses in Jerusalem first, and then *in all Judea and in Samaria,* and then *to the uttermost part of the earth* (ch. 1:8), and this method they observe. Through persecution may not drive us off from our work, yet it may send us, as a hint of Providence, to work elsewhere. The preachers were all scattered *except the apostles,* who, probably, were directed by the Spirit to continue at Jerusalem yet for some time, they being, by the special providence of God, screened from the storm, and by the special grace of God enabled to face the storm. They tarried at Jerusalem, that they might be ready to go where their assistance was most needed by the other preachers that were sent to break the ice; as Christ ordered his disciples to go to those places where he himself designed to go, Lu. 10:1. The apostles continued longer together at Jerusalem than one would have thought, considering the command and commission given them, to *go into all the world,* and to *disciple all nations.* See *ch.* 15:6; Gal. 1:17. But what was done by the evangelists whom they sent forth was reckoned as done by them.

Verses 4–13

Samson's riddle is here again unriddled: *Out of the eater comes forth meat, and out of the strong sweetness.* The persecution that was designed to extirpate the church was by the overruling providence of God made an occasion of the enlargement of it. Christ had said, *I am come to send fire on the earth;* and they thought, by scattering those who were kindled with that fire, to have put it out, but instead of this they did but help to spread it.

I. Here is a general account of what was done by them all (v. 4): *They went every where, preaching the word.* They did not go to hide themselves for fear of suffering, no, nor to show themselves as proud of their sufferings; but they went up and down to scatter the knowledge of Christ in every place where they were scattered. They went every where, into the way of the Gentiles, and the cities of the Samaritans, which before they were forbidden to go into, Mt. 10:5. They did not keep together in a body, though this might have been a strength to them; but they scattered into all parts, not to take their ease, but to find out work. They went *evangelizing* the world, preaching the word of the gospel; it was this which filled them, and which they endeavoured to fill the country with, those of them that were preachers in their preaching, and others in their common converse. They were now in a country where they were no strangers, for Christ and his disciples had conversed much in the regions of Judea; so that they had a foundation laid there for them to build upon; and it would be requisite to let the people there know what that doctrine which Jesus had preached there some time ago was come to, and that it was not lost and forgotten, as perhaps they were made to believe.

II. A particular account of what was done by Philip. We shall hear of the progress and success of others of them afterwards (ch. 11:19), but here must attend the motions of Philip, not Philip the apostle, but Philip the deacon, who was chosen and ordained to serve tables, but having *used the office of a deacon well he purchased to himself a good degree, and great boldness in the faith,* 1 Tim. 3:13. Stephen was advanced to the degree of a martyr, Philip to the degree of an evangelist, which when he entered upon, being obliged by it to *give himself to the word and prayer,* he was, no doubt, discharged from the office of a deacon; for how could he serve tables at Jerusalem, which by that office he was obliged to do, when he was preaching in Samaria? And it is probable that two others were chosen in the room of Stephen and Philip. Now observe,

1. What wonderful success Philip had in his preaching, and what reception he met with.

(1.) The place he chose was the city of Samaria, the head city of Samaria, the metropolis of that country, which stood where the city of Samaria had formerly stood, of the building of which we read, 1 Ki. 16:24, now called *Sebaste.* Some think it was the same with Sychem or Sychar, that city of

Samaria where Christ was, Jn. 4:5. Many of that city then believed in Christ, though he did no miracle among them (v. 39, 41), and now Philip, three years after, carries on the work then begun. The Jews would have no dealings with the Samaritans; but Christ sent his gospel to slay all enmities, and particularly that between the Jews and the Samaritans, by making them one in his church.

(2.) The doctrine he preached was Christ; for he determined to know nothing else. He *preached Christ to them; he proclaimed Christ to them* (so the word signifies), as a king, when he comes to the crown, is proclaimed throughout his dominions. The Samaritans had an expectation of the Messiah's coming, as appears by Jn. 4:25. Now Philip tells them that he is come, and that the Samaritans are welcome to him. Ministers' business is to preach Christ — Christ, and him crucified — Christ, and him glorified.

(3.) The proofs he produced for the confirmation of his doctrine were miracles, v. 6. To convince them that he had his commission from heaven (and therefore not only they might venture upon what he said, but they were bound to yield to it), he shows them this broad seal of heaven annexed to it, which the God of truth would never put to a lie. The miracles were undeniable; they heard and saw the miracles which he did. They heard the commanding words he spoke, and saw the amazing effects of them immediately; that he spoke, and it was done. And the nature of the miracles was such as suited the intention of his commission, and gave light and lustre to it. [1.] He was sent to break the power of Satan; and, in token of this, unclean spirits, being charged in the name of the Lord Jesus to remove, *came out of many that were possessed with them, v.* 7. As far as the gospel prevails, Satan is forced to quit his hold of men and his interest in them, and then those are restored to themselves, and to their right mind again, who, while he kept possession, were distracted. Wherever the gospel gains the admission and submission it ought to have, evil spirits are dislodged, and particularly *unclean spirits,* all inclinations to the lusts of the flesh, which war against the soul; for God has called us from uncleanness to holiness, 1 Th. 4:7. This was signified by the casting of these unclean spirits out of the bodies of people, who, it is here said, came out *crying with a loud voice,* which signifies that they came out with great reluctancy, and sorely against their wills, but were forced to acknowledge themselves overcome by a superior power, Mk. 1:26; 3:11; 9:26. [2.] He was sent to heal the minds of men, to cure a distempered world, and to put it into a good state of health; and, in token of this, *many that were taken with palsies, and that were lame, were healed.* Those distempers are specified that were most difficult to be cured by the course of nature (that the miraculous cure might be the more illustrious), and those that were most expressive of the disease of sin and that moral impotency which the souls of men labour under as to the service of God. The grace of God in the gospel is designed for the healing of those that are spiritually lame and paralytic, and cannot help themselves, Rom. 5:6.

(4.) The acceptance which Philip's doctrine, thus proved, met with in Samaria (v. 6): *The people with one accord gave heed to those things which Philip spoke,* induced thereto by the miracles which served at first to gain attention, and so by degrees to gain assent. There then begin to be some hopes of people when they begin to take notice of what is said to them concerning the things of their souls and eternity — when they begin to give heed to the word of God, as those that are well pleased to hear it, desirous to understand and remember it, and that look upon themselves as concerned in it. The common people gave heed to Philip, *oi ochloi — a multitude of them,* not here and there one, but with one accord; they were all of a mind, that it was fit the doctrine of the gospel should be enquired into, and an impartial hearing given to it.

(5.) The satisfaction they had in attending on, and attending to, Philip's preaching, and the success it had with many of them (v. 8): *There was great joy in that city;* for (v. 12) they *believed Philip, and were baptized* into the faith of Christ, the generality of them, *both men and women.* Observe, [1.] Philip preached *the things concerning the kingdom of God,* the constitution of that kingdom, the laws and ordinances of it, the liberties and privileges of it, and the obligations we are all under to be the loyal subjects of that kingdom; and he preached the name of Jesus Christ, as king of that kingdom — his *name, which is above every name.* He preached it up in its commanding power and influence — all that by which

he has made himself known. [2.] The people not only gave heed to what he said, but at length believed it, were fully convinced that it was of God and not of men, and gave up themselves to the direction and government of it. As to this mountain, on which they had hitherto worshipped God, and placed a great deal of religion in it, they were now as much weaned from it as every they had been wedded to it, and become *the true worshippers, who worship the Father in spirit and in truth,* and in the name of Christ, the true temple, Jn. 4:20–23. [3.] When they believed, without scruple (though they were Samaritans) and without delay *they were baptized,* openly professed the Christian faith, promised to adhere to it, and then, by washing them with water, were solemnly admitted into the communion of the Christian church, and owned as brethren by the disciples. *Men* only were capable of being admitted into the Jewish church by circumcision; but, to show that *in Jesus Christ there is neither male nor female* (Gal. 3:28), but both are alike welcome to him, the initiating ordinance is such as women are capable of, for they are numbered with God's spiritual Israel, though not with Israel according to the flesh, Num. 1:2. And hence it is easily gathered that women are to be admitted to the Lord's supper, though it does not appear that there were any among those to whom it was first administered. [4.] This occasioned great joy; each one rejoiced for himself, as he in the parable who *found the treasure hid in the field;* and they all rejoiced for the benefit hereby brought to their city, and that it came without opposition, which it would scarcely have done if Samaria had been within the jurisdiction of the chief priests. Note, The bringing of the gospel to any place is just matter of joy, of great joy, to that place. Hence the spreading of the gospel in the world is often prophesied of in the Old Testament as the diffusing of joy among the nations: *Let the nations be glad and sing for joy,* Ps. 67:4; 1 Th. 1:6. The gospel of Christ does not make men melancholy, but fills them with joy, if it be received as it should be; for it is *glad tidings of great joy to all people,* Lu. 2:10.

2. What there was in particular at this city of Samaria that made the success of the gospel there more than ordinarily wonderful.

(1.) That Simon Magus had been busy there, and had gained a great interest among the people, and *yet they believed the things that Philip spoke.* To unlearn that which is bad proves many times a harder task than to learn that which is good. These Samaritans, though they were not idolaters as the Gentiles, nor prejudiced against the gospel by traditions received from their fathers, yet had of late been drawn to follow Simon, a conjurer (For so *Magus* signifies) who made a mighty noise among them, and had strangely *bewitched them.* We are told,

[1.] How strong the delusion of Satan was by which they were brought into the interests of this great deceiver. He had been for some time, nay, for a *long time, in this city, using sorceries;* perhaps he came there by the instigation of the devil, soon after our Saviour had been there, to undo what he had been doing there; for it was always Satan's way to crush a good work in its bud and infancy, 2 Co. 11:3; 1 Th. 3:5. Now,

First, Simon assumed to himself that which was considerable: *He gave out that he himself was some great one,* and would have all people to believe so and to pay him respect accordingly; and then, as to every thing else, they might do as they pleased. He had no design to reform their lives, nor improve their worship and devotion, only to make them believe that he was, *tis megas — some divine person.* Justin Martyr says that he would be worshipped as *prōton theon — the chief god.* He gave out himself to be *the Son of God, the Messiah,* so some think; or to be an angel, or a prophet. Perhaps he was uncertain within himself what title of honour to pretend to; but he would be thought *some great one.* Pride, ambition, and an affectation of grandeur, have always been the cause of abundance of mischief both to the world and to the church.

Secondly, The people ascribed to him what he pleased. 1. *They all gave heed to him, from the least to the greatest,* both young and old, both poor and rich, both governors and governed. *To him they had regard* (v. 10, 11), and perhaps the more because the time fixed for the coming of the Messiah had now expired, which had raised a general expectation of the appearing of some great one about this time. Probably he was a native of their country, and therefore they embraced him the more cheerfully, that by giving honour to him they might reflect it upon themselves. 2. They said of him, *This man is the great power of God — the power of God, that great power* (so it might be read), that power which made the world. See how ignorant inconsiderate people mistake that which is done by the power of Satan, as if it were done by the power of God. Thus, in the Gentile world, devils pass for deities; and in the antichristian kingdom *all the world wonders after a beast,* to whom the dragon gives his power, and *who opens his mouth in blasphemy against God,* Rev. 13:2–5. 3. They were brought to it by his sorceries: *He bewitched the people of Samaria* (v. 9), *bewitched them with sorceries* (v. 11), that is, either, (1.) By his magic arts *he bewitched the minds of the people,* at least some of them, who drew in others. Satan, by God's permission, filled their hearts to follow Simon. *O foolish Galatians,* saith Paul, *who hath bewitched you?* Gal. 3:1. These people are said to be bewitched by Simon, because they were so strangely infatuated to believe a lie. Or, (2.) By his magic arts he did *many signs and lying wonders,* which seemed to be miracles, but really were not so: like those of the magicians of Egypt, and those of *the man of sin,* 2 Th. 2:9. When they knew no better, they were influenced by his sorceries; but, when they were acquainted with Philip's real miracles, they saw plainly that the one was real and the other a sham, and that there was as much difference as between Aaron's rod and those of the magicians. *What is the chaff to the wheat?* Jer. 23:28.

Thus, notwithstanding the influence Simon Magus had had upon them, and the unwillingness there generally is in people to own themselves in an error, and to retract it, yet, when they saw the difference between Simon and Philip, they quitted Simon, gave heed no longer to him, but to Philip: and thus you see,

[2.] How strong the power of Divine grace is, by which they were brought to Christ, who is truth itself, and was, as I may say, the great undeceiver. By that grace working with the word those that had been led captive by Satan *were brought into obedience to Christ.* Where Satan, as a *strong man armed,* kept possession of the palace, and thought himself safe, Christ, as a *stronger than he,* dispossessed him, and *divided the spoil; led captivity captive,* and made those the trophies of his victory whom the devil had triumphed over. Let us not despair of the worst, when even those whom Simon Magus had bewitched were brought to believe.

(2.) Here is another thing yet more wonderful, that Simon Magus himself became a convert to the faith of Christ, in show and profession, for a time. *Is Saul also among the prophets?* Yes (v. 13), *Simon himself believed also.* He was convinced that Philip preached a true doctrine, because he saw it confirmed by real miracles, of which he was the better able to judge because he was conscious to himself of the trick of his own pretended ones. [1.] The present conviction went so far that *he was baptized,* was admitted, as other believers were, into the church by baptism; and we have no reason to think that Philip did amiss in baptizing him, no, nor in baptizing him quickly. Though he had been a very wicked man, a sorcerer, a pretender to divine honours, yet, upon his solemn profession of repentance for his sin and faith in Jesus Christ, he was baptized. For, as great wickedness before conversion keeps not true penitents from the benefits of God's grace, so neither should it keep professing ones from church-fellowship. Prodigals, when they return, must be joyfully welcomed home, though we cannot be sure but that they will play the prodigal again. Nay, though he was now but a hypocrite, and really in *the gall of bitterness and bond of iniquity* all this while, and would soon have been found to be so if he had been tried awhile, yet Philip baptized him; for it is God's prerogative to know the heart. The church and its ministers must go by a judgment of charity, as far as there is room for it. It is a maxim in the law, *Donec contrarium patet, semper praesumitur meliori parti — We must hope the best as long as we can.* And it is a maxim in the discipline of the church, *De secretis non judicat ecclesia — The secrets of the heart God only judges.* [2.] The present conviction lasted so long that he continued with Philip. Though afterwards he apostatized from Christianity, yet not quickly. He courted Philip's acquaintance, and now he that had given out himself to be some great one is content to sit at the feet of a preacher of the gospel. Even bad men, very bad, may sometimes be in a good frame, very good; and those whose hearts still go after their covetousness may possibly not only come before God as his people come, but continue with them. [3.] The present conviction was wrought and kept up by the mira-

cles; he wondered to see himself so far outdone in signs and miracles. Many wonder at the proofs of divine truths who never experience the power of them.

Verses 14–25

God had wonderfully owned Philip in his work as an evangelist at Samaria, but he could do no more than an evangelist; there were some peculiar powers reserved to the apostles, for the keeping up of the dignity of their office, and here we have an account of what was done by two of them there — Peter and John. The twelve kept together at Jerusalem (v. 1), and thither these good tidings were brought them *that Samaria had received the word of God* (v. 14), that a great harvest of souls was gathered, and was likely to be gathered in to Christ there. The word of God was not only preached to them, but received by them; they bade it welcome, admitted the light of it, and submitted to the power of it: *When they heard it, they sent unto them Peter and John.* If Peter had been, as some say he was, the prince of the apostles, he would have sent some of them, or, if he had seen cause, would have gone himself of his own accord; but he was so far from this that he submitted to an order of the house, and, as a servant to the body, went whither they sent him. Two apostles were sent, the two most eminent, to Samaria, 1. To encourage Philip, to assist him, and strengthen his hands. Ministers in a higher station, and that excel in gifts and graces, should contrive how they may be helpful to those in a lower sphere, and contribute to their comfort and usefulness. 2. To carry on the good work that was begun among the people, and, with those heavenly graces that had enriched them, to confer upon them spiritual gifts. Now observe,

I. How they advanced and improved those of them that were sincere. It is said (v. 16), *The Holy Ghost was as yet fallen upon none of them,* in those extraordinary powers which were conveyed by the descent of the Spirit upon the day of pentecost. They were none of them endued with the gift of tongues, which seems then to have been the most usual immediate effect of the pouring out of the Spirit. See *ch.* 10:45, 46. This was both an eminent sign to those that believed not, and of excellent service to those that did. This, and other such gifts, they had not, *only they were baptized in the name of the Lord Jesus,* and so engaged in him and interested in him, which was necessary to salvation, and in this they had joy and satisfaction (v. 8), though they could not speak with tongues. Those that are indeed given up to Christ, and have experienced the sanctifying influences and operations of the Spirit of grace, have great reason to be thankful, and no reason to complain, though they have not those gifts that are for ornament, and would make them bright. But it is intended that they should go on to the perfection of the present dispensation, for the greater honour of the gospel. We have reason to think that Philip had received these gifts of the Holy Ghost himself, but had not a power to confer them; the apostles must come to do this; and they did it not upon all that were baptized, but upon some of them, and, it should seem, such as were designed for some office in the church, or at least to be eminent active members of it; and upon some of them *one gift of the Holy Ghost,* and upon others *another.* See 1 Co. 12:4, 8; 14:26. Now in order to this, 1. *The apostles prayed for them,* v. 15. The Spirit is given, not to ourselves only (Lu. 11:13), but to others also, in answer to prayer: *I will put my Spirit within you* (Eze. 36:27), *but I will for this be enquired of,* v. 37. We may take encouragement from this example in praying to God to give the renewing graces of the Holy Ghost to those whose spiritual welfare we are concerned for — for our children, for our friends, for our ministers. We should pray, and pray earnestly, *that they may receive the Holy Ghost;* for this includes all blessings. 2. They laid their hands on them, to signify that their prayers were answered, and *that the gift of the Holy Ghost was conferred upon them;* for, upon the use of this sign, *they received the Holy Ghost, and spoke with tongues.* The laying on of hands was anciently used in blessing, by those who blessed with authority. Thus the apostles blessed these new converts, ordained some to be ministers, and confirmed others in their Christianity. We cannot now, nor can any, thus give the Holy Ghost by the laying on of hands; but this may intimate to us that those whom we pray for we should use our endeavours with.

II. How they discovered and discarded him that was a hypocrite among them, and this was Simon Magus; for they knew how to *separate between the precious and the vile.* Now observe here,

1. The wicked proposal that Simon made, by which his hypocrisy was discovered (v. 18, 19): *When he saw that through laying on of the apostles' hands the Holy Ghost was given* (which should have confirmed his faith in the doctrine of Christ, and increased his veneration for the apostles). it gave him a notion of Christianity as no other than an exalted piece of sorcery, in which he thought himself capable of being equal to the apostles, and therefore *offered them money, saying, Give me also this power.* He does not desire them to lay their hands on him, that he might receive the Holy Ghost himself (for he did not foresee that any thing was to be got by that), but that they would convey to him a power to bestow the gift upon others. He was ambitious to have the honour of an apostle, but not at all solicitous to have the spirit and disposition of a Christian. He was more desirous to gain honour to himself than to do good to others. Now, in making this motion, (1.) He put a great affront upon the apostles, as if they were mercenary men, would do any thing for money, and loved it as well as he did; whereas they had left what they had, for Christ, so far were they from aiming to make it more. — (2.) He put a great affront upon Christianity, as if the miracles that were wrought for the proof of it were done by magic arts, only of a different nature from what he himself had practised formerly. (3.) He showed that, like Balaam, he aimed at the rewards of divination; for he would not have offered money for this power if he had not hoped to get money by it. (4.) He showed that he had a very high conceit of himself, and that he had never his heart truly humbled. Such a wretch as he had been before his baptism should have asked, like the prodigal, to be made as one of the hired servants. But, as soon as he is admitted into the family, no less a place will serve him than to be one of the stewards of the household, and to be entrusted with a power which Philip himself had not, but the apostles only.

2. The just rejection of his proposal, and the cutting reproof Peter gave him for it, v. 20–23.

(1.) Peter shows him his crime (v. 20): *Thou hast thought that the gift of God may be purchased with money;* and thus, [1.] He had overvalued the wealth of this world, as if it were an equivalent for any thing, and as if, because, as Solomon saith, *it answers all things,* relating to the life that now is, it would answer all things relating to the other life, and would purchase the pardon of sin, the gift of the Holy Ghost, and eternal life. [2.] He had undervalued the gift of the Holy Ghost and put it upon a level with the common gifts of nature and providence. He thought the power of an apostle might as well be had for a good fee as the advice of a physician or a lawyer, which was the greatest despite that could be done to the Spirit of grace. All the buying and selling of pardons and indulgences in the church of Rome is the product of this same wicked *thought, that the gift of God may be purchased with money,* when the offer of divine grace so expressly runs, *without money and without price.*

(2.) He shows him his character, which is inferred from his crime. From every thing that a man says or does amiss we cannot infer that he is a hypocrite in the profession he makes of religion; but this of Simon's was such a fundamental error as could by no means consist with a state of grace; his offering money (and that got by sorcery too) was an incontestable evidence that he was yet under the power of a worldly and carnal mind, and was yet that *natural man which receiveth not the things of the Spirit of God, neither can he know them.* And therefore Peter tells him plainly, [1.] That his heart was *not right in the sight of God,* v. 21. "Though thou professest to believe, and art baptized, yet thou art not sincere." We are as our hearts are; if they be not right, we are wrong; and they are open in the sight of God, who knows them, judges them, and judges of us by them. Our hearts are that which they are in the sight of God, who cannot be deceived; and if they be not right in his sight, whatever our pretensions be, our religion is vain, and will stand us in no stead: our great concern is to approve ourselves to him in our integrity, for otherwise we cheat ourselves into our own ruin. Some refer this particularly to the proposal he made; what he asked is denied him, because his *heart is not right in the sight of God* in asking it. He does not aim at the glory of God nor the honour of Christ in it, but to make a hand of it for himself; he *asks, and has not, because he asks amiss, that he may consume it upon his lusts,* and be still thought some great one. [2.] That he is in *the gall of bitterness, and in the bond of iniquity: I perceive that thou art so,* v. 23. This is plain dealing, and plain dealing is best when we are dealing about souls and eternity. Simon had got a great name among the people, and of late a good name too among God's people, and yet Peter here gives him a black character. Note, It is possible for a man to continue under the power of sin, and yet to put on a form of godliness. *I perceive it,* saith Peter. It was not so much by the spirit of discerning, with which Peter was endued, that he perceived this, as by Simon's discovery of it in the proposal he made. Note, The disguises of hypocrites many times are soon seen through; the nature of the wolf shows itself notwithstanding the cover of the sheep's clothing. Now the character here given of Simon is really the character of all wicked people. *First,* They are *in the gall of bitterness* — odious to God, as that which is bitter as gall is to us. Sin is an abominable thing, which the Lord hates, and sinners are by it made abominable to him; they are vicious in their own nature. Indwelling sin is *a root of bitterness,* that *bears gall and wormwood,* Deu. 29:18. The faculties are corrupted, and the mind embittered against all good, Heb. 12:15. It intimates likewise the pernicious consequences of sin; the *end is bitter as wormwood. Secondly,* They are *in the bond of iniquity* — bound over to the judgment of God by the guilt of sin, and bound under the dominion of Satan by the power of sin; led captive by him at his will, and it is a sore bondage, like that in Egypt, making the life bitter.

(3.) He reads him his doom in two things: —

[1.] He shall sink with his worldly wealth, which he overvalued: *Thy money perish with thee. First,* Hereby Peter rejects his offer with the utmost disdain and indignation: "Dost thou think thou canst bribe us to betray our trust, and to put the power we are entrusted with into such unworthy hands? Away with thee and thy money too; we will have nothing to do with either. *Get thee behind me, Satan.*" When we are tempted with money to do an evil thing, we should see what a perishing thing money is, and scorn to be biassed by it. — It is the character of the upright man that he shakes his hands from holding, from touching bribes, Isa. 33:15. *Secondly,* He warns him of his danger of utter destruction if he continued in this mind: "Thy money will perish and thou wilt lose it, and all that thou canst purchase with it. As *meats for the belly and the belly for meats* (1 Co. 6:13), so goods for money and money for goods, *but God shall destroy both it and them* — they perish in the using; but this is not the worst of it: *thou wilt perish with it, and it with thee;* and it will be an aggravation of thy ruin, and a heavy load upon thy perishing soul, that thou hadst money, which might have been made to turn to a good account (Lu. 16:9), which might have been laid at the apostles' feet, as a charity, and would have been accepted, but was thrust into their hands as a bribe, and was rejected. *Son, remember this.*"

[2.] He shall come short of the spiritual blessings which he undervalued (*v.* 21): *"Thou hast neither part nor lot in this matter;* thou hast nothing to do with the gifts of the Holy Ghost, thou dost not understand them, thou art excluded from them, hast put a bar in thine own door; thou canst not receive the Holy Ghost thyself, nor power to confer the Holy Ghost upon others, for *thy heart is not right in the sight of God,* if thou thinkest that Christianity is a trade to live by in this world, and therefore *thou hast no part nor lot* in the eternal life in the other world which the gospel offers." Note, *First,* There are many who profess the Christian religion, and yet have *no part nor lot in the matter, no part in Christ* (Jn. 13:8), *no lot in the heavenly Canaan. Secondly,* They are those whose *hearts are not right in the sight of God,* are not animated by a right spirit, nor guided by a right rule, nor directed to the right end.

(4.) He gives him good counsel, notwithstanding, *v.* 22. Though he was angry with him, yet he did not abandon him; and, though he would have him see his case to be very bad, yet he would not have him think it desperate; *yet now there is hope in Israel.* Observe,

[1.] What it is that he advises him to: He must do his first works. *First,* He must *repent,* — must see his error and retract it, — must change his mind and way, — must be humbled and ashamed for what he has done. His repentance must be particular: "Repent of this, own thyself guilty in this, and be sorry for it." He must lay a load upon himself for it, must not extenuate it, by calling it a mistake, or misguided zeal, but must aggravate it by calling it *wickedness,* his wickedness, the fruit of his own corruption. Those that have said and done amiss must, as far as they can, unsay it and undo it again by repentance. *Secondly,* He must *pray* to God, must pray that God would give him repentance, and pardon upon repentance. Penitents must pray, which implies a desire towards God, and a confidence in Christ. Simon Magus, as great a man as he thinks himself, shall not be courted into the apostles' communion (how much soever some would think it a reputation to them) upon any other terms than those upon which other sinners are admitted — repentance and prayer.

[2.] What encouragement he gives him to do this: *If perhaps the thought of thy heart,* this wicked thought of thine, *may be forgiven thee.* Note, *First,* There may be a great deal of wickedness in the thought of the heart, its false notions, and corrupt affections, and wicked projects, which must be repented of, or we are undone. *Secondly,* The thought of the heart, though ever so wicked, shall be forgiven, upon our repentance, and not laid to our charge. When Peter here puts a *perhaps* upon it, the doubt is of the sincerity of his repentance, not of his pardon if his repentance be sincere. *If indeed the thought of thy heart may be forgiven,* so it may be read. Or it intimates that the greatness of his sin might justly make the pardon doubtful, though the promise of the gospel had put the matter out of doubt, in case he did truly repent: like that (Lam. 3:29), *If so be there may be hope.*

[3.] Simon's request to them to pray for him, *v.* 24. He was startled and put into confusion by that which Peter said, finding that resented thus which he thought would have been embraced with both arms; and he cries out, *Pray you to the Lord for me, that none of the things which you have spoken come upon me.* Here was, *First,* Something well — that he was affected with the reproof given him, and terrified by the character given of him, enough to make the stoutest heart to tremble; and, this being so, he begged the prayers of the apostles for him, wishing to have an interest in them, who, he believed, had a good interest in heaven. *Secondly,* Something wanting. He begged of them to pray for him, but did not pray for himself, as he ought to have done; and, in desiring them to pray for him, his concern is more that the judgments he had made himself liable to might be prevented than that his corruptions might be mortified, and his heart, by divine grace, be made right in the sight of God; like Pharaoh, who would have Moses entreat the Lord for him, that he would take away this death only, not that he would take away this sin, this hardness of heart, Ex. 8:8; 10:17. Some think that Peter had denounced some particular judgments against him, as against Ananias and Sapphira, which, upon this submission of his, at the apostle's intercession, were prevented; or, from what is related, he might infer that some token of God's wrath would fall upon him, which he thus dreaded and deprecated.

Lastly, Here is the return of the apostles to Jerusalem, when they had finished the business they came about; for as yet they were not to disperse; but, though they came hither to do that work which was peculiar to them as apostles, yet, opportunity offering itself, they applied themselves to that which was common to all gospel ministers. 1. There, in the city of Samaria, they were preachers: *They testified the word of the Lord,* solemnly attested the truth of the gospel, and confirmed what the other ministers preached. They did not pretend to bring them any thing new, though they were apostles, but bore their testimony to the word of the Lord as they had received it. 2. In their road home they were itinerant preachers; as they passed through many villages of the Samaritans they preached the gospel. Though the congregations there were not so considerable as those in the cities, either for number or figure, yet their souls were as precious, and the apostles did not think it below them to preach the gospel to them. God has a regard to the inhabitants of his villages in Israel (Jdg. 5:11), and so should we.

Verses 26–40

We have here the story of the conversion of an Ethiopian eunuch to the faith of Christ, by whom, we have reason to think, the knowledge of Christ was sent into that country where he lived, and that scripture fulfilled, *Ethiopia shall soon stretch out her hands* (one of the first of the nations) *unto God,* Ps. 68:31.

I. Philip the evangelist is directed into the road where he would meet with this Ethiopian, *v.* 26. When the churches in Samaria were settled, and had ministers appointed them, the apostles went back to Jerusalem; but Philip stays, expecting to be employed in breaking up fresh ground in the country. And here we have, 1. Direction given him by an angel (probably in a dream or vision of the night) what course to steer: *Arise, and go towards the south.* Though angels were not employed to preach the gospel, they were often employed in carrying messages to ministers for advice and encouragement, as *ch.* 5:19. We cannot now expect such guides in our way; but doubtless there is a special providence of God conversant about the removes and settlements of ministers, and one way or other he will direct those who sincerely desire to follow him into that way in which he will own them: *he will guide them with his eye.* Philip must *go southward, to the way that leads from Jerusalem to Gaza,* through the desert or wilderness of Judah. He would never have thought of going thither, into a desert, into a common road through the desert; small probability of finding work there! Yet thither he is sent, according to our Saviour's parable, fore-telling the call of the Gentiles, *Go you into the highways, and the hedges,* Mt. 22:9. Sometimes God opens a door of opportunity to his ministers in places very unlikely. 2. His obedience to this direction (*v.* 27): *He arose and went,* without objecting, or so much as asking, "What business have I there?" Or, "What likelihood is there of doing good there?" *He went out, not knowing whither he went,* or whom he was to meet.

II. An account is given of this eunuch (*v.* 27), who and what he was, on whom this distinguishing favour was bestowed. 1. He was a foreigner, *a man of Ethiopia.* There were two Ethiopias, one in Arabia, but that lay east from Canaan; it should seem this was Ethiopia in Africa, which lay south, beyond Egypt, a great way off from Jerusalem; for *in Christ those that were afar off were made nigh,* according to the promise, *that the ends of the earth should see the great salvation.* The Ethiopians were looked upon as the meanest and most despicable of the nations, blackamoors, as if nature had stigmatized them; yet the gospel is sent to them, and divine grace looks upon them, *though they are black, though the sun has looked upon them.* 2. He was a person of quality, a great man in his own country, *a eunuch,* not in body, but in office — lord chamberlain or steward of the household; and either by the dignity of his place or by his personal character, which commanded respect, he was *of great authority,* and bore a mighty sway *under Candace queen of the Ethiopians,* who probably was successor to the queen of Sheba, who is called *the queen of the south,* that country being governed by queens, to whom *Candace* was a common name, as *Pharaoh* to the kings of Egypt. He *had the charge of all her treasure;* so great a trust did she repose in him. *Not many mighty, not many noble, are called;* but some are. 3. He was a proselyte to the Jewish religion, for *he came to Jerusalem to worship.* Some think that he was a proselyte of righteousness, who was circumcised, and kept the feasts; others that he was only a proselyte of the gate, a Gentile, but who had renounced idolatry, and worshipped the God of Israel occasionally in the court of the Gentiles; but, if so, then Peter was not the first that preached the gospel to the Gentiles, as he says he was. Some think that there were remains of the knowledge of the true God in this country, ever since the queen of Sheba's time; and probably the ancestor of this eunuch was one of her attendants, who transmitted to his posterity what he learned at Jerusalem.

III. Philip and the eunuch are brought together into a close conversation; and now Philip shall know the meaning of his being sent into a desert, for there he meets with a chariot, that shall serve for a synagogue, and one man, the conversion of whom shall be in effect, for aught he knows, the conversion of a whole nation.

1. Philip is ordered to fall into company with this traveller that is going home from Jerusalem towards Gaza, thinking he has done all the business of his journey, when the great business which the overruling providence of God designed in it was yet undone. He had been at Jerusalem, where the apostles were preaching the Christian faith, and multitudes professing it, and yet there he had taken no notice of it, and made no enquiries after it — nay, it should seem, had slighted it, and turned his back upon it; yet the grace of God pursues him, overtakes him in the desert, and there overcomes him. Thus God is often *found of those that sought him not,* Isa. 65:1. Philip has this order, not by an angel, as before, but by the Spirit whispering it in his ear (*v.* 29): *"Go near, and join thyself to this chariot;* go so near as that gentleman may take notice of thee." We should study to do good to those we light in company with upon the road: thus the lips of the righteous may feed many. We should not be so shy of all strangers as some affect to be. Of those of whom we know nothing else we know this, that they have souls.

2. He finds him reading in his Bible, as he sat in his char-

iot (*v.* 28): He *ran to him, and heard him read;* he read out, for the benefit of those that were with him, *v.* 30. He not only relieved the tediousness of the journey, but redeemed time by reading, not philosophy, history, nor politics, much less a romance or a play, but the scriptures, *the book of Esaias;* that book Christ read in (Lu. 4:17) and the eunuch here, which should recommend it particularly to our reading. Perhaps the eunuch was now reading over again those portions of scripture which he had heard read and expounded at Jerusalem, that he might recollect what he had heard. Note, (1.) It is the duty of every one of us to converse much with the holy scriptures. (2.) Persons of quality should abound more than others in the exercises of piety, because their example will influence many, and they have their time more at command. (3.) It is wisdom for men of business to redeem time for holy duties; time is precious, and it is the best husbandry in the world to gather up the fragments of time, that none be lost, to fill up every minute with something that will turn to a good account. (4.) When we are returning from public worship we should use means in private for the keeping up of the good affections there kindled, and the preserving of the good impressions there made, 1 Chr. 29:18. (5.) Those that are diligent in searching the scriptures are in a fair way to improve in knowledge; for *to him that hath shall be given.*

3. He puts a fair question to him: *Understandest thou what thou readest?* Not by way of reproach, but with design to offer him his service. Note, What we read and hear of the word of God it highly concerns us to understand, especially what we read and hear concerning Christ; and therefore we should often ask ourselves whether we understand it or no: *Have you understood all these things?* Mt. 13:51. And have you understood them aright? We cannot profit by the scriptures unless we do in some measure understand them, 1 Co. 14:16, 17. And, blessed by God, what is necessary to salvation is easy to be understood.

4. The eunuch in a sense of his need of assistance, desires Philip's company (*v.* 31): *"How can I understand,* says he, *except some one guide me?* Therefore pray come up, and sit with me." (1.) He speaks as one that had very low thoughts of himself, and his own capacity and attainments. He was so far from taking it as an affront to be asked whether he understood what he read, though Philip was a stranger, on foot, and probably looked mean (which many a less man would have done, and have called him an impertinent fellow, and bid him go about his business, what was it to him?) that he takes the question kindly, makes a very modest reply, *How can I?* We have reason to think he was an intelligent man, and as well acquainted with the meaning of scripture as most were, and yet he modestly confesses his weakness. Note, Those that would learn must see their need to be taught. The prophet must first own that he knows not what these are, and then the angel will tell him, Zec. 4:13. (2.) He speaks as one very desirous to be taught, to have some one to guide him. Observe, He read the scripture, though there were many things in it which he did not understand. Though there are many things in the scriptures which are *dark and hard to be understood,* nay, which are often misunderstood, yet we must not therefore throw them by, but study them for the sake of those things that are easy, which is the likeliest way to come by degrees to the understanding of those things that are difficult: for knowledge and grace grow gradually. (3.) He invited Philip to *come up and sit with him;* not as Jehu took Jonadab into his chariot, to come and see his zeal for the Lord of hosts (2 Ki. 10:16), but rather, "Come, see my ignorance, and instruct me." He will gladly do Philip the honour to take him into the coach with him, if Philip will do him the favour to expound a portion of scripture to him. Note, In order to our right understanding of the scripture, it is requisite we should have some one to guide us; some good books, and some good men, but, above all, the Spirit of grace, to lead us into all truth.

IV. The portion of scripture which the eunuch recited, with some hints of Philip's discourse upon it. The preachers of the gospel had a very good handle to take hold of those by who were conversant with the scriptures of the Old Testament and received them, especially when they found them actually engaged in the study of them, as the eunuch was here.

1. The chapter he was reading was the fifty-third of Isaiah, two verses of which are here quoted (*v.* 32, 33), part of the seventh and eighth verses; they are set down according to the Septuagint version, which in some things differs from the original Hebrew. Grotius thinks the eunuch read it in the Hebrew, but that Luke takes the Septuagint translation, as readier to the language in which he wrote; and he supposes that the eunuch had learned from the many Jews that were in Ethiopia both their religion and language. But, considering that the Septuagint version was made in Egypt, which was the next country adjoining to Ethiopia, and lay between it and Jerusalem, I rather think that translation was most familiar to him: it appears by Isa. 20:4 that there was much communication between those two nations — Egypt and Ethiopia. The greatest variation from the Hebrew is that what in the original is, *He was taken from prison and from judgment* (hurried with the utmost violence and precipitation from one judgment-seat to another; or, *From force and from judgment he was taken away;* that is, It was from the fury of the people, and their continual clamours, and the judgment of Pilate thereupon, that he was taken away), is here read, *In his humiliation his judgment was taken away.* He appeared so mean and despicable in their eyes that they denied him common justice, and against all the rules of equity,. to the benefit of which every man is entitled, they declared him innocent, and yet condemned him to die; nothing criminal can be proved upon him, but he is down, and down with him. Thus *in his humiliation his judgment was taken away;* so, the sense is much the same with that of the Hebrew. So that these verses foretold concerning the Messiah, (1.) That he should die, should be *led to the slaughter,* as sheep that were offered in sacrifice — that his life should be taken from among men, taken from the earth. With what little reason then was the death of Christ a stumbling-block to the unbelieving Jews, when it was so plainly foretold by their own prophets, and was so necessary to the accomplishment of his undertaking! Then is the offence of the cross ceased. (2.) That he should die wrongfully, should die by violence, should be hurried out of his life, and *his judgment shall be taken away* — no justice done to him; for he must be *cut off, but not for himself.* (3.) That he should die patiently. Like *a lamb dumb before the shearer,* nay, and before the butcher too, *so he opened not his mouth.* Never was there such an example of patience as our Lord Jesus was in his sufferings; when he was accused, when he was abused, he was silent, *reviled not again, threatened not.* (4.) That yet he should live for ever, to ages which cannot be numbered;; for so I understand those words, *Who shall declare his generation?* The Hebrew word properly signifies *the duration of one life,* Eccl. 1:4. Now who can conceive or express how long he shall continue, notwithstanding this; *for his life is taken* only *from the earth;* in heaven he shall live to endless and innumerable ages, as it follows in Isa. 53:10, *He shall prolong his days.*

2. The eunuch's question upon this is, *Of whom speaketh the prophet this? v.* 34. He does not desire Philip to give him some critical remarks upon the words and phrases, and the idioms of the language, but to acquaint him with the general scope and design of the prophecy, to furnish him with a key, in the use of which he might, by comparing one thing with another, be led into the meaning of the particular passage. Prophecies had usually in them something of obscurity, till they were explained by the accomplishment of them, as this now was. It is a material question he asks, and a very sensible one: "Does the prophet speak this of himself, in expectation of being used, being misused, as the other prophets were? or does he speak it *of some other man,* in his own age, or in some age to come?" Though the modern Jews will not allow it to be spoken of the Messiah, yet their ancient doctors did so interpret it; and perhaps the eunuch knew this, and did partly understand it so himself, only he proposed this question, to draw on discourse with Philip; for the way to improve in learning is to consult the learned. As *they must enquire the law at the mouth of the priests* (Mal. 2:7), so they must enquire the gospel, especially that part of the treasure which is hid in the field of the Old Testament, at the mouth of the ministers of Christ. The way to receive good instructions is to ask good questions.

3. Philip takes this fair occasion given him to open to him the great mystery of the gospel concerning *Jesus Christ, and him crucified.* He *began at this scripture,* took this for his text (as Christ did another passage of the same prophecy, Lu. 4:21), and *preached unto him Jesus, v.* 35. This is all the account given us of Philip's sermon, because it was the same in effect with Peter's sermons, which we have had before. The business of gospel ministers is to preach Jesus, and this is the preaching that is likely to do good. It is probable that Philip had now occasion for his gift of tongues, that he might preach Christ to this Ethiopian in the language of his own country. And here we have an instance of speaking of the things of God, and speaking of them to good purpose, not only as we *sit in the house,* but *as we walk by the way,* according to that rule, Deu. 6:7.

V. The eunuch is baptized in the name of Christ, *v.* 36–38. It is probable that the eunuch had heard at Jerusalem of the doctrine of Christ, so that it was not altogether new to him. But, if he had, what could that do towards this speedy conquest that was made of his heart for Christ. It was a powerful working of the Spirit with and by Philip's preaching that gained the point. Now here we have,

1. The modest proposal which the eunuch made of himself for baptism (*v.* 36): *As they went on their way,* discoursing of Christ, the eunuch asking more questions and Philip answering them to his satisfaction, they *came unto a certain water,* a well, river, or pond, the sight of which made the eunuch think of being baptized. Thus God, by hints of providence which seem casual, sometimes puts his people in mind of their duty, of which otherwise perhaps they would not have thought. The eunuch knew not how little a while Philip might be with him, nor where he might afterwards enquire for him. He could not expect his travelling with him to his next stage, and therefore, if Philip think fit, he will take the present convenience which offers itself of being baptized: *"See, here is water,* which perhaps we may not meet with a great while again; *what doth hinder me to be baptized?* Canst thou show any cause why I should not be admitted a disciple and follower of Christ by baptism?" Observe, (1.) He does not demand baptism, does not say, "Here is water and here I am resolved I will be baptized;" for, if Philip have any thing to offer to the contrary, he is willing to waive it for the present. If he think him not fit to be baptized, or if there be any thing in the institution of the ordinance which will not admit such a speedy administration of it, he will not insist upon it. The most forward zeal must submit to order and rule. But, (2.) He does desire it, and, unless Philip can show cause why not, he desires it now, and is not willing to defer it. Note, In the solemn dedicating and devoting of ourselves to God, it is good to make haste, and not to delay; for the present time is the best time, Ps. 119:60. Those who have received the thing signified by baptism should not put off receiving the sign. The eunuch feared lest the good affections now working in him should cool and abate, and therefore was willing immediately to bind his soul with the baptismal bonds unto the Lord, that he might bring the matter to an issue.

2. The fair declaration which Philip made him of the terms upon which he might have the privilege of baptism (*v.* 37): *"If thou believest with all thy heart, thou mayest;* that is, If thou believest this doctrine which I have preached to thee concerning Jesus, if thou receivest the record God has given concerning him, and set to thy seal that it is true." He must believe with all his heart, for with the heart man believeth, not with the head only, by an assent to gospel truths in the understanding; but with the heart, by a consent of the will to gospel terms. "If thou do indeed believe with all thy heart, thou art by that united to Christ, and, if thou give proofs and evidences that thou dost so, thou mayest by baptism be joined to the church."

3. The confession of faith which the eunuch made in order to his being baptized. It is very short, but it is comprehensive and much to the purpose, and what was sufficient: *I believe that Jesus Christ is the Son of God.* He was before a worshipper of the true God, so that all he had to do now was to *receive Christ Jesus the Lord.* (1.) He believes that Jesus is *the Christ,* the true Messiah promised, the *anointed One.* (2.) That Christ is *Jesus — a Saviour,* the only Saviour of his people from their sins. And, (3.) That this Jesus Christ is the *Son of God,* that he has a divine nature, as the Son is of the same nature with the Father; and that, being the Son of God, he is the *heir of all things.* This is the principal peculiar doctrine of Christianity, and whosoever believe this with all their hearts, and confess it, they and their seed are to be baptized.

4. The baptizing of him hereupon. The eunuch ordered his coachman to stop, *commanded the chariot to stand still.* It was the best baiting place he ever met with in any of his journeys. *They went down both into the water,* for they had no convenient vessels with them, being upon a journey, wherewith to take up water, and must therefore go down into it; not that they stripped off their clothes, and went naked into the water, but, going barefoot according to the custom, they went perhaps up to the ankles or mid-leg into the water,

and Philip sprinkled water upon him, according to the prophecy which this eunuch had probably but just now read, for it was but a few verses before those which Philip found him upon, and was very apposite to his case (Isa. 52:15): *So shall he sprinkle many nations, kings* and great men *shall shut their mouths at him,* shall submit to him, and acquiesce in him, *for that which had not* before *been told them shall they see, and that which they had not heard shall they consider.* Observe, Though Philip had very lately been deceived in Simon Magus, and had admitted him to baptism, though he afterwards appeared to be no true convert, yet he did not therefore scruple to baptize the eunuch upon his profession of faith immediately, without putting him upon a longer trial than usual. If some hypocrites crowd into the church, who afterwards prove a grief and scandal to us, yet we must not therefore make the door of admission any straiter than Christ has made it; they shall answer for their apostasy, and not we.

VI. Philip and the eunuch are separated presently; and this is as surprising as the other parts of the story. One would have expected that the eunuch should either have stayed with Philip, or have taken him along with him into his own country, and, there being so many ministers in those parts, he might be spared, and it would be worth while: but God ordered otherwise. As soon as they had *come up out of the water,* before the eunuch went into his chariot again, *the Spirit of the Lord caught away Philip* (*v.* 39), and did not give him time to make an exhortation to the eunuch, as usual after baptism, which it is probable the one intended and the other expected. But his sudden departure was sufficient to make up the want of that exhortation, for it seems to have been miraculous, and that he was *caught up* in the air in the eunuch's sight, and so carried out of his sight; and the working of this miracle upon Philip was a confirmation of his doctrine, as much as the working of a miracle by him would have been. He was *caught away, and the eunuch saw him no more,* but, having lost his minister, returned to the use of his Bible again. Now here we are told,

1. How the eunuch was disposed: He *went on his way rejoicing.* He pursued his journey. Business called him home, and he must hasten to it; for it was no way inconsistent with his Christianity, which places no sanctity nor perfection in men's being hermits or recluses, but is a religion which men may and ought to carry about with them into the affairs of this life. But he went on rejoicing; so far was he from reflecting upon this sudden revolution and change, or advancement rather, in his religion, with any regret, that his second thoughts confirmed him abundantly in it, and he went on, *rejoicing with joy unspeakable and full of glory;* he was never better pleased in all his life. He rejoiced, (1.) That he himself was joined to Christ and had an interest in him. And, (2.) That he had these good tidings to bring to his countrymen, and a prospect of bringing them also, by virtue of his interest among them, into fellowship with Christ; for he returned, not only a Christian, but a minister. Some copies read this verse thus: *And, when they were come up out of the water, the Holy Spirit fell upon the eunuch* (without the ceremony of the apostle's imposition of hands), *but the angel of the Lord caught away Philip.*

2. How Philip was disposed of (*v.* 40): *He was found at Azotus* or *Ashdod,* formerly a city of the Philistines; there the angel or Spirit of the Lord dropped him, which was about thirty miles from Gaza, whither the eunuch was going, and where Dr. Lightfoot thinks he took ship, and went by sea into his own country. But Philip, wherever he was, would not be idle. *Passing through, he preached in all the cities* till he came to Cesarea, and there he settled, and, for aught that appears, had his principal residence ever after; for at Cesarea we find him in a house of his own, *ch.* 21:8. He that had been faithful in working for Christ as an itinerant at length gains a settlement.

CHAPTER 9

In this chapter we have, I. The famous story of St. Paul's conversion from being an outrageous persecutor of the gospel of Christ to be an illustrious professor and preacher of it. I. How he was first awakened and wrought upon by an appearance of Christ himself to him as he was going upon an errand of persecution to Damascus: and what a condition he was in while he lay under the power of those convictions and terrors (*v.* 1–9). 2. How he was baptized by Ananias, by immediate directions from heaven (*v.* 10–19). 3. How he immediately commenced doctor, and preached the faith of Christ, and proved what he preached (*v.* 20–22). 4. How he was persecuted, and narrowly escaped with his life (*v.* 23–25). 5. How he was admitted among the brethren at Jerusalem: how he preached, and was persecuted there (*v.* 26–30). 6. The rest and quietness which the churches enjoyed for some time after this (*v.* 31). II. The cure wrought by Peter on Eneas, who had long been laid up with a palsy (*v.* 32–35). III. The raising of Tabitha from death to life, at the prayer of Peter (*v.* 36–43).

Verses 1–9

We found mention made of Saul twice or thrice in the story of Stephen, for the sacred penman longed to come to his story; and now we are come to it, not quite taking leave of Peter but from henceforward being mostly taken up with Paul the apostle of the Gentiles, as Peter was of the circumcision. His name in Hebrew was *Saul — desired,* though as remarkably little in stature as his namesake king Saul was tall and stately; one of the ancients calls him, *Homo tricubitalis — but four feet and a half in height;* his Roman name which he went by among the citizens of Rome was *Paul — little.* He was born in Tarsus, a city of Cilicia, a free city of the Romans, and himself a freeman of that city. His father and mother were both native Jews; therefore he calls himself a *Hebrew of the Hebrews;* he was of the tribe of Benjamin, which adhered to Judah. His education was in the schools of Tarsus first, which was a little Athens for learning; there he acquainted himself with the philosophy and poetry of the Greeks. Thence he was sent to the university at Jerusalem, to study divinity and the Jewish law. His tutor was Gamaliel, an eminent Pharisee. He had extraordinary natural parts, and improved mightily in learning. He had likewise a handicraft trade (being bred to tent-making), which was common with those among the Jews who were bred scholars (as Dr. Lightfoot saith), for the earning of their maintenance, and the avoiding of idleness. This is the young man on whom the grace of God wrought this mighty change here recorded, about a year after the ascension of Christ, or little more. We are here told,

I. How bad he was, how very bad, before his conversion; just before he was an inveterate enemy to Christianity, did his utmost to root it out, by persecuting all that embraced it. In other respects he was well enough, as *touching the righteousness which is of the law, blameless,* a man of no ill morals, but a blasphemer of Christ, a persecutor of Christians, and injurious to both, 1 Tim. 1:13. And so ill informed was his conscience that he thought he ought to do what he did against the name of Christ (*ch.* 26:9) and that he did God service in it, as was foretold, Jn. 16:2. Here we have,

1. His general enmity and rage against the Christian religion (*v.* 1): He *yet breathed out threatenings and slaughter against the disciples of the Lord.* The persons persecuted were the disciples of the Lord; because they were so, under that character he hated and persecuted them. The matter of the persecution was threatenings and slaughter. There is persecution in threatenings (*ch.* 4:17, 21); they terrify and break the spirit: and though we say, Threatened folks live long, yet those whom Saul threatened, if he prevailed not thereby to frighten them from Christ, he slew them, he persecuted them to death, *ch.* 22:4. His breathing out threatenings and slaughter intimates that it was natural to him, and his constant business. He even breathed in this as in his element. He breathed it out with heat and vehemence; his very breath, like that of some venomous creatures, was pestilential. He breathed death to the Christians, wherever he came; he puffed at them in his pride (Ps. 12:4, 5), spit his venom at them in his rage. Saul yet breathing thus intimates, (1.) That he still persisted in it; not satisfied with the blood of those he had slain, he still cries, *Give, give.* (2.) That he should shortly be of another mine; as yet he breathes out threatenings and slaughter, but he has not long to live such a life as this, that breath will be stopped shortly.

2. His particular design upon the Christians at Damascus; thither was the gospel now lately carried by those that fled from the persecution at Stephen's death, and thought to be safe and quiet there, and were connived at by those in power there: but Saul cannot be easy if he knows a Christian is quiet; and therefore, hearing that the Christians in Damascus were so, he resolves to give them disturbance. In order to this, he applies to the high priest for a commission (*v.* 1) to go to Damascus, *v.* 2. The high priest needed not to be stirred up to persecute the Christians, he was forward enough to do it; but it seems the young persecutor drove more furiously than the old one. Leaders in sin are the worst of sinners; and the proselytes which the scribes and Pharisees make often prove seven times more the children of hell than themselves. He saith (*ch.* 22:5) that this commission was had from the whole estate of the elders: and proud enough this furious bigot was to have a commission directed to him, with the seal of the great sanhedrim affixed to it. Now the commission was to empower him to enquire among the synagogues, or congregations, of the Jews that were at Damascus, whether there were any that belonged to them that inclined to favour this new sect or heresy, that believed in Christ; and if he found any such, whether men or women, to bring them up prisoners to Jerusalem, to be proceeded against according to law by the great council there. Observe, (1.) The Christians are here said to be *those of this way; those of the way,* so it is in the original. Perhaps the Christians sometimes called themselves so, from Christ *the Way;* or, because they looked on themselves as but in the way, and not yet at home; or, the enemies thus represented it as a way by itself, a by-way, a party, a faction. (2.) The high priest and sanhedrim claimed a power over the Jews in all countries, and had a deference paid to their authority in matters of religion, by all their synagogues, even those that were not of the jurisdiction of the civil government of the Jewish nation. And such a sovereignty the Roman pontiff now claims as the Jewish pontiff then did, though he has not so much to show for it. (3.) By this commission, all that worshipped God in the way that they called heresy, though agreeing exactly with the original institutes even of the Jewish church, whether they were men or women, were to be prosecuted. Even the weaker sex, who in a case of this nature might deserve excuse, or at least compassion, shall find neither with Saul any more than they do with the popish persecutors. (4.) He was ordered to bring them all bound to Jerusalem as criminals of the first magnitude, which, as it would be the more likely to terrify them, so it would be to magnify Saul, as having the command of the forces that were to carry them up, and opportunity of breathing out threatenings and slaughter. Thus was Saul employed when the grace of God wrought that great change in him. Let not us then despair of renewing grace for the conversion of the greatest sinners, nor let such despair of the pardoning mercy of God for the greatest sin; for Paul himself obtained mercy, that he might be a monument, 1 Tim. 1:13.

II. How suddenly and strangely a blessed change was wrought in him, not in the use of any ordinary means, but by miracles. The conversion of Paul is one of the wonders of the church. Here is,

1. The place and time of it: *As he journeyed, he came near to Damascus;* and there, Christ met with him.

(1.) He was in the way, travelling upon his journey; not in the temple, nor in the synagogue, nor in the meeting of the Christians, but by the way. The work of conversion is not tied to the church, though ordinarily public administrations are made use of. Some are reclaimed in slumberings on the bed (Job 33:15–17), and some in travelling upon the road alone: Thoughts are as free, and there is as good an opportunity of communing with our own hearts there, as upon the bed; and there the Spirit may set in with us, for that wind blows where it listeth. Some observe that Saul was spoken to abroad in the open air that there might be no suspicion of imposture, nor of a trick put upon him in it.

(2.) He was near Damascus, almost at his journey's end, ready to enter the city, the chief city of Syria. Some observe that he who was to be the apostle of the Gentiles was converted to the faith of Christ in a Gentile country. Damascus had been infamous for persecuting God's people formerly — they threshed Gilead with threshing instruments of iron (Amos 1:3), and now it was likely to be so again.

(3.) He was in a wicked way, pursuing his design against the Christians at Damascus, and pleasing himself with the thought that he should devour this new-born child of Christianity there. Note, Sometimes the grace of God works upon sinners when they are at the worst, and hotly engaged in the most desperate sinful pursuits, which is much for the glory both of God's pity and of his power.

(4.) The cruel edict and decree he had with him drew near to be put in execution; and now it was happily prevented, which may be considered, [1.] As a great kindness to the poor saints at Damascus, who had notice of his coming, as appears by what Ananias said (*v.* 13, 14), and were apprehensive of their danger from him, and trembled as poor lambs at the approach of a ravening wolf; Saul's conversion was their security for the present. Christ has many ways of delivering the godly out of temptation, and sometimes does it by a change wrought in their persecutors, either restraining their wrathful spirits (Ps. 76:10) and mollifying them for a time, as the Old-Testament Saul, who relented towards David more than once (1 Sa. 24:16; 26:21), or renewing their spirits, and fixing upon them durable impressions, as upon the New-Testament Saul here. [2.] It was also a very great mercy to Saul himself to be hindered from executing his wicked design, in which if he had now proceeded, perhaps it had been the filling up of the measure of his iniquity. Note, It is to be valued as a signal token of the divine favour if God, either by the inward operations of his grace or the outward occurrences of his providence, prevent us from prosecuting and executing a sinful purpose, 1 Sa. 25:32.

2. The appearance of Christ to him in his glory. Here it is only said that there *shone round about him a light from heaven;* but it appears from what follows (*v.* 17) that the Lord Jesus was in this light, and appeared to him by the way. He saw that just One (*ch.* 22:14), and see *ch.* 26:13. Whether he saw him at a distance, as Stephen saw him, in the heavens, or nearer in the air, is not certain. It is not inconsistent with what is said of the heavens receiving Christ till the end of time (*ch.* 3:21) to suppose that he did, upon such an extraordinary occasion as this, make a personal visit, but a very short one, to this lower world; it was necessary to Paul's being an apostle that he should see the Lord, and so he did, 1 Co. 9:1; 15:8. (1.) This light shone upon him *suddenly — exaiphnēs,* when Paul never thought of any such thing, and without any previous warning. Christ's manifestations of himself to poor souls are many times sudden and very surprising, and he anticipates them with the blessings of his goodness. This the disciples that Christ called to himself found. *Or ever I was aware,* Cant. 6:12. (2.) It was a light from Heaven, the fountain of light, from the God of heaven, the Father of lights. It was a light above the brightness of the sun (*ch.* 26:13), for it was visible at mid-day, and outshone the sun in his meridian strength and lustre, Isa. 24:23. (3.) It shone *round about him,* not in his face only, but on every side of him; let him turn which way he will, he finds himself surrounded with the discoveries of it. And this was designed not only to startle him, and awaken his attention (for well may he expect to hear when he is thus made to see something very extraordinary), but to signify the enlightening of his understanding with the knowledge of Christ. The devil comes to the soul in darkness; by this he gets and keeps possession of it. But Christ comes to the soul in light, for he is himself the light of the world, bright and glorious to us, as light. The first thing in this new creation, as in that of the world, is light, 2 Co. 4:6. Hence all Christians are said to be *children of the light and of the day,* Eph. 5:8.

3. The arresting of Saul, and his detachment: *He fell to the earth, v.* 4. Some think that he was on foot, and that this light, which perhaps was accompanied with a thunderclap, so terrified him that he could not keep his feet, but fell upon his face, usually a posture of adoration, but here of astonishment. It is probable that he was mounted, as Balaam, when he went to curse Israel, and perhaps better mounted than he; for Saul was now in a public post, was in haste, and the journey was long, so that it is not likely he should travel on foot. The sudden light would frighten the beast he rode on, and make it throw him; and it was God's good providence that his body got no hurt by the fall: but angels had a particular charge concerning him, to keep all his bones, so that not one of them was broken. It appears (*ch.* 26:14) that all that were with him fell to the earth as well as he, but the design was upon him. This may be considered, (1.) As the effect of Christ's appearing to him, and of the light which shone round about him. Note, Christ's manifestations of himself to poor souls are humbling; they lay them very low, in mean thoughts of themselves, and a humble submission to the will of God. Now *mine eyes see thee,* saith Job, *I abhor myself. I saw the Lord,* saith Isaiah, *sitting upon a throne, and I said, Woe is me, for I am undone.* (2.) As a step towards this intended advancement. He is designed not only to be a Christian, but to be a minister, an apostle, a great apostle, and therefore he must thus be cast down. Note, Those whom Christ designs for the greatest honours are commonly first laid low. Those who are designed to excel in knowledge and grace are commonly laid low first, in a sense of their own ignorance and sinfulness. Those whom God will employ are first struck with a sense of their unworthiness to be employed.

4. The arraigning of Saul. Being by the fall taken into custody, and as it were set to the bar, he heard a voice saying to him (and it was distinguishing, to him only, for though those that were with him heard a sound, *v.* 7, yet they knew not the words, *ch.* 22:9), *Saul, Saul, why persecutest thou me?* Observe here,

(1.) Saul not only saw a light from heaven, but heard a voice from heaven; wherever the glory of God was seen, the word of God was heard (Ex. 20:18); and to Moses (Num. 7:89); and to the prophets. God's manifestations of himself were never dumb shows, for he magnifies his word above all his name, and what was seen was alway designed to make way for what was said. Saul heard a voice. Note, Faith comes by hearing; hence the Spirit is said to be received by the hearing of faith, Gal. 3:2. The voice he heard was the voice of Christ. When he *saw that just One, he heard the voice of his mouth, ch.* 22:14. Note, The word we hear is likely to profit us when we hear it as the voice of Christ, 1 Th. 2:13. *It is the voice of my beloved;* no voice but his can reach the heart. Seeing and hearing are the two learning senses; Christ here, by both these doors, entered into Saul's heart.

(2.) What he heard was very awakening.

[1.] He was called by his name, and that doubled: *Saul, Saul.* Some think, in calling him Saul, he hints at that great persecutor of David whose name he bore. He was indeed a second Saul, and such an enemy to the Son of David as the other was to David. Calling him by his name intimates the particular regard that Christ had to him: *I have surnamed thee, though thou hast not known me,* Isa. 45:4 See Ex. 33:12. His calling him by name brought the conviction home to his conscience, and put it past dispute to whom the voice spoke this. Note, What God speaks in general is then likely to do us good when we apply it to ourselves, and insert our own names into the precepts and promises which are expressed generally, as if God spoke to us by name, and when he saith, *Ho, every one,* he had said, *Ho, such a one: Samuel, Samuel; Saul, Saul.* The doubling of it, *Saul, Saul,* intimates, *First,* The deep sleep that Saul was in; he needed to be called again and again, as Jer. 22:29, *O earth, earth, earth. Secondly,* The tender concern that the blessed Jesus had for him, and for his recovery. He speaks as one in earnest; it is like *Martha, Martha* (Lu. 10:41), or *Simon, Simon* (Lu. 22:31), or *O Jerusalem, Jerusalem,* Mt. 23:37. He speaks to him as to one in imminent danger, at the pit's brink, and just ready to drop in: "*Saul, Saul,* dost thou know whither thou art going, or what thou art doing?"

[2.] The charge exhibited against him is, *Why persecutest thou me?* Observe here, *First,* Before Saul was made a saint, he was made to see himself a sinner, a great sinner, a sinner against Christ. Now he was made to see that evil in himself which he never saw before; sin revived and he died. Note, A humbling conviction of sin is the first step towards a saving conversion from sin. *Secondly,* He is convinced of one particular sin, which he was most notoriously guilty of, and had justified himself in, and thereby way is made for his conviction of all the rest. *Thirdly,* The sin he is convinced of is persecution: *Why persecutest thou me?* It is a very affectionate expostulation, enough to melt a heart of stone. Observe, 1. The person sinning: "It is thou; thou, that art not one of the ignorant, rude, unthinking crowd, that will run down any thing they hear put into an ill name, but thou that hast had a liberal learned education, has good parts and accomplishments, hast the knowledge of the scriptures, which, if duly considered, would show thee the folly of it. It is worse in thee than in another." 2. The person sinned against: "It is I, who never did thee any harm, who came from heaven to earth to do thee good, who was not long since crucified for thee; and was not that enough, but must I afresh be crucified by thee?" 3. The kind and continuance of the sin. It was persecution, and he was at this time engaged in it: "Not only thou hast persecuted, but thou persecutest, thou persistest in it." He was not at this time hauling any to prison, nor killing them; but this was the errand he came upon to Damascus; he was now projecting it, and pleasing himself with the thought of it. Note, Those that are designing mischief are, in God's account, doing mischief. 4. The question put to him upon it: "Why dost thou do it?" (1.) It is complaining language. "Why dealest thou thus unjustly, thus unkindly, with my disciples?" Christ never complained so much of those who persecuted him in his own person as he did here of those who persecuted him in his followers. He complains of it as it was Saul's sin: "Why art thou such an enemy to thyself, to thy God?" Note, The sins of sinners are a very grievous burden to the Lord Jesus. He is grieved for them (Mk. 3:5), he is pressed under them, Amos 2:13. (2.) It is convincing language: "Why dost thou thus: Canst thou give any good reason for it?" Note, It is good for us often to ask ourselves why we do so and so, that we may discern what an unreasonable thing sin is: and of all sins none so unreasonable, so unaccountable, as the sin of persecuting the disciples of Christ, especially when it is discovered to be, as certainly it is, persecuting Christ. Those have no knowledge who eat up God's people, Ps. 14:4. *Why persecutest thou me?* He thought he was persecuting only a company of poor, weak, silly people, that were an offence and eye-sore to the Pharisees, little imagining that is was one in heaven that he was all this while insulting; for surely, if he had known, he would not have persecuted the Lord of glory. Note, Those who persecute the saints persecute Christ himself, and he takes what is done against them as done against himself, and accordingly will be the judgment in the great day, Mt. 25:45.

5. Saul's question upon his indictment, and the reply to it, *v.* 5.

(1.) He makes enquiry concerning Christ: *Who art thou, Lord?* He gives no direct answer to the charge preferred against him, being convicted by his own conscience, and self-condemned. If God contend with us for our sins, we are not able to answer for one of a thousand, especially such a one as the sin of persecution. Convictions of sin, when they are set home with power upon the conscience, will silence all excuses and self-justifications. *Though I were righteous, yet would I not answer.* But he desires to know who is his judge; the compellation is respectful: *Lord.* He who had been a blasphemer of Christ's name now speaks to him as his Lord. The question is proper: *Who art thou?* This implies his present unacquaintedness with Christ; he knew not his voice as his own sheep do, but he desired to be acquainted with him; he is convinced by this light which encloses him that it is one from heaven that speaks to him, and he has a veneration for every thing that appears to him to come from heaven; and therefore, *Lord, who art thou? What is thy name?* Jdg. 13:17; Gen. 32:29. Note, there is some hope of people when they begin to enquire after Jesus Christ.

(2.) He has an answer immediately, in which we have,

[1.] Christ's gracious revelation of himself to him. He is always ready to answer the serious enquiries of those who covet an acquaintance with him: *I am Jesus whom thou persecutest.* The name of Jesus was not unknown to him; his heart had risen against it many a time, and gladly would he bury it in oblivion. He knew it was the name that he persecuted, but little did he think to hear it from heaven, or from the midst of such a glory as now shone round about him. Note, Christ brings souls into fellowship with himself by manifesting himself to them. He said, *First, I am Jesus, a Saviour; I am Jesus of Nazareth,* so it is, *ch.* 22:8. Saul used to call him so when he blasphemed him: "I am that very Jesus whom thou usedst to call in scorn *Jesus of Nazareth.*" And he would show that now that he is in his glory he is not ashamed of his humiliation. *Secondly, "I am that Jesus whom thou persecutest,* and therefore it will be at thy peril if thou persist in this wicked course." There is nothing more effectual to awaken and humble the soul than to see sin to be against Christ, an affront to him, and a contradiction to his designs.

[2.] His gentle reproof of him: *It is hard for thee to kick against the pricks,* or *goads* — to spurn at the spur. It is hard, it is in itself an absurd and evil thing, and will be of fatal consequence to him that does it. Those kick at the goad that stifle and smother the convictions of conscience, that rebel against God's truths and laws, that quarrel with his providences, and that persecute and oppose his ministers, because they reprove them, and their words are as goads and as nails. Those that revolt more and more when they are stricken by the word or rod of God, that are enraged at reproofs and fly in the face of their reprovers, kick against the pricks and will have a great deal to answer for.

6. His surrender of himself to the Lord Jesus at length, *v.* 6. See here,

(1.) The frame and temper he was in, when Christ had been dealing with him. [1.] He trembled, as one in a great fright. Note, Strong convictions, set home by the blessed Spirit, will make an awakened soul to tremble. How can those choose but tremble that are made to see the eternal God provoked against them, the whole creation at war with them, and their own souls upon the brink of ruin! [2.] He was astonished, was filled with amazement, as one brought into a new world, that knew not where he was. Note, The convincing, converting, work of Christ is astonishing to the awakened soul, and fills it with admiration. "What is this that God has done with me, and what will he do?"

(2.) His address to Jesus Christ, when he was in this frame: *Lord, what wilt thou have me to do?* This may be taken, [1.] As a serious request for Christ's teachings: "Lord, I see I have hitherto been out of the way; thou hast shown me my error, set me to rights; thou hast discovered sin to me, discover to me the way to pardon and peace." It is like that, *Men and brethren, what must we do?* Note, A serious desire to be instructed by Christ in the way of salvation is an evidence of a good work begun in the soul. Or, [2.] As a sincere resignation of himself to the direction and government of the Lord Jesus. This was the first word that grace spoke in Paul, and with this began a spiritual life: Lord Jesus, *What wilt thou have me to do?* Did not he know what he had to do? Had he not his commission in his pocket? And what had he to do but to execute it? No, he had done enough of this work already, and resolves now to change his master, and employ himself better. Now it is not, What will the high priest and the elders have me to do? What will my own wicked appetites and passions have me to do? But, *What wilt thou have me to do?* The great change in conversion is wrought upon the will, and consists in the resignation of that to the will of Christ.

(3.) The general direction Christ gave him, in answer to this: *Arise, go into the city of Damascus,* which thou art now near to, *and it shall be told thee what thou must do.* It is encouragement enough to have further instruction promised him, but, [1.] He must not have it yet; it shall be told him shortly what he must do, but, for the present, he must pause upon what has been said to him, and improve that. Let him consider awhile what he has done in persecuting Christ, and be deeply humbled for that, and then he shall be told what he has further to do. [2.] He must not have it in this way, by a voice from heaven, for it is plain that he cannot bear it; he trembles, and is astonished. He shall be told therefore what he must do by a man like himself, whose terror shall not make him afraid, nor his hand be heavy upon him, which Israel desired at mount Sinai. Or, it is an intimation that Christ would take some other time to manifest himself further to him, when he was more composed, and this fright pretty well over. Christ manifests himself to his people by degrees; and both what he does and would he have them to do, though they know not now, they shall know hereafter.

7. How far his fellow travellers were affected with this, and what impression it made upon them. They fell to the earth, as he did, but rose without being bidden, which he did not, but lay still till it was said to him, *Arise;* for he lay under a heavier load than any of them did; but when they were up, (1.) *They stood speechless,* as men in confusion, and that was all, *v.* 7. They were going on the same wicked errand that Paul was, and perhaps, to the best of their power, were as spiteful as he; yet we do not find that any of them were converted, though they saw the light, and were struck down and struck dumb by it. No external means will of themselves work a change in the soul, without the Spirit and grace of God, which distinguish between some and others; among these that journeyed together, one is taken, and the others left. *They stood speechless;* none of them said, *Who art thou, Lord?* or, *What wilt thou have me to do?* as Paul did, but none of God's children are born dumb. (2.) *They heard a voice, but saw no man;* they heard Paul speak, but saw not him to whom he spoke, nor heard distinctly what was said to him: which reconciles it with what is said of this matter, *ch.* 22:9, where it is said, *They saw the light and were afraid* (which they might do and yet see no man in the light, as Paul did), and *that they heard not the voice of him that spoke to Paul,* so as to understand what he said, though they did hear a confused noise. Thus those who came hither to be the instruments of Paul's rage against the church serve for witnesses of the power of God over him.

8. What condition Saul was in after this, *v.* 8, 9. (1.) *He arose from the earth,* when Christ commanded him, but probably not without help, the vision had made him so faint and weak, I will not say like Belshazzar, when the joints of his loins were loosed and his knees smote one against another, but like Daniel, when upon the sight of a vision no strength remained in him, Dan. 10:16–17. (2.) *When his eyes were opened,* he found that his sight was gone, and *he saw no man,* none of the men that were with him, and began now to be busy about him. It was not so much this glaring light that, *by dazzling his eyes, had dimmed them — Nimium sensibile laedit sensum;* for then those with him would have lost their sight too; but it was a sight of Christ, whom the rest saw not, that had this effect upon him. Thus a believing sight of the glory of God in the face of Christ dazzles the eyes to all things here below. Christ, in order to the further discovery of himself and his gospel to Paul, took him off from the sight of other things, which he must look off, that he may look unto Jesus, and to him only. (3.) *They led him by the hand into Damascus;* whether to a public house, or to some friend's house, is not certain; but thus he who thought to have led the disciples of Christ prisoners and captives to Jerusalem was himself led a prisoner and a captive to Christ into Damascus. He was thus taught what need he had of the grace of Christ to lead his soul (being naturally blind and apt to mistake) into all truth. (4.) He lay *without sight,* and without food, *neither did eat nor drink for three days, v.* 9. I do not think, as some do, that now he had his rapture into the third heavens, which he speaks of, 2 Co. 12. So far from this that we have reason to think he was all this time rather in the belly of hell, suffering God's terrors for his sins, which were now set in order before him: he was in the dark concerning his own spiritual state, and was so wounded in spirit for sin that he could relish neither meat nor drink.

Verses 10–22

As for God, his work is perfect; if he begin, he will make an end: a good work was begun in Saul, when he was brought to Christ's feet, in that word, *Lord, what wilt thou have me to do?* And never did Christ leave any that were brought to that. Though Saul was sadly mortified when he lay three days blind, yet he was not abandoned. Christ here takes care of the work of his own hands. He that hath torn will heal — that hath smitten will bind up — that hath convinced will comfort.

I. Ananias is here ordered to go and look after him, to heal and help him; for he that causeth grief will have compassion.

1. The person employed is *Ananias, a certain disciple at Damascus,* not lately driven thither from Jerusalem, but a native of Damascus; for it is said (*ch.* 22:12) *that he had a good report of all the Jews who dwelt there, as a devout man according to the law;* he had lately embraced the gospel, and given up his name to Christ, and, as it should seem, officiated as a minister, at least *pro hac vice — on this occasion,* though it does not appear that he was apostolically ordained. But why were not some of the apostles from Jerusalem sent for upon this great occasion, or Philip the evangelist, who had lately baptized the eunuch, and might have been fetched hither by the Spirit in a little time? Surely, because Christ would employ variety of hands in eminent services, that the honours might not be monopolized nor engrossed by a few, — because he would put work into the hands, and thereby put honour upon the heads, of those that were mean and obscure, to encourage them, — and because he would direct us to make much of the ministers that are where our lot is cast, if they have ordained mercy to be faithful, though they are not of the most eminent.

2. The direction given him is to go and enquire at such a house, probably an inn, for one *Saul of Tarsus.* Christ, in a vision, called to Ananias by name, *v.* 10. It is probable it was not the first time that he had heard the words of God, and seen the visions of the Almighty; for, without terror or confusion, he readily answers, *"Behold I am here, Lord,* ready to go wherever thou sendest me, and to do whatever thou biddest me." *Go then,* saith Christ, *into the street which is called Straight, and enquire in the house of Judas* (where strangers used to lodge) *for one called Saul of Tarsus.* Note, Christ very well knows where to find out those that are his, in their distresses: when their relations, it may be, know not what is become of them, they have a friend in heaven, that knows in what street, in what house, nay, and which is more, in what frame they are: he knows their souls in adversity.

3. Two reasons are given him why he must go and enquire for this stranger, and offer him his service: —

(1.) Because he prays, and his coming to him must answer his prayer. This is a reason, [1.] Why Ananias needed not to be afraid of him, as we find he was, *v.* 13, 14. There is no question, saith Christ, but he is a true convert, *for behold he prayeth. Behold* denotes the certainty of it: "Assure thyself it is so; go and see." Christ was so pleased to find Paul praying that he must have others to take notice of it: *Rejoice with me, for I have found the sheep which I had lost.* It denotes also the strangeness of it: "Behold, and wonder, that he who but the other day breathed nothing but threatenings and slaughter, now breathes nothing but prayer." But was it such a strange thing for Saul to pray? Was he not a Pharisee? and have we not reason to think he did, as the rest of them did, make long prayers in the synagogues and the corners of the streets? Yes; but now he began to pray after another manner than he had done; then he said his prayers, now he prayed them. Note, Regenerating grace evermore sets people on praying; you may as soon find a living man without breath as a living Christian without prayer; if breathless, lifeless; and so, if prayerless, graceless. [2.] As a reason why Ananias must go to him with all speed. It is no time to linger, *for behold he prayeth:* if the child cry, the tender nurse will hasten to it with the breast. Saul here, like Ephraim, is bemoaning himself, as a bullock unaccustomed to the yoke, and kicking against the goad. "Oh! go to him quickly, and tell him he is a dear son, a pleasant child, and *since I spoke against him,* for persecuting me, *I do earnestly remember him still."* Jer. 31:18–20. Observe what condition Saul was now in. He was under conviction of sin, trembling and astonished; the setting of sin in order before us should drive us to prayer. He was under a bodily affliction, blind and sick; and, *Is any afflicted? Let him pray.* Christ had promised him that it should be further told him what he should do (*v.* 6), and he prays that one may be sent to him to instruct him. Note, What God has promised we must pray for; he will for this be enquired of, and particularly for divine instruction.

(2.) Because he hath seen in a vision such a man coming to him, to restore him to his sight; and Ananias's coming to him must answer his dream, for it was of God (*v.* 12): *He hath seen in a vision a man named Ananias,* and just such a man as thou art, *coming in* seasonably for his relief, *and putting his hand on him that he might receive his sight.* Now this vision which Paul had may be considered, [1.] As an immediate answer to his prayer, and the keeping up of that communion with God which he had entered into by prayer. He had, in prayer, spread the misery of his own case before God, and God presently manifests himself and the kind intentions of his grace to him; and it is very encouraging to know God's thoughts to us-ward. [2.] As designed to raise his expectations, and to make Ananias's coming more welcome to him. He would readily receive him as a messenger from God when he was told beforehand, in vision, that one of that name would come to him. See what a great thing it is to bring a spiritual physician and his patient together: here were two visions in order to it. When God, in his providence, does it without visions, brings a messenger to the afflicted soul, an interpreter, one among a thousand, to show unto man his uprightness, it must be acknowledged with thankfulness to his praise.

II. Ananias objects against going to him, and the Lord answers the objection. See how condescendingly the Lord admits his servant to reason with him.

1. Ananias pleads that this Saul was a notorious persecutor of the disciples of Christ, *v.* 13, 14. (1.) He had been so at Jerusalem: *"Lord, I have heard by many of this man,* what a malicious enemy he is to the gospel of Christ: all those that were scattered upon the late persecution, many of whom are come to Damascus, tell *how much evil he hath done to thy saints in Jerusalem,* that he was the most virulent, violent persecutor of all, and a ringleader in the mischief — what havoc he has made in the church: there was no man they were more afraid of, no, not the high priest himself, than of Saul; nay," (2.) "His errand to Damascus at this time is to persecute us Christians: *Here he has authority from the chief priests to bind all that call on thy name,* to treat the worshippers of Christ as the worst of criminals." Now, why does Ananias object this. Not, "There-fore I do not owe him so much service. Why should I do him a kindness who has done and designed us so much unkindness?" No, Christ has taught us another lesson, to render good for evil, and pray for our persecutors; but if he be such a persecutor of Christians, [1.] Will it be safe for Ananias to go to him? Will he not throw himself like a lamb into the mouth of a lion? And, if he thus bring himself into trouble, he will be blamed for his indiscretion. [2.] Will it be to any purpose to go to him? Can such a hard heart ever be softened, or such an Ethiopian ever change his skin?

2. Christ overrules the objection (*v.* 15, 16): "Do not tell me how bad he has been, I know it very well; but go thy way

with all speed, and give him all the help thou canst, *for he is a chosen vessel,* or instrument, unto me; I design to put confidence in him, and then thou needest not fear him." He was a vessel in which the gospel-treasure should be lodged, in order to the conveyance of it to many; an earthen vessel (2 Co. 4:7), but a chosen vessel. The vessel God uses he himself chooses; and it is fit he should himself have the choosing of the instruments he employs (Jn. 15:16): *You have not chosen me, but I have chosen you.* He is a vessel of honour, and must not be neglected in his present forlorn condition, nor thrown away as a despised broken vessel, or a vessel in which there is no pleasure. He is designed, (1.) For eminent services: *He is to bear my name before the Gentiles,* is to be the apostle of the Gentiles, and to carry the gospel to heathen nations. Christ's name is the standard to which souls must be gathered, and under which they must be enlisted, and Saul must be a standard-bearer. He must bear Christ's name, must bear witness to it before kings, king Agrippa and Caesar himself; nay, he must bear it before the children of Israel, though there were so many hands already at work about them. (2.) For eminent sufferings (*v.* 16): *I will show him how great things he must suffer for my name's sake.* He that has been a persecutor shall be himself persecuted. Christ's showing him this intimates either his bringing him to these trials (as Ps. 60:3), *Thou hast shown thy people hard things,* or his giving notice of them beforehand, that they might be no surprise to him. Note, Those that bear Christ's name must expect to bear the cross for his name; and those that do most for Christ are often called out to suffer most for him. Saul must suffer great things, this, one would think, was a cold comfort for a young convert; but it is only like telling a soldier of a bold and brave spirit, when he is enlisted, that he shall take the field, and enter upon action, shortly. Saul's sufferings for Christ shall redound so much to the honour of Christ and the service of the church, shall be so balanced with spiritual comforts and recompensed with eternal glories, that it is no discouragement to him to be told how great things he must suffer for Christ's name's sake.

III. Ananias presently goes on Christ's errand to Saul, and with good effect. He had started an objection against going to him, but, when an answer was given to it, he dropped it, and did not insist upon it. When difficulties are removed, what have we to do but to go on with our work, and not hang upon an objection?

1. Ananias delivered his message to Saul, *v.* 17. Probably he found him in bed, and applied to him as a patient. (1.) *He put his hands on him.* It was promised, as one of the signs that should follow those that believe, that they should lay hands on the sick, and they should recover (Mk. 16:18), and it was for that intent that he put his hands on him. Saul came to lay violent hands upon the disciples at Damascus, but here a disciple lays a helping healing hand upon him. *The bloodthirsty hate the upright, but the just seek his soul.* (2.) He called him *brother,* because he was made a partaker of the grace of God, though not yet baptized; and his readiness to own him as a brother intimated to him God's readiness to own him as a son, though he had been a blasphemer of God and a persecutor of his children. (3.) He produces his commission from the same hand that had laid hold on him by the way, and now had him in custody. "That *same Jesus that appeared unto thee in the way as thou camest,* and convinced thee of thy sin in persecuting him, has now sent me to thee to comfort thee." *Una eademque manus vulnus opemque tulit — The hand that wounded heals.* "His light struck thee blind, but he *hath sent me to thee that thou mightest receive thy sight;* for the design was not to blind thine eyes, but to dazzle them, that thou mightest see things by another light: he that then put clay upon thine eyes hath sent me to wash them, that they may be cured." Ananias might deliver his message to Saul very appositely in the prophet's words (Hos. 6:1, 2): *Come and turn to the Lord, for he hath torn and he will heal thee; he hath smitten, and he will bind thee up; now after two days he will revive thee, and the third day he will raise thee up, and thou shalt live in his sight.* Corrosives shall be no more applied, but lenitives. (4.) He assures him that he shall not only have his sight restored, but be filled with the Holy Ghost: he must himself be an apostle, and must in nothing come behind the chief of the apostles, and therefore must receive the Holy Ghost immediately, and not, as others did, by the interposition of the apostles; and Ananias's putting his hands upon him before he was baptized was for the conferring of the Holy Ghost.

2. Ananias saw the good issue of his mission. (1.) In Christ's favour to Saul. At the word of Ananias, Saul was discharged from his confinement by the restoring of his sight; for Christ's commission to open the prison to those that were bound (Isa. 61:1) is explained by the giving of sight to the blind, Lu. 4:18; Isa. 42:7. Christ's commission is to open the blind eyes, and to bring out the prisoners from the prison. Saul is delivered from the spirit of bondage by receiving sight (*v.* 18), which was signified by the falling of scales from his eyes; and this immediately, and forthwith: the cure was sudden, to show that it was miraculous. This signified the recovering of him, [1.] From the darkness of his unconverted state. When he persecuted the church of God, and walked in the spirit and way of the Pharisees, he was blind; he saw not the meaning either of the law or of the gospel, Rom. 7:9. Christ often told the Pharisees that they were blind, and could not make them sensible of it; they said, *We see,* Jn. 9:41. Saul is saved from his Pharisaical blindness, by being made sensible of it. Note, Converting grace opens the eyes of the soul, and makes the scales to fall from them (*ch.* 26:18), to open men's eyes, and turn them from darkness to light: this was what Saul was sent among the Gentiles to do, by the preaching of the gospel, and therefore must first experience it in himself. [2.] From the darkness of his present terrors, under the apprehension of guilt upon his conscience, and the wrath of God against him. This filled him with confusion, during those three days he sat in darkness, like Jonah for three days in the belly of hell; but now the scales fell from his eyes, the cloud was scattered, and the Sun of righteousness rose upon his soul, with healing under his wings. (2.) In Saul's subjection to Christ: He was baptized, and thereby submitted to the government of Christ, and cast himself upon the grace of Christ. Thus he was entered into Christ's school, hired into his family, enlisted under his banner, and joined himself to him for better for worse. The point was gained: it is settled; Saul is now a disciple of Christ, not only ceases to oppose him, but devotes himself entirely to his service and honour.

IV. The good work that was begun in Saul is carried on wonderfully; this new-born Christian, though he seemed *as one born out of due time,* yet presently comes to maturity.

1. He received his bodily strength, *v.* 19. He had continued three days fasting, which, with the mighty weight that was all that time upon his spirits, had made him very weak; but, *when he had received meat, he was strengthened, v.* 19. The Lord is for the body, and therefore care must be taken of it, to keep it in good plight, that it may be fit to serve the soul in God's service, and that Christ may be magnified in it, Phil. 1:20.

2. He associated with the disciples that were at Damascus, fell in with them, conversed with them, went to their meetings, and joined in communion with them. He had lately *breathed out threatenings and slaughter against them,* but now breathes love and affection to them. Now *the wolf dwells with the lamb,* and *the leopard lies down with the kid,* Isa. 11:6. Note, Those that take God for their God take his people for their people. Saul associated with the disciples, because now he saw an amiableness and excellency in them, because he loved them, and found that he improved in knowledge and grace by conversing with them; and thus he made profession of his Christian faith, and openly declared himself a disciple of Christ, by associating with those that were his disciples.

3. *He preached Christ in the synagogues, v.* 20. To this he had an extraordinary call, and for it an extraordinary qualification, God having immediately revealed his Son to him and in him, that he might preach him, Gal. 1:15, 16. He was so full of Christ himself, that *the Spirit within him constrained him* to preach him to others, and, like Elihu, *to speak that he might be refreshed,* Job 32:20. Observe, (1.) Where he preached — in the synagogues of the Jews, for they were to have the first offer made them. The synagogues were their places of concourse; there he met with them together, and there they used to preach against Christ and to punish his disciples, by the same token that Paul himself *had punished them oft in every synagogue* (*ch.* 26:11), and therefore there he would face the enemies of Christ where they were most daring, and openly profess Christianity where he had most opposed it. (2.) What he preached: *He preached Christ.* When he began to be a preacher, he fixed this for his principle, which he stuck to ever after: *We preach not ourselves, but Christ Jesus our Lord;* nothing but Christ, and him crucified. He preached concerning Christ, *that he is the Son of God,*

his beloved Son, in whom he is well pleased, and with us in him, and not otherwise. (3.) How people were affected with it (*v.* 21): *All that heard him were amazed, and said, "Is not this he that destroyed those who called on this name in Jerusalem,* and now does he call on this name himself, and persuade others to call upon it, and strengthen the hands of those that do?" *Quantum mutatus ab illo! — Oh how changed! Is Saul also among the prophets?* Nay, did he not come hither for that intent, to seize all the Christians he could find, and *bring them bound to the chief priests?* Yes, he did. Who would have thought then that he would ever preach Christ as he does? Doubtless this was looked upon by many as a great confirmation of the truth of Christianity, that one who had been such a notorious persecutor of it came, on a sudden, to be such an intelligent, strenuous, and capacious preacher of it. This miracle upon the mind of such a man outshone the miracles upon men's bodies; and giving a man such another heart was more than giving men to speak with other tongues.

4. He confuted and confounded those that opposed the doctrine of Christ, *v.* 22. He signalized himself, not only in the pulpit, but in the schools, and showed himself supernaturally enabled, not only to preach the truth, but to maintain and defend it when he had preached it. (1.) He increased in strength. He became more intimately acquainted with the gospel of Christ, and his pious affections grew more strong. He grew more bold and daring and resolute in defence of the gospel: *He increased the more* for the reflections that were cast upon him (*v.* 21), in which his new friends upbraided him as having been a persecutor, and his old friends upbraided him as being now a turncoat; but Saul, instead of being discouraged by the various remarks made upon his conversion, was thereby so much the more emboldened, finding he had enough at hand wherewith to answer the worst they could say to him. (2.) He ran down his antagonists, and *confounded the Jews who dwelt in Damascus;* he silenced them, and shamed them — answered their objections to the satisfaction of all indifferent persons, and pressed them with arguments which they could make no reply to. In all his discourses with the Jews he was still *proving that this Jesus is very Christ, is the Christ, the anointed of God, the true Messiah promised to the fathers.* He was proving it, *symbibazōn — affirming it and confirming it,* teaching with persuasion. And we have reason to think he was instrumental in converting many to the faith of Christ, and building up the church at Damascus, which he went thither to make havoc of. Thus *out of the eater came forth meat, and out of the strong sweetness.*

Verses 23–31

Luke here makes no mention of Paul's journey into Arabia, which he tells us himself was immediately after his conversion, Gal. 1:16, 17. As soon as God *had revealed his Son in him, that he might preach him,* he went not up to Jerusalem, to receive instructions from the apostles (as any other convert would have done, that was designed for the ministry), but he went to Arabia, where there was new ground to break up, and where he would have opportunity of teaching, but not learning; thence he returned to Damascus, and there, three years after his conversion, this happened, which is here recorded.

I. He met with difficulties at Damascus, and had a narrow escape of being killed there. Observe, 1. What his danger was (*v.* 23): *The Jews took counsel to kill him,* being more enraged at him than at any other of the preachers of the gospel, not only because he was more lively and zealous in his preaching than any of them, and more successful, but because he had been such a remarkable deserter, and his being a Christian was a testimony against them. It is said (*v.* 24), *The Jews watched the gates day and night to kill him;* they incensed the governor against him, as a dangerous man, who therefore kept the city with a guard to apprehend him, at his going out or coming in, 2 Co. 11:32. Now Christ showed Paul *what great things he must suffer for his name* (*v.* 16), when here was presently the government in arms against him, which was a great thing, and, as all his other sufferings afterwards, helped to make him considerable. Saul was no sooner a Christian than a preacher, no sooner a preacher than a sufferer; so quickly did he rise to the summit of his preferment. Note, Where God gives great grace he commonly exercises it with great trials. 2. How he was delivered. (1.) The design against him was discovered: *Their lying in wait was known of Saul,* by some intelligence, whether from heaven or from men we are not told. (2.) The disciples contrived to help him away — hid him, it is likely, by day; and in the night, the gates being watched, that he could not get away through them, *they let him down by the wall, in a basket,* as he himself relates it (2 Co. 11:33), *so he escaped out of their hands.* This story, as it shows us that when we enter into the way of God we must look for temptation, and prepare accordingly, so it shows us *that the Lord knows how to deliver the godly out of temptation, and will with the temptation also make a way to escape, that we may* not be by it deterred nor driven from the way of God.

II. He met with difficulties at Jerusalem the first time he went thither, *v.* 26. He came to Jerusalem. This is thought to be that journey to Jerusalem of which he himself speaks (Gal. 1:18): *After three years I went up to Jerusalem,* saith he, *to see Peter, and abode with him fifteen days.* But I rather incline to think that this was a journey before that, because *his coming in* and *going out, his preaching and disputing* (*v.* 28, 29), seem to be more than would consist with his fifteen days' stay (for that was no more) and to require a longer time; and, besides, now he came a stranger, but then he came, *historēsai — to confer with Peter,* as one he was intimate with; however, it might possibly be the same. Now observe,

1. How shy his friends were of him (*v.* 26): *When he came to Jerusalem,* he did not go to the chief priests and the Pharisees (he had taken his leave of them long since), but *he assayed to join himself to the disciples.* Wherever he came, he owned himself one of that despised persecuted people, and associated with them. They were now in his eyes *the excellent ones of the earth, in whom was all his delight.* He desired to be acquainted with them, and to be admitted into communion with them; but they looked strange upon him, shut the door against him, and would not go about any of their religious exercises if he were by, for *they were afraid of him.* Now might Paul be tempted to think himself in an ill case, when the Jews had abandoned and persecuted him, and the Christians would not receive and entertain him. Thus does he fall into divers temptations, and needs the armour of righteousness, as we all do, both on the right hand and on the left, that we may not be discouraged either by the unjust treatment of our enemies or the unkind treatment of our friends. (1.) See what was the cause of their jealousy of him: *They believed not that he was a disciple,* but only pretended to be so, and came among them as a spy or an informer. They knew what a bitter persecutor he had been, with what fury he went to Damascus some time ago; they had heard nothing of him since, and therefore thought he was but a wolf in sheep's clothing. The disciples of Christ had need to be cautious whom they admit into communion with them. *Believe not every spirit.* There is need of the wisdom of the serpent, to keep the mean between the extremes of suspicion on the one hand and credulity on the other; yet methinks it is safer to err on the charitable side, because it is an adjudged case that it is better the tares should be found among the wheat than that the wheat should any of it be rooted up and thrown out of the field. (2.) See how it was removed (*v.* 27): *Barnabas took him to the apostles* themselves, who were not so scrupulous as the inferior disciples, *to whom he first assayed to join himself, and he declared to them,* [1.] What Christ had done for him: *He had shown himself to him in the way* and spoken to him; and what he said. [2.] What he had since done for Christ: *He had preached boldly at Damascus in the name of Jesus.* How Barnabas came to know this, more than the rest of them, we are not told; whether he had himself been at Damascus, or had had letters thence, or discoursed with some of that city, by which he came to the knowledge of this; or whether he had formerly been acquainted with Paul in the Grecian synagogues, or at the feet of Gamaliel, and had such an account of his conversion from himself as he saw cause enough to give credit to: but so it was that, being satisfied himself, he gave satisfaction to the apostles concerning him, he having brought no testimonials from the disciples at Damascus, thinking *he needed not, as some others, epistles of commendation,* 2 Co. 3:1. Note, The introducing of a young convert into the communion of the faithful is a very good work, and one which, as we have opportunity, we should be ready to do.

2. How sharp his enemies were upon him. (1.) He was admitted into the communion of the disciples, which was no little provocation to his enemies. It vexed the unbelieving Jews to see Saul a trophy of Christ's victory, and a captive to his grace, who had been such a champion for their cause — to see him *coming in, and going out, with the apostles* (*v.* 28), and to hear them glorying in him, or rather glorifying God in him. (2.) He appeared vigorous in the cause of Christ, and this was yet more provoking to them (*v.* 29): *He spoke boldly in the name of the Lord Jesus.* Note, Those that speak for Christ have reason to speak boldly; for they have a good cause, and speak for one who will at last speak for himself and them too. The Grecians, or Hellenist Jews, were most offended at him, because he had been one of them; and they drew him into a dispute, in which, no doubt, he was too hard for them, as he had been for the Jews at Damascus. One of the martyrs said, Though she could not dispute for Christ, she could die for Christ; but Paul could do both. Now the Lord Jesus divided the spoils of the strong man armed in Saul. For that same natural quickness and fervour of spirit which, while he was in ignorance and unbelief, made him a furious bigoted persecutor of the faith, made him a most zealous courageous defender of the faith. (3.) This brought him into peril of his life, with which he narrowly escaped: *The Grecians,* when they found they could not deal with him in disputation, contrived to silence him another way; *they went about to slay him,* as they did Stephen when *they could not resist the Spirit by which he spoke, ch.* 6:10. That is a bad cause that has recourse to persecution for its last argument. But notice was given of this conspiracy too, and effectual care taken to secure this young champion (*v.* 30): *When the brethren knew* what was designed against him *they brought him down to Cesarea.* They remembered how the putting of Stephen to death, upon his disputing with the Grecians, had been the beginning of a sore persecution; and therefore were afraid of having such a vein opened again, and hastened Paul out of the way. He that flies may fight again. He that fled from Jerusalem might do service at Tarsus, the place of his nativity; and thither they desired him by all means to go, hoping he might there go on in his work with more safety than at Jerusalem. Yet it was also by direction from heaven that he left Jerusalem at this time, as he tells us himself (*ch.* 22:17, 18), that Christ now appeared to him, and ordered him to *go quickly out of Jerusalem,* for he must be sent *to the Gentiles, v.* 15. Those by whom God has work to do shall be protected from all the designs of their enemies against them till it be done. Christ's witnesses cannot be slain till they have *finished their testimony.*

III. The churches had now a comfortable gleam of liberty and peace (*v.* 31): *Then had the churches rest. Then,* when Saul was converted, so some; when that persecutor was taken off, those were quiet whom he used to irritate, and then those were quiet whom he used to molest. Or, *then,* when he had gone from Jerusalem, the fury of the Grecian Jews was a little abated, and they were the more willing to bear with the other preachers now that Saul had gone out of the way. Observe,

1. *The churches had rest.* After a storm comes a calm. Though we are always to expect troublesome times, yet we may expect that they shall not last always. This was a breathing-time allowed them, to prepare them for the next encounter. The churches that were already planted were mostly in Judea, Galilee, and Samaria, within the limits of the holy land. There were the first Christian churches, where Christ had himself laid the foundation.

2. They made a good use of this lucid interval. Instead of growing more secure and wanton in the day of their prosperity, they abounded more in their duty, and made a good use of their tranquillity. (1.) They *were edified,* were built up in their most holy faith; the more free and constant enjoyment they had of the means of knowledge and grace, the more they increased in knowledge and grace. (2.) They *walked in the fear of the Lord* — were more exemplary themselves for a holy heavenly conversation. They so lived that all who conversed with them might say, Surely the fear of God reigns in those people. (3.) They *walked in the comfort of the Holy Ghost* — were not only faithful, but cheerful, in religion; they stuck to the ways of the Lord, and sang in those ways. *The comfort of the Holy Ghost* was their consolation, and that which they made their chief joy. They had recourse to the comfort of the Holy Ghost, and lived upon that, not only in days of trouble and affliction, but in days of rest and prosperity. The comforts of the earth, when they had the most free and full enjoyment of them, could not content them without the comfort of the Holy Ghost. Observe the connection of these two: when they walked *in the fear of the Lord,* then they walked *in the comfort of the Holy Ghost.* Those are most likely to walk cheerfully that walk circumspectly.

3. God blessed it to them for their increase in number: They *were multiplied.* Sometimes the church multiplies the more for its being afflicted, as Israel in Egypt; yet if it were always so, the saints of the Most High would be worn out. At other times its rest contributes to its growth, as it enlarges the opportunity of ministers, and invites those in who at first are afraid of suffering. Or, *then,* when *they walked in the fear of God and his comforts, they were multiplied.* Thus those that will not be won by the word may be won by the conversation of professors.

Verses 32–35

Here we have, I. The visit Peter made to the churches that were newly planted by the dispersed preachers, *v.* 32. 1. He *passed through all quarters.* As an apostle, he was not to be the resident pastor of any one church, but the itinerant visitor of many churches, to confirm the doctrine of inferior preachers, to confer *the Holy Ghost on those that believed,* and to ordain ministers. He passed *dia pantōn — among them all,* who pertained to the churches of Judea, Galilee, and Samaria, mentioned in the foregoing chapter. He was, like his Master, always upon the remove, and *went about doing good;* but still his head-quarters were at Jerusalem, for there we shall find him imprisoned, *ch.* 12:2. *He came to the saints at Lydda.* This seems to be the same with *Lod,* a city in the tribe of Benjamin, mentioned 1 Chr. 8:12; Ezra 2:33. The Christians are called *saints,* not only some particular eminent ones, as saint Peter and saint Paul, but every sincere professor of the faith of Christ. These are the saints on the earth, Ps. 16:3.

II. The cure Peter wrought on *Eneas,* a man that had been bedridden eight years, *v.* 33. 1. His case was very deplorable: *He was sick of the palsy,* a dumb palsy, perhaps a dead palsy. The disease was extreme, for *he kept his bed;* it was inveterate, for he kept his bed *eight years;* and we may suppose that both he himself and all about him despaired of relief for him, and concluded upon no other than that he must still keep his bed till he removed to his grave. Christ chose such patients as this, whose disease was incurable in a course of nature, to show how desperate the case of fallen mankind was when he undertook their cure. When we were without strength, as this poor man, *he sent his word to heal us.* 2. His cure was very admirable, *v.* 34. (1.) Peter interested Christ in his case, and engaged him for his relief: *Eneas, Jesus Christ maketh thee whole.* Peter does not pretend to do it himself by any power of his own, but declares it to be Christ's act and deed, directs him to look up to Christ for help, and assures him of an *immediate* cure — not, "He *will* make thee," but, "He *does* make thee, whole;" and a *perfect* cure — not, "He makes thee *easy,*" but "He makes thee *whole.*" He does not express himself by way of prayer to Christ that he would make him whole, but as one having authority from Christ, and that knew his mind, he declares him made whole. (2.) He ordered him to bestir himself, to exert himself: *"Arise and make thy bed,* that all may see thou art thoroughly cured." Let none say that because it is Christ that by the power of his grace works all our works in us therefore we have no work, no duty, to do; for, though Jesus Christ makes thee whole, yet thou must arise and make use of the power he gives thee: *"Arise, and make thy bed,* to be to thee no longer a bed of sickness, but a bed of rest." (3.) Power went along with this word: he arose immediately, and no doubt very willingly made his own bed.

III. The good influence this had upon many (*v.* 35): *All that dwelt at Lydda and Saron saw him, and turned to the Lord.* We can scarcely think that every individual person in those countries took cognizance of the miracle, and was wrought upon by it; but many, the generality of the people in the town of Lydda and in the country of Saron, or Sharon, a fruitful plain or valley, of which it was foretold, *Sharon shall be a fold of flocks,* Isa. 65:10. 1. They all made enquiry into the truth of the miracle, did not overlook it, but saw him that was healed, and saw that it was a miraculous cure that was wrought upon him by the power of Christ, in his name, and with a design to confirm and ratify that doctrine of Christ which was now preached to the world. 2. They all submitted to the convincing proof and evidence there was in this of the divine origin of the Christian doctrine, and *turned to the Lord,* to the Lord Jesus. They turned from Judaism to Christianity; they embraced the doctrine of Christ, and submitted to his ordinances, and turned themselves over to him to be ruled and taught and saved by him.

Verses 36–43

Here we have another miracle wrought by Peter, for the confirming of the gospel, and which exceeded the former — the raising of Tabitha to life when she had been for some time dead. Here is,

I. The life, and death, and character of Tabitha, on whom this miracle was wrought, *v.* 36, 37. 1. She lived at Joppa, a sea-port town in the tribe of Dan, where Jonah took shipping to go to Tarshish, now called *Japho.* 2. Her name was *Tabitha,* a Hebrew name, the Greek for which is *Dorcas,* both signifying a *doe,* or *hind,* or *deer,* a pleasant creature. *Naphtali* is compared to *a hind let loose, giving goodly words;* and the wife to the kind and tender husband is as the loving *hind,* and as the pleasant *roe,* Prov. 5:19. 3. She was a disciple, one that had embraced the faith of Christ and was baptized; and not only so, but was eminent above many for works of charity. She showed her faith by her works, her good works, which she was full of, that is, in which she abounded. Her head was full of cares and contrivances which way she should do good. She *devised liberal things,* Isa. 32:8. Her hands were full of good employment; she made a business of doing good, was never idle, having learned to *maintain good works* (Tit. 3:8), to keep up a constant course and method of them. She was *full of good works,* as a tree that is full of fruit. Many are full of good words, who are empty and barren in good works; but Tabitha was a great doer, no great talker: *Non magna loquimur, sed vivimus — We do not talk great things, but we live them.* Among other good works, she was remarkable for her *alms-deeds, which she did,* not only her works of piety, which are good works and the fruits of faith, but works of charity and beneficence, flowing from love to her neighbour and a holy contempt of this world. Observe, She is commended not only for the alms which she gave, but for the alms-deeds which she did. Those that have not estates wherewith to give in charity may yet be able to do in charity, working with their hands, or walking with their feet, for the benefit of the poor. And those who will not do a charitable deed, whatever they may pretend, if they were rich would not bestow a charitable gift. She was full of alms-deeds, *hōn epoiei — which she made;* there is an emphasis upon her *doing* them, because what her hand found to do of this kind she did with all her might, and persevered in. They were alms-deeds, not which she purposed and designed and said she would do, but which she did; not which she began to do, but which she did, which she went through with, which she performed the doing of, 2 Co. 8:11; 9:7. This is the life and character of a certain disciple,; and should be of all the disciples of Christ; for, if we thus bear much fruit, then are we his disciples indeed, Jn. 15:8. 4. She was removed in the midst of her usefulness (*v.* 37): *In those days she fell sick, and died.* It is promised to those who consider the poor, not that they shall never be sick, but that the Lord will *strengthen them upon the bed of languishing,* at least with strength in their souls, and so will *make all their bed in their sickness,* will make it easy, Ps. 41:1, 3. They cannot hope that they shall never die *(merciful men are taken away,* and merciful women too, witness Tabitha), but they may hope that they shall *find mercy of the Lord in that day,* 2 Tim. 1:18. 5. Her friends and those about her did not presently bury her, as usual, because they were in hopes Peter would come and raise her to life again; but they *washed the dead body,* according to the custom, which, it is said, was with warm water, which, if there were any life remaining in the body, would recover it; so that this was done to show that she was really and truly dead. They tried all the usual methods to bring her to life, and could not. *Conclamatum est — the last cry was uttered.* They *laid her out* in her grave-clothes *in an upper chamber,* which Dr. Lightfoot thinks was probably the public meeting-room for the believers of that town; and they laid the body there, that Peter, if he would come, might raise her to life the more solemnly in that place.

II. The request which her Christian friends sent to Peter to come to them with all speed, not to attend the funeral, but, if it might be, to prevent it, *v.* 38. Lydda, where Peter now was, was nigh to Joppa, and the disciples at Joppa had heard that Peter was there, and that he had raised Eneas from a bed of languishing; and therefore they *sent him two men,* to make the message the more solemn and respectful, *desiring him that he would not delay to come to them;* not telling him the occasion, lest he should modestly decline coming upon so great an errand as to raise the dead: if they can but get him to them, they will leave it to him. Their friend was dead, and it was too late to send for a physician, but not too late to send for Peter. *Post mortem medicus — a physician after death,* is an absurdity, but not *Post mortem apostolus — an apostle after death.*

III. The posture in which he found the survivors, when he came to them (*v.* 30): *Peter arose and went with them.* Though they did not tell him what they wanted him for, yet he was willing to go along with them, believing it was upon some good account or other that he was sent for. Let not faithful ministers grudge to be at every body's beck, as far as they have ability, when the great apostle *made himself the servant of all,* 1 Co. 9:19. He found the corpse laid in the upper chamber, and attended by widows, probably such as were in the communion of the church, poor widows; there they were,

1. Commending the deceased — a good work, when there was that in them which was truly commendable, and worthy of imitation, and when it is done modestly and soberly, and without flattery of the survivors or any sinister intention, but purely for the glory of God and the exciting of others to that which is virtuous and praiseworthy. The commendation of Tabitha was like her own virtues, not in word, but in deed. Here were no encomiums of her in orations, nor poems inscribed to her memory; but *the widows showed the coats and garments which she made* for them, and bestowed upon them *while she was with them.* It was the comfort of Job, while he lived, that the loins of the poor blessed him, because they were warmed with the fleece of his sheep, Job 31:20. And here it was the credit of Tabitha, when she was dead, that the backs of the widows praised her for the garments which she made them. And those are certainly best praised *whose own works praise them in the gates,* whether the words of others do or no. It is much more honourable to clothe a company of decrepit widows with needful clothing for night and day, who will pray for their benefactors when they do not see them, than to clothe a company of lazy footmen with rich liveries, who perhaps behind their backs will curse those that clothe them (Eccl. 7:21); and it is what all that are wise and good will take a greater pleasure in, for goodness is true greatness, and will pass better in the account shortly. Observe, (1.) Into what channel Tabitha turned much of her charity. Doubtless there were other instances of her alms-deeds which she did, but this was now produced; she did, as it should seem with her own hands, *make coats and garments* for poor widows, who perhaps with their own labour could make a shift to get their bread, but could not earn enough to buy clothes. And this is an excellent piece of charity, *If thou seest the naked, that thou cover him* (Isa. 58:7), and not think it enough to say, *Be ye warmed,* James 2:15, 16. (2.) What a grateful sense the poor had of her kindness: *They showed the coats,* not ashamed to own that they were indebted to her for the clothes on their backs. Those are horribly ungrateful indeed who have kindness shown them and will not make at least an acknowledgment of it, by showing the kindness that is done them, as these widows here did. Those who receive alms are not obliged so industriously to conceal it, as those are who give alms. When the poor reflect upon the rich as uncharitable and unmerciful, they ought to reflect upon themselves, and consider whether they are not unthankful and ungrateful. Their showing the coats and garments which Dorcas made tended to the praise not only of her charity, but of her industry, according to the character of the virtuous woman, that she *lays her hands to the spindle,* or at least to the needle, and then *stretches out her hand to the poor,* and *reaches forth her hands to the needy,* of what she has worked; and, when God and the poor have thus had their due, *she makes herself coverings of tapestry* and *her* own *clothing is silk and purple,* Prov. 31:19–22.

2. They were here lamenting the loss of her: The widows stood by Peter, weeping. When the merciful are taken away, it should be laid to heart, especially by those to whom they have been in a particular manner merciful. They need not weep for her; she is taken from the evil to come, *she rests from her labours and her works follow her,* besides those she leaves behind her: but they weep for themselves and for their children, who will soon find the want of such a good woman, that has not left her fellow. Observe, They take notice of what good Dorcas did *while she was with them,* but now she is gone from them, and this is their grief. Those that are charitable will find that the *poor they have always with them;* but it is well if those that are poor find that they have always the charitable with them. We must make a good use of the lights that yet a little while are with us, because they will not be always with us, will not be long with us: and when they are gone we shall think what they did when they were with us. It should seem, the widows wept before Peter, as an inducement to him, if he could do any thing, to have compassion on them and help them, and restore one to them that used to have compassion on them. When charitable people are dead, there is no praying them to life again; but, when they are sick, this piece of gratitude is owing to them, to pray for their recovery, that, if it be the will of God, those may be spared to live who can ill be spared to die.

IV. The manner in which she was raised to life. 1. Privately: She was laid in the upper room where they used to have their public meetings, and, it should seem, there was great crowding about the dead body, in expectation of what would be done; *but Peter put them all forth,* all the weeping widows, all but some few relations of the family, or perhaps the heads of the church, to join with him in prayer; as Christ did, Mt. 9:25. Thus Peter declined every thing that looked like vainglory and ostentation; they came to see, but he did not come to be seen. He put them all forth, that he might with the more freedom pour out his soul before God in prayer upon this occasion, and not be disturbed with their noisy and clamorous lamentations. 2. By prayer. In his healing Eneas there was an implied prayer, but in this greater work he addressed himself to God by solemn prayer, as Christ when he raised Lazarus; but Christ's prayer was with the authority of a Son, who *quickens whom he will;* Peter's with the submission of a servant, who is under direction, and therefore he *knelt down and prayed.* 3. By the word, a quickening word, a word which is spirit and life: *He turned to the body,* which intimates that when he prayed he turned from it; lest the sight of it should discourage his faith, he looked another way, to teach us, like Abraham, *against hope, to believe in hope,* and overlook the difficulties that lie in the way, *not considering the body as now dead,* lest we should *stagger at the promise,* Rom. 4:19, 20. But, when he had prayed, he *turned to the body,* and spoke in his Master's name, according to his example: *"Tabitha, arise;* return to life again." Power went along with this word, and she came to life, *opened her eyes* which death had closed. Thus, in the raising of dead souls to spiritual life, the first sign of life is the opening of the eyes of the mind, *ch.* 26:18. When she saw Peter, she sat up, to show that she was really and truly alive; and (*v.* 41) *he gave her his hand and lifted her up,* not as if she laboured under any remaining weakness, but thus he would as it were welcome her to life again, and give her the right hand of fellowship among the living, from whom she had been cut off. And, *lastly,* he *called the saints and widows,* who were all in sorrow for her death, and *presented her alive* to them, to their great comfort, particularly of the widows, who laid her death much to heart (*v.* 41); to them he presented her, as Elijah (1 Ki. 17:23), and Elisha (2 Ki. 4:36), and Christ (Lu. 7:15), presented the dead sons alive to their mothers. The greatest joy and satisfaction are expressed by life from the dead.

V. The good effect of this miracle. 1. Many were by it convinced of the truth of the gospel, that is was from heaven, and not of men, and believed in the Lord, *v.* 42. The thing was *known throughout all Joppa;* it would be in every body's mouth quickly, and, it being a town of seafaring men, the notice of it would be the sooner carried thence to other countries, and though some never minded it many were wrought upon by it. This was the design of miracles, to confirm a divine revelation. 2. Peter was hereby induced to continue some time in this city, *v.* 43. Finding that a door of opportunity was opened for him there, he tarried there many days, till he was sent thence, and sent for thence upon business to another place. He tarried not in the house of Tabitha, though she was rich, lest he should seem to seek his own glory; but he took up his lodgings with one Simon a tanner, an ordinary tradesman, which is an instance of his condescension and humility: and hereby he has taught us not to *mind high things, but to condescend to those of low estate,* Rom. 12:16. And, though Peter might seem to be buried in obscurity here in the house of a poor tanner by the sea-side, yet hence God fetched him to a noble piece of service, which is recorded in the next chapter; for *those that humble themselves shall be exalted.*

CHAPTER 10

It is a turn very new and remarkable which the story of this chapter gives to the Acts of the apostles; hitherto, both at Jerusalem and every where else where the ministers of Christ came, they preached the gospel only to the Jews, or those Greeks that were circumcised and proselyted to the Jews' religion; but now, "Lo, we turn to the Gentiles;" and to them the door of faith is here opened: good news indeed to us sinners of the Gentiles. The apostle Peter is the man that is first employed to admit uncircumcised Gentiles into the Christian church; and Cornelius, a Roman centurion or colonel, is the first that with his family and friends is so admitted. Now here we are told, I. How Cornelius was directed by a vision to send for Peter, and did send for him accordingly (*v.* 1–8). II. How Peter was directed by a vision to go to Cornelius, though he was a Gentile, without making any scruple of it, and did go accordingly (*v.* 9–23). III. The happy interview between Peter and Cornelius at Cesarea (*v.* 24–33). IV. The sermon Peter preached in the house of Cornelius to him and to his friends (*v.* 34–43). V. The baptizing of Cornelius and his friends with the Holy Ghost first, and then with water (*v.* 44–48).

Verses 1–8

The bringing of the gospel to the Gentiles, and the bringing of those who had been strangers and foreigners to be fellow-citizens with the saints, and of the household of God, were such a mystery to the apostles themselves, and such a surprise (Eph. 3:3, 6), that it concerns us carefully to observe all the circumstances of the beginning of this great work, this part of the *mystery of godliness — Christ preached to the Gentiles, and believed on in this world,* 1 Tim. 3:16. It is not unlikely that some Gentiles might before now have stepped into a synagogue of the Jews, and heard the gospel preached; but the gospel was never yet designedly preached to the Gentiles, nor any of them baptized — Cornelius was the first; and here we have,

I. An account given us of this Cornelius, who and what he was, who was the first-born of the Gentiles to Christ. We are here told that he was a great man and a good man — two characters that seldom meet, but here they did; and where they do meet they put a lustre upon each other: goodness makes greatness truly valuable, and greatness makes goodness much more serviceable. 1. Cornelius was an officer of the army, *v.* 1. He was at present quartered in Cesarea, a strong city, lately re-edified and fortified by Herod the Great, and called *Cesarea* in honour of Augustus Caesar. It lay upon the sea-shore, very convenient for the keeping up of a correspondence between Rome and its conquests in those parts. The Roman governor or pro-consul ordinarily resided here, *ch.* 23:23, 24; 25:6. Here there was a band, or cohort, or regiment, of the Roman army, which probably was the governor's life-guard, and is here called *the Italian band,* because, that they might be the more sure of their fidelity, they were all native Romans, or Italians. Cornelius had a command in this part of the army. His name, *Cornelius* was much used among the Romans, among some of the most ancient and noble families. He was an officer of considerable rank and figure, a centurion. We read of one of that rank in our Saviour's time, of whom he gave a great commendation, Mt. 8:10. When a Gentile must be pitched upon to receive the gospel first, it is not a Gentile philosopher, much less a Gentile priest (who are bigoted to their notions and worship, and prejudiced against the gospel of Christ), but a Gentile soldier, who is a man of more free thought; and he that truly is so, when the Christian doctrine is fairly set before him, cannot but receive it and bid it welcome. Fishermen, unlearned and ignorant men, were the first of the Jewish converts, but not so of the Gentiles; for the world shall know that the gospel has that in it which may recommend it to men of polite learning and a liberal education, as we have reason to think this centurion was. Let not soldiers and officers of the army plead that their employment frees them from the restraints which some others are under, and, giving them an opportunity of living more at large, may excuse them if they be not religious; for here was an officer of the army that embraced Christianity, and yet was neither turned out of his place nor turned himself out. And, *lastly,* it was a mortification to the Jews that not only the Gentiles were taken into the church, but that the first who was taken in was an officer of the Roman army, which was to them *the abomination of desolation.* 2. He was, according to the measure of the light he had, a religious man. It is a very good character that is given of him, *v.* 2. He was no idolater, no worshipper of false gods or images, nor allowed himself in any of those immoralities to which the greater part of the Gentile world were given up, to punish them for their idolatry. (1.) He was possessed with a principle of regard to the true and living God. He was *a devout man and one that feared God.* He believed in one God, the Creator of heaven and earth, and had a reverence for his glory and authority, and a dread of offending him by sin; and, though he was a soldier, it was no diminution to the credit of his valour to tremble before God. (2.) He kept up religion in his family. He *feared God with all his house.* He would not admit any idolaters under his roof, but took care that not himself only, but all his, should serve the Lord. Every good man will do what he can that those about him may be good too. (3.) He was a very charitable man: He *gave much alms to the people,* the people of the Jews, notwithstanding the singularities of their religion. Though he was a Gentile, he was willing to contribute to the relief of one that was a real object of charity, without asking what religion he was of. (4.) He was much in prayer: He *prayed to God always.* He kept up stated times for prayer, and was constant to them. Note, Wherever the fear of God rules in the heart, it will appear both in works of charity and of piety, and neither will excuse us from the other.

II. The orders given him from heaven, by the ministry of an angel, to send for Peter to come to him, which he would never have done if he had not been thus directed to do it. Observe,

1. How, and in what way, these orders were given him. He had a vision, in which an angel delivered them to him. It was about the *ninth hour of the day,* at three of the clock in the afternoon, which is with us an hour of business and conversation; but then, because it was in the temple the time of offering the evening sacrifice, it was made by devout people an *hour of prayer,* to intimate that all our prayers are to be offered up in the virtue of the great sacrifice. Cornelius was now at prayer: so he tells us himself, *v.* 30. Now here we are told, (1.) That an angel of God *came in to him.* By the brightness of his countenance, and the manner of his coming in, he knew him to be something more than a man, and therefore nothing less than an angel, an express from heaven. (2.) That he *saw him evidently* with his bodily eyes, not in a dream presented to his imagination, but in a vision presented to his sight; for his greater satisfaction, it carried its own evidence along with it. (3.) That he called him by his name, *Cornelius,* to intimate the particular notice God took of him. (4.) That this put Cornelius for the present into some confusion (*v.* 4): *When he looked on him he was afraid.* The wisest and best men have been struck with fear upon the appearance of any extra-ordinary messenger from heaven; and justly, for sinful man knows that he has no reason to expect any good tidings thence. And therefore Cornelius cries, "*What is it, Lord?* What is the matter?" This he speaks as one afraid of something amiss, and longing to be eased of that fear, by knowing the truth; or as one desirous to know the mind of God, and ready to comply with it, as Joshua: *What saith my Lord unto his servant?* And Samuel: *Speak, for thy servant heareth.*

2. What the message was that was delivered to him.

(1.) He is assured that God accepts him in walking according to the light he had (*v.* 4): *Thy prayers and thine alms are come up for a memorial before God.* Observe, Prayers and alms must go together. We must follow our prayers with alms; for the fast that God hath chosen is to *draw out the soul to the hungry,* Isa. 58:6, 7. It is not enough to pray that what we have may be sanctified to us, but we must *give alms of such things as we have;* and then, behold, all things are clean to us, Lu. 11:41. And we must follow our alms with our prayers that God would graciously accept them, and that they may be blessed to those to whom they are given. Cornelius prayed, and gave alms, not as the Pharisees, *to be seen of men,* but in sincerity, as unto God; and he is here told that they were *come up for a memorial before God.* They were upon record in heaven, in the book of remembrance that is written there for all that fear God, and shall be remembered to his advantage: "Thy prayers shall be answered, and thine alms recompensed." The sacrifices under the law are said to be *for a memorial.* See Lev. 2:9, 16; 5:12; 6:15. And prayers and alms are our spiritual offerings, which God is pleased to take cognizance of, and have regard to. The divine revelation communicated to the Jews, as far as the Gentiles were concerned in it, not only as it directed and improved the light and law of nature, but as it promised a Messiah to come, Cornelius believed and submitted to. What he did he did in that faith, and was accepted of God in it; for the Gentiles, to whom the law of Moses came, were not obliged to become circumcised Jews, as those to whom the gospel of Christ comes are to become baptized Christians.

(2.) He is appointed to enquire after a further discovery of divine grace, now lately made to the world, *v.* 5, 6. He must *send* forthwith *to Joppa, and enquire for one Simon Peter; he lodgeth at the house of one Simon a tanner; his house is by the sea side,* and, if he be sent for, he will come; and *when he comes he shall tell thee what thou oughtest to do,* in answer to thy question, *What is it, Lord?* Now here are two things very surprising, and worthy our consideration: — [1.] Cornelius prays and gives alms in the fear of God, is religious himself and keeps up religion in his family, and all this so as to be accepted of God in it, and yet there is something further that he ought to do — he ought to embrace the Christian religion, now that God has established it among men. Not, He may do it if he pleases; it will be an improvement and entertainment to him. But, He must do it; it is indispensably necessary to his acceptance with God for the future, though he has been accepted in his services hitherto. He that believed the promise of the Messiah must now believe the performance of that promise. Now that God has given a further record concerning his Son than what had been given in the Old-Testament prophecies he requires that we receive this when it is brought to us; and now neither our prayers nor our alms can come up for a memorial before God unless we believe in Jesus Christ, for it is that further which we ought to do. *This is his commandment, that we believe.* Prayers and alms are accepted from those that believe that the Lord is God, and have not opportunity of knowing more; but, from those to whom it is preached that Jesus is Christ, it is necessary to the acceptance of their persons, prayers, and alms, that they believe this, and rest upon him alone for acceptance. [2.] Cornelius has now an angel from heaven talking to him, and yet he must not receive the gospel of Christ from this angel, nor be told by him what he ought to do, but all that the angel has to say is, "Send for Peter, and he shall tell thee." As the former observation puts a mighty honour upon the gospel, so does this upon the gospel ministry: it was not to the highest of angels, but to those who were less that the least of all saints, that this grace was given, *to preach among the Gentiles the unsearchable riches of Christ* (Eph. 3:8), that the excellency of the power might be of God, and the dignity of an institution of Christ supported; for *unto the angels hath he not put in subjection the world to come* (Heb. 2:5), but to the Son of man as the sovereign, and the sons of men as his agents and ministers of state, whose *terrors shall not make us afraid, nor their hand be heavy upon us,* as this angel's now was to Cornelius. And as it was an honour to the apostle that he must preach that which an angel might not, so it was a further honour that an angel was despatched on purpose from heaven to order him to be sent for. To bring a faithful minister and a willing people together is a work worthy of an angel, and what therefore the greatest of men should be glad to be employed in.

III. His immediate obedience to these orders, *v.* 7, 8. He sent with all speed to Joppa, to fetch Peter to him. Had he himself only been concerned, he would have gone to Joppa to him. But he had a family, and kinsmen, and friends (*v.* 24), a little congregation of them, that could not go with him to Joppa, and therefore he sends for Peter. Observe, 1. When he sent: As soon as ever the *angel which spoke unto him had departed,* without dispute or delay, he was obedient to the heavenly vision. He perceived, by what the angel said, he was to have some further work prescribed him, and he longed to have it told him. He made haste, and delayed not, to do this commandment. In any affair wherein our souls are concerned it is good for us not to lose time. 2. Whom he sent: *Two of his household servants,* who all feared God, *and a devout soldier,* one of those *that waited on him continually.* Observe, a devout centurion had devout soldiers. A little devotion commonly goes a great way with soldiers, but there would be more of it in the soldiers if there were but more of it in the commanders. Officers in an army, that have such a great power over the soldiers, as we find the centurion had (Mt. 8:9), have a great opportunity of promoting religion, at least of restraining vice and profaneness, in those under their command, if they would but improve it. Observe, When this centurion had to choose some of his soldiers to attend his person, and to be always about him, he pitched upon such of them as were devout; they shall be preferred and countenanced, to encourage others to be so. He went by David's rule (Ps. 101:6), *Mine eye shall be upon the faithful in the land, that they may dwell with me.* 3. What instructions he gave them (*v.* 8): *He declared all these things unto them,* told them of the vision he had, and the orders given him to send for Peter, because Peter's coming was a thing in which they were concerned, for they had souls to save as well as he. Therefore he does not only tell them where to find Peter (which he might have thought it enough to do — the *servant knows not what his Lord doeth),* but he tells them on what errand he was to come, that they might importune him.

Verses 9–18

Cornelius had received positive orders from heaven to send for Peter, whom otherwise he had not heard of, or at least not heeded; but here is another difficulty that lies in the way of bringing them together — the question is whether Peter will come to Cornelius when he is sent for; not as if he thought it below him to come at a beck, or as if he were afraid to preach his doctrine to a polite man as Cornelius was: but it sticks at a point of conscience. Cornelius is a very worthy man, and has many good qualities, but he is a Gentile, he is not circumcised; and, because God in his law had forbidden his people to associate with idolatrous nations, they would not keep company with any but those of their own religion, though they were ever so deserving, and they carried the matter so far that they made even the involuntary touch of a Gentile to contract a ceremonial pollution, Jn. 18:28. Peter had not got over this stingy bigoted notion of his countrymen, and therefore will be shy of coming to Cornelius. Now, to remove this difficulty, he has a vision here, to prepare him to receive the message sent him by Cornelius, as Ananias had to prepare him to go to Paul. The scriptures of the Old Testament had spoken plainly of the bringing in of the Gentiles into the church. Christ had given plain intimations of it when he ordered them to *teach all nations;* and yet even Peter himself, who knew so much of his Master's mind, could not understand it, till it was here revealed by vision, *that the Gentiles should be fellow-heirs,* Eph. 3:6. Now here observe,

I. The circumstances of this vision.

1. It was when the messengers sent from Cornelius were now *nigh the city, v.* 9. Peter knew nothing of their approach, and they knew nothing of his praying; but he that knew both him and them was preparing things for the interview, and facilitating the end of their negotiation. To all God's purposes *there is a time,* a proper time; and he is pleased often to bring things to the minds of his ministers, which they had not thought of, just then when they have occasion to use them.

2. It was when *Peter went up upon the house-top to pray,* about noon. (1.) Peter was much in prayer, much in secret prayer, though he had a great deal of public work upon his hands. (2.) He prayed *about the sixth hour,* according to David's example, who, not only *morning and evening,* but *at noon,* addressed himself to God by prayer, Ps. 55:17. From morning to night we should think to be too long to be without meat; yet who thinks it is too long to be without prayer? (3.) He prayed *upon the house-top;* thither he retired for privacy, where he could neither hear nor be heard, and so might avoid both distraction and ostentation. There, upon the roof of the house, he had a full view of the heavens, which might assist his pious adoration of the God he prayed to; and there he had also a full view of the city and country, which might assist his pious compassion of the people he prayed for. (4.) He had this vision immediately after he had prayed, as an answer to his prayer for the spreading of the gospel, and because the ascent of the heart to God in prayer is an excellent preparative to receive the discoveries of the divine grace and favour.

3. It was when he became *very hungry,* and was waiting for his dinner (*v.* 10); probably he had not that day eaten before, though doubtless he had prayed before; and now *he would have eaten, ēthele geusasthai — he would have tasted,* which intimates his great moderation and temperance in eating. When he was very hungry, yet he would be content with a little, with a taste, and would not *fly upon the spoil.* Now this hunger was a proper inlet to the vision about meats, as Christ's hunger in the wilderness was to Satan's temptation to turn stones into bread.

II. The vision itself, which was not so plain as that to Cornelius, but more figurative and enigmatical, to make the deeper impression. 1. He *fell into a trance or ecstasy,* not of terror, but of contemplation, with which he was so entirely swallowed up as not only not to be regardful, but not to be sensible, of external things. He quite lost himself to this world, and so had his mind entirely free for converse with divine things; as Adam in innocency, when the deep sleep fell upon him. The more clear we get of the world, the more near we get to heaven: whether Peter was now *in the body or out of the body* he could not himself tell, much less can we, 2 Co. 12:2, 3. See Gen. 15:12; Acts 22:17. 2. He *saw heaven opened,* that he might be sure that his authority to go to Cornelius was indeed from heaven — that it was a divine light which altered his sentiments, and a divine power which gave him his commission. The opening of the heavens signified the opening of a mystery that had been hid, Rom. 16:25. 3. He saw *a great sheet full of all manner of living creatures, which descended from heaven, and was let down to him to the earth,* that is, to the roof of the house where he now was. Here were not only beasts of the earth, but fowls of the air, which might have flown away, laid at his feet; and not only tame beasts, but wild. Here were no fishes of the sea, because there were none of them in particular unclean, but whatever had fins and scales was allowed to be eaten. Some make this sheet, thus filled, to represent the church of Christ. It comes down from heaven, from heaven opened, not only to send it down (Rev. 21:2), but to receive souls sent up from it. It is knit at the four corners, to receive those from all parts of the world that are willing to be added to it; and to retain and keep those safe that are taken into it, that they may not fall out; and in this we find some of all countries, nations, and languages, without any distinction of Greek or Jew, or any disadvantage put upon Barbarian or Scythian, Col. 3:11. The net of the gospel encloses all, both bad and good, those that before were clean and unclean. Or it may be applied to the bounty of the divine Providence, which, antecedently to the prohibitions of the ceremonial law, had given to man a liberty to use all the creatures, to which by the cancelling of that law we are now restored. By this vision we are taught to see all the benefit and service we have from the inferior creatures coming down to us from heaven; it is the gift of God who made them, made them fit for us, and then gave to man a right to them, and dominion over them. Lord, what is man that he should be thus magnified! Ps. 8:4–8. How should it double our comfort in the creatures, and our obligations to serve God in the use of them, to see them thus let down to us out of heaven! 4. He was ordered by a voice from heaven to make use of this plenty and variety which God had sent him (*v.* 13): *"Rise, Peter, kill and eat:* without putting any difference between clean and unclean, take which thou hast most mind to." The distinction of meats which the law made was intended to put a difference between Jew and Gentile, that it might be difficult to them to dine and sup with a Gentile, because they would have that set before them which they were not allowed to eat; and now the taking off of that prohibition was a plain allowance to converse with the Gentiles, and to be free and familiar with them. Now they might fare as they fared, and therefore might eat with them, and be fellow-commoners with them. 5. He stuck to his principles, and would by no means hearken to the motion, though he was hungry (*v.* 14): *Not so, Lord.* Though hunger will break through stone walls, God's laws should be to us a stronger fence than stone walls, and not so easily broken through. And he will adhere to God's laws, though he has a countermand by a voice from heaven, not knowing at first but that *Kill, and eat,* was a command of trial whether he would adhere to the more sure word, the written law; and if so his answer had been very good, *Not so, Lord.* Temptations to eat forbidden fruit must not be parleyed with, but peremptorily rejected; we must startle at the thought of it: *Not so, Lord.* The reason he gives is, *"For I have never eaten any thing that is common or unclean;* hitherto I have kept my integrity in this matter, and will still keep it." If God, by his grace, has preserved us from gross sin unto this day, we should use this as an argument with ourselves to abstain *from all appearance of evil.* So strict were the pious Jews in this matter, that the seven brethren, those glorious martyrs under Antiochus, choose rather to be tortured to death in the most cruel manner that ever was than to eat swine's flesh, because it was forbidden by the law. No wonder then that Peter says it with so much pleasure, that his conscience could witness for him that he had never gratified his appetite with any forbidden food. 6. God, by a second voice from heaven, proclaimed the repeal of the law in this case (*v.* 15): *What God hath cleansed, that call thou not common.* He that made the law might alter it when he pleased, and reduce the matter to its first state. God had, for reasons suited to the Old-Testament dispensation, restrained the Jews from eating such and such meats, to which, while that dispensation lasted, they were obliged in conscience to submit; but he has now, for reasons suited to the New-Testament dispensation, taken off that restraint, and set the matter at large — has cleansed that which was before polluted to us, and we ought to make use of, and *stand fast in, the liberty wherewith Christ has made us free,* and not call that common or unclean which God has now declared clean. Note, We ought to welcome it as a great mercy that by the gospel of Christ we are freed from the distinction of meats, which was made by the law of Moses, and that now *every creature of God is good, and nothing to be refused;* not so much because hereby we gain the use of swine's flesh, hares, rabbits, and other pleasant and wholesome food for our bodies, but chiefly because conscience is hereby freed from a yoke in things of this nature, *that we might serve God without fear.* Though the gospel has made duties which were not so by the law of nature, yet it has not, like the law of Moses, made sins that were not so. Those who command to abstain from some kinds of meat at some times of the year, and place religion in it, call that common which God hath cleansed, and in that error, more than in any truth, are the successors of Peter. 7. *This was done thrice, v.* 16. The sheet was drawn up a little way, and let down again the second time, and so the third time, with the same call to him, to kill, and eat, and the same reason, that what God hath cleansed we must not call common; but whether Peter's refusal was repeated the second and third time is not certain; surely it was not, when his objection had the first time received such a satisfactory answer. The trebling of Peter's vision, like the doubling of Pharaoh's dream, was to show that *the thing was certain,* and engage him to take so much the more notice of it. The instructions given us in the things of God, whether by the ear in the preaching of the word, or by the eye in sacraments, need to be often repeated; *precept must be upon precept, and line upon line.* But at last *the vessel was received up into heaven.* Those who make this vessel to represent the church, including both Jews and Gentiles, as this did both clean and unclean creatures, make this very aptly to signify the admission of the believing Gentiles into the church, and into heaven too, into the Jerusalem above. Christ *has opened the kingdom of heaven to all believers,* and there we shall find, besides *those that are sealed out of all the tribes of Israel,* an *innumerable company out of every nation* (Rev. 7:9); but they are such as God has cleansed.

III. The providence which very opportunely explained this vision, and gave Peter to understand the intention of it, *v.* 17, 18. 1. What Christ did, Peter knew not just then (Jn. 13:7): *He doubted within himself what this vision which he had seen should mean.* He had no reason to doubt the truth of it, that it was a heavenly vision; all his doubt was concerning the meaning of it. Note, Christ reveals himself to his people by degrees, and not all at once; and leaves them to doubt awhile, to ruminate upon a thing, and debate it to and fro in their own minds, before he clears it up to them. 2. Yet he was made to know presently, for *the men who were sent from Cornelius* were just now come to *the house,* and were at *the gate enquiring whether Peter lodged there;* and by their errand it will appear what was the meaning of this vision. Note, God knows what services are before us, and therefore how to prepare us; and we then better know the meaning of what he has taught us when we find what occasion we have to make use of it.

Verses 19–33

We have here the meeting between Peter the apostle, and Cornelius the centurion. Though Paul was designed to be the apostle of the Gentiles, and to gather in the harvest among them, and Peter to be the apostle of the circumcision, yet it is ordered that Peter shall break the ice, and reap the first-fruits of the Gentiles, that the believing Jews, who retained too much of the old leaven of ill-will to the Gentiles, might be the better reconciled to their admission into the church, when they were first brought in by their own apostle, which Peter urges against those that would have imposed circumcision upon the Gentile converts (*ch.* 15:7), *You know that God made choice among us that the Gentiles by my mouth should hear the word of the gospel.* Now here,

I. Peter is directed by the Spirit to go along with Cornelius's messengers (*v.* 19, 20), and this is the exposition of the vision; now the riddle is unriddled: *While Peter thought on the vision;* he was musing upon it, and then it was opened to him. Note, Those that would be taught the things of God must think on those things; those that would understand the scriptures must meditate in them day and night. He was at a loss about it, and then had it explained, which encourages us, when we know not what to do, to have our eyes up unto God for direction. Observe, 1. Whence he had the direction. The Spirit said to him what he should do. It was not spoken to him by an angel, but spoken in him by the Spirit, secretly whispering it in his ear as it were, as God spoke to Samuel (1 Sa. 9:15), or impressing it powerfully upon his mind, so that he knew it to be a divine afflatus or inspiration, according to the promise, Jn. 16:13. 2. What the direction was. (1.) He is told, before any of the servants could come up to tell him, that three men below want to speak with him (*v.* 19), and he must arise from his musings, leave off thinking of the vision, and go down to them, *v.* 20. Those that are searching into the meaning of the words of God, and the visions of the Almighty, should not be always poring, no, nor always praying, but should sometimes look abroad, look about them, and they may meet with that which will be of use to them in their enquiries; for the scripture is in the fulfilling every day. (2.) He is ordered to *go along with the messengers to Cornelius,* though he was a Gentile, *doubting nothing.* He must not only go, but go cheerfully, without reluctance or hesitation, or any scruple concerning the lawfulness of it; not doubting whether he might go, no, nor whether he ought to go; for it was his duty *"Go with them, for I have sent them:* and I will bear thee out in going along with them, however thou mayest be censured for it." Note, When we see our call clear to any service, we should not suffer ourselves to be perplexed with doubts and scruples concerning it arising from former prejudices or prepossessions, or a fear of men's censure. *Let every man be fully persuaded in his own mind, and prove his own work.*

II. He receives both them and their message: *He went down to them, v.* 21. So far was he from going out of the way, or refusing to be spoken with, as one that was shy of them, or making them tarry, as one that took state upon him, that he went to them himself, told them he was the person they were enquiring for. And 1. He favourably receives their message; with abundance of openness and condescension he asks what their business is, what they have to say to him: *What is the cause wherefore you are come?* and they tell him their errand (*v.* 22): *"Cornelius,* an officer of the Roman army, a very honest gentleman, and one who has more religion than most of his neighbours, *who fears God above many* (Neh. 7:2), who, though he is not a Jew himself, has carried it so well that he is *of good report among all the people of the Jews* — they will all give him a good word, for a conscientious, sober, charitable man, so that it will be no discredit to thee to be seen in his company — he *was warned from God," echrēmatisthē — "he had an oracle from God,* sent to him by an angel" (and the lively oracles of the law of Moses were given by the disposition of angels), "by which he was ordered to send for thee to his house (where he is expecting thee, and ready to bid thee welcome), *and to hear words of thee:* they know not what words, but they are such as he may hear from thee, and not from any one else so well." *Faith comes by hearing.* When Peter repeats this, he tells us more fully, they are *words whereby thou and all thy house shall be saved, ch.* 11:14. "Come to him, for an angel bade him send for thee: come to him, for he is ready to hear and receive the saving words thou hast to bring to him." 2. He kindly entertained the messengers (*v.* 23): *He called them in, and lodged them.* He did not bid them go and refresh and repose themselves in an inn at their own charge, but was himself at the charge of entertaining them in his own quarters. What was getting ready for him (*v.* 10) they should be welcome to share in; he little thought what company he should have when he bespoke his dinner, but God foresaw it. Note, It becomes Christians and ministers to be hospitable, and ready, according as their ability is, and there is occasion for it, *to entertain strangers.* Peter lodged them, though they were Gentiles, to show how readily he complied with the design of the vision in eating with Gentiles; for he immediately took them to eat with him. Though they were two of them servants, and the other a common soldier, yet Peter thought it not below him to take them into his house. Probably he did it that he might have some talk with them about Cornelius and his family; for the apostles, though they had instructions from the Spirit, yet made use of other information, as they had occasion for it.

III. He *went with them* to Cornelius, whom he found ready to receive and entertain him. 1. Peter, when he went with them, was *accompanied by certain brethren from Joppa,* where he now was, *v.* 23. Six of them went along with him, as we find, *ch.* 11:12. Either Peter desired their company, that they might be witnesses of his proceeding cautiously with reference to the Gentiles, and of the good ground on which he went, and therefore he invited them (*ch.* 11:12), or they offered their service to attend him, and desired they might have the honour and happiness of being his fellow travellers. This was one way in which the primitive Christians very much showed their respect to their ministers: they accompanied them in their journeys, to keep them in countenance, to be their guard, and, as there was occasion, to minister to them; with a further prospect not only of doing them service, but of being edified by their converse. It is a pity that those who have skill and will to do good to others by their discourse should want an opportunity for it by travelling alone. 2. Cornelius, when he was ready to receive him, *had got some friends together of Cesarea.* It seems, it was above a day's journey, nearly two, from Joppa to Cesarea; for it was *the day after* they set out that *they entered into Cesarea* (*v.* 24), and the afternoon of that day, *v.* 30. It is probable that they travelled on foot; the apostles generally did so. Now when they came into the house of Cornelius Peter found, (1.) That he was expected, and this was an encouragement to him. *Cornelius waited for them,* and such a guest was worth waiting for; nor can I blame him if he waited with some impatience, longing to know what that mighty thing was which an angel bade him expect to hear from Peter. (2.) That he was expected by many, and this was a further encouragement to him. As Peter brought some with him to partake of the spiritual gift he had now to dispense, so *Cornelius had called together,* not only his own family, but *kinsmen and near friends,* to partake with him of the heavenly instructions he expected from Peter, which would give Peter a larger opportunity of doing good. Note, We should not covet to eat our spiritual morsels alone, Job 31:17. It ought to be both given and taken as a piece of kindness and respect to our kindred and friends to invite them to join with us in religious exercises, to go with us to hear a sermon. What Cornelius ought to do he thought his kinsmen and friends ought to do too; and therefore let them come and hear it at the first hand, that it may be no surprise to them to see him change upon it.

IV. Here is the first interview between Peter and Cornelius, in which we have, 1. The profound and indeed undue respect and honour which Cornelius paid to Peter (*v.* 25): *He met him as he was coming in,* and instead of taking him in his arms, and embracing him as a friend, which would have been very acceptable to Peter, *he fell down at his feet, and worshipped him;* some think, as a prince and a great man, according to the usage of the eastern countries; others think, as an incarnate deity, or as if he took him to be the Messiah himself. His worshipping a man was indeed culpable; but, considering his present ignorance, it was excusable, nay, and it was an evidence of something in him that was very commendable — and that was a great veneration for divine and heavenly things: no wonder if, till he was better informed, he took him to be the Messiah, and therefore worshipped him, whom he was ordered to send for by an angel from heaven. But the worshipping of his pretended successor, who is not only a man, but a sinful man, the man of sin himself, is altogether inexcusable, and such an absurdity as would be incredible if we were not told before that all *the world would worship the beast,* Rev. 13:4. 2. Peter's modest and indeed just and pious refusal of this honour that was done him (*v.* 26): *He took him up* into his arms, with his own hands (though time was when he little thought he should ever either receive so much respect from or show so much affection to an uncircumcised Gentile), *saying, "Stand up, I myself also am a man,* and therefore not to be worshipped thus." The good angels of the churches, like the good angels of heaven, cannot bear to have the least of that honour shown to them which is due to God only. *See thou do it not,* saith the angel to John (Rev. 19:10; 22:9), and in like manner the apostle to Cornelius. How careful was Paul *that no man should think of him above what he saw in him!* 2 Co. 12:6. Christ's faithful servants could better bear to be vilified than to be deified. Peter did not entertain a surmise that his great respect for him, though excessive, might contribute to the success of his preaching, and therefore if he will be deceived let him be deceived; no, let him know that Peter is a man, that *the treasure is in earthen vessels,* that he may value the treasure for its own sake.

V. The account which Peter and Cornelius give to each other, and to the company, of the hand of Heaven in bringing them together: *As he talked with him — synomilōn autō, he went in, v.* 27. Peter went in, talking familiarly with Cornelius, endeavouring, by the freedom of his converse with him, to take off something of that dread which he seemed to have of him; and, when he came in, *he found many that were come together,* more than he expected, which added solemnity, as well as opportunity of doing good, to this service. Now,

1. Peter declares the direction God gave to him to come to those Gentiles, *v.* 28, 29. They knew it had never been allowed by the Jews, but always looked upon as an *unlawful thing, athemiton — an abomination, for a man that is a Jew,* a native Jew as I am, *to keep company or come unto one of another nation,* a stranger, an uncircumcised Gentile. It was not made so by the law of God, but by the decree of their wise men, which they looked upon to be no less binding. They did not forbid them to converse or traffic with Gentiles in the street or shop, or upon the exchange, but to eat with them. Even in Joseph's time, the Egyptians and Hebrews could not eat together, Gen. 43:32. The three children *would not defile themselves with the king's meat,* Dan. 1:8. They might not come into the house of a Gentile, for they looked upon it to be ceremonially polluted. Thus scornfully did the Jews look upon the Gentiles, who were not behindhand with them in contempt, as appears by many passages in the Latin poets. *"But now,"* saith Peter, *"God hath shown me,* by a vision, *that I should not call any man common or unclean,* nor refuse to converse with any man for the sake of his country." Peter, who had taught his new converts to *save themselves from the untoward generation of wicked men* (*ch.* 2:40), is now himself taught to join himself with the towardly generation of devout Gentiles. Ceremonial characters were abolished, that more regard might be had to moral ones. Peter thought it necessary to let them know how he came to change his mind in this matter, and that it was by a divine revelation, lest he should be upbraided with it as having used lightness. God having thus taken down the partition-wall, (1.) He assures them of his readiness to do them all the good offices he could; that, when he kept at a distance, it was not out of any personal disgust to them, but only because he wanted leave from heaven, and, having now received permission, he was at their service: *"Therefore came I unto you without gainsaying, as soon as I was sent for,* ready to preach the same gospel to you that I have preached to the Jews." The disciples of Christ could not but have some notion of the preaching of the gospel to the Gentiles, but they imagined it must be only to those Gentiles that were first proselyted to the Jewish religion, which mistake Peter acknowledges was not rectified. (2.) He enquires wherein he might be serviceable to them: *"I ask, therefore, for what intent you have sent for me?* What do you expect from me, or what business have you with me?" Note, Those that desire the help of God's ministers ought to look well to it that they propose right ends to themselves in it, and do it with a good intention.

2. Cornelius declares the directions God gave to him to send for Peter, and that it was purely in obedience to those directions that he had sent for him. Then we are right in our aims, in sending for and attending on a gospel-ministry, when we did it with a regard to the divine appointment instituting that ordinance and requiring us to make use of it. Now,

(1.) Cornelius gives an account of the angel's appearing to him, and ordering him to send for Peter; not as glorying in it, but as that which warranted his expectation of a message from heaven by Peter. [1.] He tells how this vision found him employed (*v.* 30): *Four days ago I was fasting until this hour,* this hour of the day that it is now when Peter came, about the middle of the afternoon. By this it appears that religious fasting, in order to the greater seriousness and solemnity of praying, was used by devout people who were not Jews; *the king of Nineveh proclaimed a fast,* Jonah 3:5. Some give these words another sense: *From four days ago I have been fasting until this hour;* as if he had eaten no meat, or at least no meal, from that time to this. But it comes in as an introduction to the story of the vision; and therefore the former must be the meaning. *He was at the ninth hour praying in his house,* not in the synagogue, but at home. *I will that men pray* wherever they dwell. His praying in his house intimates that it was not a secret prayer in his closet, but in a more public room of his house, with his family about him; and perhaps after prayer he retired, and had this vision. Observe, *At the ninth hour of the day,* three of the clock in the afternoon, most people were travelling or trading, working in the fields, visiting their friends, taking their pleasure, or taking a nap after dinner; yet then Cornelius was at his devotions, which shows how much he made religion his business; and then it was that he had this message from heaven. Those that would hear comfortably from God must be much in speaking to him. [2.] He describes the messenger that brought him this message from heaven: *There stood a man before me in bright clothing,* as Christ's was when he was transfigured, and that of the two angels who appeared at Christ's resurrection (Lu. 24:4), and at his ascension (*ch.* 1:10), showing their relation to the world of light. [3.] He repeats the message that was sent to him (*v.* 31, 32), just as we had it, *v.* 4–6. Only here it is said, *thy prayer is heard.* We are not told what his prayer was; but if this message was an answer to it, and it should seem it was, we may suppose that finding the deficiency of natural light, and that it left him at a loss how to obtain the pardon of his sin and the favour of God, he prayed that God would make some further discoveries of himself and of the way of salvation to him. "Well," saith the angel, *"send for Peter,* and he shall give thee such a discovery."

(2.) He declares his own and his friends' readiness to receive the message Peter had to deliver (*v.* 33): *Immediately therefore I sent to thee,* as I was directed, *and thou hast well done that thou hast come* to us, though we are Gentiles. Note, Faithful ministers do well to come to people that are willing and desirous to receive instruction from them; to come when they are sent for; it is as good a deed as they can do. Well, Peter is come to do his part; but will they do theirs? Yes. "Thou art here prepared to speak, and we are here prepared to hear," 1 Sa. 3:9, 10. Observe, [1.] Their religious attendance upon the word: *"We are all here present before God;* we are here in a religious manner, are here as worshippers" (they thus compose themselves into a serious solemn frame of spirit): *"therefore,* because thou art come to us by such a warrant, on such an errand, because we have such a price in our hand as we never had before and perhaps may never have again, we are ready now at this time of worship, here in this place of worship" (though it was in a private house): *"we are present, paresmen — we are at the business,* and are ready to come at a call." If we would have God's special presence at an ordinance, we must be there with a special presence, an ordinance presence: *Here I am. "We are all present,* all that were invited; we, and all that belong to us; we, and all that is within us." The whole of the man must be present; not the body here, and the heart, with the fool's eyes, in the ends of the earth. But that which makes it indeed a religious attendance is, *We are present before God.* In holy ordinances we present ourselves unto the Lord, and we must be as before him, as those that see his eye upon us. [2.] The intention of this attendance: *"We are present to hear all things that are commanded thee of God,* and given thee in charge to be delivered to us." Observe, *First,* Peter was there to preach all things that were commanded him of God; for, as he had an ample commission to preach the gospel, so he had full instructions what to preach. *Secondly,* They were ready to hear, not whatever he pleased to say, but what he was commanded of God to say. The truths of Christ were not communicated to the apostles to be published or stifled as they thought fit, but entrusted with them to be published to the world. "We are ready to hear *all,* to come at the beginning of the service and stay to the end, and be attentive all the while, else how can we hear all? We are desirous to hear all that thou art commissioned to preach, though it be ever so displeasing to flesh and blood, and ever so contrary to our former notions or present secular interests. We are ready to hear all, and therefore let nothing be kept back that is profitable for us."

Verses 34–43

We have here Peter's sermon preached to Cornelius and his friends: that is, an abstract or summary of it; for we have reason to think that he did with many other words testify and exhort to this purport. It is intimated that he expressed himself with a great deal of solemnity and gravity, but with freedom and copiousness, in that phrase, *he opened his mouth, and spoke, v.* 34. *O ye Corinthians, our mouth is open to you,* saith Paul, 2 Co. 6:11. "You shall find us communicative, if we but find you inquisitive." Hitherto the mouths of the apostles had been shut to the uncircumcised Gentiles, they had nothing to say to them; but now God gave unto them, as he did to Ezekiel, *the opening of the mouth.* This excellent sermon of Peter's is admirably suited to the circumstances of those to whom he preached it; for it was a new sermon.

I. Because they were Gentiles to whom he preached. He shows that, notwithstanding this, they were interested in the gospel of Christ, which he had to preach, and entitled to the benefit of it, upon an equal footing with the Jews. It was necessary that this should be cleared, or else with what comfort could either he preach or they hear? He therefore lays down this as an undoubted principle, *that God is no respecter of persons; doth not know favour in judgment,* as the Hebrew phrase is; which magistrates are forbidden to do (Deu. 1:17; 16:19; Prov. 24:23), and are blamed for doing, Ps. 82:2. And it is often said of God that he doth not respect persons, Deu. 10:17; 2 Chr. 19:7; Job 34:19; Rom. 2:11; Col. 3:25; 1 Pt. 1:17. He doth not give judgment in favour of a man for the sake of any external advantage foreign to the merits of the cause. God never perverts judgment upon personal regards and considerations, nor countenances a wicked man in a wicked thing for the sake of his beauty, or stature, his country, parentage, relations, wealth, or honour in the world. God, as a benefactor, gives favours arbitrarily and by sovereignty (Deu. 7:7, 8; 9:5, 6; Mt. 20:10); but he does not, as a judge, so give sentence; *but in every nation,* and under ever denomination, *he that fears God and works righteousness is accepted of him, v.* 35. The case is plainly thus: —

1. God never did, nor ever will, justify and save a wicked Jew that lived and died impenitent, though he was *of the seed of Abraham,* and a *Hebrew of the Hebrews,* and had all the honour and advantages that attended circumcision. He does and will render *indignation and wrath, tribulation and anguish, upon every soul of man that doeth evil;* and *of the Jew first,* whose privileges and professions, instead of screening him from the judgment of God, will but aggravate his guilt and condemnation. See Rom. 2:3, 8, 9, 17. Though God has favoured the Jews, above other nations, with the dignities of visible church-membership, yet he will not therefore accept of any particular persons of that dignity, if they allow themselves in immoralities contradictory to their profession; and particularly in persecution, which was now, more than any other, the national sin of the Jews.

2. He never did, nor ever will, reject or refuse an honest Gentile, who, though he has not the privileges and advantages that the Jews have, yet, like Cornelius, fears God, and worships him, and works righteousness, that is, is just and charitable towards all men, who lives up to the light he has, both in a sincere devotion and in a regular conversation. Whatever nation he is of, though ever so far remote from kindred to the seed of Abraham, though ever so despicable, nay, though in ever so ill a name, that shall be no prejudice to him. God judges of men by their hearts, not by their country or parentage; and, wherever he finds an upright man, he will be found an upright God, Ps. 18:25. Observe, *Fearing God, and working righteousness,* must go together; for, as righteousness towards men is a branch of true religion, so religion towards God is a branch of universal righteousness. Godliness and honesty must go together, and neither will excuse for the want of the other. But, where these are predominant, no doubt is to be made of acceptance with God. Not that any man, since the fall, can obtain the favour of God otherwise than through the mediation of Jesus Christ, and by the grace of God in him; but those that have not the knowledge of him, and therefore cannot have an explicit regard to him, may yet receive grace from God for his sake, *to fear God and to work righteousness;* and wherever God gives grace to do so, as he did to Cornelius, he will, through Christ, accept the work of his own hands. Now, (1.) This was always a truth, before Peter perceived it, *that God respecteth no man's person;* it was the fixed rule of judgment from the beginning: *If thou doest well, shalt thou not be accepted? And, if not well, sin,* and the punishment of it, *lie at the door,* Gen. 4:7. God will not ask in the great day what country men were of, but what they were, what they did, and how they stood affected towards him and towards their neighbours; and, if men's personal characters received neither advantage nor disadvantage from the great difference that existed between Jews and Gentiles, much less from any less difference of sentiments and practices that may happen to be among Christians themselves, as those *about meats and days,* Rom. 14. It is certain *the kingdom of God is not meat and drink, but righteousness, and peace, and joy in the Holy Ghost;* and he that in these things serveth Christ is accepted of God, and ought to be approved of men; for dare we reject those whom God doth not? (2.) Yet now it was made more clear than it had been; this great truth had been darkened by the covenant of peculiarity made with Israel, and the badges of distinction put upon them; the ceremonial law was a wall of partition between them and other nations; it is true that in it *God favoured that nation* (Rom. 3:1, 2; 9:4), and thence particular persons among them were ready to infer that they were sure of God's acceptance, though they lived as they listed, and that no Gentile could possibly be accepted of God. God had said a great deal by the prophets to prevent and rectify this mistake, but now at length he doth it effectually, by abolishing the covenant of peculiarity, repealing the ceremonial law, and so setting the matter at large, and placing both Jew and Gentile upon the same level before God; and Peter is here made to perceive it, by comparing the vision which he had with that which Cornelius had. Now *in Christ Jesus,* it is plain, *neither circumcision availeth any thing, nor uncircumcision,* Gal. 5:6; Col. 3:11.

II. Because they were Gentiles inhabiting a place within the confines of the land of Israel, he refers them to what they themselves could not but know concerning the life and doctrine, the preaching and miracles, the death and sufferings of our Lord Jesus: for these were things the report of which spread into every corner of the nation, *v.* 37, etc. It facilitates the work of ministers, when they deal with such as have some knowledge of the things of God, to which they may appeal, and on which they may build.

1. They knew in general, *the word,* that is, the gospel, *which God sent to the children of Israel: That word, I say, you know, v.* 37. Though the Gentiles were not admitted to hear it (Christ and his disciples were *not sent but to the lost sheep of the house of Israel),* yet they could not but hear of it: it was all the talk both of city and country. We are often told in the gospels how the fame of Christ went into all parts of Canaan, when he was on earth, as afterwards the fame of his gospel went into all parts of the world, Rom. 10:18. That word, that divine word, that word of power and grace, *you know.* (1.) What the purport of this word was. God by it *published the glad tidings of peace by Jesus Christ,* so it should be read — ***euangelizomenos eirēnēv.*** It is God himself that proclaims *peace,* who justly might have proclaimed war. He lets the world of mankind know that he is willing to be at peace with them through Jesus Christ; in him he was *reconciling the world to himself.* (2.) To whom it was sent — to the children of Israel, in the first place. The prime offer is made to them; this all their neighbours heard of, and were ready to envy them those advantages of the gospel, more than they ever envied them those of their law. *Then said they among the heathen, The Lord hath done great things for them,* Ps. 126:2.

2. They knew the several matters of fact relating to this word of the gospel sent to Israel. (1.) They knew the baptism of repentance which John preached by way of introduction to it, and in which the gospel first began, Mk. 1:1. They knew what an extraordinary man John was, and what a direct tendency his preaching had to *prepare the way of the Lord.* They knew what great flocking there was to his baptism, what an interest he had, and what he did. (2.) They knew that immediately after John's baptism the gospel of Christ, that word of *peace, was published throughout all Judea,* and that it took its rise from Galilee. The twelve apostles, and seventy disciples, and our Master himself, published these glad tidings in all parts of the land; so that we may suppose there was not a town or village in all the land of Canaan but had had the gospel preached in it. (3.) They knew that Jesus of Nazareth, when he was here upon earth, *went about doing good.* They knew what a benefactor he was to that nation, both to the souls and the bodies of men; how he made it his business to do good to all, and never did hurt to any. He was not idle, but still doing; not selfish, but doing good; did not confine himself to one place, nor wait till people came to him to seek his help, but went to them, went about from place to place, and wherever he came he was doing good. Hereby he showed *that he was sent of God, who is good and does good;* and does good because he is good: and who hereby *left not himself without witness* to the world, *in that he did good, ch.* 14:17. And in this he hath set us an example of indefatigable industry in serving God and our generation; for we came into the world that we might do all the good we

can in it; and therein, like Christ, we must always abide and abound. (4.) They knew more particularly that he *healed all that were oppressed of the devil,* and helped them from under his oppressing power. By this it appeared not only that he was sent of God, as it was a kindness to men, but that he was sent to *destroy the works of the devil;* for thus he obtained many a victory over him. (5.) They knew that the Jews put him to death; they *slew* him by *hanging him on a tree.* When Peter preached to the Jews, he said *whom you slew;* but now that he preached to the Gentiles it is whom *they* slew; they, to whom he had done and designed so much good. All this they knew; but lest they should think it was only a report, and was magnified, as reports usually are, more than the truth, Peter, for himself and the rest of the apostles, attested it (*v.* 39): *We are witnesses,* eye-witnesses, of *all things which he did;* and ear-witnesses of the doctrine which he preached, *both in the land of the Jews and in Jerusalem,* in city and country.

3. They did know, or might know, by all this, that he had a commission from heaven to preach and act as he did. This he still harps upon in his discourse, and takes all occasions to hint it to them. Let them know, (1.) That this Jesus *is Lord of all;* it comes in in a parenthesis, but is the principal proposition intended to be proved, that Jesus Christ, by whom peace is made between God and man, *is Lord of all;* not only as *God over all blessed for evermore,* but as Mediator, *all power both in heaven and on earth* is put into his hand, and all judgment committed to him. He is Lord of angels; they are all his humble servants. He is Lord of the powers of darkness, for he hath triumphed over them. He is king of nations, has a power over all flesh. He is king of saints, all the children of God are his scholars, his subjects, his soldiers. (2.) That *God anointed him with the Holy Ghost and with power;* he was both authorized and enabled to do what he did by a divine anointing, whence he was called *Christ — the Messiah, the anointed One.* The Holy Ghost descended upon him at his baptism, and he was full of power both in preaching and working miracles, which was the seal of a divine mission. (3.) That *God was with him, v.* 38. His works were wrought in God. God not only sent him, but was present with him all along, owned him, stood by him, and carried him on in all his services and sufferings. Note, Those whom God anoints he will accompany; he will himself be with those to whom he has given his Spirit.

III. Because they had had no more certain information concerning this Jesus, Peter declares to them his resurrection from the dead, and the proofs of it, that they might not think that when he was slain there was an end of him. Probably, they had heard at Cesarea some talk of his having risen from the dead; but the talk of it was soon silenced by that vile suggestion of the Jews, that *his disciples came by night and stole him away.* And therefore Peter insists upon this as the main support of that word which preacheth peace by Jesus Christ. 1. The power by which he arose is incontestably divine (*v.* 40): *Him God raised up the third day,* which not only disproved all the calumnies and accusations he was laid under by men, but effectually proved God's acceptance of the satisfaction he made for the sin of man by the blood of his cross. He did not break prison, but had a legal discharge. *God raised him up.* 2. The proofs of his resurrection were incontestably clear; for God *showed him openly. He gave him to be made manifest — edōken auton emphanē genesthai,* to be visible, evidently so; so he appears, as that it appears beyond contradiction to be him, and not another. It was such a showing of him as amounted to a demonstration of the truth of his resurrection. He showed him not publicly indeed (it was not open in this sense), but evidently; *not to all the people,* who had been the witnesses of his death. By resisting all the evidences he had given them of his divine mission in his miracles, they had forfeited the favour of being eye-witnesses of this great proof of it. Those who immediately forged and promoted that lie of his being stolen away were justly given up to strong delusions to believe it, and not suffered to be undeceived by his being shown to all the people; and so much the greater shall be the blessedness of those *who have not seen, and yet have believed — Nec ille se in vulgus edixit, ne impii errore, liberarentur; ut et fides non praemio mediocri destinato difficultate constaret — He showed not himself to the people at large, lest the impious among them should have been forthwith loosed from their error, and that faith, the reward of which is so ample, might be exercised with a degree of difficulty.* — Tertul. Apol. cap. 11. But, though all the people did not see him, a sufficient number saw him to attest the truth of his resurrection. The testator's declaring his last will and testament needs not to be before all the people; it is enough that it be done before a competent number of credible witnesses; so the resurrection of Christ was proved before sufficient witnesses. (1.) They were not so by chance, but they were *chosen before of God* to be witnesses of it, and, in order to this, had their education under the Lord Jesus, and intimate converse with him, that, having known him so intimately before, they might the better be assured it was he. (2.) They had not a sudden and transient view of him, but a great deal of free conversation with him: *They did eat and drink with him after he rose from the dead.* This implies that they saw him eat and drink, witness their dining with him at the sea of Tiberias, and the two disciples supping with him at Emmaus; and this proved that he had a true and real body. But this was not all; they saw him without any terror or consternation, which might have rendered them incompetent witnesses, for they saw him so frequently, and he conversed with them so familiarly, that *they did eat and drink with him.* It is brought as a proof of the clear view which the nobles of Israel had of the glory of God (Ex. 24:11), that *they saw God, and did eat and drink.*

IV. He concludes with an inference from all this, that therefore that which they all ought to do was to believe in this Jesus: he was sent to tell Cornelius what he must do, and it is this; his praying and his giving alms were very well, but one thing he lacked, he must believe in Christ. Observe,

1. Why he must believe in him. Faith has reference to a testimony, and the Christian faith is *built upon the foundation of the apostles and prophets,* it is built upon the testimony given by them. (1.) By the apostles. Peter as foreman speaks for the rest, that *God commanded them,* and gave them in charge, to *preach to the people, and to testify* concerning Christ; so that their testimony was not only credible, but authentic, and what we may venture upon. Their testimony is God's testimony; and they are his witnesses to the world. They do not only say it as matter of news, but testify it as matter of record, by which men must be judged. (2.) By the prophets of the Old Testament, whose testimony beforehand, not only concerning his sufferings, but concerning the design and intention of them, very much corroborates the apostles' testimony concerning them (*v.* 43): *To him give all the prophets witness.* We have reason to think that Cornelius and his friends were no strangers to the writings of the prophets. Out of the mouth of these two clouds of witnesses, so exactly agreeing, *this word is established.*

2. What they must believe concerning him. (1.) That we are all accountable to Christ as our Judge; this the apostles were commanded to testify to the world, that this Jesus is *ordained of God to be the Judge of the quick and dead, v.* 42. He is empowered to prescribe the terms of salvation, that rule by which we must be judged, to give laws both to *quick and dead,* both to Jew and Gentile; and he is appointed to determine the everlasting condition of all the children of men at the great day, of those that shall be found alive and of those that shall be raised from the dead. He hath assured us of this, *in that he hath raised him from the dead* (*ch.* 17:31), so that it is the great concern of every one of us, in the belief of this, to seek his favour, and to make him our friend. (2.) That if we believe in him we shall all be justified by him as our righteousness, *v.* 43. The prophets, when they spoke of the death of Christ, did witness this, *that through his name,* for his sake, and upon the account of his merit, *whosoever believeth in him,* Jew or Gentile, *shall receive remission of sins.* This is the great thing we need, without which we are undone, and which the convinced conscience is most inquisitive after, which the carnal Jews promised themselves from their ceremonial sacrifices and purifications, yea, and the heathen too from their atonements, but all in vain; it is to be had only through the name of Christ, and only by those that believe in his name; and those that do so may be assured of it; their sins shall be pardoned, and there shall be no condemnation to them. And the remission of sins lays a foundation for all other favours and blessings, by taking that out of the way which hinders them. If sin be pardoned, all is well, and shall end everlastingly well.

Verses 44–48

We have here the issue and effect of Peter's sermon to Cornelius and his friends. He did not labour in vain among them, but they were all brought home to Christ. Here we have,

I. God's owning Peter's word, by conferring the Holy Ghost upon the hearers of it, and immediately upon the hearing of it (*v.* 44): *While Peter was yet speaking these words,* and perhaps designed to say more, he was happily superseded by visible indications that *the Holy Ghost,* even in his miraculous gifts and powers, *fell on all those who heard the word,* even as he did on the apostles at first; so Peter saith, *ch.* 11:15. Therefore some think it was with a rushing mighty wind, and in cloven tongues, as that was. Observe, 1. When the Holy Ghost fell upon them — while Peter was preaching. Thus God bore witness to what he said, and accompanied it with a divine power. Thus were the *signs of an apostle wrought among them,* 2 Co. 12:12. Though Peter could not give the Holy Ghost, yet the Holy Ghost being given along with the word of Peter, by this it appeared he was sent of God. The Holy Ghost fell upon others after they were baptized, for their confirmation; but upon these Gentiles before they were baptized: as Abraham was justified by faith, being yet in uncircumcision, to show that God is not tied to a method, nor confines himself to external signs. The Holy Ghost fell upon those that were neither circumcised nor baptized; for *it is the Spirit that quickeneth, the flesh profiteth nothing.* 2. How it appeared that the Holy Ghost had fallen upon them (*v.* 46): *They spoke with tongues* which they never learned, perhaps the Hebrew, the holy tongue; as the preachers were enabled to speak the vulgar tongues, that they might communicate the doctrine of Christ to the hearers, so, probably, the hearers were immediately taught the sacred tongue, that they might examine the proofs which the preachers produced out of the Old Testament in the original. Or their being enabled to speak with tongues intimated that they were all designed for ministers, and by this first descent of the Spirit upon them were qualified to preach the gospel to others, which they did but now receive themselves. But, observe, when they spoke with tongues, they *magnified God,* they spoke of Christ and the benefits of redemption, which Peter had been preaching to the glory of God. Thus did they on whom the Holy Ghost first descended, c. 2:11. Note, Whatever gift we are endued with, we ought to honour God with it, and particularly the gift of speaking, and all the improvements of it. 3. What impression it made upon the believing Jews that were present (*v.* 45): *Those of the circumcision who believed were astonished* — those six that came along with Peter; it surprised them exceedingly, and perhaps gave them some uneasiness, because *upon the Gentiles also was poured out the gift of the Holy Ghost,* which they thought had been appropriated to their own nation. Had they understood the scriptures of the Old Testament, which pointed at this, it would not have been such an astonishment to them; but by our mistaken notions of things we create difficulties to ourselves in the methods of divine providence and grace.

II. Peter's owning God's work in baptizing those on whom the Holy Ghost fell. Observe, 1. Though they had received the Holy Ghost, yet it was requisite they should be baptized; though God is not tied to instituted ordinances, we are; and no extraordinary gifts set us above them, but rather oblige us so much the more to conform to them. Some in our days would have argued "These are baptized with the *Holy Ghost* and therefore what need have they to be baptized with *water?* It is below them." No; it is not below them, while water-baptism is an ordinance of Christ, and the door of admission into the visible church, and a seal of the new covenant. 2. Though they were Gentiles, yet, having received the Holy Ghost, they might be admitted to baptism (*v.* 47): *Can any man,* though ever so rigid a Jew, *forbid water, that these should not be baptized, who have received the Holy Ghost as well as we?* The argument is conclusive; can we deny the sign to those who have received the thing signified? Are not those on whom God has bestowed the grace of the covenant plainly entitled to the seals of the covenant? Surely those that have *received the Spirit as well as we* ought to receive baptism as well as we; for it becomes us to follow God's indications, and to take those into communion with us whom he hath taken into communion with himself. God hath promised to pour his Spirit upon the seed of the faithful, upon their offspring; and who then can forbid water, that they should not be baptized, who have *received the promise of the Holy Ghost as well as we?* Now it appears why the Spirit was given them before they were baptized — because otherwise Peter could not have persuaded himself to baptize them, any more than to have preached to them, if he had not been ordered to do it by a vision; at least he could not have avoided the censure of *those of the circumcision that believed.* Thus is there one unusual step of divine grace taken after another to bring the Gentiles into the church. How well is it for us that the grace of a good God is so much more extensive than the charity of some good men! 3. Peter did not baptize them himself, but *commanded them to be baptized, v.* 48. It is probable that some of the brethren who came with him did it by his order, and that he declined it for the same reason that Paul did — lest those that were baptized by him should think the better of themselves for it, or he should seem to *have baptized in his own name,* 1 Co. 1:15. the apostles received the commission to *go and disciple all nations by baptism.* But is was to prayer and the ministry of the word that they were to *give* themselves. And Paul says that he was sent, *not to baptize but to preach,* which was the more noble and excellent work. The business of baptizing was therefore ordinarily devolved upon the inferior ministers; these acted by the orders of the apostles, who might therefore be said to do it. *Qui per alterum facit, per seipsum facere dicitur — What a man does by another, he may be said to do by himself.*

III. Their owning both Peter's word and God's work in their desire for further advantage by Peter's ministry: *They prayed him to tarry certain days.* They could not press him to reside constantly among them — they knew that he had work to do in other places, and that for the present he was expected at Jerusalem; yet they were not willing he should go away immediately, but earnestly begged he would stay for some time among them, that they might be further instructed by him in the things pertaining to the kingdom of God. Note, 1. Those who have some acquaintance with Christ cannot but covet more. 2. Even those that have received the Holy Ghost must see their need of the ministry of the word.

CHAPTER 11

In this chapter we have, I. Peter's necessary vindication of what he did in receiving Cornelius and his friends into the church, from the censure he lay under for it among the brethren, and their acquiescence in it (*v.* 1–18). II. The good success of the gospel at Antioch, and the parts adjacent (*v.* 19–21). III. The carrying on of the good work that was begun at Antioch, by the ministry of Barnabas first, and afterwards of Paul in conjunction with him, and the lasting name of Christian first given to the disciples there (*v.* 22–26). IV. A prediction of an approaching famine, and the contribution that was made among the Gentile converts for the relief of the poor saints in Judea, upon that occasion (*v.* 27–30).

Verses 1–18

The preaching of the gospel to Cornelius was a thing which we poor sinners of the Gentiles have reason to reflect upon with a great deal of joy and thankfulness; for it was the bringing of light to us who sat in darkness. Now it being so great a surprize to the believing as well as the unbelieving Jews, it is worth while to enquire how it was received, and what comments were made upon it. And here we find,

I. Intelligence was presently brought of it to the church in Jerusalem, and thereabouts; for Cesarea was not so far from Jerusalem but that they might presently hear of it. Some for good-will, and some for ill-will, would spread the report of it; so that before he himself had returned to Jerusalem *the apostles and* the *brethren* there and *in Judea heard that the Gentiles also had received the word of God,* that is, the gospel of Christ, which is not only a word of God, but the word of God; for it is the summary and centre of all divine revelation. They received Christ; *for his name is called the Word of God,* Rev. 19:13. Not only that the Jews who were dispersed into the Gentile countries, and the Gentiles who were proselyted to the Jewish religion, but that the Gentiles also themselves, with whom it had hitherto been thought unlawful to hold common conversation, were taken into church-communion, that they had *received the word of God.* That is, 1. That the word of God was preached to them, which was a greater honour put upon them than they expected. Yet I wonder this should seem strange to those who were themselves commissioned to *preach the gospel to every creature.* But thus often are the prejudices of pride and bigotry held fast against the clearest discoveries of divine truth. 2. That it was entertained and submitted to by them, which was a better work wrought upon them than they expected. It is likely they had got a notion that if the gospel were preached to the Gentiles it would be to no purpose, because the proofs of the gospel were fetched so much out of the Old Testament, which the Gentiles did not receive: they looked upon them as not inclined to religion, nor likely to receive the im-

pressions of it; and therefore were surprized to hear that they had received the word of the Lord. Note, We are too apt to despair of doing good to those who yet, when they are tried, prove very tractable.

II. That offence was taken at it by the believing Jews (*v.* 2, 3): *When Peter had himself come up to Jerusalem, those that were of the circumcision,* those Jewish converts that still retained a veneration for circumcision, *contended with him.* They charged it upon him as a crime that he *went in to men uncircumcised, and did eat with them;* and thereby they think he has stained, if not forfeited, the honour of his apostleship, and ought to come under the censure of the church: so far were they from looking upon him as infallible, or as the supreme head of the church that all were accountable to, and he to none. See here, 1. How much it is the bane and damage of the church, to monopolize it, and to exclude those from it, and from the benefit of the means of grace, that are not in every thing as we are. There are narrow souls that are for engrossing the riches of the church, as there are that would engross the riches of the world, and would be *placed alone in the midst of the earth.* These men were of Jonah's mind, who, in a jealousy for his people, was angry that the Ninevites received the word of God, and justified himself in it. 2. Christ's ministers must not think it strange if they be censured and quarrelled with, not only by their professed enemies, but by their professing friends; not only for their follies and infirmities, but for their good actions seasonably and well done; but, if we have proved our own work, we may have rejoicing in ourselves, as Peter had, whatever reflections we may have from our brethren. Those that are zealous and courageous in the service of Christ must expect to be censured by those who, under pretence of being cautious, are cold and indifferent. Those who are of catholic, generous, charitable principles, must expect to be censured by such as are conceited and strait-laced, who say, *Stand by thyself, I am holier than thou.*

III. Peter gave such a full and fair account of the matter of fact as was sufficient, without any further argument or apology, both to justify him, and to satisfy them (*v.* 4): *He rehearsed the matter from the beginning,* and laid it before them in order, and then could appeal to themselves whether he had done amiss; for it appeared all along God's own work, and not his.

1. He takes it for granted that if they had rightly understood how the matter was they would not have contended with him, and commended him. And it is a good reason why we should be moderate in our censures, and sparing of them, because if we rightly understood that which we are so forward to run down perhaps we should see cause to run in with it. When we see others do that which looks suspicious, instead of contending with them, we should enquire of them what ground they went upon; and, if we have not an opportunity to do that, should ourselves put the best construction upon it that it will bear, and *judge nothing before the time.*

2. He is very willing to stand right in their opinion, and takes pains to give them satisfaction. He does not insist upon his being the chief of the apostles, for he was far from the thought of that supremacy which his pretended successors claim. Nor does he think it enough to tell them that he is satisfied himself in the grounds he went upon, and they need not trouble themselves about it; but he is ready to *give a reason of the hope that is in him* concerning the Gentiles, and why he had receded from his former sentiments, which were the same with theirs. It is a debt we owe both to ourselves and to our brethren to set those actions of ours in a true light which at first looked ill and gave offence, that we may remove stumbling-blocks out of our brethren's way. Let us now see what Peter pleads in his own defence.

(1.) That he was instructed by a vision no longer to keep up the distinctions which were made by the ceremonial law; he relates the vision (*v.* 5, 6), as we had it before *ch.* 10:9, etc. The sheet which was there said to be *let down to the earth* he here says came *even to him,* which circumstance intimates that it was particularly designed for instruction to him. We should thus see all God's discoveries of himself, which he has made to the children of men, coming even to us, applying them by faith to ourselves. Another circumstance here added is that when the sheet *came to him he fastened his eyes upon it, and considered it, v.* 6. If we would be led into the knowledge of divine things, we must fix our minds upon them, and consider them. He tells them what orders he had to eat of all sorts of meat without distinction, asking

no questions for conscience' sake, *v.* 7. It was not till after the flood (as it should seem) that man was allowed to eat flesh at all, Gen. 9:3. That allowance was afterwards limited by the ceremonial law; but now the restrictions were taken off, and the matter set at large again. It was not the design of Christ to abridge us in the use of our creature-comforts by any other law than that of sobriety and temperance, and preferring the meat that endures to eternal life before that which perishes. He pleads that he was as averse to the thoughts of conversing with Gentiles, or eating of their dainties, as they could be, and therefore refused the liberty given him: *Not so, Lord; for nothing common or unclean has at any time entered into my mouth, v.* 8. But he was told from heaven that the case was now altered, that God had cleansed those persons and things which were before polluted; and therefore that he must no longer call them common, nor look upon them as unfit to be meddled with by the peculiar people (*v.* 9); so that he was not to be blamed for changing his thoughts, when God had changed the thing. In things of this nature we must act according to our present light; yet must not be so wedded to our opinion concerning them as to be prejudiced against further discoveries, when the matter may either be otherwise or appear otherwise; and God may reveal even this unto us, Phil. 3:15. And, that they might be sure he was not deceived in it, he tells them it was done three times (*v.* 10), the same command given, to kill and eat, and the same reason, because that which God hath cleansed is not to be called common, repeated a second and third time. And, further to confirm him that it was a divine vision, the things he saw did not vanish away into the air, but *were drawn up again into heaven,* whence they were let down.

(2.) That he was particularly directed by the Spirit to go along with the messengers that Cornelius sent. And, that it might appear that the vision was designed to satisfy him in this matter, he observes to them the time when the messengers came — immediately after he had that vision; yet, lest this should not be sufficient to clear his way, the Spirit bade him *go with the men* that were then sent from Cesarea to him, *nothing doubting* (*v.* 11, 12); though they were Gentiles he went to, and went with, yet he must make no scruple of going along with them.

(3.) That he took some of his brethren along with him, who were of the circumcision, that they might be satisfied as well as he; and these he had brought up from Joppa, to witness for him with what caution he proceeded, forseeing the offence that would be taken at it. He did not act separately, but with advice; not rashly, but upon due deliberation.

(4.) That Cornelius had a vision too, by which he was directed to send for Peter (*v.* 13): *He showed us how he had seen a angel in his house,* that bade him *send to Joppa for one Simon, whose surname is Peter.* See how good it is for those that have communion with God, and keep up a correspondence with heaven, to compare notes, and communicate their experiences to each other; for hereby they may strengthen one another's faith: Peter is the more confirmed in the truth of his vision by Cornelius's, and Cornelius by Peter's. Here is something added in what the angel said to Cornelius; before it was, *Send for Peter, and he shall speak to thee, he shall tell thee what thou oughtest to do* (ch. 10:6, 32); but here it is, *"He shall tell thee words whereby thou and thy house shall be saved* (*v.* 14), and therefore it is of vast concern to thee, and will be of unspeakable advantage, to send for him."* Note, [1.] The words of the gospel are words whereby we may be saved, eternally saved; not merely by hearing them and reading them, but by believing and obeying them. They set the salvation before us, and show us what it is; they open the way of salvation to us, and, if we follow the method prescribed us by them, we shall certainly be saved from wrath and the curse, and be for ever happy. [2.] Those that embrace the gospel of Christ will have salvation brought by it to their families: *"Thou and all thy house shall be saved;* thou and thy children shall be taken into covenant, and have the means of salvation; thy house shall be as welcome to the benefit of the salvation, upon their believing, as thou thyself, even the meanest servant thou hast. *This day is salvation come to this house,"* Lu. 19:9. Hitherto salvation was of the Jews (Jn. 4:22), but now salvation is brought to the Gentiles as much as ever it was with the Jews; the promises, privileges, and means of it are conveyed to all nations as amply and fully, to all intents and purposes, as ever it had been appropriated to the Jewish nation.

(5.) That which put the matter past all dispute was the

descent of the Holy Ghost upon the Gentile hearers; this completed the evidence that it was the will of God that he should take the Gentiles into communion. [1.] The fact was plain and undeniable (*v.* 15): "*As I began to speak*" (and perhaps he felt some secret reluctance in his own breast, doubting whether he was in the right to preach to the uncircumcised), "presently *the Holy Ghost fell on them* in as visible signs *as on us at the beginning,* in which there could be no fallacy." Thus God attested what was done, and declared his approbation of it; that preaching is certainly right with which the Holy Ghost is given. The apostle supposes this, when he thus argues with the Galatians: *Received you the Spirit by the works of the law, or by the hearing of faith?* Gal. 3:2. [2.] Peter was hereby put in mind of a saying of his Master's, when he was leaving them (*ch.* 1:5): *John baptized with water; but you shall be baptized with the Holy Ghost, v.* 16. This plainly intimated, *First,* that the Holy Ghost was the gift of Christ, and the product and performance of his promise, that great promise which he left with them when he went to heaven. It was therefore without doubt from him that this gift came; and the filling of them with the Holy Ghost was his act and deed. As it was promised by his mouth, so it was performed by his hand, and was a token of his favour. *Secondly,* That the gift of the Holy Ghost was a kind of baptism. Those that received it were baptized with it in a more excellent manner than any of those that even the Baptist himself baptized with water. [3.] Comparing that promise, so worded, with this gift just now conferred, when the question was started, whether these persons should be baptized or no, he concluded that the question was determined by Christ himself (*v.* 17): "*Forasmuch then as God gave them the like gift as he did to us* — gave it to us as *believing in the Lord Jesus Christ,* and to them upon their believing in him — *What was I, that I could withstand God?* Could I refuse to baptize them with water, whom God had baptized with the Holy Ghost? Could I deny the sign to those on whom he had conferred the thing signified? *But, as for me, who was I?* What! able to forbid God? Did it become me to control the divine will, or to oppose the counsels of Heaven?" Note, Those who hinder the conversion of souls withstand God; and those take too much upon them who contrive how to exclude from their communion those whom God has taken into communion with himself.

IV. This account which Peter gave of the matter satisfied them, and all was well. Thus, when the two tribes and a half gave an account to Phinehas and the princes of Israel of the true intent and meaning of their building themselves an altar on the banks of Jordan, the controversy was dropped, and it pleased them that it was so, Jos. 22:30. Some people, when they have fastened a censure upon a person, will stick to it, though afterwards it appear ever so plainly to be unjust and groundless. It was not so here; for these brethren, though they were of the circumcision, and their bias went the other way, yet, when they heard this, 1. They let fall their censures: they held their peace, and said no more against what Peter had done; they laid their hand upon their mouth, because now they perceived that God did it. Now those who prided themselves in their dignities as Jews began to see that God was staining their pride, by letting in the Gentiles to share, and to share equally, with them. And now that prophecy was fulfilled, *Thou shalt no more be haughty because of my holy mountain,* Zep. 3:11. 2. They turned them into praises. They not only held their peace from quarrelling with Peter, but opened their mouths to glorify God for what he had done by and with Peter's ministry; they were thankful that their mistake was rectified, and that God had shown more mercy to the poor Gentiles than they were inclined to show them, saying, *Then hath God also to the Gentiles granted repentance unto life!* He hath granted them not only the means of repentance, in opening a door of entrance for his ministers among them, but the grace of repentance, in having given them his Holy Spirit, who, wherever he comes to be a Comforter, first convinces, and gives a sight of sin and sorrow for it, and then a sight of Christ and joy in him. Note, (1.) Repentance, if it be true, is unto life. It is to spiritual life; all that truly repent of their sins evidence it by living a new life, a holy, heavenly, and divine life. Those that by repentance die unto sin thenceforward live unto God; and then, and not till then, we begin to live indeed, and it shall be to eternal life. All true penitents shall live, that is, they shall be restored to the favour of God, which is life, which is better than life; they shall be comforted with the assurance of the pardon of their sins, and shall have the earnest of eternal life, and at length

the fruition of it. (2.) Repentance is God's gift; it is not only his free grace that accepts it, but his mighty grace that works it in us, that *takes away the heart of stone, and gives us a heart of flesh. The sacrifice of God is a broken spirit;* it is he that provides himself this lamb. (3.) Wherever God designs to give life he gives repentance; for this is a necessary preparative for the comforts of a sealed pardon and a settled peace in this world, and for the seeing and enjoying of God in the other world. (4.) It is a great comfort to us that God has exalted his Son Jesus, not only to *give repentance to Israel, and the remission of sins* (*ch.* 5:31), but to the Gentiles also.

Verses 19–26

We have here an account of the planting and watering of a church at Antioch, the chief city of Syria, reckoned afterwards the third most considerable city of the empire, only Rome and Alexandria being preferred before it, next to whose patriarch that of Antioch took place. It stood where Hamath or Riblah did, which we read of in the Old Testament. It is suggested that Luke, the penman of this history, as well as Theophilus, to whom he dedicates it, was of Antioch, which may be the reason why he takes more particular notice of the success of the gospel at Antioch, as also because there it was that Paul began to be famous, towards the story of whom he is hastening. Now concerning the church at Antioch observe,

I. The first preachers of the gospel there were such as were dispersed from Jerusalem by persecution, that persecution which arose five or six years ago (as some compute), at the time of Stephen's death (*v.* 19): *They travelled as far as Phenice* and other places *preaching the word.* God suffered them to be persecuted, that thereby they might be dispersed in the world, sown as seed to God, in order to their bringing forth much fruit. Thus what was intended for the hurt of the church was made to work for its good; as Jacob's curse of the tribe of Levi (*I will divide them in Jacob, and scatter them in Israel*) was turned into a blessing. The enemies designed to scatter and lose them, Christ designed to scatter and use them. Thus the wrath of man is made to praise God. Observe,

1. Those that *fled from persecution* did not flee from their work; though for the time they declined suffering, yet they did not decline service; nay, they threw themselves into a larger field of opportunity than before. Those that persecuted the preachers of the gospel hoped thereby to prevent their carrying it to the Gentile world; but it proved that they did but hasten it the sooner. *Howbeit, they meant not so, neither did their heart think so.* Those that were persecuted in one city fled to another; but they carried their religion along with them, not only that they might take the comfort of it themselves, but that they might communicate it to others, thus showing that when they got out of the way it was not because they were afraid of suffering, but because they were willing to reserve themselves for further service.

2. They pressed forward in their work, finding that the *good pleasure of the Lord prospered in their hands.* When they had preached successfully in Judea, Samaria, and Galilee, they got out of the borders of the land of Canaan, and travelled into Phoenicia, into the island of Cyprus, and into Syria. Though the further they travelled the more they exposed themselves, yet they travelled on; *plus ultra — further still,* was their motto; grudging no pains, and dreading no perils, in carrying on so good a work, and serving so good a Master.

3. They *preached the word to none but to the Jews only* who were dispersed in all those parts, and had synagogues of their own, in which they met with them by themselves, and preached to them. They did not yet understand that the Gentiles were to be fellow-heirs, and of the same body; but left the Gentiles either to turn Jews, and so come into the church, or else remain as they were.

4. They particularly applied themselves to the Hellenist Jews, here called the Grecians, that were at Antioch. Many of the preachers were natives of Judea and Jerusalem; but some of them were by birth of Cyprus and Cyrene, as Barnabas himself (*ch.* 4:36), and Simon (Mk. 15:21), but had their education in Jerusalem; and these, being themselves Grecian Jews, had a particular concern for those of their own denomination and distinction, and applied themselves closely to them at Antioch. Dr. Lightfoot says that they were there called *Hellenists,* or *Grecians,* because they were Jews of the corporation or enfranchisement of the city; for Antioch was

a Syrogrecian city. To them they preached the Lord Jesus. This was the constant subject of their preaching; what else should the ministers of Christ preach, but Christ — Christ, and him crucified — Christ, and him glorified?

5. They had wonderful success in their preaching, *v.* 21. (1.) Their preaching was accompanied with a divine power: *The hand of the Lord was with them,* which some understand of the power they were endued with to work miracles for the confirming of their doctrine; in these the Lord *was working with them, for he confirmed the word with signs following* (Mk. 16:20); in these God *bore them witness,* Heb. 2:4. But I rather under-stand it of the power of divine grace working on the hearts of the hearers, and opening them, as Lydia's heart was opened, because many saw the miracles who were not converted; but when by the Spirit the understanding was enlightened, and the will bowed to the gospel of Christ, that was a day of power, in which volunteers were enlisted under the banner of the Lord Jesus, Ps. 110:3. *The hand of the Lord was with them,* to bring that home to the hearts and consciences of men which they could but speak to the outward ear. Then the word of the Lord gains its end, when the hand of the Lord goes along with it, to write it in their heart. Then people are brought to believe the report of the gospel, when with it the *arm of the Lord is revealed* (Isa. 53:1), when God *teaches with a strong hand,* Isa. 8:11. These were not apostles, but ordinary ministers, yet they had the hand of the Lord with them, and did wonders. (2.) Abundance of good was done: *A great number believed, and turned unto the Lord* — many more than could have been expected, considering the outward disadvantages they laboured under: some of all sorts of people were wrought upon, and brought into obedience to Christ. Observe, What the change was. [1.] They believed; they were convinced of the truth of the gospel, and subscribed to the record God had given in it concerning his Son. [2.] The effect and evidence of this was that they *turned unto the Lord.* They could not be said to turn from the service of idols, for they were Jews, worshippers of the true God only; but they turned from a confidence in the righteousness of the law, to rely only upon the righteousness of Christ, the righteousness which is by faith; they turned from a loose, careless, carnal way of living, to live a holy, heavenly, spiritual, and divine life; they turned from worshipping God in show and ceremony, to worship him *in spirit and in truth.* They turned to the Lord Jesus, and he became all in all with them. This was the work of conversion wrought upon them, and it must be wrought upon every one of us. It was the fruit of their faith. All that sincerely believe will turn to the Lord; for, whatever we profess or pretend, we do not really believe the gospel if we do not cordially embrace Christ offered to us in the gospel.

II. The good work thus begun at Antioch was carried on to great perfection; and the church, thus founded, grew to be a flourishing one, by the ministry of Barnabas and Saul, who built upon the foundation which the other preachers had laid, and *entered into their labours,* Jn. 4:37, 38.

1. The church at Jerusalem sent Barnabas thither, to nurse this new-born church, and to strengthen the hands both of preachers and people, and put a reputation upon the cause of Christ there.

(1.) They heard the good news, that the gospel was received at Antioch, *v.* 22. The apostles there were inquisitive how the work went on in the countries about; and, it is likely, kept up a correspondence with all parts where preachers were, so that *tidings of these things,* of the great numbers that were converted at Antioch, soon *came to the ears of the church that was in Jerusalem.* Those that are in the most eminent stations in the church ought to concern themselves for those in a lower sphere.

(2.) They despatched Barnabas to them with all speed; they desired him to go, and assist and encourage these hopeful beginnings. They *sent him forth* as an envoy from them, and a representative of their whole body, to congratulate them upon the success of the gospel among them, as matter of rejoicing both to preachers and hearers, and with both they rejoiced. He must go *as far as Antioch.* It was a great way, but, far as it was, he was willing to undertake the journey for a public service. It is probable that Barnabas had a particular genius for work of this kind, was active and conversable, loved to be in motion, and delighted in doing good abroad as much as others in doing good at home, was as much of Zebulun's spirit, who rejoiced *in his going out,* as others are of Issachar's, who rejoiced *in his tent;* and, his talent lying this way, he was fittest to be employed in this work. God gives various gifts for various services.

(3.) Barnabas was wonderfully pleased to find that the gospel got ground, and that some of his countrymen, men of Cyprus (of which country he was, *ch.* 4:36) were instrumental in it (*v.* 23): *When he came, and had seen the grace of God,* the tokens of God's good-will to the people of Antioch and the evidences of his good work among them, *he was glad.* He took time to make his observations, and not only in their public worship, but in their common conversations and in their families, he saw the grace of God among them. Where the grace of God is it will be seen, as the *tree is known by its fruits;* and, where it is seen, it ought to be owned. What we see which is good in any we must call God's grace in them, and give that grace the glory of it; and we ought ourselves to take the comfort of it, and make it the matter of our rejoicing. We must be glad to see the grace of God in others, and the more when we see it where we did not expect it.

(4.) He did what he could to fix them, to confirm those in the faith who were converted to the faith. He *exhorted them — parekalei.* It is the same word with that by which the name of Barnabas is interpreted (*ch.* 4:36), *hyios paraklēseōs — a son of exhortation;* his talent lay that way, and he traded with it; let him that *exhorteth attend to exhortation,* Rom. 12:8. Or, being *a son of consolation* (for so we render the word), he *comforted or encouraged them with purpose of heart to cleave to the Lord.* The more he rejoiced in the beginning of the good work among them, the more earnest he was with them to proceed according to these good beginnings. Those we have comfort in we should exhort. Barnabas was glad for what he saw of the grace of God among them, and therefore was the more earnest with them to persevere. [1.] To *cleave to the Lord.* Note, Those that have *turned to the Lord* are concerned to *cleave unto the Lord,* not to fall off from following him, not to flag and tire in following him. To cleave to the Lord Jesus is to live a life of dependence upon him and devotedness to him: not only to hold him fast, but to hold fast by him, to *be strong in the Lord and in the power of his might.* [2.] To cleave to him with purpose of heart, with an intelligent, firm, and deliberate resolution, founded upon good grounds, and fixed upon that foundation, Ps. 108:1. It is to bind our souls with a bond to be the Lord's, and to say as Ruth, *Entreat me not to leave* him, or to return from following after him.

(5.) Herein he gave a proof of his good character (*v.* 24): *He was a good man, and full of the Holy Ghost, and of faith,* and approved himself so upon this occasion. [1.] He showed himself to be a man of a very sweet, affable, courteous disposition, that had himself the art of obliging, and could teach others. He was not only a righteous man, but a *good man,* a good-tempered man. Ministers that are so recommend themselves and their doctrine very much to the good opinion of those that are without. He was a good man, that is, a charitable man; so he had approved himself, when he sold an estate, and gave the money to the poor, *ch.* 4:37. [2.] By this it appeared that he was richly endued with the gifts and graces of the Spirit. The goodness of his natural disposition would not have qualified him for this service if he had not been *full of the Holy Ghost, and so full of power by the Spirit of the Lord.* [3.] He was full of faith, full of the Christian faith himself, and therefore desirous to propagate it among others; full of the grace of faith, and full of the fruits of that faith that works by love. He was *sound in the faith,* and therefore pressed them to be so.

(6.) He was instrumental to do good, by bringing in those that were without, as well as by building up those that were within: *Much people were added to the Lord,* and thereby added to the *church;* many were turned to the Lord before, yet more are to be turned; it is *done as thou hast commanded, and yet there is room.*

2. Barnabas went to fetch Saul, to join with him in the work of the gospel at Antioch. The last news we heard of him was that, when his life was sought at Jerusalem, he was sent away to Tarsus, the city where he was born, and, it should seem, he continued there ever since, doing good, no doubt. But now Barnabas takes a journey to Tarsus on purpose to see what had become of him, to tell him what a door of opportunity was opened at Antioch, and to desire him to come and spend some time with him there, *v.* 25, 26. And here also it appears that Barnabas was a good sort of a man in two things: — (1.) That he would take so much pains to bring an active useful man out of obscurity. It was he that introduced Saul to the disciples at Jerusalem, when they were shy of him; and it was he that brought him out of the corner into which he was driven, into a more public station. It is a very good work to fetch a candle from under a bushel, and to set it in a candlestick. (2.) That he would bring in Saul at Antioch, who, being a *chief speaker* (*ch.* 14:12), and probably a more popular preacher, would be likely to eclipse him there, by outshining him; but Barnabas is very willing to be eclipsed when it is for the public service. If God by his grace inclines us to do what good we can, according to the ability we have, we ought to rejoice if others that have also larger capacities have larger opportunities, and do more good than we can do. Barnabas brought Saul to Antioch, though it might be the lessening of himself, to teach us to seek the things of Christ more than our own things.

3. We are here further told,

(1.) What service was now done to the church at Antioch. Paul and Barnabas continued there a whole year, presiding in their religious assemblies, and preaching the gospel, *v.* 26. Observe, [1.] The church frequently assembled. The religious assemblies of Christians are appointed by Christ for his honour, and the comfort and benefit of his disciples. God's people of old frequently came together, *at the door of the tabernacle of the congregation;* places of meeting are now multiplied, but they must come together, though it be with difficulty and peril. [2.] Ministers were the masters of those assemblies, and held those courts in Christ's name to which all that hold by, from, and under him, owe suit and service. [3.] *Teaching the people* is one part of the work of ministers, when they preside in religious assemblies. They are not only to be the people's mouth to God in prayer and praise, but God's mouth to the people in opening the scriptures, and teaching out of them the good knowledge of the Lord. [4.] It is a great encouragement to ministers when they have opportunity of teaching much people, of casting the net of the gospel where there is a large shoal of fish, in hopes that the more may be enclosed. [5.] Preaching is not only for the conviction and conversion of those that are without, but for the instruction and edification of those that are within. A constituted church must have its teachers.

(2.) What honour was now put upon the church *at Antioch: There the disciples were first called Christians;* it is probable they called themselves so, incorporated themselves by that title, whether by some solemn act of the church or ministers, or whether this name insensibly obtained there by its being frequently used in their praying and preaching, we are not told; but it should seem that two such great men as Paul and Barnabas continuing there so long, being exceedingly followed, and meeting with no opposition, Christian assemblies made a greater figure there than any where, and became more considerable, which was the reason of their being called *Christians* first there, which, if there were to be a mother-church to rule over all other churches, would give Antioch a better title to the honour than Rome can pretend to. Hitherto those who gave up their names to Christ were called *disciples, learners, scholars,* trained up under him, in order to their being employed by him; but henceforward they were called *Christians.* [1.] Thus the reproachful names which their enemies had hitherto branded them with would, perhaps, be superseded and disused. They called them *Nazarenes* (*ch.* 24, 5), *the men of that way, that by-way,* which had no name; and thus they prejudiced people against them. To remove the prejudice, they gave themselves a name which their enemies could not but say was proper. [2.] Thus those who before their conversion had been distinguished by the names of Jews and Gentiles might after their conversion be called by one and the same name, which would help them to forget their former dividing names, and prevent their bringing their former marks of distinction, and with them the seeds of contention, into the church. Let not one say, "I was a *Jew;*" nor the other, "I was a *Gentile;*" when both the one and the other must now say, "I am a *Christian.*" [3.] Thus they studied to do honour to their Master, and showed that they were not ashamed to own their relation to him, but gloried in it; as the scholars of Plato called themselves *Platonists,* and so the scholars of other great men. They took their denomination not from the name of his person, *Jesus,* but of his office, *Christ — anointed,* so putting their creed into their names, *that Jesus is the Christ;* and they were willing all the world should know that this is the truth they will live and die by. Their enemies will turn this name to their reproach, and impute it to them as their crime, but they will glory in it: *If this be to be vile, I will be yet more vile.* [4.] Thus they now owned their dependence upon Christ, and their receivings from him; not only that they believed in him who is *the anointed,* but that through him they themselves had *the anointing,* 1 Jn. 2:20, 27. And God is said to have *anointed us in Christ,* 2 Co. 1:21. [5.] Thus they laid upon themselves, and all that should ever profess that name, a strong and lasting obligation to submit to the laws of Christ, to follow the example of Christ, and to devote themselves entirely to the honour of Christ — *to be to him for a name and a praise.* Are we Christians? Then we ought to think, and speak, and act, in every thing as becomes Christians, and to do nothing to the reproach of that worthy name by which we are called; that that may not be said to us which Alexander said to a soldier of his own name that was noted for a coward, *Aut nomen, aut mores muta — Either change thy name or mend thy manners.* And as we must look upon ourselves as Christians, and carry ourselves accordingly, so we must look upon others as Christians, and carry ourselves towards them accordingly. A Christian, though not in every thing of our mind, should be loved and respected for his sake whose name he bears, because he belongs to Christ. [6.] Thus *the scripture was fulfilled,* for so it was written (Isa. 62:2) concerning the gospel-church, *Thou shalt be called by a new name, which the mouth of the Lord shall name.* And it is said to the corrupt and degenerate church of the Jews, *The Lord God shall slay thee, and call his servants by another name,* Isa. 65:15.

Verses 27–30

When our Lord Jesus *ascended on high he gave gifts unto men,* not only *apostles and evangelists, but prophets,* who were enabled by the Spirit to foresee and foretel things to come, which not only served for a confirmation of the truth of Christianity (for all that these prophets foretold came to pass, which proved that *they were sent of God,* Deu. 18:22; Jer. 28:9), but was also of great use to the church, and served very much for its guidance. Now here we have,

I. A visit which some of these prophets made to Antioch (*v.* 27): *In these days,* during that year that Barnabas and Saul lived at Antioch, there *came prophets from Jerusalem to Antioch:* we are not told how many, nor is it certain whether these were any of those prophets that we afterwards find *in the church at Antioch, ch.* 13:1. 1. They came from Jerusalem, probably because they were not now so much regarded there as they had been; they saw their work in a manner done there, and therefore thought it time to be gone. Jerusalem had been infamous for *killing the prophets* and abusing them, and therefore is now justly deprived of these prophets. 2. They came to Antioch, because they heard of the flourishing state of that church, and there they hoped they might be of some service. Thus should *every one as he hath received the gift minister the same.* Barnabas came to exhort them, and they, having received the exhortation well, now have prophets sent them *to show them things to come,* as Christ had promised, Jn. 16:13. Those that are faithful in their little shall be entrusted with more. The best understanding of scripture-predictions is to be got in the way of obedience to scripture-instructions.

II. A particular prediction of a famine approaching, delivered by one of these prophets, his name *Agabus;* we read of him again prophesying Paul's imprisonment, *ch.* 21:10, 11. Here he stood up, probably in one of their public assemblies, and prophesied, *v.* 28. Observe, 1. Whence he had his prophecy. What he said was not of himself, nor a fancy of his own, nor an astronomical prediction, nor a conjecture upon the present workings of second causes, but *he signified it by the Spirit, the Spirit of prophecy, that there should be* a famine; as Joseph, by the Spirit enabling him, understood Pharaoh's dreams, foretold the famine in Egypt, and Elijah the famine in Israel in Ahab's time. Thus God revealed his secrets to his servants the prophets. 2. What the prophecy was: *There should be great dearth throughout all the world,* by unseasonable weather, that corn should be scarce and dear, so that many of the poor should perish for want of bread. This should be not in one particular country, but *through all the world,* that is, all the Roman empire, which they in their pride, like Alexander before them, called *the world.* Christ had foretold in general *that there should be famines* (Mt. 24:7; Mk. 13:8; Lu. 21:11); but Agabus foretels one very remarkable famine now at hand. 3. The accomplishment of it: *It came to pass in the days of Claudius Caesar;* it began in the second year of his reign, and continued to the fourth, if not longer. Several of the Roman historians make mention of it, as does also Josephus. God sent them the bread of life, and they rejected it, loathed the plenty of that manna; and therefore God justly broke the staff of bread, and punished them with famine; and herein he was righteous. They were barren, and did not bring forth to God, and therefore God made the earth barren to them.

III. The good use they made of this prediction. When they were told of a famine at hand, they did not do as the Egyptians, hoard up corn for themselves; but, as became Christians, laid by for charity to relieve others, which is the best preparative for our own sufferings and want. It is promised to those that *consider the poor that God will preserve them, and keep them alive, and they shall be blessed upon the earth,* Ps. 41:1, 2. And *those who show mercy, and give to the poor, shall not be ashamed in the evil time, but in the days of famine they shall be satisfied,* Ps. 37:19, 21. The best provision we can lay up against a dear time is to lay up an interest in these promises, by doing good, and communicating, Lu. 12:33. Many give it as a reason why they should be sparing, but the scripture gives it as a reason why we should be liberal, *to seven, and also to eight,* because *we know not what evil shall be upon the earth,* Eccl. 11:2. Observe,

1. What they determined — that *every man, according to his ability,* should *send relief to the brethren that dwelt in Judea, v.* 29. (1.) The persons that were recommended to them as objects for charity were *the brethren that dwelt in Judea.* Though we must, as we have opportunity, *do good to all men,* yet we must have a special regard *to the household of faith,* Gal. 6:10. No poor must be neglected, but God's poor most particularly regarded. The care which every particular church ought to take of their own poor we were taught by the early instance of that in the church at Jerusalem, where the ministration was so constant *that none lacked,* ch. 4:34. But the communion of saints in that instance is here extended further, and provision is made by the church at Antioch for the relief of the poor in Judea, whom they call their brethren. It seems it was the custom of the Jews of the dispersion to send money to those Jews who dwelt in Judea, for the relief of the poor that were among them, and to make collections for that purpose (Tully speaks of such a thing in his time, *Orat. pro Flacco),* which supposes there were many poor in Judea, more than in other countries, so that the rich among them were not able to bear the charge of keeping them from starving; either because their land had become *barren,* though it had been a fruitful land, *for the iniquity of those that dwelt therein,* or because they had no traffic with other nations. Now we may suppose that the greatest part of those who turned Christians in that country were the poor (Mt. 11:5, *The poor are evangelized),* and also that when the poor turned Christians they were put out of the poor's book, and cut off from their shares in the public charity; and it were easy to foresee that if there came a famine it would go very hard with them; and, if any of them should perish for want, it would be a great reproach to the Christian profession; and therefore this early care was taken, upon notice of this famine coming, to send them a stock beforehand, lest, if it should be deferred till the famine came, it should be too late. (2.) The agreement there was among the disciples about it, that *every man* should contribute, *according to his ability,* to this good work. The Jews abroad, in other countries, grew rich by trade, and many of the rich Jews became Christians, whose abundance ought to be a *supply to the want of their poor brethren* that were at a great distance; for the case of such ought to be considered, and not theirs only that live among us. Charitable people are traders with what God has given them, and the merchants find their account in sending effects to countries that lie very remote; and so should we in giving alms to those afar off that need them, which therefore we should be forward to do when we are called to it. *Every man determined to send* something, more or less, *according to his ability,* what he could spare from the support of himself and his family, and *according as God had prospered him.* What may be said to be *according to our ability* we must judge for ourselves, but must be careful *that we judge righteous judgment.*

2. What they did — they did as they determined (v. 30). *Which also they did.* They not only talked of it, but they did it. Many a good motion of that kind is made and commended, but is not prosecuted, and so comes to nothing. But this was pursued, the collection was made, and was so considerable that they thought it worth while *to send Barnabas and*

Saul to Jerusalem, to carry it *to the elders* there, though they would want their labours in the mean time at Antioch. They sent it, (1.) *To the elders,* the presbyters, the ministers or pastors, *of the churches in Judea,* to be by them distributed according to the necessity of the receivers, as it had been contributed according to the ability of the givers. (2.) It was sent *by Barnabas and Saul,* who perhaps wanted an occasion to go to Jerusalem, and therefore were willing to take this. Josephus tells us that at this time king Irates sent his charity to the chief men of Jerusalem, for the poor of that country; and Helena, queen of the Adiabeni, being now at Jerusalem, and hearing of many that died of famine there, and in the country about, sent for provisions from Cyprus and Alexandria, and distributed them among the people; so says Dr. Lightfoot, who also computes, by the date of Paul's rapture, "fourteen years before he wrote the second Epistle to the Corinthians" (2 Co. 12:1, 2), that it was in this journey of his *to Jerusalem, with these alms and offerings,* that he had his *trance* in the temple (which he speaks of, ch. 22:17), and in that *trance was rapt up into the third heaven;* and then it was that Christ told him he would send him thence *unto the Gentiles,* which accordingly he did as soon as ever he came back to Antioch. It is no disparagement, in an extraordinary case, for ministers of the gospel to be messengers of the church's charity, though to undertake the constant care of that matter would ordinarily be too great a diversion from more needful work *to those who have given themselves to prayer and the ministry of the word.*

CHAPTER 12

In this chapter we have the story, I. Of the martyrdom of James the apostle, and the imprisonment of Peter by Herod Agrippa, who now reigned as king in Judea (v. 1–4). II. The miraculous deliverance of Peter out of prison by the ministry of an angel, in answer to the prayers of the church for him (v. 6–19). III. The cutting off of Herod in the height of his pride by the stroke of an angel, the minister of God's justice (v. 20–23); and this was done while Barnabas and Saul were at Jerusalem, upon the errand that the church of Antioch sent them on, to carry their charity; and therefore in the close we have an account of their return to Antioch (v. 24, 25).

Verses 1–4

Ever since the conversion of Paul, we have heard no more of the agency of the priests in persecuting the saints at Jerusalem; perhaps that wonderful change wrought upon him, and the disappointment it gave to their design upon the Christians at Damascus, had somewhat mollified them, and brought them under the check of Gamaliel's advice — to *let those men alone,* and see what would be the issue; but here the storm arises from another point. The civil power, not now, as usual (for aught that appears) stirred up by the ecclesiastics, acts by itself in the persecution. But Herod, though originally of an Edomite family, yet seems to have been a proselyte to the Jewish religion; for Josephus says he was zealous for the Mosaic rites, a bigot for the ceremonies. He was not only (as Herod Antipas was) tetrarch of Galilee, but had also the government of Judea committed to him by Claudius the emperor, and resided most at Jerusalem, where he was at this time. Three things we are here told he did: —

I. He *stretched forth his hands to vex certain of the church, v.* 1. His stretching forth his hands to it intimates that his hands had been tied up by the restraints which perhaps his own conscience held him under in this matter; but now he broke through them, and stretched forth his hands deliberately, and of malice prepense. *Herod laid hands upon some of the church to afflict them,* so some read it; he employed his officers to seize them, and take them into custody, in order to their being prosecuted. See how he advances gradually. 1. He began with some of the members of the church, certain of them that were of less note and figure; played first at small game, but afterwards flew at the apostles themselves. His spite was at the church, and, with regard to those he gave trouble to, it was not upon any other account, but because they belonged to the church, and so belonged to Christ. 2. He began with vexing them only, or afflicting them, imprisoning them, fining them, spoiling their houses and goods, and other ways molesting them; but afterwards he proceeded to greater instances of cruelty. Christ's suffering servants are thus trained up by less troubles for greater, *that tribulation may work patience, and patience experience.*

II. He *killed James the brother of John with the sword, v.* 2. We are here to consider, 1. Who the martyr was: it was *James the brother of John;* so called to distinguish him from the other James the brother of Joses. This was called *Jaco-*

bus major — James the greater; that, minor-the less. This who was here crowned with martyrdom was one of the first three of Christ's disciples, one of those that were *the witnesses of his transfiguration and agony,* whereby he was prepared for martyrdom; he was one of those whom Christ called *Boanerges — Sons of thunder;* and perhaps by his powerful awakening preaching he had provoked Herod, or those about him, as John Baptist did the other Herod, and that was the occasion of his coming into this trouble. He was one of those sons of Zebedee whom Christ told *that they should drink of the cup that he was to drink of, and be baptized with the baptism that he was to be baptized with,* Mt. 20:23. And now those words of Christ were made good in him; but it was in order to his sitting at Christ's right hand; for *if we suffer with him, we shall reign with him.* He was one of the twelve who were commissioned *to disciple all nations;* and to take him off now, before he had removed from Jerusalem, was like Cain's killing Abel when the world was to be peopled, and one man was then more than many at another time. To kill an apostle now was killing he knew not how many. But why would God permit it? If *the blood of his saints,* much more the blood of apostles, *is precious in his eyes,* and therefore, we may be sure, is not shed but upon a valuable consideration. Perhaps God intended hereby to awaken the rest of the apostles to disperse themselves among the nations, and not to nestle any longer at Jerusalem. Or it was to show that though the apostles were appointed *to plant the gospel in the world,* yet if they were taken off God could do his work without them, and would do it. The apostle died a martyr, to show the rest of them what they must expect, that they might prepare accordingly. The tradition that they have in the Romish church, that this James had been before this in Spain, and had planted the gospel there, is altogether groundless; nor is there any certainty of it, or good authority for it. 2. What kind of death he suffered: He was slain *with the sword,* that is, his head was *cut off with a sword,* which was looked upon by the Romans to be a more disgraceful way of being beheaded than with an axe; so Lorinus. Beheading was not ordinarily used among the Jews; but, when kings gave verbal orders for private and sudden executions, this manner of death was used, as most expeditious; and it is probable that this Herod killed James, as the other Herod killed John Baptist, privately *in the prison.* It is strange that we have not a more full and particular account of the martyrdom of this great apostle, as we had of Stephen. But even this short mention of the thing is sufficient to let us know that the first preachers of the gospel were so well assured of the truth of it that they sealed it with their blood, and thereby have encouraged us, if at any time we are called to it, *to resist unto blood too.* The Old-Testament martyrs were *slain with the sword* (Heb. 11:37), and Christ *came not to send peace, but a sword* (Mt. 10:34), in preparation for which we must arm ourselves *with the sword of the Spirit,* which is the word of God, and then we need not fear *what* the sword of *men can do unto us.*

III. He imprisoned Peter, of whom he had heard most, as making the greatest figure among the apostles and whom therefore he would be proud of the honour of taking off. Observe here, 1. When he had beheaded James, *he proceeded further,* he added, *to take Peter also.* Note, Blood to the blood-thirsty does but make them more so, and the way of persecution, as of other sins, is downhill; when men are in it, they cannot easily stop themselves; when they are in they find they must on. *Male facta male factis tegere ne perpluant — One evil deed is covered with another, so that there is no passage through them.* Those that take one bold step in a sinful way give Satan advantage against them to tempt them to take another, and provoke God to leave them to them-selves, to go from bad to worse. It is therefore our wisdom to take heed of the beginnings of sin. 2. He did this *because he saw it pleased the Jews.* Observe, The Jews made themselves guilty of the blood of James by showing themselves well pleased with it afterwards, though they had not excited Herod to it. There are accessaries *ex post facto — after the fact;* and those will be reckoned with as persecutors who take pleasure in others' persecuting, who delight to see good men ill used, and cry, Aha, so would we have it, or at least secretly approve of it. For bloody persecutors, when they perceive themselves applauded for that which every one ought to cry shame upon them for, are encouraged to go on, and have their hands strengthened and their hearts hardened, and the checks of their own consciences smothered; nay, it is as strong a temptation to them to do the like as it was here to Herod, *because he saw it pleased the Jews.* Though he had no reason to fear displeasing them if he did not, as Pilate condemned Christ, yet he hoped to please them by doing it, and so to make an interest among them, and make amends for displeasing them in something else. Note, Those make themselves an easy prey to Satan who make it their business to please men. 3. Notice is taken of the time when Herod laid hold on Peter: *Then were the days of unleavened bread.* It was at the feast of the passover, when their celebrating the memorial of their typical deliverance should have led them to the acceptance of their spiritual deliverance; instead of this, they, under pretence of zeal for the law, were most violently fighting against it, and, in *the days of unleavened bread,* were most soured and embittered *with the old leaven of malice and wickedness.* At the passover, when *the Jews came from all parts to Jerusalem to keep the feast,* they irritated one another against the Christians and Christianity, and were then more violent than at other times. 4. Here is an account of Peter's imprisonment (*v.* 4): *When he* had laid hands on him, and, it is likely, examined him, *he put him in prison,* into the inner prison; some say, into the same prison into which he and the other apostles were cast some years before, and were rescued out of it by an angel, *ch.* 5:18. He was *delivered to four quaternions of soldiers,* that is, to sixteen, who were to be a guard upon him, four at a time, that he should not make his escape, nor be rescued by his friends. Thus they thought they had him fast. 5. Herod's design was, *after Easter, to bring him forth unto the people.* (1.) He would make a spectacle of him. Probably he had put James to death privately, which the people had complained of, not because it was an unjust thing to put a man to death without giving him a public hearing, but because it deprived them of the satisfaction of seeing him executed; and therefore Herod, now he knows their minds, will gratify them with the sight of Peter in bonds, of Peter upon the block, that they may feed their eyes with such a pleasing spectacle. And very ambitious surely he was to please the people who was willing thus to please them! (2.) He would do this *after Easter, meta to pascha — after the passover,* certainly so it ought to be read, for it is the same word that is always so rendered; and to insinuate the introducing of a gospel-feast, instead of the passover, when we have nothing in the New Testament of such a thing, is to mingle Judaism with our Christianity. Herod would not condemn him till the passover was over, some think, for fear lest he should have such an interest among the people that they should demand the release of him, according to the custom of the feast: or, after the hurry of the feast was over, and the town was empty, he would entertain them with Peter's public trial and execution. Thus was the plot laid, and both Herod and the people long to have the feast over, that they may gratify themselves with this barbarous entertainment.

Verses 5–19

We have here an account of Peter's deliverance out of prison, by which the design of Herod against him was defeated, and his life preserved for further service, and a stop given to this bloody torrent. Now,

I. One thing that magnified his deliverance was that it was a signal answer to prayer (*v.* 5): *Peter was kept in prison* with a great deal of care, so that it was altogether impossible, either by force or by stealth, to get him out. *But prayer was made without ceasing of the church unto God for him,* for prayers and tears are the church's arms; therewith she fights, not only against her enemies, but for her friends: and to these means they have recourse. 1. The delay of Peter's trial gave them time for prayer. It is probable that James was hurried off so suddenly and so privately that they had not time to pray for him, God so ordering it that they should not have space to pray, when he designed they should not have the thing they prayed for. James must be offered upon the sacrifice and service of their faith, and therefore prayer for him is restrained and prevented; but Peter must be continued to them, and therefore prayer for him is stirred up, and time is given them for it, by Herod's putting off the prosecution. *Howbeit, he meant not so, neither did his heart think so.* 2. They were very particular in their prayers for him, that it would please God, some way or other, to defeat Herod's purpose, and to snatch the lamb out of the jaws of the lion. The death of James alarmed them to a greater fervency in their prayer for Peter; for, if they be broken thus with breach upon breach, they fear that the enemy will make a full end. Stephen is not, and James is not, and will they take Peter also? All these things are against them; this will be sorrow upon sorrow, Phil. 2:27. Note, Though the death and sufferings of Christ's ministers may be made greatly to serve the interests of Christ's kingdom, yet it is the duty and concern of the church earnestly to pray for their life, liberty, and tranquillity; and sometimes Providence orders it that they are brought into imminent danger, to stir up prayer for them. 3. *Prayer was made without ceasing;* it was, *proseuchē ektenēs — fervent prayer.* It is the word that is used concerning Christ's praying in his agony *more earnestly;* it is *the fervent prayer of the righteous man, that* is effectual, and *availeth much.* Some think it denotes the constancy and continuance of their prayers; so we take it: *They prayed without ceasing.* It was an extended prayer; they prayed for his release in their public assemblies (private ones, perhaps, *for fear of the Jews);* then they went home, and prayed for it in their families; then retired into their closets, and prayed for it there; so *they prayed without ceasing:* or first one knot of them, and then another, and then a third, kept a day of prayer, or rather a night of prayer, for him, *v.* 12. Note, Times of public distress and danger should be praying times with the church; we must pray always, but then especially.

II. Another thing that magnified his deliverance was that *when the king's commandment and decree drew near to be put in execution,* then his deliverance was wrought, as Esth. 9:1, 2. Let us observe when his deliverance came. 1. It was the very night before Herod designed to bring him forth, which made it to be so much the greater consolation to his friends and confusion to his enemies. It is probable some who had an interest in Herod, or those about him, had been improving it to get a discharge for Peter, but in vain; Herod resolves he shall die. And now they despair of prevailing in this way, for to-morrow is *the day set for the bringing of him forth;* and, it is likely, they will make as quick work with him as with his Master; and now God opened a door of escape for him. Note, God's time to help is when things are brought to the last extremity, when there is none shut up nor left (Deu. 32:36), and for this reason it has been said, "The worse the better." When Isaac is bound upon the altar, and the knife in the hand, and the hand stretched out to slay him, then *Jehovah-jireh, the Lord will provide.* 2. It was when he was *fast bound with two chains, between two soldiers;* so that if he offer to stir he wakes them; and, besides this, though the prison-doors, no doubt, were locked and bolted, yet, to make sure work, *the keepers before the door kept the prison,* that no one might so much as attempt to rescue him. Never could the art of man do more to secure a prisoner. Herod, no doubt, said, as Pilate (Mt. 27:65), *make it as sure as you can.* When men will think to be too hard for God, God will make it appear that he is too hard for them. 3. It was when he was *sleeping between the soldiers,* fast asleep; (1.) Not terrified with his danger, though it was very imminent, and there was no visible way for his escape. There was but a step between him and death, and yet he could lay himself down in peace, and sleep — sleep in the midst of his enemies — sleep when, it may be, they were awake, having a good cause that he suffered for, and a good conscience that he suffered with, and being assured that God would issue his trial that way that should be most for his glory. Having *committed his cause to him that judgeth righteously, his soul dwells at ease;* and even in prison, between two soldiers, God gives him sleep, as he doth to his beloved. (2.) Not expecting his deliverance. He did not keep awake, looking to the right hand, or to the left, for relief, but lay asleep, and was perfectly surprised with his deliverance. Thus the church (Ps. 126:1): *We were like those that dream.*

III. It also magnified his deliverance very much that an *angel was sent from heaven* on purpose to rescue him, which made his escape both practicable and warrantable. This angel brought him a legal discharge, and enabled him to make use of it.

1. *The angel of the Lord came upon him; epestē — stood over him.* He seemed as one abandoned by men, yet not forgotten of his God; *The Lord thinketh upon him.* Gates and guards kept all his friends from him, but could not keep the angels of God from him: and *they invisibly encamp round about those that fear God, to deliver them* (Ps. 34:7), *and therefore they need not fear, though a host of enemies encamp against them,* Ps. 27:3. Wherever the people of God are, and however surrounded, they have a way open heavenward, nor can any thing intercept their intercourse with God.

2. *A light shone in the prison.* Though it is a dark place, and in the night, Peter shall see his way clear. Some observe that we do not find in the Old Testament that where angels appeared *the light shone round about them;* for that was a dark dispensation, and the glory of angels was then veiled. But in the New Testament, when mention is made of the appearing of the angels, notice is taken of the light that they appeared in; for it is by the gospel that the upper world is brought to light. The soldiers to whom Peter was chained were either struck into a deep sleep for the present (as Saul and his soldiers were when David carried off his spear and cruise of water), or, if they were awake, the appearance of the angel made them to *shake, and to become as dead men,* as it was with the guard set on Christ's sepulchre.

3. The angel awoke Peter, by giving him *a blow on his side,* a gentle touch, enough to rouse him out of his sleep, though so fast asleep that the light that shone upon him did not awaken him. When good people slumber in a time of danger, and are not awakened by the light of the word, and the discoveries it gives them, let them expect to be smitten on the side by some sharp affliction; better be raised up so than left asleep. The language of this stroke was, *Arise up quickly;* not as if the angel feared coming short by his delay, but Peter must not be indulged in it. When David hears *the sound of the going on the tops of the mulberry trees, then he must rise up quickly, and bestir himself.*

4. *His chains fell off from his hands.* It seems they had handcuffed him, to make him sure, but *God loosed his bands;* and, if they fall off from his hands, it is as well as if he had the strength of Samson to break them like threads of tow. Tradition makes a mighty rout about these chains, and tells a formal story that one of the soldiers kept them for a sacred relic, and they were long after presented to Eudoxia the empress, and I know not what miracles are said to have been wrought by them; and the Romish church keeps a feast on the first of August yearly in remembrance of Peter's chains, *festum vinculorum Petri — The feast of Peter's chains;* whereas this was at the passover. Surely they are thus fond of Peter's chains in hope with them to enslave the world!

5. He was ordered to dress himself immediately, and follow the angel; and he did so, *v.* 8, 9. When Peter was awake he knew not what to do but as the angel directed him. (1.) He must *gird himself;* for those that slept in their clothes ungirded themselves, so that they had nothing to do, when they got up, but to fasten their girdles. (2.) He *must bind on his sandals,* that he might be fit to walk. Those whose bonds are loosed by the power of divine grace must have *their feet shod with the preparation of the gospel of peace.* (3.) He must *cast his garments about him,* and come away as he was, and follow the angel; and he might go with a great deal of courage and cheerfulness who had a messenger from heaven for his guide and guard. He *went out, and followed him.* Those who are delivered out of a spiritual imprisonment must follow their deliverer, as Israel when they went out of the house of bondage did; they *went out, not knowing whither they went,* but whom they followed. Now it is said, when Peter went out after the angel, *he knew not that it was true which was done by the angel,* that it was really a matter of fact, *but thought he saw a vision;* and, if he did, it was not the first he had seen: but by this it appears that a heavenly vision was so plain, and carried so much of its own evidence along with it, that it was difficult to distinguish between what was done in fact and what was done in vision. *When the Lord brought back the captivity of his people we were like those that dream,* Ps. 126:1. Peter was so; he thought the news was too good to be true.

6. He was led safely by the angel out of danger, *v.* 10. Guards were kept at one pass and at another, which they were to make their way through when they were out of the prison, and they did so without any opposition; nay, for aught that appears, without any discovery: either their eyes were closed; or their hands were tied, or their hearts failed them; so it was that the angel and Peter safely *passed the first and second ward.* Those watchmen represented the watchmen of the Jewish church, on whom God had *poured out a spirit of slumber, eyes that they should not see and ears that they should not hear,* Rom. 11:8. His *watchmen are blind, sleeping, lying down, and loving to slumber.* But still there is an iron gate, after all, that will stop them, and, if the guards can but recover themselves, there they may recover their prison-

er, as Pharaoh hoped to retake Israel at the Red Sea. However, up to that gate they march, and, like the Red Sea before Israel, it *opened to them.* They did not so much as put a hand to it, but it opened *of its own accord,* by an invisible power; and thus was fulfilled in the letter what was figuratively promised to Cyrus (Isa. 45:1, 2): *I will open before him the two-leaved gates, will break in pieces the gates of brass, and cut in sunder the bars of iron.* And probably the iron gate shut again of itself, that none of the guards might pursue Peter. Note, When God will work salvation for his people, no difficulties in their way are insuperable; but even gates of iron are made to open of their own accord. This iron gate led him into the city out of the castle or tower; whether within the gates of the city or without is not certain, so that, when they were through this, they were got into the street. This deliverance of Peter represents to us our redemption by Christ, which is often spoken of as the setting of prisoners free, not only the proclaiming of liberty to the captives, but the *bringing of them out of the prison-house.* The application of the redemption in the conversion of souls is the *sending forth of the prisoners, by the blood of the covenant, out of the pit wherein is no water,* Zec. 9:11. The grace of God, like this angel of the Lord, brings light first into the prison, by the opening of the understanding, smites the sleeping sinner on the side by the awakening of the conscience, causes the chains to fall off from the hands by the renewing of the will, and then gives the word of command, *Gird thyself, and follow me.* Difficulties are to be passed through, and the opposition of Satan and his instruments, a first and second ward, an untoward generation, from which we are concerned to save ourselves; and we shall be saved by the grace of God, if we put ourselves under the divine conduct. And at length the iron gate shall be opened to us, to enter into the New Jerusalem, where we shall be perfectly freed from all the marks of our captivity, and brought into the *glorious liberty of the children of God.*

7. When this was done, *the angel departed from him,* and left him to himself. He was out of danger from his enemies, and needed no guard. He knew where he was, and how to find out his friends, and needed no guide, and therefore his heavenly guard and guide bids him farewell. Note, Miracles are not to be expected when ordinary means are to be used. When Peter has now no more wards to pass, nor iron gates to get through, he needs only the ordinary invisible ministration of the angels, who encamp round about those that fear God, and deliver them.

IV. Having seen how his deliverance was magnified, we are next to see how it was manifested both to himself and others, and how, being made great, it was made known. We are here told,

1. How Peter came to himself, and so came himself to the knowledge of it, *v.* 11. So many strange and surprising things coming together upon a man just awoke out of sleep put him for the present into some confusion; so that he knew not where he was, nor what he did, nor whether it was fancy or fact; but at length Peter *came to himself,* was thoroughly awake, and found that it was not a dream, but a real thing: *"Now I know of a surety,* now I know *alēthōs — truly,* now I know that it is truth, and not an illusion of the fancy. Now I am well satisfied concerning it *that the Lord Jesus hath sent his angel,* for angels are subject to him and go on his errands, and by him *hath delivered me out of the hands of Herod,* who thought he had me fast, and so hath disappointed *all the expectation of the people of the Jews,* who doubted not to see Peter cut off the next day, and hoped it was the one neck of Christianity, in which it would all be struck off at one blow." For this reason it was a cause of great expectation, among not only the common people, but the great people of the Jews. Peter, when he recollected himself, *perceived of a truth* what great things God had done for him, which at first he could not believe for joy. Thus souls who are delivered out of a spiritual bondage are not at first aware what God has wrought in them. Many have the truth of grace that want the evidence of it. They are questioning whether there be indeed this change wrought in them, or whether they have not been all this while in a dream. But *when the Comforter comes, whom the Father will send* sooner or later, he will let them know of a surety what a blessed change is wrought in them, and what a happy state they are brought into.

2. How Peter came to his friends, and brought the knowledge of it to them. Here is a particular account of this, and it is very interesting.

(1.) He *considered the thing* (*v.* 12), considered how imminent his danger was, how great his deliverance; and now what has he to do? What improvement must he make of this deliverance? What must he do next? God's providence leaves room for the use of our prudence; and, though he has undertaken to perform and perfect what he has begun, yet he expects we should consider the thing.

(2.) He went directly to a friend's house, which, it is likely, lay near to the place where he was; it was the house of Mary, a sister of Barnabas, and mother of John Mark, whose house, it should seem, was frequently made use of for the private meeting of the disciples, either because it lay obscure, or because she was more forward than others were to open her doors to them; and, no doubt, it was, like the house of Obededom, blessed for the ark's sake. A church in the house makes it a little sanctuary.

(3.) There he found *many* that were *gathered together praying,* at the dead time of the night, praying for Peter, who was the next day to come upon his trial, that God would find out some way or other for his deliverance. Observe, [1.] They continued in prayer, in token of their importunity; they did not think it enough once to have presented his case to God, but they did it again and again. Thus *men ought always to pray, and not to faint.* As long as we are kept waiting for a mercy we must continue praying for it. [2.] It should seem that now when the affair came near to a crisis, and the very next day was fixed for the determining of it, they were more fervent in prayer than before; and it was a good sign that God intended to deliver Peter when he thus stirred up a spirit of prayer for his deliverance, for he never *said to the seed of Jacob, Seek ye my face in vain.* [3.] They gathered together for prayer on this occasion; though this would made them obnoxious to the government if they were discovered, yet they know what an encouragement Christ gave to joint-prayer, Mt. 18:19, 20. And it was always the practice of God's praying people to unite their forces in prayer, as 2 Chr. 20:4; Esth. 4:16. [4.] They were many that were got together for this work, as many perhaps as the room would hold; and first one prayed, and then another, of those who gave themselves to the word and prayer, the rest joining with them; or, if they had not ministers among them, no doubt but there were many private Christians that knew how to pray, and to pray pertinently, and to continue long in prayer when the affections of those who joined were so stirred as to keep pace with them upon such an occasion. This was in the night, when others were asleep, which was an instance both of their prudence and of their zeal. Note, It is good for Christians to have private meetings for prayer, especially in times of distress, and not to let fall nor forsake such assemblies. [5.] Peter came to them when they were thus employed, which was an immediate present answer to their prayer. It was as if God should say, "You are praying that Peter may be restored to you; now here he is." *While they are yet speaking, I will hear,* Isa. 65:24. Thus the angel was sent with an answer of peace to Daniel's prayer, *while he was praying,* Dan. 9:20, 21. *Ask, and it shall be given.*

(4.) He knocked at the gate, and had much ado to get them to let him in (*v.* 13–16): *Peter knocked at the door of the gate,* designing by it to awaken them out of their sleep, and, for aught that appears, not knowing that he disturbed them in their devotions. Yet, if his friends were permitted to speak with him in private in the prison, it is possible he might know of this appointment, and it was this which he recollected and considered when he determined to go to that house, where he knew he should find many of his friends together. Now when he knocked there, [1.] A *damsel came to hearken;* not to open the door till she knew who was there, a friend or a foe, and what their business was, fearing informers. Whether this damsel was one of the family or one of the church, whether a servant or a daughter, does not appear; it should seem, by her being named, that she was of note among the Christians, and more zealously affected to the better part than most of her age. [2.] She knew Peter's voice, having often heard him pray, and preach, and discourse, with a great deal of pleasure. But, instead of letting him in immediately out of the cold, *she opened not the gate for gladness.* Thus sometimes, in a transport of affection to our friends, we do that which is unkind. In an ecstasy of joy she forgets herself, and *opened not the gate.* [3.] She ran in, and probably went up to an upper room where they were together, and told them that Peter was certainly at the gate, though she had not courage enough to open the gate, for fear she should be deceived, and it should be the enemy. But, when she spoke of Peter's being there, they said, *"Thou art mad;* it is impossible it should be he, for he is in prison." Sometimes that which we most earnestly wish for we are most backward to believe, because we are afraid of imposing upon ourselves, as the disciples, who, when Christ had risen, *believed not for joy.* However, she stood to it that it was he. Then said they, *It is his angel, v.* 15. *First,* "It is a *messenger* from him, that makes use of his name;" so some take it; *angelos* often signifies no more than *a messenger.* It is used of John's messengers (Lu. 7:24, 27), of Christ's, Lu. 9:52. When the damsel was confident it was Peter, because she knew his voice, they thought it was because he that stood at the door had called himself Peter, and therefore offer this solution of the difficulty, "It is one that comes with an errand from him, and thou didst mistake as if it had been he himself." Dr. Hammond thinks this the easiest way of understanding it. *Secondly,* "It is his *guardian angel,* or some other angel that has assumed his shape and voice, and stands at the gate in his resemblance." Some think that they supposed his angel to appear as a presage of his death approaching; and this agrees with a notion which the vulgar have, that sometimes before persons have died *their ward has been seen,* that is, some spirit exactly in their likeness for countenance and dress, when they themselves have been at the same time in some other place; they call it their *ward,* that is, their angel, who is their guard. If so, they concluded this an ill omen, that their prayers were denied, and that the language of the apparition was, "Let it suffice you, Peter must die, say no more of that matter." And, if we understand it so, it only proves that they had then such an opinion of a man's *ward* being seen a little before his death, but does not prove that there is such a thing. Others think they took this to be an angel from heaven, sent to bring them a grant to their prayers. But why should they imagine that angel to assume the voice and shape of Peter, when we find not any thing like it in the appearance of angels? Perhaps they herein spoke the language of the Jews, who had a fond conceit that every good man has a particular tutelar angel, that has the charge of him, and sometimes personates him. the heathen called it a *good genius,* that attended a man; but, since no other scripture speaks of such a thing, this alone is too weak to bear the weight of such a doctrine. We are sure that the angels are *ministering spirits* for the good of *the heirs of salvation,* that they have a *charge concerning them,* and *pitch their tents round about them;* and we need not be solicitous that every particular saint should have his guardian angel, when we are assured he has a guard of angels.

(5.) At length they let him in (*v.* 16): *He continued knocking* though they delayed to open to him, and at last they admitted him. The iron gate which opposed his enlargement opened of itself, without so much as once knocking at it; but the door of his friend's house that was to welcome him does not open of its own accord, but must be knocked at, long knocked at; lest Peter should be puffed up by the honours which the angel did him, he meets with this mortification, by a seeming slight which his friends put upon him. But, *when they saw him, they were astonished,* were filled with wonder and joy in him, as much as they were but just now with sorrow and fear concerning him. It was both surprising and pleasing to them in the highest degree.

(6.) Peter gave them an account of his deliverance. When he came to the company that were gathered together with so much zeal to pray for him, they gathered about him with no less zeal to congratulate him on his deliverance; and herein they were so noisy that when Peter himself begged them to consider what peril he was yet in, if they should be overheard, he could not make them hear him, but was forced to *beckon to them with the hand to hold their peace,* and had much ado thereby to command silence, while *he declared unto them how the Lord Jesus had* by an angel *brought him out of prison;* and it is very likely, having found them praying for his deliverance, he did not part with them till he and they had together solemnly given thanks to God for his enlargement; or, if he could not stay to do it, it is probable they staid together to do it; for what is won by prayer must be worn with praise; and God must always have the glory of that which we have the comfort of. When David declares *what God had done for his soul,* he blesses God who had not turned away his prayer, Ps. 66:16, 20.

(7.) Peter sent the account to others of his friends: *Go, show these things to James, and to the brethren with him,* who perhaps were met together in another place at the same time, upon the same errand to the throne of grace, which is one way of keeping up the communion of saints and wrestling with God in prayer — acting in concert, though at a distance, like Esther and Mordecai. He would have James and his company to know of his deliverance, not only that they might be eased of their pain and delivered from their fears concerning Peter, but that they might return thanks to God with him and for him. Observe, Though Herod had slain one James with the sword, yet here was another James, and that in Jerusalem too, that stood up in his room to preside among the brethren there; for, when God has work to do, he will never want instruments to do it with.

(8.) Peter had nothing more to do for the present than to shift for his own safety, which he did accordingly: He *departed, and went into another place more obscure,* and therefore more safe. He knew the town very well, and knew where to find a place that would be a shelter to him. Note, Even the Christian law of self-denial and suffering for Christ has not abrogated and repealed the natural law of self-preservation, and care for our own safety, as far as God gives an opportunity of providing for it by lawful means.

V. Having seen the triumph of Peter's friends in his deliverance, let us next observe the confusion of his enemies thereupon, which was so much the greater because people's expectation was so much raised of the putting of him to death. 1. The guards were in the utmost consternation upon it, for they knew how highly penal it was to them to let a prisoner escape that they had charge of (*v.* 18): *As soon as it was day,* and they found the prisoner gone, there was *no small stir or strife,* as some read it, *among the soldiers, what had become of Peter;* he is gone, and nobody knows how or which way. They thought themselves as sure as could be of him but last night; yet now the bird is flown, and they can hear no tale nor tidings of him. This set them together by the ears; one says, "It was your fault;" the other, "Nay, but it was yours;" having no other way to clear themselves, but by accusing one another. With us, if but a prisoner for debt escape, the sheriff must answer for the debt. Thus have the persecutors of the gospel of Christ been often filled with vexation to see its cause conquering, notwithstanding the opposition they have given to it. 2. Houses were searched in vain for the rescued prisoner (*v.* 19): *Herod sought for him, and found him not.* Who can find whom God hath hidden? Baruch and Jeremiah are safe, though searched for, because *the Lord has hidden them,* Jer. 36:26. In times of public danger, all believers have God for *their hiding-place,* which is such a secret, that there the ignorant world cannot find them; such a strength, that the impotent world cannot reach them. 3. The keepers were reckoned with for a permissive escape: *Herod examined the keepers,* and finding that they could give no satisfactory account how Peter got away, *he commanded that they should be put to death,* according to the Roman law, and that 1 Ki. 20:39, *If by any means he be missing, then shall thy life go for his life.* It is probable that these keepers had been more severe with Peter than they needed to be (as the jailor, *ch.* 16:24), and had been abusive to him, and to others that had been their prisoners upon the like account; and now justly are they put to death for that which was not their fault, and by him too that had set them to work to *vex the church.* When the wicked are thus snared in the work of their own hands, the Lord is known by the judgments which he executes. Or, if they had not thus made themselves obnoxious to the justice of God, and it be thought hard that innocent men should suffer thus for that which was purely the act of God, we may easily admit the conjectures of some, that though they were *commanded to be put to death,* to please the Jews, who were sadly disappointed by Peter's escape, yet they were not executed; but Herod's death, immediately after, prevented it. 4. Herod himself retired upon it: *He went down from Judea to Cesarea, and there abode.* He was vexed to the heart, as a lion disappointed of his prey; and the more because he had so much raised the *expectation of the people of the Jews* concerning Peter, had told them how he would very shortly gratify them with the sight of Peter's head in a charger, which would oblige them as much as John Baptist's did Herodias; it made him ashamed to be robbed of this boasting, and to see himself, notwithstanding his confidence, disabled to make his words good. This is such a mortification to his proud spirit that he cannot bear to stay in Judea, but away he goes to Cesarea. Josephus mentions this coming of Herod to Cesarea, at the end of the third year of his reign over all Judea (*Antiq.* 19.343), and says, he came thither to solemnize the plays that were kept there, by a vast concourse of the nobility and gentry of the kingdom, for the health of Caesar, and in honour of him.

Verses 20–25

In these verses we have,

I. The death of Herod. God reckoned with him, not only for his putting James to death, but for his design and endeavour to put Peter to death; for sinners will be called to an account, not only for the wickedness of their deeds, but for the wickedness of their endeavours (Ps. 28:4), for the mischief they have done and the mischief they would have done. It was but a little while that Herod lived after this. Some sinners God makes quick work with. Observe,

1. How the measure of his iniquity was filled up: it was *pride* that did it; it is this that commonly goes more immediately *before destruction,* and a *haughty spirit before a fall.* Nebuchadnezzar had been a very bloody man, and a great persecutor; but the word that was in the king's mouth when the judgments of God fell upon him was a proud word: *Is not this great Babylon that I have built?* Dan. 4:30, 31. It is the glory of God to *look on every one that is proud, and bring him low,* Job 40:12. The instance of it here is very remarkable, and shows how God *resists the proud.*

(1.) The men of Tyre and Sidon had, it seems, offended Herod. Those cities were now under the Roman yoke, and they had been guilty of some misdemeanours which Herod highly resented, and was resolved they should feel his resentment. Some very small matter would serve such a proud imperious man as Herod was for a provocation, where he was disposed to pick a quarrel. He was highly displeased with this people, and they must be made to know that his wrath was as the *roaring of a lion, as messengers of death.*

(2.) The offenders truckled, being convinced, if not that they had done amiss, yet that it was in vain to contend with such a potent adversary, who, right or wrong, would be too hard for them; they submitted and were willing upon any terms to *make peace with him.* Observe, [1.] The reason why they were desirous to have the matter accommodated: *Because their country was nourished by the king's country.* Tyre and Sidon were trading cities, and had little land belonging to them, but were always supplied with corn from the land of Canaan; *Judah and Israel traded in their market, with wheat, and honey, and oil,* Eze. 27:17. Now if Herod should make a law to prohibit the exportation of corn to Tyre and Sidon (which they knew not but a man so revengeful as he might soon do, not caring how many were famished by it), their country would be undone; so that it was their interest to keep in with him. And is it not then our wisdom to make our peace with God, and humble ourselves before him, who have a much more constant and necessary dependence upon him than one country can have upon another? for *in him we live, and move, and have our being.* [2.] The method they took to prevent a rupture: *They made Blastus the king's chamberlain their friend,* probably with bribes and good presents; that is usually the way for men to make courtiers their friends. And it is the hard fate of princes that they must have not only their affairs, but their affections too, governed by such mercenary tools; yet such men as Herod, that will not be governed by reason, had better be so governed than by pride and passion. Blastus had Herod's ear, and has the art of mollifying his resentments; and a time is fixed for the ambassadors of Tyre and Sidon to come and make a public submission, to beg his majesty's pardon, throw themselves upon his clemency, and promise never again to offend in the like manner; and that which will thus feed his pride shall serve to cool his passion.

(3.) Herod appeared in all the pomp and grandeur he had: He was *arrayed in his royal apparel* (*v.* 21), *and sat upon his throne.* Josephus gives an account of this splendid appearance which Herod made upon this occasion. — *Antiq.* 19.344. He says that Herod at this time wore a robe of cloth of silver, so richly woven, and framed with such art, that when the sun shone it reflected the light with such a lustre as dazzled the eyes of the spectators, and struck an awe upon them. Foolish people value men by their outward appearance; and no better are those who value themselves by the esteem of such, who court it, and recommend themselves to it as Herod did, who thought to make up the want of a royal heart with his *royal apparel; and sat upon his throne,* as if that gave him a privilege to trample upon all about him as his footstool.

(4.) He made a speech to the men of Tyre and Sidon, a fine oration, in which, probably, after he had aggravated their fault, and commended their submission, he concluded with an assurance that he would pass by their offence and receive them into his favour again — proud enough that he had it in his power *whom he would to keep alive,* as well as *whom he would to slay;* and probably he kept them in suspense as to what their doom should be, till he made this oration to them, that the act of grace might come to them with the more pleasing surprise.

(5.) The people applauded him, the people that had a dependence upon him, and had benefit by his favour, they *gave a shout;* and this was what they shouted, *It is the voice of a god, and not of a man, v.* 22. God is great and good, and they thought such was Herod's greatness in his apparel and throne, and such his goodness in forgiving them, that he was worthy to be called no less than a god; and perhaps his speech was delivered with such an air of majesty, and a mixture of clemency with it, as affected the auditors thus. Or, it may be, it was not from any real impression made upon their minds, or any high or good thoughts they had indeed conceived of him; but, how meanly soever they thought of him, they were resolved thus to curry favour with him, and strengthen the new-made peace between him and them. Thus great men are made an easy prey to flatterers if they lend an ear to them, and encourage them. Grotius here observes that, though magistrates are called *gods* (Ps. 82:1), yet *kings or monarchs, that is, single persons, are not, lest countenance should thereby be given to the Gentiles, who gave divine honours to their kings alive and dead, as here; but they are a college of senators, or a bench of judges, that are called gods. — In collegio toto senatorum non idem erat periculi; itaque eos, non autem reges, invenimus dictos elohim.* Those that live by sense vilify God, as if he were *altogether such a one as themselves,* and deify men, as if they were gods; having *their persons in admiration, because of advantage.* This is not only a great affront to God, giving that glory to others which is due to him alone, but a great injury to those who are thus flattered, as it makes them forget themselves, and so puffs them up with pride that they are in the utmost danger possible of falling into the condemnation of the devil.

(6.) These undue praises he took to himself, pleased himself with them, and prided himself in them; and this was his sin. We do not find that he had given any private orders to his confidants to begin such a shout, or to put those words into the mouths of the people, nor that he returned them thanks for the compliment and undertook to answer their opinion of him. But his fault was that he said nothing, did not rebuke their flattery, nor disown the title they had given him, nor *give God the glory* (*v.* 23); but he took it to himself, was very willing it should terminate in himself, and that he should be thought a god and have divine honours paid him. *Si populus vult decipi, decipiatur — if the people will be deceived, let them.* And it was worse in him who was a Jew, and professed to believe in one God only, than it was in the heathen emperors, who had gods many and lords many.

2. How his iniquity was punished: *Immediately* (*v.* 23) *the angel of the Lord smote him* (by the order of Christ, for to him all judgment is committed), *because he gave not God the glory* (for God is jealous for his own honour, and will be glorified upon those whom he is not glorified by); and *he was eaten of worms* above ground, *and gave up the ghost.* Now he was reckoned with for vexing the church of Christ, killing James, imprisoning Peter, and all the other mischiefs he had done. Observe in the destruction of Herod,

(1.) It was no less than an angel that was the agent — *the angel of the Lord,* that angel that was ordered and commissioned to do it, or that angel that used to be employed in works of this nature, the destroying angel: or *the angel,* that is, that angel that delivered Peter in the former part of the chapter — that angel smote Herod. For those ministering spirits are the ministers either of divine justice or of divine mercy, as God is pleased to employ them. The angel smote him with a sore disease just at that instant when he was strutting at the applauses of the people, and adoring his own shadow. Thus the king of Tyre said in his pride, *I am a god, I sit in the seat of God; and set his heart as the heart of God;* but he shall be *a man, and no God,* a weak mortal man, *in the hand of him that slayeth him* (Eze. 28:2–9), so Herod here. Potent princes must know, not only that God is omnipotent, but that angels also are greater in power and might than they. The angel *smote him, because he gave not the glory to God;* angels are jealous for God's honour, and as soon as ever they have commission are ready to smite those that usurp his prerogatives, and rob God of his honour.

(2.) It was no more than a worm that was the instrument of Herod's destruction: He was *eaten of worms, genomenos skōlēkobrōtos — he became worm-eaten,* so it must be read; rotten he was, and he became like a piece of rotten wood. The body in the grave is destroyed by worms, but Herod's body putrefied while he was yet alive, and bred the worms which began to feed upon it betimes; so Antiochum, that great persecutor, died. See here, [1.] What vile bodies those are which we carry about with us; they carry about with them the seeds of their own dissolution, by which they will soon be destroyed whenever God does but speak the word. Surprising discoveries have of late been made by microscopes of the multitude of worms that there are in human bodies, and how much they contribute to the diseases of them, which is a good reason why we should not be proud of our bodies, or of any of their accomplishments, and why we should not pamper our bodies, for this is but feeding the worms, and feeding them for the worms. [2.] See what weak and contemptible creatures God can make the instruments of his justice, when he pleases. Pharaoh is plagued with lice and flies, Ephraim consumed as with a moth, and Herod eaten with worms. [3.] See how God delights not only to bring down proud men, but to bring them down in such a way as is most mortifying, and pours most contempt upon them. Herod is not only destroyed, but destroyed by worms, that the pride of his glory may be effectually stained. This story of the death of Herod is particularly related by Josephus, a Jew, *Antiq.* 19.343–350: "That Herod came down to Cesarea, to celebrate a festival in honour of Caesar; that the second day of the festival he went in the morning to the theatre, clothed with that splendid robe mentioned before; that his flatterers saluted him as a god, begged that he would be propitious to them; that hitherto they had reverenced him as a man, but now they would confess to be in him something more excellent than a mortal nature. That he did not refuse nor correct this impious flattery (so the historian expresses it); But, presently after, looking up, he saw an owl perched over his head, and was at the same instant seized with a most violent pain in his bowels, and gripes in his belly, which were exquisite from the very first; that he turned his eyes upon his friends, and said to this purpose: 'Now I, whom you called a god, and therefore immortal, must be proved a man, and mortal.' That his torture continued without intermission, or the least abatement, and then he died in the fifty-fourth year of his age, when he had been king seven years."

II. The progress of the gospel after this. 1. *The word of God grew and multiplied,* as seed sown, which comes up with a great increase, thirty, sixty, a hundred fold; wherever the gospel was preached, multitudes embraced it, and were added to the church by it, *v.* 24. After the death of James, the word of God grew; for the church, the more it was afflicted, the more it multiplied, like Israel in Egypt. The courage and comfort of the martyrs, and God's owning them, did more to invite people to Christianity, than their sufferings did to deter them from it. After the death of Herod the word of God gained ground. When such a persecutor was taken off by a dreadful judgment, many were thereby convinced that the cause of Christianity was doubtless the cause of Christ, and therefore embraced it. 2. Barnabas and Saul returned to Antioch as soon as they had despatched the business they were sent upon: *When they had fulfilled their ministry,* had paid in their money to the proper persons, and taken care about the due distribution of it to those for whom it was collected, they *returned from Jerusalem.* Though they had a great many friends there, yet at present their work lay at Antioch; and where our business is there we should be, and no longer from it than is requisite. When a minister is called abroad upon any service, when he has fulfilled that ministry, he ought to remember that he has work to do at home, which wants him there and calls him thither. Barnabas and Saul, when they went to *Antioch, took with them John, whose surname was Mark,* at whose mother's house they had that meeting for prayer which we read of *v.* 12. She was sister to Barnabas. It is probable that Barnabas lodged there, and perhaps Paul with him, while they were at Jerusalem, and it was that that occasioned the meeting there at that time (for wherever Paul was he would have some good work doing), and their intimacy in that family while they were at Jerusalem occasioned their taking a son of that family with them when they returned, to be trained up under them, and employed by them, in the service of the gospel. Educating young men for the ministry, and entering them into it, is a very good work for elder ministers to take care of, and of good service to the rising generation.

CHAPTER 13

We have not yet met with any things concerning the spreading of the gospel to the Gentiles which bears any proportion to the largeness of that commission, "Go, and disciple all nations." The door was opened in the baptizing of Cornelius and his friends; but since then we had the gospel preached to the Jews only, *ch.* 11:19. It should seem as if the light which began to shine upon the Gentile world had withdrawn itself. But here in this chapter that work, that great good work, is revived in the midst of the years; and though the Jews shall still have the first offer of the gospel made to them, yet, upon their refusal, the Gentiles shall have their share of the offer of it. Here is, I. The solemn ordination of Barnabas and Saul, by divine direction, to the ministry, to the great work of spreading the gospel among the nations about (and it is probable that other apostles or apostolical men dispersed themselves by order from Christ, upon the same errand (*v.* 1–3). II. Their preaching the gospel in Cyprus, and the opposition they met with there from Elymas the sorcerer (*v.* 4–13). III. The heads of a sermon which Paul preached to the Jews at Antioch in Pisidia, in their synagogue, which is given us as a specimen of what they usually preached to the Jews, and the method they took with them (*v.* 14–41). IV. The preaching of the gospel to the Gentiles at their request, and upon the Jews' refusal of it, wherein the apostles justified themselves against the displeasure which the Jews conceived at it, and God owned them (*v.* 42–49). V. The trouble which the infidel Jews gave to the apostles, which obliged them to remove to another place (*v.* 50–52), so that the design of this chapter is to show how cautiously, how gradually, and with what good reason the apostles carried the gospel into the Gentile world, and admitted the Gentiles into the church, which was so great an offence to the Jews, and which Paul is so industrious to justify in his epistles.

Verses 1–3

We have here a divine warrant and commission to Barnabas and Saul to go and preach the gospel among the Gentiles, and their ordination to that service by the imposition of hands, with fasting and prayer.

I. Here is an account of the present state of the church at Antioch, which was planted, *ch.* 11:20.

1. How well furnished it was with good ministers; there were there *certain prophets and teachers* (*v.* 1), men that were eminent for gifts, graces, and usefulness. Christ, when he *ascended on high,* gave *some prophets and some teachers* (Eph. 4:11); these were both. Agabus seems to have been a prophet and not a teacher, and many were teachers who were not prophets; but those here mentioned were at times divinely inspired, and had instructions immediately from heaven upon special occasions, which gave them the title of prophets; and withal they were stated teachers of the church in their religious assemblies, expounded the scriptures, and opened the doctrine of Christ with suitable applications. These were the prophets, and scribes, or teachers, which Christ promised to send (Mt. 23:34), such as were every way qualified for the service of the Christian church. Antioch was a great city, and the Christians there were many, so that they could not all meet in one place; it was therefore requisite they should have many teachers, to preside in their respective assemblies, and to deliver God's mind to them. Barnabas is first named, probably because he was the eldest, and Saul last, probably because he was the youngest; but afterwards the last became first, and Saul more eminent in the church. Three others are mentioned. (1.) *Simeon,* or Simon, who for distinction-sake was called *Niger, Simon the Black,* from the color of his hair; like him that with us was surnamed the Black Prince. (2.) *Lucius* of Cyrene, who some think (and Dr. Lightfoot inclines to it) was the same with this Luke that wrote the Acts, originally a Cyrenian, and educated in the Cyrenian college or synagogue at Jerusalem, and there first receiving the gospel. (3.) *Manaen,* a person of some quality, as it should seem, for he was *brought up with Herod the tetrarch,* either nursed of the same milk, or bred at the same school, or pupil to the same tutor, or rather one that was his constant colleague and companion — that in every part of his education was his comrade and intimate, which gave him a fair prospect of preferment at court, and yet for Christ's sake he quitted all the hopes of it; like Moses, who, *when he had come to years, refused to be called the son of Pharaoh's daughter.* Had he joined in with Herod, with whom he was brought up, he might have had Blastus's place, and have been his chamberlain; but it is better to be fellow-sufferer with a saint than fellow-persecutor with a tetrarch.

2. How well employed they were (*v.* 2): *They ministered to the Lord, and fasted.* Observe, (1.) Diligent faithful teachers do truly minister unto the Lord. Those that instruct Christians serve Christ; they really do him honour, and carry on the interest of his kingdom. Those that minister to the church in praying and preaching (both which are included here), *minister unto the Lord,* for they are the church's servants for Christ's sake; to him they must have an eye in their ministrations, and from him they shall have their recompence. (2.) Ministering to the Lord, in one way or other, ought to be the stated business of churches and their teachers; to this work time ought to be set apart, nay, it is set apart, and in this work we ought to spend some part of every day. What have we to do as Christians and ministers but to *serve the Lord Christ?* Col. 3:24; Rom. 14:18. (3.) Religious *fasting* is of use in our ministering to the Lord, both as a sign of our humiliation and a means of our mortification. Though it was not so much practised by the disciples of Christ, *while the bridegroom was with them,* as it was by the disciples of John and of the Pharisees; yet, after the bridegroom was taken away, they abounded in it, as those that had well learned to deny themselves and to endure hardness.

II. The orders given by the Holy Ghost for the setting apart of Barnabas and Saul, while they were engaged in public exercises, the ministers of the several congregations in the city joining in one solemn fast or day of prayer: The *Holy Ghost said,* either by a voice from heaven, or by a strong impulse on the minds of those of them that were prophets, *Separate me Barnabas and Saul for the work whereunto I have called them.* He does not specify the work, but refers to a former call of which they themselves knew the meaning, whether others did or no: as for Saul, he was particularly told that he must *bear Christ's name to the Gentiles* (*ch.* 9:15), that *he must be sent to the Gentiles* (*ch.* 22:21); the matter was settled between them at Jerusalem before this, that as Peter, James, and John laid out themselves among those of the circumcision, so Paul and Barnabas should *go to the heathen,* Gal. 2:7–9. Barnabas, it is likely, knew himself designed for this service as well as Paul. Yet they would not thrust themselves into this harvest, though it appeared plenteous, till they received their orders from the Lord of the harvest: *Thrust in thy sickle for the harvest is ripe,* Rev. 14:15. The orders were, *Separate me Barnabas and Saul.* Observe here, 1. Christ by his Spirit has the nomination of his ministers; for it is by the Spirit of Christ that they are qualified in some measure for his services, inclined to it, and taken off from other cares inconsistent with it. There are some whom the Holy Ghost has separated for the service of Christ, has distinguished from others as men that are offered and that willingly offer themselves to the temple service; and concerning them directions are given to those who are competent judges of the sufficiency of the abilities and the sincerity of the inclination: *Separate* them. 2. Christ's ministers are separated to him and to the Holy Ghost: *Separate them to me;* they are to be employed in Christ's work and under the Spirit's guidance, to the glory of God the Father. 3. All that are separated to Christ as his ministers are separated to work; Christ keeps no servants to be idle. *If any man desires the office of a bishop, he desires a good work;* that is what he is separated to, *to labour in the word and doctrine.* They are separated to take pains, not to take state. 4. The work of Christ's ministers, to which they are to be separated, is work that is already settled, and that which all Christ's ministers hitherto have been called to, and which they themselves have first been, by an external call, directed to and have chosen.

III. Their ordination, pursuant to these orders: not to the ministry in general (Barnabas and Saul had both of them been ministers long before this), but to a particular service in the ministry, which had something peculiar in it, and which required a fresh commission, which commission God saw fit at this time to transmit by the hands of *these prophets and teachers,* for the giving of this direction to the church, that teachers should ordain teachers (for prophets we are not now any longer to expect), and that those who have the dispensing of the oracles of Christ committed to them should, for the benefit of posterity, *commit the same to faithful men, who shall be able also to teach others,* 2 Tim. 2:2. So here, Simeon, and Lucius, and Manaen, faithful teachers at this time in the church of Antioch, *when they had fasted and prayed, laid their hands on Barnabas and Saul, and sent them away* (*v.* 3), according to the directions received. Observe, 1. They prayed for them. When good men are going forth about good work, they ought to be solemnly and particularly prayed for, especially by their brethren that are their fellow-labourers and fellow-soldiers. 2. They joined fasting with their prayers, as they did in their other ministrations, *v.* 3. Christ has taught us this by his abstaining from sleep (a night-fast, if I may so call it) the night before he sent forth his apostles, that he might spend it in prayer. 3. They laid their hands on them. Hereby, (1.) They gave them their manumission, dismission, or discharge from the present service they were engaged in, in the church of Antioch, acknowledging that they went off not only fairly and with consent, but honourably and with a good report. (2.) They implored a blessing upon them in their present undertaking, begged that God would be with them, and give them success; and, in order to this, that *they might be filled with the Holy Ghost* in their work. This very thing is explained *ch.* 14:26, where it is said, concerning Paul and Barnabas, that from *Antioch they had been recommended to the grace of God for the work which they fulfilled.* As it was an instance of the humility of Barnabas and Saul that they submitted to the imposition of the hands of those that were their equals, or rather their inferiors; so it was of the good disposition of the other teachers that they did not envy Barnabas and Saul the honour to which they were preferred, but cheerfully committed it to them, with hearty prayers for them; and *they sent them away* with all expedition, out of a concern for those countries where they were to break up fallow ground.

Verses 4–13

In these verses we have,

I. A general account of the coming of Barnabas and Saul to the famous island of Cyprus; and perhaps thitherward they steered their course because Barnabas was a native of that country (*ch.* 4:36), and he was willing they should have the first-fruits of his labours, pursuant to his new commission. Observe, 1. Their being sent forth by the Holy Ghost was the great thing that encouraged them in this undertaking, *v.* 4. If the Holy Ghost send them forth, he will go along with them, strengthen them, carry them on in their work, and give them success; and then they fear no colours, but can cheerfully venture upon a stormy sea from Antioch, which was now to them a quiet harbour. 2. They came to Seleucia, the sea-port town opposite to Cyprus, thence crossed the sea to Cyprus, and in that island the first city they came to was Salamis, a city on the east side of the island (*v.* 5); and, when they had sown good seed there, *thence they* went onward *through the isle* (*v.* 6) till they came to Paphos, which lay on the western coast. 3. *They preached the word of God* wherever they came, *in the synagogues of the Jews;* so far were they from excluding them that they gave them the preference, and so left those among them who believed not inexcusable; *they would have gathered them, but they would not.* They did not act clandestinely, nor preach the Messiah to others unknown to them, but laid their doctrine open to the censure of the rulers of their synagogues, who might, if they had any thing to say, object against it. Nor would they have acted separately, but in concert with them, if they had not driven them out from them, and from their synagogues. 4. *They had John for their minister;* not their servant in common things, but their assistant in the things of God, either to prepare their way in places where they designed to come or to carry on their work in places where they had begun it, or to converse familiarly with those to whom they preached publicly, and explain things to them; and such a one might be many ways of use to them, especially in a strange country.

II. A particular account of their encounter with *Elymas the sorcerer,* whom they met with at Paphos, where the governor resided; a place famous for a temple built to Venus there, thence called *Paphian Venus;* and therefore there was more than ordinary need that *the Son of God* should there *be manifested to destroy the works of the devil.*

1. There the *deputy,* a Gentile, *Sergius Paulus* by name, encouraged the apostles, and was willing to hear their message. He was governor *of the country,* under the Roman emperor; proconsul or propraetor, such a one as we should call *lord lieutenant of the island.* He had the character of *a prudent man,* an intelligent, considerate man, that was ruled by reason, not passion nor prejudice, which appeared by this, that, having a character of Barnabas and Saul, he sent for them, *and desired to hear the word of God.* Note, When that which we hear has a tendency to lead us to God, it is prudence to desire to hear more of it. Those are wise people, however they may be ranked among the foolish of this world, who are inquisitive after the mind and will of God. Though he was a great man, and a man in authority, and the preachers of the gospel were men that made no figure, yet, if they have a message from God, let him know what it is, and, if it appear to be so, he is ready to receive it.

2. There Elymas, a Jew, a *sorcerer,* opposed them, and did all he could to obstruct their progress. This justified the apostles in *turning to the Gentiles,* that this Jew was so malignant against them.

(1.) This Elymas was a pretender *to the gift of prophecy, a sorcerer, a false-prophet* — one that would be taken for a divine, because he was skilled in the arts of divination; he was a conjurer, and took on him to tell people their fortune, and to discover things lost, and probably was in league with the devil for this purpose; *his name was Barjesus — the son of Joshua;* it signifies *the son of salvation;* but the Syriac calls him, *Bar-shoma — the son of pride; filius inflationis — the son of inflation.*

(2.) He was hanging on at court, *was with the deputy* of the country. It does not appear that the deputy called for him, as he did for Barnabas and Saul; but he thrust himself upon him, aiming, no doubt, to make a hand of him, and get money by him.

(3.) He made it his business to withstand Barnabas and Saul, as the magicians of Egypt, in Pharaoh's court, *withstood* Moses and Aaron, 2 Tim. 3:8. He set up himself to be a messenger from heaven, and denied that they were. And *thus he sought to turn away the deputy from the faith* (*v.* 8), to keep him from receiving the gospel, which he saw him inclined to do. Note, Satan is in a special manner busy with great men and men of power, to keep them from being religious; because he knows that their example, whether good or bad, will have an influence upon many. And those who are in any way instrumental to prejudice people against the truths and ways of Christ are doing the devil's work.

(4.) Saul (who is here for the first time called Paul) fell upon him for this with a holy indignation. *Saul, who is also called Paul, v.* 9. Saul was his name as he was a Hebrew, and of the tribe of Benjamin; Paul was his name as he was a citizen of Rome. Hitherto we have had him mostly conversant among the Jews, and therefore called by his Jewish name; but now, when he is sent forth among the Gentiles, he is called by his Roman name, to put somewhat of a reputation upon him in the Roman cities, Paulus being a very common name among them. But some think he was never called Paul till now that he was instrumental in the conversion of Sergius Paulus to the faith of Christ, and that he took the name Paulus as a memorial of this victory obtained by the gospel of Christ, as among the Romans he that had conquered a country took his denomination from it, as *Germanicus, Britannicus, Africanus;* or rather, Sergius Paulus himself gave him the name Paulus in token of his favour and respect to him, as Vespasian gave his name Flavius to Josephus the Jew. Now of Paul it is said,

[1.] That he was *filled with the Holy Ghost* upon this occasion, filled with a holy zeal against a professed enemy of Christ, which was one of the graces of the Holy Ghost — *a spirit of burning;* filled with power to denounce the wrath of God against him, which was one of the gifts of the Holy Ghost — *a spirit of judgment.* He felt a more than ordinary fervour in his mind, as the prophet did when he was *full of power by the Spirit of the Lord* (Mic. 3:8), and another prophet when *his face was made harder than flint* (Eze. 3:9), and another when his *mouth was made like a sharp sword,* Isa. 49:2. What Paul said did not come from any personal resentment, but from the strong impressions which the Holy Ghost made upon his spirit.

[2.] He *set his eyes upon him,* to face him down, and to show a holy boldness, in opposition to his wicked impudence. He set his eyes upon him, as an indication that the eye of the heart-searching God was upon him, and saw through and through him; nay, *that the face of the Lord was against him,* Ps. 34:16. He fixed his eyes upon him, to see if he could discern in his countenance any marks of remorse for what he had done; for, if he could have discerned the least sign of this, it would have prevented the ensuing doom.

[3.] He gave him his true character, not in passion, but by the Holy Ghost, who knows men better than they know themselves, *v.* 10. He describes him to be, *First,* An agent for hell; and such there have been upon this earth (the seat of the war between *the seed of the woman and of the serpent)* ever since Cain *who was of that wicked one,* an incarnate devil, *slew his brother,* for no other reason than because *his own works were evil and his brother's righteous.* This Elymas, though called *Bar-jesus — a son of Jesus,* was really a *child of the devil,* bore his image, did his lusts, and served his interests, Jn. 8:44. In two things he resembled the devil as a child does his father: — 1. In craftiness. *The serpent was more subtle than any beast of the field* (Gen. 3:1), and Elymas, though void of all wisdom, was *full of all subtlety,* expert in all the arts of deceiving men and imposing upon them. 2. In malice. He was *full of all mischief* — a spiteful ill-conditioned man, and a sworn implacable enemy to God and goodness. Note, A fulness of subtlety and mischief together make a man indeed a child of the devil. *Secondly,* An adversary to heaven. If he be a child of the devil, it follows of course that he is *an enemy to all righteousness,* for the devil is so. Note, Those that are enemies to the doctrine of Christ are enemies to all righteousness, for in it all righteousness is summed up and fulfilled.

[4.] He charged upon him his present crime, and expostulated with him upon it: *"Wilt thou not cease to pervert the right ways of the Lord,* to misrepresent them, to put false colours upon them, and so to discourage people from entering into them, and walking in them?" Note, *First,* The ways of the Lord are right: they are all so, they are perfectly so. The ways of the Lord Jesus are right, the only right ways to heaven and happiness. *Secondly,* There are those who pervert these right ways, who not only wander out of these ways themselves (as Elihu's penitent, who owns, *I have perverted that which was right and it profited me not),* but mislead others, and suggest to them unjust prejudices against these ways: as if the doctrine of Christ were uncertain and precarious, the laws of Christ unreasonable and impractical, and the service of Christ unpleasant and unprofitable, which is an unjust perverting of the right ways of the Lord, and making them seem crooked ways. *Thirdly,* Those who pervert the right ways of the Lord are commonly so hardened in it that, though the equity of those ways be set before them by the most powerful and commanding evidence, yet they will not cease to do it. *Etsi suaseris, non persuaseris — You may advise, but you will never persuade;* they will have it their own way; *they have loved strangers, and after them they will go.*

[5.] He denounced the judgment of God upon him, in a present blindness (*v.* 11): *"And now, behold, the hand of the Lord is upon thee,* a righteous hand. God is now about to lay hands on thee, and make thee his prisoner, for thou art taken in arms against him; *thou shalt be blind, not seeing the sun for a season."* This was designed both for the proof of his crime, as it was a miracle wrought to confirm the right ways of the Lord, and consequently to show the wickedness of him who would not cease to pervert them, as also for the punishment of his crime. It was a suitable punishment; he shut his eyes, the eyes of his mind, against the light of the gospel, and therefore justly were the eyes of his body shut against the light of the sun; he sought to blind the deputy (as an agent for *the god of this world, who blindeth the minds of those that believe not, lest the light of the gospel should shine unto them,* 2 Co. 4:4), and therefore is himself struck blind. Yet it was a moderate punishment: he was only struck blind, when he might most justly have been struck dead; and it was only *for a season;* if he will repent, and give glory to God, by making confession, his sight shall be restored; nay, it should seem, though he do not, yet his sight shall be restored, to try if he will be led to repentance either by the judgments of God or by his mercies.

[6.] This judgment was immediately executed: *There fell on him a mist and a darkness,* as on the Sodomites when they persecuted Elisha. This silenced him presently, filled him with confusion, and was an effectual confutation of all he said against the doctrine of Christ. Let not him any more pretend to be a guide to the deputy's conscience who is himself struck blind. It was also an earnest to him of a much sorer punishment if he repent not; for he is one of those *wandering stars to whom is reserved the blackness of darkness for ever,* Jude 13. Elymas did himself proclaim the truth of the miracle, when *he went about seeking some to lead him by the hand;* and where now is all his skill in sorcery, upon which he had so much valued himself, when he can neither find his way nor find a friend that will be so kind as to lead him!

3. Notwithstanding all the endeavours of Elymas *to turn away the deputy from the faith,* he was brought to believe, and this miracle, wrought upon the magician himself (like *the boils of Egypt,* which *were upon the magicians, so that they could not stand before Moses,* Ex. 9:11), contributed to it. The deputy was a very sensible man, and observed something uncommon, and which intimated its divine original, (1.)

In Paul's preaching: he was *astonished at the doctrine of the Lord,* the Lord Christ, — the doctrine that *is from him,* the discoveries he has made of the Father, — the doctrine that *is concerning him,* his person, natures, offices, undertaking. Note, The doctrine of Christ has a great deal in it that is astonishing; and the more we know of it the more reason we shall see to wonder and stand amazed at it. (2.) In this miracle: *When he saw what was done,* and how much Paul's power transcended that of the magician, and how plainly Elymas was baffled and confounded, he believed. It is not said that he was baptized, and so made a complete convert, but it is probable that he was. Paul would not do his business by the halves; *as for God, his work is perfect.* When he became a Christian, he neither laid down his government, nor was turned out of it, but we may suppose, as a Christian magistrate, by his influence helped very much to propagate Christianity in that island. The tradition of the Romish church, which has taken care to find bishoprics for all the eminent converts we read of in *the Acts,* has made this Sergius Paulus bishop of Narbon in France, left there by Paul in his journey to Spain.

III. Their departure from the island of Cyprus. It is probable that they did a great deal more there than is recorded, where an account is given only of that which was extraordinary — the conversion of the deputy. When they had done what they had to do, 1. They quitted the country, and *went to Perga.* Those that went were *Paul and his company,* which, it is probable, was increased in Cyprus, many being desirous to accompany him. *Anachthentes hoi peri ton Paulon — Those that were about Paul loosed from Paphos,* which supposes that he went too; but such an affection had his new friends for him that they were always about him, and by their good will would be never from him. 2. Then John *Mark quitted them, and returned to Jerusalem,* without the consent of Paul and Barnabas; either he did not like the work, or he wanted to go and see his mother. It was his fault, and we shall hear of it again.

Verses 14–41

Perga in Pamphylia was a noted place, especially for a temple there erected to the goddess Diana, yet nothing at all is related of what Paul and Barnabas did there, only that *thither they came* (*v.* 13), and *thence they departed, v.* 14. But the history of the apostles' travels, as that of Christ's, passes by many things worthy to have been recorded, because, *if all had been written, the world could not have contained the books.* But the next place we find them in is another Antioch, said to be in Pisidia, to distinguish it from that Antioch in Syria from which they were sent out. Pisidia was a province of the Lesser Asia, bordering upon Pamphylia; this Antioch, it is likely, was the metropolis of it. Abundance of Jews lived there, and to them *the gospel was to be first preached;* and Paul's sermon to them is what we have in these verses, which, it is likely, is the substance of what was preached by the apostles generally to the Jews in all places; for in dealing with them the proper way was to show them how the New Testament, which they would have them to receive, exactly agreed with the Old Testament, which they not only received, but were zealous for. We have here,

I. The appearance which Paul and Barnabas made in a religious assembly of the Jews at Antioch, *v.* 14. Though they had lately had such good success with a Roman deputy, yet, *when they came to Antioch,* they did not enquire for the chief magistrate, nor make their court to him, but they applied to the Jews, which is a further proof of their good affection to them and their desire of their welfare. 1. They observed their time of worship, *on the sabbath day,* the Jewish sabbath. *The first day of the week* they observed among themselves as a Christian sabbath; but, if they will meet the Jews, it must be on the seventh-day sabbath, which therefore, upon such occasions, they did as yet sometimes observe. For, though it was by the death of Christ that the ceremonial law died, yet it was in the ruins of Jerusalem that it was to be buried; and therefore, though the morality of the fourth commandment was entirely transferred to the Christian sabbath, yet it was not incongruous to join with the Jews in their sabbath sanctification. 2. They met them in their place of worship, *in the synagogue.* Note, Sabbath days should be kept holy in solemn assemblies; they are instituted chiefly for public worship. *The sabbath day is a holy convocation,* and for that reason *no servile work must be done therein.* Paul and Barnabas were strangers; but, wherever we come, we must enquire out God's faithful worshippers, and join with them (as these apostles here did), as those that desire to keep up a communion with all saints; though they were strangers, yet they were admitted into the synagogue, and to sit down there. Care should be taken in places of public worship that strangers be accommodated, even the poorest; for, of those of whom we know nothing else, we know this, that they have precious souls, for which our charity binds us to be concerned.

II. The invitation given them to preach. 1. The usual service of the synagogue was performed (*v.* 15): *The law and the prophets were read,* a portion of each, the lessons for the day. Note, When we come together to worship God, we must do it not only by prayer and praise, but by the reading and hearing of the word of God; hereby we *give him the glory due to his name,* as our Lord and Lawgiver. 2. When that was done, they were asked by *the rulers of the synagogue* to give them a sermon (*v.* 15): They sent a messenger to them with the respectful message, *Men and brethren, if you have any word of exhortation for the people, say on.* It is probable that the rulers of the synagogue had met with them, and been in private conversation with them before; and, if they had not an affection to the gospel, yet they had at least the curiosity to hear Paul preach; and therefore not only gave him permission, but begged the favour of him that he would speak a *word of exhortation to the people.* Note, (1.) The bare reading of the scriptures in the public assemblies is not sufficient, but they should be expounded, and the people exhorted out of them. This is spreading the net, and assisting people in doing that which is necessary to the making of the word profitable to them — that is, the applying of it to themselves. (2.) Those that preside, and have power, in public assemblies, should provide for a word of exhortation to the people, whenever they come together. (3.) Sometimes a word of exhortation from a strange minister may be of great use to the people, provided he be well approved. It is likely Paul did *often preach in the synagogue,* when he was not thus invited to it by the rulers of the synagogues; for he often preached *with much contention,* 1 Th. 2:2. But these were more noble, more generous, than the rulers of the synagogues generally were.

III. The sermon Paul preached in the synagogue of the Jews, at the invitation of the rulers of the synagogue. He gladly embraced the opportunity given him to preach Christ to his countrymen the Jews. He did not object to them that he was a stranger, and that it was none of his business; nor object to himself, that he might get ill-will by preaching Christ among the Jews; but *stood up,* as one prepared and determined to speak, *and beckoned with his hand,* to excite and prepare them to hear. He waved his hand as an orator, not only desiring silence and attention, but endeavouring to move affection, and to show himself in earnest. Perhaps, upon the moving of them *to give an exhortation to the people,* there were those in the synagogue that were ready to mutiny against the rulers, and opposed the toleration of Paul's preaching, and that occasioned some tumult and commotion, which Paul endeavoured to quiet by that decent motion of his hand; as also by his modest desire of a patient impartial hearing: *"Men of Israel,* that are *Jews* by birth, *and you that fear God,* that are proselyted to the Jewish religion, *give audience;* let me beg your attention a little, for I have something to say to you which concerns your everlasting peace, and would not say it in vain." Now this excellent sermon is recorded, to show that those who preached the gospel to the Gentiles did it not till they had first used their utmost endeavours with the Jews, to persuade them to come in and take the benefit of it; and that they had no prejudice at all against the Jewish nation, nor any desire *that they should perish, but rather that they should turn and live.* Every thing is touched in this sermon that might be proper either to convince the judgment or insinuate into the affections of the Jews, to prevail with them to receive and embrace Christ as the promised Messiah.

1. He owns them to be God's favourite people, whom he had taken into special relation to himself, and for whom he had done great things. Probably *the Jews of the dispersion,* that lived in other countries, being more in danger of mingling with the nations, were more jealous of their peculiarity than those that lived in their own land were; and therefore Paul is here very careful to take notice of it, to their honour.

(1.) That *the God of the whole earth* was, in a particular manner, *the God of this people Israel,* a God *in covenant with them,* and that he had given them a revelation of his mind and will, such as he *had not given to any other nation or people;* so that hereby they were distinguished from, and dignified above, all their neighbours, having peculiar precepts to be governed by, and peculiar promises to depend upon.

(2.) That he had *chosen their fathers* to be his friends: Abraham was called *the friend of God;* to be his prophets, by whom he would reveal his mind to his church, and to be the trustees of his covenant with the church. He puts them in mind of this, to let them know that the reason why God favoured them, though undeserving, and ill deserving, was because he would adhere to the choice he had made of *their fathers,* Deu. 7:7, 8. *They were beloved* purely *for the fathers' sakes,* Rom. 11:28.

(3.) That he had *exalted that people,* and put a great deal of honour upon them, had advanced them into a people, and raised them from nothing, *when they dwelt as strangers in the land of Egypt,* and had nothing in them to recommend them to the divine favour. They ought to remember this, and to infer hence that God was no debtor to them; for it was *ex mero motu — out of his mere good pleasure,* and not upon a valuable consideration, that they had the grant of the divine favour; and therefore it was revocable at pleasure; and God did them no wrong if he at length plucked up the hedge of their peculiarity. But they were debtors to him, and obliged to receive such further discoveries as he should make to his church.

(4.) That he had *with a high hand brought them out of Egypt,* where they were not only strangers, but captives, had delivered them at the expense of a great many miracles, both of mercy to them and judgment on their oppressors *(signs and wonders,* Deu. 4:34), and at the expense of a great many lives, *all the first-born of Egypt, Pharaoh, and all his host, in the Red Sea; I gave Egypt for thy ransom, gave men for thee.* Isa. 43:3, 4.

(5.) That *he had suffered their manners forty years in the wilderness, v.* 18, *Etropophorēsen.* Some think it should be read, *etrophophorēsen — he educated them,* because this is the word the Septuagint use concerning the fatherly care God took of that people, Deu. 1:31. Both may be included; for, [1.] God made a great deal of provision for them for forty years in the wilderness: miracles were their daily bread, and kept them from starving: *They lacked not any thing.* [2.] He exercised a great deal of patience with them. They were a provoking, murmuring, unbelieving people; and yet he bore with them, did not deal with them as they deserved, but suffered his anger many a time to be turned away by the prayer and intercession of Moses. So many years as we have each of us lived in this world, we must own that God has thus been as a tender father to us, has supplied our wants, has *fed us all our life long unto this day,* has been indulgent to us, a God of pardons (as he was to Israel, Neh. 9:17), and *not extreme to mark what we have done amiss;* we have tried his patience, and yet not tired it. Let not the Jews insist too much upon the privileges of their peculiarity, for they have forfeited them a thousand times.

(6.) That he had put them in possession of the land of Canaan (*v.* 19): *When he had destroyed seven nations in the land of Canaan,* that were doomed to be rooted out to make room for them, *he divided their land to them by lot,* and put them in possession of it. This was a signal favour of God to them, and he owns that hereby a great honour was put upon them, from which he would not in the least derogate.

(7.) That he had raised up men, inspirited from heaven, to deliver them out of the hands of those that invaded their rights, and oppressed them after their settlement in Canaan, *v.* 20, 21. [1.] He *gave them judges,* men qualified for public service, and, by an immediate impulse upon their spirits, called to it, *pro re nata — as the occasion required.* Though they were a provoking people, and were never in servitude but their sin brought them to it, yet upon their petition a deliverer was raised up. The critics find some difficulty in computing *these four hundred and fifty years.* From the *deliverance out of Egypt* to David's expulsion of *the Jebusites from the stronghold of Zion,* which completed the casting out of the heathen nations, *was four hundred and fifty years;* and most of that time they were under judges. Others thus: The government of the judges, from the death of Joshua to the death of Eli, was just *three hundred and thirty-nine years,* but it is said to be [*ōs*] as it were *four hundred and fifty years,* because the years of their servitude to the several nations that oppressed them, though really they were included in the years of the judges, are yet mentioned in the history as if they had been distinct from them. Now these, all put together, make *one hundred and eleven years,* which added to the *three hundred and thirty nine,* make them *four hundred and fifty;* as so many, though not really so many. [2.] He governed them by a *prophet, Samuel,* a man divinely inspired to preside in their affairs. [3.] He *afterwards* at their request *set a king over them* (*v.* 21), *Saul, the son of Cis.* Samuel's government and his lasted *forty years,* which was a kind of transition from the theocracy to the kingly government. [4.] At last, he made David their king, *v.* 22. *When God had removed Saul,* for his mal-administration, *he raised up unto them David to be their king,* and made *a covenant of royalty with him, and with his seed.* When he had removed one king, he did not leave them as sheep without a shepherd, but soon raised up another, raised him up from a mean and low estate, *raised him up on high,* 2 Sa. 23:1. He quotes the testimony God gave concerning him, *First,* That his choice was divine: *I have found David,* Ps. 89:20. God himself pitched upon him. Finding implies seeking; as if God had ransacked all the families of Israel to find a man fit for his purpose, and this was he. *Secondly,* That his character was divine: *A man after my own heart,* such a one as I would have, one on whom the image of God is stamped, and therefore one in whom God is well pleased and whom he approves. This character was given of him before he was first anointed, 1 Sa. 13:14. *The Lord hath sought out a man after his own heart,* such a one as he would have. *Thirdly,* That his conduct was divine, and under divine direction: *He shall fulfil all my will.* He shall desire and endeavour to do the will of God, and shall be enabled to do it, and employed in the doing of it, and go through with it. Now all this seems to show not only the special favour of God to the people of Israel (with the acknowledgment of which the apostle is very willing to oblige them) but the further favours of another nature which he designed them, and which were now, by the preaching of the gospel, offered to them. Their deliverance out of Egypt, and settlement in Canaan, *were types and figures of good things to come.* The changes of their government showed that it *made nothing perfect,* and therefore must give way to the spiritual kingdom of the Messiah, which was now in the setting up, and which, if they would admit it and submit to it, would be *the glory of their people Israel;* and therefore they needed not conceive any jealousy at all of the preaching of the gospel, as if it tended in the least to damage the true excellences of the Jewish church.

2. He gives them a full account of our Lord Jesus, passing from David to the Son of David, and shows that this Jesus is his promised Seed (*v.* 23): *Of this man's seed,* from that *root of Jesse,* from that *man after God's own heart, hath God, according to his promise, raised unto Israel a Saviour — Jesus,* who carries salvation in his name.

(1.) How welcome should the preaching of the gospel of Christ be to the Jews, and how should they embrace it, as *well worthy of all acceptation,* when it brought them the tidings, [1.] Of a Saviour, to deliver *them out of the hands of their enemies,* as the judges of old, who were therefore called *saviours;* but this *a Saviour* to do that for them which, it appears by the history, those could not do — *to save them from their sins,* their worst enemies. [2.] A Saviour of God's raising up, that has his commission from heaven. [3.] Raised up *to be a Saviour unto Israel,* to them in the first place: *He was sent to bless them;* so far was the gospel from designing the gathering of them. [4.] Raised up *of the seed of David,* that ancient royal family, which the people of Israel gloried so much in, and which at this time, to the great disgrace of the whole nation, was buried in obscurity. It ought to be a great satisfaction to them *that God had raised up this horn of salvation for them in the house of his servant David,* Lu. 1:69. [5.] Raised up *according to his promise,* the promise to David (Ps. 132:11), the promise to the Old-Testament church in the latter times of it: *I will raise unto David a righteous branch,* Jer. 23:5. This promise was it *to which the twelve tribes hoped to come* (*ch.* 26:7); why then should they entertain it so coldly, now that it was brought to them? Now,

(2.) Concerning this Jesus, he tells them,

[1.] That John the Baptist was his harbinger and forerunner, that great man whom all acknowledged to be a prophet. Let them not say that the Messiah's coming was a surprise upon them, and that this might excuse them if they took time to consider whether they should entertain him or no; for they had sufficient warning by John, who *preached before his coming, v.* 24. Two things he did: — *First,* He made way for his entrance, by preaching *the baptism of repentance,* not to a few select disciples, but *to all the people of Israel.* He showed them their sins, *warned them of the wrath to come, called them to repentance,* and *to bring forth fruits meet for repentance,* and bound those to this who were willing to be bound by the solemn rite or sign of baptism; and by this he *made ready a people prepared for the Lord Jesus,* to whom his grace would be acceptable when they were thus brought to know themselves. *Secondly,* He gave notice of his approach (*v.* 25): *As he fulfilled his course,* when he was going on vigorously in his work, and had had wonderful success in it, and an established interest: "Now," saith he to those that attended his ministry, "*Whom think you that I am?* What notions have you of me, what expectations from me? You may be thinking that I am *the Messiah,* whom you expect; but you are mistaken, *I am not he* (see Jn. 1:20), but he is at the door; *behold, there cometh one* immediately *after me,* who will so far exceed me upon all accounts, *that I am not worthy* to be employed in the meanest office about him, no, not to help him on and off with his shoes — *whose shoes of his feet I am not worthy to loose,* and you may guess who that must be."

[2.] That the rulers and people of the Jews, who should have welcomed him, and been his willing, forward, faithful subjects, were his persecutors and murderers. When the apostles preach Christ as *the Saviour,* they are so far from concealing his ignominious death, and drawing a veil over it, that they always *preach Christ crucified,* yea, and (though this added much to the reproach of his sufferings) crucified by his own people, by *those that dwelt in Jerusalem,* the holy city — the royal city, and *their rulers, v.* 27. *First,* Their sin was *that though they found no cause of death in him,* could not prove him, no, nor had any colour to suspect him, guilty of any crime (the judge himself that tried him, when he had heard all they could say against him, declared he *found no fault with him), yet they desired Pilate that he might be slain* (*v.* 28), and presented their address against Christ with such fury and outrage that they compelled Pilate to crucify him, not only contrary to his inclination, but contrary to his conscience; they condemned him *to so great a death,* though they could not convict him of the least sin. Paul cannot charge this upon his hearers, as Peter did (*ch.* 2:23): *You have with wicked hands crucified and slain him;* for these, though Jews, were far enough off; but he charges it upon the Jews at Jerusalem and the rulers, to show what little reason those Jews of the dispersion had to be so jealous for the honour of their nation as they were, when it had brought upon itself such a load and stain of guilt as this, and how justly they might have been cut off from all benefit by the Messiah, who had thus abused him, and yet they were not; but, notwithstanding all this, the preaching of this gospel shall begin at Jerusalem. *Secondly,* The reason of this was because *they knew him not, v.* 27. They knew not who he was, nor what errand he came into the world upon; for, *if they had known, they would not have crucified the Lord of glory.* Christ owned this in extenuation of their crime: *They know not what they do;* and so did Peter: *I wot that through ignorance you did this, ch.* 3:17. It was also because they knew not the voice of the prophets though they heard them read every sabbath day. They did not understand nor consider that it was foretold that the Messiah should suffer, or else they would never have been the instruments of his suffering. Note, Many that read the prophets do not know the voice of the prophets, do not understand the meaning of the scriptures; they have the sound of the gospel in their ears, but not the sense of it in their heads, nor the savour of it in their hearts. And *therefore* men do not know Christ, nor know how to carry it towards him, because they do not know the voice of the prophets, who *testified beforehand concerning Christ. Thirdly,* God overruled them, for the accomplishment of the prophecies of the Old-Testament: *Because they knew not the voice of the prophets,* which warned them not to touch God's Anointed, *they fulfilled them in condemning him;* for so it was written that *Messiah the prince shall be cut off, but not for himself.* Note, It is possible that men may be fulfilling scripture prophecies, even when they are breaking scripture precepts, particularly in the persecution of the church, as in the persecution of Christ. And this justifies the reason which is sometimes given for the obscurity of scripture prophecies, that, if they were too plain and obvious, the accomplishment of them would thereby be prevented. So Paul saith here, *Because they knew not the voice of the prophets,* therefore *they have fulfilled them,* which implies that if they had understood them they would not have fulfilled them. *Fourthly,* All that was foretold concerning the sufferings of the Messiah was fulfilled in Christ (*v.* 29): *When they had fulfilled all* the rest *that was written of him,* even to the giving of him vinegar to drink in his thirst, then they fulfilled what was foretold concerning his being buried. They *took him down from the tree, and laid him in a sepulchre.* This is taken notice of here as that which made his resurrection the more illustrious. Christ was separated from this world, as those that are buried have nothing more to do with this world, nor this world with them; and therefore our complete separation from sin is represented by our being *buried with Christ.* And a good Christian will be willing to be buried alive with Christ. They laid him in a sepulchre, and thought they had him fast.

[3.] That he *rose again from the dead,* and saw no corruption. This was the great truth that was to be preached; for it is the main pillar, by which the whole fabric of the gospel is supported, and therefore he insists largely upon this, and shows,

First, That he rose by consent. When he was imprisoned in the grave for our debt, he did not break prison, but had a fair and legal discharge from the arrest he was under (*v.* 30): *God raised him from the dead,* sent an angel on purpose to roll away the stone from the prison-door, returned to him the spirit which at his death he had committed into the hands of his Father, and quickened him by the Holy Ghost. His enemies laid him in a sepulchre, with design he should always lay there; but God said, *No;* and it was soon seen whose purpose should stand, his or theirs.

Secondly, That there was sufficient proof of his having risen (*v.* 31): *He was seen many days,* in divers places, upon divers occasions, by those that were most intimately acquainted with him; for they *came up with him from Galilee to Jerusalem,* were his constant attendants, and *they are his witnesses unto the people.* They were appointed to be so, have attested the thing many a time, and are ready to attest it, though they were to die for the same. Paul says nothing of his own seeing him, which was more convincing to himself than it could be when produced to others.

Thirdly, That the resurrection of Christ was the performance of the promise made to the partiarchs; it was not only true news, but good news: "In declaring this, we *declare unto you glad tidings* (*v.* 32, 33), which should be in a particular manner acceptable to you Jews. So far are we from designing to put any slur upon you, or do you any wrong, that the doctrine we preach, if you receive it aright, and understand it, brings you the greatest honour and satisfaction imaginable; for it is in the resurrection of Christ that *the promise which was made to your fathers is fulfilled to you.*" He acknowledges it to be the dignity of the Jewish nation that *to them pertained the promises* (Rom. 9:4), that they were the heirs of the promise, as they were the children of the patriarchs to whom the promises were first made. The great promise of the Old Testament was that of the Messiah, *in whom all the families of the earth should be blessed,* and not the family of Abraham only; though it was to be the peculiar honour of that family that he should be raised up of it, yet it was to be the common benefit of all families that he should be raised up to them. Note, 1. God hath *raised up Jesus,* advanced him, and exalted him; *raised* him *again* (so we read it), meaning *from the dead.* We may take in both senses. God raised up Jesus to be a prophet at his baptism, to be a priest to make atonement at his death, and to be a king to rule over all at his ascension; and *his raising him up from the dead* was the confirmation and ratification of all these commissions, and proved him raised of God to these offices. 2. This is the fulfilling of the promises made to the fathers, the promise of sending the Messiah, and of all those benefits and blessings which were to be had with him and by him: "This is he that should come, and in him you have all that God promised in the Messiah, though not all that you promised yourselves." Paul puts himself into the number of the Jews to whom the promise was fulfilled: *To us their children.* Now, if those who preached the gospel brought them *these glad tidings,* instead of looking upon them as enemies to their nation, they ought to caress them as their best friends, and embrace their doctrine with both arms; for if they valued the promise so much, and themselves by it, much more the performance. And the preaching of the gospel to the Gentiles, which was the great thing that the Jews found themselves aggrieved at, was so far from infringing the promise made to them that the promise itself, that *all the families of the earth* should be blessed in the Messiah, could not otherwise be accomplished.

Fourthly, That the resurrection of Christ was the great proof of his being the Son of God, and confirms what was written in the second Psalm (thus ancient was the order in which the Psalms are now placed), *Thou art my Son, this day have I begotten thee.* That the resurrection of Christ from the dead was designed to evidence and evince this is plain from that of the apostle (Rom. 1:4): *He was declared to be the Son of God with power, by the resurrection from the dead.* When he was first raised up out of obscurity, God declared concerning him by a voice from heaven, *This is my beloved Son* (Mt. 3:17), which has a plain reference to that in the second Psalm, *Thou art my Son.* Abundance of truth there is couched in those words: that this Jesus was *begotten of the Father before all worlds* — was *the brightness of his glory and the express image of his person,* as the son is of the father's, — that he was the *logos,* the *eternal thought of the eternal mind,* — that he was conceived by the power of the Holy Ghost in the womb of the virgin; for upon this account, also, *that holy thing was called the Son of God* (Lu. 1:35), that he was God's agent in creating and governing the world, and in redeeming it and reconciling it to himself, and *faithful as a son in his own house,* and as such was *heir of all things.* Now all this, which was declared at Christ's baptism and again at his transfiguration, was undeniably proved by his resurrection. The decree which was so long before declared was then confirmed; and the reason why it was impossible he should be held by the bands of death was because he was the Son of God, and consequently had *life in himself,* which he could not lay down but with a design to resume it. When his eternal generation is spoken of, it is not improper to say, *This day have I begotten thee;* for *from everlasting to everlasting* is with God as it were one and the same eternal day. Yet it may also be accommodated to his resurrection, in a subordinate sense, "This day have I made it to appear that I have begotten thee, and this day have I begotten all that are given to thee;" for it is said (1 Pt. 1:3) that *the God and Father of our Lord Jesus Christ,* as our God and Father, *hath begotten us again to a lively hope, by the resurrection of Jesus Christ from the dead.*

Fifthly, That his being raised the third day, so as not to see corruption, and to a heavenly life, so as no more to return to corruption, that is, to the state of the dead, as others did who were raised to life, further confirms his being the Messiah promised.

a. He rose to die no more; so it is expressed, Rom. 6:9: *As concerning that he raised him up from the dead, now no more to return to corruption,* that is, to the grave, which is called *corruption,* Job 17:14. Lazarus came out of the grave with his grave-clothes on, because he was to use them again; but Christ, having no more occasion for them, left them behind. Now this was the fulfilling of that scripture (Isa. 55:3), *I will give you the sure mercies of David; ta hosia Dabid ta pista — the holy things of David, the faithful things;* for in the promise made to David, and in him to Christ, great stress is laid upon the faithfulness of God (Ps. 89:1, 2, 5, 24, 33), and upon the oath God had sworn *by his holiness,* Ps. 89:35. Now this makes them sure mercies indeed that he who is entrusted with the dispensing of them has risen to die no more; so that he ever lives to see his own will executed, and the blessings he hath purchased for us given out to us. As, if Christ had died and had not risen again, so if he had risen to die again, we had come short of the sure mercies, or at least could not have been sure of them.

b. He rose so soon after he was dead that his body did not see corruption; for it is not till the third day that the body begins to change. Now this was promised to David; it was one of *the sure mercies of David,* for it was said to him in Ps. 16:10, *Neither wilt thou suffer thy Holy One to see corruption, v.* 35. God had promised to David that he would raise up the Messiah of his seed, who should therefore be a man, but should not, like other men, see corruption. This promise could not have its accomplishment in David, but looked forward to Christ.

(*a.*) It could not be accomplished in David himself (*v.* 36), for *David, after he had served his own generation, by the will of God,* who raised him up to be what he was, *fell asleep, and was laid to his fathers, and saw corruption.* Here we have a short account of the life, death, and burial, of the patriarch David, and his continuance under the power of death. [*a.*] His life: *He served his own generation, by the will of God,* before he slept the sleep of death. David was a useful good man; he did good in the world *by the will of God.* He made God's precepts his rule; he *served his own generation* so as therein to serve God; he so *served* and *pleased men (as whatever the king did pleased the people,* 2 Sa. 3:36), as still to keep himself the faithful servant of God. See Gal. 1:10. He served the good of men, but did not serve the will of men. Or, by the will of God's providence so ordering it, qualifying him for, and calling him to, a public station, he *served his own generation;* for every creature is that to us which God makes it to be. David was a great blessing to the age wherein he lived; he was the *servant* of his generation: many are the curse, and plague, and burden of their generation. Even those that are in a lower and narrower sphere must look upon it that they live to *serve their generation;* and those that will do good in the world must make themselves *servants of all,* 1 Co. 9:19. We were not born for ourselves, but are members of communities, to which we must study to be serviceable. Yet here is the difference between David and Christ, that David was to serve only his own generation, that generation in which he lived, and therefore when he had done what he had to do, and written what he had to write, he died, and continued in the grave; but Christ (not by his writings or words upon record only as David, but by his personal agency) was to serve *all* generations, must ever live to reign over the house of Jacob, not as David, for forty years, but for all ages, as long as the sun and moon endure, Ps. 89:29, 36, 37. His throne must be as the days of heaven, and all generations must be blessed in him, Ps. 72:17. [*b.*] His death: *He fell asleep.* Death is a sleep, a quiet rest, to those who, while they lived, laboured in the service of God and their generation. Observe, He did not fall asleep till he had served his generation, till he had done the work for which God raised him up. God's servants have their work assigned them; and, when they have *accomplished as a hireling their day,* then, and not till then, they are called to rest. God's witnesses never die till they have finished their testimony; and then *the sleep,* the death, *of the labouring man will be sweet.* David was not permitted to build the temple, and therefore when he had made preparation for it, which was the service he was designed to, he fell asleep, and left the work to Solomon. [*c.*] His burial: *He was laid to his fathers.* Though he was buried in *the city of David* (1 Ki. 2:10), and not in the sepulchre of Jesse his father in Bethlehem, yet he might be said to be *laid to his fathers;* for the grave, in general, is the habitation of our fathers, of those that are gone before us, Ps. 49:19. [*d.*] His continuance in the grave: *He saw corruption.* We are sure he did not rise again; this Peter insists upon when he freely speaks of the patriarch David (*ch.* 2:29): *He is both dead and buried, and his sepulchre is with us unto this day.* He saw corruption, and therefore that promise could not have its accomplishment in him. But,

(*b.*) It was accomplished in the Lord Jesus (*v.* 37): *He whom God raised again saw no corruption;* for it was in him that the sure mercies were to be reserved for us. He rose the third day, and therefore did not see corruption then; and he rose to die no more, and therefore never did. Of him therefore the promise must be understood, and no other.

c. Having given them this account of the Lord Jesus, he comes to make application of it.

(*a.*) In the midst of his discourse, to engage their attention, he had told his hearers that they were concerned in all this (*v.* 26): *"To you is the word of this salvation sent,* to you first. If you by your unbelief make it a word of rejection to you, you may thank yourselves; but it is sent to you for a word of salvation; if it be not so, it is your own fault." Let them not peevishly argue that because it was sent to the Gentiles, who had no communion with them, therefore it was not sent to them; for to them it was sent in the first place. *"To you men* this is sent, and not to the angels that sinned. To you living men, and not to the congregation of the dead and damned, whose day of grace is over." He therefore speaks to them with tenderness and respect: You are *men and brethren;* and so we are to look upon all those that stand fair with us for the great salvation as having the word of salvation sent to them. Those to whom he does by warrant from heaven here bring the *word of salvation* are, [*a.*] The native Jews, Hebrews of the Hebrews, as Paul himself was: *"Children of the stock of Abraham,* though a degenerate race, yet to you is this word of salvation sent; nay, it is therefore sent to you, to save you from your sins." It is an advantage to be of a good stock; for, though salvation does not always follow the children of godly parents, yet the word of salvation does: *Abraham will command his children and his house-hold after him.* [*b.*] The proselytes, the Gentiles by birth, that were in some degree brought over to the Jews' religion: *"Whosoever among you that feareth God.* You that have a sense of natural religion, and have subjected yourselves to the laws of that, and taken hold of the comforts of that, *to you is the word of this salvation sent;* you need the further discoveries and directions of revealed religion, are prepared for them, and will bid them welcome, and therefore shall certainly be welcome to take the benefit of them."

(*b.*) In the close of his discourse he applies what he had said concerning Christ to his hearers. He had told them a long story concerning *this Jesus;* now they would be ready to ask, What is all this to us? And he tells them plainly what it is to them.

[*a.*] It will be their unspeakable advantage if they embrace Jesus Christ, and believe this word of salvation. It will relieve them where their greatest danger lies; and that is from the guilt of their sins: *"Be it known unto you therefore, men and brethren* — we are warranted to proclaim it to you, and you are called to take notice of it." He did not stand up to preach before them, but to preach to them, and not without hopes of prevailing with them; for they are men, reasonable creatures, and capable of being argued with; they are *brethren,* spoken to, and dealt with, by men like themselves; not only of the same nature, but of the same nation. It is proper for the preachers of the gospel to call their hearers brethren, as speaking familiarly to them, and with an affectionate concern for their welfare, and as being equally interested with them in the gospel they preach. Let all that hear the gospel of Christ know these two things: — *1st,* That it is an act of indemnity granted by the King of kings to the children of men, who stand attainted at his bar of treason against his crown and dignity; and it is for and in consideration of the mediation of Christ between God and man that this act of grace is passed and proclaimed (*v.* 38): *"Through this man,* who died and rose again, *is preached unto you the forgiveness of sins.* We have to tell you, in God's name, that your sins, though many and great, may be forgiven, and how it is come about that they may be so, without any injury to God's honour, and how you may obtain the forgiveness of your sins. We are to preach repentance for the remission of sins, and divine grace giving both *repentance and remission of sins.* The remission of sins is *through this man.* By his merit it was purchased, in his name it is offered, and by his authority it is bestowed; and therefore you are concerned to be acquainted with him, and interested in him. We preach to you *the forgiveness of sins.* That is the salvation we bring you, the word of God; and therefore you ought to bid us welcome and look upon us as your friends, and messengers of good tidings." *2ndly,* That it does that for us which the law of Moses could not do. The Jews were jealous for the law, and because it prescribed expiatory and pacificatory sacrifices, and a great variety of purifications, fancied they might be justified by it before God. "No," saith Paul, "be it known to you that it is by Christ only that *those who believe in him,* and none else, are *justified from all things,* from all the guilt and stain of sin, *from which you could not be justified by the law of Moses"* (*v.* 39); therefore they ought to entertain and embrace the gospel, and not to adhere to the law in opposition to it, because the gospel is perfective, not destructive, of the law. Note, 1. The great concern of sinners it to be justified, to be acquitted from guilt and accepted as righteous in God's sight. 2. Those who are truly justified are acquitted from all their guilt; for if any be left charged upon the sinner he is undone. 3. It was impossible for a sinner to be justified by the law of Moses. Not by his moral law, for we have all broken it, and are transgressing it daily, so that instead of justifying us it condemns us. Not by his remedial law, for it was not possible that the *blood of bulls and goats should take away sin,* should satisfy God's offended justice, or pacify the sinner's wounded conscience. It was but a ritual and typical institution. See Heb. 9:9; 10:1, 4. 4. By Jesus Christ we obtain a complete justification; for by him a complete atonement was made for sin. We are justified, not only by him as our Judge, but by him as our righteousness, *the Lord our righteousness.* 5. All that believe in Christ, that rely upon him and give up themselves to be ruled by him, are justified by him, and none but they. 6. What the law *could not do* for us, *in that it was weak,* that the gospel of Christ does; and therefore it was folly, out of a jealousy for the law of Moses and the honour of that institution, to conceive a jealousy of the gospel of Christ and the designs of that more perfect institution.

[b.] It is at their utmost peril if they reject the gospel of Christ, and turn their backs upon the offer now made them (v. 40, 41): *"Beware therefore;* you have a fair invitation given you, look to yourselves, lest you either neglect or oppose it." Note, those to whom the gospel is preached must see themselves upon their trial and good behaviour, and are concerned to beware lest they be found refusers of the grace offered. "Beware lest you not only come short of the blessings and benefits spoken of in the prophets as coming upon those that believe, but fall under the doom spoken of in the prophets as coming upon those that persist in unbelief: *lest that come upon you which is spoken of."* Note, The threatenings are warnings; what we are told will come upon impenitent sinners is designed to awaken us to beware lest it should come upon us. Now the prophecy referred to we have Hab. 1:5, where the destruction of the Jewish nation by the Chaldeans is foretold as an incredible unparalleled destruction; and this is here applied to the destruction that was coming upon that nation by the Romans, for their rejecting the gospel of Christ. The apostle follows the Septuagint translation, which reads, *Behold, you despisers* (for, *behold, you among the heathen);* because it made the text more apposite to his purpose. *1st,* "Take heed lest the guilt come upon you which was spoken of in the prophets — the guilt of despising the gospel and the tenders of it, and despising the Gentiles that were advanced to partake of it. Beware lest it be said to you, *Behold, you despisers."* Note, It is the ruin of many that they despise religion, they look upon it as a thing below them, and are not willing to stoop to it. *2ndly,* "Take heed lest the judgment come upon you which was spoken of in the prophets: that *you shall wonder and perish,* that is, wonderfully perish; your perdition shall be amazing to yourselves and all about you." Those that will not wonder and be saved shall wonder and perish. Those that enjoyed the privileges of the church, and flattered themselves with a conceit that these would save them, will wonder when they find their vain presumption overruled and that their privileges do but make their condemnation the more intolerable. Let the unbelieving Jews expect that God will *work a work in their days which you shall in no wise believe, though a man declare it unto you.* This may be understood as a prediction, either, 1. Of their sin, that they should be incredulous, that that great work of God, the redemption of the world by Christ, though it should be in the most solemn manner declared unto them, yet they would *in no wise believe it,* Isa. 53:1, *Who hath believed our report?* Though it was of God's working, to whom nothing is impossible, and of his declaring, who cannot lie, yet they would not give credit to it. Those that had the honour and advantage to have this work wrought in their days had not the grace to believe it. Or, 2. Of their destruction. The dissolving of the Jewish polity, the taking of the kingdom of God from them and giving it to the Gentiles, the destruction of their holy house and city, and the dispersion of their people, was a work which one would not have believed should have ever been done, considering how much they had been the favourites of Heaven. The calamities that were brought upon them were such as were never before brought upon any people, Mt. 24:21. It was said of their destruction by the Chaldeans, and it was true of their last destruction, *All the inhabitants of the world would not have believed that the enemy would have entered into the gates of Jerusalem as they did,* Lam. 4:12. Thus is there a *strange punishment to the workers of iniquity,* especially to the despisers of Christ, Job 31:3.

Verses 42–52

The design of this story being to vindicate the apostles, especially Paul (as he doth himself at large, Rom. 11), from the reflections of the Jews upon him for preaching the gospel to the Gentiles, it is here observed that he proceeded therein with all the caution imaginable, and upon due consideration, of which we have here an instance.

I. There were some of the Jews that were so incensed against the preaching of the gospel, not to the Gentiles, but to themselves, that they would not bear to hear it, but *went out of the synagogue* while Paul was preaching (v. 42), in contempt of him and his doctrine, and to the disturbance of the congregation. It is probable they whispered among themselves, exciting one another to it, and did it by consent. Now this bespoke, 1. An open infidelity, as plain a profession of

unbelief as coming to hear the gospel is of faith. They thus publicly avowed their contempt of Christ and of his doctrine and law, were not ashamed, neither could they blush; and they thus endeavoured to beget prejudices in the minds of others against the gospel; they went out to draw others to follow their pernicious ways. 2. An obstinate infidelity. They went out of the synagogue, not only to show that they did not believe the gospel, but because they were resolved they would not, and therefore got out of the hearing of those things that had a tendency to convince them. They stopped their ears like the deaf adder. Justly therefore was the gospel taken from them, when they first took themselves from it, and turned themselves out of the church before they were turned out of it. For it is certainly true that God never leaves any till they first leave him.

II. The Gentiles were as willing to hear the gospel as those rude and ill-conditioned Jews were to get out of the hearing of it: *They besought that these words,* or words to this effect, *might be preached to them the next sabbath;* in the *week between,* so some take it; on the second and fifth days of the week, which in some synagogues were their lecture days. But it appears (v. 44) that it was the next sabbath day that they came together. They begged, 1. That the same offer might be made to them that was made to the Jews. Paul in this sermon had brought the word of salvation to the Jews and proselytes, but had taken no notice of the Gentiles; and therefore they begged that forgiveness of sins through Christ might be preached to them, as it was to the Jews. The Jews' leavings, nay, loathings, were their longings. This justifies Paul in his preaching to them, that he was invited to it, as Peter was sent for to Cornelius. Who could refuse to break the bread of life to those who begged so hard for it, and to give that to the poor at the door which the children at the table threw under their feet? 2. That the same instructions might be given to them. They had heard the doctrine of Christ, but did not understand it at the first hearing, nor could they remember all that they had heard, and therefore they begged it might be preached to them again. Note, It is good to have the word of Christ repeated to us. What we have heard we should desire to hear again, that it may take deep root in us, and the nail that is driven may be clenched and be as *a nail in a sure place.* To hear *the same things* should not be grievous, because it is safe, Phil. 3:1. It aggravates the bad disposition of the Jews that the Gentiles desired to hear that often which they were not willing to hear once; and commends the good disposition of the Gentiles that they did not follow the bad example which the Jews set them.

III. There were some, nay, there were many, both of Jews and proselytes, that were wrought upon by the preaching of the gospel. Those who aggravated the matter of the Jews' rejection by the preaching of the gospel, cried out, as is usual in such cases, "They have cast away, and cast off, all the people of God." "Nay," says Paul, "it is not so; for abundance of the Jews have embraced Christ, and are taken in;" himself for one, Rom. 11:1, 5. So it was here: *Many of the Jews and religious proselytes followed Paul and Barnabas,* and received further instructions and encouragement from them. 1. They submitted to the grace of God, and were admitted to the benefit and comfort of it, which is implied in their being exhorted to continue in it. They *followed Paul and Barnabas;* they became their disciples, or rather the disciples of Christ, whose agents they were. Those that join themselves to Christ will join themselves to his ministers, and follow them. And Paul and Barnabas, though they were sent to the Gentiles, yet bade those of the Jews welcome that were willing to come under their instructions, such hearty well-wishers were they to all the Jews and their friends, if they pleased. 2. They were exhorted and encouraged to persevere herein: *Paul and Barnabas, speaking to them* with all the freedom and friendship imaginable, *persuaded them to continue in the grace of God,* to hold fast that which they had received, to continue in their belief of the gospel of grace, their dependence upon the Spirit of grace, and their attendance upon the means of grace. And the grace of God shall not be wanting to those who thus continue in it.

IV. There was a cheerful attendance upon the preaching of the gospel the *next sabbath day* (v. 44): *Almost the whole city* (the generality of whom were Gentiles) *came together to hear the word of God.* 1. It is probable that Paul and Barnabas were not idle in the week-days, but took all opportunities in the week between (as some think the Gentiles desired) to bring them acquainted with Christ, and to raise their

expectations from him. They did a great deal of service to the gospel in private discourse and conversation, as well as in their public sermons. Wisdom cried in the chief places of concourse, and the opening of the gates, as well as in the synagogues, Prov. 1:20, 21. 2. This brought a vast concourse of people to the synagogue on the sabbath day. Some came out of curiosity, the thing being new; others longing to see what the Jews would do upon the second tender of the gospel to them; and many who had heard something of the word of God came to hear more, and to hear it, *not as the word of men but as the word of God,* by which we must be ruled and judged. Now this justified Paul in preaching to the Gentiles, that he met with the most encouraging auditors among them. There *the fields were white to the harvest,* and therefore why should he not there put in his sickle?

V. The Jews were enraged at this; and not only would not receive the gospel themselves, but were filled with indignation at those that crowded after it (v. 45): *When the Jews saw the multitudes,* and considered what an encouragement it was to Paul to go on in his work when he saw the people thus flying like doves to their windows, and what probability there was that among these multitudes some would be, without doubt, wrought upon, and probably the greater part, to embrace Christ — this *filled them with envy.* 1. They grudged the interest the apostles had in the people, were vexed to see the synagogue so full when they were going to preach. This was the same spirit that worked in the Pharisees towards Christ; they were cut to the heart when they saw *the whole world go after him.* When the kingdom of heaven was opened they not only would not go in themselves, but were angry with those that did. 2. They opposed the doctrine the apostles preached: *They spoke against those things that were spoken by Paul,* cavilled at them, started objections against them, finding some fault or other with every thing he said, *contradicting and blaspheming; antelegon antilegontes — contradicting, they contradicted.* They did it with the utmost spite and rage imaginable: they persisted in their contradiction, and nothing would silence them, they contradicted for contradiction-sake, and denied that which was most evident; and, when they could find no colour of objection, they broke out into ill language against Christ and his gospel, blaspheming him and it. From the language of the carnal man that receives not the things of the Spirit of God, and therefore contradicts them, they proceed to the language of incarnate devils, and blaspheme them. Commonly those who begin with contradicting end with blaspheming.

VI. The apostles hereupon solemnly and openly declare themselves discharged from their obligations to the Jews, and at liberty to bring the word of salvation to the Gentiles, even by the tacit consent of the Jews themselves. Never let the Jew lay the fault of the carrying of the kingdom of God to the Gentiles upon the apostles, for that complaint of theirs is for ever silenced by their own act and deed, for what they did here is for ever a bar to it. "Tender and refusal (we say) are good payment in law." The Jews had the tender of the gospel, and did refuse it, and therefore ought not to say any thing against the Gentiles having it. In declaring this, it is said (v. 46), *Paul and Barnabas waxed bold,* more bold than they had been while they were shy of looking favourably upon the Gentiles, for fear of giving offence to the Jews, and laying a stumbling-block in their way. Note, There is a time for the preachers of the gospel to show as much of the boldness of the lion as of the wisdom of the serpent and the harmlessness of the dove. When the adversaries of Christ's cause begin to be daring, it is not for its advocates to be timid. While there is any hope of working upon those that oppose themselves they must be *instructed with meekness* (2 Tim. 2:25); but, when that method has long been tried in vain, we must wax bold, and tell them what will be the issue of their opposition. The impudence of the enemies of the gospel, instead of frightening, should rather embolden its friends; for they are sure that they have a good cause, and they know in whom they have trusted to bear them out. Now Paul and Barnabas, having made the Jews a fair offer of gospel grace, here give them fair notice of their bringing it to the Gentiles, *if by any means* (as Paul says Rom. 11:14) *they might provoke them to emulation.* 1. They own that the Jews were entitled to the first offer: *"It was necessary that the word of God should first have been spoken to you,* to whom the promise was made, to you *of the lost sheep of the house of Israel,* to whom Christ reckoned himself first sent." And his charge to the preachers of his gospel to *begin at Jerusalem* (Lu. 24:47) was a tacit direction to all that went into other countries to begin with the Jews, *to whom pertained the giving of the law,* and therefore the preaching of the gospel. *Let the children first be served,* Mk. 7:27. 2. They charge them with the refusal of it: "*You put it from you;* you will not accept of it; nay, you will not so much as bear the offer of it, but take it as an affront to you." If men put the gospel from them, God justly takes it from them; why should manna be given to those that loathe it and call it *light bread,* or the privileges of the gospel forced on those that put them away, and say, *We have no part in David?* Herein they *judge themselves unworthy of everlasting life.* In one sense we must all judge ourselves unworthy of everlasting life, for there is nothing in us, nor done by us, by which we can pretend to merit it, and we must be made sensible of this; but here the meaning is, "You discover, or make it to appear, that you are not meet for eternal life; you throw away all your claims and give up your pretensions to it; since you will not take it from his hands, into whose hand the Father has given it, *krinete, you do,* in effect, *pass this judgment* upon yourselves, and *out of your own mouth you shall be judged;* you will not have it by Christ, by whom alone it is to be had, and so shall your doom be, you shall not have it at all." 3. Upon this they ground their preaching the gospel to the uncircumcised: "Since you will not accept eternal life as it is offered, our way is plain, *Lo, we turn to the Gentiles.* If one will not, another will. If those that were first invited to the wedding-feast will not come, we must invite out of the highways and hedges those that will, for *the wedding must be furnished with guests.* If he that is next of kin will not do the kinsman's part, he must not complain that another will," Ruth 4:4. 4. They justify themselves in this by a divine warrant (*v.* 47): "*For so hath the Lord commanded us;* the Lord Jesus gave us directions to witness to him in Jerusalem and Judea first, and after that *to the utmost part of the earth,* to preach the gospel to *every creature,* to *disciple all nations.*" This is according to what was foretold in the Old-Testament. When the Messiah, in the prospect of the Jews' infidelity, was ready to say, *I have laboured in vain,* he was told, to his satisfaction, that though *Israel were not gathered,* yet *he should be glorious,* that his blood should not be shed in vain, nor his purchase made in vain, nor his doctrine preached in vain, nor his Spirit sent in vain, — "*For I have set thee,* not only raised thee up, but established thee, to be *a light of the Gentiles,* not only a shining light for a time, but a standing light, set thee for a light, *that thou shouldst be for salvation unto the ends of the earth.*" Note, (1.) Christ is not only the Saviour, but the salvation, is himself our righteousness, and life, and strength. (2.) Wherever Christ is designed to be salvation, he is set up to be a light; he enlightens the understanding, and so saves the soul. (3.) He is, and is to be, light and salvation to the Gentiles, to the ends of the earth. Those of every nation shall be welcome to him, some of every nation have heard of him (Rom. 10:18), and all nations shall at length become his kingdom. This prophecy has had its accomplishment in part in the setting up of the kingdom of Christ in this island of ours, which lies, as it were, in the *ends of the earth,* a corner of the world, and shall be accomplished more and more when the time comes for the *bringing in of the fulness of the Gentiles.*

VII. The Gentiles cheerfully embraced that which the Jews scornfully rejected, *v.* 48, 49. Never was land lost for want of heirs; *through the fall of the Jews, salvation is come to the Gentiles:* the *casting off of them was the reconciling of the world, and the diminishing of them the riches of the Gentiles;* so the apostle shows at large, Rom. 11:11, 12, 15. The Jews, the natural branches, were broken off, and the Gentiles, that were branches of the wild olive, were thereupon grafted in, *v.* 17, 19. Now here we are told how the Gentiles welcomed this happy turn in their favour.

1. They took the comfort of it: *When they heard this they were glad.* It was good news to them that they might have admission into covenant and communion with God by a clearer, nearer, and better way than submitting to the ceremonial law, and being proselyted to the Jewish religion, — that the partition-wall was taken down and they were as welcome to the benefits of the Messiah's kingdom as the Jews themselves, and might share in their promise, without coming under their yoke. This was indeed *glad tidings of great joy to all people.* Note, Our being put into a possibility of salvation, and a capacity for it, ought to be the matter of our rejoicing; when the Gentiles did but hear that the offers of grace should be made them, the word of grace preached to them, and the

means of grace afforded them, *they were glad.* "Now there is some hope for us." Many grieve under doubts whether they have an interest in Christ or no, when they should be rejoicing that they have an interest in him; the golden sceptre is held out to them, and they are invited to come and touch the top of it.

2. They gave God the praise of it: *They glorified the word of the Lord;* that is, Christ (so some), the essential Word; they entertained a profound veneration for him, and expressed the high thoughts they had of him. Or, rather, *the gospel;* the more they knew of it, the more they admired it. Oh! what a light, what a power, what a treasure, does this gospel bring along with it! How excellent are its truths, its precepts, its promises! How far transcending all other institutions! How plainly divine and heavenly is its origin! Thus they *glorified the word of the Lord,* and it is this which he has himself *magnified above all his name* (Ps. 138:2), and will *magnify* and *make honourable,* Isa. 42:21. They glorified the word of the Lord, (1.) Because now the knowledge of it was diffused and not confined to the Jews only. Note, It is the glory of the word of the Lord that the further it spreads the brighter it shines, which shows it to be not like the light of the candle, but like that of the sun when he goes forth in his strength. (2.) Because now the knowledge of it was brought to them. Note, Those speak best of the honour of the word of the Lord that speak experimentally, that have themselves been subdued by its power, and comforted by its sweetness.

3. Many of them became, not only professors of the Christian faith, but sincerely obedient to the faith: *As many as were ordained to eternal life believed.* God by his Spirit wrought true faith in those for whom he had in his councils from everlasting designed a happiness to everlasting. (1.) Those believed to whom God gave grace to believe, whom by a secret and mighty operation he brought into subjection to the gospel of Christ, and made willing in the day of his power. Those came to Christ whom the Father drew, and to whom the Spirit made the gospel call effectual. It is called *the faith of the operation of God* (Col. 2:12), and is said to be *wrought by the same power that raised up Christ,* Eph. 1:19, 20. (2.) God gave this grace to believe to all those among them who were ordained to eternal life (for *whom he had predestinated, them he also called,* Rom. 8:30); or, *as many as were disposed to eternal life,* as many as had a concern about their eternal state, and aimed to make sure of eternal life, believed in Christ, in whom God hath treasured up that life (1 Jn. 5:11), and who is the only way to it; and it was the grace of God that wrought it in them. Thus all those captives, and those only, took the benefit of Cyrus's proclamation, *whose spirit God had raised up to build the house of the Lord which is in Jerusalem,* Ezra 1:5. Those will be brought to believe in Christ that by his grace are well disposed to eternal life, and make this their aim.

4. When they believed they did what they could to spread the knowledge of Christ and his gospel among their neighbours (*v.* 49): *And the word of the Lord was published throughout all the region.* When it was received with so much satisfaction in the chief city, it soon spread into all parts of the country. Those new converts were themselves ready to communicate to others that which they were so full of themselves. *The Lord gave the word, and then great was the company of those that published it,* Ps. 68:11. Those that have become acquainted with Christ themselves will do what they can to bring others acquainted with him. Those in great and rich cities that have received the gospel should not think to engross it, as if, like learning and philosophy, it were only to be the entertainment of the more polite and elevated part of mankind, but should do what they can to get it published in the country among the ordinary sort of people, the poor and unlearned, who have souls to be saved as well as they.

VIII. Paul and Barnabas, having sown the seeds of a Christian church there, quitted the place, and went to do the like else-where. We read not any thing of their working miracles here, to confirm their doctrine, and to convince people of the truth of it; for, though God then did ordinarily make use of that method of conviction, yet he could, when he pleased, do his work without it; and begetting faith by the immediate influence of his Spirit was itself the greatest miracle to those in whom it was wrought. Yet, it is probable that they did work miracles, for we find they did in the next place they came to, *ch.* 14:3. Now here we are told,

1. How *the unbelieving Jews* expelled the apostles out of that country. They first turned their back upon them, and

then *lifted up the heel against them* (*v.* 50): They raised persecution against Paul and Barnabas, excited the mob to persecute them in *their* way by insulting their persons as they went along the streets; excited the magistrates to persecute them in *their* way, by imprisoning and punishing them. When *they could not resist the wisdom and spirit wherewith they spoke,* they had recourse to these brutish methods, the last refuge of an obstinate infidelity. Satan and his agents are most exasperated against the preachers of the gospel when they see them go on successfully, and therefore then will be sure to raise persecution against them. Thus it has been the common lot of the best men in the world to suffer ill for doing well, to be persecuted instead of being preferred for the good services they have done to mankind. Observe, (1.) What method the Jews took to give them trouble: *They stirred up the devout and honourable women* against them. They could not make any considerable interest themselves, but they applied to some ladies of quality in the city, that were well affected to the Jewish religion, and were proselytes of the gate, therefore called *devout women.* These, according to the genius of their sex, were zealous in their way, and bigoted; and it was easy, by false stories and misrepresentations, to incense them against the gospel of Christ, as if it had been destructive of all religion, of which really it is perfective. It is good to see honourable women devout, and well affected to religious worship: The less they have to do in the world, the more they should do for their souls, and the more time they should spend in communion with God; but it is sad when, under colour of devotion to God, they conceive an enmity to Christ, as those here mentioned. What! women persecutors! Can they forget the tenderness and compassion of their sex? What! honourable women! Can they thus stain their honour, and disgrace themselves, and do so mean a thing? But, which is strangest of all, devout women! Will they kill Christ's servants, and think therein they do God service? Let those therefore that have zeal see that it be according to knowledge. By these devout and honourable women they stirred up likewise *the chief men of the city,* the magistrates and the rulers, who had power in their hands and set them against the apostles, and they had so little consideration as to suffer themselves to be made the tools of this ill-natured party, who *would neither go into the kingdom of heaven themselves nor suffer those who were entering to go in.* (2.) How far they carried it, so far that *they expelled them out of their coasts;* they banished them, ordered them to be carried, as we say, from constable to constable, till they were forced out of their jurisdiction; so that it was not by fear, but downright violence, that they were driven out. This was one method which the overruling providence of God took to keep the first planters of the church from staying too long at a place; as Mt. 10:23, *When they persecute you in one city flee to another,* that thus you may the sooner *go over the cities of Israel.* This was likewise a method God took to make those that were well disposed the more warmly affected towards the apostles; for it is natural to us to pity those that are persecuted, to think the better of those that suffer when we know they suffer unjustly, and to be the more ready to help them. The expelling of the apostles out of their coasts made people inquisitive what evil they had done, and perhaps raised them more friends than conniving at them in their coasts would have done.

2. How the apostles abandoned and rejected the unbelieving Jews (*v.* 51): *They shook off the dust of their feet against them.* When they went out of the city they used this ceremony in the sight of those that sat in the gate; or, when they went out of the borders of their country, in the sight of those that were sent to see the country rid of them. Hereby, (1.) They declared that they would have no more to do with them, would take nothing that was theirs; for *they sought not theirs, but them.* Dust they are, and let them keep their dust to themselves, it shall not cleave to them. (2.) They expressed their detestation of their infidelity, and that, though they were Jews by birth, yet, having rejected the gospel of Christ, they were in their eyes no better than heathen and profane. As Jews and Gentiles, if they believe, are equally acceptable to God and good men; so, if they do not, they are equally abominable. (3.) Thus they set them at defiance, and expressed their contempt of them and their malice, which they looked upon as impotent. It was as much as to say, "Do your worst, we do not fear you; we know whom we serve and whom we have trusted." (4.) Thus they left a testimony behind them that they had had a fair offer made them of the grace of the gospel, which shall be proved against them in the day of judgment.

This dust will prove that the preachers of the gospel had been among them, but were expelled by them. Thus Christ had ordered them to do, and for this reason, Mt. 10:14; Lu. 9:5. When *they left them, they came to Iconium,* not so much for safety, as for work.

3. What frame they left the new converts in *at Antioch* (*v.* 52): *The disciples,* when they saw with what courage and cheerfulness Paul and Barnabas not only bore the indignities that were done them, but went on with their work notwithstanding, they were in like manner inspirited. (1.) They were very cheerful. One would have expected that when Paul and Barnabas were expelled out of their coasts, and perhaps forbidden to return upon pain of death, the disciples would have been full of grief and full of fear, looking for no other than that, if the planters of Christianity go, the plantation would soon come to nothing; or that it would be their turn next to be banished the country, and to them it would be more grievous, for it was their own. But no; *they were filled with joy* in Christ, had such a satisfactory assurance of Christ's carrying on and perfecting his own work in them and among them, and that either he would screen them from trouble or bear them up under it, that all their fears were swallowed up in their believing joys. (2.) They were courageous, wonderfully animated with a holy resolution to cleave to Christ, whatever difficulties they met with. This seems especially to be meant by *their being filled with the Holy Ghost,* for the same expression is used of Peter's boldness (*ch.* 4:8), and Stephen's (*ch.* 7:55), and Paul's, *ch.* 13:9. The more we relish the comforts and encouragements we meet with in the power of godliness, and the fuller our hearts are of them, the better prepared we are to face the difficulties we meet with in the profession of godliness.

CHAPTER 14

We have, in this chapter, a further account of the progress of the gospel, by the ministry of Paul and Barnabas among the Gentiles; it goes on conquering and to conquer, yet meeting with opposition, as before, among the unbelieving Jews. Here is, I. Their successful preaching of the gospel for some time at Iconium, and their being driven thence by the violence of their persecutors, both Jews and Gentiles, and forced into the neighbouring countries (*v.* 1–7). II. Their healing a lame man at Lystra, and the profound veneration which the people conceived of them thereupon, which they had much ado to keep from running into an extreme (*v.* 8–18). III. The outrage of the people against Paul, at the instigation of the Jews, the effect of which was that they stoned him, as they thought, to death; but he was wonderfully restored to life (*v.* 19, 20). IV. The visit which Paul and Barnabas made to the churches which they had planted, to confirm them, and put them into order (*v.* 21–23). V. They return to Antioch, whence they were sent forth; the good they did by the way, and the report they made to the church of Antioch of their expedition, and, if I may so say, of the campaign they had made (*v.* 24–28).

Verses 1–7

In these verses we have,

I. The preaching of the gospel in Iconium, whither the apostles were forced to retire from Antioch. As the blood of the martyrs has been the seed of the church, so the banishment of the confessors has helped to scatter that seed. Observe, 1. How they made the first offer of the gospel *to the Jews in their synagogues;* thither they went, not only as to a place of meeting, but as to a place of meeting with them, to whom, wherever they came, they were to apply themselves in the first place. Though the Jews at Antioch had used them barbarously, yet they did not therefore decline preaching the gospel to the Jews at Iconium, who perhaps might be better disposed. Let not those of any denomination be condemned in the gross, nor some suffer for others' faults; but let us do good to those who have done evil to us. Though *the bloodthirsty hate the upright, yet the just seek their soul* (Prov. 29:10), seek the salvation of it. 2. How the apostles concurred herein. Notice is taken of this, that *they went both together into the synagogue,* to testify their unanimity and mutual affection, that people might say, *See how they love one another,* and might think the better of Christianity, and that they might strengthen one another's hands and confirm one another's testimony, and *out of the mouth of two witnesses every word might be established.* They did not go one one day and another another, nor one go at the beginning and the other some time after; but they went in both together.

II. The success of their preaching there: *They so spoke that a great multitude,* some hundreds perhaps, if not thousands, *both of the Jews and also of the Greeks,* that is the Gentiles, *believed.* Observe here, 1. That the gospel was now preached to Jews and Gentiles together, and those of each denomination that believed came together into the church. In the close of the foregoing chapter it was preached first to the Jews, and some of them believed, and then to the Gentiles, and some of them believed; but here they are put together, being put upon the same level. The Jews have not so lost their preference as to be thrown behind, only the Gentiles are brought to stand upon even terms with them; *both are reconciled to God in one body* (Ephes. 2:16), and both together admitted into the church without distinction. 2. There seems to have been something remarkable in the manner of the apostles' preaching here, which contributed to their success: *They so spoke that a great multitude believed* — so plainly, so convincingly, with such an evidence and *demonstration of the Spirit,* and *with such power;* they so spoke, so warmly, so affectionately, and with such a manifest concern for the souls of men, that one might perceive they were not only convinced, but filled, with the things they spoke of, and that what they spoke came from the heart and therefore was likely to reach to the heart; they so spoke, so earnestly and so seriously, so boldly and courageously, that those who heard them could not but say that *God was with them of a truth.* Yet the success was not to be attributed to the manner of their preaching, but to the Spirit of God, who made use of that means.

III. The opposition that their preaching met with there, and the trouble that was created them; lest they should be puffed up with the multitude of their converts, there was given them this thorn in the flesh. 1. Unbelieving Jews were the first spring of their trouble here, as elsewhere (*v.* 2): they *stirred up the Gentiles.* The influence which the gospel had upon many of the Gentiles, and their embracing it, as it provoked some of the Jews to a holy jealousy and stirred them up to receive the gospel too (Rom. 11:14), so it provoked others of them to a wicked jealousy, and exasperated them against the gospel. Thus as good instructions, so good examples, which to some are a savour of life unto life, to others are a savour of death unto death. See 2 Co. 2:15, 16. 2. Disaffected Gentiles, irritated by the unbelieving Jews, were likely to be the instruments of their trouble. The Jews, by false suggestions, which they were continually buzzing in the ears of the Gentiles, made *their minds evil affected against the brethren,* whom of themselves they were inclined to think favourably of. They not only took occasion in all companies, as it came in their way, but made it their business to go purposely to such as they had any acquaintance with, and said all that their wit or malice could invent to beget in them not only a mean but an ill opinion of Christianity, telling them how destructive it would certainly be to their pagan theology and worship; and, for their parts, they would rather be Gentiles than Christians. Thus they soured and embittered their spirits against both the converters and the converted. *The old serpent* did, by their poisonous tongues, infuse his venom against *the seed of the woman* into the minds of these Gentiles, and this was a *root of bitterness in them, bearing gall and wormwood.* It is no wonder if those who are ill affected towards good people wish ill to them, speak ill of them, and contrive ill against them; it is all owing to ill will. *Ekakōsan, they molested* and vexed the minds of the Gentiles (so some of the critics take it); they were continually teasing them with their impertinent solicitations. The tools of persecutors have a dog's life, set on continually.

IV. Their continuance in their work there, notwithstanding this opposition, and God's owning them in it, *v.* 3. We have here, 1. The apostles working for Christ, faithfully and diligently, according to the trust committed to them. Because the minds of *the Gentiles were evil affected against them,* one would think that therefore they should have withdrawn, and hastened out of the way, or, if they had preached, should have preached cautiously, for fear of giving further provocation to those who were already enough enraged. No; on the contrary, therefore *they abode there a long time, speaking boldly in the Lord.* The more they perceived the spite and rancour of the town against the new converts, the more they were animated to go on in their work, and the more needful they saw it to continue among them, *to confirm them in the faith, and to comfort them. They spoke boldly,* and were not afraid of giving offence to the unbelieving Jews. What God said to the prophet, with reference to the unbelieving Jews in his day, was now made good to the apostles: *I have made thy face strong against their faces,* Eze. 3:7–9. But observe what it was that animated them: *They spoke boldly in the Lord,* in his strength, and trusting in him to bear them out; not depending upon any thing in themselves. *They were strong in the Lord, and in the power of his might.* 2. Christ working with the apostles, according to his promise, *Lo, I am with you always.* When they went on in his name and strength, he failed not to give testimony to the word of his grace. Note, (1.) The gospel is a word of grace, the assurance of God's good will to us and the means of his good work in us. It is the word of Christ's grace, for it is in him alone that we find favour with God. (2.) Christ himself has attested this word of grace, who is *the Amen, the faithful witness;* he has assured us that it is the word of God, and that we may venture our souls upon it. As it was said in general concerning the first preachers of the gospel that they had *the Lord working with them, and confirming the word by signs following* (Mk. 16:20), so it is said particularly concerning the apostles here *that the Lord confirmed their testimony, in granting signs and wonders to be done by their hands* — in the miracles they wrought in the kingdom of nature — as well as the wonders done by their word, in the greater miracles wrought on men's minds by the power of divine grace. The Lord was with them, while they were with him, and abundance of good was done.

V. The division which this occasioned in the city (*v.* 4): *The multitude of the city was divided* into two parties, and both active and vigorous. Among the rulers and persons of rank, and among the common people, there were some that held with the unbelieving Jews, and others that held with the apostles. Barnabas is here reckoned an apostle, though not one of the twelve, nor called in the extra-ordinary manner that Paul was, because set apart by special designation of *the Holy Ghost to the service of the Gentiles.* It seems, this business of the preaching of the gospel was so universally taken notice of with concern that every person, even of *the multitude of the city,* was either for it or against it; none stood neuter. "Either for us or for our adversaries, for God or Baal, for Christ or Beelzebub." 1. We may here see the meaning of Christ's prediction that he *came not to send peace upon earth, but rather division,* Lu. 12:51–53. If all would have given in unanimously into his measures, there would have been universal concord; and, could men have agreed in this, there would have been no dangerous discord nor disagreement in other things; but, disagreeing here, the breach was wide as the sea. Yet the apostles must not be blamed for coming to Iconium, although before they came the city was united, and now it was divided; for it is better that part of the city go to heaven than all to hell. 2. We may here take the measures of our expectations; let us not think it strange if the preaching of the gospel occasion division, nor be offended at it; it is better to be reproached and persecuted as dividers for swimming against the stream than yield ourselves to be carried down the stream that leads to destruction. Let us hold with the apostles, and not fear those that hold with the Jews.

VI. The attempt made upon the apostles by their enemies. Their evil affection against them broke out at length into violent outrages, *v.* 5. Observe, 1. Who the plotters were: *Both the Gentiles and the Jews, with their rulers.* The Gentiles and Jews were at enmity with one another, and yet united against Christians, like Herod and Pilate, Sadducees and Pharisees, against Christ; and like *Gebal and Ammon and Amalek, of old,* against Israel. If the church's enemies can thus unite for its destruction, shall not its friends, laying aside all personal feuds, unite for its preservation? 2. What the plot was. Having now got *the rulers* on their side, they doubted not but to carry their point, and their design was *to use the apostles despitefully,* to expose them to disgrace, and then *to stone them,* to put them to death; and thus they hoped to sink their cause. They aimed to take away both their reputation and their life, and this was all they had to lose which men could take from them, for they had neither lands nor goods.

VII. The deliverance of the apostles out of the hands of those *wicked and unreasonable men, v.* 6, 7. They got away, upon notice given them of the design against them, or the beginning of the attempt upon them, of which they were soon aware, and they made an honourable retreat (for it was not an inglorious flight) to *Lystra and Derbe;* and there, 1. They found safety. Their persecutors in Iconium were for the present satisfied that they were thrust out of their borders, and pursued them no further. God has shelters for his people in a storm; nay, he is, and will be, himself their hiding place. 2. They found work, and this was what they went for. When the door of opportunity was shut against them at Iconium, it was opened at *Lystra* and *Derbe.* To these cities they went, and there, and *in the region that lieth round about, they preached the gospel.* In times of persecution ministers may see cause to quit the spot, when yet they do not quit the work.

Verses 8–18

In these verses we have,

I. A miraculous cure wrought by Paul at Lystra upon a cripple that had been lame from his birth, such a one as was miraculously cured by Peter and John, *ch.* 3:2. That introduced the gospel among the Jews, this among the Gentiles; both that and this were designed to represent the impotency of all the children of men in spiritual things: they are lame from their birth, till the grace of God puts strength into them; for it was when we were yet *without strength* that *Christ died for the ungodly,* Rom. 5:6. Observe here, 1. The deplorable case of the poor cripple (*v.* 8): He was *impotent in his feet, disabled* (so the word is) to such a degree that it was impossible he should set his foot to the ground, to lay any stress upon it. It was well known that he had been so *from his mother's womb,* and that he *never had walked,* nor could *stand up.* We should take occasion hence to thank God for the use of our limbs; and those who are deprived of it may observe that their case is not singular. 2. The expectation that was raised in him of a cure (*v.* 9): He heard Paul preach, and, it is likely, was much affected with what he heard, believed that the messengers, having their commission thence, had a divine power going along with them, and were therefore able to cure him of his lameness. This Paul was aware of, by the spirit of discerning that he had, and perhaps the aspect of his countenance did in part witness for him: *Paul perceived that he had faith to be healed;* desired it, hoped for it, had such a thing in his thoughts, which it does not appear that the lame man Peter healed had, for he expected no more than an *alms.* There *was not found such great faith in Israel* as was among the Gentiles, Mt. 8:10. 3. The cure wrought: *Paul, perceiving that he had faith to be healed,* brought *the word and healed him,* Ps. 107:20. Note, God will not disappoint the desires that are of his own kindling, nor the hopes of his own raising. Paul spoke to him *with a loud voice,* either because he was at some distance, or to show that the true miracles, wrought by the power of Christ, were far unlike the lying wonders wrought by deceivers, *that peeped, and muttered, and whispered,* Isa. 8:19. God saith, *I have not spoken in secret, in a dark place of the earth,* Isa. 45:19. Paul spoke to him with a loud voice, that the people about might take notice, and have their expectations raised of the effect. It does not appear that this cripple was a beggar; it is said (*v.* 8) *that he sat,* not that he sat begging. But we may imagine how melancholy it was to him to see other people walking about him, and himself disabled; and therefore how welcome Paul's word was to him, *"Stand upright on thy feet;* help thyself, and God shall help thee; try whether thou hast strength, and thou shalt find that thou hast." Some copies read it, *I say unto thee, in the name of the Lord Jesus Christ, Stand upright on thy feet.* It is certain that this is implied, and very probably was expressed, by Paul, and *power went along with this word;* for presently *he leaped and walked,* leaped up from the place where he sat, and not only *stood upright,* but to show that he was perfectly cured, and that immediately, he walked to and fro before them all. Herein the scripture was fulfilled, that when *the wilderness of the Gentile world is made to blossom as the rose then shall the lame man leap as a hart,* Isa. 35:1, 6. Those that by the grace of God are cured of their spiritual lameness must show it by leaping with a holy exultation and walking in a holy conversation.

II. The impression which this cure made upon the people: they were amazed at it, had never seen nor heard the like, and fell into an ecstacy of wonder. Paul and Barnabas were strangers, exiles, refugees, in their country; every thing concurred to make them mean and despicable: yet the working of this one miracle was enough to make them in the eyes of this people truly great and honourable, though the multitude of Christ's miracles could not screen him from the utmost contempt among the Jews. We find here, 1. The people take them for gods (*v.* 11): *They lifted up their voices* with an air of triumph, saying in their own language (for it was the common people that said it), *in the speech of Lycaonia,* which was a dialect of the Greek, *The gods are come down to us in the likeness of men.* They imagined that Paul and Barnabas had dropped down to them out of the clouds, and that they were some divine powers, no less than gods, though in the likeness of men. This notion of the thing agreed well enough with the pagan theology, and the fabulous account they had of the visits which their gods made to this lower world; and proud enough they were to think that they should have a visit made to them. They carried this notion so far here that they pretended to tell which of their gods they were, according to the ideas their poets had given them of the gods (*v.* 12): *They called Barnabas Jupiter;* for, if they will have him to be a god, it is as easy to make him the prince of their gods as not. It is probable that he was the senior, and the more portly comely man, that had something of majesty in his countenance. And *Paul they called Mercury,* who was the messenger of the gods, that was sent on their errands; for Paul, though he had not the appearance that Barnabas had, was *the chief speaker,* and had a greater command of language, and perhaps appeared to have something mercurial in his temper and genius. *Jupiter* used to take *Mercury* along with him, they said, and, if he make a visit to their city, they will suppose he does so now. 2. The priest thereupon prepares *to do sacrifice to them, v.* 13. The temple of Jupiter was, it seems, before the gate of their city, as its protector and guardian; and the priest of that idol and temple, hearing the people cry out thus, took the hint presently, and thought it was time for him to bestir himself to do his duty: many a costly sacrifice he had offered to the image of Jupiter, but if Jupiter be among them *himself — in propria persona,* it concerns him to do him the utmost honours imaginable; and the people are ready to join with him in it. See how easily vain minds are carried away with a popular outcry. If the crowd give a shout, Here is Jupiter, the priest of Jupiter takes the first hint, and offers his service immediately. When Christ, the Son of God, came down, and appeared in the likeness of men, and did many, very many miracles, yet they were so far from doing sacrifice to him that they made him a sacrifice to their pride and malice: *He was in the world, and the world knew him not; he came to his own, and his own received him not;* but Paul and Barnabas, upon the working of one miracle, are immediately deified. The same power of the god of this world which prejudices the carnal mind against truth makes errors and mistakes to find easy admission; and both ways his turn is served. They *brought oxen,* to be sacrificed *to them, and garlands,* with which to crown the sacrifices. These garlands were made up of flowers and ribbons; and they gilded the horns of the oxen they sacrificed.

> Victimae ad supplicium saginantur,
> hostiae ad poenam corenantur.
>
> So beasts for sacrifice do feed,
> First to be crown'd, and then to bleed.
> — So Octavius in Minutius Felix.

III. Paul and Barnabas protest against this undue respect paid them, and with much ado prevent it. Many of the heathen emperors called themselves *gods,* and took a pride in having divine honours paid them: but Christ's ministers, though real benefactors to mankind, while these tyrants only pretended to be so, refused those honours when they were so tendered. Whose successor therefore he is who *sits in the temple of God,* and shows *that he is god* (2 Th. 2:4), and who is adored as *our lord god,* the pope, it is easy to say. Observe,

1. The holy indignation which Paul and Barnabas conceived at this: *When they heard this, they rent their clothes.* We do not find that they rent their clothes when the people vilified them, and spoke of stoning them; they could bear this without disturbance: but when they deified them, and spoke of worshipping them, they could not bear it, but rent their clothes, as being more concerned for God's honour than their own.

2. The pains they took to prevent it. They did not connive at it, nor say, "If people will be deceived, let them be deceived," much less suggest to themselves and one another that it might contribute both to the safety of their persons and the success of their ministry if they suffered the people to continue in this mistake, and so they might make a good hand of an ill thing. No, God's truth needs not the service of man's lie. Christ had put honour enough upon them in making them apostles, they needed not assume either the honour of princes or the honour of gods; they appeared with much more magnificent titles when they were called *the ambassadors of Christ,* and *the stewards of the mysteries of God,* than when they were called Jupiter and Mercury. Let us see how they prevented it.

(1.) *They ran in among the people,* as soon as they heard of it, and would not so much as stay awhile to see what the people would do. Their running in, like servants, among the people, showed that they were far from looking upon themselves as gods, or taking state upon them; they did not stand still, expecting honours to be done them, but plainly declined them by thrusting themselves into the crowd. They ran in, as men in earnest, with as much concern as Aaron *ran in between the living and the dead,* when the plague was begun.

(2.) They reasoned with them, *crying out,* that all might hear, *"Sirs, why do you these things?"* Why do you go about to make gods of us? It is the most absurd thing you can do; for,

[1.] "Our nature will not admit it: *We also are men of like passions with you" homoiopatheis*: it is the same word that is used concerning Elias, Jam. 5:18, where we render it, *subject to like passions as we are.* "We are men, and therefore you wrong yourselves if you expect that from us which is to be had in God only; and you wrong God if you give that honour to us, or to any other man, which is to be given to God only. We not only have such bodies as you see, but *are of like passions with you,* have *hearts fashioned like as other men* (Ps. 33:15); for, *as in water face answers to face, so doth the heart of man to man,* Prov. 27:19. We are naturally subject to the same infirmities of the human nature, and liable to the same calamities of the human life; not only men, but sinful men and suffering men, and therefore will not be deified."

[2.] "Our doctrine is directly against it. Must we be added to the number of your gods whose business it is to abolish the gods you have? *We preach unto you that you should turn from these vanities unto the living God.* If we should suffer this, we should confirm you in that which it is our business to convert you from:" and so they take this occasion to show them how just and necessary it was that they should *turn to God from idols,* 1 Th. 1:9. When they preached to the Jews, who hated idolatry, they had nothing to do but to preach the grace of God in Christ, and needed not, as the prophets in dealing with their fathers, to preach against idolatry: but, when they had to do with the Gentiles, they must rectify their mistakes in natural religion, and bring them off from the gross corruptions of that. See here what they preached to the Gentiles.

First, That the gods which they and their fathers worshipped, and all the ceremonies of their worship of them were *vanities,* idle things, unreasonable, unprofitable, which no rational account could be given of, nor any real advantage gained from. Idols are often called vanities in the Old Testament, Deu. 32:21; 1 Ki. 10:13; Jer. 14:22. *An idol is nothing in the world* (1 Co. 8:4): it is not at all what it is pretended to be, it is a cheat, it is a counterfeit; it deceives those that trust to it and expect relief from it. Therefore *turn from these vanities,* turn from them with abhorrence and detestation, as Ephraim did (Hos. 14:8): *"What have I to do any more with idols?* I will never again be thus imposed upon."

Secondly, That the God to whom they would have them *turn* is *the living God.* They had hitherto worshipped dead images, that were utterly unable to help them (Isa. 64:9), or (as they now attempted) dying men, that would soon be disabled to help them; but now they are persuaded to worship a living God, who has life in himself, and life for us, and lives for evermore.

Thirdly, That this God is the creator of the world, the fountain of all being and power: "He *made heaven and earth, and the sea, and all things therein,* even those things which you worship as gods, so that he *is the God* of your gods. You worship gods which you made, the creatures of your own fancy, and the work of your own hands. We call you to worship the true God, and cheat not yourselves with pretenders; worship the Sovereign Lord of all, and disparage not yourselves in bowing down to his creatures and subjects."

Fourthly, That the world owed it to his patience that he had not destroyed them long ere this for their idolatry (*v.* 16): *In times past,* for many ages, unto this day, he *suffered all nations to walk in their own ways.* These idolaters, that were called from the service of other gods, might think, "Have we not served these gods hitherto, and our fathers before us, time out of mind; and why may we not as well go on to serve them still?" — No, your serving them was a trial of God's patience, and it was a miracle of mercy that you were not cut off for it. But, though he did not destroy you for it while you were in ignorance, and knew no better (*ch.* 17:30) yet now that he has sent his gospel into the world, and by it has made a clear discovery of himself and his will to *all nations,* and not to the Jews only, if you still continue in your idolatry he will not bear with you as he has done. All the nations that had not the benefit of divine revelation, that is, all but the Jews, *he suffered to walk in their own ways*, for they had nothing to check them, or control them, but their own consciences, their own thoughts (Rom. 2:15), no scriptures, no prophets; and then they were the more excusable if they mistook their way: but now that God has sent a revelation into the world which is to be published to *all nations* the case is altered. We may under-stand it as a judgment upon all nations that *God suffered them to walk in their own ways, gave them up to their own hearts' lusts;* but now the time is come when *the veil of the covering spread over all nations should be taken off* (Isa. 25:7), and now you will no longer be excused in these vanities, but must turn from them. Note, 1. God's patience with us hitherto should *lead us to repentance,* and not encourage us to presume upon the continuance of it, while we continue to provoke him. 2. Our having done ill while we were in ignorance will not bear us out in doing ill when we are better taught.

Fifthly, That even when they were not under the direction and correction of the word of God, yet they might have known, and should have known, to do better by the works of God, *v.* 17. Though the Gentiles had not the *statutes and judgments* that the Jews had to witness for God against all pretenders, no tables of testimony or tabernacle of testimony, yet *he left not himself without witness;* besides *the witness* for God within them (the dictates of natural conscience), they had *witnesses* for God round about them — the bounty of common providence. Their having no scriptures did in part excuse them, and therefore God did not destroy them for their idolatry, as he did the Jewish nation. This however did not wholly excuse them, but that notwithstanding this they were highly criminal and deeply guilty before God; for there were other *witnesses* for God, sufficient to inform them that he and he only is to be worshipped, and that to him they owed all their services from whom they received all their comforts, and therefore that they were guilty of the highest injustice and ingratitude imaginable, in alienating them from him. God, having *not left himself without witness,* has not left us without a guide, and so has left us without excuse; for whatever is a witness for God is a witness against us, if we give that glory to any other which is due to him only. 1. The bounties of common providence witness to us that there is a God, for they are all dispensed wisely and with design. The *rain and fruitful seasons* could not come by chance, nor *are there any of the vanities of the heathen that can give rain,* neither can *the heavens* of themselves *give showers,* Jer. 14:22. All the powers of nature witness to us a sovereign power in the God of nature, from whom they are derived, and on whom they depend. It is not the heaven that gives us rain, but God that gives us rain from heaven, he is the Father of the rain, Job 38:28. 2. The benefits we have by these bounties witness to us that we ought to make our acknowledgments not to the creatures who are made serviceable to us, but to the Creator who makes them so. *He left not himself without witness, in that he did good.* God seems to reckon the instances of his *goodness* to be more pregnant, cogent proofs of his title to our homage and adoration than the evidences of his *greatness;* for his goodness is his glory. *The earth is full of his goodness; his tender mercies are over all his works;* and therefore *they praise him,* Ps. 145:9, 10. God does us good, in preserving to us his air to breathe in, his ground to go upon, the light of his sun to see by; but, because the most sensible instance of the goodness of Providence to each of us in particular is that of the daily provision made by it of meat and drink for us, the apostle chooses to insist upon that, and shows how God does us good, (1.) In preparing it for us, and that by a long train of causes which depend upon him as the first cause: *The heavens hear the earth; the earth hears the corn, and wine, and oil; and they hear Jezreel.* Hos. 2:21, 22. He does us good in giving us rain from heaven, — rain for us to drink, for if there were no rain there would be no springs of water and we should soon die for thirst, — rain for our land to drink, for our meat as well as drink we have from the rain; in giving us this, he *gives us fruitful seasons. If the heavens be as iron, the earth* will soon *be as brass,* Lev. 26:19. *This is the river of God* which *greatly enriches the earth,* and by *it* God *prepares us corn,* Ps. 65:9–13. Of all the common operations of providence, the heathen chose to form their notion of the supreme God by that which bespeaks terror, and is proper to strike an awe of him upon us, and this was *the thunder;* and therefore they called Jupiter *the thunderer,* and represented him with a thunderbolt in his hand; and it

appears by Ps. 29:3 that this ought not to be overlooked; but the apostle here, to engage us to worship God, sets before us his beneficence, that we may have good thoughts of him in every thing wherein we have to do with him — may love him and delight in him, as one that does good, does good to us, does good to all, in giving *rain from heaven and fruitful seasons;* and if at any time rain be withheld, or the seasons be unfruitful, we may thank ourselves; it is our sin *that turns away these good things from us* which were coming to us, and stops the current of God's favours. (2.) In giving us the comforts of it. It is he *that fills our hearts with food and gladness.* God *is rich in mercy to all* (Rom. 10:12): *he gives us richly all things to enjoy* (1 Tim. 6:17), is not only a benefactor, but a bountiful one, not only *gives us the things we need,* but *gives us to enjoy them* (Eccl. 2:24): *He fills our hearts with food,* that is, he gives us food to our hearts' content, or according to our hearts' desire; not merely for necessity, but plenty, dainty, and variety. Even those nations that had lost the knowledge of him, and worshipped other gods, yet he *filled their houses, filled their mouths, filled their bellies* (Job 22:18; Ps. 17:14) *with good things.* The Gentiles that *lived without God in the world,* yet lived upon God, which Christ urges as a reason why we should *do good to those that hate us,* Mt. 5:44, 45. Those heathen had *their hearts filled with food;* this was their felicity and satisfaction, they desired no more; but *these things will not fill the soul* (Eze. 7:19), nor will those that know how to value their own souls be satisfied with them; but the apostles put themselves in as sharers in the divine beneficence. We must all own that God fills our hearts with food and gladness; not only *food,* that we may live, but *gladness,* that we may live cheerfully; to him we owe it that we do not *all our days eat in sorrow.* Note, We must thank God, not only for our food, but for our gladness — that he gives us leave to be cheerful, cause to be cheerful, and hearts to be cheerful. And, if *our hearts be filled with food and gladness,* they ought to be filled with love and thankfulness, and enlarged in duty and obedience, Deu. 8:10; 28:47.

Lastly, The success of this prohibition which the apostles gave to *the people (v.* 18): By *these sayings,* with much ado, they *restrained the people from doing sacrifice to them,* so strongly were these idolaters set upon their idolatry. It was not enough for the apostles to refuse to be deified (this would be construed only a pang of modesty), but they resented it, they showed the people the evil of it, and all little enough, for they could *scarcely* restrain them from it, and some of them were ready to blame the priest, that he did not go on with his business notwithstanding. We may see here what gave rise to the pagan idolatry; it was terminating those regards in the instruments of our comfort which should have passed through them to the Author. Paul and Barnabas had cured a cripple, and therefore the people deified them, instead of glorifying God for giving them such power, which should make us very cautious that we do not give that honour to another, or take it to ourselves, which is due to God only.

Verses 19–28

We have here a further account of the services and sufferings of Paul and Barnabas.

I. How Paul was stoned and left for dead, but miraculously came to himself again, *v.* 19, 20. They fell upon Paul rather than Barnabas, because Paul, being the chief speaker, galled and vexed them more than Barnabas did. Now observe here, 1. How the people were incensed against Paul; not by any injury they pretended he had done them (if they took it for an affront that he would not let them misplace divine honours upon him, when they considered themselves they would easily forgive him that wrong), but *there came certain Jews from Antioch,* hearing, it is likely, and vexed to hear, what respect was shown to Paul and Barnabas at Lystra; and they incensed the people against them, as factious, seditious, dangerous persons, not fit to be harboured. See how restless the rage of the Jews was against the gospel of Christ; they could not bear that it should have footing any where. 2. To what degree they were incensed by these barbarous Jews: they were irritated to such a degree that the mob rose and *stoned Paul,* not by a judicial sentence, but in a popular tumult; they threw stones at him, with which they knocked him down, and then *drew him out of the city,* as one not fit to live in it, or drew him out upon a sledge or in a cart, to bury him, *supposing he had been dead.* So strong is the bias of the corrupt and carnal heart to that which is evil, even in contrary extremes, that, as it is with great difficulty that

men are restrained from evil on one side, so it is with great ease that they are persuaded to evil on the other side. See how fickle and mutable the minds of carnal worldly people are, that do not know and consider things. Those that but the other day would have treated the apostles as more than men now treat them as worse than brutes, as the worst of men, as the worst of male-factors. To-day *Hosanna,* to-morrow *Crucify;* to-day sacrificed to, to-morrow sacrificed. We have an instance of a change the other way, *ch.* 28. *This man is a murderer, v.* 4; no doubt *he is a god, v.* 6. Popular breath turns like the wind. If Paul would have been Mercury, he might have been enthroned, nay, he might have been enshrined; but, if he will be a faithful minister of Christ, he shall be stoned, and thrown out of the city. Thus those who easily submit to strong delusions hate to receive the truth in the love of it. 3. How he was delivered by the power of God: When he was *drawn out of the city, the disciples stood round about him, v.* 20. It seems there were some here at Lystra that became disciples, that found the mean between deifying the apostles and rejecting them; and even these new converts had courage to own Paul when he was thus run down, though they had reason enough to fear that the same that stoned him would stone them for owning him. They stood round about him, as a guard to him against the further outrage of the people — stood about him to see whether he were alive or dead; and all of a sudden *he rose up.* Though he was not dead, yet he was ill crushed and bruised, no doubt, and fainted away; he was in a *deliquium,* so that it was not without a miracle that he came so soon to himself, and was so well as to be able to go into the city. Note, God's faithful servants, though they may be brought within a step of death, and may be looked upon as dead both by friends and enemies, shall not die as long as he has work for them to do. They *are cast down, but not destroyed,* 2 Co. 4:9.

II. How they went on with their work, notwithstanding the opposition they met with. All the stones they threw at Paul could not beat him off from his work: They *drew him out of the city (v.* 19) but, as one that set them at defiance, he *came into the city* again, to show that he did not fear them; *none even of these things move him.* However, their being persecuted here is a known indication to them to seek for opportunities of usefulness elsewhere, and therefore for the present they quit Lystra.

1. They went to break up and sow fresh ground at *Derbe.* Thither the next day *Paul and Barnabas departed,* a city not far off; there they preached the gospel, there they *taught many, v.* 21. And it should seem that Timothy was of that city, and was one of the disciples that now attended Paul, had met him at Antioch and accompanied him in all this circuit; for, with reference to this story, Paul tells him how fully *he had known the afflictions he endured at Antioch, Iconium, and Lystra,* 2 Tim. 3:10, 11. Nothing is recorded that happened at Derbe.

2. They returned, and went over their work again, watering what they had sown; and, having staid as long as they thought fit at Derbe, they came back to Lystra, to Iconium, and Antioch, the cities where they had preached, *v.* 21. Now, as we have had a very instructive account of the methods they took in laying the foundation, and beginning the good work, so here we have the like of their building upon that foundation, and carrying on that good work. Let us see what they did,

(1.) They *confirmed the souls of the disciples;* that is, they inculcated that upon them which was proper to confirm them, *v.* 22. Young converts are apt to waver, and a little thing shocks them. Their old acquaintances beg they will not leave them. Those that they look upon to be wiser than themselves set before them the absurdity, indecency, and danger, of a change. They were allured, by the prospect of preferment, to stick to the traditions of their fathers; they are frightened with the danger of swimming against the stream. All this tempts them to think of making a retreat in time; but the apostles come and tell them that *this is the true grace of God wherein they stand,* and therefore they must stand to it that there is no danger like that of losing their part in Christ, no advantage like that of keeping their hold of him; that, whatever their trials may be, they shall have strength from Christ to pass through them; and, whatever their losses may be, they shall be abundantly recompensed. And this *confirms the souls of the disciples;* it fortifies their pious resolutions, in the strength of Christ, to adhere to Christ whatever it may cost them. Note, [1.] Those that are converted need to be confirmed; those that are planted need to be rooted. Ministers' work is to establish saints as well as to awaken sinners. *Non minor est virtus quam quoerere parta tueri — To retain is sometimes as difficult as to acquire.* Those that were instructed in the truth must know the certainty of the things in which they have been instructed; and those that are resolved must be fixed in their resolutions. [2.] True confirmation is confirmation of the soul; it is not binding the body by severe penalties on apostates, but binding the soul. The best ministers can do this only by pressing those things which are proper to bind the soul; it is the grace of God, and nothing less, that can effectually *confirm the souls of the disciples,* and prevent their apostasy.

(2.) *They exhorted them to continue in the faith;* or, as it may be read, *they encouraged them.* They told them it was both their duty and interest to persevere; to abide in the belief of Christ's being the Son of God, and the Saviour of the world. Note, Those that are in the faith are concerned to *continue in the faith,* notwithstanding all the temptations they may be under to desert it, from the smiles or frowns of this world. And it is requisite that they should often be exhorted to do so. Those that are continually surrounded with temptations to apostasy have need to be continually attended with pressing exhortations to perseverance.

(3.) That which they insisted most upon was *that we must through much tribulation enter into the kingdom of God.* Not only *they* must, but *we* must; it must be counted upon that all who will go to heaven must expect tribulation and persecution in their way thither. But is this the way to *confirm the souls of the disciples,* and to engage them to *continue in the faith?* One would think it would rather shock them, and make them weary. No, as the matter is fairly stated and taken entire, it will help to confirm them, and fix them for Christ. It is true they will meet with tribulation, with much tribulation; that is the worst of it: but then, [1.] It is so appointed. They must undergo it, there is no remedy, the matter is already fixed, and cannot be altered. He that has the sovereign disposal of us has determined it to be our lot that all that *will live godly in Christ Jesus should suffer persecution;* and he that has the sovereign command over us has determined this to be our duty, that all that will be Christ's disciples must *take up their cross.* When we gave up our names to Jesus Christ it was what we agreed to; when we sat down and counted the cost, if we reckoned aright, it was what we counted upon; so that if *tribulation and persecution arise because of the word* it is but what we had notice of before, it must be so: *he performeth the thing that is appointed for us.* The matter is fixed unalterably; and *shall the rock be* for us *removed out of its place?* [2.] It is the lot of the leaders in Christ's army, as well as of the soldiers. It is not only *you,* but *we,* that (if it be thought a hardship) are subject to it; therefore, as your own sufferings must not be a stumbling-block to you, so neither must ours; see 1 Th. 3:3. *Let none be moved by our afflictions, for you yourselves know that we are appointed thereunto.* As Christ did not put the apostles upon any harder service than what he underwent before them, so neither did the apostles put the ordinary Christians. [3.] It is true we must count upon *much tribulation,* but this is encouraging, that we shall get through it; we shall not be lost and perish in it. It is a Red Sea, but the Lord has opened a way through it, for *the redeemed of the Lord to pass over.* We must go down to trouble, but we shall come up again. [4.] We shall not only get through it, but get through it *into the kingdom of God;* and the joy and glory of the end will make abundant amends for all the difficulties and hardships we may meet with in the way. It is true *we must go by the cross,* but it is as true that if we keep in the way, and do not turn aside nor turn back, we shall *go to the crown,* and the believing prospect of this will make the tribulation easy and pleasant.

(4.) *They ordained them elders,* or presbyters, *in every church.* Now at this second visit they settled them in some order, formed them into religious societies under the guidance of a settled ministry, and settled that distinction between those that are taught in the word and those that teach. [1.] Every church had its governors or presidents, whose office it was to pray with the members of the church, and to preach to them in their solemn assemblies, to administer all gospel ordinances to them, and to take the oversight of them, *to instruct the ignorant, warn the unruly, comfort the feeble-minded, and convince gainsayers.* It is requisite that every particular church should have one or more such to preside

in it. [2.] Those governors were then elders, that had in their qualification the wisdom and gravity of seniors, and had in their commission the authority and command of seniors: not to make new laws (this is the prerogative of the Prince, the great Lawgiver; the government of the church is an absolute monarchy, and the legislative power entirely in Christ), but to see to the observance and execution of the laws Christ has made; and so far they are to be obeyed and submitted to. [3.] These elders were *ordained.* The qualifications of such as were proposed or proposed themselves (whether the apostles or the people put them up) were judged of by the apostles, as most fit to judge; and they, having *devoted* themselves, were solemnly set *apart* to the work of the ministry, and bound to it. [4.] These elders were ordained to them, to the disciples, to their service, for their good. Those that are in the faith have need to be built up in it, and have need of the elders' help therein — the *pastors and teachers,* who are *to edify the body of Christ.*

(5.) *By prayer* joined with *fasting* they *commended them to the Lord,* to the Lord Jesus, *on whom they believed.* Note, [1.] Even when persons are brought to believe, and that sincerely, yet ministers' care concerning them is not over; there is need of watching over them still, instructing and admonishing them still; there is still that lacking in their faith which needs to be perfected. [2.] The ministers that take most care of those that believe must after all commend them to the Lord, and put them under the protection and guidance of his grace: *Lord, keep them through thine own name.* To his custody they must commit themselves, and their ministers must commit them. [3.] It is by prayer that they must be commended to the Lord. Christ, in his prayer (Jn. 17), commended his disciples to his Father: *Thine they were, and thou gavest them to me. Father, keep them.* [4.] It is a great encouragement to us, in commending the disciples to the Lord, that we can say, "It is he in whom they believed; we commit to him those who have committed themselves to him, and who know they have *believed in one who is able to keep what they* and we have *committed to him against* that day," 2 Tim. 1:12. [5.] It is good to join fasting with prayer, in token of our humiliation for sin, and in order to add vigour to our prayers. [6.] When we are parting with our friends, the best farewell is to commend them to the Lord, and to leave them with him.

3. They went on preaching the gospel in other places where they had been, but, as it should seem had not made so many converts as that now at their return they could form them into churches; therefore thither they came to pursue and carry on conversion-work. From Antioch they *passed through Pisidia,* the province in which that Antioch stood; thence they came into the province of *Pamphylia,* the head-city of which was *Perga,* where they had been before (*ch.* 13:13), and came thither again to *preach the word* (*v.* 25), making a second offer, to see if they were now better disposed than they were before to receive the gospel. What success they had there we are not told, but that thence they *went down to Attalia,* a city of Pamphylia, on the sea-coast. They staid not long at a place, but wherever they came endeavoured to lay a foundation which might afterwards be built upon, and to sow the seeds which would in time produce a great increase. Now Christ's parables were explained, in which he compared the kingdom of heaven to a little leaven, which in time leavened the whole lump, — to a grain of mustard-seed, which, though very inconsiderable at first, grew to a great tree, — and to the seed which a man sowed in his ground, and it sprung up he knew not how.

III. How they at length came back to Antioch in Syria, whence they had been sent forth upon this expedition. From Attalia they came by sea to Antioch, *v.* 26. And we are here told,

1. Why they came thither: because *thence they had been recommended to the grace of God,* and such a value did they put upon a solemn recommendation to the grace of God, though they had themselves a great interest in heaven, that they never thought they could show respect enough to those who had so recommended them. The brethren having recommended them to the grace of God, for the work *which they fulfilled,* now that they had fulfilled it they thought they owed them an account of it, that they might help them by their praises, as they had been helped by their prayers.

2. What account they gave them of their negociation (*v.* 27): They *gathered the church together.* It is probable that there were more Christians at Antioch than ordinarily met, or could meet, in one place, but on this occasion they called

together the *leading men* of them; as the heads of the tribes are often called the *congregation* of Israel, so the ministers and principal members of the church at Antioch are called the *church.* Or perhaps as many of the people as the place would hold came together on this occasion. Or some met at one time, or in one place, and others at another. But when they had called them together, they gave them an account of two things: — (1.) Of the tokens they had had of the divine presence with them in their labours: *They rehearsed all that God had done with them.* They did not tell what *they* had done (this would have savoured of vain-glory), but what God had done with them and by them. Note, The praise of all the little good we do at any time must be ascribed to God; for it is he that not only worketh in us both to will and to do, but then worketh with us to make what we do successful. God's grace can do any thing without ministers' preaching; but ministers' preaching, even Paul's, can do nothing without God's grace; and the operations of that grace must be acknowledged in the efficacy of the word. (2.) Of the fruit of their labours among the heathen. They told how *God had opened the door of faith unto the Gentiles;* had not only ordered them to be invited to the gospel feast, but had inclined the hearts of many of them to accept the invitation. Note, [1.] There is no entering into the kingdom of Christ but by the door of faith; we must firmly believe in Christ, or we have no part in him. [2.] It is God that opens the door of faith, that opens to us the truths we are to believe, opens our hearts to receive them, and makes this a wide door, and an effectual, into the church of Christ. [3.] We have reason to be thankful that God has *opened the door of faith to the Gentiles,* has both sent them his gospel, which is *made known to all nations for the obedience of faith* (Rom. 16:26), and has also given them hearts to entertain the gospel. Thus the gospel was spread, and it shone more and more, and none was able to shut this door which God had opened; not all the powers of hell and earth.

3. How they disposed of themselves for the present: *There they abode a long time with the disciples* (*v.* 28), longer than perhaps at first they intended, not because they *feared their enemies,* but because they *loved their friends,* and were loth to part from them.

CHAPTER 15

Hitherto we have, with a great deal of pleasure, attended the apostles in their glorious travels for the propagating of the gospel in foreign parts, have seen the bounds of the church enlarged by the accession both of Jews and Gentiles to it; and thanks be to that God who always caused them to triumph. We left them, in the close of the foregoing chapter, reposing themselves at Antioch, and edifying the church there with the rehearsal of their experiences, and it is a pity they should ever be otherwise employed; but in this chapter we find other work (not so pleasant) cut out for them. The Christians and ministers are engaged in controversy, and those that should have been now busied in enlarging the dominions of the church have as much as they can do to compose the divisions of it; when they should have been making war upon the devil's kingdom they have much ado to keep the peace in Christ's kingdom. Yet this occurrence and the record of it are of great use to the church, both for warning to us to expect such unhappy discords among Christians, and direction to us what method to take for accommodating them. Here is, I. A controversy raised at Antioch by the judaizing teachers, who would have the believing Gentiles brought under the yoke of circumcision and the ceremonial law (*v.* 1, 2). II. A consultation held with the church at Jerusalem about this matter, and the sending of delegates thither for that purpose, which occasioned the starting of the same question there (*v.* 3–5). III. An account of what passed in the synod that was convened upon this occasion (*v.* 6). What Peter said (*v.* 7–11). What Paul and Barnabas discoursed of (*v.* 12). And, lastly, what James proposed for the settling of this matter (*v.* 13–21). IV. The result of this debate, and the circular letter that was written to the Gentile converts, directing them how to govern themselves with respect to Jews (*v.* 22–29). V. The delivering of this determination to the church at Antioch, and the satisfaction it gave them (*v.* 30–35). VI. A second expedition designed by Paul and Barnabas to preach to the Gentiles, in which they quarrelled about their assistant, and separated upon it, one steering one course and the other another (*v.* 36–41).

Verses 1–5

Even when things go on very smoothly and pleasantly in a state or in a church, it is folly to be secure, and to think the mountain stands strong and cannot be moved; some uneasiness or other will arise, which is not foreseen, cannot be prevented, but must be prepared for. If ever there was a heaven upon earth, surely it was in the church at Antioch at this time, when there were so many excellent ministers there, and blessed Paul among them, building up that church in her most holy faith. But here we have their peace disturbed, and differences arising. Here is,

I. A new doctrine started among them, which occasioned

this division, obliging the Gentile converts to submit to circumcision and the ceremonial law, v. 1. Many that had been proselytes to the Jewish religion became Christians; and they would have such as were proselyted to the Christian religion to become Jews.

1. The persons that urged this were *certain men who came down from Judea;* some think such as had been of the Pharisees (v. 5), or perhaps of those priests who were *obedient to the faith, ch.* 6:7. They came from Judea, pretending perhaps to be sent by the apostles at Jerusalem, at least to be countenanced by them. Having a design to spread their notions, they came to Antioch, because that was the headquarters of those that preached to the Gentiles, and the rendezvous of the Gentile converts; and, if they could but make an interest there, this leaven would soon be diffused to all the churches of the Gentiles. They insinuated themselves into an acquaintance with the brethren, pretended to be very glad that they had embraced the Christian faith, and congratulated them on their conversion; but tell them that *yet one thing they lack,* they must be circumcised. Note, Those that are ever so well taught have need to stand upon their guard that they be not untaught again, or ill taught.

2. The position they laid down, the thesis they gave, was this, that except the Gentiles who turned Christians were *circumcised after the manner of Moses,* and thereby bound themselves to all the observances of the ceremonial law, *they could not be saved.* As to this, (1.) Many of the Jews who embraced the faith of Christ, yet continued very *zealous for the law, ch.* 21:20. They knew it was from God and its authority was sacred, valued it for its antiquity, had been bred up in the observance of it, and it is probable had been often devoutly affected in their attendance on these observances; they therefore kept them up after they were by baptism admitted into the Christian church, kept up the distinction of meats, and used the ceremonial purifyings from ceremonial pollutions, attend the temple service, and celebrated the feasts of the Jews. Herein they were connived at, because the prejudices of education are not to be overcome all at once, and in a few years the mistake would be effectually rectified by the destruction of the temple and the total dissolution of the Jewish church, by which the observance of the Mosaic ritual would become utterly impracticable. But it did not suffice them that they were herein indulged themselves, they must have the Gentile converts brought under the same obligations. Note, There is a strange proneness in us to make our opinion and practice a rule and a law to every body else, to judge of all about us by our standard, and to conclude that because we do well all do wrong that do not just as we do. (2.) Those Jews who believed that Christ was the Messiah, as they could not get clear of their affection to the law, so they could not get clear of the notions they had of the Messiah, that he should set up a temporal kingdom in favour of the Jewish nation, should make this illustrious and victorious; it was a disappointment to them that there was as yet nothing done towards this in the way they expected. But now that they hear the doctrine of Christ is received among the Gentiles, and his kingdom begins to be set up in the midst of them, if they can but persuade those that embrace Christ to embrace the law of Moses too they hope their point will be gained, the Jewish nation will be made as considerable as they can wish, though in another way; and "Therefore by all means let the brethren be pressed to be *circumcised and keep the law,* and then with our religion our dominion will be extended, and we shall in a little time be able to shake off the Roman yoke; and not only so, but to put it on the necks of our neighbours, and so shall have such a kingdom of the Messiah as we promised ourselves." Note, It is no wonder if those who have wrong notions of the kingdom of Christ take wrong measures for the advancement of it, and such as really tend to the destruction of it, as these do. (3.) The controversy about the circumcising of the Gentile proselytes had been on foot among the Jews long before this. This is observed by Dr. Whitby out of Josephus — *Antiq.* 20.38–45: "That when Izates, the son of Helen queen of Adiabene, embraced the Jews' religion, Ananias declared he might do it without circumcision; but Eleazar maintained that it was a great impiety to remain uncircumcised." And when two eminent Gentiles fled to Josephus (as he relates in the history of his own life) "the zealots among the Jews were urgent for their circumcision; but Josephus dissuaded them from insisting upon it." Such has been the difference in all ages between bigotry and moderation. (4.) It is observable what a mighty

stress they laid upon it; they do not only say, "You ought to *be circumcised after the manner of Moses,* and it will be good service to the kingdom of the Messiah if you be; it will best accommodate matters between you and the Jewish converts, and we shall take it very kindly if you will, and shall converse the more familiarly with you;" but, "*Except you be circumcised you cannot be saved.* If you be not herein of our mind and way, you will never go to heaven, and therefore of course you must go to hell." Note, it is common for proud impostors to enforce their own inventions under pain of damnation; and to tell people that unless they believe just as they would have them believe, and do just as they would have them do, they cannot be saved, it is impossible they should; not only their case is hazardous, but it is desperate. Thus the Jews tell their brethren that except they be of their church, and come into their communion, and conform to the ceremonies of their worship, though otherwise good men and believers in Christ, yet they cannot be saved; salvation itself cannot save them. None are in Christ but those that are within their pale. We ought to see ourselves well warranted by the word of God before we say, "Except you do so and so, you cannot be saved."

II. The opposition which Paul and Barnabas gave to this schismatical notion, which engrossed salvation to the Jews, now that Christ has opened the door of salvation to the Gentiles (v. 2): *They had no small dissension and disputation with them.* They would by no means yield to this doctrine, but appeared and argued publicly against it. 1. As faithful servants of Christ, they would not see his truths betrayed. They knew that Christ came to free us from the yoke of the ceremonial law, and to take down that wall of partition between Jews and Gentiles and unite them both in himself; and therefore could not bear to hear of circumcising the Gentile converts, when their instructions were only to baptize them. The Jews would unite with the Gentiles, that is, they would have them to conform in every thing to their rites, and then, and not till then they will look upon them as their brethren; and no thanks to them. But, this not being the way in which Christ designed to unite them, it is not to be admitted. 2. As spiritual fathers to the Gentile converts, they would not see their liberties encroached upon. They had told the Gentiles that if they believed in Jesus Christ they should be saved; and now to be told that this was not enough to save them, except they were circumcised and kept the law of Moses, this was such a discouragement to them at setting out, and would be such a stumbling-block in their way, as might almost tempt them to think of returning into Egypt again; and therefore the apostles set themselves against it.

III. The expedient pitched upon for preventing the mischief of this dangerous notion, and silencing those that vented it, as well as quieting the minds of the people with reference to it. They determined that Paul and Barnabas, and some others of their number, should *go to Jerusalem to the apostles and elders,* concerning this doubt. Not that the church at Antioch had any doubt concerning it: they knew the liberty wherewith Christ had made them free; but they sent the case to Jerusalem, 1. Because those who taught this doctrine came from Jerusalem, and pretended to have directions from the apostles there to urge circumcision upon the Gentile converts; it was therefore very proper to send to Jerusalem about it, to know if they had any such direction from the church there. And it was soon found to be all wrong, which yet pretended to be of apostolical right. It was true that these *went out from them* (v. 24), but they never had any such orders from them. 2. Because those who were taught this doctrine would be the better confirmed in their opposition to it, and in the less danger of being shocked and disturbed by it, if they were sure that *the apostles and elders at Jerusalem* (which was the Christian church that of all others retained the most affection to the law of Moses) were against it; and, if they could but have this under their hands, it would be the likeliest means to silence and shame these incendiaries, who had pretended to have it from them. 3. Because the apostles at Jerusalem were fittest to be consulted in a point not yet fully settled; and being most eminent for an infallible spirit, peculiar to them as apostles, their decision would be likely to end the controversy. It was owing to the subtlety and malice of the great enemy of the church's peace (as it appears by Paul's frequent complaints of these *judaizing teachers,* these *false apostles,* these *deceitful workers,* these *enemies of the cross of Christ),* that it had not this effect.

IV. Their journey to Jerusalem upon this errand, v. 3. Where we find, 1. That they were honoured at parting: *They were brought on their way by the church,* which was then much used as a token of respect to useful men, and is directed to be done *after a godly sort,* 3 Jn. 6. Thus the church showed their favour to those who witnessed against these encroachments on the liberties of the Gentile converts, and stood up for them. 2. That they did good as they went along. They were men that would not lose time, and therefore visited the churches by the way; they passed through Phenice and Samaria, and as they went *declared the conversion of the Gentiles,* and what wonderful success the gospel had had among them, which *caused great joy to all the brethren.* Note, The progress of the gospel is and ought to be a matter of great joy. *All the brethren,* the faithful brethren in Christ's family, rejoice when more are born into the family; for the family will be never the poorer for the multitude of its children. In Christ and heaven there is portion enough, and inheritance enough for them all.

V. Their hearty welcome at Jerusalem, v. 4. 1. The good entertainment their friends gave them: They were *received of the church, and of the apostles and elders,* were embraced as brethren, and had audience as messengers of the church at Antioch; they received them with all possible expressions of love and friendship. 2. The good entertainment they gave their friends: They *declared all things that God had done with them,* gave them an account of the success of their ministry among the Gentiles, not what they had done, but *what God had done with them,* what he had by his grace in them enabled them to do, and what he had by his grace in their hearers enabled them to receive. As they went they had planted, as they came back they had watered; but in both they were ready to own it was God that gave the increase. Note, It is a great honour to be employed for God, to be workers for him; for those that are so have him a worker with them, and he must have all the glory.

VI. The opposition they met with from the same party at Jerusalem, v. 5. When Barnabas and Paul gave an account of the multitude of the Gentiles, and of the great harvest of souls gathered in to Christ there, and all about them congratulated them upon it, *there rose up certain of the sect of the Pharisees,* who received the tidings very coldly, and, though they believed in Christ, yet were not satisfied in the admission of these converts, but thought it was needful to circumcise them. Observe here, 1. That those who have been most prejudiced against the gospel yet have been captivated by it; so mighty has it been through God to the pulling down of strong-holds. When Christ was here upon earth, few or none of the rulers and of the Pharisees believed on him; but now there are those of the sect of the Pharisees who believed, and many of them, we hope, in sincerity. 2. That it is very hard for men suddenly to get clear of their prejudices: those that had been Pharisees, even after they became Christians, retained some of the old leaven. All did not so, witness Paul, but some did; and they had such a jealousy for the ceremonial law, and such a dislike of the Gentiles, that they could not admit the Gentiles into communion with them, unless they would be circumcised, and thereby engage themselves to keep the law of Moses. This was, in their opinion, needful; and for their parts they would not converse with them unless they submitted to it.

Verses 6–21

We have here a council called, not by writ, but by consent, on this occasion (v. 6): *The apostles and presbyters came together, to consider this matter.* They did not give their judgment separately, but came together to do it, that they might hear one another's sense in this matter; for in the multitude of counsellors there is safety and satisfaction. They did not give their judgment rashly, but considered of this matter. Though they were clear concerning it in their own minds, yet they would take time to consider of it, and to hear what might be said by the adverse party. Nor did the apostles give their judgment concerning it without the elders, the inferior ministers, to whom they thus condescended, and on whom they thus put an honour. Those that are most eminent in gifts and graces, and are in the most exalted stations in the church, ought to show respect to their juniors and inferiors; for, though *days should speak,* yet *there is a spirit in man,* Job 32:7, 8. Here is a direction to the pastors of the churches, when difficulties arise, to come together in solemn meetings for mutual advice and encouragement, that they may know one another's mind, and strengthen one another's hands, and may act in concert. Now here we have,

I. Peter's speech in this synod. He did not in the least pretend to any primacy or headship in this synod. He was not master of this assembly, nor so much as chairman or moderator, *pro hac vice — on this occasion;* for we do not find that either he spoke first, to open the synod *(there having been much disputing* before he *rose up),* nor that he spoke last, to sum up the cause and collect the suffrages; but he was a faithful, prudent zealous member of this assembly, and offered that which was very much to the purpose, and which would come better from him than from another, because he had himself been the first that preached the gospel to the Gentiles. *There had been much disputing, pro and con,* upon this question, and liberty of speech allowed, as ought to be in such cases; those of the sect of the Pharisees were some of them present, and allowed to say what they could in defence of those of their opinion at Antioch, which probably was answered by some of the elders; such questions ought to be fairly disputed before they are decided. When both sides had been heard, *Peter rose up,* and addressed himself to the assembly, *Men and brethren,* as did James afterwards, *v.* 13. And here,

1. He put them in mind of the call and commission he had some time ago *to preach the gospel to the Gentiles;* he wondered there should be any difficulty made of a matter already settled: *You know that aph' hēmerōn archaiōn — from the beginning of the days* of the gospel, many years ago, *God made choice* among us apostles of one to preach the gospel to the Gentiles, and I was the person chosen, *that the Gentiles by my mouth should hear the word, and believe, v.* 7. You know I was questioned about it and cleared myself to the universal satisfaction; every body rejoiced that *God had granted to the Gentiles repentance unto life,* and nobody said a word of circumcising them, nor was there any thought of such a thing. See *ch.* 11:18. "Why should the Gentiles who hear the word of the gospel by Paul's mouth be compelled to submit to circumcision, any more than those that heard it by my mouth? Or why should the terms of their admission now be made harder than they were then?"

2. He puts them in mind how remarkably God owned him in preaching to the Gentiles, and gave testimony to their sincerity in embracing the Christian faith (*v.* 8): *"God, who knows the hearts,* and therefore is able to judge infallibly of men, *bore them witness* that they were his indeed, by *giving them the Holy Ghost;* not only the graces and comforts, but the extraordinary miraculous gifts of the Holy Ghost, *even as he did unto us* apostles." See *ch.* 11:15–17. Note, *The Lord knows those that are his,* for he knows men's hearts; and we are as our hearts are. Those to whom God *gives the Holy Ghost,* he thereby *bears witness* to that they are his; hence we are said to be *sealed* with that Holy Spirit of promise — *marked* for God. God had bidden the Gentiles welcome to the privilege of communion with him, without requiring them to be circumcised and to keep the law; and there-fore shall not we admit them into communion with us but upon those terms? "God has *put no difference between us and them* (*v.* 9); they, though Gentiles, are as welcome to the grace of Christ and the throne of grace as we Jews are; why then should we set them at a distance, as if we were holier than they?" Isa. 65:5. Note, We ought not to make any conditions of our brethren's acceptance with us but such as God has made the conditions of their acceptance with him, Rom. 14:3. Now the Gentiles were fitted for communion with God, in *having their hearts purified by faith,* and that faith God's own work in them; and therefore why should we think them unfit for communion with us, unless they will submit to the ceremonial purifying enjoined by the law to us? Note, (1.) *By faith the heart is purified;* we are not only justified, and conscience purified, but the work of sanctification is begun and carried on. (2.) Those that have their hearts purified by faith are therein made so nearly to resemble one another, that, whatever difference there may be between them, no account is to be made of it; for the faith of all the saints is alike precious, and has like precious effects (2 Peter 1:1), and those that by it are united to Christ are so to look upon themselves as joined to one another as that all distinctions, even that between Jew and Gentile, are merged and swallowed up in it.

3. He sharply reproves those teachers (some of whom, it is likely, were present) who went about to bring the Gentiles under the obligation of the law of Moses, *v.* 10. The thing is so plain that he cannot forbear speaking of it with some

warmth: *"Now therefore,* since God has owned them for his, *why tempt you God to put a yoke upon the neck of the disciples,* of the believing Gentiles and their children" (for circumcision was a yoke upon their infant seed, who are here reckoned among the disciples), *"a yoke which neither our fathers nor we were able to bear?"* Here he shows that in this attempt, (1.) They offered a very great affront to God: "You tempt him, by calling that in question which he has already settled and determined by no less an indication than that of the gift of the Holy Ghost; you do, in effect, ask, 'Did he know what he did? Or was he in earnest in it? Or will he abide by his own act?' Will you try whether God, who designed the ceremonial law for the people of the Jews only, will now, in its last ages, bring the Gentiles too under the obligation of it, to gratify you?" Those tempt God who prescribe to him, and say that people cannot be saved but upon such and such terms, which God never appointed; as if the God of salvation must come into their measures. (2.) They offered a very great wrong to the disciples: Christ came to proclaim *liberty to the captives,* and they go about to enslave those whom he has made free. See Neh. 5:8. The ceremonial law was a heavy yoke; they and their fathers found it difficult to be borne, so numerous, so various, so pompous, were the institutions of it. The distinction of meats was a heavy yoke, not only as it rendered conversation less pleasant, but as it embarrassed conscience with endless scruples. The ado that was made about even unavoidable touch of a grave or a dead body, the pollution contracted by it, and the many rules about purifying from that pollution, were a heavy burden. This yoke Christ came to ease us of, and called those that were *weary and heavy laden* under it to come and take his yoke upon them, his easy yoke. Now for these teachers to go about to lay that yoke upon the neck of the Gentiles from which he came to free even the Jews was the greatest injury imaginable to them.

4. Whereas the Jewish teachers had urged that circumcision was necessary to salvation, Peter shows it was so far from being so that both Jews and Gentiles were to be saved purely *through the grace of our Lord Jesus Christ,* and in no other way (*v.* 11): *We believe to be saved through that grace* only; *pisteuomen sōthēnai — We hope to be saved;* or, *We believe unto salvation in the same manner as they — kath' hon tropon kakeinoi.* "We that are circumcised believe to salvation, and so do those that are uncircumcised; and, as our circumcision will be no advantage to us, so their uncircumcision will be no disadvantage to them; for we must depend upon the grace of Christ for salvation, and must apply that grace by faith, as well as they. There is not one way of salvation for the Jews and another for the Gentiles; *neither circumcision avails any thing nor uncircumcision* (that is neither here nor there), *but faith which works by love,* Gal. 5:6. Why should we burden them with the law of Moses, as necessary to their salvation, when it is not that, but the gospel of Christ, that is necessary both to our salvation and theirs?"

II. An account of what Barnabas and Paul said in this synod, which did not need to be related, for they only gave in a narrative of what was recorded in the foregoing chapters, *what miracles and wonders God had wrought among the Gentiles by them, v.* 12. This they had given in to the church *at Antioch* (ch. 14:27), *to their brethren by the way* (ch. 15:3), and now again to the synod; and it was very proper to be given in here. That which was contended for was that the Gentiles ought to submit to the law of Moses; now, in opposition to this, Paul and Barnabas undertake to show, by a plain relation of matters of fact, that God owned the preaching of the pure gospel to them without the law, and therefore to press the law upon them now was to undo what God had done. Observe, 1. What account they gave; they declared, or opened in order, and with all the magnifying and affecting circumstances, what glorious miracles, what signs and wonders, *God had wrought among the Gentiles by them,* what confirmation he had given to their preaching by miracles wrought in the kingdom of nature, and what success he had given to it by miracles wrought in the kingdom of grace. Thus God had honoured these apostles whom Jewish teachers condemned, and had thus honoured the Gentiles whom they contemned. What need had they of any other advocate when God himself pleaded their cause? The conversion of the Gentiles was itself a wonder, all things considered, no less than a miracle. Now if *they received the Holy Ghost by the hearing of faith,* why should they be embarrassed with *the works of the law?* See Gal. 3:2. 2. What attention was given to them: *All the multitude* (who, though they had not voted, yet came together to hear what was said) *kept silence, and gave audience to Paul and Barnabas;* it should seem they took more notice of their narrative than they did of all the arguments that were offered. As in natural philosophy and medicine nothing is so satisfactory as experiments, and in law nothing is so satisfactory as cases adjudged, so in the things of God the best explication of the word of grace is the accounts given of the operations of the Spirit of grace; to these the multitude will with silence give audience. Those that fear God will most readily hear those that can tell them *what God has done for their souls,* or by their means, Ps. 66:16.

III. The speech which James made to the synod. He did not interrupt Paul and Barnabas, though, it is likely, he had before heard their narrative, but let them go on with it, for the edification of the company, and that they might have it from the first and best hand; but, *after they had held their peace,* then James stood up. *You may all prophesy one by one,* 1 Co. 14:31. God is the God of order. He let Paul and Barnabas say what they had to say, and then he made the application of it. The hearing of variety of ministers may be of use when one truth does not drive out, but clench, another.

1. He addresses himself respectfully to those present: *"Men and brethren, hearken unto me.* You are men, and therefore, it is to be hoped, will hear reason; you are my brethren, and therefore will hear me with candour. We are all brethren, and equally concerned in this cause that nothing be done to the dishonour of Christ and the uneasiness of Christians."

2. He refers to what Peter had said concerning the conversion of the Gentiles (*v.* 14): *"Simeon"* (that is, Simon Peter) *"hath declared,* and opened the matter to you — *how God at the first did visit the Gentiles,* in Cornelius and his friends, who were the first-fruits of the Gentiles — how, when the gospel began first to spread, presently the Gentiles were invited to come and take the benefit of it;" and James observes here, (1.) That the *grace of God* was the origin of it; it was *God that visited the Gentiles;* and it was a kind visit. Had they been left to themselves, they would never have visited him, but the acquaintance began on his part; he not only *visited and redeemed his people,* but visited and redeemed those that were *lo ammi — not a people.* (2.) that the glory of God was the end of it: it was *to take out of them a people for his name,* who should glorify him, and in whom he would be glorified. As of old he took the Jews, so now the Gentiles, *to be to him for a name, and for a praise, and for a glory,* Jer. 13:11. Let all the people of God remember that therefore they are thus dignified in God, that God may be glorified in them.

3. He confirms this with a quotation out of the Old Testament: he could not prove the calling of the Gentiles by a vision, as Peter could, nor by miracles wrought by his hand, as Paul and Barnabas could, but he would prove that it was foretold in the Old Testament, and therefore it must be fulfilled, *v.* 15. *To this agree the words of the prophets;* most of the Old-Testament prophets spoke more or less of the calling in of the Gentiles, even Moses himself, Rom. 10:19. It was the general expectation of the pious Jews that the Messiah should be *a light to enlighten the Gentiles* (Lu. 2:32): but James waives the more illustrious prophecies of this, and pitches upon one that seemed more obscure: *It is written,* Amos 9:11, 12, where is foretold, (1.) The setting up of the kingdom of the Messiah (*v.* 16): *I will raise up the tabernacle of David, that is fallen.* The covenant was made with David and his seed; but the house and family of David are here called his *tabernacle,* because David in his beginning was a shepherd, and dwelt in tents, and his house, that had been as a stately palace, had become a mean and despicable tabernacle, reduced in a manner to its small beginning. This tabernacle was ruined and *fallen down;* there had not been for many ages a king of the house of David; *the sceptre had departed from Judah,* the royal family was sunk and buried in obscurity, and, as it should seem, not enquired after. But God *will return, and will build it again,* raise it out of its ruins, a phoenix out of its ashes; and this was now lately fulfilled, when our Lord Jesus was raised out of that family, had *the throne of his father David given him,* with a promise *that he should reign over the house of Jacob for ever,* Lu. 1:32, 33. And, when *the tabernacle of David* was thus rebuilt in Christ, all the rest of it was, not many years after, wholly extirpated and cut off, as was also the nation of the Jews itself, and all their genealogies were lost. The church of Christ may be called the tabernacle of David. This may sometimes be brought very

low, and may seem to be in ruins, but it shall be built again, its withering interests shall revive; it is *cast down, but not destroyed:* even dry bones are made to live. (2.) The bringing in of the Gentiles as the effect and consequence of this (*v.* 17): *That the residue of men might seek after the Lord;* not the Jews only, who thought they had the monopoly of the tabernacle of David, but *the residue of men,* such as had hitherto been left out of the pale of the visible church; they must now, upon this re-edifying of the tabernacle of David, be brought *to seek after the Lord,* and to enquire how they may obtain his favour. When David's tabernacle is set up, they *shall seek the Lord their God,* and *David their king,* Hos. 3:5; Jer. 30:9. *Then Israel shall possess the remnant of Edom* (so it is in the Hebrew); but the Jews called all the Gentiles *Edomites,* and therefore the Septuagint leave out the particular mention of Edom, and read it just as it is here, *that the residue of men might seek* (James here adds, *after the Lord), and all the Gentiles,* or heathen, *upon whom my name is called.* The Jews were for many ages so peculiarly favoured that the residue of men seemed neglected; but now God will have an eye to them, and his name shall be called upon by the Gentiles; his name shall be declared and published among them, and they shall be brought both to know his name and to call upon it: they shall call themselves the people of God, and he shall call them so; and thus, by consent of both parties, *his name is called upon them.* This promise we may depend upon the fulfilling of in its season; and now it begins to be fulfilled, for it is added, *saith the Lord, who doeth this; who doeth all these things* (so the Seventy); and the apostle here: *he saith it who doeth it,* who therefore said it because he was determined to do it; and who therefore does it because he hath said it; for though with us saying and doing are two things they are not so with God. The uniting of *Jews and Gentiles in one body,* and all those things that were done in order to it, which were here foretold, were, [1.] What God did: *This was the Lord's doing,* whatever instruments were employed in it: and, [2.] It was what God delighted in, and was well pleased with; for he is the God of the Gentiles, as well as the Jews, and it is his honour *to be rich in mercy to all that call upon him.*

4. He resolves it into the purpose and counsel of God (*v.* 18): *Known unto God are all his works from the beginning of the world.* He not only foretold the calling of the Gentiles many ages ago by the prophets (and therefore it ought not to be a surprise or stumbling-block to us), but he foresaw and foreordained it in his eternal counsels, which are unquestionably wise and unalterably firm. It is an excellent maxim here laid down concerning all God's works, both of providence and grace, in the natural and spiritual kingdom, that they were all *known unto him from the beginning of the world,* from the time he first began to work, which supposes his knowing them (as other scriptures speak) *from before the foundation of the world,* and therefore from all eternity. Note, Whatever God does, he did before design and determine to do; for he works all, not only according to his will, but *according to the counsel of his will:* he not only *does whatever he determined* (Ps. 135:6), which is more than we can do (our purposes are frequently broken off, and our measures broken), but he *determined whatever he does.* Whatever he may say, to prove us, *he himself knows what he will do.* We know not our works beforehand, but must *do as occasion shall serve,* 1 Sa. 10:7. What we shall do in such or such a case we cannot tell till it comes to the setting to; but *known unto God are all his works;* in the volume of his book (called *the scriptures of truth,* Dan. 10:21) they are all written in order, without any erasure or interlining (Ps. 40:7); and all God's works will, in the day of review, be found to agree exactly with his counsels, without the least error or variation. We are poor short-sighted creatures; the wisest men can see but a little way before them, and not at all with any certainty; but this is our comfort, that, whatever uncertainty we are at, there is an infallible certainty in the divine prescience: *known unto God are all his works.*

5. He gives his advice what was to be done in the present case, as the matter now stood with reference *to the Gentiles* (*v.* 19): *My sentence is; egō krinō — I give it as my opinion,* or judgment; not as having authority over the rest, but as being an adviser with them. Now his advice is,

(1.) That circumcision and the observance of the ceremonial law be by no means imposed upon the Gentile converts; no, not so much as recommended nor mentioned to them. "There are many from among the Gentiles that are turned to God in Christ, and we hope there will be many more. Now I am clearly for using them with all possible tenderness, and putting no manner of hardship or discouragement upon them," *mē parenochlein — "not to give them any molestation nor disturbance,* nor suggest any thing to them that may be disquieting, or raise scruples in their minds, or perplex them." Note, Great care must be taken not to discourage nor disquiet young converts with matters of *doubtful disputation.* Let the essentials of religion, which an awakened conscience will readily receive, be first impressed deeply upon them, and these will satisfy them and make them easy; and let not things foreign and circumstantial be urged upon them, which will but trouble them. *The kingdom of God,* in which they are to be trained up, *is not meat and drink,* neither the opposition nor the imposition of indifferent things, which will but trouble them; *but it is righteousness, and peace, and joy in the Holy Ghost,* which we are sure will trouble nobody.

(2.) That yet it would be well that in some things, which gave most offence to the Jews, the Gentiles should comply with them. Because they must not humour them so far as to be circumcised, and keep the whole law, it does not therefore follow that they must act in a continual contradiction to them, and study how to provoke them. It will please the Jews (and, if a little thing will oblige them, better do so than cross them) if the Gentile converts abstain, [1.] *From pollutions of idols, and from fornication,* which are two bad things, and always to be abstained from; but writing to them particularly and expressly to abstain from them (because in these things the Jews were jealous of the Gentile converts, lest they should transgress) would very much gratify the Jews; not but that the apostles, both in preaching and writing to the Gentiles that embraced Christianity, were careful to warn against, *First, Pollutions of idols,* that they should have no manner of fellowship with idolaters in their idolatrous worships, and particularly not in the feasts they held upon their sacrifices. See 1 Co. 10:14, etc.; 2 Co. 6:14, etc. *Secondly, Fornication, and all manner of uncleanness.* How large, how pressing, is Paul in his cautions against this sin! 1 Co. 6:9–15; Eph. 5:3, etc. But the Jews, who were willing to think the worst of those they did not like, suggested that these were things in which the Gentiles, even after conversion, allowed themselves, and the apostle of the Gentiles connived at it. Now, to obviate this suggestion, and to leave no room for this calumny, James advises that, besides the private admonitions which were given them by their ministers, they should be publicly warned *to abstain from pollutions of idols and from fornication* — that herein they should be very circumspect, and should avoid all appearances of these two evils, which would be in so particular a manner offensive to the Jews. [2.] *From things strangled, and from blood,* which, though not evil in themselves, as the other two, nor designed to be always abstained from, as those were, had been forbidden by *the precepts of Noah* (Gen. 9:4.), before the giving of the law of Moses; and the Jews had a great dislike to them, and to all those that took a liberty to use them; and therefore, to avoid giving offence, let the Gentile converts abridge themselves of their liberty herein, 1 Co. 8:9, 13. Thus we must *become all things to all men.*

6. He gives a reason for his advice — that great respect ought to be shown to the Jews for they have been so long accustomed to the solemn injunctions of the ceremonial law that they must be borne with, if they cannot presently come off from them (*v.* 21): *For Moses hath of old those that preach him in every city,* his writings (a considerable part of which is the ceremonial law) *being read in the synagogues every sabbath day.* "You cannot blame them if they have a great veneration for the law of Moses; for besides that they are very sure God spoke to Moses," (1.) "Moses is continually preached to them, and they are called upon *to remember the law of Moses,"* Mal. 4:4. Note, Even that word of God which is written to us should also be preached: those that have the scriptures have still need of ministers to help them to understand and apply the scriptures. (2.) "His writings are read in a solemn religious manner, *in their synagogues,* and on *the sabbath day,* in the place and at the time of their meetings for the worship of God; so that from their childhood they have been trained up in a regard to the law of Moses; the observance of it is a part of their religion." (3.) "This has been done *of old time;* they have received from their fathers an honour for Moses; they have antiquity for it." (4.) "This had been done *in every city,* wherever there are any Jews, so that none of them can be ignorant what stress that law laid upon these things: and therefore, though the gospel has set us free from these things, yet they cannot be blamed if they are loth to part with them, and cannot of a sudden be persuaded to look upon those things as needless and indifferent which they, and their fathers before them, had been so long taught, and taught of God too, to place religion in. We must therefore give them time, must meet them half-way; they must be borne with awhile, and brought on gradually, and we must comply with them as far as we can without betraying our gospel liberty." Thus does this apostle show the spirit of a moderator, that is, a spirit of moderation, being careful to give no offence either to Jew or Gentile, and contriving, as much as may be, to please both sides and provoke neither. Note, We are not to think it strange if people be wedded to customs which they have had transmitted to them from their fathers, and which they have been educated in an opinion of as sacred; and therefore allowances must be made in such cases, and not rigour used.

Verses 22–35

We have here the result of the consultation that was held at Jerusalem about the imposing of the ceremonial law upon the Gentiles. Much more, it is likely, was said about it than is here recorded; but at length it was brought to a head, and the advice which James gave was universally approved and agreed to *nemine contradicente — unanimously;* and letters were accordingly sent by messengers of their own to the Gentile converts, acquainting them with their sentiments in this matter, which would be a great confirmation to them against the false teachers. Now observe here,

I. The choice of the delegates that were to be sent with Paul and Barnabas on this errand; not as if they had any suspicion of the fidelity of these great men, and could not trust them with their letters, nor as if they thought that those to whom they sent them would suspect them to have altered any thing in their letter; no, their charity thought no such evil concerning men of such tried integrity; but,

1. They thought fit *to send men of their own company to Antioch, with Paul and Barnabas, v.* 22. This was agreed to by *the apostles and elders, with the whole church,* who, it is likely, undertook to bear their charges, 1 Co. 9:7. They sent these messengers, (1.) To show their respect to the church at Antioch, as a sister-church, though a younger sister, and that they looked upon it as upon the same level with them; as also that they were desirous further to know their state. (2.) To encourage Paul and Barnabas, and to make their journey home the more pleasant (for it is likely they travelled on foot) by sending such excellent men to bear them company; *amicus pro vehiculo — a friend instead of a carriage.* (3.) To put a reputation upon the letters they carried, that it might appear a solemn embassy, and so much the more regard might be paid to the message, which was likely to meet with opposition from some. (4.) To keep up *the communion of the saints,* and cultivate an acquaintance between churches and ministers that were at a distance from each other, and to show *that, though they were many, yet they were one.*

2. Those they sent were not inferior persons, who might serve to carry the letters, and attest the receipt of them from the apostles; but *they were chosen men, and chief men among the brethren,* men of eminent gifts, graces, and usefulness; for these are the things which denominate men chief among the brethren, and qualify them to be the messengers of the churches. They are here named: *Judas,* who was called *Barsabas* (probably the brother of that Joseph who was called *Barsabas,* that was a candidate for the apostleship, *ch.* 1:23), *and Silas.* The character which these men had in the church at Jerusalem would have some influence upon those that came from Judea, as those false teachers did, and engage them to pay the more deference to the message that was sent by them.

II. The drawing up of the letters, circular letters, that were to be sent to the churches, to notify the sense of the synod in this matter.

1. Here is a very condescending obliging preamble to this decree, *v.* 23. There is nothing in it haughty or assuming, but, (1.) That which intimates the humility of the apostles, that they join *the elders and brethren* in commission with them, the ministers, the ordinary Christians, whom they had advised with in this case, as they used to do in other cases. Though never men were so qualified as they were for a monarchical power and authority in the church, nor had such a

commission as they had, yet their decrees run not, "We, the apostles, Christ's vicars upon earth, and pastors of all the pastors of the churches" (as the pope styles himself), "and sole judges in all matters of faith;" but *the apostles, and elders, and brethren,* agree in their orders. Herein they remembered the instructions their Master gave them (Mt. 23:8): *Be not you called Rabbi; for you are all brethren.* (2.) That which bespeaks their respect to the churches they wrote to; they *send* to them *greeting,* wish them health and happiness and joy, and call them *brethren of the Gentiles,* thereby owning their admission into the church, and giving them the right hand of fellowship: "You are our brethren, though Gentiles; for we meet in Christ, *the first born among many brethren,* in God our common Father." Now that *the Gentiles are fellow-heirs and of the same body,* they are to be countenanced and encouraged, and called brethren.

2. Here is a just and severe rebuke to the judaizing teachers (*v.* 24): "*We have heard that certain who went out from us have troubled you with words,* and we are very much concerned to hear it; now this is to let them know that those who preached this doctrine were false teachers, both as they produced a false commission and as they taught a false doctrine." (1.) They did a great deal of wrong to the apostles and ministers at Jerusalem, in pretending that they had instructions from them to impose the ceremonial law upon the Gentiles, when there was no colour for such a pretension. "They *went out from us* indeed — they were such as belonged to our church, of which, when they had a mind to travel, we gave them perhaps a testimonial; but, as for their urging the law of Moses upon you, we *gave* them *no such commandment,* nor had we ever thought of such a thing, nor given them the least occasion to use our names in it." It is no new thing for apostolical authority to be pleaded in defence of those doctrines and practices for which yet the apostles gave neither command nor encouragement. (2.) They did a great deal of wrong to the Gentile converts, in saying, *You must be circumcised, and must keep the law.* [1.] It perplexed them: "*They have troubled you with words,* have occasioned disturbance and disquietment to you. You depended upon those who told you, *If you believe in the Lord Jesus Christ you shall be saved;* and now you are startled by those that tell you *you must keep the law of Moses or you cannot be saved,* by which you see yourselves drawn into a snare. They trouble you with words — words, and nothing else — mere words — sound, but no substance." How has the church been troubled with words, by the pride of men that loved to hear themselves talk! [2.] It endangered them; they *subverted* their souls, put them into disorder, and pulled down that which had been built up. They took them off from pursuing pure Christianity, and minding the business of that, by filling their heads with the necessity of circumcision, and the law of Moses, which were nothing to the purpose.

3. Here is an honourable testimony given of the messengers by whom these letters were sent.

(1.) Of Paul and Barnabas, whom these judaizing teachers had opposed and censured as having done their work by the halves, because they had brought the Gentile converts to Christianity only, and not to Judaism. Let them say what they will of these men, [1.] "They are men that are dear to us; they are *our beloved Barnabas and Paul* — men whom we have a value for, a kindness for, a concern for." Sometimes it is good for those that are of eminence to express their esteem, not only for the despised truth of Christ, but for the despised preachers and defenders of that truth, to encourage them, and weaken the hands of their opposers. [2.] "They are men that have signalized themselves in the service of Christ, and therefore have deserved well of all the churches: they are men *that have hazarded their lives for the name of our Lord Jesus Christ* (*v.* 26), and therefore are worthy of double honour, and cannot be suspected of having sought any secular advantage to themselves; for they have ventured their all for Christ, have engaged in the most dangerous services, as good soldiers of Christ, and not only in laborious services." It is not likely that such faithful confessors should be unfaithful preachers. Those that urged circumcision did it to avoid persecution (Gal. 6:12, 13); those that opposed it knew they thereby exposed themselves to persecution; and which of these were most likely to be in the right?

(2.) Of Judas and Silas: "*They are chosen men* (*v.* 25), and they are men that have heard our debates, and are perfectly apprized of the matter, and will *tell you the same things by mouth,*" *v.* 27. What is of use to us it is good to have both in writing and by word of mouth, that we may have the advantage both of reading and of hearing it. The apostles refer them to the bearers for a further account of their judgment and their reasons, and the bearers will refer them to their letters for the certainty of the determination.

4. Here is the direction given what to require from the Gentile converts, where observe,

(1.) The matter of the injunction, which is according to the advice given by James, that, to avoid giving offence to the Jews, [1.] They should never eat any thing that they knew had been offered in sacrifice to an idol, but look upon it as, though clean in itself, yet thereby polluted to them. This prohibition was afterwards in part taken off, for they were allowed to eat whatever was sold in the shambles, or set before them at their friend's table, though it had been offered to idols, except when there was danger of giving offence by it, that is, of giving occasion either to a weak Christian to think the worse of our Christianity, or to a wicked heathen to think the better of his idolatry; and in these cases it is *good to forbear,* 1 Co. 10:25, etc. This to us is an antiquated case. [2.] *That they should not eat blood,* nor drink it; but avoid every thing that looked cruel and barbarous in that ceremony which had been of so long standing. [3.] *That they should not eat any thing that was strangled,* or died of itself, or had not the blood let out. [4.] That they should be very strict in censuring those that *were guilty of fornication,* or marrying within the degrees prohibited by the Levitical law, which, some think, is principally intended here. See 1 Co. 5:1. Dr. Hammond states this matter thus: The judaizing teachers would have the Gentile converts submit to all that those submitted to whom they called the proselytes of righteousness, *to be circumcised and keep the whole law;* but the apostles required no more of them than what was required of the proselytes of the gate, which was to observe *the seven precepts of the sons of Noah,* which, he thinks, are here referred to. But the only ground of this decree being in complaisance to the rigid Jews that had embraced the Christian faith, and, except in that one case of scandal, all meats being pronounced free and indifferent to all Christians as soon as the reason of the decree ceased, which, at furthest, was after the destruction of Jerusalem, the obligation of it ceased likewise. "These things are in a particular manner offensive to the Jews, and therefore do not disoblige them herein for the present; in a little time the Jews will incorporate with the Gentiles, and then the danger is over."

(2.) The manner in which it is worded. [1.] They express themselves with something of authority, that what they wrote might be received with respect, and deference paid to it: *It seemed good to the Holy Ghost, and to us,* that is, to us under the guidance of the Holy Ghost, and by direction from him: not only the apostles, but others, were endued with spiritual gifts extraordinary, and knew more of the mind of God than any since those gifts ceased can pretend to; their infallibility gave an incontestable authority to their decrees, and they would not order any thing because *it seemed good to them,* but that they knew it first *seemed good to the Holy Ghost.* Or it refers to what the Holy Ghost had determined in this matter formerly. When the Holy Ghost descended upon the apostles, he endued them with the gift of tongues, in order to their preaching the gospel to the Gentiles, which was a plain indication of God's purpose to call them in. When the Holy Ghost descended upon Cornelius and his friends, upon Peter's preaching, it was plain that Christ designed the taking down of the Jewish pale, within which they fancied the spirit had been enclosed. [2.] They express themselves with abundance of tenderness and fatherly concern. *First,* They are afraid of burdening them: We will *lay upon you no greater burden.* So far were they from delighting to impose upon them that they dreaded nothing so much as imposing too far upon them, so as to discourage them at their setting out. *Secondly,* They impose upon them *no other than necessary things.* "The avoiding of *fornication* is necessary to all Christians at all times; the avoiding of *things strangled,* and of *blood,* and of *things offered to idols,* is necessary at this time, for the keeping up of a good understanding between you and the Jews, and the preventing of offence;" and as long as it continues necessary for that end, and no longer, it is enjoined. Note, Church-rulers should impose only necessary things, things which Christ has made our duty, which have a real tendency to the edification of the church, and, as here, to the uniting of good Christians. If they impose things only to show their own authority, and to try people's obedience, they forget that they have not authority to make new laws, but only to see that the laws of Christ be duly executed, and to enforce the observance of them. *Thirdly,* They enforce their order with a commendation of those that shall comply with it, rather than with the condemnation of those that shall transgress it. They do not conclude, "From which if you do not keep yourselves, you shall be an anathema, you shall be cast out of the church, and accursed," according to the style of after-councils, and particularly that of Trent; but "*From which if you keep yourselves,* as we do not question but you will, *you will do well;* it will be for the glory of God, the furtherance of the gospel, the strengthening of the hands of your brethren, and your own credit and comfort." It is all sweetness and love and good humour, such as became the followers of him who, when he called us to take his yoke upon us, assured us we should find him *meek and lowly in heart.* The difference of the style of the true apostles from that of the false is very observable. Those that were for imposing the ceremonial laws were positive and imperious: *Except you keep it, you cannot be saved* (*v.* 1), you are excommunicated *ipso facto — at once, and delivered to Satan.* The apostles of Christ, who only recommend necessary things, are mild and gentle: "*From which if you keep yourselves, you will do well,* and as becomes you. *Fare ye well;* we are hearty well-wishers to your honour and peace."

III. The delivering of the letters, and how the messengers disposed of themselves.

1. *When they were dismissed,* had had their audience of leave of the apostles (it is probable that they were dismissed with prayer, and a solemn blessing in the name of the Lord, and with instructions and encouragements in their work), *They then came to Antioch;* they staid no longer at Jerusalem than till their business was done, and then came back, and perhaps were met at their return by those that brought them on their way at their setting out; for those that have taken pains in public service ought to be countenanced and encouraged.

2. As soon as they came to Antioch, *they gathered the multitude together, and delivered the epistle to them* (*v.* 30, 31), that they might all know what it was that was forbidden them, and might observe these orders, which would be no difficulty for them to do, most of them having been, before their conversion to Christ, proselytes of the gate, who had laid themselves under these restrictions already. But this was not all; it was that they might know that *no more* than this was forbidden them, that it was no longer a sin to eat swine's flesh, no longer a pollution to touch a grave or a dead body.

3. The people were wonderfully pleased with the orders that came from Jerusalem (*v.* 31): *They rejoiced for the consolation;* and a great consolation it was to the multitude, (1.) That they were confirmed in their freedom from the yoke of the ceremonial law, and were not burdened with that, as those upstart teachers would have had them to be. It was a comfort to them to hear that the carnal ordinances were no longer imposed on them, which perplexed the conscience, but could not purify nor pacify it. (2.) That those who troubled their minds with an attempt to force circumcision upon them were hereby for the present silenced and put to confusion, the fraud of their pretensions to an apostolical warrant being now discovered. (3.) That the Gentiles were hereby encouraged to receive the gospel, and those that had received it to adhere to it. (4.) That the peace of the church was hereby restored, and that removed which threatened a division. All this was consolation which they rejoiced in, and blessed God for.

4. They got the strange ministers that came from Jerusalem to give them each a sermon, and more, *v.* 32. Judas and Silas, *being prophets also themselves,* endued with the Holy Ghost, and called to the work, and being likewise entrusted by the apostles to deliver some things relating to this matter by word of mouth, *exhorted the brethren with many words,* and *confirmed them.* Even those that had the constant preaching of Paul and Barnabas, yet were glad of the help of Judas and Silas; the diversity of the gifts of ministers is of use to the church. Observe what is the work of ministers with those that are in Christ. (1.) To confirm them, by bringing them to see more reason both for their faith in Christ and their obedience to him; to confirm their choice of Christ and their resolutions for Christ. (2.) To exhort them to perseverance, and to the particular duties required of them: to quicken them to that which is good, and direct them in it. They comforted the brethren (so it may be rendered), and

this would contribute to the confirming of them; for the joy of the Lord will be our strength. They exhorted them with many words; they used a very great copiousness and variety of expression. One word would affect one, and another another; and therefore, though what they had to say might have been summed up in a few words, yet it was for the edification of the church that they used *many words, dia logou pollou — with much speech, much reasoning; precept must be upon precept.*

5. The dismission of the Jerusalem ministers, *v.* 33. When they had *spent some time among them* (so it might be read), *poiēsantes chronon — having made some stay,* and having made it to good purpose, not having trifled away time, but having filled it up, they were let go in peace from the brethren at Antioch, to the apostles at Jerusalem, with all possible expressions of kindness and respect; they thanked them for their coming and pains, and the good service they had done, wished them their health and a good journey home, and committed them to the custody of the peace of God.

6. The continuance of Silas, notwithstanding, together with Paul and Barnabas, at Antioch. (1.) Silas, when it came to the setting to, would not go back with Judas to Jerusalem, but let him go home by himself, and chose rather to *abide still at Antioch, v.* 34. And we have no reason at all to blame him for it, though we know not the reason that moved him to it. I am apt to think the congregations at Antioch were both more large and more lively than those at Jerusalem, and that this tempted him to stay there, and he did well: so did Judas, who, notwithstanding this, returned to his post of service at Jerusalem. (2.) Paul and Barnabas, though their work lay chiefly among the Gentiles, yet continued for some time in Antioch, being pleased with the society of the ministers and people there, which, it should seem by divers passages, was more than ordinarily inviting. They continued there, not to take their pleasure, but *teaching and preaching the word of God.* Antioch, being the chief city of Syria, it is probable there was a great resort of Gentiles thither from all parts upon one account or other, as there was of Jews to Jerusalem; so that in preaching there they did in effect preach to many nations, for they preached to those who would carry the report of what they preached to many nations, and thereby prepare them for the apostles' coming in person to preach to them. And thus they were not only not idle at Antioch, but were serving their main intention. (3.) There were *many others also* there, labouring at the same oar. The multitude of workmen in Christ's vineyard does not give us a writ of ease. Even where there are many others labouring in the word and doctrine, yet there may be opportunity for us; the zeal and usefulness of others should excite us, not lay us asleep.

Verses 36–41

We have seen one unhappy difference among the brethren, which was of a public nature, brought to a good issue; but here we have a private quarrel between two ministers, no less men than Paul and Barnabas, not compromised indeed, yet ending well.

I. Here is a good proposal Paul made to Barnabas to go and review their work among the Gentiles and renew it, to take a circuit among the churches they had planted, and see what progress the gospel made among them. Antioch was now a safe and quiet harbour for them: they had there no adversary nor evil occurrent; but Paul remembered that they only put in there to refit and refresh themselves, and therefore begins now to think of putting to sea again; and, having been in winter quarters long enough, he is for taking the field again, and making another campaign, in a vigorous prosecution of this holy war against Satan's kingdom. Paul remembered that the work appointed him was afar off among the Gentiles, and therefore he is here meditating a second expedition among them to do the same work, though to encounter the same difficulties; and this *some days after,* for his active spirit could not bear to be long out of work; no, nor his bold and daring spirit to be long out of danger. Observe, 1. To whom he makes this proposal — to Barnabas, his old friend and fellow-labourer; he invites his company and help in this work. We have need one of another, and may be in many ways serviceable one to another; and therefore should be forward both to borrow and lend assistance. Two are better than one. Every soldier has his comrade. 2. For whom the visit is designed: "Let us not presently begin new work, nor break up new ground; but let us take a view of the fields we have sown. *Come, and let us get up early to the vineyards, let us see if the vine flourish,* Cant. 7:12. *Let us go again and visit our brethren in every city where we have preached the word of the Lord.*" Observe, He calls all the Christians brethren, and not ministers only; for, *Have we not all one Father?* He has a concern for them in *every city,* even where the brethren were fewest and poorest, and most persecuted and despised; yet let us visit them. Wherever we have *preached the word of the Lord,* let us go and water the seed sown. Note, Those that have preached the gospel should visit those to whom them have preached it. As we must look after our praying, and hear what answer God gives to that; so we must look after our preaching, and see what success that has. Faithful ministers cannot but have a particular tender concern for those to whom they have preached the gospel, that they may not bestow upon them labour in vain. See 1 Th. 3:5, 6. 3. What was intended in this visit: "Let us *see how they do," pōs echousi — how it is with them.* It was not merely a compliment that he designed, nor did he take such a journey with a bare *How do you do?* No, he would visit them that he might acquaint himself with their case, and impart unto them such spiritual gifts as were suited to it; as the physician visits his recovering patient, that he may prescribe what is proper for the perfecting of his cure, and the preventing of a relapse. Let us see how they do, that is, (1.) What spirit they are of, how they stand affected, and how they behave themselves; it is probable that they frequently heard from them, "But let us go and see them; let us go and see whether they hold fast what we preached to them, and live up to it, that we may endeavour to reduce them if we find them wandering, to confirm them if we find them wavering, and to comfort them if we find them steady." (2.) What state they are in, whether the churches have rest and liberty, or whether they are not in trouble or distress, that we may rejoice with them if they rejoice, and caution them against security, and may weep with them if they weep, and comfort them under the cross, and may know the better how to pray for them.

II. The disagreement between Paul and Barnabas about an assistant; it was convenient to have a young man with them that should attend on them and minister to them, and be a witness of their *doctrine, manner of life, and patience,* and that should be fitted and trained up for further service, by being occasionally employed in the present service. Now, 1. Barnabas would have his nephew John, whose surname was Mark, to go along with them, *v.* 37. He determined to take him, because he was his relation, and, it is likely, was brought up under him, and he had a kindness for him, and was solicitous for his welfare. We should suspect ourselves of partiality, and guard against it in preferring our relations. 2. Paul opposed it (*v.* 38): *He thought not good to take him with them, ouk ēxiou — he did not think him worthy* of the honour, nor fit for the service, who had *departed from them,* clandestinely as it should seem, without their knowledge, or wilfully, without their consent, from Pamphylia (*ch.* 13:13), and *went not with them to the work,* because he was either lazy and would not take the pains that must be taken, or cowardly and would not run the hazard. He run his colours just as they were going to engage. It is probable that he promised very fair now that he would not do so again. But Paul thought it was not fit he should be thus honoured who had forfeited his reputation, nor thus employed who had betrayed his trust; at least, not till he had been longer tried. If a man deceive me once, it is his fault; but, if twice, it is my own, for trusting him. Solomon saith, *Confidence in an unfaithful man in time of trouble is like a broken tooth, and a foot out of joint,* which will hardly be used again, Prov. 25:19.

III. The issue of this disagreement: it came to such a height that they separated upon it. The contention, the *paroxysm* (so the word is), the fit of passion which this threw them both into, was so sharp that they *departed asunder one from the other.* Barnabas was peremptory that he would not go with Paul unless they took John Mark with them; Paul was as peremptory that he would not go if John did go with them. Neither would yield, and therefore there is no remedy but they must part. Now here is that which is very humbling, and just matter of lamentation, and yet very instructive. For we see, 1. That the best of men are but men, *subject to like passions* as we are, as these two good men had expressly owned concerning themselves (*ch.* 14:15), and now it appeared too true. I doubt there was (as usually there is in such contentions) a *fault on both sides;* perhaps Paul was too severe upon the young man, and did not allow his fault the extenuation it was capable of, did not consider what a useful woman his mother was in Jerusalem (*ch.* 12:12), nor make the allowances he might have made to Barnabas's natural affection. But it was Barnabas's fault that he took this into consideration, in a case wherein the interest of Christ's kingdom was concerned, and indulged it too much. And they were certainly both in fault to be hot as to let the contention be sharp (it is to be feared they gave one another some hard words), as also to be so stiff as each to stick resolutely to his opinion, and neither to yield. It is a pity that they did not refer the matter to a third person, or that some friend did not interpose to prevent its coming to an open rupture. Is there never a wise man among them to interpose his good offices, and to accommodate the matter, and to put them in mind of the Canaanite and the Perizzite that were *now in the land,* and that not only Jews and heathens, but the false brethren among themselves, would warm their hands at the flames of the contention between Paul and Barnabas? We must own it was their infirmity, and is recorded for our admonition; not that we must make use of it to excuse our own intemperate heats and passions, or to rebate the edge of our sorrow and shame for them; we must not say, "What if I was in a passion, were not Paul and Barnabas so?" No; but it must check our censures of others, and moderate them. If good men are soon put into a passion, we must make the best of it, it was the infirmity once of two of the best men that ever the world had. Repentance teaches us to be severe in reflections upon ourselves; but charity teaches us to be candid in our reflections upon others. It is only Christ's example that is a copy without a blot. 2. That we are not to think it strange if there be differences among wise and good men; we were told before that such offences would come, and here is an instance of it. Even those that are united to one and the same Jesus, and sanctified by one and the same Spirit, have different apprehensions, different opinions, different views, and different sentiments in points of prudence. It will be so while we are in this state of darkness and imperfection; we shall never be all of a mind till we come to heaven, where light and love are perfect. That is *charity* which *never fails.* 3. That these differences often prevail so far as to occasion separations. Paul and Barnabas, who were not separated by the persecutions of the unbelieving Jews, nor the impositions of the believing Jews, were yet separated by an unhappy disagreement between themselves. O the mischief that even the poor and weak remainders of pride and passion, that are found even in good men, do in the world, do in the church! Now wonder the consequences are so fatal where they reign.

IV. The good that was brought out of this evil — meat out of the eater, and sweetness out of the strong. It was strange that even the sufferings of the apostles (as Phil. 1:12), but much more strange that even the quarrels of the apostles, should tend to the *furtherance of the gospel of Christ;* yet so it proved here. God would not permit such things to be, if he knew not how to make them to serve his own purposes. 1. More places are hereby visited. Barnabas went one way; he sailed to Cyprus (*v.* 39), that famous island where they began their work (*ch.* 13:4), and which was *his own country, ch.* 4:36. Paul went another way into Cilicia, which was *his own country, ch.* 21:39. Each seems to be influenced by his affection to his native soil, as usual *(Nescio quâ natale solum dulcedine cunctos ducit — There is something that attaches us all to our native soil),* and yet God served his own purposes by it, for the diffusing of gospel light. 2. More hands are hereby employed in the ministry of the gospel among the Gentiles; for, (1.) John Mark, who had been an unfaithful hand, is not rejected, but is again made use of, against Paul's mind, and, for aught we know, proves a very useful and successful hand, though many think it was not the same with that Mark that wrote the gospel, and founded the church at Alexandria, and whom Peter calls his son, 1 Pt. 5:13. (2.) Silas who was a new hand, and never yet employed in that work, nor intended to be, but to return to the service of the church at Jerusalem, had not God changed his mind (*v.* 33, 34), he is brought in, and engaged in that noble work.

V. We may further observe, 1. That the church at Antioch seem to countenance Paul in what he did. Barnabas sailed with his nephew to Cyprus, and no notice was taken of him, nor a *bene discessit — a recommendation* given him. Note, Those that in their service of the church are swayed by private affections and regards forfeit public honours and respect. But, when Paul departed, he was *recommended by the breth-*

ren to the grace of God. They thought he was in the right in refusing to make use of John Mark, and could not but blame Barnabas for insisting upon it, though he was one who had deserved well of the church (*ch.* 11:22) before they knew Paul; and therefore they prayed publicly for Paul, and for the success of his ministry, encouraged him to go on in his work, and, though they could do nothing themselves to further him, they transferred the matter to the grace of God, leaving it to that grace both to work upon him and to work with him. Note, Those are happy at all times, and especially in times of disagreement and contention, who are enabled so to carry themselves as not to forfeit their interest in the love and prayers of good people. 2. That yet Paul afterwards seems to have had, though not upon second thoughts, yet upon further trial, a better opinion of John Mark than now he had; for he writes to Timothy (2 Tim. 4:11), *Take Mark and bring him with thee, for he is profitable to me for the ministry;* and he writes to the Colossians concerning Marcus, sister's son to Barnabas, that *if he came to them* they should *receive him,* bid him welcome, and employ him (Col. 4:10), which teaches us, (1.) That even those whom we justly condemn we should condemn moderately, and with a great deal of temper, because we know not but afterwards we may see cause to think better of them, and both to make use of them and make friendship with them, and we should so regulate our resentments that if it should prove so we may not afterwards be ashamed of them. (2.) That even those whom we have justly condemned, if afterwards they prove more faithful, we should cheerfully receive, forgive and forget, and put a confidence in, and, as there is occasion, give a good word to. 3. That Paul, though he wanted his old friend and companion in the kingdom and patience of Jesus Christ, yet went on cheerfully in his work (*v.* 41): *He went through Syria and Cilicia,* countries which lay next to Antioch, *confirming the churches.* Though we change our colleagues, we do not change our principal president. And observe, Ministers are well employed, and ought to think themselves so, and be satisfied, when they are made use of confirming those that believe, as well as in converting those that believe not.

CHAPTER 16

It is some rebuke to Barnabas that after he left Paul we hear no more of him, of what he did or suffered for Christ. But Paul, as he was recommended by the brethren to the grace of God, so his services for Christ after this are largely recorded; we are to attend him in this chapter from place to place, wherever he came doing good, either watering or planting, beginning new work or improving what was done. Here is, I. The beginning of his acquaintance with Timothy, and taking him to be his assistant (*v.* 1–3). II. The visit he made to the churches for their establishment (*v.* 4, 5). III. His call to Macedonia (after a restraint he had been under from going to some other places), and his coming to Philippi, the chief city of Macedonia, with his entertainment there (*v.* 6–13). IV. The conversion of Lydia there (*v.* 14, 15). V. The casing of an evil spirit out of a damsel (*v.* 16–18). VI. The accusing and abusing of Paul and Silas for it, their imprisonment, and the indignities done them (*v.* 19–24). VII. The miraculous conversion of the jailer to the faith of Christ (*v.* 25–34). VIII. The honourable discharge of Paul and Silas by the magistrates (*v.* 35–40).

Verses 1–5

Paul was a spiritual father, and as such a one we have him here adopting Timothy, and taking care of the education of many others who had been begotten to Christ by his ministry: and in all he appears to have been a wise and tender father. Here is,

I. His taking Timothy into his acquaintance and under his tuition. One thing designed in the book of the Acts is to help us to understand Paul's epistles, two of which are directed to Timothy; it was therefore necessary that in the history of Paul we should have some account concerning him. And we are here accordingly told, 1. That he was a disciple, one that belonged to Christ, and was baptized, probably in his infancy, when his mother became a believer, as Lydia's household was baptized upon her believing, *v.* 15. Him, that was a disciple of Christ, Paul took to be his disciple, that he might further train him up in the knowledge and faith of Christ; he took him to be brought up for Christ. 2. That his mother was a Jewess originally, *but believed in Christ;* her name was *Eunice,* his grandmother's name was *Lois.* Paul speaks of them both with great respect, as women of eminent virtue and piety, and commends them especially for their unfeigned faith (2 Tim. 1:5), their sincerely embracing and adhering to the doctrine of Christ. 3. That his father was a Greek, a Gentile. The marriage of a Jewish woman to a Gentile husband (though some would make a difference) was prohibited as much as the marriage of a Jewish man to a Gentile wife, Deu. 7:3. Thou shalt no more *give thy daughter to his son than take his daughter to thy son;* yet this seems to have been limited to the nations that lived among them in Canaan, whom they were most in danger of infection from. Now because his father was a Greek he was not circumcised: for the entail of the covenant and the seal of it, as of other entails in that nation, went by the father, not by the mother; so that his father being no Jew he was not obliged to circumcision, nor entitled to it, unless when he grew up he did himself desire it. But, observe, though his mother could not prevail to have him circumcised in his infancy, because his father was of another mind and way, yet she educated him in the fear of God, that though he wanted the sign of the covenant he might not want the thing signified. 4. That he had gained a very good character among the Christians: he was *well reported of by the brethren* that were at Lystra and Iconium; he had not only an unblemished reputation, and was free from scandal, but he had a bright reputation, and great encomiums were given of him, as an extraordinary young man, and one from whom great things were expected. Not only those in the place where he was born, but those in the neighbouring cities, admired him, and spoke honourably of him. He had a name for good things with good people. 5. That Paul would have him *to go forth with him,* to accompany him, to give attendance on him, to receive instruction from him, and to join with him in the work of the gospel — to preach for him when there was occasion, and to be left behind in places where he had planted churches. Paul had a great love for him, not only because he was an ingenious young man, and one of great parts, but because he was a serious young man, and one of devout affections: for Paul was always *mindful of his tears,* 2 Tim. 1:4. 6. That Paul took him and circumcised him, or ordered it to be done. This was strange. Had not Paul opposed those with all his might that were for imposing circumcision upon the Gentile converts? Had he not at this time the decrees of the council at Jerusalem with him, which witnessed against it? He had, and yet circumcised Timothy, not, as those teachers designed in imposing circumcision, to oblige him to keep the ceremonial law, but only to render his conversation and ministry passable, and, if it might be, acceptable among the Jews that abounded in those quarters. He knew Timothy was a man likely to do a great deal of good among them, being admirably qualified for the ministry, if they were not invincibly prejudiced against him; and therefore, that they might not shun him as one unclean, because uncircumcised, he took him and *circumcised him.* Thus *to the Jews he became as a Jew, that he might gain the Jews,* and *all things to all men, that he might gain some.* He was against those who made circumcision necessary to salvation, but used it himself when it was conducive to edification; nor was he rigid in opposing it, as they were in imposing it. Thus, though he went not in this instance according to the letter of the decree, he went according to the spirit of it, which was a spirit of tenderness towards the Jews, and willingness to bring them off gradually from their prejudices. Paul made no difficulty of taking Timothy to be his companion, though he was uncircumcised; but the Jews would not hear him if he were, and therefore Paul will humour them herein. It is probable that it was at this time that Paul laid his hands on Timothy, for the conferring of the gift of the Holy Ghost upon him, 2 Tim. 1:6.

II. His confirming the churches which he had planted (*v.* 4, 5): *He went through the cities* where he had *preached the word of the Lord,* as he intended (*ch.* 15:36), to enquire into their state. And we are told,

1. That they delivered them copies of the decrees of the Jerusalem synod, to be a direction to them in the government of themselves, and that they might have wherewith to answer the judaizing teachers, and to justify themselves in adhering to the *liberty with which Christ had made them free.* All the churches were concerned in that decree, and therefore it was requisite they should all have it well attested. Though Paul had for a particular reason circumcised Timothy, yet he would not have that drawn into a precedent; and therefore he *delivered the decrees* to the churches, to be religiously observed; for they must abide by the rule, and not be drawn from it by a particular example.

2. That this was of very good service to them. (1.) The churches were hereby *established in the faith, v.* 5. They were confirmed particularly in their opinion against the imposing of the ceremonial law upon the Gentiles; the great assurance and heat wherewith the judaizing teachers pressed the necessity of circumcision, and the plausible arguments they produced for it, had shocked them, so that they began to waver concerning it. But when they saw the testimony, not only of the apostles and elders, but of the Holy Ghost in them, against it, they were established, and did not longer waver about it. Note, Testimonies to truth, though they may not prevail to convince those that oppose it, may be of very good use to establish those that are in doubt concerning it, and to fix them. Nay, the design of this decree being to set aside the ceremonial law, and the carnal ordinances of that, they were by it established in the Christian faith in general, and were the more firmly assured that it was of God, because it set up a spiritual way of serving God, as more suited to the nature both of God and man; and, besides, that spirit of tenderness and condescension which appeared in these letters plainly showed that the apostles and elders were herein under the guidance of him who is love itself. (2.) They *increased in number daily.* The imposing of the yoke of the ceremonial law upon their converts was enough to frighten people from them. If they had been disposed to turn Jews, they could have done that long since, before the apostles came among them; but, if they cannot be interested in the Christian privileges without submitting to the Jews' yoke, they will be as they are. But, if they find there is no danger of their being so enslaved, they are ready to embrace Christianity, and join themselves to the church. And thus the church *increased in numbers daily;* not a day passed but some or other gave up their names to Christ. And it is a joy to those who heartily wish well to the honour of Christ, and the welfare of the church and the souls of men, to see such an increase.

Verses 6–15

In these verses we have,

I. Paul's travels up and down to do good. 1. He and Silas his colleague went throughout Phrygia and the region of Galatia, where, it should seem, the gospel was already planted, but whether by Paul's hand or no is not mentioned; it is likely it was, for in his epistle to the Galatians he speaks of his *preaching the gospel to them at the first,* and how very acceptable he was among them, Gal. 4:13–15. And it appears by that epistle that the judaizing teachers had then done a great deal of mischief to these churches of Galatia, had prejudiced them against Paul and drawn them from the gospel of Christ, for which he there severely reproves them. But probably that was a great while after this. 2. They were forbidden at this time to preach the gospel in Asia (the country properly so called), because it did not need, other hands being at work there; or because the people were not yet prepared to receive it, as they were afterwards (*ch.* 19:10), when *all those that dwelt in Asia heard the word of the Lord;* or, as Dr. Lightfoot suggests, because at this time Christ would employ Paul in a piece of new work, which was to preach the gospel to a Roman colony at Philippi, for hitherto the Gentiles to whom he had preached were Greeks. The Romans were more particularly hated by the Jews than other Gentiles; their armies were the *abomination of desolation;* and therefore there is this among other things extraordinary in his call thither that he is forbidden to preach the gospel in Asia and other places, in order to his preaching it there, which is an intimation that the light of the gospel would in aftertimes be directed more westward than eastward. It was the Holy Ghost that forbade them, either by secret whispers in the minds of both of them, which, when they came to compare notes, they found to be the same, and to come from the same Spirit; or by some prophets who spoke to them from the Spirit. The removals of ministers, and the dispensing of the means of grace by them, are in a particular manner under a divine guidance and direction. We find an Old-Testament minister forbidden to preach at all (Eze. 3:26): *Thou shalt be dumb.* But these New-Testament ministers are only forbidden to preach in one place, while they are directed to another where there is more need. 3. They would have gone into Bithynia, but were not permitted: *the Spirit suffered them not, v.* 7. They came to Mysia, and, as it should seem, preached the gospel there; for though it was a very mean contemptible country, even to a proverb *(Mysorum ultimus,* in Cicero, is *a most despicable man),* yet the apostles disdained not to visit it, owning themselves debtors both *to the wise and to the unwise,* Rom. 1:14. In Bithynia was the city of Nice, where the first general council was held against the Arians; into these countries Peter sent his epistle (1 Pt. 1:1); and there were flourishing churches here, for, though they had not the gospel sent them now, they had it in their turn, not long after. Observe, Though their judgment and inclination were to go into Bithynia, yet, having then extraordinary ways of knowing the mind of God, they were overruled by them, contrary to their own mind. We must now follow providence, and submit to the guidance of that pillar of cloud and fire; and, if this *suffer us not* to do what we assay to do, we ought to acquiesce, and believe it for the best. *The Spirit of Jesus* suffered them not; so many ancient copies read it. The servants of the Lord Jesus ought to be always under the check and conduct of the *Spirit of the Lord Jesus,* by whom he governs men's minds. 4. They *passed by Mysia,* or passed *through it* (so some), sowing good seed, we may suppose, as they went along; and they came down to Troas, the city of Troy, so much talked of, or the country thereabouts, which took its denomination from it. Here a church was planted; for here we find one in being, *ch.* 20:6, 7, and probably planted at this time, and in a little time. It should seem that at Troas Luke fell in with Paul, and joined himself to his company; for henceforward, for the most part, when he speaks of Paul's journeys, he puts himself into the number of his retinue, *we* went, *v.* 10.

II. Paul's particular call to Macedonia, that is, to Philippi, the chief city, inhabited mostly by Romans, as appears, *v.* 21. Here we have,

1. The vision Paul had, *v.* 9. Paul had many visions, sometimes to encourage, sometimes, as here, to direct him in his work. An angel appeared to him, to intimate to him that it was the will of Christ he should go to Macedonia. Let him not be discouraged by the embargo laid upon him once and again, by which his designs were crossed; for, though he shall not go where he has a mind to go, he shall go where God has work for him to do. Now observe, (1.) The person Paul saw. There stood by him *a man of Macedonia,* who by his habit or dialect seemed so to Paul, or who told him he was so. The angel, some think, assumed the shape of such a man; or, as others think, impressed upon Paul's fancy, when between asleep and awake, the image of such a man: he dreamt he saw such a one. Christ would have Paul directed to Macedonia, not as the apostles were at other times, by a messenger from heaven, to send him thither, but by a messenger thence to call him thither, because in this way he would afterwards ordinarily direct the motions of his ministers, by inclining the hearts of those who needed them to invite them. Paul shall be called to Macedonia by a man of Macedonia, and by him speaking in the name of the rest. Some make this man to be the tutelar angel of Macedonia, supposing angels to have charge of particular places as well as persons, and that so much is intimated Dan. 10:20, where we read of the *princes of Persia and Grecia,* that seem to have been angels. But there is no certainty of this. There was presented either to Paul's eyes or to his mind a man of Macedonia. The angel must not preach the gospel himself to the Macedonians, but must bring Paul to them. Nor must he by the authority of an angel order him to go, but in the person of a Macedonian court him to come. A man of Macedonia, not a magistrate of the country, much less a priest (Paul was not accustomed to receive invitations from such) but an ordinary inhabitant of that country, a plain man, that carried in his countenance marks of probity and seriousness, that did not come to banter Paul nor trifle with him, but in good earnest and with all earnestness to importune his assistance. (2.) The invitation given him. This honest Macedonian *prayed him, saying, Come over into Macedonia, and help us;* that is, "Come and preach the gospel to us; let us have the benefit of thy labours." [1.] *"Thou hast helped many;* we have heard of those in this and the other country to whom thou hast been very useful; and why may we not put in for a share? O come and help us." The benefits others have received from the gospel should quicken our enquiries, our further enquiries, after it. [2.] "It is thy business, and it is thy delight, to help poor souls; thou art a physician for the sick, that art to be ready at the call of every patient; O come and help us." [3.] "We have need of thy help, as much as any people; we in Macedonia are as ignorant and as careless in religion as any people in the world are, are as idolatrous and as vicious as any, and as ingenious and industrious to ruin ourselves as any; and therefore, O come, come with all speed among us. *If thou canst do any thing, have compassion on us, and help us."* [4.] "Those few among us that have any sense of divine things, and any concern for their own souls and the souls of others, have done what can be done, by the help of natural light; I have done my part for one. We have carried the matter as far as it will go, to persuade our neighbours to fear and worship God, but we can do little good among them. *O come come, thou over, and help us.* The gospel thou preachest has arguments and powers beyond those we have yet been furnished with." [5.] "Do not only help us with thy prayers here: this will not do; thou must come over and help us." Note, People have great need of help for their souls, and it is their duty to look out for it and invite those among them that can help them.

2. The interpretation made of the vision (*v.* 10): They *gathered assuredly from this that the Lord had called them to preach the gospel* there; and they were ready to go wherever God directed. Note, We may sometimes infer a call of God from a call of man. If a man of Macedonia says, *Come and help us,* Paul thence gathers assuredly that God says, Go an help them. Ministers may go on with great cheerfulness and courage in their work when they perceive Christ calling them, not only to preach the gospel, but to preach it at this time, in this place, to this people.

III. Paul's voyage to Macedonia hereupon: He *was not disobedient to the heavenly vision,* but followed this divine direction much more cheerfully, and with more satisfaction, than he would have followed any contrivance or inclination of his own. 1. Thitherward he turned his thoughts. Now that he knows the mind of God in the matter he is determined, for this is all he wanted; now he thinks no more of Asia, nor Bithynia, but *immediately we endeavoured to go into Macedonia.* Paul only had the vision, but he communicated it to his companions, and they all, upon the credit of this, resolved for Macedonia. As Paul will follow Christ, so all his will follow him, or rather follow Christ with him. They are getting things in readiness for this expedition immediately, without delay. Note, God's calls must be complied with immediately. As our obedience must not be disputed, so it must not be deferred; do it to-day, lest thy heart be hardened. Observe, They could not immediately go into Macedonia; but they immediately endeavoured to go. If we cannot be so quick as we would be in our performances, yet we may be in our endeavours, and this shall be accepted. 2. Thitherward he steered his course. They *set sail* by the first shipping and with the first fair wind *from Troas;* for they may be sure they have done what they had to do there when God calls them to another place. They *came with a straight course,* a prosperous voyage, *to Samothracia;* the *next day they came to Neapolis,* a city on the confines of Thrace and Macedonia; and at last they landed at *Philippi,* a city so called from Philip king of Macedon, the father of Alexander the Great; it is said (*v.* 12) to be, (1.) *The chief city of that part of Macedonia;* or, as some read it, *the first city,* the first they came to when they came from Troas. As an army that lands in a country of which they design to make themselves masters begin with the reduction of the first place they come to, so did Paul and his assistants: they began with the first city, because, if the gospel were received there, it would the more easily spread thence all the country over. (2.) It was a colony. The Romans not only had a garrison, but the inhabitants of the city were Romans, the magistrates at least, and the governing part. There were the greatest numbers and variety of people, and therefore the most likelihood of doing good.

IV. The cold entertainment which Paul and his companions met with at Philippi. One would have expected that having such a particular call from God thither they would have had a joyful welcome there, as Peter had with Cornelius when the angel sent him thither. Where was the man of Macedonia that begged Paul to come thither with all speed? Why did not he stir up his countrymen, some of them at least, to go and meet him? Why was not Paul introduced with solemnity, and the keys of the city put into his hand? Here is nothing like this; for, 1. It is a good while before any notice at all is taken of him: *We were in that city abiding certain days,* probably at a public house and at their own charge, for they had no friend to invite them so much as to a meal's meat, till Lydia welcomed them. They had made all the haste they could thither, but, now that they are there, they are almost tempted to think they might as well have staid where they were. But so it was ordered for their trial whether they could bear the pain of silence and lying by, when this was their lot. Those eminent and useful men are not fit to live in this world that know not how to be slighted and overlooked. Let not ministers think it strange if they be first strongly invited to a place, and then looked shyly upon when they come. 2. When they have an opportunity of preaching it is in an obscure place, and to a mean and small auditory, *v.* 13. There was no synagogue of the Jews there, for aught that appears, to be a door of entrance to them, and they never went to the idol-temples of the Gentiles, to preach to the auditories there; but here, upon enquiry, they found out a little meeting of good women, *that were proselytes of the gate,* who would be thankful to them if they would give them a sermon. The place of this meeting is out of the city; there it was connived at, but would not be suffered any where within the walls. It was a place *where prayer was wont to be made; proseuchē — where an oratory or house of prayer was* (so some), a chapel, or smaller synagogue. But I rather take it, as we read it, where prayer was appointed or accustomed to be. Those that worshipped the true God, and would not worship idols, met there to pray together, and, according to the description of the most ancient and universal devotion, *to call upon the name of the Lord.* Each of them prayed apart every day; this was always the practice of those that worshipped God: but, besides this, *they came together on the sabbath day.* Though they were but a few and discountenanced by the town, though their meeting was at some distance, though, for aught that appears, there were none but women, yet a solemn assembly the worshippers of God must have, if by any means it be possible, on the sabbath day. When we cannot do as we would we must do as we can; if we have not synagogues, we must be thankful for more private places, and resort to them, *not forsaking the assembling of ourselves together,* according as our opportunities are. This place is said to be *by a river side,* which perhaps was chosen, as befriending contemplation. Idolaters are said *to take their lot among the smooth stones of the stream,* Isa. 57:6. But these proselytes had in their eye, perhaps, the example of those prophets who had their visions, one by the *river of Chebar* (Eze. 1:1), another by *the great river Hiddekel,* Dan. 10:4. Thither Paul and Silas and Luke went, and *sat down,* to instruct the congregation, that they might the better pray with them. They *spoke unto the women who resorted thither,* encouraged them in practising according to the light they had, and led them on further to the knowledge of Christ.

V. The conversion of *Lydia,* who probably was the first that was wrought upon there to believe in Christ, though not the last. In this story of *the Acts,* we have not only the conversion of places recorded, but of many particular persons; for such is the worth of souls that the reducing of one to God is a great matter. Nor have we only the conversions that were effected by miracle, as Paul's, but some that were brought about by the ordinary methods of grace, as Lydia's here. Observe,

1. Who this convert was that there is such particular notice taken of. Four things are recorded of her: —

(1.) Her name, *Lydia.* It is an honour to her to have her name recorded here in the book of God, so that *wherever the scriptures are read there shall this be told concerning her.* Note, The names of the saints are precious with God, and should be so with us; we cannot have our names recorded in the Bible, but, if God open our hearts, we shall find them *written in the book of life,* and this is better (Phil. 4:3) and more to *be rejoiced in,* Lu. 10:20.

(2.) Her calling. She was *a seller of purple,* either of purple dye or of purple cloth or silk. Observe, [1.] She had a calling, an honest calling, which the historian takes notice of to her praise; she was none of those women that the apostle speaks of (1 Tim. 5:13), *who learn to be idle, and not only idle, etc.* [2.] It was a mean calling. She was *a seller of purple,* not a wearer of purple, few such are called. The notice here taken of this is an intimation to those who are employed in honest callings, if they be honest in the management of them, not to be ashamed of them. [3.] Though she had a calling to mind, yet she was a worshipper of God, and found time to improve advantages for her soul. The business of our particular callings may be made to consist very well with the business of religion, and therefore it will not excuse us from religious exercises alone, and in our families, or in solemn assemblies, to say, We have shops to look after, and a trade to mind; for have we not also a God to serve and a soul to look after? Religion does not call us from our business in the world, but directs us in it. Every thing in its time and place.

(3.) The place she was of — *of the city of Thyatira,* which was a great way from Philippi; there she was born and bred, but either married at Philippi, or brought by her trade to settle there. The providence of God, as it always appoints, so it often removes, *the bounds of our habitation,* and sometimes makes the change of our outward condition or place of our abode wonderfully subservient to the designs of his grace concerning our salvation. Providence brings Lydia to Philippi, to be under Paul's ministry, and there, where she met with it, she made a good use of it; so should we improve opportunities.

(4.) Her religion before the Lord opened her heart. [1.] She worshipped God according to the knowledge she had; she was one of the devout women. Sometimes the grace of God wrought upon those who, before their conversion, were very wicked and vile, publicans and harlots; *such were some of you,* 1 Co. 6:11. But sometimes it fastened upon those who were of a good character, who had some good in them, as the eunuch, Cornelius, and Lydia. Note, It is not enough to be worshippers of God, but we must be believers in Jesus Christ, for there is no coming to God as a Father, but by him as Mediator. But those who worshipped God according to the light they had stood fair for the discoveries of Christ, and his grace to them; for *to him that has shall be given:* and to them Christ would be welcome; for those that know what it is to worship God see their need of Christ, and know what use to make of his mediation. [2.] She heard the apostles. Here, where prayer was made, when there was an opportunity, *the word was preached;* for hearing the word of God is a part of religious worship, and how can we expect God should hear our prayers if we will not hearken to his word? Those that worshipped God according to the light they had looked out for further light; we must improve *the day of small things,* but must not rest in it.

2. What the work was that was wrought upon her: *Whose heart the Lord opened.* Observe here, (1.) The author of this work: it was *the Lord,* — the Lord Christ, to whom this judgment is committed, — the Spirit of the Lord, who is the sanctifier. Note, Conversion-work is God's work; it is he *that works in us both to will and to do;* not as if we had nothing to do, but of ourselves, without God's grace, we can do nothing; nor as if God were in the least chargeable with the ruin of those that perish, but the salvation of those that are saved must be wholly ascribed to him. (2.) The seat of this work; it is in the heart that the change is made, it is to the heart that this blessed turn is given; it was the heart of Lydia that was wrought upon. Conversion-work is heart-work; it is a *renewing of the heart, the inward man, the spirit of the mind.* (3.) The nature of the work; she had not only her heart touched, but her heart opened. An unconverted soul is shut up, and fortified against Christ, *straitly shut up,* as Jericho against Joshua, Jos. 6:1. Christ, in dealing with the soul, knocks at the door that is shut against him (Rev. 3:20); and, when a sinner is effectually persuaded to embrace Christ, *then the heart is opened for the King of glory to come in* — the understanding is open to receive the divine light, the will opened to receive the divine law, and the affections opened to receive the divine love. When the heart is thus opened to Christ, the ear is opened to his word, the lips opened in prayer, the hand opened in charity, and the steps enlarged in all manner of gospel obedience.

3. What were the effects of this work on the heart. (1.) She took great notice of the word of God. Her heart was so *opened that she attended to the things that were spoken by Paul;* she not only gave attendance on Paul's preaching, but gave attention to it; *she applied to herself* (so some read it) *the things that were spoken by Paul;* and then only the word does us good, and makes an abiding impression upon us, when we apply it to ourselves. Now this was an evidence of the opening of her heart, and was the fruit of it; wherever the heart is opened by the grace of God, it will appear by a diligent attendance on, and attention to, the word of God, both for Christ's sake, whose word it is, and for our own sakes, who are so nearly interested in it. (2.) She gave up her name to Jesus Christ, and took upon her the profession of his holy religion; *She was baptized,* and by this solemn rite was admitted a member of the church of Christ; and with her *her household* also was baptized, those of them that were infants in her right, for if *the root be holy so are the branches,* and those that were grown up by her influence and authority. She and her household were baptized by the same rule that Abraham and his household were circumcised, because the seal of the covenant belongs to the covenanters and their seed. (3.) She was very kind to the ministers, and very desirous to be further instructed by them in *the things pertaining to the kingdom of God: She besought us saying "If you have judged me to be faithful to the Lord,* if you take me to be a sincere Christian, manifest your confidence in me by this, *come into my house, and abide there."* Thus she desired an opportunity, [1.] To testify her gratitude to those who had been the instruments of divine grace in this blessed change that was wrought upon her. When her heart was open to Christ, her house was open to his ministers for his sake, and they were welcome to the best entertainment she had, which she did not think too good for those of whose spiritual things she had reaped so plentifully. Nay, they are not only welcome to her house, but she is extremely pressing and importunate with them: *She constrained us;* which intimates that Paul was very backward and unwilling to go, because he was afraid of being burdensome to the families of the young converts, and would study *to make the gospel of Christ without charge* (1 Co. 9:18; Acts 20:34), that those who were without might have no occasion given them to reproach the preachers of the gospel as designing, self-seeking men, and that those who were within might have no occasion to complain of the expenses of their religion: but Lydia will have no nay; she will not believe that they take her to be a sincere Christian unless they will oblige her herein; like Abraham inviting the angels (Gen. 18:3), *If now I have found favour in thy sight, pass not away from thy servant.* [2.] She desired an opportunity of receiving further instruction. If she might but have them for awhile in her family, she might hear them daily (Prov. 8:34), and not merely on sabbath days at the meeting. In her own house she might not only hear them, but ask them questions; and she might have them to pray with her daily, and to bless her household. Those that know something of Christ cannot but desire to know more, and seek opportunities of increasing their acquaintance with his gospel.

Verses 16–24

Paul and his companions, though they were for some time buried in obscurity at Philippi, yet now begin to be taken notice of.

I. *A damsel that had a spirit of divination* caused them to be taken notice of, by proclaiming them to be the servants of God. Observe,

1. The account that is given of this damsel: She was *pythonissa, possessed with* such *a spirit of divination* as that damsel was by whom the oracles of Apollo at Delphos were delivered; she was actuated by an evil spirit, that dictated ambiguous answers to those who consulted her, which served to gratify their vain desire of knowing things to come, but often deceived them. In those times of ignorance, infidelity, and idolatry, the devil, by the divine permission, thus led men captive at his will; and he could not have gained such adoration from them as he had, if he had not pretended to give oracles to them, for by both his usurpation is maintained as the god of this world. This damsel *brought her masters much gain by soothsaying;* many came to consult this witch for the discovery of robberies, the finding of things lost, and especially to be told their fortune, and none came but with the rewards of divination in their hands, according to the quality of the person and the importance of the case. Probably there were many that were thus kept for fortune-tellers, but, it should seem, this was more in repute than any of them; for, while others brought some gain, this *brought much gain to her masters,* being consulted more than any other.

2. The testimony which this damsel gave to Paul and his companions: She *met them* in the street, as they were going to prayer, to the house of prayer, or rather to the work of prayer there, *v.* 16. They went thither publicly, every body knew whither they were going, and what they were going to do. If what she did was likely to be any distraction to them, or a hindrance in their work, it is observable how subtle Satan is, that great tempter, in taking the opportunity to give us diversion when we are going about any religious exercises, to ruffle us and to put us out of temper when we need to be most composed. When she met with them she followed them, crying, *"These men,* how contemptible soever they look and are looked upon, are great men, for they *are the servants of the most high God,* and men that should be very welcome to us, for *they show unto us the way of salvation,* both the salvation that will be our happiness, and the way to it that will be our holiness."

Now, (1.) This witness is true; it is a comprehensive encomium on the faithful preachers of the gospel, and makes their feet beautiful, Rom. 10:15. Though they are *men subject to like passions as we are,* and *earthen vessels,* yet, [1.] "They are *the servants of the most high God;* they attend on him, are employed by him, and are devoted to his honour, as servants; they come to us on his errands, the message they bring is from him, and they serve the purposes and interest of his kingdom. The gods we Gentiles worship are inferior beings, therefore not gods, but these men belong to the supreme *Numen, to the most high God,* who is over all men, over all gods, who made us all, and to whom we are all accountable. They are his servants, and therefore it is our duty to respect them, and harken to them for their Master's sake, and it is at our peril if we affront them." [2.] "They *show unto us the way of salvation."* Even the heathen had some notion of the miserable deplorable state of mankind, and their need of salvation, and it was what they made some enquiries after. "Now," saith she, "these men are the men that show us what we have in vain sought for in our superstitious profitless application to our priests and oracles." Note, God has, in the gospel of his Son, plainly shown us the way of salvation, has told us what we must do that we may be delivered from the misery to which by sin we have exposed ourselves.

But, (2.) How came this testimony from the mouth of one that had a spirit of divination? Is Satan divided against himself? Will he cry up those whose business it is to pull him down? We may take it either, [1.] As extorted from this spirit of divination for the honour of the gospel by the power of God; as the devil was forced to say of Christ (Mk. 1:24): *I know thee who thou art, the Holy One of God.* The truth is sometimes magnified by the confession of its adversaries, in which they are witnesses against themselves. Christ would have this testimony of the damsel to rise up in judgment against those at Philippi who slighted and persecuted the apostles; though the gospel needed no such testimony, yet it shall serve to add to their commendation that the damsel whom they looked upon as an oracle in other things proclaimed the apostles God's servants. Or, [2.] As designed by the evil spirit, that subtle serpent, to the dishonour of the gospel; some think she designed hereby to gain credit to herself and her prophecies, and so to increase her master's profit by pretending to be in the interest of the apostles, who, she thought, had a growing reputation, or to curry favour with Paul, that he might not separate her and her familiar. Others think that Satan, who can transform himself into an angel of light, and can say anything to serve a turn, designed hereby to disgrace the apostles; as if these divines were of the same fraternity with their diviners, because they were witnessed to by them, and then the people might as well adhere to those they had been used to. Those that were most likely to receive the apostles' doctrine were such as were prejudiced against these spirits of divination, and therefore would, by this testimony, be prejudiced against the gospel; and, as for those who regarded these diviners, the devil thought himself sure of them.

II. Christ caused them to be taken notice of, by giving them power to cast the devil out of this damsel. She continued *many days* clamouring thus (*v.* 18); and, it should seem, Paul took no notice of her, not knowing but it might be ordered of God for the service of his cause, that she should thus witness concerning his ministers; but finding perhaps that it did them a prejudice, rather than any service, he soon silenced her, by casting the devil out of her. 1. He was *grieved.* It troubled him to see the damsel made an instrument of Satan to deceive people, and to see the people imposed upon by her divinations. It was a disturbance to him to hear a sacred truth so profaned, and good words come out of such a wicked mouth with such and evil design. Perhaps they were spoken in an ironical bantering way, as ridiculing the apostles' pretensions, and mocking them, as when Christ's persecutors complimented him with *Hail, king of the Jews;* and then justly might Paul be grieved, as any good man's heart would be, to hear any good truth of God bawled out in the streets in a canting jeering way. 2. He *commanded the evil spirit to come out of her. He turned* with a holy indignation, angry both at the flatteries and at the reproaches of *the unclean spirit, and said, I command thee in the name of Jesus Christ to come out of her;* and by this he will show *that these men are the servants of the living God,* and are able to prove themselves so, without her testimony: her silence shall demonstrate it more than her speaking could do. Thus Paul shows *the way of salvation* indeed, that it is by breaking *the power of Satan, and chaining him up, that he may not deceive the world* (Rev. 20:3), and that this salvation is to be obtained *in the name of Jesus Christ* only, as in his name the devil was now cast out and by no other. It was a great blessing to the country when Christ by a word cast the devil out of those in whom he frightened people and molested them *so that no man might pass by that way* (Mt. 8:28); but it was a much greater kindness to the country when Paul now, in Christ's name, cast the devil out of one who deceived people and imposed upon their credulity. Power went along with the word of Christ, before which Satan could not stand, but was forced to quit his hold, and in this case it was a strong hold: *He came out the same hour.*

III. The masters of the damsel that was dispossessed caused them to be taken notice of, by bringing them before the magistrates for doing it, and laying it to their charge as their crime. The preachers of the gospel would never have had an opportunity of speaking to the magistrates if they had not been brought before them as evil doers. Observe here,

1. That which provoked them was, that, the damsel being restored to herself, *her masters saw that the hope of their gain was gone, v.* 19. See here what evil *the love of money is the root of!* If the preaching of the gospel ruin the craft of the silversmiths (*ch.* 19:24), much more the craft of the soothsayers; and therefore here is a great outcry raised, when Satan's power to deceive is broken: the priests hated the gospel because it turned men from the blind service of dumb idols, and so the hope of their gains was gone. The power of Christ, which appeared in dispossessing the woman, and the great kindness done to her in delivering her out of Satan's hand, made no impression upon them when they apprehended that they should hereby lose money.

2. The course they took with them was to incense the higher powers against them, as men fit to be punished: *They caught them* as they went along, and, with the utmost fury and violence, *dragged them into the marketplace,* where public justice was administered. (1.) They brought them *to the rulers,* their justices of peace, to do by them as men taken into the hands of the law, the *duumviri.* (2.) From them they hurried them *to the magistrates,* the praetors or governors of the city, *tois stratēgois — the officers of the army,* so the word signifies; but it is taken in general for the judges or chief rulers: to them they brought their complaint.

3. The charge they exhibited against them was that they were the troublers of the land, *v.* 20. They take it for granted that these men are Jews, a nation at this time as much an *abomination to the Romans* as they had long ago been to the Egyptians. Piteous was the case of the apostles, when it was turned to their reproach that they were Jews, and yet the Jews were their most violent persecutors! (1.) The general charge against them is *that they troubled the city,* sowed discord, and disturbed the public peace, and occasioned riots and tumults, than which nothing could be more false and unjust, as was Ahab's character of Elijah (1 Ki. 18:17): *Art thou he that troubleth Israel?* If they troubled the city, it was but like the angel's troubling the water of Bethesda's pool, in order to healing — shaking, in order to a happy settlement. Thus those that rouse the sluggards are exclaimed against for troubling them. (2.) The proof of this charge is their teaching customs not proper to be admitted by a Roman colony, *v.* 21. The Romans were always very jealous of innovations in religion. Right or wrong, they would adhere to that, how vain soever, which they had received by tradition from their fathers. No foreign nor upstart deity must be allowed, without the approbation of the senate; the gods of their country must be their gods, true or false. This was one of the laws of the twelve tables. *Hath a nation changed their gods?* It incensed them against the apostles that they taught a religion destructive of polytheism and idolatry, and preached to them to turn from those vanities. This the Romans could not bear: "If this grow upon us, in a little while we shall lose our religion."

IV. The magistrates, by their proceedings against them, caused them to be taken notice of.

1. By countenancing the persecution they raised the mob upon them (*v.* 22): *The multitude rose up together against them,* and were ready to pull them to pieces. It has been the artifice of Satan to make God's ministers and people odious to the commonalty, by representing them as dangerous men, who aimed at the destruction of the constitution and the changing of the customs, when really there has been no ground for such an imputation.

2. By going on to an execution they further represented them as the vilest malefactors: *They rent off their clothes,* with rage and fury, not having patience till they were taken off, in order to their being scourged. This the apostle refers to when he speaks of *their being treated at Philippi,* 1 Th. 2:2. The magistrates commanded that they should be whipped as vagabonds, by the lictors or beadles who attended the praetors, and carried rods with them for that purpose; this was one of those three times that Paul was beaten with rods, according to the Roman usage, which was not under the compassionate limitation of the number of stripes not to exceed forty, which was provided by the Jewish law. It is here said that *they laid many stripes upon them* (*v.* 23), without counting how many, because they seemed vile unto them, Deu. 25:3. Now, one would think, this might have satiated their cruelty; if they must be whipped, surely they must be discharged. No, they are imprisoned, and it is probable the present purpose was to try them for their lives, and put them to death; else why should there be such care taken to prevent their escape? (1.) The judges made their commitment very strict: They *charged the jailer to keep them safely,* and have a very watchful eye upon them, as if they were dangerous men, that either would venture to break prison themselves or were in confederacy with those that would attempt to rescue them. Thus they endeavoured to render them odious, that they might justify themselves in the base usage they had given them. (2.) The jailer made their confinement very severe (*v.* 24): *Having received such a charge,* though he might have kept them safely enough in the outer prison, yet *he thrust them into the inner prison.* He was sensible that the magistrates had a great indignation against these men, and were inclined to be severe with them, and therefore he thought to ingratiate himself with them, by exerting his power likewise against them to the uttermost. When magistrates are cruel, it is no wonder that the officers under them are so too. *He put them into the inner prison,* the dungeon, into which none were usually put but condemned malefactors, dark at noon-day, damp and cold, dirty, it is likely, and every way offensive, like that into which Jeremiah was let down (Jer. 38:6); and, as if this were not enough, *he made their feet fast in the stocks.* Perhaps, having heard a report of the escape of *the preachers of the gospel out of prison, when the doors were fast barred* (*ch.* 5:19; 12:9), he thought he would be wiser than other jailers had been, and therefore would effectually secure them by fastening them in the stocks; and they were not the first of God's messengers that had their feet in the stocks; Jeremiah was so treated, and publicly too, in *the high-gate of Benjamin* (Jer. 20:2); Joseph had his *feet hurt with fetters,* Ps. 105:18. Oh what hard usage have God's servants met with, as in the former days, so in the latter times! Witness the Book of Martyrs, martyrs in queen Mary's time.

Verses 25–34

We have here the designs of the persecutors of Paul and Silas baffled and broken.

I. The persecutors designed to dishearten and discourage the preachers of the gospel, and to make them sick of the cause and weary of their work; but here we find them both hearty and heartened.

1. They were themselves hearty, wonderfully hearty; never were poor prisoners so truly cheerful, nor so far from laying their hard usage to heart. Let us consider what their case was. The praetors among the Romans had rods carried before them, and axes bound upon them, the *fasces and secures.* Now they had felt the smart of the rods, *the ploughers had ploughed upon their backs, and made long furrows.* The many stripes they had laid upon them were very sore, and one might have expected to hear them complaining of them, of the rawness and soreness of their backs and shoulders. Yet this was not all; they had reason to fear the axes next. Their master was first scourged and then crucified; and they might expect the same. In the mean time they were in the inner prison, their feet in the stocks, which, some think, not only held them, but hurt them; and yet, *at midnight,* when they should have been trying, if possible, to get a little rest, they *prayed and sang praises to God.* (1.) They prayed together, prayed to God to support them and comfort them in their afflictions, to visit them, as he did Joseph in the prison, and to be with them, — prayed that their consolations in Christ might abound, as their afflictions for him did, — prayed that even their bonds and stripes might turn to the furtherance of the gospel, — prayed for their persecutors, that God would forgive them and turn their hearts. This was not at an hour of prayer, but at midnight; it was not in a house of prayer, but in a dungeon; yet it was seasonable to pray, and the prayer was acceptable. As in the dark, so out of the depths, we may cry unto God. No place, no time, amiss for prayer, if the heart be lifted up to God. Those that are companions in suffering should join in prayer. *Is any afflicted? Let him pray.* No trouble, how grievous soever, should indispose us for prayer. (2.) *They sang praises to God.* They praised God; for we must *in every thing give thanks.* We never want matter for praise, if we do not want a heart. And what should put the heart of a child of God out of tune for this duty if a dungeon and a pair of stocks will not do it? They praised God that they were counted worthy to suffer shame for his name, and that they were so wonderfully supported and borne up under their sufferings, and felt divine consolations so sweet, so strong, in their souls. Nay, *they not only praised God, but they sang praises to him,* in some psalm, or hymn, or spiritual song, either one of David's, or some modern composition, or one of their own, as *the Spirit gave them utterance.* As our rule is that the afflicted should pray, and therefore, being in affliction, they prayed; so our rule is that the merry should sing psalms (James 5:13), and therefore, being merry in their affliction, *merry after a godly sort, they sang psalms.* This proves that the singing of psalms is a gospel ordinance, and ought to be used by all good Christians; and that it is instituted, not only for the expressing of their joys in a day of triumph, but for the balancing and relieving of their sorrows in a day of trouble. It was at midnight that they sang psalms, according to the example of the sweet psalmist of Israel (Ps. 119:62): *At midnight will I rise to give thanks unto thee.* (3.) Notice is here taken of the circumstance that *the prisoners heard them.* If the prisoners did not hear them pray, yet *they heard them sing praises.* [1.] It intimates how hearty they were in singing praises to God; they sang so loud that, though they were in the dungeon, they were heard all the prison over; nay, so loud that they woke the prisoners: for we may suppose, being at midnight, they were all asleep. We should sing psalms with all our heart. The saints are called upon to sing aloud upon their beds, Ps. 149:5. But gospel grace carries the matter further, and gives us an example of those that sang aloud in the prison, in the stocks. [2.] Though they knew the prisoners would hear them, yet they sang aloud, as those that were not ashamed of their Master, nor of his service. Shall those that would sing psalms in their families plead, in excuse for their omission of the duty, that they are afraid their neighbours should hear them, when those that sing profane songs roar them our, and care not who hears them? [3.] The prisoners were made to hear the prison-songs of Paul and Silas, that they might be prepared for the miraculous favour shown to them all for the sake of Paul and Silas, when *the prison-doors were thrown open.* By this extraordinary comfort with which they were filled it was published that he whom they preached was *the consolation of Israel.* Let the prisoners that mean to oppose him hear and tremble before him; let those that are faithful to him hear and triumph, and take of the comfort that is spoken to the prisoners of hope, Zec. 9:12.

2. God heartened them wonderfully by his signal appearances for them, *v.* 26. (1.) There was immediately a great earthquake; how far it extended we are not told, but it was such a violent shock in this place *that the very foundations of the prison were shaken.* While the prisoners were hearkening to the midnight devotions of Paul and Silas, and perhaps laughing at them and making a jest of them, this earthquake would strike a terror upon them, and convince them that those men were the favourites of Heaven, and such as God owned. We had *the house of prayer shaken,* in answer to prayer, and as a token of God's acceptance of it, *ch.* 4:31. Here *the prison shaken.* The Lord was in these earthquakes, to show his resentment of the indignities done to his servants, to testify to those whose confidence is in the earth the weakness and instability of that which they confide, and to teach people *that, though the earth be moved, yet they need not fear.* (2.) The prison-doors were thrown open, and the prisoners' fetters were knocked off: *Every man's bands were loosed.* Perhaps the prisoners, when they heard Paul and Silas pray and sing psalms, admired them, and spoke honourably of them, and said what the damsel had said of them, Surely, *these men are the servants of the living God.* To recompense them for, and confirm them in, their good opinion of them, they share in the miracle, and have *their bands loosed;* as afterwards God gave to Paul all *those that were in the ship with him* (*ch.* 27:24), so now he gave him all those that were in the prison with him. God hereby signified to these prisoners, as Grotius observes, that the apostles, in preaching the

gospel, were public blessings to mankind, as they *proclaimed liberty to the captives, and the opening of the prison-doors to those that were bound,* Isa. 61:1. *Et per eos solvi animorum vincula — and as by them the bonds of souls were unloosed.*

II. The persecutors designed to stop the progress of the gospel, that no more might embrace it; thus they hoped to ruin the meeting by the river side, that no more hearts should be opened there; but here we find converts made in the prison, that house turned into a meeting, the trophies of the gospel's victories erected there, and the jailer, their own servant, become a servant of Christ. It is probable that some of the prisoners, if not all, were converted; surely the miracle wrought on their bodies, in loosing their bands, was wrought on their souls too. See Job 36:8–10; Ps. 107:14, 15. But it is only the conversion of the jailer that is recorded.

1. He is afraid he shall lose his life, and Paul makes him easy as to this care, *v.* 27, 28. (1.) He *awoke out of his sleep.* It is probable that the shock of the earthquake woke him, and the opening of the prison-doors, and the prisoners' expressions of joy and amazement, when in the dark they found their bands loosed, and called to tell one another what they felt: this was enough to awaken the jailer, whose place required that he should not be hard to wake. This waking him out of his sleep signified the awakening of his conscience out of its spiritual slumber. The call of the gospel is, *Awake, thou that sleepest* (Eph. 5:14), like that of Jonah, 1:6. (2.) He saw the prison-doors open, and supposed, as well he might, that the prisoners had fled; and then what would become of him? He knew the Roman law in that case, and it was executed not long ago upon the keepers out of whose hands Peter escaped, *ch.* 12:19. It was according to that of the prophet, 1 Ki. 20:39, 42, *Keep this man; if he be missing, thy life shall go for his life.* The Roman lawyers after this, in their readings upon the law, *De custodia reorum — The custody of criminals* (which appoints that the keeper should undergo the same punishment that should have been inflicted on the prisoner if he let him escape), take care to except an escape by miracle. (3.) In his fright *he drew his sword,* and was going *to kill himself,* to prevent a more terrible death, and expected one, a pompous ignominious death, which he knew he was liable to for letting his prisoners escape and not looking better to them; and the extraordinarily strict charge which the magistrates gave him concerning Paul and Silas made him conclude they would be very severe upon him if they were gone. The philosophers generally allowed self-murder. Seneca prescribes it as the last remedy which those that are in distress may have recourse to. The Stoics, notwithstanding their pretended conquest of the passions, yielded thus far to them. And the Epicureans, who indulged the pleasures of sense, to avoid its pains chose rather to put an end to it. This jailer thought there was no harm in anticipating his own death; but Christianity proves itself to be of God by this, that it keeps us to the law of our creation — revives, enforces, and establishes it, obliges us to be just to our own lives, and teaches us cheerfully to resign them to our graces, but courageously to hold them out against our corruptions. (4.) Paul stopped him from his proceeding against himself (*v.* 28): He *cried with a loud voice,* not only to make him hear, but to make him heed, *saying, Do not practise any evil to thyself; Do thyself no harm.* All the cautions of the word of God against sin, and all appearances of it and approaches to it, have this tendency, "*Do thyself no harm.* Man, woman, do not wrong thyself, nor ruin thyself; hurt not thyself, and then none else can hurt thee; do not sin, for nothing else can hurt thee." Even as to the body, we are cautioned against those sins which do harm to it, and are taught to *hate our own flesh, but to nourish and cherish it.* The jailer needs not fear being called to an account for the escape of his prisoners, for *they are all here.* It was strange that some of them did not slip away, when the prison-doors were opened, and they were loosed from their bands; but their amazement held them fast, and, being sensible it was by the prayers of Paul and Silas that they were loosed, they would not stir unless they stirred; and God showed his power in binding their spirits, as much as in loosing their feet.

2. He is afraid he shall lose his soul, and Paul makes him easy as to this care too. One concern leads him to another, and a much greater; and, being hindered from hastening himself out of this world, he begins to think, if he had pursued his intention, whither death would have brought him, and what would have become of him on the other side death — a very proper thought for such as have been snatched as a brand out of the fire, when there was but a step between them and death. Perhaps the heinousness of the sin he was running into helped to alarm him.

(1.) Whatever was the cause, he was put into a great consternation. The Spirit of God, that was sent to convince, in order to his being a Comforter, struck a terror upon him, and startled him. Whether he took care to shut the prison-doors again we are not told. Perhaps he forgot this as the woman of Samaria, when Christ had impressed convictions on her conscience, *left her water-pot* and forgot her errand to the well; for *he called for a light* with all speed, and *sprang in* to the inner prison, *and came trembling to Paul and Silas.* Those that have sin set in order before them, and are made to know their abominations, cannot but tremble at the apprehension of their misery and danger. This jailer, when he was thus made to tremble, could not apply to a more proper person than to Paul, for it had once been his own case; he had been once a persecutor of good men, as this jailer was — had cast them into prison, as he kept them — and when, like him, he was made sensible of it, *he trembled, and was astonished;* and therefore he was able to speak the more feelingly to the jailer.

(2.) In this consternation, he applied to Paul and Silas for relief. Observe, [1.] How reverent and respectful his address to them is: *He called for a light,* because they were in the dark, and that they might see what a fright he was in; *he fell down before them,* as one amazed at the badness of his own condition, and ready to sink under the load of his terror because of it; he fell down before them, as one that had upon his spirit an awe of them, and of the image of God upon them, and of their commission from God. It is probable that he had heard what the damsel said of them, that they were *the servants of the living God, who showed to them the way of salvation,* and as such he thus expressed his veneration for them. He fell down before them, to beg their pardon, as a penitent, for the indignities he had done them, and to beg their advice, as a supplicant, what he should do. He gave them a title of respect, *Sirs, kyrioi — lords, masters;* just now it was, *Rogues* and *villains,* and he was their master; but now, *Sirs, lords,* and they are his masters. Converting grace changes people's language of and to good people and good ministers; and, to such as are thoroughly convinced of sin, the very feet of those that bring tidings of Christ are beautiful; yea, though they are disgracefully fastened in the stocks. [2.] How serious his enquiry is: *What must I do to be saved? First,* His salvation is now his great concern, and lies nearest his heart, which before was the furthest thing from his thoughts. Not, What shall I do to be preferred, to be rich and great in the world? but, *What shall I do to be saved? Secondly,* He does not enquire concerning others, what they must do; but concerning himself, "What must I do?" It is his own precious soul that he is in care about: "Let others do as they please; tell me what I must do, what course I must take." *Thirdly,* He is convinced that something must be done, and done by him too, in order to his salvation: that it is not a thing of course, a thing that will do itself, but a thing about which we must strive, wrestle, and take pains. He asks not, "What may be done for me?" but, "What shall I do, that, being *now in fear and trembling,* I may *work out my salvation?"* as Paul speaks in his epistle to the church at Philippi, of which this jailer was, perhaps with respect to his trembling enquiry here, intimating that he must not only ask after salvation (as he had done), but *work out his salvation with* a holy *trembling,* Phil. 2:12. *Fourthly,* He is willing to do any thing: "Tell me what I must do, and I am here ready to do it. Sirs, put me into any way, if it be but the right way, and a sure way; though narrow, and thorny, and uphill, yet I will walk in it." Note, Those who are thoroughly convinced of sin, and truly concerned about their salvation, will surrender at discretion to Jesus Christ, will give him a blank to write what he pleases, will be glad to have Christ upon his own terms, Christ upon any terms. *Fifthly,* He is inquisitive what he should do, is desirous to know what he should do, and asks those that were likely to tell him. *If you will enquire, enquire ye,* Isa. 21:12. Those that set their faces Zionward must ask the way thither, Jer. 50:5. We cannot know it of ourselves, but God has made it known to us by his word, has appointed his ministers to assist us in consulting the scriptures, and has promised *to give his Holy Spirit to those that ask him,* to be their guide in the way of salvation. *Sixthly,* He *brought them out,* to put this question to them, that their answer might not be by duress or compulsion, but that they might prescribe to him, though he was their keeper, with the same liberty as they did to others. He brings them out of the dungeon, in hopes they will bring him out of a much worse.

(3.) They very readily directed him what he must do, *v.* 31. They were always ready to answer such enquiries; though they are cold, and sore, and sleepy, they do not adjourn this cause to a more convenient time and place, do not bod him come to them the next sabbath at their meeting-place by the river side, and they will tell him, but they strike while the iron is hot, take him now when he is in a good mind, lest the conviction should wear off. Now that God begins to work, it is time for them to set in as *workers together with God.* They do not upbraid him with his rude and ill carriage towards them, and his going beyond his warrant; all this is forgiven and forgotten, and they are as glad to show him the way to heaven as the best friend they have. They did not triumph over him, though he trembled; they gave him the same directions they did to others, *Believe in the Lord Jesus Christ.* One would think they should have said, "Repent of thy abusing us, in the first place." No, that is overlooked and easily passed by, if he will but believe in Christ. This is an example to ministers to encourage penitents, to meet those that are coming to Christ and take them by the hand, not to be hard upon any for unkindness done to them, but to seek Christ's honour more than their own. Here is the sum of the whole gospel, the covenant of grace in a few words: *Believe in the Lord Jesus Christ, and thou shalt be saved, and thy house.* Here is, [1.] The happiness promised: "*Thou shalt be saved;* not only rescued from eternal ruin, but brought to eternal life and blessedness. Though thou art a *poor man,* an under-jailer or turnkey, mean and of low condition in the world, yet this shall be no bar to thy salvation. Though a great sinner, though a persecutor, yet thy heinous transgressions shall be all forgiven through the merits of Christ; and thy hard embittered heart shall be softened and sweetened by the grace of Christ, and thus thou shalt neither die for thy crime nor die of thy disease." [2.] The condition required: *Believe in the Lord Jesus Christ.* We must admit the record that God hath given in his gospel concerning his Son, and assent to it as faithful, and well *worthy of all acceptation.* We must approve the method God has taken of reconciling the world to himself by a Mediator; and accept of Christ as he is offered to us, and give up ourselves to be ruled and taught and saved by him. This is the only way and a sure way to salvation. No other way of salvation than by Christ, and no other way of our being saved by Christ than by believing in him; and no danger of coming short if we take this way, for it is the way that God has appointed, and he is faithful that has promised. It is the gospel that is to be preached to every creature, *He that believes shall be saved.* [3.] The extension of this to his family: *Thou shalt be saved, and thy house;* that is, "God will be in Christ a God to thee and to thy seed, as he was to Abraham. Believe, and salvation shall *come to thy house,* as Lu. 19:9. Those of thy house that are infants shall be admitted into the visible church with thee, and thereby put into a fair way for salvation; those that are grown up shall have the means of salvation brought to them, and, be they ever so many, let them believe in Jesus Christ and they shall be saved; they are all welcome to Christ upon the same terms."

(4.) They proceeded to instruct him and his family in the doctrine of Christ (*v.* 32): They *spoke unto him the word of the Lord.* He was, for aught that appears, an utter stranger to Christ, and therefore it is requisite he should be told who this Jesus is, that he may believe in him, Jn. 9:36. And, the substance of the matter lying in a little compass, they soon told him enough to make his being baptized a reasonable service. Christ's ministers should have the word of the Lord so ready to them, and so richly dwelling in them, as to be able to give instructions offhand to any that desire to hear and receive them, for their direction in the way of salvation. They spoke the word not only to him, but to *all that were in his house.* Masters of families should take care that all under their charge partake of the means of knowledge and grace, and that the word of the Lord be spoken to them; for the souls of the poorest servants are as precious as those of their masters, and are bought with the same price.

(5.) The jailer and his family were immediately baptized, and thereby took upon them the profession of Christianity, submitted to its laws, and were admitted to its privileges, upon their declaring solemnly, as the eunuch did, that they believed that *Jesus Christ is the Son of God:* He was *baptized, he and all his, straightway.* Neither he nor any of his family desired time to consider whether they should come into baptismal bonds or no; nor did Paul and Silas desire time to try their sincerity and to consider whether they should baptize them or no. But the Spirit of grace worked such a strong faith in them, all on a sudden, as superseded further debate; and Paul and Silas knew by the Spirit that it was a work of God that was wrought in them: so that there was no occasion for demur. This therefore will not justify such precipitation in ordinary cases.

(6.) The jailer was hereupon very respectful to Paul and Silas, as one that knew not how to make amends for the injury he had done to them, much less for the kindness he had received from them: He *took them the same hour of the night,* would not let them lie a minute longer in the inner prison; but, [1.] He *washed their stripes,* to cool them, and abate the smart of them; to clean them from the blood which the stripes had fetched. It is probable that he bathed them with some healing liquor, as the good Samaritan helped the wounded man by *pouring in oil and wine.* [2.] He *brought them into his house,* bade them welcome to the best room he had, and prepared his best bed for them. Now nothing was thought good enough for them, as before nothing bad enough. [3.] He *set meat before them,* such as his house would afford, and they were welcome to it, by which he expressed the welcome which his soul gave to the gospel. They had spoken to him the word of the Lord, had broken the bread of life to him and his family; and he, having reaped so plentifully of their spiritual things, thought it was but reasonable that they should reap of his carnal things, 1 Co. 9:11. What have we houses and tables for but as we have opportunity to serve God and his people with them?

(7.) The voice of rejoicing with that of salvation was heard in the jailer's house; never was such a truly merry night kept there before: *He rejoiced, believing in God, with all his house.* There was none in his house that refused to be baptized, and so made a jar in the harmony; but they were unanimous in embracing the gospel, which added much to the joy. Or it may be read, *He, believing in God, rejoiced all the house over; panoiki* — he went to every apartment, expressing his joy. Observe, [1.] His believing in Christ is called believing *in God,* which intimates that Christ is God, and that the design of the gospel is so far from being to draw us from God (saying, *Go serve other gods,* Deu. 13:2) that it has a direct tendency to bring us to God. [2.] His faith produced joy. Those that by faith have given up themselves to God in Christ as theirs have a great deal of reason to rejoice. The eunuch, when he was converted,, *went on his way rejoicing;* and here the jailer rejoiced. The conversion of the nations is spoken of in the Old Testament as their rejoicing, Ps. 67:4; 96:11. For, *believing, we rejoice with joy unspeakable, and full of glory.* Believing in Christ is rejoicing in Christ. [3.] He signified his joy to all about him. Out of the abundance of the joy in his heart, his mouth spoke to the glory of God, and their encouragement who believed in God too. Those who have themselves tasted the comforts of religion should do what they can to bring others to the taste of them. One cheerful Christian should make many.

Verses 35–40

In these verses we have,

I. Orders sent for the discharge of Paul and Silas out of prison *v.* 35, 36. 1. The magistrates that had so basely abused them the day before gave the orders; and their doing it so early, *as soon as it was day,* intimates that either they were sensible the terrific earthquake they felt at midnight was intended to plead the cause of their prisoners, or their consciences had smitten them for what they had done and made them very uneasy. While the persecuted were singing in the stocks, the persecutors were full of tossings to and fro upon their beds, through anguish of mind, complaining more of the lashes of their consciences than the prisoners did of the lashes on their backs, and more in haste to give them a discharge than they were to petition for one. Now God caused his servants to be *pitied of those that had carried them captives,* Ps. 106:46. The magistrates sent *sergeants, rabdouchous — those that had the rods,* the vergers, the tipstaves, the beadles, those that had been employed in beating them, that they might go and ask them forgiveness. The order was, *Let those men go.* It is probable that they designed further mischief to them, but God turned their hearts, and, as he had made their wrath hitherto to praise him, so the remainder thereof he did restrain, Ps. 76:10. 2. The jailer brought them the news (*v.* 36): *The magistrates have sent to let you go.* Some think the jailer had betimes transmitted an account to the magistrates of what had passed in his house that night, and so had obtained this order for the discharge of his prisoners: *Now therefore depart.* Not that he was desirous to part with them as his guests, but as his prisoners; they shall still be welcome to his house, but he is glad they are at liberty from his stocks. God could by his grace as easily have converted the magistrates as the jailer, and have brought them to faith and baptism; but God hath *chosen the poor of this world,* James 2:5.

II. Paul's insisting upon the breach of privilege which the magistrates had been guilty of, *v.* 37. Paul said to the sergeants, *"They have beaten us openly, uncondemned, being Romans, and have cast us into prison* against all law and justice, and *now do they thrust us out privily,* and think to make us amends with this for the injury done us? *Nay, verily; but let them come themselves and fetch us our,* and own that they have done us wrong." It is probable that the magistrates had some intimation that they were Romans, and were made sensible that their fury had carried them further than the law would bear them out; and that this was the reason why they gave orders for their discharge. Now observe,

1. Paul did not plead this before he was beaten, though it is probable that it might have prevented it, lest he should seem to be afraid of suffering for the truth which he had preached. Tully, in one of his orations, against Verres, tells of one Ganius, who was ordered by Verres to be beaten in Sicily, that all the while he was under the lash he cried out nothing but *Civis Romanus sum — I am a citizen of Rome;* Paul did not do so; he had nobler things than this to comfort himself with in his affliction.

2. He did plead it afterwards, to put an honour upon his sufferings and upon the cause he suffered for, to let the world know that the preachers of the gospel were not such despicable men as they were commonly looked upon to be, and that they merited better treatment. He did it likewise to mollify the magistrates towards the Christians at Philippi, and to gain better treatment for them, and beget in the people a better opinion of the Christian religion, when they saw that Paul had a fair advantage against their magistrates, might have brought his action against them and had them called to an account for what they had done, and yet did not take the advantage, which was very much to the honour of that worthy name by which he was called. Now here,

(1.) Paul lets them know how many ways they had run themselves into a premunire, and that he had law enough to know it. [1.] They had *beaten* those that were Romans; some think that Silas was a Roman citizen as well as Paul; others that this does not necessarily follow. Paul was a citizen, and Silas was his companion. Now both the *lex Procia* and the *lex Sempronia* did expressly forbid *liberum corpus Romani civis, virgis aut aliis verberibus caedi — the free body of a Roman citizen to be beaten with rods or otherwise.* Roman historians give instances of cities that had their charters taken from them for indignities done to Roman citizens; we shall afterwards find Paul making use of this plea, *ch.* 22:25, 26. To tell them they had beaten those who were the messengers of Christ and the favourites of Heaven would have had no influence upon them; but to tell them they have abused Roman citizens will put them into a fright: so common is it for people to be more afraid of Caesar's wrath than of Christ's. He that affronts a Roman, a gentleman, a nobleman, though ignorantly, and through mistake, thinks himself concerned to cry *Peccavi — I have done wrong,* and make his submission; but he that persecutes a Christian because he belongs to Christ stands to it, and thinks he may do it securely, though God hath said, *He that toucheth them toucheth the apple of my eye,* and Christ has warned us of the danger of *offending his little ones.* [2.] They had beaten them *uncondemned; indicta causa — without a fair hearing,* had not calmly examined what was said against them, much less enquired what they had to say for themselves. It is a universal rule of justice, *Causâ cognitâ possunt multi absolvi, incognitâ nemo condemnari potest — Many may be acquitted in consequence of having had a hearing, while without a hearing no one can be condemned.* Christ's servants would not have been abused as they have been if they and their cause might but have had an impartial trial. [3.] It was an aggravation of this that they had done it openly, which, as it was so much the greater disgrace to the sufferers, so it was the bolder defiance to justice and the law. [4.] They had *cast them into prison,* without showing any cause of their commitment, and in an arbitrary manner, by a verbal order. [5.] They now *thrust them out privily;* they had not indeed the impudence to stand by what they had done, but yet had not the honesty to own themselves in a fault.

(2.) He insists upon it that they should make them an acknowledgment of their error, and give them a public discharge, to make it the more honourable, as they had done them a public disgrace, which made that the more disgraceful: *"Let them come themselves, and fetch us out,* and give a testimony to our innocency, and that we have done nothing worthy of stripes or of bonds." It was not a point of honour that Paul stood thus stiffly upon, but a point of justice, and not to himself so much as to his cause: "Let them come and stop the clamours of the people, by confessing that we are not the troublers of the city."

III. The magistrates' submission, and the reversing of the judgment given against Paul and Silas, *v.* 38, 39. 1. The magistrates were frightened when they were told (though it may be they knew it before) that Paul was a Roman. They feared when they heard it, lest some of his friends should inform the government of what they had done, and they should fare the worse for it. The proceedings of persecutors have often been illegal, even by the law of nations, and often inhuman, against the law of nature, but always sinful, and against God's law. 2. They *came and besought them* not to take advantage of the law against them, but to overlook the illegality of what they had done and say no more of it: they *brought them out* of the prison, owning that they were wrongfully put into it, and desired them that they would peaceably and quietly *depart out of the city.* Thus Pharaoh and his servants, who had set God and Moses at defiance, came to Moses, and *bowed down themselves to him, saying, Get thee out,* Ex. 11:8. God can make the enemies of his people ashamed of their envy and enmity to them, Isa. 26:11. Jerusalem is sometimes made a burdensome stone to those that heave at it, which they would gladly get clear of, Zec. 12:3. Yet, if the repentance of these magistrates had been sincere, they would not have desired them to depart out of their city (as the Gadarenes desired to be rid of Christ), but would have courted their stay, and begged of them to continue in their city, to show them the way of salvation. But many are convinced that Christianity is not to be persecuted who yet are not convinced that it ought to be embraced, or at least are not persuaded to embrace it. They are compelled to do honour to Christ and his servants, *to worship before their feet, and to know that he has loved them* (Rev. 3:9), and yet do not go so far as to have benefit by Christ, or to come in for a share in his love.

IV. The departure of Paul and Silas from Philippi, *v.* 40. They went out of the prison when they were legally discharged, and not till then, though they were illegally committed, and then, 1. They took leave of their friends: they *went to the house of Lydia,* where probably the disciples had met to pray for them, and there they *saw the brethren,* or visited them at their respective habitations (which was soon done, they were so few); and they *comforted them,* by telling them (saith an ancient Greek commentary) what God had done for them, and how he had owned them in the prison. They encouraged them to keep close to Christ, and hold fast the profession of their faith, whatever difficulties they might meet with, assuring them that all would then end well, everlastingly well. Young converts should have a great deal said to them to comfort them, for *the joy of the Lord will be* very much *their strength.* 2. They quitted the town: *They departed.* I wonder they should do so; for, now that they had had such an honourable discharge from their imprisonment, surely they might have gone on at least for some time in their work without danger; but I suppose they went away upon that principle of their Master's (Mk. 1:38). *Let us go into the next towns, that I may preach there also, for therefore came I forth.* Paul and Silas had an extraordinary call to Philippi; and yet, when they have come thither, they see little of the fruit of their labours, and are soon driven thence. Yet they did not come in vain. Though the beginnings here were *small, the latter end greatly increased;* now they laid the foundation of a church at Philippi, which became very eminent, had its bishops and deacons, and people that were more generous to Paul than any other church, as appears by his epistle to the Philippians, *ch.* 1:1; 4:25. Let not ministers be discouraged, though they see not the fruit of their labours presently; the seed sown seems to be lost under the clods, but it shall come up again in a plentiful harvest in due time.

CHAPTER 17

We have here a further account of the travels of Paul, and his services and sufferings for Christ. He was not like a candle upon a table, that gives light only to one room, but like the sun that goes its circuit to give light to many. He was called into Macedonia, a large kingdom, *ch.* 16:9. He began with Philippi, because it was the first city he came to; but he must not confine himself to this. We have him here, I. Preaching and persecuted at Thessalonica, another city of Macedonia (*v.* 1–9). II. Preaching at Berea, where he met with an encouraging auditory, but was driven thence also by persecution (*v.* 10–15). III. Disputing at Athens, the famous university of Greece (*v.* 16–21), and the account he gave of natural religion, for the conviction of those that were addicted to polytheism and idolatry, and to lead them to the Christian religion (*v.* 22–31), together with the success of this sermon (*v.* 32–34).

Verses 1–9

Paul's two epistles to the Thessalonians, the first two he wrote by inspiration, give such a shining character of that church, that we cannot but be glad here in the history to meet with an account of the first founding of the church there.

I. Here is Paul's coming to Thessalonica, which was the chief city of this country, called at this day *Salonech,* in the Turkish dominions. Observe, 1. Paul went on with his work, notwithstanding the ill usage he had met with at Philippi; he did not fail, nor was discouraged. He takes notice of this in his first epistle to the church here (1 Th. 2:2): *After we were shamefully treated at Philippi, yet we were bold in our God to speak unto you the gospel of God.* The opposition and persecution that he met with made him the more resolute. Note of these things moved him; he could never have held out, and held on, as he did, if he had not been animated by a spirit of power from on high. 2. He did but *pass through Amphipolis and Apollonia,* the former a city near Philippi, the latter near Thessalonica; doubtless he was under divine direction, and was told by the Spirit (who, as the wind, bloweth where he listeth) what places he should pass through, and what he should rest in. Apollonia was a city of Illyricum, which, some think, illustrates that of Paul, that he had preached the gospel *from Jerusalem, and round about unto Illyricum* (Rom. 15:19), that is, to the borders of Illyricum where he now was; and we may suppose though he is said only to *pass through* these cities, yet that he staid so long in them as to publish the gospel there, and to prepare the way for the entrance of other ministers among them, whom he would afterwards send.

II. His preaching to the Jews first, in their synagogue at Thessalonica. He found a synagogue of the Jews there (*v.* 1), which intimates that one reason why he passed through those other cities mentioned, and did not continue long in them, was because there were no synagogues in them. But, finding one in Thessalonica, by it he made his entry. 1. It was always his manner to begin with the Jews, to make them the first offer of the gospel, and not to turn to the Gentiles till they had refused it, that their mouths might be stopped from clamouring against him because he preached to the Gentiles; for if they received the gospel they would cheerfully embrace the new converts; if they refused it, they might thank themselves if the apostles carried it to those that would bid it welcome. That command of beginning at Jerusalem was justly construed as a direction, wherever they came, to begin with the Jews. 2. He met them in their synagogue on the sabbath day, in their place and at their time of meeting, and thus he would pay respect to both. Sabbaths and solemn assemblies are always very precious to those to whom Christ is precious, Ps. 84:10. It is good being in the house of the Lord on his day. This was Christ's manner, and Paul's manner, and has been the manner of all the saints, the *good old way* which they have walked in. 3. He *reasoned with them out of the scriptures.* They agreed with him to receive the scriptures of the Old Testament: so far they were of a mind. But they received the scripture, and therefore thought they had reason to reject Christ; Paul received the scripture, and therefore saw great reason to embrace Christ. It was therefore requisite, in order to their conviction, that he should, by reasoning with them, the Spirit setting with him, convince them that his inferences from the scripture were right and theirs were wrong. Note, The preaching of the gospel should be both scriptural preaching and rational; such Paul's was, for he *reasoned out of the scriptures:* we must take the scriptures for our foundation, our oracle, and touchstone, and then reason out of them and upon them, and against those who,

though they pretend zeal for the scriptures, as the Jews did, yet wrest them to their own destruction. Reason must not be set up in competition with the scripture, but it must be made use of in explaining and applying the scripture. 4. He continued to do this *three sabbath days* successively. If he could not convince them the first sabbath, he would try the second and the third; for *precept must be upon precept, and line upon line.* God waits for sinners' conversion, and so must his ministers; all the labourers come not into the vineyard at the first hour, nor at the first call, nor are wrought upon so suddenly as the jailer. 5. The drift and scope of his preaching and arguing was to prove that *Jesus is the Christ;* this was that which he opened and alleged, *v.* 3. He first explained his thesis, and opened the terms, and then alleged it, and laid it down, as that which he would abide by, and which he summoned them in God's name to subscribe to. Paul had an admirable method of discourse; and showed he was himself both well apprized of the doctrine he preached and thoroughly understood it, and that he was fully assured of the truth of it, and therefore he opened it like one that believed it. He showed them, (1.) That it was necessary the Messiah should *suffer, and die, and rise again,* that the Old-Testament prophecies concerning the Messiah made it necessary he should. The great objection which the Jews made against Jesus being the Messiah was his ignominious death and sufferings. The *cross of Christ was to the Jews a stumbling-block,* because it did by no means agree with the idea they had framed of the Messiah; but Paul here alleges and makes it out undeniably, not only that it was possible he might be the Messiah, though he suffered, but that, being the Messiah, it was necessary he should suffer. He could not be made perfect but by sufferings; for, if he had not died, he could not have risen again from the dead. This was what Christ himself insisted upon (Lu. 24:26): *Ought not Christ to have suffered these things, and to enter into his glory?* And again (*v.* 46): *Thus it is written, and* therefore *thus it behoved Christ to suffer, and to rise from the dead.* He must needs have suffered for us, because he could not otherwise purchase redemption for us; and he must needs have risen again because he could not otherwise apply the redemption to us. (2.) That Jesus is the Messiah: *"This Jesus whom I preach unto you, and call upon you to believe in, is Christ,* is the Christ, is the anointed of the Lord, is he that should come, and you are to look for no other; for God has both by his word and by his works (the two ways of his speaking to the children of men), by the scriptures and by miracles, and the gift of the Spirit to make both effectual, borne witness to him." Note, [1.] Gospel ministers should preach Jesus; he must be their principal subject; their business is to bring people acquainted with him. [2.] That which we are to preach concerning Jesus is that he is Christ; and therefore we may hope to be saved by him and are bound to be ruled by him.

III. The success of his preaching there, *v.* 4. 1. Some of the Jews believed, notwithstanding their rooted prejudices against Christ and his gospel, and they *consorted with Paul and Silas:* they not only associated with them as friends and companions, but they gave up themselves to their direction, as their spiritual guides; they put themselves into their possession as an inheritance into the possession of the right owner, so the word signifies; they first *gave themselves to the Lord,* and then to them *by the will of God,* 2 Co. 8:5. They adhered to Paul and Silas, and attended them wherever they went. Note, Those that believe in Jesus Christ come into communion with his faithful ministers, and associate with them. 2. Many more of the devout Greeks, and of the chief women, embraced the gospel. These were proselytes of the gate, the *godly among the Gentiles* (so the Jews called them), such as, though they did not submit to the law of Moses, yet renounced idolatry and immorality, worshipped the true God only, and did not man any wrong. These were *hoi sebomenoi Hellēnes — the worshipping Gentiles;* as in America they call those of the natives that are converted to the faith of Christ the *praying* Indians. These were admitted to join with the Jews in their synagogue-worship. Of these *a great multitude believed,* more of them than of the thorough-paced Jews, who were wedded to the ceremonial law. And not a few of the chief women of the city, that were devout and had a sense of religion, embraced Christianity. Particular notice is taken of this, for an example to the ladies, the chief women, and an encouragement to them to employ themselves in the exercises of devotion and to submit themselves to the commanding power of Christ's holy religion, in all the instances

of it; for this intimates how acceptable it will be to God, what an honour to Christ, and what great influence it may have upon many, besides the advantages of it to their own souls. No mention is here made of their preaching the gospel to the Gentile idolaters at Thessalonica, and yet it is certain that they did, and that great numbers were converted; nay, it should seem that of the Gentile converts that church was chiefly composed, though notice is not taken of them here; for Paul writes to the Christians there as having *turned to God from idols* (1 Th. 1:9), and that at the first entering in of the apostles among them.

IV. The trouble that was given to Paul and Silas at Thessalonica. Wherever they preached, they were sure to be persecuted; bonds and afflictions awaited them in every city. Observe,

1. Who were the authors of their trouble: the *Jews who believed not, who were moved with envy, v.* 5. The Jews were in all places the most inveterate enemies to the Christians, especially to those Jews that turned Christians, against whom they had a particular spleen, as deserters. Now see what that division was which Christ came to send upon earth; some of the Jews believed the gospel and pitied and prayed for those that did not; while those that did not envied and hated those that did. St. Paul in his epistle to this church takes notice of the rage and enmity of the Jews against the preachers of the gospel, as their measure-filling sin. 1 Th. 2:15, 16.

2. Who were the instruments of the trouble: the Jews made use of *certain lewd persons of the baser sort,* whom they picked up and got together, and who must undertake to give the sense of the city against the apostles. All wise and sober people looked upon them with respect, and valued them, and none would appear against them but such as were the scum of the city, a company of vile men, that were given to all manner of wickedness. Tertullian pleads this with those that opposed Christianity, that the enemies of it were generally the worst of men: *Tales semper nobis insecutores, injusti, impii, turpes, quos, et ipsi damnare consuestis — Our persecutors are invariably unjust, impious, infamous, whom you yourselves have been accustomed to condemn.* — Apologia, cap. 5. It is the honour of religion that those who hate it are generally the *lewd fellows of the baser sort,* that are lost to all sense of justice and virtue.

3. In what method they proceeded against them. (1.) They *set the city in an uproar,* made a noise to put people in a fright, and then every body ran to see what the matter was; they began a riot, and then the mob was up presently. See who are the troublers of Israel — not the faithful preachers of the gospel, but the enemies of it. See how the devil carries on his designs; he sets cities in an uproar, sets souls in an uproar, and then fishes in troubled waters. (2.) They *assaulted the house of Jason,* where the apostles lodged, with a design *to bring them out to the people,* whom they had incensed and enraged against them, and by whom they hoped to see them pulled to pieces. The proceedings here were altogether illegal; of Jason's house must be searched, it ought to be done by the proper officers, and not without a warrant: "A man's house," the law says, "is his castle," and for them in a tumultuous manner to assault a man's house, to put him and his family in fear, was but to show to what outrages men are carried by a spirit of persecution. If men have offended, magistrates are appointed to enquire into the offence, and to judge of it; but to make the rabble judges and executioners too (as these Jews designed to do) was to make truth fall in the street, to set servants on horseback, and leave princes to walk as servants on the earth — to depose equity, and enthrone fury. (3.) When they could not get the apostles into their hands (whom they would have punished as vagabonds, and incensed the people against as strangers that came to spy out the land, and devour its strength, and eat the bread out of their mouths), then they fall upon an honest citizen of their own, who entertained the apostles in his house, his name *Jason,* a converted Jew, and drew him out with some others of the brethren to the rulers of the city. The apostles were advised to withdraw, for they were more obnoxious, *Currenti cede furori — Retire before the torrent.* But their friends were willing to expose themselves, being better able to weather this storm. *For a good man,* for such good men as the apostles were, *some would even dare to die.* (4.) They accused them to the rulers, and represented them a dangerous persons, not fit to be tolerated; the crime charged upon Jason is receiving and harbouring the apostles (*v.* 7), countenancing them and promoting their interest. And what was the

apostles' crime, that it should be no less than misprision of treason to give them lodging? Two very black characters are here given them, enough to make them odious to the people and obnoxious to the magistrates, if they had been just: — [1.] That they were enemies to the public peace, and threw every thing into disorder wherever they came: *Those that have turned the world upside down are come hither also.* In one sense it is true that wherever the gospel comes in its power to any place, to any soul, it works such a change there, gives such a wide change to the stream, so directly contrary to what it was, that it may be said to turn the world upside down in that place, in that soul. The love of the world is rooted out of the heart, and the way of the world contradicted in the life; so that the world turned upside down there. But in the sense in which they meant it, it is utterly false; they would have it thought that the preachers of the gospel were incendiaries and mischief makers wherever they came, that they sowed discord among relations, set neighbours together by the ears, obstructed commerce, and inverted all order and regularity. Because they persuaded people to turn from vice to virtue, from idols to the living and true God, from malice and envy to love and peace, they are charged with turning the world upside down, when it was only the kingdom of the devil in the world that they thus overturned. Their enemies *set the city in an uproar,* and then laid the blame upon them; as Nero set Rome on fire, and then charged it upon the Christians. If Christ's faithful ministers, even those that are most quiet in the land, be thus invidiously misrepresented and miscalled, let them not think it strange nor be exasperated by it; we are not better than Paul and Silas, who were thus abused. The accusers cry out, "They are *come hither also;* they have been doing all the mischief they could in other places, and now they have brought the infection hither; it is therefore time for us to bestir ourselves and make head against them." [2.] That they were enemies to the established government, and disaffected to that, and their principles and practices were destructive to monarchy and inconsistent with the constitution of the state (*v.* 7): They all *do contrary to the decrees of Caesar;* not to any particular decree, for there was as yet no law of the empire against Christianity, but contrary to Caesar's power in general to make decrees; for they say, *There is another king, one Jesus,* not only a king of the Jews, as our Saviour was himself charged before Pilate, but *Lord of all;* so Peter called him in the first sermon he preached to the Gentiles, *ch.* 10:36. It is true the Roman government, both while it was a commonwealth and after it came into the Caesar's hands, was very jealous of any governor under their dominion taking upon him the title of king, and there was an express law against it. But Christ's *kingdom was not of this world.* His followers said indeed, Jesus is a king, but not an earthly king, not a rival with Caesar, nor his ordinances interfering with the decrees of Caesar, but who had made it a law of his kingdom to *render unto Caesar the things that are Caesar's.* There was nothing in the doctrine of Christ that tended to the dethroning of princes, nor the depriving them of any of their prerogatives. The Jews knew this very well, and it was against their consciences that they brought such a charge against the apostles; and of all people it ill became the Jews to do it, who hated Caesar and his government, and sought the ruin of him and it, and who expected a Messiah that should be a temporal prince, and overturn the thrones of kingdoms, and were therefore opposing our Lord Jesus because he did not appear under that character. Thus those have been most spiteful in representing God's faithful people as enemies to Caesar, and hurtful to kings and provinces, who have been themselves setting up *imperium in imperio — a kingdom within a kingdom,* a power not only in competition with Caesar's but superior to it, that of the papal supremacy.

4. The great uneasiness which this gave to this city (*v.* 8): *They troubled the people and the rulers of the city, when they heard these things.* They had no ill opinion of the apostles or their doctrine, could not apprehend any danger to the state from them, and therefore were willing to connive at them; but, if they be represented to them by the prosecutors as enemies to Caesar, they will be obliged to take cognizance of them, and to suppress them, for fear of the government, and this troubled them. Claudius, who then held the reins of government, is represented by Suetonius as a man very jealous of the least commotion and timorous to the last degree, which obliged the rulers under him to be watchful against every thing that looked dangerous, or gave the least cause of sus-

picion; and therefore it troubled them to be brought under a necessity of disturbing good men.

5. The issue of this troublesome affair. The magistrates had no mind to prosecute the Christians. Care was taken to secure the apostles; they absconded, and fled, and kept out of their hands; so that nothing was to be done but to discharge Jason and his friends upon bail, *v.* 9. The magistrates here were not so easily incensed against the apostles as the magistrates at Philippi were, but were more considerate and of better temper; so they *took security of Jason and the other,* bound them to their good behavior; and perhaps they gave bond for Paul and Silas, that they should be forthcoming when they were called for, if any thing should afterwards appear against them. Among the persecutors of Christianity, as there have been instances of the madness and rage of brutes, so there have been likewise of the prudence and temper of men; moderation has been a virtue.

Verses 10–15

In these verses we have,

I. Paul and Silas removing to Berea, and employed in preaching the gospel there, *v.* 10. They had proceeded so far at Thessalonica that the foundations of a church were laid, and others were raised up to carry on the work that was begun, against whom the rulers and people were not so much prejudiced as they were against Paul and Silas; and therefore when the storm rose they withdrew, taking this as an indication to them that they must quit that place for the present. That command of Christ to his disciples, *When they persecute you in one city flee to another,* intends their flight to be not so much for their own safety ("flee to another, to hide there") as for the carrying on of their work ("flee to another, to preach there"), as appears by the reason given — *You shall not have gone over the cities of Israel till the Son of man come,* Mt. 10:23. Thus out of the eater came forth meat, and the devil was outshot in his own bow; he thought by persecuting the apostles to stop the progress of the gospel, but it was so overruled as to be made to further it. See here, 1. The care that the brethren took of Paul and Silas, when they perceived how the plot was laid against them: They *immediately sent them away by night,* incognito, *to Berea.* This could be no surprise to the young converts; *For when we were with you* (saith Paul to them, 1 Th. 3:4), when we came first among you, *we told you that we should suffer tribulation, even as it came to pass, and you know.* It should seem that Paul and Silas would willingly have staid, and faced the storm, if the brethren would have let them; but they would rather be deprived of the apostles' help than expose their lives, which, it should seem, were dearer to their friends than to themselves. They *sent them away by night,* under the covert of that, as if they had been evil doers. 2. The constancy of Paul and Silas in their work. Though they fled from Thessalonica, they did not flee from the service of Christ. When *they came to Berea, they went into the synagogue of the Jews,* and made their public appearance there. Though the Jews at Thessalonica had been their spiteful enemies, and, for aught they knew, the Jews at Berea would be so too, yet they did not therefore decline paying their respect to the Jews, either in revenge for the injuries they had received or for fear of what they might receive. If others will not do their duty to us, yet we ought to do ours to them.

II. The good character of the Jews in Berea (*v.* 11): *These were more noble than those in Thessalonica.* The Jews in the synagogue at Berea were better disposed to receive the gospel than the Jews in the synagogue at Thessalonica; they were not so bigoted and prejudiced against it, not so peevish and ill-natured; they *were more noble, eugenesteroi — better bred.*

1. They had a freer thought, and lay more open to conviction, were willing to hear reason, and admit the force of it, and to subscribe to that which appeared to them to be truth, though it was contrary to their former sentiments. This was more noble.

2. They had a better temper, were not so sour, and morose, and ill-conditioned towards all that were not of their mind, As they were ready to come into a unity with those that by the power of truth they were brought to concur with, so they continued in charity with those that they saw cause to differ from. This was more noble. They neither prejudged the cause, nor were moved with envy at the managers of it, as the Jews at Thessalonica were, but very generously gave both it and them a fair hearing, without passion or partial-

ity; for, (1.) *They received the word with all readiness of mind;* they were very willing to hear it, presently apprehended the meaning of it, and did not shut their eyes against the light. *They attended to the things that were spoken by Paul,* as Lydia did, and were very well pleased to hear them. They did not pick quarrels with the word, nor find fault, nor seek occasion against the preachers of it; but bade it welcome, and put a candid construction upon every thing that was said. Herein *they were more noble than the Jews in Thessalonica,* but walked in the same spirit, and in the same steps, with the Gentiles there, of whom it is said *that they received the word with joy of the Holy Ghost,* and *turned to God from idols,* 1 Th. 1:6–9. This was true nobility. The Jews gloried much in their being Abraham's seed, thought themselves well-born and that they could not be better born. But they are here told who among them were the most noble and the best-bred men — those that were most disposed to receive the gospel, and had the high and conceited thoughts in them subdued, and *brought into obedience to Christ.* They were the most noble, and, if I may so say, the most gentleman-like men. *Nobilitas sola est atque unica virtus — Virtue and piety are true nobility,* true honour; and, without these, *Stemmata quid prosunt? — What are pedigrees and pompous titles worth?* (2.) *They searched the scriptures daily whether those things were so.* Their readiness of mind to receive the word was not such as that they took things upon trust, swallowed them upon an implicit faith: no; but since Paul reasoned out of the scriptures, and referred them to the Old Testament for the proof of what he said, they had recourse to their Bibles, turned to the places to which he referred them, read the context, considered the scope and drift of them, compared them with other places of scripture, examined whether Paul's inferences from them were natural and genuine and his arguments upon them cogent, and determined accordingly. Observe, [1.] The doctrine of Christ does not fear a scrutiny. We that are advocates for his cause desire no more than that people will not say, *These things are not so,* till they have first, without prejudice and partiality, examined whether they be so or no. [2.] The New Testament is to be examined by the Old. The Jews received the Old Testament, and those that did so, if they considered things aright, could not but see cause sufficient to receive the New, because in it they see all the prophecies and promises of the Old fully and exactly accomplished. [3.] Those that read and receive the scriptures must *search them* (Jn. 5:39), must study them, and take pains in considering them, both that they may find out the truth contained in them, and may not mistake the sense of them and so run into error, or remain in it; and that they may find out the whole truth contained in them, and may not rest in a superficial knowledge, in the outward court of the scriptures, but may have an intimate acquaintance with the mind of God revealed in them. [4.] Searching the scriptures must be our daily work. Those that heard *the word in the synagogue on the sabbath day* did not think this enough, but were searching it every day in the week, that they might improve what they ha heard the sabbath before, and prepare for what they were to hear the sabbath after. [5.] Those are truly noble, and are in a fair way to be more and more so, that make the scriptures their oracle and touchstone, and consult them accordingly. Those that rightly study the scriptures, and *meditate therein day and night,* have their minds filled with noble thoughts, fixed to noble principles, and formed for noble aims and designs. *These are more noble.*

III. The good effect of the preaching of the gospel at Berea: it had the desired success; the people's hearts being prepared, a great deal of work was done suddenly, *v.* 12. 1. Of the Jews there were many that believed. At Thessalonica there were only *some of them that believed* (*v.* 4), but at Berea, where they heard with unprejudiced minds, many believed, many more Jews than at Thessalonica. Note, God gives grace to those whom he first inclines to make a diligent use of the means of grace, and particularly to search the scriptures. 2. Of the Greeks likewise, the Gentiles, many believed, both of *the honourable women,* the ladies of quality, *and of men not a few,* men of the first rank, as should seem by their being mentioned with the honourable women. The wives first embraced the gospel, and then they persuaded their husbands to embrace it. *For what knowest thou, O wife, but thou shalt save thy husband?* 1 Co. 7:16.

IV. The persecution that was raised against Paul and Silas at Berea, which forced Paul thence. 1. *The Jews at Thessalonica* were the mischief-makers at *Berea.* They *had notice that the word of God was preached at Berea* (for envy and jealousy bring quick intelligence), and likewise that the Jews there were not so inveterately set against it as they were. They came thither also, to turn the world upside down there, *and they stirred up the people,* and incensed them against the preachers of the gospel; as if they had such a commission from the prince of darkness to go from place to place to oppose the gospel as the apostles had to go from place to place to preach it. Thus we read before that the Jews of Antioch and Iconium came to Lystra on purpose to incense the people against the apostles, *ch.* 14:19. See how restless Satan's agents are in their opposition to the gospel of Christ and the salvation of the souls of men. This is an instance of the enmity that is in the serpent's seed against the seed of the woman; and we must not think it strange if persecutors at home extend their rage to stir up persecution abroad. 2. This occasioned Paul's removal to Athens. By seeking to extinguish this divine fire which Christ had already kindled, they did but spread it the further and the faster; so long Paul staid at Berea, and such success he had there, that there were brethren there, and sensible active men too, which appeared by the care they took of Paul, *v.* 14. They were aware of the coming of the persecuting Jews from Thessalonica, and that they were busy in irritating the people against Paul; and, fearing what it would come to, they lost no time, but *immediately sent Paul away,* against whom they were most prejudiced and enraged, hoping that this would pacify them, while they retained Silas and Timothy there still, who, now that Paul had broken the ice, might be sufficient to carry on the work without exposing him. They *sent Paul to go even to the sea,* so some; *to go as it were to the sea,* so we read it; *hōs epi tēn thalassan.* He went out from Berea, in that road which went to the sea, that the Jews, if they enquired after him, might think he had gone to a great distance; but he went by land to Athens, in which there was no culpable dissimulation at all. *Those that conducted Paul* (as his guides and guards, he being both a stranger in the country and one that had many enemies) *brought him to Athens.* The Spirit of God, influencing his spirit, directed him to that famous city, — famous of old for its power and dominion, when the Athenian commonwealth coped with the Spartan, — famous afterwards for learning; it was the rendezvous of scholars. Those who wanted learning went thither to show it. It was a great university, much resorted to from all parts, and therefore, for the better diffusing of gospel light, Paul is sent thither, and is not ashamed nor afraid to show his face among the philosophers there, and there to preach Christ crucified, though he knew it would be as much foolishness to the Greeks as it was to the Jews a stumbling-block. 3. He ordered *Silas and Timothy to come to him to Athens,* when he found there was a prospect of doing good there; or because, there being none there that he knew, he was solitary and melancholy without them. Yet it should seem that, great as was the haste he was in for them, he ordered Timothy to go about Thessalonica, to bring him an account of the affairs of that church; for he says (1 Th. 3:1, 2), *We thought it good to be left at Athens alone, and sent Timotheus to establish you.*

Verses 16–21

A scholar that has acquaintance, and is in love, with the learning of the ancients, would think he should be very happy if he were where Paul now was, at Athens, in the midst of the various sects of philosophers, and would have a great many curious questions to ask them, for the explication of the remains we have of the Athenian learning; but Paul, though bred a scholar, and an ingenious active man, does not make this any of his business at Athens. He has other work to mind: it is not the improving of himself in their philosophy that he aims at, he has learned to call it a vain thing, and is above it (Col. 2:8); his business is, in God's name, to correct their disorders in religion, and *to turn them from the service of idols,* and of Satan in them, to the *service of the true and living God* in Christ.

I. Here is the impression which the abominable ignorance and superstition of the Athenians made upon Paul's spirit, *v.* 16. Observe, 1. The account here given of that city: it was *wholly given to idolatry.* This agrees with the account which the heathen writers give of it, that there were more idols in Athens than there were in all Greece besides put together, and that they had twice as many sacred feasts as others had. Whatever strange gods were recommended to them, they admitted them, and allowed them a temple and an altar, *so that*

they had almost as many gods as men — *facilius possis deum quam hominem invenire.* And this city, after the empire became Christian, continued incurably addicted to idolatry, and all the pious edicts of the Christian emperors could not root it out, till, by the irruption of the Goths, that city was in so particular a manner laid waste that there are now scarcely any remains of it. It is observable that there, where human learning most flourished, idolatry most abounded, and the most absurd and ridiculous idolatry, which confirms that of the apostle, that when *they professed themselves to be wise they became fools* (Rom. 1:22), and, in the business of religion, were of all other the most *vain in their imaginations. The world by wisdom knew not God,* 1 Co. 1:21. They might have reasoned against polytheism and idolatry; but, it seems, the greatest pretenders to reason were the greatest slaves to idols: so necessary was it to the re-establishing even of natural religion that there should be a divine revelation, and that centering in Christ. 2. The disturbance which the sight of this gave to Paul. Paul was not willing to appear publicly till Silas and Timothy came to him, that out of the mouth of two or three witnesses the word might be established; but in the mean time *his spirit was stirred within him.* He was filled with concern for the glory of God, which he saw given to idols, and with compassion to the souls of men, which he saw thus enslaved to Satan, *and led captive by him at his will.* He beheld these transgressors, and was grieved; and horror took hold of him. He had a holy indignation at the heathen priests, that led the people such an endless trace of idolatry, and at their philosophers, that knew better, and yet never said a word against it, but themselves went down the stream.

II. The testimony that he bore against their idolatry, and his endeavours to bring them to the knowledge of the truth. He did not, as Witsius observes, in the heat of his zeal break into the temples, pull down their images, demolish their altars, or fly in the face of their priests; nor did he run about the streets crying, "You are all the bond-slaves of the devil," though it was too true; but he observed decorum, and kept himself within due bounds, doing that only which became a prudent man. 1. He *went to the synagogue of the Jews,* who, though enemies to Christianity, were free from idolatry, and joined with them in that among them which was good, and took the opportunity given him there of disputing for Christ, *v.* 17. He discoursed *with the Jews,* reasoned fairly with them, and put it to them what reason they could give why, since they expected the Messiah, they would not receive Jesus. There he met with the devout persons that had forsaken the idol temples, but rested in the Jews' synagogue, and he talked with these to lead them on to the Christian church, to which the Jews' synagogue was but as a porch. 2. He entered into conversation with all that came in his way about matters of religion: *In the market — en tē agora,* in the exchange, or place of commerce, *he disputed daily,* as he had occasion, *with those that met with him,* or that he happened to fall into company with, that were heathen, and never came to the Jews' synagogue. The zealous advocates for the cause of Christ will be ready to plead it in all companies, as occasion offers. The ministers of Christ must not think it enough to speak a good word for Christ once a week, but should be daily speaking honourably of him to such as meet with them.

III. The enquiries which some of the philosophers made concerning Paul's doctrine. Observe,

1. Who they were that encountered him, that entered into discourse with him, and opposed him: *He disputed with all that met him, in the places of concourse,* or rather of discourse. Most took no notice of him, slighted him, and never minded a word he said; but there were some of the philosophers that thought him worth making remarks upon, an they were those whose principles were most directly contrary to Christianity. (1.) *The Epicureans,* who *thought God altogether such a one as themselves,* an idle inactive being, that minded nothing, nor put any difference between good and evil. They would not own, either that God made the world or that he governs it; nor that man needs to make any conscience of what he says or does, having no punishment to fear nor rewards to hope for, all which loose atheistical notions Christianity is levelled against. The Epicureans indulged themselves in all the pleasures of sense, and placed their happiness in them, in what Christ has taught us in the first place to deny ourselves. (2.) *The Stoics,* who thought themselves altogether as good as God, and indulged themselves as much in the pride of life as the Epicureans did in the lusts of the flesh and of the eye; they made their virtuous man to be no

way inferior to God himself, nay to be superior. *Esse aliquid quo sapiens antecedat Deum — There is that in which a wise man excels God,* so Seneca: to which Christianity is directly opposite, as it teaches us to deny ourselves and abase ourselves, and to come off from all confidence in ourselves, that Christ may be all in all.

2. What their different sentiments were of him; such there were as there were of Christ, *v.* 18. (1.) *Some called him a babbler,* and thought he spoke, without any design, whatever came uppermost, as men of crazed imaginations do: *What will this babbler say? ho spermologos houtos — this scatterer of words,* that goes about, throwing here one idle word or story and there another, without any intendment or signification; or, *this picker up of seeds.* Some of the critics tell us that the term is used for *a little sort of bird,* that is worth nothing at all, either for the spit or for the cage, *that picks up the seeds that lie uncovered, either in the field or by the way-side, and hops here and there for that purpose — Avicula parva quae semina in triviis dispersa colligere solet;* such a pitiful contemptible animal they took Paul to be, or supposed he went from place to place venting his notions to get money, a penny here and another there, as that bird picks up here and there a grain. They looked upon him as an idle fellow, and regarded him, as we say, no more than a ballad-singer. (2.) *Others* called him *a setter forth of strange gods,* and thought he spoke with design to make himself considerable by that means. And, if he had strange gods to set forth, he could not bring them to a better market than to Athens. He did not, as many did, directly set forth new gods, nor avowedly; but they thought he seemed to do so, *because he preached unto then Jesus, and the resurrection.* From his first coming among them he ever and anon harped upon these two strings, which are indeed the principal doctrines of Christianity — Christ and a future state — Christ our way, and heaven our end; and, though he did not call these gods, yet they thought he meant to make them so. *Ton Iēsoun kai tēn anastasin,* "Jesus they took for a new god, and *anastasis,* the resurrection, for a new goddess." Thus they lost the benefit of the Christian doctrine by dressing it up in a pagan dialect, as if believing in Jesus, and looking for the resurrection, were the worshipping of new demons.

3. The proposal they made to give him a free, full, fair, and public hearing, *v.* 19, 20. They had heard some broken pieces of his doctrine, and are willing to have a more perfect knowledge of it. (1.) They look upon it as strange and surprising, and very different from the philosophy that had for many ages been taught and professed at Athens. "It is a new doctrine, which we do not understand the drift and design of. *Thou bringest certain strange things to our ears,* which we never heard of before, and know not what to make of now." By this it should seem that, among all the learned books they had, they either had not, or heeded not, the books of Moses and the prophets, else the doctrine of Christ would not have been so perfectly new and strange to them. There was but one book in the world that was of divine inspiration, and that was the only book they were strangers to, which, if they would have given a due regard to it, would, in its very first page, have determined that great controversy among them about the origin of the universe. (2.) They desired to know more of it, only because it was new and strange: *"May we know what this new doctrine is?* Or, is it (like the mysteries of the gods) to be kept as a profound secret? If it may be, we would gladly know, and desire thee to tell us, *what these things mean,* that we may be able to pass a judgment upon them." This was a fair proposal; it was fit they should know what this doctrine was before they embraced it; and they were so fair as not to condemn it till they had had some account of it. (3.) The place they brought him to, in order to this public declaration of his doctrine; it was *to Areopagus,* the same word that is translated (*v.* 22) *Mars' Hill;* it was the town-house, or guildhall of their city, where the magistrates met upon public business, and the courts of justice were kept; and it was as the theatre in the university, or the schools, where learned men met to communicate their notions. The court of justice which sat here was famous for its equity, which drew appeals to it from all parts; if any denied a God, he was liable to the censure of this court. Diagoras was by them put to death, as a contemner of the gods; nor might any new God be admitted without their approbation. Hither they brought Paul to be tried, not as a criminal but as a candidate.

4. The general character of the people of that city given

upon this occasion (*v.* 21): *All the Athenians,* that is natives of the place, and strangers who sojourned there for their improvement, *spent their time in nothing else but either to tell or to hear some new thing,* which comes in as the reason why they were inquisitive concerning Paul's doctrine, not because it was *good,* but because it was *new.* It is a very sorry character which is here given of these people, yet many transcribe it. (1.) They were all for conversation. St. Paul exhorts his pupil to *give attendance to reading and meditation* (1 Tim. 4:13, 15), but these people despised those old-fashioned ways of getting knowledge, and preferred that of telling and hearing. It is true that good company is of great use to a man, and will polish one that has laid a good foundation in study; but that knowledge will be very flashy and superficial which is got by conversation only. (2.) They affected novelty; they were for *telling and hearing some new thing.* They were for new schemes and new notions in philosophy, new forms and plans of government in politics, and, in religion, for new gods that came newly up (Deu. 32:17), new demons, new-fashioned images and altars (2 Ki. 16:10); they were given to change. Demosthenes, an orator of their own, had charged this upon them long before, in one of his Philippics, that their common question in the markets, or wherever they met, was *ei ti le etai neōteron — whether there was any news.* (3.) They meddled in other people's business, and were inquisitive concerning that, and never minded their own. Tattlers are always *busy bodies,* 1 Tim. 5:13. (4.) *They spent their time in nothing else,* and a very uncomfortable account those must needs have to make of their time who thus spend it. Time is precious, and we are concerned to be good husbands of it, because eternity depends upon it, and it is hastening apace into eternity, but abundance of it is wasted in unprofitable converse. To tell or hear the new occurrences of providence concerning the public in our own or other nations, and concerning our neighbours and friends, is of good use now and then; but to set up for newsmongers, and to spend our time in nothing else, is to lose that which is very precious for the gain of that which is worth little.

Verses 22–31

We have here St. Paul's sermon at Athens. Divers sermons we have had, which the apostles preached to the Jews, or such Gentiles as had an acquaintance with and veneration for the Old Testament, and were worshippers of the true and living God; and all they had to do with them was to open and allege *that Jesus is the Christ;* but here we have a sermon to heathens, that worshipped false gods, and were without the true God in the world, and to them the scope of their discourse was quite different from what it was to the other. In the former case their business was to lead their hearers by prophecies and miracles to the knowledge of the Redeemer, and faith in him; in the latter it was to lead them by the common works of providence to the knowledge of the Creator, and the worship of him. One discourse of this kind we had before to the rude idolaters of Lystra that deified the apostles (*ch.* 14:15); this recorded here is to the more polite and refined idolaters at Athens, and an admirable discourse it is, and every way suited to his auditory and the design he had upon them.

I. He lays down this, as the scope of his discourse, that he aimed to bring them to *the knowledge of the only living and true God,* as the sole and proper object of their adoration. He is here obliged to lay the foundation, and to instruct them in the first principle of all religion, that there is a God, and that God is but one. When he preached against the gods they worshipped, he had no design to draw them to atheism, but to the service of the true Deity. Socrates, who had exposed the pagan idolatry, was indicted in this very court, and condemned, not only because he did not esteem those to be gods whom the city esteemed to be so, but because he introduced new demons; and this was the charge against Paul. Now he tacitly owns the former part of the charge, but guards against the latter, by declaring that he does not introduce any new gods, but reduce them *to the knowledge of one God, the Ancient of days.* Now,

1. He shows them that they needed to be instructed herein; for they had lost the knowledge of the true God that made them, in the worship of false gods that they had made *(Deos qui rogat ille facit — He who worships the gods makes them): I perceive that in all things you are too superstitious.* The crime he charges upon them is giving that glory to others which is due to God only, that they feared and worshipped demons, spirits that they supposed inhabited the images to which they directed their worship. "It is time for you to be told that *there is but one God* who are multiplying deities above any of your neighbours, and mingle your idolatries with all your affairs. *You are in all things too superstitious — deisidaimonesteroi,* you easily admit every thing that comes under a show of religion, but it is that which corrupts it more and more; I bring you that which will reform it." Their neighbours praised them for this as a pious people, but Paul condemns them for it. Yet it is observable how he mollifies the charge, does not aggravate it, to provoke them. He uses a word which among them was taken in a good sense: *You are every way more than ordinarily religious,* so some read it; *you are very devout in your way.* Or, if it be taken in a bad sense, it is mitigated: "You are as it were (*hōs*) more superstitious than you need be;" and he says no more than what he himself perceived; *theōrō — I see it, I observe it.* They charged Paul with setting forth new demons: "Nay," says he, "you have demons enough already; I will not add to the number of them."

2. He shows them that they themselves had given a fair occasion for the declaring of this one true God to them, by *setting up an altar,* To *the unknown God,* which intimated an acknowledgment that there was a God who was yet to them *an unknown God;* and it is sad to think that at Athens, a place which was supposed to have the monopoly of wisdom, the true God was an unknown God, the only God that was unknown. "Now you ought to bed Paul welcome, for this is the God whom he comes to make known to you, the God whom you tacitly complain that you are ignorant of." There, where we are sensible we are defective and come short, just there, the gospel takes us up, and carries us on.

(1.) Various conjectures the learned have concerning this *altar dedicated to the unknown God.* [1.] Some think the meaning is, *To the God whose honour it is to be unknown,* and that they intended the God of the Jews, whose name is ineffable, and whose nature is unsearchable. It is probable they had heard from the Jews, and from the writings of the Old Testament, of the God of Israel, who had proved himself to be above all gods, but was *a God hiding himself,* Isa. 45:15. The heathen called the Jews' God, *Deus incertus, incertum Mosis Numen — an uncertain God, the uncertain Deity of Moses,* and the God without name. Now *this God,* says Paul, *this God, who cannot by searching be found out to perfection, I now declare unto you.* [2.] Others think the meaning is, *To the God whom it is our unhappiness not to know,* which intimates that they would think it their happiness to know him. Some tell us that upon occasion of a plague that raged at Athens, when they had sacrificed to all their gods one after another for the staying of the plague, they were advised to let some sheep go where they pleased, and, where they lay down, to build an altar, *tō prosēkonti Theō — to the proper God, or the God to whom that affair of staying the pestilence did belong;* and, because they knew not how to call him, they inscribed it, *To the unknown God.* Others, from some of the best historians of Athens, tell us they had many altars inscribed, *To the gods of Asia, Europe, and Africa — To the unknown God:* and some of the neighbouring countries used to swear *by the God that was unknown at Athens;* so Lucian.

(2.) Observe, how modestly Paul mentions this. That he might not be thought a spy, nor one that had intruded himself more than became a stranger into the knowledge of their mysteries, he tells them that he observed it *as he passed by, and saw their devotions,* or *their sacred things.* It was public, and he could not forbear seeing it, and it was proper enough to make his remarks upon the religion of the place; and observe how prudently and ingeniously he takes occasion from this to bring in his discourse of the true God. [1.] He tells them that the God he preached to them was one that they did already worship, and therefore he was not a setter forth of new or strange gods: "As you have a dependence upon him, so he has had some kind of homage from you." [2.] He was one whom they ignorantly worshipped, which was a reproach to them, who were famous all the world over for their knowledge. "Now," says he, "I come to take away *that reproach,* that you may worship him understandingly whom how you worship ignorantly; and it cannot but be acceptable to have your blind devotion turned into a reasonable service, that you may not worship *you know not what.*"

II. He confirms his doctrine of one living and true God, by his works of creation and providence: "The God whom I declare unto you to be the sole object of your devotion, and call you to the worship of, is *the God that made the world* and governs it; and, by the visible proofs of these, you may be led to this invisible Being, and be convinced of his *eternal power and Godhead.*" The Gentiles in general, and the Athenians particularly, in their devotions were governed, not by their philosophers, many of whom spoke clearly and excellently well of one supreme *Numen,* of his infinite perfections and universal agency and dominion (witness the writings of Plato, and long after of Cicero); but by their poets, and their idle fictions. Homer's works were the Bible of the pagan theology, or demonology rather, not Plato's; and the philosophers tamely submitted to this, rested in their speculations, disputed them among themselves, and taught them to their scholars, but never made the use they ought to have made of them in opposition to idolatry; so little certainty were they at concerning them, and so little impression did these things make upon them! Nay, they ran themselves into the superstition of their country, and thought they ought to do so. *Eamus ad communem errorem — Let us embrace the common error.* Now Paul here sets himself, in the first place, to reform the philosophy of the Athenians (he corrects the mistakes of that), and to give them right notions of *the one only living and true God,* and then to carry the matter further than they ever attempted for the reforming of their worship, and the bringing them off from their polytheism and idolatry. Observe what glorious things Paul here says of that God whom he served, and would have them to serve.

1. *He is the God that made the world, and all things therein; the Father almighty, the Creator of heaven and earth.* This was admitted by many of the philosophers; but those of Aristotle's school denied it, and maintained "that the world was from eternity, and every thing always was from eternity, and every thing always was what now it is." Those of the school of Epicurus fancied "that the world was made by a fortuitous concourse of atoms, which, having been in perpetual motion, at length accidently jumped into this frame." Against both these Paul here maintains that God by the operations of an infinite power, according to the contrivance of an infinite wisdom, in the beginning of time made the world and all things therein, the origin of which was owing, not as they fancied to an eternal matter, but to an eternal mind.

2. He is therefore *Lord of heaven and earth,* that is, he is the rightful owner, proprietor, and possessor, of all the beings, powers, and riches of the upper and lower world, material and immaterial, visible and invisible. This follows from his making heaven and earth. If he created all, without doubt he has the disposing of all: and, where he gives being, he has an indisputable right to give law.

3. He is, in a particular manner, the Creator of men, of all men (*v.* 26): *He made of one blood all nations of men.* He made the first man, he makes every man, is the former of every man's body and the Father of every man's spirit. He has made the nations of men, not only all men in the nations, but as nations in their political capacity; he is their founder, and disposed them into communities for their mutual preservation and benefit. He made them all of one blood, of one and the same nature; *he fashions their heart alike.* Descended from one and the same common ancestor, in Adam they are all akin, so they are in Noah, that hereby they might be engaged in mutual affection and assistance, as fellow-creatures and brethren. *Have we not all one Father? Hath not one God created us?* Mal. 2:10. *He hath made them to dwell on all the face of the earth,* which, as a bountiful benefactor, *he has given,* with all its fulness, *to the children of men.* He made them not to live in one place, but to be dispersed over all the earth; one nation therefore ought not to look with contempt upon another, as the Greeks did upon all other nations; for those on all the face of the earth are of the same blood. The Athenians boasted that they sprung out of their own earth, were *aborigines,* and nothing akin by blood to any other nation, which proud conceit of themselves the apostle here takes down.

4. That he is the great benefactor of the whole creation (*v.* 25): *He giveth to all life, and breath, and all things.* He not only *breathed into the first man the breath of life,* but still breathes it into every man. He gave us these souls he formed the spirit of man within him. He not only gave us our life and breath, when he brought us into being, but he is continually giving them to us; his providence is a continued creation; he *holds our souls in life;* every moment our

breath goes forth, but he graciously gives it us again the next moment; it is no only *his air that we breathe in, but it is in his hand that our breath is,* Dan. 5:23. He *gives to all the children of men their life and breath;* for as the meanest of the children of men live upon him, and receive from him, so the greatest, the wisest philosophers and mightiest potentates, cannot live without him. *He gives to all,* not only to all the children of men, but to the inferior creatures, to all animals, *every thing wherein is the breath of life* (Gen. 6:17); they have their life and breath from him, and where he gives life and breath he gives all things, all other things needful for the support of life. *The earth is full of his goodness,* Ps. 104:24, 27.

5. That he is the sovereign disposer of all the affairs of the children of men, according to the counsel of his will (*v.* 26): *He hath determined the times before appointed, and the bounds of their habitation.* See here, (1.) The sovereignty of God's disposal concerning us: he *hath determined* every event, *horisas,* the matter is fixed; the disposals of Providence are incontestable and must not be disputed, unchangeable and cannot be altered. (2.) The wisdom of his disposals; he hath *determined* what was *before appointed.* The determinations of the Eternal Mind are not sudden resolves, but the counterparts of an eternal counsel, the copies of divine decrees. *He performeth the thing that is appointed for me,* Job 23:14. *Whatever comes forth from God was before all worlds hid in God.* (3.) The things about which his providence is conversant; these are time and place: the times and places of our living in this world are determined and appointed by the God that made us. [1.] *He has determined the times* that are concerning us. Times to us seem changeable, but God has fixed them. *Our times are in his hand,* to lengthen or shorten, embitter or sweeten, as he pleases. He has appointed and determined the time of our coming into the world, and the time of our continuance in the world; our time to be born, and our time to die (Eccl. 3:1, 2), and all that little that lies between them — the time of all our concernments in this world. Whether they be prosperous times or calamitous times, it is he that has determined them; and on him we must depend, with reference to the times that are yet before us. [2.] He has also *determined and appointed the bounds of our habitation.* He that *appointed the earth to be a habitation for the children of men* has appointed to the children of men a distinction of habitations upon the earth, has instituted such a thing as property, to which he has set bounds to keep us from trespassing one upon another. The particular habitations in which our lot is cast, the place of our nativity and of our settlement, are of God's determining and appointing, which is a reason why we should accommodate ourselves to the habitations we are in, and make the best of that which is.

6. That *he is not far from every one of us, v.* 27. He is every where present, not only is *at our right hand, but has possessed our reins* (Ps. 139:13), has his eye upon us at all times, and knows us better than we know ourselves. Idolaters made images of God, that they might have him with them in those images, the absurdity of which the apostle here shows; for he in an infinite Spirit, *that is not far from any of us,* and never the nearer, but in one sense the further off from us, for our pretending to realize or presentiate him to ourselves by any image. He is nigh unto us, both to receive the homage we render him and to give the mercies we ask of him, wherever we are, though near no altar, image, or temple. The Lord of all, as *he is rich* (Rom. 10:12), so *he is nigh* (Deu. 4:7), *to all that call upon him.* He that wills us to *pray every where,* assures us that he is no where far from us; whatever country, nation, or profession we are of, whatever our rank and condition in the world are, be we in a palace or in a cottage, in a crowd or in a corner, in a city or in a desert, in the depths of the sea or afar off upon the sea, this is certain, *God is not far from every one of us.*

7. That *in him we live, and move, and have our being, v.* 28. We have a necessary and constant dependence upon his providence, as the streams have upon the spring, and the beams upon the sun. (1.) *In him we live;* that is, the continuance of our lives is owing to him and the constant influence of his providence; *he is our life, and the length of our days.* It is not only owing to his patience and pity that our forfeited lives are not cut off, but it is owing to his power, and goodness, and fatherly care, that our frail lives are prolonged. There needs not a positive act of his wrath to destroy us; if he suspend the positive acts of his goodness, we die of ourselves. (2.) *In him we move;* it is by the uninterrupted concourse of his providence that our souls move in their outgoings and operations, that our thoughts run to and fro about a thousand subjects, and our affections run out towards their proper objects. It is likewise by him that our souls move our bodies; we cannot stir a hand, or foot, or a tongue, but by him, who, as he is the first cause, so he is the first mover. (3.) *In him we have our being;* not only from him we had it at first, but in him we have it still; to his continued care and goodness we owe it, not only that we have a being and are not sunk into nonentity, but that we have our being, have this being, were and still are of such a noble rank of beings, capable of knowing and enjoying God; and are not thrust into the meanness of brutes, nor the misery of devils.

8. That upon the whole matter we are *God's offspring;* he is *our Father that begat us* (Deu. 32:6, 18), and he hath *nourished and brought us up as children,* Isa. 1:2. The confession of an adversary in such a case is always looked upon to be of use as *argumentum ad hominem — an argument to the man,* and therefore the apostle here quotes a saying of one of the Greek poets, Aratus, a native of Cilicia, Paul's countryman, who, in his *Phenomena,* in the beginning of his book, speaking of the heathen *Jupiter,* that is, in the poetical dialect, the supreme *God,* says this of him, *tou gar kai genos esmen — for we are also his offspring.* And he might have quoted other poets to the purpose of what he was speaking, that *in God we live and move:* —

Spiritus intus alit, totamque infusa per artus
Mens agitat molem.
This active mind, infus'd through all the space,
Unites and mingles with the mighty mass.
— *Virgil,* Aeneid 6

Est Deus in nobis, agitante calescimus illo.
'Tis the Divinity that warms our hearts.
— *Ovid,* Fast. 6

Jupiter est quodeunque vides,
Quocunque moveris.
Where'er you look, where'er you rove
'The spacious scene is full of Jove.
— *Lucan,* lib. 2

But he chooses this of Aratus, as having much in a little. By this it appears not only that Paul was himself a scholar, but that human learning is both ornamental and serviceable to a gospel minister, especially for the convincing of those that are without; for it enables him to beat them at their own weapons, and to cut off Goliath's head with his own sword. How can the adversaries of truth be beaten out of their strong-holds by those that do not know them? It may likewise shame God's professing people, who forget their relation to God, and walk contrary to it, that a heathen poet could say of God, *We are his offspring,* formed by him, formed for him, more the care of his providence than ever any children were the care of their parents; and therefore are obliged to obey his commands, and acquiesce in his disposals, and *to be unto him for a name and a praise.* Since in him and upon him we live, we ought to live to him; since in him we move, we ought to move towards him; and since in him we have our being, and from him we receive all the supports and comforts of our being, we ought to consecrate our being to him, and to apply to him for a new being, a better being, an eternal well-being.

III. From all these great truths concerning God, he infers the absurdity of their idolatry, as the prophets of old had done. If this be so, 1. Then God cannot be represented by an image. If we are *the offspring of God,* as we are spirits in flesh, then certainly he who is *the Father of our spirits* (and they are the principal part of us, and that part of us by which we are denominated God's offspring) is himself a Spirit, and we ought not to think that the Godhead is *like unto gold, or silver, or stone, graven by art and man's device, v.* 29. We wrong God, and put an affront upon him, if we think so. God honoured man in making his soul after his own likeness; but man dishonours God if he makes him after the likeness of his body. The Godhead is spiritual, infinite, immaterial, incomprehensible, and therefore it is a very false and unjust conception which an image gives us of God, be the matter ever so rich, *fold or silver;* be the shape ever so curious, and be it ever so well *graven by art or man's device,* its countenance, posture, or dress, ever so significant, it is a teacher of lies. 2. Then *he dwells not in temples made with hands, v.* 24. He is not invited to any temple men can build for him, nor confined to any. A temple brings him never the nearer to us, nor keeps him ever the longer among us. A temple is convenient for us to come together in to worship God; but God needs not any place of rest or residence, nor the magnificence and splendour of any structure, to add to the glory of his appearance. A pious, upright heart, *a temple not made with hands,* but by *the Spirit of God,* is that which *he dwells in,* and *delights to dwell in.* See 1 Ki. 8:27; Isa. 66:1, 2. 3. Then he is *not worshipped, therapeuetai,* he is *not served,* or *ministered unto, with men's hands, as though he needed any thing, v.* 25. He that made all, and maintains all, cannot be benefited by any of our services, nor needs them. If we receive and derive all from him, he is all-sufficient, and therefore cannot but be self-sufficient, and independent. What need can God have of our services, or what benefit can he have by them, when he has all perfection in himself, and we have nothing that is good but what we have from him? The philosophers, indeed, were sensible of this truth, that God has no need of us or our services; but the vulgar heathen built temples and offered sacrifices to their gods, with an opinion that they needed houses and food. See Job 35:5–8; Ps. 50:8, etc. 4. Then it concerns us all to enquire after God (*v.* 27): *That they should seek the Lord,* that is, fear and worship him in a right manner. Therefore God has kept the children of men in a constant dependence upon him for life and all the comforts of life, that he might keep them under constant obligations to him. We have plain indications of God's presence among us, his presidency over us, the care of his providence concerning us, and his bounty to us, that we might be put upon enquiring, *Where is God our Maker, who giveth songs in the night, who teacheth us more than the beasts of the earth, and maketh us wiser than the fowls of heaven?* Job 35:10, 11. Nothing, one would think, should be more powerful with us to convince us that there is a God, and to engage us to seek his honour and glory in our services, and to seek our happiness in his favour and love, than the consideration of our own nature, especially the noble powers and faculties of our own souls. If we reflect upon these, and contemplate these, we may perceive both our relation and obligation to a God above us. Yet so dark is this discovery, in comparison with that by divine revelation, and so unapt are we to receive it, that those who have no other could but *haply feel after God* and *find him.* (1.) It was very uncertain whether they could by this searching *find out God;* it is but a peradventure: *if haply* they might. (2.) If they did find out something of God, yet it was but some confused notions of him; they did but feel after him, as men in the dark, or blind men, who lay hold on a thing that comes in their way, but know not whether it be that which they are in quest of or no. It is a very confused notion which this poet of theirs has of the relation between God and man, and very general, that *we are his offspring:* as was also that of their philosophers. Pythagoras said, *Theion genos esti brotoios — Men have a sort of a divine nature.* And Heraclitus *(apud Lucian)* being asked, *What are men?* answered, *Theoi thnētoi — Mortal gods;* and, *What are the gods?* answered, *athanatoi anthrōpoi — Immortal men.* And Pindar saith (*Nemean, Ode* 6), *En andrōn hen theōn genos — God and man are near a-kin.* It is true that by the knowledge of ourselves we may be led to the knowledge of God, but it is a very confused knowledge. This is but feeling after him. We have therefore reason to be thankful that by the gospel of Christ we have notices given us of God much clearer than we could have by the light of nature; we do not now feel after him, but *with open face behold, as in a glass, the glory of God.*

IV. He proceeds to call them all to repent of their idolatries, and to turn from them, *v.* 30, 31. This is the practical part of Paul's sermon before the university; having declared God to them (*v.* 23), he properly presses upon them *repentance towards God,* and would also have taught them *faith towards our Lord Jesus Christ,* if they had had the patience to hear him. Having shown them the absurdity of their worshiping other gods, he persuades them to go on no longer in that foolish way of worship, but to return from it to the living and true God. Observe,

1. The conduct of God towards the Gentile world before the gospel came among them: *The times of this ignorance God winked at.* (1.) They were times of great ignorance. Human learning flourished more than ever in the Gentile world just before Christ's time; but in the things of God they were grossly ignorant. Those are ignorant indeed who either know not God or worship him ignorantly; idolatry was owing to ignorance. (2.) These times of ignorance God winked at. Understand it, [1.] As an act of divine justice. God despised

or neglected these times of ignorance, and did not send them his gospel, as now he does. It was very provoking to him to see his glory thus given to another; and he detested and hated these times. So some take it. Or rather, [2.] As an act of divine patience and forbearance. He winked at these times; he did not restrain them from these idolatries by sending prophets to them, as he did to Israel; he did not punish them in their idolatries, as he did Israel; but gave them the gifts of his providence, *ch.* 14:16, 17. *These things thou hast done, and I kept silence,* Ps. 50:21. He did not give them such calls and motives to repentance as he does now. He *let them alone.* Because they did not improve the light they had, but were willingly ignorant, he did not send them greater lights. Or, he was not quick and severe with them, but was long-suffering towards them, because they did it ignorantly, 1 Tim. 1:13.

2. The charge God gave to the Gentile world by the gospel, which he now sent among them: *He now commandeth all men every where to repent* — to change their mind and their way, to be ashamed of their folly and to act more wisely, to break off the worship of idols and bind themselves to the worship of the true God. Nay, it is to turn with sorrow and shame from every sin, and with cheerfulness and resolution to every duty. (1.) This is God's command. It had been a great favour if he had only told us that there was room left for repentance, and we might be admitted to it; but he goes further, he interposes his own authority for our good, and has made that our duty which is our privilege. (2.) It is his command to *all men, every where,* — to men, and not to angels, that need it not, — to men, and not to devils, that are excluded the benefit of it, — to all men in all places; all men have made work for repentance, and have cause enough to repent, and all men are invited to repent, and shall have the benefit of it. The apostles are commissioned to preach this every where. The prophets were sent to command the Jews to repent; but the apostles were sent to preach *repentance and remission of sins to all nations.* (3.) Now in gospel times it is more earnestly commanded, because more encouraged than it had been formerly. Now the way of remission is more opened than it had been, and the promise more fully confirmed; and therefore now he expects we should all repent. "Now repent; now at length, now in time, repent; for you have too long gone on in sin. Now in time repent, for it will be too late shortly."

3. The great reason to enforce this command, taken from the judgment to come. God commands us to repent, *because he hath appointed a day in which he will judge the world in righteousness* (*v.* 31), and has now under the gospel made a clearer discovery of a state of retribution in the other world than ever before. Observe, (1.) The God that made the world will judge it; he that gave the children of men their being and faculties will call them to an account for the use they have made of them, and recompense them accordingly, whether the body served the soul in serving God or the soul was a drudge to the body in making provision for the flesh; and *every man shall receive according to the things done in the body,* 2 Co. 5:10. The God that now governs the world will judge it, will reward the faithful friends of his government and punish the rebels. (2.) There is a day appointed for this general review of all that men have done in time, and a final determination of their state for eternity. The day is fixed in the counsel of God, and cannot be altered; but it is his there, and cannot be known. A day of decision, a day of recompence, a day that will put a final period to all the days of time. (3.) The world will be judged in righteousness; for God is not unrighteous, who taketh vengeance; far be it from him that he should do iniquity. His knowledge of all men's characters and actions is infallibly true, and therefore his sentence upon them incontestably just. And, as there will be no appeal from it, so there will be no exception against it. (4.) God will judge the world *by that man whom he hath ordained,* who can be no other than the Lord Jesus, to whom all judgment is committed. By him God made the world, by him he redeemed it, by him he governs it, and by him he will judge it. (5.) God's raising Christ from the dead is the great proof of his being appointed and ordained the Judge of quick and dead. His doing him that honour evidenced his designing him this honour. His raising him from the dead was the beginning of his exaltation, his judging the world will be the perfection of it; and he that begins will make an end. God hath *given assurance unto all men,* sufficient ground for their faith to build upon, both that there is a judgment to come and that Christ will be their judge; the matter is not left doubtful, but is of unquestionable certainty. Let all his enemies be assured of it, and tremble before him; let all his friends be assured of it, and triumph in him. (6.) The consideration of the judgment to come, and of the great hand Christ will have in that judgment, should engage us all to repent of our sins and turn from them to God. This is the only way to make the Judge our friend in that day, which will be a terrible day to all who live and die impenitent; but true penitents will then *lift up their heads with joy, knowing that their redemption draws nigh.*

Verses 32–34

We have here a short account of the issue of Paul's preaching at Athens.

I. Few were the better: the gospel had as little success at Athens as any where; for the pride of the philosophers there, as of the Pharisees at Jerusalem, prejudiced them against the gospel of Christ. 1. Some ridiculed Paul and his preaching. They heard him patiently till he came to speak of the resurrection of the dead (*v.* 32), and then some of them began to hiss him: they *mocked.* What he had said before was somewhat like what they had sometimes heard in their own schools, and some notion they had of a resurrection, as it signifies a future state; but, if he speak of a *resurrection of the dead,* though it be of the resurrection of Christ himself, it is altogether incredible to them, and they cannot bear so much as to hear of it, as being contrary to a principle of their philosophy: *A privatione ad habitum non datur regressus — Life when once lost is irrecoverable.* They had deified their heroes after their death, but never thought of their being raised from the dead, and therefore they could by no means reconcile themselves to this doctrine of Christ's being raised from the dead; how can this be? This great doctrine, which is the saints' joy, is their jest; when it was but mentioned to them they mocked, and made a laughing matter of it. We are not to think it strange if sacred truths of the greatest certainty and importance are made the scorn of profane wits. 2. Others were willing to take time to consider of it; they said, *We will hear thee again of this matter.* They would not at present comply with what Paul said, nor oppose it; but *we will hear thee again of this matter,* of the resurrection of the dead. It should seem, they overlooked what was plain and uncontroverted, and shifted off the application and the improvement of that, by starting objections against what was disputable, and would admit a debate. Thus many lose the benefit of the practical doctrine of Christianity, by wading beyond their depth into controversy, or, rather, by objecting against that which has some difficulty in it; whereas, if any man were disposed and determined to *do the will of God,* as far as it is discovered to him, he should *know of the doctrine of Christ,* that it is *of God, and not of man,* Jn. 7:17. Those that would not yield to the present convictions of the word thought to get clear of them, as Felix did, by putting them off to another opportunity; they will hear of it again some time or other, but they know not when; and thus the devil cozens them of all their time, by cozening them of the present time. 3. Paul thereupon left them for the present to consider of it (*v.* 33): *He departed from amongst them,* as seeing little likelihood of doing any good with them at this time; but, it is likely, with a promise to those that were willing to hear him again that he would meet them whenever they pleased.

II. Yet there were some that were wrought upon, *v.* 34. If some would not, others would. 1. There were certain men that adhered to him, and believed. When he departed from amongst them, they would not part with him so; wherever he went, they would follow him, with a resolution to adhere to the doctrine he preached, which they believed. 2. Two are particularly named; one was an eminent man, *Dionysius the Areopagite,* one of that high court or great council that sat in Areopagus, or Mars' Hill — a judge, a senator, one of those before whom Paul was summoned to appear; his judge becomes his convert. The account which the ancients give of this Dionysius is that he was bred at Athens, had studied astrology in Egypt, where he took notice of the miraculous eclipse at our Saviour's passion, — that, returning to Athens, he became a senator, disputed with Paul, and was by him converted from his error and idolatry; and, being by him thoroughly instructed, was made the first bishop of Athens. So *Eusebius, lib.* 5, *cap.* 4; *lib.* 4, *cap.* 22. The *woman named Damaris* was, as some think, the wife of Dionysius; but, rather, some other person of quality; and, though there was not so great a harvest gathered in at Athens as there was at other places, yet, these few being wrought upon there, Paul had no reason to say he had *laboured in vain.*

CHAPTER 18

In this chapter we have, I. Paul's coming to Corinth, his private converse with Aquila and Priscilla, and his public reasonings with the Jews, from whom, when they rejected him, he turned to the Gentiles (*v.* 1–6). II. The great success of his ministry there, and the encouragement Christ gave him in a vision to continue his labours there, in hopes of further success (*v.* 7–11). III. The molestations which after some time he met with there from the Jews, which he got pretty well through by the coldness of Gallio, the Roman governor, in the cause (*v.* 12–17). IV. The progress Paul made through many countries, after he had continued long at Corinth, for the edifying and watering of the churches which he had founded and planted, in which circuit he made a short visit to Jerusalem (*v.* 18–23). V. An account of Apollo's improvement in knowledge, and of his usefulness in the church (*v.* 24–28).

Verses 1–6

We do not find that Paul was much persecuted at Athens, nor that he was driven thence by any ill usage, as he was from those places where the Jews had or could make any interest; but this reception at Athens being cold, and little prospect of doing good there, he departed from Athens, leaving the care of those there who believed with Dionysius; and thence he came to Corinth, where he was now instrumental in planting a church that became on many accounts considerable. Corinth was the chief city of Achaia, now a province of the empire, a rich and splendid city. *Non cuivis homini contingit adire Corinthum — It is not permitted every man to see Corinth.* The country thereabouts at this day is called *the Morea.* Now here we have,

I. Paul working for his living, *v.* 2, 3. 1. Though he was bred a scholar, yet he was master of a handicraft trade. He was a tent-maker, an upholsterer; he made tents for the use of soldiers and shepherds, of cloth or stuff, or (as some say tents were then generally made) of leather or skins, as the outer covering of the tabernacle. Hence to live in tents was to live *sub pellibus — under skins.* Dr. Lightfoot shows that it was the custom of the Jews to bring up their children to some trade, yea, though they gave them learning or estates. Rabbi Judah says, "He that teaches not his son a trade is as if he taught him to be a thief." And another says, "He that has a trade in his hand is as a vineyard that is fenced." An honest trade, by which a man may get his bread, is not to be looked upon by any with contempt. Paul, though a Pharisee, and bred up at the feet of Gamaliel, yet, having in his youth learned to make tents, did not by disuse lose the art. 2. Though he was entitled to a maintenance from the churches he had planted, and from the people to whom he preached, yet he worked at his calling to get bread, which is more to his praise who did not ask for supplies than to theirs who did not supply him unasked, knowing what straits he was reduced to. See how humble Paul was, and wonder that so great a man could stoop so low; but he had learned condescension of his Master, who came not to be ministered to, but to minister. See how industrious he was, and how willing to take pains. He that had so much excellent work to do with his mind, yet, when there was occasion, did not think it below him to work with his hands. Even those that are redeemed from the curse of the law are not exempt from that sentence, *In the sweat of thy face thou shalt eat bread.* See how careful Paul was to recommend his ministry, and to prevent prejudices against it, even the most unjust and unreasonable; he therefore maintained himself with his own labour that he might not make the gospel of Christ *burdensome,* 2 Co. 11:7, etc.; 2 Th. 3:8, 9. 3. Though we may suppose he was master of his trade, yet he did not disdain to work at journey-work: He *wrought with Aquila and Priscilla,* who *were of that calling,* so that he got no more than day-wages, a bare subsistence. Poor tradesmen must be thankful if their callings bring them in a maintenance for themselves and their families, though they cannot do as the rich merchants that raise estates by their callings. 4. Though he was himself a great apostle, yet he chose to work with Aquila and Priscilla, because he found them to be very intelligent in the things of God, as appears afterwards (*v.* 26), and he owns that they had been his *helpers in Christ Jesus,* Rom. 16:3. This is an example to those who are going to service to seek for those services in which they may have the best help for their souls. Choose to work with those that are likely to be helpers in Christ Jesus. It is good to be in company and to have conversation with those that will further us in the knowledge of Christ, and to put ourselves under the influence of such as are resolved that they will serve the Lord. Concerning this Aquila we are here told, (1.) That he was a Jew, but born in Pontus, *v.* 2. Many of the Jews of the dispersion were seated in that country, as appears 1 Pt. 1:1. (2.) That he was lately come from Italy to Corinth. It seems he often changed his habitation; this is not the world we can propose ourselves a settlement in. (3.) That the reason of his leaving Italy was because by a late edict of the emperor Claudius Caesar all Jews were banished from Rome; for the Jews were generally hated, and every occasion was taken to put hardship and disgrace upon them. God's heritage was as a *speckled bird, the birds round about were against her,* Jer. 12:9. Aquila, though a Christian, was banished because he had been a Jew; and the Gentiles had such confused notions of the thing that they could not distinguish between a Jew and a Christian. Suetonius, in the life of Claudius, speaks of this decree in the ninth year of his reign, and says, The reason was because the Jews were *a turbulent people — assiduo tumultuantes;* and that it was *impulsore Christo — upon the account of Christ;* some zealous for him, others bitter against him, which occasioned great heats, such as gave umbrage to the government, and provoked the emperor, who was a timorous jealous man, to order them all to be gone. If Jews persecute Christians, it is not strange if heathens persecute them both.

II. We have here Paul preaching to the Jews, and dealing with them to bring them to the faith of Christ, both the native *Jews and the Greeks,* that is, those that were more or less proselyted to the Jewish religion, and frequented their meetings.

1. He *reasoned with them in the synagogue* publicly *every sabbath.* See in what way the apostles propagated the gospel, not by force and violence, by fire and sword, not by demanding an implicit consent, but by fair arguing; they drew with the cords of a man, gave a reason for what they said, and gave a liberty to object against it, having satisfactory answers ready. God invites us to come and reason with him (Isa. 1:18), and challenges sinners to *produce their cause,* and *bring forth their strong reasons,* Isa. 41:21. Paul was a rational as well as a scriptural preacher.

2. *He persuaded them — epeithe.* It denotes, (1.) The urgency of his preaching. He did not only dispute argumentatively with them, but he followed his arguments with affectionate persuasions, begging of them for God's sake, for their own soul's sake, for their children's sake, not to refuse the offer of salvation made to them. Or, (2.) The good effect of his preaching. He persuaded them, that is, he prevailed with them; so some understand it. *In sententiam suam adducebat — He brought them over to his own opinion.* Some of them were convinced by his reasonings, and yielded to Christ.

3. He was yet more earnest in this matter when his fellow-labourers, his seconds, came up with him (*v.* 5): *When Silas and Timothy had come from Macedonia,* and had brought him good tidings from the churches there, and were ready to assist him here, and strengthened his hands, then Paul was more than before *pressed in spirit,* which made him more than ever pressing in his preaching. He was grieved for the obstinacy and infidelity of his countrymen the Jews, was more intent than ever upon their conversion, and the *love of Christ constrained him* to it (2 Co. 5:14): it is the word that is used here, it *pressed him in spirit* to it. And, being thus pressed, he *testified to the Jews* with all possible solemnity and seriousness, as that which he was perfectly well assured of himself, and attested to them as a *faithful saying, and worthy of all acceptation, that Jesus is the Christ,* the Messiah promised to the fathers and expected by them.

III. We have him here abandoning the unbelieving Jews, and turning from them to the Gentiles, as he had done in other places, *v.* 6.

1. Many of the Jews, and indeed the most of them, persisted in their contradiction to the gospel of Christ, and would not yield to the strongest reasonings nor the most winning persuasions; they *opposed themselves* and *blasphemed;* they *set themselves in battle array* (so the word signifies) against the gospel; they joined hand in hand to stop the progress of it. They resolved they would not believe it themselves, and would do all they could to keep others from believing it. They could not argue against it, but what was wanting in reason they made up in ill language: they *blasphemed,* spoke reproachfully of Christ, and in him of God himself, as Rev. 13:5, 6. To justify their infidelity, they broke out into downright blasphemy.

2. Paul hereupon declared himself discharged from them, and left them to perish in their unbelief. He that was *pressed in spirit* to *testify to them* (*v.* 5), when they opposed that testimony, and persisted in their opposition, was pressed in spirit to testify against them (*v.* 6), and his zeal herein also he showed by a sign: he *shook his raiment,* shaking off the dust from it (as before they *shook off the dust from their feet, ch.* 13:51), for a testimony against them. thus he cleared himself from them, but threatened the judgments of God against them. As Pilate by washing his hands signified the devolving of the guilt of Christ's blood from himself upon the Jews, so Paul by shaking his raiment signified what he said, if possible to affect them with it. (1.) He had done his part, and was clean from the blood of their souls; he had, like a faithful watchman, given them warning, and thereby had *delivered his soul,* though he could not prevail to deliver theirs. He had tried all methods to work upon them, but all in vain, so that if they perish in their unbelief their blood is not to be required at his hands; here, and *ch.* 20:26, he plainly refers to Eze. 33:8, 9. It is very comfortable to a minister to have the testimony of his conscience for him, that he has faithfully discharged his trust by warning sinners. (2.) They would certainly perish if they persisted in their unbelief, and the blame would lie wholly upon themselves: "Your *blood be upon your own heads,* you will be your own destroyers, your nation will be ruined in this world, and particular persons will be ruined in the other world, and *you alone shall bear it.*" If any thing would frighten them at last into a compliance with the gospel, surely this would.

3. Having given them over, yet he does not give over his work. Though Israel be not gathered, Christ and his gospel shall be glorious: *Henceforth I will go unto the Gentiles;* and the Jews cannot complain, for they had the first offer, and a fair one, made to them. The guests that were first invited will not come, and the provision must not be lost; guests must be had therefore *from the highways and the hedges.* "We *would have gathered* the Jews (Mt. 23:37), would have *healed them* (Jer. 51:9), and they would not; but Christ must not be a head without a body, nor a foundation without a building, and therefore, if they will not, we must try whether others will." Thus the fall and diminishing of the Jews became the riches of the Gentiles; and Paul said this to their faces, not only because it was what he could justify, but to *provoke them to jealousy,* Rom. 11:12, 14.

Verses 7–11

Here we are told,

I. That Paul changed his quarters. Christ directed his disciples,, when he sent them forth, not to *go from house to house* (Lu. 10:7), but there might be occasion to do it, as Paul did here. He departed out of the synagogue, being driven out by the perverseness of the unbelieving Jews, and he *entered into a certain man's house, named Justus, v.* 7. It should seem, he went to this man's house, not to lodge, for he continued with Aquila and Priscilla, but to preach. When the Jews would not let him go on peaceably with his work in their meeting, this honest man opened his doors to him, and told him he should be welcome to preach there; and Paul accepted the proposal. It was not the first time that God's ark had taken up its lodging in a private house. When Paul could not have liberty to preach in the synagogue, he preached in a house, without any disparagement to his doctrine. But observe the account of this man and his house. 1. The man was next door to a Jew; he was one that *worshipped God;* he was not an idolater, though he was a Gentile, but was a worshipper of the God of Israel, and him only, as Cornelius. That Paul might give the less offence to the Jews, though he had abandoned them, he set up his meeting in this man's house. Even when he was under a necessity of breaking off from them to turn to the Gentiles, yet he would study to oblige them. 2. The house was next door to the synagogue, it *joined close to it,* which some perhaps might interpret as done with design to draw people from the synagogue to the meeting; but I rather think it was done in charity, to show that he would come as near to them as he could, and was ready to return to them if they were but willing to receive his message, and would not contradict and blaspheme as they had done.

II. That Paul presently saw the good fruit of his labours, both among Jews and Gentiles. 1. *Crispus* a Jew, an eminent one, the *chief ruler of the synagogue, believed on the Lord Jesus, with all his house, v.* 8. It was for the honour of the gospel that there were some rulers, and persons of the first rank both in church and state, that embraced it. This would leave the Jews inexcusable, that the ruler of their synagogue, who may be supposed to have excelled the rest in knowledge of the scriptures and zeal for their religion, believed the gospel, and yet they opposed and blasphemed it. Not only he, but his house, believed, and, probably, were baptized with him by Paul, 1 Co. 1:14. 2. Many of the Corinthians, who were Gentiles (and some of them persons of bad character, as appears, 1 Co. 6:11, *such were some of you), hearing, believed, and were baptized.* First, they heard, for *faith comes by hearing.* Some perhaps came to hear Paul under some convictions of conscience that the way they were in was not right; but it is probable that the most came only for curiosity, because it was a new doctrine that was preached; but, hearing, *they believed,* by the power of God working upon them; and, *believing,* they were *baptized,* and so fixed for Christ, took upon them the profession of Christianity, and became entitled to the privileges of Christians.

III. That Paul was encouraged by a vision to go on with his work at Corinth (*v.* 9): *The Lord Jesus spoke to Paul in the night by a vision;* when he was musing on his work, *communing with his own heart upon his bed,* and considering whether he should continue here or no, what method he should take here, and what probability there was of doing good, then Christ appeared very seasonably to him, and *in the multitude of his thoughts within him* delighted his soul with divine consolations. 1. He renewed his commission and charge to preach the gospel: *"Be not afraid of the Jews;* though they are very outrageous, and perhaps the more enraged by the conversion of the chief ruler of their synagogue. Be not afraid of the magistrates of the city, for they have no power against thee but what is given them from above. It is the cause of heaven thou art pleading, do it boldly. *Be not afraid of their words, nor dismayed at their looks;* but *speak, and hold not thy peace;* let slip no opportunity of speaking to them; *cry aloud, spare not.* Do not hold thy peace from speaking for fear of them, nor hold thy peace in speaking" (if I may so say); "do not speak shyly and with caution, but plainly and fully and with courage. Speak out; use all the liberty of spirit that becomes an ambassador for Christ." 2. He assured him of his presence with him, which was sufficient to animate him, and put life and spirit into him: *"Be not afraid, for I am with thee,* to protect thee, and bear thee out, and to deliver thee from all thy fears; *speak, and hold not thy peace, for I am with thee,* to own what thou sayest, to work with thee, and to confirm the word by signs following." The same promise that ratified the general commission (Mt. 28:19, 20), *Lo I am with you always,* is here repeated. Those that have Christ with them need not to fear, and ought not to shrink. 3. He gave him a warrant of protection to save him harmless: *"No man shall set on thee to hurt thee;* thou shalt be delivered out of the hands of wicked and unreasonable men and shalt not be driven hence, as thou wast from other places, by persecution." He does not promise that no man should set on him (for the next news we hear is that he is set upon, and *brought to the judgment-seat, v.* 12), but, *"No man shall set on thee to hurt thee;* the remainder of their wrath shall be restrained; thou shalt not be beaten and imprisoned here, as thou wast at Philippi." Paul met with coarser treatment at first than he did afterwards, and was now *comforted according to the time wherein he had been afflicted.* Trials shall not last always, Ps. 66:10–12. Or we may take it more generally: *"No man shall set on thee, tou kakōsai se — to do evil* to thee; whatever trouble they may give thee, there is no real evil in it. They may kill thee, but they cannot hurt thee; for *I am with thee,"* Ps. 23:4; Isa. 41:10. 4. He gave him a prospect of success: *"For I have much people in this city.* Therefore no man shall prevail to obstruct thy work, therefore I will be with thee to own thy work, and therefore do thou go on vigorously and cheerfully in it; for there are many in this city that are to be effectually called by thy ministry, in whom thou shalt *see of the travail of thy soul." Laos esti moi polys — There is to me a great people here.* The Lord knows those that are his, yea, and those that shall be his; for it is by his work upon them that they become his, and *known unto him are all his works.* "I have them, though they yet know me not, though yet they are let captive by Satan at his will; for the Father has given them to me, to be a seed to serve me; I have them written in the book of life; I have their names down, and of all that were given me I will lose none; I have them, for I am sure to have them;" *whom he did predestinate, those he called. In this city,* though it be a very profane wicked city, full of impurity, and the more so for a temple of Venus there, to which there was a great resort, yet in this heap, that seems to be all chaff, there is wheat; in this ore, that seems to be all dross, there is gold. Let us not despair concerning any place, when even in Corinth Christ had *much people.*

IV. That upon this encouragement he made a long stay there (v. 11): He *continued at Corinth a year and six months,* not to take his ease, but to follow his work, *teaching the word of God among them;* and, it being a city flocked to from all parts, he had opportunity there of preaching the gospel to strangers, and sending notice of it thence to other countries. He staid so long, 1. For the bringing in of those that were without. Christ had many people there, and by the power of his grace he could have had them all converted in one month or week, as at the first preaching of the gospel, when thousands were enclosed at one cast of the net; but God works variously. The people Christ has at Corinth must be called in by degrees, some by one sermon, others by another;; *we see not yet all things put under Christ.* Let Christ's ministers go on in their duty, though their work be not done all at once; nay, though it be done but a little at a time. 2. For the building up of those that were within. Those that are converted have still need to be *taught the word of God,* and particular need at Corinth to be taught it by Paul himself; for no sooner was the good seed sown in that field than the enemy came and sowed tares, the false apostles, those deceitful workers, of whom Paul in his epistles to the Corinthians complains so much. When the hands of Jewish persecutors were tied, who were professed enemies to the gospel, Paul had a more vexatious trouble created him, and the church more mischievous damage done it, by the tongue of judaizing preachers, who, under colour of the Christian name, undermined the very foundations of Christianity. Soon after Paul came to Corinth, it is supposed, he wrote the first epistle to the Thessalonians, which in order of time was the first of all the epistles he wrote by divine inspiration; and the second epistle to the same church was written not long after. Ministers may be serving Christ, and promoting the great ends of their ministry, by writing good letters, as well as by preaching good sermons.

Verses 12–17

We have here an account of some disturbance given to Paul and his friends at Corinth, but no great harm done, nor much hindrance given to the work of Christ there.

I. Paul is accused by the Jews before the Roman governor, v. 12, 13. The governor was *Gallio, deputy of Achaia,* that is, proconsul; for Achaia was a consular province of the empire. This Gallio was elder brother to the famous Seneca; in his youth he was called Novatus, but took the name of Gallio upon his being adopted into the family of Julius Gallio; he is described by Seneca, his brother, to be a man of great ingenuous and great probity, and a man of wonderful good temper; he was called *Dulcis Gallio — Sweet Gallio,* for his sweet disposition; and is said to have been universally beloved. Now observe, 1. How rudely Paul is apprehended, and brought before Gallio; *The Jews made insurrection with one accord against Paul.* They were the ringleaders of all the mischief against Paul, and they entered into a confederacy to do him a mischief. They were unanimous in it: they came upon him *with one accord;* hand joined in hand to do this wickedness. They did it with violence and fury: *They made an insurrection* to the disturbance of the public peace, and hurried Paul away to *the judgment-seat,* and, for aught that appears, allowed him no time to prepare for his trial. 2. How falsely Paul is accused before Gallio (v. 13): *This fellow persuades men to worship God contrary to the law.* They could not charge him with persuading men not to worship God at all, or to worship other gods (Deu. 13:2): but only to worship God in a way contrary to the law. The Romans allowed the Jews in their provinces the observance of their own law; and what then? Must those therefore be prosecuted as criminals who worship God in any other way? Does their toleration include a power of imposition? But the charge was unjust; for their own law had in it a promise of a prophet whom God would raise up to them, and him they should hear. Now Paul persuaded them to believe in this prophet, who was come, and to hear him, which was according to the law; for he came not *to destroy the law, but to fulfil it.* The law relating to the temple-service those Jews at Corinth could not observe, because of their distance from Jerusalem, and there was no part

of their synagogue-worship which Paul contradicted. Thus when people are taught to worship God in Christ, and to worship him in the Spirit, they are ready to quarrel, as if they were taught to worship him contrary to the law; whereas this is indeed perfective of the law.

II. Gallio, upon the first hearing, or rather without any hearing at all, dismisses the cause, and will not take any cognizance of it, v. 14, 15. Paul was going about to make his defence, and to show that he did not teach men to worship God contrary to the law; but the judge, being resolved not to pass any sentence upon this cause, would not give himself the trouble of examining it. Observe,

1. He shows himself very ready to do the part of a judge in any matter that it was proper for him to take cognizance of. He *said to the Jews,* that were the prosecutors, *"If it were a matter of wrong, or wicked lewdness,* — if you could charge the prisoner with theft or fraud, with murder or rapine, or any act of immorality, — I should think myself bound *to bear with you* in your complaints, though they were clamorous and noisy;" for the rudeness of the petitioners was no good reason, if their cause was just, why they should not have justice done them. It is the duty of magistrates to right the injured, and to animadvert upon the injurious; and, if the complaint be not made with all the decorum that might be, yet they should hear it out. But,

2. He will by no means allow them to make a complaint to him of a thing that was not within his jurisdiction (v. 15): *"If it be a question of words and names, and of your law, look you to it:* end it among yourselves as you can, but *I will be no judge of such matters;* you shall neither burden my patience with the hearing of it, nor burden my conscience with giving judgment upon it;" and therefore, when they were urgent and pressing to be heard, *he drove them from the judgment-seat* (v. 16), and ordered another cause to be called. Now, (1.) Here was something right in Gallio's conduct, and praise-worthy — that he would not pretend to judge of things he did not understand; that he left the Jews to themselves in matters relating to their own religion, but yet would not let them, under pretence of that, run down Paul, and abuse him; or, at least, would not himself be the tool of their malice, to give judgment against him. He looked upon the matter to be not within his jurisdiction, and therefore would not meddle in it. But, (2.) It was certainly wrong to speak so slightly of a law and religion which he might have known to be of God, and with which he ought to have acquainted himself. In what way God is to be worshipped, whether Jesus be the Messiah, whether the gospel be a divine revelation, were not *questions of words and names,* as he scornfully and profanely called them. They are questions of vast importance, and in which, if he had understood them himself aright, he would have seen himself nearly concerned. He speaks as if he boasted of his ignorance of the scriptures, and took a pride in it; as if it were below him to take notice of the law of God, or make any enquiries concerning it.

III. The abuse done to Sosthenes, and Gallio's unconcernedness in it, v. 17. 1. The parties put a great contempt upon the court, when *they took Sosthenes and beat him before the judgment-seat.* Many conjectures there are concerning this matter, because it is uncertain who this Sosthenes was, and who the Greeks were that abused him. It seems most probable that Sosthenes was a Christian, and Paul's particular friend, that appeared for him on this occasion, and probably had taken care of his safety, and conveyed him away, when Gallio dismissed the cause; so that, when they could not light on Paul, they fell foul on him who protected him. It is certain that there was one Sosthenes that was a friend of Paul, and well known at Corinth; it is likely he was a minister, for Paul calls him his brother, and joins him with himself in his first epistle to the church at Corinth (1 Co. 1:1), as he does Timothy in his second, and it is probable that this was he; he is said to be a *ruler of the synagogue,* either joint-ruler with Crispus (v. 8), or a ruler of one synagogue, as Crispus was of another. As for the Greeks that abused him, it is very probable that they were either Hellenist Jews, or Jewish Greeks, those that joined with the Jews in opposing the gospel (v. 4, 6), and that the native Jews put them on to do it, thinking it would in them be less offensive. They were so enraged against Paul that they beat Sosthenes; and so enraged against Gallio, because he would not countenance the prosecution, that they beat him before the judgment-seat, whereby they did, in effect, tell him that they cared not for him; if he would not be their executioner, they would be their own judges. 2.

The court put no less a contempt upon the cause, and the persons too. But *Gallio cared for none of these things.* If by this be meant that he cared not for the affronts of bad men, it was commendable. While he steadily adhered to the laws and rules of equity, he might despise their contempts; but, if it be meant (as I think it is) that he concerned not himself for the abuses done to good men, it carries his indifference too far, and gives us but an ill character of him. Here is *wickedness* done *in the place of judgment* (which Solomon complains of, Eccl. 3:16), and nothing done to discountenance and suppress it. Gallio, as a judge, ought to have protected Sosthenes, and restrained and punished the Greeks that assaulted him. For a man to be mobbed in the street or in the market, perhaps, may not be easily helped; but to be so in his court, the judgment-seat, the court sitting and not concerned at it, is an evidence that *truth is fallen in the street, and equity cannot enter;* for *he that departeth from evil maketh himself a prey,* Isa. 59:14, 15. Those that see and hear of the sufferings of God's people, and have no sympathy with them, nor concern for them, do not pity and pray for the, it being all one to them whether the interests of religion sink or swim, are of the spirit of Gallio here, who, when a good man was abused before his face, *cared for none of these things;* like those that were *at ease in Zion,* and *were not grieved for the affliction of Joseph* (Amos 6:6), like *the king and Haman, that sat down to drink when the city Shushan was perplexed,* Esth. 3:15.

Verses 18–23

We have here Paul in motion, as we have had him at Corinth for some time at rest, but in both busy, very busy, in the service of Christ; if he sat still, if he went about, still it was to do good. Here is,

I. Paul's departure from Corinth, v. 18. 1. He did not go away till some time after the trouble he met with there; from other places he had departed when the storm arose, but not from Corinth, because there it had no sooner risen than it fell again. Some tell us that Gallio did privately countenance Paul, and took him into his favour, and that this occasioned a correspondence between Paul and Seneca, Gallio's brother, which some of the ancients speak of. *After this he tarried there yet a good while,* some think, beyond *the year and a half* mentioned, v. 11. While he found he laboured not in vain, he continued labouring. 2. When he went, he took leave of the brethren solemnly, and with much affection, with suitable comforts and counsels, and prayers at parting, commending what was good, reproving what was otherwise, and giving them necessary cautions against the wiles of the false apostles; and his farewell sermon would leave impressions upon them. 3. He took *with him Priscilla and Aquila,* because they had a mind to accompany him; for they seemed disposed to remove, and not inclined to stay long at a place, a disposition which may arise from a good principle, and have good effects, and therefore ought not to be condemned in others, though it ought to be suspected in ourselves. There was a great friendship contracted between them and Paul, and therefore, when he went, they begged to go along with him. 4. At Cenchrea, which was hard by Corinth, the port where those that went to sea from Corinth took ship, either Paul or Aquila (for the original does not determine which) had his head shaved, to discharge himself from the vow of a Nazarite: *Having shorn his head at Cenchrea; for he had a vow.* Those that lived in Judea were, in such a case, bound to do it at the temple: but those who lived in other countries might do it in other places. The Nazarite's head was to be shaved when either his consecration was accidentally polluted, in which case he must begin again, or *when the days of his separation were fulfilled* (Num. 6:9; 13:18), which, we suppose, was the case here. Some throw it upon Aquila, who was a Jew (v. 2), and retained perhaps more of his Judaism than was convenient; but I see no harm in admitting it concerning Paul, for concerning him we must admit the same thing (ch. 21:24, 26), not only in compliance for a time with the Jews, to whom he *became as a Jew* (1 Co. 9:20), *that he might win upon them,* but because the vow of the Nazarites, though ceremonial, and as such ready to vanish away, had yet a great deal of moral and very pious significance, and therefore was fit to die the last of all the Jewish ceremonies. The Nazarites are joined with the prophets (Amos 2:11), and were very much *the glory of Israel* (Lam. 4:7), and therefore it is not strange if Paul bound himself for some time with the vow of a Nazarite from wine and strong drink, and from being trimmed, to recommend himself to the Jews; and from this he now discharged himself.

II. Paul's calling *at Ephesus,* which was the metropolis of the Lesser Asia, and a sea-port. 1. *There he left Aquila and Priscilla;* not only because they would be but burdensome to him in his journey, but because they might be serviceable to the interests of the gospel at Ephesus. Paul intended shortly to settle there for some time, and he left Aquila and Priscilla there in the mean time, for the same end as Christ sent his disciple before to every place where he himself would come, to prepare his way. Aquila and Priscilla might, by private conversation, being very intelligent judicious Christians, dispose the minds of many to give Paul, when he should come among them, a favourable reception, and to understand his preaching; therefore he calls them his *helpers in Christ Jesus,* Rom. 16:3. 2. There he preached *to the Jews in their synagogue;* though he did but call there in his journey, yet he would not go without giving them a sermon. *He entered into the synagogue,* not as a hearer, but as a preacher, for *there he reasoned with the Jews.* Though he had abandoned the Jews at Corinth, who opposed themselves, and blasphemed, yet he did not, for their sakes, decline the synagogues of the Jews in other places, but still made the first offer of the gospel to them. We must not condemn a whole body or denomination of men, for the sake of some that conduct themselves ill. 3. The Jews at Ephesus were so far from driving Paul away that they courted his stay with them (*v.* 20): *They desired him to tarry longer with them,* to instruct them, in the gospel of Christ. These were more noble, and better bred, than those Jews at Corinth, and other places, and it was a sign that God had not quite cast away his people, but had a remnant among them. 4. Paul would not stay with them now: *He consented not; but bade them farewell.* He had further to go; he *must by all means keep this feast at Jerusalem;* not that he thought himself bound in duty to it (he knew the laws of the feasts were no longer binding), but he had business t Jerusalem (whatever it was) which would be best done at the time of the feast, when there was a general rendezvous of all the Jews from all parts; which of the feasts it was we are not told, probably it was the passover, which was the most eminent. 5. He intimated his purpose, after this journey, to come and spend some time at Ephesus, being encouraged by their kind invitation to hope that he should do good among them. It is good to have opportunities in reserve, when one good work is over to have another to apply ourselves to: *I will return again to you,* but he inserts that necessary proviso, *if God will.* Our times are in God's hand; we purpose, but he disposes; and therefore we must make all our promises with submission to the will of God. *If the Lord will, we shall live, and do this or that. I will return again to you, if the Spirit suffer me* (*ch.* 16:7); this was included in Paul's case; not only if providence permit, but if God do not otherwise direct my motions.

III. Paul's visit to Jerusalem; a short visit it was, but it served as a token of respect to that truly mother-church. 1. He came by sea to the port that lay next to Jerusalem. *He sailed from Ephesus* (*v.* 21), *and landed at Caesarea, v.* 22. He chose to go by sea, for expedition and for safety, and that he might *see the works of the Lord, and his wonders in the deep.* Joppa had been the port for Jerusalem, but Herod having improved Caesarea, and the port at Joppa being dangerous, that was generally made use of. 2. He went *up, and saluted the church,* by which, I think, is plainly meant the church at Jerusalem, which is emphatically called *the church,* because there the Christian church began, *ch.* 15:4. Paul thought it requisite to show himself among them, that they might not think his success among them, that they might not think his success among the Gentiles had made him think himself either above them or estranged from them, or that the honour God had put upon him made him unmindful of the honour he owed to them. His going to salute the church at Jerusalem intimates, (1.) That it was a very friendly visit that he made them, in pure kindness, to enquire into their state, and to testify his hearty good-will to them. Note, The increase of our new friends should not make us forget our old ones, but it should be a pleasure to good men, and good ministers, to revive former acquaintance. The ministers at Jerusalem were constant residents, Paul was a constant itinerant; but he took care to keep up a good correspondence with them, that they might rejoice with him in his going out, and he might rejoice with them in their tents, and they might both congratulate and wish well to one another's comfort and success. (2.) That it was but a short visit. He went *up, and saluted them,* perhaps *with the holy kiss,* and made no stay among them. It was designed but for a transient interview, and yet Paul undertook this long journey for that. This is not the world we are to be together in. God's people are *the salt of the earth,* dispersed and scattered; yet it is good to see one another sometimes, if it be but to see one another, that we may confirm mutual love, may the better keep up our spiritual communion with one another at a distance, and may long the more for that heavenly Jerusalem in which we hope to be together for ever.

IV. His return through those countries where he had formerly preached the gospel. 1. *He went and spent some time in Antioch,* among his old friends there, whence he was first sent out to preach among the Gentiles, *ch.* 13:1. He went down to Antioch, to refresh himself with the sight and conversation of the ministers there; and a very good refreshment it is to a faithful minister to have for awhile the society of his brethren; for, *as iron sharpeneth iron, so doth a man the countenance of his friend.* Paul's coming to Antioch would bring to remembrance the former days, which would furnish him with matter for fresh thanksgiving. 2. *Thence he went over the country of Galatia and Phrygia in order,* where he had preached the gospel, and planted churches, which, though very briefly mentioned (*ch.* 16:6), was yet a glorious work, as appears by Gal. 4:14, 15, where Paul speaks of his preaching the gospel to the Galatians at the first, and their receiving him *as an angel of God.* These country churches (for such they were [Gal. 1:2], and we read not of any city in Galatia where a church was) Paul visited *in order* as they lay, watering what he had been instrumental to plant, and *strengthening all the disciples.* His very coming among them, and owning them, were a great strengthening to them and their ministers. Paul's countenancing them was encouraging them; but that was not all: he preached that to them which strengthened them, which confirmed their faith in Christ, their resolutions for Christ, and their pious affections to him. Disciples need to be strengthened, for they are compassed about with infirmity; ministers must do what they can to strengthen them, to strengthen them all, by directing them to Christ, and bringing them to live upon him, whose strength is perfected in their weakness, and who is himself their strength and song.

Verses 24–28

The sacred history leaves Paul upon his travels, and goes here to meet Apollos at Ephesus, and to give us some account of him, which was necessary to our understanding some passages in Paul's epistles.

I. Here is an account of his character, when he came to Ephesus.

1. He was *a Jew, born at Alexandria* in Egypt, but of Jewish parents; for there were abundance of Jews in that city, since the dispersion of the people, as it was foretold (Deu. 28:68): *The Lord shall bring thee into Egypt again.* His name was not *Apollo,* the name of one of the heathen gods, but *Apollos,* some think the same with *Apelles,* Rom. 16:10.

2. He was a man of excellent good parts, and well fitted for public service. He was *an eloquent man, and mighty in the scriptures* of the Old Testament, in the knowledge of which he was, as a Jew, brought up. (1.) He had a great command of language: he was *an eloquent man;* he was *anēr logios — a prudent man,* so some; *a learned man,* so others; *historiarum peritus — a good historian,* which is an excellent qualification for the ministry: he was one that could speak well, so it properly signifies; he was *an oracle of a man;* he was famous for speaking pertinently and closely, fully and fluently, upon any subject. (2.) He had a great command of scripture-language, and this was the eloquence he was remarkable for. He *came to Ephesus,* being *mighty in the scriptures,* so the words are placed; having an excellent faculty of expounding scripture, he came to Ephesus, which was a public place, to trade with that talent, for the honour of God and the good of many. He was not only ready in the scriptures, able to quote texts off-hand, and repeat them, and tell you where to find them (many of the carnal Jews were so, who were therefore said to have the *form of knowledge,* and *the letter of the law);* but he was *mighty in the scriptures.* He understood the sense and meaning of them, he knew how to make use of them and to apply them, how to reason out of the scriptures, and to reason strongly; a convincing, commanding, confirming power went along with all his expositions and applications of the scripture. It is probable he had given proof of his knowledge of the scriptures, and his abilities in them, in many synagogues of the Jews.

3. He *was instructed in the way of the Lord;* that is, he had some acquaintance with the doctrine of Christ, had obtained some general notions of the gospel and the principles of Christianity, *that Jesus is the Christ,* and *that prophet that should come into the world;* the first notice of this would be readily embraced by one that was so mighty in the scripture as Apollos was, and therefore understood *the signs of the times.* He *was instructed, katēchēmenos — he was catechised* (so the word is), either by his parents or by ministers; he was taught something of Christ and the way of salvation by him. Those that are to teach others must first be themselves taught the word of the Lord, not only to talk of it, but to walk in it. It is not enough to have our tongues tuned to the word of the Lord, but we must have our feet directed into the way of the Lord.

4. Yet he *knew only the baptism of John;* he was instructed in the gospel of Christ as far as John's ministry would carry him, and no further; he knew *the preparing of the way of the Lord* by *that voice crying in the wilderness,* rather than the way of the Lord itself. We cannot but think he had heard of Christ's death and resurrection, but he was not let into the mystery of them, had not had opportunity of conversing with any of the apostles since the pouring out of the Spirit; or he had himself been baptized *only with the baptism of John,* but was not baptized with the Holy Ghost, as the disciples were at the day of pentecost.

II. We have here the employment and improvement of his gifts at Ephesus; he came thither, seeking opportunities of doing and getting good, and he found both.

1. He there made a very good use of his gifts in public. He came, probably, recommended to the synagogue of the Jews as a fit man to be a teacher there, and according to the light he had, and *the measure of the gift given to him,* he was willing to be employed (*v.* 25): *Being fervent in the Spirit, he spoke and taught diligently the things of the Lord.* Though he had not the miraculous gifts of the Spirit, as the apostles had, he made use of the gifts he had; *for the dispensation of the Spirit,* whatever the measure of it is, *is given to every man to profit withal.* And our Savior, by a parable, designed to teach his ministers that though they had but one talent they must not bury that. We have seen how Apollos was qualified with a good head and a good tongue: he was *an eloquent man, and mighty in the scriptures;* he had laid in a good stock of useful knowledge, and had an excellent faculty of communicating it. Let us now see what he had further to recommend him as a preacher; and his example is recommended to the intimation of all preachers. (1.) He was a lively affectionate preacher; as he had a good head, so he had a good heart; he was *fervent in Spirit.* He had in him a great deal of divine fire as well as divine light, was burning as well as shining. He was full of zeal for the glory of God, and the salvation of precious souls. This appeared both in his forwardness to preach when he was called to it by *the rulers of the synagogue,* and in his fervency in his preaching. He preached as one in earnest, and that had his heart in his work. What a happy composition was here! Many are fervent in spirit, but are weak in knowledge, in scripture-knowledge — have far to seek for proper words and are full of improper ones; and, on the other hand, many are eloquent enough, and mighty in the scriptures, and learned, and judicious, but they have no life or fervency. Here was a complete *man of God, thoroughly furnished for his work;* both eloquent and fervent, full both of divine knowledge and of divine affections. (2.) He was an industrious laborious preacher. *He spoke and taught diligently.* He took pains in his preaching, what he delivered was elaborate; and he did not offer that to God, or to the synagogue, that either cost nothing or cost *him* nothing. He first worked it upon his own heart, and then laboured to impress it on those he preached to: *he taught diligently, akribōs — accurately, exactly;* every thing he said was well-weighed. (3.) He was an evangelical preacher. Though he knew only the baptism of John, yet that was the beginning of the gospel of Christ, and to that he kept close; for he taught the things of the Lord, of the Lord Christ, the things that tended to make way for him, and to set him up. The things pertaining to the kingdom of the Messiah were the subjects he chose to insist upon; not the things of the ceremonial law, though those would be pleasing to his Jewish auditors; not the things of the Gentile philosophy, though he could have discoursed very well on those things; but the things of the

Lord. (4.) He was a courageous preacher: *He began to speak boldly in the synagogue,* as one who, having put confidence in God, did not fear the face of man; he spoke as one that knew the truth of what he said, and had no doubt of it, and that knew the worth of what he said and was not afraid to suffer for it; *in the synagogue,* where the Jews not only were present, but had power, there he preached the things of God, which he knew they were prejudiced against.

2. He there made a good increase of his gifts in private, not so much in study, as in conversation with *Aquila and Priscilla.* If Paul or some other apostle or evangelist had been at Ephesus, he would have instructed him; but, for want of better help, *Aquila and Priscilla* (who were tent-makers) *expounded to him the way of God more perfectly.* Observe, (1.) Aquila and Priscilla heard him preach in the synagogue. Though in knowledge he was much inferior to them, yet, having excellent gifts for public service, they encouraged his ministry, by a diligent and constant attendance upon it. Thus young ministers, that are hopeful, should be countenanced by grown Christians, for it becomes them to fulfil all righteousness. (2.) Finding him defective in his knowledge of Christianity, *they took him to them,* to lodge in the same house with them, and *expounded to him the way of God,* the way of salvation by Jesus Christ, *more perfectly.* They did not take occasion from what they observed of his deficiency either to despise him themselves, or to disparage him to others; did not call him a young raw preacher, not fit to come into a pulpit, but considered the disadvantages he had laboured under, as knowing only the baptism of John; and, having themselves got great knowledge in the truths of the gospel by their long intimate conversation with Paul, they communicated what they knew to him, and gave him a clear, distinct, and methodical account of those things which before he had but confused notions of. [1.] See here an instance of that which Christ has promised, that *to him that hath shall be given;* he that has, and uses what he has, shall have more. He that diligently traded with the talent he had doubled it quickly. [2.] See an instance of truly Christian charity in Aquila and Priscilla; they did good according to their ability. Aquila, though a man of great knowledge, yet did no undertake to speak in the synagogue, because he had not such gifts for public work as Apollos had; but he furnished Apollos with matter, and then left him to clothe it with acceptable words. Instructing young Christians and young ministers privately in conversation, who mean well, and perform well, as far as they go, is a piece of very good service, both to them and to the church. [3.] See an instance of great humility in Apollos. He was a very bright young man, of great parts and learning, newly come from the university, a popular preacher, and one mightily cried up and followed; and yet, finding that Aquila and Priscilla were judicious serious Christians, that could speak intelligently and experimentally of the things of God, though they were but mechanics, poor tent-makers, he was glad to receive instructions from them, to be shown by them his defects and mistakes, and to have his mistakes rectified by them, and his deficiencies made up. Young scholars may gain a great deal by converse with old Christians, as young students in the law may by old practitioners. Apollos, though he *was instructed in the way of the Lord,* did not rest in the knowledge he had attained, nor thought he understood Christianity as well as any man (which proud conceited young men are apt to do), but was willing to have it expounded to him more perfectly. Those that know much should covet to know more, and what they know to know it better, pressing forward towards perfection. [4.] Here is an instance of a good woman, though not permitted to speak in the church or in the synagogue, yet doing good with the knowledge God had given her in private converse. Paul will have *the aged women to be teachers of good things* Tit. 2:3, 4.

III. Here is his preferment to the service of the church of Corinth, which was a larger sphere of usefulness than Ephesus at present was. Paul had set wheels a-going in Achaia and particularly at Corinth, the county-town. Many were stirred up by his preaching to receive the gospel, and they needed to be confirmed; and many were likewise irritated to oppose the gospel, and they needed to be confuted. Paul was gone, was called away to other work, and now there was a fair occasion in this vacancy for Apollos to set in, who was fitted rather to water than to plant, to build up those that were within than to bring in those that were without. Now here we have,

1. His call to this service, not by a vision, as Paul was called to Macedonia, no, nor so much as by the invitation of those he was to go to; but, (1.) He himself inclined to go: *He was disposed to pass into Achaia;* having heard of the state of the churches there, he had a mind to try what good he could do among them. Though there were those there who were eminent for spiritual gifts, yet Apollos thought there might be some work for him, and God disposed his mind that way. (2.) His friends encouraged him to go, and approved of his purpose; and, he being a perfect stranger there, they gave him a testimonial or letters of recommendation, exhorting the disciples in Achaia to entertain him and employ him. In this way, among others, the communion of churches is kept up, by the recommending of members and ministers to each other, when ministers, as Apollos here, are disposed to remove. Though those at Ephesus had a great loss of his labours, they did not grudge those in Achaia the benefit of them; but, on the contrary, used their interest in them to introduce him; for the churches of Christ, though they are many, yet they are one.

2. His success in this service, which both ways answered his intention and expectation; for,

(1.) Believers were greatly edified, and those that had received the gospel were very much confirmed: *He helped those much who had believed through grace.* Note, [1.] Those who believe in Christ, it is through grace that they believe; it is *not of themselves, it is God's gift to them;* it is his work in them. [2.] Those who through grace do believe, yet still have need of help; as long as they are here in this world there are remainders of unbelief, and something lacking in their faith to be perfected, and the work of faith to be fulfilled. [3.] Faithful ministers are capable of being in many ways helpful to those who through grace do believe, and it is their business to help them, to help them much; and, when a divine power goes along with them, they will be helpful to them.

(2.) Unbelievers were greatly mortified. Their objections were fully answered, the folly and sophistry of their arguments were discovered, so that they had nothing to say in defence of the opposition they made to the gospel; their mouths were stopped, and their faces filled with shame (*v.* 28): *He mightily convinced the Jews, and that publicly,* before the people; he did it, *eutonōs — earnestly,* and with a great deal of vehemence; he took pains to do it; his heart was upon it, as one that was truly desirous both to serve the cause of Christ and to save the souls of men. He did it effectually and to universal satisfaction. He did it *levi negotio — with facility.* The case was so plain, and the arguments were so strong on Christ's side, that it was an easy matter to baffle all that the Jews could say against it. Though they were so fierce, yet their cause was so weak that he made nothing of their opposition. Now that which he aimed to convince them of was *that Jesus is the Christ,* that he is *the Messiah promised to the fathers, who should come,* and they were to look for not other. If the Jews were but convinced of this — that Jesus is Christ, even their own law would teach them to hear him. Note, The business of ministers is to preach Christ: *We preach not ourselves, but Christ Jesus the Lord.* The way he took to convince them was *by the scriptures;* thence he fetched his arguments; for the Jews owned the scriptures to be of divine authority, and it was easy for him, who was mighty in the scriptures, from them to show that Jesus is the Christ. Note, Ministers must be able not only to preach the truth, but to prove it and defend it, and to convince gainsayers with meekness and yet with power, instructing those that oppose themselves; and this is real service to the church.

CHAPTER 19

We left Paul in his circuit visiting the churches (*ch.* 18:23), but we have not forgotten, nor has he, the promise he made to his friends at Ephesus, to return to them, and make some stay there; now this chapter shows us his performance of that promise, his coming to Ephesus, and his continuance there two years; we are here told, I. How he laboured there in the word and doctrine, how he taught some weak believers that had gone no further than John's baptism (*v.* 1–7), how he taught three months in the synagogue of the Jews (*v.* 8), and, when he was driven thence, how he taught the Gentiles a long time in a public school (*v.* 9, 10), and how he confirmed his doctrine by miracles (*v.* 11, 12). II. What was the fruit of his labour, particularly among the conjurors, the worst of sinners: some were confounded, that did but make use of his name (*v.* 13–17), but others were converted, that received and embraced his doctrine (*v.* 18–20). III. What projects he had of further usefulness (*v.* 21, 22), and what trouble at length he met with at Ephesus from the silversmiths, which forced him thence to pursue the measures he had laid; how a mob was raised by Demetrius to cry up Diana (*v.* 23–34), and how it was suppressed and dispersed by the town-clerk (*v.* 35–41).

Verses 1–7

Ephesus was a city of great note in Asia, famous for a temple built there to Diana, which was one of the wonders of the world: thither *Paul came to preach the gospel while Apollos was at Corinth* (*v.* 1); while he was watering there, Paul was planting here, and grudged not that Apollos entered into his labours and was building upon his foundation, but rejoiced in it, and went on in the new work that was cut out for him at Ephesus with the more cheerfulness and satisfaction, because he knew that such an able minister of the New Testament as Apollos was now at Corinth, carrying on the good work there. Though there were those that made him the head of a party against Paul (1 Co. 1:12), yet Paul had no jealousy of him, nor any way disliked the affection the people had for him. Paul having gone through the country of Galatia and Phrygia, having *passed through the upper coasts,* Pontus and Bithynia, that lay north, at length *came to Ephesus,* where he had left Aquila and Priscilla, and there found them. At his first coming, he met with some disciples there, who professed faith in Christ as the true Messiah, but were as yet in the first and lowest form in the school of Christ, under his usher John the Baptist. They were in number *about twelve* (*v.* 7); they were much of the standing that Apollos was of when he came to Ephesus (for he *knew only the baptism of John, ch.* 18:25), but they had not opportunity of being acquainted with Aquila and Priscilla, or had not been so long in Ephesus or were not so willing to receive instruction as Apollos was, otherwise they might have had the way of God expounded to them more perfectly, as Apollos had. Observe here,

I. How Paul catechised them. He was told, probably by Aquila and Priscilla, that they were believers, that they did own Christ, and had given up their names to him; now Paul hereupon takes them under examination.

1. They did believe in the Son of God; but Paul enquires whether they had *received the Holy Ghost,* — whether they believed in the spirit, whose operations on the minds of men, for conviction, conversion, and comfort, were revealed some time after the doctrine of Jesus being the Christ, — whether they had been acquainted with, and had admitted, this revelation? This was not all; extraordinary gifts of the Holy Ghost were conferred upon the apostles and other disciples presently after Christ's ascension, which was frequently repeated upon occasion; had they participated in these gifts? *"Have you received the Holy Ghost since you believed?* Have you had that seal of the truth of Christ's doctrine in yourselves?" We are not now to expect any such extraordinary gifts as they had then. The canon of the New Testament being long since completed and ratified, we depend upon that as the most sure word of prophecy. But there are graces of the Spirit given to all believers, which are as earnests to them, 2 Co. 1:22; 5:5; Eph. 1:13, 14. Now it concerns us all who profess the Christian faith seriously to enquire whether we have received the Holy Ghost or not. The Holy Ghost is promised to all believers, to all petitioners (Lu. 11:13); but many are deceived in this matter, thinking they have received the Holy Ghost when really they have not. As there are pretenders to the gifts of the Holy Ghost, so there are to his graces and comforts; we should therefore strictly examine ourselves, Have we received the Holy Ghost since we believed? The tree will be known by its fruits. Do we bring forth the fruits of the Spirit? Are we led by the Spirit? Do we walk in the Spirit? Are we under the government of the Spirit?

2. They owned their ignorance in this matter: *"Whether there be a Holy Ghost* is more than we know. That there is a promise of the Holy Ghost we know from the scriptures of the Old Testament, and that this promise will be fulfilled in its season we doubt not; but so much have we been out of the way of intelligence in this matter that we have not so much as heard whether the Holy Ghost be indeed yet given as a spirit of prophecy." They knew (as Dr. Lightfoot observes) that, according to the tradition of their nation, after the death of Ezra, Haggai, Zechariah, and Malachi, *the Holy Ghost departed from Israel, and went up;* and they professed that they had never heard of his return. They spoke as if they expected it, and wondered they did not hear of it, and were ready to welcome the notice of it. The gospel light, like that of the morning, shone more and more, gradually; not only clearer and clearer, in the discovery of truths not before heard of, but further and further, in the discovery of them to persons that had not before heard of them.

3. Paul enquired how they came to be baptized, if they

knew nothing of the Holy Ghost; for, if they were baptized by any of Christ's ministers, they were instructed concerning the Holy Ghost, and were baptized in his name. "Know you not that Jesus being glorified, consequently the Holy Ghost is given? *unto what then were you baptized?* This is strange and unaccountable. What! baptized, and yet know nothing of the Holy Ghost? Surely your baptism was a nullity, if you know nothing of the Holy Ghost; for it is the receiving of the Holy Ghost that is signified and sealed by that washing of regeneration. Ignorance of the Holy Ghost is as inconsistent with a sincere profession of Christianity as ignorance of Christ is." Applying it to ourselves, it intimates that those are baptized to no purpose, and have received the grace of God therein in vain, that do not receive and submit to the Holy Ghost. It is also an enquiry we should often make, not only to whose honour we were born, but into whose service we were baptized, that we may study to answer the ends both of our birth and of our baptism. Let us often consider unto what we were baptized, that we may live up to our baptism.

4. They own that they were baptized *unto John's baptism — eis to Iōannou baptisma* that is, as I take it, they were baptized in the name of John, not by John himself (he was far enough from any such thought), but by some weak, well-meaning disciple of his, that ignorantly kept up his name as the head of a party, retaining the spirit and notion of those disciples of his that were jealous of the growth of Christ's interest, and complained to him of it, Jn. 3:26. Some one or more of these, that found themselves much edified by John's baptism of *repentance for the remission of sins,* not thinking that the kingdom of heaven, which he spoke of as at hand, was so very near as it proved, ran away with that notion, rested in what they had, and thought they could not do better than to persuade others to do so too; and so, ignorantly, in a blind zeal for John's doctrine, they baptized here and there one in John's name, or, as it is here expressed, *unto John's baptism,* looking no further themselves, nor directing those that they baptized any further.

5. Paul explains to them the true intent and meaning of John's baptism, as principally referring to Jesus Christ, and so rectifies the mistake of those who had baptized them into the baptism of John, and had not directed them to look any further, but to rest in that. Those that have been left in ignorance, or led into error, by any infelicities of their education, should not therefore be despised nor rejected by those who are more knowing and orthodox, but should be compassionately instructed, and better taught, as these disciples were by Paul. (1.) He owns that John's baptism was a very good thing, as far as it went: *John verily baptized with the baptism of repentance.* By this baptism he required people to be sorry for their sins, and to confess them and turn from them; and to bring any to this is a great point gained. But, (2.) He shows them that John's baptism had a further reference, and he never designed that those he baptized should rest there, but told them that they should believe on him who should come after him, that is, on Christ Jesus, — that his baptism of repentance was designed only to prepare the way of the Lord, and to dispose them to receive and entertain Christ, whom he left them big with expectations of; nay, whom he directed them to: *Behold the Lamb of God.* "John was a great and good man; but he was only the harbinger, — Christ is the Prince. His baptism was the porch which you were to pass through, not the house you were to rest in; and therefore it was all wrong for you to be baptized into the baptism of John."

6. When they were thus shown the error they were led into, they thankfully accepted the discovery, and *were baptized in the name of the Lord Jesus, v.* 5. As for Apollos, of whom it was said (*ch.* 18:25) that he *knew the baptism of John* — that he rightly understood the meaning of it when he was baptized with it, though he knew that *only* — yet, when he understood the way of God more perfectly, he was no again baptized, any more than Christ's first disciples that had been baptized with John's baptism and knew it referred to the Messiah at the door (and, with an eye to this, submitted to it), were baptized again. But to these disciples, who received it only with an eye to John and looked no further, as if he were their saviour, it was such a fundamental error as was as fatal to it as it would have been for any to be baptized in the name of Paul (1 Co. 1:13); and therefore, when they came to understand things better, they desired to be *baptized in the name of the Lord Jesus,* and were so: not by Paul himself, as we have reason to think, but by some of those who attended him. It does not therefore follow hence that there was not an agreement between John's baptism and Christ's, or that they were not for substance the same; much less does it follow that those who have been once baptized *in the name of the Father, Son, and Holy Ghost* (which is the appointed form of Christ's baptism), may be again baptized in the same name; for those that were baptized *in the name of the Lord Jesus* had never been so baptized before.

II. How Paul conferred the extraordinary gifts of the Holy Ghost upon them, *v.* 6. 1. Paul solemnly *prayed to God* to give them those gifts, signified by his *laying his hands on them,* which was a gesture used in blessing by the patriarchs, especially in conveying the great trust of the promise, as Gen. 48:14. The Spirit being the great promise of the New Testament, the apostles conveyed it by the imposition of hands: "The Lord bless thee with that blessing, that blessing of blessings," Isa. 44:3. 2. God granted the thing he prayed for: *The Holy Ghost came upon them* in a surprising overpowering manner, and *they spoke with tongues and prophesied,* as the apostles did and the first Gentile converts, *ch.* 10:44. This was intended to introduce the gospel at Ephesus, and to awaken in the minds of men an expectation of some great things from it; and some think that it was further designed to qualify these twelve men for the work of the ministry, and that these twelve were the elders of Ephesus, to whom Paul committed the care and government of that church. They had the Spirit of prophesy, that they might understand the mysteries of the kingdom of God themselves, and the gift of tongues, that they might preach them to every nation and language. Oh, what a wonderful change was here made on a sudden in these men! those that but just now had *not so much as heard that there was any Holy Ghost* are now themselves filled with the Holy Ghost; for the Spirit, like the wind, blows where and when he listeth.

Verses 8–12

Paul is here very busy at Ephesus to do good.

I. He begins, as usual, in the Jews' synagogue, and makes the first offer of the gospel to them, that he might gather in the *lost sheep of the house of Israel,* who were now scattered upon the mountains. Observe,

1. Where he preached to them: in their synagogue (*v.* 8), as Christ used to do. He went and joined them in their synagogue-worship, to take off their prejudices against him, and to ingratiate himself with them, while there was any hope of winning upon them. Thus he would bear his testimony to public worship on sabbath days. Where there were no Christian assemblies yet formed, he frequented the Jewish assemblies, while the Jews were not as yet wholly cast off. Paul went into the synagogue, because there he had them together, and had them, it might be hoped, in a good frame.

2. What he preached to them: *The things concerning the kingdom of God* among men, the great things which concerned God's dominion over all men and favour to them, and men's subjection to God and happiness in God. He showed them their obligations to God and interest in him, as the Creator, by which the kingdom of God was set up, — the violation of those obligations, and the forfeiture of that interest, by sin, by which the kingdom of God was pulled down, — and the renewing of those obligations and the restoration of man to that interest again, by the Redeemer, whereby the kingdom of God was again set up. Or, more particularly, *the things concerning the kingdom of the Messiah,* which the Jews were in expectation of, and promised themselves great matters from; he opened the scriptures which spoke concerning this, gave them a right notion of this kingdom, and showeth them their mistakes about it.

3. How he preached to them. (1.) He preached argumentatively: he disputed; gave reasons, scripture-reasons, for what he preached, and answered objections, for the convincing of men's judgments and consciences, that they might not only believe, but might see cause to believe. He preached *dialegomenos — dialogue-wise;* he put questions to them and received their answers, gave them leave to put questions to him and answered them. (2.) He preached affectionately: he persuaded; he used not only logical arguments, to enforce what he said upon their understandings, but rhetorical motives, to impress what he said upon their affections, showing them that the things he preached concerning the kingdom of God were things concerning themselves, which they were nearly concerned in, and therefore ought to concern themselves about, 2 Co. 5:11, *We persuade men.* Paul was a moving preacher, and was a master of the art of persuasion. (3.) He preached undauntedly, and with a holy resolution: he spoke boldly, as one that had not the least doubt of the things he spoke of, nor the least distrust of him he spoke from, nor the least dread of those he spoke to.

4. How long he preached to them: *For the space of three months,* which was a competent time allowed them to consider of it; in that time among them that belonged to the election of grace were called in, and the rest were left inexcusable. Thus long Paul preached the gospel *with much contention* (1 Th. 2:2), yet he *did not fail, nor was discouraged.*

5. What success his preaching had among them. (1.) There were some that were persuaded to believe in Christ; some think this is intimated in the word *persuading* — he prevailed with them. But, (2.) Many continued in their infidelity, and were confirmed in their prejudices against Christianity. When Paul called on them before, and preached only some general things to them, they courted his stay among them (*ch.* 18:20); but now that he settled among them, and his word came more closely to their consciences, they were soon weary of him. [1.] They had an invincible aversion to the gospel of Christ themselves: they were *hardened, and believed not;* they were resolved they would not believe, though the truth shone in their faces with ever such a convincing light and evidence. Therefore they believed not, because they were hardened. [2.] They did their utmost to raise and keep up in others an aversion to the gospel; they not only entered not into the kingdom of God themselves, but neither did they suffer those that were entering to go in; for *they spoke evil of that way before the multitude,* to prejudice them against it. Though they could not show any manner of evil in it, yet they said all manner of evil concerning it. These sinners, like the angels that sinned, became Satans, adversaries and devils, false accusers.

II. When he had carried the matter as far as it would go in the synagogue of the Jews, and found that their opposition grew more obstinate, he left the synagogue, because he could not safely, or rather because he could not comfortably and successfully, continue in communion with them. Though their worship was such as he could join in, and they had not silenced him, nor forbidden him to preach among them, yet they drove him from them by their railing at those things which he spoke *concerning the kingdom of God:* they hated to be reformed, hated to be instructed, and therefore *he departed from them.* Here we are sure there was a separation and no schism; for there was a just cause for it and a clear call to it. Now observe,

1. When Paul departed from the Jews he took the disciples with him, and *separated them, to save them from that untoward generation* (according to the charge Peter gave to his new converts, *ch.* 2:40); lest they should be infected with the poisonous tongues of those blasphemers, he separated those who believed, to be the foundation of a Christian church, now that they were a competent number to be incorporated, that others might attend with them upon the preaching of the gospel, and might, upon their believing, be added to them. When Paul departed there needed no more to separate the disciples; let him go where he will, they will follow him.

2. When Paul separated from the synagogue he set up a meeting of his own, he *disputed daily in the school of one Tyrannus.* He left the synagogue of the Jews, that he might go on with the more freedom in his work; still he disputed for Christ and Christianity, and was ready to answer all opponents whatsoever in defence of them; and he had by this separation a double advantage. (1.) That now his opportunities were more frequent. In the synagogue he could only preach every sabbath day (*ch.* 13:42), but now he disputed daily, he set up a lecture every day, and thus redeemed time: those whose business would not permit them to come one day might come another day; and those were welcome who *watched daily at these gates of wisdom, and waited daily at the posts of her doors.* (2.) That now they were more open. To the synagogue of the Jews none might come, nor could come, but Jews or proselytes; Gentiles were excluded; but, when he set up a meeting in the school of Tyrannus, both Jews and Greeks attended his ministry, *v.* 10. Thus, as he describes this gate of opportunity at Ephesus (1 Co. 16:8, 9), *a wide door and an effectual* was *opened to him,* though *there were many adversaries.* Some think this school of Tyrannus was a divinity-school of the Jews, and such a one they commonly had in their great cities besides their synagogue; they

called it *Bethmidrash, the house of enquiry,* or of *repetition;* and they went to that on the sabbath day, after they had been in the synagogue. They go *from strength to strength,* from the *house of the sanctuary to the house of doctrine.* If this was such a school, it shows that though Paul left the synagogue he left it gradually, and still kept as near it as he could, as he had done, *ch.* 18:7. But others think it was a philosophy-school of the Gentiles, belonging to one Tyrannus, or a retiring place (for so the word *scholē* sometimes signifies) belonging to a principal man or governor of the city; some convenient place it was, which Paul and the disciples had the use of, either for love or money.

3. Here he continued his labours for *two years,* read his lectures and disputed daily. These two years commence from the end of the *three months* which he spent in the synagogue (*v.* 8); after they were ended, he continued for some time in the country about, preaching; therefore he might justly reckon it in all three years, as he does, *ch.* 20:31.

4. The gospel hereby spread far and near (*v.* 10): *All those that dwelt in Asia heard the word of the Lord Jesus;* not only all that dwelt in Ephesus, but all that dwelt in that large province called *Asia,* of which Ephesus was the head city — *Asia the Less* it was called. There was great resort to Ephesus from all parts of the country, for law, traffic, religion, and education, which gave Paul an opportunity of sending the report of the gospel to all the towns and villages of that country. They all heard the *word of the Lord Jesus.* The gospel is Christ's word, it is a word concerning Christ. This they heard, or at least heard of it. Some of all sects, some out of all parts both in city and country, embraced this gospel, and entertained it, and by them it was communicated to others; and so they all *heard the word of the Lord Jesus,* or might have heard it. Probably Paul sometimes made excursions himself into the country, to preach the gospel, or sent his missionaries or assistants that attended him, and thus the word of the Lord was *heard throughout that region.* Now *those that sat in darkness saw a great light.*

III. God confirmed Paul's doctrine by miracles, which awakened people's enquiries after it, fixed their affection to it, and engaged their belief of it, *v.* 11, 12. I wonder we have not read of any miracle wrought by Paul since the casting of the evil spirit out of the damsel at Philippi; why did he not work miracles at Thessalonica, Berea, and Athens? Or, if he did, why are they not recorded? Was the success of the gospel, without miracles in the kingdom of nature, itself such a miracle in the kingdom of grace, and the divine power which went along with it such a proof of its divine original, that there needed no other? It is certain that at Corinth he wrought many miracles, though Luke has recorded none, for he tells them (2 Co. 12:12) that the signs of his apostleship were among them, *in wonders and mighty deeds.* But here at Ephesus we have a general account of the proofs of this kind which he gave his divine mission. 1. They were *special miracles — Dynameis ou tychousas.* God exerted powers that were not according to the common course of nature: *Virtutes non vulgares.* Things were done which could by no means be ascribed either to chance or second causes. Or, they were not only (as all miracles are) *out of the common road,* but they were even uncommon miracles, such miracles as had not been wrought by the hands of any other of the apostles. The opposers of the gospel were so prejudiced that any miracles would not serve their turn; therefore God wrought *virtutes non quaslibet* (so they render it), *something above the common road of miracles.* 2. It was not Paul that wrought them *(What is Paul, and what is Apollos?)* but it was God that *wrought them by the hand of Paul.* He was but the instrument, God was the principal agent.

3. He not only cured the sick that were brought to him, or to whom he was brought, but *from his body were brought to the sick handkerchiefs or aprons;* they got Paul's handkerchiefs, or his aprons, that is, say some, the aprons he wore when he worked at his trade, and the application of them to the sick cured them immediately. Or, they brought the sick people's handkerchiefs, or their girdles, or caps, or head-dresses, and laid them for awhile to Paul's body, and then took them to the sick. The former is more probable. Now was fulfilled that word of Christ to his disciples, *Greater works than these shall you do.* We read of one that was cured by the touch of Christ's garment when it was upon him, and he perceived that *virtue went out of him;* but here were people cured by Paul's garments when they were taken from him. Christ gave his apostles power *against unclean spirits and against all manner of sickness* (Mt. 10:1), and accordingly we find here that those to whom Paul sent relief had it in both those cases: *for the diseases departed from them* and the *evil spirits went out of them,* which were both significant of the great design and blessed effect of the gospel, and the healing of spiritual disease, and freeing the souls of men from the power and dominion of Satan.

Verses 13–20

The preachers of the gospel were sent forth to carry on a war against Satan, and therein Christ went forth *conquering and to conquer.* The casting of evil spirits out of those that were possessed was one instance of Christ's victory over Satan; but, to show in how many ways Christ triumphed over that great enemy, we have here in these verses two remarkable instances of the conquest of Satan, not only in those that were violently possessed by him, but in those that were voluntarily devoted to him.

I. Here is the confusion of some of Satan's servants, some *vagabond Jews,* that were *exorcists,* who made use of Christ's name profanely and wickedly in their diabolical enchantments, but were made to pay dearly for their presumption. Observe,

1. The general character of those who were guilty of this presumption. They were Jews, but *vagabond* Jews, were of the Jewish nation and religion, but went about from town to town to get money by conjuring. They strolled about to tell people their fortunes, and pretended by spells and charms to cure diseases, and bring people to themselves that were melancholy or distracted. They called themselves exorcists, because in doing their tricks they used forms of adjuration, by such and such commanding names. The superstitious Jews, to put a reputation upon these magic arts, wickedly attributed the invention of them to Solomon. So Josephus (*Antiq.* 8.45–46) says that Solomon composed charms by which diseases were cured, and devils driven out so as never to return; and that these operations continued common among the Jews to his time. And Christ seems to refer to this (Mt. 12:27), *By whom do your children cast them out?*

2. A particular account of some at Ephesus that led this course of life and came thither in their travels; they were *seven sons of one Sceva, a Jew, and chief of the priests, v.* 14. It is sad to see the house of Jacob thus degenerated, much more the house of Aaron, the family that was in a peculiar manner consecrated to God; it is truly sad to see any of that race in league with Satan. Their father was a chief of the priests, head of one of the twenty-four courses of priests. One would think the temple would find both employment and encouragement enough for the sons of a chief priest, if they had been twice as many. But probably it was a vain, rambling, rakish humour that led them to turn mountebanks, and wander all the world over to cure mad folks.

3. The profaneness they were guilty of: *They took upon them to call over evil spirits the name of the Lord Jesus;* not as those who had a veneration for Christ and a confidence in his name, as we read of some who cast out devils in Christ's name and yet did not follow with his disciples (Lu. 9:49), whom he would not have to be discouraged; but as those who were willing to try all methods to carry on their wicked trade, and, it should seem, had this design: — If the evil spirits should yield to an adjuration in the name of Jesus by those that did not believe in him, they would say it was no confirmation of his doctrine to those that did; for it was all one whether they believed it or no. If they should not yield to it, they would say the name of Christ was not so powerful as the other names they used, to which the devils had often by collusion yielded. They said, *We adjure you by Jesus whom Paul preaches;* not, "whom we believe in, or depend upon, or have any authority from," but *whom Paul preaches;* as if they had said, "We will try what that name will do." The exorcists in the Romish church, who pretend to cast the devil out of melancholy people by spells and charms which they understand not, and which, not having any divine warrant, cannot be used in faith, are the followers of these vagabond Jews.

4. The confusion they were put to in their impious operations. Let them not be deceived, God is not mocked, nor shall the glorious name of Jesus be prostituted to such a vile purpose as this; *what communion hath Christ with Belial?* (1.) The evil spirit gave them a sharp reply (*v.* 15): *"Jesus I know, and Paul I know; but who are you?* I know that Jesus has conquered principalities and powers, and that Paul has authority in his name to cast out devils; but what power have you to command us in his name, or who gave you any such power? What have you to do to declare the power of Jesus, or to take his covenant and commands into your mouths, seeing you hate his instructions?" Ps. 50:16, 17. This was extorted out of the mouth of the evil spirit by the power of God, to gain honour to the gospel, and to put those to shame that made a bad use of Christ's name. Antichristian powers and factions pretend a mighty zeal for Jesus and Paul, and to have authority from them; but, when the matter comes to be looked into, it is a mere worldly secular interest that is to be thus supported; nay, it is an enmity to true religion: *Jesus we know, and Paul we know; but who are you?* (2.) *The man in whom the evil spirit was* gave them a warm reception, fell foul upon them, *leaped upon them* in the height of his frenzy and rage, *overcame them* and all their enchantments, *prevailed against them,* and was every way too hard for them; so that *they fled out of the house,* not only *naked,* but *wounded;* their clothes pulled off their backs, and their heads broken. This is written for a warning to all those who name the name of Christ, but do not depart from iniquity. The same enemy that overcomes them with his temptations will overcome them with his terrors; and their adjuring him in Christ's name to let them alone will be no security to them. If we resist the devil by a true and lively faith in Christ, he will flee from us; but if we think to resist him by the bare using of Christ's name, or any part of his word, as a spell or charm, he will prevail against us.

5. The general notice that was taken of this, and the good impression it made upon many (*v.* 17): *This was known to all the Jews and Greeks also dwelling at Ephesus.* It was the common talk of the town; and the effect of it was, (1.) That men were terrified: *fear fell on them all.* In this instance they saw the malice of the devil whom they served, and the power of Christ whom they opposed; and both were awful considerations. They saw that the name of Christ was not to be trifled with, nor his religion compounded with pagan superstitions. (2.) That God was glorified; *the name of the Lord Jesus,* by which his faithful servants cast out devils and cured diseases, without any resistance, *was the more magnified;* for now it appeared to be a name above every name.

II. Here is the conversion of others of Satan's servants, with the evidences of their conversion.

1. Those that had been guilty of wicked practices confessed them, *v.* 18. Many that had believed and were baptized, but had not then been so particular as they might have been in the confession of their sins, were so terrified with these instances of the magnifying of the name of Jesus Christ that they came to Paul, or some of the other ministers that were with him, and confessed what evil lives they had led, and what a great deal of secret wickedness their own consciences charged them with, which the world knew not of — secret frauds and secret filthiness; *they showed their deeds,* took shame to themselves and gave glory to God and warning to others. These confessions were not extorted from them, but were voluntary, for the ease of their consciences, upon which the late miracles had struck a terror. Note, Where there is true contrition for sin there will be an ingenuous confession of sin to God in every prayer, and to man whom we have offended when the case requires it.

2. Those that had conversed with wicked books burnt them (*v.* 19): *Many also of those who used curious arts, ta perierga — impertinent things; multa nihil ad se pertinentia satagentes — busy bodies* (so the word is used, 2 Th. 3:11; 1 Tim. 5:13), that traded in the study of magic and divination, in books of judicial astrology, casting nativities, telling fortunes, raising and laying spirits, interpreting dreams, predicting future events, and the like, to which some think are to be added *plays, romances, love-books, and unchaste and immodest poems — histrionica, amatoria, saltatoria.* — Stres. These, having their consciences more awakened than ever to see the evil of those practices in which these books instructed them, *brought their books together, and burnt them before all men.* Ephesus was notorious for the use of these curious arts; hence spells and charms were called *Literae Ephesiae.* Here people furnished themselves with all those sorts of books, and, probably, had tutors to instruct them in those *black* arts. It was therefore much for the honour of Christ and his gospel to have such a noble testimony borne against those *curious* arts, in a place where they were so much in vogue. It is taken for granted that they were convinced of the evil of these curious arts, and resolved to deal in them no longer; but they did not think this enough unless

they burnt their books. (1.) Thus they showed a holy indignation at the sins they had been guilty of; as the idolaters, when they were brought to repentance, said to their idols, *Get you hence* (Isa. 30:22), and cast even those of silver and gold *to the moles and to the bats,* Isa. 2:20. They thus took a pious revenge on those things that had been the instruments of sin to them, and proclaimed the force of their convictions of the evil of it, and that those very things were now detectable to them, as much as ever they had been delectable. (2.) Thus they showed their resolution never to return to the use of those arts, and the books which related to them, again. They were so fully convinced of the evil and danger of them that they would not throw the books by, within reach of a recall, upon supposition that it was possible they might change their mind; but, being stedfastly resolved never to make use of them, they burnt them. (3.) Thus they put away a temptation to return to them again. Had they kept the books by them, there was danger lest, when the heat of the present conviction was over, they should have the curiosity to look into them, and so be in danger of liking them and loving them again, and therefore they burnt them. Note, Those that truly repent of sin will keep themselves as far as possible from the occasions of it. (4.) Thus they prevented their doing mischief to others. If Judas had been by he would have said, "Sell them, and give the money to the poor;" or, "Buy Bibles and good books with it." But then who could tell into whose hands these dangerous books might fall, and what mischief might be done by them? it was therefore the safest course to commit them all to the flames. Those that are recovered from sin themselves will do all they can to keep others from falling into it, and will be much more afraid of laying an occasion of sin in the way of others. (5.) Thus they showed a contempt of the wealth of this world; for the price of the books was cast up, probably by those that persuaded them not to burn them, and it was found to be *fifty thousand pieces of silver,* which some compute to be fifteen hundred pounds of our money. It is probable that the books were scarce, perhaps prohibited, and therefore dear. Probably they had cost them so much; yet, being the devil's books, though they had been so foolish as to buy them, they did not think this would justify them in being so wicked as to sell them again. (6.) Thus they publicly testified their joy for their conversion from these wicked practices, as Matthew did by the great feast he made when Christ had called him from the receipt of custom. These converts joined together in making this bonfire, and made it before all men. They might have burnt the books privately, every one in his own house, but they chose to do it together, by consent, and to do it at the high cross (as we say), that Christ and his grace in them might be the more magnified, and all about them the more edified.

III. Here is a general account of the progress and success of the gospel in and about Ephesus (*v.* 20): *So mightily grew the word of God, and prevailed.* It is a blessed sight to see the word of God growing and prevailing mightily, as it did here. 1. To see it grow extensively, by the addition of many to the church. When still more and more are wrought upon by the gospel, and wrought up into a conformity to it, then it grows; when those that were least likely to yield to it, and that had been most stiff in their opposition to it, are captivated and brought into obedience to it, then it may be said to *grow mightily.* 2. To see it prevail extensively, by the advancement in knowledge and grace of those that are added to the church; when strong corruptions are mortified, vicious habits changed, evil customs of long standing broken off, and pleasant, gainful, fashionable sins are abandoned, then it prevails mightily; and Christ in it goes on conquering and to conquer.

Verses 21–41

I. Paul is here brought into some trouble at Ephesus, just when he is forecasting to go thence, and to cut out work for himself elsewhere. See here,

1. How he laid his purpose of going to other places, *v.* 21, 22. He was a man of vast designs for God, and was for making his influences as widely diffusive as might be. Having spent above two years at Ephesus, (1.) He designed a visit to the churches of Macedonia and Achaia, especially of Philippi and Corinth, the chief cities of those provinces, *v.* 21. There he had planted churches, and now is concerned to visit them. He *purposed in the spirit,* either in his own spirit, not communicating his purpose as yet, but keeping it to himself; or by the direction of the Holy Spirit, who was his guide in all his motions, and by whom he was led. He purposed to go and see how the work of God went on in those places, that he might rectify what was amiss and encourage what was good. (2.) Thence he designed to go to Jerusalem, to visit the brethren there, and give an account to them of the prospering of the good pleasure of the Lord in his hand; and thence he intended to go to Rome, to go and *see Rome;* not as if he designed only the gratifying of his curiosity with the sight of that ancient famous city, but because it was an expression people commonly used, that they would go and see Rome, would look about them there, when that which he designed was to see the Christians there, and to do them some service, Rom. 1:11. The good people at Rome were the glory of the city which he longed for a sight of. Dr. Lightfoot supposes that it was upon the death of the emperor Claudius, who died the second year of Paul's being at Ephesus, that Paul thought of going to Rome, because while he lived the Jews were forbidden Rome, *ch.* 18:2. (3.) He sent Timothy and Erastus into Macedonia, to give them notice of the visit he intended them, and to get their collection ready for the poor saints at Jerusalem. Soon after he wrote *the first epistle to the Corinthians,* designing to follow it himself, as appears 1 Co. 4:17, 19, *I have sent to you Timotheus; but I will myself come to you shortly, if the Lord will.* For the present, he staid in Asia, in the country about Ephesus, founding churches.

2. How he was seconded in his purpose, and obliged to pursue it by the troubles which at length he met with at Ephesus. It was strange that he had been quiet there so long; yet it should seem he had met with trouble there not recorded in this story, for in his epistle written at this time he speaks of his having *fought with beasts at Ephesus* (1 Co. 15:32), which seems to be meant of his being put to fight with wild beasts in the theatre, according to the barbarous treatment they sometimes gave the Christians. And he speaks of the trouble which came to them in Asia, near Ephesus, when he *despaired of life,* and *received a sentence of death within himself,* 2 Co. 1:8, 9.

II. But, in the trouble here related, he was worse frightened than hurt. In general, *there arose no small stir about that way, v.* 23. Some historians say that the famous impostor Apollonius Tyanaeus, who set up for a rival with Christ, and gave out himself, as Simon Magus, to be *some great one,* was at Ephesus about this time that Paul was there. But it seems the opposition he gave to the gospel was so insignificant that St. Luke did not think it worth taking notice of. The disturbance he gives an account of was of another nature: let us view the particulars of it. Here is,

1. A great complaint against Paul and the other preachers of the gospel for drawing people off from the worship of Diana, and so spoiling the trade of the silversmiths that worked for Diana's temple.

(1.) The complainant is Demetrius, a silversmith, a principal man, it is likely, of the trade, and one that would be thought to understand and consult the interests of it more than others of the company. Whether he worked in other sorts of plate or no we are not told; but the most advantageous branch of his trade was *making silver shrines for Diana, v.* 24. Some think these were medals stamped with the effigies of Diana, or her temple, or both; others think they were representations of the temple, with the image of Diana in it in miniature, all of silver, but so small that people might carry them about with them, as the papists do their crucifixes. Those that came from far to pay their devotions at the temple of Ephesus, when they went home bought these little temples or shrines, to carry home with them, for the gratifying of the curiosity of their friends, and to preserve in their own minds the idea of that stately edifice. See how craftsmen, and crafty men too above the rank of silversmiths, make an advantage to themselves of people's superstition, and serve their worldly ends by it.

(2.) The persons he appeals to are not the magistrates, but the mob; he called the *craftsmen* together, *with the workmen of like occupation* (a company of mechanics, who had no sense of any thing but their worldly interest), and these he endeavoured to incense against Paul, who would be actuated as little by reason and as much by fury as he could desire.

(3.) His complaint and representation are very full. [1.] He lays it down for a principle that the art and mystery of making silver shrines for the worshippers of Diana was very necessary to be supported and kept up (*v.* 25): *"You know that by this craft we have* not only our subsistence, and our necessary food, but *our wealth.* We grow rich, and raise estates. We live great, and have wherewithal to maintain our pleasures; and therefore, whatever comes of it, we must not suffer this craft to grow into contempt." Note, It is natural for men to be jealous for that, whether right or wrong, by which they get their wealth; and many have, for this reason alone, set themselves against the gospel of Christ, because it calls men off from those crafts which are unlawful, how much wealth soever is to be obtained by them. [2.] He charges it upon Paul that he had dissuaded men from worshipping idols. The words, as they are laid in the indictment, are, that he had asserted, *Those are no gods which are made with hands, v.* 26. Could any truth be more plain and self-evident than this, or any reasoning more cogent and convincing than that of the prophets, *The workman made it, therefore it is not God?* The first and most genuine notion we have of God is, that he had his being of himself, and depends upon none; but that all things have their being from him, and their dependence on him: and then it must follow that those are no gods which are the creatures of men's fancy and the work of men's hands. Yet this must be looked upon as an heretical and atheistical notion, and Paul as a criminal for maintaining it; not that they could advance any thing against this doctrine itself, but that the consequence of it was that not only at Ephesus, the chief city, but almost throughout all Asia, among the country people, who were their best customers, and whom they thought they were surest of, he had *persuaded and turned away much people* from the worship of Diana; so that there was not now such a demand for the silver shrines as had been, nor were such good rates given for them. There are those who will stickle for that which is most grossly absurd and unreasonable, and which carries along with it its own conviction of falsehood, as this does, *that those are gods which are made with hands,* if it have but human laws, and worldly interest and prescription, on its side. [3.] He reminds them of the danger which their trade was in of going to decay. Whatever touches this touches them in a sensible tender part: "If this doctrine gains credit, we are all undone, and may even shut up shop; *this our craft will be set at nought,* will be convicted, and put into an ill name as superstition, and a cheat upon the world, and every body will run it down. *This our part"* (so the word is), "our interest or share of trade and commerce," ***kindyneuei hēmin to meros,*** "will not only come into danger of being lost, but it will bring us into danger, and we shall become not only beggars, but malefactors." [4.] He pretends a mighty zeal for Diana, and a jealousy for her honour: *Not only this our craft is in danger;* if that were all, he would not have you think that he would have spoken with so much warmth, but all his care is lest *the temple of the great goddess Diana should be despised, and her magnificence should be destroyed;* and he would not, for all the world, see the diminution of the honour of that goddess, *whom all Asia and the world worship.* See what the worship of Diana had to plead for itself, and what was the utmost which the most zealous bigots for it had to say in its behalf. *First,* That it had pomp on its side; the magnificence of the temple was the thing that charmed them, the thing that chained them; they could not bear the thoughts of any thing that tended to the diminution, much less to the destruction, of that. *Secondly,* That it had numbers on its side; *All Asia and the world worship* it; and therefore it must needs be the right way of worship, let Paul say what he will to the contrary. Thus, because *all the world wonders after the beast,* therefore *the dragon, the devil, the god of this world, gives him his power, and his seat, and great authority,* Rev. 13:2, 3.

2. The popular resentment of this complaint. The charge was managed by a craftsman, and was framed to incense the common people, and it had the desired effect; for on this occasion they showed, (1.) A great displeasure against the gospel and the preachers of it. *They were full of wrath* (*v.* 28), *full of fury and indignation,* so the word signifies. The craftsmen went stark mad when they were told that their trade and their idol were both in danger. (2.) A great jealousy for the honour of their goddess: *They cried out, "Great is Diana of the Ephesians;* and we are resolved to stand by her, and live and die in the defence of her. Are there any that expose her to contempt, or threaten her destruction? Let us alone to deal with them. Let Paul say ever so much to prove that those are no gods which are made with hands, we will abide by it that, whatever becomes of other gods and goddesses, *Great is Diana of the Ephesians.* We must and will stand up for the religion of our country, which we have received by

tradition from our fathers." Thus all people *walked every one in the name of his god,* and all thought well of their own; much more should the servants of the true God do so, who can say, *This God is our God for ever and ever.* (3.) A great disorder among themselves (*v.* 29): *The whole city was full of confusion* — he common and natural effect of intemperate zeal for a false religion; it throws all into confusion, dethrones reason, and enthrones passion; and men run together, not only not knowing one another's minds, but not knowing their own.

3. The proceedings of the mob under the power of these resentments, and how far they were carried.

(1.) They laid hands on some of Paul's companions, and hurried them into the theatre (*v.* 29), some think with design there to make them *fight with beasts,* as Paul had sometimes done; or perhaps they intended only to abuse them, and to make them a spectacle to the crowd. Those whom they seized were *Gaius and Aristarchus,* of both of whom we read elsewhere. *Gaius was of Derbe, ch.* 20:4. *Aristarchus* is also there spoken of, and Col. 4:10. They came with Paul *from Macedonia,* and this was their only crime, that they were Paul's companions in travel, both in services and sufferings.

(2.) *Paul,* who had escaped being seized by them, when he perceived his friends in distress for his sake, *would have entered in unto the people,* to sacrifice himself, if there were no other remedy, rather than his friends should suffer upon his account; and it was an evidence of a generous spirit, and that he loved his neighbour as himself.

(3.) He was persuaded from it by the kindness of his friends, who overruled him. [1.] *The disciples suffered him not,* for it better became him to offer it than it would have become them to suffer it. They had reason to say to Paul, as David's servants did to him, when he was for exposing himself in a piece of public service, *Thou art worth ten thousand of us,* 2 Sa. 18:3. [2.] Others of his friends interposed, to prevent his throwing himself thus into the mouth of danger. They would treat him much worse than Gaius and Aristarchus, looking upon him as the ringleader of the party; and therefore better let them bear the brunt of the storm than that he should venture into it, *v.* 31. They were *certain of the chief of Asia, the princes of Asia — Asiarchai.* The critics tell us they were the chief of their priests; or, as others, the chief of their players. Whether they were converts to the Christian faith (and some such there were even of their priests and governors), or whether they were only well-wishers to Paul, as an ingenuous good man, we are not told, only that they were *Paul's friends.* Dr. Lightfoot suggests that they kept up a respect and kindness for him ever since he fought with beasts in their theatre, and were afraid he should be abused so again. Note, It is a friendly part to take more care of the lives and comforts of good men than they do themselves. It would be a very hazardous adventure for Paul to go into the theatre; it was a thousand to one that it would cost him his life; and therefore Paul was overruled by his friends to obey the law of self-preservation, and has taught us to keep out of the way of danger as long as we can without going out of the way of duty. We may be called to lay down our lives, but not to throw away our lives. It would better become Paul to venture into a synagogue than into a theatre.

(4.) The mob was in a perfect confusion (*v.* 32): *Some cried one thing and some another,* according as their fancies and passions, and perhaps the reports they received, led them. Some cried, Down with the Jews; others, Down with Paul; but *the assembly was confused,* as not understanding one another's minds. They contradicted one another, and were ready to fly in one another's faces for it, but they did not understand their own; for the truth was *the greater part knew not wherefore they had come together.* They knew not what began the riot, nor who, much less what business they had there; but, upon such occasions, the greatest part come only to enquire what the matter is: they follow the cry, follow the crowd, increase like a snow-ball, and where there are many there will be more.

(5.) The Jews would have interested themselves in this tumult (in other places they had been the first movers of such riots) but now at Ephesus they had not interest enough to raise the mob, and yet, when it was raised, they had ill-will enough to set in with it (*v.* 35): *They drew Alexander out of the multitude,* called him out to speak on the behalf of the Jews against Paul and his companions: "You have heard what Demetrius and the silversmiths have to say against them, as enemies to their religion; give us leave now to tell you what we have to say against him as an enemy to our religion." *The Jews put him forward* to do this, encouraged him, and told him they would stand by him and second him; and this they looked upon as necessary in their own defence, and therefore what he designed to say is called his apologizing to the people, not for himself in particular, but for the Jews in general, whom the worshippers of Diana looked upon to be as much their enemies as Paul was. Now they would have them know that they were as much Paul's enemies as they were; and those who are thus careful to distinguish themselves from the servants of Christ now, and are afraid of being taken for them, shall have their doom accordingly in the great day. *Alexander beckoned with the hand,* desiring to be heard against Paul; for it had been strange if a persecution had been carried on against the Christians and there were not Jews at one end or the other of it: if they could not begin the mischief, they would help it forward, and so make themselves partakers of other men's sins. Some think this Alexander had been a Christian, but had apostatized to Judaism, and therefore was drawn out as a proper person to accuse Paul; and that he was the *Alexander the coppersmith* that did Paul so much evil (2 Tim. 4:14), and whom he had *delivered unto Satan,* 1 Tim. 1:20.

(6.) This occasioned the prosecutors to drop the prosecution of Paul's friends, and to turn it into acclamations in honour of their goddess (*v.* 34): *When they knew that he was a Jew,* and, as such, an enemy to the worship of Diana (for the Jews had now an implacable hatred to idols and idolatry), whatever he had to say for Paul or against him, they were resolved not to hear him, and therefore set the mob a shouting, *"Great is Diana of the Ephesians;* whoever runs her down, be he Jew or Christian, we are resolved to cry her up. *She is Diana of the Ephesians,* our Diana; and it is our honour and happiness to have her temple with us; and she is great, a famous goddess, and universally adored. There are other Dianas, but Diana of the Ephesians is beyond them all, because her temple is more rich and magnificent than any of theirs." This was all the cry for *two hours* together; and it was thought a sufficient confutation of Paul's doctrine, *that those are not gods which are made with hands.* Thus the most sacred truths are often run down with nothing else but noise and clamour and popular fury. It was said of old concerning idolaters that they were *mad upon their idols;* and here is an instance of it. Diana made the Ephesians great, for the town was enriched by the vast concourse of people from all parts to Diana's temple there, and therefore they are concerned by all means possible to keep up her sinking reputation with, *Great is Diana of the Ephesians.*

4. The suppressing and dispersing of these rioters, by the prudence and vigilance of *the town-clerk;* he is called, *grammateus — the scribe,* or *secretary,* or *recorder;* "the register of their games," the Olympic games (so others), whose business it was to preserve the names of the victors and the prizes they won. With much ado he, at length, stilled the noise, so as to be heard, and then made a pacific speech to them, and gave us an instance of that of Solomon, *The words of wise men are heard in quiet more than the cry of him that rules among fools,* as Demetrius did. Eccl. 9:17.

(1.) He humours them with an acknowledgment that Diana was the celebrated goddess of the Ephesians, *v.* 35. They needed not to be so loud and strenuous in asserting a truth which nobody denied, or could be ignorant of: Every one *knows that the city of the Ephesians is a worshipper of the great goddess Diana;* is *neōkoros;* not only that the inhabitants were worshippers of this goddess, but the city, as a corporation, was, by its charter, entrusted with the worship of Diana, to take care of her temple, and to accommodate those who came thither to do her homage. Ephesus is *the aeditua* (they say that is the most proper word), or *the sacrist, of the great goddess Diana.* The city was more the patroness and protectress of Diana than Diana was of the city. Such great care did idolaters take for the keeping up of the worship of gods made with hands, while the worship of the true and living God is neglected, and few nations or cities glory in patronizing and protecting that. The temple of Diana at Ephesus was a very rich and sumptuous structure, but, it should seem, the *image* of Diana in the temple, because they thought it sanctified the temple, was had in greater veneration than the temple, for they persuaded the people that it *fell down from Jupiter,* and therefore was none of the gods that were made with men's hands. See how easily the credulity of superstitious people is imposed upon by the fraud of designing men. Because this image of Diana had been set up time out of mind, and nobody could tell who made it, they made the people believe it fell down from Jupiter. "Now *these things,"* says the town-clerk very gravely (but whether seriously or no, and as one that did himself believe them, may be questioned), *"cannot be spoken against;* they have obtained such universal credit that you need not fear contradiction, it can do you no prejudice." Some take it thus: "Seeing the image of Diana fell down from Jupiter, as we all believe, then what is said against gods made with hands does not at all affect us."

(2.) He cautions them against all violent and tumultuous proceedings, which their religion did not need, nor could receive any real advantage from (*v.* 36): *You ought to be quiet, and to do nothing rashly.* A very good rule this is to be observed at all times, both in private and public affairs; not to be hasty and precipitate in our motions, but to deliberate and take time to consider: not to put ourselves or others into a heat, but to be calm and composed, and always keep reason in the throne and passion under check. This word should be ready to us, to command the peace with, when we ourselves or those about us are growing disorderly: *We ought to be quiet, and to do nothing rashly;* to do nothing in haste, which we may repent of at leisure.

(3.) He wipes off the odium that had been cast upon Paul and his associates, and tells them, they were not the men that they were represented to them to be (*v.* 37): *"You have brought hither these men,* and are ready to pull them to pieces; but have you considered what is their transgression and what is their offence? What can you prove upon them? They are not robbers of churches, you cannot charge them with sacrilege, or the taking away of any dedicated thing. They have offered no violence to Diana's temple or the treasures of it; nor are they *blasphemers of your goddess;* they have not given any opprobrious language to the worshippers of Diana, nor spoken scurrilously of her or her temple. Why should you prosecute those *with all this violence* who, though they are not of your mind, yet do not inveigh with any bitterness against you? Since they are calm, why should you be hot?" It was the idol in the heart that they levelled all their force against, by reason and argument; if they can but get that down, the idol in the temple will fall of course. Those that preach against idolatrous churches have truth on their side, and ought vigorously to maintain it and press it on men's consciences; but let them not be robbers of those churches *(on the prey laid they not their hand,* Est. 9:15, 16), nor blasphemers of those worships; with meekness instructing, not with passion and foul language reproaching, those that oppose themselves; for God's truth, as it needs not man's lie, so it needs not man's intemperate heat. *The wrath of man worketh not the righteousness of God.*

(4.) He turns them over to the regular methods of the law, which ought always to supersede popular tumults, and in civilized well-governed nations will do so. A great mercy it is to live in a country where provision is made for the keeping of the peace, and the administration of public justice, and the appointing of a remedy for every wrong; and herein we of this nation are as happy as any people. [1.] If the complaint be of a private injury, let them have recourse to the judges and courts of justice, which are kept publicly at stated times. If Demetrius and the company of the silversmiths, that have made all this rout, find themselves aggrieved, or any privilege they are legally entitled to infringed or entrenched upon, let them bring their action, take out a process, and the matter shall be fairly tried, and justice done: *The law is open, and there are deputies;* there is a proconsul and his delegate, whose business it is to hear both sides, and to determine according to equity; and in their determination all parties must acquiesce, and not be their own judges, nor appeal to the people. Note, *The law is good if a man use it lawfully,* as the last remedy both for the discovery of a right disputed and the recovery of a right denied. [2.] If the complaint be of a public grievance, relating to the constitution, it must be redressed, not by a confused rabble, but by a convention of the states (*v.* 39): *If you enquire any thing concerning other matters,* that are of common concern, *it shall be determined in a lawful assembly* of the aldermen and common-council, called together in a regular way by those in authority. Note, Private persons should not intermeddle in public matters, so as to anticipate the counsels of those whose business it is to take cognizance of them; we have enough to do to mind our own business.

(5.) He makes them sensible of the danger they are in, and of the premunire they have run themselves into by this riot (*v.* 40): "It is well if we be not *called in question for this day's uproar,* if we be not complained of at the emperor's court, as a factious and seditious city, and if a *quo warranto* be not brought against us and our charter taken away; for *there is no cause whereby we may give an account of this concourse,* we have nothing to say in excuse of it. We cannot justify ourselves in breaking the peace by saying that others broke it first, and we only acted defensively; we have no colour for any such plea, and therefore let the matter go no further, for it has gone too far already." Note, Most people stand in awe of men's judgment more than of the judgment of God. How well were it if we would thus still the tumult of our disorderly appetites and passions, and check the violence of them, with the consideration of the account we must shortly give to the Judge of heaven and earth for all these disorders! *We are in danger to be called in question for this day's uproar* in our hearts, in our houses; and how shall we answer it, there being no cause, no just cause, or no proportionable one, whereby we may give an account of this concourse, and of this heat and violence? As we must repress the inordinacy of our appetites, so also of our passions, with this, that *for all these things God will bring us unto judgment* (Eccl. 11:9), and we are concerned to manage ourselves *as those that must give account.*

(6.) When he has thus shown them the absurdity of their riotous meeting, and the bad consequences that might follow from it, he advises them to separate with all speed (*v.* 41): he *dismissed the assembly,* ordered the crier perhaps to give notice that all manner of persons should peaceably depart and go about their own business, and they did so. See here, [1.] How the overruling providence of God preserves the public peace, by an unaccountable power over the spirits of men. Thus the world is kept in some order, and men are restrained from being as the fishes of the sea, where the greater devour the less. Considering what an impetuous furious thing, what an ungovernable untameable wild beast the mob is, when it is up, we shall see reason to acknowledge God's goodness that we are not always under the tyranny of it. *He stills the noise of the sea, noise of her waves, and* (which is no less an instance of his almighty power) *the tumult of the people,* Ps. 65:7. [2.] See how many ways God has of protecting his people. Perhaps this town-clerk was no friend at all to Paul, nor to the gospel he preached, yet his human prudence is made to serve the divine purpose. *Many are the troubles of the righteous, but the Lord delivereth them out of them all.*

CHAPTER 20

In this chapter we have, I. Paul's travels up and down about Macedonia, Greece, and Asia, and his coming at length to Troas (*v.* 1–6). II. A particular account of his spending one Lord's day at Troas, and his raising Eutychus to life there (*v.* 7–12). III. His progress, or circuit, for the visiting of the churches he had planted, in his way towards Jerusalem, where he designed to be by the next feast of pentecost (*v.* 13–16). IV. The farewell sermon he preached to the presbyters at Ephesus, now that he was leaving that country (*v.* 17–35). V. The very sorrowful parting between him and them (*v.* 36–38). And in all these we find Paul very busy to serve Christ, and to do good to the souls of men, not only in the conversion of heathen, but in the edification of Christians.

Verses 1–6

These travels of Paul which are thus briefly related, if all in them had been recorded that was memorable and worthy to be written in letters of gold, *the world would not contain the books that would have been* written; and therefore we have only some general hints of occurrences, which therefore ought to be the more precious. Here is,

I. Paul's departure from Ephesus. He had tarried there longer than he had done at any one place since he had been ordained to the apostleship of the Gentiles; and now it was time to think of removing, for he must *preach in other cities also;* but after this, to the end of the scripture-history of his life (which is all we can depend upon), we never find him breaking up fresh ground again, nor preaching *the gospel where Christ had not been named,* as hitherto he had done (Rom. 15:20), for in the close of the next chapter we find him made a prisoner, and so continued, and so left, at the end of this book. 1. Paul left Ephesus soon after the uproar had ceased, looking upon the disturbance he met with there to be an indication of Providence to him not to stay there any longer, *v.* 1. His removal might somewhat appease the rage of his adversaries, and gain better quarter for the Christians there. *Currenti cede furori — It is good to lie by in a storm.* Yet some think that before he now left Ephesus he wrote *the first epistle to the Corinthians,* and that his *fighting with beasts at Ephesus,* which he mentions in that epistle, was a figurative description of this uproar; but I rather take that literally. 2. He did not leave them abruptly and in a fright, but took leave of them solemnly: *He called unto him the disciples,* the principal persons of the congregation, *and embraced them, took leave of them* (saith the Syriac) *with the kiss of love,* according to the usage of the primitive church. Loving friends know not how well they love one another till they come to part, and then it appears how near they lay to one another's hearts.

II. His visitation of the Greek churches, which he had planted, and more than once watered, and which appear to have laid very near his heart. 1. He went first *to Macedonia* (*v.* 1), according to his purpose before the uproar (*ch.* 19:21); there he visited the churches of Philippi and Thessalonica, and *gave them much exhortation, v.* 2. Paul's visits to his friends were preaching visits, and his preaching was large and copious: *He gave them much exhortation;* he had a great deal to say to them, and did not stint himself in time; he exhorted them to many duties, in many cases, and (as some read it) *with many reasonings.* He enforced his exhortation with a great variety of motives and arguments. 2. He staid *three months in Greece* (*v.* 2, 3), that is, *in Achaia,* as some think, for thither also he purposed to go, to Corinth, and thereabouts (*ch.* 19:21), and, no doubt, there also he gave the disciples much exhortation, to direct and confirm them, and engage them to cleave to the Lord.

III. The altering of his measures; for we cannot always stand to our purposes. Accidents unforeseen put us upon new counsels, which oblige us to purpose with a proviso. 1. *Paul was about to sail into Syria, to Antioch,* whence he was first sent out into the service of the Gentiles, and which therefore in his journeys he generally contrived to take in his way; but he changed his mind, and resolved *to return to Macedonia,* the same way he came. 2. The reason was because the Jews, expecting he would steer that course as usual, had way-laid him, designing to be the death of him; since they could not get him out of the way by stirring up both mobs and magistrates against him, which they had often attempted, they contrived to assassinate him. Some think they *laid wait for him,* to rob him of the money that he was carrying to Jerusalem for the relief of the poor saints there; but, considering how very spiteful the Jews were against him, I suppose they thirsted for his blood more than for his money.

IV. His companions in his travels when he went into Asia; they are here named, *v.* 4. Some of them were ministers, whether they were all so or no is not certain. *Sopater of Berea,* it is likely, is the same with *Sosipater,* who is mentioned Rom. 16:21. *Timothy* is reckoned among them, for though Paul, when he departed from Ephesus (*v.* 1), left Timothy there, and afterwards wrote his first epistle to him thither, to direct him as an evangelist how to settle the church there, and in what hands to leave it (see 1 Tim. 1:3; 3:14, 15), which epistle was intended for direction to Timothy what to do, not only at Ephesus where he now was, but also at other places where he should be in like manner left, or whither he should be sent to reside as an evangelist (and not to him only, but to the other evangelists that attended Paul, and were in like manner employed); yet he soon followed him, and accompanied him, with others here named. Now, one would think, this was no good husbandry, to have all these worthy men accompanying Paul, for there was more need of them where Paul was not than where he was; but so it was ordered, 1. That they might assist him in instructing such as by his preaching were awakened and startled; wherever Paul came, the waters were stirred, and then there was need of many hands to help the cripples in. It was time to strike when the iron was hot. 2. That they might be trained up by him, and fitted for future service, *might fully know his doctrine and manner of life,* 2 Tim. 3:10. Paul's bodily presence was weak and despicable, and therefore these friends of his accompanied him, to put a reputation upon him, to keep him in countenance, and to intimate to strangers, who would be apt to judge by the sight of the eye, that he had a great deal in him truly valuable, which was not discovered upon the outward appearance.

V. His coming to Troas, where he had appointed a general rendezvous of his friends. 1. They went before, and staid for him at Troas (*v.* 5), designing to go along with him to Jerusalem, as Trophimus particularly did, *ch.* 21:29. We should not think it hard to stay awhile for good company in a journey. 2. Paul made the best of his way thither; and, it should seem, Luke was now in company with him; for he says *We sailed from Philippi* (*v.* 6), and the first time we find him in his company was here at Troas, *ch.* 16:11. *The days of unleavened bread* are mentioned only to describe the time, not to intimate that Paul kept the passover after the manner of the Jews; for just about this time he had written in his first epistle to the church at Corinth, and taught, that Christs is our Passover, and a Christian life our feast of unleavened bread (1 Co. 5:7, 8), and when the substance was come the shadow was done away. He *came to them to Troas,* by sea, *in five days,* and when he was there staid but *seven days.* There is no remedy, but a great deal of time will unavoidably be lost in travelling to and fro, by those who go about doing good, yet it shall not be put upon the score of lost time. Paul thought it worth while to bestow *five days* in going to Troas, though it was but for an opportunity of *seven days'* stay there; but he knew, and so should we, how to redeem even journeying time, and make it turn to some good account.

Verses 7–12

We have here an account of what passed at Troas the last of the seven days that Paul staid there.

I. There was a solemn religious assembly of the Christians that were there, according to their constant custom, and the custom of all the churches. 1. *The disciples came together, v.* 7. Though they read, and meditated, and prayed, and sung psalms, apart, and thereby kept up their communion with God, yet that was not enough; they must come together to worship God in concert, and so keep up their communion with one another, by mutual countenance and assistance, and testify their spiritual communion with all good Christians. There ought to be stated times for the disciples of Christ to come together; though they cannot all come together in one place, yet as many as can. 2. They *came together upon the first day of the week,* which they called *the Lord's day* (Rev. 1:10), the Christian sabbath, celebrated to the honour of Christ and the Holy Spirit, in remembrance of the resurrection of Christ, and the pouring out of the Spirit, both on the first day of the week. This is here said to be the day when the disciples came together, that is, when it was their practice to come together in all the churches. Note, The first day of the week is to be religiously observed by all the disciples of Christ; and it is a sign between Christ and them, for by this it is known that they are his disciples; and it is to be observed in solemn assemblies, which are, as it were, the courts held in the name of our Lord Jesus, and to his honour, by his ministers, the stewards of his courts, to which all that hold from and under him owe suit and service, and at which they are to make their appearance, as tenants at their Lord's courts, and the first day of the week is appointed to be the court-day. 3. *They were gathered together in an upper chamber* (*v.* 8); they had no temple nor synagogue to meet in, no capacious stately chapel, but met in a private house, in a garret. As they were few, and did not need, so they were poor, and could not build, a large meeting-place; yet they came together, in that despicable inconvenient place. It will be no excuse for our absenting ourselves from religious assemblies that the place of them is not so decent nor so commodious as we would have it to be. 4. They *came together to break bread,* that is, to celebrate the ordinance of the Lord's supper, that one instituted sign of breaking the bread being put for all the rest. *The bread which we break is the communion of the body of Christ,* 1 Co. 10:16. In the breaking of the bread, not only the breaking of Christ's body for us, to be a sacrifice for our sins, is commemorated, but the breaking of Christ's body to us, to be food and a feast for our souls, is signified. In the primitive times it was the custom of many churches to receive the Lord's supper every Lord's day, celebrating the memorial of Christ's death in the former, with that of his resurrection in the latter; and both in concert, in a solemn assembly, to testify their joint concurrence in the same faith and worship.

II. In this assembly Paul gave them a sermon, a long sermon, a farewell sermon, *v.* 7. 1. He gave them a sermon: he *preached to them.* Though they were disciples already, yet it was very necessary they should have the word of God preached to them, in order to their increase in knowledge and grace. Observe, The preaching of the gospel ought to accompany the sacraments. *Moses read the book of the covenant in the audience of the people, and then sprinkled the blood of the covenant, which the Lord had made with them concerning all these words,* Ex. 24:7, 8. What does the seal signify without a writing? 2. It was a farewell sermon, he being *ready to depart on the morrow.* When he was gone, they might have the same gospel preached, but not as he preached it; and therefore they must make the best use of him that they could while they had him. Farewell sermons are usually in a particular manner affecting both to the preacher and to the hearers. 3. It was a very long sermon: He *continued his speech until midnight;* for he had a great deal to say, and knew not that ever he should have another opportunity of preaching to them. After they had received the Lord's supper, he preached to them the duties they had thereby engaged themselves to, and the comforts they were interested in, and in this he was very large and full and particular. There may be occasion for ministers to preach, not only *in season, but out of season.* We know some that would have reproached Paul for this as a long-winded preacher, that tired his hearers; but they were willing to hear: he saw them so, and therefore continued his speech. He *continued it till midnight;* perhaps they met in the evening for privacy, or in conformity to the example of the disciples who came together on the first Christian sabbath in the evening. It is probable he had preached to them in the morning, and yet thus lengthened out his evening sermon even till midnight; we wish we had the heads of this long sermon, but we may suppose it was for substance the same with his epistles. The meeting being continued till midnight, there were candles set up, *many lights* (*v.* 8), that the hearers might turn to the scriptures Paul quoted, and see *whether these things were so;* and that this might prevent the reproach of their enemies, who said they met in the night for works of darkness.

III. *A young man* in the congregation, that slept at sermon, was killed by a fall *out of the window, but raised to life again;* his name signifies *one that had good fortune — Eutychus, bene fortunatus;* and he answered his name. Observe,

1. The infirmity with which he was overtaken. It is probable his parents brought him, though but a boy, to the assembly, out of a desire to have him well instructed in the things of God by such a preacher as Paul. Parents should bring their children to hear sermons as soon as they can hear with understanding (Neh. 8:2), even *the little ones,* Deu. 29:11. Now this youth was to be blamed, (1.) That he presumptuously *sat in the window,* unglazed perhaps, and so exposed himself; whereas, if he could have been content to sit on the floor, he had been safe. Boys that love to climb, or otherwise endanger themselves, to the grief of their parents, consider not how much it is also an offence to God. (2.) That he slept, nay, he *fell into a deep sleep when Paul was preaching,* which was a sign he did not duly attend to the things that Paul spoke of, though they were weighty things. The particular notice taken of his sleeping makes us willing to hope none of the rest slept, though it was sleeping time and after supper; but this youth fell fast asleep, he was *carried away with it* (so the word is), which intimates that he strove against it, but was overpowered by it, and at last sunk down with sleep.

2. The calamity with which he was seized herein: *He fell down from the third loft, and was taken up dead.* Some think that the hand of Satan was in it, by the divine permission, and that he designed it for a disturbance to this assembly and a reproach to Paul and it. Others think that God designed it for a warning to all people to take heed of sleeping when they are hearing the word preached; and certainly we are to make this use of it. We must look upon it as an evil thing, as a bad sign of our low esteem of the word of God, and a great hindrance to our profiting by it. We must be afraid of it, do what we can to prevent our being sleepy, not compose ourselves to sleep, but get our hearts affected with the word we hear to such a degree as may drive sleep far enough. Let us *watch and pray, that we enter not into this temptation,* and by it into worse. Let the punishment of Eutychus strike an awe upon us, and show us how jealous God is in the matters of his worship; *Be not deceived, God is not mocked.* See how severely God visited an iniquity that seemed little, and but in a youth, and say, *Who is able to stand before this holy Lord God?* Apply to this story that lamentation (Jer. 9:20, 21), *Hear the word of the Lord, for death is come up into our windows, to cut off the children from without and the young men from the streets.*

3. The miraculous mercy shown him in his recovery to *life again, v.* 10. It gave a present distraction to the assembly, and an interruption to Paul's preaching; but it proved an occasion of that which was a great confirmation to his preaching, and helped to set it home and make it effectual. (1.) *Paul fell on the dead body, and embraced it,* thereby expressing a great compassion to, and an affectionate concern for, this young man, so far was he from saying, "He was well enough served for minding so little what I said!" Such tender spirits as Paul had are much affected with sad accidents of this kind, and are far from judging and censuring those that fall under them, as if those on whom *the tower of Siloam fell were sinners above all that dwelt at Jerusalem; I tell you, nay.* But this was not all; his falling on him and embracing him were in imitation of Elijah (1 Ki. 17:21), and Elisha (2 Ki. 4:34), in order to the raising of him to life again; not that this could as a means contribute any thing to it, but as a sign it represented the descent of that divine power upon the dead body, for the putting of life into it again, which at the same time he inwardly, earnestly, and in faith prayed for. (2.) He assured them that he had returned to life, and it would appear presently. Various speculations, we may suppose, this ill accident had occasioned in the congregation, but Paul puts an end to them all: *"Trouble not yourselves,* be not in any disorder about it, let it not put you into any hurry, *for his life is in him;* he is not dead, but sleepeth: lay him awhile upon a bed, and he will come to himself, for he is now alive." Thus, when Christ raised Lazarus, he said, *Father, I thank thee that thou hast heard me.* (3.) He returned to his work immediately after this interruption (*v.* 11): *He came up again* to the meeting, they broke bread together in a love-feast, which usually attended the eucharist, in token of their communion with each other, and for the confirmation of friendship among them; and *they talked a long while, even till break of day.* Paul did not now go on in a continued discourse, as before, but he and his friends fell into a free conversation, the subject of which, no doubt, was good, and to the use of edifying. Christian conference is an excellent means of promoting holiness, comfort, and Christian love. They knew not when they should have Paul's company again, and therefore made the best use they could of it when they had it, and reckoned a night's sleep well lost for that purpose. (4.) Before they parted *they brought the young man alive* into the congregation, every one congratulating him upon his return to life from the dead, and *they were not a little comforted, v.* 12. It was matter of great rejoicing among them, not only to the relations of the young man, but to the whole society, as it not only prevented the reproach that would otherwise have been cast upon them, but contributed very much to the credit of the gospel.

Verses 13–16

Paul is hastening towards Jerusalem, but strives to do all the good he can by the way, *ōs en parodō,* "as it were by the by." He had called at Troas, and done good there; and now he makes a sort of coasting voyage, the merchants would call it a trading voyage, going from place to place, and no doubt endeavouring to make every place he came to the better for him, as every good man should do.

I. He sent his companions by sea to Assos, but he himself was *minded to go afoot, v.* 13. He had decreed or determined within himself that whatever importunity should be used with him to the contrary, urging either his ease or his credit, or the conveniency of a ship that offered itself, or the company of his friends, he would foot it to Assos: and, if the land-way which Paul took was the shorter way, yet it is taken notice of by the ancients as a rough way (Homer, Iliad 6, and Eustathius upon him, say, it was enough to *kill one* to go *on foot* to Assos. — *Lorin. in locum*); yet that way Paul would take, 1. That he might call on his friends by the way, and do good among them, either converting sinners or edifying saints; and in both he was serving his great Master, and carrying on his great work. Or, 2. That he might be alone, and might have the greater freedom of converse with God and his own heart in solitude. He loved his companions, and delighted in their company, yet he would show hereby that he did not need it, but could enjoy himself alone. Or, 3. That he might inure himself to hardship, and not seem to indulge his ease. Thus he would by voluntary instances of mortification and self-denial *keep under the body, and bring it into subjection,* that he might make his sufferings for Christ, when he was called out to them, the more easy, 2 Tim. 2:3. We should use ourselves to deny ourselves.

II. At Assos he went on board with his friends. There they *took him in;* for by this time he had enough of his walk, and was willing to betake himself to the other way of travelling; or perhaps he could not go any further by land, but was obliged to go by water. When Christ sent his disciples away by ship, and tarried behind himself, yet he came to them, and they took him in, Mk. 6:45, 51.

III. He made the best of his way to Jerusalem. His ship passed by *Chios* (*v.* 15), touched at *Samos* (these are places of note among the Greek writers, both poets and historians); they tarried awhile at *Trogyllium,* the sea-port next to Samos; *and the next day* they came *to Miletus,* the sea-port that lay next to Ephesus; for (*v.* 16) he had determined not to go to Ephesus at this time, because he could not go thither without being urged by his friends whose importunity he could not resist, to make some stay with them there; and, because he was resolved not to stay, he would not put himself into a temptation to stay; *for he hasted, if it were possible for him, to be at Jerusalem on the day of pentecost.* He had been at Jerusalem about four or five years ago (*ch.* 18:21, 22), and now he was going thither again to pay his continued respects to that church, with which he was careful to keep a good correspondence, that he might not be thought alienated from it by his commission to preach among the Gentiles. He aimed to be there by the feast of pentecost because it was a time of concourse, which would give him an opportunity of propagating the gospel among the Jews and proselytes, who came from all parts to worship at the feast: and the feast of pentecost had been particularly made famous among the Christians by the pouring out of the Spirit. Note, Men of business must fit themselves, and it will contribute to the expediting of it, to set time (with submission to Providence) and strive to keep it, contriving to do that first which we judge to be most needful, and not suffering ourselves to be diverted from it. It is a pleasure to us to be with our friends; it diverts us, nothing more; but we must not by it be diverted from our work. When Paul has a call to Jerusalem, he will not loiter away the time in Asia, though he had more and kinder friends there. This is not the world we are to be together in; we hope to be so in the other world.

Verses 17–35

It should seem the ship Paul and his companions were embarked in for Jerusalem attended him on purpose, and staid or moved as he pleased; for when he came to Miletus, he went ashore, and tarried thee so long as to send for the elders of Ephesus to come to him thither; for if he had gone up to Ephesus, he could never have got away from them. These elders, or presbyters, some think, were those twelve who received the Holy Ghost by Paul's hands, *ch.* 19:6. But, besides these, it is probable that Timothy had ordained other elders there for the service of that church, and the country about; these Paul sent for, that he might instruct and encourage them to go on in the work to which they had laid their hands. And what instructions he gave to them they would give to the people under their charge.

It is a very pathetic and practical discourse with Paul here takes leave of these elders, and has in it much of the excellent spirit of this good man.

I. He appeals to them concerning both his life and doctrine, all the time he had been in and about Ephesus (*v.* 18): *"You know after what manner I have been with you,* and how I have done the work of an apostle among you." He mentions this as a confirmation of his commission and consequently of the doctrine he had preached among them. They all knew him to be a man of serious, gracious, heavenly spirit, that he was no designing self-seeking man, as seducers are; he could not have been carried on with so much evenness and constancy in his services and sufferings, but by the power of divine grace. The temper of his mind, and the tenour both of his preaching and conversation, were such as plainly proved that God was with him of a truth, and that he was actuated and animated by a better spirit than his own. — He likewise makes this reference to his own conduct as an instruction to them, in whose hands the work was now left, to follow his example: *"You know after what manner I have been with you,* how I have conducted myself as a minister; in like manner be you with those that are committed to your charge when I am gone (Phil. 4:9), *what you have seen in me* that is good *do."*

1. His spirit and conversation were excellent and exemplary; they knew after what manner he had been among them, and how he had had his conversation towards them, in simplicity and godly sincerity (2 Co. 1:12), how holily, just-

ly, and unblamably he behaved himself, and how gentle he was towards them, 1 Th. 2:7, 10. (1.) He had conducted himself well all along, *from the very first day that he came into Asia* — at all seasons; the manner of his entering in among them was such as nobody could find fault with. He appeared from the first day they knew him to be a man that aimed not only to do well, but to do good, wherever he came. He was a man that was consistent with himself, and all of a piece; take him where you would he was the same at all seasons, he did not turn with the wind nor change with the weather, but was uniform like a die, which, throw it which way you will, lights on a square side. (2.) He had made it his business to serve the Lord, to promote the honour of God and the interest of Christ and his kingdom among them. He never served himself, nor made himself a servant of men, of their lusts and humours, nor was he a time-server; but he made it his business to serve the Lord. In his ministry, in his whole conversation, he proved himself what he wrote himself, Paul *a servant of Jesus Christ,* Rom. 1:1. (3.) He had done his work *with all humility of mind — meta pasēs tapeinophrosynēs,* that is, in all works of condescension, modesty, and self-abasement. Though he was one that God had put a great deal of honour upon, and done a great deal of good by, yet he never took state upon him, nor kept people at a distance, but conversed as freely and familiarly with the meanest, for their good, as if he had stood upon a level with them. He was willing to stoop to any service, and to make himself and his labours as cheap as they could desire. Note, Those that would in any office serve the Lord acceptably to him, and profitably to others, must do it with all humility of mind, Mt. 20:26, 27. (4.) He had always been very tender, affectionate, and compassionate, among them; he had *served the Lord with many tears.* Paul was herein like his Master; often in tears; in his praying, he *wept and made supplication,* Hos. 12:5. In his preaching, what he had told them before he told them again, *even weeping,* Phil. 3:18. In his concern for them, though his acquaintance with them was but of a late standing, yet so near did they lie to his heart that he *wept with those that wept,* and mingled his tears with theirs upon every occasion, which was very endearing. (5.) He had struggled with many difficulties among them. He went on in his work in the face of much opposition, *many temptations,* trials of his patience and courage, such discouragements as perhaps were sometimes *temptations* to him, as to Jeremiah in a like case to say, *I will not speak any more in the name of the Lord,* Jer. 20:8, 9. These befel him *by the lying in wait of the Jews,* who still were plotting some mischief or other against him. Note, Those are the faithful servants of the Lord that continue to serve him in the midst of troubles and perils, that care not what enemies they make, so that they can but approve themselves to their Master, and make him their friend. Paul's tears were owing to his temptations; his afflictions helped to excite his good affections.

2. His preaching was likewise such as it should be, *v.* 20, 21. He came to Ephesus to preach the gospel of Christ among them, and he had been faithful both to them and to him that appointed him. (1.) He was a plain preacher, and one that delivered his message so as to be understood. This is intimated in two words, *I have shown you, and have taught you.* He did not amuse them with nice speculations, nor lead them into, and then lose them in, the clouds of lofty notions and expressions; but he showed them the plain truths of the gospel, which were of the greatest consequence and importance, and taught them as children are taught. "I have shown you the right way to happiness, and taught you to go in it." (2.) He was a powerful preacher, which is intimated in his *testifying* to them; he preached as one upon oath, that was himself fully assured of the truth of what he preached and was desirous to convince them of it and to influence and govern them by it. He preached the gospel, not as a hawker proclaims news in the street (it is all one to him whether it be true or false), but as a conscientious witness gives in his evidence at the bar, with the utmost seriousness and concern. Paul preached the gospel as a testimony to them if they received it, but as a testimony against them if they rejected it. (3.) He was a profitable preacher, one that in all his preaching aimed at doing good to those he preached to; he studied that which was *profitable unto them,* which had a tendency to make them wise and good, wiser and better, to inform their judgments and reform their hearts and lives. He preached *ta sympheronta,* such things as *brought with them* divine light, and heat, and power to their souls. It is not enough not to preach that which is hurtful, which leads into error or hardens in sin, but we must preach that which is profitable. *We do all things, dearly beloved, for your edifying.* Paul aimed to preach not that which was pleasing, but that which was profitable, and to please only in order to profit. God is said to teach his people to profit, Isa. 48:17. Those teach for God that teach people to profit. (4.) He was a painstaking preacher, very industrious and indefatigable in his work; he preached *publicly, and from house to house.* He did not confine himself to a corner when he had opportunity of preaching in the great congregation; nor did he confine himself to the congregation when there was occasion for private and personal instruction. He was neither afraid nor ashamed to preach the gospel publicly, nor did he grudge to bestow his pains privately, among a few, when there was occasion for it. He preached publicly to the flock that came together into the green pastures, and went from house to house to seek those that were weak and had wandered, and did not think that the one would excuse him from the other. Ministers should in their private visits, and as they go from house to house, discourse of those things which they have taught publicly, repeat them, inculcate them, and explain them, if it be needful, asking, *Have you understood all these things?* And, especially, they should help persons to apply the truth to themselves and their own case. (5.) He was a faithful preacher. He not only preached that which was profitable, but he preached every thing that he thought might be profitable, and kept back nothing, though the preaching of it might either cost him more pains or be disobliging to some and expose him to their ill-will. He declined not preaching whatever he thought might be profitable, though it was not fashionable, nor to some acceptable. He did not keep back reproofs, when they were necessary and would be profitable, for fear of offending; nor did he keep back the preaching of the cross, though he knew it was to the Jews a stumbling-block and to the Greeks foolishness, as the Roman missionaries in China lately did. (6.) He was a catholic preacher. He *testified both to the Jews and also to the Greeks.* Though he was born and bred a Jew, and had an entire affection for that nation, and was trained up in their prejudices against the Gentiles, yet he did not therefore confine himself to the Jews and avoid the Gentiles; but preached as readily to them as to the Jews, and conversed as freely with them. And, on the other hand, though he was called to be the apostle of the Gentiles, and the Jews had an implacable enmity against him upon that score, had done him many an ill turn, and here at Ephesus were continually plotting against him, yet he did not therefore abandon them as reprobates, but continued to deal with them for their good. Ministers must preach the gospel with impartiality; for they are ministers of Christ for the universal church. (7.) He was a truly Christian evangelical preacher. He did not preach philosophical notions, or matters of doubtful disputation, nor did he preach politics, or intermeddle at all with affairs of state or the civil government; but he preached faith and repentance, the two great gospel graces, the nature and necessity of them; these he urged upon all occasions. [1.] *Repentance towards God;* that those who by sin had gone away from God, and were going further and further from him into a state of endless separation from him, should by true repentance look towards God, turn towards him, move towards him, and hasten to him. He preached repentance as God's great command (*ch.* 17:30), which we must obey — *that men should repent, and turn to God, and do works meet for repentance* (so he explains it, *ch.* 26:20); and he preached it as Christ's gift, in order to the *remission of sins* (*ch.* 5:31), and directed people to look up to him for it. [2.] *Faith towards our Lord Jesus Christ.* We must be repentance look towards God as our end; and by faith towards Christ as our way to God. Sin must by repentance be abandoned and forsaken, and then Christ must by faith be relied on for the pardon of sin. Our repentance towards God is not sufficient, we must have a true faith in Christ as our Redeemer and Saviour, consenting to him as our Lord and our God. For there is no coming to God, as penitent prodigals to a Father, but in the strength and righteousness of Jesus Christ as Mediator.

Such a preacher as this they all knew Paul had been; and, if they will carry on the same work, they must walk in the same spirit, in the same steps.

II. He declares his expectation of sufferings and afflictions in his present journey to Jerusalem, *v.* 22–24. Let them not think that he quitted Asia now for fear of persecution; nor, he was so far from running away like a coward from the post of danger that he was now like a hero hastening to the high places of the field, where the battle was likely to be hottest: *Now, behold, I go bound in the spirit to Jerusalem,* which may be understood either, (1.) Of the certain foresight he had of trouble before him. Though he was not yet bound in body, he was bound in spirit; he was in full expectation of trouble, and made it his daily business to prepare for it. He was bound in spirit, as all good Christians are poor in spirit, endeavouring to accommodate themselves to the will of God if they should be reduced to poverty. Or, (2.) Of the strong impulse he was under from the Spirit of God working upon his spirit to go this journey: *"I go bound in the spirit,* that is, firmly resolved to proceed, and well assured that it is by a divine direction and influence that I am so, and not from any humour or design of my own. I go led by the Spirit, and bound to follow him wherever he leads me."

1. He does not know particularly the things that shall befal him at Jerusalem. Whence the trouble shall spring, what shall be the occasion of it, what the circumstances and to what degree it shall arise, God had not thought fit to reveal to him. It is good for us to be kept in the dark concerning future events, that we may be always waiting on God and waiting for him. When we go abroad, it should be with this thought, we know not the things that shall befal us, nor what a day, or a night, or an hour, may bring forth; and therefore must refer ourselves to God, let him do with us as seemeth good in his eyes, and study to stand complete in his whole will.

2. Yet he does know in general that thee is a storm before him; for the prophets in every city he passed through told him, by the Holy Ghost, that bonds and afflictions awaited him. Besides the common notice given to all Christians and ministers to expect and prepare for sufferings, Paul had particular intimations of an extraordinary trouble, greater and longer than any he had yet met with, that was now before him.

3. He fixes a brave and heroic resolution to go on with his work, notwithstanding. It was a melancholy peal that was rung in his ears in every city, that *bonds and afflictions did abide him;* it was a hard case for a poor man to labour continually to do good, and to be so ill treated for his pains. Now it is worth while to enquire how he bore it. He was flesh and blood as well as other men; he was so, and yet by the grace of God he was enabled to go on with his work, and to look with a gracious and generous contempt upon all the difficulties and discouragements he met with in it. Let us take it from his own mouth here (*v.* 24), where he speaks not with obstinacy nor ostentation, but with a holy humble resolution: *"None of these things move me;* all my care is to proceed and to persevere in the way of my duty, and to finish well." Paul is here an example,

(1.) Of holy courage and resolution in our work, notwithstanding the difficulties and oppositions we meet with in it; he saw them before him, but he made nothing of them: *None of these things move me; oudenos logon poioumai — I make no account of them.* He did not lay these things to heart, Christ and heaven lay there. None of these things moved him. [1.] They did not drive him off from his work; he did not tack about, and go back again, when he saw the storm rise, but went on resolutely, preaching there, where he knew how dearly it would cost him. [2.] They did not deprive him of his comfort, nor make him drive on heavily in his work. In the midst of troubles he was as one unconcerned. In his patience he possessed his soul, and, when he was as sorrowful, yet he was always rejoicing, and in all things more than a conqueror. Those that have their conversation in heaven can look down, not only upon the common troubles of this earth but upon the threatening rage and malice of hell itself, and say that none of these things moved them, as knowing that none of these things can hurt them.

(2.) Of a holy contempt of life, and the continuance and comforts of it: *Neither count I my life dear to myself.* Life is sweet, and is naturally dear to us. *All that a man has will he give for his life;* but all that a man has, and life too, will he give who understands himself aright and his own interest, rather than lose the favour of God and hazard eternal life. Paul was of this mind. Though to an eye of nature life is superlatively valuable, yet to an eye of faith it is comparatively despicable; it is not so dear but it can be cheerfully parted with for Christ. This explains Lu. 14:26, where we are required to hate our own lives, not in a hasty passion, as Job and Jeremiah, but in a holy submission to the will of God, and a resolution to die for Christ rather than to deny him.

(3.) Of a holy concern to go through with the work of life, which should be much more our care than to secure either the outward comforts of it or the countenance of it. Blessed Paul counts not his life dear in comparison with this, and resolves in the strength of Christ, *non propter vitam vivendi perdere causas — that he never will, to save his life, lose the ends of living.* He is willing to spend his life in labour, to hazard his life in dangerous services, to waste it in toilsome services; nay, to lay down his life in martyrdom, so that he may but answer the great intentions of his birth, of his baptism, and of his ordination to the apostleship. Two things this great and good man is in care about, and if he gain them it is no matter to him what becomes of life: — [1.] That he may be found faithful to the trust reposed in him, that he may *finish the ministry which he has received of the Lord Jesus,* may do the work which he was sent into the world about, or, rather, which he was sent into the church about, — that he may complete the service of his generation, may make full proof of his ministry, — that he may go through the business of it, and others may reap the advantage of it, to the utmost of what was designed, — that he may, as is said of the two witnesses, *finish his testimony* (Rev. 11:7), and may not do his work by halves. Observe, *First,* The apostleship was a ministry both to Christ and to the souls of men; and those that were called to it considered more the ministry of it than the dignity or dominion of it; and, if the apostles did so, much more ought the pastors and teachers to do so, and to be in the church as those who serve. *Secondly,* This ministry was *received from the Lord Jesus.* He entrusted them with it, and from him they received their charge; for him they do their work, in his name, in his strength; and to him they must give up their account. It was Christ that put them into the ministry (1 Tim. 1:12); it is he that carries them on in their ministry, and from him they have strength to do their service and bear up under the hardships of it. *Thirdly,* The work of this ministry was to *testify the gospel of the grace of God,* to publish it to the world, to prove it, and to recommend it; and, being the gospel of the grace of God, it has enough in it to recommend itself. It is a proof of God's good-will to us, and a means of his good work in us; it shows him gracious towards us, and tends to make us gracious, and so is the gospel of the grace of God. Paul made it the business of his life to testify this, and desired not to live a day longer than he might be instrumental to spread the knowledge and savour and power of this gospel. [2.] That he may finish well. He cares not when the period of his life comes, nor how, be it ever so soon, ever so sudden, ever so sad, as to outward circumstances, so that he may but *finish his course with joy. First,* He looks upon his life as *a course, a race,* so the word is. Our life is *a race set before us,* Heb. 12:1. This intimates that we have our labours appointed us, for we were not sent into the world to be idle; and our limits appointed us, for we were not sent into the world to be here always, but to pass through the world, nay, to run through it, and it is soon run through; I may add, to *run the gauntlet* through it. *Secondly,* He counts upon the finishing of his course, and speaks of it as sure and near, and that which he had his thoughts continually upon. Dying is the end of our race, when we come off either with honour or shame. *Thirdly,* He is full of care to finish it well, which implies a holy desire of obtaining and a holy fear of coming short. "Oh! that I may but finish my course with joy; and then all will be well, perfectly and eternally well." *Fourthly,* He thinks nothing too much to do, nor too hard to suffer, so that he may but finish well, finish with joy. We must look upon it as the business of our life to provide for a joyful death, that we may not only die safely, but die comfortably.

III. Counting upon it that this was the last time they should see him, he appeals to their consciences concerning his integrity, and demands of them a testimony to it.

1. He tells them that he was now taking his last leave of them (*v.* 25): *I know that you all, among whom I have* been conversant *preaching the kingdom of God,* though you may have letters from me, shall never see my face again. When any of us part with our friends, we may say, and should say, "We know not that ever we shall see one another again: our friends may be removed, or we ourselves may." But Paul here speaks it with assurance, by the Spirit of prophecy, that these Ephesians should *see his face no more;* and we cannot think that he who spoke so doubtfully of that which he was not sure of *(not knowing the things that shall befal me there, v.* 22) would speak this with so much confidence, especially when he foresaw what a trouble it would be to his friends here, unless he had had a special warrant from the Spirit to say it, to whom I think those do wrong who suppose that, notwithstanding this, Paul did afterwards come to Ephesus, and see them again. He would never have said thus solemnly, *Now, behold, I know it,* if he had not known it *for certain.* Not but that he foresaw that he had a great deal of time and work yet before him, but he foresaw that his work would be cut out for him in other places, and in these parts he had no more to do. Here he had for a great while gone about preaching the kingdom of God, preaching down the kingdom of sin and Satan, and preaching up the authority and dominion of God in Christ, preaching the kingdom of glory as the end and the kingdom of grace as the way. Many a time they had been glad to see his face in the pulpit, and saw it *as it had been the face of an angel.* If the feet of these messengers of peace were beautiful upon the mountains, what were their faces? But now they shall see his face no more. Note, We ought often to think of it, that those who now are preaching to us the kingdom of God will shortly be removed and we shall see their faces no more: *the prophets, do they live for ever?* Yet a little while is their light with us; it concerns us therefore to improve it while we have it, that when we shall see their faces no more on earth, yet we may hope to look them in the face with comfort in the great day.

2. He appeals to them concerning the faithful discharge of his ministry among them (*v.* 26): *"Wherefore,* seeing my ministry is at an end with you, it concerns both you and me to reflect, and look back;" and, (1.) He challenges them to prove him unfaithful, or to have said or done any thing by which he had made himself accessory to the ruin of any precious soul: *I am pure from the blood of all men,* the blood of souls. This plainly refers to that of the prophet (Eze. 33:6), where the blood of him that perishes by the sword of the enemy is said to be required at the hand of the unfaithful watchman that did not give warning: "You cannot say but I have given warning, and therefore no man's blood can be laid at my door." If a minister has approved himself faithful, he may have this rejoicing in himself, *I am pure from the blood of all men,* and ought to have this testimony from others. (2.) He therefore leaves the blood of those that perish upon their own heads, because they had fair warning given them, but they would not take it. (3.) He charges these ministers to look to it that they took care and pains, as he had done: *"I am pure from the blood of all men,* see that you keep yourselves so too. *I take you to record this day" — en tē sēmeron hēmera,* "I call this day to witness to you:" so Streso. As sometimes the heaven and earth are appealed to, so here this day shall be a witness, this parting day.

3. He proves his own fidelity with this (*v.* 27): *For I have not shunned to declare unto you all the counsel of God.* (1.) He had preached to them nothing but the counsel of God, and had not added any inventions of his own; "it was pure gospel, and nothing else, the will of God concerning your salvation." The gospel is the counsel of God; it is admirably contrived by his wisdom, it is unalterably determined by his will, and it is kindly designed by his grace for our glory, 1 Co. 2:7. This counsel of God it is the business of ministers to declare as it is revealed, and not otherwise nor any further. (2.) He had preached to them the whole counsel of God. As he had preached to them the whole counsel of God. As he had preached to them the gospel pure, so he had preached it to them entire; he had gone over a body of divinity among them, that, having the truths of the gospel opened to them methodically from first to last in order, they might the better understand them, by seeing them in their several connections with, and dependences upon, one another. (3.) He had not shunned to do it; had not wilfully nor designedly avoided the declaring of any part of the counsel of God. He had not, to save his own pains, declined preaching upon the most difficult parts of the gospel, nor, to save his own credit, declined preaching upon the most plain and easy parts of it; he had not shunned preaching those doctrines which he knew would be provoking to the watchful enemies of Christianity, or displeasing to the careless professors of it, but faithfully took his work before him, whether they would hear or forbear. And thus it was that he kept himself pure from the blood of all men.

IV. He charges them as ministers to be diligent and faithful in their work.

1. He commits the care of the church at Ephesus, that is, the saints, the Christians that were there and thereabouts (Eph. 1:1), to them, who, though doubtless they were so numerous that they could not all meet in one place, but worshipped God in several congregations, under the conduct of several ministers, are yet called here *one flock,* because they not only agreed in one faith, as they did with all Christian churches, but in many instances they kept up communion one with another. To these elders or presbyters the apostle here, upon the actual foresight of his own final leaving them, commits the government of this church, and tells them that not he, but *the Holy Ghost, had made them overseers, episkopous — bishops of the flock.* "You that are presbyters are bishops of the Holy Ghost's making, that are to take the oversight of this part of the church of God," 1 Pt. 5:1, 2; Tit. 1:5, 7. While Paul was present at Ephesus, he presided in all the affairs of that church, which made the elders loth to part with him; but now this eagle *stirs up the nest, flutters over her young;* now that they begin to be fledged they must learn to fly themselves, and to act without him, for the Holy Ghost had made them overseers. They took not this honour to themselves, nor was it conferred upon them by any prince or potentate, but the Holy Ghost in them qualified them for, and enriched them to, this great undertaking, the *Holy Ghost fell upon them, ch.* 19:6. The Holy Ghost also directed those that chose, and called, and ordained, them to this work in answer to prayer.

2. He commanded them to mind the work to which they were called. Dignity calls for duty; if the Holy Ghost has made them *overseers of the flock,* that is, shepherds, they must be true to their trust. (1.) They must take heed to themselves in the first place, must have a very jealous eye upon all the motions of their own souls, and upon all they said and did, must walk circumspectly, and know how to behave themselves aright in the house of God, in which they were now advanced to the office of stewards: "You have many eyes upon you, some to take example by you, others to pick quarrels with you, and therefore you ought to *take heed to yourselves."* Those are not likely to be skilful or faithful keepers of the vineyards of others that do not keep their own. (2.) *"Take heed to the flock,* to all the flock, some to one part of it, others to another, according as your call and opportunity are, but see that no part of it be neglected among you." Ministers must not only take heed to their own souls, but must have a constant regard to the souls of those who are under their charge, as shepherds have to their sheep, that they may receive no damage: *"Take heed to all the flock,* that none of them either of themselves wander from the fold or be seized by the beasts of prey; that none of them be missing, or miscarry, through your neglect." (3.) They must feed the church of God, must do all the parts of the shepherd's office, must lead the sheep of Christ into the green pastures, must lay meat before them, must do what they can to heal those that are distempered and have no appetite to their meat, must feed them with wholesome doctrine, with a tender evangelical discipline, and must see that nothing is wanting that is necessary in order to their being nourished up to eternal life. There is need of pastors, not only to gather the church of God by bringing in of those that are without, but to *feed it* by building up those that are within. (4.) They must watch (*v.* 31), as shepherds keep watch over their flocks by night, must be awake and watchful, must not give way to spiritual sloth and slumber, but must stir up themselves to their business and closely attend it. *Watch thou in all things* (2 Tim. 4:5), watch against every thing that will be hurtful to the flock, and watch to every thing that will be advantageous to it; improve every opportunity of doing it a kindness.

3. He gives them several good reasons why they should mind the business of their ministry.

(1.) Let them consider the interest of their Master, and his concern for the flock that was committed to their charge, *v.* 28. It is *the church which he has purchased with his own blood.* [1.] "It is his own; you are but his servants to take care of it for him. It is your honour that you are employed for God, who will own you in his service; but then your carelessness and treachery are so much the worse if you neglect your work, for you wrong God and are false to him. From him you received the trust, and to him you must give up your account, and therefore *take heed to yourselves.* And, if it be the church of God, he expects you should show your love to him by feeding his sheep and lambs." [2.] He has purchased it. The world is God's by right of creation, but the church is his by right of redemption, and therefore it ought to be dear to us, for it was dear to him, because it cost him dear, and we cannot better show it than by feeding his sheep and his lambs. [3.] This church of God is what he has purchased; not as Israel of old, when he *gave men for them, and people for their life* (Isa. 43:3, 4), but *with his own blood.* This proves that Christ is God, for he is called so here, where yet he is said to purchase the church *with his own blood;* the blood was his as man, yet so close is the union between the divine and human nature that it is here called the blood of God, for it was the blood of him who is God, and his being so put such dignity and worth into it as made it both a valuable ransom of us from evil, and a valuable purchase for us of all good, nay, a purchase of us to Christ, to be to him a peculiar people: *Thine they were, and thou gavest them to me.* In consideration of this, therefore, *feed the church of God,* because it is purchased at so dear a rate. Did Christ lay down his life to purchase it, and shall his ministers be wanting in any care and pains to feed it? Their neglect of its true interest is a contempt of his blood that purchased it.

(2.) Let them consider the danger that the flock was in of being made a prey to its adversaries, *v.* 29, 30. "If the flock be thus precious upon the account of its relation to God, and its redemption by Christ, then you are concerned to take heed both to yourselves and to it." Here are reasons for both. [1.] *Take heed to the flock,* for wolves are abroad, that seek to devour (*v.* 29): *I know this, that after my departure grievous wolves shall enter in among you. First,* Some understand it of persecutors, that will inform against the Christians, and incense the magistrates against them, and will have no compassion on the flock. They thought, because, while Paul was with them, the rage of the Jews was most against him, that, when he had gone out of the country, they would be quiet: "No," says he, *"after my departure* you will find the persecuting spirit still working, therefore take heed to the flock, confirm them in the faith, comfort and encourage them, that they may not either leave Christ for fear of suffering or lose their peace and comfort in their sufferings." Ministers must take a more ordinary care of the flock in times of persecution. *Secondly,* It is rather to be understood of seducers and false teachers. Probably Paul has an eye to those of the circumcision, who preached up the ceremonial law; these he calls *grievous wolves,* for though they came in sheep's clothing, nay, in shepherds' clothing, they made mischief in the congregations of Christians, sowed discord among them, drew away many from the pure gospel of Christ, and did all they could to blemish and defame those that adhered to it; not sparing the most valuable members of the flock, stirring up those whom they could influence to bite and devour them (Gal. 5:15); therefore they are called dogs (Phil. 3:2), as here wolves. While Paul was at Ephesus, they kept away, for they durst not face him; but, when he was gone, then they entered in among them, and sowed their tares where he had sown the good seed. "Therefore take heed to the flock, and do all you can to establish them in the truth, and to arm them against the insinuations of the false teachers." [2.] *Take heed to yourselves,* for some shepherds will apostatise (*v.* 30): *"Also of your ownselves,* among the members, nay, perhaps, among the ministers of your own church, among you that I am now speaking to (though I am willing to hope it does not go so far as that), *shall men arise speaking perverse things,* things contrary to the right rule of the gospel, and destructive of the great intentions of it. Nay, they will pervert some sayings of the gospel, and wrest them to make them patronize their errors, 2 Pt. 3:16. Even those that were well thought of among you, and that you had confidence in, will grow proud, and conceited, and opinionative, and will refine upon the gospel, and will pretend with more nice and curious speculations to advance you to a higher form; but it is to *draw away disciples after them,* to make a party for themselves, that shall admire them, and be led by them, and pin their faith upon their sleeve." Some read it, *to draw away disciples after them* — those that are already disciples of Christ, draw them from him to follow them. "Therefore, take heed to yourselves; when you are told that some of you shall betray the gospel, you are each of you concerned to ask, *Is it I?* and to look well to yourselves." This was there fulfilled in *Phygellus and Hermogenes,* who turned away from Paul and the doctrine he had preached (2 Tim. 1:15), and in *Hymeneus and Philetus,* who *concerning the truth erred, and overthrew the faith of some* (2 Tim. 2:18), which explains the expression here. But, though there were some such seducers in the church of Ephesus, yet it should seem by Paul's Epistle to that church (wherein we do not find such complaints and reprehensions as we meet with in some other of his epistles) that that church was not so much infested with false teachers, at least not so much infected with their false doctrine, as some other churches were; but its peace and purity were preserved by the blessing of God on the pains and vigilance of these presbyters, to whom the apostle, in the actual foresight and consideration of the rise of heresies and schisms, as well as of his own death, committed the government of this church.

(3.) Let them consider the great pains that Paul had taken in planting this church (*v.* 31): *"Remember that for the space of three years"* (for so long he had been preaching in Ephesus, and the parts adjacent) *"I ceased not to warn every one night and day with tears;* and be not you negligent in building upon that foundation which I was so diligent to lay." [1.] Paul, like a faithful watchman, had warned them, and, by the warnings he gave men of the danger of their continuing in their Judaism and heathenism, he prevailed with them to embrace Christianity. [2.] He warned every one; besides the public warnings he gave in his preaching, he applied himself to particular persons according as he saw their case called for it, which he had something to say peculiar to. [3.] He was constant in giving warning; he *warned night and day;* his time was filled up with his work. In the night, when he should have been reposing himself, he was dealing with those he could not get to speak with in the day about their souls. [4.] He was indefatigable in it; he *ceased not* to warn. Though they were ever so obstinate against his warnings, yet he did not cease to warn, not knowing but that at length they might, by the grace of God, be overcome; though they were ever so pliable to his warnings, yet he did not think this would be a sufficient excuse for him to desist, but still he warned those that were righteous as not to turn from their righteousness, as he had warned them when they were wicked to turn from their wickedness, Eze. 3:18–21. [5.] He spoke to them about their souls with a great deal of affection and concern: he *warned them with tears.* As he had served the Lord, so he had served them, *with many tears, v.* 19. He warned them with tears of compassion, thereby showing how much he was himself affected with their misery and danger in a sinful state and way, that he might affect them with it. Thus Paul had begun the good work at Ephesus, thus free had he been of his pains; and why then should they be sparing of their pains in carrying it on?

V. He recommends them to divine direction and influence (*v.* 32): *"And now, brethren,* having given you this solemn charge and caution, *I commend you to God.* Now that I have said what I have to say, The Lord be with you; I must leave you, but I leave you in good hands." They were in care what would become of them, how they should go on in their work, break through their difficulties, and what provision would be made for them and their families. In answer to all these perplexities, Paul directs them to look up to God with an eye of faith, and beseeches God to look down on them with an eye of favour.

1. See here to whom he commends them. He calls them brethren, not only as Christians, but as ministers, and thereby encourages them to hope in God, as he had done; for they and he were brethren. (1.) He commends them to God, begs of God to provide for them, to take care of them, and to supply all their needs, and encourages them to cast all their care upon him, with an assurance that he cared for them: "Whatever you want, go to God, let your eye be ever towards him, and your dependence upon him, in all your straits and difficulties; and let this be your comfort, that you have a God to go to, a God all sufficient." *I commend you to God,* that is, to his providence, and to the protection and care of that. It is enough that, from whomsoever we are separated, still we have God nigh unto us, 1 Pt. 4:19. (2.) He commends them *to the word of his grace,* by which some understand Christ: he is *the word* (Jn. 1:1), *the word of life,* because life is treasured up for us in him (1 Jn. 1:1), and in the same sense he is here called *the word of God's grace,* because *from his fulness we receive grace for grace.* He commends them to Christ, puts them into his hand, as being his servants, whom he would in a particular manner take care of. Paul commends them not only to God and to his providence, but to Christ and his grace as Christ himself did his disciples when he was leaving them: *You believe in God, believe also in me.* It comes to much the same thing, if by the word of his grace we understand the gospel of Christ, for it is Christ in the word that is nigh unto us for our support and encouragement, and his word is spirit and life: "You will find much relief by acting faith on the providence of God, but much more by acting faith on the promises of the gospel." He commends them to the word of Christ's grace, which he spoke to his disciples when he sent them forth, the commission he gave them, with assurance that he would be with them *always to the end of the world:* "Take hold of that word, and God give you the benefit and comfort of it, and you need no more." He commends them to the word of God's grace, not only as the foundation of their hope and the fountain of their joy, but as the rule of their walking: *"I commend you to God,* as your Master, whom you are to serve, and I have found him a good Master, *and to the word of his grace,* as cutting you out your work, and by which you are to govern yourselves; observe the precepts of this word, and then live upon the promises of it."

2. See here what he commends them to the word of God's grace for, not so much for a protection from their enemies, or a provision for their families, as for the spiritual blessings which they most needed and ought most to value. They had received the gospel of the grace of God, and were entrusted to preach it. Now he recommends them to that, (1.) For their edification: *"It is able* (the Spirit of grace working with it and by it) *to build you up,* and you may depend upon this, while you keep close to it, and are deriving daily from it. Though you are already furnished with good gifts, yet this is able to build you up; there is that in it with which you need to be better acquainted and more affected." Note, Ministers, in preaching the word of grace, must aim at their own edification as well as at the edification of others. The most advanced Christians, while they are in this world, are capable of growing, and they will find the word of grace to have still more and more in it to contribute to their growth. It is still able to build them up. (2.) For their glorification: *It is able to give you an inheritance among all those who are sanctified.* The word of God's grace gives it, not only as it gives the knowledge of it (for *life and immortality are brought to light by the gospel),* but as it gives the promise of it, the promise of a God *that cannot lie,* and which is *yea and amen in Christ;* and by the word, as the ordinary vehicle, the Spirit of grace is given (*ch.* 10:44), to be the seal of the promise, and the earnest of the eternal life promised; and thus it is the word of God's grace that gives us the inheritance. Note, [1.] Heaven is an inheritance which gives an indefeasible right to all the heirs; it is an inheritance like that of the Israelites in Canaan, which was by promise and yet by lot, but was *sure to all the seed.* [2.] This inheritance is entailed upon and secured to all those, and those only, that are sanctified; for as those cannot be welcome guests to the holy God, or the holy society above, that are unsanctified, so really heaven would be no heaven to them; but *to all that are sanctified,* that are born again, and on whom the image of God is renewed, it is as sure as almighty power and eternal truth can make it. Those therefore that would make out a title to that inheritance must make it sure that they are among the sanctified, are joined to them and incorporated with them, and partake of the same image and nature; for we cannot expect to be among the glorified hereafter unless we be among the sanctified here.

VI. He recommends himself to them as an example of indifference to this world, and to every thing in it, which, if they would walk in the same spirit and in the same steps, they would find to contribute greatly to their easy and comfortable passage through it. He had recommended them to God, and to the word of his grace, for spiritual blessings, which, without doubt, are the best blessings; but what shall they do for food for their families, an agreeable subsistence for themselves, and portions for their children? "As to these," Paul says, "do as I did;" and how was that? He here tells them,

1. That he never aimed at worldly wealth (*v.* 33): *"I have coveted no man's silver, or gold, or apparel;* nor do you, and then you will be easy." There were many in Ephesus, and many of those that had embraced the Christian faith, who were rich, had a great deal of money, and plate, and rich furniture, and wore very good clothes, and made a very good appearance. Now, (1.) Paul was not ambitious to live like them. We may take it in this sense: *"I never coveted to have so much silver and gold at command* as I see others have, nor to wear such rich clothes as I see others wear. I neither condemn them nor envy them. I can live comfortably and usefully without living great." The false apostles desired *to make a fair show in the flesh* (Gal. 6:12), to make a figure in the world; but Paul did not do so. *He knew how to want and how to be abased.*

(2.) He was not greedy to receive from them, silver, or gold, or apparel; so far from being always craving that he was not so much as coveting, nor desired them to allow him so and so for his pains among them, but was *content with such things as he had;* he never *made a gain of them,* 2 Co. 12:17. He could not only say with Moses (Num. 16:15), and with Samuel (1 Sa. 12:3, 5), *Whose ox have I taken? Or whom have I defrauded?* But, "Whose kindness have I coveted, or asked? Or to whom have I been burdensome?" He protests against desiring a gift, Phil. 4:17.

2. That he had worked for his living, and taken a great deal of pains to get bread (*v.* 34) *"Yea, you yourselves know,* and have been eye-witnesses of it, *that these hands of mine have ministered to my necessities, and to those that were with me;* you have seen me busy early and late, cutting out tents and making them up;" and, they being commonly made of leather, it was very hard work. Observe, (1.) Paul was sometimes reduced to necessities, and the want of the common supports of life, though he was so great a favourite of Heaven and so great a blessing to this earth. What an unthinking, unkind, and ungrateful world is this, that could let such a man as Paul be poor in it! (2.) He desired no more than to have his necessities supplied; he did not work at his calling to enrich himself, but to maintain himself with food and raiment. (3.) When he was to earn his bread, he did it by a manual occupation. Paul had a head and a tongue that he might have got money by, but they were these hands, saith he, *that ministered to my necessities.* What a pity was it that those hands by the laying on of which the Holy Ghost had been so often conferred, those hands by which God had wrought special miracles, and both these at Ephesus too (*ch.* 19:6, 11), should there be obliged to lay themselves to the needle and shears, the awl and tacking-end, in tent-making, purely to get bread! Paul puts these presbyters (and others in them) in mind of this, that they may not think it strange if they be thus neglected, and yet to go on in their work, and make the best shift they can to live; the less encouragement they have from men, the more they shall have from God. (4.) He worked not only for himself, but for the support of those also that were with him. This was hard indeed. It had better become them to have worked for him (to maintain him as their tutor) than he for them. But so it is; those that are willing to take the labouring oar will find those about them willing they should have it. If Paul will work for the maintenance of his companions, he is welcome to do it.

3. That even then, when he worked for the supply of his own necessities, yet he spared something out of what he got for the relief of others; for this he here obliges them to do (*v.* 35): *"I have shown you all things,* that is, in all the parts of your duty I have set you your copy and given you a good example, and particularly in this, *that so labouring you ought to support the weak."* Some understand it of their supporting the faith of weak believers, by removing the prejudices which some conceived against Christianity, as if the preachers of it made a gainful trade of their preaching, and the gospel was only a trick to get money by, and pick people's pockets. "Now, that you may *cut off occasion from those that seek occasion to reproach us,* and so may support the weak among us, you will do well, for the present, to get your livelihood by the labour of your hands, and not to depend upon your ministry." But I rather understand it of their helping to support the sick, and the poor, and those that could not labour, because it agrees with Paul's exhortation (Eph. 4:28): *Let him labour, working with his hands, that he may have to give to him that needeth.* We must labour in an honest employment, not only that we may be able to live, but that we may be able to give. This might seem a hard saying, and therefore Paul backs it with a saying of our Master's, which he would have them always to remember. These words our Lord Jesus said; it should seem, they were words he often used to his disciples. When he himself did so much good gratis, and bade them to do so too (Mt. 10:8, 9), he added this saying, which, though nowhere recorded by the evangelists, yet Paul had by word of mouth from Peter, or some other of the disciples; and an excellent saying it is, and has something of a paradox in it: *It is more blessed to give than to receive.* "It is" (saith Dr. Tillotson) "a particular endearment of this admirable saying of our Saviour's to us, that, being omitted by the evangelists, and in danger of being lost and forgotten, it was thus happily retrieved by St. Paul, and recorded by St. Luke." It is more blessed to give to others than to receive from others; not only more blessed to be rich, and so on the giving hand, than to be poor, and so on the receiving hand (every one will own this); but more blessed to do good with what we have, be it much or little, than to increase it and make it more. The sentiment of the children of this world is contrary to this; they are afraid of giving. "This giving," they say, "undoes us all;" but they are in hope of getting. *Every one for his gain from his quarter,* Isa. 56:11. Clear gain is with them the most blessed thing that can be; but Christ tells us, *It is more blessed* (more excellent in itself, an evidence of a more excellent disposition of mind, and the way to a better blessedness at last) *to give than to receive.* It makes us more like to God, who gives to all, and receives from none; and to the Lord Jesus, *who went about doing good.* It is more blessed to give our pains than to receive pay for it, and what we should delight to do if the necessities of ourselves and families would admit it. It is more pleasant to do good to the grateful, but it is more honourable to do good to the ungrateful, for then we have God to be our paymaster, who will reward in the resurrection of the just what has not otherwise been recompensed.

Verses 36–38

After the parting sermon that Paul preached to the elders of Ephesus, which was very affecting, we have here the parting prayer and tears, which were yet more affecting; we can scarcely read the account here given of them, and meditate upon them with dry eyes.

I. They parted with prayer (*v.* 36): *And, when he had thus spoken, he kneeled down, and prayed with them all.* And, no doubt, it was a prayer every way suited to the present mournful occasion. He committed them to God in this prayer, prayed that he would not leave them, but continue his presence with them. 1. It was a joint prayer. He not only prayed for them, but prayed with them, *prayed with them all;* that they might put up the same petitions for themselves and one another that he put up to God for them all, and that they might learn what to ask of God for themselves when he was gone. Public prayers are so far from being intended to supersede our own secret prayers, and make them needless, that they are designed to quicken and encourage them, and to direct us in them. When we are alone we should pray over the prayers that our ministers have put up with us. 2. It was a humble reverent prayer. This was expressed by the posture they used: *He kneeled down, and prayed with them,* which is the most proper gesture in prayer, and significant both of adoration and of petition, especially petition for the forgiveness of sin. Paul used it much: *I bow my knees,* Eph. 3:14. 3. It was a prayer after sermon; and, we may suppose, he prayed over what he had preached. He had committed the care of the church at Ephesus to those elders, and now he prays that God would enable them faithfully to discharge this great trust reposed in them, and would give them those measures of wisdom and grace which it required; he prayed for the flock, and all that belonged to it, *that the great Shepherd of the sheep* would take care of them all, and keep them from being a prey to the grievous wolves. Thus he taught these ministers to pray for those they preached to, *that they might not labour in vain.* 4. It was a parting prayer, which might be likely to leave lasting impressions, as the farewell sermon did. It is good for friends, when they part, to part with prayer, that by praying together just at parting they may be enabled to pray the more feelingly one for another when they are separated, which is one part of our Christian duty, and an improvement of the communion of saints. The Lord watch between us, and watch over us both, when we are absent one from the other, is a good parting prayer (Gen. 31:49), as also that our next meeting may be either nearer heaven or in heaven. Paul here followed the example of Christ, who, when he took leave of his disciples, after he had preached to them, prayed with them all, Jn. 17:1.

II. They parted with tears, abundance of tears, and most affectionate embraces, *v.* 37, 38. 1. *They all wept sorely.* We have reason to think the Paul himself began; though he was determined to go, and saw his call clear to other work, yet he was sorry in his heart to leave them, and many a tear it cost him. He that was so often in tears while he was with them (*v.* 19, 31), no doubt shed many at parting, so watering what he had sown among them. But the notice is taken of their tears: *They all wept sorely;* there was not a dry eye among them, and it is probable the affectionate expressions Paul used in prayer set them a-weeping. These were tears of love and mutual endearment, like those of Jonathan and David, when they were forced to part, and *wept one with another, until* (as if they wept for strife) *David exceeded,* 1 Sa. 20:41. 2. *They fell upon Paul's neck, and kissed him,* all, one after another, each bewailing his own loss: "How can I part with this invaluable man, this blessed Paul," says one, "in whom my life is a manner bound up?" — "Farewell, my dear friend," says another, "a thousand thanks to thee, and ten thousand to God for thee, and for all the pains thou hast taken with me for my good." "And must we part?" says another: "must I lose my spiritual father, nurse, and guide?" — "What will become of us now?" says another, "when we shall no more have him to apply to, and receive direction from? What shall I do, if the Lord take away my master from my head? *My father, my father, the chariots of Israel, and the horsemen thereof.*" Note, Those that are most loving are commonly best beloved. Paul, who was a most affectionate friend himself, had friends that were very affectionate to him. These tears at parting with Paul were a grateful return for all the tears he had shed in preaching to them and praying with them. *He that watereth shall be watered also himself.* 3. That which cut them to the heart thus, and made this place such a *Bochim, such a place of weepers,* was, *that word which Paul spoke, that* he was certain *they should see his face no more.* If he had given them directions to follow him, as he did to those that were his usual companions, or any intimation that he would come hereafter and make them a visit, they could have borne this parting pretty well; but when they are told that they shall see his face no more in this world, that it is a final farewell they are now giving and taking, this makes it a great mourning; it makes farewell just like a funeral, and puts them into this passion of weeping. There were other things for which they sorrowed — that they should lose the benefit of his public performances, and see him no longer presiding in their assemblies, should have none of his personal counsels and comforts; and, we hope, they sorrowed for their own sin, in not profiting more by his labours while they had him among them, and which had provoked God to order his remove. But that which gave the most sensible accent to their grief was *that they should see his face no more.* When our friends are separated from us by death, this is the consideration with which we raise up our mourning, that we shall see their faces no more; but we complain of this as those that have no hope, for if our friends died in Christ, and we live to him, they are gone to see God's face, to behold his glory, with the reflection of which their faces shine, and we hope to be with them shortly. Though we shall see their faces no more in this world, we hope to see them again in a better world, and to be there together for ever and with the Lord.

III. They *accompanied him unto the ship,* partly to show their respect for him (they would bring him on his way as far as they could), and partly that they might have a little more of his company and conversation; if it must be the last interview, they will have as much of him as they can, and see the last of him. And we have reason to think that when they came to the water-side, and he was about to go on board, their tears and embraces were repeated; for loth to part bids oft farewell. But this was a comfort to both sides, and soon turned this tide of passion, that the presence of Christ both went with him and staid with them.

CHAPTER 21

We have, with a great deal of pleasure, attended the apostle in his travels throughout the Gentile nations to preach the gospel, and have seen a great harvest of souls gathered in to Christ; there we have seen likewise what persecutions he endured; yet still out of them all the Lord presently delivered him, 2 Tim. 3:11. But now we are to attend him to Jerusalem, and there into lasting bonds; the days of his service now seem to be over, and nothing to remain but days of suffering, days of darkness, for they are many. It is a thousand pities that such a workman should be laid aside; yet so it is, and we must not only acquiesce, as his friends then did, saying, "The will of the Lord be done;" but we must believe, and shall find reason to do so, that Paul in the prison, and at the bar, is as truly glorifying God, and serving Christ's interest, as Paul in the pulpit was. In this chapter we have, I. A journal of Paul's voyage from Ephesus to Caesarea, the next sea-port to Jerusalem, some places he touched at, and his landing there (*v.* 1–7). II. The struggles he had with his friends at Caesarea, who mightily opposed his going up to Jerusalem, but could not prevail (*v.* 8–14). III. Paul's journey from Caesarea to Jerusalem, and the kind entertainment which the Christians there gave him (*v.* 15–17). IV. His compliance with the persuasions of the brethren there, who advised him so far to compliment the Jews as to go and purify that it might appear he was no such enemy to the Mosaic rites and ceremonies as he was reported to be (*v.* 18–26). V. The turning of this very thing against him by the Jews, and the apprehending of him in the temple as a criminal thereupon (*v.* 27–30). VI. The narrow escape he had of being pulled to pieces by the rabble, and the taking of him into fair and legal custody by the chief captain, who permitted him to speak for himself to the people (*v.* 31–40). And so we have him made a prisoner, and shall never have him otherwise to the end of the history of this book.

Verses 1–7

We may observe here,

I. How much ado Paul had to get clear from Ephesus, intimated in the first words of the chapter, *after we had gotten from them,* that is, were drawn from them as by violence. It was a force put upon both sides; Paul was loth to leave them, and they were loth to part with him, and yet there was no remedy, but so it must be. When good people are taken away by death, they are, as it were, gotten from their friends here below, who struggled hard to have detained them if possible.

II. What a prosperous voyage they had thence. Without any difficulty, *they came with a straight course,* by direct sailing, *to Coos,* a famous Grecian island, — *the next day to Rhodes,* talked of for the Colossus there, — *thence to Patara,* a famous port, the metropolis of Lycia (*v.* 1); here they very happily *found a ship sailing over into Phenicia,* the very course they were steering, *v.* 2. Providence must be acknowledged when things happen thus opportunely, and we are favoured by some little circumstances that contribute to the expediting of our affairs; and we must say, *It is God that maketh our way perfect.* This ship that was bound for Phenicia (that is, Tyre) they took the convenience of, *went on board, and set sail* for Tyre. In this voyage *they discovered Cyprus,* the island that Barnabas was of, and which he took care of, and therefore Paul did not visit it, but *we left it on the left hand* (*v.* 3), *sailed* upon the coast of *Syria, and* at length *landed at Tyre,* that celebrated mart of the nations, so it had been, but was now reduced; yet something of a trade it had still, *for there the ship was to unlade her burden,* and did so.

III. The halt that Paul made at Tyre; when he had arrived there, he was upon the coast of the land of Israel, and found now that he could compass the remainder of his journey within the time he had fixed.

1. *At Tyre he found disciples,* some that had embraced the gospel, and professed the Christian faith. Observe, Wherever Paul came, he enquired what disciples were there, found them out, and associated with them; for we know what is the usage with birds of a feather. When Christ was upon earth, though he went sometimes into the coast of Tyre, yet he never went thither to preach the gospel there; nor did he think fit to afford to Tyre and Sidon the advantages which Chorazin and Bethsaida had, though he knew that if they had had them they would have made a better improvement of them, Lu. 10:13, 14. But, after the enlarging of the gospel-commission, Christ was preached at Tyre, and had disciples there; and to this, some think, that prophecy concerning Tyre had reference (Isa. 23:18), *Her merchandise and her hire shall be holiness to the Lord.*

2. Paul, *finding those disciples at Tyre, tarried there seven days,* they urging him to stay with them as long as he could. He staid seven days at Troas (*ch.* 20:6), and here so many days at Tyre, that he might be sure to spend one Lord's day with them, and so might have an opportunity of preaching publicly among them; for it is the desire of good men to do good wherever they come, and where we find disciples we may either benefit them or be benefited by them.

3. The disciples at Tyre were endowed with such gifts that they could by the Spirit foretel the troubles Paul would meet with at Jerusalem; for *the Holy Ghost witnessed it in every city, ch.* 20:23. Being a thing that would be so much talked of when it came to pass, God saw fit to have it much prophesied of before, that people's faith, instead of being offended, might be confirmed. And withal they were endowed with such graces that foreseeing his troubles, out of love to him and concern for the church, especially the churches of the Gentiles, that could ill spare him, they begged of him *that he would not go up to Jerusalem,* for they hoped the decree was conditional: If he go up, he will come into trouble there; as the prediction to David *that the men of Keilah will deliver him up* (that is, if he *venture himself with them);* and therefore they said to him, *by the Spirit, that he should not go up,* because they concluded it would be most for the glory of God that he should continue at liberty; and it was not at all their fault to think so, and consequently to dissuade him; but it was their mistake, for his trial would be for the glory of God and the furtherance of the gospel, and he knew it; and the importunity that was used with him, to dissuade him from it, renders his pious and truly heroic resolution the more illustrious.

4. The disciples of Tyre, though they were none of Paul's converts, yet showed a very great respect to Paul, whose usefulness in the church they had heard so much of when he departed from Tyre. Though they had had but seven days' acquaintance with him, yet, as if he had been some great man, they all came together, *with their wives and children,* solemnly to take leave of him, to beg his blessing, and to bring him as far on his way as the sea would permit them. Note, (1.) We should pay respect, not only to our own ministers, that are over us in the Lord, and admonish us, and, for their work's sake among us, *esteem them highly in love,* but we must, as there is occasion, testify our love and respect to all the faithful ministers of Christ, both for his sake whose ministers they are, and for their work's sake among others. (2.) We must, in a particular manner, honour those whom God hath singularly honoured, by making them eminently useful in their generation. (3.) It is good to train up children in a respect to good people and good ministers. This was particularly remarkable at Tyre, which we have not met with any where else, that they brought their wives and children to attend Paul, to do him the more honour and to receive benefit by his instructions and prayers; and as angry notice was taken of the children of the idolaters of Bethel, that mocked a prophet, so, no doubt, gracious notice was taken of the children of the disciples at Tyre, that honoured an apostle, as Christ accepted the hosannas of the little children. (4.) We should be good husbands of our opportunities, and make the utmost we can of them for the good of our souls. *They brought Paul on his way,* that they might have so much the more of his company and his prayers. Some refer us to Ps. 45:12, as a prediction of this, *The daughter of Tyre shall be there with a gift;* for it is probable that they made some presents to Paul at parting, as usual to our friends that are going to sea, *ch.* 28:10.

5. They parted with prayer, as Paul and the Ephesians elders had done, *ch.* 20:36. Thus Paul has taught us by example, as well as rule, to pray always, to pray without ceasing. *We kneeled down on the shore and prayed.* Paul prayed for himself, prayed for them, prayed for all the churches; as he was much in prayer so he was mighty in prayer. They prayed upon the shore, that their last farewell might be sanctified and sweetened with prayer. Those that are going to sea should, when they quit the shore, commit themselves to God by prayer, and put themselves under his protection, as those that hope, even when they leave the *terra firma,* to find firm footing for their faith in the providence and promise of God. They kneeled down on the shore, though we may suppose it either stony or dirty, and there prayed. Paul would *that men should pray every where,* and so he did himself; and, where he lifted up his prayer, he bowed his knees. Mr. George Herbert says, *Kneeling never spoiled silk stockings.*

6. They parted at last (*v.* 6): *When we had taken our leave one of another,* with the most affectionate embraces and expressions of love and grief, *we took ship* to be gone, and *they returned home again,* each complaining that this is a parting world. Observe how they disposed of themselves: "We, that had a journey before us, took ship, thankful that we had a ship to carry us; and those, who had no occasions to call them abroad returned home again, thankful that they had a home to go to." *Rejoice Zebulun in thy going out, and Issachar in thy tents.* Paul left his blessing behind him with those that returned home, and those that staid sent their prayers after those that went to sea.

IV. Their arrival at Ptolemais, which was not far from Tyre (*v.* 27): *We came to Ptolemais,* which some think is the same place with Accho, which we find in the tribe of Asher, Jdg. 1:31. Paul begged leave to go ashore there, *to salute the brethren,* to enquire of their state, and to testify his good will to them; though he could not stay long with them, yet he would not pass by them without paying his respects to them, and he *abode with them one day,* perhaps it was a Lord's day; better a short stay than no visit.

Verses 8–14

We have here Paul and his company arrived at length at Caesarea, where he designed to make some stay, it being the place where the gospel was first preached to the Gentiles, and *the Holy Ghost fell upon them, ch.* 10:1, 44. Now here we are told,

I. Who it was that entertained Paul and his company *at Caesarea.* He seldom had occasion to go to a public house, but, wherever he came, some friend or other took him in, and bade him welcome. Observe, those that had sailed together parted when the voyage was accomplished, according as their business was. "Those that were concerned in the cargo staid where the ship was *to unlade her burden* (*v.* 3); others, when they came to Ptolemais, went as their occasions led them; but we that were of Paul's company went where he went, and came to Caesarea." Those that travel together through this world will separate at death, and then it will appear who are of Paul's company and who are not. Now at Caesarea.

1. They were entertained by Philip the evangelist, whom we left at Caesarea many years ago, after he had baptized the eunuch (*ch.* 8:40), and there we now find him again. (1.) He was originally a deacon, one of the seven that were chosen to serve tables, *ch.* 6:5. (2.) He was now and had long been an evangelist, one that went about to plant and water churches, as the apostles did, and gave himself, as they did, *to the word and prayer;* thus, having *used the office of a deacon well, he purchased to himself a good degree;* and, having been *faithful in a few things, was made ruler over many things.* (3.) He had a house at Caesarea, fit to entertain Paul and all his company, and he bade him and them very welcome to it; *We entered into the house of Philip the evangelist, and we abode with him.* Thus does it become Christians and ministers, according as their ability is, to *use hospitality one to another, without grudging,* 1 Pt. 4:9.

2. This Philip *had four maiden daughters, who did prophesy, v.* 9. It intimates that they prophesied of Paul's troubles at Jerusalem, as others had done, and dissuaded him from going; or perhaps they prophesied for his comfort and encouragement, in reference to the difficulties that were before him. Here was a further accomplishment of that prophecy, Joel 2:28, of such a plentiful pouring out of the Spirit upon all flesh that their *sons and their daughters should prophesy,* that is, foretel things to come.

II. A plain and full prediction of the sufferings of Paul, by a noted prophet, *v.* 10, 11. 1. Paul and his company tarried many days at Caesarea, perhaps Cornelius was yet living there, and (though Philip lodged them) yet might be many ways kind to them, and induce them to stay there. What cause Paul saw to tarry so long there, and to make so little haste at the latter end of his journey to Jerusalem, when he seemed so much in haste at the beginning of it, we cannot tell; but we are sure he did not stay either there or any where else to be idle; he measured his time by days, and numbered them. 2. *Agabus the prophet came to Caesarea from Judea;* this was he of whom we read before, who came *from Jerusalem to Antioch,* to foretel a general famine, *ch.* 11:27, 28. See how God dispenseth his gifts variously. To Paul was given the word of wisdom and knowledge, as an apostle, by the Spirit, and the gifts of healing; to Agabus, and to Philip's daughters, was given prophecy, by the same Spirit — the foretelling of things to come, which came to pass according to the prediction. See 1 Co. 12:8, 10. So that that which was the most eminent gift of the Spirit under the Old Testament, the foretelling of things to come, was under the New Testament quite outshone by other gifts, and was bestowed upon those that were of less note in the church. It should seem as if Agabus came on purpose to Caesarea, to meet Paul with this prophetic intelligence. 3. He foretold Paul's bonds at Jerusalem, (1.) By a sign, as the prophets of old did, Isaiah (*ch.* 20:3), Jeremiah (*ch.* 13:1; 27:2), Ezekiel (*ch.* 4:1; 12:3), and many others. *Agabus took Paul's girdle,* when he laid it by, or perhaps took it from about him, and with it *bound* first *his own hands, and then his own feet,* or perhaps bound his hands and feet together; this was designed both to confirm the prophecy (it was as sure to be done as if it were done already) and to affect those about him with it, because that which we see usually makes a greater impression upon us than that which we only hear of. (2.) By an explication of the sign: *Thus saith the Holy Ghost,* the Spirit of prophecy, *So shall the Jews at Jerusalem bind the man that owneth this girdle, and,* as they dealt with his Master (Mt. 20:18, 19), *shall deliver him into the hands of the Gentiles,* as the Jews in other places had all along endeavoured to do, by accusing him to the Roman governors. Paul had this express warning given him of his troubles, that he might prepare for them, and that when they came they might be no surprise nor terror to him; the general notice given us *that through much tribulation we must enter into the kingdom of God* should be of the same use to us.

III. The great importunity which his friends used with him to dissuade him from going forward to Jerusalem, *v.* 12. "Not only those of that place, but we that were of Paul's company, and among the rest Luke himself, who had heard this often before, and seen Paul's resolution notwithstanding, besought him with tears that he would not go up to Jerusalem, but steer his course some other way." Now, 1. Here appeared a commendable affection to Paul, and a value for him, upon account of his great usefulness in the church. Good men that are very active sometimes need to be dissuaded from overworking themselves, and good men that are very bold need to be dissuaded from exposing themselves too far. *The Lord is for the body,* and so we must be. 2. Yet there was a mixture of infirmity, especially in those of Paul's company, who knew he undertook this journey by divine direction, and had seen with what resolution he had before broken through the like opposition. But we see in them the infirmity incident to us all; when we see trouble at a distance, and have only a general notice of it, we can make light of it; but when it comes near we begin to shrink, and draw back. *Now that it toucheth thee thou art troubled,* Job 4:5.

IV. The holy bravery and intrepidity with which Paul persisted in his resolution, *v.* 13.

1. He reproves them for dissuading him. Here is a quarrel of love on both sides, and very sincere and strong affections clashing with each other. They love him dearly, and therefore oppose his resolution; he loves them dearly, and therefore chides them for opposing it: *What mean you to weep and to break my heart?* They were an offence to him, as Peter was to Christ, when, in a like case, he said, *Master, spare thyself.* Their weeping about him *broke his heart.* (1.) It. was a temptation to him, it shocked him, it began to weaken and slacken his resolution, and caused him to entertain thoughts of tacking about: "I know I am appointed to suffering, and you ought to animate and encourage me, and to say that which will strengthen my heart; but you, with your tears, break my heart, and discourage me. What do you mean by doing thus? Has not our Master told us to take up our cross? And would you have me to avoid mine?" (2.) It was a trouble to him that they should so earnestly press him to that in which he could not gratify them without wronging his conscience. Paul was of a very tender spirit. As he was much in tears himself, so he had a compassionate regard to the tears of his friends; they made a great impression upon him, and would bring him almost to yield to any thing. But now it breaks his heart, when he is under a necessity of denying the request of his weeping friends. It was an unkind kindness, a cruel pity, thus to torment him with their dissuasions, and to add affliction to his grief. When our friends are called out to sufferings, we shall show our love rather by comforting them than by sorrowing for them. But observe, These Christians at Caesarea, if they could have foreseen the particulars of that event, the general notice of which they received with so much heaviness, would have been better reconciled to it for their own sakes; for, when Paul was made a prisoner at Jerusalem, he was presently sent to Caesarea, the very place where he now was (*ch.* 23:33), and there he continued at least *two years* (*ch.* 24:27), and he was a prisoner at large, as appears (*ch.* 24:23), orders being given that he should have liberty to go among his friends, and his friends to come to him; so that the church at Caesarea had much more of Paul's company and help when he was imprisoned than they could have had if he had been at liberty. That which we oppose, as thinking it to operate much against us, may be overruled by the providence of God to work for us, which is a reason why we should follow providence, and not fear it.

2. He repeats his resolution to go forward, notwithstanding: *"What mean you to weep thus? I am ready* to suffer whatever is appointed for me. I am fully determined to go, whatever comes of it, and therefore it is to no purpose for you to oppose it. I am willing to suffer, and therefore why are you unwilling that I should suffer? Am not I nearest myself, and fittest to judge for myself? If the trouble found me unready, it would be a trouble indeed, and you might well weep at the thoughts of it. But, blessed be God, it does not. It is very welcome to me, and therefore should not be such a terror to you. For my part, *I am ready," etoimōs echō — I have myself in a readiness,* as soldiers for an engagement. "I expect trouble, I count upon it, it will be no surprise to me. I was told at first *what great things I must suffer," ch.* 9:16. "I am *prepared* for it, by a clear conscience, a firm confidence in God, a holy contempt of the world and the body, a lively faith in Christ, and a joyful hope of eternal life. I can *bid it welcome,* as we do a friend that we look for, and have made preparation for. I can, through grace, not only bear it, but rejoice in it." Now, (1.) See how far his resolution extends: You are told that I must be bound at Jerusalem, and you would have me keep away for fear of this. I tell you, *"I am ready not only to be bound, but,* if the will of God be so, *to die at Jerusalem;* not only to lose my liberty, but to lose my life." It is our wisdom to think of the worst that may befal us, and to prepare accordingly, that we may *stand complete in all the will of God.* (2.) See what it is that carries him out thus, that makes him willing to suffer and die: it is *for the name of the Lord Jesus.* All that a man has will he give for his life; but life itself will Paul give for the service and honour of the name of Christ.

V. The patient acquiescence of his friends in his resolution, *v.* 14. 1. They submitted to the wisdom of a good man. They had carried the matter as far as they could with decency; but, *"when he would not be persuaded, we ceased* our importunity. Paul knows best his own mind, and what he has to do, and it becomes us to leave it to himself, and not to censure him for what he does, nor to say he is rash, and wilful, and humoursome, and has a spirit of contradiction, as some people are apt to judge of those that will not do just as they would have them do. No doubt, Paul has a good reason for his resolution, though he sees cause to keep it to himself, and God has gracious ends to serve in confirming him in it." It is good manners not to over-press those in their own affairs that will not be persuaded. 2. They submitted to the will of a good God: *We ceased,* saying, *The will of the Lord be done.* They did not resolve his resolution into his stubbornness, but into his willingness to suffer, and God's will that he should. *Father in heaven, thy will be done,* as it is a rule to our prayers and to our practice, so it is to our patience. This may refer, (1.) To Paul's present firmness; he is inflexible, and unpersuadable, and in this they see the will of the Lord done. "It is he that has wrought this fixed resolution in him, and therefore we acquiesce in it." Note, In the turning of the hearts of our friends or ministers, this way or that way (and it may be quite another way than we could wish), we should eye the hand of God, and submit to that. (2.) To his approaching sufferings: "If there be no remedy, but Paul will run himself into bonds, the will of the Lord Jesus be done. We have done all that we could do on our parts to prevent it, and now we leave it to God, we leave it to Christ, to whom the Father has committed all judgment, and therefore we do, not as we will, but as he will." Note, When we see trouble coming, and particularly that of our ministers' being silenced or removed from us, it becomes us to say, *The will of the Lord be done.* God is wise, and knows how to make all work for good, and therefore "welcome his holy will." Not only, "The will of the Lord must be done, and there is no remedy;" but, "Let the will of the Lord be done, for his will is his wisdom, and he doeth all according to the counsel of it; let him therefore do with us and ours as seemeth good in his eyes." When a trouble is come, this must allay our griefs, that the will of the Lord is done; when we see it coming, this must silence our fears, that the will of the Lord shall be done, to which we must say, *Amen,* let it be done.

Verses 15–26

In these verses we have,

I. Paul's journey to Jerusalem from Caesarea, and the company that went along with him. 1. They *took up their carriages,* their bag and baggage, and as it should seem, like poor travellers or soldiers, were their own porters; so little had they of change of raiment. *Omnia mea mecum porto — My property is all about me.* Some think they had with them the money that was collected in the churches of Macedonia and Achaia for the poor saints at Jerusalem. If they could have persuaded Paul to go some other way, they would gladly have gone along with him; but if, notwithstanding their dissuasive, he will go to Jerusalem, they do no say, "Let him go by himself then;" but as Thomas, in a like case, when Christ would go into danger at Jerusalem, *Let us go and die with him,* Jn. 11:16. Their resolution to cleave to Paul was like that of Ittai to cleave to David (2 Sa. 15:21): *In what place my Lord the king shall be, whether in death or life, there also will thy servant be.* Thus Paul's boldness emboldened them. 2. Certain of the disciples of Caesarea went along with them. Whether they designed to go however, and took this opportunity of going with so much good company, or whether they went on purpose to see if they could do Paul any service and if possible prevent his trouble, or at least minister to him in it, does not appear. The less while that Paul is likely to enjoy his liberty the more industrious they are to improve every opportunity of conversation with him. Elisha kept close to Elijah when he knew the time was at hand that he should be taken up. 3. They brought with them an honest old gentleman that had a house of his own at Jerusalem, in which he would gladly entertain Paul and his company, *one Mnason of Cyprus* (*v.* 16), *with whom we should lodge.* Such a great concourse of people there was to the feast that it was a hard matter to get lodgings; the public houses would be taken up by those of the better sort, and it was looked upon as a scandalous thing for those that had private houses to let their rooms out at those times, but they must freely accommodate strangers with them. Every one then would choose his friends to be his guests, and Mnason took Paul and his company to be his lodgers; though he had heard what trouble Paul was likely to come into, which might bring those that entertained him into trouble too, yet he shall be welcome to him, whatever comes of it. This Mnason is called an *old disciple* — a disciple *from the beginning;* some think, one of the seventy disciples of Christ, or one of the first converts after the pouring out of the Spirit, or one of the first that was converted by the preaching of the gospel in Cyprus, *ch.* 13:4. However it was, it seems he had been long a Christian, and was now in years. Note, It is an honourable thing to be an old disciple of Jesus Christ, to have been enabled by the grace of God to continue long in a course of duty, stedfast in the faith, and growing more and more prudent and experienced to a good old age. And with these old disciples one would choose to lodge; for the multitude of their years will teach wisdom.

II. Paul's welcome at Jerusalem. 1. Many of the brethren there *received him gladly, v.* 17. As soon as they had notice that he was come to town, they went to his lodgings at Manson's house, and congratulated him on his safe arrival, and told him they were glad to see him, and invited him to their houses, accounting it an honour to be known to one that was such an eminent servant of Christ. Streso observes that the word here used concerning the welcome they gave to the apostles, *asmenōs apodechein,* is used concerning the welcome of the apostles' doctrine, *ch.* 2:41. They *gladly received his word.* We think if we had Paul among us we should gladly receive him; but it is a question whether we should or no it, having his doctrine, we do not gladly receive that. 2. They paid a visit to James and the elders of the church, at a church-meeting (*v.* 18): *"The day following, Paul went unto James,* and took us with him, that were his companions, to introduce us into acquaintance with the church at Jerusalem." It should seem that James was now the only apostle that was resident at Jerusalem; the rest had dispersed themselves to preach the gospel in other places. But still they forecasted to have an apostle at Jerusalem, perhaps sometimes one and sometimes another, because there was a great resort thither from all parts. James was now upon the spot, and all the elders or presbyters that were the ordinary pastors of the church, both to preach and govern, were present. Paul saluted them all, paid his respects to them, enquired concerning their welfare, and gave them the right hand of fellowship. He *saluted them,* that is, he wished them all health and happiness, and prayed to God to bless them. The proper signification of salutation is, wishing salvation to you: *salve,* or *salus tibi sit;* like *peace be unto you.* And such mutual salutations, or good wishes, very well become Christians, in token of their love to each other and joint regard to God.

III. The account they had from him of his ministry among the Gentiles, and their satisfaction in it. 1. He gave them a narrative of the success of the gospel in those countries where he had been employed, knowing it would be very acceptable to them to hear of the enlarging of Christ's kingdom: *He declared particularly what things God had wrought among the Gentiles by his ministry, v.* 19. Observe how modestly he speaks, not what things he had wrought (he was but the instrument), but what God had wrought by his ministry. It was *not I, but the grace of God which was with me.* He planted and watered, but God gave the increase. He declared it particularly, that the grace of God might appear the more illustrious in the circumstances of his success. Thus David will tell others what God has done for his soul (Ps. 66:16), as Paul here what God has done by his hand, and both that their friends may help them to be thankful. 2. Hence they took occasion to give praise to God (*v.* 20): *When they heart it, they glorified the Lord.* Paul ascribed it all to God, and to God they gave the praise of it. They did not break out into high encomiums of Paul, but left it to his Master to say to him, *Well done, good and faithful servant;* but they gave glory to the grace of God, which was extended to the Gentiles. Note, The conversion of sinners ought to be the matter of our joy and praise as it is of the angels'. God had honoured Paul more than any of them, in making his usefulness more extensive, yet they did not envy him, nor were they jealous of his growing reputation, but, on the contrary, *glorified the Lord.* And they could not do more to encourage Paul to go on cheerfully in his work than to glorify God for his success in it; for, if God be praised, Paul is pleased.

IV. The request of James and the elders of the church at Jerusalem to Paul, or their advice rather, that he would gratify the believing Jews by showing some compliance with the ceremonial law, and appearing publicly in the temple to offer sacrifice, which was not a thing in itself sinful; for the ceremonial law, though it was by no means to be imposed upon the Gentile converts (as the false teachers would have it, and thereby endeavoured to subvert the gospel), yet it was not become unlawful as yet to those that had been bred up in the observance of it, but were far from expecting justification by it. It was dead, but not buried; dead, but not yet deadly. And, being not sinful, they thought it was a piece of prudence in Paul to conform thus far. Observe the counsel they give to Paul herein, not as having authority over him, but an affection for him.

1. They desired him to take notice of the great numbers there were of the Jewish converts: *Thou seest, brother, how many thousands of the Jews there are who believe.* They called him brother, for they looked upon him as a joint-commissioner with them in gospel-work. Though they were of the circumcision and he the apostle of the Gentiles, though they were conformists and he a nonconformist, yet they were brethren, and owned the relation. Thou hast been in some of our assemblies, and seest how numerous they are: *how many myriads of Jews believe.* The word signifies, not thousands, but *ten thousands.* Even among the Jews, who were most prejudiced against the gospel, yet there were great multitudes that received it; for the grace of God can break down the strongest holds of Satan. The number of the names at first was but one hundred and twenty, yet now many thousands. Let none therefore despise the day of small things; for, though the beginning be small, God can make the latter end greatly to increase. Hereby it appeared that God had not quite cast away his people the Jews, for among them there was a remnant, an election, that obtained (see Rom. 11:1, 5, 7): *many thousands that believed.* And this account which they could give to Paul of the success of the gospel among the Jews was, no doubt, as grateful to Paul as the account which he gave them of the conversion of the Gentiles was to them; for his heart's desire and prayer to God for the Jews was *that they might be saved.*

2. They informed him of a prevailing infirmity these believing Jews laboured under, of which they could not yet be cured: *They are all zealous of the law.* They believe in Christ as the true Messiah, they rest upon his righteousness and submit to his government; but they know the law of Moses was of God, they have found spiritual benefit in their attendance on the institutions of it, and therefore they can by no means think of parting with it, no, nor of growing cold to it. And perhaps they urged Christ's being *made under the law,* and observing it (which was designed to be our deliverance from the law), as a reason for their continuance under it. This was a great weakness and mistake, to be so fond of the shadows when the substance was come, to keep their necks under a yoke of bondage when Christ had come to make them free. But see, (1.) The power of education and long usage, and especially of a ceremonial law. (2.) The charitable allowance that must be made in consideration of these. These Jews that believed were not therefore disowned and rejected as no Christians because they were for the law, nay, were zealous for it, while it was only in their own practice, and they did not impose it upon others. Their being zealous of the law was capable of a good construction, which charity would put upon it; and it was capable of a good excuse, considering what they were brought up in, and among whom they lived.

3. They gave him to understand that these Jews, who were so zealous of the law, were ill-affected to him, *v.* 21. Paul himself, though as faithful a servant as any Christ ever had, yet could not get the good word of all that belonged to Christ's family: *"They are informed of thee* (and form their opinion of thee accordingly) that thou not only dost not teach the Gentiles to observe the law, as some would have had thee (we have prevailed with them to drop that), but *dost teach all the Jews who are* dispersed *among the Gentiles to forsake Moses, not to circumcise their children nor to walk after the customs* of our nation, which were of divine appointment, so far as they might be observed even among the Gentiles, at a distance from the temple, — not to observe the fasts and feasts of the church, not to wear their phylacteries, nor abstain from unclean meats." Now, (1.) It was true that Paul preached the abrogation of the law of Moses, taught them that it was impossible to be justified by it, and therefore we are not bound up any longer to the observance of it. But, (2.) It was false that he taught them to forsake Moses; for the religion he preached tended not to destroy the law, but to fulfil it. He preached Christ *(the end of the law for righteousness),* and repentance and faith, in the exercise of which we are to make great use of the law. The Jews among the Gentiles whom Paul taught were so far from forsaking Moses that they never understood him better, nor ever embraced him so heartily as now when they were taught to make use of him as a *schoolmaster to bring them to Christ.* But even the believing Jews, having got this notion of Paul, that he was an enemy to Moses, and perhaps giving too much regard to the unbelieving Jews too, were much exasperated against him. Their ministers, the elders here present, loved and honoured him, and approved of what he did, and called him brother, but the people could hardly be induced to entertain a favourable thought of him; for it is certain the least judicious are the most censorious, the weak-headed are the hot-headed. They could not distinguish upon Paul's doctrine as they ought to have done, and therefore condemned it in the gross, through ignorance.

4. They therefore desired Paul that he would by some public act, now that he had come to Jerusalem, make it to appear that the charge against him was false, and that he did not teach people to forsake Moses and to break the customs of the Jewish church, for he himself retained the use of them.

(1.) They conclude that something of this kind must be done: *"What is it therefore?* What must be done? The *multitude will hear that thou art come* to town." This is an inconvenience that attends men of fame, that their coming and going are taken notice of more than other people's, and will be talked of, by some for good-will and by others for ill-will. "When they hear thou art come, *they must needs come together,* they will expect that we call them together, to advise with them whether we should admit thee to preach among us as a brother or no; or, they will come together of themselves expecting to hear thee." Now something must be done to satisfy them that Paul does not teach the people to forsake Moses, and they think it necessary, [1.] For Paul's sake, that his reputation should be cleared, and that so good a man may not lie under any blemish, nor so useful a man labour under any disadvantage which may obstruct his usefulness. [2.] For the people's sake, that they may not continue prejudiced against so good a man, nor lose the benefit of his ministry by those prejudices. [3.] For their own sake, that since they knew it was their duty to own Paul their doing it might not be turned to their reproach among those that were under their charge.

(2.) They produce a fair opportunity which Paul might take to clear himself: *"Do this that we say unto thee,* take our advice in this case. *We have four men,* Jews who believe, of our own churches, and *they have a vow on them,* a vow of Nazariteship for a certain time; their time has now expired (*v.* 23), and they are to offer their offering according to the law, when they shave the head of their separation, a he-lamb for a burnt-offering, a ewe-lamb for a sin-offering, and a ram for a peace-offering, with other offerings pertinent to them, Num. 6:13–20. Many used to do this together, when their vow expired about the same time, either for the greater expedition or for the greater solemnity. Now Paul having so far of late complied with the law as to take upon him the vow of a Nazarite, and to signify the expiration of it by shaving his head at Cenchrea (*ch.* 18:18), according to the custom of those who lived at a distance from the temple, they desire him but to go a little further, and to join with these four in offering the sacrifices of a Nazarite: *'Purify thyself with them* according to the law; and be willing not only to take that trouble, but to be at charges with them, in buying sacrifices for this solemn occasion, and to join with them in the sacrifice." This, they think, will effectually stop the mouth of calumny, and every one will be convinced that the report was false, that Paul was not the man he was represented to be, did not teach the Jews to forsake Moses, but that he himself, being originally a Jew, walked orderly, and kept the law; and then all would be well.

5. They enter a protestation that this shall be no infringement at all of the decree lately made in favour of the Gentile converts, nor do they intend by this in the least to derogate from the liberty allowed them (*v.* 25): *"As touching the Gentiles* who *believe, we have written and concluded,* and resolve to abide by it, *that they observe no such things;* we would not have them to be bound up by the ceremonial law by any means, but only that they keep themselves from *things offered to idols, and from blood, and from things strangled, and from fornication;* but let not them be tied to the Jewish sacrifices or purifications, nor any of their rites and ceremonies." They knew how jealous Paul was for the preservation of the liberty of the converted Gentiles, and therefore expressly covenant to abide by that. Thus far is their proposal.

V. Here is Paul's compliance with it. He was willing to gratify them in this matter. Though he would not be persuaded not to go to Jerusalem, yet, when he was there, he was persuaded to do as they there did, *v.* 26. *Then Paul took the men,* as they advised, and the very *next day, purifying himself with them,* and not *with multitude nor tumult,* as he himself pleads (*ch.* 24:18), he *entered into the temple,* as other devout Jews that came upon such errands did, to signify the accomplishment of the days of purification to the priests; desiring the priest would appoint a time when the offering should be offered for every one of them, one for each. Ainsworth, on Num. 6:18, quotes out of Maimonides a passage which gives some light to this: *If a man say, Upon me behalf the oblations of a Nazarite,* or, *Upon me be half the shaving of a Nazarite, then he brings half the offerings by what Nazarite he will, and that Nazarite pays his offering out of that which is his.* So Paul did here; he contributed what he vowed to the offerings of these Nazarites, and some think bound himself to the law of Nazariteship, and to an attendance at the temple with fastings and prayers for seven days, not designing that the offering should be offered till them, which was what he signified to the priest. Now it has been questioned whether James and the elders did well to give Paul this advice, and whether he did well to take it. 1. Some have blamed this occasional conformity of Paul's, as indulging the Jews too much in their adherence to the ceremonial law, and a discouragement of those who stood fast in the liberty wherewith Christ had made them free. Was it not enough for James and the elders of Jerusalem to connive at this mistake in the Jewish converts themselves, but must they wheedle Paul to countenance them in it? Had it not been better, when they had told Paul how zealous the believing Jews were for the law, if they had desired, whom God had endued with such excellent gifts, to take pains with their people to convince them of their error, and to show them that they were made free from the law by their marriage to Christ? Rom. 7:4. To urge him to encourage them in it by his example seems to have more in it of fleshly wisdom than of the grace of God. Surely Paul knew what he had to do better than they could teach him. But, 2. Others think the advice was prudent and good, and Paul's following it was justifiable enough, as the case stood. It was Paul's avowed principle, *To the Jews became I as a Jew, that I might gain the Jews,* 1 Co. 9:20. He had circumcised Timothy, to please the Jews; though he would not constantly observe the ceremonial law, yet, to gain an opportunity of doing good, and to show how far he could comply, he would occasionally go to the temple and join in the sacrifices there. Those that are weak in the faith are to be borne with, when those that undermine the faith must be opposed. It is true, this compliance of Paul's sped ill to him, for this very thing by which he hoped to pacify the Jews did but provoke them, and bring him into trouble; yet this is not a sufficient ground to go upon in condemning it: Paul might do well, and yet suffer for it. But perhaps the wise God overruled both their advice and Paul's compliance with it to serve a better purpose than was intended; for we have reason to think that when the believing Jews, who had endeavoured by their zeal for the law to recommend themselves to the good opinion of those who believed not, saw how barbarously they used Paul (who endeavoured to oblige them), they were by this more alienated from the ceremonial law than they could have been by the most argumentative or affecting discourses. They saw it was in vain to think of pleasing men that would be pleased with nothing else but the rooting out of Christianity. Integrity and uprightness will be more likely to preserve us than sneaking compliances. And when we consider what a great trouble it must needs be to James and the presbyters, in the reflection upon it, that they had by their advice brought Paul into trouble, it should be a warning to us not to press men to oblige us by doing any thing contrary to their own mind.

Verses 27–40

We have here Paul brought into a captivity which we are not likely to see the end of; for after this he is either hurried from one bar to another, or lies neglected, first in one prison and then in another, and can neither be tried nor bailed. When we see the beginning of a trouble, we know not either how long it will last or how it will issue.

I. We have here Paul seized, and laid hold on.

1. He was seized in the temple, when he was there attending the days of his purifying, and the solemn services of those days, *v.* 27. Formerly he had been well known in the temple, but now he had been so long in his travels abroad that he had become a stranger there; so that it was not till *the seven days were almost ended* that he was taken notice of by those that had an evil eye towards him. In the temple, where he should have been protected, as in a sanctuary, he was most violently set upon by those who did what they could to have his blood mingled with his sacrifices — in the temple, where he should have been welcomed as one of the greatest ornaments of it that ever had been there since the Lord of the temple left it. The temple, which they themselves pretended such a mighty zeal for, yet did they themselves thus profane. Thus is the church polluted by none more than by popish persecutors, under the colour of the church's name and interest.

2. The informers against him were the Jews of Asia, not those of Jerusalem — the Jews of the dispersion, who knew him best, and who were most exasperated against him. Those who seldom came up to worship at the temple in Jerusalem themselves, but contentedly lived at a distance from it, in pursuit of their private advantages, yet appeared most zealous for the temple, as if thereby they would atone for their habitual neglect of it.

3. The method they took was to raise the mob, and to incense them against him. They did not go to the high priest, or the magistrates of the city, with their charge (probably because they expected not to receive countenance from them), but *they stirred up all the people,* who were at this time more than ever disposed to any thing that was tumultuous and seditious, riotous and outrageous. Those are fittest to be employed against Christ and Christianity that are governed least by reason and most by passion; therefore Paul described the Jewish persecutors to be not only wicked, but absurd unreasonable men.

4. The arguments wherewith they exasperated the people against him were popular, but very false and unjust. They cried out, *"Men of Israel, help.* If you are indeed men of Israel, true-born Jews, that have a concern for your church and your country, now is your time to show it, by helping to seize an enemy to both." Thus *they cried after him as after a thief* (Job 30:5), or after a mad dog. Note, The enemies of Christianity, since they could never prove it to be an ill thing, have been always very industrious, right or wrong, to put it into an ill name, and so run it down by outrage and outcry. It had become men of Israel to help Paul, who preached up him who was so much the *glory of his people Israel;* yet here the popular fury will not allow them to be men of Israel, unless they will help against him. This was like, *Stop thief,* or Athaliah's cry, *Treason, treason;* what is wanting in right is made up in noise.

5. They charge upon him both bad doctrine and bad practice, and both against the Mosaic ritual.

(1.) They charge upon him bad doctrine; not only that he holds corrupt opinions himself, but that he vents and publishes them, though not here at Jerusalem, yet in other places, nay in all places, he teaches all men, every where; so artfully is the crime aggravated, as if, because he was an itinerant, he was a ubiquitary: "He spreads to the utmost of his power certain damnable and heretical positions," [1.] Against the people of the Jews. He had taught that Jews and Gentiles stand on the same level before God, *and neither circumcision avails any thing nor uncircumcision;* nay, he had taught against the unbelieving Jews that they were rejected (and therefore had separated from them and their synagogues), and this is interpreted to be speaking against the whole nation, as if no doubt but *they were the people, and wisdom must die with them* (Job 12:2), whereas God, though he had cast them off, yet had not *cast away his people,* Rom. 11:1. They were *Lo-ammi, not a people* (Hos. 1:9), and yet pretended to be the only people. Those commonly seem most jealous for the church's name that belong to it in name only. [2.] Against the law. His teaching men to believe the gospel as the end of the law, and the perfection of it, was interpreted his preaching against the law; whereas it was so far from making void the law that it established it, Rom. 3:31. [3.] Against *this place,* the temple. Because he taught men to pray every where, he was reproached as an enemy to the temple, and perhaps because he sometimes mentioned the destruction of Jerusalem and the temple, and of the Jewish nation, which his Master had foretold. Paul had himself been active in persecuting Stephen, and putting him to death for words spoken *against this holy place,* and now the same thing is laid to his charge. He that was then made use of as the tool is now set up as the butt of Jewish rage and malice.

(2.) They charge upon him bad practices. To confirm their charge against him, as teaching people against this holy place, they charge it upon him that he had himself polluted it, and by an overt-act showed his contempt of it, and a design to make it common. He *has brought Gentiles also into the temple,* into the inner court of the temple, which none that were uncircumcised were admitted, under any pretence, to come into; there was written upon the wall that enclosed this inner court, in Greek and Latin, *It is a capital crime for strangers to enter.* — Josephus *Antiq.* 15.417. Paul was himself a Jew, and had right to enter into the court of the Jews. And they, seeing some with him there that joined with him in his devotions, concluded that Trophimus an Ephesian, who was a Gentile, was one of them. Why? Did they see him there? Truly no; but they had seen him with Paul in the streets of the city, which was no crime at all, and therefore they affirm that he was with Paul in the inner court of the temple, which was a heinous crime. They had seen him with him in the city, and therefore they supposed that Paul had brought him with him into the temple, which was utterly false. See here, [1.] Innocency is no fence against calumny and false accusation. It is no new thing for those that mean honestly, and act regularly, to have things laid to their charge which they know not, nor ever thought of. [2.] *Evil men dig up mischief,* and go far to seek proofs of their false accusations, as they did here, who, because they saw a Gentile with Paul in the city, will thence infer that he was with him in the temple. This was a strained innuendo indeed, yet by such unjust and groundless suggestions have wicked men thought to justify themselves in the most barbarous outrages committed upon the *excellent ones of the earth.* [3.] It is common for malicious people to improve that against those that are wise and good with which they thought to have obliged them and ingratiated themselves with them. Paul thought to recommend himself to their good opinion by going into the temple, he had not been so maligned by them. This is the genius of ill-nature; *for my love, they are my adversaries,* Ps. 109:4; 69:10.

We have Paul in danger of being pulled in pieces by the rabble. They will not be at the pains to have him before the high priest, or the sanhedrim; that is a roundabout way: the execution shall be of a piece with the prosecution, all unjust and irregular. They cannot prove the crime upon him, and therefore dare not bring him upon a fair trial; nay, so greedily do they thirst after his blood that they have not patience to proceed against him by a due course of law, though they were ever so sure to gain their point; and therefore, as those who neither feared God nor regarded man, they resolved to knock him on the head immediately.

1. All the city was in an uproar, *v.* 30. The people, who though they had little holiness themselves, yet had a mighty veneration for the holy place, when they heard a hue-and-cry from the temple, were up in arms presently, being resolved to stand by that with their lives and fortunes. *All the city was moved,* when they were called to from the temple, *Men of Israel, help,* with as much violence as if the old complaint were revived (Ps. 79:1), *O God, the heathen are come into thine inheritance, thy holy temple have they defiled.* Just such a zeal the Jews here show for God's temple as the Ephesians did for Diana's temple, when Paul was informed against as an enemy to that (*ch.* 19:29): *The whole city was full of confusion.* But God does not reckon himself at all honoured by those whose zeal for him transports them to such irregularities, and who, while they pretend to act for him, act in such a brutish barbarous manner.

2. They drew Paul out of the temple, and shut the doors between the outer and inner court of the temple, or perhaps the doors of the outer court. In dragging him furiously out of the temple, (1.) They showed a real detestation of him as one not fit to be suffered in the temple, nor to worship there, nor to be looked upon as a member of the Jewish nation; as if his sacrifice had been an abomination. (2.) They pretended a veneration for the temple; like that of good Jehoiada, who would not have Athaliah to be *slain in the house of the Lord,* 2 Ki. 11:15. See how absurd these wicked men were; they condemned Paul for drawing people from the temple, and yet, when he himself was very devoutly worshipping in the temple, they drew him out of it. The officers of the temple shut the doors, either, [1.] Lest Paul should find means to get back and take hold of the horns of the altar, and so protect himself by that sanctuary from their rage. Or rather, [2.] Lest the crowd should by the running in of more to them be thrust back into the temple, and some outrage should be committed, to the profanation of that holy place. Those that made no conscience of doing so ill a thing as the murdering of a good man for well-doing, yet would be thought to scruple doing it in a holy place, or at a holy time: *Not in the temple, as Not on the feast-day.*

3. They went about to kill him (*v.* 31), for they fell a beating him (*v.* 32), resolving to beat him to death by blows without number, a punishment which the Jewish doctors allowed in some cases (not at all to the credit of their nation), and called *the beating of the rebels.* Now was Paul, like a lamb, thrown into a den of lions, and made an easy prey to them, and, no doubt, he was still of the same mind as when he said, *I am ready not only to be bound, but to die at Jerusalem,* to die so great a death.

III. We have here Paul rescued out of the hands of his Jewish enemies by a Roman enemy. 1. Tidings were brought of the tumult, and that the mob was up, *to the chief captain of the band,* the governor of the castle, or, whoever he was, the now commander-in-chief of the Roman forces that were quartered in Jerusalem. Somebody that was concerned not for Paul, but for the public peace and safety, gave this information to the colonel, who had always a jealous and watchful eye upon these tumultuous Jews, and he is the man that must be instrumental to save Paul's life, when never a friend he had was capable of doing him any service. 2. The tribune, or chief captain, got his forces together with all possible expedition, and went to suppress the mob: *He took soldiers* and *centurions,* and *ran down to them.* Now at the feast, as at other such solemn times, the guards were up, and the militia more within call than at other times, and so he had them near at hand, and *he ran down unto the multitude;* for at such times delays are dangerous. Sedition must be crushed at first, lest it grow headstrong. 3. The very sight of the Roman general frightened them from beating Paul; for they knew they were doing what they could not justify, and were in danger of being called in question for this day's uproar, as the town clerk told the Ephesians. They were deterred from that by the power of the Romans from which they ought to have been restrained by the justice of God and the dread of his wrath. Note, God often makes the earth to help the woman (Rev. 12:16), and those to be a protection to his people who yet have no affection for his people; they have only a compassion for sufferers, and are zealous for the public peace. The shepherd makes use even of his dogs for the defence of his sheep. It is Streso's comparison here. See here how these wicked people were frightened away at the very sight of the chief captain; for the *king that sitteth on the throne of judgment scattereth away all evil with his eyes.* The governor takes him into custody. He rescued him, not out of a concern for him, because he thought him innocent, but out of a concern for justice, because he ought not to be put to death without trial; and because he knew not how dangerous the consequence might be to the Roman government of such tumultuous proceedings were not timely suppressed, nor what such an outrageous people might do if once they knew their own strength: he therefore takes Paul out of the hands of the mob into the hands of the law (*v.* 33): *He took him, and command-*

ed him to be bound with two chains, that the people might be satisfied he did not intend to discharge him, but to examine him, *for he demanded of* those who were so eager against him *who he was, and what he had done.* This violent taking of him out of the hands of the multitude, though there was all the reason in the world for it, yet they laid to the charge of the chief captain as his crime (*ch.* 24:7): *The chief captain Lysias came with great violence, and took him out of our hands,* which refers to this rescue as appears by comparing *ch.* 23:27, 28, where the chief captain gives an account of it to Felix.

IV. The provision which the chief captain made, with much ado, to bring Paul to speak for himself. One had almost as good enter into a struggle with the winds and the waves, as with such a mob as was here got together; and yet Paul made a shift to get liberty of speech among them.

1. There was no knowing the sense of the people; for when the chief captain enquired concerning Paul, having perhaps never heard of his name before (such strangers were the great ones to the excellent ones of the earth, and affected to be so), *some cried one thing, and some another,* among the multitude; so that it was impossible for the chief captain to know their mind, when really they knew not either one another's mind or their own, when every one pretended to give the sense of the whole body. Those that will hearken to the clamours of the multitude will know nothing for a certainty, any more than the builders of Babel, when their tongues were confounded.

2. There was no quelling the rage and fury of the people; for when *the chief captain commanded that Paul should be carried into the castle,* the tower of Antonia, where the Roman soldiers kept garrison, near the temple, the soldiers themselves had much ado to get him safely thither out of the noise, the people were so violent (*v.* 35): *When he came upon the stairs,* leading up to the castle, the soldiers were forced to take him up in their arms, and carry him (which they might easily do, for he was a little man, and his bodily presence weak), to keep him from the people, who would have pulled him limb from limb if they could. When they could not reach him with their cruel hands, they followed him with their *sharp arrows, even bitter words: They followed, crying, Away with him, v.* 36. See how the most excellent persons and things are often run down by a popular clamour. Christ himself was so, with, *Crucify him, crucify him,* though they could not say what evil he had done. *Take him out of the land of the living* (so the ancients expound it), chase him out of the world.

3. Paul at length begged leave of the chief captain to speak to him (*v.* 37): *As he was to be led into the castle,* with a great deal of calmness and composedness in himself, and a great deal of mildness and deference to those about him, *he said unto the chief captain, "May I speak unto thee?* Will it be no offence, nor construed as a breach of rule, if I give thee some account of myself, since my persecutors can give no account of me?" What a humble modest question was this! Paul knew how to speak to the greatest of men, and had many a time spoken to his betters, yet he humbly begs to leave to speak to this commander, and will not speak till he has obtained leave: *May I speak unto thee?*

4. The chief captain tells him what notion he had of him: *Canst thou speak Greek?* I am surprised to hear thee speak a learned language; for, *Art not thou that Egyptian who made an uproar?* The Jews made the uproar, and then would have it thought that Paul had given them occasion for it, by beginning first; for probably some of them whispered this in the ear of the chief captain. See what false mistaken notions of good people and good ministers many run away with, and will not be at the pains to have the mistake rectified. It seems, there had lately been an insurrection somewhere in that country, headed by an Egyptian, who took on him to be a prophet. Josephus mentions this story, that "an Egyptian raised a seditious party, promised to show them the fall of *the walls of Jerusalem from the mount of Olives,* and that they should enter the city upon the ruins." The captain here says *that he led out into the wilderness four thousand men that were murderers* — desperadoes, banditti, raparees, cutthroats. What a degeneracy was there in the Jewish nation, when there were found there so many that had such a character, and could be drawn into such an attempt upon the public peace! But Josephus says that "Felix the Roman president went out against them, killed four hundred, and took two hundred prisoners, and the rest were dispersed." — *Antiq.* 20.171; *Wars* 2.263. And Eusebius speaks of it, *Hist.* 2:20. It happened in the thirteenth year of Claudius, a little before those days, about three years ago. The ringleader of this rebellion, it seems, had made his escape, and the chief captain concluded that one who lay under so great an odium as Paul seemed to lie under, and against whom there was so great an outcry, could not be a criminal of less figure than this Egyptian. See how good men are exposed to ill-will by mistake.

5. Paul rectifies his mistake concerning him, by informing him particularly what he was; not such a vagabond, a scoundrel, a rake, as that Egyptian, who could give no good account of himself. No: *I am a man who is a Jew* originally, and no Egyptian — a Jew both by nation and religion; *I am of Tarsus, a city of Cilicia,* of honest parents and a liberal education (Tarsus was a university), and, besides that, *a citizen of no mean city.* Whether he means Tarsus or Rome is not certain; they were neither of them mean cities, and he was a freeman of both. Though the chief captain had put him under such an invidious suspicion, that he was that Egyptian, he kept his temper, did not break out into any passionate exclamations against the times he lived in or the men he had to do with, did not render railing for railing, but mildly denied the charge, and owned what he was.

6. He humbly desired a permission from the chief captain, whose prisoner he now was, to speak to the people. He does not demand it as a debt, though he might have done so, but sues for it as a favour, which he will be thankful for: *I beseech thee, suffer me to speak to the people.* The chief captain rescued him with no other design than to give him a fair hearing. Now, to show that his cause needs no art to give it a plausible colour, he desires he may have leave immediately to defend himself; for it needed no more than to be set in a true light; nor did he depend only on the goodness of his cause, but upon the goodness and fidelity of his patron, and that promise of his to all his advocates, *that it should be given them in that same hour what they should speak.*

7. He obtained leave to plead his own cause, for he needed not to have counsel assigned him, when the Spirit of the Father was ready to dictate to him, Mt. 10:20. *The chief captain gave him license* (*v.* 40), so that now he could speak with a good grace, and with the more courage; he had, I will not say that favour, but that justice, done him by the chief captain, which he could not obtain from his countrymen the Jews; for they would not hear him, but the captain would, though it were but to satisfy his curiosity. This licence being obtained, (1.) The people were attentive to hear: *Paul stood on the stairs,* which gave a little man like Zaccheus some advantage, and consequently some boldness, in delivering himself. A sorry pulpit it was, and yet better than none; it served the purpose, though it was not, like Ezra's pulpit of wood, made for the purpose. There he *beckoned with the hand unto the people,* made signs to them to be quiet and to have a little patience, for he had something to say to them; and so far he gained his point that every one cried hush to his neighbour, and there was made a profound silence. Probably the chief captain also intimated his charge to all manner of people to keep silence; if the people were not required to give audience, it was to no purpose at all that Paul was allowed to speak. When the cause of Christ and his gospel is to be pleaded, there ought to be a great silence, that we may *give the more earnest heed,* and all little enough. (2.) Paul addressed himself to speak, well assured that he was serving the interest of Christ's kingdom as truly and effectually as if he had been preaching in the synagogue: he *spoke unto them in the Hebrew tongue,* that is, in their own vulgar tongue, which was the language of their country, to which he hereby owned not only an abiding relation, but an abiding respect.

CHAPTER 22

In the close of the foregoing chapter we had Paul bound, according to Agabus's prophecy of the hard usage he should receive from the Jews at Jerusalem, yet he had his tongue set at liberty, by the permission the chief captain gave him to speak for himself; and so intent he is upon using that liberty of speech which is allowed him, to the honour of Christ and the service of his interest, that he forgets the bonds he is in, makes no mention of them, but speaks of the great things Christ had done for him with as much ease and cheerfulness as if nothing had been done to ruffle him or put him into disorder. We have here, I. His address to the people, and their attention to it (*v.* 1, 2). II. The account he gives of himself. 1. What a bigoted Jew he had been in the beginning of his time (*v.* 3–5). 2. How he was miraculously converted and brought over to the faith of Christ (*v.* 6–11). 3. How he was confirmed and baptized by the ministry of Ananias (*v.* 12–16). 4. How he was afterwards called, by an immediate warrant from heaven, to be the apostle of the Gentiles (*v.* 17–21). III. The interruption given him upon this by the rabble, who could not bear to hear any thing said in favour of the Gentiles, and the violent passion they flew into upon it (*v.* 22, 23). IV. Paul's second rescue out of the hands of the rabble, and the further course which the chief captain took to find out the true reason of this mighty clamour against Paul (*v.* 24, 25). V. Paul's pleading his privilege as a Roman citizen, by which he was exempted from this barbarous method of inquisition (*v.* 26–29). VI. The chief captain's removing the cause into the high priest's court, and Paul's appearing there (*v.* 30).

Verses 1–2

Paul had, in the last verse of the foregoing chapter, gained a great point, by commanding so profound a silence after so loud a clamour. Now here observe,

I. With what an admirable composure and presence of mind he addresses himself to speak. Never was poor man set upon in a more tumultuous manner, nor with more rage and fury; and yet, in what he said, 1. There appears o fright, but his mind is sedate and composed. Thus he makes his own words good, *None of these things move me;* and David's (Ps. 3:6), *I will not be afraid of ten thousands of people that have set themselves against me round about.* 2. There appears no passion. Though the suggestions against him were all frivolous and unjust, though it would have vexed any man alive to be charged with profaning the temple just then when he was contriving and designing to show his respect to it, yet he breaks out into no angry expressions, but is *led as a lamb to the slaughter.*

II. What respectful titles he gives even to those who thus abused him, and how humbly he craves their attention: *"Men, brethren, and fathers, v.* 1. *To you, O men, I call;* men, that should hear reason, and be ruled by it; men, from whom one may expect humanity. You, *brethren* of the common people; you, *fathers* of the priests." Thus he lets them know that he was one of them, and had not renounced his relation to the Jewish nation, but still had a kindness and concern for it. Note, Though we must not give flattering titles to any, yet we ought to give titles of due respect to all; and those we would do good to we should endeavour not to provoke. Though he was rescued out of their hands, and was taken under the protection of the chief captain, yet he does not fall foul upon them, with, *Hear now, you rebels;* but compliments them with, *Men, brethren, and fathers.* And observe, he does not exhibit a charge against them, does not recriminate, Hear now what I have to say against you, but, Hear now what I have to say for myself: *Hear you my defence;* a just and reasonable request, for every man that is accused has a right to answer for himself, and has not justice done him if his answer be not patiently and impartially heard.

III. The language he spoke in, which recommended what he said to the auditory; *He spoke in the Hebrew tongue,* that is, the vulgar language of the Jews, which, at this time, was not the pure Old-Testament Hebrew, but the Syriac, a dialect of the Hebrew, or rather a corruption of it, as the Italian of the Latin. However, 1. It showed his continued respect to his countrymen, the Jews. Though he had conversed so much with the Gentiles, yet he still retained the Jews' language, and could talk it with ease; by this it appears he is a Jew, *for his speech betrayeth him.* 2. What he said was the more generally understood, for that was the language every body spoke, and therefore to speak in that language was indeed to appeal to the people, by which he might have somewhat to insinuate into their affections; and therefore, *when they heard that he spoke in the Hebrew tongue, they kept the more silence.* How can it be thought people should give any attention to that which is spoken to them in a language they do not understand? The chief captain was surprised to hear him speak Greek (*ch.* 21:37), the Jews were surprised to hear him speak Hebrew, and both therefore think the better of him. But how would they have been surprised if they had enquired, as they ought to have done, and found in what variety of tongues *the Spirit gave him utterance!* 1 Co. 14:18, *I speak with tongues more than you all.* But the truth is, many wise and good men are therefore slighted only because they are not known.

Verses 3–21

Paul here gives such an account of himself as might serve not only to satisfy the chief captain that he was not that Egyptian he took him to be, but the Jews also that he was not that enemy to their church and nation, to their law and temple, they took him to be, and that what he did in preaching Christ, and particularly in preaching him to the Gentiles, he did by a divine commission. He here gives them to understand,

I. What his extraction and education were. 1. That he was one of their own nation, *of the stock of Israel, of the seed of Abraham, a Hebrew of the Hebrews,* not of any obscure family, or a renegado of some other nation: "No, *I am verily a man who is a Jew, anēr Ioudaios — a Jewish man;* I am a man, and therefore ought not to be treated as a beast; a man who is a Jew, not a barbarian; I am a sincere friend to your nation, for I am one of it, and should defile my own nest if I should unjustly derogate from the honour of your law and your temple." 2. That he was born in a creditable reputable place, *in Tarsus, a city of Cilicia,* and was by his birth a freeman of that city. He was not born in servitude, as some of the Jews of the dispersion, it is likely, were; but he was a gentleman born, and perhaps could produce his certificate of his freedom in that ancient and honourable city. This was, indeed, but a small matter to make any boast of, and yet it was needful to be mentioned at this time to those who insolently trampled upon him, as if he were to be ranked with the children of fools, yea, the children of base men, Job 30:8. 3. That he had a learned and liberal education. He was not only a Jew, and a gentleman, but a scholar. He *was brought up* in Jerusalem, the principal seat of the Jewish learning, and *at the feet of Gamaliel,* whom they all knew to be an eminent doctor of the Jewish law, of which Paul was designed to be himself a teacher; and therefore he could not be ignorant of their law, nor be thought to slight it because he did not know it. His parents had brought him very young to this city, designing him for a Pharisee; and some think his being brought up at the feet of Gamaliel intimates, not only that he was one of his pupils, but that he was, above any other, diligent and constant in attending his lectures, observant of him, and obsequious to him, in all he said, as *Mary,* that *sat at Jesus' feet, and heard his word.* 4. That he was in his early days a very forward and eminent professor of the Jews' religion; his studies and learning were all directed that way. So far was he from being principled in his youth with any disaffection to the religious usages of the Jews that there was not a young man among them who had a greater and more entire veneration for them than he had, was more strict in observing them himself, or more hot in enforcing them upon others. (1.) He was an intelligent professor of their religion, and had a clear head. He minded his business at Gamaliel's feet, and was there *taught according to the perfect manner of the law of the fathers.* What departures he had made from the law were not owing to any confused or mistaken notions of it, for he understood it to a nicety, *kata akribeian — according to the most accurate and exact method.* He was not trained up in the principles of the latitudinarians, had nothing in him of a Sadducee, but was of that sect that was most studious in the law, kept most close to it, and, to make it more strict than it was, added to it the traditions of the elders, the law of the fathers, the law which was given to them, and which they gave to their children, and so it was handed down to us. Paul had as great a value for antiquity, and tradition, and the authority of the church, as any of them had; and there was never a Jew of them all that understood his religion better than Paul did, or could better give an account of it or a reason for it. (2.) He was an active professor of their religion, and had a warm heart: *I was zealous towards God, as you all are this day.* Many that are very well skilled in the theory of religion are willing to leave the practice of it to others, but Paul was as much a zealot as a rabbi. He was zealous against every thing that the law prohibited, and for every thing that the law enjoined; and this was zeal towards God, because he thought it was for the honour of God and the service of his interests; and here he compliments his hearers with a candid and charitable opinion of them, *that they all were this day zealous towards God; he bears them record* (Rom. 10:2), *that they have a zeal for God, but not according to knowledge.* In hating him, and casting him out, they said, *Let the Lord be glorified* (Isa. 66:5), and, though this did by no means justify their rage, yet it enabled those that prayed, *Father, forgive them,* to plead, as Christ did, *For they know not what they do.* And when Paul owns that he had been zealous for God in the law of Moses, *as they were this day,* he intimates his hope that they might be zealous for God, in Christ, as he was this day.

II. What a fiery furious persecutor he had been of the Christian religion in the beginning of his time, *v.* 4, 5. He mentions this to make it the more plainly and evidently to appear that the change which was wrought upon him, when he was converted to the Christian faith, was purely the effect of a divine power; for he was so far from having any previous inclinations to it, or favourable opinions of it, that immediately before that sudden change was wrought in him he had the utmost antipathy imaginable to Christianity, and was filled with rage against it to the last degree. And perhaps he mentions it to justify God in his present trouble; how unrighteous soever those were that persecuted him, God was righteous, who permitted them to do it, for time was when he was a persecutor; and he may have a further view in it to invite and encourage those people to repent, for he himself had been *a blasphemer, and a persecutor,* and yet obtained mercy. Let us view Paul's picture of himself when he was a persecutor. 1. He hated Christianity with a mortal enmity: *I persecuted this way unto the death,* that is, "Those that walked in this way I aimed, if possible, to be the death of." *He breathed out slaughter against them, ch.* 9:1. When *they were put to death, he gave his voice against them, ch.* 26:10. Nay, he persecuted not only those that walked in this way, but the way itself, Christianity, which was branded as a byway, a sect; he aimed to persecute this to the death, to be the ruin of this religion. He *persecuted it to the death,* that is, he could have been willing himself to die in his opposition to Christianity, so some understand it. He would contentedly have lost his life, and would have thought it well laid out, in defence of the laws and traditions of the fathers. 2. He did all he could to frighten people from this way, and out of it, by *binding and delivering into prison both men and women;* he filled the jails with Christians. Now that he himself was bound, he lays a particular stress upon this part of his charge against himself, that he had bound the Christians, and carried them to prison; he likewise reflects upon it with a special regret that he had imprisoned not only the men, but the women, the weaker sex, who ought to be treated with particular tenderness and compassion. 3. He was employed by the great sanhedrim, the high priest, and all the estate of the elders, as an agent for them, in suppressing this new sect; so much had he already signalized himself for his zeal against it, *v.* 5. The high priest can witness for him that he was ready to be employed in any service against the Christians. When they heard that many of the Jews at Damascus had embraced the Christian faith, to deter others from doing the like they resolved to proceed against them with the utmost severity, and could not think of a fitter person to be employed in that business, nor one more likely to go through with it, than Paul. They therefore sent him, and letters by him, to the Jews at Damascus, here called *the brethren,* because they all descended from one common stock, and were of one family in religion too, ordering them to be assisting to Paul in seizing those among them that had turned Christians, and bringing them up prisoners to Jerusalem, in order to their being punished as deserters from the faith and worship of the God of Israel; and so might either be compelled to retract, or be put to death for a terror to others. Thus did Saul make *havoc of the church,* and was in a fair way, if he had gone on awhile, to ruin it, and root it out. "Such a one," says Paul, "I was at first, just such as you now are. I know the heart of a persecutor, and therefore pity you, and pray that you may know the heart of a convert, as God soon made me to do. *And who was I that I could withstand God?*"

III. In what manner he was converted and made what he now was. It was not from any natural or external causes; he did not change his religion from an affectation of novelty, for he was then as well affected to antiquity as he used to be; nor did it arise from discontent because he was disappointed in his preferment, for he was now, more than ever, in the way of preferment in the Jewish church; much less could it arise from covetousness, or ambition, or any hope of mending his fortune in the world by turning Christian, for it was to expose himself to all manner of disgrace and trouble; nor had he any conversation with the apostles or any other Christians, by whose subtlety and sophistry he might be thought to have been wheedled into this change. No, it was the Lord's doing, and the circumstances of the doing of it were enough to justify him in the change, to all those who believe there is a supernatural power; and none can condemn him for it, without reflecting upon that divine energy by which he was herein overruled. He relates the story of his conversion here very particularly, as we had it before (*ch.* 9), aiming to show that it was purely the act of God. 1. He was a fully bent upon persecuting the Christians just before Christ arrested him as ever. He *made his journey, and was come nigh to Damascus* (*v.* 6), and had no other thought than to execute the cruel design he was sent upon; he was not conscious of the least compassionate relentings towards the poor Christians, but still represented them to himself as heretics, schismatics, and dangerous enemies both to church and state. 2. It was *a light from heaven* that first startled him, *a great light,* which *shone suddenly round about him,* and the Jews knew that God is light, and his angels angels of light, and that such a light as this shining at noon, and therefore exceeding that of the sun, must be from God. Had it shone in upon him into some private room, there might have been a cheat in it, but it shone upon him in the open road, at high noon, and so strongly *that it struck him to the ground* (*v.* 7), and all *that were with him, ch.* 26:14. They could not deny but that surely the Lord was in this light. 3. It was a voice *from heaven* that first begat in him awful thoughts of Jesus Christ, of whom before he had had nothing but hateful spiteful thoughts. The voice called to him by name, to distinguish him from *those that journeyed with him, Saul, Saul, why persecutest thou me?* And when he asked, *Who art thou, Lord?* it was answered, *I am Jesus of Nazareth, whom thou persecutest, v.* 8. By which it appeared that this Jesus of Nazareth, whom they also were now persecuting, was one that spoke from heaven, and they knew it was dangerous resisting one that did so, Heb. 12:25. 4. Lest it should be objected, "How came this light and voice to work such a change upon him, and not upon those that journeyed with him?" (though, it is very probable, it had a good effect upon them, and that they thereupon became Christians), he observes *that his fellow travellers saw indeed the light, and were afraid* they should be consumed with fire from heaven, their own consciences, perhaps, now telling them that the way they were in was not good, but like Balaam's when he was going to curse Israel, and therefore they might expect to meet an angel with a flaming glittering sword; but, though the light made them afraid, they heard not the voice of him that spoke to Paul, that is, they did not distinctly hear the words. Now faith comes by hearing, and therefore that change was now presently wrought upon him that heard the words, and heard them directed to himself, which was not wrought upon those who only saw the light; and yet it might afterwards be wrought upon them too. 5. He assures them that when he was thus startled he referred himself entirely to a divine guidance; he did not hereupon presently cry out, "Well, I will be a Christian," but, *"What shall I do, Lord?* Let the same voice from heaven that has stopped me in the wrong way guide me into the right way, *v.* 10. Lord, tell me what I shall do, and I will do it." And immediately he had directions to go to Damascus, and there he should hear further from him that now spoke to him: "No more needs to be said from heaven, *there it shall be told thee,* by a man like thyself, in the name of him that now speaks to thee, *all things which are appointed for thee to do."* The extraordinary ways of divine revelation, by visions, and voices, and the appearance of angels, were designed, both in the Old Testament and in the New, only to introduce and establish the ordinary method by the scriptures and a standing ministry, and therefore were generally superseded when these were settled. The angel did not preach to Cornelius himself, but bade him send for Peter; so the voice here tells not Paul what he shall do, but bids him go to Damascus, and there it shall be told him. 6. As a demonstration of the greatness of that light which fastened upon him, he tells them of the immediate effect it had upon his eye-sight (*v.* 11): *I could not see for the glory of that light.* It struck him blind for the present. *Nimium sensibile laedit sensum — Its radiance dazzled him.* Condemned sinners are struck blind, as the Sodomites and Egyptians were, by the power of darkness, and it is a lasting blindness, like that of the unbelieving Jews; but convinced sinners are struck blind, as Paul here was, not by darkness, but by light: they are for the present brought to be at a loss within themselves, but it is in order to their being enlightened, as the putting of clay upon the eyes of the blind man was the designed method of his cure. Those that were with Paul had not the light so directly darted into their faces as Paul had unto his, and therefore they were not blinded, as he was; yet, considering the issue, who would not rather have chosen his lot than theirs? They, having their sight, led *Paul by the hand into the city.* Paul, being a Pharisee, was proud of his spiritual eyesight.

The Pharisees said, *Are we blind also?* Jn. 9:40. Nay, they were confident *that they themselves were guides to the blind,* and *lights to those that were in darkness,* Rom. 2:19. Now Paul was thus struck with bodily blindness to make him sensible of his spiritual blindness, and his mistake concerning himself, when he was *alive without the law,* Rom. 7:9.

IV. How he was confirmed in the change he had made, and further directed what he should do, by Ananias who lived at Damascus.

Observe, 1. The character here given of Ananias. He was not a man that was any way prejudiced against the Jewish nation or religion, but was himself *a devout man according to the law;* if not a Jew by birth, yet one that had been proselyted to the Jewish religion, and therefore called a devout man, and thence advanced further to the faith of Christ; and he conducted himself so well that he had a *good report of all the Jews that dwelt at Damascus.* This was the first Christian that Paul had any friendly communication with, and it was not likely that he should instil into him any such notions as they suspected him to espouse, injurious to the law or to this holy place.

2. The cure immediately wrought by him upon Paul's eyes, which miracle was to confirm Ananias's mission to Paul, and to ratify all that he should afterwards say to him. He *came to him* (*v.* 13); and, to assure him that he came to him from Christ (the very same who had torn and would heal him, had smitten, but would bind him up, had taken away his sight, but would restore it again, with advantage), he *stood by him, and said, Brother Saul, receive thy sight.* Power went along with this word, and *the same hour,* immediately, he recovered his sight, and *looked up upon him,* ready to receive from him the instructions sent by him.

3. The declaration which Ananias makes to him of the favour, the peculiar favour, which the Lord Jesus designed him above any other.

(1.) In the present manifestation of himself to him (*v.* 14): *The God of our fathers has chosen thee.* This powerful call is the result of a particular choice; his calling God the God of our fathers intimates that Ananias was himself a Jew by birth, that observed the law of the fathers, and lived upon the promise made unto the fathers; and he gives a reason why he said *Brother Saul,* when he speaks of God as the God of our fathers: *This God of our fathers has chosen thee that thou shouldst,* [1.] *Know his will,* the will of his precept that is to be done by thee, the will of his providence that is to be done concerning thee. He hath chosen thee that thou shouldst know it in a more peculiar manner; not of man nor by man, but immediately by *the revelation of Christ,* Gal. 1:1, 12. Those whom God hath chosen he hath chosen to know his will, and to do it. [2.] *That thou shouldst see that Just One, and shouldst hear the voice of his mouth,* and so shouldst know his will immediately from himself. This was what Paul was, in a particular manner, chosen to above others; it was a distinguishing favour, that he should see Christ here upon earth after his ascension into heaven. Stephen saw him *standing at the right hand of God,* but Paul saw him standing at his right hand. This honour none had but Paul. Stephen saw him, but we do not find that he heard the voice of his mouth, as Paul did, who says, *he was last of all seen of me, as of one born out of due time,* 1 Co. 15:8. Christ is here called *that Just One;* for he is Jesus Christ the righteous, and suffered wrongfully. Observe, Those whom God has chosen to know his will must have an eye to Christ, and must see him, and hear the voice of his mouth; for it is by him that God has made known his will, his good-will to us, and he has said, *Hear you him.*

(2.) In the after-manifestation of himself by him to others (*v.* 15): *"Thou shalt be his witness,* not only a monument of his grace, as a pillar may be, but a witness *viva voce — by word of mouth;* thou shalt publish his gospel, as that which thou hast experienced the power of, and been delivered into, the mould of; *thou shalt be his witness unto all men,* Gentiles as well as Jews, *of what thou hast seen and heard,* now at the very first." And finding Paul so particularly relating the manner of his conversation in his apologies for himself, here and *ch.* 26, we have reason to think that he frequently related the same narrative in his preaching for the conversion of others; he told them what God had done for his soul, to encourage them to hope that he would do something for their souls.

4. The counsel and encouragement he gave him to join himself to the Lord Jesus by baptism (*v.* 16): *Arise, and be baptized,* He had in his circumcision been given up to God, but he must now by baptism be given up to God in Christ — must embrace the Christian religion and the privileges of it, in submission to the precepts of it. This must now be done immediately upon his conversion, and so was added to his circumcision: but to the seed of the faithful it comes in the room of it; for it is, as that was to Abraham and his believing seed, *a seal of the righteousness which is by faith.* (1.) The great gospel privilege which by baptism we have sealed to us is the remission of sins: *Be baptized and wash away thy sins;* that is, "Receive the comfort of the pardon of thy sins in the through Jesus Christ and lay hold of his righteousness for that purpose, and receive power against sin for the mortifying of thy corruption;" for our being washed includes our being both justified and sanctified, 1 Co. 6:11. Be baptized, and rest not in the sign, but make sure of the thing signified, the putting away of the filth of sin. (2.) The great gospel duty which by our baptism we are bound to is *to call on the name of the Lord, the Lord Jesus;* to acknowledge him to be our Lord and our God, and to apply to him accordingly; to give honour to him, to put all our petitions in his hand. To *call on the name of Jesus Christ our Lord* (Son of David, have mercy on us) is the periphrasis of a Christian, 1 Co. 1:2. We must *wash away our sins, calling on the name of the Lord;* that is, we must seek for the pardon of our sins in Christ's name, and in dependence on him and his righteousness. In prayer, we must not any longer call God the God of Abraham, but the Father of our Lord Jesus Christ, and in him our Father; in every prayer, our eye must be to Christ. (3.) We must do this quickly. *Why tarriest thou?* Our covenanting with God in Christ is needful work, that must not be deferred. The case is so plain that it is needless to deliberate; and the hazard so great that it is folly to delay. Why should not that be done at the present time that must be done some time, or we are undone?

V. How he was commissioned to go and preach the gospel to the Gentiles. This was the great thing for which they were so angry at him, and therefore it was requisite he should for this, in a special manner, produce a divine warrant; and here he does it. This commission he did not receive presently upon his conversion, for this was *at Jerusalem,* whither he did not go till *three years after,* or more (Gal. 1:18); and whether it was then, or afterwards, that he had this vision here spoken of, we are not certain. But, to reconcile them, if possible, to his preaching the gospel among the Gentiles, he tells them, 1. That he received his orders to do it when he was at prayer, begging of God to appoint him his work and to show him the course he should steer; and (which was a circumstance that would have some weight with those he was now speaking to) he was *at prayer in the temple,* which was to be called *a house of prayer for all people;* not only in which all people should pray, but in which all people should be prayed for. Now as Paul's praying in the temple was an evidence, contrary to their malicious suggestion, that he had a veneration for the temple, though he did not make an idol of it as they did; so God's giving him this commission there in the temple was an evidence that the sending him to the Gentiles would be no prejudice to the temple, unless the Jews by their infidelity made it so. Now it would be a great satisfaction to Paul afterwards, in the execution of this commission, to reflect upon it that he received it when he was at prayer. 2. He received it in a vision. He fell *into a trance* (*v.* 17), his external senses, for the present, locked up; he was in an ecstasy, as when he was *caught up into the third heaven,* and was not at that time sensible whether he was *in the body or out of the body.* In this trance he saw Jesus Christ, not with the eyes of his body, as at his conversion, but represented to the eye of his mind (*v.* 18): *I saw him saying unto me.* Our eye must be upon Christ when we are receiving the law from his mouth; and we must not only hear him speak, but see him speaking to us. 3. Before Christ gave him a commission to go to the Gentiles, he told him it was to no purpose for him to think of doing any good at Jerusalem; so that they must not blame him, but themselves, if he be sent to the Gentiles. Paul came to Jerusalem full of hopes that, by the grace of God, he might be instrumental to bring those to the faith of Christ who had stood it out against the ministry of the other apostles; and perhaps this was what he was now praying for, that he, having had his education at Jerusalem and being well known there, might be employed in gathering the children of Jerusalem to Christ that were not yet gathered, which he thought he had particular advantages for doing of. But Christ crosses the measures he had laid: *"Make haste,"* says he, *"and get thee quickly out of Jerusalem;"* for, though thou thinkest thyself more likely to work upon them than others, thou wilt find they are more prejudiced against thee than against any other, and therefore *"will not receive thy testimony concerning me."* As God knows before who will receive the gospel, so he knows who will reject it. 4. Paul, notwithstanding this, renewed his petition that he might be employed at Jerusalem, because they knew, better than any did, what he had been before his conversion, and therefore must ascribe so great a change in him to the power of almighty grace, and consequently give the greater regard to his testimony; thus he reasoned, both with himself and with the Lord, and thought he reasoned justly (*v.* 19, 20): *"Lord,"* says he, *"they know* that I was once of their mind, that I was as bitter an enemy as any of them to such as believed on thee, that I irritated the civil power against them, and *imprisoned them,* and turned the edge of the spiritual power against them too, and *beat them in every synagogue."* And therefore they will not impute my preaching Christ to education nor to any prepossession in his favour (as they do that of other ministers), but will the more readily regard what I say because they know I have myself been one of them: particularly in Stephen's case; they know that when he was stoned I was standing by, I was aiding and abetting and *consenting to his death,* and in token of this *kept the clothes of those that stoned him.* Now "Lord," says he, "if I appear among them, preaching the doctrine that Stephen preached and suffered for, they will no doubt receive my testimony." "No," says Christ to him, "they will not; but will be more exasperated against thee as a deserter from, than against others whom they look upon only as strangers to, their constitution." 5. Paul's petition for a warrant to preach the gospel at Jerusalem is overruled, and he has peremptory orders to go among the Gentiles (*v.* 21): *Depart, for I will send thee far hence, unto the Gentiles.* Note, God often gives gracious answers to the prayers of his people, not in the thing itself that they pray for, but in something better. Abraham prays, *O that Ishmael may live before thee;* and God hears him for Isaac. So Paul here prays that he may be an instrument of converting souls at Jerusalem: "No," says Christ, "but thou shalt be employed among the Gentiles, and *more shall be the children of the desolate than those of the married wife."* It is God that appoints his labourers both their day and their place, and it is fit they should acquiesce in his appointment, though it may cross their own inclinations. Paul hankers after Jerusalem: to be a preacher there was the summit of his ambition; but Christ designs him greater preferment. He shall not enter into other men's labours (as the other apostles did, Jn. 4:38), but shall break up new ground, and *preach the gospel where Christ was not named,* Rom. 15:20. So often does Providence contrive better for us than we for ourselves; to the guidance of that we must therefore refer ourselves. *He shall choose our inheritance for us.* Observe, Paul shall not go to preach among the Gentiles without a commission: *I will send thee.* And, if Christ send him, his Spirit will go along with him, he will stand by him, will carry him on, and bear him out, and give him to see the fruit of his labours. Let not Paul set his heart upon Jerusalem, for he must be sent far hence; his call must be quite another way, and his work of another kind. And it might be a mitigation of the offence of this to the Jews that he did not set up a Gentile church in the neighbouring nations; others did this in their immediate vicinity; he was sent to places at a distance, a vast way off, where what he did could not be thought an annoyance to them.

Now, if they would lay all this together, surely they would see that they had no reason to be angry with Paul for preaching among the Gentiles, or construe it as an act of ill-will to his own nation, for he was compelled to it, contrary to his own mind, by an overruling command from heaven.

Verses 22–30

Paul was going on with this account of himself, had shown them his commission to preach among the Gentiles without any peevish reflections upon the Jews, and we may suppose designed next to show how he was afterwards, by a special direction of the Holy Ghost at Antioch, separated to this service, how tender he was of the Jews, how respectful to them, and how careful to give them the precedency in all places whither he came, and to unite Jews and Gentiles in one body; and then to show how wonderfully God had owned him, and what good service had been done to the interest of God's kingdom among men in general, without damage to any of the true interests of the Jewish church in particular. But, whatever he designs to say, they resolve he shall say no more to them: *They gave him audience to this word.* Hitherto they had heard him with patience and some attention. But when he speaks of being sent to the Gentiles, though it was what Christ himself said to him, they cannot bear it, not so much as to hear the Gentiles named, such an enmity had they to them, and such a jealousy of them. Upon the mention of this, they have no manner of patience, but forget all rules of decency and equity; thus were they *provoked to jealousy by those that were no people,* Rom. 10:19.

Now here we are told how furious and outrageous the people were against Paul, for mentioning the Gentiles as taken into the cognizance of divine grace, and so justifying his preaching among them.

I. They interrupted him, by lifting up their voice, to put him into confusion, and that nobody might hear a word he said. Galled consciences kick at the least touch; and those who are resolved not to be rules by reason commonly resolve not to hear it if they can help it. And the spirit of enmity against the gospel of Christ commonly shows itself in silencing the ministers of Christ and his gospel, and stopping their mouths, as the Jews did Paul's here. Their fathers had said to the best of seers, *See not,* Isa. 30:10. And so they to the best of speakers, *Speak not. Forbear, wherefore shouldst thou be smitten?* 2 Chr. 25:16.

II. They clamoured against him as one that was unworthy of life, much more of liberty. Without weighing the arguments he had urged in his own defence, or offering to make any answer to them, they cried out with a confused noise, *"Away with such a fellow* as this *from the earth,* who pretends to have a commission to preach to the Gentiles; why, *it is not fit that he should live."* Thus the men that have been the greatest blessings of their age have been represented not only as the burdens of the earth, but the plague of their generation. He that was worthy of the greatest honours of life is condemned as not worthy of life itself. See what different sentiments God and men have of good men, and yet they both agree in this that they are not likely to live long in this world. Paul says of the godly Jews that they were men of *whom the world was not worthy,* Heb. 11:38. And therefore they must be removed, that the world may be justly punished with the loss of them. The ungodly Jews here say of Paul that it was not fit he should live; and therefore he must be removed, that the world may be eased of the burden of him, as of the two witnesses, Rev. 11:10.

III. They went stark mad against Paul, and against the chief captain for not killing him immediately at their request, or throwing him as a pry into their teeth, that they might devour him (*v.* 23); as men whose reason was quite lost in passion, they cried out like roaring lions or raging bears, and howled like the evening wolves; they *cast off their clothes* with fury and violence, as much as to say that thus they would tear him if they could but come at him. Or, rather, they thus showed how ready they were to stone him; those that stoned Stephen threw off their clothes, *v.* 20. Or, they *rent their clothes,* as if he had spoken blasphemy; and *threw dust into the air,* in detestation of it; or signifying how ready they were to throw stones at Paul, if the chief captain would have permitted them. But why should we go about to give a reason for these experiences of fury, which they themselves could not account for? All they intended was to make the chief captain sensible how much they were enraged and exasperated at Paul, so that he could not do any thing to gratify them more than to let them have their will against him.

IV. The chief captain took care for his safety, by ordering him to be brought into the castle, *v.* 24. A prison sometimes has been a protection to good men from popular rage. Paul's hour was not yet come, he had not finished his testimony, and therefore God raised up one that took care of him, when none of his friends durst appear on his behalf. *Grant not, O Lord, the desire of the wicked.*

V. He ordered him the torture, to force from him a confession of some flagrant crimes which had provoked the people to such an uncommon violence against him. *He ordered that he should be examined by scourging* (as now in some countries by the rack), that *he might know wherefore they cried so against him.* Herein he did not proceed fairly; he should have singled out some of the clamorous tumultuous complainants, and taken them into the castle as breakers of the peace, and should have examined them, and by scourging too, what they had to lay to the charge of a man that could give so good an account of himself, and did not appear to have done any thing worthy of death or of bonds. It was proper to ask them, but not at all proper to ask Paul, *wherefore they cried so against him.* He could tell that he had given them no just cause to do it; if there were any cause, let them produce it. No man is bound to accuse himself, though he be guilty, much less ought he to be compelled to accuse himself when he is innocent. Surely the chief captain did not know the Jewish nation when he concluded that he must needs have done something very bad whom they cried out against. Had they not just thus cried out against our Lord Jesus, *Crucify him, crucify him,* when they had not one word to say in answer to the judge's question, *Why, what evil has he done?* Is this a fair or just occasion to scourge Paul, that a rude tumultuous mob cry out against him, but cannot tell why or wherefore, and therefore he must be forced to tell?

VI. Paul pleaded his privilege as a Roman citizen, by which he was exempted from all trials and punishments of this nature (*v.* 25): *As they bound him with thongs,* or leathern bands, to the whipping post, as they used to bind the vilest of malefactors in bridewell from whom they would extort a confession, he made no outcry against the injustice of their proceedings against an innocent man, but very mildly let them understand the illegality of their proceedings against him as a citizen of Rome, which he had done once before at Philippi after he had been scourged (*ch.* 16:37), but here he makes use of it for prevention. He *said to the centurion that stood by,* "You know the law; pray *is it lawful for you* who are yourselves Romans to *scourge a man that is a Roman, and uncondemned?"* The manner of his speaking plainly intimates what a holy security and serenity of mind this good man enjoyed, not disturbed either with anger or fear in the midst of all those indignities that were done him, and the danger he was in. The Romans had a law (it was called *lex Sempronia*), that if any magistrate did chastise or condemn a freeman of Rome, *indicta causa — without hearing him speak for himself, and deliberating upon the whole of his case,* he should be liable to the sentence of the people, who were very jealous of their liberties. It is indeed the privilege of every man not to have wrong done him, except it be proved he has done wrong; as it is of every Englishman by *Magna Charta* not to be dis-seized of his life or freehold, but by a verdict of twelve men of his peers.

VII. The chief captain was surprised at this, and put into a fright. He had taken Paul to be a vagabond Egyptian, and wondered he could speak Greek (*ch.* 21:37), but is much more surprised now he finds that he is as good a gentleman as himself. How many men of great worth and merit are despised because they are not known, are looked upon and treated as the offscouring of all things, when those that count them so, if they knew their true character, would own them to be of the excellent ones of the earth! The chief captain had centurions, under-officers, attending him, *ch.* 21:32. One of these reports this matter to the chief captain (*v.* 26): *Take heed what thou doest, for this man is a Roman,* and what indignity is done to him will be construed an offence against the majesty of the Roman people, as they loved to speak. They all knew what a value was put upon this privilege of the Roman citizens. Tully extols it in one of his orations against Verres, *O nomen dulce libertatis, O jus eximium nostrae civitatis! O lex Porcia! O leges Semproniae; facinus est vincere Romanum civem, scelus verberare — O Liberty! I love thy charming name; and these our Porcian and Sempronian laws, how admirable! It is a crime to bind a Roman citizen, but an unpardonable one to beat him.* "Therefore" (says the centurion) "let us look to ourselves; if this man be a Roman, and we do him any indignity, we shall be in danger to lose our commissions at least." Now, 1. The chief captain would be satisfied of the truth of this from his own mouth (*v.* 27): *"Tell me, art thou a Roman?* Art thou entitled to the privileges of a Roman citizen?" "Yes," says Paul, *"I am;"* and perhaps produced some ticket or instrument which proved it; for otherwise they would scarcely have taken his word. 2. The chief captain very freely compares notes with him upon this matter, and it appears that the privilege Paul had as a Roman citizen was of the two more honourable than the colonel's; for the colonel owns that his was purchased: "I am a freeman of Rome; but *with a great sum obtained I this freedom,* it cost me dear, how came you by it?" "Why truly," says Paul, *"I was free-born."* Some think he became entitled to this freedom by the place of his birth, as a native of Tarsus, a city privileged by the emperor with the same privileges that Rome itself enjoyed; others rather think it was by his father or grandfather having served in the war between Caesar and Antony, or some other of the civil wars of Rome, and being for some signal piece of service rewarded with a freedom of the city, and so Paul came to be free-born; and here he pleads it for his own preservation, for which end not only we may but we ought to use all lawful means. 3. This put an immediate stop to Paul's trouble. Those that were appointed to examine him by scourging quitted the spot; they *departed from him* (*v.* 29), lest they should run themselves into a snare. Nay, and the colonel himself, though we may suppose him to have a considerable interest, was afraid when he heard he was a Roman, because, though he had not beaten him, yet he had bound him in order to his being beaten. Thus many are restrained from evil practices by the fear of man who would not be restrained from them by the fear of God. See here the benefit of human laws and magistracy, and what reason we have to be thankful to God for them; for even when they have given no countenance nor special protection to God's people and ministers, yet, by the general support of equity and fair dealing between man and man, they have served to check the rage of wicked and unreasonable illegal men, who otherwise would know no bounds, and to say, *Hitherto it shall come, but no further; here shall its proud waves by stayed.* And therefore this service we owe to all in authority, to pray for them, because this benefit we have reason to expect from them, whether we have it or no, as long as we are quiet and peaceable — to live *quiet and peaceable lives in all godliness and honesty,* 1 Tim. 2:1, 2. 4. The governor, the next day, brought Paul before the sanhedrim, *v.* 30. He first *loosed him from his bands,* that those might not prejudge his cause, and that he might not be charged with having pinioned a Roman citizen, and then summoned the chief priests and all their council to come together to take cognizance of Paul's case, for he found it to be a matter of religion, and therefore looked upon them to be the most proper judges of it. Gallio in this case discharged Paul; finding it to be a matter of their law, he drove the prosecutors from the judgement-seat (*ch.* 18:16), and would not concern himself at all in it; but this Roman, who was a military man, kept Paul in custody, and appealed from the rabble to the general assembly. Now, (1.) We may hope that hereby he intended Paul's safety, as thinking, if he were an innocent and inoffensive man, though the multitude might be incensed against him, yet the chief priests and elders would do him justice, and clear him; for they were, or should be, men of learning and consideration, and their court governed by rules of equity. When the prophet could find no good among the poorer sort of people, he concluded that it was because they *knew not the way of the Lord, nor the judgments of their God,* and promised himself that he should speed better among the great men, as the chief captain here did, but soon found himself disappointed there: these have *altogether broken the yoke, and burst the bonds,* Jer. 5:4, 5. But, (2.) That which he is here said to aim at is the gratifying of his own curiosity: He *would have known the certainty wherefore he was accused of the Jews.* Had he sent for Paul to his own chamber, and talked freely with him, he might soon have learned from him that which would have done more than satisfy his enquiry, and which might have persuaded him to be a Christian. But it is too common for great men to affect to set that at a distance from them which might awaken their consciences, and to desire to have no more of the knowledge of God's ways than may serve them to talk of.

CHAPTER 23

The close of the foregoing chapter left Paul in the high priest's court, into which the chief captain (whether to his advantage or no I know not) had removed his cause from the mob; and, if his enemies act there against him with less noise, yet it is with more subtlety. Now here we have, I. Paul's protestation of his own integrity, and of a civil respect to the high priest, however he had upon a sudden spoken warmly to him, and justly (*v.* 1–5). II. Paul's prudent contrivance to get himself clear of them, by setting the Pharisees and Sadducees at variance one with another (*v.* 6–9). III. The governor's seasonable interposal to rescue him out of their hands likewise (*v.* 10). IV. Christ's more comfortable appearing to him, to animate him against those difficulties that lay before him, and to tell him what he must expect (*v.* 11). V. A bloody conspiracy of some desperate Jews to kill Paul, and their drawing in the chief priests and the elders to be aiders and abettors with them in it (*v.* 12–15). VI. The discovery of this conspiracy to Paul, and by him to the chief captain, who perceived so much of their inveterate malice against Paul that he had reason enough to believe the truth of it (*v.* 16–22). VII. The chief captain's care of Paul's safety, by which he prevented the execution of the design; he sent him away immediately under a strong guard from Jerusalem to Caesarea, which was now the residence of Felix, the Roman governor, and there he safely arrived (*v.* 23–35).

Verses 1–5

Perhaps when Paul was brought, as he often was *(corpus cum causa — the person and the cause together),* before heathen magistrates and councils, where he and his cause were slighted, because not at all understood, he thought, if he were brought before the sanhedrim at Jerusalem, he should be able to deal with them to some good purpose, and yet we do not find that he works at all upon them. Here we have,

I. Paul's protestation of his own integrity. Whether the chief priest put any question to him, or the chief captain made any representation of his case to the court, we are not told; but Paul appeared here,

1. With a good courage. He was not at all put out of countenance upon his being brought before such an august assembly, for which in his youth he had conceived such a veneration; nor did he fear their calling him to an account about the letters they gave him to Damascus, to persecute the Christians there, though (for aught we know) this was the first time he had ever seem them since; but *he earnestly beheld the council.* When Stephen was brought before them, they thought to have faced him down, but could not, such was his holy confidence; they *looked stedfastly on him, and his face was as that of an angel, ch.* 6:15. Now that Paul was brought before them he thought to have faced them down, but could not, such was their wicked impudence. However, now was fulfilled in him what God promised to Ezekiel (*ch.* 3:8, 9): *I have made thy face strong against their faces; fear them not, neither be dismayed at their looks.*

2. With a good conscience, and that gave him a good courage.

— Hic murus aheneus esto,
Nil conscire sibi —
Be this thy brazen bulwark of defence,
Still to preserve thy conscious innocence.

He said, *"Men and brethren, I have lived in all good conscience before God unto this day.* However I may be reproached, my heart does not reproach me, but witnesses for me." (1.) He had always been a man inclined to religion; he never was a man that lived at large, but always put a difference between moral good and evil; even in his unregenerate state, he was, *as touching the righteousness that was in the law, blameless.* He was no unthinking man, who never considered what he did, no designing man, who cared not what he did, so he could but compass his own ends. (2.) Even when he persecuted the church of God, he thought he ought to do it, and that he did God service in it. Though his conscience was misinformed, yet he acted according to the dictates of it. See *ch.* 26:9. (3.) He seems rather to speak of the time since his conversion, since he left the service of the high priest, and fell under their displeasure for so doing; he does not say, From my beginning until this day; but, "All the time in which you have looked upon me as a deserter, an apostate, and an enemy to your church, even *to this day,* I have *lived in all good conscience before God;* whatever you may think of me, I have in every thing approved myself to God, and lived honestly," Hob. 13:18. He had aimed at nothing but to please God and do his duty, in those things for which they were so incensed against him; in all he had done towards the setting up of the kingdom of Christ, and the setting of it up among the Gentiles, he had acted conscientiously. See here the character of an honest man. [1.] He sets God before him, and lives as in his sight, and under his eyes, and with an eye to him. *Walk before me, and be thou upright.* [2.] He makes conscience of what he says and does, and, though he may be under some mistakes, yet, according to the best of his knowledge, he abstains from that which is evil and cleaves to that which is good. [3.] He is universally conscientious; and those that are not so are not at all truly conscientious; is so in *all manner of conversation:* "I have lived in all good conscience; have had my whole conversation under the direction and dominion of conscience." [4.] He continues so, and perseveres in it: "I have lived so *until this day."* Whatever changes pass over him, he is still the same, strictly conscientious. And those who thus live in all good conscience before God may, like Paul here, *lift up their face without spot;* and, if their hearts condemn them not, may have confidence both towards God and man, as Job had when he *still held fast his integrity,* and Paul himself, whose rejoicing was this, the testimony of his conscience.

II. The outrage of which Ananias the high priest was guilty: he *commanded those that stood by,* the beadles that attended the court, *to smite him on the mouth* (*v.* 2), to give him a dash on the teeth, either with a hand or with a rod. Our Lord Jesus was thus despitefully used in this court, by one of the servants (Jn. 18:22), as was foretold, Mic. 5:1, *They shall smite the Judge of Israel upon the cheek.* But here was an order of court for the doing of it, and, it is likely, it was done. 1. The high priest was highly offended at Paul; some think, because he looked so boldly and earnestly at the council, as if he would face them down; others because he did not address himself particularly to him as president, with some title of honour and respect, but spoke freely and familiarly to them all, as men and brethren. His protestation of his integrity was provocation enough to one who was resolved to run him down and make him odious. When he could charge him with no crime, he thought it was crime enough that he asserted his own innocency. 2. In his rage he ordered him to be smitten, so to put disgrace upon him, and to be smitten on the mouth, as having offended with his lips, and in token of his enjoining him silence. This brutish and barbarous method he had recourse to when he *could not answer the wisdom and spirit wherewith he spoke.* Thus Zedekiah smote Micaiah (1 Ki. 22:24), and Pashur smote Jeremiah (Jer. 20:2), when they spoke in the name of the Lord. If therefore we see such indignities done to good men, nay, if they be done to us for well doing and well saying, we must not think it strange; Christ will give those the *kisses of his mouth* (Cant. 1:2) who for his sake receive blows on the mouth. And though it may be expected that, as Solomon says, *every man should kiss his lips that giveth a right answer* (Prov. 24:26), yet we often see the contrary.

III. The denunciation of the wrath of God against the high priest for this *wickedness in the place of judgment* (Eccl. 3:16): it agrees with what follows there, *v.* 17, with which Solomon comforted himself *(I said in my heart, God shall judge the righteous and the wicked): God shall smite thee, thou whited wall, v.* 3. Paul did not speak this in any sinful heat or passion, but in a holy zeal against the high priest's abuse of his power, and with something of a prophetic spirit, not at all with a spirit of revenge. 1. He gives him his due character: *Thou whited wall;* that is, thou hypocrite — a mud-wall, trash and dirt and rubbish underneath, but plastered over, or whitewashed. It is the same comparison in effect with that of Christ, when he compares the Pharisees to whited sepulchres, Mt. 23:27. Those that daubed with untempered mortar failed not to daub themselves over with something that made them look not only clean, but gay. 2. He reads him his just doom: *"God shall smite thee,* shall bring upon thee his sore judgments, especially spiritual judgments." Grotius thinks this was fulfilled soon after, in his removal from the office of the high priest, either by death or deprivation, for he finds another in that office a little while after this; probably he was smitten by some sudden stroke of divine vengeance. Jeroboam's hand was withered when it was stretched out against a prophet. 3. He assigns a good reason for that doom: "For *sittest thou* there as president in the supreme judicature of the church, pretending *to judge me after the law,* to convict and condemn me by the law, and yet *commandest me to be smitten* before any crime is proved upon me, which is *contrary to the law?"* No man must be beaten unless he be *worthy to be beaten,* Deu. 25:2. It is against all law, human and divine, natural and positive, to hinder a man from making his defense, and to condemn him unheard. When Paul was beaten by the rabble, he could say, *Father, forgive them, they know not what they do;* but it is inexcusable in a high priest that is appointed to judge according to the law.

IV. The offence which was taken at this bold word of Paul's (*v.* 4): *Those that stood by said, Revilest thou God's high priest?* It is a probable conjecture that those who blamed Paul for what he said were believing Jews, who were zealous for the law, and consequently for the honour of the high priest, and therefore took it ill that Paul should thus reflect upon him, and checked him for it. See here then, 1. What a hard game Paul had to play, when his enemies were abusive to him, and his friends were so far from standing by him, and appearing for him, that they were ready to find fault with his management. 2. How apt even the disciples of Christ themselves are to overvalue outward pomp and power. As because the temple had been God's temple, and a magnificent structure, there were those who followed Christ that could not bear to have any thing said that threatened the destruction of it; so because the high priest had been God's high priest, and was a man that made a figure, though he was an inveterate enemy to Christianity, yet these were disgusted at Paul for giving him his due.

V. The excuse that Paul made for what he had said, because he found it was a stumbling-block to his weak brethren, and might prejudice them against him in other things. These Jewish Christians, though weak, yet were brethren, so he calls them here, and, in consideration of that, is almost ready to recall his words; for *who is offended,* saith he, *and I burn not?* 2 Co. 11:29. His fixed resolution was rather to abridge himself in the use of his Christian liberty than give offence to a weak brother; rather than do this, he will *eat no flesh while the world stands,* 1 Co. 8:13. And so here though he had taken the liberty to tell the high priest his own, yet, when he found it gave offence, he cried *Peccavi — I have done wrong.* He wished he had not done it; and though he did not beg the high priest's pardon, nor excuse it to him, yet he begs their pardon who took offence at it, because this was not a time to inform them better, nor to say what he could say to justify himself. 1. He excuses it with this, that he did not consider when he said it to whom he spoke (*v.* 5): *I wist not, brethren, that he was the high priest — ouk ēdein.* "I did not just then think of the dignity of his place, or else I would have spoken more respectfully to him." I see not how we can with any probability think that Paul did not know him to be the high priest, for Paul had been seven days in the temple at the time of the feast, where he could not miss of seeing the high priest; and his telling him that *he sat to judge him after the law* shows that he knew who he was; but, says he, I did not consider it. Dr. Whitby puts this sense upon it, that the prophetic impulse that was upon him, and inwardly moved him to say what he did, did not permit him to notice that it was the high priest, lest this law might have restrained him from complying with that impulse; but the Jews acknowledged that prophets might use a liberty in speaking of rulers which others might not, as Isa. 1:10, 23. Or (as he quotes the sense of Grotius and Lightfoot) Paul does not go about to excuse what he had said in the least, but rather to justify it; "I own that God's high priest is not to be reviled, but I do not own this Ananias to be high priest. He is a usurper; he came to the office by bribery and corruption, and the Jewish rabbin say that he who does so is neither a judge nor to be honoured as such." Yet, 2. He takes care that what he had said should not be drawn into a precedent, to the weakening of the obligation of that law in the least: *For it is written,* and it remains a law in full force, *Thou shalt not speak evil of the ruler of thy people.* It is for the public good that the honour of magistracy should be supported, and not suffer for the miscarriages of those who are entrusted with it, and therefore that decorum be observed in speaking both of and to princes and judges. Even in Job's time it was not thought fit to *say to a king, Thou art wicked, or to princes, You are ungodly,* Job 34:18. Even when we do well, and suffer for it, we must *take it patiently,* 1 Pt. 2:20. Not as if great men may not hear of their faults, and public grievances be complained of by proper persons and in a decent manner, but there must be a particular tenderness for the honour and reputation of those in authority more than of other people, because the law of God requires a particular reverence to be paid to them, as God's vicegerents; and it is of dangerous consequence to have those any way countenanced who *despise dominions,* and *speak evil of dignities,* Jude 8. *Curse not the king, no not in thy thought,* Eccl. 10:20.

Verses 6–11

Many are the troubles of the righteous, but some way or other *the Lord delivereth them out of them all.* Paul owned he had experienced the truth of this in the persecutions he had undergone among the Gentiles (see 2 Tim. 3:11): *Out of them all the Lord delivered me.* And now he finds that he who has delivered does and will deliver. He that delivered him in the foregoing chapter from the tumult of the people here delivers him from that of the elders.

I. His own prudence and ingenuity stand him in some stead, and contribute much to his escape. Paul's greatest honour, and that upon which he most valued himself, was that he was a Christian, and an apostle of Christ; and all his other honours he despised and made nothing of, in comparison with this, *counting them but dung, that he might win Christ;* and yet he had sometimes occasion to make use of his other honours, and they did him service. His being a citizen of Rome saved him in the foregoing chapter from his being scourged by the chief captain as a vagabond, and here his being a Pharisee saved him from being condemned by the sanhedrim, as an apostate from the faith and worship of the God of Israel. It will consist very well with our willingness to suffer for Christ to use all lawful methods, nay, and arts too, both to prevent suffering and to extricate ourselves out of it. The honest policy Paul used here for his own preservation was to divide his judges, and to set them at variance one with another about him; and, by incensing one part of them more against him, to engage the contrary part for him.

1. The great council was made up of Sadducees and Pharisees, and Paul perceived it. He knew the characters of many of them ever since he lived among them, and saw those among them whom he knew to be Sadducees, and others whom he knew to be Pharisees (*v.* 6): *One part were Sadducees and the other Pharisees,* and perhaps nearly an equal part. Now these differed very much from one another, and yet they ordinarily agreed well enough to do the business of the council together. (1.) The Pharisees were bigots, zealous for the ceremonies, not only those which God had appointed, but those which were enjoined by the tradition of the elders. They were great sticklers for the authority of the church, and for enforcing obedience to its injunctions, which occasioned many quarrels between them and our Lord Jesus; but at the same time they were very orthodox in the faith of the Jewish church concerning the world of spirits, the resurrection of the dead, and the life of the world to come. (2.) The Sadducees were deists — no friends to the scripture, or divine revelation. The books of Moses they admitted as containing a good history and a good law, but had little regard to the other books of the Old Testament; see Mt. 22:23. The account here given of these Sadducees is, [1.] That they *deny the resurrection;* not only the return of the body to life, but a future state of rewards and punishments. They had neither hope of eternal happiness nor dread of eternal misery, nor expectation of any thing on the other side death; and it was upon these principles that they said, *It is in vain to serve God,* and called the proud happy, Mal. 3:14, 15. [2.] That they denied the existence of angels and spirits, and allowed of no being but matter. They thought that God himself was corporeal, and had parts and members as we have. When they read of angels in the Old Testament, they supposed them to be messengers that God made and sent on his errands as there was occasion, or that they were impressions on the fancies of those they were sent to, and no real existences — that they were this, or that, or any thing rather than what they were. And, as for the souls of men, they looked upon them to be nothing else but the temperament of the humours of the body, or the animal spirits, but denied their existence in a state of separation from the body, and any difference between the soul of a man and of a beast. These, no doubt, pretended to be free-thinkers, but really thought as meanly, absurdly, and slavishly, as possible. It is strange how men of such corrupt and wicked principles could come into office, and have a place in the great sanhedrim; but many of them were of quality and estate, and they complied with the public establishment, and so got in and kept in. But they were generally stigmatized as heretics, were ranked with the Epicureans, and were prayed against and excluded from eternal life. The prayer which the modern Jews use against Christians, Witsius thinks, was designed by Gamaliel, who made it, against the Sadducees; and that they meant them in their usual imprecation, *Let the name of the wicked rot.* But how degenerate was the character and how miserable the state of the Jewish church, when such profane men as these were among their rulers!

2. In this matter of difference between the Pharisees and Sadducees Paul openly declared himself to be on the Pharisees' side against the Sadducees (*v.* 6): He *cried out,* so as to be heard by all, *"I am a Pharisee,* was bred a Pharisee, nay, I was born one, in effect, for I was the *son of a Pharisee,* my father was one before me, and thus far I am still a Pharisee that I *hope for the resurrection of the dead,* and I may truly say that, if the matter were rightly understood, it would be found that this is it for which I am now *called in question."* When Christ was upon earth the Pharisees set themselves most against him, because he witnessed against their traditions and corrupt glosses upon the law; but, after his ascension, the Sadducees set themselves most against his apostles, because they *preached through Jesus the resurrection of the dead, ch.* 4:1, 2. And it is said (*ch.* 5:17) that they were *the sect of the Sadducees* that were *filled with indignation* at them, because they preached that life and immortality which is *brought to light by the gospel.* Now here, (1.) Paul owns himself a Pharisee, so far as the Pharisees were in the right. Though as Pharisaism was opposed to Christianity he set himself against it, and against all its traditions that were set up in competition with the law of God or in contradiction to the gospel of Christ, yet, as it was opposed to Sadducism, he adhered to it. We must never think the worse of any truth of God, nor be more shy of owning it, for its being held by men otherwise corrupt. If the Pharisees will hope for the resurrection of the dead, Paul will go along with them in that hope, and be one of them, whether they will or no. (2.) He might truly say that being persecuted, as a Christian, this was the thing he was called in question for. Perhaps he knew that the Sadducees, though they had not such an interest in the common people as the Pharisees had, yet had underhand incensed the mob against him, under pretence of his having preached to the Gentiles, but really because he had preached the hope of the resurrection. However, being called in question for his being a Christian, he might truly say he was called in question for the hope of the resurrection of the dead, as he afterwards pleaded, *ch.* 24:15, and *ch.* 26:6, 7. Though Paul preached against the traditions of the elders (as his Master had done), and therein opposed the Pharisees, yet he valued himself more upon his preaching the resurrection of the dead, and a future state, in which he concurred with the Pharisees.

3. This occasioned a division in the council. It is probable that the high priest sided with the Sadducees (as he had done *ch.* 5:17, and made it to appear by his rage at Paul, *v.* 2), which alarmed the Pharisees so much the more; but so it was, there arose a *dissension between the Pharisees and the Sadducees* (*v.* 7), for this word of Paul's made the Sadducees more warm and the Pharisees more cool in the prosecution of him; so that *the multitude was divided; eschisthē — there was a schism,* a quarrel among them, and the edge of their zeal began to turn from Paul against one another; nor could they go on to act against him when they could not agree among themselves, or prosecute him for breaking the unity of the church when there was so little among them of the unity of the spirit. All the cry had been against Paul, but now there arose a great cry against one another, *v.* 9. So much did a fierce furious spirit prevail among all orders of the Jews at this time that every thing was done with clamour and noise; and in such a tumultuous manner were the great principles of their religion stickled for, by which they received little service, for *the wrath of man worketh not the righteousness of God.* Gainsayers may be convinced by fair reasoning, but never by a great cry.

4. The Pharisees hereupon (would one think it?) took Paul's part (*v.* 9): *They strove, diemachonto — They fought, saying, We find no evil in this man.* He had conducted himself decently and reverently in the temple, and had attended the service of the church; and, though it was but occasionally, yet it showed that he was not such an enemy to it as he was said to be. He had spoken very handsomely in his own defence, and given a good account of himself, and had now declared himself orthodox in the great principles of religion, as well as regular and conscientious in his conversation; and therefore they cannot see that he has *done any thing worthy of death of bonds.* Nay, they go further, *"If a spirit or an angel hath spoken to him* concerning Jesus, and put him upon preaching as he does, though we may not be so far satisfied as to give credit to him, yet we ought to be cautioned not to oppose him, *lest we be found fighting against God;"* as Gamaliel, who was himself a Pharisee, had argued, *ch.* 5:39. Now here, (1.) We may observe, to the honour of the gospel, that it was witnessed to even by its adversaries, and confessions, not only of its innocency, but of its excellency, were extorted sometimes by the power of truth even from those that persecuted it. Pilate found no fault in Christ though he put him to death, nor Festus in Paul though he detained him in bonds; and the Pharisees here supposed it possible that Paul might have a commission sent him for heaven by an angel to do what he did; and yet it should seem, as elders, they after this joined with the high priest in prosecuting him, *ch.* 24:1. They sinned against the knowledge which they not only had, but sometimes owned, as Christ had said of them, *They have both seen and hated both me and my Father,* Jn. 15:24. Yet, (2.) We will hope that some of them at least did henceforward conceive a better opinion of Paul than they had had, and were favourable to him, having had such a satisfactory account both of his conversation in all good conscience and of his faith touching another world; and then it must be observed to their honour that their zeal for the traditions of the elders, which Paul had departed from, was so far swallowed up in a zeal for the great and fundamental doctrines of religion, to which Paul still adhered, that if he will heartily join with them against the Sadducees, and adhere to the hope of the resurrection of the dead, they will not think his shaking off the ceremonial law to be an evil in him, but charitably hope that he walks according to the light God has given him by some angel or spirit, and are so far from persecuting him that they are ready to patronize and protect him. The persecuting Pharisees of the church of Rome are not of this spirit: for let a man be ever so sincere and zealous for all the articles of the Christian faith, yet, if he lay not his neck under the yoke of their church's authority, they find evil enough in him to persecute him unto the death.

II. The chief captain's care and conduct stand him in more stead; for when he has thrown this bone of contention between the Pharisees and Sadducees (which set them together by the ears, and gained a fair testimony from the Pharisees), yet he is never the nearer, but is in danger of being pulled in pieces by them — the Pharisees pulling to have him et at liberty, and the Sadducees pulling to have him put to death, or thrown to the people, like Daniel into the den of lions; so that the chief captain is forced to come with his soldiers and rescue him, as he had done, *ch.* 21:32, and *ch.* 22:24. 1. See here Paul's danger. Between his friends and his enemies he had like to have been pulled to pieces, the one hugging him to death, the other crushing him to death, such violences are those liable to that are eminent, and that are become remarkable, as Paul was, who was by some so much beloved and by others so much maligned. 2. His deliverance: *The chief captain ordered his soldiers to go down* from the upper wards, and *to take them by force from among them,* out of that apartment in *the temple* where he had ordered the council to meet, and *to bring him into the castle,* or tower of Antonio; for he saw he could make nothing of them towards the understanding of the merits of his cause.

III. Divine consolations stood him in most stead of all. The chief captain had rescued him out of the hands of cruel men, but still he had him in custody, and what might be the issue he could not tell. The castle was indeed a protection to him, but withal it was a confinement; and, as it was now his preservation from so great a death, it might be his reservation for a greater. We do not find that any of the apostles or elders at Jerusalem came to him; either they had not courage or they had not admission. Perhaps, in the night following, Paul was full of thoughts and cares what should become of him, and how his present troubles might be turned to answer some good purpose. Then did the Lord Jesus make him a kind visit, and, thought at midnight, yet a very seasonable one (*v.* 11): *The Lord stood by him,* came to his bed-side, though perhaps it was but a bed of straw, to show him that he was all the day long with him really as sure as he was in the night with him visibly. Note, Whoever is against us, we need not fear if the Lord stand by us; if he undertake our protection, we may set those that seek our ruin at defiance. *The Lord is with those that uphold my soul,* and then nothing can come amiss. 1. Christ bids him have a good heart upon it: *"Be of good cheer, Paul;* be not discouraged; let not what has happened sadden thee, nor let what may yet be before thee frighten thee." Note, It is the will of Christ that his servants who are faithful should be always cheerful. Perhaps Paul, in the reflection, began to be jealous of himself whether he had done well in what he said to the council the day before; but Christ, by his word, satisfies him that God approved of his conduct. Or, perhaps, it troubled him that his friends did not come to him; but Christ's visit did itself speak, though he had not said, *Be of good cheer, Paul.* 2. It is a strange argument which he makes use of to encourage him: *As thou hast testified of me in Jerusalem, so must thou bear witness also at Rome.* One would think this was but cold comfort: "As thou hast undergone a great deal of trouble for me so thou must undergo a great deal more;" and yet this was designed to encourage him; for hereby he is given to understand, (1.) That he had been serving Christ as a witness for him in what he had hitherto endured. It was for no fault that he was buffeted, and it was not his former persecuting of the church that was now remembered against him, however he might remember it against himself, but he was still going on with his work. (2.) That he had not yet finished his testimony, nor was, by his imprisonment, laid aside as useless, but was only reserved for further service. Nothing disheartened Paul so much as the thought of being taken off from doing service to Christ and good to souls: *Fear not,* says Christ, *I have not done with thee,* (3.) Paul seems to have had a particular fancy, and an innocent one, to go to Rome, to preach the gospel there, though it was already preached, and a church planted there; yet, being a citizen of Rome, he longed for a journey thither, and had designed it (*ch.* 19:21): *After I have been at Jerusalem, I must also see Rome.* And he had written to the Romans some time ago *that he longed to see them,* Rom. 1:11. Now he was ready to conclude that this had broken his measures, and he should never see Rome; but even in that Christ tells him he should be gratified, since he desired it for the honour of Christ and to do good.

Verses 12–35

We have here the story of a plot against the life of Paul; how it was laid, how it was discovered, and how it was defeated.

I. How this plot was laid. They found they could gain nothing by popular tumult, or legal process, and therefore have a recourse to the barbarous method of assassination; they will come upon him suddenly, and stab him, if they can but get him within their reach. So restless is their malice against this good man that, when one design fails, they will turn another stone. Now observe here,

1. Who they were that formed this conspiracy. They were *certain Jews* that had the utmost degree of indignation against him because he was the apostle of the Gentiles, *v.* 12. *And they were more than forty* that were in the design, *v.* 13. *Lord, how are they increased that trouble me!*

2. When the conspiracy was formed: *When it was day. Satan had filled their hearts* in the night to purpose it, and, as soon as it was day, they got together to prosecute it; answering to the account which the prophet gives of some who *work evil upon their beds, and when the morning is light they practise it,* and are laid under a woe for it, Mic. 2:1. In the night Christ appeared to Paul to protect him, and, when it was day, here were forty men appearing against him to destroy him; they were not up so soon but Christ was up before them *God shall help her, and that right early,* Ps. 46:5.

3. What the conspiracy was. These men *banded together* in a league, perhaps they called it a *holy* league; they engaged to stand by one another, and every one, to his power, to be aiding and assisting to murder Paul. It was strange that so many could so soon be got together, and that in Jerusalem too, who were so perfectly lost to all sense of humanity and honour as to engage in so bloody a design. Well might the prophet's complaint be renewed concerning Jerusalem (Isa. 1:21): *Righteousness has lodged in it, but now murderers.* What a monstrous idea must these men have formed of Paul, before they could be capable of forming such a monstrous design against him; they must be made to believe that he was the worst of men, an enemy to God and religion, and the curse and plague of his generation; when really his character was the reverse of all this! What laws of truth and justice so sacred, so strong which malice and bigotry will not break through!

4. How firm they made it, as they thought, that none of them might fly off, upon conscience of the horror of the fact, at second thoughts: *They bound themselves under an anathema,* imprecating the heaviest curses upon themselves, their souls, bodies, and families, if they did not kill Paul, and so quickly *that they would not eat nor drink till they had done it.* What a complication of wickedness is here! To design to kill an innocent man, a good man, a useful man, a man that had done them no harm, but was willing to do them all the good he could, was *going in the way of Cain,* and proved them to be of *their father the devil, who was a murderer from the beginning;* yet, as if this had been a small matter, (1.) They bound themselves to it. To incline to do evil, and intend to do it, is bad; but to engage to do it is much worse. This is entering into covenant with the devil; it is swearing allegiance to the prince of darkness; it is leaving no room for repentance; nay, it is bidding defiance to it. (2.) They bound one another to it, and did all they could, not only to secure the damnation of their own souls, but of theirs whom they drew into the association. (3.) They showed a great contempt of the providence of God, and a presumption upon it, in that they bound themselves to do such a thing within so short a time as they could continue fasting, without any proviso or reserve for the disposal of an overruling Providence. When we say, *To-morrow we will do this or that,* be it ever so lawful and good, forasmuch as *we know not what shall be on the morrow,* we must add, *If the Lord will.* But with what face could they insert a proviso for the permission of God's providence when they knew that what they were about was directly against the prohibitions of God's work? (4.) They showed a great contempt of their own souls and bodies; of their own souls in imprecating a curse upon them if they did not proceed in this desperate enterprise (what a woeful dilemma did they throw themselves upon! God certainly meets them with his curse if they do go on in it, and they desire he would if they do not!) — and of their own bodies too (for wilful sinners are the destroyers of both) in tying themselves out from the necessary supports of life till they had accomplished a thing which they could never lawfully do, and perhaps not possibly do. Such language of hell those speak that wish God to damn them, and the devil to take them, if they do not do so and so. *As they love cursing, so shall it come unto them.* Some think the meaning of this curse was, they would either kill Paul, as an Achan, an accursed thing, a troubler of the camp; or, if they did not do it, they would make themselves accursed before God in his stead. (5.) They showed a most eager desire to compass this matter, and an impatience till was done: not only like David's enemies, *that were mad against him,* and *sworn against him* (Ps. 102:8), but like the servants of Job against his enemy: *O that we had of this flesh! we cannot be satisfied,* Job 31:31. Persecutors are said to *eat up God's people as they eat bread;* it is as much a gratification to them as meat to one that is hungry, Ps. 14:4.

5. What method they took to bring it about. There is no getting near Paul in the castle. He is there under the particular protection of the government, and is imprisoned, not, as others are, lest he should do harm, but lest he should have harm done him; and therefore the contrivance is that the chief priests and elders must desire the governor of the castle to let Paul come to them to the coucil-chamber, to be further examined (they have some questions to ask him, or something to say to him), and the, in his passage from the castle to the council, they would put an end to all disputes about Paul by killing him; thus the plot was laid, *v.* 14, 15. Having been all day employed in engaging one another to this wickedness, towards evening they come to the principal members of the great sanhedrim, and, though they might have concealed their mean design and yet might have moved them upon some other pretence to send for Paul, they are so confident of their approbation of this villainy, that they are not ashamed nor afraid to own to them *that they have bound themselves under a great curse,* without consulting the priests first whether they might lawfully do it, *that they will eat nothing* the next day *till they have killed Paul.* They design to breakfast the next morning upon his blood. They doubt not but the chief priests will not only countenance them in the design, but will lend them a helping hand, and be their tools to get them an opportunity of killing Paul; nay, and tell a lie for them too, pretending to *the chief captain that they would enquire something more perfectly concerning him,* when they meant no such thing. What a mean, what an ill opinion had they of their priests, when they could apply to them on such an errand as this! And yet, vile as the proposal was which was made to them (for aught that appears), the priests and elders consented to it, and at the first work, without boggling at it in the least, promised to gratify them. Instead of reproving them, as they ought, for their wicked conspiracy, they bolstered them up in it, because it was against Paul whom they hated; and thus they made themselves partakers of the crime as much as if they had been the first in the conspiracy.

II. How the plot was discovered. We do not find that the plotters, though they took an oath of fidelity, took an oath of secrecy, either because they thought it did not need it (they would every one keep his own counsel) or because they thought they could accomplish it, though it should take wind and be known; but Providence so ordered it that it was brought to light, and so as effectually to be brought to nought. See here,

1. How it was discovered to Paul, *v.* 16. There was a youth that was related to Paul, *his sister's son,* whose mother probably lived in Jerusalem; and some how or other, we are not told how, *he heard of their lying in wait,* either overheard them talking of it among themselves, or got intelligence from some that were in the ploy: and *he went into the castle,* probably, as he used to do, to attend on his uncle, and bring him what he wanted, which gave him a free access to him and *he told Paul* what he heard. Note, God has many ways of bringing *to light the hidden works of darkness;* though the contrivers of them *dig deep to hide them from the Lord,* he can made a *bird of the air to carry the voice* (Eccl. 10:20), or the conspirators' own tongues to betray them.

2. How it was discovered to the chief captain by the young man that told it to Paul. This part of the story is related very particularly, perhaps because the penman was an eye-witness of the prudent and successful management of this affair, and remembered it with a great deal of pleasure. (1.) Paul had got a good interest in the officers that attended, by his prudent peaceable deportment. He could call one of the centurions to him, though a centurion was one in authority, that had soldiers under him, and used to call, not to be called to, and he was ready to come at his call (*v.* 17); and he desired that he would introduce this young man to the chief captain, to give in an information of something that concerned the honour of the government. (2.) The centurion very readily gratified him, *v.* 18. He did not send a common soldier with him, but went himself to keep the young man in countenance, to recommend his errand to the chief captain, and to show his respect to Paul: *"Paul the prisoner* (this was his title now) *called me to him, and prayed me to bring this young man to thee;* what his business is I know not, but *he has something to say to thee."* Note, It is true charity to poor prisoners to act for them as well as to give to them. *"I was sick and in prison,* and you went on an errand for me," will pass as well in the account as, *"I was sick and in prison, and you came unto me,* to visit me, or sent me a token." Those that have acquaintance and interest should be ready to use them for the assistance of those that are in distress. This centurion helped to save Paul's life by this piece of civility, which should engage us to be ready to do the like when there is occasion. *Open thy mouth for the dumb,* Prov. 31:8. Those that cannot give a good gift to God's prisoners may yet speak a good word for them. (3.) The chief captain received the information with a great deal of condescension and tenderness, *v.* 19. He *took the young man by the hand,* as a friend or father, to encourage him, that he might not be put out of countenance, but might be assured of a favourable audience. The notice that is taken of this circumstance should encourage great men to take themselves easy of access to the meanest, upon any errand which may give them an opportunity of doing good — *to condescend to those of low estate.* This familiarity to which this Roman tribune or colonel admitted Paul's nephew is here upon record to his honour. Let no man think he disparages himself by his humility or charity. He *went with him aside privately,* that none might hear his business, *and asked him, "What is it that thou hast to tell me?* Tell me wherein I can be serviceable to Paul." It is probable that the chief captain was the more obliging in this case because he was sensible he had run himself into a premunire in binding Paul, against his privilege as a Roman citizen, which he was willing now to atone for. (4.) The young man delivered his errand to the chief captain very readily and handsomely (*v.* 20, 21). *"The Jews"* (he does not say who, lest he should invidiously reflect upon *the chief priests and the elders;* and his business was to save his uncle's life, not to accuse his enemies) *"have agreed to desire thee that thou wouldest bring down Paul to-morrow into the council,* presuming that, being so short a distance, thou wilt send him without a guard; *but do not thou yield unto them,* we have reason to believe thou wilt not when thou knowest the truth; *for there lie in wait for him of them more than forty me,* who have sworn to be the death of him, *and now are they ready looking for a promised from thee,* but I have happily got the start of them." (5.) The captain dismissed the young man with a charge of secrecy: *See that thou tell no man that thou hast shown these things unto me, v.* 22. The favours of great men are not always to be boasted of; and not fit to be employed in business. If it should be known that the chief captain had this information brought to him, perhaps they would compass and imagine the death of Paul some other way; "therefore keep it private."

III. How the plot was defeated: The chief captain, finding how implacable and inveterate the malice of the Jews was against Paul, how restless they were in their designs to do him a mischief, and how near he was to become himself accessory to it as a minister, resolves to send him away with all speed out of their reach. He received the intelligence with horror and indignation at the baseness and bloody-mindedness of these Jews; and seemed afraid lest, if he should detain Paul in his castle here, under ever so strong a guard, they would find some way or other to compass their end notwithstanding, either beating the guards or burning the castle; and, whatever came of it, he would, if possible, protect Paul, because he looked upon it that he did not deserve such treatment. What a melancholy observation is it, that the Jewish *chief priests,* when they knew of this assassination-plot, should countenance it, and assist in it, while a Roman *chief captain,* purely from a natural sense of justice and humanity, when he knows it, sets himself to baffle it, and puts himself to a great deal of trouble to do it effectually!

1. He orders a considerable detachment of the Roman forces under his command to get ready *to go to Caesarea* with all expedition, and to bring Paul thither *to Felix the governor,* where he might sooner expect to have justice done him than by the great sanhedrim at Jerusalem. I see not but the chief captain might, without any unfaithfulness to the duty of his place, have set Paul at liberty, and given him leave to shift for his own safety, for he was never legally committed to his custody as a criminal, he himself owns *that nothing was laid to his charge worthy of bonds* (*v.* 29), and he ought to have had the same tenderness for his liberty that he had for his life; but he feared that this would have incensed the Jews too much against him. Or perhaps, finding Paul to be a very extraordinary man, he was proud to have him his prisoner, and under his protection; and the mighty parade with which he sent him off intimates as much. *Two centurions,* or captains of the hundreds, are employed in this business, *v.* 23, 24. They must *get ready two hundred soldiers,* probably those under their own command, *to go to Caesarea;* and with these *seventy horse, and two hundred spearmen* besides, which some think were the *chief captain's* guards; whether they were horse or foot is not certain, most probably foot, as pikemen for the protection of the horse. See how justly God brought the Jewish nation under the Roman yoke, when such a party of the Roman army was necessary to restrain them from the most execrable villanies! There needed not all this force, there needed not any of it, to keep Paul from being rescued by his friends; ten times this force would not have kept him from being rescued by an angel, if it had pleased God to work his deliverance that way, as he had sometimes done; but, (1.) The chief captain designed hereby to expose the Jews, as a headstrong tumultuous people, that would not be kept within the bounds of duty and decency by the ordinary ministers of justice, but needed to be awed by such a train as this; and, hearing how many were in the conspiracy against Paul, he thought less would not serve to defeat their attempt. (2.) God designed hereby to encourage Paul; for, being thus attended, he was not only kept safely in the hands of his friends, but out of the hands of his enemies. Yet Paul did not desire such a guard, any more than Ezra did (Ezra 8:22), and for the same reason, because he trusted in God's all-sufficiency; it was owing, however, to the governor's own care. But he was also made considerable; thus his *bonds in Christ* were made manifest all the country over (Phil. 1:13); and, son great an honour having been put upon them before by the prediction of them, it was agreeable enough that they should be thus honourably attended, *that the brethren in the Lord might wax the more confident by his bonds,* when they same him rather guarded as the patriot of his country than guarded against as the pest of his country, and so great a preacher made so great a prisoner. When his enemies hate him, and I doubt his friends neglect him, then does a Roman tribune patronise him, and carefully provide, [1.] For his ease: *Let them provide beasts, that they may set Paul on.* Had his Jewish persecutors ordered his removal by *habeas corpus* to Caesarea, they would have made him run on foot, or dragged him thither in a cart, or on a sledge, or have horsed him behind one of the troopers; but the chief captain treats him like a gentleman, though he was his prisoner, and orders him a good horse to ride upon, not at all afraid that he should ride away. Nay, the order being that they should provide, not a beast, but beasts, to set Paul on, we must either suppose that he was allowed so great a piece of state as to have a led horse, or more, that if he did not like one he might take to another; or (as some expositors conjecture) that he had beasts assigned him for his friends and companions, as many as pleased to go along with him, to divert him in his journey, and to minister to him. [2.] For his security. They have a strict charge given them by their commander in chief *to bring him safely to Felix the governor,* to whom he is consigned, and who was supreme in all civil affairs among the Jews, as this chief captain was in military affairs. The Roman historians speak much of this Felix, as a man of mean extraction, but that raised himself by his shifts to be governor of Judea, in the execution of which office, Tacitus, *Hist.* 5, says this of him: *Per omnem saevitiam ac libidinem jus regium servili ingenio exercuit — He used royal power with a servile genius, and in connection with all the varieties of cruelty and lust.* To the judgement of such a man as this is poor Paul turned over; and yet better so than in the hands of *Ananias the high priest!* Now, a prisoner, thus upon his deliverance by course of law, ought to be protected as well as a prince.

2. The chief captain orders, for the greater security of Paul, that he be taken away at *the third hour of the night,* which some understand of three hours after sun-set, that, it being now after *the feast of pentecost* (that is, in the midst of summer), they might have the cool of the night to march in. Others understand it of *three hours after midnight, in the third watch, about three in the morning,* that they might have the day before them, and might get out of Jerusalem before Paul's enemies were stirring, and so might prevent any popular tumult, and leave them to roar when they rose, like a lion disappointed of his prey.

3. *He writes a letter to Felix the governor* of this province, by which he discharges himself from any further care about Paul, and leaves the whole matter with Felix. This letter is here inserted *totidem verbis — verbatim, v.* 25. It is probable that Luke the historian had a copy of it by him, having attended Paul in this remove. Now in this epistle we may observe,

(1.) The compliments he passes upon *the governor, v.* 26. He is *the most excellent governor Felix,* this title being given him of course, his excellency, etc. He sends him *greeting,* wishes him all health and prosperity; may he rejoice, may he ever rejoice.

(2.) The just and fair account which he gives him of Paul's case: [1.] That he was one that the Jews had a pique against: *They had taken him,* and would *have killed him;* and perhaps Felix knew the temper of the Jews so well that he did not think much the worse of him for that, *v.* 27. [2.] That he had protected him because he was a Roman: "When they were about to kill him, *I came with an army,* a considerable body of men, *and rescued him;*" which action for a citizen of Rome would recommend him to the Roman governor. [3.] That he could not understand the merits of his cause, nor what it was that made him so odious to the Jews, and obnoxious to their ill-will. He took the proper method to know: he *brought him forth into their council* (*v.* 28), to be examined there, hoping that, either from their complaints or his own confession, he would learn something of the ground of all this clamour, but he found *that he was accused of questions of their law* (*v.* 29), about *the hope of the resurrection of the dead, v.* 6. This chief captain was a man of sense and honour, and had good principles in him of justice and humanity; and yet see how slightly he speaks of another world, and the great things of that world, as if that were a question, which is of undoubted certainty, and which both sides agreed in, except the Sadducees; and as if that were a question only *of their law,* which is of the utmost concern to all mankind! Or perhaps he refers rather to the question about their rituals than about their doctrinals, and the quarrel he perceived they had with him was for lessening the credit and obligation of their ceremonial law, which he looked upon as a thing not worth speaking of. The Romans allowed the nations they conquered the exercise of their own religion, and never offered to impose theirs upon them; yet, as conservators of the public peace, they wound not suffer them, under colour of their religion, to abuse their neighbours. [4.] That thus far he understood that there was *nothing laid to his charge worthy of death or of bonds,* much less proved or made out against him. The Jews had, by their wickedness, made themselves odious to the world, had polluted their own honour and profaned their own crown, had brought disgrace upon their church, their law, and their holy place, and then they cry out against Paul, as having diminished the reputation of them; and was this a crime *worthy of death or bonds?*

(3.) His referring Paul's case to Felix (*v.* 30): *"When it was told me that the Jews laid wait for the man,* to kill him, without any legal process against him, *I sent straightaway to thee,* who art the most proper person to head the cause, and give judgment upon it, and let *his accusers* go after him, if they please, and *say before thee what they have against him,* for, being bred a soldier, I will never pretend to be a judge, and so *farewell."*

4. Paul was accordingly conducted to Caesarea; the soldiers got him safely out of Jerusalem by night, and left the conspirators to consider whether they should east and drink or no before they had killed Paul; and, if they would not repent of the wickedness of their oath as it was against Paul, they were now at leisure to repent of the rashness of it as it was against themselves; if any of them did starve themselves to death, in consequence of their oath and vexation at their disappointment, they fell unpitied. Paul was conducted to *Antipatris,* which was seventeen miles from Jerusalem, and about the mid-way to Caesarea, *v.* 31. Thence *the two hundred foot-soldiers,* and *the two hundred spearmen, returned* back to Jerusalem, to their quarters in *the castle;* for, having conducted Paul out of danger, there needed not strong a guard, but *the horsemen* might serve to bring him to Caesarea, and would do it with more expedition; this they did, not only to save their own labour, but their master's charge; and it is an example to servants, not only to act obediently according to their masters' orders, but to act prudently, so as may be most for their masters' interest.

5. He was delivered into the hands of Felix, as his prisoner, *v.* 33. The officers *presented the letter,* and *Paul with it, to Felix,* and so discharged themselves of their trust. Paul had never affected acquaintance or society with great men, but with the disciples, wherever he came; yet Providence overrules his sufferings so as by them to give him an opportunity of witnessing to Christ before great men; and so Christ had foretold concerning his disciples, *that they should be brought before rulers and kings for his sake, for a testimony against them,* Mk. 13:9. *The governor* enquired *of what province* of the empire the prisoner originally was, and was told *that he was a native of Cilicia, v.* 34; and, (1.) He promises him a speedy trial (*v.* 35): *"I will hear thee when thing accusers have come,* and will have an ear open to both sides, as becomes a judge." (2.) He ordered him into custody, that he should *be kept* a prisoner *in Herod's judgment-hall,* in some apartment belonging to that palace which was denominated from Herod the Great, who built it. There he had opportunity of acquainting himself with great men that attended the governor's court, and, no doubt, he improved what acquaintance he got there to the best purposes.

CHAPTER 24

We left Paul a prisoner at Caesarea, in Herod's judgment-hall, expecting his trial to come on quickly; for in the beginning of his imprisonment his affairs moved very quickly, but afterwards very slowly. In this chapter we have his arraignment and trial before Felix the governor at Caesarea; here is, I. The appearing of the prosecutors against him, and the setting of the prisoner to the bar (*v.* 1, 2). II. The opening of the indictment against him by Tertullus, who was of counsel for the prosecutors, and the aggravating of the charge, with abundance of compliments to the judge, and malice to the prisoner (*v.* 2–8). III. The corroborating of the charge by the testimony of the witnesses, or rather the prosecutors themselves (*v.* 9). IV. The prisoner's defence, in which, with all due deference to the governor (*v.* 10), he denies the charge, and challenges them to prove it (*v.* 11–13), owns the truth, and makes an unexceptionable profession of his faith, which he declares was it that they hated him for (*v.* 14–16), and gives a more particular account of what had passed from their first seizing him, challenging them to specify any ill they had found in him (*v.* 17–21). V. The adjourning of the cause, and the continuing of the prisoner in custody (*v.* 22, 23). VI. The private conversation that was between the prisoner and the judge, by which the prisoner hoped to do good to the judge and the judge thought to get money by the prisoner, but both in vain (*v.* 24–26). VII. The lengthening out of Paul's imprisonment for two years, till another governor came (*v.* 27), where he seems as much neglected as there had been ado about him.

Verses 1–9

We must suppose *that Lysias, the chief captain,* when he had *sent away Paul to Caesarea,* gave notice to the chief priests, and others that had appeared against Paul, that if they had any thing to accuse him of they must follow him to Caesarea, and there they would find hi, and a judge ready to hear them — thinking, perhaps, they would not have given themselves so much trouble; but what will not malice do?

I. We have here the cause followed against Paul, and it is vigorously carried on. 1. Here is no time lost, for they are ready for a hearing *after five days;* all other business is laid aside immediately, to prosecute Paul; so intent are evil men to do evil! Some reckon *these five days* from Paul's being first seized, and with most probability, for he says here (*v.* 11) *that it was but twelve days since he came up to Jerusalem,* and he had *spent seven in his purifying the temple,* so that these five must be reckoned from the last of those. 2. Those who had been his judges do themselves appear here as his prosecutors. *Ananias* himself *the high priest,* who had sat to judge him, now stands to inform against him. One would wonder, (1.) That he should thus disparage himself, and forget the dignity of his place. She *the high priest* turn informer, and leave all his business in *the temple at Jerusalem,* to go to be called as a prosecutor in *Herod's judgment-hall?* Justly did God make *the priests contemptible and base,* when they made themselves so, Mal. 2:9. (2.) That he should thus discover himself and his enmity against Paul!. If men of the first rank have a malice against any, they think it policy to employ others against them, and to play least in sight themselves, because of the odium that commonly attends it; but Ananias is not shamed to own himself a sworn enemy to Paul. *The elders* attended him, to signify their concurrence with him, and to invigorate the prosecution; for they could not find any attorneys or solicitors that would follow it with so much violence as they desired. The pains that evil men take in an evil matter, their contrivances, their condescensions, and their unwearied industry, should shame us out of our coldness and backwardness, and out indifference in that which is good.

II. We have here the cause pleaded against Paul. The prosecutors brought *with them a certain orator named Tertullus,* a Roman, skilled in the Roman law and language, and therefore fittest to be employed in a cause before *the Roman governor,* and most likely to gain favour. The high priest and elders, though they had their own hearts spiteful enough, did not think their own tongues sharp enough, and therefore retained Tertullus, who probably was noted for a satirical wit, to be of counsel for them; and, no doubt, they gave him a good fee, probably out of the treasury of the temple, which they had the command of, it being a cause wherein the church was concerned and which therefore must not be starved. Paul is set to the bas before Felix the governor: *He was called forth, v.* 2. Tertullus's business is, on the behalf of the prosecutors, to open the information against him, and he is a man that will say any thing for his fee; mercenary tongues will do so. No cause so unjust but can find advocates to plead it; and yet we hope many advocates are so just as not knowingly to patronise an unrighteous cause, but Tertullus was none of these: his speech (or at least an abstract of it, for it appears, by Tully's orations, that the Roman lawyers, on such occasions, used to make long harangues) is here reported, and it is made up of flattery and falsehood; it calls evil good, and good evil.

1. One of the worst of men is here applauded as one of the best of benefactors, only because he was the judge. Felix is represented by the historians of his own nation, as well as by Josephus the Jew, as a very bad man, who, depending upon his interest in the court, allowed himself in all manner of wickedness, was a great oppressor, very cruel, and very covetous, patronising and protecting assassins. — Joseph. *Antiq.* 20.162–165. And yet Tertullus here, in the name of the high priest and elders, and probably by particular directions from them and according to the instructions of his breviate, compliments him, and extols him to the sky, as if he were so good a magistrate as never was the like: and this comes the worse from the high priest and the elders, because he had given a late instance of his enmity to their order; for Jonathan the high priest, or one of the chief priests, having offended him by too free an invective against the tyranny of his government, he had him murdered by some villains whom he hired for that purpose who afterwards did the like for others, as they were hired: *Cujus facinoris quia nemo ultor extitit, invitati hac licentia sicarii multos confodiebant, alios propter privatas inimicitias, alios conducti pecunia, etiam in ipso templo — No one being found to punish such enormous wickedness, the assassins, encouraged by this impunity, stabbed several persons, some from personal malice, some for hire, and that even in the temple itself.* An yet, to engage him to gratify their malice against Paul, and to return them that kindness for their kindness in overlooking all this, they magnify him as the greatest blessing to their church and nation that ever came among them.

(1.) They are very ready to own it (*v.* 2): "*By thee we,* of the church, *enjoy great quietness,* and we look upon thee as our patron and protector, *and very worthy deeds are done,* from time to time, *to the whole nation of the Jews, by thy providence* — thy wisdom, and care, and vigilance." To give him his due, he had been instrumental to suppress the in-

surrection of that Egyptian of whom the chief captain spoke (*ch.* 21:38); but will the praise of that screen him from the just reproach of his tyranny and oppression afterwards? See here, [1.] The unhappiness of great men, and a great unhappiness it is, to have their services magnified beyond measure, and never to be faithfully told of their faults; and hereby they are hardened and encouraged in evil. [2.] The policy of bad men, by flattering princes in what they do amiss to draw them in to do worse. The bishops of Rome got themselves confirmed in their exorbitant church power, and have been assisted in persecuting the servants of Christ, by flattering and caressing usurpers and tyrants, and so making them the tools of their malice, as the high priest, by his compliments, designed to make Felix here.

(2.) They promise to retain a grateful sense of it (*v.* 3): "*We accept it always, and in all places,* every where and at all times we embrace it, we admire it, *most noble Felix, with all thankfulness.* We will be ready, upon any occasion, to witness for thee, that thou art a wise and good governor, and very serviceable to the country." And, if it had been true that he was such a governor, it had been just that they should thus accept his good offices with all thankfulness. The benefits which we enjoy by government, especially by the administration of wise and good governors, are what we ought to be thankful for, both to God and man. This is part of the honour due to magistrates, to acknowledge the quietness we enjoy under their protection, and the worthy deeds done by their prudence.

(3.) They therefore expect his favour in this cause, *v.* 4. They pretend a great care not to intrench upon his time: We will *not be further tedious to thee;* and yet to be very confident of his patience: *I pray thee that thou wouldest hear us of thy clemency a few words.* All this address is only *ad captandam benefolentiam* — *to induce him to give countenance to their cause;* and they were so conscious to themselves that it would soon appear to have more malice than matter in it that they found it necessary thus to insinuate themselves into his favour. Every body knew that the high priest and the elders were enemies to the Roman government, and were uneasy under all the marks of that yoke, and therefore, in their hearts, hated Felix; and yet, to gain their ends against Paul, they, by their counsel, show him all this respect, as they did to Pilate and Caesar when they were persecuting our Saviour. Princes cannot always judge of the affections of their people by their applauses; flattery is one thing, and true loyalty is another.

2. One of the best of men is here accused as one of the worst of malefactors, only because he was the prisoner. After a flourish of flattery, in which you cannot see matter for words, he comes to his business, and it is to inform his excellency concerning the prisoner at the bar; and this part of his discourse is as nauseous for its raillery as the former part is for its flattery. I pity the man, and believe he has no malice against Paul, nor does he think as he speaks in calumniating him, any more than he did in courting Felix; but, a I cannot but be sorry that a man of wit and sense should have such a saleable tongue (as one calls it), so I cannot but be angry at those dignified men that had such malicious hearts as to put such words into his mouth. Two things Tertullus here complains of to Felix, in the name of the high priest and the elders: —

(1.) That the peace of the nation was disturbed by Paul. They could not have baited Christ's disciples if they had not first dressed them up in the skins of wild beasts, nor have given them as they did the vilest of treatment if they had not first represented them as the vilest of men, though the characters they gave of them were absolutely false and there was not the least colour nor foundation for them. Innocence, may excellence and usefulness, are no fence against calumny, no, nor against the impressions of calumny upon the minds both of magistrates and multitudes to excite their fury and jealousy; for, be the representation ever so unjust, when it is enforced, as here it was, with gravity and pretence of sanctity, and with assurance and noise, something will stick. The old charge against God's prophets was that they were the troublers of the land, and against God's Jerusalem that it was a rebellious city, hurtful to kings and provinces (Ezra 4:15, 19), and against our Lord Jesus that he perverted the nation, and forbade to give tribute to Caesar. It is the very same against Paul here; and, though utterly false, is averred with all the confidence imaginable. They do not say, "We suspect him to be a dangerous man, and have taken him up upon that sus-

picion;" but, as if the thing were past dispute, "*We have found him* to be so; we have often and long found him so;" as if he were a traitor and rebel already convicted. And yet, after all, there is not a word of truth in this representation; but, if Paul's just character be enquired into, it will be found directly the reverse of this.

[1.] Paul was a useful man, and a great blessing to his country, a man of exemplary candour and goodness, blessing to all, and provoking to none; and yet he is here called *a pestilent fellow* (*v.* 5): "*We have found him, loimon — pestem — the plague* of the nation, a walking pestilence, which supposes him to be a man of a turbulent spirit, malicious and ill-natured, and one that threw all things in disorder wherever he came." They would have it thought that he had dome a more mischief in his time than a plague could do, — that the mischief he did was spreading and infectious, and that he made others as mischievous as himself, — that it was of as fatal consequence as the plague is, killing and destroying, and laying all waste, — that it was as much to be dreaded and guarded against as a plague is. Many a good sermon he had preached, and many a good work he had done, and for these he is called a pestilent fellow.

[2.] Paul was a peace-maker, was a preacher of that gospel which has a direct tendency to *slay all enmities,* and to establish true and lasting peace; he lived peaceably and quietly himself, and taught others to do so too, and yet is here represented as *a mover of sedition among all the Jews throughout all the world.* The Jews were disaffected to the Roman government; those of them that were most bigoted were the most so. This Felix knew, and had therefore a watchful eye upon them. Now they would fain make him believe that this Paul was the man that made them so, whereas they themselves were the men that sowed the seeds of faction and sedition among them: and they knew it; and the reason why they hated Christ and his religion was because he did not go about to head them in a opposition to the Romans. The Jews were every where much set against Paul, and stirred up the people to clamour against him; they moved sedition in all places where he came, and then cast the blame unjustly upon him as if he had been the mover of the sedition; as Nero not long after set Rome on fire, and then said the Christians did it.

[3.] Paul was a man of catholic charity, who did not affect to be singular, but made himself the servant of all for their good; and yet he is here charged as being a *ringleader of the sect of the Nazarenes,* a standard-bearer of that sect, so the word signifies. When Cyprian was condemned to die for being a Christian, this was inserted in hi sentence, that he was *auctor iniqui nominis et signifer — The author and standard-bearer of a wicked cause.* Now it was true that Paul was an active leading man in propagating Christianity. But, *First,* It was utterly false that this was a sect; he did not draw people to a party or private opinion, nor did he make his own opinions their rule. True Christianity establishes that which is of common concern to all mankind, publishes good-will to men, and shows us God in Christ reconciling the world to himself, and therefore cannot be thought to take its rise from such narrow opinions and private interests as sects owe their origin to. True Christianity has a direct tendency to the uniting of the children of men, and the gathering of them together in one; and, as far as it obtains its just power and influence upon the minds of men, will make them meek and quiet, and peaceable and loving, and every way easy, acceptable, and profitable one to another, and therefore is far from being a sect, which is supposed to lead to division and to sow discord. True Christianity aims at no worldly benefit or advantage, and therefore must by no means be called a sect. Those that espouse a sect are governed in it by their secular interest, they aim at wealth and honour; but the professors of Christianity are so far from this that they expose themselves thereby to the loss and ruin of all that is dear to them in this world. *Secondly,* It is invidiously called *the sect of the Nazarenes,* by which Christ was represented as of Nazareth, whence no good thing was expected to arise; whereas he was of Bethlehem, where the Messiah was to be born. Yet he was pleased to call himself, *Jesus of Nazareth, ch.* 22:8. And the scripture has put an honour on the name, Mt. 2:23. And therefore, though intended for a reproach, the Christians had not reason to be ashamed of sharing with their Master in it. *Thirdly,* It was false that Paul was the author of standard-bearer of this sect; for he did not draw people to himself, but to Christ — did not preach himself, but Christ Jesus.

[4.] Paul had a veneration for the temple, as it was the

place which God had chosen to put his name there, and had lately himself with reverence attended the temple-service; and yet it is here charged upon him that he went about to *profane the temple*, and that he designedly put contempt upon it, and violated the laws of it, *v.* 6. Their proof of this failed; for that they alleged as matter of act was utterly false, and they knew it, *ch.* 21:29.

(2.) That the course of justice against Paul was obstructed by the chief captain. [1.] They pleaded that they *took him, and would have judged him according to their law.* This was false; they did not go about to judge him according to their law, but, contrary to all law and equity, went about to *beat him to death* or to *pull him to pieces*, without hearing what he had to say for himself — went about, under pretence of having him into their court, to throw him into the hands of ruffians that lay in wait to destroy him. Was this judging him according to their law? It is easy for men, when they know what they should have done, to say, this they would have done, when they meant nothing less. [2.] They reflected upon the chief captain as having done them an injury in rescuing Paul out of their hands; whereas he therein not only did him justice, but them the greatest kindness that could be, in preventing the guilt they were bringing upon themselves: *The chief captain Lysias came upon us and with great violence* (but really no more than was necessary) *took him out of our hands, v.* 7. See how persecutors are enraged at their disappointments, which they ought to e thankful for. When David in a heat of passion was going upon a bloody enterprise, he thanked Abigail for stopping him, and God for sending her to do it, so soon did he correct and recover himself. But these cruel men justify themselves, and reckon him their enemy who kept them (as David there speaks) from shedding blood with their own hands. [3.] They referred the matter to Felix and his judgment, yet seeming uneasy that they were under a necessity of doing so, the chief captain having obliged them to it (*v.* 8): "It was he that forced us to give your excellency this trouble, and ourselves too; for," *First,* "He commanded his accusers to come to thee,* that though mightest hear the charge, when it might as well have been ended in the inferior court." *Secondly,* "He has left it to thee to examine him, and try what thou canst get out of him, and whether thou canst by his confession come to the knowledge of those things which we lay to his charge."

III. The assent of the Jews to this charge which Tertullus exhibited (*v.* 9): *They confirmed it, saying that those things were so.* 1. Some think this expresses the proof of their charge by witnesses upon oath, that were examined as to the particulars of it, and attested them. And no wonder if, when they had found an orator that would say it, they found witnesses that would swear it, for money. 2. It rather seems to intimate the approbation which the high priest and the elders gave to what Tertullus said. Felix asked them, "Is this your sense, and is it all that you have to say?" And they answered, "Yes it is;" and so they made themselves guilty of all the falsehood that was in his speech. Those that have not the wit and parts to do mischief with that some others have, that cannot make speeches and hold disputes against religion, yet make themselves guilty of the mischiefs others do, by assenting to that which others do, and saying, These things are so, repeating and standing by what is said, to *pervert the right ways of the Lord.* Many that have not learning enough to plead for Baal yet have wickedness enough to vote for Baal.

Verses 10–21

We have here Paul's defence of himself, in answer to Tertullus's charge, and there appears in it a great deal of the spirit of wisdom and holiness, and an accomplishment of Christ's promise to his followers that when they were before governors and kings, for his sake, it should be *given them in that same hour what they should speak.* Though Tertullus had said a great many provoking things, yet Paul did not interrupt him, but let him go on to the end of his speech, according to the rules of decency and the method in courts of justice, that the plaintiff be allowed to finish his evidence before the defendant begins his plea. And when he had done, he did not presently fly out into passionate exclamations against the iniquity of the times and the men *(O tempora! O mores! — Oh the degeneracy of the times!)* but he waited for a permission from the judge to speak in his turn, and had it. The *governor beckoned to him to speak, v.* 10. And now he also may have leave to speak out, under the protection of the governor, which was more than he could hitherto obtain. And,

when he did speak, he made no reflections at all upon Tertullus, who he knew spoke for his fee, and therefore despised what he said, and levelled his defence against those that employed him. And here,

I. He addressed himself very respectfully to the governor, and with a confidence that he would do him justice. Here are not such flattering compliments as Tertullus soothed him up with, but, which was more truly respectful, a profession that he *answered for himself cheerfully,* and with good assurance *before him,* looking upon him, though not as one that was his friend, yet as one that would be fair and impartial. He thus expresses his expectation that he would be so, to engage him to be so. It was likewise the language of one that was conscious to himself of his own integrity, and whose heart did not reproach him, whoever did. He did not stand trembling at the bar; on the contrary, he was very cheerful when he had one to be his judge that was not a party, but an indifferent person. Nay, when he considers who his judge is, he *answers the more cheerfully;* and why so? He does not say, "Because I know thee to be a judge of inflexible justice and integrity, that hatest bribes, and in giving judgment fearest God, and regardest not man;" for he could not justly say this of him, and therefore would not say it, though it were to gain his favour ever so much; but, *I the more cheerfully answer from myself,* because *I know thou hast been many years a judge to this nation,* and this was very true, and being so, 1. He could say of his own knowledge that there had not formerly been any complaints against Paul. Such clamours as they raised are generally against old offenders; but, though he had long say judge there, he never had Paul brought before him till now; and therefore he was not so dangerous a criminal as he was represented to be. 2. He was well acquainted with the Jewish nation, and with their temper and spirit. He knew how bigoted they were to their own way, what furious zealots they were against all that did not comply with them, how peevish and perverse they generally were, and therefore would make allowances for that in their accusation of him, and not regard that which he had reason to think came so much from part-malice. Though he did not know him, he knew his prosecutors, and by this might guess what manner of man he was.

II. He denies the facts that he was charged with, upon which their character of him was grounded. *Moving sedition,* and *profaning the temple,* were the crimes for which he stood indicted, crimes which they knew the Roman governors were not accustomed to enquire into, and therefore they hoped that the governor would return him back to them to be judged by their law, and this was all they wished for. But Paul desires that though he would not enquire into the crimes he would protect one that was unjustly charged with them from those whom he knew to be spiteful and ill-natured enough. Now he would have him to understand (and what he said he was ready, if required, to make out by witnesses),

1. That he came up to Jerusalem on purpose to worship God in peace and holiness, so far was he from any design to move sedition among the people or to profane the temple. He came to keep up his communion with the Jews, not to put any affront upon them.

2. That it was but twelve days since he came up to Jerusalem, and he came up to Jerusalem, and he had been six days a prisoner; he was alone, and it could not be supposed that in so short a time he could do the mischief they charged upon him. And, as for what he had done in other countries, they knew nothing of it but by uncertain report, by which the matter was very unfairly represented.

3. That he had demeaned himself at Jerusalem very quietly and peaceably, and had made no manner of stir. If it had been true (as they alleged) that he was a *mover of sedition among all the Jews,* surely he would have been industrious to make a party at Jerusalem: but he did not do so. He was in the temple, attending the public service there. He was in the synagogues where the law was read and opened. He went about in the city among his relations and friends, and conversed freely in the places of concourse; and he was a man of a great genius and an active spirit, and yet they could not charge him with offering any thing either against the faith or against the peace of the Jewish church. (1.) He had nothing in him of a contradicting spirit, as the movers of sedition have; he had no disposition to quarrel or oppose. They never found him *disputing with any man,* either affronting the learned with captious cavils or perplexing the weak and simple with curious subtleties. He was ready, if asked, to give

a reason of his own hope, and to give instruction to others; but he never picked a quarrel with any man about his religion, nor made that the subject of debate, and controversy, and perverse dispute, which ought always to be treated of with humility and reverence, with meekness and love. (2.) He had nothing in him of a turbulent spirit: "They never found me *raising up the people,* by incensing them against their governors in church or state or suggesting to them fears and jealousies concerning public affairs, nor by setting them at variance one with another or sowing discord among them." He behaved as became a Christian and minister, with love and quietness, and due subjection to lawful authority. The weapons of his warfare were not carnal, not did he ever mention or think of such a thing as taking up arms for the propagating of the gospel or the defence of the preachers of it; though he could have made, perhaps, as strong a party among the common people as his adversaries, yet he never attempted it.

4. That as to what they had charged him with, of moving sedition in other countries, he was wholly innocent, and they could not make good the charge (*v.* 13): *Neither can the prove the things whereof the now accuse me.* Hereby, (1.) He maintains his own innocency; for when he says, They cannot prove it, he means, The matter is not so. He was no enemy to the public peace; he had done no real prejudice, but a great deal of real service, and would gladly have done more, to the nation of the Jews. He was so far from having any antipathy to them that he had the strongest affection imaginable for them, and a most passionate desire for their welfare, *Rom.* 9:1–3. (2.) He bemoans his own calamity, that he was accused of those things which could not be proved against him. And it has often been the lot of very worthy good men to be thus injured, to have things laid to their charge which they are the greatest distance from and abhor the though of. But, while they are lamenting this calamity, this may be their rejoicing, even the *testimony of their consciences* concerning their integrity. (3.) He shows the iniquity of his prosecutors, who said that which they knew they could not prove, and thereby did him wrong in his name, liberty, and life, and did the judge wrong too, in imposing upon him, and doing what in them lay to pervert his judgment. (4.) He appeals to the equity of his judge, and awakens him to look about him, that he might not be drawn into a snare by the violence of the prosecution. The judge must give sentence *secundum allegata et probata — according to that which is not only alleged but proved,* and therefore must enquire, and search, and ask diligently, whether the thing be true and certain (Deu. 13:14); he cannot otherwise give a right judgment.

III. He gives a fair and just account of himself, which does at once both clear him from crime and likewise intimate what was the true reason of their violence in prosecuting him.

1. He acknowledges himself to be one whom they looked upon as a heretic, and that was the reason of their spleen against him. The chief captain had observed, and the governor now cannot but observe, an uncommon violence and fury in his prosecutors, which they know not what to make of, but, guessing at the crime by the cry, conclude he must needs have been a very bad man only for that reason. Now Paul here unriddles the matter: I confess that *in the way which they call heresy* — or a *sect, so worship I the God of my fathers.* The controversy is in a matter of religion, and such controversies are commonly managed with most fury and violence. Note, It is no new thing for the right way of worshipping God to be called heresy; and for the best of God's servants to be stigmatized and run down as sectaries. The reformed churches are called heretical ones by those who themselves hate to be reformed, and are themselves heretics. Let us therefore never be driven off from any good way by its being put into an ill name; for true and pure Christianity is never the worse, nor to be the worse thought of, for its being called heresy; no, not though it be called so by the high priest and the elders.

2. He vindicates himself from this imputation. They call Paul a heretic, but he is not so; for,

(1.) He *worships the God of his fathers,* and therefore is right in the object of his worship. He does not say, *Let us go after other gods, which we have not known, and let us serve them,* as the false prophet is supposed to do, Deu. 13:2. If so, they might justly call his way heresy, a drawing of them aside into a by-path, and a dangerous one; but he worships the God of Abraham, Isaac, and Jacob, not only the God whom they worshipped, but the God who took them into covenant with himself, and was and would be called their God. Paul adheres to that covenant, and sets up no other in opposition to it. The *promise made unto the fathers* Paul preached as *fulfilled to the children* (*ch.* 13:32, 33), and so directed both his own devotions and those of others to God, as the *God of their fathers.* He also refers to the practice of all his pious ancestors: *I worship* the same God that all my fathers worshipped. His religion was so far from being chargeable with novelty that it gloried in its antiquity, and in an uninterrupted succession of its professors. Note, It is very comfortable in our worshipping God to have an eye to him as the God of our fathers. Our fathers trusted in him, and were owned by him, and he engaged to be their God, and the God of their seed. He approved himself theirs, and therefore, if we serve him as they did, he will be ours; what an emphasis is laid upon this, *He is my father's God, and I will exalt him!* Ex. 15:2.

(2.) He *believes all things which are written in the law and the prophets,* and therefore is right in the rule of his worship. His religion is grounded upon, and governed by, the holy scriptures; they are his oracle and touchstone, and he speaks and acts according to them. He receives the scriptures entire, and believes all things that are there written; and he receives them pure, for he says no other things than what are contained in them, as he explains himself, *ch.* 26:22. He sets not up any other rule of faith, or practice but the scriptures — not tradition, nor the authority of the church, nor the infallibility of any man or company of men on earth, nor the light within, nor human reason; but divine revelation, as it is in the scripture, is that which he resolves to live and die by, and therefore he is not a heretic.

(3.) He has his eye upon a future state, and is a believing expectant of that, and therefore is right in the end of his worship. Those that turn aside to heresy have a regard to this world, and some secular interest, but Paul aims to make heaven of his religion, and neither more nor less (*v.* 15): "*I have hope towards God,* all my expectation is from him, and therefore all my desire is towards him and all my dependence upon him; my hope is towards God and not towards the world, towards another world and not towards this. I depend upon God and upon his power, that *there shall be a resurrection of the dead* at the end of time, of all, both *the just and unjust;* and the great thing I aim at in my religion is to obtain a joyful and happy resurrection, a share in the resurrection of the just." Observe here, [1.] That there shall be a resurrection of the dead, the dead bodies of men, of all men from the beginning to the end of time. It is certain, not only that the soul does not die with the body, but that the body itself shall live again; we have not only another life to live when our present life is at an end, but there is to be another world, which shall commence when this world is at an end, into which all the children of men must enter at once by a resurrection from the dead, as they entered into this, one after another, by their birth. [2.] It shall be a resurrection *both of the just and of the unjust,* the sanctified and the unsanctified, of those that did well, and to them our Saviour has told us that it will be a *resurrection of life;* and of those that did evil, and to them that it will be a resurrection of condemnation, Jn. 5:29. See Dan. 12:2. This implies that it will be a resurrection to a final judgment, by which all the children of men will be determined to everlasting happiness or misery in a world of retribution, according to what they were and what they did in this state of probation and preparation. The just shall rise by virtue of their union with Christ as their head; the unjust shall rise by virtue of Christ's dominion over them as their Judge. [3.] God is to be depended upon for the resurrection of the dead: I have *hope towards God,* and in God, that there shall be a resurrection; it shall be effected by the almighty power of God, in performance of the word which God hath spoken; so that those who doubt of it betray their ignorance both of the scriptures and of the power of God, Mt. 22:29. [4.] The resurrection of the dead is a fundamental article of our creed, as it was also of that of the Jewish church. It is what *they themselves also allow;* nay, it was the expectation of the ancient patriarchs, witness Job's confession of his faith; but it is more clearly revealed and more fully confirmed by the gospel, and therefore those who believed it should have been thankful to the preachers of the gospel for their explications and proofs of it, instead of opposing them. [5.] In all our religion we ought to have an eye to the other world, and to serve God in all instances with a confidence in him *that there will be a resurrection of the dead,* doing all in preparation for that, and expecting our recompence in that.

(4.) His conversation is of a piece with his devotion (*v.* 16): *And herein do I exercise myself, to have always a conscience void of offence towards God and towards men.* Prophets and their doctrine were to be tried by their fruits. Paul was far from having made shipwreck of a good conscience, and therefore it is not likely he has made shipwreck of the faith, the mystery of which is best held in a pure conscience. This protestation of Paul's is to the same purport with that which he made before the high priest (*ch.* 23:1): *I have lived in all good conscience;* and this was his rejoicing. Observe, [1.] What was Paul's aim and desire: To *have a conscience void of offence.* Either, *First,* "A conscience not offending; not informing me wrong, nor flattering me, nor dealing deceitfully with me, nor in any thing misleading me." Or, *Secondly,* A conscience not offended; it is like Job's resolution, *"My heart shall not reproach me,* that is, I will never give it any occasion to do so. This is what I am ambitious of, to keep upon good terms with my own conscience, that it may have no cause either to question the goodness of my spiritual state or to quarrel with me for any particular action. I am as careful not to offend my conscience as I am not to offend a friend with whom I daily converse; nay, as I am not to offend a magistrate whose authority I am under, and to whom I am accountable; for conscience is God's deputy in my soul." [2.] What was his care and endeavour, in pursuance of this: "*I exercise myself — askō.* I make it my constant business, and govern myself by this intention; I discipline myself, and live by rule" (those that did so were called *ascetics,* from the word here used), "abstain from many a thing which my inclination leads me to, and abound in all the exercises of religion that are most spiritual, with this in my eye, that I may keep peace with my own conscience." [3.] The extent of this care: *First,* To all times: *To have always a conscience void of offence,* always void of gross offence; for though Paul was conscious to himself that he *had not yet attained perfection,* and the evil that he would not do yet he did, yet he was *innocent from the great transgression.* Sins of infirmity are uneasy to conscience, but they do not wound it, and waste it, as presumptuous sins do; and, though offence may be given to conscience, yet care must be taken that it be not an abiding offence, but that by the renewed acts of faith and repentance the matter may be taken up again quickly. This however we must always exercise ourselves in, and, though we come short, we must follow after. *Secondly,* To all things: *Both towards God, and towards man.* His conscientious care extended itself to the whole of his duty, and he was afraid of breaking the law of love either to God or his neighbour. Conscience, like the magistrate, is *custos utriusque tabulae — the guardian of each table.* We must be very cautious that we do not think, or speak, or do any thing amiss, either against God or man, 2 Co. 8:21. [4.] The inducement to it: *Herein, en toutō, for this cause;* so it may be read. "Because I look for the resurrection of the dead and the life of the world to come, therefore I thus exercise myself." The consideration of the future state should engage us to be universally conscientious in our present state.

IV. Having made confession of his faith, he gives a plain and faithful account of his case, and of the wrong done him by his persecutors. Twice he had been rescued by the chief captain out of the hands of the Jews, when they were ready to pull him to pieces, and he challenges them to prove him guilty of any crime either time.

1. In the temple. Here they fell furiously upon him as an enemy to their nation and the temple, *ch.* 21:28. But was there any colour for the charge? No, but evidence sufficient against it, (1.) It was very hard to accuse him as an *enemy to their nation,* when after long absence from Jerusalem he came to *bring alms to his nation,* money which (though he had need enough himself of it) he had collected among his friends, for the relief of the poor at Jerusalem. He not only had no malice to that people, but he had a very charitable concern for them, and was ready to do them all good offices; and were they his adversaries for his love? Ps. 109:4. (2.) It was very hard to accuse him of having profaned the temple when he brought offerings to the temple, and was himself at charges therein (*ch.* 21:24), and was found *purifying himself in the temple,* according to the law (*v.* 18), and that in a very quiet decent manner, *neither with multitude nor with tumult.* Though he was a man so much talked of, he was far from coveting to show himself when he came to Jerusalem, or to be crowded after, but went to the temple, as much as was possible, *incognito.* They were Jews from Asia, his enemies, that caused him to be taken notice of; they had not pretence to make

a tumult and raise a multitude against him, for he had neither multitude nor tumult for him. And as to what was perhaps suggested to Felix that he had brought Greeks into the temple, contrary to their law, and the governor ought to reckon with him for that, the Romans having stipulated with the nations that submitted to them to preserve them in their religion, he challenges them to prove it (*v.* 19): "Those Jews of Asia ought to have been *here before thee,* that they might have been examined, whether *they had aught against me,* that they would stand by and swear to;" for some that will not scruple to tell a lie have such heavings of conscience that they scruple confirming it with an oath.

2. In the council: "Since the Jews of Asia are not here to prove any thing upon me done amiss in the temple, let *these same* that are *here,* the high priest and the elders, say whether they have *found any evil doing in me,* or whether I was guilty of any misdemeanor *when I stood before the council,* when also they were ready to pull me in pieces, *v.* 20. When I was there, they could not take offence at any thing I said; for all I said was, *Touching the resurrection of the dead I am called in question by you this day* (*v.* 21), which gave no offence to any one but the Sadducees. This I hope was no crime, that I stuck to that which is the faith of the whole Jewish church, excepting those whom they themselves call heretics."

Verses 22–27

We have here the result of Paul's trial before Felix, and what was the consequence of it.

I. Felix adjourned the cause, and took further time to consider of it (*v.* 22): He *had a more perfect knowledge of that way* which the Jews called heresy than the high priest and the elders thought he had. He understood something of the Christian religion; for, living at Caesarea, where Cornelius, a Roman centurion, was, who was a Christian, from him and others he had got a notion of Christianity, that it was not such an evil thing as it was represented. He himself knew some of that way to be honest good men, and very conscientious, and therefore he put off the prosecutors with an excuse: "*When the chief captain shall come down* hither, *I will know the uttermost of your matter,* or I shall know the truth, whether this Paul did go about to raise sedition or no; you are parties, he is an indifferent person. Either Paul deserves to be punished for raising the tumult, or you do for doing it yourselves and then charging it upon him; and I will hear what he says, and determine accordingly between you." Now, 1. It was a disappointment to the high priest and the elders that Paul was not condemned, or remitted to their judgment, which they wished for and expected. But thus sometimes God restrains the wrath of his people's enemies by the agency, not of their friends, but of such as are strangers to them. And though they be so, if they have but some *knowledge of their way,* they cannot but appear for their protection. 2. It was an injury to Paul that he was not released. Felix ought to have *avenged him of his adversaries,* when he so plainly saw there was nothing but malice in the prosecution, and to have delivered *him out of the hand of the wicked,* according to the duty of a judge, Ps. 82:4. But he was a judge that neither feared God nor regarded man, and what good could be expected from him? It is a wrong not only to deny justice, but to delay it.

II. He detained the prisoner in custody, and would not take bail for him; else here at Caesarea Paul had friends enough that would gladly have been his security. Felix thought a man of such a public character as Paul was had many friends, as well as many enemies, and he might have an opportunity of obliging them, or making a hand of them, if he did not presently release him, and yet did show him countenance; and therefore, 1. He continued him a prisoner, commanded a centurion or captain to keep him, *v.* 23. He did not commit him to the common jail, but, being first made an army-prisoner, he shall still be so. 2. Yet he took care he should be *a prisoner at large — in libera custodia;* his keeper must let him have liberty, not bind him nor lock him up, but make his confinement as easy to him as possible; let him have the liberty of the castle, and, perhaps, he means liberty to take the air, or go abroad upon his parole; and Paul was such an honest man that they might take his word for his return. The high priest and the elders grudged him his life, but Felix generously allows him a sort of liberty; for he had not those prejudices against him and his way that they had. He also gave orders that none of his friends should be hindered from coming to him; the centurion must not forbid any of his acquaintances from ministering to him; and a man's prison is as it were his own house if he has but his friends about him.

III. He had frequent conversation with him afterwards in private, once particularly, not long after his public trial, *v.* 24, 25. Observe,

1. With what design *Felix sent for Paul.* He had a mind to have some talk with him *concerning the faith in Christ,* the Christian religion; he had some knowledge of that way, but he desired to have an account of it from Paul, who was so celebrated a preacher of that faith, above the rest. Those that would enlarge their knowledge must discourse with men of their own profession, and those that would be acquainted with any profession should consult those that excel in the knowledge of it; and therefore Felix had a mind to talk with Paul more freely than he could in open court, where he observed Paul upon his guard, *concerning the faith of Christ;* and this only to satisfy his curiosity, or rather the curiosity of *his wife Drusilla, who was a Jewess,* daughter of Herod Agrippa, that was eaten of worms. Being educated in the Jewish religion, she was more inquisitive concerning the Christian religion, which pretended to be the perfection of that, and desired to hear Paul discourse of it. But it was no great matter what religion she was of; for, whatever it was, she was a reproach and scandal to it — a Jewess, but an adulteress; she was another man's wife when Felix took her to be his wife, and she lived with him in whoredom and was noted for an impudent woman, yet she desires to hear *concerning the faith of Christ.* Many are fond of new notions and speculations in religion, and can hear and speak of them with pleasure, who yet hate to come under the power and influence of religion, can be content to have their judgments informed but not their lives reformed.

2. What the account was which Paul gave him of the Christian religion; by the idea he had of it, he expected to be amused with a mystical divinity, but, as Paul represents it to him, he is alarmed with a practical divinity. Paul, being asked *concerning the faith in Christ, reasoned* (for Paul was always a rational preacher) concerning *righteousness, temperance, and judgment to come.* It is probable that he mentioned the peculiar doctrines of Christianity concerning the death and resurrection of the Lord Jesus, and his being *the Mediator between God and man;* but he hastened to his application, in which he designed to come home to the consciences of his hearers.

(1.) He discoursed with clearness and warmth *of righteousness, temperance, and judgment to come;* and here he showed, [1.] That the faith in Christ is designed to enforce upon the children of men the great laws of justice and temperance. *The grace of God teacheth us to live soberly and righteously,* Tit. 2:12. Justice and temperance were celebrated virtues among the heathen moralists; if the doctrine Paul preaches, which Felix has heard of as proclaiming liberty, will but free him from an obligation to these, he will readily embrace it: *"No,"* says Paul, "it is so far from doing so that it strengthens the obligations of those sacred laws; it binds all under the highest penalties to be *honest in all their dealings,* and to *render to all their due;* to *deny themselves,* and *to keep under the body, and bring it into subjection."* The world and the flesh being in our baptism renounced, all our pursuits of the world and all our gratifications of the desires of the body are to be under the regulations of religion. *Paul reasoned of righteousness and temperance,* to convince Felix of his unrighteousness and intemperance, of which he had been notoriously guilty, that, seeing the odiousness of them, and his obnoxiousness to the wrath of God for them (Eph. 5:6), he might enquire concerning the faith of Christ, with a resolution to embrace it. [2.] That by the doctrine of Christ is discovered to us the judgment to come, by the sentence of which the everlasting state of all the children of men will be finally and irreversibly determined. Men have their day now, Felix hath his; but God's day is coming, *when everyone shall give account of himself to God, the Judge of all.* Paul reasoned concerning this; that is, he showed what reason we have to believe *that there is a judgment to come,* and what reason we have, in consideration thereof, to be religious.

(2.) From this account of the heads of Paul's discourse we may gather, [1.] That Paul in his preaching had no respect to persons, for the word of God, which he preached, has not: he urged the same convictions and instructions upon the Roman governor that he did upon other people. [2.] That Paul in his preaching aimed at the consciences of men, and came close to them, sought not to please their fancy nor to gratify their curiosity, but led them to a sight of their sins and a sense of their duty and interest. [3.] That Paul preferred the serving of Christ, and the saving of souls, before his own safety. He lay at the mercy of Felix, who had power (as Pilate said) *to crucify him* (or, which was as bad, to deliver him back to the Jews), *and he had power to release him.* Now when Paul had his ear, and had him in a good humour, he had a fair opportunity of ingratiating himself with him, and obtaining a release, nay, and of incensing him against his prosecutors: and, on the contrary, if he disobliged him, and put him out of humour, he might do himself a great diskindness by it; but he is wholly negligent of these considerations, and is intent upon doing good, at least discharging his duty. [4.] That Paul was willing to take pains, and run hazards, in his work, even where there was little probability of doing good. Felix and Drusilla were such hardened sinners that it was not at all likely they should be brought to repentance by Paul's preaching, especially under such disadvantages; and yet Paul deals with them as one that did not despair of them. Let the watchman give fair warning, and then they have delivered their own souls, though they should not prevail to deliver the souls they watch for.

3. What impressions Paul's discourse made upon this great but wicked man: *Felix trembled, emphobos genomenos — being put into a fright,* or made *a terror to himself, a magor-missabib,* as Pashur, Jer. 20:3, 4. Paul never trembled before him, but he was made to tremble before Paul. "If this be so, as Paul says, what will become of me in another world? If the unrighteous and intemperate will be condemned in the judgment to come, I am undone, for ever undone, unless I lead a new course of life." We do not find that Drusilla trembled, though she was equally guilty, for she was a Jewess, and depended upon the ceremonial law, which she adhered to the observance of, to justify her; but Felix for the present could fasten upon nothing to pacify his conscience, and therefore trembled. See here, (1.) The power of the word of God, when it comes with commission; it is searching, it is startling, it can strike a terror into the heart of the most proud and daring sinner, by *setting his sins in order before him,* and showing him *the terrors of the Lord.* (2.) The workings of natural conscience; when it is startled and awakened, it fills the soul with horror and amazement at its own deformity and danger. Those that are themselves *the terror of the mighty in the land of the living* have hereby been made a terror to themselves. A prospect of the judgment to come is enough to make the stoutest heart to tremble, as when it comes indeed it will make *the mighty men and the chief captains* to call in vain *to rocks and mountains to shelter them.*

4. How Felix struggled to get clear of these impressions, and to shake off the terror of his convictions; he did by them as he did by Paul's prosecutors (*v.* 25), *he deferred them;* he said, *Go thy way for this time, when I have a convenient season I will call for thee.* (1.) He trembled and that was all. Paul's trembling (*ch.* 9:6), and the *jailer's* (*ch.* 16:29), ended in their conversion, but this of Felix did not. Many are startled by the word of God who are not effectually changed by it. Many are in fear of the consequences of sin, and yet continue in love and league with sin. (2.) He did not fight against his convictions, nor fly in the face of the word or of the preacher of it, to be revenged on them for making his conscience fly in his face; he did not say to Paul, as Amaziah to the prophet, *Forbear, why shouldst thou be smitten?* He did not threaten him with a closer confinement, or with death, for touching him (as John Baptist did Herod) in the sore place. But, (3.) He artfully shifted off his convictions by putting off the prosecution of them to another time. He has nothing to object against what Paul has said; it is weighty and worth considering. But, like a sorry debtor, he begs a day; Paul has spent himself, and has tired him and his lady, and therefore, *"Go thy way for this time* — break off here, business calls me away; but *when I have a convenient season,* and have nothing else to do, *I will call for thee,* and hear what thou hast further to say." Note, [1.] Many lose all the benefit of their convictions for want of striking while the iron is hot. If Felix, now that he trembled, had but asked, as Paul and the jailer did when they trembled, *What shall I do?* he might have been brought to the faith of Christ, and have been a *Felix* indeed, *happy* for ever; but, by dropping his convictions now, he lost them for ever, and himself with them. [2.] In the affairs of our souls, delays are dangerous; nothing is of more fatal consequence than men's putting off their conversion from time to time. They will repent, and turn to God, but not yet; the matter is adjourned to some more convenient season, when such a business or affair is compassed, when they are so much older; and then convictions cool and wear off, good purposes prove to no purpose, and they are more hardened than ever in their evil way. Felix put off this matter to a more convenient season, but we do not find that this more convenient season ever came; for the devil cozens us of all our time by cozening us of the present time. The present season is, without doubt, the most convenient season. *Behold, now is the accepted time. To-day if you will hear his voice.*

IV. After all, he detained him a prisoner, and left him so, when two years after he was removed from the government, *v.* 26, 27. He was convinced in his conscience that Paul had done *nothing worthy of death or of bonds,* and yet had not the honesty to release him. To little purpose had Paul reasoned with him about righteousness, though he then trembled at the thought of his own iniquity, who could thus persist in such a palpable piece of injustice. But here we are told what principles he was governed by herein; and they were such as make the matter yet much worse. 1. The love of money. He would not release Paul because he hoped to make his market of him, and that at length his friends would make a purse to purchase his liberty, and then he would satisfy his conscience by releasing him when he could withal satisfy his covetousness by it; but he cannot find in his heart to do his duty as a judge, unless he can get money by it: *He hoped that money would have been given him of Paul,* or somebody for him, and then he would have loosed him, and set him at liberty. In hopes of this, he detains him a prisoner, and *sends for him the oftener, and communes with him;* not any more about the faith of Christ (he had had enough of that, and of the judgment to come; Paul must not return to those subjects, nor go on with them), but about his discharge, or ransom rather, out of his present captivity. He cannot for shame ask Paul what he will give him to release him, but he sends for him to feel his pulse, and gives him an opportunity to ask why he would take to release him. And now we see what became of his promise both to Paul and to himself, that he would hear more of Christ at some other convenient season. Here were many seasons convenient enough to have talked that matter through, but nothing is done in it; all his business now is to get money by Paul, not to get the knowledge of Christ by him. Note, It is just with God to say concerning those who trifle with their convictions, and think they can have the grace of God at command when they please, *My Spirit shall no more strive with them.* When men will not hear God's voice *to-day, while it is called to-day,* the heart is commonly *hardened by the deceitfulness of sin.* Paul was but a poor man himself, *silver and gold he had none* to give, to purchase his liberty; but Felix knew there were those who wished well to him who were able to assist him. He having lately collected a great deal of money for the poor saints to relieve them, it might also be expected that the rich saints should contribute some to release him, and I wonder it was not done. Though Paul is to be commended that he would not offer money to Felix, nor beg money of the churches (his great and generous soul disdained both), yet I know not whether his friends are to be commended, nay, whether they can be justified, in not doing it for him. They ought to have solicited the governor as pressingly for him as his enemies did against him: and if a *gift was necessary to make room for them* (as Solomon speaks) and to bring them before great men, they might lawfully have done it. I ought not to bribe a man to do an unjust thing, but, if he will not do me justice without a fee, it is but doing myself justice to give it to him; and, if they might do it, it was a shame they did not do it. I blush for them, that they would let such an eminent and useful man as Paul lie in the jail, when a little money would have fetched him out, and restored him to his usefulness again. The Christians here at Caesarea, where he now was, had parted with their tears to prevent his going to the prison (*ch.* 21:13), and could they not find in their hearts to part with their money to help him out? Yet there might be a providence of God in it; Paul's bonds must be for the furtherance of the gospel of Christ, and therefore he must continue in bonds. However, this will not excuse Felix, who ought to have released an innocent man, without demanding or accepting any thing for it: the judge that will not do right without a bribe will no doubt do wrong for a bribe. 2. Men-pleasing. Felix was recalled from his government about *two years after this,* and Porcius Festus was put in his place, and one should have expected he would have at least concluded his government with this act of justice, the release of Paul, but he did not; he *left Paul bound,* and the reason here given is because he was *willing to do the Jews a pleasure.* Though he would not deliver him *to death, to please them,* yet he would continue him a prisoner rather than offend them; and he did it in hope hereby to atone for the many offences he had done against them. He did not think Paul had either interest or inclination to complain of him at court, for detaining him so long in custody, against all law and equity; but he was jealous of the high priest and elders, that they would be his accusers to the emperor for the wrongs he had done them, and therefore hopes by gratifying them in this matter to stop their mouths. Thus those who do some base things are tempted to do more to screen themselves and bear them out. If Felix had not injured the Jews, he needed not to have done this to please them; but, when he had done it, it seems he did not gain his point. The Jews, notwithstanding this, accused him to the emperor, and some historians say he was sent bound to Rome by Festus; and, if so, surely his remembering how light he had made of Paul's bonds would help to make his own chain heavy. Those that aim to please God by doing good will have what they aim at; but so will not those that seek to please men by doing evil.

CHAPTER 25

Some think that Felix was turned out, and Festus succeeded him, quickly after Paul's imprisonment, and that the two years mentioned in the close of the foregoing chapter are to be reckoned from the beginning of Nero's reign; but it seems more natural to compute them from Paul's being delivered into the hands of Felix. However, we have here much the same management of Paul's case as we had in the foregoing chapter; cognizance is here taken of it, I. By Festus the governor; it is brought before him by the Jews (*v.* 1-3). The hearing of it is appointed to be, not at Jerusalem, as the Jews desired, out at Caesarea (*v.* 4-6). The Jews appear against Paul and accuse him (*v.* 7), but he stands upon his own innocency (*v.* 8); and to avoid the removing of the cause to Jerusalem, to which he was pressed to consent, he at length appeals to Caesar (*v.* 9-12). II. By king Agrippa, to whom Festus relates his case (*v.* 13-21), and Agrippa desires he might have the hearing of it himself (*v.* 22). The court is accordingly set, and Paul brought to the bar (*v.* 23), and Festus opens the cause (*v.* 24-27), to introduce Paul's defence in the next chapter.

Verses 1-12

We commonly say, "New lords, new laws, new customs;" but here was a new governor, and yet Paul had the same treatment from him that he had from the former, and no better. Festus, like Felix, is not so just to him as he should have been, for he does not release him; and yet not so unjust to him as the Jews would have had him to be, for he will not condemn him to die, nor expose him to their rage. Here is,

I. The pressing application which the high priest and other Jews used with the governor to persuade him to abandon Paul; for to send him to Jerusalem was in effect to abandon him. 1. See how speedy they were in their applications to Festus concerning Paul. As soon as ever he *had come into the province,* and had taken possession of the government, into which, probably, he was installed at Caesarea, within *three days he went up to Jerusalem,* to show himself there, and presently the priests were upon him to proceed against Paul. He staid *three days at Caesarea,* where Paul was a prisoner, and we do not find that in that time Paul made any application to him to release him, though, no doubt, he could have made good friends, that he might hope to have prevailed by; but as soon as ever he comes up to Jerusalem the priests are in all haste to make an interest with him against Paul. See how restless a thing malice is. Paul more patiently bears the lengthening out of his imprisonment than his enemies do the delay of his prosecution even to the death. 2. See how spiteful they were in their application. They *informed the governor against Paul* (*v.* 2) before he was brought upon a fair trial, that so they might, if possible, prejudge the cause with the governor, and make him a party who was to be the judge. But this artifice, though base enough, they could not confide in; for the governor would be sure to hear him himself, and then all their informations against him would fall to the ground; and therefore they form another project much more base, and that is to assassinate Paul before he came upon his trial. These inhuman hellish methods, which all the world profess at least to abhor, have these persecutors recourse to, to gratify their malice against the gospel of Christ, and this too under colour of zeal for Moses. *Tantum religio potuit suadere malorum — Such was their dire religious zeal.* 3. See how specious the pretence was. Now that *the governor was himself at Jerusalem they desired he would send for Paul thither,* and try him there, which would save the prosecutors a great deal of labour, and looked most reasonable, because he was charged with having profaned the temple at Jerusalem, and it is usual for criminals to be tried in the court where the fact was committed; but that which they designed was to way-lay him as he was brought up, and to murder him upon the road, supposing that he would not be brought up under so strong a guard as he was sent down with, or that the officers that were to bring him up might be bribed to give them an opportunity for their wickedness. It is said, *They desired favour against Paul.* The business of prosecutors is to demand justice against one that they suppose to be a criminal, and, if he be not proved so, it is as much justice to acquit him as it is to condemn him if he be. But to desire favour against a prisoner, and from the judge too, who ought to be of counsel for him, is a very impudent thing. The favour ought to be for the prisoner, *in favorem vitae — to favour his life,* but here they desire it against him. They will take it as a favour if the governor will but condemn Paul, though they can prove no crime upon him.

II. The governor's resolution that Paul shall take his trial at Caesarea, where he now is, *v.* 4, 5. See how he manages the prosecutors. 1. He will not do them the kindness to send for him to Jerusalem; no, he gave orders *that Paul should be kept at Caesarea.* It does not appear that he had any suspicion, much less any certain information, of their bloody design to murder him by the way, as the chief priests had when he sent him to Caesarea (*ch.* 23:30); but perhaps he was not willing so far to oblige the high priest and his party, or he would maintain the honour of his court at Caesarea and require their attendance there, or he was not willing to be at the trouble or charge of bringing Paul up; whatever was his reason for refusing it, God made use of it as a means of preserving Paul out of the hands of his enemies. Perhaps now they were more careful to keep their conspiracy secret than they had been before, that the discovery of it might not be now, as it was then, the defeat of it. But though God does not, as then, bring it to light, yet he finds another way, as effectual, to bring it to nought, by inclining the heart of the governor, for some other reasons, not to remove Paul to Jerusalem. God is not tied to one method, in working out salvation for his people. He can suffer the designs against them to be concealed, and yet not suffer them to be accomplished; and can make even the carnal policies of great men to serve his gracious purposes. 2. Yet he will do them the justice to hear what they have to say against Paul, if they will go down to Caesarea, and appear against him there: *"Let those among you who are able,* able in body and purse for such a journey, or able in mind and tongue to manage the prosecution *—let those among you* who are fit to be managers, *go down with me, and accuse this man;* or, those who are competent witnesses, who are able to prove any thing criminal upon him, let them go and give in their evidence, if there be any such wickedness in him as you charge upon him." Festus will not take it for granted, as they desire he should, that there is wickedness in him, till it is proved upon him, and he has been heard in his own defence; but, if he be guilty, it lies upon them to prove him so.

III. Paul's trial before Festus. Festus staid *at Jerusalem about ten days,* and then *went down to Caesarea,* and the prosecutors, it is likely, in his retinue; for he said they should *go down with him;* and, since they are so eager in the prosecution, he is willing this cause should be first called; and, that they may hasten home, he will despatch it *the next day.* Expedition in administering justice is very commendable, provided more haste be not made than good speed. Now here we have, 1. The court set, and the prisoner called to the bar. Festus *sat in the judgment-seat,* as he used to do when any cause was brought before him that was of consequence, and he *commanded Paul to be brought,* and to make his appearance, *v.* 6. Christ, to encourage his disciples and keep up their spirits under such awful trials of their courage as this was to Paul, promised them that the day should come when they *should sit on thrones, judging the tribes of Israel.* 2. The prosecutors exhibiting their charges against the prisoner (*v.* 7): *The Jews stood round about,* which intimates that they were many. *Lord, how are they increased that trouble me!* It intimates also that they were unanimous, they stood by one another, and resolved to hold together; and that they were intent upon the prosecution, and eager in clamouring against Paul. They *stood round about,* if possible, to frighten the judge into a compliance with their malicious design, or, at least, to frighten the prisoner, and to put him out of countenance; but in vain: he had too just and strong an assurance to be frightened by them. *They compassed me about like bees, but they are quenched as the fire of thorns,* Ps. 118:12. *When they stood round about him, they brought many and grievous accusations against Paul,* so it should be read. They charged him with high crimes and misdemeanors. The articles of impeachment were many, and contained things of a very heinous nature. They represented him to the court as black and odious as their wit and malice could contrive; but when they had opened the cause as they thought fit, and came to the evidence, there they failed: *they could not prove* what they alleged against him, for it was all false, and the complaints were groundless and unjust. Either the fact was not as they opened it, or there was no fault in it; *they laid to his charge things that he knew not,* nor they neither. It is no new thing for the most excellent ones of the earth to have all manner of evil said against them falsely, not only *in the song of the drunkards,* and upon *the seat of the scornful,* but even *before the judgment-seat.* 3. The prisoner's insisting upon his own vindication, *v.* 8. Whoever reproaches him, his own heart does not, and therefore his own tongue shall not; *though he die, he will not remove his integrity from him.* When it came to his turn to speak *for himself,* he insisted upon his general plea, Not guilty: *Neither against the law of the Jews, nor against the temple, nor yet against Caesar, have I offended any thing at all.* (1.) He had not violated the law of the Jews, nor taught any doctrine destructive of it. *Did he make void the law by faith? No, he established the law.* Preaching Christ, *the end of the law,* was no offence against the law. (2.) He had not profaned the temple, nor put any contempt at all upon the temple-service; his helping to set up the gospel temple did not at all offend against that temple which was a type of it. (3.) He had not offended against Caesar, nor his government. By this it appears that now his cause being brought before the government, to curry favour with the governor and that they might seem friends to Caesar, they had charged him with some instances of disaffection to the present higher powers, which obliged him to purge himself as to that matter, and to protest that he was no enemy to Caesar, not so much as those were who charged him with being so.

IV. Paul's appeal to the emperor, and the occasion of it. This gave the cause a new turn. Whether he had before designed it, or whether it was a sudden resolve upon the present provocation, does not appear; but God puts it into his heart to do it, for the bringing about of that which he had said to him, *that he must bear witnesss to Christ at Rome,* for there the emperor's court was, *ch.* 23:11. We have here,

1. The proposal which Festus made to Paul to go and take his trial at Jerusalem, *v.* 9. *Festus* was *willing to do the Jews a pleasure,* inclined to gratify the prosecutors rather than the prisoner, as far as he could go with safety against one that was a citizen of Rome, and therefore asked him whether he would be willing to go up to Jerusalem, and clear himself there, where he had been accused, and where he might have his witnesses ready to vouch for him and confirm what he said. He would not offer to turn him over to the high priest and the sanhedrim, as the Jews would have had him; but, *Wilt thou go thither, and be judged of these things before me?* The president, if he had pleased, might have ordered him thither, but he would not do it without his own consent, which, if he could have wheedled him to give it, would have taken off the odium of it. In suffering times, the prudence of the Lord's people is tried as well as their patience; being sent forth therefore as sheep in the midst of wolves, they have need to be wise as serpents.

2. Paul's refusal to consent to it, and his reasons for it. He knew, if he were removed to Jerusalem, notwithstanding the utmost vigilance of the president, the Jews would find some means or other to be the death of him; and therefore desires to be excused, and pleads, (1.) That, as a citizen of Rome, it was most proper for him to be tried, not only by the president, but in that which was properly his court, which sat at Caesarea: *I stand at Caesar's judgment-seat, where I ought to be judged,* in the city which is the metropolis of the province. The court being held in Caesar's name, and by his authority and commission, before one that was delegated by him, it might well be said to be his judgment seat, as, with us, all writs run in the name of the sovereign, in whose name all courts are held. Paul's owning that he ought to be judged at Caesar's judgment-seat plainly proves that Christ's ministers are not exempted from the jurisdiction of the civil powers, but ought to be subject to them, as far as they can with

a good conscience; and, if they be guilty of a real crime, to submit to their censure; if innocent, yet to submit to their enquiry, and to clear themselves before them. (2.) That, as a member of the Jewish nation, he had done nothing to make himself obnoxious to them: *To the Jews have I done no wrong, as thou very well knowest.* It very well becomes those that are innocent to plead their innocency, and to insist upon it; it is a debt we owe to our own good name, not only not to bear false witness against ourselves, but to maintain our own integrity against those who bear false witness against us. (3.) That he was willing to abide by the rules of the law, and to let that take its course, *v.* 11. If he be guilty of any capital crime that deserves death, he will not offer either to make resistance or to make his escape, will neither flee from justice nor fight with it: "I refuse not to die, but will accept of the punishment of my iniquity." Not that all who have committed any thing worthy of death are obliged to accuse themselves, and offer themselves to justice; but, when they are accused and brought to justice, they ought to submit, and to say both God and the government are righteous; as it is necessary that some should be made examples. But, if he be innocent, as he protests he is, *"If there be none of these things whereof these accuse me,* — if the prosecution be malicious and they are resolved to have my blood right or wrong, — *no man may deliver me unto them,* no, not the governor himself, without palpable injustice; for it is his business as much to protect the innocent as to punish the guilty;" and he claims his protection.

3. His appealing to court. Since he is continually in danger of the Jews, and one attempt made after another to get him into their hands, *whose tender mercies were cruel,* he flies to the *dernier resort — the last refuge* of oppressed innocency, and takes sanctuary there, since he cannot have justice done him in any other way: *"I appeal unto Caesar.* Rather than be delivered to the Jews" (which Festus seems inclined to consent to) "let me be delivered to Nero." When David had divers times narrowly escaped the rage of Saul, and concluded he was such a restless enemy that he should *one day perish by his hands,* he came to this resolution, being in a manner compelled to it, *There is nothing better for me than to take shelter in the land of the Philistines,* 1 Sa. 27:1. So Paul here. But it is a hard case that a son of Abraham must be forced to appeal to a Philistine, to a Nero, from those who call themselves the seed of Abraham, and shall be safer in Gath or Rome than in Jerusalem. *How is the faithful city become a harlot!*

V. The judgment given upon the whole matter. Paul is neither released nor condemned. His enemies hoped the cause would be ended in his death; his friends hoped it would be ended in his deliverance; but it proved neither so nor so, they are both disappointed, the thing is left as it was. It is an instance of the slow steps which Providence sometimes takes, not bringing things to an issue so soon as we expect, by which we are often made ashamed both of our hopes and of our fears, and are kept still waiting on God. The cause had before been adjourned to another time, now to another place, to another court, that Paul's *tribulation might work patience.* 1. The president takes advice upon the matter: *He conferred with the council — meta tou symbouliou,* not with the council of the Jews (that is called *synedrion*), but with his own counsellors, who were always ready to assist the governor with their advice. *In multitude of counsellors there is safety;* and judges should consult both with themselves and others before they pass sentence. 2. He determines to send him to Rome. Some think Paul meant not an appeal to Caesar's person, but only to his court, the sentence of which he would abide by, rather than be remitted to the Jew's council, and that Festus might have chosen whether he would have sent him to Rome, or, at least, whether he would have joined issue with him upon the appeal. But it should seem, by what Agrippa said (*ch.* 26:32), that *he might have been set at liberty if he had not appealed to Caesar* — that, by the course of the Roman law, a Roman citizen might appeal at any time to a superior court, even to the supreme, as causes with us are removed by *certiorari,* and criminals by *habeas corpus,* and as appeals are often made to the house of peers. Festus, therefore, either of choice or of course, comes to this resolution: *Hast thou appealed unto Caesar? Unto Caesar thou shalt go.* He found there was something very extraordinary in the case, which he was therefore afraid of giving judgment upon, either one way or other, and the knowledge of which he thought would be an entertainment to the emperor, and therefore he transmitted it to his cognizance. In our judgment before God those that by justifying themselves appeal to the law, to the law they shall go, and it will condemn them; but those that by repentance and faith appeal to the gospel, to the gospel they shall go, and it will save them.

Verses 13–27

We have here the preparation that was made for another hearing of Paul before King Agrippa, not in order to his giving judgment upon him, but in order to his giving advice concerning him, or rather only to gratify his curiosity. Christ had said, concerning his followers, *that they should be brought before governors and kings.* In the former part of this chapter Paul was brought before Festus the governor, here before Agrippa the king, for a testimony to both. Here is,

I. The kind and friendly visit which king Agrippa made to Festus, now upon his coming into the government in that province (*v.* 13): *After certain days, king Agrippa came to Caesarea.* Here is royal visit. Kings usually think it enough to send their ambassadors to congratulate their friends, but here was a king that came himself, that made the majesty of a prince yield to the satisfaction of a friend; for personal converse is the most pleasant among friends. Observe,

1. Who the visitants were. (1.) King Agrippa, the son of that Herod (surnamed *Agrippa*) who killed James the apostle, and was himself eaten of worms, and great grandson of Herod the Great, under whom Christ was born. Josephus calls this *Agrippa the younger;* Claudius the emperor made him king of Chalcis, and *tetrarch of Trachonitis and Abylene,* mentioned Lu. 3:1. The Jewish writers speak of him, and (as Dr. Lightfoot tells us) among other things relate this story of him, "That reading the law publicly, in the latter end of the year of release, as was enjoined, the king, when he came to those words (Deu. 17:15), *Thou shalt not set a stranger king over thee, who is not of thy brethren,* the tears ran down his cheeks, for he was not of the seed of Israel, which the congregation observing, cried out, Be of good comfort, king Agrippa, thou art our brother; for he was of their religion, though not of their blood." (2.) Bernice came with him. She was his own sister, now a widow, the widow of his uncle Herod, king of Chalcis, after whose death she lived with this brother of hers, who was suspected to be too familiar with her, and, after she was a second time married to Polemon king of Cilicia, she got to be divorced from him, and returned to her brother king Agrippa. Juvenal (*Sat.* 6) speaks of a diamond ring which Agrippa gave to Bernice, his incestuous sister: —

> — Berenices
> In digito factus pretiosior; hunc dedit olim
> Barbarus incestae, dedit hunc Agrippa sorori.
>
> That far-famed gem which on the finger glow'd
> Of Bernice (dearer thence), bestowed
> By an incestuous brother. — Gifford

And both Tacitus and Suetonius speak of a criminal intimacy afterwards between her and Titus Vespasian. Drusilla, the wife of Felix, was another sister. Such lewd people were the great people generally in those times! *Say not that the former days were better.*

2. What the design of this visit was: they *came to salute Festus,* to give him joy of his new promotion, and to wish him joy in it; they came to compliment him upon his accession to the government, and to keep up a good correspondence with him, that Agrippa, who had the government of Galilee, might act in concert with Festus, who had the government of Judea; but it is probable they came as much to divert themselves as to show respect to him, and to share in the entertainments of his court, and to show their fine clothes, which would do vain people no good if they did not go abroad.

II. The account which Festus gave to king Agrippa of Paul and his case, which he gave.

1. To entertain him, and give him some diversion. It was a very remarkable story, and worth any man's hearing, not only as it was surprising and entertaining, but, if it were truly and fully told, very instructive and edifying; and it would be particularly acceptable to Agrippa, not only because he was a judge, and there were some points of law and practice in it well worth his notice, but much more as he was a Jew, and there were some points of religion in it much more deserving his cognizance.

2. To have his advice. *Festus* was but newly come to be a judge, at least to be a judge in these parts, and therefore was diffident of himself and of his own ability, and willing to have the counsel of those that were older and more experienced, especially in a matter that had so much difficulty in it as Paul's case seemed to have, and therefore he declared it to the king. Let us now see the particular account he gives to king Agrippa concerning Paul, *v.* 14–21.

(1.) He found him a prisoner when he came into the government of this province; and therefore could not of his own knowledge give an account of his cause from the beginning: *There is a certain man left in bonds by Felix;* and therefore, if there were any thing amiss in the first taking of him into custody, Festus is not to answer for that, for he found him in bonds. When *Felix, to do the Jews a pleasure, left Paul bound,* though he knew him to be innocent, he knew not what he did, knew not but he might fall into worse hands than he did fall into, though they were none of the best.

(2.) That the Jewish sanhedrim were extremely set against him: "The *chief priests and the elders informed me* against him as a dangerous man, and not fit to live, and desired he might therefore be condemned to die." These being great pretenders to religion, and therefore to be supposed men of honour and honesty, Festus thinks he ought to give credit to them; but Agrippa knows them better than he does, and therefore Festus desires his advice in this matter.

(3.) That he had insisted upon the Roman law in favour of the prisoner, and would not condemn him unheard (*v.* 16): *"It is not the manner of the Romans,* who herein govern themselves by the law of nature and the fundamental rules of justice, to *deliver any man to die,* to grant him to destruction" (so the word is), "to gratify his enemies with his destruction, *before the accused has the accusers face to face,* to confront their testimony, and have both licence and time given him to answer for himself." He seems to upbraid them as if they reflected upon the Romans and their government in asking such a thing, or expecting that they would condemn a man without trying him: "No," says he, "I would have you to know, whatever you may allow of among yourselves, the Romans allow not of such a piece of injustice among them." *Audi et alteram partem — Hear the other side,* had become a proverb among them. This rule we ought to be governed by in our private censures in common conversation; we must not give men bad characters, nor condemn their words and actions, till we have heard what is to be said in their vindication. See Jn. 7:51.

(4.) That he had brought him upon his trial, according to the duty of his place, *v.* 17. That he had been expeditious in it, and the prosecutors had not reason to complain of his being dilatory, for *as soon as ever they had come* (and we are sure they lost no time) *without any delay, on the morrow,* he had brought on the cause. He had likewise tried him in the most solemn manner: He *sat on the judgment-seat,* as they used to do in weightier causes, while those that were of small moment they judged *de plano — upon even ground.* He called a great court on purpose for the trial of Paul, that the sentence might be definitive, and the cause ended.

(5.) That he was extremely *disappointed* in the charge they brought against him (*v.* 18, 19): *When the accusers stood up against him,* and opened their indictment, *they brought no accusations of such things as I supposed.*

[1.] He supposed by the eagerness of their prosecution, and their urging it thus upon the Roman governors one after another, *First,* That they had something to accuse him of that was dangerous either to private property or the public peace, — that they would undertake to prove him a robber, or a murderer, or a rebel against the Roman power, —that he had been in arms to head a sedition, — that if he were not that Egyptian who lately made an uproar, and commanded a party of cut-throats, as the chief captain supposed him to be, yet he was one of the same kidney. Such were the outcries against the primitive Christians, so loud, so fierce, that the standers-by, who judged of them by those outcries, could not but conclude them the worst of men; and to represent them so was the design of that clamour, as it was against our Saviour. *Secondly,* That they had something to accuse him of that was cognizable in the Roman courts, and which the governor was properly the judge of, as Gallio expected (*ch.* 18:14); otherwise it was absurd and ridiculous to trouble him with it, and really an affront to him.

[2.] But to his great surprise he finds the matter is neither so nor so; they had *certain questions against him,* instead of proofs and evidences against him. The worst they had to say against him was disputable whether it was a crime or no — moot-points, that would bear an endless debate, but had no tendency to fasten any guilt upon him, questions fitter for the schools than for the judgment-seat. And they were questions *of their own superstition*, so he calls their religion; or, rather, so he calls that part of their religion which Paul was charged with doing damage to. The Romans protected their religion according to their law, but not their superstition, nor the tradition of their elders. But the great question, it seems, was *concerning one Jesus that was dead, whom Paul affirmed to be alive*. Some think the superstition he speaks of was the Christian religion, which Paul preached, and that he had the same notion of it that the Athenians had, that it was the introducing of a new demon, even Jesus. See how slightly this Roman speaks of Christ, and of his death and resurrection, and of the great controversy between the Jews and the Christians whether he were the Messiah promised or no, and the great proof of his being the Messiah, his resurrection from the dead, as if it were no more than this, There was one Jesus that was dead, and Paul affirmed he was alive. In many causes issue is joined upon this question, whether such a person that has been long absent be living or dead, and proofs are brought on both sides; and Festus will have it thought that this is a matter of no more moment. Whereas this Jesus, whom he prides himself in being thus ignorant of, as if he were below his notice, is he that *was dead, and is alive, and lives for evermore, and has the keys of hell and of death*, Rev. 1:18. What Paul affirmed concerning Jesus, that he is alive, is a matter of such vast importance that if it be not true we are all undone.

(6.) That therefore he had proposed to Paul that the cause might be adjourned to the Jewish courts, as best able to take cognizance of an affair of this nature (*v.* 20): *"Because I doubted of such manner of questions,* and thought myself unfit to judge of things I did not understand, *I asked him whether he would go to Jerusalem*, appear before the great sanhedrim, *and there be judged of these matters."* He would not force him to it, but would be glad if Paul would consent to it, that he might not have his conscience burdened with a cause of this nature.

(7.) That Paul had chosen rather to remove his cause to Rome than to Jerusalem, as expecting fairer play from the emperor than from the priests: "He *appealed to be reserved to the hearing of Augustus* (*v.* 21), having no other way to stop proceedings here in this inferior court; and therefore I *commanded him to be kept* a close prisoner *till I might send him to Caesar*, for I did not see cause to refuse his appeal, but rather was pleased with it."

III. The bringing of him before Agrippa, that he might have the hearing of his cause.

1. The king desired it (*v.* 22): "I thank you for your account of him, but *I would also hear the man myself*." Agrippa knows more of this matter, of the cause and of the person, than Festus does; he has heard of Paul, and knows of what vast concern this question is, which Festus makes such a jest of, whether Jesus be alive or no. And nothing would oblige him more than to hear Paul. Many great men think it below them to take cognizance of the matters of religion, except they can hear them like themselves in the judgment-seat. Agrippa would not for all the world have gone to a meeting to hear Paul preach, any more than Herod to hear Jesus; and yet they are both glad to have them brought before them, only to satisfy their curiosity. Perhaps Agrippa desired to hear him himself, that he might be in a capacity to do him a kindness, and yet did him none, only put some credit upon him.

2. Festus granted it: *To-morrow thou shalt hear him*. There was a good providence in this, for the encouragement of Paul, who seemed buried alive in his imprisonment, and deprived of all opportunities of doing good. We know not of any of his epistles that bore date from his prison at Caesarea. What opportunity he had of doing good to his friends that visited him, and perhaps to a little congregation of them that visited him every Lord's-day, was but a low and narrow sphere of usefulness, so that he seemed to be thrown by as a *despised broken vessel, in which there was no pleasure;* but this gives him an opportunity of preaching Christ to a great congregation, and (which is more) to a congregation of great ones. Felix heard him in private concerning the faith of Christ. But Agrippa and Festus agree he shall be heard in public. And we have reason to think that his sermon in the next chapter, though it might not be so instrumental as some other of his sermons for the conversion of souls, redounded as much to the honour of Christ and Christianity as any sermon he ever preached in his life.

3. Great preparation was made for it (*v.* 23): *The next day there was a great appearance in the place of hearing,* Paul and his cause being much talked of, and the more for their being much talked against.

(1.) Agrippa and Bernice took this opportunity to show themselves in state, and to make a figure, and perhaps for that end desired the occasion, that they might see and be seen; for *they came with great pomp*, richly dressed, with gold and pearls, and costly array; with a great retinue of footmen in rich liveries, which made a splendid show, and dazzled the eyes of the gazing crowd. They came *meta pollēs phantasias — with great fancy*, so the word is. Note, Great pomp is but great fancy. It neither adds any read excellency, nor gains any real respect, but feeds a vain humour, which wise men would rather mortify than gratify. It is but a show, a dream, a fantastical thing (so the word signifies), superficial, and *it passeth away*. And the pomp of this appearance would put one for ever out of conceit with pomp, when the pomp which Agrippa and Bernice appeared in was, [1.] Stained by their lewd characters, and all the beauty of it sullied, and all virtuous people that knew them could not but contemn them in the midst of all this pomp as vile persons, Ps. 15:4. [2.] Out-shone by the real glory of the poor prisoner at the bar. What was the honour of their fine clothes, compared with that of his wisdom, and grace, and holiness, his courage and constancy in suffering for Christ! His bonds in so good a cause were more glorious than their chains of gold, and his guards than their equipage. Who would be fond of worldly pomp that here sees so bad a woman loaded with it and so good a man loaded with the reverse of it?

(2.) The chief captains and principal men of the city took this opportunity to pay their respects to Festus and to his guests. It answered the end of a ball at court, it brought the fine folks together in their fine clothes, and served for an entertainment. It is probable that Festus sent Paul notice of it overnight, to be ready for a hearing the next morning before Agrippa. And such confidence had Paul in the promise of Christ, that it should be *given him in that same hour what he should speak,* that he complained not of the short warning, nor was put into confusion by it. I am apt to think that those who were to appear in pomp perplexed themselves more with care about their clothes than Paul, who was to appear as a prisoner, did with care about his cause; for he knew whom he had believed, and who stood by him.

IV. The speech with which Festus introduced the cause, when the court, or rather the audience, was set, which is much to the same purport with the account he had just now given to Agrippa. 1. He addressed himself respectfully to the company: *"King Agrippa, and all men who are here present with us."* He speaks *to all the men — pantes andres*, as if he intended a tacit reflection upon Bernice, a woman, for appearing in a meeting of this nature; he does not refer any thing to her judgment nor desire her counsel; but, *"All you that are present that are men* (so the words are placed), I desire you to take cognizance of this matter." The word used is that which signifies men in distinction from women; what had Bernice to do here? 2. he represents the prisoner as one that the Jews had a very great spite against; not only the rulers, but *the multitude of them, both at Jerusalem and here at Caesarea,* cry out *that he ought not to live any longer,* for they think he has lived too long already, and if he live any longer it will be to do more mischief. They could not charge him with any capital crime, but they wanted to have him out of the way. 3. He confesses the prisoner's innocency; and it was much for the honour of Paul and his bonds that he had such a public acknowledgement as this from the mouth of his judge (*v.* 25): *I found that he had committed nothing worthy of death.* Upon a full hearing of the case, it appeared there was no evidence at all to support the indictment: and therefore, though he was inclinable enough to favour the prosecutors, yet his own conscience brought in Paul *not guilty*. And why did he not discharge him then, for he stood upon his deliverance? Why, truly, because he was so much clamoured against, and he feared the clamour would turn upon himself if he should release him. It is a pity but every man that has a conscience should have courage to act according to it. Or perhaps because there was so much smoke that he concluded there could not but be some fire, which would appear at last, and he would detain him a prisoner in expectation of it. 4. He acquaints them with the present state of the case, that the prisoner had appealed to the emperor himself (whereby he put ann honour upon his own cause, as

knowing it not unworthy the cognizance of the greatest of men), and that he had admitted his appeal: *I have determined to send him*. And thus the cause now stood. 5. He desires their assistance in examining the matter calmly and impartially, now that there was no danger of their being interrupted, as he had been with the noisiness and outrage of the prosecutors — that he might have at least such an insight into the cause as was necessary to his stating it to the emperor, *v.* 26, 27. (1.) He thought it *unreasonable to send a prisoner,* especially so far as Rome, *and not withal to signify the crimes laid against him,* that the matter might be prepared as much as possible, and put in a readiness for the emperor's determination; for he is supposed to be a man of great business, and therefore every affair must be laid before him in as little compass as possible. (2.) He could not as yet write *any thing certain* concerning Paul; so confused were the informations that were given in against him, and so inconsistent, that Festus could make nothing at all of them. He therefore desired Paul might thus be publicly examined, that he might be advised by them what to write. See what a great deal of trouble and vexation those were put to, and to what delay, nay, and to what hazard, in the administration of public justice, who live at such a distance from Rome, and yet were subject to the emperor of Rome. The same was this nation of ours put to (which is about as far distant from Rome the other way) when it was in ecclesiastical affairs subject to the pope of Rome, and appeals were upon all occasions made to his court; and the same mischiefs, and a thousand worse, would those bring upon us who would again entangle us in that yoke of bondage.

CHAPTER 26

We left Paul at the bar, and Festus, and Agrippa, and Bernice, and all the great men of the city of Caesarea, upon the bench, or about it, waiting to hear what he had to say for himself. Now in this chapter we have, I. The account he gives of himself, in answer to the calumnies of the Jews. And in this, 1. His humble address to king Agrippa, and the compliment he passed upon him (*v.* 1–3). 2. His account of his origin, and education, his profession as a Pharisee, and his adherence still to that which was then the main article of his creed, in distinction from the Sadducees, the "resurrection of the dead," however in rituals he had since departed from it (*v.* 3–8). 3. Of his zeal against the Christian religion, and the professors of it, in the beginning of his time (*v.* 9–11). 4. Of his miraculous conversion to the faith of Christ (*v.* 12–16). 5. Of the commission he received from heaven to preach the gospel to the Gentiles (*v.* 17, 18). 6. Of his proceedings pursuant to that commission, which had given this mighty offence to the Jews (*v.* 19–21). 7. Of the doctrine which he had made it his business to preach to the Gentiles, which was so far from destroying the law and the prophets that it showed the fulfilling of both (*v.* 22, 23). II. The remarks that were made upon his apology. 1. Festus thought he never heard a man talk so madly, and slighted him as crazed (*v.* 24). In answer to him, he denies the charge, and appeals to king Agrippa (*v.* 25–27). 2. King Agrippa, being more closely and particularly dealt with, thinks he never heard a man talk more rationally and convincingly, and owns himself almost his convert (*v.* 28), and Paul heartily wishes him so (*v.* 29). 3. They all agreed that he was an innocent man, that he ought to be set at liberty, and that it was a pity he was provoked to put a bar in his own door by appealing to Caesar (*v.* 30–32).

Verses 1–11

Agrippa was the most honourable person in the assembly, having the title of king bestowed upon him, though otherwise having only the power of other governors under the emperor, and, though not here superior, yet senior, to Festus; and therefore, Festus having opened the cause, Agrippa, as the mouth of the court, intimates to Paul a licence given him to *speak for himself, v.* 1. Paul was silent till he had this liberty allowed him; for those are not the most forward to speak that are best prepared to speak and speak best. This was a favour which the Jews would not allow him, or not without difficulty; but Agrippa freely gives it to him. And Paul's cause was so good that he desired no more than to have liberty to speak for himself; he needed no advocate, no Tertullus, to speak for him. Notice is taken of his gesture: He *stretched forth his hand*, as one that was under no consternation at all, but had perfect freedom and command of himself; it also intimates that he was in earnest, and expected their attention while he answered for himself. Observe, He did not insist upon his having appealed to Caesar as an excuse for being silent, did not say, "I will be examined no more till I come to the emperor himself;" but cheerfully embraced the opportunity of doing honour to the cause he suffered for. If we must be ready to give *a reason of the hope that is in us to every man that asketh us,* much more to every man in authority, 1 Pt. 3:15. Now in this former part of the speech,

I. Paul addressed himself with a very particular respect to Agrippa, *v.* 2, 3. He answered cheerfully before Felix, because he knew he had been *many years a judge to that nation, ch.* 24:10. But his opinion of Agrippa goes further. Observe, 1. Being accused of the Jews, and having many base things laid to his charge, he is glad he has an opportunity of clearing himself; so far is he from imagining that his being an apostle exempted him from the jurisdiction of the civil powers. Magistracy is an ordinance of God, which we have all benefit by, and therefore must all be subject to. 2. Since he is forced to answer for himself, he is glad it is before king Agrippa, who, being himself a proselyte to the Jewish religion, understood all matters relating to it better than the other Roman governors did: *I know thee to be expert in all customs and questions which are among the Jews.* It seems, Agrippa was a scholar, and had been particularly conversant in the Jewish learning, was expert in the customs of the Jewish religion, and knew the nature of them, and that they were not designed to be either universal or perpetual. He was expert also in the questions that arose upon those customs, in determining which the Jews themselves were not all of a mind. Agrippa was well versed in the scriptures of the Old-Testament, and therefore could make a better judgment upon the controversy between him and the Jews concerning Jesus being the Messiah than another could. It is an encouragement to a preacher to have those to speak to that are intelligent, and can discern things that differ. When Paul says, *Judge you what I say,* yet he *speaks as to wise men,* 1 Co. 10:15. 3. He therefore begs that he would *hear him patiently, makrothymōs — with long suffering.* Paul designs a long discourse, and begs that Agrippa will hear him out, and not be weary; he designs a plain discourse, and begs that he will hear him with mildness, and not be angry. Paul had some reason to fear that as Agrippa, being a Jew, was well versed in the Jewish customs, and therefore the more competent judge of his cause, so he was soured in some measure with the Jewish leaven, and therefore prejudiced against Paul as the apostle of the Gentiles; he therefore says this to sweeten him: *I beseech thee, hear me patiently.* Surely the least we can expect, when we preach the faith of Christ, is to be heard patiently.

II. He professes that though he was hated and branded as a apostate, yet he still adhered to all that good which he was first educated and trained up in; his religion was always built upon the *promise of God made unto the fathers;* and this he still built upon.

1. See here what his religion was in his youth: His *manner of life* was *well known, v.* 4, 5. He was not indeed born among his own nation, but he was bred among them at Jerusalem. Though he had of late years been conversant with the Gentiles (which had given great offence to the Jews), yet at his setting out in the world he was intimately acquainted with the Jewish nation, and entirely in their interests. His education was neither foreign nor obscure; it was among his own nation at Jerusalem, where religion and learning flourished. All the Jews knew it, all that could remember so long, for Paul made himself remarkable betimes. Those that *knew him from the beginning* could testify for him that he was a Pharisee, that he was not only of the Jewish religion, and an observer of all the ordinances of it, but that he was of the *most strict sect of that religion,* most nice and exact in observing the institutions of it himself, and most rigid and critical in imposing them upon others. He was not only called a Pharisee, but he *lived a Pharisee.* All that knew him knew very well that never any Pharisee conformed more punctually to the rules of his order than he did. Nay, and he was of the better sort of Pharisees; for he was brought up at the feet of Gamaliel, who was an eminent rabbi of the school of house of Hillel, which was in much greater reputation for religion than the school or house of Samai. Now if Paul was a Pharisee, and lived a Pharisee, (1.) Then he was a scholar, a man of learning, and not an ignorant, illiterate, mechanic; the Pharisees knew the law, and were well versed in it, and in the traditional expositions of it. It was a reproach to the other apostles that they had not had an academical education, but were bred fishermen, *ch.* 4:13. Therefore, that the unbelieving Jews might be left without excuse, here is an apostle raised up that had sat at the feet of their most eminent doctors. (2.) Then he was a moralist, a man of virtue, and not a rake or loose debauched young man. If he lived like a Pharisee, he was no drunkard nor fornicator; and, being a young Pharisee, we may hope he was no extortioner, nor had yet learned the arts which the crafty covetous old Pharisees had of devouring the houses of poor widows; but he was, *as touching the righteousness which is in the law, blameless.* He was not chargeable with any instance of open vice and profaneness; and therefore, as he could not be thought to have deserted his religion because he did not know it (for he was a learned man), so he could not be thought to have deserted it because he did not love it, or was disaffected to the obligations of it, for he was a virtuous man, and not inclined to any immorality. (3.) Then he was orthodox, sound in the faith, and not a deist or sceptic, or a man of corrupt principles that led to infidelity. He was a Pharisee, in opposition to a Sadducee; he received those books of the Old Testament which the Sadducees rejected, believed a world of spirits, the immortality of the soul, the resurrection of the body, and the rewards and punishments of the future state, all which the Sadducees denied. They could not say, He quitted his religion for want of a principle, or for want of a due regard to divine revelation; no, he always had a veneration for the ancient *promise made of God unto the fathers,* and built his hope upon it.

Now though Paul knew very well that all this would not justify him before God, nor make a righteousness for him yet he knew it was for his reputation among the Jews, and an argument *ad hominem — such as Agrippa would feel,* that he was not such a man as they represented him to be. Though he counted it but loss that he might win Christ, yet he mentioned it when it might serve to honour Christ. He knew very well that all this while he was a stranger to the spiritual nature of the divine law, and to heart-religion, and that except his righteousness exceeded this he should never go to heaven; yet he reflects upon it with some satisfaction that he had not been before his conversion an atheistical, profane, vicious man, but, according to the light he had, had *lived in all good conscience before God.*

2. See here what his religion is. He has not indeed such a zeal for the ceremonial law as he had in his youth. The sacrifices and offerings appointed by that, he thinks, are superseded by the great sacrifice which they typified; ceremonial pollutions and purifications from them he makes no conscience of, and thinks the Levitical priesthood is honourably swallowed up in the priesthood of Christ; but for the main principles of his religion he is as zealous for them as ever, and more so, and resolves to live and die by them.

(1.) His religion is built upon the *promise made of God unto the fathers.* It is built upon divine revelation, which he receives and believes, and ventures his soul upon; it is built upon divine grace, and that grace manifested and conveyed by promise. The promise of God is the guide and ground of his religion, the promise *made to the fathers,* which was more ancient than the ceremonial law, *that covenant which was confirmed before of God in Christ, and which the law, that was not till four hundred and thirty years after, could not disannul,* Gal. 3:17. Christ and heaven are the two great doctrines of the gospel — that *God has given to us eternal life, and this life is in his Son.* Now these two are the matter of the *promise made unto the fathers.* It may look back as far as the promise made to father Adam, concerning the seed of the woman, and those discoveries of a future state which the first patriarchs acted faith upon, and were saved by that faith; but it respects chiefly the promise made to father Abraham, that *in his seed all the families of the earth should be blessed,* and that *God would be a God to him, and to his seed after him:* the former meaning Christ, the latter heaven; for, if God had not *prepared for them a city,* he would have been ashamed to have called himself *their God.* Heb. 11:16.

(2.) His religion consists in the hopes of this promise. He places it not, as they did, in meats and drinks, and the observance of carnal ordinances (God had often shown what little account he made of them), but in a believing dependence upon God's grace in the covenant, and upon the promise, which was the great charter by which the church was first incorporated. [1.] He had hope in Christ as the promised seed; he hoped to be blessed in him, to receive the blessing of God and to be truly blessed. [2.] He had hopes of heaven; this is expressly meant, as appears by comparing *ch.* 24:15, *That there shall be a resurrection of the dead.* Paul had no confidence in the flesh, but in Christ; no expectation at all of great things in this world, but of greater things in the other world than any this world can pretend to; he had his eye upon a future state.

(3.) Herein he concurred with all the pious Jews; his faith was not only according to the scripture, but according to the testimony of the church, which was a support to it. Though they set him up as a mark, he was not singular: *"Our twelve tribes,* the body of the Jewish church, *instantly serving God day and night,* hope to *come to this promise,* that is, to the good promised." The people of Israel are called *the twelve tribes,* because so they were at first; and, though we read not of the return of the ten tribes in a body, yet we have reason to think many particular persons, more or less of every tribe, returned to their own land; perhaps, by degrees, the greater part of those that were carried away. Christ speaks of the *twelve tribes,* Mt. 19:28. Anna was of the tribe of Asher, Lu. 2:36. James directs his epistle to the *twelve tribes scattered abroad,* Jam. 1:1. "Our twelve tribes, which make up the body of our nation, to which I and others belong. Now all the Israelites profess to believe in this promise, both of Christ and heaven, and hope to come to the benefits of them. They all hope for a Messiah to come, and we that are Christians hope in a Messiah already come; so that we all agree to build upon the same promise. They look for the *resurrection of the dead* and *the life of the world to come,* and this is what I look for. Why should I be looked upon as advancing something dangerous and heterodox, or as an apostate from the faith and worship of the Jewish church, when I agree with them in this fundamental article? I hope to come to the same heaven at last that they hope to come to; and, if we expect to meet so happily in our end, why should we fall out so unhappily by the way?" Nay, the Jewish church not only hoped to come to this promise, but, in the hope of it, they *instantly served God day and night.* The temple-service, which consisted in a continual course of religious duties, morning and evening, day and night, from the beginning of the year to the end of it, and was kept up by the priests and Levites, and the *stationary men,* as they called them, who continually attended there to lay their hands upon the public sacrifices, as the representatives of all the twelve tribes, this service was kept up in the profession of faith in the promise of eternal life, and, in expectation of it, *Paul instantly serves God day and night* in the gospel of his Son; the twelve tribes by their representatives do so in the law of Moses, but he and they do it in hope of the same promise: "Therefore they ought not to look upon me as a deserter from their church, so long as I hold by the same promise that they hold by." Much more should Christians, who hope in the same Jesus, for the same heaven, though differing in the modes and ceremonies of worship, hope the best one of another, and live together in holy love. Or it may be meant of particular persons who continued in the communion of the Jewish church, and were very devout in their way, serving God with great intenseness, and a close application of mind, and constant in it, *night and day,* as Anna, who *departed not from the temple, but served God* (it is the same word here used) *in fastings and prayers night and day,* Lu. 2:37. "In this way they hope to come to the promise, and I hope they will." Note, Those only can upon good grounds hope for eternal life that are diligent and constant in the service of God; and the prospect of that eternal life should engage us to diligence and constancy in all religious exercises. We should go on with our work with heaven in our eye. And of those that *instantly serve God day and night,* though not in our way, we ought to judge charitably.

(4.) This was what he was now suffering for — for preaching that doctrine which they themselves, if they did but understand themselves aright, must own: *I am judged for the hope of the promise made unto the fathers.* He stuck to the promise, against the ceremonial law, while his persecutors stuck to the ceremonial law, against the promise: "It is *for this hope's sake, king Agrippa, that I am accused of the Jews* — because I do that which I think myself obliged to do by the hope of this promise." It is common for men to hate and persecute the power of that religion in others which yet they pride themselves in the form of. Paul's hope was what *they themselves also allowed* (*ch.* 24:15), and yet they were thus enraged against him for practising according to that hope. But it was his honour that when he suffered as a Christian he suffered *for the hope of Israel, ch.* 28:20.

(5.) This was what he would persuade all that heard him cordially to embrace (*v.* 8): *Why should it be thought a thing incredible with you that God should raise the dead?* This seems to come in somewhat abruptly; but it is probable Paul said much more than is here recorded, and that he explained the *promise made to the fathers* to be the promise of the resurrection and eternal life, and proved that he was in the right way of pursuing his hope of that happiness because he believed in Christ who had *risen from the dead,* which was a pledge and earnest of that resurrection which the fathers hoped for. Paul is therefore earnest to *know the power of Christ's resurrection,* that by it he might *attain to the resurrection of the dead;* see Phil. 3:10, 11. Now many of his hearers were Gentiles, most of them perhaps, Festus particularly, and we may suppose, when they heard him speak so much of Christ's resurrection, and of the resurrection from the dead, which the twelve tribes hoped for, that they mocked, as the Athenians did, began to smile at it, and whispered to one another what an absurd thing it was, which occasioned Paul thus to reason with them. *What! is it thought incredible with you that God should raise the dead?* So it may be read. *If it be marvellous in your eyes, should it be marvellous in mine eyes, saith the Lord of hosts?* Zec. 8:6. If it be above the power of nature, yet it is not above the power of the God of nature. Note, There is no reason why we should think it at all incredible that God should raise the dead. We are not required to believe any thing that is incredible, any thing that implies a contradiction. There are motives of credibility sufficient to carry us through all the doctrines of the Christian religion, and this particularly of the resurrection of the dead. Has not God an infinite almighty power, to which nothing is impossible? Did not he make the world at first out of nothing, with a word's speaking? Did he not form our bodies, form them out of the clay, and breathe into us the breath of life at first? and cannot the same power form them again out of their own clay, and put life into them again? Do we not see a kind of resurrection in nature, at the return of every spring? Has the sun such a force to raise dead plants, and should it seem incredible to us that God should raise dead bodies?

III. He acknowledges that while he continued a Pharisee he was a bitter enemy to Christians and Christianity, and thought he ought to be so, and continued so to the moment that Christ wrought that wonderful change in him. This he mentions,

1. To show that his becoming a Christian and a preacher was not the product and result of any previous disposition or inclination that way, or any gradual advance of thought in favour of the Christian doctrine; he did not reason himself into Christianity by a chain of arguments, but was brought into the highest degree of an assurance of it, immediately from the highest degree of prejudice against it, by which it appeared that he was made a Christian and a preacher by a supernatural power; so that his conversion in such a miraculous way was not only to himself, but to others also, a convincing proof of the truth of Christianity.

2. Perhaps he designs it for such an excuse of his persecutors as Christ made for his, when he said, *They know not what they do.* Paul himself once thought he did what he ought to do when he persecuted the disciples of Christ, and he charitably thinks they laboured under the like mistake. Observe,

(1.) What a fool he was in his opinion (*v.* 9): He *thought with himself that he ought to do many things,* every thing that lay in his power, *contrary to the name of Jesus of Nazareth,* contrary to his doctrine, his honour, his interest. That name did not harm, yet, because it agreed not with the notion he had of the kingdom of the Messiah, he was for doing all he could against it. He thought he did God good service in persecuting those who called on the name of Jesus Christ. Note, It is possible for those to be confident they are in the right who yet are evidently in the wrong; and for those to think they are doing their duty who are wilfully persisting in the greatest sin. Those that hated their brethren, and cast them out, said, *Let the Lord be glorified,* Isa. 66:5. Under colour and pretext of religion, the most barbarous and inhuman villanies have been not only justified, but sanctified and magnified, Jn. 16:2.

(2.) What a fury he was in his practice, *v.* 10, 11. There is not a more violent principle in the world than conscience misinformed. When Paul thought it his duty to do all he could against the name of Christ, he spared no pains nor cost in it. He gives an account of what he did of that kind, and aggravates it as one that was truly penitent for it: *I was a blasphemer, a persecutor,* 1 Tim. 1:13. [1.] He filled the jails with Christians, as if they had been the worst of criminals, designing hereby not only to terrify them, but to make them odious to the people. He was *the devil that cast some of them into prison* (Rev. 2:10), took them into custody, in order to their being prosecuted. *Many of the saints did I shut up in prison* (*ch.* 26:10), *both men and women, ch.* 8:3. [2.] He made himself the tool of the chief priests. Herein from them he *received authority,* as an inferior officer, to put their laws in execution, and proud enough he was to be a man in authority for such a purpose. [3.] He was very officious to vote, unasked for, the putting of Christians to death, particularly Stephen, to whose death Saul was consenting (*ch.* 8:1), and so made himself *particeps criminis — partaker of the crime.* Perhaps he was, for his great zeal, though young, made a member of the sanhedrim, and there voted for the condemning of Christians to die; or, after they were condemned, he justified what was done, and commended it, and so made himself guilty *ex post facto — after the deed was committed,* as if he had been a judge or jury-man. [4.] He brought them under punishments of an inferior nature, *in the synagogues,* where they were *scourged* as transgressors of the rules of the synagogue. He had a hand in the punishing of many; nay, it should seem the same persons were by his means *often punished,* as he himself was five times, 2 Co. 11:24. [5.] He not only punished them for their religion, but, taking a pride in triumphing over men's consciences, he forced them to abjure their religion, by putting them to the torture: *"I compelled them to blaspheme* Christ, and to say he was a deceiver and they were deceived in him — compelled them to deny their Master, and renounce their obligations to him." Nothing will lie heavier upon persecutors than forcing men's consciences, how much soever they may now triumph in the proselytes they have made by their violences. [6.] His rage swelled so against Christians and Christianity that Jerusalem itself was too narrow a stage for it to act upon, but, being *exceedingly mad against them, he persecuted them even to strange cities.* He was mad at them, to see how much they had to say for themselves, notwithstanding all he did against them, mad to see them multiply the more for their being afflicted. He was *exceedingly mad;* the stream of his fury would admit no banks, no bounds, but he was as much a terror to himself as he was to them, so great was his vexation within himself that he could not prevail, as well as his indignation against them. Persecutors are mad men, and some of them *exceedingly mad.* Paul was mad to see that those in other cities were not so outrageous against the Christians, and therefore made himself busy where he had no business, and persecuted the Christians even in strange cities. There is not a more restless principle than malice, especially that which pretends conscience.

This was Paul's character, and this his manner of life in the beginning of his time; and therefore he could not be presumed to be a Christian by education or custom, or to be drawn in by hope of preferment, for all imaginable external objections lay against his being a Christian.

Verses 12–23

All who believe a God, and have a reverence for his sovereignty, must acknowledge that those who speak and act by his direction, and by warrant from him, are not to be opposed; for that *is fighting against God.* Now Paul here, by a plain and faithful narrative of matters of fact, makes it out to this august assembly that he had an immediate call from heaven to preach the gospel of Christ to the Gentile world, which was the thing that exasperated the Jews against him. He here shows,

I. That he was made a Christian by a divine power, notwithstanding all his prejudices against that way. He was brought into it on a sudden by the hand of heaven; not compelled to confess Christ by outward force, as he had compelled others to blaspheme him, but by a divine and spiritual energy, by a revelation of Christ from above, both to him and in him: and this when he was in the full career of his sin, going to Damascus, to suppress Christianity by persecuting the Christians there, as hot as ever in the cause, his persecuting fury not in the least spent nor tired, nor was he tempted to give it up by the failing of his friends, for he had at this time as ample an *authority and commission from the chief priests* to persecute Christianity as ever he had, when he was obliged by a superior power to give up that, and accept another commission to preach up Christianity. Two things bring about this surprising change, a vision from heaven and a voice from heaven, which conveyed the knowledge of Christ to him by the two learning senses of seeing and hearing.

1. He saw a heavenly vision, the circumstances of which were such that it could not be a *delusion — deciptio visus,* but it was without doubt a divine appearance. (1.) He *saw a great light, a light from heaven,* such as could not be produced by any art, for it was not in the night, but *at mid day;* it was not in a house where tricks might have been played with him, but it was *in the way,* in the open air; it was such a light as was *above the brightness of the sun,* outshone and eclipsed that (Isa. 24:23), and this could not be the product of Paul's own fancy, for it *shone round about those that journeyed with him:* they were all sensible of their being surrounded with this inundation of light, which made the sun itself to be in their eyes a less light. The force and power of this light appeared in the effects of it; they all fell to the earth upon the sight of it, such a mighty consternation did it put them into; this light was lightning for its force, yet did not pass away as lightning, but continued to shine round about them. In Old-Testament times God commonly manifested himself in the thick darkness, and made that his pavilion, 2 Chr. 6:1. He spoke to Abraham in a great darkness (Gen. 15:12), for that was a dispensation of darkness; but now that *life and immortality were brought to light by the gospel* Christ appeared in a great light. In the creation of grace, as of the world, the first thing created is light, 2 Co. 4:6. (2.) Christ himself appeared to him (*v.* 16): *I have appeared to thee for this purpose.* Christ was in this light, though those that travelled with Paul saw the light only, and not Christ in the light. It is not every knowledge that will serve to make us Christians, but it must be *the knowledge of Christ.*

2. He heard a heavenly voice, an articulate one, *speaking to him;* it is here said to be *in the Hebrew tongue* (which was not taken notice of before), his native language, the language of his religion, to intimate to him that though he must be sent among the Gentiles, yet he must not forget that he was a Hebrew, nor make himself a stranger to the Hebrew language. In what Christ said to him we may observe, (1.) That he called him by his name, and repeated it *(Saul, Saul),* which would surprise and startle him; and the more because he was now in a strange place, where he thought nobody knew him. (2.) That he convinced him of sin, of that great sin which he was now in the commission of, the sin of persecuting the Christians, and showed him the absurdity of it. (3.) That he interested himself in the sufferings of his followers: *Thou persecutest me* (*v.* 14), and again, It is *Jesus whom thou persecutest, v.* 15. Little did Paul think, when he was trampling upon those that he looked upon as the burdens and blemishes of this earth, that he was insulting one that was so much the glory of heaven. (4.) That he checked him for his wilful resistance of those convictions: *It is hard for thee to kick against the pricks,* or goads, *as a bullock unaccustomed to the yoke.* Paul's spirit at first perhaps began to rise, but he is told it is at his peril, and then he yields. Or, it was spoken by way of caution: "Take heed lest thou resist these convictions, for they are designed to affect thee, not to affront thee." (5.) That, upon his enquiry, Christ made himself known to him. Paul asked (*v.* 15), *"Who art thou, Lord?* Let me know who it is that speaks to me from heaven, that I may answer him accordingly?" And he said, *"I am Jesus;* he whom thou hast despised, and hated, and vilified; I bear that name which thou hast made so odious, and the naming of it criminal." Paul thought Jesus was buried in the earth, and, though stolen out of his own sepulchre, yet laid in some other. All the Jews were taught to say so, and therefore he is amazed to hear him speak from heaven, to see him surrounded with all this glory whom he had loaded with all possible ignominy. This convinced him that the doctrine of Jesus was divine and heavenly, and not only not to be opposed, but to be cordially embraced: *That Jesus is the Messiah,* for he has not only *risen from the dead,* but he has *received from God the Father honour and glory;* and this is enough to make him a Christian immediately, to quit the society of the persecutors, whom the Lord from heaven thus appears against, and to join himself with the society of the persecuted, whom the Lord from heaven thus appears for.

II. That he was made a minister by a divine authority: *That the same Jesus that appeared to him in that glorious light* ordered him *to go and preach the gospel to the Gentiles;* he did not run without sending, nor was he sent by men like himself, but by him whom the Father sent, Jn. 20:21. What is said of his being an apostle is here joined immediately to that which was said to him by the way, but it appears by *ch.* 9:15, and 22:15, 17, etc., that it was spoken to him afterwards; but he puts the two together for brevity-sake: *Rise, and stand upon thy feet.* Those whom Christ, by the light of his gospel, casts down in humiliation for sin, shall find that it is in order to their rising and standing upon their feet, in spiritual grace, strength, and comfort. If Christ has torn, it is that he may heal; if he has cast down, it is that he may raise up. *Rise then, and shake thyself from the dust* (Isa. 52:2), help thyself, and Christ shall help thee. He must stand up, for Christ shall help thee. He must stand up, for Christ has work for him to do — has an errand, and a very great errand, to send him upon: *I have appeared to thee to make thee a minister.* Christ has the making of his own ministers; they have both their qualifications and their commissions from him. Paul thanks Christ Jesus who put him into the ministry, 1 Tim. 1:12. Christ appeared to him to make him a minister. One way or other, Christ will manifest himself to all those whom he makes his ministers; for how can those preach him who do not know him? And how can those know him to whom he does not by his spirit make himself known? Observe,

1. The office to which Paul is appointed: he is made a minister, to attend on Christ, and act for him, as a witness — to give evidence in his cause, and attest the truth of his doctrine. He must testify *the gospel of the grace of God;* Christ appeared to him that he might appear for Christ before men.

2. The matter of Paul's testimony: he must give an account to the world, (1.) *Of the things which he had seen,* now at this time, must tell people of Christ's manifesting himself to him by the way, and what he said to him. He saw these things that he might publish them, and he did take all occasions to publish them, as here, and before, *ch.* 22. (2.) *Of those things in which he would appear to him.* Christ now settled a correspondence with Paul, which he designed afterwards to keep up, and only told him now that he should hear further from him. Paul at first had but confused notions of the gospel, till Christ appeared to him and gave him fuller instructions. *The gospel he preached he received from Christ* immediately (Gal. 1:12); but he received it gradually, some at one time and some at another, as there was occasion. Christ often appeared to Paul, oftener, it is likely, than is recorded, and still taught him, *that he might still teach the people knowledge.*

3. The spiritual protection he was taken under, while he was thus employed as Christ's witness: all the powers of darkness could not prevail against him till he had finished his testimony (*v.* 17), *delivering thee from the people of the Jews and from the Gentiles.* Note, Christ's witnesses are under his special care, and, though they may fall into the hands of the enemies, yet he will take care to deliver them out of their hands, and he knows how to do it. Christ had shown Paul at this time *what great things he must suffer* (*ch.* 9:16), and yet tells him here he will *deliver him from the people.* Note, Great sufferings are reconcilable to the promise of the deliverance of God's people, for it is not promised that they shall be kept from trouble, but kept through it; and sometimes God delivers them into the hands of their persecutors that he may have the honour of delivering them out of their hands.

4. The special commission given him to go among the Gentiles, and the errand upon which he is sent to them; it was some years after Paul's conversion before he was *sent to the Gentiles,* or (for aught that appears) knew any thing of his being designed for that purpose (see *ch.* 22:21); but at length he is ordered to steer his course that way.

(1.) There is great work to be done among the Gentiles, and Paul must be instrumental in doing it. Two things must be done, which their case calls for the doing of: — [1.] A world that sits in darkness must be enlightened; those must be brought to *know the things that belong to their everlasting peace* who are yet ignorant of them, to know God as their end, and Christ as their way, who as yet know nothing of either. He is *sent to open their eyes, and to turn them from darkness to light.* His preaching shall not only make known to them those things which they had not before heard of, but shall be the vehicle of that divine grace and power by which their understandings shall be enlightened to receive those things, and bid them welcome. Thus he shall open their eyes, which before were shut against the light, and they shall be willing to understand themselves, their own case and interest. Christ opens the heart by opening the eyes, does not lead men blindfold, but gives them to see their own way. He is sent not only to open their eyes for the present, but to keep them open, *to turn them from darkness to light,* that is, from following false and blind guides, their oracles, divinations, and superstitious usages, received by tradition from their fathers, and the corrupt notions and ideas they had of their gods, to follow a divine revelation of unquestionable certainty and truth. This was turning them from darkness to light, from the ways of darkness to those on which the light shines. The great design of the gospel is to instruct the ignorant, and to rectify the mistakes of those who are in error, that things may be set and seen in a true light. [2.] A world that lies in wickedness, in the wicked one, must be sanctified and reformed; it is not enough for them to have their eyes opened, they must have their hearts renewed; not enough to be turned from darkness to light, but they must be turned from the power of Satan unto God, which will follow of course; for Satan rules by the power of darkness, and God by the convincing evidence of light. Sinners are under the power of Satan; idolaters were so in a special manner, they paid their homage to devils. All sinners are under the influence of his temptations, yield themselves captives to him, are at his beck; converting grace turns them from under the dominion of Satan, and brings them into subjection to God, to conform to the rules of his word and comply with the dictates and directions of his Spirit, *translates them out of the kingdom of darkness into the kingdom of his dear Son.* When gracious dispositions are strong in the soul (as corrupt and sinful dispositions had been), it is then turned from the power of Satan unto God.

(2.) There is a great happiness designed for the Gentiles by this work — *that they may receive forgiveness of sins, and inheritance among those who are sanctified;* they are turned from the darkness of sin to the light of holiness, from the slavery of Satan to the service of God; not that God may be a gainer by them, but that they may be gainers by him. [1.] That they may be restored to his favour, which by sin they have forfeited and thrown themselves out of: *That they may receive forgiveness of sins.* They are delivered from the dominion of sin, that they may be saved from that death which is the wages of sin. Not that they may merit forgiveness as a debt of reward, but that they may receive it as a free gift, that they may be qualified to receive the comfort of it. They are persuaded to lay down their arms, and return to their allegiance, that they may have the benefit of the act of indemnity, and may plead it in arrest of the judgment to be given against them. [2.] That they may be happy in the fruition of him; not only that they may have their sins pardoned, but *that they may have an inheritance among those who are sanctified by faith that is in me.* Note, *First,* Heaven is an inheritance, it descends to all the children of God; for, *if children, then heirs. That they may have, klēron — a lot* (so it might be read), alluding to the inheritances of Canaan, which were appointed by lot, and that also is the act of God, *the disposal thereof is of the Lord. That they may have a right,* so some read it; not by merit, but purely by grace. *Secondly,* All that are effectually turned from sin to God are not only pardoned, but preferred — have not only their attainder reversed, but a patent of honour given to them, and a grant of a rich inheritance. And the forgiveness of sins makes way for this inheritance, by taking that out of the way which alone hindered. *Thirdly,* All that shall be saved hereafter are sanctified now; those that have the heavenly inheritance must have it in this way, they must be prepared and made meet for it. None can be happy that are not holy; nor shall any be saints in heaven that are not first saints on earth. *Fourthly,* We need no more to make us happy than to have our lot among those that are sanctified, to fare as they fare; this is having our lot among the chosen, for they are chosen to salvation through sanctification. Those who are sanctified shall be glorified. Let us therefore now cast in our lot among them, by coming into the communion of saints, and be willing to take our lot with them, and share with them in their afflictions, which (how grievous soever) our lot with them in the inheritance will abundantly make amends for. *Fifthly,* We are sanctified and saved by faith in Christ. Some refer it to the word next before, *sanctified by faith,* for faith purifies the heart, and applies to the soul those precious promises, and subjects the soul to the influence of that grace, by which we partake of a divine nature. Others refer it to the receiving of both pardon and the inheritance; it is by faith accepting the grant: it comes all to one; for it is by faith that we are justified, sanctified, and glorified. *By faith, tē eis eme — that faith which is in me;* it is emphatically expressed. That faith which not only receives divine revelation in general, but which in a particular manner fastens upon Jesus Christ and his mediation, by which we rely upon Christ as *the Lord our righteousness,* and resign ourselves to him as the Lord our ruler. This is that by which we receive *the remission of sins, the gift of the Holy Ghost, and eternal life.*

III. That he had discharged his ministry, pursuant to his commission, by divine aid, and under divine direction and protection. God, who called him to be an apostle, owned him in his apostolical work, and carried him on in it with enlargement and success.

1. God gave him a heart to comply with the call (*v.* 19): *I was not disobedient to the heavenly vision,* for any one would say he ought to be obedient to it. Heavenly visions have a commanding power over earthly counsels, and it is at our peril if we be disobedient to them; yet if Paul had conferred with flesh and blood, and been swayed by his secular interest, he would have done as Jonah did, gone any where rather than upon this errand; but God *opened his ear, and he was not rebellious.* He accepted the commission, and, having with it received his instructions, he applied himself to act accordingly.

2. God enabled him to go through a great deal of work, though in it he grappled with a great deal of difficulty, *v.* 20. He applied himself to the preaching of the gospel with all vigour. (1.) He began at Damascus, where he was converted, for he resolved to lose no time, *ch.* 9:20. (2.) When he came to Jerusalem, where he had his education, he there witnessed for Christ, where he had most furiously set himself against him, *ch.* 9:29. (3.) He preached *throughout all the coasts of Judea,* in the country towns and villages, as Christ had done; he made the first offer of the gospel to the Jews, as Christ had appointed, and did not leave them till they had wilfully thrust the gospel from them; and laid out himself for the good of their souls, labouring more abundantly than any of the apostles, nay perhaps then all put together.

3. His preaching was all practical. He did not go about to fill people's heads with airy notions, did not amuse them with nice speculations, nor set them together by the ears with matters of doubtful disputation, but he showed them, declared it, demonstrated it, that they ought, (1.) *To repent of their sins,* to be sorry for them and to confess them, and enter into covenant against them; they ought to *bethink themselves,* so the word *metanoein* properly signifies; they ought to change their mind and change their way, and undo what they had done amiss. (2.) *To turn to God.* They must not only conceive an antipathy to sin, but they must come into a conformity to God — must not only turn from that which is evil, but turn to that which is good; they must turn to God, in love and affection, and return to God in duty and obedience, and turn and return from the world and the flesh; this is that which is required from the whole revolted degenerate race of mankind, both Jews and Gentiles; *epistrephein epi ton Theon — to turn back to God, even to him:* to turn to him as our chief good and highest end, as our ruler and portion, turn our eye to him, turn our heart to him, and turn our feet unto his testimonies. (3.) *To do works meet for repentance.* This was what John preached, who was the first gospel preacher, Mt. 3:8. Those that profess repentance must practise it, must live a life of repentance, must in every thing carry it as becomes penitents. It is not enough to speak penitent words, but we must do works agreeable to those words. As true faith, so true repentance, will work. Now what fault could be found with such preaching as this? Had it not a direct tendency to reform the world, and to redress its grievances, and to revive natural religion?

4. The Jews had no quarrel with him but upon this account, that he did all he could to persuade people to be religious, and to bring them to God by bringing them to Christ (*v.* 21): It was for these causes, and no other, *that the Jews caught me in the temple, and went about to kill me;* and let any one judge whether these were crimes worthy of death or of bonds. He suffered ill, not only for doing well himself, but for doing good to others. They attempted to kill him; it was his precious life that they hunted for, and hated, because it was a useful life; they caught him in the temple worshipping God, and there they set upon him, as if the better place the better deed

5. He had no help but from heaven; supported and carried on by that, he went on in this great work (*v.* 22): *"Having therefore obtained help of God, I continue unto this day; hestēka — I have stood,* my life has been preserved, and my work continued; I have stood my ground, and have not been beaten off; I have stood to what I said, and have not been afraid nor ashamed to persist in it." It was now above twenty years since Paul was converted, and all that time he had been

very busy preaching the gospel in the midst of hazards; and what was it that bore him up? Not any strength of his own resolutions, but *having obtained help of God;* for therefore, because the work was so great and he had so much opposition, he could not otherwise have gone on in it, but by help obtained of God. Note, Those who are employed in work for God shall obtain help from God; for he will not be wanting in necessary assistances to his servants. And our continuance to this day must be attributed to help obtained of God; we had sunk, if he had not borne us up — had fallen off, if he had not carried us on; and it must be acknowledged with thankfulness to his praise. Paul mentions it as an evidence that he had his commission from God that from him he had ability to execute it. The preachers of the gospel could never have done, and suffered, and prospered, as they did, if they had not had immediate help from heaven, which they would not have had if it had not been the cause of God that they were now pleading.

6. He preached no doctrine but what agreed with the scriptures of the Old Testament: He *witnessed both to small and great,* to young and old, rich and poor, learned and unlearned, obscure and illustrious, all being concerned in it. It was an evidence of the condescending grace of the gospel that it was witnessed to the meanest, and the poor were welcome to the knowledge of it; and of the incontestable truth and power of it that it was neither afraid nor ashamed to show itself to the greatest. The enemies of Paul objected against him that he preached something more than *that men should repent, and turn to God, and do works meet for repentance.* These indeed were but what the prophets of the old Testament had preached; but, besides these, he had preached Christ, and his death, and his resurrection, and this was what they quarrelled with him for, as appears by *ch.* 25:19, *that he affirmed Jesus to be alive:* "And so I did," says Paul, "and so I do, but therein also I say *no other than that which Moses and the prophets said should come;* and what greater honour can be done to them than to show that what they foretold is accomplished, and in the appointed season too — that what they said should come is come, and at the time they prefixed?" Three things they prophesied, and Paul preached: — (1.) *That Christ should suffer,* that the Messiah should be a *sufferer — pathētos;* not only a man, and capable of suffering, but that, as Messiah, he should be appointed to sufferings; that his ignominious death should be not only consistent with, but pursuant of, his undertaking. The cross of Christ was a stumbling-block to the Jews, and Paul's preaching it was the great thing that exasperated them; but Paul stands to it that, in preaching that, he preached the fulfilling of the Old-Testament predictions, and therefore they ought not only not to be offended at what he preached, but to embrace it, and subscribe to it. (2.) *That he should be the first that should rise from the dead;* not the first in time, but the first in influence — *that he should be the chief of the resurrection, the head, or principal one, prōtos ex anastaseōs,* in the same sense that he is called *the first-begotten from the dead* (Rev. 1:5), and *the first-born from the dead,* Col. 1:18. He opened the womb of the grave, as the first-born are said to do, and made way for our resurrection; and he is said *to be the first-fruits of those that slept* (1 Co. 15:20), for he sanctified the harvest. He was the first that rose from the dead to die no more; and, to show that the resurrection of all believers is in virtue of his, just when he arose *many dead bodies of saints arose, and went into the holy city,* Mt. 27:52, 53. (3.) *That he should show light unto the people, and to the Gentiles,* to the people of the Jews in the first place, for he was to be *the glory of his people Israel.* To them he showed light by himself, and then to the Gentiles by the ministry of his apostles, for he was *to be a light to enlighten those who sat in darkness.* In this Paul refers to his commission (*v.* 18), *To turn them from darkness to light.* He rose from the dead on purpose that he might show light to the people, that he might give a convincing proof of the truth of his doctrine, and might send it with so much the greater power, both among Jews and Gentiles. This also was foretold by the Old-Testament prophets, *that the Gentiles should be brought to the knowledge of God by the Messiah;* and what was there in all this that the Jews could justly be displeased at?

Verses 24–32

We have reason to think that Paul had a great deal more to say in defence of the gospel he preached, and for the honour of it, and to recommend it to the good opinion of this noble audience; he had just fallen upon that which was the life of the cause — the death and resurrection of Jesus Christ, and here he is in his element; now he warms more than before, his mouth is opened towards them, his heart is enlarged. Lead him but to this subject, and let him have leave to go on, and he will never know when to conclude; for the power of Christ's death, and the fellowship of his sufferings, are with him inexhaustible subjects. It was a thousand pities then that he should be interrupted, as he is here, and that, being permitted to speak for himself (*v.* 1), he should not be permitted to say all he designed. But it was a hardship often put upon him, and is a disappointment to us too, who read his discourse with so much pleasure. But there is no remedy, the court thinks it is time to proceed to give in their judgment upon his case.

I. Festus, the Roman governor, is of opinion that the poor man is crazed, and that Bedlam is the fittest place for him. he is convinced that he is no criminal, no bad man, that should be punished, but he takes him to be a lunatic, a distracted man, that should be pitied, but at the same time should not be heeded, nor a word he says regarded; and thus he thinks he has found out an expedient to excuse himself both from condemning Paul as a prisoner and from believing him as a preacher; for, if he be not *compos mentis — in his senses,* he is not to be either condemned or credited. Now here observe,

1. What it was that Festus said of him (*v.* 24): *He said with a loud voice,* did not whisper it to those that sat next him; if so, it had been the more excusable, but (without consulting Agrippa, to whose judgment he had seemed to pay profound deference, *ch.* 25:26), *said aloud,* that he might oblige Paul to break off his discourse, and might divert the auditors from attending to it *"Paul, thou art beside thyself,* thou talkest like a madman, like one with a heated brain, that knowest not what thou sayest;" yet he does not suppose that a guilty conscience had disturbed his reason, nor that his sufferings, and the rage of his enemies against him, had given any shock to it; but he puts the most candid construction that could be upon his delirium: *Much learning hath made thee mad,* thou hast cracked thy brains with studying. This he speaks, not so much in anger, as in scorn and contempt. He did not understand what Paul said; it was above his capacity, it was all a riddle to him, and therefore he imputes it all to a heated imagination. *Si non vis intelligi, debes negligi — If thou art not willing to be understood, thou oughtest to be neglected.* (1.) He owns Paul to be a scholar, and a man of learning, because he could so readily refer to what Moses and the prophets wrote, books that he was a stranger to; and even this is turned to his reproach. The apostles, who were fishermen, were despised because they had no learning; Paul, who was a university-man, and bred a Pharisee, is despised as having too much learning, more than did him good. Thus the enemies of Christ's ministers will always have something or other to upbraid them with. (2.) He reproaches him as a madman. The prophets of the Old Testament were thus stigmatized, to prejudice people against them by putting them into an ill-name: *Wherefore came this mad fellow unto thee?* said the captains of the prophet, 2 Ki. 9:11; Hos. 9:7. John Baptist and Christ were represented as having a devil, as being crazed. It is probable that Paul now spoke with more life and earnestness than he did in the beginning of his discourse, and used more gestures that were expressive of his zeal, and therefore Festus put this invidious character upon him, which perhaps never a one in the company but himself thought of. It is not so harmless a suggestion as some make it to say concerning those that are zealous in religion above others that they are crazed.

2. How Paul cleared himself from this invidious imputation, which whether he had ever lain under before is not certain; it should seem, it had been said of him by the false apostles, for he ways (2 Co. 5:13), *If we be beside ourselves,* as they say we are, *it is to God;* but he was never charged with this before *the Roman governor,* and therefore he must say something to this. (1.) He denies the charge, with due respect indeed to the governor, but with justice to himself, protesting that there was neither ground nor colour for it (*v.* 25): *"I am not mad, most noble Festus,* nor ever was, nor any thing like it; the use of my reason, thanks be to God, has been all my days continued to me, and at this time I do not ramble, *but speak the words of truth and soberness,* and know what I say." Observe, Though Festus gave Paul this base and contemptuous usage, not becoming a gentlemen, much less a judge, yet Paul is so far from resenting it, and being provoked by it, that he gives him all possible respect, compliments him with his title of honour, *most noble Festus,* to teach us not to render railing for railing, nor one invidious character for another, but to speak civilly to those who speak slightly of us. It becomes us, upon all occasions, to speak the words of truth and soberness, and then we may despise the unjust censures of men. (2.) He appeals to Agrippa concerning what he spoke (*v.* 26): *For the king knows of these things,* concerning Christ, and his death and resurrection, and the prophecies of the Old Testament, which had their accomplishment therein. He therefore *spoke freely before him,* who knew these were no fancies, but matters of fact, knew something of them, and therefore would be willing to know more: *For I am persuaded that none of these things are hidden from him;* no, not that which he had related concerning his own conversion, and the commission he had received to preach the gospel. Agrippa could not but have heard of it, having been so long conversant among the Jews. *This thing was not done in a corner;* all the country rang of it; and any of the Jews present might have witnessed for him that they had heard it many a time from others, and therefore it was unreasonable to censure him as a distracted man for relating it, much more for speaking of the death and resurrection of Christ, which was so universally spoken of. Peter tells Cornelius and his friends (*ch.* 10:37), *That word you know which was published throughout all Judea* concerning Christ; and therefore Agrippa could not be ignorant of it, and it was a shame for Festus that he was so.

II. Agrippa is so far from thinking him a madman that he thinks he never heard a man argue more strongly, nor talk more to the purpose.

1. Paul applies himself closely to Agrippa's conscience. Some think Festus was displeased at Paul because he kept his eye upon Agrippa, and directed his discourse to him all along, and that therefore he gave him that interruption, *v.* 24. But, if that was the thing that affronted him, Paul regards it not: he will speak to those who understand him, and whom he is likely to fasten something upon, and therefore still addresses *Agrippa;* and, because he had mentioned Moses and the prophets as confirming the gospel he preached, he refers Agrippa to them (*v.* 27): *"King Agrippa, believest thou the prophets?* Dost thou receive the scriptures of the Old Testament as a divine revelation, and admit them as foretelling good things to come?" He does not stay for an answer, but, in compliment to Agrippa, takes it for granted: *I know that thou believest;* for every one knew that Agrippa professed the Jews' religion, as his fathers had done, and therefore both knew the writings of the prophets and gave credit to them. Note, It is good dealing with those who have acquaintance with the scriptures and believe them; for such one has some hold of.

2. Agrippa owns there was a great deal of reason in what Paul said (*v.* 28): *Almost thou persuadest me to be a Christian.* Some understand this as spoken ironically, and read it thus, *Wouldst thou in so little a time persuade me to be a Christian?* But, taking it so, it is an acknowledgement that Paul spoke very much to the purpose, and that, whatever others thought of it, to his mind there came a convincing power along with what he said: "Paul, thou art too hasty, thou canst not think to make a convert of me all of a sudden." Others take it as spoken seriously, and as a confession that he was in a manner, or within a little, convinced that Christ was the Messiah; for he could not but own, and had many a time thought so within himself, that the prophecies of the Old Testament had had their accomplishment in him; and now that it is urged thus solemnly upon him he is ready to yield to the conviction, he begins to sound a parley, and to think of rendering. He is as near being persuaded to believe in Christ as Felix, when he trembled, was to leave his sins: he sees a great deal of reason for Christianity; the proofs of it, he owns, are strong, and such as he cannot answer; the objections against it trifling, and such as he cannot for shame insist upon; so that if it were not for his obligations to the ceremonial law, and his respect to the religion of his fathers and of his country, or his regard to his dignity as a king and to his secular interests, he would turn Christian immediately. Note, Many are almost persuaded to be religious who are not quite persuaded; they are under strong convictions of their duty, and of the excellency of the ways of God, but yet are overruled by some external inducements, and do not pursue their convictions.

3. Paul, not being allowed time to pursue his argument, concludes with a compliment, or rather a pious wish that all his hearers were Christians, and this wish turned into a prayer: *euxaimēn an tō Theō — I pray to God for it* (*v.* 29); it was *his heart's desire and prayer to God for them all that they might be saved,* Rom. 10:1. *That not only thou but all that hear me this day* (for he has the same kind design upon them all) *were both almost, and altogether, such as I am, except these bonds.* Hereby, (1.) He professes his resolution to cleave to his religion, as that which he was entirely satisfied in, and determined to live and die by. In wishing that they were all as he was, he does in effect declare against ever being as they were, whether Jews or Gentiles, how much soever it might be to his worldly advantage. He adheres to the instruction God gave to the prophet (Jer. 15:19), *Let them return unto thee, but return not thou unto them.* (2.) He intimates his satisfaction not only in the truth, but in the benefit and advantage of Christianity; he had so much comfort in it for the present, and was so sure it would end in his eternal happiness, that he could not wish better to the best friend he had in the world than to wish him such a one as he was, a faithful zealous disciple of Jesus Christ. *Let my enemy be as the wicked,* says Job, *ch.* 27:7. Let my friend be as the Christian, says Paul. (3.) He intimates his trouble and concern that Agrippa went no further than being almost such a one as he was, almost a Christian, and not altogether one; for he wishes that he and the rest of them might be not only almost (what good would that do?) but altogether such as he was, sincere thorough-paced Christians. (4.) He intimates that it was the concern, and would be the unspeakable happiness, of every one of them to become *true Christians* — that there is grace enough in Christ for all, be they ever so many — enough for each, be they ever so craving. (5.) He intimates the hearty good-will he bore to them all; he wishes them, [1.] As well as he wished his own soul, that they might be as happy in Christ as he was. [2.] Better than he now was as to his outward condition, for he excepts these bonds; he wishes they might all be comforted Christians as he was, but not persecuted Christians as he was — that they might taste as much as he did of the advantages that attended religion, but not so much of its crosses. They had made light of his imprisonment, and were in no concern for him. Felix detained him in bonds to gratify the Jews. Now this would have tempted many a one to wish them all in his bonds, that they might know what it was to be confined as he was, and then they would know the better how to pity him; but he was so far from this that, when he wished them in bonds to Christ, he desired they might never be in bonds for Christ. Nothing could be said more tenderly nor with a better grace.

III. They all agree that Paul is an innocent man, and is wronged in his prosecution. 1. The court broke up with some precipitation (*v.* 30): *When he had spoken* that obliging word (*v.* 29), which moved them all, the king was afraid, if he were permitted to go on, he would say something yet more moving, which might work upon some of them to appear more in his favour than was convenient, and perhaps might prevail with them to turn Christians. The king himself found his own heart begin to yield, and durst not trust himself to hear more, but, like Felix, dismissed Paul for this time. They ought in justice to have asked the prisoner whether he had any more to say for himself; but they thought he had said enough, and therefore *the king rose up, and the governor, and Bernice, and those that sat with them,* concluding the case was plain, and with this they contented themselves, when Paul had more to say which would have made it plainer. 2. They all concurred in an opinion of Paul's innocency, *v.* 31. The court withdrew to consult of the matter, to know one another's minds upon it, and *they talked among themselves,* all to the same purport, *that this man does nothing worthy of bonds* — he is not a dangerous man, whom it is prudent to confine. After this, Nero made a law for the putting of those to death who professed the Christian religion, but as yet there was no law of that kind among the Romans, and therefore no transgression; and this judgment of theirs is a testimony against that wicked law which Nero made not long after this, that Paul, the most active zealous Christian that ever was, was adjudged, even by those that were no friends to his way, to have *done nothing worthy of death, or of bonds.* Thus was he made manifest in the conscience of those who yet would not receive his doctrine; and the clamours of the hot-headed Jews, who cried out, *Away with him, it is not fit he should live,* were shamed by the moderate counsels of this court. 3. *Agrippa* gave his judgment *that he might have been set at liberty, if he had not himself appealed to Caesar* (*v.* 32), but by that appeal he had put a bar in his own door. Some think that by the Roman law this was true, that, when a prisoner had appealed to the supreme court, the inferior courts could no more discharge him than they could condemn him; and we suppose the law was so, if the prosecutors joined issue upon the appeal, and consented to it. But it does not appear that in Paul's case the prosecutors did so; he was forced to do it, to screen himself from their fury, when he saw the governor did not take the care he ought to have done for his protection. And therefore others think that Agrippa and Festus, being unwilling to disoblige the Jews by setting him at liberty, made this serve for an excuse of their continuing him in custody, when they themselves knew they might have justified the discharging of him. Agrippa, who was but almost persuaded to be a Christian, proves no better than if he had not been at all persuaded. And now I cannot tell, (1.) Whether Paul repented of his having appealed to Caesar, and wished he had not done it, blaming himself for it as a rash thing, now he saw that was the only thing that hindered his discharge. He had reason perhaps to reflect upon it with regret, and to charge himself with imprudence and impatience in it, and some distrust of the divine protection. He had better have appealed to God than to Caesar. It confirms what Solomon says (Eccl. 6:12), *Who knows what is good for man in this life?* What we think is for our welfare often proves to be a trap; such short-sighted creatures are we, and so ill-advised in leaning, as we do, to our own understanding. Or, (2.) Whether, notwithstanding this, he was satisfied in what he had done, and was easy in his reflections upon it. His appealing to Caesar was lawful, and what became a Roman citizen, and would help to make his cause considerable; and forasmuch as when he did it it appeared to him, as the case then stood, to be for the best, though afterwards it appeared otherwise, he did not vex himself with any self-reproach in the matter, but believed there was a providence in it, and it would issue well at last. And besides, he was told in a vision that he must *bear witness to Christ at Rome, ch.* 23:11. And it is all one to him whether he goes thither a prisoner or at his liberty; he knows *the counsel of the Lord shall stand,* and says, *Let it stand. The will of the Lord be done.*

CHAPTER 27

This whole chapter is taken up with an account of Paul's voyage towards Rome, when he was sent thither a prisoner by Festus the governor, upon his appeal to Caesar. I. The beginning of the voyage was well enough, it was calm and prosperous (*v.* 1–8). II. Paul gave them notice of a storm coming, but could not prevail with them to lie by (*v.* 9–11). III. As they pursued their voyage, they met with a great deal of tempestuous weather, which reduced them to such extremity that they counted upon nothing but being cast away (*v.* 12–20). IV. Paul assured them that though they would not be advised by him to prevent their coming into this danger, yet, by the good providence of God, they should be brought safely through it, and none of them should be lost (*v.* 21–26). V. At length they were at midnight thrown upon an island, which proved to be Malta, and then they were in the utmost danger imaginable, but were assisted by Paul's counsel to keep the mariners in the ship, and encouraged by his comforts to eat their meat, and have a good heart on it (*v.* 27–36). VI. Their narrow escape with their lives, when they came to shore, when the ship was wrecked, but all the persons wonderfully preserved (*v.* 37–44).

Verses 1–11

It does not appear how long it was after Paul's conference with Agrippa that he was sent away for Rome, pursuant to his appeal to Caesar; but it is likely they took the first convenience they could hear of to do it; in the mean time Paul is in the midst of his friends at Caesarea — they comforts to him, and he a blessing to them. But here we are told,

I. How Paul was shipped off for Italy: a long voyage, but there is no remedy. He has appealed to Caesar, and to Caesar he must go: *It was determined that we should sail into Italy,* for to Rome they must go by sea; it would have been a vast way about to go by land. Hence, when the Roman conquest of the Jewish nation is foretold, it is said (Num. 24:24), *Ships shall come from Chittim,* that is, *Italy, and shall afflict Eber,* that is, the Hebrews. It was determined by the counsel of God, before it was determined by the counsel of Festus, that Paul should go to Rome; for, whatever man intended, God had work for him to do there. Now here we are told, 1. Whose custody he was committed to — to *one named Julius, a centurion of Augustus's band,* as Cornelius was of the Italian band, or legion, *ch.* 10:1. He had soldiers under him, who were a guard upon Paul, that he might not make his escape, and likewise to protect him, that he might have no mischief done him. 2. What bottom he embarked in: they went on board a ship of Adramyttium (*v.* 2), a sea-port of Africa, whence this ship brought African goods, and, as it should seem, made a coasting voyage for Syria, where those goods came to a good market. 3. What company he had in this voyage, there were some prisoners who were committed to the custody of the same centurion, and who probably had appealed to Caesar too, or were upon some other account removed to Rome, to be tried there, or to be examined as witnesses against some prisoners there; perhaps some notorious offenders, like Barabbas, who were therefore ordered to be brought before the emperor himself. Paul was linked with these, as Christ with the thieves that were crucified with him, and was obliged to take his lot with them in this voyage; and we find in this chapter (*v.* 42) that for their sakes he had like to have been killed, but for his sake they were preserved. Note, It is no new thing for the innocent to be numbered among the transgressors. But he had also some of his friends with him, Luke particularly, the penman of this book, for he puts himself in all along, *We* sailed into Italy, and, *We* launched, *v.* 2. Aristarchus a Thessalonian is particularly named, as being now in his company. Dr. Lightfoot thinks that Trophimus the Ephesian went off with him, but that he left him sick at Miletum (2 Tim. 4:20), when he passed by those coasts of Asia mentioned here (*v.* 2), and that there likewise he left Timothy. It was a comfort to Paul to have the society of some of his friends in this tedious voyage, with whom he might converse freely, though he had so much loose profane company about him. Those that go long voyages at sea are commonly necessitated to sojourn, as it were, in Mesech and Kedar, and have need of wisdom, that they may do good to the bad company they are in, may make them better, or at lest be made never the worse by them.

II. What course they steered, and what places they touched at, which are particularly recorded for the confirming of the truth of the history to those who lived at that time, and could by their own knowledge tell of their being at such and such a place. 1. They touched at Sidon, not far off from where they went on board; thither they came *the next day.* And that which is observable here is, that *Julius the centurion* was extraordinarily civil to Paul. It is probable that he knew his case, and was one of the *chief captains, or principal men,* that heard him plead his own cause before Agrippa (*ch.* 25:23), and was convinced of his innocency, and the injury done him; and therefore, though Paul was committed to him as a prisoner, he treated him as a friend, as a scholar, as a gentleman, and as a man that had an interest in heaven: He *gave him liberty,* while the business of the ship detained it at Sidon, *to go among his friends* there, *to refresh himself;* and it would be a great refreshment to him. Julius herein gives an example to those in power to be respectful to those whom they find worthy of their respect, and in using their power to make a difference. A Joseph, a Paul, are not to be used as common prisoners. God herein encourages those that suffer for him to trust in him; for he can put it into the hearts of those to befriend them from whom they least expect it — can cause them to be pitied, nay, can cause them to be prized and valued, even in the eyes of those that carry them captive, Ps. 106:46. And it is likewise an instance of Paul's fidelity. He did not go about to make his escape, which he might have easily done; but, being out upon his parole of honour, he faithfully returns to his imprisonment. If the centurion is so civil as to take his word, he is so just and honest as to keep his word. 2. They thence *sailed under Cyprus, v.* 4. If the wind had been fair, they had gone forward by direct sailing, and had left Cyprus on the right hand; but, the wind not favouring them, they were driven to oblique sailing with a side wind, and so compassed the island, in a manner, and left it on the left hand. Sailors must do as they can, when they cannot do as they would, and make the best of their wind, whatever point it is in; so must we all in our passage over the ocean of this world. When the winds are contrary yet we must be getting forward as well as we can. 3. At a port called Myra they changed their ship; that which they were in, it is probable, having business no further, they went on board a vessel of Alexandria bound for Italy, *v.* 5, 6. Alexandria was now the chief city of Egypt, and great trading there was between that city and Italy; from Alexandria they carried corn to Rome, and the East-India goods and Persian which they imported at the Red Sea they exported again to all parts of the Mediterranean, and especially to Italy. And it was a particular favour shown to the Alexandrian ships in the ports of Italy that they were not obliged to strike sail, as other ships were, when they came into port. 4. With much ado they made *The Fair Havens,* a port of the island of Crete, *v.* 7, 8. They *sailed slowly many days,* being becalmed, or having the wind against them. It was a great while before they made the point of Cnidus, a port of Caria, and were forced to sail under Crete, as before under Cyprus; much difficulty they met with in passing by Salmone, a promontory on the eastern shore of the island of Crete. Though the voyage hitherto was not tempestuous, yet it was very tedious. They many that are not driven backward in their affairs by cross providences, yet sail slowly, and do not get forward by favourable providences. And many good Christians make this complaint in the concerns of their souls, that they do not rid ground in their way of heaven, but have much ado to keep their ground; they move with many stops and pauses, and lie a great while wind-bound. Observe, The place they came to was called *The Fair Havens.* Travellers say that it is known to this day by the same name, and that it answers the name from the pleasantness of its situation and prospect. And yet, (1.) It was not the harbour they were bound for; it was a fair haven, but it was not their haven. Whatever agreeable circumstances we may be in in this world, we must remember we are not at home, and therefore we must arise and depart; for, though it be a fair haven, it is not the desired haven, Ps. 107:30. (2.) It was not a *commodious haven to winter in,* so it is said, *v.* 12. It had a fine prospect, but it lay exposed to the weather. Note, Every fair haven is not a safe haven; nay, there may be most danger where there is most pleasure.

III. What advice Paul gave them with reference to that part of their voyage they had before them — it was to be content to winter where they were, and not to think of stirring till a better season of the year. 1. It was now a bad time for sailing; they had lost a deal of time while they were struggling with contrary winds. Sailing was now dangerous, because *the fast was already past,* that is, the famous yearly fast of the Jews, the day of atonement, which was on the tenth day of the seventh month, *a day to afflict the soul* with fasting; it was about the 20th of our September. That yearly fast was very religiously observed; but (which is strange) we never have any mention made in all the scripture history of the observance of it, unless it be meant here, where it serves only to describe the season of the year. Michaelmas is reckoned by mariners as a bad time of the year to be at sea as any other; they complain of their Michaelmas-blasts; it was that time now with these distressed voyagers. *The harvest was past, the summer was ended;* they had not only lost time, but lost the opportunity. 2. Paul put them in mind of it, and gave them notice of their danger (*v.* 10): "*I perceive*" (either by notice from God, or by observing their wilful resolution to prosecute the voyage notwithstanding the peril of the season) — "that *this voyage will be with hurt and damage;* you that have effects on board are likely to lose them, and it will be a miracle of mercy if our lives be given us for a prey." There were some good men in the ship, and many more bad men: but in things of this nature *all things come alike to all,* and *there is one event to the righteous and to the wicked.* If both be in the same ship, they both are in the same danger. 3. They would not be advised by Paul in this matter, *v.* 11. They thought him impertinent in interposing in an affair of this nature, who did not understand navigation; and the centurion to whom it was referred to determine it, though himself a passenger, yet, being a man in authority, takes upon him to overrule, though he had not been oftener at sea perhaps than Paul, nor was better acquainted with these seas, for Paul had planted the gospel in Crete (Tit. 1:5), and knew the several parts of the island well enough. But the centurion gave more regard to the opinion of the master and owner of the ship than to Paul's; for every man is to be credited in his own profession ordinarily: but such a man as Paul, who was so intimate with Heaven, was rather to be regarded in seafaring matters than the most celebrated sailors. Note, Those know not what dangers they run themselves into who will be governed more by human prudence than by divine revelation. The centurion was very civil to Paul (*v.* 3), and yet would not be governed by his advice. Note, Many will show respect to good ministers that will not take their advice, Eze. 33:31.

Verses 12–20

In these verses we have,

I. The ship putting to sea again, and pursuing her voyage

at first with a promising gale. Observe, 1. What induced them to leave the fair havens: it was because they thought the harbour not *commodious to winter in;* it was pleasant enough in summer but in the winter they lay bleak. Or perhaps it was upon some other account incommodious; provisions perhaps were scarce and dear there; and they ran upon a mischief to avoid an inconvenience, as we often do. Some of the ship's crew, or of the council that was called to advise in this matter, were for staying there, rather than venturing to sea now that the weather was so uncertain: it is better to be safe in an incommodious harbour than to be lost in a tempestuous sea. But they were outvoted when it was put to the question, and the *greater part advised to depart thence also;* yet they aimed not to go far, but only to another port of the same island, here called *Phenice,* and some think it was so called because the Phenicians frequented it much, the merchants of Tyre and Sidon. It is here described to lie towards the south-west and north-west. Probably the haven was between the two promontories or juttings-out of land into the sea, one of which pointed to the north-west and the other to the south-west, by which it was guarded against the east winds. Thus hath the wisdom of the Creator provided for the relief and safety of those who *go down to the sea in ships, and do business in great waters.* In vain had nature provided for us the waters to sail on, if it had not likewise provided for us natural harbours to take shelter in. 2. What encouragement they had at first to pursue their voyage. They set out with a fair wind (*v.* 13), the *south wind blew softly,* upon which they should gain their point, and so they sailed close by the coast of Crete and were not afraid of running upon the rocks or quicksands, because the wind blew so gently. Those who put to sea with ever so fair a gale know not what storms they may yet meet with, and therefore must not be secure, nor take it for granted that they have obtained their purpose, when so many accidents may happen to cross their purpose. *Let not him that girdeth on the harness boast as though he had put it off.*

II. The ship in a storm presently, a dreadful storm. They looked at second causes, and took their measures from the favourable hints they gave, and imagined that because the south wind now blew softly it would always blow so; in confidence of this, they ventured to sea, but were soon made sensible of their folly in giving more credit to a smiling wind than to the word of God in Paul's mouth, by which they had fair warning given them of a storm. Observe,

1. What their danger and distress was, (1.). There *arose against them a tempestuous wind,* which was not only contrary to them, and directly in their teeth, so that they could not get forward, but a violent wind, which raised the waves, like that which was sent forth in pursuit of Jonah, though Paul was following God, and going on in his duty, and not as Jonah running away from God and his duty. This wind the sailors called *Euroclydon,* a north-east wind, which upon those seas perhaps was observed to be in a particular manner troublesome and dangerous. It was a sort of whirlwind, for the ship is said to be caught by it, *v.* 15. It was God that commanded this wind to rise, designing to bring glory to himself, and reputation to Paul, out of it; stormy winds being brought *out of his treasuries* (Ps. 135:7), they *fulfil his word,* Ps. 148:8. (2.) The ship was *exceedingly tossed* (*v.* 18); it was kicked like a football from wave to wave; its passengers (as it is elegantly described, Ps. 107:26, 27) *mount up to the heavens, go down again to the depths, reel to and fro, stagger like a drunken man, and are at their wits' end.* The ship could not possibly *bear up into the wind,* could not make her way in opposition to the wind; and therefore they folded up their sails, which in such a storm would endanger them rather than to them any service, and so *let the ship drive, Not whither it would, but whither it was impelled by the impetuous waves* — *Non quo voluit, sed quo rapit impetus undae.* Ovid. Trist. It is probable that they were very near the heaven of Phenice when this tempest arose, and thought they should presently be in a quiet haven, and were pleasing themselves with the thought of it, and wintering there, and lo, of a sudden, they are in this distress. Let us therefore always rejoice with trembling, and never expect a perfect security, nor a perpetual security, till we come to heaven. (3.) They saw neither sun nor stars for many days. This made the tempest the more terrible, that they were all in the dark; and the use of the loadstone for the direction of sailors not being then found out (so that they had no guide at all, when they could see neither sun nor stars) made the case the more hazardous.

Thus melancholy sometimes is the condition of the people of God upon a spiritual account. They *walk in darkness and have no light.* Neither sun nor stars appear; they cannot dwell, nay, they cannot fasten, upon any thing comfortable or encouraging; thus it may be with them, and yet light is sown for them. (4.) They had abundance of winter-weather: *No small tempest — cheimōn ouk oligos,* cold rain, and snow, and all the rigours of that season of the year, so that they were ready to perish for cold; and all this continued many days. See what hardships those often undergo who are much at sea, besides the hazards of life they run; and yet to get gain there are still those who make nothing of all this; and it is an instance of divine Providence that it disposes some to this employment, notwithstanding the difficulties that attend it, for the keeping up of commerce among the nations, and the isles of the Gentiles particularly; and Zebulun can as heartily rejoice in his going out as Issachar in his tents. Perhaps Christ therefore chose ministers from among seafaring men, because they had been used to endure hardness.

2. What means they used for their own relief: they betook themselves to all the poor shifts (for I can call them no better) that sailors in distress have recourse to. (1.) When they could not make head against the wind, they let the ship run adrift, finding it was to no purpose to ply either the oar or the sail. When it is fruitless to struggle, it is wisdom to yield. (2.) They nevertheless did what they could to avoid the present danger; there was a little island called Clauda, and when they were near that, though they could not pursue their voyage, they took care to prevent their shipwreck, and therefore so ordered their matters that they did not run against the island, but quietly ran under it, *v.* 16. (3.) When they were afraid they should scarcely save the ship, they were busy to save the boat, which they did with much ado. They had *much work to come by the boat* (*v.* 16), but at last they took it up, *v.* 17. This might be of use in any exigence, and therefore they made hard shift to get it into the ship to them. (4.) They used means which were proper enough in those times, when the art of navigation was far short of the perfection it is now come to; they *undergirded the ship, v.* 17. They bound the ship under the bottom of it with strong cables, to keep it from bulging in the extremity of the tempest. (5.) For fear of falling *into the quicksands* they *struck sail,* and then let the ship go as it would. It is strange how a ship will live at sea (so they express it), even in very stormy weather, if it have but sea-room; and, when the sailors cannot make the shore, it is their interest to keep as far off it as they can. (6.) The next day they lightened the ship of its cargo, threw the goods and the merchandises overboard (as Jonah's mariners did, *ch.* 1:5), being willing rather to be poor without them than to perish with them. *Skin for skin, and all that a man has, will he give for his life.* See what the wealth of this world is; how much soever it is courted as a blessing, the time may come when it will be a burden, not only too heavy to be carried safe of itself, but heavy enough to sink him that has it. Riches are often *kept by the owners thereof to their hurt* (Eccl. 5:13); and parted with to their good. But see the folly of the children of this world, they can be thus prodigal of their goods when it is for the saving of their lives, and yet how sparing of them in works of piety and charity, and in suffering for Christ, though they are told by eternal Truth itself that those shall be recompensed more than a thousand fold *in the resurrection of the just.* Those went upon a principle of faith who *took joyfully the spoiling of their goods, knowing in themselves that they had in heaven a better and a more enduring substance,* Heb. 10:34. Any man will rather make shipwreck of his goods than of his life; but many will rather make *shipwreck of faith and a good conscience* than of their goods. (7.) The third day they *cast out the tacklings of the ship* —the utensils of it, *Armamenta* (so some render it), as if it were a ship of force. With us it is common to heave the guns overboard in the extremity of a storm; but what heavy artillery they had then which it was necessary to lighten the ship of I do not know; and I question whether it was not then a vulgar error among seamen thus to throw every thing into the sea, even that which would be of great use in a storm, and no great weight.

3. The despair which at last they were brought to (*v.* 20): *All hope that we should be saved was then taken away.* The storm continued, and they saw no symptoms of its abatement; we have known very blustering weather to continue for some weeks. The means they had used were ineffectual,

so that they were at their wits' end; and such was the consternation that this melancholy prospect put them into that they had no heart either to eat or drink. They had provision enough on board (*v.* 38), but such bondage were they under, through fear of death, that they could not admit the supports of life. Why did not Paul, by the power of Christ, and in his name, lay this storm? Why did he not say to the winds and waves, *Peace, be still,* as his Master had done? Surely it was because the apostles wrought miracles for the confirmation of their doctrine, not for the serving of a turn for themselves or their friends.

Verses 21–44

We have here the issue of the distress of Paul and his fellow-travellers; they escaped with their lives and that was all, and that was for Paul's sake. We are here told (*v.* 37) what number there were on board — mariners, merchants, soldiers, prisoners, and other passengers, in all two hundred and seventy-six souls; this is taken notice of to make us the more concerned for them in reading the story, that they were such a considerable number, whose lives were now in the utmost jeopardy, and one Paul among them worth more than all the rest. We left them in despair, giving up themselves for gone. Whether they *called every man on his God,* as Jonah's mariners did, we are not told; it is well if this laudable practice in a storm was not gone out of fashion and made a jest of. However, Paul among these seamen was not, like Jonah among his, the cause of the storm, but the comforter in the storm, and as much a credit to the profession of an apostle as Jonah was a blemish to the character of a prophet. Now here we have,

I. The encouragement Paul gave them, by assuring them, in the name of God, that their lives should all be saved, even when, in human appearance, all hope that they should be saved was taken away. Paul rescued them from their despair first, that they might not die of that, and starve themselves in that, and then they were in a fair way to be rescued from their distress. *After long abstinence,* as if they were resolved not to eat till they knew whether they should live or die, *Paul stood forth in the midst of them.* During the distress hitherto Paul hid himself among them, was one of the crowd, helped with the rest to *throw out the tackling* (*v.* 19), but now he distinguished himself, and, though a prisoner, undertook to be their counsellor and comforter.

1. He reproves them for not taking his advice, which was to stay where they were, in the road of Lasea (*v.* 8): *"You should have hearkened to me and not have loosed from Crete,* where we might have made a shift to winter well enough, and then we should not have *gained this harm and loss,* that is, we should have escaped them." Harm and loss in the world, if sanctified to us, may be truly said to be gain; for if they wean us from present things, and awaken us to think of a future state, we are truly gainers by them. Observe, They did not hearken to Paul when he warned them of their danger, and yet if they will but acknowledge their folly, and repent of it, he will speak comfort and relief to them now that they are in danger, so compassionate is God to those that are in misery, though they bring themselves into it by their own incogitancy, nay, by their own wilfulness, and contempt of admonition. Paul, before administering comfort, will first make them sensible of their sin in not hearkening to him, by upbraiding them with their rashness, and probably, when he tells them of their gaining harm and loss, he reflects upon what they promised themselves by proceeding on their voyage, that they should gain so much time, gain this and the other point: "But," says he, "you have gained nothing but harm and loss; how will you answer it?" That which they are blamed for is their loosing from Crete, where they were safe. Note, Most people bring themselves into inconvenience, because they do not know when they are well off, but gain harm and loss by aiming against advice to better themselves.

2. He assures them that though they should lose the ship yet they should none of them lose their lives: "You see your folly in not being ruled by me:" he does not say, "Now therefore expect to fare accordingly, you may thank yourselves if you be all lost, those that will not be counselled cannot be helped." No, "Yet now there is hope in Israel concerning this thing; your case is sad, but it is not desperate, now, *I exhort you to be of good cheer."* Thus we say to sinners that are convinced of their sin and folly, and begin to see and bewail their error, *"You should have hearkened unto us,* and should have had nothing to do with sin; yet now we *exhort you to be of good cheer:* though you would not take our advice when we said, *Do not presume,* yet take it now when we say, *Do not despair."* They had given up the cause, and would use no further means, because *all hope that they should be saved was taken away.* Now Paul quickens them to bestir themselves yet in working for their own safety, by telling them that it they would resume their vigour they should secure their lives. He gives them this assurance when they were brought to the last extremity, for now it would be doubly welcome to them to be told that not a life should be lost when they were ready to conclude they must inevitably be all lost. He tells them, (1.) That they must count upon the loss of the ship. Those who were interested in that and the goods were probably those greater part that were for pushing forward the voyage and running the venture, notwithstanding Paul's admonition, and they are made to pay for their rashness. Their ship shall be wrecked. Many a stately, strong, rich, gallant ship is lost in the mighty waters in a little time; *for vanity of vanities, all is vanity and vexation of spirit.* But, (2.) *Not a life shall be lost.* This would be good news to those that were ready to die for fear of dying, and whose guilty consciences made death look very terrible to them.

3. He tells them what ground he had for this assurance, that it is not a banter upon them, to put them into humour, nor a human conjecture, he has a divine revelation for it, and is as confident of it as that God is true, being fully satisfied that he has his word for it. An angel of the Lord appeared to him in the night, and told him that for his sake they should all be preserved (*v.* 23–25), which would double the mercy of their preservation, that they should have it not only by providence, but by promise, and as a particular favour to Paul. Now observe here,

(1.) The solemn profession Paul makes of relation to God, the God from whom he had this favourable intelligence: It is he *whose I am, and whom I serve.* He looks upon God, [1.] As his rightful owner, who has a sovereign incontestable title to him, and dominion over him: *Who I am.* Because God made us and not we ourselves, therefore we are not our own but his. His we are by creation, for he made us; by preservation, for he maintains us; by redemption, for he bought us. We are more his than our own. [2.] As his sovereign ruler and master, who, having given him being, has right to give him law: *Whom I serve.* Because his we are, therefore we are bound to serve him, to devote ourselves to his honour and employ ourselves in his work. It is Christ that Paul here has an eye to; he is God, and the angels are his and go on his errands. Paul often calls himself a *servant of Jesus Christ;* he is his, and him he serves, both as a Christian and as an apostle; he does not say, "Whose *we* are, and whom we serve," for most that were present were strangers to him, but, "Whose *I am,* and whom *I serve,* whatever others do; nay, whom I am now in the actual service of, going to Rome, not as you are, upon worldly business, but to appear as a witness for Christ." Now this he tells the company, that, seeing their relief coming from his God whose he was and whom he served, they might thereby be drawn in to take him for their God, and to serve him likewise; for the same reason Jonah said to his mariners, *I fear the Lord, the God of heaven, who has made the sea and the dry land,* Jonah 1:9.

(2.) The account he gives of the vision he had: *There stood by me this night an angel of God,* a divine messenger who used formerly to bring him messages from heaven; he *stood by him,* visibly appeared to him, probably when he was awake upon his bed. Though he was *afar off upon the sea* (Ps. 65:5), *on the uttermost parts of the sea* (Ps. 139:9), yet this could not intercept his communion with God, nor deprive him of the benefit of divine visits. Thence he can direct a prayer to God, and thither God can direct an angel to him. He knows not where he is himself, yet God's angel knows where to find him out. The *ship is tossed* with winds and waves, hurried to and fro with the utmost violence, and yet the angel finds a way into it. No storms nor tempests can hinder the communications of God's favour to his people, for he is a very present help, a help at hand, even when the *sea roars and is troubled,* Ps. 46:1, 3. We may suppose that Paul, being a prisoner, had not a cabin of his own in the ship, much less a bed in the captain's cabin, but was put down into the hold (any dark or dirty place was thought good enough for him in common with the rest of the prisoners), and yet there the angel of God stood by him. Meanness and poverty set none at a distance from God and his favour. Jacob, when he has no pillow but a stone, no curtains but the clouds, yet has a vision of angels. Paul had this vision but *this last night.* He had himself been assured by a former vision that he should go to Rome (*ch.* 23:11), from which he might infer that he himself should be safe; but he has this fresh vision to assure him of the safety of those with him.

(3.) The encouragements that were given him in the vision, *v.* 14. [1.] He is forbidden to fear. Though all about him are at their wits' end, and lost in despair, yet, *Fear not, Paul;* fear not *their fear, nor be afraid,* Isa. 8:12. Let the *sinners in Zion be afraid,* but let not the saints be afraid, no, not at sea, in a storm; for *the Lord of hosts is with them,* and their *place of defence shall be the munitions of rocks,* Isa. 33:14–16. [2.] He is assured that for his part he shall come safely to Rome: *Thou must be brought before Caesar.* As the rage of the most potent enemies, so the rage of the most stormy sea, cannot prevail against God's witnesses till they have finished their testimony. Paul must be preserved in this danger, for he is reserved for further service. This is comfortable for the faithful servants of God in straits and difficulties, that as long as God has any work for them to do their lives shall be prolonged. [3.] That for his sake all that were in the ship with him should be delivered too from perishing in this storm: *God hath given thee all those that sail with thee.* The angel that was ordered to bring him this message could have singled him out from this wretched crew, and those that were his friends too, and have carried them safely to shore, and have left the rest to perish, because they would not take Paul's counsel. But God chooses rather, by preserving them all for his sake, to show what great blessings good men are to the world, than by delivering him only to show how good men are distinguished from the world. *God has given thee all those that sail with thee,* that is, spares them in answer to thy prayers, or for thy sake. Sometimes good men deliver *neither sons nor daughters, but their own souls only,* Eze. 14:18. But Paul here delivers a whole ship's crew, almost three hundred souls. Note, God often spares wicked people for the sake of the godly; as Zoar for Lot's sake, and as Sodom might have been, if there had been ten righteous persons in it. The good people are hated and persecuted in the world as if they were not worthy to live in it, yet really it is tor their sakes that the world stands. If Paul had thrust himself needlessly into bad company, he might justly have been cast away with them, but, God calling him into it, they are preserved with him. And it is intimated that it was a great favour to Paul, and he looked upon it to be so, that others were saved for his sake: *They are given thee.* There is no greater satisfaction to a good man than to know that he is a public blessing.

4. He comforts them with the same comforts wherewith he himself was comforted (*v.* 25): *"Wherefore, Sirs, be of good cheer,* you shall see even this will end well; *for I believe God,* and depend upon his word, *that it shall be even as it was told me."* He would not require them to give credit to that to which he did not himself give credit; and therefore solemnly professes that he believes it himself, and the belief of it makes him easy: "I doubt not but it shall be as it was told me." Thus he *staggers not at the promise of God through unbelief. Hath God spoken, and shall he not make it good?* No doubt he can, no doubt he will; for *he is not a man that he should lie.* And shall it be as God hath said? Then be of good cheer, be of good courage. God is ever faithful, and therefore let all that have an interest in his promise be ever cheerful. if with God saying and doing are not two things, then with us believing and enjoying should not.

5. He gives them a sign, telling them particularly what this tempestuous voyage would issue in (*v.* 26): *"We must be cast upon a certain island,* and that will both break the ship and save the passengers; and so the prediction in both respects will be fulfilled." The pilot had quitted his post, the ship was left to run at random, they knew not what latitude they were in, much less how to steer their course; and yet Providence undertakes to bring them to an island that shall be a refuge for them. When the church of God, like this ship, is *tossed with tempests, and not comforted,* when *there is none to guide her of all her sons,* yet God can bring her safely to shore, and will do it.

II. Their coming at length to an anchor upon an unknown shore, *v.* 27–29. 1. They had been a full fortnight in the storm, continually expecting death: *The fourteenth night,* and not sooner, *they came near land;* they were *that night driven up and down in Adria,* not in the Adriatic Gulf on which Venice stands, but in the Adriatic Sea, a part of the Mediterranean, containing both the Sicilian and Ionian seas, and extending to the African shore; in this sea they were tossed, and knew not whereabouts they were. 2. *About midnight the mariners apprehended that they drew near to some shore,* which confirmed what Paul had told them, that they must be driven upon some island. To try whether it was so or no, *they sounded,* in order to their finding the depth of the water, for the water would be shallower as they drew nearer to shore; by the first experiment *they found they drew twenty fathoms deep of water,* and by *the next fifteen fathoms,* which was a demonstration that they were near some shore; God has wisely ordered such a natural notice to sailors in the dark, that they may be cautious. 3. They took the hint, and, fearing rocks near the shore, *they cast anchor, and wished for the day;* they durst not go forward for fear of rocks, and yet would not go back in hope of shelter, but they would wait for the morning, and heartily wished for it; who can blame them when the affair came to a crisis? When they had light, there was no land to be seen; now that there was land near them, they had no light to see it by; no marvel then they wished for day. When those that fear God *walk in darkness, and have no light,* yet let them not say, *The Lord has forsaken us,* or, *Our God has forgotten us;* but let them do as these mariners did, cast anchor, and wish for the day, and be assured that the day will dawn. *Hope is an anchor of the soul, sure and stedfast, entering into that within the veil.* Hold fast by that, think not of putting to sea again, but abide by Christ, and wait till the day break, and the shadows flee away.

III. The defeating of the sailors' attempt to quit the ship; here was a new danger added to their distress, which they narrowly escaped. Observe, 1. The treacherous design of the seamen, and that was to leave the sinking ship, which, though a piece of wisdom in others, yet in those that were entrusted with the care of it was the basest fraud that could be (*v.* 30): *They were about to flee out of the ship,* concluding no other than that when it ran ashore it must be broken all to pieces; having the command of the boat, the project was to get all of them into that, and so save themselves, and leave all the rest to perish. To cover this vile design, they pretended they would *cast anchors out of the fore-ship,* or carry them further off, and in order to this *they let down the boat,* which they had taken in (*v.* 16, 17), and were *going into it,* having agreed among themselves, when they were in to make straight for the shore. The treacherous seamen are like the treacherous shepherd, who flees when he sees the danger coming, and there is most need of his help, Jn. 10:12. Thus true is that of Solomon, *Confidence in an unfaithful man in time of trouble is like a broken tooth or a foot out of joint.* Let us therefore cease from man. Paul had, in God's name, assured them that they should come safely to land, but they will rather trust their own refuge of lies than God's word and truth. 2. Paul's discovery of it, and protestation against it, *v.* 31. They all saw them preparing to go into the boat, but were deceived by the pretence they made; only Paul saw through it, and gave notice to the centurion and the soldiers concerning it, and told them plainly, *Except these abide in the ship, you cannot be saved.* The skill of a mariner is seen in a storm, and, in the distress of the ship, then is the proper time for him to exert himself. Now the greatest difficulty of all was before them, and therefore the seamen were now more necessary than ever yet; it was indeed not by any skill of theirs *that they were brought to land,* for it was quite beyond their skill, but, now that they are near land, they must use their art to bring the ship to it. When God has done that for us which we could not, we must then in his strength help ourselves. Paul speaks humanly, when he says, *You cannot be saved except these abide in the ship;* and he does not at all weaken the assurances he had divinely given that they should infallibly be saved. God, who appointed the end, *that they should be saved,* appointed the means, that they should be saved by the help of these seamen; though, if they had gone off, no doubt God would have made his word good some other way. Paul speaks as a prudent man, not as a prophet, when he says, These are necessary to your preservation. Duty is ours, events are God's; and we do not trust God, but tempt him, when we say, "We put ourselves under his protection," and do not use proper means, such as are within our power, for our own preservation. 3. The effectual defeat of it by the soldiers, *v.* 32. It was not time to stand arguing the case with the seamen, and therefore they made no more ado, *but cut the ropes of the boat,* and though it might otherwise have done them service in their present distress, they chose rather *to let it fall off,* and lose it, than suffer it to do them this disservice. And now the seamen, being forced to stay in the ship whether they would or no, are forced likewise to work for the safety of the ship as hard as they could, because if the rest perish they must perish with them.

IV. The new life which Paul put into the company, by cheerfully inviting them to take some refreshment, and by the repeated assurances he gave them that they should all of them have their lives given them for a prey. Happy they who had such a one as Paul in their company, who not only had correspondence with Heaven, but was of a hearty lively spirit with those about him, that sharpened the countenance of his friend, as iron sharpens iron. Such a friend in distress, when *without are fightings and within are fears,* is a friend indeed. *Ointment and perfume rejoice the heart; so doth the sweetness of a man's friend by hearty counsel,* Prov. 27:9. Such was Paul's here to his companions in tribulation. The day was coming on: those that wish for the day, let them wait awhile, and they shall have what they wish for. The dawning of the day revived them a little, and then Paul got them together. 1. He chid them for their neglect of themselves, that they had so far given way to fear and despair as to forget or not to mind their food: *This is the fourteenth day that you have tarried, and continued fasting, having taken nothing;* and that is not well, *v.* 33. Not that they had all, or any of them, continued fourteen days without any food, but they had not had any set meal, as they used to have, all that time; they ate very little, next to nothing. Or, "*You have continued fasting,* that is, you have lost your stomach; you have had no appetite at all to your food, nor any relish of it, through prevailing fear and despair." A very disconsolate state is thus expressed (Ps. 102:4), *I forget to eat my bread.* It is a sin to starve the body, and to deny it its necessary supports; he is an unnatural man indeed *that hateth his own flesh, and does not nourish and cherish it;* and it is a sore evil under the sun to have a sufficiency of the good things of this life, and not to have power to use them, Eccl. 6:2. If this arise from the sorrow of the world, and from any inordinate fear or trouble, it is so far from excusing it that it is another sin, it is discontent, it is distrust of God, it is all wrong. What folly is it to die for fear of dying! But thus *the sorrow of the world works death,* while joy in God is life and peace in the greatest distresses and dangers. 2. He courts them to their food (*v.* 34): "*Wherefore I pray you to take some meat.* We have a hard struggle before us, must get to shore as well as we can; if our bodies be weak through fasting, we shall not be able to help ourselves." The angel bade Elijah, *Arise and eat,* for otherwise he would find *the journey too great for him,* 1 Ki. 19:7. So Paul will have these people eat, or otherwise the waves will be too hard for them: *I pray you, parakalō,* "*I exhort you,* if you will be ruled by me, take some nourishment; though you have no appetite to it, though you have fasted away your stomach, yet let reason bring you to it, *for this is for your health,* or rather *your preservation, or safety, at this time;* it is for your salvation, you cannot without nourishment have strength to shift for your lives." As *he that will not labour, let him not eat;* so he that means to labour must eat. Weak and trembling Christians, that give way to doubts and fears about their spiritual state, continue fasting from the Lord's supper, and fasting from divine consolations, and then complain they cannot go on in their spiritual work and warfare; and it is owing to themselves. If they would feed and feast as they ought, upon the provision Christ has made for them, they would be strengthened, and it would be for their souls' health and salvation. 3. He assures them of their preservation: *There shall not a hair fall from the head of any of you.* It is a proverbial expression, denoting a complete indemnity. It is used 1 Ki. 1:51; Lu. 21:18. "You cannot eat for fear of dying; I tell you, you are sure of living, and therefore eat. You will come to shore wet and cold, but sound wind and limb; your hair wet, but not a hair lost." 4. He himself spread their table for them; for none of them had any heart to do it, they were all so dispirited: *When he had thus spoken, he took bread,* fetched it from the ship's stores, to which every one might safely have access when none of them had an appetite. They were not reduced to short allowance, as sailors sometimes are when they are kept longer at sea than they expected by distress of weather; they had plenty, but what good did that do them, when they had no stomach? We have reason to be thankful to God that we have not only food to our appetite, but appetite to our food; that our soul abhors not even dainty meat (Job 33:20), through sickness or sorrow. 5. He was chaplain to the ship, and they had reason to be proud of their chaplain. *He gave thanks to God in presence of them all.* We have reason to think he had often prayed with Luke and Arisatarchus, and what others there were among them that were Christians, that they prayed daily together; but whether he had before this prayed with the whole company promiscuously is not certain. Now *he gave thanks to God, in presence of them all,* that they were alive, and had been preserved hitherto, and that they had a promise that their lives should be preserved in the imminent peril now before them; he gave thanks for the provision they had, and begged a blessing upon it. We must *in every thing give thanks;* and must particularly have an eye to God in receiving our food, for *it is sanctified to us by the word of God and prayer,* and is *to be received with thanksgiving.* Thus the curse is taken off from it, and we obtain a covenant-right to it and a covenant-blessing upon it, 1 Tim. 4:3–5. And *it is not by bread alone that man lives, but by the word of God,* which must be met with prayer. *He gave thanks in presence of them all,* not only to show that he served a Master he was not ashamed of, but to invite them into his service too. If we crave a blessing upon our meat, and give thanks for it in a right manner, we shall not only keep up a comfortable communion with God ourselves, but credit our profession, and recommend it to the good opinion of others. 6. He set them a good example: *When he had given thanks, he broke the bread* (it was sea-biscuit) and *he began to eat.* Whether they would be encouraged or no, he would; if they would be sullen, and, like froward children, refuse their victuals because they had not every thing to their mind, he would eat his meat, and be thankful. Those that teach others are inexcusable if they do not themselves do as they teach, and the most effectual way of preaching is by example. 7. It had a happy influence upon them all (*v.* 36): *Then were they all of good cheer.* They then ventured to believe the message God sent them by Paul when they plainly perceived that Paul believed it himself, who was in the same common danger with them. Thus God sends good tidings to the perishing world of mankind by those who are of themselves, and in the same common danger with themselves, who are sinners too, and must be saved, if ever they be saved, in the same way in which they persuade others to venture; for it is a common salvation which they bring the tidings of; and it is an encouragement to people to commit themselves to Christ as their Saviour when those who invite them to do so make it to appear that they do so themselves. It is here upon this occasion that the number of the persons is set down, which we took notice of before: *they were in all two hundred threescore and sixteen souls.* See how many may be influenced by the good example of one. *They did all eat,* nay, *they did all eat enough* (*v.* 38), they were satiated with food, or filled with it; *they made a hearty meal.* This explains the meaning of *their fasting before for fourteen days;* not that they did not eat during all that time, but they never had enough all that time, as they had now. 8. They once more lightened the ship, that it might escape the better in the shock it was now to have. They had before thrown *the wares and the tackle overboard,* and now *the wheat,* the victuals and provisions they had; better they should sink the food than that it should sink them. See what good reason our Saviour had to call our bodily food meat that perishes. We may ourselves be under a necessity of throwing that away to save our lives which we had gathered and laid up for the support of our lives. It is probable that the ship was overloaded with the multitude of the passengers (for this comes in just after the account of the number of them) and that this obliged them so often to lighten the ship.

V. Their putting to shore, and the staving of the ship in the adventure. It was about break of day when they ate their meat, and when it was quite day they began to look about them; and here we are told, 1. *That they knew not where they were;* they could not tell what country it was they were now upon the coast of, whether it was Europe, Asia, or Africa, for each had shores washed by the Adriatic Sea. It is probable that these seamen had often sailed this way, and thought they knew every country they came near perfectly well, and yet here they were at a loss. *Let not the wise man then glory in his wisdom,* since it may perhaps fail him thus egregiously even in his own profession. 2. *They observed a creek with a level shore, into which they hoped to thrust the ship, v.* 39. Though they knew not what country it was, nor whether the inhabitants were friends or foes, civil or barbarous, they determined to cast themselves upon their mercy; it was dry land, which would be very welcome to those that had been so long at sea. It was a pity but they had had some help from the shore, a pilot sent them, that knew the coast, who might steer their ship in, or another second ship, to take some of the men on board. Those who live on the sea-coast have often opportunity of succouring those who are in distress at sea, and of saving precious lives, and they ought to do their utmost in order to it, with all readiness and cheerfulness; for it is a great sin, and very provoking to God, *to forbear to deliver those that are driven unto death, and are ready to be slain;* and it will not serve for an excuse to say, *Behold, we knew it not,* when either we did, or might, and should, have *known* it, Prov. 24:11, 12. I have been told there are some, and in our own nation too, who when from the sea-coast they see a ship in distress and at a loss will, by misguiding fires or otherwise, purposely lead them into danger, that the lives may be lost, and they may have the plunder of the ship. One can scarcely believe that any of the human species can possibly be so wicked, so barbarously inhuman, and can have so much of the devil in them; if there be, *let them know of a truth that they shall have judgment without mercy who have shown no mercy.* 3. They made straight to the shore with wind and tide (*v.* 40): *They took up the anchors, the four anchors which they cast out of the stern, v.* 29. Some think that they took pains to weigh them up, hoping they should have use for them again at the shore; others that they did it with such precipitation that they were forced to cut the cables and leave them; the original will admit either. *They then committed themselves to the sea,* the wind standing fair to carry them into the port, and *they loosed the rudder-bands,* which were fastened during the storm for the greater steadiness of the ship, but, now that they were *putting into the port, were loosed,* that the pilot might steer with the greater freedom; *they then hoisted up the main-sail to the wind, and made towards shore.* The original words here used for the *rudder-bands* and the *main-sail* find the critics a great deal of work to accommodate them to the modern terms; but they need not give us any difficulty who are content to know that when they saw the shore they hastened to it as fast as they could, and perhaps made more haste than good speed. And should not a poor soul that has long been struggling with winds and tempests in this world long to put into the safe and quiet haven of everlasting rest? Should it not get clear from all that which fastens it to this earth, and straitens the out-goings of its pious and devout affections heavenward? And should it not hoist up the main-sail of faith to the wind of the Spirit, and so with longing desires make to shore? 4. They made a shift among them *to run the ship aground,* in a shelf or bed of sand, as it should seem, or an isthmus, or neck of land, washed with the sea on both sides, and therefore two seas are said to meet upon it, and *there the forepart stuck fast;* and then, when it had no liberty to play, as a ship has when it rides at anchor, but remained immovable, *the hinder part* would soon be broken of course *by the violence of the waves.* Whether the seamen did not do their part, being angry that they were disappointed in their design to escape, and therefore wilfully ran the ship aground, or whether we may suppose that they did their utmost to save it, but God in his providence overruled, for the fulfilling of Paul's word, *that the ship must be lost* (*v.* 22), I cannot say; but this we are sure of *that God will confirm the word of his servants, and perform the counsel of his messengers,* Isa. 44:26. The ship, that had strangely weathered the storm in the vast ocean, where it had room to roll, is dashed to pieces when it sticks fast. Thus if the heart fixes in the world, in love and affection, and adherence to it, it is lost. Satan's temptations beat against it, and it is gone; but, as long as it keeps above the world, though it be tossed with its cares and tumults, there is hope of it. They had the shore in view, and yet suffered shipwreck in the harbour, to teach us never to be secure.

VI. A particular danger that Paul and the rest of the prisoners were in, besides their share in the common calamity, and their deliverance from it. 1. In this critical moment, when every man hung in doubt of his life, *the soldiers advised the killing of the prisoners* that were committed to their custody, and whom they were to give an account of, *lest any of them should swim out and escape, v.* 42. There was no great danger of that, for they could not escape far, weak and weary as they were; and, under the eye of so many soldiers that had the charge of them, it was not likely they should attempt it; and if it should so happen, though they might be obnoxious to the law for a permissive escape, yet in such a case as this equity would certainly relieve them. But it was a brutish barbarous motion, and so much the worse that they were thus prodigal of other people's lives when without a miracle of mercy they must lose their own. 2. The centurion, for Paul's sake, quashed this motion presently. Paul, who was his prisoner, had found favour with him, as Joseph with the captain of the guard. Julius, though he despised Paul's advice (*v.* 11), yet afterwards saw a great deal of cause to respect him, and therefore, being *willing to save Paul,* he prevented the execution of that bloody project, and *in favorem vitae — from a regard to his life,* he kept them from their purpose. It does not appear that they were any of them malefactors convicted, but only suspected, and waiting their trial, and in such a case as this better ten guilty ones should escape than one that was innocent be slain. As God had saved all in the ship for Paul's sake, so here the centurion saves all the prisoners for his sake; such a diffusive good is a good man.

VII. The saving of the lives of all the persons in the ship, by the wonderful providence of God. When the ship broke under them, surely *there was but a step between them and death;* and yet infinite mercy interposed, and that step was not stepped. 1. Some were saved by swimming: *The centurion commanded his soldiers* in the first place, *as many of them as could swim, to get to land* first, and to be ready to receive the prisoners, and prevent their escape. The Romans trained up their youth, among other exercises, to that of swimming, and it was often of service to them in their wars: Julius Caesar was a famous swimmer. It may be very useful to these who deal much at sea, but otherwise perhaps more lives have been lost by swimming in sport, and learning to swim, than have been saved by swimming for need. 2. The rest with much ado scrambled to the shore, some on boards that they had loose with them in the ship, and others on the *broken pieces of the ship,* every one making the best shift he could for himself and his friends, and the more busy because they were assured their labour should not be in vain; but *so it came to pass* that through the good providence of God none of them miscarried, none of them were by accident turned off, but they *escaped all safely to land.* See here an instance of the special providence of God in the preservation of people's lives, and particularly in the deliverance of many from perils by water, ready to sink, and yet kept from sinking, *the deep from swallowing them up* and *the water-floods from overflowing them,* the storm turned into a calm. They were rescued from the dreaded sea, and brought to the desired haven. *O that men would praise the Lord for his goodness!* Ps. 107:30, 31. Here was an instance of the performance of a particular word of promise which God gave, that all the persons in this ship should be saved for Paul's sake. Though there be great difficulty in the way of the promised salvation, yet it shall without fail be accomplished; and even the wreck of the ship may furnish out means for the saving of the lives, and, when all seems to be gone, all proves to be safe, though it be *on boards, and broken pieces of the ship.*

CHAPTER 28

We are the more concerned to take notice of and to improve what is here recorded concerning blessed Paul because, after the story of this chapter, we hear no more of him in the sacred history, though we have a great deal of him yet before us in his epistles. We have attended him through several chapters from one judgment-seat to another, and could at last have taken leave of him with the more pleasure if we had left him at liberty; but in this chapter we are to condole with him, and yet congratulate him. I. We condole with him as a poor shipwrecked passenger, stripped of all; and yet congratulate him, 1. As singularly owned by his God in his distress, preserved himself from receiving hurt by a viper that fastened on his hand (*v.* 1–6), and being made an instrument of much good in the island on which they were cast, in healing many that were sick, and particularly the father of Publius, the chief man of the island (*v.* 7–9). 2. As much respected by the people there (*v.* 10). II. We condole with him as a poor confined prisoner, carried to Rome under the notion of a criminal removed by "habeas corpus" (*v.* 11–16), and yet we congratulate him, 1. Upon the respect shown him by the Christians at Rome, who came a great way to meet him (*v.* 15). 2. Upon the favour he found with the captain of the guard, into whose custody he was delivered, who suffered him to dwell by himself, and did not put him in the common prison (*v.* 16). 3. Upon the free conference he had with the Jews at Rome, both about his own affair (*v.* 17–22) and upon the subject of the Christian religion in general (*v.* 23), the issue of which was that God was glorified, many were edified, the rest left inexcusable, and the apostles justified in preaching the gospel to the Gentiles (*v.* 24–29). 4. Upon the undisturbed liberty he had to preach the gospel to all comers in his own house for two years together (*v.* 30–31).

Verses 1–10

What a great variety of places and circumstances do we find Paul in! He was a planet, and not a fixed star. Here we have him in an island to which, in all probability, he had never come if he had not been thrown upon it by a storm; and yet it seems God has work for him to do here. Even stormy winds fulfil God's counsel, and an ill wind indeed it is that blows nobody any good; this ill wind blew good to the island of Melita; for it gave them Paul's company for three months, who was a blessing to every place he came to. This island was called Melita, lying between Sicily and Africa, twenty miles long, and twelve broad; it lies furthest from the continent of any island in the Mediterranean; it is about sixty miles from Sicily. It has been famous since for the knights of Malta, who, when the Turks overran that part of Christendom, made a noble stand, and gave some check to the progress of their arms. Now here we have,

I. The kind reception which the inhabitants of this island gave to the distressed strangers that were shipwrecked on their coast (*v.* 2): *The barbarous people showed us no little kindness.* God had promised that there should be no loss of any man's life; and, *as for God, his work is perfect.* If they had escaped the sea, and when they came ashore had perished for cold or want, it had been all one; therefore Providence continues its care of them, and what benefits we receive by the hand of man must be acknowledged to come from the hand of God; for every creature is that to us, and no more, that he makes it to be, and when he pleases, as he can make enemies to be at peace, so he can make strangers to be friends, friends in need, and those are friends indeed — friends *in adversity,* and that is *the time that a brother is born for.* Observe, 1. The general notice taken of the kindness which the natives of Malta showed to Paul and his company. They are called *barbarous people,* because they did not, in language and customs, conform either to the Greeks or Romans, who looked (superciliously enough) upon all but themselves as barbarians, though otherwise civilized enough, and perhaps in some cases more civil than they. These barbarous people, however they were called so, were full of humanity: They *showed us not little kindness.* So far were they from making a prey of this shipwreck, as many, I fear, who are called Christian people, would have done, that they laid hold of it as an opportunity of showing mercy. *The Samaritan* is a better neighbour to the poor wounded man *than the priest or Levite.* And verily we have not found greater humanity among Greeks, or Romans, or Christians, than among these barbarous people; and it is written for our imitation, that we may hence learn to be compassionate to those that are in distress and misery, and to relieve and succour them to the utmost of our ability, as those *that know we ourselves are also in the body.* We should be ready *to entertain strangers, as Abraham, who sat at his tent door to invite passengers in* (Heb. 13:2), but especially strangers in distress, as these were. *Honour all men.* If Providence hath so *appointed the bounds of our habitation* as to give us an opportunity of being frequently serviceable to persons at a loss, we should not place it among the inconveniences of our lot, but the advantages of it; because *it is more blessed to give than to receive.* Who knows but these barbarous people had their lot cast in this island for such a time as this! 2. A particular instance of their kindness: *They kindled a fire,* in some large hall or other, and *they received us everyone* — made room for us about the fire, and bade us all welcome, without asking either what country we were of or what religion. In swimming *to the shore,* and coming on *the broken pieces of the ship,* we must suppose that they were sadly wet, that they had not a dry thread on them; and, as if that were not enough, to complete the deluge, waters from above met those from below, and it rained so hard that this would wet them to the skin presently; and *it was a cold rain too,* so that they wanted nothing so much as a good fire (for they had eaten heartily but just before on ship-board), and this they got for them presently, *to warm them, and dry their clothes.* It is sometimes as much a piece of charity to poor families to supply them with fuel as with food or raiment. *Be you warmed,* is as necessary as *Be you filled.* When in the extremities of bad weather we find ourselves fenced against the rigours of the season, by the accommodations of a warm house, bed, clothes, and a good fire, we should think how many lie exposed *to the present rain, and to the cold,* and pity them, and pray for them, and help them if we can.

II. The further danger that Paul was in by a viper's fastening on his hand, and the unjust construction that the people put upon it. Paul is among strangers, and appears one of the meanest and most contemptible of the company, therefore God distinguishes him, and soon causes him to be taken notice of.

1. When the fire was to be made, and too be made bigger, that so great a company might all have the benefit of it, Paul was as busy as any of them in gathering sticks. *v.* 3. Though he was free from all, and of greater account than any of them, *yet he made himself servant of all.* Paul was an industrious active man, and loved to be doing when any thing was to be done, and never contrived to take his ease. Paul was a humble self-denying man, and would stoop to any thing by which he might be serviceable, even to the gathering of sticks to make a fire of. We should reckon nothing below us but sin, and be willing to condescend to the meanest offices, if there be occasion, for the good of our brethren. The people were ready to help them; yet Paul, wet and cold as he is, will not throw it all upon them, but will help himself. Those that receive benefit by the fire should help to carry fuel to it.

2. The sticks being old dry rubbish, it happened there was a viper among them, that lay as dead till it came to the heat, and then revived, or lay quiet till it felt the fire, and then was provoked, and flew at him that unawares threw it into the fire, and *fastened upon his hand, v.* 3. Serpents and such venomous creatures commonly lie among sticks; hence we read of him *that leans on the wall, and a serpent bites him,* Amos 5:19. It was so common that people were by it frightened from tearing hedges (Eccl. 10:8): *Whoso breaketh a hedge, a serpent shall bite him.* As there is a snake under the green grass, so there is often under the dry leaves. See how many perils human life is exposed to, and what danger we are in from the inferior creatures, which have many of them become enemies to men, since men became rebels to God; and what a mercy it is that we are preserved from them as we are. We often meet with that which is mischievous where we expect that which is beneficial; and many come by hurt when they are honestly employed, and in the way of their duty.

3. The barbarous people concluded that Paul, being a prisoner, was certainly a murderer, who had appealed to Rome, to escape justice in his own country, and that this viper was sent by divine justice to be the avenger of blood; or, if they were not aware that he was a prisoner, they supposed that he was in his flight; and *when they saw the venomous animal hand on his hand,* which it seems he could not, or would not, immediately throw off, but let it hang, they concluded, *"No doubt this man is a murderer,* has shed innocent blood, and therefore, *though he has escaped the sea, yet* divine *vengeance* pursues him, and fastens upon him now that he is pleasing himself with the thoughts of that escape, and will *not suffer him to live."* Now in this we may see,

(1.) Some of the discoveries of natural light. They were barbarous people, perhaps had no books nor learning among them, and yet they knew naturally, [1.] That there is a God that governs the world, and a providence that presides in all occurrences, that things do not come to pass by chance, no, not such a thing as this, but by divine direction. [2.] That evil pursues sinners, that there are good works which God will reward and wicked works which he will punish; there is a divine *nemesis — a vengeance,* which sooner or later will reckon for enormous crimes. They believe not only that there is a God, but that this God hath said, *Vengeance is mine, I will repay,* even to death. [3.] That murder is a heinous crime, and which shall not long go unpunished, that *whoso sheds man's blood,* if his blood be not shed by man (by the magistrate, as it ought to be) it shall be shed by the righteous Judge of heaven and earth, who is the avenger of wrong. Those that think they shall go unpunished in any evil way will be judged out of the mouth of these barbarians, who could say, without book, *Woe to the wicked, for it shall be ill with them, for the reward of their hands shall be given them.* Those who, because they have escaped many judgments are secure, and say, *We shall have peace though we go on,* and have their hearts so much the more *set to do evil because sentence against their evil works is not executed speedily,* may learn from these illiterate people that, though malefactors have escaped the vengeance of the sea, yet there is no outrunning divine justice, *vengeance suffers not to live.* In Job's time you might ask *those that to by the way,* ask the next body you met, and they would tell you that *the wicked is reserved to the day of destruction.*

(2.) Some of the mistakes of natural light, which needed to be rectified by divine revelation. In two things their knowledge was defective: — [1.] That they thought all wicked people were punished in this life; that divine vengeance never suffers great and notorious sinners, such as murderers are, to live long; but that, if *they come up out of the pit, they shall be taken in the snare* (Jer. 48:43, 44), if *they flee from a lion, a bear shall meet them* (Amos 5:19), if they escape being drowned, a viper shall fasten upon them; whereas it is not so. The wicked, even murderers, sometimes *live, become old, yea, are mighty in power;* for the day of vengeance is to come in the other world, *the great day of wrath;* and though some are made examples of in this world, to prove that there is a God and a providence, yet many are left unpunished, to prove that there is a judgment to come. [2.] That they thought all who were remarkably afflicted in this life were wicked people; that a man on whose hand a viper fastens may thence be judged to be a murderer, as if those on whom the tower in Siloam fell must needs be greater sinners than all in Jerusalem. This mistake Job's friends went upon, in their judgment upon his case; but divine revelation sets this matter in a true light — that all things come ordinarily alike to all, that good men are oftentimes greatly afflicted in this life, for the exercise and improvement of their faith and patience.

4. When he shook off the viper from his hand, yet they expected that divine vengeance would ratify the censure they had passed, and *that he would have swollen* and burst, through the force of the poison, or *that he would have fallen down dead suddenly.* See how apt men are, when once they have got an ill opinion of a man, though ever so unjust, to abide by it, and to think that God must necessarily confirm and ratify their peevish sentence. It was well they did not knock him down themselves, when they saw he did not swell and fall down; but so considerate they are as to let Providence work, and to attend the motions of it.

III. Paul's deliverance from the danger, and the undue construction the people put upon this. The viper's fastening on his hand was a trial of his faith; and it was found to praise, and honour, and glory: for, 1. It does not appear that it put him into any fright or confusion at all. He did not shriek or start, nor, as it would be natural for us to do, throw it off with terror and precipitation; for he suffered it to hang on so long that the people had time to take notice of it and to make their remarks upon it. Such a wonderful presence of mind he had, and such a composure, as no man could have upon such a sudden accident, but by the special aids of divine grace, and the actual belief and consideration of that word of Christ concerning his disciples (Mk. 16:18), *They shall take up serpents.* This it is to have *the heart fixed, trusting in God.* 2. He carelessly *shook off the viper into the fire,* without any difficulty, calling for help, or any means used to loosen its hold; and it is probable that it was consumed in the fire. Thus, in the strength of the grace of Christ, believers shake off the temptations of Satan, with a holy resolution, saying, as Christ did, *Get thee behind me, Satan; The Lord rebuke thee;* and thus they *keep themselves, that the wicked one toucheth them not,* so as to fasten upon them, 1 Jn. 5:18. When we despise the censures and reproaches of men, and look upon them with a holy contempt, having the testimony of conscience for us, then we do, as Paul here, *shake off the viper into the fire.* It does us no harm, except we fret at it, or be deterred by it from our duty, or be provoked to render railing for railing. 3. He was none the worse. Those that thought it would have been his death *looked a great while, but saw no harm at all come to him.* God hereby intended to make him remarkable among these barbarous people, and so to make way for the entertainment of the gospel among them. It is reported that after this no venomous creature would live in that island, any more than in Ireland; but I do not find that the matter of fact is confirmed, though the popish writers speak of it with assurance. 4. They then magnified him as much as before they had vilified him: *They changed their minds, and said that he was a god* — an immortal god; for they thought it impossible that a mortal man should have a viper hang on his hand so long and be never the worse. See the uncertainty of popular opinion, how it turns with the wind, and how apt it is to run into extremes both ways; from *sacrificing to Paul and Barnabas to stoning them;* and here, from condemning him as a murderer to idolizing him as a god.

IV. The miraculous cure of an old gentleman that was ill of a fever, and of others that were otherwise diseased, by Paul. And, with these confirmations of the doctrine of Christ, no doubt there was a faithful publication of it. Observe, 1. The

kind entertainment which *Publius, the chief man of the island,* gave to these distressed strangers; he had a considerable estate in the island, and some think was governor, and he *received them and lodged them three days very courteously,* that they might have time to furnish themselves in other places at the best hand. It is happy when God gives a large heart to those to whom he has given a large estate. It became him, who was the chief man of the island, to be most hospitable and generous, — who was the richest man, to be rich in good works. 2. The illness of *the father of Publius:* He *lay sick of a fever and a bloody flux,* which often go together, and, when they do, are commonly fatal. Providence ordered it that he should be ill just at this time, that the cure of him might be a present recompence to Publius for his generosity, and the cure of him by miracle a recompence particularly for his kindness to Paul, whom he received in the name of a prophet, and had this prophet's reward. 3. His cure: Paul took cognizance of his case, and though we do not find he was urged to it, for they had no thought of any such thing, yet he entered in, not as a physician to heal him by medicines, but as an apostle to heal him by miracle; and he prayed to God, in Christ's name, for his cure, and then laid his hands on him, and he was perfectly well in an instant. Though he must needs be in years, yet he recovered his health, and the lengthening out of his life yet longer would be a mercy to him. 4. The cure of many others, who were invited by this cure to apply to Paul. If he can heal diseases so easily, so effectually, he shall soon have patients enough; and he *bade them all welcome,* and sent them away with what they came for. He did not plead that he was a stranger there, thrown accidentally among them, under no obligations to them and waiting to be gone by the first opportunity, and therefore might be excused from receiving their applications. No, a good man will endeavour to do good wherever the providence of God casts him. Paul reckoned himself a debtor, not only to the Greeks, but to the Barbarians, and thanked God for an opportunity of being useful among them. Nay, he was particularly obliged to these inhabitants of Malta for the seasonable shelter and supply they had afforded him, and hereby he did in effect discharge his quarters, which should encourage us to entertain strangers, for some thereby have entertained angels and some apostles unawares. God will not be behind-hand with any for kindness shown to his people in distress. We have reason to think that Paul with these cures preached the gospel to them, and that, coming thus confirmed and recommended, it was generally embraced among them. And, if so, never were any people so enriched by a shipwreck on their coasts as these Maltese were.

V. The grateful acknowledgement which even these barbarous people made of the kindness Paul had done them, in preaching Christ unto them. They were civil to him, and to the other ministers that were with him, who, it is likely, were assisting to him in preaching among them, *v.* 10. 1. They *honoured us with many honours.* They showed them all possible respect; they saw God honoured them, and therefore they justly thought themselves obliged to honour them, and thought nothing too much by which they might testify the esteem they had for them. Perhaps they made them free of their island by naturalizing them, and admitted them members of their guilds and fraternities. The faithful preachers of the gospel are worthy of a double honour, especially when they succeeded in their labours. 2. *When we departed, they loaded us with such things as were necessary;* or, they put on board such things as we had occasion for. Paul could not labour with his hands here, for he had nothing to work upon, and therefore accepted the kindness of the good people of Melita, not as a fee for his cures (freely he had received, and freely he gave), but as the relief of his wants, and theirs that were with him. And, having reaped of their spiritual things, it was but just they should make them those returns, 1 Co. 9:11.

Verses 11–16

We have here the progress of Paul's voyage towards Rome, and his arrival there at length. A rough and dangerous voyage he had hitherto had, and narrowly escaped with his life; but after a storm comes a calm: the latter part of his voyage was easy and quiet.

> Per varios casus, per tot discrimina rerum,
> Tendimus ad Latium —
>
> Through various hazards and events we move
> To Latium.

Tendimus ad coelum.
We make for heaven.
— Dabit Deus his quoque finem.
To these a period will be fixed by Heaven.

We have here,

I. Their leaving Malta. That island was a happy shelter to them, but it was not their home; when they are refreshed they must put to sea again. The difficulties and discouragements we have met with in our Christian course must not hinder us from pressing forward. Notice is here taken, 1. Of the time of their departure: *After three months,* the three winter months. Better lie by, though they lay upon charges, than go forward while the season was dangerous. Paul had warned them against venturing to sea in winter weather, and they would not take the warning; but, now that they had learned it by the difficulties and dangers they had gone through, he needed not to warn them: their learning did them good when they had paid dearly for it. Experience is therefore called the mistress of fools, because those are fools that will not learn till experience has taught them. 2. Of the ship in which they departed. It was in a ship of Alexandria; so was that which was cast away, *ch.* 27:6. This ship had *wintered in that isle,* and was safe. See what different issues there are of men's undertakings in this world. Here were two ships, both of Alexandria, both bound for Italy, both thrown upon the same island, but one is wrecked there and the other is saved. Such occurrences may often be observed. Providence sometimes favours those that deal in the world, and prospers them, that people may be encouraged to set their hands to worldly business; at other times Providence crosses them, that people may be warned not to set their hearts upon it. Events are thus varied, that we may learn both how to want and how to abound. The historian takes notice of the sign of the ship, which probably gave it its name: it was *Castor and Pollux.* Those little foolish pagan deities, which the poets had made to preside over storms and to protect seafaring men, as gods of the sea, were painted or graven upon the fore-part of the ship, and thence the ship took its name. I suppose this is observed for no other reason than for the better ascertaining of the story, that ship being well known by that name and sign by all that dealt between Egypt and Italy. Dr. Lightfoot thinks that Luke mentions this circumstance to intimate the men's superstition, that they hoped they should have better sailing under this badge than they had had before.

II. Their landing in or about Italy, and the pursuing of their journey towards Rome. 1. They landed first at Syracuse in Sicily, the chief city of that island. There they *tarried three days,* probably having some goods to put ashore, or some merchandise to make there; for it seems to have been a trading voyage that this ship made. Paul had now his curiosity gratified with the sight of places he had often heard of and wished to see, particularly Syracuse, a place of great antiquity and note; and yet, it should seem, there were no Christians there. 2. From Syracuse they came to Rhegium, a city in Italy, directly opposite to Messina in Sicily, belonging to the kingdom of Calabria or Naples. There, it seems they staid one day; and a very formal story the Romish legends tell of Paul's preaching here at this time, and the fish coming to the shore to hear him, — that with a candle he set a stone pillar on fire, and by that miracle convinced the people of the truth of his doctrine, and they were many of them baptized, and he ordained Stephen, one of his companions in this voyage, to be their bishop, — and all this, they tell you, was done in this one day; whereas it does not appear that they did so much as go ashore, but only came to an anchor in the road. 3. From Rhegium they came to Puteoli, a sea-port town not far from Naples, now called *Pozzolana.* The ship of Alexandria was bound for that port, and therefore there Paul, and the rest that were bound for Rome, were put ashore, and went the remainder of their way by land. At Puteoli they *found brethren,* Christians. Who brought the knowledge of Christ hither we are not told, but here it was, so wonderfully did the leaven of the gospel diffuse itself. God has many that serve and worship him in places where we little think he has. And observe, (1.) Though it is probable there were but few brethren in Puteoli, yet Paul found them out; either they heard of him, or he enquired them out, but as it were by instinct they got together. Brethren in Christ should find out one another, and keep up communion with each other, as those of the same country do in a foreign land. (2.) They desired Paul and his companions to *tarry with them seven days,* that is, to forecast to stay at least one Lord's day with them, and to assist them in their public worship that day. They knew not whether ever they should see Paul at Puteoli again, and therefore he must not go without giving them a sermon or two, or more. And Paul was willing to allow them so much of his time; and the centurion under whose command Paul now was, perhaps having himself friends or business at Puteoli, agreed to stay one week there, to oblige Paul. 4. From Puteoli they went forward towards Rome; whether they travelled on foot, or whether they had beasts provided for them to ride on (as *ch.* 23:24), does not appear; but to Rome they must go, and this was their last stage.

III. The meeting which the Christians at Rome gave to Paul. It is probable that notice was sent to them by the Christians at Puteoli, as soon as ever Paul had come thither, how long he intended to stay there, and when he would set forward for Rome, which gave an opportunity for this interview. Observe,

1. The great honour they did to Paul. They had heard much of his fame, what use God had made of him, and what eminent service he had done to the kingdom of Christ in the world, and to what multitudes of souls he had been a spiritual father. They had heard of his sufferings, and how God had owned him in them, and therefore they not only longed to see him, but thought themselves obliged to show him all possible respect, as a glorious advocate for the cause of Christ. He had some time ago written a long epistle to them, and a most excellent one, *the epistle to the Romans,* in which he had not only expressed his great kindness for them, but had given them a great many useful instructions, in return for which they show him this respect. They *went to meet him,* that they might bring him in state, as ambassadors and judges make their public entry, though he was a prisoner. Some of them went as far as *Appiiforum,* which was fifty-one miles from Rome; others to a place called the *Three Taverns,* which was twenty-eight miles (some reckon it thirty-three miles) from Rome. They are to be commended for it, that they were so far from being ashamed of him, or afraid of owning him, because he was a prisoner, that for that very reason they counted him worthy of double honour, and were the more careful to show him respect.

2. The great comfort Paul had in this. Now that he was drawing near to Rome, and perhaps heard at Puteoli what character the emperor Nero now had, and what a tyrant he had of late become, he began to have some melancholy thoughts about his appeal to Caesar, and the consequences of it. He was drawing near to Rome, where he had never been, where there were few that knew him or that he knew, and what things might befal him here he could not tell; but he began to grow dull upon it, till he met with these good people that came from Rome to show him respect; and *when he saw them,* (1.) He *thanked God.* We may suppose he thanked them for their civility, told them again and again how kindly he took it; but this was not all: he *thanked God.* Note, If our friends be kind to us, it is God that makes them so, that puts it into their hearts, and into the power of their hands, to be so, and we must give him the glory of it. He thanked God, no doubt, for the civility and generosity of the barbarous people at Melita, but much more for the pious care of the Christian people at Rome for him. When he saw so many Christians that were of Rome, he thanked God that the gospel of Christ had had such wonderful success there in the metropolis of the empire. When we go abroad, or but look abroad, into the world, and meet with those, even in strange places, that bear up Christ's name, and fear God, and serve him, we should lift up our hearts to heaven in thanksgiving; blessed be God that there are so many excellent ones on this earth, bad as it is. Paul had thanked God for the Christians at Rome before he had ever seen them, upon the report he had heard concerning them (Rom. 1:8): *I thank my God for you all.* But now that he saw them (and perhaps they appeared more fashionable and genteel people than most he had conversed with, or more grave, serious, and intelligent, than most) *he thanked God.* But this was not all: (2.) He *took courage.* It put new life into him, cheered up his spirits, and banished his melancholy, and now he can enter Rome a prisoner as cheerfully as ever he had entered Jerusalem at liberty. he finds there are those there who love and value him, and whom he may both converse with and consult with as his friends, which will take off much of the tediousness of his imprisonment, and the terror of his appearing before Nero. Note, it is an encouragement to those who are travelling towards heaven to meet with their fellow travellers, who are their *companions in the kingdom and patience of Jesus Christ.* When we see the numerous and serious assemblies of good Christians, we should not only give thanks to God, but take courage to ourselves. And this is a good reason why respect should be shown to good ministers, especially when they are in sufferings, and have contempt put upon them, that it encourages them, and makes both their sufferings and their services more easy. Yet it is observable that though the Christians at Rome were now so respectful to Paul, and he had promised himself so much from their respect, yet they failed him when he most needed them; for he says (2 Tim. 4:16), *At my first answer, no man stood with me, but all men forsook me.* They could easily take a ride of forty or fifty miles to go and meet Paul, for the pleasantness of the journey; but to venture the displeasure of the emperor and the disobliging of other great men, by appearing in defence of Paul and giving evidence for him, here they desire to be excused; when it comes to this, they will rather ride as far out of town to miss him as now they did to meet him, which is an intimation to us to cease from man, and to encourage ourselves in the Lord our God. The courage we take from his promises will never fail us, when we shall be ashamed of that which we took from men's compliments. *Let God be true, but every man a liar.*

IV. The delivering of Paul into custody at Rome, *v.* 16. He is now come to his journey's end. And, 1. He is still a prisoner. He had longed to see Rome, but, when he comes there, he is delivered, with other prisoners, to the *captain of the guard,* and can see no more of Rome than he will permit him. How many great men had made their entry into Rome, crowned and in triumph, who really were the plagues of their generation! But here a good man makes his entry into Rome, chained and triumphed over as a poor captive, who was really the greatest blessing to his generation. This thought is enough to put one for ever out of conceit with this world. 2. Yet he has some favour shown him. He is a prisoner, but not a close prisoner, not in the common jail: *Paul was suffered to dwell by himself,* in some convenient private lodgings which his friends there provided for him, and a soldier was appointed to be his guard, who, we hope, was civil to him, and let him take all the liberty that could be allowed to a prisoner, for he must be very ill-natured indeed that could be so to such a courteous obliging man as Paul. Paul, being suffered to dwell by himself, could the better enjoy himself, and his friends, and his God, than if he had been lodged with the other prisoners. Note, This may encourage God's prisoners, that he can give them favour in the eyes of those that carry them captive (Ps. 106:46), as Joseph in the eyes of his keeper (Gen. 39:21), and Jehoiachin in the eyes of the king of Babylon, 2 Ki. 25:27, 28. When God does not deliver his people presently out of bondage, yet, if he either make it easy to them or them easy under it, they have reason to be thankful.

Verses 17–22

Paul, with a great deal of expense and hazard, is brought a prisoner to Rome, and when he has come nobody appears to prosecute him or lay any thing to his charge; but he must call his own cause; and here he represents it to the chief of the Jews at Rome. It was not long since, by an edict of Claudius, all the Jews were banished from Rome, and kept out till his death; but, in the five years since then, many Jews had come thither, for the advantage of trade, though it does not appear that they were allowed any synagogue there or place of public worship; but these *chief of the Jews* were those of best figure among them, the most distinguished men of that religion, who had the best estates and interests. *Paul called them together,* being desirous to stand right in their opinion, and that there might be a good understanding between him and them. And here we are told,

I. What he said to them, and what account he gave them of his cause. He speaks respectfully to them, calls them men and brethren, and thereby intimates that he expects to be treated by them both as a man and as a brother, and engages to treat them as such and to tell them nothing but the truth; for *we are members one of another — all we are brethren.* Now, 1. He professes his own innocency, and that he had not given any just occasion to the Jews to bear him such an ill will as generally they did: "I have *committed nothing against the people* of the Jews, have done nothing to the prejudice of their religion or civil liberties, have added no affliction to their present miseries, they know I have not; nor have

I committed any thing *against the customs of our fathers,* either by abrogating or by innovating in religion." It is true Paul did not impose the customs of the fathers upon the Gentiles: they were never intended for them. But it is as true that he never opposed them in the Jews, but did himself, when he was among them, conform to them. He never quarrelled with them for practising according to the usages of their own religion, but only for their enmity to the Gentiles, Gal. 2:12. Paul had the testimony of his conscience for him that he had done his duty to the Jews. 2. He modestly complains of the hard usage he had met with — that, though he had given them no offence, yet *he was delivered prisoner from Jerusalem into the hands of the Romans.* If he had spoken the whole truth in this matter, it would have looked worse than it did upon the Jews, for they would have murdered him without any colour of law or justice if the Romans had not protected him; but, however, they accused him as a criminal, before Felix the governor, and, demanding judgment against him, were, in effect delivering him prisoner into the hands of the Romans, when he desired no more than a fair and impartial trial by their own law. 3. He declares the judgment of the Roman governors concerning him, *v.* 18. They examined him, enquired into his case, heard what was to be said against him, and what he had to say for himself. The chief captain examined him, so did Felix, and Festus, and Agrippa, and they could find no cause of death in him; nothing appeared to the contrary but that he was an honest, quiet, conscientious, good man, and therefore they would never gratify the Jews with a sentence of death upon him; but, on the contrary, would have let him go, and have let him go on in his work too, and have given him no interruption, for they all heard him and liked his doctrine well enough. It was for the honour of Paul that those who most carefully examined his case acquitted him, and none condemned him but unheard, and such as were prejudiced against him. 4. He pleads the necessity he was under to remove himself and his cause to Rome; and that it was only in his own defence, and not with any design to recriminate, or exhibit a cross bill against the complainants, (*v.* 19): *When the Jews spoke against it,* and entered a caveat against his discharge, designing, if they could not have him condemned to die, yet to have him made a prisoner for life, he was *constrained to appeal unto Caesar,* finding that the governors, one after another, stood so much in awe of the Jews that they could not discharge him, for fear of making him their enemies, which made it necessary for him to pray the assistance of the higher powers. This was all he aimed at in this appeal; not to accuse his nation, but only to vindicate himself. Every man has a right to plead in his own defence, who yet ought not to find fault with his neighbours. It is an invidious thing to accuse, especially to accuse a nation, such a nation. Paul made intercession for them, but never against them. The Roman government had at this time an ill opinion of the Jewish nation, as factious, turbulent, disaffected, and dangerous; and it had been an easy thing for a man with such a fluent tongue as Paul had, a citizen of Rome, and so injured as he was, to have exasperated the emperor against the Jewish nation. But Paul would not for ever so much do such a thing; he was for making the best of every body, and not making bad worse. 5. He puts his sufferings upon the true footing, and gives them such an account of the reason of them as should engage them not only not to join with his persecutors against him, but to concern themselves for him, and to do what they could on his behalf (*v.* 20): "*For this cause I have called for you,* not to quarrel with you, for I have no design to incense the government against you, but to *see you and speak with you* as my countrymen, and men that I would keep up a correspondence with, because *for the hope of Israel I am bound with this chain.*" He carried the mark of his imprisonment about with him, and probably was chained to the soldier that kept him; and it was, (1.) Because he preached that the Messiah was come, who was the hope of Israel, he whom Israel hoped for. "Do not all the Jews agree in this, that the Messiah will be the glory of his people Israel? And therefore he is to be hoped for, and this Messiah I preach, and prove he is come. They would keep up such a hope of a Messiah yet to come as must end in a despair of him; I preach such a hope in a Messiah already come as must produce a joy in him." (2.) Because he preached that the resurrection of the dead would come. This also was the hope of Israel; so he had called it, *ch.* 23:6; 24:15; 26:6, 7. "They would have you still expect a Messiah that would free you from the Roman yoke, and make you great and prosperous upon earth, and it is this that occupies their thoughts; and they are angry at me for directing their expectations to the great things of another world, and persuading them to embrace a Messiah who will secure those to them, and not external power and grandeur. I am for bringing you to the spiritual and eternal blessedness upon which our fathers by faith had their eye, and this is what they hate me for, — because I would take you off from that which is the cheat of Israel, and will be its shame and ruin, the notion of a temporal Messiah, and lead you to that which is the true and real hope of Israel, and the genuine sense of all the promises made to the fathers, a spiritual kingdom of holiness and love set up in the hearts of men, to be the pledge of, and preparative for, the joyful resurrection of the dead and the life of the world to come."

II. What was their reply. They own, 1. That they had nothing to say in particular against him; nor had any instructions to appear as his prosecutors before the emperor, either by letter or word of mouth (*v.* 21): "*We have neither received letters out of Judea concerning thee* (have no orders to prosecute thee) *nor have any of the brethren* of the Jewish nation that have lately come up to Rome (as many occasions drew the Jews thither now that their nation was a province of that empire) *shown or spoken any harm of thee.*" This was very strange, that that restless and inveterate rage of the Jews which had followed Paul wherever he went should not follow him to Rome, to get him condemned there. Some think they told a lie here, and had orders to prosecute him, but durst not own it, being themselves obnoxious to the emperor's displeasure, who though he had not, like his predecessors, banished them all from Rome, yet gave them no countenance there. But I am apt to think that what they said was true, and Paul now found he had gained the point he aimed at in appealing to Caesar, which was to remove his cause into a court to which they durst not follow it. This was David's policy, and it was his security (1 Sa. 27:1): *There is nothing better for me than to escape into the land of the Philistines, and Saul shall despair of me, to seek me any more in any coasts of Israel; so shall I escape out of his hands:* and it proved so, *v.* 4. *When Saul heard that David had fled to Gath, he sought no more again for him.* Thus did Paul by his appeal: he fled to Rome, where he was out of their reach; and they said, "Even let him go." 2. That they desired to know particularly concerning the doctrine he preached, and the religion he took so much pains to propagate in the face of so much opposition (*v.* 22): "*We desire to hear of thee what thou thinkest — ha phroneis* what thy opinions or sentiments are, what are those things which thou art so wise about, and hast such a relish of and such a zeal for; for, though we know little else of Christianity, we know *it is a sect every where spoken against.*" Those who said this scornful spiteful word of the Christian religion were Jews, *the chief of the Jews at Rome,* who boasted of their knowledge (Rom. 2:17), and yet this was all they knew concerning the Christian religion, that it was a *sect every where spoken against.* They put it into an ill name, and then ran it down. (1.) They looked upon it to be a sect, and this was false. True Christianity establishes that which is of common concern to all mankind, and is not built upon such narrow opinions and private interests as sects commonly owe their original to. It aims at no worldly benefit or advantage as sects do; but all its gains are spiritual and eternal. And, besides, it has a direct tendency to the uniting of the children of men, and not the dividing of them, and setting them at variance, as sects have. (2.) They said it was every where spoken against, and this was too true. All that they conversed with spoke against it, and therefore they concluded every body did: most indeed did. It is, and always has been, the lot of Christ's holy religion to be every where spoken against.

Verses 23–29

We have here a short account of a long conference which Paul had with the Jews at Rome about the Christian religion. Though they were so far prejudiced against it, because it was every where spoken against, as to call it *a sect,* yet they were willing to give it a hearing, which was more than the Jews at Jerusalem would do. It is probable that these Jews at Rome, being men of larger acquaintance with the world and more general conversation, were more free in their enquiries than the bigoted Jews at Jerusalem were, and would not answer this matter before they heard it.

I. We are here told how Paul managed this conference in defence of the Christian religion. The Jews appointed the time, a day was set for this dispute, that all parties concerned might have sufficient notice, *v.* 23. Those Jews seemed well disposed to receive conviction, and yet it did not prove that they all were so. Now when the day came,

1. There were *many got together to Paul.* Though he was a prisoner and could not come out to them, yet they were willing to come to him to his lodging. And the confinement he was now under, if duly considered, instead of prejudicing them against his doctrine, ought to confirm it to them; for it was a sign not only that he believed it, but that he thought it worth suffering for. One would visit such a man as Paul in his prison rather than not have instruction from him. And he made room for them in his lodging, not fearing to give offence to the government, so that he might do good to them.

2. He was very large and full in his discourse with them, seeking their conviction more than his own vindication. (1.) He expounded, or explained, the kingdom of God to them, — showed them the nature of that kingdom and the glorious purposes and designs of it, that it is heavenly and spiritual, seated in the minds of men, and shines not in external pomp, but in purity of heart and life. That which kept the Jews in their unbelief was a misunderstanding of the kingdom of God, as if it came with observation; let but that be expounded to them, and set in a true light, and they will be brought into obedience to it. (2.) He not only expounded the kingdom of God, but he testified it, — plainly declared it to them, and confirmed it by incontestable proofs, that the kingdom of God by the Messiah's administration was come, and was now set up in the world. He attested the extraordinary powers in the kingdom of grace by which bore his testimony to it from his own experience of its power and influence upon him, and the manner of his being brought into subjection to it. (3.) He not only expounded and testified the kingdom of God, but he persuaded them, urged it upon their consciences and pressed them with all earnestness to embrace the kingdom of God, and submit to it, and not to persist in an opposition to it. He followed his doctrine (the explication and confirmation of it) with a warm and lively application to his hearers, which is the most proper and profitable method of preaching. (4.) He persuaded them concerning Jesus. The design and tendency of his whole discourse were to bring them to Christ, to convince them of his being the Messiah, and to engage them to believe in him as he is offered in the gospel. He urged upon them, *ta peri tou Iēsou — the things concerning Jesus,* the prophecies of him, which he read to them *out of the law of Moses and out of the prophets,* as pointing at the Messiah, and showed how they had all had their accomplishment in this Jesus. They being Jews, he dealt with them out of the scriptures of the Old Testament, and demonstrated that these were so far from making against Christianity that they were the great proofs of it; so that, if we compare the history of the New Testament with the prophecy of the Old, we must conclude that this Jesus is he that should come, and we are to look for no other.

3. He was very long; for he continued his discourse, and it should seem to have been a continued discourse, from *morning till evening;* perhaps it was a discourse eight or ten hours long. The subject was curious — he was full of it —it was of vast importance — he was in good earnest, and his heart was upon it — he knew not when he should have such another opportunity, and therefore, without begging pardon for tiring their patience, he kept them all day; but it is probable that he spent some of the time in prayer with them and for them.

II. What was the effect of this discourse. One would have thought that so good a cause as that of Christianity, and managed by such a skilful hand as Paul's, could not but carry the day, and that all the hearers would have yielded to it presently; but it did not prove so: the child Jesus is set for the fall of some and the rising again of others, a foundation stone to some and a stone of stumbling to others. 1. *They did not agree among themselves, v.* 25. Some of them thought Paul was in the right, others would not admit it. This is that division which Christ came to send, that fire which he came to kindle, Lu. 12:49, 51. Paul preached with a great deal of plainness and clearness, and yet his hearers could not agree about the sense and evidence of what he preached. 2. *Some believed the things that were spoken, and some believed not, v.* 24. There was the disagreement. Such as this has always been the success of the gospel; to some it has been *a savour of life unto life,* to others *a savour of death unto death.* Some are wrought upon by the word, and others hardened; some receive the light, and others shut their eyes against it. So it was among Christ's hearers, and the spectators of his miracles, some believed and some blasphemed. If all had believed, there had been no disagreement; so that all the blame of the division lay upon those who would not believe.

III. The awakening word which Paul said to them at parting. He perceived by what they muttered that there were many among them, and perhaps the greater part, that were obstinate, and would not yield to the conviction of what he said; and they were getting up to be gone, they had had enough of it: "Hold," says Paul, "take one word with you before you go, and consider of it when you come home: what do you think will be the effect of your obstinate infidelity? What will you do in the end hereof? What will it come to?"

1. "You will by the righteous judgment of God be sealed up under unbelief. You harden your own hearts, and God will harden them as he did Pharaoh's; and this is what was prophesied of concerning you. Turn to that scripture (Isa. 6:9, 10), and read it seriously, and tremble lest the case there described should prove to be your case." As there are in the Old Testament gospel promises, which will be accomplished in all that believe, so there are gospel threatenings of spiritual judgments, which will be fulfilled in those that believe not; and this is one. it is part of the commission given to Isaiah the prophet; he is sent to make those worse that would not be made better. *Well spoke the Holy Ghost by Esaias the prophet unto our fathers.* What was spoken by JEHOVAH is here said to be spoken by the Holy Ghost, which proves that the Holy Ghost is God; and what was spoken to Isaiah is here said to be spoken by him to their fathers, for he was ordered to tell the people what God said to him; and, though what is there said had in it much of terror to the people and of grief to the prophet, yet it is here said to be well spoken. Hezekiah said concerning a message of wrath, *Good is the word of the Lord which thou hast spoken,* Isa. 39:8. And *he that believes not shall be damned* is gospel, as well as, *He that believes shall be saved,* Mk. 16:16. Or this may be explained by that of our Saviour (Mt. 15:7), *"Well did Esaias prophesy of you.* The Holy Ghost said to your fathers, that which would be fulfilled in you, *Hearing you shall hear, and shall not understand."* (1.) "That which was their great sin against God is yours; and that is this, you will not see. You shut your eyes against the most convincing evidence possible, and will not admit the conclusion, though you cannot deny the premises: *Your eyes you have closed,"* v. 27. This intimates an obstinate infidelity, and a willing slavery to prejudice. "As your fathers would not see God's hand lifted up against them in his judgments (Isa. 26:11), so you will not see God's hand stretched out to you in gospel grace." It was true of these unbelieving Jews that they were prejudiced against the gospel; they did not see, because they were resolved they would not, and none so blind as those that will not see. They would not prosecute their convictions, and for this reason would not admit them. They have purposely *closed their eyes, lest they should see with their eyes* the great things which belong to their everlasting peace, should see the glory of God, the amiableness of Christ, the deformity of sin, the beauty of holiness, the vanity of this world, and the reality of another. They will not be changed and governed by these truths, and therefore will not receive the evidence of them, *lest they should hear with their ears* that which they are loth to hear, the wrath of God revealed from heaven against them, and the will of God revealed from heaven to them. They stop their ears, like the deaf adder, that *will not hearken to the voice of the charmer, charm he ever so wisely.* Thus their fathers did; they *would not hear,* Zec. 7:11, 12. And that which they are afraid of in shutting up their eyes and ears, and barricading (as it were) both their learning senses against him that made both the hearing ear and the seeing eye, is, *lest they should understand with their heart, and should be converted, and I should heal them.* They kept their mind in the dark, or at least in a constant confusion and tumult, lest, if they should admit a considerate sober thought, they should understand with their heart how much it is both their duty and their interest to be religious, and so by degrees the truth should be too hard for them, and they should be converted from the evil ways which they take pleasure in, to those exercises to which they have now an aversion. Observe, God's method is to bring people first to see and he and so to understand with their hearts, and then to convert them, and bow their wills, and so heal them, which is the regular way of dealing with a rational soul;

and therefore Satan prevents the conversion of souls to God by blinding the mind and darkening the understanding, 2 Co. 4:4. And the case is very sad when the sinner joins with him herein, and puts out his own eyes. *Ut liberius peccent, libenter ignorant — They plunge into ignorance, that they may sin the more freely.* They are in love with their disease, and are afraid lest God should heal them; like Babylon of old, We would have healed her, and she would not be healed, Jer. 51:9. This was the sin. (2.) "That which was the great judgment of God upon them for this sin is his judgment upon you, and that is, you shall be blind. God will give you up to a judicial infatuation: *Hearing you shall hear* — you shall have the word of God preached to you over and over — *but you shall not understand* it; because you will not give your minds to understand it, God will not give you strength and grace to understand it. *Seeing you shall see* — you shall have abundance of miracles and signs done before your eyes — *but you shall not perceive* the convincing evidence of them. Take heed lest what Moses said to your fathers should be true of you (Deu. 29:4), *The Lord has not given you a heart to perceive, and eyes to see, and ears to hear, unto this day;* and what Isaiah said to the men of his generation (Isa. 29:10–12), *The Lord has poured out upon you the spirit of deep sleep, and has closed your eyes."* What with their resisting the grace of God and rebelling against the light, and God's withdrawing and withholding his grace and light from them, — what with their not receiving the love of the truth, and God's giving them up for that to strong delusions, to believe a lie, — what with their wilful and what with their judicial hardness, *the heart of this people is waxed gross, and their ears are dull of hearing.* They are stupid and senseless, and not wrought upon by all that can be said to them. No physic that can be given them operates upon them, nor will reach them, and therefore their disease must be adjudged incurable, and their case desperate. How should those be happy that will not be healed of a disease that makes them miserable? And how should those be healed that will not be converted to the use of the methods of cure? And how should those be converted that will not be convinced either of their disease or of their remedy? And how should those be convinced that *shut their eyes and stop their ears?* Let all that hear the gospel, and do not heed it, tremble at this doom; for, when once they are thus given up to hardness of heart, they are already in the suburbs of hell; for who shall heal them, if God do not?

2. "Your unbelief will justify God in sending the gospel to the Gentile world, which is the thing you look upon with such a jealous eye (v. 28): therefore seeing you put the grace of God away from you, and will not submit to the power of divine truth and love, seeing you will not be converted and healed in the methods which divine wisdom has appointed, *therefore be it known unto you that the salvation of God is sent unto the Gentiles,* that salvation which was of the Jews only (Jn. 4:22), the offer of it is made to them, the means of it afforded to them, and they stand fairer for it than you do; it is sent to them, and they will hear it, and receive it, and be happy in it." Now Paul designs hereby, (1.) To abate their displeasure at the preaching of the gospel to the Gentiles, by showing them the absurdity of it. They were angry that the salvation of God was sent to the Gentiles, and thought it was too great a favour done to them; but, if they thought that salvation of so small a value as not to be worthy of their acceptance, surely they could not grudge it to the Gentiles as too good for them, nor envy them for it. The salvation of God was sent into the world, the Jews had the first offer of it, it was fairly proposed to them, it was earnestly pressed upon them, but they refused it; they would not accept the invitation which was given to them first to the wedding-feast and therefore must thank themselves if other guests be invited. If they will not strike the bargain, nor come up to the terms, they ought not to be angry at those that will. They cannot complain that the Gentiles took it over their heads, or out of their hands, for they had quite taken their hands off it, nay, *they had lifted up the heel against it;* and therefore it is their fault, for *it is through their fall that salvation is come to the Gentiles,* Rom. 11:11. (2.) To improve their displeasure at the favour done to the Gentiles to their advantage, and to bring good out of that evil; for when he had spoken of this very thing in his epistle to the Romans, the benefit which the Gentiles had by the unbelief and rejection of the Jews, he says, he took notice of it on purpose that he might provoke his dear countrymen the Jews *to a holy emulation, and might save some of them,* Rom. 11:14. The Jews

have rejected the gospel of Christ, and pushed it off to the Gentiles, but it is not yet too late to repent of their refusal, and to accept of the salvation which they did make light of; they may say No, and take it, as the elder brother in the parable, who, when he was bidden to *go work in the vineyard,* first said, *I will not,* and yet *afterwards repented and went,* Mt. 21:29. Is the gospel sent to the Gentiles? Let us go after it rather than come short of it. And will they hear it, who are thought to be out of hearing, and have been so long like the idols they worshipped, *that have ears and hear not?* And shall not we hear it, whose privilege it is to have God so nigh to us in all that we call upon him for? Thus he would have them to argue, and to be shamed into the belief of the gospel by the welcome it met with among the Gentiles. And, if it had not that effect upon them, it would aggravate their condemnation, as it did that of the scribes and Pharisees, who, when they saw the publicans and harlots submit to John's baptism, did not afterwards thereupon repent of their folly, *that they might believe him,* Mt. 21:32.

IV. The breaking up of the assembly, as it should seem, in some disorder. 1. They turned their backs upon Paul. Those of them that believed not were extremely nettled at that last word which he said, that they should be judicially blinded, and that the light of the gospel should shine among those that sat in darkness. *When Paul had said these words,* he had said enough for them, and *they departed,* perhaps not so much enraged as some others of their nation had been upon the like occasion, but stupid and unconcerned, no more affected, either with those terrible words in the close of his discourse or all the comfortable words he had spoken before, than the seats they sat on. They departed, many of them with a resolution never to hear Paul preach again, nor trouble themselves with further enquiries about this matter. 2. They set their faces one against another; for they had great disputes among themselves. There was not only a quarrel between those who believed and those who believed not, but even among those who believed not there were debates. Those that agreed to depart from Paul, yet agreed not in the reasons why they departed, but had *great reasoning among themselves.* Many have great reasoning who yet do not reason right, can find fault with one another's opinions, and yet not yield to truth. Nor will men's reasoning among themselves convince them, without the grace of God to open their understandings.

Verses 30–31

We are here taking our leave of the history of blessed Paul; and therefore, since God saw it not fit that we should know any more of him, we should carefully take notice of every particular of the circumstances in which we must here leave him.

I. It cannot but be a trouble to us that we must leave him in bonds for Christ, nay, and that we have no prospect given us of his being set at liberty. *Two whole years* of that good man's life are here spent in confinement, and, for aught that appears, he was never enquired after, all that time, by those whose prisoner he was. He appealed to Caesar, in hope of a speedy discharge from his imprisonment, the governors having signified to his imperial majesty concerning the prisoner *that he had done nothing worthy of death or bonds,* and yet he is detained a prisoner. So little reason have we to trust in men, especially despised prisoners in great men; witness the case of Joseph, whom *the chief butler remembered not, but forgot,* Gen. 40:23. Yet some think that though it be not mentioned here, yet it was in the former of these two years, and early too in that year, that he was first brought before Nero, and then his bonds in Christ were manifest in Caesar's court, as he says, Phil. 1:13. And at this first answer it was that *no man stood by him,* 2 Tim. 4:16. But it seems, instead of being set at liberty upon this appeal, as he expected, he hardly escaped out of the emperor's hands with his life; he calls it a deliverance out of the mouth of the lion, 2 Tim. 4:17, and his speaking there of his first answer intimates that since that he had a second, in which he had come off better, and yet was not discharged. During these two years' imprisonment he wrote his epistle to the Galatians, then his second epistle to Timothy, then those to the Ephesians, Philippians, Colossians, and to Philemon, in which he mentions several things particularly concerning his imprisonment; and, lastly, his epistle to the Hebrews just after he was set at liberty, as Timothy also was, who, coming to visit him, was upon some account or other made his fellow-prisoner (*with whom,* writes Paul to the Hebrews, 13:23, *if he come shortly, I will see you*), but how or by what means he obtained his liberty we are not told, only that two years he was a prisoner. Tradition says that after his discharge he went from Italy to Spain, thence to Crete, and so with Timothy into Judea, and thence went to visit the churches in Asia, and at length came a second time to Rome, and there was beheaded in the last year of Nero. But Baronius himself owns that there is no certainty of any thing concerning him betwixt his release from this imprisonment and his martyrdom; but it is said by some that Nero, having, when he began to play the tyrant, set himself against the Christians, and persecuted them (and he was the first of the emperors that made a law against them, as Tertullian says, *Apol.* cap. 5), the church at Rome was much weakened by that persecution, and this brought Paul the second time to Rome, to re-establish the church there, and to comfort the souls of the disciples that were left, and so he fell a second time into Nero's hand. And Chrysostom relates that a young woman that was one of Nero's misses (to speak modishly) being converted, by Paul's preaching, to the Christian faith, and so brought off from the lewd course of life she had lived, Nero was incensed against Paul for it, and ordered him first to be imprisoned, and then put to death. But to keep to this short account here given of it, 1. It would grieve one to think that such a useful man as Paul was should be so long in restraint. Two years he was a prisoner under Felix (*ch.* 24:27), and, besides all the time that passed between that and his coming to Rome, he is here two years more a prisoner under Nero. How many churches might Paul have planted, how many cities and nations might he have brought over to Christ, in these five years' time (for so much it was at least), if he had been at liberty! But God is wise, and will show that he is not debtor to the most useful instruments he employs, but can and will carry on his own interest, both without their services and by their sufferings. Even Paul's bonds fell out *to the furtherance of the gospel,* Phil. 1:12–14. 2. Yet even Paul's imprisonment was in some respects a kindness to him, for these *two years he dwelt in his own hired house,* and that was more, for aught I know, than ever he had done before. He had always been accustomed to sojourn in the houses of others, now he has a house of his own — his own while he pays the rent of it; and such a retirement as this would be a refreshment to one who had been all his days an itinerant. He had been accustomed to be always upon the remove, seldom staid long at a place, but now he lived for two years in the same house; so that the bringing of him into this prison was like Christ's call to his disciples *to come into a desert place, and rest awhile,* Mk. 6:31. When he was at liberty, he was in continual fear by reason of *the lying in wait of the Jews* (*ch.* 20:19), but now his prison was his castle. Thus *out of the eater came forth meat, and out of the strong sweetness.*

II. Yet it is a pleasure to us (for we are sure it was to him) that, though we leave him in bonds for Christ, yet we leave him at work for Christ, and this made his bonds easy that he was not by them bound out from serving God and doing good. His prison becomes a temple, a church, and then it is to him a palace. His hands are tied, but, thanks be to God, his mouth is not stopped; a faithful zealous minister can better bear any hardship than being silenced. Here is Paul a prisoner, and yet a preacher; he is bound, but the word of the Lord is not bound. When he wrote his epistle to the Romans, he said *he longed to see them, that he might impart unto them some spiritual gift* (Rom. 1:11); he was glad *to see some of them* (*v.* 15), but it would not be half his joy unless he could impart to them some spiritual gift, which here he has an opportunity to do, and then he will not complain of his confinement. Observe,

1. To whom he preached: to all that had a mind to hear him, whether Jews or Gentiles. Whether he had liberty to go to other houses to preach does not appear; it is likely not; but whoever would had liberty to come to his house to hear, and they were welcome: *He received all that came to him.* Note, Ministers' doors should be open to such as desire to receive instruction from them, and they should be glad of an opportunity to advise those that are in care about their souls. Paul could not preach in a synagogue, or any public place of meeting that was sumptuous and capacious, but he preached in a poor cottage of his own. Note, When we cannot do what we would in the service of God we must do what we can. Those ministers that have but little hired houses should rather preach in them, if they may be allowed to do that, than be silent. *He received all that came to him,* and was not afraid of the greatest, nor ashamed of the meanest. He was ready to preach on the first day of the week to Christians, on the seventh day to Jews, and to all who would come on any day of the week; and he might hope the better to speed because *they came in unto him,* which supposed a desire to be instructed and a willingness to learn, and where these are it is probable that some good may be done.

2. What he preached. He does not fill their heads with curious speculations, nor with matters of state and politics, but he keeps to his text, minds his business as an apostle. (1.) He is God's ambassador, and therefore *preaches the kingdom of God,* does all he can to preach it up, negotiates the affairs of it, in order to the advancing of all its true interests. He meddles not with the affairs of the kingdoms of men; let those treat of them whose work it is. He preaches the kingdom of God among men, and the word of that kingdom; the same that he defended in his public disputes, *testifying the kingdom of God* (*v.* 23), he enforced in his public preaching, as that which, if received aright, will make us all wise and good, wiser and better, which is the end of preaching. (2.) He is an agent for Christ, a friend of the bridegroom, and therefore *teaches those things which concern the Lord Jesus Christ* — the whole history of Christ, his incarnation, doctrine, life, miracles, death, resurrection, ascension; all that relates to the mystery of godliness. Paul stuck still to his principle — to know and preach *nothing but Christ, and him crucified.* Ministers, when in their preaching they are tempted to diverge from that which is their main business, should reduce themselves with this question, What does this concern the Lord Jesus Christ? What tendency has it to bring us to him, and to keep us walking in him? *For we preach not ourselves, but Christ.*

3. With what liberty he preached. (1.) Divine grace gave him a liberty of spirit. He preached *with all confidence,* as one that was himself well assured of the truth of what he preached — that it was what he durst stand by; and of the worth of it — that it was what he durst suffer for. He was *not ashamed of the gospel of Christ.* (2.) Divine Providence gave him a liberty of speech: *No man forbidding him,* giving him any check for what he did or laying any restraint upon him. The Jews that used to forbid him to speak to the Gentiles had no authority here; and the Roman government as yet took no cognizance of the profession of Christianity as a crime. Herein we must acknowledge the hand of God, [1.] Setting bounds to the rage of persecutors; where he does not turn the heart, yet he can tie the hand and bridle the tongue. Nero was a bloody man, and there were many, both Jews and Gentiles, in Rome, that hated Christianity; and yet so it was, unaccountably, that Paul though a prisoner was connived at in preaching the gospel, and it was not construed a breach of the peace. Thus God makes *the wrath of men to praise him, and restrains the remainder of it,* Ps. 76:10. Though there were so many that had it in their power to forbid Paul's preaching (even the common soldier that kept him might have done it), yet God so ordered it, *that no man did forbid him.* [2.] See God here providing comfort for the relief of the persecuted. Though it was a very low and narrow sphere of opportunity that Paul was here placed in, compared with what he had been in, yet, such as it was, he was not molested nor disturbed in it. Though it was not a wide door that was opened to him, yet it was kept open, and no man was suffered to shut it; and it was to many an effectual door, so that there were saints even in Caesar's household, Phil. 4:22. When the city of our solemnities is thus made a quiet habitation at any time, and we are fed from day to day with the bread of life, no man forbidding us, we must give thanks to God for it and prepare for changes, still longing for that holy mountain in which there shall never be any pricking brier nor grieving thorn.

AN EXPOSITION, WITH PRACTICAL OBSERVATIONS, OF

THE EPISTLE OF ST. PAUL TO THE ROMANS

If we may compare scripture with scripture, and take the opinion of some devout and pious persons, in the Old Testament David's Psalms, and in the New Testament Paul's Epistles, are stars of the first magnitude, that differ from the other stars in glory. The whole scripture is indeed an epistle from heaven to earth: but in it we have upon record several particular epistles, more of Paul's than of any other, for he was the chief of the apostles, and laboured more abundantly than they all. His natural parts, I doubt not, were very pregnant; his apprehension was quick and piercing; his expressions were fluent and copious; his affections, wherever he took, very warm and zealous, and his resolutions no less bold and daring: this made him, before his conversion, a very keen and bitter persecutor; but when the strong man armed was dispossessed, and the stronger than he came to divide the spoil and to sanctify these qualifications, he became the most skilful zealous preacher; never any better fitted to win souls, nor more successful. Fourteen of his epistles we have in the canon of scripture; many more, it is probable, he wrote in the course of his ministry, which might be profitable enough for doctrine, for reproof, etc., but, not being given by inspiration of God, they were not received as canonical scripture, nor handed down to us. Six epistles, said to be Paul's, written to Seneca, and eight of Seneca's to him, are spoken of by some of the ancients [*Sixt. Senens. Biblioth. Sanct.* lib. 2] and are extant; but, upon the first view, they appear spurious and counterfeit.

This epistle to the Romans is placed first, not because of the priority of its date, but because of the superlative excellency of the epistle, it being one of the longest and fullest of all, and perhaps because of the dignity of the place to which it is written. Chrysostom would have this epistle read over to him twice a week. It is gathered from some passages in the epistle that it was written *Anno Christi* 56, from Corinth, while Paul made a short stay there in his way to Troas, Acts 20:5, 6. He commendeth to the Romans Phebe, a servant of the church at Cenchrea (*ch.* 16), which was a place belonging to Corinth. He calls Gaius his *host,* or the man with whom he lodged (*ch.* 16:23), and he was a Corinthian, not the same with Gaius of Derbe, mentioned Acts 20. Paul was now going up to Jerusalem, with the money that was given to the poor saints there; and of that he speaks, *ch.* 15:26. The great mysteries treated of in this epistle must needs produce in this, as in other writings of Paul, many things dark and hard to be understood, 2 Peter 3:16. The method of this (as of several other of the epistles) is observable; the former part of it doctrinal, in the first eleven chapters; the latter part practical, in the last five: to inform the judgment and to reform the life. And the best way to understand the truths explained in the former part is to abide and abound in the practice of the duties prescribed in the latter part; for, if any man will do his will, he shall know of the doctrine, Jn. 7:17.

I. The doctrinal part of the epistles instructs us,

1. Concerning the way of salvation (1.) The foundation of it laid in justification, and that not by the Gentiles' works of nature (*ch.* 1), nor by the Jews' works of the law (*ch.* 2, 3), for both Jews and Gentiles were liable to the curse; but only by faith in Jesus Christ, *ch.* 3:21, etc.; *ch.* 4. (2.) The steps of this salvation are, [1.] Peace with God, *ch.* 5. [2.] Sanctification, *ch.* 6, 7. [3.] Glorification, *ch.* 8.

2. Concerning the persons saved, such as belong to the election of grace (*ch.* 9), Gentiles and Jews, *ch.* 10, 11. By this is appears that the subject he discourses of were such as were then the present truths, as the apostle speaks, 2 Peter 1:12. Two things the Jews then stum-

bled at — justification by faith without the works of the law, and the admission of the Gentiles into the church; and therefore both these he studied to clear and vindicate.

II. The practical part follows, wherein we find, 1. Several general exhortations proper for all Christians, *ch.* 12. 2. Directions for our behaviour, as members of civil society, *ch.* 13. 3. Rules for the conduct of Christians to one another, as members of the Christian church, *ch.* 14 and *ch.* 15:1–14.

III. As he draws towards a conclusion, he makes an apology for writing to them (*ch.* 15:14–16), gives them an account of himself and his own affairs (*v.* 17–21), promises them a visit (*v.* 22–29), begs their prayers (*v.* 30–33), sends particular salutations to many friends there (*ch.* 16:1–16), warns them against those who caused divisions (*v.* 17–20), adds the salutations of his friends with him (*v.* 21–23), and ends with a benediction to them and a doxology to God (*v.* 24–27).

CHAPTER 1

In this chapter we may observe, I. The preface and introduction to the whole epistle, to *v.* 16. II. A description of the deplorable condition of the Gentile world, which begins the proof of the doctrine of justification by faith, here laid down at *v.* 17. The first is according to the then usual formality of a letter, but intermixed with very excellent and savoury expressions.

Verses 1–7

In this paragraph we have,

I. The person who writes the epistle described (*v.* 1): *Paul, a servant of Jesus Christ;* this is his title of honour, which he glories in, not as the Jewish teachers, *Rabbi, Rabbi;* but a servant, a more immediate attendant, a steward in the house. *Called to be an apostle.* Some think he alludes to his old name Saul, which signifies *one called for,* or *enquired after:* Christ sought him to make an apostle of him, Acts 9:15. He here builds his authority upon his call; he did not run without sending, as the false apostles did; *klētos apostolos — called an apostle,* as if this were the name he would be called by, though he acknowledged himself not meet to be called so, 1 Co. 15:9. *Separated to the gospel of God.* The Pharisees had their name from separation, because they *separated themselves to the study of the law,* and might be called *aphōrismenoi eis ton nomon;* such a one Paul had formerly been; but now he had changed his studies, was *aphōrismenos eis to Euangelion,* a gospel Pharisee, separated by the counsel of God (Gal. 1:15), *separated from his mother's womb,* by an immediate direction of the Spirit, and a regular ordination according to that direction (Acts 13:2, 3), by a dedication of himself to this work. He was an entire devotee to the gospel of God, the gospel which has God for its author, the origin and extraction of it divine and heavenly.

II. Having mentioned the gospel of God, he digresses, to give us an encomium of it.

1. The antiquity of it. It was *promised before* (*v.* 2); it was no novel upstart doctrine, but of ancient standing in the promises and prophecies of the old Testament, which did all unanimously point at the gospel, the morning-beams that ushered in the sun of righteousness; this not by word of mouth only, but in the scriptures.

2. The subject-matter of it: it is concerning Christ, *v.* 3, 4. The prophets and apostles all bear witness to him; he is the true treasure hid in the field of the scriptures. Observe, When Paul mentions Christ, how he heaps up his names and titles, *his Son Jesus Christ our Lord,* as one that took a pleasure in speaking of him; and, having mentioned him, he cannot go on in his discourse without some expression of love and honour, as here, where in one person he shows us his two distinct natures. (1.) His human nature: *Made of the seed of David* (*v.* 3), that is, born of the virgin Mary, who was of the house of David (Lu. 1:27), as was Joseph his supposed father, Lu. 2:4. David is here mentioned, because of the special promises made to him concerning the Messiah, especially his kingly office; 2 Sa. 7:12; Ps. 132:11, compared with Lu. 1:32, 33. (2.) His divine nature: *Declared to be the Son of God* (*v.* 4), the Son of God by eternal generation, or, as it is here explained, *according to the Spirit of holiness. According to the flesh,* that is, his human nature, *he was of the seed of David;* but, *according to the Spirit of holiness,* that is, the divine nature (as he is said to be *quickened by the Spirit,* 1 Pt. 3:18, compared with 2 Co. 13:4), he is the Son of God. The great proof or demonstration of this is *his resurrection from the dead,* which proved it effectually and undeniably. The sign of the prophet Jonas, Christ's resurrection, was intended for the last conviction, Mt. 12:39, 40. Those that would not be convinced by that would be convinced by nothing. So that we have here a summary of the gospel doctrine concerning Christ's two natures in one person.

3. The fruit of it (*v.* 5); *By whom,* that is, by Christ manifested and made known in the gospel, *we (Paul and the rest of the ministers) have received grace and apostleship,* that is, the favour to be made apostles, Eph. 3:8. The apostles were made a spectacle to the world, led a life of toil, and trouble, and hazard, *were killed all the day long,* and yet Paul reck-

ons the apostleship a favour: we may justly reckon it a great favour to be employed in any work or service for God, whatever difficulties or dangers we may meet with in it. This apostleship was received *for obedience to the faith,* that is, to bring people to that obedience; as Christ, so his ministers, received that they might give. Paul's was for this obedience *among all nations,* for he was the *apostle of the Gentiles, ch.* 11:13. Observe the description here given of the Christian profession: it is *obedience to the faith.* It does not consist in a notional knowledge or a naked assent, much less does it consist in perverse disputings, but in obedience. This obedience to the faith answers the *law of faith,* mentioned ch. 3:27. The act of faith is the obedience of the understanding to God revealing, and the product of that is the obedience of the will to God commanding. To anticipate the ill use which might be made of the doctrine of justification by faith without the works of the law, which he was to explain in the following epistle, he here speaks of Christianity as an obedience. Christ has a yoke. *"Among whom are you, v.* 6. You Romans in this stand upon the same level with other Gentile nations of less fame and wealth; you are all one in Christ." The gospel salvation is a common salvation, Jude 3. No respect of persons with God. *The called of Jesus Christ;* all those, and those only, are brought to an obedience of the faith that are effectually called of Jesus Christ.

III. The persons to whom it is written (*v.* 7): *To all that are in Rome, beloved of God, called to be saints;* that is, to all the professing Christians that were in Rome, whether Jews or Gentiles originally, whether high or low, bond or free, learned or unlearned. Rich and poor meet together in Christ Jesus. Here is, 1. The privilege of Christians: They are *beloved of God,* they are members of that body which is beloved, which is God's *Hephzibah,* in which his delight is. We speak of God's love by his bounty and beneficence, and so he hath a common love to all mankind and a peculiar love for true believers; and between these there is a love he hath for all the body of visible Christians. 2. The duty of Christians; and that is to be holy, for hereunto are they called, *called to be saints,* called to salvation through sanctification. Saints, and only saints, are beloved of God with a special and peculiar love. *Klētois hagiois — called saints,* saints in profession; it were well if all that are called saints were saints indeed. Those that are called saints should labour to answer to the name; otherwise, though it is an honour and a privilege, yet it will be of little avail at the great day to have been called saints, if we be not really so.

IV. The apostolical benediction (*v.* 7): *Grace to you and peace.* This is one of the tokens in every epistle; and it hath not only the affection of a good wish, but the authority of a blessing. The priests under the law were to bless the people, and so are gospel ministers, in the name of the Lord. In this usual benediction observe, 1. The favours desired: *Grace and peace.* The Old-Testament salutation was, *Peace be to you;* but now grace is prefixed — *grace,* that is, the favour of God towards us or the work of God in us; both are previously requisite to true peace. All gospel blessings are included in these two: *grace and peace. Peace,* that is all good; peace with God, peace in your own consciences, peace with all that are about you; all these founded in grace. 2. The fountain of those favours, *from God our Father, and the Lord Jesus Christ.* All good comes, (1.) From God as a Father; he hath put himself into that relation to engage and encourage our desires and expectations; we are taught, when we come for grace and peace, to call him our Father. (2.) *From the Lord Jesus Christ,* as Mediator, and the great feoffee in trust for the conveying and securing of these benefits. We have them from his fulness, peace from the fulness of his merit, grace from the fulness of his Spirit.

Verses 8–15

We may here observe,

I. His thanksgivings for them (*v.* 8): *First, I thank my God.* It is good to begin every thing with blessing God, to make that *the alpha and omega* of every song, *in every thing to*

give thanks. — My God. He speaks this with delight and triumph. In all our thanksgivings, it is good for us to eye God as our God; this makes every mercy sweet, when we can say of God, "He is mine in covenant." *— Through Jesus Christ.* All our duties and performances are pleasing to God only through Jesus Christ, praises as well as prayers. *— For you all.* We must express our love to our friends, not only by praying for them, but by praising God for them. God must have the glory of all the comfort we have in our friends; for every creature is that to us, and no more, which God makes it to be. Many of these Romans Paul had no personal acquaintance with, and yet he could heartily rejoice in their gifts and graces. When some of the Roman Christians met him (Acts 28:15), he thanked God for them, and took courage; but here his true catholic love extends itself further, and he *thanks God for them all;* not only for those among them that were his helpers in Christ, and that bestowed much labour upon him (of whom he speaks *ch.* 16:3, 6), but for them all. *— That your faith is spoken of.* Paul travelled up and down from place to place, and, wherever he came, he heard great commendations of the Christians at Rome, which he mentions, not to make them proud, but to quicken them to answer the general character people gave of them, and the general expectation people had from them. The greater reputation a man hath for religion, the more careful he should be to preserve it, because *a little folly spoils him that is in reputation,* Eccl. 10:1. *— Throughout the whole world,* that is, the Roman empire, into which the Roman Christians, upon Claudius's edict to banish all the Jews from Rome, were scattered abroad, but had now returned, and, it seems, left a very good report behind them, wherever they had been, in all the churches. There was this good effect of their sufferings: if they had not been persecuted, they had not been famous. This was indeed a good name, a name for good things with God and good people. As the elders of old, so these Romans, *obtained a good report through faith,* Heb. 11:2. It is a desirable thing to be famous for faith. The faith of the Roman Christians came to be thus talked of, not only because it was excelling in itself, but because it was eminent and observable in its circumstances. Rome was a city upon a hill, every one took notice of what was done there. Thus those who have many eyes upon them have need to walk circumspectly, for what they do, good or bad, will be spoken of. The church of Rome was then a flourishing church; but since that time how is the gold become dim! How is the most fine gold changed! Rome is not what it was. She was then espoused a *chaste virgin to Christ,* and excelled in beauty; but she has since *degenerated, dealt treacherously, and embraced the bosom of a stranger;* so that (as that good old book, *the Practice of Piety,* makes appear in no less than twenty-six instances) even *the epistle to the Romans* is now an epistle *against* the Romans; little reason has she therefore to boast of her former credit.

II. His prayer for them, *v.* 9. Though a famous flourishing church, yet they had need to be prayed for; they *had not yet attained.* Paul mentions this as an instance of his love to them. One of the greatest kindnesses we can do our friends, and sometimes the only kindness that is in the power of our hands, is, by prayer to recommend them to the loving-kindness of God. From Paul's example here we may learn, 1. Constancy in prayer: *Always without ceasing.* He did himself observe the same rules he gave to others, Eph. 6:18; 1 Th. 5:17. Not that Paul did nothing else but pray, but he kept up stated times for the solemn performance of that duty, and those very frequent, and observed without fail. 2. Charity in prayer: *I make mention of you.* Though he had not particular acquaintance with them, nor interest in them, yet he prayed for them; not only for all saints in general, but he made express mention of them. It is not unfit sometimes to be express in our prayers for particular churches and places; not to inform God, but to affect ourselves. We are likely to have the most comfort in those friends that we pray most for. Concerning this he makes a solemn appeal to the searcher of hearts: *For God is my witness.* It was in a weighty matter, and in a thing known only to God and his own heart, that he used this asseveration. It is very comfortable to be able to call God to witness to our sincerity and constancy in the discharge of a duty. God is particularly a witness to our secret prayers, the matter of them, the manner of the performance; then our Father sees in secret, Mt. 6:6. *God, whom I serve with my spirit.* Those that serve God with their spirits may, with a humble confidence, appeal to him; hypocrites who rest in bodily exercise cannot. His particular prayer, among many other petitions he put up for them, was that he might have an opportunity of paying them a visit (*v.* 10): *Making request, if by any means,* etc. Whatever comfort we desire to find in any creature, we must have recourse to God for it by prayer; for *our times are in his hand,* and all our ways at his disposal. The expressions here used intimate that he was very desirous of such an opportunity: *if by any means;* that he had long and often been disappointed: *now at length;* and yet that he submitted it to the divine Providence: *a prosperous journey by the will of God.* As in our purposes, so in our desires, we must still remember to insert this, *if the Lord will,* James 4:15. Our journeys are prosperous or otherwise according to the will of God, comfortable or not as he pleases.

III. His great desire to see them, with the reasons of it, *v.* 11–15. He had heard so much of them that he had a great desire to be better acquainted with them. Fruitful Christians are as much the joy as barren professors are the grief of faithful ministers. Accordingly, he *often purposed to come, but was let hitherto* (*v.* 13), for man purposeth, but God disposeth. He was hindered by other business that took him off, by his care of other churches, whose affairs were pressing; and Paul was for doing that first, not which was most pleasant (then he would have gone to Rome), but which was most needful —a good example to ministers, who must not consult their own inclinations so much as the necessity of their people's souls. Paul desired to visit these Romans,

1. That they might be edified (*v.* 11): *That I may impart unto you.* He received, that he might communicate. Never were full breasts so desirous to be drawn out to the sucking infant as Paul's head and heart were to be imparting spiritual gifts, that is, preaching to them. A good sermon is a good gift, so much the better for being a spiritual gift. — *To the end you may be established.* Having commended their flourishing he here expresses his desire of their establishment, that as they grew upward in the branches they might grow downward in the root. The best saints, while they are in such a shaking world as this, have need to be more and more established; and spiritual gifts are of special use for our establishment.

2. That he might be comforted, *v.* 12. What he heard of their flourishing in grace was so much a joy to him that it must needs be much more so to behold it. Paul could take comfort in the fruit of the labours of other ministers. — *By the mutual faith both of you and me,* that is, our mutual faithfulness and fidelity. It is very comfortable when there is a mutual confidence between minister and people, they confiding in him as a faithful minister, and he in them as a faithful people. Or, the mutual work of faith, which is love; they rejoiced in the expressions of one another's love, or communicating their faith one to another. It is very refreshing to Christians to compare notes about their spiritual concerns; thus are they sharpened, *as iron sharpens iron.* — *That I might have some fruit, v.* 13. Their edification would be his advantage, it would be fruit abounding to a good account. Paul minded his work, as one that believed the more good he did the greater would his reward be.

3. That he might discharge his trust as the apostle of the Gentiles (*v.* 14): *I am a debtor.* (1.) His receivings made him a debtor; for they were talents he was entrusted with to trade for his Master's honour. We should think of this when we covet great things, that all our receivings put us in debt; we are but stewards of our Lord's goods. (2.) His office made him a debtor. He was a debtor as he was an apostle; he was called and sent to work, and had engaged to mind it. Paul had improved his talent, and laboured in his work, and done as much good as ever any man did, and yet, in reflection upon it, he still writes himself debtor; for, *when we have done all, we are but unprofitable servants.* — *Debtor to the Greeks, and to the barbarians,* that is, as the following words explain it, *to the wise and to the unwise.* The Greeks fancied themselves to have the monopoly of wisdom, and looked upon all the rest of the world as barbarians, comparatively so; not cultivated with learning and arts as they were. Now Paul was a debtor to both, looked upon himself as obliged to do all the good he could both to the one and to the other. Accordingly, we find him paying his debt, both in his preaching and in his writing, doing good *both to Greeks and barbarians,* and suiting his discourse to the capacity of each. You may observe a difference between his sermon at Lystra among the plain Lycaonians (Acts 14:15, etc.) and his sermon at Athens among the polite philosophers, Acts 17:22, etc. He delivered both as debtor to each, giving to each their portion. Though a plain preacher, yet, as debtor to the wise, he speaks wisdom among those that are perfect, 1 Co. 2:6. For these reasons he was ready, if he had an opportunity, *to preach the gospel at Rome, v.* 15. Though a public place, though a perilous place, where Christianity met with a great deal of opposition, yet Paul was ready to run the risk at Rome, if called to it: *I am ready — prothymon.* It denotes a great readiness of mind, and that he was very forward to it. What he did was not for filthy lucre, but of a ready mind. It is an excellent thing to be ready to meet every opportunity of doing or getting good.

Verses 16–18

Paul here enters upon a large discourse of justification, in the latter part of this chapter laying down his thesis, and, in order to the proof of it, describing the deplorable condition of the Gentile world. His transition is very handsome, and like an orator: he was ready to preach the gospel at Rome, though a place where the gospel was run down by those that called themselves the wits; *for,* saith he, *I am not ashamed of it, v.* 16. There is a great deal in the gospel which such a man as Paul might be tempted to be ashamed of, especially that he whose gospel it is was a man hanged upon a tree, that the doctrine of it was plain, had little in it to set it off among scholars, the professors of it were mean and despised, and every where spoken against; yet Paul was not ashamed to own it. I reckon him a Christian indeed that is neither ashamed of the gospel nor a shame to it. The reason of this bold profession, taken from the nature and excellency of the gospel, introduces his dissertation.

I. The proposition, *v.* 16, 17. The excellency of the gospel lies in this, that it reveals to us,

1. The salvation of believers as the end: *It is the power of God unto salvation.* Paul is not ashamed of the gospel, how mean and contemptible soever it may appear to a carnal eye; for *the power of God works by it the salvation of all that believe;* it shows us *the way of salvation* (Acts 16:17), and is the great charter by which salvation is conveyed and made over to us. But, (1.) *It is through the power of God;* without that power the gospel is but a dead letter; the revelation of the gospel is the revelation of *the arm of the Lord* (Isa. 53:1), as power went along with the word of Christ to heal diseases. (2.) It is to those, and those only, that believe. Believing interests us in the gospel salvation; to others it is hidden. The medicine prepared will not cure the patient if it be not taken. — *To the Jew first. The lost sheep of the house of Israel* had the first offer made them, both by Christ and his apostles. *You first* (Acts 3:26), but upon their refusal the apostles turned to the Gentiles, Acts 13:46. Jews and Gentiles now stand upon the same level, both equally miserable without a Saviour, and both equally welcome to the Saviour, Col. 3:11. Such doctrine as this was surprising to the Jews, who had hitherto been the peculiar people, and had looked with scorn upon the Gentile world; but the long-expected Messiah proves *a light to enlighten the Gentiles,* as well as *the glory of his people Israel.*

2. The justification of believers as the way (*v.* 17): *For therein,* that is, in this gospel, which Paul so much triumphs in, *is the righteousness of God revealed.* Our misery and ruin being the product and consequent of our iniquity, that which will show us the way of salvation must needs show us the way of justification, and this the gospel does. The gospel makes known a righteousness. While God is a just and holy God, and we are guilty sinners, it is necessary we should have a righteousness wherein to appear before him; and, blessed be God, there is such a righteousness brought in by Messiah the prince (Dan. 9:24) and *revealed in the gospel;* a *righteousness,* that is, a gracious method of reconciliation and acceptance, notwithstanding the guilt of our sins. This evangelical righteousness, (1.) Is called the *righteousness of God;* it is of God's appointing, of God's approving and accepting. It is so called to cut off all pretensions to a righteousness resulting from the merit of our own works. It is the righteousness of Christ, who is God, resulting from a satisfaction of infinite value. (2.) It is said to be *from faith to faith,* from the faithfulness of God revealing to the faith of man receiving (so some); from the faith of dependence upon God, and dealing with him immediately, as Adam before the fall, to the faith of dependence upon a Mediator, and so dealing with God (so others); from the first faith, by which we are put into a justified state, to after faith, by which we live, and are continued in that state: and the faith that justifies us is no less than our taking Christ for our Saviour, and becoming true Christians, according to the tenour of the baptismal covenant; from faith engrafting us into Christ, to faith deriving virtue from him as our root: both implied in the next words, *The just shall live by faith. Just by faith,* there is faith justifying us; *live by faith,* there is faith maintaining us; and so *there is a righteousness from faith to faith.* Faith is all in all, both in the beginning and progress of a Christian life. It is not from faith to works, as if faith put us into a justified state, and then works preserved and maintained us in it, but it is all along from faith to faith, as 2 Co. 3:18, *from glory to glory;* it is increasing, continuing, persevering faith, faith pressing forward, and getting ground of unbelief. To show that this is no novel upstart doctrine, he quotes for it that famous scripture in the Old Testament, so often mentioned in the New (Hab. 2:4): *The just shall live by faith.* Being justified by faith he shall live by it both the life of grace and of glory. The prophet there had placed himself upon the watch-tower, expecting some extraordinary discoveries (*v.* 1), and the discovery was of the certainty of the appearance of the promised Messiah in the fulness of time, not withstanding seeming delays. This is there called *the vision,* by way of eminence, as elsewhere *the promise;* and while that time is coming, as well as when it has come, *the just shall live by faith.* Thus is the evangelical righteousness from faith to faith — from Old-Testament faith in a Christ to come to New-Testament faith in a Christ already come.

II. The proof of this proposition, that both Jews and Gentiles stand in need of a righteousness wherein to appear before God, and that neither the one nor the other have nay of their own to plead. Justification must be either by faith or works. It cannot be by works, which he proves at large by describing the works both of Jews and Gentiles; and therefore he concludes it must be by faith, *ch.* 3:20, 28. The apostle, like a skilful surgeon, before he applies the plaster, searches the wound — endeavours first to convince of guilt and wrath, and then to show the way of salvation. This makes the gospel the more welcome. We must first see the righteousness of God condemning, and then the righteousness of God justifying will appear *worthy of all acceptation.* In general (*v.* 18), *the wrath of God is revealed.* The light of nature and the light of the law reveal the wrath of God from sin to sin. It is well for us that the gospel reveals the justifying righteousness of God from faith to faith. The antithesis is observable. Here is,

1. The sinfulness of man described; he reduceth it to two heads, *ungodliness and unrighteousness;* ungodliness against the laws of the first table, unrighteousness against those of the second.

2. The cause of that sinfulness, and that is, *holding the truth in unrighteousness.* Some *communes notitae,* some ideas they had of the being of God, and of the difference of good and evil; but they held them in unrighteousness, that is, they knew and professed them in a consistency with their wicked courses. They held the truth as a captive or prisoner, that it should not influence them, as otherwise it would. An unrighteous wicked heart is the dungeon in which many a good truth is detained and buried. *Holding fast the form of sound words in faith and love* is the root of all religion (2 Tim. 1:13), but holding it fast in unrighteousness is the root of all sin.

3. The displeasure of God against it: *The wrath of God is revealed from heaven;* not only in the written word, *which is given by inspiration of God* (the Gentiles had not that), but in the providences of God, his judgments executed upon sinners, which do not spring out of the dust, or fall out by chance, nor are they to be ascribed to second causes, but they are a revelation from heaven. Or *wrath from heaven is revealed;* it is not the wrath of a man like ourselves, *but wrath from heaven,* therefore the more terrible and the more unavoidable.

Verses 19–32

In this last part of the chapter the apostle applies what

he had said particularly to the Gentile world, in which we may observe,

I. The means and helps they had to come to the knowledge of God. Though they had not such a knowledge of his law as Jacob and Israel had (Ps. 147:20), yet among them *he left not himself without witness* (Acts 14:17): *For that which may be known,* etc., v. 19, 20. Observe,

1. What discoveries they had: *That which may be known of God is manifest, en autois — among them;* that is, there were some even among them that had the knowledge of God, were convinced of the existence of one supreme *Numen.* The philosophy of Pythagoras, Plato, and the Stoics, discovered a great deal of the knowledge of God, as appears by abundance of testimonies. *That which may be known,* which implies that there is a great deal which may not be known. The being of God may be apprehended, but cannot be comprehended. We cannot by searching find him out, Job 11:7–9. Finite understandings cannot perfectly know an infinite being; but, blessed be God, there is that which may be known, enough to lead us to our chief end, the glorifying and enjoying of him; and these things revealed belong to us and to our children, while secret things are not to be pried into, Deu. 29:29.

2. Whence they had these discoveries: *God hath shown it to them.* Those common natural notions which they had of God were imprinted upon their hearts by the God of nature himself, who is the *Father of lights.* This sense of a Deity, and a regard to that Deity, are so connate with the human nature that some think we are to distinguish men from brutes by these rather than by reason.

3. By what way and means these discoveries and notices which they had were confirmed and improved, namely, by the work of creation (v. 20); *For the invisible things of God,* etc.

(1.) Observe what they knew: *The invisible things of him, even his eternal power and Godhead.* Though God be not the object of sense, yet he hath discovered and made known himself by those things that are sensible. The power and Godhead of God are invisible things, and yet are clearly seen in their products. He works in secret (Job 23:8, 9; Ps. 139:15; Eccl. 11:5), but manifests what he has wrought, and therein makes known his power and Godhead, and others of his attributes which natural light apprehends in the idea of a God. They could not come by natural light to the knowledge of the three persons in the Godhead (though some fancy they have found footsteps of this in Plato's writings), but they did come to the knowledge of the Godhead, at least so much knowledge as was sufficient to have kept them from idolatry. This was that truth which they held in unrighteousness.

(2.) How they knew it: *By the things that are made,* which could not make themselves, nor fall into such an exact order and harmony by any casual hits; and therefore must have been produced by some first cause or intelligent agent, which first cause could be no other than an eternal powerful God. See Ps. 19:1; Isa. 40:26; Acts 17:24. The workman is known by his work. The variety, multitude, order, beauty, harmony, different nature, and excellent contrivance, of the things that are made, the direction of them to certain ends, and the concurrence of all the parts to the good and beauty of the whole, do abundantly prove a Creator and his eternal power and Godhead. Thus did the light shine in the darkness. And *this from the creation of the world.* Understand it either, [1.] As the topic from which the knowledge of them is drawn. To evince this truth, we have recourse to the great work of creation. And some think this *ktisis kosmou, this creature of the world* (as it may be read), is to be understood of man, the *ktisis kat' exochēn — the most remarkable creature* of the lower world, called *ktisis,* Mk. 16:15. The frame and structure of human bodies, and especially the most excellent powers, faculties, and capacities of human souls, do abundantly prove that there is a Creator, and that he is God. Or, [2.] As the date of the discovery. It as old as the creation of the world. In this sense *apo ktiseōs* is most frequently used in scripture. These notices concerning God are not any modern discoveries, hit upon of late, but ancient truths, which were from the beginning. The way of the acknowledgement of God is a good old way; it was from the beginning. Truth got the start of error.

II. Their gross idolatry, notwithstanding these discoveries that God made to them of himself; described here, v. 21–23, 25. We shall the less wonder at the inefficacy of these natural discoveries to prevent the idolatry of the Gentiles if we remember how prone even the Jews, who had scrip-

ture light to guide them, were to idolatry; so miserably are the degenerate sons of men plunged in the mire of sense. Observe,

1. The inward cause of their idolatry, v. 21, 22. They are therefore without excuse, in that they did know God, and from what they knew might easily infer that it was their duty to worship him, and him only. Though some have greater light and means of knowledge than others, yet all have enough to leave them inexcusable. But the mischief of it was that, (1.) They *glorified him not as God.* Their affections towards him, and their awe and adoration of him, did not keep pace with their knowledge. To glorify him as God is to glorify him only; for there can be but one infinite: but they did not so glorify him, for they set up a multitude of other deities. To glorify him as God is to worship him with spiritual worship; but they made images of him. Not to glorify God as God is in effect not to glorify him at all; to respect him as a creature is not to glorify him, but to dishonour him. (2.) *Neither were they thankful;* not thankful for the favours in general they received from God (insensibleness of God's mercies is at the bottom of our sinful departures from him); not thankful in particular for the discoveries God was pleased to make of himself to them. Those that do not improve the means of knowledge and grace are justly reckoned unthankful for them. (3.) *But they became vain in their imaginations, en tois dialogismois — in their reasonings,* in their practical inferences. They had a great deal of knowledge of general truths (v. 19), but no prudence to apply them to particular cases. Or, in their notions of God, and the creation of the world, and the origination of mankind, and the chief good; in these things, when they quitted the plain truth, they soon disputed themselves into a thousand vain and foolish fancies. The several opinions and hypotheses of the various sects of philosophers concerning these things were so many vain imaginations. When truth is forsaken, errors multiply *in infinitum — infinitely.* (4.) *And their foolish heart was darkened.* The foolishness and practical wickedness of the heart cloud and darken the intellectual powers and faculties. Nothing tends more to the blinding and perverting of the understanding than the corruption and depravedness of the will and affections. (5.) *Professing themselves to be wise, they became fools, v. 22.* This looks black upon the philosophers, the pretenders to wisdom and professors of it. Those that had the most luxuriant fancy, in framing to themselves the idea of a God, fell into the most gross and absurd conceits: and it was the just punishment of their pride and self-conceitedness. It has been observed that the most refined nations, that made the greatest show of wisdom, were the arrantest fools in religion. The barbarians adored the sun and moon, which of all others was the most specious idolatry; while the learned Egyptians worshipped an ox and an onion. The Grecians, who excelled them in wisdom, adored diseases and human passions. The Romans, the wisest of all, worshipped the furies. And at this day the poor Americans worship the thunder; while the ingenious Chinese adore the devil. Thus the *world by wisdom knew not God,* 1 Co. 1:21. As a profession of wisdom is an aggravation of folly, so a proud conceit of wisdom is the cause of a great deal of folly. Hence we read of few philosophers who were converted to Christianity; and Paul's preaching was no where so laughed at and ridiculed as among the learned Athenians, Acts 17:18–32. *Phaskontes einai — conceiting themselves* to be wise. The plain truth of the being of God would not content them; they thought themselves above that, and so fell into the greatest errors.

2. The outward acts of their idolatry, v. 23–25. (1.) Making images of God (v. 23), by which, as much as in them lay, they *changed the glory of the incorruptible God.* Compare Ps. 106:20; Jer. 2:11. They ascribed a deity to the most contemptible creatures, and by them represented God. It was the greatest honour God did to man that he made man in the image of God; but it is the greatest dishonour man has done to God that he has made God in the image of man. This was what God so strictly warned the Jews against, Deu. 4:15, etc. This the apostle shows the folly of in his sermon at Athens, Acts 17:29. See Isa. 40:18, etc.; 44:10, etc. This is called (v. 25) *changing the truth of God into a lie.* As it did dishonour his glory, so it did misrepresent his being. Idols are called lies, for they belie God, as if he had a body, whereas he is a Spirit, Jer. 23:14; Hos. 7:1. *Teachers of lies,* Hab. 2:18. (2.) Giving divine honour to the creature: *Worshipped and served the creature, para ton ktisavta — besides the Creator.* They did

own a supreme *Numen* in their profession, but they did in effect disown him by the worship they paid to the creature; for God will be all or none. Or, *above* the Creator, paying more devout respect to their inferior deities, stars, heroes, demons, thinking the supreme God inaccessible, or above their worship. The sin itself was their worshipping the creature at all; but this is mentioned as an aggravation of the sin, that they worshipped the creature more than the Creator. This was the general wickedness of the Gentile world, and became twisted in with their laws and government; in compliance with which even the wise men among them, who knew and owned a supreme God and were convinced of the nonsense and absurdity of their polytheism and idolatry, yet did as the rest of their neighbours did. *Seneca,* in his book *De Superstitione,* as it is quoted by *Aug. de Civit. Dei,* lib. 6, cap. 10 (for the book itself is lost), after he had largely shown the great folly and impiety of the vulgar religion, in divers instances of it, yet concludes, *Quae omnia sapiens servabit tanquam legibus jussa, non tanquam diis grata — All which a wise man will observe as established by law, not imagining them grateful to the gods.* And afterwards, *Omnem istam ignobilem deorum turbam, quam longo aevo longa superstitio congessit, sic adorabimus, ut meminerimus cultum ejus magis ad morem quam ad rem pertinere — All this ignoble rout of gods, which ancient superstition has amassed together by long prescription, we will so adore as to remember that the worship of them is rather a compliance with custom than material in itself.* Upon which Augustine observes, *Colebat quod reprehendebat, agebat quod arguebat, quod culpabat adorabat — He worshipped that which he censured, he did that which he had proved wrong, and he adored what he found fault with.* I mention this thus largely because methinks it doth fully explain that of the apostle here (v. 18): *Who hold the truth in unrighteousness.* It is observable that upon the mention of the dishonour done to God by the idolatry of the Gentiles the apostle, in the midst of his discourse, expresses himself in an awful adoration of God: *Who is blessed for ever. Amen.* When we see or hear of any contempt cast upon God or his name, we should thence take occasion to think and speak highly and honourably of him. In this, as in other things, the worse others are, the better we should be. *Blessed for ever,* notwithstanding these dishonours done to his name: though there are those that do not glorify him, yet he is glorified, and will be glorified to eternity.

III. The judgments of God upon them for this idolatry; not many temporal judgments (the idolatrous nations were the conquering ruling nations of the world), but spiritual judgments, giving them up to the most brutish and unnatural lusts. *Paredōken autous — He gave them up;* it is thrice repeated here, v. 24, 26, 28. Spiritual judgments are of all judgments the sorest, and to be most dreaded. Observe,

1. By whom they were given up. God gave them up, in a way of righteous judgment, as the just punishment of their idolatry — taking off the bridle of restraining grace — leaving them to themselves — letting them alone; for his grace is his own, he is debtor to no man, he may give or withhold his grace at pleasure. Whether this giving up be a positive act of God or only privative we leave to the schools to dispute: but this we are sure of that it is no new thing for God to give men up to their own hearts' lusts, to send them strong delusions, to let Satan loose upon them, nay, to lay stumbling-blocks before them. And yet God is not the author of sin, but herein infinitely just and holy; for, though the greatest wickedness follow upon this giving up, the fault of that is to be laid upon the sinner's wicked heart. If the patient be obstinate, and will not submit to the methods prescribed, but wilfully takes and does that which is prejudicial to him, the physician is not to be blamed if he give him up as in a desperate condition; and all the fatal symptoms that follow are not to be imputed to the physician, but to the disease itself and to the folly and wilfulness of the patient.

2. To what they were given up.

(1.) *To uncleanness and vile affections, v. 24, 26, 27.* Those that would not entertain the more pure and refined notices of natural light, which tend to preserve the honour of God, justly forfeited those more gross and palpable sentiments which preserve the honour of human nature. *Man being in honour,* and refusing to understand the God that made him, thus becomes worse than the *beasts that perish,* Ps. 49:20. Thus one, by the divine permission, becomes the punishment of another; but it is (as it said here) *through the lusts of their own hearts* — there all the fault is to be laid. Those who dishonoured God were given up to dishonour themselves. A man cannot be delivered up to a greater slavery than to be given up to his own lusts. Such are given over, like the Egyptians (Isa. 19:4), into the hand of a cruel lord. The particular instances of their uncleanness and vile affections are their unnatural lusts, for which many of the heathen, even of those among them who passed for wise men, as Solon and Zeno, were infamous, against the plainest and most obvious dictates of natural light. The crying iniquity of Sodom and Gomorrah, for which God rained hell from heaven upon them, became not only commonly practised, but avowed, in the pagan nations. Perhaps the apostle especially refers to the abominations that were committed in the worship of their idol-gods, in which the worst of uncleannesses were prescribed for the honour of their gods; dunghill service for dunghill gods: the unclean spirits delight in such ministrations. In the church of Rome, where the pagan idolatries are revived, images worshipped, and saints only substituted in the room of demons, we hear of these same abominations going barefaced, licensed by the pope (*Fox's Acts and Monuments,* vol. 1, p. 808), and not only commonly perpetrated, but justified and pleaded for by some of their cardinals: the same spiritual plagues for the same spiritual wickednesses. See what wickedness there is in the nature of man. How abominable and filthy is man! *Lord, what is man?* says David; what a vile creature is he when left to himself! How much are we beholden to the restraining grace of God for the preserving any thing of the honour and decency of the human nature! For, were it not for this, man, who was made but little lower than the angels, would make himself a great deal lower than the devils. This is said to be that *recompence of their error which was meet.* The Judge of all the earth does right, and observes a meetness between the sin and the punishment of it.

(2.) To a reprobate mind in these abominations, *v.* 28.

[1.] They *did not like to retain God in their knowledge.* The blindness of their understandings was caused by the wilful aversion of their wills and affections. They did not retain God in their knowledge, because they did not like it. They would neither know nor do any thing but just what pleased themselves. It is just the temper of carnal hearts; the pleasing of themselves is their highest end. There are many that have God in their knowledge, they cannot help it, the light shines so fully in their faces; but they do not retain him there. They *say to the Almighty, Depart* (Job 21:14), and they therefore do not retain God in their knowledge because it thwarts and contradicts their lusts; they do not like it. In their knowledge — *en epignōsei.* There is a difference between *gnōsis* and *epignōsis,* the *knowledge* and the *acknowledgement* of God; the pagans knew God, but did not, would not, acknowledge him.

[2.] Answerable to this wilfulness of theirs, in gainsaying the truth, God gave them over to a wilfulness in the grossest sins, here called a *reprobate mind — eis adokimon noun,* a mind void of all sense and judgment to discern things that differ, so that they could not distinguish their right hand from their left in spiritual things. See whither a course of sin leads, and into what a gulf it plunges the sinner at last; hither fleshly lusts have a direct tendency. *Eyes full of adultery cannot cease from sin,* 2 Pt. 2:14. This reprobate mind was a blind scared conscience, past feeling, Eph. 4:19. When the judgment is once reconciled to sin, the man is in the suburbs of hell. At first Pharaoh hardened his heart, but afterwards God hardened Pharaoh's heart. Thus wilful hardness is justly punished with judicial hardness. — *To do those things which are not convenient.* This phrase may seem to bespeak a diminutive evil, but here it is expressive of the grossest enormities; things that are not agreeable to men, but contradict the very light and law of nature. And here he subjoins a black list of those unbecoming things which the Gentiles were guilty of, being delivered up to a reprobate mind. No wickedness so heinous, so contrary to the light of nature, to the law of nations, and to all the interests of mankind, but a reprobate mind will comply with it. By the histories of those times, especially the accounts we have of the then prevailing dispositions and practices of the Romans when the ancient virtue of that commonwealth was so degenerated, it appears that these sins here mentioned were then and there reigning national sins. No fewer than twenty-three several sorts of sins and sinners are here specified, *v.* 29–31. Here the devil's seat is; his name is legion, for they are many. It was time to have the gospel preached among them, for the world had need of reformation.

First, Sins against the first table: *Haters of God.* Here is the devil in his own colours, sin appearing sin. Could it be imagined that rational creatures should hate the chief good, and depending creatures abhor the fountain of their being? And yet so it is. Every sin has in it a hatred of God; but some sinners are more open and avowed enemies to him than others, Zec. 11:8. *Proud men and boasters* cope with God himself, and put those crowns upon their own heads which must be cast before his throne.

Secondly, Sins against the second table. These are especially mentioned, because in these things they had a clearer light. In general here is a charge of unrighteousness. This is put first, for every sin is unrighteousness; it is withholding that which is due, perverting that which is right; it is especially put for second-table sins, doing as we would not be done by. Against the fifth commandment: *Disobedient to parents,* and *without natural affection — astorgous,* that is parents unkind and cruel to their children. Thus, when duty fails on one side, it commonly fails on the other. Disobedient children are justly punished with unnatural parents; and, on the contrary, unnatural parents with disobedient children. Against the sixth commandment: *Wickedness* (doing mischief for mischief's sake), *maliciousness, envy, murder, debate* (*eridos — contention*), *malignity, despiteful, implacable, unmerciful;* all expressions of that hatred of our brother which is heart-murder. Against the seventh commandment: *Fornication;* he mentions no more, having spoken before of other uncleannesses. Against the eighth commandment: *Unrighteousness, covetousness.* Against the ninth commandment: *Deceit, whisperers, back-biters, covenant-breakers,* lying and slandering. Here are two generals not before mentioned — *inventors of evil things, and without understanding;* wise to do evil, and yet having no knowledge to do good. The more deliberate and politic sinners are in inventing evil things, the greater is their sin: so quick of invention in sin, and yet without understanding (stark fools) in the thoughts of God. Here is enough to humble us all, in the sense of our original corruption; for every heart by nature has in it the seed and spawn of all these sins. In the close he mentions the aggravations of the sins, *v.* 32. 1. They *knew the judgment of God;* that is, (1.) They knew the law. The judgment of God is that which his justice requires, which, because he is just, he judgeth meet to be done. (2.) They knew the penalty; so it is explained here: They knew *that those who commit such things were worthy of death,* eternal death; their own consciences could not but suggest this to them, and yet they ventured upon it. It is a great aggravation of sin when it is committed against knowledge (James 4:17), especially against the knowledge of the judgment of God. It is daring presumption to run upon the sword's point. It argues the heart much hardened, and very resolutely set upon sin. 2. They *not only do the same, but have pleasure in those that do them.* The violence of some present temptation may hurry a man into the commission of such sins himself in which the vitiated appetite may take a pleasure; but to be pleased with other people's sins is to love sin for sin's sake: it is joining in a confederacy for the devil's kingdom and interest. *Syneudokousi*: they do not only commit sin, but they defend and justify it, and encourage others to do the like. Our own sins are much aggravated by our concurrence with, and complacency in, the sins of others.

Now lay all this together, and then say whether the Gentile world, lying under so much guilt and corruption, could be justified before God by any works of their own.

CHAPTER 2

The scope of the first two chapters of this epistle may be gathered from *ch.* 3:9, "We have before proved both Jews and Gentiles that they are all under sin." This we have proved upon the Gentiles (*ch.* 1), now in this chapter he proves it upon the Jews, as appears by *v.* 17, "thou art called a Jew." I. He proves in general that Jews and Gentiles stand upon the same level before the justice of God, to *v.* 11. II. He shows more particularly what sins the Jews were guilty of, notwithstanding their profession and vain pretensions (*v.* 17 to the end).

Verses 1–16

In the former chapter the apostle had represented the state of the Gentile world to be as bad and black as the Jews were ready enough to pronounce it. And now, designing to show that the state of the Jews was very bad too, and their sin in many respects more aggravated, to prepare his way he sets himself in this part of the chapter to show that God would proceed upon equal terms of justice with Jews and Gentiles; and now with such a partial hand as the Jews were apt to think he would use in their favour.

I. He arraigns them for their censoriousness and self-conceit (*v.* 1): *Thou art inexcusable, O man, whosoever thou art that judgest.* As he expresses himself in general terms, the admonition may reach those *many masters* (Jam. 3:1), of whatever nation or profession they are, that assume to themselves a power to censure, control, and condemn others. But he intends especially the Jews, and to them particularly he applies this general charge (*v.* 21), *Thou who teachest another teachest thou not thyself?* The Jews were generally a proud sort of people, that looked with a great deal of scorn and contempt upon the poor Gentiles, as not worthy to be set with the dogs of their flock; while in the mean time they were themselves as bad and immoral — though not idolaters, as the Gentiles, yet sacrilegious, *v.* 22. *Therefore thou art inexcusable.* If the Gentiles, who had but the light of nature, were inexcusable (*ch.* 1:20), much more the Jews, who had the light of the law, the revealed will of God, and so had greater helps than the Gentiles.

II. He asserts the invariable justice of the divine government, *v.* 2, 3. To drive home the conviction, he here shows what a righteous God that is with whom we have to do, and how just in his proceedings. It is usual with the apostle Paul, in his writings, upon mention of some material point, to make large digressions upon it; as here concerning the justice of God (*v.* 2), That the *judgment of God is according to truth,* — according to the eternal rules of justice and equity, — according to the heart, and not according to the outward appearance (1 Sa. 16:7), — according to the works, and not with respect to persons, is a doctrine which we are all sure of, for he would not be God if he were not just; but it behoves those especially to consider it who condemn others for those things which they themselves are guilty of, and so, while they practise sin and persist in that practice, think to bribe the divine justice by protesting against sin and exclaiming loudly upon others that are guilty, as if preaching against sin would atone for the guilt of it. But observe how he puts it to the sinner's conscience (*v.* 3): *Thinkest thou this, O man?* O man, a rational creature, a dependent creature, made by God, subject under him, and accountable to him. The case is so plain that we may venture to appeal to the sinner's own thoughts: "Canst thou think that *thou shalt escape the judgment of God?* Can the heart-searching God be imposed upon by formal pretences, the righteous Judge of all so bribed and put off?" The most plausible politic sinners, who acquit themselves before men with the greatest confidence, cannot *escape the judgment of God,* cannot avoid being judged and condemned.

III. He draws up a charge against them (*v.* 4, 5) consisting of two branches: —

1. Slighting the goodness of God (*v.* 4), *the riches of his goodness.* This is especially applicable to the Jews, who had singular tokens of the divine favour. Means are mercies, and the more light we sin against the more love we sin against. Low and mean thoughts of the divine goodness are at the bottom of a great deal of sin. There is in every wilful sin an interpretative contempt of the goodness of God; it is spurning at his bowels, particularly the goodness of his patience, his forbearance and long-suffering, taking occasion thence to be so much the more bold in sin, Eccl. 8:11. *Not knowing,* that is, not considering, not knowing practically and with application, that *the goodness of God leadeth thee,* the design of it is to lead thee, *to repentance.* It is not enough for us to know that God's goodness leads to repentance, but we must know that it leads *us — thee* in particular. See here what method God takes to bring sinners to repentance. He leads them, not drives them like beasts, but leads them like rational creatures, allures them (Hos. 2:14); and it is goodness that leads, bands of love, Hos. 11:4. Compare Jer. 31:3. The consideration of the goodness of God, his common goodness to all (the goodness of his providence, of his patience, and of his offers), should be effectual to bring us all to repentance; and the reason why so many continue in impenitency is because they do not know and consider this.

2. Provoking the wrath of God, *v.* 5. The rise of this provocation is a *hard and impenitent heart;* and the ruin of sinners is their walking after such a heart, being led by it. To sin is to walk in the way of the heart; and when that is a hard and impenitent heart (contracted hardness by long custom, besides that which is natural), how desperate must the course needs be! The provocation is expressed by *treasuring up*

wrath. Those that go on in a course of sin are treasuring up unto themselves wrath. A treasure denotes abundance. It is a treasure that will be spending to eternity, and yet never exhausted; and yet sinners are still adding to it as to a treasure. Every wilful sin adds to the score, and will inflame the reckoning; it brings a *branch to their wrath,* as some read that (Eze. 8:17), they *put the branch to their nose.* A treasure denotes secrecy. The treasury or magazine of wrath is the heart of God himself, in which it lies hid, as treasures in some secret place sealed up; see Deu. 32:34; Job 14:17. But withal it denotes reservation to some further occasion; as the treasures of the hail are reserved against the day of battle and war, Job 38:22, 23. These treasures will be broken open like the fountains of the great deep, Gen. 7:11. They are treasured up *against the day of wrath,* when they will be dispensed by the wholesale, poured out by full vials. Though the present day be a day of patience and forbearance towards sinners, yet there is a day of wrath coming — wrath, and nothing but wrath. Indeed, every day is to sinners a day of wrath, for God is *angry with the wicked every day* (Ps. 7:11), but there is the *great day of wrath* coming, Rev. 6:17. And that day of wrath will be *the day of the revelation of the righteous judgment of God.* The wrath of God is not like our wrath, a heat and passion; no, fury is not in him (Isa. 27:4): but it is a righteous judgment, his will to punish sin, because he hates it as contrary to his nature. This righteous judgment of God is now many times concealed in the prosperity and success of sinners, but shortly it will be manifested before all the world, these seeming disorders set to rights, and the heavens shall declare his righteousness, Ps. 50:6. *Therefore judge nothing before the time.*

IV. He describes the measures by which God proceeds in his judgment. Having mentioned the righteous judgment of God in *v.* 5, he here illustrates that judgment, and the righteousness of it, and shows what we may expect from God, and by what rule he will judge the world. The equity of distributive justice is the dispensing of frowns and favours with respect to deserts and without respect to persons: such is the righteous judgment of God.

1. He will *render to every man according to his deeds* (*v.* 6), a truth often mentioned in scripture, to prove that the Judge of all the earth does right.

(1.) In dispensing his favours; and this is mentioned twice here, both in *v.* 7 and *v.* 10. For he delights to show mercy. Observe,

[1.] The objects of his favour: *Those who by patient continuance,* etc. By this we may try our interest in the divine favour, and may hence be directed what course to take, that we may obtain it. Those whom the righteous God will reward are, *First,* Such as fix to themselves the right end, that *seek for glory, and honour, and immortality;* that is, the glory and honour which are immortal — acceptance with God here and for ever. There is a holy ambition which is at the bottom of all practical religion. This is seeking the kingdom of God, looking in our desires and aims as high as heaven, and resolved to take up with nothing short of it. This seeking implies a loss, sense of that loss, desire to retrieve it, and pursuits and endeavours consonant to those desires. *Secondly,* Such as, having fixed the right end, adhere to the right way: *A patient continuance in well-doing.* 1. There must be well-doing, working good, *v.* 10. It is not enough to know well, and speak well, and profess well, and promise well, but we must do well: do that which is good, not only for the matter of it, but for the manner of it. We must do it well. 2. A continuance in well-doing. Not for a fit and a start, like the morning cloud and the early dew; but we must endure to the end: it is perseverance that wins the crown. 3. A patient continuance. This patience respects not only the length of the work, but the difficulties of it and the oppositions and hardships we may meet with in it. Those that will do well and continue in it must put on a great deal of patience.

[2.] The product of his favour. He will render to such eternal life. Heaven is life, eternal life, and it is the reward of those that patiently continue in well-doing; and it is called (*v.* 10) *glory, honour, and peace.* Those that seek for glory and honour (*v.* 7) shall have them. Those that seek for the vain glory and honour of this world often miss of them, and are disappointed; but those that seek for immortal glory and honour shall have them, and not only *glory and honour,* but *peace.* Worldly glory and honour are commonly attended with trouble; but heavenly glory and honour have peace with them, undisturbed everlasting peace.

(2.) In dispensing his frowns (*v.* 8, 9). Observe, [1.] The objects of his frowns. In general those that do evil, more particularly described to be *such as are contentious and do not obey the truth.* Contentious against God. every wilful sin is a quarrel with God, it is *striving with our Maker* (Isa. 45:9), the most desperate contention. The Spirit of God strives with sinners (Gen. 6:3), and impenitent sinners strive against the Spirit, rebel against the light (Job 24:13), hold fast deceit, strive to retain that sin which the Spirit strives to part them from. *Contentious, and do not obey the truth.* The truths of religion are not only to be known, but to be obeyed; they are directing, ruling, commanding; truths relating to practice. Disobedience to the truth is interpreted a striving against it. *But obey unrighteousness* — do what unrighteousness bids them do. Those that refuse to be the servants of truth will soon be the slaves of unrighteousness. [2.] The products or instances of these frowns: *Indignation and wrath, tribulation and anguish.* These are the wages of sin. *Indignation and wrath* the causes — *tribulation and anguish* the necessary and unavoidable effects. And this *upon the soul;* souls are the vessels of that wrath, the subjects of that tribulation and anguish. Sin qualifies the soul for this wrath. The soul is that in or of man which is alone immediately capable of this indignation, and the impressions or effects of anguish therefrom. Hell is eternal tribulation and anguish, the product of wrath and indignation. This comes of contending with God, of setting briers and thorns before a consuming fire, Isa. 27:4. Those that will not bow to his golden sceptre will certainly be broken by his iron rod. Thus will God render to every man according to his deeds.

2. *There is no respect of persons with God, v.* 11. As to the spiritual state, there is a respect of persons; but not as to outward relation or condition. Jews and Gentiles stand upon the same level before God. This was Peter's remark upon the first taking down of the partition-wall (Acts 10:34), that God is no respecter of persons; and it is explained in the next words, that *in every nation he that fears God, and works righteousness, is accepted of him.* God does not save men with respect to their external privileges or their barren knowledge and profession of the truth, but according as their state and disposition really are. In dispensing both his frowns and favours it is both to Jew and Gentile. If to *the Jews first,* who had greater privileges, and made a greater profession, yet *also to the Gentiles,* whose want of such privileges will neither excuse them from the punishment of their ill-doing nor bar them out from the reward of their well-doing (see Col. 3:11); for shall not the Judge of all the earth do right?

V. He proves the equity of his proceedings with all, when he shall actually come to Judge them (*v.* 12–16), upon this principle, that that which is the rule of man's obedience is the rule of God's judgment. Three degrees of light are revealed to the children of men: —

1. The light of nature. This the Gentiles have, and by this they shall be judged: *As many as have sinned without law shall perish without law;* that is, the unbelieving Gentiles, who had no other guide but natural conscience, no other motive but common mercies, and had not the law of Moses nor any supernatural revelation, shall not be reckoned with for the transgression of the law they never had, nor come under the aggravation of the Jews' sin against and judgment by the written law; but they shall be judged by, as they sin against, the law of nature, not only as it is in their hearts, corrupted, defaced, and imprisoned in unrighteousness, but as in the uncorrupt original the Judge keeps by him. Further to clear this (*v.* 14, 15), in a parenthesis, he evinces that the light of nature was to the Gentiles instead of a written law. He had said (*v.* 12) they had *sinned without law,* which looks like a contradiction; for where there is no law there is no transgression. But, says he, though they had not the written law (Ps. 147:20), they had that which was equivalent, not to the ceremonial, but to the moral law. They *had the work of the law.* He does not mean that work which the law commands, as if they could produce a perfect obedience; but that work which the law does. The work of the law is to direct us what to do, and to examine us what we have done. Now, (1.) They had that which directed them what to do by the light of nature: by the force and tendency of their natural notions and dictates they apprehended a clear and vast difference between good and evil. They *did by nature the things contained in the law.* They had a sense of justice and equity, honour and purity, love and charity; the light of nature taught obedience to parents, pity to the miserable, conservation of public peace and order, forbade murder, stealing, lying, perjury, etc. Thus they were a *law unto themselves.* (2.) They had that which examined them as to what they had done: *Their conscience also bearing witness.* They had that within them which approved and commended what was well done and which reproached them for what was done amiss. Conscience is a witness, and first or last will bear witness, though for a time it may be bribed or brow-beaten. It is instead of a thousand witnesses, testifying of that which is most secret; and their *thoughts accusing or excusing,* passing a judgment upon the testimony of conscience by applying the law to the fact. Conscience is that candle of the Lord which was not quite put out, no, not in the Gentile world. The heathen have witnessed to the comfort of a good conscience.

> — Hic murus ahoncus esto,
> Nil conscire sibi —
>
> Be this thy brazen bulwark of defence,
> Still to preserve thy conscious innocence. — Hos.

and to the terror of a bad one:

> — Quos diri consein facti
> Mens habet attonitos, et surdo verbere cuodit —
>
> No lash is heard, and yet the guilty heart
> Is tortur'd with a self-inflicted smart — Juv. Sat. 13.

Their *thoughts the meanwhile, metaxy allēlōn — among themselves,* or one with another. The same light and law of nature that witnesses against sin in them, and witnessed against it in others, accused or excused one another. *Vicissim,* so some read it, *by turns;* according as they observed or broke these natural laws and dictates, their consciences did either acquit or condemn them. All this did evince that they had that which was to them instead of a law, which they might have been governed by, and which will condemn them, because they were not so guided and governed by it. So that the guilty Gentiles are left without excuse. God is justified in condemning them. They cannot plead ignorance, and therefore are likely to perish if they have not something else to plead.

2. The light of the law. This the Jews had, and by this they shall be judged (*v.* 12): *As many as have sinned in the law shall be judged by the law.* They sinned, not only having the law, but *en nomō — in the law,* in the midst of so much law, in the face and light of so pure and clear a law, the directions of which were so very full and particular, and the sanctions of it so very cogent and enforcing. These shall be judged *by the law;* their punishment shall be, as their sin is, so much the greater for their having the law. *The Jew first, v.* 9. It shall be more tolerable for Tyre and Sidon. Thus Moses did accuse them (Jn. 5:45), and they fell under the many stripes of him that knew his master's will, and did it not, Lu. 12:47. The Jews prided themselves very much in the law; but, to confirm what he had said, the apostle shows (*v.* 13) that their having, and hearing, and knowing the law, would not justify them, but their doing it. The Jewish doctors bolstered up their followers with an opinion that all that were Jews, how bad soever they lived, should have a place in the world to come. This the apostle here opposes: it was a great privilege that they had the law, but not a saving privilege, unless they lived up to the law they had, which it is certain the Jews did not, and therefore they had need of a righteousness wherein to appear before God. We may apply it to the gospel: it is not hearing, but doing that will save us, Jn. 13:17; James 1:22.

3. The light of the gospel: and according to this those that enjoyed the gospel shall be judge (*v.* 16): *According to my gospel;* not meant of any fifth gospel written by Paul, as some conceit; or of the gospel written by *Luke,* as Paul's amanuensis (*Euseb. Hist.* lib 3, cap. 8), but the gospel in general, called Paul's because he was a preacher of it. As many as are under that dispensation shall be judged according to that dispensation, Mk. 16:16. Some refer those words, *according to my gospel,* to what he says of the day of judgment: "There will come a day of judgment, according as I have in my preaching often told you; and that will be the day of the final judgment both of Jews and Gentiles." It is good for us to get acquainted with what is revealed concerning that day. (1.) There is a day set for a general judgment. The day, the great day, his day that is coming, Ps. 37:13. (2.) The judgment of that day will be put into the hands of Jesus Christ. God shall judge by Jesus Christ, Acts 17:31. It will be part of the reward of his humiliation. Nothing speaks more terror to sinners, or more comfort to saints, than this, that Christ shall be the Judge. (3.) The secrets of men shall then be judged. Secret services shall be then rewarded, secret sins shall be

then punished, hidden things shall be brought to light. That will be the great discovering day, when that which is now done in corners shall be proclaimed to all the world.

Verses 17–29

In the latter part of the chapter the apostle directs his discourse more closely to the Jews, and shows what sins they were guilty of, notwithstanding their profession and vain pretensions. He had said (*v.* 13) that not the hearers but the doers of the law are justified; and he here applies that great truth to the Jews. Observe,

I. He allows their profession (*v.* 17–20) and specifies their particular pretensions and privileges in which they prided themselves, that they might see he did not condemn them out of ignorance of what they had to say for themselves; no, he knew the best of their cause.

1. They were a peculiar people, separated and distinguished from all others by their having the written law and the special presence of God among them. (1.) *Thou art called a Jew;* not so much in parentage as profession. It was a very honourable title. Salvation was of the Jews; and this they were very proud of, to be a people by themselves; and yet many that were so called were the vilest of men. It is no new thing for the worst practices to be shrouded under the best names, for many of the synagogue of Satan to say they are Jews (Rev. 2:9), for a generation of vipers to boast they have *Abraham to their father,* Mt. 3:7–9. (2.) *And restest in the law;* that is, they took a pride in this, that they had the law among them, had it in their books, read it in their synagogues. They were mightily puffed up with this privilege, and thought this enough to bring them to heaven, though they did not live up to the law. To rest in the law, with a rest of complacency and acquiescence, is good; but to rest in it with a rest of pride, and slothfulness, and carnal security, is the ruin of souls. *The temple of the Lord,* Jer. 7:4. *Bethel their confidence,* Jer. 48:13. *Haughty because of the holy mountain,* Zep. 3:11. It is a dangerous thing to rest in external privileges, and not to improve them. (3.) *And makest thy boast of God.* See how the best things may be perverted and abused. A believing, humble, thankful glorying in God, is the root and summary of all religion, Ps. 34:2; Isa. 45:15; 1 Co. 1:31. But a proud vainglorious boasting in God, and in the outward profession of his name, is the root and summary of all hypocrisy. Spiritual pride is of all kinds of pride the most dangerous.

2. They were a knowing people (*v.* 18): *and knowest his will, to* thelēma — *the will.* God's will is the will, the sovereign, absolute, irresistible will. The world will then, and not till then, be set to rights, when God's will is the only will, and all other wills are melted into it. They did not only know the truth of God, but the will of God, that which he would have them to do. It is possible for a hypocrite to have a great deal of knowledge in the will of God. — *And approvest the things that are more excellent* — dokimazeis ta diapheronta. Paul prays for it for his friends as a very great attainment, Phil. 1:10. *Eis to dokimazein hymas ta diapheronta.* Understand it, (1.) Of a good apprehension in *the things of God,* reading it thus, *Thou discernest things that differ,* knowest how to distinguish between good and evil, to separate between the precious and the vile (Jer. 15:19), to make a difference between the unclean and the clean, Lev. 11:47. Good and bad lie sometimes so near together that it is not easy to distinguish them; but the Jews, having the touchstone of the law ready at hand, were, or at least thought they were, able to distinguish, to cleave the hair in doubtful cases. A man may be a good casuist and yet a bad Christian — accurate in the notion, but loose and careless in the application. Or, we may, with *De Dieu,* understand *controversies* by the *ta diapheronta.* A man may be well skilled in the controversies of religion, and yet a stranger to the power of godliness. (2.) Of a warm affection to the things of God, as we read it, *Approvest the things that are excellent.* There are excellences in religion which a hypocrite may approve of: there may be a consent of the practical judgment *to the law, that it is good,* and yet that consent overpowerd by the lusts of the flesh, and of the mind: —

— Video meliora proboque
Deteriora sequor.

I see the better, but pursue the worse.

and it is common for sinners to make that approbation an excuse which is really a very great aggravation of a sinful course. They got this acquaintance with, and affection to, that which is good, but being *instructed out of the law,* katēchou-

menos — *being catechised.* The word signifies an early instruction in childhood. It is a great privilege and advantage to be well catechised betimes. It was the custom of the Jews to take a great deal of pains in teaching their children when they were young, and all their lessons were *out of the law;* it were well if Christians were but as industrious to teach their children *out of the gospel.* Now this is called (*v.* 20), *The form of knowledge, and of the truth in the law,* that is, the show and appearance of it. Those whose knowledge rests in an empty notion, and does not make an impression on their hearts, have only the form of it, like a picture well drawn and in good colours, but which wants life. A form of knowledge produces but a form of godliness, 2 Tim. 3:5. A form of knowledge may deceive men, but cannot impose upon the piercing eye of the heart-searching God. A form may be the vehicle of the power; but he that takes up with that only is *like sounding brass and a tinkling cymbal.*

3. They were a teaching people, or at least thought themselves so (*v.* 19, 20): *And art confident that thou thyself art a guide of the blind.* Apply it, (1.) To the Jews in general. They thought themselves guides to the poor blind Gentiles that sat in darkness, were very proud of this, that whoever would have the knowledge of God must be beholden to them for it. All other nations must come to school to them, to learn what is good, and what the Lord requires; for they had the lively oracles. (2.) To their rabbis, and doctors, and leading men among them, who were especially those that judged others, *v.* 1. These prided themselves much in the possession they had got of Moses's chair, and the deference which the vulgar paid to their dictates; and the apostle expresses this in several terms, *a guide of the blind, a light of those who are in darkness, an instructor of the foolish, a teacher of babes,* the better to set forth their proud conceit of themselves, and contempt of others. This was a string they loved to be harping upon, heaping up titles of honour upon themselves. The best work, when it is prided in, is unacceptable to God. It is good to instruct the foolish, and to teach the babes: but considering our own ignorance, and folly, and inability to make these teachings successful without God, there is nothing in it to be proud of.

II. He aggravates their provocations (*v.* 21–24) from two things: —

1. That they sinned against their knowledge and profession, did that themselves which they taught others to avoid: *Thou that teachest another, teachest thou not thyself?* Teaching is a piece of that charity which begins at home, though it must not end there. It was the hypocrisy of the Pharisees *that they did not do as they taught* (Mt. 23:3), but pulled down with their lives what they built up with their preaching; for who will believe those who do not believe themselves? Examples will govern more than rules. The greatest obstructors of the success of the word are those whose bad lives contradict their good doctrine, who in the pulpit preach so well that it is a pity they should ever come out, and out of the pulpit live so ill that it is a pity they should ever come in. He specifies three particular sins that abound among the Jews: — (1.) Stealing. This is charged upon some that declared God's statutes (Ps. 50:16, 18), *When thou sawest a thief, then thou consentedst with him.* The Pharisees are charged with devouring widows' houses (Mt. 23:14), and that is the worst of robberies. (2.) Adultery, *v.* 22. This is likewise charged upon that sinner (Ps. 50:18), *Thou hast been partaker with adulterers.* Many of the Jewish rabbin are said to have been notorious for this sin. (3.) Sacrilege — robbing in holy things, which were then by special laws dedicated and devoted to God; and this is charged upon those that professed to abhor idols. So the Jews did remarkably, after their captivity in Babylon; that furnace separated them for ever from the dross of their idolatry, but they dealt very treacherously in the worship of God. It was in the latter days of the Old-Testament church that they were charged *with robbing God in tithes and offerings* (Mal. 3:8, 9), converting that to their own use, and to the service of their lusts, which was, in a special manner, set apart for God. And this is almost equivalent to idolatry, though this sacrilege was cloaked with the abhorrence of idols. Those will be severely reckoned with another day who, while they condemn sin in others, do the same, or as bad, or worse, themselves.

2. That they dishonoured God by their sin, *v.* 23, 24. While God and his law were an honour to them, which they boasted of and prided themselves in, they were a dishonour to God and his law, by giving occasion to those that were without

to reflect upon their religion, as if that did countenance and allow of such things, which, as it is their sin who draw such inferences (for the faults of professors are not to be laid upon professions), so it is their sin who give occasion for those inferences, and will greatly aggravate their miscarriages. This was the condemnation in David's case, *that he had given great occasion to the enemies of the Lord to blaspheme,* 2 Sa. 12:14. And the apostle here refers to the same charge against their forefathers: *As it is written,* v. 24. He does not mention the place, because he wrote this to those that were instructed in the law (in labouring to convince, it is some advantage to deal with those that have knowledge and are acquainted with the scripture), but he seems to point at Isa. 52:5; Eze. 36:22, 23; and 2 Sa. 12:14. It is a lamentation that those who were made *to be to God for a name and for a praise* should be to him a shame and dishonour. The great evil of the sins of professors is the dishonour done to God and religion by their profession. *"Blasphemed through you;* that is, you give the occasion for it, it is through your folly and carelessness. The reproaches you bring upon yourselves reflect upon your God, and religion is wounded through your sides." A good caution to professors to walk circumspectly. See 1 Tim. 6:1.

III. He asserts the utter insufficiency of their profession to clear them from the guilt of these provocations (*v.* 25–20): *Circumcision verily profiteth, if thou keep the law;* that is, obedient Jews shall not lose the reward of their obedience, but will gain this by their being Jews, that they have a clearer rule of obedience than the Gentiles have. God did not give the law nor appoint circumcision in vain. This must be referred to the state of the Jews before the ceremonial polity was abolished, otherwise circumcision to one that professed faith in Christ was forbidden, Gal. 5:1. But he is here speaking to the Jews, whose Judaism would benefit them, if they would but live up to the rules and laws of it; but if not *"thy circumcision is made uncircumcision;* that is, thy profession will do thee no good; thou wilt be no more justified than the uncircumcised Gentiles, but more condemned for sinning against greater light." The uncircumcised are in scripture branded as *unclean* (Isa. 52:1), as *out of the covenant,* (Eph. 2:11, 12) and wicked Jews will be dealt with as such. See Jer. 9:25, 26. Further to illustrate this,

1. He shows that the uncircumcised Gentiles, if they live up to the light they have, stand upon the same level with the Jews; if *they keep the righteousness of the law* (*v.* 26), *fulfil the law* (*v.* 27); that is, by submitting sincerely to the conduct of natural light, perform the matter of the law. Some understand it as putting the case of a perfect obedience to the law: "If the Gentiles could perfectly keep the law, they would be justified by it as well as the Jews." But it seems rather to be meant of such an obedience as some of the Gentiles did attain to. The case of Cornelius will clear it. Though he was a Gentile, and uncircumcised, yet, *being a devout man, and one that feared God with all his house* (Acts 10:2), he was accepted, *v.* 4. Doubtless, there were many such instances: and *they were the uncircumcision, that kept the righteousness of the law;* and of such he says, (1.) That they were accepted with God, as if they had been circumcised. *Their uncircumcision was counted for circumcision.* Circumcision was indeed *to the Jews* a commanded duty, but it was not to all the world a necessary condition of justification and salvation. (2.) That their obedience was a great aggravation of the disobedience of the Jews, who had the letter of the law, *v.* 27. *Judge thee,* that is, help to add to thy condemnation, who *by the letter and circumcision dost transgress.* Observe, To carnal professors the law is but the letter; they read it as a bare writing, but are not ruled by it as a law. They did transgress, not only notwithstanding the letter and circumcision, but by it, that is, they thereby hardened themselves in sin. External privileges, if they do not do us good, do us hurt. The obedience of those that enjoy less means, and make a less profession, will help to condemn those that enjoy greater means, and make a greater profession, but do not live up to it.

2. He describes the true circumcision, *v.* 28, 29. (1.) It is *not that which is outward in the flesh and in the letter.* This is not to drive us off from the observance of external institutions (they are good in their place), but from trusting to them and resting in them as sufficient to bring us to heaven, taking up with a name to live, without being alive indeed. *He is not a Jew,* that is, shall not be accepted of God as the seed of believing Abraham, nor owned as having answered the intention of the law. To be Abraham's children is to do

the works of Abraham, Jn. 8:39, 40. (2.) It is *that which is inward, of the heart, and in the spirit.* It is the heart that God looks at, the circumcising of the heart that renders us acceptable to him. See Deu. 30:6. This is *the circumcision that is not made with hands,* Col. 2:11, 12. *Casting away the body of sin.* So it is in the spirit, in our spirit as the subject, and wrought by God's Spirit as the author of it. (3.) The praise thereof, though it be *not of men,* who judge according to outward appearance, yet it is *of God,* that is, God himself will own and accept and crown this sincerity; for *he seeth not as man seeth.* Fair pretences and a plausible profession may deceive men: but God cannot be so deceived; he sees through shows to realities. This is alike true of Christianity. He is not a Christian that is one outwardly, nor is that baptism which is outward in the flesh; but he is a Christian that is one inwardly, and baptism is that of the heart, in the spirit, and not in the letter, whose praise is not of men but of God.

CHAPTER 3

The apostle, in this chapter, carries on his discourse concerning justification. He had already proved the guilt both of Gentiles and Jews. Now in this chapter, I. He answers some objections that might be made against what he had said about the Jews (*v.* 1–8). II. He asserts the guilt and corruption of mankind in common, both Jews and Gentiles (*v.* 9–18). III. He argues thence that justification must needs be by faith, and not by the law, which he gives several reasons for (*v.* 19 to the end). The many digressions in his writings render his discourse sometimes a little difficult, but his scope is evident.

Verses 1–18

I. Here the apostle answers several objections, which might be made, to clear his way. No truth so plain and evident but wicked wits and corrupt carnal hearts will have something to say against it; but divine truths must be cleared from cavil.

Object. 1. If Jew and Gentile stand so much upon the same level before God, *what advantage then hath the Jew?* Hath not God often spoken with a great deal of respect for the Jews, as a non-such people (Deu. 33:29), a holy nation, a peculiar treasure, the seed of Abraham his friend: Did not he institute circumcision as a badge of their church-membership, and a seal of their covenant-relation to God? Now does not this levelling doctrine deny them all such prerogatives, and reflect dishonour upon the ordinance of circumcision, as a fruitless insignificant thing.

Answer. The Jews are, notwithstanding this, a people greatly privileged and honoured, have great means and helps, though these be not infallibly saving (*v.* 2): *Much every way.* The door is open to the Gentiles as well as the Jews, but the Jews have a fairer way up to this door, by reason of their church-privileges, which are not to be undervalued, though many that have them perish eternally for not improving them. He reckons up many of the Jews' privileges Rom. 9:4, 5; here he mentions but one (which is indeed *instar omnium — equivalent to all*), *that unto them were committed the oracles of God,* that is, the scriptures of the Old Testament, especially the law of Moses, which is called *the lively oracles* (Acts 7:38), and those types, promises, and prophecies, which relate to Christ and the gospel. The scriptures are the oracles of God: they are a divine revelation, they come from heaven, are of infallible truth, and of eternal consequence as oracles. The Septuagint call the Urim and Thummim the *logia — the oracles.* The scripture is our breast-plate of judgment. We must have recourse to the law and to the testimony, as to an oracle. The gospel is called the oracles of God, Heb. 5:12; 1 Pt. 4:11. Now these oracles were committed to the Jews; the Old Testament was written in their language; Moses and the prophets were of their nation, lived among them, preached and wrote primarily to and for the Jews. They were committed to them as trustees for succeeding ages and churches. The Old Testament was deposited in their hands, to be carefully preserved pure and uncorrupt, and so transmitted down to posterity. The Jews were the Christians' library-keepers, were entrusted with that sacred treasure for their own use and benefit in the first place, and then for the advantage of the world; and, in preserving the letter of the scripture, they were very faithful to their trust, did not lose one iota or tittle, in which we are to acknowledge God's gracious care and providence. The Jews had the means of salvation, but they had not the monopoly of salvation. Now this he mentions with a *chiefly, prōton men gar —* this was their prime and principal privilege. The enjoyment of God's word and ordinances is the chief happiness of a people, is to be put in the *imprimis* of their advantages, Deu. 4:8; 33:3; Ps. 147:20.

Object. 2. Against what he had said of the advantages the Jews had in the lively oracles, some might object the unbelief of many of them. To what purpose were the oracles of God committed to them, when so many of them, notwithstanding these oracles, continued strangers to Christ, and enemies to his gospel? *Some did not believe, v.* 3.

Answer. It is very true that some, nay most of the present Jews, do not believe in Christ; *but shall their unbelief make the faith of God without effect?* The apostle startles at such a thought: *God forbid!* The infidelity and obstinacy of the Jews could not invalidate and overthrow those prophecies of the Messiah which were contained in the oracles committed to them. Christ will be glorious, *though Israel be not gathered,* Isa. 49:5. God's words shall be accomplished, his purposes performed, and all his ends answered, though there be a generation that by their unbelief go about to make God a liar. *Let God be true but every man a liar;* let us abide by this principle, that God is true to every word which he has spoken, and will let none of his oracles fall to the ground, though thereby we give the lie to man; better question and overthrow the credit of all the men in the world than doubt of the faithfulness of God. What David said in his haste (Ps. 116:11), that all men are liars, Paul here asserts deliberately. Lying is a limb of that old man which we every one of us come into the world clothed with. All men are fickle, and mutable, and given to change, *vanity and a lie* (Ps. 62:9), *altogether vanity,* Ps. 39:5. All men are liars, compared with God. It is very comfortable, when we find every man a liar (no faith in man), that God is faithful. When *they speak vanity every one with his neighbour,* it is very comfortable to think *that the words of the Lord are pure words,* Ps. 12:2, 6. For the further proof of this he quotes Ps. 51:4, *That thou mightest be justified,* the design of which is to show, 1. That God does and will preserve his own honour in the world, notwithstanding the sins of men. 2. That it is our duty, in all our conclusions concerning ourselves and others, to justify God and to assert and maintain his justice, truth, and goodness, however it goes. David lays a load upon himself in his confession, that he might justify God, and acquit him from any injustice. So here, Let the credit or reputation of man shift for itself, the matter is not great whether it sink or swim; let us hold fast this conclusion, how specious soever the premises may be to the contrary, that *the Lord is righteous in all his ways, and holy in all his works.* Thus is God justified in his sayings, and cleared when he judges (as it is Ps. 51:4), or when *he is judged,* as it is here rendered. When men presume to quarrel with God and his proceedings, we may be sure the sentence will go on God's side.

Object. 3. Carnal hearts might hence take occasion to encourage themselves in sin. He had said that the universal guilt and corruption of mankind gave occasion to the manifestation of God's righteousness in Jesus Christ. Now it may be suggested, If all our sin be so far from overthrowing God's honour that it commends it, and his ends are secured, so that there is no harm done, is it not unjust for God to punish our sin and unbelief so severely? If the unrighteousness of the Jews gave occasion to the calling in of the Gentiles, and so to God's greater glory, why are the Jews so much censured? *If our unrighteousness commend the righteousness of God, what shall we say? v.* 5. What inference may be drawn from this? *Is God unrighteous, mē adikos ho Theos — Is not God unrighteous* (so it may be read, more in the form of an objection), *who taketh vengeance?* Unbelieving hearts will gladly take any occasion to quarrel with equity of God's proceedings, and to condemn him that is most just, Job 34:17. *I speak as a man,* that is, I object this as the of carnal hearts; it is suggested like a man, a vain, foolish, proud creature.

Answer. God forbid; far be it from us to imagine such a thing. Suggestions that reflect dishonour upon God and his justice and holiness are rather to be startled at than parleyed with. Get thee behind me, Satan; never entertain such a thought. *For then how shall God judge the world? v.* 6. The argument is much the same with that of Abraham (Gen. 18:25): *Shall not the Judge of all the earth do right?* No doubt, he shall. If he were not infinitely just and righteous, he would be unfit to be the judge of all the earth. *Shall even he that hateth right govern?* Job 34:17. Compare *v.* 18, 19. The sin has never the less of malignity and demerit in it though God bring glory to himself out of it. It is only accidentally that sin commends God's righteousness. No thanks to the sinner for that, who intends no such thing. The consideration of God's judging the world should for ever silence all our doubtings of, and reflections upon, his justice and equity. It is not for us to arraign the proceedings of such an absolute Sovereign. The sentence of the supreme court, whence lies no appeal, is not to be called in question.

Object. 4. The former objection is repeated and prosecuted (*v.* 7, 8), for proud hearts will hardly be beaten out of their refuge of lies, but will hold fast the deceit. But his setting off the objection in its own colours is sufficient to answer it: *If the truth of God has more abounded through my lie.* He supposes the sophisters to follow their objection thus: "If my lie, that is, my sin" (for there is something of a lie in every sin, especially in the sins of professors) "have occasioned the glorifying of God's truth and faithfulness, why *should I be judged* and condemned *as a sinner, and not rather* thence take encouragement to go on in my sin, that grace may abound?" an inference which at first sight appears too black to be argued, and fit to be cast out with abhorrence. Daring sinners take occasion to boast in mischief, because the *goodness of God endures continually,* Ps. 52:1. *Let us do evil that good may come* is oftener in the heart than in the mouth of sinners, so justifying themselves in their wicked ways. Mentioning this wicked thought, he observes, in a parenthesis, that there were those who charged such doctrines as this upon Paul and his fellow-ministers: Some affirm that we say so. It is no new thing for the best of God's people and ministers to be charged with holding and teaching such things as they do most detest and abhor; and it is not to be thought strange, when our Master himself was said to be in league with Beelzebub. Many have been reproached as if they had said that the contrary of which they maintain: it is an old artifice of Satan thus to cast dirt upon Christ's ministers, *Fortiter calumniari, aliquid adhaerebit — Lay slander thickly on, for some will be sure to stick.* The best men and the best truths are subject to slander. Bishop Sanderson makes a further remark upon this, *as we are slanderously reported —blasphēmoumetha.* Blasphemy in scripture usually signifies the highest degree of slander, speaking ill of God. The slander of a minister and his regular doctrine is a more than ordinary slander, it is a kind of blasphemy, not for his person's sake, but for his calling's sake and his work's sake, 1 Th. 5:13.

Answer. He says no more by way of confutation but that, whatever they themselves may argue, the damnation of those is just. Some understand it of the slanderers; God will justly condemn those who unjustly condemn his truth. Or, rather, it is to be applied to those who embolden themselves in sin under a pretence of God's getting glory to himself out of it. Those who deliberately do evil that good may come of it will be so far from escaping, under the shelter of that excuse, that it will rather justify their damnation, and render them the more inexcusable; for sinning upon such a surmise, and in such a confidence, argues a great deal both of the wit and of the will in the sin — a wicked will deliberately to choose the evil, and a wicked wit to palliate it with the pretence of good arising from it. Therefore their damnation is just; and, whatever excuses of this kind they may now please themselves with, they will none of them stand good in the great day, but God will be justified in his proceedings, and all flesh, even the proud flesh that now lifts up itself against him, shall be silent before him. Some think Paul herein refers to the approaching ruin of the Jewish church and nation, which their obstinacy and self-justification in their unbelief hastened upon them apace.

II. Paul, having removed these objections, next revives his assertion of the general guilt and corruption of mankind in common, both of Jews and Gentiles, *v.* 9–18. *"Are we better than they,* we Jews, to whom were committed the oracles of God? Does this recommend us to God, or will this justify us? No, by no means." Or, "Are we Christians (Jews and Gentiles) so much better antecedently than the unbelieving part as to have merited God's grace? Alas! no: before free grace made the difference, those of us that had been Jews and those that had been Gentiles were all alike corrupted." They *are all under sin.* Under the guilt of sin: under it as under a sentence; — under it as under a bond, by which they are bound over to eternal ruin and damnation; — under it as under a burden (Ps. 38:4) that will sink them to the lowest hell: we are guilty before God, *v.* 19. Under the government and dominion of sin: under it as under a tyrant and cruel task-master, enslaved to it; — under it as under a yoke; — under the power of it, sold to work wickedness. And this he had proved, *pro-*

ētiasametha. It is a law term: *We have charged them with it,* and have made good our charge; we have proved the indictment, we have convicted them by the notorious evidence of the fact. This charge and conviction he here further illustrates by several scriptures out of the Old Testament, which describe the corrupt depraved state of all men, till grave restrain or change them; so that herein as in a glass we may all of us behold our natural face. The 10th, 11th, and 12th verses are taken from Ps. 14:1–3, which are repeated as containing a very weighty truth, Ps. 53:1–3. The rest that follows here is found in the Septuagint translation of the 14th Psalm, which some think the apostle chooses to follow as better known; but I rather think that Paul took these passages from other places of scripture here referred to, but in later copies of the Septuagint they were all added in Ps. 14 from this discourse of Paul. It is observable that, to prove the general corruption of nature, he quotes some scriptures which speak of the particular corruptions of particular persons, as of Doeg (Ps. 140:3), of the Jews (Isa. 59:7, 8), which shows that the same sins that are committed by one are in the nature of all. The times of David and Isaiah were some of the better times, and yet to their days he refers. What is said Ps. 14 is expressly spoken of *all the children of men,* and that upon a particular view and inspection made by God himself. The *Lord looked down,* as upon the old world, Gen. 6:5. And this judgment of God was according to truth. He who, when he himself had made all, looked upon every thing that he had made, and behold all was very good, now that man had marred all, looked, and behold all was very bad. Let us take a view of the particulars. Observe,

1. That which is habitual, which is two-fold: —

(1.) An habitual defect of every thing that is good. [1.] *There is none righteous,* none that has an honest good principle of virtue, or is governed by such a principle, none that retains any thing of that image of God, consisting in righteousness, wherein man was created; *no, not one;* implying that, if there had been but one, God would have found him out. When all the world was corrupt, God had his eye upon one righteous Noah. Even those who through grace are justified and sanctified were none of them righteous by nature. No righteousness is born with us. The man after God's own heart owns himself conceived in sin. [2.] *There is none that understandeth, v.* 11. The fault lies in the corruption of the understanding; that is blinded, depraved, perverted. Religion and righteousness have so much reason on their side that if people had but any understanding they would be better and do better. But they do not understand. Sinners are fools. [3.] *None that seeketh after God,* that is, none that has any regard to God, any desire after him. Those may justly be reckoned to have no understanding that do not seek after God. The carnal mind is so far from seeking after God that really it is enmity against him. [4.] *They are together become unprofitable, v.* 12. Those that have forsaken God soon grow good for nothing, useless burdens of the earth. Those that are in a state of sin are the most unprofitable creatures under the sun; for it follows, [5.] *There is none that doeth good;* no, not a just man upon the earth, that doeth good, and sinneth not, Eccl. 7:23. Even in those actions of sinners that have some goodness in them there is a fundamental error in the principle and end; so that it may be said, There is none that doeth good. *Malum oritur ex quolibet defectu — Every defect is the source of evil.*

(2.) An habitual defection to every thing that is evil: *They are all gone out of the way.* No wonder that those miss the right way who do not seek after God, the highest end. God made man in the way, set him in right, but he hath forsaken it. The corruption of mankind is an apostasy.

2. That which is actual. And what good can be expected from such a degenerate race? He instances,

(1.) In their words (*v.* 13, 14), in three things particularly: — [1.] Cruelty: *Their throat is an open sepulchre,* ready to swallow up the poor and innocent, waiting an opportunity to do mischief, like the old serpent seeking to devour, whose name is Abaddon and Apollyon, the destroyer. And when they do not openly avow this cruelty, and vent it publicly, yet they are underhand intending mischief: the *poison of asps is under their lips* (Jam. 3:8), the most venomous and incurable poison, with which they blast the good name of their neighbour by reproaches, and aim at his life by false witness. These passages are borrowed from Ps. 5:9 and 140:3. [2.] Cheating: *With their tongues they have used deceit.* Herein they show themselves the devil's children, for he is a liar, and the father of lies. They *have used* it: it intimates that they make a trade of lying; it is their constant practice, especially belying the ways and people of God. [3.] Cursing: reflecting upon God, and blaspheming his holy name; wishing evil to their brethren: *Their mouth is full of cursing and bitterness.* This is mentioned as one of the great sins of the tongue, Jam. 3:9. But those that thus love cursing shall have enough of it, Ps. 109:17–19. How many, who are called Christians, do by these sin evince that they are still under the reign and dominion of sin, still in the condition that they were born in.

(2.) In their ways (*v.* 15–17): *Their feet are swift to shed blood;* that is, they are very industrious to compass any cruel design, ready to lay hold of all such opportunities. Wherever they go, *destruction and misery* go along with them; these are their companions — destruction and misery to the people of God, to the country and neighbourhood where they live, to the land and nation, and to themselves at last. Besides the destruction and misery that are at the end of their ways (death is the end of these things), destruction and misery are in their ways; their sin is its own punishment: a man needs no more to make him miserable than to be a slave to his sins. — *And the way of peace have they not known;* that is, they know not how to preserve peace with others, nor how to obtain peace for themselves. They may talk of peace, such a peace as is in the devil's palace, while he keeps it, but they are strangers to all true peace; they know not the things that belong to their peace. These are quoted from Prov. 1:16; Isa. 59:7, 8.

(3.) The root of all this we have: *There is no fear of God before their eyes, v.* 18. The fear of God is here put for all practical religion, which consists in an awful and serious regard to the word and will of God as our rule, to the honour and glory of God as our end. Wicked people have not this before their eyes; that is, they do not steer by it; they are governed by other rules, aim at other ends. This is quoted from Ps. 36:1. Where no fear of God is, no good is to be expected. The fear of God is would lay a restraint upon our spirits, and keep them right, Neh. 5:15. When once fear is cast off, prayer is restrained (Job 15:4), and then all goes to wreck and ruin quickly. So that we have here a short account of the general depravity and corruption of mankind; and may say, O Adam! what hast thou done? God made man upright, but thus he hath sought out many inventions.

Verses 19–31

From all this Paul infers that it is in vain to look for justification by the works of the law, and that it is to be had only by faith, which is the point he has been all along proving, from *ch.* 1:17, and which he lays down (*v.* 28) as the summary of his discourse, with a *quod erat demonstrandum — which was to be demonstrated. We conclude that a man is justified by faith, without the deeds of the law;* not by the deeds of the first law of pure innocence, which left no room for repentance, nor the deeds of the law of nature, how highly soever improved, nor the deeds of the ceremonial law (the blood of bulls and goats could not take away sin), nor the deeds of the moral law, which are certainly included, for he speaks of that law by which is the knowledge of sin and those works which might be matter of boasting. Man, in his depraved state, under the power of such corruption, could never, by any works of his own, gain acceptance with God; but it must be resolved purely into the free grace of God, given through Jesus Christ to all true believers that receive it as a free gift. If we had never sinned, our obedience to the law would have been our righteousness: "Do this, and live." But having sinned, and being corrupted, nothing that we can do will atone for our former guilt. It was by their obedience to the moral law that the Pharisees looked for justification, Lu. 18:11. Now there are two things from which the apostle here argues: the guiltiness of man, to prove that we cannot be justified by the works of the law, and the glory of God, to prove that we must be justified by faith.

I. He argues from man's guiltiness, to show the folly of expecting justification by the works of the law. The argument is very plain: we can never be justified and saved by the law that we have broken. A convicted traitor can never come off by pleading the statute of 25 *Edward* III, for that law discovers his crime and condemns him: indeed, if he had never broken it, he might have been justified by it; but now it is past that he has broken it, and there is no way of coming off but by pleading the act of indemnity, upon which he has surrendered and submitted himself, and humbly and penitently claiming the benefit of it and casting himself upon it. Now concerning the guiltiness of man,

1. He fastens it particularly upon the Jews; for they were the men that made their boast of the law, and set up for justification by it. He had quoted several scriptures out of the Old Testament to show this corruption: Now, says he (*v.* 19), *this that the law says, it says to those who are under the law;* this conviction belongs to the Jews as well as others, for it is written in their law. The Jews boasted of their being under the law, and placed a great deal of confidence in it: "But," says he, "the law convicts and condemns you — you see it does." That *every mouth may be stopped* — that all boasting may be silenced. See the method that God takes both in justifying and condemning: he stops every mouth; those that are justified have their mouths stopped by a humble conviction; those that are condemned have their mouths stopped too, for they shall at last be convinced (Jude 15), and sent speechless to hell, Mt. 22:12. *All iniquity shall stop her mouth,* Ps. 107:42.

2. He extends it in general to all the world: *That all the world may become guilty before God.* If the world likes in wickedness (1 Jn. 5:19), to be sure it is guilty. — *May become guilty;* that is, may be proved guilty, liable to punishment, all by nature *children of wrath,* Eph. 2:3. They must all plead guilty; those that stand most upon their own justification will certainly be cast. Guilty before God is a dreadful word, before an all-seeing God, that is not, nor can be, deceived in his judgment — before a just and righteous judge, who will by no means clear the guilty. All are guilty, and therefore all have need of a righteousness wherein to appear before God. *For all have sinned* (*v.* 23); all are sinners by nature, by practice, and *have come short of the glory of God* — have failed of that which is the chief end of man. *Come short,* as the archer comes short of the mark, as the runner comes short of the prize; so come short, as not only not to win, but to be great losers. *Come short of the glory of God.* (1.) Come short of glorifying God. See *ch.* 1:21, *They glorified him not as God.* Man was placed at the head of the visible creation, actively to glorify that great Creator whom the inferior creatures could glorify only objectively; but man by sin comes short of this, and, instead of glorifying God, dishonours him. It is a very melancholy consideration, to look upon the children of men, who were made to glorify God, and to think how few there are that do it. (2.) Come short of glorying *before God.* There is no boasting of innocency: if we go about to glory before God, to boast of any thing we are, or have, or do, this will be an everlasting estoppel — that we have all sinned, and this will silence us. We may glory before men, who are shortsighted, and cannot search our hearts, — who are corrupt, as we are, and well enough pleased with sin; but there is no glorying before God, who cannot endure to look upon iniquity. (3.) Come short of being glorified by God. Come short of justification, or acceptance with God, which is glory begun — come short of the holiness or sanctification which is the glorious image of God upon man, and have overthrown all hopes and expectations of being glorified with God in heaven by any righteousness of their own. It is impossible now to get to heaven in the way of spotless innocency. That passage is blocked up. There is a cherub and a flaming sword set to keep that way to the tree of life.

3. Further to drive us off from expecting justification by the law, he ascribes this conviction to the law (*v.* 20): *For by the law is the knowledge of sin.* That law which convicts and condemns us can never justify us. The law is the straight rule, that *rectum* which is *index sui et obliqui — that which points out the right and the wrong;* it is the proper use and intendment of the law to open our wound, and therefore not likely to be the remedy. That which is searching is not sanative. Those that would know sin must get the knowledge of the law in its strictness, extent, and spiritual nature. If we compare our own hearts and lives with the rule, we shall discover wherein we have turned aside. Paul makes this use of the law, *ch.* 7:9, *Therefore by the deeds of the law shall no flesh be justified in his sight.* Observe, (1.) *No flesh shall be justified,* no man, no corrupted man (Gen. 6:3), *for that he also is flesh,* sinful and depraved; therefore not justified, because we are flesh. The corruption that remains in our nature will for ever obstruct any justification by our own works, which, coming from flesh, must needs taste of the cask, Job 14:4. (2.) Not justified in his sight. He does not deny that justification which was by the deeds of the law in the sight of the church: they were, in their church-estate, as embodied

in a polity, a holy people, a nation of priests; but as the conscience stands in relation to God, *in his sight,* we cannot be justified by the deeds of the law. The apostle refers to Ps. 143:2.

II. He argues from God's glory to prove that justification must be expected only by faith in Christ's righteousness. There is no justification by the works of the law. Must guilty man then remain eternally under wrath? Is there no hope? Is the wound become incurable because of transgression? No, blessed be God, it is not (*v.* 21, 22); there is another way laid open for us, *the righteousness of God without the law is manifested* now under the gospel. Justification may be obtained without the keeping of Moses's law: and this is called *the righteousness of God,* righteousness of his ordaining, and providing, and accepting, — righteousness which he confers upon us; as the Christian armour is called *the armour of God,* Eph. 6:11.

1. Now concerning this righteousness of God observe, (1.) That it is manifested. The gospel-way of justification is a highway, a plain way, it is laid open for us: the brazen serpent is lifted up upon the pole; we are not left to grope our way in the dark, but it is manifested to us. (2.) It is *without the law.* Here he obviates the method of the judaizing Christians, who would needs join Christ and Moses together — owning Christ for the Messiah, and yet too fondly retaining the law, keeping up the ceremonies of it, and imposing it upon the Gentile converts: no, says he, it is without the law. The righteousness that Christ hath brought in is a complete righteousness. (3.) Yet *it is witnessed by the law and the prophets;* that is, there were types, and prophecies, and promises, in the Old Testament, that pointed at this. The law is so far from justifying us that it directs us to another way of justification, points at Christ as our righteousness, to whom bear all the prophets witness. See Acts 10:43. This might recommend it to the Jews, who were so fond of the law and the prophets. (4.) It is by the *faith of Jesus Christ,* that faith which hath Jesus Christ for its object — an *anointed Saviour,* so Jesus Christ signifies. Justifying faith respects Christ as a Saviour in all his three anointed offices, as prophet, priest, and king — trusting in him, accepting of him, and adhering to him, in all these. It is by this that we become interested in that righteousness which God has ordained, and which Christ has brought in. (5.) It is *to all, and upon all, those that believe.* In this expression he inculcates that which he had been often harping upon, that Jews and Gentiles, if they believe, stand upon the same level, and are alike welcome to God through Christ; *for there is no difference.* Or, it is *eis pantas — to all,* offered to all in general; the gospel excludes none that do not exclude themselves; but it is *epi pantas tous pisteuontas, upon all that believe,* not only tendered to them, but put upon them as a crown, as a robe; they are, upon their believing, interested in it, and entitled to all the benefits and privileges of it.

2. But now how is this for God's glory?

(1.) It is for the glory of his grace (*v.* 24): *Justified freely by his grace — dōrean tē autou chariti.* It is *by his grace,* not by the grace wrought in us as the papists say, confounding justification and sanctification, but by the gracious favour of God to us, without any merit in us so much as foreseen. And, to make it the more emphatic, he says it is *freely by his grace,* to show that it must be understood of grace in the most proper and genuine sense. It is said that *Joseph found grace* in the sight of his master (Gen. 39:4), but there was a reason; he saw that what he did prospered. There was something in Joseph to invite that grace; but the grace of God communicated to us comes *freely, freely;* it is free grace, mere mercy; nothing in us to deserve such favours: no, it is all *through the redemption that is in Jesus Christ.* It comes freely to us, but Christ bought it, and paid dearly for it, which yet is so ordered as not to derogate from the honour of free grace. Christ's purchase is no bar to the freeness of God's grace; for grace provided and accepted this vicarious satisfaction.

(2.) It is for the glory of his justice and righteousness (*v.* 25, 26): *Whom God hath set forth to be a propitiation,* etc. Note, [1.] Jesus Christ is the great propitiation, or propitiatory sacrifice, typified by the *hilastērion,* or *mercy-seat,* under the law. He is our throne of grace, in and through whom atonement is made for sin, and our persons and performances are accepted of God, 1 Jn. 2:2. He is all in all in our reconciliation, not only the maker, but the matter of it — our priest, our sacrifice, our altar, our all. God was in Christ as in his mercy-seat, reconciling the world unto himself. [2.] *God hath set him forth* to be so. God, the party offended, makes the first overtures towards a reconciliation, appoints the daysman; *proetheto — fore-ordained* him to this, in the counsels of his love from eternity, appointed, anointed him to it, qualified him for it, and has exhibited him to a guilty world as their propitiation. See Mt. 3:17, and 17:5. [3.] That *by faith in his blood* we become interested in this propitiation. Christ is the propitiation; there is the healing plaster provided. Faith is the applying of this plaster to the wounded soul. And this faith in the business of justification hath a special regard to *the blood of Christ,* as that which made the atonement; for such was the divine appointment that without blood there should be no remission, and no blood but his would do it effectually. Here may be an allusion to the sprinkling of the blood of the sacrifices under the law, as Ex. 24:8. Faith is the bunch of hyssop, and the blood of Christ is the blood of sprinkling. [4.] That all who by faith are interested in this propitiation have *the remission of their sins that are past.* It was for this that Christ was set forth to be a propitiation, in order to remission, to which the reprieves of his patience and forbearance were a very encouraging preface. *Through the forbearance of God.* Divine patience has kept us out of hell, that we might have space to repent, and get to heaven. Some refer the *sins that are past* to the sins of the Old-Testament saints, which were pardoned for the sake of the atonement which Christ in the fulness of time was to make, which looked backward as well as forward. *Past through the forbearance of God.* It is owing to the divine forbearance that we were not taken in the very act of sin. Several Greek copies make *en tēanochē tou Theou — through the forbearance of God,* to begin *v.* 26, and they denote two precious fruits of Christ's merit and God's grace: — Remission: *dia tēn paresin — for the remission;* and reprieves: the *forbearance* of God. It is owing to the master's goodness and the dresser's mediation that barren trees are let alone in the vineyard; and in both God's righteousness is declared, in that without a mediator and a propitiation he would not only not pardon, but not so much as forbear, not spare a moment; it is owning to Christ that there is ever a sinner on this side hell. [5.] That God does in all this *declare his righteousness.* This he insists upon with a great deal of emphasis: *To declare, I say, at this time his righteousness.* It is repeated, as that which has in it something surprising. He declares his righteousness, *First,* In the propitiation itself. Never was there such a demonstration of the justice and holiness of God as there was in the death of Christ. It appears that he hates sin, when nothing less than the blood of Christ would satisfy for it. Finding sin, though but imputed, upon his own Son, he did not spare him, because he had made himself sin for us, 2 Co. 5:21. The iniquities of us all being laid upon him, though he was the Son of his love, yet it pleased the Lord to bruise him, Isa. 53:10. *Secondly,* In the pardon upon that propitiation; so it follows, by way of explication: *That he might be just, and the justifier of him that believeth.* Mercy and truth are so met together, righteousness and peace have so kissed each other, that it is now become not only an act of grace and mercy, but an act of righteousness, in God, to pardon the sins of penitent believers, having accepted the satisfaction that Christ by dying made to his justice for them. It would not comport with his justice to demand the debt of the principal when the surety has paid it and he has accepted that payment in full satisfaction. See 1 Jn. 1:9. He is just, that is, faithful to his word.

(3.) It is for God's glory; for boasting is thus excluded, *v.* 27. God will have the great work of the justification and salvation of sinners carried on from first to last in such a way as to exclude boasting, that no flesh may glory in his presence, 1 Co. 1:29–31. Now, if justification were by the works of the law, boasting would not be excluded. How should it? If we were saved by our own works, we might put the crown upon our own heads. But the *law of faith,* that is, the way of justification by faith, doth for ever exclude boasting; for faith is a depending, self-emptying, self-denying grace, and casts every crown before the throne; therefore it is most for God's glory that thus we should be justified. Observe, He speaks of *the law of faith.* Believers are not left lawless: faith is a law, it is a working grace, wherever it is in truth; and yet, because it acts in a strict and close dependence upon Jesus Christ, it excludes boasting.

From all this he draws this conclusion (*v.* 28): *That a man is justified by faith without the deeds of the law.*

III. In the close of the chapter he shows the extent of this privilege of justification by faith, and that it is not the peculiar privilege of the Jews, but pertains to the Gentiles also; for he had said (*v.* 22) that there is no difference: and as to this, 1. He asserts and proves it (*v.* 29, 39): *Is he the God of the Jews only?* He argues from the absurdity of such a supposition. Can it be imagined that a God of infinite love and mercy should limit and confine his favours to that little perverse people of the Jews, leaving all the rest of the children of men in a condition eternally desperate? This would by no means agree with the idea we have of the divine goodness, for his *tender mercies are over all his works;* therefore it is one God of grace that *justifies the circumcision by faith, and the uncircumcision through faith,* that is, both in one and the same way. However the Jews, in favour of themselves, will needs fancy a difference, really there is no more difference than between *by* and *through,* that is, no difference at all. 2. He obviates an objection (*v.* 31), as if this doctrine did nullify the law, which they knew came from God: "No," says he, "though we do say that the law will not justify us, yet we do not therefore say that it was given in vain, or is of no use to us; no, *we establish the right use of the law,* and secure its standing, by fixing it on the right basis. The law is still of use to convince us of what is past, and to direct us for the future; though we cannot be saved by it as a covenant, yet we own it, and submit to it, as a rule in the hand of the Mediator, subordinate to the law of grace; and so are so far from overthrowing that we establish the law." Let those consider this who deny the obligation of the moral law on believers.

CHAPTER 4

The great gospel doctrine of justification by faith without the works of the law was so very contrary to the notions the Jews had learnt from those that sat in Moses' chair, that it would hardly go down with them; and therefore the apostle insists very largely upon it, and labours much in the confirmation and illustration of it. He had before proved it by reason and argument, now in this chapter he proves it by example, which in some places serves for confirmation as well as illustration. The example he pitches upon is that of Abraham, whom he chooses to mention because the Jews gloried much in their relation to Abraham, put it in the first rank of their external privileges that they were Abraham's seed, and truly they had Abraham for their father. Therefore this instance was likely to be more taking and convincing to the Jews than any other. His argument stands thus: "All that are saved are justified in the same way as Abraham was; but Abraham was justified by faith, and not by works; therefore all that are saved are so justified;" for it would easily be acknowledged that Abraham was the father of the faithful. Now this is an argument, not only *à pari* — from an equal case, as they say, but *à fortiori* — from a stronger case. If Abraham, a man so famous for works, so eminent in holiness and obedience, was nevertheless justified by faith only, and not by those works, how much less can any other, especially any of those that spring from him, and come so far short of him in works, set up for a justification by their own works? And it proves likewise, *ex abundanti* — the more abundantly, as some observe, that we are not justified, no not by those good works which flow from faith, as the matter of our righteousness; for such were Abraham's works, and are we better than he? The whole chapter is taken up with his discourse upon this instance, and there is this in it, which hath a particular reference to the close of the foregoing chapter, where he has asserted that, in the business of justification, Jews and Gentiles stand upon the same level. Now in this chapter, with a great deal of cogency of argument, I. He proves that Abraham was justified not by works, but by faith (*v.* 1–8). II. He observes when and why he was so justified (*v.* 9–17). III. He describes and commends that faith of his (*v.* 17–22). IV. He applies all this to us (*v.* 22–25). And, if he had now been in the school of Tyrannus, he could not have disputed more argumentatively.

Verses 1–8

Here the apostle proves that Abraham was justified not by works, but by faith. Those that of all men contended most vigorously for a share in righteousness by the privileges they enjoyed, and the works they performed, were the Jews, and therefore he appeals to the case of Abraham their father, and puts his own name to the relation, being a Hebrew of the Hebrews: *Abraham our father.* Now surely his prerogative must needs be as great as theirs who claim it as his seed according to the flesh. Now *what has he found?* All the world is seeking; but, while the most are wearying themselves for very vanity, none can be truly reckoned to have found, but those who are justified before God; and thus Abraham, like a wise merchant, seeking goodly pearls, found this one pearl of great price. What has he found, *kata sarka — as pertaining to the flesh,* that is, by circumcision and his external privileges and performances? These the apostle calls *flesh,* Phil. 3:3. Now what did he get by these? Was he justified by them? Was it the merit of his works that recommended him to God's acceptance? No, by no means, which he proves by several arguments.

I. If he had been justified by works, room would have been

left for boasting, which must for ever be excluded. If so, *he hath whereof to glory* (*v.* 2), which is not to be allowed. "But," might the Jews say, "was not his name made great (Gen. 12:2), and then might not he glory?" Yes, but not before God; he might deserve well of men, but he could never merit of God. Paul himself had *whereof to glory before men,* and we have him sometimes glorying in it, yet with humility; but nothing to glory in before God, 1 Co. 4:4; Phil. 3:8, 9. So Abraham. Observe, He takes it for granted that man must not pretend to glory in any thing before God; no, not Abraham, as great and as good a man as he was; and therefore he fetches an argument from it: it would be absurd for him *that glorieth to glory in any but the Lord.*

II. It is expressly said that Abraham's faith was counted to him for righteousness. *What saith the scripture? v.* 3. In all controversies in religion this must be our question, *What saith the scripture?* It is not what this great man, and the other good man, say, but What saith the scripture? Ask counsel at this Abel, and so end the matter, 2 Sa. 2:18. *To the law, and to the testimony* (Isa. 8:20), thither is the last appeal. Now the scripture saith that *Abraham believed, and this was counted to him for righteousness* (Gen. 15:6); therefore he had not whereof to glory before God, it being purely of free grace that it was so imputed, and having not in itself any of the formal nature of a righteousness, further than as God himself was graciously pleased so to count it to him. It is mentioned in Genesis, upon occasion of a very signal and remarkable act of faith concerning the promised seed, and is the more observable in that it followed upon a grievous conflict he had had with unbelief; his faith was now a victorious faith, newly returned from the battle. It is not the perfect faith that is required to justification (there may be acceptable faith where there are remainders of unbelief), but the prevailing faith, the faith that has the upper hand of unbelief.

III. If he had been justified by faith, the reward would have been *of debt, and not of grace,* which is not to be imagined. This is his argument (*v.* 4, 5): Abraham's reward was God himself; so he had told him but just before (Gen. 15:1), *I am thy exceeding great reward.* Now, if Abraham had merited this by the perfection of his obedience, it had not been an act of grace in God, but Abraham might have demanded it with as much confidence as ever any labourer in the vineyard demanded the penny he had earned. But this cannot be; it is impossible for man, much more guilty man, to make God a debtor to him, Rom. 11:35. No, God will have free grace to have all the glory, grace for grace's sake, Jn. 1:16. And therefore *to him that worketh not* — that can pretend to no such merit, nor show any worth or value in his work, which may answer such a reward, but disclaiming any such pretension casts himself wholly upon the free grace of God in Christ, by a lively, active, obedient faith — to such a one *faith is counted for righteousness,* is accepted of God as the qualification required in all those that shall be pardoned and saved. *Him that justifieth the ungodly,* that is, him that was before ungodly. His former ungodliness was no bar to his justification upon his believing: *ton asebē — that ungodly one,* that is, Abraham, who, before his conversion, it should seem, was carried down the stream of the Chaldean idolatry, Jos. 24:2. No room therefore is left for despair; though God clears not the impenitent guilty, yet through Christ he justifies the ungodly.

IV. He further illustrates this by a passage out of the Psalms, where David speaks of the remission of sins, the prime branch of justification, as constituting the happiness and blessedness of a man, pronouncing blessed, not the man who has no sin, or none which deserved death (for then, while man is so sinful, and God so righteous, where would be the blessed man?) but *the man to whom the Lord imputeth not sin,* who though he cannot plead, Not guilty, pleads the act of indemnity, and his plea is allowed. It is quoted from Ps. 32:1, 2, where observe, 1. The nature of forgiveness. It is the remission of a debt or a crime; it is the covering of sin, as a filthy thing, as the nakedness and shame of the soul. God is said *to cast sin behind his back, to hide his face from it,* which, and the like expressions, imply that the ground of our blessedness is not our innocency, or our not having sinned (a thing is, and is filthy, though covered; justification does not make the sin not to have been, or not to have been sin), but God's not laying it to our charge, as it follows here: it is God's *not imputing sin* (*v.* 8), which makes it wholly a gracious act of God, not dealing with us in strict justice as we have deserved, not entering into judgment, not marking iniquities, all which being purely acts of grace, the acceptance and the reward cannot be expected as debts; and therefore Paul infers (*v.* 6) that it is the imputing of righteousness without works. 2. The blessedness of it: *Blessed are they.* When it is said, *Blessed are the undefiled in the way, blessed is the man that walketh not in the counsel of the wicked,* etc., the design is to show the characters of those that are blessed; but when it is said, *Blessed are those whose iniquities are forgiven,* the design is to show what that blessedness is, and what the ground and foundation of it. Pardoned people are the only blessed people. The sentiments of the world are, Those are happy that have a clear estate, and are out of debt to man; but the sentence of the word is, Those are happy that have their debts to God discharged. O how much therefore is it our interest to make it sure to ourselves that our sins are pardoned! For this is the foundation of all other benefits. So and so I will do for them; for I will be merciful, Heb. 8:12.

Verses 9–17a

St. Paul observes in this paragraph when and why Abraham was thus justified; for he has several things to remark upon that. It was before he was circumcised, and before the giving of the law; and there was a reason for both.

I. It was before he was circumcised, *v.* 10. His faith was counted to him for righteousness while he was in uncircumcision. It was imputed, Gen. 15:6, and he was not circumcised till *ch.* 17. Abraham is expressly said to be justified by faith *fourteen years,* some say *twenty-five years, before he was circumcised.* Now this the apostle takes notice of in answer to the question (*v.* 9), *Cometh this blessedness then on the circumcision only, or on the uncircumcision also?* Abraham was pardoned and accepted in uncircumcision, a circumstance which, as it might silence the fears of the poor uncircumcised Gentiles, so it might lower the pride and conceitedness of the Jews, who gloried in their circumcision, as if they had the monopoly of all happiness. Here are two reasons why Abraham was justified by faith in uncircumcision: —

1. That circumcision might be *a seal of the righteousness of faith, v.* 11. The tenour of the covenants must first be settled before the seal can be annexed. Sealing supposes a previous bargain, which is confirmed and ratified by that ceremony. After Abraham's justification by faith had continued several years only a grant by parole, for the confirmation of Abraham's faith God was pleased to appoint a sealing ordinance, and Abraham received it; though it was a bloody ordinance, yet he submitted to it, and even received it as a special favour, *the sign of circumcision,* etc. Now we may hence observe, (1.) The nature of sacraments in general: they are signs and seals — signs to represent and instruct, seals to ratify and confirm. They are signs of absolute grace and favour; they are seals of the conditional promises; nay, they are mutual seals: God does in the sacraments seal to us to be to us a God, and we do therein seal to him to be to him a people. (2.) The nature of circumcision in particular: it was the initiating sacrament of the Old Testament; and it is here said to be, [1.] *A sign* — a sign of that original corruption which we are all born with, and which is cut off by spiritual circumcision, — a commemorating sign of God's covenant with Abraham, — a distinguishing sign between Jews and Gentiles, — a sign of admission into the visible church, — a sign prefiguring baptism, which comes in the room of circumcision, now under the gospel, when (the blood of Christ being shed) all bloody ordinances are abolished; it was *an outward and sensible sign of an inward and spiritual grace signified thereby.* [2.] *A seal of the righteousness of the faith.* In general, it was a seal of the covenant of grace, particularly of justification by faith — the covenant of grace, called *the righteousness which is of faith* (*ch.* 10:6), and it refers to an Old-Testament promise, Deu. 30:12. Now if infants were then capable of receiving a seal of the covenant of grace, which proves that they then were within the verge of that covenant, how they come to be now cast out of the covenant and incapable of the seal, and by what severe sentence they were thus rejected and incapacitated, those are concerned to make out that not only reject, but nullify and reproach, the baptism of the seed of believers.

2. *That he might be the father of all those that believe.* Not but that there were those that were justified by faith before Abraham; but of Abraham first it is particularly observed, and in him commenced a much clearer and fuller dispensation of the covenant of grace than any that had been before extant; and there he is called *the father of all that believe,* because he was so eminent a believer, and so eminently justified by faith, as Jabal was the father of shepherds and Jubal of musicians, Gen. 4:20, 21. *The father of all those that believe;* that is, a standing *pattern of faith,* as parents are examples to their children; and a standing precedent of justification by faith, as the liberties, privileges, honours, and estates, of the fathers descend to their children. Abraham was the father of believers, because to him particularly the *magna charta* was renewed. (1.) The father of believing Gentiles, *though they be not circumcised.* Zaccheus, a publican, if he believe, is reckoned a son of Abraham, Lu. 19:9. Abraham being himself uncircumcised when he was justified by faith, uncircumcision can never be a bar. Thus were the doubts and fears of the poor Gentiles anticipated and no room left to question but that righteousness might be imputed to them also, Col. 3:11; Gal. 5:6. (2.) The father of believing Jews, not merely as circumcised, and of the seed of Abraham according to the flesh, but because believers, because they *are not of the circumcision only* (that is, are not only circumcised), *but walk in the steps of that faith* — have not only the sign, but the thing signified — not only are of Abraham's family, but follow the example of Abraham's faith. See here who are the genuine children and lawful successors of those that were the church's fathers: not those that sit in their chairs, and bear their names, but those that tread in their steps; this is the line of succession, which holds, notwithstanding interruptions. It seems, then, those were most loud and forward to call Abraham father that had least title to the honours and privileges of his children. Thus those have most reason to call Christ Father, not that bear his name in being Christians in profession, but that tread in his steps.

II. It was before the giving of the law, *v.* 13–16. The former observation is levelled against those that confined justification to the circumcision, this against those that expected it by the law; now the promise was made to Abraham long before the law. Compare Gal. 3:17, 18. Now observe,

1. What that promise was — *that he should be the heir of the world,* that is, of the land of Canaan, the choicest spot of ground in the world, — or the father of many nations of the world, who sprang from him, besides the Israelites, —or the heir of the comforts of the life which now is. The meek are said to *inherit the earth,* and the world is theirs. Though Abraham had so little of the world in possession, yet he was heir of it all. Or, rather, it points at Christ, the seed here mentioned; compare Gal. 3:16, *To thy seed, which is Christ.* Now Christ is the heir of the world, the ends of the earth are his possession, and it is in him that Abraham was so. And it refers to that promise (Gen. 12:3), *In thee shall all the families of the earth be blessed.*

2. How it was made to him: *Not through the law, but through the righteousness of faith. Not through the law,* for that was not yet given: but it was upon that believing which was counted to him for righteousness; it was upon his trusting God, in his leaving his own country when God commanded him, Heb. 11:8. Now, being by faith, it could not be by the law, which he proves by the opposition there is between them (*v.* 14, 15): *If those who are of the law be heirs;* that is, those, and those only, and they by virtue of the law (the Jews did, and still do, boast that they are the rightful heirs of the world, because to them the law was given), then *faith is made void;* for, if it were requisite to an interest in the promise that there should be a perfect performance of the whole law, then the promise can never take its effect, nor is it to any purpose for us to depend upon it, since the way to life by perfect obedience to the law, and spotless sinless innocency, is wholly blocked up, and the law in itself opens no other way. This he proves, *v.* 15. *The law worketh wrath* — wrath in us to God; it irritates and provokes that carnal mind which is enmity to God, as the damming up of a stream makes it swell —wrath in God against us. It works this, that is, it discovers it, or our breach of the law works it. Now it is certain that we can never expect the inheritance by a law that worketh wrath. How the law works wrath he shows very concisely in the latter part of the verse: *Where no law is there is no transgression,* an acknowledged maxim, which implies, Where there is a law there is transgression and that transgression is provoking, and so the law worketh wrath.

3. Why the promise was made to him by faith; for three reasons, *v.* 16. (1.) *That it might be by grace,* that grace might have the honour of it; *by grace, and not by the law; by grace, and not of debt, nor of merit;* that *Grace, grace,* might be cried to every stone, especially to the top-stone, in this building.

Faith hath particular reference to grace granting, as grace hath reference to faith receiving. *By grace,* and therefore *through faith,* Eph. 2:8. For God will have every crown thrown at the feet of grace, free grace, and every song in heaven sung to that tune, *Not unto us, O Lord, not unto us, but unto thy name be the praise.* (2.) *That the promise might be sure.* The first covenant, being a covenant of works, was not sure: but, through man's failure, the benefits designed by it were cut off; and therefore, the more effectually to ascertain and ensure the conveyance of the new covenant, there is another way found out, *not by works* (were it so, the promise would not be sure, because of the continual frailty and infirmity of the flesh), *but by faith,* which receives all from Christ, and acts in a continual dependence upon him, as the great trustee of our salvation, and in whose keeping it is safe. The covenant is therefore sure, because it is so well ordered in all things, 2 Sa. 23:5. (3.) *That it might be sure to all the seed.* If it had been *by the law,* it had been limited to the Jews, *to whom pertained the glory, and the covenants, and the giving of the law* (*ch.* 9:4); but therefore it was by faith that Gentiles as well as Jews might become interested in it, the spiritual as well as the natural seed of faithful Abraham. God would contrive the promise in such a way as might make it most extensive, to comprehend all true believers, that circumcision and uncircumcision might break no squares; and for this (*v.* 17) he refers us to Gen. 17:5, where the reason of the change of his name from *Abram — a high father, to Abraham — the high father of a multitude,* is thus rendered: *For a father of many nations have I made thee;* that is, all believers, both before and since the coming of Christ in the flesh, should take Abraham for their pattern, and call him *father.* The Jews say Abraham was the father of all proselytes to the Jewish religion. *Behold, he is the father of all the world, which are gathered under the wings of the Divine Majesty.* — Maimonides.

Verses 17b–22

Having observed when Abraham was justified by faith, and why, for the honour of Abraham and for example to us who call him father, the apostle here describes and commends the faith of Abraham, where observe,

I. Whom he believed: *God who quickeneth.* It is God himself that faith fastens upon: *other foundation can no man lay.* Now observe what in God Abraham's faith had an eye to —to that, certainly, which would be most likely to confirm his faith concerning the things promised: — 1. *God who quickeneth the dead.* It was promised that he should be *the father of many nations,* when he and his wife were now as good as dead (Heb. 11:11, 12), and therefore he looks upon God as a God that could breathe life into dry bones. He that quickeneth the dead can do any thing, can give a child to Abraham when he is old, can bring the Gentiles, who are *dead in trespasses and sins,* to a divine and spiritual life, Eph. 2:1. Compare Eph. 1:19, 20. 2. *Who calleth things which are not as though they were;* that is, creates all things by the word of his power, as in the beginning, Gen. 1:3; 2 Co. 4:6. The justification and salvation of sinners, the espousing of the Gentiles that had not been a people, were a gracious calling of things which are not as though they were, giving being to things that were not. This expresses the sovereignty of God and his absolute power and dominion, a mighty stay to faith when all other props sink and totter. It is the holy wisdom and policy of faith to fasten particularly on that in God which is accommodated to the difficulties wherewith it is to wrestle, and will most effectually answer the objections. It is faith indeed to build upon the all-sufficiency of God for the accomplishment of that which is impossible to anything but that all-sufficiency. Thus Abraham became *the father of many nations before him whom he believed,* that is, in the eye and account of God; or *like him whom he believed;* as God was a common Father, so was Abraham. It is by faith in God that we become accepted of him, and conformable to him.

II. How he believed. He here greatly magnifies the strength of Abraham's faith, in several expressions. 1. *Against hope, he believed in hope, v.* 18. There was a hope against him, a natural hope. All the arguments of sense, and reason, and experience, which in such cases usually beget and support hope, were against him; no second causes smiled upon him, nor in the least favoured his hope. But, against all those inducements to the contrary, he believed; for he had a hope for him: *He believed in hope,* which arose, as his faith did, from the consideration of God's all-sufficiency. *That he might become the father of many nations.* Therefore God, by his almighty grace, enabled him thus to believe against hope, that he might pass for a pattern of great and strong faith to all generations. It was fit that he who was to be the father of the faithful should have something more than ordinary in his faith — that in him faith should be set in its highest elevation, and so the endeavours of all succeeding believers be directed, raised, and quickened. Or this is mentioned as the matter of the promise that he believed; and he refers to Gen. 15:5, *So shall thy seed be,* as the stars of heaven, so innumerable, so illustrious. This was that which he believed, when it was counted to him for righteousness, *v.* 6. And it is observable that this particular instance of his faith was *against hope,* against the surmises and suggestions of his unbelief. He had just before been concluding hardly that he should go childless, that one born in his house was his heir (*v.* 2, 3); and this unbelief was a foil to his faith, and bespeaks it a believing against hope. 2. *Being not weak in faith, he considered not his own body, v.* 19. Observe, His own body was now dead — become utterly unlikely to beget a child, though the new life and vigour that God gave him continued after Sarah was dead, witness his children by Keturah. When God intends some special blessing, some child of promise, for his people, he commonly puts a sentence of death upon the blessing itself, and upon all the ways that lead to it. Joseph must be enslaved and imprisoned before he be advanced. But Abraham did not consider this, *sy katenoēse — he did not dwell in his thoughts upon it.* He said indeed, *Shall a child be born to him that is a hundred years old?* Gen. 17:17. But that was the language of his admiration and his desire to be further satisfied, not of his doubting and distrust; his faith passed by that consideration, and thought of nothing but the faithfulness of the promise, with the contemplation whereof he was swallowed up, and this kept up his faith. *Being not weak in faith, he considered not.* It is mere weakness of faith that makes a man lie poring upon the difficulties and seeming impossibilities that lie in the way of a promise. Though it may seem to be the wisdom and policy of carnal reason, yet it is the weakness of faith, to look into the bottom of all the difficulties that arise against the promise. 3. *He staggered not at the promise of God through unbelief* (*v.* 20), and he therefore staggered not because he considered not the frowns and discouragements of second causes; *sy diekrithē — he disputed not;* he did not hold any self-consultation about it, did not take time to consider whether he should close with it or no, did not hesitate nor stumble at it, but by a resolute and peremptory act of his soul, with a holy boldness, ventured all upon the promise. He took it not for a point that would admit of argument or debate, but presently determined it as a ruled case, did not at all hang in suspense about it: he *staggered not through unbelief.* Unbelief is at the bottom of all our staggerings at God's promises. It is not the promise that fails, but our faith that fails when we stagger. 4. He *was strong in faith, giving glory to God, enedynamōthē — he was strengthened* in faith, his faith *got ground by exercise — crescit eundo.* Though weak faith shall not be rejected, the bruised reed not broken, the smoking flax not quenched, yet strong faith shall be commended and honoured. The strength of his faith appeared in the victory it won over his fears. And hereby he gave glory to God; for, as unbelief dishonours God by making him a liar (1 Jn. 5:10), so faith honours God by setting to its seal that he is true, Jn. 3:33. Abraham's faith gave God the glory of his wisdom, power, holiness, goodness, and especially of his faithfulness, resting upon the word that he had spoken. Among men we say, "He that trusts another, gives him credit, and honours him by taking his word;" thus Abraham gave glory to God by trusting him. We never hear our Lord Jesus commending any thing so much as great faith (Mt. 8:10 and 15:28): therefore God gives honour to faith, great faith, because faith, great faith, gives honour to God. 5. He was *fully persuaded that what God had promised he was able to perform, plērophorētheis — was carried on with the greatest confidence* and assurance; it is a metaphor taken from ships that come into the harbour with full sail. Abraham saw the storms of doubts, and fears, and temptations likely to rise against the promise, upon which many a one would have shrunk back, and lain by for fairer days, and waited a smiling gale of sense and reason. But Abraham, having taken God for his pilot, and the promise for his card and compass, resolves to weather his point, and like a bold adventurer sets up all his sails, breaks through all the difficulties, regards neither winds nor clouds, but trusts to the strength of his bottom and the wisdom and faithfulness of his pilot, and bravely makes to the harbour, and comes home an unspeakable gainer. Such was his full persuasion, and it was built on the omnipotence of God: *He was able.* Our waverings rise mainly from our distrust of the divine power; and therefore to fix us it is requisite we believe not only that he is faithful, but that he is able, that hath promised. *And therefore it was imputed to him for righteousness, v.* 22. Because with such a confidence he ventured his all in the divine promise, God graciously accepted him, and not only answered, but out-did, his expectation. This way of glorifying God by a firm reliance on his bare promise was so very agreeable to God's design, and so very conducive to his honour, that he graciously accepted it as a righteousness, and justified him, though there was not that in the thing itself which could merit such an acceptance. This shows why faith is chosen to be the prime condition of our justification, because it is a grace that of all others gives glory to God.

Verses 23–25

In the close of the chapter, he applies all to us; and, having abundantly proved that Abraham was justified by faith, he here concludes that his justification was to be the pattern or sampler of ours: *It was not written for his sake alone.* It was not intended only for an historical commendation of Abraham, or a relation of something peculiar to him (as some antipaedobaptists will needs understand that circumcision was a *seal of the righteousness of the faith, v.* 11, only to Abraham himself, and no other); no, the scripture did not intend hereby to describe some singular way of justification that belonged to Abraham as his prerogative. The accounts we have of the Old-Testament saints were not intended for histories only, barely to inform and divert us, but for precedents to direct us, for ensamples (1 Co. 10:11) for *our learning, ch.* 15:4. And this particularly concerning Abraham was written *for us also,* to assure us what that righteousness is which God requireth and accepteth to our salvation, — for us also, that are man and vile, that come so far short of Abraham in privileges and performances, us Gentiles as well as the Jews, for the blessing of Abraham comes upon the Gentiles through Christ, — for us on whom the ends of the world are come, as well as for the patriarchs; for the grace of God is the same yesterday, to-day, and for ever. His application of it is but short. Only we may observe,

I. Our common privilege; it shall be imputed to us, that is, righteousness shall. The gospel way of justification is by an imputed righteousness, *mellei logizesthai — it shall be imputed;* he uses a future verb, to signify the continuation of this mercy in the church, that as it is the same now so it will be while God has a church in the world, and there are any of the children of men to be justified; for there is a fountain opened that is inexhaustible.

II. Our common duty, the condition of this privilege, and that is believing. The proper object of this believing is a divine revelation. The revelation to Abraham was concerning a Christ to come; the revelation to us is concerning a Christ already come, which difference in the revelation does not alter the case. Abraham believed the power of God in raising up an Isaac from the dead womb of Sarah; we are to believe the same power exerted in a higher instance, the resurrection of Christ from the dead. The resurrection of Isaac was in a figure (Heb. 11:19); the resurrection of Christ was real. Now we are to believe on him that raised up Christ; not only believe his power, that he could do it, but depend upon his grace in raising up Christ as our surety; so he explains it, *v.* 25, where we have a brief account of the meaning of Christ's death and resurrection, which are the two main hinges on which the door of salvation turns. 1. He was *delivered for our offences.* God the Father delivered him, he delivered up himself as a sacrifice for sin. He died indeed as a malefactor, because he died for sin; but it was not his own sin, but the sins of the people. He died to make atonement for our sins, to expiate our guilt, to satisfy divine justice. 2. He was *raised again for our justification,* for the perfecting and completing of our justification. By the merit of his death he paid our debt, in his resurrection he took out our acquittance. When he was buried he lay a prisoner in execution for our debt, which as a surety he had undertaken to pay; on the third day an angel was sent to roll away the stone, and so to discharge the prisoner, which was the greatest assurance possible that divine justice was satisfied, the debt paid, or else he would never have released the prisoner: and therefore the apostle puts a special emphasis on Christ's resurrection; it is Christ that died, *yea, rather that has risen again, ch.* 8:34. So that upon the whole matter it is very evident that we are not justified by the merit of our own works, but by a fiducial obediential dependence upon Jesus Christ and his righteousness, as the condition on our part of our right to impunity and salvation, which was the truth that Paul in this and the foregoing chapter had been fixing as the great spring and foundation of all our comfort.

CHAPTER 5

The apostle, having made good his point, and fully proved justification by faith, in this chapter proceeds in the explication, illustration, and application of that truth. I. He shows the fruits of justification (*v.* 1–5). II. He shows the fountain and foundation of justification in the death of Jesus Christ, which he discourses of at large in the rest of the chapter.

Verses 1–5

The precious benefits and privileges which flow from justification are such as should quicken us all to give diligence to make it sure to ourselves that we are justified, and then to take the comfort it renders to us, and to do the duty it calls for from us. The fruits of this tree of life are exceedingly precious.

I. *We have peace with God, v.* 1. It is sin that breeds the quarrel between us and God, creates not only a strangeness, but an enmity; the holy righteous God cannot in honour be at peace with a sinner while he continues under the guilt of sin. Justification takes away the guilt, and so makes way for peace. And such are the benignity and good-will of God to man that, immediately upon the removing of that obstacle, the peace is made. By faith we lay hold of God's arm and of his strength, and so are at peace, Isa. 27:4, 5. There is more in this peace than barely a cessation of enmity, there is friendship and loving-kindness, for God is either the worst enemy or the best friend. Abraham, being justified by faith, was called *the friend of God* (Jam. 2:23), which was his honour, but not his peculiar honour: Christ has called his disciples *friends,* Jn. 15:13–15. And surely a man needs no more to make him happy than to have God his friend! But this is *through our Lord Jesus Christ* — through him as the great peace-maker, *the Mediator between God and man,* that blessed Day's-man that has laid his hand upon us both. Adam, in innocency, had peace with God immediately; there needed no such mediator. But to guilty sinful man it is a very dreadful thing to think of God out of Christ; *for he is our peace,* Eph. 2:14, not only the maker, but the matter and maintainer, of our peace, Col. 1:20.

II. *We have access by faith into this grace wherein we stand, v.* 2. This is a further privilege, not only peace, but grace, that is, this favour. Observe, 1. The saints' happy state. It is a state of grace, God's loving-kindness to us and our conformity to God; he that hath God's love and God's likeness is in a state of grace. Now into this grace we have access *prosagōgēn — an introduction,* which implies that we were not born in this state; we are *by nature children of wrath,* and *the carnal mind is enmity against God;* but we are brought into it. We could not have got into it of ourselves, nor have conquered the difficulties in the way, but we have a manuduction, a leading by the hand, — are led into it as blind, or lame, or weak people are led, — are introduced as pardoned offenders, — are introduced by some favourite at court to kiss the king's hand, as strangers, that are to have audience, are conducted. *Prosagōgēn eschēkamen — We have had access.* He speaks of those that have been already brought out of a state of nature into a state of grace. Paul, in his conversion, had this access; then he was made nigh. Barnabas introduced him *to the apostles* (Acts 9:27), and there were others *that led him by the hand to Damascus* (*v.* 8), but it was Christ that introduced and led him by the hand into this grace. *By whom we have access by faith.* By Christ as the author and principal agent, by faith as the means of this access. Not by Christ in consideration of any merit or desert of ours, but in consideration of our believing dependence upon him and resignation of ourselves to him. 2. Their happy standing in this state: *wherein we stand.* Not only wherein we are, but wherein we stand, a posture that denotes our discharge from guilt; *we stand in the judgment* (Ps. 1:5), not cast, as convicted criminals, but our dignity and honour secured, not thrown to the ground, as abjects. The phrase denotes also our progress; while we stand, we are going. We must not lie down, as if we had already attained, but stand as those that are pressing forward, stand as servants attending on Christ our master. The phrase denotes, further, our perseverance: we stand firmly and safely, upheld by the power of God; stand as soldiers stand, that keep their ground, not borne down by the power of the enemy. It denotes not only our admission to, but our confirmation in, the favour of God. It is not in the court of heaven as in earthly courts, where high places are slippery places: but we stand in a humble confidence of this very thing *that he who has begun the good work will perform it,* Phil. 1:6.

III. *We rejoice in hope of the glory of God.* Besides the happiness in hand, there is a happiness in hope, *the glory of God,* the glory which God will put upon the saints in heaven, glory which will consist in the vision and fruition of God. 1. Those, and those only, that have access by faith into the grace of God now may hope for the glory of God hereafter. There is no good hope of glory but what is founded in grace; grace is glory begun, the earnest and assurance of glory. *He will give grace and glory,* Ps. 84:11. 2. Those who hope for the glory of God hereafter have enough to rejoice in now. It is the duty of those that hope for heaven to rejoice in that hope.

IV. *We glory in tribulations also;* not only notwithstanding our tribulations (these do not hinder our rejoicing in hope of the glory of God), but even in our tribulations, as they are working for us the weight of glory, 2 Co. 4:17. Observe, What a growing increasing happiness the happiness of the saints is: *Not only so.* One would think such peace, such grace, such glory, and such a joy in hope of it, were more than such poor undeserving creatures as we are could pretend to; and yet it is *not only so:* there are more instances of our happiness — *we glory in tribulations also,* especially tribulations for righteousness' sake, which seemed the greatest objection against the saints' happiness, whereas really their happiness did not only consist with, but take rise from, those tribulations. *They rejoiced that they were counted worthy to suffer,* Acts 5:41. This being the hardest point, he sets himself to show the grounds and reasons of it. How come we to glory in tribulations? Why, because tribulations, by a chain of causes, greatly befriend hope, which he shows in the method of its influence. 1. *Tribulation worketh patience,* not in and of itself, but the powerful grace of God working in and with the tribulation. It proves, and by proving improves, patience, as parts and gifts increase by exercise. It is not the efficient cause, but yields the occasion, as steel is hardened by the fire. See how God brings meat out of the eater, and sweetness out of the strong. That which worketh patience is matter of joy; for patience does us more good than tribulations can do us hurt. Tribulation in itself worketh impatience; but, as it is sanctified to the saints, it worketh patience. 2. *Patience experience, v.* 4. It works an experience of God, and the songs he gives in the night; the patient sufferers have the greatest experience of the divine consolations, which abound as afflictions abound. It works an experience of ourselves. It is by tribulation that we make an experiment of our own sincerity, and therefore such tribulations are called trials. It works, *dokimēn — an approbation,* as he is approved that has passed the test. Thus Job's tribulation wrought patience, and that patience produced an approbation, that still he *holds fast his integrity,* Job 2:3. 3. *Experience hope.* He who, being thus tried, comes forth as gold, will thereby be encouraged to hope. This experiment, or approbation, is not so much the ground, as the evidence, of our hope, and a special friend to it. Experience of God is a prop to our hope; he that hath delivered doth and will. Experience of ourselves helps to evidence our sincerity. 4. This *hope maketh not ashamed;* that is, it is a hope that will not deceive us. Nothing confounds more than disappointment. Everlasting shame and confusion will be caused by the perishing of the expectation of the wicked, *but the hope of the righteous shall be gladness,* Prov. 10:28. See Ps. 22:5; 71:1. Or, It maketh not ashamed of our sufferings. Though *we are counted as the offscouring of all things, and trodden under foot as the mire in the streets,* yet, having hopes of glory, we are not ashamed of these sufferings. It is in a good cause, for a good Master, and in good hope; and therefore we are not ashamed. We will never think ourselves disparaged by sufferings that are likely to end so well. *Because the love of God is shed abroad.* This hope will not disappoint us, because it is sealed with the Holy Spirit as a Spirit of love. It is the gracious work of the blessed Spirit to shed abroad the love of God in the hearts of all the saints. *The love of God,* that is, the sense of God's love to us, drawing out love in us to him again. Or, The great effects of his love: (1.) Special grace; and, (2.) The pleasant gust or sense of it. *It is shed abroad,* as sweet ointment, perfuming the soul, as rain watering it and making it fruitful. The ground of all our comfort and holiness, and perseverance in both, is laid in the *shedding abroad of the love of God in our hearts;* it is this which constrains us, 2 Co. 5:14. Thus are we drawn and held by the bonds of love. Sense of God's love to us will make us not ashamed, either of our hope in him or our sufferings for him.

Verses 6–21

The apostle here describes the fountain and foundation of justification, laid in the death of the Lord Jesus. The streams are very sweet, but, if you run them up to the spring-head, you will find it to be Christ's dying for us; it is in the precious stream of Christ's blood that all these privileges come flowing to us: and therefore he enlarges upon this instance of the love of God which is shed abroad. Three things he takes notice of for the explication and illustration of this doctrine: —1. The persons he died for, *v.* 6–8. 2. The precious fruits of his death, *v.* 9–11. 3. The parallel he runs between the communication of sin and death by the first Adam and of righteousness and life by the second Adam, *v.* 12, to the end.

I. The character we were under when Christ died for us.

1. *We were without strength* (*v.* 6), in a sad condition; and, which is worse, altogether unable to help ourselves out of that condition — lost, and no visible way open for our recovery — our condition deplorable, and in a manner desperate; and, therefore our salvation is here said to come *in due time.* God's time to help and save is when those that are to be saved are without strength, that his own power and grace may be the more magnified, Deu. 32:36. It is the manner of God to help at a dead lift,

2. *He died for the ungodly;* not only helpless creatures, and therefore likely to perish, but guilty sinful creatures, and therefore deserving to perish; not only mean and worthless, but vile and obnoxious, unworthy of such favour with the holy God. Being ungodly, they had need of one to die for them, to satisfy for guilt, and to bring in a righteousness. This he illustrates (*v.* 7, 8) as an unparalleled instance of love; herein God's thoughts and ways were above ours. Compare Jn. 15:13, 14, *Greater love has no man.* (1.) One would hardly *die for a righteous man,* that is, an innocent man, one that is unjustly condemned; every body will pity such a one, but few will put such a value upon his life as either to hazard, or much less to deposit, their own in his stead. (2.) It may be, one might perhaps be persuaded *to die for a good man,* that is, a useful man, who is more than barely a righteous man. Many that are good themselves yet do but little good to others; but those that are useful commonly get themselves well beloved, and meet with some that in a case of necessity would venture to be their ***antipsychoi*** *— would engage life for life,* would be their bail, body for body. Paul was, in this sense, a very good man, one that was very useful, and he met with some that for his life laid down their own necks, *ch.* 16:4. And yet observe how he qualifies this: it is but some that would do so, and it is a daring act if they do it, it must be some bold venturing soul; and, after all, it is but a *peradventure.* (3.) *But Christ died for sinners* (*v.* 8), neither righteous nor good; not only such as were useless, but such as were guilty and obnoxious; not only such as there would be no loss of should they perish, but such whose destruction would greatly redound to the glory of God's justice, being malefactors and criminals that ought to die. Some think he alludes to a common distinction the Jews had of their people into ***ndyqym*** *— righteous,* ***hsdym*** *— merciful* (compare Isa. 17:1), and ***rssym*** *— wicked.* Now herein *God commended his love,* not only proved or evidenced his love (he might have done that at a cheaper rate), but magnified it and made it illustrious. This circumstance did greatly magnify and advance his love, not only put it past dispute, but rendered it the object of the greatest wonder and admiration: "Now my creatures shall see that I love them, I will give them such an instance of it as shall be without parallel." *Commendeth his love,* as merchants commend their goods when they would put them off. This commending of his love was in order to the shedding abroad of his love in our hearts by the Holy Ghost. He evinces his love in the most winning, affecting, endearing way imaginable. *While we were yet sinners,* implying that we were not to be always sinners, there should be a change wrought; for he died to save us, not in our sins, but from our sins; but we were yet sinners when he died for us. (4.) Nay, which is more, *we were enemies* (*v.* 10), not only malefactors, but traitors and

rebels, in arms against the government; the worst kind of malefactors and of all malefactors the most obnoxious. The carnal mind is not only an enemy to God, but enmity itself, *ch.* 8:7; Col. 1:21. This enmity is a mutual enmity, God loathing the sinner, and the sinner loathing God, Zec. 11:8. And that for such as these Christ should die is such a mystery, such a paradox, such an unprecedented instance of love, that it may well be our business to eternity to adore and wonder at it. This is a commendation of love indeed. Justly might he who had thus loved us make it one of the laws of his kingdom that we should love our enemies.

II. The precious fruits of his death.

1. Justification and reconciliation are the first and primary fruit of the death of Christ: *We are justified by his blood* (*v.* 9), *reconciled by his death, v.* 10. Sin is pardoned, the sinner accepted as righteous, the quarrel taken up, the enmity slain, an end made of iniquity, and an everlasting righteousness brought in. This is done, that is, Christ has done all that was requisite on his part to be done in order hereunto, and, immediately upon our believing, we are actually put into a state of justification and reconciliation. *Justified by his blood.* Our justification is ascribed to the blood of Christ because *without blood there is no remission* Heb. 9:22. *The blood is the life,* and that must go to make atonement. In all the propitiatory sacrifices, the sprinkling of the blood was of the essence of the sacrifice. It was *the blood that made an atonement for the soul,* Lev. 17:11.

2. Hence results salvation from wrath: *Saved from wrath* (*v.* 9), *saved by his life, v.* 10 When that which hinders our salvation is taken away, the salvation must needs follow. Nay, the argument holds very strongly; if God justified and reconciled us when we were enemies, and put himself to so much charge to do it, much more will he save us when we are justified and reconciled. He that has done the greater, which is of enemies to make us friends, will certainly the less, which is when we are friends to use us friendly and to be kind to us. And therefore the apostle, once and again, speaks of it with a *much more.* He that hath digged so deep to lay the foundation will no doubt build upon that foundation. — *We shall be saved from wrath,* from hell and damnation. It is the wrath of God that is the fire of hell; *the wrath to come,* so it is called, 1 Th. 1:10. The final justification and absolution of believers at the great day, together with the fitting and preparing of them for it, are the salvation from wrath here spoken of; it is the perfecting of the work of grace. — *Reconciled by his death, saved by his life.* His life here spoken of is not to be understood of his life in the flesh, but his life in heaven, that life which ensued after his death. Compare *ch.* 14:9. *He was dead, and is alive,* Rev. 1:18. We are reconciled by Christ humbled, we are saved by Christ exalted. The dying Jesus laid the foundation, in satisfying for sin, and slaying the enmity, and so making us salvable; thus is the partition-wall broken down, atonement made, and the attainder reversed; but it is the living Jesus that perfects the work: *he lives to make intercession,* Heb. 7:25. It is Christ, in his exaltation, that by his word and Spirit effectually calls, and changes, and reconciles us to God, is our Advocate with the Father, and so completes and consummates our salvation. Compare *ch.* 4:25 and 8:34. Christ dying was the testator, who bequeathed us the legacy; but Christ living is the executor, who pays it. Now the arguing is very strong. He that puts himself to the charge of purchasing our salvation will not decline the trouble of applying it.

3. All this produces, as a further privilege, our *joy in God, v.* 11. God is now so far from being a terror to us that he is our *joy, and our hope in the day of evil,* Jer. 17:17. *We are reconciled and saved from wrath.* Iniquity, blessed be God, *shall not be our ruin. And not only so,* there is more in it yet, a constant stream of favours; we not only go to heaven, but go to heaven triumphantly; not only get into the harbour, but come in with full sail: *We joy in God,* not only saved from his wrath, but solacing ourselves in his love, and this through Jesus Christ, who is the Alpha and the Omega, the foundation-stone and the top-stone of all our comforts and hopes — not only *our salvation, but our strength and our song;* and all this (which he repeats as a string he loved to be harping upon) by virtue of the atonement, for by him we Christians, we believers, have now, now in gospel times, or now in this life, *received the atonement,* which was typified by the sacrifices under thee law, and is an earnest of our happiness in heaven. True believers do by Jesus Christ receive the atonement. Receiving the atonement is our actual reconciliation to God in justification, grounded upon Christ's satisfaction. To *receive the atonement* is, (1.) To give our consent to the atonement, approving of, and agreeing to, those methods which Infinite Wisdom has taken of saving a guilty world by the blood of a crucified Jesus, being willing and glad to be saved in a gospel way and upon gospel terms. (2.) To take the comfort of the atonement, which is the fountain and the foundation of our joy in God. Now *we joy in God,* now we do indeed *receive the atonement, kauchōmenoi — glorying* in it. God hath received the atonement (Mt. 3:17; 17:5; 28:2): if we but receive it, the work is done.

III. The parallel that the apostle runs between the communication of sin and death by the first Adam and of righteousness and life by the second Adam (*v.* 12, to the end), which not only illustrates the truth he is discoursing of, but tends very much to the commending of the love of God and the comforting of the hearts of true believers, in showing a correspondence between our fall and our recovery, and not only a like, but a much greater power in the second Adam to make us happy, than there was in the first to make us miserable. Now, for the opening of this, observe,

1. A general truth laid down as the foundation of his discourse — that Adam was a type of Christ (*v.* 14): *Who is the figure of him that was to come.* Christ is therefore called the *last Adam,* 1 Co. 15:45. Compare *v.* 22. In this Adam was a type of Christ, that in the covenant-transactions that were between God and him, and in the consequent events of those transactions, Adam was a public person. God dealt with Adam and Adam acted as such a one, as a common father and factor, root and representative, of and for all his posterity; so that what he did in that station, as agent for us, we may be said to have done in him, and what was done to him may be said to have been done to us in him. Thus Jesus Christ, the Mediator, acted as a public person, the head of all the elect, dealt with God for them, as their father, factor, root, and representative — died for them, rose for them, entered within the veil for them, did all for them. When Adam failed, we failed with him; when Christ performed, he performed for us. Thus was Adam *typos tou mellontos — the figure of him that was to come,* to come to repair that breach which Adam had made.

2. A more particular explication of the parallel, in which observe,

(1.) How Adam, as a public person, communicated sin and death to all his posterity (*v.* 12): *By one man sin entered.* We see the world under a deluge of sin and death, full of iniquities and full of calamities. Now, it is worth while to enquire what is the spring that feeds it, and you will find it to be the general corruption of nature; and at what gap it entered, and you will find it to have been Adam's first sin. It was *by one man,* and he the first man (for if any had been before him they would have been free), that one man from whom, as from the root, we all spring. [1.] By him *sin entered.* When God pronounced all very good (Gen. 1:31) there was no sin in the world; it was when Adam ate forbidden fruit that sin made its entry. Sin had before entered into the world of angels, when many of them revolted from their allegiance and left their first estate; but it never entered into the world of mankind till Adam sinned. Then it entered as an enemy, to kill and destroy, as a thief, to rob and despoil; and a dismal entry it was. Then entered the guilt of Adam's sin imputed to posterity, and a general corruption and depravedness of nature. *Eph' hō — for that* (so we read it), rather *in whom, all have sinned.* Sin entered into the world by Adam, for in him we all sinned. As, 1 Co. 15:22, *in Adam all die;* so here, *in him all have sinned;* for it is agreeable to the law of all nations that the acts of a public person be accounted theirs whom they represent; and what a whole body does every member of the same body may be said to do. Now Adam acted thus as a public person, by the sovereign ordination and appointment of God, and yet that founded upon a natural necessity; for God, as the author of nature, had made this the law of nature, that man should beget in his own likeness, and so the other creatures. In Adam therefore, as in a common receptacle, the whole nature of man was reposited, from him to flow down in a channel to his posterity; for all mankind are made *of one blood* (Acts 17:26), so that according as this nature proves through his standing or falling, before he puts it out of his hands, accordingly it is propagated from him. Adam therefore sinning and falling, the nature became guilty and corrupt, and is so derived. Thus in him all have sinned. [2.] *Death by sin,* for death is the wages of sin. Sin, when it is finished, brings forth death. When sin came, of course death came with it. Death is here put for all that misery which is the due desert of sin, temporal, spiritual, eternal death. If Adam had not sinned, he had not died; the threatening was, *In the day thou eatest thou shall surely die,* Gen. 2:17. [3.] *So death passed,* that is, a sentence of death was passed, as upon a criminal, *diēlthen — passed through* all men, as an infectious disease passes through a town, so that none escape it. It is the universal fate, without exception: death passes upon all. There are common calamities incident to human life which do abundantly prove this. *Death reigned, v.* 14. He speaks of death as a mighty prince, and his monarchy the most absolute, universal, and lasting monarchy. None are exempted from its sceptre; it is a monarchy that will survive all other earthly rule, authority, and power, for it is the last enemy, 1 Co. 15:26. Those sons of Belial that will be subject to no other rule cannot avoid being subject to this. Now all this we may thank Adam for; from him sin and death descend. Well may we say, as that good man, observing the change that a fit of sickness had made in his countenance, *O Adam!* what hast thou done?

Further, to clear this, he shows that sin did not commence with the law of Moses, but was *in the world until,* or *before,* that law; therefore that law of Moses is not the only rule of life, for there was a rule, and that rule was transgressed, before the law was given. It likewise intimates that we cannot be justified by our obedience to the law of Moses, any more than we were condemned by and for our disobedience to it. Sin was in the world before the law; witness Cain's murder, the apostasy of the old world, the wickedness of Sodom. His inference hence is, Therefore there was a law; for *sin is not imputed where there is no law.* Original sin is a want of conformity to, and actual sin is a transgression of, the law of God: therefore all were under some law. His proof of it is, *Death reigned from Adam to Moses, v.* 14. It is certain that death could not have reigned if sin had not set up the throne for him. This proves that sin was in the world before the law, and original sin, for death reigned over those that had not sinned any actual sin, that *had not sinned after the similitude of Adam's transgression,* never sinned in their own persons as Adam did — which is to be understood of infants, that were never guilty of actual sin, and yet died, because Adam's sin was imputed to them. This reign of death seems especially to refer to those violent and extraordinary judgments which were long before Moses, as the deluge and the destruction of Sodom, which involved infants. It is a great proof of original sin that little children, who were never guilty of any actual transgression, are yet liable to very terrible diseases, casualties, and deaths, which could by no means be reconciled with the justice and righteousness of God if they were not chargeable with guilt.

(2.) How, in correspondence to this, Christ, as a public person, communicates righteousness and life to all true believers, who are his spiritual seed. And in this he shows not only wherein the resemblance holds, but, *ex abundanti,* wherein the communication of grace and love by Christ *goes beyond* the communication of guilt and wrath by Adam. Observe,

[1.] Wherein the resemblance holds. This is laid down most fully, *v.* 18, 19.

First, By the offence and disobedience of one many were made sinners, and judgment came upon all men to condemnation. Here observe, 1. That Adam's sin was disobedience, disobedience to a plain and express command: and it was a command of trial. The thing he did was therefore evil because it was forbidden, and not otherwise; but this opened the door to other sins, though itself seemingly small. 2. That the malignity and poison of sin are very strong and spreading, else the guilt of Adam's sin would not have reached so far, nor have been so deep and long a stream. Who would think there should be so much evil in sin? 3. That by Adam's sin many are made sinners: *many,* that is, all his posterity; said to be many, in opposition to the one that offended, *Made sinners, katestathēsav.* It denotes the making of us such by a judicial act: we were cast as sinners by due course of law. 4. That judgment is come to condemnation upon all those that by Adam's disobedience were made sinners. Being convicted, we are condemned. All the race of mankind lie under a sentence, like an attainder upon a family. There is judgment given and recorded against us in the court of heaven; and, if the judgment be not reversed, we are likely to sink under it to eternity.

Secondly, In like manner, *by the righteousness and obe-*

dience of one (and that one is Jesus Christ, the second Adam), *are many made righteous,* and so the *free gift comes upon all.* It is observable how the apostle inculcates this truth, and repeats it again and again, as a truth of very great consequence. Here observe, 1. The nature of Christ's righteousness, how it is brought in; it is by his obedience. The disobedience of the first Adam ruined us, the obedience of the second Adam saves us, — his obedience to the law of mediation, which was that he should fulfil all righteousness, and then make his soul an offering for sin. By his obedience to this law he wrought out a righteousness for us, satisfied God's justice, and so made way for us into his favour. 2. The fruit of it. (1.) There is a *free gift come upon all men,* that is, it is made and offered promiscuously to all. The salvation wrought is a *common salvation;* the proposals are general, the tender free; whoever will may come, and take of these waters of life. This free gift is to all believers, upon their believing, *unto justification of life.* It is not only a justification that frees from death, but that entitles to life. (2.) *Many shall be made righteous* — many compared with one, or as many as belong to the election of grace, which, though but a few as they are scattered up and down in the world, yet will be a great many when they come all together. *Katastathēsontai — they shall be constituted* righteous, as by letters patent. Now the antithesis between these two, our ruin by Adam and our recovery by Christ, is obvious enough.

[2.] Wherein the communication of grace and love by Christ goes beyond the communication of guilt and wrath by Adam; and this he shows, *v.* 15–17. It is designed for the magnifying of the riches of Christ's love, and for the comfort and encouragement of believers, who, considering what a wound Adam's sin has made, might begin to despair of a proportionable remedy. His expressions are a little intricate, but this he seems to intend: — *First,* If guilt and wrath be communicated, much more shall grace and love; for it is agreeable to the idea we have of the divine goodness to suppose that he should be more ready to save upon an imputed righteousness than to condemn upon an imputed guilt: *Much more the grace of God, and the gift by grace.* God's goodness is, of all his attributes, in a special manner his glory, and it is that grace that is the root (his favour to us in Christ), and the gift is by grace. We know that God is rather inclined to show mercy; punishing is his strange work. *Secondly,* If there was so much power and efficacy, as it seems there was, in the sin of a man, who was of the earth, earthy, to condemn us, much more are there power and efficacy in the righteousness and grace of Christ, who is the Lord from heaven, to justify and save us. The *one man* that saves us is Jesus Christ. Surely Adam could not propagate so strong a poison but Jesus Christ could propagate as strong an antidote, and much stronger. 3. It is but the guilt of one single offence of Adam's that is laid to our charge: *The judgment was ex henos eis katakrima, by one,* that is, by one offence, *v.* 16, 17. *Margin.* But from Jesus Christ we receive and derive an *abundance of grace, and of the gift of righteousness.* The stream of grace and righteousness is deeper and broader than the stream of guilt; for this righteousness does not only take away the guilt of that one offence, but of many other offences, even of all. God in Christ forgives all trespasses, Col. 2:13. 4. By Adam's sin *death reigned;* but by Christ's righteousness there is not only a period put to the reign of death, but believers are preferred to *reign of life, v.* 17. In and by the righteousness of Christ we have not only a charter of pardon, but a patent of honour, are not only freed from our chains, but, like Joseph, advanced to the second chariot, and made unto our God kings and priests — not only pardoned, but preferred. See this observed, Rev. 1:5, 6; 5:9, 10. We are by Christ and his righteousness entitled to, and instated in, more and greater privileges than we lost by the offence of Adam. The plaster is wider than the wound, and more healing than the wound is killing.

IV. In the last two verses the apostle seems to anticipate an objection which is expressed, Gal. 3:19, *Wherefore then serveth the law?* Answer, 1. *The law entered that the offence might abound.* Not to make sin to abound the more in itself, otherwise than as sin takes occasion by the commandment, but to discover the abounding sinfulness of it. The glass discovers the spots, but does not cause them. When the commandment came into the world sin revived, as the letting of a clearer light into a room discovers the dust and filth which were there before, but were not seen. It was like the searching of a wound, which is necessary to the cure. *The offence, to paraptōma — that offence,* the sin of Adam, the extending of the guilt of it to us, and the effect of the corruption in us, are the abounding of that offence which appeared upon the entry of the law. 2. *That grace might much more abound* — that the terrors of the law might make gospel-comforts so much the sweeter. Sin abounded among the Jews; and, to those of them that were converted to the faith of Christ, did not grace much more abound in the remitting of so much guilt and the subduing of so much corruption? The greater the strength of the enemy, the greater the honour of the conqueror. This abounding of grace he illustrates, *v.* 21. As the reign of a tyrant and oppressor is a foil to set off the succeeding reign of a just and gentle prince and to make it the more illustrious, so doth the reign of sin set off the reign of grace. *Sin reigned unto death;* it was a cruel bloody reign. But *grace reigns* to life, *eternal life,* and this *through righteousness,* righteousness imputed to us for justification, implanted in us for sanctification; and both by *Jesus Christ our Lord,* through the power and efficacy of Christ, the great prophet, priest, and king, of his church.

CHAPTER 6

The apostle having at large asserted, opened, and proved, the great doctrine of justification by faith, for fear lest any should suck poison out of that sweet flower, and turn that grace of God into wantonness and licentiousness, he, with a like zeal, copiousness of expression, and cogency of argument, presses the absolute necessity of sanctification and a holy life, as the inseparable fruit and companion of justification; for, wherever Jesus Christ is made of God unto any soul righteousness, he is made of God unto that soul sanctification, 1 Co. 1:30. The water and the blood came streaming together out of the pierced side of the dying Jesus. And what God hath thus joined together let not us dare to put asunder.

Verses 1–23

The apostle's transition, which joins this discourse with the former, is observable: "*What shall we say then? v.* 1. What use shall we make of this sweet and comfortable doctrine? Shall we do evil that good may come, as some say we do? *ch.* 3:8. *Shall we continue in sin that grace may abound?* Shall we hence take encouragement to sin with so much the more boldness, because the more sin we commit the more will the grace of God be magnified in our pardon? Is this a use to be made of it?" No, it is an abuse, and the apostle startles at the thought of it (*v.* 2): "*God forbid;* far be it from us to think such a thought." He entertains the objection as Christ did the devil's blackest temptation (Mt. 4:10): *Get thee hence, Satan.* Those opinions that give any countenance to sin, or open a door to practical immoralities, how specious and plausible soever they be rendered, by the pretension of advancing free grace, are to be rejected with the greatest abhorrence; for the truth as it is in Jesus is a truth *according to godliness,* Tit. 1:1. The apostle is very full in pressing the necessity of holiness in this chapter, which may be reduced to two heads: — His exhortations to holiness, which show the nature of it; and his motives or arguments to enforce those exhortations, which show the necessity of it.

I. For the first, we may hence observe the nature of sanctification, what it is, and wherein it consists. In general it has two things in it, mortification and vivification — dying to sin and living to righteousness, elsewhere expressed by putting off the old man and putting on the new, ceasing to do evil and learning to do well.

1. Mortification, putting off the old man; several ways this is expressed. (1.) We must *live no longer in sin* (*v.* 2), we must not be as we have been nor do as we have done. The time past of our life must suffice, 1 Peter 4:3. Though there are none that live without sin, yet, blessed be God, there are those that do not live in sin, do not live in it as their element, do not make a trade of it: this is to be sanctified. (2.) *The body of sin must be destroyed, v.* 6. The corruption that dwelleth in us is the body of sin, consisting of many parts and members, as a body. This is the root to which the axe must be laid. We must not only cease from the acts of sin (this may be done through the influence of outward restraints, or other inducements), but we must get the vicious habits and inclinations weakened and destroyed; not only cast away the idols of iniquity out of the heart. — *That henceforth we should not serve sin.* The actual transgression is certainly in a great measure prevented by the crucifying and killing of the original corruption. Destroy the body of sin, and then, though there should be Canaanites remaining in the land, yet the Israelites will not be slaves to them. It is the body of sin that sways the sceptre, wields the iron rod; destroy this, and the yoke is broken. The destruction of Eglon the tyrant is the deliverance of oppressed Israel from the Moabites. (3.) *We must be dead indeed unto sin, v.* 11. As the death of the oppressor is a release, so much more is the death of the oppressed, Job 3:17, 18. Death brings a writ of ease to the weary. Thus must we be dead to sin, obey it, observe it, regard it, fulfil its will no more than he that is dead doth his *quandam* task-masters — be as indifference to the pleasures and delights of sin as a man that is dying is to his former diversions. He that is dead is separated from his former company, converse, business, enjoyments, employments, is not what he was, does not what he did, has not what he had. Death makes a mighty change; such a change doth sanctification make in the soul, it cuts off all correspondence with sin. (4.) *Sin must not reign in our mortal bodies that we should obey it, v.* 12. Though sin may remain as an outlaw, though it may oppress as a tyrant, yet let it not reign as a king. Let it not make laws, nor preside in councils, nor command the militia; let it not be uppermost in the soul, so that we should obey it. Though we may be sometimes overtaken and overcome by it, yet let us never be obedient to it in the lusts thereof; let not sinful lusts be a law to you, to which you would yield a consenting obedience. *In the lusts thereof — en tais epithymiais autou.* It refers to the body, not to sin. Sin lies very much in the gratifying of the body, and humouring that. And there is a reason implied in the phrase *your mortal body;* because it is a mortal body, and hastening apace to the dust, therefore let not sin reign in it. It was sin that made our bodies mortal, and therefore do not yield obedience to such an enemy. (5.) We must not *yield our members as instruments of unrighteousness, v.* 13. The members of the body are made use of by the corrupt nature as tools, by which the wills of the flesh are fulfilled; but we must not consent to that abuse. The members of the body are fearfully and wonderfully made; it is a pity they should be the devil's tools of *unrighteousness unto sin,* instruments of the sinful actions, according to the sinful dispositions. Unrighteousness is unto sin; the sinful acts confirm and strengthen the sinful habits; one sin begets another; it is like the letting forth of water, therefore leave it before it be meddled with. The members of the body may perhaps, through the prevalency of temptation, be forced to be instruments of sin; but do not yield them to be so, do not consent to it. This is one branch of sanctification, the mortification of sin.

2. Vivification, or living to righteousness; and what is that? (1.) It is to *walk in newness of life, v.* 4. Newness of life supposes newness of heart, for out of the heart are the issues of life, and there is not way to make the stream sweet but by making the spring so. Walking, in scripture, is put for the course and tenour of the conversation, which must be new. Walk by new rules, towards new ends, from new principles. Make a new choice of the way. Choose new paths to walk in, new leaders to walk after, new companions to walk with. Old things should pass away, and all things become new. The man is what he was not, does what he did not. (2.) It is to be *alive unto God through Jesus Christ our Lord, v.* 11. To converse with God, to have a regard to him, a delight in him, a concern for him, the soul upon all occasions carried out towards him as towards an agreeable object, in which it takes a complacency: this is to be alive to God. The love of God reigning in the heart is the life of the soul towards God. *Anima est ubi amat, non ubi animat — The soul is where it loves, rather than where it lives.* It is to have the affections and desires alive towards God. Or, *living* (our live in the flesh) *unto God,* to his honour and glory as our end, by his word and will as our rule — in all our ways to acknowledge him, and to have our eyes ever towards him; this is to live unto God. — *Through Jesus Christ our Lord.* Christ is our spiritual life; there is no living to God but through him. He is the Mediator; there can be no comfortable receivings from God, nor acceptable regards to God, but in and through Jesus Christ; no intercourse between sinful souls and a holy God, but by the mediation of the Lord Jesus. Through Christ as the author and maintainer of this life; through Christ as the head from whom we receive vital influence; through Christ as the root by which we derive sap and nourishment, and so live. In living to God, Christ is all in all. (3.) It is to *yield ourselves to God, as those that are alive from the dead, v.* 13. The very life and being of holiness lie in the dedication of ourselves to the Lord, giving our own selves to the Lord, 2 Co. 8:5. "Yield yourselves to him, not only as the conquered yields to the conqueror, because he can stand it out no longer; but

as the wife yields herself to her husband, to whom her desire is, as the scholar yields himself to the teacher, the apprentice to his master, to be taught and ruled by him. Not yield your estates to him, but yield yourselves; nothing less than your whole selves;" *parastēsate eautous — accommodate vos ipsos Deo — accommodate yourselves to God;* so *Tremellius*, from the *Syriac.* "Not only submit to him, but comply with him; not only present yourselves to him once for all, but be always ready to serve him. Yield yourselves to him as wax to the seal, to take any impression, to be, and have, and do, what he pleases." When Paul said, *Lord, what wilt thou have me to do?* (Acts 9:6) he was then yielded to God. *As those that are alive from the dead.* To yield a dead carcase to a living God is not to please him, but to mock him: "Yield yourselves as those that are alive and good for something, a *living sacrifice,*" *ch.* 12:1. The surest evidence of our spiritual life is the dedication of ourselves to God. It becomes those that are alive from the dead (it may be understood of a death in law), that are justified and delivered from death, to give themselves to him that hath so redeemed them. (4.) It is to yield *our members as instruments of righteousness to God.* The members of our bodies, when withdrawn from the service of sin, are not to lie idle, but to be made use of in the service of God. When the strong man armed is dispossessed, let him whose right it is divide the spoils. Though the powers and faculties of the soul be the immediate subjects of holiness and righteousness, yet the members of the body are to be instruments; the body must be always ready to serve the soul in the service of God. Thus (*v.* 19), *"Yield your members servants to righteousness unto holiness.* Let them be under the conduct and at the command of the righteous law of God, and that principle of inherent righteousness which the Spirit, as sanctifier, plants in the soul." *Righteousness unto holiness,* which intimates growth, and progress, and ground obtained. As every sinful act confirms the sinful habit, and makes the nature more and more prone to sin (hence the members of a natural man are here said to be servants to *iniquity unto iniquity* — one sin makes the heart more disposed for another), so every gracious act confirms the gracious habit: serving righteousness is unto holiness; one duty fits us for another; and the more we do the more we may do for God. Or serving righteousness, *eis hagiasmon — as an evidence of sanctification.*

II. The motives or arguments here used to show the necessity of sanctification. There is such an antipathy in our hearts by nature to holiness that it is no easy matter to bring them to submit to it: it is the Spirit's work, who persuades by such inducements as these set home upon the soul.

1. He argues from our sacramental conformity to Jesus Christ. Our baptism, with the design and intention of it, carried in it a great reason why we should die to sin, and live to righteousness. Thus we must improve our baptism as a bridle of restraint to keep us in from sin, as a spur of constraint to quicken us to duty. Observe this reasoning.

(1.) In general, we are *dead to sin,* that is, in profession and in obligation. Our baptism signifies our cutting off from the kingdom of sin. We profess to have no more to do with sin. We are dead to sin by a participation of virtue and power for the killing of it, and by our union with Christ and interest in him, in and by whom it is killed. All this is in vain if we persist in sin; we contradict a profession, violate an obligation, return to that to which we were dead, like walking ghosts, than which nothing is more unbecoming and absurd. For (*v.* 7) *he that is dead is freed from sin;* that is, he that is dead to it is freed from the rule and dominion of it, as the servant that is dead is freed from his master, Job 3:19. Now shall we be such fools as to return to that slavery from which we are discharged? When we are delivered out of Egypt, shall we talk of going back to it again?

(2.) In particular, being *baptized into Jesus Christ, we were baptized into his death, v.* 3. We were baptized *eis Christon — unto Christ,* as 1 Co. 10:2, *eis Mōsēn — unto Moses.* Baptism binds us to Christ, it binds us apprentice to Christ as our teacher, it is our allegiance to Christ as our sovereign. Baptism is *externa ansa Christi — the external handle of Christ,* by which Christ lays hold on men, and men offer themselves to Christ. Particularly, we were baptized into his death, into a participation of the privileges purchased by his death, and into an obligation both to comply with the design of his death, which was to redeem us from all iniquity, and to conform to the pattern of his death, that, as Christ died for sin, so we should die to sin. This was the profession and promise of our baptism, and we do not do well if we do not answer this profession, and make good this promise.

[1.] Our conformity to the death of Christ obliges us to die unto sin; thereby we know the *fellowship of his sufferings,* Phil. 3:10. Thus we are here said to be *planted together in the likeness of is death* (*v.* 5), *tō homoiōmati,* not only a conformity, but a conformation, as the engrafted stock is planted together into the likeness of the shoot, of the nature of which it doth participate. Planting is in order to life and fruitfulness: we are planted in the vineyard in a likeness to Christ, which likeness we should evidence in sanctification. Our creed concerning Jesus Christ is, among other things, that he was *crucified, dead, and buried;* now baptism is a sacramental conformity to him in each of these, as the apostle here takes notice. *First, Our old man is crucified with him, v.* 6. The death of the cross was a slow death; the body, after it was nailed to the cross, gave many a throe and many a struggle: but it was a sure death, long in expiring, but expired at last; such is the mortification of sin in believers. It was a cursed death, Gal. 3:13. Sin dies as a malefactor, devoted to destruction; it is an accursed thing. Though it be a slow death, yet this must needs hasten it that it is an old man that is crucified; not in the prime of its strength, but decaying: that which waxeth old is ready to vanish away, Heb. 8:13. *Crucified with him — synestaurōthē,* not in respect of time, but in respect of causality. The crucifying of Christ for us has an influence upon the crucifying of sin in us. *Secondly,* We are dead with Christ, *v.* 8. Christ was obedient to death: when he died, we might be said to die with him, as our dying to sin is an act of conformity both to the design and to the example of Christ's dying for sin. Baptism signifies and seals our union with Christ, our engrafting into Christ; so that we are dead with him, and engaged to have no more to do with sin than he had. *Thirdly, We are buried with him by baptism, v.* 4. Our conformity is complete. We are in profession quite cut off from all commerce and communion with sin, as those that are buried are quite cut off from all the world; not only not of the living, but no more among the living, have nothing more to do with them. Thus must we be, as Christ was, separate from sin and sinners. We are buried, namely, in profession and obligation: we profess to be so, and we are bound to be so: it was our covenant and engagement in baptism; we are sealed to be the Lord's, therefore to be cut off from sin. Why this burying in baptism should so much as allude to any custom of dipping under water in baptism, any more than our baptismal crucifixion and death should have any such references, I confess I cannot see. It is plain that it is not the sign, but the thing signified, in baptism, that the apostle here calls being buried with Christ, and the expression of burying alludes to Christ's burial. As Christ was buried, that he might rise again to a new and more heavenly life, so we are in baptism buried, that is, cut off from the life of sin, that we may rise again to a new life of faith and love.

[2.] Our conformity to the resurrection of Christ obliges us to rise again to newness of life. This is *the power of his resurrection* which Paul was so desirous to know, Phil. 3:10. Christ was raised up *from the dead by the glory of the Father,* that is, by the power of the Father. The power of God is his glory; it is glorious power, Col. 1:11. Now in baptism we are obliged to conform to that pattern, to be planted in the *likeness of his resurrection* (*v.* 5), to *live with him, v.* 8. See Col. 2:12. Conversion is the first resurrection from the death of sin to the life of righteousness; and this resurrection is conformable to Christ's resurrection. This conformity of the saints to the resurrection of Christ seems to be intimated in the rising of so many of the bodies of the saints, which, though mentioned before by anticipation, is supposed to have been concomitant with Christ's resurrection, Mt. 27:52. We have all risen with Christ. In two things we must conform to the resurrection of Christ: — *First,* He rose to die no more, *v.* 9. We read of many others that were raised from the dead, but they rose to die again. But, when Christ rose, he rose to die no more; therefore he left his grave-clothes behind him, whereas Lazarus, who was to die again, brought them out with him, as one that should have occasion to use them again: but over Christ *death has no more dominion;* he was dead indeed, but he is alive, and so alive that he lives for evermore, Rev. 1:18. Thus we must rise from the grave of sin never again to return to it, nor to have any more fellowship with the works of darkness, having quitted that grave, that land of darkness as darkness itself. *Secondly,* He rose to live unto God (*v.* 10), to live a heavenly life, to receive that glory which was set before him. Others that were raised from the dead returned to the same life in every respect which they had before lived; but so did not Christ: he rose again to leave the world. *Now I am no more in the world,* Jn. 13:1; 17:11. He rose to *live to God,* that is, to intercede and rule, and all to the glory of the Father. Thus must we rise to live to God: this is what he calls *newness of life* (*v.* 4), to live from other principles, by other rules, with other aims, than we have done. A life devoted to God is a new life; before, self was the chief and highest end, but now God. To live indeed is to live to God, with our eyes ever towards him, making him the centre of all our actions.

2. He argues from the precious promises and privileges of the new covenant, *v.* 14. It might be objected that we cannot conquer and subdue sin, it is unavoidably too hard for us: "No," says he, "you wrestle with an enemy that may be dealt with and subdued, if you will but keep your ground and stand to your arms; it is an enemy that is already foiled and baffled; there is strength laid up in the covenant of grace for your assistance, if you will but use it. *Sin shall not have dominion.*" God's promises to us are more powerful and effectual for the mortifying of sin than our promises to God. Sin may struggle in a believer, and may create him a great deal of trouble, but it shall not have dominion; it may vex him, but shall not rule over him. *For we are not under the law, but under grace,* not under the law of sin and death, but under the law of the spirit of life, which is in Christ Jesus: we are actuated by other principles than we have been: new lords, new laws. Or, not under the covenant of works, which requires brick, and gives no straw, which condemns upon the least failure, which runs thus, "Do this, and live; do it not, and die;" but under the covenant of grace, which accepts sincerity as our gospel perfection, which requires nothing but what it promises strength to perform, which is herein well ordered, that every transgression in the covenant does not put us out of covenant, and especially that it does not leave our salvation in our own keeping, but lays it up in the hands of the Mediator, who undertakes for us that sin shall not have dominion over us, who hath himself condemned it, and will destroy it; so that, if we pursue the victory, we shall come off more than conquerors. Christ rules by the golden sceptre of grace, and he will not let sin have dominion over those that are willing subjects to that rule. This is a very comfortable word to all true believers. If we were under the law, we were undone, for the law curses every one that continues not in every thing; but we are under grace, grace which accepts the willing mind, which is not extreme to mark what we do amiss, which leaves room for repentance, which promises pardon upon repentance; and what can be to an ingenuous mind a stronger motive than this to have nothing to do with sin? Shall we sin against so much goodness, abuse such love? Some perhaps might suck poison out of this flower, and disingenuously use this as an encouragement to sin. See how the apostle starts at such a thought (*v.* 15): *Shall we sin because we are not under the law, but under grace? God forbid.* What can be more black and ill-natured than from a friend's extraordinary expressions of kindness and good-will to take occasion to affront and offend him? To spurn at such bowels, to spit in the face of such love, is that which, between man and man, all the world would cry out shame on.

3. He argues from the evidence that this will be of our state, making for us, or against us (*v.* 16): *To whom you yield yourselves servants to obey, his servants you are.* All the children of men are either the servants of God, or the servants of sin; these are the two families. Now, if we would know to which of these families we belong, we must enquire to which of these masters we yield obedience. Our obeying the laws of sin will be an evidence against us that we belong to that family on which death is entailed. As, on the contrary, our obeying the laws of Christ will evidence our relation to Christ's family.

4. He argues from their former sinfulness, *v.* 17–21, where we may observe,

(1.) What they had been and done formerly. We have need to be often reminded of our former state. Paul frequently remembers it concerning himself, and those to whom he writes. [1.] *You were the servants of sin.* Those that are now the servants of God would do well to remember the time when they were the servants of sin, to keep them humble, penitent, and watchful, and to quicken them in the service of God. It is a reproach to the service of sin that so many thousands have quitted the service, and shaken off the yoke; and never any that sincerely deserted it, and gave themselves to the service of God, have returned to the former drudgery. *"God be thanked that you were so,* that is, that though you were so, yet you have obeyed. You were so; God be thanked that we can speak of it as a thing past: you were so, but you are not now so. Nay, your having been so formerly tends much to the magnifying of divine mercy and grace in the happy change. God be thanked that the former sinfulness is such a foil and such a spur to your present holiness." [2.] *You have yielded your members servants to uncleanness, and to iniquity unto iniquity, v.* 19. It is the misery of a sinful state that the body is made a drudge to sin, than which there could not be a baser or a harder slavery, like that of the prodigal that was sent into the fields to feed swine. *You have yielded.* Sinners are voluntary in the service of sin. The devil could not force them into the service, if they did not yield themselves to it. This will justify God in the ruin of sinners, that they sold themselves to work wickedness: it was their own act and deed. *To iniquity unto iniquity.* Every sinful act strengthens and confirms the sinful habit: to iniquity as the work unto iniquity as the wages. Sow the wind, and reap the whirlwind; growing worse and worse, more and more hardened. This he speaks *after the manner of men,* that is, he fetches a similitude from that which is common among men, even the change of services and subjections. [3.] *You were free from righteousness* (*v.* 20); not free by any liberty given, but by a liberty taken, which is licentiousness: *"You were* altogether void of that which is good, — void of any good principles, motions, or inclinations, — void of all subjection to the law and will of God, of all conformity to his image; and this you were highly pleased with, as a freedom and a liberty; but a freedom from righteousness is the worst kind of slavery."

(2.) How the blessed change was made, and wherein it did consist.

[1.] *You have obeyed from the heart that form of doctrine which was delivered to you, v.* 17. This describes conversion, what it is; it is our conformity to, and compliance with, the gospel which was delivered to us by Christ and his ministers. — *Margin. Whereto you were delivered; eis hon paredothēte — into which you were delivered.* And so observe, *First,* The rule of grace, *that form of doctrine — typon didachēs.* The gospel is the great rule both of truth and holiness; it is the stamp, grace is the impression of that stamp; it is the form of healing words, 2 Tim. 1:13. *Secondly,* The nature of grace, as it is our conformity to that rule. 1. It is to *obey from the heart.* The gospel is a doctrine not only to be believed, but to be obeyed, and that from the heart, which denotes the sincerity and reality of that obedience; not in profession only, but in power — from the heart, the innermost part, the commanding part of us. 2. It is to be *delivered into it,* as into a mould, as the wax is cast into the impression of the seal, answering it line for line, stroke for stroke, and wholly representing the shape and figure of it. To be a Christian indeed is to be transformed into the likeness and similitude of the gospel, our souls answering to it, complying with it, conformed to it — understanding, will, affections, aims, principles, actions, all according to that form of doctrine.

[2.] *Being made free from sin, you became servants of righteousness* (*v.* 18), *servants to God, v.* 22. Conversion is, *First,* A freedom from the service of sin; it is the shaking off of that yoke, resolving to have no more to do with it. *Secondly,* A resignation of ourselves to the service of God and righteousness, to God as our master, to righteousness as our work. When we are made free from sin, it is not that we may live as we list, and be our own masters; no: when we are delivered out of Egypt, we are, as Israel, led to the holy mountain, to receive the law, and are there brought into the bond of the covenant. Observe, We cannot be made the servants of God till we are freed from the power and dominion of sin; we cannot serve two masters so directly opposite one to another as God and sin are. We must, with the prodigal, quit the drudgery of the citizen of the country, before we can come to our Father's house.

(3.) What apprehensions they now had of their former work and way. He appeals to themselves (*v.* 21), whether they had not found the service of sin, [1.] An unfruitful service: *"What fruit had you then?* Did you ever get any thing by it? Sit down, and cast up the account, reckon your gains, what fruit had you then?" Besides the future losses, which are infinitely great, the very present gains of sin are not worth mentioning. *What fruit?* Nothing that deserves the name of fruit. The present pleasure and profit of sin do not deserve to be called fruit; they are but chaff, ploughing iniquity, sowing vanity, and reaping the same. [2.] It is an unbecoming service; it is that of which we *are now ashamed* — ashamed of the folly, ashamed of the filth, of it. Shame came into the world with sin, and is still the certain product of it — either the shame of repentance, or, if not that, eternal shame and contempt. Who would wilfully do that which sooner or later he is sure to be ashamed of?

5. He argues from the end of all these things. it is the prerogative of rational creatures that they are endued with a power of prospect, are capable of looking forward, considering the latter end of things. To persuade us from sin to holiness here are blessing and cursing, good and evil, life and death, set before us; and we are put to our choice. (1.) The end of sin is death (*v.* 21): *The end of those things is death.* Though the way may seem pleasant and inviting, yet the end is dismal: at the last it bites; it will be bitterness in the latter end. *The wages of sin is death, v.* 23. Death is as due to a sinner when he hath sinned as wages are to a servant when he hath done his work. This is true of every sin. There is no sin in its own nature venial. Death is the wages of the least sin. Sin is here represented either as the work for which the wages are given, or as the master by whom the wages are given; all that are sin's servants and do sin's work must expect to be thus paid. (2.) If the fruit be unto holiness, if there be an active principle of true and growing grace, the end will be everlasting life — a very happy end! — Though the way be up-hill, though it be narrow, and thorny, and beset, yet everlasting life at the end of it is sure. So, *v.* 23, *The gift of God is eternal life.* Heaven is life, consisting in the vision and fruition of God; and it is eternal life, no infirmities attending it, no death to put a period to it. This is the gift of God. The death is the wages of sin, it comes by desert; but the life is a gift, it comes by favour. Sinners merit hell, but saints do not merit heaven. There is no proportion between the glory of heaven and our obedience; we must thank God, and not ourselves, if ever we get to heaven. And this gift is *through Jesus Christ our Lord.* It is Christ that purchased it, prepared it, prepares us for it, preserves us to it; he is *the Alpha and Omega,* All in all in our salvation.

CHAPTER 7

We may observe in this chapter, I. Our freedom from the law further urged as an argument to press upon us sanctification (*v.* 1–6). II. The excellency and usefulness of the law asserted and proved from the apostle's own experience, notwithstanding (*v.* 7–14). III. A description of the conflict between grace and corruption in the heart (*v.* 14, 15, to the end).

Verses 1–6

Among other arguments used in the foregoing chapter to persuade us against sin, and to holiness, this was one (*v.* 14), that *we are not under the law;* and this argument is here further insisted upon and explained (*v.* 6): *We are delivered from the law.* What is meant by this? And how is it an argument why sin should not reign over us, and why we should walk in newness of life? 1. We are delivered from the power of the law which curses and condemns us for the sin committed by us. The sentence of the law against us is vacated and reversed, by the death of Christ, to all true believers. The law saith, *The soul that sins shall die;* but we are delivered from the law. *The Lord has taken away thy sin, thou shalt not die.* We are *redeemed from the curse of the law,* Gal. 3:13. 2. We are delivered from that power of the law which irritates and provokes the sin that dwelleth in us. This the apostle seems especially to refer to (*v.* 5): *The motions of sins which were by the law.* The law, by commanding, forbidding, threatening, corrupt and fallen man, but offering no grace to cure and strengthen, did but stir up the corruption, and, like the sun shining upon a dunghill, excite and draw up the filthy steams. We being lamed by the fall, the law comes and directs us, but provides nothing to heal and help our lameness, and so makes us halt and stumble the more. Understand this of the law not as a rule, but as a covenant of works. Now each of these is an argument why we should be holy; for here is encouragement to endeavours, though in many things we come short. We are under grace, which promises strength to do what it commands, and pardon upon repentance when we do amiss. This is the scope of these verses in general, that, in point of profession and privilege, we are under a covenant of grace, and not under a covenant of works — under the gospel of Christ, and not under the law of Moses. The difference between a law-state and a gospel-state he had before illustrated by the similitude of rising to a new life, and serving a new master; now here he speaks of is under the similitude of being married to a new husband.

I. Our first marriage was to the law, which, according to the law of marriage, was to continue only during the life of the law. The law of marriage is binding till the death of one of the parties, no matter which, and no longer. The death of either discharges both. For this he appeals to themselves, as persons knowing the law (*v.* 1): *I speak to those that know the law.* It is a great advantage to discourse with those that have knowledge, for such can more readily understand and apprehend a truth. Many of the Christians at Rome were such as had been Jews, and so were well acquainted with the law. One has some hold of knowing people. *The law hath power over a man as long as he liveth;* in particular, the law of marriage hath power; or, in general, every law is so limited —the laws of nations, of relations, of families, etc. 1. The obligation of laws extends no further; by death the servant who, while he lived, was under the yoke, is *freed from his master,* Job 3:19. 2. The condemnation of laws extends no further; death is the finishing of the law. *Actio moritur cum personâ — The action expires with the person.* The severest laws could but kill the body, and after that there is no more that they can do. Thus while we were alive to the law we were under the power of it — while we were in our Old-Testament state, before the gospel came into the world, and before it came with power into our hearts. Such is the law of marriage (*v.* 2), the woman is bound to her husband during life, so bound to him that she cannot marry another; if she do, she shall be reckoned an adulteress, *v.* 3. It will make her an adulteress, not only to be defiled by, but to be married to, another man; for that is so much the worse, upon this account, that it abuses an ordinance of God, by making it to patronise the uncleanness. Thus were we married to the law (*v.* 5): *When we were in the flesh,* that is, in a carnal state, under the reigning power of sin and corruption — in the flesh as in our element — then *the motions of sins which were by the law did work in our members,* we were carried down the stream of sin, and the law was but as an imperfect dam, which made the stream to swell the higher, and rage the more. Our desire was towards sin, as that of the wife towards her husband, and sin ruled over us. We embraced it, loved it, devoted all to it, conversed daily with it, made it our care to please it. We were under a law of sin and death, as the wife under the law of marriage; and the product of this marriage was fruit brought forth unto death, that is, actual transgressions were produced by the original corruption, such as deserve death. Lust, having conceived by the law (which is the strength of sin, 1 Co. 15:56), *bringeth forth sin, and sin, when it is finished, bringeth forth death,* Jam. 1:15. This is the posterity that springs from this marriage to sin and the law. This comes of the motions of sin working in our members. And this continues during life, while the law is alive to us, and we are alive to the law.

II. Our second marriage is to Christ: and how comes this about? Why,

1. We are freed, by death, from our obligation to the law as a covenant, as the wife is from her obligation to her husband, *v.* 3. This resemblance is not very close, nor needed it to be. *You are become dead to the law, v.* 4. He does not say, "The law is dead" (some think because he would avoid giving offence to those who were yet zealous for the law), but, which comes all to one, *You are dead to the law.* As the crucifying of the world to us, and of us to the world, amounts to one and the same thing, so doth the law dying, and our dying to it. We are *delivered from the law* (*v.* 6), *katērgēthēmen — we are nulled* as to the law; our obligation to it as a husband is cassated and made void. And then he speaks of the law being dead as far as it was a law of bondage to us: *That being dead wherein we were held;* not the law itself, but its obligation to punishment and its provocation to sin. It is dead, it has lost its power; and this (*v.* 4) *by the body of Christ,* that is, by the sufferings of Christ in his body, by his crucified body, which abrogated the law, answered the demands of it, made satisfaction for our violation of it, purchased for us a covenant of grace, in which righteousness and strength are laid up for us, such as were not, nor could be, by the law. We are dead to the law by our union with the mystical body of Christ. By being incorporated into Christ in our baptism professedly, in our believing powerfully and effectually, we are dead to the law, have no more to do with

it than the dead servant, that is free from his master, hath to do with his master's yoke.

2. We are married to Christ. The day of our believing is the day of our espousals to the Lord Jesus. We enter upon a life of dependence on him and duty to him: *Married to another, even to him who is raised from the dead,* a periphrasis of Christ and very pertinent here; for as our dying to sin and the law is in conformity to the death of Christ, and the crucifying of his body, so our devotedness to Christ in newness of life is in conformity to the resurrection of Christ. We are married to the raised exalted Jesus, a very honourable marriage. Compare 2 Co. 11:2; Eph. 5:29. Now we are thus married to Christ, (1.) *That we should bring forth fruit unto God, v.* 4. One end of marriage is fruitfulness: God instituted the ordinance that he might seek a *godly seed,* Mal. 2:15. The wife is compared to the fruitful vine, and children are called the fruit of the womb. Now the great end of our marriage to Christ is our fruitfulness in love, and grace, and every good work. This is fruit unto God, pleasing to God, according to his will, aiming at his glory. As our old marriage to sin produced fruit unto death, so our second marriage to Christ produces fruit unto God, fruits of righteousness. Good works are the children of the new nature, the products of our union with Christ, as the fruitfulness of the vine is the product of its union with the root. Whatever our professions and pretensions may be, there is no fruit brought forth to God till we are married to Christ; it is in Christ Jesus that we are created unto good works, Eph. 2:10. The only fruit which turns to a good account is that which is brought forth in Christ. This distinguishes the good works of believers from the good works of hypocrites and self-justifiers that they are brought forth in marriage, done in union with Christ, in the name of the Lord Jesus, Col. 3:17. This is, without controversy, one of the great mysteries of godliness. (2.) *That we should serve in newness of spirit, and not in the oldness of the letter, v.* 6. Being married to a new husband, we must change our way. Still we must serve, but it is a service that is perfect freedom, whereas the service of sin was a perfect drudgery: we must now serve in newness of spirit, by new spiritual rules, from new spiritual principles, in spirit and in truth, Jn. 4:24. There must be a renovation of our spirits wrought by the spirit of God, and in that we must serve. *Not in the oldness of the letter;* that is, we must not rest in mere external services, as the carnal Jews did, who gloried in their adherence to the letter of the law, and minded not the spiritual part of worship. The letter is said to kill with its bondage and terror, but we are delivered from that yoke that we may serve God without fear, in holiness and righteousness, Lu. 1:74, 75. We are under the dispensation of the Spirit, and therefore must be spiritual, and serve in the spirit. Compare with this 2 Co. 3:3, 6, etc. It becomes us to worship within the veil, and no longer in the outward court.

Verses 7–14a

To what he had said in the former paragraph, the apostle here raises an objection, which he answers very fully: *What shall we say then? Is the law sin?* When he had been speaking of the dominion of sin, he had said so much of the influence of the law as a covenant upon that dominion that it might easily be misinterpreted as a reflection upon the law, to prevent which he shows from his own experience the great excellency and usefulness of the law, not as a covenant, but as a guide; and further discovers how sin took occasion by the commandment. Observe in particular,

I. The great excellency of the law in itself. Far be it from Paul to reflect upon the law; no, he speaks honourably of it. 1. It is *holy, just, and good, v.* 12. The law in general is so, and every particular commandment is so. Laws are as the law-makers are. God, the great lawgiver, is holy, just, and good, therefore his law must needs be so. The matter of it is holy: it commands holiness, encourages holiness; it is holy, for it is agreeable to the holy will of God, the original of holiness. It is just, for it is consonant to the rules of equity and right reason: the ways of the Lord are right. It is good in the design of it; it was given for the good of mankind, for the conservation of peace and order in the world. It makes the observers of it good; the intention of it was to better and reform mankind. Wherever there is true grace there is an assent to this — that the law is holy, just, and good. 2. *The law is spiritual* (*v.* 14), not only in regard to the effect of it, as it is a means of making us spiritual, but in regard to the extent of it; it reaches our spirits, it lays a restraint upon, and gives a direction to, the motions of the inward man; *it is a discerner of the thoughts and intents of the heart,* Heb. 4:12. It forbids spiritual wickedness, heart-murder, and heart-adultery. It commands spiritual service, requires the heart, obliges us to worship God in the spirit. It is a spiritual law, for it is given by God, who is a Spirit and the Father of spirits; it is given to man, whose principal part is spiritual; the soul is the best part, and the leading part of the man, and therefore the law to the man must needs be a law to the soul. Herein the law of God is above all other laws, that it is a spiritual law. Other laws may forbid *compassing and imagining,* etc., which are treason in the heart, but cannot take cognizance thereof, unless there be some overt act; but the law of God takes notice of the iniquity regarded in the heart, though it go no further. *Wash thy heart from wickedness,* Jer. 4:14. *We know this:* Wherever there is true grace there is an experimental knowledge of the spirituality of the law of God.

II. The great advantage that he had found by the law. 1. It was discovering: *I had not known sin but by the law, v.* 7. As that which is straight discovers that which is crooked, as the looking-glass shows us our natural face with all its spots and deformities, so there is no way of coming to that knowledge of sin which is necessary to repentance, and consequently to peace and pardon, but by comparing our hearts and lives with the law. Particularly he came to the knowledge of the sinfulness of lust by the law of the tenth commandment. By lust he means sin dwelling in us, sin in its first motions and workings, the corrupt principle. This he came to know when the law said, *Thou shalt not covet.* The law spoke in other language than the scribes and Pharisees made it to speak in; it spoke in the spiritual sense and meaning of it. By this he knew that lust was sin and a very sinful sin, that those motions and desires of the heart towards sin which never came into act were sinful, exceedingly sinful. Paul had a very quick and piercing judgment, all the advantages and improvements of education, and yet never attained the right knowledge of indwelling sin till the Spirit by the law made it known to him. There is nothing about which the natural man is more blind than about original corruption, concerning which the understanding is altogether in the dark till the Spirit by the law reveal it, and make it known. Thus *the law is a schoolmaster, to bring us to Christ,* opens and searches the wound, and so prepares it for healing. Thus sin by the commandment does appear sin (*v.* 13); it appears in its own colours, appears to be what it is, and you cannot call it by a worse name than its own. Thus by the commandment it becomes *exceedingly sinful;* that is, it appears to be so. We never see the desperate venom or malignity there is in sin, till we come to compare it with the law, and the spiritual nature of the law, and then we see it to be an evil and a bitter thing. 2. It was humbling (*v.* 9): *I was alive.* He thought himself in a very good condition; he was alive in his own opinion and apprehension, very secure and confident of the goodness of his state. Thus he was *once, pote — in times past,* when he was a Pharisee; for it was the common temper of that generation of men that they had a very good conceit of themselves; and Paul was then like the rest of them, and the reason was he was then *without the law.* Though brought up at the feet of Gamaliel, a doctor of the law, though himself a great student in the law, a strict observer of it, and a zealous stickler for it, yet *without the law.* He had the letter of the law, but he had not the spiritual meaning of it — the shell, but not the kernel. He had the law in his hand and in his head, but he had it not in his heart; the notion of it, but not the power of it. There are a great many who are spiritually dead in sin, that yet are alive in their own opinion of themselves, and it is their strangeness to the law that is the cause of the mistake. *But when the commandment came,* came in the power of it (not to his eyes only, but to his heart), *sin revived,* as the dust in a room rises (that is, appears) when the sun-shine is let into it. Paul then saw that in sin which he had never seen before; he then saw sin in its causes, the bitter root, the corrupt bias, the bent to backslide, — sin in its colours, deforming, defiling, breaking a righteous law, affronting an awful Majesty, profaning a sovereign crown by casting it to the ground, — sin in its consequences, sin with death at the heels of it, sin and the curse entailed upon it. "Thus sin revived, and then I died; I lost that good opinion which I had had of myself, and came to be of another mind. *Sin revived, and I died;* that is, the Spirit, but the commandment, convinced me that I was in a state of sin, and in a state of death because of sin." Of this excellent use is the law; it is a lamp and a light; it converts the soul, opens the eyes, prepares the way of the Lord in the desert, rends the rocks, levels the mountains, makes ready a people prepared for the Lord.

III. The ill use that his corrupt nature made of the law notwithstanding. 1. *Sin, taking occasion by the commandment, wrought in me all manner of concupiscence, v.* 8. Observe, Paul had in him all manner of concupiscence, though one of the best unregenerate men that ever was; as touching the righteousness of the law, blameless, and yet sensible of all manner of concupiscence. And it was sin that wrought it, indwelling sin, his corrupt nature (he speaks of a sin that did work sin), and it took occasion by the commandment. The corrupt nature would not have swelled and raged so much if it had not been for the restraints of the law; as the peccant humours in the body are raised, and more inflamed, by a purge that is not strong enough to carry them off. It is incident to corrupt nature, *in vetitum niti — to lean towards what is forbidden.* Ever since Adam ate forbidden fruit, we have all been fond of forbidden paths; the diseased appetite is carried out most strongly towards that which is hurtful and prohibited. *Without the law sin was dead,* as a snake in winter, which the sunbeams of the law quicken and irritate. 2. It *deceived men.* Sin puts a cheat upon the sinner, and it is a fatal cheat, *v.* 11. *By it* (by the commandment) *slew me.* There being in the law no such express threatening against sinful lustings, sin, that is, his won corrupt nature, took occasion thence to promise him impunity, and to say, as the serpent to our first parents, *You shall not surely die.* Thus it deceived and slew him. 3. It *wrought death in me by that which is good, v.* 13. That which works concupiscence works death, for sin bringeth forth death. Nothing so good but a corrupt and vicious nature will pervert it, and make it an occasion of ins; no flower so sweet by sin will such poison out of it. Now in this sin appears sin. The worst thing that sin does, and most like itself, is the perverting of the law, and taking occasion from it to be so much the more malignant. Thus the commandment, which was ordained to life, was intended as a guide in the way to comfort and happiness, proved unto death, through the corruption of nature, *v.* 10. Many a precious soul splits upon the rock of salvation; and the same word which to some is an occasion of life unto life is to others an occasion of death unto death. The same sun that makes the garden of flowers more fragrant makes the dunghill more noisome; the same heat that softens wax hardens clay; and the same child was set for the fall and rising again of many in Israel. The way to prevent this mischief is to bow our souls to the commanding authority of the word and law of God, not striving against, but submitting to it.

Verses 14b–25

Here is a description of the conflict between grace and corruption in the heart, between the law of God and the law of sin. And it is applicable two ways: — 1. To the struggles that are in a convinced soul, but yet unregenerate, in the person of whom it is supposed, by some, that Paul speaks. 2. To the struggles that are in a renewed sanctified soul, but yet in a state of imperfection; as other apprehend. And a great controversy there is of which of these we are to understand the apostle here. So far does the evil prevail here, when he speaks of one sold under sin, doing it, not performing that which is good, that it seems difficult to apply it to the regenerate, who are described to walk not after the flesh, but after the Spirit; and yet so far does the good prevail in hating sin, consenting to the law, delighting in it, serving the law of God with the mind, that it is more difficult to apply it to the unregenerate that are dead in trespasses and sins.

I. Apply it to the struggles that are felt in a convinced soul, that is yet in a state of sin, knows his Lord's will, but does it not, approves the things that are more excellent, being instructed out of the law, and yet lives in the constant breach of it, *ch.* 2:17–23. Though he has that within him that witnesses against the sin he commits, and it is not without a great deal of reluctancy that he does commit it, the superior faculties striving against it, natural conscience warning against it before it is committed and smiting for it afterwards, yet the man continues a slave to his reigning lusts. It is not thus with every unregenerate man, but with those only that are convinced by the law, but not changed by the gospel. The apostle had said (*ch.* 6:14), *Sin shall not have dominion, because you are not under the law, but under grace,* for the proof of which he here shows that a man under the law, and not under grace, may be, and is, under the dominion of sin. The law may discover sin, and convince of sin, but it cannot conquer and subdue sin, witness the predominancy of sin in many that are under very strong legal convictions. It discovers the defilement, but will not wash it off. It makes a man weary and heavy laden (Mt. 11:28), burdens him with his sin; and yet, if rested in, it yields no help towards the shaking off of that burden; this is to be had only in Christ. The law may make a man cry out, *O wretched man that I am! who shall deliver me?* and yet leave him thus fettered and captivated, as being too weak to deliver him (*ch.* 8:3), give him a spirit of bondage to fear, *ch.* 8:15. Now a soul advanced thus far by the law is in a fair way towards a state of liberty by Christ, though many rest here and go no further. Felix trembled, but never came to Christ. It is possible for a man to go to hell with his eyes open (Num. 24:3, 4), illuminated with common convictions, and to carry about with him a self-accusing conscience, even in the service of the devil. He may *consent to the law that it is good,* delight to know God's ways (as they, Isa. 58:2), may have that within him that witnesses against sin and for holiness; and yet all this overpowered by the reigning love of sin. Drunkards and unclean persons have some faint desires to leave off their sins, and yet persist in them notwithstanding, such is the impotency and such the insufficiency of their convictions. Of such as these there are many that will needs have all this understood, and contend earnestly for it: though it is very hard to imagine why, if the apostle intended this, he should speak all along in his own person; and not only so, but in the present tense. Of his own state under conviction he had spoken at large, as of a thing past (*v.* 7, etc.): *I died; the commandment I found to be unto death;* and if here he speaks of the same state as his present state, and the condition he was now in, surely he did not intend to be so understood: and therefore,

II. It seems rather to be understood of the struggles that are maintained between grace and corruption in sanctified souls. That there are remainders of indwelling corruption, even where there is a living principle of grace, is past dispute; that this corruption is daily breaking forth in sins of infirmity (such as are consistent with a state of grace) is no less certain. If we say that we have no sin, we deceive ourselves, 1 Jn. 1:8, 10. That true grace strives against these sins and corruptions, does not allow of them, hates them, mourns over them, groans under them as a burden, is likewise certain (Gal. 5:17): *The flesh lusteth against the spirit, and the spirit against the flesh; and these are contrary the one to the other, so that you cannot do the things that you would.* These are the truths which, I think, are contained in this discourse of the apostle. And his design is further to open the nature of sanctification, that it does not attain to a sinless perfection in this life; and therefore to quicken us to, and encourage us in, our conflicts with remaining corruptions. Our case is not singular, that which we do sincerely strive against, shall not be laid to our charge, and through grace the victory is sure at last. The struggle here is like that between Jacob and Esau in the womb, between the Canaanites and Israelites in the land, between the house of Saul and the house of David; but great is the truth and will prevail. Understanding it thus, we may observe here,

1. What he complains of — the remainder of indwelling corruptions, which he here speaks of, to show that the law is insufficient to justify even a regenerate man, that the best man in the world hath enough in him to condemn him, if God should deal with him according to the law, which is not the fault of the law, but of our own corrupt nature, which cannot fulfil the law. The repetition of the same things over and over again in this discourse shows how much Paul's heart was affected with what he wrote, and how deep his sentiments were. Observe the particulars of this complaint. (1.) *I am carnal, sold under sin, v.* 14. He speaks of the Corinthians as carnal, 1 Co. 3:1. Even where there is spiritual life there are remainders of carnal affections, and so far a man may be *sold under sin;* he does not sell himself to work wickedness, as Ahab did (1 Ki. 21:25), but he was sold by Adam when he sinned and fell — sold, as a poor slave that does his master's will against his own will — sold under sin, because conceived in iniquity and born in sin. (2.) *What I would, that I do not; but what I hate, that do I, v.* 15. And to the same purport, *v.* 19, 21, *When I would do good, evil is present with me.* Such was the strength of corruptions, that he could not attain that perfection in holiness which he desired and breathed after. Thus, while he was pressing forward towards perfection, yet he acknowledges that he had not already attained, neither was already perfect, Phil. 3:12. Fain he would be free from all sin, and perfectly do the will of God, such was his settled judgment; but his corrupt nature drew him another way: it was like a clog, that checked and kept him down when he would have soared upward, like the bias in a bowl, which, when it is thrown straight, yet draws it aside. (3.) *In me, that is in my flesh, dwelleth no good, v.* 18. Here he explains himself concerning the corrupt nature, which he calls flesh; and as far as that goes there is no good to be expected, any more than one would expect good corn growing upon a rock, or on the sand which is by the sea-side. As the new nature, as far as that goes, cannot commit sin (1 Jn. 3:9), so the flesh, the old nature, as far as that goes, cannot perform a good duty. How should it? For the flesh serveth the law of sin (*v.* 25), it is under the conduct and government of that law; and, while it is so, it is not likely to do any good. The corrupt nature is elsewhere called flesh (Gen. 6:3, Jn. 3:6); and, though there may be good things dwelling in those that have this flesh, yet, as far as the flesh goes, there is no good, the flesh is not a subject capable of any good. (4.) *I see another law in my members warring against the law of my mind, v.* 23. The corrupt and sinful inclination is here compared to a law, because it controlled and checked him in his good motions. It is said to be seated in his members, because, Christ having set up his throne in his heart, it was only the rebellious members of the body that were the instruments of sin — in the sensitive appetite; or we may take it more generally for all that corrupt nature which is the seat not only of sensual but of more refined lusts. This wars against the law of the mind, the new nature; it draws the contrary way, drives on a contrary interest, which corrupt disposition and inclination are as great a burden and grief to the soul as the worst drudgery and captivity could be. *It brings me into captivity.* To the same purport (*v.* 25), *With the flesh I serve the law of sin;* that is, the corrupt nature, the unregenerate part, is continually working towards sin. (5.) His general complaint we have in *v.* 24, *O wretched man that I am! who shall deliver me from the body of this death?* The thing he complains of is a body of death; either the body of flesh, which is a mortal dying body (while we carry this body about with us, we shall be troubled with corruption; when we are dead, we shall be freed from sin, and not before), or the body of sin, the old man, the corrupt nature, which tends to death, that is, to the ruin of the soul. Or, comparing it to a dead body, the touch of which was by the ceremonial law defiling, if actual transgressions be dead works (Heb. 9:14), original corruption is a dead body. It was as troublesome to Paul as if he had had a dead body tied to him, which he must have carried about with him. This made him cry out, *O wretched man that I am!* A man that had learned in every state to be content yet complains thus of his corrupt nature. Had I been required to speak of Paul, I should have said, "O blessed man that thou art, an ambassador of Christ, a favourite of heaven, a spiritual father of thousands!" But in his own account he was a wretched man, because of the corruption of nature, because he was not so good as he fain would be, had not yet attained, neither was already perfect. Thus miserably does he complain. *Who shall deliver me?* He speaks like one that was sick of it, that would give any thing to be rid of it, looks to the right hand and to the left for some friend that would part between him and his corruptions. The remainders of indwelling sin are a very grievous burden to a gracious soul.

2. What he comforts himself with. The case was sad, but there were some allays. Three things comforted him: —

(1.) That his conscience witnessed for him that he had a good principle ruling and prevailing in him, notwithstanding. It is well when all does not go one way in the soul. The rule of this good principle which he had was the law of God, to which he here speaks of having a threefold regard, which is certainly to be found in all that are sanctified, and no others. [1.] *I consent unto the law that it is good, v.* 16, *symphēmi — I give my vote* to the law; here is the approbation of the judgment. Wherever there is grace there is not only a dread of the severity of the law, but a consent to the goodness of the law. "It is a good in itself, it is good for me." This is a sign that the law is written in the heart, that the soul is delivered into the mould of it. To consent to the law is so far to approve of it as not to wish it otherwise constituted than it is. The sanctified judgment not only concurs to the equity of the law, but to the excellency of it, as convinced that a conformity to the law is the highest perfection of human nature, and the greatest honour and happiness we are capable of. [2.] *I delight in the law of God after the inward man, v.* 22. His conscience bore witness to a complacency in the law. He delighted not only in the promises of the word, but in the precepts and prohibitions of the word; *synēdomai* expresses a becoming *delight.* He did herein concur in affection with all the saints. All that are savingly regenerate or born again do truly delight in the law of God, delight to know it, to do it — cheerfully submit to the authority of it, and take a complacency in that submission, never better pleased than when heart and life are in the strictest conformity to the law and will of God. *After the inward man;* that is, *First,* The mind or rational faculties, in opposition to the sensitive appetites and wills of the flesh. The soul is the inward man, and that is the seat of gracious delights, which are therefore sincere and serious, but secret; it is the renewing of the inward man, 2 Co. 4:16. *Secondly,* The new nature. The new man is called the *inner man* (Eph. 3:16), the *hidden man of the heart,* 1 Pt. 3:4. Paul, as far as he was sanctified, had a delight in the law of God. [3.] *With the mind I myself serve the law of God, v.* 25. It is not enough to consent to the law, and to delight in the law, but we must serve the law; our souls must be entirely delivered up into the obedience of it. Thus it was with Paul's mind; thus it is with every sanctified renewed mind; this is the ordinary course and way; thitherward goes the bent of the soul. *I myself — autos egō,* plainly intimating that he speaks in his own person, and not in the person of another.

(2.) That the fault lay in that corruption of his nature which he did really bewail and strive against: *It is no more I that do it, but sin that dwelleth in me.* This he mentions twice (*v.* 17, 20), not as an excuse for the guilt of his sin (it is enough to condemn us, if we were under the law, that the sin which does the evil dwelleth in us), but as a salvo for his evidences, that he might not sink in despair, but take comfort from the covenant of grace, which accepts the willingness of the spirit, and has provided pardon for the weakness of the flesh. He likewise herein enters a protestation against all that which this indwelling sin produced. Having professed his consent to the law of God, he here professes his dissent from the law of sin. "It is not I; I disown the fact; it is against my mind that it is done." As when in the senate the major part are bad, and carry every thing the wrong way, it is indeed the act of the senate, but the honest party strive against it, bewail what is done, and enter their protestation against it; so that it is no more they that do it. — *Dwelleth in me,* as the Canaanites among the Israelites, though they were put under tribute: dwelleth in me, and is likely to dwell there, while I live.

(3.) His great comfort lay in Jesus Christ (*v.* 25): *I thank God, through Jesus Christ our Lord.* In the midst of his complaints he breaks out into praises. It is a special remedy against fears and sorrows to be much in praise: many a poor drooping soul hath found it so. And, in all our praises, this should be the burden of the son, "Blessed be God for Jesus Christ." *Who shall deliver me?* says he (*v.* 24), as one at a loss for help. At length he finds an all-sufficient friend, even Jesus Christ. When we are under the sense of the remaining power of sin and corruption, we shall see reason to bless God through Christ (for, as he is the mediator of all our prayers, so he is of all our praises) — to bless God for Christ; it is he that stands between us and the wrath due to us for this sin. If it were not for Christ, this iniquity that dwells in us would certainly be our ruin. He is our advocate with the Father, and through him God pities, and spares, and pardons, and lays not our iniquities to our charge. It is Christ that has purchased deliverance for us in due time. Through Christ death will put an end to all these complaints, and waft us to an eternity which we shall spend without sin or sigh. *Blessed be God that giveth us this victory through our Lord Jesus Christ!*

CHAPTER 8

The apostle, having fully explained the doctrine of justification, and pressed the necessity of sanctification, in this chapter applies himself to the consolation of the Lord's people. Ministers are helpers of the joy of the saints. "Comfort ye, comfort ye my people," so runs our commission, Isa. 40:1. It is the will of God that his people should be a comforted people. And we have here such a draught of the gospel charter, such a display of the unspeakable privileges of true believers, as may furnish us with abundant matter for joy and peace in believing, that by all these immutable things, in which it is impossible for God to lie, we might have strong consolation. Many of the people of God have, accordingly, found this chapter a well-spring of comfort to their souls, living and dying, and have sucked and been satisfied from these breasts of consolation, and with joy drawn water out of these wells of salvation. There are three things in this chapter: I. The particular instances of Christians' privileges (v. 1–28). II. The ground thereof laid in predestination (v. 29, 30). III. The apostle's triumph herein, in the name of all the saints (v. 31 to the end).

Verses 1–9

I. The apostle here beings with one signal privilege of true Christians, and describes the character of those to whom it belongs: *There is therefore now no condemnation to those that are in Christ Jesus, v. 1.* This is his triumph after that melancholy complaint and conflict in the foregoing chapter — sin remaining, disturbing, vexing, but, blessed be God, not ruining. The complaint he takes to himself, but humbly transfers the comfort with himself to all true believers, who are all interested in it. 1. It is the unspeakable privilege and comfort of all those that are in Christ Jesus that there is therefore now no condemnation to them. He does not say, "There is no accusation against them," for this there is; but the accusation is thrown out, and the indictment quashed. He does not say, "There is nothing in them that deserves condemnation," for this there is, and they see it, and own it, and mourn over it, and condemn themselves for it; but it shall not be their ruin. He does not say, "There is no cross, no affliction to them or no displeasure in the affliction," for this there may be; but *no condemnation.* They may be chastened of the Lord, but not condemned with the world. Now this arises from their being in Christ Jesus; by virtue of their union with him through faith they are thus secured. They are in Christ Jesus, as in their city of refuge, and so are protected from the avenger of blood. He is their advocate, and brings them off. There is therefore no condemnation, because they are interested in the satisfaction that Christ by dying made to the law. In Christ, God does not only not condemn them, but is well pleased with them, Mt. 17:5. 2. It is the undoubted character of all those who are so in Christ Jesus as to be freed from condemnation that *they walk not after the flesh but after the Spirit.* Observe, The character is given from their walk, not from any one particular act, but from their course and way. And the great question is, What is the principle of the walk, the flesh or the spirit, the old or the new nature, corruption or grace? Which of these do we mind, for which of these doe we make provision, by which of these are we governed, which of these do we take part with?

II. This great truth, thus laid down, he illustrates in the following verses; and shows how we come by this great privilege, and how we may answer this character.

1. How we come by these privileges — the privilege of justification, that *there is no condemnation to us* — the privilege of sanctification, that *we walk after the Spirit, and not after the flesh,* which is no less our privilege than it is our duty. How comes it about?

(1.) The law could not do it, v. 3. It could neither justify nor sanctify, neither free us from the guilt nor from the power of sin, having not the promises either of pardon or grace. The law made nothing perfect: *It was weak.* Some attempt the law made towards these blessed ends, but, alas! it was weak, it could not accomplish them: yet that weakness was not through any defect in the law, but *through the flesh,* through the corruption of human nature, by which we became incapable either of being justified or sanctified by the law. We had become unable to keep the law, and, in case of failure, the law, as a covenant of works, made no provision, and so left us as it found us. Or understand it of the ceremonial law; that was a plaster not wide enough for the wound, it could never take away sin, Heb. 10:4.

(2.) *The law of the Spirit of life in Christ Jesus* does it, v. 2. The covenant of grace made with us in Christ is a treasury of merit and grace, and thence we receive pardon and a new nature, *are freed from the law of sin and death,* that is, both from the guilt and power of sin — from the course of the law, and the dominion of the flesh. We are under another covenant, another master, another husband, under the *law of the Spirit,* the law that gives the Spirit, spiritual life to qualify us for eternal. The foundation of this freedom is laid in Christ's undertaking for us, of which he speaks v. 3, *God sending his own Son.* Observe, When the law failed, God provided another method. Christ comes to do that which the law could not do. Moses brought the children of Israel to the borders of Canaan, and then died, and left them there; but Joshua did that which Moses could not do, and put them in posses-

sion of Canaan. Thus what the law could not do Christ did. The best exposition of this verse we have Heb. 10:1–10. To make the sense of the words clear, which in our translation is a little intricate, we may read it thus, with a little transposition: — *God sending his own Son in the likeness of sinful flesh, and a sacrifice for sin, condemned sin in the flesh, which the law could not do, in that it was weak through the flesh,* etc. v. 4. Observe, [1.] How Christ appeared: *In the likeness of sinful flesh.* Not sinful, for he was holy, harmless, undefiled; but in the likeness of that flesh which was sinful. He took upon him that nature which was corrupt, though perfectly abstracted from the corruptions of it. His being circumcised, redeemed, baptized with John's baptism, bespeaks the likeness of sinful flesh. The bitings of the fiery serpents were cured by a serpent of brass, which had the shape, through free from the venom, of the serpents that bit them. It was great condescension that he who was God should be made in the likeness of flesh; but much greater that he who was holy should be made in the likeness of sinful flesh. *And for sin,* — here the best Greek copies place the comma. God sent him, *en homoiōmati sarkos hamartias, kai peri hamartias* — *in the likeness of sinful flesh, and as a sacrifice for sin.* The Septuagint call a sacrifice for sin no more than *peri hamartias* — *for sin;* so Christ was a sacrifice; he was sent to be so, Heb. 9:26. [2.] What was done by this appearance of his: Sin *was condemned,* that is, God did therein more than ever manifest his hatred of sin; and not only so, but for all that are Christ's both the damning and the domineering power of sin is broken and taken out of the way. He that is condemned can neither accuse nor rule; his testimony is null, and his authority null. Thus by Christ is sin condemned; though it live and remain, its life in the saints is still but like that of a condemned malefactor. It was by the condemning of sin that death was disarmed, and the devil, who had the power of death, destroyed. The condemning of sin saved the sinner from condemnation. Christ was made sin for us (2 Co. 5:21), and, being so made, when he was condemned sin was condemned in the flesh of Christ, condemned in the human nature: So was sanctification made to divine justice, and way made for the salvation of the sinner. [3.] The happy effect of this upon us (v. 4): *That the righteousness of the law might be fulfilled in us.* Both in our justification and in our sanctification, the righteousness of the law if fulfilled. A righteousness of satisfaction for the breach of the law is fulfilled by the imputation of Christ's complete and perfect righteousness, which answers the utmost demands of the law, as the mercy-seat was as long and as broad as the ark. A righteousness of obedience to the commands of the law is fulfilled in us, when by the Spirit the law of love is written upon the heart, and that love is the fulfilling of the law, ch. 13:10. Though the righteousness of the law is not fulfilled by us, yet, blessed be God, it is fulfilled in us; there is that to be found upon and in all true believers which answers the intention of the law. *Us who walk not after the flesh, but after the Spirit.* This is the description of all those that are interested in this privilege — they act from spiritual and not from carnal principles; as for others, the righteousness of the law will be fulfilled upon them in their ruin. Now,

2. Observe how we may answer to this character, v. 5, etc.

(1.) By looking to our minds. How may we know whether we are after the flesh or after the Spirit? By examining what we mind, the things of the flesh or the things of the spirit. Carnal pleasure, worldly profit and honour, the things of sense and time, are the things of the flesh, which unregenerate people mind. The favour of God, the welfare of the soul, the concerns of eternity, are the things of the Spirit, which those that are after the Spirit do mind. The man is as the mind is. The mind is the forge of thoughts. *As he thinketh in his heart, so is he,* Prov. 23:7. Which way do the thoughts move with most pleasure? On what do they dwell with most satisfaction? The mind is the seat of wisdom. Which way go the projects and contrivances? whether are we more wise for the world or for our souls? *phronousi ta tēs sarkos* — *they savour the things of the flesh;* so the word is rendered, Mt. 16:23. It is a great matter what our savour is, what truths, what tidings, what comforts, we do most relish, and are most agreeable to us. Now, to caution us against this carnal-mindedness, he shows the great misery and malignity of it, and compares it with the unspeakable excellency and comfort of spiritual-mindedness. [1.] It is death, v. 6. It is spiritual death, the certain way to eternal death. It is the death of the soul; for it is its alienation from God, in union and communion with

whom the life of the soul consists. A carnal soul is a dead soul, dead as a soul can die. She that *liveth in pleasure is dead* (1 Tim. 5:6), not only dead in law as guilty, but dead in state as carnal. Death includes all misery; carnal souls are miserable souls. But to be *spiritually minded, phronēma tou pneumatos — a spiritual savour* (the wisdom that is from above, a principle of grace) is *life and peace;* it is the felicity and happiness of the soul. The life of the soul consists in its union with spiritual things by the mind. A sanctified soul is a living soul, and that life is peace; it is a very comfortable life. All the paths of spiritual wisdom are paths of peace. It is life and peace in the other world, as well as in this. Spiritual-mindedness is eternal life and peace begun, and an assuring earnest of the perfection of it. [2.] It is enmity to God (v. 7), and this is worse than the former. The former speaks the carnal sinner a dead man, which is bad; but this speaks him a devil of a man. It is not only an enemy, but enmity itself. It is not only the alienation of the soul from God, but the opposition of the soul against God; it rebels against his authority, thwarts his design, opposes his interest, spits in his face, spurns at his bowels. Can there be a greater enmity? An enemy may be reconciled, but enmity cannot. How should this humble us for and warn us against, carnal-mindedness! Shall we harbour and indulge that which is enmity to God our creator, owner, ruler, and benefactor? To prove this, he urges that *it is not subject to the law of God, neither indeed can be.* The holiness of the law of God, and the unholiness of the carnal mind, are as irreconcilable as light and darkness. The carnal man may, by the power of divine grace, be made subject to the law of God, but the *carnal mind* never can; this must be broken and expelled. See how wretchedly the corrupt will of man is enslaved to sin; as far as the carnal mind prevails, there is no inclination to the law of God; therefore wherever there is a change wrought it is by the power of God's grace, not by the freedom of man's will. Hence he infers (v. 8), *Those that are in the flesh cannot please God.* Those that are in a carnal unregenerate state, under the reigning power of sin, cannot do the things that please God, wanting grace, the pleasing principle, and an interest in Christ, the pleasing Mediator. The very *sacrifice of the wicked is an abomination,* Prov. 15:8. Pleasing God is our highest end, of which those that are in the flesh cannot but fall short; they cannot please him, nay, they cannot but displease him. We may know our state and character,

(2.) By enquiring whether we have the Spirit of God and Christ, or not (v. 9): *You are not in the flesh, but in the Spirit.* This expresses states and conditions of the soul vastly different. All the saints have flesh and spirit in them; but to be in the flesh and to be in the Spirit are contrary. It denotes our being overcome and subdued by one of these principles. As we say, A man is *in love,* or *in drink,* that is, overcome by it. Now the great question is whether we are in the flesh or in the Spirit; and how may we come to know it? Why, by enquiring whether the Spirit of God dwell in us. The Spirit dwelling in us is the best evidence of our being in the Spirit, for the indwelling is mutual (1 Jn. 4:16): *Dwelleth in God, and God in him.* The Spirit visits many that are unregenerate with his motions, which they resist and quench; but in all that are sanctified he dwells; there he resides and rules. He is there as a man at his own house, where he is constant and welcome, and has the dominion. Shall we put this question to our own hearts, Who dwells, who rules, who keeps house, here? Which interest has the ascendant? To this he subjoins a general rule of trial: *If any man has not the Spirit of Christ, he is none of his.* To be Christ's (that is, to be a Christian indeed, one of his children, his servants, his friends, in union with him) is a privilege and honour which many pretend to that have no part nor lot in the matter. None are his but those that have his Spirit; that is, [1.] That are spirited as he was spirited — are meek, and lowly, and humble, and peaceable, and patient, and charitable, as he was. We cannot tread in his steps unless we have his spirit; the frame and disposition of our souls must be conformable to Christ's pattern. [2.] That are actuated and guided by the Holy Spirit of God, as a sanctifier, teacher, and comforter. Having the Spirit of Christ is the same with having the Spirit of God to dwell in us. But those two come much to one; for all that are actuated by the Spirit of God as their rule are conformable to the spirit of Christ as their pattern. Now this description of the character of those to whom belongs this first privilege of freedom from condemnation is to be applied to all the other privileges that follow.

Verses 10–16

In these verses the apostle represents two more excellent benefits, which belong to true believers.

I. Life. The happiness is not barely a negative happiness, not to be condemned; but it is positive, it is an advancement to a life that will be the unspeakable happiness of the man (*v.* 10, 11): *If Christ be in you.* Observe, If the Spirit be in us, Christ is in us. He dwells in the heart by faith, Eph. 3:17. Now we are here told what becomes of the bodies and souls of those in whom Christ is.

1. We cannot say but that *the body is dead;* it is a frail, mortal, dying body, and it will be dead shortly; it is a house of clay, whose foundation is in the dust. The life purchased and promised does not immortalize the body in its present state. It is dead, that is, it is appointed to die, it is under a sentence of death: as we say one that is condemned is a dead man. In the midst of life we are in death: be our bodies ever so strong, and healthful, and handsome, they are as good as dead (Heb. 11:12), and this *because of sin.* It is sin that kills the body. This effect the first threatening has (Gen. 3:19): *Dust thou art.* Methinks, were there no other argument, love to our bodies should make us hate sin, because it is such an enemy to our bodies. The death even of the bodies of the saints is a remaining token of God's displeasure against sin.

2. But the spirit, the precious soul, that is life; it is now spiritually alive, nay, it is life. Grace in the soul is its new nature; the life of the saint lies in the soul, while the life of the sinner goes no further than the body. When the body dies, and returns to the dust, *the spirit if life;* not only living and immortal, but swallowed up of life. Death to the saints is but the freeing of the heaven-born spirit from the clog and load of this body, that it may be fit to partake of eternal life. When Abraham was dead, yet God was the God of Abraham, for even then his spirit was life, Mt. 22:31, 32. See Ps. 49:15. And this *because of righteousness.* The righteousness of Christ imputed to them secures the soul, the better part, from death; the righteousness of Christ inherent in them, the renewed image of God upon the soul, preserves it, and, by God's ordination, at death elevates it, and improves it, and makes it meet to partake of the inheritance of the saints in light. The eternal life of the soul consists in the vision and fruition of God, and both assimilating, for which the soul is qualified by the righteousness of sanctification. I refer to Ps. 17:15, *I will behold thy face in righteousness.*

3. There is a life reserved too for the poor body at last: *He shall also quicken your mortal bodies, v.* 11. The Lord is for the body; and though at death it is cast aside as a despised broken vessel, a vessel in which is no pleasure, yet God will have a desire to the work of his hands (Job 14:15), will remember his covenant with the dust, and will not lose a grain of it; but the body shall be reunited to the soul, and clothed with a glory agreeable to it. Vile bodies shall be newly fashioned, Phil. 3:21; 1 Co. 15:42. Two great assurances of the resurrection of the body are mentioned: — (1.) The resurrection of Christ: He *that raised up Christ from the dead shall also quicken.* Christ rose as the head, and first-fruits, and forerunner of all the saints, 1 Co. 15:20. The body of Christ lay in the grave, under the sin of all the elect imputed, and broke through it. O grave, then, where is thy victory? It is in the virtue of Christ's resurrection that we shall rise. (2.) The indwelling of the Spirit. The same Spirit that raiseth the soul now will raise the body shortly: *By his Spirit that dwelleth in you.* The bodies of the saints are the temples of the Holy Ghost, 1 Co. 3:16; 6:19. Now, though these temples may be suffered for awhile to lie in ruins, yet they shall be rebuilt. The tabernacle of David, which has fallen down, shall be repaired, whatever great mountains may be in the way. The Spirit, breathing upon dead and dry bones, will make them live, and the saints even in their flesh shall see God. Hence the apostle by the way infers how much it is our duty to walk not after the flesh, but after the Spirit, *v.* 12, 13. Let not our life be after the wills and motions of the flesh. Two motives he mentions here: — [1.] We are not debtors to the flesh, neither by relation, gratitude, nor any other bond or obligation. We owe no suit nor service to our carnal desires; we are indeed bound to clothe, and feed, and take care of the body, as a servant to the soul in the service of God, but no further. We are not debtors to it; the flesh never did us so much kindness as to oblige us to serve it. It is implied that we are debtors to Christ and to the Spirit: there we owe our all, all we have and all we can do, by a thousand bonds and obligations. Being delivered from so great a death by so great a ransom, we are deeply indebted to our deliverer. See 1 Co. 6:19, 20. [2.] Consider the consequences, what will be at the end of the way. Here are life and death, blessing and cursing, set before us. *If you live after the flesh, you shall die;* that is, die eternally. It is the pleasing, and serving, and gratifying, of the flesh, that are the ruin of souls; that is, the second death. Dying indeed is the soul's dying: the death of the saints is but a sleep. But, on the other hand, *You shall live,* live and be happy to eternity; that is the true life: *If you through the Spirit mortify the deeds of the body,* subdue and keep under all fleshly lusts and affections, deny yourselves in the pleasing and humouring of the body, and this through the Spirit; we cannot do it without the Spirit working it in us, and the Spirit will not do it without our doing our endeavour. So that in a word we are put upon this dilemma, either to displease the body or destroy the soul.

II. The *Spirit of adoption* is another privilege belonging to those that are in Christ Jesus, *v.* 14–16.

1. All that are Christ's are taken into the relation of Children to God, *v.* 14. Observe, (1.) Their property: They are *led by the Spirit of God,* as a scholar in his learning is led by his tutor, as a traveller in his journey is led by his guide, as a soldier in his engagements is led by his captain; not driven as beasts, but led as rational creatures, drawn with the cords of a man and the bands of love. It is the undoubted character of all true believers that they are led by the Spirit of God. Having submitted themselves in believing to his guidance, they do in their obedience follow that guidance, and are sweetly led into all truth and all duty. (2.) Their privilege: *They are the sons of God,* received into the number of God's children by adoption, owned and loved by him as his children.

2. And those that are the sons of God have the Spirit,

(1.) To work in them the disposition of children.

[1.] *You have not received the spirit of bondage again to fear, v.* 15. Understand it, *First,* Of that spirit of bondage which the Old-Testament church was under, by reason of the darkness and terror of that dispensation. The veil signified bondage, 2 Co. 3:15. Compare *v.* 17. The Spirit of adoption was not then so plentifully poured out as now; for the law opened the wound, but little of the remedy. Now you are not under that dispensation, you have not received that spirit. *Secondly,* Of that spirit of bondage which many of the saints themselves were under at their conversion, under the convictions of sin and wrath set home by the Spirit; as those in Acts 2:37, the jailer (Acts 16:30), Paul, Acts 9:6. Then the Spirit himself was to the saints a spirit of bondage: "But," says the apostle, "with you this is over." "God as a Judge," says Dr. Manton, "by the spirit of bondage, sends us to Christ as Mediator, and Christ as Mediator, by the spirit of adoption, sends us back again to God as a Father." Though a child of God may come under fear of bondage again, and may be questioning his sonship, yet the blessed Spirit is not again a spirit of bondage, for then he would witness an untruth.

[2.] But you *have received the Spirit of adoption.* Men may give a charter of adoption; but it is God's prerogative, when he adopts, to give a spirit of adoption — the nature of children. The Spirit of adoption works in the children of God a filial love to God as a Father, a delight in him, and a dependence upon him, as a Father. A sanctified soul bears the image of God, as the child bears the image of the father. *Whereby we cry, Abba, Father.* Praying is here called *crying,* which is not only an earnest, but a natural expression of desire; children that cannot speak vent their desires by crying. Now, the Spirit teaches us in prayer to come to God as a Father, with a holy humble confidence, emboldening the soul in that duty. *Abba, Father. Abba* is a Syriac word signifying *father* or *my father; patēr,* a Greek work; and why both, *Abba, Father?* Because Christ said so in prayer (Mk. 14:36), *Abba, Father:* and we have received the Spirit of the Son. It denotes an affectionate endearing importunity, and a believing stress laid upon the relation. Little children, begging of their parents, can say little but *Father, Father,* and that is rhetoric enough. It also denotes that the adoption is common both to Jews and Gentiles: the Jews call him *Abba* in their language, the Greeks may call him *patēr* in their language; for in Christ Jesus there is neither Greek nor Jew.

(2.) To witness to the relation of children, *v.* 16. The former is the work of the Spirit as a Sanctifier; this as a Comforter. *Beareth witness with our spirit.* Many a man has the witness of his own spirit to the goodness of his state who has not the concurring testimony of the Spirit. Many speak peace to themselves to whom the God of heaven does not speak peace. But those that are sanctified have God's Spirit witnessing with their spirits, which is to be understood not of any immediate extraordinary revelation, but an ordinary work of the Spirit, in and by the means of comfort, speaking peace to the soul. This testimony is always agreeable to the written word, and is therefore always grounded upon sanctification; for the Spirit in the heart cannot contradict the Spirit in the word. The Spirit witnesses to none the privileges of children who have not the nature and disposition of children.

Verses 17–25

In these words the apostle describes a fourth illustrious branch of the happiness of believers, namely, a title to the future glory. This is fitly annexed to our sonship; for as the adoption of sons entitles us to that glory, so the disposition of sons fits and prepares us for it. *If children, then heirs, v.* 17. In earthly inheritances this rule does not hold, only the first-born are heirs; but the church is a church of first-born, for they are all heirs. Heaven is an inheritance that all the saints are heirs to. They do not come to it as purchasers by any merit or procurement of their own; but as heirs, purely by the act of God; for God makes heirs. The saints are heirs though in this world they are heirs under age; see Gal. 4:1, 2. Their present state is a state of education and preparation for the inheritance. How comfortable should this be to all the children of God, how little soever they have in possession, that, being heirs, they have enough in reversion! But the honour and happiness of an heir lie in the value and worth of that which he is heir to: we read of those that inherit the wind; and therefore we have here an abstract of the premises. 1. *Heirs of God.* The Lord himself is the portion of the saints' inheritance (Ps. 16:5), a goodly heritage, *v.* 6. The saints are spiritual priests, that have the Lord for their inheritance, Num. 18:20. The vision of God and the fruition of God make up the inheritance the saints are heirs to. God himself will be with them, and will be their God, Rev. 21:3. 2. *Joint-heirs with Christ.* Christ, as Mediator, is said to be the heir of all things (Heb. 1:2), and true believers, by virtue of their union with him, *shall inherit all things,* Rev. 21:7. Those that now partake of the Spirit of Christ, as his brethren, shall, as his brethren, partake of his glory (Jn. 17:24), shall sit down with him upon his throne, Rev. 3:21. Lord, what is man, that thou shouldst thus magnify him! Now this future glory is further spoken of as the reward of present sufferings and as the accomplishment of present hopes.

I. As the reward of the saints' present sufferings; and it is a rich reward: *If so be that we suffer with him* (*v.* 17), or *forasmuch as we suffer with him.* The state of the church in this world always is, but was then especially, an afflicted state; to be a Christian was certainly to be a sufferer. Now, to comfort them in reference to those sufferings, he tells them that they suffered with Christ — for his sake, for his honour, and for the testimony of a good conscience, and should be glorified with him. Those that suffered with David in his persecuted state were advanced by him and with him when he came to the crown; see 2 Tim. 2:12. See the gains of suffering for Christ; though we may be losers for him, we shall not, we cannot, be losers by him in the end. This the gospel is filled with the assurances of. Now, that suffering saints may have strong supports and consolations from their hopes of heaven, he holds the balance (*v.* 18), in a comparison between the two, which is observable. 1. In one scale he puts the *sufferings of this present time.* The sufferings of the saints are but sufferings of this present time, strike no deeper than the things of time, last no longer than the present time (2 Co. 4:17), light affliction, and but for a moment. So that on the sufferings he writes *tekel,* weighed in the balance and found light. 2. In the other scale he puts the glory, and finds that a weight, an exceeding and eternal weight: *Glory that shall be revealed.* In our present state we come short, not only in the enjoyment, but in the knowledge of that glory (1 Co. 2:9; 1 Jn. 3:2): it shall be revealed. It surpasses all that we have yet seen and known: present vouchsafements are sweet and precious, very precious, very sweet; but there is something to come, something behind the curtain, that will outshine all. *Shall be revealed in us;* not only revealed to us, to be seen, but revealed in us, to be enjoyed. The kingdom of God is within you, and will be so to eternity. 3. He concludes the sufferings *not worthy to be compared with the glory — ouk axia pros tēn doxan.* They cannot merit that glory; and, if suffering for Christ will not merit, much less will doing. They should not at all deter and frighten us from the diligent and earnest pursuit of that glory. The sufferings are small and short, and concern the body only; but the glory is rich and great, and concerns the soul, and is eternal. This he reckons. *I reckon — logizomai.* It is not a rash and sudden determination, but the product of a very serious and deliberate consideration. he had reasoned the case within himself, weighed the arguments on both sides, and thus at last resolves the point. O how vastly different is the sentence of the word from the sentiment of the world concerning the sufferings of this present time! *I reckon,* as an arithmetician that is balancing an account. He first sums up what is disbursed for Christ in the sufferings of this present time, and finds they come to very little; he then sums up what is secured to us by Christ in the glory that shall be revealed, and this he finds to be an infinite sum, transcending all conception, the disbursement abundantly made up and the losses infinitely countervailed. And who would be afraid then to suffer for Christ, who as he is before-hand with us in suffering, so he will not be behind-hand with us in recompence? Now Paul was as competent a judge of this point as ever any mere man was. He could reckon not by art only, but by experience; for he knew both. He knew what the sufferings of this present time were; see 2 Co. 11:23–28. He knew what the glory of heaven is; see 2 Co. 12:3, 4. And, upon the view of both, he gives this judgment here. There is nothing like a believing view of the glory which shall be revealed to support and bear up the spirit under all the sufferings of this present time. The reproach of Christ appears riches to those who have respect to the recompence of reward, Heb. 11:26.

II. As the accomplishment of the saints' present hopes and expectations, *v.* 19, etc. As the saints are suffering for it, so they are waiting for it. Heaven is therefore sure; for God by his Spirit would not raise and encourage those hopes only to defeat and disappoint them. He will establish that word unto his servants on which he has caused them to hope (Ps. 119:49), and heaven is therefore sweet; for, if hope deferred makes the heart sick, surely when the desire comes it will be a tree of life, Prov. 13:12. Now he observes an expectation of this glory,

1. In the creatures *v.* 19–22. That must needs be a great, a transcendent glory, which all the creatures are so earnestly expecting and longing for. This observation in these verses has some difficulty in it, which puzzles interpreters a little; and the more because it is a remark not made in any other scripture, with which it might be compared. By the *creature* here we understand, not as some do the Gentile world, and their expectation of Christ and the gospel, which is an exposition very foreign and forced, but the whole frame of nature, especially that of this lower world — the whole creation, the compages of inanimate and sensible creatures, which, because of their harmony and mutual dependence, and because they all constitute and make up one world, are spoken of in the singular number as the *creature.* The sense of the apostle in these four verses we may take in the following observations: — (1.) That there is a present vanity to which the creature, by reason of the sin of man, is made subject, *v.* 20. When man sinned, the ground was cursed for man's sake, and with it all the creatures (especially of this lower world, where our acquaintance lies) became subject to that curse, became mutable and mortal. *Under the bondage of corruption, v.* 21. There is an impurity, deformity, and infirmity, which the creature has contracted by the fall of man: the creation is sullied and stained, much of the beauty of the world gone. There is an enmity of one creature to another; they are all subject to continual alteration and decay of the individuals, liable to the strokes of God's judgments upon man. When the world was drowned, and almost all the creatures in it, surely then it was subject to vanity indeed. The whole species of creatures is designed for, and is hastening to, a total dissolution by fire. And it is not the least part of their vanity and bondage that they are used, or abused rather, by men as instruments of sin. The creatures are often abused to the dishonour of their Creator, the hurt of his children, or the service of his enemies. When the creatures are made the food and fuel of our lusts, they are subject to vanity, they are captivated by the law of sin. And this *not willingly,* not of their own choice. All the creatures desire their own perfection and consummation; when they are made instruments of sin it is not willingly. Or, They are thus captivated, not for any sin of their own, which they had committed, but for man's sin: *By reason of him who hath subjected the same.* Adam did it meritoriously; the creatures being delivered to him, when he by sin delivered himself he delivered them likewise into the bondage of corruption. God did it judicially; he passed a sentence upon the creatures for the sin of man, by which they became subject. And this yoke (poor creatures) they bear in hope that it will not be so always. *Ep' elpidi hoti kai,* etc. — *in hope that the creature itself;* so many Greek copies join the words. We have reason to pity the poor creatures that for our sin have become subject to vanity. (2.) That the creatures *groan and travail in pain* together under this vanity and corruption, *v.* 22. It is a figurative expression. Sin is a burden to the whole creation; the sin of the Jews, in crucifying Christ, set the earth a quaking under them. The idols were a burden to the weary beast, Isa. 46:1. There is a general outcry of the whole creation against the sin of man: the stone crieth out of the wall (Hab. 2:11), the land cries, Job 31:38. (3.) That the creature, that is now thus burdened, shall, at the time of the restitution of all things, be *delivered from this bondage into the glorious liberty of the children of God* (*v.* 21) — they shall no more be subject to vanity and corruption, and the other fruits of the curse; but, on the contrary, this lower world shall be renewed: when there will be new heavens there will be a new earth (2 Pt. 3:13; Rev. 21:1); and there shall be a glory conferred upon all the creatures, which shall be (in the proportion of their natures) as suitable and as great an advancement as the glory of the children of God shall be to them. The fire at the last day shall be a refining, not a destroying annihilating fire. What becomes of the souls of brutes, that go downwards, none can tell. But it should seem by the scripture that there will be some kind of restoration of them. And if it be objected, What use will they be of to glorified saints? we may suppose them of as much use as they were to Adam in innocency; and if it be only to illustrate the wisdom, power, and goodness of their Creator, that is enough. Compare with this Ps. 96:10–13; 98:7–9. *Let the heavens rejoice before the Lord, for he cometh.* (4.) That the creature doth therefore earnestly expect and wait for the *manifestation of the children of God, v.* 19. Observe, At the second coming of Christ there will be a manifestation of the children of God. Now the saints are God's hidden ones, the wheat seems lost in a heap of chaff; but then they shall be manifested. It does not yet appear what we shall be (1 Jn. 3:2), but then the glory shall be revealed. The children of God shall appear in their own colours. And this redemption of the creature is reserved till then; for, as it was with man and for man that they fell under the curse, so with man and for man they shall be delivered. All the curse and filth that now adhere to the creature shall be done away then when those that have suffered with Christ upon earth shall reign with him upon the earth. This the whole creation looks and longs for; and it may serve as a reason why now a good man should be merciful to his beast.

2. In the saints, who are new creatures, *v.* 23–25. Observe, (1.) The grounds of this expectation in the saints. It is our having received *the first-fruits of the Spirit,* which both quickens our desires and encourages our hopes, and both ways raises our expectations. The first-fruits did both sanctify and ensure the lump. Grace is the first-fruits of glory, it is glory begun. We, having received such clusters in this wilderness, cannot but long for the full vintage in the heavenly Canaan. *Not only they* — not only the creatures which are not capable of such a happiness as the first-fruits of the Spirit, but even we, who have such present rich receivings, cannot but long for something more and greater. In having the first-fruits of the Spirit we have that which is very precious, but we have not all we would have. *We groan within ourselves,* which denotes the strength and secrecy of these desires; not making a loud noise, as the hypocrites howling upon the bed for corn and wine, but with silent groans, which pierce heaven soonest of all. Or, *We groan among ourselves.* It is the unanimous vote, the joint desire, of the whole church, all agree in this: *Come, Lord Jesus, come quickly.* The groaning denotes a very earnest and importunate desire, the soul pained with the delay. Present receivings and comforts are consistent with a great many groans; not as the pangs of one dying, but as the throes of a woman in travail — groans that are symptoms of life, not of death. (2.) The object of this expectation. What is it we are thus desiring and waiting for? What would we have? *The adoption, to wit, the redemption of our body.* Though the soul be the principal part of the man, yet the Lord has declared himself for the body also, and has provided a great deal of honour and happiness for the body. The resurrection is here called *the redemption of the body.* It shall then be rescued from the power of death and the grave, and the bondage of corruption; and, though a vile body, yet it shall be refined and beautified, and made like that glorious body of Christ, Phil. 3:21; 1 Co. 15:42. This is called *the adoption.* [1.] It is the adoption manifested before all the world, angels and men. Now are we the sons of God, but it does not yet appear, the honour is now clouded; but then God will publicly own all his children. The deed of adoption, which is now written, signed, and sealed, will then be recognized, proclaimed, and published. As Christ was, so the saints will be, declared to be the sons of God with power, by the resurrection from the dead, *ch.* 1:4. It will then be put past dispute. [2.] It is the adoption perfected and completed. The children of God have bodies as well as souls; and, till those bodies are brought into the glorious liberty of the children of God, the adoption is not perfect. But then it will be complete, when the Captain of our salvation shall bring the many sons to glory, Heb. 2:10. This is that which we expect, in hope of which our flesh rests, Ps. 16:9, 10. All the days of our appointed time we are waiting, till this change shall come, when he shall call, and we shall answer, and he will have a desire to the work of his hands, Job 14:14, 15. (3.) The agreeableness of this to our present state, *v.* 24, 25. Our happiness is not in present possession: *We are saved by hope.* In this, as in other things, God hath made our present state a state of trial and probation — that our reward is out of sight. Those that will deal with God must deal upon trust. It is acknowledged that one of the principal graces of a Christian is hope (1 Co. 13:13), which necessarily implies a good thing to come, which is the object of that hope. Faith respects the promise, hope the thing promised. Faith is the evidence, hope the expectation, of things not seen. Faith is the mother of hope. *We do with patience wait.* In hoping for this glory we have need of patience, to bear the sufferings we meet with in the way to it and the delays of it. Our way is rough and long; but he that shall come will come, and will not tarry; and therefore, though he seem to tarry, it becomes us to wait for him.

Verses 26–28

The apostle here suggests two privileges more to which true Christians are entitled: —

I. The help of the Spirit in prayer. While we are in this world, hoping and waiting for what we see not, we must be praying. Hope supposes desire, and that desire offered up to God is prayer; we groan. Now observe,

1. Our weakness in prayer: *We know not what we should pray for as we ought.* (1.) As to the matter of our requests, we know not what to ask. We are not competent judges of our own condition. *Who knows what is good for a man in this life?* Eccl. 6:12. We are short-sighted, and very much biassed in favour of the flesh, and apt to separate the end from the way. *You know not what you ask,* Mt. 20:22. We are like foolish children, that are ready to cry for fruit before it is ripe and fit for them; see Lu. 9:54, 55. (2.) As to the manner, we know not how to pray as we ought. It is not enough that we do that which is good, but we must do it well, seek in a due order; and here we are often at a loss — graces are weak, affections cold, thoughts wandering, and it is not always easy to *find the heart to pray,* 2 Sa. 7:27. The apostle speaks of this in the first person: *We know not.* He puts himself among the rest. Folly, and weakness, and distraction in prayer, are what all the saints are complaining of. If so great a saint as Paul knew not what to pray for, what little reason have we to go forth about that duty in our own strength!

2. The assistances which the Spirit gives us in that duty. He *helps our infirmities,* meant especially of our praying infirmities, which most easily beset us in that duty, against which the Spirit helps. The Spirit in the world helps; many rules and promises there are in the word for our help. The Spirit in the heart helps, dwelling in us, working in us, as a Spirit of grace and supplication, especially with respect to the infirmities we are under when we are in a suffering state, when our faith is most apt to fail; for this end the Holy Ghost was poured out. *Helpeth, synantilambanetai — heaves with us, over against us,* helps as we help one that would lift up a burden, by lifting over against him at the other end — helps with us, that is, with us doing our endeavour, putting forth the strength we have. We must not sit still, and expect that the Spirit should do all; when the Spirit goes before us we must bestir ourselves. We cannot without God, and he will not without us. What help? Why, the *Spirit itself makes inter-*

cession for us, dictates our requests, indites our petitions, draws up our plea for us. Christ intercedes for us in heaven, the Spirit intercedes for us in our hearts; so graciously has God provided for the encouragement of the praying remnant. The Spirit, as an enlightening Spirit, teaches us what to pray for, as a sanctifying Spirit works and excites praying graces, as a comforting Spirit silences our fears, and helps us over all our discouragements. The Holy Spirit is the spring of all our desires and breathings towards God. Now this intercession which the Spirit makes is, (1.) *With groanings that cannot be uttered.* The strength and fervency of those desires which the Holy Spirit works are hereby intimated. There may be praying in the Spirit where there is not a word spoken; as Moses prayed (Ex. 14:15), and Hannah, 1 Sa. 1:13. It is not the rhetoric and eloquence, but the faith and fervency, of our prayers, that the Spirit works, as an intercessor, in us. *Cannot be uttered;* they are so confused, the soul is in such a hurry with temptations and troubles, we know not what to say, nor how to express ourselves. Here is the Spirit interceding with groans that cannot be uttered. When we can but cry, *Abba, Father,* and refer ourselves to him with a holy humble boldness, this is the work of the Spirit. (2.) *According to the will of God, v.* 27. The Spirit in the heart never contradicts the Spirit in the word. Those desires that are contrary to the will of God do not come from the Spirit. The Spirit interceding in us evermore melts our wills into the will of God. *Not as I will, but as thou wilt.*

3. The sure success of these intercessions: *He that searches the heart knoweth what is the mind of the Spirit, v.* 27. To a hypocrite, all whose religion lies in his tongue, nothing is more dreadful than that God searches the heart and sees through all his disguises. To a sincere Christian, who makes heart-work of his duty, nothing is more comfortable than that God searches the heart, for then he will hear and answer those desires which we want words to express. He knows what we have need of before we ask, Mt. 6:8. He knows what is the mind of his own Spirit in us. And, as he always hears the Son interceding for us, so he always hears the Spirit interceding in us, because his intercession is according to the will of God. What could have been done more for the comfort of the Lord's people, in all their addresses to God? Christ had said, "Whatever you ask the Father according to his will he will give it you." But how shall we learn to ask according to his will? Why, the Spirit will teach us that. Therefore it is that the seed of Jacob never seek in vain.

II. The concurrence of all providences for the good of those that are Christ's, *v.* 28. It might be objected that, notwithstanding all these privileges, we see believers compassed about with manifold afflictions; though the Spirit makes intercession for them, yet their troubles are continued. It is very true; but in this the Spirit's intercession is always effectual, that, however it goes with them, all this is working together for their good. Observe here.

1. The character of the saints, who are interested in this privilege; they are here described by such properties as are common to all that are truly sanctified. (1.) *They love God.* This includes all the out-goings of the soul's affections towards God as the chief good and highest end. It is our love to God that makes every providence sweet, and therefore profitable. Those that love God make the best of all he does, and take all in good part. (2.) *They are the called according to his purpose,* effectually called according to the eternal purpose. The call is effectual, not according to any merit or desert of ours, but according to God's own gracious purpose.

2. The privilege of the saints, that *all things work together for good to them,* that is, all the providences of God that concern them. All that God performs he performs for them, Ps. 57:2. Their sins are not of his performing, therefore not intended here, though his permitting sin is made to work for their good, 2 Chr. 32:31. But all the providences of God are theirs — merciful providences, afflicting providences, personal, public. They are all for good; perhaps for temporal good, as Joseph's troubles; at least, for spiritual and eternal good. That is good for them which does their souls good. Either directly or indirectly, every providence has a tendency to the spiritual good of those that love God, breaking them off from sin, bringing them nearer to God, weaning them from the world, fitting them for heaven. *Work together.* They work, as physic works upon the body, various ways, according to the intention of the physician; but all for the patient's good. *They work together,* as several ingredients in a medicine concur to answer the intention. God hath set the one over against the other (Eccl. 7:14): *synergei,* a very singular, with a noun plural, denoting the harmony of Providence and its uniform designs, all the wheels as one wheel, Eze. 10:13. *He worketh all things together for good;* so some read it. It is not from any specific quality in the providences themselves, but from the power and grace of God working in, with, and by, these providences. All this *we know* — know it for a certainty, from the word of God, from our own experience, and from the experience of all the saints.

Verses 29–30

The apostle, having reckoned up so many ingredients of the happiness of true believers, comes here to represent the ground of them all, which he lays in predestination. These precious privileges are conveyed to us by the charter of the covenant, but they are founded in the counsel of God, which infallibly secures the event. That Jesus Christ, the purchaser, might not labour in vain, nor spend his strength and life for nought and in vain, there is a remnant given him, a seed that he shall see, so that the good pleasure of the Lord shall prosper in his hands. For the explication of this he here sets before us the order of the causes of our salvation, a golden chain, which cannot be broken. There are four links of it: —

I. *Whom he did foreknow he also did predestinate to be conformed to the image of his Son.* All that God designed for glory and happiness as the end he decreed to grace and holiness as the way. Not, whom he did foreknow to be holy those he predestinated to be so. The counsels and decrees of God do not truckle to the frail and fickle will of men; no, God's foreknowledge of the saints is the same with that everlasting love wherewith he is said to have loved them, Jer. 31:3. God's knowing his people is the same with his owning them, Ps. 1:6; Jn. 10:14; 2 Tim. 2:19. See *ch.* 11:2. Words of knowledge often in scripture denote affection; so here: *Elect according to the foreknowledge of God,* 1 Pt. 1:2. And the same word is rendered *fore-ordained,* 1 Pt. 1:20. *Whom he did foreknow,* that is, whom he designed for his friends and favourites. *I know thee by name,* said God to Moses, Ex. 33:12. Now those whom god thus foreknew he did predestinate to be conformed to Christ. 1. Holiness consists in our conformity to the image of Christ. This takes in the whole of sanctification, of which Christ is the great pattern and sampler. To be spirited as Christ was, to walk and live as Christ did, to bear our sufferings patiently as Christ did. Christ is the express image of his Father, and the saints are conformed to the image of Christ. Thus it is by the mediation and interposal of Christ that we have God's love restored to us and God's likeness renewed upon us, in which two things consists the happiness of man. 2. All that God hath from eternity foreknown with favour he hath predestinated to this conformity. It is not we that can conform ourselves to Christ. Our giving ourselves to Christ takes rise in God's giving us to him; and, in giving us to him, he predestinated us to be conformable to his image. It is a mere cavil therefore to call the doctrine of election a licentious doctrine, and to argue that it gives encouragement to sin, as if the end were separated from the way and happiness from holiness. None can know their election but by their conformity to the image of Christ; for all that are chosen are chosen to sanctification (2 Th. 2:13), and surely it cannot be a temptation to any to be conformed to the world to believe that they were predestinated to be conformed to Christ. 3. That which is herein chiefly designed is the honour of Jesus Christ, that he might be the *first-born among many brethren;* that is, that Christ might have the honour of being the great pattern, as well as the great prince, and in this, as in other things, might have pre-eminence. It was in the first-born that all the children were dedicated to God under the law. The first-born was the head of the family, on whom all the rest did depend: now in the family of the saints Christ must have the honour of being the first-born. And blessed be God that there are many brethren; though they seem but a few in one place at one time, yet, when they come all together, they will be a great many. There is, therefore, a certain number predestinated, that the end of Christ's undertaking might be infallibly secured. Had the event been left at uncertainties in the divine counsels, to depend upon the contingent turn of man's will, Christ might have been the first-born among but few or no brethren — a captain without soldiers and a prince without subjects — to prevent which, and to secure to him many brethren, the decree is absolute, the thing ascertained, that he might be sure to see his seed, there is a remnant predestinated to be conformed to his image, which decree will certainly have its accomplishment in the holiness and happiness of that chosen race; and so, in spite of all the opposition of the powers of darkness, Christ will be the first-born among many, very many brethren.

II. *Whom he did predestinate those he also called,* not only with the external call (so many are called that were not chosen, Mt. 20:16; 22:14), but with the internal and effectual call. The former comes to the ear only, but this to the heart. All that God did from eternity predestinate to grace and glory he does, in the fulness of time, effectually call. The call is then effectual when we come at the call; and we then come at the call when the Spirit draws us, convinces the conscience of guilt and wrath, enlightens the understanding, bows the will, persuades and enables us to embrace Christ in the promises, makes us willing in the day of his power. It is an effectual call from self and earth to God, and Christ, and heaven, as our end — from sin and vanity to grace, and holiness, and seriousness as our way. This is the gospel call. *Them he called,* that the purpose of God, according to election, might stand: we are called to that to which we were chosen. So that the only way to make our election sure is to make sure our calling, 2 Pt. 1:10.

III. *Whom he called those he also justified.* All that are effectually called are justified, absolved from guilt, and accepted as righteous through Jesus Christ. They are *recti in curia — right in court;* no sin that ever they have been guilty of shall come against them, to condemn them. The book is crossed, the bond cancelled, the judgment vacated, the attainder reversed; and they are no longer dealt with as criminals, but owned and loved as friends and favourites. Blessed is the man whose iniquity is thus forgiven. None are thus justified but those that are effectually called. Those that stand it out against the gospel call abide under guilt and wrath.

IV. *Whom he justified those he also glorified.* The power of corruption being broken in effectual calling, and the guilt of sin removed in justification, all that which hinders is taken out of the way, and nothing can come between that soul and glory. Observe, It is spoken of as a thing done: *He glorified,* because of the certainty of it; he *hath* saved us, and called us with a holy calling. In the eternal glorification of all the elect, God's design of love has its full accomplishment. This was what he aimed at all along — to bring them to heaven. Nothing less than that glory would make up the fulness of his covenant relation to them as God; and therefore, in all he does for them, and in them, he has this in his eye. Are they chosen? It is to salvation. Called? It is to his kingdom and glory. Begotten again? It is to an inheritance incorruptible. Afflicted: It is to work for them this exceeding and eternal weight of glory. Observe, The author of all these is the same. It is God himself that predestinated, calleth, justifieth, glorifieth; so *the Lord alone did lead him, and there was no strange God with him.* Created wills are so very fickle, and created powers so very feeble, that, if any of these did depend upon the creature, the whole would shake. But God himself hath undertaken the doing of it from first to last, that we might abide in a constant dependence upon him and subjection to him, and ascribe all the praise to him — that every crown may be cast before the throne. This is a mighty encouragement to our faith and hope; for, as for God, his way, his work, is perfect. He that hath laid the foundation will build upon it, and the top-stone will at length be brought forth with shoutings, and it will be our eternal work to cry, Grace, grace to it.

Verses 31–39

The apostle closes this excellent discourse upon the privileges of believers with a holy triumph, in the name of all the saints. Having largely set forth the mystery of God's love to us in Christ, and the exceedingly great and precious privileges we enjoy by him, he concludes like an orator: *What shall we then say to these things?* What use shall we make of all that has been said? He speaks as one amazed and swallowed up with the contemplation and admiration of it, wondering at the height and depth, and length and breadth, of the love of Christ, which passeth knowledge. The more we know of other things the less we wonder at them; but the further we are led into an acquaintance with gospel mysteries the more we are affected with the admiration of them. If Paul was at a loss what to say to these things, no marvel if we be. And what does he say? Why, if ever Paul rode in a triumphant chariot on this side of heaven, here it was: with such a holy height and bravery of spirit, with such a fluency and copiousness of expression, does he here comfort himself and all the people of God, upon the consideration of these privileges. In general, he here makes a challenge, throws down the gauntlet, as it were, dares all the enemies of the saints to do their worst: *If God be for us, who can be against us?* The ground of the challenge is God's being for us; in this he sums up all our privileges. This includes all, that *God is for us;* not only reconciled to us, and so not against us, but in covenant with us, and so engaged for us — all his attributes for us, his promises for us. All that he is, and has, and does, is for his people. He performs all things for them. He is for them, even when he seems to act against them. And, if so, *who can be against us,* so as to prevail against us, so as to hinder our happiness? Be they ever so great and strong, ever so many, ever so might, ever so malicious, what can they do? While God is for us, and we keep in his love, we may with a holy boldness defy all the powers of darkness. Let Satan do his worst, he is chained; let the world do its worst, it is conquered: principalities and powers are spoiled and disarmed, and triumphed over, in the cross of Christ. Who then dares fight against us, while God himself is fighting for us? And this we say to these things, this is the inference we draw from these premises. More particularly.

I. We have supplies ready in all our wants (*v.* 32): *He that spared,* etc. Who can be against us, to strip us, to deprive us of our comforts? Who can cut off our streams, while we have a fountain to go to? 1. Observe what God has done for us, on which our hopes are built: *He spared not his own Son.* When he was to undertake our salvation, the Father was willing to part with him, did not think him too precious a gift to bestow for the salvation of poor souls; now we may know that he loves us, in that he hath not withheld his Son, his own Son, his only Son, from us, as he said of Abraham, Gen. 22:12. If nothing less will save man, rather than man shall perish let him go, though it were out of his bosom. Thus did he *deliver him up for us all,* that is, for all the elect; *for us all,* not only for our good, but in our stead, as a sacrifice of atonement to be a propitiation for sin. When he had undertaken it, he did not spare him. Though he was his own Son, yet, being made sin for us, it pleased the Lord to bruise him. ***Ouk epheisato*** *— he did not abate* him a farthing of that great debt, but charged it home. *Awake, O sword.* He did not *spare his own Son that served him,* that he might spare us, though we have done him so much disservice. 2. What we may therefore expect he will do: He will *with him freely give us all things.* (1.) It is implied that he will give us Christ, for other things are bestowed with him: not only with him given for us, but with him given to us. He that put himself to so much charge to make the purchase for us surely will not hesitate at making the application to us. (2.) He will with him freely give us all things, all things that he sees to be needful and necessary for us, all good things, and more we should not desire, Ps. 34:10. And Infinite Wisdom shall be the judge whether it be good for us and needful for us or no. *Freely give* — freely, without reluctancy; he is ready to give, meets us with his favours; — and freely, without recompence, without money, and without price. *How shall he not?* Can it be imagined that he should do the greater and not do the less? that he should give so great a gift for us when we were enemies, and should deny us any good thing, now that through him we are friends and children? Thus may we by faith argue against our fears of want. he that hath prepared a crown and kingdom for us will be sure to give us enough to bear our charges in the way to it. He that hath designed us for the inheritance of sons when we come to age will not let us want necessaries in the mean time.

II. We have an answer ready to all accusations and a security against all condemnations (*v.* 33, 34): *Who shall lay any thing?* Doth the law accuse them? Do their own consciences accuse them? Is the devil, the accuser of the brethren, accusing them before our God day and night? This is enough to answer all those accusations, *It is God that justifieth.* Men may justify themselves, as the Pharisees did, and yet the accusations may be in full force against them; but, if God justifies, this answers all. He is the judge, the king, the party offended, and his judgment is according to truth, and sooner or later all the world will be brought to be of his mind; so that we may challenge all our accusers to come and put in their charge. This overthrows them all; it is God, the righteous faithful God, that justifieth. *Who is he that condemneth?* Though they cannot make good the charge yet they will be ready to condemn; but we have a plea ready to move in arrest of judgment, a plea which cannot be overruled. *It is Christ that died,* etc. It is by virtue of our interest in Christ, our relation to him, and our union with him, that we are thus secured. 1. His death: *It is Christ that died.* By the merit of his death he paid our debt; and the surety's payment is a good plea to an action of debt. It is Christ, an able all-sufficient Saviour. 2. His resurrection: *Yea, rather, that has risen again.* This is a much greater encouragement, for it is a convincing evidence that divine justice was satisfied by the merit of his death. His resurrection was his acquittance, it was a legal discharge. Therefore the apostle mentions it with a *yea, rather.* If he had died, and not risen again, we had been where we were. 3. His sitting at the right hand of God: He is *even at the right hand of God* — a further evidence that he has done his work, and a mighty encouragement to us in reference to all accusations, that we have a friend, such a friend, in court. At *the right hand of God,* which denotes that he is ready there — always at hand; and that he is ruling there — all power is given to him. Our friend is himself the judge. 4. The intercession which he makes there. He is there, not unconcerned about us, not forgetful of us, but *making intercession.* He is agent for us there, an advocate for us, to answer all accusations, to put in our plea, and to prosecute it with effect, to appear for us and to present our petitions. And is not this abundant matter for comfort? What shall we say to these things? Is this the manner of men, O Lord God? What room is left for doubting and disquietment? Why art thou cast down, O my soul? Some understand the accusation and condemnation here spoken of of that which the suffering saints met with from men. The primitive Christians had many black crimes laid to their charge — heresy, sedition, rebellion, and what not? For these the ruling powers condemned them: "But no matter for that" (says the apostle); "while we stand right at God's bar it is of no great moment how we stand at men's. To all the hard censures, the malicious calumnies, and the unjust and unrighteous sentences of men, we may with comfort oppose our justification before God through Christ Jesus as that which doth abundantly countervail," 1 Co. 4:3, 4.

III. We have good assurance of our preservation and continuance in this blessed state, *v.* 35, to the end. The fears of the saints lest they should lose their hold of Christ are often very discouraging and disquieting, and create them a great deal of disturbance; but here is that which may silence their fears, and still such storms, that nothing can separate them. We have here from the apostle,

1. A daring challenge to all the enemies of the saints to separate them, if they could, from the love of Christ. *Who shall?* None shall, *v.* 35–37. God having manifested his love in giving his own Son for us, and not hesitating at that, can we imagine that any thing else should divert or dissolve that love? Observe here,

(1.) The present calamities of Christ's beloved ones supposed — that they meet with *tribulation* on all hands, are in *distress,* know not which way to look for any succour and relief in this world, are followed with *persecution* from an angry malicious world that always hated those whom Christ loved, pinched with *famine,* and starved with *nakedness,* when stripped of all *creature-comforts,* exposed to the greatest *perils,* the *sword* of the magistrate drawn against them, ready to be sheathed in their bowels, bathed in their blood. Can a case be supposed more black and dismal? It is illustrated (*v.* 36) by a passage quoted from Ps. 44:22, *For thy sake we are killed all the day long,* which intimates that we are not to think strange, no not concerning the fiery bloody trial. We see the Old-Testament saints had the same lot; so persecuted they the prophets that were before us. *Killed all the day long,* that is, continually exposed to and expecting the fatal stroke. There is still every day, and all the day long, one or other of the people of God bleeding and dying under the rage of persecuting enemies. *Accounted as sheep for the slaughter;* they make no more of killing a Christian than of butchering a sheep. Sheep are killed, not because they are hurtful while they live, but because they are useful when they are dead. They kill the Christians to please themselves, to be food to their malice. *They eat up my people as they eat bread,* Ps. 14:4.

(2.) The inability of all these things to separate us from the love of Christ. Shall they, can they, do it? No, by no means. All this will not cut the bond of love and friendship that is between Christ and true believers. [1.] Christ doth not, will not, love us the less for all this. All these troubles are very consistent with the strong and constant love of the Lord Jesus. They are neither a cause nor an evidence of the abatement of his love. When Paul was whipped, and beaten, and imprisoned, and stoned, did Christ love him ever the less? Were his favours intermitted? his smiles any whit suspended? his visits more shy? By no means, but the contrary. These things separate us from the love of other friends. When Paul was brought before Nero all men forsook him, but then the Lord stood by him, 2 Tim. 4:16, 17. Whatever persecuting enemies may rob us of, they cannot rob us of the love of Christ, they cannot intercept his love-tokens, they cannot interrupt nor exclude his visits: and therefore, let them do their worst, they cannot make a true believer miserable. [2.] We do not, will not, love him the less for this; and that for this reason, because we do not think that he loves us the less. Charity thinks no evil, entertains no misgiving thoughts, makes no hard conclusions, no unkind constructions, takes all in good part that comes from love. A true Christian loves Christ never the less though he suffer for him, thinks never the worse of Christ through he lose all for him.

(3.) The triumph of believers in this (*v.* 37): *Nay, in all these things we are more than conquerors.*

[1.] We are conquerors: though killed all the day long, yet conquerors. A strange way of conquering, but it was Christ's way; thus he triumphed over principalities and powers in his cross. It is a surer and a nobler way of conquest by faith and patience than by fire and sword. The enemies have sometimes confessed themselves baffled and overcome by the invincible courage and constancy of the martyrs, who thus overcame the most victorious princes by not loving their lives to the death, Rev. 12:11.

[2.] We are more than conquerors. In our patiently bearing these trials we are not only conquerors, but more than conquerors, that is, triumphers. Those are more than conquerors that conquer, *First,* With little loss. Many conquests are dearly bought; but what do the suffering saints lose? Why, they lose that which the gold loses in the furnace, nothing but the dross. It is no great loss to lose things which are not — a body that is of the earth, earthy. *Secondly,* With great gain. The spoils are exceedingly rich; glory, honour, and peace, a crown of righteousness that fades not away. In this the suffering saints have triumphed; not only have not been separated from the love of Christ, but have been taken into the most sensible endearments and embraces of it. As afflictions abound, consolations much more abound, 2 Co. 1:5. There is one more than a conqueror, when pressed above measure. He that embraced the stake, and said, "Welcome the cross of Christ, welcome everlasting life," — he that dated his letter from the delectable orchard of the Leonine prison, — he that said, "In these flames I feel no more pain than if I were upon a bed of down," — she who, a little before her martyrdom, being asked how she did, said, "Well and merry, and going to heaven," — those that have gone smiling to the stake, and stood singing in the flames — these were more than conquerors.

[3.] It is only *through Christ that loved us,* the merit of his death taking the sting out of all these troubles, the Spirit of his grace strengthening us, and enabling us to bear them with holy courage and constancy, and coming in with special comforts and supports. Thus we are conquerors, not in our own strength, but in the grace that is in Christ Jesus. We are conquerors by virtue of our interest in Christ's victory. He hath overcome the world for us (Jn. 16:33), both the good things and the evil things of it; so that we have nothing to do but to pursue the victory, and to divide the spoil, and so are more than conquerors.

2. A direct and positive conclusion of the whole matter: *For I am persuaded, v.* 38, 39. It denotes a full, and strong, and affectionate persuasion, arising from the experience of the strength and sweetness of the divine love. And here he enumerates all those things which might be supposed likely to separate between Christ and believers, and concludes that it could not be done. (1.) *Neither death nor life* — neither the terrors of death on the one hand nor the comforts and pleasures of life on the other, neither the fear of death nor the hope of life. Or, We shall not be separated from that love either in death or in life. (2.) *Nor angels, nor principalities, nor powers.* Both the good angels and the bad are called principalities and powers: the good, Eph. 1:21; Col. 1:16; the bad, Eph. 6:12; Col. 2:15. And neither shall do it. The good angels will not, the bad shall not; and neither can. The good angels are engaged friends, the bad are restrained enemies. (3.) *Nor things present, nor things to come* — neither the sense of trou-

bles present nor the fear of troubles to come. Time shall not separate us, eternity shall not. Things present separate us from things to come, and things to come separate and cut us off from things present; but neither from the love of Christ, whose favour is twisted in with both present things and things to come. (4.) *Nor height, nor depth* — neither the height of prosperity and preferment, nor the depth of adversity and disgrace; nothing from heaven above, no storms, no tempests; nothing on earth below, no rocks, no seas, no dungeons. (5.) *Nor any other creature* — any thing that can be named or thought of. It will not, it cannot, separate us from the love of God, which is in Christ Jesus our Lord. It cannot cut off or impair our love to God, or God's to us; nothing does it, can do it, but sin. Observe, The love that exists between God and true believers is through Christ. He is the Mediator of our love: it is in and through him that God can love us and that we dare love God. This is the ground of the stedfastness of the love; therefore God rests in his love (Zep. 3:17), because Jesus Christ, in whom he loves us, is the same yesterday, to-day, and for ever.

Mr. Hugh Kennedy, an eminent Christian of Ayr, in Scotland, when he was dying, called for a Bible; but, finding his sight gone, he said, "Turn me to the eighty of the Romans, and set my finger at these words, *I am persuaded that neither death nor life,*" etc. "Now," said he, "is my finger upon them?" And, when they told him it was, without speaking any more, he said, "Now, God be with you, my children; I have breakfasted with you, and shall sup with my Lord Jesus Christ this night;" and so departed.

CHAPTER 9

The apostle, having plainly asserted and largely proved that justification and salvation are to had by faith only, and not by the works of the law, by Christ and not by Moses, comes in this and the following chapters to anticipate an objection which might be made against this. If this be so, then what becomes of the Jews, of them all as a complex body, especially those of them that do not embrace Christ, nor believe the gospel? By this rule they must needs come short of happiness; and then what becomes of the promise made to the fathers, which entailed salvation upon the Jews? Is not that promise nullified and made of none effect? Which is not a thing to be imagined concerning any word of God. That doctrine therefore, might they say, is not to be embraced, from which flows such a consequence as this. That the consequence of the rejection of the unbelieving Jews follows from Paul's doctrine he grants, but endeavours to soften and mollify (*v.* 1–5). But that from this it follows that the word of God takes no effect he denies (*v.* 6), and proves the denial in the rest of the chapter, which serves likewise to illustrate the great doctrine of predestination, which he had spoken of (*ch.* 8:28) as the first wheel which in the business of salvation sets all the other wheels a-going.

Verses 1–5

We have here the apostle's solemn profession of a great concern for the nation and people of the Jews — that he was heartily troubled that so many of them were enemies to the gospel, and out of the way of salvation. For this he had *great heaviness and continual sorrow.* Such a profession as this was requisite to take off the odium which otherwise he might have contracted by asserting and proving their rejection. It is wisdom as much as may be to mollify those truths which sound harshly and seem unpleasant: dip the nail in oil, it will drive the better. The Jews had a particular pique at Paul above any of the apostles, as appears by the history of the Acts, and therefore were the more apt to take things amiss of him, to prevent which he introduces his discourse with this tender and affectionate profession, that they might not think he triumphed or insulted over the rejected Jews or was pleased with the calamities that were coming upon them. Thus Jeremiah appeals to God concerning the Jews of his day, whose ruin was hastening on (Jer. 17:16), *Neither have I desired the woeful day, thou knowest.* Nay, Paul was so far from desiring it that he most pathetically deprecates it. And lest this should be thought only a copy of his countenance, to flatter and please them,

I. He asserts it with a solemn protestation (*v.* 1): *I say the truth in Christ,* "I speak it as a Christian, one of God's people, children that will not lie, as one that knows not how to give flattering title." Or, "I appeal to Christ, who searches the heart, concerning it." He appeals likewise to his own conscience, which was instead of a thousand witnesses. That which he was going to assert was not only a great and weighty thing (such solemn protestations are not to be thrown away upon trifles), but it was likewise a secret; it was concerning a sorrow in his heart to which none was a capable competent witness but God and his own conscience. — *That I have great heaviness, v.* 2. He does not say for what; the very mention of it was unpleasant and invidious; but it is plain that he means for the rejection of the Jews.

II. He backs it with a very serious imprecation, which he was ready to make, out of love to the Jews. *I could wish;* he does not say, I do wish, for it was no proper means appointed for such an end; but, if it were, *I could wish that myself were accursed from Christ for my brethren* — a very high pang of zeal and affection for his countrymen. He would be willing to undergo the greatest misery to do them good. Love is apt to be thus bold, and venturous, and self-denying. Because the glory of God's grace in the salvation of many is to be preferred before the welfare and happiness of a single person, Paul, if they were put in competition, would be content to forego all his own happiness to purchase theirs. 1. He would be content to be cut off from the land of the living, in the most shameful and ignominious manner, as an anathema, or a devoted person. They thirsted for his blood, persecuted him as the most obnoxious person in the world, the curse and plague of his generation, 1 Co. 4:13; Acts 22:22. "Now," says Paul, "I am willing to bear all this, and a great deal more, for your good. Abuse me as much as you will, count and call me at your pleasure; your unbelief and rejection create in my heart a heaviness so much greater than all these troubles can that I could look upon them not only as tolerable, but as desirable, rather than this rejection." 2. He would be content to be excommunicated from the society of the faithful, to be separated from the church, and from the communion of saints, as a heathen man and a publican, if that would do them any good. he could wish himself no more remembered among the saints, his name blotted out of the church-records; though he had been so great a planter of churches, and the spiritual father of so many thousands, yet he would be content to be disowned by the church, cut off from all communion with it, and have his name buried in oblivion or reproach, for the good of the Jews. It may be, some of the Jews had a prejudice against Christianity for Paul's sake; such a spleen they had at him that they hated the religion he was of: "If this stumble you," says Paul, "I could wish I might be cast out, not embraced as a Christian, so you might but be taken in." Thus Moses (Ex. 32:33), in a like holy passion of concern, *Blot me, I pray thee, out of the book which thou hast written.* 3. Nay, some think that the expression goes further, and that he could be content to be cut off from all his share of happiness in Christ, if that might be a means of their salvation. It is a common charity that begins at home; this is something higher, and more noble and generous.

III. He gives us the reason of this affection and concern. 1. Because of their relation to them: *My brethren, my kinsmen, according to the flesh.* Though they were very bitter against him upon all occasions, and gave him the most unnatural and barbarous usage, yet thus respectfully does he speak of them. It shows him to be a man of a forgiving spirit. *Not that I had aught to accuse my nation of,* Acts 28:19. *My kinsmen.* Paul was a Hebrew of the Hebrews. We ought to be in a special manner concerned for the spiritual good of our relations, our brethren and kinsmen. To them we lie under special engagements, and we have more opportunity of doing good to them; and concerning them, and our usefulness to them, we must in a special manner give account.

2. Especially because of their relation to God (*v.* 4, 5): *Who are Israelites,* the seed of Abraham, God's friend, and of Jacob his chosen, taken into the covenant of peculiarity, dignified and distinguished by visible church-privileges, many of which are here mentioned: — (1.) *The adoption;* not that which is saving, and which entitled to eternal happiness, but that which was external and typical, and entitled them to the land of Canaan. *Israel is my son,* Ex. 4:22. (2.) *And the glory;* the ark with the mercy-seat, over which God dwelt between the cherubim — this was the glory of Israel, 1 Sa. 4:21. The many symbols and tokens of the divine presence and guidance, the cloud, the Shechinah, the distinguishing favours conferred upon them — these were the glory. (3.) *And the covenants* — the covenant made with Abraham, and often renewed with his seed upon divers occasions. There was a covenant at Sinai (Ex. 24), in the plains of Moab (Deu. 29), at Shechem (Jos. 24), and often afterwards; and still these pertained to Israel. Or, the covenant of peculiarity, and in that, as in the type, the covenant of grace. (4.) *And the giving of the law.* It was to them that the ceremonial and judicial law were given, and the moral law in writing pertained to them. It is a great privilege to have the law of God among us, and it is to be accounted so, Ps. 147:19, 20. This was the grandeur of Israel, Deu. 4:7, 8. (5.) *And the service of God.* They had the ordinances of God's worship among them — the temple, the altars, the priests, the sacrifices, the feasts, and the institutions relating to them. They were in this respect greatly honoured, that, while other nations were worshipping and serving stocks, and stones, and devils, and they knew not what other idols of their own invention, the Israelites were serving the true God in the way of his own appointment. (6.) *And the promises* — particular promises added to the general covenant, promises relating to the Messiah and the gospel state. Observe, The promises accompany the giving of the law, and the service of God; for the comfort of the promises is to be had in obedience to that law and attendance upon that service. (7.) *Whose are the fathers* (*v.* 5), Abraham, Isaac, and Jacob, those men of renown, that stood so high in the favour of God. The Jews stand in relation to them, are their children, and proud enough they are of it: *We have Abraham to our father.* It was for the father's sake that they were taken into covenant, *ch.* 11:28. (8.) But the greatest honour of all was that *of them as concerning the flesh* (that is, as to his human nature) *Christ came;* for he took on him the seed of Abraham, Heb. 2:16. As to his divine nature, he is the Lord from heaven; but, as to his human nature, he is of the seed of Abraham. This was the great privilege of the Jews, that Christ was of kin to them. Mentioning Christ, he interposes a very great word concerning him, that he is *over all, God blessed for ever.* Lest the Jews should think meanly of him, because he was of their alliance, he here speaks thus honourably concerning him: and it is a very full proof of the Godhead of Christ; he is not only over all, as Mediator, but he is God blessed for ever. Therefore, how much sorer punishment were they worthy of that rejected him! It was likewise the honour of the Jews, and one reason why Paul had a kindness for them, that, seeing God blessed for ever would be a man, he would be a Jew; and, considering the posture and character of that people at that time, it may well be looked upon as a part of his humiliation.

Verses 6–13

The apostle, having made his way to that which he had to say, concerning the rejection of the body of his countrymen, with a protestation of his own affection for them and a concession of their undoubted privileges, comes in these verses, and the following part of the chapter, to prove that the rejection of the Jews, by the establishment of the gospel dispensation, did not at all invalidate the word of God's promise to the patriarchs: *Not as though the word of God hath taken no effect* (*v.* 6), which, considering the present state of the Jews, which created to Paul so much *heaviness and continual sorrow* (*v.* 2), might be suspected. We are not to ascribe inefficacy to any word of God: nothing that he has spoken does or can fall to the ground; see Isa. 55:10, 11. The promises and threatenings shall have their accomplishment; and, one way or other, he will magnify the law and make it honourable. This is to be understood especially of the promise of God, which by subsequent providences may be to a wavering faith very doubtful; but it is not, it cannot be, made of no effect; at the end it will speak and not lie.

Now the difficulty is to reconcile the rejection of the unbelieving Jews with the word of God's promise, and the external tokens of the divine favour, which had been conferred upon them. This he does in four ways: — 1. By explaining the true meaning and intention of the promise, *v.* 6–13. 2. By asserting and proving the absolute sovereignty of God, in disposing of the children of men, *v.* 14–24. 3. By showing how this rejection of the Jews, and the taking in of the Gentiles, were foretold in the Old Testament, *v.* 25–29. 4. By fixing the true reason of the Jews' rejection, *v.* 30, to the end.

In this paragraph the apostle explains the true meaning and intention of the promise. When we mistake the word, and misunderstand the promise, no marvel if we are ready to quarrel with God about the accomplishment; and therefore the sense of this must first be duly stated. Now he here makes it out that, when God said he would be *a God to Abraham, and to his seed* (which was the famous promise made unto the fathers), he did not mean it of all his seed according to the flesh, as if it were a necessary concomitant of the blood of Abraham; but that he intended it with a limitation only to such and such. And as from the beginning it was appropriated to Isaac and not to Ishmael, to Jacob and not to Esau, and yet for all this the word of God was not made of no effect; so now the same promise is appropriated to believing Jews that embrace Christ and Christianity, and, though it throws off multitudes that refuse Christ, yet the promise is not therefore defeated and invalidated, any more than it was by the typical rejection of Ishmael and Esau.

I. He lays down this proposition — that *they are not all Israel who are of Israel* (v. 6), *neither because they are,* etc. v. 7. Many that descended from the loins of Abraham and Jacob, and were of that people who were surnamed by the name of Israel, yet were very far from being Israelites indeed, interested in the saving benefits of the new covenant. They are not all really Israel that are so in name and profession. It does not follow that, because they are the seed of Abraham, therefore they must needs be the children of God, though they themselves fancied so, boasted much of, and built much upon, their relation to Abraham, Mt. 3:9; Jn. 8:38, 39. But it does not follow. Grace does not run in the blood; nor are saving benefits inseparably annexed to external church privileges, though it is common for people thus to stretch the meaning of God's promise, to bolster themselves up in a vain hope.

II. He proves this by instances; and therein shows not only that some of Abraham's seed were chosen, and others not, but that God therein wrought according to the counsel of his own will; and not with regard to that law of commandments to which the present unbelieving Jews were so strangely wedded.

1. He specifies the case of Isaac and Ishmael, both of them the seed of Abraham; and yet Isaac only taken into covenant with God, and Ishmael rejected and cast out. For this he quotes Gen. 21:12, *In Isaac shall thy seed be called,* which comes in there as a reason why Abraham must be willing to cast out the bond-woman and her son, because the covenant was to be established with Isaac, Gen. 17:19. And yet the word which God had spoken, that he would be a God to Abraham and to his seed, did not therefore fall to the ground; for the blessings wrapt up in that great word, being communicated by God as a benefactor, he was free to determine on what head they should rest, and accordingly entailed them upon Isaac, and rejected Ishmael. This he explains further (v. 8, 9), and shows what God intended to teach us by this dispensation. (1.) That the children of the flesh, as such, by virtue of their relation to Abraham according to the flesh, are not therefore the children of God, for then Ishmael had put in a good claim. This remark comes home to the unbelieving Jews, who boasted of their relation to Abraham according to the flesh, and looked for justification in a fleshly way, by those carnal ordinances which Christ had abolished. They had confidence in the flesh, and looked for justification in a fleshly way, by those carnal ordinances which Christ had abolished. They had confidence in the flesh, Phil. 3:3. Ishmael was a child of the flesh, conceived by Hagar, who was young and fresh, and likely enough to have children. There was nothing extraordinary or supernatural in his conception, as there was in Isaac's; he was born after the flesh (Gal. 4:29), representing those that expect justification and salvation by their own strength and righteousness. (2.) That the *children of the promise are counted for the seed.* Those that have the honour and happiness of being counted for the seed have it not for the sake of any merit or desert of their own, but purely by virtue of the promise, in which God hath obliged himself of his own good pleasure to grant the promised favour. Isaac was a child of promise; this his proves, v. 9, quoted from Gen. 18:10. he was a child promised (so were many others), and he was also conceived and born by force and virtue of the promise, and so a proper type and figure of those who are now counted for the seed, even true believers, who are born, not of the will of the flesh, nor of the will of man, but of God — of the incorruptible seed, even the word of promise, by virtue of the special promise of a new heart: see Gal. 4:28. It was through faith that Isaac was conceived, Heb. 11:11. Thus were the great mysteries of salvation taught under the Old Testament, not in express words, but by significant types and dispensations of providence, which to them then were not so clear as they are to us now, when the veil is taken away, and the types are expounded by the antitypes.

2. The case of Jacob and Esau (v. 10–13), which is much stronger, to show that the carnal seed of Abraham were not, as such, interested in the promise, but only such of them as God in sovereignty had appointed. There was a previous difference between Ishmael and Isaac, before Ishmael was cast out: Ishmael was the son of the bond-woman, born long before Isaac, was of a fierce and rugged disposition, and had mocked or persecuted Isaac, to all which it might be supposed God had regard when he appointed Abraham to cast him out. But, in the case of Jacob and Esau, it was neither so nor so, they were both the sons of Isaac by one mother; they were conceived *hex henos — by one conception; hex henos koitou,* so some copies read it. The difference was made between them by the divine counsel before they were born, or had done any good or evil. Both lay struggling alike in their mother's womb, when it was said, *The elder shall serve the younger,* without respect to good or bad works done or foreseen, *that the purpose of God according to election might stand* — that this great truth may be established, that God chooses some and refuses others as a free agent, by his own absolute and sovereign will, dispensing his favours or withholding them as he pleases. This difference that was put between Jacob and Esau he further illustrates by a quotation from Mal. 1:2, 3, where it is said, not of Jacob and Esau the person, but the Edomites and Israelites their posterity, *Jacob have I loved, and Esau have I hated.* The people of Israel were taken into the covenant of peculiarity, had the land of Canaan given them, were blessed with the more signal appearances of God for them in special protections, supplies, and deliverances, while the Edomites were rejected, had no temple, altar, priests, nor prophets — no such particular care taken of them nor kindness shown to them. Such a difference did God put between those two nations, that both descended from the loins of Abraham and Isaac, as at first there was a difference put between Jacob and Esau, the distinguishing heads of those two nations. So that all this choosing and refusing was typical, and intended to shadow forth some other election and rejection. (1.) Some understand it of the election and rejection of conditions or qualifications. As God chose Isaac and Jacob, and rejected Ishmael and Esau, so he might and did choose faith to be the condition of salvation and reject the works of the law. Thus Arminius understands it, *De rejectis et assumptis talibus, certa qualitate notatis — Concerning such as are rejected and such as are chosen, being distinguished by appropriate qualities;* so John Goodwin. But this very much strains the scripture; for the apostle speaks all along of persons, he has mercy on whom (he does not say on what kind of people) he will have mercy, besides that against this sense those two objections (v. 14, 19) do not at all arise, and his answer to them concerning God's absolute sovereignty over the children of men is not at all pertinent if no more be meant than his appointing the conditions of salvation. (2.) Others understand it of the election and rejection of particular person — some loved, and others hated, from eternity. But the apostle speaks of Jacob and Esau, not in their own persons, but as ancestors — Jacob the people, and Esau the people; nor does God condemn any, or decree so to do, merely because he will do it, without any reason taken from their own deserts. (3.) Others therefore understand it of the election and rejection of people considered complexly. His design is to justify God, and his mercy and truth, in calling the Gentiles, and taking them into the church, and into covenant with himself, while he suffered the obstinate part of the Jews to persist in unbelief, and so to un-church themselves — thus hiding from their eyes the things that belonged to their peace. The apostle's reasoning for the explication and proof of this is, however, very applicable to, and, no doubt (as is usual in scripture) was intended for the clearing of the methods of God's grace towards particular person, for the communication of saving benefits bears some analogy to the communication of church-privileges. The choosing of Jacob the younger, and preferring him before Esau the elder (so crossing hands), were to intimate that the Jews, though the natural seed of Abraham, and the first-born of the church, should be laid aside; and the Gentiles, who were as the younger brother, should be taken in in their stead, and have the birthright and blessing. The Jews, considered as a body politic, a nation and people, knit together by the bond and cement of the ceremonial law, the temple and priesthood, the centre of their unity, had for many ages been the darlings and favourites of heaven, a kingdom of priests, a holy nation, dignified and distinguished by God's miraculous appearances among them and for them. Now that the gospel was preached, and Christian churches were planted, this national body was thereby abandoned, their church-polity dissolved; and Christian churches (and in process of time Christian nations), embodied in like manner, become their successors in the divine favour, and those special privileges and protections which were the products of that favour. To clear up the justice of God in this great dispensation is the scope of the apostle here.

Verses 14–24

The apostle, having asserted the true meaning of the promise, comes here to maintain and prove the absolute sovereignty of God, in disposing of the children of men, with reference to their eternal state. And herein God is to be considered, not as a rector and governor, distributing rewards and punishments according to his revealed laws and covenants, but as an owner and benefactor, giving to the children of men such grace and favour as he has determined in and by his secret and eternal will and counsel: both the favour of visible church-membership and privileges, which is given to some people and denied to others, and the favour of effectual grace, which is given to some particular persons and denied to others.

Now this part of his discourse is in answer to two objections.

I. It might be objected, *Is there unrighteousness with God?* If God, in dealing with the children of men, do thus, in an arbitrary manner, choose some and refuse others, may it not be suspected that there is unrighteousness with him? This the apostle startles at the thought of: *God forbid!* Far be it from us to think such a thing; shall not the judge of all the earth do right? Gen. 18:25; ch. 3:5, 6. He denies the consequences, and proves the denial.

1. In respect of those to whom he shows mercy, v. 15, 16. He quotes that scripture to show God's sovereignty in dispensing his favours (Ex. 33:19): *I will be gracious to whom I will be gracious.* All God's reasons of mercy are taken from within himself. All the children of men being plunged alike into a state of sin and misery, equally under guilt and wrath, God, in a way of sovereignty, picks out some from this fallen apostatized race, to be vessels of grace and glory. He dispenses his gifts to whom he will, without giving us any reason: according to his own good pleasure he pitches upon some to be monuments of mercy and grace, preventing grace, effectual grace, while he passes by others. The expression is very emphatic, and the repetition makes it more so: *I will have mercy on whom I will have mercy.* It imports a perfect absoluteness in God's will; he will do what he will, and giveth not account of any of his matters, nor is it fit he should. As these great words, *I am that I am* (Ex. 3:14) do abundantly express the absolute independency of his being, so these words, *I will have mercy on whom I will have mercy,* do as fully express the absolute prerogative and sovereignty of his will. To vindicate the righteousness of God, in showing mercy to whom he will, the apostle appeals to that which God himself had spoken, wherein he claims this sovereign power and liberty. God is a competent judge, even in his own case. Whatsoever God does, or is resolved to do, is both by the one and the other proved to be just. *Eleēsō on han heleō — I will have mercy on whom I will have mercy.* When I begin, I will make an end. Therefore God's mercy endures for ever, because the reason of it is fetched from within himself; therefore his gifts and callings are without repentance. Hence he infers (v. 16), *It is not of him that willeth.* Whatever good comes from God to man, the glory of it is not to be ascribed to the most generous desire, nor to the most industrious endeavour, of man, but only and purely to the free grace and mercy of God. In Jacob's case it was *not of him that willeth, nor of him that runneth;* it was not the earnest will and desire of Rebecca that Jacob might have the blessing; it was not Jacob's haste to get it (for he was compelled to run for it) that procured him the blessing, but only the mercy and grace of God. Wherein the holy happy people of God differ from other people, it is God and his grace that make them differ. Applying this general rule to the particular case that Paul has before him, the reason why the unworthy, undeserving, ill-deserving Gentiles are called, and grafted into the church, while the greatest part of the Jews are left to perish in unbelief, is not because those Gentiles were better deserving or better disposed for such a favour, but because of God's free grace that made that difference. The Gentiles did neither will it, nor run for it, for they *sat in darkness,* Mt. 4:16. In darkness, therefore not willing what they knew not; *sitting* in darkness, a contented posture, therefore not running to meet it, but anticipated with these invaluable blessings of goodness. Such is the method of God's grace towards all that

partake of it, for he is found of those that sought him not (Isa. 65:1); in this preventing, effectual, distinguishing grace, he acts as a benefactor, whose grace is his own. Our eye therefore must not be evil because his is good; but, of all the grace that we or others have, he must have the glory: *Not unto us,* Ps. 115:1.

2. In respect of those who perish, *v.* 17. God's sovereignty, manifested in the ruin of sinners, is here discovered in the instance of Pharaoh; it is quoted from Ex. 9:16. Observe,

(1.) What God did with Pharaoh. He raised him up, brought him into the world, made him famous, gave him the kingdom and power, — set him up as a beacon upon a hill, as the mark of all his plagues (compare Ex. 9:14) — hardened his heart, as he had said he would (Ex. 4:21): *I will harden his heart,* that is, withdraw softening grace, leave him to himself, let Satan loose against him, and lay hardening providences before him. Or, by raising him up may be meant the intermission of the plagues which gave Pharaoh respite, and the reprieve of Pharaoh in those plagues. In the Hebrew, *I have made thee stand,* continued thee yet in the land of the living. Thus doth God raise up sinners, make them for himself, even for the day of evil (Prov. 16:4), raise them up in outward prosperity, external privileges (Mt. 11:23), sparing mercies.

(2.) What he designed in it: *That I might show my power in thee.* God would, by all this, serve the honour of his name, and manifest his power in baffling the pride and insolence of that great and daring tyrant, who bade defiance to Heaven itself, and trampled upon all that was just and sacred. If Pharaoh had not been so high and might, so bold and hardy, the power of God had not been so illustrious in the ruining of him; but the taking off of the spirit of such a prince, who hectored at that rate, did indeed proclaim God glorious in holiness, fearful in praises, doing wonders, Ex. 15:11. This is Pharaoh, and all his multitude.

(3.) His conclusion concerning both these we have, *v.* 18. *He hath mercy on whom he will have mercy, and whom he will he hardeneth.* The various dealings of God, by which he makes some to differ from others, must be resolved into his absolute sovereignty. He is debtor to no man, his grace is his own, and he may give it or withhold it as it pleaseth him; we have none of us deserved it, nay, we have all justly forfeited it a thousand times, so that herein the work of our salvation is admirably well ordered that those who are saved must thank God only, and those who perish must thank themselves only, Hos. 13:9. We are bound, as God hath bound us, to do our utmost for the salvation of all we have to do with; but God is bound no further than he has been pleased to bind himself by his own covenant and promise, which is his revealed will; and that is that he will receive, and not cast out, those that come to Christ; but the drawing of souls in order to that coming is a preventing distinguishing favour to whom he will. Had he mercy on the Gentiles? It was because he would have mercy on them. Were the Jews hardened? It was because it was his own pleasure to deny them softening grace, and to give them up to their chosen affected unbelief. *Even so, Father, because it seemed good unto thee.* That scripture excellently explains this, Lu. 10:21, and, as this, shows the sovereign will of God in giving or withholding both the means of grace and the effectual blessing upon those means.

II. It might be objected, *Why doth he yet find fault? For who hath resisted his will? v.* 19. Had the apostle been arguing only for God's sovereignty in appointing and ordering the terms and conditions of acceptance and salvation, there had not been the least colour for this objection; for he might well find fault if people refused to come up to the terms on which such a salvation is offered; the salvation being so great, the terms could not be hard. But there might be colour for the objection against his arguing for the sovereignty of God in giving and withholding differencing and preventing grace; and the objection is commonly and readily advanced against the doctrine of distinguishing grace. If God, while he gives effectual grace to some, denies it to others, why doth he find fault with those to whom he denies it? If he hath rejected the Jews, and hid from their eyes the things that belong to their peace, why doth he find fault with them for their blindness? If it be his pleasure to discard them as not a people, and not obtaining mercy, their knocking off themselves was no resistance of his will. This objection he answers at large,

1. By reproving the objector (*v.* 20): *Nay but, O man.* This is not an objection fit to be made by the creature against his Creator, by man against God. The truth, as it is in Jesus, is that which abases man as nothing, less than nothing, and advances God as sovereign Lord of all. Observe how contemptibly he speaks of man, when he comes to argue with God his Maker: "*Who art thou,* thou that art so foolish, so feeble, so short-sighted, so incompetent a judge of the divine counsels? Art thou able to fathom such a depth, dispute such a case, to trace that way of God which is in the sea, his path in the great waters?" *That repliest against God.* It becomes us to submit to him, not to reply against him; to lie down under his hand, not to fly in his face, nor to charge him with folly. *Ho antapokrinomenos — That answerest again.* God is our master, and we are his servants; and it does not become servants to answer again, Tit. 2:9.

2. By resolving all into the divine sovereignty. We are the thing formed, and he is the former; and it does not become us to challenge or arraign his wisdom in ordering and disposing of us into this or that shape of figure. The rude and unformed mass of matter hath no right to this or that form, but is shaped at the pleasure of him that formeth it. God's sovereignty over us is fitly illustrated by the power that the potter hath over the clay; compare Jer. 18:6, where, by a like comparison, God asserts his dominion over the nation of the Jews, when he was about to magnify his justice in their destruction by Nebuchadnezzar.

(1.) He gives us the comparison, *v.* 21. The potter, out of the same lump, may make either a fashionable vessel, and a vessel fit for creditable and honourable uses, or a contemptible vessel, and a vessel in which is no pleasure; and herein he acts arbitrarily, as he might have chosen whether he would make any vessel of it at all, or whether he would leave it in the hole of the pit, out of which it was dug.

(2.) The application of the comparison, *v.* 22–24. Two sorts of vessels God forms out of the great lump of fallen mankind: — [1.] *Vessels of wrath* — vessels filled with wrath, as a vessel of wine is a vessel filled with wine; *full of the fury of the Lord,* Isa. 51:20. In these God is willing to show his wrath, that is, his punishing justice, and his enmity to sin. This must be shown to all the world, God will make it appear that he hates sin. He will likewise make his power known, *to dynaton autou.* It is a power of strength and energy, an inflicting power, which works and effects the destruction of those that perish; it is a destruction that proceeds from the *glory of his power,* 2 Th. 1:9. The eternal damnation of sinners will be an abundant demonstration of the power of God; for he will act in it himself immediately, his wrath preying as it were upon guilty consciences, and his arm stretched out totally to destroy their well-being, and yet at the same instant wonderfully to preserve the being of the creature. In order to this, God *endured them with much long-suffering* — exercised a great deal of patience towards them, let them alone to fill up the measure of sin, to grow till they were ripe for ruin, and so they became *fitted for destruction,* fitted by their own sin and self-hardening. The reigning corruptions and wickedness of the soul are its preparedness and disposedness for hell: a soul is hereby made combustible matter, fit for the flames of hell. When Christ said to the Jews (Mt. 23:32), *Fill you up then the measure of your father, that upon you may come all the righteous blood* (*v.* 35), he did, as it were, endure them with much long-suffering, that they might, by their own obstinacy and wilfulness in sin, fit themselves for destruction. [2.] *Vessels of mercy* — filled with mercy. The happiness bestowed upon the saved remnant is the fruit, not of their merit, but of God's mercy. The spring of all the joy and glory of heaven is that mercy of God which endures for ever. Vessels of honour must to eternity own themselves vessels of mercy. Observe, *First,* What he designs in them: *To make known the riches of his glory,* that is, of his goodness; for God's goodness is his greatest glory, especially when it is communicated with the greatest sovereignty. *I beseech thee show me thy glory,* says Moses, Ex. 33:18. *I will make all my goodness to pass before thee,* says God (*v.* 19), and that given out freely: *I will be gracious to whom I will be gracious.* God makes known his glory, this goodness of his, in the preservation and supply of all the creatures: the earth is full of his goodness, and the year crowned with it; but when he would demonstrate the riches of his goodness, unsearchable riches, he does it in the salvation of the saints, that will be to eternity glorious monuments of divine grace. *Secondly,* What he does for them he does before *prepare them to glory.* Sanctification is the preparation of the soul for glory, making it meet to partake of the inheritance of the saints in light. This is God's work. We can destroy ourselves fast enough, but we cannot save ourselves. Sinners fit themselves for hell, but it is God that prepares saints for heaven; and all those that God designs for heaven hereafter he prepares and fits for heaven now: he works them to the self-same thing, 2 Co. 5:5. And would you know who these *vessels of mercy are?* Those whom he hath called (*v.* 24); for whom he did predestinate those he also called with an effectual call: and these not of the Jews only, but of the Gentiles; for, the partition-wall being taken down, the world was laid in common, and not (as it had been) God's favour appropriated to the Jews, and they put a degree nearer his acceptance than the rest of the world. They now stood upon the same level with the Gentiles; and the question is not now whether of the seed of Abraham or no, that is neither here nor there, but whether or no called according to his purpose.

Verses 25–29

Having explained the promise, and proved the divine sovereignty, the apostle here shows how the rejection of the Jews, and the taking in of the Gentiles, were foretold in the Old Testament, and therefore must needs be very well consistent with the promise made to the fathers under the Old Testament. It tends very much to the clearing of a truth to observe how the scripture is fulfilled in it. The Jews would, no doubt, willingly refer it to the Old Testament, the scriptures of which were committed to them. Now he shows how this, which was so uneasy to them, was there spoken of.

I. By the prophet Hosea, who speaks of the taking in of a great many of the Gentiles, Hos. 2:23 and Hos. 1:10. The Gentiles had not been the people of God, not owning him, nor being owned by him in that relation: "But," says he, "*I will call them my people,* make them such and own them as such, notwithstanding all their unworthiness." A blessed change! Former badness is no bar to God's present grace and mercy. — *And her beloved which was not beloved.* Those whom God calls his people he calls beloved: he loves those that are his own. And lest it might be supposed that they should become God's people only by being proselyted to the Jewish religion, and made members of that nation, he adds, from Hos. 1:10, *In the place where it was said,* etc., *there shall they be called.* They need not be embodied with the Jews, nor go up to Jerusalem to worship; but, wherever they are scattered over the face of the earth, there will God own them. Observe the great dignity and honour of the saints, that they are called the children of the living God; and his calling them so makes them so. Behold, what manner of love! This honour have all his saints.

II. By the prophet Isaiah, who speaks of the casting off of many of the Jews, in two places.

1. One is Isa. 10:22, 23, which speaks of the saving of a remnant, that is, but a remnant, which, though in the prophecy it seems to refer to the preservation of a remnant from the destruction and desolation that were coming upon them by Sennacherib and his army, yet is to be understood as looking further, and sufficiently proves that it is no strange thing for God to abandon to ruin a great many of the seed of Abraham, and yet maintain his word of promise to Abraham in full force and virtue. This is intimated in the supposition that the number of children of Israel was as the sand of the sea, which was part of the promise made to Abraham, Gen. 22:17. And yet only a remnant shall be saved; for many are called, but few are chosen. In this salvation of the remnant we are told (*v.* 28) from the prophet, (1.) That he will complete the work: *He will finish the work.* When God begins he will make an end, whether in ways of judgment or of mercy. The rejection of the unbelieving Jews god would finish in their utter ruin by the Romans, who soon after this quite took away their place and nation. The assuming of Christian churches into the divine favour, and the spreading of the gospel in other nations, was a work which God would likewise finish, and be known by his name JEHOVAH. As for God, his work is perfect. Margin, *He will finish the account.* God, in his eternal counsels, has taken an account of the children of men, allotted them to such or such a condition, to such a share of privileges; and, as they come into being, his dealings with them are pursuant to these counsels: and he will finish the account, complete the mystical body, call in as many as belong to the election of grace, and then the account will be finished. (2.) That he will contract it; not only finish it, but finish it quickly. Under the Old Testament he seemed to tarry, and to make a longer and more tedious work of it. The wheels moved but slowly towards the extent of the church; but now

he will *cut it short,* and make a short work upon the earth. Gentile converts were now flying as a cloud. But he will cut it short *in righteousness,* both in wisdom and in justice. Men, when they cut short, do amiss; they do indeed despatch causes; but, when God cuts short, it is always in righteousness. So the fathers generally apply it. Some understand it of the evangelical law and covenant, which Christ has introduced and established in the world: he has in that finished the work, put an end to the types and ceremonies of the Old Testament. Christ said, *It is finished,* and then the veil was rent, echoing as it were to the word that Christ said upon the cross. And he will cut it short. *The work* (it is *logos — the word,* the law) was under the Old Testament very long; a long train of institutions, ceremonies, conditions: but now it is cut short. Our duty is now, under the gospel, summed up in much less room than it was under the law; the covenant was abridged and contracted; religion is brought into a less compass. And it is in righteousness, in favour to us, in justice to his own design and counsel. With us contractions are apt to darken things: —

— Brevis esse laboro, Obscurus fio —

I strive to be concise, but prove obscure.

but it is not so in this case. Though it be cut short, it is clear and plain; and, because short, the more easy.

2. Another is quoted from Isa. 1:9, where the prophet is showing how in a time of general calamity and destruction God would preserve a seed. This is to the same purport with the former; and the scope of it is to show that it was no strange thing for God to leave the greatest part of the people of the Jews to ruin, and to reserve to himself only a small remnant: so he had done formerly, as appears by their own prophets; and they must not wonder if he did so now. Observe, (1.) What God is. He is *the Lord of sabaoth,* that is, the Lord of hosts — a Hebrew word retained in the Greek, as James 5:4. All the host of heaven and earth are at his beck and disposal. When God secures a seed to himself out of a degenerate apostate world, he acts as Lord of sabaoth. It is an act of almighty power and infinite sovereignty. (2.) What his people are; they are a *seed,* a small number. The corn reserved for next year's seedings is but little, compared with that which is spent and eaten. But they are a useful number — the seed, the substance, of the next generation, Isa. 6:13. It is so far from being an impeachment of the justice and righteousness of God that so many perish and are destroyed, that it is a wonder of divine power and mercy that all are not destroyed, that there are any saved; for even those that are left to be a seed, if God had dealt with them according to their sins, had perished with the rest. This is the great truth which this scripture teacheth us.

Verses 30–33

The apostle comes here at last to fix the true reason of the reception of the Gentiles, and the rejection of the Jews. There was a difference in the way of their seeking, and therefore there was that different success, though still it was the free grace of God that made them differ. He concludes like an orator, *What shall we say then?* What is the conclusion of the whole dispute?

I. Concerning the Gentiles observe, 1. How they had been alienated from righteousness: the followed not after it; they knew not their guilt and misery, and therefore were not at all solicitous to procure a remedy. In their conversion preventing grace was greatly magnified: God was *found of those that sought him not,* Isa. 65:1. There was nothing in them to dispose them for such a favour more than what free grace wrought in them. Thus doth God delight to dispense grace in a way of sovereignty and absolute dominion. 2. How they attained to righteousness, notwithstanding: *By faith;* not by being proselyted to the Jewish religion, and submitting to the ceremonial law, but by embracing Christ, and believing in Christ, and submitting to the gospel. They attained to that by the short cut of believing sincerely in Christ for which the Jews had been long in vain beating about the bush.

II. Concerning the Jews observe, 1. How they missed their end: they *followed after the law of righteousness* (*v.* 31) — they talked much of justification and holiness, seemed very ambitious of being the people of God and the favourites of heaven, but they did not attain to it, that is, the greatest part of them did not; as many as stuck to their old Jewish principles and ceremonies, and pursued a happiness in those observances, embracing the shadows now that the substance was come, these fell short of acceptance with God, were not owned as his people, nor went to their house justified. 2. How they mistook their way, which was the cause of their missing the end, *v.* 32, 33. They sought, but not in the right way, not in the humbling way, not in the instituted appointed way. *Not by faith,* not by embracing the Christian religion, and depending upon the merit of Christ, and submitting to the terms of the gospel, which were the very life and end of the law. But they sought by the *works of the law;* as if they were to expect justification by their observance of the precepts and ceremonies of the law of Moses. This was the *stumbling-stone at which they stumbled.* They could not get over this corrupt principle which they had espoused, That the law was given them for no end but that merely by their observance of it, and obedience to it, they might be justified before God: and so they could by no means be reconciled to the doctrine of Christ, which brought them off from that to expect justification through the merit and satisfaction of another. Christ himself is to some a stone of stumbling, for which he quotes Isa. 8:14; 28:16. It is sad that Christ should be set for the fall of any, and yet it is so (Lu. 2:34), that ever poison should be sucked out of the balm of Gilead, that the foundation-stone should be to any a stone of stumbling, and the rock of salvation a rock of offence; so he is to multitudes; so he was to the unbelieving Jews, who rejected him, because he put an end to the ceremonial law. But still there is a remnant that do believe on him; and they *shall not be ashamed,* that is, their hopes and expectations of justification by him shall not be disappointed, as theirs are who expect it by the law. So that, upon the whole, the unbelieving Jews have no reason to quarrel with God for rejecting them; they had a fair offer of righteousness, and life, and salvation, made to them upon gospel terms, which they did not like, and would not come up to; and therefore, if they perish, they may thank themselves — their blood is upon their own heads.

CHAPTER 10

The dissolving of the peculiar church-state of the Jews, and the rejection of that polity by the repealing of their ceremonial law, the vacating of all the institutions of it, the abolishing of their priesthood, the burning of their temple, and the taking away of their place and nation, and in their room the substituting and erecting of a catholic church-state among the Gentile nations, though to us, now that these things have long since been done and completed, they may seem no great matter, yet to those who lived when they were doing, who knew how high the Jews had stood in God's favour, and how deplorable the condition of the Gentile world had been for many ages, it appeared very great and marvellous, and a mystery hard to be understood. The apostle, in this chapter, as in the foregoing and that which follows, is explaining and proving it; but with several very useful digressions, which a little interrupt the thread of his discourse. To two great truths I would reduce this chapter: — I. That there is a great difference between the righteousness of the law, which the unbelieving Jews were wedded to, and the righteousness of faith offered in the gospel (*v.* 1–11). II. That there is no difference between Jews and Gentiles; but, in point of justification and acceptance with God, the gospel sets them both upon the same level (*v.* 12 to the end).

Verses 1–11

The scope of the apostle in this part of the chapter is to show the vast difference between the righteousness of the law and the righteousness of faith, and the great pre-eminence of the righteousness of faith above that of the law; that he might induce and persuade the Jews to believe in Christ, aggravate the folly and sin of those that refused, and justify God in the rejection of such refusers.

I. Paul here professes his good affection to the Jews, with the reason of it (*v.* 1, 2), where he gives them a good wish, and a good witness.

1. A good wish (*v.* 1), a wish that they might be saved — saved from the temporal ruin and destruction that were coming upon them — saved from the wrath to come, eternal wrath, which was hanging over their heads. It is implied in this wish that they might be convinced and converted; he could not pray in faith that they might be saved in their unbelief. Though Paul preached against them, yet he prayed for them. Herein he was merciful, as God is, who is *not willing that any should perish* (2 Pt. 3:9), desires not the death of sinners. It is our duty truly and earnestly to desire the salvation of our own. This, he says, was *his heart's desire and prayer,* which intimates, (1.) The strength and sincerity of his desire. It was *his heart's desire;* it was not a formal compliment, as good wishes are with many from the teeth outward, but a real desire. This it was before it was his prayer. The soul of prayer is the heart's desire. Cold desires do but beg denials; we must even breathe out our souls in every prayer. (2.) The offering up of this desire to God. It was not only his heart's desire, but it was his prayer. There may be desires in the heart, and yet no prayer, unless those desires be presented to God. Wishing and woulding, if that be all, are not praying.

2. A good witness, as a reason of his good wish (*v.* 2): *I bear them record that they have a zeal of God.* The unbelieving Jews were the most bitter enemies Paul had in the world, and yet Paul gives them as good a character as the truth would bear. We should say the best we can even of our worst enemies; this is blessing those that curse us. Charity teaches us to have the best opinion of persons, and to put the best construction upon words and actions, that they will bear. We should take notice of that which is commendable even in bad people. *They have a zeal of God.* Their opposition to the gospel is from a principle of respect to the law, which they know to have come from God. There is such a thing as a blind misguided zeal: such was that of the Jews, who, when they hated Christ's people and ministers, and cast them out, said, *Let the Lord be glorified* (Isa. 66:5); nay, they killed them, and thought they did God good service, Jn. 16:2.

II. He here shows the fatal mistake that the unbelieving Jews were guilty of, which was their ruin. Their zeal was *not according to knowledge.* It is true God gave them that law for which they were so zealous; but they might have known that, by the appearance of the promised Messiah, an end was put to it. He introduced a new religion and way of worship, to which the former must give place. He proved himself the Son of God, gave the most convincing evidence that could be of his being the Messiah; and yet they did not know and would not own him, but shut their eyes against the clear light, so that their zeal for the law was blind. This he shows further, *v.* 3, where we may observe,

1. The nature of their unbelief. They *have not submitted themselves to the righteousness of God,* that is, they have not yielded to gospel-terms, nor accepted the tender of justification by faith in Christ, which is made in the gospel. Unbelief is a non-submission to the righteousness of God, standing it out against the gospel proclamation of indemnity. *Have not submitted.* In true faith, there is need of a great deal of submission; therefore the first lesson Christ teaches is to deny ourselves. It is a great piece of condescension for a proud heart to be content to be beholden to free grace; we are loth to sue *sub forma pauperis — as paupers.*

2. The causes of their unbelief, and these are two: — (1.) Ignorance of God's righteousness. They did not understand, and believe, and consider, the strict justice of God, in hating and punishing sin, and demanding satisfaction, did not consider what need we have of a righteousness wherein to appear before him; if they had, they would never have stood out against the gospel offer, nor expected justification by their own works, as if they could satisfy God's justice. Or, being ignorant of God's way of justification, which he has now appointed and revealed by Jesus Christ. They did not know it, because they would not; they shut their eyes against the discoveries of it, and love darkness rather. (2.) A proud conceit of their own righteousness: *Going about to establish their own* — a righteousness of their own devising, and of their own working out, by the merit of their works, and by their observance of the ceremonial law. They thought they needed not to be beholden to the merit of Christ, and therefore depended upon their own performances as sufficient to make up a righteousness wherein to appear before God. They could not with Paul disclaim a dependence upon this (Phil. 3:9), *Not having my own righteousness.* See an instance of this pride in the Pharisee, Lu. 18:10, 11. Compare *v.* 14.

III. He here shows the folly of that mistake, and what an unreasonable thing it was for them to be seeking justification by the works of the law, now that Christ had come, and had brought in an everlasting righteousness; considering,

1. The subserviency of the law to the gospel (*v.* 4): *Christ is the end of the law for righteousness.* The design of the law was to lead people to Christ. The moral law was but for the searching of the wound, the ceremonial law for the shadowing forth of the remedy; but Christ is the end of both. See 2 Co. 3:7, and compare Gal. 3:23, 24. The use of the law was to direct people for righteousness to Christ. (1.) Christ is the end of the ceremonial law; he is the period of it, because he is the perfection of it. When the substance comes, the shadow is gone. The sacrifices, and offerings, and purifications appointed under the Old Testament, prefigured Christ, and pointed at him; and their inability to take away sin discovered the necessity of a sacrifice that should, by being once

offered, take away sin. (2.) Christ is the end of the moral law in that he did what the law could not do (*ch.* 8:3), and secured the great end of it. The end of the law was to bring men to perfect obedience, and so to obtain justification. This is now become impossible, by reason of the power of sin and the corruption of nature; but Christ is the end of the law. The law is not destroyed, nor the intention of the lawgiver frustrated, but, full satisfaction being made by the death of Christ for our breach of the law, the end is attained, and we are put in another way of justification. Christ is thus the end of the law for righteousness, that is, for justification; but it is only to *every one that believeth.* Upon our believing, that is, our humble consent to the terms of the gospel, we become interested in Christ's satisfaction, and so are justified through the redemption that is in Jesus.

2. The excellency of the gospel above the law. This he proves by showing the different constitution of these two.

(1.) What is the righteousness which is of the law? This he shows, *v.* 5. The tenour of it is, *Do, and live.* Though it directs us to a better and more effectual righteousness in Christ, yet in itself, considered as a law abstracted from its respect to Christ and the gospel (for so the unbelieving Jews embraced and retained it), it owneth nothing as a righteousness sufficient to justify a man but that of perfect obedience. For this he quotes that scripture (Lev. 18:5), *You shall therefore keep my statutes and my judgments, which if a man do, he shall live in them.* To this he refers likewise, Gal. 3:12, *The man that doeth them, shall live in them. Live,* that is, be happy, not only in the land of Canaan, but in heaven, of which Canaan was a type and figure. The doing supposed must be perfect and sinless, without the least breach or violation. The law which was given upon Mount Sinai, though it was not a pure covenant of works (for who then could be saved under that dispensation?) yet, that is might be the more effectual to drive people to Christ and to make the covenant of grace welcome, it had a very great mixture of the strictness and terror of the covenant of works. Now, was it not extreme folly in the Jews to adhere so closely to this way of justification and salvation, which was in itself so hard, and by the corruption of nature now become impossible, when there was a new and a living way opened?

(2.) What is that righteousness which is of faith, *v.* 6, etc. This he describes in the words of Moses, in Deuteronomy, in the *second law* (so Deuteronomy signifies), where there was a much clearer revelation of Christ and the gospel than there was in the first giving of the law: he quotes it from Deu. 30:11-14, and shows,

[1.] That it is not at all hard or difficult. The way of justification and salvation has in it no such depths or knots as may discourage us, no insuperable difficulties attending it; but, as was foretold, it is a high-way, Isa. 35:8. We are not put to climb for it — it is not in heaven; we are not put to dive for it — it is not in the deep. *First,* We need not go to heaven, to search the records there, or to enquire into the secrets of the divine counsel. It is true Christ is in heaven; but we may be justified and saved without going thither, to fetch him thence, or sending a special messenger to him. *Secondly,* We need not go to the deep, to fetch Christ out of the grave, or from the state of the dead: *Into the deep, to bring up Christ from the dead.* This plainly shows that Christ's descent into the *deep,* or into *hadēs,* was no more than his going into the state of the dead, in allusion to Jonah. It is true that Christ was in the grave, and it is as true that he is now in heaven; but we need not perplex and puzzle ourselves with fancied difficulties, nor must we create to ourselves such gross and carnal ideas of these things as if the method of salvation were impracticable, and the design of the revelation were only to amuse us. No, salvation is not put at so vast a distance from us.

[2.] But it is very plain and easy: *The word is nigh thee.* When we speak of looking upon Christ, and receiving Christ, and feeding upon Christ, it is not Christ in heaven, nor Christ in the deep, that we mean; but Christ in the promise, Christ exhibited to us, and offered, in the word. Christ is nigh thee, for the word is nigh thee: nigh thee indeed: it is *in thy mouth, and in thy heart;* there is no difficulty in understanding, believing, and owning it. The work thou hast to do lies within thee: *the kingdom of God is within you,* Lu. 17:21. Thence thou must fetch thy evidences, not out of the records of heaven. *It is,* that is, it is promised that it shall be, *in thy mouth* (Isa. 59:21), *and in thy heart,* Jer. 31:33. All that which is done for us is already done to our hands. Christ is come down from

heaven; we need not go to fetch him. He is come up from the deep; we need not perplex ourselves how to bring him up. There is nothing now to be done, but a work in us; this must be our care, to look to our heart and mouth. Those that were under the law were to do all themselves, *Do this, and live;* but the gospel discovers the greatest part of the work done already, and what remains cut short in righteousness, salvation offered upon very plain and easy terms, brought to our door, as it were, in the word which is nigh us. It is in our mouth — we are reading it daily; it is in our heart — we are, or should be, thinking of it daily. Even *the word of faith;* the gospel and the promise of it, called the word of faith because it is the object of faith about which it is conversant, the word which we believe; — because it is the precept of faith, commanding it, and making it the great condition of justification; — and because it is the ordinary means by which faith is wrought and conveyed. Now what is this word of faith? We have the tenour of it, *v.* 9, 10, the sum of the gospel, which is plain and easy enough. Observe,

First, What is promised to us: *Thou shalt be saved.* It is salvation that the gospel exhibits and tenders — saved from guilt and wrath, with the salvation of the soul, an eternal salvation, which Christ is the author of, a Saviour to the uttermost.

Secondly, Upon what terms.

a. Two things are required as conditions of salvation: — (a.) *Confessing the Lord Jesus* — openly professing relation to him and dependence on him, as our prince and Saviour, owning Christianity in the face of all the allurements and affrightments of this world, standing by him in all weathers. Our Lord Jesus lays a great stress upon this confessing of him before men; see Mt. 10:32, 33. It is the product of many graces, evinces a great deal of self-denial, love to Christ, contempt of the world, a mighty courage and resolution. It was a very great thing, especially, when the profession of Christ or Christianity hazarded estate, honour, preferment, liberty, life, and all that is dear in this world, which was the case in the primitive times. (b.) *Believing in the heart that God raised him from the dead.* The profession of faith with the mouth, if there be not the power of it in the heart, is but a mockery; the root of it must be laid in an unfeigned assent to the revelation of the gospel concerning Christ, especially concerning his resurrection, which is the fundamental article of the Christian faith, for thereby he was declared to be the Son of God with power, and full evidence was given that God accepted his satisfaction.

b. This is further illustrated (*v.* 10), and the order inverted, because there must first be faith in the heart before there can be an acceptable confession with the mouth. (a.) Concerning faith: It is *with the heart that man believeth,* which implies more than an assent of the understanding, and takes in the consent of the will, an inward, hearty, sincere, and strong consent. It is not believing (not to be reckoned so) if it be not with the heart. This is *unto righteousness.* There is the righteousness of justification and the righteousness of sanctification. Faith is to both; it is the condition of our justification (*ch.* 5:1), and it is the root and spring of our sanctification; in it it is begun; by it it is carried on, Acts 15:9. (b.) Concerning profession: It is *with the mouth that confession is made* — confession to God in prayer and praise (*ch.* 15:6), confession to men by owning the ways of God before others, especially when we are called to it in a day of persecution. It is fit that God should be honoured with the mouth, for he made man's mouth (Ex. 4:11), and at such a time has promised to give his faithful people a *mouth and wisdom,* Lu. 21:15. It is part of the honour of Christ that every tongue shall confess, Phil. 2:11. And this is said to be *unto salvation,* because it is the performance of the condition of that promise, Mt. 10:32. Justification by faith lays the foundation of our title to salvation; but by confession we build upon that foundation, and come at last to the full possession of that to which we were entitled. So that we have here a brief summary of the terms of salvation, and they are very reasonable; in short this, that we must devote, dedicate, and give up, to God, our souls and our bodies — our souls in believing with the heart, and our bodies in confessing with the mouth. This do, and thou shalt live. For this (*v.* 11) he quotes Isa. 28:16, *Whosoever believeth on him shall not be ashamed; ou kataischyn-thēsetai.* That is, [a.] He will not be ashamed to own that Christ in whom he trusts; he that believes in the heart will not be ashamed to confess with the mouth. It is sinful shame that makes people deny Christ, Mk. 8:38. He that believeth

will not make haste (so the prophet has it) — will not make haste to run away from the sufferings he meets with in the way of his duty, will not be ashamed of a despised religion. [b.] He shall not be ashamed of his hope in Christ; he shall not be disappointed of his end. It is our duty that we must not, it is our privilege that we shall not, be ashamed of our faith in Christ. He shall never have cause to repent his confidence in reposing such a trust in the Lord Jesus.

Verses 12-21

The first words express the design of the apostle through these verses, that there is no difference between Jews and Gentiles, but they stand upon the same level in point of acceptance with God. In Jesus Christ there is neither Greek nor Jews, Col. 3:11. God doth not save any nor reject any because they are Jews, nor because they are Greeks, but doth equally accept both upon gospel terms: *There is no difference.* For the proof of this he urges two arguments: —

I. That God is the same to all: *The same Lord over all is rich unto all.* There is not one God to the Jews who is more kind, and another to the Gentiles who is less kind; but he is the same to all, a common father to all mankind. When he proclaimed his name, *The Lord, the Lord god, gracious and merciful,* he thereby signified not only what he was to the Jews, but what he is and will be to all his creatures that seek unto him: not only good, but rich, plenteous in goodness: he hath wherewith to supply them all, and he is free and ready to give out to them; he is both able and willing: not only rich, but rich unto us, liberal and bountiful in dispensing his favours *to all that call upon him.* Something must be done by us, that we may reap of this bounty; and it is as little as can be, we must call upon him. He will for this be enquired of (Eze. 36:37), and surely that which is not worth the asking is not worth the having. We have nothing to do but to draw out by prayer, as there is occasion.

II. That the promise is the same to all (*v.* 13): *Whoever shall call* — one as well as another, without exception. This extent, this undifferencing extent, of the promise both to Jews and Gentiles he thinks should not be surprising, for it was foretold by the prophet, Joel 2:32. Calling upon the name of the Lord is here put for all practical religion. What is the life of a Christian but a life of prayer? It implies a sense of our dependence on him, an entire dedication of ourselves to him, and a believing expectation of our all from him. He that thus calls upon him shall be saved. It is but ask and have; what would we have more? for the further illustration of this he observes,

1. How necessary it was that the gospel should be preached to the Gentiles, *v.* 14, 15. This was what the Jews were so angry with Paul for, that he was the apostle of the Gentiles, and preached the gospel to them. Now he shows how needful it was to bring them within the reach of the forementioned promise, an interest in which they should not envy to any of their fellow-creatures. (1.) *They cannot call on him in whom they have not believed.* Except they believe that he is God, they will not call upon him by prayer; to what purpose should they? The grace of faith is absolutely necessary to the duty of prayer; we cannot pray aright, nor pray to acceptation, without it. He that comes to God by prayer must believe, Heb. 11:6. Till they believed the true God, they were calling upon idols, O Baal, hear us. (2.) *They cannot believe in him of whom they have not heard.* some way or other the divine revelation must be made known to us, before we can receive it and assent to it; it is not born with us. In hearing is included reading, which is tantamount, and by which many are brought to believe (Jn. 20:31): *These things are written that you may believe.* But hearing only is mentioned, as the more ordinary and natural way of receiving information. (3.) *They cannot hear without a preacher;* how should they? Somebody must tell them what they are to believe. Preachers and hearers are correlates; it is a blessed thing when they mutually rejoice in each other — the hearers in the skill and faithfulness of the preacher, and the preacher in the willingness and obedience of the hearers. (4.) *They cannot preach except they be sent,* except they be both commissioned and in some measure qualified for their preaching work. How shall a man act as an ambassador, unless he have both his credentials and his instructions from the prince that sends him? This proves that to the regular ministry there must be a regular mission and ordination. It is God's prerogative to send ministers; he is the Lord of the harvest, and therefore to him we must *pray that he would send forth labourers,* Mt.

9:38. He only can qualify men for, and incline them to, the work of the ministry. But the competency of that qualification, and the sincerity of that inclination, must not be left to the judgment of every man for himself: the nature of the thing will by no means admit this; but, for the preservation of due order in the church, this must needs be referred and submitted to the judgment of a competent number of those who are themselves in that office and of approved wisdom and experience in it, who, as in all other callings, are presumed the most able judges, and who are empowered to set apart such as they find so qualified and inclined to this work of the ministry, that by this preservation of the succession the name of Christ may endure for ever and his throne as the days of heaven. And those that are thus set apart, not only may, but must preach, as those that are sent.

2. How welcome the gospel ought to be to those to whom it was preached, because it showed the way to salvation, *v.* 15. For this he quotes Isa. 52:7. The like passage we have, Nah. 1:15, which, if it point at the glad tidings of the deliverance of Israel out of Babylon in the type, yet looks further to the gospel, the good news of our salvation by Jesus Christ. Observe, (1.) What the gospel is: It is *the gospel of peace;* it is the word of reconciliation between God and man. *On earth peace,* Lu. 2:14. Or, peace is put in general for all good; so it is explained here; it is *glad tidings of good things.* The things of the gospel are good things indeed, the best things; tidings concerning them are the most joyful tidings, the best news that ever came from heaven to earth. (2.) What the work of ministers is: To preach this gospel, to *bring these glad tidings;* to *evangelize peace* (so the original is), to evangelize good things. Every good preacher is in this sense an evangelist: he is not only a messenger to carry the news, but an ambassador to treat; and the first gospel preachers were angels, Lu. 2:13, etc. (3.) How acceptable they should therefore be to the children of men for their work's sake: *How beautiful are the feet,* that is, how welcome are they! Mary Magdalene expressed her love to Christ by kissing his feet, and afterwards by holding him by the feet, Mt. 28:9. And, when Christ was sending forth his disciples, he washed their feet. Those that preach the gospel of peace should see to it that their feet (their life and conversation) be beautiful: the holiness of ministers' lives is the beauty of their feet. *How beautiful!* namely, in the eyes of those that hear them. Those that welcome the message cannot but love the messengers. See 1 Th. 5:12, 13.

3. He answers an objection against all this, which might be taken from the little success which the gospel had in many places (*v.* 16): *But they have not all obeyed the gospel.* All the Jews have not, all the Gentiles have not; far the greater part of both remain in unbelief and disobedience. Observe, The gospel is given us not only to be known and believed, but to be obeyed. It is not a system of notions, but a rule of practice. This little success of the word was likewise foretold by the prophet (Isa. 53:1): *Who hath believed our report?* Very few have, few to what one would think should have believed it, considering how faithful a report it is and how well worthy of all acceptation, — very few to the many that persist in unbelief. It is no strange thing, but it is a very sad and uncomfortable thing, for the ministers of Christ to bring the report of the gospel, and not to be believed in it. Under such a melancholy consideration it is good for us to go to God and make our complaint to him. *Lord, who hath believed,* etc. In answer to this,

(1.) He shows that the word preached is the ordinary means of working faith (*v.* 17): *So then, ara — however;* though many that hear do not believe, yet those that believe have first heard. *Faith cometh by hearing.* It is the summary of what he had said before, *v.* 14. The beginning, progress, and strength of faith, are by hearing. The word of God is therefore called *the word of faith:* it begets and nourishes faith. God gives faith, but it is by the word as the instrument. *Hearing* (that hearing which works faith) is *by the word of God.* It is not hearing the enticing words of man's wisdom, but hearing the word of God, that will befriend faith, and hearing it as the word of God. See 1 Th. 2:13.

(2.) That those who would not believe the report of the gospel, yet, having heard it, were thereby left inexcusable, and may thank themselves for their own ruin, *v.* 18, *to the end.*

[1.] The Gentiles have heard it (*v.* 18): *Have they not heard?* Yes, more or less, they have either heard the gospel, or at least heard of it. *Their sound went into all the earth;* not only a confused sound, but their *words* (more distinct and intelligible notices of these things) are *gone unto the ends of the world.* The commission which the apostles received runs thus: *Go you into all the world — preach to every creature — disciple all nations;* and they did with indefatigable industry and wonderful success pursue that commission. See the extent of Paul's province, *ch.* 15:19. To this remote island of Britain, one of the utmost corners of the world, not only the sound, but the words, of the gospel came within a few years after Christ's ascension. It was in order to this that the gift of tongues was at the very first poured so plentifully upon the apostles, Acts 2. In the expression here he plainly alludes to Ps. 19:4, which speaks of the notices which the visible works of God in the creation give to all the world of the power and Godhead of the Creator. As under the Old Testament God provided for the publishing of the work of creation by the sun, moon, and stars, so now for the publishing of the work of redemption to all the world by the preaching of gospel ministers, who are therefore called *stars.*

[2.] The Jews have heard it too, *v.* 19–21. For this he appeals to two passages of the Old Testament, to show how inexcusable they are too. *Did not Israel know* that the Gentiles were to be called in? They might have known it from Moses and Isaiah.

First, One is taken from Deu. 32:21, *I will provoke you to jealousy.* The Jews not only had the offer, but saw the Gentiles accepting it and benefitted by that acceptance, witness their vexation at the event. They had the refusal: *To you first,* Acts 3:26. In all places where the apostles came still the Jews had the first offer, and the Gentiles had but their leavings. If one would not, another would. Now this provoked them to jealousy. They, as the elder brother in the parable (Lu. 15) envied the reception and entertainment of the prodigal Gentiles upon their repentance. The Gentiles are here called *no people,* and *a foolish nation,* that is, not the professing people of God. How much soever there be of the wit and wisdom of the world, those that are not the people of God are, and in the end will be found to be, a foolish people. Such was the state of the Gentile world, who yet were made the people of God, and Christ to them the wisdom of God. What a provocation it was to the Jews to see the Gentiles taken into favour we may see, Acts 13:45; 17:5, 13, and especially Acts 22:22. It was an instance of the great wickedness of the Jews that they were thus enraged; and this in Deuteronomy is the matter of a threatening. God often makes people's sin their punishment. A man needs no greater plague than to be left to eh impetuous rage of his own lusts.

Secondly, Another is taken from Isa. 65:1, 2, which is very full, and in it Esaias is very bold — bold indeed, to speak so plainly of the rejection of his own countrymen. Those that will be found faithful have need to be very bold. Those that are resolved to please God must not be afraid to displease any man. Now Esaias speaks boldly and plainly,

a. Of the preventing grace and favour of God in the reception and entertainment of the Gentiles (*v.* 20): *I was found of those that sought me not.* The prescribed method is, Seek and find; this is a rule for us, not a rule for God, who is often found of those that do not seek. His grace is his own, distinguishing grace his own, and he dispenses it in a way of sovereignty, gives of withholds it at pleasure — anticipates us with the blessings, the riches choicest blessings, of his goodness. Thus he manifested himself to the Gentiles, by sending the light of the gospel among them, when they were so far from seeking him and asking after him that they were following after lying vanities, and serving dumb idols. Was not this our own particular case? Did not God begin in love, and manifest himself to us when we did not ask after him? And was not that a time of love indeed, to be often remembered with a great deal of thankfulness?

b. Of the obstinacy and perverseness of Israel, notwithstanding the fair offers and affectionate invitations they had, *v.* 21. Observe,

(*a.*) God's great goodness to them: *All day long I have stretched forth my hands.* [*a.*] His offers: *I have stretched forth my hands,* offering them life and salvation with the greatest sincerity and seriousness that can be, with all possible expressions of earnestness and importunity, showing them the happiness tendered, setting it before them with the greatest evidence, reasoning the case with them. Stretching forth the hands is the gesture of those that require audience (Acts 26:1), or desire acceptance, Prov. 1:24. Christ was crucified with his hands stretched out. *Stretched forth my hands* as offering reconciliation — come let us shake hands and be friends; and our duty is to give the hand to him, 2 Chr. 30:8. [*b.*] His patience in making these offers: *All day long.* The patience of God towards provoking sinners is admirable. He waits to be gracious. The time of God's patience is here called a day, lightsome as a day and fit for work and business, but limited as a day, and a night at the end of it. he bears long, but he will not bear always.

(*b.*) Their great badness to him. They were a *disobedient gainsaying people.* One word in the Hebrew, in Isaiah, is here well explained by two; not only disobedient to the call, not yielding to it, but gainsaying, and quarrelling with it, which is much worse. Many that will not accept of a good proposal will yet acknowledge that they have nothing to say against it: but the Jews who believed not rested not there, but contradicted and blasphemed. God's patience with them was a very great aggravation of their disobedience, and rendered it the more exceedingly sinful; as their disobedience advanced the honour of God's patience and rendered it the more exceedingly gracious. It is a wonder of mercy in God that his goodness is not overcome by man's badness; and it is a wonder of wickedness in man that his badness is not overcome by God's goodness.

CHAPTER 11

The apostle, having reconciled that great truth of the rejection of the Jews with the promise made unto the fathers, is, in this chapter, further labouring to mollify the harshness of it, and to reconcile it to the divine goodness in general. It might be said, "Hath God then cast away his people?" The apostles therefore sets himself, in this chapter, to make a reply to this objection, and that two ways: — I. He shows at large what the mercy is that is mixed with this wrath (*v.* 1–32). II. He infers thence the infinite wisdom and sovereignty of God, with the adoration of which he concludes this chapter and subject (*v.* 33–36).

Verses 1–32

The apostle proposes here a plausible objection, which might be urged against the divine conduct in casting off the Jewish nation (*v.* 1): *"Hath God cast away his people?* Is the rejection total and final? Are they all abandoned to wrath and ruin, and that eternal? Is the extent of the sentence so large as to be without reserve, or the continuance of it so long as to be without repeal? Will he have no more a peculiar people to himself?" In opposition to this, he shows that there was a great deal of goodness and mercy expressed along with this seeming severity, particularly he insists upon three things: — 1. That, though some of the Jews were cast off, yet they were not all so. 2. That, though the body of the Jews were cast off, yet the Gentiles were taken in. And, 3. That, though the Jews were cast off at present, yet in God's due time they should be taken into his church again.

I. The Jews, it is true, were many of them cast off, but not all. The supposition of this he introduces with a *God forbid.* He will by no means endure such a suggestions. God had made a distinction between some of them and others.

1. There was a chosen remnant of believing Jews, that obtained righteousness and life by faith in Jesus Christ, *v.* 1–7. These are said to be such as he *foreknew* (*v.* 2), that is, had thoughts of love to, before the world was; for whom he thus foreknew he did predestinate. her lies the ground of the difference. They are called the *election* (*v.* 7), that is, the elect, God's chosen ones, whom he calls the election, because that which first distinguished them from the dignified them above others was God's electing love. Believers are the *election,* all those and those only whom God hath chosen. Now,

(1.) He shows that he himself was one of them: *For I also am an Israelite;* as if he had said, "Should I say that all the Jews are rejected, I should cut off my own claims, and see myself abandoned." Paul was a chosen vessel (Acts 9:15), and yet he was of the *seed of Abraham,* and particularly of the tribe of Benjamin, the least and youngest of all the tribes of Israel.

(2.) He suggests that as in Elias's time, so now, this chosen remnant was really more and greater than one would think it was, which intimates likewise that it is no new nor unusual thing for God's grace and favour to Israel to be limited and confined to a remnant of that people; for so it was in Elijah's time. The scripture saith it of Elias, *en lia — in the story of Elias,* the great reformer of the Old Testament. Observe, [1.] His mistake concerning Israel; as if their apostasy in the days of Ahab was so general that he himself was the only faithful servant God had in the world. He refers to 1 Ki. 19:14, where (it is here said) *he maketh intercession to God against Israel.* A strange kind of intercession: *entyn-*

chanei tō Theō kata tou Israēl — He deals with God against *Israel;* so it may be read; so *entynchanō* is translated, Acts 25:24. The Jews *enetychon moi* — have dealt with me. In prayer we deal with God, commune with him, discourse with him: it is said of Elijah (Jam. 5:17) that he *prayed in praying.* We are then likely to pray in praying, to make a business of that duty, when we pray as those that are dealing with God in the duty. Now Elijah in this prayer spoke as if there were one left faithful in Israel but himself. See to what a low ebb the profession of religion may sometimes be brought, and how much the face of it may be eclipsed, that the most wise and observing men may give it up for gone. So it was in Elijah's time. That which makes the show of a nation is the powers and the multitude. The powers of Israel were then persecuting powers: They have *killed thy prophets, and digged down thine altars,* and they *seek my life.* The multitude of Israel were then idolatrous: *I am left alone.* Thus those few that were faithful to God were not only lost in the crowd of idolaters, but crushed and driven into corners by the rage of persecutors. *When the wicked rise, a man is hidden,* Prov. 28:12. — *Digged down thine altars;* not only neglected them, and let them go out of repair, but digged them down. When altars were set up for Baal, it is no wonder if God's altars were pulled down; they could not endure that standing testimony against their idolatry. This was his intercession *against Israel;* as if he had said, "Lord, is not this a people ripe for ruin, worthy to be cast off? What else canst thou do for thy great name?" It is a very sad thing for any person or people to have the prayers of God's people against them, especially of God's prophets, for God espouses, and sooner or later will visibly own, the cause of his praying people. [2.] The rectifying of this mistake by the answer of God (*v.* 4): *I have reserved.* Note, *First,* Things are often much better with the church of God than wise and good men think they are. They are ready to conclude hardly, and to give up all for gone, when it is not so. *Secondly,* In times of general apostasy, there is usually a remnant that keep their integrity — some, though but a few; all do not go one way. *Thirdly,* That when there is a remnant who keep their integrity in times of general apostasy it is God that reserves to himself that remnant. If he had left them to themselves, they had gone down the stream with the rest. It is his free and almighty grace that makes the difference between them and others. — *Seven thousand:* a competent number to bear their testimony against the idolatry of Israel, and yet, compared with the many thousands of Israel, a very small number, one of a city, and two of a tribe, like the grape-gleanings of the vintage. Christ's flock is but a little flock; and yet, when they come all together at last, they will be a great and innumerable multitude, Rev. 7:9. Now the description of this remnant is that *they had not bowed the knee to the image of Baal,* which was then the reigning sin of Israel. In court, city, and country, Baal had the ascendant; and the generality of people, more or less, paid their respect to Baal. The best evidence of integrity is a freedom from the present prevailing corruptions of the times and places that we live in, to swim against the stream when it is strong. Those God will own for his faithful witnesses that are bold in bearing their testimony to the *present* truth, 2 Pt. 1:12. This is thank-worthy, not to bow to Baal when every body bows. Sober singularity is commonly the badge of true sincerity. [3.] The application of this instance to the case in hand: *Even so at this present time, v.* 5–7. God's methods of dispensation towards his church are as they used to be. As it has been, so it is. In Elijah's time there was a remnant, and so there is now. If then there was a remnant left under the Old Testament, when the displays of grace were less clear and the pourings out of the Spirit less plentiful, much more now under the gospel, when the grace of God, which bringeth salvation, appears more illustrious. — *A remnant,* a few of many, a remnant of believing Jews when the rest were obstinate in their unbelief. This is called *a remnant according to the election of grace;* they are such as were chosen from eternity in the counsels of divine love to be vessels of grace and glory. Whom he did predestinate those he called. If the difference between them and others be made purely by the grace of God, as certainly it is *(I have reserved them,* saith he, *to myself),* then it must needs be according to the election; for we are sure that whatever God does he does it according to the counsel of his own will. Now concerning this remnant we may observe, *First,* Whence it takes its rise, from the free grace of God (*v.* 6), that grace which excludes works. The eternal election, in which the difference between some and others is first founded, is

purely of grace, free grace; not for the sake of works done or foreseen; if so, it would not be *grace. Gratia non est ullo modo gratia, si non sit omni modo gratuita — It is not grace, properly so called, if it be not perfectly free.* Election is purely according to the good pleasure of his will, Eph. 1:5. Paul's heart was so full of the freeness of God's grace that in the midst of his discourse he turns aside, as it were, to make this remark, *If of grace, then not of works.* And some observe that faith itself, which in the matter of justification if opposed to works, is here included in them; for faith has a peculiar fitness to receive the free grace of God for our justification, but not to receive that grace for our election. *Secondly,* What it obtains: that which Israel, that is, the body of that people, in van sought for (*v.* 7): *Israel hath not obtained that which he seeketh for,* that is, justification, and acceptance with God (see *ch.* 9:31), but the *election have obtained it.* In them the promise of God has its accomplishment, and God's ancient kindness for that people is remembered. He calls the remnant of believers, not the elect, but the *election,* to show that the sole foundation of all their hopes and happiness is laid in election. They were the persons whom God had in his eye in the counsels of his love; they are the election; they are God's choice. Such was the favour of God to the chosen remnant. But,

2. *The rest were blinded, v.* 7. Some are chosen and called, and the call is made effectual. But others are left to perish in their unbelief; nay, they are made worse by that which should have made them better. The gospel, which to those that believed was the savour of life unto life, to the unbelieving was the savour of death unto death. The same sun softens wax and hardens clay. Good old Simeon foresaw that the child Jesus was set for the fall, as well as for the rising again, of many in Israel, Lu. 2:34. — *Were blinded; epōrōthēsan — they were hardened;* so some. They were seared, and made brawny and insensible. They could neither see the light, nor feel the touch, of gospel grace. Blindness and hardness are expressive of the same senselessness and stupidity of spirit. They shut their eyes, and would not see; this was their sin: and then God, in a way of righteous judgment, blinded their eyes, that they could not see; this was their punishment. This seemed harsh doctrine: to qualify it, therefore, he vouches two witnesses out of the Old Testament, who speak of such a thing.

(1.) Isaiah, who spoke of such a judgment in his day, *ch.* 29:10; 6:9. The *spirit of slumber,* that is, an indisposedness to mind either their duty or interest. They are under the power of a prevailing unconcernedness, like people that are slumbering and sleeping; not affected with any thing that is said or done. They were resolved to continue as they were, and would not stir. The following words explain what is meant by the spirit of slumber: *Eyes, that they should not see, and ears, that they should not hear.* They had the faculties, but in the things that belonged to their peace they had not the use of those faculties; they were quite infatuated, they saw Christ, but they did not believe in him; they heard his word, but they did not receive it; and so both their hearing and their seeing were in vain. It was all one as if they had neither seen nor heard. Of all judgments spiritual judgments are the sorest, and most to be dreaded, though they make the least noise. — *Unto this day.* Ever since Esaias prophesied, this hardening work has been in the doing; some among them have been blind and senseless. Or, rather, ever since the first preaching of the gospel: though they have had the most convincing evidences that could be of the truth of it, the most powerful preaching, the fairest offers, the clearest calls from Christ himself, and from his apostles, yet to this day they are blinded. It is still true concerning multitudes of them, even to this day in which we live; they are hardened and blinded, the obstinacy and unbelief go by succession from generation to generation, according to their own fearful imprecation, which entailed the curse: *His blood be upon us and upon our children.*

(2.) David (*v.* 9, 10), quoted from Ps. 69:22, 23, where David having in the Spirit foretold the sufferings of Christ from his own people the Jews, particularly that of their giving him *vinegar to drink (v.* 21, which was literally fulfilled, Mt. 27:48), an expression of the greatest contempt and malice that could be, in the next words, under the form of an imprecation, he foretels the dreadful judgments of God upon them for it: *Let their table become a snare,* which the apostle here applies to the present blindness of the Jews, and the offence they took at the gospel, which increased their hardness. This teach-

es us how to understand other prayers of David against his enemies; they are to be looked upon as prophetic of the judgments of God upon the public and obstinate enemies of Christ and his kingdom. His prayer that it might be so was a prophecy that it should be so, and not the private expression of his own angry resentments. It was likewise intended to justify God, and to clear his righteousness in such judgments. He speaks here, [1.] Of the ruin of their comforts: *Let their table be made a snare,* that is, as the psalmist explains it, Let that which should be for their welfare be a trap to them. The curse of God will turn meat into poison. It is a threatening like that in Mal. 2:2, *I will curse your blessings.* Their table a snare, that is, an occasion of sin and an occasion of misery. Their very food, that should nourish them, shall choke them. [2.] Of the ruin of their powers and faculties (*v.* 10), their eyes darkened, their backs bowed down, that they can neither find the right way, nor, if they could, are they able to walk in it. The Jews, after their national rejection of Christ and his gospel, became infatuated in their politics, so that their very counsels turned against them, and hastened their ruin by the Romans. They looked like a people designed for slavery and contempt, their backs bowed down, to be ridden and trampled upon by all the nations about them. Or, it may be understood spiritually; their backs are bowed down in carnality and worldly-mindedness. *Curvae in terris animae — They mind earthly things.* This is an exact description of the state and temper of the present remainder of that people, than whom, if the accounts we have of them be true, there is not a more worldly, wilful, blind, selfish, ill-natured, people in the world. They are manifestly to this day under the power of this curse. Divine curses will work long. It is a sign we have our eyes darkened if we are bowed down in worldly-mindedness.

II. Another thing which qualified this doctrine of the rejection of the Jews was that though they were cast off and unchurched, yet the Gentiles were taken in (*v.* 11–14), which he applies by way of caution to the Gentiles, *v.* 17–22.

1. The rejection of the Jews made room for the reception of the Gentiles. The Jews' leavings were a feast for the poor Gentiles (*v.* 11): "*Have they stumbled that they should fall?* Had God no other end in forsaking and rejecting them than their destruction?" He startles at this, rejecting the thought with abhorrence, as usually he does when any thing is suggested which seems to reflect upon the wisdom, or righteousness, or goodness of God: *God forbid!* no, *through their fall salvation is come to the Gentiles.* Not but that salvation might have come to the Gentiles if they had stood; but by the divine appointment it was so ordered that the gospel should be preached to the Gentiles upon the Jews' refusal of it. Thus in the parable (Mt. 22:8, 9), *Those that were* first *bidden were not worthy — Go ye therefore into the highways,* Lu. 14:21. And so it was in the history (Acts 13:46): *It was necessary that the word of God should first have been spoken to you; but, seeing you put it from you, lo, we turn to the Gentiles;* so Acts 18:6. God will have a church in the world, will have the wedding furnished with guests; and, if one will not come, another will, or why was the offer made? The Jews had the refusal, and so the tender came to the Gentiles. See how Infinite Wisdom brings light out of darkness, good out of evil, meat out of the eater, and sweetness out of the strong. To the same purport he says (*v.* 12), *The fall of them was the riches of the world,* that is, it hastened the gospel so much the sooner into the Gentile world. The gospel is the greatest riches of the place where it is; it is better than thousands of gold and silver. Or, The riches of the Gentiles was the multitude of converts among them. True believers are God's jewels. To the same purport (*v.* 15): *The casting away of them is the reconciling of the world.* God's displeasure towards them made way for his favour towards the Gentiles. God was in Christ *reconciling the world,* 2 Co. 5:19. And therefore he took occasion from the unbelief of the Jews openly to disavow and disown them, though they had been his peculiar favourites, to show that in dispensing his favours he would now no longer act in such a way of peculiarity and restriction, but that in every nation he that feared God and wrought righteousness should be accepted of him, Acts 10:34, 35.

2. The use that the apostle makes of this doctrine concerning the substitution of the Gentiles in the room of the Jews.

(1.) As a kinsman to the Jews, here is a word of excitement and exhortation to them, to stir them up to receive and embrace the gospel-offer. This God intended in his favour to the Gentiles, to provoke the Jews to jealousy (*v.* 11), and Paul endeavours to enforce it accordingly (v. 14): *If by any means I might provoke to emulation those who are my flesh.* "Shall the despised Gentiles run away with all the comforts and privileges of the gospel, and shall not we repent of our refusal, and now at last put in for a share? Shall not we believe and obey, and be pardoned and saved, as well as the Gentiles?" See an instance of such an emulation in Esau, Gen. 28:6–9. There is a commendable emulation in the affairs of our souls: why should not we be as holy and happy as any of our neighbours? In this emulation there needs no suspicion, undermining or countermining; for the church has room enough, and the new covenant grace and comfort enough, for us all. The blessings are not lessened by the multitudes of the sharers. — *And might save some of them.* See what was Paul's business, to save souls; and yet the utmost he promises himself is but to save some. Though he was such a powerful preacher, spoke and wrote with such evidence and demonstration of the Spirit, yet of the many he dealt with he could but save some. Ministers must think their pains well bestowed if they can but be instrumental to save some.

(2.) As an apostle to the Gentiles, here is a word of caution for them: "*I speak to you Gentiles.* You believing Romans, you hear what riches of salvation are come to you by the fall of the Jews, but take heed lest you do any thing to forfeit it." Paul takes this, as other occasions, to apply his discourse to the Gentiles, because he was the apostle of the Gentiles, appointed for the service of their faith, to plant and water churches in the Gentile nations. This was the purport of his extraordinary mission, Acts 22:21, *I will send thee far hence unto the Gentiles;* compare Acts 9:15. It was likewise the intention of his ordination, Gal. 2:9. Compare Acts 13:2. It ought to be our great and special care to do good to those that are under our charge: we must particularly mind that which is our own work. It was an instance of God's great love to the poor Gentiles that he appointed Paul, who in gifts and graces excelled all the apostles, to be the apostle of the Gentiles. The Gentile world was a wider province; and the work to be done in it required a very able, skilful, zealous, courageous workman: such a one was Paul. God calls those to special work whom he either sees or makes fit for it. — *I magnify my office.* There were those that vilified it, and him because of it. It was because he was the apostle of the Gentiles that the Jews were so outrageous against him (Acts 22:21, 22), and yet he thought never the worse of it, though it set him up as the butt of all the Jewish rage and malice. It is a sign of true love to Jesus Christ to reckon that service and work for him truly honourable which the world looks upon with scorn, as mean and contemptible. The office of the ministry is an office to be *magnified.* Ministers are ambassadors for Christ, and stewards of the mysteries of God, and for their work's sake are to be esteemed highly in love. — *My office; tēn diakonian mou — my ministry,* my service, not my lordship and dominion. It was not the dignity and power, but the duty and work, of an apostle, that Paul was so much in love with. Now two things he exhorts the Gentiles to, with reference to the rejected Jews: —

[1.] To have a respect for the Jews, notwithstanding, and to desire their conversion. This is intimated in the prospect he gives them of the advantage that would accrue to the church by their conversion, v. 12, 15. It would be as life from the dead; and therefore they must not insult and triumph over those poor Jews, but rather pity them, and desire their welfare, and long for the receiving of them in again.

[2.] To take heed to themselves, lest they should stumble and fall, as they Jews had done, v. 17–22. Here observe,

First, The privilege which the Gentiles had by being taken into the church. They were grafted in (v. 17), as a branch of a wild olive into a good olive, which is contrary to the way and custom of the husbandman, who grafts the good olive into the bad; but those that God grafts into the church he finds wild and barren, and good for nothing. Men graft to mend the tree; but God grafts to mend the branch. 1. The church of God is an olive-tree, flourishing and fruitful as an olive (Ps. 52:8; Hos. 14:6), the fruit useful for the honour both of God and man, Jdg. 9:9. 2. Those that are out of the church are as wild olive-trees, not only useless, but what they do produce is sour and unsavoury: *Wild by nature, v. 24.* This was the state of the poor Gentiles, that wanted church privileges, and in respect of real sanctification; and it is the natural state of every one of us, to be wild by nature. 3. Conversion is the grafting in of wild branches into the good olive. We must be cut off from the old stock, and be brought into union with

a new root. 4. Those that are grafted into the good olive-tree partake of the root and fatness of the olive. It is applicable to a saving union with Christ; all that are by a lively faith grafted into Christ partake of him as the branches of the root — receive from his fulness. But it is here spoken of a visible church-membership, from which the Jews were as branches broken off; and so the Gentiles were grafted in, *autois — among those* that continued, or in the room of those that were broken off. The Gentiles, being grafted into the church, partake of the same privileges that the Jews did, *the root and fatness.* The olive-tree is the visible church (called so Jer. 11:16); the root of this tree was Abraham, not the root of communication, so Christ only is the root, but the root of administration, he being the first with whom the covenant was so solemnly made. Now the believing Gentiles partake of this root: *he also is a son of Abraham* (Lu. 19:9), the *blessing of Abraham comes upon the Gentiles* (Gal. 3:14), the same fatness of the olive-tree, the same for substance, special protection, lively oracles, means of salvation, a standing ministry, instituted ordinances; and, among the rest, the visible church-membership of their infant seed, which was part of the fatness of the olive-tree that the Jews had, and cannot be imagined to be denied to the Gentiles.

Secondly, A caution not to abuse these privileges. 1. "Be not proud (v. 18): *Boast not against the branches.* Do not therefore trample upon the Jews as a reprobate people, nor insult over those that are broken off, much less over those that do continue." Grace is given, not to make us proud, but to make us thankful. The law of faith excludes all boasting either of ourselves or against others. "Do not say (v. 19): *They were broken off that I might be grafted in;* that is, do not think that thou didst merit more at the hand of God than they, or didst stand higher in his favour." "But remember, *thou bearest not the root, but the root thee.* Though thou art grafted in, thou art still but a branch borne by the root; nay, and an engrafted branch, brought into the good olive *contrary to nature* (v. 24), not free-born, but by an act of grace enfranchised and naturalized. Abraham, the root of the Jewish church, is not beholden to thee; but thou art greatly obliged to him, as the trustee of the covenant and the father of many nations. Therefore, *if thou boast,* know (this word must be supplied to clear the sense) *thou bearest not the root but the root thee.*" 2. "Be not secure (v. 20): *Be not high-minded, but fear.* Be not too confident of your own strength and standing." A holy fear is an excellent preservative against high-mindedness: happy is the man that thus feareth always. We need not fear but God will be true to his word; all the danger is lest we be false to ours. *Let us therefore fear,* Heb. 4:1. The church of Rome now boasts of a patent of perpetual preservation; but the apostle here, in his epistle to that church when she was in her infancy and integrity, enters an express caveat against that boast, and all claims of that kind. — *Fear* what? "Why fear lest thou commit a forfeiture as they have done, lest thou lose the privileges thou now enjoyest, as they have lost theirs." The evils that befal others should be warnings to us. *Go* (saith God to Jerusalem Jer. 7:12), and *see what I did to* Shiloh; so now, let all the churches of God go and see what he did to Jerusalem, and what is become of the day of their visitation, that we may hear and fear, and take heed of Jerusalem's sin. The patent which churches have of their privileges is not for a certain term, nor entailed upon them and their heirs; but it runs as long as they carry themselves well, and no longer. Consider, (1.) "How they were broken off. It was not undeservedly, by an act of absolute sovereignty and prerogative, but *because of unbelief.* It seems, then, it is possible for churches that have long stood by faith to fall into such a state of infidelity as may be their ruin. Their unbelief did not only provoke God to cut them off, but they did by this cut themselves off; it was not only the meritorious, but the formal cause of their separation. "Now, thou art liable to the same infirmity and corruption that they fell by." Further observe, They were *natural branches* (v. 21), not only interested in Abraham's covenant, but descending from Abraham's loins, and so born upon the premises, and thence had a kind of tenant-right: yet, when they sunk into unbelief, God did not spare them. Prescription, long usage, the faithfulness of their ancestors, would not secure them. It was in vain to plead, though they insisted much upon it, that they were Abraham's seed, Mt. 3:9; Jn. 8:33. It is true they were the husbandmen to whom the vineyard was first let out; but, when they forfeited it, it was justly taken from them, Mt. 21:41, 43. This is called here *severity, v. 22.* God laid righteousness to the

line and judgment to the plummet, and dealt with them according to their sins. Severity is a word that sounds harshly; and I do not remember that it is any where else in scripture ascribed to God; and it is here applied to the unchurching of the Jews. God is most severe towards those that have been in profession nearest to him, if they rebel against him, Amos 3:2. Patience and privileges abused turn to the greatest wrath. Of all judgments, spiritual judgments are the sorest; for of these he is here speaking, v. 8. (2.) "How thou standest, thou that art engrafted in." He speaks to the Gentile churches in general, though perhaps tacitly reflecting on some particular person, who might have expressed some such pride and triumph in the Jews' rejection. "Consider then," [1.] "By what means thou standest: *By faith,* which is a depending grace, and fetches in strength from heaven. Thou dost not stand in any strength of thy own, of which thou mightest be confident: thou art no more than the free grace of God makes thee, and his grace is his own, which he gives or withholds at pleasure. That which ruined them was unbelief, and by faith thou standest; therefore thou hast no faster hold than they had, thou standest on no firmer foundation than they did." [2.] "On what terms (v. 22): *Towards thee goodness, if thou continue in his goodness,* that is, continue in a dependence upon and compliance with the free grace of God, the want of which it was that ruined the Jews — if thou be careful to keep up thine interest in the divine favour, by being continually careful to please God and fearful of offending him." The sum of our duty, the condition of our happiness, is to keep ourselves in the love of God. *Fear the Lord and his goodness.* Hos. 3:5.

III. Another thing that qualified this doctrine of the Jews' rejection is that, though for the present they are cast off, yet the rejection is not final; but, when the fulness of time is come, they will be taken in again. They are not cast off for ever, but mercy is remembered in the midst of wrath. Let us observe,

1. How this conversion of the Jews is here described. (1.) It is said to be their fulness (v. 12), that is, the addition of them to the church, the filling up again of that place which became vacant by their rejection. This would be the enriching of the world (that is, the church in the world) with a great deal of light and strength and beauty. (2.) It is called the receiving of them. The conversion of a soul is the receiving of that soul, so the conversion of a nation. They shall be received into favour, into the church, into the love of Christ, whose arms are stretched out for the receiving of all those that will come to him. And this will be as *life from the dead* — so strange and surprising, and yet withal so welcome and acceptable. The conversion of the Jews will bring great joy to the church. See Lu. 15:32, *He was dead, and is alive;* and therefore *it was meet we should make merry and be glad.* (3.) It is called the *grafting of them in again* (v. 23), into the church, from which they had been broken off. That which is grafted in receives sap and virtue from the root; so does a soul that is truly grafted into the church receive life, and strength, and grace from Christ the quickening root. They shall be *grafted into their own olive-tree* (v. 24), that is, into the church of which they had formerly been the most eminent and conspicuous members, to retrieve those privileges of visible church-membership which they had so long enjoyed, but have now sinned away and forfeited by their unbelief. (4.) It is called the *saving of all Israel, v. 26.* True conversion may well be called salvation; it is salvation begun. See Acts 2:47. The adding of them to the church is the saving of them: *tous sōzomenous,* in the present tense, *are saved.* When conversion-work goes on, salvation-work goes on.

2. What it is grounded upon, and what reason we have to look for it.

(1.) Because of the holiness of the first-fruits and the root, v. 16. Some by the first-fruits understand those of the Jews that were already converted to the faith of Christ and received into the church, who were as the first-fruits dedicated to God, as earnests of a more plentiful and sanctified harvest. A good beginning promises a good ending. Why may we not suppose that others may be savingly wrought upon as well as those who are already brought in? Others by the first-fruits understand the same with the root, namely, the patriarchs, Abraham, Isaac, and Jacob, from whom the Jews descended, and with whom, as the prime trustees, the covenant was deposited: and so they were the root of the Jews, not only as a people, but as a church. Now, if they were holy, which is not meant so much of inherent as of federal holiness —

if they were in the church and in the covenant — then we have reason to conclude that God hath a kindness for the *lump* — the body of that people; and for the *branches* — the particular members of it. The Jews are in a sense a holy nation (Ex. 19:6), being descended from holy parents. Now it cannot be imagined that such a holy nation should be totally and finally cast off. This proves that the seed of believers, as such, are within the pale of the visible church, and within the verge of the covenant, till they do, by their unbelief, throw themselves out; for, *if the root be holy, so are the branches.* Though real qualifications are not propagated, yet relative privileges are. Though a wise man does not beget a wise man, yet a free man begets a free man. Though grace does not run in the blood, yet external privileges do (till they are forfeited), even to a thousand generations. Look how they will answer it another day that cut off the entail, by turning the seed of the faithful out of the church, and so not allowing the blessing of Abraham to come upon the Gentiles. The Jewish branches are reckoned holy, because the root was so. This is expressed more plainly (*v.* 28): *They are beloved for the fathers' sakes.* In this love to the fathers the first foundation of their church-state was laid (Deu. 4:37): *Because he loved they fathers, therefore he chose their seed after them.* And the same love would revive their privileges, for still the ancient loving-kindness is remembered; they are *beloved for the fathers' sakes.* It is God's usual method of grace. Kindness to the children for the father's sake is therefore called the *kindness of God,* 2 Sa. 9:3, 7. Though, as concerning the gospel (namely, in the present dispensation of it), they are enemies to it *for your sakes,* that is, for the sake of the Gentiles, against whom they have such an antipathy; yet, when God's time shall come, this will wear off, and God's love to their fathers will be remembered. See a promise that points at this, Lev. 26:42. The iniquity of the fathers is visited but to the third and fourth generation; but there is mercy kept for thousands. Many fare the better for the sake of their godly ancestors. It is upon this account that the church is called their own *olive-tree.* Long it had been their own peculiar, which is some encouragement to us to hope that there may be room for them in it again, for old acquaintance-sake. That which hath been may be again. Though particular persons and generations wear off in unbelief, yet there having been a national church-membership, though for the present suspended, we may expect that it will be revived.

(2.) Because of the power of God (*v.* 23): *God is able to graft them in again.* The conversion of souls is a work of almighty power; and when they seem most hardened, and blinded, and obstinate, our comfort is that God is able to work a change, able to graft those in that have been long cast out and withered. When the house is kept by the strong man armed, with all his force, yet God is stronger than he, and is able to dispossess him. The condition of their restoration is faith: *If they abide not still in unbelief.* So that nothing is to be done but to remove that unbelief that is the great obstacle; and God is able to take that away, though nothing less than an almighty power will do it, the same power that raised up Christ from the dead, Eph. 1:19, 29. Otherwise, can these dry bones live?

(3.) Because of the grace of God manifested to the Gentiles. Those that have themselves experienced the grace of God, preventing, distinguishing grace, may thence take encouragement to hope well concerning others. This is his argument (*v.* 24): "If thou wast grafted into a good olive, that was wild by nature, much more shall these that were the natural branches, and may therefore be presumed somewhat nearer to the divine acceptance." This is a suggestion very proper to check the insolence of those Gentile Christians that looked with disdain and triumph upon the condition of the rejected Jews, and trampled upon them; as if he had said, "Their condition, bad as it is, is not so bad as yours was before your conversion; and therefore why may it not be made as good as yours is?" This is his argument (*v.* 30, 31): *As you in times past have not,* etc. It is good for those that have found mercy with God to be often thinking what they were in time past, and how they obtained that mercy. This would help to soften our censures of those that still continue in unbelief, and quicken our prayers for them. He argues further from the occasion of the Gentiles' call, that is, the unbelief of the Jews; thence it took rise: *"You have obtained mercy through their unbelief;* much more shall they obtain mercy through your mercy. If the putting out of their candle was the lighting of yours, by that power of God which brings good out of evil, much more shall the continued light of your candle, when God's time shall come, be a means of lighting theirs again." *"That through your mercy they might obtain mercy,"* that is, that they may be beholden to you, as you have been to them." He takes it for granted that the believing Gentiles would do their utmost endeavour to work upon the Jews — that, when God had persuaded Japhet, Japhet would be labouring to persuade Shem. True grace hates monopolies. Those that have found mercy themselves should endeavour that through their mercy others also may obtain mercy.

(4.) Because of the promises and prophecies of the Old Testament, which point at this. He quotes a very remarkable one, *v.* 26, from Isa. 59:20, 21. Where we may observe, [1.] The coming of Christ promised: *There shall come out of Zion the deliverer.* Jesus Christ is the great deliverer, which supposes mankind in a state of misery and danger. In Isaiah it is, *the Redeemer shall come to Zion.* There he is called the Redeemer; here the deliverer; he delivers in a way of redemption, by a price. There he is said to come to Zion, because when the prophet prophesied he was yet to come into the world, and Zion was his first head-quarters. Thither he came, there he took up his residence: but, when the apostle wrote this, he had come, he had been in Zion; and he is speaking of the fruits of his appearing, which shall come *out of Zion;* thence, as from the spring, issued forth those streams of living water which in the everlasting gospel watered the nations. *Out of Zion went forth the law,* Isa. 2:3. Compare Lu. 24:47. [2.] The end and purpose of this coming: *He shall turn away ungodliness from Jacob.* Christ's errand into the world was to turn away ungodliness, to turn away the guilt by the purchase of pardoning mercy, and to turn away the power by the pouring out of renewing grace, to save his people from their sins (Mt. 1:21), to separate between us and our sins, that iniquity might not be our ruin, and that it might not be our ruler. Especially to turn it away from Jacob, which is that for the sake of which he quotes the text, as a proof of the great kindness God intended for the seed of Jacob. What greater kindness could he do them than to turn away ungodliness from them, to take away that which comes between them and all happiness, take away sin, and then make way for all good? This is the blessing that Christ was sent to bestow upon the world, and to tender it to the Jews in the first place (Acts 3:26), to turn people from their iniquities. In Isaiah it is, *The Redeemer shall come to Zion, and unto those that turn from transgression in Jacob,* which shown who in Zion were to have a share in and to reap benefit by the deliverance promised, those and those only that leave their sins and turn to God; to them Christ comes as a Redeemer, but as an avenger to those that persist in impenitence. See Deu. 30:2, 3. Those that turn from sin will be owned as the true citizens of Zion (Eph. 2:19), the right Jacob, Ps. 24:4, 6. Putting both these readings together, we learn that none have an interest in Christ but those that turn from their sins, nor can any turn from their sins but by the strength of the grace of Christ. — *For this is my covenant with them* — this, that the deliverer shall come to them — this, that my Spirit shall not depart from them, as it follows, Isa. 59:21. God's gracious intentions concerning Israel were made the matter of a covenant, which the God that cannot lie could not but be true and faithful to. They were the *children of the covenant,* Acts 3:25. The apostle adds, *When I shall take away their sins,* which some think refers to Isa. 27:9, or only to the foregoing words, to *turn away ungodliness.* Pardon of sin is laid as the foundation of all the blessings of the new covenant (Heb. 8:12): *For I will be merciful.* Now from all this he infers that certainly God had great mercy in store for that people, something answerable to the extent of these rich promises: and he proves his inference (*v.* 29) by this truth: *For the gifts and callings of God are without repentance.* Repentance is sometimes taken for a change of mind, and so God never repents, for he is in one mind and who can turn him? Sometimes for a change of way, and that is here understood, intimating the constancy and unchangeableness of that love of God which is founded in election. Those gifts and callings are immutable; whom he so loves, he loves to the end. We find God repenting that he had given man a being (Gen. 6:6, *It repented the Lord that he had made man),* and repenting that he had given a man honour and power (1 Sa. 15:11, *It repenteth me that I have set up Saul to be king);* but we never find God repenting that he had given a man grace, or effectually called him; those gifts and callings are without repentance.

3. The time and extent of this conversion, when and where it is to be expected. It is called a mystery (*v.* 25), that which was not obvious, and which one would not expect upon the view of the present state of that people, who appeared generally so obstinate against Christ and Christianity that it was a riddle to talk of their unanimous conversion. The conversion of the Gentiles is called a mystery, Eph. 3:3, 6, 9. The case of the rejected Jews seemed as bad now as that of the Gentiles had been. The work of conversion was carried on in a mystery. Now he would have them know so much of this mystery as to keep them humble: lest *you be wise in your own conceit,* that is, lest you be so much puffed up with your church-membership, and trample upon the Jews. Ignorance is the cause of our self-conceitedness. *I would not have you ignorant, lest you be wise in your own conceits.* Observe, (1.) Their present state: *Blindness, in part, is happened to Israel, v.* 25. Here is something to qualify it, that it is but in part; there is a remnant that see the things which belong to their peace, though part, the far greater part, are in blindness, *v.* 7, 8. To the same purport (*v.* 32): *God has concluded them all in unbelief,* shut them up as in a prison, given them over to their own hearts' lusts. Shutting up is sometimes put for conviction, as Gal. 3:22. They all stand before God convicted of unbelief. They would not believe. "Why then," saith God, "you shall not." They peremptorily refused to submit to Christ and his government, which refusal of theirs was, as it were, entered upon record in the court of heaven, and was conclusive against them. (2.) When this blessed change should be: when the *fulness of the Gentiles shall come in,* when the gospel has had its intended success, and made its progress in the Gentile world; compare *v.* 12. The Jews shall continue in blindness, till God hath performed his whole work among the Gentiles, and then their turn will come next to be remembered. This was the purpose and ordination of God, for wise and holy ends; things should not be ripe for the Jews' conversion till the church was replenished with the Gentiles, that it might appear that God's taking them again was not because he had need of them, but of his own free grace. (3.) The extent of it: *All Israel shall be saved, v.* 26. He will *have mercy upon all, v.* 32. Not every individual person, but the body of the people. Not that ever they should be restored to their covenant of peculiarity again, to have their priesthood, and temple, and ceremonies again (an end is put to all those things); but they should be brought to believe in Christ the true Messiah whom they crucified, and be incorporated in the Christian church, and become one sheep-fold with the Gentiles under Christ the great Shepherd. But the question is concerning the accomplishment of all this. [1.] Some think it is done already, when before, and in, and after, the destruction of Jerusalem by the Romans, multitudes of the Jews were convinced of their infidelity, and turned Christians; so many that, considering how many millions of them were cut off in the destruction, we may reasonably conclude that of those who survived the greater part were Christians, and embodied in the Christian church, and it was a very inconsiderable number that persisted obstinately. For many ages Judea had, as other Christian provinces, their ministers and churches, and a face of religion. And most of this work, they suppose, was done towards the close of the ministry of the apostles, when the Gentiles had generally come in. [2.] Others think that it is yet to have its accomplishment towards the end of the world — that those Jews which yet wonderfully remain distinct from the rest of the nations by their names, customs, and religion, and are very numerous, especially in the Levant parts, shall, by the working of the Spirit with the word, be convinced of their sin, and brought generally to embrace the Christian faith, and to join in with the Christian churches, which will contribute much to their strength and beauty. Alas! who shall live when God doeth this?

Verses 33–36

The apostle having insisted so largely, through the greatest part of this chapter, upon reconciling the rejection of the Jews with the divine goodness, he concludes here with the acknowledgment and admiration of the divine wisdom and sovereignty in all this. Here the apostle does with great affection and awe adore,

I. The secrecy of the divine counsels: *O the depth!* in these proceedings towards the Jews and Gentiles; or, in general, the whole mystery of the gospel, which we cannot fully comprehend. — *The riches of the wisdom and knowledge of God,* the abundant instances of his wisdom and knowledge in contriving and carrying on the work of our redemption by Christ, a depth which the angels pry into, 1 Pt. 1:12. Much more may it puzzle any human understanding to give an account of the methods, and reasons, and designs, and compass of it. Paul was as well acquainted with the mysteries of the kingdom of God as ever any mere man was; and yet he confesses himself at a loss in the contemplation, and, despairing to find the bottom, he humbly sits down at the brink, and adores the depth. Those that know most in this state of imperfection cannot but be most sensible of their own weakness and short-sightedness, and that after all their researches, and all their attainments in those researches, while they are here they cannot order their speech by reason of darkness. Praise is silent to thee, Ps. 65:1. — *The depth of the riches.* Men's riches of all kinds are shallow, you may soon see the bottom; but God's riches are deep (Ps. 36:6): *Thy judgments are a great deep.* There is not only depth in the divine counsels, but riches too, which denotes an abundance of that which is precious and valuable, so complete are the dimensions of the divine counsels; they have not only depth and height, but *breadth and length* (Eph. 3:18), and that passing knowledge, *v.* 19. — *Riches of the wisdom and knowledge of God.* His seeing all things by one clear, and certain, and infallible view — all things that are, or ever were, or ever shall be, — that all is naked and open before him: there is his knowledge. His ruling and ordering all things, directing and disposing them to his own glory, and bringing about his own purposes and counsels in all; this is his *wisdom.* And the vast extent of both these is such a depth as is past our fathoming, and we may soon lose ourselves in the contemplation of them. Such *knowledge is too wonderful for me,* Ps. 139:6. Compare *v.* 17, 18. — *How unsearchable are his judgments!* that is, his counsels and purposes: and his *ways,* that is, the execution of these counsels and purposes. We know not what he designs. When the wheels are set in motion, and Providence has begun to work, yet we know not what he has in view; it is *past finding out.* This does not only overturn all our positive conclusions about the divine counsels, but it also checks all our curious enquiries. Secret things belong not to us, Deu. 29:29. God's way is in the sea, Ps. 77:19. Compare Job 23:8, 9; Ps. 97:2. What he does we know not now, Jn. 13:7. We cannot give a reason of God's proceedings, nor by searching find out God. See Job 5:9; 9:10. The judgments of his mouth, and the way of our duty, blessed be God, are plain and easy, it is a high-way; but the judgments of his hands, and the ways of his providence, are dark and mysterious, which therefore we must not pry into, but silently adore and acquiesce in. The apostle speaks this especially with reference to that strange turn, the casting off of the Jews and the entertainment of the Gentiles, with a purpose to take in the Jews again in due time; these were strange proceedings, the choosing of some, the refusing of others, and neither according to the probabilities of human conjecture. Even so, Father, because it seemed good in thing eyes. These are methods unaccountable, concerning which we must say, *O the depth! — Past finding out, anexichniastoi — cannot be traced.* God leaves no prints nor footsteps behind him, does not make a path to shine after him; but his paths of providence are new every morning. He does not go the same way so often as to make a track of it. *How little a portion is heard of him!* Job 26:14. It follows (*v.* 34), *For who hath known the mind of the Lord?* Is there any creature made of his cabinet-council, or laid, as Christ was, in the bosom of the Father? Is there any to whom he has imparted his counsels, or that is able, upon the view of his providences, to know the way that he takes? There is so vast a distance and disproportion between God and man, between the Creator and the creature, as for ever excludes the thought of such an intimacy and familiarity. The apostle makes the same challenge (1 Co. 2:16): *For who hath known the mind of the Lord?* And yet there he adds, *But we have the mind of Christ,* which intimates that through Christ true believers, who have his Spirit, know so much of the mind of God as is necessary to their happiness. He that knew the mind of the Lord has declared him, Jn. 1:18. And so, though we know not the mind of the Lord, yet, if we have the mind of Christ, we have enough. *The secret of the Lord is with those that fear him,* Ps. 25:14. *Shall I hide from Abraham the thing which I do?* See Jn. 15:15. — *Or who has been his counsellor?* He needs no counsellor, for he is infinitely wise; nor is any creature capable of being his counsellor; this would be like lighting a candle to the sun. This seems to refer to that scripture (Isa. 40:13, 14), *Who hath directed the Spirit of the Lord, or, being his counsellor, hath*

taught him? With whom took he counsel? etc. It is the substance of God's challenge to Job concerning the work of creation (Job 38), and is applicable to all the methods of his providence. It is nonsense for any man to prescribe to God, or to teach him how to govern the world.

II. The sovereignty of the divine counsels. In all these things God acts as a free agent, does what he will, because he will, and gives not account of any of his matters (Job 23:13; 33:13), and yet there is no unrighteousness with him. To clear which,

1. He challenges any to prove God a debtor to him (*v.* 35): *Who hath first given to him?* Who is there of all the creatures that can prove God is beholden to him? Whatever we do for him, or devote to him, it must be with that acknowledgment, which is for ever a bar to such demands (1 Chr. 29:14): *Of thine own we have given thee.* All the duties we can perform are not requitals, but rather restitutions. If any can prove that God is his debtor, the apostle here stands bound for the payment, and proclaims, in God's name, that payment is ready: *It shall be recompensed to him again.* It is certain God will let nobody lose by him; but never any one yet durst make a demand of this kind, or attempt to prove it. This is here suggested, (1.) To silence the clamours of the Jews. When God took away their visible church-privileges from them, he did but take his own: and may he not do what he will with his own — give or withhold his grace where and when he pleases? (2.) To silence the insultings of the Gentiles. When God sent the gospel among them, and gave so many of them grace and wisdom to accept of it, it was not because he owed them so much favour, or that they could challenge it as a debt, but of his own good pleasure.

2. He resolves all into the sovereignty of God (*v.* 36): *For of him, and through him, and to him, are all things,* that is, God is all in all. All things in heaven and earth (especially those things which relate to our salvation, the things which belong to our peace) are of him by way of creation, through him by way of providential influence, that they may be to him in their final tendency and result. Of God as the spring and fountain of all, through Christ, God-man, as the conveyance, to God as the ultimate end. These three include, in general, all God's causal relations to his creatures: of him as the first efficient cause, through him as the supreme directing cause, to him as the ultimate final cause; for the Lord hath made all for himself, Rev. 4:11. If all be of him and through him, there is all the reason in the world that all should be to him and for him. It is a necessary circulation; if the rivers received their waters from the sea, they return them to the sea again, Eccl. 1:7. To do all to the glory of God is to make a virtue of necessity; for all shall in the end be to him, whether we will or no. And so he concludes with a short doxology: *To whom be glory for ever, Amen.* God's universal agency as the first cause, the sovereign ruler, and the last end, ought to be the matter of our adoration. Thus all his works do praise him objectively; but his saints do bless him actively; they hand that praise to him which all the creatures do minister matter for, Ps. 145:10. Paul had been discoursing at large of the counsels of God concerning man, sifting the point with a great deal of accuracy; but, after all, he concludes with the acknowledgment of the divine sovereignty, as that into which all these things must be ultimately resolved, and in which alone the mind can safely and sweetly rest. This is, if not the scholastic way, yet the Christian way, of disputation. Whatever are the premises, let god's glory be the conclusion; especially when we come to talk of the divine counsels and actings, it is best for us to turn our arguments into awful and serious adorations. The glorified saints, that see furthest into these mysteries, never dispute, but praise to eternity.

CHAPTER 12

The apostle, having at large cleared and confirmed the prime fundamental doctrines of Christianity, comes in the next place to press the principal duties. We mistake our religion if we look upon it only as a system of notions and a guide to speculation. No, it is a practical religion, that tends to the right ordering of the conversation. It is designed not only to inform our judgments, but to reform our hearts and lives. From the method of the apostle's writing in this, as in some other of the epistles (as from the management of the principal ministers of state in Christ's kingdom) the stewards of the mysteries of God may take direction how to divide the word of truth: not to press duty abstracted from privilege, nor privilege abstracted from duty; but let both go together, with a complicated design, they will greatly promote and befriend each other. The duties are drawn from the privileges, by way of

inference. The foundation of Christian practice must be laid in Christian knowledge and faith. We must first understand how we receive Christ Jesus the Lord, and then we shall know the better how to walk in him. There is a great deal of duty prescribed in this chapter. The exhortations are short and pithy, briefly summing up what is good, and what the Lord our God in Christ requires of us. It is an abridgment of the Christian directory, an excellent collection of rules for the right ordering of the conversation, as becomes the gospel. It is joined to the foregoing discourse by the word "therefore." It is the practical application of doctrinal truths that is the life of preaching. He had been discoursing at large of justification by faith, and of the riches of free grace, and the pledges and assurances we have of the glory that is to be revealed. Hence carnal libertines would be apt to infer,"Therefore we may live as we list, and walk in the way of our hearts and the sight of our eyes." Now this does not follow; the faith that justifies is a faith that "works by love." And there is no other way to heaven but the way of holiness and obedience. Therefore what God hath joined together let no man put asunder. The particular exhortations of this chapter are reducible to the three principal heads of Christian duty: our duty to God t ourselves, and to our brother. The grace of God teaches us, in general, to live "godly, soberly, and righteously;" and to deny all that which is contrary hereunto. Now this chapter will give us to understand what godliness, sobriety, and righteousness, are though somewhat intermixed.

Verses 1–21

We may observe here, according to the scheme mentioned in the contents, the apostle's exhortations,

I. Concerning our duty to God, We see what is godliness.

1. It is to surrender ourselves to God, and so to lay a good foundation. We must first give our own selves unto the Lord, 2 Co. 8:5. This is here pressed as the spring of all duty and obedience, *v.* 1, 2. Man consists of body and soul, Gen. 2:7; Eccl. 12:7.

(1.) The body must be presented to him, *v.* 1. *The body is for the Lord, and the Lord for the body,* 1 Co. 6:13, 14. The exhortation is here introduced very pathetically: *I beseech you, brethren.* Though he was a great apostle, yet he calls the meanest Christians *brethren,* a term of affection and concern. He uses entreaty; this is the gospel way: *As though God did beseech you by us,* 2 Co. 5:20. Though he might with authority command, yet for love's sake he rather beseeches, Philem. *v.* 8, 9. The *poor useth entreaty,* Prov. 18:23. This is to insinuate the exhortation, that it might come with the more pleasing power. Many are sooner wrought upon if they be accosted kindly, are more easily led than driven. Now observe,

[1.] The duty pressed — to present our *bodies a living sacrifice,* alluding to the sacrifices under the law, which were presented or set before God at the altar, ready to be offered to him. *Your bodies* — your whole selves; so expressed because under the law the bodies of beasts were offered in sacrifice, 1 Co. 6:20. Our bodies and spirits are intended. The offering was sacrificed by the priest, but presented by the offerer, who transferred to God all his right, title, and interest in it, by laying his hand on the head of it. Sacrifice is here taken for whatsoever is by God's own appointment dedicated to himself; see 1 Pt. 2:5. We are temple, priest, and sacrifice, as Christ was in his peculiar sacrificing. There were sacrifices of atonement and sacrifices of acknowledgment. Christ, who was once offered to bear the sins of many, is the only sacrifice of atonement; but our persons and performances, tendered to God through Christ our priest, are as sacrifices of acknowledgment to the honour of God. Presenting them denotes a voluntary act, done by virtue of that absolute despotic power which the will has over the body and all the members of it. It must be a free-will offering. Your bodies; not your beasts. Those legal offerings, as they had their power from Christ, so they had their period in Christ. The presenting of the body to God implies not only the avoiding of the sins that are committed with or against the body, but the using of the body as a servant of the soul in the service of God. It is to *glorify God with our bodies* (1. Cor. 6:20), to engage our bodies in the duties of immediate worship, and in a diligent attendance to our particular callings, and be willing to suffer for God with our bodies, when we are called to it. It is to yield the members of our bodies as instruments of righteousness, ch. 6:13. Though bodily exercise alone profits little, yet in its place it is a proof and product of the dedication of our souls to God. *First,* Present them a living sacrifice; not killed, as the sacrifices under the law. A Christian makes his body a sacrifice to God, though he does not give it to be burned. A body sincerely devoted to God is a living sacrifice. A living sacrifice, by way of allusion — that which was dead of itself might not be eaten, much less sacrificed, Deu. 14:21; and by ways of opposition — "The sacrifice was to be slain, but you may be sacrificed, and yet live on" —

an unbloody sacrifice. The barbarous heathen sacrificed their children to their idol-gods, not living, but slain sacrifices: but God will have mercy, and not such sacrifice, though life is forfeited to him. A *living* sacrifice, that is, inspired with the spiritual life of the soul. It is Christ living in the soul by faith that makes the body a living sacrifice, Gal. 2:20. Holy love kindles the sacrifices, puts life into the duties; see *ch.* 6:13. *Alive,* that is, to God, *v.* 11. *Secondly,* They must be holy. There is a relative holiness in every sacrifice, as dedicated to God. But, besides this, there must be that real holiness which consists in an entire rectitude of heart and life, by which we are conformed in both to the nature and will of God: even our bodies must not be made the instruments of sin and uncleanness, but set apart for God, and put to holy uses, as the vessels of the tabernacle were holy, being devoted to God's service. It is the soul that is the proper subject of holiness; but a sanctified soul communicates a holiness to the body it actuates and animates. That is holy which is according to the will of God; when the bodily actions are no, the body is holy. They are the *temples of the Holy Ghost,* 1 Co. 6:19. *Possess the body in sanctification,* 1 Th. 4:4, 5.

[2.] The arguments to enforce this, which are three: — *First,* Consider the mercies of God: *I beseech you by the mercies of God.* An affectionate obtestation, and which should melt us into a compliance: *dia tōn oiktirmōn tou Theou.* This is an argument most sweetly cogent. There is the mercy that is in God and the mercy that is from God — mercy in the spring and mercy in the streams: both are included here; but especially gospel-mercies (mentioned *ch.* 11), the transferring of what the Jews forfeited and lost by their unbelief unto us Gentiles (Eph. 3:4–6): the sure mercies of David, Isa. 55:3. God is a merciful God, therefore let us present our bodies to him; he will be sure to use them kindly, and knows how to consider the frames of them, for he is of infinite compassion. We receive from him every day the fruits of his mercy, particularly mercy to our bodies: he made them, he maintains them, he bought them, he has put a great dignity upon them. It is of the Lord's mercies that we are not consumed, that our souls are held in life; and the greatest mercy of all is that Christ hath made not his body only, but his soul, an offering for sin, that he gave himself for us and gives himself to us. Now surely we cannot but be studying what we shall render to the Lord for all this. And what shall we render? Let us render ourselves as an acknowledgment of all these favours — all we are, all we have, all we can do; and, after all, it is but very poor returns for very rich receivings: and yet, because it is what we have, *Secondly,* It is *acceptable to God.* The great end we should all labour after is to be accepted of the Lord (2 Co. 5:9), to have him well-pleased with our persons and performances. Now these living sacrifices are acceptable to God; while the sacrifices of the wicked, though fat and costly, are an abomination to the Lord. It is God's great condescension that he will vouchsafe to accept of any thing in us; and we can desire no more to make us happy; and, if the presenting of ourselves will but please him, we may easily conclude that we cannot bestow ourselves better. *Thirdly,* It is our *reasonable service.* There is an act of reason in it; for it is the soul that presents the body. Blind devotion, that has ignorance for the mother and nurse of it, is fit to be paid only to those dunghill-gods that have eyes and see not. Our God must be served in the spirit and with the understanding. There is all the reason in the world for it, and no good reason can possibly be produced against it. *Come now, and let us reason together,* Isa. 1:18. God does not impose upon us any thing hard or unreasonable, but that which is altogether agreeable to the principles of right reason. *Tēn logikēn latreian hymōn — your service according to the word;* so it may be read. The word of God does not leave out the body in holy worship. That service only is acceptable to God which is according to the written word. It must be gospel worship, spiritual worship. That is a reasonable service which we are able and ready to give a reason for, in which we understand ourselves. God deals with us as with rational creatures, and will have us so to deal with him. Thus must the body be presented to God.

(2.) The mind must be renewed for him. This is pressed (*v.* 2): *"Be you transformed by the renewing of your mind;* see to it that there be a saving change wrought in you, and that it be carried on." Conversion and sanctification are the renewing of the mind, a change not of the substance, but of the qualities of the soul. It is the same with making a new heart and a new spirit — new dispositions and inclinations, new sympathies and antipathies; the understanding enlightened, the conscience softened, the thoughts rectified; the will bowed to the will of God, and the affections made spiritual and heavenly: so that the man is not what he was — old things are passed away, all things are become new; he acts from new principles, by new rules, with new designs. The mind is the acting ruling part of us; so that the renewing of the mind is the renewing of the whole man, for out of it are the *issues of life,* Prov. 4:23. The progress of sanctification, dying to sin more and more and living to righteousness more and more, is the carrying on of this renewing work, till it be perfected in glory. This is called the *transforming* of us; it is like putting on a new shape and figure. *Metamorphousthe — Be you metamorphosed.* The transfiguration of Christ is expressed by this word (Mt. 17:2), when he put on a heavenly glory, which made his face to shine like the sun; and the same word is used 2 Co. 3:18, where we are said to be *changed into the same image from glory to glory.* This transformation is here pressed as a duty; not that we can work such a change ourselves: we could as soon make a new world as make a new heart by any power of our own; it is God's work, Eze. 11:19; 36:26, 27. But *be you transformed,* that is, "use the means which God hath appointed and ordained for it." It is God that turns us, and then we are turned; but we must *frame our doings to turn,* Hos. 5:4. "Lay your souls under the changing transforming influences of the blessed Spirit; seek unto God for grace in the use of all the means of grace." Though the new man be created of God, yet we must put it on (Eph. 4:24), and be pressing forward towards perfection. Now in this verse we may further observe,

[1.] What is the great enemy to this renewing, which we must avoid; and that is, conformity to this world: *Be not conformed to this world.* All the disciples and followers of the Lord Jesus must be nonconformists to this world. *Mē syschēmatizesthe — Do not fashion yourselves* according to the world. We must not conform to the things of the world; they are mutable, and the fashion of them is passing away. Do not conform either to the lusts of the flesh or the lusts of the eye. We must not conform to the men of the world, of that world which lies in wickedness, not walk according *to the course of this world* (Eph. 2:2); that is, we must not follow a multitude to do evil, Ex. 23:2. If sinners entice us, we must not consent to them, but in our places witness against them. Nay, even in things indifferent, and which are not in themselves sinful, we must so far not conform to the custom and way of the world as not to act by the world's dictates as our chief rule, nor to aim at the world's favours as our highest end. True Christianity consists much in a sober singularity. Yet we must take heed of the extreme of affected rudeness and moroseness, which some run into. In civil things, the light of nature and the custom of nations are intended for our guidance; and the rule of the gospel in those cases is a rule of direction, not a rule of contrariety.

[2.] What is the great effect of this renewing, which we must labour after: *That you may prove what is that good, and acceptable, and perfect will of God.* by the will of God here we are to understand his revealed will concerning our duty, what the Lord our God requires of us. This is the will of God in general, even our sanctification, that will which we pray may be done by us as it is done by the angels; especially his will as it is revealed in the New Testament, where he hath in these last days spoken to us by his Son. *First,* The will of God is *good, and acceptable, and perfect;* three excellent properties of a law. It is good (Mic. 6:8); it is exactly consonant to the eternal reason of good and evil. It is good in itself. It is good for us. Some think the evangelical law is here called good, in distinction from the ceremonial law, which consisted of *statutes that were not good,* Eze. 20:25. It is acceptable, it is pleasing to God; that and that only is so which is prescribed by him. The only way to attain his favour as the end is to conform to his will as the rule. It is perfect, to which nothing can be added. The revealed will of God is a sufficient rule of faith and practice, containing all things which tend to the perfection of the man of God, to furnish us thoroughly to every good work, 2 Tim. 3:16, 17. *Secondly,* That it concerns Christians to prove what is that will of God which is good, and acceptable, and perfect; that is, to know it with judgment and approbation, to know it experimentally, to know the excellency of the will of God by the experience of a conformity to it. It is to approve *things that are excellent* (Phil. 1:10); it is *dokimazein* (the same word that is used here) *to try* things that differ, in doubtful cases readily to apprehend what the will of God is and to close in with it. It is to be *of quick understanding in the fear of the Lord,* Isa. 11:3. *Thirdly,* That those are best able to prove what is the good, and acceptable, and perfect will of God, who are transformed by the renewing of their mind. A living principle of grace is in the soul, as far as it prevails, an unbiassed unprejudiced judgment concerning the things of God. It disposes the soul to receive and entertain the revelations of the divine will. The promise is (Jn. 7:17), *If any man will do his will, he shall know of the doctrine.* A good wit can dispute and distinguish about the will of God; while an honest, humble heart, that has spiritual senses exercised, and is delivered into the mould of the word, loves it, and practises it, and has the relish and savour of it. Thus to be godly is to surrender ourselves to God.

2. When this is done, to serve him in all manner of gospel obedience. Some hints of this we have here (*v.* 11, 12), *Serving the Lord.* Wherefore do we present ourselves to him, but that we may serve him? Acts 27:23, *Whose I am;* and then it follows, *whom I serve.* To be religious is to serve God. How? (1.) We must make a business of it, and not be slothful in that business. *Not slothful in business.* There is the business of the world, that of our particular calling, in which we must not be slothful, 1 Th. 4:11. But this seems to be meant of the business of serving the Lord, our Father's business, Lu. 2:49. Those that would approve themselves Christians indeed must make religion their business — must choose it, and learn it, and give themselves to it; they must love it, and employ themselves in it, and abide by it, as their great and main business. And, having made it our business, we must not be slothful in it: not desire our own ease, and consult that, when it comes in competition with our duty. We must not drive on slowly in religion. Slothful servants will be reckoned with us wicked servants. (2.) We must be *fervent in spirit, serving the Lord.* God must be served with the spirit (*ch.* 1:9; Jn. 4:24), under the influences of the Holy Spirit. Whatever we do in religion it is pleasing to God no further than it is done with our spirits wrought upon by the Spirit of God. And there must be fervency in the spirit — a holy zeal, and warmth, and ardency of affection in all we do, as those that love God not only with the heart and soul, but with all our hearts, and with all our souls. This is the holy fire that kindles the sacrifice, and carries it up to heaven, an offering of a sweet-smelling savour. — *Serving the Lord. Tō kairō douleuontes* (so some copies read it), *serving the time,* that is, improving your opportunities and making the best of them, complying with the present seasons of grace. (3.) *Rejoicing in hope.* God is worshipped and honoured by our hope and trust in him, especially when we rejoice in that hope, take a complacency in that confidence, which argues a great assurance of the reality and a great esteem of the excellency of the good hoped for. (4.) *Patient in tribulation.* Thus also God is served, not only by working for him when he calls us to work, but by sitting still quietly when he calls us to suffer. Patience for God's sake, and with an eye to his will and glory, is true piety. Observe, Those that rejoice in hope are likely to be patient in tribulation. It is a believing prospect of the joy set before us that bears up the spirit under all outward pressure. (5.) *Continuing instant in prayer.* Prayer is a friend to hope and patience, and we do in it serve the Lord. *Proskarterountes.* It signifies both fervency and perseverance in prayer. We should not be cold in the duty, nor soon weary of it, Lu. 18:1; 1 Th. 5:17; Eph. 6:18; Col. 4:2. This is our duty which immediately respects God.

II. Concerning our duty which respects ourselves; this is sobriety.

1. A sober opinion of ourselves, *v.* 3. It is ushered in with a solemn preface: *I say, through the grace given unto me:* the grace f wisdom, by which he understood the necessity and excellency of this duty; the grace of apostleship, by which he had authority to press and enjoin it. "I say it, who am commissioned to say it, in God's name. I say it, and it is not for you to gainsay it." It is said to every one of us, one as well as another. Pride is a sin that is bred in the bone of all of us, and we have therefore each of us need to be cautioned and armed against it. — *Not to think of himself more highly than he ought to think.* We must take heed of having too great an opinion of ourselves, or putting too high a valuation upon our own judgments, abilities, persons, performances. We must not be self-conceited, nor esteem too much our own wisdom and other attainments, not think ourselves to be something, Gal. 6:3. There is a high thought of ourselves which we may

and must have to think ourselves too good to be the slaves of sin and drudges to this world. But, on the other hand, we should think soberly, that is, we must have a low and modest opinion of ourselves and our own abilities, our gifts and graces, according to what we have received from God, and not otherwise. We must not be confident and hot in matters of doubtful disputation; not stretch ourselves beyond our line; not judge and censure those that differ from us; not desire to make a fair show in the flesh. These and the like are the fruits of a sober opinion of ourselves. The words will bear yet another sense agreeable enough. *Of himself* is not in the original; therefore it may be read, *That no man be wise above what he ought to be wise, but be wise unto sobriety.* We must not exercise ourselves in things too high for us (Ps. 131:1, 2), not intrude into those things which we have not seen (Col. 2:18), those secret things which belong not to us (Deu. 29:29), not covet to be wise above what is written. There is a knowledge that puffs up, which reaches after forbidden fruit. We must take heed of this, and labour after that knowledge which tends to sobriety, to the rectifying of the heart and the reforming of the life. Some understand it of the sobriety which keeps us in our own place and station, from intruding into the gifts and offices of others. See an instance of this sober modest care in the exercise of the greatest spiritual gifts, 2 Co. 10:13–15. To this head refers also that exhortation (v. 16), *Be not wise in your own conceits.* It is good to be wise, but it is bad to think ourselves so; for there is more hope of a fool than of him that is wise in his own eyes. It was an excellent thing for Moses to have his face shine and not know it. Now the reasons why we must have such a sober opinion of ourselves, our own abilities and attainments, are these: —

(1.) Because whatever we have that is good, *God hath dealt* it to us; every good and perfect gift *comes from above,* James 1:17. What have we that we have not received? And, if we have received it, why then do we boast? 1 Co. 4:7. The best and most useful man in the world is no more, no better, than what the free grace of God makes him every day. When we are thinking of ourselves, we must remember to think not how we attained, as though our might and the power of our hand had gotten us these gifts; but think how kind God hath been to us, for it is he that gives us power to do any thing that is good, and in him is all our sufficiency.

(2.) Because God deals out his gifts in a certain measure: According to *the measure of faith.* Observe, The measure of spiritual gifts he calls the measure of faith, for this is the radical grace. What we have and do that is good is so far right and acceptable as it is founded in faith, and flows from faith, and no further. Now faith, and other spiritual gifts with it, are dealt by measure, according as Infinite Wisdom sees meet for us. Christ had the Spirit given him without measure, Jn. 3:34. But the saints have it by measure; see Eph. 4:7. Christ, who had gifts without measure, was meek and lowly; and shall we, that are stinted, be proud and self-conceited?

(3.) Because God has dealt out gifts to others as well as to us: *Dealt to every man.* Had we the monopoly of the Spirit, or a patent to be sole proprietors of spiritual gifts, there might be some pretence for this conceitedness of ourselves; but others have their share as well as we. God is a common Father, and Christ a common root, to all the saints, who all drive virtue from him; and therefore it ill becomes us to lift up ourselves, and to despise others, as if we only were the people in favour with heaven, and wisdom should die with us. This reasoning he illustrates by a comparison taken from the members of the natural body (as 1 Co. 12:12; Eph. 4:16): *As we have many members in one body,* etc. v. 4, 5. Here observe, [1.] All the saints make up one body in Christ, who is the head of the body, and the common centre of their unity. Believers lie not in the world as a confused disorderly heap, but are organized and knit together, as they are united to one common head, and actuated and animated by one common Spirit. [2.] Particular believers are members of this body, constituent parts, which speak them less than the whole, and in relation to the whole, deriving life and spirits from the head. Some members in the body are bigger and more useful than others, and each receives spirits from the head according to its proportion. if the little finger should receive as much nourishment as the leg, how unseemly and prejudicial would it be! We must remember that we are not the whole; we think above what is meet if we think so; we are but parts and members. [3.] All *the members have not the same office* (v. 4), but each hath its respective place and work assigned it. The office of the eye is to see, the office of the hand is to work, etc. So in the mystical body, some are qualified for, and called to, one sort of work; others are, in like manner, fitted for, and called to, another sort of work. Magistrates, ministers, people, in a Christian commonwealth, have their several offices, and must not intrude one upon another, nor clash in the discharge of their several offices. [4.] Each member hath its place and office, for the good and benefit of the whole, and of every other member. We are not only members of Christ, but we are *members one of another, v.* 5. We stand in relation one to another; we are engaged to do all the good we can one to another, and to act in conjunction for the common benefit. See this illustrated at large, 1 Co. 12:14, etc. Therefore we must not be puffed up with a conceit of our own attainments, because, whatever we have, as we received it, so we received it not for ourselves, but for the good of others.

2. A sober use of the gifts that God hath given us. As we must not on the one hand be proud of our talents, so on the other hand we must not bury them. Take heed lest, under a pretence of humility and self-denial, we be slothful in laying out ourselves for the good of others. We must not say, "I am nothing, therefore I will sit still, and do nothing;" but, "I am nothing in myself, and therefore I will lay out myself to the utmost in the strength of the grace of Christ." He specifies the ecclesiastical offices appointed in particular churches, in the discharge of which each must study to do his own duty, for the preserving of order and the promotion of edification in the church, each knowing his place and fulfilling it. *Having then gifts.* The following induction of particulars supplies the sense of this general. *Having gifts,* let us use them. Authority and ability for the ministerial work are the gift of God. — *Gifts differing.* The immediate design is different, though the ultimate tendency of all is the same. *According to the grace, charismata kata tēn charin.* The free grace of God is the spring and original of all the gifts that are given to men. It is grace that appoints the office, qualifies and inclines the person, works both to will and to do. There were in the primitive church extraordinary gifts of tongues, of discerning, of healing; but he speaks here of those that are ordinary. Compare 1 Co. 12:4; 1 Tim. 4:14; 1 Pt. 4:10. Seven particular gifts he specifies (v. 6–8), which seem to be meant of so many distinct offices, used by the prudential constitution of many of the primitive churches, especially the larger. There are two general ones here expressed by prophesying and ministering, the former the work of the bishops, the latter the work of the deacons, which were the only two standing officers, Phil. 1:1. But the particular work belonging to each of these might be, and it should seem was, divided and allotted by common consent and agreement, that it might be done the more effectually, because that which is every body's work is nobody's work, and he despatches his business best that is *vir unius negotii — a man of one business.* Thus David sorted the Levites (1 Chr. 23:4, 5), and in this wisdom is profitable to direct. The five latter will therefore be reduced to the two former.

(1.) *Prophecy. Whether prophecy, let us prophesy according to the proportion of faith.* It is not meant of the extraordinary gifts of foretelling things to come, but the ordinary office of preaching the word: so *prophesying* is taken, 1 Co. 14:1–3, etc.; 11:4; 1 Th. 5:20. The work of the Old-Testament prophets was not only to foretel future things, but to warn the people concerning sin and duty, and to be their remembrancers concerning that which they knew before. And thus gospel preachers are prophets, and do indeed, as far as the revelation of the word goes, foretel things to come. Preaching refers to the eternal condition of the children of men, points directly at a future state. Now those that preach the word must do it *according to the proportion of faith — kata tēn analogian tēs pisteōs,* that is, [1.] As to the manner of our prophesying, it must be according to the proportion of the grace of faith. He had spoken (v. 3) of the measure of faith dealt to every man. Let him that preaches set all the faith he hath on work, to impress the truths he preaches upon his own heart in the first place. As people cannot hear well, so ministers cannot preach well, without faith. First believe and then speak, Ps. 116:10; 2 Co. 4:13. And we must remember the proportion of faith — that, though all men have not faith, yet a great many have besides ourselves; and therefore we must allow others to have a share of knowledge and ability to instruct, as well as we, even those that in less things differ from us. *"Hast thou faith? Have it to thyself;* and do not make it a ruling rule to others, remembering that thou hast but thy proportion." [2.] As to the matter of our prophesying, it must be according to the proportion of the doctrine of faith, as it is revealed in the holy scriptures of the Old and New Testament. By this rule of faith the Bereans tried Paul's preaching, Acts 17:11. Compare Acts 26:22; Gal. 1:9. There are some staple-truths, as I may call them, some *prima axiomata — first axioms,* plainly and uniformly taught in the scripture, which are the touchstone of preaching, by which (though we must not despise prophesying) we must *prove all things,* and then *hold fast that which is good,* 1 Th. 5:20, 21. Truths that are more dark must be examined by those that are more clear; and then entertained when they are found to agree and comport with the analogy of faith; for it is certain one truth can never contradict another. See here what ought to be the great care of preachers — to preach sound doctrine, according to the form of wholesome words, Tit. 2:8; 2 Tim. 1:13. It is not so necessary that the prophesying be according to the proportion of art, the rules of logic and rhetoric; but it is necessary that it be according to the proportion of faith: for it is the word of faith that we preach. Now there are two particular works which he that prophesieth hath to mind — teaching and exhorting, proper enough to be done by the same person at the same time, and when he does the one let him mind that, when he does the other let him do that too as well as he can. If, by agreement between the ministers of a congregation, this work be divided, either constantly or interchangeably, so that one teaches and the other exhorts (that is, in our modern dialect, one expounds and the other preaches), let each do his work according to the proportion of faith. *First,* let him that teacheth wait on teaching. Teaching is the bare explaining and proving of gospel truths, without practical application, as in the expounding of the scripture. *Pastors and teachers* are the same office (Eph. 4:11), but the particular work is somewhat different. Now he that has a faculty of teaching, and has undertaken that province, let him stick to it. It is a good gift, let him use it, and give his mind to it. *He that teacheth, let him be in his teaching;* so some supply it, *Ho didaskōn, en tē didaskalia.* Let him be frequent and constant, and diligent in it; let him abide in that which is his proper work, and be in it as his element. See 1 Tim. 4:15, 16, where it is explained by two words, *en toutois isthi,* and *epimene autois, be in these things* and *continue in them. Secondly,* Let him that *exhorteth* wait on *exhortation.* Let him give himself to that. This is the work of the pastor, as the former of the teacher; to apply gospel truths and rules more closely to the case and condition of the people, and to press upon them that which is more practical. Many that are very accurate in teaching may yet be very cold and unskilful in exhorting; and on the contrary. The one requires a clearer head, the other a warmer heart. Now where these gifts are evidently separated (that the one excels in the one and the other in the other) it conduces to edification to divide the work accordingly; and, whatsoever the work is that we undertake, let us mind it. To wait on our work is to bestow the best of our time and thoughts upon it, to lay hold of all opportunities for it, and to study not only to do it, but to do it well.

(2.) *Ministry.* If a man hath *diakonian — the office of a deacon,* or assistant to the pastor and teacher, let him use that office well — a churchwarden (suppose), an elder, or an overseer of the poor; and perhaps there were more put into these offices, and there was more solemnity in them, and a greater stress of care and business lay upon them in the primitive churches, than we are now well aware of. It includes all those offices which concern the *ta exō* of the church, *the outward business of the house of God.* See Neh. 11:16. *Serving tables,* Acts 6:2. Now let him on whom this care of ministering is devolved attend to it with faithfulness and diligence; particularly, [1.] *He that giveth, let him do it with simplicity.* Those church-officers that were the stewards of the church's alms, collected money, and distributed it according as the necessities of the poor were. Let them do it *en aplotēti — liberally* and faithfully; not converting what they receive to their own use, nor distributing it with any sinister design, or with respect of person: not froward and peevish with the poor, nor seeking pretences to put them by; but with all sincerity and integrity, having no other intention in it than to glorify God and do good. Some understand it in general of all almsgiving: He that hath wherewithal, let him give, and give plentifully and liberally; so the word is translated, 2 Co. 8:2; 9:13. God loves a cheerful bountiful giver. [2.] *He that ruleth with diligence.* It should seem, he means those that were assistants to the pastors in exercising church-discipline, as their eyes, and hands, and mouth, in the government of the church, or those ministers that in the congregation did chiefly undertake and apply themselves to this ruling work; for we find those ruling that laboured in the word and doctrine, 1 Tim. 5:17. Now such must do it with diligence. The word denotes both care and industry to discover what is amiss, to reduce those that go astray, to reprove and admonish those that have fallen, to keep the church pure. Those must take a great deal of pains that will approve themselves faithful in the discharge of this trust, and not let slip any opportunity that may facilitate and advance that work. [3.] *He that showeth mercy with cheerfulness.* Some think it is meant in general of all that in any thing show mercy: Let them be willing to do it, and take a pleasure in it; God loves a cheerful giver. But it seems to be meant of some particular church-officers, whose work it was to take care of the sick and strangers; and those were generally widows that were in this matter servants to the church — deaconesses (1 Tim. 5:9, 10), though others, it is likely, might be employed. Now this must be done with cheerfulness. A pleasing countenance in acts of mercy is a great relief and comfort to the miserable; when they see it is not done grudgingly and unwillingly, but with pleasant looks and gentle words, and all possible indications of readiness and alacrity. Those that have to do with such as are sick and sore, and commonly cross and peevish, have need to put on not only patience, but cheerfulness, to make the work the more easy and pleasant to them, and the more acceptable to God.

III. Concerning that part of our duty which respects our brethren, of which we have many instances, in brief exhortations. Now all our duty towards one another is summer up in one word, and that a sweet work, *love.* In that is laid the foundation of all our mutual duty; and therefore the apostle mentions this first, which is the livery of Christ's disciples, and the great law of our religion: *Let love be without dissimulation;* not in compliment and pretence, but in reality; *not in word and tongue only,* 1 Jn. 3:18. The right love is love unfeigned; not as the kisses of an enemy, which are deceitful. We should be glad of an opportunity to *prove the sincerity of our love,* 2 Co. 8:8. More particularly, there is a love owing to our friends, and to our enemies. He specifies both.

1. To our friends. He that hath friends must show himself friendly. There is a mutual love that Christians owe, and must pay.

(1.) An affectionate love (*v.* 10): *Be kindly affectioned one to another, with brotherly love, philostorgoi* — it signifies not only love, but a readiness and inclination to love, the most genuine and free affection, kindness flowing out as from a spring. It properly denotes the love of parents to their children, which, as it is the most tender, so it is the most natural, of any, unforced, unconstrained; such must our love be to one another, and such it will be where there is a new nature and the law of love is written in the heart. This kind affection puts us on to express ourselves both in word and action with the greatest courtesy and obligingness that may be. — *One to another.* This may recommend the grace of love to us, that, as it is made our duty to love others, so it is as much their duty to love us. And what can be sweeter on this side heaven than to love and be beloved? He that thus watereth shall be watered also himself.

(2.) A respectful love: *In honour preferring one another.* Instead of contending for superiority, let us be forward to give to others the pre-eminence. This is explained, Phil. 2:3, *Let each esteem other better than themselves.* And there is this good reason for it, because, if we know our own hearts, we know more evil by ourselves than we do by any one else in the world. We should be forward to take notice of the gifts, and graces, and performances of our brethren, and value them accordingly, be more forward to praise another, and more pleased to hear another praised, than ourselves; *tē timē allēlous proēgoumenoi — going before,* or *leading one another in honour;* so some read it: not in taking honour, but in giving honour. "Strive which of you shall be most forward to pay respect to those to whom it is due, and to perform all Christian offices of love (which are all included in the word honour) to your brethren, as there is occasion. Let all your contention be which shall be most humble, and useful, and condescending." So the sense is the same with Tit. 3:14, *Let them learn, proistasthai — to go before in good works.* For though we must prefer others (as our translation reads it), and put on others, as more capable and deserving than ourselves, yet we must not make that an excuse for our lying by and doing nothing, nor under a pretence of honouring others, and their serviceableness and performances, indulge ourselves in ease and slothfulness. Therefore he immediately adds (*v.* 11), *Not slothful in business.*

(3.) A liberal love (*v.* 13): *Distributing to the necessities of saints.* It is but a mock love which rests in the verbal expressions of kindness and respect, while the wants of our brethren call for real supplies, and it is in the power of our hands to furnish them. [1.] It is no strange thing for saints in this world to want necessaries for the support of their natural live. In those primitive times prevailing persecutions must needs reduce many of the suffering saints to great extremities; and still the poor, even the poor saints, we have always with us. Surely the things of this world are not the best things; if they were, the saints, who are the favourites of heaven, would not be put off with so little of them. [2.] It is the duty of those who have wherewithal to *distribute,* or (as it might better be read) to *communicate* to those necessities. It is not enough to draw out the soul, but we must draw out the purse, to the hungry. See Jam. 2:15, 16; 1 Jn. 3:17. *Communicating — koinōnountes.* It intimates that our poor brethren have a kind of interest in that which God hath given us; and that our reliving them should come from a sense and fellow-feeling of their wants, as though we suffered with them. The charitable benevolence of the Philippians to Paul is called their communicating with his affliction, Phil. 4:14. We must be ready, as we have ability and opportunity, to relieve any that are in want; but we are in a special manner bound to communicate to the saints. There is a common love owing to our fellow-creatures, but a special love owing to our fellow-christians (Gal. 6:10), *Especially to those who are of the household of faith. Communicating, tais mneiais — to the memories* of the saints; so some of the ancients read it, instead of *tais chreiais.* There is a debt owing to the memory of those who through faith and patience inherit the promises — to value it, to vindicate it, to embalm it. Let the memory of the just be blessed; so some read Prov. 10:7. He mentions another branch of this bountiful love: *Given to hospitality.* Those who have houses of their own should be ready to entertain those who go about doing good, or who, for fear of persecution, are forced to wander for shelter. They had not then so much of the convenience of common inns as we have; or the wandering Christians durst not frequent them; or they had not wherewithal to bear the charges, and therefore it was a special kindness to bid them welcome on free-cost. Nor is it yet an antiquated superseded duty; as there is occasion, we must welcome strangers, for we know not the heart of a stranger. *I was a stranger, and you took me in,* is mentioned as one instance of the mercifulness of those that shall obtain mercy: *tēn philoxenian diōkontes — following* or *pursuing* hospitality. It intimates, not only that we must take opportunity, but that we must seek opportunity, thus to show mercy. As Abraham, who sat at the tent-door (Gen. 18:1), and Lot, who sat in the gate of Sodom (Gen. 19:1), expecting travellers, whom they might meet and prevent with a kind invitation, and so they entertained angels unawares, Heb. 13:2.

(4.) A sympathizing love (*v.* 15): *Rejoice with those that do rejoice, and weep with those that weep.* Where there is a mutual love between the members of the mystical body, there will be such a fellow-feeling. See 1 Co. 12:26. True love will interest us in the sorrows and joys of one another, and teach us to make them our own. Observe the common mixture in this world, some rejoicing, and others weeping (as the people, Ezra 3:12, 13), for the trial, as of other graces, so of brotherly love and Christian sympathy. Not that we must participate in the sinful mirths or mournings of any, but only in just and reasonable joys and sorrows: not envying those that prosper, but rejoicing with them; truly glad that others have the success and comfort which we have not; not despising those that are in trouble, but concerned for them, and ready to help them, as being ourselves in the body. This is to do as God does, who not only has *pleasure in the prosperity of his servants* (Ps. 35:27), but is likewise *afflicted in all their afflictions,* Isa. 63:9.

(5.) A united love: *"Be of the same mind one towards another* (*v.* 16), that is, labour, as much as you can, to agree in apprehension; and, wherein you come short of this, yet agree in affection; endeavour to be all one, not affecting to clash, and contradict, and thwart one another; but keep the unity of the Spirit in the bond of peace, Phil. 2:2; 3:15, 16; 1 Co. 1:10; *to auto eis allēlous phronountes — wishing the same good* to others that you do to yourselves;" so some understand it. This is to love our brethren as ourselves, desiring their welfare as our own.

(6.) A condescending love: *Mind not high things, but condescend to men of low estate, v.* 16. True love cannot be without lowliness, Eph. 4:1, 2; Phil. 2:3. When our Lord Jesus washed his disciples' feet, to teach us brotherly love (Jn. 13:5; 14:34), it was designed especially to intimate to us that to love one another aright is to be willing to stoop to the meanest offices of kindness for the good of one another. Love is a condescending grace: *Non bene conveniunt — majestas et amor — Majesty and love do but ill assort with each other.* Observe how it is pressed here. [1.] *Mind not high things.* We must not be ambitious of honour and preferment, nor look upon worldly pomp and dignity with any inordinate value or desire but rather with a holy contempt. When David's advancements were high, his spirit was humble (Ps. 131:1): *I do not exercise myself in great matters.* The Romans, living in the imperial city, which reigned over the kings of the earth (Rev. 17:18), and was at that time in the meridian of its splendour, were perhaps ready to take occasion thence to think the better of themselves. Even the holy seed were tainted with this leaven. Roman Christians, as some citizens do upon the country; and therefore the apostle so often cautions them against high-mindedness; compare *ch.* 11:20. They lived near the court, and conversed daily with the gaiety and grandeur of it: "Well," saith he, "do not mind it, be not in love with it." [2.] *Condescend to men of low estate — Tois tapeinois synapagomenoi. First,* It may be meant of *mean things,* to which we must condescend. If our condition in the world be poor and low, our enjoyments coarse and scanty, our employments despicable and contemptible, yet we must bring our minds to it, and acquiesce in it. So the margin: *Be contented with mean things.* Be reconciled to the place which God in his providence hath put us in, whatever it be. We must account nothing below us but sin: stoop to mean habitations, mean fare, mean clothing, mean accommodations when they are our lot, and not grudge. Nay, we must be carried with a kind of impetus, by the force of the new nature (so the word *synapagomai* properly signifies, and it is very significant), towards mean things, when God appoints us to them; as the old corrupt nature is carried out towards high things. We must accommodate ourselves to mean things. We should make a low condition and mean circumstances more the centre of our desires than a high condition. *Secondly,* It may be meant of *mean persons;* so we read it (I think both are to be included) *Condescend to men of low estate.* We must associate with, and accommodate ourselves to, those that are poor and mean in the world, if they be such as fear God. David, though a king upon the throne, was a companion for all such, Ps. 119:63. We need not be ashamed to converse with the lowly, while the great God overlooks heaven and earth to look at such. True love values grace in rags as well as in scarlet. A jewel is a jewel, though it lie in the dirt. The contrary to this condescension is reproved, Jam. 2:1–4. *Condescend;* that is, suit yourselves to them, stoop to them for their good; as Paul, 1 Cor. 9:19, etc. Some think the original word is a metaphor taken from travellers, when those that are stronger and swifter of foot stay for those that are weak and slow, make a halt, and take them with them; thus must Christians be tender towards their fellow travellers. As a means to promote this, he adds, *Be not wise in your own conceits;* to the same purport with *v.* 3. We shall never find in our hearts to condescend to others while we find there so great a conceit of ourselves: and therefore this must needs be mortified. *Mē ginesthe phronimoi par' heautois — "Be not wise by yourselves,* be not confident of the sufficiency of your own wisdom, so as to despise others, or think you have no need of them (Prov. 3:7), nor be shy of communicating what you have to others. We are members one of another, depend upon one another, are obliged to one another; and therefore, *Be not wise by yourselves,* remembering it is the merchandise of wisdom that we profess; now merchandise consists in commerce, receiving and returning."

(7.) A love that engages us, as much as lies in us, *to live peaceably with all men, v.* 18. Even those with whom we cannot live intimately and familiarly, by reason of distance in degree or profession, yet we must with such live peaceably; that is, we must be harmless and inoffensive, not giving others occasion to quarrel with us; and we must be gall-less and unrevengeful, not taking occasion to quarrel with them. Thus must we labour to preserve the peace, that it be not broken, and to piece it again when it is broken. The wisdom from above is pure and peaceable. Observe how the exhortation is limited. It is not expressed so as to oblige us to impossibilities: *If it be possible, as much as lies in you.* Thus Heb. 12:14, *Follow peace.* Eph. 4:3, *Endeavouring to keep.* Study the things that make for peace. — *If it be possible.* It is not possible to preserve the peace when we cannot do it without offending God and wounding conscience: *Id possumus quod jure possumus — That is possible which is possible without incurring blame.* The wisdom that is from above is first pure and then peaceable, Jam. 3:17. Peace without purity is the peace of the devil's palace. — *As much as lieth in you.* There must be two words to the bargain of peace. We can but speak for ourselves. We may be unavoidably striven with; as Jeremiah, who was a *man of contention* (Jer. 15:10), and this we cannot help; our care must be that nothing be wanting on our parts to preserve the peace, Ps. 120:7. I am for peace, though, when I speak, they are for war.

2. To our enemies. Since men became enemies to God, they have been found very apt to be enemies one to another. Let but the centre of love be once forsaken, and the lines will either clash and interfere, or be at an uncomfortable distance. And, of all men, those that embrace religion have reason to expect to meet with enemies in a world whose smiles seldom concur with Christ's. Now Christianity teaches us how to behave towards our enemies; and in this instruction it quite differs from all other rules and methods, which generally aim at victory and dominion; but this at inward peace and satisfaction. Whoever are our enemies, that wish us ill and seek to do us ill, our rule is to do them no hurt, but all the good we can.

(1.) To do them no hurt (*v.* 17): *Recompense to no man evil for evil,* for that is a brutish recompence, and befitting only those animals which are not conscious either of any being above them or of any state before them. Or, if mankind were made (as some dream) in a state of war, such recompences as these were agreeable enough; but we have not so learned God, who does so much for his enemies (Mt. 5:45), much less have we so learned Christ, who died for us when we were enemies (*ch.* 5:8, 10), so loved that world which hated him without a cause. — *"To no man;* neither to Jew nor Greek; not to one that has been thy friend, for by recompensing evil for evil thou wilt certainly lose him; not to one that has been thine enemy, for by not recompensing evil for evil thou mayest perhaps gain him." To the same purport, *v.* 19, *Dearly beloved, avenge not yourselves.* And why must this be ushered in with such an affectionate compellation, rather than any other of the exhortations of this chapter? Surely because this is intended for the composing of angry spirits, that are hot in the resentment of a provocation. He addresses himself to such in this endearing language, to mollify and qualify them. Any thing that breathes love sweetens the blood, lays the storm, and cools the intemperate heat. Would you pacify a brother offended? Call him dearly beloved. Such a soft word, fitly spoken, may be effectual to turn away wrath. *Avenge not yourselves;* that is, when any body has done you any ill turn, do not desire nor endeavour to bring the like mischief or inconvenience upon him. it is not forbidden to the magistrate to do justice to those that are wronged, by punishing the wrong-doer; nor to make and execute just and wholesome laws against malefactors; but it forbids private revenge, which flows from anger and ill-will; and this is fitly forbidden, for it is presumed that we are incompetent judges in our own case. Nay, if persons wronged in seeking the defence of the law, and magistrates in granting it, act from any particular personal pique or quarrel, and not from a concern that public peace and order be maintained and right done, even such proceedings, though seemingly regular, will fall under this prohibited self-revenging. See how strict the law of Christ is in this matter, Mt. 5:38–40. It is forbidden not only to take it into our own hands to avenge ourselves, but to desire and thirst after event that judgment in our case which the law affords, for the satisfying of a revengeful humour. This is a hard lesson to corrupt nature; and therefore he subjoins, [1.] A remedy against it: *Rather give place unto wrath.* Not to our own wrath; to give place to this is to give place to the devil, Eph. 4:26, 27. We must resist, and stifle, and smother, and suppress this; but, *First,* To the wrath of our enemy. "Give place to it, that is, be of a yielding temper; do not answer wrath with wrath, but with love rather. *Yielding pacifies great offences,* Eccl. 10:4. Receive affronts and injuries, as a stone is received into a heap of wool, which gives way to it, and so it does not rebound back, nor go any further." So it explains that of our Saviour (Mt. 5:39), *Whosoever shall smite thee on thy right cheek, turn to him the other also.* Instead of meditating how to revenge one wrong, prepare to receive another. When men's passions are up, and the stream is strong, let it have its course, lest by an unseasonable opposition it be made to rage and swell the more. When others are angry, let us be calm; this is a remedy against revenge, and seems to be the genuine sense. But, *Secondly,* Many apply it to the wrath of God: "Give place to this, make room for him to take the throne of judgment, and let him alone to deal with thine adversary." [2.] A reason against it: *For it is written, Vengeance is mine.* We find it written, Deu. 32:35. God is the sovereign King, the righteous Judge, and to him it belongs to administer justice; for, being a God of infinite knowledge, by him actions are weighed in unerring balances; and, being a God of infinite purity, he hates sin and cannot endure to look upon iniquity. Some of this power he hath trusted in the hands of the civil magistrates (Gen. 9:6; *ch.* 13:4); their legal punishments therefore are to be looked upon as a branch of God's revengings. This is a good reason why we should not avenge ourselves; for, if vengeance be God's, then, *First,* We may not do it. We step into the throne of God if we do and take his work out of his hand. *Secondly,* We need not do it. For God will, if we meekly leave the matter with him; he will avenge us as far as there is reason or justice for it, and further we cannot desire it. See Ps. 38:14, 15, *I heard not, for thou wilt hear;* and if God hears what need is there for me to hear?

(2.) We must not only not to hurt to our enemies, but our religion goes higher, and teaches us to do them all the good we can. It is a command peculiar to Christianity, and which does highly commend it: *Love your enemies,* Mt. 5:44. We are here taught to show that love to them both in word and deed.

[1.] In word: *Bless those who persecute you, v.* 14. It has been the common lot of God's people to be persecuted, either with a powerful hand or with a spiteful tongue. Now we are here taught to bless those that so persecute us. *Bless* them; that is, *First,* "Speak well of them. If there be any thing in them that is commendable and praiseworthy, take notice of it, and mention it to their honour." *Secondly,* "Speak respectfully to them, according as their place is, not rendering railing for railing, and bitterness for bitterness." And, *Thirdly,* We must wish well to them, and desire their good, so far from seeking any revenge. Nay, *Fourthly,* We must offer up that desire to God, by prayer for them. If it be not in the power of our hand to do any thing else for them, yet we can testify our good-will by praying for them, for which our master hath given us not only a rule, but an example to back that rule, Lu. 23:34 — *Bless, and curse not.* It denotes a thorough good-will in all the instances and expressions of it; not, "bless them when you are at prayer, and curse them at other times;" but, "bless them always, and curse not at all." Cursing ill becomes the mouths of those whose work it is to bless God, and whose happiness it is to be blessed of him.

[2.] In deed (*v.* 20): *"If thine enemy hunger,* as thou hast ability and opportunity, be ready and forward to show him any kindness, and do him any office of love for his good; and be never the less forward for his having been thine enemy, but rather the more, that thous mayest thereby testify the sincerity of thy forgiveness of him." It is said of archbishop Cranmer that the way for a man to make him his friend was to do him an ill turn. The precept is quoted from Prov. 25:21, 22; so that, high as it seems to be, the Old Testament was not a stranger to it. Observe here, *First,* What we must do. We must do good to our enemies. *"If he hunger,* do not insult over him, and say, Now God is avenging me of him, and pleading my cause; do not make such a construction of his wants. But *feed him." Then,* when he has need of thy help, and thou hast an opportunity of starving him and trampling upon him, then *feed him* (*psōmize auton,* a significant word) — "feed him abundantly, nay, feed him carefully and indulgently:" *frustulatim pasce — feed him with small pieces,* "feed him, as we do children and sick people, with much tenderness. Contrive to do it so as to express thy love. *If he thirst, give him drink: potize auton — drink to him,* in token of reconciliation and friendship. So confirm your love to him." *Secondly,* Why we must do this. Because in so doing thou shalt heap *coals of fire on his head.* Two senses are given of this, which I think are both to be taken in disjunctively. *Thou shalt heap coals of fire on his head;* that is, "Thou shalt either," 1. "Melt him into repentance and friendship, and mollify his spirit towards thee" (alluding to those who melt metals; they not only put fire under them, but heap fire upon them; thus Saul was melted and conquered with the kindness of David, 1 Sa. 24:16; 26:21) — "thou wilt win a friend by it, and if thy kindness have not that effect then," 2. "It will aggravate his condemnation, and make his malice against thee the more inexcusable. Thou wilt hereby hasten upon him the tokens of God's wrath and vengeance." Not that this must be our intention in showing him kindness, but, for our encouragement, such will be the effect. To this purpose is the exhortation in the last verse, which suggests a paradox not easily understood by the world, that in all matters of strife and contention those that revenge are the conquered, and those that forgive are the conquerors. (1.) *"Be not overcome of evil.* Let not the evil of any provocation that is given you have such a power over you, or make such an impression upon you, as to dispossess you of yourselves, to disturb your peace, to destroy your love, to ruffle and discompose your spirits, to transport you to any indecencies, or to bring you to study or attempt any revenge." He that cannot quietly bear an injury is perfectly conquered by it. (2.) *"But overcome evil with good,* with the good of patience and forbearance, nay, and of kindness and beneficence to those that wrong you. Learn to defeat their ill designs against you, and either to change them, or at least to preserve your own peace." He that hath this rule over his spirit is better than the mighty.

3. To conclude, there remain two exhortations yet untouched, which are general, and which recommend all the rest as good in themselves, and of good report.

(1.) As good in themselves (*v.* 9): *Abhor that which is evil, cleave to that which is good.* God hath shown us what is good: these Christian duties are enjoined; and that is evil which is opposite to them. Now observe, [1.] We must not only not do evil, but we must *abhor that which is evil.* We must hate sin with an utter and irreconcilable hatred, have an antipathy to it as the worst of evils, contrary to our new nature, and to our true interest — hating all the appearances of sin, even the garment spotted with the flesh. [2.] We must not only do that which is good, but we must cleave to it. It denotes a deliberate choice of, a sincere affection for, and a constant perseverance in, that which is good. "So cleave to it as not to be allured nor affrighted from it, cleave *to him that is good,* even to the Lord (Acts 11:23), with a dependence and acquiescence." It is subjoined to the precept of brotherly love, as directive of it; we must love our brethren, but not love them so much as for their sakes to commit any sin, or omit any duty; not think the better of any sin for the sake of the person that commits it, but forsake all the friends in the world, to cleave to God and duty.

(2.) As of good report (*v.* 17): *"Provide things honest in the sight of all men;* that is, not only do, but study and forecast and take care to do, that which is amiable and creditable, and recommends religion to all with whom you converse." See Phil. 4:8. These acts of charity and beneficence are in a special manner of good report among men, and therefore are to be industriously regarded by all that consult the glory of God and the credit of their profession.

CHAPTER 13

There are three good lessons taught us in this chapter, where the apostle enlarges more upon his precepts than he had done in the foregoing chapter, finding them more needful to be fully pressed. I. A lesson of subjection to lawful authority (*v.* 1–6). II. A lesson of justice and love to our brethren (*v.* 7–10). III. A lesson of sobriety and godliness in ourselves (*v.* 11 to the end).

Verses 1–6

We are here taught how to conduct ourselves towards magistrates, and those that are in authority over us, called here the *higher powers,* intimating their authority (they are powers), and their dignity (they are higher powers), including not only the king as supreme, but all inferior magistrates under him: and yet it is expressed, not by the persons that are in that power, but the place of power itself, in which they are. However the persons themselves may be wicked, and of those vile persons whom the citizen of Zion contemneth (Ps. 15:4), yet the just power which they have must be submitted to and obeyed. The apostle had taught us, in the foregoing chapter, not to avenge ourselves, nor to recompense evil for evil; but, lest it should seem as if this did cancel the ordinance of a civil magistracy among Christians, he takes occasion to assert the necessity of it, and of the due infliction of punishment upon evil doers, however it may look like recompensing evil for evil. Observe,

I. The duty enjoined: *Let every soul be subject.* Every soul — every person, one as well as another, not excluding the clergy, who call themselves spiritual persons, however the church of Rome may not only exempt such from subjection to the civil powers, but place them in authority above them, making the greatest princes subject to the pope, who thus exalteth himself above all that is called God. — *Every soul.* Not that our consciences are to be subjected to the will of any man. It is God's prerogative to make laws immediately to bind conscience, and we must render to God the things that are God's. But it intimates that our subjection must be free and voluntary, sincere and hearty. *Curse not the king, no, not in thy thought,* Eccl. 10:20. To compass and imagine are treason begun. The subjection of soul here required includes inward honour (1 Pt. 2:17) and outward reverence and respect, both in speaking to them and in speaking of them — obedience to their commands in things lawful and honest, and in other things a patient subjection to the penalty without resistance — a conformity in every thing to the place and duty of subjects, bringing our minds to the relation and condition, and the inferiority and subordination of it. "They are *higher powers;* be content they should be so, and submit to them accordingly." Now there was good reason for the pressing of this duty of subjection to civil magistrates, 1. Because of the reproach which the Christian religion lay under in the world, as an enemy to public peace, order, and government, as a sect that turned the world upside down, and the embracers of it as enemies to Caesar, and the more because the leaders were Galileans — an old slander. Jerusalem was represented as a *rebellious city, hurtful to kings and provinces,* Ezra 4:15, 16. Our Lord Jesus was so reproached, though he told them his kingdom was not of this world: no marvel, then, if his followers have been loaded in all ages with the like calumnies, called *factious, seditious,* and *turbulent,* and looked upon as the troublers of the land, their enemies having found such representations needful for the justifying of their barbarous rage against them. The apostle therefore, for the obviating of this reproach and the clearing of Christianity from it, shows that obedience to civil magistrates is one of the laws of Christ, whose religion helps to make people good subjects; and it was very unjust to charge upon Christianity that faction and rebellion to which its principles and rules are so directly contrary. 2. Because of the temptation which the Christians lay under to be otherwise affected to civil magistrates, some of them being originally Jews, and so leavened with a principle that it was unmeet for any of the seed of Abraham to be subject to one of another nation — their king must be of their brethren, Deu. 17:15. Besides, Paul had taught them that they were *not under the law,* they were made free by Christ. Lest this liberty should be turned into licentiousness, and misconstrued to countenance faction and rebellion, the apostle enjoins obedience to civil government, which was the more necessary to be pressed now because the magistrates were heathens and unbelievers, which yet did not destroy their civil power and authority. Besides, the civil powers were persecuting powers; the body of the law was against them.

II. The reasons to enforce this duty. Why must we be subject?

1. For *wrath's sake.* Because of the danger we run ourselves into by resistance. Magistrates bear the sword, and to oppose them is to hazard all that is dear to us in this world; for it is to no purpose to contend with him that bears the sword. The Christians were then in those persecuting times obnoxious to the sword of the magistrate for their religion, and they needed not make themselves more obnoxious by their rebellion. The least show of resistance or sedition in a Christian would soon be aggravated and improved, and would be very prejudicial to the whole society; and therefore they had more need than others to be exact in their subjection, that those who had so much occasion against them in the matter of their God might have no other occasion. To this head must that argument be referred (*v.* 2), *Those that resist shall receive to themselves damnation: krima lēpsontai,* they shall be called to an account for it. God will reckon with them for it, because the resistance reflects upon him. The magistrates will reckon with them for it. They will come under the lash of the law, and will find the higher powers too high to be trampled upon, all civil governments being justly strict and severe against treason and rebellion; so it follows (*v.* 3), *Rulers are a terror.* This is a good argument, but it is low for a Christian.

2. We must be subject, *not only for wrath, but for conscience' sake;* not so much *formidine poenae — from the fear of punishment,* as *virtutis amore — from the love of virtue.* This makes common civil offices acceptable to God, when they are done for *conscience' sake,* with an eye to God, to his providence putting us into such relations, and to his precept making subjection the duty of those relations. Thus the same thing may be done from a very different principle. Now to oblige conscience to this subjection he argues, *v.* 1–4, 6,

(1.) From the institution of magistracy: *There is no power but of God.* God as the ruler and governor of the world hath appointed the ordinance of magistracy, so that all civil power is derived from him as from its original, and he hath by his providence put the administration into those hands, whatever they are that have it. By him kings reign, Prov. 8:15. The usurpation of power and the abuse of power are not of God, for he is not the author of sin; but the power itself is. As our natural powers, though often abused and made instruments of sin, are from God's creating power, so civil powers are from God's governing power. The most unjust and oppressive princes in the world have no power but what is given them from above (Jn. 19:11), the divine providence being in a special manner conversant about those changes and revolutions of governments which have such an influence upon states and kingdoms, and such a multitude of particular persons and smaller communities. Or, it may be meant of government in general: it is an instance of God's wisdom, power, and goodness, in the management of mankind, that he has disposed them into such a state as distinguishes between governors and governed, and has not left them like the fishes of the sea, where the greater devour the less. He did herein consult the benefit of his creatures. — *The powers that be:* whatever the particular form and method of government are — whether by monarchy, aristocracy, or democracy — wherever the governing power is lodged, it is an ordinance of God, and it is to be received and submitted to accordingly; though immediately an ordinance of man (1 Pt. 2:13), yet originally an ordinance of God. — *Ordained of God — tetagmenai;* a military word, signifying not only the ordination of magistrates, but the subordination of inferior magistrates to the supreme, as in an army; for among magistrates there is a diversity of gifts, and trusts, and services. Hence it follows (*v.* 2) that whosoever *resisteth the power resisteth the ordinance of God.* There are other things from God that are the greatest calamities; but magistracy is from God as an ordinance, that is, it is a great law, and it is a great blessing: so that the children of Belial, that will not endure the yoke of government, will be found breaking a law and despising a blessing. Magistrates are therefore called gods (Ps. 82:6), because they bear the image of God's authority. And those who spurn at their power reflect upon God himself. This is not at all applicable to the particular rights of kings and kingdoms, and the branches of their constitution; nor can any certain rule be fetched from this for the modelling of the original contracts between the governors and governed; but it is intended for direction to private persons in their private capacity, to behave themselves quietly and peaceably in the sphere in which God has set them, with a due regard to the civil powers which God in his providence has set over them, 1 Tim. 2:1, 2. Magistrates are here again and again called God's ministers. he is the *minister of God, v.* 4, 6. Magistrates are in a more peculiar manner God's servants; the dignity they have calls for duty. Though they are lords to us, they are servants to God, have work to do for him, and an account to render to him. In the administration of public justice, the determining of quarrels, the protecting of the innocent, the righting of the wronged, the punishing of offenders, and the preserving of national peace and order, that every man may not do what is right in his own eyes — in these things it is that magistrates act as God's ministers. As the killing of an inferior magistrate, while he is actually doing his duty, is accounted treason against the prince, so the resisting of any magistrates in the discharge of these duties of their place is the resisting of an ordinance of God.

(2.) From the intention of magistracy: *Rulers are not a terror to good works, but to the evil,* etc. Magistracy was designed to be,

[1.] A terror to evil works and evil workers. They bear the sword; not only the sword of war, but the sword of justice. They are *heirs of restraint,* to put offenders to shame; Laish wanted such, Jdg. 18:7. Such is the power of sin and corruption that many will not be restrained from the greatest enormities, and such as are most pernicious to human society, by any regard to the law of God and nature or the wrath to come; but only by the fear of temporal punishments, which the wilfulness and perverseness of degenerate mankind have made necessary. Hence it appears that laws with penalties for the lawless and disobedient (1 Tim. 1:9) must be constituted in Christian nations, and are agreeable with, and not contradictory to, the gospel. When men are become such beasts, such ravenous beasts, one to another, they must be dealt with accordingly, taken and destroyed *in terrorem — to deter others.* The horse and the mule must thus be held in with bit and bridle. In this work the magistrate is the *minister of God, v.* 4. He acts as God's agent, to whom vengeance belongs; and therefore must take heed of infusing into his judgments any private personal resentments of his own. — *To execute wrath upon him that doeth evil.* In this the judicial processes of the most vigilant faithful magistrates, though some faint resemblance and prelude of the judgments of the great day, yet come far short of the judgment of God: they reach only to the evil act, can execute wrath only on him that *doeth* evil: but God's judgment extends to the evil thought, and is a discerner of the intents of the heart. — *He beareth not the sword in vain.* It is not for nothing that God hath put such a power into the magistrate's hand; but it is intended for the restraining and suppressing of disorders. And therefore, *"If thou do that which is evil,* which falls under the cognizance and censure of the civil magistrate, *be afraid;* for civil powers have quick eyes and long arms." It is a good thing when the punishment of malefactors is managed as an ordinance of God, instituted and appointed by him. *First,* As a holy God, that hates sin, against which, as it appears and puts up its head, a public testimony is thus borne. *Secondly,* As King of nations, and the God of peace and order, which are hereby preserved. *Thirdly,* As the protector of the good, whose persons, families, estates, and names, are by this means hedged about. *Fourthly,* As one that desires not the eternal ruin of sinners, but by the punishment of some would terrify others, and so prevent the like wickedness, that others may hear and fear, and do no more presumptuously. Nay, it is intended for a kindness to those that are punished, that by the destruction of the flesh the spirit may be saved in the day of the Lord Jesus.

[2.] A praise to those that do well. Those that keep in the way of their duty shall have the commendation and protection of the civil powers, to their credit and comfort. "Do that which is good (*v.* 3), and thou needest not be *afraid of the power,* which, though terrible, reaches none but those that by their own sin make themselves obnoxious to it; the fire burns only that which is combustible: nay, thou shalt have praise of it." This is the intention of magistracy, and therefore we must, for conscience' sake, be subject to it, as a constitution designed for the public good, to which all private interests must give way. But pity it is that ever this gracious intention should be perverted, and that those who bear the sword, while they countenance and connive at sin, should be a terror to those who do well. But so it is, when the vilest men are exalted (Ps. 12:1, 8); and yet even then the blessing and benefit of a common protection, and a face of government and order, are such that it is our duty in that case rather to submit to persecution for well-doing, and to take it patiently, than by any irregular and disorderly practices to attempt a redress. Never did sovereign prince pervert the ends of government as Nero did, and yet to him Paul appealed, and under him had the protection of the law and the inferior magistrates more than once. Better a bad government than none at all.

(3.) From our interest in it: "He is *the minister of God to thee for good.* Thou hast the benefit and advantage of the government, and therefore must do what thou canst to preserve it, and nothing to disturb it." Protection draws allegiance. If we have protection from the government, we owe subjection to it; by upholding the government, we keep up our own hedge. This subjection is likewise consented to by the tribute we pay (*v.* 6): *"For this cause pay you tribute,* as a testimony of your submission, and an acknowledgment that in conscience you think it to be due. You do by paying taxes contribute your share to the support of the power; if therefore you be not subject, you do but pull down with one hand what you support with the other; and is that conscience?" "By your paying tribute you not only own the magistrate's authority, but the blessing of that authority to yourselves, a sense of which you thereby testify, giving him that as a recompence for the great pains he takes in the government; for honour is a burden: and, if he do as he ought, *he is attending continually upon this very thing,* for it is enough to take up all a man's thoughts and time, in consideration of which fatigue, we pay tribute, and must be subject." — *Pay you tribute, phorous seleite.* He does not say, "You give it as an alms," but, "You pay it as a just debt, or lend it to be repaid in all the blessings and advantages of public government, of which you reap the benefit." This is the lesson the apostle teaches, and it becomes all Christians to learn and practise it, that the godly in the land may be found (whatever others are) the quiet and the peaceable in the land.

Verses 7–10

We are here taught a lesson of justice and charity.

I. Of justice (*v.* 7): *Render therefore to all their dues,* especially to magistrates, for this refers to what goes before; and likewise to all with whom we have to do. To be just is to give to all their due, to give every body his own. What we have we have as stewards; others have an interest in it, and must have their dues. "Render to God his due in the first place, to yourselves, to you families, your relations, to the commonwealth, to the church, to the poor, to those that you have dealings with in buying, selling, exchanging, etc. Render to all their dues; and that readily and cheerfully, not tarrying till you are by law compelled to it." He specifies, 1. Due taxes: *Tribute to whom tribute is due, custom to whom custom.* Most of the countries where the gospel was first preached were subject at this time to the Roman yoke, and were made provinces of the empire. He wrote this to the Romans, who, as they were rich, so they were drained by taxes and impositions, to the just and honest payment of which they are here pressed by the apostle. Some distinguish between tribute and custom, understanding by the former constant standing taxes, and by the latter those which were occasionally required, both which are to be faithfully and conscientiously paid as they become legally due. Our Lord was born when his mother went to be taxed; and he enjoined the payment of tribute to Caesar. Many, who in other things seem to be just, yet make no conscience of this, but pass it off with a false ill-favoured maxim, that it is no sin to cheat the king, directly contrary to Paul's rule, *Tribute to whom tribute is due.* 2. Due respect: *Fear to whom fear, honour to whom honour.* This sums up the duty which we owe not only to magistrates, but to all superiors, parents, masters, all that are over us in the Lord, according to the fifth commandment: *Honour thy father and mother.* Compare Lev. 19:3, *You shall fear every man his mother and his father;* not with a fear of amazement, but a loving, reverent, respectful, obediential fear. Where there is not this respect in the heart to our superiors, no other duty will be paid aright. 3. Due payment of debts (*v.* 8): *"Owe no man any thing;* that is, do not continue in any one's debt, while you are able to pay it, further than by, at least, the tacit consent of the person to whom you are indebted. Give every one his own. Do not spend that upon yourselves, which you owe to others." The *wicked borroweth, and payeth not again,* Ps. 37:21. Many that are very sensible of the trouble think little of the sin of being in debt.

II. Of charity: *Owe no man any thing; opheilete — you do owe* no man any thing; so some read it: "Whatever you owe to any relation, or to any with whom you have to do, it is eminently summer up and included in this debt of love. But to *love one another,* this is a debt that must be always in the paying, and yet always owing." Love is a debt. The law of God and the interest of mankind make it so. It is not a thing which we are left at liberty about, but it is enjoined us, as the principle and summary of all duty owing one to another; for love *is the fulfilling of the law;* not perfectly, but it is a good step towards it. It is inclusive of all the duties of the second table, which he specifies, *v.* 9, and these suppose the love of God. See 1 Jn. 4:20. If the love be sincere, it is accepted as the *fulfilling of the law.* Surely we serve a good master, that has summed up all our duty in one word, and that a short word and a sweet word — *love,* the beauty and harmony of the universe. Loving and being loved is all the pleasure, joy, and happiness, of an intelligent being. *God is love* (1 Jn. 4:16), and love is his image upon the soul: where it is, the soul is well moulded, and the heart fitted for every good work. Now, to prove that love is the fulfilling of the law, he gives us, 1. An induction of particular precepts, *v.* 9. He specifies the last five of the ten commandments, which he observes to be all summed up in this royal law, *Thou shalt love thy neighbour as thyself* — with an *as* of quality, not of equality — "with the same sincerity that thou lovest thyself, though not in the same measure and degree." He that loves his neighbour as himself will be desirous of the welfare of his neighbour's body, goods, and good name, as of his own. On this is built that golden rule of doing as we would be done by. Were there no restraints of human laws in these things, no punishments incurred (which the malignity of human nature hath made necessary), the law of love would of itself be effectual to prevent all such wrongs and injuries, and to keep peace and good order among us. In the enumeration of these commandments, the apostle puts the seventh before the sixth, and mentions this first, *Thou shalt not commit adultery;* for though this commonly goes under the name of love (pity it is that so good a word should be so abused) yet it is really as great a violation of it as killing and stealing is, which shows that true brotherly love is love to the souls of our brethren in the first place. He that tempts others to sin, and defiles their minds and consciences, though he may pretend the most passionate love (Prov. 7:15, 18), does really hate them, just as the devil does, who wars against the soul. 2. A general rule concerning the nature of brotherly love: *Love worketh no ill* (*v.* 10) — he that walks in love, that is actuated and governed by a principle of love, *worketh no ill;* he neither practises nor contrives any ill *to his neighbour,* to any one that he has any thing to do with: *ouk ergazetai.* The projecting of evil is in effect the performing of it. Hence devising iniquity is called *working evil* upon the bed, Mic. 2:1. Love intends and designs no ill to any body, is utterly against the doing of that which may turn to the prejudice, offence, or grief of any. It *worketh no ill;* that is, it prohibits the working of any ill: more is implied than is expressed; it not only worketh no ill, but it worketh all the good that may be, deviseth liberal things. For it is a sin not only to devise evil against thy neighbour, but to withhold good from those to whom it is due; both are forbidden together, Prov. 3:27–29. This proves that love is the fulfilling of the law, answers all the end of it; for what else is that but to restrain us from evil-doing, and to constrain us to well-doing? Love is a living active principle of obedience to the whole law. The whole law is written in the heart, if the law of love be there.

Verses 11–14

We are here taught a lesson of sobriety and godliness in ourselves. Our main care must be to look to ourselves. Four things we are here taught, as a Christian's directory for his day's work: when to awake, how to dress ourselves, how to walk, and what provision to make.

I. When to awake: *Now it is high time to awake* (*v.* 11), to awake out of the sleep of sin (for a sinful condition is a sleeping condition), out of the sleep of carnal security, sloth and negligence, out of the sleep of spiritual death, and out of the sleep of spiritual deadness; both the wise and foolish virgins slumbered and slept, Mt. 25:5. We have need to be often excited and stirred up to awake. The word of command to all Christ's disciples is, *Watch. "Awake* — be concerned about your souls and your eternal interest; take heed of sin, be ready to, and serious in, that which is good, and live in a constant expectation of the coming of our Lord. Considering," 1. "The time we are cast into: *Knowing the time.* Consider what time of day it is with us, and you will see it is high time to awake. It is gospel time, it is the accepted time, it is working time; it is a time when more is expected than was in the times of that ignorance which God winked at, when people sat in darkness. It is high time to awake; for the sun has been up a great while, and shines in our faces. Have we this light to sleep in? See 1 Th. 5:5, 6. It is high time to awake; for others are awake and up about us. Know the time to be a busy time; we have a great deal of work to do, and our Master is calling us to it again and again. Know the time to be a perilous time. We are in the midst of enemies and snares. It is high time to awake, for the Philistines are upon us; our neighbour's house is on fire, and our own in danger. It is time to awake, for we have slept enough (1 Pt. 4:3), high time indeed, for *behold the bridegroom cometh."* 2. "The salvation we are upon the brink of: *Now is our salvation nearer than when we believed* — than when we first believed, and so took upon us the profession of Christianity. The eternal happiness we chose for our portion is now nearer to us than it was when we became Christians. Let us mind our way and mend our pace, for we are now nearer our journey's end than we were when we had our first love. The nearer we are to our centre the quicker should our motion be. Is there but a step between us and heaven, and shall we be so very slow and dull in our Christian course, and move so heavily? The more the days are shortened, and the more grace is increased, the nearer is our salvation, and the more quick and vigorous we should be in our spiritual motions."

II. How to dress ourselves. This is the next care, when we are awake and up: "The *night is far spent, the day is at hand;* therefore it is time to dress ourselves. Clearer discoveries will be quickly made of gospel grace than have been yet made, as light gets ground. The night of Jewish rage and cruelty is just at an end; their persecuting power is near a period; the day of our deliverance from them is at hand, that day of redemption which Christ promised, Lu. 21:28. And the day of our complete salvation, in the heavenly glory, is at hand. Observe then,"

1. "What we must put off; put off our night-clothes, which it is a shame to appear abroad in: *Cast off the works of darkness."* Sinful works are works of darkness; they come from the darkness of ignorance and mistake, they covet the darkness of privacy and concealment, and they end in the darkness of hell and destruction. "Let us therefore, who are of the day, cast them off; not only cease from the practice of them, but detest and abhor them, and have no more to do with them. Because eternity is just at the door, let us take heed lest we be found doing that which will then make against us," 2 Pt. 3:11, 14.

2. "What we must put on." Our care must be *wherewithal we shall be clothed,* how shall we dress our souls? (1.) *Put on the armour of light.* Christians are soldiers in the midst of enemies, and their life a warfare, therefore their array must be armour, that they may stand upon their defence — the *armour of God,* to which we are directed, Eph. 6:13, etc. A Christian may reckon himself undressed if he be unarmed. The graces of the Spirit are this armour, to secure the soul from Satan's temptations and the assaults of this present evil world. This is called the armour of light, some think alluding to the bright glittering armour which the Roman soldiers used to wear; or such armour as it becomes us to wear in the day-light. The graces of the Spirit are suitable splendid ornaments, are in the sight of God of great price. (2.) *Put on the Lord Jesus Christ, v.* 14. This stands in opposition to a great many base lusts, mentioned *v.* 13. *Rioting and drunkenness* must be cast off: one would think it should follows, but, "Put on sobriety, temperance, chastity," the opposite virtues: no, *"Put on Christ,* this includes all. Put on the righteousness of Christ for justification; be found in him (Phil. 3:9) as a man is found in his clothes; put on the priestly garments of the elder brother, that in them you may obtain the blessing. Put on the spirit and grace of Christ for sanctification; put on the *new man* (Eph. 4:24); get the habit of grace confirmed, the acts of it quickened." Jesus Christ is the best clothing for Christians to adorn themselves with, to arm themselves with; it is decent, distinguishing, dignifying, and defending. Without Christ, we are naked, deformed; all other things are filthy rages, fig-leaves, a sorry shelter. God has provided us coats of skins — large, strong, warm, and durable. By baptism we have in profession put on Christ, Gal. 3:27. Let us do it in truth and sincerity. *The Lord Jesus Christ.* "Put him on as Lord to rule you, as Jesus to save you, and in both as Christ, anointed and appointed by the Father to this ruling saving work."

III. How to walk. When we are up and dressed, we are not to sit still in an affected closeness and privacy, as monks and hermits. What have we good clothes for, but to appear abroad in them? — *Let us walk.* Christianity teaches us how to walk so as to please God, whose eye is upon us: 1 Th. 4:1, *Walk honestly as in the day.* Compare Eph. 5:8, *Walk as children of light.* Our conversation must be as becomes the gospel. *Walk honestly; euschēmonōs — decently* and becomingly, so as to credit your profession, and to adorn the doctrine of God our Saviour, and recommend religion in its beauty to others. Christians should be in a special manner careful to conduct themselves well in those things wherein men have an eye upon them, and to study that which is lovely and of good report. Particularly, here are three pairs of sins we are cautioned against: — 1. We must not walk in *rioting and drunkenness;* we must abstain from all excess in eating and drinking. We must not give the least countenance to revelling, nor indulge our sensual appetite in any private excesses. Christians must not overcharge their hearts with surfeiting and drunkenness, Lu. 21:34. This is not walking as in the day; for those that are *drunk are drunk in the night,* 1 Th. 5:7. 2. *Not in chambering and wantonness;* not in any of those lusts of the flesh, those works of darkness, which are forbidden in the seventh commandment. Downright adultery and fornication are the chambering forbidden. Lascivious thoughts and affections, lascivious looks, words, books, sons, gestures, dances, dalliances, which lead to, and are degrees of, that uncleanness, are the wantonness here forbidden — whatsoever transgresseth the pure and sacred law of chastity and modesty. 3. Not in *strife and envying.* These are also works of darkness; for, though the acts and instances of strife and envy are very common, yet none are willing to own the principles, or to acknowledge themselves envious and contentious. it may be the lot of the best saints to be envied and striven with; but to strive and to envy ill becomes the disciples and followers of the peaceable and humble Jesus. Where there are riot and drunkenness, there usually are chambering and wantonness, and strife and envy. Solomon puts them all together, Prov. 23:29, etc. Those that tarry long at the wine (*v.* 30) have contentions and wounds without cause (*v.* 29) and their eyes behold strange women, *v.* 33.

IV. What provision to make (*v.* 14): *"Make not provision for the flesh.* Be not careful about the body." Our great care must be to provide for our souls; but must we take no care about our bodies? Must we not provide for them, when they need it? Yes, but two things are here forbidden: — 1. Perplexing ourselves with an inordinate care, intimated in these words, *pronoian mē poieisthe.* "Be not solicitous in forecasting for the body; do not stretch your wits, nor set your thoughts upon the tenter-hooks, in making this provision; be not careful and cumbered about it; do not *take thought,"* Mt. 6:31. It forbids an anxious encumbering care. 2. Indulging ourselves in an irregular desire. We are not forbidden barely to provide for the body (it is a lamp that must be supplied with oil), but we are forbidden to fulfil the lusts thereof. The necessities of the body must be considered, but the lusts of it must not be gratified. Natural desires must be answered, but wanton appetites must be checked and denied. To ask meat for our necessities is duty: we are taught to pray for daily bread; but to ask meat for our lusts is provoking, Ps. 78:18. Those who profess to walk in the spirit must not fulfil the lusts of the flesh, Gal. 5:16.

CHAPTER 14

The apostle having, in the former chapter, directed our conduct one towards another in civil things, and prescribed the sacred laws of justice, peaceableness, and order, to be observed by us as members of the commonwealth, comes in this and part of the following chapter in like manner to direct our demeanour one towards another in sacred things, which pertain more immediately to conscience and religion, and which we observe as members of the church. Particularly, he gives rules how to manage our different apprehensions about indifferent things, in the management of which, it seems, there was something amiss among the Roman Christians, to whom he wrote, which he here labours to redress. But the rules are general, and of standing use in the church, for the preservation of that Christian love which he had so earnestly pressed in the foregoing chapter as the fulfilling of the law. It is certain that nothing is more threatening, nor more often fatal, to Christian societies, than the contentions and divisions of their members. By these wounds the life and soul of religion expire. Now in this chapter we are furnished with the sovereign balm of Gilead; the blessed apostle prescribes like a wise physician. "Why then is not the hurt of the daughter of my people recovered," but because his directions are not followed? This chapter, rightly understood, made use of, and lived up to, would set things to rights, and heal us all.

Verses 1–23

We have in this chapter,

I. An account of the unhappy contention which had broken out in the Christian church. Our Master had foretold that offences would come; and, it seems, so they did, for want of that wisdom and love which would have prevented discord, and kept up union among them.

1. There was a difference among them about the distinction of meats and days; these are the two things specified. There might be other similar occasions of difference, while these made the most noise, and were most taken notice of. The case was this: The members of the Christian church at Rome were some of them originally Gentiles, and others of them Jews. We find Jews at Rome believing, Acts 28:24. Now those that had been Jews were trained up in the observance of the ceremonial appointments touching meats and days. This, which had been bred in the bone with them, could hardly be got out of the flesh, even after they turned Christians; especially with some of them, who were not easily weaned from what they had long been wedded to. They were not well instructed touching the cancelling of the ceremonial law by the death of Christ, and therefore retained the ceremonial institutions, and practised accordingly; while other Christians that understood themselves better, and knew their Christian liberty, made no such difference. (1.) Concerning meats (*v.* 2): *One believeth that he may eat all things* — he is well satisfied that the ceremonial distinction of meats into clean and unclean is no longer in force, but that every creature of God is good, and nothing to be refused; nothing *unclean of itself, v.* 14. This he was assured of, not only from the general tenour and scope of the gospel, but particularly from the revelation which Peter, the apostle of the circumcision (and therefore more immediately concerned in it), had to this purport, Acts 10:15, 28. This the strong Christian is clear in, and practises accordingly, eating what is set before him, and asking no question for conscience' sake, 1 Co. 10:27. On the other hand, *another, who is weak,* is dissatisfied in this point, is not clear in his Christian liberty, but rather inclines to think that the meats forbidden by the law remain still unclean; and therefore, to keep at a distance from them, he will eat no flesh at all, but *eateth herbs,* contenting himself with only the fruits of the earth. See to what degrees of mortification and self-denial a tender conscience will submit. None know but those that experience it how great both the restraining and the constraining power of conscience is. (2.) Concerning days, *v.* 5. Those who thought themselves still under some kind of obligation to the ceremonial law esteemed *one day above another* — kept up a respect to the times of the passover, pentecost, new moons, and feasts of tabernacles; thought those days better than other days, and solemnized them accordingly with particular observances, binding themselves to some religious rest and exercise on those days. Those who knew that all these things were abolished and done away by Christ's coming esteemed every day alike. We must understand it with an exception of the Lord's day, which all Christians unanimously observed; but they made no account, took no notice, of those antiquated festivals of the Jews. Here the apostle speaks of the distinction of meats and days as a thing indifferent, when it went no further than the opinion and practice of some particular persons, who had been trained up all their days to such observances, and therefore were the more excusable if they with difficulty parted with them. But in the epistle to the Galatians, where he deals with those that were originally Gentiles, but were influenced by some judaizing teachers, not only to believe such a distinction and to practise accordingly, but to lay a stress upon it as necessary to salvation, and to make the observance of the Jewish festivals public and congregational, here the case was altered, and it is charged upon them as the frustrating of the design of the gospel, falling from grace, Gal. 4:9–11. The Romans did it out of weakness, the Galatians did it out of wilfulness and wickedness; and therefore the apostle handles them thus differently. This epistle is supposed to have been written some time before that to the Galatians. The apostle seems willing to let the ceremonial law wither by degrees, and to let it have an honourable burial; now these weak Romans seem to be only following it weeping to its grave, but those Galatians were raking it out of its ashes.

2. It was not so much the difference itself that did the mischief as the mismanagement of the difference, making it a bone of contention. (1.) Those who were strong, and knew their Christian liberty, and made use of it, despised the weak, who did not. Whereas they should have pitied them, and helped them, and afforded them meek and friendly instruction, they trampled upon them as silly, and humoursome, and superstitious, for scrupling those things which they knew to be lawful: so apt are those who have knowledge to be puffed up with it, and to look disdainfully and scornfully upon their brethren. (2.) Those who were weak, and durst not use their Christian liberty, judged and censured the strong, who did, as if they were loose Christians, carnal professors, that cared not what they did, but walked at all adventures, and stuck at nothing. They judged them as breakers of the law, contemners of God's ordinance, and the like. Such censures as these discovered a great deal of rashness and uncharitableness, and would doubtless tend much to the alienating of affection. Well, this was the disease, and we see it remaining in the church to this day; the like differences, in like manner mismanaged, are still the disturbers of the church's peace. But,

II. We have proper directions and suggestions laid down for allaying this contention, and preventing the ill consequences of it. The apostle, as a wise physician, prescribes proper remedies for the disease, which are made up of rules and reasons. Such gentle methods does he take, with such cords of a man does he draw them together; not by excommunicating, suspending, and silencing either side, but by persuading them both to a mutual forbearance: and as a faithful daysman he lays his hand upon them both, reasoning the case with the strong that they should not be so scornful, and with the weak that they should not be so censorious. If the contending parties will but submit to this fair arbitration, each abate of his rigour, and sacrifice their differences to their graces, all will be well quickly. Let us observe the rules he gives, some to the strong and some to the weak, and some to both, for they are interwoven; and reduce the reasons to their proper rules.

1. Those who are weak must be *received, but not to doubtful disputations, v.* 1. Take this for a general rule; spend your zeal in those things wherein you and all the people of God are agreed, and do not dispute about matters that are doubtful. *Receive him, proslambavesthe — take him to you,* bid him welcome, receive him with the greatest affection and tenderness; *porrigite manum* (so the Syriac): *lend him your hand,* to help him, to fetch him to you, to encourage him. Receive him into your company, and converse, and communion, entertain him with readiness and condescension, and treat him with all possible endearments. Receive him: not to quarrel with him, and to argue about uncertain points that are in controversy, which will but confound him, and fill his head with empty notions, perplex him, and shake his faith. Let not your Christian friendship and fellowship be disturbed with such vain janglings and strifes of words. — *Not to judge his doubtful thoughts* (so the margin), "not to pump out his weak sentiments concerning those things which he is in doubt about, that you may censure and condemn him." Receive him, not to expose him, but to instruct and strengthen him. See 1 Co. 1:10; Phil. 3:15, 16.

2. Those who are strong must by no means despise the weak; nor those who are weak judge the strong, *v.* 3. This is levelled directly against the fault of each party. It is seldom that any such contention exists but there is a fault on both sides, and both must mend. He argues against both these jointly: we must not despise nor judge our brethren. Why so?

(1.) Because God hath received them; and we reflect upon him if we reject those whom he hath received. God never cast off any one that had true grace, though he was but weak in it; never broke the bruised reed. Strong believers and weak believers, those that eat and those that eat not, if they be true believers, are accepted of God. It will be good for us to put this question to ourselves, when we are tempted to behave scornfully towards our brethren, to disdain and censure them: "Hast not God owned them; and, if he has, dare I disown them?" "Nay, God doth not only receive him, but *hold him up, v.* 4. You think that he who eateth will fall by his presumption, or that he who eateth not will sink under the weight of his own fears and scruples; but if they have true faith, and an eye to God, the one in the intelligent use of his Christian liberty and the other in the conscientious forbearance of it, they shall be held up — the one in his integrity, and the other in his comfort. This hope is built upon the power of God, for *God is able to make him stand;* and, being able, no doubt he is willing to exert that power for the preservation of those that are his own." In reference to spiritual difficulties and dangers (our own and others), much of our hope and comfort are grounded upon the divine power, 1 Pt. 1:5; Jude 24.

(2.) Because they are servants to their own master (*v.* 4): *Who art thou that judgest another man's servant?* We reckon it a piece of ill manners to meddle with other people's servants, and to find fault with them and censure them. Weak and strong Christians are indeed our brethren, but they are not our servants. This rash judging is reproved, Jam. 3:1, under the notion of being many masters. We make ourselves our brethren's masters, and do in effect usurp the throne of God, when we take upon us thus to judge them, especially to judge their thoughts and intentions, which are out of our view, to judge their persons and state, concerning which it is hard to conclude by those few indications which fall within our cognizance. God sees not as man sees; and he is their master, and not we. In judging and censuring our brethren, we meddle with that which does not belong to us: we have work enough to do at home; and, if we must needs be judging, let us exercise our faculty upon our own hearts and ways.

— *To his own master he stands or falls;* that is, his doom will be according to his master's sentence, and not according to ours. How well for us is it that we are not to stand nor fall by the judgment one of another, but by the righteous and unerring judgment of God, which is according to truth! "While thy brother's cause is before thy judgment, it is *coram non judice — before one who is not the judge;* the court of heaven is the proper court for trial, where, and where only, the sentence is definitive and conclusive; and to this, if his heart be upright, he may comfortably appeal from thy rash censure."

(3.) Because both the one and the other, if they be true believers, and are right in the main, have an eye to God, and do approve themselves to God in what they do, *v.* 6. He *that regards the day* — that makes conscience of the observance of the Jewish fasts and festivals, not imposing it upon others, nor laying a stress upon it, but willing to be as he thinks on the surer side, as thinking there is no harm in resting from worldly labours, and worshipping God on those days — it is well. We have reason to think, because in other things he conducts himself like a good Christian, that in this also his eye is single, and that *he regardeth it unto the Lord;* and God will accept of his honest intention, though he be under a mistake about the observance of days; for the sincerity and uprightness of the heart were never rejected for the weakness and infirmity of the head: so good a master do we serve. On the other hand, he *that regards not the day* — that does not make a difference between one day and another, does not call one day holy and another profane, one day lucky and another unlucky, but esteems every day alike — he does not do it out of a spirit of opposition, contradiction, or contempt of his brother. If he be a good Christian, he does not, he dares not, do it from such a principle; and therefore we charitably conclude that to the *Lord he does not regard it.* he makes no such difference of days only because he knows God hath made none; and therefore intends his honour in endeavouring to dedicate ever day to him. So for the other instance: *He that eateth* whatever is set before him, though it be blood, though it be swine's flesh, if it be food convenient for him, he *eateth to the Lord.* He understands the liberty that God has granted him, and uses it to the glory of God, with an eye to his wisdom and goodness in enlarging our allowance now under the gospel, and taking off the yoke of legal restraints; and he *giveth God thanks* for the variety of food he has, and the liberty he has to eat it, and that in those things his conscience is not fettered. On the other hand, *he that eatest not* those meats which were forbidden by the ceremonial law, *to the Lord he eateth not.* It is for God's sake, because he is afraid of offending God by eating that which he is sure was once prohibited; and he *giveth God thanks too* that there is enough besides. If he conscientiously deny himself that which he takes to be forbidden fruit, yet he blesses God that of other trees in the garden he may freely eat. Thus, while both have an eye to God in what they do, and approve themselves to him in their integrity, why should either of them be judged or despised? Observe, Whether we eat flesh, or eat herbs, it is a thankful regard to God, the author and giver of all our mercies, that sanctifies and sweetens it. Bishop Sanderson, in his 34th sermon, upon 1 Tim. 4:4, justly makes this observation: It appears by this that *saying grace* (as we commonly call it, perhaps from 1 Co. 10:30) before and after meat was the common known practice of the church, among Christians of all sorts, weak and strong: an ancient, commendable, apostolical, Christian practice, derived down from Christ's example through all the ages of the church, Mt. 14:19; 15:36; Lu. 9:16; Jn. 6:11; Mt. 26:26, 27; Acts 27:35. Blessing the creatures in the name of God before we use them, and blessing the name of God for them after, are both included; for **eulogein** and **eucharistein** are used promiscuously. To clear this argument against rash judging and despising, he shows how essential it is to true Christianity to have a regard to God and not to ourselves, which therefore, unless the contrary do manifestly appear, we must presume concerning those that in minor things differ from us. Observe his description of true Christians, taken from their end and aim (*v.* 7, 8), and the ground of it, *v.* 9.

[1.] Our end and aim: not self, but the Lord. As the particular end specifies the action, so the general scope and tendency specify the state. if we would know what way we walk in, we must enquire what end we walk towards. *First,* Not to self. We have learned to deny ourselves; this was our first lesson: *None of us liveth to himself.* This is a thing in which all the people of God are one, however they differ in other things; though some are weak and others are strong, yet both agree in this, not to live to themselves. Not one that hath given up his name to Christ is allowedly a self-seeker; it is contrary to the foundation of true Christianity. We neither *live to ourselves nor die to ourselves.* We are not our own masters, nor our own proprietors — we are not at our own disposal. The business of our lives is not to please ourselves, but to please God. The business of our deaths, to which we are every day exposed and delivered, is not to make ourselves talked of; we run not such hazards out of vain-glory, while we are dying daily. When we come to die actually, neither is that to ourselves; it is not barely that we would be unclothed, and eased of the burden of the flesh, but it is to the Lord, that we may depart and be with Christ, may be present with the Lord. *Secondly,* But *to the Lord* (*v.* 8), to the Lord Christ, to whom all power and judgment are committed, and in whose name we are taught, as Christians, to do every thing we do (Col. 3:17), with an eye to the will of Christ as our rule, to the glory of Christ as our end, Phil. 1:21. Christ is the gain we aim at, living and dying. We live to glorify him in all the actions and affairs of life; we die, whether a natural or a violent death, to glorify him, and to go to be glorified with him. Christ is the centre, in which all the lines of life and death do meet. This is true Christianity, which makes Christ all in all. So that, *whether we live or die, we are the Lord's,* devoted to him, depending on him, designed and designing for him. Though some Christians are weak and others strong, — though of different sizes, capacities, apprehensions, and practices, in minor things, yet they are all the Lord's — all eying, and serving, and approving themselves to Christ, and are accordingly owned and accepted of him. Is it for us then to judge or despise them, as if we were their masters, and they were to make it their business to please us, and to stand or fall by our dooms?

[2.] The ground of this, *v.* 9. It is grounded upon Christ's absolute sovereignty and dominion, which were the fruit and end of his death and resurrection. *To this end he both died, and rose, and revived* (he, having risen, entered upon a heavenly life, the glory which he had before) *that he might be Lord both of dead and living* — that he might be universal monarch, Lord of all (Acts 10:36), all the animate and inanimate creatures; for he is head over all things to the church. He is Lord of those that are living to rule them, of those that are dead to receive them and raise them up. This was that *name above every name* which God gave him as the reward of his humiliation, Phil. 2:8, 9. It was after he had died and risen that he said, *All power is given unto me* (matt. 28:18), and presently he exerts that power in issuing out commissions, *v.* 19, 20. Now if Christ paid so dearly for his dominion over souls and consciences, and has such a just and undisputed right to exercise that dominion, we must not so much as seem to invade it, nor intrench upon it, by judging the consciences of our brethren, and arraigning them at our bar. When we are ready to reproach and reflect upon the name and memory of those that are dead and gone, and to pass a censure upon them (which some the rather do, because such judgments of the dead are more likely to pass uncontrolled and uncontradicted), we must consider that Christ is Lord of the dead, as well as of the living. If they are dead, they have already given up their account, and let that suffice. And this leads to another reason against judging and despising,

(4.) Because both the one and the other must shortly give an account, *v.* 10–12. A believing regard to the judgment of the great day would silence all these rash judgings: *Why dost thou* that art weak *judge thy brother* that is strong? And *why dost thou* that art strong *set at nought thy brother* that is weak? Why is all this clashing, and contradicting, and censuring, among Christians? *We shall all stand before the judgment-seat of Christ,* 2 Co. 5:10. Christ will be the judge, and he has both authority and ability to determine men's eternal state according to their works, and before him we shall stand as persons to be tried, and to give up an account, expecting our final doom from him, which will be eternally conclusive. To illustrate this (*v.* 11), he quotes a passage out of the Old Testament, which speaks of Christ's universal sovereignty and dominion, and that established with an oath: *As I live* (saith the Lord), *every knee shall bow to me.* It is quoted from Isa. 45:23. There it is, *I have sworn by myself;* here it is, *As I live.* So that whenever God saith *As I live,* it is to be interpreted as swearing by himself; for it is God's prerogative to have life in himself: there is a further ratification of it there, *The word is gone out of my mouth.* It is a prophecy, in general, of Christ's dominion; and here very fully applied to the judgment of the great day, which will be the highest and most illustrious exercise of that dominion. Here is a proof of Christ's Godhead: he is the Lord and he is God, equal with the Father. Divine honour is due to him, and must be paid. It is paid to God through him as Mediator. God will judge the world by him, Acts 17:31. The bowing of the knee to him, and the confession made with the tongue, are but outward expressions of inward adoration and praise. *Every knee* and *every tongue,* either freely or by force.

[1.] All his friends do it freely, are made willing in the day of his power. Grace is the soul's cheerful, entire, and avowed subjection to Jesus Christ. *First,* Bowing to him — the understanding bowed to his truths, the will to his laws, the whole man to his authority; and this expressed by the bowing of the knee, the posture of adoration and prayer. It is proclaimed before our Joseph, *Bow the knee,* Gen. 41:43. Though bodily exercise alone profits little, yet, as it is guided by inward fear and reverence, it is accepted. *Secondly,* Confessing to him — acknowledging his glory, grace, and greatness — acknowledging our own meanness and vileness, confessing our sins to him; so some understand it.

[2.] All his foes shall be constrained to do it, whether they will or no. When he shall come in the clouds, and every eye shall see him, then, and not till then, will all those promises which speak of his victories over his enemies and their subjection to him have their full and complete accomplishment; then his foes shall be his footstool, and all his enemies shall lick the dust. hence he concludes (*v.* 12), *Every one of us shall give account of himself to God.* We must not give account for others, nor they for us; but every one for himself. We must give account how we have spent our time, how we have improved our opportunities, what we have done and how we have done it. And therefore, *First,* We have little to do to judge others, for they are not accountable to us, nor are we accountable for them (Gal. 2:6): *Whatsoever they were, it maketh no matter to me, God accepteth no man's person.* Whatever they are, and whatever they do, they must give account to their own master, and not to us; if we can in any thing be helpers of their joy, it is well; but we have not dominion over their faith. And, *Secondly,* We have the more to do to judge ourselves. We have an account of our own to make up, and that is enough for us; let every *man prove his own work* (Gal. 6:4), state his own accounts, search his own heart and life; let this take up his thoughts, and he that is strict in judging himself and abasing himself will not be apt to judge and despise his brother. let all these differences be referred to the arbitration of Christ at the great day.

(5.) Because the stress of Christianity is not to be laid upon these things, nor are they at all essential to religion, either on the one side or on the other. This is his reason (*v.* 17, 18), which is reducible to this branch of exhortation. Why should you spend your zeal either for or against those things which are so minute and inconsiderable in religion? Some make it a reason why, in case of offence likely to be taken, we should refrain the use of our Christian liberty; but it seems directed in general against that heat about those things which he observed on both sides. *The kingdom of God is not meat,* etc. Observe here,

[1.] The nature of true Christianity, what it is: it is here called, *The kingdom of God;* it is a religion intended to rule us, a kingdom: it stands in a true and hearty subjection to God's power and dominion. The gospel dispensation is in a special manner called *the kingdom of God,* in distinction from the legal dispensation, Mt. 3:2; 4:17. *First,* It is *not meat and drink:* it does not consist either in using or in abstaining from such and such meats and drinks. Christianity gives no rule in that case, either in one way or another. The Jewish religion consisted much in meats and drinks (Heb. 9:10), abstaining from some meats religiously (Lev. 11:2), eating other meats religiously, as in several of the sacrifices, part of which were to be eaten before the Lord: but all those appointments are now abolished and are no more, Col. 2:21, 22. The matter is left at large. Every *creature of God is good,* 1 Tim. 4:4. So, as to other things, it is neither circumcision nor uncircumcision (Gal. 5:6; 6:15; 1 Co. 7:19), it is not being of this party and persuasion, of this or the other opinion in minor things, that will recommend us to God. It will not be asked at the great day, "Who ate flesh, and who ate herbs?" "Who kept holy days, and who did not?" Nor will it be asked, "Who was conformist and who was non-conformist?" But it will be asked, "Who feared God and worked righteousness, and who did not?" Nothing more destructive to true Christianity than placing it in modes, and forms, and circumstantials, which eat out the essentials. *Secondly, It is righteousness, and peace, and joy in the Holy Ghost.* These are some of the essentials of Christianity, things in which all the people of God are agreed, in the pursuit of which we must spend our zeal, and which we must mind with an excelling care. Righteousness, peace, and joy, are very comprehensive words; and each of them includes much, both of the foundation and the super-structure of religion. Might I limit the sense of them, it should be thus: — As to God, our great concern is *righteousness* — to appear before him justified by the merit of Christ's death, sanctified by the Spirit of his grace; for the righteous Lord loveth righteousness. As to our brethren, it is *peace* — to live in peace and love, and charity with them, following peace with all men: Christ came into the world to be the great peace-maker. As to ourselves, it is *joy in the Holy Ghost* — that spiritual joy which is wrought by the blessed Spirit in the hearts of believers, which respects God as their reconciled Father and heaven as their expected home. Next to our compliance with God, the life of religion consists in our complacency in him; to delight ourselves always in the Lord. Surely we serve a good Master, who makes peace and joy so essential to our religion. Then and then only we may expect peace and joy in the Holy Ghost when the foundation is laid in righteousness, Isa. 32:17. *Thirdly,* It is in these things to *serve Christ* (v. 18), to do all this out of respect to Christ himself as our Master, to his will as our rule and to his glory as our end. That which puts an acceptableness upon all our good duties is a regard to Christ in the doing of them. We are to serve his interests and designs in the world, which are in the first place to reconcile us one to another. What is Christianity but the serving of Christ? And we may well afford to serve him who for us and for our salvation took upon him the form of a servant.

[2.] The advantages of it. He that duly observeth these things, *First,* Is acceptable to God. God is well pleased with such a one, though he be not in every thing just of our length. He has the love and favour of God; his person, his performances, are accepted of God, and we need no more to make us happy. If God now accepts thy works, thou may-est eat thy bread with joy. Those are most pleasing to God that are best pleased with him; and they are those that abound most in peace and joy in the Holy Ghost. *Secondly,* He is approved of men — of all wise and good men, and the opinion of others is not to be regarded. The persons and things which are acceptable to God should be approved of us. Should not we be pleased with that which God is pleased with? What is it to be sanctified, but to be of God's mind? Observe, The approbation of men is not to be slight-ed; for we must provide things honest in the sight of all men, and study those things that are lovely and of good report: but the acceptance of God is to be desired and aimed at in the first place, because, sooner or later, God will bring all the world to be of his mind.

3. Another rule here given is this, that in these doubtful things every one not only may, but must, walk according to the light that God hath given him. This is laid down *v.* 5, *Let every man be fully persuaded in his own mind;* that is, "Practise according to your own judgment in these things, and leave others to do so too. Do not censure the practice of others; let them enjoy their own opinion; if they be per-suaded in their own mind that they ought to do so and so, do not condemn them, but, if your sober sentiments be oth-erwise, do not make their practice a rule to you, any more than you must prescribe yours as a rule to them. Take heed of acting contrary to the dictates of a doubting conscience. First be persuaded that what you do is lawful, before you ven-ture to do it." In doubtful things, it is good keeping on the sure side of the hedge. If a weak Christian doubts whether it be lawful to eat flesh, while he remains under that doubt he had best forbear, till he be fully persuaded in his own mind. We must not pin our faith upon any one's sleeve, nor make the practice of others our rule; but follow the dictates of our own understanding. To this purport he argues, *v.* 14 and 23, which two verses explain this, and give us a rule not to act against the dictates,

(1.) Of a mistaken conscience, *v.* 14. If a thing be indiffer-ent, so that it is not in itself a sin not to do it, if we really think it a sin to do it it is to us a sin, though not to others, because we act against our consciences, though mistaken and

misinformed. He specifies the case in hand, concerning the difference of meats. Observe,

[1.] His own clearness in this matter. "*I know and am per-suaded* — I am fully persuaded, I am acquainted with my Christian liberty, and am satisfied in it, without any doubt or scruple, that there *is nothing unclean of itself,* that is, no kind of meat that lies under any ceremonial uncleanness, nor is forbidden to be eaten, if it be food proper for human bod-ies." Several kinds of meat were forbidden to the Jews, that in that, as in other things, they might be a peculiar and sep-arate people, Lev. 11:44; Deu. 14:2, 3. Sin had brought a curse upon the whole creation: *Cursed is the ground for thy sake;* the use of the creatures and dominion over them were for-feited, so that to man they were all unclean (Tit. 1:15), in to-ken of which God in the ceremonial law prohibited the use of some, to show what he might have done concerning all; but now that Christ has removed the curse the matter is set at large again, and that prohibition is taken away. Therefore Paul says that he was persuaded by the Lord Jesus, not only as the author of that persuasion, but as the ground of it; it was built upon the efficacy of Christ's death, which removed the curse, took off the forfeiture, and restored our right to the creature in general, and consequently put a period to that particular distinguishing prohibition. So that now there is nothing unclean of itself, every creature of God is good; noth-ing *common:* so the margin, *ouden koinon;* nothing which is common to others to eat, from the use of which the pro-fessors of religion are restrained: nothing profane; in this sense the Jews used the word *common.* It is explained by the word *akatharton,* Acts 10:14, nothing *common or unclean.* It was not only from the revelation made to Peter in this matter, but from the tenour and tendency of the whole gospel, and from the manifest design of Christ's death in gen-eral, that Paul learned to count nothing common or unclean. This was Paul's own clearness, and he practised accordingly.

[2.] But here is a caution he gives to those who had not that clearness in this matter which he had: *To him that es-teemeth any thing to be unclean,* though it be his error, yet *to him it is unclean.* This particular case, thus determined, gives a general rule, That he who does a thing which he ver-ily believes to be unlawful, however the thing be in itself, to him it is a sin. This arises from that unchangeable law of our creation, which is, that our wills, in all their choices, motions, and directions, should follow the dictates of our understand-ings. This is the order of nature, which order is broken if the understanding (though misguided) tell us that such a thing is a sin, and yet we will do it. This is a *will* to do evil; for, if it appears to us to be sin, there is the same pravity and corruption of the will in the doing of it as if really it were a sin; and therefore we ought not to do it. Not that it is in the power of any man's conscience to alter the nature of the action in itself, but only as to himself. It must be understood likewise with this proviso, though men's judgments and opin-ions may make that which is good in itself to become evil to them, yet they cannot make that which is evil in itself to become good, either in itself or to them. If a man were ver-ily persuaded (it is Dr. Sanderson's instance, sermon on *ch.* 14:23) that it were evil to ask his father's blessing, that mis-persuasion would make it become evil to him: but, if he should be as verily persuaded that it were good to curse his father, this would not make it become good. The Pharisees taught people to plead conscience, when they made *corban* an excuse for denying relief to their parents, Mt. 15:5, 6. But this would not serve any more than Paul's erroneous con-science would justify his rage against Christianity (Acts 26:9), or theirs, Jn. 16:2.

(2.) Nor must we act against the dictates of a doubting conscience. In those indifferent things which we are sure it is no sin not to do, and yet are not clear that it is lawful to do them, we must not do them while we continue under those doubts; for he *that doubteth is damned if he eat* (v. 23), that is, it turns into sin to him; he is *damned, katakekritai — he is condemned* of his own conscience, because he *eateth not of faith,* because he does that which he is not fully per-suaded he may lawfully do. He is not clear that it is lawful for him to eat swine's flesh (suppose), and yet is drawn, not-withstanding his doubts, to eat it, because he sees others do it, because he would gratify his appetite with it, or because he would not be reproached for his singularity. Here his own heart cannot but condemn him as a transgressor. our rule is, to walk as far as we have attained, not further, Phil. 3:15, 16. — *For whatsoever is not of faith is sin.* Taking it in gen-

eral, it is the same with that of the apostle (Heb. 11:6), *With-out faith it is impossible to please God.* Whatever we do in religion, it will not turn to any good account, except we do it from a principle of faith, with a believing regard to the will of Christ as our rule, to the glory of Christ as our end, and to the righteousness of Christ as our plea. Here it seems to be taken more strictly; whatever is not of faith (that is, what-ever is done while we are not clearly persuaded of the law-fulness of it), is a sin against conscience. He that will venture to do that which his own conscience suggests to him to be unlawful, when it is not so in itself, will by a like temptation be brought to do that which his conscience tells him is un-lawful when it is really so. The spirit of a man is the candle of the Lord, and it is a dangerous thing to debauch and put a force upon conscience, though it be under a mistake. This seems to be the meaning of that aphorism, which sounds somewhat darkly (v. 22), *Happy is he that condemns not him-self in that thing which he allows.* Many a one allows himself in practice to do that which yet in his judgment and con-science he condemns himself for — allows it for the sake of the pleasure, profit, or credit of it — allows it in conformity to the custom; and yet whilst he does it, and pleas for it, his own heart gives him the lie, and his conscience condemns him for it. Now, happy is the man who so orders his con-versation as not in any action to expose himself to the chal-lenges and reproaches of his own conscience — that does not make his own heart his adversary, as he must needs do who does that which he is not clear he may lawfully do. He is happy that has peace and quietness within, for the testi-mony of conscience will be a special cordial in troublesome times. Though men condemn us, it is well enough if our own hearts condemn us not, 1 Jn. 3:21.

4. Another rule here prescribed is to those who are clear in these matters, and know their Christian liberty, yet to take heed of using it so as to give offence to a weak brother. This is laid down *v.* 13, *Let us not judge one another any more.* "Let it suffice that you have hitherto continued in this un-charitable practice, and do so no more." The better to insin-uate the exhortation, he puts himself in; Let us not; as if he had said, "It is what I have resolved against, therefore do you leave it: but *judge this rather,* instead of censuring the prac-tice of others, let us look to our own, that no *man put a stumbling-block, or an occasion to fall, in his brother's way," — proskomma, ē skandalon.* We must take heed of say-ing or doing any thing which may occasion our brother to stumble or fall; the one signifies a less, the other a greater degree of mischief and offence — that which may be an occasion,

(1.) Of grief to our brother, "One that is weak, and thinks it unlawful to eat such and such meats, will be greatly trou-bled to see thee eat them, out of a concern for the honour of the law which he thinks forbids them, and for the good of thy soul which he thinks is wronged by them, especially when thou dost it wilfully and with a seeming presumption, and not with that tenderness and that care to give satisfac-tion to thy weak brother which would become thee." Chris-tians should take heed of grieving one another, and of sad-dening the hearts of Christ's little ones. See Mt. 18:6, 10.

(2.) Of guilt to our brother. The former is a *stumbling-block,* that gives our brother a great shake, and is a hindrance and discouragement to him; but this is an *occasion to fall.* "If thy weak brother, purely by thy example and influence, without any satisfaction received concerning his Christian lib-erty, be drawn to act against his conscience and to walk con-trary to the light he has, and so to contract guilt upon his soul, though the thing were lawful to thee, yet not being so to him (he having not yet *thereto attained),* thou art to be blamed for giving the occasion." See this case explained, 1 Co. 8:9–11. To the same purport (v. 21) he recommends it to our care not to give offence to any one by the use of lawful things: *It is good neither to eat flesh nor to drink wine;* these are things lawful indeed and comfortable, but not necessary to the support of human life, and therefore we may, and must, deny ourselves in them, rather than give offence. *It is good* — pleasing to God, profitable to our brother, and no harm to ourselves. Daniel and his fellows were in better liking with pulse and water than those were who ate the portion of the king's meat. It is a generous piece of self-denial, for which we have Paul's example (1 Co. 8:13), *If meat make my broth-er to offend;* he does not say, *I will eat no meat,* that is to destroy himself; but *I will eat no flesh,* that is to deny him-self, *while the world stands.* This is to be extended to all such indifferent things whereby thy brother stumbleth, or is offended, is involved either in sin or in trouble: or *is made weak* — his graces weakened, his comforts weakened, his resolutions weakened. *Is made weak,* that is, takes occasion to show his weakness by his censures and scruples. We must not weaken those that are weak; that is to quench the smoking flax and to break the bruised reed. Observe the motives to enforce this caution.

[1.] Consider the royal law of Christian love and charity, which is hereby broken (*v.* 15): *If thy brother be grieved with thy meat* — be troubled to see thee eat those things which the law of Moses did forbid, which yet thou mayest lawfully do; possibly thou art ready to say, "Now he talks foolishly and weakly, and it is no great matter what he says." We are apt, in such a case, to lay all the blame on that side. But the reproof is here given to the stronger and more knowing Christian: *Now walkest thou not charitably.* Thus the apostle takes part with the weakest, and condemns the defect in love on the one side more than the defect in knowledge on the other side; agreeably to his principles elsewhere, that the way of love is the *more excellent way,* 1 Co. 12:31. Knowledge puffeth up, but charity edifieth, 1 Co. 8:1–3. *Now walkest thou not charitably.* Charity to the souls of our brethren is the best charity. True love would make us tender of their peace and purity, and beget a regard to their consciences as well as to our own. Christ deals gently with those that have true grace, though they are weak in it.

[2.] Consider the design of Christ's death: *Destroy not him with thy meat for whom Christ died, v.* 15. *First,* Drawing a soul to sin threatens the destruction of that soul. By shaking his faith, provoking his passion, and tempting him to act against the light of his own conscience, thou dost, as much as in thee lies, destroy him, giving him an occasion to return to Judaism. *Mē apollye.* It denotes an utter destruction. The beginning of sin is as the letting forth of water; we are not sure that it will stop any where on this side of eternal destruction. *Secondly,* The consideration of the love of Christ in dying for souls should make us very tender of the happiness and salvation of souls, and careful not to do any thing which may obstruct and hinder them. Did Christ quit a life for souls, such a life, and shall not we quit a morsel of meat for them? Shall we despise those whom Christ valued at so high a rate? Did he think it worth while to deny himself so much for them as to die for them, and shall not we think it worth while to deny ourselves so little for them as abstaining from flesh comes to? — *with thy meat.* Thou pleadest that it is thy own meat, and thou mayest do what thou wilt with it; but remember that, though the meat is thine, the brother offended by it is Christ's, and a part of his purchase. While thou destroyest thy brother thou art helping forward the devil's design, for he is the great destroyer; and, as much as in thee lies, thou art crossing the design of Christ, for he is the great Saviour, and dost not only offend thy brother, but offend Christ; for the work of salvation is that which his heart is upon. But are any destroyed for whom Christ died? If we understand it of the sufficiency and general intendment of Christ's death, which was to save all upon gospel terms, no doubt but multitudes are. If of the particular determination of the efficacy of his death to the elect, then, though none that were given to Christ shall perish (Jn. 6:39), yet thou mayest, as much as is in thy power, destroy such. No thanks to thee if they be not destroyed; by doing that which has a tendency to it, thou dost manifest a great opposition to Christ. Nay, and thou mayest utterly destroy some whose profession may be so justifiable that thou art bound to believe, in a judgment of charity, that Christ died for them. Compare this with 1 Co. 8:10, 11.

[3.] Consider the work of God (*v.* 20): *"For meat destroy not the work of God* — the work of grace, particularly the work of faith in thy brother's soul." The works of peace and comfort are destroyed by such an offence given; take heed of it therefore; do not undo that which God hath done. You should work together with God, do not countermine his work. *First,* The work of grace and peace is the work of God; it is wrought by him, it is wrought for him; it is a good work of his beginning, Phil. 1:6. Observe, The same for whom Christ died (*v.* 15) are here called the work of God; besides the work that is wrought for us there is a work to be wrought in us, in order to our salvation. Every saint is God's workmanship, his husbandry, his building, Eph. 2:10; 1 Co. 3:9. *Secondly,* We must be very careful to do nothing which tends to the destruction of this work, either in ourselves or others. We must deny ourselves in our appetites, inclinations, and in the use of Christian liberty, rather than obstruct and prejudice our own or others' grace and peace. Many do for meat and drink destroy the work of God in themselves (nothing more destructive to eh soul than pampering and pleasing the flesh, and fulfilling the lusts of it), so likewise in others, by wilful offence given. Think what thou destroyest — *the work of God,* whose work is honourable and glorious; think for what thou destroyest it — *for meat,* which was but for the belly, and the belly for it.

[4.] Consider the evil of giving offence, and what an abuse it is of our Christian liberty. He grants that *all things indeed are pure.* We may lawfully eat flesh, even those meats which were prohibited by the ceremonial law; but, if we abuse this liberty, it turns into sin to us: *It is evil to him that eats with offence.* Lawful things may be done unlawfully. — *Eats with offence,* either carelessly or designedly giving offence to his brethren. It is observable that the apostle directs his reproof most against those who gave the offence; not as if those were not to be blamed who causelessly and weakly took the offence from their ignorance of Christian liberty, and the want of that charity which is not easily provoked and which thinketh no evil (he several times tacitly reflects upon them), but he directs his speech to the strong, because they were better able to bear the reproof, and to begin the reformation. For the further pressing of this rule, we may here observe two directions which have relation to it: — *First, Let not then your good be evil spoken of* (*v.* 16) — take heed of doing any thing which may give occasion to others to speak evil, either of the Christian religion in general, or of your Christian liberty in particular. The gospel is your good; the liberties and franchises, the privileges and immunities, granted by it, are your good; your knowledge and strength of grace to discern and use your liberty in things disputed are your good, a good which the weak brother hath not. Now let not this be evil spoken of. It is true we cannot hinder loose and ungoverned tongues from speaking evil of us, and of the best things we have; but we must not (if we can help it) give them any occasion to do it. Let not the reproach arise from any default of ours; as 1 Tim. 4:12, *Let no man despise thee,* that is, do not make thyself despicable. So here, Do not use your knowledge and strength in such a manner as to give occasion to people to call it presumption and loose walking, and disobedience to God's law. We must deny ourselves in many cases for the preservation of our credit and reputation, forbearing to do that which we rightly know we may lawfully do, when our doing it may be a prejudice to our good name; as, when it is suspicious and has the appearance of evil, or when it becomes scandalous among good people, or has any way a brand upon it. In such a case we must rather cross ourselves than shame ourselves. Though it be but a little folly, it may be like a dead fly, very prejudicial to one that is in reputation for wisdom and honour, Eccl. 10:1. We may apply it more generally. We should manage all our good duties in such a manner that they may not be evil spoken of. That which for the matter of it is good and unexceptionable may sometimes, by mismanagement, be rendered liable to a great deal of censure and reproach. Good praying, preaching, and discourse, may often, for want of prudence in ordering the time, the expression, and other circumstances to edification, be evil spoken of. It is indeed their sin who do speak evil of that which is good for the sake of any such circumstantial errors, but it is our folly if we give any occasion to do so. As we tender the reputation of the good we profess and practise, let us so order it that it may not be evil spoken of. *Secondly, Hast thou faith? Have it to thyself before God, v.* 22. It is not meant of justifying faith (that must not be hid, but manifested by our works), but of a knowledge and persuasion of our Christian liberty in things disputed. "Hast thou clearness in such a particular? Art thou satisfied that thou mayest eat all meats, and observe all days (except the Lord's day) alike? *Have it to thyself,* that is, enjoy the comfort of it in thy own bosom, and do not trouble others by the imprudent use of it, when it might give offence, and cause thy weak brother to stumble and fall." In these indifferent things, though we must never contradict our persuasion, yet we may sometimes conceal it, when the avowing of it will do more hurt than good. *Have it to thyself* — a rule to thyself (not to be imposed upon others, or made a rule to them), or a rejoicing to thyself. Clearness in doubtful matters contributes very much to our comfortable walking, as it frees us from those scruples, jealousies, and suspicions, which those who have not such clearness are entangled in endlessly. Compare Gal. 6:4, *Let every man prove his own work,* that is, bring it to the touchstone of the word and try it by that so exactly as to be well satisfied in what he does; and then he *shall have rejoicing in himself alone, and not in another.* Paul had faith in these things: *I am persuaded that there is nothing unclean of itself;* but he had it to himself, so as not to use his liberty to the offence of others. How happy were it for the church if those that have a clearness in disputable things would be satisfied to have it to themselves before God, and not impose those things upon others, and make them terms of communions, than which nothing is more opposite to Christian liberty, nor more destructive both to the peace of churches and the peace of consciences. That healing method is not the less excellent for being common: in things necessary let there be unity, things unnecessary let there be liberty, and in both let there be charity, then all will be well quickly. — *Have it to thyself before God.* The end of such knowledge is that, being satisfied in our liberty, we may have a conscience void of offence towards God, and let that content us. That is the true comfort which we have before God. Those are right indeed that are so in God's sight.

5. There is one rule more laid down here; and it is general: *Let us therefore follow after the things which make for peace, and things wherewith one may edify another, v.* 19. Here is the sum of our duty towards our brethren. (1.) We must study mutual peace. Many wish for peace, and talk loudly for it, that do not follow the things that make for peace, but the contrary. Liberty in things indifferent, condescension to those that are weak and tender, zeal in the great things of God wherein we are all agreed; these are things that make for peace. Meekness, humility, self-denial, and love, and the springs of peace, the things that make for our peace. WE are not always so happy as to obtain peace; there are so many that delight in war: but the God of peace will accept us if we follow after the things that make for peace, that is, if we do our endeavour. (2.) We must study mutual edification. The former makes way for this. We cannot edify one another, while we are quarrelling and contending. There are many ways by which we might edify one another, if we did but seriously mind it; by good counsel, reproof, instruction, example, building up not only ourselves, but one another, in our most holy faith. We are God's building, God's temple, and have need to be edified; and therefore must study to promote the spiritual growth one of another. None so strong but they may be edified; none so weak but may edify; and, while we edify others, we benefit ourselves.

CHAPTER 15

The apostle, in this chapter, continues the discourse of the former, concerning mutual forbearance in indifferent things; and so draws towards a conclusion of the epistle. Where such differences of apprehension, and consequently distances of affection, are among Christians, there is need of precept upon precept, line upon line, to allay the heat, and to beget a better temper. The apostle, being desirous to drive the nail home, as a nail in a sure place, follows his blow, unwilling to leave the subject till he has some hopes of prevailing, to which end he orders the cause before them and fills his mouth with the most pressing arguments. We may observe, in this chapter, I. His precepts to them. II. His prayers for them. III. His apology for writing to them. IV. His account of himself and his own affairs. V. His declaration of his purpose to come and see them. VI. His desire of a share in their prayers.

Verses 1–4

The apostle here lays down two precepts, with reasons to enforce them, showing the duty of the strong Christian to consider and condescend to the weakest.

I. We must *bear the infirmities of the weak, v.* 1. We all have our infirmities; but the weak are more subject to them than others — the weak in knowledge or grace, the bruised reed and the smoking flax. We must consider these; not trample upon them, but encourage them, and bear with their infirmities. If through weakness they judge and censure us, and speak evil of us, we must bear with them, pity them, and not have our affections alienated from them. Alas! it is their weakness, they cannot help it. Thus Christ bore with his weak disciples, and apologised for them. But there is more in it; we must also bear their infirmities by sympathizing with them, concerning ourselves for them, ministering strength to them, as there is occasion. This is bearing one another's burdens.

II. We must not please ourselves, but our neighbour, *v.* 1, 2. We must deny our own humour, in consideration of our brethren's weakness and infirmity.

1. Christians must not please themselves. We must not

make it our business to gratify all the little appetites and desires of our own heart; it is good for us to cross ourselves sometimes, and then we shall the better bear others crossing of us. We shall be spoiled (as Adonijah was) if we be always humoured. The first lesson we have to learn is to deny ourselves, Mt. 16:24.

2. Christians must please their brethren. The design of Christianity is to soften and meeken the spirit, to teach us the art of obliging and true complaisance; not to be servants to the lust of any, but to the necessities and infirmities of our brethren — to comply with all that we have to do with as fare as we can with a good conscience. Christians should study to be pleasing. As we must not please ourselves in the use of our Christian liberty (which was allowed us, not for our own pleasure, but for the glory of God and the profit and edification of others), so we must please our neighbour. How amiable and comfortable a society would the church of Christ be if Christians would study to please one another, as now we see them commonly industrious to cross, and thwart, and contradict one another! — *Please his neighbour,* not in every thing, it is not an unlimited rule; but *for his good,* especially for the good of his soul: not please him by serving his wicked wills, and humouring him in a sinful way, or consenting to his enticements, or suffering sin upon him; this is a base way of pleasing our neighbour to the ruin of his soul: if we thus please men, we are not the servants of Christ; but please him for his good; not for our own secular good, or to make a prey of him, but for his spiritual good. — *To edification,* that is, not only for his profit, but for the profit of others, to edify the body of Christ, by studying to oblige one another. The closer the stones lie, and the better they are squared to fit one another, the stronger is the building. Now observe the reason why Christians must please one another: *For even Christ pleased not himself.* The self-denial of our Lord Jesus is the best argument against the selfishness of Christians. Observe,

(1.) That Christ pleased not himself. He did not consult his own worldly credit, ease, safety, nor pleasure; he had not where to lay his head, lived upon alms, would not be made a king, detested no proposal with greater abhorrence than that, *Master, spare thyself,* did not *seek his own will* (Jn. 5:30), washed his disciples' feet, endured the contradiction of sinners against himself, troubled himself (Jn. 11:33), did not consult his own honour, and, in a word, emptied himself, and made himself of no reputation: and all this for our sakes, to bring in a righteousness for us, and to set us an example. His whole life was a self-denying self-displeasing life. He bore the *infirmities of the weak,* Heb. 4:15.

(2.) That herein the scripture was fulfilled: *As it is written, The reproaches of those that reproached thee fell on me.* This is quoted out of Ps. 69:9, the former part of which verse is applied to Christ (Jn. 2:17), *The zeal of thine house hath eaten me up;* and the latter part here; for David was a type of Christ, and his sufferings of Christ's sufferings. It is quoted to show that Christ was so far from pleasing himself that he did in the highest degree displease himself. Not as if his undertaking, considered on the whole, were a task and grievance to him, for he was very willing to it and very cheerful in it; but in his humiliation the content and satisfaction of natural inclination were altogether crossed and denied. He preferred our benefit before his own ease and pleasure. This the apostle chooses to express in scripture language; for how can the things of the Spirit of God be better spoken of than in the Spirit's own words? And this scripture he alleges, *The reproaches of those that reproached thee fell on me.* [1.] The shame of those reproaches, which Christ underwent. Whatever dishonour was done to God was a trouble to the Lord Jesus. He was grieved for the hardness of people's hearts, beheld a sinful place with sorrow and tears. When the saints were persecuted, Christ so far displeased himself as to take what was done to them as done against himself: *Saul, Saul, why persecutest thou me?* Christ also did himself endure the greatest indignities; there was much of reproach in his sufferings. [2.] The sin of those reproaches, for which Christ undertook to satisfy; so many understand it. Every sin is a kind of reproach to God, especially presumptuous sins; now the guilt of these fell upon Christ, when he was made sin, that is, a sacrifice, a sin-offering for us. When the Lord laid upon him the iniquities of us all, and he bore our sins in his own body upon the tree, they fell upon him as upon our surety. *Upon me be the curse.* This was the greatest piece of self-displacency that could be: considering his infinite spotless purity and holiness, the infinite love of the Father to him, and his eternal concern for his Father's glory, nothing could be more contrary to him, nor more against him, than to be made sin and a curse for us, and to have the reproaches of God fall upon him, especially considering for whom he thus displeased himself, for strangers, enemies, and traitors, the *just for the unjust,* 1 Pt. 3:18. This seems to come in as a reason why we should bear the infirmities of the weak. We must not please ourselves, for Christ pleased not himself; we must bear the infirmities of the weak, for Christ bore the reproaches of those that reproached God. He bore the guilt of sin and the curse for it; we are only called to bear a little of the trouble of it. he bore the presumptuous sins of the wicked; we are called only to bear the infirmities of the weak. — *Even Christ; kai gar ho Christos.* Even he who was infinitely happy in the enjoyment of himself, who needed not us nor our services, — even he who thought it no robbery to be equal with God, who had reason enough to pleas himself, and no reason to be concerned, much less to be crossed, for us, — even he pleased not himself, even he bore our sins. And should not we be humble, and self-denying, and ready to consider one another, who are members one of another?

(3.) That therefore we must go and do likewise: *For whatsoever things were written aforetime were written for our learning.* [1.] That which is written of Christ, concerning his self-denial and sufferings, is *written for our learning;* he hath left us an example. If Christ denied himself, surely we should deny ourselves, from a principle of ingenuousness and of gratitude, and especially of conformity to his image. The example of Christ, in what he did and said, is recorded for our imitation. [2.] That which is written in the scriptures of the Old Testament in the general is written for our learning. What David had said in his own person Paul had just now applied to Christ. Now lest this should look like a straining of the scripture, he gives us this excellent rule in general, that all the scriptures of the Old Testament (much more those of the New) were written for our learning, and are not to be looked upon as of private interpretation. What happened to the Old-Testament saint happened to them for ensample; and the scriptures of the Old Testament have many fulfillings. The scriptures are left for a standing rule to us: they are *written,* that they might remain for our use and benefit. *First,* For our learning. There are many things to be learned out of the scriptures; and that is the best learning which is drawn from these fountains. Those are the most learned that are most mighty in the scriptures. We must therefore labour, not only to understand the literal meaning of the scripture, but to learn out of it that which will do us good; and we have need of help therefore not only to roll away the stone, but to draw out the water, for in many places the well is deep. Practical observations are more necessary than critical expositions. *Secondly, That we through patience and comfort of the scriptures might have hope.* That hope which hath eternal life for its object is here proposed as the end of scripture-learning. The scripture was written that we might know what to hope for from God, and upon what grounds, and in what way. This should recommend the scripture to us that it is a special friend to Christian hope. Now the way of attaining this hope is *through patience and comfort of the scripture.* Patience and comfort suppose trouble and sorrow; such is the lot of the saints in this world; and, were it not so, we should have no occasion for patience and comfort. But both these befriend that hope which is the life of our souls. Patience works experience, and experience hope, which maketh not ashamed, *ch.* 5:3–5. The more patience we exercise under troubles the more hopefully we may look through our troubles; nothing more destructive to hope than impatience. And the *comfort of the scriptures,* that comfort which springs from the word of God (that is the surest and sweetest comfort) is likewise a great stay to hope, as it is an earnest in hand of the good hoped for. The Spirit, as a comforter, is the earnest of our inheritance.

Verses 5–6

The apostle, having delivered two exhortations, before he proceeds to more, intermixes here a prayer for the success of what he had said. Faithful ministers water their preaching with their prayers, because, whoever sows the seed, it is God that gives the increase. We can but speak to the ear; it is God's prerogative to speak to the heart. Observe,

I. The title he gives to God: *The God of patience and consolation,* who is both the author and the foundation of all the patience and consolation of the saints, from whom it springs and on whom it is built. He gives the grace of patience; he confirms and keeps it up as the God of consolation; for the comforts of the Holy Ghost help to support believers, and to bear them up with courage and cheerfulness under all their afflictions. When he comes to beg the pouring out of the spirit of love and unity he addresses himself to God as the God of patience and consolation; that is, 1. As a God that bears with us and comforts us, is not extreme to mark what we do amiss, but is ready to comfort those that are cast down — to teach us so to testify our love to our brethren, and by these means to preserve and maintain unity, by being patient one with another and comfortable one to another. Or, 2. As a God that gives us patience and comfort. He had spoken (*v.* 4) of patience and comfort of the scriptures; but here he looks up to God as the God of patience and consolation: it comes through the scripture as the conduit-pipe, but from God as the fountain-head. The more patience and comfort we receive from God, the better disposed we are to love one another. Nothing breaks the peace more than an impatient, and peevish, and fretful melancholy temper.

II. The mercy he begs of God: *Grant you to be like-minded one towards another, according to Christ Jesus.* 1. The foundation of Christian love and peace is laid in like-mindedness, a consent in judgment as far as you have attained, or at least a concord and agreement in affection. *To auto phronein — to mind the same thing,* all occasions of difference removed, and all quarrels laid aside. 2. This like-mindedness must be *according to Christ Jesus,* according to the precept of Christ, the royal law of love, according to the pattern and example of Christ, which he had propounded to them for their imitation, *v.* 3. Or, "Let Christ Jesus be the centre of your unity. Agree in the truth, not in any error." It was a cursed concord and harmony of those who were of one mind to give their power and strength to the beast (Rev. 17:13); this was not a like-mindedness according to Christ, but against Christ; like the Babel-builders, who were one in their rebellion, Gen. 11:6. The method of our prayer must be first for truth, and then for peace; for such is the method of the wisdom that is from above: *it is first pure, then peaceable.* This is to be like-minded according to Christ Jesus. 3. Like-mindedness among Christians, according to Christ Jesus, is the gift of God; and a precious gift it is, for which we must earnestly seek unto him. He is the *Father of spirits,* and fashions the hearts of men alike (Ps. 33:15), opens the understanding, softens the heart, sweetens the affections, and gives the grace of love, and the Spirit as a Spirit of love, to those that ask him. We are taught to pray that the will of God may be done on earth as it is done in heaven — now there it is done unanimously, among the angels, who are one in their praises and services; and our desire must be that the saints on earth may be so too.

III. The end of his desire: that God may be glorified, *v.* 6. This is his plea with God in prayer, and is likewise an argument with them to seek it. We should have the glory of God in our eye in every prayer; therefore our first petition, as the foundation of all the rest, must be, *Hallowed be thy name.* Like-mindedness among Christians is in order to our glorifying God, 1. *With one mind and one mouth.* It is desirable that Christians should agree in every thing, that so they may agree in this, to praise God together. It tends very much to the glory of God, who is one, and his name one, when it is so. It will not suffice that there be one mouth, but there must be one mind, for God looks at the heart; nay, there will hardly be one mouth where there is not one mind, and God will scarcely be glorified where there is not a sweet conjunction of both. One mouth in confessing the truths of God, in praising the name of God — one mouth in common converse, not jarring, biting, and devouring one another — one mouth in the solemn assembly, one speaking, but all joining. 2. As *the Father of our Lord Jesus Christ.* This is his New-Testament style. God must be glorified as he has now revealed himself in the face of Jesus Christ, according to the rules of the gospel, and with an eye to Christ, in whom he is our Father. The unity of Christians glorifies *God as the Father of our Lord Jesus Christ,* because it is a kind of counter-part or representation of the oneness that is between the Father and the Son. We are warranted so to speak of it, and, with that in our eye, to desire it, and pray for it, from Jn. 17:21, *That they all may be one, as thou, Father, art in me, and I in thee:* a high expression of the honour and sweetness of the saints' unity. And it follows, *The the world may believe that thou hast sent me;* and so God may be glorified as the Father of our Lord Jesus Christ.

Verses 7–12

The apostle here returns to his exhortation to Christians. What he says here (*v.* 7) is to the same purport with the former; but the repetition shows how much the apostle's heart was upon it. "Receive one another into your affection, into your communion, and into your common conversation, as there is occasion." He had exhorted the strong to receive the weak (*ch.* 14:1), here, *Receive one another;* for sometimes the prejudices of the weak Christian make him shy of the strong, as much as the pride of the strong Christian makes him shy of the weak, neither of which ought to be. Let there be a mutual embracing among Christians. Those that have received Christ by faith must receive all Christians by brotherly love; though poor in the world, though persecuted and despised, though it may be matter of reproach and danger to you to receive them, though in the less weighty matters of the law they are of different apprehensions, though there may have been occasion for private piques, yet, laying aside these and the like considerations, *receive you one another.* Now the reason why Christians must receive one another is taken, as before, from the condescending love of Christ to us: *As Christ also received us, to the glory of God.* Can there be a more cogent argument? Has Christ been so kind to us, and shall we be so unkind to those that are his? Was he so forward to entertain us, and shall we be backward to entertain our brethren? Christ has received us into the nearest and dearest relations to himself: has received us into his fold, into his family, into the adoption of sons, into a covenant of friendship, yea, into a marriage-covenant with himself; he has received us (though we were strangers and enemies, and had played the prodigal) into fellowship and communion with himself. Those words, *to the glory of God,* may refer both to Christ's receiving us, which is our pattern, and to our receiving one another, which is our practice according to that pattern.

I. Christ hath received us to the glory of God. The end of our reception by Christ is that we might glorify God in this world, and be glorified with him in that to come. It was the glory of God, and our glory in the enjoyment of God, that Christ had in his eye when he condescended to receive us. We are called to an eternal glory by Christ Jesus, Jn. 17:24. See to what he received us — to a happiness transcending all comprehension; see for what he received us — for his Father's glory; he had this in his eye in all the instances of his favour to us.

II. We must receive one another to the glory of God. This must be our great end in all our actions, that God may be glorified; and nothing more conduces to this than the mutual love and kindness of those that profess religion; compare *v.* 6, *That you may with one mind and one mouth glorify God.* That which was a bone of contention among them was a different apprehension about meats and drinks, which took rise in distinction between Jews and Gentiles. Now, to prevent and make up this different, he shows how Jesus Christ has received both Jews and Gentiles; in him they are both one, *one new man,* Eph. 2:14–16. Now it is a rule, *Quae conveniunt in aliquo tertio, inter se conveniunt — Things which agree with a third thing agree with each other.* Those that agree in Christ, who is the Alpha and the Omega, the first and the last, and the great centre of unity, may well afford to agree among themselves. This coalescence of the Jews and Gentiles in Christ and Christianity was a thing that filled and affected Paul so much that he could not mention it without some enlargement and illustration.

1. He received the Jews, *v.* 8. Let not any think hardly or scornfully therefore of those that were originally Jews, and still, through weakness, retain some savour of their old Judaism; for, (1.) Jesus Christ was a *minister of the circumcision.* That he was a *minister, diakonos — a servant,* bespeaks his great and exemplary condescension, and puts an honour upon the ministry: but that he was a minister of the circumcision, was himself circumcised and made under the law, and did in his own person preach the gospel to the Jews, who were of the circumcision — this makes the nation of the Jews more considerable than otherwise they appear to be. Christ conversed with the Jews, blessed them, looked upon himself as primarily sent to the *lost sheep of the house of Israel, laid hold of the seed of Abraham* (Heb. 2:16, *margin*), and by them, as it were, caught at the whole body of mankind. Christ's personal ministry was appropriated to them, though the apostles had their commission enlarged. (2.) He was so for the truth of God. That which he preached to them was the truth; for he came into the world to bear witness to the truth, Jn. 18:37. And he is himself the truth, Jn. 14:6. Or, for the truth of God, that is, to make good the promises given to the patriarchs concerning the special mercy God had in store for their seed. It was not for the merit of the Jews, but for the truth of God, that they were thus distinguished — that God might approve himself true to this word which he had spoken. — *To confirm the promises made unto the fathers.* The best confirmation of promises is the performance of them. It was promised that in the seed of Abraham all the nations of the earth should be blessed, that Shiloh should come from between the feet of Judah, that out of Israel should he proceed that should have the dominion, that out of Zion should go forth the law, and many the like. There were many intermediate providences which seemed to weaken those promises, providences which threatened the fatal decay of that people; but when Messiah the Prince appeared in the fulness of time, as a minister of the circumcision, all these promises were confirmed, and the truth of them was made to appear; for in Christ all the promises of God, both those of the Old Testament and those of the New, are Yea, and in him Amen. Understanding by *the promises made to the fathers* the whole covenant of grace, darkly administered under the Old Testament, and brought to a clearer light now under the gospel, it was Christ's great errand to confirm that covenant, Dan. 9:27. He confirmed it by shedding the blood of the covenant.

2. He received the Gentiles likewise. This he shows, *v.* 9–12.

(1.) Observe Christ's favour to the Gentiles, in taking them in to praise God — the work of the church on earth and the wages of that in heaven. One design of Christ was that the Gentiles likewise might be converted that they might be one with the Jews in Christ's mystical body. A good reason why they should not think the worse of any Christian for his having been formerly a Gentile; for Christ has received him. He invites the Gentiles, and welcomes them. Now observe how their conversion is here expressed: *That the Gentiles might glorify God for his mercy.* A periphrasis of conversion. [1.] They shall have matter for praise, even the mercy of God. Considering the miserable and deplorable condition that the Gentile world was in, the receiving of them appears more as an act of mercy than the receiving of the Jews. Those that were *Lo-ammi — not a people,* were *Lo-ruhama — not obtaining mercy,* Hos. 1:6, 9; 2:23. The greatest mercy of God to any people is the receiving of them into covenant with himself: and it is good to take notice of God's mercy in receiving us. [2.] They shall have a heart for praise. They shall glorify God for his mercy. Unconverted sinners do nothing to glorify God; but converting grace works in the soul a disposition to speak and do all to the glory of God; God intended to reap a harvest of glory from the Gentiles, who had been so long turning his glory into shame.

(2.) The fulfilling of the scriptures in this. The favour of God to the Gentiles was not only mercy, but truth. Though there were not promises directly given to them, as to the fathers of the Jews, yet there were many prophesies concerning them, which related to the calling of them, and the embodying of them in the church, some of which he mentions because it was a thing that the Jews were hardly persuaded to believe. Thus, by referring them to the Old Testament, he labours to qualify their dislike of the Gentiles, and so to reconcile the parties at variance. [1.] It was foretold that the Gentiles should have the gospel preached to them: *"I will confess to thee among the Gentiles* (*v.* 9), that is, thy name shall be known and owned in the Gentile world, there shall gospel grace and love be celebrated." This is quoted from Ps. 18:49, *I will give thanks unto thee, O Lord, among the heathen.* A thankful explication and commemoration of the name of God are an excellent means of drawing others to know and praise God. Christ, in and by his apostles and ministers, whom he sent to disciple all nations, did confess to God among the Gentiles. The exaltation of Christ, as well as the conversion of sinners, is set forth by the praising of God. Christ's declaring God's name to his brethren is called *his praising God in the midst of the congregation,* Ps. 22:22. Taking these words as spoken by David, they were spoken when he was old and dying, and he was not likely to confess to God among the Gentiles; but when David's psalms are read and sung among the Gentiles, to the praise and glory of God, it may be said that David is *confessing to God among the Gentiles, and singing to his name.* He that was the sweet psalmist of the Gentiles. Converting grace makes people greatly in love with David's psalms. Taking them as spoken by Christ, the Son of David, it may be understood of his spiritual indwelling by faith in the hearts of all the praising saints. If any confess to God among the Gentiles, and sing to his name, it is not they, but Christ and his grace in them. *I live, yet not I, but Christ liveth in me;* so, I praise, yet not I, but Christ in me. [2.] That the Gentiles should *rejoice with his people, v.* 10. This is quoted from that song of Moses, Deu. 32:43. Observe, Those who were incorporated among his people are said to rejoice with his people. No greater joy can come to any people than the coming of the gospel among them in power. Those Jews that retain a prejudice against the Gentiles will by no means admit them to any of their joyful festivities; for (say they) a stranger intermeddleth not with the joy, Prov. 14:10. But, the partition-wall being taken down, the Gentiles are welcome to rejoice with his people. Being brought into the church, they share in its sufferings, are companions in patience and tribulation, to recompense which they share in the joy. [3.] That they should praise God (*v.* 11): *Praise the Lord, all ye Gentiles.* This is quoted out of that short psalm, Ps. 117:1. Converting grace sets people a praising God, furnishes with the richest matter for praise, and gives a heart to it. The Gentiles had been, for many ages, praising their idols of wood and stone, but now they are brought to praise the Lord; and this David in spirit speaks of. In calling upon all the nations to praise the Lord, it is intimated that they shall have the knowledge of him. [4.] That they should believe in Christ (*v.* 12), quoted from Isa. 11:10, where observe, *First,* The revelation of Christ, as the Gentiles' king. He is here called *the root of Jesse,* that is, such a branch from the family of David as is the very life and strength of the family: compare Isa. 11:1. Christ was David's Lord, and yet withal he was the Son of David (Mt. 22:45), for he was the *root and offspring of David,* Rev. 22:16. Christ, as God, was David's root; Christ, as man, was David's offspring. — *And he that shall rise to reign over the Gentiles.* This explains the figurative expression of the prophet, he shall *stand for an ensign of the people.* When Christ rose from the dead, when he ascended on high, it was to reign over the Gentiles. *Secondly,* The recourse of the Gentiles to him: *In him shall the Gentiles trust.* Faith is the soul's confidence in Christ and dependence on him. The prophet has it, *to him shall the Gentiles seek.* The method of faith is first to seek unto Christ, as to one proposed to us for a Saviour; and, finding him able and willing to save, then to trust in him. Those that know him will trust in him. Or, this seeking to him is the effect of a trust in him; seeking him by prayer, and pursuant endeavours. We shall never seek to Christ till we trust in him. Trust is the mother; diligence in the use of means the daughter. Jews and Gentiles being thus united in Christ's love, why should they not be united in one another's love?

Verse 13

Here is another prayer directed to God, as the God of hope; and it is, as the former (*v.* 5, 6), for spiritual blessings: these are the blest blessings, and to be first and chiefly prayed for.

I. Observe how he addresses himself to God, as the *God of hope.* It is good in prayer to fasten upon those names, titles, and attributes of God, which are most suitable to the errand we come upon, and will best serve to encourage our faith concerning it. Every word in the prayer should be a plea. Thus should the cause be skilfully ordered, and the mouth filled with arguments. God is the God of hope. He is the foundation on which our hope is built, and he is the builder that doth himself raise it: he is both the object of our hope, and the author of it. That hope is but fancy, and will deceive us, which is not fastened upon God (as the goodness hoped for, and the truth hoped in), and which is not of his working in us. We have both together, Ps. 119:49. *Thy word* — there is God the object; *on which thou hast caused me to hope* — there is God the author of our hope, 1 Pt. 1:3.

II. What he asks of God, not for himself, but for them.

1. *That they might be filled with all joy and peace in believing.* Joy and peace are two of those things in which the kingdom of God consists, *ch.* 14:17. Joy in God, peace of conscience, both arising from a sense of our justification; see *ch.* 5:1, 2. Joy and peace in our own bosoms would promote a cheerful unity and unanimity with our brethren. Observe, (1.)

How desirable this joy and peace are: they are filling. Carnal joy puffs up the soul, but cannot fill it; therefore in laughter the heart is sad. True, heavenly, spiritual joy is filling to the soul; it has a satisfaction in it, answerable to the soul's vast and just desires. Thus does God satiate and replenish the weary soul. Nothing more than this joy, only more of it, even the perfection of it in glory, is the desire of the soul that hath it, Ps. 4:6, 7; 36:8; 63:5; 65:4. (2.) How it is attainable. [1.] By prayer. We must go to God for it; he will for this be enquired of. Prayer fetches in spiritual joy and peace. [2.] By believing; that is the means to be used. It is vain, and flashy, and transient joy, that is the product of fancy; true substantial joy is the fruit of faith. *Believing, you rejoice with joy unspeakable,* 1 Pt. 1:8. It is owing to the weakness of our faith that we are so much wanting in joy and peace. Only believe; believe the goodness of Christ, the love of Christ, the promises of the covenant, and the joys and glories of heaven; let faith be the substance and evidence of these things, and the result must needs be joy and peace. Observe, It is *all* joy and peace — all sorts of true joy and peace. When we come to God by prayer we must enlarge our desires; we are not straitened in him, why should we be straitened in ourselves? Ask for all joy; open thy mouth wide, and he will fill it.

2. That they might *abound in hope through the power of the Holy Ghost.* The joy and peace of believers arise chiefly from their hopes. What is laid out upon them is but little, compared with what is laid up for them; therefore the more hope they have the more joy and peace they have. We do then abound in hope when we hope for great things from God, and are greatly established and confirmed in these hopes. Christians should desire and labour after an abundance of hope, such hope as will not make ashamed. This is through the power of the Holy Ghost. The same almighty power that works grace begets and strengthens this hope. Our own power will never reach it; and therefore where this hope is, and is abounding, the blessed Spirit must have all the glory.

Verses 14–16

Here, I. He commends these Christians with the highest characters that could be. He began his epistle with their praises (ch 1:8), *Your faith is spoken of throughout the world,* thereby to make way for his discourse: and, because sometimes he had reproved them sharply, he now concludes with the like commendation, to qualify them, and to part friends. This he does like an orator. It was not a piece of idle flattery and compliment, but a due acknowledgment of their worth, and of the grace of God in them. We must be forward to observe and commend in others that which is excellent and praise-worthy; it is part of the present recompence of virtue and usefulness, and will be of use to quicken others to a holy emulation. It was a great credit to the Romans to be commended by Paul, a man of such great judgment and integrity, too skilful to be deceived and too honest to flatter. Paul had no personal acquaintance with these Christians, and yet he says he was persuaded of their excellencies, though he knew them only be hearsay. As we must not, on the one hand, be so simple as to believe every word; so, on the other hand, we must not be so skeptical as to believe nothing; but especially we must be forward to believe good concerning others: in this case charity hopeth all things, and believeth all things, and (if the probabilities be any way strong, as here they were) is persuaded. It is safer to err on this side. Now observe what it was that he commended them for. 1. That they *were full of goodness;* therefore the more likely to take in good part what he had written, and to account it a kindness; and not only so, but to comply with it, and to put it in practice, especially that which relates to their union and to the healing of their differences. A good understanding of one another, and a good will to one another, would soon put an end to strife. 2. *Filled with all knowledge.* Goodness and knowledge together! A very rare and an excellent conjunction; the head and the heart of the new man. All knowledge, all necessary knowledge, all the knowledge of those things which belong to their everlasting peace. 3. *Able to admonish one another.* To this there is a further gift requisite, even the gift of utterance. Those that have goodness and knowledge should communicate what they have for the use and benefit of others. "You that excel so much in good gifts may think you have no need of any instructions of mine." It is a comfort to faithful ministers to see their work superseded by the gifts and graces of their people. How gladly would ministers leave off their admonishing work, if people were able and willing to admonish one another! Would to God that all the Lord's people were prophets. But that which is every body's work is nobody's work; and therefore,

II. He clears himself from the suspicion of intermeddling needlessly with that which did not belong to him, *v.* 15. Observe how affectionately he speaks to them: *My brethren* (*v.* 14), and again, *brethren, v.* 15. He had himself, and taught others, the art of obliging. He calls them all his brethren, to teach them brotherly love one to another. Probably he wrote the more courteously to them because, being Roman citizens living near the court, they were more genteel, and made a better figure; and therefore Paul, who became all things to all men, was willing, by the respectfulness of his style, to please them for their good. He acknowledges he had written *boldly in some sort — tolmēroteron apo merous,* in a manner that looked like boldness and presumption, and for which some might perhaps charge him with taking too much upon him. But then consider,

1. He did it only as their remembrancer: *As putting you in mind.* such humble thoughts had Paul of himself, though he excelled in knowledge, that he would not pretend to tell them that which they did not know before, but only to remind them of that in which they had formerly been by others instructed. So Peter, 2 Pt. 1:12; 3:1. People commonly excuse themselves from hearing the word with this, that the minister can tell them nothing but what they knew before. If it be so, yet have they not need to know it better, and to be put in mind of it?

2. He did it as the apostle of the Gentiles. It was in pursuance of his office: *Because of the grace* (that is, the *apostleship, ch.* 1:5) *given to me of God,* to be the minister *of Jesus Christ to the Gentiles, v.* 16. Paul reckoned it a great favour, and an honour that God had put upon him, in putting him into that office, *ch.* 1:13. Now, because of this grace given to him, he thus laid out himself among the Gentiles, that he might not receive that grace of God in vain. Christ received that he might give; so did Paul; so have we talents which must not be buried. Places and offices must be filled up with duty. It is good for ministers to be often remembering the grace that is given unto them of God. *Minister verbi es, hoc age — You are a minister of the word; give yourself wholly to it,* was Mr. Perkins's motto. Paul was a minister. Observe here, (1.) Whose minister he was: the *minister of Jesus Christ,* 1 Co. 4:1. He is our Master; his we are, and him we serve. (2.) To whom: to the Gentiles. So God had appointed him, Acts 22:21. So Peter and he had agreed, Gal. 2:7–9. These Romans were Gentiles: "Now," says he, "I do not thrust myself upon you, nor seek any lordship over you; I am appointed to it: if you think I am rude and bold, my commission is my warrant, and must bear me out." (3.) What he ministered: the *gospel of God; hierourgounta to euangelion — ministering as about holy things* (so the word signifies), executing the office of a Christian priest, more spiritual, and therefore more excellent, than the Levitical priesthood. (4.) For what end: *that the offering up* (or sacrificing) *of the Gentiles might be acceptable* — that god might have the glory which would redound to his name by the conversion of the Gentiles. Paul laid out himself thus to bring about something that might be acceptable to God. Observe how the conversion of the Gentiles is expressed: it is the *offering up of the Gentiles;* it is *prosphora tōn ethnōn — the oblation of the Gentiles,* in which the Gentiles are looked upon either, [1.] As the priests, offering the oblation of prayer and praise and other acts of religion. Long had the Jews been the holy nation, the kingdom of priests, but now the Gentiles are made priests unto God (Rev. 5:10), by their conversion to the Christian faith consecrated to the service of God, that the scripture may be fulfilled, *In ever place incense shall be offered, and a pure offering,* Mal. 1:11. The converted Gentiles are said to be *made nigh* (Eph. 2:13) — the periphrasis of priests. Or, [2.] The Gentiles are themselves the sacrifice offered up to God by Paul, in the name of Christ, a living sacrifice, holy, acceptable to God, *ch.* 12:1. A sanctified soul is offered up to God in the flames of love, upon Christ the altar. Paul gathered in souls by his preaching, not to keep them to himself, but to offer them up to God: *Behold, I, and the children that God hath given me.* And it is an acceptable offering, *being sanctified by the Holy Ghost.* Paul preached to them, and dealt with them; but that which made them sacrifices to God was their sanctification; and this was not his work, but the work of the Holy Ghost. None are acceptably offered to God but those that are sanctified: unholy things can never be pleasing to the holy God.

Verses 17–21

The apostle here gives some account of himself and of his own affairs. Having mentioned his ministry and apostleship, he goes on further to magnify his office in the efficacy of it, and to mention to the glory of God the great success of his ministry and the wonderful things that God had done by him, for encouragement to the Christian church at Rome, that they were not alone in the profession of Christianity, but though, compared with the multitude of their idolatrous neighbours, they were but a little flock, yet, up and down the country, there were many that were their companions in the kingdom and patience of Jesus Christ. It was likewise a great confirmation of the truth of the Christian doctrine that it had such strange success, and was so far propagated by such weak and unlikely means, such multitudes captivated to the obedience of Christ by the foolishness of preaching. Therefore Paul gives them this account, which he makes the matter of his glorying; not vain glory, but holy gracious glorying, which appears by the limitations; it is *through Jesus Christ.* Thus does he centre all his glorying in Christ; he teaches us so to do, 1 Co. 1:31. *Not unto us,* Ps. 115:1. And it is *in those things which pertain to God.* The conversion of souls is one of those things that pertain to God, and therefore is the matter of Paul's glorying; not the things of the flesh. *Whereof I may glory, echō oun kauchēsin en Christō Iēsou ta pros Theon.* I would rather read it thus: *Therefore I have a rejoicing in Christ Jesus* (it is the same word that is used, 2 Co. 1:12, and Phil. 3:3, where it is the character of the circumcision that they *rejoice — kauchōmenoi,* in Christ Jesus) *concerning the things of God;* or those things that are offered to God — the living sacrifices of the Gentiles, *v.* 16. Paul would have them to rejoice with him in the extent and efficacy of his ministry, of which he speaks not only with the greatest deference possible to the power of Christ, and the effectual working of the Spirit as all in all; but with a protestation of the truth of what he said (*v.* 18): *I will not dare to speak of any of those things which Christ hath not wrought by me.* He would not boast of things without his line, nor take the praise of another man's work, as he might have done when he was writing to distant strangers, who perhaps could not contradict him; but (says he) I dare not do it: a faithful man dares not lie, however he be tempted, dares be true, however he be terrified. now, in this account of himself, we may observe,

I. His unwearied diligence and industry in his work. He was one that laboured *more abundantly than they all.*

1. He preached in many places: *From Jerusalem,* whence the law went forth as a lamp that shineth, and *round about unto Illyricum,* many hundred miles distant from Jerusalem. We have in the book of the Acts an account of Paul's travels. There we find him, after he was sent forth to preach to the Gentiles (Acts 13), labouring in that blessed work in Seleucia, Cyprus, Pamphylia, Pisidia, and Lycaonia (Acts 13 and 14), afterwards travelling through Syria and Cilicia, Phrygia, Galatia, Mysia, Troas, and thence called over to Macedonia, and so into Europe, Acts 15 and 16. Then we find him very busy at Thessalonica, Berea, Athens, Corinth, Ephesus, and the parts adjacent. Those that know the extent and distance of these countries will conclude Paul an active man, rejoicing as a strong man to run a race. Illyricum is the country now called Sclavonia, bordering upon Hungary. Some take it for the same with Bulgaria; others for the lower Pannonia: however, it was a great way from Jerusalem. Now it might be suspected that if Paul undertook so much work, surely he did it by the halves. "No," says he, *"I have fully preached the Gospel of Christ* — have given them a full account of the truth and terms of the gospel, have not shunned to declare the whole counsel of God (Acts 20:27), have kept back nothing that was necessary for them to know." *Filled the gospel,* so the word is; *peplērōkenai to euangelion,* filled it as the net is filled with fishes in a large draught; or filled the gospel, that is, filled them with the gospel. Such a change does the gospel make that, when it comes in power to any place, it fills the place. Other knowledge is airy, and leaves souls empty, but he knowledge of the gospel is filling.

2. He preached in places that had not heard the gospel before, *v.* 20, 21. He broke up the fallow ground, laid the first stone in many places, and introduced Christianity where nothing had reigned for many ages but idolatry and witchcraft, and all sorts of diabolism. Paul broke the ice, and therefore must needs meet with the more difficulties and discouragements in his work. Those who preached in Judea had upon this account a much easier task than Paul, who was the apos-

tle of the Gentiles; for they entered into the labours of others, Jn. 4:38. Paul, being a hardy man, was called out to the hardest work; there were many instructors, but Paul was the great father — many that watered, but Paul was the great planter. Well, he was a bold man that made the first attack upon the palace of the strong man armed in the Gentile world, that first assaulted Satan's interest there, and Paul was that man who ventured the first onset in many places, and suffered greatly for it. He mentions this as a proof of his apostleship; for the office of the apostles was especially to bring in those that were without, and to lay the foundations of the new Jerusalem; see Rev. 21:14. Not but that Paul preached in many places where others had been at work before him; but he principally and mainly laid himself out for the good of those that sat in darkness. He was in care not to *build upon another man's foundation,* lest he should thereby disprove his apostleship, and give occasion to those who sought occasion to reflect upon him. He quotes a scripture for this out of Isa. 52:15, *To whom he was not spoken of, they shall see. That which had not been told them, shall they see;* so the prophet has it, much to the same purport. This made the success of Paul's preaching the more remarkable. The transition from darkness to light is more sensible than the after-growth and increase of that light. And commonly the greatest success of the gospel is at its first coming to a place; afterwards people become sermon-proof.

II. The great and wonderful success that he had in his work: It was effectual to *make the Gentiles obedient.* The design of the gospel is to bring people to be *obedient;* it is not only a truth to be believed, but a law to be obeyed. This Paul aimed at in all his travels; not his own wealth and honour (if he had, he had sadly missed his aim), but the conversion and salvation of souls: this his heart was upon, and for this he travailed in birth again. Now how was this great work wrought? 1. Christ was the principal agent. He does not say, "which I worked," but "which Christ wrought by me," *v.* 18. Whatever good we do, it is not we, but Christ by us, that does it; the work is his, the strength his; he is all in all, he works all our works, Phil. 2:13; Isa. 26:12. Paul takes all occasions to own this, that the whole praise might be transmitted to Christ. 2. Paul was a very active instrument: *By word and deed,* that is, by his preaching, and by the miracles he wrought to confirm his doctrine; or his preaching and his living. Those ministers are likely to win souls that preach both by word and deed, by their conversation showing forth the power of the truths they preach. This is according to Christ's example, who began both to do and teach, Acts 1:1. — *Through mighty signs and wonders: en dynamei sēmeiōn — by the power,* or in the strength, of signs and wonders. These made the preaching of the word so effectual, being the appointed means of conviction, and the divine seal affixed to the gospel-charter, Mk. 16:17, 18. 3. The *power of the Spirit of God* made this effectual, and crowned all with the desired success, *v.* 19. (1.) The power of the Spirit in Paul, as in the other apostles, for the working of those miracles. Miracles were wrought by the power of the Holy Ghost (Acts 1:8), therefore reproaching the miracles is called the blasphemy against the Holy Ghost. Or, (2.) The power of the Spirit in the hearts of those to whom the word was preached, and who saw the miracles, making these means effectual to some and not to others. It is the Spirit's operation that makes the difference. Paul himself, as great a preacher as he was, with all his might signs and wonders, could not make one soul obedient further than the power of the Spirit of God accompanied his labours. It was the Spirit of the Lord of hosts that made those great mountains plain before this Zerubbabel. This is an encouragement to faithful ministers, who labour under the sense of great weakness and infirmity, that it is all one to the blessed Spirit to work by many, or by those that have on power. The same almighty Spirit that wrought with Paul often perfects strength in weakness, and ordains praise out of the mouths of babes and sucklings. This success which he had in preaching is that which he here rejoices in; for the converted nations were his joy and crown of rejoicing: and he tells them of it, not only that they might rejoice with him, but that they might be the more ready to receive the truths which he had written to them, and to own him whom Christ had thus signally owned.

Verses 22–29

St. Paul here declares his purpose to come and see the Christians at Rome. Upon this head his matter is but common and ordinary, appointing a visit to his friends; but the manner of his expression is gracious and savoury, very instructive, and for our imitation. We should learn by it to speak of our common affairs in the language of Canaan. Even our common discourse should have an air of grace; by this it will appear what country we belong to. it should seem that Paul's company was very much desired at Rome. He was a man that had as many friends and as many enemies as most men ever had: he passed through evil report and good report. No doubt they had heard much of him at Rome, and longed to see him. Should the apostle of the Gentiles be a stranger at Rome, the metropolis of the Gentile world? Why as to this he excuses it that he had not come yet, he promises to come shortly, and gives a good reason why he could not come now.

I. He excuses it that he never came yet. Observe how careful Paul was to keep in with his friends, and to prevent or anticipate any exceptions against him; not as one that lorded it over God's heritage. 1. He assures them that he had a great desire to see them; not to see Rome, though it was now in its greatest pomp and splendour, nor to see the emperor's court, nor to converse with the philosophers and learned men that were then at Rome, though such conversation must needs be very desirable to so great a scholar as Paul was, but *to come unto you* (*v.* 3), a company of poor despised saints in Rome, hated of the world, but loving God, and beloved of him. These were the men that Paul was ambitious of an acquaintance with at Rome; they were the excellent ones in whom he delighted, Ps. 16:3. And he had a special desire to see them, because of the great character they had in all the churches for faith and holiness; they were men that excelled in virtue, and therefore Paul was so desirous to come to them. This desire Paul had had for many years, and yet could never compass it. The providence of God wisely overrules the purposes and desires of men. God's dearest servants are not always gratified in every thing that they have a mind to. Yet all that delight in God have the desire of their heart fulfilled (Ps. 37:4), though all the desires in their heart be not humoured. 2. He tells them that the reason why he could not come to them was because he had so much work cut out for him elsewhere. *For which cause,* that is, because of his labours in other countries, he was so much *hindered.* God had opened a wide door for him in other places, and so turned him aside. Observe in this, (1.) The gracious providence of God conversant in a special manner about his ministers, casting their lot, not according to their contrivance, but according to his own purpose. Paul was several times crossed in his intentions; sometimes hindered by Satan (as 1 Th. 2:18), sometimes forbidden by the Spirit (Acts 16:7), and here diverted by other work. Man purposes but God disposes, Prov. 16:9; 19:21; Jer. 10:23. Ministers purpose, and their friends purpose concerning them, but God overrules both, and orders the journeys, removals, and settlements, of his faithful ministers as he pleases. The stars are in the right hand of Christ, to shine where he sets them. The gospel does not come by chance to any place, but by the will and counsel of God. (2.) The gracious prudence of Paul, in bestowing his time and pains where there was most need. Had Paul consulted his own ease, wealth, and honour, the greatness of the word would never have hindered him from seeing Rome, but would rather have driven him thither, where he might have had more preferment and taken less pains. But Paul sought the things of Christ more than his own things, and therefore would not leave his work of planting churches, no, not for a time, to go and see Rome. The Romans were whole, and needed not the physician as other poor places that were sick and dying. While men and women were every day dropping into eternity, and their precious souls perishing for lack of vision, it was no time for Paul to trifle. There was now a gale of opportunity, the fields were white unto the harvest; such a season slipped might never be retrieved; the necessities of poor souls were pressing, and called aloud, and therefore Paul must be busy. It concerns us all to do that first which is most needful. True grace teaches us to prefer that which is necessary before that which is unnecessary, Lu. 10:41, 42. And Christian prudence teaches us to prefer that which is more necessary before that which is less so. This Paul mentions as a sufficient satisfying reason. We must not take it ill of our friends if they prefer necessary work, which is pleasing to God, before unnecessary visits and compliments, which may be pleasing to us. In this, as in other things, we must deny ourselves.

II. He promised to come and see them shortly, *v.* 23, 24, 29. *Having no more place in these parts,* namely, in Greece, where he then was. The whole of that country being more or less leavened with the savour of the gospel, churches being planted in the most considerable towns and pastors settled to carry on the work which Paul had begun, he had little more to do there. He had driven the chariot of the gospel to the sea-coast, and having thus conquered Greece he is ready to wish there were another Greece to conquer. Paul was one that went through with his work, and yet then did not think of taking his ease, but set himself to contrive more work, to devise liberal things. Here was a workman that needed not to be ashamed. Observe,

1. How he forecasted his intended visit. His project was to see them in his way to Spain. It appears by this that Paul intended a journey into Spain, to plant Christianity there. The difficulty and peril of the work, the distance of the place, the danger of the voyage, the other good works (though less needful, he thinks) which Paul might find to do in other places, did not quench the flame of his holy zeal for the propagating of the gospel, which did even eat him up, and make him forget himself. But it is not certain whether ever he fulfilled his purpose, and went to Spain. Many of the best expositors think he did not, but was hindered in this as he was in others of his purposes. He did indeed come to Rome, but he was brought thither a prisoner, and there was detained two years; and whither he went after is uncertain: but several of his epistles which he wrote in prison intimate his purpose to go eastward, and not towards Spain. However, Paul, forasmuch as it was in thine heart to bring the light of the gospel into Spain, thou didst well, in that it was in thine heart; as God said to David, 2 Chr. 6:8. The grace of God often with favour accepts the sincere intention, when the providence of God in wisdom prohibits the execution. And do not we serve a good Master then? 2 Co. 8:12. Now, in his way to Spain he proposed to come to them. Observe his prudence. It is wisdom for every one of us to order our affairs so that we may do the most work in the least time. Observe how doubtfully he speaks: *I trust to see you:* not, "I am resolved I will," but, "I hope I shall." We must purpose all our purposes and make all our promises in like manner with a submission to the divine providence; not boasting ourselves of to-morrow, because we know not what a day may bring forth, Prov. 27:1; James 4:13–15.

2. What he expected in his intended visit. (1.) What he expected from them. He expected they would bring him on his way towards Spain. It was not a stately attendance, such as princes have but a loving attendance, such as friends give, that Paul expected. Spain was then a province of the empire, well known to the Romans, who had a great correspondence with it, and therefore they might be helpful to Paul in his voyage thither; and it was not barely their accompanying him part of the way, but their furthering him in his expedition, that he counted upon: not only out of their respect to Paul, but out of respect to the souls of those poor Spaniards that Paul was going to preach to. It is justly expected from all Christians that they should lay out themselves for the promoting and furthering of every good work, especially that blessed work of the conversion of souls, which they should contrive to make as easy as may be to their ministers, and as successful as may be to poor souls. (2.) What he expected in them: to *be somewhat filled with their company.* That which Paul desired was their company and conversation. The good company of the saints is very desirable and delightful. Paul was himself a man of great attainments in knowledge and grace, taller by head and shoulders than other Christians in these things, and yet see how he pleased himself with the thoughts of good company; for as iron sharpens iron so does a man the countenance of his friend. He intimates that he intended to make some stay with them, for he would be filled with their company; not just look at them, and away: and yet he thinks their converse so pleasant that he should never have enough of it; it is but somewhat filled, he thought he should leave them with a desire of more of their company. Christian society, rightly managed and improved, is a heaven upon earth, a comfortable earnest of our gathering together unto Christ at the great day. Yet observe, It is but somewhat filled, *apo merous — in part.* The satisfaction we have in communion with the saints in this world is but partial; we are but somewhat filled. It is partial compared with our communion with Christ; that, and that only, will completely satisfy, that will fill the soul. It is partial compared with the communion we hope to have with the saints

in the other world. When we shall sit down with Abraham, and Isaac, and Jacob, with all the saints, and none but saints, and saints made perfect, we shall have enough of that society, and be quite filled with that company. (3.) What he expected from God with them, *v.* 29. He expected to come *in the fulness of the blessing of the gospel of Christ.* Observe, Concerning what he *expected* from *them* he speaks doubtfully: *I trust to be brought on my way, and to be filled with your company.* Paul had learnt not to be too confident of the best. These very men slipped from him afterwards, when he had occasion to use them (2 Tim. 4:16), *At my first answer, no man stood by me;* none of the Christians at Rome. The Lord teach us to cease from man. But concerning what he expected from God he speaks confidently. It was uncertain whether he should come or no, but *I am sure when I do come I shall come in the fulness,* etc. We cannot expect too little from man, nor too much from God. Now Paul expected that God would bring him to them, loaded with blessings, so that he should be an instrument of doing a great deal of good among them, and fill them with the blessings of the gospel. Compare *ch.* 1:11, *That I may impart unto you some spiritual gift.* The blessing of the gospel of Christ is the best and most desirable blessing. When Paul would raise their expectation of something great and good in his coming, he directs them to hope for the blessings of the gospel, spiritual blessings, knowledge, and grace, and comfort. There is then a happy meeting between people and ministers, when they are both under the fulness of the blessing. The blessing of the gospel is the treasure which we have in earthen vessels. When ministers are fully prepared to give out, and people fully prepared to receive, this blessing, both are happy. Many have the gospel who have not the blessing of the gospel, and so they have it in vain. The gospel will not profit, unless God bless it to us; and it is our duty to wait upon him for that blessing, and for the fulness of it.

III. He gives them a good reason why he could not come and see them now, because he had other business upon his hands, which required his attendance, upon which he must first make a journey to Jerusalem, *v.* 25–28. He gives a particular account of it, to show that the excuse was real. He was going to Jerusalem, as the messenger of the church's charity to the poor saints there. Observe what he says,

1. Concerning this charity itself. And he speaks of that upon this occasion probably to excite the Roman Christians to do the like, according to their ability. Examples are moving, and Paul was very ingenious at begging, not for himself, but for others. Observe, (1.) For whom it was intended: *For the poor saints which are at Jerusalem, v.* 26. It is no strange thing for saints to be poor. Those whom God favours the world often frowns upon; therefore riches are not the best things, nor is poverty a curse. It seems, the saints at Jerusalem were poorer than other saints, either because the wealth of that people in general was now declining, as their utter ruin was hastening on (and, to be sure, if any must be kept poor, the saints must), or because the famine that was over all the world in the days of Claudius Caesar did in a special manner prevail in Judea, a dry country; and, God having called the poor of this world, the Christians smarted most by it. This was the occasion of that contribution mentioned Acts 11:28–30. Or, because the saints at Jerusalem suffered most by persecution; for of all people the unbelieving Jews were most inveterate in their rage and malice against the Christians, wrath having come upon them to the uttermost, 1 Th. 2:16. The Christian Hebrews are particularly noted too as having had their good spoiled (Heb. 10:34), in consideration of which this contribution was made for them. Though the saints at Jerusalem were at a great distance form them, yet they thus extended their bounty and liberality to them, to teach us as we have ability, and as there is occasion, to stretch out the hand of our charity to all that are of the household of faith, though in places distant from us. Though in personal instances of poverty every church should take care to maintain their own poor (for such poor we have always with us), yet sometimes, when more public instances of poverty are presented as objects of our charity, though a great way off from us, we must extend our bounty, as the sun his beams; and, with the virtuous woman, *stretch out our hands to the poor, and reach forth our hands to the needy,* Prov. 31:20. (2.) By whom it was collected: *By those of Macedonia* (the chief of whom were the Philippians) *and Achaia* (the chief of whom were the Corinthians), two flourishing churches, though yet in their infancy, newly converted to Christianity. And I wish the observation did not hold that people are commonly more liberal at their first acquaintance with the gospel than they are afterwards, that, as well as other instances of the first love and the love of the espousals, being apt to cool and decay after a while. It seems those of Macedonia and Achaia were rich and wealthy, while those at Jerusalem were poor and needy, Infinite Wisdom ordering it so that some should have what others want, and so this mutual dependence of Christians one upon another might be maintained. — *It pleased them.* This intimates how ready they were to it — they were not pressed nor constrained to it, but they did it of their own accord; and how cheerful they were in it — they took a pleasure in doing good; and God loves a cheerful giver. — *To make a certain contribution; koinōnian tina — a communication,* in token of the communion of saints, and their fellow-membership, as in the natural body one member communicates to the relief, and succour, and preservation of another, as there is occasion. Every thing that passes between Christians should be a proof and instance of that common union which they have one with another in Jesus Christ. Time was when the saints at Jerusalem were on the giving hand, and very liberal they were, when they laid their estates at the apostles' feet for charitable uses, and took special care that the Grecian widows should not be neglected in the daily ministration, Acts 6:1, etc. And now that the providence of God had turned the scale, and made them necessitous, they found the Grecians kind to them; for the merciful shall obtain mercy. We should give a portion to seven, and also to eight, because we know not what evil may be on the earth, which may make us glad to be beholden to others. (3.) What reason there was for it (*v.* 27): *And their debtors they are.* Alms are called righteousness, Ps. 112:9. Being but stewards of what we have, we owe it where our great Master (by the calls of providence, concurring with the precepts of the word) orders us to dispose of it: but here there was a special debt owing; the Gentiles were greatly beholden to the Jews, and were bound in gratitude to be very kind to them. From the stock of Israel came Christ himself, according to the flesh, who is the light to enlighten the Gentiles; out of the same stock came the prophets, and apostles, and first preachers of the gospel. The Jews, having had the lively oracles committed to them, were the Christians' library-keepers — *out of Zion went forth the law, and the word of the Lord from Jerusalem;* their political church-state was dissolved, and they were cut off, that the Gentiles might be admitted in. Thus did the Gentiles partake of their spiritual things, and receive the gospel of salvation as it were at second-hand from the Jews; and therefore *their duty is,* they are bound in gratitude to *minister unto them in carnal things:* it is the least they can do: *leitourgēsai — to minister as unto God in holy tings;* so the word signifies. A conscientious regard to God in works of charity and almsgiving makes them an acceptable service and sacrifice to God, and fruit abounding to a good account. Paul mentions this, probably, as the argument he had used with them to persuade them to it, and it is an argument of equal cogency to other Gentile churches.

2. Concerning Paul's agency in this business. He could himself contribute nothing; silver and gold he had none, but lived upon the kindness of his friends; yet he *ministered unto the saints* (*v.* 25) by stirring up others, receiving what was gathered, and transmitting it to Jerusalem. Many good works of that kind stand at a stay for want of some one active person to lead in them, and to set the wheels a going. Paul's labour in this work is not to be interpreted as any neglect of his preaching-work, nor did Paul leave the word of God, to serve tables; for, besides this, Paul had other business in this journey, to visit and confirm the churches, and took this by the bye; this was indeed a part of the trust committed to him, in which he was concerned to approve himself faithful (Gal. 2:10): *They would that we should remember the poor.* Paul was one that laid out himself to do good every way, like his Master, to the bodies as well as to the souls of people. Ministering to the saints is good work, and is not below the greatest apostles. This Paul had undertaken, and therefore he resolves to go through with it, before he fell upon other work (*v.* 28): *When I have sealed to them this fruit.* He calls the alms *fruit,* for it is one of the fruits of righteousness; it sprang from a root of grace in the givers, and redounded to the benefit and comfort of the receivers. And his sealing it intimates his great care about it, that what was given might be kept entire, and not embezzled, but disposed of according to the design of the givers. Paul was very solicitous to approve himself faithful in the management of this matter: an excellent pattern for ministers to write after, that the ministry may in nothing be blamed.

Verses 30–33

Here we have, I. St. Paul's desire of a share in the prayers of the Romans for him, expressed very earnestly, *v.* 30–32. Though Paul was a great apostle, yet he begged the prayers of the meanest Christians, not here only, but in several other of the epistles. He had prayed much for them, and this he desires as the return of his kindness. Interchanging prayers is an excellent token of the interchanging of loves. Paul speaks like one that knew himself, and would hereby teach us how to value the effectual fervent prayer of the righteous. How careful should we be lest we do any thing to forfeit our interest in the love and prayers of god's praying people!

1. Observe why they must pray for him. He begs it with the greatest importunity. He might suspect they would forget him in their prayers, because they had no personal acquaintance with him, and therefore he urges it so closely, and begs it with the most affectionate obtestations, by all that is sacred and valuable: *I beseech you,* (1.) *"For the Lord Jesus Christ's sake.* He is my Master, I am going about his work, and his glory is interested in the success of it: if you have any regard to Jesus Christ, and to his cause and kingdom, pray for me. You love Christ, and own Christ; for his sake then do me this kindness." (2.) *"For the love of the Spirit.* As a proof and instance of that love which the Spirit works in the hearts of believers one to another, pray for me; as a fruit of that communion which we have one with another by the Spirit though we never saw one another. If ever you experienced the Spirit's love to you, and would be found returning your love to the Spirit, be not wanting in this office of kindness."

2. How they must pray for him: *That you strive together.* (1.) That *you strive in prayer.* We must put forth all that is within us in that duty; pray with fixedness, faith, and fervency; wrestle with God, as Jacob did; pray in praying, as Elias did (Jam. 5:17), and stir up ourselves to take hold on God (Isa. 64:7); and this is not only when we are praying for ourselves, but when we are praying for our friends. True love to our brethren should make us as earnest for them as sense of our own need makes us for ourselves. (2.) That you strive together with me. When he begged their prayers for him, he did not intend thereby to excuse his praying for himself; no, *"Strive together with me,* who am wrestling with God daily, upon my own and my friends' account." He would have them to ply the same oar. Paul and these Romans were distant in place, and likely to be so, and yet they might join together in prayer; those who are put far asunder by the disposal of God's providence may yet meet together at the throne of his grace. Those who beg the prayers of others must not neglect to pray for themselves.

3. What they must beg of God for him. He mentions particulars; for, in praying both for ourselves and for our friends, it is good to be particular. *What wilt thou that I shall do for thee?* So says Christ, when he holds out the golden sceptre. Though he knows our state and wants perfectly, he will know them from us. He recommends himself to their prayers, with reference to three things: — (1.) The dangers which he was exposed to: *That I may be delivered from those that do not believe in Judea.* The unbelieving Jews were the most violent enemies Paul had and most enraged against him, and some prospect he had of trouble from them in this journey; and therefore they must pray that God would deliver him. We may, and must, pray against persecution. This prayer was answered in several remarkable deliverances of Paul, recorded Acts 21, 22, 23, and 24. (2.) His services: *Pray that my service which I have for Jerusalem may be accepted of the saints.* Why, was there any danger that it would not be accepted? Can money be otherwise than acceptable to the poor? Yes, there was some ground of suspicion in this case; for Paul was the apostle of the Gentiles, and as the unbelieving Jews looked spitefully at him, which was their wickedness, so those that believed were shy of him upon that account, which was their weakness. He does not say, "Let them choose whether they will accept it or no; if they will not, it shall be better bestowed;" but, "Pray that it may be accepted." As God must be sought unto for the restraining of the ill will of our enemies, so also for the preserving and increasing of the good will of our friends; for God has the hearts both of the one and of the other in his hands. (3.) His journey to them. To

engage their prayers for him, he interests them in his concerns (*v.* 32): *That I may come unto you with joy.* If his present journey to Jerusalem proved unsuccessful, his intended journey to Rome would be uncomfortable. If he should not do good, and prosper, in one visit, he thought he should have small joy of the next: may *come with joy, by the will of God.* All our joy depends upon the will of God. The comfort of the creature is in every thing according to the disposal of the Creator.

II. Here is another prayer of the apostle for them (*v.* 33): *Now the God of peace be with you all, Amen.* The Lord of hosts, the God of battle, is the God of peace, the author and lover of peace. He describes God under this title here, because of the divisions among them, to recommend peace to them; if God be the God of peace, let us be men of peace. The Old-Testament blessing was, *Peace be with you;* now, *The god of peace be with you.* Those who have the fountain cannot want any of the streams. *With you all;* both weak and strong. To dispose them to a nearer union, he puts them altogether in this prayer. Those who are united in the blessing of God should be united in affection one to another.

CHAPTER 16

Paul is now concluding this long and excellent epistle, and he does it with a great deal of affection. As in the main body of the epistle he appears to have been a very knowing man, so in these appurtenances of it he appears to have been a very loving man. So much knowledge and so much love are a very rare, but (where they exist) a very excellent and amiable-composition; for what is heaven but knowledge and love made perfect? It is observable how often Paul speaks as if he were concluding, and yet takes fresh hold again. One would have thought that solemn benediction which closed the foregoing chapter should have ended the epistle; and yet here he begins again, and in this chapter he repeats the blessing (*v.* 20), "The grace of our Lord Jesus Christ be with you, Amen." And yet he has something more to say; nay, again he repeats the blessing (*v.* 24), and yet has not done; an expression of his tender love. These repeated benedictions, which stand for valedictions, speak Paul loth to part. Now, in this closing chapter, we may observe, I. His recommendation of one friend to the Roman Christians, and his particular salutation of several among them (*v.* 1–16). II. A caution to take heed of those who caused divisions (*v.* 17–20). III. Salutations added from some who were with Paul (*v.* 21–24). IV. He concludes with a solemn celebration of the glory of God (*v.* 25–27).

Verses 1–16

Such remembrances as these are usual in letters between friends; and yet Paul, by the savouriness of his expressions, sanctifies these common compliments.

I. Here is the recommendation of a friend, by whom (as some think) this epistle was sent — one *Phebe, v.* 1, 2. It should seem that she was a person of quality and estate, who had business which called her to Rome, where she was a stranger; and therefore Paul recommends her to the acquaintance of the Christians there: an expression of his true friendship to her. Paul was as well skilled in the art of obliging as most men. True religion, rightly received, never made any man uncivil. Courtesy and Christianity agree well together. It is not in compliment to her, but in sincerity, that,

1. He gives a very good character of her. (1.) As a sister to Paul: *Phebe our sister;* not in nature, but in grace; not in affinity or consanguinity, but in pure Christianity: his own sister in the faith of Christ, loving Paul, and beloved of him, with a pure and chaste and spiritual love, as a sister; for there is neither male nor female, but all are one in Christ Jesus, Gal. 3:28. Both Christ and his apostles had some of their best friends among the devout (and upon that account honourable) women. (2.) As a *servant to the church at Cenchrea: diakonon,* a servant by office, a stated servant, not to preach the word (that was forbidden to women), but in acts of charity and hospitality. Some think she was one of the widows that ministered to the sick and were taken into the church's number, 1 Tim. 5:9. But those were old and poor, whereas Phebe seems to have been a person of some account; and yet it was no disparagement to her to be a servant to the church. Probably they used to meet at her house, and she undertook the care of entertaining the ministers, especially strangers. Every one in his place should strive to serve the church, for therein he serves Christ, and it will turn to a good account another day. Cenchrea was a small sea-port town adjoining to Corinth, about twelve furlongs distant. Some think there was a church there, distinct from that at Corinth, though, being so near, it is very probable that the church of Corinth is called *the church of Cenchrea,* because their place of meeting might be there, on account of the great opposition to them in the city (Acts 18:12), as at Philippi they met out of the city by the water-side, Acts 16:13. So the reformed church of Paris might be called *the church at Charenton,* where they formerly met, out of the city. (3.) As a *succourer of many,* and particularly of Paul, *v.* 2. She relieved many that were in want and distress — a good copy for women to write after that have ability. she was kind to those that needed kindness, intimated in her succouring them; and her bounty was extensive, she was a succourer of many. Observe the gratitude of Paul in mentioning her particular kindness to him: *And to myself also.* Acknowledgment of favours is the least return we can make. It was much to her honour that Paul left this upon record; for wherever this epistle is read her kindness to Paul is told for a memorial of her.

2. He recommends her to their care and kindness, as one worthy to be taken notice of with peculiar respect. (1.) *"Receive her in the Lord.* Entertain her; bid her welcome." This pass, under Paul's hand, could not but recommend her to any Christian church. *"Receive her in the Lord,"* that is, "for the Lord's sake; receive her as a servant and friend of Christ." *As it becometh saints* to receive, who love Christ, and therefore love all that are his for his sake; or, as *becometh saints* to be received, with love and honour and the tenderest affection. There may be occasion sometimes to improve our interest in our friends, not only for ourselves, but for others also, *interest* being a price in the hand for doing good. (2.) *Assist her in whatsoever business she has need of you.* Whether she had business of trade, or law-business at the court, is not material; however being a woman, a stranger, a Christian, she had need of help: and Paul engaged them to be assistant to her. It becomes Christians to be helpful one to another in their affairs, especially to be helpful to strangers; for we are members one of another and we know not what need of help we may have ourselves. Observe, Paul bespeaks help for one that had been so helpful to many; he that watereth shall be watered also himself.

II. Here are commendations to some particular friends among those to whom he wrote, more than in any other of the epistles. Though the care of all the churches came upon Paul daily, enough to distract an ordinary head, yet he could retain the remembrance of so many; and his heart was so full of love and affection as to send salutations to each of them with particular characters of them, and expressions of love to them and concern for them. *Greet* them, *salute* them; it is the same word, *aspasasthe.* "Let them know that I remember them, and love them, and wish them well." There is something observable in several of these salutations.

1. Concerning Aquila and Priscilla, a famous couple, that Paul had a special kindness for. They were originally of Rome, but were banished thence by the edict of Claudius, Acts 18:2. At Corinth, Paul became acquainted with them, wrought with them at the trade of tent-making; after some time, when the edge of that edict was rebated, they returned to Rome, and thither he now sends commendations to them. He calls them his *helpers in Christ Jesus,* by private instructions and converse furthering the success of Paul's public preaching, one instance of which we have in their instructing Apollos, Acts 18:26. Those are helpers to faithful ministers that lay out themselves in their families and among their neighbours to do good to souls. Nay, they did not only do much, but they ventured much, for Paul: They have *for my life laid down their own necks.* They exposed themselves to secure Paul, hazarded their own lives for the preservation of his, considering how much better they might be spared than he. Paul was in a great deal of danger at Corinth, while he sojourned with them; but they sheltered him, though they thereby made themselves obnoxious to the enraged multitudes, Acts 18:12, 17. It was a good while ago that they had done Paul this kindness; and yet he speaks as feelingly of it as if it had been but yesterday. *To whom* (says he) *not only I give thanks, but also all the churches of the Gentiles;* who were all beholden to these good people for helping to save the life of him that was the apostle of the Gentiles. Paul mentions this, to engage the Christians at Rome to be the more kind to Aquila and Priscilla. He sends likewise greeting to the *church in their house, v.* 5. It seems then, a church in a house is no such absurd thing as some make it to be. Perhaps there was a congregation of Christians that used to meet at their house at stated times; and then, no doubt, it was, like the house of Obed-Edom, blessed for the ark's sake. Others think that the church was no more than a religious, pious, well-governed family, that kept up the worship of God. Religion, in the power of it, reigning in a family, will turn a house into a church. And doubtless it had a good influence upon this that Priscilla the good wife of the family was so very eminent and forward in religion, so eminent that she is often named first. A virtuous woman, that looks well to the ways of her household, may do much towards the advancement of religion in a family. When Priscilla and Aquila were at Ephesus, though but sojourners there, yet there also they had a church in their house, 1 Co. 16:19. A truly godly man will be careful to take religion along with him wherever he goes. When Abraham removed his tent, he renewed his altar, Gen. 13:18.

2. Concerning Epenetus, *v.* 5. He calls him his *well-beloved.* Where the law of love is in the heart the law of kindness will be in the tongue. Endearing language should pass among Christians to express love, and to engage love. So he calls Amplias, *beloved in the Lord,* with true Christian love for Christ's sake; and Stachys, his *beloved:* a sign that Paul had been in the third heaven, he was so much made up of love. Of Epenetus it is further said that he was the *first-fruit of Achaia unto Christ;* not only one of the most eminent believers in that country, but one of the first that was converted to the faith of Christ: one that was offered up to God by Paul, as the first-fruits of his ministry there; an earnest of a great harvest; for in Corinth, the chief city of Achaia, God had much people, Acts 18:10. Special respect is to be paid to those that set out early, and come to work in the vineyard at the first hour, at the first call. The *household of Stephanas* is likewise said to be the *first-fruits of Achaia,* 1 Co. 16:15. Perhaps Epenetus was one of that household; or, at least, he was one of the *first three;* not the first alone, but one of the first fleece of Christians, that the region of Achaia afforded.

3. Concerning Mary, and some others who were laborious in that which is good, industrious Christians: *Mary,* who *bestowed much labour on us.* True love never sticks at labour, but rather takes a pleasure in it; where there is much love there will be much labour. Some think this Mary had been at some of those places where Paul was, though now removed to Rome, and had personally ministered to him; others think Paul speaks of her labour as bestowed upon him because it was bestowed upon his friends and fellow-labourers, and he took what was done to them as done to himself. He says of Tryphena and Tryphosa, two useful women in their places, that they laboured in the Lord (*v.* 12), and of the beloved Persis, another good woman, that she laboured much in the Lord, more than others, abounding more in the work of the Lord.

4. Concerning Andronicus and Junia, *v.* 7. Some take them for a man and his wife, and the original will well enough bear it; and, considering the name of the latter, this is more probable than that they should be two men, as others think, and brethren. Observe, (1.) They were Paul's *cousins,* akin to him; so was Herodion, *v.* 11. Religion does not take away, but rectifies, sanctifies, and improves, our respect to our kindred, engaging us to lay out ourselves most for their good, and to rejoice in them the more, when we find them related to Christ by faith. (2.) They were his fellow-prisoners. Partnership in suffering sometimes does much towards the union of souls and the knitting of affections. We do not find in the story of the Acts any imprisonment of Paul before the writing of this epistle, but that at Philippi, Acts 16:23. But Paul was *in prisons more frequent* (2 Co. 11:23), in some of which, it seems, he met with his friends Andronicus and Junia, yoke-fellows, as in other things, so in suffering for Christ and bearing his yoke. (3.) They were *of note among the apostles,* not so much perhaps because they were persons of estate and quality in the world as because they were eminent for knowledge, and gifts, and graces, which made them famous among the apostles, who were competent judges of those things, and were endued with a spirit of discerning not only the sincerity, but the eminency, of Christians. (4.) *Who also were in Christ before me,* that is, were converted to the Christian faith. In time they had the start of Paul, though he was converted the next year after Christ's ascension. How ready was Paul to acknowledge in others any kind of precedency!

5. Concerning Apelles, who is here said to be *approved in Christ* (*v.* 10), a high character! He was one of known integrity and sincerity in his religion, one that had been tried; his friends and enemies had tried him, and he was as gold. he was of approved knowledge and judgment, approved courage and constancy; a man that one might trust and repose a confidence in.

6. Concerning Aristobulus and Narcissus; notice is taken of their household, *v.* 10, 11. Those of their household who *are in the Lord* (as it is limited, *v.* 11), that were Christians.

How studious was Paul to leave none out of his salutations that he had any knowledge of or acquaintance with! Aristobulus and Narcissus themselves, some think, were absent, or lately dead; others think they were unbelievers, and such as did not themselves embrace Christianity; so Pareus: and some think this Narcissus was the same with one of that name who is frequently mentioned in the life of Claudius, as a very rich man that had a great family, but was very wicked and mischievous. It seems, then, there were some good servants, or other retainers, even in the family of a wicked man, a common case, 1 Tim. 6:1. Compare *v.* 2. The poor servant is called, and chosen, and faithful, while the rich master is passed by, and left to perish in unbelief. Even so, Father, because it seemed good unto thee.

7. Concerning Rufus (*v.* 13), *chosen in the Lord.* He was a choice Christian, whose gifts and graces evinced that he was eternally chosen in Christ Jesus. He was one of a thousand for integrity and holiness. — *And his mother and mine,* his mother by nature and mine by Christian love and spiritual affection; as he calls Phebe his sister, and teaches Timothy to treat the elder women as mothers, 1 Tim. 5:2. This good woman, upon some occasion or other, had been as a mother to Paul, in caring for him, and comforting him; and Paul here gratefully owns it, and calls her mother.

8. Concerning the rest this is observable, that he salutes the *brethren who are with them* (*v.* 14), and the *saints who are with them* (*v.* 15), with them in family-relations, with them in the bond of Christian communion. It is the good property of saints to delight in being together; and Paul thus joins them together in his salutations to endear them one to another. Lest any should find themselves aggrieved, as if Paul had forgotten them, he concludes with the remembrance of the rest, as brethren and saints, though not named. In Christian congregations there should be smaller societies linked together in love and converse, and taking opportunities of being often together. Among all those to whom Paul sends greeting here is not a word of Peter, which gives occasion to suspect that he was not bishop of Rome, as the Papists say he was; for, if he was, we cannot but suppose him resident, or at least how could Paul write so long an epistle to the Christians there, and take no notice of him?

Lastly, He concludes with the recommendation of them to the love and embraces one of another: *Salute one another with a holy kiss.* Mutual salutations, as they express love, so they increase and strengthen love, and endear Christians one to another: therefore Paul here encourages the use of them, and only directs that they may be holy — a chaste kiss, in opposition to that which is wanton and lascivious; a sincere kiss, in opposition to that which is treacherous and dissembling, as Judas's, when he betrayed Christ with a kiss. He adds, in the close, a general salutation to them all, in the name of the churches of Christ (*v.* 16): *"The churches of Christ salute you;* that is, the churches which I am with, and which I am accustomed to visit personally, as knit together in the bonds of the common Christianity, desire me to testify their affection to you and good wishes for you." This is one way of maintaining the communion of saints.

Verses 17–20

The apostle having endeavoured by his endearing salutations to unite them together, it was not improper to subjoin a caution to take heed of those whose principles and practices were destructive to Christian love. And we may observe,

I. The caution itself, which is given in the most obliging manner that could be: *I beseech you, brethren.* He does not will and command, as one that lorded it over God's heritage, but for love's sake beseeches. How earnest, how endearing, are Paul's exhortations! He teaches them, 1. To see their danger: Mark those who cause divisions *and offences.* Our Master had himself foretold that divisions and offences would come, but had entailed a woe on those by whom they come (Mt. 18:7), and against such we are here cautioned. Those who burden the church with dividing and offending impositions, who uphold and enforce those impositions, who introduce and propagate dividing and offending notions, which are erroneous or justly suspected, who out of pride, ambition, affectation of novelty, or the like, causelessly separate from their brethren, and by perverse disputes, censures, and evil surmisings, alienate the affections of Christians one from another — these cause divisions and offences, contrary to, or different from (for that also is implied, it is *para tēn didachēn*), the *doctrine which we have learned.* Whatever varies from the form of sound doctrine which we have in the scriptures opens a door to divisions and offences. If truth be once deserted, unity and peace will not last long. Now, *mark* those that thus cause divisions, *skopein.* Observe them, the method they take, the end they drive at. There is need of a piercing watchful eye to discern the danger we are in from such people; for commonly the pretences are plausible, when the projects are very pernicious. Do not look only at the divisions and offences, but run up those streams to the fountain, and mark those that cause them, and especially that in them which causes these divisions and offences, those lusts on each side whence come these wars and fightings. A danger discovered is half prevented. 2. To shun it: *"Avoid them.* Shun all necessary communion and communication with them, lest you be leavened and infected by them. Do not strike in with any dividing interests, nor embrace any of those principles or practices which are destructive to Christian love and charity, or to the truth which is according to godliness. — *Their word will eat as doth a canker."* Some think he especially warns them to take heed of the judaizing teachers, who, under convert of the Christian name, kept up the Mosaical ceremonies, and preached the necessity of them, who were industrious in all places to draw disciples after them, and whom Paul in most of his epistles cautions the churches to take heed of.

II. The reasons to enforce this caution.

1. Because of the pernicious policy of these seducers, *v.* 18. The worse they are, the more need we have to watch against them. Now observe his description of them, in two things: — (1.) The master they serve: not *our Lord Jesus Christ.* Though they call themselves Christians, they do not serve Christ; do not aim at his glory, promote his interest, nor do his will, whatever they pretend. How many are there who call Christ Master and Lord, that are far from serving him! But they *serve their own belly* — their carnal, sensual, secular interests. It is some base lust or other that they are pleasing; pride, ambition, covetousness, luxury, lasciviousness, these are the designs which they are really carrying on. Their *God is their belly,* Phil. 3:19. What a base master do they serve, and how unworthy to come in competition with Christ, that serve their own bellies, that make gain their godliness, and the gratifying of a sensual appetite the very scope and business of their lives, to which all other purposes and designs must truckle and be made subservient. (2.) The method they take to compass their design: *By good words and fair speeches they deceive the hearts of the simple.* Their words and speeches have a show of holiness and zeal for God (it is an easy thing to be godly from the teeth outward), and show of kindness and love to those into whom they instil their corrupt doctrines, accosting them courteously when they intend them the greatest mischief. Thus by good words and fair speeches the serpent beguiled Eve. Observe, They corrupt their heads by deceiving their hearts, pervert their judgments by slyly insinuating themselves into their affections. We have a great need therefore to keep our hearts with all diligence, especially when seducing spirits are abroad.

2. Because of the peril we are in, through our proneness and aptness to be inveigled and ensnared by them: "For *your obedience has come abroad unto all men* — you are noted in all the churches for a willing, tractable, complying people." And, (1.) Therefore, because it was so, these seducing teachers would be the more apt to assault them. The devil and his agents have a particular spite against flourishing churches and flourishing souls. The ship that is known to be richly laden is most exposed to privateers. The adversary and enemy covets such a prey, therefore look to yourselves, 2 John *v.* 8. "The false teachers hear that you are an obedient people, and therefore they will be likely to come among you, to see if you will be obedient to them." It has been the common policy of seducers to set upon those who are softened by convictions, and begin to enquire what they shall do, because such do most easily receive the impressions of their opinions. Sad experience witnesses how many who have begun to ask the way to Zion, with their faces thitherward, have fatally split upon this rock, which proves it to be much the duty of ministers, with a double care, to feed the lambs of the flock, to lay a good foundation, and gently to lead those that are with young. (2.) Though it were so, yet they were in danger from these seducers. This Paul suggests with a great deal of modesty and tenderness; not as one suspicious of them, but as one solicitous for them: "You *obedience has come abroad unto all men;* we grant this and rejoice in it: *I am glad therefore on your behalf."* Thus does he insinuate their commendation, the better to make way for the caution. A holy jealousy of our friends may very well comport with a holy joy in them. "You think yourselves a very happy people, and so do I too: but for all that you must not be secure: *I would have you wise unto that which is good, and simple concerning evil.* You are a willing good-natured people, but you had best take heed of being imposed upon by those seducers." A pliable temper is good when it is under good government; but otherwise it may be very ensnaring; and therefore he gives two general rules: — [1.] To be *wise unto that which is good,* that is, to be skilful and intelligent in the truths and ways of God. "Be wise to try the spirits, to prove all things, and then to hold fast that only which is good." There is need of a great deal of wisdom in our adherence to good truths, and good duties, and good people, lest in any of these we be imposed upon and deluded. *Be ye therefore wise as serpents* (Mt. 10:16), wise to discern that which is really good and that which is counterfeit; wise to distinguish things that differ, to improve opportunities. While we are in the midst of so many deceivers, we have great need of that wisdom of the prudent which is to understand his way, Prov. 14:8. [2.] To be *simple concerning evil* — so wise as not to be *deceived,* and yet so simple as not to be deceivers. It is a holy simplicity, not to be able to contrive, nor palliate, nor carry on, any evil design; *akeraious — harmless,* unmixed, inoffensive. *In malice be you children,* 1 Co. 14:20. The wisdom of the serpent becomes Christians, but not the subtlety of the old serpent. We must withal *be harmless as doves.* That is a wisely simple man that knows not how to do any thing against the truth. Now Paul was the more solicitous for the Roman church, that it might preserve its integrity, because it was so famous; it was a city upon a hill, and many eyes were upon the Christians there, so that an error prevailing there would be a bad precedent, and have an ill influence upon other churches: as indeed it has since proved in fact, the great apostasy of the latter days taking its rise from that capital city. The errors of leading churches are leading errors. When the bishop of Rome fell as a *great star* from heaven (Rev. 8:10), *his tail drew a third part of the stars* after him, Rev. 12:4.

3. Because of the promise of God, that we shall have victory at last, which is given to quicken and encourage, not to supersede, our watchful cares and vigorous endeavours. It is a very sweet promise (*v.* 20): *The God of peace shall bruise Satan under your feet.*

(1.) The titles he gives to God: *The God of peace,* the author and giver of all good. When we come to God for spiritual victories, we must not only eye him as the Lord of hosts, whose all power is, but as the God of peace, a God at peace with us, speaking peace to us, working peace in us, creating peace for us. Victory comes from God more as the God of peace than as the God of war; for, in all our conflicts, peace is the thing we must contend for. God, as the God of peace, will restrain and vanquish all those that cause divisions and offences, and so break and disturb the peace of the church.

(2.) The blessing he expects from God — a victory over Satan. If he mean primarily those false doctrines and seducing spirits spoken of before, of which Satan was the prime founder and author, yet doubtless, it comprehends all the other designs and devices of Satan against souls, to defile, disturb, and destroy them, all his attempts to keep us from the purity of heaven, the peace of heaven here, and the possession of heaven hereafter. Satan tempting and troubling, acting as a deceiver and as a destroyer, the *God of peace* will *bruise under our feet.* He had cautioned them before against simplicity: now they, being conscious of their own great weakness and folly, might think, "How shall we evade and escape these snares that are laid for us? Will not these adversaries of our souls be at length too hard for us?" "No," says he, "fear not; though you cannot overcome in your own strength and wisdom, yet the God of peace will do it for you; and through him that loved us we shall be more than conquerors." [1.] The victory shall be complete: *He shall bruise Satan under your feet,* plainly alluding to the first promise the Messiah made in paradise (Gen. 3:15), that the seed of the woman should break the serpent's head, which is in the fulfilling every day, while the saints are enabled to resist and overcome the temptations of Satan, and will be perfectly fulfilled when, in spite of all the powers of darkness, all that belong to the election of grace shall be brought triumphantly to glory. When Joshua had conquered the kings of Canaan, he called the captains of Israel to set their feet upon the necks of those kings (Jos. 10:24), so will Christ, our Joshua, enable all his faithful servants and soldiers to set their feet upon Satan's neck, to trample upon, and triumph over, their spiritual enemies. Christ hath overcome for us; disarmed the strong man armed, broken his power, and we have nothing to do but to pursue the victory and divide the spoil. Let this quicken us to our spiritual conflict, to fight the good fight of faith — we have to do with a conquered enemy, and the victory will be perfect shortly. [2.] The victory shall be speedy: He shall do it *shortly*. Yet a little while, and he that shall come will come. He hath said it, *Behold, I come quickly*. When Satan seems to have prevailed, and we are ready to give up all for lost, then will the God of peace cut the work short in righteousness. It will encourage soldiers when they know the war will be at an end quickly, in such a victory. Some refer it to the happy period of their contentions in true love and unity; others to the period of the church's persecutions in the conversion of the powers of the empire to Christianity, when the bloody enemies of the church were subdued and trampled on by Constantine, and the church under his government. It is rather to be applied to the victory which all the saints shall have over Satan when they come to heaven, and shall be for ever out of his reach, together with the present victories which through grace they obtain in earnest of that. Hold out therefore, faith and patience, yet a little while; when we have once got through the Red Sea, we shall see our spiritual enemies dead on the shore, and triumphantly sing the song of Moses and the song of the Lamb. To this therefore he subjoins the benediction, *The grace of our Lord Jesus Christ be with you* — the good-will of Christ towards you, the good work of Christ in you. This will be the best preservative against the snares of heretics and schismatics, and false teachers. If the grace of Christ be with us, who can be against us so as to prevail? *Be strong therefore in the grace which is in Christ Jesus*. Paul, not only as a friend, but as a minister and an apostle, who had received grace for grace, thus with authority blesses them with this blessing, and repeats it, *v.* 24.

Verses 21–24

As the Apostle had before sent his own salutations to many of this church, and that of the churches round him to them all, he here adds an affectionate remembrance of them from some particular persons who were now with him, the better to promote acquaintance and fellowship among distant saints, and that the subscribing of these worthy names, known to them, might the more recommend this epistle. He mentions, 1. Some that were his particular friends, and probably known to the Roman Christians: *Timotheus my workfellow*. Paul sometimes calls Timothy his son, as an inferior; but here he styles him his work-fellow, as one equal with him, such a respect does he put upon him: and *Lucius*, probably Lucius of Cyrene, a noted man in the church of Antioch (Acts 13:1), as Jason was at Thessalonica, where he suffered for entertaining Paul (Acts 17:5, 6): and *Sosipater*, supposed to be the same with Sopater of Berea, mentioned Acts 20:4. These Paul calls his kinsmen; not only more largely, as they were Jews, but as they were in blood or affinity nearly allied to him. It seems, Paul was of a good family, that he met with so many of his kindred in several places. It is a very great comfort to see the holiness and usefulness of our kindred. 2. One that was Paul's amanuensis (*v.* 22): *I Tertius, who wrote this epistle*. Paul made use of a scribe, not out of state nor idleness, but because he wrote a bad hand, which was not very legible, which he excuses, when he writes to the Galatians with his own hand (Gal. 6:11): *pēlikois grammasi — with what kind of letters*. Perhaps this Tertius was the same with Silas; for Silas (as some think) signifies *the third* in Hebrew, as *Tertius* in Latin. Tertius either wrote as Paul dictated, or transcribed it fairly over out of Paul's foul copy. The least piece of service done to the church, and the ministers of the church, shall not pass without a remembrance and a recompence. It was an honour to Tertius that he had a hand, though but as a scribe, in writing this epistle. 3. Some others that were of note among the Christians (*v.* 23): *Gaius my host*. It is uncertain whether this was Gaius of Derbe (Acts 20:4), or Gaius of Macedonia (Acts 19:29), or rather Gaius of Corinth (1 Co. 1:14), and whether any of these was he to whom John wrote his third epistle. However, Paul commends him for his great hospitality; not only my host, but of the *whole church* — one that entertained them all as there was occasion, opened his doors to their church-meetings, and eased

the rest of the church by his readiness to treat all Christian stranger that came to them. *Erastus, the chamberlain of the city* is another; he means the city of Corinth, whence this epistle was dated. It seems he was a person of honour and account, one in public place, steward or treasurer. Not many mighty, not many noble, are called, but some are. His estate, and honour, and employment, did not take him off from attending on Paul and laying out himself for the good of the church, it should seem, in the work of the ministry; for he is joined with Timothy (Acts 19:22), and is mentioned 2 Tim. 4:20. It was no disparagement to the chamberlain of the city to be a preacher of the gospel of Christ. *Quartus* is likewise mentioned, and called a brother; for as one is our Father, even Christ, so all we are brethren.

Verses 25–27

Here the apostle solemnly closes his epistle with a magnificent ascription of glory to the blessed God, as one that terminated all in the praise and glory of God, and studied to return all to him, seeing all is of him and from him. He does, as it were, breathe out his soul to these Romans in the praise of God, choosing to make that the end of his epistle which he made the end of his life. Observe here,

I. A description of the gospel of God, which comes in in a parenthesis; having occasion to speak of it as the means by which the power of God establishes souls, and the rule of that establishment: *To establish you according to my gospel*. Paul calls it his gospel, because he was the preacher of it and because he did so much glory in it. Some think he means especially that declaration, explication, and application, of the doctrine of the gospel, which he had now made in this epistle; but it rather takes in all the preaching and writing of the apostles, among whom Paul was a principal labourer. Through their word (Jn. 17:20), the word committed to them. Ministers are the ambassadors, and the gospel is their embassy. Paul had his head and heart so full of the gospel that he could scarcely mention it without a digression to set forth the nature and excellency of it.

1. It is the *preaching of Jesus Christ*. Christ was the preacher of it himself; it began to be spoken by the Lord, Heb. 2:3. So pleased was Christ with his undertaking for our salvation that he would himself be the publisher of it. Or, Christ is the subject-matter of it; the sum and substance of the whole gospel is Jesus Christ and him crucified. We preach not ourselves, says Paul, but Christ Jesus the Lord. That which establishes souls is the plain preaching of Jesus Christ.

2. It is the revelation of the mystery which was kept secret since the world began, and by the scriptures of the prophets made known. The subject-matter of the gospel is a mystery. Our redemption and salvation by Jesus Christ, in the foundation, method, and fruits of it, are, without controversy, a great mystery of godliness, 1 Tim. 3:16. This bespeaks the honour of the gospel; it is no vulgar common thing, hammered out by any human wit, but it is the admirable product of the eternal wisdom and counsel of God, and has in it such an inconceivable height, such an unfathomable depth, as surpass knowledge. It is a mystery which the angels desire to look into, and cannot find the bottom of. And yet, blessed be God, there is as much of this mystery made plain as will suffice to bring us to heaven, if we do not wilfully neglect so great salvation. Now,

(1.) This mystery was kept secret since the world began: *chronois aiōniois sesigēmenou*. It was *wrapped up in silence from eternity*; so some — *a temporibus aeternis*; it is no new and upstart notion, no late invention, but took rise from the days of eternity and the purposes of God's everlasting love. Before the foundation of the world was laid, the mystery was hid in God, Eph. 3:9. Or, *since the world began*, so we translate it. During all the times of the Old-Testament this mystery was comparatively kept secret in the types and shadows of the ceremonial law, and the dark predictions of the prophets, which pointed at it, but so that they could not stedfastly look to the end of those things, 2 Co. 3:13. Thus it was hid from ages and generations, even among the Jews, much more among the Gentiles that sat in darkness and had no notices at all of it. Even the disciples of Christ themselves, before his resurrection and ascension, were very much in the dark about the mystery of redemption, and their notion of it was very much clouded and confused; such a secret was it for many ages. But,

(2.) It is now made manifest. The veil is rent, the shadows of the evening are done away, and life and immortality are

brought to light by the gospel, and the Sun of righteousness has risen upon the world. Paul does not pretend to have the monopoly of this discovery, as if he alone knew it; no, it is made manifest to many others. But how is it made manifest by the scriptures of the prophets? Surely, because now the event has given the best exposition to the prophecies of the Old Testament. Being accomplished, they are explained. The preaching of the prophets, as far as it related to this mystery, was in a great measure dark and unintelligible in the ages wherein they lived; but the scriptures of the prophets, the things which they left in writing, are now not only made plain in themselves, but by them this mystery is made known to all nations. The Old Testament does not only borrow light from, but return light to, the revelation of the New Testament. If the New Testament explains the Old, the Old Testament, by way of requital, very much illustrates the New. Thus the Old-Testament prophets prophesy again, now their prophecies are fulfilled, *before many people, and nations, and tongues*. I refer to Rev. 10:11, which this explains. Now Christ appears to have been the treasure hid in the field of the Old Testament. To him bear *all the prophets witness*. See Lu. 24:27.

(3.) It is manifested *according to the commandment of the everlasting God* — the purpose, counsel, and decree of God from eternity, and the commission and appointment given first to Christ and then to the apostles, in the fulness of time. They received commandment from the Father to do what they did in preaching the gospel. Lest any should object, "Why was this mystery kept secret so long, and why made manifest now?" — he resolves it into the will of God, who is an absolute sovereign, and gives not an account of any of his matters. The commandment of the everlasting God was enough to bear out the apostles and ministers of the gospel in their preaching. *The everlasting God*. This attribute of eternity is here given up to God very emphatically. [1.] He is from everlasting, which intimates that though he had kept this mystery secret since the world began, and had but lately revealed it, yet he had framed and contrived it from everlasting, before the worlds were. The oaths and covenants in the written word are but the copy of the oath and covenant which were between the Father and the Son from eternity: those the extracts, these the original. And, [2.] He is to everlasting, intimating the eternal continuance to us. We must never look for any new revelation, but abide by this, for this is according to the commandment of the everlasting God. Christ, in the gospel, is the same yesterday, to-day, and for ever.

(4.) It is *made known to all nations for the obedience of faith*. The extent of this revelation he often takes notice of; that whereas hitherto in Judah only God was known, now Christ is salvation to the ends of the earth, to all nations. And the design of it is very observable; it is for the obedience of faith — that they may believe and obey it, receive it and be rules by it. The gospel is revealed, not to be talked of and disputed about, but to be submitted to. The obedience of faith is that obedience which is paid to the word of faith (see that phrase, Acts 6:7), and which is produced by the grace of faith. See here what is the right faith — even that which works in obedience; and what is the right obedience — even that which springs from faith; and what is the design of the gospel — to bring us to both.

II. A doxology to that God whose gospel it is, ascribing glory to him for ever (*v.* 27), acknowledging that he is a glorious God, and adoring him accordingly, with the most awful affections, desiring and longing to be at this work with the holy angels, where we shall be doing it to eternity. This is praising God, ascribing glory to him for ever. Observe,

1. The matter of this praise. In thanking God, we fasten upon his favours to us; in praising and adoring God, we fasten upon his perfections in himself. Two of his principal attributes are here taken notice of: — (1.) His power (*v.* 25): *To him that is of power to establish you*. It is no less than a divine power that establishes the saints. Considering the disposition there is in them to fall, the industry of their spiritual enemies that seek to overthrow them, and the shaking times into which their lot is cast, no less than an almighty power will establish them. That power of God which is put forth for the establishment of the saints is and ought to be the matter of our praise, as Jude 24, *To him that is able to keep you from falling*. In giving God the glory of this power we may, and must, take to ourselves the comfort of it — that whatever our doubts, and difficulties, and fears, may be, our God, whom we serve, is of power to establish us. See 1 Pt. 1:5; Jn. 10:29.

(2.) His wisdom (*v.* 27): *To God only wise.* Power to effect without wisdom to contrive, and wisdom to contrive without power to effect, are alike vain and fruitless; but both together, and both infinite, make a perfect being. He is only wise; not the Father only wise, exclusive of the Son, but Father, Son, and Holy Ghost, three persons and one God, only wise, compared with the creatures. Man; the wisest of all the creatures in the lower world, is born like a wild ass's colt; nay, the angels themselves are charged with folly, in comparison with God. He only is perfectly and infallibly wise; he only is originally wise, in and of himself; for he is the spring and fountain of all the wisdom of the creatures, the Father of all the lights of wisdom that any creature can pretend to (James 1:17): with him are strength and wisdom, the deceived and deceiver are his.

2. The Mediator of this praise: *Through Jesus Christ. To God only wise through Jesus Christ;* so some. It is in and through Christ that God is manifested to the world as the only wise God; for he is the wisdom of God, and the power of God. Or rather, as we read it, *glory through Jesus Christ.* All the glory that passes from fallen man to God, so as to be accepted of him, must go through the hands of the Lord Jesus, in whom alone it is that our persons and performances are, or can be, pleasing to God. Of his righteousness therefore we must make mention, even of his only, who, as he is the Mediator of all our prayers, so he is, and I believe will be to eternity, the Mediator of all our praises.

AN EXPOSITION, WITH PRACTICAL OBSERVATIONS, OF

THE FIRST EPISTLE OF ST. PAUL TO THE CORINTHIANS

Corinth was a principal city of Greece, in that particular division of it which was called *Achaia.* It was situated on the isthmus (or neck of land) that joined Peloponnesus to the rest of Greece, on the southern side, and had two ports adjoining, one at the bottom of the Corinthian Gulf, called *Lechaeum,* not far from the city, whence they traded to Italy and the west, the other at the bottom of the Sinus Saronicus, called *Cenchrea,* at a more remote distance, whence they traded to Asia. From this situation, it is no wonder that Corinth should be a place of great trade and wealth; and, as affluence is apt to produce luxury of all kinds, neither is it to be wondered at if a place so famous for wealth and arts should be infamous for vice. It was in a particular manner noted for fornication, insomuch that a *Corinthian woman* was a proverbial phrase for a strumpet, and *korinthiazein, korinthiasesthai — to play the Corinthian,* is to play the whore, or indulge whorish inclinations. Yet in this lewd city did Paul, by the blessing of God on his labours, plant and raise a Christian church, chiefly among the Gentiles, as seems very probable from the history of this matter, Acts 18:1–18, compared with some passages in this epistle, particularly 12:2, where the apostle tells them, *You know that you wee Gentiles, carried away to those dumb idols even as you were led,* though it is not improbable that many Jewish converts might be also among them, for we are told that *Crispus, the chief ruler of the synagogue, believed on the Lord, with all his house,* Acts 18:8. He continued in this city nearly two years, as is plain from Acts 18:11 and 18 compared, and laboured with great success, being encouraged by a divine vision assuring him God *had much people in that city,* Acts 18:9, 10. Nor did he use to stay long in a place where his ministry met not with acceptance and success.

Some time after he left them he wrote this epistle to them, to water what he had planted and rectify some gross disorders which during his absence had been introduced, partly from the interest some false teacher or teachers had obtained amongst them, and partly from the leaven of their old maxims and manners, that had not been thoroughly purged out by the Christian principles they had entertained. And it is but too visible how much their wealth had helped to corrupt their manners, from the several faults for which the apostle reprehends them. Pride, avarice, luxury, lust (the natural offspring of a carnal and corrupt mind), are all fed and prompted by outward affluence. And with all these either the body of this people or some particular persons among them are here charged by the apostle. Their pride discovered itself in their parties and factions, and the notorious disorders they committed in the exercise of their spiritual gifts. And this vice was not wholly fed by their wealth, but by the insight they had into the Greek learning and philosophy. Some of the ancients tell us that the city abounded with rhetoricians and philosophers. And these were men naturally vain, full of self-conceit, and apt to despise the plain doctrine of the gospel, because it did not feed the curiosity of an inquisitive and disputing temper, nor please the ear with artful speeches and a flow of fine words. Their avarice was manifest in their law-suits and litigations about *meum — mine,* and *tuum — thine,* before heathen judges. Their luxury appeared in more instances than one, in their dress, in their debauching themselves even at the Lord's table, when the rich, who were most faulty on this account, were guilty also of a very proud and criminal contempt of their poor brethren. Their lust broke out in a most flagrant and infamous instance, such as had not been named among the Gentiles, not spoken of without detestation — that a man should have his father's wife, either as his wife, or so as to commit fornication with her. This indeed seems to be the fault of a particular person; but the whole church were to blame that they had his crime in no greater abhorrence, that they could endure one of such very corrupt morals and of so flagitious a behaviour among them. But their participation in his sin was yet greater, if, as some of the ancients tell us, they were puffed up on behalf of the great learning and eloquence of this incestuous person. And it is plain from other passages of the epistle that they were not so entirely free from their former lewd inclinations as not to need very strict cautions and strong arguments against fornication: see 6:9–20. The pride of their learning had also carried many of them so far as to disbelieve or dispute against the doctrine of the resurrection. It is not improbable that they treated this question problematically, as they did many questions in philosophy, and tried their skill by arguing it *pro* and *con.*

It is manifest from this state of things that there was much that deserved reprehension, and needed correction, in this church. And the apostle, under the direction and influence of the Holy Spirit, sets himself to do both with all wisdom and faithfulness, and with a due mixture of tenderness and authority, as became one in so elevated and important a station in the church. After a short introduction at the beginning of the epistle, he first blames them for their discord and factions, enters into the origin and source of them, shows them how much pride and vanity, and the affectation of science, and learning, and eloquence, flattered by false teachers, contributed to the scandalous schism; and prescribes humility, and submission to divine instruction, the teaching of God by his Spirit, both by external revelation and internal illumination, as a remedy for the evils that abounded amongst them. He shows them the vanity of their pretended science and eloquence on many accounts. This he does through the first four chapters. In the fifth he treats of the case of the incestuous person, and orders him to be put out from among them. Nor is what the ancients say improbable, that this incestuous person was a man in great esteem, and head of one party at least among them. The apostle seems to tax them with being puffed up on his account, 5:2. In the sixth chapter he blames them for their law-suits, carried on before heathen judges, when their disputes about property should have been amicably determined amongst themselves, and in the close of the chapter warns them against the sin of fornication, and urges his caution with a variety of arguments. In the seventh chapter he gives advice upon a case of conscience, which some of that church had proposed to him in an epistle, about marriage, and shows it to be appointed of God as a remedy against fornication, that the ties of it were not dissolved, though a husband or wife continued a heathen, when the other became a Christian; and, in short, that Christianity made no change in men's civil states and relations. He gives also some directions here about virgins, in answer, as is probable, to the Corinthians' enquiries. In the eighth he directs them about meats offered to idols, and cautions them against abusing their Christian liberty. From this he also takes occasion, in the ninth chapter, to expatiate a little on his own conduct upon this head of liberty. For, though he might have insisted on a maintenance from the churches where he ministered, he waived this demand, that *he might make the gospel of Christ without charge,* and did in other things comply with and suit himself to the tempers and circumstances of those among whom he laboured, for their good. In the tenth chapter he dissuades them, from the example of the Jews, against having communion with idolaters, by eating of their sacrifices, inasmuch as they could not be at once partakers of the Lord's table and the table of devils, though they were not bound to enquire concerning meat sold in the shambles, or set before them at a feast made by unbelievers, whether it were a part of the idol-sacrifices or no, but were at liberty to eat without asking questions. In the eleventh chapter he gives direction about their habit in public worship, blames them for their gross irregularities and scandalous disorders in receiving the Lord's supper, and solemnly warns them against the abuse of so sacred an institution. In the twelfth chapter he enters on the consideration of spiritual gifts, which were poured forth in great abundance on this church, upon which they were not a little elated. He tells them, in this chapter, that all came from the same original, and were all directed to the same end. They issued from one Spirit, and were intended for the good of the church, and must be abused when they were not made to minister to this purpose. Towards the close he informs them that they were indeed valuable gifts, but he could recommend to them something far more excellent, upon which he breaks out, in the thirteenth chapter, into the commendation and characteristics of charity. And them, in the fourteenth, he directs them how to keep up decency and order in the churches in the use of their spiritual gifts, in which they seem to have been exceedingly irregular, through pride of their gifts and a vanity of showing them. The fifteenth chapter is taken up in confirming and explaining the great doctrine of the resurrection. The last chapter consists of some particular advices and salutations; and thus the epistle closes.

CHAPTER 1

In this chapter we have, I. The preface or introduction to the whole epistle (*v.* 1–9). II. One principal occasion of writing it hinted, namely, their divisions and the origin of them (*v.* 10–13). III. An account of Paul's ministry among them, which was principally preaching the gospel (*v.* 14–17). IV. The manner wherein he preached the gospel, and the different success of it, with an account how admirably it was fitted to bring glory to God and beat down the pride and vanity of men (*v.* 17 to the end).

Verses 1–9

We have here the apostle's preface to his whole epistle, in which we may take notice,

I. Of the inscription, in which, according to the custom of writing letters then, the name of the person by whom it was written and the persons to whom it was written are both inserted. 1. It is an epistle from Paul, the apostle of the Gentiles, to the church of Corinth, which he himself had planted, though there were some among them that now questioned his apostleship (*ch.* 9:1, 2), and vilified his person and ministry, 2 Co. 10:10. The most faithful and useful ministers are not secure from this contempt. He begins with challenging this character: *Paul, called to be an apostle of Jesus Christ, through the will of God.* He had not taken this honour to himself, but had a divine commission for it. It was proper at any time, but necessary at this time, to assert his character, and magnify his office, when false teachers made a merit of running him down, and their giddy and deluded followers were so apt to set them up in competition with him. It was not pride in Paul, but faithfulness to his trust, in this juncture, to maintain his apostolical character and authority. And, to make this more fully appear, he joins Sosthenes with him in writing, who was a minister of a lower rank. Paul, and Sosthenes his brother, not a fellow-apostle, but a fellow-minister, once a ruler of the Jewish synagogue, afterwards a convert to Christianity, a Corinthian by birth, as is most probable, and dear to this people, for which reason Paul, to ingratiate himself with them, joins them with himself in his first salutations. There is no reason to suppose he was made a partaker of the apostle's inspiration, for which reasons he speaks, through the rest of the epistle, in his own name, and in the singular number. Paul did not in any case lessen his apostolical authority, and yet he was ready upon all occasions to do a kind and condescending thing for their good to whom he ministered. The persons to whom this epistle was directed were *the church of God that was at Corinth, sanctified in Christ Jesus, and called to be saints.* All Christians are thus far sanctified in Christ Jesus, that they are by baptism dedicated and devoted to him, they are under strict obligations to be holy, and they make profession of real sanctity. If they be not truly holy, it is their own fault and reproach. Note, It is the design of Christianity to sanctify us in Christ. *He gave himself for us, to redeem us from all iniquity, and purify us to himself a peculiar people, zealous of good works.* In conjunction with the church at Corinth, he directs the epistle *to all that in every place call on the name of Christ Jesus our Lord, both theirs and ours.* Hereby Christians are distinguished from the profane and atheistical, that they dare not live without prayer; and hereby they are distinguished from Jews and Pagans, that they call on the name of Christ. He is their common head and Lord. Observe, In every place in the Christian world there are some that call on the name of Christ. God hath a remnant in all places; and we should have a common concern for and hold communion with all that call on Christ's name.

II. Of the apostolical benediction. *Grace be to you, and peace, from God our Father, and from the Lord Jesus Christ.* An apostle of the prince of peace must be a messenger and minister of peace. This blessing the gospel brings with it, and this blessing every preacher of the gospel should heartily wish and pray may be the lot of all among whom he ministers. Grace and peace — the favour of God, and reconciliation to him. It is indeed the summary of all blessings. *The Lord lift up his countenance upon thee, and give thee peace,* was the form of benediction under the Old Testament (Num. 6:26), but this advantage we have by the gospel, 1. That we are directed how to obtain that peace from God: it is in and by Christ. Sinners can have no peace with God, nor any good from him, but through Christ. 2. We are told what must qualify us for this peace; namely, grace: first grace, then peace. God first reconciles sinners to himself, before he bestows his peace upon them.

III. Of the apostle's thanksgiving to God on their behalf. Paul begins most of his epistles with thanksgiving to God for his friends and prayer for them. Note, The best way of manifesting our affection to our friends is by praying and giving thanks for them. It is one branch of the communion of saints to give thanks to God mutually for our gifts, graces, and comforts. He gives thanks, 1. For their conversion to the faith of Christ: *For the grace which was given you through Jesus Christ, v.* 4. He is the great procurer and disposer of the favours of God. Those who are united to him by faith, and made to partake of his Spirit and merits, are the objects of divine favour. God loves them, bears them hearty good-will, and bestows on them his fatherly smiles and blessings. 2. For the abundance of their spiritual gifts. This the church of Corinth was famous for. They did not come behind any of the churches in any gift, *v.* 7. He specifies *utterance and knowledge, v.* 5. Where God has given these two gifts, he has given great capacity for usefulness. Many have the flower of utterance that have not the root of knowledge, and their converse is barren. Many have the treasure of knowledge, and want utterance to employ it for the good of others, and then it is in a manner wrapped up in a napkin. But, where God gives both, a man is qualified for eminent usefulness. When the church of Corinth was enriched with all utterance and all knowledge, it was fit that a large tribute of praise should be rendered to God, especially when these gifts were a testimony to the truth of the Christian doctrine, a confirmation of the testimony of Christ among them, *v.* 6. They were *signs and wonders and gifts of the Holy Ghost,* by which God did bear witness to the apostles, both to their mission and doctrine (Heb. 2:4), so that the more plentifully they were poured forth on any church the more full attestation was given to that doctrine which was delivered by the apostles, the more confirming evidence they had of their divine mission. And it is no wonder that when they had such a foundation for their faith they should live in expectation of the coming of their Lord Jesus Christ, *v.* 7. It is the character of Christians that they wait for Christ's second coming; all our religion has regard to this: we believe it, and hope for it, and it is the business of our lives to prepare for it, if we are Christians indeed. And the more confirmed we are in the Christian faith the more firm is our belief of our Lord's second coming, and the more earnest our expectation of it.

IV. Of the encouraging hopes the apostle had of them for the time to come, founded on the power and love of Christ, and the faithfulness of God, *v.* 8, 9. He who had begun a good work in them, and carried it on thus far, would not leave it unfinished. Those that wait for the coming of our Lord Jesus Christ will be kept by him, and confirmed to the end; and those that are so *will be blameless in the day of Christ:* not upon the principle of strict justice, but gracious absolution; not in rigour of law, but from rich and free grace. How desirable is it to be confirmed and kept of Christ for such a purpose as this! How glorious are the hopes of such a privilege, whether for ourselves or others! To be kept by the power of Christ from the power of our own corruption and Satan's temptation, that we may appear without blame in the great day! O glorious expectation, especially when the faithfulness of God comes in to support our hopes! He *who hath called us into the fellowship of his Son is faithful, and will do it,* 1 Th. 5:24. He who hath brought us into near and dear relation to Christ, into sweet and intimate communion with Christ, is faithful; he may be trusted with our dearest concerns. Those that come at his call shall never be disappointed in their hopes in him. If we approve ourselves faithful to God, we shall never find him unfaithful to us. *He will not suffer his faithfulness to fail,* Ps. 89:33.

Verses 10–13

Here the apostle enters on his subject.

I. He extorts them to unity and brotherly love, and reproves them for their divisions. He had received an account from some that wished them well of some unhappy differences among them. It was neither ill-will to the church, nor to their ministers, that prompted them to give this account; but a kind and prudent concern to have these heats qualified by Paul's interposition. He writes to them in a very engaging way: *"I beseech you, brethren, by the name of our Lord Jesus Christ;* if you have any regard to that dear and worthy name by which you are called, be unanimous. *Speak all the same thing;* avoid *divisions or schisms"* (as the original is), "that is, all alienation of affection from each other. *Be perfectly joined together in the same mind,* as far as you can. In the great things of religion be of a mind: but, when there is not a unity of sentiment, let there be a union of affections. The consideration of being agreed in greater things should extinguish all feuds and divisions about minor ones."

II. He hints at the origin of these contentions. Pride lay at the bottom, and this made them factious. *Only of pride cometh contention,* Prov. 13:10. They quarrelled about their ministers. Paul and Apollos were both faithful ministers of Jesus Christ, and helpers of their faith and joy: but those who were disposed to be contentious broke into parties, and set their ministers at the head of their several factions: some cried up Paul, perhaps as the most sublime and spiritual teacher; others cried up Apollos, perhaps as the most eloquent speaker; some Cephas, or Peter, perhaps for the authority of his age, or because he was the apostle of the circumcision; and some were for none of them, but Christ only. So liable are the best things in the world to be corrupted, and the gospel and its institutions, which are at perfect harmony with themselves and one another, to be made the engines of variance, discord, and contention. This is no reproach to our religion, but a very melancholy evidence of the corruption and depravity of human nature. Note, How far will pride carry Christians in opposition to one another! Even so far as to set Christ and his own apostles at variance, and make them rivals and competitors.

III. He expostulates with them upon their discord and quarrels: *"Is Christ divided?* No, there is but one Christ, and therefore Christians should be on one heart. *Was Paul crucified for you?* Was he your sacrifice and atonement? Did I ever pretend to be your saviour, or any more than his minister? Or, *were you baptized in the name of Paul?* Were you devoted to my service, or engaged to be my disciples, by that sacred rite? Did I challenge that right in you, or dependence from you, which is the proper claim of your God and Redeemer?" No; ministers, however instrumental they are of good to us, are not to be put in Christ's stead. They are not to usurp Christ's authority, nor encourage any thing in the people that looks like transferring his authority to them. He is our Saviour and sacrifice, he is our Lord and guide. And happy were it for the churches if there were no name of distinction among them, as Christ is not divided.

Verses 14–16

Here the apostle gives an account of his ministry among them. He thanks God he had baptized but a few among them, *Crispus,* who had been a ruler of a synagogue at Corinth (Acts 18:8), *Gaius, and the household of Stephanas,* besides whom, he says, he did not remember that he had baptized any. But how was this a proper matter for thankfulness? Was it not a part of the apostolical commission to baptize all nations? And could Paul give thanks to God for his own neglect of duty? He is not to be understood in such a sense as if he were thankful for not having baptized at all, but for not having done it in present circumstances, lest it should have had this very bad construction put upon it — that he had baptized in his own name, made disciples for himself, or set himself up as the head of a sect. He left it to other ministers to baptize, while he set himself to more useful work, and filled up his time with preaching the gospel. This, he thought, was more his business, because the more important business of the two. He had assistants that could baptize, when none could discharge the other part of his office so well as himself. In this sense he says, *Christ sent him not to baptize, but to preach the gospel* — not so much to baptize as to preach. Note, Ministers should consider themselves sent and set apart more especially to that service in which Christ will be most honoured and the salvation of souls promoted, and for which they are best fitted, though no part of their duty is to be neglected. The principal business Paul did among them was to preach *the gospel* (*v.* 17), *the cross* (*v.* 18), *Christ crucified, v.* 23. Ministers are the soldiers of Christ, and are to erect and display the banner of the cross. He did not preach his own fancy, but the gospel — the glad tidings of peace, and reconciliation to God, through the mediation of a crucified Redeemer. This is the sum and substance of the gospel. Christ crucified is the foundation of all our joys. By his death we live. This is what Paul preached, what all ministers should preach, and what all the saints live upon.

Verses 17–31

We have here,

I. The manner in which Paul preached the gospel, and the cross of Christ: *Not with the wisdom of words* (*v.* 17), *the enticing words of man's wisdom* (*ch.* 2:4), the flourish of oratory, or the accuracies of philosophical language, upon which the Greeks so much prided themselves, and which seem to have been the peculiar recommendations of some of the heads of the faction in this church that most opposed this apostle. He did not preach the gospel in this manner, lest *the cross of Christ should be of no effect,* lest the success should be ascribed to the force of art, and not of truth; not to the plain doctrine of a crucified Jesus, but to the powerful oratory of those who spread it, and hereby the honour of the cross be diminished or eclipsed. Paul had been bred up himself in Jewish learning at the feet of Gamaliel, but in preaching the cross of Christ he laid his learning aside. He preached a crucified Jesus in plain language, and told the people that that Jesus who was crucified at Jerusalem was the Son of God and Saviour of men, and that all who would be saved must repent of their sins, and believe in him, and submit to his government and laws. This truth needed no artificial dress; it shone out with the greatest majesty in its own light, and prevailed in the world by its divine authority, and the demonstration of the Spirit, without any human helps. The plain preaching of a crucified Jesus was more powerful than all the oratory and philosophy of the heathen world.

II. We have the different effects of this preaching: To those who perish it is foolishness, *but to those who are saved it is the power of God, v.* 18. *It is to the Jews a stumbling-block,* and to the Greeks foolishness; but unto those who are called, both Jews and Greeks, Christ the power of God and the wisdom of God, v. 23, 24. 1. Christ crucified is a stumbling-block to the Jews. They could not get over it. They had a conceit that their expected Messiah was to be a great temporal prince, and therefore would never own one who made so mean an appearance in life, and died so accursed a death, for their deliverer and king. They despised him, and looked upon him as execrable, because he was hanged on a tree, and because he did not gratify them with a sign to their mind, though his divine power shone out in innumerable miracles. The Jews require a sign, v. 22. See Mt. 12:38. 2. He was to the Greeks foolishness. They laughed at the story of a crucified Saviour, and despised the apostles' way of telling it. They sought for wisdom. They were men of wit and reading, men that had cultivated arts and sciences, and had, for some ages, been in a manner the very mint of knowledge and learning. There was nothing in the plain doctrine of the cross to suit their taste, nor humour their vanity, nor gratify a curious and wrangling temper: they entertained it therefore with scorn and contempt. What, hope to be saved by one that could not save himself! And trust in one who was condemned and crucified as a malefactor, a man of mean birth and poor condition in life, and cut off by so vile and opprobrious a death! This was what the pride of human reason and learning could not relish. The Greeks thought it little better than stupidity to receive such a doctrine, and pay this high regard to such a person: and thus were they justly left to perish in their pride and obstinacy. Note, It is just with God to leave those to themselves who pour such proud contempt on divine wisdom and grace. 3. To those who are called and saved *he is the wisdom of God, and the power of God.* Those who are called and sanctified, who receive the gospel, and are enlightened by the Spirit of God, discern more glorious discoveries of God's wisdom and power in the doctrine of Christ crucified than in all his other works. Note, Those who are saved *are reconciled to the doctrine of the cross,* and led into an experimental acquaintance with the mysteries of Christ crucified.

III. We have here the triumphs of the cross over human wisdom, according to the ancient prophecy (Isa. 29:14): *I will destroy the wisdom of the wise, and bring to nothing the understanding of the prudent. Where is the wise? Where is the scribe? Where is the disputer of this world? Hath not God made foolish the wisdom of this world? v.* 19, 20, All the valued learning of this world was confounded, baffled, and eclipsed, by the Christian revelation and the glorious triumphs of the cross. The heathen politicians and philosophers, the Jewish rabbis and doctors, the curious searchers into the secrets of nature, were all posed and put to a nonplus. This scheme lay out of the reach of the deepest statesmen and philosophers, and the greatest pretenders to learning both among the Jews and Greeks. When God would save the world, he took a way by himself; and good reason, for *the world by wisdom knew not God, v.* 21. All the boasted science of the heathen world did not, could not, effectually bring home the world to God. In spite of all their wisdom, ignorance still prevailed, iniquity still abounded. Men were puffed up by their imaginary knowledge, and rather further alienated from God; and therefore *it pleased him, by the foolishness of preaching, to save those that believe.* By the *foolishness of preaching* — not such in truth, but in vulgar reckoning.

1. The thing preached was foolishness in the eyes of worldly-wise men. Our living through one who died, our being blessed by one who was made a curse, our being justified by one who was himself condemned, was all folly and inconsistency to men blinded with self-conceit and wedded to their own prejudices and the boasted discoveries of their reason and philosophy.

2. The manner of preaching the gospel was foolishness to them too. None of the famous men for wisdom or eloquence were employed to plant the church or propagate the gospel. A few fishermen were called out, and sent upon this errand. These were commissioned to disciple the nations: these vessels chosen to convey the treasure of saving knowledge to the world. There was nothing in them that at first view looked grand or august enough to come from God; and the proud pretenders to learning and wisdom despised the doctrine for the sake of those who dispensed it. And yet *the foolishness of God is wiser than men, v.* 25. Those methods of divine conduct that vain men are apt to censure as unwise and weak have more true, solid, and successful wisdom in them, than all the learning and wisdom that are among

men: "*You see your calling, brethren, how that not many wise men after the flesh, not many mighty, not many noble, are called, v.* 26, etc. You see the state of Christianity; not many men of learning, or authority, or honourable extraction, are called." There is a great deal of meanness and weakness in the outward appearance of our religion. For, (1.) Few of distinguished character in any of these respects were chosen for the work of the ministry. God did not choose philosophers, nor orators, nor statesmen, nor men of wealth and power and interest in the world, to publish the gospel of grace and peace. Not the wise men after the flesh, though men would apt to think that a reputation for wisdom and learning might have contributed much to the success of the gospel. Not the mighty and noble, however men might be apt to imagine that secular pomp and power would make way for its reception in the world. But God seeth not as man seeth. He hath chosen the foolish things of the world, the weak things of the world, the base and despicable things of the world, men of mean birth, of low rank, of no liberal education, to be the preachers of the gospel and planters of the church. *His thoughts are not as our thoughts, nor his ways as our ways.* He is a better judge than we what instruments and measures will best serve the purposes of his glory. (2.) Few of distinguished rank and character were called to be Christians. As the teachers were poor and mean, so generally were the converts. Few of the wise, and mighty, and noble, embraced the doctrine of the cross. The first Christians, both among Jews and Greeks, were weak, and foolish, and base; men of mean furniture as to their mental improvements, and very mean rank and condition as to their outward estate; and yet what glorious discoveries are there of divine wisdom in the whole scheme of the gospel, and in this particular circumstance of its success!

IV. We have an account how admirably all is fitted, 1. To beat down the pride and vanity of men. God hath chosen *the foolish things of the world to confound the wise* — men of no learning to confound the most learned; *the weak things of the world to confound the might* — men of mean rank and circumstances to confound and prevail against all the power and authority of earthly kings; *and base things, and things which are despised* — things which men have in the lowest esteem, or in the utmost contempt, to pour contempt and disgrace on all they value and have in veneration; *and things which are not, to bring to nought (to abolish) things that are* — the conversion of the Gentiles (of whom the Jews had the most contemptuous and vilifying thoughts) was to open a way to the abolishing of that constitution of which they were so fond, and upon which they valued themselves so much as for the sake of it to despise the rest of the world. It is common for the Jews to speak of the Gentiles under this character, as *things that are not.* Thus, in the apocryphal book of Esther, she is brought in praying that God would not give his sceptre to those *who are not,* Esth. 14:11. Esdras, in one of the apocryphal books under his name, speaks to God *of the heathen as those who are reputed as nothing,* 2 Esdras 6:56, 57. And the apostle Paul seems to have this common language of the Jews in his view when he calls Abraham *the father of us all before him whom he believed, God, who calleth those things that are not as though they were,* Rom. 4:17. The gospel is fitted to bring down the pride of both Jews and Greeks, to shame the boasted science and learning of the Greeks, and to take down that constitution on which the Jews valued themselves and despised all the world besides, *that no flesh should glory in his presence* (v. 29), that there might be no pretence for boasting. Divine wisdom alone had the contrivance of the method of redemption; divine grace alone revealed it, and made it known. It lay, in both respects, out of human reach. And the doctrine and discovery prevailed, in spite of all the opposition it met with from human art or authority: so effectually did God veil the glory and disgrace the pride of man in all. The gospel dispensation is a contrivance to humble man. But, 2. It is as admirably fitted to glorify God. There is a great deal of power and glory in the substance and life of Christianity. Though the ministers were poor and unlearned, and the converts generally of the meanest rank, yet the hand of the Lord went along with the preachers, and was mighty in the hearts of the hearers; and Jesus Christ was made both to ministers and Christians what was truly great and honourable. All we have we have from God as the fountain, and in and through Christ as the channel of conveyance. He is made of God to us *wisdom, righteousness, sanctification, and redemption* (v. 30): all we need, or can de-

sire. We are foolishness, ignorant and blind in the things of God, with all our boasted knowledge; and he is made wisdom to us. We are guilty, obnoxious to justice; and he is made righteousness, our great atonement and sacrifice. We are depraved and corrupt; and he is made sanctification, the spring of our spiritual life; from him, the head, it is communicated to all the members of his mystical body by his Holy Spirit. We are in bonds, and he is made redemption to us, our Saviour and deliverer. Observe, Where Christ is made righteousness to any soul, he is also made sanctification. He never discharges from the guilt of sin, without delivering from the power of it; and he is made righteousness and sanctification, that he may in the end be made complete redemption, may free the soul from the very being of sin, and loose the body from the bonds of the grave: and what is designed in all is *that all flesh may glory in the Lord, v.* 31. Observe, It is the will of God that all our glorifying should be in the Lord: and, our salvation being only through Christ, it is thereby effectually provided that it should be so. Man is humbled, and God glorified and exalted, by the whole scheme.

CHAPTER 2

The apostle proceeds with his argument in this chapter, and, I. Reminds the Corinthians of the plain manner wherein he delivered the gospel to them (v. 1–5). But yet, II. Shows them that he had communicated to them a treasure of the truest and highest wisdom, such as exceeded all the attainments of learned men, such as could never have entered into the heart of man if it had not been revealed, nor can be received and improved to salvation but by the light and influence of that Spirit who revealed it (v. 6 to the end).

Verses 1–5

In this passage the apostle pursues his design, and reminds the Corinthians how he acted when he first preached the gospel among them.

I. As to the matter or subject he tell us (v. 2), *He determined to know nothing among them but Jesus Christ and him crucified* — to make a show of no other knowledge than this, to preach nothing, to discover the knowledge of nothing, but Jesus Christ, and him crucified. Note, Christ, in his person and offices, is the sum and substance of the gospel, and ought to be the great subject of a gospel minister's preaching. His business is to display the banner of the cross, and invite people under it. Any one that heard Paul preach found him to harp so continually on this string that he would say he knew nothing but Christ and him crucified. Whatever other knowledge he had, this was the only knowledge he discovered, and showed himself concerned to propagate among his hearers.

II. The manner wherein he preached Christ is here also observable. 1. Negatively. *He came not among them with excellency of speech or wisdom, v.* 1. His speech and preaching were not with enticing words of man's wisdom, v. 4. He did not affect to appear a fine orator or a deep philosopher; nor did he insinuate himself into their minds, by a flourish of words, or a pompous show of deep reason and extraordinary science and skill. He did not set himself to captivate the ear by fine turns and eloquent expressions, nor to please and entertain the fancy with lofty flights of sublime notions. Neither his speech, nor the wisdom he taught, savoured of human skill: he learnt both in another school. Divine wisdom needed not to be set off with such human ornaments. 2. Positively. He came among them *declaring the testimony of God, v.* 1. He published a divine revelation, and gave in sufficient vouchers for the authority of it, both by its consonancy to ancient predictions and by present miraculous operations; and there he left the matter. Ornaments of speech and philosophical skill and argument could add no weight to what came recommended by such authority. *He was also among them in weakness and fear, and in much trembling;* and yet *his speech and preaching were in demonstration of the Spirit and of power, v.* 3, 4. His enemies in the church of Corinth spoke very contemptuously of him: *His bodily presence, say they, is weak, and his speech contemptible,* 2 Co. 10:10. Possibly he had a little body, and a low voice; but, though he had not so good an elocution as some, it is plain that he was no mean speaker. The men of Lystra looked on him to be the heathen god Mercury, come down to them in the form of a man, because he was the chief speaker, Acts 14:12. Nor did he want courage nor resolution to go through his work; he was *in nothing terrified by his adversaries.* Yet he was no boaster. He did not proudly vaunt himself, like his opposers. He acted in his office with much modesty, concern, and care. He behaved with great humility among them; not as one grown vain with the honour and authority conferred on him, but as one concerned to approve himself faithful, and fearful of himself, lest he should mismanage in his trust. Observe, None know the fear and trembling of faithful ministers, who are zealous over souls with a godly jealousy; and a deep sense of their own weakness is the occasion of this fear and trembling. They know how insufficient they are, and are therefore fearful for themselves. But, though Paul managed with this modesty and concern, yet he spoke with authority: *In the demonstration of the Spirit and of power.* He preached the truths of Christ in their native dress, with plainness of speech. He laid down the doctrine as the Spirit delivered it; and left the Spirit, by his external operation in signs and miracles, and his internal influences on the hearts of men, to demonstrate the truth of it, and procure its reception.

III. Here is the end mentioned for which he preached Christ crucified in this manner: *That your faith should not stand in the wisdom of man, but the power of God* (*v.* 5) — that they might not be drawn by human motives, nor overcome by mere human arguments, lest it should be said that either rhetoric or logic had made them Christians. But, when nothing but Christ crucified was plainly preached, the success must be founded, not on human wisdom, but divine evidence and operation. The gospel was so preached that God might appear and be glorified in all.

Verses 6–16

In this part of the chapter the apostle shows them that though he had not come to them with the excellency of human wisdom, with any of the boasted knowledge and literature of the Jews or Greeks, yet he had communicated to them a treasure of the truest and the highest wisdom: *We speak wisdom among those who are perfect* (*v.* 6), among those who are well instructed in Christianity, and come to some maturity in the things of God. Those that receive the doctrine as divine, and, having been illuminated by the Holy Spirit, have looked well into it, discover true wisdom in it. They not only understand the plain history of Christ, and him crucified, but discern the deep and admirable designs of the divine wisdom therein. Though what we preach is foolishness to the world, it is wisdom to them. They are made wise by it, and can discern wisdom in it. Note, Those who are wise themselves are the only proper judges of what is wisdom; *not* indeed *the wisdom of this world, nor of the princes of this world,* but *the wisdom of God in a mystery* (*v.* 6, 7); not worldly wisdom, but divine; not such as the men of this world could have discovered, nor such as worldly men, under the direction of pride, and passion, and appetite, and worldly interest, and destitute of the Spirit of God, can receive. Note, How different is the judgment of God from that of the world! *He seeth not as man seeth.* The wisdom he teaches is of a quite different kind from what passes under that notion in the world. It is not the wisdom of politicians, nor philosophers, nor rabbis (see *v.* 6), not such as they teach nor such as they relish; *but the wisdom of God in a mystery, the hidden wisdom of God* — what he had a long time kept to himself, and concealed from the world, and the depth of which, now it is revealed, none but himself can fathom. *It is the mystery which hath been hid from ages and generations, though now made manifest to the saints* (Col. 1:26), hid in a manner entirely from the heathen world, and made mysterious to the Jews, by being wrapped up in dark types and distant prophecies, but revealed and made known to us by the Spirit of God. Note, See the privilege of those who enjoy the gospel revelation: to them types are unveiled, mysteries made plain, prophecies interpreted, and the secret counsels of God published and laid open. The wisdom of God in a mystery is now made manifest to the saints. Now, concerning this wisdom, observe,

I. The rise and origin of it: *It was ordained of God, before the world, to our glory, v.* 7. It was ordained of God; he had determined long ago to reveal and make it known, from many ages past, from the beginning, nay, from eternity; and that to our glory, *the glory of us,* either us apostles or us Christians. It was a great honour put upon the apostles, to be entrusted with the revelation of this wisdom. It was a great and honourable privilege for Christians to have this glorious wisdom discovered to them. And the wisdom of God discovered to them. And the wisdom of God discovered in the gospel, the divine wisdom taught by the gospel, prepares for our everlasting glory and happiness in the world to come. The counsels of God concerning our redemption are dated from eternity, and designed for the glory and happiness of the saints. And what deep wisdom was in these counsels! Note, The wisdom of God is both employed and displayed for the honour of the saints — employed from eternity, and displayed in time, to make them glorious both here and hereafter, in time and to eternity. What honour does he put on his saints!

II. The ignorance of the great men of the world about it: *Which none of the princes of this world knew* (*v.* 8), the principal men in authority and power, or in wisdom and learning. The Roman governor, and the guides and rulers of the Jewish church and nation, seem to be the persons here chiefly meant. These were the princes of this world, or this age, who, had they known this true and heavenly wisdom, would not have crucified the Lord of glory. This Pilate and the Jewish rulers literally did when our Redeemer was crucified upon the sentence of the one and the clamorous demands of the other. Observe, Jesus Christ is the Lord of Glory, a title much too great for any creature to bear: and the reason why he was hated was because he was not known. Had his crucifiers known him, known who and what he was, they would have withheld their impious hands, and not have taken and slain him. This he pleaded with his Father for their pardon: *Father, forgive them, for they know not what they do,* Lu. 23:34. Note, There are many things which people would not do if they knew the wisdom of God in the great work of redemption. They act as they do because they are blind or heedless. They know not the truth, or will not attend to it.

III. It is such wisdom as could not have been discovered without a revelation, according to what the prophet Isaiah says (Isa. 64:4), *Eye hath not seen, nor ear heard, nor have entered into the heart of man the things which God hath prepared for those that love him — for him that waiteth for him,* that waiteth for his mercy, so the Septuagint. It was a testimony of love to God in the Jewish believers to live in expectation of the accomplishment o evangelical promises. Waiting upon God is an evidence of love to him. *Lo, this is our God, we have waited for him,* Isa. 25:9. Observe, There are things which God hath prepared for those that love him, and wait for him. There are such things prepared in a future life for them, things which sense cannot discover, no present information can convey to our ears, nor can yet enter our hearts. *Life and immortality are brought to light through the gospel,* 2 Tim. 1:10. But the apostle speaks here of the subject-matter of the divine revelation under the gospel. These are such as eye hath not seen nor ear heard. Observe, The great truths of the gospel are things lying out of the sphere of human discovery: *Eye hath not seen, nor ear heard them, nor have they entered into the heart of man.* Were they objects of sense, could they be discovered by an eye of reason, and communicated by the ear to the mind, as matters of common human knowledge may, there had been no need of a revelation. But, lying out of the sphere of nature, we cannot discover them but by the light of revelation. And therefore we must take them as they lie in the scriptures, and as God has been pleased to reveal them.

IV. We here see by whom this wisdom is discovered to us: *God hath revealed them to us by his Spirit, v.* 10. The scripture is given by inspiration of God. *Holy men spoke of old as they were moved by the Holy Ghost,* 2 Pt. 1:21. And the apostles spoke by inspiration of the same Spirit, as he taught them, and gave them utterance. Here is a proof of the divine authority of the holy scriptures. Paul wrote what he taught: and what he taught was revealed of God by his Spirit, *that Spirit that searches all things, yea, the deep things of God, and knows the things of God, as the spirit of a man that is in him knows the things of a man, v.* 11. A double argument is drawn from these words in proof of the divinity of the Holy Ghost: — 1. Omniscience is attributed to him: *He searches all things, even the deep things of God.* He has exact knowledge of all things, and enters into the very depths of God, penetrates into his most secret counsels. Now who can have such a thorough knowledge of God but God? 2. This allusion seems to imply that the Holy Spirit is as much in God as a man's mind is in himself. Now the mind of the man is plainly essential to him. He cannot be without his mind. Now can God be without his Spirit. He is as much and as intimately one with God as the man's mind is with the man. The man knows his own mind because his mind is one with himself. The Spirit of God knows the things of God because he is one with God. And as no man can come at the knowledge of what is in another man's mind till he communicates and reveals it, so neither can we know the secret counsels and purposes of God till they are made known to us by his Holy Spirit. We cannot know them at all till he had proposed them objectively (as it is called) in the external revelation; we cannot know or believe them to salvation till he enlightens the faculty, opens the eye of the mind, and gives us such a knowledge and faith of them. And it was by this Spirit that the apostles had received the *wisdom of God in a mystery,* which they spoke. *"Now we have received not the spirit of the world, but the Spirit which is of God, that we might know the things freely given to us of God* (*v.* 12); not the spirit which is in the *wise men of the world* (*v.* 6), nor in the *rulers of the world* (*v.* 8), but the *Spirit which is of God,* or proceedeth from God. We have what we deliver in the name of God by inspiration from him; and it is by his gracious illumination and influence that *we know the things freely given to us of God* unto salvation" — that is, "the great privileges of the gospel, which are the free gift of God, distributions of mere and rich grace." Though these things are given to us, and the revelation of this gift is made to us, we cannot know them to any saving purpose till we have the Spirit. The apostles had the revelation of these things from the Spirit of God, and the saving impression of them from the same Spirit.

V. We see here in what manner this wisdom was taught or communicated: *Which things we speak, not in the words which man's wisdom teaches, but which the Holy Ghost teaches, v.* 13. They had received the wisdom they taught, not from the wise men of the world, but from the Spirit of God. Nor did they put a human dress on it, but plainly declared the doctrine of Christ, in terms also taught them by the Holy Spirit. He not only gave them the knowledge of these things, but gave them utterance. Observe, The truths of God need no garnishing by human skill or eloquence, but look best in the words which the Holy Ghost teaches. The Spirit of God knows much better how to speak of the things of God than the best critics, orators, or philosophers. *Comparing spiritual things with spiritual* — one part of revelation with another, the revelation of the gospel with that of the Jews, the discoveries of the New Testament with the types and prophecies of the Old. The comparing of matters of revelation with matters of science, things supernatural with things natural and common, is going by a wrong measure. Spiritual things, when brought together, will help to illustrate one another; but, if the principles of human art and science are to be made a test of revelation, we shall certainly judge amiss concerning it, and the things contained in it. Or, *adapting spiritual things to spiritual* — speaking of spiritual matters, matters of revelation, and the spiritual life, in language that is proper and plain. The language of the Spirit of God is the most proper to convey his meaning.

VI. We have an account how this wisdom is received.

1. *The natural man receiveth not the things of God, for they are foolishness to him, neither can he know them, because they are spiritually discerned, v.* 14. The *natural man, the animal man.* Either, (1.) The man under the power of corruption, and never yet illuminated by the Spirit of God, such as Jude calls *sensual, not having the Spirit, v.* 19. Men unsanctified receive not the things of God. The understanding, through the corruption of nature by the fall, and through the confirmation of this disorder by customary sin, is utterly unapt to receive the rays of divine light; it is prejudiced against them. The truths of God are foolishness to such a mind. The man looks on them as trifling and impertinent things, not worth his minding. *The light shineth in darkness, and the darkness comprehendeth it not,* Jn. 1:5. Not that the natural faculty of discerning is lost, but evil inclinations and wicked principles render the man unwilling to enter into the mind of God, in the spiritual matters of his kingdom, and yield to their force and power. It is the quickening beams of the Spirit of truth and holiness that must help the mind to discern their excellency, and to so thorough a conviction of their truth as heartily to receive and embrace them. Thus the natural man, the man destitute of the Spirit of God, cannot know them, because they are spiritually discerned. Or, (2.) The natural man, that is, the wise man of the world (*ch.* 1:19, 20), the wise man after the flesh, or according to the flesh (*v.* 26), one who hath the wisdom of the world, man's wisdom (*ch.* 2:4–6), a man, as some of the ancients, that would learn all truth by his own ratiocinations, receive nothing by faith, nor own any need of supernatural assistance. This was very much the character of the pretenders to philosophy and the Grecian learning and wisdom in that day. Such a man receives not the things of the Spirit of God. Revelation is not with him

a principle of science; he looks upon it as delirium and dotage, the extravagant thought of some deluded dreamer. It is no way to wisdom among the famous masters of the world; and for that reason he can have no knowledge of things revealed, because they are only spiritually discerned, or made known by the revelation of the Spirit, which is a principle of science or knowledge that he will not admit.

2. *But he that is spiritual judgeth all things, yet he himself is judged,* or discerned, *of no man, v.* 15. Either, (1.) He who is sanctified and made spiritually-minded (Rom. 8:6) judgeth all things, or discerneth all things — he is capable of judging about matters of human wisdom, and has also a relish and savour of divine truths; he sees divine wisdom, and experiences divine power, in gospel revelations and mysteries, which the carnal and unsanctified mind looks upon as weakness and folly, as things destitute of all power and not worthy any regard. It is the sanctified mind that must discern the real beauties of holiness; but, by the refinement of its facilities, they do not lose their power of discerning and judging about common and natural things. The spiritual man may judge of all things, natural and supernatural, human and divine, the deductions of reason and the discoveries of revelation. But he himself is judged or discerned of NO MAN. God's saints are his hidden ones, Ps. 83:3. *Their life is hid with Christ in God,* Col. 3:3. The carnal man knows no more of a spiritual man than he does of other spiritual things. He is a stranger to the principles, pleasures, and actings, of the divine life. The spiritual man does not lie open to his observation. Or, (2.) *He that is spiritual* (who has had divine revelations made to him, receives them as such, and founds his faith and religion upon them) can judge both of common things and things divine; he can discern what is, and what is not, the doctrine of the gospel and of salvation, and whether a man preaches the truths of God or not. He does not lose the power of reasoning, nor renounce the principles of it, by founding his faith and religion on revelation. But *he himself is judged of no man* — can be judged, so as to be confuted, by no man; nor can any man who is not spiritual, not under a divine *afflatus* himself (see *ch.* 14:37), or not founding his faith on a divine revelation, discern or judge whether what he speaks be true or divine, or not. In short, he who founds all his knowledge upon principles of science, and the mere light of reason, can never be a judge of the truth or falsehood of what is received by revelation. *For who hath known the mind of the Lord, that he may instruct him* (*v.* 16), that is, the *spiritual man?* Who can enter so far into the mind of God as to instruct him who has the Spirit of God, and is under his inspiration? He only is the person to whom God immediately communicates the knowledge of his will. And who can inform or instruct him in the mind of God who is so immediately under the conduct of his own Spirit? Very few have known any thing of the mind of God by a natural power. *But,* adds the apostle, *we have the mind of Christ;* and the mind of Christ is the mind of God. He is God, and the principal messenger and prophet of God. And the apostles were empowered by his Spirit to make known his mind to us. And in the holy scriptures the mind of Christ, and the mind of God in Christ, are fully revealed to us. Observe, It is the great privilege of Christians that they have the mind of Christ revealed to them by his Spirit.

CHAPTER 3

In this chapter the apostle, I. Blames the Corinthians for their carnality and divisions (*v.* 1–4). II. He instructs them how what was amiss among them might be rectified, by remembering, 1. That their ministers were no more than ministers (*v.* 5). 2. That they were unanimous, and carried on the same design (*v.* 6–10). 3. That they built on one and the same foundation (*v.* 11–15). III. He exhorts them to give due honour to their bodies, by keeping them pure (*v.* 16, 17), and to humility and self-diffidence (*v.* 18–21). IV. And dehorts them from glorying in particular ministers, because of the equal interest they had in all (*v.* 22 to the end).

Verses 1–4

Here, I. Paul blames the Corinthians for their weakness and nonproficiency. Those who are sanctified are so only in part: there is still room for growth and increase both in grace and knowledge, 2 Pt. 3:18. Those who through divine grace are renewed to a spiritual life may yet in many things be defective. The apostle tells *them he could not speak to them as unto spiritual* men, *but as unto carnal* men, *as to babes in Christ, v.* 1. They were so far from forming their maxims and measures upon the ground of divine revelation, and entering into the spirit of the gospel, that is was but too evident they were much under the command of carnal and corrupt affections. They were still mere babes in Christ. They had received some of the first principles of Christianity, but had not grown up to maturity of understanding in them, or of faith and holiness; and yet it is plain, from several passages in this epistle, that the Corinthians were very proud of their wisdom and knowledge. Note, It is but too common for persons of very moderate knowledge and understanding to have a great measure of self-conceit. The apostle assigns their little proficiency in the knowledge of Christianity as a reason why he had communicated no more of the deep things of it to them. They could not bear such food, they needed to be fed with milk, not with meat, *v.* 2. Note, It is the duty of a faithful minister of Christ to consult the capacities of his hearers and teach them as they can bear. And yet it is natural for babes to grow up to men; and babes in Christ should endeavour to grow in Stature, and become men in Christ. It is expected that their advances in knowledge should be in proportion to their means and opportunities, and their time of professing religion, that they may be able to bear discourses on the mysteries of our religion, and not always rest in plain things. It was a reproach to the Corinthians that they had so long sat under the ministry of Paul and had made no more improvement in Christian knowledge. Note, Christians are utterly to blame who do not endeavour to grow in grace and knowledge.

II. He blames them for their carnality, and mentions their contention and discord about their ministers as evidence of it: *For you are yet carnal; for whereas there are among you envyings, and strifes, and divisions, are you not carnal, and walk as men? v.* 3. They had mutual emulations, and quarrels, and factions among them, upon the account of their ministers, *while one said, I am of Paul; and another, I am of Apollos, v.* 4. These were proofs of their being carnal, that fleshly interests and affections too much swayed them. Note, Contentions and quarrels about religion are sad evidences of remaining carnality. True religion makes men peaceable and not contentious. Factious spirits act upon human principles, not upon principles of true religion; they are guided by their own pride and passions, and not by the rules of Christianity: *Do you not walk as men?* Note, It is to be lamented that many who should walk as Christians, that is, above the common rate of men, do indeed walk as men, live and act too much like other men.

Verses 5–10

Here the apostle instructs them how to cure this humour, and rectify what was amiss among them upon this head,

I. By reminding them that the ministers about whom they contended were but ministers: *Who then is Paul, and who is Apollos, but ministers by whom you believed? Even as the Lord gave to every man, v.* 5. They are but ministers, mere instruments used by the God of all grace. Some of the factious people in Corinth seem to have made more of them, as if they were lords of their faith, authors of their religion. Note, We should take care not to deify ministers, nor put them into the place of God. Apostles were not the authors of our faith and religion, though they were authorized and qualified to reveal and propagate it. They acted in this office as God gave to every man. Observe, All the gifts and powers that even apostles discovered and exerted in the work of the ministry were from God. They were intended to manifest their mission and doctrine to be divine. It was perfectly wrong, upon their account, to transfer that regard to the apostles which was solely to be paid to the divine authority by which they acted, and to God, from whom they had their authority. *Paul had planted and Apollos had watered, v.* 6. Both were useful, one for one purpose, the other for another. Note, God makes use of variety of instruments, and fits them to their several uses and intentions. Paul was fitted for planting work, and Apollos for watering work, but God gave the increase. Note, The success of the ministry must be derived from the divine blessing: *Neither he that planteth is any thing, nor he that watereth, but God who giveth the increase, v.* 7. Even apostolical ministers are nothing of themselves, can do nothing with efficacy and success unless God give the increase. Note, The best qualified and most faithful ministers have a just sense of their own insufficiency, and are very desirous that God should have all the glory of their success. Paul and Apollos are nothing at all in their own account, but God is all in all.

II. By representing to them the unanimity of Christ's ministers: *He that planteth and he that watereth are one* (*v.* 8), employed by one Master, entrusted with the same revelation, busied in one work, and engaged in one design — in harmony with one another, however they may be set in opposition to each other by factious party-makers. They have their different gifts from one and the same Spirit, for the very same purposes; and they heartily carry on the same design. Planters and waterers are but fellow-labourers in the same work. Note, All the faithful ministers of Christ are one in the great business and intention of their ministry. They may have differences of sentiment in minor things; they may have their debates and contests; but they heartily concur in the great design of honouring God and saving souls, by promoting true Christianity in the world. All such may expect a glorious recompence of their fidelity, and in proportion to it: *Every man shall receive his own reward, according to his own labour.* Their business is one, but some may mind it more than others: their end or design is one, but some may pursue it more closely than others: their Master also is one, and yet this good and gracious Master may make a difference in the rewards he gives, according to the different service they do: *Every one's own work shall have its own reward.* Those that work hardest shall fare best. Those that are most faithful shall have the greatest reward; and glorious work it is in which all faithful ministers are employed. *They are labourers with God, synergoi — co-workers, fellow-labourers* (*v.* 9), not indeed in the same order and degree, but in subordination to him, as instruments in his hand. They are engaged in his business. They are working together with God, in promoting the purposes of his glory, and the salvation of precious souls; and he who knows their work will take care they do not labour in vain. Men may neglect and vilify one minister while they cry up another, and have no reason for either: they may condemn when they should commend, and applaud what they should neglect and avoid; but the judgment of God is according to truth. He never rewards but upon just reason, and he ever rewards in proportion to the diligence and faithfulness of his servants. Note, Faithful ministers, when they are ill used by men, should encourage themselves in God. And it is to God, the chief agent and director of the great work of the gospel, to whom those that labour with him should endeavour to approve themselves. They are always under his eye, employed in his husbandry and building; and therefore, to be sure, he will carefully look over them: "*You are God's husbandry, you are God's building;* and therefore are neither of Paul nor of Apollos; neither belong to one nor the other, but to God: they only plant and water you, but it is the divine blessing on his own husbandry that alone can make it yield fruit. You are not our husbandry, but God's. We work under him, and with him, and for him. It is all for God that we have been doing among you. You are God's husbandry and building." He had employed the former metaphor before, and now he goes on to the other of a building: *According to the grace of God which is given unto me, as a wise master-builder, I have laid the foundation, and another buildeth thereon.* Paul here calls himself a wise master-builder, a character doubly reflecting honour on him. It was honourable to be a master-builder in the edifice of God; but it added to his character to be a wise one. Persons may be in an office for which they are not qualified, or not so thoroughly qualified as this expression implies Paul was. But, though he gives himself such a character, it is not to gratify his own pride, but to magnify divine grace. He was a wise master-builder, but the grace of God made him such. Note, It is no crime in a Christian, but much to his commendation, to take notice of the good that is in him, to the praise of divine grace. Spiritual pride is abominable: it is making use of the greatest favours of God to feed our own vanity, and make idols of ourselves. But to take notice of the favours of God to promote our gratitude to him, and to speak of them to his honour (be they of what sort they will), is but a proper expression of the duty and regard we own him. Note, Ministers should not be proud of their gifts or graces; but the better qualified they are for their work, and the more success they have in it, the more thankful should they be to God for his distinguishing goodness: *I have laid the foundation, and another buildeth thereon.* As before he had said, *I have planted, Apollos watered.* It was Paul that laid the foundation of a church among them. He had *begotten them through the gospel, ch.* 4:15. Whatever instructors they had besides, *they had not many fathers.* He would derogate from none that had done service among them, nor would he be robbed of his own honour and respect. Note,

Faithful ministers may and ought to have a concern for their own reputation. Their usefulness depends much upon it. *But let every man take heed how he buildeth thereon.* This is a proper caution; there may be very indifferent building on a good foundation. It is easy to err here; and great care should be used, not only to lay a sure and right foundation, but to erect a regular building upon it. Nothing must be laid upon it but what the foundation will bear, and what is of a piece with it. Gold and dirt must not be mingled together. Note, Ministers of Christ should take great care that they do not build their own fancies or false reasonings on the foundation of divine revelation. What they preach should be the plain doctrine of their Master, or what is perfectly agreeable with it.

Verses 11–15

Here the apostle informs us what foundation he had laid at the bottom of all his labours among them — *even Jesus Christ, the chief corner-stone,* Eph. 2:20. Upon this foundation all the faithful ministers of Christ build. Upon this rock all the Christians found their hopes. Those that build their hopes of heaven on any other foundation build upon the sand. *Other foundation can no man lay besides what is laid — even Jesus Christ.* Note, The doctrine of our Saviour and his mediation is the principal doctrine of Christianity. It lies at the bottom, and is the foundation, of all the rest. Leave out this, and you lay waste all our comforts, and leave no foundation for our hopes as sinners. It is in Christ *only that God is reconciling a sinful world to himself,* 2 Co. 5:19. But of those that hold the foundation, and embrace the general doctrine of Christ's being the mediator between God and man, there are two sorts: —

I. Some build upon this foundation *gold, silver, and precious stones* (*v.* 12), namely, those who receive and propagate the pure truths of the gospel, who hold nothing but the *truth as it is in Jesus,* and preach nothing else. This is building well upon a good foundation, making all of apiece, when ministers not only depend upon Christ as the great prophet of the church, and take him for their guide and infallible teacher, but receive and spread the doctrines he taught, in their purity, without any corrupt mixtures, without adding or diminishing.

II. Others *build wood, hay, and stubble,* on this foundation; that is, though they adhere to the foundation, they depart from the mind of Christ in many particulars, substitute their own fancies and inventions in the room of his doctrines and institutions, and build upon the good foundation what will not abide the test when the day of trial shall come, and the fire must make it manifest, as wood, hay, and stubble, will not bear the trial by fire, but must be consumed in it. There is a time coming when a discovery will be made of what men have built on this foundation: *Every man's work shall be made manifest,* shall be laid open to view, to his own view and that of others. Some may, in the simplicity of their hearts, build wood and stubble on the good foundation, and know not, all the while, what they have been doing; but in the day of the Lord their own conduct shall appear to them in its proper light. Every man's work shall be made manifest to himself, and made manifest to others, both those that have been misled by him and those that have escaped his errors. Now we may be mistaken in ourselves and others; but there is a day coming that will cure all our mistakes, and show us ourselves, and show us our actions in the true light, without covering or disguise: *For the day shall declare it* (that is, every man's work), *because it shall be revealed by fire; and the fire shall try every man's work, of what sort it is, v.* 13. The day shall declare and make it manifest, the last day, the great day of trial; see *ch.* 4:5. Though some understand it of the time when the Jewish nation was destroyed and their constitution thereby abolished, when the superstructure which judaizing teachers would have raised on the Christian foundation was manifested to be no better than hay and stubble, that would not bear the trial. The expression carries in it a plain allusion to the refiner's art, in which the fire separates and distinguishes the dross from the gold and silver; as it also will silver and gold and precious stones, that will endure the fire, from wood and hay and stubble, that will be consumed in it. Note, There is a day coming that will as nicely distinguish one man from another, and one man's work from another's, as the fire distinguishes gold from dross, or metal that will bear the fire from other materials that will be consumed in it. In that day, 1. Some men's works will *abide the trial* — will be found standard. It will appear that they not only held the foundation, but that they built regularly and well upon it — that they laid on proper materials, and in due form and order. The foundation and the superstructure were all of a piece. The foundation-truths, and those that had a manifest connection with them, were taught together. It may not be so easy to discern this connection now, nor know what works will abide the trial then; but that day will make a full discovery. And such a builder shall not, cannot fail of a reward. He will have praise and honour in that day, and eternal recompence after it. Note, Fidelity in the ministers of Christ will meet with a full and ample reward in a future life. Those who spread true and pure religion in all the branches of it, and whose work will abide in the great day, shall receive a reward. And, Lord, how great! how much exceeding their deserts! 2. There are others *whose works shall be burnt* (*v.* 15), whose corrupt opinions and doctrines, or vain inventions and usages in the worship of God, shall be discovered, disowned, and rejected, in that day — shall be first manifested to be corrupt, and then disapproved of God and rejected. Note, The great day will pluck off all disguises, and make things appear as they are: *He whose work shall be burnt will suffer loss.* If he have built upon the right foundation wood and hay and stubble, he will suffer loss. His weakness and corruption will be the lessening of his glory, though he may in the general have been an honest and an upright Christian. This part of his work will be lost, turning no way to his advantage, though he himself may be saved. Observe, Those who hold the foundation of Christianity, though they build hay, wood, and stubble, upon it, may be saved. This may help to enlarge our charity. We should not reprobate men for their weakness: for nothing will damn men but wickedness. He shall be saved, *yet so as by fire,* saved out of the fire. He himself shall be snatched out of that flame which will consume his work. This intimates that it will be difficult for those that corrupt and deprave Christianity to be saved. God will have no mercy on their works, though he may pluck them as brands out of the burning. On this passage of scripture the papists found their doctrine of purgatory, which is certainly hay and stubble: a doctrine never originally fetched from scripture, but invented in barbarous ages, to feed the avarice and ambition of the clergy, at the cost of those who would rather part with their money than their lusts, for the salvation of their souls. It can have no countenance from this text, (1.) Because this is plainly meant of a figurative fire, not of a real one: for what real fire can consume religious rites or doctrines? (2.) Because this fire is to *try men's works, of what sort they are;* but purgatory-fire is not for trial, not to bring men's actions to the test, but to punish for them. They are supposed to be venial sins, not satisfied for in this life, for which satisfaction must be made by suffering the fire of purgatory. (3.) Because this fire is to *try every man's works,* those of Paul and Apollos, as well as those of others. Now, no papists will have the front to say apostles must have passed through purgatory fires.

Verses 16–17

Here the apostle resumes his argument and exhortation, founding it on his former allusion, *You are God's building, v.* 9, and here, *Know you not that you are the temple of God, and the Spirit of God dwelleth in you? If any man defile* (corrupt and destroy) *the temple of God, him shall God destroy* (the same word is in the original in both clauses); *for the temple of God is holy, which temple you are.* It looks from other parts of the epistle, where the apostle argues to the very same purport (see *ch.* 6:13–20), as if the false teachers among the Corinthians were not only loose livers, but taught licentious doctrines, and what was particularly fitted to the taste of this lewd city, on the head of fornication. Such doctrine was not to be reckoned among hay and stubble, which would be consumed while the person who laid them on the foundation escaped the burning; for it tended to corrupt, to pollute, and destroy the church, which was a building erected for God, and consecrated to him, and therefore should be kept pure and holy. Those who spread principles of this sort would provoke God to destroy them. Note, Those who spread loose principles, that have a direct tendency to pollute the church of God, and render it unholy and unclean, are likely to bring destruction on themselves. It may be understood also as an argument against their discord and factious strifes, division being the way to destruction. But what I have been mentioning seems to be the proper meaning of the passage: *Know you not that you are the temple of God, and that the Spirit of God dwelleth in you?* It may be understood of the church of Corinth collectively, or of every single believer among them; Christian churches are temples of God. He dwells among them by his Holy Spirit. *They are built together for a habitation of God through the Spirit,* Eph. 2:22. Every Christian is a living temple of the living God. God dwelt in the Jewish temple, took possession of it, and resided in it, by that glorious cloud that was the token of his presence with that people. So Christ by his Spirit dwells in all true believers. The temple was devoted and consecrated to God, and set apart from every common to a holy use, to the immediate service of God. So all Christians are separated from common uses, and set apart for God and his service. They are sacred to him — a very good argument this against all fleshly lusts, and all doctrines that give countenance to them. If we are the temples of God, we must do nothing that shall alienate ourselves from him, or corrupt and pollute ourselves, and thereby unfit ourselves for his use; and we must hearken to no doctrine nor doctor that would seduce us to any such practices. Note, Christians are holy by profession, and should be pure and clean both in heart and conversation. We should heartily abhor, and carefully avoid, what will defile God's temple, and prostitute what ought to be sacred to him.

Verses 18–20

Here he prescribes humility, and a modest opinion of themselves, for the remedy of the irregularities in the church of Corinth, the divisions and contests among them: *"Let no man deceive himself, v.* 18. Do not be led away from the truth and simplicity of the gospel by pretenders to science and eloquence, by a show of deep learning, or a flourish of words, by rabbis, orators, or philosophers." Note, We are in great danger of deceiving ourselves when we have too high an opinion of human wisdom and arts; plain and pure Christianity will be likely to be despised by those who can suit their doctrines to the corrupt taste of their hearers, and set them off with fine language, or support them with a show of deep and strong reasoning. But *he who seems to be wise must become a fool that he may be wise.* He must be sensible of his own ignorance, and lament it; he must distrust his own understanding, and not lean on it. To have a high opinion of our wisdom is but to flatter ourselves, and self-flattery is the very next step to self-deceit. The way to true wisdom is to sink our opinion of our own to a due level, and be willing to be taught of God. He must become a fool who would be truly and thoroughly wise. The person who resigns his own understanding, that he may follow the instruction of God, is in the way to true and everlasting wisdom. *The meek will he guide in judgment, the meek will he teach his way,* Ps. 25:9. He that has a low opinion of his own knowledge and powers will submit to better information; such a person may be informed and improved by revelation: but the proud man, conceited of his own wisdom and understanding, will undertake to correct even divine wisdom itself, and prefer his own shallow reasonings to the revelations of infallible truth and wisdom. Note, We must abase ourselves before God if we would be either truly wise or good: *For the wisdom of this world is foolishness with God, v.* 19. The wisdom which worldly men esteem (policy, philosophy, oratory) *is foolishness with God.* It is so in a way of comparison with his wisdom. *He chargeth his angels with folly* (Job 4:18), and much more the wisest among the children of men. *His understanding is infinite,* Ps. 147:5. There can be no more comparison between his wisdom and ours than between his power and being and ours. There is no common measure by which to compare finite and infinite. And much more is the wisdom of man foolishness with God when set in competition with his. How justly does he despise, how easily can he baffle and confound it! *He taketh the wise in their own craftiness* (Job 5:13), he catches them in their own nets, and entangles them in their own snares: he turns their most studies, plausible, and promising schemes against themselves, and ruins them by their own contrivance. Nay, *He knows the thoughts of the wise, that they are vain* (*v.* 20), that they are vanity, Ps. 94:11. Note, God has a perfect knowledge of the thoughts of men, the deepest thoughts of the wisest men, their most secret counsels and purposes: nothing is hidden from him, but *all things are naked and bare* before him, Heb. 4:13. And he knows them to be vanity. The thoughts of the wisest men in the world have a great mixture of vanity, of weakness and folly, in them; and before God their wisest and best thoughts are very vanity, compared, I mean, with his thoughts of things. And should not all this teach us modesty, diffidence in ourselves, and a deference to the wisdom of God, make us thankful for his revelations, and willing to be taught of God, and not be led away by specious pretences to human wisdom and skill, from the simplicity of Christ, or a regard to his heavenly doctrine? Note, He who would be wise indeed must learn of God, and not set his own wisdom up in competition with God's.

Verses 21–23

Here the apostle founds an exhortation against overvaluing their teachers on what he had just said, and on the consideration that they had an equal interest in all their ministers: *Therefore let no man glory in men* (*v.* 21) — forget that their ministers are men, or pay that deference to them that is due only to God, set them at the head of parties, have them in immoderate esteem and admiration, and servilely and implicitly follow their directions and submit to their dictates, and especially in contradiction to God and the truths taught by his Holy Spirit. Mankind are very apt to make the mercies of God cross their intentions. The ministry is a very useful and very gracious institution, and faithful ministers are a great blessing to any people; yet the folly and weakness of people may do much mischief by what is in itself a blessing. They may fall into factions, side with particular ministers, and set them at their head, glory in their leaders, and be carried by them they know not whither. The only way to avoid this mischief is to have a modest opinion of ourselves, a due sense of the common weakness of human understanding, and an entire deference to the wisdom of God speaking in his word. Ministers are not to be set up in competition with one another. All faithful ministers are serving one Lord and pursuing one purpose. They were appointed of Christ, for the common benefit of the church: *"Paul, and Apollos, and Cephas, are all yours.* One is not to be set up against another, but all are to be valued and used for your own spiritual benefit." Upon this occasion also he gives in an inventory of the church's possessions, the spiritual riches of a true believer: *"All is yours* — ministers of all ranks, ordinary and extraordinary. Nay the world itself is yours." Not that saints are proprietors of the world, but it stands for their sake, they have as much of it as Infinite Wisdom sees to be fit for them, and they have all they have with the divine blessing. *"Life is yours,* that you may have season and opportunity to prepare for the life of heaven; and *death is yours,* that you may go to the possession of it. It is the kind messenger that will fetch you to your Father's house. *Things present* are yours, for your support on the road; *things to come* are yours, to enrich and regale you for ever at your journey's end." Note, If we belong to Christ, and are true to him, all good belongs to us, and is sure to us. All is ours, time and eternity, earth and heaven, life and death. *We shall want no good thing,* Ps. 84:11. But it must be remembered, at the same time, *that we are Christ's,* the subjects of his kingdom, his property. He is Lord over us, and we must own his dominion, and cheerfully submit to his command and yield themselves to his pleasure, if we would have all things minister to our advantage. All things are ours, upon no other ground than our being Christ's. Out of him we are without just title or claim to any thing that is good. Note, Those that would be safe for time, and happy to eternity, must be Christ's. *And Christ is God's.* He is the Christ of God, anointed of God, and commissioned by him, to bear the office of a Mediator, and to act therein for the purposes of his glory. Note, All things are the believer's, that Christ might have honour in his great undertaking, and God in all might have the glory. God in Christ reconciling a sinful world to himself, and shedding abroad the riches of his grace on a reconciled world, is the sum and substance of the gospel.

CHAPTER 4

In this chapter the apostle, I. Directs them how to account of him and his fellow-ministers, and therein, tacitly at least, reproves them for their unworthy carriage towards him (*v.* 1–6). II. He cautions them against pride and self-elation, and hints at the many temptations they had to conceive too highly of themselves, and despise him and other apostles, because of the great diversity in their circumstances and condition (*v.* 7–13). III. He challenges their regard to him as their father in Christ (*v.* 14–16). IV. He tells them of his having sent Timothy to them, and of his own purpose to come to them shortly, however some among them had pleased themselves, and grown vain, upon the quite contrary expectation (*v.* 17 to the end).

Verses 1–6

Here, I. The apostle challenges the respect due to him on account of his character and office, in which many among them had at least very much failed: *Let a man so account of us as of the ministers of Christ, and stewards of the mysteries of God* (*v.* 1), though possibly others might have valued them too highly, by setting him up as the head of a party, and professing to be his disciples. In our opinion of ministers, as well as all other things, we should be careful to avoid extremes. Apostles themselves were, 1. Not to be overvalued, for they were ministers, not masters; stewards, not lords. They were servants of Christ, and no more, though they were servants of the highest rank, that had the care of his household, that were to provide food for the rest, and appoint and direct their work. Note, It is a very great abuse of their power, and highly criminal in common ministers, to lord it over their fellow-servants, and challenge authority over their faith or practice. For even apostles were but servants of Christ, employed in his work, and sent on his errand, and dispensers of the mysteries of God, or those truths which had been hidden from the world in ages and generations past. They had no authority to propagate their own fancies, but to spread Christian faith. 2. Apostles were not to be undervalued; for, though they were ministers, they were ministers of Christ. The character and dignity of their master put an honour on them. Though they are but stewards, they are not stewards of the common things of the world, but of divine mysteries. They had a great trust, and for that reason had an honourable office. They were stewards of God's household, high-stewards in his kingdom of grace. They did not set up for masters, but they deserved respect and esteem in this honourable service. Especially,

II. When they did their duty in it, and approved themselves faithful: *It is required in stewards that a man be found faithful* (*v.* 2), trustworthy. The stewards in Christ's family must appoint what he hath appointed. They must not set their fellow-servants to work for themselves. They must not require any thing from them without their Master's warrant. They must not feed them with the chaff of their own inventions, instead of the wholesome food of Christian doctrine and truth. They must teach what he hath commanded, and not the doctrines and commandments of men. They must be true to the interest of their Lord, and consult his honour. Note, The ministers of Christ should make it their hearty and continual endeavour to approve themselves trustworthy; and when they have the testimony of a good conscience, and the approbation of their Master, they must slight the opinions and censures of their fellow-servants: *But with me,* saith the apostle, *it is a small thing that I should be judged of you, or of man's judgment, v.* 3. Indeed, reputation and esteem among men are a good step towards usefulness in the ministry; and Paul's whole argument upon this head shows he had a just concern for his own reputation. But he that would make it his chief endeavour to please men would hardly approve himself a faithful servant of Christ, Gal. 1:10. He that would be faithful to Christ must despise the censures of men for his sake. He must look upon it as a very little thing (if his Lord approves him) what judgment men form of him. They may think very meanly or very hardly of him, while he is doing his duty; but it is not by their judgment that he must stand or fall. And happy is it for faithful ministers that they have a more just and candid judge than their fellow-servants; one who knows and pities their imperfections, though he has none of his own. It is better to *fall into the hands of God than into the hands of men,* 2 Sa. 24:14. The best of men are too apt to judge rashly, and harshly, and unjustly; but his judgment is always according to truth. It is a comfort that men are not to be our final judges. Nay, we are not thus to judge ourselves: *"Yea, I judge not myself. For though I know nothing by myself,* cannot charge myself with unfaithfulness, *yet I am not thereby justified,* this will not clear me of the charge; *but he that judgeth me is the Lord.* It is his judgment that must determine me. By his sentence I must abide. Such I am as he shall find and judge me to be." Note, It is not judging well of ourselves, justifying ourselves, that will prove us safe and happy. Nothing will do this but the acceptance and approbation of our sovereign Judge. *Not he that commendeth himself is approved, but he whom the Lord commendeth,* 2 Co. 10:18.

III. The apostle takes occasion hence to caution the Corinthians against censoriousness — the forward and severe judging of others: *Therefore judge nothing before the time, until the Lord come, v.* 5. It is judging out of season, and judging at an adventure. He is not to be understood of judging by persons in authority, within the verge of their office, nor of private judging concerning facts that are notorious; but of judging persons' future state, or the secret springs and principles of their actions, or about facts doubtful in themselves. To judge in these cases, and give decisive sentence, is to assume the seat of God and challenge his prerogative. Note, How bold a sinner is the forward and severe censurer! How ill-timed and arrogant are his censures! But there is one who will judge the censurer, and those he censures, without prejudice, passion, or partiality. And there is a time coming when men cannot fail judging aright concerning themselves and others, by following his judgment. This should make them now cautious of judging others, and careful in judging themselves. There is a time coming when *the Lord will bring to light the hidden things of darkness, and make manifest the counsels of the hearts* — deeds of darkness that are now done in secret, and all the secret inclinations, purposes, and intentions, of the hidden man of the heart. Note, There is a day coming that will dispel the darkness and lay open the face of the deep, will fetch men's secret sins into open day and discover the secrets of their hearts: *The day shall declare it.* The judge will bring these things to light. The Lord Jesus Christ will manifest the counsels of the heart, of all hearts. Note, The Lord Jesus Christ must have the knowledge of the counsels of the heart, else he could not make them manifest. This is a divine prerogative (Jer. 17:10), and yet it is what our Saviour challenges to himself in a very peculiar manner (Rev. 2:23): *All the churches shall know that I am HE who searcheth the reins and hearts, and I will give to every one of you according to your works.* Note, We should be very careful how we censure others, when we have to do with a Judge from whom we cannot conceal ourselves. Others do not lie open to our notice, but we lie all open to his: and, when he shall come to judge, *every man shall have praise of God. Every man,* that is, every one qualified for it, every one who has done well. Though none of God's servants can deserve any thing from him, though there be much that is blamable even in their best services, yet shall their fidelity be commended and crowned by him; and should they be condemned, reproached, or vilified, by their fellow-servants, he will roll away all such unjust censures and reproaches, and show them in their own amiable light. Note, Christians may well be patient under unjust censures, when they know such a day as this is coming, especially when they have their consciences testifying to their integrity. But how fearful should they be of loading any with reproaches now whom their common Judge shall hereafter commend.

IV. The apostle here lets us into the reason why he had used his own name and that of Apollos in this discourse of his. He had done *it in a figure,* and *he had done it for their sakes.* He chose rather to mention his own name, and the name of a faithful fellow-labourer, than the names of any heads of factions among them, that hereby he might avoid what would provoke, and so procure for his advice the greater regard. Note, Ministers should use prudence in their advices and admonitions, but especially in their reproofs, lest they lose their end. The advice the apostle would by this means inculcate was *that they might learn not to think of men above what is written* (above what he had been writing), *nor be puffed up for one against another* (*v.* 6). Apostles were not to be esteemed other than planters or waterers in God's husbandry, master-builders in his building, stewards of his mysteries, and servants of Christ. And common ministers cannot bear these characters in the same sense that apostles did. Note, We must be very careful not to transfer the honour and authority of the Master to his servant. *We must call no man Master on earth; one is our Master, even Christ,* Mt. 23:8, 10. We must not think of them above what is written. Note, The word of God is the best rule by which to judge concerning men. And again, judging rightly concerning men, and not judging more highly of them than is fit, is one way to prevent quarrels and contentions in the churches. Pride commonly lies at the bottom of these quarrels. Self-conceit contributes very much to our immoderate esteem of our teachers, as well as ourselves. Our commendation of our own taste and judgment commonly goes along with our unreasonable applause, and always with a factious adherence to one teacher, in opposition to others that may be equally faithful and well qualified. But to think modestly of ourselves, and not above what is written of our teachers, is the most effectual means to prevent quarrels and contests, sidings and parties, in the church. We shall not be puffed up for one against another if we remember that they are all instruments employed by God in his husbandry and building, and endowed by him with their various talents and qualifications.

Verses 7–13

Here the apostle improves the foregoing hint to a caution against pride and self-conceit, and sets forth the temptations the Corinthians had to despise him, from the difference of their circumstances.

I. He cautions them against pride and self-conceit by this consideration, that all the distinction made among them was owing to God: *Who maketh thee to differ? And what hast thou that thou didst not receive? v.* 7. Here the apostle turns his discourse to the ministers who set themselves at the head of these factions, and did but too much encourage and abet the people in those feuds. What had they to glory in, when all their peculiar gifts were from God? They had received them, and could not glory in them as their own, without wronging God. At the time when they reflected on them to feed their vanity, they should have considered them as so many debts and obligations to divine bounty and grace. But it may be taken as a general maxim: We have no reason to be proud of our attainments, enjoyments, or performances; all that we have, or are, or do, that is good, is owing to the free and rich grace of God. Boasting is for ever excluded. There is nothing we have that we can properly call our own: all is received from God. It is foolish in us therefore, and injurious to him, to boast of it; those who receive all should be proud of nothing, Ps. 115:1. Beggars and dependents may glory in their supports; but to glory in themselves is to be proud at once of meanness, impotence, and want. Note, Due attention to our obligations to divine grace would cure us of arrogance and self-conceit.

II. He presses the duty of humility upon them by a very smart irony, or at least reproves them for their pride and self-conceit: *"You are full, you are rich, you have reigned as kings without us.* You have not only a sufficiency, but an affluence, of spiritual gifts; nay, you can make them the matter of your glory *without us,* that is, in my absence, and without having any need of me." There is a very elegant gradation from sufficiency to wealth, and thence to royalty, to intimate how much the Corinthians were elated by the abundance of their wisdom and spiritual gifts, which was a humour that prevailed among them while the apostle was away from them, and made them forget what an interest he had in all. See how apt pride is to overrate benefits and overlook the benefactor, to swell upon its possessions and forget from whom they come; nay, it is apt to behold them in a magnifying-glass: *"You have reigned as kings,"* says the apostle, "that is, in your own conceit; and *I would to God you did reign, that we also might reign with you.* I wish you had as much of the true glory of a Christian church upon you as you arrogate to yourselves. I should come in then for a share of the honour: *I should reign with you:* I should not be overlooked by you as now I am, but valued and regarded as a minister of Christ, and a very useful instrument among you." Note, Those do not commonly know themselves best who think best of themselves, who have the highest opinion of themselves. The Corinthians might have reigned, and the apostle with them, if they had not been blown up with an imaginary royalty. Note, Pride is a great prejudice to our improvement. He is stopped from growing wiser or better who thinks himself at the height; not only full, but rich, nay, a king.

III. He comes to set forth his own circumstances and those of the other apostles, and compares them with theirs. 1. To set forth the case of the apostles: *For I think it hath pleased God to set forth us the apostles last, as it were appointed to death. For we are made a spectacle to the world, and to angels, and to men.* Paul and his fellow-apostles were exposed to great hardships. Never were any men in this world so hunted and worried. They carried their lives in their hands: *God hath set forth us the apostles last, as it were appointed to death, v.* 9. An allusion is made to some of the bloody spectacles in the Roman amphitheatres, where men were exposed to fight with wild beasts, or to cut one another to pieces, to make diversion for the populace, where the victor did not escape with his life, though he should destroy his adversary, but was only reserved for another combat, and must be devoured or cut in pieces at last; so that such wretched criminals (for they were ordinarily condemned persons that were thus exposed) might very properly be called *epithanatioi — persons devoted or appointed to death.* They are said to be set forth last, because the meridian gladiators, those who combated one another in the after-part of the day, were most exposed, being obliged to fight naked; so that (as Seneca says, *epist.* 7) this was perfect butchery, and those exposed to beasts in the morning were treated mercifully in comparison with these. The general meaning is that the apostles were exposed to continual danger of death, and that of the worst kinds, in the faithful discharge of their office. God had set them forth, brought them into view, as the Roman emperors brought their combatants into the arena, the place of show, though not for the same purposes. They did it to please the populace, and humour their own vanity, and sometimes a much worse principle. The apostles were shown to manifest the power of divine grace, to confirm the truth of their mission and doctrine, and to propagate religion in the world. These were ends worthy of God — noble views, fit to animate them to the combat. But they had like difficulties to encounter, and were in a manner as much exposed as these miserable Roman criminals. Note, The office of an apostle was, as an honourable, so a hard and hazardous one: *"For we are made a spectacle to the world, and to angels, and to men, v.* 9. A *show.* We are brought into the theatre, brought out to the public view of the world. Angels and men are witnesses to our persecutions, sufferings, patience, and magnanimity. They all see that we suffer for our fidelity to Christ, and how we suffer; how great and imminent are our dangers, and how bravely we encounter them; how sharp our sufferings, and how patiently we endure them, by the power of divine grace and our Christian principles. Ours is hard work, but honourable; it is hazardous, but glorious. God will have honour from us, religion will be credited by us. The world cannot but see and wonder at our undaunted resolution, our invincible patience and constancy." And how contentedly could they be exposed, both to sufferings and scorn, for the honour of their Master! Note, The faithful ministers and disciples of Christ should contentedly undergo any thing for his sake and honour. 2. He compares his own case with that of the Corinthians: *"We are fools for Christ's sake, but you are wise in Christ; we are weak, but you are strong; you are honourable, but we are despised, v.* 10. *We are fools for Christ's sake;* such in common account, and we are well content to be so accounted. We can pass for fools in the world, and be despised as such, so that the wisdom of God and the honour of the gospel may by this means be secured and displayed." Note, Faithful ministers can bear being despised, so that the wisdom of God and the power of his grace be thereby displayed. *"But you are wise in Christ.* You have the fame of being wise and learned Christians, and you do not a little value yourselves upon it. We are under disgrace for delivering the plain truths of the gospel, and in as plain a manner: you are in reputation for your eloquence and human wisdom, which among many make you pass for wise men in Christ. *We are weak, but you are strong.* We are suffering for Christ's sake" (so being weak plainly signifies, 2 Co. 12:10), "when you are in easy and flourishing circumstances." Note, All Christians are not alike exposed. Some suffer greater hardships than others who are yet engaged in the same warfare. The standard-bearers in an army are most struck at. So ministers in a time of persecution are commonly the first and greatest sufferers. Or else, "We pass upon the world for persons of but mean endowments, mere striplings in Christianity; but you look upon yourselves, and are looked upon by others, as men, as those of a much more advanced growth and confirmed strength." Note, Those are not always the greatest proficients in Christianity who think thus of themselves, or pass for such upon others. It is but too easy and common for self-love to commit such a mistake. The Corinthians may think themselves, and be esteemed by others, as wiser and stronger men in Christ than the apostles themselves. But O! how gross is the mistake!

IV. He enters into some particularities of their sufferings: *Even to this present hour;* that is, after all the service we have been doing among you and other churches, *we hunger and thirst, and are naked, and are buffeted, and have no certain dwelling-place, and labour, working with our own hands, v.* 11, 12. Nay, they were *made as the filth of the world, and the off-scouring of all things, v.* 13. They were forced to labour with their own hands to get subsistence, and had so much, and so much greater, business to mind, that they could not attend enough to this, to get a comfortable livelihood, but were exposed to hunger, thirst, and nakedness — many times wanted meat, and drink, and clothes. They were driven about the world, without having any fixed abode, any settled habitation. Poor circumstances indeed, for the prime ministers of our Saviour's kingdom to have no house nor home, and to be destitute of food and raiment! But yet no poorer than his who had not *where to lay his head,* Lu. 9:58. But O glorious charity and devotion, that would carry them through all these hardships! How ardently did they love God, how vehemently did they thirst for the salvation of souls! Theirs was voluntary, it was pleasing poverty. They thought they had a rich amends for all the outward good things they wanted, if they might but serve Christ and save souls. Nay, though they *were made the filth of the world, and the off-scouring of all things.* They were treated as men not fit to live, *perikatharmata.* It is reasonably thought by the critics that an allusion is here made to a common custom of many heathen nations, to offer men in sacrifice in a time of pestilence, or other like grievous calamity. These were ordinarily the vilest of men, persons of the lowest rank and worst character. Thus, in the first ages, Christians were counted the source of all public calamities, and were sacrificed to the people's rage, if not to appease their angry deities. And apostles could not meet with better usage. They suffered in their persons and characters as the very worst and vilest men, as the most proper to make such a sacrifice: or else as the very dirt of the world, that was to be swept away: nay, as the *off-scouring of all things,* the dross, the filings of all things. They were the common-sewer into which all the reproaches of the world were to be poured. To be the off-scouring of any thing is bad, but what is it to be the off-scouring of all things! How much did the apostles resemble their Master, *and fill up that which was behind of his afflictions, for his body's sake, which is the church!* Col. 1:24. They suffered for him, and they suffered after his example. Thus poor and despised was he in his life and ministry. And every one who would be faithful in Christ Jesus must prepare for the same poverty and contempt. Note, Those may be very dear to God, and honourable in his esteem, whom men may think unworthy to live, and use and scorn as the very dirt and refuse of the world. *God seeth not as man seeth,* 1 Sa. 16:7.

V. We have here the apostles' behaviour under all; and the return they made for this mal-treatment: *Being reviled, we bless; being persecuted, we suffer it; being defamed, we entreat, v.* 12, 13. They returned blessings for reproaches, and entreaties and kind exhortations for the rudest slanders and defamation, and were patient under the sharpest persecutions. Note, The disciples of Christ, and especially his ministers, should hold fast their integrity, and keep a good conscience, whatever opposition of hardships they meet with from the world. Whatever they suffer from men, they must follow the example, and fulfil the will and precepts, of their Lord. They must be content, with him and for him, to be despised and abused.

Verses 14–16

Here Paul challenges their regard to him as their father. He tells them, 1. That what he had written was not for their reproach, but admonition; not with the gall of an enemy, but the bowels of a father (*v.* 14): *I write not to shame you, but as my beloved children I warn you.* Note, In reproving for sin, we should have a tender regard to the reputation, as well as the reformation, of the sinner. We should aim to distinguish between them and their sins, and take care not to discover any spite against them ourselves, nor expose them to contempt and reproach in the world. Reproofs that expose commonly do but exasperate, when those that kindly and affectionately warn are likely to reform. When the affections of a father mingle with the admonitions of a minister, it is to be hoped that they may at once melt and mend; but to lash like an enemy or executioner will provoke and render obstinate. To expose to open shame is but the way to render shameless. 2. He shows them upon what foundation he claimed paternal relation to them, and called them his sons. They might have other pedagogues or instructors, but he was their father; *for in Christ Jesus he had begotten them by the gospel, v.* 15. They were made Christians by his ministry. He had laid the foundation of a church among them. Others could only build upon it. Whatever other teachers they had, he was their spiritual father. He first brought them off from pagan idolatry to the faith of the gospel and the worship of the true and living God. He was the instrument of their new birth, and therefore claimed the relation of a father to them, and felt the bowels of a father towards them. Note, There commonly is, and always ought to be, an endeared affection between faithful ministers and those they beget in Christ Jesus through the gospel. They should love like parents and children. 3. We have here the special advice he urges on them: *Wherefore I beseech you be you followers of me, v.* 16. This he elsewhere explains and limits (*ch.* 11:1): *"Be you followers of me, as I also am of Christ.* Follow me as far as I follow Christ. Come up as close as you can to my example in those instances wherein I endeavour to copy after his pattern. Be my disciples, as far as I manifest myself to be a faithful minister and disciple of Christ, and no further. I would not have you be my disciples, but his. But I hope I have approved myself a faithful steward of the mysteries of Christ, and a faithful servant of my master Christ; so far follow me, and tread in my steps." Note, Ministers should so live that their people may take pattern from them, and live after their copy. They should guide them by their lives as well as their lips, go before them in the way to heaven, and not content themselves with pointing it out. Note, As ministers are to set a pattern, others must take it. They should follow them as far as they are satisfied that they follow Christ in faith and practice.

Verses 17–21

Here, I. He tells them of his having sent Timothy to them, *to bring them into remembrance of his ways in Christ, as he taught every where in every church* (*v.* 17) — to remind them of his ways in Christ, to refresh their memory as to his preaching and practice, what he taught, and how he lived among them. Note, Those who have had ever so good teaching are apt to forget, and need to have their memories refreshed. The same truth, taught over again, if it give no new light, may make new and quicker impression. He also lets them know that *his teaching was the same every where, and in every church.* He had not one doctrine for one place and people, and another for another. He kept close to his instructions. What *he received of the Lord, that he delivered, ch.* 11:23. This was the gospel revelation, which was the equal concern of all men, and did not very from itself. He therefore taught the same things in every church, and lived after the same manner in all times and places. Note, The truth of Christ is one and invariable. What one apostle taught every one taught. What one apostle taught at one time and in one place, he taught at all times and in all places. Christians may mistake and differ in their apprehensions, but Christ and Christian truth *are the same yesterday, today, and for ever,* Heb. 13:8. To render their regard to Timothy the greater, he gives them his character. He was *his beloved son,* a spiritual child of his, as well as themselves. Note, Spiritual brotherhood should engage affection as well as what is common and natural. The children of one father should have one heart. But he adds, *"He is faithful in the Lord* — trustworthy, as one that feared the Lord. He will be faithful in the particular office he has now received of the Lord, the particular errand on which he comes; not only from me, but from Christ. He knows what I have taught, and what my conversation has been in all places, and, you may depend upon it, he will make a faithful report." Note, It is a great commendation of any minister that he is faithful in the Lord, faithful to his soul, to his light, to his trust from God; this must go a great way in procuring regard to his message with those that fear God.

II. He rebukes the vanity of those who imagined he would not come to them, by letting them know this was his purpose, though he had sent Timothy: *"I will come to you shortly,* though some of you are so vain as to think I will not." But he adds, *if the Lord will.* It seems, as to the common events of life, apostles knew no more than other men, nor were they in these points under inspiration. For, had the apostle certainly known the mind of God in this matter, he would not have expressed himself with this certainty. But he sets a good example to us in it. Note, All our purposes must be formed with a dependence on Providence, and a reserve for the overruling purposes of God. *If the Lord will, we shall live, and do this and that,* Jam. 4:15.

III. He lets them know what would follow upon his coming to them: *I will know, not the speech of those that are puffed up, but the power, v.* 19. He would bring the great pretenders among them to a trial, would know what they were, not by their rhetoric or philosophy, but by the authority and efficacy of what they taught, whether they could confirm it by miraculous operations, and whether it was accompanied with divine influences and saving effects on the minds of men. For, adds he, *the kingdom of God is not in word, but in power.* It is not set up, nor propagated, nor established, in the hearts of men, by plausible reasonings nor florid discourses, but by the external power of the Holy Spirit in miraculous operations at first, and the powerful influence of divine truth on the minds and manners of men. Note, It is a good way in the general to judge of a preacher's doctrine, to see whether the effects of it upon men's hearts to be truly divine. That is most likely to come from God which in its own nature is most fit, and in event is found to produce most likeness to God, to spread piety and virtue, to change men's hearts and mend their manners.

IV. He puts it to their choice how he should come among them, *whether with a rod or in love and the spirit of meekness* (*v.* 21); that is, according as they were they would find him. If they continued perverse among themselves and with him, it would be necessary to come with a rod; that is, to exert his apostolical power in chastising them, by making some examples, and inflicting some diseases and corporal punishments, or by other censures for their faults. Note, Stubborn offenders must be used with severity. In families, in Christian communities, paternal pity and tenderness, Christian love and compassion, will sometimes force the use of the rod. But this is far from being desirable, if it may be prevented. And therefore the apostle adds that it was in their own option whether he should come with a rod or in a quite different disposition and manner: *Or in love and the spirit of meekness.* As much as if he had said, "Take warning, cease your unchristian feuds, rectify the abuses among you, and return to your duty, and you shall find me as gentle and benign as you can with. It will be a force upon my inclination to proceed with severity. I had rather come and display the tenderness of a father among you than assert his authority. Do but your duty, and you have no reason to avoid my presence." Note, It is a happy temper in a minister to have the spirit of love and meekness predominant, and yet to maintain his just authority.

CHAPTER 5

In this chapter the apostle, I. Blames them for their indulgence in the case of the incestuous person, and orders him to be excommunicated, and delivered to Satan (*v.* 1–6). II. He exhorts them to Christian purity, by purging out the old leaven (*v.* 7, 8). And, III. Directs them to shun even the common conversation of Christians who were guilty of any notorious and flagitious wickedness (*v.* 9 to the end).

Verses 1–6

Here the apostle states the case; and,

I. Lets them know what was the common or general report concerning them, that one of their community was guilty of fornication, *v.* 1. It was told in all places, to their dishonour, and the reproach of Christians. And it was the more reproachful because it could not be denied. Note, The heinous sins of professed Christians are quickly noted and noised abroad. We should walk circumspectly, for many eyes are upon us, and many mouths will be opened against us if we fall into any scandalous practice. This was not a common instance of fornication, but *such as was not so much as named among the Gentiles, that a man should have his father's wife* — either marry her while his father was alive, or keep her as his concubine, either when he was dead or while he was alive. In either of these cases, his criminal conversation with her might be called *fornication;* but had his father been dead, and he, after his decease, married to her, it had been incest still, but neither fornication nor adultery in the strictest sense. But to marry her, or keep her as a concubine, while his father was alive, though he had repudiated her, or she had deserted him, whether she were his own mother or not, was incestuous fornication: *Scelus incredibile* (as Cicero calls it), *et prater unum in omni vitâ inauditum* (Orat. pro Cluent.), when a woman had caused her daughter to be put away, and was married to her husband. *Incredible wickedness!* says the orator; *such I never heard of in all my life besides.* Not that there were no such instances of incestuous marriages among the heathens; but, whenever they happened, they gave a shock to every man of virtue and probity among them. They could not think of them without horror, nor mention them without dislike and detestation. Yet such a horrible wickedness was committed by one in the church of Corinth, and, as is probable, a leader of one of the factions among them, a principal man. Note, The best churches are, in this state of imperfection, liable to very great corruptions. Is it any wonder when so horrible a practice was tolerated in an apostolical church, a church planted by the great apostle of the Gentiles?

II. He greatly blames them for their own conduct hereupon: *They were puffed up* (*v.* 2), *they gloried,* 1. Perhaps on account of this very scandalous person. He might be a man of great eloquence, of deep science, and for this reason very greatly esteemed, and followed, and cried up, by many among them. They were proud that they had such a leader. Instead of mourning for his fall, and their own reproach upon his account, and renouncing him and removing him from the society, they continued to applaud him and pride themselves in him. Note, Pride or self-esteem often lies at the bottom of our immoderate esteem of others, and this makes us as blind to their faults as to our own. It is true humility that will bring a man to a sight and acknowledgement of his errors. The proud man either wholly overlooks or artfully disguises his faults, or endeavours to transform his blemishes into beauties. Those of the Corinthians that were admirers of the incestuous person's gifts could overlook or extenuate his horrid practices. Or else, 2. It may intimate to us that some of the opposite party were puffed up. They were proud of their own standing, and trampled upon him that fell. Note, It is a very wicked thing to glory over the miscarriages and sins of others. We should lay them to heart, and mourn for them, not be puffed up with them. Probably this was one effect of the divisions among them. The opposite party made their advantage of this scandalous lapse, and were glad of the opportunity. Note, It is a sad consequence of divisions among Christians that it makes them apt to rejoice in iniquity. The sins of others should be our sorrow. Nay, churches should mourn for the scandalous behaviour of particular members, and, if they be incorrigible, should remove them. He that had done this wicked deed should have been taken away from among them.

III. We have the apostle's direction to them how they should now proceed with this scandalous sinner. He would have him excommunicated and delivered to Satan (*v.* 3–5); *as absent in body, yet present in spirit, he had judged already as if he had been present;* that is, he had, by revelation and the miraculous gift of discerning vouchsafed him by the Spirit, as perfect a knowledge of the case, and had hereupon come to the following determination, not without special authority from the Holy Spirit. He says this to let them know that, though he was at a distance, he did not pass an unrighteous sentence, nor judge without having as full cognizance of the case as if he had been on the spot. Note, Those who would appear righteous judges to the world will take care to inform them that they do not pass sentence without full proof and evidence. The apostle adds, *him who hath so done this deed.* The fact was not only heinously evil in itself, and horrible to the heathens, but there were some particular circumstances that greatly aggravated the offence. He had so committed the evil as to heighten the guilt by the manner of doing it. Perhaps he was a minister, a teacher, or a principal man among them. By this means the church and their profession were more reproached. Note, In dealing with scandalous sinners, not only are they to be charged with the fact, but the aggravating circumstances of it. Paul had judged that *he should be delivered to Satan* (*v.* 5), and this was to be done *in the name of Christ,* with the power of Christ, and in a full assembly, where the apostle would be also present in spirit, or by his spiritual gift of discerning at a distance. Some think that this is to be understood of a mere ordinary excommunication, and that delivering him to Satan for the destruction of the flesh is only meant of disowning him, and casting him out of the church, that by this means he might be brought to repentance, and his flesh might be mortified. Christ and Satan divide the world: and those that live in sin, when they profess relation to Christ, belong to another master, and by excommunication should be delivered up to him; and this in the name of Christ. Note, Church-censures are Christ's ordinances, and should be dispensed in his name. It was to be done also *when they were gathered together,* in full assembly. The more public the more solemn, and the more solemn the more likely to have a good effect on the offender. Note, Church-censures on notorious and incorrigible sinners should be passed with great solemnity. Those who sin in this manner *are to be rebuked before all, that all may fear,* 1 Tim. 5:20. Others think the apostle is not to be understood of mere excommunication, but of a miraculous power or authority they had of delivering a scandalous sinner into the power of Satan, to have bodily diseases inflicted, and to be tormented by him with bodily pains, which is the meaning of the *destruction of the flesh.* In this sense the destruction of the flesh has been a happy occasion of the salvation of the spirit. It is probable that this was a mixed case. It was an extraordinary instance: and the church was to proceed against him by just censure; the apostle, when they did so, put forth an act of extraordinary power, and gave him up to Satan, nor for his destruction, but for his deliverance, at least for the destruction of the flesh, that the soul might be saved. Note, The great end of church-censures is the good of those who fall under them, their spiritual and eternal good. It is that their spirit may be saved in the day of the Lord Jesus, *v.* 5. Yet it is not merely a regard to their benefit that is to be had in proceeding against them. For,

IV. He hints the danger of contagion from this example: *Your glorying is not good. Know you not that a little leaven leaveneth the whole lump?* The bad example of a man in rank and reputation is very mischievous, spreads the contagion far and wide. It did so, probably, in this very church and case: see 2 Co. 12:21. They could not be ignorant of this. The experience of the whole world was for it; *one scabbed sheep infects a whole flock.* A little heaven will quickly spread the ferment through a great lump. Note, Concern for their purity and preservation should engage Christian churches to remove gross and scandalous sinners.

Verses 7–8

Here the apostle exhorts them to purity, by purging out the old leaven. In this observe,

I. The advice itself, addressed either, 1. To the church in general; and so purging out the old leaven, that they might be a new lump, refers to the *putting away from themselves that wicked person, v.* 13. Note, Christian churches should be pure and holy, and not bear such corrupt and scandalous members. They are to be unleavened, and should endure no such heterogeneous mixture to sour and corrupt them. Or, 2. To each particular member of the church. And so it implies that they should purge themselves from all impurity of heart and life, especially from this kind of wickedness, to which the Corinthians were addicted to a proverb. See the *argument* at the beginning. This old leaven was in a particular manner to be purged out, that they might become a new lump. Note, Christians should be careful to keep themselves clean, as well as purge polluted members out of their society. And they should especially avoid the sins to which they themselves were once most addicted, and the reigning vices of the places and the people where they live. They were also to purge themselves from malice and wickedness — all ill-will and mischievous subtlety. This is leaven that sours the mind to a great degree. It is not improbable that this was intended as a check to some who gloried in the scandalous behaviour of the offender, both out of pride and pique. Note, Christians should be careful to keep free from malice and mischief. Love is the very essence and life of the Christian religion. It is the fairest image of God, *for God is love* (1 Jn. 4:16), and therefore it is no wonder if it be the greatest beauty and ornament of a Christian. But malice is murder in its principles: He that hates his brother is a murderer (1 Jn. 3:15), he bears the image and proclaims him the offspring of him *who was a murderer from the beginning,* Jn. 8:44. How hateful should every thing be to a Christian that looks like malice and mischief.

II. The reason with which this advice is enforced: *For Christ our passover is sacrificed for us, v.* 7. This is the great doctrine of the gospel. The Jews, after they had killed the passover, kept the feast of unleavened bread. So must we; not for seven days only, but all our days. We should die with our Saviour to sin, be planted into the likeness of his death by mortifying sin, and into the likeness of his resurrection by rising again to newness of life, and that internal and external. We must have new hearts and new lives. Note, The whole life of a Christian must be a feast of unleavened bread. His common conversation and his religious performances must be holy. *He must purge out the old leaven, and keep the feast of unleavened bread of sincerity and truth.* He must be without guilt in his conduct towards God and man. And the more there is of sincerity in our own profession, the less shall we censure that of others. Note, On the whole, The sacrifice of our Redeemer is the strongest argument with a gracious heart for purity and sincerity. How sincere a regard did he show to our welfare, in dying for us! and how terrible a proof was his death of the detestable nature of sin, and God's displeasure against it! Heinous evil, that could not be expiated but with the blood of the Son of God! And shall a Christian love the murderer of his Lord? God forbid.

Verses 9–13

Here the apostle advises them to shun the company and converse of scandalous professors. Consider,

I. The advice itself: *I wrote to you in a letter not to company with fornicators, v.* 9. Some think this was an epistle written to them before, which is lost. Yet we have lost nothing by it, the Christian revelation being entire in those books of scripture which have come down to us, which are all that were intended by God for the general use of Christians, or he could and would in his providence have preserved more of the writings of inspired men. Some think it is to be understood of this very epistle, that he had written this advice before he had full information of their whole case, but thought it needful now to be more particular. And therefore on this occasion he tells them that if any man called a brother, any one professing Christianity, and being a member of a Christian church, were *a fornicator, or covetous, or an idolater, or a railer,* that they should not *keep company with him, nor so much as eat with such a one.* They were to avoid all familiarity with him; they were to have no commerce with him; they were to have no commerce with him: but, that they might shame him, and bring him to repentance, must disclaim and shun him. Note, Christians are to avoid the familiar conversation of fellow-christians that are notoriously wicked, and under just censure for their flagitious practices. Such disgrace the Christian name. They may call themselves *brethren in Christ,* but they are not Christian brethren. They are only fit companions for the brethren in iniquity; and to such company they should be left, till they *mend their ways and doings.*

II. How he limits this advice. He does not forbid the Christians the like commerce with scandalously wicked heathens. He does not forbid their eating nor conversing with the *fornicators of this world,* etc. They know no better. They profess no better. The gods they serve, and the worship they render to many of them, countenance such wickedness. *"You must needs go out of the world* if you will have no conversation with such men. Your Gentile neighbours are generally vicious and profane; and it is impossible, as long as you are in the world, and have any worldly business to do, but you must fall into their company. This cannot be wholly avoided." Note, Christians may and ought to testify more respect to loose worldlings than to loose Christians. This seems a paradox. Why should we shun the company of a profane or loose Christian, rather than that of a profane or loose heathen?

III. The reason of this limitation is here assigned. It is impossible the one should be avoided. Christians must have gone out of the world to avoid the company of loose heathens. But this was impossible, as long as they had business in the world. While they are minding their duty, and doing their proper business, God can and will preserve them from contagion. Besides, they carry an antidote against the infection of their bad example, and are naturally upon their guard. They are apt to have a horror at their wicked practices. But the dread of sin wears off by familiar converse with wicked Christians. Our own safety and preservation are a reason of this difference. But, besides, heathens were such as Christians had nothing to do to judge and censure, and avoid upon a censure passed; for *they are without* (*v.* 12), and must be left to *God's judgment, v.* 13. But, as to members of the church, they are within, are professedly bound by the laws and rules of Christianity, and not only liable to the judgment of God, but to the censures of those who are set over them, and the fellow-members of the same body, when they transgress those rules. Every Christian is bound to judge them unfit for communion and familiar converse. They are to be punished, by having this mark of disgrace put upon them, that they may be shamed, and, if possible, reclaimed thereby: and the more because the sins of such much more dishonour God than the sins of the openly wicked and profane can do. The church therefore is obliged to clear herself from all confederacy with them, or connivance at them, and to bear testimony against their wicked practices. Note, Though the church has nothing to do with those without, it must endeavour to keep clear of the guilt and reproach of those within.

IV. How he applies the argument to the case before him: *"Therefore put away from among yourselves that wicked person, v.* 13. Cast him out of your fellowship, and avoid his conversation."

CHAPTER 6

In this chapter the apostle, I. Reproves them for going to law with one another about small matters, and bringing the cause before heathen judges (*v.* 1–8). II. He takes occasion hence to warn them against many gross sins, to which they had been formerly addicted (*v.* 9–11). III. And, having cautioned them against the abuse of their liberty, he vehemently dehorts them from fornication, by various arguments (*v.* 12 to the end).

Verses 1–8

Here the apostle reproves them for going to law with one another before heathen judges for little matters; and therein blames all *vexatious law-suits.* In the previous chapter he had directed them to punish heinous sins among themselves by church-censures. Here he directs them to determine controversies with one another by church-counsel and advice, concerning which observe,

I. The fault he blames them for: it was going to law. Not but that *the law is good, if a man use it lawfully.* But, 1. *Brother went to law with brother* (*v.* 6), one member of the church with another. The near relation could not preserve peace and good understanding. The bonds of fraternal love were broken through. *And a brother offended,* as Solomon says, *is harder to be won than a strong city;* their contentions are like the bars of a castle, Prov. 18:19. Note, Christians should not contend with one another, for they are brethren. This, duly attended to, would prevent law-suits, and put an end to quarrels and litigations. 2. They brought the matter before the heathen magistrates: *they went to law before the unjust, not before the saints* (*v.* 1), brought the controversy before unbelievers (*v.* 6), and did not compose it among themselves, Christians and saints, at least in profession. This tended much to the reproach of Christianity. It published at once their folly and unpeaceableness; whereas they pretended to be the children of wisdom, and the followers of the Lamb, the meek and lowly Jesus, the *prince of peace.* And therefore, says the apostle, *"Dare any of you,* having a controversy with another, go to law, implead him, bring the matter to a hearing before the unjust?" Note, Christians should not dare to do any thing that tends to the reproach of their Christian name and profession. 3. Here is at least an intimation that they went to law for trivial matters, things of little value; for the apostle blames them that they did not suffer wrong rather than go to law (*v.* 7), which must be understood of matters not very important. In matters of great damage to ourselves or families, we may use lawful means to right ourselves. We are not bound to sit down and suffer the injury tamely, without stirring for our own relief; but, in matters of small consequence, it is better to put up with the wrong. Christians should be of a forgiving temper. And it is more for their ease and honour to suffer small injuries and inconveniences than seem to be contentious.

II. He lays before them the aggravations of their fault: *Do you not know that the saints shall judge the world* (*v.* 2), *shall judge angels? v.* 3. And are they unworthy *to judge the smallest matters, the things of this life?* It was a dishonour to their Christian character, a forgetting of their real dignity, as saints, for them to carry little matters, about the things of life, before heathen magistrates. When they were to judge the world, nay, to judge, it is unaccountable that they could not determine little controversies among one another. By judging the world and angels, some think, is to be understood, their being assessors to Christ in the great judgment-day; it being said of our Saviour's disciples that they should at that day *sit on twelve thrones, judging the twelve tribes of Israel,* Mt. 19:28. And elsewhere we read of our *Lord's coming with ten thousand of his saints to execute judgment on all,* etc., Jude 14, 15. *He will come to judgment with all his saints,* 1 Th. 3:13. They themselves are indeed to be judged (see Mt. 25:31–41), but they may first be acquitted, and then advanced to the bench, to approve and applaud the righteous judgment of Christ both on men and angels. In no other sense can they be judges. They are not partners in their Lord's commission, but they have the honour to sit by, and see his proceeding against the wicked world, and approve it. Others understand this judging of the world to be meant when the empire should become Christian. But it does not appear that the Corinthians had knowledge of the empire's becoming Christian; and, if they had, in what sense could Christian emperors be said to judge angels? Others understand it of their condemning the world by their faith and practice, and casting out evil angels by miraculous power, which was not confined to the first ages, nor to the apostles. The first sense seems to be most natural; and at the same time it gives the utmost force to the argument. "Shall Christians have the honour to sit with the sovereign Judge at the last day, whilst he passes judgment on sinful men and evil angels, and are they not worthy to judge of the trifles about which you contend before heathen magistrates? Cannot they make up your mutual differences? Why must you bring them before heathen judges? When you are to judge them, as it fit to appeal to their judicature? Must you, about *the affairs of this life, set those to judge who are of no esteem in the church?*" (so some read, and perhaps most properly, *v.* 4), *heathen* magistrates, *exouthenēmenous,* the *things that are not, ch.* 1:28. "Must those be called in to judge in your controversies of whom you ought to entertain so low an opinion? Is this not shameful?" *v.* 5. Some who read it as our translators make it an ironical speech: "If you have such controversies depending, set those to judge who are of least esteem among yourselves. The meanest of your own members are able surely to determine these disputes. Refer the matters in variance to any, rather than go to law about them before heathen judges. They are trifles not worth contending about, and may easily be decided, if you have first conquered your own spirits, and brought them into a truly Christian temper. *Bear and forbear,* and the men of meanest skill among you may end your quarrels. *I speak it to your shame,*" *v.* 5. Note, It is a shame that little quarrels should grow to such a head among Christians, that they cannot be determined by arbitration of the brethren.

III. He puts them on a method to remedy this fault. And this twofold: — 1. By referring it to some to make it up: *"Is it so that there is no wise man among you, no one able to judge between his brethren? v.* 5. You who value yourselves so much upon your wisdom and knowledge, who are so puffed up upon your extraordinary gifts and endowments, is there none among you fit for this office, none that has wisdom enough to judge in these differences? Must brethren quarrel, and the heathen magistrate judge, in a church so famous as yours for knowledge and wisdom? It is a reproach to you that quarrels should run so high, and none of your wise men interpose to prevent them." Note, Christians should never engage in law-suits till all other remedies have been tried in vain. Prudent Christians should prevent, if possible, their disputes, and not courts of judicature decide them, especially in matters of no great importance. 2. By suffering wrong rather than taking this method to right themselves: *It is utterly a fault among you to go to law in this matter:* it is always a fault of one side to go to law, except in a case where the title is indeed dubious, and there is a friendly agreement of both parties to refer it to the judgment of those learned in the law to decide it. And this is referring it, rather than contending about it, which is the thing the apostle here seems chiefly to condemn: *Should you not rather take wrong, rather suffer yourselves to be defrauded?* Note, A Christian should rather put up with a little injury than tease himself, and provoke others, by a litigious contest. The peace of his own mind, and the calm of his neighbourhood, are more worth than victory in such a contest, or reclaiming his own right, especially when the quarrel must be decided by those who are enemies to religion. But the apostle tells them they were so far from bearing injuries *that they actually did wrong, and defrauded, and that their brethren.* Note, It is utterly a fault to wrong and defraud any; but it is an aggravation of this fault to defraud our Christian brethren. The ties of mutual love ought to be stronger between them than between others. And *love worketh no ill to his neighbour,* Rom. 13:10. Those who love the brotherhood can never, under the influence of this principle, hurt or injure them.

Verses 9–11

Here he takes occasion to warn them against many heinous evils, to which they had been formerly addicted.

I. He puts it to them as a plain truth, of which they could not be ignorant, that such sinners should not inherit the kingdom of God. The meanest among them must know thus much, that *the unrighteous shall not inherit the kingdom of God* (*v.* 9), shall not be owned as true members of his church on earth, nor admitted as glorious members of the church in heaven. All unrighteousness is sin; and all reigning sin, nay, every actual sin committed deliberately, and not repented of, shuts out of the kingdom of heaven. He specifies several sorts of sins: against the first and second commandments, as *idolaters;* against the seventh, as *adulterers, fornicators, effeminate,* and *Sodomites;* against the eighth, as *thieves* and *extortioners,* that by force or fraud wrong their neighbours; against the ninth, as *revilers;* and against the tenth, as *covetous and drunkards,* as those who are in a fair way to break all the rest. Those who knew any thing of religion must know that heaven could never be intended for these. The scum of the earth are no ways fit to fill the heavenly mansions. Those who do the devil's work can never receive God's wages, at least no other than *death, the just wages of sin,* Rom. 6:23.

II. Yet he warns them against deceiving themselves: *Be not deceived.* Those who cannot but know the fore-mentioned truth are but too apt not to attend to it. Men are very much inclined to flatter themselves that *God is such a one as themselves,* and that they may live in sin and yet die in Christ, may lead the life of the devil's children and yet go to heaven with the children of God. But this is all a gross cheat. Note, It is very much the concern of mankind that they do not cheat themselves in the matters of their souls. We cannot hope to sow to the flesh and yet reap everlasting life.

III. He puts them in mind what a change the gospel and grace of God had made in them: *Such were some of you* (*v.* 11), such notorious sinners as he had been reckoning up. The Greek word is *tauta — such things* were some of you, very monsters rather than men. Note, Some that are eminently good after their conversion have been as remarkably wicked before. *Quantum mutatus ab illo! How glorious a change does grace make!* It changes the vilest of men into saints and the children of God. Such were some of you, but you are not what you were. *You are washed, you are sanctified, you are justified in the name of Christ, and by the Spirit of our God.* Note, The wickedness of men before conversion is no bar to their regeneration and reconciliation to God. The blood of Christ, and *the washing of regeneration,* can purge away all guilt and defilement. Here is a rhetorical change of the natural order: *You are sanctified, you are justified.* Sanctification is mentioned before justification: and yet the name of Christ, by which we are justified, is placed before the Spirit of God, by whom we are sanctified. Our justification is owing to the merit of Christ; our sanctification to the operation of the Spirit: but both go together. Note, None are cleansed from the guilt of sin, and reconciled to God through Christ, but those who are also sanctified by his Spirit. All who are made righteous in the sight of God are made holy by the grace of God.

Verses 12–20

The twelfth verse and former part of the thirteenth seem to relate to that early dispute among Christians about the distinction of meats, and yet to be prefatory to the caution that follows against fornication. The connection seems plain enough if we attend to the famous determination of the apostles, Acts 15, where the prohibition of certain foods was joined with that of fornication. Now some among the Corinthians seem to have imagined that they were as much at liberty in the point of fornication as of meats, especially because it was not a sin condemned by the laws of their country. They were ready to say, even in the case of fornication, *All things are lawful for me.* This pernicious conceit Paul here sets himself to oppose: he tells them that many things lawful in themselves were not expedient at certain times, and under particular circumstances; and Christians should not barely consider what is in itself lawful to be done, but what is fit for them to do, considering their profession, character, relations, and hopes: they should be very careful that by carrying this maxim too far they be not brought into bondage, either to a crafty deceiver or a carnal inclination. *All things are lawful for me,* says he, *but I will not be brought under the power of any, v.* 12. Even in lawful things, he would not be subject to the impositions of a usurped authority: so far was he from apprehending that in the things of God it was lawful for any power on earth to impose its own sentiments. Note, There is a liberty wherewith Christ has made us free, in which we must stand fast. But surely he would never carry this liberty so far as to put himself into the power of any bodily appetite. Though all meats were supposed lawful, he would not become a glutton nor a drunkard. And much less would he abuse the maxim of lawful liberty to countenance the sin of fornication, which, though it might be allowed by the Corinthian laws, was a trespass upon the law of nature, and utterly unbecoming a Christian. He would not abuse this maxim about eating and drinking to encourage any intemperance, nor indulge a carnal appetite: *"Though meats are for the belly and the belly for meats* (*v.* 13), though the belly was made to receive food, and food was originally ordained to fill the belly, yet if it be not convenient for me, and much more if it be inconvenient, and likely to enslave me, if I am in danger of being subjected to my belly and appetite, I will abstain. *But God shall destroy both it and them,* at least as to their mutual relation. There is a time coming when the human body will need no further recruits of food." Some of the ancients suppose that this is to be understood of abolishing the belly as well as the food; and that though the same body will be raised at the great day, yet not with all the same members, some being utterly unnecessary in a future state, as the belly for instance, when the man is never to hunger, nor thirst, nor eat, nor drink more. But, whether this be true or no, there is a time coming when the need and use of food shall be abolished. Note, The expectation we have of being without bodily appetites in a future life is a very good argument against being under their power in the present life. This seems to me the sense of the apostle's argument; and that this passage is plainly to be connected with his caution against fornication, though some make it a part of the former argument against litigious law-suits, especially before heathen magistrates and the enemies of true religion. These suppose that the apostle argues that though it may be lawful to claim our rights yet it is not always expedient, and it is utterly unfit for Christians to put themselves into the power of infidel judges, lawyers, and solicitors, on these accounts. But this connection seems not so natural. The transition to his arguments against fornication, as I have laid it, seems very natural: *But the body is not for fornication, but for the Lord, and the Lord for the body, v.* 13. Meats and the belly are for one another; not so fornication and the body.

I. The body is not for fornication, but for the Lord. This is the first argument he uses against this sin, for which the heathen inhabitants of Corinth were infamous, and the converts to Christianity retained too favourable an opinion of it. It is making things to cross their intention and use. The *body is not for fornication;* it was never formed for any such purpose, *but for the Lord,* for the service and honour of God. It is to be an instrument *of righteousness to holiness* (Rom. 6:19), and therefore is never to be made an instrument of uncleanness. It is to be a member of Christ, and therefore must not be made the member of a harlot, *v.* 15. And *the Lord is for the body,* that is, as some think, Christ is to be Lord of the body, to have property in it and dominion over it, having assumed a body and been made to partake of our nature, that he might be head of his church, and head over all things, Heb. 2:5, 18. Note, We must take care that we do not use what belongs to Christ as if it were our own, and much less to his dishonour.

II. Some understand this last passage, *The Lord is for the body,* thus: He is for its resurrection and glorification, according to what follows, *v.* 14, which is a second argument against this sin, the honour intended to be put on our bodies: *God hath both raised up our Lord, and will raise us up by his power* (*v.* 14), by the power of him who *shall change our vile body, and make it like to his glorious body by that power whereby he is able to subdue all things to himself,* Phil. 3:21. It is an honour done to the body that Jesus Christ was raised from the dead: and it will be an honour to our bodies that they will be raised. Let us not abuse those bodies by sin, and make them vile, which, if they be kept pure, shall, notwithstanding their present vileness, be made like to *Christ's glorious body.* Note, The hopes of a resurrection to glory should restrain Christians from dishonouring their bodies by fleshly lusts.

III. A third argument is the honour already put on them: *Know you not that your bodies are the members of Christ? v.* 15. If the soul be united to Christ by faith, the whole man is become a member of his mystical body. The body is in union with Christ as well as the soul. How honourable is this to the Christian! His very flesh is a part of the mystical body of Christ. Note, It is good to know in what honourable relations we stand, that we may endeavour to become them. *But now,* says the apostle, *shall I take the members of Christ, and make them the members of a harlot? God forbid.* Or, *take away* the members of Christ? Would not this be a gross abuse, and the most notorious injury? Would it not be dishonouring Christ, and dishonouring ourselves to the very last degree? What, make a Christ's members the members of a harlot, prostitute them to so vile a purpose! The thought is to be abhorred. God forbid. *Know you not that he who is joined to a harlot is one body* with hers? *For two,* says he, *shall be one flesh. But he who is joined to the Lord is one spirit, v.* 16,

17. Nothing can stand in greater opposition to the honourable relations and alliances of a Christian man than this sin. He is joined to the Lord in union with Christ, and made partaker by faith of his Spirit. One spirit lives and breathes and moves in the head and members. Christ and his faithful disciples are one, Jn. 17:21, 22. *But he that is joined to a harlot is one body, for two shall be one flesh,* by carnal conjunction, which was ordained of God only to be in a married state. Now shall one in so close a union with Christ as to be one spirit with him yet be so united to a harlot as to become one flesh with her? Were not this a vile attempt to make a union between Christ and harlots? And can a greater indignity he offered to him or ourselves? Can any thing be more inconsistent with our profession or relation? Note, The sin of fornication is a great injury in a Christian to his head and lord, and a great reproach and blot on his profession. It is no wonder therefore that the apostle should say, *"Flee fornication* (*v.* 18), avoid it, keep out of the reach of temptations to it, of provoking objects. Direct the eyes and mind to other things and thoughts." *Alia vitia pugnando, sola libido fugiendo vincitur — Other vices may be conquered in fight, this only by flight;* so speak many of the fathers.

IV. A fourth argument is that it is a sin against our own bodies. *Every sin that a man does is without the body; he that committeth fornication sinneth against his own body* (*v.* 18); every sin, that is, every other sin, every external act of sin besides, is without the body. It is not so much an abuse of the body as of somewhat else, as of wine by the drunkard, food by the glutton, etc. Nor does it give the power of the body to another person. Nor does it so much tend to the reproach of the body and render it vile. This sin is in a peculiar manner styled uncleanness, pollution, because no sin has so much external turpitude in it, especially in a Christian. He sins against his own body; he defiles it, he degrades it, making it one with the body of that vile creature with whom he sins. He casts vile reproach on what he Redeemer has dignifies to the last degree by taking it into union with himself. Note, We should not make our present vile bodies more vile by sinning against them.

V. The fifth argument against this sin is that the bodies of Christians are *the temples of the Holy Ghost which is in them, and which they have of God, v.* 19. He that is joined to Christ is one spirit. He is yielded up to him, is consecrated thereby, and set apart for his use, and is hereupon possessed, and occupied, and inhabited, by his Holy Spirit. This is the proper notion of a temple — a place where God dwells, and sacred to his use, by his own claim and his creature's surrender. Such temples real Christians are of the Holy Ghost. Must he not therefore be God? But the inference is plain that hence we are not our own. We are yielded up to God, and possessed by and for God; nay, and this is virtue of a purchase made of us: *You are bought with a price.* In short, our bodies were made for God, they were purchased for him. If we are Christians indeed they are yielded to him, and he inhabits and occupies them by his Spirit: so that our bodies are not our own, but his. And shall we desecrate his temple, defile it, prostitute it, and offer it up to the use and service of a harlot? Horrid sacrilege! This is robbing God in the worst sense. Note, The temple of the Holy Ghost must be kept holy. Our bodies must be kept as his whose they are, and fit for his use and residence.

VI. The apostle argues from the obligation we are under *to glorify God both with our body and spirit, which are his, v.* 20. He made both, he bought both, and therefore both belong to him and should be used and employed for him, and therefore should not be defiled, alienated from him, and prostituted by us. No, they must be kept as vessels fitted for our Master's use. We must look upon our whole selves as holy to the Lord, and must use our bodies as property which belongs to him and is sacred to his use and service. We are to honour *him with our bodies and spirits, which are his;* and therefore, surely, must abstain from fornication; and not only from the outward act, but from the *adultery of the heart,* as our Lord calls it, Mt. 5:28. Body and spirit are to be kept clean, that God may be honoured by both. But God is dishonoured when either is defiled by so beastly a sin. Therefore flee fornication, nay, and every sin. Use your bodies for the glory and service of their Lord and Maker. Note, We are not proprietors of ourselves, nor have power over ourselves, and therefore should not use ourselves according to our own pleasure, but according to his will, and for his glory, *whose we are, and whom we should serve,* Acts 27:23.

CHAPTER 7

In this chapter the apostle answers some cases proposed to him by the Corinthians about marriage. He, I. Shows them that marriage was appointed as a remedy against fornication, and therefore that persons had better marry than burn (*v.* 1–9). II. He gives direction to those who are married to continue together, though they might have an unbelieving relative, unless the unbeliever would part, in which case a Christian would not be in bondage (*v.* 10–16). III. He shows them that becoming Christians does not change their external state; and therefore advises every one to continue, in the general, in that state in which he was called (*v.* 17–24). IV. He advises them, by reason of the present distress, to keep themselves unmarried; hints the shortness of time, and how they should improve it, so as to grow dead and indifferent to the comforts of the world; and shows them how worldly cares hinder their devotions, and distract them in the service of God (*v.* 25–35). V. He directs them in the disposal of their virgins (*v.* 36–38). VI. And closes the chapter with advice to widows how to dispose of themselves in that state (*v.* 39, 40).

Verses 1–9

The apostle comes now, as a faithful and skilful casuist, to answer some cases of conscience which the Corinthians had proposed to him. Those were *things whereof they wrote to him, v.* 1. As the lips of ministers should *keep knowledge,* so the people should *ask the law at their mouths.* The apostle was as ready to resolve as they were to propose their doubts. In the former chapter, he warns them to avoid fornication; here he gives some directions about marriage, the remedy God had appointed for it. He tells them in general,

I. That it was good, in that juncture of time at least, to abstain from marriage altogether: *It is good for a man not to touch a woman* (not to take her to wife), by good here not understanding what is so conformable to the mind and will of God as if to do otherwise were sin, an extreme into which many of the ancients have run in favour of celibacy and virginity. Should the apostle be understood in this sense, he would contradict much of the rest of his discourse. But it is good, that is, either abstracting from circumstances there are many things in which the state of celibacy has the advantage above the marriage state; or else *at this juncture,* by reason of the distress of the Christian church, it would be a convenience for Christians to keep themselves single, provided they have the gift of continency, and at the same time can keep themselves chaste. The expression also may carry in it an intimation that Christians must avoid all occasions of this sin, and flee all fleshly lusts, and incentives to them; must neither look on nor touch a woman, so as to provoke lustful inclinations. Yet,

II. He informs them that marriage, and the comforts and satisfactions of that state, are by divine wisdom prescribed for preventing fornication (*v.* 2), *Porneias — Fornications,* all sorts of lawless lust. To avoid these, *Let every man,* says he, *have his own wife, and every woman her own husband;* that is, marry, and confine themselves to their own mates. And, when they are married, let each render the other *due benevolence* (*v.* 3), consider the disposition and exigency of each other, and render conjugal duty, which is owing to each other. For, as the apostle argues (*v.* 4), in the married state neither person has power over his own body, but has delivered it into the power of the other, the wife hers into the power of the husband, the husband his into the power of the wife. Note, Polygamy, or the marriage of more persons than one, as well as adultery, must be a breach of marriage-covenants, and a violation of the partner's rights. And therefore they should not defraud one another of the use of their bodies, nor any other of the comforts of the conjugal state, appointed of God for keeping *the vessel in sanctification and honour,* and preventing the lusts of uncleanness, except it be *with mutual consent* (*v.* 5) and *for a time* only, while they employ themselves in some extraordinary duties of religion, *or give themselves to fasting and prayer.* Note, Seasons of deep humiliation require abstinence from lawful pleasures. But this separation between husband and wife must not be for a continuance, lest they expose themselves to Satan's temptations, by reason of their incontinence, or inability to contain. Note, Persons expose themselves to great danger by attempting to perform what is above their strength, and at the same time not bound upon them by any law of God. If they abstain from lawful enjoyments, they may be ensnared into unlawful ones. The remedies God hath provided against sinful inclinations are certainly best.

III. The apostle limits what he had said about *every man's having his own wife,* etc. (*v.* 2): *I speak this by permission, not of command.* He did not lay it as an injunction upon every man to marry without exception. Any man might marry. No law of God prohibited the thing. But, on the other hand, not law bound a man to marry so that he sinned if he did not; I mean, unless his circumstances required it for preventing the lust of uncleanness. It was a thing in which men, by the laws of God, were in a great measure left at liberty. And therefore Paul did not bind every man to marry, though every man had an allowance. No, he *could wish all men were as himself* (*v.* 7), that is, single, and capable of living continently in that state. There were several conveniences in it, which at that season, if not at others, made it more eligible in itself. Note, It is a mark of true goodness to wish all men as happy as ourselves. But it did not answer the intentions of divine Providence as well for all men to have as much command of this appetite as Paul had. It was a gift vouchsafed to such persons as Infinite Wisdom thought proper: *Every one hath his proper gift of God, one after this manner and another after that.* Natural constitutions vary; and, where there may not be much difference in the constitution, different degrees of grace are vouchsafed, which may give some a greater victory over natural inclination than others. Note, The gifts of God, both in nature and grace, are variously distributed. Some have them after this manner and some after that. Paul could wish all men were as himself, but *all men cannot receive such a saying, save those to whom it is given,* Mt. 19:11.

IV. He sums up his sense on this head (*v.* 9, 10): *I say therefore to the unmarried and widows,* to those in a state of virginity or widowhood, *It is good for them if they abide even as I.* There are many conveniences, and especially at this juncture, in a single state, to render it preferable to a married one. It is convenient therefore *that the unmarried abide as I,* which plainly implies that Paul was at that time unmarried. *But, if they cannot contain, let them marry; for it is better to marry than to burn.* This is God's remedy for lust. The fire may be quenched by the means he has appointed. And marriage, with all its inconveniences, is much better than to burn with impure and lustful desires. *Marriage is honourable in all;* but it is a duty in those who cannot contain nor conquer those inclinations.

Verses 10–16

In this paragraph the apostle gives them direction in a case which must be very frequent in that age of the world, especially among the Jewish converts; I mean whether they were to live with heathen relatives in a married state. Moses's law permitted divorce; and there was a famous instance in the Jewish state, when the people were obliged to put away their idolatrous wives, Ezra 10:3. This might move a scruple in many minds, whether converts to Christianity were not bound to put away or desert their mates, continuing infidels. Concerning this matter the apostle here gives direction. And,

I. In general, he tells them that marriage, by Christ's command, is for life; and therefore those who are married must not think of separation. The wife *must not depart from the husband* (*v.* 10), nor the *husband put away his wife, v.* 11. This *I command,* says the apostle; *yet not I, but the Lord.* Not that he commanded any thing of his own head, or upon his own authority. Whatever he commanded was the Lord's command, dictated by his Spirit and enjoined by his authority. But his meaning is that the Lord himself, with his own mouth, had forbidden such separations, Mt. 5:32; 19:9; Mk. 10:11; Lu. 16:18. Note, Man and wife cannot separate at pleasure, nor dissolve, when they will, their matrimonial bonds and relation. They must not separate for any other cause than what Christ allows. And therefore the apostle advises that if any woman had been separated, either by a voluntary act of her own or by an act of her husband, she should continue unmarried, and seek reconciliation with her husband, that they might cohabit again. Note, Husbands and wives should not quarrel at all, or should be quickly reconciled. They are bound to each other for life. The divine law allows of no separation. They cannot throw off the burden, and therefore should set their shoulders to it, and endeavour to make it as light to each other as they can.

II. He brings the general advice home to the case of such as had an unbelieving mate (*v.* 12): *But to the rest speak I, not the Lord;* that is, the Lord had not so expressly spoken to this case as to the former divorce. It does not mean that the apostle spoke without authority from the Lord, or decided this case by his own wisdom, without the inspiration of the Holy Ghost. He closes this subject with a declaration to the contrary (*v.* 40), I think *also that I have the Spirit of God.* But, having thus prefaced his advice, we may attend,

1. To the advice itself, which is that if an unbelieving husband or wife were pleased to dwell with a Christian relative, the other should not separate. The husband should not put away an unbelieving wife, nor the wife leave an unbelieving husband, *v.* 12, 13. The Christian calling did not dissolve the marriage covenant, but bind it the faster, by bringing it back to the original institution, limiting it to two persons, and binding them together for life. The believer is not by faith in Christ loosed from matrimonial bonds to an unbeliever, but is at once bound and made apt to be a better relative. But, though a believing wife or husband should not separate from an unbelieving mate, yet if the unbelieving relative desert the believer, and no means can reconcile to a cohabitation, in such *a case a brother or sister is not in bondage* (*v.* 15), not tied up to the unreasonable humour, and bound servilely to follow or cleave to the malicious deserter, or not bound to live unmarried after all proper means for reconciliation have been tried, at least of the deserter contract another marriage or be guilty of adultery, which was a very easy supposition, because a very common instance among the heathen inhabitants of Corinth. In such a case the deserted person must be free to marry again, and it is granted on all hands. And some think that such a malicious desertion is as much a dissolution of the marriage-covenant as death itself. For how is it possible that *the two shall be one flesh* when the one is maliciously bent to part from or put away the other? Indeed, the deserter seems still bound by the matrimonial contract; and therefore the apostle says (*v.* 11), *If the woman depart from her husband* upon the account of his infidelity, *let her remain unmarried.* But the deserted party seems to be left more at liberty (I mean supposing all the proper means have been used to reclaim the deserter, and other circumstances make it necessary) to marry another person. It does not seem reasonable that they should be still bound, when it is rendered impossible to perform conjugal duties or enjoy conjugal comforts, through the mere fault of their mate: in such a case marriage would be a state of servitude indeed. But, whatever liberty be indulged Christians in such a case as this, they are not allowed, for the mere infidelity of a husband or wife, to separate; but, if the unbeliever be willing, they should continue in the relation, and cohabit as those who are thus related. This is the apostle's general direction.

2. We have here the reasons of this advice. (1.) Because the relation or state is sanctified by the holiness of either party: *For the unbelieving husband is sanctified by the wife, and the unbelieving wife by the husband* (*v.* 14), or *hath been sanctified.* The relation itself, and the conjugal use of each other, are sanctified to the believer. *To the pure all things are pure,* Tit. 1:15. Marriage is a divine institution; it is a compact for life, by God's appointment. Had converse and congress with unbelievers in that relation defiled the believer, or rendered him or her offensive to God, the ends of marriage would have been defeated, and the comforts of it in a manner destroyed, in the circumstances in which Christians then were. But the apostle tells them that, though they were yoked with unbelievers, yet, if they themselves were holy, marriage was to them a holy state, and marriage comforts, even with an unbelieving relative, were sanctified enjoyments. It was no more displeasing to God for them to continue to live as they did before, with their unbelieving or heathen relation, than if they had become converts together. If one of the relatives had become holy, nothing of the duties or lawful comforts of the married state could defile them, and render them displeasing to God, though the other were a heathen. He is sanctified for the wife's sake. She is sanctified for the husband's sake. Both are one flesh. He is to be reputed clean who is one flesh with her that is holy, and *vice versâ: Else were your children unclean, but now are they holy* (*v.* 14), that is, they would be heathen, out of the pale of the church and covenant of God. They would not be of the holy seed (as the Jews are called, Isa. 6:13), but common and unclean, in the same sense as heathens in general were styled in the apostle's vision, Acts 10:28. This way of speaking is according to the dialect of the Jews, among whom a child begotten by parents yet heathens, was said to be begotten *out of holiness;* and a child begotten by parents made proselytes was said to be begotten *intra sanctitatem — within the holy enclosure.* Thus Christians are called commonly *saints;* such they are by profession, separated to be a peculiar people of God, and as such distinguished from the world; and therefore the children born to Christians, though married to unbelievers, are not to be reckoned as part of the world, but

of the church, a holy, not a common and unclean seed. "Continue therefore to live even with unbelieving relatives; for, if you are holy, the relation is so, the state is so, you may make a holy use even of an unbelieving relative, in conjugal duties, and your seed will be holy too." What a comfort is this, where both relatives are believers! (2.) Another reason is that *God hath called Christians to peace, v.* 15. The Christian religion obliges us to act peaceably in all relations, natural and civil. We are bound, *as much as in us lies, to live peaceably with all men* (Rom. 12:18), and therefore surely to promote the peace and comfort of our nearest relatives, those with whom we are one flesh, nay, though they should be infidels. Note, It should be the labour and study of those who are married to make each other as easy and happy as possible. (3.) A third reason is that it is possible for the believing relative to be an instrument of the other's salvation (*v.* 16): *What knowest thou, O wife, whether thou shalt save thy husband?* Note, It is the plain duty of those in so near a relation to seek the salvation of those to whom they are related. "Do not separate. There is other duty now called for. The conjugal relation calls for the most close and endeared affection; it is a contract for life. And should a Christian desert a mate, when an opportunity offers to give the most glorious proof of love? Stay, and labour heartily for the conversion of thy relative. Endeavour to save a soul. Who knows but this may be the event? It is not impossible. And, though there be no great probability, saving a soul is so good and glorious a service that the bare possibility should put one on exerting one's self." Note, Mere possibility of success should be a sufficient motive with us to use our diligent endeavours for saving the souls of our relations. *"What know I but I may save his soul?* should move me to attempt it."

Verses 17–24

Here the apostle takes occasion to advise them to continue in the state and condition in which Christianity found them, and in which they became converts to it. And here,

I. He lays down this rule in general — *as God hath distributed to every one.* Note, Our states and circumstances in this world are distributions of divine Providence. *This fixes the bounds of men's habitations,* and orders their steps. God setteth up and pulleth down. And again, *As the Lord hath called every one, so let him walk.* Whatever his circumstances or condition was when he was converted to Christianity, let him abide therein, and suit his conversation to it. The rules of Christianity reach every condition. And in every state a man may live so as to be a credit to it. Note, It is the duty of every Christian to suit his behaviour to his condition and the rules of religion, to be content with his lot, and conduct himself in his rank and place as becomes a Christian. The apostle adds that this was a general rule, to be observed at all times and in all places; *So ordain I in all churches.*

II. He specifies particular cases; as, 1. That of circumcision. *Is any man called being circumcised? Let him not be uncircumcised. Is any man called being uncircumcised? Let him not be circumcised.* It matters not whether a man be a Jew or Gentile, within the covenant of peculiarity made with Abraham or without it. He who is converted, being a Jew, has no need to give himself uneasiness upon that head, and wish himself uncircumcised. Nor, is he who is converted from Gentilism under an obligation to be circumcised: nor should he be concerned because he wants that mark of distinction which did heretofore belong to the people of God. For, as the apostle goes on, *circumcision is nothing, and uncircumcision is nothing, but keeping the commandments of God, v.* 19. In point of acceptance with God, it is neither here nor there whether men be circumcised or not. Note, It is practical religion, sincere obedience to the commands of God, on which the gospel lays stress. External observances without internal piety are as nothing. Therefore let every man abide *in the calling* (the state) *wherein he was called, v.* 20. 2. That of servitude and freedom. It was common in that age of the world for many to be in a state of slavery, bought and sold for money, and so the property of those who purchased them. "Now," says the apostle, *"art thou called being a servant? Care not for it.* Be not over-solicitous about it. It is not inconsistent with thy duty, profession, or hopes, as a Christian. *Yet, if thou mayest be made free, use it rather," v.* 21. There are many conveniences in a state of freedom above that of servitude: a man has more power over himself, and more command of his time, and is not under the control of another lord; and therefore liberty is the more eligible state. But men's

outward condition does neither hinder nor promote their acceptance with God. For he that is called *being a servant is the Lord's freed-man — apeleutheros, as he that is called being free is the Lord's servant.* Though he be not discharged from his master's service, he is freed from the dominion and vassalage of sin. Though he be not enslaved to Christ, yet he is bound to yield himself up wholly to his pleasure and service; and yet that service is perfect freedom. Note, Our comfort and happiness depend on what we are to Christ, not what we are in the world. The goodness of our outward condition does not discharge us from the duties of Christianity, nor the badness of it debar us from Christian privileges. He who is a slave may yet be a Christian freeman; he who is a freeman may yet be Christ's servant. He is bought with a price, and should not therefore be the servant of man. Not that he must quit the service of his master, or not take all proper measures to please him (this were to contradict the whole scope of the apostle's discourse); but he must not be so the servant of men but that Christ's will must be obeyed, and regarded, more than his master's. He has paid a much dearer price for him, and has a much fuller property in him. He is to be served and obeyed without limitation or reserve. Note, The servants of Christ should be at the absolute command of no other master besides himself, should serve no man, any further than is consistent with their duty to him. *No man can serve two masters.* Though some understand this passage of persons being bought out of slavery by the bounty and charity of fellow-Christians; and read the passage thus, *Have you been redeemed out of slavery with a price? Do not again become enslaved;* just as before he had advised that, if in slavery they had any prospect of being made free, they should choose it rather. This meaning the words will bear, but the other seems the more natural. See *ch.* 6:20.

III. He sums up his advice: *Let every man wherein he is called abide therein with God, v.* 24. This is to be understood of the state wherein a man is converted to Christianity. No man should make his faith or religion an argument to break through any natural or civil obligations. He should quietly and comfortably abide in the condition in which he is; and this he may well do, when he may abide therein with God. Note, The special presence and favour of God are not limited to any outward condition or performance. He may enjoy it who is circumcised; and so may he who is uncircumcised. He who is bound may have it as well as he who is free. In this respect *there is neither Greek nor Jew, circumcision nor uncircumcision, barbarian nor Scythian, bond nor free,* Col. 3:11. The favour of God is not bound.

Verses 25–35

The apostle here resumes his discourse, and gives directions to virgins how to act, concerning which we may take notice,

I. Of the manner wherein he introduces them: *"Now concerning virgins I have no commandment of the Lord, v.* 25. I have no express and universal law delivered by the Lord himself concerning celibacy; but *I give my judgment, as one who hath obtained mercy of the Lord to be faithful,"* namely, in the apostleship. He acted faithfully, and therefore his direction was to be regarded as a rule of Christ: for he gave judgment as one who was a faithful apostle of Christ. Though Christ had before delivered no universal law about that matter, he now gives direction by an inspired apostle, one who had obtained mercy of the Lord to be faithful. Note, Faithfulness in the ministry is owing to the grace and mercy of Christ. It is what Paul was ready to acknowledge upon all occasions: *I laboured more abundantly than they all; yet not I, but the grace of God which was with me, ch.* 15:10. And it is a great mercy which those obtain from God who prove faithful in the ministry of his word, either ordinary or extraordinary.

II. The determination he gives, which, considering the present distress, was that a state of celibacy was preferable: *It is good for a man so to be,* that is, *to be single. I suppose,* says the apostle, or it is my opinion. It is worded with modesty, but delivered, notwithstanding, with apostolic authority. It is not the mere opinion of a private man, but the very determination of the Spirit of God in an apostle, though it be thus spoken. And it was thus delivered to give it the more weight. Those that were prejudiced against the apostle might have rejected this advice had it been given with a mere authoritative air. Note, Ministers do not lose their authority by prudent condescensions. They must become all things to all

…ys he, *for the present distress.* Christians, at the first planting of their religion, were grievously persecuted. Their enemies were very bitter against them, and treated them very cruelly. They were continually liable to be tossed and hurried by persecution. This being the then state of things, he did not think it so advisable for Christians that were single to change conditions. The married state would bring more care and cumber along with it (*v.* 33, 34), and would therefore make persecution more terrible, and render them less able to bear it. Note, Christians, in regulating their conduct, should not barely consider what is lawful in itself, but what may be expedient for them.

III. Notwithstanding he thus determines, he is very careful to satisfy them that he does not condemn marriage in the gross, nor declare it unlawful. And therefore, though he says, "If thou *art loosed from a wife* (in a single state, whether bachelor or widower, virgin or widow) *do not seek a wife,* do not hastily change conditions;" yet he adds, "*If thou art bound to a wife, do not seek to be loosed.* It is thy duty to continue in the married relation, and do the duties of it." And though such, if they were called to suffer persecution, would find peculiar difficulties in it; yet, to avoid these difficulties, they must not cast off nor break through the bonds of duty. Duty must be done, and God trusted with events. But to neglect duty is the way to put ourselves out of the divine protection. He adds therefore, *I thou marry thou hast not sinned; or if a virgin marry she hath not sinned: but such shall have trouble in the flesh.* Marrying is not in itself a sin, but marrying at that time was likely to bring inconvenience upon them, and add to the calamities of the times; and therefore he thought it advisable and expedient that such as could contain should refrain from it; but adds that he would not lay celibacy on them as a yoke, nor, by seeming to urge it too far, draw them into any snare; and therefore says, *But I spare you.* Note, How opposite in this are the papist casuists to the apostle Paul! They forbid many to marry, and entangle them with vows of celibacy, whether they can bear the yoke or no.

IV. He takes this occasion to give general rules to all Christians to carry themselves with a holy indifferency towards the world, and every thing in it. 1. *As to relations:* Those *that had wives must be as though they had none;* that is, they must not set their hearts too much on the comforts of the relation; they must be as though they had none. They know not how soon they shall have none. This advice must be carried into every other relation. Those that have children should be as though they had none. Those that are their comfort now may prove their greatest cross. And soon may the flower of all comforts be cut down. 2. As to afflictions: *Those that weep must be as though they wept not;* that is, we must not be dejected too much with any of our afflictions, nor indulge ourselves in the sorrow of the world, but keep up a holy joy in God in the midst of all our troubles, so that even in sorrow the heart may be joyful, and the end of our grief may be gladness. *Weeping may endure for a night, but joy will come in the morning.* If we can but get to heaven at last, *all tears shall be wiped from our eyes;* and the prospect of it now should make us moderate our sorrows and refrain our tears. 3. As to worldly enjoyments: *Those that rejoice should be as though they rejoiced not;* that is, they should not take too great a complacency in any of their comforts. They must be moderate in their mirth, and sit loose to the enjoyments they most value. Here is not their rest, nor are these things their portion; and therefore their hearts should not be set on them, nor should they place their solace or satisfaction in them. 4. As to worldly traffic and employment: *Those that buy must be as though they possessed not.* Those that prosper in trade, increase in wealth, and purchase estates, should hold these possessions as though they held them not. It is but setting their hearts on that which is not (Prov. 23:5) to do otherwise. Buying and possessing should not too much engage our minds. They hinder many people altogether from minding the better part. Purchasing land and trying oxen kept the guests invited from the wedding-supper, Lu. 14:18, 19. And, when they do not altogether hinder men from minding their chief business, they do very much divert them from a close pursuit. Those are most likely to run so as to obtain the prize who ease their minds of all foreign cares and cumbrances. 5. As to all worldly concerns: *Those that use this world as not abusing it, v.* 31. The world may be used, but must not be abused. It is abused when it is not used to those purposes for which it is given, to honour God and do good to men — it is made fuel to lust — when, instead of being a servant, it is made our master, our idol, and has that room in our affections which should be reserved for God. And there is great danger of abusing it in all these respects, if our hearts are too much set upon it. We must keep the world as much as may be out of our hearts, that we may not abuse it when we have it in our hands.

V. He enforces these advices with two reasons: — 1. *The time is short, v.* 29. We have but little time to continue in this world; but a short season for possessing and enjoying worldly things; *kairos synestalmenos.* It is contracted, reduced to a narrow compass. It will soon be gone. It is just ready to be wrapped up in eternity. Therefore do not set your hearts on worldly enjoyments. Do not be overwhelmed with worldly cares and troubles. Possess what you must shortly leave without suffering yourselves to be possessed by it. Why should your hearts be much set on what you must quickly resign? 2. *The fashion of this world passeth away* (*v.* 31), *schēma — the habit,* figure, appearance, of the world, passeth away. It is daily changing countenance. It is in a continual flux. It is not so much a world as the appearance of one. All is show, nothing solid in it; and it is transient show too, and will quickly be gone. How proper and powerful an argument is this to enforce the former advice! How irrational is it to be affected with the images, the fading and transient images, of a dream! *Surely man walketh in a vain show* (Ps. 39:6), in an image, amidst the faint and vanishing appearances of things. And should he be deeply affected, or grievously afflicted, with such a scene?

VI. He presses his general advice by warning them against the embarrassment of worldly cares: *But I would have you without carefulness, v.* 32. Indeed to be careless is a fault; a wise concern about worldly interests is a duty; but to be careful, full of care, to have an anxious and perplexing care about them, is a sin. All that care which disquiets the mind, and distracts it in the worship of God, is evil; for God must *be attended upon without distraction, v.* 35. The whole mind should be engaged when God is worshipped. The work ceases while it diverts to any thing else, or is hurried and drawn hither and thither by foreign affairs and concerns. Those who are engaged in divine worship should attend to this very thing, should make it their whole business. But how is this possible when the mind is swallowed up of the cares of this life? Note, It is the wisdom of a Christian so to order his outward affairs, and choose such a condition in life, as to be without distracting cares, that he may attend upon the Lord with a mind at leisure and disengaged. This is the general maxim by which the apostle would have Christians govern themselves. In the application of it Christian prudence must direct. That condition of life is best for every man which is best for his soul, and keeps him most clear of the cares and snares of the world. By this maxim the apostle solves the case put to him by the Corinthians, whether it were advisable to marry? To this he says, That, by reason of the present distress, and it may be in general, at that time, when Christians were married to infidels, and perhaps under a necessity of being so, if married at all: I say, in these circumstances, to continue unmarried would be the way to free themselves from any cares and incumbrances, and allow them more vacation for the service of God. Ordinarily, the less care we have about the world the more freedom we have for the service of God. Now the married state at that time (if not at all times) did bring most worldly care along with it. *He that is married careth for the things of the world, that he may please his wife, v.* 33. *And she that is married careth for the things of the world, how she may please her husband.* But the unmarried man and woman mind the things of the Lord, that they may please the Lord, and be holy both in body and spirit, *v.* 32, 34. Not but the married person may be holy both in body and spirit too. Celibacy is not in itself a state of greater purity and sanctity than marriage; but the unmarried would be able to make religion more their business at that juncture, because they would have less distraction from worldly cares. Marriage is that condition of life that brings care along with it, though sometimes it brings more than at others. It is the constant care of those in that relation to please each other; though this is more difficult to do at some reasons, and in some cases, than in others. At that season, therefore, the apostle advises that those who were single should abstain from marriage, if they were under no necessity to change conditions. And, where the same reason is plain at other times, …e rule is as fit to be observed. And the very same rule must determine persons for marriage where there is the same reason, that is, if in the unmarried state persons are likely to be more distracted in the service of God than if they were married, which is a case supposable in many respects. This is the general rule, which every one's discretion must apply to his own particular case; and by it should he endeavour to determine, whether it be for marriage or against. That condition of life should be chosen by the Christian in which it is most likely he will have the best helps, and the fewest hindrances, in the service of God and the affairs of his own salvation.

Verses 36–38

In this passage the apostle is commonly supposed to give advice about the disposal of children in marriage, upon the principle of his former determination. In this view the general meaning is plain. It was in that age, and those parts of the world, and especially among the Jews, reckoned a disgrace for a woman to remain unmarried past a certain number of years: it gave a suspicion of somewhat that was not for her reputation. "Now," says the apostle, "if any man thinks he behaves unhandsomely towards his daughter, and that it is not for her credit to remain unmarried, when she is of full age, and that upon this principle it is needful to dispose of her in marriage, he may use his pleasure. It is no sin in him to dispose of her to a suitable mate. But if a man has determined in himself to keep her a virgin, and stands to this determination, and is under no necessity to dispose of her in marriage, but is at liberty, with her consent, to pursue his purpose, he does well in keeping her a virgin. In short, he that gives her in marriage does well; but he that keeps her single, if she can be easy and innocent in such a state, does what is better; that is, more convenient for her in the present state of things, if not at all times and seasons." Note, 1. Children should be at the disposal of their parents, and not dispose of themselves in marriage. Yet, 2. Parents should consult their children's inclinations, both to marriage in general and to the person in particular, and not reckon they have uncontrollable power to do with them, and dictate to them, as they please. 3. It is our duty not only to consider what is lawful, but in many cases, at least, what is fit to be done, before we do it.

But I think the apostle is here continuing his former discourse, and advising unmarried persons, who are at their own disposal, what to do, the man's virgin being meant of his virginity. *Tērein tēn heautou parthenon* seems to be rather meant of preserving his own virginity than keeping his daughter a virgin, though it be altogether uncommon to use the word in this sense. Several other reasons may be seen in Locke and Whitby, by those who will consult them. And it was a common matter of reproach among Jews and civilized heathens, for a man to continue single beyond such a term of years, though all did not agree in limiting the single life to the same term. The general meaning of the apostle is the same, that it was no sin to marry, if a man thought there was a necessity upon, to avoid popular reproach, much less to avoid the hurrying fervours of lust. But he that was in his own power, stood firm in his purpose, and found himself under no necessity to marry, would, at that season, and in the circumstances of Christians at that time, at least, make a choice every way most for his own conveniency, ease, and advantage, as to his spiritual concerns. And it is highly expedient, if not a duty, for Christians to be guided by such a consideration.

Verses 39–40

The whole is here closed up with advice to widows: *As long as the husband liveth the wife is bound by the law,* confined to one husband, and bound to continue and cohabit with him. Note, The marriage-contract is for life; death only can annul the bond. *But, the husband being dead, she is at liberty to marry whom she will.* There is no limitation by God's law to be married only for such a number of times. It is certain, from this passage, that second marriages are not unlawful; for then the widow could not be at liberty to marry whom she pleased, nor to marry a second time at all. But the apostle asserts she has such a liberty, when her husband is dead, only with a limitation that *she marry in the Lord.* In our choice of relations, and change of conditions, we should always have an eye to God. Note, Marriages are likely to have God's blessing only when they are made in the

Lord, when persons are guided by the fear of God, and the laws of God, and act in dependence on the providence of God, in the change and choice of a mate — when they can look up to God, and sincerely seek his direction, and humbly hope for his blessing upon their conduct. *But she is happier,* says the apostle, *if she so abide* (that is, continue a widow) *in my judgment; and I think I have the Spirit of God, v.* 40. At this juncture, at least, if not ordinarily, it will be much more for the peace and quiet of such, and give them less hindrance in the service of God, to continue unmarried. And this, he tells them, was by inspiration of the Spirit. "Whatever your false apostles may think of me, I think, and have reason to know, that I have the Spirit of God." Note, Change of condition in marriage is so important a matter that it ought not to be made but upon due deliberation, after careful consideration of circumstances, and upon very probable grounds, at least, that it will be a change to advantage in our spiritual concerns.

CHAPTER 8

The apostle, in this chapter, answers another case proposed to him by some of the Corinthians, about eating those things that had been sacrificed to idols. I. He hints at the occasion of this case, and gives a caution against too high an esteem of their knowledge (*v.* 1–3). II. He asserts the vanity of idols, the unity of the Godhead, and the sole mediation of Christ between God and man (*v.* 4–6). III. He tells them that upon supposition that it were lawful in itself to eat of things offered to idols (for that they themselves are nothing), yet regard must be had to the weakness of Christian brethren, and nothing done that would lay a stumbling block before them, and occasion their sin and destruction (*v.* 7 to the end).

Verses 1–3

The apostle comes here to the case of things that had been offered to idols, concerning which some of them sought satisfaction: a case that frequently occurred in that age of Christianity, when the church of Christ was among the heathen, and the Israel of God must live among the Canaanites. For the better understanding of it, it must be observed that it was a custom among the heathens to make feasts on their sacrifices, and not only to eat themselves, but invite their friends to partake with them. These were usually kept in the temple, where the sacrifice was offered (*v.* 10), and, if any thing was left when the feast ended, it was usual to carry away a portion to their friends; what remained, after all, belonged to the priests, who sometimes sold it in the markets. See *ch.* 10:25. Nay, feasts, as Athenaeus informs us, were always accounted, among the heathen, sacred and religious things, so that they were wont to sacrifice before all their feasts; and it was accounted a very profane thing among them, *athyta esthiein,* to eat at their private tables any meat whereof they had not first sacrificed on such occasions. In this circumstance of things, while Christians lived among idolaters, had many relations and friends that were such, with whom they must keep up acquaintance and maintain good neighbourhood, and therefore have occasion to eat at their tables, what should they do if any thing that had been sacrificed should be set before them? What, if they should be invited to feast with them in their temples? It seems as if some of the Corinthians had imbibed an opinion that even this might be done, because they knew an idol was nothing in the world, *v.* 4. The apostle seems to answer more directly to the case (*ch.* 10), and here to argue, upon supposition of their being right in this thought, against their abuse of their liberty to the prejudice of others; but he plainly condemns such liberty in *ch.* 10. The apostle introduces his discourse with some remarks about knowledge that seem to carry in them a censure of such pretences to knowledge as I have mentioned: *We know,* says the apostle, *that we all have knowledge* (*v.* 1); as if he had said, "You who take such liberty are not the only knowing persons; we who abstain know as much as you of the vanity of idols, and that they are nothing; but we know too that the liberty you take is very culpable, and that even lawful liberty must be used with charity and not to the prejudice of weaker brethren." *Knowledge puffeth up, but charity edifieth, v.* 1. Note, 1. The preference of charity to conceited knowledge. That is best which is fitted to do the greatest good. Knowledge, or at least a high conceit of it, is very apt to swell the mind, to fill it with wind, and so puff it up. This tends to no good to ourselves, but in many instances is much to the hurt of others. But true love, and tender regard to our brethren, will put us upon consulting their interest, and acting as may be for their edification. Observe, 2. That there is no evidence of ignorance more common than a conceit of knowledge: *If any man think that he knoweth any thing, he knoweth nothing yet as he ought to know.* He that knows most best understands his own ignorance, and the imperfection of human knowledge. He that imagines himself a knowing man, and is vain and conceited on this imagination, has reason to suspect that he knows nothing aright, *nothing as he ought to know it.* Note, It is one thing to know truth, and another to know it as we ought, so as duly to improve our knowledge. Much may be known when nothing is known to any good purpose, when neither ourselves nor others are the better for our knowledge. And those who think they know any thing, and grow fain hereupon, are of all men most likely to make no good use of their knowledge; neither themselves nor others are likely to be benefited by it. *But,* adds the apostle, *if any man love God, the same is known* of God. If any man love God, and is thereby influenced to love his neighbour, the same is known of God; that is, as some understand it, is made by him to know, is taught of God. Note, Those that love God are most likely to be taught of God, and be made by him to know as they ought. Some understand it thus: He shall be approved of God; he will accept him and have pleasure in him. Note, The charitable person is most likely to have God's favour. Those who love God, and for his sake love their brethren and seek their welfare, are likely to be beloved of God; and how much better is it to be approved of God than to have a vain opinion of ourselves!

Verses 4–6

In this passage he shows the vanity of idols: *As to the eating of things that have been sacrificed to idols, we know that an idol is nothing in the world;* or, there is no idol in the world; or, an idol can do nothing in the world: for the form of expression in the original is elliptical. The meaning in the general is, that heathen idols have no divinity in them; and therefore the Old Testament they are commonly called *lies* and *vanities,* or *lying vanities.* They are merely imaginary gods, and many of them no better than imaginary beings; they have no power to pollute the creatures of God, and thereby render them unfit to be eaten by a child or servant of God. *Every creature of God is good, if it be received with thanksgiving,* 1 Tim. 4:4. It is not in the power of the vanities of the heathens to change its nature. — *And there is no other God but one.* Heathen idols are not gods, nor to be owned and respected as gods, for there is no other God but one. Note, the unity of the Godhead is a fundamental principle in Christianity, and in all right religion. The gods of the heathens must be nothing in the world, must have no divinity in them, nothing of real godhead belonging to them; for there is no other God but one. Others may be called gods: *There are that are called gods, in heaven and earth, gods many, and lords many;* but they are falsely thus called. The heathens had many such, some in heaven and some on earth, celestial deities, that were of highest rank and repute among them, and terrestrial ones, men made into gods, that were to mediate for men with the former, and were deputed by them to preside over earthly affairs. These are in scripture commonly called *Baalim.* They had gods of higher and lower degree; nay, many in each order: *gods many, and lords many;* but all titular deities and mediators: so called, but not such in truth. All their divinity and mediation were imagery. For, 1. *To us there is but one God,* says the apostle, *the Father, of whom are all things, and we in or for him.* We Christians are better informed; we well know there is but one God, the fountain of being, the author of all things, maker, preserver, and governor of the whole world, of whom and for whom are all things. Not one God to govern one part of mankind, or one rank and order of men, and another to govern another. One God made all, and therefore has power over all. All things are of him, and we, and all things else, are for him. Called the *Father* here, not in contradistinction to the other persons of the sacred Trinity, and to exclude them from the Godhead, but in contradistinction to all creatures that were made by God, and whose formation is attributed to each of these three in other places of scripture, and not appropriated to the Father alone. God the Father, as *Fons et fundamentum Trinitatis — as the first person in the Godhead, and the original of the other two,* stands here for the Deity, which yet comprehends all three, the name God being sometimes in scripture ascribed to the Father, *kat' exochēn,* or *by way of eminency,* because he is *fons et principiam Deitatis* (as Calvin observes), *the fountain of the Deity* in the other two, they having it by communication from him: so that there is but one God the Father, and yet the Son is God too, but is not another God, the Father, with his Son and Spirit, being the one God, but not without them, or so as to exclude them from the Godhead. 2. There is to us but one Lord, one Mediator between God and men, even Jesus Christ. Not many mediators, as the heathen imagined, but one only, by whom all things were created and do consist, and to whom all our hope and happiness are owing — the man Christ Jesus; but a man in personal union with the divine Word, or God the Son. This very man hath God made both Lord and Christ, Acts 2:36. Jesus Christ, in his human nature and mediatorial state, has a delegated power, a name given him, though above every name, that at his name every knee should bow, and every tongue confess that he is Lord. And thus he is the only Lord, the only Mediator, that Christians acknowledge, the only person who comes between God and sinners, administers the world's affairs under God, and mediates for men with God. All the lords of this sort among heathens are merely imaginary ones. Note, It is the great privilege of us Christians that we know the true God, and true Mediator between God and man: *the true God, and Jesus Christ whom he hath sent,* Jn. 17:3.

Verses 7–13

The apostle, having granted, and indeed confirmed, the opinion of some among the Corinthians, that idols were nothing, proceeds now to show them that their inference from this assumption was not just, namely, that therefore they might go into the idol-temple, and eat of the sacrifices, and feast there with their heathen neighbours. He does not indeed here so much insist upon the unlawfulness of the thing in itself as the mischief such freedom might do to weaker Christians, persons that had not the same measure of knowledge with these pretenders. And here,

I. He informs them that every Christian man, at that time, was not so fully convinced and persuaded that an idol was nothing. *Howbeit, there is not in every man this knowledge; for some, with conscience of the idol, unto this hour, eat it as a thing offered unto an idol;* with conscience of the idol; that is, some confused veneration for it. Though they were converts to Christianity, and professed the true religion, they were not perfectly cured of the old leaven, but retained an unaccountable respect for the idols they had worshipped before. Note, Weak Christians may be ignorant, or have but a confused knowledge of the greatest and plainest truths. Such were those of the one God and one Mediator. And yet some of those who were turned form heathenism to Christianity among the Corinthians seem to have retained a veneration for their idols, utterly irreconcilable with those great principles; so that when an opportunity offered to eat things offered to idols they did not abstain, to testify their abhorrence of idolatry, nor eat with a professed contempt of the idol, bu declaring they looked upon it to be nothing; and *so their conscience, being weak, was defiled;* that is, they contracted guilt; they ate out of respect to the idol, with an imagination that it had something divine in it, and so committed idolatry: whereas the design of the gospel was to turn men from dumb idols to the living God. They were weak in their understanding, not thoroughly apprized of the vanity of idols; and, while they ate what was sacrificed to them out of veneration for them, contracted the guilt of idolatry, and so greatly polluted themselves. This seems to be the sense of the place; though some understand it of weak Christians defiling themselves by eating what was offered to an idol with an apprehension that thereby it became unclean, and made those so in a moral sense who should eat it, every one not having a knowledge that the idol was nothing, and therefore that it could not render what was offered to it in this sense unclean. Note, We should be careful to do nothing that may occasion weak Christians to defile their consciences.

II. He tells them that mere eating and drinking had nothing in them virtuous nor criminal, nothing that could make them better nor worse, pleasing nor displeasing to God: *Meat commendeth us not to God; for neither if we eat are we the better, nor if we eat not are we the worse, v.* 8. It looks as if some of the Corinthians made a merit of their eating what had been offered to idols, and that in their very temples too (*v.* 10), because it plainly showed that they thought the idols nothing. But eating and drinking are in themselves actions indifferent. It matters little what we eat. What goes into the man of this sort neither purifies nor defiles. Flesh offered to idols may in itself be as proper for food as any other; and the bare eating, or forbearing to eat, has no virtue in it. Note, be a *stumbling-block to the weak* (*v.* 9), it might occasion their falling into idolatrous actions, perhaps their falling off from Christianity and revolting again to heathenism. "If a man see thee, who hast knowledge (hast superior understanding to his, and hereupon concedest that thou hast a liberty to sit at meat, or feast, in an idol's temple, because an idol, thou sayest, is nothing), shall not one who is less thoroughly informed in this matter, and thinks an idol something, be emboldened to eat what was offered to the idol, not as common food, but sacrifice, and thereby be guilty of idolatry?" Such an occasion of falling they should be careful of laying before their weak brethren, whatever liberty or power they themselves had. The apostle backs this caution with two considerations: — 1. The danger that might accrue to weak brethren, even those weak brethren for whom Christ died. We must deny ourselves even what is lawful rather than occasion their stumbling, and endanger their souls (*v.* 11): *Through thy knowledge shall thy weak brother perish, for whom Christ died?* Note, Those whom Christ hath redeemed with his most precious blood should be very precious and dear to us. If he had such compassion as to die for them, that they might not perish, we should have so much compassion for them as to deny ourselves, for their sakes, in various instances, and not use our liberty to their hurt, to occasion their stumbling, or hazard their ruin. That man has very little of the spirit of the Redeemer who had rather his brother should perish than himself be abridged, in any respect, of his liberty. He who hath the Spirit of Christ in him will love those whom Christ loved, so as to die for them, and will study to promote their spiritual and eternal warfare, and shun every thing that would unnecessarily grieve them, and much more every thing that would be likely to occasion their stumbling, or falling into sin. 2. The hurt done to them Christ takes as done to himself: *When you sin so against the weak brethren and wound their consciences, you sin against Christ, v.* 12. Note, Injuries done to Christians are injuries to Christ, especially to babes in Christ, to weak Christians; and most of all, involving them in guilt: wounding their consciences is wounding him. He has a particular care of the lambs of the flock: *He gathers them in his arm and carries them in his bosom,* Isa. 60:11. Strong Christians should be very careful to avoid what will offend weak ones, or lay a stumbling-block in their way. Shall we be void of compassion for those to whom Christ has shown so much? Shall we sin against Christ who suffered for us? Shall we set ourselves to defeat his gracious designs, and help to ruin those whom he died to save?

IV. He enforces all with his own example (*v.* 13): *Wherefore if meat make my brother to offend I will eat no flesh while the world standeth, lest I make my brother to offend.* He does not say that he will never eat more. This were to destroy himself, and to commit a heinous sin, to prevent the sin and fall of a brother. Such evil must not be done that good may come of it. But, though it was necessary to eat, it was not necessary to eat flesh. And therefore, rather than occasion sin in a brother, he would abstain from it as long as he lived. He had such a value for the soul of his brother that he would willingly deny himself in a matter of liberty, and forbear any particular food, which he might have lawfully eaten and might like to eat, rather than lay a stumbling-block in a weak brother's way, and occasion him to sin, by following his example, without being clear in his mind whether it were lawful or no. Note, We should be very tender of doing any thing that may be an occasion of stumbling to others, though it may be innocent in itself. Liberty is valuable, but the weakness of a brother should induce, and sometimes bind, us to waive it. We must not rigorously claim nor use our own rights, to the hurt and ruin of a brother's soul, and so to the injury of our Redeemer, who died for him. When it is certainly foreseen that my doing what I may forbear will occasion a fellow-christian to do what he ought to forbear, I shall offend, scandalize, or lay a stumbling-block in his way, which to do is a sin, however lawful the thing itself be which is done. And,

ural reason and the Mosaical law, and asserts it also to be a constitution of Christ (*v.* 3–14). III. He shows that he had willingly waived this privilege and power for their benefit (*v.* 15–18). IV. He specifies several other things, in which he had denied himself for the sake of other men's spiritual interest and salvation (*v.* 19–23). And, V. Concludes his argument by showing what animated him to this course, even the prospect of an incorruptible crown (*v.* 24 to the end.)

Verses 1–2

Blessed Paul, in the work of his ministry, not only met with opposition from those without, but discouragement from those within. He was under reproach; false brethren questioned his apostleship, and were very industrious to lessen his character and sink his reputation; particularly here at Corinth, a place to which he had been instrumental in doing much good, and from which he had deserved well; and yet there were those among them who upon these heads created him great uneasiness. Note, It is no strange nor new thing for a minister to meet with very unkind returns for great good-will to a people, and diligent and successful services among them. Some among the Corinthians questioned, if they did not disown, his apostolical character. To their cavils he here answers, and in such a manner as to set forth himself as a remarkable example of that self-denial, for the good of others, which he had been recommending in the former chapter. And, 1. He asserts his apostolical mission and character: *Am I not an apostle? Have I not seen Jesus Christ our Lord?* To be a witness of his resurrection was one great branch of the apostolical charge. "Now," says Paul, "have not I seen the Lord, though not immediately after his resurrection, yet since his ascent?" See *ch.* 4:8. *"Am I not free?* Have I not the same commission, and charge, and powers, with the other apostles? What respect, or honour, or subsistence, can they challenge, which I am not at liberty to demand as well as they?" It was not because he had no right to live of the gospel that he maintained himself with his own hands, but for other reasons. 2. He offers the success of his ministry among them, and the good he had done to them, as a proof of his apostleship: *"Are not you my work in the Lord?* Through the blessing of Christ on my labours, have not I raised a church among you? *The seal of my apostleship are you in the Lord.* Your conversion by my means is a confirmation from God of my mission." Note, The ministers of Christ should not think it strange to be put upon the proof of their ministry by some who have had experimental evidence of the power of it and the presence of God with it. 3. He justly upbraids the Corinthians with their disrespect: *"Doubtless, if I am not an apostle to others, I am so to you, v.* 2. I have laboured so long, and with so much success, among you, that you, above all others, should own and honour my character, and not call it in question." Note, It is no new thing for faithful ministers to meet with the worst treatment where they might expect the best. This church at Corinth had as much reason to believe, and as little reason to question, his apostolical mission, as any; they had as much reason, perhaps more than any church, to pay him respect. He had been instrumental in bringing them to the knowledge and faith of Christ; he laboured long among them, nearly two years, and he laboured to good purpose, *God having much people among them.* See Acts 18:10, 11. It was aggravated ingratitude for this people to call in question his authority.

Verses 3–14

Having asserted his apostolical authority, he proceeds to claim the rights belonging to his office, especially that of being maintained by it.

I. These he states, *v.* 3–6. *"My answer to those that do examine me* (that is, enquire into my authority, or the reasons of my conduct, if I am an apostle) is this: *Have we not power to eat and drink* (*v.* 4), or a right to maintenance? *Have we not power to lead about a sister, a wife, as well as other apostles, and the brethren of the Lord, and Cephas;* and, not only to be maintained ourselves, but have them maintained also?" Though Paul was at that time single, he had a right to take

them, which none could have over any but wives. Now the apostles, who worked for their bread, do n to have been in a capacity to buy or have servants to c with them. Not to observe that it would have raised susp cion to have carried about even women-servants, and much more other women to whom they were not married, for which the apostles would never give any occasion. The apostle therefore plainly asserts he had a right to marry as well as other apostles, and claim a maintenance for his wife, nay, and his children too, if he had any, from the churches, without labouring with his own hands to procure it. *Or I only and Barnabas, have not we power to for bear working? v.* 6. In short, the apostle here claims a maintenance from the churches, both for him and his. This was due from them, and what he might claim.

II. He proceeds, by several arguments, to prove his claim. 1. From the common practice and expectations of mankind. Those who addict and give themselves up to any way of business in the world expect to live out of it. Soldiers expect to be paid for their service. Husbandmen and shepherds expect to get a livelihood out of their labours. If they plant vineyards, and dress and cultivate them, it is with expectation of fruit; if they feed a flock, it is with the expectation of being fed and clothed by it! *Who goeth a warfare at any time at his own charge? Who planteth a vineyard, and eateth not the fruit thereof? Who feedeth a flock, and eateth not the milk thereof? v.* 7–9. Note, It is very natural, and very reasonable, for ministers to expect a livelihood out of their labours. 2. He argues it out of the Jewish law: *Say I these things as a man? Or saith not the law the same also? v.* 8. Is this merely a dictate of common reason and according to common usage only? No, it is also consonant to the old law. God had therein ordered that the ox should not be muzzled while he was treading out the corn, nor hindered from eating while he was preparing the corn for man's use, and treading it out of the ear. But this law was not chiefly given out of God's regard to oxen, or concern for them, but to teach mankind that all due encouragement should be given to those who are employed by us, or labouring for our good — that the labourers should taste of the fruit of their labours. *Those who plough should plough in hope; and those who thresh in hope should be partakers of their hope, v.* 10. The law saith this about oxen for our sakes. Note, Those that lay themselves out to do our souls good should not have their mouths muzzled, but have food provided for them. 3. He argues from common equity: *If we have sown unto you spiritual things, is it a great thing if we shall reap your carnal things?* What they had sown was much better than they expected to reap. They had taught them the way to eternal life, and laboured heartily to put them in possession of it. It was no great matter, surely, while they were giving themselves up to this work, to expect a support of their own temporal life. They had been instruments of conveying to them the greater spiritual blessings; and had they no claim to as great a share in their carnal things as was necessary to subsist them? Note, Those who enjoy spiritual benefits by the ministry of the word should not grudge a maintenance to such as are employed in this work. If they have received a real benefit, one would think they could not grudge them this. What, get so much good by them, and yet grudge to do so little good to them! Is this grateful or equitable? 4. He argues from the maintenance they afforded others: *"If others are partakers of this power over you, are not we rather?* You allow others this maintenance, and confess their claim just; but who has so just a claim as I from the church of Corinth? Who has given greater evidence of the apostolic mission? Who had laboured so much for your good, or done like service among you?" Note, Ministers should be valued and provided for according to their worth. *"Nevertheless,"* says the apostle, *"we have not used this power; but suffer all things, lest we should hinder the gospel of Christ.* We have not insisted on our right, but have rather been in straits to serve the interests of the gospel, and promote the salvation of souls." He renounced his right, rather than by claiming it he would hinder his success. He denied himself, for fear of giving offence; but asserted his right lest his self-denial should prove prejudicial to the ministry. Note, He is likely to plead most effectually for the rights of others who shows a generous disregard to his own. It is plain, in this case, that justice, and not self-love, is the principle by which he is actuated. 5. He argues from the old Jewish establishment: *"Do you not know that those who minister about holy things live of the things of the temple, and those who wait at the altar are partakers with the altar? v.* 13. And, if the Jewish priesthood was maintained out of the holy things that were then offered, shall not Christ's ministers have a maintenance out of their ministry? Is there not as much reason that we should be maintained as they?" He asserts it to be the institution of Christ: *"Even so hath the Lord ordained that those who preach the gospel should live of the gospel (v.* 14), should have a right to a maintenance, though not bound to demand it, and insist upon it." It is the people's duty to maintain their minister, by Christ's appointment, though it be not a duty bound on every minister to call for or accept it. He may waive his right, as Paul did, without being a sinner; but those transgress an appointment of Christ who deny or withhold it. Those who preach the gospel have a right to live by it; and those who attend on their ministry, and yet take no thought about their subsistence, fail very much in their duty to Christ, and respect owing to them.

Verses 15–18

Here he tells them that he had, notwithstanding, waived his privilege, and lays down his reason for doing it.

I. He tells them that he had neglected to claim his right in times past: *I have used none of these things, v.* 15. He neither ate nor drank himself at their cost, nor led about a wife to be maintained by them, nor forbore working to maintain himself. From others he received a maintenance, but not from them, for some special reasons. Nor did he write this to make his claim now. Though he here asserts his right, yet he does not claim his due; but denies himself for their sakes, and the gospel.

II. We have the reason assigned of his exercising this self-denial. He would not have his glorying made void: *It were better for his to die than that any man should make his glorying void, v.* 15. This glorying did imply nothing in it of boasting, or self-conceit, or catching at applause, but a high degree of satisfaction and comfort. It was a singular pleasure to him to preach the gospel without making it burdensome; and he was resolved that among them he would not lose this satisfaction. His advantages for promoting the gospel were his glory, and he valued them above his rights, or his very life: *Better were it for him to die than to have his glorying made void,* than to have it justly said that he preferred his wages to his work. No, he was ready to deny himself for the sake of the gospel. Note, It is the glory of a minister to prefer the success of his ministry to his interest, and deny himself, that he may serve Christ, and save souls. Not that in so doing he does more than he ought; he is still acting within the bounds of the law of charity. But he acts upon truly noble principles, he brings much honour to God in so doing; and those that honour him he will honour. It is what God will approve and commend, what a man may value himself for and take comfort in, though he cannot make a merit of it before God.

III. He shows that this self-denial was more honourable in itself, and yielded him much more content and comfort, than his preaching did: *"Though I preach the gospel, I have nothing whereof to glory; for necessity is laid upon me; yea, woe is unto me, if I preach not the gospel, v.* 16. It is my charge, my business; it is the work for which I am constituted an apostle, ch.* 1:17. This is a duty expressly bound upon me. It is not in any degree a matter of liberty. *Necessity is upon me.* I am false and unfaithful to my trust, I break a plain and express command, and *woe be to me, if I do not preach the gospel."* Those who are set apart to the office of the ministry have it in charge to preach the gospel. Woe be to them if they do not. From this none is excepted. But it is not given in charge to all, nor any preacher of the gospel, to do his work gratis, to preach and have no maintenance out of it. It is not said, "Woe be to him if he do not preach the gospel, and yet maintain himself." In this point he is more at liberty. It may be his duty to preach at some seasons, and under some circumstances, without receiving a maintenance for it; but he has, in the general, a right to it, and may expect it from those among whom he labours. When he renounces this right for the sake of the gospel and the souls of men, though he does not supererogate, yet he denies himself, waives his privilege and right; he does more than his charge and office in general, and at all times, obliges him to. Woe be to him if he do not preach the gospel; but it may sometimes be his duty to insist on his maintenance for so doing, and whenever he forbears to claim it he parts with his right, though a man may sometimes be bound to do so by the general duties of love to God and charity to men. Note, It is a high attainment in religion to renounce our own rights for the good of others; this will entitle to a peculiar reward from God. For,

IV. The apostle here informs us that doing our duty with a willing mind will meet with a gracious recompence from God: *If I do this thing,* that is, either preach the gospel or take no maintenance, *willingly, I have a reward.* Indeed, it is willing service only that is capable of reward from God. It is not the bare doing of any duty, but the doing of it heartily (that is, willingly and cheerfully) that God has promised to reward. Leave the heart out of our duties, and God abhors them: they are but the carcasses, without the life and spirit, of religion. Those must preach willingly who would be accepted of God in this duty. They must make their business a pleasure, and not esteem it a drudgery. And those who, out of regard to the honour of God or good of souls, give up their claim to a maintenance, should do this duty willingly, if they would be accepted in it or rewarded for it. But whether the duty of the office be done willingly or with reluctance, whether the heart be in it or averse from it, all in office have a trust and charge from God, for which they must be accountable. Ministers have a dispensation of the gospel, or *stewardship — oikonomia* (Lu. 16:2), committed to them. Note, Christ's willing servants shall not fail of a recompence, and that proportioned to their fidelity, zeal, and diligence; and his slothful and unwilling servants shall all be called to an account. Taking his name, and professing to do his business, will make men accountable at his bar. And how sad an account have slothful servants to give!

V. The apostle sums up the argument, by laying before them the encouraging hope he had of a large recompence for his remarkable self-denial: *What is my reward then? v.* 18. What is it I expect a recompence from God for? *That when I preach the gospel I may make it without charge, that I abuse not my power in the gospel.* Or, "not so to claim my rights as to make them destroy the great intentions and ends of my office, but renounce them for the sake of these." It is an abuse of power to employ it against the very ends for which it is given. And the apostle would never use his power, or privilege of being maintained by his ministry, so as to frustrate the ends of it, but would willingly and cheerfully deny himself for the honour of Christ and the interest of souls. That ministers who follows his example may have cheerful expectations of a full recompence.

Verses 19–23

The apostle takes occasion from what he had before discoursed to mention some other instances of his self-denial and parting with his liberty for the benefit of others.

I. He asserts his liberty (*v.* 19): *Though I be free from all men.* He was free-born, a citizen of Rome. He was in bondage to none, nor depended upon any for his subsistence; *yet he made himself a servant to all, that he might gain the more.* He behaved as a servant; he laboured for their good as a servant; he was careful to please, as a servant to his master; he acted in many cases as if he had no privileges; and this that he might gain the more, or make the more converts to Christianity. He made himself a servant, that they might be made free.

II. He specifies some particulars wherein he made himself a servant to all. He accommodated himself to all sorts of people. 1. *To the Jews, and those under the law, he became a Jew,* and as under the law, to gain them. Though he looked on the ceremonial law as a yoke taken off by Christ, yet in many instances he submitted to it, that he might work upon the Jews, remove their prejudices, prevail with them to hear the gospel, and win them over to Christ. 2. *To those that are without the law as without law* that is, to the Gentiles, whether converted to the Christian faith or not. In innocent things he could comply with people's usages or humours for their advantage. He would reason with the philosophers in their own way. And, as to converted Gentiles, he behaved among them as one that was not under the bondage of the Jewish laws, as he had asserted and maintained concerning them, though he did not act as a lawless person, but as one who was bound by the laws of Christ. He would transgress no laws of Christ to please or humour any man; but he would accommodate himself to all men, where he might do it lawfully, to gain some. Paul was the apostle of the Gentiles, and so, one would have thought, might have excused himself from complying with the Jews; and yet, to do them good, and win them over to Christ, he did, in innocent things, neglect the power he had to do otherwise, and conformed to some of their usages and laws. And though he might, by virtue of that character, have challenged authority over the Gentiles, yet he accommodated himself, as much as he innocently might, to their prejudices and ways of thinking. Doing good was the study and business of his life; and, so that he might reach this end, he did not stand on privileges and punctilios. 3. *To the weak he became as weak, that he might gain the weak, v.* 22. He was willing to make the best of them. He did not despise nor judge them, but became as one of them, forbore to use his liberty for their sake, and was careful to lay no stumbling-block in their way. Where any, through the weakness of their understanding, or the strength of their prejudices, were likely to fall into sin, or fall off from the gospel into heathen idolatry, through his use of his liberty, he refrained himself. He denied himself for their sakes, that he might insinuate into their affections, and gain their souls. In short, *he became all things to all men, that he might by all means* (all lawful means) *gain some.* He would not sin against God to save the soul of his neighbour, but he would very cheerfully and readily deny himself. The rights of God he could not give up, but he might resign his own, and he very often did so for the good of others.

III. He assigns his reason for acting in this manner (*v.* 23): *This I do for the gospel's sake, and that I may be partaker thereof with you;* that is, for the honour of Christ, whose the gospel is, and for the salvation of souls, for which it was designed, and that he and they might communicate in the privileges of it, or partake together of them. For these ends did he thus condescend, deny himself as to his liberty, and accommodate himself to the capacities and usages of those with whom he had to do, where he lawfully might. Note, A heart warmed with zeal for God, and breathing after the salvation of men, will not plead and insist upon rights and privileges in bar to this design. Those manifestly abuse their power in the gospel who employ it not to edification but destruction, and therefore breathe nothing of its spirit.

Verses 24–27

In these verses the apostle hints at the great encouragement he had to act in this manner. He had a glorious prize, an incorruptible crown, in view. Upon this head he compares himself to the racers and combatants in the Isthmian games, an allusion well known to the Corinthians, because they were celebrated in their neighbourhood: *"Know you not that those who run in a race run all, but one obtaineth the prize? v.* 24. All run at your games, but only one gets the race and wins the crown." And here,

I. He excites them to their duty: *"So run that you may obtain.* It is quite otherwise in the Christian race than in your races; only one wins the prize in them. You may all run so as to obtain. You have great encouragement, therefore, to persist constantly, and diligently, and vigorously, in your course. There is room for all to get the prize. You cannot fail if you run well. Yet there should be a noble emulation; you should endeavour to outdo one another. And it is a glorious contest who shall get first to heaven, or have the best rewards in that blessed world. I make it my endeavour to run; so do you, as you see me go before you." Note, It is the duty of Christians to follow their ministers closely in the chase of eternal glory, and the honour and duty of ministers to lead them in the way.

II. He directs them in their course, by setting more fully to view his own example, still carrying on the allusion. 1. Those that ran in their games were kept to a set diet: *"Every man that strives for the mastery is temperate in all things, v.* 23. The fighters and wrestlers in your exercises are kept to strict diet and discipline; nay, they keep themselves to it. They do not indulge themselves, but restrain themselves from the food they eat and so from the liberties they use on other occasions. And should not Christians much more abridge themselves of their liberty, for so glorious an end as winning the race, and obtaining the prize set before them? They close combat, or brandish them by way of flourish. There is no room for any such exercise in the Christian warfare. Christians are ever in close combat. There enemies make fierce and hearty opposition, and are ever at hand; and for this reason they must lay about them in earnest, and never drop the contest, nor flag and faint in it. They must fight, not as those that beat the air, but must strive against their enemies with all their might. One enemy the apostle here mentions, namely, the body; this must be kept under, beaten black and blue, as the combatants were in these Grecian games, and thereby brought into subjection. By the body we are to understand fleshly appetites and inclinations. These the apostle set himself to curb and conquer, and in this the Corinthians were bound to imitate him. Note, Those who would aright pursue the interests of their souls must beat down their bodies, and keep them under. They must combat hard with fleshly lusts, and not indulge a wanton appetite, and long for heathenish sacrifices, nor eat them, to please their flesh, at the hazard of their brethren's souls. The body must be made to serve the mind, not suffered to lord over it.

III. The apostle presses this advice on the Corinthians by proper arguments drawn from the same contenders. 1. They take pains, and undergo all those hardships, *to obtain a corruptible crown* (*v.* 25), *but we an incorruptible.* Those who conquered in these games were crowned only with the withering leaves or boughs of trees, of olive, bays, or laurel. But Christians have an incorruptible crown in view, a crown of glory that never fadeth away, an inheritance incorruptible, reserved in heaven for them. And would they yet suffer themselves to be outdone by these racers or wrestlers? Can they use abstinence in diet, exert themselves in racing, expose their bodies to so much hardship in a combat, who have no more in view than the trifling huzzas of a giddy multitude, or a crown of leaves? And shall not Christians, who hope for the approbation of the sovereign Judge, and a crown of glory from his hands, stretch forward in the heavenly race, and exert themselves in beating down their fleshly inclinations, and the strong-holds of sin? 2. The racers in these games run at uncertainty. All run, but one receives the prize, *v.* 24. Every racer, therefore, is at a great uncertainty whether he shall win it or no. But the Christian racer is at no such uncertainty. Every one may run here so as to obtain; but then he must run within the lines, he must keep to the path of duty prescribed, which, some think, is the meaning of *running not as uncertainly, v.* 26. He who keeps within the limits prescribed, and keeps on in his race, will never miss his crown, though others may get theirs before him. And would the Grecian racers keep within their bounds, and exert themselves to the very last, when one only could win, and all must be uncertain which that one would be? And shall not Christians be much more exact and vigorous when all are sure of a crown when they come to the end of their race? 3. He sets before himself and them the danger of yielding to fleshly inclinations, and pampering the body and its lusts and appetites: *I keep my body under, lest that by any means, when I have preached to others, I myself should be a castaway* (*v.* 27), *rejected, disapproved, adokimos,* one to whom the *brabeutēs — the judge* or *umpire* of the race, will not decree the crown. The allusion to the games runs through the whole sentence. Note, A preacher of salvation may yet miss it. He may show others the way to heaven, and never get thither himself. To prevent this, Paul took so much pains in subduing and keeping under bodily inclinations, lest by any means he himself, who had preached to others, should yet miss the crown, be disapproved and rejected by his sovereign Judge. A holy fear of himself was necessary to preserve the fidelity of an apostle; and how much more necessary is it to our preservation? Note, Holy fear of ourselves, and not presumptuous confidence, is the best security against apostasy from God, and final rejection by him.

... which cannot consist with having fellowship with God (*v.* 15–22). III. He lets them yet know that though they must not eat of things sacrificed to idols as such, and out of any regard to the idol, yet they might buy such flesh in the markets, or eat it at the table of heathen acquaintances, without asking any questions; for that the heathens' abuse of them did not render the creatures of God unfit to be the food of his servants. Yet liberty of this kind must be used with a due regard to weak consciences, and no offence given by it t Jew nor Gentile, nor to the church of God (*v.* 23 to the end).

Verses 1–5

In order to dissuade the Corinthians from communion with idolaters, and security in any sinful course, he sets before them the example of the Jews, the church under the Old Testament. They enjoyed great privileges, but, having been guilty of heinous provocations, they fell under very grievous punishments. In these verses he reckons up their privileges, which, in the main, were the same with ours.

I. He prefaces this discourse with a note of regard: *"Moreover, brethren, I would not that you should be ignorant.* I would not have you without the knowledge of this matter; it is a thing worthy both of your knowledge and attention. It is a history very instructive and monitory." Judaism was Christianity under a veil, wrapt up in types and dark hints. The gospel was preached to them, in their legal rites and sacrifices. And the providence of God towards them, and what happened to them notwithstanding these privileges, may and ought to be warnings to us.

II. He specifies some of their privileges. He begins, 1. With their deliverance from Egypt: *"Our fathers,* that is, the ancestors of us Jews, were *under the cloud, and all passed through the sea.* They were all under the divine covering and conduct." The cloud served for both purposes: it sometimes contracted itself into a cloudy pillar, shining on one side to show them their way, dark on the other to hide them from their pursuing enemies; and sometimes spread itself over them as a mighty sheet, to defend them from the burning sun in the sandy desert, Ps. 105:39. They were miraculously conducted through the Red Sea, where the pursuing Egyptians were drowned: it was a lane to them, but a grave to these: a proper type of our redemption by Christ, who saves us by conquering and destroying his enemies and ours. They were very dear to God, and much in his favour, when he would work such miracles for their deliverance, and take them so immediately under his guidance and protection. 2. They had sacraments like ours. (1.) *They were all baptized unto Moses in the cloud, and in the sea* (*v.* 2), or into Moses, that is, brought under obligation to Moses's law and covenant, as we are by baptism under the Christian law and covenant. It was to them a typical baptism. (2.) *They did all eat of the same spiritual meat, and drink of the same spiritual drink,* that we do. The manna on which they fed was a type of Christ crucified, the bread which came down from heaven, which whoso eateth shall live forever. Their drink was a stream fetched from a rock which followed them in all their journeyings in the wilderness; and this rock was Christ, that is, in type and figure. He is the rock on which the Christian church is built; and of the streams that issue from him do all believers drink, and are refreshed. Now all the Jews did eat of this meat, and drink of this rock, called here a spiritual rock, because it typified spiritual things. These were great privileges. One would think that this should have saved them; that all who ate of that spiritual meat, and drank of that spiritual drink, should have been holy and acceptable to God. Yet was it otherwise: *With many of them God was not well pleased; for they were overthrown in the wilderness, v.* 5. Note, Men may enjoy many and great spiritual privileges in this world, and yet come short of eternal life. Many of those *who were baptized unto Moses in the cloud and sea,* that is, had their faith of his divine commission confirmed by these miracles, were yet overthrown in the wilderness, and never saw the promised land. Let none presume upon their great privileges, or profession of the truth; these will not secure heavenly happiness, nor prevent judgments here on earth, except the *root of the matter* be in us.

lust after evil things, as they lusted, v. 6. God fed them with manna, but they must have flesh, Num. 11:4. They had food for their supply, but, not content with this, they asked *meat for their lusts,* Ps. 16:14. Carnal desires get head by indulgence, and therefore should be observed and checked in their first rise: if once they prevail, and bear sway in us, we know not whither they will carry us. This caution stands first, because carnal appetites indulged are the root and source of much sin. 2. He warns against idolatry (*v.* 7): *Neither be you idolaters, as were some of them; as it is written, The people sat down to eat and drink, and rose up to play.* The sin of the golden calf is referred to, Ex. 32:6. They first sacrificed to their idol, then feasted on the sacrifices, and then danced before it. Though only eating and drinking are mentioned here, yet the sacrifice is supposed. The apostle is speaking to the case of the Corinthians, who were tempted to feast on the heathen sacrifices, things offered to idols, though they do not seem to have been under any temptation to offer sacrifice themselves. Even eating and drinking of the sacrifices before the idol, and as things sacrificed, was idolatry, which, by the example of the Israelites, they should be warned to avoid. 3. He cautions against fornication, a sin to which the inhabitants of Corinth were in a peculiar manner addicted. They had a temple among them dedicated to Venus (that is, to lust), with above a thousand priestesses belonging to it, all common prostitutes. How needful was a caution against fornication to those who lived in so corrupt a city, and had been used to such dissolute manners, especially when they were under temptations to idolatry too! and spiritual whoredom did in many cases lead to bodily prostitution. Most of the gods whom the heathens served were represented as patterns of lewdness; and much lewdness was committed in the very worship of many of them. Many of the Jewish writers, and many Christians after them, think that such worship was paid to Baal-Peor; and that fornication was committed with the daughters of Moab in the worship of that idol. They were enticed by these women both to spiritual and corporal whoredom; first to feast on the sacrifice, if not to do more beastly acts, in honour of the idol, and then to defile themselves with strange flesh (Num. 25), which brought on a plague, that in one day slew twenty-three thousand, besides those who fell by the hand of public justice. Note, Whoremongers and adulterers God will judge, in whatever external relation they may stand to him, and whatever outward privileges he may bestow upon them. Let us fear the sins of Israel, if we would shun their plagues. 4. He warns us against *tempting Christ (as some of them tempted, and were destroyed of serpents, v.* 9), or provoking him to jealousy, *v.* 22. He was with the church in the wilderness; he was the angel of the covenant, who went before them. But he was greatly grieved and provoked by them in many ways: *They spoke against him and Moses, Wherefore have you brought us out of Egypt to die in the wilderness?* for which reason God sent fiery serpents among them (Num. 21:5, 6), by which many of them were stung mortally. And it is but just to fear that such as tempt Christ under the present dispensation will be left by him in the power of the old serpent. 5. He warns against murmuring: *Neither murmur you as some of them also murmured, and were destroyed of the destroyer* (*v.* 10), by a destroying angel, an executioner of divine vengeance. They quarrelled with God, and murmured against Moses his minister, when any difficulties pressed them. When they met with discouragements in the way to Canaan, they were very apt to fly in the face of their leaders, were for displacing them, and going back to Egypt under the conduct of others of their own choosing. Something like this seems to have been the case of the Corinthians; they murmured against Paul, and in him against Christ, and seem to have set up other teachers, who would indulge and soothe them in their inclinations, and particularly in a revolt to idolatry. Rather let them feast on idol sacrifices than bear the reproach, or expose themselves to the ill-will, of heathen neighbours. Such conduct was very provoking to God, and was likely to bring upon them swift destruction, as it did on the Israelites, Num. 14:37. Note, Murmuring against divine disposals and commands is a sin that greatly provokes, especially when it grows to such a head as to issue in apostasy, and a revolt from him and his good ways.

II. The apostle subjoins to these particular cautions a more general one (v. 11): *All these things happened to them for ensamples, and were written for our admonition.* Not only the laws and ordinances of the Jews, but the providences of God towards them, were typical. Their sins against God, and backslidings from him, were typical of the infidelity of many under the gospel. God's judgments on them were types of spiritual judgments now. Their exclusion from the earthly Canaan typified the exclusion of many under the gospel out of the heavenly Canaan, for their unbelief. Their history was written, to be a standing monitor to the church, even under the last and most perfect dispensation: *To us, on whom the end of the world is come,* the concluding period of God's gracious government over men. Note, Nothing in scripture is written in vain. God had wise and gracious purposes towards us in leaving the Jewish history upon record; and it is our wisdom and duty to receive instruction from it. Upon this hint the apostle grounds a caution (v. 12): *Let him that thinketh he standeth take heed lest he fall.* Note, The harms sustained by others should be cautious to us. He that thinks he stands should not be confident and secure, but upon his guard. Others have fallen, and so may we. And then we are most likely to fall when we are most confident of our own strength, and thereupon most apt to be secure, and off our guard. Distrust of himself, putting him at once upon vigilance and dependence on God, is the Christian's best security against all sin. Note, He who thinks he stands is not likely to keep his footing, if he fears no fall, nor guards against it. God has not promised to keep us from falling, if we do not look to ourselves: his protection supposes our own care and caution.

III. But to this word of caution he adds a word of comfort, v. 13. Though it is displeasing to God for us to presume, it is not pleasing to him for us to despair. If the former be a great sin, the latter is far from being innocent. Though we must fear and take heed lest we fall, yet should we not be terrified and amazed; for either our trials will be proportioned to our strength, or strength will be supplied in proportion to our temptations. We live indeed in a tempting world, where we are compassed about with snares. Every place, condition, relation, employment, and enjoyment, abounds with them; yet what comfort may we fetch from such a passage! For, 1. *"No temptation,"* says the apostle, *"hath yet taken you, but such as is common to man,* what is human; that is, such as you may expect from men of such principles as heathens, and such power; or else such as is common to mankind in the present state; or else such as the spirit and resolution of mere men may bear you through." Note, The trials of common Christians are but common trials: others have the like burdens and the like temptations; what they bear up under, and break through, we may also. 2. *God is faithful.* Though Satan be a deceiver, God is true. Men may be false, and the world may be false; but God is faithful, and our strength and security are in him. He keepeth his covenant, and will never disappoint the filial hope and trust of his children. 3. He is wise as well as faithful, and will proportion our burden to our strength. *He will not suffer us to be tempted above what we are able.* He knows what we can bear, and what we can bear up against; and he will, in his wise providence, either proportion our temptations to our strength or make us able to grapple with them. He will take care that we be not overcome, if we rely upon him, and resolve to approve ourselves faithful to him. We need not perplex ourselves with the difficulties in our way when God will take care that they shall not be too great for us to encounter, especially. 4. When he will make them to issue well. *He will make a way to escape,* either the trial itself, or at least the mischief of it. There is no valley so dark but he can find a way through it, no affliction so grievous but he can prevent, or remove, or enable us to support it, and in the end overrule it to our advantage.

IV. And upon this argument he grounds another caution against idolatry: *Wherefore, my dearly beloved, flee from idolatry.* Observe, 1. How he addresses them: *My dearly beloved.* It is out of tender affection to them that he presses this advice upon them. 2. The matter of his advice: *"Flee idolatry;* shun it, and all approaches towards it." Idolatry is the most heinous injury and affront to the true God; it is transferring his worship and honour to a rival. 3. The ground of this ad-

vice: "Seeing you have such encouragement to trust God, and to be faithful, do you approve yourselves men, be not shaken by any discouragements your heathen enemies may lay before you. God will succour and assist, help you in your trials, and help you out of them; and therefore be not guilty of any idolatrous compliances." Note, We have all the encouragement in the world to flee sin and prove faithful to God. We cannot fall by a temptation if we cleave fast to him.

Verses 15–22

In this passage the apostle urges the general caution against idolatry, in the particular case of eating the heathen sacrifices as such, and out of any religious respect to the idol to whom they were sacrificed.

I. He prefaces his argument with an appeal to their own reason and judgment: *"I speak to wise men, judge you what I say,* v. 15. You are great pretenders to wisdom, to close reasoning and argument; I can leave it with your own reason and conscience whether I do not argue justly." Note, It is no dishonour to an inspired teacher, nor disadvantage to his argument, to appeal for the truth of it to the reason and consciences of his hearers. It comes upon them with the greater force when it comes with this conviction. Paul, an inspired apostle, would yet, in some cases, leave it with the Corinthians to judge whether what he taught was not conformable to their own light and sense.

II. He lays down his argument from the Lord's supper: *The cup which we bless, is it not the communion of the blood of Christ? The bread which we break, is it not the communion of the body of Christ?* Is not this sacred rite an instrument of communion with God? Do we not therein profess to be in friendship, and to have fellowship, with him? Is it not a token whereby we professedly hold communion with Christ, whose body was broken, and blood shed, to procure remission of our sins, and the favour of God? And can we be in alliance with Christ, or friendship with God, without being devoted to him? In short, the Lord's supper is a feast on the sacrificed body and blood of our Lord, *epulum ex oblatis.* And to eat of the feast is to partake of the sacrifice, and so to be his guests to whom the sacrifice was offered, and this in token of friendship with him. Thus to partake of the Lord's table is to profess ourselves his guests and covenant people. This is the very purpose and intention of this symbolical eating and drinking; it is holding communion with God, and partaking of those privileges, and professing ourselves under those obligations, which result from the death and sacrifice of Christ; and this in conjunction with all true Christians, with whom we have communion also in this ordinance. *Because the bread is one, we, being many, are one body, for we are made partakers of one bread,* or loaf (v. 17), which I think is thus more truly rendered: "By partaking of one broken loaf, the emblem of our Saviour's broken body, who is the only true bread that came down from heaven, we coalesce into one body, become members of him and one another." Those who truly partake by faith have this communion with Christ, and one another; and those who eat the outward elements make profession of having this communion, of belonging to God and the blessed fraternity of his people and worshippers. This is the true meaning of this holy rite.

III. He confirms this from the Jewish worship and customs: *Behold Israel after the flesh: are not those who eat of the sacrifices partakers of the altar,* that is, of the sacrifice offered upon it? Those who were admitted to eat of the offerings were reckoned to partake of the sacrifice itself, as made for them, and to be sanctified thereby; and therefore surely to worship God, and be in alliance or covenant with him, even the God of Israel, to whom the sacrifice was made: this was a symbol or token of holding communion with him.

IV. He applies this to the argument against feasting with idolaters on their sacrifices, and to prove those that do so idolaters. This he does, 1. By following the principle on which they would argue it to be lawful, namely, that an idol was nothing. Many of them were nothing at all, none of them had any divinity in them. What was sacrificed to idols was nothing, no way changed from what it was before, but was every whit as fit for food, considered in itself. They indeed seem to argue that, because an idol was nothing, what was offered was no sacrifice, but common and ordinary food, of which they might therefore eat with as little scruple. Now the apostle allows that the food was not changed as to its nature, was as fit to be eaten as common food, where it was set before any who knew not of its having been offered to an idol. But,

2. He proves that the eating of it as a part of a heathen sacrifice was, (1.) A partaking with them in their idolatry. *It was having fellowship with devils,* because what the Gentiles sacrificed they sacrificed to devils; and to feast with them upon these sacrifices was to partake in the sacrifice, and therefore to worship the god to whom it was made, and have fellowship or communion with him just as he who eats the Lord's supper is supposed to partake in the Christian sacrifice; or as those who ate the Jewish sacrifices partook of what was offered on their altar. But heathens sacrificed to devils: "Therefore do not feast on their sacrifices. Doing it is a token of your having fellowship with the demons to whom they are offered. I would not have you be in communion with devils." (2.) It was a virtual renouncing of Christianity: *You cannot drink the cup of the Lord, and the cup of devils: you cannot be partakers of the Lord's table, and the table of devils,* v. 21. To partake of this Christian feast was to have communion with Christ: to partake of the feasts made in honour of the heathen idols, and made of things sacrificed to them, was to have communion with devils. Now this was to compound contraries; it was by no means consistent. Communion with Christ, and communion with devils, could never be had at once. One must be renounced, if the other was maintained. He who held communion with Christ must renounce that with devils; he who held communion with devils must by that very deed renounce communion with Christ. And what a manifest self-contradiction must that man's conduct be that would partake of the Lord's table, and yet partake of the table of demons! God and mammon can never be served together, nor fellowship be at once had with Christ and Satan. Those who communicate with devils must virtually renounce Christ. This may also intimate that such as indulge themselves in gluttony or drunkenness, and by so doing make their own table the table of devils, or keep up fellowship with Satan by a course of known and wilful wickedness, cannot partake truly of the cup and table of the Lord. They may use the sign, but do not the thing signified thereby. For a man can never be at once in communication with Christ and his church and yet in fellowship with Satan. Note, How much reason have we to look to it that every sin and idol be renounced by us, when we eat and drink at the Lord's table.

V. He warns them, upon the whole, against such idolatry, by signifying to them that God is a jealous God (v. 22): *Do we provoke the Lord to jealousy? Are we stronger than he?* It is very probable that many among the Corinthians made light of being at these heathen feasts, and thought there was no harm in it. But the apostle bids them beware. The reason with which the second commandment is enforced is, *I am a jealous God.* God cannot endure a rival in matter of worship; nor give his glory, nor suffer it to be given, to another. Those who have fellowship with other gods provoke him to jealousy, Deu. 32:16. And, before this be done, persons should consider whether they are stronger than he. It is a dangerous thing to provoke God's anger, unless we could withstand his power. But *who can stand before him when he is angry?* Nah. 1:6. This should be considered by all who continue in the love and liking of sin, and in league with it, while yet they profess to keep up communion with Christ. Is not this the way to provoke his jealousy and indignation? Note, Attention to the greatness of God's power should restrain us from provoking his jealousy, from doing any thing to displease him. Shall we rouse almighty wrath? And how shall we withstand it? Are we a match for God? Can we resist his power, or control it? And, if not, shall we arm it against us, by provoking him to jealousy? No, let us fear his power, and let this restrain us from all provocation.

Verses 23–33

In this passage the apostle shows in what instances, notwithstanding, Christians might lawfully eat what had been sacrificed to idols. They must not eat it out of religious respect to the idol, nor go into his temple, and hold a feast there, upon what they knew was an idol-sacrifice; nor perhaps out of the temple, if they knew it was a feast held upon a sacrifice, but there were cases wherein they might without sin eat what had been offered. Some such the apostle here enumerates. — But,

I. He gives a caution against abusing our liberty in lawful things. That may be lawful which is not expedient, which will not edify. A Christian must not barely consider what is lawful, but what is expedient, and for the use of edification. A

lawfully done. Circumstances may make that a sin which in itself is none. These must be weighed, and the expediency of an action, and its tendency to edification, must be considered before it be done. Note, The welfare of others, as well as our own convenience, must be consulted in many things we do, if we would do them well.

II. He tells them that what was *sold in the shambles they might eat without asking questions*. The priest's share of heathen sacrifices was thus frequently offered for sale, after it had been offered in the temple. Now the apostle tells them they need not be so scrupulous as to ask the butcher in the market whether the meat he sold had been offered to an idol? It was there sold as common food, and as such might be bought and used; *for the earth is the Lord's, and the fulness thereof* (v. 26), and the fruit and products of the earth were designed by him, the great proprietor, for the use and subsistence of mankind, and more especially of his own children and servants. *Every creature of God is good, and nothing to be refused, if it be received with thanksgiving; for it is sanctified by the word of God and prayer,* 1 Tim. 4:4, 5. *To the pure all things are pure,* Tit. 1:15. Note, Though it is sinful to use any food in an idolatrous manner, it is no sin, after such abuse, to apply it, in a holy manner, to its common use.

III. He adds that if they were invited by any heathen acquaintances to a feast, *they might go, and eat what was set before them, without asking questions* (v. 27), nay, though they knew things sacrificed to idols were served up at such entertainments, as well as sold in the shambles. Note, The apostle does not prohibit their going to a feast upon the invitation of those that believed not. There is a civility owing even to infidels and heathens. Christianity does by no means bind us up from the common offices of humanity, nor allow us an uncourteous behaviour to any of our own kind, however they may differ from us in religious sentiments or practices. And when Christians were invited to feast with infidels they were not to ask needless questions about the food set before them, but eat without scruple. Needless enquiries might perplex their minds and consciences, for which reason they were to be avoided. Any thing fit to be eaten, that was set before them at a common entertainment, they might lawfully eat. And why then should they scrupulously enquire whether what was set before them had been sacrificed? It is to be understood of civil feasting, not religious; for the latter among the heathens was feasting upon their sacrifices, which he had condemned before as a participation in their idolatrous worship. At a common feast they might expect common food; and they needed not to move scruples in their own minds whether what was set before them was otherwise or no. Note, Though Christians should be very careful to know and understand their duty, yet they should not, by needless enquiries, perplex themselves.

IV. Yet, even at such an entertainment, he adds, if any should say it was a thing that had been offered to idols, they should refrain: *Eat not, for his sake that showed it, and for conscience' sake*. Whether it were the master of the feast or any of the guests, whether it were spoken in the hearing of all or whispered in the ear, they should refrain for his sake who suggested this to them, whether he were an infidel or an infirm Christian; and for conscience' sake, out of regard to conscience, that they might show a regard to it in themselves, and keep up a regard to it in others. This he backs with the same reason as the former: *For the earth is the Lord's*. There is food enough provided by our common Lord, of which we maya eat without scruple. The same doctrine may be variously improved, as here: "The earth is the Lord's, therefore you may eat any thing without scruple that is set before you as common food; and yet, because the earth is the Lord's, eat nothing that will give offence, lay a stumbling-block before others, and encourage some in idolatry, or tempt others to eat when they are not clear in their own mind that it is lawful, and so sin, and wound their own consciences." Note, Christians should be very cautious of doing what may thus prej-

unjust to reproach me for using it. This must be understood abstracted from the scandal given by eating in the circumstance mentioned. Though some understand it to mean, "Why should I, by using the liberty I have, give occasion to those who are scandalized to speak evil of me?" According to that advice of the apostle (Rom. 14:16), *Let not your good be evil spoken of*. Note, Christians should take care not to use their liberty to the hurt of others, nor their own reproach.

VI. The apostle takes occasion from this discourse to lay down a rule for Christians' conduct, and apply it to this particular case (v. 31, 32), namely, that in eating and drinking, and in all we do, we should aim at the glory of God, at pleasing and honouring him. This is the fundamental principle of practical godliness. The great end of all practical religion must direct us where particular and express rules are wanting. Nothing must be done against the glory of God, and the good of our neighbours, connected with it. Nay, the tendency of our behaviour to the common good, and the credit of our holy religion, should give direction to it. And therefore nothing should be done by us to offend any, *whether Jew, or Gentile, or the church, v.* 32. The Jews should not be unnecessarily grieved nor prejudiced, who have such an abhorrence of idols that they reckon every thing offered to them thereby defiled, and that it will pollute and render culpable all who partake of it; nor should heathens be countenanced in their idolatry by any behaviour of ours, which they may construe as homage or honour done to their idols; nor young converts from Gentilism take any encouragement from our conduct to retain any veneration for the heathen gods and worship, which they have renounced: nor should we do any thing that may be a means to pervert any members of the church from their Christian profession or practice. Our own humour and appetite must not determine our practice, but the honour of God and the good and edification of the church. We should not so much consult our own pleasure and interest as the advancement of the kingdom of God among men. Note, A Christian should be a man devoted to God, and of a public spirit.

VII. He presses all upon them by his own example: *Even as I please all men* (or study to do it) *in all things* (that I lawfully can), *not seeking my own profit, but that of many, that they may be saved, v.* 33. Note, A preacher may press his advice home with boldness and authority when he can enforce it with his own example. He is most likely to promote a public spirit in others who can give evidence of it in himself. And it is highly commendable in a minister to neglect his own advantage that he may promote the salvation of his hearers. This shows that he has a spirit suitable to his function. It is a station for public usefulness, and can never be faithfully discharged by a man of a narrow spirit and selfish principles.

CHAPTER 11

In this chapter the apostle blames, and endeavours to rectify, some great indecencies and manifest disorders in the church of Corinth; as, I. The misconduct of their women (some of whom seem to have been inspired) in the public assembly, who laid by their veils, the common token of subjection to their husbands in that part of the world. This behaviour he reprehends, requires them to keep veiled, asserts the superiority of the husband, yet so as to remind the husband that both were made for mutual help and comfort (v 1–16). II. He blames them for their discord and neglect and contempt of the poor, at the Lord's supper (v. 17–22). III. To rectify these scandalous disorders, he sets before them the nature and intentions of this holy institution, directs them how they should attend on it, and warns them of the danger of a conduct to indecent as theirs, and of all unworthy receiving (v. 23 to the end).

Verses 1–16

Paul, having answered the cases put to him, proceeds in this chapter to the redress of grievances. The first verse of the chapter is put, by those who divided the epistle into chapters, as a preface to the rest of the epistle, but seems to have been a more proper close to the last, in which he had enforced the cautions he had given against the abuse of liberty, by his own example: *Be ye followers of me, as I also*

blindly neither. He encourages neither implicit faith nor obedience. He would be followed himself no further than he followed Christ. Christ's pattern is a copy without a blot; so is no man's else. Note, We should follow no leader further than he follows Christ. Apostles should be left by us when they deviate from the example of their Master. He passes next to reprehend and reform an indecency among them, of which the women were more especially guilty, concerning which observe,

I. How he prefaces it. He begins with a commendation of what was praiseworthy in them (v. 2): *I praise you, that you remember me in all things, and keep the ordinances as I delivered them to you*. Many of them, it is probable, did this in the strictest sense of the expression: and he takes occasion thence to address the body of the church under this good character; and the body might, in the main, have continued to observe the ordinances and institutions of Christ, though in some things they deviated from, and corrupted, them. Note, When we reprove what is amiss in any, it is very prudent and fit to commend what is good in them; it will show that the reproof is not from ill-will, and a humour of censuring and finding fault; and it will therefore procure the more regard to it.

II. How he lays the foundation for his reprehension by asserting the superiority of the man over the woman: *I would have you know that the head of every man is Christ, and the head of the woman is the man, and the head of Christ is God*. Christ, in his mediatorial character and glorified humanity, is at the head of mankind. He is not only first of the kind, but Lord and Sovereign. He has a name above every name: though in this high office and authority he has a superior, God being his head. And as God is the head of Christ, and Christ the head of the whole human kind, so the man is the head of the tow sexes: not indeed with such dominion as Christ has over the kind or God has over the man Christ Jesus; but a superiority and headship he has, and the woman should be in subjection and not assume or usurp the man's place. This is the situation in which God has placed her; and for that reason she should have a mind suited to her rank, and not do any thing that looks like an affectation of changing places. Something like this the women of the church of Corinth seem to have been guilty of, who were under inspiration, and prayed and prophesied even in their assemblies, *v.* 5. It is indeed an apostolical canon, that the women *should keep silence in the churches* (ch. 14:34; 1 Tim. 2:12), which some understand without limitation, as if a woman under inspiration also must keep silence, which seems very well to agree with the connection of the apostle's discourse, ch. 14. Others with a limitation: though a woman might not from her own abilities pretend to teach, or so much as question and debate any thing in the church yet when under inspiration the case was altered, she had liberty to speak. Or, though she might not preach even by inspiration (because teaching is the business of a superior), yet she might pray or utter hymns by inspiration, even in the public assembly. She did not show any affectation of superiority over the man by such acts of public worship. It is plain the apostle does not in this place prohibit the thing, but reprehend the manner of doing it. And yet he might utterly disallow the thing and lay an unlimited restraint on the woman in another part of the epistle. These things are not contradictory. It is to his present purpose to reprehend the manner wherein the women prayed and prophesied in the church, without determining in this place whether they did well or ill in praying or prophesying. Note, The manner of doing a thing enters into the morality of it. We must not only be concerned to do good, but that the good we do be well done.

III. The thing he reprehends is the woman's praying or prophesying uncovered, or the man's doing either covered, *v.* 4, 5. To understand this, it must be observed that it was a signification either of shame or subjection for persons to be veiled, or covered, in the eastern countries, contrary to the custom of ours, where the being bare-headed betokens subjection, and being covered superiority and dominion. And this will help us the better to understand,

IV. The reasons on which he grounds his reprehension. 1. *The man that prays or prophesies with his head covered dishonoureth his head,* namely, Christ, the head of every man (*v.* 3), by appearing in a habit unsuitable to the rank in which God has placed him. Note, We should, even in our dress and habits, avoid every thing that may dishonour Christ. *The woman,* on the other hand, *who prays or prophesies with her head uncovered dishonoureth her head,* namely, the man, *v.* 3. She appears in the dress of her superior, and throws off the token of her subjection. She might, with equal decency, cut her hair short, or cut it close, which was the custom of the man in that age. This would be in a manner to declare that she was desirous of changing sexes, a manifest affectation of that superiority which God had conferred on the other sex. And this was probably the fault of these prophetesses in the church of Corinth. It was doing a thing which, in that age of the world, betokened superiority, and therefore a tacit claim of what did not belong to them but the other sex. Note, The sexes should not affect to change places. The order in which divine wisdom has placed persons and things is best and fittest: to endeavour to amend it is to destroy all order, and introduce confusion. The woman should keep to the rank God has chosen for her, and not dishonour her head; for this, in the result, is to dishonour God. If she was made out of the man, and for the man, and made to be the glory of the man, she should do nothing, especially in public, that looks like a wish of having this order inverted. 2. Another reason against this conduct is that *the man is the image and glory of God,* the representative of that glorious dominion and headship which God has over the world. It is the man who is set at the head of this lower creation, and therein he bears the resemblance of God. The woman, on the other hand, *is the glory of the man* (*v.* 7): she is his representative. Not but she has dominion over the inferior creatures, as she is a partaker of human nature, and so far is God's representative too, but it is at second-hand. She is the image of God, inasmuch as she is the image of the man: *For the man was not made out of the woman, but the woman out of the man, v.* 8. The man was first made, and made head of the creation here below, and therein the image of the divine dominion; and the woman was made out of the man, and shone with a reflection of his glory, being made superior to the other creatures here below, but in subjection to her husband, and deriving that honour from him out of whom she was made. 3. *The woman was made for the man,* to be his help-meet, *and not the man for the woman.* She was naturally, therefore, made subject to him, because made for him, for his use, and help, and comfort. And she who was intended to be always in subjection to the man should do nothing, in Christian assemblies, that looks like an affectation of equality. 4. *She ought to have power on her head, because of the angels.* Power, that is, a veil, the token, not of her having the power or superiority, but being under the power of her husband, subjected to him, and inferior to the other sex. Rebekah, when she met Isaac, and was delivering herself into his possession, put on her veil, in token of her subjection, Gen. 24:65. Thus would the apostle have the women appear In Christian assemblies, even though they spoke there by inspiration, *because of the angels,* that is, say some, because of the evil angels. The woman *was first in the transgression, being deceived by the devil* (1 Tim. 2:14), which increased her subjection to man, Gen. 3:16. Now, believe evil angels will be sure to mix in all Christian assemblies, therefore should women wear the token of their shamefacedness and subjection, which in that age and country, was a veil. Others say because of the good angels. Jews and Christians have had an opinion that these ministering spirits are many of them present in their assemblies. Their presence should restrain Christians from all indecencies in the worship of God. Note, We should learn from all to behave in the public assemblies of divine worship so as to express a reverence for God, and a content and satisfaction with that rank in which he has placed us.

V. He thinks fit to guard his argument with a caution lest the inference be carried too far (*v.* 11, 12): *Nevertheless, neither is the man without the woman, nor the woman without the man in the Lord.* They were made for one another. *It is not good for him to be alone* (Gen. 2:18), and therefore was a woman made, and made for the man; and the man was intended to be a comfort, and help, and defence, to the woman, though not so directly and immediately made for her. They were made to be a mutual comfort and blessing, not one a slave and the other a tyrant. *Both were to be one flesh* (Gen. 2:24), and this for the propagation of a race of mankind. They are reciprocal instruments of each other's production. As the woman was first formed out of the man, the man is ever since propagated by the woman (*v.* 12), all by the divine wisdom and power of the First Cause so ordaining it. The authority and subjection should be no greater than are suitable to two in such near relation and close union to each other. Note, As it is the will of God that the woman know her place, so it is his will also that the man abuse not his power.

VI. He enforces his argument from the natural covering provided for the woman (*v.* 13–15): *"Judge in yourselves —* consult your own reason, hearken to what nature suggests *— is it comely for a woman to pray to God uncovered?* Should there not be a distinction kept up between the sexes in wearing their hair, since nature has made one? Is it not a distinction which nature has kept up among all civilized nations? The woman's hair is a natural covering; to wear it long is a glory to her; but for a man to have long hair, or cherish it, is a token of softness and effeminacy." Note, It should be our concern, especially in Christian and religious assemblies, to make no breach upon the rules of natural decency.

VII. He sums up all by referring those who were contentious to the usages and customs of the churches, *v.* 16. Custom is in a great measure the rule of decency. And the common practice of the churches is what would have them govern themselves by. He does not silence the contentious by mere authority, but lets them know that they would appear to the world as very odd and singular in their humour if they would quarrel for a custom to which all the churches of Christ were at that time utter strangers, or against a custom in which they all concurred, and that upon the ground of natural decency. It was the common usage of the churches for women to appear in public assemblies, and join in public worship, veiled; and it was manifestly decent that they should do so. Those must be very contentious indeed who would quarrel with this, or lay it aside.

Verses 17–22

In this passage the apostle sharply rebukes them for much greater disorders than the former, in their partaking of the Lord's supper, which was commonly done in the first ages, as the ancients tell us, with a love-feast annexed, which gave occasion to the scandalous disorders which the apostle here reprehends, concerning which observe,

I. The manner in which he introduces his charge: *"Now in this that I declare to you I praise you not, v.* 17. I cannot commend, but must blame and condemn you." It is plain, from the beginning of the chapter, that he was willing and pleased to commend as far as he could. But such scandalous disorders, in so sacred an institution, as they were guilty of, called for a sharp reprehension. They quite turned the institution against itself. It was intended to make them better, to promote their spiritual interests; but it really made them worse. *They came together, not for the better, but for the worse.* Note, The ordinances of Christ, if they do not make us better, will be very apt to make us worse; if they do not do our souls good, they do us harm; if they do not melt and mend, they will harden. Corruptions will be confirmed in us, if the proper means do not work a cure of them.

II. He enters upon his charge against them in more particulars than one. 1. He tells them that, upon coming together, they fell into *divisions, schisms — schismata.* Instead of concurring unanimously in celebrating the ordinance, they fell a quarrelling with one another. Note, There may be schism where there is no separation of communion. Persons may come together in the same church, and sit down at the same table of the Lord, and yet be schismatics. Uncharitableness, alienation of affection, especially if it grows up to discord, and feuds, and contentions, constitute schism. Christians may separate from each other's communion, and yet be uncharitable one towards another; they may continue in the same communion, and yet be uncharitable. This latter is schism, rather than the former. The apostle had heard a report of the Corinthians' divisions, and he tells them he had too much reason to believe it. For, adds he, there must be heresies also; not only quarrels, but factions, and perhaps such corrupt opinions as strike at the foundation of Christianity, and all sound religion. Note, No marvel there should be breaches of Christian love in the churches, when such offences will come as shall make shipwreck of faith and a good conscience. Such offences must come. Note that men are necessitated to be guilty of them; but the event is certain, and God permits them, that those who are approved (such honest hearts as will bear the trial) may be set to view, and appear faithful by their constant adherence to the truths and ways of God, notwithstanding the temptations of seducers. Note, The wisdom of God can make the wickedness and errors of others a foil to the piety and integrity of the saints. 2. He charges them not only with discord and division, but with scandalous disorder: *For in eating every one taketh before the other his own supper; and one is hungry, and another is drunken, v.* 21. Heathens used to drink plentifully at their feasts upon their sacrifices. Many of the wealthier Corinthians seem to have taken the same liberty at the Lord's table, or at least at their *Agapai,* or *love-feasts,* that were annexed to the supper. They would not stay for one another; the rich despised the poor, and ate and drank up the provisions they themselves brought, before the poor were allowed to partake; and thus some wanted, while others had more than enough. This was profaning a sacred institution, and corrupting a divine ordinance, to the last degree. What was appointed to feed the soul was employed to feed their lusts and passions. What should have been a bond of mutual amity and affection was made an instrument of discord and disunion. The poor were deprived of the food prepared for them, and the rich turned a feast of charity into a debauch. This was scandalous irregularity.

III. The apostle lays the blame of this conduct closely on them, 1. By telling them that their conduct perfectly destroyed the purpose and use of such an institution: *This is not to eat the Lord's supper, v.* 20. It was coming to the Lord's table, and not coming. They might as well have staid away. Thus to eat the outward elements was not to eat Christ's body. Note, There is a careless and irregular eating of the Lord's supper which is as none at all; it will turn to no account, but to increase guilt. Such an eating was that of the Corinthians; their practices were a direct contradiction to the purposes of this sacred institution. 2. Their conduct carried in it a contempt of God's house, or of the church, *v.* 22. If they had a mind to feast, they might do it at home in their own houses; but to come to the Lord's table, and cabal and quarrel, and keep the poor from their share of the provision there made for them as well as rich, was such an abuse of the ordinance, and such a contempt of the poorer members of the church more especially, as merited a very sharp rebuke. Such a behaviour tended much to the shame and discouragement of the poor, whose souls were as dear to Christ, and cost him as much, as those of the rich. Note, Common meals may be managed after a common manner, but religious feasts should be attended religiously. Note, also, It is a heinous evil, and severely to be censured, for Christians to treat their fellow-christians with contempt and insolence, but especially at the Lord's table. This is doing what they can to pour contempt on divine ordinances. And we should look carefully to it that nothing in our behaviour at the Lord's table have the appearance of contemning so sacred an institution.

Verses 23–34

To rectify these gross corruptions and irregularities, the apostle sets the sacred institution here to view. This should be the rule in the reformation of all abuses.

I. He tells us how he came by the knowledge of it. He was not among the apostles at the first institution; but *he had received from the Lord what he delivered to them, v.* 23. He had the knowledge of this matter by revelation from Christ: and what he had received he communicated, without varying from the truth a tittle, without adding or diminishing.

II. He gives us a more particular account of the institution than we meet with elsewhere. We have here an account,

1. Of the author — our Lord Jesus Christ. The king of the church only has power to institute sacraments.

2. The time of the institution: *It was the very night wherein he was betrayed;* just as he was entering on his sufferings which are therein to be commemorated.

3. The institution itself. Our Saviour took bread, and when he had given thanks, or *blessed* (as it is in Mt. 26:26), *he broke, and said, Take, eat; this is my body, broken for you; this do in remembrance of me. And in like manner he took the cup, when he had supped, saying, This cup is the New Testament in my blood; this do, as oft as you drink it, in remembrance of me, v.* 24, 25. Here observe,

(1.) The materials of this sacrament; both, [1.] As to the

Bread and the cup are both made use of, because it is a holy feast. Nor is it here, or any where, made necessary, that any particular liquor should be in the cup. In one evangelist, indeed, it is plain that wine was the liquor used by our Saviour, though it was, perhaps, mingled with water, according to the Jewish custom; *vide* Lightfoot on Mt. 26. But this by no means renders it unlawful to have a sacrament where persons cannot come at wine. In every place of scripture in which we have an account of this part of the institution it is always expressed by a figure. The cup is put for what was in it, without once specifying what the liquor was, in the words of the institution. [2.] The things signified by these outward signs; they are Christ's body and blood, his body broken, his blood shed, together with all the benefits which flow from his death and sacrifice: *it is the New Testament in his blood.* His blood is the seal and sanction of all the privileges of the new covenant; and worthy receivers take it as such, at this holy ordinance. They have the New Testament, and their own title to all the blessings of the new covenant, confirmed to them by his blood.

(2.) We have here the sacramental actions, the manner in which the materials of the sacrament are to be used. [1.] Our Saviour's actions, which are taking the bread and cup, giving thanks, breaking the bread, and giving about both the one and the other. [2.] The actions of the communicants, which were to take the bread and eat, to take the cup and drink, and both in remembrance of Christ. But the external acts are not the whole nor the principal part of what is to be done at this holy ordinance; each of them has a significancy. Our Saviour, having undertaken to make an offering of himself to God, and procure, by his death, the remission of sins, with all other gospel benefits, for true believers, did, at the institution, deliver his body and blood, with all the benefits procured by his death, to his disciples, and continues to do the same every time the ordinance is administered to the true believers. This is here exhibited, or set forth, as the food of souls. And as food, though ever so wholesome or rich, will yield no nourishment without being eaten, here the communicants are to take and eat, or to receive Christ and feed upon him, his grace and benefits, and by faith convert them into nourishment to their souls. They are to take him as their Lord and life, yield themselves up to him, and live upon him. *He is our life,* Col. 3:4.

(3.) We have here an account of the ends of this institution. [1.] It was appointed to be done *in remembrance of Christ,* to keep fresh in our minds an ancient favour, his dying for us, as well as to remember an absent friend, even Christ interceding for us, in virtue of his death, at God's right hand. The best of friends, and the greatest acts of kindness, are here to be remembered, with the exercise of suitable affections and graces. The motto on this ordinance, and the very meaning of it, is, *When this you see, remember me.* [2.] It was *to show forth Christ's death,* to declare and publish it. It is not barely in remembrance of Christ, of what he has done and suffered, that this ordinance was instituted; but to commemorate, to celebrate, his glorious condescension and grace in our redemption. We declare his death to be our life, the spring of all our comforts and hopes. And we glory in such a declaration; we show forth his death, and spread it before God, as our accepted sacrifice and ransom. We set it in view of our own faith, for our own comfort and quickening; and we own before the world, by this very service, that we are the disciples of Christ, who trust in him alone for salvation and acceptance with God.

(4.) It is moreover hinted here, concerning this ordinance, [1.] That it should be frequent: *As often as you eat this bread,* etc. Our bodily meals return often; we cannot maintain life and health without this. And it is fit that this spiritual diet should be taken often tool The ancient churches celebrated this ordinance every Lord's day, if not every day when they assembled for worship. [2.] That it must be perpetual. It is to be celebrated *till the Lord shall come;* till he shall come

III. He lays before the Corinthians the danger of receiving unworthily, of prostituting this institution as they did, and using it to the purposes of feasting and faction, with intentions opposite to its design, or a temper of mind altogether unsuitable to it; or keeping up the covenant with sin and death, while they are there professedly renewing and confirming their covenant with God. 1. It is great guilt which such contract. They shall *be guilty of the body and blood of the Lord* (*v.* 27), of violating this sacred institution, of despising his body and blood. They act as if they *counted the blood of the covenant, wherewith they are sanctified, an unholy thing,* Heb. 10:29. They profane the institution, and in a manner crucify their Saviour over again. Instead of being cleansed by his blood, they are guilty of his blood. 2. It is a great hazard which they run: *They eat and drink judgment to themselves, v.* 29. They provoke God, and are likely to bring down punishment on themselves. No doubt but they incur great guilt, and so render themselves liable to damnation, to spiritual judgments and eternal misery. Every sin is in its own nature damning; and therefore surely so heinous a sin as profaning such a holy ordinance is so. And it is profaned in the grossest sense by such irreverence and rudeness as the Corinthians were guilty of. But fearful believers should not be discouraged from attending at this holy ordinance by the sound of these words, as if they bound upon themselves the sentence of damnation by coming to the table of the Lord unprepared. Thus sin, as well as all others, leaves room for forgiveness upon repentance; and the Holy Spirit never indited this passage of scripture to deter serious Christians from their duty, though the devil has often made this advantage of it, and robbed good Christians of their choicest comforts. The Corinthians came to the Lord's table as to a common feast, *not discerning the Lord's body* — not making a difference or distinction between that and common food, but setting both on a level: nay, they used much more indecency at this sacred feast than they would have done at a civil one. This was very sinful in them, and very displeasing to God, and brought down his judgments on them: *For this cause many are weak and sickly among you, and many sleep.* Some were punished with sickness, and some with death. Note, A careless and irreverent receiving of the Lord's supper may bring temporal punishments. Yet the connection seems to imply that even those who were thus punished were in a state of favour with God, at least many of them: *They were chastened of the Lord, that they should not be condemned with the world, v.* 32. Now divine chastening is a sign of divine love: *Whom the Lord loveth he chasteneth* (Heb. 12:6), especially with so merciful a purpose, to prevent their final condemnation. In the midst of judgment, God remembers mercy: he frequently punishes those whom he tenderly loves. It is kindness to use the rod to prevent the child's ruin. He will visit such iniquity as this under consideration with stripes, and yet make those stripes the evidence of his lovingkindness. Those were in the favour of God who yet so highly offended him in this instance, and brought down judgments on themselves; at least many of them were; for they were punished by him out of fatherly good-will, punished now that they might not perish for ever. Note, It is better to bear trouble in this world than to be miserable to eternity. And God punishes his people now, to prevent their eternal woe.

IV. He points out the duty of those who would come to the Lord's table. 1. In general: *Let a man examine himself* (*v.* 28), try and approve himself. Let him consider the sacred intention of this holy ordinance, its nature, and use, and compare his own views in attending on it and his disposition of mind for it; and, when he has approved himself to his own conscience in the sight of God, then let him attend. Such self-examination is necessary to a right attendance at this holy ordinance. Note, Those who, through weakness of understanding, cannot try themselves, are by no means fit to eat of this bread and drink of this cup; nor those who, upon a fair trial, have just ground to charge themselves with impenitency, unbelief, and alienation from the life of God. Those

verity of our heavenly Father. We must not judge others, lest we be judged (Mt. 7:1); but we must judge ourselves, to prevent our being judged and condemned by God. We may be critical as to ourselves, but should be very candid in judging others.

V. He closes all with a caution against the irregularities of which they were guilty (*v.* 33, 34), charging them to avoid all indecency at the Lord's table. They were to eat for hunger and pleasure only at home, and not to change the holy supper to a common feast; and much less eat up the provisions before those who could bring none did partake of them, lest they should come together for condemnation. Note, Our holy duties, through our own abuse, may prove matter of condemnation. Christians may keep Sabbaths, hear sermons, attend at sacraments, and only aggravate guilt, and bring on a heavier doom. A sad but serious truth! O! let all look to it that they do not come together at any time to God's worship, and all the while provoke him, and bring down vengeance on themselves. Holy things are to be used in a holy manner, or else they are profaned. What else was amiss in this matter, he tells them, he would rectify when he came to them.

CHAPTER 12

In this chapter the apostle, I. Considers the case of spiritual gifts, which were very plentifully poured out on the Corinthian church. He considers their original, that they are from God; their variety and use, that they were all intended for one and the same general end, the advancement of Christianity and the church's edification (*v.* 1–11). II. He illustrates this by an allusion to a human body, in which all the members have a mutual relation and subserviency, and each has its proper place and use (*v.* 12–26). III. He tells us that the church is the body of Christ, and the members are variously gifted for the benefit of the whole body, and each particular member (*v.* 27–30). And them, IV. Closes with an exhortation to seek somewhat more beneficial than these gifts (*v.* 31).

Verses 1–11

The apostle comes now to treat of spiritual gifts, which abounded in the church of Corinth, but were greatly abused. What these gifts were is at large told us in the body of the chapter; namely, extraordinary offices and powers, bestowed on ministers and Christians in the first ages, for conviction of unbelievers, and propagation of the gospel. Gifts and graces, *charismata* and *charis,* greatly differ. Both indeed were freely given of God. But where grace is given it is for the salvation of those who have it. Gifts are bestowed for the advantage and salvation of others. And there may be great gifts where there is not a dram of grace, but persons possessed of them are utterly out of the divine favour. They are great instances of divine benignity to men, but do not by themselves prove those who have them to be the objects of divine complacency. This church was rich in gifts, but there were many things scandalously out of order in it. Now concerning these spiritual gifts, that is, the extraordinary powers they had received from the Spirit,

I. The apostle tells them he would not have them ignorant either of their original or use. They came from God, and were to be used for him. It would lead them far astray if they were ignorant of one or the other of these. Note, Right information is of great use as to all religious practice. It is wretched work which gifted men make who either do not know or do not advert to the nature and right use of the gifts with which they are endowed.

II. He puts them in the mind of the sad state out of which they had been recovered: *You were Gentiles, carried away to dumb idols, even as you were led, v.* 2. While they were so, they could have no pretensions to be spiritual men, nor to have spiritual gifts. While they were under the conduct of the spirit of Gentilism, they could not be influenced by the Spirit of Christ. If they well understood their former condition, they could not but know that all true spiritual gifts were from God. Now concerning this observe, 1. Their former character: they *were Gentiles.* Not God's peculiar people, but of the nations whom he had in a manner abandoned. The Jews were, before, his chosen people, distinguished from the rest of the world by his favour. To them the knowledge and worship of the true God were in a manner confined. The rest of the world were strangers to the covenant of promise, aliens from the commonwealth of Israel, and in a manner without God, Eph. 2:12. Such Gentiles were the body of the Corinthians, before their conversion to Christianity. What a change was here! Christian Corinthians were once Gentiles. Note, It is of great use to the Christian, and a proper consideration to stir him up both to duty and thankfulness, to think what once he was: *You were Gentiles.* 2. The conduct they were under: *Carried away to these dumb idols, even as you were led.* They were hurried upon the grossest idolatry, the worship even of stocks and stones, through the force of a vain imagination, and the fraud of their priests practising on their ignorance, for, whatever were the sentiments of their philosophers, this was the practice of the herd. The body of the people paid their homage and worship to dumb idols, *that had ears but could not hear, and mouths but could not speak,* Ps. 115:5, 6. Miserable abjectness of mind! And those who despised these gross conceptions of the vulgar yet countenanced them by their practice. O dismal state of Gentilism! Could the Spirit of God be among such stupid idolators, or they be influenced by it? How did the prince of this world triumph in the blindness of mankind! How thick a mist had he cast over their minds!

III. He shows them how they might discern those gifts that were from the Spirit of God, true spiritual gifts: *No man, speaking by the Spirit, calls Jesus accursed.* Thus did both Jews and Gentiles: they blasphemed him as an impostor, and execrated his name, and deemed it abominable. And yet many Jews, who were exorcists and magicians, went about, pretending to work wonders by the Spirit of God (vid. Lightfoot's *Horae in loc.*), and many among the Gentiles pretended to inspiration. Now the apostle tells them none could act under the influence, nor by the power, of the Spirit of God, who disowned and blasphemed Christ: for the Spirit of God bore uncontrollable witness to Christ by prophecy, miracles, his resurrection from the dead, the success of his doctrine among men, and its effect upon them; and could never so far contradict itself as to declare him accursed. And on the other hand *no man could say Jesus was the Lord* (that is, live by this faith, and work miracles to prove it), *but it must be by the Holy Ghost.* To own this truth before men, and maintain it to the death, and live under the influence of it, could not be done without the sanctification of the Holy Ghost. No man can call Christ *Lord,* with a believing subjection to him and dependence upon him, unless that faith be wrought by the Holy Ghost. No man can confess this truth in the day of trial but by the Holy Ghost animating and encouraging him. Note, We have as necessary a dependence on the Spirit's operation and influence for our sanctification and perseverance as on the mediation of Christ for our reconciliation and acceptance with God: and no man could confirm this truth with a miracle but by the Holy Ghost. No evil spirit would lend assistance, if it were in his power, to spread a doctrine and religion so ruinous to the devil's kingdom. The substance of what the apostle asserts and argues here is that whatever pretences there were to inspiration or miracles, among those who were enemies to Christianity, they could not be from the Spirit of God; but no man could believe this with his heart, nor prove with a miracle that Jesus was Christ, but by the Holy Ghost: so that the extraordinary operations and powers among them did all proceed from the Spirit of God. He adds,

IV. These spiritual gifts, though proceeding from the same Spirit, are yet various. They have one author and original, but are themselves of various kinds. A free cause may produce variety of effects; and the same giver may bestow various gifts, *v.* 4. *There are diversities of gifts,* such as revelations, tongues, prophecy, interpretations of tongues; *but the same Spirit.* There are differences of administrations, or different offices, and officers to discharge them, different ordinances and institutions (see *v.* 28–30), but the same Lord, who appointed all, *v.* 6. *There are diversities of operations,* or miraculous powers, called *energēmata dynameōn* (*v.* 10), as here *energēmata, but it is the same God that worketh all in all.* There are various gifts, administrations, and operations, but all proceed from one God, one Lord, one Spirit; that is, from Father, Son, and Holy Ghost, the spring and origin of all spiritual blessings and bequests: all issue from the same fountain; all have the same author. However different they may be in themselves, in this they agree; all are from

God. And several of the kinds are here specified, *v.* 8–10. Several persons had their several gifts, some one, some another, all from and by the same Spirit. To one was given the *word of wisdom;* that is, say some, a knowledge of the mysteries of the gospel, and ability to explain them, an exact understanding of the design, nature, and doctrines, of the Christian religion. Others say an uttering of grave sentences, like Solomon's proverbs. Some confine this word of wisdom to the revelations made to and by the apostles. — *To another the word of knowledge, by the same Spirit;* that is, say some, the knowledge of mysteries (*ch.* 2:13): wrapped up in the prophecies, types, and histories of the Old Testament: say others, a skill and readiness to give advice and counsel in perplexed cases. — *To another faith, by the same Spirit;* that is, the faith of miracles, or a faith in the divine power and promise, whereby they were enabled to trust God in any emergency, and go on in the way of their duty, and own and profess the truths of Christ, whatever was the difficulty or danger. — *To another the gift of healing, by the same Spirit;* that is, healing the sick, either by laying on of hands, or anointing with oil, or with a bare word. — *To another the working of miracles;* the efficacies of powers, *energēmata dynameōn,* such as raising the dead, restoring the blind to sight, giving speech to the dumb, hearing to the deaf, and the use of limbs to the lame. — *To another prophecy,* that is, ability to foretel future events, which is the more usual sense of prophecy; or to explain scripture by a peculiar gift of the Spirit. See *ch.* 14:24. — *To another the discerning of Spirits,* power to distinguish between true and false prophets, or to discern the real and internal qualifications of any person for an office, or to discover the inward workings of the mind by the Holy Ghost, as Peter did those of Ananias, Acts 5:3. — *To another divers kinds of tongues,* or ability to speak languages by inspiration. — *To another the interpretation of tongues,* or ability to render foreign languages readily and properly into their own. With such variety of spiritual gifts were the first ministers and churches blessed.

V. The end for which these gifts were bestowed: *The manifestation of the Spirit is given to every man to profit withal, v.* 7. The Spirit was manifested by the exercise of these gifts; his influence and interest appeared in them. But they were not distributed for the mere honour and advantage of those who had them, but for the benefit of the church, to edify the body, and spread and advance the gospel. Note, Whatever gifts God confers on any man, he confers them that he may do good with them, whether they be common or spiritual. The outward gifts of his bounty are to be improved for his glory, and employed in doing good to others. No man has them merely for himself. They are a trust put into his hands, to profit withal; and the more he profits others with them, the more abundantly will they turn to his account in the end, Phil. 4:17. Spiritual gifts are bestowed, that men may with them profit the church and promote Christianity. They are not given for show, but for service; not for pomp and ostentation, but for edification; not to magnify those that have them, but to edify others.

VI. The measure and proportion in which they are given: *All these worketh one and the same Spirit, dividing to every man as he will.* It is according to the sovereign pleasure of the donor. What more free than a gift? And shall not the Spirit of God do what he will with his own? May he not give to what persons he pleases, and in what proportion he pleases; one gift to one man, and another to another; to one more, and another fewer, as he thinks fit? Is he not the best judge how his own purpose shall be served, and his own donatives bestowed? It is not as men will, nor as they may think fit, but as the Spirit pleases. Note, The Holy Ghost is a divine person. He works divine effects and divides divine gifts a he will, by his own power, and according to his own pleasure, without dependence or control. But though he distributes these gifts freely and uncontrollably, they are intended by him, not for private honour and advantage, but for public benefit, for the edification of the body, the church.

Verses 12–26

The apostle here makes out the truth of what was above asserted, and puts the gifted men among the Corinthians in mind of their duty, by comparing the church of Christ to a human body.

I. By telling us that one body may have many members, and that the many members of the same body make but one body (*v.* 12): *As the body is one, and hath many members,*

and all members of that one body, being many, are one body, so also is Christ; that is, Christ mystical, as divines commonly speak. Christ and his church making one body, as head and members, this body is made up of many parts or members, yet but one body; for all the members are *baptized into the same body, and made to drink of the same Spirit, v.* 13. Jews and Gentiles, bond and free, are upon a level in this: all are baptized into the same body, and made partakers of the same Spirit. Christians become members of this body by baptism: they are baptized into one body. The outward rite is of divine institution, significant of the new birth, called therefore *the washing of regeneration,* Tit. 3:5. But it is by the Spirit, by the renewing of the Holy Ghost, that we are made members of Christ's body. It is the Spirit's operation, signified by the outward administration, that makes us members. And by communion at the other ordinance we are sustained; but then it is not merely by drinking the wine, but by drinking into one Spirit. The outward administration is a means appointed of God for our participation in this great benefit; but it is baptism by the Spirit, it is internal renovation and drinking into one Spirit, partaking of his sanctifying influence from time to time, that makes us true members of Christ's body, and maintains our union with him. Being animated by one Spirit makes Christians one body. Note, All who have the spirit of Christ, without difference, are the members of Christ, whether Jew or Gentile, bond or free; and none but such. And all the members of Christ make up one body; the members many, but the body one. They are one body, because they have one principle of life; all are quickened and animated by the same Spirit.

II. Each member has its particular form, place, and use. 1. The meanest member makes a part of the body. The foot and ear are less useful, perhaps, than the hand and eye; but because one is not a hand, and the other an eye, shall they say, therefore, that they do not belong to the body? *v.* 15, 16. So every member of the body mystical cannot have the same place and office; but what then? Shall it hereupon disown relation to the body? Because it is not fixed in the same station, or favoured with the same gifts as others, shall it say, "I do not belong to Christ?" No, the meanest member of his body is as much a member as the noblest, and as truly regarded by him. All his members are dear to him. 2. There must be a distinction of members in the body: *Were the whole body eye, where were the hearing? Were the whole ear, where were the smelling? v.* 17. *If all were one member, where were the body? v.* 19. *They are many members,* and for that reason must have distinction among them, *and yet are but one body, v.* 20. One member of a body is not a body; this is made up of many; and among these many there must be a distinction, difference of situation, shape, use, etc. So it is in the body of Christ; its members must have different uses, and therefore have different powers, and be in different places, some having one gift, and others a different one. Variety in the members of the body contributes to the beauty of it. What a monster would a body be if it were all ear, or eye, or arm! So it is for the beauty and good appearance of the church that there should be diversity of gifts and offices in it. 3. The disposal of members in a natural body, and their situation, are as God pleases: *But now hath God set the members, every one of them, in the body, as it hath pleased him, v.* 18. We may plainly perceive the divine wisdom in the distribution of the members; but it was made according to the counsel of his will; he distinguished and distributed them as he pleased. So is it also in the members of Christ's body: they are chosen out to such stations, and endued with such gifts, as God pleases. He who is sovereign Lord of all disposes his favours and gifts as he will. And who should gainsay his pleasure? What foundation is here for repining in ourselves, or envying others? We should be doing the duties of our own place, and not murmuring in ourselves, nor quarrelling with others, that we are not in theirs. 4. All the members of the body are, in some respect, useful and necessary to each other: *The eye cannot say to the hand, I have no need of thee; nor the head to the feet, I have no need of your:* nay, those members of the body *which seem to be more feeble* (the bowels, etc.) *are necessary* (*v.* 21, 22); God has so fitted and tempered them together that they are all necessary to one another, and to the whole body; there is no part redundant and unnecessary. Every member serves some good purpose or other: it is useful to its fellow-members, and necessary to the good state of the whole body. Nor is there a member of the body of Christ but may and ought to be useful to his fellow-members, and at some times, and in some cases, is needful to them. None should despise and envy another, seeing God has made the distinction between them as he pleased, yet so as to keep them all in some degree of mutual dependence, and make them valuable to each other, and concerned for each other, because of their mutual usefulness. Those who excel in any gift cannot say that they have no need of those who in that gift are their inferiors, while perhaps, in other gifts, they exceed them. Nay, the lowest members of all have their use, and the highest cannot do well without them. The eye has need of the hand, and the head of the feet. 5. Such is the man's concern for his whole body that *on the less honourable members more abundant honour is bestowed, and our uncomely parts have more abundant comeliness.* Those parts which are not fit, like the rest, to be exposed to view, which are either deformed or shameful, we most carefully clothe and cover; whereas the comely parts have no such need. The wisdom of Providence has so contrived and tempered things that the most abundant regard and honour should be paid to that which most wanted it, *v.* 24. So should the members of Christ's body behave towards their fellow-members: instead of despising them, or reproaching them, for their infirmities, they should endeavour to cover and conceal them, and put the best face upon them that they can. 6. Divine wisdom has contrived and ordered things in this manner that the members of the body should not be schismatics, divided from each other and acting upon separate interests, but well affected to each other, tenderly concerned for each other, having a fellow-feeling of each other's griefs and a communion in each other's pleasures and joys, *v.* 25, 26. God has tempered the members of the body natural in the manner mentioned, that *there might be no schism in the body* (*v.* 25), no rupture nor disunion among the members, nor so much as the least mutual disregard. This should be avoided also in the spiritual body of Christ. There should be no schism in this body, but the members should be closely united by the strongest bonds of love. All decays of this affection are the seeds of schism. Where Christians grow cold towards each other, they will be careless and unconcerned for each other. And this mutual disregard is a schism begun. The members of the natural body are made to have a care and concern for each other, to prevent a schism in it. So should it be in Christ's body; the members should sympathize with each other. As in the natural body the pain of the one part afflicts the whole, the ease and pleasure of one part affects the whole, so should Christians reckon themselves honoured in the honours of their fellow-christians, and should suffer in their sufferings. Note, Christian sympathy is a great branch of Christian duty. We should be so far from slighting our brethren's sufferings that we should suffer with them, so far from envying their honours that we should rejoice with them and reckon ourselves honoured in them.

Verses 27–31

I. Here the apostle sums up the argument, and applies this similitude to the church of Christ, concerning which observe,

1. The relation wherein Christians stand to Christ and one another. The church, or whole collective body of Christians, in all ages, is his body. Every Christian is a member of his body, and every other Christian stands related to him as a fellow-member (*v.* 27): *Now you are the body of Christ, and members in particular,* or particular members. Each is a member of the body, not the whole body; each stands related to the body as a part of it, and all have a common relation to one another, dependence upon one another, and should have a mutual care and concern. Thus are the members of the natural body, thus should the members of the mystical body be, disposed. Note, Mutual indifference, and much more contempt, and hatred, and envy, and strife, are very unnatural in Christians. It is like the members of the same body being destitute of all concern for one another, or quarrelling with each other. This is the apostle's scope in this argument. He endeavours in it to suppress the proud, vaunting, and contentious spirit, that had prevailed among the Corinthians, by reason of their spiritual gifts.

2. The variety of offices instituted by Christ, and gifts or favours dispensed by him (*v.* 28): *God hath set some in the church; first, apostles,* the chief ministers entrusted with all the powers necessary to found a church, and make an entire revelation of God's will. *Secondarily, prophets,* or persons enabled by inspiration, as the evangelists did. *Thirdly, teachers,* those who labour in word and doctrine, whether with pastoral charge or without it. After that, *miracles,* or miracle-workers. *The gifts of healing,* or those who had power to heal diseases; *helps,* or such as had compassion on the sick and weak, and ministered to them; *governments,* or such as had the disposal of the charitable contributions of the church, and dealt them out to the poor; *diversities of tongues,* or such as could speak divers languages. Concerning all these observe, (1.) The plenteous variety of these gifts and offices. What a multitude are they! A good God was free in his communications to the primitive church; he was no niggard of his benefits and favours. No, he provided richly for them. They had no want, but a store — all that was necessary, and even more; what was convenient for them too. (2.) Observe the order of these offices and gifts. They are here placed in their proper ranks. Those of most value have the first place. Apostles, prophets, and teachers, were all intended to instruct the people, to inform them well in the things of God, and promote their spiritual edification: without them, neither evangelical knowledge nor holiness could have been promoted. But the rest, however fitted to answer the great intentions of Christianity, had no such immediate regard to religion, strictly so called. Note, God does, and we should, value things according to their real worth: and the use of things is the best criterion of their real worth. Those are most valuable that best answer the highest purposes. Such were apostolical powers, compared with theirs who had only the gift of healing and miracles. What holds the last and lowest rank in this enumeration is diversity of tongues. It is by itself the most useless and insignificant of all these gifts. Healing diseases, relieving the poor, helping the sick, have their use: but how vain a thing is it to speak languages, if a man does it merely to amuse or boast himself! This may indeed raise the admiration, but cannot promote the edification, of the hearers, nor do them any good. And yet it is manifest from *ch.* 14 that the Corinthians valued themselves exceedingly on this gift. Note, How proper a method it is to beat down pride to let persons know the true value of what they pride themselves in! It is but too common a thing for men to value themselves most on what is least worth: and it is of great use to bring them to a sober mind by letting them know how much they are mistaken. (3.) The various distribution of these gifts, not all to one, nor to every one alike. All members and officers had not the same rank in the church, nor the same endowments (*v.* 29, 30): *Are all apostles? Are all prophets?* This were to make the church a monster: all one as if the body were all ear or all eye. Some are fit for one office and employment, and some for another; and the Spirit distributes to every one as he will. We must be content with our own rank and share, if they be lower and less than those of others. We must not be conceited of ourselves, and despise others, if we are in the higher rank and have greater gifts. Every member of the body is to preserve its own rank, and do its own office; and all are to minister to one another, and promote the good of the body in general, without envying, or despising, or neglecting, or ill-using, any one particular member. How blessed a constitution were the Christian church, if all the members did their duty!

II. He closes this chapter with an advice (as the generality read it) and a hint. 1. An advice to covet the best gifts, *charismata ta kreittona — dona potiora, praestantiora,* either the most valuable in themselves or the most serviceable to others; and these are, in truth, most valuable in themselves, though men may be apt to esteem those most that will raise their fame and esteem highest. Those are truly best by which God will be most honoured and his church edified. Such gifts should be most earnestly coveted. Note, We should desire that most which is best, and most worth. Grace is therefore to be preferred before gifts; and, of gifts, those are to be preferred which are of greatest use. But some read this passage, not as an advice, but a charge: *zēloute, You are envious* at each other's gifts. In *ch.* 13:4, the same word is thus translated. You quarrel and contend about them. This they certainly did. And this behaviour the apostle here reprehends, and labours to rectify. *Only of pride cometh contention.* These contests in the church of Corinth sprang from this original. It was a quarrel about precedency (as most quarrels among Christians are, with whatever pretences they are gilded over); and it is no wonder that a quarrel about precedence should extinguish charity. When all would stand in the first rank, no wonder if they jostle, or throw down, or thrust back, their brethren. Gifts may be valued for their use, but they are mischievous when made the fuel of pride and contention. This therefore the apostle endeavours to prevent. 2. By giving them the hint of a more excellent way, namely, of charity, of mutual love and good-will. This was the only right way to quiet and cement them, and make their gifts turn to the advantage and edification of the church. This would render them kind to each other, and concerned for each other, and therefore calm their spirits, and put an end to their little piques and contests, their disputes about precedency. Those would appear to be in the foremost rank, according to the apostle, who had most of true Christian love. Note, True charity is greatly to be preferred to the most glorious gifts. To have the heart glow with mutual love is vastly better than to glare with the most pompous titles, offices, or powers.

CHAPTER 13

In this chapter the apostle goes on to show more particularly what that more excellent way was of which he had just before been speaking. He recommends it, I. By showing the necessity and importance of it (*v.* 1–3). II. By giving a description of its properties and fruits (*v.* 4–7). III. By showing how much it excels the best of gifts and other graces, by its continuance, when they shall be no longer in being, or of any use (*v.* 8 to the end).

Verses 1–3

Here the apostle shows what more excellent way he meant, or had in view, in the close of the former chapter, namely, *charity,* or, as it is commonly elsewhere rendered, *love — agapē*: not what is meant by charity in our common use of the word, which most men understand of alms-giving, but love in its fullest and most extensive meaning, true love to God and man, a benevolent disposition of mind towards our fellow-christians, growing out of sincere and fervent devotion to God. This living principle of all duty and obedience is the more excellent way of which the apostle speaks, preferable to all gifts. Nay, without this the most glorious gifts are nothing, of no account to us, of no esteem in the sight of God. He specifies, 1. The gift of tongues: *Though I speak with the tongues of men and of angels, and have not charity, I am become as sounding brass, or a tinkling cymbal, v.* 1. Could a man speak all the languages on earth, and that with the greatest propriety, elegance, and fluency, could he talk like an angel, and yet be without charity, it would be all empty noise, mere unharmonious and useless sound, that would neither profit nor delight. It is not talking freely, nor finely, nor learnedly, of the things of God, that will save ourselves, or profit others, if we are destitute of holy love. It is the charitable heart, not the voluble tongue, that is acceptable with God. The apostle specifies first this gift because hereupon the Corinthians seemed chiefly to value themselves and despise their brethren. 2. Prophecy, and the understanding of mysteries, and all knowledge. This without charity is as nothing, *v.* 2. Had a man ever so clear an understanding of the prophecies and types under the old dispensation, ever so accurate a knowledge of the doctrines of Christianity, nay, and this by inspiration, from the infallible dictates and illumination of the Spirit of God, without charity he would be nothing; all this would stand him in no stead. Note, A clear and deep head is of no signification, without a benevolent and charitable heart. It is not great knowledge that God sets a value upon, but true and hearty devotion and love. 3. Miraculous faith, the faith of miracles, or the faith by which persons were enabled to work miracles: *Had I all faith* (the utmost degree of this kind of faith), *that I could remove mountains* (or say to them, "Go hence into the midst of the sea," and have my command obeyed, Mk. 11:23), *and had no charity, I am nothing.* The most wonder-working faith, to which nothing is in a manner impossible, is itself nothing without charity. Moving mountains is a great achievement in the account of men; but one dram of charity is, in God's account, of much greater worth than all the faith of this sort in the world. Those may do many wondrous works in Christ's name whom yet he will disown, and bid depart from him, as workers of iniquity, Mt. 7:22, 23. Saving faith is ever in conjunction with charity, but the faith of miracles may be without it. 4. The outward acts of charity: *Bestowing his goods to feed the poor, v.* 3. Should all a man has be laid out in this manner, if he had no charity, it would profit him nothing. There may be an open and lavish hand, where there is no liberal and charitable heart. The external act of giving alms may proceed from a very ill principle. Vain-glorious ostentation, or a proud conceit of merit, may put a man to large expense this way who has no true love to God nor men. Our doing good to others will do none to us, if it be not well done, namely, from a principle of devotion and charity, love to God, and good-will to men. Note, If we leave charity out of religion, the most costly services will be of no avail to us. If we give away all we have, while we withhold the heart from God, it will not profit. 5. Even sufferings, and even those of the most grievous kind: *If we give our bodies to be burnt, without charity, it profiteth nothing, v.* 3. Should we sacrifice our lives for the faith of the gospel, and be burnt to death in maintenance of its truth, this will stand us in no stead without charity, unless we be animated to these sufferings by a principle of true devotion to God, and sincere love to his church and people, and good-will to mankind. The outward carriage may be plausible, when the invisible principle is very bad. Some men have thrown themselves into the fire to procure a name and reputation among men. It is possible that the very same principle may have worked up some to resolution enough to die for their religion who never heartily believed and embraced it. But vindicating religion at the cost of our lives will profit nothing if we feel not the power of it; and true charity is the very heart and spirit of religion. If we feel none of its sacred heat in our hearts, it will profit nothing, though we be burnt to ashes for the truth. Note, The most grievous sufferings, the most costly sacrifices, will not recommend us to God, if we do not love the brethren; should we give our own bodies to be burnt, it would not profit us. How strange a way of recommending themselves to God are those got into who hope to do it by burning others, by murdering, and massacring, and tormenting their fellow-christians, or by any injurious usage of them! *My soul, enter not thou into their secrets.* If I cannot hope to recommend myself to God by giving my own body to be burnt while I have no charity, I will never hope to do it by burning or maltreating others, in open defiance to all charity.

Verses 4–7

The apostle gives us in these verses some of the properties and effects of charity, both to describe and commend it, that we may know whether we have this grace and that if we have not we may fall in love with what is so exceedingly amiable, and not rest till we have obtained it. It is an excellent grace, and has a world of good properties belonging to it. As,

I. *It is long suffering* — *makrothymei.* It can endure evil, injury, and provocation, without being filled with resentment, indignation, or revenge. It makes the mind firm, gives it power over the angry passions, and furnishes it with a persevering patience, that shall rather wait and wish for the reformation of a brother than fly out in resentment of his conduct. It will put up with many slights and neglects from the person it loves, and wait long to see the kindly effects of such patience on him.

II. *It is kind* — *chrēsteuetai.* It is benign, bountiful; it is courteous and obliging. *The law of kindness is in her lips;* her heart is large, and her hand open. She is ready to show favours and to do good. She seeks to be useful; and not only seizes on opportunities of doing good, but searches for them. This is her general character. She is patient under injuries, and apt and inclined to do all the good offices in her power. And under these two generals all the particulars of the character may be reduced.

III. Charity suppresses envy: *It envieth not;* it is not grieved at the good of others; neither at their gifts nor at their good qualities, their honours not their estates. If we love our neighbour we shall be so far from envying his welfare, or being displeased with it, that we shall share in it and rejoice at it. His bliss and sanctification will be an addition to ours, instead of impairing or lessening it. This is the proper effect of kindness and benevolence: envy is the effect of ill-will. The prosperity of those to whom we wish well can never grieve us; and the mind which is bent on doing good to all can never with ill to any.

IV. Charity subdues pride and vain-glory; *It vaunteth not itself, is not puffed up,* is not bloated with self-conceit, does not swell upon its acquisitions, nor arrogate to itself that honour, or power, or respect, which does not belong to it. It is not insolent, apt to despise others, or trample on them, or treat them with contempt and scorn. Those who are animated with a principle of true brotherly love will in honour prefer one another, Rom. 12:10. They will *do nothing out of a spirit of contention or vain-glory, but in lowliness of mind will esteem others better than themselves,* Phil. 2:3. True love will give us an esteem of our brethren, and raise our value for them; and this will limit our esteem of ourselves, and prevent the tumours of self-conceit and arrogance. These ill qualities can never grow out of tender affection for the brethren, nor a diffusive benevolence. The word rendered in our translation *vaunteth itself* bears other significations; nor is the proper meaning, as I can find, settled; but in every sense and meaning true charity stands in opposition to it. The Syriac renders it, *non tumultuatur — does not raise tumults* and disturbances. Charity calms the angry passions, instead of raising them. Others render it, *Non perperà et perversè agit — It does not act insidiously with any,* seek to ensnare them, nor tease them with needless importunities and addresses. It is not froward, nor stubborn and untractable, nor apt to be cross and contradictory. Some understand it of dissembling and flattery, when a fair face is put on, and fine words are said, without any regard to truth, or intention of good. Charity abhors such falsehood and flattery. Nothing is commonly more pernicious, nor more apt to cross the purposes of true love and good will.

V. Charity is careful not to pass the bounds of decency; *ouk aschēmonei — it behaveth not unseemly;* it does nothing indecorous, nothing that in the common account of men is base or vile. It does nothing out of place or time; but behaves towards all men as becomes their rank and ours, with reverence and respect to superiors, with kindness and condescension to inferiors, with courtesy and good-will towards all men. It is not for breaking order, confounding ranks bringing all men on a level; but for keeping up the distinction God has made between men, and acting decently in its own station, and minding its own business, without taking upon it to mend, or censure, or despise, the conduct of others. Charity will do nothing that misbecomes it.

VI. Charity is an utter enemy to selfishness: *Seeketh not its own,* does not inordinately desire nor seek its own praise, or honour, or profit, or pleasure. Indeed self-love, in some degree, is natural to all men, enters into their very constitution. And a reasonable love of self is by our Saviour made the measure of our love to others, that charity which is here described, *Thou shalt love thy neighbour as thyself.* The apostle does not mean that charity destroys all regard to self; he does not mean that the charitable man should never challenge what is his own, but utterly neglect himself and all his interests. Charity must then root up that principle which is wrought into our nature. But charity never seeks its own to the hurt of others, or with the neglect of others. It often neglects its own for the sake of others; prefers their welfare, and satisfaction, and advantage, to its own; and it ever prefers the weal of the public, of the community, whether civil or ecclesiastical, to its private advantage. It would not advance, nor aggrandize, nor enrich, nor gratify itself, at the cost and damage of the public.

VII. It tempers and restrains the passions. *Ou paroxynetai — is not exasperated.* It corrects a sharpness of temper, sweetens and softens the mind, so that it does not suddenly conceive, nor long continue, a vehement passion. Where the fire of love is kept in, the flames of wrath will not easily kindle, nor long keep burning. Charity will never be angry without a cause, and will endeavour to confine the passions within proper limits, that they may not exceed the measure that is just, either in degree or duration. Anger cannot rest in the bosom where love reigns. It is hard to be angry with those we love, but very easy to drop our resentments and be reconciled.

VIII. Charity *thinks no evil.* It cherishes no malice, nor gives way to revenge: so some understand it. It is not soon, nor long, angry; it is never mischievous, nor inclined to revenge; it does not suspect evil of others, *ou logizetai to kakon — it does not reason out* evil, charge guilt upon them by inference and *innuendo,* when nothing of this sort appears open. True love is not apt to be jealous and suspicious; it will hide faults that appear, and draw a veil over them, instead of hunting and raking out those that lie covered and concealed: it will never indulge suspicion without proofs, but will rather incline to darken and disbelieve evidence against the person it affects. It will hardly give into an ill opinion of another, and it will do it with regret and reluctance when the evidence cannot be resisted; hence it will never be forward to suspect ill, and reason itself into a bad opinion upon mere appearances, nor give way to suspicion without any. It will not make the worst construction of things, but put the best face that it can on circumstances that have no good appearance.

IX. The matter of its joy and pleasure is here suggested: 1. Negatively: *It rejoiceth not in iniquity.* It takes no pleasure in doing injury or hurt to any. It thinks not evil of any, without very clear proof. It wishes ill to none, much less will it hurt or wrong any, and least of all make this matter of its delight, rejoice in doing harm and mischief. Nor will it rejoice at the faults and failings of others, and triumph over them, either out of pride or ill-will, because it will set off its own excellences or gratify its spite. The sins of others are rather the grief of a charitable spirit than its sport or delight; they will touch it to the quick, and stir all its compassion, but give it no entertainment. It is the very height of malice to take pleasure in the misery of a fellow-creature. And is not falling into sin the greatest calamity that can befal one? How inconsistent is it with Christian charity, to rejoice at such fall! 2. Affirmatively: *It rejoiceth in the truth,* is glad of the success of the gospel, commonly called *the truth,* bu way of emphasis, in the New Testament; and rejoices to see men moulded into an evangelical temper by it, and made good. It takes no pleasure in their sins, but is highly delighted to see them do well, to approve themselves men of probity and integrity. It gives it much satisfaction to see truth and justice prevail among men, innocency cleared, and mutual faith and trust established, and to see piety and true religion flourish.

X. *It beareth all things, it endureth all things, panta stegei, panta hypomenei.* Some read the first, *covers all things.* So the original also signifies. *Charity will cover a multitude of sins,* 1 Pt. 4:8. It will draw a veil over them, as far as it can consistently with duty. It is not for blazing nor publishing the faults of a brother, till duty manifestly demands it. Necessity only can extort this from the charitable mind. Though such a man be free to tell his brother his faults in private, he is very unwilling to expose him by making them public. Thus we do by our own faults, and thus charity would teach us to do by the faults of others; not publish them to their shame and reproach, but cover them from public notice as long as we can, and be faithful to God and to others. Or, it *beareth all things,* — will pass by and put up with injuries, without indulging anger or cherishing revenge, will be patient upon provocation, and long patient, *panta hypomenei* — holds firm, though it be much shocked, and borne hard upon; sustains all manner of injury and ill usage, and bears up under it, such as curses, contumacies, slanders, prison, exile, bonds, torments, and death itself, for the sake of the injurious, and of others; and perseveres in this firmness. Note, What a fortitude and firmness fervent love will give the mind! What cannot a lover endure for the beloved and for his sake! How many slights and injuries will he put up with! How many hazards will he run and how many difficulties encounter!

XI. Charity believes and hopes well of others: *Believeth all things; hopeth all things.* Indeed charity does by no means destroy prudence, and, out of mere simplicity and silliness, believe every word, Prov. 14:15. Wisdom may dwell with love, and charity be cautious. But it is apt to believe well of all, to entertain a good opinion of them when there is no appearance to the contrary; nay, to believe well when there may be some dark appearances, if the evidence of ill be not clear. All charity is full of candour, apt to make the best of every thing, and put on it the best face and appearance? it will judge well, and believe well, as far as it can with any reason, and will rather stretch its faith beyond appearances for the support of a kind opinion; but it will go into a bad one with the upmost reluctance, and fence against it as much as it fairly and honestly can. And when, in spite of inclination, it cannot believe well of others, it will yet hope well, and continue to hope as long as there is any ground for it. It will not presently conclude a case desperate, but wishes the amendment of the worst of men, and is very apt to hope for what it wishes. How well-natured and amiable a thing is Christian charity? How lovely a mind is that which is tinctured throughout with such benevolence, and has it diffused over its whole frame! Happy the man who has this heavenly fire glowing in his heart, flowing out of his mouth, and diffusing its warmth over all with whom he has to do! How lovely a thing would Christianity appear to the world, if those who profess it were more actuated and animated by this divine principle, and paid a due regard to a command on which its blessed author laid a chief stress! *A new commandment give I to you, that you love one another, as I have loved you, that you also love one another,* Jn. 13:34. *By this shall all men know that you are my disciples, v.* 35. Blessed Jesus! how few of thy professed disciples are to be distinguished and marked out by this characteristic!

Verses 8–13

Here the apostle goes on to commend charity, and show how much it is preferable to the gifts on which the Corinthians were so apt to pride themselves, to the utter neglect, and almost extinction, of charity. This he makes out,

I. From its longer continuance and duration: *Charity never faileth.* It is a permanent and perpetual grace, lasting as eternity; whereas the extraordinary gifts on which the Corinthians valued themselves were of short continuance. They were only to edify the church on earth, and that but for a time, not during its whole continuance in this world; but in heaven would be all superseded, which yet is the very seat and element of love. *Prophecy must fail,* that is, either the prediction of things to come (which is its most common sense) or the interpretation of scripture by immediate inspiration. *Tongues will cease,* that is, the miraculous power of speaking languages without learning them. There will be but one language in heaven. There is no confusion of tongues in the region of perfect tranquility. And *knowledge will vanish away.* Not that, in the perfect state above, holy and happy souls shall be unknowing, ignorant: it is a very poor happiness that can consist with utter ignorance. The apostle is plainly speaking of miraculous gifts, and therefore of knowledge to be had out of the common way (see *ch.* 14:6), a knowledge of mysteries supernaturally communicated. Such knowledge was to vanish away. Some indeed understand it of common knowledge acquired by instruction, taught and learnt. This way of knowing is to vanish away, though the knowledge itself, once acquired, will not be lost. But it is plain that the apostle is here setting the grace of charity in opposition to supernatural gifts. And it is more valuable, because more durable; *it* shall last, when *they* shall be no more; *it* shall enter into heaven, where *they* will have no place, because they will be of no use, though, in a sense, even our common knowledge may be said to cease in heaven, by reason of the improvement that will then be made in it. The light of a candle is perfectly obscured by the sun shining in its strength.

II. He hints that these gifts are adapted only to a state of imperfection: *We know in part, and we prophesy in part, v.* 9. Our best knowledge and our greatest abilities are at present like our condition, narrow and temporary. Even the knowledge they had by inspiration was but in part. How little a portion of God, and the unseen world, was heard even by apostles and inspired men! How much short do others come of them! But these gifts were fitted to the present imperfect state of the church, valuable in themselves, but not to be compared with charity, because they were to vanish with the imperfections of the church, nay, and long before, whereas charity was to last for ever.

III. He takes occasion hence to show how much better it will be with the church hereafter than it can be here. A state of perfection is in view (*v.* 10): *When that which is perfect shall come, then that which is in part shall be done away.* When the end is once attained, the means will of course be abolished. There will be no need of tongues, and prophecy, and inspired knowledge, in a future life, because then the church will be in a state of perfection, complete both in knowledge and holiness. God will be known then clearly, and in a manner by intuition, and as perfectly as the capacity of glorified minds will allow; not by such transient glimpses, and little portions, as here. The difference between these two states is here pointed at in two particulars: 1. The present state is a state of childhood, the future that of manhood: *When I was a child, I spoke as a child* (that is, as some think, spoke with tongues), *I understood as a child; ephronoun — sapiebam* (that is, "I prophesied, I was taught the mysteries of the kingdom of heaven, in such an extraordinary way as manifested I was not out of my childish state"), *I thought,* or reasoned, *elogizomēn, as a child; but, when I became a man, I put away childish things.* Such is the difference between earth and heaven. What narrow views, what confused and indistinct notions of things, have children, in comparison of grown men! And how naturally do men, when reason is ripened and matured, despise and relinquish their infant thoughts, put them away, reject them, esteem as nothing! Thus shall we think of our most valued gifts and acquisitions in this world, when we come to heaven. We shall despise our childish folly, in priding ourselves in such things when we are grown up to men in Christ. 2. Things are all dark and confused now, in comparison of what they will be hereafter: *Now we see through a glass darkly* (*ev ainigmati, in a riddle*), *then face to face; now we know in part, but then we shall know as we are known.* Now we can only discern things at a great distance, as through a telescope, and that involved in clouds and obscurity; but hereafter the things to be known will be near and obvious, open to our eyes; and our knowledge will be free from all obscurity and error. God is to be seen *face to face;* and we *are to know him as we are known by him;* not indeed as perfectly, but in some sense in the same manner. We are known to him by mere inspection; he turns his eye towards us, and sees and searches us throughout. We shall then fix our eye on him, *and see him as he is,* 1 Jn. 3:2. We shall know how we are known, enter into all the mysteries of divine love and grace. O glorious change! To pass from darkness to light, from clouds to the clear sunshine of our Saviour's face, and in God's own light to see light! Ps. 36:9. Note, It is the light of heaven only that will remove all clouds and darkness from the face of God. It is at best but twilight while we are in this world; there it will be perfect and eternal day.

IV. To sum up the excellences of charity, he prefers it not only to gifts, but to other graces, to faith and hope (*v.* 13): *And now abide faith, hope, and charity; but the greatest of these is charity.* True grace is much more excellent than any spiritual gifts whatever. And faith, hope, and love, are the three principal graces, of which charity is the chief, being the end to which the other two are but means. This is the divine nature, the soul's felicity, or its complacential rest in God, and holy delight in all his saints. And it is everlasting work, when faith and hope shall be no more. Faith fixes on the divine revelation, and assents to that: hope fastens on future felicity, and waits for that: and in heaven faith well be swallowed up in vision, and hope in fruition. There is no room to believe and hope, when we see and enjoy. But love fastens on the divine perfections themselves, and the divine image on the creatures, and our mutual relation both to God and them. These will all shine forth in the most glorious splendours in another world, and there will love be made perfect; there we shall perfectly love God, because he will appear amiable for ever, and our hearts will kindle at the sight, and glow with perpetual devotion. And there shall we perfectly love one another, when all the saints meet there, when none but saints are there, and saints made perfect. O blessed state! How much surpassing the best below! O amiable and excellent grace of charity! How much does it exceed the most valuable gift, when it outshines every grace, and is the everlasting consummation of them! When faith and hope are at an end, true charity will burn for ever with the brightest flame. Note, Those border most upon the heavenly state and perfection whose hearts are fullest of this divine principle, and burn with the most fervent charity. It is the surest offspring of God, and bears his fairest impression. For God is love, 1 Jn. 4:8, 16. And where God is to be seen as he is, and face to face, there charity is in its greatest height — there, and there only, will it be perfected.

CHAPTER 14

In this chapter the apostle directs them about the use of their spiritual gifts, preferring those that are best and fitted to do the greatest good. I. He begins with advising them of all spiritual gifts to prefer prophesying, and shows that this is much better than speaking with tongues (*v.* 1–5). II. He goes on to show them how unprofitable the speaking of foreign languages is, and useless to the church; it is like piping in one tone, like sounding a trumpet without any certain note, like talking gibberish; whereas gifts should be used for the good of the church (*v.* 6–14). III. He advises that worship should be celebrated so that the most ignorant might understand, and join in prayer and praise, and presses the advice by his own example (*v.* 15–20). IV. He informs them that tongues were a sign for unbelievers rather than those that believe; and represents the advantage of prophecy above speaking with tongues, from the different suggestions they would give to the mind of an unbeliever coming into their assemblies (*v.* 21–25). V. He blames them for the disorder and confusion they had brought into the assembly, by their vanity and ostentation of their gifts; and directs them in using the gifts both of tongues and prophecy (*v.* 26–33). VI. He forbids women speaking in the church; and closes this subject by requiring them to perform every thing in the public worship with order and decency (*v.* 34 to the end).

Verses 1–5

The apostle, in the foregoing chapter, had himself preferred, and advised the Corinthians to prefer, Christian charity to all spiritual gifts. Here he teaches them, among spiritual gifts, which they should prefer, and by what rules they should make comparison. He begins the chapter,

I. With an exhortation to charity (*v.* 1): *Follow after charity,* pursue it. The original, *diōkete,* when spoken of a thing, signifies a singular concern to obtain it; and is commonly taken in a good and laudable sense. It is an exhortation to obtain charity, to get this excellent disposition of mind upon any terms, whatever pains or prayers it may cost: as if he had said, "In whatever you fail, see you do not miss of this; the principal of all graces is worth your getting at any rate."

II. He directs them which spiritual gift to prefer, from a principle of charity: *"Desire spiritual gifts, but rather that you may prophesy,* or chiefly that you may prophesy." While they were in close pursuit of charity, and made this Christian disposition their chief scope, they might be zealous of spiritual gifts, be ambitious of them in some measure, but especially of prophesying, that is, of interpreting scripture. This preference would most plainly discover that they were indeed upon such pursuit, that they had a due value for Christian charity, and were intent upon it. Note, Gifts are fit objects of our desire and pursuit, in subordination to grace and charity. That should be sought first and with the greatest earnestness which is most worth.

III. He assigns the reasons of this preference. And it is remarkable here that he only compares prophesying with speaking with tongues. It seems, this was the gift on which the Corinthians principally valued themselves. This was more ostentatious than the plain interpretation of scripture, more fit to gratify pride, but less fit to pursue the purposes of Christian charity; it would not equally edify nor do good to the souls of men. For, 1. He that spoke with tongues must wholly speak between God and himself; for, whatever mysteries might be communicated in his language, none of his own countrymen could understand them, because they did not understand the language, *v.* 2. Note, What cannot be understood can never edify. No advantage can be reaped from the most excellent discourses, if delivered in unintelligible language, such as the audience can neither speak nor understand: but he that prophesies speaks to the advantage of his hearers; they may profit by his gift. Interpretation of scripture will be for their edification; they may be exhorted and comforted by it, *v.* 3. And indeed these two must go together. Duty is the proper way to comfort; and those that would be comforted must bear being exhorted. 2. He that speaks with tongues may edify himself, *v.* 4. He may understand and be affected with what he speaks; and so every minister should; and he that is most edified himself is in the disposition and fitness to do good to others by what he speaks; but he that speaks with tongues, or language unknown, can only edify himself; others can reap no benefit from his speech. Whereas the end of speaking in the church is to edify the church (*v.* 4), to which prophesying, or interpreting scripture by inspiration or otherwise, is immediately adapted. Note, That is the best and most eligible gift which best answers the purposes of charity and does most good; not that which can edify ourselves only, but that which will edify the church. Such is prophesying, or preaching, and interpreting scripture, compared with speaking in an unknown tongue. 3. Indeed, no gift is to be despised, but the best gifts are to be preferred. *I could wish,* says the apostle, *that you all spoke with tongues, but rather that you prophesied, v.* 5. Every gift of God is a favour from God, and may be improved for his glory, and as such is to be valued and thankfully received; but then those are to be most valued that are most useful. *Greater is he that prophesieth than he that speaketh with tongues, unless he interpret, that the church may receive edifying, v.* 5. Benevolence makes a man truly great. *It is more blessed to give than to receive.* And it is true magnanimity to study and seek to be useful to others, rather than to raise their admiration and draw their esteem. Such a man has a large soul, copious and diffused in proportion to his benevolence and bent of mind for public good. Greater is he who interprets scripture to edify the church than he who speaks tongues to recommend himself. And what other end he who spoke with tongues could have, unless he interpreted what he spoke, is not easy to say, Note, That makes most for the honour of a minister which is most for the church's edification, not that which shows his gifts to most advantage. He acts in a narrow sphere, while he aims at himself; but his spirit and character increase in proportion to his usefulness, I mean his own intention and endeavours to be useful.

Verses 6–14

In this paragraph he goes on to show how vain a thing the ostentation of speaking unknown and unintelligible language must be. It was altogether unedifying and unprofitable (*v.* 6): *If I come to you speaking with tongues, what will it profit you, unless I speak to you by revelation, or by knowledge, or by prophesying, or by doctrine?* It would signify nothing to utter any of these in an unknown tongue. An apostle, with all his furniture, could not edify, unless he spoke to the capacity of his hearers. New revelations, the most clear explications of old ones, the most instructive discourses in themselves, would be unprofitable in a language not understood. Nay, interpretations of scripture made in an unknown tongue would need to be interpreted over again, before they could be of any use.

I. He illustrates this by several allusions. 1. To a pipe and a harp playing always in one tone. Of what use can this be to those who are dancing? If there be no distinction of sounds, how should they order their steps or motions? Unintelligible language is like piping or harping without distinction of sounds: it gives no more direction how a man should order his conversation than a pipe with but one stop or a harp with but one string can direct a dancer how he should order his steps, *v.* 7. 2. To a trumpet giving an *uncertain sound, adēlon phōnēn,* a sound not manifest; either not the proper sound for the purpose, or not distinct enough to be discerned from every other sound. If, instead of sounding on onset, it sounded a retreat, or sounded one knew not what, who would prepare for the battle? To talk in an unknown language in a Christian assembly is altogether as vain and to no purpose as for a trumpet to give no certain sound in the field or day of battle. The army in one case, and the congregation in the other, must be all in suspense, and at a perfect nonplus. To speak words that have no significancy to those who hear them is to leave them ignorant of what is spoken; it is speaking to the air, *v.* 9. Words without a meaning can convey no notion nor instruction to the mind; and words not understood have no meaning with those who do not understand them: to talk to them in such language is to waste our breath. 3. He compares the speaking in an unknown tongue to the gibberish of barbarians. There are, as he says (*v.* 10), many kinds of voices in the world, none of which is without its proper signification. This is true of the several languages spoken by different nations. All of them have their proper signification. Without this they would be *phōnai aphōnoi — a voice, and no voice.* For that is no language, nor can it answer the end of speaking, which has no meaning. But whatever proper signification the words of any language may have in themselves, and to those who understand them, they are perfect gibberish to men of another language, who understand them not. In this case, speaker and hearers are barbarians to each other (*v.* 11), they talk and hear only sounds without sense; for this is to be a barbarian. For thus says the polite Ovid, when banished into Pontus,

> Barbarus hic ego sum, quia non intelligor ulli,
> I am a barbarian here, none understand me.

To speak in the church in an unknown tongue is to talk gibberish; it is to play the barbarian; it is to confound the audience, instead of instructing them; and for this reason is utterly vain and unprofitable.

II. Having thus established his point, in the two next verses he applies, 1. By advising them to be chiefly desirous of those gifts that were most for the church's edification, *v.* 12. "Forasmuch as you are zealous of spiritual gifts, this way it will become commendable zeal, be zealous to edify the church, to promote Christian knowledge and practice, and covet those gifts most that will do the best service to men's souls." This is the great rule he gives, which, 2. He applies to the matter in hand, that, if they did speak a foreign language, they should beg of God the gift of interpreting it, *v.* 13. That these were different gifts, see *ch.* 12:10. Those might speak and understand a foreign language who could not readily translate it into their own: and yet was this necessary to the church's edification; for the church must understand, that it might be edified, which yet it could not do till the foreign language was translated into its own. Let him therefore pray for the gift of interpreting what he speaks in an unknown tongue; or rather covet and ask of God the gift of interpreting than of speaking in a language that needs interpretation, this being most for the church's benefit, and therefore among the gifts that excel; *vide v.* 12. Some understand it, "Let him pray so as to interpret what he utters in prayer in a language unintelligible without it." The sum is that they should perform all religious exercises in their assemblies so that all might join in them and profit by them. 3. He enforces this advice with a proper reason, that, if *he prayed in an unknown tongue, his spirit might pray,* that is, a spiritual gift might be exercised in prayer, or his own mind might be devoutly engaged, *but his understanding would be unfruitful* (*v.* 14), that is, the sense and meaning of his words would be unfruitful, he would not be understood, nor therefore would others join with him in his devotions. Note, It should be the concern of such as pray in public to pray intelligibly, not in a foreign language, nor in a language that, if it be not foreign, is above the level of his audience. Language that is most obvious and easy to be understood is the most proper for public devotion and other religious exercises.

Verses 15–20

The apostle here sums up the argument hitherto, and,

I. Directs them how they should sing and pray in public (*v.* 15): *What is it then? I will pray with the spirit, and I will pray with the understanding also. I will sing with the spirit,* etc. He does not forbid their praying or singing under a divine *afflatus,* or when they were inspired for this purpose, or had such a spiritual gift communicated to them; but he would have them perform both so as to be understood by others, that others might join with them. Note, Public worship should be performed so as to be understood.

II. He enforces the argument with several reasons.

1. That otherwise the unlearned could not say Amen to their prayers or thanksgivings, could not join in the worship, for they did not understand it, *v.* 16. He who fills up or occupies the place of the unlearned, that is, as the ancients interpret it, the body of the people, who, in most Christian assemblies, are illiterate; how should they say *Amen* to prayers in an unknown tongue? How should they declare their consent and concurrence? This is saying *Amen,* So be it. *God grant the thing we have requested;* or, We join in the confession that has been made of sin, and in the acknowledgment that has been made of divine mercies and favours. This is the import of saying *Amen.* All should say *Amen* inwardly; and it is not improper to testify this inward concurrence in public prayers and devotions, by an audible *Amen.* The ancient Christians said *Amen* aloud. *Vide* Just. Mart. *apol.* 2. *propè fin.* Now, how should the people say *Amen* to what they did not understand? Note, There can be no concurrence in those prayers that are not understood. The intention of public devotions is therefore entirely destroyed if they are performed in an unknown tongue. He who performs may pray well, and give thanks well, but not in that time and place, because others are not, cannot be, edified (*v.* 17) by what they understand not.

2. He alleges his own example, to make the greater impression, concerning which observe, (1.) That he did not come behind any of them in this spiritual gift: *"I thank my God, I speak with tongues more than you all* (*v.* 18); not only more than any single person among you, but more than all together." It was not envy at their better furniture that made Paul depreciate what they so highly valued and so much vaunted of; he surpassed them all in this very gift of tongues, and did not vilify their gift because he had it not. This spirit of envy is too common in the world. But the apostle took care to guard against this misconstruction of his purpose, by letting them know there was more ground for them to envy him upon this head than for him to envy them. Note, When we beat down men's unreasonable value for themselves, or any of their possessions or attainments, we should let them see, if possible, that this does not proceed from an envious and grudging spirit. We miss our aim if they can fairly give our conduct this invidious turn. Paul could not be justly censured, nor suspected for any such principle in this whole argument. He spoke more language than they all. Yet, (2.) He had rather *speak five words with understanding,* that is, so as to be understood, and instruct and edify others, *than ten thousand words in an unknown tongue, v.* 19. He was so far from valuing himself upon talking languages, or making ostentation of his talents of this kind, that he had rather speak five intelligible words, to benefit others, than make a thousand, ten thousand fine discourses, that would do no one else any good, because they did not understand them. Note, A truly Christian minister will value himself much more upon doing the least spiritual good to men's souls than upon procuring the greatest applause and commendation to himself. This is true grandeur and nobleness of spirit; it is acting up to his character; it is approving himself the servant of Christ, and not a vassal to his own pride and vanity.

3. He adds a plain intimation that the fondness then discovered for this gift was but too plain an indication of the immaturity of their judgment: *Brethren, be not children in understanding; in malice be you children, but in understanding be men, v.* 20. Children are apt to be struck with novelty and strange appearances. They are taken with an outward show, without enquiring into the true nature and worth of things. Do not you act like them, and prefer noise and show to worth and substance; show a greater ripeness of judgment, and act a more manly part; be like children in nothing but an innocent and inoffensive disposition. A double rebuke is couched in this passage, both of their pride upon account of their gifts, and their arrogance and haughtiness towards each other, and the contests and quarrels proceeding from them. Note, Christians should be harmless and inoffensive as children, void of all guile and malice; but should have wisdom and knowledge that are ripe and mature. They should not be unskilful in the word of righteousness (Heb. 5:13), though they should be unskilful in all the arts of mischief.

Verses 21–25

In this passage the apostle pursues the argument, and reasons from other topics; as,

I. Tongues, as the Corinthians used them, were rather a token of judgment from God than mercy to any people (*v.* 21): *In the law* (that is, the Old Testament) *it is written, With men of other tongues and other lips will I speak to this people; and yet for all this they will not hear me, saith the Lord,* Isa. 28:11. Compare Deu. 28:46, 49. To both these passages, it is thought, the apostle refers. Both are delivered by way of threatening, and one is supposed to interpret the other. The meaning in this view is that it is an evidence that a people ar abandoned of God when he gives them up to this sort of instruction, to the discipline of those who speak in another language. And surely the apostle's discourse implies, "You should not be fond of the tokens of divine displeasure. God can have no gracious regards to those who are left merely to this sort of instruction, and taught in language which they cannot understand. They can never be benefited by such teaching as this; and, when they are left to it, it is a sad sign that God gives them over as past cure." And should Christians covet to be in such a state, or to bring the churches into it? Yet thus did the Corinthian preachers in effect, who would always deliver their inspirations in an unknown tongue.

II. Tongues were rather a sign to unbelievers than to believers, *v.* 22. They were a spiritual gift, intended for the conviction and conversion of infidels, that they might be brought into the Christian church; but converts were to be built up in Christianity by profitable instructions in their own language. The gift of tongues was necessary to spread Christianity, and gather churches; it was proper and intended to convince unbelievers of that doctrine which Christians had already embraced; but prophesying, and interpreting scripture in their own language, were most for the edification of such as did already believe: so that speaking with tongues in Christians assemblies was altogether out of time and place; neither one nor the other was proper for it. Note, That gifts may be rightly used, it is proper to know the ends which they are intended to serve. To go about the conversion of infidels, as the apostles did, had been a vain undertaking without the gift of tongues, and the discovery of this gift; but, in an assembly of Christians already converted to the Christian faith, to make use and ostentation of this gift would be perfectly impertinent, because it would be of no advantage to the assembly; not for conviction of truth, because they had already embraced it; not for their edification, because they did not understand, and could not get benefit without understanding, what they heard.

III. The credit and reputation of their assemblies among unbelievers required them to prefer prophesying before speaking with tongues. For, 1. If, when they were all assembled for Christian worship, their ministers, or all employed in public worship, should talk unintelligible language, and infidels should drop in, they would conclude them to be mad, to be no better than a parcel of wild fanatics. Who in their right senses could carry on religious worship in such a manner? Or what sort of religion is that which leaves out sense and understanding? Would not this make Christianity ridiculous to a heathen, to hear the ministers of it pray, or preach, or perform any other religious exercise, in a language that neither he nor the assembly understood? Note, The Christian religion is a sober and reasonable thing in itself, and should not, by the ministers of it, be made to look wild or senseless. Those disgrace their religion, and vilify their own character, who do any thing that has this aspect. But, on the other hand, 2. If, instead of speaking with tongues, those who minister plainly interpret scripture, or preach, in language intelligible and proper, the great truths and rules of the gospel, a heathen or unlearned person, coming in, will probably be convinced, and become a convert to Christianity (*v.* 24, 25); his conscience will be touched, the secrets of his heart will be revealed to him, he will be condemned by the truth he hears, and so will be brought to confess his guilt, to pay his homage to God, and own that he is indeed among you, present in the assembly. Note, Scripture-truth, plainly and duly taught, has a marvellous aptness to awaken the conscience, and touch the heart. And is not this much more for the honour of our religion than that infidels should conclude the ministers of it a set of madmen, and their religious exercises only fits of frenzy? This last would at once cast contempt on them and their religion too. Instead of procuring applause for them, it would render them ridiculous, and involve their profession in the same censure: whereas prophesying would certainly edify the church, much better keep up their credit, and might probably convince and convert infidels who might occasionally hear them. Note, Religious exercises in Christian assemblies should be such as are fit to edify the faithful, and convince, affect, and convert unbelievers. The ministry was not instituted to make ostentation of gifts and parts, but to save souls.

Verses 26–33

In this passage the apostle reproves them for their disorder, and endeavours to correct and regulate their conduct for the future.

I. He blames them for the confusion they introduced into the assembly, by ostentation of their gifts (*v.* 26): *When you come together every one hath a psalm, hath a doctrine, hath a tongue,* etc.; that is, "You are apt to confound the several parts of worship; and, while one has a psalm to utter by inspiration, another has a doctrine, or revelation;" or else, "You are apt to be confused in the same branch of worship, many of you having psalms or doctrines to propose at the same time, without staying for one another. Is not this perfect uproar? Can this be edifying? And yet all religious exercises in public assemblies should have this view, *Let all things be done to edifying.*"

II. He corrects their faults, and lays down some regulations for their future conduct. 1. As to speaking in an unknown tongue, he orders that no more than two or three should do it at one meeting, and this not altogether, but successively, one after another. And even this was not to be done unless there were some one to interpret (*v.* 27, 28), some other interpreter besides himself, who spoke; for to speak in an unknown tongue what he himself was afterwards to interpret could only be for ostentation. But, if another were present who could interpret, two miraculous gifts might be exercised at once, and thereby the church edified, and the faith of the hearers confirmed at the same time. But, if there were none to interpret, he was to be silent in the church, and only exercise his gift between God and himself (*v.* 28), that is (as I think) in private, at home; for all who are present at public worship should join in it, and not be at their private devotions in public assemblies. Solitary devotions are out of time and place when the church has met for social worship. 2. As to prophesying he orders, (1.) That two or three only should speak at one meeting (*v.* 20), and this successively, not all at once; and that the other should examine and judge what he delivered, that is, discern and determine concerning it, whether it were of divine inspiration or not. There might be false prophets, mere pretenders to divine inspiration; and the true prophets were to judge of these, and discern and discover who was divinely inspired, and by such inspiration interpreted scripture, and taught the church, and who was not — what was of divine inspiration and what was not. This seems to be the meaning of this rule. For where a prophet was known to be such, and under the divine *afflatus,* he could not be judged; for this were to subject even the Holy Spirit to the judgment of men. He who was indeed inspired, and known to be so, was above all human judgment. (2.) He orders that, if any assistant prophet had a revelation, while another was prophesying, the other should hold his peace, be silent (*v.* 30), before the inspired assistant uttered his revelation. Indeed, it is by many understood that the former speaker should immediately hold his peace. But this seems unnatural, and not so well to agree with the context. For why must one that was speaking by inspiration be immediately silent upon another man's being inspired, and suppress what was dictated to him by the same Spirit? Indeed, he who had the new revelation might claim liberty of speech in his turn, upon producing his vouchers; but why must liberty of speech be taken from him who was speaking before, and his mouth stopped, when he was delivering the dictates of the same Spirit, and could produce the same vouchers? Would the Spirit of God move one to speak, and, before he had delivered what he had to say, move another to interrupt him, and put him to silence? This seems to me an unnatural thought. Nor is it more agreeable to the context, and the reason annexed (*v.* 31): *That all might prophesy, one by one,* or one after another, which could not be where any one was interrupted and silenced before he had done prophesying; but might easily be if he who was afterwards inspired forbore to deliver his new revelation till the former prophet had finished what he had to say. And, to confirm this sense, the apostle quickly adds, *The spirits of the prophets are subject to the prophets* (*v.* 33); that is, the spiritual gifts they have leave them still possessed of their reason, and capable of using their own judgment in the exercise of them. Divine inspirations are not, like the diabolical possessions of heathen priests, violent and ungovernable, and prompting them to act as if they were beside themselves; but are sober and calm, and capable of regular conduct. The man inspired by the Spirit of God may still act the man, and observe the rules of natural order and decency in delivering his revelations. His spiritual gift is thus far subject to his pleasure, and to be managed by his discretion.

III. The apostle gives the reasons of these regulations. As, 1. That they would be for the church's benefit, their instruction and consolation. It is that *all may learn, and all may be comforted or exhorted,* that the prophets were to speak in the orderly manner the apostle advises. Note, The instruction, edification, and comfort of the church, is that for which God instituted the ministry. And surely ministers should, as much as possible, fit their ministrations to these purposes. 2. He tells them, *God is not the God of confusion, but of peace and good order, v.* 33. Therefore divine inspiration should by no means throw Christian assemblies into confusion, and break through all rules of common decency, which yet would be unavoidable if several inspired men should all at once utter what was suggested to them by the Spirit of God, and not wait to take their turns. Note, The honour of God requires that things should be managed in Christian assemblies so as not to transgress the rules of natural decency. If they are managed in a tumultuous and confused manner, what a notion must this give of the God who is worshipped, to considerate observers! Does it look as if he were the God of peace and order, and an enemy to confusion? Things should be managed so in divine worship that no unlovely nor dishonourable notion of God should be formed in the minds of observers. 3. He adds that things were thus orderly managed in all the other churches: *As in all the churches of the saints* (*v.* 33); they kept to these rules in the exercise of their spiritual gifts, which was a manifest proof that the church of Corinth might observe the same regulations. And it would be perfectly scandalous for them, who exceeded most churches in spiritual gifts, to be more disorderly than any in the exercise of them. Note, Though other churches are not to be our rule, yet the regard they pay to the rules of natural decency and order should restrain us from breaking these rules. Thus far they may be proposed as examples, and it is a shame not to follow them.

Verses 34–35

Here the apostle, 1. Enjoins silence on their women in public assemblies, and to such a degree that they must not ask questions for their own information in the church, but ask their husbands at home. *They are to learn in silence with all subjection; but,* says the apostle, *I suffer them not to teach,* 1 Tim. 2:11, 12. There is indeed an intimation (*ch.* 11:5) as if the women sometimes did pray and prophecy in their assemblies, which the apostle, in that passage, does not simply condemn, but the manner of performance, that is, praying or prophesying with the head uncovered, which, in that age and country, was throwing off the distinction of sexes, and setting themselves on a level with the men. But here he seems to forbid all public performances of theirs. They are not permitted to speak (*v.* 34) in the church, neither in praying nor prophesying. The connection seems plainly to include the latter, in the limited sense in which it is taken in this chapter, namely, for preaching, or interpreting scripture by inspiration. And, indeed, for a woman to prophesy in this sense were to teach, which does not so well befit her state of subjection. A teacher of others has in that respect a superiority over them, which is not allowed the woman over the man, nor must she therefore be allowed to teach in a congregation: *I suffer them not to teach.* But praying, and uttering hymns inspired, were not teaching. And seeing there were women who had spiritual gifts of this sort in that age of the church (see Acts 22:9), and might be under this impulse in the assembly, must they altogether suppress it? Or why should they have this gift, if it must never be publicly exercised? For these reasons, some think that these general prohibitions are only to be understood in common cases; but that upon extraordinary occasions, when women were under a divine *afflatus,* and known to be so, they might have liberty of speech. They were not ordinarily to teach, nor so much as to debate and ask questions in the church, but learn in silence there; and, if difficulties occurred, *ask their own husbands at home.* Note, As it is the woman's duty to learn in subjection, it is the man's duty to keep up his superiority, by being able to instruct her; if it be her duty to ask her husband at home, it is his concern and duty to endeavour at lest to be able to answer her enquiries; if it be a shame for her to speak in the church, where she should be silent, it is a shame for him to be silent when he should speak, and not be able to give an answer, when she asks him at home. 2. We have here the reason of this injunction: It is God's law and commandment that they should be under obedience (*v.* 34); they are placed in subordination to the man, and it is a shame for them to do any thing that looks like an affectation of changing ranks, which speaking in public seemed to imply, at least in that age, and among that people, as would public teaching much more: so that the apostle concludes it was a shame for women to speak in the church, in the assembly. Shame is the mind's uneasy reflection on having done an indecent thing. And what more indecent than for a woman to quit her rank, renounce the subordination of her sex, or do what in common account had such aspect and appearance? Note, Our spirit and conduct should be suitable to our rank. The natural distinctions God has made, we should observe. Those he has placed in subjection to others should not set themselves on a level, nor affect or assume superiority. The woman was made subject to the man, and she should keep her station and be content with it. For this reason women must be silent in the churches, not set up for teachers; for this is setting up for superiority over the man.

Verses 36–40

In these verses the apostle closes his argument, 1. With a just rebuke of the Corinthians for their extravagant pride and self-conceit: they so managed with their spiritual gifts as no church did like them; they behaved in a manner by themselves, and would not easily endure control nor regulation. Now, says the apostle, to beat down this arrogant humour, *"Came the gospel out from you? Or came it to you only? v.* 36. Did Christianity come our of Corinth? was its original among you? Or, if not, is it now limited and confined to you? are you the only church favoured with divine revelations, that you will depart from the decent usages of all other churches, and, to make ostentation of your spiritual gifts, bring confusion into Christian assemblies? How intolerably assuming is this behaviour! Pray bethink yourselves." When it was needful or proper the apostle could rebuke with all authority; and surely his rebukes, if ever, were proper here. Note, Those must be reproved and humbled whose spiritual pride and self-conceit throw Christian churches and assemblies into confusion, though such men will hardly bear even the rebukes of an apostle. 2. He lets them know that what he said to them was the command of God; nor durst any true prophet, any one really inspired, deny it (*v.* 37): *"If any man think himself a prophet, or spiritual, let him acknowledge,* etc., nay, let him be tried by this very rule. If he will not own what I deliver on this head to be the will of Christ, he himself never had the Spirit of Christ. The Spirit of Christ can never contradict itself; if it speak in me, and in them, it must speak the same things in both. If their revelations contradict mine, they do not come from the same Spirit; either I or they must be false prophets. *By this therefore you may know them.* If they say that my directions in this matter are no divine commandments, you may depend upon it they are not divinely inspired. But if any continue after all, through prejudice or obstinacy, uncertain or ignorant whether they or I speak by the Spirit of God, they must be left under the power of this ignorance. If their pretences to inspiration can stand in competition with the apostolical character and powers which I have, I have lost all my authority and influence; and the persons who allow of this competition against me are out of the reach of conviction, and must be left to themselves." Note, It is just with God to leave those to the blindness of their own minds who wilfully shut out the light. Those who would be ignorant in so plain a case were justly left under the power of their mistake. 3. He sums up all in two general advices: — (1.) That though they should not despise the gift of tongues, nor altogether disuse it, under the regulations mentioned, yet they should prefer prophesying. This is indeed the scope of the whole argument. It was to be preferred to the other, because it was the more useful gift. (2.) He charges them to let all things be done decently and in order (*v.* 40), that is, that they should avoid every thing that was manifestly indecent and disorderly. Not that they should hence take occasion to bring into the Christian church and worship any thing that a vain mind might think ornamental to it, or that would help to set it off. Such indecencies and disorders as he had remarked upon were especially to be shunned. They must do nothing that was manifestly childish (*v.* 20), or that would give occasion to say they were mad (*v.* 23), nor must they act so as to breed confusion, *v.* 33. This would be utterly indecent; it would make a tumult and mob of a Christian assembly. But they were to do things in order; they were to speak one after another, and not all at once; take their turns, and not interrupt one another. To do otherwise was to destroy the end of a Christians ministry, and all assemblies for Christian worship. Note, Manifest indecencies and disorders are to be carefully kept out of all Christian churches, and every part of divine worship. They should have nothing in them that is childish, absurd, ridiculous, wild, or tumultuous; but all parts of divine worship should be carried on in a manly, grave, rational, composed, and orderly manner. God is not to be dishonoured, nor his worship disgraced, by our unbecoming and disorderly performance of it and attendance at it.

CHAPTER 15

In this chapter the apostle treats of that great article of Christianity — the resurrection of the dead. I. He establishes the certainty of our Saviour's resurrection (*v.* 1–11). II. He, from this truth, sets himself to refute those who said, There is no resurrection of the dead (*v.* 12–19). III. From our Saviour's resurrection he establishes the resurrection of the dead and confirms the Corinthians in the belief of it by some other considerations (*v.* 20–34). IV. He answers an objection against this truth, and takes occasion thence to show what a vast change will be made in the bodies of believers at the resurrection (*v.* 35–50). V. He informs us what a change will be made in those who shall be living at the sound of the last trumpet, and the complete conquest the just shall then obtain over death and the grave (*v.* 51–57). And, VI. He sums up the argument with a very serious exhortation to Christians, to be resolved and diligent in their Lord's service, because they know they shall be so gloriously rewarded by him (*v.* 58).

Verses 1–11

It is the apostle's business in this chapter to assert and establish the doctrine of the resurrection of the dead, which some of the Corinthians flatly denied, *v.* 12. Whether they turned this doctrine into allegory, as did Hymeneus and Philetus, by saying it was already past (2 Tim. 2:17, 18), and several of the ancient heretics, by making it mean no more than a changing of their course of life; or whether they rejected it as absurd, upon principles of reason and science; it seems they denied it in the proper sense. And they disowned a future state of recompences, by denying the resurrection of the dead. Now that heathens and infidels should deny this truth does not seem so strange; but that Christians, who had their religion by revelation, should deny a truth so plainly discovered is surprising, especially when it is a truth of such importance. It was time for the apostle to confirm them in this truth, when the staggering of their faith in this point was likely to shake their Christianity; and they were yet in great danger of having their faith staggered. He begins with an epitome or summary of the gospel, what he had preached among them, namely, the death and resurrection of Christ. Upon this foundation the doctrine of the resurrection of the dead is built. Note, Divine truths appear with greatest evidence when they are looked upon in their mutual connection. The foundation may be strengthened, that the superstructure may be secured. Now concerning the gospel observe,

I. What a stress he lays upon it (*v.* 1, 2): *Moreover, brethren, I declare unto you the gospel which I preached to you.* 1. It was what he constantly preached. His word was not yea and nay: he always preached the same gospel, and taught the same truth. He could appeal to his hearers for this. Truth is in its own nature invariable; and the infallible teachers of divine truth could never be at variance with themselves or one another. The doctrine which Paul had heretofore taught, he still taught. 2. It was what they had received; they had been convinced of the faith, believed it in their hearts, or at least made profession of doing so with their mouths. It was no strange doctrine. It was that very gospel in which, or by which, they had hitherto stood, and must continue to stand. If they gave up this truth, they left themselves no ground to stand upon, no footing in religion. Note, The doctrine of Christ's death and resurrection is at the foundation of Christianity. Remove this foundation, and the whole fabric falls, all our hopes for eternity sink at once. And it is by holding this truth firmly that Christians are made to stand in a day of trial, and kept faithful to God. 3. It was that alone by which they could hope for salvation (*v.* 2), for there is *no salvation in any other name; no name given under heaven by which we may be saved, but by the name of Christ.* And there is no salvation in his name, but upon supposition of his death and resurrection. These are the saving truths of our holy religion. The crucifixion of our Redeemer and his conquest over death are the very source of our spiritual life and hopes. Now concerning these saving truths observe, (1.) They must be retained in mind, they must be held fast (so the word is translated, Heb. 10:23): *Let us hold fast the profession of our faith.* Note, The saving truths of the gospel must be fixed in our mind, revolved much in our thoughts, and maintained and held fast to the end, if we would be saved. They will not save us, if we do not attend to them, and yield to their power, and continue to do so to the end. *He only that endureth to the end shall be saved,* Mt. 10:22. (2.) We believe in vain, unless we continue and persevere in the faith of the gospel. We shall be never the better for a temporary faith; nay, we shall aggravate our guilt by relapsing into infidelity. And in vain is it to profess Christianity, or our faith in Christ, if we deny the resurrection; for this must imply and involve the denial of his resurrection; and, take away this, you make nothing of Christianity, you leave nothing for faith or hope to fix upon.

II. Observe what this gospel is, on which the apostle lays such stress. It was that doctrine which he had received, and delivered to them, *en prōtois — among the first, the principal.* It was a doctrine of the first rank, a most necessary truth, That Christ died for our sins, and was buried, and rose again: or, in other words, that *he was delivered for our offences and rose again for our justification* (Rom. 4:25), that he was offered in sacrifice for our sins, and rose again, to show that he had procured forgiveness for them, and was accepted of God in this offering. Note, Christ's death and resurrection are the very sum and substance of evangelical truth. Hence we derive our spiritual life now, and here we must found our hopes of everlasting life hereafter.

III. Observe how this truth is confirmed,

1. By Old-Testament predictions. He died for our sins, according to the scriptures; he was buried, and rose from the dead, according to the scriptures, according to the scripture-prophecies, and scripture-types. Such prophecies as Ps. 16:10; Isa. 53:4–6; Dan. 9:26, 27; Hos. 6:2. Such scripture-types as Jonah (Mt. 12:4), as Isaac, who is expressly said by the apostle to have been *received from the dead in a figure,* Heb. 11:19. Note, It is a great confirmation of our faith of the gospel to see how it corresponds with ancient types and prophecies.

2. By the testimony of many eye-witnesses, who saw Christ after he had risen from the dead. He reckons up five several appearances, beside that to himself. He *was seen of Cephas, or Peter, then of the twelve,* called so, though Judas was no longer among them, because this was their usual number; then he was *seen of above five hundred brethren at once,* many of whom were living when the apostle wrote this epistle, though some had fallen asleep. This was in Galilee, Mt. 28:10. After that, he was seen of James singly, and then by all the apostles when he was taken up into heaven. This was on mount Olivet, Lu. 24:50. Compare Acts 1:2, 5–7. Note, How uncontrollably evident was Christ's resurrection from the dead, when so many eyes saw him at so many different times alive, and when he indulged the weakness of one disciple so far as to let him handle him, to put his resurrection out of doubt! And what reason have we to believe those who were so steady in maintaining this truth, though they hazarded all that was dear to them in this world, by endeavouring to assert and propagate it! Even Paul himself was last of all favoured with the sight of him. It was one of the peculiar offices of an apostle to be a witness of our Saviour's resurrection (Lu. 24:48); and, when Paul was called to the apostolical office, he was made an evidence of this sort; the Lord Jesus appeared to him by the way to Damascus, Acts 9:17. Having mentioned this favour, Paul takes occasion from it to make a humble digression concerning himself. He was highly favoured of God, but he always endeavoured to keep up a mean opinion of himself, and to express it. So he does here, by observing, (1.) That he was *one born out of due time* (*v.* 8), an abortive, *ektrōma,* a child dead born, and out of time. Paul resembled such a birth, in the suddenness of his new birth, in that he was not matured for the apostolic function, as the others were, who had personal converse with our Lord. He was called to the office when such conversation was not to be had, he was out of time for it. He had not known nor followed the Lord, nor been formed in his family, as the others were, for this high and honourable function. This was in Paul's account a very humbling circumstance. (2.) By owning himself inferior to the other apostles: *Not meet to be called an apostle.* The least, because the last of them; called latest to the office, and not worthy to be called an apostle, to have either the office or the title, because he had been *a persecutor of the church of God, v.* 9. Indeed, he tells us elsewhere that he was *not a whit behind the very chief apostles* (2 Co. 11:5) — for gifts, graces, service, and sufferings, inferior to none of them. Yet some circumstances in his case made him think more meanly of himself than of any of them. Note, A humble spirit, in the midst of high attainments, is a great ornament to any man; it sets his good qualities off to much greater advantage. What kept Paul low in an especial manner was the remembrance of his former wickedness, his raging and destructive zeal against Christ and him members. Note, How easily God can bring a good out of the greatest evil! When sinners are by divine grace turned into saints, he makes the remembrance of their former sins very serviceable, to make them humble, and diligent, and faithful. (3.) By ascribing all that was valuable in him to divine grace: *But by the grace of God I am what I am, v.* 10. It is God's prerogative to say, *I am that I am;* it is our privilege to be able to say, "By God's grace we are what we are." We are nothing but what God makes us, nothing in religion but what his grace makes us. All that is good in us is a stream from this fountain. Paul was sensible of this, and kept humble and thankful by this conviction; so should we. Nay, though he was conscious of his own diligence, and zeal, and service, so that he could say of himself, *the grace of God was not given him in vain, but he laboured more abundantly than they all:* he thought himself so much more the debtor to divine grace. *Yet not I, but the grace of God which was with me.* Note, Those who have the grace of God bestowed on them should take care that it be not in vain. They should cherish, and exercise, and exert, this heavenly principle. So did Paul, and therefore laboured with so much heart and so much success. And yet the more he laboured, and the more good he did, the more humble he was in his opinion of himself, and the more disposed to own and magnify the favour of God towards him, his free and unmerited favour. Note, A humble spirit will be very apt to own and magnify the grace of God. A humble spirit is commonly a gracious one. Where pride is subdued there it is reasonable to believe grace reigns.

After this digression, the apostle returns to his argument, and tells them (*v.* 11) that he not only preached the same gospel himself at all times, and in all places, but that all the apostles preached the same: *Whether it were they or I, so we preached, and so you believed.* Whether Peter, or Paul, or any other apostle, had converted them to Christianity, all maintained the same truth, told the same story, preached the same doctrine, and confirmed it by the same evidence. All agreed in this that Jesus Christ, and him crucified and slain, and then rising from the dead, was the very sum and substance of Christianity; and this all true Christians believe. All the apostles agreed in this testimony; all Christians agree in the belief of it. By this faith they live. In this faith they die.

Verses 12–19

Having confirmed the truth of our Saviour's resurrection,

the apostle goes on to refute those among the Corinthians who said there would be none: *If Christ be preached that he rose from the dead, how say some among you that there is no resurrection of the dead? v.* 12. It seems from this passage, and the course of the argument, there were some among the Corinthians who thought the resurrection an impossibility. This was a common sentiment among the heathens. But against this the apostle produces an incontestable fact, namely, the resurrection of Christ; and he goes on to argue against them from the absurdities that must follow from their principle. As,

I. *If there be* (can be) *no resurrection of the dead, then Christ has not risen* (*v.* 13); and again, *"If the dead rise not,* cannot be raised or recovered to life, *then is Christ not raised, v.* 16. And yet it was foretold in ancient prophecies that he should rise; and it has been proved by multitudes of eyewitnesses that he had risen. And will you say, will any among you dare to say, that is not, cannot be, which God long ago said should be, and which is now undoubted matter of fact?"

II. It would follow hereupon that the preaching and faith of the gospel would be vain: *If Christ be not risen, then is our preaching vain, and your faith vain, v.* 14. This supposition admitted, would destroy the principal evidence of Christianity; and so, 1. Make preaching vain. "*We* apostles should *be found false witnesses of God;* we pretend to be God's witnesses for truth, and to work miracles by his power in confirmation of it, and are all the while deceivers, liars for God, if in his name, and by power received from him, we go forth, and publish and assert a thing false in fact, and impossible to be true. And does not this make us the vainest men in the world, and our office and ministry the vainest and most useless thing in the world? What end could we propose to ourselves in undertaking this hard and hazardous service, if we knew our religion stood on no better foundation, nay, if we were not well assured of the contrary? What should we preach for? Would not our labour be wholly in vain? We can have no very favourable expectations in this life; and we could have none beyond it. If Christ be not raised, the gospel is a jest; it is chaff and emptiness." 2. This supposition would make the faith of Christians vain, as well as the labours of ministers: *If Christ be not raised, your faith is vain; you are yet in your sins* (*v.* 17), yet under the guilt and condemnation of sin, because it is through his death and sacrifice for sin alone that forgiveness is to be had. *We have redemption through his blood, the forgiveness of sins,* Eph. 1:7. No remission of sins is to be had but through the shedding of his blood. And had his blood been shed, and his life taken away, without ever being restored, what evidence could we have had that through him we should have justification and eternal life? Had he remained under the power of death, how could he have delivered us from its power? And how vain a thing is faith in him, upon this supposition! He must rise for our justification who was delivered for our sins, or in vain we look for any such benefit by him. There had been no justification nor salvation if Christ had not risen. And must not faith in Christ be vain, and of no signification, if he be still among the dead?

III. Another absurdity following from this supposition is that *those who have fallen asleep in Christ have perished.* if there be no resurrection, they cannot rise, and therefore are lost, even those who have died in the Christian faith, and for it. It is plain from this that those among the Corinthians who denied the resurrection meant thereby a state of future retribution, and not merely the revival of the flesh; they took death to be the destruction and extinction of the man, and not merely of the bodily life; for otherwise the apostle could not infer the utter loss of those who slept in Jesus, from the supposition that they would never rise more or that they had no hopes in Christ after life; for they might have hope of happiness for their minds if these survived their bodies, and this would prevent the limiting of their hopes in Christ to this life only. "Upon supposition there is no resurrection in your sense, no after-state and life, then dead Christians are quite lost. How vain a thing were our faith and religion upon this supposition!" And this,

IV. Would infer that Christ's ministers and servants were *of all men most miserable,* as having *hope in him in this life only* (*v.* 19), which is another absurdity that would follow from asserting no resurrection. Their condition who hope in Christ would be worse than that of other men. *Who hope in Christ.* Note, All who believe in Christ have hope in him; all who believe in him as a Redeemer hope for redemption and salvation by him; but if there be no resurrection, or state of future recompence (which was intended by those who denied the resurrection at Corinth), their hope in him must be limited to this life: and, if all their hopes in Christ lie within the compass of this life, they are in a much worse condition than the rest of mankind, especially at that time, and under those circumstances, in which the apostles wrote; for then they had no countenance nor protection from the rulers of the world, but were hated and persecuted by all men. Preachers and private Christians therefore had a hard lot if in this life only they had hope in Christ. Better be any thing than a Christian upon these terms; for in this world they are hated, and hunted, and abused, stripped of all worldly comforts and exposed to all manner of sufferings: they fare much harder than other men in this life, and yet have no further nor better hopes. And is it not absurd for one who believes in Christ to admit a principle that involves so absurd an inference? Can that man have faith in Christ who can believe concerning him that he will leave his faithful servants, whether ministers or others, in a worse state than his enemies? Note, It were a gross absurdity in a Christian to admit the supposition of no resurrection or future state. It would leave no hope beyond this world, and would frequently make his condition the worst in the world. Indeed, the Christian is by his religion crucified to this world, and taught to live upon the hope of another. Carnal pleasures are insipid to him in a great degree; and spiritual and heavenly pleasures are those which he affects and pants after. How sad is his case indeed, if he must be dead to worldly pleasures and yet never hope for any better!

Verses 20–34

In this passage the apostle establishes the truth of the resurrection of the dead, the holy dead, the dead in Christ,

I. On the resurrection of Christ. 1. Because he is indeed *the first-fruits of those that slept, v.* 20. He has truly risen himself, and he has risen in this very quality and character, as the first-fruits of those who sleep in him. As he has assuredly risen, so in his resurrection there is as much an earnest given that the dead in him shall rise as there was that the Jewish harvest in general should be accepted and blessed by the offering and acceptance of the first-fruits. The whole lump was made holy by the consecration of the first-fruits (Rom. 11:16), and the whole body of Christ, all that are by faith united to him, are by his resurrection assured of their own. As he has risen, they shall rise; just as the lump is holy because the first fruits are so. He has not risen merely for himself, but as head of the body, the church; and *those that sleep in him God will bring with him,* 1 Th. 4:14. Note, Christ's resurrection is a pledge and earnest of ours, if we are true believers in him; because he has risen, we shall rise. We are a part of the consecrated lump, and shall partake of the acceptance and favour vouchsafed the first-fruits. This is the first argument used by the apostle in confirmation of the truth; and it is, 2. Illustrated by a parallel between the first and second Adam. For, since by man came death, it was every way proper that by man should come deliverance from it, or, which is all one, a resurrection, *v.* 21. And so, *as in Adam all die, in Christ shall all be made alive;* as through the sin of the first Adam all men became mortal, because all derived from him the same sinful nature, so through the merit and resurrection of Christ shall all who are made to partake of the Spirit, and the spiritual nature, revive, and become immortal. All who die through the sin of Adam; all who are raised, in the sense of the apostle, rise through the merit and power of Christ. But the meaning is not that, as all men died in Adam, so all men, without exception, shall be made alive in Christ; for the scope of the apostle's argument restrains the general meaning. Christ rose as the first-fruits; therefore *those that are Christ's* (*v.* 23) shall rise too. Hence it will not follow that all men without exception shall rise too; but it will fitly follow that all who thus rise, rise in virtue of Christ's resurrection, and so that their revival is owing to the man Christ Jesus, as the mortality of all mankind was owing to the first man; and so, as by man came death, by man came deliverance. Thus it seemed fit to the divine wisdom that, as the first Adam ruined his posterity by sin, the second Adam should raise his seed to a glorious immortality. 3. Before he leaves the argument he states that there will be an order observed in their resurrection. What that precisely will be we are nowhere told, but in the general only here that there will be order observed. Possibly those may rise first who have held the highest rank, and done the most eminent service, or suffered the most grievous evils, or cruel deaths, for Christ's sake. It is only here said that the first-fruits are supposed to rise first, and afterwards all who are Christ's, when he shall come again. Not that Christ's resurrection must in fact go before the resurrection of any of his, but it must be laid as the foundation: as it was not necessary that those who lived remote from Jerusalem must go thither and offer the first-fruits before they could account the lump holy, yet they must be set apart for this purpose, till they could be offered, which might be done at any time from pentecost till the feast of dedication. See Bishop Patrick on Num. 24:2. The offering of the first-fruits was what made the lump holy; and the lump was made holy by this offering, though it was not made before the harvest was gathered in, so it were set apart for that end, and duly offered afterwards. So Christ's resurrection must, in order of nature, precede that of his saints, though some of these might rise in order of time before him. It is because he has risen that they rise. Note, Those that are Christ's must rise, because of their relation to him.

II. He argues from the continuance of the mediatorial kingdom till all Christ's enemies are destroyed, the last of which is death, *v.* 24–26. He has risen, and, upon his resurrection, was invested with sovereign empire, *had all power in heaven and earth put into his hands* (Mt. 28:18), *had a name given him above every name, that every knee might bow to him, and every tongue confess him Lord.* Phil. 2:9–11. And the administration of this kingdom must continue in his hands till all opposing *power, and rule, and authority, be put down* (*v.* 24), *till all enemies are put under his feet* (*v.* 25), and *till the last enemy is destroyed,* which is death, *v.* 26.

1. This argument implies in it all these particulars: — (1.) That our Saviour rose from the dead to have all power put into his hands, and have and administer a kingdom, as Mediator: *For this end he died, and rose, and revived, that he might be Lord both of the dead and living,* Rom. 14:9. (2.) That this mediatorial kingdom is to have an end, at least as far as it is concerned in bringing his people safely to glory, and subduing all his and their enemies: *Then cometh the end, v.* 24. (3.) That it is not to have an end till all opposing power be put down, and all enemies brought to his feet, *v.* 24, 25. (4.) That, among other enemies, death must be destroyed (*v.* 26) or abolished; its powers over its members must be disannulled. Thus far the apostle is express; but he leaves us to make the inference that therefore the saints must rise, else death and the grave would have power over them, nor would our Saviour's kingly power prevail against the last enemy of his people and annul its power. When saints shall live again, and die no more, then, and not till then, will death be abolished, which must be brought about before our Saviour's mediatorial kingdom is delivered up, which yet must be in due time. The saints therefore shall live again and die no more. This is the scope of the argument; but,

2. The apostle drops several hints in the course of it which it will be proper to notice: as, (1.) That our Saviour, as man and mediator between God and man, has a delegated royalty, a kingdom given: *All things are put under him, he excepted that did put all things under him, v.* 27. As man, all his authority must be delegated. And, though his mediation supposes his divine nature, yet as Mediator he does not so explicitly sustain the character of God, but a middle person between God and man, partaking of both natures, human and divine, as he was to reconcile both parties, God and man, and receiving commission and authority from God the Father to act in this office. The Father appears, in this whole dispensation, in the majesty and with the authority of God: the Son, made man, appears as the minister of the Father, though he is God as well as the Father. Nor is this passage to be understood of the eternal dominion over all his creatures which belongs to him as God, but of a kingdom committed to him as Mediator and God-man, and that chiefly after his resurrection, when, having overcome, he sat down with his Father on his throne, Rev. 3:21. Then was the prediction verified, *I have set my king upon my holy hill of Zion* (Ps. 2:6), placed him on his throne. This is meant by the phrase so frequent in the writings of the New Testament, of *sitting at the right hand of God* (Mk. 16:19; Rom. 8:34; Col. 3:1 etc.), *on the right hand of power* (Mk. 14:62; Lu. 22:69), *on the right hand of the throne of God* (Heb. 12:2), *on the right hand of the throne of the Majesty in the heavens,* Heb. 8:1. Sitting down in this seat is taking upon him the exercise of his mediatorial power and royalty, which was done upon his ascension into heaven, Mk. 16:19. And it is spoken of in scripture as a recompence made him for his deep humiliation and self-

abasement, in becoming man, and dying for man the accursed death of the cross, Phil. 2:6–12. Upon his ascension, he was made head over all things to the church, had power given him to govern and protect it against all its enemies, and in the end destroy them and complete the salvation of all that believe in him. This is not a power appertaining to Godhead as such; it is not original and unlimited power, but power given and limited to special purposes. And though he who has it is God, yet, inasmuch as he is somewhat else besides God, and in this whole dispensation acts not as God, but as Mediator, not as the offended Majesty, but as one interposing in favour of his offending creatures, and this by virtue of his consent and commission who acts and appears always in that character, he may properly be said to have this power given him; he may reign as God, with power unlimited, and yet may reign as Mediator, with a power delegated, and limited to these particular purposes. (2.) That this delegated royalty must at length *be delivered up to the Father,* from whom it was received (*v.* 24); for it is a power received for particular ends and purposes, a power to govern and protect his church till all the members of it be gathered in, and the enemies of it for ever subdued and destroyed (*v.* 25, 26), and when these ends shall be obtained the power and authority will not need to be continued. The Redeemer must reign till his enemies be destroyed, and the salvation of his church and people accomplished; and, when this end is attained, then will he deliver up the power which he had only for this purpose, though he may continue to reign over his glorified church and body in heaven; and in this sense it may notwithstanding be said that *he shall reign for ever and ever* (Rev. 11:15), *that he shall reign over the house of Jacob for ever, and of his kingdom there shall be no end* (Lu. 1:33), *that his dominion is an everlasting dominion, which shall not pass away,* Dan. 7:14. See also Mich. 4:7. (3.) The Redeemer shall certainly reign till the last enemy of his people be destroyed, till death itself be abolished, till his saints revive and recover perfect life, never to be in fear and danger of dying any more. He shall have all power in heaven and earth till then — *he who loved us, and gave himself for us, and washed us from our sins in his own blood* — he who is so nearly related to us, and so much concerned for us. What support should this be to his saints in every hour of distress and temptation! *He is alive who was dead, and liveth for ever,* and doth reign, and will continue to reign, till the redemption of his people be completed, and the utter ruin of their enemies effected. (4.) When this is done, *and all things are put under his feet, then shall the Son become subject to him that put all things under him, that God may be all in all, v.* 28. The meaning of this I take to be that then the man Christ Jesus, who hath appeared in so much majesty during the whole administration of his kingdom, shall appear upon giving it up to be a subject of the Father. Things are in scripture many times said *to be* when they are *manifested* and *made to appear;* and this delivering up of the kingdom will make it manifest that he who appeared in the majesty of the sovereign king was, during this administration, a subject of God. The glorified humanity of our Lord Jesus Christ, with all the dignity and power conferred on it, was no more than a glorious creature. This will appear when the kingdom shall be delivered up; and it will appear to the divine glory, that God may be all in all, that the accomplishment of our salvation may appear altogether divine, and God alone may have the honour of it. Note, Though the human nature must be employed in the work of our redemption, yet God was all in all in it. *It was the Lord's doing and should be marvellous in our eyes.*

III. He argues for the resurrection, from the case of those who were baptized for the dead (*v.* 29): *What shall those do who are baptized for the dead, if the dead rise not at all? Why are they baptized for the dead?* What shall they do if the dead rise not? What have they done? How vain a thing hath their baptism been! Must they stand by it, or renounce it? why are they baptized for the dead, if the dead rise not? ***hyper tōn nekrōn.*** But what is this baptism for the dead? It is necessary to be known, that the apostle's argument may be understood; whether it be only *argumentum ad hominem,* or *ad rem;* that is, whether it conclude for the thing in dispute universally, or only against the particular persons who were baptized for the dead. But who shall interpret this very obscure passage, which, though it consists of no more than three words, besides the articles, has had more than three times three senses put on it by interpreters? It is not agreed what is meant by baptism, whether it is to be taken in a proper or figurative sense, and, if in a proper sense, whether it is to be understood or Christian baptism properly so called, or some other ablution. And as little is it agreed who are the dead, or in what sense the preposition ***hyper*** is to be taken. Some understand the dead of our Saviour himself; *vide* Whitby *in loc.* Why are persons baptized in the name of a dead Saviour, a Saviour who remains among the dead, if the dead rise not? But it is, I believe, and instance perfectly singular for ***hoi nekroi*** to mean no more than one dead person; it is a signification which the words have nowhere else. And the ***hoi baptizomenoi*** *(the baptized)* seem plainly to mean some particular persons, not Christians in general, which yet must be the signification if the ***hoi nekroi*** *(the dead)* be understood of our Saviour. Some understand the passage of the martyrs: Why do they suffer martyrdom for their religion? This is sometimes called the baptism of blood by ancients, and, by our Saviour himself, baptism indefinitely, Mt. 20:22; Lu. 12:50. But in what sense can those who die martyrs for their religion be said to be baptized (that is, die martyrs) for the dead? Some understand it of a custom that was observed, as some of the ancients tell us, among many who professed the Christian name in the first ages, of baptizing some in the name and stead of catechumens dying without baptism. But this savoured of such superstition that, if the custom had prevailed in the church so soon, the apostle would hardly have mentioned it without signifying a dislike of it. Some understand it of baptizing over the dead, which was a custom, they tell us, that early obtained; and this to testify their hope of the resurrection. This sense is pertinent to the apostle's argument, but it appears not that any such practice was in use in the apostle's time. Others understand it of those who have been baptized for the sake, or on occasion, of the martyrs, that is, the constancy with which they died for their religion. Some were doubtless converted to Christianity by observing this: and it would have been a vain thing for persons to have become Christians upon this motive, if the martyrs, by losing their lives for religion, became utterly extinct, and were to live no more. But the church at Corinth had not, in all probability, suffered much persecution at this time, or seem many instances of martyrdom among them, nor had many converts been made by the constancy and firmness which the martyrs discovered. Not to observe that ***hoi nekroi*** seems to be too general an expression to mean only the martyred dead. It is as easy an explication of the phrase as any I have met with, and as pertinent to the argument, to suppose the ***hoi nekroi*** to mean some among the Corinthians, who had been taken off by the hand of God. We read that *many were sickly among them, and many slept* (*ch.* 11:30), because of their disorderly behaviour at the Lord's table. These executions might terrify some into Christianity; as the miraculous earthquake did the jailer, Acts 16:29, 30, etc. Persons baptized on such an occasion might be properly said to be baptized for the dead, that is, on their account. And the ***hoi baptizomenoi*** *(the baptized)* and the ***hoi nekroi*** *(the dead)* answer to one another; and upon this supposition the Corinthians could not mistake the apostle's meaning. "Now," says he, "what shall they do, and why were they baptized, if the dead rise not? You have a general persuasion that these men have done right, and acted wisely, and as they ought, on this occasion; but why, if the dead rise not, seeing they may perhaps hasten their death, by provoking a jealous God, and have no hopes beyond it?" But whether this be the meaning, or whatever else be, doubtless the apostle's argument was good and intelligible to the Corinthians. And his next is as plain to us.

IV. He argues from the absurdity of his own conduct and that of other Christians upon this supposition,

1. It would be a foolish thing for them to run so many hazards (*v.* 30): *"Why stand we in jeopardy every hour?* Why do we expose ourselves to continual peril — we Christians, especially we apostles?" Every one knows that it was dangerous being a Christian, and much more a preacher and an apostle, at that time. "Now," says the apostle, "what fools are we to run these hazards, if we have no better hopes beyond death, if when we die we die wholly, and revive no more!" Note, Christianity were a foolish profession if it proposed no hopes beyond this life, at least in such hazardous times as attended the first profession of it; it required men to risk all the blessings and comforts of this life, and to face and endure all the evils of it, without any future prospects. And is this a character of his religion fit for a Christian to endure? And must he not fix this character on it if he give up his future hopes, and deny the resurrection of the dead? This argument the apostle brings home to himself: *"I protest,"* says he, *"by your rejoicing in Jesus Christ,* by all the comforts of Christianity, and all the peculiar succours and supports of our holy faith, that *I die daily," v.* 31. He was in continual danger of death, and carried his life, as we say, in his hand. And why should he thus expose himself, if he had no hopes after life? To live in daily view and expectation of death, and yet have no prospect beyond it, must be very heartless and uncomfortable, and his case, upon this account, a very melancholy one. He had need be very well assured of the resurrection of the dead, or he was guilty of extreme weakness, in hazarding all that was dear to him in this world, and his life into the bargain. He had encountered very great difficulties and fierce enemies; he had *fought with beasts at Ephesus* (*v.* 32), and was in danger of being pulled to pieces by an enraged multitude, stirred up by Demetrius and the other craftsmen (Acts 19:24, etc.), though some understand this literally of Paul's being exposed to fight with wild beasts in the amphitheatre, at a Roman show in that city. And Nicephorus tells a formal story to this purport, and of the miraculous complaisance of the lions to him when they came near him. But so remarkable a trial and circumstance of his life, methinks, would not have been passed over by Luke, and much less by himself, when he gives us so large and particular a detail of his sufferings, 2 Co. 11:24, *ad fin.* When he mentioned that he was five times scourged of the Jews, thrice beaten with rods, once stoned, thrice shipwrecked, it is strange that he should not have said that he was once exposed to fight with the beasts. I take it, therefore, that this fighting with beasts is a figurative expression, that the beasts intended were men of a fierce and ferine disposition, and that this refers to the passage above cited. "Now," says he, "what advantage have I from such contests, if the dead rise not? Why should I die daily, expose myself daily to the danger of dying by violent hands, if the dead rise not? And if *post mortem nihil — if I am to perish by death,* and expect nothing after it, could any thing be more weak?" Was Paul so senseless? Had he given the Corinthians any ground to entertain such a thought of him? If he had not been well assured that death would have been to his advantage, would he, in this stupid manner, have thrown away his life? Could any thing but the sure hopes of a better life after death have extinguished the love of life in him to this degree? *"What advantageth it me, if the dead rise not?* What can I propose to myself?" Note, It is very lawful and fit for a Christian to propose advantage to himself by his fidelity to God. Thus did Paul. Thus did our blessed Lord himself, Heb. 12:2. And thus we are bidden to do after his example, and have our fruit to holiness, that our end may be everlasting life. This is the very end of our faith, even the salvation of our souls (1 Pt. 1:9), not only what it will issue in, but what we should aim at.

2. It would be a much wiser thing to take the comforts of this life: *Let us eat and drink, for to-morrow we die* (*v.* 32); let us turn epicures. Thus this sentence means in the prophet, Isa. 22:13. Let us even live like beasts, if we must die like them. This would be a wiser course, if there were no resurrection, no after-life or state, than to abandon all the pleasures of life, and offer and expose ourselves to all the miseries of life, and live in continual peril of perishing by savage rage and cruelty. This passage also plainly implies, as I have hinted above, that those who denied the resurrection among the Corinthians were perfect Sadducees, of whose principles we have this account in the holy writings, that they say, *There is no resurrection, neither angel nor spirit* (Acts 23:8), that is, "Man is all body, there is nothing in him to survive the body, nor will that, when once he is dead, ever revive again." Such Sadducees were the men against whom the apostle argued; otherwise his arguments had no force in them; for, though the body should never revive, yet, as long as the mind survived it, he might have much advantage from all the hazards he ran for Christ's sake. Nay, it is certain that the mind is to be the principal seat and subject of the heavenly glory and happiness. But, if there were no hopes after death, would not every wise man prefer an easy comfortable life before such a wretched one as the apostle led; nay, and endeavour to enjoy the comforts of life as fast as possible, because the continuance of it is short? Note, Nothing but the hopes of better things hereafter can enable a man to forego all the comforts and pleasures here, and embrace poverty, contempt, misery, and death. Thus did the apostles and primitive Christians; but how wretched was their case,

and how foolish their conduct, if they deceived themselves, and abused the world with vain and false hopes!

V. The apostle closes his argument with a caution, exhortation, and reproof. 1. A caution against the dangerous conversation of bad men, men of loose lives and principles: *Be not deceived,* says he; *evil communications corrupt good manners, v.* 33. Possibly, some of those who said that there was no resurrection of the dead were men of loose lives, and endeavoured to countenance their vicious practices by so corrupt a principle; and had that speech often in their mouths *Let us eat and drink, for to-morrow we die.* Now, the apostle grants that their talk was to the purpose if there was no future state. But, having confuted their principle, he now warns the Corinthians how dangerous such men's conversation must prove. He tells them that they would probably be corrupted by them, and fall in with their course of life, if they gave into their evil principles. Note, Bad company and conversation are likely to make bad men. Those who would keep their innocence must keep good company. Error and vice are infectious: and, if we would avoid the contagion, we must keep clear of those who have taken it. *He that walketh with wise men shall be wise; but a companion of fools shall be destroyed,* Prov. 13:20. 2. Here is an exhortation to break off their sins, and rouse themselves, and lead a more holy and righteous life (*v.* 34): *Awake to righteousness,* or *awake righteously, eknēpsate dikaiōs, and sin not,* or sin no more. "Rouse yourselves, break off your sins by repentance: renounce and forsake every evil way, correct whatever is amiss, and do not, by sloth and stupidity, be led away into such conversation and principles as will sap your Christian hopes, and corrupt your practice." The disbelief of a future state destroys all virtue and piety. But the best improvement to be made of the truth is to cease from sin, and set ourselves to the business of religion, and that in good earnest. If there will be a resurrection and a future life, we should live and act as those who believe it, and should not give into such senseless and sottish notions as will debauch our morals, and render us loose and sensual in our lives. 3. Here is a reproof, and a sharp one, to some at least among them: *Some of you have not the knowledge of God; I speak this to your shame.* Note, It is a shame in Christians not to have the knowledge of God. The Christian religion gives the best information that can be had about God, his nature, and grace, and government. Those who profess this religion reproach themselves, by remaining without the knowledge of God; for it must be owing to their own sloth, and slight of God, that they are ignorant of him. And is it not a horrid shame for a Christian to slight God, and be so wretchedly ignorant in matters that so nearly and highly concern him? Note, also, It must be ignorance of God that leads men into the disbelief of a resurrection and future life. Those who know God know that he will not abandon his faithful servants, nor leave them exposed to such hardships and sufferings without any recompence or reward. They know he is not unfaithful nor unkind, to forget their labour and patience, their faithful services and cheerful sufferings, or let their *labour be in vain.* But I am apt to think that the expression has a much stronger meaning; that there were atheistical people among them who hardly owned a God, or one who had any concern with or took cognizance of human affairs. These were indeed a scandal and shame to any Christian church. Note, Real atheism lies at the bottom of men's disbelief of a future state. Those who own a God and a providence, and observe how unequal the distributions of the present life are, and how frequently the best men fare worst, can hardly doubt an after state, where every thing will be set to rights.

Verses 35–50

The apostle comes now to answer a plausible and principal objection against the doctrine of the resurrection of the dead, concerning which observe the proposal of the objection: *Some man will say, How are the dead raised up? And with what body do they come? v.* 35. The objection is plainly two-fold. *How are they raised up?* that is, "By what means? How can they be raised? What power is equal to this effect?" It was an opinion that prevailed much among the heathens, and the Sadducees seem to have been in the same sentiment, that it was not within the compass of divine power, *mortales aeternitate donare, aut revocare defunctos — to make mortal men immortal, or revive and restore the dead.* Such sort of men those seem to have been who among the Corinthians denied the resurrection of the dead, and object here, "How are they raised? How should they be raised? Is it not utterly impossible?" The other part of the objection is about the quality of their bodies, who shall rise: *"With what body will they come?* Will it be with the same body, with like shape, and form, and stature, and members, and qualities, or various?" The former objection is that of those who opposed the doctrine, the latter the enquiry of curious doubters.

I. To the former the apostle replies by telling them this was to be brought about by divine power, that very power which they had all observed to do something very like it, year after year, in the death and revival of the corn; and therefore it was an argument of great weakness and stupidity to doubt whether the resurrection of the dead might not be effected by the same power: *Thou fool! that which thou sowest is not quickened unless it die, v.* 36. It must first corrupt, before it will quicken and spring up. It not only sprouts after it is dead, but it must die that it may live. And why should any be so foolish as to imagine that the man once dead cannot be made to live again, by the same power which every year brings the dead grain to life? This is the substance of the apostle's answer to the first question. Note, It is a foolish thing to question the divine power to raise the dead, when we see it every day quickening and reviving things that are dead.

II. But he is longer in replying to the second enquiry.

1. He begins by observing that there is a change made in the grain that is sown: It is *not that body which shall be* that is sown, but *bare grain,* of wheat or barley, etc.; but God gives it such a body as he will, and in such way as he will, only so as to distinguish the kinds from each other. Every seed sown has its *proper body,* is constituted of such materials, and figured in such a manner, as are proper to it, proper to that kind. This is plainly in the divine power, though we no more know how it is done than we know how a dead man is raised to life again. It is certain the grain undergoes a great change, and it is intimated in this passage that so will the dead, when they rise again, and live again, in their bodies, after death.

2. He proceeds hence to observe that there is a great deal of variety among others bodies, as there is among plants: as, (1.) In bodies of flesh: *All flesh is not the same;* that of men is of one kind, that of beasts another, another that of fishes, and that of birds another, *v.* 39. There is a variety in all the kinds, and somewhat peculiar in every kind, to distinguish it from the other. (2.) In bodies celestial and terrestrial there is also a difference; and what is for the glory of one is not for the other; for the true glory of every being consists in its fitness for its rank and state. Earthly bodies are not adapted to the heavenly regions, nor heavenly bodies fitted to the condition of earthly beings. Nay, (3.) There is a variety of glory among heavenly bodies themselves: *There is one glory of the sun, and another of the moon, and another of the stars; for one star differs from another star in glory, v.* 41. All this is to intimate to us that the bodies of the dead, when they rise, will be so far changed, that they will be fitted for the heavenly regions, and that there will be a variety of glories among the bodies of the dead, when they shall be raised, as there is among the sun, and moon, and stars, nay among the stars themselves. All this carries an intimation along with it that it must be as easy to divine power to raise the dead, and recover their mouldered bodies, as out of the same materials to form so many different kinds of flesh and plants, and, for aught we know, celestial bodies as well as terrestrial ones. The sun and stars may, for aught we know, be composed of the same materials as the earth we tread on, though as much refined and changed by the divine skill and power. And can he, out of the same materials, form such various beings, and yet not be able to raise the dead? Having thus prepared the way, he comes,

3. To speak directly to the point: *So also,* says he, *is the resurrection of the dead;* so (as the plant growing out of the putrefied grain), so as no longer to be a terrestrial but a celestial body, and varying in glory from the other dead, who are raised, as one star does from another. But he specifies some particulars: as, (1.) *It is sown in corruption, it is raised in incorruption. It is sown.* Burying the dead is like sowing them; it is like committing the seed to the earth, that it may spring out of it again. And our bodies, which are sown, are corruptible, liable to putrefy and moulder, and crumble to dust; but, when we rise, they will be out of the power of the grave, and never more be liable to corruption. (2.) *It is sown in dishonour, it is raised in glory.* Ours is at present a vile body, Phil. 3:21. Nothing is more loathsome than a dead body; it is thrown into the grave as a despised and broken vessel, in which there is no pleasure. But at the resurrection a glory will be put upon it; it will be made like the glorious body of our Saviour; it will be purged from all the dregs of earth, and refined into an ethereal substance, and shine out with a splendour resembling his. (3.) *It is sown in weakness, it is raised in power.* It is laid in the earth, a poor helpless thing, wholly in the power of death, deprived of all vital capacities and powers, of life and strength: it is utterly unable to move or stir. But when we arise our bodies will have heavenly life and vigour infused into them; they will be hale, and firm, and durable, and lively, and liable no more to any infirmity, weakness, or decay. (4.) *It is sown a natural,* or *animal* body, *sōma psychikon,* a body fitted to the low condition and sensitive pleasures and enjoyments of this life, which are all gross in comparison of the heavenly state and enjoyments. But when we rise it will be quire otherwise; our body will rise spiritual. Not that body would be changed into spirit: this would be a contradiction in our common conceptions; it would be as much as to say, Body changed into what is not body, matter made immaterial. The expression is to be understood comparatively. We shall at the resurrection have bodies purified and refined to the last degree, made light and agile; and, though they are not changed into spirit, yet made fit to be perpetual associates of spirits made perfect. And why should it not be as much in the power of God to raise incorruptible, glorious, lively, spiritual bodies, out of the ruins of those vile, corruptible, lifeless, and animal ones, as first to make matter out of nothing, and then, out of the same mass of matter, produce such variety of beings, both in earth and heaven? *To God all things are possible;* and this cannot be impossible.

4. He illustrates this by a comparison of the first and second Adam: *There is an animal body,* says he, *and there is a spiritual body;* and then goes into the comparison in several instances. (1.) As we have our natural body, the animal body we have in this world, from the first Adam, we expect our spiritual body from the second. This is implied in the whole comparison. (2.) This is but consonant to the different characters these two persons bear: *The first Adam was made a living soul,* such a being as ourselves, and with a power of propagating such beings as himself, and conveying to them a nature and animal body like his own, but none other, nor better. The *second Adam is a quickening Spirit;* he is the resurrection and the life, Jn. 11:25. He hath life in himself, and quickeneth whom he will, Jn. 5:20, 21. *The first man was of the earth,* made out of the earth, and was earthy; his body was fitted to the region of his abode: *but the second Adam is the Lord from heaven;* he who came down from heaven, and giveth life to the world (Jn. 6:33); he who came down from heaven and was in heaven at the same time (Jn. 3:13); the Lord of heaven and earth. If the first Adam could communicate to us natural and animal bodies, cannot the second Adam make our bodies spiritual ones? If the deputed lord of this lower creation could do the one, cannot the Lord from heaven, the Lord of heaven and earth, do the other? (3.) We must first have natural bodies from the first Adam before we can have spiritual bodies from the second (*v.* 49); we *must bear the image of the earthy before we can bear the image of the heavenly.* Such is the established order of Providence. We must have weak, frail, mortal bodies by descent from the first Adam, before we can have lively, spiritual, and immortal ones by the quickening power of the second. We must die before we can live to die no more. (4.) Yet if we are Christ's, true believers in him (for this whole discourse relates to the resurrection of the saints), it is as certain that we shall have spiritual bodies as it is now that we have natural or animal ones. By these we are as the first Adam, earthy, we bear his image; by those we shall be as the second Adam, have bodies like his own, heavenly, and so bear him image. And we are as certainly intended to bear the one as we have borne the other. As surely therefore as we have had natural bodies, we shall have spiritual ones. The dead in Christ shall not only rise, but shall rise thus gloriously changed.

5. He sums up this argument by assigning the reason of this change (*v.* 50): *Now this I say that flesh and blood cannot inherit the kingdom of God; nor doth corruption inherit incorruption.* The natural body is flesh and blood, consisting of bones, muscles, nerves, veins, arteries, and their several fluids; and, as such, it is of a corruptible frame and form, liable to dissolution, to rot and moulder. But no such thing shall inherit the heavenly regions; for this were for corrup-

tion to inherit incorruption, which is little better than a contradiction in terms. The heavenly inheritance is incorruptible, and never fadeth away, 1 Pt. 1:4. How can this be possessed by flesh and blood, which is corruptible and will fade away? It must be changed into ever-during substance, before it can be capable of possessing the heavenly inheritance. The sum is that the bodies of the saints, when they shall rise again, will be greatly changed from what they are now, and much for the better. They are now corruptible, flesh and blood; they will be then incorruptible, glorious, and spiritual bodies, fitted to the celestial world and state, where they are ever afterwards to dwell, and have their eternal inheritance.

Verses 51–57

To confirm what he had said of this change,

I. He here tells them what had been concealed from or unknown to them till then — that all the saints would not die, but all would be changed. Those that are alive at our Lord's coming will be caught up into the clouds, without dying, 1 Th. 4:11. But it is plain from this passage that it will not be without changing from corruption to incorruption. The frame of their living bodies shall be thus altered, as well as those that are dead; and this *in a moment, in the twinkling of an eye, v.* 52. What cannot almighty power effect? That power that calls the dead into life can surely thus soon and suddenly change the living; for changed they must be as well as the dead, because flesh and blood cannot inherit the kingdom of God. This is the mystery which the apostle shows the Corinthians: *Behold, I show you a mystery;* or bring into open light a truth dark and unknown before. Note, There are many mysteries shown to us in the gospel; many truths that before were utterly unknown are there made known; many truths that were but dark and obscure before are there brought into open day, and plainly revealed; and many things are in part revealed that will never be fully known, nor perhaps clearly understood. The apostle here makes known a truth unknown before, which is that the saints living at our Lord's second coming will not die, but be changed, that this change will be made in a moment, in the twinkling of an eye, and *at the sound of the last trump;* for, as he tells us elsewhere, the *Lord himself shall descend with a shout, with a voice of the archangel, and with the trump of God* (1 Th. 4:16), so here, *the trumpet must sound.* It is the loud summons of all the living and all the dead, to come and appear at the tribunal of Christ. At this summons the graves shall open, the dead saints shall rise incorruptible, and the living saints be changed to the same incorruptible state, *v.* 52.

II. He assigns the reason of this change (*v.* 53): *For this corruptible must put on incorruption, and this mortal must put on immortality.* How otherwise could the man be a fit inhabitant of the incorruptible regions, or be fitted to possess the eternal inheritance? How can that which is corruptible and mortal enjoy what is incorruptible, permanent, and immortal? This corruptible body must be made incorruptible, this mortal body must be changed into immortal, that the man may be capable of enjoying the happiness designed for him. Note, It is this corruptible that must put on incorruption; the demolished fabric that must be reared again. What is sown must be quickened. Saints will come in their own bodies (*v.* 38), not in other bodies.

III. He lets us know what will follow upon this change of the living and dead in Christ: *Then shall be brought to pass that saying, Death is swallowed up in victory;* or, *He will swallow up death in victory.* Isa. 25:8. For *mortality shall be then swallowed up of life* (2 Co. 5:4), and death perfectly subdued and conquered, and saints for ever delivered from its power. Such a conquest shall be obtained over it that it shall for ever disappear in those regions to which our Lord will bear his risen saints. And therefore will the saints hereupon sing their *epinikion,* their *song of triumph.* Then, when this mortal shall have put on immortality, will death be swallowed up, for ever swallowed up, *eis nikos.* Christ hinders it from swallowing his saints when they die; but, when they rise again, death shall, as to them, be swallowed for ever. And upon this destruction of death will they break out into a song of triumph.

1. They will glory over death as a vanquished enemy, and insult this great and terrible destroyer: *"O death! where is thy sting?* Where is now thy sting, thy power to hurt? What mischief hast thou done us? We are dead; but behold we live again, and shall die no more. Thou art vanquished and disarmed, and we are out of the reach of thy deadly dart. Where now is thy fatal artillery? Where are thy stores of death? We fear no further mischiefs from thee, nor heed thy weapons, but defy thy power, and despise thy wrath. And, *O grave! where is thy victory?* Where now is thy victory? What has become of it? Where are the spoils and trophies of it? Once we were thy prisoners, but the prison-doors are burst open, the locks and bolts have been forced to give way, our shackles are knocked off, and we are for ever released. Captivity is taken captive. The imaginary victor is conquered, and forced to resign his conquest and release his captives. Thy triumphs, grave, are at an end. The bonds of death are loosed, and we are at liberty, and are never more to be hurt by death, nor imprisoned in the grave." In a moment, the power of death, and the conquests and spoils of the grave, are gone; and, as to the saints, the very signs of them will not remain. Where are they? Thus will they raise themselves, when they become immortal, to the honour of their Saviour and the praise of divine grace: they shall glory over vanquished death.

2. The foundation for this triumph is here intimated, (1.) In the account given whence death had its power to hurt: *The sting of death is sin.* This gives venom to his dart: this alone puts it into the power of death to hurt and kill. Sin unpardoned, and nothing else, can keep any under his power. And the *strength of sin is the law;* it is the divine threatening against the transgressors of the law, the curse there denounced, that gives power to sin. Note, Sin is the parent of death, and gives it all its hurtful power. *By one man sin entered into the world, and death by sin,* Rom. 5:12. It is its cursed progeny and offspring. (2.) In the account given of the victory saints obtain over it through Jesus Christ, *v.* 56. *The sting of death is sin;* but Christ, by dying, has taken out this sting. He has made atonement for sin; he has obtained remission of it. It may hiss therefore, but it cannot hurt. *The strength of sin is the law;* but the curse of the law is removed by our Redeemer's *becoming a curse for us.* So that sin is deprived of its strength and sting, through Christ, that is, by his incarnation, suffering, and death. Death may seize a believer, but cannot sting him, cannot hold him in his power. There is a day coming when the grave shall open, the bands of death be loosed, the dead saints revive, and become incorruptible and immortal, and put out of the reach of death for ever. And then will it plainly appear that, as to them, death will have lost its strength and sting; and all by the mediation of Christ, by his dying in their room. By dying, he conquered death, and spoiled the grave; and, through faith in him, believers become sharers in his conquests. They often rejoice beforehand, in the hope of this victory; and, when they arise glorious from the grave, they will boldly triumph over death. Note, It is altogether owing to the grace of God in Christ that sin is pardoned and death disarmed. The law puts arms into the hand of death, to destroy the sinner; but pardon of sin takes away this power from the law, and deprives death of its strength and sting. It is *by the grace of God, through the redemption which is in Christ Jesus, that we are freely justified,* Rom. 3:24. It is no wonder, therefore, (3.) If this triumph of the saints over death should issue in thanksgiving to God: *Thanks be to God, who giveth us the victory through Christ Jesus, our Lord, v.* 57. The way to sanctify all our joy is to make it tributary to the praise of God. Then only do we enjoy our blessings and honours in a holy manner when God has his revenue of glory out of it, and we are free to pay it to him. And this really improves and exalts our satisfaction. We are conscious at once of having done our duty and enjoyed our pleasure. And what can be more joyous in itself than the saints' triumph over death, when they shall rise again? And shall they not then rejoice in the Lord, and be glad in the God of their salvation? Shall not their souls magnify the Lord? When he shows *such wonders to the dead, shall they not arise and praise him?* Ps. 88:10. Those who remain under the power of death can have no heart to praise; but such conquests and triumphs will certainly tune the tongues of the saints to thankfulness and praise — praise for the victory (it is great and glorious in itself), and for the means whereby it is obtained (it is given of God through Christ Jesus), a victory obtained not by our power, but the power of God; not given because we are worthy, but because Christ is so, and has by dying obtained this conquest for us. Must not this circumstance endear the victory to us, and heighten our praise to God? Note, How many springs of joy to the saints and thanksgiving to God are opened by the death and resurrection, the sufferings and conquests, of our Redeemer! With what acclamations will saints rising from the dead applaud him! How will the heaven of heavens resound his praises for ever! *Thanks be to God* will be the burden of their song; and angels will join the chorus, and declare their consent with a loud Amen, Hallelujah.

Verse 58

In this verse we have the improvement of the whole argument, in an exhortation, enforced by a motive resulting plainly from it.

I. An exhortation, and this threefold: — 1. That they should be stedfast — *hedraioi,* firm, fixed in the faith of the gospel, that gospel which he had preached and they had received, namely, *That Christ died for our sins, and arose again the third day, according to the scriptures* (*v.* 3, 4), and fixed in the faith of the glorious resurrection of the dead, which, as he had shown, had so near and necessary a connection with the former. "Do not let your belief of these truths be shaken or staggered. They are most certain, and of the last importance." Note, Christians should be stedfast believers of this great article of the resurrection of the dead. It is evidently founded on the death of Christ. *Because he lives, his servants shall live also,* Jn. 14:19. And it is of the last importance; a disbelief of a future life will open a way to all manner of licentiousness, and corrupt men's morals to the last degree. It will be easy and natural to infer hence that we may live like beasts, and eat and drink, for to-morrow we die. 2. He exhorts them to be *immovable,* namely, in their expectation of this great privilege of being raised incorruptible and immortal. Christians should not be moved away from this hope of this gospel (Col. 1:23), this glorious and blessed hope; they should not renounce nor resign their comfortable expectations. They are not vain, but solid hopes, built upon sure foundations, the purchase and power of their risen Saviour, and the promise of God, to whom it is impossible to lie — hopes that shall be their most powerful supports under all the pressures of life, the most effectual antidotes against the fears of death, and the most quickening motives to diligence and perseverance in Christian duty. Should they part with these hopes? Should they suffer them to be shaken? Note, Christians should live in the most firm expectation of a blessed resurrection. This hope should be an anchor to their souls, firm and sure, Heb. 6:19. 3. He exhorts them *to abound in the work of the Lord,* and that *always,* in the Lord's service, in obeying the Lord's commands. They should be diligent and persevering herein, and going on towards perfection; they should be continually making advances in true piety, and ready and apt for every good work. The most cheerful duty, the greatest diligence, the most constant perseverance, become those who have such glorious hopes. Can we too much abound in zeal and diligence in the Lord's work, when we are assured of such abundant recompences in a future life? What vigour and resolution, what constancy and patience, should those hopes inspire! Note, Christians should not stint themselves as to their growth in holiness, but be always improving in sound religion, and abounding in the work of the Lord.

II. The motive resulting from the former discourse is that their *labour shall not be in vain in the Lord;* nay, they know it shall not. They have the best grounds in the world to build upon: they have all the assurance that can rationally be expected: as surely as Christ is risen, they shall rise; and Christ is as surely risen as the scriptures are true, and the word of God. The apostles saw him after his death, testified this truth to the world in the face of a thousand deaths and dangers, and confirmed it by miraculous powers received from him. Is there any room to doubt a fact so well attested? Note, True Christians have undoubted evidence that their labour will not be in vain in the Lord; not their most diligent services, nor their most painful sufferings; they will not be in vain, not be vain and unprofitable. Note, The labour of Christians will not be lost labour; they may lose for God, but they will lose nothing by him; nay, there is more implied than is expressed in this phrase: it means that they shall be abundantly rewarded. He will never be found unjust to forget their labour of love, Heb. 6:10. Nay, he will do exceedingly abundantly above what they can now ask or think. Neither the services they do for him, nor the sufferings they endure for him here, are worthy to be compared with the joy hereafter to be revealed in them, Rom. 8:18. Note, Those who serve God have good wages; they cannot do too much nor suffer too much for so good a Master. If they serve him now, they shall see him hereafter; if they suffer for him on earth, they shall reign with him in heaven; if they die for his sake, they shall rise again from the dead, be crowned with glory, honour, and immortality, and inherit eternal life.

CHAPTER 16

In this chapter the apostle, I. Gives directions about some charitable collection to be made in this church, for the afflicted and impoverished churches in Judea (*v.* 1–4). II. He talks of paying them a visit (*v.* 5–9). III. He recommends Timothy to them, and tells them Apollos intended to come to them (*v.* 10–12). IV. He presses them to watchfulness, constancy, charity, and to pay a due regard to all who helped him and his fellow-labourers in their work (*v.* 13–19). V. After salutations from others, and his own, he closes the epistle with a solemn admonition to them, and his good wishes for them (*v.* 20 to the end).

Verses 1–4

In this chapter Paul closes this long epistle with some particular matters of less moment; but, as all was written by divine inspiration, it is all profitable for our instruction. He begins with directing them about a charitable collection on a particular occasion, the distresses and poverty of Christians in Judea, which at this time were extraordinary, partly through the general calamities of that nation and partly through the particular sufferings to which they were exposed. Now concerning this observe,

I. How he introduces his direction. It was not a peculiar service which he required of them; he had given similar *orders to the churches of Galatia, v.* 1. He desired them only to conform to the same rules which he had given to other churches on a similar occasion. *He did not desire that others should be eased and they burdened,* 2 Co. 8:13. He also prudently mentions these orders of his to the churches of Galatia, to excite emulation, and stir them up to be liberal, according to their circumstances, and the occasion. Those who exceeded most churches in spiritual gifts, and, as it is probable, in worldly wealth (see the argument), surely would not suffer themselves to come behind any in their bounty to their afflicted brethren. Note, The good examples of other Christians and churches should excite in us a holy emulation. It is becoming a Christian not to bear to be outdone by a fellow-christian in any thing virtuous and praise-worthy, provided this consideration only makes him exert himself, not envy others; and the more advantages we have above others the more should we endeavour to exceed them. The church of Corinth should not be outdone in this service of love by the churches of Galatia, which do not appear to have been enriched with equal spiritual gifts nor outward ability.

II. The direction itself, concerning which observe,

1. The manner in which the collection was to be made: *Every one was to lay by in store* (*v.* 2), have a treasury, or fund, with himself, for this purpose. The meaning is that he should lay by as he could spare from time to time, and by this means make up a sum for this charitable purpose. Note, It is a good thing to lay up in store for good uses. Those who are rich in this world should be rich in good works, 1 Tim. 6:17, 18. The best way to be so is to appropriate of their income, and have a treasury for this purpose, a stock for the poor as well as for themselves. By this means they will be ready to every good work as the opportunity offers; and many who labour with their own hands for a livelihood should so work that they may have to give to him that needeth, Eph. 4:28. Indeed their treasury for good works can never be very large (though, according to circumstances, it may considerably vary); but the best way in the world for them to get a treasury for this purpose is to lay by from time to time, as they can afford. Some of the Greek fathers rightly observe here that this advice was given for the sake of the poorer among them. They were to lay by from week to week, and not bring in to the common treasury, that by this means their contributions might be easy to themselves, and yet grow into a fund for the relief of their brethren. "Every little," as the proverb says, "would make a mickle." Indeed all our charity and benevolence should be free and cheerful, and for that reason should be made as easy to ourselves as may be. And what more likely way to make us easy in this matter than thus to lay by? We may cheerfully give when we know that we can spare, and that we have been laying by in store that we may.

2. Here is the measure in which they are to lay by: *As God hath prospered them; ti an euodōtai,* as he has been prospered, namely, by divine Providence, as God has been pleased to bless and succeed his labours and business. Note, All our business and labour are that to us which God is pleased to make them. It is not the diligent hand that will make rich by itself, without the divine blessing, Prov. 10:4, 22. Our prosperity and success are from God and not from ourselves; and he is to be owned in all and honoured with all. It is his bounty and blessing to which we owe all we have; and whatever we have is to be used, and employed, and improved, for him. His right to ourselves and all that is ours is to be owned and yielded to him. And what argument more proper to excite us to charity to the people and children of God than to consider all we have as his gift, as coming from him? Note, When God blesses and prospers us, we should be ready to relieve and comfort his needy servants; when his bounty flows forth upon us, we should not confine it to ourselves, but let it stream out to others. The good we receive from him should stir us up to do good to others, to resemble him in our beneficence; and therefore the more good we receive from God the more we should do good to others. They were to lay by as God had blessed them, in that proportion. The more they had, through God's blessing, gained by their business or labour, their traffic or work, the more they were to lay by. Note, God expects that our beneficence to others should hold some proportion to his bounty to us. All we have is from God; the more he gives (circumstances being considered), the more he enables us to give, and the more he expects we should give, that we should give more than others who are less able, that we should give more than ourselves when we were less able. And, on the other hand, from him to whom God gives less he expects less. He is no tyrant nor cruel taskmaster, to exact brick without straw, or expect men shall do more good than he gives ability. Note, *Where there is a willing mind he accepts according to what a man hath, and not according to what he hath not* (2 Co. 8:12); but as he prospers and blesses us, and puts us in a capacity to do good, he expects we should. The greater ability he gives, the more enlarged should our hearts be, and the more open our hands; but, where the ability is less, the hands cannot be as open, however willing the mind and however large the heart; nor does God expect it.

3. Here is the time when this is to be done: *The first day of the week, kata mian sabbatōn* (Lu. 24:1), the Lord's day, the Christian holiday, when public assemblies were held and public worship was celebrated, and the Christian institutions and mysteries (as the ancients called them) were attended upon; then let every one lay by him. It is a day of holy rest; and the more vacation the mind has from worldly cares and toils the more disposition has it to show mercy: and the other duties of the day should stir us up to the performance of this; works of charity should always accompany works of piety. True piety towards God will beget kind and friendly dispositions towards men. *This commandment have we from him that he who loveth God love his brother also,* 1 Jn. 4:21. Works of mercy are the genuine fruits of true love to God, and therefore are a proper service on his own day. Note, God's day is a proper season on which to lay up for charitable uses, or lay out in them, according as he has prospered us; it is paying tribute for the blessings of the past week, and it is a proper way to procure his blessing on the work of our hands for the next.

4. We have here the disposal of the collections thus made: the apostle would have every thing ready against he came, and therefore gave direction as before: *That there be no gatherings when I come, v.* 2. But, when he came, as to the disposal of it, he would leave it much to themselves. The charity was theirs, and it was fit they should dispose of it in their own way, so it answered its end, and was applied to the right use. Paul no more pretended to lord it over the purses of his hearers than over their faith; he would not meddle with their contributions without their consent. (1.) He tells them that they should give letters of credence, and send messengers of their own with their liberality, *v.* 3. This would be a proper testimony of their respect and brotherly love to their distressed brethren, to send their gift by members of their own body, trusty and tenderhearted, who would have compassion on their suffering brethren, and a Christian concern for them, and not defraud them. It would argue that they were very hearty in this service, when they should send some of their own body on so long and hazardous a journey or voyage, to convey their liberality. Note, We should not only charitably relieve our poor fellow-christians but do it in such a way as will best signify our compassion to them and care of them. (2.) He offers to go with their messengers, if they think proper, *v.* 4. His business, as an apostle, was not to serve tables, but to give himself to the word and prayer; yet he was never wanting to set on foot, or help forward, a work of charity, when an opportunity offered. He would go to Jerusalem, to carry the contributions of the church at Corinth to their suffering brethren, rather than they should go without them, or the charity of the Corinthians fail of a due effect. It was no hindrance to his preaching work, but a great furtherance to the success of it, to show such a tender and benign disposition of mind. Note, Ministers are doing their proper business when they are promoting or helping in works of charity. Paul stirs up the Corinthians to gather for the relief of the churches in Judea, and he is ready to go with their messengers, to convey what is gathered; and he is still in the way of his duty, in the business of his office.

Verses 5–9

In this passage the apostle notifies and explains his purpose of visiting them, concerning which, observe, 1. His purpose: he intended to pass out of Asia, where he now was (*vide v.* 8, 19) and to go through Macedonia into Achaia, where Corinth was, and to stay some time with them, and perhaps the winter, *v.* 5, 6. He had long laboured in this church, and done much good among them, and had his heart set upon doing much more (if God saw fit), and therefore he had it in his thoughts to see them, and stay with them. Note, The heart of a truly Christian minister must be much towards that people among whom he has long laboured, and with remarkable success. No wonder that Paul was willing to see Corinth and stay with them as long as the other duties of his office would permit. Though some among this people despised him, and made a faction against him, doubtless there were many who loved him tenderly, and paid him all the respect due to an apostle and their spiritual father. And is it any wonder that he should be willing to visit them, and stay with them? And as to the rest, who now manifested great disrespect, he might hope to reduce them to a better temper, and thereby rectify what was out of order in the church, by staying among them for some time. It is plain that he hoped for some good effect, because he says he intended to stay, *that they might bring him on his journey whithersoever he went* (*v.* 6); not that they might accompany him a little way on the road, but expedite and furnish him for his journey, help and encourage him to it, and provide him for it. He is to be understood of being brought forward in his journey after a godly sort (as it is expressed, 3 Jn. 6), so that nothing might be wanting to him, as he himself speaks, Tit. 3:13. His stay among them, he hoped, would cure their factious humour, and reconcile them to himself and their duty. Note, It was a just reason for an apostle to make his abode in a place that he had a prospect of doing good. 2. His excuse for not seeing them now, because it would be *only by the way* (*v.* 7), *en parodō — in transitu — en passant: it would only be a transient visit.* He would not see them because he could not stay with them. Such a visit would give neither him nor them any satisfaction or advantage; it would rather raise the appetite than regale it, rather heighten their desires of being together than satisfy them. He loved them so much that he longed for an opportunity to stay with them, take up his abode among them for some length of time. This would be more pleasing to himself, and more serviceable to them, than a cursory visit in his way; and therefore he would not see them now, but another time, when he could tarry longer. 3. We have the limitation of this purpose: *I trust to tarry awhile with you, if the Lord permit, v.* 7. Though the apostles wrote under inspiration, they did not know thereby how God would dispose of them. Paul had a purpose of coming to Corinth, and staying there, and hoped to do good thereby. This was not a purpose proceeding from any extraordinary motion or impulse of the Spirit of God; it was not the effect of inspiration; for had it been such he could not have spoken of it in this manner. A purpose formed thus in him must have been the purpose of God, signified to him by his Spirit; and could he say he would come to Corinth upon this view only, if God permit, that is, that he would execute God's own purpose concerning himself, with God's permission? It is to be understood then of a common purpose, formed in his own spirit. And concerning all our purposes it is fit we should say, "We will execute them if the Lord permit." Note, All our purposes must be made with submission to the divine providence. We should say, *If the Lord will, we shall live, and do this and that,* James 4:15. It is not in us to effect our own designs, without the divine leave. It is by God's power and permission, and under his direction, that we must do every thing. Heathens have concurred in acknowledging this concern of Providence in all our actions and concerns; surely we should readily own it, and frequently and seriously attend to it. 4. We have his purpose expressed of staying at Ephesus for the present. He says he would stay there till pentecost, *v.* 8. It is very probable that at the time of writing this epistle he was in Ephesus, from this passage, compared with *v.* 19, where he says, *The churches of Asia salute you.* A proper salutation from Ephesus, but hardly so proper had he been at Philippi, as the subscription to this epistle in our common copies has it. *"The churches of Macedonia salute you"* had been much more properly inserted in the close of a letter from Philippi, than the other. But, 5. We have the reason given for his staying at Ephesus for the present: *Because a great door, and effectual, was opened to him, and there were many adversaries, v.* 9. A great door and effectual was opened to him; many were prepared to receive the gospel at Ephesus, and God gave him great success among them; he had brought over many to Christ, and he had great hope of bringing over many more. For this reason he determined to stay awhile at Ephesus. Note, Success, and a fair prospect of more, was a just reason to determine an apostle to stay and labour in a particular place. And there were many adversaries, because a great door, and an effectual, was opened. Note, Great success in the work of the gospel commonly creates many enemies. The devil opposes those most, and makes them most trouble, who most heartily and successfully set themselves to destroy his kingdom. There were many adversaries; and therefore the apostle determined to stay. Some think he alludes in this passage to the custom of the Roman Circus, and the doors of it, at which the charioteers were to enter, as their antagonists did at the opposite doors. True courage is whetted by opposition; and it is no wonder that the Christian courage of the apostle should be animated by the zeal of his adversaries. They were bent to ruin him, and prevent the effect of his ministry at Ephesus; and should he at this time desert his station, and disgrace his character and doctrine? No, the opposition of adversaries only animated his zeal. He was in nothing daunted by his adversaries; but the more they raged and opposed the more he exerted himself. Should such a man as he flee? Note, Adversaries and opposition do not break the spirits of faithful and successful ministers, but only enkindle their zeal, and inspire them with fresh courage. Indeed, to labour in vain is heartless and discouraging. This damps the spirits, and breaks the heart. But success will give life and vigour to a minister, though enemies rage, and blaspheme, and persecute. It is not the opposition of enemies, but the hardness and obstinacy of his hearers, and the backslidings and revolt of professors, that damp a faithful minister, and break his heart.

Verses 10–12

In this passage,

I. He recommends Timothy to them, in several particulars. As, 1. He bids them take care that he should *be among them without feat, v.* 10. Timothy was sent by the apostle to correct the abuses which had crept in among them; and not only to direct, but to blame, and censure, and reprove, those who were culpable. They were all in factions, and no doubt the mutual strife and hatred ran very high among them. There were some very rich, as it is probable; and many very proud, upon account both of their outward wealth and spiritual gifts. Proud spirits cannot easily bear reproof. It was reasonable therefore to think young Timothy might be roughly used; hence the apostle warns them against using him ill. Not but that he was prepared for the worst; but, whatever his firmness and prudence might be, it was their duty to behave themselves well towards him, and not discourage and dishearten him in his Lord's work. They should not fly out into resentment at his reproof. Note, Christians should bear faithful reproofs from their ministers, and not terrify and discourage them from doing their duty. 2. He warns them against despising him, *v.* 11. He was but a young man, and alone, as Ecumenius observes. He had no one to back him, and his own youthful face and years commanded but little reverence; and therefore the great pretenders to wisdom among them might be apt to entertain contemptuous thoughts of him. "Now," says the apostle, "guard against this." Not that he distrusted Timothy; he knew that Timothy would do nothing to bring contempt on his character, nothing to make his youth despicable. But pride was a reigning sin among the Corinthians, and such a caution was but too necessary. Note, Christians should be very careful not to pour contempt on any, but especially on ministers, the faithful ministers of Christ. These, whether young or old, are to be had in high esteem for their works sake. 3. He tells them they should give him all due encouragement, use him well while he was with them; and, as an evidence of this, they should send him away in friendship, and well prepared for his journey back again to Paul. This, as I have before observed, is the meaning of bringing him on his journey in peace, *v.* 11. Note, Faithful ministers are not only to be well received by a people among whom they may for a season minister, but are to be sent away with due respect.

II. He assigns the reasons why they should behave thus towards Timothy. 1. Because he was employed in the same work as Paul, and acted in it by the same authority, *v.* 10. He did not come on Paul's errand among them, nor to do his work, but the work of the Lord. Though he was not an apostle, he was assistant to one, and was sent upon this very business by a divine commission. And therefore to vex his spirit would be to grieve the Holy Spirit; to despise him would be to despise him that sent him, not Paul, but Paul's Lord and theirs. Note, Those who work the work of the Lord should be neither terrified nor despised, but treated with all tenderness and respect. Such are all the faithful ministers of the word, though not all in the same rank and degree. Pastors and teachers, as well as apostles and evangelists, while they are doing their duty, are to be treated with honour and respect. 2. Another reason is implied; as they were to esteem him for his work's sake, so also for Paul's sake, who had sent him to Corinth; not of his own errand indeed, but to work the work of the Lord: *Conduct him forth in peace, that he may come to me, for I look for him with the brethren* (*v.* 11); or *I with the brethren look for him* (the original will bear either), ***ekdechomai gar auton meta tōn adelphōn*** — "I am expecting his return, and his report concerning you; and shall judge by your conduct towards him what your regard and respect for me will be. Look to it that you send him back with no evil report." Paul might expect from the Corinthians, that a messenger from him, upon such an errand, should be regarded, and well treated. His services and success among them, his authority with them as an apostle, would challenge this at their hands. They would hardly dare to send back Timothy with a report that would grieve or provoke the apostle. "I and the brethren expect his return, wait for the report he is to make; and therefore do not use him ill, but respect him, regard his message, and let him return in peace."

III. He informs them of Apollos's purpose to see them. 1. He himself had greatly desired him to come to them, *v.* 12. Though one party among them had declared for Apollos against Paul (if that passage is to be understood literally, *vide ch.* 4:6), yet Paul did not hinder Apollos from going to Corinth in his own absence, nay, he pressed him to go thither. He had no suspicions of Apollos, as if he would lessen Paul's interest and respect among them, to the advancement of his own. Note, Faithful ministers are not apt to entertain jealousies of each other, nor suspect of such selfish designs. True charity and brotherly love think no evil. And where should these reign, if not in the breasts of the ministers of Christ? 2. Apollos could not be prevailed on for the present to come, but would at a more convenient season. Perhaps their feuds and factions might render the present season improper. He would not go to be set at the head of a party and countenance the dividing and contentious humour. When this had subsided, through Paul's epistle to them and Timothy's ministry among them, he might conclude a visit would be more proper. Apostles did not vie with each other, but consulted each other's comfort and usefulness. Paul intimates his great regard to the church of Corinth, when they had used him ill, by entreating Apollos to go to them; and Apollos shows his respect to Paul, and his concern to keep up his character and authority, by declining the journey till the Corinthians were in better temper. Note, It is very becoming the ministers of the gospel to have and manifest a concern for each other's reputation and usefulness.

Verses 13–18

In this passage the apostle gives,

I. Some general advices; as, 1. That they should watch (*v.* 13), be wakeful and upon their guard. A Christian is always in danger, and therefore should ever be on the watch; but the danger is greater at some times and under some circumstances. The Corinthians were in manifest danger upon many accounts: their feuds ran high, the irregularities among them were very great, there were deceivers got among them, who endeavoured to corrupt their faith in the most important articles, those without which the practice of virtue and piety could never subsist. And surely in such dangerous circumstances it was their concern to watch. Note, If a Christian would be secure, he must be on his guard; and the more his danger the greater vigilance is needful for his security. 2. He advises them to *stand fast in the faith,* to keep their ground, adhere to the revelation of God, and not give it up for the wisdom of the world, nor suffer it to be corrupted by it — stand for the faith of the gospel, and maintain it even to death; and stand in it, so as to abide in the profession of it, and feel and yield to its influence. Note, A Christian should be fixed in the faith of the gospel, and never desert nor renounce it. It is by this faith alone that he will be able to keep his ground in an hour of temptation; it is by faith that we stand (2 Co. 1:24); it is by this that we must overcome the world (1 Jn. 5:4), both when it fawns and when it frowns, when it tempts and when it terrifies. We must stand therefore in the faith of the gospel, if we would maintain our integrity. 3. He advises them to act like men, and be strong: "Act the manly, firm, and resolved part: behave strenuously, in opposition to the bad men who would divide and corrupt you, those who would split you into factions or seduce you from the faith: be not terrified nor inveigled by them; but show yourselves men in Christ, by your steadiness, by your sound judgment and firm resolution." Note, Christians should be manly and firm in all their contests with their enemies, in defending their faith, and maintaining their integrity. They should, in an especial manner, be so in those points of faith that lie at the foundation of sound and practical religion, such as were attacked among the Corinthians: these must be maintained with solid judgment and strong resolution. 4. He advises them to do every thing in charity, *v.* 14. Our zeal and constancy must be consistent with charity. When the apostle would have us play the man for our faith or religion, he puts in a caution against playing the devil for it. We may defend our faith, but we must, at the same time, maintain our innocence, and not devour and destroy, and think with ourselves that the wrath of man will work the righteousness of God, James 1:24. Note, Christians should be careful that charity not only reign in their hearts, but shine out in their lives, nay, in their most manly defences of the faith of the gospel. There is a great difference between constancy and cruelty, between Christian firmness and feverish wrath and transport. Christianity never appears to so much advantage as when the charity of Christians is most conspicuous when they can bear with their mistaken brethren, and oppose the open enemies of their holy faith in love, when every thing is done in charity, when they behave towards one another, and towards all men, with a spirit of meekness and good will.

II. Some particular directions how they should behave towards some that had been eminently serviceable to the cause of Christ among them.

1. He gives us their character (1.) The household of Stephanas is mentioned by him, and their character is, that they were the first-fruits of Achaia, the first converts to Christianity in that region of Greece in which Corinth was. Note, It is an honourable character to any man to be early a Christian, betimes in Christ. But they had moreover addicted themselves to the ministry of the saints, to serve the saints. They have *disposed and devoted themselves* — ***etaxan heautous,*** to serve the saints, to do service to the saints. It is not meant of the ministry of the word properly, but of serving them in other respects, supplying their wants, helping and assisting them upon all occasions, both in their temporal and spiritual concerns. The family of Stephanas seems to have been a family of rank and importance in those parts, and yet they willingly offered themselves to this service. Note, It is an honour to persons of the highest rank to devote themselves to the service of the saints. I do not mean to change ranks, and become proper servants to the inferiors, but freely and voluntarily to help them, and do good to them in all their concerns. (2.) He mentions Stephanas, and Fortunatus, and Achaicus, as coming to him from the church of Corinth. The account he gives of them is that they supplied the deficiencies of the church towards him, and by so doing *refreshed his spirit and theirs, v.* 17, 18. They gave him a more perfect account of the state of the church by word of mouth than he could acquire by their letter, and by that means much quieted his mind, and upon their return from him would quiet the minds

of the Corinthians. Report had made their cause much worse than it was in fact, and their letters had not explained it sufficiently to give the apostle satisfaction; but he had been made more easy by converse with them. It was a very good office they did, by truly stating facts, and removing the ill opinion Paul had received by common fame. They came to him with a truly Christian intention, to set the apostle right, and give him as favourable sentiments of the church as they could, as peace-makers. Note, It is a great refreshment to the spirit of a faithful minister to hear better of a people by wise and good men of their own body than by common report, to find himself misinformed concerning them, that matters are not so bad as they had been represented. It is a grief to him to hear ill of those he loves; it gladdens his heart to hear the report thereof is false. And the greater value he has for those who give him this information, and the more he can depend upon their veracity, the greater is his joy.

2. Upon this account of the men, he directs how they should behave towards them; and, (1.) He would have them acknowledged (*v.* 11), that is, owned and respected. They deserve it for their good offices. Those who serve the saints, those who consult the honour and good esteem of the churches, and are concerned to wipe off reproaches from them, and take off from the ill opinion fame had propagated, are to be valued, and esteemed, and loved. Those who discover so good a spirit cannot easily be over-valued. (2.) He advises that they should *submit themselves to such, and to all who helped with the apostles, and laboured, v.* 16. This is not to be understood of subjection to proper superiors, but of a voluntary acknowledgment of their worth. They were persons to whom they owed peculiar respect, and whom they should have in veneration. Note, It is a venerable character which those bear who serve the saints and labour hard to help the success of the gospel, who countenance and encourage the faithful ministers of Christ, and endeavour to promote their usefulness. Such should be had in honourable esteem.

Verses 19–24

The apostle closes his epistle,

I. With salutations to the church of Corinth, first from those of Asia, from *Priscilla* and *Aquila* (who seem to have been at this time inhabitants of Ephesus, *vid.* Acts 18:26), *with the church in their house* (*v.* 19), and from *all the brethren* (*v.* 20) at Ephesus, where, it is highly probable at least, he then was. All these saluted the church at Corinth, by Paul. Note, Christianity does by no means destroy civility and good manners. Paul could find room in an epistle treating of very important matters to send the salutations of friends. Religion should promote a courteous and obliging temper towards all. Those misrepresent and reproach it who would take any encouragement from it to be sour and morose. Some of these *salute them much in the Lord.* Note, Christian salutations are not empty compliments; they carry in them real expressions of good-will, and are attended with hearty recommendations to the divine grace and blessing. Those who salute in the Lord wish their brethren all good from the Lord, and breathe out their good wishes in fervent prayers. We read also of a church in a private family, *v.* 19. It is very probable that the family itself is called *the church in their house.* Note, Every Christian family should in some respects be a Christian church. In some cases (as, for instance, were they cast away on a foreign shore, where there are no other Christians), they should be a church themselves, if large enough, and live in the use

of all ordinances; but in common cases they should live under the direction of Christian rules, and daily offer up Christian worship. Wherever two or three are gathered together, and Christ is among them, there is a church. To these salutations he subjoins, 1. An advice, that *they should greet one another with a holy kiss* (*v.* 20), or with sincere good-will, a tacit reproof of their feuds and factions. When the churches of Asia, and the Christian brethren so remote, did so heartily salute them in the Lord, and own and love them as brethren, and expressed so much good-will to them, it would be a shame for them not to own and love one another as brethren. Note, The love of the brethren should be a powerful incentive to mutual love. When the other churches of Christ love us all, we are very culpable if we do not love one another. 2. He subjoins his own salutation: *The salutation of me Paul with my own hand, v.* 21. His *amanuensis,* it is reasonable to think, wrote the rest of his epistle from his mouth, but at the close it was fit that himself should sign it, that they might know it to be genuine; and therefore it is added (2 Th. 3:17), *Which is my token in every epistle,* the mark of its being genuine; so he wrote in every epistle which he did not wholly pen, as he did that to the Galatians, Gal. 6:11. Note, Those churches to whom apostolical letters were sent were duly certified of their being authentic and divine. Nor would Paul be behind the rest of the brethren in respect to the Corinthians; and therefore, after he has given their salutations, he adds his own.

II. With a very solemn warning to them: *If any man love not the Lord Jesus Christ, let him be Anathema, Maran-atha, v.* 22. We sometimes need words of threatening, that we may fear. *Blessed is he,* says the wise man, *who feareth always.* Holy fear is a very good friend both to holy faith and holy living. An how much reason have all Christians to fear falling under this doom! *If any man love not the Lord Jesus Christ, let him be Anathema, Maran-atha.* Here observe, 1. The person described, who is liable to this doom: *He that loveth not the Lord Jesus Christ.* A *meiōsis,* as some think; he who blasphemes Christ disowns his doctrine, slights and contemns his institutions, or, through pride of human knowledge and learning, despises his revelations. It stands here as a warning to the Corinthians and a rebuke of their criminal behaviour. It is an admonition to them not to be led away from the simplicity of the gospel, or those principles of it which were the great motives to purity of life, by pretenders to science, by the wisdom of the world, which would call their religion folly, and its most important doctrines absurd and ridiculous. Those men had a spite at Christ; and, if the Corinthians give ear to their seducing speeches, they were in danger of apostatizing from him. Against this he gives them here a very solemn caution. "Do not give into such conduct, if you would escape the severest vengeance." Note, Professed Christians will, by contempt of Christ, and revolt from him, bring upon themselves the most dreadful destruction. Some understand the words as they lie, in their plain and obvious meaning, for such as are without holy and sincere affection for the Lord Jesus Christ. Many who have his name much in their mouths have no true love to him in their hearts, will not have him to rule over them (Lu. 19:27), no, not though they have very towering hopes of being saved by him. And none love him in truth who do not love his laws and keep his commandments. Note, There are many Christians in name who do not love Christ Jesus the Lord in sincerity. But can any thing be more criminal or provoking? What, not love the most glorious lover in the world! Him who loved us, and gave himself for us, who shed his blood for us, to testify his love to us, and that after heinous wrong and provocation! What had we a power of loving for, if we are unmoved with such love as this, and without affection to such a Saviour? But, 2. We have here the doom of the person described: "*Let him be Anathema, Maran-atha,* lie under the heaviest and most dreadful curse. Let him be separated from the people of God, from the favour of God, and delivered up to his final, irrevocable, and inexorable vengeance" *Maran-atha* is a Syriac phrase, and signifies *The Lord cometh.* That very Lord whom they do not love, to whom they are inwardly and really disaffected whatever outward profession they make, is coming to execute judgment. And to be exposed to his wrath, to be divided to his left hand, to be condemned by him, how dreadful! If he will destroy, who can save? Those who fall under his condemning sentence must perish, and that for ever. Note, Those who love not the Lord Jesus Christ must perish without remedy. *The wrath of God abides on every one who believes not on the Son,* Jn. 3:36. And true faith in Christ will evermore be productive of sincere love to him. Those who love him not cannot be believers in him.

III. With his good wishes for them and expressions of good-will to them. 1. With his good wishes: *The grace of our Lord Jesus Christ be with you, v.* 23. As much as if he had said, "Though I warn you against falling under his displeasure, I heartily wish you an interest in his dearest love and his eternal favour." The grace of our Lord Jesus Christ comprehends in it all that is good, for time or eternity. To wish our friends may have this grace with them is wishing them the utmost good. And this we should wish all our friends and brethren in Christ. We can wish them nothing more, and we should wish them nothing less. We should heartily pray that they may value, and seek, and obtain, and secure, the grace and good-will of their Lord and Judge. Note, The most solemn warnings are the result of the tenderest affection and the greatest good-will. We may tell our brethren and friends with great plainness and pathos that, if they love not the Lord Jesus Christ, they must perish, while we heartily wish the grace of Christ may be with them. Nay, we may give them this warning that they may prize and lay hold of this grace. Note also, How much true Christianity enlarges our hearts; it makes us wish those whom we love the blessings of both worlds; for this is implied in wishing the grace of Christ to be with them. And therefore it is no wonder that the apostle should close all, 2. With the declaration of his love to them in Christ Jesus: *My love be with you all, in Christ Jesus, Amen, v.* 24. He had dealt very plainly with them in this epistle, and told them of their faults with just severity; but, to show that he was not transported with passion, he parts with them in love, makes solemn profession of his love to them, nay, to them all in Christ Jesus, that is, for Christ's sake. He tells them that his heart was with them, that he truly loved them; but lest this, after all, should be deemed flattery and insinuation, he adds that his affection was the result of his religion, and would be guided by the rules of it. His heart would be with them, and he would bear them dear affection as long as their hearts were with Christ, and they bore true affection to his cause and interest. Note, We should be cordial lovers of all who are in Christ, and who love him in sincerity. Not but we should love all men, and wish them well, and do them what good is in our power; but *those* must have our dearest affection who are dear to Christ, and lovers of him. May our love be with all those who are in Christ Jesus! Amen.

AN EXPOSITION, WITH PRACTICAL OBSERVATIONS, OF

THE SECOND EPISTLE OF ST. PAUL TO THE CORINTHIANS

In his former epistle the apostle had signified his intentions of *coming to Corinth, as he passed through Macedonia* (16:5); but, being providentially hindered for some time, he writes this second epistle to them about a year after the former; and there seem to be these two urgent occasions: — 1. The case of the incestuous person, who lay under censure, required that with all speed he should be restored and received again into communion. This therefore he gives directions about (*ch.* 2), and afterwards (*ch.* 7) he declares the satisfaction he had upon the intelligence he received of their good behaviour in that affair. 2. There was a contribution now making for the poor saints at Jerusalem, in which he exhorts the Corinthians to join (*ch.* 8, 9).

There are divers other things very observable in this epistle; for example, I. The account the apostle gives of his labours and success in preaching the gospel in several places, *ch.* 2. II. The comparison he makes between the Old and New Testament dispensation, *ch.* 3. III. The manifold sufferings that he and his fellow-labourers met with, and the motives and encouragements for their diligence and patience, *ch.* 4, 5. IV. The caution he gives the Corinthians against mingling with unbelievers, *ch.* 6. V. The way and manner in which he justifies himself and his apostleship from the opprobrious insinuations and accusations of false teachers, who endeavoured to ruin his reputation at Corinth, *ch.* 10–12, and throughout the whole epistle.

CHAPTER 1

After the introduction (*v.* 1, 2) the apostle begins with the narrative of his troubles and God's goodness, which he had met with in Asia, by way of thanksgiving to God (*v.* 3–6), and for the edification of the Corinthians (*v.* 7–11). Then he attests his and his fellow-labourers' integrity (*v.* 12–14), and afterwards vindicates himself from the imputation of levity and inconstancy (*v.* 15–24).

Verses 1–2

This is the introduction to this epistle, in which we have,

I. The inscription; and therein, 1. The person from whom it was sent, namely, Paul, who calls himself *an apostle of Jesus Christ by the will of God.* The apostleship itself was ordained by Jesus Christ, according to the will of God; and Paul was called to it by Jesus Christ, according to the will of God. He joins Timotheus with himself in writing this epistle; not because he needed his assistance, but that out of the mouth of two witnesses the word might be established; and this dignifying Timothy with the title of *brother* (either in the common faith, or in the work of the ministry) shows the humility of this great apostle, and his desire to recommend Timothy (though he was then a young man) to the esteem of the Corinthians, and give him a reputation among the churches. 2. The persons to whom this epistle was sent, namely, *the church of God at Corinth:* and not only to them, but also *to all the saints in all Achaia,* that is, to all the Christians who lived in the region round about. Note, In Christ Jesus no distinction is made between the inhabitants of city and country; all Achaia stands upon a level in his account.

II. The salutation or apostolical benediction, which is the same as in his former epistle; and therein the apostle desires the two great and comprehensive blessings, grace and peace, for those Corinthians. These two benefits are fitly joined together, because there is no good and lasting peace without true grace; and both of them come *from God our Father, and from the Lord Jesus Christ,* who is the procurer and dispenser of those benefits to fallen man, and is prayed to as God.

Verses 3–6

After the foregoing preface, the apostle begins with the narrative of God's goodness to him and his fellow-labourers in their manifold tribulations, which he speaks of by way of thanksgiving to God, and to advance the divine glory (*v.* 3–6); and it is fit that in all things, and in the first place, God be glorified. Observe,

I. The object of the apostle's thanksgiving, to whom he offers up blessing and praise, namely, the blessed God, who only is to be praised, whom he describes by several glorious and amiable titles. 1. *The God and Father of our Lord Jesus Christ: ho Theos kai patēr tou Kyriou hēmōn Iēsou Christou.* God is the Father of Christ's divine nature by eternal generation, of his human nature by miraculous conception in the womb of the virgin, and of Christ as God-man, and our Redeemer, by covenant-relation, and in and through him as Mediator our God and our Father, Jn. 20:17. In the Old Testament we often meet with this title, *The God of Abraham, and of Isaac, and of Jacob,* to denote God's covenant-relation to them and their seed; and in the New Testament God is styled *the God and Father of our Lord Jesus Christ,* to denote his covenant-relation to the Mediator and his spiritual seed, Gal. 3:16. 2. *The Father of mercies.* There is a multitude of tender mercies in God essentially, and all mercies are from God originally: mercy in his genuine offspring and his delight. *He delighteth in mercy,* Mic. 7:18. 3. *The God of all comfort;* from his proceedeth the COMFORTER, Jn. 15:26. He giveth the earnest of the Spirit in our hearts, *v.* 22. All our comforts come from God, and our sweetest comforts are in him.

II. The reasons of the apostle's thanksgivings, which are these: —

1. The benefits that he himself and his companions had received from God; for God *had comforted* them *in all their tribulations, v.* 4. In the world they had trouble, but in Christ they had peace. The apostles met with many tribulations, but they found comfort in them all: their sufferings (which are called *the sufferings of Christ, v.* 5, because Christ sympathized with his members when suffering for his sake) did abound, but their consolation by Christ did abound also. Note, (1.) Then are we qualified to receive the comfort of God's mercies when we set ourselves to give him the glory of them. (2.) Then we speak best of God and his goodness when we

speak from our own experience, and, in telling others, tell God also what he has done for our souls.

2. The advantage which others might receive; for God intended that they *should be able to comfort others* in trouble (*v.* 4), by communicating to them their experiences of the divine goodness and mercy; and the sufferings of good men have a tendency to this good end (*v.* 6) when they are endued with faith and patience. Note, (1.) What favours God bestows on us are intended not only to make us cheerful ourselves, but also that we may be useful to others. (2.) If we do imitate the faith and patience of good men in their afflictions, we may hope to partake of their consolations here and their salvation hereafter.

Verses 7–11

In these verses the apostle speaks for the encouragement and edification of the Corinthians; and tells them (*v.* 7) of his persuasion or stedfast hope that they should receive benefit by the troubles he and his companions in labour and travel had met with, that their faith should not be weakened, but their consolations increased. In order to this he tells them, 1. What their sufferings had been (*v.* 8): *We would not have you ignorant of our trouble.* It was convenient for the churches to know what were the sufferings of their ministers. It is not certain what particular troubles in Asia are here referred to; whether the tumult raised by Demetrius at Ephesus, mentioned Acts 19, or the fight with beasts at Ephesus, mentioned in the former epistle (*ch.* 15), or some other trouble; for the apostle was in deaths often. This however is evident, that they were great tribulations. They *were pushed out of measure,* to a very extraordinary degree, above the common strength of men, or of ordinary Christians, to bear up under them, insomuch that they *despaired even of life* (*v.* 8), and thought they should have been killed, or have fainted away and expired. 2. What they did in their distress: *They trusted in God.* And they were brought to this extremity in order *that they should not trust in themselves but in God, v.* 9. Note, God often brings his people into great straits, that they may apprehend their own insufficiency to help themselves, and may be induced to place their trust and hope in his all-sufficiency. Our extremity is God's opportunity. *In the mount will the Lord be seen;* and we may safely trust in *God, who raiseth the dead, v.* 9. God's raising the dead is a proof of his almighty power. He that can do this can do any thing, can do all things, and is worthy to be trusted in at all times. Abraham's faith fastened upon this instance of the divine power: *He believed God who quickeneth the dead,* Rom. 4:17. If we should be brought so low as to despair even of life, yet we may then trust in God, who can bring back not only from the gates, but from the jaws, of death. 3. What the deliverance was that they had obtained; and this was seasonable and continued. Their hope and trust were not in vain, nor shall any who trust in him be ashamed. God had delivered them, and did still deliver them, *v.* 10. *Having obtained help of God, they continued to that day,* Acts 26:22. 4. What use they made of this deliverance: *We trust that he will yet deliver us* (*v.* 10), that God will deliver to the end, and *preserve to his heavenly kingdom.* Note, Past experiences are great encouragements to faith and hope, and they lay great obligations to trust in God for time to come. We reproach our experiences if we distrust God in future straits, who hath delivered as in former troubles. David, even when a young man, and when he had but a small stock of experiences, argued after the manner of the apostle here, 1 Sa. 17:37. 5. What was desired of the Corinthians upon this account: *That they would help together by prayer for them* (*v.* 11), by social prayer, agreeing and joining together in prayer on their behalf. Note, our trusting in God must not supersede the use of any proper and appointed means; and prayer is one of those means. We should pray for ourselves and for one another. The apostle had himself a great interest in the throne of grace, yet he desires the help of others' prayers. If we thus help one another by our prayers, we may hope for an occasion of *giving thanks by many* for answer of prayer. And it is our duty not only to help one another with prayer, but in praise and thanksgiving, and thereby to make suitable returns for benefits received.

Verses 12–14

The apostle in these verses attests their integrity by the sincerity of their conversation. This he does not in a way of boasting and vain-glory, but as one good reason for desiring

the help of prayer, as well as for the more comfortably trusting in God (Heb. 13:18), and for the necessary vindication of himself from the aspersions of some persons at Corinth, who reproached his person and questioned his apostleship. Here,

I. He appeals to the testimony of conscience with rejoicing (*v.* 12), in which observe, 1. The witness appealed to, namely, conscience, which is instead of a thousand witnesses. This God's deputy in the soul, and the voice of conscience is the voice of God. They rejoiced in the testimony of conscience, when their enemies reproached them, and were enraged against them. Note, The testimony of conscience for us, if that be right and upon good grounds, will be matter of rejoicing at all times and in all conditions. 2. The testimony this witness gave. And here take notice, Conscience witnessed, (1.) Concerning their conversation, their constant course and tenour of life: by that we may judge of ourselves, and not by this or that single act. (2.) Concerning the nature or manner of their conversation; that it was in simplicity and godly sincerity. This blessed apostle was a true Israelite, a man of plain dealing; you might know where to have him. He was not a man who seemed to be one thing and was another, but a man of sincerity. (3.) Concerning the principle they acted from in all their conversation, both in the world and towards these Corinthians; and that was not fleshly wisdom, nor carnal politics and worldly views, but it was the grace of God, a vital gracious principle in their hearts, that cometh from God, and tendeth to God. Then will our conversation be well ordered when we live and act under the influence and command of such a gracious principle in the heart.

II. He appeals to the knowledge of the Corinthians with hope and confidence, *v.* 13, 14. Their conversation did in part fall under the observation of the Corinthians; and these knew how they behaved themselves, *how holily, and justly, and unblamably;* they never found any thing in them unbecoming an honest man. This they had acknowledged in part already, and he doubted not but they would still do so to the end, that is, that they would never have any good reason to think or say otherwise of him, but that he was an honest man. And so there would be mutual rejoicing in one another. *We are your rejoicing, even as you also are ours in the day of the Lord Jesus.* Note, It is happy when ministers and people do rejoice in each other here; and this joy will be complete in that day when the great Shepherd of the sheep shall appear.

Verses 15–24

The apostle here vindicates himself from the imputation of levity and inconstancy, in that he did not hold his purpose of coming to them at Corinth. His adversaries there sought all occasions to blemish his character, and reflect upon his conduct; and, it seemed, they took hold of this handle to reproach his person and discredit his ministry. Now, for his justification,

I. He avers the sincerity of his intention (*v.* 15–17), and he does this in confidence of their good opinion of him, and that they would believe him, when he assured them he *was minded,* or did really intend, *to come* to them, and that with the design, not that he might receive, but that they might receive a *second benefit,* that is, a further advantage by his ministry. He tells them that he had not herein *used lightness* (*v.* 17), that, as he aimed not at any secular advantage to himself (for his purpose was not *according to the flesh,* that is, with carnal views and aims), so it was not a rash and inconsiderate resolution that he had taken up, for he had laid his measures thus of *passing by them to Macedonia, and coming again to them from Macedonia in his way to Judea* (*v.* 16), and therefore they might conclude that it was for some weighty reasons that he had altered his purpose; and that with him there was not yea yea, and nay nay, *v.* 17. He was not to be accused of levity and inconstancy, nor a contradiction between his words and intentions. Note, Good men should be careful to preserve the reputation of sincerity and constancy; they should not resolve but upon mature deliberation, and they will not change their resolves but for weighty reasons.

II. He would not have the Corinthians to infer that his gospel was false or uncertain, nor that it was contradictory in itself, nor unto truth, *v.* 18, 19. For if it had been so, that he had been fickle in his purposes, or even false in the promises he made of coming to them (which he was not justly to be accused of, and so some understand his expression, *v.* 18, *Our word towards you was not yea and nay),* yet it would not follow that the gospel preached not only by him, but also by others in full agreement with him, was either false or doubtful. For *God is true, and the Son of God, Jesus Christ,* is true. The true God, and eternal life. Jesus Christ, whom the apostle preached, is not *yea* and *nay,* but in him was *yea* (*v.* 19), nothing but infallible truth. And the promises of God in Christ are not yea and nay, but yea and amen, *v.* 20. There is an inviolable constancy and unquestionable sincerity and certainty in all the parts of the gospel of Christ. If in the promises that the ministers of the gospel make as common men, and about their own affairs, they see cause sometimes to vary from them, yet the promises of the gospel covenant, which they preach, stand firm and inviolable. Bad men are false; good men are fickle; but *God is true,* neither fickle nor false. The apostle, having mentioned the stability of the divine promises, makes a digression to illustrate this great and sweet truth, that all the promises of God are yea and amen. For, 1. They are the promises of the God of truth (*v.* 20), of him *that cannot lie,* whose truth as well as mercy endureth for ever. 2. They are made in Christ Jesus (*v.* 20), the Amen, the true and faithful witness; he hath purchased and ratified the covenant of promises, and is the *surety of the covenant,* Heb. 7:22. 3. They are confirmed by the Holy Spirit. He does establish Christians in the faith of the gospel; he has anointed them with his sanctifying grace, which in scripture is often compared to oil; he has sealed them, for their security and confirmation; and he is given *as an earnest in their hearts, v.* 21, 22. An earnest secures the promise, and is part of the payment. The illumination of the Spirit is an earnest of everlasting life; and the comforts of the Spirit are an earnest of everlasting joy. Note, The veracity of God, the mediation of Christ, and the operation of the Spirit, are all engaged that the promises shall be sure to all the seed, and the accomplishment of them shall be to the *glory of God* (*v.* 20) for the glory of his rich and sovereign grace, and never-failing truth and faithfulness.

III. The apostle gives a good reason why he did not come to Corinth, as was expected, *v.* 23. It was that he might spare them. They ought therefore to own his kindness and tenderness. He knew there were things amiss among them, and such as deserved censure, but was desirous to show tenderness. He assures them that this is the true reason, after this very solemn manner: *I call God for a record upon my soul* — a way of speaking not justifiable where used in trivial matters; but this was very justifiable in the apostle, for his necessary vindication, and for the credit and usefulness of his ministry, which was struck at by his opposers. He adds, to prevent mistakes, that he did not pretend to have any dominion over their faith, *v.* 24. Christ only is the Lord of our faith; he is the *author and finisher of our faith,* Heb. 12:2. He reveals to us what we must believe. Paul, and Apollos, and the rest of the apostles, were *but ministers by whom they believed* (1 Co. 3:5), and so the *helpers of their joy,* even the joy of faith. For by faith we stand firmly, and live safely and comfortably. Our strength and ability are owing to faith, and our comfort and joy must flow from faith.

CHAPTER 2

In this chapter the apostle proceeds in the account of the reasons why he did not come to Corinth (*v.* 1–4). Then he writes concerning the incestuous person who lay under censure; and gives direction for restoring him, together with the reasons for their so doing (*v.* 5–11), and afterwards informs them of his labours and success in preaching the gospel in several places (*v.* 12–17).

Verses 1–4

In these verses, 1. The apostle proceeds in giving an account of the reason why he did not come to Corinth, as was expected; namely, because he was unwilling to grieve them, or be grieved by them, *v.* 1,2. *He had determined not to come to them in heaviness,* which yet he would have done had he come and found scandal among them not duly animadverted upon: this would have been cause of grief both to him and them, for their sorrow or joy at meeting would have been mutual. If he had made them sorry, that would have been a sorrow to himself, for there would have been none to have made him glad. But his desire was to have a cheerful meeting with them, and not to have it embittered by any unhappy occasion of disagreeing. 2. He tells them it was to the same intent that he wrote his former epistle, *v.* 3, 4. (1) *That he might not have sorrow from those of whom he ought to rejoice;* and that he had written to them in confidence of their doing what was requisite, in order to their benefit and his comfort. The particular thing referred to, as appears by the following verses, was the case of the incestuous person about whom he had written in the first epistle, *ch.* 5. Nor was the apostle disappointed in his expectation. (2.) He assures them that he did not design to grieve them, but to testify his love to them, and that he wrote to them with much *anguish and affliction* in his own heart, and with great affection to them. He had *written with tears, that they might know his abundant love to them.* Note, [1.] Even in reproofs, admonitions, and acts of discipline, faithful ministers show their love. [2.] Needful censures, and the exercise of church-discipline towards offenders, are a grief to tender-spirited ministers, and are administered with regret.

Verses 5–11

In these verses the apostle treats concerning the incestuous person who had been excommunicated, which seems to be one principal cause of his writing this epistle. Here observe, 1. He tells them that the crime of that person had grieved him *in part;* and that he was grieved also with a part of them, who, notwithstanding this scandal had been found among them, were *puffed up and had not mourned,* 1 Co. 5:2. However, he was unwilling to lay too heavy a charge upon the whole church, especially seeing they had cleared themselves in that matter by observing the directions he had formerly given them. 2. He tells them that the punishment which had been inflicted upon this offender was sufficient, *v.* 6. The desired effect was obtained, for the man was humbled, and they had shown the proof of their obedience to his directions. 3. He therefore directs them, with all speed, to restore the excommunicated person, or to receive him again to their communion, *v.* 7, 8. This is expressed several ways. He beseeches them to forgive him, that is, to release him from church-censures, for they could not remit the guilt or offence against God; and also to comfort him, for in many cases the comfort of penitents depends upon their reconciliation not only with God, but with men also, whom they have scandalized or injured. They must also confirm their love to him; that is, they should show that their reproofs and censures proceeded from love to his person, as well as hatred to his sin, and that their design was to reform, not to ruin him. Or thus: If his fall had weakened their love to him, that they could not take such satisfaction in him as formerly; yet, now that he was recovered by repentance, they must renew and confirm their love to him. 4. He uses several weighty arguments to persuade them to do thus, as, (1.) The case of the penitent called for this; for he was in danger of being *swallowed up with over-much sorrow, v.* 7. He was so sensible of this fault, and so much afflicted under his punishment, that he was in danger of falling into despair. When sorrow is excessive it does hurt; and even sorrow for sin is too great when it unfits for other duties, and drives men to despair. (2.) They had shown obedience to his directions in passing a censure upon the offender and now he would have them comply with his desire to restore him, *v.* 9. (3.) He mentions his readiness to forgive this penitent, and concur with them in this matter. *"To whom you forgive I forgive also, v.* 10. I will readily concur with you in forgiving him." And this he would do for their sakes, for love to them and for their advantage; and for Christ's sake, or in his name, as his apostle, and in conformity to his doctrine and example, which are so full of kindness and tender mercy towards all those who truly repent. (4.) He gives another weighty reason (*v.* 11): *Lest Satan get an advantage against us.* Not only was there danger lest Satan should get an advantage against the penitent, by driving him to despair; but against the churches also, and the apostles or ministers of Christ, by representing them as too rigid and severe, and so frightening people from coming among them. In this, as in other things, *wisdom is profitable to direct,* so to manage according as the case may be that the *ministry may not be blamed,* for indulging sin on the one hand, or for too great severity towards sinners on the other hand. Note, Satan is a subtle enemy, and uses many stratagems to deceive us; and we should not be *ignorant of his devices:* he is also a watchful adversary, ready to take all advantages against us, and we should be very cautious lest we give him any occasion so to do.

Verses 12–17

After these directions concerning the excommunicated person the apostle makes a long digression, to give the Corinthians an account of his travels and labours for the furtherance of the gospel, and what success he had therein, declaring at the same time how much he was concerned for them in their affairs, how he *had no rest in his spirit,* when he found not Titus at Troas (*v.* 13), as he expected, from whom he hoped to have understood more perfectly how it fared with them. And we find afterwards (*ch.* 7:5–7) that when the apostle had come into Macedonia he was comforted by the coming of Titus, and the information he gave him concerning them. So that we may look upon all that we read from this second chapter, *v.* 12, to *ch.* 7:5, as a kind of parenthesis. Observe here,

I. Paul's unwearied labour and diligence in his work, *v.* 12, 13. He travelled from place to place, to preach the gospel. He went to Troas from Philippi by sea (Acts 20:6), and thence he went to Macedonia; so that he was prevented from passing by Corinth, as he had designed, *ch.* 1:16. But, though he was prevented in his design as to the place of working, yet he was unwearied in his work.

II. His success in his work: A *great door was opened to him of the Lord, v.* 12. He had a great deal of work to do wherever he came, and had good success in his work; for God *made manifest the savour of his knowledge* by him in every place where he came. He had an opportunity to open the door of his mouth freely, and God opened the hearts of his hearers, as the heart of Lydia (Acts 16:14), and the apostle speaks of this as a matter of thankfulness to God and of rejoicing to his soul: *Thanks be to God, who always causeth us to triumph in Christ.* Note, 1. A believer's triumphs are all in Christ. In ourselves we are weak, and have neither joy nor victory; but in Christ we may rejoice and triumph. 2. True believers have constant cause of triumph in Christ, for they are more than conquerors through him who hath loved them, Rom. 8:37. 3. God causeth them to triumph in Christ. It is God who has given us matter for triumph, and hearts to triumph. To him therefore be the praise and glory of all. 4. The good success of the gospel is a good reason for a Christian's joy and rejoicing.

III. The comfort that the apostle and his companions in labour found, even when the gospel was not successful to the salvation of some who heard it, *v.* 15–17. Here observe,

1. The different success of the gospel, and its different effects upon several sorts of persons to whom it is preached. The success is different; for some are saved by it, while others perish under it. Nor is this to be wondered at, considering the different effects the gospel has. For, (1.) Unto some it is a *savour of death unto death.* Those who are willingly ignorant, and wilfully obstinate, disrelish the gospel, as men dislike an ill savour, and therefore they are blinded and hardened by it: it stirs up their corruptions, and exasperates their spirits. They reject the gospel, to their ruin, even to spiritual and eternal death. (2.) Unto others the gospel is a *savour of life unto life.* To humble and gracious souls the preaching of the word is most delightful and profitable. As it is sweeter than honey to the taste, so it is more grateful than the most precious odours to the senses, and much more profitable; for as it quickened them at first, *when they were dead in trespasses and sins,* so it makes them more lively, and will end in eternal life.

2. The awful impressions this matter made upon the mind of the apostle, and should also make upon our spirits: *Who is sufficient for these things? v.* 16. *Tis hikanos* — who is *worthy* to be employed in such weighty work, a work of such vast importance, because of so great consequence? Who is able to perform such a difficult work, that requires so much skill and industry? The work is great and our strength is small; yea, of ourselves we have no strength at all; *all our sufficiency is of God.* Note, If men did seriously consider what great things depend upon the preaching of the gospel, and how difficult the work of the ministry is, they would be very cautious how they enter upon it, and very careful to perform it well.

3. The comfort which the apostle had under this serious consideration, (1.) Because faithful ministers shall be accepted of God, whatever their success be: *We are,* if faithful, *unto God a sweet savour of Christ* (*v.* 15), in those who are saved and in those also who perish. God will accept of sincere intentions, and honest endeavours, though with many they are not successful. Ministers shall be accepted, and recompensed, not according to their success, but according to their fidelity. *Though Israel be not gathered, yet shall I be glorious in the eyes of the Lord,* Isa. 49:5. (2.) Because his conscience witnessed to his faithfulness, *v.* 17. Though many *did corrupt*

the word of God, yet the apostle's conscience witnessed to his fidelity. He did not mix his own notions with the doctrines and institutions of Christ; he durst not add to, nor diminish from, the word of God; he was faithful in dispensing the gospel, as he received it from the Lord, and had no secular turn to serve; his aim was to approve himself to God, remembering that his eye was always upon him; he therefore spoke and acted always as in the sight of God, and therefore in sincerity. Note, What we do in religion is not of God, does not come from God, will not reach to God, unless it be done in sincerity, as in the sight of God.

CHAPTER 3

The apostle makes an apology for his seeming to commend himself, and is careful not to assume too much to himself, but to ascribe all praise unto God (*v.* 1–5). He then draws a comparison between the Old Testament and the New, and shows the excellency of the later above the former (*v.* 6–11), whence he infers what is the duty of gospel ministers, and the advantage of those who live under the gospel above those who lived under the law (*v.* 12 to the end).

Verses 1–5

In these verses,

I. The apostle makes an apology for seeming to commend himself. He thought it convenient to protest his sincerity to them, because there were some at Corinth who endeavoured to blast his reputation; yet he was not desirous of vain-glory. And he tells them, 1. That he neither needed nor desired any verbal commendation to them, nor letters testimonial from them, as some others did, meaning the false apostles or teachers, *v.* 1. His ministry among them had, without controversy, been truly great and honourable, how little soever his person was in reality, or how contemptible soever some would have him thought to be. 2. The Corinthians themselves were his real commendation, and a good testimonial for him, that God was with him of a truth, that he was sent of God: *You are our epistle, v.* 2. This was the testimonial he most delighted in, and what was most dear to him — they were written *in his heart;* and this he could appeal to upon occasion, for it was, or might be, *known and read of all men.* Note, There is nothing more delightful to faithful ministers, nor more to their commendation, than the success of their ministry, evidenced in the hearts and lives of those among whom they labour.

II. The apostle is careful not to assume too much to himself, but to ascribe all the praise to God. Therefore, 1. He says they were the *epistle of Christ, v.* 3. The apostle and others were but instruments, Christ was the author of all the good that was in them. The law of Christ was written in their hearts, and the love of Christ shed abroad in their hearts. This epistle was not written with *ink, but with the Spirit of the living God;* nor was it written in *tables of stone,* as the law of God given to Moses, but on the *heart;* and that heart not a stony one, but a heart of flesh, upon the *fleshy* (not *fleshly,* as fleshliness denotes sensuality) *tables of the heart,* that is, upon hearts that are softened and renewed by divine grace, according to that gracious promise, *I will take away the stony heart, and I will give you a heart of flesh,* Eze. 36:26. This was the good hope the apostle had concerning these Corinthians (*v.* 4) that their hearts were like the ark of the covenant, containing the tables of the law and the gospel, written with the finger, that is, by the Spirit, of the living God. 2. He utterly disclaims the taking of any praise to themselves, and ascribes all the glory to God: *"We are not sufficient of ourselves, v.* 5. We could never have made such good impressions on your hearts, nor upon our own. Such are our weakness and inability that we cannot of ourselves think a good thought, much less raise any good thoughts or affections in other men. *All our sufficiency is of God;* to him therefore are owing all the praise and glory of that good which is done, and from him we must receive grace and strength to do more." This is true concerning ministers and all Christians; the best are no more than what the grace of God makes them. Our hands are not sufficient for us, but our sufficiency is of God; and his grace is sufficient for us, to furnish us for every good word and work.

Verses 6–11

Here the apostle makes a comparison between the Old Testament and the New, the law of Moses and the gospel of Jesus Christ, and values himself and his fellow-labourers by this, that *they were able ministers of the New Testament,* that God had made them so, *v.* 6. This he does in answer to the accusations of false teachers, who magnify greatly the law of Moses.

I. He distinguishes between the letter and the spirit even of the New Testament, *v.* 6. As able ministers of the New Testament, they were ministers not merely of the letter, to read the written word, or to preach the letter of the gospel only, but they were ministers of the Spirit also; the Spirit of God did accompany their ministrations. The *letter killeth;* this the letter of the law does, for that is the ministration of death; and if we rest only in the letter of the gospel we shall be never the better for so doing, for even that will be a *savour of death unto death;* but the Spirit of the gospel, going along with the ministry of the gospel, giveth life spiritual and life eternal.

II. He shows the difference between the Old Testament and the New, and the excellency of the gospel above the law. For, 1. The Old-Testament dispensation was the *ministration of death* (*v.* 7), whereas that of the New Testament is the *ministration of life.* The law discovered sin, and the wrath and curse of God. This showed us a God above us and a God against us; but the gospel discovers grace, and *Emmanuel,* God with us. Upon this account the gospel is more glorious than the law; and yet that had a glory in it, witness the shining of Moses's face (an indication thereof) when he came down from the mount with the tables in his hand, that reflected rays of brightness upon his countenance. 2. The law was the *ministration of condemnation,* for that condemned and cursed every one who *continued not in all things written therein to do them;* but the gospel is the *ministration of righteousness:* therein the righteousness of God by faith is revealed. This shows us that the just shall live by his faith. This reveals the grace and mercy of God through Jesus Christ, for obtaining the remission of sins and eternal life. The gospel therefore so much exceeds in glory that in a manner it eclipses the glory of the legal dispensation, *v.* 10. As the shining of a burning lamp is lost, or not regarded, when the sun arises and goes forth in his strength; so there was no glory in the Old Testament, in comparison with that of the New. 3. The law is done away, but the gospel does and shall *remain, v.* 11. Not only did the glory of Moses's face go away, but the glory of Moses's law is done away also; yea, the law of Moses itself is now abolished. That dispensation was only to continue for a time, and then to vanish away; whereas the gospel shall remain to the end of the world, and is always fresh and flourishing and remains glorious.

Verses 12–18

In these verses the apostle draws two inferences from what he had said about the Old and New Testament: —

I. Concerning the duty of the ministers of the gospel to use great plainness or clearness of speech. They ought not, like Moses, to put a veil upon their faces, or obscure and darken those things which they should make plain. The gospel is a more clear dispensation than the law; the things of God are revealed in the New Testament, not in types and shadows, and ministers are much to blame if they do not set spiritual things, and gospel-truth and grace, in the clearest light that is possible. Though the Israelites could not look *stedfastly to the end* of what was commanded, but is now abolished, yet we may. We may see the meaning of those types and shadows by the accomplishment, seeing the veil is done away in, Christ and he is come, who was the end of the law for righteousness to all those who believe, and whom Moses and all the prophets pointed to, and wrote of.

II. Concerning the privilege and advantage of those who enjoy the gospel, above those who lived under the law. For, 1. Those who lived under the legal dispensation had their minds blinded (*v.* 14), and there was a *veil upon their hearts, v.* 15. Thus it was formerly, and so it was especially as to those who remained in Judaism after the coming of the Messiah and the publication of his gospel. Nevertheless, the apostle tells us, there is a time coming when this *veil also shall be taken away,* and *when it* (the body of that people) *shall turn to the Lord, v.* 16. Or, when any particular person is converted to God, then the veil of ignorance is taken away; the blindness of the mind, and the hardness of the heart, are cured. 2. The condition of those who enjoy and believe the gospel is much more happy. For, (1.) They have liberty: *Where the Spirit of the Lord is,* and where he worketh, as he does under the gospel-dispensation, *there is liberty* (*v.* 17), freedom from the yoke of the ceremonial law, and from the servitude of corruption; liberty of access to God, and freedom of speech in prayer. The heart is set at liberty, and enlarged, to run the ways of God's commandments. (2.) They have *light;* for with *open face we behold the glory of the Lord, v.* 18. The Israelites saw the glory of God in a cloud, which was dark and dreadful; but Christians see the glory of the Lord as in a glass, more clearly and comfortably. It was the peculiar privilege of Moses for God to converse with him face to face, in a friendly manner; but now all true Christians see him more clearly with open face. He showeth them his glory. (3.) This light and liberty *are transforming;* we are changed into the *same image, from glory to glory* (*v.* 18), from one degree of glorious grace unto another, till grace here be consummated in glory for ever. How much therefore should Christians prize and improve these privileges! We should not rest contented without an experimental knowledge of the transforming power of the gospel, by the operation of the Spirit, bringing us into a conformity to the temper and tendency of the glorious gospel of our Lord and Saviour Jesus Christ.

CHAPTER 4

In this chapter we have an account, I. Of the constancy of the apostle and his fellow-labourers in their work. Their constancy in declared (*v.* 1), their sincerity is vouched (*v.* 2), an objection is obviated (*v.* 3, 4), and their integrity proved (*v.* 5–7). II. Of their courage and patience under their sufferings. Where see what their sufferings were, together with their allays (*v.* 8–12), and what it was that kept them from sinking and fainting under them (*v.* 13 to the end).

Verses 1–7

The apostle had, in the foregoing chapter, been *magnifying his office,* upon the consideration of the excellency or glory of that gospel about which he did officiate; and now in this chapter his design is to vindicate their ministry from the accusation of false teachers, who charged them as deceitful workers, or endeavoured to prejudice the minds of the people against them on account of their sufferings. He tells them, therefore, how they believed, and how they showed their value for their office as ministers of the gospel. They were not puffed up with pride, but spurred on to great diligence: *"Seeing we have this ministry,* are so much distinguished and dignified, we do not take state upon ourselves, nor indulge in idleness, but are excited to the better performance of our duty."

I. Two things in general we have an account of: — Their constancy and sincerity in their work and labour, concerning which observe, 1. Their constancy and perseverance in their work are declared: *"We faint not* (*v.* 1) under the difficulty of our work, nor do we desist from our labour." And this their stedfastness was owing to the *mercy of God.* From the same mercy and grace from which they received the apostleship (Rom. 1:5), they received strength to persevere in the work of that office. Note, As it is great mercy and grace to be called to be saints, and especially to be *counted faithful, and be put into the ministry* (1 Tim. 1:12), so it is owing to the mercy and grace of God if we continue faithful and persevere in our work with diligence. The best men in the world would faint in their work, and under their burdens, if they did not receive mercy from God. *By the grace of God I am what I am,* said this great apostle in his former epistle to these Corinthians, *ch.* 15:10. And that mercy which has helped us out, and helped us on, hitherto, we may rely upon to help us even to the end. 2. Their sincerity in their work is avouched (*v.* 2) in several expressions: *We have renounced the hidden things of dishonesty.* The things of dishonesty are hidden things, that will not bear the light; and those who practise them are, or should be, ashamed of them, especially when they are known. Such things the apostle did not allow of, but did renounce and avoid with indignation: *Not walking in craftiness,* or in disguise, acting with art and cunning, but in great simplicity, and with open freedom. They had no base and wicked designs covered with fair and specious pretences of something that was good. Nor did they in their preaching *handle the word of God deceitfully;* but, as he said before, they used *great plainness of speech,* and did not make their ministry serve a turn, or truckle to base designs. They had not cheated the people with falsehood instead of truth. Some think the apostle alludes to the deceit which treacherous gamesters use, or that of hucksters in the market, who mix bad wares with good. The apostles acted not like such persons, but they *manifested the truth to every man's conscience,* declaring nothing but what in their own conscience they believed to be true, and what might serve for the conviction of their consciences who heard them, who were to judge for themselves, and to give an account for themselves.

And all this they did *as in the sight of God,* desirous thus to commend themselves to God, and to the consciences of men, by their undisguised sincerity. Note, A stedfast adherence to the truths of the gospel will commend ministers and people; and sincerity or uprightness will preserve a man's reputation, and the good opinion of wise and good men concerning him.

II. An objection is obviated, which might be thus formed: "If it be thus, how then does it come to pass, that the gospel is hid, and proves ineffectual, as to some who hear it?" To which the apostle answers, by showing that this was not the fault of the gospel, nor of the preachers thereof. But the true reasons of this are, 1. *Those are lost souls* to whom the gospel is hid, or is ineffectual, *v.* 3. Christ came to *save that which was lost* (Mt. 17:11), and the gospel of Christ is sent to save such; and, if this do not find and save them, they are lost for ever; they must never expect any thing else to save them, for there is no other method or means of salvation. The hiding of the gospel therefore from souls is both an evidence and cause of their ruin. 2. *The god of this world hath blinded their minds, v.* 4. They are under the influence and power of the devil, who is here called *the god of this world,* and elsewhere *the prince of this world,* because of the great interest he has in this world, the homage that is paid to him by multitudes in this world, and the great sway that, by divine permission, he bears in the world, and in the hearts of his subjects, or rather slaves. And as he is the prince of darkness, and ruler of the darkness of this world, so he darkens the understandings of men, and increases their prejudices, and supports his interest by keeping them in the dark, blinding their minds with ignorance, and error, and prejudices, that they should not *behold the light of the glorious gospel of Christ, who is the image of God.* Observe, (1.) Christ's design by his gospel is to make a glorious discovery of God to the minds of men. Thus, as the image of God, he demonstrates the power and wisdom of God, and the grace and mercy of God for their salvation. But, (2.) The design of the devil is to keep men in ignorance; and, when he cannot keep the light of the gospel out of the world, he makes it his great business to keep it out of the hearts of men.

III. A proof of their integrity is given, *v.* 5. They made it their business to preach Christ, and not themselves: *We preach not ourselves.* Self was not the matter nor the end of the apostles' preaching: they did not give their own notions and private opinions, nor their passions and prejudices, for the word and will of God; nor did they seek themselves, to advance their own secular interest or glory. But they *preached Christ Jesus the Lord;* and thus it did become them and behove them to do, as being Christ's servants. Their business was to make their Master known to the world as the Messiah, or the Christ of God, and as Jesus, the only Saviour of men, and as the rightful Lord, and to advance his honour and glory. Note, All the lines of Christian doctrine centre in Christ; and in preaching Christ we preach all we should preach. "As to *ourselves,*" says the apostle, *"we preach,* or declare, that *we are your servants for Jesus' sake."* This was no compliment, but a real profession of a readiness to do good to their souls, and to promote their spiritual and eternal interest, and that for *Jesus' sake;* not for their own sake or their own advantage, but for Christ's sake, that they might imitate his great example, and advance his glory. Note, Ministers should not be of proud spirits, *lording it over God's heritage,* who are servants to the souls of men: yet, at the same time, they must avoid the meanness of spirit implied in becoming the servants of the humours or the lusts of men; if they should thus *seek to please men, they would not be the servants of Christ,* Gal. 1:10. And there was good reason, 1. Why they should preach Christ. For by gospel light we have the *knowledge of the glory of God,* which shines in the *face of Jesus Christ, v.* 6. And the light of this *Sun of righteousness* is more glorious than that light which God commanded to shine out of darkness. It is a pleasant thing for the eye to behold the sun in the firmament; but it is more pleasant and profitable when the gospel shines in the heart. Note, As light was the first-born of the first creation, so it is in the new creation: the illumination of the Spirit is his first work upon the soul. The grace of God created such a light in the soul that those who *were sometimes darkness are made light in the Lord,* Eph. 5:8. 2. Why they should not preach themselves: because they were but earthen vessels, things of little or no worth or value. Here seems to be an allusion to the lamps which Gideon's soldiers carried in earthen pitchers, Jud. 7:16. The treasure of gospel light and grace is put into earthen vessels. The ministers of the gospel are weak and frail creatures, and *subject to like passions* and infirmities as other men; they are mortal, and soon broken in pieces. And God has so ordered it that the weaker the vessels are the stronger his power may appear to be, that the treasure itself should be valued the more. Note, There is an excellency of power in the gospel of Christ, to enlighten the mind, to convince the conscience, to convert the soul, and to rejoice the heart; but all this power is from God the author, and not from men, who are but instruments, so that God in all things must be glorified.

Verses 8–18

In these verses the apostle gives an account of their courage and patience under all their sufferings, where observe,

I. How their sufferings, and patience under them, are declared, *v.* 8–12. The apostles were great sufferers; therein they followed their Master: Christ had told them *that in the world they should have tribulation,* and so they had; yet they met with wonderful support, great relief, and many allays of their sorrows. *"We are,"* says the apostle, *"troubled on every side,* afflicted many ways, and we meet with almost all sorts of troubles; *yet not distressed, v.* 8. We are not hedged in nor cooped up, because we can see help in God, and help from God, and have liberty of access to God." Again, "We are *perplexed,* often uncertain, and in doubt what will become of us, and not always without anxiety in our minds on this account; *yet not in despair* (*v.* 8), even in our greatest perplexities, knowing that God is able to support us, and to deliver us, and in him we always place our trust and hope." Again, "We are *persecuted* by men, pursued with hatred and violence from place to place, as men not worthy to live; yet *not forsaken* of God," *v.* 9. Good men may be sometimes forsaken of their friends, as well as persecuted by their enemies; but God will never leave them nor forsake them. Again, "We are sometimes dejected, or *cast down;* the enemy may in a great measure prevail, and our spirits begin to fail us; there may be fears within, as well as fightings without; yet we are *not destroyed," v.* 9. Still they were preserved, and kept their heads above water. Note, Whatever condition the children of God may be in, in this world, they have a *"but not"* to comfort themselves with; their case sometimes is bad, yea very bad, but not so bad as it might be. The apostle speaks of their sufferings as constant, and as a counterpart of the sufferings of Christ, *v.* 10. The sufferings of Christ were, after a sort, re-acted in the sufferings of Christians; thus did they *bear about the dying of the Lord Jesus* in their body, setting before the world the great example of a suffering Christ, *that the life of Jesus might also be made manifest,* that is, that people might see the power of Christ's resurrection, and the efficacy of grace in and from the living Jesus, manifested in and towards them, who did yet live, though they were always *delivered to death* (*v.* 11), and though *death worked in them* (*v.* 12), they being exposed to death, and ready to be swallowed up by death continually. So great were the sufferings of the apostles that, in comparison with them, other Christians were, even at this time, in prosperous circumstances: *Death worketh in us; but life in you, v.* 12.

II. What it was that kept them from sinking and fainting under their sufferings, *v.* 13–18. Whatever the burdens and troubles of good men may be, they have cause enough not to faint.

1. Faith kept them from fainting: *We have the same spirit of faith* (*v.* 13), that faith which is of the operation of the Spirit; the same faith by which the saints of old did and suffered such great things. Note, The grace of faith is a sovereign cordial, and an effectual antidote against fainting-fits in troublous times. The spirit of faith will go far to bear up the spirit of a man under his infirmities; and as the apostle had David's example to imitate, who said (Ps. 116:10), *I have believed, and therefore have I spoken,* so he leaves us his example to imitate: *We also believe,* says he, *and therefore speak.* Note, As we receive help and encouragement from the good words and examples of others, so we should be careful to give a good example to others.

2. Hope of the resurrection kept them from sinking, *v.* 14. They knew that Christ was raised, and that his resurrection was an earnest and assurance of theirs. This he had treated of largely in his former epistle to these Corinthians, *ch.* 15. And therefore their hope was firm, being well grounded, that he who raised up Christ the head will also raise up all his members. Note, The hope of the resurrection will encourage us in a suffering day, and set us above the fear of death; for what reason has a good Christian to fear death, that dies in hope of a joyful resurrection?

3. The consideration of the glory of God and the benefit of the church, by means of their sufferings, kept them from fainting, *v.* 15. Their sufferings were for the church's advantage (*ch.* 1:6), and thus did redound to God's glory. For, when the church is edified, then God is glorified; and we may well afford to bear sufferings patiently and cheerfully when we see others are the better for them — if they are instructed and edified, if they are confirmed and comforted. Note, The sufferings of Christ's ministers, as well as their preaching and conversation, are intended for the good of the church and the glory of God.

4. The thoughts of the advantage their souls would reap by the sufferings of their bodies kept them from fainting: *Though our outward man perish, our inward man is renewed day by day, v.* 16. Here note, (1.) We have every one of us an outward and an inward man, a body and a soul. (2.) If the outward man perish, there is no remedy, it must and will be so, it was made to perish. (3.) It is our happiness if the decays of the outward man do contribute to the renewing of the inward man, if afflictions outwardly are gain to us inwardly, if when the body is sick, and weak, and perishing, the soul is vigorous and prosperous. The best of men have need of further renewing of the inward man, even day by day. Where the good work is begun there is more work to be done, for carrying it forward. And as in wicked men things grow every day worse and worse, so in godly men they grow better and better.

5. The prospect of eternal life and happiness kept them from fainting, and was a mighty support and comfort. As to this observe, (1.) The apostle and his fellow-sufferers saw their afflictions working towards heaven, and that they would end at last (*v.* 17), whereupon they weighed things aright in the balance of the sanctuary; they did as it were put the heavenly glory in one scale and their earthly sufferings in the other; and, pondering things in their thoughts, they found afflictions to be light, and the glory of heaven to be *a far more exceeding weight.* That which sense was ready to pronounce heavy and long, grievous and tedious, faith perceived to be light and short, and but for a moment. On the other hand, the worth and weight of the crown of glory, as they are exceedingly great in themselves, so they are esteemed to be by the believing soul — far exceeding all his expressions and thoughts; and it will be a special support in our sufferings when we can perceive them appointed as the way and preparing us for the enjoyment of the future glory. (2.) Their faith enabled them to make this right judgment of things: *We look not at the things which are seen, but at the things which are not seen, v.* 18. It is by faith that we see God, who is invisible (Heb. 11:27), and by this we look to an unseen heaven and hell, and faith is the *evidence of things not seen.* Note, [1.] There are unseen things, as well as things that are seen. [2.] There is this vast difference between them: unseen things are eternal, seen things but temporal, or temporary only. [3.] By faith we not only discern these things, and the great difference between them, but by this also we take our aim at unseen things, and chiefly regard them, and make it our end and scope, not to escape present evils, and obtain present good, both of which are temporal and transitory, but to escape future evil and obtain future good things, which though unseen, are real, and certain, and eternal; and faith is *the substance of things hoped for,* as well as the evidence of things not seen, Heb. 11:1.

CHAPTER 5

The apostle proceeds in showing the reasons why they did not faint under their afflictions, namely, their expectation, desire, and assurance of happiness after death (*v.* 1–5), and deduces an inference for the comfort of believers in their present state (*v.* 6–8), and another to quicken them in their duty (*v.* 9–11). Then he makes an apology for seeming to commend himself, and gives a good reason for his zeal and diligence (*v.* 12–15), and mentions two things that are necessary in order to our living to Christ, regeneration and reconciliation (*v.* 16 to the end).

Verses 1–11

The apostle in these verses pursues the argument of the former chapter, concerning the grounds of their courage and patience under afflictions. And,

I. He mentions their expectation, and desire, and assurance, of eternal happiness after death, *v.* 1–5. Observe particularly,

1. The believer's expectation of eternal happiness after

death, v. 1. He does not only know, or is well assured by faith of the truth and reality of the thing itself — that there is another and a happy life after this present life is ended, but he has good hope through grace of his interest in that everlasting blessedness of the unseen world: "We know that we have a building of God, we have a firm and well-grounded expectation of the future felicity." Let us take notice, (1.) What heaven is in the eye and hope of a believer. He looks upon it as a house, or habitation, a dwelling-place, a resting-place, a hiding-place, our Father's house, where there are many mansions, and our everlasting home. It is a house in the heavens, in that high and holy place which as far excels all the palaces of this earth as the heavens are high above the earth. It is a building of God, whose builder and maker is God, and therefore is worthy of its author; the happiness of the future state is what God hath prepared for those that love him. It is eternal in the heavens, everlasting habitations, not like the earthly tabernacles, the poor cottages of clay in which our souls now dwell, which are mouldering and decaying, and whose foundations are in the dust. (2.) When it is expected this happiness shall be enjoyed — immediately after death, so soon as our house of this earthly tabernacle is dissolved. Note, [1.] That the body, this earthly house, is but a tabernacle, that must be dissolved shortly; the nails or pins will be drawn, and the cords be loosed, and then the body will return to dust as it was. [2.] When this comes to pass, then comes the house not made with hands. The spirit returns to God who gave it; and such as have walked with God here shall dwell with God for ever.

2. The believer's earnest desire after this future blessedness, which is expressed by this word, stenazomen — we groan, which denotes, (1.) A groaning of sorrow under a heavy load; so believers groan under the burden of life: In this we groan earnestly, v. 2. We that are in this tabernacle groan, being burdened, v. 4. The body of flesh is a heavy burden, the calamities of life are a heavy load. But believers groan because burdened with a body of sin, and the many corruptions that are still remaining and raging in them. This makes them complain, O wretched man that I am! Rom. 7:24. (2.) There is a groaning of desire after the happiness of another life; and thus believers groan: Earnestly desiring to be clothed upon with our house which is from heaven (v. 2), to obtain a blessed immortality, that mortality might be swallowed up of life (v. 4), that being found clothed, we may not be naked (v. 3), that, if it were the will of God, we might not sleep, but be changed; for it is not desirable in itself to be unclothed. Death considered merely as a separation of soul and body is not to be desired, but rather dreaded; but, considered as a passage to glory, the believer is willing rather to die than live, to be absent from the body, that he may be present with the Lord (v. 1), to leave this body that he may go to Christ, and to put off these rags of mortality that he may put on the robes of glory. Note, [1.] Death will strip us of the clothing of flesh, and all the comforts of life, as well as put an end to all our troubles here below. Naked we came into this world, and naked shall we go out of it. But, [2.] Gracious souls are not found naked in the other world; no, they are clothed with garments of praise, with robes of righteousness and glory. They shall be delivered out of all their troubles, and shall have washed their robes and made them white in the blood of the Lamb, Rev. 7:14.

3. The believer's assurance of his interest in this future blessedness, on a double account: — (1.) From the experience of the grace of God, in preparing and making him meet for this blessedness. He that hath wrought us for the selfsame thing is God, v. 5. Note, All who are designed for heaven hereafter are wrought or prepared for heaven while they are here; the stones of that spiritual building and temple above are squared and fashioned here below. And he that hath wrought us for this is God, because nothing less than a divine power can make a soul partaker of a divine nature; no hand less than the hand of God can work us for this thing. A great deal is to be done to prepare our souls for heaven, and that preparation of the heart is from the Lord. (2.) The earnest of the Spirit gave them this assurance: for an earnest is part of payment, and secures the full payment. The present graces and comforts of the Spirit are earnests of everlasting grace and comfort.

II. The apostle deduces an inference for the comfort of believers in their present state and condition in this world, v. 6-8. Here observe, 1. What their present state or condition is: they are absent from the Lord (v. 6); they are pilgrims

and strangers in this world; they do but sojourn here in their earthly home, or in this tabernacle; and though God is with us here, by his Spirit, and in his ordinances, yet we are not with him as we hope to be: we cannot see his face while we live: For we walk by faith, not by sight, v. 7. We have not the vision and fruition of God, as of an object that is present with us, and as we hope for hereafter, when we shall see as we are seen. Note, Faith is for this world, and sight is reserved for the other world: and it is our duty, and will be our interest, to walk by faith, till we come to live by sight. 2. How comfortable and courageous we ought to be in all the troubles of life, and in the hour of death: Therefore we are, or ought to be, always confident (v. 6), and again (v. 8), We are confident, and willing rather to be absent from the body. True Christians, if they duly considered the prospect faith gives them of another world, and the good reasons of their hope of blessedness after death, would be comforted under the troubles of life, and supported in the hour of death: they should take courage, when they are encountering the last enemy, and be willing rather to die than live, when it is the will of God that they should put off this tabernacle. Note, As those who are born from above long to be there, so it is but being absent from the body, and we shall very soon be present with the Lord — but to die, and be with Christ — but to close our eyes to all things in this world, and we shall open them in a world of glory. Faith will be turned into sight.

III. He proceeds to deduce an inference to excite and quicken himself and others to duty, v. 9-11. So it is that well-grounded hopes of heaven will be far from giving the least encouragement to sloth and sinful security; on the contrary, they should stir us up to use the greatest care and diligence in religion: Wherefore, or because we hope to be present with the Lord, we labour and take pains, v. 9. Philotimoumetha — We are ambitious, and labour as industriously as the most ambitious men do to obtain what they aim at. Here observe, 1. What it was that the apostle was thus ambitious of — acceptance with God. We labour that, living and dying, whether present in the body or absent from the body, we may be accepted of him, the Lord (v. 9), that we may please him who hath chosen us, that our great Lord may say to us, Well done. This they coveted as the greatest favour and the highest honour: it was the summit of their ambition. 2. What further quickening motives they had to excite their diligence, from the consideration of the judgment to come, v. 10, 11. There are many things relating to this great matter that should awe the best of men into the utmost care and diligence in religion; for example, the certainty of this judgment, for we must appear; the universality of it, for we must all appear; the great Judge before whose judgment-seat we must appear, the Lord Jesus Christ, who himself will appear in flaming fire; the recompence to be then received, for things done in the body, which will be very particular (unto every one), and very just, according to what we have done, whether good or bad. The apostle calls this awful judgment the terror of the Lord (v. 11), and, by the consideration thereof, was excited to persuade men to repent, and live a holy life, that, when Christ shall appear terribly, they may appear before him comfortably. And, concerning his fidelity and diligence, he comfortably appeals unto God, and the consciences of those he wrote to: We are made manifest unto God, and I trust also are made manifest in your consciences.

Verses 12-15

Here observe, I. The apostle makes an apology for seeming to commend himself and his fellow-labourers (v. 13), and tells them, 1. It was not to commend themselves, nor for their own sakes, that he had spoken of their fidelity and diligence in the former verses; nor was he willing to suspect their good opinion of him. But, 2. The true reason was this, to put an argument in their mouths wherewith to answer his accusers, who made vain boastings, and gloried in appearances only; that he might give them an occasion to glory on their behalf, or to defend them against the reproaches of their adversaries. And if the people can say that the word has been manifested to their consciences, and been effectual to their conversion and edification, this is the best defence they can make for the ministry of the word, when they are vilified and reproached.

II. He gives good reasons for their great zeal and diligence. Some of Paul's adversaries had, it is likely, reproached him for his zeal and fervour, as if he had been a madman, or, in the language of our days, a fanatic; they imputed all to en-

thusiasm, as the Roman governor told him, Much learning has made thee mad, Acts 26:24. But the apostle tells them, 1. It was for the glory of God, and the good of the church, that he was thus zealous and industrious: "Whether we be beside ourselves, or whether we be sober (whether you or others do think the one or the other), it is to God, and for his glory: and it is for your cause, or to promote your good," v. 13. If they manifested the greatest ardour and vehemency at some times, and used the greatest calmness in strong reasonings at other times, it was for the best ends; and in both methods they had good reason for what they did. For, 2. The love of Christ constrained them, v. 14. They were under the sweetest and strongest constraints to do what they did. Love has a constraining virtue to excite ministers and private Christians in their duty. Our love to Christ will have this virtue; and Christ's love to us, which was manifested in this great instance of his dying for us, will have this effect upon us, if it be duly considered and rightly judged of. For observe how the apostle argues for the reasonableness of love's constraints, and declares, (1.) What we were before, and must have continued to be, had not Christ died for us: We were dead, v. 14. If one died for all, then were all dead; dead in law, under sentence of death; dead in sins and trespasses, spiritually dead. Note, This was the deplorable condition of all those for whom Christ died: they were lost and undone, dead and ruined, and must have remained thus miserable for ever if Christ had not died for them. (2.) What such should do, for whom Christ died; namely, that they should live to him. This is what Christ designed, that those who live, who are made alive unto God by means of his death, should live to him that died for them, and rose again for their sakes also, and that they should not live to themselves, v. 15. Note, We should not make ourselves, but Christ, the end of our living and actions: and it was one end of Christ's death to cure us of this self-love, and to excite us always to act under the commanding influence of his love. A Christian's life should be consecrated to Christ; and then do we live as we ought to live when we live to Christ, who died for us.

Verses 16-21

In these verses the apostle mentions two things that are necessary in order to our living to Christ, both of which are the consequences of Christ's dying for us; namely, regeneration and reconciliation.

I. Regeneration, which consists of two things; namely, 1. Weanedness from the world: "Henceforth we know no man after the flesh, v. 16. We do not own nor affect any person or thing in this world for carnal ends and outward advantage: we are enabled, by divine grace, not to mind nor regard this world, nor the things of this world, but to live above it. The love of Christ is in our hearts, and the world is under our feet." Note, Good Christians must enjoy the comforts of this life, and their relations in this world, with a holy indifference. Yea, though we have known Christ after the flesh, yet, says the apostle, we know him no more. It is questioned whether Paul had seen Christ in the flesh. However, the rest of the apostles had, and so might some among those he was now writing to. However, he would not have them value themselves upon that account; for even the bodily presence of Christ is not to be desired nor doted upon by his disciples. We must live upon his spiritual presence, and the comfort it affords. Note, Those who make images of Christ, and use them in their worship, do not take the way that God has appointed for strengthening their faith and quickening their affections; for it is the will of God that we should not know Christ any more after the flesh. 2. A thorough change of the heart: For if any man be in Christ, if any man be a Christian indeed, and will approve himself such, he is, or he must be, a new creature, v. 17. Some read it, Let him be a new creature. This ought to be the care of all who profess the Christian faith, that they be new creatures; not only that they have a new name, and wear a new livery, but that they have a new heart and new nature. And so great is the change the grace of God makes in the soul, that, as it follows, old things are passed away — old thoughts, old principles, and old practices, are passed away; and all these things must become new. Note, Regenerating grace creates a new world in the soul; all things are new. The renewed man acts from new principles, by new rules, with new ends, and in new company.

II. Reconciliation, which is here spoken of under a double notion: —

1. As an unquestionable privilege, v. 18, 19. Reconcilia-

tion supposes a quarrel, or breach of friendship; and sin has made a breach, it has broken the friendship between God and man. The heart of the sinner is filled with enmity against God, and God is justly offended with the sinner. Yet, behold, there may be a reconciliation; the offended Majesty of heaven is willing to be reconciled. And observe, 1. He has appointed the Mediator of reconciliation. He has reconciled us to himself by Jesus Christ, *v.* 18. God is to be owned from first to last in the undertaking and performance of the Mediator. All things relating to our reconciliation by Jesus Christ are of God, who by the mediation of Jesus Christ has reconciled the world to himself, and put himself into a capacity of being actually reconciled to offenders, without any wrong or injury to his justice or holiness, and does not impute to men their trespasses, but recedes from the rigour of the first covenant, which was broken, and does not insist upon the advantage he might justly take against us for the breach of that covenant, but is willing to enter into a new treaty, and into a new covenant of grace, and, according to the tenour thereof, freely to forgive us all our sins, and justify freely by his grace all those who do believe. 2. He has appointed the *ministry of reconciliation, v.* 18. By the inspiration of God the scriptures were written, which contain the word of reconciliation, showing us that peace was made by the blood of the cross, that reconciliation is wrought, and directing us how we may be interested therein. And he has appointed the office of the ministry, which is a *ministry of reconciliation:* ministers are to open and proclaim to sinners the terms of mercy and reconciliation, and persuade them to comply therewith. For,

2. Reconciliation is here spoken of as our indispensable duty, *v.* 20. As God is willing to be reconciled to us, we ought to be reconciled to God. And it is the great end and design of the gospel, that word of reconciliation, to prevail upon sinners to lay aside their enmity against God. Faithful ministers are Christ's ambassadors, sent to treat with sinners on peace and reconciliation: they come in God's name, with his entreaties, and act in Christ's stead, doing the very thing he did when he was upon this earth, and what he wills to be done now that he is in heaven. Wonderful condescension! Though God can be no loser by the quarrel, nor gainer by the peace, yet by his ministers he beseeches sinners to lay aside their enmity, and accept of the terms he offers, that they would be reconciled to him, to all his attributes, to all his laws, and to all his providences, to believe in the Mediator, to accept the atonement, and comply with his gospel, in all the parts of it and in the whole design of it. And for our encouragement so to do the apostle subjoins what should be well known and duly considered by us (*v.* 21), namely, (1.) The purity of the Mediator: *He knew no sin.* (2.) The sacrifice he offered: *He was made sin;* not a sinner, but *sin,* that is, a sin-offering, a sacrifice for sin. (3.) The end and design of all this: that *we might be made the righteousness of God in him,* might be justified freely by the grace of God through the redemption which is in Christ Jesus. Note, [1.] As Christ, who knew no sin of his own, was made sin for us, so we, who have no righteousness of our own, are made the righteousness of God in him. [2.] Our reconciliation to God is only through Jesus Christ, and for the sake of his merit: on him therefore we must rely, and make mention of his righteousness and his only.

CHAPTER 6

In this chapter the apostle gives an account of his general errand to all to whom he preached; with the several arguments and methods he used (*v.* 1–10). Then he addresses himself particularly to the Corinthians, giving them good cautions with great affection and strong arguments (*v.* 11–18).

Verses 1–10

In these verses we have an account of the apostle's general errand and exhortation to all to whom he preached in every place where he came, with the several arguments and methods he used. Observe,

I. The errand or exhortation itself, namely, to comply with the gospel offers of reconciliation — that, being favoured with the gospel, they would not receive this *grace of God in vain, v.* 1. The gospel is a word of grace sounding in our ears; but it will be in vain for us to hear it, unless we believe it, and comply with the end and design of it. And as it is the duty of the ministers of the gospel to exhort and persuade their hearers to accept of grace and mercy which are offered to

them, so they are honoured with this high title of *co-workers with God.* Note, 1. They must work; and must work for God and his glory, for souls and their good: and they are workers with God, yet under him, as instruments only; however, if they be faithful, they may hope to find God working with them, and their labour will be effectual. 2. Observe the language and way of the spirit of the gospel: it is not with roughness and severity, but with all mildness and gentleness, to beseech and entreat, to use exhortations and arguments, in order to prevail with sinners and overcome their natural unwillingness to be reconciled to God and to be happy for ever.

II. The arguments and method which the apostle used. And here he tells them,

1. The present time is the only proper season to accept of the grace that is offered, and improve that grace which is afforded: NOW *is the accepted time,* NOW *is the day of salvation, v.* 2. The gospel day is a day of salvation, the means of grace the means of salvation, the offers of the gospel the offers of salvation, and the present time the only proper time to accept of these offers: *To-day, while it is called to-day.* The morrow is none of ours: we know not what will be on the morrow, nor where we shall be; and we should remember that present seasons of grace are short and uncertain, and cannot be recalled when they are past. It is therefore our duty and interest to improve them while we have them, and no less than our salvation depends upon our so doing.

2. What caution they used not to give offence that might hinder the success of their preaching: *Giving no offence in any thing, v.* 3. The apostle had great difficulty to behave prudently and inoffensively towards the Jews and Gentiles, for many of both sorts watched for his halting, and sought occasion to blame him and his ministry, or his conversation; therefore he was very cautious not to give offence to those who were so apt to take offence, that he might not offend the Jews by unnecessary zeal against the law, nor the Gentiles by unnecessary compliances with such as were zealous for the law. He was careful, in all his words and actions, not to give offence, or occasion of guilt or grief. Note, When others are too apt to take offence, we should be cautious lest we give offence; and ministers especially should be careful lest they do any thing that may bring blame on their ministry or render that unsuccessful.

3. Their constant aim and endeavor in all things to approve themselves faithful, as became the ministers of God, *v.* 4. We see how much stress the apostle upon all occasions lays on fidelity in our work, because much of our success depends upon that. His eye was single, and his heart upright, in all his ministrations; and his great desire was to be the servant of God, and to approve himself so. Note, Ministers of the gospel should look upon themselves as God's servants or ministers, and act in every thing suitably to that character. So did the apostle, (1.) By much patience in afflictions. He was a great sufferer, and met with many afflictions, was often in necessities, and wanted the conveniences, if not the necessaries, of life; in distresses, being straitened on every side, hardly knowing what to do; in stripes often (*ch.* 11:24); in imprisonments; in tumults raised by the Jews and Gentiles against him; in labours, not only in preaching the gospel, but in travelling from place to place for that end, and working with his hands to supply his necessities; in watchings and in fastings, either voluntary or upon a religious account, or involuntary for the sake of religion: but he exercised much patience in all, *v.* 4, 5. Note, [1.] It is the lot of faithful ministers often to be reduced to great difficulties, and to stand in need of much patience. [2.] Those who would approve themselves to God must approve themselves faithful in trouble as well as in peace, not only in doing the work of God diligently, but also in bearing the will of God patiently. (2.) By acting from good principles. The apostle went by a good principle in all he did, and tells them what his principles were (*v.* 6, 7); namely, pureness; and there is no piety without purity. A care to keep ourselves unspotted from the world is necessary in order to our acceptance with God. Knowledge was another principle; and zeal without this is but madness. He also acted with *long-suffering and kindness,* being not easily provoked, but bearing with the hardness of men's hearts, and hard treatment from their hands, to whom he kindly endeavoured to do good. He acted under the influence of the Holy Ghost, from the noble principle of unfeigned love, according to the rule of the word of truth, under the supports and assistances of the power of God, having on the armour of righteousness (a consciousness of universal righteousness and holiness),

which is the best defence against the temptations of prosperity on the right hand, and of adversity on the left. (3.) By a due temper and behaviour under all the variety of conditions in this world, *v.* 8–10. We must expect to meet with many alterations of our circumstances and conditions in this world; and it will be a great evidence of our integrity if we preserve a right temper of mind, and duly behave ourselves, under them all. The apostles met with honour and dishonour, good report and evil report: good men in this world must expect to meet with some dishonour and reproaches, to balance their honour and esteem; and we stand in need of the grace of God to arm us against the temptations of honour on the one hand, so as to bear good report without pride, and of dishonour on the other hand, so as to bear reproaches without impatience or recrimination. It should seem that persons differently represented the apostles in their reports; that some represented them as the best, and others as the worst, of men: by some they were counted deceivers, and run down as such; by others as true, preaching the gospel of truth, and men who were true to the trust reposed in them. They were slighted by the men of the world as unknown, men of no figure or account, not worth taking notice of; yet in all the churches of Christ they were well known, and of great account: they were looked upon as dying, being killed all the day long, and their interest was thought to be a dying interest; "and yet behold," says the apostle, "we live, and live comfortably, and bear up cheerfully under all our hardships, and go on conquering and to conquer." They were chastened, and often fell under the lash of the law, yet not killed: and though it was thought that they were sorrowful, a company of mopish and melancholy men, always sighing and mourning, yet they were always rejoicing in God, and had the greatest reason to rejoice always. They were despised as poor, upon the account of their poverty in this world; and yet they made many rich, by preaching the unsearchable riches of Christ. They were thought to have nothing, and silver and gold they had none, houses and lands they had none; yet they possessed all things: they had nothing in this world, but they had a treasure in heaven. Their effects lay in another country, in another world. They had nothing in themselves, but possessed all things in Christ. Such a paradox is a Christian's life, and through such a variety of conditions and reports lies our way to heaven; and we should be careful in all these things to approve ourselves to God.

Verses 11–18

The apostle proceeds to address himself more particularly to the Corinthians, and cautions them against mingling with unbelievers. Here observe,

I. How the caution is introduced with a profession, in a very pathetic manner, of the most tender affection to them, *even like that of a father to his children, v.* 11–13. Though the apostle was happy in a great fluency of expressions, yet he seemed to want words to express the warm affections he had for these Corinthians. As if he had said, "O ye Corinthians, to whom I am now writing, I would fain convince you how well I love you: we are desirous to promote the spiritual and eternal welfare of all to whom we preach, yet *our mouth is open unto you, and our heart is enlarged unto* you, in a special manner." And, because his heart was thus enlarged with love to them, therefore he opened his mouth so freely to them in kind admonitions and exhortations: *"You are not,"* says he, *"straitened in us;* we would gladly do you all the service we can, and promote your comfort, as helpers of your faith and your joy; and, if it be otherwise, the fault is in yourselves; it is because you are straitened in yourselves, and fail in suitable returns to us, through some misapprehensions concerning us; and all we desire as a recompense is only that you would be proportionably affected towards us, as children should love their father." Note, It is desirable that there should be a mutual good affection between ministers and their people, and this would greatly tend to their mutual comfort and advantage.

II. The caution or exhortation itself, not to mingle with unbelievers, not to be *unequally yoked* with them, *v.* 14. Either,

1. In stated relations. It is wrong for good people to join in affinity with the wicked and profane; these will draw different ways, and that will be galling and grievous. Those relations that are our choice must be chosen by rule; and it is good for those who are themselves the children of God to join with those who are so likewise; for there is more dan-

ger that the bad will damage the good than hope that the good will benefit the bad.

2. In common conversation. We should not yoke ourselves in friendship and acquaintance with wicked men and unbelievers. Though we cannot wholly avoid seeing, and hearing, and being with such, yet we should never choose them for our bosom-friends.

3. Much less should we join in religious communion with them; we must not join with them in their idolatrous services, nor concur with them in their false worship, nor any abominations; we must not confound together the table of the Lord and the table of devils, the house of God and the house of Rimmon. The apostle gives several good reasons against this corrupt mixture. (1.) It is a very great absurdity, *v.* 14, 15. It is an unequal yoking of things together that will not agree together; as bad as for the Jews to have ploughed with an ox and an ass or to have sown divers sorts of grain intermixed. What an absurdity is it to think of joining righteousness and unrighteousness, or mingling light and darkness, fire and water, together! Believers are, and should be, righteous; but unbelievers are unrighteous. Believers are made light in the Lord, but unbelievers are in darkness; and what comfortable communion can these have together? Christ and Belial are contrary one to the other; they have opposite interests and designs, so that it is impossible there should be any concord or agreement between them. It is absurd, therefore, to think of enlisting under both; and, if the believer has part with an infidel, he does what in him lies to bring Christ and Belial together. (2.) It is a dishonour to the Christian's profession (*v.* 16); for Christians are by profession, and should be in reality, the *temples of the living God* — dedicated to, and employed for, the service of God, who has promised to reside in them, *to dwell and walk in them,* to stand in a special relation to them, and take a special care of them, that he will be their God and they shall be his people. Now there can be no agreement between *the temple of God and idols.* Idols are rivals with God for his honour, and God is a jealous God, and will not give his glory to another. (3.) There is a great deal of danger in communicating with unbelievers and idolators, danger of being defiled and of being rejected; therefore the exhortation is (*v.* 17) *to come out from among them,* and keep at a due distance, *to be separate,* as one would avoid the society of those who have the leprosy or the plague, for fear of taking infection, and not *to touch the unclean thing,* lest we be defiled. Who can touch pitch, and not be defiled by it? We must take care not to defile ourselves by converse with those who defile themselves with sin; so is the will of God, as we ever hope to be received, and not rejected, by him. (4.) It is base ingratitude to God for all the favours he has bestowed upon believers and promised to them, *v.* 18. God has promised to be a Father to them, and that they shall be his sons and his daughters; and is there a greater honour or happiness than this? How ungrateful a thing then must it be if those who have this dignity and felicity should degrade and debase themselves by mingling with unbelievers! *Do we thus requite the Lord, O foolish and unwise?*

CHAPTER 7

This chapter begins with an exhortation to progressive holiness and a due regard to the ministers of the gospel (*v.* 1–4). Then the apostle returns from a long digression to speak further of the affair concerning the incestuous person, and tells them what comfort he received in his distress about that matter, upon his meeting with Titus (*v.* 5–7), and how re rejoiced in their repentance, with the evidences thereof (*v.* 8–11). And, lastly, he concludes with endeavouring to comfort the Corinthians, upon whom his admonitions had had so good an effect (*v.* 12–16).

Verses 1–4

These verses contain a double exhortation: —

I. To make a progress in holiness, or *to perfect holiness in the fear of God, v.* 1. This exhortation is given with most tender affection to those who were dearly beloved, and enforced by strong arguments, even the consideration of those exceedingly great and precious promises which were mentioned in the former chapter, and which the Corinthians had an interest in and a title to. The promises of God are strong inducements to sanctification, in both the branches thereof; namely, 1. The dying unto sin, or mortifying our lusts and corruptions: we must *cleanse ourselves from all filthiness of flesh and spirit.* Sin is filthiness, and there are defilements of body and mind. There are sins of the flesh, that are committed with the body, and sins of the spirit, spiritual wickednesses; and we must cleanse ourselves from the filthiness of both, for God is to be glorified both with body and soul. 2. The living unto righteousness and holiness. If we hope God is our Father, we must endeavour to be *partakers of his holiness,* to be holy as he is holy, and perfect as our Father in heaven is perfect. We must be still perfecting holiness, and not be contented with sincerity (which is our gospel perfection), without aiming at sinless perfection, though we shall always come short of it while we are in this world; and this we must do in the *fear of God,* which is the root and principle of all religion, and there is no holiness without it. Note, Faith and hope in the promises of God must not destroy our fear of God, *who taketh pleasure in those that fear him and hope in his mercy.*

II. To show a due regard to the ministers of the gospel: *Receive us, v.* 2. Those who labour in the word and doctrine should *be had in reputation,* and *be highly esteemed for their work's sake:* and this would be a help to making progress in holiness. If the ministers of the gospel are thought contemptible because of their office, there is danger lest the gospel itself be contemned also. The apostle did not think it any disparagement to court the favour of the Corinthians; and, though we must flatter none, yet we must be gentle towards all. He tells them, 1. He had done nothing to forfeit their esteem and good-will, but was cautious not to do any thing to deserve their ill-will (*v.* 2): *"We have wronged no man:* we have done you no harm, but always designed your good." *I have coveted no man's silver, nor gold, nor apparel,* said he to the elders of Ephesus, Acts 20:33. *"We have corrupted no man,* by false doctrines or flattering speeches. *We have defrauded no man;* we have not sought ourselves, nor to promote our own secular interests by crafty and greedy measures, to the damage of any persons." This is an appeal like that of Samuel, 1 Sa. 12. Note, Then may ministers the more confidently expect esteem and favour from the people when they can safely appeal to them that they are guilty of nothing that deserves disesteem or displeasure. 2. He did not herein reflect upon them for want of affection to him, *v.* 3, 4. So tenderly and cautiously did the apostle deal with the Corinthians, among whom there were some who would be glad of any occasion to reproach him, and prejudice the minds of others against him. To prevent any insinuations against him on account of what he had said, as if he intended to charge them with wronging him, or unjust accusations of him for having wronged them, he assures them again of his great affection to them, insomuch that he could spend his last breath at Corinth, and *live and die with them,* if his business with other churches, and his work as an apostle (which was not to be confined to one place only), would permit him to do so. An he adds it was his great affection to them that made him use such *boldness* or freedom of *speech towards them,* and caused him to *glory,* or make his boast of them, in all places, and upon all occasions, being *filled with comfort, and exceedingly joyful in all their tribulations.*

Verses 5–11

There seems to be a connection between *ch.* 2:13 (where the apostle said he had no rest in his spirit when he found not Titus at Troas) and the fifth verse of this chapter: and so great was his affection to the Corinthians, and his concern about their behaviour in relation to the incestuous person, that, in his further travels, he still had no rest till he heard from them. And now he tells them,

I. How he was distressed, *v.* 5. He was troubled when he did not meet with Titus at Troas, and afterwards when for some time he did not meet with him in Macedonia: this was a grief to him, because he could not hear what reception he met with at Corinth, nor how their affairs went forward. And, besides this, they met with other troubles, with incessant storms of persecutions; there were *fightings without,* or continual contentions with, and opposition from, Jews and Gentiles; and there were *fears within,* and great concern for such as had embraced the Christian faith, lest they should be corrupted or seduced, and give scandal to others, or be scandalized.

II. How he was comforted, *v.* 6, 7. Here observe, 1. The very coming of Titus was some comfort to him. It was matter of joy to see him, whom he long desired and expected to meet with. The very coming of Titus and his company, who was dear to him as his *own son in the common faith* (Tit. 1:4), was a great comfort to the apostle in his travels and troubles. But, 2. The good news which Titus brought concerning the Corinthians was matter of greater consolation. He found Titus to be comforted in them; and this filled the apostle with comfort, especially when he acquainted him with their earnest desire to give good satisfaction in the things about which the apostle had written to them; and of their mourning for the scandal that was found among them and the great grief they had caused to others, and their fervent mind or great affection towards the apostle, who had dealt so faithfully with them in reproving their faults: so true is the observation of Solomon (Prov. 28:23), *He that rebuketh a man afterwards shall find more favour than he that flattereth with his tongue.* 3. He ascribes all his comfort to God as the author. It was God who comforted him by the coming of Titus, even the God of all comfort: *God, who comforteth those that are cast down, v.* 6. Note, We should look above and beyond all means and instruments, unto God, as the author of all the consolation and the good that we enjoy.

III. How greatly he rejoiced at their repentance, and the evidences thereof. The apostle was sorry that he had grieved them, that some pious persons among them laid to heart very greatly what he said in his former epistle, or that it was needful he should make those sorry whom he would rather have made glad, *v.* 8. But now he rejoiced, when he found they had *sorrowed to repentance, v.* 9. Their sorrow in itself was not the cause of his rejoicing; but the nature of it, and the effect of it (*repentance unto salvation, v.* 10), made him rejoice; for now it appeared that they had received damage by him in nothing. Their sorrow was *but for a season;* it was turned into joy, and that joy was durable. Observe here,

1. The antecedent of true repentance is godly sorrow; this worketh repentance. It is not repentance itself, but it is a good preparative to repentance, and in some sense the cause that produces repentance. The offender had great sorrow, he was in danger of being *swallowed up with overmuch sorrow;* and the society was greatly sorrowful which before was puffed up: and this sorrow of theirs was after a godly manner, or according to God (as it is in the original), that is, it was according to the will of God, tended to the glory of God, and was wrought by the Spirit of God. It was a godly sorrow, because a sorrow for sin, as an offence against God, an instance of ingratitude, and a forfeiture of God's favour. There is a great difference between this sorrow of a godly sort and the sorrow of this world. Godly sorrow produces repentance and reformation, and will end in salvation; but worldly sorrow worketh death. The sorrows of worldly men for worldly things will bring down gray hairs the sooner to the grave, and such a sorrow even for sin, as Judas had will have fatal consequences, as his had, which wrought death. Note, (1.) Repentance will be attended with salvation. Therefore, (2.) True penitents will never repent that they have repented, nor of any thing that was conducive thereto. (3.) Humiliation and godly sorrow are previously necessary in order to repentance, and both of them are from God, the giver of all grace.

2. The happy fruits and consequences of true repentance are mentioned (*v.* 11); and those *fruits that are meet for repentance* are the best evidences of it. Where the heart is changed, the life and actions will be changed too. The Corinthians made it evident that their sorrow was a godly sorrow, and such as wrought repentance, because it wrought in them great carefulness about their souls, and to avoid sin, and please God; it wrought also a clearing of themselves, not by insisting upon their own justification before God, especially while they persisted in their sin, but by endeavours to put away the accursed thing, and so free themselves from the just imputation of approving the evil that had been done. It wrought indignation at sin, at themselves, at the tempter and his instruments; it wrought fear, a fear of reverence, a fear of watchfulness, and a fear of distrust, not a distrust of God, but of themselves; an awful fear of God, a cautious fear of sin, and a jealous fear of themselves. It wrought vehement desires after a thorough reformation of what had been amiss, and of reconciliation with God whom they had offended. It wrought zeal, a mixture of love and anger, a zeal for duty, and against sin. It wrought, lastly, revenge against sin and their own folly, by endeavours to make all due satisfaction for injuries that might be done thereby. And thus *in all things had they approved themselves to be clear in that matter.* Not that they were innocent, but that they were penitent, and therefore clear of guilt before God, who would pardon and not punish them; and they ought no longer to be reproved, much less to be reproached, by men, for what they had truly repented of.

Verses 12–16

In these verses the apostle endeavours to comfort the Corinthians, upon whom his admonitions had had such good effect. And in order thereto, 1. He tells them he had a good design in his former epistle, which might be thought severe, *v.* 12. It was not chiefly *for his cause that did the wrong,* not only for his benefit, much less merely that he should be punished; nor was it merely *for his cause that suffered wrong,* namely, the injured father, and that he might have what satisfaction could be given him; but it was also to manifest his great and sincere concern and *care for them,* for the whole church, lest that should suffer by letting such a crime, and the scandal thereof, remain among them without due remark and resentment. 2. He acquaints them with the joy of Titus as well as of himself upon the account of their repentance and good behaviour. Titus was rejoiced, and his spirit refreshed, with their comfort, and this comforted and rejoiced the apostle also (*v.* 13); and, as Titus was comforted while he was with them, so when he remembered his reception among them, expressing their obedience to the apostolical directions, and their fear and trembling at the reproofs that were given them, the thoughts of these things inflamed and increased his affections to them, *v.* 15. Note, Great comfort and joy follow upon godly sorrow. As sin occasions general grief, so repentance and reformation occasion general joy. Paul was glad, and Titus was glad, and the Corinthians were comforted, and the penitent ought to be comforted; and well may all this joy be on earth, when there is joy in heaven over one sinner that repenteth. 3. He concludes this whole matter with expressing the entire confidence he had in them: He was not ashamed of his boasting concerning them to Titus (*v.* 14); for he was not disappointed in his expectation concerning them, which he signified to Titus, and he could now with great joy declare what confidence he still had in them as to all things, that he did not doubt of their good behaviour for the time to come. Note, It is a great comfort and joy to a faithful minister to have to do with a people whom he can confide in, and who he has reason to hope will comply with every thing he proposes to them that is for the glory of God, the credit of the gospel, and their advantage.

CHAPTER 8

In this and the following chapter Paul is exhorting and directing the Corinthians about a particular work of charity — to relieve the necessities of the poor saints at Jerusalem and in Judea, according to the good example of the churches in Macedonia, Rom. 15:26. The Christians at Jerusalem, through war, famine, and persecution, had become poor, many of them had fallen into decay, and perhaps most of them were but poor when they first embraced Christianity; for Christ said, "The poor receive the gospel." Now Paul, though he was the apostle of the Gentiles, had a fonder regard, and kind concern, for those among the Jews who were converted to the Christian faith; and, though many of them had not so much affection to the Gentile converts as they ought to have had, yet the apostle would have the Gentiles to be kind to them, and stirred them up to contribute liberally for their relief. Upon this subject he is very copious, and writes very affectingly. In this eighth chapter he acquaints the Corinthians with, and commends, the good example of the Macedonians in this work of charity, and that Titus was sent to Corinth to collect their bounty (*v.* 1–6). He the proceeds to urge this duty with several cogent arguments (*v.* 7–15), and commends the persons who were employed in this affair (*v.* 16–24).

Verses 1–6

Observe here,

I. The apostle takes occasion from the good example of the churches of Macedonia, that is, of Philippi, Thessalonica, Berea, and others in the region of Macedonia, to exhort the Corinthians and the Christians in Achaia to the good work of charity. And,

1. He acquaints them with their great liberality, which he calls *the grace of God bestowed on the churches, v.* 1. Some think the words should be rendered, *the gift of God given in or by the churches.* He certainly means the charitable gifts of these churches, which are called the grace or gifts of God, either because they were very large, or rather because their charity to the poor saints did proceed from God as the author, and was accompanied with true love to God, which also was manifested this way. The grace of God must be owned as the root and fountain of all the good that is in us, or done by us, at any time; and it is great grace and favour from God, and bestowed on us, if we are made useful to others, and are forward to any good work.

2. He commends the charity of the Macedonians, and sets it forth with good advantage. He tells them, (1.) They were but in a low condition, and themselves in distress, yet they contributed to the relief of others. *They were in great tribulation and deep poverty, v.* 2. It was a time of great affliction with them, as may be seen, Acts 18:17. The Christians in these parts met with ill treatment, which had reduced them to deep poverty; yet, as they had abundance of joy in the midst of tribulation, they abounded in their liberality; they gave out of a little, trusting in God to provide for them, and make it up to them. (2.) They gave very largely, with *the riches of liberality* (*v.* 2), that is, as liberally as if they had been rich. It was a large contribution they made, all things considered; it was *according to,* yea *beyond, their power* (*v.* 3), as much as could well be expected from them, if not more. Note, Though men may condemn the indiscretion, yet God will accept the pious zeal, of those who in real works of piety and charity do rather beyond their power. (3.) They were very ready and forward to this good work. *They were willing of themselves* (*v.* 3), and were so far from needing that Paul should urge and press them with many arguments that they *prayed him with much entreaty to receive the gift, v.* 4. It seems Paul was backward to undertake this trust, for *he would give himself to the word and prayer;* or, it may be, he was apprehensive how ready his enemies would be to reproach and blacken him upon all occasions, and might take a handle against him upon account of so large a sum deposited in his hands, to suspect or accuse him of indiscretion and partiality in the distribution, if not of some injustice. Note, How cautious ministers should be, especially in money-matters, not to give occasion to those who seek occasion to speak reproachfully! (4.) Their charity was founded in true piety, and this was the great commendation of it. They performed this good work in a right method: *First they gave themselves to the Lord, and then* they gave unto us their contributions, *by the will of God* (*v.* 5), that is, according as it was the will of God they should do, or to be disposed of as the will of God should be, and for his glory. This, it seems, exceeded the expectation of the apostle; it was more than he hoped for, to see such warm and pious affections shining in these Macedonians, and this good work performed with so much devotion and solemnity. They solemnly, jointly, and unanimously, made a fresh surrender of themselves, and all they had, unto the Lord Jesus Christ. They had done this before, and now they do it again upon this occasion; sanctifying their contributions to God's honour, by first giving themselves to the Lord. Note, [1.] We should give ourselves to God; we cannot bestow ourselves better. [2.] When we give ourselves to the Lord, we then give him all we have, to be called for and disposed of according to his will. [3.] Whatever we use or lay out for God, it is only giving to him what is his own. [4.] What we give or bestow for charitable uses will not be accepted of God, nor turn to our advantage, unless we first give ourselves to the Lord.

II. The apostle tells them that Titus was desired to go and make a collection among them (*v.* 6), and Titus, he knew, would be an acceptable person to them. He had met with a kind reception among them formerly. They had shown good affection to him, and he had a great love for them. Besides, Titus had already begun this work among them, therefore he was desired to finish it. So that he was, on all accounts, a proper person to be employed; and, when so good a work had already prospered in so good a hand, it would be a pity if it should not proceed and be finished. Note, It is an instance of wisdom to use proper instruments in a work we desire to do well; and the work of charity will often succeed the best when the most proper persons are employed to solicit contributions and dispose of them.

Verses 7–15

In these verses the apostle uses several cogent arguments to stir up the Corinthians to this good work of charity.

I. He urges upon them the consideration of their eminence in other gifts and graces, and would have them excel in this of charity also, *v.* 7. Great address and much holy art are here used by the apostle. When he would persuade the Corinthians to this good thing, he commends them for other good things that were found in them. Most people love to be complimented, especially when we ask a gift of them for ourselves or others; and it is a justice we owe to those in whom God's grace shines to give them their due commendation. Observe here, What it was that the Corinthians abounded in. Faith is mentioned first, for that is the root; and, as *without faith it is impossible to please God* (Heb. 11:6), so those who abound in faith will abound in other graces and good works also; and this will work and show itself by love. To their faith was added utterance, which is an excellent gift, and redounds much to the glory of God and the good of the church. Many have faith who want utterance. But these Corinthians excelled most churches in spiritual gifts, and particularly in utterance; and yet this was not in them, as in too many, both the effect and evidence of ignorance; for with their utterance there appeared knowledge, abundance of knowledge. They had a treasury of things new and old, and in their utterance they brought out of this treasury. They abounded also in all diligence. Those who have great knowledge and ready utterance are not always the most diligent Christians. Great talkers are not always the best doers; but these Corinthians were diligent to do, as well as know and talk, well. And further, they had abundant love to their minister; and were not like too many, who, having gifts of their own, are but too apt to slight their ministers, and neglect them. Now to all these good things the apostle desires them to add this grace also, to abound in charity to the poor; that, where so much good was found, there should be found yet more good. Before the apostle proceeds to another argument he takes care to prevent any misapprehensions of his design to impose on them, or to bind heavy burdens upon them by his authority; and tells them (*v.* 8) he does not speak by commandment, or in a way of authority. I give *my advice, v.* 10. He took occasion from the forwardness of others to propose what would be expedient for them, and would prove the sincerity of their love, or be the genuine effect and evidence thereof. Note, A great difference should be made between plain and positive duty, and the improvement of a present opportunity of doing or getting good. Many a thing which is good for us to do, yet can not be said to be, by express and indispensable commandment, our duty at this or that time.

II. Another argument is taken from the consideration of the grace of our Lord Jesus Christ. The best arguments for Christian duties are those that are taken from the love of Christ, *that constraineth us.* The example of the churches of Macedonia was such as the Corinthians should imitate; but the example of our Lord Jesus Christ should have much greater influence. And *you know,* saith the apostle, *the grace of our Lord Jesus Christ* (*v.* 9), *that though he was rich,* as being God, equal in power and glory with the Father, rich in all the glory and blessedness of the upper world, *yet for your sakes he became poor;* not only did become man for us, but he became poor also. He was born in poor circumstances, lived a poor life, and died in poverty; and this was for our sakes, that we thereby might be made rich, rich in the love and favour of God, rich in the blessings and promises of the new covenant, rich in the hopes of eternal life, being heirs of the kingdom. This is a good reason why we should be charitable to the poor out of what we have, because we ourselves live upon the charity of the Lord Jesus Christ.

III. Another argument is taken from their good purposes, and their forwardness to begin this good work. As to this he tells them, 1. It was expedient for them to perform what they purposed, and finish what they had begun, *v.* 10, 11. What else did their good purposes and good beginnings signify? Good purposes, indeed, are good things; they are like buds and blossoms, pleasant to behold, and give hopes of good fruit; but they are lost, and signify nothing, without performances. So good beginnings are amiable; but we shall lose the benefit unless there be perseverance, and we bring forth fruit to perfection. Seeing therefore the Corinthians had shown a readiness to will, he would have them be careful also in the performance, according to their ability. For, 2. This would be acceptable to God. *This willing mind is accepted* (*v.* 12), when accompanied with sincere endeavours. When men purpose that which is good, and endeavour, according to their ability, to perform also, God will accept of what they have, or can do, and not reject them for what they have not, and what is not in their power to do: and this is true as to other things besides the work of charity. But let us note here that this scripture will by no means justify those who think good meanings are enough, or that good purposes, and the profession of a willing mind, are sufficient to save them. It is accepted, indeed, where there is a performance as far as we are able, and when Providence hinders the performance, as in David's case concerning building a house for the Lord, 2 Sa. 7.

IV. Another argument is taken from the discrimination which the divine Providence makes in the distribution of the things of this world, and the mutability of human affairs, *v.* 13–15. The force of the arguing seems to be this: — Providence gives to some more of the good things of this world, and to some less, and that with this design, that those who have a greater *abundance may supply those who are in want,* that there may be room for charity. And further, considering the mutability of human affairs, and how soon there may be an alteration, so that those who now have an abundance may stand in need of being supplied themselves in their wants, this should induce them to be charitable while they are able. It is the will of God that, by our mutually supplying one another, there should *be some sort of equality;* not an *absolute* equality indeed, or such a levelling as would destroy property, for in such a case there could be no exercise of charity. But as in works of charity there should be an equitable proportion observed, that the burden should not lie too heavy on some, while others are wholly eased, so all should think themselves concerned to supply those who are in want. This is illustrated by the instance of gathering and distributing manna in the wilderness, concerning which (as we may read, Ex. 16) it was the duty of every family, and all in the family, to gather what they could, which, when it was gathered, was put into some common receptacle for each family, whence the master of the family distributed to every one as he had occasion, to some more than they were able, through age and infirmity, to gather up; to others less than they gathered, because they did not need so much: and thus *he that had gathered much* (more than he had occasion for) had nothing over, when a communication was made to him *that had gathered little,* who by this method had no lack. Note, Such is the condition of men in this world that we mutually depend on one another, and should help one another. Those who have ever so much of this world have no more than food and raiment; and those who have but a little of this world seldom want these; nor, indeed, should those who have abundance suffer others to want, but be ready to afford supply.

Verses 16–24

In these verses the apostle commends the brethren who were sent to them to collect their charity; and as it were, gives them letters credential, that, if they *were enquired after* (*v.* 23), if any should be inquisitive or suspicious concerning them, it might be known who they were and how safely they might be trusted.

I. He commends Titus, 1. For his earnest care and great concern of heart for them, and desire in all things to promote their welfare. This is mentioned with thankfulness to God (*v.* 16), and it is cause of thankfulness if God hath put it into the hearts of any to do us or others any good. 2. For his readiness to this present service. He accepted the office, and was forward to go upon this good errand, *v.* 17. Asking charity for the relief of others is by many looked upon as a thankless office; yet it is a good office, and what we should not be shy of when we are called to it.

II. He commends another brother, who was sent with Titus. It is generally thought that this was Luke. He is commended, 1. As a man whose *praise was in the gospel through all the churches, v.* 18. His ministerial services of several kinds were well known, and he had approved himself praiseworthy in what he had done. 2. As one chosen of the churches (*v.* 19) and joined with the apostle in his ministration. This was done, it is most likely, at the motion and request of Paul himself; for this reason, *that no man might blame him in that abundance which was administered by him* (*v.* 20), so cautious was the apostle to avoid all occasions that evil-minded men might lay hold on to blacken him. He would not give occasion to any to accuse him of injustice or partiality in this affair, and thought it to be his duty, as it is the duty of all Christians, *to provide for things honest, not only in the sight of the Lord, but also in the sight of men;* that is, to act so prudently as to prevent, as far as we can, all unjust suspicions concerning us, and all occasions of scandalous imputations. Note, We live in a censorious world, and should cut off occasion from those who seek occasion to speak reproachfully. It is the crime of others if they reproach or censure us without occasion; and it is our imprudence at least if we give them any occasion, when there may not be a just cause for them so to do.

III. He commends also another brother who was joined with the two former in this affair. This brother is thought to be Apollos. Whoever he was, he had *approved himself diligent in many things;* and therefore was fit to be employed in this affair. Moreover, he had great desire to this work, because of the confidence or good opinion he had of the Corinthians (*v.* 22), and it is a great comfort to see those employed in good works who have formerly approved themselves diligent.

IV. He concludes this point with a general good character of them all (*v.* 23), as *fellow-labourers with him* for their welfare; as the *messengers of the churches;* as the *glory of Christ,* who were to him for a name and a praise, who brought glory to Christ as instruments and had obtained honour from Christ to be counted faithful and employed in his service. Wherefore, upon the whole, he exhorts them to show their liberality, answerable to the great expectation others had concerning them at this time, that these messengers of the churches, and the churches themselves, might see a full *proof of their love* to God and to their afflicted brethren, and that it was with good reason the apostle had even *boasted on their behalf, v.* 24. Note, The good opinion others entertain of us should be an argument with us to do well.

CHAPTER 9

In this chapter the apostle seems to excuse his earnestness in pressing the Corinthians to the duty of charity (*v.* 1–5), and proceeds to give directions about the acceptable way and manner of performing it, namely, bountifully, deliberately, and freely; and gives good encouragement for so doing (*v.* 6 to the end).

Verses 1–5

In these verses the apostle speaks very respectfully to the Corinthians, and with great skill; and, while he seems to excuse his urging them so earnestly to charity, still presses them thereto, and shows how much his heart was set upon this matter.

I. He tells them it was needless to press them with further arguments to afford relief to their poor brethren (*v.* 1), being satisfied he had said enough already to prevail with those of whom he had so good an opinion. For, 1. *He knew their forwardness* to every good work, and how they had begun this good work a year ago, insomuch that, 2. He had boasted of their zeal to the Macedonians, and this had provoked many of them to do as they had done. Wherefore he was persuaded, that, as they had begun well, they would go on well; and so, commending them for what they had done, he lays an obligation on them to proceed and persevere.

II. He seems to apologize for sending Titus and the other brethren to them. He is unwilling they should be offended at him for this, as if he were too earnest, and pressed too hard upon them; and tells the true reasons why he sent them, namely, 1. That, having this timely notice, they might be fully ready (*v.* 3), and not surprised with hasty demands, when he should come to them. When we would have others to do that which is good we must act towards them prudently and tenderly, and give them time. 2. That he might not be ashamed of his boasting concerning them, if they should be found unready, *v.* 3, 4. He intimates that some from Macedonia might *haply come with him:* and, if the collection should not then be made, this would make him, not to say them, ashamed, considering the boasting of the apostle concerning them. Thus careful was he to preserve their reputation and his own. Note, Christians should consult the reputation of their profession, and endeavour to *adorn the doctrine of God our Saviour.*

Verses 6–15

Here we have,

I. Proper directions to be observed about the right and acceptable manner of bestowing charity; and it is of great concernment that we not only do what is required, but do it as is commanded. Now, as to the manner in which the apostle would have the Corinthians give, observe, 1. It should be bountifully; this was intimated, *v.* 5, that a liberal contribution was expected, a matter of bounty, not what savoured of covetousness; and he offers to their consideration that men who expect a good return at harvest are not wont to pinch and spare in sowing their seed, for the return is usually proportionable to what they sow, *v.* 6. 2. It should be deliberately *Every man, according as he purposes in his heart, v.* 7. Works of charity, like other good works, should be done with thought and design; whereas some do good only by accident. They comply, it may be hastily, with the importunity of others, without any good design, and give more than they intended, and then repent of it afterwards. Or possibly, had they duly considered all things, they would have given more. Due deliberation, as to this matter of our own circumstances, and those of the persons we are about to relieve, will be very helpful to direct us how liberal we should be in our contributions for charitable uses. 3. It should be freely, whatever we give, be it more or less: *Not grudgingly, nor of necessity,* but cheerfully, *v.* 7. Persons sometimes will give merely to satisfy the importunity of those who ask their charity, and what they give is in a manner squeezed or forced from them, and this unwillingness spoils all they do. We ought to give more freely than the modesty of some necessitous persons will allow them to ask: we should not only deal out bread, but draw out our souls to the hungry, Isa. 58:10. We should give liberally, with an open hand, and cheerfully, with an open countenance, being glad we have ability and an opportunity to be charitable.

II. Good encouragement to perform this work of charity in the manner directed. Here the apostle tells the Corinthians,

1. They themselves would be no losers by what they gave in charity. This may serve to obviate a secret objection in the minds of many against this good work who are ready to think they may want what they give away; but such should consider that what is given to the poor in a right manner is far from being lost; as the precious seed which is cast into the ground is not lost, though it is buried there for a time, for it will spring up, and bear fruit; the sower shall receive it again with increase, *v.* 6. Such good returns may those expect who give freely and liberally in charity. For, (1.) God loveth a cheerful giver (*v.* 7), and what may not those hope to receive who are the objects of the divine love? Can a man be a loser by doing that with which God is pleased? May not such a one be sure that he shall some way or other be a gainer? Nay, are not the love and favour of God better than all other things, *better than life* itself? (2.) God is able to make our charity redound to our advantage, *v.* 8. We have no reason to distrust the goodness of God, and surely we have no reason to question his power; he is *able to make all grace abound* towards us, and abound in us; to give a large increase of spiritual and temporal good things. He can cause us to have a sufficiency in all things, to be content with what we have, to make up what we give, to be able to give yet more: as it is written (Ps. 112:9) concerning the charitable man, *He hath dispersed abroad. He hath given to the poor. His righteousness,* that is, his almsgiving, *endureth for ever.* The honour of it is lasting, the reward of it eternal, and he is still able to live comfortably himself and to give liberally to others. (3.) The apostle puts up a prayer to God in their behalf that they might be gainers, and not losers, *v.* 10, 11. Here observe, [1.] To whom the prayer is made — to God, *who ministereth seed to the sower,* who by his providence giveth such an increase of the fruits of the earth that we have not only bread sufficient to eat for one year, but enough to sow again for a future supply: or thus, It is God who giveth us not only a competency for ourselves, but that also wherewith we may supply the wants of others, and so should be as seed to be sown. [2.] For what he prayeth. There are several things which he desires for them, namely, that they may have *bread for their food,* always a competency for themselves, *food convenient,* — that God will *multiply their seed sown,* that they may still be able to do more good, — and that there may be *an increase of the fruits of righteousness,* that they may reap plentifully, and have the best and most ample returns of their charity, so as to be *enriched in every thing to all bountifulness* (*v.* 11), — that upon the whole they may find it true that they shall be no losers, but great gainers. Note, Works of charity are so far from impoverishing us that they are the proper means truly to enrich us, or make us truly rich.

2. While they would be no losers, the poor distressed saints would be gainers; for this service would *supply their wants, v.* 12. If we have reason to think them to be saints, whom we believe to be of the household of faith, whose wants are great, how ready should we be to do them good! Our goodness can not extend unto God, but we should freely extend it to these *excellent ones of the earth,* and thus show that we delight in them.

3. This would redound to the praise and glory of God. Many thanksgivings would be given to God on this account, by the apostle, and by those who were employed in this ministration, *v.* 11. These would bless God, who had made them happy instruments in so good a work, and rendered them successful in it. Besides these, others also would be thankful; the poor, who were supplied in their wants, would not fail to be very thankful to God, and bless God for them; and all who wished well to the gospel would *glorify God for this experiment,* or proof *of subjection to the gospel of Christ,* and

true love to all men, *v.* 13. Note, (1.) True Christianity is a subjection to the gospel, a yielding of ourselves to the commanding influence of its truths and laws. (2.) We must evince the sincerity of our subjection to the gospel by works of charity. (3.) This will be for the credit of our profession, and to the praise and glory of God.

4. Those whose wants were supplied would make the best return they were able, by sending up many prayers to God for those who had relieved them, *v.* 14. And thus should we recompense the kindnesses we receive when we are not in a capacity of recompensing them in any other way; and, as this is the only recompence the poor can make, so it is often greatly for the advantage of the rich.

Lastly, The apostle concludes this whole matter with this doxology, *Thanks be to God for his unspeakable gift, v.* 15. Some think that by this unspeakable gift he means the gift of grace bestowed on the churches, in making them able and willing to supply the necessities of the saints, which would be attended with unspeakable benefit both to the givers and receivers. It should seem rather that he means Jesus Christ, who is indeed the unspeakable gift of God unto this world, a gift we have all reason to be very thankful for.

CHAPTER 10

There was no place in which the apostle Paul met with more opposition from false apostles than at Corinth; he had many enemies there. Let not any of the ministers of Christ think it strange if they meet with perils, not only from enemies, but from false brethren; for blessed Paul himself did so. Though he was so blameless and inoffensive in all his carriage, so condescending and useful to all, yet there were those who bore him ill-will, who envied him, and did all they could to undermine him, and lesson his interest and reputation. Therefore he vindicates himself from their imputation, and arms the Corinthians against their insinuations. In this chapter the apostle, in a mild and humble manner, asserts the power of his preaching, and to punish offenders (*v.* 1–6). He then proceeds to reason the case with the Corinthians, asserting his relation to Christ, and his authority as an apostle of Christ (*v.* 7–11), and refuses to justify himself, or to act by such rules as the false teachers did, but according to the better rules he had fixed for himself (*v.* 12 to the end).

Verses 1–6

Here we may observe,

I. The mild and humble manner in which the blessed apostle addresses the Corinthians, and how desirous he is that no occasion may be given him to use severity. 1. He addresses them in a very mild and humble manner: *I Paul myself beseech you, v.* 1. We find, in the introduction to this epistle, he joined Timothy with himself; but now he speaks only for himself, against whom the false apostles had particularly levelled their reproaches; yet in the midst of the greatest provocations he shows humility and mildness, from the consideration of the *meekness and gentleness of Christ,* and desires this great example may have the same influence on the Corinthians. Note, When we find ourselves tempted or inclined to be rough and severe towards any body, we should think of the meekness and gentleness of Christ, that appeared in him in the days of his flesh, in the design of his undertaking, and in all the acts of his grace towards poor souls. How humbly also does this great apostle speak of himself, as *one in presence base among them!* So his enemies spoke of him with contempt, and he seems to acknowledge it; while others thought meanly, and spoke scornfully of him, he had low thoughts of himself, and spoke humbly of himself. Note, We should be sensible of our own infirmities, and think humbly of ourselves, even when men reproach us for them.

2. He is desirous that no occasion may be given to use severity, *v.* 2. *He beseeches them* to give no occasion for him to be bold, or to exercise his authority against them in general, as he had resolved to do against some who unjustly charged him as *walking according to the flesh,* that is, regulating his conduct, even in his ministerial actions, according to carnal policy or with worldly views. This was what the apostle had renounced, and this is contrary to the spirit and design of the gospel, and was far from being the aim and design of the apostle. Hereupon,

II. He asserts the power of his preaching and his power to punish offenders.

1. The power of his preaching, *v.* 3, 5. Here observe, (1.) The work of the ministry is a warfare, not *after the flesh* indeed, for it is a spiritual warfare, with spiritual enemies and for spiritual purposes. And though ministers walk in the flesh, or live in the body, and in the common affairs of life act as other men, yet in their work and warfare they must not go by the maxims of the flesh, nor should they design to please

the flesh: this must be crucified with its affections and lusts; it must be mortified and kept under. (2.) The doctrines of the gospel and discipline of the church are the weapons of this warfare; and these are not carnal: outward force, therefore, is not the method of the gospel, but strong persuasions, by the power of truth and the meekness of wisdom. A good argument this is against persecution for conscience' sake: conscience is accountable to God only; and people must be persuaded to God and their duty, not driven by force of arms. And so the weapons of our warfare are mighty, or very powerful; the evidence of truth is convincing and cogent. This indeed is through God, or owing to him, because they are his institutions, and accompanied with his blessing, which makes all opposition to fall before his victorious gospel. We may here observe, [1.] What opposition is made against the gospel by the powers of sin and Satan in the hearts of men. Ignorance, prejudices, beloved lusts, are Satan's strong-holds in the souls of some; vain imaginations, carnal reasonings, and high thoughts, or proud conceits, in others, *exalt themselves against the knowledge of God,* that is, by these ways the devil endeavours to keep men from faith and obedience to the gospel, and secures his possession of the hearts of men, as his own house or property. But then observe, [2.] The conquest which the word of God gains. These strong-holds are pulled down by the gospel as the means, through the grace and power of God accompanying it as the principal efficient cause. Note, The conversion of the soul is the conquest of Satan in that soul.

2. The apostle's power to punish offenders (and that in an extraordinary manner) is asserted in *v.* 6. The apostle was a prime-minister in the kingdom of Christ, and chief officer in his army, and *had in readiness* (that is, he had power and authority at hand) *to revenge all disobedience,* or to punish offenders in a most exemplary and extraordinary manner. The apostle speaks not of personal revenge, but of punishing disobedience to the gospel, and disorderly walking among church-members, by inflicting church-censures. Note, Though the apostle showed meekness and gentleness, yet he would not betray his authority; and therefore intimates that when he would commend those whose obedience was fulfilled or manifested others would fall under severe censures.

Verses 7–11

In these verses the apostle proceeds to reason the case with the Corinthians, in opposition to those who despised him, judged him, and spoke hardly of him: *"Do you,"* says he, *"look on things after the outward appearance? v.* 7. Is this a fit measure or rule to make an estimate of things or persons by, and to judge between me and my adversaries?" In outward appearance, Paul was mean and despicable with some; he did not make a figure, as perhaps some of his competitors might do: but this was a false rule to make a judgment by. It should seem that some boasted mighty things of themselves, and made a fair show. But there are often false appearances. A man may seem to be learned who has not learned Christ, and appear virtuous when he has not a principle of grace in his heart. However, the apostle asserts two things of himself: —

I. His relation to Christ: *If any man trust to himself that he is Christ's, even so are we Christ's, v.* 7. It would seem by this that Paul's adversaries boasted of their relation to Christ as his ministers and servants. Now the apostle reasons thus with the Corinthians: "Suppose it to be so, allowing what they say to be true (and let us observe that, in fair arguing, we should allow all that may be reasonably granted, and should not think it impossible but those who differ from us very much may yet belong to Christ, as well as we), allowing them," might the apostle say, "what they boast of, yet they ought also to allow this to us, that *we also are Christ's.*" Note, 1. We must not, by the most charitable allowances we make to others who differ from us, cut ourselves off from Christ, nor deny our relation to him. For, 2. There is room in Christ for many; and those who differ much from one another may yet be one in him. It would help to heal the differences that are among us if we would remember that, how confident soever we may be that we belong to Christ, yet, at the same time, we must allow that those who differ from us may belong to Christ too, and therefore should be treated accordingly. We must not think that we are the people, and that none belong to Christ but ourselves. This we may plead for ourselves, against those who judge us and despise us that, how weak soever we are, yet, as they are Christ's, so are we: we profess the same faith,

we walk by the same rule, we build upon the same foundation, and hope for the same inheritance.

II. His authority from Christ as an apostle. This he had mentioned before (*v.* 6), and now he tells them that he might speak of it again, and that with some sort of boasting, seeing it was a truth, that the *Lord had given it to him,* and it was more than his adversaries could justly pretend to. It was certainly what he should not be ashamed of, *v.* 8. Concerning this observe, 1. The nature of his authority: it was for *edification, and not for destruction.* This indeed is the end of all authority, civil and ecclesiastical, and was the end of that extraordinary authority which the apostles had, and of all church-discipline. 2. The caution with which he speaks of his authority, professing that his design was not to terrify them with big words, nor by angry letters, *v.* 9. Thus he seems to obviate an objection that might have been formed against him, *v.* 10. But the apostle declares he did not intend to frighten those who were obedient, nor did he write any thing in his letters that he was not able to make good by deeds against the disobedient; and he would have his adversaries *know this* (*v.* 11), that he would, by the exercise of his apostolical power committed to him, make it appear to have a real efficacy.

Verses 12–18

In these verses observe,

I. The apostle refuses to justify himself, or to act by such rules as the false apostles did, *v.* 12. He plainly intimates that they took a wrong method to commend themselves, in *measuring themselves by themselves, and comparing themselves among themselves,* which was *not wise.* They were pleased, and did pride themselves, in their own attainments, and never considered those who far exceeded them in gifts and graces, in power and authority; and this made them haughty and insolent. Note, If we would compare ourselves with others who excel us, this would be a good method to keep us humble; we should be pleased and thankful for what we have of gifts or graces, but never pride ourselves therein, as if there were none to be compared with us or that did excel us. The apostle would not be of the number of such vain men: let us resolve that we will not make ourselves of that number.

II. He fixes a better rule for his conduct, namely, *not to boast of things without his measure,* which was the measure *God had distributed* to him, *v.* 13. His meaning is, either that he would not boast of more gifts or graces, or power and authority, than God had really bestowed on him; or, rather, that he would not act beyond his commission as to persons or things, nor go beyond the line prescribed to him, which he plainly intimates the false apostles did, while they *boasted of other men's labors.* The apostle's resolution was to keep within his own province, and that compass of ground which God had marked out for him. His commission as an apostle was to preach the gospel every where, especially among the Gentiles, and he was not confined to one place; yet he observed the directions of Providence, and the Holy Spirit, as to the particular places whither he went or where he did abide.

III. He acted according to this rule: *We stretch not ourselves beyond our measure, v.* 14. And, particularly, he acted according to this rule in preaching at Corinth, and in the exercise of his apostolical authority there; for he came thither by divine direction, and there he converted many to Christianity; and, therefore, in boasting of them as his charge, he acted not contrary to his rule, he boasted not of *other men's labours, v.* 15.

IV. He declares his success in observing this rule. His hope was that their faith was increased, and that others beyond them, even in the remoter parts of Achaia, would embrace the gospel also; and in all this he exceeded not his commission, nor acted in another man's line.

V. He seems to check himself in this matter, as if he had spoken too much in his own praise. The unjust accusations and reflections of his enemies had made it needful he should justify himself; and the wrong methods they took gave him good occasion to mention the better rule he had observed: yet he is afraid of boasting, or taking any praise to himself, and therefore he mentions two things which ought to be regarded: — 1. *He that glorieth should glory in the Lord, v.* 17. If we are able to fix good rules for our conduct, or act by them, or have any good success in so doing, the praise and glory of all are owing unto God. Ministers in particular must be careful not to glory in their performances, but must give God the glory of their work, and the success thereof. 2. *Not he that commendeth himself is approved, but he whom the Lord commendeth, v.* 18. Of all flattery, self-flattery is the worst, and self-applause is seldom any better than self-flattery and self-deceit. At the best, self-commendation is no praise, and it is oftentimes as foolish and vain as it is proud; therefore, instead of praising or commending ourselves, we should strive to approve ourselves to God, and his approbation will be our best commendation.

CHAPTER 11

In this chapter the apostle goes on with his discourse, in opposition to the false apostles, who were very industrious to lessen his interest and reputation among the Corinthians, and had prevailed too much by their insinuations. I. He apologizes for going about to commend himself, and gives the reason for what he did (*v.* 1–4). II. He mentions, in his own necessary vindication, his equality with the other apostles, and with the false apostles in this particular of preaching the gospel to the Corinthians freely, without wages (*v.* 5–15). III. He makes another preface to what he was about further to say in his own justification (*v.* 16–21). And, IV. He gives a large account of his qualifications, labours, and sufferings, in which he exceeded the false apostles (*v.* 22 to the end).

Verses 1–4

Here we may observe, 1. The apology the apostle makes for going about to commend himself. He is loth to enter upon this subject of self-commendation: *Would to God you could bear with me a little in my folly, v.* 1. He calls this folly, because too often it is really no better. In his case it was necessary; yet, seeing others might apprehend it to be folly in him, he desires them to bear with it. Note, As much against the grain as it is with a proud man to acknowledge his infirmities, so much is it against the grain with a humble man to speak in his own praise. It is no pleasure to a good man to speak well of himself, yet in some cases it is lawful, namely, when it is for the advantage of others, or for our own necessary vindication; as thus it was here. For, 2. We have the reasons for what the apostle did. (1.) To preserve the Corinthians from being corrupted by the insinuations of the false apostles, *v.* 2, 3. He tells them *he was jealous over them with godly jealousy;* he was afraid lest their faith should be weakened by hearkening to such suggestions as tended to lessen their regard to his ministry, by which they were brought to the Christian faith. He had *espoused them to one husband,* that is, converted them to Christianity (and the conversion of a soul is its marriage to the Lord Jesus); and he was desirous to *present them as a chaste virgin* — pure, and spotless, and faithful, not having *their minds corrupted* with false doctrines by false teachers, as *Eve was beguiled by the subtlety of the serpent.* This godly jealousy in the apostle was a mixture of love and fear; and faithful ministers cannot but be afraid and concerned for their people, lest they should lose that which they have received, and turn from what they have embraced, especially when *deceivers have gone abroad,* or have *crept in among them.* (2.) To vindicate himself against the false apostles, forasmuch as they could not pretend they had another Jesus, or another Spirit, or another gospel, to preach to them, *v.* 4. If this had been the case, there would have been some colour of reason to bear with them, or to hearken to them. But seeing there is but one Jesus, one Spirit, and one gospel, that is, or at least that ought to be, preached to them and received by them, what reason could there be why the Corinthians should be prejudiced against him, who first converted them to the faith, by the artifices of any adversary? It was a just occasion of jealousy that such persons designed to preach another Jesus, another Spirit, and another gospel.

Verses 5–15

After the foregoing preface to what he was about to say, the apostle in these verses mentions,

I. His equality with the other apostles — that *he was not a whit behind the very chief of the apostles, v.* 5. This he expresses very modestly: *I suppose so.* He might have spoken very positively. The apostleship, as an office, was equal in all the apostles; but the apostles, like other Christians, differed one from another. These *stars differed one from another in glory,* and Paul was indeed of the first magnitude; yet he speaks modestly of himself, and humbly owns his personal infirmity, that he was *rude in speech,* had not such a graceful delivery as some others might have. Some think that he was a man of very low stature, and that his voice was proportionably small; others think that he may have had some impediment in his speech, perhaps a stammering tongue. However, he was not rude *in knowledge;* he was not unacquainted with the best rules of oratory and the art of persuasion, much less was he ignorant of the mysteries of the kingdom of heaven, as had been *thoroughly manifested among them.*

II. His equality with the false apostles in this particular — the preaching of the gospel unto them freely, without wages. This the apostle largely insists on, and shows that, as they could not but own him to be a minister of Christ, so they ought to acknowledge he had been a good friend to them. For, 1. He had preached the gospel to them freely, *v.* 7–10. He had proved at large, in his former epistle to them, the lawfulness of ministers' receiving maintenance from the people, and the duty of the people to give them an honourable maintenance; and here he says he himself had *taken wages of other churches* (*v.* 8), so that he had a right to have asked and received from them: yet he waived his right, and chose rather to abase himself, by working with his hands in the trade of tent-making to maintain himself, than be burdensome to them, that they might *be exalted,* or encouraged to receive the gospel, which they had so cheaply; yea, he chose rather to be supplied from Macedonia than to be chargeable unto them. 2. He informs them of the reason of this his conduct among them. It was not because *he did not love them* (*v.* 11), or was unwilling to receive tokens of their love (for love and friendship are manifested by mutual giving and receiving), but it was to avoid offence, that *he might cut off occasion from those that desired occasion.* He would not give occasion for any to accuse him of worldly designs in preaching the gospel, or that he intended to make a trade of it, to enrich himself; and that others who opposed him at Corinth might not in this respect gain an advantage against him: that wherein *they gloried,* as to this matter, *they might be found even as he, v.* 12. It is not improbable to suppose that the chief of the false teachers at Corinth, or some among them, were rich, and taught (or deceived) the people freely, and might accuse the apostle or his fellow-labourers as mercenary men, who received hire or wages, and therefore the apostle kept to his resolution not to be chargeable to any of the Corinthians.

III. The false apostles are charged *as deceitful workers* (*v.* 13), and that upon this account, because they would *transform themselves* into the likeness of the apostles of Christ, and, though they were the ministers of Satan, would seem to be the *ministers of righteousness.* They would be as industrious and as generous in promoting error as the apostles were in preaching truth; they would endeavour as much to undermine the kingdom of Christ as the apostles did to establish it. There were counterfeit prophets under the Old Testament, who wore the garb and learned the language of the prophets of the Lord. So there were counterfeit apostles under the New Testament, who seemed in many respects like the true apostles of Christ. And no marvel (says the apostle); hypocrisy is a thing not to be much wondered at in this world, especially when we consider the great influence Satan has upon the minds of many, who *rules in the hearts of the children of disobedience.* As he can turn himself into any shape, and put on almost any form, and look sometimes *like an angel of light,* in order to promote his kingdom of darkness, so he will teach his ministers and instruments to do the same. But it follows, *Their end is according to their works* (*v.* 15); the end will discover them to be deceitful workers, and their work will end in ruin and destruction.

Verses 16–21

Here we have a further excuse that the apostle makes for what he was about to say in his own vindication. 1. He would not have them think he was guilty of folly, in saying what he said to vindicate himself: *Let no man think me a fool, v.* 16. Ordinarily, indeed, it is unbecoming a wise man to be much and often speaking in his own praise. Boasting of ourselves is usually not only a sign of a proud mind, but a mark of folly also. However, says the apostle, yet *as a fool receive me;* that is, if you count it folly in me to *boast a little,* yet give due regard to what I shall say. 2. He mentions a caution, to prevent the abuse of what he should say, telling them that what he spoke, *he did not speak after the Lord, v.* 17. He would not have them think that boasting of ourselves, or glorying in what we have, is a thing commanded by the Lord in general unto Christians, nor yet that this is always necessary in our own vindication; though it may be lawfully used, because not contrary to the Lord, when, strictly speaking, it is not after the Lord. It is the duty and practice of Christians, in obedience to the command and example of the Lord, rather to humble and abase themselves; yet prudence must direct in what circumstances it is needful to do that which we may do lawfully, even speak of what God has wrought for us, and in us, and by us too. 3. He gives a good reason why they should suffer him to boast a little; namely, because they suffered others to do so who had less reason. *Seeing many glory after the flesh* (of carnal privileges, or outward advantages and attainments), *I will glory also, v.* 18. But he would not glory in those things, though he had as much or more reason than others to do so. But he gloried in his infirmities, as he tells them afterwards. The Corinthians thought themselves wise, and might think it an instance of wisdom to bear with the weakness of others, and therefore suffered others to do what might seem folly; therefore the apostle would have them bear with him. Or these words, *You suffer fools gladly, seeing you yourselves are wise* (*v.* 19), may be ironical, and then the meaning is this: "Notwithstanding all your wisdom, you willingly suffer yourselves to be *brought into bondage* under the Jewish yoke, or suffer others to tyrannize over you; nay, to *devour you,* or make a prey of you, and *take of you* hire for their own advantage, and to *exalt themselves* above you, and lord it over you; nay, even to *smite you on the face,* or impose upon you to your very faces (*v.* 20), upbraiding you while they reproach me, as if you had been very weak in showing regard to me," *v.* 21. Seeing this was the case, that the Corinthians, or some among them, could so easily bear all this from the false apostles, it was reasonable for the apostle to desire, and expect, they should bear with what might seem to them an indiscretion in him, seeing the circumstances of the case were such as made it needful that *whereinsoever any were bold* he should be *bold also, v.* 21.

Verses 22–33

Here the apostle gives a large account of his own qualifications, labours, and sufferings (not out of pride or vainglory, but to the honour of God, who had enabled him to do and suffer so much for the cause of Christ), and wherein he excelled the false apostles, who would lessen his character and usefulness among the Corinthians. Observe,

I. He mentions the privileges of his birth (*v.* 22), which were equal to any they could pretend to. He was a Hebrew of the Hebrews; of a family among the Jews that never intermarried with the Gentiles. He was also an Israelite, and could boast of his being descended from the beloved Jacob as well as they, and was also of the seed of Abraham, and not of the proselytes. It should seem from this that the false apostles were of the Jewish race, who gave disturbance to the Gentile converts.

II. He makes mention also of his apostleship, that he was more than an ordinary minister of Christ, *v.* 23. God had counted him faithful, and had put him into the ministry. He had been a useful minister of Christ unto them; they had found full proofs of his ministry: *Are they ministers of Christ? I am more so.*

III. He chiefly insists upon this, that he had been an extraordinary sufferer for Christ; and this was what he gloried in, or rather he gloried in the grace of God that had enabled him to be more *abundant in labours,* and to endure very great sufferings, such as *stripes above measure, frequent imprisonments,* and *often* the dangers of *death, v.* 23. Note, When the apostle would prove himself an extraordinary minister, he proves that he had been an extraordinary sufferer. Paul was the apostle of the Gentiles, and for that reason was hated of the Jews. They did all they could against him; and among the Gentiles also he met with hard usage. Bonds and imprisonments were familiar to him; never was the most notorious malefactor more frequently in the hands of public justice than Paul was for righteousness' sake. The jail and the whipping-post, and all other hard usages of those who are accounted the worst of men, were what he was accustomed to. As to the Jews, whenever he fell into their hands, they never spared him. *Five times* he fell under their lash, and received *forty stripes save one, v.* 24. Forty stripes was the utmost their law allowed (Deu. 25:3), but it was usual with them, that they might not exceed, to abate one at least of that number. And to have the abatement of one only was all the favour that ever Paul received from them. The Gentiles were not tied up to that moderation, and among them *he was thrice beaten with rods,* of which we may suppose once was at Philippi, Acts 16:22. *Once he was stoned* in a popular tumult, and was taken up for dead, Acts 14:19. He says that *thrice* he suffered shipwreck; and we may believe him, though the sacred history gives a relation but of one. *A night and a day he had been in the deep* (v. 25), in some deep dungeon or other, shut up as a prisoner. Thus he was all his days a constant confessor; perhaps scarcely a year of his life, after his conversion, passed without suffering some hardship or other for his religion; yet this was not all, for, wherever he went, he went in perils; he was exposed to perils of all sorts. If he journeyed by land, or voyaged by sea, he was in perils of robbers, or enemies of some sort; the Jews, his own countrymen, sought to kill him, or do him a mischief; the heathen, to whom he was sent, were not more kind to him, for among them he was in peril. If he was in the city, or in the wilderness, still he was in peril. He was in peril not only among avowed enemies, but among those also who called themselves brethren, but were false brethren, v. 26. Besides all this, he had great weariness and painfulness in his ministerial labours, and these are things that will come into account shortly, and people will be reckoned with for all the care and pains of their ministers concerning them. Paul was a stranger to wealth and plenty, power and pleasure, preferment and ease; he was in *watchings often*, and exposed to *hunger and thirst;* in *fastings often,* it may be out of necessity; and endured *cold and nakedness,* v. 27. Thus was he, who was one of the greatest blessings of the age, used as if he had been the burden of the earth, and the plague of his generation. And yet this is not all; for, as an apostle, the *care of all the churches* lay on him, v. 28. He mentions this last, as if this lay the heaviest upon him, and as if he could better bear all the persecutions of his enemies than the scandals that were to be found in the churches he had the oversight of. *Who is weak, and I am not weak? Who is offended, and I burn not? v.* 29. There was not a weak Christian with whom he did not sympathize, nor any one scandalized, but he was affected therewith. See what little reason we have to be in love with the pomp and plenty of this world, when this blessed apostle, one of the best of men that ever lived, excepting Jesus Christ, felt so much hardship in it. Nor was he ashamed of all this, but, on the contrary, it was what he accounted his honour; and therefore, much against the grain as it was with him to glory, yet, says he, *if I must needs glory,* if my adversaries will oblige me to it in my own necessary vindication, *I will glory in these my infirmities, v.* 30. Note, Sufferings for righteousness' sake will, the most of any thing, redound to our honour.

In the last two verses, he mentions one particular part of his sufferings out of its place, as if he had forgotten it before, or because the deliverance God wrought for him was most remarkable; namely, the danger he was in at Damascus, soon after he was converted, and not settled in Christianity, at least in the ministry and apostleship. This is recorded, Acts 9:24, 25. This was his first great danger and difficulty, and the rest of his life was a piece with this. And it is observable that, lest it should be thought he spoke more than was true, the apostle confirms this narrative with a solemn oath, or appeal to the omniscience of God, v. 31. It is a great comfort to a good man that *the God and Father of our Lord Jesus Christ,* who is an omniscient God, knows the truth of all he says, and knows all he does and all he suffers for his sake.

CHAPTER 12

In this chapter the apostle proceeds in maintaining the honour of his apostleship. He magnified his office when there were those who vilified it. What he says in his own praise was only in his own justification and the necessary defence of the honour of his ministry, the preservation of which was necessary to its success. First, He makes mention of the favour God had shown him, the honour done him, the methods God took to keep him humble, and the use he made of this dispensation (v. 1–10). Then he addresses himself to the Corinthians, blaming them for what was faulty among them, and giving a large account of his behaviour and kind intentions towards them (v. 11 to the end).

Verses 1–10

Here we may observe,

I. The narrative the apostle gives of the favours God had shown him, and the honour he had done him; for doubtless he himself is the man in Christ of whom he speaks. Concerning this we may take notice, 1. Of the honour itself which was done to the apostle: he was *caught up into the third heaven, v.* 2. When this was we cannot say, whether it was during those three days that he lay without sight at his conversion or at some other time afterwards, much less can we pretend to say *how* this was, whether by a separation of his soul from his body or by an extraordinary transport in the depth of contemplation. It would be presumption for us to deter-

mine, if not also to enquire into, this matter, seeing the apostle himself says, *Whether in the body or out of the body, I cannot tell.* It was certainly a very extraordinary honour done him: in some sense he was caught up into the *third heaven,* the heaven of the blessed, above the aerial heaven, in which the fowls fly, above the starry heaven, which is adorned with those glorious orbs: it was into the third heaven, where God most eminently manifests his glory. We are not capable of knowing all, nor is it fit we should know very much, of the particulars of that glorious place and state; it is our duty and interest to give diligence to make sure to ourselves a mansion there; and, if that be cleared up to us, then we should long to be removed thither, to abide there for ever. This third heaven is called paradise (v. 4), in allusion to the earthly paradise out of which Adam was driven for his transgression; it is called the paradise of God (Rev. 2:7), signifying to us that by Christ we are restored to all the joys and honours we lost by sin, yea, to much better. The apostle does not mention what he saw in the third heaven or paradise, but tells us that *he heard unspeakable words,* such as it is not possible for a man to utter — such are the sublimity of the matter and our unacquaintedness with the language of the upper world: nor was it lawful to utter those words, because, while we are here in this world, we have a more sure word of prophecy than such visions and revelations. 2 Pt. 1:19. We read of the tongue of angels as well as men, and Paul knew as much of that as ever any man upon earth did, and yet preferred charity, that is, the sincere love of God and our neighbour. This account which the apostle gives us of his vision should check our curious desires after forbidden knowledge, and teach us to improve the revelation God has given us in his word. Paul himself, who had been in the third heaven, did not publish to the world what he had heard there, but adhered to the doctrine of Christ: on this foundation the church is built, and on this we must build our faith and hope. 2. The modest and humble manner in which the apostle mentions this matter is observable. One would be apt to think that one who had had such visions and revelations as these would have boasted greatly of them; but, says he, *It is not expedient for me doubtless to glory, v.* 1. He therefore did not mention this immediately, nor till *above fourteen years* after, v. 2. And then it is not without some reluctancy, as a thing which in a manner he was forced to by the necessity of the case. Again, he speaks of himself in the third person, and does not say, I am the man who was thus honoured above other men. Again, his humility appears by the check he seems to put upon himself (v. 6), which plainly shows that he delighted not to dwell upon this theme. Thus was he, who was not behind the chief of the apostles in dignity, very eminent for his humility. Note, It is an excellent thing to have a lowly spirit in the midst of high advancements; and those who abase themselves shall be exalted.

II. The apostle gives an account of the methods God took to keep him humble, and to prevent his *being lifted up above measure;* and this he speaks of to balance the account that was given before of the visions and revelations he had had. Note, When God's people communicate their experiences, let them always remember to take notice of what God has done to keep them humble, as well as what he has done in favour to them and for their advancement. Here observe,

1. The apostle was pained with a thorn in the flesh, and buffeted with a messenger of Satan, v. 7. We are much in the dark what this was, whether some great trouble or some great temptation. Some think it was an acute bodily pain or sickness; others think it was the indignities done him by the false apostles, and the opposition he met with from them, particularly on the account of his speech, which was contemptible. However this was, God often brings this good out of evil, that the reproaches of our enemies help to hide pride from us; and this is certain, that what the apostle calls a thorn in his flesh was for a time very grievous to him: but the thorns Christ wore for us, and with which he was crowned, sanctify and make easy all the thorns in the flesh we may at any time be afflicted with; for *he suffered, being tempted, that he might be able to succour those that are tempted.* Temptations to sin are most grievous thorns; they are messengers of Satan, to buffet us. Indeed it is a great grievance to a good man to be so much as tempted to sin.

2. The design of this was to keep the apostle humble: *Lest he should be exalted above measure, v.* 7. Paul himself knew he *had not yet attained, neither was already perfect;* and yet he was in danger of being lifted up with pride. If God love

us, he will hide pride from us, and keep us from being exalted above measure; and spiritual burdens are ordered, to cure spiritual pride. This thorn in the flesh is said to be a messenger of Satan, which he did not send with a good design, but on the contrary, with ill intentions, to discourage the apostle (who had been so highly favoured of God) and hinder him in his work. But God designed this for good, and he overruled it for good, and made this messenger of Satan to be so far from being a hindrance that it was a help to the apostle.

3. The apostle prayed earnestly to God for the removal of this sore grievance. Note, Prayer is a salve for every sore, a remedy for every malady; and when we are afflicted with thorns in the flesh we should give ourselves to prayer. Therefore we are sometimes tempted that we may learn to pray. The apostle *besought the Lord thrice, that it might depart from him, v.* 8. Note, Though afflictions are sent for our spiritual benefit, yet we may pray to God for the removal of them: we ought indeed to desire also that they may reach the end for which they are designed. The apostle prayed earnestly, and repeated his requests; he besought the Lord *thrice,* that is, often. So that if an answer be not given to the first prayer, nor to the second, we must hold on, and hold out, till we receive an answer. Christ himself prayed to his Father thrice. As troubles are sent to teach us to pray, so they are continued to teach us to continue instant in prayer.

4. We have an account of the answer given to the apostle's prayer, that, although the trouble was not removed, yet an equivalent should be granted: *My grace is sufficient for thee.* Note, (1.) Though God accepts the prayer of faith, yet he does not always answer it in the letter; as he sometimes grants in wrath, so he sometimes denies in love. (2.) When God does not remove our troubles and temptations, yet, if he gives us grace sufficient for us, we have no reason to complain, nor to say that he deals ill by us. It is a great comfort to us, whatever thorns in the flesh we are pained with, that God's grace is sufficient for us. Grace signifies two things: — [1.] The goodwill of God towards us, and this is enough to enlighten and enliven us, sufficient to strengthen and comfort us, to support our souls and cheer up our spirits, in all afflictions and distresses. [2.] The good work of God in us, the grace we receive from the fulness that is in Christ our head; and from him there shall be communicated that which is suitable and seasonable, and sufficient for his members. Christ Jesus understands our case, and knows our need, and will proportion the remedy to our malady, and not only strengthen us, but glorify *himself. His strength is made perfect in our weakness.* Thus his grace is manifested and magnified; he ordains his praise out of the mouths of babes and sucklings.

III. Here is the use which the apostle makes of this dispensation: *He gloried in his infirmities* (v. 9), and took pleasure in them, v. 10. He does not mean his sinful infirmities (those we have reason to be ashamed of and grieved at), but he means his afflictions, his reproaches, necessities, persecutions, and distresses for Christ's sake, v. 10. And the reason of his glory and joy on account of these things was this — they were fair opportunities for Christ to manifest the power and sufficiency of his grace resting upon him, by which he had so much experience of the strength of divine grace that he could say, *When I am weak, then am I strong.* This is a Christian paradox: when we are weak in ourselves, then we are strong in the grace of our Lord Jesus Christ; when we see ourselves weak in ourselves, then we go out of ourselves to Christ, and are qualified to receive strength from him, and experience most of the supplies of divine strength and grace.

Verses 11–21

In these verses the apostle addresses himself to the Corinthians two ways: —

I. He blames them for what was faulty in them; namely, that they had not stood up in his defence as they ought to have done, and so made it the more needful for him to insist so much on his own vindication. They in manner compelled him to commend himself, who *ought to have been commended of them v.* 11. And had they, or some among them, not failed on their part, it would have been less needful for him to have said so much on his own behalf. He tells them further that they in particular had good reason to speak well of him, as being *in nothing behind the very chief apostles,* because he had given them full proof and evidence of his apostleship; for *the signs of an apostle were wrought among them in all patience, in signs, and wonders, and mighty deeds.*

Note, 1. It is a debt we owe to good men to stand up in the defence of their reputation; and we are under special obligations to those we have received benefit by, especially spiritual benefit, to own them as instruments in God's hand of good to us, and to vindicate them when they are calumniated by others. 2. How much soever we are, or ought to be, esteemed by others, we ought always to think humbly of ourselves. See an example of this in this great apostle, who thought himself to be nothing, though in truth he was not behind the greatest apostles — so far was he from seeking praise from men, though he tells them their duty to vindicate his reputation — so far was he from applauding himself, when he was forced to insist upon his own necessary self-defence.

II. He gives a large account of his behaviour and kind intentions towards them, in which we may observe the character of a faithful minister of the gospel. 1. He was not willing to be burdensome to them, nor did he seek theirs, but them. He says (*v.* 13) he had not been burdensome to them, for the time past, and tells them (*v.* 14) he would not be burdensome to them for the time to come, when he should come to them. He spared their purses, and did not covet their money: *I seek not yours but you.* He sought not to enrich himself, but to save their souls: he did not desire to make a property of them to himself, but to gain them over to Christ, whose servant he was. Note, Those who aim at clothing themselves with the fleece of the flock, and take no care of the sheep, are hirelings, and not good shepherds. 2. He would gladly spend and be spent for them (*v.* 15); that is, he was willing to take pains and to suffer loss for their good. He would spend his time, his parts, his strength, his interest, his all, to do them service; nay, so spend as to be spent, and be like a candle, which consumes itself to give light to others. 3. He did not abate in his love to them, notwithstanding their unkindness and ingratitude to him; and therefore was contented and glad to take pains with them, though *the more abundantly he loved them the less he was loved, v.* 15. This is applicable to other relations: if others be wanting in their duty to us it does not follow therefore that we may neglect our duty to them. 4. He was careful not only that he himself should not be burdensome, but that none he employed should. This seems to be the meaning of what we read, *v.* 16–18. If it should be objected by any that though he did not himself burden them, *yet, being crafty, he caught them with guile,* that is, he sent those among them who pillaged them, and afterwards he shared with them in the profit: "This was not so," says the apostle; "I did not make a gain of you myself, nor by any of those whom I sent; nor did Titus, nor any others — We walked by the same spirit and in the same steps." They all agreed in this matter to do them all the good they could, without being burdensome to them, to promote the gospel among them and make it as easy to them as possible. Or, this may be read with an interrogation, as utterly disclaiming any guile in himself and others towards them. 5. He was a man who did all things for edifying, *v.* 19. This was his great aim and design, to do good, to lay the foundation well, and then with care and diligence to build the superstructure. 6. He would not shrink from his duty for fear of displeasing them, though he was so careful to make himself easy to them. Therefore he was resolved to be faithful in reproving sin, though he was therein *found to be such as they would not, v.* 20. The apostle here mentions several sins that are too commonly found among professors of religion, and are very reprovable: *debates, envyings, wraths, strifes, backbitings, whisperings, swellings, tumults;* and, though those who are guilty of these sins can hardly bear to be reproved for them, yet faithful ministers must not fear offending the guilty by sharp reproofs, as they are needful, in public and in private. 7. He was grieved at the apprehension that he should find scandalous sins among them not duly repented of. This, he tells them, would be the cause of great humiliation and lamentation. Note, (1.) The falls and miscarriages of professors cannot but be a humbling consideration to a good minister; and God sometimes takes this way to humble those who might be under temptation to be lifted up: *I fear lest my God will humble me among you.* (2.) We have reason to bewail those who sin and do not repent, to *bewail many that have sinned, and have not repented, v.* 21. If these have not, as yet, grace to mourn and lament their own case, their case is the more lamentable; and those who love God, and love them, should mourn for them.

CHAPTER 13

In this chapter the apostle threatens to be severe against obstinate sinners, and assigns the reason thereof (*v.* 1–6); then he makes a suitable prayer to God on the behalf of the Corinthians, with the reasons inducing him thereto (*v.* 7–10), and concludes his epistle with a valediction and a benediction (*v.* 11–14).

Verses 1–6

In these verses observe,

I. The apostle threatens to be severe against obstinate sinners when he should come to Corinth, having now sent to them a first and second epistle, with proper admonitions and exhortations, in order to reform what was amiss among them. Concerning this we may notice, 1. The caution with which he proceeded in his censures: he was not hasty in using severity, but gave a first and second admonition. So some understand his words (*v.* 1): *This is the third time I am coming to you,* referring to his first and second epistles, by which he admonished them, as if he were present with them, though in person he was absent, *v.* 2. According to this interpretation, these two epistles are the witnesses he means in the first verse, referring rather to the direction of our Saviour (Mt. 17:16) concerning the manner how Christians should deal with offenders before they proceed to extremity than to the law of Moses (Deu. 17:6; 19:15) for the behaviour of judges in criminal matters. We should go, or send, to our brother, once and again, to tell him of his fault. Thus the apostle had told these Corinthians before, in his former epistle, and now he tells them, or *writes to those who heretofore had sinned, and to all others,* giving warning unto all before he came in person *the third time,* to exercise severity against scandalous offenders. Others think that the apostle had designed and prepared for his journey to Corinth twice already, but was providentially hindered, and now informs them of his intentions a third time to come to them. However this be, it is observable that he kept an account how often he endeavoured, and what pains he took with these Corinthians for their good: and we may be sure that an account is kept in heaven, and we must be reckoned with another day for the helps we have had for our souls, and how we have improved them. 2. The threatening itself: *That if* (or when) *he came again* (in person) *he would not spare* obstinate sinners, and such as were impenitent, in their scandalous enormities. He had told them before, he feared *God would humble him among them,* because he should find some who *had sinned and had not repented;* and now he declares he would not spare such, but would inflict church-censures upon them, which are thought to have been accompanied in those early times with visible and extraordinary tokens of divine displeasure. Note, Though it is God's gracious method to bear long with sinners, yet he will not bear always; at length he will come, and will not spare those who remain obstinate and impenitent, notwithstanding all his methods to reclaim and reform them.

II. The apostle assigns a reason why he would be thus severe, namely, for *a proof of Christ's speaking in him,* which they *sought after, v.* 3. The evidence of his apostleship was necessary for the credit, confirmation, and success, of the gospel he preached; and therefore such as denied this were justly and severely to be censured. It was the design of the false teachers to make the Corinthians call this matter into question, of which yet they had not weak, but strong and mighty proofs (*v.* 3), notwithstanding the mean figure he made in the world and the contempt which by some was cast upon him. Even as Christ himself *was crucified through weakness,* or appeared in his crucifixion as a weak and contemptible person, *but liveth by the power of God,* or in his resurrection and life manifests his divine power (*v.* 4), so the apostles, how mean and contemptible soever they appeared to the world, did yet, as instruments, manifest the power of God, and particularly the power of his grace, in converting the world to Christianity. And therefore, as a proof to those who among the *Corinthians sought a proof of* Christ's speaking in the apostle, he puts them upon proving their Christianity (*v.* 5): *Examine yourselves,* etc. Hereby he intimates that, if they could prove their own Christianity, this would be a proof of his apostleship; for if they were in the faith, if Jesus Christ was in them, this was a proof that Christ spoke in him, because it was by his ministry that they did believe. He had been not only an instructor, but a father to them. He had begotten them again by the gospel of Christ. Now it could not be imagined that a divine power should go along with his ministrations if he had not his commission from on high. If therefore they could prove themselves *not to be reprobates,* not to be rejected of Christ, *he trusted they would know that he was not a reprobate* (*v.* 6), not disowned by Christ. What the apostle here says of the duty of the Corinthians to *examine themselves,* etc., with the particular view already mentioned, is applicable to the great duty of all who call themselves Christians, to examine themselves concerning their spiritual state. We should examine whether we be in the faith, because it is a matter in which we may be easily deceived, and wherein a deceit is highly dangerous: we are therefore concerned to *prove our own selves,* to put the question to our own souls, whether Christ be in us, or not; and *Christ is in us, except we be reprobates:* so that either we are true Christians or we are great cheats; and what a reproachful thing is it for a man not to know himself, not to know his own mind!

Verses 7–10

Here we have,

I. The apostle's prayer to God on the behalf of the Corinthians, that they might *do no evil, v.* 7. This is the most desirable thing we can ask of God, both for ourselves and for our friends, to be kept from sin, that we and they may do no evil; and it is most needful that we often pray to God for his grace to keep us, because without this we cannot keep ourselves. We are more concerned to pray that we may not do evil than that we may not suffer evil.

II. The reasons why the apostle put up this prayer to God on behalf of the Corinthians, which reasons have a special reference to their case, and the subject-matter about which he was writing to them. Observe, he tells them, 1. It was not so much for his own personal reputation as for the honour of religion: *"Not that we should appear approved, but that you should do that which is honest,* or decent, and for the credit of religion, though we should be reproached and vilified, and accounted as reprobates," *v.* 7. Note, (1.) The great desire of faithful ministers of the gospel is that the gospel they preach may be honoured, however their persons may be vilified. (2.) The best way to adorn our holy religion is *to do that which is honest,* and of good report, to walk as becomes the gospel of Christ. 2. Another reason was this: that they might be free from all blame and censure when he should come to them. This is intimated in *v.* 8, *We can do nothing against the truth, but for the truth.* If therefore they did not do evil, nor act contrary to their profession of the gospel, the apostle had no power nor authority to punish them. He had said before (*ch.* 10:8) and says here (*v.* 10) that the power which the Lord had given him was to edification, not to destruction; so that, although the apostle had great powers committed to him for the credit and advancement of the gospel, yet he could not do anything to the disparagement of the truth, nor the discouragement of those who obeyed it. He could not, that is, he would not, he dared not, he had no commission to act against the truth; and it is remarkable how the apostle did rejoice in this blessed impotency: *"We are glad,"* says he (*v.* 9), *"when we are weak and you are strong;* that is, that we have no power to censure those who are strong in faith and fruitful in good works." Some understand this passage thus: "Though we are weak through persecutions and contempt, we bear it patiently, and also joyfully, while we see that you are strong, that you are prosperous in holiness, and persevering in well-doing." For, 3. He desired their perfection (*v.* 9); that is, that they might be sincere, and aim at perfection (sincerity is our gospel-perfection), or else he wished there might be a thorough reformation among them. He not only desired that they might be kept from sin, but also that they might grow in grace, and increase in holiness, and that all that was amiss among them might be rectified and reformed. This was the great end of his writing this epistle, and that freedom he used with them by *writing these things* (those friendly admonitions and warnings), *being absent, that so, being present, he should not use sharpness* (*v.* 10), that is, not proceed to the utmost extremity in the exercise of the power which the Lord had given him as an apostle, *to revenge all disobedience, ch.* 10:6.

Verses 11–14

Thus the apostle concludes this epistle with,

I. A valediction. He gives them a parting farewell, and takes his leave of them for the present, with hearty good wishes for their spiritual welfare. In order to this,

1. He gives them several good exhortations. (1.) To be per-

fect, or to be knit together in love, which would tend greatly to their advantage as a church, or Christian society. (2.) To be of good comfort under all the sufferings and persecutions they might endure for the cause of Christ or any calamities and disappointments they might meet with in the world. (3.) To be of one mind, which would greatly tend to their comfort; for the more easy we are with our brethren the more ease we shall have in our own souls. The apostle would have them, as far as was possible, to be of the same opinion and judgment; however, if this could not be attained, yet, (4.) He exhorts them to live in peace, that difference in opinion should not cause an alienation of affections — that they should be at peace among themselves. He would have all the schisms that were among them healed, that there should be no more contention and wrath found among them, to prevent which they should avoid *debates, envyings, backbitings, whisperings,* and such like enemies to peace.

2. He encourages them with the promise of God's presence among them: *The God of love and peace shall be with you, v.* 11. Note, (1.) God is the God of love and peace.

He is the author of peace, and lover of concord. He hath loved us, and is willing to be at peace with us; he commands us to love him, and to be reconciled to him, and also that we love one another, and be at peace among ourselves. (2.) God will be with those who live in love and peace. He will love those who love peace; he will dwell with them here, and they shall dwell with him for ever. Such shall have God's gracious presence here, and be admitted to his glorious presence hereafter.

3. He gives directions to them to salute each other, and sends kind salutations to them from those who were with him, *v.* 12, 13. He would have them testify their affection to one another by the sacred rite of a kiss of charity, which was then used, but has long been disused, to prevent all occasions of wantonness and impurity, in the more declining and degenerate state of the church.

II. The apostolical benediction (*v.* 14): *The grace of the Lord Jesus Christ, and the love of God, and the communion of the Holy Ghost, be with you all.* Thus the apostle concludes his epistle, and thus it is usual and proper to dismiss worshipping assemblies. This plainly proves the doctrine of the gospel, and is an acknowledgment that Father, Son, and Spirit, are three distinct persons, yet but one God; and herein the same, that they are the fountain of all blessings to men. It likewise intimates our duty, which is to have an eye by faith to Father, Son, and Holy Ghost — to live in a continual regard to the three persons in the Trinity, into whose name we were baptized, and in whose name we are blessed. This is a very solemn benediction, and we should give all diligence to inherit this blessing. The grace of Christ, the love of God, and the communion (or communication) of the Holy Ghost: the grace of Christ as Redeemer, the love of God who sent the Redeemer, and all the communications of this grace and love, which come to us by the Holy Ghost; it is the communications of the Holy Ghost that qualify us for an interest in the grace of Christ, and the love of God: and we can desire no more to make us happy than the grace of Christ, the love of God, and the communion of the Holy Ghost. *Amen.*

AN EXPOSITION, WITH PRACTICAL OBSERVATIONS, OF
THE EPISTLE OF ST. PAUL TO THE GALATIANS

This epistle of Paul is directed not to the church or churches of a single city, as some others are, but of a country or province, for so Galatia was. It is very probable that these Galatians were first converted to the Christian faith by his ministry; or, if he was not the instrument of planting, yet at least he had been employed in watering these churches, as is evident from this epistle itself, and also from Acts 18:23, where we find him going over all the country of Galatia and Phrygia in order, strengthening all the disciples. While he was with them, they had expressed the greatest esteem and affection both for his person and ministry; but he had not been long absent from them before some judaizing teachers got in among them, by whose arts and insinuations they were soon drawn into a meaner opinion both of the one and of the other. That which these false teachers chiefly aimed at was to draw them off from the truth as it is in Jesus, particularly in the great doctrine of justification, which they grossly perverted, by asserting the necessity of joining the observance of the law of Moses with faith in Christ in order to it: and, the better to accomplish this their design, they did all they could to lessen the character and reputation of the apostle, and to raise up their own on the ruins of his, representing him as one who, if he was to be owned as an apostle, yet was much inferior to others, and particularly who deserved not such a

regard as Peter, James, and John, whose followers, it is likely, they pretended to be: and in both these attempts they had but too great success. This was the occasion of his writing this epistle, wherein he expresses his great concern that they had suffered themselves to be so soon turned aside from the faith of the gospel, vindicates his own character and authority as an apostle against the aspersions of his enemies, showing that his mission and doctrine were both divine, and that he was not, upon any account, *behind the very chief of the apostles,* 2 Co. 11:5. He then sets himself to assert and maintain the great gospel doctrine of justification by faith without the works of the law, and to obviate some difficulties that might be apt to arise in their minds concerning it: and, having established this important doctrine, he exhorts them to stand fast in the liberty wherewith Christ had made them free, cautions them against the abuse of this liberty, gives them several very needful counsels and directions and then concludes the epistle by giving them a just description of those false teachers by whom they had been ensnared, and, on the contrary, of his own temper and behaviour. In all this his great scope and design were to recover those who had been perverted, to settle those who might be wavering, and to confirm such among them as had kept their integrity.

CHAPTER 1

In this chapter, after the preface or introduction (*v.* 1–5), the apostle severely reproves these churches for their defection from the faith (*v.* 6–9), and then proves his own apostleship, which his enemies had brought them to question, I. From his end and design in preaching the gospel (*v.* 10). II. From his having received it by immediate revelation (*v.* 11, 12). For the proof of which he acquaints them, 1. What his former conversation was (*v.* 13, 14). 2. How he was converted, and called to the apostleship (*v.* 15, 16). 3. How he behaved himself afterwards (*v.* 16 to the end).

Verses 1–5

In these verses we have the preface or introduction to the epistle, where observe,

I. The person or persons from whom this epistle is sent — from Paul *an apostle,* etc., *and all the brethren that were with him.* 1. The epistle is sent from Paul; he only was the penman of it. And, because there were some among the Galatians who endeavoured to lessen his character and authority, in the front of it he gives a general account both of his office and of the manner in which he was called to it, which afterwards, in this and the following chapter, he enlarges more upon. As to his office, he was an apostle. He is not afraid to style himself so, though his enemies would scarcely allow him this title: and, to let them see that he did not assume this character without just ground, he acquaints them how he was called to this dignity and office, and assures them that his commission to it was wholly divine, for he was an apostle, *not of man, neither by man;* he had not the common call of an ordinary minister, but an extraordinary call from heaven to this office. He neither received his qualification for it, nor his designation to it, by the mediation of men, but had both the one and the other directly from above; for he was an apostle *by Jesus Christ,* he had his instructions and commission immediately from him, and consequently from *God the Father,* who was one with him in respect of his divine nature,

and who had appointed him, as Mediator, to be the apostle and high priest of our profession, and as such to authorize others to this office. He adds, *Who raised him from the dead,* both to acquaint us that herein God the Father gave a public testimony to Christ's being his Son and the promised Messiah, and also that, as his call to the apostleship was immediately from Christ, so it was after his resurrection from the dead, and when he had entered upon his exalted state; so that he had reason to look upon himself, not only as standing upon a level with the other apostles, but as in some sort preferred above them; for, whereas they were called by him when on earth, he had his call from him when in heaven. Thus does the apostle, being constrained to it by his adversaries, magnify his office, which shows that though men should by no means be proud of any authority they are possessed of, yet at certain times and upon certain occasions it may become needful to assert it. But, 2. He joins all the brethren that were with him in the inscription of the epistle, and writes in their name as well as his own. By *the brethren that were with him* may be understood either the Christians in common of that place where he now was, or such as were employed as ministers of the gospel. These, notwithstanding his own superior character and attainments, he is ready to own as his brethren; and, though he alone wrote the epistle, yet he joins them with himself in the inscription of it. Herein, as he shows his own great modesty and humility, and how remote he was from an assuming temper, so he might do this to dispose these churches to a greater regard to what he wrote, since hereby it would appear that he had their concurrence with him in the doctrine which he had preached, and was now about to confirm, and that it was no other than what was both published and professed by others as well as himself.

II. To whom this epistle is sent — *to the churches of Galatia.* There were several churches at that time in this country, and it should seem that all of them were more or less corrupted through the arts of those seducers who had crept in among them; and therefore Paul, on whom *came daily the care of all the churches,* being deeply affected with their state, and concerned for their recovery to the faith and establishment in it, writes this epistle to them. He directs it to all of them, as being all more or less concerned in the matter of it; and he gives them the name of *churches,* though they had done enough to forfeit it, for corrupt churches are never allowed to be churches: no doubt there were some among them who still continued in the faith, and he was not without hope that others might be recovered to it.

III. The apostolical benediction. *v.* 3. Herein the apostle, and the brethren who were with him, wish these churches *grace and peace from God the Father, and from the Lord Jesus Christ.* This is the usual blessing wherewith he blesses the churches in the name of the Lord — *grace and peace.* Grace includes God's good-will towards us and his good work upon us; and peace implies in it all that inward comfort, or outward prosperity, which is really needful for us; and they come from God the Father as the fountain, through Jesus Christ as the channel of conveyance. Both these the apostle wishes for these Christians. But we may observe, First grace, and then peace, for there can be no true peace without grace. Having mentioned the Lord Jesus Christ, he cannot pass without enlarging upon his love; and therefore adds (*v.* 4), *Who gave himself for our sins, that he might deliver,* etc. Jesus Christ gave himself for our sins, as a great sacrifice to make atonement for us; this the justice of God required, and to this he freely submitted for our sakes. One great end hereof was *to deliver us from this present evil world;* not only to redeem us from the wrath of God, and the curse of the law, but also to recover us from the corruption that is in the world through lust, and to rescue us from the vicious practices and customs of it, unto which we are naturally enslaved; and possibly also to set us free from the Mosaic constitution, for so *aiōn houtos* is used, 1 Co. 2:6, 8. From this we may note, 1. This present world is an evil world: it has become so by the sin of man, and it is so on account of the sin and sorrow with which it abounds and the many snares and temptations to which we are exposed as long as we continue in it. But, 2. Jesus Christ has died to deliver us from this present evil world, not presently to remove his people out of it, but to rescue them from the power of it, to keep them from the evil of it, and in due time to possess them of another and better world. This, the apostle informs us, he has done *according to the will of God and our Father.* In offering up himself a sacrifice for this end and purpose, he acted by the appointment of the Father, as well as with his own free consent; and therefore we have the greatest reason to depend upon the efficacy and acceptableness of what he has done and suffered for us; yea, hence we have encouragement to look upon God as our Father, for thus the apostle here represents him: as he is the Father of our Lord Jesus, so in and through him he is also the Father of all true believers, as our blessed Saviour himself acquaints us (Jn. 20:17), when he tells his disciples that he was ascending to his Father and their Father.

The apostle, having thus taken notice of the great love wherewith Christ hath loved us, concludes this preface with a solemn ascription of praise and glory to him (*v.* 5): *To whom be glory for ever and ever. Amen.* Intimating that on this account he is justly entitled to our highest esteem and regard. Or this doxology may be considered as referring both to God the Father and our Lord Jesus Christ, from whom he had just before been wishing grace and peace. They are both the proper objects of our worship and adoration, and all honour and glory are perpetually due to them, both on account of their own infinite excellences, and also on account of the blessings we receive from them.

Verses 6–9

Here the apostle comes to the body of the epistle; and he begins it with a more general reproof of these churches for their unsteadiness in the faith, which he afterwards, in some following parts of it, enlarges more upon. Here we may observe,

I. How much he was concerned at their defection: *I marvel,* etc. It filled him at once with the greatest surprise and sorrow. Their sin and folly were that they did not hold fast the doctrine of Christianity as it had been preached to them, but suffered themselves to be removed from the purity and simplicity of it. And there were several things by which their defection was greatly aggravated; as, 1. That they were *removed from him that had called them;* not only from the apostle, who had been the instrument of calling them into the fellowship of the gospel, but from God himself, by whose order and direction the gospel was preached to them, and they were invited to a participation of the privileges of it: so that herein they had been guilty of a great abuse of his kindness and mercy towards them. 2. That they had been *called into the grace of Christ.* As the gospel which had been preached to them was the most glorious discovery of divine grace and mercy in Christ Jesus; so thereby they had been called to partake of the greatest blessings and benefits, such as justification, and reconciliation with God here, and eternal life and happiness hereafter. These our Lord Jesus has purchased for us at the expense of his precious blood, and freely bestows upon all who sincerely accept of him: and therefore, in proportion to the greatness of the privilege they enjoyed, such were their sin and folly in deserting it and suffering themselves to be drawn off from the established way of obtaining these blessings. 3. That they were *so soon removed.* In a very little time they lost that relish and esteem of this grace of Christ which they seemed to have, and too easily fell in with those who taught justification by the works of the law, as many did, who had been bred up in the opinions and notions of the Pharisees, which they mingled with the doctrine of Christ, and so corrupted it; and this, as it was an instance of their weakness, so it was a further aggravation of their guilt. 4. That they were removed to *another gospel, which yet was not another.* Thus the apostle represents the doctrine of these judaizing teachers; he calls it another gospel, because it opened a different way of justification and salvation from that which was revealed in the gospel, namely, by works, and not by faith in Christ. And yet he adds, *"Which is not another* — you will find it to be no gospel at all — not really another gospel, but the perverting of the gospel of Christ,

and the overturning of the foundations of that" — whereby he intimates that those who go about to establish any other way to heaven than what the gospel of Christ has revealed are guilty of a gross perversion of it, and in the issue will find themselves wretchedly mistaken. Thus the apostle endeavours to impress upon these Galatians a due sense of their guilt in forsaking the gospel way of justification; and yet at the same time he tempers his reproof with mildness and tenderness towards them, and represents them as rather drawn into it by the arts and industry of some that troubled them than as coming into it of their own accord, which, though it did not excuse them, yet was some extenuation of their fault. And hereby he teaches us that, in reproving others, as we should be faithful, so we should also be gentle, and endeavour *to restore them in the spirit of meekness,* ch. 6:1.

II. How confident he was that the gospel he had preached to them was the only true gospel. He was so fully persuaded of this that he pronounced an anathema upon those who pretended to preach any other gospel (*v.* 8), and, to let them see that this did not proceed from any rashness or intemperate zeal in him, he repeated it, *v.* 9. This will not justify our thundering out anathemas against those who differ from us in minor things. It is only against those who forge a new gospel, who overturn the foundation of the covenant of grace, by setting up the works of the law in the place of Christ's righteousness, and corrupting Christianity with Judaism, that Paul denounces this. He puts the case: "Suppose we should preach any other gospel; nay, suppose an angel from heaven should:" not as if it were possible for an angel from heaven to be the messenger of a lie; but it is expressed so the more to strengthen what he was about to say. "If you have any other gospel preached to you by any other person, under our name, or under colour of having it from an angel himself, you must conclude that you are imposed upon: and whoever preaches another gospel lays himself under a curse, and is in danger of laying you under it too."

Verses 10–24

What Paul had said more generally, in the preface of this epistle, he now proceeds more particularly to enlarge upon. There he had declared himself to be an apostle of Christ; and here he comes more directly to support his claim to that character and office. There were some in the churches of Galatia who were prevailed with to call this in question; for those who preached up the ceremonial law did all they could to lessen Paul's reputation, who preached the pure gospel of Christ to the Gentiles: and therefore he here sets himself to prove the divinity both of his mission and doctrine, that thereby he might wipe off the aspersions which his enemies had cast upon him, and recover these Christians into a better opinion of the gospel he had preached to them. This he gives sufficient evidence of,

I. From the scope and design of his ministry, which was *not to persuade men, but God,* etc. The meaning of this may be either that in his preaching the gospel he did not act in obedience to men, but God, who had called him to this work and office; or that his aim therein was to bring persons to the obedience, not of men, but of God. As he professed to act by a commission from God; so that which he chiefly aimed at was to promote his glory, by recovering sinners into a state of subjection to him. And as this was the great end he was pursuing, so, agreeably hereunto, *he did not seek to please men.* He did not, in his doctrine, accommodate himself to the humours of persons, either to gain their affection or to avoid their resentment; but his great care was to approve himself to God. The judaizing teachers, by whom these churches were corrupted, had discovered a very different temper; they mixed works with faith, and the law with the gospel, only to please the Jews, whom they were willing to court and keep in with, that they might escape persecution. But Paul was a man of another spirit; he was not so solicitous to please them, nor to mitigate their rage against him, as to alter the doctrine of Christ either to gain their favour or to avoid their fury. And he gives this very good reason for it, that, *if he yet pleased men, he would not be the servant of Christ.* These he knew were utterly inconsistent, and that no man could serve two such masters; and therefore, though he would not needlessly displease any, yet he dared not allow himself to gratify men at the expense of his faithfulness to Christ. Thus, from the sincerity of his aims and intentions in the discharge of his office, he proves that he was truly an apostle of Christ. And from this his temper and behaviour we may note, 1. That

the great end which ministers of the gospel should aim at is to bring men to God. 2. That those who are faithful will not seek to please men, but to approve themselves to God. 3. That they must not be solicitous to please men, if they would approve themselves faithful servants to Christ. But, if this argument should not be thought sufficient, he goes on to prove his apostleship,

II. From the manner wherein he received the gospel which he preached to them, concerning which he assures them (*v.* 11, 12) that he had it not by information from others, but by revelation from heaven. One thing peculiar in the character of an apostle was that he had been called to, and instructed for, this office immediately by Christ himself. And in this he here shows that he was by no means defective, whatever his enemies might suggest to the contrary. Ordinary ministers, as they receive their call to preach the gospel by the mediation of others, so it is by means of the instruction and assistance of others that they are brought to the knowledge of it. But Paul acquaints them that he had his knowledge of the gospel, as well as his authority to preach it, directly from the Lord Jesus: the gospel which he preached was not *after man; he neither received it of man, nor was he taught it by man,* but by immediate inspiration, or revelation from Christ himself. This he was concerned to make out, to prove himself an apostle: and to this purpose,

1. He tells them what his education was, and what, accordingly, his conversation in time past had been, *v.* 13, 14. Particularly, he acquaints them that he had been brought up in the Jewish religion, and *that he had profited in it above many his equals of his own nation* — that *he had been exceedingly zealous of the traditions of the elders,* such doctrines and customs as had been invented by their fathers, and conveyed down from one generation to another; yea, to such a degree that, in his zeal for them, *he had beyond measure persecuted the church of God, and wasted it.* He had not only been a rejecter of the Christian religion, notwithstanding the many evident proofs that were given of its divine origin; but he had been a persecutor of it too, and had applied himself with the utmost violence and rage to destroy the professors of it. This Paul often takes notice of, for the magnifying of that free and rich grace which had wrought so wonderful a change in him, whereby of so great a sinner he was made a sincere penitent, and from a persecutor had become an apostle. And it was very fit to mention it here; for it would hence appear that he was not led to Christianity, as many others are, purely by education, since he had been bred up in an enmity and opposition to it; and they might reasonably suppose that it must be something very extraordinary which had made so great a change in him, which had conquered the prejudices of his education, and brought him not only to profess, but to preach, that doctrine, which he had before so vehemently opposed.

2. In how wonderful a manner he was turned from the error of his ways, brought to the knowledge and faith of Christ, and appointed to the office of an apostle, *v.* 15, 16. This was not done in an ordinary way, nor by ordinary means, but in an extraordinary manner; for, (1.) God had *separated him hereunto from his mother's womb:* the change that was wrought in him was in pursuance of a divine purpose concerning him, whereby he was appointed to be a Christian and an apostle, before he came into the world, or had done either good or evil. (2.) he was *called by his grace.* All who are savingly converted are called by the grace of God; their conversion is the effect of his good pleasure concerning them, and is effected by his power and grace in them. But there was something peculiar in the case of Paul, both in the suddenness and in the greatness of the change wrought in him, and also in the manner wherein it was effected, which was not by the mediation of others, as the instruments of it, but by Christ's personal appearance to him, and immediate operation upon him, whereby it was rendered a more special and extraordinary instance of divine power and favour. (3.) He had Christ *revealed in him.* He was not only revealed to him, but in him. It will but little avail us to have Christ revealed to us if he is not also revealed in us; but this was not the case of Paul. It pleased God *to reveal his Son in him,* to bring him to the knowledge of Christ and his gospel by special and immediate revelation. And, (4.) It was with this design, that he should preach him among the heathen; not only that he should embrace him himself, but preach him to others; so that he was both a Christian and an apostle by revelation.

3. He acquaints them how he behaved himself hereupon, from *v.* 16, to the end. Being thus called to his work and office, *he conferred not with flesh and blood.* This may be taken more generally, and so we may learn from it that, when God calls us by his grace, we must not consult flesh and blood. But the meaning of it here is that he did not consult men; he did not apply to any others for their advice and direction; *neither did he go up to Jerusalem, to those that were apostles before him,* as though he needed to be approved by them, or to receive any further instructions or authority from them: but, instead of that, he steered another course, and *went into Arabia,* either as a place of retirement proper for receiving further divine revelations, or in order to preach the gospel there among the Gentiles, being appointed to be the apostle of the Gentiles; and thence *he returned again to Damascus,* where he had first begun his ministry, and whence he had with difficulty escaped the rage of his enemies, Acts 9. It was not till *three years after* his conversion that *he went up to Jerusalem, to see Peter;* and when he did so he made but a very short stay with him, no more than *fifteen days;* nor, while he was there, did he go much into conversation; for *others of the apostles he saw none, but James, the Lord's brother.* So that it could not well be pretended that he was indebted to any other either for his knowledge of the gospel or his authority to preach it; but it appeared that both his qualifications for, and his call to, the apostolic office were extraordinary and divine. This account being of importance, to establish his claim to this office, to remove the unjust censures of his adversaries, and to recover the Galatians from the impressions they had received to his prejudice, he confirms it by a solemn oath (*v.* 20), declaring, as in the presence of God, that what he had said was strictly true, and that he had not in the least falsified in what he had related, which, though it will not justify us in solemn appeals to God upon every occasion, yet shows that, in matters of weight and moment, this may sometimes not only be lawful, but duty. After this he acquaints them that *he came into the regions of Syria and Cilicia:* having made this short visit to Peter, he returns to his work again. He had no communication at that time with the *churches of Christ in Judea,* they had not so much as *seen his face; but, having heard that he who persecuted them in times past now preached the faith which he once destroyed, they glorified God* because of him; thanksgivings were rendered by many unto God on that behalf; the very report of this mighty change in him, as it filled them with joy, so it excited them to give glory to God on the account of it.

CHAPTER 2

The apostle, in this chapter, continues the relation of his past life and conduct, which he had begun in the former; and, by some further instances of what had passed between him and the other apostles, makes it appear that he was not beholden to them either for his knowledge of the gospel or his authority as an apostle, as his adversaries would insinuate; but, on the contrary, that he was owned and approved even by them, as having an equal commission with them to this office. I. He particularly informs them of another journey which he took to Jerusalem many years after the former, and how he behaved himself at that time (*v.* 1–10). And, II. Gives them an account of another interview he had with the apostle Peter at Antioch, and how he was obliged to behave himself towards him there. From the subject-matter of that conversation, he proceeds to discourse on the great doctrine of justification by faith in Christ, without the works of the law, which it was the main design of this epistle to establish, and which he enlarges more upon in the two following chapters.

Verses 1–10

It should seem, by the account Paul gives of himself in this chapter, that, from the very first preaching and planting of Christianity, there was a difference of apprehension between those Christians who had first been Jews and those who had first been Gentiles. Many of those who had first been Jews retained a regard to the ceremonial law, and strove to keep up the reputation of that; but those who had first been Gentiles had no regard to the law of Moses, but took pure Christianity as perfective of natural religion, and resolved to adhere to that. Peter was the apostle to them; and the ceremonial law, though dead with Christ, yet not being as yet buried, he connived at the respect kept up for it. But Paul was the apostle of the Gentiles; and, though he was a Hebrew of the Hebrews, yet he adhered to pure Christianity. Now in this chapter he tells us what passed between him and the other apostles, and particularly between him and Peter hereupon.

In these verses he informs us of another journey which he took to Jerusalem, and of what passed between him and the other apostles there, *v.* 1–10. Here he acquaints us,

I. With some circumstances relating to this his journey thither. As particularly, 1. With the time of it: that it was not till *fourteen years* after the former (mentioned *ch.* 1:18), or, as others choose to understand it, from his conversion, or from the death of Christ. It was an instance of the great goodness of God that so useful a person was for so many years preserved in his work. And it was some evidence that he had no dependence upon the other apostles, but had an equal authority with them, that he had been so long absent from them, and was all the while employed in preaching and propagating pure Christianity, without being called into question by them for it, which it may be thought he would have been, had he been inferior to them, and his doctrine disapproved by them. 2. With his companions in it: *he went up with Barnabas, and took with him Titus also.* If the journey here spoken of was the same with that recorded Acts 15 (as many think), then we have a plain reason why Barnabas went along with him; for he was chosen by the Christians at Antioch to be his companion and associate in the affair he went about. But, as it does not appear that Titus was put into the same commission with him, so the chief reason of his taking him along with him seems to have been to let those at Jerusalem see that he was neither ashamed nor afraid to own the doctrine which he had constantly preached; for though Titus had now become not only a convert to the Christian faith, but a preacher of it too, yet he was by birth a Gentile and uncircumcised, and therefore, by making him his companion, it appeared that their doctrine and practice were of a piece, and that as he had preached the non-necessity of circumcision, and observing the law of Moses, so he was ready to own and converse with those who were uncircumcised. 3. With the reason of it, which was a divine revelation he had concerning it: *he went up be revelation;* not of his own head, much less as being summoned to appear there, but by special order and direction from Heaven. It was a privilege with which this apostle was often favoured to be under a special divine direction in his motions and undertakings; and, though this is what we have no reason to expect, yet it should teach us, in every thing of moment we go about, to endeavour, as far as we are capable, to see our way made plain before us, and to commit ourselves to the guidance of Providence.

II. He gives us an account of his behaviour while he was at Jerusalem, which was such as made it appear that he was not in the least inferior to the other apostles, but that both his authority and qualifications were every way equal to theirs. He particularly acquaints us,

1. That *he there communicated the gospel to them, which he preached among the Gentiles, but privately,* etc. Here we may observe both the faithfulness and prudence of our great apostle. (1.) His faithfulness in giving them a free and fair account of the doctrine which he had all along preached among the Gentiles, and was still resolved to preach — that of pure Christianity, free from all mixtures of Judaism. This he knew was a doctrine that would be ungrateful to many there, and yet he was not afraid to own it, but in a free and friendly manner lays it open before them and leaves them to judge whether or no it was not the true gospel of Christ. And yet, (2.) He uses prudence and caution herein, for fear of giving offence. He chooses rather to do it in a more private than in a public way, and *to those that were of reputation,* that is, to the apostles themselves, or to the chief among the Jewish Christians, rather than more openly and promiscuously to all, because, when he came to Jerusalem, *there were multitudes that believed, and yet continued zealous for the law,* Acts 21:20. And the reason of this his caution was *lest he should run, or had run, in vain,* lest he should stir up opposition against himself and thereby either the success of his past labours should be lessened, or his future usefulness be obstructed; for nothing more hinders the progress of the gospel than differences of opinion about the doctrines of it, especially when they occasion quarrels and contentions among the professors of it, as they too usually do. It was enough to his purpose to have his doctrine owned by those who were of greatest authority, whether it was approved by others or not. And therefore, to avoid offence, he judges it safest to communicate it privately to them, and not in public to the whole church. This conduct of the apostle may teach all, and especially ministers, how much need they have of prudence, and how careful they should be to use it upon all occasions, as far as is consistent with their faithfulness.

2. That in his practice he firmly adhered to the doctrine which he had preached. Paul was a man of resolution, and would adhere to his principles; and therefore, though he had Titus with him, who was a Greek, yet he would not suffer him to be circumcised, because he would not betray the doctrine of Christ, as he had preached it to the Gentiles. It does not appear that the apostles at all insisted upon this; for, though they connived at the use of circumcision among the Jewish converts, yet they were not for imposing it upon the Gentiles. But there were others who did, whom the apostle here calls *false brethren,* and concerning whom he informs us that they were *unawares brought in,* that is, into the church, or into their company, and that they came only to *spy out their liberty which they had in Christ Jesus,* or to see whether Paul would stand up in defence of that freedom from the ceremonial law which he had taught as the doctrine of the gospel, and represented as the privilege of those who embraced the Christian religion. Their design herein was *to bring them into bondage,* which they would have effected could they have gained the point they aimed at; for, had they prevailed with Paul and the other apostles to have circumcised Titus, they would easily have imposed circumcision upon other Gentiles, and so have brought them under the bondage of the law of Moses. But Paul, seeing their design, would by no means yield to them; he would not *give place by subjection, no, not for an hour,* not in this one single instance; and the reason of it was *that the truth of the gospel might continue with them* — that the Gentile Christians, and particularly the Galatians, might have it preserved to them pure and entire, and not corrupted with the mixtures of Judaism, as it would have been had he yielded in this matter. Circumcision was at that time a thing indifferent, and what in some cases might be complied with without sin; and accordingly we find even Paul himself sometimes giving way to it, as in the case of Timothy, Acts 16:3. But when it is insisted on as necessary, and his consenting to it, though only in a single instance, is likely to be improved as giving countenance to such an imposition, he has too great a concern for the purity and liberty of the gospel, to submit to it; he would not yield to those who were for the Mosaic rites and ceremonies, but would stand fast in the liberty wherewith Christ hath made us free, which conduct of his may give us occasion to observe that what under some circumstances may lawfully be complied with, yet, when that cannot be done without betraying the truth, or giving up the liberty, of the gospel, it ought to be refused.

3. That, though he conversed with the other apostles, yet he did not receive any addition to his knowledge or authority from them, *v.* 6. By *those who seemed to be somewhat* he means the other apostles, particularly James, Peter, and John, whom he afterwards mentions by name, *v.* 9. And concerning these he grants that they were deservedly had in reputation by all, that they were looked upon (and justly too) as pillars of the church, who were set not only for its ornament, but for its support, and that on some accounts they might seem to have the advantage of him, in that they had seen Christ in the flesh, which he had not, and were apostles before him, yea, even while he continued a persecutor. But yet, *whatever they were, it was no matter to him.* This was no prejudice to his being equally an apostle with them; for God does not accept the persons of men on the account of any such outward advantages. As he had called them to this office, so he was at liberty to qualify others for it, and to employ them in it. And it was evident in this case that he had done so; for *in conference they added nothing to him,* they told him nothing but what he before knew by revelation, nor could they except against the doctrine which he communicated to them, whence it appeared that he was not at all inferior to them, but was as much called and qualified to be an apostle as they themselves were.

4. That the issue of this conversation was that the other apostles were fully convinced of his divine mission and authority, and accordingly acknowledged him as their fellow-apostle, *v.* 7–10. They were not only satisfied with his doctrine, but they saw a divine power attending him, both in preaching it and in working miracles for the confirmation of it: *that he who wrought effectually in Peter to the apostleship of the circumcision, the same was mighty in him towards the Gentiles.* And hence they justly concluded *that the gospel of the uncircumcision was committed to Paul, as the gospel of the circumcision was to Peter.* And therefore, *perceiving the grace that was given to him* (that he was designed

to the honour and office of an apostle as well as themselves) *they gave unto him and Barnabas the right hand of fellowship,* a symbol whereby they acknowledged their equality with them, and agreed that *these should go to the heathen, while they continued to preach to the circumcision,* as judging it most agreeable to the mind of Christ, and most conducive to the interest of Christianity, so to divide their work. And thus this meeting ended in an entire harmony and agreement; they approved both Paul's doctrine and conduct, they were fully satisfied in him, heartily embraced him as an apostle of Christ, and had nothing further to add, *only that they would remember the poor,* which of his own accord *he was very forward to do.* The Christians of Judea were at that time labouring under great wants and difficulties; and the apostles, out of their compassion to them and concern for them, recommend their case to Paul, that he should use his interest with the Gentile churches to procure a supply for them. This was a reasonable request; *for, if the Gentiles were made partakers of their spiritual things, it was their duty to minister to them in carnal things,* as Rom. 15:27. And he very readily falls in with it, whereby he showed his charitable and catholic disposition, how ready he was to own the Jewish converts as brethren, though many of them could scarcely allow the like favour to the converted Gentiles, and that mere difference of opinion was no reason with him why he should not endeavour to relieve and help them. Herein he has given us an excellent pattern of Christian charity, and has taught us that we should by no means confine it to those who are just of the same sentiments with us, but be ready to extend it to all whom we have reason to look upon as the disciples of Christ.

Verses 11–21

I. From the account which Paul gives of what passed between him and the other apostles at Jerusalem, the Galatians might easily discern both the falseness of what his enemies had insinuated against him and their own folly and weakness in departing from that gospel which he had preached to them. But to give the greater weight to what he had already said, and more fully to fortify them against the insinuations of the judaizing teachers, he acquaints them with another interview which he had with the apostle Peter at Antioch, and what passed between them there, *v.* 11–14. Antioch was one of the chief churches of the Gentile Christians, as Jerusalem was of those Christians who turned from Judaism to the faith of Christ. There is no colour of reason for the supposition that Peter was bishop of Antioch. If he had, surely Paul would not have withstood him in his own church, as we here find he did; but, on the contrary, it is here spoken of as an occasional visit which he made thither. In their other meeting, there had been good harmony and agreement. Peter and the other apostles had both acknowledged Paul's commission and approved his doctrine, and they parted very good friends. But in this Paul finds himself obliged to appose Peter, for *he was to be blamed,* a plain evidence that he was not inferior to him, and consequently of the weakness of the pope's pretence to supremacy and infallibility, as the successor of Peter. Here we may observe,

1. Peter's fault. When he came among the Gentile churches, he complied with them, and did eat with them, though they were not circumcised, agreeably to the instructions which were given in particular to him (Acts 10), when he was warned by the heavenly vision *to call nothing common or unclean.* But, when there came some Jewish Christians from Jerusalem, he grew more shy of the Gentiles, only to humour those of the circumcision and for fear of giving them offence, which doubtless was to the great grief and discouragement of the Gentile churches. Then *he withdrew, and separated himself.* His fault herein had a bad influence upon others, for *the other Jews also dissembled with him;* though before they might be better disposed, yet now, from his example, they took on them to scruple eating with the Gentiles, and pretended they could not in conscience do it, because they were not circumcised. And (would you think it?) Barnabas himself, one of the apostles of the Gentiles, and one who had been instrumental in planting and watering the churches of the Gentiles, *was carried away with their dissimulation.* Here note, (1.) The weakness and inconstancy of the best of men, when left to themselves, and how apt they are to falter in their duty to God, out of an undue regard to the pleasing of men. And, (2.) The great force of bad examples, especially the examples of great men and good men, such as are in reputation for wisdom and honour.

2. The rebuke which Paul gave him for his fault. Notwithstanding Peter's character, yet, when he observes him thus behaving himself to the great prejudice both of the truth of the gospel and the peace of the church, he is not afraid to reprove him for it. Paul adhered resolutely to his principles, when others faltered in theirs; he was as good a Jew as any of them (for he was a Hebrew of the Hebrews), but he would magnify his office as the apostle of the Gentiles, and therefore would not see them discouraged and trampled upon. *When he saw that they walked not uprightly, according to the truth of the gospel* — that they did not live up to that principle which the gospel taught, and which they had professed to own and embrace, namely, that by the death of Christ the partition-wall between Jew and Gentile was taken down, and the observance of the law of Moses was no longer in force — when he observed this, as Peter's offence was public, so he publicly reproved him for it: *He said unto him before them all, If thou, being a Jew, livest after the manner of the Gentiles, and not as do the Jews, why compellest thou the Gentiles to live as do the Jews?* Herein one part of his conduct was a contradiction to the other; for if he, who was a Jew, could himself sometimes dispense with the use of the ceremonial law, and live after the manner of the Gentiles, this showed that he did not look upon the observance of it as still necessary, even for the Jews themselves; and therefore that he could not, consistently with his own practice, impose it upon the Gentile Christians. And yet Paul charges him with this, yea, represents him as compelling the Gentiles to live as did the Jews — not by open force and violence, but this was the tendency of what he did; for it was in effect to signify this, that the Gentiles must comply with the Jews, or else not be admitted into Christian communion.

II. Paul having thus established his character and office, and sufficiently shown that he was not inferior to any of the apostles, no, not to Peter himself, from the account of the reproof he gave him he takes occasion to speak of that great fundamental doctrine of the gospel — That justification is only by faith in Christ, and not by the works of the law (though some think that all he says to the end of the chapter is what he said to Peter at Antioch), which doctrine condemned Peter for his symbolizing with the Jews. For, if it was the principle of his religion that the gospel is the instrument of our justification and not the law, then he did very ill in countenancing those who kept up the law, and were for mixing it with faith in the business of our justification. This was the doctrine which Paul had preached among the Galatians, to which he still adhered, and which it is his great business in this epistle to mention and confirm. Now concerning this Paul acquaints us,

1. With the practice of the Jewish Christians themselves: *"We,"* says he, *"who are Jews by nature, and not sinners of the Gentiles* (even we who have been born and bred in the Jewish religion, and not among the impure Gentiles), *knowing that a man is not justified by the works of the law, but by the faith of Jesus Christ, even we ourselves have believed in Jesus Christ, that we might be justified by the faith of Christ, and not by the works of the law.* And, if we have thought it necessary to seek justification by the faith of Christ, why then should we hamper ourselves with the law? What did we believe in Christ for? Was it not that we might be justified by the faith of Christ? And, if so, is it not folly to go back to the law, and to expect to be justified either by the merit of moral works or the influence of any ceremonial sacrifices or purifications? And if it would be wrong in us who are Jews by nature to return to the law, and expect justification by it, would it not be much more so to require this of the Gentiles, who were never subject to it, since *by the works of the law no flesh shall be justified?"* To give the greater weight to this he adds (*v.* 17), *"But if, while we seek to be justified by Christ, we ourselves also are found sinners, is Christ the minister of sin?* If, while we seek justification by Christ alone, and teach others to do so, we ourselves are found giving countenance or indulgence to sin, or rather are accounted sinners of the Gentiles, and such as it is not fit to have communion with, unless we also observe the law of Moses, *is Christ the minister of sin?* Will it not follow that he is so, if he engage us to receive a doctrine that gives liberty to sin, or by which we are so far from being justified that we remain impure sinners, and unfit to be conversed with?" This, he intimates, would be the consequence, but he rejects it with abhorrence: *"God forbid,"* says he, "that we should entertain such a thought of Christ, or of his doctrine, that thereby he should direct us into a way of justification that is defective and ineffectual, and leave those who embrace it still unjustified, or that would give the least encouragement to sin and sinners." This would be very dishonourable to Christ, and it would be very injurious to them also. *"For,"* says he (*v.* 18), *"if I build again the things which I destroyed* — if I (or any other), who have taught that the observance of the Mosaic law is not necessary to justification, should now, by word or practice, teach or intimate that it is necessary — *I make myself a transgressor;* I own myself to be still an impure sinner, and to remain under the guilt of sin, notwithstanding my faith in Christ; or I shall be liable to be charged with deceit and prevarication, and acting inconsistently with myself." Thus does the apostle argue for the great doctrine of justification by faith without the works of the law from the principles and practice of the Jewish Christians themselves, and from the consequences that would attend their departure from it, whence it appeared that Peter and the other Jews were much in the wrong in refusing to communicate with the Gentile Christians, and endeavouring to bring them under the bondage of the law.

2. He acquaints us what his own judgment and practice were. (1.) That he was dead to the law. Whatever account others might make of it, yet, for his part, he was dead to it. He knew that the moral law denounced a curse against all that continue not in all things written therein, to do them; and therefore he was dead to it, as to all hope of justification and salvation that way. And as for the ceremonial law, he also knew that it was now antiquated and superseded by the coming of Christ, and therefore, the substance having come, he had no longer any regard to the shadow. He was thus dead to the law, *through the law itself;* it discovered itself to be at an end. By considering the law itself, he saw that justification was not to be expected by the works of it (since none could perform a perfect obedience to it) and that there was now no further need of the sacrifices and purifications of it, since they were done away in Christ, and a period was put to them by his offering up himself a sacrifice for us; and therefore, the more he looked into it the more he saw that there was no occasion for keeping up that regard to it which the Jews pleaded for. But, though he was thus *dead to the law,* yet he did not look upon himself as *with law.* He had renounced all hopes of justification by the works of it, and was unwilling any longer to continue under the bondage of it; but he was far from thinking himself discharged from his duty to God; on the contrary, he was dead to the law, *that he might live unto God.* The doctrine of the gospel, which he had embraced, instead of weakening the bond of duty upon him, did but the more strengthen and confirm it; and therefore, though he was dead to the law, yet it was only in order to his living a new and better life to God (as Rom. 7:4, 6), such a life as would be more agreeable and acceptable to God than his observance of the Mosaic law could now be, that is, a life of faith in Christ, and, under the influence thereof, of holiness and righteousness towards God. Agreeably hereunto he acquaints us, (2.) That, as he was dead to the law, so he was alive unto God through Jesus Christ (*v.* 20): *I am crucified with Christ,* etc. And here in his own person he gives us an excellent description of the mysterious life of a believer. [1.] He is crucified, and yet he lives; the old man is crucified (Rom. 6:6), but the new man is living; he is dead to the world, and dead to the law, and yet alive to God and Christ; sin is mortified, and grace quickened. [2.] *He lives, and yet not he.* This is strange: *I live, and yet not I;* he lives in the exercise of grace; he has the comforts and the triumphs of grace; and yet that grace is not from himself, but from another. Believers see themselves living in a state of dependence. [3.] *He is crucified with Christ,* and yet *Christ lives in him;* this results from his mystical union with Christ, by means of which he is interested in the death of Christ, so as by virtue of that to die unto sin; and yet interested in the life of Christ, so as by virtue of that to live unto God. [4.] *He lives in the flesh,* and yet *lives by faith;* to outward appearance he lives as other people do, his natural life is supported as others are; yet he has a higher and nobler principle that supports and actuates him, that of faith in Christ, and especially as eyeing the wonders of his love in giving himself for him. Hence it is that, though he lives in the flesh, yet he does not live after the flesh. Note, Those who have true faith live by that faith; and the great thing which faith fastens upon is Christ's loving us and giving himself for us. The great evidence of Christ's loving us

is his giving himself for us; and this is that which we are chiefly concerned to mix faith with, in order to our living to him.

Lastly, The apostle concludes this discourse with acquainting us that by the doctrine of justification by faith in Christ, without the works of the law (which he asserted, and others opposed), he avoided two great difficulties, which the contrary opinion was loaded with: — 1. *That he did not frustrate the grace of God,* which the doctrine of the justification by the works of the law did; for, as he argues (Rom. 11:6), *If it be of works, it is no more of grace.* 2. That he did not frustrate the death of Christ; whereas, *if righteousness come by* the law, then it must follow *that Christ has died in vain;* for, if we look for salvation by the law of Moses, then we render the death of Christ needless: for to what purpose should he be appointed to die, if we might have been saved without it?

CHAPTER 3

The apostle in this chapter, I. Reproves the Galatians for their folly, in suffering themselves to be drawn away from the faith of the gospel, and endeavours, from several considerations, to impress them with a sense of it. II. He proves the doctrine which he had reproved them for departing from — that of justification by faith without the works of the law, 1. From the example of Abraham's justification. 2. From the nature and tenour of the law. 3. From the express testimony of the Old Testament; and, 4. From the stability of the covenant of God with Abraham. Lest any should hereupon say, "Wherefore then serveth the law?" he answers, (1.) It was added because of transgressions. (2.) It was given to convince the world of the necessity of a Saviour. (3.) It was designed as a schoolmaster, to bring us to Christ. And then he concludes the chapter by acquainting us with the privilege of Christians under the gospel state.

Verses 1–5

The apostle is here dealing with those who, having embraced the faith of Christ, still continued to seek for justification by the works of the law; that is, who depended upon their own obedience to the moral precepts as their righteousness before God, and, wherein that was defective, had recourse to the legal sacrifices and purifications to make it up. These he first sharply reproves, and then endeavours, by the evidence of truth, to convince them. This is the right method, when we reprove any for a fault or an error, to convince them that it is an error, that it is a fault.

He reproves them, and the reproof is very close and warm: he calls them *foolish Galatians, v.* 1. Though as Christians they were Wisdom's children, yet as corrupt Christians they were foolish children. Yea, he asks, *Who hath bewitched you?* whereby he represents them as enchanted by the arts and snares of their seducing teachers, and so far deluded as to act very unlike themselves. That wherein their folly and infatuation appeared was that *they did not obey the truth;* that is, they did not adhere to the gospel way of justification, wherein they had been taught, and which they had professed to embrace. Note, It is not enough to know the truth, and to say we believe it, but we must obey it too; we must heartily submit to it, and stedfastly abide by it. Note, also, Those are spiritually bewitched who, when the truth as it is in Jesus is plainly set before them, will not thus obey it. Several things proved and aggravated the folly of these Christians.

1. *Jesus Christ had been evidently set forth as crucified among them;* that is, they had had the doctrine of the cross preached to them, and the sacrament of the Lord's supper administered among them, in both which Christ crucified had been set before them. Now, it was the greatest madness that could be for those who had acquaintance with such sacred mysteries, and admittance to such great solemnities, not to obey the truth which was thus published to them, and signed and sealed in that ordinance. Note, The consideration of the honours and privileges we have been admitted to as Christians should shame us out of the folly of apostasy and backsliding.

2. He appeals to the experiences they had had of the working of the Spirit upon their souls (*v.* 2); he puts them in mind that, upon their becoming Christians, *they had received the Spirit,* that many of them at least had been made partakers not only of the sanctifying influences, but of the miraculous gifts, of the Holy Spirit, which were eminent proofs of the truth of the Christian religion and the several doctrines of it, and especially of this, that justification is by Christ only, and not by the works of the law, which was one of the peculiar and fundamental principles of it. To convince them of the folly of their departing from this doctrine, he desires to know how they came by these gifts and graces: Was it *by the works of the law,* that is, the preaching of the necessity of these in order to justification? This they could not say, for that doctrine had not then been preached to them, nor had they, as Gentiles, any pretence to justification in that way. Or was it by the *hearing of faith,* that is, the preaching of the doctrine of faith in Christ as the only way of justification? This, if they would say the truth, they were obliged to own, and therefore must be very unreasonable if they should reject a doctrine of the good effects of which they had had such experience. Note, (1.) It is usually by the ministry of the gospel that the Spirit is communicated to persons. And, (2.) Those are very unwise who suffer themselves to be turned away from the ministry and doctrine which have been blessed to their spiritual advantage.

3. He calls upon them to consider their past and present conduct, and thence to judge whether they were not acting very weakly and unreasonably (*v.* 3, 4): he tells them that *they had begun in the Spirit,* but now were seeking *to be made perfect by the flesh;* they had embraced the doctrine of the gospel, by means of which they had received the Spirit, and wherein only the true way of justification is revealed. And thus they had begun well; but now they were turning to the law, and expected to be advanced to higher degrees of perfection by adding the observance of it to faith in Christ, in order to their justification, which could end in nothing but their shame and disappointment: for this, instead of being an improvement upon the gospel, was really a perversion of it; and, while they sought to be justified in this way, they were so far from being more perfect Christians that they were more in danger of becoming no Christians at all; hereby they were pulling down with one hand what they had built with the other, and undoing what they had hitherto done in Christianity. Yea, he further puts them in mind that they had not only embraced the Christian doctrine, but suffered for it too; and therefore their folly would be the more aggravated, if now they should desert it: for in this case all that they had suffered would be in vain — it would appear that they had been foolish in suffering for what they now deserted, and their sufferings would be altogether in vain, and of no advantage to them. Note, (1.) It is the folly of apostates that they lose the benefit of all they have done in religion, or suffered for it. And, (2.) It is very sad for any to live in an age of services and sufferings, of sabbaths, sermons, and sacraments, in vain; in this case former righteousness shall not be mentioned.

4. He puts them in mind that they had had ministers among them (and particularly himself) who came with a divine seal and commission; for they had *ministered the Spirit to them, and wrought miracles among them:* and he appeals to them whether they did it *by the works of the law or by the hearing of faith,* whether the doctrine that was preached by them, and confirmed by the miraculous gifts and operations of the Spirit, was that of justification by the works of the law or by the faith of Christ; they very well knew that it was not the former, but the latter; and therefore must needs be inexcusable in forsaking a doctrine which had been so signally owned and attested, and exchanging it for one that had received no such attestations.

Verses 6–18

The apostle having reproved the Galatians for not obeying the truth, and endeavoured to impress them with a sense of their folly herein, in these verses he largely proves the doctrine which he had reproved them for rejecting, namely, that of justification by faith without the works of the law. This he does several ways.

I. From the example of Abraham's justification. This argument the apostle uses, Rom. 4. *Abraham believed God, and that was accounted to him for righteousness* (*v.* 6); that is, his faith fastened upon the word and promise of God, and upon his believing he was owned and accepted of God as a righteous man: as on this account he is represented as the father of the faithful, so the apostle would have us to know *that those who are of faith are the children of Abraham* (*v.* 7), not according to the flesh, but according to the promise; and, consequently, that they are justified in the same way that he was. Abraham was justified by faith, and so are they. To confirm this, the apostle acquaints us that the promise made to Abraham (Gen. 12:3), *In thee shall all nations be blessed,* had a reference hereunto, *v.* 8. The scripture is said to *foresee,* because he that indited the scripture did foresee, that God would justify the heathen world in the way of faith; and therefore in Abraham, that is, in the seed of Abraham, which is Christ, not the Jews only, but the Gentiles also, should be blessed; not only blessed in the seed of Abraham, but blessed as Abraham was, being justified as he was. This the apostle calls *preaching the gospel to Abraham;* and thence infers (*v.* 9) that *those who are of faith,* that is, true believers, of what nation soever they are, *are blessed with faithful Abraham.* They are blessed with Abraham the father of the faithful, by the promise made to him, and therefore by faith as he was. It was through faith in the promise of God that he was blessed, and it is only in the same way that others obtain this privilege.

II. He shows that we cannot be justified but by faith fastening on the gospel, because the law condemns us. If we put ourselves upon trial in that court, and stand to the sentence of it, we are certainly cast, and lost, and undone; *for as many as are of the works of the law are under the curse,* as many as depend upon the merit of their own works as their righteousness, as plead not guilty, and insist upon their own justification, the cause will certainly go against them; *for it is written, Cursed is every one that continueth not in all things which are written in the book of the law, to do them, v.* 10, and Deu. 27:26. The condition of life, by the law, is perfect, personal, and perpetual, obedience; the language of it is, *Do this and live;* or, as *v.* 12, *The man that doeth them shall live in them:* and for every failure herein the law denounces a curse. Unless our obedience be universal, continuing in all things that are written in the book of the law, and unless it be perpetual too (if in any instance at any time we fail and come short), we fall under the curse of the law. The curse is wrath revealed, and ruin threatened: it is a separation unto all evil, and this is in full force, power, and virtue, against all sinners, and therefore against all men; for all have sinned and become guilty before God: and if, as transgressors of the law, we are under the curse of it, it must be a vain thing to look for justification by it. But, though this is not to be expected from the law, yet the apostle afterwards acquaints us that there is a way open to our escaping this curse, and regaining the favour of God, namely, through faith in Christ, who (as he says, *v.* 13) *hath redeemed us from the curse of the law,* etc. A strange method it was which Christ took to redeem us from the curse of the law; it was *by his being himself made a curse for us.* Being made sin for us, he was made a curse for us; not separated from God, but laid for the present under that infamous token of the divine displeasure upon which the law of Moses had put a particular brand, Deu. 21:23. The design of this was *that the blessing of Abraham might come on the Gentiles through Jesus Christ* — that all who believed on Christ, whether Jews or Gentiles, might become heirs of Abraham's blessing, and particularly of that great promise of the Spirit, which was peculiarly reserved for the times of the gospel. Hence it appeared that it was not by putting themselves under the law, but by faith in Christ, that they become the people of God and heirs of the promise. Here note, 1. The misery which as sinners we are sunk into — we are under the curse and condemnation of the law. 2. The love and grace of our Lord Jesus Christ towards us — he has submitted to be made a curse for us, that he might redeem us from the curse of the law. 3. The happy prospect which we now have through him, not only of escaping the curse, but of inheriting the blessing. And, 4. That it is only through faith in him that we can hope to obtain this favour.

III. To prove that justification is by faith, and not by the works of the law, the apostle alleges the express testimony of the Old Testament, *v.* 11. The place referred to is Habak. 2:4, where it is said, *The just shall live by faith;* it is again quoted, Rom. 1:17, and Heb. 10:38. The design of it is to show that those only are just or righteous who do truly live, who are freed from death and wrath, and restored into a state of life in the favour of God; and that it is only through faith that persons become righteous, and as such obtain this life and happiness — that they are accepted of God, and enabled to live to him now, and are entitled to an eternal life in the enjoyment of him hereafter. Hence the apostle says, *It is evident that no man is justified by the law in the sight of God.* Whatever he may be in the account of others, yet he is not so in the sight of God; for *the law is not of faith* — that says nothing concerning faith in the business of justification, nor does it give life to those who believe; but the language of it is, *The man that doeth them shall live in them,* as Lev. 18:5. It requires perfect obedience as the condition of life, and therefore now can by no means be the rule of our justification. This argument of the apostle's may give us occasion to remark that justification by faith is no new doctrine, but what was established and taught in the church of God long before the times of the gospel. Yea, it is the only way where-in any sinners ever were, or can be, justified.

IV. To this purpose the apostle urges the stability of the covenant which God made with Abraham, which was not vacated nor disannulled by the giving of the law to Moses, v. 15, etc. Faith had the precedence of the law, for Abraham was justified by faith. It was a promise that he built upon, and promises are the proper objects of faith. God entered into covenant with Abraham (v. 8), and this covenant was firm and steady; even men's covenants are so, and therefore much more his. When a deed is executed, or articles of agreement are sealed, both parties are bound, and it is too late then to settle things otherwise; and therefore it is not to be supposed that by the subsequent law the covenant of God should be vacated. The original word *diathēkē* signifies both a covenant and a testament. Now the promise made to Abraham was rather a testament than a covenant. When a testament has become of force by the death of the testator, it is not capable of being altered; and therefore, the promise that was given to Abraham being of the nature of a testament, it remains firm and unalterable. But, if it should be said that a grant or testament may be defeated for want of persons to claim the benefit of it (v. 16), he shows that there is no danger of that in this case. Abraham is dead, and the prophets are dead, but the covenant is made with Abraham and his seed. And he gives us a very surprising exposition of this. We should have thought it had been meant only of the people of the Jews. "Nay," says the apostle, "it is in the singular number, and points at a single person — *that seed is Christ*," So that the covenant is still in force; for Christ abideth for ever in his person, and in his spiritual seed, who are his by faith. And if it be objected that the law which was given by Moses did disannul this covenant, because that insisted so much upon works, and there was so little in it of faith or of the promised Messiah, he answers that the subsequent law could not disannul the previous covenant or promise (v. 18): *If the inheritance be of the law, it is no more of promise; but*, says he, *God gave it to Abraham by promise*, and therefore it would be inconsistent with his holiness, wisdom, and faithfulness, by any subsequent act to set aside the promise, and so alter the way of justification which he had thus established. If the inheritance was given to Abraham by promise, and thereby entailed upon his spiritual seed, we may be sure that God would not retract that promise; for he is not a man that he should repent.

Verses 19–29

The apostle having just before been speaking of the promise made to Abraham, and representing that as the rule of our justification, and not the law, lest they should think he did too much derogate from the law, and render it altogether useless, he thence takes occasion to discourse of the design and tendency of it, and to acquaint us for what purposes it was given. It might be asked, "If that promise be sufficient for salvation, wherefore then serveth the law? Or, Why did God give the law by Moses?" To this he answers,

I. The law *was added because of transgressions, v.* 19. It was not designed to disannul the promise, and to establish a different way of justification from that which was settled by the promise; but *it was added* to it, annexed on purpose to be subservient to it, and it was so *because of transgressions.* The Israelites, though they were chosen to be God's peculiar people, were sinners as well as others, and therefore the law was given to convince them of their sin, and of their obnoxiousness to the divine displeasure on the account of it; *for by the law is the knowledge of sin* (Rom. 3:20), and *the law entered that sin might abound,* Rom. 5:20. And it was also intended to restrain them from the commission of sin, to put an awe upon their minds, and be a curb upon their lusts, that they should not run into that excess of riot to which they were naturally inclined; and yet at the same time it was designed to direct them to the true and only way whereby sin was to be expiated, and wherein they might obtain the pardon of it; namely, through the death and sacrifice of Christ, which was the special use for which the law of sacrifices and purifications was given.

The apostle adds that the law was given for this purpose *till the seed should come to whom the promise was made;* that is, either till Christ should come (the principle seed referred to in the promise, as he had before shown), or till the gospel dispensation should take place, when Jews and Gentiles, without distinction, should, upon believing, become the

seed of Abraham. The law was added because of transgressions, till this fulness of time, or this complete dispensation, should come. But when the seed came, and a fuller discovery of divine grace in the promise was made, then the law, as given by Moses, was to cease; that covenant, being found faulty, was to give place to another, and a better, Heb. 8:7, 8. And though the law, considered as the law of nature, is always in force, and still continues to be of use to convince men of sin and to restrain them from it, yet we are now no longer under the bondage and terror of that legal covenant. The law then was not intended to discover another way of justification, different from that revealed by the promise, but only to lead men to see their need of the promise, by showing them the sinfulness of sin, and to point them to Christ, through whom alone they could be pardoned and justified.

As a further proof that the law was not designed to vacate the promise, the apostle adds, *It was ordained by angels in the hand of a mediator.* It was given to different persons, and in a different manner from the promise, and therefore for different purposes. The promise was made to Abraham, and all his spiritual seed, including believers of all nations, even of the Gentiles as well as the Jews; but the law was given to the Israelites as a peculiar people, and separated from the rest of the world. And, whereas the promise was given immediately by God himself, the law was given *by the ministry of angels, and the hand of a mediator.* Hence it appeared that the law could not be designed to set aside the promise; for (v. 20), *A mediator is not a mediator of one,* of one party only; *but God is one,* but one party in the promise or covenant made with Abraham: and therefore it is not to be supposed that by a transaction which passed only between him and the nation of the Jews he should make void a promise which he had long before made to Abraham and all his spiritual seed, whether Jews or Gentiles. This would not have been consistent with his wisdom, nor with his truth and faithfulness. Moses was only a mediator between God and the spiritual seed of Abraham; and therefore the law that was given by him could not affect the promise made to them, much less be subversive of it.

II. The law was given to convince men of the necessity of a Saviour. The apostle asks (v. 21), as what some might be willing to object, "*Is the law then against the promises of God?* Do they really clash and interfere with each other? Or do you not set the covenant with Abraham, and the law of Moses, at variance with one another?" To this he answers, *God forbid;* he was far from entertaining such a thought, nor could it be inferred from what he had said. The law is by no means inconsistent with the promise, but subservient to it, as the design of it is to discover men's transgressions, and to show them the need they have of a better righteousness than that of the law. That consequence would much rather follow from their doctrine than from his; *for, if there had been a law given that could have given life, verily righteousness would have been by the law,* and in that case the promise would have been superseded and rendered useless. But that in our present state could not be, *for the scripture hath concluded all under sin* (v. 22), or declared that all, both Jew and Gentile, are in a state of guilt, and therefore unable to attain to righteousness and justification by the works of the law. The law discovered their wounds, but could not afford them a remedy: it showed that they were guilty, because it appointed sacrifices and purifications, which were manifestly insufficient to take away sin: and therefore the great design of it was *that the promise by faith of Jesus Christ might be given to those that believe,* that being convinced of their guilt, and the insufficiency of the law to effect a righteousness for them, they might be persuaded to believe on Christ, and so obtain the benefit of the promise.

III. The law was designed for *a schoolmaster, to bring men to Christ, v.* 24. In the foregoing verse, the apostle acquaints us with the state of the Jews under the Mosaic economy, that *before faith came,* or before Christ appeared and the doctrine of justification by faith in him was more fully discovered, *they were kept under the law,* obliged, under severe penalties, to a strict observance of the various precepts of it; and at that time they were shut up, held under the terror and discipline of it, as prisoners in a state of confinement: the design of this was that hereby they might be disposed more readily to embrace the *faith which should afterwards be revealed,* or be persuaded to accept Christ when he came into the world, and to fall in with that better dispensation he was to introduce, whereby they were to be freed from bondage

and servitude, and brought into a state of greater light and liberty. Now, in that state, he tells them, *the law was their schoolmaster, to bring them to Christ, that they might be justified by faith.* As it declared the mind and will of God concerning them, and at the same time denounced a curse against them for every failure in their duty, so it was proper to convince them of their lost and undone condition in themselves, and to let them see the weakness and insufficiency of their own righteousness to recommend them to God. And as it obliged them to a variety of sacrifices, etc., which, though they could not of themselves take away sin, were typical of Christ, and of the great sacrifice which he was to offer up for the expiation of it, so it directed them (though in a more dark and obscure manner) to him as their only relief and refuge. And thus it was their schoolmaster, to instruct and govern them in their state of minority, or, as the word *paidagōgos* most properly signifies, their *servant,* to lead and conduct them to Christ (as children were wont to be led to school by those servants who had the care of them); that they might be more fully instructed by him as their schoolmaster, in the true way of justification and salvation, which is only by faith in him, and of which he was appointed to give the fullest and clearest discoveries. But lest it should be said, If the law was of this use and service under the Jewish, why may it not continue to be so under the Christian state too, the apostle adds (v. 25) that *after faith has come,* and the gospel dispensation has taken place, under which Christ, and the way of pardon and life through faith in him, are set in the clearest light, *we are no longer under a schoolmaster* — we have no such need of the law to direct us to him as there was then. Thus the apostle acquaints us for what uses and purposes the law served; and, from what he says concerning this matter, we may observe,

1. The goodness of God to his people of old, in giving the law to them; for though, in comparison of the gospel state, it was a dispensation of darkness and terror, yet it furnished them with sufficient means and helps both to direct them in their duty to God and to encourage their hopes in him.

2. The great fault and folly of the Jews, in mistaking the design of the law, and abusing it to a very different purpose from that which God intended in the giving of it; for they expected to be justified by the works of it, whereas it was never designed to be the rule of their justification, but only a means of convincing them of their guilt and of their need of a Saviour, and of directing them to Christ, and faith in him, as the only way of obtaining this privilege. See Rom. 9:31, 32; 10:3, 4.

3. The great advantage of the gospel state above the legal, under which we not only enjoy a clearer discovery of divine grace and mercy than was afforded to the Jews of old, but are also freed from the state of bondage and terror under which they were held. We are not now treated as children in a state of minority, but as sons grown up to a full age, who are admitted to greater freedoms, and instated in larger privileges, than they were. This the apostle enlarges upon in the following verses. For, having shown for what intent the law was given, in the close of the chapter he acquaints us with our privilege by Christ, where he particularly declares,

(1.) That *we are the children of God by faith in Christ Jesus, v.* 26. And here we may observe, [1.] The great and excellent privilege which real Christians enjoy under the gospel: *They are the children of God;* they are no longer accounted servants, but *sons;* they are not now kept at such a distance, and under such restraints, as the Jews were, but are allowed a nearer and freer access to God than was granted to them; yea, they are admitted into the number, and have a right to all the privileges, of his children. [2.] How they come to obtain this privilege, and that is *by faith in Christ Jesus.* Having accepted him as their Lord and Saviour, and relying on him alone for justification and salvation, they are hereupon admitted into this happy relation to God, and are entitled to the privileges of it; for (Jn. 1:12) *as many as received him, to them gave he power to become the sons of God, even to those that believe on his name.* And this faith in Christ, whereby they became the children of God, he reminds us (v. 27), was what they professed in baptism; for he adds, *As many of you as have been baptized into Christ have put on Christ.* Having in baptism professed their faith in him, they were thereby devoted to him, and had, as it were, put on his livery, and declared themselves to be his servants and disciples; and having thus become the members of Christ, they were through him owned and accounted as the children of

God. Here note, *First,* Baptism is now the solemn rite of our admission into the Christian church, as circumcision was into that of the Jews. Our Lord Jesus appointed it to be so, in the commission he gave to his apostles (Mt. 28:19), and accordingly it was their practice to baptize those whom they had discipled to the Christian faith; and perhaps the apostle might take notice of their baptism here, and of their becoming the children of God through faith in Christ, professed therein, to obviate a further objection, which the false teachers might be apt to urge in favour of circumcision. They might be ready to say, "Though it should be allowed that the law, as given at mount Sinai, was abrogated by the coming of Christ the promised seed, yet why should circumcision be set aside too, when that was given to Abraham together with the promise, and long before the giving of the law by Moses?" But this difficulty is sufficiently removed when the apostle says, *Those who are baptized into Christ have put on Christ;* for thence it appears that under the gospel baptism comes in the room of circumcision, and that those who by baptism are devoted to Christ, and do sincerely believe in him, are to all intents and purposes as much admitted into the privileges of the Christian state as the Jews were by circumcision into those of the legal (Phil. 3:3), and therefore there was no reason why the use of that should still be continued. Note, *Secondly,* In our baptism we put on Christ; therein we profess our discipleship to him, and are obliged to behave ourselves as his faithful servants. Being baptized into Christ, we are baptized into his death, that as he died and rose again, so, in conformity thereunto, we should die unto sin, and walk in newness of life (Rom. 6:3, 4); it would be of great advantage to us did we oftener remember this.

(2.) That this privilege of being the children of God, and of being by baptism devoted to Christ, is now enjoyed in common by all real Christians. The law indeed made a difference between Jew and Greek, giving the Jews on many accounts the pre-eminence: that also made a difference between *bond and free,* master and servant, and between *male and female,* the males being circumcised. But it is not so now; they all stand on the same level, *and are all one in Christ Jesus;* as the one is not accepted on the account of any national or personal advantages he may enjoy above the other, so neither is the other rejected for the want of them; but all who sincerely believe on Christ, of what nation, or sex, or condition, soever they be, are accepted of him, and become the children of God through faith in him.

(3.) That, *being Christ's, we are Abraham's seed, and heirs according to the promise.* Their judaizing teachers would have them believe that they must be circumcised and keep the law of Moses, or they could not be saved: "No," says the apostle, "there is no need of that; for *if you be Christ's,* if you sincerely believe on him, who is the promised seed, in whom all the nations of the earth were to be blessed, you therefore become the true *seed of Abraham,* the father of the faithful, and as such *are heirs according to the promise,* and consequently are entitled to the great blessings and privileges of it." And therefore upon the whole, since it appeared that justification was not to be attained by the works of the law, but only by faith in Christ, and that the law of Moses was a temporary institution and was given for such purposes as were only subservient to and not subversive of the promise, and that now, under the gospel, Christians enjoy much greater and better privileges than the Jews did under that dispensation, it must needs follow that they were very unreasonable and unwise, in hearkening to those who at once endeavoured to deprive them of the truth and liberty of the gospel.

CHAPTER 4

The apostle, in this chapter, is still carrying on the same general design as in the former — to recover these Christians from the impressions made upon them by the judaizing teachers, and to represent their weakness and folly in suffering themselves to be drawn away from the gospel doctrine of justification, and to be deprived of their freedom from the bondage of the law of Moses. For this purpose he makes use of various considerations; such as, I. The great excellence of the gospel state above the legal (*v.* 1–7). II. The happy change that was made in them at their conversion (*v.* 8–11). III. The affection they had had for him and his ministry (*v.* 12–16). IV. The character of the false teachers by whom they had been perverted (*v.* 17, 18). V. The very tender affection he had for them (*v.* 19, 20). VI. The history of Isaac and Ishmael, by a comparison taken from which he illustrates the difference between such as rested in Christ and such as trusted in the law. And in all these, as he uses great plainness and faithfulness with them, so he expresses the tenderest concern for them.

Verses 1–7

In this chapter the apostle deals plainly with those who hearkened to the judaizing teachers, who cried up the law of Moses in competition with the gospel of Christ, and endeavored to bring them under the bondage of it. To convince them of their folly, and to rectify their mistake herein, in these verses he prosecutes the comparison of a child under age, which he had touched upon in the foregoing chapter, and thence shows what great advantages we have now, under the gospel, above what they had under the law. And here.

I. He acquaints us with the state of the Old-Testament church: it was like a child under age, and it was used accordingly, being kept in a state of darkness and bondage, in comparison of the greater light and liberty which we enjoy under the gospel. That was indeed a dispensation of grace, and yet it was comparatively a dispensation of darkness; for as the heir, in his minority, is *under tutors and governors till the time appointed of his father,* by whom he is educated and instructed in those things which at present he knows little of the meaning of, though afterwards they are likely to be of great use to him; so it was with the Old-Testament church — the Mosaic economy, which they were under, was what they could not fully understand the meaning of; for, as the apostle says (2 Co. 3:13), *They could not stedfastly look to the end of that which is abolished.* But to the church, when grown up to maturity, in gospel days, it becomes of great use. And as that was a dispensation of darkness, so of bondage too; for *they were in bondage under the elements of the world,* being tied to a great number of burdensome rites and observances, by which, as by a kind of first rudiments, they were taught and instructed, and whereby they were kept in a state of subjection, like a child under tutors and governors. The church then lay more under the character of *a servant,* being obliged to do every thing according to the command of God, without being fully acquainted with the reason of it; but the service under the gospel appears to be more reasonable than that was. The time appointed of the Father having come, when the church was to arrive at its full age, the darkness and bondage under which it before lay are removed, and we are under a dispensation of greater light and liberty.

II. He acquaints us with the much happier state of Christians under the gospel-dispensation, *v.* 4–7. *When the fulness of time had come,* the time appointed of the Father, when he would put an end to the legal dispensation, and set up another and a better in the room of it, *he sent forth his Son,* etc. The person who was employed to introduce this new dispensation was no other than the Son of God himself, the only-begotten of the Father, who, as he had been prophesied of and promised from the foundation of the world, so in due time he was manifested for this purpose. He, in pursuance of the great design he had undertaken, submitted to be *made of a woman* — there is his incarnation; and to be *made under the law* — there is his subjection. He who was truly God for our sakes became man; and he who was Lord of all consented to come into a state of subjection and to take upon him the form of a servant; and one great end of all this was *to redeem those that were under the law* — to save us from that intolerable yoke and to appoint gospel ordinances more rational and easy. He had indeed something more and greater in his view, in coming into the world, than merely to deliver us from the bondage of the ceremonial law; for he came in our nature, and consented to suffer and die for us, that hereby he might redeem us from the wrath of God, and from the curse of the moral law, which, as sinners, we all lay under. But that was one end of it, and a mercy reserved to be bestowed at the time of his manifestation; then the more servile state of the church was to come to a period, and a better to succeed in the place of it; for he was sent to redeem us, *that we might receive the adoption of sons* — that we might no longer be accounted and treated as servants, but as sons grown up to maturity, who are allowed greater freedoms, and admitted to larger privileges, than while they were under tutors and governors. This the course of the apostle's argument leads us to take notice of, as one thing intended by this expression, though no doubt it may also be understood as signifying that gracious adoption which the gospel so often speaks of as the privilege of those who believe in Christ. Israel was God's son, his first-born, Rom. 9:4. But now, under the gospel, particular believers receive the adoption; and, as an earnest and evidence of it, they have together therewith the Spirit of adoption, putting them upon the duty of prayer, and enabling them in prayer to eye God as a Father (*v.* 6): *Because you are sons, God hath sent forth the Spirit of his Son into your hearts, crying Abba, Father.* And hereupon (*v.* 7) the apostle concludes this argument by adding, *Wherefore thou art no more a servant, but a son; and, if a son, then an heir of God through Christ;* that is, Now, under the gospel state, we are no longer under the servitude of the law, but, upon our believing in Christ, become the sons of God; we are thereupon accepted of him, and adopted by him; and, being the sons, we are also heirs of God, and are entitled to the heavenly inheritance (as he also reasons Rom. 8:17), and therefore it must needs be the greatest weakness and folly to turn back to the law, and to seek justification by the works of it. From what the apostle says in these verses, we may observe,

1. The wonders of divine love and mercy towards us, particularly of God the Father, in sending his Son into the world to redeem and save us, — of the Son of God, in submitting so low, and suffering so much, for us, in pursuance of that design, — and of the Holy Spirit, in condescending to dwell in the hearts of believers for such gracious purposes.

2. The great and invaluable advantages which Christians enjoy under the gospel; for, (1.) We receive *the adoption of sons.* Whence note, It is the great privilege which believers have through Christ that they are adopted children of the God of heaven. We who by nature are children of wrath and disobedience have become by grace children of love. (2.) We receive *the Spirit of adoption.* Note, [1.] All who have the privilege of adoption have the Spirit of adoption — all who are received into the number partake of the nature of the children of God; for he will have all his children to resemble him. [2.] The Spirit of adoption is always the Spirit of prayer, and it is our duty in prayer to eye God as a Father. Christ has taught us in prayer to eye God as our Father in heaven. [3.] If we are his sons, then his heirs. It is not so among men, with whom the eldest son is heir; but all God's children are heirs. Those who have the nature of sons shall have the inheritance of sons.

Verses 8–11

In these verses the apostle puts them in mind of what they were before their conversion to the faith of Christ, and what a blessed change their conversion had made upon them; and thence endeavours to convince them of their great weakness in hearkening to those who would bring them under the bondage of the law of Moses.

I. He reminds them of their past state and behaviour, and what they were before the gospel was preached to them. Then *they knew not God;* they were grossly ignorant of the true God, and the way wherein he is to be worshipped: and at that time they were under the worst of slaveries, for *they did service to those which by nature were no gods,* they were employed in a great number of superstitious and idolatrous services to those who, though they were accounted gods, were yet really no gods, but mere creatures, and perhaps of their own making, and therefore were utterly unable to hear and help them. Note, 1. Those who are ignorant of the true God cannot but be inclined to false gods. Those who forsook the God who made the world, rather than be without gods, worshipped such as they themselves made. 2. Religious worship is due to none but to him who is by nature God; for, when the apostle blames the doing service to such as by nature were no gods, he plainly shows that he only who is by nature God is the proper object of our religious worship.

II. He calls upon them to consider the happy change that was made in them by the preaching of the gospel among them. Now *they had known God* (they were brought to the knowledge of the true God and of his Son Jesus Christ, whereby they were recovered out of the ignorance and bondage under which they before lay) *or rather were known of God;* this happy change in their state, whereby they were turned from idols to the living God, and through Christ had received the adoption of sons, was not owing to themselves, but to him; it was the effect of his free and rich grace towards them, and as such they ought to account it; and therefore hereby they were laid under the greater obligation to adhere to the liberty wherewith he had made them free. Note, All our acquaintance with God begins with him; we know him, because we are known of him.

III. Hence he infers the unreasonableness and madness of their suffering themselves to be brought again into a state of bondage. He speaks of it with surprise and deep concern of mind that such as they should do so: *How turn you again,* etc., says he, *v.* 9. "How is it that you, who have been taught to worship God in the gospel way, should not be persuaded to comply with the ceremonial way of worship? that you, who have been acquainted with a dispensation of light, liberty, and love, as that of the gospel is, should now submit to a dispensation of darkness, and bondage, and terror, as that of the law is?" This they had the less reason for, since they had never been under the law of Moses, as the Jews had been; and therefore on this account they were more inexcusable than the Jews themselves, who might be supposed to have some fondness for that which had been of such long standing among them. Besides, what they suffered themselves to be brought into bondage to were but *weak and beggarly elements,* such things as had no power in them to cleanse the soul, nor to afford any solid satisfaction to the mind, and which were only designed for that state of pupillage under which the church had been, but which had now come to a period; and therefore their weakness and folly were the more aggravated, in submitting to them, and in symbolizing with the Jews in observing their various festivals, here signified by *days, and months, and times, and years.* Here note, 1. It is possible for those who have made great professions of religion to be afterwards drawn into very great defections from the purity and simplicity of it, for this was the case of these Christians. And, 2. The more mercy God has shown to any, in bringing them into an acquaintance with the gospel, and the liberties and privileges of it, the greater are their sin and folly in suffering themselves to be deprived of them; for this the apostle lays a special stress upon, that after they had known God, or rather were known of him, they desired to be in bondage under the weak and beggarly elements of the law.

IV. Hereupon he expresses his fears concerning them, *lest he had bestowed on them labour in vain.* He had been at a great deal of pains about them, in preaching the gospel to them, and endeavouring to confirm them in the faith and liberty of it; but now they were giving up these, and thereby rendering his labour among them fruitless and ineffectual, and with the thoughts of this he could not but be deeply affected. Note, 1. A great deal of the labour of faithful ministers is labour in vain; and, when it is so, it cannot but be a great grief to those who desire the salvation of souls. Note, 2. The labour of ministers is in vain upon those who begin in the Spirit and end in the flesh, who, though they seem to set out well, yet afterwards turn aside from the way of the gospel. Note, 3. Those will have a great deal to answer for upon whom the faithful ministers of Jesus Christ bestow labour in vain.

Verses 12–16

That these Christians might be the more ashamed of their defection from the truth of the gospel which Paul had preached to them, he here reminds them of the great affection they formerly had for him and his ministry, and puts them upon considering how very unsuitable their present behaviour was to what they then professed. And here we may observe,

I. How affectionately he addresses himself to them. He styles them brethren, though he knew their hearts were in a great measure alienated from him. He desires that all resentments might be laid aside, and that they would bear the same temper of mind towards him which he did to them; he would have them *to be as he was, for he was as they were,* and moreover tells them that *they had not injured him at all.* He had no quarrel with them upon his own account. Though, in blaming their conduct, he had expressed himself with some warmth and concern of mind he assured them that it was not owing to any sense of personal injury or affront (as they might be ready to think), but proceeded wholly from a zeal for the truth and purity of the gospel, and their welfare and happiness. Thus he endeavours to mollify their spirits towards him, that so they might be the better disposed to receive the admonitions he was giving them. Hereby he teaches us that in reproving others we should take care to convince them that our reproofs do not proceed from any private pique or resentment, but from a sincere regard to the honour of God and religion and their truest welfare; for they are then likely to be most successful when they appear to be most disinterested.

II. How he magnifies their former affection to him, that hereby they might be the more ashamed of their present behaviour towards him. To this purpose, 1. He puts them in mind of the difficulty under which he laboured when he came first among them: *I knew,* says he, *how, through infirmity of the flesh, I preached the gospel unto you at the first.* What this *infirmity of the flesh* was, which in the following words he expresses by *his temptation that was in his flesh* (though, no doubt, it was well known to those Christians to whom he wrote), we can now have no certain knowledge of: some take it to have been the persecutions which he suffered for the gospel's sake; others, to have been something in his person, or manner of speaking, which might render his ministry less grateful and acceptable, referring to 2 Co. 10:10, and to *ch.* 12:7–10. But, whatever it was, it seems it made no impression on them to his disadvantage. For, 2. He takes notice that, notwithstanding this his infirmity (which might possibly lessen him in the esteem of some others), they did not despise nor reject him on the account of it, but, on the contrary, *received him as an angel of God, even as Christ Jesus.* They showed a great deal of respect to him, he was a welcome messenger to them, even as though an angel of God or Jesus Christ himself had preached to them; yea, so great was their esteem of him, that, if it would have been any advantage to him, *they could have plucked out their own eyes, and have given them to him.* Note, How uncertain the respects of people are, how apt they are to change their minds, and how easily they are drawn into contempt of those for whom they once had the greatest esteem and affection, so that they are ready to pluck out the eyes of those for whom they would before have plucked out their own! We should therefore labour to be accepted of God, *for it is a small thing to be judged of man's judgment,* 1 Co. 4:3.

III. How earnestly he expostulates with them hereupon: *Where is then,* says he, *the blessedness you spoke of?* As if he had said, "Time was when you expressed the greatest joy and satisfaction in the glad tidings of the gospel, and were very forward in pouring out your blessings upon me as the publisher of them; whence is it that you are now so much altered, that you have so little relish of them or respect for me? You once thought yourselves happy in receiving the gospel; have you now any reason to think otherwise?" Note, Those who have left their first love would do well to consider, Where is now the blessedness they once spoke of? What has become of that pleasure they used to take in communion with God, and in the company of his servants? The more to impress upon them a just shame of their present conduct, he again asks (*v.* 16), *"Am I become your enemy, because I tell you the truth?* How is it that I, who was heretofore your favourite, am now accounted your enemy? Can you pretend any other reason for it than that I have told you the truth, endeavoured to acquaint you with, and to confirm you in, the truth of the gospel? And, if not, how unreasonable must your disaffection be!" Note, 1. It is no uncommon thing for men to account those their enemies who are really their best friends; for so, undoubtedly, those are, whether ministers or others, who tell them the truth, and deal freely and faithfully with them in matters relating to their eternal salvation, as the apostle now did with these Christians. 2. Ministers may sometimes create enemies to themselves by the faithful discharge of their duty; for this was the case of Paul, he was accounted their enemy for telling them the truth. 3. Yet ministers must not forbear speaking the truth, for fear of offending others and drawing their displeasure upon them. 4. They may be easy in their own minds, when they are conscious to themselves that, if others have become their enemies, it is only for telling them the truth.

Verses 17–18

The apostle is still carrying on the same design as in the foregoing verse, which was, to convince the Galatians of their sin and folly in departing from the truth of the gospel: having just before been expostulating with them about the change of their behaviour towards him who endeavoured to establish them in it, he here gives them the character of those false teachers who made it their business to draw them away from it, which if they would attend to, they might soon see how little reason they had to hearken to them: whatever opinion they might have of them, he tells them they were designing men, who were aiming to set up themselves, and who, under their specious pretences, were more consulting their own interest than theirs: *"They zealously affect you,"* says he; "they show a mighty respect for you, and pretend a great deal of affection to you, *but not well;* they do it not with any good design, they are not sincere and upright in it, for *they would exclude you, that you might affect them.* That which they are chiefly aiming at is to engage your affections to them; and, in order to this, they are doing all they can to draw off your affections from me and from the truth, that so they may engross you to themselves." This, he assures them, was their design, and therefore they must needs be very unwise in hearkening to them. Note, 1. There may appear to be a great deal of zeal where yet there is but little truth and sincerity. 2. It is the usual way of seducers to insinuate themselves into people's affections, and by that means to draw them into their opinions. 3. Whatever pretences such may make, they have usually more regard to their own interest than that of others, and will not stick at ruining the reputation of others, if by that means they can raise their own. On this occasion the apostle gives us that excellent rule which we have, *v.* 18, *It is good to be zealously affected always in a good thing.* What our translation renders *in a good man,* and so consider the apostle as pointing to himself; this sense, they think, is favoured both by the preceding context and also by the words immediately following, *and not only when I am present with you,* which may be as if he had said, "Time was when you were zealously affected towards me; you once took me for a good man, and have now no reason to think otherwise of me; surely then it would become you to show the same regard to me, now that I am absent from you, which you did when I was present with you." But, if we adhere to our own translation, the apostle here furnishes us with a very good rule to direct and regulate us in the exercise of our zeal: there are two things which to this purpose he more especially recommends to us: — (1.) That it be exercised only upon that which is good; for zeal is then only good when it is in a good thing: those who are zealously affected to that which is evil will thereby only to do so much the more hurt. And, (2.) That herein it be constant and steady: it is good to be zealous always in a good thing; not for a time only, or now and then, like the heat of an ague-fit, but, like the natural heat of the body, constant. Happy would it be for the church of Christ if this rule were better observed among Christians!

Verses 19–20

That the apostle might the better dispose these Christians to bear with him in the reproofs which he was obliged to give them, he here expresses his great affection to them, and the very tender concern he had for their welfare: he was not like them — one thing when among them and another when absent from them. Their disaffection to him had not removed his affection from them; but he still bore the same respect to them which he had formerly done, nor was he like their false teachers, who pretended a great deal of affection to them, when at the same time they were only consulting their own interest; but he had a sincere concern for their truest advantage; he sought not theirs, but them. They were too ready to account him their enemy, but he assures them that he was their friend; nay, not only so, but that he had the bowels of a parent towards them. He calls them *his children,* as he justly might, since he had been the instrument of their conversion to the Christian faith; yea, he styles them his *little children,* which, as it denotes a greater degree of tenderness and affection to them, so it may possibly have a respect to their present behaviour, whereby they showed themselves too much like little children, who are easily wrought upon by the arts and insinuations of others. He expresses his concern for them, and earnest desire of their welfare and soul-prosperity, by the pangs of a travailing woman: *He travailed in birth for them:* and the great thing which he was in so much pain about, and which he was so earnestly desirous of, was not so much that they might affect him as *that Christ might be formed in them,* that they might become Christians indeed, and be more confirmed and established in the faith of the gospel. From this we may note, 1. The very tender affection which faithful ministers bear towards those among whom they are employed; it is like that of the most affectionate parents to their little children. 2. That the chief thing they are longing and even travailing in birth for, on their account, is that Christ may be formed in them; not so much that they may gain their affections, much less that they may make a prey of them, but that they may be renewed in the spirit of their minds, wrought into the image of Christ, and more fully settled and confirmed in the Christian faith and life: and how unreasonably must those people act who suffer themselves to be prevailed upon to desert or dislike such ministers! 3. That Christ is not fully formed in men till they are brought off from trusting in their own righteousness, and made to rely only upon him and his righteousness.

As further evidence of the affection and concern which the apostle had for these Christians, he adds (*v.* 20) that *he desired to be then present with them* — that he would be glad of an opportunity of being among them, and conversing with them, and that thereupon he might find occasion *to change his voice* towards them; for at present *he stood in doubt of them.* He knew not well what to think of them. He was not so fully acquainted with their state as to know how to accommodate himself to them. He was full of fears and jealousies concerning them, which was the reason of his writing to them in such a manner as he had done; but he would be glad to find that matters were better with them than he feared, and that he might have occasion to commend them, instead of thus reproving and chiding them. Note, Though ministers too often find it necessary to reprove those they have to do with, yet this is no grateful work to them; they had much rather there were no occasion for it, and are always glad when they can see reason to change their voice towards them.

Verses 21–31

In these verses the apostle illustrates the difference between believers who rested in Christ only and those judaizers who trusted in the law, by a comparison taken from the story of Isaac and Ishmael. This he introduces in such a manner as was proper to strike and impress their minds, and to convince them of their great weakness in departing from the truth, and suffering themselves to be deprived of the liberty of the gospel: *Tell me,* says he, *you that desire to be under the law, do you not hear the law?* He takes it for granted that they did hear the law, for among the Jews it was wont to be read in their public assemblies every sabbath day; and, since they were so very fond of being under it, he would have them duly to consider what is written therein (referring to what is recorded Gen. 16 and 21), for, if they would do this, they might soon see how little reason they had to trust in it. And here, 1. He sets before them the history itself (*v.* 22, 23): *For it is written, Abraham had two sons,* etc. Here he represents the different state and condition of these two sons of Abraham — that the one, Ishmael, *was by a bond-maid,* and the other, Isaac, *by a free-woman;* and that whereas the former *was born after the flesh,* or by the ordinary course of nature, the other *was by promise,* when in the course of nature there was no reason to expect that Sarah should have a son. 2. He acquaints them with the meaning and design of this history, or the use which he intended to make of it (*v.* 24–27): *These things,* says he, *are an allegory,* wherein, besides the literal and historical sense of the words, the Spirit of God might design to signify something further to us, and that was, That these two, Agar and Sarah, *are the two covenants,* or were intended to typify and prefigure the two different dispensations of the covenant. The former, Agar, represented that which was given from mount Sinai, and *which gendereth to bondage,* which, though it was a dispensation of grace, yet, in comparison of the gospel state, was a dispensation of bondage, and became more so to the Jews, through their mistake of the design of it, and expecting to be justified by the works of it. *For this Agar is mount Sinai in Arabia* (mount Sinai was then called Agar by the Arabians), *and it answereth to Jerusalem which now is, and is in bondage with her children;* that is, it justly represents the present state of the Jews, who, continuing in their infidelity and adhering to that covenant, are still in bondage with their children. But the other, Sarah, was intended to prefigure Jerusalem which is above, or the state of Christians under the new and better dispensation of the covenant, which is free both from the curse of the moral and the bondage of the ceremonial law, and *is the mother of us all* — a state into which all, both Jews and Gentiles, are admitted, upon their believing in Christ. And to this greater freedom and enlargement of the church under the gospel dispensation, which was typified by Sarah the mother of the promised seed, the apostle refers that of the prophet, Isa. 54:1, where it is written, *Rejoice, thou barren that bearest not; break forth and cry, thou that travailest not; for the desolate hath many more children than she who hath a husband.* 3. He applies the history thus explained to the present case (*v.* 28); *Now we, brethren,* says he, *as Isaac was, are the children of the promise.* We Christians, who have accepted Christ, and rely upon him, and look for justification and salvation by him alone, as hereby we become the spiritual, though we are not the natural, seed of Abraham, so we are entitled to the promised inheritance and interested in the blessings of it. But lest these Christians should be stumbled at the opposition they might meet with from the Jews, who were so tenacious of their law as to be ready to persecute those who would not submit to it, he tells them that this was no more than what was pointed to in the type; for *as then he that was born after the flesh persecuted him that was born after the Spirit,* they must expect it would be *so now.* But, for their comfort in this case, he desires them to consider what the scripture saith (Gen. 21:10), *Cast out the bond-woman and her son, for the son of the bond-woman shall not be heir with the son of the free-woman.* Though the judaizers should persecute and hate them, yet the issue would be that Judaism would sink, and wither, and perish; but true Christianity should flourish and last for ever. And then, as a general inference from the whole of the sum of what he had said, he concludes (*v.* 31), *So then, brethren, we are not children of the bond-woman, but of the free.*

CHAPTER 5

In this chapter the apostle comes to make application of his foregoing discourse. He begins it with a general caution, or exhortation (*v.* 1), which he afterwards enforces by several considerations (*v.* 2–12). He then presses them to serious practical godliness, which would be the best antidote against the snares of their false teachers; particularly, I. That they should not strive with one another (*v.* 13–15). II. That they would strive against sin, where he shows, 1. That there is in every one a struggle between flesh and spirit (*v.* 17). 2. That it is our duty and interest, in this struggle, to side with the better part (*v.* 16, 18). 3. He specifies the works of the flesh, which must be watched against and mortified, and the fruits of the Spirit, which must be brought forth and cherished, and shows of what importance it is that they be so (*v.* 19–24). And then concludes the chapter with a caution against pride and envy.

Verses 1–12

In the former part of this chapter the apostle cautions the Galatians to take heed of the judaizing teachers, who endeavoured to bring them back under the bondage of the law. He had been arguing against them before, and had largely shown how contrary the principles and spirit of those teachers were to the spirit of the gospel; and now this is as it were the general inference or application of all that discourse. Since it appeared by what had been said that we can be justified only by faith in Jesus Christ, and not by the righteousness of the law, and that the law of Moses was no longer in force, nor Christians under any obligation to submit to it, therefore he would have them to *stand fast in the liberty wherewith Christ hath made us free, and not to be again entangled with the yoke of bondage.* Here observe, 1. Under the gospel we are enfranchised, we are brought into a state of liberty, wherein we are freed from the yoke of the ceremonial law and from the curse of the moral law; so that we are no longer tied to the observance of the one, nor tied up to the rigour of the other, which curses every one that continues not in all things written therein to do them, *ch.* 3:10. 2. We owe this liberty to Jesus Christ. It is he who *has made us free;* by his merits he has satisfied the demands of the broken law, and by his authority as a king he has discharged us from the obligation of those carnal ordinances which were imposed on the Jews. And, 3. It is therefore our duty to *stand fast in this liberty,* constantly and faithfully to adhere to the gospel and to the liberty of it, and not to suffer ourselves, upon any consideration, *to be again entangled in the yoke of bondage,* nor persuaded to return back to the law of Moses. This is the general caution or exhortation, which in the following verses the apostle enforces by several reasons or arguments. As,

I. That their submitting to circumcision, and depending on the works of the law for righteousness, were an implicit contradiction of their faith as Christians and a forfeiture of all their advantages by Jesus Christ, *v.* 2–4. And here we may observe, 1. With what solemnity the apostle asserts and declares this: *Behold, I Paul say unto you* (*v.* 2), and he repeats it (*v.* 3), *I testify unto you;* as it he had said, "I, who have proved myself an apostle of Christ, and to have received my authority and instructions from him, do declare, and am ready to pawn my credit and reputation upon it, *that if you be circumcised Christ shall profit you nothing,* etc.," wherein he shows that what he was now saying was not only a matter of great importance, but what might be most assuredly depended on. He was so far from being a preacher of circumcision (as some might report him to be) that he looked upon it as a matter of the greatest consequence that they did not submit to it. 2. What it is which he so solemnly, and with so much assurance, declares; it is that, *if they were circumcised, Christ would profit them nothing,* etc. We are not to suppose that it is mere circumcision which the apostle is here speaking of, or that it was his design to say that none who are circumcised could have any benefit by Christ; for all the Old-Testament saints had been circumcised, and he himself had consented to the circumcising of Timothy. But he is to be understood as speaking of circumcision in the sense in which the judaizing teachers imposed it, who taught *that except they were circumcised, and kept the law of Moses, they could not be saved,* Acts 15:1. That this is his meaning appears from *v.* 4, where he expresses the same thing by their being *justified by the law,* or seeking justification by the works of it. Now in this case, if they submitted to circumcision in this sense, he declares that *Christ would profit them nothing, that they were debtors to do the whole law,* that *Christ had become of no effect to them,* and that *they were fallen from grace.* From all these expressions it appears that thereby they renounced that way of justification which God had established; yea, that they laid themselves under an impossibility of being justified in his sight, for they became debtors to do the whole law, which required such an obedience as they were not capable of performing, and denounced a curse against those who failed in it, and therefore condemned, but could not justify them; and, consequently, that having thus revolted from Christ, and built their hopes upon the law, Christ would profit them nothing, nor be of any effect to them. Thus, as by being circumcised they renounced their Christianity, so they cut themselves off from all advantage by Christ; and therefore there was the greatest reason why they should stedfastly adhere to that doctrine which they had embraced, and not suffer themselves to be brought under this yoke of bondage. Note, (1.) Though Jesus Christ is able to save to the uttermost, yet there are multitudes whom he will profit nothing. (2.) All those who seek to be justified by the law do thereby render Christ of no effect to them. By building their hopes on the works of the law, they forfeit all their hopes from him; for he will not be the Saviour of any who will not own and rely upon him as their only Saviour.

II. To persuade them to stedfastness in the doctrine and liberty of the gospel, he sets before them his own example, and that of other Jews who had embraced the Christian religion, and acquaints them what their hopes were, namely, That *through the Spirit they were waiting for the hope of righteousness by faith.* Though they were Jews by nature, and had been bred up under the law, yet being, through the Spirit, brought to the knowledge of Christ, they had renounced all dependence on the works of the law, and looked for justification and salvation only by faith in him; and therefore it must needs be the greatest folly in those who had never been under the law to suffer themselves to be brought into subjection to it, and to found their hopes upon the works of it. Here we may observe, 1. What it is that Christians are waiting for: it is *the hope of righteousness,* by which we are chiefly to understand the happiness of the other world. This is called the hope of Christians, as it is the great object of their hope, which they are above every thing else desiring and pursuing; and the hope of righteousness, as their hopes of it are founded on righteousness, not their own, but that of our Lord Jesus: for, though a life of righteousness is the way that leads to this happiness, yet it is the righteousness of Christ alone which has procured it for us, and on account of which we can expect to be brought to the possession of it. 2. How they hope to obtain this happiness, namely, by faith, that is, in our Lord Jesus Christ, not by the works of the law, or any thing they can do to deserve it, but only by faith, receiving and relying upon him as the Lord our righteousness. It is in this way only that they expect either to be entitled to it here or possessed of it hereafter. And, 3. Whence it is that they are thus waiting for the hope of righteousness: it is *through the Spirit.* Herein they act under the direction and influence of the Holy Spirit; it is under his conduct, and by his assistance, that they are both persuaded and enabled to believe on Christ, and to look for the hope of righteousness through him. When the apostle thus represents the case of Christians, it is implied that if they expected to be justified and saved in any other way they were likely to meet with a disappointment, and therefore that they were greatly concerned to adhere to the doctrine of the gospel which they had embraced.

III. He argues from the nature and design of the Christian institution, which was to abolish the difference between Jew and Gentile, and to establish faith in Christ as the way of our acceptance with God. He tells them (*v.* 6) that *in Christ Jesus*, or under the gospel dispensation, *neither circumcision availeth any thing nor uncircumcision.* Though, while the legal state lasted, there was a difference put between Jew and Greek, between those who were and those who were not circumcised, the former being admitted to those privileges of the church of God from which the other were excluded, yet it was otherwise in the gospel state: Christ, who is *the end of the law,* having come, now it was neither here nor there whether a man were circumcised or uncircumcised; he was neither the better for the one nor the worse for the other, nor would either the one or the other recommend him to God; and therefore as their judaizing teachers were very unreasonable in imposing circumcision upon them, and obliging them to observe the law of Moses, so they must needs be very unwise in submitting to them herein. But, though he assures them that neither circumcision nor uncircumcision would avail to their acceptance with God, yet he informs them what would do so, and that is *faith, which worketh by love:* such a faith in Christ as discovers itself to be true and genuine by a sincere love to God and our neighbour. If they had this, it mattered not whether they were circumcised or uncircumcised, but without it nothing else would stand them in any stead. Note, 1. No external privileges nor profession will avail to our acceptance with God, without a sincere faith in our Lord Jesus. 2. Faith, where it is true, is a working grace: it works by love, love to God and love to our brethren; and faith, thus working by love, is all in all in our Christianity.

IV. To recover them from their backslidings, and engage them to greater stedfastness for the future, he puts them in mind of their good beginnings, and calls upon them to consider whence it was that they were so much altered from what they had been, *v.* 7.

1. He tells them that *they did run well;* at their first setting out in Christianity they had behaved themselves very commendably, they had readily embraced the Christian religion, and discovered a becoming zeal in the ways and work of it; as in their baptism they were devoted to God, and had declared themselves the disciples of Christ, so their behaviour was agreeable to their character and profession. Note, (1.) The life of a Christian is a race, wherein he must run, and hold on, if he would obtain the prize. (2.) It is not enough that we run in this race, by a profession of Christianity, but we must run well, by living up to that profession. Thus these Christians had done for awhile, but they had been obstructed in their progress, and were either turned out of the way or at least made to flag and falter in it. Therefore,

2. He asks them, and calls upon them to ask themselves, *Who did hinder you?* How came it to pass that they did not hold on in the way wherein they had begun to run so well? He very well knew who they were, and what it was that hindered them; but he would have them to put the question to themselves, and seriously consider whether they had any good reason to hearken to those who gave them this disturbance, and whether what they offered was sufficient to justify them in their present conduct. Note, (1.) Many who set out fair in religion, and run well for awhile — run within the bounds appointed for the race, and run with zeal and alacrity too — are yet by some means or other hindered in their progress, or turned out of the way. (2.) It concerns those who have run well, but now begin either to turn out of the way or to tire in it, to enquire what it is that hinders them. Young converts must expect that Satan will be laying stumbling blocks in their way, and doing all he can to divert them from the course they are in; but, whenever they find themselves in danger of being turned out of it, they would do well to consider who it is that hinders them. Whoever they were that hindered these Christians, the apostle tells them that by hearkening to them they were kept from *obeying the truth,* and were thereby in danger of losing the benefit of what they had done in religion. The gospel which he had preached to them, and which they had embraced and professed, he assures them was the truth; it was therein only that the true way of justification and salvation was fully discovered, and, in order to their enjoying the advantage of it, it was necessary that they should obey it, that they should firmly adhere to it, and continue to govern their lives and hopes according to the directions of it. If therefore they should suffer themselves to be drawn away from it they must needs be guilty of the greatest weakness and folly. Note, [1.] The truth is not only to be believed, but to be obeyed, to be received not only in the light of it, but in the love and power of it.

[2.] Those do not rightly obey the truth, who do not stedfastly adhere to it. [3.] There is the same reason for our obeying the truth that there was for our embracing it: and therefore those act very unreasonably who, when they have begun to run well in the Christian race, suffer themselves to be hindered, so as not to persevere in it.

V. He argues for their stedfastness in the faith and liberty of the gospel from the ill rise of that persuasion whereby they were drawn away from it (*v.* 8): *This persuasion,* says he, *cometh not of him that calleth you.* The opinion or persuasion of which the apostle here speaks was no doubt that of the necessity of their being circumcised, and keeping the law of Moses, or of their mixing the works of the law with faith in Christ in the business of justification. This was what the judaizing teachers endeavoured to impose upon them, and what they had too easily fallen into. To convince them of their folly herein, he tells them that this persuasion did not come of him that called them, that is, either of God, by whose authority the gospel had been preached to them and they had been called into the fellowship of it, or of the apostle himself, who had been employed as the instrument of calling them hereunto. It could not come from God, for it was contrary to that way of justification and salvation which he had established; nor could they have received it from Paul himself; for, whatever some might pretend, he had all along been an opposer and not a preacher of circumcision, and, if in any instance he had submitted to it for the sake of peace, yet he had never pressed the use of it upon Christians, much less imposed it upon them as necessary to salvation. Since then this persuasion did not come of him that had called them, he leaves them to judge whence it must arise, and sufficiently intimates that it could be owing to none but Satan and his instruments, who by this means were endeavouring to overthrow their faith and obstruct the progress of the gospel, and therefore that the Galatians had every reason to reject it, and to continue stedfast in the truth which they had before embraced. Note, 1. In order to our judging aright of the different persuasions in religion which there are among Christians, it concerns us to enquire whether they come of him that calleth us, whether or no they are founded upon the authority of Christ and his apostles. 2. If, upon enquiry, they appear to have no such foundation, how forward soever others may be to impose them upon us, we should by no means submit to them, but reject them.

VI. The danger there was of the spreading of this infection, and the ill influence it might have upon others, are a further argument which the apostle urges against their complying with their false teachers in what they would impose on them. It is possible that, to extenuate their fault, they might be ready to say that there were but few of those teachers among them who endeavoured to draw them into this persuasion and practice, or that they were only some smaller matters wherein they complied with them — that though they submitted to be circumcised, and to observe some few rites of the Jewish laws, yet they had by no means renounced their Christianity and gone over to Judaism. Or, suppose their complying thus far was as faulty as he could represent it, yet perhaps they might further say that there were but few among them who had done so, and therefore he needed not be so much concerned about it. Now, to obviate such pretences as these, and to convince them that there was more danger in it than they were aware of, he tells them (*v.* 9) that *a little leaven leaveneth the whole lump* — that the whole lump of Christianity may be tainted and corrupted by one such erroneous principle, or that the whole lump of the Christian society may be infected by one member of it, and therefore that they were greatly concerned not to yield in this single instance, or, if any had done so, to endeavour by all proper methods to purge out the infection from among them. Note, It is dangerous for Christian churches to encourage those among them who entertain, especially who set themselves to propagate, destructive errors. This was the case here. The doctrine which the false teachers were industrious to spread, and which some in these churches had been drawn into, was subversive of Christianity itself, as the apostle had before shown; and therefore, though the number either of the one or the other of these might be but small, yet, considering the fatal tendency of it and the corruption of human nature, whereby others were too much disposed to be infected with it, he would not have them on that account to be easy and unconcerned, but remember that *a little leaven leaveneth the whole lump.* If these were indulged the contagion

might soon spread further and wider; and, if they suffered themselves to be imposed upon in this instance, it might soon issue in the utter ruin of the truth and liberty of the gospel.

VII. That he might conciliate the greater regard to what he had said, he expresses the hopes he had concerning them (*v.* 10): *I have confidence in you,* says he, *through the Lord, that you will be none otherwise minded.* Though he had many fears and doubts about them (which was the occasion of his using so much plainness and freedom with them), yet he hoped that through the blessing of God upon what he had written they might be brought to be of the same mind with him, and to own and abide by that truth and that liberty of the gospel which he had preached to them, and was now endeavouring to confirm them in. Herein he teaches us that we ought to hope the best even of those concerning whom we have cause to fear the worst. That they might be the less offended at the reproofs he had given them for their unstedfastness in the faith, he lays the blame of it more upon others than themselves; for he adds, *But he that troubleth you shall bear his judgment, whosoever he be.* He was sensible that there were *some that troubled them, and would pervert the gospel of Christ* (as *ch.* 1:7), and possibly he may point to some one particular man who was more busy and forward than others, and might be the chief instrument of the disorder that was among them; and to this he imputes their defection or inconstancy more than to any thing in themselves. This may give us occasion to observe that, in reproving sin and error, we should always distinguish between the leaders and the led, such as set themselves to draw others thereinto and such as are drawn aside by them. Thus the apostle softens and alleviates the fault of these Christians, even while he is reproving them, that he might the better persuade them to return to, and stand fast in, the liberty wherewith Christ had made them free: but as for him or those that troubled them, whoever he or they were, he declares they *should bear their judgment,* he did not doubt but God would deal with them according to their deserts, and out of his just indignation against them, as enemies of Christ and his church, he wishes that *they were even cut off* — not cut off from Christ and all hopes of salvation by him, but cut off by the censures of the church, which ought to witness against those teachers who thus corrupted the purity of the gospel. Those, whether ministers or others, who set themselves to overthrow the faith of the gospel, and disturb the peace of Christians, do thereby forfeit the privileges of Christian communion and deserve to be cut off from them.

VIII. To dissuade these Christians from hearkening to their judaizing teachers, and to recover them from the ill impressions they had made upon them, he represents them as men who had used very base and disingenuous methods to compass their designs, for they had misrepresented him, that they might the more easily gain their ends upon them. That which they were endeavouring was to bring them to submit to circumcision, and to mix Judaism with their Christianity; and, the better to accomplish this design, they had given out among them that Paul himself was a preacher of circumcision: for when he says (*v.* 11), *And I brethren, if I yet preach circumcision,* it plainly appears that they had reported him to have done so, and that they had made use of this as an argument to prevail with the Galatians to submit to it. It is probable that they grounded this report upon his having circumcised Timothy, Acts 16:3. But, though for good reasons he had yielded to circumcision in that instance, yet that he was a preacher of it, and especially in that sense wherein they imposed it, he utterly denies. To prove the injustice of that charge upon him, he offers such arguments as, if they would allow themselves to consider, could not fail to convince them of it. 1. If he would have preached circumcision, he might have avoided persecution. If I yet preach circumcision, says he, *why do I yet suffer persecution?* It was evident, and they could not but be sensible of it, that he was hated and persecuted by the Jews; but what account could be given of this their behaviour towards him, if he had so far symbolized with them as to preach up circumcision, and the observance of the law of Moses, as necessary to salvation? This was the great point they were contending for; and, if he had fallen in with them herein, instead of being exposed to their rage he might have been received into their favour. When therefore he was suffering persecution from them, this was a plain evidence that he had not complied with them; yea, that he was so far from preaching the doctrine he was charged with, that, rather than do so, he was willing to expose himself to the greatest hazards. 2. If he had yielded to the Jews herein, *then would the offence of the cross have ceased.* They would not have taken so much offence against the doctrine of Christianity as they did, nor would he and others have been exposed to so much suffering on the account of it as they were. He informs us (1 Co. 1:23) that the preaching of the cross of Christ (or the doctrine of justification and salvation only by faith in Christ crucified) *was to the Jews a stumbling-block.* That which they were most offended at in Christianity was, that thereby circumcision, and the whole frame of the legal administration, were set aside, as no longer in force. This raised their greatest outcries against it, and stirred them up to oppose and persecute the professors of it. Now if Paul and others could have given into this opinion, that circumcision was still to be retained, and the observance of the law of Moses joined with faith in Christ as necessary to salvation, then their offence against it would have been in a great measure removed, and they might have avoided the sufferings they underwent for the sake of it. But though others, and particularly those who were so forward to asperse him as a preacher of this doctrine, could easily come into it, yet so could not he. He rather chose to hazard his ease and credit, yea his very life itself, than thus to corrupt the truth and give up the liberty of the gospel. Hence it was that the Jews continued to be so much offended against Christianity, and against him as the preacher of it. Thus the apostle clears himself from the unjust reproach which his enemies had cast upon him, and at the same time shows how little regard was due to those men who could treat him in such an injurious manner, and how much reason he had to wish that they were even cut off.

Verses 13–26

In the latter part of this chapter the apostle comes to exhort these Christians to serious practical godliness, as the best antidote against the snares of the false teachers. Two things especially he presses upon them: —

I. That they should not strive with one another, but love one another. He tells them (*v.* 13) that *they had been called unto liberty,* and he would have them to stand fast in the liberty wherewith Christ had made them free; but yet he would have them be very careful that they did not *use this liberty as an occasion to the flesh* — that they did not thence take occasion to indulge themselves in any corrupt affections and practices, and particularly such as might create distance and disaffection, and be the ground of quarrels and contentions among them: but, on the contrary, he would have them *by love to serve one another,* to maintain that mutual love and affection which, notwithstanding any minor differences there might be among them, would dispose them to all those offices of respect and kindness to each other which the Christian religion obliged them to. Note, 1. The liberty we enjoy as Christians is not a licentious liberty: though Christ has redeemed us from the curse of the law, yet he has not freed us from the obligation of it; the gospel is a *doctrine according to godliness* (1 Tim. 6:3), and is so far from giving the least countenance to sin that it lays us under the strongest obligations to avoid and subdue it. 2. Though we ought to stand fast in our Christian liberty, yet we should not insist upon it to the breach of Christian charity; we should not use it as an occasion of strife and contention with our fellow Christians, who may be differently minded from us, but should always maintain such a temper towards each other as may dispose us by love to serve one another. To this the apostle endeavours to persuade these Christians, and there are two considerations which he sets before them for this purpose: — (1.) *That all the law is fulfilled in one word, even in this, Thou shalt love thy neighbour as thyself, v.* 14. Love is the sum of the whole law; as love to God comprises the duties of the first table, so love to our neighbour those of the second. The apostle takes notice of the latter here, because he is speaking of their behaviour towards one another; and, when he makes use of this as an argument to persuade them to mutual love, he intimates both that this would be a good evidence of their sincerity in religion and also the most likely means of rooting out those dissensions and divisions that were among them. It will appear that we are the disciples of Christ indeed when we have love one to another (Jn. 13:35); and, where this temper is kept up, if it do not wholly extinguish those unhappy discords that are among Christians, yet at least it will so far accommodate them that the fatal consequences of them will be prevented. (2.) The sad and dangerous tendency of a contrary behaviour (*v.* 15): *But,* says he, if instead of serving one another in love, and therein fulfilling the law of God, *you bite and devour one another, take heed that you be not consumed one of another.* If, instead of acting like men and Christians, they would behave themselves more like brute beasts, in tearing and rending one another, they could expect nothing as the consequence of it, but that they would be consumed one of another; and therefore they had the greatest reason not to indulge themselves in such quarrels and animosities. Note, Mutual strifes among brethren, if persisted in, are likely to prove a common ruin; those that devour one another are in a fair way to be consumed one of another. Christian churches cannot be ruined but by their own hands; but if Christians, who should be helps to one another and a joy one to another, be as brute beasts, biting and devouring each other, what can be expected but that the God of love should deny his grace to them, and the Spirit of love should depart from them, and that the evil spirit, who seeks the destruction of them all, should prevail?

II. That they should all strive against sin; and happy would it be for the church if Christians would let all their quarrels be swallowed up of this, even a quarrel against sin — if, instead of biting and devouring one another on account of their different opinions, they would all set themselves against sin in themselves and the places where they live. This is what we are chiefly concerned to fight against, and that which above every thing else we should make it our business to oppose and suppress. To excite Christians hereunto, and to assist them herein, the apostle shows,

1. That there is in every one a struggle between the flesh and the spirit (*v.* 17): *The flesh* (the corrupt and carnal part of us) *lusts* (strives and struggles with strength and vigour) *against the spirit:* it opposes all the motions of the Spirit, and resists every thing that is spiritual. On the other hand, *the spirit* (the renewed part of us) strives *against the flesh,* and opposes the will and desire of it: and hence it comes to pass *that we cannot do the things that we would.* As the principle of grace in us will not suffer us to do all the evil which our corrupt nature would prompt us to, so neither can we do all the good that we would, by reason of the oppositions we meet with from that corrupt and carnal principle. Even as in a natural man there is something of this struggle (the convictions of his conscience and the corruption of his own heart strive with one another; his convictions would suppress his corruptions, and his corruptions silence his convictions), so in a renewed man, where there is something of a good principle, there is a struggle between the old nature and the new nature, the remainders of sin and the beginnings of grace; and this Christians must expect will be their exercise as long as they continue in this world.

2. That it is our duty and interest in this struggle to side with the better part, to side with our convictions against our corruptions and with our graces against our lusts. This the apostle represents as our duty, and directs us to the most effectual means of success in it. If it should be asked, What course must we take that the better interest may get the better? he gives us this one general rule, which, if duly observed, would be the most sovereign remedy against the prevalence of corruption; and that is to walk in the Spirit (*v.* 16): *This I say, then, Walk in the Spirit, and you shall not fulfil the lust of the flesh.* By the *Spirit* here may be meant either the Holy Spirit himself, who condescends to dwell in the hearts of those whom he has renewed and sanctified, to guide and assist them in the way of their duty, or that gracious principle which he implants in the souls of his people and which lusts against the flesh, as that corrupt principle which still remains in them does against it. Accordingly the duty here recommended to us is that we set ourselves to act under the guidance and influence of the blessed Spirit, and agreeably to the motions and tendency of the new nature in us; and, if this be our care in the ordinary course and tenour of our lives, we may depend upon it that, though we may not be freed from the stirrings and oppositions of our corrupt nature, we shall be kept from fulfilling it in the lusts thereof; so that though it remain in us, yet it shall not obtain a dominion over us. Note, The best antidote against the poison of sin is to walk in the Spirit, to be much in conversing with spiritual things, to mind the things of the soul, which is the spiritual part of man, more than those of the body, which is his carnal part, to commit ourselves to the guidance of the word, wherein the Holy Spirit makes known the will of God concerning us, and in the way of our duty to act in a dependence on his aids and influences. And, as this would be the best means of preserving them from fulfilling the lusts of the flesh, so it would be a good evidence that they were Christians indeed; for, says the apostle (*v.* 18), *If you be led by the Spirit, you are not under the law.* As if he had said, "You must expect a struggle between flesh and spirit as long as you are in the world, that the flesh will be lusting against the spirit as well as the spirit against the flesh; but if, in the prevailing bent and tenour of your lives, you be *led by the Spirit,* — if you act under the guidance and government of the Holy Spirit and of that spiritual nature and disposition he has wrought in you, — if you make the word of God your rule and the grace of God your principle, — it will hence appear that you are not under the law, not under the condemning, though you are still under the commanding, power of it; for *there is now no condemnation to those that are in Christ Jesus, who walk not after the flesh, but after the Spirit;* and *as many as are led by the Spirit of God, they are the sons of God,*" Rom. 8:1–14.

3. The apostle specifies the works of the flesh, which must be watched against and mortified, and the fruits of the Spirit, which must be cherished and brought forth (*v.* 19, etc.); and by specifying particulars he further illustrates what he is here upon. (1.) He begins with *the works of the flesh,* which, as they are many, so they are manifest. It is past dispute that the things he here speaks of are the works of the flesh, or the product of corrupt and depraved nature; most of them are condemned by the light of nature itself, and all of them by the light of scripture. The particulars he specifies are of various sorts; some are sins against the seventh commandment, such as *adultery, fornication, uncleanness, lasciviousness,* by which are meant not only the gross acts of these sins, but all such thoughts, and words, and actions, as have a tendency towards the great transgression. Some are sins against the first and second commandments, as *idolatry* and *witchcraft.* Others are sins against our neighbour, and contrary to the royal law of brotherly love, such as *hatred, variance, emulations, wrath, strife,* which too often occasion *seditions, heresies, envyings,* and sometimes break out into *murders,* not only of the names and reputation, but even of the very lives, of our fellow-creatures. Others are sins against ourselves, such as *drunkenness and revellings;* and he concludes the catalogue with an *et cetera,* and gives fair warning to all to take care of them, as they hope to see the face of God with comfort. Of these and *such like,* says he, *I tell you before, as I have also told you in times past,* that *those who do such things,* how much soever they may flatter themselves with vain hopes, *shall not inherit the kingdom of God.* These are sins which will undoubtedly shut men out of heaven. The world of spirits can never be comfortable to those who plunge themselves in the filth of the flesh; nor will the righteous and holy God ever admit such into his favour and presence, unless they be first *washed and sanctified, and justified in the name of our Lord Jesus, and by the Spirit of our God,* 1 Co. 6:11. (2.) He specifies the fruits of the Spirit, or the renewed nature, which as Christians we are concerned to bring forth, *v.* 22, 23. And here we may observe that as sin is called *the work of the flesh,* because the flesh, or corrupt nature, is the principle that moves and excites men to it, so grace is said to be *the fruit of the Spirit,* because it wholly proceeds from the Spirit, as the fruit does from the root: and whereas before the apostle had chiefly specified those works of the flesh which were not only hurtful to men themselves but tended to make them so to one another, so here he chiefly takes notice of those fruits of the Spirit which had a tendency to make Christians agreeable one to another, as well as easy to themselves; and this was very suitable to the caution or exhortation he had before given (*v.* 13), that they should *not use their liberty as an occasion to the flesh, but by love serve one another.* He particularly recommends to us, *love,* to God especially, and to one another for his sake, — *joy,* by which may be understood cheerfulness in conversation with our friends, or rather a constant delight in God, — *peace,* with God and conscience, or a peaceableness of temper and behaviour towards others, — *long-suffering,* patience to defer anger, and a contentedness to bear injuries, — *gentleness,* such a sweetness of temper, and especially towards our inferiors, as disposes us to be affable and courteous, and easy to be entreated when any have wronged us, — *goodness* (kindness, beneficence), which shows itself in a readiness to do good to all as we have opportunity, — *faith,* fidelity, justice, and honesty, in what we profess and promise to others, — *meekness,* wherewith to govern our passions

and resentments, so as not to be easily provoked, and, when we are so, to be soon pacified, — and *temperance,* in meat and drink, and other enjoyments of life, so as not to be excessive and immoderate in the use of them. Concerning these things, or those in whom these fruits of the Spirit are found, the apostle says, *There is no law against them,* to condemn and punish them. Yea, hence it appears that they are not under the law, but under grace; for these fruits of the Spirit, in whomsoever they are found, plainly show that such are *led by the Spirit,* and consequently that they are not *under the law,* as *v.* 18. And as, by specifying these works of the flesh and fruits of the Spirit, the apostle directs us both what we are to avoid and oppose and what we are to cherish and cultivate, so (*v.* 24) he informs us that this is the sincere care and endeavour of all real Christians: *And those that are Christ's,* says he (those who are Christians indeed, not only in show and profession, but in sincerity and truth), *have crucified the flesh with the affections and lusts.* As in their baptism they were obliged hereunto (for, being baptized into Christ, they were baptized into his death, Rom. 6:3), so they are now sincerely employing themselves herein, and, in conformity to their Lord and head, are endeavouring to die unto sin, as he had died for it. They have not yet obtained a complete victory over it; they have still flesh as well as Spirit in them, and that has its affections and lusts, which continue to give them no little disturbance, but as it does not now *reign in their mortal bodies, so as that they obey it in the lusts thereof* (Rom. 6:12), so they are seeking the utter ruin and destruction of it, and to put it to the same shameful and ignominious, though lingering death, which our Lord Jesus underwent for our sakes. Note, If we should approve ourselves to be Christ's, such as are united to him and interested in him, we must make it our constant care and business to crucify the flesh with its corrupt affections and lusts. Christ will never own those as his who yield themselves the servants of sin. But though the apostle here only mentions the crucifying of the flesh with the affections and lusts, as the care and character of real Christians, yet, no doubt, it is also implied that, on the other hand, we should show forth those fruits of the Spirit which he had just before been specifying; this is no less our duty than that, nor is it less necessary to evidence our sincerity in religion. It is not enough that we cease to do evil, but we must learn to do well. Our Christianity obliges us not only to die unto sin, but to live unto righteousness; not only to oppose the works of the flesh, but to bring forth the fruits of the Spirit too. If therefore we would make it appear that we do indeed belong to Christ, this must be our sincere care and endeavour as well as the other; and that it was the design of the apostle to represent both the one and the other of these as our duty, and as necessary to support our character as Christians, may be gathered from what follows (*v.* 25), where he adds, *If we live in the Spirit, let us also walk in the Spirit;* that is, "If we profess to have received the Spirit of Christ, or that we are renewed in the Spirit of Christ, or that we are renewed in the spirit of our minds, and endued with a principle of spiritual life, let us make it appear by the proper fruits of the Spirit in our lives." He had before told us that the Spirit of Christ is a privilege bestowed on all the children of God, *ch.* 4:6. "Now," says he, "if we profess to be of this number, and as such to have obtained this privilege, let us show it by a temper and behaviour agreeable hereunto; let us evidence our good principles by good practices." Our conversation will always be answerable to the principle which we are under the guidance and government of: as *those that are after the flesh do mind the things of the flesh,* so *those that are after the Spirit do mind the things of the Spirit,* Rom. 8:5. If therefore we would have it appear that we are Christ's, and that we are partakers of his Spirit, it must be by our *walking not after the flesh, but after the spirit.* We must set ourselves in good earnest both to mortify the deeds of the body, and to walk in newness of life.

4. The apostle concludes this chapter with a caution against pride and envy, *v.* 26. He had before been exhorting these Christians *by love to serve one another* (*v.* 13), and had put them in mind of what would be the consequence if, instead of that, they did *bite and devour one another, v.* 15. Now, as a means of engaging them to the one and preserving them from the other of these, he here cautions them against being desirous of vain-glory, or giving way to an undue affectation of the esteem and applause of men, because this, if it were indulged, would certainly lead them to provoke one another and to envy one another. As far as this temper pre-

vails among Christians, they will be ready to slight and despise those whom they look upon as inferior to them, and to be put out of humour if they are denied that respect which they think is their due from them, and they will also be apt to envy those by whom their reputation is in any danger of being lessened: and thus a foundation is laid for those quarrels and contentions which, as they are inconsistent with that love which Christians ought to maintain towards each other, so they are greatly prejudicial to the honour and interest of religion itself. This therefore the apostle would have us by all means to watch against. Note, (1.) The glory which comes from men is vain-glory, which, instead of being desirous of, we should be dead to. (2.) An undue regard to the approbation and applause of men is one great ground of the unhappy strifes and contentions that exist among Christians.

CHAPTER 6

This chapter chiefly consists of two parts. In the former the apostle gives us several plain and practical directions, which more especially tend to instruct Christians in their duty to one another, and to promote the communion of saints in love (*v.* 1–10). In the latter he revives the main design of the epistle, which was to fortify the Galatians against the arts of their judaizing teachers, and confirm them in the truth and liberty of the gospel, for which purpose he, I. Gives them the true character of these teachers, and shows them from what motives, and with what views, they acted (*v.* 11–14). And, II. On the other hand he acquaints them with his own temper and behaviour. From both these they might easily see how little reason they had to slight him, and to fall in with them. And then he concludes the epistle with a solemn benediction.

Verses 1–10

The apostle having, in the foregoing chapter, exhorted Christians *by love to serve one another* (*v.* 13), and also cautioned us (*v.* 26) against a temper which, if indulged, would hinder us from showing the mutual love and serviceableness which he had recommended, in the beginning of this chapter he proceeds to give some further directions, which, if duly observed, would both promote the one and prevent the other of these, and render our behaviour both more agreeable to our Christian profession and more useful and comfortable to one another: particularly,

I. We are here taught to deal tenderly with those who are overtaken in a fault, *v.* 1. He puts a common case: *If a man be overtaken in a fault,* that is, be brought to sin by the surprise of temptation. It is one thing to overtake a fault by contrivance and deliberation, and a full resolution in sin, and another thing to be overtaken in a fault. The latter is the case here supposed, and herein the apostle shows that great tenderness should be used. *Those who are spiritual,* by whom is meant, not only the ministers (as if none but they were to be called spiritual persons), but other Christians too, especially those of the higher form in Christianity; these must *restore such a one with the spirit of meekness.* Here observe, 1. The duty we are directed to — to restore such; we should labour, by faithful reproofs, and pertinent and seasonable councils, to bring them to repentance. The original word, *katartizete,* signifies *to set in joint,* as a dislocated bone; accordingly we should endeavour to set them in joint again, to bring them to themselves, by convincing them of their sin and error, persuading them to return to their duty, comforting them in a sense of pardoning mercy thereupon, and having thus recovered them, confirming our love to them. 2. The manner wherein this is to be done: *With the spirit of meekness;* not in wrath and passion, as those who triumph in a brother's falls, but with meekness, as those who rather mourn for them. Many needful reproofs lose their efficacy by being given in wrath; but when they are managed with calmness and tenderness, and appear to proceed from sincere affection and concern for the welfare of those to whom they are given, they are likely to make a due impression. 3. A very good reason why this should be done with meekness: *Considering thyself, lest thou also be tempted.* We ought to deal very tenderly with those who are overtaken in sin, because we none of us know but it may some time or other be our own case. We also may be tempted, yea, and overcome by the temptation; and therefore, if we rightly consider ourselves, this will dispose us to do by others as we desire to be done by in such a case.

II. We are here directed *to bear one another's burdens, v.* 2. This may be considered either as referring to what goes before, and so may teach us to exercise forbearance and compassion towards one another, in the case of those weaknesses, and follies, and infirmities, which too often attend us — that, though we should not wholly connive at them, yet we should

not be severe against one another on account of them; or as a more general precept, and so it directs us to sympathize with one another under the various trials and troubles that we may meet with, and to be ready to afford each other the comfort and counsel, the help and assistance, which our circumstances may require. To excite us hereunto, the apostle adds, by way of motive, that so we shall *fulfil the law of Christ.* This is to act agreeably to the law of his precept, which is the law of love, and obliges us to a mutual forbearance and forgiveness, to sympathy with and compassion towards each other; and it would also be agreeable to his pattern and example, which have the force of a law to us. He bears with us under our weaknesses and follies, he is *touched with a fellow-feeling of our infirmities;* and therefore there is good reason why we should maintain the same temper towards one another. Note, Though as Christians we are freed from the law of Moses, yet we are under the law of Christ; and therefore, instead of laying unnecessary burdens upon others (as those who urged the observance of Moses's law did), it much more becomes us to fulfil the law of Christ by bearing one another's burdens. The apostle being aware how great a hindrance pride would be to the mutual condescension and sympathy which he had been recommending, and that a conceit of ourselves would dispose us to censure and contemn our brethren, instead of bearing with their infirmities and endeavouring to restore them when overtaken with a fault, he therefore (*v.* 3) takes care to caution us against this; he supposes it as a very possible thing (and it would be well if it were not too common) for a man to think himself to be something — to entertain a fond opinion of his own sufficiency, to look upon himself as wiser and better than other men, and as fit to dictate and prescribe to them — when in truth he is nothing, has nothing of substance or solidity in him, or that can be a ground of the confidence and superiority which he assumes. To dissuade us from giving way to this temper he tells us that such a one does but deceive himself; while he imposes upon others, by pretending to what he has not, he puts the greatest cheat upon himself, and sooner or later will find the sad effects of it. This will never gain him that esteem, either with God or good men, which he is ready to expect; he is neither the freer from mistakes nor will he be the more secure against temptations for the good opinion he has of his own sufficiency, but rather the more liable to fall into them, and to be overcome by them; for *he that thinks he stands has need to take heed lest he fall.* Instead therefore of indulging such a vain-glorious humour, which is both destructive of the love and kindness we owe to our fellow-christians and also injurious to ourselves, it would much better become us to accept the apostle's exhortation (Phil. 2:3), *Do nothing through strife nor vain-glory; but in lowliness of mind let each esteem others better than himself.* Note, Self-conceit is but self-deceit: as it is inconsistent with that charity we owe to others (for *charity vaunteth not itself, is not puffed up,* 1 Co. 13:4), so it is a cheat upon ourselves; and there is not a more dangerous cheat in the world than self-deceit. As a means of preventing this evil,

III. We are advised every one to prove his own work, *v.* 4. By our own work is chiefly meant our own actions or behaviour. These the apostle directs us to prove, that is seriously and impartially to examine them by the rule of God's word, to see whether or no they are agreeable to it, and therefore such as God and conscience do approve. This he represents as the duty of every man; instead of being forward to judge and censure others, it would much more become us to search and try our own ways; our business lies more at home than abroad, with ourselves than with other men, *for what have we to do to judge another man's servant?* From the connection of this exhortation with what goes before it appears that if Christians did duly employ themselves in this work they might easily discover those defects and failings in themselves which would soon convince them how little reason they have either to be conceited of themselves or severe in their censures of others; and so it gives us occasion to observe that the best way to keep us from being proud of ourselves is to prove our own selves: the better we are acquainted with our own hearts and ways, the less liable shall we be to despise and the more disposed to compassionate and help others under their infirmities and afflictions. That we may be persuaded to this necessary and profitable duty of proving our own work, the apostle urges two considerations very proper for this purpose: —

1. This is the way to *have rejoicing in ourselves alone.* If

we set ourselves in good earnest to *prove our own work*, and, upon the trial, can approve ourselves to God, as to our sincerity and uprightness towards him, then may we expect to have comfort and peace in our own souls, having the testimony of our own consciences for us (as 2 Co. 1:12), and this, he intimates, would be a much better ground of joy and satisfaction than to be able to rejoice *in another*, either in the good opinion which others may have of us or in having gained over others to our opinion, which the false teachers were wont to glory in (as we see *v.* 13), or by comparing ourselves with others, as, it should seem, some did, who were ready to think well of themselves, because they were not so bad as some others. Too many are apt to value themselves upon such accounts as these; but the joy that results thence is nothing to that which arises from an impartial trial of ourselves by the rule of God's word, and our being able thereupon to approve ourselves to him. Note, (1.) Though we have nothing in ourselves to boast of, yet we may have the matter of rejoicing in ourselves: our works can merit nothing at the hand of God; but, if our consciences can witness for us that they are such as he for Christ's sake approves and accepts, we may upon good ground rejoice therein. (2.) The true way to have *rejoicing in ourselves* is to be much in *proving our own works*, in examining ourselves by the unerring rule of God's word, and not by the false measures of what others are, or may think of us. (3.) It is much more desirable to have matter of glorying in ourselves than in another. If we have the testimony of our consciences that we are accepted of God, we need not much concern ourselves about what others think or say of us; and without this the good opinion of others will stand us in little stead.

2. The other argument which the apostle uses to press upon us this duty of proving our own work is that every man shall bear his own burden (*v.* 5), the meaning of which is that at the great day every one shall be reckoned with according as his behaviour here has been. He supposes that there is a day coming when we must all give an account of ourselves to God; and he declares that then the judgment will proceed, and the sentence pass, not according to the sentiments of the world concerning us, or any ungrounded opinion we may have had of ourselves, or upon our having been better or worse than others, but according as our state and behaviour have really been in the sight of God. And, if there be such an awful time to be expected, when he will *render to every one according to his works*, surely there is the greatest reason why we should prove our own works now: if we must certainly be called to an account hereafter, surely we ought to be often calling ourselves to an account here, to see whether or no we are such as God will own and approve then: and, as this is our duty, so if it were more our practice we should entertain more becoming thoughts both of ourselves and our fellow-christians, and instead of bearing hard upon one another, on account of any mistakes or failings we may be guilty of, we should be more ready to fulfil that law of Christ by which we must be judged in bearing one another's burdens.

IV. Christians are here exhorted to be free and liberal in maintaining their ministers (*v.* 6): *Let him that is taught in the word communicate to him that teacheth, in all good things.* Here we may observe, 1. The apostle speaks of it as a thing known and acknowledged, that, as there are some to be taught, so there are others who are appointed to teach them. The office of the ministry is a divine institution, which does not lie open in common to all, but is confined to those only whom God has qualified for it and called to it: even reason itself directs us to put a difference between the teachers and the taught (for, if all were teachers, there would be none to be taught), and the scriptures sufficiently declare that it is the will of God we should do so. 2. It is the word of God wherein ministers are to teach and instruct others; that which they are to preach is *the word*, 2 Tim. 4:2. That which they are to declare is *the counsel of God*, Acts 20:27. They are not *lords of our faith, but helpers of our joy*, 2 Co. 1:24. It is the word of God which is the only rule of faith and life; this they are concerned to study, and to open, and improve, for the edification of others, but they are no further to be regarded than as they speak according to this rule. 3. It is the duty of those who are taught in the word to support those who are appointed to teach them; for they are *to communicate to them in all good things*, freely and cheerfully to contribute, of the good things with which God has blessed them, what is needful for their comfortable subsistence. Ministers are *to give attendance to reading, to exhortation, to doctrine*

(1 Tim. 4:13); they are not to *entangle themselves with the affairs of this life* (2 Tim. 2:4), and therefore it is but fit and equitable that, while they are *sowing to others spiritual things, they should reap their carnal things*. And this is the appointment of God himself; for as, under the law, *those who ministered about holy things lived of the things of the temple, so hath the Lord ordained that those who preach the gospel should live of the gospel*, 1 Co. 9:11, 13, 14.

V. Here is a caution to take heed of mocking God, or of deceiving ourselves, by imagining that he can be imposed upon by mere pretensions or professions (*v.* 7): *Be not deceived, God is not mocked*. This may be considered as referring to the foregoing exhortation, and so the design of it is to convince those of their sin and folly who endeavoured by any plausible pretences to excuse themselves from doing their duty in supporting their ministers: or it may be taken in a more general view, as respecting the whole business of religion, and so as designed to take men off from entertaining any vain hopes of enjoying its rewards while they live in the neglect of its duties. The apostle here supposes that many are apt to excuse themselves from the work of religion, and especially the more self-denying and chargeable parts of it, though at the same time they may make a show and profession of it; but he assures them that *this their way is their folly*, for, though hereby they may possibly impose upon others, yet they do but deceive themselves if they think to impose upon God, who is perfectly acquainted with their hearts as well as actions, and, as he cannot be deceived, so he will not be mocked; and therefore, to prevent this, he directs us to lay down as a rule to ourselves, *That whatsoever a man soweth that shall he also reap;* or that according as we behave ourselves now, so will our account be in the great day. Our present time is seed-time: in the other world there will be a great harvest; and, as the husbandman reaps in the harvest according as he sows in the seedness, so we shall reap then as we sow now. And he further informs us (*v.* 8) that, as there are two sorts of seedness, sowing to the flesh and sowing to the Spirit, so accordingly will the reckoning be hereafter: *If we sow to the flesh, we shall of the flesh reap corruption*. If we sow the wind, we shall reap the whirlwind. Those who live a carnal sensual life, who instead of employing themselves to the honour of God and the good of others, spend all their thoughts, and care, and time, about the flesh, must expect no other fruit of such a course than corruption — a mean and short-lived satisfaction at present, and ruin and misery at the end of it. But, on the other hand, *those who sow to the Spirit*, who under the guidance and influence of the Spirit do live a holy and spiritual life, a life of devotedness to God and of usefulness and serviceableness to others, may depend upon it that *of the Spirit they shall reap life everlasting* — they shall have the truest comfort in their present course, and an eternal life and happiness at the end of it. Note, Those who go about to mock God do but deceive themselves. Hypocrisy in religion is the greatest folly as well as wickedness, since the God we have to do with can easily see through all our disguises, and will certainly deal with us hereafter, not according to our professions, but our practices.

VI. Here is a further caution given us, *not to be weary in well doing, v.* 9. As we should not excuse ourselves from any part of our duty, so neither should we grow weary in it. There is in all of us too great a proneness to this; we are very apt to flag and tire in duty, yea to fall off from it, particularly that part of it to which the apostle has here a special regard, that of doing good to others. This therefore he would have us carefully to watch and guard against; and he gives this very good reason for it, because *in due season we shall reap, if we faint not*, where he assures us that there is a recompence of reward in reserve for all who sincerely employ themselves in well doing; that this reward will certainly be bestowed on us in the proper season — if not in this world, yet undoubtedly in the next; but then that it is upon supposition that we faint not in the way of our duty; if we grow weary of it, and withdraw from it, we shall not only miss of this reward, but lose the comfort and advantage of what we have already done; but, if we hold on and hold out in well-doing, though our reward may be delayed, yet it will surely come, and will be so great as to make us an abundant recompence for all our pains and constancy. Note, Perseverance in well-doing is our wisdom and interest, as well as our duty, for to this only is the reward promised.

VII. Here is an exhortation to all Christians to do good

in their places (*v.* 10): As we have therefore an opportunity, etc. It is not enough that we be good to others, if we would approve ourselves to be Christians indeed. The duty here recommended to us is the same that is spoken of in the foregoing verses; and, as there the apostle exhorts us to sincerity and perseverance in it, so here he directs us both as to the objects and rule of it. 1. The objects of this duty are more generally all men. We are not to confine our charity and beneficence within too narrow bounds, as the Jews and judaizing Christians were apt to do, but should be ready to extend it to all who partake of the same common nature with us, as far as we are capable and they stand in need of us. But yet, in the exercise of it, we are to have a special regard to the household of faith, or to those who profess the same common faith, and are members of the same body of Christ, with us: though others are not to be excluded, yet these are to be preferred. The charity of Christians should be extensive charity: but yet therein a particular respect is to be had to good people. God does good to all, but in an especial manner he is good to his own servants; and we must in doing good be *followers of God as dear children*. 2. The rule which we are to observe in doing good to others is *as we have opportunity*, which implies, (1.) That we should be sure to do it while we have opportunity, or while our life lasts, which is the only season wherein we are capable of doing good to his own servants; and we must in doing good be *followers of God as dear children*. 2. The rule which we are to observe in doing good to others is *as we have opportunity*, which implies, (1.) That we should be sure to do it while we have opportunity, or while our life lasts, which is the only season wherein we are capable of doing good to others. If therefore we would behave ourselves aright in this matter, we must not, as too many do, neglect it in our life-time, and defer it till we come to die, under a pretence of doing something of this nature then: for, as we cannot be sure that we shall then have an opportunity for it, so neither, if we should, have we any ground to expect that what we do will be so acceptable to God, much less that we can atone for our past neglects by leaving something behind us for the good of others, when we can no longer keep it ourselves. But we should take care to do good in our life-time, yea, to make this the business of our lives. And, (2.) That we be ready to improve every opportunity for it: we should not content ourselves in having done some good already; but, whenever fresh occasions offer themselves, as far as our capacity reaches we should be ready to embrace them too, for we are directed to *give a portion to seven and also to eight*, Eccl. 11:2. Note, [1.] As God has made it our duty to do good to others, so he takes care in his providence to furnish us with opportunities for it. *The poor we have always with us*, Mt. 26:11. [2.] Whenever God gives us an opportunity of being useful to others, he expects we should improve it, according to our capacity and ability. [3.] We have need of godly wisdom and discretion to direct us in the exercise of our charity or beneficence, and particularly in the choice of the proper objects of it; for, though none who stand in need of us are to be wholly overlooked, yet there is a difference to be made between some and others.

Verses 11–18

The apostle, having at large established the doctrine of the gospel, and endeavoured to persuade these Christians to a behaviour agreeable to it, seems as if he intended here to have put an end to the epistle, especially when he had acquainted them that, as a particular mark of his respect for them, he had written this large letter with his own hand, and had not made use of another as his amanuensis, and only subscribed his name to it, as he was wont to do in his other epistles: but such is his affection to them such his concern to recover them from the bad impressions made upon them by their false teachers, that he cannot break off till he has once again given them the true character of those teachers, and an account of his own contrary temper and behaviour, that by comparing these together they might the more easily see how little reason they had to depart from the doctrine he had taught them and to comply with theirs.

I. He gives them the true character of those teachers who were industrious to seduce them, in several particulars. As, 1. They were men who *desired to make a fair show in the flesh, v.* 12. They were very zealous for the externals of religion, forward to observe, and to oblige others to observe, the rites of the ceremonial law, though at the same time they had little or no regard to real piety; for, as the apostle says of them in the following verse, *neither do they themselves keep the law.* Proud, vain, and carnal hearts desire nothing more than to make a fair show in the flesh, and they can easily be content with so much religion as will help them to keep up such a fair show; but frequently those have least of the substance of religion who are most solicitous to make a show of it. 2. They were men who were afraid of suffering, for they constrained the Gentile Christians to be circumcised, *only lest they should suffer persecution for the cross of Christ.* It was not so much out of a regard to the law as to themselves; they were willing to sleep in a whole skin, and to save their worldly cargo, and cared not though they made shipwreck of faith and a good conscience. That which they chiefly aimed at was to please the Jews, and to keep up their reputation among them, and so to prevent the trouble that Paul, and other faithful professors of the doctrine of Christ, lay open to. And, 3. Another part of their character was that they were men of a party spirit, and who had no further zeal for the law than as it subserved their carnal and selfish designs; for they desired to have these Christians circumcised, *that they might glory in their flesh* (*v.* 13), that they might say they had gained them over to their side, and made proselytes of them, of which they carried the mark in their flesh. And thus, while they pretended to promote religion, they were the greatest enemies of it; for nothing has been more destructive to the interest of religion than men-siding and party-making.

II. He acquaints us, on the other hand, with his own temper and behaviour, or makes profession of his own faith, hope, and joy; particularly,

1. That his principle glory was in the cross of Christ: *God forbid,* says he, *that I should glory, save in the cross of our Lord Jesus Christ, v.* 14. By the cross of Christ is here meant his sufferings and death on the cross, or the doctrine of salvation by a crucified Redeemer. This was what the Jews stumbled at and the Greeks accounted foolishness; and the judaizing teachers themselves, though they had embraced Christianity, yet were so far ashamed of it that in compliance with the Jews, and to avoid persecution from them, they were for mixing the observance of the law of Moses with faith in Christ, as necessary to salvation. But Paul had a very different opinion of it; he was so far from being offended at the cross of Christ, or ashamed of it, or afraid to own it, that he gloried in it; yea, he desired to glory in nothing else, and rejected the thought of setting up anything in competition with it, as the object of his esteem, with the utmost abhorrence; *God forbid,* etc. This was the ground of all his hope as a Christian: this was the doctrine which, as an apostle, he was resolved to preach; and, whatever trials his firm adherence to it might bring upon him, he was ready, not only to submit to them, but to rejoice in them. Note, The cross of Christ is a good Christian's chief glory, and there is the greatest reason why we should glory in it, for to it we owe all our joys and hopes.

2. That he was dead to the world. By Christ, or by the cross of Christ, *the world was crucified to him, and he to the world;* he had experienced the power and virtue of it in weaning him from the world, and this was one great reason of his glorying in it. The false teachers were men of a worldly temper, their chief concern was about their secular interests, and therefore they accommodated their religion thereunto. But Paul was a man of another spirit; as the world had no kindness for him, so neither had he any great regard to it; he had got above both the smiles and the frowns of it, and had become as indifferent to it as one who is dying out of it. This is a temper of mind that all Christians should be labouring after; and the best way to attain it is to converse much with the cross of Christ. The higher esteem we have of him the meaner opinion shall we have of the world, and the more we contemplate the sufferings our dear Redeemer met with from the world the less likely shall we be to be in love with it.

3. That he did not lay the stress of his religion on one side or the other of the contesting interests, but on sound Christianity, *v.* 15. There was at that time an unhappy division among Christians; circumcision and uncircumcision had become names by which they were distinguished from each other; for (*ch.* 2:9, 12) the Jewish Christians are called *the circumcision,* and *those of the circumcision.* The false teachers were very zealous for circumcision; yea, to such a degree as to represent it as necessary to salvation, and therefore they did all they could to constrain the Gentile Christians to submit to it. In this they had carried the matter much further than others did; for, though the apostles connived at the use of it among the Jewish converts, yet they were by no means for imposing it upon the Gentiles. But what they laid so great a stress upon Paul made very little account of. It was indeed of great importance to the interest of Christianity that circumcision should not be imposed on the Gentile converts, and therefore this he had set himself with the utmost vigour to oppose; but as for mere circumcision or uncircumcision, whether those who embraced the Christian religion had been Jews or Gentiles, and whether they were for or against continuing the use of circumcision, so that they did not place their religion in it — this was comparatively a matter of little moment with him; for he very well knew that *in Jesus Christ,* that is, in his account, or under the Christian dispensation, *neither circumcision availed any thing nor uncircumcision,* as to men's acceptance with God, *but a new creature.* Here he instructs us both wherein real religion does not and wherein it does consist. It does not consist in circumcision or uncircumcision, in our being in this or the other denomination of Christians; but it consists in our being new creatures; not in having a new name, or putting on a new face, but in our being renewed in the spirit of our minds and having Christ formed in us: this is of the greatest account with God, and so it was with the apostle. If we compare this text with some others, we may more fully see what it is that renders us most acceptable to God, and about which we should therefore be chiefly concerned. Here we are told that it is *a new creature,* and in *ch.* 5:6 that it is *faith which worketh by love,* and in 1 Co. 7:19 that it is *the keeping of the commandments of God,* from all which it appears that it is a change of mind and heart, whereby we are disposed and enabled to believe in the Lord Jesus and to live a life of devotedness to God; and that where this inward, vital, practical religion is wanting, no outward professions, nor particular names, will ever stand us in any stead, or be sufficient to recommend us to him. Were Christians duly concerned to experience this in themselves, and to promote it in others, if it did not make them lay aside their distinguishing names, yet it would at least take them off from laying so great a stress upon them as they too often do. Note, Christians should take care to lay the stress of their religion where God has laid it, namely, on those things which are available to our acceptance with him; so we see the apostle did, and it is our wisdom and interest herein to follow his example. The apostle having shown what was of chief consideration in religion, and what he laid the greatest stress upon, namely, not a mere empty name or profession, but a sound and saving change, in *v.* 16 he pronounces a blessing upon all those who walk according to this rule: *And as many as walk according to this rule peace be upon them, and mercy upon the Israel of God.* The rule which he here speaks of may signify more generally the whole word of God, which is the complete and perfect rule of faith and life, or that doctrine of the gospel, or way of justification and salvation, which he had laid down in this epistle, namely, by faith in Christ without the works of the law; or it may be considered as more immediately referring to the new creature, of which he had just before been speaking. The blessings which he desires for those who walk according to this rule, or which he gives them the hope and prospect of (for the words may be taken either as a prayer or a promise), are *peace and mercy* — peace with God and conscience, and all the comforts of this life as far as they are needful for them, and mercy, or an interest in the free love and favour of God in Christ, which are the spring and fountain of all other blessings. A foundation is laid for these in that gracious change which is wrought in them; and while they behave themselves as new creatures, and govern their lives and hopes by the rule of the gospel, they may most assuredly depend upon them. These, he declares, shall be the portion of *all the Israel of God,* by whom he means all sincere Christians, whether Jews or Gentiles, all who are Israelites indeed, who, though they may not be the natural, yet are become the spiritual seed of Abraham; these, being heirs of his faith, are also heirs together with him of the same promise, and consequently entitled to the peace and mercy here spoken of. The Jews and judaizing teachers were for confining these blessings to such as were circumcised and kept the law of Moses; but, on the contrary, the apostle declares that they belong to all who walk according to the rule of the gospel, or of the new creature, even to all the Israel of God, intimating that those only are the true Israel of God who walk according to this rule, and not that of circumcision, which they insisted so much upon, and therefore that this was the true way to obtain peace and mercy. Note, (1.) Real Christians are such as walk by rule; not a rule of their own devising, but that which God himself has prescribed to them. (2.) Even those who walk according to this rule do yet stand in need of the mercy of God. But, (3.) All who sincerely endeavour to walk according to this rule may be assured that peace and mercy will be upon them: this is the best way to have peace with God, ourselves, and others; and hereupon, as we may be sure of the favour of God now, so we may be sure that we shall find mercy with him hereafter.

4. That he had cheerfully suffered persecution for the sake of Christ and Christianity, *v.* 17. As the cross of Christ, or the doctrine of salvation by a crucified Redeemer, was what he chiefly gloried in, so he had been willing to run all hazards rather than he would betray this truth, or suffer it to be corrupted. The false teachers were afraid of persecution, and this was the great reason why they were zealous for circumcision, as we see, *v.* 12. But this was the least of Paul's concern; he was not moved at any of the afflictions he met with, *nor did he count his life dear to him, so that he might finish his course with joy, and the ministry which he had received of the Lord Jesus, to testify the gospel of the grace of God,* Acts 20:24. He had already suffered much in the cause of Christ, for *he bore in his body the marks of the Lord Jesus,* the scars of those wounds which he had sustained from persecuting enemies, for his steady adherence to him, and that doctrine of the gospel which he had received from him. As from this it appeared that he was firmly persuaded of the truth and importance of it, and that he was far from being a favourer of circumcision, as they had falsely reported him to be, so hereupon, with a becoming warmth and vehemence, suitable to his authority as an apostle and to the deep concern of mind he was under, he insists upon it that no man should henceforth trouble him, namely by opposing his doctrine or authority, or by any such calumnies and reproaches as had been cast upon him; for as, both from what he had said and what he had suffered, they appeared to be highly unjust and injurious, so also those were very unreasonable who either raised or received them. Note, (1.) It may justly be presumed that men are fully persuaded of those truths in the defence of which they are willing to suffer. And (2.) It is very unjust to charge those things upon others which are contrary not only to their profession, but their sufferings too.

III. The apostle, having now finished what he intended to write for the conviction and recovery of the churches of Galatia, concludes the epistle with his apostolical benediction, *v.* 18. He calls them his brethren, wherein he shows his great humility, and the tender affection he had for them, notwithstanding the ill treatment he had met with from them; and takes his leave of them with this very serious and affectionate prayer, that *the grace of our Lord Jesus Christ may be with their spirit.* This was a usual farewell wish of the apostle's, as we see, Rom. 16:20, 24, and 1 Co. 16:23. And herein he prays that they might enjoy the favour of Christ, both in its special effects and its sensible evidences, that they might receive from him all that grace which was needful to guide them in their way, to strengthen them in their work, to establish them in their Christian course, and to encourage and comfort them under all the trials of life and the prospect of death itself. This is fitly called *the grace of our Lord Jesus Christ,* as he is both the sole purchaser and the appointed dispenser of it; and though these churches had done enough to forfeit it, by suffering themselves to be drawn into an opinion and practice highly dishonourable to Christ, as well as dangerous to them, yet, out of his great concern for them, and knowing of what importance it was to them, he earnestly desires it on their behalf; yea, that it might *be with their spirit,* that they might continually experience the influences of it upon their souls, disposing and enabling them to act with sincerity and uprightness in religion. We need desire no more to make us happy than the grace of our Lord Jesus Christ. This the apostle begs for these Christians, and therein shows us what we are chiefly concerned to obtain; and, both for their and our encouragement to hope for it, he adds his *Amen.*

AN EXPOSITION, WITH PRACTICAL OBSERVATIONS, OF

THE EPISTLE OF ST. PAUL TO THE EPHESIANS

Some think that this epistle to the Ephesians was a circular letter sent to several churches, and that the copy directed to the Ephesians happened to be taken into the canon, and so it came to bear that particular inscription. And they have been induced the rather to think this because it is the only one of all Paul's epistles that has nothing in it peculiarly adapted to the state or case of that particular church; but it has much of common concernment to all Christians, and especially to all who, having been Gentiles in times past, were converted to Christianity. But then it may be observed, on the other hand, that the epistle is expressly inscribed (1:1) *to the saints which are at Ephesus;* and in the close of it he tells them that he had sent Tychicus unto them, whom, in 2 Tim. 4:12, he says he had sent to Ephesus. It is an epistle that bears date out of a prison: and some have observed that what this apostle wrote when he was a prisoner had the greatest relish and savour in it of the things of God. When his tribulations did abound, his consolations and experiences did much more abound, whence we may observe that the afflictive exercises of God's people, and particularly of his ministers, often tend to the advantage of others as well as to their own. The apostle's design is to settle and establish the Ephesians in the truth, and further to acquaint them with the mystery of the gospel, in order to it. In the former part he represents the great privilege of the Ephesians, who, having been in time past idolatrous heathens, were now converted to Christianity and received into covenant with God, which he illustrates from a view of their deplorable state before their conversion, *ch.* 1–3. In the latter part (which we have in the 4th, 5th, and 6th chapters) he instructs them in the principal duties of religion, both personal and relative, and exhorts and quickens them to the faithful discharge of them. Zanchy observes that we have here an epitome of the whole Christian doctrine, and of almost all the chief heads of divinity.

CHAPTER 1

In this chapter we have, I. The introduction to the whole epistle, which is much the same as in others (*v.* 1, 2). II. The apostle's thanksgivings and praises to God for his inestimable blessings bestowed on the believing Ephesians (*v.* 3–14). III. His earnest prayers to God in their behalf (*v.* 15–23). This great apostle was wont to abound in prayers and in thanksgivings to almighty God, which he generally so disposes and orders that at the same time they carry with them and convey the great and important doctrines of the Christian religion, and the most weighty instructions to all those who seriously peruse them.

Verses 1–2

Here is, 1. The title St. Paul takes to himself, as belonging to him — *Paul, an apostle of Jesus Christ,* etc. He reckoned it a great honour to be employed by Christ, as one of his messengers to the sons of men. The apostles were prime officers in the Christian church, being extraordinary ministers appointed for a time only. They were furnished by their great Lord with extraordinary gifts and the immediate assistance of the Spirit, that they might be fitted for publishing and spreading the gospel and for governing the church in its infant state. Such a one Paul was, and that not *by the will* of man conferring that office upon him, nor by his own intrusion into it; but *by the will of God,* very expressly and plainly intimated to him, he being immediately called (as the other apostles were) by Christ himself to the work. Every faithful minister of Christ (though his call and office are not of so extraordinary a nature) may, with our apostle, reflect on it as an honour and comfort to himself that he is what he is *by the will of God.* 2. The persons to whom this epistle is sent: *To the saints who are at Ephesus,* that is, to the Christians who were members of the church at Ephesus, the metropolis of Asia. He calls them saints, for such they were in profession, such they were bound to be in truth and reality, and many of them were such. All Christians must be saints; and, if they come not under that character on earth, they will never be saints in glory. He calls them *the faithful in Christ Jesus,* believers in him, and firm and constant in their adherence to him and to his truths and ways. Those are not saints who are not faithful, believing in Christ, firmly adhering to him, and true to the profession they make of relation to their Lord. Note, It is the honour not only of ministers, but of private Christians too, to have obtained mercy of the Lord to be faithful. — *In Christ Jesus,* from whom they derive all their grace and spiritual strength, and in whom their persons, and all that they perform, are made accepted. 3. The apostolical benediction: *Grace be to you,* etc. This is the token in every epistle; and it expresses the apostle's good-will to his friends, and a real desire of their welfare. By *grace* we are to understand the free and undeserved love and favour of God, and those graces of the Spirit which proceed from it; by *peace* all other blessings, spiritual and temporal, the fruits and product of the former. No peace without grace. No peace, nor grace, but *from God the Father, and from the Lord Jesus Christ.* These peculiar blessings proceed from God, not as a Creator, but as a Father by special relation: and they come from our Lord Jesus Christ, who, having purchased them for his people, has a right to bestow them upon them. Indeed the saints, and the faithful in Christ Jesus, had already received grace and peace; but the increase of these is very desirable, and the best saints stand in need of fresh supplies of the graces of the Spirit, and cannot but desire to improve and grow: and therefore they should pray, each one for himself and all for one another, that such blessings may still abound unto them.

After this short introduction he comes to the matter and body of the epistle; and, though it may seem somewhat peculiar in a letter, yet the Spirit of God saw fit that his discourse of divine things in this chapter should be cast into prayers and praises, which, as they are solemn addresses to God, so they convey weighty instructions to others. Prayer may preach; and praise may do so too.

Verses 3–14

He begins with thanksgivings and praise, and enlarges with a great deal of fluency and copiousness of affection upon the exceedingly great and precious benefits which we enjoy by Jesus Christ. For the great privileges of our religion are very aptly recounted and enlarged upon in our praises to God.

I. In general he blesses God for *spiritual blessings, v.* 3, where he styles him *the God and Father of our Lord Jesus Christ;* for, as Mediator, the Father was his God; as God, and the second person in the blessed Trinity, God was his Father. It bespeaks the mystical union between Christ and believers, that the God and Father of our Lord Jesus Christ is their God and Father, and that in and through him. All blessings come from God as the Father of our Lord Jesus Christ. No good can be expected from a righteous and holy God to sinful creatures, but by his mediation. *He hath blessed us with all spiritual blessings.* Note, Spiritual blessings are the best blessings with which God blesses us, and for which we are to bless him. He blesses us by bestowing such things upon us as make us really blessed. We cannot thus bless God again; but must do it by praising, and magnifying, and speaking well of him on that account. Those whom God blesses with some he blesses with all spiritual blessings; to whom he gives Christ, he freely gives all these things. It is not so with temporal blessings; some are favoured with health, and not with riches; some with riches, and not with health, etc. But, where God blesses with spiritual blessings, he blesses with all. They are *spiritual blessings in heavenly places;* that is, say some, in the church, distinguished from the world, and called out of it. Or it may be read, *in heavenly things,* such as come from heaven, and are designed to prepare men for it, and to secure their reception into it. We should hence learn to mind spiritual and heavenly things as the principal things, spiritual and heavenly blessings as the best blessings, with which we cannot be miserable and without which we cannot but be so. *Set not your affections on things on the earth, but on those things which are above.* These we are blessed with in Christ; for, as all our services ascend to God through Christ, so all our blessings are conveyed to us in the same way, he being the Mediator between God and us.

II. The particular spiritual blessings with which we are blessed in Christ, and for which we ought to bless God, are (many of them) here enumerated and enlarged upon. 1. Election and predestination, which are the secret springs whence the others flow, *v.* 4, 5, 11. *Election,* or choice, respects that lump or mass of mankind out of which some are chosen, from which they are separated and distinguished. Predestination has respect to the blessings they are designed for; particularly *the adoption of children,* it being the purpose of God that in due time we should become his adopted children, and so have a right to all the privileges and to the inheritance of children. We have here the date of this act of love: it was *before the foundation of the world;* not only before God's people had a being, but before the world had a beginning; for they were chosen in the counsel of God from all eternity. It magnifies these blessings to a high degree that they are the products of eternal counsel. The alms which you give to beggars at your doors proceed from a sudden resolve; but the provision which a parent makes for his children is the result of many thoughts, and is put into his last will and testament with a great deal of solemnity. And, as this magnifies divine love, so it secures the blessings to God's elect; for *the purpose of God according to election shall stand.* He acts in pursuance of his eternal purpose in bestowing spiritual blessings upon his people. *He hath blessed us — according as he hath chosen us in him,* in Christ the great head of the election, who is emphatically called *God's elect, his chosen;* and in the chosen Redeemer an eye of favour was cast upon them. Observe here one great end and design of this choice: *chosen — that we should be holy;* not because he foresaw they would be holy, but because he determined to make them so. All who are chosen to happiness as the end are chosen to holiness as the means. Their sanctification, as well as their salvation, is the result of the counsels of divine love. — *And without blame before him* — that their holiness might not be merely external and in outward appearance, so as to prevent blame from men, but internal and real, and what God himself, who *looketh at the heart,* will account such, such holiness as proceeds from love to God and to our fellow-creatures, this charity being the principle of all true holiness. The original word signifies such an innocence as no man can carp at; and therefore some understand it of that perfect holiness which the saints shall attain in the life to come, which will be eminently before God, they being in his immediate presence for ever. Here is also the rule and the fontal cause of God's election: it is *according to the good pleasure of his will* (*v.* 5), not for the sake of any thing in them foreseen, but because it was his sovereign will, and a thing highly pleasing to him. It is *according to the purpose,* the fixed and unalterable will, *of him who worketh all things after the counsel of his own will* (*v.* 11), who powerfully accomplishes whatever concerns his elect, as he has wisely and freely fore-ordained and decreed, the last and great end and design of all which is his own glory: *To the praise of the glory of his grace* (*v.* 6), that we should be to the praise of his glory (*v.* 12), that is, that we should live and behave ourselves in such a manner that his rich grace might be magnified, and appear glorious, and worthy of the highest praise. *All is of God, and from him, and through him,* and therefore all must be to him, and centre in his praise. Note, The glory of God is his own end, and it should be ours in all that we do. This passage has been understood by some in a very different sense, and with a special reference to the conversion of these Ephesians to Christianity. Those who have a mind to see what is said to this purpose may consult Mr. Locke, and other well-known writers, on the place. 2. The next spiritual blessing the apostle takes notice of is acceptance with God through Jesus Christ: *Wherein,* or by which grace, *he hath made us accepted in the beloved, v.* 6. Jesus Christ is the beloved of his Father (Mt. 3:17), as well as of angels and saints. It is our great privilege to be accepted of God, which implies his love to us and his taking us under his care and into his family. We cannot be thus accepted of God, but in and through Jesus Christ. He loves his people for the sake of the beloved. 3. Remission of sins, and redemption through the blood of Jesus, *v.* 7. No remission without redemption. It was by reason of sin that we were captivated, and we cannot be released from our captivity but by the remission of our sins. This redemption we have in Christ, and this remission through his blood. The guilt and the stain of sin could be no otherwise removed than by the blood of Jesus. All our spiritual blessings flow down to us in that stream. This great benefit, which comes freely to us, was dearly bought and paid for by our blessed Lord; and yet it is according to the riches of God's grace. Christ's satisfaction and God's rich grace are very consistent in the great affair of man's redemption. God was satisfied by Christ as our substitute and surety; but it was rich grace that would accept of a surety, when he might have executed the severity of the law upon the transgressor, and it was rich grace to provide such a surety as his own Son, and freely to deliver him up, when nothing of that nature could have entered into our thoughts, nor have been any otherwise found out for us. In this instance he has not only manifested riches of grace, but *has abounded towards us in all wisdom and prudence* (*v.* 8), wisdom in contriving the dispensation, and prudence in executing the counsel of his will, as he has done. How illustrious have the divine wisdom and prudence rendered themselves, in so happily adjusting the matter between justice and mercy in this grand affair, in securing the honour of God and his law, at the same time that the recovery of sinners and their salvation are ascertained and made sure! 4. Another privilege which the apostle here blesses God for is divine revelation — that God hath *made known to us the mystery of his will* (*v.* 9), that is, so much of his good-will to men, which had been concealed for a long time, and is still concealed from so great a part of the world: this we owe to Christ, who, having lain in the bosom of the Father from eternity, came to declare his will to the children of men. *According to his good pleasure,* his secret counsels concerning man's redemption, *which he had purposed,* or resolved upon, merely in and from himself, and not for any thing in them. In this revelation, and in his *making known unto us the mystery of his will,* the wisdom and the prudence of God do abundantly shine forth. It is described (*v.* 13) *as the word of truth, and the gospel of our salvation.* Every word of it is true. It contains and instructs us in the most weighty and important truths, and it is confirmed and sealed by the very oath of God, whence we should learn to *betake ourselves to it in all our searches after divine truth.* It is the gospel of our salvation: it publishes the glad tidings of salvation, and contains the offer of it: it points out the way that leads to it; and the blessed Spirit renders the reading and the ministration of it effectual to the salvation of souls. O, how ought we to prize this glorious gospel and to bless God for it! This is the light shining in a dark place, for which we have reason to be thankful, and to which we should take heed. 5. Union in and with Christ is a great privilege, a spiritual blessing, and the foundation of many others. *He gathers together in one all things in Christ, v.* 10. All the lines of divine revelation meet in Christ; all religion centres in him. Jews and Gentiles were united to each other by being both united to Christ. *Things in heaven and things on earth* are gathered together in him; peace made, correspondence settled, between heaven and earth, through him. The innumerable company of angels become one with the church through Christ: this God *purposed in himself,* and it was his design in that dispensation which was to be accomplished by his sending Christ in the fulness of time, at the exact time that God had prefixed and settled. 6. The eternal inheritance is the great blessing with which we are blessed in Christ: *In whom also we have obtained an inheritance, v.* 11. Heaven is the inheritance, the happiness of which is a sufficient portion for a soul: it is conveyed in the way of an inheritance, being the gift of a Father to his children. *If children, then heirs.* All the blessings that we have in hand are but small if compared with the inheritance. What is laid out upon an heir in his minority is nothing to what is reserved for him when he comes to age. Christians are said to have obtained this inheritance, as they have a present right to it, and even actual possession of it, in Christ their head and representative. 7. The seal and earnest of the Spirit are of the number of these blessings. We are said to be *sealed with that Holy Spirit of promise, v.* 13. The blessed Spirit is holy himself, and he makes us holy. He is called *the Spirit of promise,* as he is the promised Spirit. By him believers are sealed; that is, separated and set apart for God, and distinguished and marked as belonging to him. The Spirit *is the earnest of our inheritance, v.* 14. The earnest is part of payment, and it secures the full sum: so is the gift of the Holy Ghost; all his influences and operations, both as a sanctifier and a comforter, are heaven begun, glory in the seed and bud. The Spirit's illumination is an earnest of everlasting light; sanctification is an earnest of perfect holiness; and his comforts are earnests of everlasting joys. He is said to be the earnest, *until the redemption of the purchased possession.* It may be called here the possession, because this earnest makes it as sure to the heirs as though they were already possessed of it; and it is purchased for them by the blood of Christ. The redemption of it is mentioned because it was mortgaged and forfeited by sin; and Christ restores it to us, and so is said to redeem it, in allusion to the law of redemption. Observe, from all this, what a gracious promise that is which secures the gift of the Holy Ghost to those who ask him.

The apostle mentions the great end and design of God in bestowing all these spiritual privileges, *that we should be to the praise of his glory who first trusted in Christ* — we to whom the gospel was first preached, and who were first converted to the faith of Christ, and to the placing of our hope and trust in him. Note, Seniority in grace is a preferment: *Who were in Christ before me,* says the apostle (Rom. 16:7); those who have for a longer time experienced the grace of Christ are under more special obligations to glorify God. They should be strong in faith, and more eminently glorify him; but this should be the common end of all. For this we were made, and for this we were redeemed; this is the great design of our Christianity, and of God in all that he has done for us: *unto the praise of his glory, v.* 14. He intends that his grace and power and other perfection should by this means become conspicuous and illustrious, and that the sons of men should magnify him.

Verses 15–23

We have come to the last part of this chapter, which consists of Paul's earnest prayer to God in behalf of these Ephesians. We should pray for the persons for whom we give thanks. Our apostle blesses God for what he had done for them, and then he prays that he would do more for them. He gives thanks for spiritual blessings, and prays for further supplies of them; for God *will for this be enquired of by the house of Israel, to do it for them.* He has laid up these spiritual blessings for us in the hands of his Son, the Lord Jesus; but then he has appointed us to draw them out, and fetch them in, by prayer. We have no part nor lot in the matter, any further than we claim it by faith and prayer. One inducement to pray for them was the good account he had of them, *of their faith in the Lord Jesus and love to all the saints, v.* 15. Faith in Christ, and love to the saints, will be attended with all other graces. Love to the saints, as such, and because they are such, must include love to God. Those who love saints, as such, love all saints, how weak in grace, how mean in the world, how fretful and peevish soever, some of them may be. Another inducement to pray for them was because they had received the earnest of the inheritance: this we may observe from the words being connected with the preceding ones by the particle *wherefore.* "Perhaps you will think that, having received the earnest, it should follow, therefore you are happy enough, and need take no further care: you need not pray for yourselves, nor I for you." No, quite the contrary. *Wherefore — I cease not to give thanks for you, making mention of you in my prayers, v.* 16. While he blesses God for giving them the Spirit, he ceases not to pray that he would give unto them the Spirit (*v.* 17), that he would give greater measures of the Spirit. Observe, Even the best of Christians need to be prayed for: and, while we hear well of our Christian friends, we should think ourselves obliged to intercede with God for them, that they may abound and increase yet more and more. Now what is it that Paul prays for in behalf of the Ephesians? Not that they might be freed from persecution; nor that they might possess the riches, honours, or pleasures of the world; but the great thing he prays for is the illumination of their understandings, and that their knowledge might increase and abound: he means it of a practical and experimental knowledge. The graces and comforts of the Spirit are communicated to the soul by the enlightening of the understanding. In this way he gains and keeps possession. Satan takes a contrary way: he gets possession by the senses and passions, Christ by the understanding. Observe,

I. Whence this knowledge must come from *the God of our Lord Jesus Christ, v.* 17. The Lord *is a God of knowledge,* and there is no sound saving knowledge but what comes from him; and therefore to him we must look for it, who is *the God of our Lord Jesus Christ* (see *v.* 3) *and the Father of glory.* It is a Hebraism. God is infinitely glorious in himself all glory is due to him from his creatures, and he is the author of all that glory with which his saints are or shall be invested. Now he gives knowledge by giving the Spirit of knowledge; for the Spirit of God is the teacher of the saints, *the Spirit of wisdom and revelation.* We have the revelation of the Spirit in the word: but will that avail us, if we have not the wisdom of the Spirit in the heart? If the same Spirit who indited the sacred scriptures do not take the veil from off our hearts, and enable us to understand and improve them, we shall be never the better. — *In the knowledge of him,* or for the acknowledgment of him; not only a speculative knowledge of Christ, and of what relates to him, but an acknowledgment of Christ's authority by an obedient conformity to him, which must be by the help of *the Spirit of wisdom and revelation.* This knowledge is first in the understanding. He prays that *the eyes of their understanding may be enlightened, v.* 18. Observe, Those who have their eyes opened, and have some understanding in the things of God, have need to be more and more enlightened, and to have their knowledge more clear, and distinct, and experimental. Christians should not think it enough to have warm affections, but they should labour to have clear understandings; they should be ambitious of being knowing Christians, and judicious Christians.

II. What it is that he more particularly desire they should grow in the knowledge of. 1. *The hope of his calling, v.* 18. Christianity is our calling. God has called us to it, and on that account it is said to be his calling. There is a hope in this calling; for those who deal with God deal upon trust. And it is a desirable thing to know what this hope of our calling is, to have such an acquaintance with the immense privileges of God's people, and the expectations they have from God, and with respect to the heavenly world, as to be quickened thereby to the utmost diligence and patience in the Christian course. We ought to labour after, and pray earnestly for, a clearer insight into, and a fuller acquaintance with, the great objects of a Christian's hopes. 2. *The riches of the glory of his inheritance in the saints.* Besides the heavenly inheritance prepared for the saints, there is a present inheritance in the saints; for grace is glory begun, and holiness is happiness in the bud. There is a glory in this inheritance, riches of glory, rendering the Christian more excellent and more truly honourable than all about him: and it is desirable to know this experimentally, to be acquainted with the principles, pleasures, and powers, of the spiritual and divine life. It may be understood of the glorious inheritance in or among the saints in heaven, where God does, as it were, lay forth all his riches, to make them happy and glorious, and where all that the saints are in possession of is transcendently glorious, as the knowledge that can be attained of this upon earth is very desirable, and must be exceedingly entertaining and delightful. Let us endeavour then, by reading, contemplation, and prayer, to know as much of heaven as we can, that we may be desiring and longing to be there. 3. *The exceeding greatness of God's power towards those who believe, v.* 19. The practical belief of the all-sufficiency of God, and of the omnipotence of divine grace, is absolutely necessary to a close and steady walking with him. It is a desirable thing to know experimentally the mighty power of that grace beginning and carrying on the work of faith in our souls. It is a difficult thing to bring a soul to believe in Christ, and to venture its all upon his righteousness, and upon the hope of eternal life. It is nothing less than an almighty power that will work this in us. The apostle speaks here with a mighty fluency and copiousness of expression, and yet, at the same time, as if he wanted words to express the *exceeding greatness of God's almighty power,* that power which God exerts towards his people, and by which *he raised Christ from the dead, v.* 20. That indeed was the great proof of the truth of the gospel to the world: but the transcript of that in ourselves (our sanctification, and rising from the death of sin, in conformity to Christ's resurrection) is the great proof to us. Though this cannot prove the truth of the gospel to another who knows nothing of the matter (there the resurrection of Christ is the proof), yet to be able to speak experimentally, as the Samaritans, *"We have heard him ourselves,* we have felt a mighty change in our hearts," will make us able to say, with the fullest satisfaction, *Now we believe, and are sure, that this is the Christ, the Son of God.* Many understand the apostle here as speaking of that *exceeding greatness of power* which God will exert for raising the bodies of believers to eternal life, even the same *mighty power which he wrought in Christ when he raised him,* etc. And how desirable a thing must it be to become at length acquainted with that power, by being raised out of the grave thereby unto eternal life!

Having said something of Christ and his resurrection, the apostle digresses a little from the subject he is upon to make some further honourable mention of the Lord Jesus and his exaltation. He sits at the Father's *right hand in the heavenly places,* etc. *v.* 20, 21. Jesus Christ is advanced above all, and he is set in authority over all, they being made subject to him. All the glory of the upper world, and all the powers of both worlds, are entirely devoted to him. The Father *hath put all things under his feet* (*v.* 22), according to the promise, Ps. 110:1. All creatures whatsoever are in subjection to him; they must either yield him sincere obedience or fall under the weight of his sceptre, and receive their doom from him. God GAVE *him to be head over all things.* It was a gift to Christ, considered as a Mediator, to be advanced to such dominion and headship, and to have such a mystical body prepared for him: and it was a gift to the church, to be provided with a head endued with so much power and authority. God *gave him to be the head over all things.* He gave him all power both in heaven and in earth. *The Father loves the Son, and hath given* ALL *things into his hands.* But that which completes the comfort of this is that he is the head over all things to the church; he is entrusted with all power, that is, that he may dispose of all the affairs of the providential kingdom in subserviency to the designs of his grace concerning his church. With this therefore we may answer the messengers of the nations, that the Lord hath founded Zion. The same power that supports the world support the church; and we are sure he loves his church, for it *is his body* (*v.* 23), his mystical body, and he will care for it. It is *the fulness of him that filleth all in all.* Jesus Christ filleth all in all; he supplies all defects in all his members, filling them with his Spirit, and even with *the fulness of God, ch.* 3:19. And yet the church is said to be his fulness, because Christ as Mediator would not be complete if he had not a church. How could he be a king if he had not a kingdom? This therefore comes in to the honour of Christ, *as Mediator, that the church is his fulness.*

CHAPTER 2

This chapter contains an account, I. Of the miserable condition of these Ephesians by nature (*v.* 1–3) and again (*v.* 11, 12). II. Of the glorious change that was wrought in them by converting grace (*v.* 4–10) and again (*v.* 13). III. Of the great and mighty privileges that both converted Jews and Gentiles receive from Christ (*v.* 14–22). The apostle endeavours to affect them with a due sense of the wonderful change which divine grace had wrought in them; and this is very applicable to that great change which the same grace works in all those who are brought into a state of grace. So that we have here a lively picture both of the misery of unregenerate men and of the happy condition of converted souls, enough to awaken and alarm those who are yet in their sins and to put them upon hastening out of that state, and to comfort and delight those whom God hath quickened, with a consideration of the mighty privileges with which they are invested.

Verses 1–3

The miserable condition of the Ephesians by nature is here in part described. Observed, 1. Unregenerate souls are dead in trespasses and sins. All those who are in their sins, are dead in sins; yea, in trespasses and sins, which may signify all sorts of sins, habitual and actual, sins of heart and of life. Sin is the death of the soul. Wherever that prevails there is a privation of all spiritual life. Sinners are dead in state, being destitute of the principles, and powers of spiritual life; and cut off from God, the fountain of life: and they are dead in law, as a condemned malefactor is said to be a dead man. 2. A state of sin is a state of conformity to this world, *v.* 2. In the first verse he speaks of their internal state, in this of their outward conversation: *Wherein,* in which trespasses and sins, *in time past you walked,* you lived and behaved yourselves in such a manner as the men of the world are used to do. 3. We are by nature bond-slaves to sin and Satan. Those who walk in trespasses and sins, and according to the course of this world, walk *according to the prince of the power of the air.* The devil, or the prince of devils, is thus described. See Mt. 12:24, 26. The legions of apostate angels are as one power united under one chief; and therefore what is called *the powers of darkness* elsewhere is here spoken of in the singular number. The air is represented as the seat of his kingdom: and it was the opinion of both Jews and heathens that the air is full of spirits, and that there they exercise and exert themselves. The devil seems to have some power (by God's permission) in the lower region of the air; there he is at hand to tempt men, and to do as much mischief to the world as he can: but it is the comfort and joy of God's people that he who is *head over all things to the church* has conquered the devil and has him in his chain. But wicked men are slaves to Satan, for they walk according to him; they conform their lives and actions to the will and pleasure of this great usurper. The course and tenour of their lives are according to his suggestions, and in compliance with his temptations; they are subject to him, and are led captive by him at his will, whereupon he is called the god of this world, and *the spirit that now worketh in the children of disobedience. The children of disobedience* are such as choose to disobey God, and to serve the devil; in these he works very powerfully and effectually. As the good Spirit works that which is good in obedient souls, so this evil spirit works that which is evil in wicked men; and he now works, not only heretofore, but even since the world has been blessed with the light of the glorious gospel. The apostle adds, *Among whom also we all had our conversation in times past,* which words refer to the Jews, whom he signifies here to have been in the like sad and miserable condition by nature, and to have been as vile and wicked as the unregenerate Gentiles themselves, and whose natural state he further describes in the next words. 4. We are by nature drudges to the flesh, and to our corrupt affections, *v.* 3. By *fulfilling the desires of the flesh and of the mind,* men contract that filthiness of flesh and spirit from which the apostle exhorts Christians to cleanse themselves, 2 Co. 7:1. The fulfilling of the desires of the flesh and of the mind includes all the sin and wickedness that are acted in and by both the inferior and the higher or nobler powers of the soul. We lived in the actual commission of all those sins to which corrupt nature inclined us. The carnal mind makes a man a perfect slave to his vicious appetite. — *The fulfilling of the wills of the flesh,* so the words may be rendered, denoting the efficacy of these lusts, and what power they have over those who yield themselves up unto them. 5. We are *by nature the children of wrath, even as others.* The Jews were so, as well as the Gentiles; and one man is as much so as another by nature, not only by custom and imitation, but from the time when we began to exist, and by reason of our natural inclinations and appetites. All men, being naturally children of disobedience, are also by nature children of wrath: God is angry with the wicked every day. Our state and course are such as deserve wrath, and would end in eternal wrath, if divine grace did not interpose. What reason have sinners then to be looking out for that grace that will make them, of children of wrath, children of God and heirs of glory! Thus far the apostle has described the misery of a natural state in these verses, which we shall find him pursuing again in some following ones.

Verses 4–10

Here the apostle begins his account of the glorious change that was wrought in them by converting grace, where observe,

I. By whom, and in what manner, it was brought about and effected. 1. Negatively: *Not of yourselves, v.* 8. Our faith, our conversion, and our eternal salvation, are not the mere product of any natural abilities, nor of any merit of our own: *Not of works, lest any man should boast, v.* 9. These things are not brought to pass by any thing done by us, and therefore all boasting is excluded; he who glories must not glory in himself, but in the Lord. There is no room for any man's boasting of his own abilities and power; or as though he had done any thing that might deserve such immense favours from God. 2. Positively: *But God, who is rich in mercy,* etc. *v.* 4. God himself is the author of this great and happy change, and his great love is the spring and fontal cause of it; hence he resolved to show mercy. Love is his inclination to do us good considered simply as creatures; mercy respects us as apostate and as miserable creatures. Observe, God's eternal love or good-will towards his creatures is the fountain whence all his mercies vouch-safed to us proceed; and that love of God is great love, and that mercy of his is rich mercy, inexpressibly great and inexhaustibly rich. And then *by grace you are saved* (*v.* 5), and *by grace are you saved through faith — it is the gift of* God, *v.* 8. Note, Every converted sinner is a saved sinner. Such are delivered from sin and wrath; they are brought into a state of salvation, and have a right given them by grace to eternal happiness. The grace that saves them is the free undeserved goodness and favour of God; and he saves them, not *by the works of the law,* but through faith in Christ Jesus, by means of which they come to partake of the great blessings of the gospel; and both that faith and that salvation on which it has so great an influence are the gift of God. The great objects of faith are made known by divine revelation, and made credible by the testimony and evidence which God hath given us; and that we believe to salvation and obtain salvation through faith is entirely owing to divine assistance and grace; God has ordered all so that the whole shall appear to be of grace. Observe,

II. Wherein this change consists, in several particulars, answering to the misery of our natural state, some of which are enumerated in this section, and others are mentioned below. 1. We who were dead are quickened (*v.* 5), we are saved from the death of sin and have a principle of spiritual life implanted in us. Grace in the soul is a new life in the soul. As death locks up the senses, seals up all the powers and faculties, so does a state of sin, as to any thing that is good. Grace unlocks and opens all, and enlarges the soul. Observe, A regenerate sinner becomes a living soul: he lives a life of sanctification, being born of God; and he lives in the sense of the law, being delivered from the guilt of sin by pardoning and justifying grace. *He hath quickened us together with Christ.* Our spiritual life results from our union with Christ; it is in him that we live: *Because I live, you shall live also.* 2. We who were buried are raised up. *v.* 6. What remains yet to be done is here spoken of as though it were already past, though indeed we are raised up in virtue of our union with him whom God hath raised from the dead. When he raised Christ from the dead, he did in effect raise up all believers together with him, he being their common head; and when he placed him at his right hand in heavenly places, he advanced and glorified them in and with him, their raised and exalted head and forerunner. — *And made us sit together in heavenly places in Christ Jesus.* This may be understood in another sense. Sinners roll themselves in the dust; sanctified souls sit in heavenly places, are raised above the world; the world is as nothing to them, compared with what it has been, and compared with what the other world is. Saints are not only Christ's freemen, but they are assessors with him; by the assistance of his grace they have ascended with him above this world to converse with another, and they live in the constant expectation of it. They are not only servants to the best of masters in the best work, but they are exalted to reign with him; they sit upon the throne with Christ, *as he has sat down with his Father on his throne.*

III. Observe what is the great design and aim of God in producing and effecting this change: And this, 1. With respect to others: *That in the ages to come he might show,* etc. (*v.* 7), that he might give a specimen and proof of his great goodness and mercy, for the encouragement of sinners in future time. Observe, The goodness of God in converting and saving sinners heretofore is a proper encouragement to others in after-time to hope in his grace and mercy, and to apply themselves to these. God having this in his design, poor sinners should take great encouragement from it. And what may we not hope for from such grace and kindness, from riches of grace, to which this change is owing? *Through Christ Jesus,* by and through whom God conveys all his favour and blessings to us. 2. With respect to the regenerated sinners themselves: *For we are his workmanship, created in Christ Jesus unto good works,* etc. *v.* 10. It appears that all is of grace, because all our spiritual advantages are from God. *We are his workmanship;* he means in respect of the new creation; not only as men, but as saints. The new man is a new creature; and God is its Creator. It is a new birth, and we are born or begotten of his will. *In Christ Jesus,* that is, on the account of what he has done and suffered, and by the influence and operation of his blessed Spirit. *Unto good works,* etc. The apostle having before ascribed this change to divine grace in exclusion of works, lest he should seem thereby to discourage good works, he here observes that though the change is to be ascribed to nothing of that nature *(for we are the workmanship of God),* yet God, in his new creation, has designed and prepared us for good works: *Created unto good works,* with a design that we should be fruitful in them. Wherever God by his grace implants good principles, they are intended to be for good works. *Which God hath before ordained,* that is, decreed and appointed. Or, the words may be read, *To which God hath before prepared us,* that is, by blessing us with the knowledge of his will, and with the assistance of his Holy Spirit; and by producing such a change in us. *That we should walk in them,* or glorify God by an exemplary conversation and by our perseverance in holiness.

Verses 11–13

In these verses the apostle proceeds in his account of the miserable condition of these Ephesians by nature. *Wherefore remember,* etc. *v.* 11. As if he had said, "You should remember what you have been, and compare it with what you now are, in order to humble yourselves and to excite your love and thankfulness to God." Note, Converted sinners ought frequently to reflect upon the sinfulness and misery of the state they were in by nature. *Gentiles in the flesh,* that is, living in the corruption of their natures, and being destitute of circumcision, the outward sign of an interest in the covenant of grace. *Who are called uncircumcision by that,* etc., that is, "You were reproached and upbraided for it by the formal Jews, who made an external profession, and who looked no further than the outward ordinance." Note, Hypocritical professors are wont to value themselves chiefly on their external privileges, and to reproach and despise others who are destitute of them. The apostle describes the misery of their case in several particulars, *v.* 12. *"At that time,* while you were Gentiles, and in an unconverted state, you were," 1. "In a Christless condition, without the knowledge of the Messiah, and without any saving interest in him or relation to him." It is true of all unconverted sinners, all those who are destitute of faith, that they have no saving interest in Christ; and it must be a sad and deplorable thing for a soul to be without a Christ. Being without Christ, they were, 2. *Aliens from the commonwealth of Israel;* they did not belong to Christ's church, and had no communion with it, that being confined to the Israelitish nation. It is no small privilege to be placed in the church of Christ, and to share with the members of it in the advantages peculiar to it. 3. *They are strangers from the covenants of promise.* The covenant of grace has ever been the same for substance, though, having undergone various additions and improvements in the several ages of the church, it is called covenants; and the covenants of promise, because it is made up of promises, and particularly contains the great promise of the Messiah, and of eternal life through him. Now the Ephesians, in their gentilism, were strangers to this covenant, having never had any information nor overture of it; and all unregenerate sinners are strangers to it, as they have no interest in it. Those who are without Christ, and so have no interest in the Mediator of the covenant, have none in the promises of the covenant. 4. They had no hope, that is, beyond this life — no well-grounded hope in God, no hope of spiritual and eternal blessings. Those who are without Christ, and strangers from the covenant, can have no good hope; for Christ and the covenant are the ground and foundation of all the Christian's hopes. They were in a state of distance and estrangement from God: *Without God in the world;* not without some general knowledge of a deity, for they worshipped idols, but living without any due regard to him, any acknowledged dependence on him, and any special interest in him. The words are, *atheists in the world;* for, though they worshipped many gods, yet they were without the true God.

The apostle proceeds *(v.* 13) further to illustrate the happy change that was made in their state: *But now, in Christ Jesus, you who sometimes were far off,* etc. They were far off from Christ, from his church, from the promises, from the Christian hope, and from God himself; and therefore from all good, like the prodigal son in the far country: this had been represented in the preceding verses. Unconverted sinners remove themselves at a distance from God, and God puts them at a distance: *He beholds the proud afar off.* "*But now in Christ Jesus,* etc., upon your conversion, by virtue of union with Christ, and interest in him by faith, you are made nigh." They were brought home to God, received into the church,

taken into the covenant, and possessed of all other privileges consequent upon these. Note, *The saints are a people near to God. Salvation is far from the wicked;* but God is a help at hand to his people; and this is *by the blood of Christ,* by the merit of his sufferings and death. Every believing sinner owes his nearness to God, and his interest in his favour, to the death and sacrifice of Christ.

Verses 14–22

We have now come to the last part of the chapter, which contains an account of the great and mighty privileges that converted Jews and Gentiles both receive from Christ. The apostle here shows that those who were in a state of enmity are reconciled. Between the Jews and the Gentiles there had been a great enmity; so there is between God and every unregenerate man. Now Jesus Christ is our peace, *v.* 14. He made peace by the sacrifice of himself; and came to reconcile, 1. Jews and Gentiles to each other. He *made both one,* by reconciling these two divisions of men, who were wont to malign, to hate, and to reproach each other before. He *broke down the middle wall of partition,* the ceremonial law, that made the great feud, and was the badge of the Jews' peculiarity, called *the partition-wall* by way of allusion to the partition in the temple, which separated the court of the Gentiles from that into which the Jews only had liberty to enter. Thus *he abolished in his flesh the enmity, v.* 15. By his sufferings in the flesh, to took away the binding power of the ceremonial law (so removing that cause of enmity and distance between them), which is here called *the law of commandments contained in ordinances,* because it enjoined a multitude of external rites and ceremonies, and consisted of many institutions and appointments about the outward parts of divine worship. *The legal ceremonies were abrogated by Christ, having their accomplishment in him.* By taking these out of the way, he formed one church of believers, whether they had been Jews or Gentiles. Thus he made *in himself of twain one new man.* He framed both these parties into one new society, or body of God's people, uniting them to himself as their common head, they being renewed by the Holy Ghost, and now concurring in a new way of gospel worship, *so making peace* between these two parties, who were so much at variance before. 2. There is an enmity between God and sinners, whether Jews and Gentiles; and Christ came to slay that enmity, and to reconcile them both to God, *v.* 16. Sin breeds a quarrel between God and men. Christ came to take up the quarrel, and to bring it to an end, by reconciling both Jew and Gentile, now collected and gathered into one body, to a provoked and an offended God: and this *by the cross,* or by the sacrifice of himself upon the cross, *having slain the enmity thereby.* He, being slain or sacrificed, slew the enmity that there was between God and poor sinners. The apostle proceeds to illustrate the great advantages which both parties gain by the mediation of our Lord Jesus Christ, *v.* 17. Christ, who purchased peace on the cross, came, partly in his own person, as to the Jews, who are here said to have been nigh, and partly in his apostles, whom he commissioned to preach the gospel to the Gentiles, who are said to have been afar off, in the sense that has been given before. *And preached peace,* or published the terms of reconciliation with God and of eternal life. Note here, When the messengers of Christ deliver his truths, it is in effect the same as if he did it immediately himself. He is said to preach by them, insomuch that he who receiveth them receiveth him, and he who despiseth them (acting by virtue of his commission, and delivering his message) despiseth and rejecteth Christ himself. Now the effect of this peace is the free access which both Jews and Gentiles have unto God (*v.* 18): *For through him,* in his name and by virtue of his mediation, *we both have access* or admission into the presence of God, who has become the common reconciled Father of both: the throne of grace is erected for us to come to, and liberty of approach to that throne is allowed us. Our access is by the Holy Spirit. Christ purchased for us leave to come to God, and the Spirit gives us a heart to come and strength to come, even grace to serve God acceptably. Observe, We draw nigh to God, through Jesus Christ, by the help of the Spirit. The Ephesians, upon their conversion, having such an access to God, as well as the Jews, and by the same Spirit, the apostle tells them, *Now therefore you are no more strangers and foreigners, v.* 19. This he mentions by way of opposition to what he had observed of them in their heathenism: they were now no longer *aliens from the commonwealth of Israel,* and no

longer what the Jews were wont to account all the nations of the earth besides themselves (namely, strangers to God), *but fellow-citizens with the saints, and of the household of God,* that is, members of the church of Christ, and having a right to all the privileges of it. Observe here, The church is compared to a city, and every converted sinner is free of it. It is also compared to a house, and every converted sinner is one of the domestics, one of the family, a servant and a child in God's house. In *v.* 20 the church is compared to a building. The apostles and prophets are *the foundation* of that building. They may be so called in a secondary sense, Christ himself being the primary foundation; but we are rather to understand it of the doctrine delivered by the prophets of the Old Testament and the apostles of the New. It follows, *Jesus Christ himself being the chief corner-stone.* In him both Jews and Gentiles meet, and constitute one church; and Christ supports the building by his strength: *In whom all the building, fitly framed together,* etc. *v.* 21. All believers, of whom it consists, being united to Christ by faith, and among themselves by Christian charity, *grow unto a holy temple,* become a sacred society, in which there is much communion between God and his people, as in the temple, they worshipping and serving him, he manifesting himself unto them, they offering up spiritual sacrifices to God and he dispensing his blessings and favours to them. Thus the building, for the nature of it, is a temple, a holy temple; for the church is the place which God hath chosen to put his name there, and it becomes such a temple by grace and strength derived from himself — *in the Lord.* The universal church being built upon Christ as the foundation-stone, and united in Christ as the corner-stone, comes at length to be glorified in him as the top-stone: *In whom you also are built together,* etc. *v.* 22. Observe, Not only the universal church is called the temple of God, but particular churches; and even every true believer is a living temple, is *a habitation of God through the Spirit.* God dwells in all believers now, they having become the temple of God through the operations of the blessed Spirit, and his dwelling with them now is an earnest of their dwelling together with him to eternity.

CHAPTER 3

This chapter consists of two parts. I. Of the account which Paul gives the Ephesians concerning himself, as he was appointed by God to be the apostle of the Gentiles (*v.* 1–13). II. Of his devout and affectionate prayer to God for the Ephesians (*v.* 14–21). We may observe it to have been very much the practice of this apostle to intermix, with his instructions and counsels, intercessions and prayers to God for those to whom he wrote, as knowing that all his instructions and teachings would be useless and vain, except God did co-operate with them, and render them effectual. This is an example that all the ministers of Christ should copy after, praying earnestly that the efficacious operations of the divine Spirit may attend their ministrations, and crown them with success.

Verses 1–13

Here we have the account which Paul gives the Ephesians concerning himself, as he was appointed by God the apostle of the Gentiles.

I. We may observe that he acquaints them with the tribulations and sufferings which he endured in the discharge of that office, *v.* 1. The first clause refers to the preceding chapter, and may be understood either of these two ways: — 1. *"For this cause,* — for having preached the doctrine contained in the foregoing chapter, and for asserting that the great privileges of the gospel belong not only to the Jews, but to believing Gentiles also, though they are not circumcised, — for this I am now a prisoner, but *a prisoner of Jesus Christ,* as I suffer in his cause and for his sake, and continue his faithful servant and the object of his special protection and care, while I am thus suffering for him." Observe, Christ's servants, if they come to be prisoners, are his prisoners; and he despises not his prisoners. He thinks never the worse of them for the bad character which the world gives them or the evil treatment that they met with in it. Paul adhered to Christ, and Christ owned him, when he was in prison. — *For you, Gentiles;* the Jews persecuted and imprisoned him because he was the apostle of the Gentiles, and preached the gospel to them. We may learn hence that the faithful ministers of Christ are to dispense his sacred truths, however disagreeable they may be to some, and whatever they themselves may suffer for doing so. Or, 2. The words may be thus understood: — *"For this cause,* — since *you are no more strangers and foreigners* (as ch. 2:19), but are united to Christ, and admitted into communion with his church, — *I Paul,* who am *the prisoner of Jesus Christ,* pray that you may be enabled to act as becomes persons thus favoured by God, and made partakers of such privileges." To this purport you find him expressing himself in *v.* 14, where, after the digression contained in the several verses intervening, he proceeds with what he began in the first verse. Observe, Those who have received grace and signal favours from God stand in need of prayer, that they may improve and advance, and continue to act as becomes them. And, seeing Paul while he was a prisoner employed himself in such prayers to God in behalf of the Ephesians, we should learn that no particular sufferings of our own should make us so solicitous about ourselves as to neglect the cases of others in our supplications and addresses to God. He speaks again of his sufferings: *Wherefore I desire that you faint not at my tribulation for you, which is your glory, v.* 13. While he was in prison, he suffered much there; and, though it was upon their account that he suffered, yet he would not have them discouraged nor dismayed at this, seeing God had done such great things for them by his ministry. What a tender concern was here for these Ephesians! The apostle seems to have been more solicitous lest they should be discouraged and faint upon his tribulations than about what he himself endured; and, to prevent this, he tells them that his sufferings were their glory, and would be so far from being a real discouragement, if they duly considered the matter, that they ministered cause to them for glorying and for rejoicing, as this discovered the great esteem and regard which God bore to them, in that he not only sent his apostles to preach the gospel to them, but even to suffer for them, and to confirm the truths they delivered by the persecutions they underwent. Observe, Not only the faithful ministers of Christ themselves, but their people too, have some special cause for joy and glorying, when they suffer for the sake of dispensing the gospel.

II. The apostle informs them of God's appointing him to the office, and eminently fitting and qualifying him for it, by a special revelation that he made unto him. 1. God appointed him to the office: *If you have heard of the dispensation of the grace of God, which is given me to you-ward, v.* 2. They could not have heard of this, and therefore he does not design to speak doubtfully of this matter. *Eige* is sometimes an affirmative particle, and we may read it, *Since you have heard,* etc. He styles the gospel *the grace of God* here (as in other places) because it is the gift of divine grace to sinful men; and all the gracious overtures that it makes, and the joyful tidings that it contains, proceed from the rich grace of God; and it is also the great instrument in the hands of the Spirit by which God works grace in the souls of men. He speaks of the dispensation of this grace given to him; he means as he was authorized and commissioned by God to dispense the doctrine of the gospel, which commission and authority were given to him chiefly for he service of the Gentiles: *to you-ward.* And again, speaking of the gospel, he says, *Whereof I was made a minister,* etc. *v.* 7 Here he again asserts his authority. He *was* MADE *a minister* — he did not make himself such; he took not to himself that honour — and he was made such *according to the gift of the grace of God unto* him. God supplied and furnished him for his work; and in the performance of it suitably assisted him with all needful gifts and graces, both ordinary and extraordinary, and that *by the effectual working of his power,* in himself more especially, and also in great numbers of those to whom he preached, by which means his labours among them were successful. Observe, What God calls men to he fits them for, and does it with an almighty power. An effectual working of divine power attends the gifts of divine grace. 2. As God appointed him to the office, so he eminently qualified him for it, by a special revelation that he made unto him. He makes mention both of the mystery that was revealed and of the revelation of it. (1.) The mystery revealed is *that the Gentiles should be fellow-heirs, and of the same body, and partakers of his promise in Christ, by the gospel* (*v.* 6); that is, that they should be joint-heirs with the believing Jews of the heavenly inheritance; and that they should be members of the same mystical body, be received into the church of Christ, and be interested in the gospel-promises, as well as the Jews, and particularly in that great promise of the Spirit. And this *in Christ,* being united to Christ, *in whom all the promises are yea and amen; and by the gospel,* that is, in the times of the gospel, as some understand it; or, *by the gospel* preached to them, which is the great instrument and means by which God works faith in Christ, as others. This was the great truth revealed to the apostles, namely, that God would call the Gentiles to salvation by faith in Christ, and that without the works of the law. (2.) Of the revelation of this truth he speaks. *v.* 3–5. Here we may observe that the coalition of Jews and Gentiles in the gospel church was a mystery, a great mystery, what was designed in the counsel of God before all worlds, but what could not be fully understood for many ages, till the accomplishment expounded the prophecies of it. It is called a mystery because the several circumstances and peculiarities of it (such as the time and manner and means by which it should be effected) were concealed and kept secret in God's own breast, till be an immediate *revelation he made them known* to his servant. See Acts 26:16–18. And it is called the mystery of Christ because it was revealed by him (Gal. 1:12), and because it relates so very much to him. Of this the apostle has given some hints *afore,* or a little before; that is, in the preceding chapters. *Whereby, when you read;* or, as those words may be read, *unto which attending* (and it is not enough for us barely to read the scriptures, unless we attend to them, and seriously consider and lay to heart what we read), *you may understand my knowledge in the mystery of Christ;* so as to perceive how God had fitted and qualified him to be an apostle to the Gentiles, which might be to them an evident token of his divine authority. *This mystery,* he says, *in other ages was not made known unto the sons of men, as it is now revealed unto his holy apostles and prophets by the Spirit* (*v.* 5); that is, "It was not so fully and clearly discovered in the ages before Christ as it is now revealed unto the prophets of this age, the prophets of the New Testament, who are immediately inspired and taught by the Spirit." Let us observe, that the conversion of the Gentile world to the faith of Christ was an adorable mystery, and we ought to bless God for it. Who would have imagined that those who had been so long in the dark, and at so great a distance, would be enlightened with the marvellous light, and be made nigh? Let us learn hence not to despair of the worst, of the worst of persons, and the worst of nations. Nothing is too hard for divine grace to do: none so unworthy but God may please to confer great grace upon them. And how much are we ourselves interested in this affair; not only as we live in a time in which the mystery is revealed, but particularly as we are a part of the nations which in times past were foreigners and strangers, and lived in gross idolatry; but are now enlightened with the everlasting gospel, and partake of its promises!

III. The apostle informs them how he was employed in this office, and that with respect to the Gentiles, and to all men.

1. With respect to the Gentiles, he *preached* to them *the unsearchable riches of Christ, v.* 8. Observe, in this verse, how humbly he speaks of himself, and how highly he speaks of Jesus Christ. (1.) How humbly he speaks of himself: *I am less than the least of all saints.* St. Paul, who was the chief of the apostles, calls himself *less than the least of all saints:* he means on account of his having been formerly a persecutor of the followers of Christ. He was, in his own esteem, as little as could be. What can be less than the least? To speak himself as little as could be, he speaks himself less than could be. Observe, Those whom God advances to honourable employments he humbles and makes low in their own eyes; and, where God gives grace to be humble, there he gives all other grace. You may also observe in what a different manner the apostle speaks of himself and of his office. While he magnifies his office, he debases himself. Observe, A faithful minister of Christ may be very humble, and think very meanly of himself, even when he thinks and speaks very highly and honourably of his sacred function. (2.) How highly he speaks of Jesus Christ: *The unsearchable riches of Christ.* There is a mighty treasury of mercy, grace, and love, laid up in Christ Jesus, and that both for Jews and Gentiles. Or, the riches of the gospel are here spoken of as the riches of Christ: the riches which Christ purchased for, and bestows upon, all believers. And they are unsearchable riches, which we cannot find the bottom of, which human sagacity could never have discovered, and men could no otherwise attain to the knowledge of them but by revelation. Now it was the apostle's business and employment to *preach* these *unsearchable riches of Christ among the Gentiles:* and it was a favour he greatly valued, and looked upon it as an unspeakable honour to him: *"Unto me is this grace given;* this special favour God has granted to such an unworthy creature as I am." And it is an unspeakable favour to the Gentile world that to them *the unsearchable riches of Christ* are preached. Though many remain poor, and are not enriched with these riches, yet it is a favour to have them preached among us, to have an offer of them made to us; and, if we are not enriched with them, it is our own fault.

2. With respect to all men, *v.* 9. His business and employment were *to make all men see* (to publish and make known to the whole world) *what is the fellowship of the mystery* (that the Gentiles who have hitherto been strangers to the church, shall be admitted into communion with it) *which from the beginning of the world hath been hid in God* (kept secret in his purpose), *who created all things by Jesus Christ:* as Jn. 1:3, *All things were made by him, and without him was not any thing made that was made;* and therefore no wonder that he saves the Gentiles as well as the Jews; for he is the common Creator of them both: and we may conclude that he is able to perform the work of their redemption, seeing he was able to accomplish the great work of creation. It is true that both the first creation, when God made all things out of nothing, and the new creation, whereby sinners are made new creatures by converting grace, are of God by Jesus Christ. The apostle adds, *To the intent that now unto the principalities and powers in heavenly places might be known, by the church, the manifold wisdom of God, v.* 10. This was one things, among others, which God had in his eye in revealing this mystery, that the good angels, who have a pre-eminence in governing the kingdoms and principalities of the world, and who are endued with great power to execute the will of God on this earth (though their ordinary residence is in heaven) may be informed, from what passes in the church and is done in and by it, *of the manifold wisdom of God;* that is, of the great variety with which God wisely dispenses things, or of his wisdom manifested in the many ways and methods he takes in ordering his church in the several ages of it, and especially in receiving the Gentiles into it. The holy angels, who look into the mystery of our redemption by Christ, could not but take notice of this branch of that mystery, that among the Gentiles is preached the unsearchable riches of Christ. And this is *according to the eternal purpose which he purposed in Christ Jesus our Lord, v.* 11. Some translate the words *kata prothesin tōn aiōnōn* thus *According to the fore-disposing of the ages which he made,* etc. So Dr. Whitby, etc. "In the first of the ages," says this author, "his wisdom seeing fit to give the promise of a Saviour to a fallen Adam: in the second age to typify and represent him to the Jews in sacred persons, rites, and sacrifices: and in the age of the Messiah, or the last age, to reveal him to the Jews, and preach him to the Gentiles." Others understand it, according to our translation, of the eternal purpose which God purposed to execute in and through Jesus Christ, the whole of what he has done in the great affair of man's redemption being in pursuance of his eternal decree about that matter. The apostle, having mentioned our Lord Jesus Christ, subjoins concerning him, *In whom we have boldness and access with confidence by the faith of him* (*v.* 12); that is, "By (or through) whom we have liberty to open our minds freely to God, as to a Father, and a well-grounded persuasion of audience and of acceptance with him; and this by means of the faith we have in him, as our great Mediator and Advocate." We may come with humble boldness to hear from God, knowing that the terror of the curse is done away; and we may expect to hear from him good words and comfortable. We may have access with confidence to speak to God, knowing that we have such a Mediator between God and us, and such an Advocate with the Father.

Verses 14–21

We now come to the second part of this chapter, which contains Paul's devout and affectionate prayer to God for his beloved Ephesians. — *For this cause.* This may be referred either to the immediately foregoing verse, *That you faint not,* etc., or, rather, the apostle is here resuming what he began at the first verse, from which he digressed in those which are interposed. Observe,

I. To whom he prays — to God, as *the Father of our Lord Jesus Christ,* of which see *ch.* 1:3.

II. His outward posture in prayer, which was humble and reverent: *I bow my knees.* Note, When we draw nigh to God, we should reverence him in our hearts, and express our reverence in the most suitable and becoming behaviour and gesture. Here, having mentioned Christ, he cannot pass without an honourable encomium of his love, *v.* 15. The universal church has a dependence upon the Lord Jesus Christ: *Of whom the whole family in heaven and earth is named.* The

Jews were wont to boast of Abraham as their father, but now Jews and Gentiles are both denominated from Christ (so some); while others understand it of the saints in heaven, who wear the crown of glory, and of saints on earth who are going on in the work of grace here. Both the one and the other make but one family, one household; and from him they are *named* CHRISTIANS, as they really are such, acknowledging their dependence upon, and their relation to, Christ.

III. What the apostle asks of God for these his friends — spiritual blessings, which are the best blessings, and the most earnestly to be sought and prayed for by every one of us, both for ourselves and for our friends. 1. Spiritual strength for the work and duty to which they were called, and in which they were employed: *That he would grant you, according to the riches of his grace, to be strengthened,* etc. *The inner man* is the heart or soul. To be *strengthened with might* is to be mightily strengthened, much more than they were at present; to be endued with a high degree of grace, and spiritual abilities for discharging duty, resisting temptations, enduring persecutions, etc. And the apostle prays that this may be *according to the riches of his glory,* or according to his glorious riches — answerable to that great abundance of grace, mercy, and power, which resides in God, and is his glory: and this by his Spirit, who is the immediate worker of grace in the souls of God's people. Observe from these things, That strength from the Spirit of God in the inner man is the best and most desirable strength, strength in the soul, the strength of faith and other graces, strength to serve God and to do our duty, and to persevere in our Christian course with vigour and with cheerfulness. And let us further observe that *as the work of grace is first begun so it is continued and carried on, by the blessed Spirit of God.* 2. The indwelling of Christ in their hearts, *v.* 17. Christ is said to dwell in his people, as he is always present with them by his gracious influences and operations. Observe, It is a desirable thing to have Christ dwell in our hearts; and if the law of Christ be written there, and the love of Christ be shed abroad there, then Christ dwells there. Christ is an inhabitant in the soul of every good Christian. Where his spirit dwells, there he swells; and he dwells in the heart by faith, by means of the continual exercise of faith upon him. Faith opens the door of the soul, to receive Christ; faith admits him, and submits to him. By faith we are united to Christ, and have an interest in him. 3. The fixing of pious and devout affections in the soul: *That you being rooted and grounded in love,* stedfastly fixed in your love to God, the Father of our Lord Jesus Christ, and to all the saints, the beloved of our Lord Jesus Christ. Many have some love to God and to his servants, but it is a flash, like the crackling of throns under a pot, it makes a great noise, but is gone presently. We should earnestly desire that good affections may be fixed in us, that we may be *rooted and grounded in love.* Some understand it of their being settled and established in the sense of God's love to them, which would inspire them with greater ardours of holy love to him, and to one another. And how very desirable is it to have a settled fixed sense of the love of God and Christ to our souls, so as to be able to say with the apostle at all times, *He has loved me!* Now the best way to attain this is to be careful that we maintain a constant love to God in our souls; this will be the evidence of the love of God to us. *We love him, because he first loved us.* In order to this he prays, 4. For their experimental acquaintance with the love of Jesus Christ. The more intimate acquaintance we have with Christ's love to us, the more our love will be drawn out to him, and to those who are his, for his sake: *That you may be able to comprehend with all saints,* etc. (*v.* 18, 19); that is, more clearly to understand, and firmly to believe, the wonderful love of Christ to his, which the saints do understand and believe in some measure, and shall understand more hereafter. Christians should not aim to comprehend above all saints; but be content that God deals with them as he uses to do with those who love and fear his name: we should desire to comprehend *with all saints,* to have so much knowledge as the saints are allowed to have in this world. We should be ambitious of coming up with *the first three;* but not of going beyond what is the measure of the stature of other saints. It is observable how magnificently the apostle speaks of the love of Christ. The dimensions of redeeming love are admirable: *The breadth, and length, and depth, and height.* By enumerating these dimensions, the apostle designs to signify the exceeding greatness of the love of Christ, the unsearchable riches of his love, which is *higher than heaven, deeper than hell, longer than the earth, and broader than the sea,* Job 11:8, 9. Some describe the particulars thus: By the breadth of it we may understand the extent of it to all ages, nations, and ranks of men; by the length of it, its continuance from everlasting to everlasting; by the depth of it, its stooping to the lowest condition, with a design to relieve and save those who have sunk into the depths of sin and misery; by its height, its entitling and raising us up to the heavenly happiness and glory. We should desire to comprehend this love: it is the character of all the saints that they do so; for they all have a complacency and a confidence in the love of Christ: *And to know the love of Christ which passeth knowledge, v.* 19. If it passeth knowledge, how can we know it? We must pray and endeavour to know something, and should still covet and strive to know more and more of it, though, after the best endeavours, none can fully comprehend it: in its full extent it surpasses knowledge. Though the love of Christ may be better perceived and known by Christians than it generally is, yet it cannot be fully understood on this side heaven. 5. He prays that they may *be filled with all the fulness of God.* It is a high expression: we should not dare to use it if we did not find it in the scriptures. It is like those other expressions, of being *partakers of a divine nature,* and of being *perfect as our Father in heaven is perfect.* We are not to understand it of his fulness as God in himself, but of his fulness as a God in covenant with us, as a God to his people: such a fulness as God is ready to bestow, who is willing to fill them all to the utmost of their capacity, and that with all those gifts and graces which he sees they need. Those who receive grace for grace from Christ's fulness may be said to be *filled with the fulness of God,* according to their capacity, all which is in order to their arriving at the highest degree of the knowledge and enjoyment of God, and an entire conformity to him.

The apostle closes the chapter with a doxology, *v.* 20, 21. It is proper to conclude our prayers with praises. Our blessed Saviour has taught us to do so. Take notice how he describes God, and how he ascribes glory to him. He describes him as a God that *is able to do exceedingly abundantly above all that we ask or think.* There is an inexhaustible fulness of grace and mercy in God, which the prayers of all the saints can never draw dry. Whatever we may ask, or think to ask, still God is still able to do more, abundantly more, exceedingly abundantly more. Open thy mouth ever so wide, still he hath wherewithal to fill it. Note, In our applications to God we should encourage our faith by a consideration of his all-sufficiency and almighty power. *According to the power which worketh in us.* As if he had said, We have already had a proof of this power of God, in what he hath wrought in us and done for us, having quickened us by his grace, and converted us to himself. The power that still worketh for the saints is according to that power that hath wrought in them. Wherever God gives of his fulness he gives to experience his power. Having thus described God, he ascribes glory to him. When we come to ask for grace from God, we ought to give glory to God. Unto him be glory in the church by Christ Jesus. In ascribing glory to God, we ascribe all excellences and perfections to him, glory being the effulgency and result of them all. Observe, The seat of God's praises is in the church. That little rent of praise which God receives from this world is from the church, a sacred society constituted for the glory of God, every particular member of which, both Jew and Gentile, concurs in this work of praising God. The Mediator of these praises is Jesus Christ. All God's gifts come from his to us through the hand of Christ; and all our praises pass from us to him through the same hand. And God should and will be praised thus *throughout all ages, world without end;* for he will ever have a church to praise him, and he will ever have his tribute of praise from his church. *Amen.* So be it; and so it will certainly be.

CHAPTER 4

We have gone through the former part of this epistle, which consists of several important doctrinal truths, contained in the three preceding chapters. We enter now on the latter part of it, in which we have the most weighty and serious exhortations that can be given. We may observe that in this, as in most others of Paul's epistles, the former part is doctrinal, and fitted to inform the minds of men in the great truths and doctrines of the gospel, the latter is practical, and designed for the direction of their lives and manners, all Christians being bound to endeavour after soundness in the faith, and regularity in life and practice. In what has gone before we have heard of Christian privileges, which are the matter of our comfort. In what follows we shall hear of Christian duties, and what the Lord our God requires of us in consideration of such privileges vouchsafed to us. The best way to understand the mysteries and partake of the privileges of which we have read before is conscientiously to practise the duties prescribed to us in what follows: as, on the other hand, a serious consideration and belief of the doctrines that have been taught us in the foregoing chapters will be a good foundation on which to build the practice of the duties prescribed in those which are yet before us. Christian faith and Christian practice mutually befriend each other. In this chapter we have divers exhortations to important duties. I. One that is more general (*v.* 1). II. An exhortation to mutual love, unity, and concord, with the proper means and motives to promote them (*v.* 2–16). III. An exhortation to Christian purity and holiness of life; and that both more general (*v.* 17–24) and in several particular instances (*v.* 25 to the end).

Verse 1

This is a general exhortation to walk as becomes our Christian profession. Paul was now a prisoner at Rome; and he was the *prisoner of the Lord,* or in the Lord, which signifies as much as for the Lord. See of this, *ch.* 3:1. He mentions this once and again, to show that he was not ashamed of his bonds, well knowing that he suffered not as an evil doer: and likewise to recommend what he wrote to them with the greater tenderness and with some special advantage. It was a doctrine he thought worth suffering for, and therefore surely they should think it worthy their serious regards and their dutiful observance. We have here the petition of a poor prisoner, one of Christ's prisoners: *"I therefore, the prisoner of the Lord, beseech you,"* etc. Considering what God has done for you, and to what a state and condition he has called you, as has been discoursed before, I now come with an earnest request to you (not to send me relief, nor to use your interest for the obtaining of my liberty, the first thing which poor prisoners are wont to solicit from their friends, but) that you would approve yourselves good Christians, and live up to your profession and calling; *That you walk worthily,* agreeably, suitably, and congruously to those happy circumstances into which the grace of God has brought you, whom he has converted from heathenism to Christianity. Observe, Christians ought to accommodate themselves to the gospel by which they are called, and to the glory to which they are called; both are their vocation. We are called Christians; we must answer that name, and live like Christians. We are called to God's kingdom and glory; that kingdom and glory therefore we must mind, and walk as becomes the heirs of them.

Verses 2–16

Here the apostle proceeds to more particular exhortations. Two he enlarges upon in this chapter: — To unity an love, purity and holiness, which Christians should very much study. We do not *walk worthy of the vocation wherewith we are called* if we be not faithful friends to all Christians, and sworn enemies to all sin.

This section contains the exhortation to mutual love, unity, and concord, with the proper means and motives to promote them. Nothing is pressed upon us more earnestly in the scriptures than this. Love is the law of Christ's kingdom, the lesson of his school, the livery of his family. Observe,

I. The means of unity: *Lowliness and meekness, long-suffering, and forbearing one another in love, v.* 2. By lowliness we are to understand humility, entertaining mean thoughts of ourselves, which is opposed to pride. By *meekness,* that excellent disposition of soul which makes men unwilling to provoke others, and not easily to be provoked or offended with their infirmities; and it is opposed to angry resentments and peevishness. *Long-suffering* implies a patient bearing of injuries, without seeking revenge. *Forbearing one another in love* signifies bearing their infirmities out of a principle of love, and so as not to cease to love them on the account of these. The best Christians have need to bear one with another, and to make the best one of another, to provoke one another's graces and not their passions. We find much in ourselves which it is hard to forgive ourselves; and therefore we must not think it much if we find that in others which we think hard to forgive them, and yet we must forgive them as we forgive ourselves. Now without these things unity cannot be preserved. The first step towards unity is humility; without this there will be no meekness, no patience, or forbearance; and without these no unity. Pride and passion break the peace, and make all the mischief. Humility and meekness restore the peace, and keep it. *Only by pride comes contention;* only by humility comes love. The more lowly-mindedness the more like-mindedness. We do not walk worthy of the vocation wherewith we are called if we be not meek and lowly of heart: for he by whom we are called, he to whom we are called, was eminent for meekness and lowliness of heart, and has commanded us therein to learn of him.

II. The nature of that unity which the apostle prescribes: it is *the unity of the Spirit, v.* 3. The seat of Christian unity is in the heart or spirit: it does not lie in one set of thoughts, nor in one form and mode of worship, but in one heart and one soul. This unity of heart and affection may be said to be of the Spirit of God; it is wrought by him, and is one of the fruits of the Spirit. This we should endeavour to keep. *Endeavouring* is a gospel word. We must do our utmost. If others will quarrel with us, we must take all possible care not to quarrel with them. If others will despise and hate us, we must not despise and hate them. *In the bond of peace.* Peace is a bond, as it unites persons, and makes them live friendly one with another. A peaceable disposition and conduct bind Christians together, whereas discord and quarrelling disband and disunite their hearts and affections. Many slender twigs, bound together, become strong. The bond of peace is the strength of society. Not that it can be imagined that all good people, and all the members of societies, should be in every thing just of the same length, and the same sentiments, and the same judgment: buy the bond of peace unites them all together, with a *non obstante* to these. As in a bundle of rods, they may be of different lengths and different strength; but, when they are tied together by one bond, they are stronger than any, even than the thickest and strongest was of itself.

III. The motives proper to promote this Christian unity and concord. The apostle urges several, to persuade us thereto.

1. Consider how many unities there are that are the joy and glory of our Christian profession. There should be one heart; for *there is one body, and one spirit, v.* 4. Two hearts in one body would be monstrous. If there be but one body, all that belong to that body should have one heart. The Catholic church is one mystical body of Christ, and all good Christians make up but one body, incorporated by one charter, that of the gospel, animated by one Spirit, the same Holy Spirit who by his gifts and graces quickens, enlivens, and governs that body. If we belong to Christ, we are all actuated by one and the same Spirit, and therefore should be one. *Even as you are called in one hope of your calling.* Hope is here put for its object, the thing hoped for, the heavenly inheritance, to the hope of which we are called. All Christians are called to the same hope of eternal life. There is one Christ that they all hope in, and one heaven that they are all hoping for; and therefore they should be of one heart. *One Lord* (*v.* 5), that is, Christ, the head of the church, to whom, by God's appointment, all Christians are immediately subject. *One faith,* that is, the gospel, containing the doctrine of the Christian faith: or, it is the same grace of faith (faith in Christ) whereby all Christians are saved. *One baptism,* by which we profess our faith, being baptized in the name of the Father, Son, and Holy Ghost; and so the same sacramental covenant, whereby we engage ourselves to the Lord Christ. *One God and Father of all, v.* 6. One God, who owns all the true members of the church for his children; for he is the Father of all such by special relation, as he is the Father of all men by creation: and he *is above all,* by his essence, and with respect to the glorious perfections of his nature, and as he has dominion over all creatures and especially over his church, *and through all,* by his providence upholding and governing them: *and in you all,* in all believers, in whom he dwells as in his holy temple, by his Spirit and special grace. If then there be so many *ones,* it is a pity but there should be one more — one heart, or one soul.

2. Consider the variety of gifts that Christ has bestowed among Christians: *But unto every one of us is given grace according to the measure of the gift of Christ.* Though the members of Christ's church agree in so many things, yet there are some things wherein they differ: but this should breed no difference of affection among them, since they are all derived from the same bountiful author and designed for the same great ends. Unto every one of us Christians is given grace, some gift of grace, in some kind or degree or other, for the mutual help of one another. Unto every one of us ministers is given grace; to some a greater measure of gifts, to others a less measure. The different gifts of Christ's ministers proved a great occasion of contention among the first Christians: one was for Paul, and another for Apollos. The apostle shows that they had no reason to quarrel about them, but all the reason in the world to agree in the joint use of them, for common edification; because all was given *according to the measure of the gift of Christ,* in such a measure as seemed best to Christ to bestow upon every one. Observe, All the ministers, and all the members of Christ, owe all the gifts and graces that they are possessed of to him; and this is a good reason why we should love one another, *because to every one of us is given grace.* All to whom Christ has given grace, and on whom he has bestowed his gifts (though they are of different sizes, different names, and different sentiments, yet), *ought to love one another.* The apostle takes this occasion to specify some of the gifts which Christ bestowed. And that they were bestowed by Christ he makes appear by those words of David wherein he foretold this concerning him (Ps. 68:18), *Wherefore he saith* (*v.* 8), that is, the Psalmist saith, *When he ascended up on high, he led captivity captive, and gave gifts unto men.* David prophesied of the ascension of Christ; and the apostle descants upon it here, and in the three following verses. *When he ascended up on high.* We may understand the apostle both of the place into which he ascended in his human nature, that is, the highest heavens, and particularly of the state to which he was advanced, he being then highly exalted, and eminently glorified, by his Father. Let us set ourselves to think of the ascension of Jesus Christ: that our blessed Redeemer, having risen from the dead, in gone to heaven, where he sits at the right hand of the Majesty on high, which completed the proof of his being the Son of God. As great conquerors, when they rode in their triumphal chariots, used to be attended with the most illustrious of their captives led in chains, and were wont to scatter their largesses and bounty among the soldiers and other spectators of their triumphs, so Christ, when he ascended into heaven, as a triumphant conqueror, *led captivity captive.* It is a phrase used in the Old Testament to signify a conquest over enemies, especially over such as formerly had led others captive; see Judges 5:12. Captivity is here put for captives, and signifies all our spiritual enemies, who brought us into captivity before. He conquered those who had conquered us; such as sin, the devil, and death. Indeed, he triumphed over these *on the cross;* but the triumph was completed at his ascension, when he became Lord over all, and had the keys of death and hades put into his hands. *And he gave gifts unto men:* in the psalm it is, *He received gifts for men.* He received for them, that he might give to them, a large measure of gifts and graces; particularly, he enriched his disciples with the gift of the Holy Ghost. The apostle, thus speaking of the ascension of Christ, takes notice that he *descended first, v.* 9. As much as if he had said, "When David speaks of Christ's ascension, he intimates the knowledge he had of Christ's humiliation on earth; for, when it is said that he ascended, this implies that he first descended: for what is it but a proof or demonstration of his having done so?" *Into the lower parts of the earth;* this may refer either to his incarnation, according to that of David, Ps. 139:15, *My substance was not hidden from thee, when I was made in secret, and curiously wrought in the lowest parts of the earth;* or, to his burial, according to that of Ps. 63:9, *Those that seek my soul to destroy it shall go into the lower parts of the earth.* He calls his death (say some of the fathers) *his descent into the lower parts of the earth.* He descended to the earth in his incarnation. He descended into the earth in his burial. *As Jonas was three days and three nights in the whale's belly, so was the Son of man in the heart of the earth. He that descended is the same also that ascended up far above all heavens* (*v.* 10), far above the airy and starry (which are the visible) heavens, into the heaven of heavens; *that he might fill all things,* all the members of his church, with gifts and graces suitable to their several conditions and stations. Observe, Our Lord humbled himself first, and then he was exalted. He descended first, and then ascended. The apostle next tells us what were Christ's gifts at his ascension: *He gave some apostles,* etc. *v.* 11. Indeed he sent forth some of these before his ascension, Mt. 10:1–5. But one was then added, Acts 1:26. And all of them were more solemnly installed, and publicly confirmed, in their office, by his visibly pouring forth the Holy Ghost in an extraordinary manner and measure upon them. Note, The great gift that Christ gave to the church at his ascension was that of the ministry of peace and reconciliation. The gift of the ministry is the fruit of Christ's ascension. And ministers have their various gifts, which are all given them by the Lord Jesus. The officers which Christ gave to his church were of two sorts — *extraordinary* ones advanced to a higher office in the church: such were *apostles, prophets,* and *evangelists.* The apostles were chief. These Christ immediately called, furnished them with extraordinary gifts and the power of working miracles, and with infallibility in delivering his truth; and, they having been the witnesses of his miracles and doctrine, he sent them forth to spread the gospel and to plant and govern churches. The prophets seem to have been such as expounded the writings of the Old Testament, and foretold things to come. The evangelists were ordained persons (2 Tim. 1:6), whom the apostles took for their companions in travel (Gal. 2:1), and sent them out to settle and establish such churches as the apostles themselves had planted (Acts 19:22), and, not being fixed to any particular place, they were to continue till recalled, 2 Tim. 4:9. And then there are *ordinary* ministers, employed in a lower and narrower sphere; as *pastors* and *teachers.* Some take these two names to signify one office, implying the duties of ruling and teaching belonging to it. Others think they design two distinct offices, both ordinary, and of standing use in the church; and then pastors are such as are fixed at the head of particular churches, with design to guide, instruct, and feed them in the manner appointed by Christ; and they are frequently called bishops and elders: and the teachers were those whose work it was also to preach the gospel and to instruct the people by way of exhortation. We see here that it is Christ's prerogative to appoint what officers and offices he pleases in his church. And how rich is the church, that had at first such a variety of officers and has still such a variety of gifts! How kind is Christ to his church! How careful of it and of its edification! When he ascended, he procured the gift of the Holy Ghost; and the gifts of the Holy Ghost are various: some have greater, others have less measures; but all for the good of the body, which brings us to the third argument,

3. Which is taken from Christ's great end and design in giving gifts unto men. The gifts of Christ were intended for the good of his church, and in order to advance his kingdom and interest among men. All these being designed for one common end is a good reason why all Christians should agree in brotherly love, and not envy one another's gifts. All are *for the perfecting of the saints* (*v.* 12); that is, according to the import of the original, to bring into an orderly spiritual state and frame those who had been as it were dislocated and disjointed by sin, and then to strengthen, confirm, and advance them therein, that so each, in his proper place and function, might contribute to the good of the whole. — *For the work of the ministry, or for the work of dispensation;* that is, that they might dispense the doctrines of the gospel, and successfully discharge the several parts of their ministerial function. — *For the edifying of the body of Christ;* that is, to build up the church, which is Christ's mystical body, by an increase of their graces, and an addition of new members. All are designed to prepare us for heaven: *Till we all come,* etc., *v.* 13. The gifts and offices (some of them) which have been spoken of are to continue in the church till the saints be perfected, which will not be *till they all come in the unity of the faith* (till all true believers meet together, by means of the same precious faith) *and of the knowledge of the Son of God,* by which we are to understand, not a bare speculative knowledge, or the acknowledging of Christ to be the Son of God and the great Mediator, but such as is attended with appropriation and affection, with all due honour, trust, and obedience. — *Unto a perfect man,* to our full growth of gifts and graces, free from those childish infirmities that we are subject to in the present world. — *Unto the measure of the stature of the fulness of Christ,* so as to be Christians of a full maturity and ripeness in all the graces derived from Christ's fulness: or, according to the measure of that stature which is to make up the fulness of Christ, which is to complete his mystical body. Now we shall never come to the perfect man, till we come to the perfect world. There is a fulness in Christ, and a fulness to be derived from him; and a certain stature of that fulness, and a measure of that stature, are assigned in the counsel of God to every believer, and we never come to that measure till we come to heaven. God's children, as long as they are in this world, are growing. Dr Lightfoot understands the apostle as speaking here of Jews and Gentiles knit in the unity of the faith and of the knowledge of the Son of God, so making a perfect man, and the measure of the stature of the fulness of Christ. The apostle further shows, in the following verses, what was God's design in his sacred institutions, and what effect they ought to have upon us. As, (1.) *That we henceforth be no more children,* etc. (*v.* 14);

that is, that we may be no longer children in knowledge, weak in the faith, and inconstant in our judgments, easily yielding to every temptation, readily complying with every one's humour, and being at every one's back. Children are easily imposed upon. We must take care of this, and of being *tossed to and fro,* like ships without ballast, *and carried about,* like clouds in the air, with such doctrines as have no truth nor solidity in them, but nevertheless spread themselves far and wide, and are therefore compared to wind. *By the sleight of men;* this is a metaphor taken from gamesters, and signifies the mischievous subtlety of seducers: *and cunning craftiness,* by which is meant their skilfulness in finding ways to seduce and deceive; for it follows, *whereby they lie in wait to deceive,* as in an ambush, in order to circumvent the weak, and draw them from the truth. Note, Those must be very wicked and ungodly men who set themselves to seduce and deceive others into false doctrines and errors. The apostle describes them here as base men, using a great deal of devilish art and cunning, in order thereunto. The best method we can take to fortify ourselves against such is to study the sacred oracles, and to pray for the illumination and grace of the Spirit of Christ, that we may know the truth as it is in Jesus, and be established in it. (2.) That we should *speak the truth in love* (*v.* 15), or follow the truth in love, or be sincere in love to our fellow-christians. While we adhere to the doctrine of Christ, which is the truth, we should live in love one with another. Love is an excellent thing; but we must be careful to preserve truth together with it. Truth is an excellent thing; yet it is requisite that we speak it in love, and not in contention. These two should go together — truth and peace. (3.) That we should *grow up into Christ in all things.* Into Christ, so as to be more deeply rooted in him. In all things; in knowledge, love, faith, and all the parts of the new man. We should grow up towards maturity, which is opposed to being children. Those are improving Christians who grow up into Christ. The more we grow into an acquaintance with Christ, faith in him, love to him, dependence upon him, the more we shall flourish in every grace. He is the head; and we should thus grow, that we may thereby honour our head. The Christian's growth tends to the glory of Christ. (4.) We should be assisting and helpful one to another, as members of the same body, *v.* 16. Here the apostle makes a comparison between the natural body and Christ's mystical body, that body of which Christ is the head: and he observes that as there must be communion and mutual communications of the members of the body among themselves, in order to their growth and improvement, so there must be mutual love and unity, together with the proper fruits of these, among Christians, in order to their spiritual improvement and growth in grace. *From whom,* says he (that is, from Christ their head, who conveys influence and nourishment to every particular member), *the whole body of Christians, fitly joined together and compacted* (being orderly and firmly united among themselves, every one in his proper place and station), *by that which every joint supplies* (by the assistance which every one of the parts, thus united, gives to the whole, or by the Spirit, faith, love, sacraments, etc., which, like the veins and arteries in the body, serve to unite Christians to Christ their head, and to one another as fellow-members), *according to the effectual working in the measure of every part* (that is, say some, according to the power which the Holy Ghost exerts to make God's appointed means effectual for this great end, in such a measure as Christ judges to be sufficient and proper for every member, according to its respective place and office in the body; or, as others, according to the power of Christ, who, as head, influences and enlivens every member; or, according to the effectual working of every member, in communicating to others of what it has received, nourishment is conveyed to all in their proportions, and according to the state and exigence of every part) *makes increase of the body,* such an increase as is convenient for the body. Observe, Particular Christians receive their gifts and graces from Christ for the sake and benefit of the whole body. *Unto the edifying of itself in love.* We may understand this two ways: — Either that all the members of the church may attain a greater measure of love to Christ and to one another; or that they are moved to act in the manner mentioned from love to Christ and to one another. Observe, Mutual love among Christians is a great friend to spiritual growth: it is in love that the body edifies itself; whereas *a kingdom divided against itself cannot stand.*

Verses 17–32

The apostle having gone through his exhortation to mutual love, unity, and concord, in the foregoing verses, there follows in these an exhortation to Christian purity and holiness of heart and life, and that both more general (*v.* 17–24) and in several particular instances, *v.* 25–32. This is solemnly introduced: *"This I say therefore, and testify in the Lord;* that is, seeing the matter is as above described, seeing you are members of Christ's body and partakers of such gifts, this I urge upon your consciences, and bear witness to as your duty in the Lord's name, and by virtue of the authority I have derived from him." Consider,

I. The more general exhortation to purity and holiness of heart and life.

1. It begins thus, *"That you henceforth walk not as other Gentiles walk* — that for the time to come you do not live, and behave yourselves, as ignorant and unconverted heathens do, who are wholly guided by an understanding employed about vain things, their idols and their worldly possessions, things which are no way profitable to their souls, and which will deceive their expectations." Converted Gentiles must not live as unconverted Gentiles do. Though they live among them, they must not live like them. Here,

(1.) The apostle takes occasion to describe the wickedness of the Gentile world, out of which regenerate Christians were snatched as brands out of the burning. [1.] Their *understandings were darkened, v.* 18. They were void of all saving knowledge; yea, ignorant of many things concerning God which the light of nature might have taught them. They sat in darkness, and they loved it rather than light: and by their ignorance they were *alienated from the life of God.* They were estranged from, and had a dislike and aversion to, a life of holiness, which is not only that way of life which God requires and approves, and by which we live to him, but which resembles God himself, in his purity, righteousness, truth, and goodness. Their wilful ignorance was the cause of their estrangement from this life of God, which begins in light and knowledge. Gross and affected ignorance is destructive to religion and godliness. And what was the cause of their being thus ignorant? It was *because of the blindness* or the hardness *of their heart.* It was not because God did not make himself known to them by his works, but because they would not admit the instructive rays of the divine light. They were ignorant because they would be so. Their ignorance proceeded from their obstinacy and the hardness of their hearts, their resisting the light and rejecting all the means of illumination and knowledge. [2.] Their consciences were debauched and seared: *Who being past feeling, v.* 19. They had no sense of their sin, nor of the misery and danger of their case by means of it; whereupon they *gave themselves over unto lasciviousness.* They indulged themselves in their filthy lusts; and, yielding themselves up to the dominion of these, they became the slaves and drudges of sin and the devil, *working all uncleanness with greediness.* They made it their common practice to commit all sorts of uncleanness, and even the most unnatural and monstrous sins, and that with insatiable desires. Observe, When men's consciences are once seared, there are no bounds to their sins. When they set their hearts upon the gratification of their lusts, what can be expected but the most abominable sensuality and lewdness, and that their horrid enormities will abound? This was the character of the Gentiles; but,

(2.) These Christians must distinguish themselves from such Gentiles: *You have not so learned Christ, v.* 20. It may be read, *But you not so; you have learned Christ.* Those who have learned Christ are saved from the darkness and defilement which others lie under; and, as they know more, they are obliged to live in a better manner than others. It is a good argument against sin that we have not so learned Christ. Learn Christ! Is Christ a book, a lesson, a way, a trade? The meaning is, "You have not so learned Christianity — the doctrines of Christ and the rules of life prescribed by him. Not so as to do as others do. *If so be,* or since, *that you have heard him* (*v.* 21), have heard his doctrine preached by us, *and have been taught by him,* inwardly and effectually, by his Spirit." Christ is the lesson; we must learn Christ: and Christ is the teacher; we are taught by him. *As the truth is in Jesus.* This may be understood two ways: either, "You have been taught the real truth, as held forth by Christ himself, both in his doctrine and in his life." Or thus, "The truth has made such an impression on your hearts, in your measure, as it did upon the heart of Jesus." The truth of Christ then appears in its beauty and power, when it appears as in Jesus.

2. Another branch of the general exhortation follows in those words, *That you put off, concerning the former conversation, the old man,* etc., *v.* 22–24. "This is a great part of the doctrine which has been taught you, and which you have learned." Here the apostle expresses himself in metaphors taken from garments. The principles, habits, and dispositions of the soul must be changed, before there can be a saving change of the life. There must be sanctification, which consists of these two things: — (1.) The old man must be put off. The corrupt nature is called a man, because, like the human body, it consists of divers parts, mutually supporting and strengthening one another. It is the old man, as old Adam, from whom we derive it. It is bred in the bone, and we brought it into the world with us. It is subtle as the old man; but in all God's saints decaying and withering as an old man, and ready to pass away. It is said to be corrupt; for sin in the soul is the corruption of its faculties: and, where it is not mortified, it grows daily worse and worse, and so tends to destruction. *According to the deceitful lusts.* Sinful inclinations and desires are deceitful lusts: they promise men happiness, but render them more miserable, and if not subdued and mortified betray them into destruction. These therefore must be put off as an old garment that we should be ashamed to be seen in: they must be subdued and mortified. These lusts prevailed against them in their *former conversation,* that is, during their state of unregeneracy and heathenism. (2.) The new man must be put on. It is not enough to shake off corrupt principles, but we must be actuated by gracious ones. We must embrace them, espouse them, and get them written on our hearts: it is not enough to cease to do evil, but we must learn to do well. *"Be renewed in the spirit of your mind* (*v.* 23); that is, use the proper and prescribed means in order to have the mind, which is a spirit, renewed more and more." *And that you put on the new man, v.* 24. By the new man is meant the new nature, the new creature, which is actuated by a new principle, even regenerating grace, enabling a man to lead a new life, that life of righteousness and holiness which Christianity requires. This new man *is created,* or produced out of confusion and emptiness, by God's almighty power, whose workmanship it is, truly excellent and beautiful. *After God,* in imitation of him, and in conformity to that grand exemplar and pattern. The loss of God's image upon the soul was both the sinfulness and misery of man's fallen state; and that resemblance which it bears to God is the beauty, the glory, and the happiness, of the new creature. *In righteousness* towards men, including all the duties of the second table; *and in holiness* towards God, signifying a sincere obedience to the commands of the first table; *true holiness* in opposition to the outward and ceremonial holiness of the Jews. We are said to put on this new man when, in the use of all God's appointed means, we are endeavouring after this divine nature, this new creature. This is the more general exhortation to purity and holiness of heart and life.

II. The apostle proceeds to some things more particular. Because generals are not so apt to affect, we are told what are those particular limbs of the old man that must be mortified, those filthy rags of the old nature that must be put off, and what are the peculiar ornaments of the new man wherewith we should adorn our Christian profession. 1. Take heed of lying, and be ever careful to speak the truth (*v.* 25): *"Wherefore,* since you have been so well instructed in your duty, and are under such obligations to discharge it, let it appear, in your future behaviour and conduct, that there is a great and real change wrought in you, particularly by *putting away lying."* Of this sin the heathen were very guilty, affirming that a profitable lie was better than a hurtful truth; and therefore the apostle exhorts them to cease from lying, from every thing that is contrary to truth. This is a part of the old man that must be put off; and that branch of the new man that must be put on in opposition to it is *speaking the truth* in all our converse with others. It is the character of God's people that they are *children who will not lie,* who dare not lie, who hate and abhor lying. All who have grace make conscience of speaking the truth, and would not tell a deliberate lie for the greatest gain and benefit to themselves. The reason here given for veracity is, *We are members one of another.* Truth is a debt we owe to one another; and, if we love one another, we shall not deceive nor lie one to another. We belong to the same society or body, which falsehood or lying tends to dissolve; and therefore we should avoid it, and speak truth. Observe, Lying is a very great sin, a peculiar violation of the obligations which Christians are under, and very injurious and hurtful to Christian society. 2. "Take heed of anger and ungoverned passions. *Be you angry, and sin not,*" *v.* 26. This is borrowed from the Septuagint translation of Ps. 4:4, where we render it, *Stand in awe, and sin not.* Here is an easy concession; for as such we should consider it, rather than as a command. *Be you angry.* This we are apt enough to be, God knows: but we find it difficult enough to observe the restriction, *and sin not.* "If you have a just occasion to be angry at any time, see that it be without sin; and therefore take heed of excess in your anger." If we would be angry and not sin (says one), we must be angry at nothing but sin; and we should be more jealous for the glory of God than for any interest or reputation of our own. One great and common sin in anger is to suffer it to burn into wrath, and then to let it rest; and therefore we are here cautioned against that. "If you have been provoked and have had your spirits greatly discomposed, and if you have bitterly resented any affront that has been offered, before night calm and quiet your spirits, be reconciled to the offender, and let all be well again: *Let not the sun go down upon your wrath.* If it burn into wrath and bitterness of spirit, O see to it that you suppress it speedily." Observe, Though anger in itself is not sinful, yet there is the upmost danger of its becoming so if it be not carefully watched and speedily suppressed. And therefore, though anger may come into the bosom of a wise man, *it rests* only *in the bosom of fools. Neither give place to the devil, v.* 27. Those who persevere in sinful anger and in wrath let the devil into their hearts, and suffer him to gain upon them, till he bring them to malice, mischievous machinations, etc. "*Neither give place to the* calumniator, or the false accuser" (so some read the words); that is, "let your ears be deaf to whisperers, talebearers, and slanderers." 3. We are here warned against the sin of stealing, the breach of the eighth commandment, and advised to honest industry and to beneficence: *Let his that stole steal no more, v.* 28. It is a caution against all manner of wrong-doing, by force or fraud. "Let those of you who, in the time of your gentilism, have been guilty of this enormity, be no longer guilty of it." But we must not only take heed of the sin, but conscientiously abound in the opposite duty: not only not steal, *but rather let him labour, working with his hands the thing that is good.* Idleness makes thieves. So Chrysostom, *To gar kleptein argias estin — Stealing is the effect of idleness.* Those who will not work, and who are ashamed to beg, expose themselves greatly to temptations to thievery. Men should therefore be diligent and industrious, not in any unlawful way, but in some honest calling: *Working the thing which is good.* Industry, in some honest way, will keep people out of temptation of doing wrong. But there is another reason why men ought to be industrious, namely, that they may be capable of doing some good, as well as that they may be preserved from temptation: *That he may have to give to him that needeth.* They must labour not only that they may live themselves, and live honestly, but they may distribute for supplying the wants of others. Observe, Even those who get their living by their labour should be charitable out of their little to those who are disabled for labour. So necessary and incumbent a duty is it to be charitable to the poor that even labourers and servants, and those who have but little for themselves, must cast their mite into the treasury. God must have his dues and the poor are his receivers. Observe further, Those alms that are likely to be acceptable to God must not be the produce of unrighteousness and robbery, but of honesty and industry. *God hates robbery for burnt-offerings.* 4. We are here warned against corrupt communication; and directed to that which is useful and edifying, *v.* 29. Filthy and unclean words and discourse are poisonous and infectious, as putrid rotten meat: they proceed from and prove a great deal of corruption in the heart of the speaker, and tend to corrupt the minds and manners of others who hear them; and therefore Christians should beware of all such discourse. It may be taken in general for all that which provokes the lusts and passions of others. We must not only put off corrupt communications, but *put on that which is good to the use of edifying.* The great use of speech is to edify those with whom we converse. Christians should endeavour to promote a useful conversation: *that it may minister grace unto the hearers;* that it may be good for, and acceptable to, the hearers, in the way of information, counsel, pertinent reproof, or the like. Observe, It is the great duty of Christians to take care that they offend not with their lips, and that they improve discourse and converse, as much as may be, for the good of others. 5. Here is another caution against wrath and anger, with further advice to mutual love and kindly dispositions towards each other, *v.* 31, 32. By *bitterness, wrath,* and *anger,* are meant violent inward resentment and displeasure against others: and, by *clamour,* big words, loud threatenings, and other intemperate speeches, by which bitterness, wrath, and anger, vent themselves. Christians should not entertain these vile passions in their hearts not be clamorous with their tongues. *Evil speaking* signifies all railing, reviling, and reproachful speeches, against such as we are angry with. And by *malice* we are to understand that rooted anger which prompts men to design and to do mischief to others. The contrary to all this follows: *Be you kind one to another.* This implies the principle of love in the heart, and the outward expressions of it, in an affable, humble, courteous behaviour. It becomes the disciples of Jesus to be kind one to another, as those who have learned, and would teach, the art of obliging. *Tender-hearted;* that is, merciful, and having tender sense of the distresses and sufferings of others, so as to be quickly moved to compassion and pity. *Forgiving one another.* Occasions of difference will happen among Christ's disciples; and therefore they must be placable, and ready to forgive, therein resembling God himself, who *for Christ's sake hath forgiven them,* and that more than they can forgive one another. Note, With God there is forgiveness; and he forgives sin for the sake of Jesus Christ, and on account of that atonement which he has made to divine justice. Note again, Those who are forgiven of God should be of a forgiving spirit, and should forgive even as God forgives, sincerely and heartily, readily and cheerfully, universally and for ever, upon the sinner's sincere repentance, as remembering that they pray, *Forgive us our trespasses, as we forgive those who trespass against us.* Now we may observe concerning all these particulars that the apostle has insisted on that they belong to the second table, whence Christians should learn the strict obligations they are under to the duties of the second table, and that he who does not conscientiously discharge them can never fear nor love God in truth and in sincerity, whatever he may pretend to.

In the midst of these exhortations and cautions the apostle interposes that general one, *And grieve not the Holy Spirit of God, v.* 30. By looking to what precedes, and to what follows, we may see what it is that grieves the Spirit of God. In the previous verses it is intimated that all lewdness and filthiness, lying, and corrupt communications that stir up filthy appetites and lusts, grieve the Spirit of God. In what follows it is intimated that those corrupt passions of bitterness, and wrath, and anger, and clamour, and evil speaking, and malice, grieve this good Spirit. By this we are not to understand that this blessed Being could properly be grieved or vexed as we are; but the design of the exhortation is that we act not towards him in such a manner as is wont to be grievous and disquieting to our fellow-creatures: we must not do that which is contrary to his holy nature and his will; we must not refuse to hearken to his counsels, nor rebel against his government, which things would provoke him to act towards us as men are wont to do towards those with whom they are displeased and grieved, withdrawing themselves and their wonted kindness from such, and abandoning them to their enemies. O provoke not the blessed Spirit of God to withdraw his presence and his gracious influences from you! It is a good reason why we should not grieve him that *by him we are sealed unto the day of redemption.* There is to be a day of redemption; the body is to be redeemed from the power of the grave at the resurrection-day, and then God's people will be delivered from all the effects of sin, as well as from all sin and misery, which they are not till rescued out of the grave: and then their full and complete happiness commences. All true believers are sealed to that day. God has distinguished them from others, having set his mark upon them; and he gives them the earnest and assurance of a joyful and glorious resurrection; and the Spirit of God is the seal. Wherever that blessed Spirit is as a sanctifier, he is the earnest of all the joys and glories of the redemption-day; and we should be undone should God take away his Holy Spirit from us.

CHAPTER 5

We had several important exhortations in the close of the foregoing chapter, and they are continued in this: particularly, I. We have here an exhortation to mutual love and charity (*v.* 1, 2). II. Against all manner of uncleanness, with proper arguments and remedies proposed against such sins: and some further cautions are added, and other duties recommended (*v.* 3–20). III. The apostle directs to the conscientious discharge of relative duties, from *v.* 21, throughout this, and in the beginning of the next chapter.

Verses 1–2

Here we have the exhortation to mutual love, or to Christian charity. The apostle had been insisting on this in the former chapter, and particularly in the last verses of it, to which the particle *therefore* refers, and connects what he had said there with what is contained in these verses, thus: "Because God, for Christ's sake, has forgiven you, therefore be you followers of God, or *imitators* of him;" for so the word signifies. Pious persons should imitate the God whom they worship, as far as he has revealed himself as imitable by them. They must conform themselves to his example, and have his image renewed upon them. This puts a great honour upon practical religion, that it is the imitating of God. We must be holy as God is holy, merciful as he is merciful, perfect as he is perfect. But there is no one attribute of God more recommended to our imitation than that of his goodness. Be you imitators of God, or resemble him, in every grace, and especially in his love, and in his pardoning goodness. God *is love; and those that dwell in love dwell in God and God in them.* Thus he has proclaimed his name, *Gracious and merciful, and abundant in goodness. As dear children,* as children (who are wont to be greatly beloved by their parents) usually resemble them in the lineaments and features of their faces, and in the dispositions and qualities of their minds; or as becomes the children of God, who are beloved and cherished by their heavenly Father. Children are obliged to imitate their parents in what is good, especially when dearly beloved by them. The character that we bear of God's children obliges us to resemble him, especially in his love and goodness, in his mercy and readiness to forgive. And those only are God's dear children who imitate him in these. It follows, *And walk in love, v.* 2. This godlike grace should conduct and influence our whole conversation, which is meant by walking in it. It should be the principle from which we act; it should direct the ends at which we aim. We should be more careful to give proof of the sincerity of our love one to another. *As Christ also hath loved us.* Here the apostle directs us to the example of Christ, whom Christians are obliged to imitate, and in whom we have an instance of the most free and generous love that ever was, that great love wherewith he hath loved us. We are all joint sharers in that love, and partakers of the comfort of it, and therefore should love one another, Christ having loved us all and given such proof of his love to us; for *he hath given himself for us.* The apostle designedly enlarges on the subject; for what can yield us more delightful matter for contemplation than this? Christ gave himself to die for us; and the death of Christ was the great sacrifice of atonement: *An offering and a sacrifice to God;* or an offering, even a sacrifice — a propitiatory sacrifice, to expiate our guilt, which had been prefigured in the legal oblations and sacrifices; and this *for a sweet-smelling savour.* Some observe that the sin-offerings were never said to be of a sweet-smelling savour; but this is said of *the Lamb of God, which taketh away the sin of the world.* As he offered himself with a design to be accepted of God, so God did accept, was pleased with, and appeased by, that sacrifice. Note, As the sacrifice of Christ was efficacious with God, so his example should be prevailing with us, and we should carefully copy after it.

Verses 3–20

These verses contain a caution against all manner of uncleanness, with proper remedies and arguments proposed: some further cautions are added, and other duties recommended. Filthy lusts must be suppressed, in order to the supporting of holy love. *Walk in love,* and *shun fornication and all uncleanness. Fornication* is folly committed between unmarried persons. *All uncleanness* includes all other sorts of filthy lusts, which were too common among the Gentiles. Or *covetousness,* which being thus connected, and mentioned as a thing which should not be *once named,* some understand it, in the chaste style of the scripture, of unnatural lust; while others take it in the more common sense, for an immoderate desire of gain or an insatiable love of riches, which is spiritual adultery; for by this the soul, which was espoused to God, goes astray from him, and embraces the bosom of a stranger, and therefore carnal worldlings are called adulterers: *You adulterers and adulteresses, know you not that the friendship of the world is enmity with God?* Now these sins must be dreaded and detested in the highest degree: *Let it not be once named among you,* never in a way of approbation nor without abhorrence, *as becometh saints,* holy persons, who are separated from the world, and dedicated unto God. The apostle not only cautions against the gross acts of sin, but against what some may be apt to make light of, and think to be excusable. *Neither filthiness* (*v.* 4), by which may be understood all wanton and unseemly gestures and behaviour; *nor foolish talking,* obscene and lewd discourse, or, more generally, such vain discourse as betrays much folly and indiscretion, and is far from edifying the hearers; *nor jesting.* The Greek word *eutrapelia* is the same which Aristotle, in his Ethics, makes a virtue: pleasantness of conversation. And there is no doubt an innocent and inoffensive jesting, which we cannot suppose the apostle here forbids. Some understand him of such scurrilous and abusive reflections as tend to expose others and to make them appear ridiculous. This is bad enough: but the context seems to restrain it to such pleasantry of discourse as is filthy and obscene, which he may also design by that *corrupt,* or putrid and rotten, communication that he speaks of, *ch.* 4:29. Of these things he says, *They are not convenient.* Indeed there is more than inconvenience, even a great deal of mischief, in them. They are so far from being profitable that they pollute and poison the hearers. But the meaning is, Those things do not become Christians, and are very unsuitable to their profession and character. Christians are allowed to be cheerful and pleasant; but they must be merry and wise. The apostle adds, *But rather giving of thanks:* so far let the Christian's way of mirth be from that of obscene and profane wit, that he may delight his mind, and make himself cheerful, by a grateful remembrance of God's goodness and mercy to him, and by blessing and praising him on account of these. Note, 1. We should take all occasions to render thanksgivings and praises to God for his kindness and favours to us. 2. A reflection on the grace and goodness of God to us, with a design to excite our thankfulness to him, is proper to refresh and delight the Christian's mind, and to make him cheerful. Dr. Hammond thinks that ***eucharistia*** may signify gracious, pious, religious discourse in general, by way of opposition to what the apostle condemns. Our cheerfulness, instead of breaking out into what is vain and sinful, and a profanation of God's name, should express itself as becomes Christians, and in what may tend to his glory. If men abounded more in good and pious expressions, they would not be so apt to utter ill and unbecoming words; for shall *blessing* and *cursing,* lewdness and thanksgivings, *proceed out of the same mouth?*

I. To fortify us against the sins of uncleanness, etc., the apostle urges several arguments, and prescribes several remedies, in what follows,

1. He urges several arguments, As, (1.) Consider that these are sins which shut persons out of heaven: *For this you know,* etc., *v.* 5. They knew it, being informed of it by the Christian religion. By *a covetous man* some understand a lewd lascivious libertine, who indulges himself in those vile lusts which were accounted the certain marks of a heathen and an idolater. Others understand it in the common acceptation of the word; and such a man is an idolater because there is spiritual idolatry in the love of this world. As the epicure makes a god of his belly, so the covetous man makes a god of his money, sets those affectations upon it, and places that hope, confidence, and delight, in worldly good, which should be reserved for God only. He serves mammon instead of God. Of these persons it is said that they *have no inheritance in the kingdom of Christ and of God;* that is, the kingdom of Christ, who is God, or the kingdom which is God's by nature, and Christ's as he is Mediator, the kingdom which Christ has purchased and which God bestows. Heaven is here described as a kingdom (as frequently elsewhere) with respect to its eminency and glory, its fulness and sufficiency, etc. In this kingdom the saints and servants of God have an inheritance; for it is the *inheritance of the saints in light.* But those who are impenitent, and allow themselves either in the lusts of the flesh or the love of the world, are not Christians indeed, and so belong not to the kingdom of grace, nor shall they ever come to the kingdom of glory. Let us then be excited to be on our guard against those sins which would exclude and shut us out of heaven. (2.) These sins bring the wrath of God upon those who are guilty of them: *"Let no man deceive you with vain words,* etc., *v.* 6. Let none flatter you, as though such things were tolerable and to be allowed of in Christians, or as though they were not very provoking and offensive unto God, or as though you might indulge yourselves in them and yet escape with impunity. These are *vain words."* Observe, Those who flatter themselves and others with hopes of impunity in sin do but put a cheat upon themselves and others. Thus Satan deceived our first parents with vain words when he said to them, *You shall not surely die.* They are *vain words* indeed; for those who trust to them will find themselves wretchedly imposed upon, *for because of these things cometh the wrath of God upon the children of disobedience.* By *children of disobedience* may be meant the Gentiles, who disbelieved, and refused to comply with, and to submit themselves to, the gospel: or, more generally, all obstinate sinners, who will not be reclaimed, but are given over to disobedience. Disobedience is the very malignity of sin. And it is by a usual Hebraism that such sinners are called children of disobedience; and such indeed they are from their childhood, going astray as soon as they are born. *The wrath of God comes upon* such because of their sins; sometimes in this world, but more especially in the next. And dare we make light of that which will lay us under the wrath of God? O no. *Be not you therefore partakers with them, v.* 7. "Do not partake with them in their sins, that you may not share in their punishment." We partake with other men in their sins, not only when we live in the same sinful manner that they do, and consent and comply with their temptations and solicitations to sin, but when we encourage them in their sins, prompt them to sin, and do not prevent and hinder them, as far as it may be in our power to do so. (3.) Consider what obligations Christians are under to live at another rate than such sinners do: *For you were sometimes darkness, but now,* etc., *v.* 8. The meaning is, "Such courses are very unsuitable to your present condition; for, whereas in your Gentile and your unregenerate state you were darkness, you have now undergone a great change." The apostle calls their former condition *darkness* in the abstract, to express the great darkness they were in. They lived wicked and profane lives, being destitute of the light of instruction without and of the illumination and grace of the blessed Spirit within. Note, A state of sin is a state of darkness. Sinners, like men in the dark, are going they know not whither, and doing they know not what. But the grace of God had produced a mighty change in their souls: *Now are you light in the Lord,* savingly enlightened by the word and the Spirit of God. *Now,* upon your believing in Christ, and your receiving the gospel. *Walk as children of light.* Children of light, according to the Hebrew dialect, are those who are in a state of light, endued with knowledge and holiness. "Now, being such, let your conversation be suitable to your condition and privileges, and accordingly live up to the obligation you are under by that knowledge and those advantages you enjoy — *Proving what is acceptable unto the Lord* (*v.* 10), examining and searching diligently what God has revealed to be his will, and making it appear that you approve it by conforming yourselves to it." Observe, We must not only dread and avoid that which is displeasing to God, but enquire and consider what will be acceptable to him, searching the scriptures with this view, thus keeping at the greatest distance from these sins.

2. The apostle prescribes some remedies against them. As, (1.) If we would not be entangled by the lusts of the flesh, we must bring forth *the fruits of the Spirit, v.* 9. This is expected from the children of light, that, being illuminated, they be also sanctified by the Spirit, and thereupon bring forth his fruit, which *is in all goodness,* an inclination to do good and to show mercy, *and righteousness,* which signifies justice in our dealings. Thus they are taken more strictly; but, more generally, all religion is goodness and righteousness. And in and with these must be *truth,* or sincerity and uprightness of heart. (2.) We must have no fellowship with sin nor sinners, *v.* 11. Sinful works are works of darkness: they come from the darkness of ignorance, they seek the darkness of concealment, and they lead to the darkness of hell. These works of darkness are *unfruitful works;* there is nothing got by them in the long run, whatever profit is pretended by sin, it will by no means balance the loss; for it issues in the utter ruin and destruction of the impenitent sinner. We must therefore *have no fellowship* with these unfruitful works; as we must not practise them ourselves, so we must not countenance others in the practice of them. There are many ways of our being accessary to the sins of others, by commendation, counsel, consent, or concealment. And, if we share with others in their sin, we must expect to share with them in their plagues. Nay, if we thus have fellowship with them, we shall be in the utmost danger of acting as they do ere long. But, rather than have fellowship with them, we must *reprove them,* implying that if we do not reprove the sins of others we have fellowship with them. We must prudently and in our places witness against the sins of others, and endeavour to convince them of their sinfulness, when we can do it seasonably and pertinently, in our words; but especially by the holiness of our lives, and a religious conversation. Reprove their sins by abounding in the contrary duties. One reason given is, *For it is a shame even to speak of those things,* etc., *v.* 12. They are so filthy and abominable that it is a shame to mention them, except in a way of reproof, much more must it be a shame to have any fellowship with them. *The things which are done of them in secret.* The apostle seems to speak here of the Gentile idolaters, and of their horrid mysteries, which abounded with detestable wickedness, and which none were permitted to divulge upon pain of death. Observe, A good man is ashamed to speak that which many wicked people are not ashamed to act; but, as far as their wickedness appears, it should be reproved by good men. There follows another reason for such reproof: *But all things that are reproved are made manifest by the light, v.* 13. The meaning of this passage may be this: "All those unfruitful works of darkness which you are called upon to reprove are laid open, and made to appear in their proper colours to the sinners themselves, by the light of doctrine or of God's word in your mouths, as faithful reprovers, or by that instructive light which is diffused by the holiness of your lives and by your exemplary walk." Observe, The light of God's word, and the exemplification of it in a Christian conversation, are proper means to convince sinners of their sin and wickedness. It follows, *For whatsoever doth make manifest is light;* that is, it is the light that discovers what was concealed before in darkness; and accordingly it becomes those who are *children of light,* who are *light in the Lord,* to discover to others their sins, and to endeavour to convince them of the evil and danger of them, thus shining as lights in the world. The apostle further urges this duty from the example of God or Christ: *Wherefore he saith,* etc. (*v.* 14); as if he had said, "In doing this, you will copy after the great God, who has set himself to awaken sinners from their sleep, and to raise them from the death of sin, that they might receive light from Christ." *He saith.* The Lord is constantly saying in his word what is more particularly expressed in Isa. 60:1. Or, Christ, by his ministers, who preach the everlasting gospel, is continually calling upon sinners to this effect: *Awake, thou that sleepest, and arise from the dead.* The same thing in the main is designed by these different expressions; and they serve to remind us of the great stupidity and the wretched security of sinners, how insensible they are of their danger, and how unapt they naturally are to spiritual motions, sensations, and actions. When God calls upon them to awake, and to arise, his meaning is that they would break off their sins by repentance, and enter on a course of holy obedience, and he encourages them to essay and do their utmost that way, by that gracious promise, *And Christ shall give thee light; or Christ shall enlighten thee,* or *shall shine upon thee.* "He shall bring thee into a state of knowledge, holiness, and comfort, assisting thee with his grace, and refreshing thy mind with joy and peace here and rewarding thee with eternal glory at length." Observe, When we are endeavouring to convince sinners, and to reform them from their sins, we are imitating God and Christ in that which is their great design throughout the gospel. Some indeed understand this as a call to sinners and to saints: to sinners to repent and turn; to saints to stir up themselves to their duty. The former must arise from their spiritual death; and the latter must awake from their spiritual deadness. (3.) Another remedy against sin is circumspection, care, or caution (*v.* 15): *See then,* etc. This may be understood either with respect to what immediately precedes, "If you are to reprove others for their sins, and would be faithful to your duty in this particular, you must look well to yourselves, and to your own behaviour and conduct" (and, indeed, those only are fit to reprove others who walk with due circumspection and care themselves): or else we have here another remedy or rather preservative from the before-mentioned sins; and this I take to be the design of the apostle, being impossible to maintain purity and holiness of heart and life without great circumspection and care. *Walk circumspectly,* or, as the word signifies, accurately, exactly, in the right way, in order to which we must be frequently consulting our rule, and the

directions we have in the sacred oracles. *Not as fools,* who walk at all adventures, and who have no understanding of their duty, nor of the worth of their souls, and through neglect, supineness, and want of care, fall into sin, and destroy themselves; *but as wise,* as persons taught of God and endued with wisdom from above. Circumspect walking is the effect of true wisdom, but the contrary is the effect of folly. It follows, *redeeming the time* (*v.* 16), literally, *buying the opportunity.* It is a metaphor taken from merchants and traders who diligently observe and improve the seasons for merchandise and trade. It is a great part of Christian wisdom to redeem the time. Good Christians must be good husbands of their time, and take care to improve it to the best of purposes, by watching against temptations, by doing good while it is in the power of their hands, and by filling it up with proper employment — one special preservative from sin. They should make the best use they can of the present seasons of grace. Our time is a talent given us by God for some good end, and it is misspent and lost when it is not employed according to his design. If we have lost our time heretofore, we must endeavour to redeem it by doubling our diligence in doing our duty for the future. The reason given is *because the days are evil,* either by reason of the wickedness of those who dwell in them, or rather "as they are troublesome and dangerous times to you who live in them." Those were times of persecution wherein the apostle wrote this: the Christians were in jeopardy every hour. When the days are evil we have one superadded argument to redeem time, especially because we know not how soon they may be worse. People are very apt to complain of bad times; it were well if that would stir them up to redeem time. *"Wherefore,"* says the apostle (*v.* 17), "because of the badness of the times, *be you not unwise,* ignorant of your duty and negligent about your souls, *but understanding what the will of the Lord is.* Study, consider, and further acquaint yourselves with the will of God, as determining your duty." Observe, Ignorance of our duty, and neglect of our souls, are evidences of the greatest folly; while an acquaintance with the will of God, and a care to comply with it, bespeak the best and truest wisdom.

II. In the three following verses the apostle warns against some other particular sins, and urges some other duties. 1. He warns against the sin of drunkenness: *And be not drunk with wine, v.* 18. This was a sin very frequent among the heathens; and particularly on occasion of the festivals of their gods, and more especially in their Bacchanalia: then they were wont to inflame themselves with wine, and all manner of inordinate lusts were consequent upon it: and therefore the apostle adds, *wherein,* or in which drunkenness, *is excess.* The word *asōtia* may signify *luxury* or *dissoluteness;* and it is certain that drunkenness is no friend to chastity and purity of life, but it virtually contains all manner of extravagance, and transports men into gross sensuality and vile enormities. Note, Drunkenness is a sin that seldom goes alone, but often involves men in other instances of guilt: it is a sin very provoking to God, and a great hindrance to the spiritual life. The apostle may mean all such intemperance and disorder as are opposite to the sober and prudent demeanor he intends in his advice, to redeem the time. 2. Instead of being filled with wine, he exhorts them to *be filled with the Spirit.* Those who are full of drink are not likely to be full of the Spirit; and therefore this duty is opposed to the former sin. The meaning of the exhortation is that men should labour for a plentiful measure of the graces of the Spirit, that would fill their souls with great joy, strength, and courage, which things sensual men expect their wine should inspire them with. We cannot be guilty of any excess in our endeavours after these: nay, we ought not to be satisfied with a little of the Spirit, but to be aspiring after measures, so as to be filled with the Spirit. Now by this means we shall come to *understand what the will of the Lord is;* for the Spirit of God is given as a Spirit of wisdom and of understanding. And because those who are filled with the Spirit will be carried out in acts of devotion, and all the proper expressions of it, therefore the apostle exhorts, 3. To sing unto the Lord, *v.* 19. Drunkards are wont to sing obscene and profane songs. The heathens, in their Bacchanalia, used to sing hymns to Bacchus, whom they called the god of wine. Thus they expressed their joy; but the joy of Christians should express itself in songs of praise to their God. In these they should *speak to themselves* in their assemblies and meetings together, for mutual edification. By *psalms* may be meant David's psalms, or such composures as were fitly sung with musical instruments. By *hymns* may be meant such others as were confined to matter of praise, as those of Zacharias, Simeon, etc. *Spiritual songs* may contain a greater variety of matter, doctrinal, prophetical, historical, etc. Observe here, (1.) The singing of psalms and hymns is a gospel ordinance: it is an ordinance of God, and appointed for his glory. (2.) Though Christianity is an enemy to profane mirth, yet it encourages joy and gladness, and the proper expressions of these in the professors of it. God's people have reason to rejoice, and to sing for joy. They are to *sing and to make melody in their hearts;* not only with their voices, but with inward affection, and then their doing this will be as delightful and acceptable to God as music is to us: and it must be with a design to please him, and to promote his glory, that we do this; and then it will be done to the Lord. 4. Thanksgiving is another duty that the apostle exhorts to, *v.* 20. We are appointed to sing psalms, etc., for the expression of our thankfulness to God; but, though we are not always singing, we should never want a disposition for this duty, as we never want matter for it. We must continue it throughout the whole course of our lives; and we should give thanks *for all things;* not only for spiritual blessings enjoyed, and eternal ones expected (for what of the former we have in hand, and for what of the other we have in hope), but for temporal mercies too; not only for our comforts, but also for our sanctified afflictions; not only for what immediately concerns ourselves, but for the instances of God's kindness and favour to others also. It is our duty in *every thing to give thanks unto God and the Father,* to God as the Father of our Lord Jesus Christ and our Father in him, in whose name we are to offer up all our prayers, and praises, and spiritual services, that they may be acceptable to God.

Verses 21–33

Here the apostle begins his exhortation to the discharge of relative duties. As a general foundation for these duties, he lays down that rule *v.* 21. There is a mutual submission that Christians owe one to another, condescending to bear one another's burdens: not advancing themselves above others, nor domineering over one another and giving laws to one another. Paul was an example of this truly Christian temper, for he *became all things to all men.* We must be of a yielding and of a submissive spirit, and ready to all the duties of the respective places and stations that God has allotted to us in the world. *In the fear of God,* that is, so far as is consistent with the fear of God, for his sake, and out of conscience towards him, and that hereby we may give proof that we truly fear him. Where there is this mutual condescension and submission, the duties of all relations will be the better performed. From *v.* 22 to the end he speaks of the duties of husbands and wives; and he speaks of these in a Christian manner, setting the church as an example of the wife's subjection, and Christ as an example of love in husbands.

I. The duty prescribed to wives is submission to their husbands in the Lord (*v.* 22), which submission includes the honouring and obeying of them, and that from a principle of love to them. They must do this in compliance with God's authority, who has commanded it, which is doing it *as unto the Lord;* or it may be understood by way of similitude and likeness, so that the sense may be, "as, being devoted to God, you submit yourselves unto him." From the former sense we may learn that by a conscientious discharge of the duties we owe to our fellow-creatures we obey and please God himself; and, from the latter, that God not only requires and insists on those duties which immediately respect himself, but such as respect our neighbours too. The apostle assigns the reason of this submission from wives: *For the husband is the head of the wife, v.* 23. The metaphor is taken from the head in the natural body, which, being the seat of reason, of wisdom, and of knowledge, and the fountain of sense and motion, is more excellent than the rest of the body. God has given the man the pre-eminence and a right to direct and govern by creation, and in that original law of the relation, *Thy desire shall be to thy husband, and he shall rule over thee.* Whatever there is of uneasiness in this, it is an effect of sin coming into the world. Generally, too, the man has (what he ought to have) a superiority in wisdom and knowledge. He is therefore the head, *even as Christ is the head of the church.* There is a resemblance of Christ's authority over the church in that superiority and headship which God has appointed to the husband. The apostle adds, *and he is the Saviour of the body.* Christ's authority is exercised over the church for the saving of her from evil, and the supplying of her with every thing good for her. In like manner should the husband be employed for the protection and comfort of his spouse; and therefore she should the more cheerfully submit herself unto him. So it follows, *Therefore as the church is subject unto Christ* (*v.* 24), with cheerfulness, with fidelity, with humility, *so let the wives be to their own husbands in every thing* — in every thing to which their authority justly extends itself, in every thing lawful and consistent with duty to God.

II. The duty of husbands (on the other hand), is to love their wives (*v.* 25); for without this they would abuse their superiority and headship, and, wherever this prevails as it ought to do, it will infer the other duties of the relation, it being a special and peculiar affection that is required in her behalf. The love of Christ to the church is proposed as an example of this, which love of his is a sincere, a pure, an ardent, and constant affection, and that notwithstanding the imperfections and failures that she is guilty of. The greatness of his love to the church appeared in his giving himself unto the death for it. Observe, As the church's subjection to Christ is proposed as an exemplar to wives, so the love of Christ to his church is proposed as a pattern to husbands; and while such exemplars are offered to both, and so much is required of each, neither has reason to complain of the divine injunctions. The love which God requires from the husband in behalf of his wife will make amends for the subjection which he demands from her to her husband; and the prescribed subjection of the wife will be an abundant return for that love of the husband which God has made her due. The apostle, having mentioned Christ's love to the church, enlarges upon it, assigning the reason why he gave himself for it, namely, that he might sanctify it in this world, and glorify it in the next: *That he might sanctify and cleanse it, with the washing of water by the word* (*v.* 26) — that he might endue all his members with a principle of holiness, and deliver them from the guilt, the pollution, and the dominion of sin. The instrumental means whereby this is affected are the instituted sacraments, particularly the washing of baptism and the preaching and reception of the gospel. *And that he might present it to himself,* etc. *v.* 27. Dr. Lightfoot thinks the apostle alludes here to the Jews' extraordinary carefulness in their washings for purification. They were careful that there should be no wrinkle to keep the flesh from the water, and no spot nor dirt which was not thoroughly washed. Others understand him as alluding to a garment come newly out of the fuller's hand, purged from spots, stretched from wrinkles, the former newly contracted, the latter by long time and custom. *That he might present it to himself* — that he might perfectly unite it to himself in the great day, *a glorious church,* perfect in knowledge and in holiness, *not having spot, nor wrinkle, nor any such thing,* nothing of deformity or defilement remaining, but being entirely amiable and pleasing in his eye, *holy and without blemish,* free from the least remains of sin. The church in general, and particular believers, will not be without spot or wrinkle till they come to glory. From this and the former verse together we may take notice that the glorifying of the church is intended in the sanctifying of it: and that those, and those only, who are sanctified now, will be glorified hereafter. — *So ought men to love their wives as their own bodies,* etc. *v.* 28. The wife being made one with her husband (not in a natural, but in a civil and in a relative sense), this is an argument why he should love her with as cordial and as ardent an affection as that which he loves himself. *For no man ever yet hated his own flesh, v.* 29 — (no man in his right senses ever hated himself, however deformed, or whatever his imperfections might be); so far from it that *he nourishes and cherishes it;* he uses himself with a great deal of care and tenderness, and is industrious to supply himself with every thing convenient or good for him, with food and clothing, etc. *Even as the Lord the church:* that is, as the Lord nourishes and cherishes the church, which he furnishes with all things that he sees needful or good for her, with whatever conduces to her everlasting happiness and welfare. The apostle adds, *For we are members of his body, of his flesh and of his bones, v.* 30. He assigns this as a reason why Christ nourishes and cherishes his church — because all who belong to it *are members of his body,* that is, of his mystical body. Or, we are members *out of his body:* all the grace and glory which the church has are from Christ, as Eve was taken out of the man. But, as one observes, it being the manner of the sacred writings to express a complex body by the enumeration of its several parts, as the heaven and earth for the world, evening and morning for the natural day, so here, by body, flesh, and bones, we are to understand himself, the meaning of the verse being that we are members of Christ. — *For this cause* (because they are one, as Christ and his church are one) *shall a man leave his father and mother;* the apostle refers to the words of Adam, when Eve was given to him for a meet help, Gen. 2:24. We are not to understand by this that a man's obligation to other relations is cancelled upon his marriage, but only that this relation is to be preferred to all others, there being a nearer union between these two than between any others, that the man must rather leave any of those than his wife. — *And they two shall be one flesh,* that is, by virtue of the matrimonial bond. *This is a great mystery, v.* 32. Those words of Adam, just mentioned by the apostle, are spoken literally of marriage; but they have also a hidden mystical sense in them, relating to the union between Christ and his church, of which the conjugal union between Adam and the mother of us all was a type: though not instituted or appointed by God to signify this, yet it was a kind of natural type, as having a resemblance to it: *I speak concerning Christ and the church.*

After this, the apostle concludes this part of his discourse with a brief summary of the duty of husbands and wives, *v.* 33. "*Nevertheless* (though there be such a secret mystical sense, yet the plain literal sense concerns you) *let every one of you in particular so love his wife even as himself,* with such a sincere, peculiar, singular, and prevailing affection as that is which he bears to himself. *And the wife see that she reverence her husband.*" Reverence consists of love and esteem, which produce a care to please, and of fear, which awakens a caution lest just offence be given. That the wife thus reverence her husband is the will of God and the law of the relation.

CHAPTER 6

In this chapter, I. The apostle proceeds in the exhortation to relative duties which he began in the former, particularly he insists on the duties of children and parents, and of servants and masters (*v.* 1–9). II. He exhorts and directs Christians how to behave themselves in the spiritual warfare with the enemies of their souls; and to the exercise of several Christian graces, which he proposes to them as so many pieces of spiritual armour, to preserve and defend them in the conflict (*v.* 10–18). III. We have here the conclusion of the epistle, in which he takes his leave of them, recommending himself to the prayers of the believing Ephesians, and praying for them (*v.* 19–24).

Verses 1–9

Here we have further directions concerning relative duties, in which the apostle is very particular.

I. The duty of children to their parents. *Come, you children, hearken to me, I will teach you the fear of the Lord.* The great duty of children is to obey their parents (*v.* 1), parents being the instruments of their being, God and nature having given them an authority to command, in subserviency to God; and, if children will be obedient to their pious parents, they will be in a fair way to be pious as they are. That obedience which God demands from their children, in their behalf, includes an inward reverence, as well as the outward expressions and acts. Obey in the Lord. Some take this as a limitation, and understand it thus: "as far as is consistent with your duty to God." We must not disobey our heavenly Father in obedience to earthly parents; for our obligation to God is prior and superior to all others. I take it rather as a reason: "Children, obey your parents; for the Lord has commanded it: obey them therefore for the Lord's sake, and with an eye to him." Or it may be a particular specification of the general duty: "Obey your parents, especially in those things which relate to the Lord. Your parents teach you good manners, and therein you must obey them. They teach you what is for your health, and in this you must obey them: but the chief things in which you are to do it are the things pertaining to the Lord." Religious parents charge their children to keep the ways of the Lord, Gen. 18:19. They command them to be found in the way of their duty towards God, and to take heed of those sins most incident to their age; in these things especially they must see that they be obedient. There is a general reason given: *For this is right,* there is a natural equity in it, God has enjoined it, and it highly becomes Christians. It is the order of nature that parents command and children obey. Though this may seem a hard saying, yet it is duty, and it must be done by such as would please God and approve themselves to him. For the proof of this the apostle quotes the law of the fifth commandment, which Christ was so far from designing to abrogate and repeal that he came

to confirm it, as appears by his vindicating it, Mt. 15:4, etc. *Honour thy father and mother* (*v.* 2), which honour implies reverence, obedience, and relief and maintenance, if these be needed. The apostle adds, *which is the first commandment with promise.* Some little difficulty arises from this, which we should not overlook, because some who plead for the lawfulness of images bring this as a proof that we are not bound by *the second commandment.* But there is no manner of force in the argument. The second commandment has not a particular promise; but only a general declaration or assertion, which relates to the whole law of God's keeping mercy for thousands. And then by this is not meant the first commandment of the decalogue that has a promise, for there is no other after it that has, and therefore it would be improper to say it is the first; but the meaning may be this: "This is a prime or chief commandment, and it has a promise; it is the first commandment in the second table, and it has a promise." The promise is, *That it may be well with thee,* etc., *v.* 3. Observe, Whereas the promise in the commandment has reference to the land of Canaan, the apostle hereby shows that this and other promises which we have in the Old Testament relating to the land of Canaan are to be understood more generally. That you may not think that the Jews only, to whom God gave the land of Canaan, were bound by the fifth commandment, he here gives it a further sense, *That it may be well with thee,* etc. Outward prosperity and long life are blessings promised to those who keep this commandment. This is the way to have it well with us, and obedient children are often rewarded with outward prosperity. Not indeed that it is always so; there are instances of such children who meet with much affliction in this life: but *ordinarily* obedience is thus rewarded, and, where it is not, it is made up with something better. Observe, 1. The gospel has its temporal promises, as well as spiritual ones. 2. Although the authority of God be sufficient to engage us in our duty, yet we are allowed to have respect to the promised reward: and, 3. Though it contains some temporal advantage, even this may be considered as a motive and encouragement to our obedience.

II. The duty of parents: *And you fathers, v.* 4. Or, you parents, 1. "*Do not provoke your children to wrath.* Though God has given you power, you must not abuse that power, remembering that your children are, in a particular manner, pieces of yourselves, and therefore ought to be governed with great tenderness and love. Be not impatient with them, use no unreasonable severities and lay no rigid injunctions upon them. When you caution them, when you counsel them, when you reprove them, do it in such a manner as not to *provoke them to wrath.* In all such cases deal prudently and wisely with them, endeavouring to convince their judgments and to work upon their reason." 2. "*Bring them up* well, *in the nurture and admonition of the Lord,* in the discipline of proper and of compassionate correction, and in the knowledge of that duty which God requires of them and by which they may become better acquainted with him. Give them a good education." It is the great duty of parents to be careful in the education of their children: "Not only bring them up, as the brutes do, taking care to provide for them; but bring them up in nurture and admonition, in such a manner as is suitable to their reasonable natures. Nay, not only bring them up as men, in nurture and admonition, but as Christians, in the admonition of the Lord. Let them have a religious education. Instruct them to fear sinning; and inform them of, and excite them to, the whole of their duty towards God."

III. The duty of servants. This also is summed up in one word, which is, *obedience.* He is largest on this article, as knowing there was the greatest need of it. These servants were generally slaves. Civil servitude is not inconsistent with Christian liberty. Those may be the Lord's freemen who are slaves to men. "*Your masters according to the flesh* (*v.* 5), that is, who have the command of your bodies, but not of your souls and consciences: God alone has dominion over these." Now, with respect to servants, he exhorts, 1. That they obey *with fear and trembling.* They are to reverence those who are over them, fearing to displease them, and trembling lest they should justly incur their anger and indignation. 2. That they be sincere in their obedience: *In singleness of heart;* not pretending obedience when they design disobedience, but serving them with faithfulness. 3. They should have an eye to Jesus Christ in all the service that they perform to their masters (*v.* 5–7), *doing service as to the Lord, and not to men;* that is, not to men only or principally. When servants, in the

discharge of the duty of their places, have an eye to Christ, this puts an honour upon their obedience, and an acceptableness into it. Service done to their earthly masters, with an eye to him, becomes acceptable service to him also. To have an eye to Christ is to remember that he sees them and is ever present with them, and that his authority obliges them to a faithful and conscientious discharge of the duties of their station. 4. They must not serve their masters *with eye-service* (*v.* 6) — that is, only when their master's eye is upon them; but they must be as conscientious in the discharge of their duty, when they are absent and out of the way, because then their Master in heaven beholds them: and therefore they must not act as *men-pleasers* — as though they had no regard to the pleasing of God, and approving themselves to him, if they can impose upon their masters. Observe, A steady regard to the Lord Jesus Christ will make men faithful and sincere in every station of life. 5. What they do they must do cheerfully: *Doing the will of God from the heart,* serving their masters as God wills they should, not grudgingly, nor by constraint, but from a principle of love to them and their concerns. This is *doing it with good-will* (*v.* 7), which will make their service easy to themselves, pleasing to their masters, and acceptable to the Lord Christ. There should be *good-will* to their masters, good-will to the families they are in; and especially a readiness to do their duty to God. Observe, Service, performed with conscience, and from a regard to God, though it be to unrighteous masters, will be accounted by Christ as service done to himself. 6. Let faithful servants trust God for their wages, while they do their duty in his fear: *Knowing that whatsoever good thing (v.* 8), how poor and mean soever it may be, considered in itself, — *the same shall he receive of the Lord,* that is, by a metonymy, the reward of the same. Though his master on earth should neglect or abuse him, instead of rewarding him, he shall certainly be rewarded by the Lord Christ, *whether he be bond or free,* whether he be a poor bond-servant or a freeman or master. Christ regards not these differences of men at present; nor will he in the great and final judgment. You think, "A prince, or a magistrate, or a minister, that does his duty here, will be sure to receive his reward in heaven: but what capacity am I, a poor servant, in, of recommending myself to the favour of God." Why, God will as certainly reward thee for the meanest drudgery that is done from a sense of duty and with an eye to himself. And what can be said more proper either to engage or to encourage servants to their duty?

IV. The duty of masters: "*And you masters, do the same things unto them* (*v.* 9); that is, act after the same manner. Be just to them, as you expect they should be to you: show the like good-will and concern for them, and be careful herein to approve yourselves to God." Observe, Masters are under as strict obligations to discharge their duty to their servants as servants are to be obedient and dutiful to them. "*Forbearing threatening; anientes — moderating* threatening, and remitting the evils with which you threaten them. Remember that your servants are made of the same mould with yourselves, and therefore be not tyrannical and imperious over them, *knowing that your Master also is in heaven:*" some copies read, both *your* and *their* Master. "You have a Master to obey who makes this your duty; and you and they are but fellow-servants in respect of Christ. You will be as punishable by him, for the neglect of your duty, or for acting contrary to it, as any others of meaner condition in the world. You are therefore to show favour to others, as ever you expect to find favour with him; and you will never be a match for him, though you may be too hard for your servants." *Neither is there respect of persons with him;* a rich, a wealthy, and a dignified master, if he be unjust, imperious, and abusive, is not a jot the nearer being accepted of God for his riches, wealth, and honour. He will call masters and servants to an impartial account for their conduct one to another, and will neither spare the former because they are more advanced nor be severe towards the latter because they are inferior and mean in the world. If both masters and servants would consider their relation and obligation to God and the account they must shortly give to him, they would be more careful of their duty to each other. Thus the apostle concludes his exhortation to relative duties.

Verses 10–18

Here is a general exhortation to constancy in our Christian course, and to encourage in our Christian warfare. Is not our life a warfare? It is so; for we struggle with the common calamities of human life. Is not our religion much more a warfare? It is so; for we struggle with the opposition of the powers of darkness, and with many enemies who would keep us from God and heaven. We have enemies to fight against, a captain to fight for, a banner to fight under, and certain rules of war by which we are to govern ourselves. *"Finally, my brethren (v. 10), it yet remains that you apply yourselves to your work and duty as Christian soldiers."* Now it is requisite that a soldier be both stout-hearted and well armed. If Christians be soldiers of Jesus Christ,

I. They must see that they be stout-hearted. This is prescribed here: *Be strong in the Lord,* etc. Those who have so many battles to fight, and who, in their way to heaven, must dispute every pass, with dint of sword, have need of a great deal of courage. *Be strong therefore,* strong for service, strong for suffering, strong for fighting. Let a soldier be ever so well armed without, if he have not within a good heart, his armour will stand him in little stead. Note, spiritual strength and courage are very necessary for our spiritual warfare. Be strong in the Lord, either in his cause and for his sake or rather in his strength. We have no sufficient strength of our own. Our natural courage is as perfect cowardice, and our natural strength as perfect weakness; but all our sufficiency is of God. In his strength we must go forth and go on. By the actings of faith, we must fetch in grace and help from heaven to enable us to do that which of ourselves we cannot do, in our Christian work and warfare. We should stir up ourselves to resist temptations in a reliance upon God's all-sufficiency and the omnipotence of his might.

II. They must be well armed: *"Put on the whole armour of God (v. 11),* make use of all the proper defensitives and weapons for repelling the temptations and stratagems of Satan — get and exercise all the Christian graces, the whole armour, that no part be naked and exposed to the enemy." Observe, Those who would approve themselves to have true grace must aim at all grace, the whole armour. It is called the armour of God, because he both prepares and bestows it. We have no armour of our own that will be armour of proof in a trying time. Nothing will stand us in stead but the armour of God. This armour is prepared for us, but we must put it on; that is, we must pray for grace, we must use the grace given us, and draw it out into act and exercise as there is occasion. The reason assigned why the Christian should be completely armed is *that he may be able to stand against the wiles of the devil* — that he may be able to hold out, and to overcome, notwithstanding all the devil's assaults, both of force and fraud, all the deceits he puts upon us, all the snares he lays for us, and all his machinations against us. This the apostle enlarges upon here, and shows,

1. What our danger is, and what need we have to put on this whole armour, considering what sort of enemies we have to deal with — the devil and all the powers of darkness: *For we wrestle not against flesh and blood,* etc., *v.* 12. The combat for which we are to be prepared is not against ordinary human enemies, not barely against men compounded of *flesh and blood,* nor against our own corrupt natures singly considered, but against the several ranks of devils, who have a government which they exercise in this world. (1.) We have to do with a subtle enemy, an enemy who uses wiles and stratagems, as *v.* 11. He has a thousand ways of beguiling unstable souls: hence he is called a serpent for subtlety, an old serpent, experienced in the art and trade of tempting. (2.) He is a powerful enemy: *Principalities,* and *powers,* and *rulers.* They are numerous, they are vigorous; and rule in those heathen nations which are yet in darkness. The dark parts of the world are the seat of Satan's empire. Yea, they are usurping princes over all men who are yet in a state of sin and ignorance. Satan's is a kingdom of darkness; whereas Christ's is a kingdom of light. (3.) They are spiritual enemies: *Spiritual wickedness in high places,* or wicked spirits, as some translate it. The devil is a spirit, a wicked spirit; and our danger is the greater from our enemies because they are unseen, and assault us ere we are aware of them. The devils are wicked spirits, and they chiefly annoy the saints with, and provoke them to, spiritual wickednesses, pride, envy, malice, etc. These enemies are said to be *in high places,* or in heavenly places, so the word is, taking heaven (as one says) for the whole *expansum,* or spreading out of the air between the earth and the stars, the air being the place from which the devils assault us. Or the meaning may be, *"We wrestle about heavenly places or heavenly things;"* so some of the ancients interpret it. Our enemies strive to prevent our as-

cent to heaven, to deprive us of heavenly blessings and to obstruct our communion with heaven. They assault us in the things that belong to our souls, and labour to deface the heavenly image in our hearts; and therefore we have need to be upon our guard against them. We have need of faith in our Christian warfare, because we have spiritual enemies to grapple with, as well as of faith in our Christian work, because we have spiritual strength to fetch in. Thus you see your danger.

2. What our duty is: to take and put on the whole armour of God, and then to stand our ground, and withstand our enemies.

(1.) We must *withstand, v.* 13. We must not yield to the devil's allurements and assaults, but oppose them. Satan is said *to stand up against us,* 1 Chr. 21:1. If he stand up against us, we must stand against him; set up, and keep up, an interest in opposition to the devil. Satan is the wicked one, and his kingdom is the kingdom of sin: to stand against Satan is to strive against sin. *That you may be able to withstand in the evil day,* in the day of temptation, or of any sore affliction.

(2.) We must stand our ground: *And, having done all, to stand.* We must resolve, by God's grace, not to yield to Satan. Resist him, and he will flee. If we distrust our cause, or our leader, or our armour, we give him advantage. Our present business is to withstand the assaults of the devil, and to stand it out; and then, having done all that is incumbent on the good soldiers of Jesus Christ, our warfare will be accomplished, and we shall be finally victorious.

(3.) We must stand armed; and this is here most enlarged upon. Here is a Christian in complete armour: and the armour is divine: *Armour of God, armour of light,* Rom. 13:12. *Armour of righteousness,* 2 Co. 6:7. The apostle specifies the particulars of this armour, both offensive and defensive. The military girdle or belt, the breast-plate, the greaves (or soldier's shoes), the shield, the helmet, and the sword. It is observable that, among them all, there is none for the back; if we turn our back upon the enemy, we lie exposed. [1.] Truth or sincerity is our girdle, *v.* 14. It was prophesied of Christ (Isa. 11:5) that *righteousness should be the girdle of his loins and faithfulness the girdle of his reins.* That which Christ was girded with all Christians must be girded with. God desires truth, that is, sincerity, in the inward parts. This is the strength of our loins; and it girds on all other pieces of our armour, and therefore is first mentioned. I know no religion without sincerity. Some understand it of the doctrine of the truths of the gospel: they should cleave to us as the girdle does to the loins, Jer. 13:11. This will restrain from libertinism and licentiousness, as a girdle restrains and keeps in the body. This is the Christian soldier's belt: ungirded with this, he is unblessed. [2.] Righteousness must be our breast-plate. The breast-plate secures the vitals, shelters the heart. The righteousness of Christ imputed to us is our breast-plate against the arrows of divine wrath. The righteousness of Christ implanted in us is our breast-plate to fortify the heart against the attacks which Satan makes against us. The apostle explains this in 1 Th. 5:8, *Putting on the breast-plate of faith and love.* Faith and love include all Christian graces; for by faith we are united to Christ and by love to our brethren. These will infer a diligent observance of our duty to God, and a righteous deportment towards men, in all the offices of justice, truth, and charity. [3.] Resolution must be as the greaves to our legs: *And their feet shod with the preparation of the gospel of peace, v.* 15. Shoes, or greaves of brass, or the like, were formerly part of the military armour (1 Sa. 17:6): the use of them was to defend the feet against the gall-traps, and sharp sticks, which were wont to be laid privily in the way, to obstruct the marching of the enemy, those who fell upon them being unfit to march. *The preparation of the gospel of peace* signifies a prepared and resolved frame of heart, to adhere to the gospel and abide by it, which will enable us to walk with a steady pace in the way of religion, notwithstanding the difficulties and dangers that may be in it. It is styled *the gospel of peace* because it brings all sorts of peace, peace with God, with ourselves, and with one another. It may also be meant of that which prepares for the entertainment of the gospel, namely, repentance. With this our feet must be shod: for by living a life of repentance we are armed against temptations to sin, and the designs of our great enemy. Dr. Whitby thinks this may be the sense of the words: "That you may be ready for the combat, be shod with the gospel of peace, endeavour after that peaceable and quiet mind which the gospel calls for. Be not easily provoked, nor

prone to quarrel: but show all gentleness and all long-suffering to all men, and this will certainly preserve you from many great temptations and persecutions, as did those shoes of brass the soldiers from those galltraps," etc. [4.] Faith must be our shield: *Above all,* or chiefly, *taking the shield of faith, v.* 16. This is more necessary than any of them. Faith is all in all to us in an hour of temptation. The breast-plate secures the vitals; but with the shield we turn every way. *This is the victory over the world, even our faith.* We are to be fully persuaded of the truth of all God's promises and threatenings, such a faith being of great use against temptations. Consider faith as it *is the evidence of things not seen and the substance of things hoped for,* and it will appear to be of admirable use for this purpose. Faith, as receiving Christ and the benefits of redemption, so deriving grace from him, is like a shield, a sort of universal defence. Our enemy the devil is here called *the wicked one.* He is wicked himself, and he endeavours to make us wicked. His temptations are called *darts,* because of their swift and undiscerned flight, and the deep wounds that they give to the soul; *fiery darts,* by way of allusion to the poisonous darts which were wont to inflame the parts which were wounded with them, and therefore were so called, as the serpents with poisonous stings are called fiery serpents. Violent temptations, by which the soul is set on fire of hell, are the darts which Satan shoots at us. Faith is the shield with which we must quench these fiery darts, wherein we should receive them, and so render them ineffectual, that they may not hit us, or at least that they may not hurt us. Observe, Faith, acted upon the word of God and applying that, acted upon the grace of Christ and improving that, quenches the darts of temptation. [5.] Salvation must be our helmet (*v.* 17); that is, *hope,* which has salvation for its object; so 1 Th. 5:8. The helmet secures the head. A good hope of salvation, well founded and well built, will both purify the soul and keep it from being defiled by Satan, and it will comfort the soul and keep it from being troubled and tormented by Satan. He would tempt us to despair; but good hope keeps us trusting in God, and rejoicing in him. [6.] The word of God is the sword of the Spirit. The sword is a very necessary and useful part of a soldier's furniture. The word of God is very necessary, and of great use to the Christian, in order to his maintaining the spiritual warfare and succeeding in it. It is called *the sword of the Spirit,* because it is of the Spirit's inditing and he renders it efficacious and powerful, and *sharper than a two-edged sword.* Like Goliath's sword, none like that; with this we assault the assailants. Scripture-arguments are the most powerful arguments to repel temptation with. Christ himself resisted Satan's temptations with, *It is written,* Mt. 4:4, 6, 7, 10. This, being hid in the heart, will preserve from sin (Ps. 119:11), and will mortify and kill those lusts and corruptions that are latent there. [7.] Prayer must buckle on all the other parts of our Christian armour, *v.* 18. We must join prayer with all these graces, for our defence against these spiritual enemies, imploring help and assistance of God, as the case requires: and we must pray always. Not as though we were to do nothing else but pray, for there are other duties of religion and of our respective stations in the world that are to be done in their place and season; but we should keep up constant times of prayer, and be constant to them. We must pray upon all occasions, and as often as our own and others' necessities call us to it. We must always keep up a disposition to prayer, and should intermix ejaculatory prayers with other duties, and with common business. Though set and solemn prayer may sometimes be unseasonable (as when other duties are to be done), yet pious ejaculations *can* never be so. We must pray *with all prayer and supplication,* with all kinds of prayer: public, private, and secret; social and solitary, solemn and sudden; with all the parts of prayer: confession of sin, petition for mercy, and thanksgivings for favours received. We must pray *in the Spirit;* our spirits must be employed in the duty and we must do it by the grace of God's good Spirit. We must *watch thereunto,* endeavouring to keep our hearts in a praying frame, and taking all occasions, and improving all opportunities, for the duty: we must watch to all the motions of our own hearts towards the duty. When God says, *Seek my face,* our hearts must comply, Ps. 27:8. This we must do *with all perseverance.* We must abide by the duty of prayer, whatever change there may be in our outward circumstances; and we must continue in it as long as we live in the world. We must persevere in a particular prayer; not cutting it short, when our hearts are disposed to enlarge, and there is time for it, and our occasions call for it. We must likewise persevere in particular requests, notwithstanding some present discouragements and repulses. And we must pray *with supplication,* not for ourselves only, but *for all saints;* for we are members one of another. Observe, None are so much saints, and in so good a condition in this world, but they need our prayers, and they ought to have them. The apostle passes hence to the conclusion of the epistle.

Verses 19–24

Here, I. He desires their prayers for him, *v.* 19. Having mentioned *supplication for all saints,* he puts himself into the number. We must pray for all saints, and particularly for God's faithful ministers. *Brethren, pray for us, that the word of the Lord may run and be glorified.* Observe what it is he would have them pray for in his behalf: *"That utterance may be given unto me;* that I may be enlarged from my present restraints, and so have liberty to propagate the faith of Christ; that I may have ability to express myself in a suitable and becoming manner; *and that I may open my mouth boldly,* that is, that I may deliver the whole counsel of God, without any base fear, shame, or partiality." *To make known the mystery of the gospel;* some understand it of that part of the gospel which concerns the calling of the Gentiles, which had hitherto, as a mystery, been concealed. But the whole gospel was a mystery, till made known by divine revelation; and it is the work of Christ's ministers to publish it. Observe, Paul had a great command of language; they called him Mercury, because he was the chief speaker (Acts 14:12), and yet he would have his friends ask of God the gift of utterance for him. He was a man of great courage, and often signalized himself for it; yet he would have them pray that God would give him boldness. He knew as well what to say as any man; yet he desires them to pray for him, that he may *speak as he ought to speak.* The argument with which he enforces his request is that for the sake of the gospel he was *an ambassador in bonds, v.* 20. He was persecuted and imprisoned for preaching the gospel; though, notwithstanding, he continued in the embassy committed to him by Christ, and persisted in preaching it. Observe, 1. It is no new thing for Christ's ministers to be in bonds. 2. It is a hard thing for them to speak boldly when that is their case. 3. The best and most eminent ministers have need of, and may receive advantage by, the prayers of good Christians; and therefore should earnestly desire them. Having thus desired their prayers,

II. He recommends Tychicus unto them, *v.* 21, 22. He sent him with this epistle, that he might acquaint them with what other churches were informed of, namely, how he did, and what he did; how he was used by the Romans in his bonds, and how he behaved himself in his present circumstances. It is desirable to good ministers both that their Christian friends should know their state and that they should be acquainted with the condition of their friends; for by this means they may the better help each other in their prayers. — *And that he might comfort their hearts,* by giving such an account of his sufferings, of the cause of them, and of the temper of his mind and his behaviour under them, as might prevent their fainting at his tribulations and even minister matter of joy and thanksgiving unto them. He tells them that Tychicus was *a beloved brother and faithful minister in the Lord.* He was a sincere Christian, and so a brother in Christ: he was a faithful minister in the work of Christ, and he was very dear to Paul, which makes Paul's love to these Christian Ephesians the more observable, in that he should now part with so good and dear a friend for their sakes, when his company and conversation must have been peculiarly delightful and serviceable to himself. But the faithful servants of Jesus Christ are wont to prefer the public good to their own private or personal interests.

III. He concludes with his good wishes and prayers for them, and not for them only, but for all the brethren, *v.* 23, 24. His usual benediction was, *Grace and peace;* here it is, *Peace be to the brethren, and love with faith.* By peace we are to understand all manner of peace — peace with God, peace with conscience, peace among themselves: and all outward prosperity is included in the word; as if he had said, "I wish the continuance and increase of all happiness to you." *And love with faith.* This in part explains what he means in the following verse by grace; not only grace in the fountain, or the love and favour of God, but grace in the streams, the grace of the Spirit flowing from that divine principle, faith and love including all the rest. It is the continuance and increase of these that he desires for them, in whom they were already begun. It follows, *from God the Father,* etc. All Grace and blessings are derived to the saints from God, through the merit and intercession of Jesus Christ our Lord. The closing benediction is more extensive than the former; for in this he prays for all true believers at Ephesus, and every where else. It is the undoubted character of all the saints that they love our Lord Jesus Christ. Our love to Christ is not acceptable, unless it be in sincerity: indeed there is no such thing as love to Christ, whatever men may pretend, where there is not sincerity. The words may be read, *Grace be with all those who love our Lord Jesus Christ in incorruption,* who continue constant in their love to him, so as not to be corrupted out of it by any baits or seductions whatsoever, and whose love to him is uncorrupted by any opposite lust, or the love of any thing displeasing to him. Grace, that is, the favour of God, and all good (spiritual and temporal), that is, the product of it, are and shall be with all those who thus love our Lord Jesus Christ. And it is, or ought to be, the desire and prayer of every lover of Christ that it may be so with all his fellow-christians. *Amen,* so be it.

AN EXPOSITION, WITH PRACTICAL OBSERVATIONS, OF

THE EPISTLE OF ST. PAUL TO THE PHILIPPIANS

Philippi was a chief city of the western part of Macedonia, *prōtē tēs meridos tēs Makedonias polis,* Acts 16:12. It took its name from Philip, the famous king of Macedon, who repaired and beautified it, and it was afterwards made a Roman colony. Near this place were the *Campi Philippici,* remarkable for the famous battles between Julius Caesar and Pompey the Great, and that between Augustus and Antony on one side and Cassius and Brutus on the other. But it is most remarkable among Christians for this epistle, which was written when Paul was a prisoner at Rome, A.D. 62. Paul seems to have had a very particular kindness for the church at Philippi, which he himself had been instrumental in planting; and, though he had *the care of all the churches,* he had, upon that account, a particular fatherly tender care of this. To those to whom God has employed us to do any good we should look upon ourselves both as encouraged and engaged to study to do more good. He looked upon them as his children, and, having *begotten them by the gospel,* he was desirous by the same gospel to nourish and nurse them up. I. He was called in an extraordinary manner to preach the gospel at Philippi, Acts 16:9. A vision appeared to Paul in the night: *There stood a man of Macedonia, and prayed him, saying, Come over into Macedonia, and help us.* He saw God going before him, and was encouraged to use all means for carrying on the good work which was begun among them, and building upon the foundation which was laid. II. At Philippi he suffered hard things; he was scourged, and put into the stocks (Acts 16:23, 24); yet he had not the less kindness for the place for the hard usage he met with there. We must never love our friends the less for the ill treatment which our enemies give us. III. The beginnings of that church were very small; Lydia was converted there, and the jailer, and a few more: yet that did not discourage him. If good be not done at first, it may be done afterwards, and the last works may be more abundant. We must not be discouraged by small beginnings. IV. It seems, by many passages in this epistle, that this church at Philippi grew into a flourishing church, and particularly that the brethren were very kind to Paul. He had reaped of their temporal things, and he made a return in spiritual things. He acknowledges the receipt of a present they had sent him (4:18), and this when no other church communicated with him as concerning giving and receiving (*v.* 15); and he gives them a prophet's, an apostle's reward, in this epistle, which is of more value than thousands of gold and silver.

CHAPTER 1

He begins with the inscription and benediction (*v.* 1, 2). He gives thanks for the saints at Philippi (*v.* 3–6). He speaks of his great affection and concern for their spiritual welfare (*v.* 7, 8), his prayers for them (*v.* 9–11), his care to prevent their offence at his sufferings (*v.* 12–20), his readiness to glorify Christ by life or death (*v.* 21–26), and then concludes with a double exhortation to strictness and constancy (*v.* 27–30).

Verses 1–2

We have here the inscription and benediction. Observe,

I. The persons writing the epistle — *Paul and Timotheus.* Though Paul was alone divinely inspired, he joins Timothy with himself, to express his own humility, and put honour upon Timothy. Those who are aged, and strong, and eminent, should pay respect to, and support the reputation of, those who are younger, and weaker, and of less note. *The servants of Jesus Christ;* not only in the common relation of his disciples, but in the peculiar work of the ministry, the high office of an apostle and an evangelist. Observe, The highest honour of the greatest apostle, and most eminent ministers, is to be the servants of Jesus Christ; not the masters of the churches, but the servants of Christ. Observe,

II. The persons to whom it is directed. 1. To *all the saints in Christ who are at Philippi.* He mentions the church before the ministers, because the ministers are for the church, for their edification and benefit, not the churches for the ministers, for their dignity, dominion, and wealth. *Not for that we have dominion over your faith, but are helpers of your joy,* 2 Co. 1:24. They are not only the servants of Christ, but the servants of the church for his sake. *Ourselves your servants for Jesus' sake,* 2 Co. 4:5. Observe, The Christians here are called saints; set apart for God, or sanctified by his Spirit, either by visible profession or real holiness. And those who are not really saints on earth will never be saints in heaven. Observe, It is directed to *all the saints,* one as well as another, even the meanest, the poorest, and those of the least gifts. Christ makes no difference; the rich and the poor meet together in him: and the ministers must not make a difference in their care and tenderness upon these accounts. We must not *have the faith of our Lord Jesus Christ with respect of persons,* James 2:1. *Saints in Christ Jesus;* saints are accepted only by virtue of their being in Christ Jesus, or as they are Christians. Out of Christ the best saints will appear sinners, and unable to stand before God. 2. It is directed to the ministers, or church-officers — *with the bishops and deacons,* the bishops or elders, in the first place, whose office it was to teach and rule, and the deacons, or overseers of the poor, who took care of the outward business of the house of God: the place, the furniture, the maintenance of the ministers, and provision for the poor. These were all the offices which were then known in the church, and which were of divine appointment. The apostle, in the direction of his epistle to a Christian church, acknowledges but two orders, which he calls bishops and deacons. And whosoever shall consider that the same characters and titles, the same qualifications, the same acts of office, and the same honour and respect, are every where ascribed throughout the New Testament to those who are called bishops and presbyters (as Dr. Hammond and other learned men allow), will find it difficult to make them a different office or distinct order of ministry in the scripture times.

III. Here is the apostolical benediction: *Grace be unto you, and peace, from God our Father, and from the Lord Jesus Christ, v.* 2. This is the same, almost word for word, in all the epistles, to teach us that we must not be shy of forms, though we are not to be tied down to them, especially such as are not scriptural. The only form in the Old Testament is that of a benediction (Num. 6:23–26), *On this wise you shall bless the children of Israel, saying unto them, The Lord bless thee and keep thee: the Lord make his face shine upon thee, and be gracious unto thee: the Lord lift up the light of his countenance upon thee, and give thee peace.* So in the New Testament, the good which is wished is spiritual good, *grace and peace* — the free favour and good-will of God, and all the blessed fruits and effects of it, and that *from God our Father, and from the Lord Jesus Christ,* jointly from them both, though in a different way. Observe, 1. No peace without grace. Inward peace springs from a sense of divine favour. 2. No grace and peace but from God our Father, the fountain and original of all blessings, the *Father of lights, from whom cometh down every good and perfect gift,* James 1:17. 3. No grace and peace from God our Father, but in and through our Lord Jesus Christ. Christ, as Mediator, is the channel of conveyance of all spiritual blessings to the church, and directs the disposal of them to all his members.

Verses 3–6

The apostle proceeds after the inscription and benediction to thanksgiving for the saints at Philippi. He tells them what it was he thanked God for, upon their account. Observe here,

I. Paul remembered them: he bore them much in his thoughts; and though they were out of sight, and he was at a distance from them, yet they were not out of his mind: or, *Upon every mention of you — epi pasē tē mneia.* As he often thought of them, so he often spoke of them, and delighted to hear them spoken of. The very mention of them was grateful to him: it is a pleasure to hear of the welfare of an absent friend.

II. He remembered them with joy. At Philippi he was maltreated; there he was scourged and put into the stocks, and for the present saw little of the fruit of his labour; and yet he remembers Philippi with joy. He looked upon his sufferings for Christ as his credit, his comfort, his crown, and was pleased at every mention of the place where he suffered. So far was he from being ashamed of them, or loth to hear of the scene of his sufferings, that he remembered it with joy.

III. He remembered them in prayer: *Always in every prayer of mine for you all, v.* 4. The best remembrance of our friends is to remember them at the throne of grace. Paul was much in prayer for his friends, for all his friends, for these particularly. It should seem, by this manner of expression, that he mentioned at the throne of grace the several churches he was interested in and concerned for particularly and by name. He had seasons of prayer for the church at Philippi. God gives us leave to be thus free with him, though, for our comfort, he knows whom we mean when we do not name them.

IV. He thanked God upon every joyful remembrance of them. Observe, Thanksgiving must have a part in every prayer; and whatsoever is the matter of our rejoicing ought to be the matter of our thanksgiving. What we have the comfort of, God must have the glory of. He thanked God, as well as made requests with joy. As holy joy is the heart and soul of thankful praise, so thankful praise is the lip and language of holy joy.

V. As in our prayers, so in our thanksgiving, we must eye God as our God: *I thank my God.* It encourages us in prayer, and enlarges the heart in praise, to see every mercy coming from the hand of God as our God. — *I thank my God upon every remembrance of you.* We must thank our God for others' graces and comforts, and gifts and usefulness, as we receive the benefit of them, and God receives glory by them. But what is the matter of this thanksgiving? 1. He gives thanks to God for the comfort he had in them: for *your fellowship in the gospel, from the first day until now, v.* 5. Observe, Gospel fellowship is a good fellowship; and the meanest Christians have fellowship in the gospel with the greatest apostles, for the gospel salvation is a *common salvation* (Jude 3), and they *obtain like precious faith* with them, 2 Pt. 1:1. Those who sincerely receive and embrace the gospel have fellowship in it *from the very first day:* a new-born Christian, if he is true-born, is interested in all the promises and privileges of the gospel from the first day of his becoming such. — *Until now.* Observe, It is a great comfort to ministers when those who begin well hold on and persevere. Some, by their *fellowship in the gospel,* understand their liberality towards propagating the gospel, and translate *koinōnia,* not *communion,* but *communication.* But, comparing it with Paul's thanksgiving on the account of other churches, it rather seems to be taken more generally for the fellowship which they had, in faith, and hope, and holy love, with all good Christians — a fellowship in gospel promises, ordinances, privileges, and hopes; and this from the *first day until now.* 2. For the confidence he had concerning them (*v.* 6): *Being confident of this very thing,* etc. Observe, The confidence of Christians is the great comfort of Christians, and we may fetch matter of praise from our hopes as well as from our joys; we must give thanks not only for what we have the present possession and evidence of, but for what we have the future prospect of. Paul speaks with much confidence concerning the good estate of others, hoping well concerning them in the judgment of charity, and being confident in the judgment of faith that if they were sincere they would be happy: *That he who has begun a good work in you will perform it unto the day of Jesus Christ.* A good work *among you — en hymin,* so it may be read: understand it, in the general, of the planting of the church among them. He who hath planted Christianity in the world will preserve it as long as the world stands. Christ will have a church till the mystery of God shall be finished and the mystical body completed. The church is built upon a rock, and the *gates of hell shall not prevail against it.* But it is rather to be applied to particular persons, and then it speaks of the certain accomplishment of the work of grace wherever it is begun. Observe here, (1.) The work of grace is a good work, a blessed work; for it makes us good, and is an earnest of good to us. It makes us like God, and fits us for the enjoyment of God. That may well be called a good work which does us the greatest good. (2.) Wherever this good work is begun it is of God's beginning: *He has begun a good work in you.* We could not begin it ourselves, for we are by nature *dead in trespasses and sins:* and what can dead men do towards raising themselves to life; or how can they begin to act till they are enlivened in the same respect in which they are said to be dead? It is God who quickens those who are thus dead, Eph. 2:1; Col. 2:13. (3.) The work of grace is but begun in this life; it is not finished here; as long as we are in this imperfect state there is something more to be done. (4.) If the same God who begins the good work did not undertake the carrying on and finishing of it, it would lie for ever unfinished. He must perform it who began it. (5.) We may be confident, or well persuaded, that God not only will not forsake, but that he will finish and crown the work of his own hands. For, *as for God, his work is perfect.* (6.) The work of grace will never be perfected *till the day of Jesus Christ,* the day of his appearance. When he shall come to judge the world, and finish his mediation, then this work will be complete, and the top-stone will be brought forth with shouting. We have the same expression, *v.* 10.

Verses 7–8

The apostle expresses the ardent affection he had for them, and his concern for their spiritual welfare: *I have you in my heart, v.* 7. He loved them as his own soul, and they lay near his heart. He thought much of them, and was in care about them. Observe, 1. Why he had them in his heart: *Inasmuch as both in my bonds, and in the defence and confirmation of the gospel, you all are partakers of my grace;* that is, they had received benefit by him and by his ministry; they were partakers of that grace of God which by him, and through his hands, was communicated to them. This makes people dear to their ministers — their receiving benefit by their ministry. Or, *"You are partakers of my grace,* you have joined with me in doing and suffering." They were partakers of his affliction by sympathy and concern, and readiness to assist him. Thus he calls being partakers of his grace; for those who suffer with the saints are and shall be comforted with them; and those shall share in the reward, who bear their part of the burden. He loved them because they adhered to him in his bonds, and in the *defence and confirmation of the gospel:* they were as ready to appear in their places, and according to their capacity, for the defence of the gospel, as the apostle was in his; and therefore he had them in his heart. Fellow sufferers should be dear one to another; those who have ventured and suffered in the same good cause of God and religion should for that reason love one another dearly: or, because *you have me at heart — dia to echein me en tē kardia hymas.* They manifested their respect for him by adhering firmly to the doctrine he preached, and readily suffering for it along with him. The truest mark of respect towards our ministers is receiving and abiding by the doctrine they preach. 2. The evidence of it: *It is meet for me to think this of you all, because I have you in my heart.* By this it appeared that he had them in his heart, because he had a good opinion of them and good hopes concerning them. Observe, It is very proper to think the best of other people, and as well as we can of them — to suppose as well of them as the matter will admit in all cases. 3. An appeal to God concerning the truth of this (*v.* 8): *For God is my record how greatly I long after you all in the bowels of Jesus Christ.* Having them in his heart, he longed after them; either he longed to see them, longed to hear from them, or he longed for their spiritual welfare and their increase and improvement in knowledge and grace. He had *joy in them* (*v.* 4), because of the good he saw and heard of among them; yet still he longed after them, to hear of more of it among them; and he *longed after them all,* not only those among them who were witty and wealthy, but even the meanest and poorest; and he *longed greatly* after them, or with strong affection and great goodwill; and this *in the bowels of Jesus Christ,* with that tender concern which Christ himself has and has shown to precious souls. Paul was herein a follower of Christ, and all good ministers should aim to be so. O the bowels of compassion which are in Jesus Christ to poor souls! It was in compassion to them that he undertook their salvation, and put himself to so vast an expense to compass it. Now, in conformity to the example of Christ, Paul had a compassion for them, and longed after them all *in the bowels of Jesus Christ.* Shall not we pity and love those souls whom Christ had such a love and pity for? For this he appeals to God: *God is my record.* It was an inward disposition of mind that he expressed towards them, to the sincerity of which God only was witness, and therefore to him he appeals. "Whether you know it or not, or are sensible of it, God, who knows the heart, knows it."

Verses 9–11

These verses contain the prayers he put up for them. Paul often let his friends know what it was he begged of God for them, that they might know what to beg for themselves and be directed in their own prayers, and that they might be encouraged to hope they should receive from God the quickening, strengthening, everlasting, comforting grace, which so powerful an intercessor as Paul asked of God for them. It is an encouragement to us to know that we are prayed for by our friends, who, we have reason to think, have an interest at the throne of grace. It was intended likewise for their direction in their walk, and that they might labour to answer his prayers for them; for by this it would appear that God had answered them. Paul, in praying thus for them, expected good concerning them. It is an inducement to us to do our duty, that we may not disappoint the expectations of praying friends and ministers. He prayed, 1. That they might be a loving people, and that good affections might abound among them; *That your love might abound yet more and more.* He means it of their love to God, and one another, and all men. Love is the fulfilling both of the law and of the gospel. Observe, Those who abound much in any grace have still need to abound more and more, because there is still something wanting in it and we are imperfect in our best attainments. 2. That they might be a knowing and judicious people: that love might abound *in knowledge and in all judgment.* It is not a blind love that will recommend us to God, but a love grounded upon knowledge and judgment. We must love God because of his infinite excellence and loveliness, and love our brethren because of what we see of the image of God upon them. Strong passions, without knowledge and a settled judgment, will not make us complete in the will of God, and sometimes do more hurt than good. The Jews had a zeal of God, but not according to knowledge, and were transported by it to violence and rage, Rom. 10:2; Jn. 16:2. 3. That they might be a discerning people. This would be the effect of their knowledge and judgment: *That you may approve the things which are excellent* (*v.* 10); or, as it is in the margin, *Try the things which differ; eis to dokimazein,* that we may approve the things which are excellent upon the trial of them, and discern their difference from other things. Observe, The truths and laws of Christ are excellent things; and it is necessary that we every one approve them, and esteem them such. We only need to try them, to approve of them; and they will easily recommend themselves to any searching and discerning mind. 4. That they might be an honest upright-hearted people: *That you may be sincere.* Sincerity is our gospel perfection, that in which we should have our conversation in the world, and which is the glory of all our graces. When the eye is single, when we are inward with God in what we do, are really what we appear to be, and mean honestly, then we are sincere. 5. That they might be an inoffensive people: that you may be *without offence until the day of Christ;* not apt to take offence; and very careful not to give offence to God or their brethren, to *live in all good conscience before God* (Acts 23:1), and to *exercise ourselves to have always a conscience void of offence towards God and towards men,* Acts 24:16. And we must continue to the end *blameless,* that we may be presented so at the *day of Christ.* He will present the church *without spot or wrinkle* (Eph. 5:27), and *present believers faultless before the presence of his glory with exceeding joy,* Jude 24. 6. That they might be a fruitful useful people (*v.* 11): *Being filled with the fruits of righteousness,* etc. From God is our fruit found, and therefore from him it must be asked. The *fruits of righteousness* are the evidences and effects of our sanctification, the duties of holiness springing from a renewed heart, the *root of the matter in us. Being filled* with them. Observe, Those who do much good should still endeavour to do more. The fruits of righteousness, brought forth for the glory of God and edification of his church, should really fill us, and wholly take us up. Fear not being emptied by bringing forth the fruits of righteousness, for you will be filled with them. These fruits are *by Jesus Christ,* by his strength and grace, for *without him we can do nothing.* He is the root of the good olive, from which it derives its fatness. We are *strong in the grace which is in Christ Jesus* (2 Tim. 2:1) and *strengthened with might by his Spirit* (Eph. 3:16), and they are *unto the glory and praise of God.* We must not aim at our own glory in our fruitfulness, but at the *praise and glory of God,* that *God may be glorified in all things* (1 Peter 4:11), and *whatsoever we do we must do all to the glory of God,* 1 Co. 10:31. It is much for the honour of God, when Christians not only are good, but do good, and *abound in good works.*

Verses 12–20

We see here the care the apostle takes to prevent their being offended at his sufferings. He was now a prisoner at Rome; this might be a stumbling-block to those who had received the gospel by his ministry. They might be tempted to think, If this doctrine were indeed of God, God would not suffer one who was so active and instrumental in preaching and propagating it to be thrown by as a despised broken vessel. They might be shy of owning this doctrine, lest they should be involved in the same trouble themselves. Now to take off the offence of the cross, he expounds this dark and hard chapter of his sufferings, and makes it very easy and intelligible, and reconcilable to the wisdom and goodness of God who employed him.

I. He suffered by the sworn enemies of the gospel, who laid him in prison, and aimed at taking away his life; but they should not be stumbled at this, for good was brought out of it, and it tended to the furtherance of the gospel (*v.* 12): *The things which happened unto me have fallen out rather unto the furtherance of the gospel.* A strange chemistry of Providence this, to extract so great a good as the enlargement of the gospel out of so great an evil as the confinement of the apostle. *"I suffer trouble as an evil-doer, even unto bonds; but the word of God is not bound,* 2 Tim. 2:9. They cannot imprison the word of God; that has its free course, though I am confined." But how was this?

1. It alarmed those who were without (*v.* 13): *"My bonds in Christ,* or for Christ, *are manifest in all the palace and in all other places.* The emperor, the courtiers, the magistrates, are convinced that I do not suffer as an evil-doer, but as an honest man, with a good conscience. They know that I suffer for Christ, and not for any wickedness." Observe, (1.) Paul's sufferings made him known at court, where perhaps he would never have otherwise been known; and this might lead some of them to enquire after the gospel for which he suffered, which they might otherwise have never heard of. (2.) When his bonds were manifest in the palace, they were manifest in all other places. *The sentiments of the court have a great influence on the sentiments of all people — Regis ad exemplum totus componitur orbis.*

2. It emboldened those who were within. As his enemies were startled at his sufferings, so his friends were encour-

aged by them. *Upright men shall be astonished at this, and the innocent shall stir up himself against the hypocrite. The righteous also shall hold on his way, and he who has clean hands shall be stronger and stronger,* Job 17:8, 9. So it was here: *Many of the brethren in the Lord waxing confident by my bonds, v.* 14. The expectation of trouble for their religion, in general, perhaps disheartened and discouraged them; but, when they saw Paul imprisoned for Christ, they were so far from being deterred from preaching Christ and praising his name, that it made them the more bold; for they could gladly suffer in Paul's company. If they should be hurried from the pulpit to the prison, they could be reconciled to it, because they would be there in such good company. Besides, the comfort which Paul had in his sufferings, his extraordinary consolations received from Christ in a suffering state, greatly encouraged them. They saw that those who served Christ served a good Master, who could both bear them up and bear them out, in their sufferings for him. *Waxing confident by my bonds. Pepoithotas.* They were more fully satisfied and persuaded by what they saw. Observe the power of divine grace; that which was intended by the enemy to discourage the preachers of the gospel was overruled for their encouragement. And *are much more bold to speak the word without fear;* they see the worst of it, and therefore are not afraid to venture. Their confidence gave them courage, and their courage preserved them from the power of fear.

II. He suffered from false friends as well as from enemies (*v.* 15, 16): *Some preach Christ even of envy and strife. The one preach Christ of contention, not sincerely.* Now this would be a stumbling-block and discouragement to some, that there were those who envied Paul's reputation in the churches, and the interest he had among the Christians, and endeavoured to supplant and undermine him. They were secretly pleased when he was laid up in prison, that they might have the better opportunity to steal away the people's affections; and they laid themselves out the more in preaching, that they might gain to themselves the reputation they envied him: *Supposing to add affliction to my bonds.* They thought hereby to grieve his spirit, and make him afraid of losing his interest, uneasy under his confinement, and impatient for release. It is sad that there should be men who profess the gospel, especially who preach it, who are governed by such principles as these, who should preach Christ in spite to Paul, and to increase the affliction of his bonds. Let us not think it strange if in these later and more degenerate ages of the church there should be any such. However, there were others who were animated by Paul's sufferings to preach Christ the more vigorously: *Some also of good will, and love:* from sincere affection to the gospel, that the work might not stand while the workman was laid up. — *Knowing that I am set for the defence of the gospel.* They knew that he was appointed to support and propagate the gospel in the world, against all the violence and opposition of its enemies, and were afraid lest the gospel should suffer by his confinement. This made them the more bold to preach the word and *supply his lack of service* to the church.

III. It is very affecting to see how easy he was in the midst of all: *Notwithstanding every way, whether in pretence or in truth, Christ is preached; and I therein do rejoice, yea, and I will rejoice, v.* 18. Note, The preaching of Christ is the joy of all who wish well to his kingdom among men. Since it may tend to the good of many, we ought to rejoice in it, though it be done in pretence, and not in reality. It is God's prerogative to judge of the principles men act upon; this is out of our line. Paul was so far from envying those who had liberty to preach the gospel while he was under confinement that he rejoiced in the preaching of it even by those who do it in pretence, and not in truth. How much more then should we rejoice in the preaching of the gospel by those who do it in truth, yea, though it should be with much weakness and some mistake! Two things made the apostle rejoice in the preaching of the gospel:

1. Because it tended to the salvation of the souls of men: *I know that this shall turn to my salvation, v.* 19. Observe, God can bring good out of evil; and what does not turn to the salvation of the ministers may yet, by the grace of God, be made to turn to the salvation of the people. What reward can those expect who preach Christ out *of strife, and envy, and contention,* and to add affliction to a faithful minister's bonds? who preach in pretence, and not in truth? And yet even this may turn to the salvation of others; and Paul's rejoicing in it turned to his salvation too. This is one of the things

which *accompany salvation* — to be able to rejoice that Christ is preached, though it be to the diminution of us and our reputation. This noble spirit appeared in John the Baptist, at the first public preaching of Christ: *"This my joy therefore is fulfilled. He must increase, but I must decrease,* Jn. 3:29, 30. Let him shine, though I be obscured; and his glory be exalted, though upon my ruins." Others understand this expression of the malice of his enemies being defeated, and contributing towards his deliverance from his confinement. *Through your prayers, and the supply of the Spirit of Christ.* Note, Whatever turns to our salvation is by the supply or the aids and assistance of the Spirit of Christ; and prayer is the appointed means of fetching in that supply. The prayers of the people may bring a supply of the Spirit to their ministers, to support them in suffering, as well as in preaching the gospel.

2. Because it would turn to the glory of Christ, *v.* 20, where he takes occasion to mention his own entire devotedness to the service and honour of Christ: *According to my earnest expectation and hope, that in nothing I shall be ashamed,* etc. Here observe, (1.) The great desire of every true Christian is that Christ may be magnified and glorified, that his name may be great, and his kingdom come. (2.) Those who truly desire that Christ may be magnified desire that he may be *magnified in their body.* They present their *bodies a living sacrifice* (Rom. 12:1), and *yield their members as instruments of righteousness unto God,* Rom. 6:13. They are willing to serve his designs, and be instrumental to his glory, with every member of their body, as well as faculty of their soul. (3.) It is much for the glory of Christ that we should serve him boldly and not be ashamed of him, with freedom and liberty of mind, and without discouragement: *That in nothing I shall be ashamed, but that with all boldness Christ may be magnified.* The boldness of Christians is the honour of Christ. (4.) Those who make Christ's glory their desire and design may make it their expectation and hope. If it be truly aimed at, it shall certainly be attained. If in sincerity we pray, *Father, glorify thy name,* we may be sure of the same answer to that prayer which Christ had: *I have glorified it, and I will glorify it again,* Jn. 12:28. (5.) Those who desire that Christ may be magnified in their bodies have a holy indifference whether it be by life or by death. They refer it to him which way he will make them serviceable to his glory, whether by their labours or sufferings, by their diligence or patience, by their living to his honour in working for him or dying to his honour in suffering for him.

Verses 21–26

We have here an account of the life and death of blessed Paul: his life was Christ, and his death was gain. Observe, 1. It is the undoubted character of every good Christian that to him to live is Christ. The glory of Christ ought to be the end of our life, the grace of Christ the principle of our life, and the word of Christ the rule of it. The Christian life is derived from Christ, and directed to him. He is the principle, rule, and end of it. 2. All those to whom to live is Christ to them to die *will be gain:* it is great gain, a present gain, everlasting gain. Death is a great loss to a carnal worldly man; for he loses all his comforts and all his hopes: but to a good Christian it is gain, for it is the end of all his weakness and misery and the perfection of his comforts and accomplishment of his hopes; it delivers him from all the evils of life, and brings him to the possession of the chief good. Or, *To me to die is gain;* that is, "to the gospel as well as to myself, which will receive a further confirmation by the seal of my blood, as it had before by the labours of my life." So Christ would be *magnified by his death, v.* 20. Some read the whole expression thus: *To me, living and dying, Christ is gain;* that is, "I desire no more, neither while I live nor when I die, but to win Christ and be found in him." It might be thought, if death were gain to him, he would be weary of life, and impatient for death. No, says he,

I. *If I live in the flesh, this is the fruit of my labour* (*v.* 22), that is, Christ is. He reckoned his labour well bestowed, if he could be instrumental to advance the honour and interest of the kingdom of Christ in the world. It is *the fruit of my labour — karpos ergou — operae pretium.* It is worth while for a good Christian and a good minister to live in the world as long as he can glorify God and do good to his church. *Yet what I shall choose I wot not; for I am in a strait betwixt two.* It was a blessed strait which Paul was in, not between two evil things, but between two good things. David was in a strait by three judgments — sword, famine, and pestilence:

Paul was in a strait between two blessings — living to Christ, and being with him. Here we have him reasoning with himself upon the matter.

1. His inclination was for death. See the power of faith and of divine grace; it can reconcile the mind to death, and make us willing to die, though death is the destruction of our present nature and the greatest natural evil. We have naturally an aversion to death, but he had an inclination to it (*v.* 23); *Having a desire to depart, and to be with Christ,* Observe, (1.) It is being with Christ which makes a departure desirable to a good man. It is not simply dying, or putting off the body, it is not of itself and for its own sake a desirable thing; but it may be necessarily connected with something else which may make it truly so. If I cannot be with Christ without departing, I shall reckon it desirable on that account to depart. (2.) As soon as ever the soul departs, it is immediately with Christ. *This day shalt thou be with me in paradise,* Lu. 23:43. *Absent from the body and present with the Lord* (2 Co. 5:8), without any interval between. *Which is far better, pollō gar mallon kreisson — very much exceeding,* or *vastly preferable.* Those who know the value of Christ and heaven will readily acknowledge it far better to be in heaven than to be in this world, to be with Christ than to be with any creature; for in this world we are compassed about with sin, born to trouble, born again to it; but, if we come to be with Christ, farewell sin and temptation, farewell sorrow and death, for ever.

2. His judgment was rather to live awhile longer in this world, for the service of the church (*v.* 24): *Nevertheless to abide in the flesh is more needful for you.* It is needful for the church to have ministers; and faithful ministers can ill be spared when the *harvest is plenteous and the labourers are few.* Observe, Those who have most reason to desire to depart should be willing to continue in the world as long as God has any work for them to do. Paul's strait was not between living in this world and living in heaven; between these two there is no comparison: but his strait was between serving Christ in this world and enjoying him in another. Still it was Christ that his heart was upon: though, to advance the interest of Christ and his church, he chose rather to tarry here, where he met with oppositions and difficulties, and to deny himself for awhile the satisfaction of his reward.

II. *And, having this confidence, I know that I shall abide and continue with you all for your furtherance and joy of faith, v.* 25. Observe here, 1. What a great confidence Paul had in the divine Providence, that it would order all for the best to him. "Having this confidence that it will be needful for you that I should abide in the flesh, I know that I shall abide." 2. Whatsoever is best for the church, we may be sure God will do. If we know what is needful for building up the body of Christ, we may certainly know what will be; for he will take care of its interests, and do what is best, all things considered, in every condition it is in. 3. Observe what ministers are continued for: *For our furtherance and joy of faith,* our further advancement in holiness and comfort. 4. What promotes our *faith and joy of faith* is very much for our furtherance in the way to heaven. The more faith the more joy, and the more faith and joy the more we are furthered in our Christian course. 5. There is need of a settled ministry, not only for the conviction and conversion of sinners, but for the edification of saints, and their furtherance in spiritual attainments.

III. *That your rejoicing may be more abundant in Jesus Christ for me, by my coming to you again, v.* 26. They rejoiced in the hope of seeing him, and enjoying his further labours among them. Observe, 1. The continuance of ministers with the church ought to be the rejoicing of all who wish well to the church, and to its interests. 2. All our joys should terminate in Christ. Our joy in good ministers should be our joy *in Christ Jesus for them;* for they are but the *friends of the bridegroom,* and are to be received in his name, and for his sake.

Verses 27–30

The apostle concludes the chapter with two exhortations:—

I. He exhorts them to strictness of conversation (*v.* 27): *Only let your conversation be as becometh the gospel of Christ.* Observe, Those who profess the gospel of Christ should have their conversation as becomes the gospel, or in a suitableness and agreeableness to it. Let it be as becomes those who believe gospel truths, submit to gospel laws, and

depend upon gospel promises; and with an answerable faith, holiness, and comfort. Let it be in all respects as those who belong to the kingdom of God among men, and are members and subjects of it. It is an ornament to our profession when our conversation is of a piece with it. — *That whether I come and see you, or else be absent, I may hear of your affairs.* He had spoken in *v.* 26 of his coming to them again, and had spoken it with some assurance, though he was now a prisoner; but he would not have them build upon that. Our religion must not be bound up in the hands of our ministers: "Whether I come or no, let me hear well of you, and do you stand fast." Whether ministers come or no, Christ is always at hand. He is nigh to us, never far from us; and hastens his second coming. *The coming of the Lord draws nigh,* James 5:8. Let me hear of you *that you stand fast in one spirit, with one mind striving together for the faith of the gospel.* Three things he desired to hear of them; and they are all such as become the gospel: — 1. It becomes those who profess the gospel to strive for it, to use a holy violence in taking the kingdom of heaven. The *faith of the gospel* is the doctrine of faith, *or* the religion of the gospel. There is that in the faith of the gospel which is worth striving for. If religion is worth any thing, it is worth every thing. There is much opposition, and there is need of striving. A man may sleep and go to hell; but he who will go to heaven must look about him and be diligent. 2. The unity and unanimity of Christians become the gospel: *Strive together,* not strive one with another; all of you must strive against the common adversary. One spirit and one mind become the gospel; for *there is one Lord, one faith, one baptism.* There may be a oneness of heart and affection among Christians, where there is diversity of judgment and apprehensions about many things. 3. Stedfastness becomes the gospel: *Stand fast in one spirit, with one mind.* Be *stedfast and immovable* by any opposition. It is a shame to religion when the professors of it are off and on, unfixed in their minds, and unstable as water; for they will never excel. Those who would strive for the faith of the gospel must stand firm to it.

II. He exhorts them to courage and constancy in suffering: *And in nothing terrified by your adversaries, v.* 28. The professors of the gospel have all along met with adversaries, especially at the first planting of Christianity. Our great care must be to keep close to our profession, and be constant to it: whatever oppositions we meet with, we must not be frightened at them, considering that the condition of the persecuted is much better and more desirable than the condition of the persecutors; for persecuting is an *evident token of perdition.* Those who oppose the gospel of Christ, and injure the professors of it, are marked out for ruin. But being persecuted is a token of salvation. Not that it is a certain mark; many hypocrites have suffered for their religion; but it is a good sign that we are in good earnest in religion, and designed for salvation, when we are enabled in a right manner to suffer for the cause of Christ. — *For to you it is given on the behalf of Christ not only to believe, but also to suffer for his name, v.* 29. Here are two precious gifts given, and both on the behalf of Christ: — 1. To believe in him. Faith is God's gift on the behalf of Christ, who purchased for us not only the blessedness which is the object of faith, but the grace of faith itself: the ability or disposition to believe is from God. 2. To suffer for the sake of Christ is a valuable gift too: it is a great honour and a great advantage; for we may be very serviceable to the glory of God, which is the end of our creation, and encourage and confirm the faith of others. And there is a great reward attending it too: *Blessed are you when men shall persecute you, for great is your reward in heaven,* Mt. 5:11, 12. And, if *we suffer with him, we shall also reign with him,* 2 Tim. 2:12. If we suffer reproach and loss for Christ, we are to reckon it a great gift, and prize it accordingly, always provided we behave under our sufferings with the genuine temper of martyrs and confessors (*v.* 30): "Having the same conflict which you saw in me, and now hear to be in me; that is, suffering in the same manner as you saw and now hear of me that I suffer." It is not simply the suffering, but the cause, and not only the cause, but the spirit, which makes the martyr. A man may suffer in a bad cause, and then he suffers justly; or in a good cause, but with a wrong mind, and then his sufferings lose their value.

CHAPTER 2

The apostle proceeds to further exhortations to several duties, to be like-minded, and lowly-minded, which he presses from the example of Christ

(*v.* 1–11), to be diligent and serious in the Christian course (*v.* 12, 13), and to adorn their Christian profession by several suitable graces (*v.* 14–18). He then concludes with particular notice and commendation of two good ministers, Timothy and Epaphroditus, whom he designed to send to them (*v.* 19–30).

Verses 1–11

The apostle proceeds in this chapter where he left off in the last, with further exhortations to Christian duties. He presses them largely to like-mindedness and lowly-mindedness, in conformity to the example of the Lord Jesus, the great pattern of humility and love. Here we may observe,

I. The great gospel precept passed upon us; that is, to love one another. This is the law of Christ's kingdom, the lesson of his school, the livery of his family. This he represents (*v.* 2) by being *like-minded, having the same love, being of one accord, of one mind.* We are of a like mind when we have the same love. Christians should be one in affection, whether they can be one in apprehension or no. This is always in their power, and always their duty, and is the likeliest way to bring them nearer in judgment. *Having the same love.* Observe, The same love that we are required to express to others, others are bound to express to us. Christian love ought to be mutual love. Love, and you shall be loved. *Being of one accord, and of one mind;* not crossing and thwarting, or driving on separate interests, but unanimously agreeing in the great things of God and keeping the *unity of the Spirit* in other differences. Here observe,

1. The pathetic pressing of the duty. He is very importunate with them, knowing what an evidence it is of our sincerity, and what a means of the preservation and edification of the body of Christ. The inducements to brotherly love are these: — (1.) "If there is any *consolation in Christ.* Have you experienced consolation in Christ? Evidence that experience by loving one another." The sweetness we have found in the doctrine of Christ should sweeten our spirits. Do we expect consolation in Christ? If we would not be disappointed, we must love one another. If we have not consolation in Christ, where else can we expect it? Those who have an interest in Christ have consolation in him, strong and everlasting consolation (Heb. 6:18; 2 Th. 2:16), and therefore ought to love one another. (2.) "*Comfort of love.* If there is any comfort in Christian love, in God's love to you, in your love to God, or in your brethren's love to us, in consideration of all this, be you like-minded. If you have ever found that comfort, if you would find it, if you indeed believe that the grace of love is a comfortable grace, abound in it." (3.) "*Fellowship of the Spirit.* If there is such a thing as communion with God and Christ by the Spirit, such a thing as the communion of saints, by virtue of their being animated and actuated by *one and the same Spirit,* be you like-minded; for Christian love and like-mindedness will preserve to us our communion with God and with one another." (4.) "*Any bowels and mercies,* in God and Christ, towards you. If you expect the benefit of God's compassions to yourselves, be you compassionate one to another. If there is such a thing as mercy to be found among the followers of Christ, if all who are sanctified have a disposition to holy pity, make it appear this way." How cogent are these arguments! One would think them enough to tame the most fierce, and mollify the hardest, heart. (5.) Another argument he insinuates is the comfort it would be to him: *Fulfil you my joy.* It is the joy of ministers to see people like-minded and living in love. He had been instrumental in bringing them to the grace of Christ and the love of God. "Now," says he, "if you have found any benefit by your participation of the gospel of Christ, if you have any comfort in it, or advantage by it, *fulfil the joy* of your poor minister, who preached the gospel to you."

2. He proposes some means to promote it. (1.) *Do nothing through strife and vain glory, v.* 3. There is no greater enemy to Christian love than pride and passion. If we do things in contradiction to our brethren, this is doing them through strife; if we do them through ostentation of ourselves, this is doing them through vain-glory: both are destructive of Christian love and kindle unchristian heats. Christ came to slay all enmities; therefore let there not be among Christians a spirit of opposition. Christ came to humble us, and therefore let there not be among us a spirit of pride. (2.) We must *esteem others in lowliness of mind better than ourselves,* be severe upon our own faults and charitable in our judgments of others, be quick in observing our own defects and infirmities, but ready to overlook and make favourable allowances for the defects of others. We must esteem the good

which is in others above that which is in ourselves; for we best know our own unworthiness and imperfections. (3.) We must interest ourselves in the concerns of others, not in a way of curiosity and censoriousness, or as *busy-bodies in other men's matters,* but in Christian love and sympathy: *Look not every man on his own things, but every man also on the things of others, v.* 4. A selfish spirit is destructive of Christian love. We must be concerned not only for our own credit, and ease, and safety, but for those of others also; and rejoice in the prosperity of others as truly as in our own. We must love our neighbour as ourselves, and make his case our own.

II. Here is a gospel pattern proposed to our imitation, and that is the example of our Lord Jesus Christ: *Let this mind be in you which was also in Christ Jesus, v.* 5. Observe, Christians must be of Christ's mind. We must bear a resemblance to his life, if we would have the benefit of his death. *If we have not the Spirit of Christ, we are none of his,* Rom. 8:9. Now what was the mind of Christ? He was eminently humble, and this is what we are peculiarly to learn of him. *Learn of me, for I am meek and lowly in heart,* Mt. 11:29. If we were lowly-minded, we should be like-minded; and, if we were like Christ, we should be lowly-minded. We must walk in the same spirit and in the same steps with the Lord Jesus, who humbled himself to sufferings and death for us; not only to satisfy God's justice, and pay the price of our redemption, but to set us an example, and that we might *follow his steps.* Now here we have the two natures and the two states of our Lord Jesus. It is observable that the apostle, having occasion to mention the Lord Jesus, and the mind which was in him, takes the hint to enlarge upon his person, and to give a particular description of him. It is a pleasing subject, and a gospel minister needs not think himself out of the way when he is upon it; any fit occasion should be readily taken.

1. Here are the two natures of Christ: his divine nature and his human nature. (1.) Here is his divine nature: *Who being in the form of God* (*v.* 6), partaking of the divine nature, as the eternal and only begotten Son of God. This agrees with Jn. 1:1, *In the beginning was the Word, and the Word was with God:* it is of the same import with being the *image of the invisible* God (Col. 1:15), and the *brightness of his glory, and express image of his person,* Heb. 1:3. *He thought it no robbery to be equal with God;* did not think himself guilty of any invasion of what did not belong to him, or assuming another's right. He said, *I and my Father are one,* Jn. 10:30. It is the highest degree of robbery for any mere man or mere creature to pretend to be equal with God, or profess himself *one with the Father.* This is for a man to rob God, not in tithes and offerings, but of the rights of his Godhead, Mal. 3:8. Some understand *being in the form of God — en morphē Theou hyparchōn,* of his appearance in a divine majestic glory to the patriarchs, and the Jews, under the Old Testament, which was often called the *glory,* and the *Shechinah.* The word is used in such a sense by the Septuagint and in the New Testament. *He appeared to the two disciples, en hetera morphē — In another form,* Mk. 16:12. *Metemorphōthē — he was transfigured* before them, Mt. 17:2. And *he thought it no robbery to be equal with God;* he did not greedily *catch at,* nor covet and affect to appear in that glory; he laid aside the majesty of his former appearance while he was here on earth, which is supposed to be the sense of the peculiar expression, *ouk harpagmon hēgēsato.* Vid. *Bishop Bull's Def.* cap. 2 sect. 4 et alibi, and *Whitby* in loc. (2.) His human nature: He was *made in the likeness of men,* and *found in fashion as a man.* He was really and truly man, *took part of our flesh and blood,* appeared in the nature and habit of man. And he voluntarily assumed human nature; it was his own act, and by his own consent. We cannot say that our participation of the human nature is so. Herein he *emptied himself,* divested himself of the honours and glories of the upper world, and of his former appearance, to clothe himself with the rags of human nature. *He was in all things like to us,* Heb. 2:17.

2. Here are his two estates, of humiliation and exaltation. (1.) His estate of humiliation. He not only took upon him the likeness and fashion of a man, but the *form of a servant,* that is, a man of mean estate. He was not only God's servant whom he had chosen, but he came to minister to men, and was among them as one who serveth in a mean and servile state. One would think that the Lord Jesus, if he would be a man, should have been a prince, and appeared in splendour. But quite the contrary: *He took upon him the form of a servant.* He was brought up meanly, probably working with his supposed father at his trade. His whole life was a life of humiliation, meanness, poverty, and disgrace; he had nowhere to lay his head, lived upon alms, was a *man of sorrows and acquainted with grief,* did not appear with external pomp, or any marks of distinction from other men. This was the humiliation of his life. But the lowest step of his humiliation was his dying the death of the cross. *He became obedient to death, even the death of the cross.* He not only suffered, but was actually and voluntarily obedient; he obeyed the law which he brought himself under as Mediator, and by which he was obliged to die. *I have power to lay down my life, and I have power to take it again: this commandment have I received of my Father,* Jn. 10:18. And he was *made under the law,* Gal. 4:4. There is an emphasis laid upon the manner of his dying, which had in it all the circumstances possible which are humbling: *Even the death of the cross,* a cursed, painful, and shameful death, — a death accursed by the law *(Cursed is he that hangeth on a tree)* — full of pain, the body nailed through the nervous parts (the hands and feet) and hanging with all its weight upon the cross, — and the death of a malefactor and a slave, not of a free-man, — exposed as a public spectacle. Such was the condescension of the blessed Jesus. (2.) His exaltation: *Wherefore God also hath highly exalted him.* His exaltation was the reward of his humiliation. Because he humbled himself, God exalted him; and he *highly exalted him, hyperypsōse,* raised him to an exceeding height. He exalted his whole person, the human nature as well as the divine; for he is spoken of as being in the form of God as well as in the fashion of man. As it respects the divine nature, it could only be the recognizing of his rights, or the display and appearance of the *glory he had with the Father before the world was* (Jn. 17:5), not any new acquisition of glory; and so the Father himself is said to be exalted. But the proper exaltation was of his human nature, which alone seems to be capable of it, though in conjunction with the divine. His exaltation here is made to consist in honour and power. In honour; so *he had a name above every name,* a title of dignity above all the creatures, men and angels. And in power: *Every knee must bow to him.* The whole creation must be in subjection to him: *things in heaven, and things in earth, and things under the earth,* the inhabitants of heaven and earth, the living and the dead. *At the name of Jesus;* not at the sound of the word, but the authority of Jesus; all should pay a solemn homage. And that *every tongue should confess that Jesus Christ is Lord* — every nation and language should publicly own the universal empire of the exalted Redeemer, and that *all power in heaven and earth is given to him,* Mt. 28:18. Observe the vast extent of the kingdom of Christ; it reaches to heaven and earth, and to all the creatures in each, to angels as well as men, and to the dead as well as the living. — *To the glory of God the Father.* Observe, It is to the glory of God the Father to confess that Jesus Christ is Lord; for it is his will that *all men should honour the Son as they honour the Father,* Jn. 5:23. Whatever respect is paid to Christ redounds to the honour of the Father. *He who receiveth me receiveth him who sent me,* Mt. 10:40.

Verses 12–13

I. He exhorts them to diligence and seriousness in the Christian course: *Work out your own salvation.* It is the salvation of our souls (1 Pt. 1:9), and our eternal salvation (Heb. 5:9), and contains deliverance from all the evils sin had brought upon us and exposed us to, and the possession of all good and whatsoever is necessary to our complete and final happiness. Observe, It concerns us above all things to secure the welfare of our souls: whatever becomes of other things, let us take care of our best interests. It is our own salvation, the salvation of our own souls. It is not for us to judge other people; we have enough to do to look to ourselves; and, though we must promote the common salvation (Jude 3) as much as we can, yet we must upon no account neglect our own. We are required to *work out our salvation, katergazesthe.* The word signifies *working thoroughly* at a thing, and taking *true pains.* Observe, We must be diligent in the use of all the means which conduce to our salvation. We must not only work at our salvation, by doing something now and then about it; but we must work out our salvation, by doing all that is to be done, and persevering therein to the end. Salvation is the great thing we should mind, and set our hearts upon; and we cannot attain salvation without the utmost care and diligence. He adds, *With fear and trembling,* that is, with great care and circumspection: "Trembling for fear lest you miscarry and come short. Be careful to do every thing in religion in the best manner, and fear lest under all your advantages you should so much as *seem to come short,"* Heb. 4:1. Fear is a great guard and preservative from evil.

II. He urges this from the consideration of their readiness always to obey the gospel: *"As you have always obeyed, not as in my presence only, but now much more in my absence, v.* 12. You have been always willing to comply with every discovery of the will of God; and that in my absence as well as presence. You make it to appear that regard to Christ, and care of your souls, sway more with you than any mode of showing respect whatsoever." They were not merely awed by the apostle's presence, but did it even *much more in his absence.* "And because *it is God who worketh in you,* do you work out your salvation. Work, for he worketh." It should encourage us to do our utmost, because our *labour shall not be in vain.* God is ready to concur with his grace, and assist our faithful endeavours. Observe, Though we must use our utmost endeavours in working out our salvation, yet still we must go forth, and go on, in a dependence upon the grace of God. His grace works in us in a way suitable to our natures, and in concurrence with our endeavours; and the operations of God's grace in us are so far from excusing, that they are intended to quicken and engage our endeavours. "And work out our salvation *with fear and trembling,* for *he worketh in you."* All our working depends upon his working in us. "Do not trifle with God by neglects and delays, lest you provoke him to withdraw his help, and all your endeavours prove in vain. Work with *fear,* for he works of his *good pleasure." — To will and to do:* he gives the whole ability. It is the grace of God which inclines the will to that which is good: and then enables us to perform it, and to act according to our principles. *Thou hast wrought all our works in us,* Isa. 26:12. *Of his good pleasure.* As there is no strength in us, so there is no merit in us. As we cannot act without God's grace, so we cannot claim it, nor pretend to deserve it. God's good will to us is the cause of his good work in us; and he is under no engagements to his creatures, but those of his gracious promise.

Verses 14–18

The apostle exhorts them in these verses to adorn their Christian profession by a suitable temper and behaviour, in several instances. 1. By a cheerful obedience to the commands of God (*v.* 14): *"Do all things,* do your duty in every branch of it, *without murmurings.* Do it, and do not find fault with it. Mind your work, and do not quarrel with it." God's commands were given to be obeyed, not to be disputed. This greatly adorns our profession, and shows we serve a good Master, whose service is freedom and whose work is its own reward. 2. By peaceableness and love one to another. "Do all things *without disputing,* wrangling, and debating one another; because the light of truth and the life of religion are often lost in the heats and mists of disputation." 3. By a blameless conversation towards all men (*v.* 15): *"That you may be blameless and harmless, the sons of God, without rebuke;* that you be not injurious to any in word or deed, and give no just occasion of offence." We should endeavour not only to be harmless, but to be blameless; not only not to do hurt, but not to come under the just suspicion of it. *Blameless and sincere;* so some read it. Blameless before men, sincere towards God. The *sons of God.* It becomes those to be blameless and harmless who stand in such a relation, and are favoured with such a privilege. The children of God should differ from the sons of men. *Without rebuke — amōmēta.* Momus was a carping deity among the Greeks, mentioned by Hesiod and Lucian, who did nothing himself, and found fault with every body and every thing. From him all carpers at other men, and rigid censurers of their works, were called *Momi.* The sense of the expression is, "Walk so circumspectly that Momus himself may have no occasion to cavil at you, that the severest censurer may find no fault with you." We should aim and endeavour, not only to get to heaven, but to get thither without a blot; and, like Demetrius, to *have a good report of all men, and of the truth,* 3 Jn. 12. *In the midst of a crooked and perverse generation;* that is, among the heathens, and those who are without. Observe, Where there is no true religion, little is to be expected but crookedness and perverseness; and the more crooked and perverse others are among whom we live, and the more apt to cavil, the more careful we should be to keep ourselves blameless and harmless. Abraham and Lot must not *strive, because the Canaanite and Perizzite dwelt in the land,* Gen. 13:7. *Among whom you shine as lights in the world.* Christ is the light of the world, and good Christians are lights in the world. When God raises up a good man in any place, he sets up a light in that place. Or it may be read imperatively: *Among whom shine you as lights:* compare Mt. 5:16, *Let your light so shine before men.* Christians should endeavour not only to approve themselves to God, but to recommend themselves to others, that they may also glorify God. They must shine as well as be sincere. — *Holding forth the word of life, v.* 16. The gospel is called the word of life because it reveals and proposes to us eternal life through Jesus Christ. *Life and immortality are brought to light by the gospel,* 2 Tim. 1:10. It is our duty not only to hold fast, but to hold forth the word of life; not only to hold it fast for our own benefit, but to hold it forth for the benefit of others, to hold it forth as the candlestick holds forth the candle, which makes it appear to advantage all around, or as the luminaries of the heavens, which shed their influence far and wide. This Paul tells them would be his joy: *"That I may rejoice in the day of Christ,"* not only rejoice in your stedfastness, but in your usefulness." He would have them think his pains well bestowed, and that *he had not run in vain, nor laboured in vain.* Observe, (1.) The work of the ministry requires the putting forth of the whole man: all that is within us is little enough to be employed in it; as in running and labouring. Running denotes vehemence and vigour, and continual pressing forward; labour denotes constancy and close application. (2.) It is a great joy to ministers when they perceive that they have not *run in vain, nor laboured in vain;* and it will be their rejoicing in the day of Christ, when their converts will be their crown. *What is our hope, or joy, or crown of rejoicing? Are not even you in the presence of our Lord Jesus Christ at his coming? For you are our glory and joy,* 1 Th. 2:19, 20. The apostle not only ran and laboured for them with satisfaction, but shows that he was ready to suffer for their good (v. 17): *Yea, and if I be offered upon the sacrifice and service of your faith, I joy and rejoice with you all.* He could reckon himself happy if he could promote the honour of Christ, the edification of the church, and the welfare of the souls of men; though it were not only by hazarding, but by laying down, his life: he could willingly be a sacrifice at their altars, to serve the faith of God's elect. Could Paul think it worth while to shed his blood for the service of the church, and shall we think it much to take a little pains? Is not that worth our labour which he thought worth his life? *If I be offered,* or *poured* out as the wine of the *drink-offerings, spendomai.* 2 Tim. 4:6, *I am now ready to be offered.* He could rejoice to seal his doctrine with his blood (v. 18): *For the same cause also do you joy and rejoice with me.* It is the will of God that good Christians should be much in rejoicing; and those who are happy in good ministers have a great deal of reason to joy and rejoice with them. If the minister loves the people, and is willing to spend and be spent for their welfare, the people have reason to love the minister and to *joy and rejoice with him.*

Verses 19–30

Paul takes particular notice of two good ministers; for though he was himself a great apostle, and *laboured more abundantly than they all,* yet he took all occasions to speak with respect of those who were far his inferiors.

I. He speaks of Timothy, whom he intended to send to the Philippians, that he might have an account of their state. See Paul's care of the churches, and the comfort he had in their well-doing. He was in pain when he had not heard of them for a good while, and therefore would send Timothy to enquire, and bring him an account: *For I have no man likeminded, who will naturally care for your state.* Timothy was a non-such. There were, no doubt, many good ministers, who were in care for the souls of those for whom they preached; but none comparable to Timothy, a man of an excellent spirit and tender heart. *Who will naturally care for your state.* Observe, It is best with us when our duty becomes in a manner natural to us. Timothy was a genuine son of blessed Paul, and walked in the same spirit and the same steps. *Naturally,* that is, sincerely, and not in pretence only: with a willing heart and upright view, so agreeably to the make of his mind. Note, 1. It is the duty of ministers to care for the state of their people and be concerned for their welfare: *I seek not yours, but you,* 2 Co. 12:14. 2. It is a rare thing to find one who does it naturally: such a one is remarkable and distinguished

among his brethren. *All seek their own, not the things which are Jesus Christ's, v.* 21. Did Paul say this in haste, as David said, *All men are liars?* Ps. 116:11. Was there so general a corruption among ministers so early that there was not one among them who cared for the state of their people? We must not understand it so: he means the generality; *all,* that is, either the most, or all in comparison of Timothy. Note, Seeking our own interest to the neglect of Jesus Christ is a very great sin, and very common among Christians and ministers. Many prefer their own credit, ease, and safety, before truth, holiness, and duty, the things of their own pleasure and reputation before the things of Christ's kingdom and his honour and interest in the world: but Timothy was none of these. — *You know the proof of him, v.* 22. Timothy was a man who had been tried, and had made *full proof of his ministry* (2 Tim. 4:5), and was faithful in all that befel him. All the churches with whom he had acquaintance knew the proof of him. He was a man as good as he seemed to be; and *served Christ so as to be acceptable to God,* and *approved of men,* Rom. 14:18. "You not only know the name of him, and the face of him, but the proof of him, and have experienced his affection and fidelity in your service," *that, as a son with a father, he hath served with me in the gospel.* He was Paul's assistant in many places where he preached, and served with him in the gospel with all the dutiful respect which a child pays to a father, and with all the love and cheerfulness with which a child is serviceable to his father. Their ministrations together were with great respect on the one side and great tenderness and kindness on the other — an admirable example to elder and younger ministers united in the same service. Paul designed to send him shortly: *Him therefore I hope to send presently, as soon as I shall see how it will go with me, v.* 23. He was now a prisoner, and did not know what would be the issue; but, according as it turned, he would dispose of Timothy. Nay, he hoped to come himself (v. 24): *But I trust in the Lord that I also myself shall come shortly.* He hoped he should soon be set at liberty, and be able to pay them a visit. Paul desired his liberty, not that he might take his pleasure, but that he might do good. — *I trust in the Lord.* He expresses his hope and confidence of seeing them, with a humble dependence and submission to the divine will. See Acts 18:21; 1 Co. 4:19; James 4:15; and Heb. 6:3.

II. Concerning Epaphroditus, whom he calls *his brother, and companion in labour, and fellow-soldier,* his Christian brother, to whom he bore a tender affection, — his companion in the work and sufferings of the gospel, who submitted to the same labours and hardships with himself, — and their messenger, one who was sent by them to him, probably to consult him about some affairs relating to their church, or to bring a present from them for his relief for he adds, and *who ministered to my wants.* He seems to be the same who is called *Epaphras,* Col. 4:12. He had an earnest desire to come to them, and Paul was willing he should. It seems, 1. Epaphroditus had been sick: *They had heard that he had been sick, v.* 26. And *indeed he was sick, nigh unto death, v.* 27. Sickness is a calamity common to men, to good men and ministers. But why did not the apostle heal him, who was endued with a power of curing diseases, as well as raising the dead? Acts 20:10. Probably because that was intended as a sign to others, and to confirm the truth of the gospel, and therefore needed not be exercised one towards another. *These signs shall follow those who believe, they shall lay hands on the sick, and they shall recover,* Mk. 16:17, 18. And perhaps they had not that power at all times, and at their own discretion, but only when some great end was to be served by it, and when God saw fit. It was proper to Christ, who had *the Spirit above measure.* 2. The Philippians were exceedingly sorry to hear of his sickness. They were full of heaviness, as well as he, upon the tidings of it: for he was one, it seems, for whom they had a particular respect and affection, and thought fit to choose out to send to the apostle. 3. It pleased God to recover and spare him: *But God had mercy on him, v.* 27. The apostle owns it is a great mercy to himself, as well as to Epaphroditus and others. Though the church was blessed at that time with extraordinary gifts, they could even then ill spare a good minister. He was sensibly touched with the thoughts of so great a loss: *Lest I should have sorrow upon sorrow;* that is, "Lest, besides the sorrow of my own imprisonment, I should have the sorrow of his death." Or perhaps some other good ministers had died lately, which had been a great affliction to him: and, if this had died now, it would have been a fresh grief to him, and *sorrow added to*

sorrow. 4. Epaphroditus was willing to pay a visit to the Philippians, that he might be comforted with those who had sorrowed for him when he was sick: *"That when you see him again you may rejoice* (v. 28), that you may yourselves see how well he has recovered, and what reason you have for the thankfulness and joy upon his account." He gave himself the pleasure of comforting them by the sight of so dear a friend. 5. Paul recommends him to their esteem and affection: *"Receive him therefore in the Lord with all gladness, and hold such in reputation:* account such men valuable, who are zealous and faithful, and let them be highly loved and regarded. Show your joy and respect by all the expressions of hearty affection and good opinion." It seems he had caught his illness in the work of God: *It was for the work of Christ that he was nigh to death, and to supply their lack of service to him.* The apostle does not blame him for his indiscretion in hazarding his life, but reckons they ought to love him the more upon that account. Observe, (1.) Those who truly love Christ, and are hearty in the interests of his kingdom, will think it very well worth their while to hazard their health and life to do him service, and promote the edification of his church. (2.) They were to receive him with joy, as newly recovered from sickness. It is an endearing consideration to have our mercies restored to us after danger of removal, and should make them the more valued and improved. What is given us in answer to prayer should be received with great thankfulness and joy.

CHAPTER 3

He cautions them against judaizing seducers (v. 1–3) and proposes his own example: and here he enumerates the privileges of his Jewish state which he rejected (v. 4–8), describes the matter of his own choice (v. 9–16), and closes with an exhortation to beware of wicked men, and to follow his example (v. 17–21).

Verses 1–3

It seems the church of the Philippians, though a faithful and flourishing church, was disturbed by the judaizing teachers, who endeavoured to keep up the law of Moses, and mix the observances of it with the doctrine of Christ and his institutions. He begins the chapter with warnings against these seducers.

I. He exhorts them to *rejoice in the Lord* (v. 1), to rest satisfied in the interest they had in him and the benefit they hoped for by him. It is the character and temper of sincere Christians to rejoice in Christ Jesus. The more we take of the comfort of our religion the more closely we shall cleave to it: the more we rejoice in Christ the more willing we shall be to do and suffer for him, and the less danger we shalt be in of being drawn away from him. The *joy of the Lord is our strength,* Neh. 8:10.

II. He cautions them to take heed of those false teachers: *To write the same thing to you to me indeed is not grievous, but for you it is safe;* that is, the same things which I have already preached to you; as if he had said, "What has been presented to your ears shall be presented to your eyes: what I have spoken formerly shall now be written; to show that I am still of the same mind." *To me indeed is not grievous.* Observe, 1. Ministers must not think any thing grievous to themselves which they have reason to believe is safe and edifying to the people. 2. It is good for us often to hear the same truths, to revive the remembrance and strengthen the impression of things of importance. It is a wanton curiosity to desire always to hear some new thing. It is a needful caution he here gives: *Beware of dogs, v.* 2. The prophet calls the false prophets dumb dogs (Isa. 56:10), to which the apostle here seems to refer. *Dogs,* for their malice against the faithful professors of the gospel of Christ, barking at them and biting them. They cried up good works in opposition to the faith of Christ; but Paul calls them evil workers: they boasted themselves to be of the circumcision; but he calls them the concision: they rent and tore the church of Christ, and cut it to pieces; or contended for an abolished rite, a mere insignificant cutting of the flesh.

III. He describes true Christians, who are indeed the circumcision, the spiritual circumcision, the peculiar of people of God, who are in covenant with him, as the Old-Testament Israelites were: *We are the circumcision, who worship God in the spirit, and rejoice in Christ Jesus, and have no confidence in the flesh.* Here are three characters: — 1. They worshipped in the spirit, in opposition to the carnal ordinances of the Old-Testament, which consist in meats, and drinks, and divers washings, etc. Christianity takes us off from these things, and teaches us to be inward with God in all the duties of religious worship. We must *worship God in spirit,* Jn. 4:24. The work of religion is to no purpose any further than the heart is employed in it. *Whatsoever we do, we must do it heartily as unto the Lord;* and we must worship God in the strength and grace of the Divine Spirit, which is so peculiar to the gospel state, which is the *ministration of the spirit,* 2 Co. 3:8. 2. They *rejoice in Christ Jesus,* and not in the peculiar privileges of the Jewish church, or what answers to them in the Christian church — mere outward enjoyments and performances. They rejoice in their relation to Christ and interest in him. God made it the duty of the Israelites to rejoice before him in the courts of his house; but now that the substance has come the shadows are done away, and we are to rejoice in Christ Jesus only. 3. They have no *confidence in the flesh,* in those carnal ordinances and outward performances. We must be taken off from trusting in our own bottom, that we may build only on Jesus Christ, the everlasting foundation. Our confidence, as well as our joy, is proper to him.

Verses 4–8

The apostle here proposes himself for an example of trusting in Christ only, and not in his privileges as an Israelite.

I. He shows what he had to boast of as a Jew and a Pharisee. Let none think that the apostle despised these things (as men commonly do) because he had them not himself to glory in. No, if he would have gloried and trusted in the flesh, he had as much cause to do so as any man: *If any other man thinketh that he hath whereof to trust in the flesh, I more, v.* 4. He had as much to boast of as any Jew of them all. 1. His birth-right privileges. He was not a proselyte, but a native Israelite: *of the stock of Israel.* And he was *of the tribe of Benjamin,* in which tribe the temple stood, and which adhered to Judah when all the other tribes revolted. Benjamin was the father's darling, and this was a favourite tribe. *A Hebrew of the Hebrews,* an Israelite on both sides, by father and mother, and from one generation to another; none of his ancestors had matched with Gentiles. 2. He could boast of his relations to the church and the covenant, for he was *circumcised the eighth day;* he had the token of God's covenant in his flesh, and was circumcised the very day which God had appointed. 3. For learning, he was a Pharisee, brought up at the feet of Gamaliel, an eminent doctor of the law: and was a scholar learned in all the learning of the Jews, taught according to the perfect manner of the laws of the fathers, Acts 22:3. He was a *Pharisee, the son of a Pharisee* (Acts 23:6), and *after the most strict sect of his religion lived a Pharisee,* Acts 26:5. 4. He had a blameless conversation: *Toughing the righteousness which is of the law, blameless:* as far as the Pharisees' exposition of the law went, and as to the mere letter of the law and outward observance of it, he could acquit himself from the breach of it and could not be accused by any. 5. He had been an active man for his religion. As he made a strict profession of it, under the title and character of a Pharisee, so he persecuted those whom he looked upon as enemies to it. *Concerning zeal, persecuting the church.* 6. He showed that he was in good earnest, though he had a zeal without knowledge to direct and govern the exercise of it: *I was zealous towards God, as you all are this day, and I persecuted this way unto the death,* Acts 22:3, 4. All this was enough to have made a proud Jew confident, and was stock sufficient to set up with for his justification. But,

II. The apostle tells us here how little account he made of these, in comparison of his interest in Christ and his expectations from him: *But what things were gain to me those have I counted loss for Christ* (*v.* 7); that is, those things which he had counted gain while he was a Pharisee, and which he had before reckoned up, *these he counted loss for Christ.* "I should have reckoned myself an unspeakable loser of, to adhere to them, I had lost my interest in Jesus Christ." He counted them loss; not only insufficient to enrich him, but what would certainly impoverish and ruin him, if he trusted to them, in opposition to Christ. Observe, The apostle did not persuade them to do any thing but what he had himself did, to quit any thing but what he had himself quitted, nor venture on any bottom but what he himself had ventured his immortal soul upon. — *Yea doubtless, and I count all things but loss for the excellency of the knowledge of Christ Jesus my Lord, v.* 8. Here the apostle explains himself. 1. He tells us what it was that he was ambitious of and reached after: it was the knowledge of Christ Jesus his Lord, a believing experimental acquaintance with Christ as Lord; not a merely notional and speculative, but a practical and efficacious knowledge of him. So knowledge is sometimes put for faith: *By his knowledge,* or the knowledge of him, *shall my righteous servant justify many,* Isa. 53:11. And it is the excellency of knowledge. There is an abundant and transcendent excellency in the doctrine of Christ, or the Christian religion above all the knowledge of nature, and improvements of human wisdom; for it is suited to the case of fallen sinners, and furnishes them with all they need and all they can desire and hope for, with all saving wisdom and saving grace. 2. He shows how he had quitted his privileges as a Jew and a Pharisee: *Yea doubtless;* his expression rises with a holy triumph and elevation, *alla men oun ge kai.* There are five particles in the original: *But indeed even also do I count all things but loss.* He had spoken before of *those things,* his Jewish privileges: here he speaks of *all things,* all worldly enjoyments and mere outward privileges whatsoever, things of a like kind or any other kind which could stand in competition with Christ for the throne in his heart, or pretend to merit and desert. There he had said that he did count them but loss; but it might be asked, "Did he continue still in the same mind, did he not repent his renouncing them?" No, now he speaks in the present tense: *Yea doubtless, I do count them but loss.* But it may be said, "It is easy to say so; but what would he do when he came to the trial?" Why he tells us that he had himself practised according to this estimate of the case: *For whom I have suffered the loss of all things.* He had quitted all his honours and advantages, as a Jew and a Pharisee, and submitted to all the disgrace and suffering which attended the profession and preaching of the gospel. When he embarked in the bottom of the Christian religion, he ventured all in it, and suffered the loss of all for the privileges of a Christian. Nay, he not only counted them loss, but dung, *skybala — offals* thrown to dogs; they are not only less valuable than Christ, but in the highest degree contemptible, when they come in competition with him. Note, The New Testament never speaks of saving grace in any terms of diminution, but on the contrary represents it as the fruits of the divine Spirit and the image of God in the soul of man; as a divine nature, and the seed of God: and faith is called precious faith; and meekness is in the *sight of God of great price,* 1 Pt. 3:4; 2 Pt. 1:1, etc.

Verses 9–14

We now heard what the apostle renounced; let us now see what he laid hold on, and resolved to cleave to, namely, Christ and heaven. He had his heart on these two great peculiarities of the Christian religion.

I. The apostle had his heart upon Christ as his righteousness. This is illustrated in several instances. 1. He desired to win Christ; and an unspeakable gainer he would reckon himself if he had but an interest in Christ and his righteousness, and if Christ became his Lord and his Saviour: *That I may win him;* as the runner wins the prize, as the sailor makes the port he is bound for. The expression intimates that we have need to strive for him and after him, and that all is little enough to win him. 2. That he *might be found in him* (*v.* 9), as the manslayer was found in the city of refuge, where he was safe from the avenger of blood, Num. 35:25. Or it alludes to a judicial appearance; so we are to be found of our Judge in peace, 2 Pt. 3:14. We are undone without a righteousness wherein to appear before God, for we are guilty. There is a righteousness provided for us in Jesus Christ, and it is a complete and perfect righteousness. None can have interest or benefit by it but those who come off from confidence in themselves, and are brought heartily to believe in him. *"Not having my own righteousness, which is of the law;* not thinking that my outward observances and good deeds are able to atone for my bad ones, or that by setting the one over against the other I can come to balance accounts with God. No, the righteousness which I depend upon is that *which is through the faith of Christ,* not a legal, but evangelical righteousness: *The righteousness which is of God by faith,* ordained and appointed of God." The Lord Jesus Christ is the Lord our righteousness, Isa. 45:24; Jer. 23:6. Had he not been God, he could not have been our righteousness; the transcendent excellence of the divine nature put such a value upon, and such a virtue into, his sufferings, that they became sufficient to satisfy for the sins of the world, and to bring in a righteousness which will be effectual to all that believe. Faith is the ordained means of actual interest and saving benefit in all the purchase of his blood. It is *by faith in his blood,* Rom. 3:25. 3. That he might know Christ (*v.* 10): *That I may know him, and the power of his resurrection, and the fellowship of his sufferings.* Faith is called knowledge, Isa. 53:11. Knowing him here is believing in him: it is an experimental knowledge of the *power of his resurrection, and the fellowship of his sufferings,* or feeling the transforming efficacy and virtue of them. Observe, The apostle was as ambitious of being sanctified as he was of being justified. He was as desirous to know the power of Christ's death and resurrection killing sin in him, and raising him up to newness of life, as he was to receive the benefit of Christ's death and resurrection in his justification. 4. That he might be conformable unto him, and this also is meant of his sanctification. We are then made conformable to his death when we die to sin, as Christ died for sin, when we are crucified with Christ, the flesh and affections of it mortified, and the *world is crucified to us,* and *we to the world, by virtue of the cross of Christ.* This is our conformity to his death.

II. The apostle had his heart upon heaven as his happiness: *If by any means I might attain to the resurrection of the dead, v.* 11.

1. The happiness of heaven is here called the resurrection of the dead, because, though the souls of the faithful, when they depart, are immediately with Christ, yet their happiness will not be complete till the general resurrection of the dead at the last day, when soul and body shall be glorified together. *Anastasis* sometimes signifies the future state. This the apostle had his eye upon; this he would attain. There will be a resurrection of the unjust, who shall arise to *shame and everlasting contempt;* and our care must be to escape that: but the joyful and glorious resurrection of saints is called *the resurrection, kat' exochēn — by eminence,* because it is in virtue of Christ's resurrection, as their head and first-fruits; whereas the wicked shall rise only by the power of Christ, as their judge. To the saints it will be indeed a resurrection, a return to bliss, and life, and glory; while the resurrection of the wicked is a rising from the grave, but a return to a second death. It is called the *resurrection of the just,* and the *resurrection of life* (Jn. 5:29), and they are *counted worthy to obtain that world and the resurrection from the dead,* Lu. 20:35.

2. This joyful resurrection the apostle pressed towards. He was willing to do any thing, or suffer any thing, that he might attain that resurrection. The hope and prospect of it carried him with so much courage and constancy through all the difficulties he met with in his work. He speaks as if they were in danger of missing it, and coming short of it. A holy fear of coming short is an excellent means of perseverance. Observe, His care to be found in Christ was in order to his attaining the resurrection of the dead. Paul himself did not hope to attain it through his own merit and righteousness, but through the merit and righteousness of Jesus Christ. "Let me be found in Christ, that I may attain the resurrection of the dead, be found a believer in him, and interested in him by faith." Observe,

(1.) He looks upon himself to be in a state of imperfection and trial: *Not as though I had already attained, or were already perfect, v.* 12. Observe, The best men in the world will readily own their imperfection in the present state. We have not yet attained, are not already perfect; there is still much wanting in all our duties, and graces, and comforts. If Paul had not attained to perfection (who had reached to so high a pitch of holiness), much less have we. Again, *Brethren, I count not myself to have apprehended* (*v.* 13), *ou logizomai.* "I make this judgment of the case; I thus reason with myself." Observe, Those who think they have grace enough give proof that they have little enough, or rather that they have none at all; because, wherever there is true grace, there is a desire of more grace, and a pressing towards the perfection of grace.

(2.) What the apostle's actings were under this conviction. Considering that he had not already attained, and had not apprehended, he pressed forward: *"I follow after* (*v.* 12), *diōkō — I pursue* with vigour, as one following after the game. I endeavour to get more grace and do more good, and never think I have done enough: *If that I may apprehend that for which also I am apprehended of Christ Jesus."* Observe, [1.] Whence our grace comes — from our being apprehended of Christ Jesus. It is not our laying hold of Christ first, but his laying hold of us, which is our happiness and salvation. *We love him because he first loved us,* 1 Jn. 4:19. Not our keeping hold of Christ, but his keeping hold of us, is our safety. We are *kept by his mighty power through faith unto salvation,* 1 Pt. 1:5. Observe, [2.] What the happiness of heaven is: it is *to apprehend that for which we are apprehended of Christ.* When Christ laid hold of us, it was to bring us to heaven; and to apprehend that for which he apprehended us is to attain the perfection of our bliss. He adds further (*v.* 13): *This one thing I do* (this was his great care and concern), *forgetting those things which are behind, and reaching forth to those things which are before.* There is a sinful forgetting of past sins and past mercies, which ought to be remembered for the exercise of constant repentance and thankfulness to God. But Paul forgot the things which were behind so as not to be content with present measures of grace: he was still for having more and more. So he *reaches forth, epekteinomenos — stretched* himself forward, bearing towards his point: it is expressive of a vehement concern.

(3.) The apostle's aim in these actings: *I press towards the mark, for the prize of the high calling of God in Christ Jesus, v.* 14. He pressed towards the mark. As he who runs a race never takes up short of the end, but is still making forwards as fast as he can, so those who have heaven in their eye must still be pressing forward to it in holy desires and hopes, and constant endeavours and preparations. The fitter we grow for heaven the faster we must press towards it. Heaven is called here the mark, because it is that which every good Christian has in his eye; as the archer has his eye fixed upon the mark he designs to hit. *For the prize of the high calling.* Observe, A Christian's calling is a high calling: it is from heaven, as its original; and it is to heaven in its tendency. Heaven is the *prize of the high calling; to brabeion — the prize* we fight for, and run for, and wrestle for, what we aim at in all we do, and what will reward all our pains. It is of great use in the Christian course to keep our eye upon heaven. This is proper to give us measures in all our service, and to quicken us every step we take; and it is of God, from whom we are to expect it. *Eternal life is the gift of God* (Rom. 6:23), but it is in Christ Jesus; through his hand it must come to us, as it is procured for us by him. There is no getting to heaven as our home but by Christ as our way.

Verses 15–16

The apostle, having proposed himself as an example, urges the Philippians to follow it. Let the same mind be in us which was in blessed Paul. We see here how he was minded; let us be like-minded, and set our hearts upon Christ and heaven, as he did. 1. He shows that this was the thing wherein all good Christians were agreed, to make Christ all in all, and set their hearts upon another world. This is that whereto we have all attained. However good Christians may differ in their sentiments about other things, this is what they are agreed in, that Christ is a Christian's all, that to win Christ and to be found in him involve our happiness both here and hereafter. And therefore let us walk by the same rule, and mind the same thing. Having made Christ our all, *to us to live must be Christ.* Let us agree to press towards the mark, and make heaven our end. 2. That this is a good reason why Christians who differ in smaller matters should yet bear with one another, because they are agreed in the main matter: "*If in any thing you be otherwise minded* — if you differ from one another, and are not of the same judgment as to meats and days, and other matters of the Jewish law — yet you must not judge one another, while you all meet now in Christ as your centre, and hope to meet shortly in heaven as your home. As for other matters of difference, lay no great stress upon them, *God shall reveal even this unto you.* Whatever it is wherein you differ, you must wait till God give you a better understanding, which he will do in his due time. In the mean time, *as far as you have attained,* you must go together in the ways of God, join together in all the great things in which you are agreed, and wait for further light in the minor things wherein you differ."

Verses 17–21

He closes the chapter with warnings and exhortations.

I. He warns them against following the examples of seducers and evil teachers (*v.* 18, 19): *Many walk, of whom I have told you often, and now tell you weeping, that they are the enemies of the cross of Christ.* Observe,

1. There are many called by Christ's name who are enemies to Christ's cross, and the design and intention of it. Their walk is a surer evidence what they are than their profession. By *their fruits you shall know them,* Mt. 7:20. The apostle warns people against such, (1.) Very frequently: *I have told you often.* We so little heed the warnings given us that we have need to have them repeated. *To write the same things is safe, v.* 1. (2.) Feelingly and affectionately: *I now tell you weeping.* Paul was upon proper occasions a weeping preacher, as Jeremiah was a weeping prophet. Observe, An old sermon may be preached with new affections; what we say often we may say again, if we say it affectionately, and are ourselves under the power of it.

2. He gives us the characters of those who were the enemies of the cross of Christ. (1.) Whose God is their belly. They minded nothing but their sensual appetites. A wretched idol it is, and a scandal for any, but especially for Christians, to sacrifice the favour of God, the peace of their conscience, and their eternal happiness to it. Gluttons and drunkards make a god of their belly, and all their care is to please it and make provision for it. The same observance which good people give to God epicures give to their appetites. Of such he says, *They serve not the Lord Jesus Christ, but their own bellies,* Rom. 16:18. (2.) They glory in their shame. They not only sinned, but boasted of it and gloried in that of which they ought to have been ashamed. Sin is the sinner's shame, especially when it is gloried in. "They value themselves for what is their blemish and reproach." (3.) They mind earthly things. Christ came by his cross to *crucify the world to us and us to the world;* and those who mind earthly things act directly contrary to the cross of Christ, and this great design of it. They relish earthly things, and have no relish of the things which are spiritual and heavenly. They set their hearts and affections on earthly things; they love them, and even dote upon them, and have a confidence and complacency in them. He gives them this character, to show how absurd it would be for Christians to follow the example of such or be led away by them; and, to deter us all from so doing, he reads their doom. (4.) Whose end is destruction. Their way seems pleasant, but death and hell are at the end of it. *What fruit had you then in those things whereof you are now ashamed? For the end of those things is death,* Rom. 6:21. It is dangerous following them, though it is going down the stream; for, if we choose their way, we have reason to fear their end. Perhaps he alludes to the total destruction of the Jewish nation.

II. He proposes himself and his brethren for an example, in opposition to these evil examples: *Brethren, be followers together of me, and mark those who walk as you have us for an example, v.* 17. Mark them out for your pattern. He explains himself (*v.* 20) by their regard to Christ and heaven: *For our conversation is in heaven.* Observe, Good Christians, even while they are here on earth, have their conversation in heaven. Their *citizenship* is there, *politeuma.* As if he had said, We stand related the that world, and are citizens of the New Jerusalem. This world is not our home, but that is. There our greatest privileges and concerns lie. And, because our citizenship is there, our conversation is there; being related to that world, we keep up a correspondence with it. The life of a Christian is in heaven, where his head is, and his home is, and where he hopes to be shortly; he *sets his affections upon things above;* and where his heart is there will his conversation be. The apostle had pressed them to follow him and other ministers of Christ: "Why," might they say, "you are a company of poor, despised, persecuted people, who make no figure, and pretend to no advantages in the world; who will follow you?" "Nay," says he, "but our conversation is in heaven. We have a near relation and a great pretension to the other world, and are not so mean and despicable as we are represented." It is good having fellowship with those who have fellowship with Christ, and conversation with those whose conversation is in heaven.

1. Because we look for the Saviour from heaven (*v.* 20): *Whence also we look for the Saviour, the Lord Jesus Christ.* He is not here, he has ascended, he has entered within the veil for us; and we expect his second coming thence, to gather in all the citizens of that New Jerusalem to himself.

2. Because at the second coming of Christ we expect to be happy and glorified there. There is good reason to have our conversation in heaven, not only because Christ is now there, but because we hope to be there shortly: *Who shall change our vile bodies, that they may be fashioned like unto his glorious body, v.* 21. There is a glory reserved for the bodies of the saints, which they will be instated in at the resurrection. The body is now at the best a *vile body, to sōma tēs tapeinōseōs hēmōn — the body of our humiliation:* it has its rise and origin from the earth, it is supported out of the earth, and is subject to many diseases and to death at last. Besides, it is often the occasion and instrument of much sin, which is called the *body of this death,* Rom. 7:24. Or it may be understood of its vileness when it lies in the grave; at the resurrection it will be found a vile body, resolved into rottenness and dust; the *dust will return to the earth as it was,* Eccl. 12:7. But it will be made a glorious body; and not only raised again to life, but raised to great advantage. Observe, (1.) The sample of this change, and that is, the glorious body of Christ; when he was transfigured upon the mount, *his face did shine as the sun, and his raiment was white as the light,* Mt. 17:2. He went to heaven clothed with a body, that he might take possession of the inheritance in our nature, and be not only the *first-born from the dead,* but the *first-born* of the *children of the resurrection.* We shall be *conformed to the image of his Son, that he may be the first-born among many brethren,* Rom. 8:29. (2.) The power by which this change will be wrought: *According to the working whereby he is able even to subdue all things unto himself.* There is an efficacy of power, an *exceeding greatness of power,* and the *working of mighty power,* Eph. 1:19. It is matter of comfort to us that he can subdue all things to himself, and sooner or later will bring over all into his interest. And the resurrection will be wrought by this power. *I will raise him up at the last day,* Jn. 6:44. Let this confirm our faith of the resurrection, that we not only have the scriptures, which assure us it shall be, but we *know the power of God,* which can effect it, Mt. 22:29. At Christ's resurrection was a glorious instance of the divine power, and therefore *he is declared to be the Son of God with power, by the resurrection from the dead* (Rom. 1:4), so will our resurrection be: and his resurrection is a standing evidence, as well as pattern, of ours. And then all the enemies of the Redeemer's kingdom will be completely conquered. Not only he *who had the power of death,* that is, *the devil* (Heb. 2:14), but the *last enemy, shall be destroyed,* that is, *death,* 1 Co. 15:26, *shall be swallowed up in victory, v.* 54.

CHAPTER 4

Exhortations to several Christian duties, as stedfastness, unanimity, joy, etc. (*v.* 1–9). The apostle's grateful acknowledgments of the Philippians' kindness to him, with expressions of his own content, and desire of their good (*v.* 10–19). He concludes the epistle with praise, salutations, and blessing (*v.* 20–23).

Verses 1–9

The apostle begins the chapter with exhortations to divers Christian duties.

I. To stedfastness in our Christian profession, *v.* 1. It is inferred from the close of the foregoing chapter: *Therefore stand fast,* etc. Seeing our *conversation is in heaven,* and we look for the Saviour to come thence and fetch us thither, *therefore let us stand fast.* Note, The believing hope and prospect of eternal life should engage us to be steady, even, and constant, in our Christian course. Observe here,

1. The compellations are very endearing: *My brethren, dearly beloved and longed for, my joy and crown;* and again, *My dearly beloved.* Thus he expresses the pleasure he took in them, the kindness he had for them, to convey his exhortations to them with so much the greater advantage. He looked upon them as his brethren, though he was a great apostle. *All we are brethren.* There is difference of gifts, graces, and attainments, yet, being renewed by the same Spirit, after the same image, we are brethren; as the children of the same parents, though of different ages, statures, and complexions. Being brethren, (1.) He loved them, and loved them dearly: *Dearly beloved;* and again, *My dearly beloved.* Warm affections become ministers and Christians towards one another. Brotherly love must always go along with brotherly relation. (2.) He loved them and longed for them, longed to see them and hear from them, longed for their welfare and was earnestly desirous of it. *I long after you all in the bowels of Jesus Christ, ch.* 1:8. (3.) He loved them and rejoiced in them. They were his joy; he had no greater joy than to hear of their spiritual health and prosperity. *I rejoiced greatly that I found of thy children walking in the truth,* 2 Jn. 4; 3 Jn. 4. (4.) he loved them and gloried in them. They were his crown as well as his joy. Never was proud ambitious man more pleased with the ensigns of honour than Paul was with the evidences of the sincerity of their faith and obedience. All this is to prepare his way to greater regard.

2. The exhortation itself: *So stand fast in the Lord.* Being in Christ, they must stand fast in him, be even and steady in their walk with him, and close and constant unto the end. Or, To *stand fast in the Lord* is to stand fast in his strength and by his grace; not trusting in ourselves, and disclaiming any sufficiency of our own. We must be *strong in the Lord, and in the power of his might,* Eph. 6:10. "So stand fast, so as you have done hitherto, stand fast unto the end, so as you are by beloved, and my joy and crown; so stand fast as those in whose welfare and perseverance I am so nearly interested and concerned."

II. He exhorts them to unanimity and mutual assistance (*v.* 2, 3): *I beseech Euodias and Syntyche that they be of the same mind in the Lord.* This is directed to some particular persons. Sometimes there is need of applying the general precepts of the gospel to particular persons and cases. Euodias and Syntyche, it seems, were at variance, either one with the other or with the church; either upon a civil account (it may be they were engaged in a law-suit) or upon a religious account — it may be they were of different opinions and sentiments. "Pray," says he, "desire them from me to be of the same mind in the Lord, to keep the peace and live in love, to be of the same mind one with another, not thwarting and contradicting, and to be of the same mind with the rest of the church, not acting in opposition to them." Then he exhorts to mutual assistance (*v.* 3), and this exhortation he directs to particular persons: *I entreat thee also, true yoke-fellow.* Who this person was whom he calls true yoke-fellow is uncertain. Some think Epaphroditus, who is supposed to have been one of the pastors of the church of the Philippians. Others think it was some eminently good woman, perhaps Paul's wife, because he exhorts his yoke-fellow to *help the women who laboured with him.* Whoever was the yoke-fellow with the apostle must be a yoke-fellow too with his friends. It seems, there were women who laboured with Paul in the gospel; not in the public ministry (for the apostle expressly forbids that, 1 Tim. 2:12, *I suffer not a woman to teach),* but by entertaining the ministers, visiting the sick, instructing the ignorant, convincing the erroneous. Thus women may be helpful to ministers in the work of the gospel. Now, says the apostle, *do thou help them.* Those who help others should be helped themselves when there is occasion. *"Help them,* that is, join with them, strengthen their hands, encourage them in their difficulties." — *With Clement also, and other my fellow-labourers.* Paul had a kindness for all his fellow-labourers; and, as he had found the benefit of their assistance, he concluded how comfortable it would be to them to have the assistance of others. Of his fellow-labourers he says, *Whose names are in the book of life;* either they were chosen of God from all eternity, or registered and enrolled in the corporation and society to which the privilege of eternal life belongs, alluding to the custom among the Jews and Gentiles of registering the inhabitants or the freemen of the city. So we read of their *names being written in heaven* (Lu. 10:20), *not blotting his name out of the book of life* (Rev. 3:5), and of *those who are written in the Lamb's book of life,* Rev. 21:27. Observe, There is a book of life; there are names in that book and not characters and conditions only. We cannot search into that book, or know whose names are written there; but we may, in a judgment of charity, conclude that those who labour in the gospel, and are faithful to the interest of Christ and souls, have their names in the book of life.

III. He exhorts to holy joy and delight in God: *Rejoice in the Lord always, and again I say, Rejoice, v.* 4. All our joy must terminate in God; and our thoughts of God must be delightful thoughts. *Delight thyself in the Lord* (Ps. 37:4), *in the multitude of our thoughts within us* (grievous and afflicting thoughts) *his comforts delight our souls* (Ps. 94:19), and our *meditation of him is sweet,* Ps. 104:34. Observe, It is our duty and privilege to rejoice in God, and to rejoice in him always; at all times, in all conditions; even when we suffer for him, or are afflicted by him. We must not think the worse of him or of his ways for the hardships we meet with in his service. There is enough in God to furnish us with matter of joy in the worst circumstance on earth. He had said it before (*ch.* 3:1): *Finally, my brethren, rejoice in the Lord.* Here he says it again, *Rejoice in the Lord always; and again I say Rejoice.* Joy in God is a duty of great consequence in the Christian life; and Christians need to be again and again called to it. If good men have not a continual feast, it is their own fault.

IV. We are here exhorted to candour and gentleness, and good temper towards our brethren: *"Let your moderation be known to all men, v.* 5. In things indifferent do not run into extremes; avoid bigotry and animosity; judge charitably concerning one another." The word *to epieikes* signifies a good disposition towards other men; and this moderation is explained, Rom. 14. Some understand it of the patient bearing of afflictions, or the sober enjoyment of worldly good; and so it well agrees with the following verse. The reason is, *the Lord is at hand.* The consideration of our Master's approach, and our final account, should keep us from smiting our fellow-servants, support us under present sufferings, and moderate our affections to outward good. "He will take vengeance on your enemies, and reward your patience."

V. Here is a caution against disquieting perplexing care (*v.* 6): *Be careful for nothing — mēden merimnate*: the same expression with that Mt. 6:25, *Take no thought for your life;* that is, avoid anxious care and distracting thought in the wants and difficulties of life. Observe, It is the duty and interest of Christians to live without care. There is a care of diligence which is our duty, and consists in a wise forecast and due concern; but there is a care of diffidence and distrust which is our sin and folly, and which only perplexes and distracts the mind. *"Be careful for nothing,* so as by your care to distrust God, and unfit yourselves for his service."

VI. As a sovereign antidote against perplexing care he recommends to us constant prayer: *In every thing by prayer and supplication, with thanksgiving, let your requests be made known to God.* Observe, 1. We must not only keep up stated times for prayer, but we must pray upon every particular emergency: *In every thing by prayer.* When any thing burdens our spirits, we must ease our minds by prayer; when our affairs are perplexed or distressed, we must seek direction and support. 2. We must join thanksgiving with our prayers and supplications. We must not only seek supplies of good, but own receipts of mercy. Grateful acknowledgments of what we have argue a right disposition of mind, and are prevailing motives for further blessings. 3. Prayer is the offering up of our desires to God, or making them known to him: *Let your requests be made known to God.* Not that God needs to be told either our wants or desires; for he knows them better than we can tell him: but he will know them from us, and have us show our regards and concern, express our value of the mercy and sense of our dependence on him. 4. The effect of this will be the *peace of God keeping our hearts, v.* 7. The *peace of God,* that is, the comfortable sense of our reconciliation to God and interest in his favour, and the hope of the heavenly blessedness, and enjoyment of God hereafter, *which passeth all understanding,* is a great good than can be sufficiently valued or duly expressed. *It has not entered into the heart of ham,* 1 Co. 2:9. This peace will *keep our hearts and minds through Christ Jesus;* it will keep us from sinning under our troubles, and from sinking under them; keep us calm and sedate, without discomposure of passion, and with inward satisfaction. *Thou wilt keep him in perfect peace whose mind is stayed on thee,* Isa. 26:3.

VII. We are exhorted to get and keep a good name, a name for good things with God and good men: *Whatsoever things are true and honest* (*v.* 8), a regard to truth in our words and engagements, and to decency and becomingness in our behaviour, suitable to our circumstances and condition of life. Whatsoever things are *just and pure,* — agreeable to the rules of justice and righteousness in all our dealings with men, and without the impurity or mixture of sin. Whatsoever things are *lovely and of good report,* that is, amiable; that will render us beloved, and make us well spoken of, as well as well thought of, by others. *If there is any virtue, if there is any praise* — any thing really virtuous of any kind and worthy of commendation. Observe, 1. The apostle would have the Christians learn any thing which was good of their heathen neighbours: *"If there be any virtue, think of these things* — imitate them in what is truly excellent among them, and let not them outdo you in any instance of goodness." We should not be ashamed to learn any good thing of bad men, or those who have not our advantages. 2. Virtue has its praise, and will have. We should walk in all the ways of virtue, and abide therein; and then, whether our praise be of men or no, it will be of God, Rom. 2:29.

In these things he proposes himself to them for an example (*v.* 9): *Those things which you have learned, and received, and heard and seen in me, do.* Observe, Paul's doctrine and life were of a piece. What they saw in him was the same thing with what they heard from him. He could propose himself as well as his doctrine to their imitation. It gives a great force to what we say to others when we can appeal to what they have seen in us. And this is the way to have the *God of peace with us* — to keep close to our duty to him. The *Lord is with us while we are with him.*

Verses 10–19

In these verses we have the thankful grateful acknowledgment which the apostle makes of the kindness of the Philippians in sending him a present for his support, now that he was a prisoner at Rome. And here,

I. He takes occasion to acknowledge their former kindnesses to him, and to make mention of them, *v.* 15, 16. Paul had a grateful spirit; for, though what his friends did for him was nothing in comparison of what he deserved from them and the obligations he had laid upon them, yet he speaks of their kindness as if it had been a piece of generous charity, when it was really far short of a just debt. If they had each of them contributed half their estates to him, they had not given him too much, since they *owed to him even their own souls;* and yet, when they send a small present to him, how kindly does he take it, how thankfully does he mention it, even in this epistle which was to be left upon record, and read in the churches, through all ages; so that wherever this epistle shall be read there shall this which they did to Paul be told for a memorial of them. Surely never was present so well repaid. He reminds them that *in the beginning of the gospel no church communicated with him as to giving and receiving but they only, v.* 15. They not only maintained him comfortably while he was with them, but when *he departed from Macedonia* they sent tokens of their kindness after him; and this when no other church did so. None besides sent after him of their carnal things, in consideration of what they had reaped of his spiritual things. In works of charity, we are ready to ask what other people do. But the church of the Philippians never considered that. It redounded so much the more to their honour that they were the only church who were thus just and generous. *Even in Thessalonica* (after he had departed from Macedonia) *you sent once and again to my necessity, v.* 16. Observe, 1. It was but little which they sent; they sent only to his necessity, just such things as he had need of; perhaps it was according to their ability, and he did not desire superfluities nor dainties. 2. It is an excellent thing to see those to whom God has abounded in the gifts of his grace abounding in grateful returns to his people and ministers, according to their own ability and their necessity: *You sent once and again.* Many people make it an excuse for their charity that they have given once; why should the charge come upon them again? But the Philippians sent once and again; they often relieved and refreshed him in his necessities. He makes this mention of their former kindness, not only out of gratitude, but for their encouragement.

II. He excuses their neglect of late. It seems, for some time they had not sent to enquire after him, or sent him any present; but *now at the last their care of him flourished again* (*v.* 10), like a tree in the spring, which seemed all the winter to be quite dead. Now, in conformity to the example of his great Master, instead of upbraiding them for their neglect, he makes an excuse for them: *Wherein you were also careful, but you lacked opportunity.* How could they lack opportunity, if they had been resolved upon it? They might have sent a messenger on purpose. But the apostle is willing to suppose, in favour of them, that they would have done it if a fair opportunity had offered. How contrary is this to the behaviour of many to their friends, by whom neglects which really are excusable are resented very heinously, when Paul excused that which he had reason enough to resent.

III. He commends their present liberality: *Notwithstanding, you have well done that you did communicate with my affliction, v.* 14. It is a good work to succour and help a good minister in trouble. Here see what is the nature of true Christian sympathy; not only to be concerned for our friends in their troubles, but to do what we can to help them. They *communicated with his affliction,* in relieving him under it. He who says, *Be you warmed, be you filled, and giveth not those things they have need of, what doth it profit?* Jam. 2:16. He rejoiced greatly in it (*v.* 10), because it was an evidence of their affection to him and the success of his ministry among them. When the fruit of their charity abounded towards the apostle, it appeared that the fruit of his ministry abounded among them.

IV. He takes care to obviate the bad use some might make

of his taking so much notice of what was sent him. It did not proceed either from discontent and distrust (*v.* 11) or from covetousness and love of the world, *v.* 12. 1. It did not come from discontent, or distrust of Providence: *Not that I speak in respect of want* (*v.* 11); not in respect of any want he felt, nor of any want he feared. As to the former, he was content with the little he had, and that satisfied him; as to the latter, he depended upon the providence of God to provide for him from day to day, and that satisfied him: so that he did not speak in respect of want any way. *For I have learned, in whatsoever state I am, therewith to be content.* We have here an account of Paul's learning, not that which he got at the feet of Gamaliel, but that which he got at the feet of Christ. He had learnt to be content; and that was the lesson he had as much need to learn as most men, considering the hardships and sufferings with which he was exercised. He was in bonds, and imprisonments, and necessities, often; but in all he had learnt to be content, that is, to bring his mind to his condition, and make the best of it. — *I know both how to be abased and I know how to abound, v.* 12. This is a special act of grace, to accommodate ourselves to every condition of life, and carry an equal temper of mind through all the varieties of our state. (1.) To accommodate ourselves to an afflicted condition — to know how to be abased, how to be hungry, how to suffer want, so as not to be overcome by the temptations of it, either to lose our comfort in God or distrust his providence, or to take any indirect course for our own supply. (2.) To a prosperous condition — to know how to abound, how to be full, so as not to be proud, or secure, or luxurious. And this is as hard a lesson as the other; for the temptations of fulness and prosperity are not less than those of affliction and want. But how must we learn it? *I can do all things through Christ who strengthens me, v.* 13. We have need of strength from Christ, to enable us to perform not only those duties which are purely Christian, but even those which are the fruit of moral virtue. We need his strength to teach us to be content in every condition. The apostle had seemed to boast of himself, and of his own strength: *I know how to be abased* (*v.* 12); but here he transfers all the praise to Christ. "What do I talk of *knowing how to be abased, and how to abound?* It is only *through Christ who strengthens me* that I can do it, not in my own strength." So we are required to be *strong in the Lord, and in the power of his might* (Eph. 6:10), and to be *strong in the grace which is in Christ Jesus* (2 Tim. 2:1); and we are *strengthened with might by his Spirit in the inner man,* Eph. 3:16. The word in the original is a participle of the present tense, *en tō endynamounti me Christō,* and denotes a present and continued act; as if he had said, "Through Christ, who is strengthening me, and does continually strengthen me; it is by his constant and renewed strength I am enabled to act in every thing; I wholly depend upon him for all my spiritual power." 2. It did not come from covetousness, or an affection to worldly wealth: "*Not because I desired a gift* (*v.* 17): that is, I welcome your kindness, not because it adds to my enjoyments, but because it adds to your account." He desired not so much for his own sake, but theirs: "*I desire fruit that may abound to your account,* that is, that you may be enabled to make such a good use of your worldly possessions that you may give an account of them with joy." It is not with any design to draw more from you, but to encourage you to such an exercise of beneficence as will meet with a glorious reward hereafter. "For my part," says he, "*I have all, and abound, v.* 18. What can a man desire more than enough? I do not desire a gift for the gift's sake, for *I have all, and abound.*" They sent him a small token, and he desired no more; he was not solicitous for a present superfluity, or a future supply: *I am full, having received from Epaphroditus the things which were sent by you.* Note, A good man will soon have enough of this world; not only of living in it, but of receiving from it. A covetous worldling, if he has ever so much, would still have more; but a heavenly Christian, though he has little, has enough.

V. The apostle assures them that God did accept, and would recompense, their kindness to him. 1. He did accept it: *It is an odour of a sweet smell, a sacrifice acceptable, well-pleasing to God.* Not a sacrifice of atonement, for none makes atonement for sin but Christ; but a sacrifice of acknowledgment, and *well-pleasing to God.* It was more acceptable to God as it was the fruit of their grace than it was to Paul as it was the supply of his want. *With such sacrifices God is well pleased,* Heb. 13:16. 2. He would recompense it: *But my God shall supply all your wants according to his riches in glory by Christ Jesus, v.* 19. He does as it were draw a bill upon the exchequer in heaven, and leaves it to God to make them amends for the kindness they had shown him. "He shall do it, not only as your God, but as my God, who takes what is done to me as done to himself. You supplied my needs, according to your poverty; and he shall supply yours, according to his riches." But still it is by Christ Jesus; through him we have grace to do that which is good, and through him we must expect the reward of it. Not of debt, but of grace; for the more we do for God the more we are indebted to him, because we receive the more from him.

Verses 20–23

The apostle concludes the epistle in these verses,

1. With praises to God: *Now unto God and our Father be glory for ever and ever, Amen, v.* 20. Observe, (1.) God is to be considered by us as our Father: *Now unto God and our Father.* It is a great condescension and favour in God to own the relation of Father to sinners, and allow us to say to him, *Our Father;* and it is a title peculiar to the gospel dispensation. It is also a great privilege and encouragement to us to consider him as our Father, as one so nearly related and who bears so tender an affection towards us. We should look upon God, under all our weaknesses and fears, not as a tyrant or an enemy, but as a Father, who is disposed to pity us and help us. (2.) We must ascribe glory to God as a Father, the glory of his own excellence and of all his mercy unto us. We must thankfully own the receipt of all from him, and give the praise of all to him. And our praise must be constant and perpetual; it must be *glory for ever and ever.*

2. With salutations to his friends at Philippi: "*Salute every saint in Christ Jesus* (*v.* 21); give my hearty love to all the Christians in your parts." He desires remembrances not only to the bishops and deacons, and the church in general, but to every particular saint. Paul had a kind affection to all good Christians.

3. He sends salutations from those who were at Rome: "*The brethren who are with me salute you;* the *ministers,* and all the saints here, send their affectionate remembrances to you. *Chiefly those who are of Caesar's household;* the Christian converts who belonged to the emperor's court." Observe, (1.) There were saints in Caesar's household. Though Paul was imprisoned at Rome, for preaching the gospel, by the emperor's command, yet there were some Christians in his own family. The gospel early obtained among some of the rich and great. Perhaps the apostle fared the better, and received some favour, by means of his friends at court. (2.) *Chiefly those,* etc. Observe, They, being bred at court, were more complaisant than the rest. See what an ornament to religion sanctified civility is.

4. The apostolical benediction, as usual: "*The grace of our Lord Jesus Christ be with you all, Amen.* The free favour and good will of Christ be your portion and happiness."

AN EXPOSITION, WITH PRACTICAL OBSERVATIONS, OF

THE EPISTLE OF ST. PAUL TO THE COLOSSIANS

Colosse was a considerable city of Phrygia, and probably not far from Laodicea and Hierapolis; we find these mentioned together, 4:13. It is now buried in ruins, and the memory of it chiefly preserved in this epistle. The design of the epistle is to warn them of the danger of the Jewish zealots, who pressed the necessity of observing the ceremonial law; and to fortify them against the mixture of the Gentile philosophy with their Christian principles. He professes a great satisfaction in their stedfastness and constancy, and encourages them to perseverance. It was written about the same time with the epistles to the Ephesians and Philippians, A.D. 62, and in the same place, while he was now a prisoner at Rome. He was not idle in his confinement, and the word of God was not bound.

This epistle, like that to the Romans, was written to those he had never seen, nor had any personal acquaintance with. The church planted at Colosse was not by Paul's ministry, but by the ministry of Epaphras or Epaphroditus, an evangelist, one whom he delegated to preach the gospel among the Gentiles; and yet, I. There was a flourishing church at Colosse, and one which was eminent and famous among the churches. One would have thought none would have come to be flourishing churches but those which Paul himself had planted; but here was a flourishing church planted by Epaphras. God is sometimes pleased to make use of the ministry of those who are of less note, and lower gifts, for doing great service to his church. God uses what hands he pleases, and is not tied to those of note, that the *excellence of the power may appear to be of God and not of men,* 2 Co. 4:7. II. Though Paul had not the planting of this church, yet he did not therefore neglect it; nor, in writing his epistles, does he make any difference between that and other churches. The Colossians, who were converted by the ministry of Epaphras, were as dear to him, and he was as much concerned for their welfare, as the Philippians, or any others who were converted by his ministry. Thus he put an honour upon an inferior minister, and teaches us not to be selfish, nor think all that honour lost which goes beside ourselves. We learn, in his example, not to think it a disparagement to us to water what others have planted, or build upon the foundation which others have laid: as he himself, as a *wise master-builder, laid the foundation, and another built thereon,* 1 Co. 3:10.

CHAPTER 1

We have here, I. The inscription, as usual (*v.* 1, 2). II. His thanksgiving to God for what he had heard concerning them — their faith, love, and hope (*v.* 3–8). III. His prayer for their knowledge, fruitfulness, and strength (*v.* 9–11). IV. An admirable summary of the Christian doctrine concerning the operation of the Spirit, the person of the Redeemer, the work of redemption, and the preaching of it in the gospel (*v.* 12–29).

Verses 1–2

I. The inscription of this epistle is much the same with the rest; only it is observable that, 1. He calls himself an *apostle of Jesus Christ by the will of God.* An apostle is a prime-minister in the kingdom of Christ, immediately called by Christ, and extraordinarily qualified; his work was peculiarly to plant the Christian church, and confirm the Christian doctrine. He attributes this not to his own merit, strength, or sufficiency; but to the free grace and good-will of God. He thought himself engaged to do his utmost, as an apostle, because he was made so by the will of God. 2. He joins Timothy in commission with himself, which is another instance of his humility; and, though he elsewhere calls him his son (2 Tim. 2:1), yet here he calls him his brother, which is an example to the elder and more eminent ministers to look upon the younger and more obscure as their brethren, and to treat them accordingly with kindness and respect. 3. He calls the Christians at Colosse *saints, and faithful brethren in Christ.* As all good ministers, so all good Christians, are brethren one to another, who stand in a near relation and owe a mutual love. Towards God they must be saints, consecrated to his honour and sanctified by his grace, bearing his image and aiming at his glory. And in both these, as saints to God and as brethren to one another, they must be faithful. Faithfulness runs through every character and relation of the Christian life, and is the crown and glory of them all.

II. The apostolical benediction is the same as usual: *Grace be unto you, and peace, from God our Father, and the Lord Jesus Christ.* He wishes them *grace and peace,* the free favour of God and all the blessed fruits of it; every kind of spiritual blessings, and that *from God our Father, and the Lord Jesus Christ;* jointly from both, and distinctly from each; as in the former epistle.

Verses 3–8

Here he proceeds to the body of the epistle, and begins with thanksgiving to God for what he had heard concerning them, though he had no personal acquaintance with them, and knew their state and character only by the reports of others.

I. He gave thanks to God for them, that they had embraced the gospel of Christ, and given proofs of their fidelity to him. Observe, In his prayers for them he gave thanks for them. Thanksgiving ought to be a part of every prayer; and whatever is the matter of our rejoicing ought to be the matter of our thanksgiving. Observe, 1. Whom he gives thanks to: *To God, even the Father of our Lord Jesus Christ.* In our thanksgiving we must have an eye to God as God (he is the object of thanksgiving as well as prayer), and is the Father of our Lord Jesus Christ, in and through whom all good comes to us. He is the Father of our Lord Jesus Christ as well as our Father; and it is a matter of encouragement, in all our addresses to God, that we can look to him as Christ's Father and our Father, as his God and our God, Jn. 20:17. Observe, 2. What he gives thanks to God for — for the graces of God in them, which were evidences of the grace of God towards them: *Since we heard of your faith in Christ Jesus, and of the love you have to all the saints; for the hope which is laid up for you in heaven, v.* 4, 5. Faith, hope, and love, are the three principal graces in the Christian life, and proper matter of our prayer and thanksgiving. (1.) He gives thanks for their faith in Christ Jesus, that they were brought to believe in him, and take upon them the profession of his religion, and venture their souls upon his undertaking. (2.) For their love. Besides the general love which is due to all men, there is a particular love owing to the saints, or those who are of the Christian *brotherhood,* 1 Pt. 2:17. We must love all the saints, bear an extensive kindness and good-will to good men, notwithstanding smaller points of difference, and many real weaknesses. Some understand it of their charity to the saints in necessity, which is one branch and evidence of Christian love. (3.) For their hope: *The hope which is laid up for you in heaven, v.* 5. The happiness of heaven is called their hope, because it is the *thing hoped for, looking for the blessed hope,* Tit. 2:13. What is laid out upon believers in this world is much; but what is laid up for them in heaven is much more. And we have reason to give thanks to God for the hope of heaven which good Christians have, or their well-grounded expectation of the future glory. Their faith in Christ, and love to the saints, had an eye to the *hope laid up for them in heaven.* The more we fix our hopes on the recompence of reward in the other world, the more free and liberal shall we be of our earthly treasure upon all occasions of doing good.

II. Having blessed God for these graces, he blesses God for the means of grace which they enjoyed: *Wherein you heard before in the word of the truth of the gospel.* They had heard in the word of the truth of the gospel concerning this *hope laid up for them in heaven.* Observe, 1. The gospel is the word of truth, and what we may safely venture our immortal souls upon: it proceeds from the God of truth and the Spirit of truth, and is a faithful saying. He calls it *the grace of God in truth, v.* 6. 2. It is a great mercy to hear this word of truth; for the great thing we learn from it is the happiness of heaven. Eternal life is brought to light by the gospel, 2 Tim. 1:10. They heard of the hope laid up in heaven in the word of the truth of the gospel. *"Which has come unto you, as it hath to all the world, and bringeth forth fruit, as it doth also in you, v.* 6. This gospel is preached and brings forth fruit in other nations; it has come to you, *as it hath to all the world,* according to the commission, *Go preach the gospel in all the nations,* and to *every creature."* Observe, (1.) All who hear the word of the gospel ought to bring forth the fruit of the gospel, that is, be obedient to it, and have their principles and lives formed according to it. This was the doctrine first preached: *Bring forth therefore fruits meet for repentance,* Mt. 3:8. And our Lord says, *If you know these things, happy are you if you do them,* Jn. 13:17. Observe, (2.) Wherever the gospel comes, it will bring forth fruit to the honour and glory of God: *It bringeth forth fruit, as it doth also in you.* We mistake, if we think to monopolize the comforts and benefits of

the gospel to ourselves. Does the gospel bring forth fruit in us? So it does in others.

III. He takes this occasion to mention the minister by whom they believed (*v.* 7, 8): *As you also learned of Epaphras, our dear fellow-servant, who is for you a faithful minister of Christ.* He mentions him with great respect, to engage their love to him. 1. He calls him his fellow-servant, to signify not only that they served the same Master, but that they were engaged in the same work. They were fellow-labourers in the work of the Lord, though one was an apostle and the other an ordinary minister. 2. He calls him his dear fellow-servant: all the servants of Christ ought to love one another, and it is an endearing consideration that they are engaged in the same service. 3. He represents him as one who was a faithful minister of Christ to them, who discharged his trust and fulfilled his ministry among them. Observe, Christ is our proper Master, and we are his ministers. He does not say who is your minister; but *who is the minister of Christ for you.* It is by his authority and appointment, though for the people's service. 4. He represents him as one who gave them a good word: *Who also declared unto us your love in the Spirit, v.* 8. He recommends him to their affection, from the good report he made of their sincere love to Christ and all his members, which was wrought in them by the Spirit, and is agreeable to the spirit of the gospel. Faithful ministers are glad to be able to speak well of their people.

Verses 9–11

The apostle proceeds in these verses to pray for them. He heard that they were good, and he prayed that they might be better. He was constant in this prayer: *We do not cease to pray for you.* It may be he could hear of them but seldom, but he constantly prayed for them. — *And desire that you may be filled with the knowledge,* etc. Observe what it is that he begs of God for them,

I. That they might be knowing intelligent Christians: *filled with the knowledge of his will, in all wisdom and spiritual understanding.* Observe, 1. The knowledge of our duty is the best knowledge. A mere empty notion of the greatest truths is insignificant. Our knowledge of the will of God must be always practical: we must know it, in order to do it. 2. Our knowledge is then a blessing indeed when it is in wisdom, when we know how to apply our general knowledge to our particular occasions, and to suit it to all emergencies. 3. Christians should endeavour to be filled with knowledge; not only to know the will of God, but to know more of it, and to *increase in the knowledge of God* (as it is *v.* 10), and to *grow in grace, and in the knowledge of our Lord and Saviour,* 2 Pt. 3:18.

II. That their conversation might be good. Good knowledge without a good life will not profit. Our understanding is then a spiritual understanding when we exemplify it in our way of living: *That you may walk worthy of the Lord unto all pleasing (v.* 10), that is, as becomes the relation we stand in to him and the profession we make of him. The agreeableness of our conversation to our religion is pleasing to God as well as to good men. We walk unto all well-pleasing when we walk in all things according to the will of God. *Being fruitful in every good work.* This is what we should aim at. Good words will not do without good works. We must abound in good works, and in every good work: not in some only, which are more easy, and suitable, and safe, but in all, and every instance of them. There must be a regular uniform regard to all the will of God. And the more fruitful we are in good works the more we shall *increase in the knowledge of God. He who doeth his will shall know of the doctrine whether it be of God,* Jn. 7:17.

III. That they might be strengthened: *Strengthened with all might according to his glorious power (v.* 11), fortified against the temptations of Satan and furnished for all their duty. It is a great comfort to us that he who undertakes to give strength to his people is a God of power and of glorious power. Where there is spiritual life there is still need of spiritual strength, strength for all the actions of the spiritual life. To be strengthened is to be furnished by the grace of God for every good work, and fortified by that grace against every evil one: it is to be enabled to do our duty, and still to hold fast our integrity. The blessed Spirit is the author of this strength; for we are *strengthened with might by his Spirit in the inward man,* Eph. 3:16. The word of God is the means of it, by which he conveys it; and it must be fetched in by prayer. It was in answer to earnest prayer that the apostle

obtained sufficient grace. In praying for spiritual strength we are not straitened in the promises, and therefore should not be straitened in our own hopes and desires. Observe, 1. He prayed that they might be strengthened with might: this seems a tautology; but he means, that they might be mightily strengthened, or strengthened with might derived from another. 2. It is with all might. It seems unreasonable that a creature should be strengthened with all might, for that is to make him *almighty;* but he means, with all that might which we have occasion for, to enable us to discharge our duty or preserve our innocence, that grace which is sufficient for us in all the trials of life and able to help us in time of need. 3. It is *according to his glorious power.* He means, according to the grace of God: but the grace of God in the hearts of believers is the power of God; and there is a glory in this power; it is an excellent and sufficient power. And the communications of strength are not according to our weakness, to whom the strength is communicated, but according to his power, from whom it is received. When God gives he gives like himself, and when he strengthens he strengthens like himself. 4. The special use of this strength was for suffering work: *That you may be strengthened unto all patience and long-suffering with joyfulness.* He prays not only that they may be *supported* under their troubles, but *strengthened* for them: the reason is there is work to be done even when we are suffering. And those who are strengthened *according to his glorious power* are strengthened, (1.) To all patience. When patience *hath its perfect work* (Jam. 1:4) then we are strengthened to all patience — when we not only bear our troubles patiently, but receive them as gifts from God, and are thankful for them. To you *it is given to suffer,* Phil. 1:29. When we bear our troubles well, though ever so many, and the circumstances of them ever so aggravating, then we bear them with all patience. And the same reason for bearing one trouble will hold for bearing another, if it be a good reason. All patience includes all the kinds of it; not only bearing patience, but waiting patience. (2.) This is even unto long-suffering, that is, drawn out to a great length: not only to bear trouble awhile, but to bear it as long as God pleases to continue it. (3.) It is with joyfulness, to rejoice in tribulation, to take joyfully the spoiling of our goods, and rejoice that we are counted worthy to suffer for his name, to have joy as well as patience in the troubles of life. This we could never do by any strength of our own, but as we are strengthened by the grace of God.

Verses 12–29

Here is a summary of the doctrine of the gospel concerning the great work of our redemption by Christ. It comes in here not as the matter of a sermon, but as the matter of a thanksgiving; for our salvation by Christ furnishes us with abundant matter of thanksgiving in every view of it: *Giving thanks unto the Father, v.* 12. He does not discourse of the work of redemption in the natural order of it; for then he would speak of the purchase of it first, and afterwards of the application of it. But here he inverts the order, because, in our sense and feeling of it, the application goes before the purchase. We first find the benefits of redemption in our hearts, and then are led by those streams to the original and fountain-head. The order and connection of the apostle's discourse may be considered in the following manner: —

I. He speaks concerning the operations of the Spirit of grace upon us. We must give thanks for them, because by these we are qualified for an interest in the mediation of the Son: *Giving thanks to the Father,* etc. *v.* 12, 13. It is spoken of as the work of the Father, because the Spirit of grace is the Spirit of the Father, and the Father works in us by his Spirit. Those in whom the work of grace is wrought must give thanks unto the Father. If we have the comfort of it, he must have the glory of it. Now what is it which is wrought for us in the application of redemption? 1. "He hath *delivered us from the power of darkness, v.* 13. He has rescued us from the state of heathenish darkness and wickedness. He hath saved us from the dominion of sin, which is darkness (1 Jn. 1:6), from the dominion of Satan, who is the *prince of darkness* (Eph. 6:12), and from the damnation of hell, which is *utter darkness,"* Mt. 25:30. They are *called out of darkness,* 1 Pt. 2:9. 2. "He hath <u>translated us into the kingdom of his dear Son,</u> brought us into the gospel-state, and made us members of the church of Christ, which is a state of light and purity. *You were once darkness, but now are you light in the Lord,* Eph. 5:8. *Who hath called you out of darkness into his marvellous light,* 1 Pt. 2:9. Those were made willing subjects of Christ who were the slaves of Satan. The conversion of a sinner is the translation of a soul into the kingdom of Christ out of the kingdom of the devil. The power of sin is shaken off, and the power of Christ submitted to. The law of the Spirit of life in Christ Jesus makes them free from the law of sin and death; and it is the kingdom of his dear Son, or the Son of his peculiar love, his beloved Son (Mt. 3:17), and eminently the beloved, Eph. 1:6. 3. "He hath not only done this, but hath *made us meet to partake of the inheritance of the saints in light, v.* 12. He hath prepared us for the eternal happiness of heaven, as the Israelites divided the promised land by lot; and has given us the earnest and assurance of it." This he mentions first because it is the first indication of the future blessedness, that by the grace of God we find ourselves in some measure prepared for it. God gives *grace and glory,* and we are here told what they both are. (1.) What that glory is. It is the *inheritance of the saints in light.* It is an inheritance, and belongs to them as children, which is the best security and the sweetest tenure: *If children, then heirs,* Rom. 8:17. And it is an inheritance of the saints — proper to sanctified souls. Those who are not saints on earth will never be saints in heaven. And it is an inheritance in light; the perfection of knowledge, holiness, and joy, by communion with God, who is light, and the Father of lights, Jam. 1:17; Jn. 1:5. (2.) What this grace is. It is a meetness for the inheritance: *"He hath made us meet to be partakers,* that is, suited and fitted us for the heavenly state by a proper temper and habit of soul; and he makes us meet by the powerful influence of his Spirit." It is the effect of the divine power to change the heart, and make it heavenly. Observe, All who are designed for heaven hereafter are prepared for heaven now. As those who live and die unsanctified go out of the world with their hell about them, so those who are sanctified and renewed go out of the world with their heaven about them. Those who have the inheritance of sons have the education of sons and the disposition of sons: they *have the Spirit of adoption, whereby they cry, Abba, Father.* Rom. 8:15. *And, because you are sons, God hath sent forth the Spirit of his Son into your hearts, crying, Abba, Father,* Gal. 4:6. This meetness for heaven is the earnest of the Spirit in our heart, which is part of payment, and assures the full payment. Those who are sanctified shall be glorified (Rom. 8:30), and will be for ever indebted to the grace of God, which hath sanctified them.

II. Concerning the person of the Redeemer. Glorious things are here said of him; for blessed Paul was full of Christ, and took all occasions to speak honourably of him. He speaks of him distinctly as God, and as Mediator. 1. As God he speaks of him, *v.* 15–17. (1.) He is the *image of the invisible God.* Not as man was made *in the image of God* (Gen. 1:27), in his natural faculties and dominion over the creatures: no, he is the *express image of his person,* Heb. 1:3. He is so the image of God as the son is the image of his father, who has a natural likeness to him; so that he who has seen him has *seen the Father,* and his *glory was the glory of the only-begotten of the Father,* Jn. 1:14; 14:9. (2.) He is the *first-born of every creature.* Not that he is himself a creature; for it is *prōtotokos pasēs ktiseōs — born* or *begotten before all the creation,* or before any creature was made, which is the scripture-way of representing eternity, and by which the eternity of God is represented to us: *I was set up from everlasting, from the beginning, or ever the earth was; when there was no depth, before the mountains were settled, while as yet he had not made the earth,* Prov. 8:23–26. It signifies his dominion over all things, as the first-born in a family is heir and lord of all, so he is the *heir of all things,* Heb. 1:2. The word, with only the change of the accent, *prōtotokós,* signifies actively the first begetter or producer of all things, and so it well agrees with the following clause. *Vid. Isidor. Peleus. epist.* 30 *lib.* 3. (3.) He is so far from beginning himself a creature that he is the Creator: *For by him were all things created, which are in heaven and earth, visible and invisible, v.* 16. He made all things out of nothing, the highest angel in heaven, as well as men upon earth. He made the world, the upper and lower world, with all the inhabitants of both. *All things were made by him, and without him was not any thing made which was made,* Jn. 1:3. He speaks here as if there were several orders of angels: *Whether thrones, or dominions, or principalities, or powers,* which must signify either different degrees of excellence or different offices and employments. *Angels, authorities, and powers,* 1 Pt. 3:22. Christ is the eternal wisdom of the Father, and the world was made in wisdom. He is the eternal Word, and the world was made by the word of God. He is the *arm of the Lord,* and the world was made by that arm. *All things are created by him and for him; di' autou kai eis auton.* Being created by him, they were created for him; being made by his power, they were made according to his pleasure and for his praise. He is the end, as well as the cause of all things. *To him are all things,* Rom. 11:36; *eis auton ta panta.* (4.) He *was before all things.* He had a being before the world was made, before the beginning of time, and therefore from all eternity. Wisdom was with the Father, and possessed by him in the beginning of his ways, before his works of old, Prov. 8:22. And in the beginning the Word was with God and was God, Jn. 1:1. He not only had a being before he was born of the virgin, but he had a being before all time. (5.) *By him all things consist.* They not only subsist in their beings, but consist in their order and dependences. He not only created them all at first, but it is by the word of his power that they are still upheld, Heb. 1:3. The whole creation is kept together by the power of the Son of God, and made to consist in its proper frame. It is preserved from disbanding and running into confusion.

2. The apostle next shows what he is as Mediator, *v.* 18, 19. (1.) He is the *head of the body the church:* not only a head of government and direction, as the king is the head of the state and has right to prescribe laws, but a head of vital influence, as the head in the natural body: for all grace and strength are derived from him: and the church is his body, *the fulness of him who filleth all in all,* Eph. 1:22, 23. (2.) He is the *beginning, the first-born from the dead, archē, prōtotokos* — the principle, the first-born from the dead; the principle of our resurrection, as well as the first-born himself. All our hopes and joys take their rise from him who is the author of our salvation. Not that he was the first who ever rose from the dead, but the first and only one who rose by his own power, and was *declared to be the Son of God, and Lord of all things.* And he is the head of the resurrection, and has given us an example and evidence of our resurrection from the dead. He rose as the first-fruits, 1 Co. 15:20. (3.) He hath in *all things the pre-eminence.* It was the will of the Father that he should have *all power in heaven and earth,* that he might be preferred above angels and all the powers in heaven (he has *obtained a more excellent name than they,* Heb. 1:4), and that in all the affairs of the kingdom of God among men he should have the pre-eminence. He has the pre-eminence in the hearts of his people above the world and the flesh; and by giving him the pre-eminence we comply with the Father's will, That *all men should honour the Son even as they honour the Father,* Jn. 5:23. (4.) All fulness dwells in him, and it pleased the Father it should do so (*v.* 19), not only a fulness of abundance for himself, but redundance for us, a fulness of merit and righteousness, of strength and grace. As the head is the seat and source of the animal spirits, so is Christ of all graces to his people. *It pleased the Father* that all fulness should dwell in him; and we may have free resort to him for all that grace for which we have occasion. He not only intercedes for it, but is the trustee in whose hands it is lodged to dispense to us: *Of his fulness we receive, and grace for grace,* grace in us answering to that grace which is in him (Jn. 1:16), and *he fills all in all,* Eph. 1:23.

III. Concerning the work of redemption. He speaks of the nature of it, or wherein it consists; and of the means of it, by which it was procured.

1. Wherein it consists. It is made to lie in two things: — (1.) In the remission of sin: *In whom we have redemption, even the forgiveness of sins, v.* 14. It was sin which sold us, sin which enslaved us: if we are redeemed, we must be redeemed from sin; and this is by forgiveness, or remitting the obligation to punishment. So Eph. 1:7, *In whom we have redemption, the forgiveness of sins, according to the riches of his grace.* (2.) In reconciliation to God. God by him *reconciled all things to himself, v.* 20. He is the Mediator of reconciliation, who procures peace as well as pardon for sinners, who brings them into a state of friendship and favour at present, and will bring all holy creatures, angels as well as men, into one glorious and blessed society at last: *things in earth, or things in heaven.* So Eph. 1:10, *He will gather together in one all things in Christ, both which are in heaven and which are on earth.* The word is *anakephalaiōsasthai — he will bring them all under one head.* The Gentiles, who were alienated, and *enemies in their minds by wicked works, yet now hath he reconciled, v.* 21. Here see what was their condition by nature, and in their Gentile state — estranged from God, and at enmity with God: and yet this *enmity is slain,* and, notwithstanding this distance, we are now reconciled. Christ has laid the foundation for our reconciliation; for he has paid the price of it, has purchased the proffer and promise of it, proclaims it as a prophet, applies it as a king. Observe, The greatest enemies to God, who have stood at the greatest distance and bidden him defiance, may be reconciled, if it by not their own fault.

2. How the redemption is procured: *it is through his blood* (*v.* 14); he has *made peace through the blood of his cross* (*v.* 20), and it is *in the body of his flesh through death, v.* 22. It was the *blood which made an atonement, for the blood is the life; and without the shedding of blood there is no remission,* Heb. 9:22. There was such a value in the blood of Christ that, on account of Christ's shedding it, God was willing to deal with men upon new terms to bring them under a covenant of grace, and *for his sake,* and in consideration of his death upon the cross, to pardon and accept to favour all who comply with them.

IV. Concerning the preaching of this redemption. Here observe,

1. To whom it was preached: *To every creature under heaven* (*v.* 23), that is, it was ordered to be preached to every creature, Mk. 16:15. It may be preached to every creature; for the gospel excludes none who do not exclude themselves. More or less it has been or will be preached to every nation, though many have sinned away the light of it and perhaps some have never yet enjoyed it.

2. By whom it was preached: *Whereof I Paul am made a minister.* Paul was a great apostle; but he looks upon it as the highest of his titles of honour to be a minister of the gospel of Jesus Christ. Paul takes all occasions to speak of his office; for he *magnified his office,* Rom. 11:13. And again in *v.* 25, *Whereof I am made a minister.* Observe here,

(1.) Whence Paul had his ministry: it was *according to the dispensation of God which was given to him* (*v.* 25), the economy or wise disposition of things in the house of God. He was steward and master-builder, and this was given to him: he did not usurp it, nor take it to himself; and he could not challenge it as a debt. He received it from God as a gift, and took it as a favour.

(2.) For whose sake he had his ministry: *"It is for you,* for your benefit: *ourselves your servants for Jesus' sake,* 2 Co. 4:5. We are Christ's ministers for the good of his people, to *fulfil the word of God* (that is, fully to preach it), of which you will have the greater advantage. The more we fulfil our ministry, or fill up all the parts of it, the greater will be the benefit of the people; they will be the more filled with knowledge, and furnished for service."

(3.) What kind of preacher Paul was. This is particularly represented.

[1.] He was a suffering preacher: *Who now rejoice in my sufferings for you, v.* 24. He suffered in the cause of Christ, and for the good of the church. He suffered for preaching the gospel to them. And, while he suffered in so good a cause, he could rejoice in his sufferings, *rejoice that he was counted worthy to suffer,* and esteem it an honour to him. *And fill up that which is behind of the afflictions of Christ in my flesh.* Not that the afflictions of Paul, or any other, were expiations for sin, as the sufferings of Christ were. There was nothing wanting in them, nothing which needed to *be filled up.* They were perfectly sufficient to answer the intention of them, the satisfaction of God's justice, in order to the salvation of his people. But the sufferings of Paul and other good ministers made them conformable to Christ; and they followed him in his suffering state: so they are said to fill up what was behind of the sufferings of Christ, as the wax fills up the vacuities of the seal, when it receives the impression of it. Or it may be meant not of Christ's sufferings, but of his suffering for Christ. He *filled that which was behind.* He had a certain rate and measure of suffering for Christ assigned him; and, as his sufferings were agreeable to that appointment, so he was still filling up more and more what was behind, or remained of them to his share.

[2.] He was a close preacher: he preached not only in public, but *from house to house,* from person to person. *Whom we preach, warning every man, and teaching every man in all wisdom, v.* 28. Every man has need to be warned and taught, and therefore let every man have his share. Observe, *First,* When we warn people of what they do amiss, we must teach them to do better: warning and teaching must go together. *Secondly,* Men must be warned and taught in all wisdom. We must choose the fittest seasons, and use the likeliest means, and accommodate ourselves to the different circumstances and capacities of those we have to do with, and teach them as they are able to bear. That which he aimed at was to *present every man perfect in Christ Jesus, teleios,* either perfect in the knowledge of the Christian doctrine (*Let us therefore, as many as are perfect, be thus minded,* Phil. 3:15; 2 Tim. 3:17), or else crowned with a glorious reward hereafter, when he will *present to himself a glorious church* (Eph. 5:27), and bring them to the *spirits of just men made perfect,* Heb. 12:23. Observe, Ministers ought to aim at the improvement and salvation of every particular person who hears them. *Thirdly,* He was a laborious preacher, and one who took pains: he was no loiter, and did not do his work negligently (*v.* 29): *Whereunto I also labour, striving according to his working, which worketh in me mightily.* He laboured and strove, used great diligence and contended with many difficulties, according to the measure of grace afforded to him and the extraordinary presence of Christ which was with him. Observe, As Paul laid out himself to do much good, so he had this favour, that the power of God wrought in him the more effectually. The more we labour in the work of the Lord the greater measures of help we may expect from him in it (Eph. 3:7): *According to the gift of the grace of God given unto me, by the effectual working of his power.*

3. The gospel which was preached. We have an account of this: *Even the mystery which hath been hid from ages, and from generations, but is now made manifest to his saints,* *v.* 26, 27. Observe, (1.) The mystery of the gospel was long hidden: it was concealed from ages and generations, the several ages of the church under the Old-Testament dispensation. They were in a state of minority, and training up for a more perfect state of things, and could not look to the end of those things which were ordained, 2 Co. 3:13. (2.) This mystery now, in the fulness of time, is made manifest to the saints, or clearly revealed and made apparent. The veil which was over Moses's face is done away in Christ, 2 Co. 3:14. The meanest saint under the gospel understands more than the greatest prophets under the law. He who is least in the kingdom of heaven is greater than they. The *mystery of Christ, which in other ages was not made known unto the sons of men, is now revealed unto his holy apostles and prophets by the Spirit,* Eph. 3:4, 5. And what is this mystery? It is the riches of God's glory among the Gentiles. The peculiar doctrine of the gospel was a mystery which was before hidden, and is now made manifest and made known. But the great mystery here referred to is the breaking down of the partition-wall between the Jew and Gentile, and preaching the gospel to the Gentile world, and making those partakers of the privileges of the gospel state who before lay in ignorance and idolatry: *That the Gentiles should be fellow-heirs, and of the same body, and partakers together of his promise in Christ by the gospel,* Eph. 3:6. This mystery, thus made known, *is Christ in you* (or among you) *the hope of glory.* Observe, Christ is the hope of glory. The ground of our hope is Christ in the word, or the gospel revelation, declaring the nature and methods of obtaining it. The evidence of our hope is Christ in the heart, or the sanctification of the soul, and its preparation for the heavenly glory.

4. The duty of those who are interested in this redemption: *If you continue in the faith, grounded and settled, and be not moved away from the hope of the gospel which you have heard,* *v.* 23. We must continue in the faith grounded and settled, and not be moved away from the hope of the gospel; that is, we must be so well fixed in our minds as not to be moved from it by any temptations. We must be stedfast and immovable (1 Co. 15:58) and *hold fast the profession of our faith without wavering,* Heb. 10:23. Observe, We can expect the happy end of our faith only when we continue in the faith, and are so far grounded and settled in it as not to be moved from it. We must not *draw back unto perdition,* but *believe unto the saving of the soul,* Heb. 10:39. We must be faithful to death, through all trials, that we may receive the *crown of life, and receive the end of our faith, the salvation of our souls,* 1 Pt. 1:9.

CHAPTER 2

I. The apostle expresses concern for the Colossians (*v.* 1–3). II. He repeats it again (*v.* 5). III. He cautions them against false teachers among the Jews (*v.* 4, 6, 7), and against the Gentile philosophy (*v.* 8–12). IV. He represents the privileges of Christians (*v.* 13–15). And, V. Concludes with a caution against the judaizing teachers, and those who would introduce the worship of angels (*v.* 16–23).

Verses 1–3

We may observe here the great concern which Paul had for these Colossians and the other churches which he had not any personal knowledge of. The apostle had never been at Colosse, and the church planted there was not of his planting; and yet he had as tender a care of it as if it had been the only people of his charge (*v.* 1): *For I would that you knew what great conflict I have for you, and for those at Laodicea, and for as many as have not seen my face in the flesh.* Observe, 1. Paul's care of the church was such as amounted to a conflict. He was in a sort of agony, and had a constant fear respecting what would become of them. Herein he was a follower of his Master, who was in an agony for us, and was *heard in that he feared.* (2.) We may keep up a communion by faith, hope, and holy love, even with those churches and fellow-christians of whom we have no personal knowledge, and with whom we have no conversation. We can think, and pray, and be concerned for one another, at the greatest distance; and those we never saw in the flesh we may hope to meet in heaven. But,

I. What was it that the apostle desired for them? *That their hearts may be comforted, being knit together in love,* etc., *v.* 2. It was their spiritual welfare about which he was solicitous. He does not say that they may be healthy, and merry, and rich, and great, and prosperous; but that their *hearts may be comforted.* Note, The prosperity of the soul is the best prosperity, and what we should be most solicitous about for ourselves and others. We have here a description of soul-prosperity.

1. When our knowledge grows to an understanding of the mystery of God, and of the Father, and of Christ, — when we come to have a more clear, distinct, methodical knowledge of the truth as it is in Jesus, then the soul prospers: *To understand the mystery,* either what was before concealed, but is now made known concerning the Father and Christ, or the mystery before mentioned, of calling the Gentiles into the Christian church, as the Father and Christ have revealed it in the gospel; and not barely to speak of it by rote, or as we have been taught it by our catechisms, but to be led into it, and enter into the meaning and design of it. This is what we should labour after, and then the soul prospers.

2. When our faith grows to a full assurance and bold acknowledgment of this mystery. (1.) To a full assurance, or a well-settled judgment, upon their proper evidence, of the great truths of the gospel, without doubting, or calling them in question, but embracing them with the highest satisfaction, as faithful sayings and worthy of all acceptation. (2.) When it comes to a free acknowledgment, and we not only believe with the heart, but are ready, when called to it, to make confession with our mouth, and are not ashamed of our Master and our holy religion, under the frowns and violence of their enemies. This is called the *riches of the full assurance of understanding.* Great knowledge and strong faith make a soul rich. This is being rich towards God, and rich in faith, and having the true riches, Lu. 12:21; 16:11; Jam. 2:5.

3. It consists in the abundance of comfort in our souls: *That their hearts might be comforted.* The soul prospers when it is filled with joy and peace (Rom. 15:13), and has a satisfaction within which all the troubles without cannot disturb, and is able to joy in the Lord when all other comforts fail, Hab. 3:17, 18.

4. The more intimate communion we have with our fellow-christians the more the soul prospers: *Being knit together in love.* Holy love knits the hearts of Christians one to another; and faith and love both contribute to our comfort. The stronger our faith is, and the warmer our love, the greater will our comfort be. Having occasion to mention Christ (*v.* 2), according to his usual way, he makes this remark to his honour (*v.* 3): *In whom are hidden all the treasures of wisdom and knowledge.* He had said (*ch.* 1:19) *that all fulness dwells in him:* here he mentions particularly the *treasures of wisdom and knowledge.* There is a fulness of wisdom in him, as he has perfectly revealed the will of God to mankind. Observe, The treasures of wisdom are hidden not from us, but for us, in Christ. Those who would be wise and knowing must make application to Christ. We must spend upon the stock which is laid up for us in him, and draw from the treasures which are hidden in him. He is the wisdom of God, and is *of God made unto us wisdom,* etc., 1 Co. 1:24, 30.

II. His concern for them is repeated (*v.* 5): *Though I am absent in the flesh, yet am I with you in the spirit, joying, and beholding your order, and the stedfastness of your faith in Christ.* Observe, 1. We may be present in spirit with those churches and Christians from whom we are absent in body; for the communion of saints is a spiritual thing. Paul had heard concerning the Colossians that they were orderly and regular; and though he had never seen them, nor was present with them, he tells them he could easily think himself among them, and look with pleasure upon their good behaviour. 2. The order and stedfastness of Christians are matter of joy to ministers; they joy when they behold their order, their regular behaviour and stedfast adherence to the Christian doctrine. 3. The more stedfast our faith in Christ is, the better order there will be in our whole conversation; for we live and walk by faith, 2 Co. 5:7; Heb. 10:38.

Verses 4–12

The apostle cautions the Colossians against deceivers (*v.* 4): *And this I say lest any man beguile you with enticing words;* and *v.* 8, *Lest any man spoil you.* He insists so much upon the perfection of Christ and the gospel revelation, to preserve them from the ensnaring insinuations of those who would corrupt their principles. Note, 1. The way in which Satan spoils souls is by beguiling them. He deceives them, and by this means slays them. He is the *old serpent who beguiled Eve through his subtlety,* 2 Co. 11:3. He could not ruin us if he did not cheat us; and he could not cheat us but by our own fault and folly. 2. Satan's agents, who aim to spoil them, beguile them with enticing words. See the danger of enticing words; how many are ruined by the flattery of those who lie in wait to deceive, and by the false disguises and fair appearances of evil principles and wicked practices. *By good words, and fair speeches, they deceive the hearts of the simple,* Rom. 16:18. "You ought to stand upon your guard against enticing words, and be aware and afraid of those who would entice you to any evil; for that which they aim at is to spoil you." *If sinners entice thee, consent thou not,* Prov. 1:10. Observe,

I. A sovereign antidote against seducers (*v.* 6, 7): *As you have therefore received Christ Jesus the Lord, so walk you in him, rooted and built up,* etc. Here note, 1. All Christians have, in profession at least, *received Jesus Christ the Lord,* received him as Christ, the great prophet of the church, anointed by God to reveal his will; as Jesus the great high priest, and Saviour from sin and wrath, by the expiatory sacrifice of himself; and as Lord, or sovereign and king, whom we are to obey and be subject to. — *Received him,* consented to him, taken him for ours in every relation and every capacity, and for all the purposes and uses of them. 2. The great concern of those who have received Christ is *to walk in him* — to make their practices conformable to their principles and their conversation agreeable to their engagements. As we have received Christ, or consented to be his, so we must walk with him in our daily course and keep up our communion with him. 3. The more closely we walk with Christ the more we are *rooted and established in the faith.* A good conversation is the best establishment of a good faith. If we walk in him, we shall be rooted in him; and the more firmly we are rooted in him the more closely we shall walk in him: *Rooted and built up.* Observe, We cannot be built up in Christ, unless we be first rooted in him. We must be united to him by a lively faith, and heartily consent to his covenant, and then we shall *grow up in him in all things.* — *As you have been taught* — "according to the rule of the Christian doctrine, in which you have been instructed." Observe, A good education has a good influence upon our establishment. We must be *established in the faith, as we have been taught, abounding therein.* Observe, Being established in the faith, we must abound therein, and improve in it more and more; and this with thanksgiving. The way to have the benefit and comfort of God's grace is to be much in giving thanks for it. We must join thanksgiving to all our improvements, and be sensible of the mercy of all our privileges and attainments. Observe,

II. The fair warning given us of our danger: *Beware lest any man spoil you through philosophy and vain deceit, after the tradition of men, after the rudiments of the world, and not after Christ,* *v.* 8. There is a philosophy which is a noble exercise of our reasonable faculties, and highly serviceable to religion, such a study of the works of God as leads us to the knowledge of God and confirms our faith in him. But there is a philosophy which is vain and deceitful, which is prejudicial to religion, and sets up the wisdom of man in competition with the wisdom of God, and while it pleases men's fancies ruins their faith; as nice and curious speculations about things above us, or of no use and concern to us; or a care of words and terms of art, which have only an empty and often a cheating appearance of knowledge. *After the tradition of men, after the rudiments of the world:* this plainly reflects upon the Jewish pedagogy or economy, as well as the Pagan learning. The Jews governed themselves by the traditions of their elders and the rudiments or elements of the world, the rites and observances which were only preparatory and introductory to the gospel state; the Gentiles mixed their maxims of philosophy with their Christian principles; and both alienated their minds from Christ. Those who pin their faith on other men's sleeves, and walk in the way of the world, have turned away from following after Christ. The deceivers were especially the Jewish teachers, who endeavoured to keep up the law of Moses in conjunction with the gospel of Christ, but really in competition with it and contradiction to it. Now here the apostle shows,

1. That we have in Christ the substance of all the shadows of the ceremonial law; for example, (1.) Had they then the Shechinah, or special presence of God, called the glory, from the visible token of it? So have we now in Jesus Christ (v. 9): *For in him dwelleth all the fulness of the Godhead bodily.* Under the law, the presence of God dwelt between the cherubim, in a cloud which covered the mercy-seat; but now it dwells in the person of our Redeemer, who partakes of our nature, and is bone of our bone and flesh of our flesh, and has more clearly declared the Father to us. It dwells in him bodily; not as the body is opposed to the spirit, but as the body is opposed to the shadow. The fulness of the Godhead dwells in the Christ really, and not figuratively; for he is both God and man. (2.) Had they circumcision, which was the seal of the covenant? In Christ we are *circumcised with the circumcision made without hands* (v. 11), by the work of regeneration in us, which is the spiritual or Christian circumcision. *He is a Jew who is one inwardly, and circumcision is that of the heart,* Rom. 2:29. This is owing to Christ, and belongs to the Christian dispensation. *It is made without hands;* not by the power of any creature, but by the power of the blessed Spirit of God. We are *born of the Spirit,* Jn. 3:5. And it is *the washing of regeneration, and renewing of the Holy Spirit,* Tit. 3:5. It consists in *putting off the body of the sins of the flesh,* in renouncing sin and reforming our lives, not in mere external rites. It is not the *putting away of the filth of the flesh, but the answer of a good conscience towards God,* 1 Pt. 3:21. And it is not enough to put away some one particular sin, but we must put off the whole body of sin. The *old man must be crucified, and the body of sin destroyed,* Rom. 6:6. Christ was circumcised, and, by virtue of our union to him, we partake of that effectual grace which puts off the *body of the sins of the flesh.* Again, The Jews thought themselves complete in the ceremonial law; but we are *complete in Christ,* v. 10. That was imperfect and defective; *if the first covenant had been faultless, there would no place have been sought for the second* (Heb. 8:7), and the *law was but a shadow of good things, and could never, by those sacrifices, make the comers thereunto perfect,* Heb. 10:1. But all the defects of it are made up in the gospel of Christ, by the complete sacrifice for sin and revelation of the will of God. *Which is the head of all principality and power.* As the Old-Testament priesthood had its perfection in Christ, so likewise had the kingdom of David, which was the eminent principality and power under the Old Testament, and which the Jews valued themselves so much upon. And he is the Lord and head of all the powers in heaven and earth, of angels and men. *Angels, and authorities, and powers are subject to him,* 1 Pt. 3:22.

2. We have communion with Christ in his whole undertaking (v. 12): *Buried with him in baptism, wherein also you have risen with him.* We are both buried and rise with him, and both are signified by our baptism; not that there is anything in the sign or ceremony of baptism which represents this burying and rising, any more than the crucifixion of Christ is represented by any visible resemblance in the Lord's supper: and he is speaking of the *circumcision made without hands;* and says it is *through the faith of the operation of God.* But the thing signified by our baptism is that we are buried with Christ, as baptism is the seal of the covenant and

an obligation to our dying to sin; and that we are raised with Christ, as it is a seal and obligation to our living to righteousness, or newness of life. God in baptism engages to be to us a God, and we become engaged to be his people, and by his grace to die to sin and to live to righteousness, or put off the old man and put on the new.

Verses 13–15

The apostle here represents the privileges we Christians have above the Jews, which are very great.

I. Christ's death is our life: *And you, being dead in your sins and the uncircumcision of your flesh, hath he quickened together with him,* v. 13. A state of sin is a state of spiritual death. Those who are in sin are dead in sin. As the death of the body consists in its separation from the soul, so the death of the soul consists in its separation from God and the divine favour. As the death of the body is the corruption and putrefaction of it, so sin is the corruption or depravation of the soul. As a man who is dead is unable to help himself by any power of his own, so an habitual sinner is morally impotent: though he has a natural power, or the power of a reasonable creature, he has not a spiritual power, till he has the divine life or a renewed nature. It is principally to be understood of the Gentile world, who *lay in wickedness.* They were *dead in the uncircumcision of their flesh,* being *aliens to the covenant of promise, and without God in the world,* Eph. 2:11, 12. By reason of their uncircumcision they were dead in their sins. It may be understood of the spiritual uncircumcision or corruption of nature; and so it shows that we are dead in law, and dead in state. Dead in law, as a condemned malefactor is called a dead man because he is under a sentence of death; so sinners by the guilt of sin are under the sentence of the law and *condemned already,* Jn. 3:18. And dead in state, by reason of the *uncircumcision of our flesh.* An unsanctified heart is called an *uncircumcised heart:* this is our state. Now through Christ we, who were dead in sins, are quickened; that is, effectual provision is made for taking away the guilt of sin, and breaking the power and dominion of it. *Quickened together with him* — by virtue of our union to him, and in conformity to him. Christ's death was the death of our sins; Christ's resurrection is the quickening of our souls.

II. Through him we have the remission of sin: *Having forgiven you all trespasses.* This is our quickening. The pardon of the crime is the life of the criminal: and this is owing to the resurrection of Christ, as well as his death; for, as he *died for our sins,* so he *rose again for our justification,* Rom. 4:25.

III. Whatever was in force against us is taken out of the way. He has obtained for us a legal discharge from the *hand-writing of ordinances, which was against us* (v. 14), which may be understood, 1. Of that obligation to punishment in which consists the guilt of sin. The curse of the law is the hand-writing against us, like the hand-writing on Belshazzar's wall. *Cursed is every one who continues not in every thing.* This was a hand-writing which was *against us, and contrary to us;* for it threatened our eternal ruin. This was removed when he *redeemed us from the curse of the law, being made a curse for us,* Gal. 3:13. He cancelled the obligation for all who repent and believe. "Upon me be the curse, my father." He vacated and disannulled the judgment which was against us. When he was nailed to the cross, the curse was as it were nailed to the cross. And our indwelling corruption is crucified with Christ, and by virtue of his cross. When we remember the dying of the Lord Jesus, and see him nailed to the cross, we should see the hand-writing against us taken out of the way. Or rather, 2. It must be understood of the ceremonial law, the *hand-writing of ordinances,* the ceremonial institutions or *the law of commandments contained in ordinances* (Eph. 2:15), which was a yoke to the Jews and a partition-wall to the Gentiles. The Lord Jesus *took it out of the way, nailed it to his cross;* that is, disannulled the obligation of it, that all might see and be satisfied that it was no more binding. When the substance came, the shadows fled away. It is abolished (2 Co. 3:13), and *that which decayeth and waxeth old is ready to vanish away,* Heb. 8:13. The expressions are in allusion to the ancient methods of cancelling a bond, either by crossing the writing or striking it through with a nail.

IV. He has obtained a glorious victory for us over the powers of darkness: *And, having spoiled principalities and powers, he made a show of them openly, triumphing over them in it,* v. 15. As the curse of the law was against us, so the power of Satan was against us. He treated with God as the Judge,

and redeemed us out of the hands of his justice by a price; but out of the hands of Satan the executioner he redeemed us by power and with a high hand. *He led captivity captive.* The devil and all the powers of hell were conquered and disarmed by the dying Redeemer. The first promise pointed at this; the bruising of the heel of Christ in his sufferings was the breaking of the serpent's head, Gen. 3:15. The expressions are lofty and magnificent: let us turn aside and see this great sight. The Redeemer conquered by dying. See his crown of thorns turned into a crown of laurels. He *spoiled them,* broke the devil's power, and conquered and disabled him, and *made a show of them openly* — exposed them to public shame, and made a show of them to angels and men. Never had the devil's kingdom such a mortal blow given to it as was given by the Lord Jesus. He tied them to his chariot-wheels, and rode forth conquering and to conquer — alluding to the custom of a general's triumph, who returned victorious. — *Triumphing over them in it;* that is, either in his cross and by his death; or, as some read it, in himself, by his own power; for he *trod the wine-press alone, and of the people there was none with him.*

Verses 16–23

The apostle concludes the chapter with exhortations to proper duty, which he infers from the foregoing discourse.

I. Here is a caution to take heed of judaizing teachers, or those who would impose upon Christians the yoke of the ceremonial law: *Let no man therefore judge you in meat nor drink,* etc., v. 16. Much of the ceremonies of the law of Moses consisted in the distinction of meats and days. It appears by Rom. 14 that there were those who were for keeping up those distinctions: but here the apostle shows that since Christ has come, and has cancelled the ceremonial law, we ought not to keep it up. "Let no man impose those things upon you, for God has not imposed them: if God has made you free, be not you again *entangled in that yoke of bondage.*" And this the rather because these things *were shadows of things to come* (v. 17), intimating that they had no intrinsic worth in them and that they are now done away. *But the body is of Christ:* the body, of which they were shadows, has come; and to continue the ceremonial observances, which were only types and shadows of Christ and the gospel, carries an intimation that Christ has not yet come and the gospel state has not yet commenced. Observe the advantages we have under the gospel, above what they had under the law: they had the shadows, we have the substance.

II. He cautions them to take heed of those who would introduce the worship of angels as mediators between God and them, as the Gentile philosophers did: *Let no man beguile you of your reward, in a voluntary humility and worshipping of angels,* v. 18. It looked like a piece of modesty to make use of the mediation of angels, as conscious to ourselves of our unworthiness to speak immediately to God; but, though it has a show of humility, it is a voluntary, not a commanded humility; and therefore it is not acceptable, yea, it is not warrantable: it is taking that honour which is due to Christ only and giving it to a creature. Besides, the notions upon which this practice was grounded were merely the inventions of men and not by divine revelation, — the proud conceits of human reason, which make a man presume to dive into things, and determine them, without sufficient knowledge and warrant: *Intruding into those things which he hath not seen, vainly puffed up by his fleshly mind* — pretending to describe the order of angels, and their respective ministries, which God has hidden from us; and therefore, though there was a show of humility in the practice, there was a real pride in the principle. They advanced those notions to gratify their own carnal fancy, and were fond of being thought wiser than other people. Pride is at the bottom of a great many errors and corruptions, and even of many evil practices, which have great show and appearance of humility. Those who do so do *not hold the head,* v. 19. They do in effect disclaim Christ, who is the only Mediator between God and man. It is the highest disparagement to Christ, who is the head of the church, for any of the members of it to make use of any intercessors with God but him. When men let go their hold of Christ, they catch at that which is next them and will stand them in no stead. — *From which all the body, by joints and bands, having nourishment ministered, and knit together, increaseth with the increase of God.* Observe, 1. Jesus Christ is not only a head of government over the church, but a head of vital influence to it. They are knit to him by joints and bands, as the several members of the body are united to the head, and receive life and nourishment from him. 2. The body of Christ is a growing body: *it increaseth with the increase of God.* The new man is increasing, and the nature of grace is to grow, where there is not an accidental hindrance. — *With the increase of God,* with an increase of grace which is from God as its author; or, in a usual Hebraism, with a large and abundant increase. — *That you may be filled with all the fulness of God,* Eph. 3:19. See a parallel expression, *Which is the head, even Christ, from whom the whole body, fitly joined together, maketh increase of the body,* Eph. 4:15, 16.

III. He takes occasion hence to warn them again: "*Wherefore, if you be dead with Christ from the rudiments of the world, why, as though living in the world, are you subject to ordinances? v.* 20. If as Christians you are dead to the observances of the ceremonial law, why are you subject to them? Such observances as, *Touch not, taste not, handle not,*" *v.* 21, 22. Under the law there was a ceremonial pollution contracted by touching a dead body, or any thing offered to an idol; or by tasting any forbidden meats, etc., *which all are to perish with the using,* having no intrinsic worth in themselves to support them, and those who used them saw them perishing and passing away; or, which tend to corrupt the Christian faith, having no other authority than the traditions and injunctions of men. — *Which things have indeed a show of wisdom in will-worship and humility.* They thought themselves wiser than their neighbours, in observing the law of Moses together with the gospel of Christ, that they might be sure in the one, at least, to be in the right; but, alas! it was but a show of wisdom, a mere invention and pretence. So they seem to neglect the body, by abstaining from such and such meats, and mortifying their bodily pleasures and appetites; but there is nothing of true devotion in these things, for the gospel teaches us to worship God in spirit and truth and not by ritual observances, and through the mediation of Christ alone and not of any angels. Observe, 1. Christians are freed by Christ from the ritual observances of Moses's law, and delivered from that yoke of bondage which God himself had laid upon them. 2. Subjection to ordinances, or human appointments in the worship of God, is highly blamable, and contrary to the freedom and liberty of the gospel. The apostle requires Christians *to stand fast in the liberty with which Christ hath made them free, and not to be entangled again with the yoke of bondage,* Gal. 5:1. And the imposition of them is invading the authority of Christ, the head of the church, and *introducing another law of commandments contained in ordinances,* when Christ has abolished the old one, Eph. 2:15. 3. Such things have only a show of wisdom, but are really folly. It is true wisdom to keep close to the appointments of the gospel, and an entire subjection to Christ, the only head of the church.

CHAPTER 3

I. The apostle exhorts us to set our hearts upon heaven and take them off from this world (*v.* 1–4). II. He exhorts to the mortification of sin, in the various instances of it (*v.* 5–11). III. He earnestly presses to mutual love and compassion (*v.* 12–17). And concludes with exhortations to relative duties, of wives and husbands, parents and children, masters and servants (*v.* 18–25).

Verses 1–4

The apostle, having described our privileges by Christ in the former part of the epistle, and our discharge from the yoke of the ceremonial law, comes here to press upon us our duty as inferred thence. Though we are made free from the obligation of the ceremonial law, it does not therefore follow that we may live as we list. We must walk the more closely with God in all the instances of evangelical obedience. He begins with exhorting them to set their hearts on heaven, and take them off from this world: *If you then have risen with Christ.* It is our privilege that we have risen with Christ; that is, have benefit by the resurrection of Christ, and by virtue of our union and communion with him are justified and sanctified, and shall be glorified. Hence he infers that we must *seek those things which are above.* We must mind the concerns of another world more than the concerns of this. We must make heaven our scope and aim, seek the favour of God above, keep up our communion with the upper world by faith, and hope, and holy love, and make it our constant care and business to secure our title to and qualifications for the heavenly bliss. And the reason is because *Christ sits at the right hand of God.* He who is our best friend and our head is advanced to the highest dignity and honour in heaven, and has gone before to secure to us the heavenly happiness; and therefore we should seek and secure what he has purchased at so vast an expense, and is taking so much care about. We must live such a life as Christ lived here on earth and lives now in heaven, according to our capacities.

I. He explains this duty (*v.* 2): *Set your affections on things above, not on things on the earth.* Observe, To seek heavenly things is to set our affections upon them, to love them and let our desires be towards them. Upon the wings of affection the heart soars upwards, and is carried forth towards spiritual and divine objects. We must acquaint ourselves with them, esteem them above all other things, and lay out ourselves in preparation for the enjoyment of them. David gave this proof of his *loving the house of God,* that he diligently sought after it, and prepared for it, Ps. 27:4. This is to be spiritually minded (Rom. 8:6), and to *seek and desire a better country, that is, a heavenly,* Heb. 11:14, 16. *Things on earth* are here set in opposition to *things above.* We must not dote upon them, nor expect too much from them, that we may set our affections on heaven; for heaven and earth are contrary one to the other, and a supreme regard to both is inconsistent; and the prevalence of our affection to one will proportionably weaken and abate our affection to the other.

II. He assigns three reasons for this, *v.* 3, 4.

1. That we are dead; that is, to present things, and as our portion. We are so in profession and obligation; for we are *buried with Christ, and planted into the likeness of his death.* Every Christian is *crucified unto the world,* and *the world is crucified unto him,* Gal. 6:14. And if we are dead to the earth, and have renounced it as our happiness, it is absurd for us to *set our affections* upon it, and *seek* it. We should be like a dead thing to it, unmoved and unaffected towards it.

2. Our true life lies in the other world: *You are dead, and your life is hid with Christ in God, v.* 3. The new man has its livelihood thence. It is born and nourished from above; and the perfection of its life is reserved for that state. It is *hid with Christ;* not hid from us only, in point of secrecy, but hid for us, denoting security. The life of a Christian *is hid with Christ. Because I live you shall live also,* Jn. 14:19. Christ is at present a hidden Christ, or one *whom we have not seen;* but this is our comfort, that our *life is hid with him,* and laid up safely with him. As we have reason to *love him whom we have not seen* (1 Pt. 1:8), so we may take the comfort of a happiness out of sight, and *reserved in heaven for us.*

3. Because at the second coming of Christ we hope for the perfection of our happiness. If we live a life of Christian purity and devotion now, *when Christ, who is our life, shall appear, we shall also appear with him in glory, v.* 4. Observe, (1.) Christ is a believer's life. *I live, yet not I, but Christ lives in me,* Gal. 2:20. He is the principle and end of the Christian's life. He lives *in* us by his Spirit, and we live to him in all we do. *To me to live is Christ,* Phil. 1:21. (2.) Christ will appear again. He is now *hid;* and the *heavens must contain* him; but he will appear in all the pomp of the upper world, with his *holy angels,* and in *his own glory and his Father's glory,* Mk. 8:38; Lu. 9:26. (3.) We shall then appear with him in glory. It will be his glory to have his redeemed with him; he will come to be glorified in his saints (2 Th. 1:10); and it will be their glory to come with him, and be with him for ever. At the second coming of Christ there will be a general meeting of all the saints; and those whose life is now *hid with Christ* shall then appear with Christ in that glory which he himself enjoys, Jn. 17:24. Do we look for such a happiness, and should we not set our affections upon that world, and live above this? What is there here to make us fond of it? What is there not there to draw our hearts to it? Our head is there, our home is there, our treasure is there, and we hope to be there for ever.

Verses 5–7

The apostle exhorts the Colossians to the mortification of sin, the great hindrance to seeking the things which are above. Since it is our duty to set our affections upon heavenly things, it is our duty to mortify our *members which are upon the earth,* and which naturally incline us to the things of the world: "Mortify them, that is, subdue the vicious habits of mind which prevailed in your Gentile state. Kill them, suppress them, as you do weeds or vermin which spread and destroy all about them, or as you kill an enemy who fights against you and wounds you." — *Your members which are upon the earth;* either the members of the body, which are the earthly part of us, and were *curiously wrought in the lower parts of the earth* (Ps. 139:15), or the corrupt affections of the mind, which lead us to earthly things, the members of the body of death, Rom. 7:24. He specifies,

I. The lusts of the flesh, for which they were before so very remarkable: *Fornication, uncleanness, inordinate affection, evil concupiscence* — the various workings of the carnal appetites and fleshly impurities, which they indulged in their former course of life, and which were so contrary to the Christian state and the heavenly hope.

II. The love of the world: *And covetousness, which is idolatry;* that is, an inordinate love of present good and outward enjoyments, which proceeds from too high a value in the mind, puts upon too eager a pursuit, hinders the proper use and enjoyment of them, and creates anxious fear and immoderate sorrow for the loss of them. Observe, Covetousness is spiritual idolatry: it is the giving of that love and regard to worldly wealth which are due to God only, and carries a greater degree of malignity in it, and is more highly provoking to God, than is commonly thought. And it is very observable that among all the instances of sin which good men are recorded in the scripture to have fallen into (and there is scarcely any but some or other, in one or other part of their life, have fallen into) there is no instance in all the scripture of any good man charged with covetousness. He proceeds to show how necessary it is to mortify sins, *v.* 6, 7. 1. Because, if we do not kill them, they will kill us: *For which things' sake the wrath of God cometh on the children of disobedience, v.* 6. See what we are all by nature more or less: we are *children of disobedience:* not only disobedient children, but under the power of sin and naturally prone to disobey. The *wicked are estranged from the womb; they go astray as soon as they are born, speaking lies,* Ps. 58:3. And, being children of disobedience, we are *children of wrath,* Eph. 2:3. The wrath of God comes upon all the children of disobedience. Those who do not obey the precepts of the law incur the penalties of it. The sins he mentions were their sins in their heathen and idolatrous state, and they were then especially the children of disobedience; and yet these sins brought judgments upon them, and exposed them to the wrath of God. 2. We should mortify these sins because they have lived in us: *In which you also walked some time, when you lived in them, v.* 7. Observe, The consideration that we have formerly lived in sin is a good argument why we should now forsake it. We have walked in by-paths, therefore let us walk in them no more. *If I have done iniquity, I will do no more,* Job 34:32. The time past our lives may suffice us to have wrought the will of the Gentiles, when we walked in lasciviousness, 1 Pt. 4:3. — *When you lived among those who did such things* (so some understand it), then you walked in those evil practices. It is a hard thing to live among those who do the works of darkness and not have fellowship with them, as it is to walk in the mire and contract no soil. Let us keep out of the way of evil-doers.

Verses 8–11

As we are to mortify inordinate appetites, so we are to mortify inordinate passions (*v.* 8): *But now you also put off all these, anger wrath, malice;* for these are contrary to the design of the gospel, as well as grosser impurities; and, though they are more spiritual wickedness, have not less malignity in them. The gospel religion introduces a change of the higher as well as the lower powers of the soul, and supports the dominion of right reason and conscience over appetite and passion. Anger and wrath are bad, but malice is worse, because it is more rooted and deliberate; it is anger heightened and settled. And, as the corrupt principles in the heart must be cut off, so the product of them in the tongue; as *blasphemy,* which seems there to mean, not so much speaking ill of God as speaking ill of men, giving ill language to them, or raising ill reports of them, and injuring their good name by any evil arts, — *filthy communication,* that is, all lewd and wanton discourse, which comes from a polluted mind in the speaker and propagates the same defilements in the hearers, — and lying: *Lie not one to another* (*v.* 9), for it is contrary both to the law of truth and the law of love, it is both unjust and unkind, and naturally tends to destroy all faith and friendship among mankind. Lying makes us like the devil (who is the *father of lies),* and is a prime part of the devil's image upon our souls; and therefore we are cautioned against this sin by this general reason: Seeing *you have put off the old man with his deeds, and have put on the new man, v.* 10. The consideration that we have by profession put away sin and espoused the cause and interest of Christ, that we have renounced all sin and stand engaged to Christ, should fortify us against this sin of lying. Those who have put off the old man have put it off with its deeds; and those who have put on the new man must put on all its deeds — not only espouse good principles but act them in a good conversation. The new man is said to be *renewed in knowledge,* because an ignorant soul cannot be a good soul. Without knowledge the heart cannot be good, Prov. 19:2. The grace of God works upon the will and affections by renewing the understanding. Light is the first thing in the new creation, as it was in the first: *after the image of him who created him.* It was the honour of man in innocence that he was made after the image of God; but that image was defaced and lost by sin, and is renewed by sanctifying grace: so that a renewed soul is something like what Adam was in the day he was created. In the privilege and duty of sanctification *there is neither Greek nor Jew, circumcision nor uncircumcision, Barbarian, Scythian, bond nor free, v.* 11. There is now no difference arising from different country or different condition and circumstance of life: it is as much the duty of the one as of the other to be holy, and as much the privilege of the one as of the other to receive from God the grace to be so. Christ came to take down all partition-walls, that all might stand on the same level before God, both in duty and privilege. And for this reason, because *Christ is all in all.* Christ is a Christian's all, his only Lord and Saviour, and all his hope and happiness. And to those who are sanctified, one as well as another and whatever they are in other respects, he is *all in all,* the *Alpha* and *Omega,* the *beginning and the end:* he is all in all things to them.

Verses 12–17

The apostle proceeds to exhort to mutual love and compassion: *Put on therefore bowels of mercy, v.* 12. We must not only put off anger and wrath (as *v.* 8), but we must put on compassion and kindness; not only cease to do evil, but learn to do well; not only not do hurt to any, but do what good we can to all.

I. The argument here used to enforce the exhortation is very affecting: *Put on, as the elect of God, holy and beloved.* Observe, 1. Those who are holy are the elect of God; and those who are the elect of God, and holy, are beloved — beloved of God, and ought to be so of all men. 2. Those who are the elect of God, holy and beloved, ought to conduct themselves in every thing as becomes them, and so as not to lose the credit of their holiness, nor the comfort of their being chosen and beloved. It becomes those who are holy towards God to be lowly and loving towards all men. Observe, What we must put on in particular. (1.) Compassion towards the miserable: *Bowels of mercy,* the tenderest mercies. Those who owe so much to mercy ought to be merciful to all who are proper objects of mercy. *Be you merciful, as your Father is merciful,* Lu. 6:36. (2.) *Kindness* towards our friends, and those who love us. A courteous disposition becomes the elect of God; for the design of the gospel is not only to soften the minds of men, but to sweeten them, and to promote friendship among men as well as reconciliation with God. (3.) *Humbleness of mind,* in submission to those above us, and condescension to those below us. There must not only be a humble demeanour, but a humble mind. *Learn of me, for I am meek and lowly in heart,* Mt. 11:29. (4.) *Meekness* towards those who have provoked us, or been any way injurious to us. We must not be transported into any indecency by our resentment of indignities and neglects: but must prudently bridle our own anger, and patiently bear the anger of others. (5.) *Long-suffering* towards those who continue to provoke us. *Charity suffereth long,* as well *as is kind,* 1 Co. 13:4. Many can bear a short provocation who are weary of bearing when it grows long. But we must suffer long both the injuries of men and the rebukes of divine Providence. If God is long-suffering to us, under all our provocations of him, we should exercise long-suffering to others in like cases. (6.) Mutual forbearance, in consideration of the infirmities and deficiencies under which we all labour: *Forbearing one another.* We have all of us something which needs to be borne with, and this is a good reason why we should bear with others in what is disagreeable to us. We need the same good turn from others which we are bound to show them. (7.) A readiness to forgive injuries: *Forgiving one another, if any man have a quarrel against any.* While we are in this world, where there is so much corruption in our hearts, and so much occasion of difference and contention, quarrels will sometimes happen, even among the elect of God, who are holy and beloved, as Paul and Barnabas had a *sharp contention, which parted them asunder one from the other* (Acts 15:39), and Paul and Peter, Gal. 2:14. But it is our duty to forgive one another in such cases; not to bear any grudge, but put up with the affront and pass it by. And the reason is: *Even as Christ forgave you, so also do you.* The consideration that we are forgiven by Christ so many offences is a good reason why we should forgive others. It is an argument of the divinity of Christ that he had *power on earth to forgive sins;* and it is a branch of his example which we are obliged to follow, if we ourselves would be forgiven. *Forgive us our trespasses, as we forgive those who trespass against us,* Mt. 6:12.

II. In order to all this, we are exhorted here to several things: — 1. To clothe ourselves with love (*v.* 14): *Above all things put on charity: epi pasi de toutois — over all things.* Let this be the upper garment, the robe, the livery, the mark of our dignity and distinction. Or, Let this be principal and chief, as the whole sum and abstract of the second table. *Add to faith virtue, and to brotherly-kindness charity,* 2 Pt. 1:5–7. He lays the foundation in faith, and the top-stone in charity, *which is the bond of perfectness,* the cement and centre of all happy society. Christian unity consists of unanimity and mutual love. 2. To submit ourselves to the government of the *peace of God* (*v.* 15): *Let the peace of God rule in your hearts,* that is, God's being at peace with you, and the comfortable sense of his acceptance and favour: or, a disposition to peace among yourselves, a peaceable spirit, that keeps the peace, and makes peace. This is called the *peace of God,* because it is of his working in all who are his. The *kingdom of God is righteousness and peace,* Rom. 14:17. "Let this peace *rule in your heart* — prevail and govern there, or as an umpire decide all matters of difference among you." — *To which you are called in one body.* We are called to this peace, to peace with God as our privilege and peace with our brethren as our duty. Being united in one body, we are called to be at peace one with another, as the members of the natural body; for *we are the body of Christ, and members in particular,* 1 Co. 12:27. To preserve in us this peaceable disposition, we must be thankful. The work of thanksgiving to God is such a sweet and pleasant work that it will help to make us sweet and pleasant towards all men. "Instead of envying one another upon account of any particular favours and excellence, be thankful for his mercies, which are common to all of you." 3. To let the *word of Christ dwell in us richly, v.* 16. The gospel is the word of Christ, which has come to us; but that is not enough, it must dwell in us, or *keep house — enoikeitō,* not as a servant in a family, who is under another's control, but as a master, who has a right to prescribe to and direct all under his roof. We must take our instructions and directions from it, and our portion of meat and strength, of grace and comfort, in due season, as from the *master of the household.* It must dwell in us; that is, be always ready and at hand to us in every thing, and have its due influence and use. We must be familiarly acquainted with it, and *know it for our good,* Job 5:27. It must dwell in us richly: not only keep house in our hearts, but keep a good house. Many have the word of Christ dwelling in them, but it dwells in them but poorly; it has no mighty force and influence upon them. Then the soul prospers when the word of God *dwells in us richly,* when we have abundance of it in us, and are full of the scriptures and of the grace of Christ. And this in all wisdom. The proper office of wisdom is to apply what we know to ourselves, for our own direction. The word of Christ must dwell in us, not in all notion and speculation, to make us doctors, but in all wisdom, to make us good Christians, and enable us to conduct ourselves in every thing as becomes Wisdom's children. 4. To teach and admonish one another. This would contribute very much to our furtherance in all grace; for we sharpen ourselves by quickening others, and improve our knowledge by communicating it for their edification. We must *admonish one another in psalms and hymns.* Observe, Singing of psalms is a gospel ordinance: *psalmois kai hymnois kai ōdais* — the Psalms of David, and spiritual hymns and odes, collected out of the scripture, and suited to special occasions, instead of their lewd and profane songs in their idolatrous worship. Religious poesy seems countenanced by these expressions and is capable of great edification. But, when we sing psalms, we make no melody unless we sing with grace in our hearts, unless we are suitably affected with what we sing and go along in it with true devotion and understanding. Singing of psalms is a teaching ordinance as well as a praising ordinance; and we are not only to quicken and encourage ourselves, but to *teach and admonish one another,* mutually excite our affections, and convey instructions. 5. All must be done in the name of Christ (*v.* 17): *And whatsoever you do in word or deed, do all in the name of the Lord Jesus,* according to his command and in compliance with his authority, by strength derived from him, with an eye to his glory, and depending upon his merit for the acceptance of what is good and the pardon of what is amiss, *Giving thanks to God and the Father by him.* Observe, (1.) We must give thanks in all things; whatsoever we do, we must still give thanks, Eph. 5:20, *Giving thanks always for all things.* (2.) The Lord Jesus must be the Mediator of our praises as well as of our prayers. *We give thanks to God and the Father in the name of the Lord Jesus Christ,* Eph. 5:20. Those who do all things in Christ's name will never want matter of thanksgiving to God, even the Father.

Verses 18–25

The apostle concludes the chapter with exhortations to relative duties, as before in the epistle to the Ephesians. The epistles which are most taken up in displaying the glory of divine grace, and magnifying the Lord Jesus, are the most particular and distinct in pressing the duties of the several relations. We must never separate the privileges and duties of the gospel religion.

I. He begins with the duties of wives and husbands (*v.* 18): *Wives, submit yourselves unto your own husbands, as it is fit in the Lord.* Submission is the duty of wives, *hypotassesthe.* It is the same word which is used to express our duty to magistrates (Rom. 13:1, *Let every soul be* subject *to the higher powers),* and is expressed by subjection and reverence, Eph. 5:24, 33. The reason is that *Adam was first formed, then Eve: and Adam was not deceived, but the woman, being deceived, was in the transgression,* 1 Tim. 2:13, 14. He was first in the creation and last in the transgression. The *head of the woman is the man;* and the *man is not of the woman, but the woman of the man; neither was the man created for the woman, but the woman for the man,* 1 Co. 11:3, 8, 9. It is agreeable to the order of nature and the reason of things, as well as the appointment and will of God. But then it is submission, not to a rigorous lord or absolute tyrant, who may do his will and is without restraints, but to a husband, and to her own husband, who stands in the nearest relation, and is under strict engagements to proper duty too. And *this is fit in the Lord,* it is becoming the relation, and what they are bound in duty to do, as an instance of obedience to the authority and law of Christ. On the other hand, *husbands must love their wives, and not be bitter against them, v.* 19. They must love them with tender and faithful affection, as Christ loved the church, and as their own bodies, and even as themselves (Eph. 5:25, 28, 33), with a love peculiar to the nearest relation and the greatest comfort and blessing of life. And they must not be bitter against them, not use them unkindly, with harsh language or severe treatment, but be kind and obliging to them in all things; for the *woman was made for the man, neither is the man without the woman,* and the *man also is by the woman,* 1 Co. 11:9, 11, 12.

II. The duties of children and parents: *Children, obey your parents in all things, for this is well-pleasing unto the Lord, v.* 20. They must be willing to do all their lawful commands, and be at their direction and disposal; as those who have a natural right and are fitter to direct them than themselves. The apostle (Eph. 6:2) requires them to honour as well as obey their parents; they must esteem them and think honourably of them, as the obedience of their lives must proceed from the esteem and opinion of their minds. And this is *well-pleasing to God,* or acceptable to him; for it is the *first commandment with promise* (Eph. 6:2), with an explicit promise annexed to it, namely, *That it shall be well with them, and they shall live long on the earth.* Dutiful children are the most likely to prosper in the world and enjoy long life. And parents must be tender, as well as children obedient (*v.* 21): *"Fathers, provoke not your children to anger, lest they be discouraged.* Let not your authority over them be exercised with rigour and severity, but with kindness and gentleness, lest you raise their passions and discourage them in their duty, and by holding the reins too tight make them fly out with greater fierceness." The bad temper and example of imprudent parents often prove a great hindrance to their children and a stumbling-block in their way; see Eph. 6:4. And it is by the tenderness of parents, and dutifulness of children, that God ordinarily furnishes his church with a seed to serve him, and propagates religion from age to age.

III. Servants and masters: *Servants, obey your masters in all things according to the flesh, v.* 22. Servants must do the duty of the relation in which they stand, and obey their master's commands in *all things* which are consistent with their duty to God their heavenly Master. *Not with eye-service, as men-pleasers* — not only when their master's eye is upon them, but when they are from under their master's eye. They must be both just and diligent. *In singleness of heart, fearing God* — without selfish designs, or hypocrisy and disguise, as those who fear God and stand in awe of him. Observe, The fear of God ruling in the heart will make people good in every relation. Servants who fear God will be just and faithful when they are from under their master's eye, because they know they are under the eye of God. See Gen. 20:11, *Because I thought, Surely the fear of God is not in this place.* Neh. 5:15, *But so did not I, because of the fear of God.* "And *whatsoever you do, do it heartily* (*v.* 23), with diligence, not idly and slothfully:" or, "Do it cheerfully, not discontented at the providence of God which put you in that relation." — *As to the Lord, and not as to men.* It sanctifies a servant's work when it is done as unto God — with an eye to his glory and in obedience to his command, and not merely as unto men, or with regard to them only. Observe, We are really doing our duty to God when we are faithful in our duty to men. And, for servants' encouragement, let them know that a good and faithful servant is never the further from heaven for his being a servant: *"Knowing that of the Lord you shall receive the reward of the inheritance, for you serve the Lord Christ, v.* 24. Serving your masters according to the command of Christ, you serve Christ, and he will be your paymaster: you will have a glorious reward at last. Though you are now servants, you will receive the inheritance of sons. But, on the other hand, *He who does wrong will receive for the wrong which he has done," v.* 25. There is a righteous God, who, if servants wrong their masters, will reckon with them for it, though they may conceal it from their master's notice. And he will be sure to punish the unjust as well as reward the faithful servant: and so if masters wrong their servants. — *And there is no respect of persons with him.* The righteous Judge of the earth will be impartial, and carry it with an equal hand towards the master and servant; not swayed by any regard to men's outward circumstances and condition of life. The one and the other will stand upon a level at his tribunal.

It is probable that the apostle has a particular respect, in all these instances of duty, to the case mentioned 1 Co. 7 of relations of a different religion, as a Christian and heathen, a Jewish convert and an uncircumcised Gentile, where there was room to doubt whether they were bound to fulfil the proper duties of their several relations to such persons. And, if it hold in such cases, it is much stronger upon Christians one towards another, and where both are of the same religion. And how happy would the gospel religion make the world, if it every where prevailed; and how much would it influence every state of things and every relation of life!

CHAPTER 4

I. He continues his account of the duty of masters, from the close of the former chapter (*v.* 1). II. He exhorts to the duty of prayer (*v.* 2–4), and to a prudent and decent conduct towards those with whom we converse (*v.* 5, 6). III. He closes the epistle with the mention of several of his friends, of whom he gives an honourable testimony (*v.* 7–18).

Verse 1

The apostle proceeds with the duty of masters to their servants, which might have been joined to the foregoing chapter, and is a part of that discourse. Here observe, 1. Justice is required of them: *Give unto your servants that which is just and equal* (*v.* 1), not only strict justice, but equity and kindness. Be faithful to your promises to them, and perform your agreements; not defrauding them of their dues, nor *keeping back by fraud the hire of the labourers,* Jam. 5:4. Require no more of them than they are able to perform; and do not lay unreasonable burdens upon them, and beyond their strength. Provide for them what is fit, supply proper food and physic, and allow them such liberties as may fit them the better for cheerful service and make it the easier to them, and this though they be employed in the meanest and lowest offices, and of another country and a different religion from yourselves. 2. A good reason for this regard: *"Knowing that you also have a Master in heaven.* You who are masters of others have a Master yourself, and are servants of another Lord. You are not lords of yourselves, and are accountable to one above you. Deal with your servants as you expect God should deal with you, and as those who believe they must give an account. You are both servants of the same Lord in the different relations in which you stand, and are equally accountable to him at last. *Knowing that your Master also is in heaven, neither is there respect of persons with him,"* Eph. 6:9.

Verses 2–4

If this be considered as connected with the foregoing verse, then we may observe that it is part of the duty which masters owe their servants to pray with them, and to pray daily with them, or *continue in prayer.* They must not only do justly and kindly by them, but act a Christian and religious part, and be concerned for their souls as well as their bodies: "As parts of your charge, and under your influence, be concerned for the blessing of God upon them, as well as the success of your affairs in their hands." And this is the duty of every one — to *continue in prayer.* "Keep up your constant times of prayer, without being diverted from it by other business; keep your hearts close to the duty, without wandering or deadness, and even to the end of it: *Watching the same."* Christians should lay hold of all opportunities for prayer, and choose the fittest seasons, which are least liable to disturbance from other things, and keep their minds lively in the duty, and in suitable frames. — *With thanksgiving,* or solemn acknowledgment of the mercies received. Thanksgiving must have a part in every prayer. — *Withal praying also for us, v.* 3. The people must pray particularly for their ministers, and bear them upon their hearts at all times at the throne of grace. As if he had said, "Do not forget us, whenever you pray for yourselves," Eph. 6:19; 1 Th. 5:25; Heb. 13:18. *That God would open to us a door of utterance,* that is, either afford opportunity to preach the gospel (so he says, *a great door and effectual is opened to me,* 1 Co. 16:9), or else give me ability and courage, and enable me with freedom and faithfulness; so Eph. 6:19, *And for me, that utterance may be given to me, that I may open my mouth boldly, to speak the mystery of Christ, for which I am also in bonds;* that is, either the deepest doctrines of the gospel with plainness, of which Christ is the principal subject (he calls it the *mystery of the gospel,* Eph. 6:19), or else he means the preaching of the gospel to the Gentile world, which he calls the *mystery hidden from ages* (*ch.* 1:26) and the *mystery of Christ,* Eph. 3:4. For this he was now in bonds. He was a prisoner at Rome, by the violent opposition of the malicious Jews. He would have them pray for him, that he might not be discouraged in his work, nor driven from it by his sufferings: *"That I may make it manifest, as I ought to speak, v.* 4. That I may make this mystery known to those who have not heard of it, and make it plain to their understanding, in such a manner as I ought to do." He had been particular in telling them what he prayed for on their behalf, *ch.* 1. Here he tells them particularly what he would have them pray for on his behalf. Paul knew as well as any man how to speak; and yet he begged their prayers for him, that he might be taught to speak. The best and most eminent Christians need the prayers of meaner Christians, and are not above asking them. The chief speakers need prayer, that God would give them a door of utterance, and that they may speak as they ought to speak.

Verses 5–6

The apostle exhorts them further to a prudent and decent conduct towards all those with whom they conversed, towards the heathen world, or those out of the Christian church among whom they lived (*v.* 5): *Walk in wisdom towards those who are without.* Be careful, in all your converse with them, to get no hurt by them, or contract any of their customs; for *evil communications corrupt good manners;* and to do not hurt to them, or increase their prejudices against religion, and give them an occasion of dislike. Yea, do them all the good you can, and by all the fittest means and in the proper seasons recommend religion to them. — *Redeeming the time;* that is, either "improving every opportunity of doing them good, and making the best use of your time in proper duty" (diligence in redeeming time very much recommends religion to the good opinion of others), or else "walking cautiously and with circumspections, to give them no advantage against you, nor expose yourselves to their malice and ill-will," Eph. 5:15, 16. *Walk circumspectly, redeeming the time, because the days are evil,* that is, dangerous, or times of trouble and suffering. And towards others, or those who are within as well as those who are without, "Let *your speech be always with grace, v.* 6. Let all your discourse be as becomes Christians, suitable to your profession — savoury, discreet, seasonable." Though it be not always of grace, it must be always with grace; and, though the matter of our discourse be that which is common, yet there must be an air of piety upon it and it must be in a Christian manner *seasoned with salt.* Grace is the salt which seasons our discourse, makes it savoury, and keeps it from corrupting. *That you may know how to answer every man.* One answer is proper for one man, and another for another man Prov. 26:4, 5. We have need of a great deal of wisdom and grace to give proper answers to every man, particularly in answering the questions and objections of adversaries against our religion, giving the reasons of our faith, and showing the unreasonableness of their exceptions and cavils to the best advantage for our cause and least prejudice to ourselves. *Be ready always to give an answer to every man who asketh you a reason of the hope that is in you, with meekness and fear,* 1 Pt. 3:15.

Verses 7–18

In the close of this epistle the apostle does several of his friends the honour to leave their names upon record, with some testimony of his respect, which will be spoken of wherever the gospel comes, and last to the end of the world.

I. Concerning Tychicus, *v.* 7. By him this epistle was sent; and he does not give them an account in writing of his present state, because Tychicus would do it by word of mouth more fully and particularly. He knew they would be glad to hear how it fared with him. The churches cannot but be concerned for good ministers and desirous to know their state. He gives him this character, *A beloved brother and faithful minister.* Paul, though a great apostle, owns a faithful minister for a brother and a beloved brother. Faithfulness in any one is truly lovely, and renders him worthy our affection and esteem. *And a fellow-servant in the Lord.* Ministers are servants to Christ, and fellow-servants to one another. They have one Lord, though they have different stations and capacities of service. Observe, It adds much to the beauty and strength of the gospel ministry when ministers are thus loving and condescending one to another, and by all just means support and advance one another's reputation. Paul sent him not only to tell them of his affairs, but to bring him an account of theirs: *Whom I have sent unto you for the same purpose, that he might know your estate, and comfort your hearts, v.* 8. He was willing to hear from them as they could be to hear from him, and thought himself as much obliged to sympathize with them as he thought them obliged to sympathize with him. It is a great comfort, under the troubles and difficulties of life, to have the mutual concern of fellow-christians.

II. Concerning Onesimus (*v.* 9): *With Onesimus, a faithful and beloved brother, who is one of you.* He was sent back from Rome along with Tychicus. This was he whom Paul had begotten in his bonds, Philem. 10. He had been servant to Philemon, and was a member, if not a minister, of their church. He was converted at Rome, whither he had fled from his master's service; and was now sent back, it is probable, with the epistle to Philemon, to introduce him again into his master's family. Observe, Though he was a poor servant, and had been a bad man, yet, being now a convert, Paul calls him a *faithful and beloved brother.* The meanest circumstance of life, and greatest wickedness of former life, make no difference in the spiritual relation among sincere Christians: they partake of the same privileges, and are entitles to the same regards. The *righteousness of God by faith of Jesus Christ is unto all and upon all those that believe; for there is no difference* (Rom. 3:22): and *there is neither Jew nor Greek, neither bond nor free, for you are all one in Christ Jesus,* Gal. 3:28. Perhaps this was some time after he was converted and sent back to Philemon, and by this time he had entered into the ministry, because Paul calls him a brother.

III. *Aristarchus, a fellow-prisoner.* Those who join in services and sufferings should be thereby engaged to one another in holy love. Paul had a particular affection for his fellow-servants and his fellow-prisoners.

IV. *Marcus, sister's son to Barnabas.* This is supposed to be the same who wrote the gospel which bears his name. *If he come unto you receive him.* Paul had a quarrel with Barnabas upon the account of this Mark, who was his nephew, and *thought not good to take him with them, because he de-*

parted from them from Pamphylia, and went not with them to the work, Acts 15:38. He would not take Mark with him, but took Silas, because Mark had deserted them; and yet Paul is not only reconciled to him himself, but recommends him to the respect of the churches, and gives a great example of a truly Christian forgiving spirit. If men have been guilty of a fault, it must not be always remembered against them. We must forget as well as forgive. *If a man be overtaken in a fault, you who are spiritual restore such a one in the spirit of meekness,* Gal. 6:1.

V. Here is one who is called *Jesus,* which is the Greek name for the Hebrew *Joshua. If Jesus had given them rest, then would he not afterwards have spoken of another day,* Heb. 4:8. *Who is called Justus.* It is probable that he changed his name for that of Justus, in honour to the name of the Redeemer. Or else Jesus was his Jewish name, for he was of the circumcision; and Justus his Roman or Latin name. *These are my fellow-labourers unto the kingdom of God, who have been a comfort unto me.* Observe, What comfort the apostle had in the communion of saints and ministers! One is his fellow-servant, another his fellow-prisoner, and all his fellow-workers, who were working out their own salvation and endeavouring to promote the salvation of others. Good ministers take great comfort in those who are their fellow-workers unto the kingdom of God. Their friendship and converse together are a great refreshment under the sufferings and difficulties in their way.

VI. *Epaphras* (*v.* 12), the same with *Epaphroditus.* He is *one of you,* one of your church; *he salutes you,* or sends his service to you, and his best affections and wishes. *Always labouring fervently for you in prayers.* Epaphras had learned of Paul to be much in prayer for his friends. Observe, 1. In what manner he prayed for them. He laboured in prayer, laboured fervently, and always laboured fervently for them. Those who would succeed in prayer must take pains in prayer; and we must be earnest in prayer, not only for ourselves, but for others also. It is the effectual fervent prayer which is the prevailing prayer, and availeth much (Jam. 5:16), and *Elias prayed earnestly that it might not rain, v.* 17. 2. What is the matter of this prayer: *That you may stand perfect and complete in all the will of God.* Observe, To stand perfect and complete in the will of God is what we should earnestly desire both for ourselves and others. We must stand complete in all the will of God; in the will of his precepts by a universal obedience, and in the will of his providence by a cheerful submission to it: and we stand perfect and complete in both by constancy and perseverance unto the end. The apostle was witness for Epaphras that he had a great zeal for them: *"I bear him record;* I can testify for him that he has a great concern for you, and that all he does for you proceeds from a warm desire for your good." And his zeal extended to all about them: to *those who are in Laodicea and Hierapolis.* He had a great concern for the Christian interest in the neighbouring places, as well as among them.

VII. *Luke* is another here mentioned, whom he calls the *beloved physician.* This is he who wrote the Gospel and Acts, and was Paul's companion. Observe, He was both a physician and an evangelist. Christ himself both taught and healed, and was the great physician as well as prophet of the church. He was the beloved physician; one who recommended himself more than ordinary to the affections of his friends. Skill in physic is a useful accomplishment in a minister and may be improved to more extensive usefulness and greater esteem among Christians.

VIII. *Demas.* Whether this was written before the second epistle to Timothy or after is not certain. There we read (2 Tim. 4:10), *Demas hath forsaken me, having loved this present world.* Some have thought that this epistle was written after; and then it is an evidence that, though Demas forsook Paul, yet he did not forsake Christ; or he forsook him but for a time, and recovered himself again, and Paul forgave him and owned him as a brother. But others think more probably that this epistle was written before the other; this in *anno* 62, that in 66, and then it is an evidence how considerable a man Demas was, who yet afterwards revolted. Many who have made a great figure in profession, and gained a great name among Christians, have yet shamefully apostatized: *They went forth from us, because they were not of us,* 1 Jn. 2:19.

IX. The *brethren in Laodicea* are here mentioned, as living in the neighbourhood of Colosse: and Paul sends salutations to them, and orders that this epistle should be read in the church of the Laodiceans (*v.* 16), that a copy of it should be sent thither, to be read publicly in their congregation. And some think Paul sent another epistle at this time to Laodicea, and ordered them to send for that from Laodicea, and read it in their church: *And that you likewise read the epistle from Laodicea.* If so, that epistle is now lost, and did not belong to the canon; for all the epistles which the apostles ever wrote were not preserved, any more than the words and actions of our blessed Lord. *There are many other things which Jesus did, which if they should be written every one, I suppose the world itself could not contain the books which would be written,* Jn. 21:25. But some think it was the epistle to the Ephesians, which is still extant.

X. *Nymphas* is mentioned (*v.* 15) as one who lived at Colosse, and had a church in his house; that is, either a religious family, where the several parts of worship were daily performed; or some part of the congregation met there, when they had no public places of worship allowed, and they were forced to assemble in private houses for fear of their enemies. *The disciples were assembled for fear of the Jews* (Jn. 20:19), and the apostle preached in his *own lodging and hired house,* Acts 28:23, 30. In the former sense it showed his exemplary piety; in the latter his zeal and public spirit.

XI. Concerning *Archippus,* who was one of their ministers at Colosse. They are bidden to admonish him to mind his work as a minister, to *take heed to it, and to fulfil it*—to be diligent and careful of all the parts of it, and to persevere in it unto the end. They must attend to the main design of their ministry, without troubling themselves or the people with things foreign to it, or of less moment. Observe, (1.) The ministry we have received is a great honour; for it is *received in the Lord,* and is by his appointment and command. (2.) Those who have received it must fulfil it, or do the full duty of it. Those betray their trust, and will have a sad account at last, who *do this work of the Lord negligently.* (3.) The people may put their ministers in mind of their duty, and excite them to it: *Say to Archippus, Take heed to the ministry,* though no doubt with decency and respect, not from pride and conceit.

XII. Concerning himself (*v.* 18): *The salutation of me Paul. Remember my bonds.* He had a scribe to write all the rest of the epistle, but these words he wrote with his own hand: *Remember my bonds.* He does not say, "Remember I am a prisoner, and send me supply;" but, "Remember I am in bonds as the apostle of the Gentiles, and let this confirm your faith in the gospel of Christ:" it adds weight to this exhortation: *I therefore, the prisoner of the Lord, beseech you to walk worthy,* Eph. 4:1. *"Grace be with you.* The favour of God, and all good, the blessed fruits and effects of it, be with you, and be your portion."

AN EXPOSITION, WITH PRACTICAL OBSERVATIONS, OF

THE FIRST EPISTLE OF ST. PAUL TO THE THESSALONIANS

Thessalonica was formerly the metropolis of Macedonia; it is now called *Salonichi,* and is the best peopled, and one of the best towns for commerce, in the Levant. The apostle Paul, being diverted from his design of going into the provinces of Asia, properly so called, and directed after an extraordinary manner to preach the gospel in Macedonia (Acts 16:9, 10), in obedience to the call of God went from Troas to Samothracia, thence to Neapolis, and thence to Philippi, where he had good success in his ministry, but met with hard usage, being cast into prison with Silas his companion in travel and labour, from which being wonderfully delivered, they comforted the brethren there, and departed. Passing through Amphipolis and Apollonia, they came to Thessalonica, where the apostle planted a church that consisted of some believing Jews and many converted Gentiles, Acts 17:1–4. But a tumult being raised in the city by the unbelieving Jews, and the lewd and baser sort of the inhabitants, Paul and Silas, for their safety, were sent away by night unto Berea, and afterwards Paul was conducted to Athens, leaving Silas and Timotheus behind him, but sent directions that they should come to him with all speed. When they came, Timotheus was sent to Thessalonica, to enquire after their welfare and to establish them in the faith (1 Th. 3:2), and, returning to Paul while he tarried at Athens, was sent again, together with Silas, to visit the churches in Macedonia. So that Paul, being left at Athens alone (1 Th. 3:1), departed thence to Corinth, where he continued a year and a half, in which time Silas and Timotheus returned to him from Macedonia (Acts 18:5), and then he wrote this epistle to the church of Christ at Thessalonica, which, though it is placed after the other epistles of this apostle, is supposed to be first in time of all Paul's epistles, and to be written about A.D. 51. The main scope of it is to express the thankfulness of this apostle for the good success his preaching had among them, to establish them in the faith, and persuade them to a holy conversation.

CHAPTER 1

After the introduction (*v.* 1) the apostle begins with a thanksgiving to God for the saving benefits bestowed on them (*v.* 2–5). And then mentions the sure evidences of the good success of the gospel among them, which was notorious and famous in several other places (*v.* 6–10).

Verse 1

In this introduction we have,

I. The inscription, where we have, 1. The persons from whom this epistle came, or by whom it was written. Paul was the inspired apostle and writer of this epistle, though he makes no mention of his apostleship, which was not doubted of by the Thessalonians, nor opposed by any false apostle among them. He joins Silvanus (or Silas) and Timotheus with himself (who had now come to him with an account of the prosperity of the churches in Macedonia), which shows this great apostle's humility, and how desirous he was to put honour upon the ministers of Christ who were of an inferior rank and standing. A good example this is to such ministers as are of greater abilities and reputation in the church than some others. 2. The persons to whom this epistle is written, namely, the church of the Thessalonians, the converted Jews and Gentiles in Thessalonica; and it is observable that this church is said to *be in God the Father and in the Lord Jesus Christ;* they had fellowship with the Father, and his Son Jesus Christ, 1 Jn. 1:3. They were a Christian church, because they believed in God the Father and in the Lord Jesus Christ. They believed the principles both of natural and revealed religion. The Gentiles among them were turned to God from idols, and the Jews among them believed Jesus to be the promised Messias. All of them were devoted and dedicated to God the Father and the Lord Jesus Christ: to God as their chief good and highest end, to Jesus Christ as their Lord and Mediator between God and man. God the Father is the original centre of all natural religion; and Jesus Christ is the author and centre of all revealed religion. *You believe in God,* says our Saviour, *believe also in me.* Jn. 14:1.

II. The salutation or apostolical benediction: *Grace be with you, and peace from God our Father and the Lord Jesus Christ.* This is the same for substance as in the other epistles. Grace and peace are well joined together; for the free grace or favour of God is the spring or fountain of all the peace and prosperity we do or can enjoy; and where there are gracious dispositions in us we may hope for peaceful thoughts in our own breasts; both grace and peace, and all spiritual blessings, come to us from God the Father and the Lord Jesus Christ; from God the original of all good, and from the Lord Jesus the purchaser of all good for us; from God in Christ, and so our Father in covenant, because he is the God and Father of our Lord Jesus Christ. Note, As all good comes from God, so no good can be hoped for by sinners but from God in Christ. And the best good may be expected from God as our Father for the sake of Christ.

Verses 2–5

I. The apostle begins with thanksgiving to God. Being about to mention the things that were matter of joy to him, and highly praiseworthy in them, and greatly for their advantage, he chooses to do this by way of thanksgiving to God, who is the author of all that good that comes to us, or is done by us, at any time. God is the object of all religious worship, of prayer and praise. And thanksgiving to God is a great duty, to be performed always or constantly; even when we do not actually give thanks to God by our words, we should have a grateful sense of God's goodness upon our minds. Thanksgiving should be often repeated; and not only should we be thankful for the favours we ourselves receive, but for the benefits bestowed on others also, upon our fellow-creatures and fellow-christians. The apostle gave thanks not only for those who were his most intimate friends, or most eminently favoured of God, but for them all.

II. He joined prayer with his praise or thanksgiving. When we in every thing by prayer and supplication make our requests known to God, we should join thanksgiving therewith, Phil. 4:6. So when we give thanks for any benefit we receive we should join prayer. We should pray always and without ceasing, and should pray not only for ourselves, but for others also, for our friends, and should make mention of them in our prayers. We may sometimes mention their names, and should make mention of their case and condition; at least, we should have their persons and circumstances in our minds, remembering them without ceasing. Note, As there is much that we ought to be thankful for on the behalf of ourselves and our friends, so there is much occasion of constant prayer for further supplies of good.

III. He mentions the particulars for which he was so thankful to God; namely,

1. The saving benefits bestowed on them. These were the grounds and reasons of his thanksgiving. (1.) Their faith and their work of faith. Their faith he tells them (*v.* 8) was very famous, and spread abroad. This is the radical grace; and their faith was a true and living faith, because a working faith. Note, Wherever there is a true faith, it will work: it will have an influence upon heart and life; it will put us upon working for God and for our own salvation. We have comfort in our own faith and the faith of others when we perceive the work of faith. *Show me thy faith by thy works,* Jam. 2:18. (2.) Their love and labour of love. Love is one of the cardinal graces; it is of great use to us in this life and will remain and be perfected in the life to come. *Faith works by love;* it shows itself in the exercise of love to God and love to our neighbour; as love will show itself by labour, it will put us upon taking pains in religion. (3.) Their hope and the patience of hope. *We are saved by hope.* This grace is compared to the soldier's helmet and sailor's anchor, and is of great use in times of danger. Wherever there is a well-grounded hope of eternal life, it will appear by the exercise of patience; in a patient bearing of the calamities of the present time and a patient waiting for the glory to be revealed. *For, if we hope for that we see not, then do we with patience wait for it,* Rom. 8:25.

2. The apostle not only mentions these three cardinal graces, faith, hope and love, but also takes notice, (1.) Of the object and efficient cause of these graces, namely, our Lord Jesus Christ. (2.) Of the sincerity of them: being in the *sight of God even our Father.* The great motive to sincerity is the apprehension of God's eye as always upon us; and it is a sign of sincerity when in all we do we endeavour to approve ourselves to God, and that is right which is so in the sight of God. Then is the work of faith, or labour of love, or patience of hope, sincere, when it is done under the eye of God. (3.) He mentions the fountain whence these graces flow, namely, God's electing love: *Knowing, brethren beloved, your election of God, v.* 4. Thus he runs up these streams to the fountain, and that was God's eternal election. Some by their election of God would understand only the temporary separation of the Thessalonians from the unbelieving Jews and Gentiles in their conversion; but this was according to the *eternal purpose of him who worketh all things according to the counsel of his own will,* Eph. 1:11. Speaking of their election, he calls them, *brethren beloved;* for the original of the brotherhood that is between Christians and the relation wherein they stand one to another is election. And it is a good reason why we should *love one another,* because we are all beloved of God, and were beloved of him in his counsels when there was not any thing in us to merit his love. The election of these Thessalonians was known to the apostles, and therefore might be known to themselves, and that by the fruits and effects thereof — their sincere faith, and hope, and love, by the successful preaching of the gospel among them. Observe, [1.] All those who in the fulness of time are effectually called and sanctified were from eternity elected and chosen to salvation. [2.] The election of God is of his own good pleasure and mere grace, not for the sake of any merit in those who are chosen. [3.] The election of God may be known by the fruits thereof. [4.] Whenever we are giving thanks to God for his grace either to ourselves or others, we should run up the streams to the fountain, and give thanks to God for his electing love, by which we are made to differ.

3. Another ground or reason of the apostle's thanksgiving is the success of his ministry among them. He was thankful on his own account as well as theirs, that he had not laboured in vain. He had the seal and evidence of his apostleship hereby, and great encouragement in his labours and sufferings. Their ready acceptance and entertainment of the gospel he preached to them were an evidence of their being elected and beloved of God. It was in this way that he knew their election. It is true he had been in the third heavens; but he had not searched the records of eternity, and found their election there, but knew this by the success of the gospel among them (*v.* 5), and he takes notice with thankfulness, (1.) That the gospel came to them also not in word only, but in power; they not only heard the sound of it, but submitted to the power of it. It did not merely tickle the ear and please the fancy, not merely fill their heads with notions and amuse their minds for awhile, but it affected their hearts: a divine power went along with it for convincing their consciences and amending their lives. Note, By this we may know our election, if we not only speak of the things of God by rote as parrots, but feel the influence of these things in our hearts, mortifying our lusts, weaning us from the world, and raising us up to heavenly things. (2.) It came in the Holy Ghost, that is, with the powerful energy of the divine Spirit. Note, Wherever the gospel comes in power, it is to be attributed to the operation of the Holy Ghost; and unless the Spirit of God accompany the word of God, to render it effectual by his power, it will be to us but as a dead letter; and the letter killeth, it is the Spirit that giveth life. (3.) The gospel came to them in much assurance. Thus did they entertain it by the power of the Holy Ghost. They were fully convinced of the truth of it, so as not to be easily shaken in mind by objections and doubts; they were willing to leave all for Christ, and to venture their souls and everlasting condition upon the verity of the gospel revelation. The word was not to them, like the sentiments of some philosophers about matters of opinion and doubtful speculation, but the object of their faith and assurance. Their *faith was the evidence of things not seen;* and the Thessalonians thus knew what manner of men the apostle and his fellow-labourers were among them, and what they did for their sake, and with what good success.

Verses 6–10

In these words we have the evidence of the apostle's success among the Thessalonians, which was notorious and famous in several places. For,

I. They were careful in their holy conversation to imitate the good examples of the apostles and ministers of Christ, *v.* 6. As the apostle took care to demean himself well, not only for his own credit's sake, but for the benefit of others, by a conversation suitable to his doctrine, that he might not pull down with one hand what he built up with the other, so the Thessalonians, who observed what manner of men they were among them, how their preaching and living were all of a piece, showed a conscientious care to be followers of them, or to imitate their good example. Herein they became also followers of the Lord, who is the perfect example we must strive to imitate; and we should be followers of others no further than they are followers of Christ, 1 Co. 11:1. The Thessalonians acted thus, notwithstanding their affliction, that much affliction which the apostles and themselves also were exposed to. They were willing to share in the sufferings that attended the embracing and professing of Christianity. They entertained the gospel, notwithstanding the troubles and hardships which attended the preachers and professors of it too. Perhaps this made the word more precious, being dear-bought; and the examples of the apostles shone very bright under their afflictions; so that the Thessalonians embraced the word cheerfully, and followed the example of the suffering apostles joyfully, *with joy in the Holy Ghost* — such solid and spiritual and lasting joy as the Holy Ghost is the author of, who, when our afflictions abound, makes our consolations much more to abound.

II. Their zeal prevailed to such a degree that they were themselves examples to all about them, *v.* 7, 8. Observe here,

1. Their example was very effectual to make good impressions upon many others. They were *typoi — stamps,* or instruments to make impression with. They had themselves received good impressions from the preaching and conversation of the apostles, and they made good impressions, and their conversation had an influence upon others. Note, Christians should be so good as by their example to influence others.

2. It was very extensive, and reached beyond the confines of Thessalonica, even to the believers of all Macedonia, and further, in Achaia; the Philippians, and others who received the gospel before the Thessalonians, were edified by their example. Note, Some who were last hired into the vineyard may sometimes outstrip those who come in before them, and become examples to them.

3. It was very famous. The word of the Lord, or its wonderful effects upon the Thessalonians, sounded, or was famous and well known, in the regions round about that city, and *in every place;* not strictly every where, but here and there, up and down in the world: so that, from the good success of the gospel among them, many others were encouraged to entertain it, and to be willing, when called, to suffer for it. Their faith was spread abroad. (1.) The readiness of their faith was famed abroad. These Thessalonians embraced the gospel as soon as it was preached to them; so that every body took notice what manner of entering in among them the apostles had, that there were no such delays as at Philippi, where it was a great while before much good was done. (2.) The effects of their faith were famous. [1.] They quitted their idolatry; they turned from their idols, and abandoned all the false worship they had been educated in. [2.] They gave themselves up to God, to the living and true God, and devoted themselves to his service. [3.] They set themselves to wait for the Son of God from heaven, *v.* 10. And this is one of the peculiarities of our holy religion, to wait for Christ's second coming, as those who believe he will come and hope he will come to our joy. The believers under the Old Testament waited for the coming of the Messiah, and believers now wait for his second coming; he is yet to come. And there is good reason to believe he will come, because God has raised him from the dead, which is full assurance unto all men that he will come to judgment, Acts 17:31. And there is good reason to hope and wait for his coming, because he has delivered us from the wrath to come. He came to purchase salvation, and will, when he comes again, bring salvation with him, full and final deliverance from sin, and death, and hell, from that wrath which is yet to come upon unbelievers, and which, when it has once come, will be yet to come, because it is *everlasting fire* prepared for the devil and his angels, Mt. 25:41.

CHAPTER 2

In this chapter the apostle puts the Thessalonians in mind of the manner of his preaching among them (*v.* 1–6). Then of the manner of his conversation among them (*v.* 7–12). Afterwards of the success of his ministry, with the effects both on himself and on them (*v.* 13–16), and then apologizes for his absence (*v.* 17–20).

Verses 1–6

Here we have an account of Paul's manner of preaching, and his comfortable reflection upon his entrance in among the Thessalonians. As he had the testimony of his own conscience witnessing to his integrity, so he could appeal to the Thessalonians how faithful he, and Silas, and Timotheus, his helpers in the work of the Lord, had discharged their office: *You yourselves, brethren, know our entrance in unto you.* Note, It is a great comfort to a minister to have his own conscience and the consciences of others witnessing for him that he set out well, with good designs and from good principles;

and that *his preaching was not in vain,* or, as some read it, *was not fain.* The apostle here comforts himself either in the success of his ministry, that it was not fruitless or in vain (according to our translation), or as others think, reflecting upon the sincerity of his preaching, that it was not vain and empty, or deceitful and treacherous. The subject-matter of the apostle's preaching was not vain and idle speculations about useless niceties and foolish questions, but sound and solid truth, such as was most likely to profit his hearers. A good example this is, to be imitated by all the ministers of the gospel. Much less was the apostle's preaching vain or deceitful. He could say to these Thessalonians what he told the Corinthians (2 Co. 4:2): *We have renounced the hidden things of dishonesty, not walking in craftiness, nor handling the word of God deceitfully.* He had no sinister or worldly design in his preaching, which he puts them in mind to have been,

I. With courage and resolution: *We were bold in our God to speak unto you the gospel of God, v.* 2. The apostle was inspired with a holy boldness, nor was he discouraged at the afflictions he met with, or the opposition that was made against him. He had met with ill usage at Philippi, as these Thessalonians well knew. There it was that he and Silas were shamefully treated, being put in the stocks; yet no sooner were they set at liberty than they went to Thessalonica, and preached the gospel with as much boldness as ever. Note, Suffering in a good cause should rather sharpen than blunt the edge of holy resolution. The gospel of Christ, at its first setting out in the world, met with much opposition; and those who preached it preached it *with contention,* with great agony, which denoted either the apostles' striving in their preaching or their striving against the opposition they met with. This was Paul's comfort; he was neither daunted in his work, nor driven from it.

II. With great simplicity and godly sincerity: *Our exhortation was not of deceit, nor of uncleanness, nor in guile, v.* 3. This, no doubt, was matter of the greatest comfort to the apostle — the consciousness of his own sincerity; and was one reason of his success. It was the sincere and uncorrupted gospel that he preached and exhorted them to believe and obey. His design was not to set up a faction, to draw men over to a party, but to promote *pure religion and undefiled before God and the Father.* The gospel he preached was without deceit, it was true and faithful; it was not fallacious, nor a cunningly-devised fable. Nor was it of uncleanness. His gospel was pure and holy, worthy of its holy author, tending to discountenance all manner of impurity. *The word of God is pure.* There should be no corrupt mixtures therewith; and, as the matter of the apostle's exhortation was thus true and pure, the manner of his speaking was without guile. He did not pretend one thing and intend another. *He believed, and therefore he spoke.* He had no sinister and secular aims and views, but was in reality what he seemed to be. The apostle not only asserts his sincerity, but subjoins the reasons and evidences thereof. The reasons are contained, *v.* 4.

1. They were stewards, *put in trust* with the gospel: and it is required of a steward that he be faithful. The gospel which Paul preached was not his own, but the gospel of God. Note, Ministers have a great favour shown them, and honour put upon them, and trust committed to them. They must not dare to corrupt the word of God: they must diligently make use of what is entrusted with them, so as God hath allowed and commanded, knowing they shall be called to an account, when they must be no longer stewards.

2. Their design was to please God and not men. God is a God of truth, and requires truth in the inward parts; and, if sincerity be wanting, all that we do cannot please God. The gospel of Christ is not accommodated to the fain fancies and lusts of men, to gratify their appetites and passions; but, on the contrary, it was designed for the mortifying of their corrupt affections, and delivering them from the power of fancy, that they might be brought under the power of faith. *If I yet pleased men, I should not be the servant of Christ,* Gal. 1:10.

3. They acted under the consideration of God's omniscience, as in the sight of him who *tries our hearts.* This is indeed the great motive to sincerity, to consider that God not only seeth all that we do, but knoweth our thoughts afar off, and searcheth the heart. He is well acquainted with all our aims and designs, as well as our actions. And it is from this God who trieth our hearts that we must receive our reward. The evidences of the apostle's sincerity follow; and they are these: — (1.) He avoided flattery: *Neither at any time used we flattering words, as you know, v.* 5. He and his fellow-labourers preached Christ and him crucified, and did not aim to gain an interest in men's affections for themselves, by glorying, and fawning and wheedling them. No, he was far from this; nor did he flatter men in their sins; nor tell them, if they would be of his party, they might live as they listed. He did not flatter them with fain hopes, nor indulge them in any evil work or way, promising them life, and so *daubing with untempered mortar.* (2.) He avoided covetousness. He did not make the ministry *a cloak,* or a covering, for *covetousness, as God was witness, v.* 5. His design was not to enrich himself by preaching the gospel; so far from this, he did not stipulate with them for bread. He was not like the false apostles, who, *through covetousness, with feigned words made merchandise* of the people, 2 Pt. 2:3. (3.) He avoided ambition and vain-glory: *Nor of men sought we glory, neither of you nor yet of others, v.* 6. They expected neither people's purses nor their caps, neither to be enriched by them nor caressed, and adored, and called Rabbi by them. This apostle exhorts the Galatians (*ch.* 5:26) *not to be desirous of vain glory;* his ambition was to obtain *that honour which comes from God,* Jn. 5:44. He tells them that they might have used greater authority as apostles, and expected greater esteem, and demanded maintenance, which is meant by the phrase of *being burdensome,* because perhaps some would have thought this too great a burden for them to bear.

Verses 7–12

In these words the apostle reminds the Thessalonians of the manner of his conversation among them. And,

I. He mentions the gentleness of their behaviour: *We were gentle among you, v.* 7. He showed great mildness and tenderness who might have acted with the authority of an apostle of Christ. Such behaviour greatly recommends religion, and is most agreeable to God's gracious dealing with sinners, in and by the gospel. This great apostle, though he abhorred and avoided flattery, was most condescending to all men. He accommodated himself to all men's capacities, *and became all things to all men.* He showed the kindness and care of a nurse that cherishes her children. This is the way to win people, rather than to rule with rigour. The word of God is indeed powerful; and as it comes often with awful authority upon the minds of men, as it always has enough in it to convince every impartial judgment, so it comes with the more pleasing power, when the ministers of the gospel recommend themselves to the affections of the people. And as a nursing mother bears with frowardness in a child, and condescends to mean offices for its good, and draws out her breast, cherishing it in her bosom, so in like manner should the ministers of Christ behave towards their people. The *servant of the Lord must not strive, but be gentle unto all men, and patient,* 2 Tim. 2:24. This gentleness and goodness the apostle expressed several ways. 1. By the most affectionate desire of their welfare: *Being affectionately desirous of you, v.* 8. The apostle had a most affectionate love to their persons, and sought them, not theirs; themselves, not their goods; and to gain them, not to be a gainer by them, or to make a merchandise of them: it was their spiritual and eternal welfare and salvation that he was earnestly desirous of. 2. By great readiness to do them good, willingly imparting to them, *not the gospel of God only, but also our own souls, v.* 8. See here the manner of Paul's preaching. He spared no pains therein. He was willing to run hazards, and venture his soul, or life, in preaching the gospel. He was willing to spend and be spent in the service of men's souls; and, as those who give bread to the hungry from a charitable principle are said to impart their souls in what they give (Isa. 18:10), so did the apostles in giving forth the bread of life; so dear were these Thessalonians in particular to this apostle, and so great was his love to them. 3. By bodily labour to prevent their charge, or that his ministry might not be expensive and burdensome to them: *You remember our labour and travail; for, labouring night and day,* etc., *v.* 9. He denied himself the liberty he had of taking wages from the churches. To the labour of the ministry he added that of his calling, as a tent-maker, that he might get his own bread. We are not to suppose that the apostle spent the whole night and day in bodily labour, or work, to supply the necessities of his body; for then he would have had no time for the work of the ministry. But he spent part of the night, as well as the day, in this work; and was willing to forego his rest in the night, that he might have an opportunity to do good to the souls of men in the day time. A good example is here set before the ministers of the gospel, to be industrious for the salvation of men's souls, though it will not follow that they are always obliged to preach freely. There is no general rule to be drawn from this instance, either that ministers may at no time work with their hands, for the supply of their outward necessities, or that they ought always to do so. 4. By the holiness of their conversation, concerning which he appeals not only to them, but to God also (*v.* 10): *You are witnesses, and God also.* They were observers of their outward conversation in public before men, and God was witness not only of their behaviour in secret, but of the inward principles from which they acted. Their behaviour was holy towards God, just towards all men, and unblamable, without giving cause of scandal or offence; and they were careful to give no offence either to those who were without, or to those who believed, that they might give no ill example; that their preaching and living might be all of a piece. Herein, said this apostle, *do I exercise myself, to have always a conscience void of offence towards God, and towards men,* Acts 24:16.

II. He mentions their faithful discharge of the work and office of the ministry, *v.* 11, 12. Concerning this also he could appeal to them as witnesses. Paul and his fellow-labourers were not only good Christians, but faithful ministers. And we should not only be good as to our general calling as Christians, but in our particular callings and relations. Paul exhorted the Thessalonians, not only informing them in their duty, but exciting and quickening them to the performance of it, by proper motives and arguments. And he comforted them also, endeavouring to cheer and support their spirits under the difficulties and discouragements they might meet with. And this he did not only publicly, but privately also, and from house to house (Acts 20:20), *and charged every one* of them by personal addresses: this, some think, is intended by the similitude of a father's charging his children. This expression also denotes the affectionate and compassionate counsels and consolations which this apostle used. He was their spiritual father; and, as he cherished them like a nursing mother, so he charged them as a father, with a father's affection rather than a father's authority. As *my beloved sons, I warn you,* 1 Co. 4:14. The manner of this apostle's exhortation ought to be regarded by ministers in particular for their imitation, and the matter of it is greatly to be regarded by them and all others; namely, that *they would walk worthy of God, who hath called them to his kingdom and glory, v.* 12. Observe, 1. What is our great gospel privilege — that God has called us to his kingdom and glory. The gospel calls us into the kingdom and state of grace here and unto the kingdom and state of glory hereafter, to heaven and happiness as our end and to holiness as the way to that end. 2. What is our great gospel duty — that we walk worthy of God, that the temper of our minds and tenour of our lives be answerable to this call and suitable to this privilege. We should accommodate ourselves to the intention and design of the gospel, and live suitably to our profession and privileges, our hopes and expectations, as becomes those who are called with such a high and holy calling.

Verses 13–16

Here observe, I. The apostle makes mention of the success of his ministry among these Thessalonians (*v.* 13), which is expressed,

1. By the manner of their receiving the word of God: *When you received the word of God, which you heard of us, you received it, not as the word of men, but (as it is in truth) the word of God.* Where note, (1.) The word of the gospel is preached by men like ourselves, men of like passions and infirmities with others: *We have this treasure in earthen vessels.* The word of God, which these Thessalonians received, they heard from the apostles. (2.) However, it is in truth the word of God. Such was the word the apostles preached by divine inspiration, and such is that which is left upon record, written in the scriptures by divine inspiration; and such is that word which in our days is preached, being either contained, or evidently founded on, or deduced from, these sacred oracles. (3.) Those are greatly to blame who give out their own fancies or injunctions for the word of God. This is the vilest way of imposing upon a people, and to deal unfaithfully. (4.) Those are also to blame who, in hearing the word, look no further than to the ministry of men, who are only, or chiefly, pleased with the elegance of the style, or the beauty of the composition, or the voice and manner in which the word is preached, and expect to receive their advantage herein. (5.)

We should receive the word of God as the word of God, with affections suitable to the holiness, wisdom, verity, and goodness, thereof. The words of men are frail and perishing, like themselves, and sometimes false, foolish, and fickle: but God's word is holy, wise, just, and faithful; and, like its author, lives and abides for ever. Let us accordingly receive and regard it.

2. By the wonderful operation of this word they received: *It effectually worketh in those that believe, v.* 13. Those who by faith receive the word find it profitable. *It does good to those that walk uprightly,* and by its wonderful effects evidences itself to be the word of God. This converts their souls, and enlightens their minds, and rejoices their hearts (Ps. 19); and such as have this inward testimony of the truth of the scriptures, the word of God, by the effectual operations thereof on their hearts, have the best evidence of their divine original to themselves, though this is not sufficient to convince others who are strangers thereto.

II. He mentions the good effects which his successful preaching had,

1. Upon himself and fellow-labourers. It was a constant cause of thankfulness: *For this cause thank we God without ceasing, v.* 13. The apostle expressed his thankfulness to God so often upon this account that he seemed to think he never could be sufficiently thankful that God had counted him faithful, and put him into the ministry, and made his ministrations successful.

2. Upon them. The word wrought effectually in them, not only to be examples unto others in faith and good works (which he had mentioned before), but also in constancy and patience under sufferings and trials for the sake of the gospel: *You became followers of the churches of God, and have suffered like things as they have done* (*v.* 14), and with like courage and constancy, with like patience and hope. Note, The cross is the Christian's mark: if we are called to suffer we are called only to be followers of the churches of God; *so persecuted they the prophets that were before you,* Mt. 5:12. It is a good effect of the gospel when we are enabled to suffer for its sake. The apostle mentions the sufferings of the churches of God, which *in Judea were in Christ Jesus.* Those in Judea first heard the gospel, and they first suffered for it: for the Jews were the most bitter enemies Christianity had, and were especially enraged against their countrymen who embraced Christianity. Note, Bitter zeal and fiery persecution will set countrymen at variance, and break through all the bonds of nature, as well as contradict all the rules of religion. In every city where the apostles went to preach the gospel the Jews stirred up the inhabitants against them. They were the ringleaders of persecution in all places; so in particular it was at Thessalonica: Acts 17:5, *The Jews that believed not, moved with envy, took unto them certain lewd fellows of the baser sort, and gathered a company, and set all the city in an uproar.* Upon this occasion, the apostle gives a character of the unbelieving Jews (*v.* 15), enough to justify their final rejection and the ruin of their place, and church, and nation, which was now approaching. (1.) They *killed the Lord Jesus,* and impudently and presumptuously wished that his blood might be on them and their children. (2.) They killed *their own prophets:* so they had done all along; their fathers had done so: they had been a persecuting generation. (3.) They hated the apostles, and did them all the mischief they could. They persecuted them, and drove and chased them from place to place: and no marvel, if they killed the Lord Jesus, that they persecuted his followers. (4.) They *pleased not God.* They had quite lost all sense of religion, and due care to do their duty to God. It was a most fatal mistake to think that they did God service by killing God's servants. Murder and persecution are most hateful to God and cannot be justified on any pretence; they are so contrary to natural religion that no zeal for any true or only pretended institution of religion can ever excuse them. (5.) They were *contrary to all men.* Their persecuting spirit was a perverse spirit; contrary to the light of nature, and contrary to humanity, contrary to the welfare of all men, and contrary to the sentiments of all men not under the power of bigotry. (6.) They had *an implacable enmity to the Gentiles,* and envied them the offers of the gospel: *Forbidding the apostles to speak to the Gentiles, that they might be saved.* The means of salvation had long been confined to the Jews. *Salvation is of the Jews,* says our Saviour. And they were envious against the Gentiles, and angry that they should be admitted to share in the means of salvation. Nothing provoked them more than our Saviour's speaking to them at any time concerning this matter; this enraged the Jews at Jerusalem, when, in his defence, Paul told them, *he was sent unto the Gentiles,* Acts 22:21. They heard him patiently till he uttered these words, but then could endure no longer, but *lifted up their voices, and said, Away with such a fellow from the earth, for it is not fit that he should live.* Thus did the Jews fill up their sins; and nothing tends more to any person or people's filling up the measure of their sins than opposing the gospel, obstructing the progress of it, and hindering the salvation of precious souls. For the sake of these things *wrath has come upon them to the uttermost;* that is, wrath was determined against them, and would soon overtake them. It was not many years after this that Jerusalem was destroyed, and the Jewish nation cut off by the Romans. Note, When the measure of any man's iniquity is full, and he has sinned to the uttermost, then comes wrath, and that to the uttermost.

Verses 17–20

In these words the apostle apologizes for his absence. Here observe, 1. He tells them they were involuntarily forced from them: *We, brethren, were taken from you, v.* 17. Such was the rage of his persecutors. He was unwillingly sent away by night to Berea, Acts 17:10. 2. Though he was absent in body, yet he was present in heart. He had still a remembrance of them, and great care for them. 3. Even his bodily absence was but for a short time, the time of an hour. Time is short, all our time on earth is short and uncertain, whether we are present with our friends or absent from them. This world is not a place where we are always, or long, to be together. It is in heaven that holy souls shall meet, and never part more. 4. He earnestly desired and endeavoured to see them again: *We endeavoured more abundantly to see your face with great desire, v.* 17. So that the apostle at least intended his absence should be but for a short time. His desire and endeavour were to return again very soon to Thessalonica. But men of business are not masters of their own time. Paul did his endeavour, and he could do no more, *v.* 18. 5. He tells them that Satan hindered his return (*v.* 18), that is, either some enemy or enemies, or the great enemy of mankind, who stirred up opposition to Paul, either in his return to Thessalonica, when he intended to return thither, or stirred up such contentions or dissensions in those places whether he went as made his presence necessary. Note, Satan is a constant enemy to the work of God, and does all he can to obstruct it. 6. He assures them of his affection and high esteem for them, though he was not able, as yet, to be present with them according to his desire. They were his *hope, and joy, and crown of rejoicing; his glory and joy.* These are expressions of great and endeared affection, and high estimation. And it is happy when ministers and people have such mutual affection and esteem of each other, and especially if they shall thus rejoice, if those that sow and those that reap shall rejoice together, *in the presence of our Lord Jesus Christ at his coming.*

The apostle here puts the Thessalonians in mind that though he could not come to them as yet, and though he should never be able to come to them, yet our Lord Jesus Christ will come, nothing shall hinder this. And further, when he shall come, all must appear in his presence, or before him. Ministers and people must all appear before him, and faithful people will be the glory and joy of faithful ministers in that great and glorious day.

CHAPTER 3

In this chapter the apostle gives further evidence of his love to the Thessalonians, reminding them of his sending Timothy to them, with the mention of his design therein and his inducements so to do (*v.* 1–5). He acquaints them also with his great satisfaction at the return of Timothy, with good tidings concerning them (*v.* 6–10). And concludes with fervent prayer for them (*v.* 11 to the end).

Verses 1–5

In these words the apostle gives an account of his sending Timothy to the Thessalonians. Though he was hindered from going to them himself, yet his love was such that he could not forbear sending Timothy to them. Though Timothy was very useful to him, and he could not well spare him, yet Paul was content, for their good, *to be left alone at Athens.* Note, Those ministers do not duly value the establishment and welfare of their people who cannot deny themselves in many things for that end. Observe,

I. The character he gives of Timothy (*v.* 2): *We sent Timotheus, our brother.* Elsewhere he calls him his son; here he calls him brother. Timothy was Paul's junior in age, his inferior in gifts and graces, and of a lower rank in the ministry: for Paul was an apostle, and Timothy but an evangelist; yet Paul calls him brother. This was an instance of the apostle's humility, and showed his desire to put honour upon Timothy and to recommend him to the esteem of the churches. He calls him also a minister of God. Note, Ministers of the gospel of Christ are ministers of God, to promote the kingdom of God among men. He calls him also his fellow-labourer in the gospel of Christ. Note, Ministers of the gospel must look upon themselves as labourers in the Lord's vineyard; they have an honourable office and hard work, yet a good work. *This is a true saying, If any man desire the office of a bishop, he desires a good work,* 1 Tim. 3:1. And ministers should look upon one another, and strengthen one another's hands, not strive and contend one with another (which will hinder their work), but strive together to carry on the great work they are engaged in, namely, to preach and publish the gospel of Christ, and to persuade people to embrace and entertain it and live suitably thereto.

II. The end and design why Paul sent Timothy: *To establish you and to comfort you concerning your faith, v.* 2. Paul had converted them to the Christian faith, and now he was desirous that they might be confirmed and comforted, that they might confirmed in the choice they had made of the Christian religion, and comforted in the profession and practice of it. Note, The more we are comforted, the more we shall be confirmed, because, when we find pleasure in the ways of God, we shall thereby be engaged to continue and persevere therein. The apostle's design was to establish and comfort the Thessalonians concerning their faith, — concerning the object of their faith, namely, the truths of the gospel, and particularly that Jesus Christ was the Saviour of the world, and so wise and good, so powerful and faithful, that they might rely upon him, — concerning the recompence of faith, which was more than sufficient to balance all their losses and reward all their labours.

III. The motive inducing Paul to send Timothy for this end, namely, a godly fear or jealousy, lest they should be moved from the faith of Christ, *v.* 3. He was desirous that no man, no one among them, should be moved or shaken in mind, that they should not apostatize or waver in the faith. And yet,

1. He apprehended there was danger, and feared the consequence.

(1.) There was danger, [1.] By reason of *affliction* and persecution for the sake of the gospel, *v.* 3. These Thessalonians could not but perceive what afflictions the apostles and preachers of the gospel met with, and this might possibly stumble them; and also those who made profession of the gospel were persecuted, and without doubt these Thessalonians themselves were afflicted. [2.] By reason of the tempter's subtlety and malice. The apostle was afraid lest by any means the tempter had tempted them, *v.* 5. The devil is a subtle and unwearied tempter, who seeks an opportunity to beguile and destroy us, and takes all advantages against us, both in a time of prosperity and adversity; and he has often been successful in his attacks upon persons under afflictions. He has often prejudiced the minds of men against religion on account of the sufferings its professors are exposed to. We have reason therefore to be jealous over ourselves and others, lest we be ensnared by him.

(2.) The consequence the apostle feared was lest his labour should be in vain. And thus it would have been, if the tempter had tempted them, and prevailed against them, to move them from the faith. They would have lost what they had wrought, and the apostle would have lost what he laboured for. Note, It is the devil's design to hinder the good fruit and effect of the preaching of the gospel. If he cannot hinder ministers from labouring in the word and doctrine, he will, if he be able, hinder them of the success of their labours. Note also, Faithful ministers are much concerned about the success of their labours. No one would willingly labour in vain; and ministers are loth to spend their strength, and pains, and time, for nought.

2. To prevent this danger, with its bad consequence, the apostle tells them what care he took in sending Timothy, (1.) To put them in mind of what he had told them before concerning suffering tribulation (*v.* 4), he says (*v.* 3), *We are appointed thereunto,* that is, unto afflictions. So is the will and purpose of God that *through many afflictions we must enter into his kingdom.* Their troubles and persecutions did not come by chance, not merely from the wrath and malice of the enemies of religion, but by the *appointment of God.* The

event only came to pass according as God had determined, and they knew he had told them before it would be; so that they should not think it strange, and, being fore-warned, they should be fore-armed. Note, The apostles were so far from flattering people with an expectation of worldly prosperity in religion that, on the contrary, they told them plainly they must count upon trouble in the flesh. And herein they followed the example of their great Master, the author or our faith. Besides, it might prove a confirmation of their faith, when they perceived that it only happened to them as was predicted before. (2.) To know their faith, that so he might inform the apostles whether they remained stedfast under all their sufferings, whether their faith failed or not, because, if their faith did not fail, they would be able to stand their ground against the tempter and all his temptations: their faith would be a *shield, to defend them against all the fiery darts of the wicked,* Eph. 6:16.

Verses 6–10

Here we have Paul's great satisfaction upon the return of Timothy with good tidings from the Thessalonians, in which we may observe,

I. The good report Timothy made concerning them, *v.* 6. Without question, he was a willing messenger of these good tidings. *Concerning their faith,* that is, concerning their stedfastness in the faith, that they were not shaken in mind, nor turned aside form the profession of the gospel. *Their love* also continued; their love to the gospel, and the ministers of the gospel. For they had a good and a kind remembrance of the apostles, and that constantly, or always. The names of the apostles were very dear to them, and the thoughts of them, and what they themselves had received from them, were very precious, insomuch that they *desired greatly to see them again,* and receive some spiritual gift from them; and there was no love lost, for the apostle was as desirous to see them. It is happy where there is such mutual love between minister and people. This tends to promote religion, and the success of the gospel. The world hates them, and therefore they should love one another.

II. The great comfort and satisfaction the apostle had in this good report concerning them (*v.* 7, 8): *Therefore, brethren, we were comforted in all our affliction and distress.* The apostle thought this good news of them was sufficient to balance all the troubles he met with. It was easy to him to bear affliction, or persecution, or fightings from without, when he found the good success of his ministry and the constancy of the converts he had made to Christianity; and his distress of mind on account of his fears within, lest he had laboured in vain, was now in a good measure over, when he understood their faith and the perseverance of it. This put new life and spirit into the apostle and made him vigorous and active in the work of the Lord. Thus he was not only comforted, but greatly rejoiced also: *Now we live, if you stand fast in the Lord, v.* 8. It would have been a killing thing to the apostles if the professors of religion had been unsteady, or proved apostates; whereas nothing was more encouraging than their constancy.

III. The effects of this were thankfulness and prayer to God on their behalf. Observe, 1. How thankful the apostle was, *v.* 9. He was full of joy, and full of praise and thanksgiving. When we are most cheerful we should be most thankful. What we rejoice in we should give thanks for. This is to rejoice before our God, to spiritualize our joy. Paul speaks as if he could not tell how to express his thankfulness to God, or his joy and rejoicing for their sakes. But he was careful God should not lose the glory of the comfort he received in the welfare of his friends. His heart was enlarged with love to them and with thanksgiving to God. He was willing to express the one and the other as well as he could. As to thankfulness to God, this especially is very imperfect in the present state; but, when we come to heaven, we shall do this work better than now we can. 2. He prayed for them night and day (*v.* 10), evening and morning, or very frequently, in the midst of the business of the day or slumber of the night lifting up his heart to God in prayer. Thus we should pray always. And Paul's prayer was fervent prayer. He prayed exceedingly, and was earnest in his supplication. Note, When we are most thankful we should always give ourselves to prayer; and those we give thanks for have yet need to be prayed for. Those whom we most rejoice in, and who are our greatest comforts, must be our constant care, while in this world of temptation and imperfection. There was something still lacking in their faith; Paul desired that this might be perfected, and to see their face in order thereunto. Note, (1.) The best of men have something wanting in their faith, if not as to the matter of it, there being some mysteries or doctrines not sufficiently known or believed by them, yet as to the clearness and certainty of their faith, there being some remaining darkness and doubtings, or at least as to the effects and operations of it, these being not so conspicuous and perfect as they should be. And, (2.) The ministry of the word and ordinances is helpful, and to be desired and used for the perfecting of that which is lacking in our faith.

Verses 11–13

In these words we have the earnest prayer of the apostle. He desired to be instrumental in the further benefit of the Thessalonians; and the only way to be so while at a distance was by prayer for them, together with his writing or sending to them. He desired that their faith might be perfected, which he could not be the proper cause or author of; for he pretended not to dominion over their faith, nor to have the donation of it, and he therefore concludes with prayer for them. Observe,

I. Whom he prays to, namely, God and Christ. Prayer is a part of religious worship, and all religious worship is due unto God only. Prayer is here made to God, even the Father and our Father; and also to Christ, even our Lord Jesus Christ. Therefore Jesus Christ our Lord is God, even as God our Father is God. Prayer is to be offered to God as our Father. So Christ taught his disciples to pray; and so the Spirit of adoption prompts them to pray, to cry, *Abba Father.* Prayer is not only to be offered in the name of Christ, but offered up to Christ himself, as our Lord and our Saviour.

II. What he prays for, with respect to himself and his fellow-labourers, and on behalf of the Thessalonians.

1. He prays that himself and fellow-labourers might have a prosperous journey to them by the will of God, that their way might be directed to them, *v.* 11. The taking of a journey to this or that place, one would think, is a thing depending so much on a man's own will, and lies so much in his own power, that Paul needed not by prayer to go to God about it. But the apostle knew that *in God we live, and move, and have our being,* that we depend upon God in all our motions and actions, as well as for the continuance of life and being, that divine Providence orders all our affairs and that it is owing thereto if we prosper therein, that God our Father directs and orders his children whither they shall go and what they shall do, that our Lord Jesus Christ in a particular manner directs the motions of his faithful ministers, those stars which he holds in his right hand. Let us acknowledge God in all our ways, and he will direct our paths.

2. He prays for the prosperity of the Thessalonians. Whether he should have an opportunity of coming to them or not, yet he earnestly prayed for the prosperity of their souls. And there are two things he desired for them, which we should desire for ourselves and friends: — (1.) That they might increase and abound in love (*v.* 12), in love to one another and in love to all men. Note, Mutual love is required of all Christians, and not only that they love one another, but that they also have a charitable disposition of mind and due concern for the welfare of all men. Love is of God, and is the fulfilling of the gospel as well as of the law. Timothy brought good tidings of their faith, yet something was lacking therein; and of their charity, yet the apostle prays that this might increase and abound. Note, We have reason to desire to grow in every grace, and have need of the Spirit's influence in order to growth in grace; and the way to obtain this is by prayer. We are beholden to God not only for the stock put into our hands at first, but for the improvement of it also. And to our prayer we must add endeavour. To excite this in the Thessalonians the apostle again mentions his love, his abounding love, towards them. The more we are beloved, the more affectionate we should be. (2.) That they might be established unblamable in holiness, *v.* 13. This spiritual benefit is mentioned as an effect of increasing and abounding love: *To the end that he* (the Lord) *may establish your hearts.* Note, The more we grow and abound in grace, and particularly in the grace of love, the more we are established and confirmed in it. Note also, Holiness is required of all those who would go to heaven, and therein we must be unblamable; that is, we must act in every thing so that we may not in the least contradict the profession we make of holiness. Our desire should be to have our hearts established in holiness before God, and be preserved safe, to the coming of the Lord Jesus Christ; and that we may be unblamable before God, even the Father, now, and be presented blameless before the throne of his glory, when the Lord Jesus shall come with all his saints. Note, [1.] The Lord Jesus will certainly come, and come in his glory. [2.] When he comes, his saints will come with him: *They shall appear with him in glory.* [3.] Then the excellency as well as the necessity of holiness will appear, because without this no hearts shall be established at that day, nor shall any one be unblamable, or avoid everlasting condemnation.

CHAPTER 4

In this chapter the apostle gives earnest exhortations to abound in holiness, with a caution against uncleanness, enforced with several arguments (*v.* 1–8). He then mentions the great duties of brotherly love, and quietness with industry in our callings (*v.* 9–12). And concludes with comforting those who mourned for their relations and friends that died in the Lord (*v.* 13–18).

Verses 1–8

Here we have,

I. An exhortation to abound in holiness, to *abound more and more* in that which is good, *v.* 1, 2. We may observe,

1. The manner in which the exhortation is given — very affectionately. The apostle entreats them as brethren; he calls them so, and loved them as such. Because his love to them was very great, he exhorts them very earnestly: *We beseech and exhort you.* The apostle was unwilling to take any denial, and therefore repeats his exhortation again and again.

2. The matter of his exhortation — that they would abound more and more in holy walking, or excel in those things that are good, in good works. Their faith was justly famed abroad, and they were already examples to other churches: yet the apostle would have them yet further to excel others, and to make further progress in holiness. Note, (1.) Those who most excel others fall short of perfection. The very best of us should *forget those things which are behind, and reach forth unto those things which are before.* (2.) It is not enough that we abide in the faith of the gospel, but we must abound in the work of faith. We must not only persevere to the end, but we should grow better, and walk more evenly and closely with God.

3. The arguments with which the apostle enforces his exhortation. (1.) They had been informed of their duty. They knew their Master's will, and could not plead ignorance as an excuse. Now as faith, so knowledge, is dead without practice. They had received of those who had converted them to Christianity, or been taught of them, *how they ought to walk.* Observe, The design of the gospel is to teach men not only what they should believe, but also how they ought to live; not so much to fill men's minds with notions as to regulate their temper and behaviour. The apostle taught them how to walk, not how to talk. To talk well without living well will never bring us to heaven: for the character of those who are in Christ Jesus is this: *They walk not after the flesh, but after the Spirit.* (2.) Another argument is that the apostle taught and exhorted them in the name, or by the authority, of the Lord Jesus Christ. He was Christ's minster and ambassador, declaring to them what was the will and command of the Lord Jesus. (3.) Another argument is this. Herein they would please God. Holy walking is most pleasing to the holy God, *who is glorious in holiness.* This ought to be the aim and ambition of every Christian, to please God and to be accepted of him. We should not be men-pleasers, nor flesh-pleasers, but should walk so as to please God. (4.) The rule according to which they ought to walk and act — *the commandments they had given them by the Lord Jesus Christ,* which were the commandments of the Lord Jesus Christ himself, because given by authority and direction from him and such as were agreeable to his will. The apostles of our Lord Jesus Christ were only commissioned by him to teach men to observe all things *whatsoever he had commanded them,* Mt. 28:20. Though they had great authority from Christ, yet that was to teach men what Christ had commanded, not to give forth commandments of their own. They did not act as lords over God's heritage (1 Pt. 5:3), nor should any do so that pretend to be their successors. The apostle could appeal to the Thessalonians, who knew what commandments he gave them, that they were no other than what he had received from the Lord Jesus.

II. A caution against uncleanness, this being a sin directly contrary to sanctification, or that holy walking to which he so earnestly exhorts them. This caution is expressed, and also enforced by many arguments,

1. It is expressed in these words: *That you should abstain from fornication* (*v.* 3), by which we are to understand all uncleanness whatsoever, either in a married or unmarried state. Adultery is of course included, though fornication is particularly mentioned. And other sorts of uncleanness are also forbidden, of which it is a shame even to speak, though they are done by too many in secret. All that is contrary to chastity in heart, speech, and behaviour, is contrary to the command of God in the decalogue, and contrary to that holiness which the gospel requires.

2. There are several arguments to enforce this caution. As, (1.) This branch of sanctification in particular is the will of God, *v.* 3. It is the will of God in general that we should be holy, because *he that called us is holy,* and because we are *chosen unto salvation through the sanctification of the Spirit;* and not only does God require holiness in the heart, but also purity in our bodies, and that we should cleanse ourselves from all *filthiness both of flesh and spirit,* 2 Co. 7:1. Whenever the body is, as it ought to be, devoted to God, and dedicated and set apart for him, it should be kept clean and pure for his service; and, as chastity is one branch of our sanctification, so this is one thing which God commands in his law, and what his grace effects in all true believers. (2.) This will be greatly for our honour: so much is plainly implied, *v.* 4. Whereas the contrary will be a great dishonour. *And his reproach shall not be wiped away,* Prov. 6:33. The body is here called the vessel of the soul, which dwells therein (so 1 Sa. 21:5), and it must be kept pure from defiling lusts. Every one should be careful in this matter, as he values his own honour and will not be contemptible on this account, that his inferior appetites and passions gain not the ascendant, tyrannizing over his reason and conscience, and enslaving the superior faculties of his soul. What can be more dishonourable than for a rational soul to be enslaved by bodily affections and brutal appetites? (3.) To indulge the lust of concupiscence is to live and act like heathens? *Even as the Gentiles who know not God, v.* 5. The Gentiles, and especially the Grecians, were commonly guilty of some sins of uncleanness which were not so evidently forbidden by the light of nature. But they did not know God, nor his mind and will, so well as Christians know, and should know, this his will, namely *our sanctification* in this branch of it. It is not so much to be wondered at, therefore, if the Gentiles indulge their fleshly appetites and lusts; but Christians should not walk as unconverted Gentiles, *in lasciviousness, lusts, excess of wine, revellings, banquetings,* etc. (1 Pt. 4:3), because those who are in Christ *have crucified the flesh with its affections and lusts.* (4.) The sin of uncleanness, especially adultery, is a great piece of injustice that God will be the avenger of; so we may understand those words, *That no man go beyond or defraud his brother* (*v.* 6), *in any matter — en tō pragmati,* in *this* matter of which the apostle is speaking in the preceding and following verses, namely, the sin of uncleanness. Some understand these words as a further warning and caution against injustice and oppression, all fraud and deceit in our dealings with men, which are certainly criminal, and contrary to the gospel. And Christians should not impose upon the ignorance and necessity of those they deal with, and so go beyond them, nor should they by equivocations or lying arts defraud them; and although this may be practised by some and lie long undiscovered, and so go unpunished among men, yet the righteous God will render a recompence. But the meaning may rather be to show the injustice and wrong that in many cases are done by the sin of uncleanness. Not only are fornication and other acts of uncleanness sins against his own body who commits them (1 Co. 6:18), not only are they very injurious to the sinner himself both in soul and body, but sometimes they are very injurious, and no less than defrauding, acts of injustice to others, particularly to those who are joined together in the marriage covenant and to their posterity. And, as this sin is of such a heinous nature, so it follows that God will be the avenger of it. *Whoremongers and adulterers God will judge,* Heb. 13:4. This the apostle had forewarned and testified by his gospel, which, as it contained exceedingly great and precious promises, so also it *revealed from heaven the wrath of God against all ungodliness and unrighteousness among men,* Rom. 1:18. (5.) The sin of uncleanness is contrary to the nature and design of our Christian calling: *For God hath called us not unto uncleanness, but unto holiness, v.* 7. The law of God forbids all impurity, and the gospel requires the greatest purity; it calls us from uncleanness unto holiness. (6.) The contempt therefore of God's law and gospel is the contempt of God himself: *He that despises despises God, not man* only. Some might possibly make light of the precepts of purity and holiness, because they heard them from men like themselves; but the apostle lets them know that they were God's commands, and to violate them was no less than to despise God. He adds, *God hath given Christians his Spirit,* intimating that all sorts of uncleanness do in an especial manner grieve the Holy Spirit, and will provoke him to withdraw from us; and also the Holy Spirit is given unto us to arm us against these sins, and to help us to mortify these deeds of the body, that we may live, Rom. 8:13.

Verses 9–12

In these words the apostle mentions the great duties,

I. Of brotherly love. This he exhorts them to increase in yet more and more. The exhortation is introduced, not with a compliment, but with a commendation, because they were remarkable in the exercise of it, which made it less needful that he should write to them about it, *v.* 9. Thus by his good opinion of them he insinuated himself into their affections, and so made way for his exhortation to them. Note, We should take notice of that in others which is good, to their praise, that by so doing we may lay engagements upon them to abound therein more and more. Observe,

1. What it is that the apostle commends in them. It was not so much their own virtue as God's grace; yet he takes notice of the evidence they gave of the grace of God in them. (1.) It was God's grace that he took special notice of: that God had taught them this good lesson: *You yourselves are taught of God to love one another, v.* 9. Whoever does that which is good is taught of God to do it, and God must have the glory. All who are savingly taught of God are taught this lesson, to love one another. This is the livery of Christ's family. Note also, The teaching of the Spirit exceeds the teaching of men; and, as no man should teach contrary to what God teaches, so none can teach so effectually as he teaches; and men's teaching is fain and useless unless God teach also. (2.) The Thessalonians gave good evidence of their being taught of God by *their love to the brethren in all Macedonia, v.* 10. They not only loved those of their own city and society, or such as were near them and just of their own sentiments, but their love was extensive. And a true Christian's is so to all the saints, though distant from him in place, and differing from him in some opinions or practices of less moment.

2. The exhortation itself is to increase more and more in this great grace and duty of brotherly love, *v.* 10. Though these Thessalonians had in some sense no need of an exhortation to brotherly love, as if it were wholly wanting, yet they must be exhorted to pray for more, and labour for more. There are none on this side heaven who love in perfection. Those who are eminent in this or any other grace have need of increase therein as well as of perseverance unto the end.

II. Of quietness and industry in their callings. Observe, 1. The apostle exhorts to these duties: that they should *study to be quiet, v.* 11. It is the most desirable thing to have a calm and quiet temper, and to be of a peaceable and quiet behaviour. This tends much to our own and others' happiness; and Christians should study how to be quiet. We should be ambitious and industrious how to be calm and quiet in our minds, in patience to possess our own souls, and to be quiet towards others; or of a meek and mild, a gentle and peaceable disposition, not given to strife, contention, or division. Satan is very busy to disquiet us; and we have that in our own hearts that disposes us to be disquiet; therefore let us study to be quiet. It follows, *Do your own business.* When we go beyond this, we expose ourselves to a great deal of inquietude. Those who are busy-bodies, meddling in other men's matters, generally have but little quiet in their own minds and cause great disturbances among their neighbours; at least they seldom mind the other exhortation, to be diligent in their own calling, *to work with their own hands;* and yet this was what the apostle commanded them, and what is required of us also. Christianity does not discharge us from the work and duty of our particular callings, but teaches us to be diligent therein. 2. The exhortation is enforced with a double argument; namely, (1.) So we shall live creditably. Thus we shall walk honestly, or decently and creditably, towards those that are without, *v.* 12. This will be to act as becomes the gospel, and will gain a good report from those that are strangers, yea, enemies to it. Note, It is a great ornament to religion when the professors of it are of meek and quiet spirits, diligent to do their own business, and not busybodies in other men's matters. (2.) We shall live comfortably, and have lack of nothing, *v.* 12. People often by their slothfulness bring themselves into narrow circumstances, and reduce themselves to great straits, and are liable to many wants, when such as are diligent in their own business live comfortably and have lack of nothing. They are not burdensome to their friends, nor scandalous to strangers. They earn their own bread, and have the greatest pleasure in so doing.

Verses 13–18

In these words the apostle comforts the Thessalonians who mourned for the death of their relations and friends that died in the Lord. His design is to dissuade them from excessive grief, or inordinate sorrow, on that account. *All grief* for the death of friends is far from being unlawful; we may weep at least for ourselves if we do not weep for them, weep for own loss, though it may be their fain. Yet we must not be immoderate in our sorrows, because,

I. This looks as if we had no hope, *v.* 13. It is to act too much like the Gentiles, who had no hope of a better life after this; whereas we Christians, who have a most sure hope, the hope of eternal life after this, *which God who cannot lie hath promised us,* should moderate all our joys and our sorrows on account of any worldly thing. This hope is more than enough to balance all our griefs upon account of any of the crosses of the present time.

II. This is an effect of ignorance concerning those who are dead, *v.* 13. There are some things which we cannot be ignorant of concerning those that are asleep; for the land they are removed to is a land of darkness, which we know but little of and have no correspondence with. To go among the dead is to go among we know not whom, and to live we know not how. Death is an unknown thing, and the state of the dead, or the state after death, we are much in the dark about; yet there are some things concerning those especially who die in the Lord that we need not, and ought not, to be ignorant of; and, if these things be really understood and duly considered, they will be sufficient to allay our sorrow concerning them.

1. They sleep in Jesus. They are asleep, *v.* 13. They have *fallen asleep in Christ,* 1 Co. 15:18. Death does not annihilate them. It is but a sleep to them. It is their rest, and undisturbed rest. They have retired out of this troublesome world, to rest from all their labours and sorrows, and they sleep in Jesus, *v.* 14. Being still in union with him, they sleep in his arms and are under his special care and protection. Their souls are in his presence, and their dust is under his care and power; so that they are not lost, nor are they losers, but great gainers by death, and their removal out of this world is into a better.

2. They shall be raised up from the dead, and awakened out of their sleep, for *God will bring them with him, v.* 14. They then are with God, and are better where they are than when they were here; and when God comes he will bring them with him. The doctrine of the resurrection and the second coming of Christ is a great antidote against the fear of death and inordinate sorrow for the death of our Christian friends; and this doctrine we have a full assurance of, because we *believe that Jesus died and rose again, v.* 14. It is taken for granted that as Christians they knew and believed this. The death and resurrection of Christ are fundamental articles of the Christian religion, and give us hope of a joyful resurrection; for *Christ, having risen from the dead, has become the first fruits of those that slept;* and therefore *those who have fallen asleep in him have not perished nor are lost,* 1 Co. 15:18, 20. His resurrection is a full confirmation of all that is said in the gospel, or by the word of the Lord, which has *brought life and immortality to light.*

3. Their state and condition shall be glorious and happy at the second coming of Christ. This the apostle informs the Thessalonians of *by the word of the Lord* (*v.* 15), by divine revelation from the Lord Jesus; for though the resurrection of the dead, and a future state of blessedness, were part of the creed of the Old-Testament saints, yet they are much more clearly revealed in and by the gospel. By this word of the Lord we know, (1.) That the Lord Jesus will come down from heaven in all the pomp and power of the upper world (*v.* 16): *The Lord himself shall descend from heaven with a shout.* He ascended into heaven after his resurrection, and passed through these material heavens into the third heaven, which must retain him till the restitution of all things; and then he will come again, and appear in his glory. He will descend

from heaven into this our air, *v.* 17. The appearance will be with pomp and power, *with a shout* — the shout of a king, and the power and authority of a mighty king and conqueror, with *the voice of the archangel;* an innumerable company of angels will attend him. Perhaps *one,* as general of those hosts of the Lord, will give notice of his approach, and the glorious appearance of this great Redeemer and Judge will be proclaimed and ushered in by the *trump of God. For the trumpet shall sound,* and this will awaken those that sleep in the dust of the earth, and will summon all the world to appear. For, (2.) The dead shall be raised: *The dead in Christ shall rise first* (*v.* 16), before those who are *found alive at Christ's coming shall be changed;* and so it appears that those who shall then *be found alive shall not prevent those that are asleep, v.* 15. The first care of the Redeemer in that day will be about his dead saints; he will raise them before the great change passes on those that shall be found alive: so that those who did not sleep in death will have no greater privilege or joy at that day than those who fell asleep in Jesus. (3.) Those that shall be found alive will then be changed. They shall *be caught up together with them in the clouds, to meet the Lord in the air, v.* 17. At, or immediately before, this rapture into the clouds, those who are alive will undergo a mighty change, which will be equivalent to dying. This change is so mysterious that we cannot comprehend it: we know little or nothing of it, 1 Co. 15:51. Only, in the general, *this mortal must put on immortality,* and these bodies will be made fit to inherit the kingdom of God, which flesh and blood in its present state are not capable of. This change will be *in a moment, in the twinkling of an eye* (1 Co. 15:52), in the very instant, or not long after the raising up of those that sleep in Jesus. And those who are raised, and thus changed, shall meet together in the clouds, and there meet with their Lord, to congratulate him on his coming, to receive the crown of glory he will then bestow upon them, and to be assessors with him in judgment, approving and applauding the sentence he will then pass upon the prince of the power of the air, and all the wicked, who shall be doomed to destruction with the devil and his angels. (4.) Here is the bliss of the saints at that day: they shall *be ever with the Lord, v.* 17. It will be some part of their felicity that all the saints shall meet together, and remain together for ever; but the principal happiness of heaven is this, *to be with the Lord,* to see him, live with him, and enjoy him, for ever. This should comfort the saints upon the death of their friends, that, although death has made a separation, yet their souls and bodies will meet again; we and they shall meet together again: we and they shall meet together again: we and they with all the saints shall meet our Lord, and be with him for ever, no more to be separated wither from him or from one another for ever. And the apostle would have us *comfort one another with these words, v.* 18. We should endeavour to support one another in times of sorrow, not deaden one another's spirits, nor weaken one another's hands, but should comfort one another; and this may be done by serious consideration and discourse on the many good lessons to be learned from the doctrine of the resurrection of the dead, the second coming of Christ, and the glory of the saints in that day.

CHAPTER 5

The apostle, having spoken in the end of the foregoing chapter concerning the resurrection, and the second coming of Christ, proceeds to speak concerning the uselessness of enquiring after the particular time of Christ's coming, which would be sudden and terrible to the wicked, but comfortable to the saints (*v.* 1–5). He then exhorts them to the duties of watchfulness, sobriety, and the exercise of faith, love, and hope, as being suitable to their state (*v.* 6–10). In the next words he exhorts them to several duties they owed to others, or to one another (*v.* 11–15), afterwards to several other Christian duties of great importance (*v.* 16–22), and then concludes this epistle (*v.* 23–28).

Verses 1–5

In these words observe,

I. The apostle tells the Thessalonians it was needless or useless to enquire about the particular time of Christ's coming: *Of the times and seasons you need not that I write unto you, v.* 1. The thing is certain that Christ will come, and there is a certain time appointed for his coming; but there was no need that the apostle should write about this, and therefore he had no revelation given him; nor should they or we enquire into this secret, *which the Father has reserved in his own power. Of that day and hour knoweth no man.* Christ himself did not reveal this while upon earth; it was not in his commission as the great prophet of the church: nor did he reveal this to his apostles; there was *no need* of this. There are times and seasons for us to do our work in: these it is our duty and interest to know and observe; but the time and season when we must give up our account we know not, nor is it needful that we should know them. Note, There are many things which our vain curiosity desires to know which there is no necessity at all of our knowing, nor would our knowledge of them do us good.

II. He tells them that the coming of Christ would be sudden, and a great surprise to most men, *v.* 2. And this is what they knew perfectly, or might know, because our Lord himself had so said: *In such an hour as you think not, the Son of man cometh,* Mt. 24:44. So Mk. 13:35, 36, *Watch you therefore, for you know not when the master of the house cometh; lest, coming suddenly, he find you sleeping.* And no doubt the apostle had told them, as of the coming of Christ, so also of his coming suddenly, which is the meaning of his coming *as a thief in the night,* Rev. 16:15. As the thief usually cometh in the dead time of the night, when he is least expected, such a *surprise* will the day of the Lord be; so sudden and surprising will be his appearance. The knowledge of this will be more useful than to know the exact time, because this should awaken us to stand upon our watch, that we may be ready whenever he cometh.

III. He tells them how terrible Christ's coming would be to the ungodly, *v.* 3. It will be to their destruction in that day of the Lord. The righteous God will bring ruin upon his and his people's enemies; and this their destruction, as it will be total and final, so, 1. It will be sudden. It will overtake them, and fall upon them, in the midst of their carnal security and jollity, when they say in their hearts, *Peace and safety,* when they dream of felicity and please themselves with vain amusements of their fancies or their senses, and think not of it, — *as travail cometh upon a woman with child,* at the set time indeed, but not perhaps just then expected, nor greatly feared. 2. It will be unavoidable destruction too: *They shall not escape;* they shall in no wise escape. There will be no means possible for them to avoid the terror nor the punishment of that day. Thee will be *no place where the workers of iniquity shall be able to hide themselves,* no shelter from the storm, nor shadow from the burning heat that shall consume the wicked.

IV. He tells them how comfortable this day will be to the righteous, *v.* 4, 5. Here observe, 1. Their character and privilege. They are not in darkness; they are the children of the light, etc. This was the happy condition of the Thessalonians as it is of all true Christians. They were not in a state of sin and ignorance as the heathen world. They were *some time darkness, but were made light in the Lord.* They were favoured with the divine revelation of things that are unseen and eternal, particularly concerning the coming of Christ, and the consequences thereof. They were the *children of the day,* for the day-star had risen upon them; yea, the Sun of righteousness had arisen on them with healing under his wings. They were no longer under the darkness of heathenism, nor under the shadows of the law, but under the gospel, which brings life and immortality to light. 2 Tim. 1:10. 2. Their great advantage on this account: that *that day should not overtake them as a thief, v.* 4. It was at least their own fault if they were surprised by that day. They had fair warning, and sufficient helps to provide against that day, and might hope to stand with comfort and confidence before the Son of man. This would be a time of *refreshing to them from the presence of the Lord,* who to *those that look for him will appear without sin unto their salvation,* and will come to them as a friend in the day, not as a thief in the night.

Verses 6–10

On what had been said, the apostle grounds seasonable exhortations to several needful duties.

I. To watchfulness and sobriety, *v.* 6. These duties are distinct, yet they mutually befriend one another. For, while we are compassed about with so many temptations to intemperance and excess, we shall not keep sober, unless we be upon our guard, and, unless we keep sober, we shall not long watch. 1. Then *let us not sleep as do others, but let us watch;* we must not be secure and careless, nor indulge spiritual sloth and idleness. We must not be off our watch, but continually upon our guard against sin, and temptation to it. The generality of men are too careless of their duty and regardless of their spiritual enemies. They say, *Peace and safety,* when they are in the greatest danger, doze away their precious moments on which eternity depends, indulging idle dreams, and have no more thoughts nor cares about another world than men that are asleep have about this. Either they do not consider the things of another world at all, because they are asleep; or they do not consider them aright, because they dream. But let us watch, and act like men that are awake, and that stand upon their guard. 2. Let us also *be sober,* or temperate and moderate. Let us keep our natural desires and appetites after the things of this world within due bounds. Sobriety is usually opposed to excess in meats and drinks, and here particularly it is opposed to drunkenness; but it also extends to all other temporal things. Thus our Saviour warned his disciples to *take heed lest their hearts should be overcharged with surfeiting and drunkenness, and cares of this life, and so that day come on them unawares,* Lu. 21:34. *Our moderation* then, as to all temporal things, *should be known to all men, because the Lord is at hand.* Besides this, watchfulness and sobriety are most suitable to the Christian's character and privilege, as being *children of the day;* because *those that sleep sleep in the night, and those that are drunken are drunken in the night, v.* 7. It is a most reproachful thing for men to sleep away the day-time, which is for work and not for sleep, to be drunken in the day, when so many eyes are upon them, to behold their shame. It was not so strange if those who had not the benefit of divine revelation suffered themselves to be lulled asleep by the devil in carnal security, and if they laid the reins upon the neck of their appetites, and indulged themselves in all manner of riot and excess; for it was night-time with them. They were not sensible of their danger, therefore they *slept;* they were not sensible of their duty, therefore they were drunk: but it ill becomes Christians to do thus. What! shall Christians, who have the light of the blessed gospel shining in their faces, be careless about their souls, and unmindful of another world? Those who have so many eyes upon them should conduct themselves with peculiar propriety.

II. To be well armed as well as watchful: to put on the whole armour of God. This is necessary in order to such sobriety as becomes us and will be a preparation for the day of the Lord, because our spiritual enemies are many, and mighty, and malicious. They draw many to their interest, and keep them in it, by making them careless, secure, and presumptuous, by making them drunk — drunk with pride, drunk with passion, drunk and giddy with self-conceit, drunk with the gratifications of sense: so that we have need to arm ourselves against their attempts, by putting on the spiritual breast-plate to keep the heart, and the spiritual helmet to secure the head; and this spiritual armour consists of three great graces of Christians, faith, love, and hope, *v.* 8. 1. We must live by faith, and this will keep us watchful and sober. If we believe that the eye of God (who is a spirit) is always upon us, that we have spiritual enemies to grapple with, that there is a world of spirits to prepare for, we shall see reason to watch and be sober. Faith will be our best defence against the assaults of our enemies. 2. We must get a heart inflamed with love; and this also will be our defence. True and fervent love to God, and the things of God, will keep us watchful and sober, and hinder our apostasy in times of trouble and temptation. 3. We must make salvation our hope, and should have a lively hope of it. This good hope, through grace, of eternal life, will be as a helmet to defend the head, and hinder our being intoxicated with the pleasures of sin, which are but for a season. If we have hope of salvation, let us take heed of doing any thing that shall shake our hopes, or render us unworthy of or unfit for the great salvation we hope for. Having mentioned salvation and the hope of it, the apostle shows what grounds and reasons Christians have to hope for this salvation, as to which observe, He says nothing of their meriting it. No, the doctrine of our merits is altogether unscriptural and antiscriptural; there is no foundation of any good hope upon that account. But our hopes are to be grounded, (1.) Upon God's appointment: because *God hath not appointed us to wrath, but to obtain salvation, v.* 9. If we would trace our salvation to the first cause, that is God's appointment. Those who live and die in darkness and ignorance, who sleep and are drunken as in the night, are, it is but too plain, *appointed to wrath;* but as for those who are of the day, if they watch and be sober, it is evident that they are *appointed to obtain salvation.* And the sureness and firmness of the divine appointment are the great support and encouragement of our hope. Were we to obtain salvation by our own merit or power, we could have but little or no hope of it; but seeing we are to obtain it by virtue of God's appointment, which we are sure cannot be shaken *(for his purpose, according to election, shall stand),* on this we build unshaken hope, especially when we consider, (2.) Christ's merit and grace, and that salvation is by our Lord Jesus Christ, who died for us. Our salvation therefore is owing to, and our hopes of it are grounded on, Christ's atonement as well as God's appointment: and, as we should think on God's gracious design and purpose, so also on Christ's death and sufferings, for this end, *that whether we wake or sleep* (whether we live or die, for death is but a sleep to believers, as the apostles had before intimated) *we should live together with Christ* live in union and in glory with him for ever. And, as it is the salvation that Christians hope for to *be for ever with the Lord,* so one foundation of their hope is their union with him. And if they are united with Christ, and live in him, and live to him, here, the sleep of death will be no prejudice to the spiritual life, much less to the life of glory hereafter. On the contrary, Christ died for us, that, living and dying, we might be his; that we might live to him while we are here, and live with him when we go hence.

Verses 11–15

In these words the apostle exhorts the Thessalonians to several duties.

I. Towards those who were nearly related one to another. Such should comfort themselves, or exhort one another, and edify one another, *v.* 11. 1. They must comfort or exhort themselves and one another; for the original word may be rendered both these ways. And we may observe, As those are most able and likely to comfort others who can comfort themselves, so the way to have comfort ourselves, or to administer comfort to others, is by compliance with the exhortation of the word. Note, We should not only be careful about our own comfort and welfare, but to promote the comfort and welfare of others also. He was a Cain that said, *Am I my brother's keeper? We must bear one another's burdens, and so fulfil the law of Christ.* 2. They must edify one another, by *following after those things whereby one may edify another,* Rom. 14:19. As Christians are lively stones built up together a spiritual house, they should endeavour to promote the good of the whole church by promoting the work of grace in one another. And it is the duty of every one of us to study that which is for the edification of those with whom we converse, *to please all men for their* real *profit.* We should communicate our knowledge and experiences one to another. We should join in prayer and praise one with another. We should set a good example one before another. And it is the duty of those especially who live in the same vicinity and family thus to comfort and edify one another; and this is the best neighbourhood, the best means to answer the end of society. Such as are nearly related together and have affection for one another, as they have the greatest opportunity, so they are under the greatest obligation, to do this kindness one to another. This the Thessalonians did *(which also you do),* and this is what they are exhorted to continue and increase in doing. Note, Those who do that which is good have need of further exhortations to excite them to do good, to do more good, as well as continue in doing what they do.

II. He shows them their duty towards their ministers, *v.* 12, 13. Though the apostle himself was driven from them, yet they had others who laboured among them, and to whom they owed these duties. The apostle here exhorts them to observe,

1. How the ministers of the gospel are described by the work of their office; and they should rather mind the work and duty they are called to than affect venerable and honourable names that they may be called by. Their work is very weighty, and very honourable and useful. (1.) Ministers must labour among their people, labour with diligence, and unto weariness (so the word in the original imports; *they must la-bour in the word and doctrine,* 1 Tim. 5:17. They are called labourers, and should not be loiterers. They must labour with their people, to instruct, comfort, and edify them. And, (2.) Ministers are to rule their people also, so the word is rendered, 1 Tim. 5:17. They must rule, not with rigour, but with love. They must not exercise dominion as temporal lords; but rule as spiritual guides, by setting a good example to the flock. They are over the people in the Lord, to distinguish them from civil magistrates, and to denote also that they are but ministers under Christ, appointed by him, and must rule the

people by Christ's laws, and not by laws of their own. This may also intimate the end of their office and all their labour; namely, the service and honour of the Lord. (3.) They must also admonish the people, and that not only publicly, but privately, as there may be occasion. They must instruct them to do well, and should reprove when they do ill. It is their duty not only to give good counsel, but also to give admonition, to give warning to the flock of the dangers they are liable to, and reprove for negligence or what else may be amiss.

2. What the duty of the people is towards their ministers. There is a mutual duty between ministers and people. If ministers should labour among the people, then, (1.) The people must know them. As the shepherd should know his flock, so the sheep must know their shepherd. They must know his person, hear his voice, acknowledge him for their pastor, and pay due regard to his teaching, ruling, and admonitions. (2.) They must esteem their ministers highly in love; they should greatly value the office of the ministry, honour and love the persons of their ministers, and show their esteem and affection in all proper ways, and this for their work's sake, because their business is to promote the honour of Christ and the welfare of men's souls. Note, Faithful ministers ought to be so far from being lightly esteemed because of their work that they should be highly esteemed on account of it. The work of the ministry is so far from being a disgrace to those who upon other accounts deserve esteem, that it puts an honour upon those who are faithful and diligent, to which otherwise they could lay no claim, and will procure them that esteem and love among good people which otherwise they could not expect.

III. He gives divers other exhortations touching the duty Christians owe to one another. 1. To *be at peace among themselves, v.* 13. Some understand this exhortation (according to the reading in some copies) as referring to the people's duty to their ministers, to live peaceably with them, and not raise nor promote dissensions at any time between minister and people, which will certainly prove a hindrance to the success of a minister's work and the edification of the people. This is certain, that ministers and people should avoid every thing that tends to alienate their affections one from another. And the people should be at peace among themselves, doing all they can to hinder any differences from rising or continuing among them, and using all proper means to preserve peace and harmony. 2. *To warn the unruly, v.* 14. There will be in all societies some who walk disorderly, who go out of their rank and station; and it is not only the duty of ministers, but of private Christians also, to warn and admonish them. Such should be reproved for their sin, warned of their danger, and told plainly of the injury they do their own souls, and the hurt they may do to others. Such should be put in mind of what they should do, and be reproved for doing otherwise. 3. *To comfort the feebleminded, v.* 14. By these are intended the timorous and faint-hearted, or such as are dejected and of a sorrowful spirit. Some are cowardly, afraid of difficulties, and disheartened at the thoughts of hazards, and losses, and afflictions; now such should be encouraged; we should not despise them, but comfort them; and who knows what good a kind and comfortable word may do them? 4. *To support the weak, v.* 14. Some are not well able to perform their work, nor bear up under their burdens; we should therefore support them, help their infirmities, and lift at one end of the burden, and so help to bear it. It is the grace of God, indeed, that must strengthen and support such; but we should tell them of that grace, and endeavour to minister of that grace to them. 5. *To be patient towards all men, v.* 14. We must bear and forbear. We must be long-suffering, and suppress our anger, if it begin to rise upon the apprehension of affronts or injuries; at least we must not fail to moderate our anger: and this duty must be exercised towards all men, good and bad, high and low. We must not be high in our expectations and demands, nor harsh in our resentments, nor hard in our impositions, but endeavour to make the best we can of every thing, and think the best we can of every body. 6. *Not to render evil for evil to any man, v.* 15. This we must look to, and be very careful about, that is, we must by all means forbear to avenge ourselves. If others do us an injury, this will not justify us in returning it, in doing the same, or the like, or any other injury to them. It becomes us to forgive, as those that are, and that hope to be, forgiven of God. 7. *Ever to follow that which is good, v.* 15. In general, we must study to do what is our duty, and pleasing to God, in all cir-

cumstances, whether men do us good turns or ill turns; whatever men do to us, we must do good to others. We must always endeavour to be beneficent and instrumental to promote the welfare of others, both among ourselves (in the first place to those that *are of the household o faith),* and then, *as we have opportunity, unto all men,* Gal. 6:10.

Verses 16–22

Here we have divers short exhortations, that will not burden our memories, but will be of great use to direct the motions of our hearts and lives; for the duties are of great importance, and we may observe how they are connected together, and have a dependence upon one another. 1. *Rejoice evermore, v.* 16. This must be understood of spiritual joy; for we must rejoice in our creature-comforts as if we rejoiced not, and must not expect to live many years, and rejoice in them all; but, if we do rejoice in God, we may do that evermore. In him our joy will be full; and it is our fault if we have not a continual feast. If we are sorrowful upon any worldly account, yet still we may always rejoice, 2 Co. 6:10. Note, A religious life is a pleasant life, it is a life of constant joy. 2. *Pray without ceasing, v.* 17. Note, The way to rejoice evermore is to pray without ceasing. We should rejoice more if we prayed more. We should keep up stated times for prayer, and continue instant in prayer. We should pray always, and not faint: pray without weariness, and continue in prayer, till we come to that world where prayer shall be swallowed up in praise. The meaning is not that men should do nothing but pray, but that nothing else we do should hinder prayer in its proper season. Prayer will help forward and not hinder all other lawful business, and every good work. 3. *In every thing give thanks, v.* 18. If we pray without ceasing, we shall not want matter for thanksgiving *in every thing.* As we must in every thing make our requests known to God by supplications, so we must not omit thanksgiving, Phil. 4:6. We should be thankful in every condition, even in adversity as well as prosperity. It is never so bad with us but it might be worse. If we have ever so much occasion to make our humble complaints to God, we never can have any reason to complain of God, and have always much reason to praise and give thanks: the apostle says, This is the *will of God in Christ Jesus concerning us, that we give thanks,* seeing God is reconciled to us in Christ Jesus; in him, through him, and for his sake, he allows us to rejoice evermore, and appoints us in every thing to give thanks. It is pleasing to God. 4. *Quench not the Spirit (v.* 19), for it is this Spirit of grace and supplication that helpeth our infirmities, that assisteth us in our prayers and thanksgivings. Christians are said to *be baptized with the Holy Ghost and with fire.* He worketh as fire, by enlightening, enlivening, and purifying the souls of men. We must be careful not to quench this holy fire. As fire is put out by withdrawing fuel, so we quench the Spirit if we do not stir up our spirits, and all that is within us, to comply with the motions of the good Spirit; and as fire is quenched by pouring water, or putting a great quantity of dirt upon it, so we must be careful not to quench the Holy Spirit by indulging carnal lusts and affections, or minding only earthly things. 5. *Despise not prophesyings (v.* 20); for, if we neglect the means of grace, we forfeit the Spirit of grace. By *prophesyings* here we are to understand the preaching of the word, the interpreting and applying of the scriptures; and this we must not despise, but should prize and value, because it is the ordinance of God, appointed of him for our furtherance and increase in knowledge and grace, in holiness and comfort. We must not despise preaching, though it be plain, and not with enticing words of men's wisdom, and though we be told no more than what we knew before. It is useful, and many times needful, to have our minds stirred up, our affections and resolutions excited, to those things that we knew before to be our interest and our duty. 6. *Prove all things, but hold fast that which is good, v.* 21. This is a needful caution, to prove all things; for, though we must put a value on preaching, we must not take things upon trust from the preacher, but try them by the law and the testimony. We must search the scriptures, whether what they say be true or not. We must not believe every spirit, but must try the spirits. But we must not be always trying, always unsettled; no, at length we must be settled, and hold fast that which is good. When we are satisfied that any thing is right, and true, and good, we must hold it fast, and not let it go, whatever opposition or whatever persecution we meet with for the sake thereof. Note, The doctrines of human infallibility, implicit faith, and blind obedience, are not the doctrines of the Bible. Every Christian has and ought to have, the judgment of discretion, and should have *his senses exercised in discerning between good and evil,* truth and falsehood, Heb. 5:13, 14. And proving all things must be in order to holding fast that which is good. We must not always be seekers, or fluctuating in our minds, *like children tossed to and fro with every wind of doctrine.* 7. *Abstain from all appearance of evil, v.* 22. This is a good means to prevent our being deceived with false doctrines, or unsettled in our faith; for our Saviour has told us (Jn. 7:17), *If a man will do his will, he shall know of the doctrine whether it be of God.* Corrupt affections indulged in the heart, and evil practices allowed of in the life, will greatly tend to promote fatal errors in the mind; whereas purity of heart, and integrity of life, will dispose men to receive the truth in the love of it. We should therefore abstain from evil, and all appearances of evil, from sin, and that which looks like sin, leads to it, and borders upon it. He who is not shy of the appearances of sin, who shuns not the occasions of sin, and who avoids not the temptations and approaches to sin, will not long abstain from the actual commission of sin.

Verses 23–28

In these words, which conclude this epistle, observe,

I. Paul's prayer for them, *v.* 23. He had told them, in the beginning of this epistle, that he always made mention of them in his prayers; and, now that he is writing to them, he lifts up his heart to God in prayer for them. Take notice, 1. To whom the apostle prays, namely, *The very God of peace.* He is the God of grace, and the God of peace and love. He is the author of peace and lover of concord; and by their peaceableness and unity, from God as the author, those things would best be obtained which he prays for. 2. The things he prays for on behalf of the Thessalonians are their sanctification, that *God would sanctify them wholly;* and their preservation, that they might be *preserved blameless.* He prays that they may be wholly sanctified, that the whole man may be sanctified, and then that the whole man, spirit, soul, and body, may be preserved: or, he prays that they may be wholly sanctified, that is, more perfectly, for the best are sanctified but in part while in this world; and therefore we should pray for and press towards complete sanctification. Where the good work of grace is begun, it shall be carried on, be protected and preserved; and all those who are sanctified in Christ Jesus shall be preserved to the coming of our Lord Jesus Christ. And because, if God did not carry on his good work in the soul, it would miscarry, we should pray to God to perfect his work, and *preserve us blameless,* free from sin and impurity, till at length we are *presented faultless before the throne of his glory with exceeding joy.*

II. His comfortable assurance that God would hear his prayer: *Faithful is he who calleth you, who will also do it, v.* 24. The kindness and love of God had appeared to them in calling them to the knowledge of his truth, and the faithfulness of God was their security that they should persevere to the end; and therefore, the apostle assures them, God would do what he desired; he would effect what he had promised; he would accomplish all the good pleasure of his goodness towards them. Note, Our fidelity to God depends upon his faithfulness to us.

III. His request of their prayers: *Brethren, pray for us, v.* 25. We should pray for one another; and brethren should thus express brotherly love. This great apostle did not think it beneath him to call the Thessalonians brethren, nor to request their prayers. Ministers stand in need of their people's prayers; and the more people pray for their ministers the more good ministers may have from God, and the more benefit people may receive by their ministry.

IV. His salutation: *Greet all the brethren with a holy kiss, v.* 26. Thus the apostle sends a friendly salutation from himself, and Silvanus, and Timotheus, and would have them salute each other in their names; and thus he would have them signify their mutual love and affection to one another by the kiss of charity (1 Pt. 5:14), which is here called a holy kiss, to intimate how cautious they should be of all impurity in the use of this ceremony, then commonly practised; as it should not be a treacherous kiss like that of Judas, so not a lascivious kiss like that of the harlot, Prov. 7:13.

V. His solemn charge for the reading of this epistle, *v.* 27. This is not only an exhortation, but an adjuration by the Lord. And this epistle was to be read to all the holy brethren. It is not only allowed to the common people to read the scriptures, and what none should prohibit, but it is their indispensable duty, and what they should be persuaded to do. In order to this, these holy oracles should not be kept concealed in an unknown tongue, but translated into the vulgar languages, that all men, being concerned to know the scriptures, may be able to read them, and be acquainted with them. The public reading of the law was one part of the worship of the sabbath among the Jews in their synagogues, and the scriptures should be read in the public assemblies of Christians also.

VI. The apostolical benediction that is usual in other epistles: *The grace of our Lord Jesus Christ be with you. Amen, v.* 28. We need no more to make us happy than to know that grace which our Lord Jesus Christ has manifested, be interested in that grace which he has purchased, and partake of that grace which dwells in him as the head of the church. This is an ever-flowing and overflowing fountain of grace to supply all our wants.

AN EXPOSITION, WITH PRACTICAL OBSERVATIONS, OF

THE SECOND EPISTLE OF ST. PAUL TO THE THESSALONIANS

This Second Epistle was written soon after the former, and seems to have been designed to prevent a mistake, which might arise from some passages in the former epistle, concerning the second coming of Christ, as if it were near at hand. The apostle in this epistle is careful to prevent any wrong use which some among them might make of those expressions of his that were agreeable to the dialect of the prophets of the Old Testament, and informs them that there were many intermediate counsels yet to be fulfilled before that day of the Lord should come, though, because it is sure, he had spoken of it as near. There are other things that he writes about for their consolation under sufferings, and exhortation and direction in duty.

CHAPTER 1

After the introduction (*v.* 1, 2) the apostle begins this epistle with an account of his high esteem for these Thessalonians (*v.* 3, 4). He then comforts them under their afflictions and persecutions (*v.* 5–10) and tells them what his prayers were to God for them (*v.* 11, 12).

Verses 1–4

Here we have,

I. The introduction (*v.* 1, 2), in the same words as in the former epistle, from which we may observe that as this apostle did not count it grievous to him to write the same things (Phil. 3:1) in his epistles that he had delivered in preaching, so he willingly wrote the same things to one church that he did to another. The occurrence of the same words in this epistle as in the former shows us that ministers ought not so much to regard the variety of expression and elegance of style as the truth and usefulness of the doctrines they preach. And great care should be taken lest, from an affectation of novelty in method and phrases, we advance new notions or doctrines, contrary to the principles of natural or revealed religion, upon which this church of the Thessalonians was built, as all true churches are; namely, *in God our Father and the Lord Jesus Christ.*

II. The apostle's expression of the high esteem he had for them. He not only had a great affection for them (as he had expressed in his former epistle, and now again in his pious wish of grace and peace for them), but he also expresses his great esteem for them, concerning which observe,

1. How his esteem of them is expressed. (1.) He glorified God on their behalf: *We are bound to thank God always for you, brethren, as it is meet, v.* 3. He chose rather to speak of what was praiseworthy in them in a way of thanksgiving to God than by commendation of them; and, as what he mentions was matter of his rejoicing, he accounted it matter of thanksgiving, and it was meet or fit it should be so, for we are bound, and it is our duty, to be thankful to God for all the good that is found in us or others: and it not only is an act of kindness to our fellow-christians, but our duty, to thank God on their behalf. (2.) He also *glories in them before the churches of God, v.* 4. The apostle never flattered his friends, but he took pleasure in commending them, and speaking well of them, to the glory of God and for the excitement and encouragement of others. Paul did not glory in his own gifts, nor in his labour among them, but he gloried in the grace of God which was bestowed upon them, and so his glorying was good, because all the commendation he gave to them, and the pleasure he took himself, centered in the praise and glory of God.

2. For what he esteemed them and thanked God; namely, the increase of their faith, and love, and patience. In his former epistle (*ch.* 1:3) he gave thanks for their faith, love, and patience; here he gives thanks for the increase of all those graces, that they were not only true Christians, but growing Christians. Note, Where there is the truth of grace there will be increase of it. *The path of the just is as the shining light, which shines more and more unto the perfect day.* And where there is the increase of grace God must have all the glory of it. We are as much indebted to him for the improvement of grace, and the progress of that good work, as we are for the first work of grace and the very beginning of it. We may be tempted to think that though when we were bad we could not make ourselves good, yet when we are good we can easily make ourselves better; but we have as much dependence on the grace of God for increasing the grace we have as for planting grace when we had it not. The matter of the apostle's thanksgiving and glorying on behalf of the Thessalonians was, (1.) That their faith grew exceedingly, *v.* 3. They were more confirmed in the truth of gospel-revelations, confided in gospel-promises, and had lively expectations of another world. The growth of their faith appeared by the works of faith; and, where faith grows, all other graces grow proportionably. (2.) Their charity abounded (*v.* 3), their love to God and man. Note, Where faith grows love will abound, for faith works by love; and not only the charity of some few of them, but of every one to each other, did abound. There were no such divisions among them as in some other churches. (3.) Their patience as well as faith increased in all their persecutions and tribulations. And patience has then its perfect work when it extends itself to all trials. There were many persecutions which the Thessalonians endured for the sake of righteousness, as well as other troubles which they met with in this calamitous life; yet they endured all these, by faith *seeing him that is invisible,* and looking to the *recompence of reward;* and endured them with patience, not with an insensibility under them, but with patience arising from Christian principles, which kept them quiet and submissive, and afforded them inward strength and support.

Verses 5–10

Having mentioned their persecutions and tribulations, which they endured principally for the cause of Christ, the apostle proceeds to offer several things for their comfort under them; as,

I. He tells them of the present happiness and advantage of their sufferings, *v.* 5. Their faith being thus tried, and patience exercised, they were improved by their sufferings, insomuch that they were *counted worthy of the kingdom of God.* Their sufferings were a manifest token of this, that they were worthy or meet to be accounted Christians indeed, seeing they could suffer for Christianity. And the truth is, Religion, if it is worth any thing, is worth every thing; and those either have no religion at all, or none that is worth having, or know not how to value it, that cannot find in their hearts to suffer for it. Besides, from their patient suffering, it appeared that, according to the righteous judgment of God, they should be counted worthy of the heavenly glory: not by worthiness of condignity, but of congruity only; not that they could merit heaven, but they were made meet for heaven. We cannot by all our sufferings, any more than by our services, merit heaven as a debt; but by our patience under our sufferings we are qualified for the joy that is promised to patient sufferers in the cause of God.

II. He tells them next of the future recompence that shall be given to persecutor and persecuted.

1. In this future recompence there will be, (1.) A punishment inflicted on persecutors: God will *recompense tribulation to those that trouble you, v.* 6. And there is nothing that more infallibly marks a man for eternal ruin than a spirit of persecution, and enmity to the name and people of God: as the faith, patience, and constancy of the saints are to them an earnest of everlasting rest and joy, so the pride, malice, and wickedness of their persecutors are to them an earnest of everlasting misery; for every man carries about with him, and carries out of the world with him, either his heaven or his hell. God will render a recompence, and will trouble those that trouble his people. This he has done sometimes in this world, witness the dreadful end of many persecutors; but especially this he will do in the other world, where the portion of the wicked must be *weeping, and wailing, and gnashing of teeth.* (2.) A reward for those that are persecuted: God will recompense their trouble with rest, *v.* 7. There is a rest that remains for the people of God, a rest from sin and sorrow. Though many may be the troubles of the righteous now, yet God will deliver them out of them all. The future rest will abundantly recompense all their present troubles. The sufferings of this present time are not worthy to be compared with the glory that shall be revealed. There is enough in heaven to countervail all that we may lose or suffer for the name of Christ in this world. The apostle says, *To you who are troubled rest with us.* In heaven, ministers and people shall rest together, and rejoice together, who suffer together here; and the meanest Christian shall rest with the greatest apostle: nay, what is far more, if we suffer for Christ, we shall also reign with him, 2 Tim. 2:12.

2. Concerning this future recompence we are further to observe,

(1.) The certainty of it, proved by the righteousness and justice of God: *It is a righteous thing with God* (*v.* 6) to render to every man according to his works. The thoughts of this should be terrible to wicked men and persecutors, and the great support of the righteous and such as are persecuted; for, seeing there is a righteous God, there will be a righteous recompence. God's suffering people will lose nothing by their sufferings, and their enemies will gain nothing by their advantages against them.

(2.) The time when this righteous recompence shall be made: *When the Lord Jesus shall be revealed from heaven, v.* 7. That will be the day of the *revelation of the righteous judgment of God;* for then will God judge the world in righteousness by that man whom he hath appointed, even Jesus Christ the righteous Judge. The righteousness of God does not so visibly appear to all men in the procedure of his providence as it will in the process of the great judgment-day. The scripture has made known to us the judgment to come, and we are bound to receive the revelation here given concerning Christ. As,

[1.] That the Lord Jesus will in that day appear from heaven. Now the heavens retain him, they conceal him; but then he will be revealed and made manifest. He will come in all the pomp and power of the upper world, *whence we look for the Saviour.*

[2.] He will be revealed with his mighty angels (*v.* 7), or the angels of his power: these will attend upon him, to grace the solemnity of that great day of his appearance; they will be the ministers of his justice and mercy in that day; they will summon the criminals to his tribunal, and gather in the elect, and be employed in executing his sentence.

[3.] He will come in flaming fire, *v.* 8. A fire goeth before him, which shall consume his enemies. The earth, and all the works that are therein, shall be burnt up, and the elements shall melt with fervent heat. This will be a trying fire, to try every man's work, — a refining fire, to purify the saints, who shall share in the purity, and partake of the felicity, of the new heaven and the new earth, — a consuming fire to the wicked. His light will be piercing, and his power consuming, to all those who in that day shall be found as chaff.

[4.] The effects of this appearance will be terrible to some and joyful to others.

First, They will be terrible to some; for he will then take vengeance on the wicked. 1. On those that sinned against the principles of natural religion, and rebelled against the light of nature, *that knew not God* (*v.* 8), though the invisible things of him are manifested in the things that are seen. 2. On those that rebel against the light of revelation, that *obey not the gospel of our Lord Jesus Christ.* And this is the condemnation, that light is come into the world, and men love darkness rather than light. This is the great crime of multitudes — the gospel is revealed to them, and they will not believe it; or, if they pretend to believe it, they will not obey it. Note, Believing the truths of the gospel is in order to our obeying the precepts of the gospel: there must be the obedience of faith. To such persons as are here mentioned the revelation of our Lord Jesus Christ will be terrible, because of their doom, which is mentioned, *v.* 9. Here observe, (1.) They will then be punished. Though sinners may be long reprieved, yet they will be punished at last. Their misery will be a proper punishment for their crimes, and only what they have deserved. They did sin's work, and must receive sin's wages. (2.) Their punishment will be no less than destruction, not of their being, but of their bliss; not that of the body alone, but both as to body and soul. (3.) This destruction will be everlasting. They shall be always dying, and yet never die. Their misery will run parallel with the line of eternity. The chains of darkness are everlasting chains, and the fire is everlasting fire. It must needs be so, since the punishment is inflicted by an eternal God, fastening upon an immortal soul, set out of the reach of divine mercy and grace. (4.) This destruction shall come from the *presence of the Lord,* that is, immediately from God himself. Here God punishes sinners by creatures, by instruments; but then he will take the work into his own hands. It will be destruction from the Almighty, more terrible than the consuming fire which consumed Nadab and Abihu, which came from before the Lord. (5.) It shall come from the *glory of his power,* or from his glorious power. Not only the justice of God, but this almighty power, will be glorified in the destruction of sinners; and who knows the power of his anger? He is able to cast into hell.

Secondly, It will be a joyful day to some, even to the saints, unto those that believe and obey the gospel. And then the apostle's testimony concerning this day will be confirmed and *believed* (*v.* 10); in that bright and blessed day, 1. Christ Jesus will be glorified and admired by his saints. They will behold his glory, and admire it with pleasure; they will glorify his grace, and admire the wonders of his power and goodness towards them, and sing hallelujahs to him in that day of his triumph, for their complete victory and happiness. 2. Christ will be glorified and admired in them. His grace and power will then be manifested and magnified, when it shall appear what he has purchased for, and wrought in, and bestowed upon, all those who believe in him. As his wrath and power will be made known in and by the destruction of his enemies, so his grace and power will be magnified in the salvation of his saints. Note, Christ's dealings with those who believe will be what the world one day shall wonder at. Now, they are a wonder to many; but how will they be wondered at in this great and glorious day; or, rather, how will Christ, whose name is Wonderful, be admired, when the mystery of God shall be finished! Christ will not be so much admired in the glorious esteem of angels that he will bring from heaven with him as in the many saints, *the many sons,* that he will bring to glory.

Verses 11–12

In these verses the apostle again tells the Thessalonians of his earnest and constant prayer for them. He could not be present with them, yet he had a constant remembrance of them; they were much upon his thoughts; he wished them well, and could not express his good-will and good wishes to them better than in earnest constant prayer to God for them: *Wherefore also we pray,* etc. Note, The believing thoughts and expectation of the second coming of Christ should put us upon prayer to God for ourselves and others. We should watch and pray, so our Saviour directs his disciples (Lu. 21:36), *Watch therefore, and pray always, that you may be counted worthy to stand before the Son of man.* Observe,

I. What the apostle prayed for, *v.* 11. It is a great concern to be well instructed what to pray for; and without divine instruction we know not what to pray for, as without divine assistance we shall not pray in such a manner as we ought. Our prayers should be suitable to our expectations. Thus the apostle prays for them, 1. That God would begin his good work of grace in them; so we may understand this expression: *That our God would count you* (or, as it might be read, *make you) worthy of this calling.* We are called with a high and holy calling; we are called to God's kingdom and glory; and no less than the inheritance of the saints is the hope of our calling, nothing less than the enjoyment of that glory and felicity which shall be revealed when Christ Jesus shall be revealed from heaven. Now, if this be our calling, our great concern should be to be worthy of it, or meet and prepared for this glory: and because we have no worthiness of our own, but what is owing purely to the grace of God, we should pray that he would make us worthy, and then count us worthy, of this calling, or that he would make us meet to partake of the inheritance of the saints in light, Col. 1:12. 2. That God would carry on the good work that is begun, and *fulfil all the good pleasure of his goodness.* The good pleasure of God denotes his gracious purposes towards his people, which flow from his goodness, and are full of goodness towards them; and it is thence that all good comes to us. If there be any good in us, it is the fruit of God's good-will to us, it is owing to the good pleasure of his goodness, and therefore is called grace. Now, there are various and manifold purposes of grace and good-will in God towards his people; and the apostle prays that all of them may be fulfilled or accomplished towards these Thessalonians. There are several good works of grace begun in the hearts of God's people, which proceed from this good pleasure of God's goodness, and we should desire that they may be completed and perfected. In particular, the apostle prays that God would fulfil in them the *work of faith with power.* Note, (1.) The fulfilling of the work of faith is in order to the fulfilling of every other good work. And, (2.) It is the power of God that not only begins, but that carries on and perfects the work of faith.

II. Why the apostle prayed for these things (*v.* 12): *That the name of the Lord Jesus may be glorified;* this is the end we should aim at in every thing we do and desire, that God and Christ in all things may be glorified. Our own happiness and that of others should be subordinate to this ultimate end. Our good works should so shine before men that others may glorify God, that Christ may be glorified in and by us, and then we shall be glorified in and with him. And this is the great end and design of the grace of our God and the Lord Jesus Christ, which is manifested to us and wrought in us. Or thus: it is according to the grace of God and Christ, that is, it is an agreeable thing, considering the grace that is manifested to us and bestowed on us, by God and Christ, that we direct all we do to the glory of our Creator and Redeemer.

CHAPTER 2

The apostle is very careful to hinder the spreading of an error into which some among them had fallen concerning the coming of Christ, as being very near (*v.* 1–3). Then he proceeds to confute the error he cautioned them against, by telling them of two great events that were antecedent to the coming of Christ — a general apostasy, and the revelation of antichrist, concerning whom the apostle tells them many remarkable things, about his name, his character, his rise, his fall, his reign, and the sin and ruin of his subjects (*v.* 4–12). He then comforts them against the terror of this apostasy, and exhorts them to stedfastness (*v.* 13–15). And concludes with a prayer for them (*v.* 16, 17).

Verses 1–3a

From these words it appears that some among the Thessalonians had mistaken the apostle's meaning, in what he had written in his former epistle about the coming of Christ, by thinking that it was near at hand, — that Christ was just ready to appear and come to judgment. Or, it may be, some among them pretended that they had the knowledge of this by particular revelation from the Spirit, or from some words they had heard from the apostle, when he was with them, or some letter he had written or they pretended he had written to them or some other person: and hereupon the apostle is careful to rectify this mistake, and to prevent the spreading of this error. Observe, If errors and mistakes arise among Christians, we should take the first opportunity to rectify them, and hinder the spreading thereof; and good men will be especially careful to suppress errors that may arise from a mistake of their words and actions, though that which was spoken or done was ever so innocent or well. We have a subtle adversary, who watches all opportunities to do mischief, and will sometimes promote errors even by means of the words of scripture. Observe,

I. How very earnest and solicitous this apostle was to prevent mistakes: *We beseech you, brethren,* etc., *v.* 1. He entreats them as brethren who might have charged them as a father charges his children: he shows great kindness and condescension, and insinuates himself into their affections. And this is the best way to deal with men when we would preserve or recover them from errors, to deal gently and affectionately with them: rough and rigorous treatment will but exasperate their spirits, and prejudice them against the reasons we may offer. He obtests and even conjures them in the most solemn manner: *By the coming of Christ,* etc. The words are in the form of an oath; and his meaning is that if they believed Christ would come, and if they desired he would come, and rejoiced in the hope of his coming, they should be careful to avoid the error, and the evil consequences of it, against which he was now cautioning them. From this form of obtestation used by the apostle, we may observe,

1. It is most certain that the Lord Jesus Christ will come to judge the world, that he will come in all the pomp and power of the upper world in the last day, to execute judgment upon all. Whatever uncertainty we are at, or whatever mistakes may arise about the time of his coming, his coming itself is certain. This has been the faith and hope of all Christians in all ages of the church; nay, it was the faith and hope of the Old-Testament saints, ever since Enoch the seventh from Adam, who said, *Behold, the Lord cometh,* etc., Jude 14.

2. At the second coming of Christ all the saints will be gathered together to him; and this mention of the gathering of the saints together unto Christ at his coming shows that the apostle speaks of Christ's coming to judgment day, and not of his coming to destroy Jerusalem. He speaks of a proper, and not a metaphorical advent: and, as it will be part of Christ's honour in that day, so it will be the completing of the happiness of his saints. (1.) That they all shall be gathered together. There will then be a general meeting of all the saints, and none but saints; all the Old-Testament saints, who got acquaintance with Christ by the dark shadows of the law, and saw this day at a distance; and all the New-Testament saints, to whom life and immortality were brought to light by the gospel; they will all be gathered together. There will then come from the four winds of heaven all that are, or ever were, or ever shall be, from the beginning to the end of time. All shall be gathered together. (2.) That they shall be gathered *together to Christ.* He will be the great centre of their unity. They shall be gathered together to him, to be attendants on him, to be assessors with him, to be presented by him to the Father, to be with him for ever, and altogether happy in his presence to all eternity. (3.) The doctrine of Christ's coming and our gathering together to him is of a great moment and importance to Christians; otherwise it would not be the proper matter of the apostle's obtestation. We ought therefore not only to believe these things, but highly to account of them also, and look upon them as things we are greatly concerned in and should be much affected with.

II. The thing itself against which the apostle cautions the Thessalonians is that they should not be deceived about the time of Christ's coming, and so *be shaken in mind, or be troubled.* Note, Errors in the mind tend greatly to weaken our faith, and cause us trouble; and such as are weak in faith and of troubled minds are oftentimes apt to be deceived, and fall a prey to seducers. 1. The apostle would not have them be deceived: *Let no man deceive you by any means, v.* 3. There are many who lie in wait to deceive, and they have many ways of deceiving; we have reason therefore to be cautious and stand upon our guard. Some deceivers will pretend new revelations, others misinterpret scripture, and others will be guilty of gross forgeries; divers means and artifices of deceit men will use; but we must be careful that no man deceive us by any means. The particular matter in which the apostle cautions them not to be deceived is about the near approach of Christ's coming, as if it was to have been in the apostle's days; and harmless as this error might seem to many, yet, because it was indeed an error, it would have proved of bad consequences to many persons. Therefore, 2. He gives them warning, and would not have them be soon shaken in mind, nor be troubled. (1.) He would not have their faith weakened. We should firmly believe the second coming of Christ, and be settled and established in the faith of this; but there was danger lest the Thessalonians, if they apprehended the coming of Christ was just at hand, upon finding that they, or others whom they too much regarded, were mistaken as to the time, should thereupon question the truth or certainty of the thing itself; whereas they ought not to waver in their minds as to this great thing, which is the faith and hope of all the saints. False doctrines are like winds, that toss the water to and fro, and they are apt to unsettle the minds of men, who are sometimes as unstable as water. Then, (2.) He would not have their comforts lessened, that they should not be troubled nor affrighted with false alarms. It is probable that the coming of Christ was represented in so much terror as to trouble many serious Christians among them, though in itself it should be matter of the believer's hope and joy; or else many might be troubled with the thought how surprising this day would be, or with the fear of their unpreparedness, or upon the reflection on their mistake about the time of Christ's coming: we should always watch and pray, but must not be discouraged nor uncomfortable at the thought of Christ's coming.

Verses 3b–12

In these words the apostle confutes the error against which he had cautioned them, and gives the reasons why they should not expect the coming of Christ as just at hand. There were several events previous to the second coming of Christ; in particular, he tells them there would be,

I. A general apostasy, *there would come a falling away first, v.* 3. By this apostasy we are not to understand a defection in the state, or from civil government, but in spiritual or religious matters, from sound doctrine, instituted worship and church government, and a holy life. The apostle speaks of some very great apostasy, not only of some converted Jews or Gentiles, but such as should be very general, though gradual, and should give occasion to the revelation of rise of *antichrist,* that *man of sin.* This, he says (*v.* 5), he had told them of when he was with them, with design, no doubt, that they should not take offence nor be stumbled at it. And let us observe that no sooner was Christianity planted and rooted in the world than there began to be a defection in the Christian church. It was so in the Old-Testament church; presently after any considerable advance made in religion there followed a defection: soon after the promise there was revolting; for example, soon after men began to call upon the name of the Lord all flesh corrupted their way, — soon after the covenant with Noah the Babel-builders bade defiance to heaven, — soon after the covenant with Abraham his seed degenerated in Egypt, — soon after the Israelites were planted in Canaan, when the first generation was worn off, they forsook God and served Baal, — soon after God's covenant with David his seed revolted, and served other gods, — soon after the return out of captivity there was a general decay of piety, as appears by the story of Ezra and Nehemiah; and therefore it was no strange thing that after the planting of Christianity there should come a falling away.

II. A revelation of that man of sin, that is (*v.* 3), antichrist would take his rise from this general apostasy. The apostle afterwards speaks of the revelation of that wicked one (*v.* 8), intimating the discovery which should be made of his wickedness, in order to his ruin: here he seems to speak of his rise, which should be occasioned by the general apostasy he had mentioned, and to intimate that all sorts of false doctrines and corruptions should centre in him. Great disputes have been as to who or what is intended by this man of sin and son of perdition: and, if it be not certain that the papal power and tyranny are principally or only intended, yet this is plain, What is here said does very exactly agree thereto. For observe,

1. The names of this person, or rather the state and power here spoken of. He is called the man of sin, to denote his egregious wickedness; not only is he addicted to, and practises, wickedness himself, but he also promotes, countenances, and commands sin and wickedness in others; and he is the son of perdition, because he himself is devoted to certain destruction, and is the instrument of destroying many others both in soul and body. These names may properly be applied, for these reasons, to the papal state; and thereto agree also,

2. The characters here given, *v.* 4. (1.) That he *opposes and exalts himself above all that is called God, or is worshipped;* and thus have the bishops of Rome not only opposed God's authority, and that of the civil magistrates, who are called gods, but have exalted themselves above God and earthly governors, in demanding greater regard to their commands than to the commands of God or the magistrate. (2.) *As God, he sits in the temple of God, showing himself that he is God.* As God was in the temple of old, and worshipped there, and is in and with his church now, so the antichrist here mentioned is some usurper of God's authority in the Christian church, who claims divine honours; and to whom can this better apply than to the bishops of Rome, to whom the most blasphemous titles have been given, as *Dominus Deus noster papa — Our Lord God the pope; Deus alter in terrâ — Another God on earth; Idem est dominium Dei et papae — The dominion of God and the pope is the same?*

3. His rise is mentioned, *v.* 6, 7. Concerning this we are to observe two things: — (1.) There was something that hindered or withheld, or *let, until it was taken away.* This is supposed to be the power of the Roman empire, which the apostle did not think fit to mention more plainly at that time; and it is notorious that, while this power continued, it prevented the advances of the bishops of Rome to that height of tyranny to which soon afterwards they arrived. (2.) This mystery of iniquity was gradually to arrive at its height; and so it was in effect that the universal corruption of doctrine and worship in the Romish church came in by degrees, and the usurpation of the bishops of Rome was gradual, not all at once; and thus the mystery of iniquity did the more easily, and almost insensibly, prevail. The apostle justly calls it a *mystery of iniquity,* because wicked designs and actions were concealed under false shows and pretences, at least they were concealed from the common view and observation. By pretended devotion, superstition and idolatry were advanced; and, by a pretended zeal for God and his glory, bigotry and persecution were promoted. And he tells us that this mystery of iniquity did even then begin, or did *already work.* While the apostles were yet living, *the enemy came, and sowed tares;* there were then the *deeds of the Nicolaitans,* persons who pretended zeal for Christ, but really opposed him. Pride, ambition, and worldly interest of church-pastors and church-rulers, as in Diotrephes and others, were the early working of the mystery of iniquity, which, by degrees, came to that prodigious height which has been visible in the church of Rome.

4. The fall or ruin of the antichristian state is declared, *v.* 8. The head of this antichristian kingdom is called *that wicked one,* or that lawless person who sets up a human power in competition with, and contradiction to, the divine dominion and power of the Lord Jesus Christ; but, as he would thus manifest himself to be the man of sin, so the revelation or discovery of this to the world would be the sure presage and the means of his ruin. The apostle assures the Thessalonians that the Lord would consume and destroy him; the consuming of him precedes his final destruction, and that is by the *Spirit of his mouth,* by his word of command; the pure word of God, accompanied with the Spirit of God, will discover this mystery of iniquity, and make the power of antichrist to consume and waste away; and in due time it will be totally and finally destroyed, and this will be by the brightness of Christ's coming. Note, The coming of Christ to destroy the wicked will be with peculiar glory and eminent lustre and brightness.

5. The apostle further describes the reign and rule of this man of sin. Here we are to observe, (1.) The manner of his coming, or ruling, and working: in general, that it is after the example of Satan, the grand enemy of souls, the great adversary of God and man. He is the great patron of error and lies, the sworn enemy of the truth as it is in Jesus and all the faithful followers of Jesus. More particularly, it is with Satanical power and deceit. A divine power is pretended for the support of this kingdom, but it is only after the working of Satan. Signs and wonders, visions and miracles, are pretended; by these the papal kingdom was first set up, and has all along been kept up, but they have false signs to support false doctrines; and lying wonders, or only pretended miracles that have served their cause, things false in fact, or fraudulently managed, to impose upon the people: and the diabolical deceits with which the antichristian state has been supported are notorious. The apostle calls it *all deceivableness of unrighteousness, v.* 10. Others may call them pious frauds, but the apostle called them unrighteous and wicked frauds; and, indeed, all fraud (which is contrary to truth) is

an impious thing. Many are the subtle artifices the man of sin has used, and various are the plausible pretences by which he had beguiled unwary and unstable souls to embrace false doctrines, and submit to his usurped dominion. (2.) The persons are described who are his willing subjects, or most likely to become such, *v.* 10. They are such as *love not the truth that they may be saved.* They heard the truth (it may be), but they did not love it; they could not bear sound doctrine, and therefore easily imbibed false doctrines; they had some notional knowledge of what was true, but they indulged some powerful prejudices, and so became a prey to seducers. Had they loved the truth, they would have persevered in it, and been preserved by it; but no wonder if they easily parted with what they never had any love to. And of these persons it is said that they perish or are lost; they are in a lost condition, and in danger to be lost for ever. For,

6. We have the *sin and ruin of the subjects* of antichrist's kingdom declared, *v.* 11, 12. (1.) Their sin is this: *They believed not the truth, but had pleasure in unrighteousness:* they did not love the truth, and therefore they did not believe it; and, because they did not believe the truth, therefore they had pleasure in unrighteousness, or in wicked actions, and were pleased with false notions. Note, An erroneous mind and vicious life often go together and help forward one another. (2.) Their ruin is thus expressed: *God shall send them strong delusions, to believe a lie.* Thus he will punish men for their unbelief, and for their dislike of the truth and love to sin and wickedness; not that God is the author of sin, but in righteousness he sometimes withdraws his grace from such sinners as are here mentioned; he gives them over to Satan, or leaves them to be deluded by his instruments; he gives them up to their own hearts' lusts, and leaves them to themselves, and then sin will follow of course, yea, the worst of wickedness, that shall end at last in eternal damnation. God is just when he inflicts spiritual judgments here, and eternal punishments hereafter, upon those who have no love to the truths of the gospel, who will not believe them, nor live suitably to them, but indulge false doctrines in their minds, and wicked practices in their lives and conversations.

Verses 13–15

Here observe, I. The consolation the Thessalonians might take against the terrors of this apostasy, *v.* 13, 14. For they were chosen to salvation, and called to the obtaining of glory. Note, When we hear of the apostasy of many, it is matter of great comfort and joy that there is a remnant according to the election of grace which does and shall persevere; and especially we should rejoice if we have reason to hope that we are of that number. The apostle reckoned himself bound in duty to be thankful to God on this account: *We are bound to give thanks to God always for you.* He had often given thanks on their behalf, and he is still abounding in thanksgiving for them; and there was good reason, because they were beloved by the Lord, as appeared in this matter — their security from apostatizing. This preservation of the saints is owing,

1. To the stability of the election of grace, *v.* 13. Therefore were they beloved of the Lord, because God had chosen them from the beginning. He had loved them with an everlasting love. Concerning this election of God we may observe, (1.) The eternal date of it — it is from the beginning; not the beginning of the gospel, but the beginning of the world, before the foundation of the world, Eph. 1:4. Then, (2.) The end to which they were chosen — salvation, complete and eternal salvation from sin and misery, and the full fruition of all good. (3.) The means in order to obtaining this end — *sanctification of the spirit and belief of the truth.* The decree of election therefore connects the end and the means, and these must not be separated. We are not the elected of God because we were holy, but that we might be holy. Being chosen of God, we must not live as we list; but, if we are chosen to salvation as the end, we must be prepared for it by sanctification as the necessary means to obtain that end, which sanctification is by the operation of the Holy Spirit as the author and by faith on our part. There must be the belief of the truth, without which there can be by true sanctification, nor perseverance in grace, nor obtaining of salvation. Faith and holiness must be joined together, as well as holiness and happiness; therefore our Saviour prayed for Peter that his faith might not fail (Lu. 22:32), and for his disciples (Jn. 17:17), *Sanctify them by thy truth; thy word is truth.*

2. To the efficacy of the gospel call, *v.* 14. As they were

chosen to salvation, so they were called thereunto by the gospel. Whom he did predestinate those he also called, Rom. 8:30. The outward call of God is by the gospel; and this is rendered effectual by the inward operation of the Spirit. Note, Wherever the gospel comes it calls and invites men to the obtaining of glory; it is a call to honour and happiness, even the *glory of our Lord Jesus Christ,* the glory he has purchased, and the glory he is possessed of, to be communicated unto those who believe in him and obey his gospel; such shall be with Christ, to behold his glory, and they shall be glorified with Christ and partake of his glory. Hereupon there follows,

II. An exhortation to stedfastness and perseverance: *Therefore, brethren, stand fast, v.* 15. Observe, He does not say, "You are chosen to salvation, and therefore you may be careless and secure;" but *therefore stand fast.* God's grace in our election and vocation is so far from superseding our diligent care and endeavour that it should quicken and engage us to the greatest resolution and diligence. So the apostle John having told those to whom he wrote that they had received the anointing which should abide in them, and that they should abide in him (in Christ), subjoins this exhortation, *Now abide in him,* 1 Jn. 2:27, 28. The Thessalonians are exhorted to stedfastness in their Christian profession, to *hold fast the traditions which they had been taught,* or the doctrine of the gospel, which had been delivered by the apostle, by word or epistle. As yet the canon of scripture was not complete, and therefore some things were delivered by the apostles in their preaching, under the guidance of the infallible Spirit, which Christians were bound to observe as coming from God; other things were afterwards by them committed to writing, as the apostle had written a former epistle to these Thessalonians; and these epistles were written as the writers were moved by the Holy Ghost. Note, There is no argument hence for regarding oral traditions in our days, now that the canon of scripture is complete, as of equal authority with the sacred writings. Such doctrines and duties as were taught by the inspired apostles we must stedfastly adhere to; but we have no certain evidence of any thing delivered by them more than what we find contained in the holy scriptures.

Verses 16–17

In these words we have the apostle's earnest prayer for them, in which observe,

I. To whom he prays: *Our Lord Jesus Christ himself, and God, even our Father.* We may and should direct our prayers, not only to God the Father, through the mediation of our Lord Jesus Christ, but also *to our Lord Jesus Christ himself;* and should pray in his name unto God, not only as his Father but as our Father in and through him.

II. From what he takes encouragement in his prayer — from the consideration of what God had already done for him and them: *Who hath loved us, and given us everlasting consolation and good hope through grace, v.* 16. Here observe, 1. The love of God is the spring and fountain of all the good we have or hope for; our election, vocation, justification, and salvation, are all owing to the love of God in Christ Jesus. 2. From this fountain in particular all our consolation flows. And the consolation of the saints is an everlasting consolation. The comforts of the saints are not dying things; they shall not die with them. The spiritual consolations God gives none shall deprive them of; and God will not take them away: because he love them with an everlasting love, therefore they shall have everlasting consolation. 3. Their consolation is founded on the hope of eternal life. They rejoice in hope of the glory of God, and are not only patient, but joyful, in tribulations; and there is good reason for these strong consolations, because the saints have good hope: their hope is grounded on the love of God, the promise of God, and the experience they have had of the power, the goodness, and the faithfulness of God, and it is good hope through grace; the free grace and mercy of God are what they hope for, and what their hopes are founded on, and not on any worth or merit of their own.

III. What it is that he asks of God for them — that *he would comfort their hearts, and establish them in every good word and work, v.* 17. God had given them consolations, and he prayed that they might have more abundant consolation. There was good hope, through grace, that they would be preserved, and he prayed that they might be established: it is observable how comfort and establishment are here joined together. Note therefore, 1. Comfort is a means of establishment; for the more pleasure we take in the word, and work,

and ways of God, the more likely we shall be to persevere therein. And, 2. Our establishment in the ways of God is a likely means in order to comfort; whereas, if we are wavering in faith, and of a doubtful mind, or if we are halting and faltering in our duty, no wonder if we are strangers to the pleasures and joys of religion. What is it that lies at the bottom of all our uneasiness, but our unsteadiness in religion? We must be established in every good word and work, in the word of truth and the work of righteousness: Christ must be honoured by our good works and good words; and those who are sincere will endeavour to do both, and in so doing they may hope for comfort and establishment, till at length their holiness and happiness be completed.

CHAPTER 3

In the close of the foregoing chapter, the apostle had prayed earnestly for the Thessalonians, and now he desires their prayers, encouraging them to trust in God, to which he subjoins another petition for them (*v.* 1–5). He then proceeds to give them commands and directions for correcting some things he was informed were amiss among them (*v.* 6–15) and concludes with benedictions and prayers (*v.* 16–18).

Verses 1–5

In these words observe,

I. The apostle desires the prayers of his friends: *Finally, brethren, pray for us, v.* 1. He always remembered them in his prayers, and would not have them forget him and his fellow-labourers, but bear them on their hearts at the throne of grace. Note, 1. This is one way by which the communion of saints is kept us, not only by their praying together, or with one another, but by their praying for one another when they are absent one from another. And thus those who are at great distance may meet together at the throne of grace; and thus those who are not capable of doing or receiving any other kindness may yet this way do and receive real and very great kindness. 2. It is the duty of people to pray for their ministers; and not only for their own pastors, but also for all good and faithful ministers. And, 3. Ministers need, and therefore should desire, the prayers of their people. How remarkable is the humility, and how engaging the example, of this great apostle, who was so mighty in prayer himself, and yet despised not the prayers of the meanest Christian, but desired an interest in them. Observe, further, what they are desired and directed to pray for; namely, (1.) For the success of the gospel ministry: *That the word of the Lord may have free course, and be glorified, v.* 1. This was the great thing that Paul was most solicitous about. He was more solicitous that God's name might be sanctified, his kingdom advanced, and his will done, than he was about his own daily bread. He desired that the word of the Lord might run (so it is in the original), that it might get ground, that the interest of religion in the world might go forward and not backward, and not only go forward, but go apace. All the forces of hell were then, and still are, more or less, raised and mustered to oppose the word of the Lord, to hinder its publication and success. We should pray, therefore, that oppositions may be removed, that so the gospel, may have free course to the ears, the hearts, and the consciences of men, that it may be glorified in the conviction and conversion of sinners, the confutation, of gainsayers, and the holy conversation of the saints. God, who magnified the law, and made it honourable, will glorify the gospel, and make that honourable, and so will glorify his own name; and good ministers and good Christians may very well be contented to be little, to be any thing, to be nothing, if Christ be magnified and his gospel be glorified. Paul was now at Athens, or, as some think, at Corinth, and would have the Thessalonians pray that he might have as good success there as he had at Thessalonica, that it might be as well with others even as it was with them. Note, If ministers have been successful in one place, they should desire to be successful in every place where they may preach the gospel. (2.) For the safety of gospel ministers. He asks their prayers, nor for preferment, but for preservation: *That we may be delivered from unreasonable and wicked men, v.* 2. Note, Those who are enemies to the preaching of the gospel, and persecutors of the faithful preachers of it, are unreasonable and wicked men. They act against all the rules and laws of reason and religion, and are guilty of the greatest absurdity and impiety. Not only in the principles of atheism and infidelity, but also in the practice of the vice and immorality, and especially in persecution, there is the greatest absurdity in the world, as well as impiety. There is need of the spiritual protection, as well as the assistance, of godly and faithful ministers, for these are as the standard-bearers, who are most struck at; and therefore all who wish well to the interest of Christ in the world should pray for them. *For all men have not faith;* that is, many do not believe the gospel; they will not embrace it themselves, and no wonder if such are restless and malicious in their endeavours to oppose the gospel, decry the ministry, and disgrace the ministers of the word; and too many have not common faith or honesty; there is no confidence that we can safely put in them, and we should pray to be delivered from those who have no conscience nor honour, who never regard what they say or do. We may sometimes be in as much or more danger from false and pretended friends as from open and avowed enemies.

II. He encourages them to trust in God. We should not only pray to God for his grace, but also place our trust and confidence in his grace, and humbly expect what we pray for. Observe,

1. What the good is which we may expect from the grace of God — establishment, and preservation from evil; and the best Christians stand in need of these benefits. (1.) That God would establish them. This the apostle had prayed for on their behalf (*ch.* 2:17), and now he encourages them to expect this favour. We stand no longer than God holds us up; unless he *hold up our goings in his paths, our feet will slide,* and we shall fall. (2.) That God will keep them from evil. We have as much need of the grace of God for our perseverance to the end as for the beginning of the good work. The evil of sin is the greatest evil, but there are other evils which God will also preserve his saints from — the evil that is in the world, yea, from all evil, to his heavenly kingdom.

2. What encouragement we have to depend upon the grace of God: *The Lord is faithful.* He is faithful to his promises, and is the Lord who cannot lie, who will not alter the thing that has gone out of his mouth. When once the promise therefore is made, performance is sure and certain. He is faithful to his relation, a faithful God and a faithful friend; we may depend upon his filling up all the relations he stands in to his people. Let it be our care to be true and faithful in our promises, and to the relations we stand in to this faithful God. He adds,

3. A further ground of hope that God would do this for them, seeing they did and would do the things they were commanded, *v.* 4. The apostle had this confidence in them, and this was founded upon his confidence in God; for there is otherwise no confidence in man. Their obedience is described by doing what he and his fellow-labourers had commanded them, which was no other thing than the commandments of the Lord; for the apostles themselves had no further commission than to teach men *to observe and to do what the Lord had commanded,* Mt. 28:20. And as the experience the apostle had of their obedience for the time past was one ground of his confidence that they would do the things commanded them for the time to come, so this is one ground to hope that *whatsoever we ask of God we shall receive of him, because we keep his commandments, and do those things that are pleasing in his sight,* 1 Jn. 3:22.

III. He makes a short prayer for them, *v.* 5. It is a prayer for spiritual blessings. Two things of the greatest importance the apostle prays for: — 1. That their hearts may be brought into the love of God, to be in love with God as the most excellent and amiable Being, the best of all beings; and this is not only most reasonable and necessary in order to our happiness, but is our happiness itself; it is a great part of the happiness of heaven itself, where this love shall be made perfect. We can never attain to this unless God by his grace direct our hearts aright, for our love is apt to go astray after other things. Note, We sustain a great deal of damage by misplacing our affections; it is our sin and our misery that we place our affections upon wrong objects. If God directs our love aright upon himself, the rest of the affections will thereby be rectified. 2. That a *patient waiting for Christ* may be joined with this love of God. There is no true love of God without faith in Jesus Christ. We must wait for Christ, which supposes our faith in him, that we believe he came once in flesh and will come again in glory: and we must expect this second coming of Christ, and be careful to get ready for it; there must be a patient waiting, enduring with courage and constancy all that we may meet with in the mean time: and we *have need of patience,* and need of divine grace to exercise Christian patience, the *patience of Christ* (as some

read the word), patience for Christ's sake and after Christ's example.

Verses 6–15

The apostle having commended their obedience for the time past, and mentioned his confidence in their obedience for the time to come, proceeds to give them commands and directions to some who were faulty, correcting some things that were amiss among them. Observe, The best society of Christians may have some faulty persons among them, and some things that ought to be reformed. Perfection is not to be found on this side heaven: but evil manners beget good laws; the disorders that Paul heard of as existing among the Thessalonians occasioned the good laws we find in these verses, which are of constant use to us, and all others whom they may concern. Observe,

I. That which was amiss among the Thessalonians, which is expressed,

1. More generally. There were some who *walked disorderly, not after the tradition they received* from the apostle, *v.* 6. Some of the brethren were guilty of this disorderly walking; they did not live regularly, nor govern themselves according to the rules of Christianity, nor agreeably to their profession of religion; not according to the precepts delivered by the apostle, which they had received, and pretended to pay a regard to. Note, It is required of those who have received the gospel, and who profess a subjection to it, that they live according to the gospel. If they do not, they are to be counted disorderly persons.

2. In particular, there were among them some *idle persons and busy-bodies, v.* 11. This the apostle was so credibly informed of that he had sufficient reason to give commands and directions with relation to such persons, how they ought to behave, and how the church should act towards them. (1.) There were some among them who were idle, *not working at all,* or doing nothing. It does not appear that they were gluttons or drunkards, but idle, and therefore disorderly people. It is not enough for any to say they do no hurt; for it is required of all persons that they do good in the places and relations in which Providence has placed them. It is probable that these persons had a notion (by misunderstanding some passages in the former epistle) concerning the near approach of the coming of Christ, which served them for a pretence to leave off the work of their callings, and live in idleness. Note, It is a great error, or abuse of religion, to make it a cloak for idleness or any other sin. If we were sure that the day of judgment were ever so near, we must, notwithstanding, do the work of the day in its day, that when our Lord comes he may find us doing. The servant who waits for the coming of his Lord aright must be working as his Lord has commanded, that all may be ready when he comes. Or, it may be, these disorderly persons pretended that the liberty wherewith Christ had made them free discharged them from the services and business of their particular callings and employments in the world: whereas they were *to abide in the same calling wherein they were called of God, and therein abide with God,* 1 Co. 7:20, 24. Industry in our particular callings as men is a duty required of us by our general calling as Christians. Or perhaps the general charity there was then among Christians to their poor brethren encouraged some to live in idleness, as knowing the church would maintain them: whatever was the cause, they were much to blame. (2.) There were busy-bodies among them: and it should seem, by the connection, that the same persons who were idle were busy-bodies also. This may seem to be a contradiction; but so it is, that most commonly those persons who have no business of their own to do, or who neglect it, busy themselves in other men's matters. If we are idle, the devil and a corrupt heart will soon find us something to do. The mind of man is a busy thing; if it be not employed in doing good, it will be doing evil. Note, Busy-bodies are disorderly walkers, such as are guilty of vain curiosity, and impertinent meddling with things that do not concern them, and troubling themselves and others with other men's matters. The apostle warns Timothy (1 Tim. 5:13) to beware of such *as learn to be idle, wandering about from house to house, and are not only idle, but tatlers also, and busy-bodies, speaking things which they ought not.*

II. The good laws which were occasioned by these evil manners, concerning which we may take notice,

1. Whose laws they are: they are commands of the apostles of our Lord, given in the name of their Lord and ours,

that is, the commands of our Lord himself. *We command you, brethren, in the name of the Lord Jesus Christ, v.* 6. Again, *We command and exhort you by our Lord Jesus Christ, v.* 12. The apostle uses words of authority and entreaty: and, where disorders are to be rectified or prevented, there is need of both. The authority of Christ should awe our minds to obedience, and his grace and goodness should allure us.

2. What the good laws and rules are. The apostle gives directions to the whole church, commands to those disorderly persons, and an exhortation to those in particular who did well among them.

(1.) His commands and directions to the whole church regard, [1.] Their behaviour towards the disorderly persons who were among them, which is thus expressed (*v.* 6), to *withdraw themselves from such,* and afterwards to *mark that man, and have no company with him, that he may be ashamed; yet not to count him as an enemy, but to admonish him as a brother.* The directions of the apostle are carefully to be observed in our conduct towards disorderly persons. We must be very cautious in church-censures and church-discipline. We must, *First,* Note that man who is suspected or charged with not obeying the word of God, or walking contrary thereto, that is, we must have sufficient proof of his fault before we proceed further. We must, *Secondly,* Admonish him in a friendly manner; we must put him in mind of his sin, and of his duty; and this should be done privately (Mt. 18:15); then, if he will not hear, we must, *Thirdly,* Withdraw from him, and not keep company with him, that is, we must avoid familiar converse and society with such, for two reasons, namely, that we may not learn his evil ways; for he who follows vain and idle persons, and keeps company with such, is in danger of becoming like them. Another reason is for the shaming, and so the reforming, of those that offend, that when idle and disorderly persons see how their loose practices are disliked by all wise and good people they may be ashamed of them, and walk more orderly. Love therefore to the persons of our offending brethren, even when we hate their vices, should be the motive of our withdrawing from them; and even those who are under the censures of the church must not be accounted as enemies (*v.* 15); for, if they be reclaimed and reformed by these censures, they will recover their credit and comfort, and right to church-privileges as brethren. [2.] Their general conduct and behaviour ought to be according to the good example the apostle and those who were with him had given them: *Yourselves know how you ought to follow us, v.* 7. Those who planted religion among them had set a good example before them; and the ministers of the gospel should be ensamples to the flock. It is the duty of Christians not only to walk according to the traditions of the apostles, and the doctrines they preached, but also according to the good example they set before them, *to be followers of them so far as they were followers of Christ.* The particular good example the apostle mentions was their diligence, which was so different from what was found in the disorderly walkers he takes notice of: "*We behaved not ourselves disorderly among you* (*v.* 7), we did not spend our time idly, in idle visits, idle talk, idle sports." They took pains in their ministry, in preaching the gospel, and in getting their own living. *Neither did we eat any man's bread for nought, v.* 8. Though he might justly have demanded a maintenance, because those who preach the gospel may of right expect to live by the gospel. This is a just debt that people owe to their ministers, and the apostle had power or authority to have demanded this (*v.* 9); but he waived his right from affection to them, and for the sake of the gospel, and that he might be an example for them to follow (*v.* 9), that they might learn how to fill up time, and always be employed in something that would turn to good account.

(2.) He commands and directs those that live idle lives to reform, and set themselves to their business. He had given commandments to this purport, as well as a good example of this, when he was among them: *Even when we were with you, this we commanded you, that if any man would not work neither should he eat, v.* 10. It was a proverbial speech among the Jews, *He who does not labour does not deserve to eat.* The labourer is worthy of his meat; but what is the loiterer worthy of? It is the will of God that every man should have a calling, and mind his calling, and make a business of it, and that none should live like useless drones in the world. Such persons do what in them lies to defeat the sentence, *In the sweat of thy face shalt thou eat thy bread.* It was not the mere humour of the apostle, who was an active stirring man himself and therefore would have every body else to be so too, but it was the command of our Lord Jesus Christ, that *with quietness we work, and eat our own bread, v.* 12. Men ought some way or other to earn their own living, otherwise they do not eat their own bread. Observe, There must be work or labour, in opposition to idleness; and there must be quietness, in opposition to being busy-bodies in other men's matters. We must study to be quiet, and do our own business. This is an excellent but rare composition, to be of an active yet quiet spirit, active in our own business and yet quiet as to other people's.

(3.) He exhorts *those that did well not to* be *weary in well-doing* (*v.* 13); as if he had said, "Go on and prosper. The Lord is with you while you are with him. See that whatever you do, that is good, you persevere therein. Hold on your way, and hold out to the end. You must never give over, nor tire in your work. It will be time enough to rest when you come to heaven, that *everlasting rest which remains for the people of God.*"

Verses 16–18

In this conclusion of the epistle we have the apostle's benediction and prayers for these Thessalonians. Let us desire them for ourselves and our friend. There are three blessings pronounced upon them, or desired for them: —

I. That God would give them peace. Note, 1. Peace is the blessing pronounced or desired. By peace we may understand all manner of prosperity; here it may signify, in particular, peace with God, peace in their own minds and consciences, peace among themselves, and peace with all men. 2. This peace is desired for them always, or in every thing; and he desired they might have all good things at all times. 3. Peace by all means: that, as they enjoyed the means of grace, they might with success use all the means and methods of peace too; for peace is often difficult, as it is always desirable. 4. That God would give them peace, who is the Lord of peace. If we have any peace that is desirable, God must give it, who is the *author of peace and lover of concord.* We shall neither have peaceable dispositions ourselves nor find men disposed to be at peace with us, unless the God of peace give us both.

II. That the presence of God might be with them: *The Lord be with you all.* We need nothing more to make us safe and happy, nor can we desire any thing better for ourselves and our friends, than to have God's gracious presence with us and them. This will be a guide and guard in every way that we may go, and our comfort in every condition we may be in. It is the presence of God that makes heaven to be heaven, and this will make this earth to be like heaven. No matter where we are if God be with us, nor who is absent if God be with us, nor who is absent if God be present with us.

III. That the *grace of our Lord Jesus Christ might be with them.* So this apostle concluded his first epistle to these Thessalonians; and it is through the grace of our Lord Jesus Christ that we may comfortably hope to have peace with God and enjoy the presence of God, for he has made those nigh that were afar off. It is this grace that is all in all to make us happy. This is what the apostle admired and magnified on all occasions, what he delighted and trusted in; and by this salutation or benediction, written with his own hand, as the token of every epistle (when the rest was written by an amanuensis), he took care lest the churches he wrote to should be imposed on by counterfeit epistles, which he knew would be of dangerous consequence.

Let us be thankful that we have the canon of scripture complete, and by the wonderful and special care of divine Providence preserved pure and uncorrupt through so many successive ages, and not dare to add to it, nor diminish from it. Let us believe the divine original of the sacred scriptures, and conform our faith and practice to this our sufficient and only rule, *which is able to make us wise unto salvation, through faith which is in Christ Jesus.* Amen.

AN EXPOSITION, WITH PRACTICAL OBSERVATIONS, OF

THE FIRST EPISTLE OF ST. PAUL TO TIMOTHY

Hitherto Paul's epistles were directed to churches; now follow some to particular persons: two to Timothy, one to Titus, and another to Philemon — all three ministers. Timothy and Titus were evangelists, an inferior order to the apostles, as appears by Eph. 4:11, *Some prophets, some apostles, some evangelists.* Their commission and work was much the same with that of the apostles, to plant churches, and water the churches that were planted; and accordingly they were itinerants, as we find Timothy was. Timothy was first converted by Paul, and therefore he calls him his *own son in the faith:* we read of his conversion, Acts 16:3.

The scope of these two epistles is to direct Timothy how to discharge his duty as an evangelist at Ephesus, where he now was, and where Paul ordered him for some time to reside, to perfect the good work which he had begun there. As for the ordinary pastoral charge of that church, he had very solemnly committed it to the presbytery, as appears from Acts 20:28, where he charges the presbyters *to feed the flock of God, which he had purchased with his own blood.*

CHAPTER 1

After the inscription (*v.* 1, 2) we have, I. The charge given to Timothy (*v.* 3, 4). II. The true end of the law (*v.* 5–11), where he shows that it is entirely agreeable to the gospel. III. He mentions his own call to be an apostle, for which he expresses his thankfulness (*v.* 12–16) IV. His doxology (*v.* 17). V. A renewal of the charge to Timothy (*v.* 18). And of Hymenaeus and Alexander (*v.* 19, 20).

Verses 1–4

Here is, I. The inscription of the epistle, from whom it is sent: *Paul an apostle of Jesus Christ,* constituted an apostle *by the commandment of God our Saviour, and Lord Jesus Christ.* His credentials were unquestionable. He had not only a commission, but a commandment, not only from God our Saviour, but from Jesus Christ: he was a preacher of the gospel of Christ, and a minister of the kingdom of Christ. Observe, God is our Saviour. — *Jesus Christ, who is our hope.* Observe, Jesus Christ is a Christian's hope; our hope is in him, all our hope of eternal life is built upon him; Christ is in us the hope of glory, Col. 1:27. He calls Timothy his own son, because he had been an instrument of his conversion, and because he had been a son that served him, served with him in the gospel, Phil. 2:22. Timothy had not been wanting in the duty of a son to Paul, and Paul was not wanting in the care and tenderness of a father to him.

II. The benediction is, *grace, mercy, and peace, from God our Father.* Some have observed that whereas in all the epistles to the churches the apostolical benediction is *grace and peace,* in these two epistles to Timothy and that to Titus it is *grace, mercy, and peace:* as if ministers had more need of God's mercy than other men. Ministers need more grace than others, to discharge their duty faithfully; and they need more mercy than others, to pardon what is amiss in them: and if Timothy, so eminent a minister, must be indebted to the mercy of God, and needed the increase and continuance of it, how much more do we ministers, in these times, who have so little of his excellent spirit!

III. Paul tells Timothy what was the end of his appointing him to this office: *I besought thee to abide at Ephesus.* Timothy had a mind to go with Paul, was loth to go from under his wing, but Paul would have it so; it was necessary for the public service: *I besought thee,* says he. Though he might assume an authority to command him, yet for love's sake he chose rather to beseech him. Now his business was to take care to fix both the ministers and the people of that church: *Charge them that they teach no other doctrine* than what they have received, that they do not add to the Christian doctrine, under pretence of improving it or making up the defects of it, that they do no alter it, but cleave to it as it was delivered to them. Observe, 1. Ministers must not only be charged to preach the true doctrine of the gospel, but charged to preach no other doctrine. *If an angel from heaven preach any other doctrine, let him be anathema,* Gal. 1:8. 2. In the times of the apostles there were attempts made to corrupt Christianity *(we are not as many, who corrupt the word,* 2 Co. 2:17), otherwise this charge to Timothy might have been spared. 3. He must not only see to it that he did not preach any other doctrine, but he must charge others that they might not add any thing of their own to the gospel, or take any thing from it, but that they preach it pure and uncorrupt. He must also take care to prevent their regarding *fables, and endless genealogies,* and strifes of words. This is often repeated in these two epistles (as *ch.* 4:7; 6:4; 2 Tim. 2:23), as well as in the epistle to Titus. As among the Jews there were some who brought Judaism into Christianity; so among the Gentiles there were some who brought paganism into Christianity. "Take heed of these," says he, "watch against them, or they will be the corrupting and ruining of religion among you, for *they minister questions rather than edifying.*" That which ministers questions is not for edifying; that which gives occasion for doubtful disputes pulls down the church rather than builds it up. And I think, by a parity of reason, every thing else that ministers questions rather than godly edifying should be disclaimed and disregarded by us, such as an uninterrupted succession in the ministry from the apostles down to these times, the absolute necessity of episcopal ordination, and of the intention of the minister to the efficacy and validity of the sacraments he ministers. These are as bad as Jewish fables and endless genealogies, for they involve us in inextricable difficulties, and tend only to shake the foundations of a Christian's hope and to fill his mind with perplexing doubts and fears. Godly edifying is the end ministers should aim at in all their discourses, that Christians may be improving in godliness and growing up to a greater likeness to the blessed God. Observe, further, Godly edifying must be in faith: the gospel is the foundation on which we build; it is by faith that we come to God at first (Heb. 11:6), and it must be in the same way, and by the same principle of faith, that we must be edified. Again, Ministers should avoid, as much as may be, what will occasion disputes; and would do well to insist on the great and practical points of religion, about which there can be no disputes; for even disputes about great and necessary truths draw off the mind from the main design of Christianity, and eat out the vitals of religion, which consist in practice and obedience as well as in faith, that we may not hold the truth in unrighteousness, but may keep the mystery of the faith in a pure conscience.

Verses 5–11

Here the apostle instructs Timothy how to guard against the judaizing teachers, or others who mingled fables and endless genealogies with the gospel. He shows the use of the law, and the glory of the gospel.

I. He shows the end and uses of the law: it is intended to promote love, *for love is the fulfilling of the law,* Rom. 13:10.

1. *The end of the commandment is charity,* or love, Rom. 13:8. The main scope and drift of the divine law are to engage us to the love of God and one another; and whatever tends to weaken either our love to God or love to the brethren tends to defeat the end of the commandment: and surely the gospel, which obliges us to love our enemies, to do good to those who hate us (Mt. 5:44) does not design to lay aside or supersede a commandment the end whereof is love; so far from it that, on the other hand, we are told that though we had all advantages and wanted charity, we are but as sounding brass and a tinkling cymbal, 1 Co. 13:1. *By this shall all men know that you are my disciples, if you love one another,* Jn. 13:35. Those therefore who boasted of their knowledge of the law, but used it only as a colour for the disturbance that they gave to the preaching of the gospel (under pretence of zeal for the law, dividing the church and distract-

ing it), defeated that which was the very end of the commandment, and that is love, love *out of a pure heart,* a heart purified by faith, purified from corrupt affections. In order to the keeping up of holy love our hearts must be cleansed from all sinful love; our love must arise *out of a good conscience,* kept without offence. Those answer the end of the commandment who are careful to keep a good conscience, from a real belief of the truth of the word of God which enjoins it, here called a *faith unfeigned.* Here we have the concomitants of that excellency grace charity; they are three: — (1.) A pure heart; there it must be seated, and thence it must take its rise. (2.) A good conscience, in which we must exercise ourselves daily, that we may not only get it, but that we may keep it, Acts 24:16. (3.) Faith unfeigned must also accompany it, for it is love without dissimulation: the faith that works by it must be of the like nature, genuine and sincere. Now some who set up for teachers of the law swerved from the very end of the commandment: they set up for disputers, but their disputes proved vain jangling; they set up for teachers, but they pretended to teach others what they themselves did not understand. If the church be corrupted by such teachers, we must not think it strange, for we see from the beginning it was so. Observe, [1.] When persons, especially ministers, swerve from the great law of charity — the end of the commandment, they will turn aside to vain jangling; when a man misses his end and scope, it is no wonder that every step he takes is out of the way. [2.] Jangling, especially in religion, is vain; it is unprofitable and useless as to all that is good, and it is very pernicious and hurtful: and yet many people's religion consists of little else but vain jangling. [3.] Those who deal much in vain jangling are fond and ambitious to be teachers of others; they desire (that is, they affect) the office of teaching. [4.] It is too common for men to intrude into the office of the ministry when they are very ignorant of those things about which they are ton speak: they understand neither what they say nor whereof they affirm; and by such learned ignorance, no doubt, they edify their hearers very much!

2. The use of the law (*v.* 8): *The law is good, if a man use it lawfully.* The Jews used it unlawfully, as an engine to divide the church, a cover to the malicious opposition they made to the gospel of Christ; they set it up for justification, and so used it unlawfully. We must not therefore think to set it aside, but use it lawfully, for the restraint of sin. The abuse which some have made of the law does not take away the use of it; but, when a divine appointment has been abused, call it back to its right use and take away the abuses, for the law is still very useful as a rule of life; though we are not under it as under a covenant of works, yet it is good to teach us what is sin and what is duty. It is not made for a righteous man, that is, it is not made for those who observe it; for, if we could keep the law, righteousness would be by the law (Gal. 3:21): but it is made for wicked persons, to restrain them, to check them, and to put a stop to vice and profaneness. It is the grace of God that changes men's hearts; but the terrors of the law may be of use to tie their hands and restrain their tongues. A righteous man does not want those restraints which are necessary for the wicked; or at least the law is not made primarily and principally for the righteous, but for sinners of all sorts, whether in a greater or less measure, *v.* 9, 10. In this black roll of sinners, he particularly mentions breaches of the second table, duties which we owe to our neighbour; against the fifth and sixth commandments, *murderers of fathers and mothers, and manslayers;* against the seventh, *whoremongers, and those that defile themselves with mankind;* against the eighth, *men-stealers;* against the ninth, *liars and perjured persons;* and then he closes his account with this, *and if there be any other thing that is contrary to sound doctrine.* Some understand this as an institution of a power in the civil magistrate to make laws against such notorious sinners as are specified, and to see those laws put in execution.

II. He shows the glory and grace of the gospel. Paul's epithets are expressive and significant; and frequently every one is a sentence: as here (*v.* 11), *According to the glorious gospel of the blessed God.* Let us learn hence, 1. To call God blessed God, infinitely happy in the enjoyment of himself and his own perfections. 2. To call the gospel the glorious gospel, for so it is: much of the glory of God appears in the works of creation and providence, but much more in the gospel, where it shines in the face of Jesus Christ. Paul reckoned it a great honour put upon him, and a great favour done him, that this glorious gospel was committed to his trust; that is, the preaching of it, for the framing of it is not committed to any man or company of men in the world. The settling of the terms of salvation in the gospel of Christ is God's own work; but the publishing of it to the world is committed to the apostles and ministers. Note here, (1.) The ministry is a trust, for the gospel was committed unto this apostle; it is an office of trust as well as of power, and the former more than the latter; for this reason ministers are called stewards, 1 Co. 4:1. (2.) It is a glorious trust, because the gospel committed to them is a glorious gospel; it is a trust of very great importance. God's glory is very much concerned in it. Lord, what a trust is committed to us! How much grace do we want, to be found faithful in this great trust!

Verses 12–17

Here the apostle, I. Returns thanks to Jesus Christ for putting him into the ministry. Observe, 1. It is Christ's work to put men into the ministry, Acts 26:16, 17. God condemned the false prophets among the Jews in these words, *I have not sent these prophets, yet they ran: I have not spoken to them, yet they prophesied,* Jer. 23:21. Ministers, properly speaking, cannot make themselves ministers; for it is Christ's work, as king and head, prophet and teacher, of his church. 2. Those whom he puts into the ministry he fits for it; whom he calls he qualifies. Those ministers who are no way fit for their work, nor have ability for it, are not of Christ's putting into the ministry, though there are different qualifications as to gifts and graces. 3. Christ gives not only ability, but fidelity, to those whom he puts into the ministry: He *counted me faithful;* and none are counted faithful but those whom he makes so. Christ's ministers are trusty servants, and they ought to be so, having so great a trust committed to them. 4. A call to the ministry is a great favour, for which those who are so called ought to give thanks to Jesus Christ: *I thank Christ Jesus our Lord, who hath put me into the ministry.*

II. The more to magnify the grace of Christ in putting him into the ministry, he gives an account of his conversion.

1. What he was before his conversion: *A blasphemer, a persecutor, and injurious.* Saul breathed out threatenings and slaughter against the disciples of the Lord, Acts 9:1. He made havoc of the church, Acts 8:3. He was a blasphemer of God, a persecutor of the saints, and injurious to both. Frequently those who are designed for great and eminent services are left to themselves before their conversion, to fall into great wickedness, that the mercy of God may be the more glorified in their remission, and the grace of God in their regeneration. The greatness of sin is no bar to our acceptance with God, no, nor to our being employed for him, if it be truly repented of. Observe here, (1.) Blasphemy, persecution, and injuriousness, are very great and heinous sins, and those who are guilty of them are sinners before God exceedingly. To blaspheme God is immediately and directly to strike at God; to persecute his people is to endeavour to wound him through their sides; and to be injurious is to be like Ishmael, whose hand was against every one, and every one was against him; for such invade God's prerogative, and encroach upon the liberties of their fellow-creatures. (2.) True penitents, to serve a good purpose, will not be backward to own their former condition before they were brought home to God: this good apostle often confessed what his former life had been, as Acts 22:4; 26:10, 11.

2. The great favour of God to him: *But I obtained mercy.* This was a blessed *but* indeed, a great favour, that so notorious a rebel should find mercy with his prince.

(1.) If Paul had persecuted the Christians wilfully, knowing them to be the people of God, for aught I know he had been guilty of the unpardonable sin; but, because he did it ignorantly and in unbelief, he obtained mercy. Note, [1.] What we do ignorantly is a less crime than what we do knowingly; yet a sin of ignorance is a sin, for he that knew not his Master's will, but did commit things worthy of stripes, shall be beaten with few stripes, Lu. 12:48. Ignorance in some cases will extenuate a crime, though it do not take it away. [2.] Unbelief is at the bottom of what sinners do ignorantly; they do not believe God's threatenings, otherwise they could not do as they do. [3.] For these reasons Paul obtained mercy: *But I obtained mercy, because I did it ignorantly, in unbelief.* [4.] Here was mercy for a blasphemer, a persecutor, and an injurious person: *"But I obtained mercy,* I a blasphemer," etc.

(2.) Here he takes notice of the abundant grace of Jesus Christ, *v.* 14. The conversion and salvation of great sinners are owing to the grace of Christ, his exceedingly abundant grace, even that grace of Christ which appears in his glorious gospel (*v.* 15): *This is a faithful saying,* etc. Here we have the sum of the whole gospel, *that Jesus Christ came into the world.* The Son of God took upon him our nature, was made flesh, and dwelt among us, Jn. 1:14. He came into the world, *not to call the righteous but sinners to repentance,* Mt. 9:13. His errand into the world was to seek and find, and so save, *those that were lost,* Lu. 19:10. The ratification of this is *that it is a faithful saying, and worthy of all acceptation.* It is good news, worthy of all acceptation; and yet not too good to be true, for it is a faithful saying. It is a faithful saying, and therefore worthy to be embraced in the arms of faith: it is worthy of all acceptation, and therefore to be received with holy love, which refers to the foregoing verse, where the grace of Christ is said to abound in faith and love. In the close of the verse Paul applies it to himself: *Of whom I am chief.* Paul was a sinner of the first rank; so he acknowledges himself to have been, for he breathed out threatenings and slaughter against the disciples of the Lord, etc., Acts 9:1, 2. Persecutors are some of the worst of sinners: such a one Paul had been. Or, *of whom I am chief,* that is, of pardoned sinners I am chief. It is an expression of his great humility; he that elsewhere calls himself the *least of all saints* (Eph. 3:8) here calls himself the chief of sinners. Observe, [1.] Christ Jesus has come into the world; the prophecies concerning his coming are now fulfilled. [2.] He came to save sinners; he came to save those who could not save and help themselves. [3.] Blasphemers and persecutors are the chief of sinners, so Paul reckoned them. [4.] The chief of sinners may become the chief of saints; so this apostle was, for he was not a whit behind the very chief apostles (2 Co. 11:5), for Christ came to save the chief of sinners. [5.] This is a very great truth, it is a faithful saying; these are true and faithful words, which may be depended on. [6.] It deserves to be received, to be believed by us all, for our comfort and encouragement.

(3.) The mercy which Paul found with God, notwithstanding his great wickedness before his conversion, he speaks of,

[1.] For the encouragement of others to repent and believe (*v.* 16): *For this cause I obtained mercy, that in me first Jesus Christ might show forth all long-suffering, for a pattern to those who should hereafter believe.* It was an instance of the long-suffering of Christ that he would bear so much with one who had been so very provoking; and it was designed for a pattern to all others, that the greatest sinners might not despair of mercy with God. Note here, *First,* Our apostle was one of the first great sinners converted to Christianity. *Secondly,* He was converted, and obtained mercy, for the sake of others as well as of himself; he was a pattern to others. *Thirdly,* The Lord Jesus Christ shows great long-suffering in the conversion of great sinners. *Fourthly,* Those who obtain mercy believe on the Lord Jesus Christ; for without faith it is impossible to please God, Heb. 11:6. *Fifthly,* Those who believe on Christ believe on him to life everlasting; they believe to the saving of the soul, Heb. 10:39.

[2.] He mentions it to the glory of God having spoken of the mercy he had found with God, he could not go on with his letter without inserting a thankful acknowledgment of God's goodness to him: *Now unto the King eternal, immortal, invisible, the only wise God, be honour and glory for ever and ever. Amen.* Observe, *First,* That grace which we have the comfort of God must have the glory of. Those who are sensible of their obligations to the mercy and grace of God will have their hearts enlarged in his praise. Here is praise ascribed to him, as *the King eternal, immortal, invisible. Secondly,* When we have found God good we must not forget to pronounce him great; and his kind thoughts of us must not at all abate our high thoughts of him, but rather increase them. God had taken particular cognizance of Paul, and shown him mercy, and taken him into communion with himself, and yet he calls him the King eternal, etc. God's gracious dealings with us should fill us with admiration of his glorious attributes. He is eternal, without beginning of days, or end of life, or change of time. He is the Ancient of days, Dan. 7:9. He is immortal, and the original of immortality; he only has immortality (1 Tim. 6:16), for he cannot die. He is invisible, for he cannot be seen with mortal eyes, dwelling in the light to which no man can approach, whom no man hath seen nor can see, 1 Tim. 6:16. He is *the only wise God* (Jude 25); he only is infinitely wise, and the fountain of all wisdom. *"To him be glory for ever and ever,"* or, "Let me be for ever employed in giving honour and glory to him, as the thousands of thousands do," Rev. 5:12, 13.

Verses 18–20

Here is the charge he gives to Timothy to proceed in his work with resolution, *v.* 18. Observe here, The gospel is a charge committed to the ministers of it; it is committed to their trust, to see that it be duly applied according to the intent and meaning of it, and the design of its great Author. It seems, there had been prophecies before concerning Timothy, that he should be taken into the ministry, and should prove eminent in the work of the ministry; this encouraged Paul to commit this charge to him. Observe, 1. The ministry is a warfare, it is a good warfare against sin and Satan: and under the banner of the Lord Jesus, who is the Captain of our salvation (Heb. 2:10), and in his cause, and against his enemies, ministers are in a particular manner engaged. 2. Ministers must war this good warfare, must execute their office diligently and courageously, notwithstanding oppositions and discouragements. 3. The prophecies which went before concerning Timothy are here mentioned as a motive to stir him up to a vigorous and conscientious discharge of his duty; so the good hopes that others have entertained concerning us should excite us to our duty: *That thou by them mightest war a good warfare.* 4. We must hold both faith and a good conscience: *Holding faith and a good conscience, v.* 19. Those that put away a good conscience will soon make shipwreck of faith. Let us live up to the directions of a renewed enlightened conscience, and keep conscience void of offence (Acts 24:16), a conscience not debauched by any vice or sin, and this will be a means of preserving us sound in the faith; we must look to the one as well a the other, for the mystery of the faith must be held in a pure conscience, *ch.* 3:9. As for those who had made shipwreck of the faith, he specifies two, *Hymeneus and Alexander,* who had made a profession of the Christian religion, but had quitted that profession; and Paul had delivered them to Satan, had declared them to belong to the kingdom of Satan, and, as some think, had, by an extraordinary power, delivered them to be terrified or tormented by Satan, *that they might learn not to blaspheme* not to contradict or revile the doctrine of Christ and the good ways of the Lord. Observe, The primary design of the highest censure in the primitive church was to prevent further sin and to reclaim the sinner. In this case it was for the destruction of the flesh, that the spirit might be saved in the day of the Lord Jesus, 1 Co. 5:5. Observe, (1.) Those who love the service and work of Satan are justly delivered over to the power of Satan: *Whom I have delivered over to Satan.* (2.) God can, if he please, work by contraries: Hymeneus and Alexander are delivered to Satan, that they may learn not to blaspheme, when one would rather think they would learn of Satan to blaspheme the more. (3.) Those who have put away a good conscience, and made shipwreck of faith, will not stick at any thing, blasphemy not excepted. (4.) Therefore let us hold faith and a good conscience, if we would keep clear of blasphemy; for, if we once let go our hold of these, we do not know where we shall stop.

CHAPTER 2

In this chapter Paul treats, I. Of prayer, with many reasons for it (*v.* 1–8). II. Of women's apparel (*v.* 9, 10). III. Of their subjection, with the reasons of it (*v.* 11–14). IV. A promise given for their encouragement in child-bearing (*v.* 15).

Verses 1–8

Here is, I. A charge given to Christians to pray for all men in general, and particularly for all in authority. Timothy must take care that this be done. Paul does not send him any prescribed form of prayer, as we have reason to think he would if he had intended that ministers should be tied to that way of praying; but, in general, that they should make *supplications, prayers, intercessions, and giving of thanks:* supplications for the averting of evil, prayers for the obtaining of good, intercessions for others, and thanksgivings for mercies already received. Paul thought it enough to give them general heads; they, having the scripture to direct them in prayer and the Spirit of prayer poured out upon them, needed not any further directions. Observe, The design of the Christian religion is to promote prayer; and the disciples of Christ must be praying people. Pray *always with all prayer,* Eph. 6:18. There must be prayers for ourselves in the first place; this is implied here. We must also pray *for all men,* for the world

of mankind in general, for particular persons who need or desire our prayers. See how far the Christian religion was from being a sect, when it taught men this diffusive charity, to pray, not only for those of their own way, but for all men. Pray for kings (*v.* 2); though the kings at this time were heathens, enemies to Christianity, and persecutors of Christians, yet they must pray for them, because it is for the public good that there should be civil government, and proper persons entrusted with the administration of it, for whom therefore we ought to pray, yea, though we ourselves suffer under them. *For kings, and all that are in authority,* that is, inferior magistrates: we must pray for them, and we must give thanks for them, pray for their welfare and for the welfare of their kingdoms, and therefore must not plot against them, that in the peace thereof we may have peace, and give thanks for them and for the benefit we have under their government, that *we may lead a quiet and peaceable life in all godliness and honesty.* Here see what we must desire for kings, that God will so turn their hearts, and direct them and make use of them, that we under them may lead a quiet and peaceable life. He does not say, "that we may get preferments under them, grow rich, and be in honour and power under them;" no, the summit of the ambition of a good Christian is to lead a quiet and peaceable life, to get through the world unmolested in a low private station. We should desire that we and others may lead a peaceable life *in all godliness and honesty,* implying that we cannot expect to be kept quiet and peaceable unless we keep in all godliness and honesty. Let us mind our duty, and then we may expect to be taken under the protection both of God and the government. *In all godliness and honesty.* Here we have our duty as Christians summed up in two words: godliness, that is, the right worshipping of God; and honesty, that is, a good conduct towards all men. These two must go together; we are not truly honest if we are not godly, and do not render to God his due; and we are not truly godly if we are not honest, for God hates robbery for burnt-offering. Here we may observe, 1. Christians are to be men much given to prayer: they ought to abound herein, and should use themselves to prayers, supplications, etc. 2. In our prayers we are to have a generous concern for others as well as for ourselves; we are to pray for all men, and to give thanks for all men; and must not confine our prayers nor thanksgiving to our own persons or families. 3. Prayer consists of various parts, of supplications, intercessions, and thanksgivings; for we must pray for the mercies we want, as well as be thankful for mercies already received; and we are to deprecate the judgments which our own sins or the sins of others have deserved. 4. All men, yea, kings themselves, and those who are in authority, are to be prayed for. They want our prayers, for they have many difficulties to encounter, many snares to which their exalted stations expose them. 5. In praying for our governors, we take the most likely course to lead a peaceable and quiet life. The Jews at Babylon were commanded to seek the peace of the city whither the Lord had caused them to be carried captives, and to pray to the Lord for it; for in the peace thereof they should have peace, Jer. 29:7. 6. If we would lead a peaceable and quiet life, we must live in all godliness and honesty; we must do our duty to God and man. *He that will love life, and see good days, let him refrain his tongue from evil, and his lips that they speak no guile; let him eschew evil, and do good; let him seek peace, and pursue it,* 1 Pt. 3:10, 11. Now the reason he gives for this is *because this is good in the sight of God our Saviour;* that is, the gospel of Christ requires this. That which is acceptable in the sight of God our Saviour we should do, and should abound in.

II. As a reason why we should in our prayers concern ourselves for all men, he shows God's love to mankind in general, *v.* 4.

1. One reason why all men are to be prayed for is because there is one God, and that God bears a good will to all mankind. There is one God (*v.* 5), and one only, there is no other, there can be no other, for there can be but one infinite. This one God *will have all men to be saved;* he desires not the death and destruction of any (Eze. 33:11), but the welfare and salvation of all. Not that he has decreed the salvation of all, for then all men would be saved; but he has a good will to the salvation of all, and none perish but by their own fault, Mt. 23:37. He will have all to be saved, *and to come to the knowledge of the truth,* to be saved in the way that he has appointed and not otherwise. It concerns us to get the knowledge of the truth, because that is the way to be saved; *Christ is the way and the truth, and so he is the life.*

2. There is one Mediator, and that mediator gave himself a ransom for all. As the mercy of God extends itself to all his works, so the mediation of Christ extends itself thus far to all the children of men that he paid a price sufficient for the salvation of all mankind; he brought mankind to stand upon new terms with God, so that they are not now under the law as a covenant of works, but as a rule of life. They are under grace; not under the covenant of innocence, but under a new covenant: *He gave himself a ransom.* Observe, The death of Christ was a ransom, a counter-price. We deserved to have died. Christ died for us, to save us from death and hell; he gave himself a ransom voluntarily, a ransom for all; so that all mankind are put in a better condition than that of devils. He died to work out a common salvation: in order hereunto, he put himself into the office of Mediator between God and man. A mediator supposes a controversy. Sin had made a quarrel between us and God; Jesus Christ is a Mediator who undertakes to make peace, to bring God and man together, in the nature of an umpire or arbitrator, a daysman who lays his hand upon u both, Job 9:33. He is a ransom that *was to be testified in due time;* that is, in the Old-Testament times, his sufferings and the glory that should follow were spoken of as things to be revealed in the last times, 1 Pt. 1:10, 11. And they are accordingly revealed, Paul himself having been ordained a preacher and an apostle, to publish to the Gentiles the glad tidings of redemption and salvation by Jesus Christ. This doctrine of Christ's mediation Paul was entrusted to preach to every creature, Mk. 16:15. He was appointed to be a teacher of the Gentiles; besides his general call to the apostleship, he was commissioned particularly to preach to the Gentiles, *in faith and truth,* or faithfully and truly. Note, (1.) It is good and acceptable in the sight of God and our Saviour that we pray for kings and for all men, and also that we lead a peaceable and quiet life; and this is a very good reason why we should do the one as well as the other. (2.) God has a good will to the salvation of all; so that it is not so much the want of a will in God to save them as it is a want of will in themselves to be saved in God's way. Here our blessed Lord charges the fault: *You will not come unto me that you may have life,* Jn. 5:40. *I would have gathered you, and you would not.* (3.) Those who are saved must come to the knowledge of the truth, for this is God's appointed way to save sinners. Without knowledge the heart cannot be good; if we do not know the truth, we cannot be ruled by it. (4.) It is observable that the unity of God is asserted, and joined with the unity of the Mediator; and the church of Rome might as well maintain a plurality of gods as a plurality of mediators. (5.) He that is a Mediator in the New-Testament sense, gave himself a ransom. Vain then is the pretence of the Romanists that there is but one Mediator of satisfaction, but many of intercession; for, according to Paul, Christ's giving himself a ransom was a necessary part of the Mediator's office; and indeed this lays the foundation for his intercession. (6.) Paul was ordained a minister, to declare this to the Gentiles, that Christ is the one Mediator between God and men, who gave himself a ransom for all. This is the substance of which all ministers are to preach, to the end of the world; and Paul magnified his office, as he was the apostle of the Gentiles, Rom. 11:13. (7.) Ministers must preach the truth, what they apprehend to be so, and they must believe it themselves; they are, like our apostle, to preach in faith and verity, and they must also be faithful and trusty.

III. A direction how to pray, *v.* 8. 1. Now, under the gospel, prayer is not to be confined to any one particular house of prayer, but men must pray every where: no place is amiss for prayer, no place more acceptable to God than another, Jn. 4:21. *Pray every where.* We must pray in our closets, pray in our families, pray at our meals, pray when we are on journeys, and pray in the solemn assemblies, whether more public or private. 2. It is the will of God that in prayer we should lift up holy hands: *Lifting up holy hands,* or pure hands, pure from the pollution of sin, washed in the fountain opened for sin and uncleanness. *I will wash my hands,* etc., Ps. 26:6. 3. We must pray in charity: *Without wrath,* or malice, or anger at any person. 4. We must pray in faith *without doubting* (Jam. 1:6), or, as some read it, *without disputing,* and then it falls under the head of charity.

Verses 9–15

I. Here is a charge, that women who profess the Christian religion should be modest, sober, silent, and submissive, as becomes their place. 1. They must be very modest in their apparel, not affecting gaudiness, gaiety, or costliness (you may read the vanity of a person's mind in the gaiety and gaudiness of his habit), because they have better ornaments with which they should *adorn themselves, with good works*. Note, Good works are the best ornament; these are, in the sight of God, of great price. Those that profess godliness should, in their dress, as well as other things, act as becomes their profession; instead of laying out their money on fine clothes, they must lay it out in works of piety and charity, which are properly called good works. 2. Women must learn the principles of their religion, learn Christ, learn the scriptures; they must not think that their sex excuses them from that learning which is necessary to salvation. 3. They must be silent, submissive, and subject, and not usurp authority. The reason given is because *Adam was first formed, then Eve* out of him, to denote her subordination to him and dependence upon him; and that she was made for him, to be a help-meet for him. And as she was last in the creation, which is one reason for her subjection, so she was first in the transgression, and that is another reason. *Adam was not deceived,* that is, not first; the serpent did not immediately set upon him, but the woman was first in the transgression (2 Co. 11:3), and it was part of the sentence, *Thy desire shall be to thy husband, and he shall rule over thee,* Gen. 3:16. But it is a word of comfort (*v.* 15) that those who continue in sobriety shall be *saved in child-bearing,* or *with* child-bearing — the Messiah, who was born of a woman, should break the serpent's head (Gen. 3:15); or the sentence which they are under for sin shall be no bar to their acceptance with Christ, *if they continue in faith, and charity, and holiness, with sobriety.*

II. Here observe, 1. The extensiveness of the rules of Christianity; they reach not only to men, but to women, not only to their persons, but also to their dress, which must be modest, like their sex; and to their outward deportment and behaviour, it must be in silence, with all subjection. 2. Women are to profess godliness as well as men; for they are baptized, and thereby stand engaged to exercise themselves to godliness; and, to their honour be it spoken, many of them were eminent professors of Christianity in the days of the apostles, as the book of Acts will inform us. 3. Women being more in danger of exceeding in their apparel, it was more necessary to caution them in this respect. 4. The best ornaments for professors of godliness are good works. 5. According to Paul, women must be learners, and are not allowed to be public teachers in the church; for teaching is an office of authority, and the woman must not usurp authority over the man, but is to be in silence. But, notwithstanding this prohibition, good women may and ought to teach their children at home the principles of religion. Timothy from a child had known the holy scriptures; and who should teach him but his mother and grandmother? 2 Tim. 3:15. Aquila and his wife Priscilla expounded unto Apollos the way of God more perfectly; but then they did it privately, for *they took him unto them,* Acts 18:26. 6. Here are two very good reasons given for the man's authority over the woman, and her subjection to the man, *v.* 13, 14. Adam was first formed, then Eve; she was created for the man, and not the man for the woman (1 Co. 11:9); then she was deceived, and brought the man into the transgression. 7. Though the difficulties and dangers of child-bearing are many and great, as they are part of the punishment inflicted on the sex for Eve's transgression, yet here is much for her support and encouragement: *Notwithstanding she shall be saved,* etc. Though in sorrow, yet she shall bring forth, and be a living mother of living children; with this proviso, that they continue in faith, and charity, and holiness, with sobriety: and women, under the circumstance of child-bearing should by faith lay hold of this promise for their support in the needful time.

CHAPTER 3

In this chapter our apostle treats of church-officers. He specifies, I. The qualifications of a person to be admitted to the office of a bishop (*v.* 1–7). II. The qualifications of deacons (*v.* 8–10), and of their wives (*v.* 11), again of the deacons (*v.* 12, 13). III. The reasons of his writing to Timothy, whereupon he speaks of the church and the foundation-truth professed therein (*v.* 14 to the end).

Verses 1–7

The two epistles to Timothy, and that to Titus, contain a scripture-plan of church-government, or a direction to ministers. Timothy, we suppose, was an evangelist who was left at Ephesus, to take care of those whom the Holy Ghost had made bishops there, that is, the presbyters, as appears by Acts

20:28, where the care of the church was committed to the presbyters, and they were called bishops. It seems they were very loth to part with Paul, especially because he told them they should *see his face no more* (Acts 20:38); for their church was but newly planted, they were afraid of undertaking the care of it, and therefore Paul left Timothy with them to set them in order. And here we have the character of a gospel minister, whose office it is, as a bishop, to preside in a particular congregation of Christians: *If a man desires the office of a bishop, he desires a good work, v.* 1. Observe,

I. The ministry is a work. However the office of a bishop may be now thought a good preferment, then it was thought a good work. 1. The office of a scripture-bishop is an office of divine appointment, and not of human invention. The ministry is not a creature of the state, and it is a pity that the minister should be at any time the tool of the state. The office of the ministry was in the church before the magistrate countenanced Christianity, for this office is one of the great gifts Christ has bestowed on the church, Eph. 4:8–11. 2. This office of a Christian bishop is a work, which requires diligence and application: the apostle represents it under the notion and character of a work; not of great honour and advantage, for ministers should always look more to their work than to the honour and advantage of their office. 3. It is a good work, a work of the greatest importance, and designed for the greatest good: the ministry is conversant about no lower concerns than the life and happiness of immortal souls; it is a good work, because designed to illustrate the divine perfections in bringing many sons to glory; the ministry is appointed to open men's eyes, and to turn them from darkness to light, and from the power of Satan unto God, etc., Acts 26:18. 4. There ought to be an earnest desire of the office in those who would be put into it; if a man desire, he should earnestly desire it for the prospect he has of bringing greater glory to God, and of doing the greatest good to the souls of men by this means. This is the question proposed to those who offer themselves to the ministry of the church of England: "Do you think you are moved by the Holy Ghost to take upon you this office?"

II. In order to the discharge of this office, the doing of this work, the workman must be qualified. 1. A minister must be blameless, he must not lie under any scandal; he must give as little occasion for blame as can be, because this would be a prejudice to his ministry and would reflect reproach upon his office. 2. He must be the husband of one wife; not having given a bill of divorce to one, and then taken another, or not having many wives at once, as at that time was too common both among Jews and Gentiles, especially among the Gentiles. 3. He must be vigilant and watchful against Satan, that subtle enemy; he must watch over himself, and the souls of those who are committed to his charge, of whom having taken the *oversight,* he must improve all opportunities of doing them good. A minister ought to be vigilant, because our adversary the devil goes about like a roaring lion, seeking whom he may devour, 1 Pt. 5:8. 4. He must be sober, temperate, moderate in all his actions, and in the use of all creature-comforts. Sobriety and watchfulness are often in scripture put together, because they mutually befriend one another: *Be sober, be vigilant.* 5. He must be of good behaviour, composed and solid, and not light, vain, and frothy. 6. He must be given to hospitality, open-handed to strangers, and ready to entertain them according to his ability, as one who does not set his heart upon the wealth of the world and who is a true lover of his brethren. 7. Apt to teach. Therefore this is a preaching bishop whom Paul describes, one who is both able and willing to communicate to others the knowledge which God has given him, one who is fit to teach and ready to take all opportunities of giving instructions, who is himself *well instructed in the things of the kingdom of heaven,* and is communicative of what he knows to others. 8. No drunkard: *Not given to wine.* The priests were not to drink wine when they went in to minister (Lev. 10:8, 9), lest they should drink and pervert the law. 9. No striker; one who is not quarrelsome, nor apt to use violence to any, but does every thing with mildness, love, and gentleness. The servant of the Lord must not strive, but be gentle towards all, etc., 2 Tim. 2:24. 10. One who is not greedy of filthy lucre, who does not make his ministry to truckle to any secular design or interest, who uses no mean, base, sordid ways of getting money, who is dead to the wealth of this world, lives above it, and makes it appear he is so. 11. He must be patient, and not a brawler, of a mild disposition. Christ, the great Shep-

herd and Bishop of souls, is so. Not apt to be angry or quarrelsome; as not a striker with his hands, so not a brawler with his tongue; for how shall men teach others to govern their tongues who do not make conscience of keeping them under good government themselves? 12. Not covetous. Covetousness is bad in any, but it is worst in a minister, whose calling leads him to converse so much with another world. 13. He must be one who keeps his family in good order: *That rules well his own house,* that he may set a good example to other masters of families to do so too, and that he may thereby give a proof of his ability to take care of the church of God: *For, if a man know not how to rule his own house, how shall he take care of the church of God.* Observe, The families of ministers ought to be examples of good to all others families. Ministers must have their children in subjection; then it is the duty of ministers' children to submit to the instructions that are given them. — *With all gravity.* The best way to keep inferiors in subjection, is to be grave with them. Not having his children in subjection with all austerity, but with all gravity. 14. He must not be a novice, not one newly brought to the Christian religion, or not one who is but meanly instructed in it, who knows no more of religion than the surface of it, for such a one is apt to be lifted up with pride: the more ignorant men are the more proud they are: *Lest, being lifted up with pride, he fall into the condemnation of the devil.* The devils fell through pride, which is a good reason why we should take heed of pride, because it is a sin that turned angels into devils. 15. He must be of good reputation among his neighbours, and under no reproach from former conversation; for the devil will make use of that to ensnare others, and work in them an aversion to the doctrine of Christ preached by those who have not had a good report.

III. Upon the whole, having briefly gone through the qualifications of a gospel-bishop, we may infer, 1. What great reason we have to cry out, as Paul does, *Who is sufficient for these things?* 2 Co. 2:16. *Hic labor, hoc opus — This is a work indeed.* What piety, what prudence, what zeal, what courage, what faithfulness, what watchfulness over ourselves, our lusts, appetites, and passions, and over those under our charge; I say, what holy watchfulness is necessary in this work! 2. Have not the best qualified and the most faithful and conscientious ministers just reason to complain against themselves, that so much is requisite by way of qualification, and so much work is necessary to be done? And, alas! how far short do the best come of what they should be and what they should do! 3. Yet let those bless God, and be thankful, whom the Lord has enabled, and counted faithful, putting them into the ministry: if God is pleased to make any in some degree able and faithful, let him have the praise and glory of it. 4. For the encouragement of all faithful ministers, we have Christ's gracious word of promise, *Lo, I am with you always, even unto the end of the world,* Mt. 28:20. And, if he be with us, he will fit us for our work in some measure, will carry us through the difficulties of it with comfort, graciously pardon our imperfections, and reward our faithfulness with a crown of glory that fadeth not away, 1 Pt. 5:4.

Verses 8–13

We have here the character of deacons: these had the care of the temporal concerns of the church, that is, the maintenance of the ministers and provision for the poor: they served tables, while the ministers or bishops gave themselves only to the ministry of the word and prayer, Acts 6:2, 4. Of the institution of this office, with that which gave occasion to it, you have an account in Acts 6:1–7. Now it was requisite that deacons should have a good character, because they were assistants to the ministers, appeared and acted publicly, and had a great trust reposed in them. They must be *grave.* Gravity becomes all Christians, but especially those who are in the office in the church. *Not doubled-tongued;* that will say one thing to one and another thing to another, according as their interests leads them: a double tongue comes from a double heart; flatterers and slanderers are double-tongued. *Not given to much wine;* for this is a great disparagement to any man, especially to a Christian, and one in office, unfits men for business, opens the door to many temptations. *Not greedy of filthy lucre;* this would especially be bad in the deacons, who were entrusted with the church's money, and, if they were covetous and greedy of filthy lucre, would be tempted to embezzle it, and convert that to their own use which was intended for the public service. *Holding the mystery of faith in a pure conscience, v.* 9. Note, The mystery of faith is best held in a pure conscience. The practical love of truth is the most powerful preservative from error and delusion. If we keep a pure conscience (take heed of every thing that debauches conscience, and draws us away from God), this will preserve in our souls the mystery of faith. *Let these also first be proved, v.* 10. It is not fit that the public trusts should be lodged in the hands of any, till they have been first proved, and found fit for the business they are to be entrusted with; the soundness of their judgments, their zeal for Christ, and the blamelessness of their conversation, must be proved. Their wives likewise must have a good character (*v.* 11); they must be of a grave behaviour, not slanderers, tale-bearers, carrying stories to make mischief and sow discord; they must be *sober and faithful in all things,* not given to any excess, but trusty in all that is committed to them. All who are related to ministers must double their care to walk as becomes the gospel of Christ, lest, if they in any thing walk disorderly, the ministry be blamed. As he said before of the bishops or ministers, so here of the deacons, they must be *the husband of one wife,* such as had not put away their wives, upon dislike, and married others; they must *rule their children and their own houses well;* the families of deacons should be examples to other families. And the reason why the deacons must be thus qualified is (*v.* 13) because, though the office of a deacon be of an inferior degree, yet it is a step towards the higher degree; and those who had served tables well the church might see cause afterwards to discharge from that service, and prefer to serve in preaching the word and in prayer. Or it may be meant of the good reputation that a man would gain by his fidelity in this office: *they will purchase to themselves great boldness in the faith that is in Christ Jesus.* Observe, 1. In the primitive church there were but two orders of ministers or officers, *bishops and deacons,* Phil. 1:1. After-ages have invented the rest. The office of the bishop, presbyter, pastor, or minister, was confined to prayer and to the ministry of the word; and the office of the deacon was confined to, or at least principally conversant about, serving tables. Clemens Romanus, in his epistle to the Christian (*cap.* 42, 44), speaks very fully and plainly to this effect, that the apostles, foreknowing, by our Lord Jesus Christ, that there would arise in the Christian church a controversy about the name *episcopacy,* appointed the forementioned orders, bishops and deacons. 2. The scripture-deacon's main employment was to serve tables, and not to preach or baptize. It is true, indeed, that Philip did preach and baptize in Samaria (Acts 8), but you read that he was an evangelist (Acts 21:8), and he might preach and baptize, and perform any other part of the ministerial office, under that character; but still the design of the deacon's office was to mind the temporal concerns of the church, such as the salaries of the ministers and providing for the poor. 3. Several qualifications were very necessary, even for these inferior officers: *The deacons must be grave,* etc. 4. Some trial should be made of persons' qualifications before they are admitted into office in the church, or have any trust committed to them: *Let these also first be proved.* 5. Integrity and uprightness in an inferior office are the way to be preferred to a higher station in the church: *They purchase to themselves a good degree.* 6. This will also give a man great boldness in the faith, whereas a want of integrity and uprightness will make a man timorous, and ready to tremble at his own shadow. *The wicked fleeth when no man pursueth, but the righteous are bold as a lion,* Prov. 28:1.

Verses 14–16

He concludes the chapter with a particular direction to Timothy. He hoped shortly to come to him, to give him further directions and assistance in his work, and to see that Christianity was well planted, and took root well, at Ephesus; he therefore wrote the more briefly to him. But he wrote *lest he should tarry long, that* Timothy *might know how to behave himself in the house of God,* how to conduct himself as became an evangelist, and the apostle's substitute. Observe,

I. Those who are employed in the house of God must see to it that they behave themselves well, lest they bring reproach upon the house of God, and that worthy name by which they are called. Ministers ought to behave themselves well, and to look not only to their praying and preaching, but to their behaviour: their office binds them to their good behaviour, for any behaviour will not do in this case. Timothy must know how to behave himself, not only in the particular church where he was now appointed to reside for some time, but being an evangelist, and the apostle's substitute, he must learn how to behave himself in other churches, where he should in like manner be appointed to reside for some time; and therefore it is not the church of Ephesus, but the catholic church, which is here called *the house of God, which is the church of the living God.* Observe here, 1. God is the living God; he is the fountain of life, he is life in himself, and he gives life, breath, and all things to his creatures; in him we live, and move, and have our being, Acts 17:25, 28. 2. The church is the house of God, he dwells there; the Lord has chosen Zion, to dwell there. "This is my rest, here will I dwell, for I have chosen it;" there may we see God's power and glory, Ps. 63:2.

II. It is the great support of the church that it is the church of the living *God,* the true God in opposition to false gods, dumb and dead idols.

1. As the church of God, it is *the pillar and ground of truth;* that is, either, (1.) The church itself is the pillar and ground of truth. Not that the authority of the scriptures depends upon that of the church, as the papists pretend, for truth is the pillar and ground of the church; but the church holds forth the scripture and the doctrine of Christ, as the pillar to which a proclamation is affixed holds forth the proclamation. *Even to the principalities and powers in heavenly places is made known by the church the manifold wisdom of God,* Eph. 3:10. (2.) Others understand it of Timothy. He, not he himself only, but he as an evangelist, he and other faithful ministers, are the pillars and ground of truth; it is their business to maintain, hold up, and publish, the truths of Christ in the church. It is said of the apostles that *they seemed to be pillars,* Gal. 2:9. [1.] Let us be diligent and impartial in our own enquiries after truth; let us buy the truth at any rate, and not think much of any pains to discover it. [2.] Let us be careful to keep and preserve it. *"Buy the truth, and sell it not* (Prov. 23:23), do not part with it on any consideration." [3.] Let us take care to publish it, and to transmit it safe and uncorrupted unto posterity. [4.] When the church ceases to be the pillar and ground of truth, we may and ought to forsake her; for our regard to truth should be greater than our regard to the church; we are no longer obliged to continue in the church than she continues to be the pillar and ground of truth.

2. But what is the truth which the churches and ministers are the pillars and grounds of? He tells us (*v.* 16) that *without controversy great is the mystery of godliness.* The learned Camero joins this with what goes before, and then it runs thus: "The pillar and ground of the truth, and *without controversy great is the mystery of godliness."* He supposes this mystery to be the pillar, etc. Observe,

(1.) Christianity is a mystery, a mystery that could not have been found out by reason or the light of nature, and which cannot be comprehended by reason, because it is above reason, though not contrary thereto. It is a mystery, not of philosophy or speculation; but of godliness, designed to promote godliness; and herein it exceeds all the mysteries of the Gentiles. It is also a revealed mystery, not shut up and sealed; and it does not cease to be a mystery because now in part revealed. But,

(2.) What is the mystery of godliness? It is Christ; and here are six things concerning Christ, which make up the mystery of godliness. [1.] That he is God manifest in the flesh: *God was manifest in the flesh.* This proves that he is God, the eternal Word, that was made flesh and was manifest in the flesh. When God was to be manifested to man he was pleased to manifest himself in the incarnation of his own Son: *The Word was made flesh,* Jn. 1:14. [2.] He is *justified in the Spirit.* Whereas he was reproached as a sinner, and put to death as a malefactor, he was raised again by the Spirit, and so was justified from all the calumnies with which he was loaded. *He was made sin for us, and was delivered for our offences;* but, being raised again, he was justified in the Spirit; that is, it was made to appear that his sacrifice was accepted, and so he rose again for our justification, as he was delivered for our offences, Rom. 4:25. He was put to death in the flesh, but quickened by the Spirit, 1 Pt. 3:18. [3.] He was *seen of angels.* They worshipped him (Heb. 1:6); they attended his incarnation, his temptation, his agony, his death, his resurrection, his ascension; this is much to his honour, and shows what a mighty interest he had in the upper world, that angels ministered to him, for he is the Lord of angels. [4.] He is *preached unto the Gentiles.* This is a great part of the mystery of godliness, that Christ was offered to the Gentiles a Redeemer and Saviour; that whereas, before, salvation was of the Jews, the partition-wall was now taken down, and the Gentiles were taken in. *I have set thee to be a light of the Gentiles,* Acts 13:47. [5.] That he was *believed on in the world,* so that he was not preached in vain. Many of the Gentiles welcomed the gospel which the Jews rejected. Who would have thought that the world, which lay in wickedness, would believe in the Son of God, would take him to be their Saviour who was himself crucified at Jerusalem? But, notwithstanding all the prejudices they laboured under, he was believed on, etc. [6.] He was *received up into glory,* in his ascension. This indeed was before he was believed on in the world; but it is put last, because it was the crown of his exaltation, and because it is not only his ascension that is meant, but his sitting at the right hand of God, where he ever lives, making intercession, and has all power, both in heaven and earth, and because, in the apostasy of which he treats in the following chapter, his remaining in heaven would be denied by those who pretend to bring him down on their altars in the consecrated wafers. Observe, *First,* He who was manifest in flesh was God, really and truly God, God by nature, and not only so by office, for this makes it to be a mystery. *Secondly,* God was manifest in flesh, real flesh. *Forasmuch as the children are partakers of flesh and blood, he also himself likewise took part of the same,* Heb. 2:14. And, what is more amazing, he was manifest in the flesh after all flesh had corrupted his way, though he himself was holy from the womb. *Thirdly,* Godliness is a mystery in all its parts and branches, from the beginning to the end, from Christ's incarnation to his ascension. *Fourthly,* It being a great mystery, we should rather humbly adore it, and piously believe it, than curiously pry into it, or be too positive in our explications of it and determinations about it, further than the holy scriptures have revealed it to us.

CHAPTER 4

Paul here foretels, I. A dreadful apostasy (*v.* 1–3). II. He treats of Christian liberty (*v.* 4, 5). III. He gives Timothy divers directions with respect to himself, his doctrine, and the people under his care (*v.* 6 to the end)

Verses 1–5

We have here a prophecy of the apostasy of the latter times, which he had spoken of as a thing expected and taken for granted among Christians, 2 Th. 2.

I. In the close of the foregoing chapter, we had the mystery of godliness summed up; and therefore very fitly, in the beginning of this chapter, we have the mystery of iniquity summed up: *The Spirit speaks expressly that in the latter times some shall depart from the faith;* whether he means the Spirit in the Old Testament, or the Spirit in the prophets of the New Testament, or both. The prophecies concerning antichrist, as well as the prophecies concerning Christ, came from the Spirit. The Spirit in both spoke expressly of a general apostasy from the faith of Christ and the pure worship of God. This should come in the *latter times,* during the Christian dispensation, for these are called the latter days; in the following ages of the church, for the mystery of iniquity now began to work. *Some shall depart from the faith,* or there shall be an apostasy from the faith. Some, not all; for in the worst of times God will have a remnant, according to the election of grace. *They shall depart from the faith,* the faith delivered to the saints (Jude 3), which was delivered at once, the sound doctrine of the gospel. *Giving heed to seducing spirits,* men who pretended to the Spirit, but were not really guided by the Spirit, 1 Jn. 4:1. *Beloved, believe not every spirit,* every one who pretends to the Spirit. Now here observe,

1. One of the great instances of the apostasy, namely, giving heed to doctrines of demons, or concerning demons; that is, those doctrines which teach the worship of saints and angels, as a middle sort of deities, between the immortal God and mortal men, such as the heathen called demons, and worshipped under that notion. Now this plainly agrees to the church of Rome, and it was one of the first steps towards that great apostasy, the enshrining of the relics of martyrs, paying divine honours to them, erecting altars, burning incense, consecrating images and temples, and making prayers and praises to the honour of saints departed. This demon-worship is paganism revived, the image of the first beast.

2. The instruments of promoting and propagating this apostasy and delusion. (1.) It will be done by hypocrisy of those that speak lies, the agents and emissaries of Satan, who promote these delusions by lies and forgeries and pretended miracles, *v.* 2. It is done by their hypocrisy, professing honour to Christ, and yet at the same time fighting against all

his anointed offices, and corrupting or profaning all his ordinances. This respects also the hypocrisy of those who have *their consciences seared with a red-hot iron,* who are perfectly lost to the very first principles of virtue and moral honesty. If men had not their consciences seared as with a hot iron, they could never maintain a power to dispense with oaths for the good of the catholic cause, could never maintain that no faith is to be kept with heretics, could never divest themselves of all remains of humanity and compassion, and clothe themselves with the most barbarous cruelty, under pretence of promoting the interest of the church. (2.) Another part of their character is that they forbid to marry, forbid their clergy to marry, and speak very reproachfully of marriage, though an ordinance of God; and that they command *to abstain from meats,* and place religion in such abstinence at certain times and seasons, only to exercise a tyranny over the consciences of men.

3. On the whole observe, (1.) The apostasy of the latter times should not surprise us, because it was expressly foretold by the Spirit. (2.) The Spirit is God, otherwise he could not certainly foresee such distant events, which as to us are uncertain and contingent, depending on the tempers, humours, and lusts of men. (3.) The difference between the predictions of the Spirit and the oracles of the heathen is remarkable; the Spirit speaks expressly, but the oracles of the heathen were always doubtful and uncertain. (4.) It is comfortable to think that in such general apostasies all are not carried away, but only some. (5.) It is common for seducers and deceivers to pretend to the Spirit, which is a strong presumption that all are convinced that this is the most likely to work in us an approbation of what pretends to come from the Spirit. (6.) Men must be hardened, and their consciences seared, before they can depart from the faith, and draw in others to side with them. (7.) It is a sign that men have departed from the faith when they will command what God has forbidden, such as saint and angel or demon-worship; and forbid what God has allowed or commanded, such as marriage and meats.

II. Having mentioned their hypocritical fastings, the apostle takes occasion to lay down the doctrine of the Christian liberty, which we enjoy under the gospel, of using God's good creatures, — that, whereas under the law there was a distinction of meats between clean and unclean (such sorts of flesh they might eat, and such they might not eat), all this is now taken away; and we are to call nothing common or unclean, Acts 10:15. Here observe, 1. We are to look upon our food as that which God has created; we have it from him, and therefore must use it for him. 2. God, in making those things, had a special regard to *those who believe and know the truth,* to good Christians, who have a covenant right to the creatures, whereas others have only a common right. 3. What God has created is to be *received with thanksgiving.* We must not refuse the gifts of God's bounty, nor be scrupulous in making differences where God has made none; but receive them, and be thankful, acknowledging the power of God the Maker of them, and the bounty of God the giver of them: *Every creature of God is good, and nothing to be refused, v.* 4. This plainly sets us at liberty from all the distinctions of meats appointed by the ceremonial law, as particularly that of swine's flesh, which the Jews were forbidden to eat, but which is allowed to us Christians, by this rule, *Every creature of God is good,* etc. Observe, God's good creatures are then good, and doubly sweet to us, when they are received with thanksgiving. — *For it is sanctified by the word of God and prayer, v.* 5. It is a desirable thing to have a sanctified use of our creature-comforts. Now they are sanctified to us, (1.) By the word of God; not only his permission, allowing us the liberty of the use of these things, but his promise to feed us with food convenient for us. This gives us a sanctified use of our creature-comforts. (2.) By prayer, which blesses our meat to us. The word of God and prayer must be brought to our common actions and affairs, and then we do all in faith. Here observe, [1.] Every creature is God's, for he made all. *Every beast in the forest is mine* (says God), *and the cattle upon a thousand hills. I know all the fowls of the mountains, and the wild beasts of the field are mine,* Ps. 50:10, 11. [2.] Every creature of God is good: when the blessed God took a survey of all his works, God saw all that was made, and, behold, it was very good, Gen. 1:31. [3.] The blessing of God makes every creature nourishing to us; man lives not by bread alone, but by every word that proceeds out of the mouth of God (Mt. 4:4), and therefore nothing ought to be refused. [4.] We ought therefore to ask his blessing by prayer, and so to sanctify the creatures we receive by prayer.

Verses 6–16

The apostle would have Timothy to instil into the minds of Christians such sentiments as might prevent their being seduced by the judaizing teachers. Observe, Those are good ministers of Jesus Christ who are diligent in their work; not that study to advance new notions, but that *put the brethren in remembrance of those things which they have received and heard. Wherefore I will not be negligent to put you always in remembrance of these things, though you knew them,* 2 Pt. 1:12. And elsewhere, *I stir up your pure minds by way of remembrance,* 2 Pt. 3:1. And, says the apostle Jude, *I will therefore put you in remembrance,* Jude 5. You see that the apostles and apostolical men reckoned it a main part of their work to put their hearers in remembrance; for we are apt to forget, and slow to learn and remember, the things of God. — *Nourished up in the words of faith and good doctrine, whereunto thou hast attained.* Observe, 1. Even ministers themselves have need to be growing and increasing in the knowledge of Christ and his doctrine: they must be nourished up in the words of faith. 2. The best way for ministers to grow in knowledge and faith is to put the brethren in remembrance; while we teach others, we teach ourselves. 3. Those whom ministers teach are brethren, and are to be treated like brethren; for ministers are not lords of God's heritage.

I. Godliness is here pressed upon him and others: *Refuse profane and old wives' sayings, v.* 7, 8, The Jewish traditions, which some people fill their heads with, have nothing to do with them. *But exercise thyself rather unto godliness;* that is, mind practical religion. Those who would be godly must exercise themselves unto godliness; it requires a constant exercise. The reason is taken from the fain of godliness; *bodily exercise profits little,* or for a little time. Abstinence from meats and marriage, and the like, though they pass for acts of mortification and self-denial, yet profit little, they turn to little account. What will it avail us to mortify the body if we do not mortify sin? Observe, 1. There is a great deal to be got by godliness; it will be of use to us in the whole of our life, for it has *the promise of the life that now is, and of that which is to come.* 2. The gain of godliness lies much in the promise: and the promises made to godly people relate to the life that now is, but especially they relate to the life that is to come. Under the Old Testament the promises were mostly of temporal blessings, but under the New Testament of spiritual and eternal blessings. If godly people have but little of the good things of the life that now is, yet it shall be made up to them in the good things of the life that is to come. 3. There were profane and old wives' fables in the days of the apostles; and Timothy, though an excellent man, was not above such a word of advice, *Refuse profane,* etc. 4. It is not enough that we refuse profane and old wives' fables, but we must exercise ourselves to godliness; we must not only cease to do evil, but we must learn to do well (Isa. 1:16, 17), and we must make a practice of exercising ourselves to godliness. And, 5. Those who are truly godly shall not be losers at last, whatever becomes of those who content themselves with bodily exercise, for godliness has the promise, etc.

II. The encouragement which we have to proceed in the ways of godliness, and to exercise ourselves to it, notwithstanding the difficulties and discouragements that we meet with in it. He had said (*v.* 8) that it *is profitable for all things, having the promise of the life which now is.* But the question is, Will the profit balance the loss? For, if it will not, it is not profit. Yes, we are sure it will. Here is another of Paul's faithful sayings, worthy of all acceptation — that all our labours and losses in the service of God and the work of religion will be abundantly recompensed, so that though we lose for Christ we shall not lose by him. *Therefore we labour and suffer reproach, because we trust in the living God, v.* 10. Observe,

1. Godly people must labour and expect reproach; they must do well, and yet expect at the same time to suffer ill: toil and trouble are to be expected by us in this world, not only as men, but as saints.

2. Those who labour and suffer reproach in the service of God and the work of religion may depend upon the living God that they shall not lose by it. Let this encourage them, *We trust in the living God.* The consideration of this, that the God who has undertaken to be our pay-master is the living God, who does himself live for ever and is the fountain of life to all who serve him, should encourage us in all our services and in all our sufferings for him, especially considering that he is *the Saviour of all men.* (1.) By his providences he protects the persons, and prolongs the lives, of the children of men. (2.) He has a general good-will to the eternal salvation of all men thus far that he is not willing that any should perish, but that all should come to repentance. He desires not the death of sinners; he is thus far the Saviour of all men that none are left in the same desperate condition that fallen angels are in. Now, if he be thus the Saviour of all men, we may hence infer that much more he will be the rewarder of those who seek and serve him; if he has such a good-will for all his creatures, much more will he provide well for those who are new creatures, who are born again. He is the Saviour of all men, but *especially of those that believe;* and the salvation he has in store for those that believe is sufficient to recompense them for all their services and sufferings. Here we see, [1.] The life of a Christian is a life of labour and suffering: *We labour and suffer.* [2.] The best we can expect to suffer in the present life is reproach for our well-doing, for our work of faith and labour of love. [3.] True Christians trust in the living God; for cursed is the man that trusts in man, or in any but the living God; and those that trust in him shall never be ashamed. *Trust in him at all times.* [4.] God is the general Saviour of all men, as he has put them into a salvable state; but he is in a particular manner the Saviour of true believers; there is then a general and a special redemption.

III. He concludes the chapter with an exhortation to Timothy,

1. To *command and teach these things* that he had now been teaching him. "Command them to exercise themselves unto godliness, teach them the profit of it, and that if they serve God they serve one who will be sure to bear them out."

2. To conduct himself with that gravity and prudence which might gain him respect, notwithstanding his youth: *"Let no man despise thy youth;* that is, give no man an occasion to despise thy youth." Men's youth will not be despised if they do not by youthful vanities and follies make themselves despicable; and this men may do who are old, who may therefore thank themselves if they be despised.

3. To confirm his doctrine by a good example: *Be thou an example of the believers,* etc. Observe, Those who teach by their doctrine must teach by their live, else they pull down with one hand what they build up with the other: they must be examples both *in word and conversation.* Their discourse must be edifying, and this will be a good example: their conversation must be strict, and this will be a good example: they must be examples *in charity,* or love to God and all good men, examples *in spirit,* that is, in spiritual-mindedness, in spiritual worship, — *in faith,* that is, in the profession of Christian faith, — and *in purity* or chastity.

4. He charges him to study hard: *Till I come, give attendance to reading, to exhortation, to doctrine, to meditation upon these things, v.* 13. Though Timothy had extraordinary gifts, yet he must use ordinary means. Or it may be meant of the public reading of the scriptures; he must *read and exhort,* that is, read and expound, read and press what he read upon them; he must expound it both by way of exhortation and by way of doctrine; he must teach them both what to do and what to believe. Observe, (1.) Ministers must teach and command the things that they are themselves taught and commanded to do; they must teach people to observe all things whatsoever Christ has commanded, Mt. 28:20. (2.) The best way for ministers to avoid being despised is to teach and practise the things that are given them in charge. No wonder if ministers are despised who do not teach these things, or who, instead of being examples of good to believers, act directly contrary to the doctrines they preach; for ministers are to be ensamples of their flock. (3.) Those ministers that are the best accomplished for their work must yet mind their studies, that they may be improving in knowledge; and they must mind also their work; they are to give attendance to reading, to exhortation, to doctrine.

5. He charges him to beware of negligence: *Neglect not the gift that is in thee, v.* 14. The gifts of God will wither if they be neglected. It may be understood either of the office to which he was advanced, or of his qualifications for that office; if of the former, it was ordination in an ordinary way; if of the latter, it was extraordinary. It seems to be the former, for it was by *laying on of hands,* etc. Here see the scripture-way of ordination: it was by the laying on of hands, and the laying on of the hands of the presbytery. Observe, Timothy

was ordained by men in office. It was an extraordinary gift that we read of elsewhere as being conferred on him by the laying on of Paul's hands, but he was invested in the office of the ministry by the laying on of the hands of the presbytery. (1.) We may note, The office of the ministry is a gift, it is the gift of Christ; when he ascended on high, he received gifts for men, and he gave some apostles, and some pastors and teachers (Eph. 4:8, 11), and this was a very kind gift to his church. (2.) Ministers ought not to neglect the gift bestowed upon them, whether by gift we are here to understand the office of the ministry or the qualifications for the office; neither the one nor the other must be neglected. (3.) Though there was a prophecy in the case of Timothy (the gift was given by prophecy), yet this was accompanied by the laying on of the hands of the presbytery, that is, a number of presbyters; the office was conveyed to him this way; and I should think here is a sufficient warrant for ordination by presbyters, since it does not appear that Paul was concerned in Timothy's ordination. It is true, extraordinary gifts were conferred on him by the laying on of the apostle's hands (2 Tim. 1:6), but, if he was concerned in his ordination, the presbytery was not excluded, for that is particularly mentioned, whence it seems pretty evident that the presbytery have the inherent power of ordination.

6. Having this work committed to him, he must *give himself wholly* to it: "Be wholly in those things, *that thy profiting may appear.*" He was a wise knowing man, and yet must still be profiting, and make it appear that he improved in knowledge. Observe, (1.) Ministers are to be much in meditation. They are to consider beforehand how and what they must speak. They are to meditate on the great trust committed to them, on the worth and value of immortal souls, and on the account they must give at the last. (2.) Ministers must be wholly in these things, they must mind these things as their principal work and business: *Give thyself wholly to them.* (3.) By this means their profiting will appear in all things, as well a to all persons; this is the way for them to profit in knowledge and grace, and also to profit others.

7. He presses it upon him to be very cautious: *"Take heed to thyself and to the doctrine,* consider what thou preachest; *continue in them,* in the truths that thou hast received; and this will be the way to *save thyself, and those that hear thee."* Observe, (1.) Ministers are engaged in saving work, which makes it a good work. (2.) The care of ministers should be in the first place to save themselves: "Save thyself in the first place, so shalt thou be instrumental to save those that hear thee." (3.) Ministers in preaching should aim at the salvation of those that hear them, next to the salvation of their own souls. (4.) The best way to answer both these ends is to take heed to ourselves, etc.

CHAPTER 5

Here the apostle, I. Directs Timothy how to reprove (*v.* 1, 2). II. Adverts to widows, both elder and younger (*v.* 3–16). III. To elders (*v.* 17–19). IV. Treats of public reproof (*v.* 20). V. Gives a solemn charge concerning ordination (*v.* 21, 22). VI. Refers to his health (*v.* 23), and states men's sins to be very different in their effects (*v.* 24, 25).

Verses 1–2

Here the apostle gives rules to Timothy, and in him to other ministers, in reproving. Ministers are reprovers by office; it is a part, though the least pleasing part, of their office; they are to preach the word, to reprove and rebuke, 2 Tim. 4:2. A great difference is to be made in our reproofs, according to the age, quality, and other circumstances, of the persons rebuked; thus, and elder in age or office must be entreated as a father; *on some have compassion, making a difference,* Jude 22. Now the rule is, 1. To be very tender in rebuking elders — elders in age, elders by office. Respect must be had to the dignity of their years and place, and therefore they must not be rebuked sharply nor magisterially; but Timothy himself, though an evangelist, must entreat them as fathers, for this would be the likeliest way to work upon them, and to win upon them. 2. The younger must be rebuked as brethren, with love and tenderness; not as desirous, to spy faults or pick quarrels, but as being willing to make the best of them. There is need of a great deal of meekness in reproving those who deserve reproof. 3. The elder women must be reproved, when there is occasion, as mothers. Hos. 2:2, *Plead with your mother, plead.* 4. The younger women must be reproved, but reproved as *sisters, with all purity.* If Timothy, so mortified a man to this world and to the flesh and lusts of it, had need of such a caution as this, much more have we.

Verses 3–16

Directions are here given concerning the taking of widows into the number of those who were employed by the church and had maintenance from the church: *Honour widows that are widows indeed.* Honour them, that is, maintain them, admit them into office. There was in those times an office in the church in which widows were employed, and that was to tend the sick and the aged, to look to them by the direction of the deacons. We read of the care taken of widows immediately upon the first forming of the Christian church (Acts 6:1), where the Grecians thought their widows were neglected in the daily ministration and provision made for poor widows. The general rule is to *honour widows that are widows indeed,* to maintain them, to relieve them with respect and tenderness.

I. It is appointed that those widows only should be relieved by the charity of the church who were pious and devout, and not wanton widows that *lived in pleasure, v.* 5, 6. She is to be reckoned a widow indeed, and it to be maintained at the church's charge, who, being *desolate, trusteth in God.* Observe, It is the duty and comfort of those who are desolate to trust in God. *Therefore* God sometimes brings his people into such straits that they have nothing else to trust to, that they may with more confidence trust in him. Widowhood is a desolate estate; but *let the widows trust in me* (Jer. 49:11), and rejoice that they have a God to trust to. Again, Those who trust in God must *continue in prayer.* If by faith we confide in God, by prayer we must give glory to God and commit ourselves to his guidance. Anna was a widow indeed, who *departed not from the temple* (Lu. 2:37), *but served God with fasting and prayer night and day.* But she is not a widow indeed *that lives in pleasure* (*v.* 6), or who lives licentiously. A jovial widow is not a widow indeed, not fit to be taken under the care of the church. *She that lives in pleasure is dead while she lives,* is no living member of the church, but as a carcase in it, or a mortified member. We may apply it more generally; those who live in pleasure are dead while they live, spiritually dead, *dead in trespasses and sins;* they are in the world to no purpose, buried alive as to the great ends of living.

II. Another rule he gives is that the church should not be charged with the maintenance of those widows who had relations of their own that were able to maintain them. This is mentioned several times (*v.* 4): *If any widow have children or nephews,* that is grandchildren or near relations, let them maintain them, and let not the church be burdened. So *v.* 16. This is called showing *piety at home* (*v.* 4), or showing piety towards their own families. Observe, The respect of children to their parents, with their care of them, is fitly called piety. This is requiting their parents. Children can never sufficiently requite their parents for the care they have taken of them, and the pains they have taken with them; but they must endeavour to do it. It is the indispensable duty of children, if their parents be in necessity, and they in ability to relieve them, to do it to the utmost of their power, *for this is good and acceptable before God.* The Pharisees taught that a gift to the altar was more acceptable to God than relieving a poor parent, Mt. 15:5. But here we are told that this *is better than all burnt-offerings and sacrifices; this is good and acceptable,* etc. He speaks of this again (*v.* 8), *If any provide not for his own,* etc. If any men or women do not maintain their own poor relations who belong to them, they do in effect *deny the faith;* for the design of Christ was to confirm the law of Moses, and particularly the law of the fifth commandment, which is, *Honour thy father and mother;* so that those deny the faith who disobey that law, much more if they provide not for their wives and children, who are parts of themselves; if they spend that upon their lusts which should maintain their families, they have denied the faith *and are worse than infidels.* One reason why this care must be taken that those who are rich should maintain their poor relations, and not burden the church with them is (*v.* 16) *that it may relieve those who are widows indeed.* Observe, Charity misplaced is a great hindrance to true charity; there should be prudence in the choice of the objects of charity, that it may not be thrown away upon those who are not properly so, that there may be the more for those who are real objects of charity.

III. He gives directions concerning the characters of the widows that were to be taken into the number to receive the church's charity: not under sixty years old, nor any who have divorced their husbands or been divorced from them and have married again; she must have been *the wife of one man,* such as had been a housekeeper, had a good name for hospitality and charity, *well reported of for good works.* Observe, Particular care ought to be taken to relieve those, when they fall into decay, who, when they had wherewithal, were ready to every good work. Here are instances of such good works as are proper to be done by good wives: *If she have brought up children:* he does not say, If she have borne children *(children are a heritage of the Lord),* that depends on the will of God; but, if she had not children of her own, yet if she had brought up children. *If she have lodged strangers,* and *washed the saints' feet;* if she have been ready to give entertainment to good Christians and good ministers, when they were in their travels for the spreading of the gospel. Washing of the feet o their friends was a part of their entertainments. *If she have relieved the afflicted* when she had ability, let her be relieved now. Observe, Those who would find mercy when they are in distress must show mercy when they are in prosperity.

IV. He cautions them to take heed of admitting into the number those who are likely to be no credit to them (*v.* 11): *The younger widows refuse:* they will be weary of their employments in the church, and of living by rule, as they must do; so they *will marry, and cast off their first faith.* You read of a first love (Rev. 2:4), and here of a first faith, that is, the engagements they gave to the church to behave well, and as became the trust reposed in them: it does not appear that by their first faith is meant their vow not to marry, for the scripture is very silent on that head; besides the apostle here advises the younger widows to marry (*v.* 14), which he would not if hereby they must have broken their vows. Dr. Whitby well observes, "If this faith referred to a promise made to the church not to marry, it could not be called their first faith." *Withal they learn to be idle, and not only idle, but tattlers,* etc., *v.* 13. Observe, It is seldom that those who are idle are idle only, they learn *to be tattlers and busy-bodies,* and to make mischief among neighbours, and sow discord among brethren. Those who had not attained to such a gravity of mind as was fit for the deaconesses (or the widows who were taken among the church's poor), let them *marry, bear children,* etc., *v.* 14. Observe, If housekeepers do not mind their business, but are tattlers, they give occasion to the adversaries of Christianity to reproach the Christian name, which, it seems, there were some instances of, *v.* 15. We learn hence, 1. In the primitive church there was care taken of poor widows, and provision made for them; and the churches of Christ in these days should follow so good an example, as far as they are able. 2. In the distribution of the church's charity, or alms, great care is to be taken that those share in the public bounty who most want it and best deserve it. A widow was not to be taken into the primitive church that had relations who were able to maintain her, or who was not well reported of for good works, but lived in pleasure: *But the younger widows refuse, for, when they have begun to wax wanton against Christ, they will marry.* 3. The credit of religion, and the reputation of Christian churches, are very much concerned in the character and behaviour of those that are taken into any employment in the church, though of a lower nature (such as the business of deaconesses), or that receive alms of the church; if they do not behave well, but are tatlers and busy-bodies, they will give occasion to the adversary to speak reproachfully. 4. Christianity obliges its professors to relieve their indigent friends, particularly poor widows, that the church may not be charged with them, that it may relieve those that are widows indeed: rich people should be ashamed to burden the church with their poor relations, when it is with difficulty that those are supplied who have no children or nephews, that is, grand-children, who are in a capacity to relieve them.

Verses 17–25

Here are directions,

I. Concerning the supporting of ministers. Care must be taken that they be honourably maintained (*v.* 17): *Let the elders that rule well be counted worthy of double honour* (that is, of double maintenance, double to what they have had, or to what others have), *especially those who labour in the word and doctrine,* those who are more laborious than others. Observe, The presbytery ruled, and the same that ruled were those *who laboured in the word and doctrine:* they had not one to preach to them and another to rule them, but the work was done by one and the same person. Some have imagined that by the *elders that rule well* the apostle means lay-elders, who were employed in ruling but not in teaching, who were concerned in church-government, but did not meddle with the administration of the word and sacraments; and I confess this is the plainest text of scripture that can be found to countenance such an opinion. But it seem a little strange that mere ruling elders should be accounted worthy of double honour, when the apostle preferred preaching to baptizing, and much more would he prefer it to ruling the church; and it is more strange that the apostle should take no notice of them when he treats of church-officers; but, as it is hinted before, they had not, in the primitive church, one to preach to them and another to rule them, but ruling and teaching were performed by the same persons, only some might labour more in the word and doctrine than others. Here we have, 1. The work of ministers; it consists principally in two things: ruling well and labouring in the word and doctrine. This was the main business of elders or presbyters in the days of the apostles. 2. The honour due to those who were not idle, but laborious in this work; they were worthy of double honour, esteem, and maintenance. He quotes a scripture to confirm this command concerning the maintenance of ministers that we might think foreign; but it intimates what a significancy there was in many of the laws of Moses, and particularly in this, *Thou shalt not muzzle the ox that treads out the corn,* Deu. 25:4. The beasts that were employed in treading out the corn (for that way they took instead of threshing it) were allowed to feed while they did the work, so that the more work they did the more food they had; therefore let the elders that labour in the word and doctrine be well provided for; *for the labourer is worthy of his reward* (Mt. 10:10), and there is all the reason in the world that he should have it. We hence learn, (1.) God, both under the law, and now under the gospel, has taken care that his ministers be well provided for. Does God take care for oxen, and will he not take care of his own servants? The ox only treads out the corn of which they make the bread that perishes; but ministers break the bread of life which endures for ever. (2.) The comfortable subsistence of ministers, as it is God's appointment that those who preach the gospel should live of the gospel (1 Co. 9:14), so it is their just due, as much as the reward of the labourer; and those who would have ministers starved, or not comfortably provided for, God will require it of them another day.

II. Concerning the accusation of ministers (*v.* 19): *Against an elder receive not an accusation, but before two or three witnesses.* Here is the scripture-method of proceeding against an elder, when accused of any crime. Observe, 1. There must be an accusation; it must not be a flying uncertain report, but an accusation, containing a certain charge, must be drawn up. Further, He is not to be proceeded against by way of enquiry; this is according to the modern practice of the inquisition, which draws up articles for men to purge themselves of such crimes, or else to accuse themselves; but, according to the advice of Paul, there must be an accusation brought against an elder. 2. This accusation is not to be received unless supported by two or three credible witnesses; and the accusation must be received before them, that is, the accused must have the accusers face to face, because the reputation of a minister is, in a particular manner, a tender thing; and therefore, before any thing be done in the least to blemish that reputation, great care should be taken that the thing alleged against him be well proved, that he be not reproached upon an uncertain surmise; "but (*v.* 20) *those that sin rebuke before all;* that is, thou needest not be so tender of other people, but rebuke them publicly." Or "those that sin before all rebuke before all, that the plaster may be as wide as the wound, and that those who are in danger of sinning by the example of their fall may take warning by the rebuke given them for it, *that others also may fear.*" Observe, (1.) Public scandalous sinners must be rebuked publicly: as their sin has been public, and committed before many, or at least come to the hearing of all, so their reproof must be public, and before all. (2.) Public rebuke is designed for the good of others, that they may fear, as well as for the good of the party rebuked; hence it was ordered under the law that public offenders should receive public punishment, that *all Israel* might *hear, and fear, and do no more wickedly.*

III. Concerning the ordination of ministers (*v.* 22): *Lay hands suddenly on no man;* it seems to be meant of the ordaining of men to the office of the ministry, which ought not to be done rashly and inconsiderately, and before due trial made of their gifts and graces, their abilities and qualifications for it. Some understand it of absolution: "Be not too hasty in laying hands on any; remit not the censure of the church to any, till time be first taken for the proof of their sincerity in their repentance, *neither be partakers of other men's sins,* implying that those who are too easy in remitting the censures of the church encourage others in the sins which are thus connived at, and make themselves thereby guilty." Observe, We have great need to watch over ourselves at all times, that we do not make ourselves partakers of other men's sins. "Keep thyself pure, not only from doing the like thyself, but from countenancing it, or being any way accessary to it, in others." Here is, 1. A caution against the rash ordination of ministers, or absolution of those who have been under church-censures: *Lay hands suddenly on no man.* 2. Those who are rash, either in the one case or the other, will make themselves partakers in other men's sins. 3. We must keep ourselves pure, if we will be pure; the grace of God makes and keeps us pure, but it is by our own endeavours.

IV. Concerning absolution, to which *v.* 24, 25, seem to refer: *Some men's sins are open beforehand, going before to judgment, and some follow after,* etc. Observe, Ministers have need of a great deal of wisdom, to know how to accommodate themselves to the variety of offences and offenders that they have occasion to deal with. Some men's sins are so plain and obvious, and not found by secret search, that there is no dispute concerning the bringing of them under the censures of the church; they *go before to judgment,* to lead them to censure. — *Others they follow after;* that is, their wickedness does not presently appear, nor till after a due search has been made concerning it. Or, as some understand it, some men's sins continue after they are censured; they are not reformed by the censure, and in that case there must be no absolution. So, also, as to the evidences of repentance: *The good works of some are manifest beforehand. And those that are otherwise,* whose good works do not appear, their wickedness *cannot be hid,* and so it will be easy to discern who are to be absolved, and who are not. Observe, 1. There are secret, and there are open sins; some men's sins are open beforehand, and going unto judgment, and some they follow after. 2. Sinners must be differently dealt with by the church. 3. The effects of church-censures are very different; some are thereby humbled and brought to repentance, so that their good works are manifest beforehand, while it is quite otherwise with others. 4. The incorrigible cannot be hid; for God will bring to light the hidden things of darkness, and make manifest the counsels of all hearts.

V. Concerning Timothy himself. 1. Here is a charge to him to be careful of his office; and a solemn charge it is: *I charge thee before God, as thou wilt answer it to God before the holy and elect angels, observe these things without partiality, v.* 21. Observe, It ill becomes ministers to be partial, and to have respect of persons, and to prefer one before another upon any secular account. He charges him, by all that is dear, *before God, and the Lord Jesus Christ, and the elect angels,* to guard against partiality. Ministers must give an account to God and the Lord Jesus Christ, whether, and how, they have observed all things given them in charge: and woe to them if they have been partial in their ministrations, out of an worldly politic view. 2. He charges him to take care of his health: *Drink no longer water,* etc. It seems Timothy was a mortified man to the pleasures of sense; he drank water, and he was a man of no strong constitution of body, and for this reason Paul advises him to use wine for the helping of his stomach and the recruiting of his nature. Observe, It is a little wine, for ministers must not be given to much wine; so much as may be for the health of the body, not so as to distemper it, for God has made wine to rejoice man's heart. Note, (1.) It is the will of God that people should take all due care of their bodies. As we are not to make them our masters, so neither our slaves; but to use them so that they may be most fit and helpful to us in the service of God. (2.) Wine is most proper for sickly and weak people, whose stomachs are often out of order, and who labour under infirmities. *Give strong drink to him that is ready to perish, and wine to those that are of heavy hearts,* Prov. 31:6. (3.) Wine should be used as a help, and not a hindrance, to our work and usefulness.

CHAPTER 6

I. He treats of the duty of servants (*v.* 1, 2). II. Of false teachers (*v.* 3–5). III. Of godliness and covetousness (*v.* 6–10). IV. What Timothy was to flee, and what to follow (*v.* 11, 12). V. A solemn charge (*v.* 13–16). VI. A charge for the rich (*v.* 17–19). And lastly, a charge to Timothy (*v.* 20, 21).

Verses 1–5

I. Here is the duty of servants. The apostle had spoken before of church-relations, here of our family-relations. Servants are here said to be *under the yoke,* which denotes both subjection and labour; they are yoked to work, not to be idle. If Christianity finds servants under the yoke, it continues them under it; for the gospel does not cancel the obligations any lie under either by the law of nature or by mutual consent. They must respect their masters, *count them worthy of all honour* (because they are their masters), of all the respect, observance, compliance, and obedience, that are justly expected from servants to their masters. Not that they were to think that of them which they were not; but as their masters they must count them worthy of all that honour which was fit for them to receive, *that the name of God be not blasphemed.* If servants that embraced the Christian religion should grow insolent and disobedient to their masters, the doctrine of Christ would be reflected on for their sakes, as if it had made men worse livers than they had been before they received the gospel. Observe, If the professors of religion misbehave themselves, *the name of God and his doctrine* are in danger of being blasphemed by those who seek occasion *to speak evil of that worthy name by which we are called.* And this is a good reason why we should all conduct ourselves well, that we may prevent the occasion which many seek, and will be very apt to lay hold of, to speak ill of religion for our sakes. Or suppose the master were a Christian, and a believer, and the servant a believer too, would not this excuse him, because *in Christ there is neither bond nor free?* No, by no means, for Jesus Christ did not come to dissolve the bond of civil relation, but to strengthen it: *Those that have believing masters, let them not despise them because they are brethren;* for this brotherhood relates only to spiritual privileges, not to any outward dignity or advantage (those misunderstood and abuse their religion who make it a pretence for denying the duties that they owe to their relations); nay, *rather do them service, because they are faithful and beloved.* They must think themselves the more obliged to serve them because the faith and love that bespeak men Christians oblige them to do good; and that is all wherein their service consists. Observe, It is a great encouragement to us in doing our duty to our relations if we have reason to think they are faithful and beloved, *and partakers of the benefit,* that is, of the benefit of Christianity. Again, Believing masters and servants are brethren, and partakers of the benefit; for in Christ Jesus there is neither bond nor free, for you are all one in Christ Jesus, Gal. 3:28. Timothy is appointed to *teach and exhort these things.* Ministers must preach not only the general duties of all, but the duties of particular relations.

II. Paul here warns Timothy to withdraw from those who corrupted the doctrine of Christ, and made it the subject off strife, debate, and controversy: *If any man teach otherwise* (*v.* 3–5), do not preach practically, do not teach and exhort that which is for the promoting of serious godliness — if he will not consent to wholesome words, words that have a direct tendency to heal the soul — if he will *not consent* to these, even the *words of our Lord Jesus Christ.* Observe, We are not required to consent to any words as wholesome words except the words of our Lord Jesus Christ; but to those we must give our unfeigned assent and consent, and *to the doctrine which is according to godliness.* Observe, The doctrine of our Lord Jesus is a doctrine according to godliness; it has a direct tendency to make people godly. But he that does not consent to the words of Christ *is proud* (*v.* 4) and contentious, ignorant, and does a great deal of mischief to the church, knowing nothing. Observe, Commonly those are most proud who know least; for with all their knowledge they do not know themselves. — *But doting about questions.* Those who fall off from the plain practical doctrines of Christianity fall in with controversies, which eat out the life and power of religion; they dote about questions *and strifes of words,* which do a great deal of mischief in the church, are the occasion of *envy, strife, railings, evil surmisings.* When men are not content with the words of the Lord Jesus Christ, and the doctrine which is according to godliness, but will frame notions of their own and impose them, and that too in their own words, which man's wisdom teaches, and not in the words which the Holy Ghost teaches (1 Co. 2:13), they sow the seeds of all mischief in the church. Hence come *perverse disputings of men of corrupt minds* (*v.* 5), disputes that are all subtlety, and no solidity. Observe, Men of corrupt minds are *destitute of the truth.* The reason why men's minds are corrupt is because they do not stick to *the truth as it is in Jesus: supposing that gain is godliness,* making religion truckle to their secular interest. From such as these Timothy is warned to withdraw himself. We observe, 1. The words of our Lord Jesus Christ are wholesome words, they are the fittest to prevent or heal the church's wounds, as well as to heal a wounded conscience; for Christ has the tongue of the learned, to speak a word in season to him that is weary, Isa. 50:4. The words of Christ are the best to prevent ruptures in the church; for none who profess faith in him will dispute the aptness or authority of his words who is their Lord and teacher, and it has never gone well with the church since the words of men have claimed a regard equal to his words, and in some cases a much greater. 2. Whoever teaches otherwise, and does not consent to these wholesome words, he is proud, knowing nothing; for pride and ignorance commonly go together. 3. Paul sets a brand only on those who consent not to the words of our Lord Jesus Christ, and the doctrine which is according to godliness; they are proud, knowing nothing: other words more wholesome he knew not. 4. We learn the sad effects of doting about questions and strifes of words; of such doting about questions comes envy, strife, evil surmisings, and perverse disputings; when men leave the wholesome words of our Lord Jesus Christ, they will never agree in other words, either of their own or other men's invention, but will perpetually wrangle and quarrel about them; and this will produce envy, when they see the words of others preferred to those they have adopted for their own; and this will be attended with jealousies and suspicions of one another, called here *evil surmisings;* then they will proceed to perverse disputings. 5. Such persons as are given to perverse disputings appear to be men of corrupt minds, and destitute of the truth; especially such as act in this manner for the sake of gain, which is all their godliness, supposing gain to be godliness, contrary to the apostle's judgment, who reckoned godliness great gain. 6. Good ministers and Christians will withdraw themselves from such. "Come out from among them, my people, and be ye separate," says the Lord: *from such withdraw thyself.*

Verses 6–12

From the mention of the abuse which some put upon religion, making it to serve their secular advantages, the apostle,

I. Takes occasion to show the excellency of contentment and the evil of covetousness.

1. The excellency of contentment, *v.* 6–8. Some account Christianity an advantageous profession for this world. In the sense they mean this is false; yet it is undoubtedly true that, though Christianity is the worst trade, it is the best calling in the world. Those that make a trade of it, merely to serve their turn for this world, will be disappointed, and find it a sorry trade; but those that mind it as their calling, and make a business of it, will find it a gainful calling, for it has the promise of the life that now is, as well as of that which is to come.

(1.) The truth he lays down is that *godliness with contentment is great gain.* Some read it, *godliness with a competency;* that is, if a man have but a little in this world, yet, if he have but enough to carry him through it, he needs desire no more, his godliness with that will be his great gain. *For a little which a righteous man has is better than the riches of many wicked,* Ps. 37:16. We read it, *godliness with contentment;* godliness is itself great gain, it is profitable to all things; and, wherever there is true godliness, there will be contentment; but those have arrived at the highest pitch of contentment with their godliness are certainly the easiest happiest people in this world. *Godliness with contentment,* that is, Christian contentment (content must come from principles of godliness) is great gain; it is all the wealth in the world. He that is godly is sure to be happy in another world; and if withal he do by contentment accommodate himself to his condition in this world he has enough. Here we have, [1.] A Christian's gain; it is godliness with contentment, this is the true way to gain, yea, it is gain itself. [2.] A Christian's gain is great: it is not like the little gain of worldlings, who are so fond of a little worldly advantage. [3.] Godliness is ever accompanied with contentment in a great or less degree; all truly godly people have learned with Paul, in whatever state they are, to be therewith content, Phil. 4:11. They are content with what God allots for them, well knowing that this is best for them. Let us all then endeavour after godliness with contentment.

(2.) The reason he gives for it is, *For we brought nothing with us into this world, and it is certain we can carry nothing out, v.* 7. This is a reason why we should be content with a little. [1.] Because we can challenge nothing as a debt that is due to us, for we came naked into the world. Whatever we have had since, we are obliged to the providence of God for it; but he that gave may take what and when he pleases. We had our beings, our bodies, our lives (which are more than meat, and which are more than raiment), when we came into the world, though we came naked, and brought nothing with us; may we not then be content while our beings and lives are continued to us, though we have not every thing we would have? We brought nothing with us into this world, and yet God provided for us, care was taken of us, we have been fed all our lives long unto this day; and therefore, when we are reduced to the greatest straits, we cannot be poorer than when we came into this world, and yet then we were provided for; therefore let us trust in God for the remaining part of our pilgrimage. [2.] We shall carry nothing with us out of this world. A shroud, a coffin, and a grave, are all that the richest man in the world can have from his thousands. Therefore why should we covet much? Why should we not be content with a little, because, how much soever we have, we must leave it behind us? Eccl. 5:15, 16.

(3.) Hence he infers, *having food and raiment, let us be therewith content, v.* 8. Food and a *covering,* including habitation as well as raiment. Observe, If God give us the necessary supports of life, we ought to be content therewith, though we have not the ornaments and delights of it. If nature should be content with a little, grace should be content with less; though we have not dainty food, though we have not costly raiment, if we have but food and raiment convenient for us we ought to be content. This was Agur's prayer: *Give me neither poverty nor riches; feed me with food convenient for me,* Prov. 30:8. Here we see, [1.] The folly of placing our happiness in these things, when we did not bring any thing into this world with us, and we can carry nothing out. What will worldlings do when death shall strip them of their happiness and portion, and they must take an everlasting farewell of all these things, on which they have so much doted? They may say with poor Micah, *You have taken away my gods; and what have I more?* Jud. 18:24. [2.] The necessaries of life are the hounds of a true Christian's desire, and with these he will endeavour to be content; his desires are not insatiable; no, a little, a few comforts of this life, will serve him, and these may hope to enjoy: *Having food and raiment.*

2. The evil of covetousness. *Those that will be rich* (that set their hearts upon the wealth of this world, and are resolved right or wrong, they will have it), *fall into temptation and a snare, v.* 9. It is not said, those that are rich, but those that will be rich, that is, that place their happiness in worldly wealth, that covet it inordinately, and are eager and violent in the pursuit of it. Those that are such *fall into temptation and a snare,* unavoidably; for, when the devil sees which way their lusts carry them, he will soon bait his hook accordingly. He knew how fond Achan would be of a wedge of gold, and therefore laid that before him. They fall into *many foolish and hurtful lusts.* Observe,

(1.) The apostle supposes that, [1.] Some will be rich; that is, they are resolved upon it, nothing short of a great abundance will satisfy. [2.] Such will not be safe nor innocent, for they will be in danger of ruining themselves for ever; they fall into temptation, and a snare, etc. [3.] Worldly lusts are foolish and hurtful, for they drown men in destruction and perdition. [4.] It is good for us to consider the mischievousness of worldly fleshly lusts. They are foolish, and therefore we should be ashamed of them, hurtful, and therefore we should be afraid of them, especially considering to what degree they are hurtful, for they *drown men in destruction and perdition.*

(2.) The apostle affirms that *the love of money is the root of all evil, v.* 10. What sins will not men be drawn to by the love of money? Particularly this was at the bottom of the apostasy of many from the faith of Christ; while they coveted money, they *erred from the faith,* they quitted their Christianity, and *pierced themselves through with many sorrows.* Observe, [1.] What is the root of all evil; the love of money: people may have money, and yet not love it; but, if they love it inordinately, it will push them on to all evil. [2.] Covetous persons will quit the faith, if that be the way to get money: *Which while some coveted after, they have erred from the faith. Demas hath forsaken me, having loved this present world,* 2 Tim. 4:10. For the world was dearer to him than Christianity. Observe, Those that err from the faith pierce themselves with many sorrows; those that depart from God do but treasure up sorrows for themselves.

II. Hence he takes occasion to caution Timothy, and to counsel him to keep in the way of God and his duty, and particularly to fulfil the trust reposed in him as a minister. He addresses himself to him as *a man of God.* Ministers are men of God, and ought to conduct themselves accordingly in every thing; they are men employed for God, devoted to his honour more immediately. The prophets under the Old Testament were called men of God. 1. He charges Timothy to take heed of the love of money, which had been so pernicious to many: *Flee these things.* It ill becomes any men, but especially men of God, to set their hearts upon the things of this world; men of God should be taken up with the things of God. 2. To arm him against the love of the world, he directs him to follow that which is good. *Follow after righteousness, godliness, faith, love, patience, meekness:* righteousness in his conversation towards men, godliness towards God, faith and love as living principles, to support him and carry him on in the practice both of righteousness and godliness. Those that follow after righteousness and godliness, from a principle of faith and love, have need to put on patience and meekness — patience to bear both the rebukes of Providence and the reproaches of men, and meekness wherewith to instruct gainsayers and pass by the affronts and injuries that are done us. Observe, It is not enough that men of God flee these things, but they must follow after what is directly contrary thereto. Further, What excellent persons men of God are who follow after righteousness! They are the excellent of the earth, and, being acceptable to God, they should be approved of men. 3. He exhorts him to do the part of a soldier: *Fight the good fight of faith.* Note, Those who will get to heaven must fight their way thither. There must be a conflict with corruption and temptations, and the opposition of the powers of darkness. Observe, It is a good fight, it is a good cause, and it will have a good issue. It is the fight of faith; we do not war after the flesh, for the weapons of our warfare are not carnal, 2 Co. 10:3, 4. He exhorts him to *lay hold on eternal life.* Observe, (1.) Eternal life is the crown proposed to us, for our encouragement to war, and to fight the good fight of faith, the good warfare. (2.) This we must lay hold on, as those that are afraid of coming short of it and losing it. Lay hold, and take heed of losing your hold. *Hold fast that which thou hast, that no man take thy crown,* Rev. 3:11. (3.) We are called to the fight, and to lay hold on eternal life. (4.) The profession Timothy and all faithful ministers make before many witnesses is a good profession; for they profess and engage to fight the good fight of faith, and to lay hold on eternal life; their calling and their own profession oblige them to this.

Verses 13–21

The apostle here charges Timothy *to keep this commandment* (that is, the whole work of his ministry, all the trust reposed in him, all the service expected from him) *without spot, unrebukable;* he must conduct himself so in his ministry that he might not lay himself open to any blame nor incur any blemish. What are the motives to move him to this?

I. He gives him a solemn charge: *I give thee charge in the sight of God that thou do this.* He charges him as he will answer it at the great day to that God whose eyes are upon us all, who sees what we are and what we do: — *God, who quickens all things,* who has life in himself and is the fountain of life. This should quicken us to the service of God that we serve a God who quickens all things. He charges him before Christ Jesus, to whom in a peculiar manner he stood related as a minister of his gospel: *Who before Pontius Pilate witnessed a good confession.* Observe, Christ died not only as a sacrifice, but as a martyr; and he witnessed a good confession when he was arraigned before Pilate, saying (Jn. 18:36, 37), *My kingdom is not of this world: I am come to bear witness unto the truth.* That good confession of his before Pilate, *My kingdom is not of this world,* should be effectual to draw off all his followers, both ministers and people, from the love of this world.

II. He reminds him of the confession that he himself had made: *Thou hast professed a good profession before many witnesses* (v. 12), namely, when he was ordained by the laying on of the hands of the presbytery. The obligation of that was still upon him, and he must live up to that, and be quickened by that, to do the work of his ministry.

III. He reminds him of Christ's second coming: *"Keep this commandment — until the appearing of our Lord Jesus Christ;* keep it as long as thou live, till Christ come at death to give thee a discharge. Keep it with an eye to his second coming, when we must all give an account of the talents we have been entrusted with," Lu. 16:2. Observe, The Lord Jesus Christ will appear, and it will be a glorious appearing, not like his first appearing in the days of his humiliation. Ministers should have an eye to this appearing of the Lord Jesus Christ in all their ministrations, and, till his appearing, they are to keep this commandment without spot, unrebukable. Mentioning the appearing of Christ, as one that loved it, Paul loves to speak of it, and loves to speak of him who shall then appear. The appearing of Christ is certain *(he shall show it),* but it is not for us to know the time and season of it, which the Father has kept in his own power: let this suffice us, that in time he will show it, in the time that he thinks fit for it. Observe,

1. Concerning Christ and God the Father the apostle here speaks great things. (1.) That God is the only Potentate; the powers of earthly princes are all derived from him, and depend upon him. The powers that exist are ordained of God, Rom. 13:1. He is the only Potentate that is absolute and sovereign, and perfectly independent. (2.) He is the blessed and the only Potentate, infinitely happy, and nothing can in the least impair his happiness. (3.) He is King of kings, and Lord of lords. All the kings of the earth derive their power from him; he gave them their crowns, they hold them under him, and he has a sovereign dominion over them. This is Christ's title (Rev. 19:16), *upon his vesture and his thigh;* for he has a name higher than the kings of the earth. (4.) He only has immortality. He only is immortal in himself, and has immortality as he is the fountain of it, for the immortality of angels and spirits derived from him. (5.) He dwells in inaccessible light, *light which no man can approach unto:* no man can get to heaven but those whom he is pleased to bring thither, and admit into his kingdom. (6.) He is invisible: *Whom no man hath seen, nor can see.* It is impossible that mortal eyes should bear the brightness of the divine glory. No man can see God and live.

2. Having mentioned these glorious attributes, he concludes with a doxology: *To him be honour and power everlasting. Amen.* God having all power and honour to himself, it is our duty to ascribe all power and honour to him. (1.) What an evil is sin, when committed against such a God, the blessed and only Potentate! The evil of it rises in proportion to the dignity of him against whom it is committed. (2.) Great is his condescension, to take notice of such mean and vile creatures as we are. What are we then, that the blessed God, the King of kings and Lord of lords, should seek after us? (3.) Blessed are those who are admitted to dwell with this great and blessed Potentate. *Happy are thy men* (says the queen of Sheba to king Solomon), *happy are these thy servants, who stand continually before thee,* 1 Ki. 10:8. Much more happy are those who are allowed to stand before the King of kings. (4.) Let us love, adore, and praise, the great God; for *who shall not fear thee, O Lord, and glorify thy name? For thou only art holy,* Rev. 15:4.

IV. The apostle adds, by way of postscript, a lesson for rich people, v. 17–19.

1. Timothy must charge those that are rich to beware of the temptations, and improve the opportunities, of their prosperous estate. (1.) He must caution them to take heed of pride. This is a sin that easily besets rich people, upon whom the world smiles. Charge them *that they be not high-minded,* or think of themselves above what is meet, or be puffed up with their wealth. (2.) He must caution them against vain confidence in their wealth. Charge them that they *trust not in uncertain riches.* Nothing is more uncertain than the wealth of this world; many have had much of it one day and been stripped of all the next. Riches make themselves wings, and fly away as an eagle, etc., Prov. 23:5. (3.) He must charge them to *trust in God, the living God,* to make him their hope, *who giveth us richly all things to enjoy.* Those who are rich must see God giving them their riches, and giving them to enjoy them richly; for many have riches, but enjoy them poorly, not having a heart to use them. (4.) He must charge them to do good with what they have (for what is the best estate worth, any more than as it gives a man an opportunity of doing so much the more good?): *That they be rich in good works.* Those are truly rich who are rich in good works. That they be *ready to distribute, willing to communicate:* not only to do it, but to do it willingly, for *God loves a cheerful giver.* (5.) He must charge them to think of another world, and prepare for that which is to come by works of charity: *Laying up in store a good foundation against the time to come,* that they may take hold on eternal life.

2. Hence we may observe, (1.) Ministers must not be afraid of the rich; be they ever so rich, they must speak to them, and charge them. (2.) They must caution them against pride, and vain confidence in their riches: *That they be not high-minded, nor trust in uncertain riches.* Stir them up to works of piety and charity: *That they do good,* etc. (3.) This is the way for the rich to lay up in store for themselves for the time to come, that they may lay hold on eternal life; in the way of well-doing we are to seek for glory, honour, and immortality, *and eternal life will be the end of all,* Rom. 2:7. (4.) Here is a lesson for ministers in the charge given to Timothy: *Keep that which is committed to thy trust.* Every minister is a trustee, and it is a treasure committed to his trust, which he has to keep. The truths of God, the ordinances of God, keep these, *avoiding profane and vain babblings;* not affecting human eloquence, which the apostle calls vain babbling, or human learning, which often opposes the truths of God, but keep close to the written word, for that is committed to our trust. Some who have been very proud of their learning, their *science, which is falsely so called,* have by that been debauched in their principles and been drawn away from the faith of Christ, which is a good reason why we should keep to the plain word of the gospel, and resolve to live and die by that. Observe, [1.] Ministers cannot be too earnestly exhorted to keep what is committed to their trust, because it is a great trust lodged with them: *O Timothy, keep that which is committed to thy trust!* as if he had said, "I cannot conclude without charging thee again; whatever thou doest, be sure to keep this trust, for it is too great a trust to be betrayed." [2.] Ministers are to avoid babblings, if they would keep what is committed to them, because they are vain and profane. [3.] That science that opposes the truth of the gospel is falsely so called; it is not true science, for if it were it would approve of the gospel and consent to it. [4.] Those who are so fond of such science are in great danger of erring concerning the faith; those who are for advancing reason above faith are in danger of leaving faith.

V. Our apostle concludes with a solemn prayer and benediction: *Grace be with thee. Amen.* Observe, this is a short, yet comprehensive prayer for our friends, for grace comprehends in it all that is good, and grace is an earnest, yea, a beginning, of glory; for, wherever God gives grace, he will give glory, and will not withhold any good thing from him who walketh uprightly. Grace be with you all. Amen.

AN EXPOSITION, WITH PRACTICAL OBSERVATIONS, OF
THE SECOND EPISTLE OF ST. PAUL TO TIMOTHY

This second epistle Paul wrote to Timothy from Rome, when he was a prisoner there and in danger of his life; this is evident from these words, *I am now ready to be offered, and the time of my departure is at hand, ch.* 4:6. It appears that his removal out of this world, in his own apprehension, was not far off, especially considering the rage and malice of his persecutors; and that he had been brought before the emperor Nero, which he calls *his first answer, when no man stood with him, but all men forsook him, ch.* 4:16. And interpreters agree that this was the last epistle he wrote. Where Timothy now was is not certain. The scope of this epistle somewhat differs from that of the former, not so much relating to his office as an evangelist as to his personal conduct and behaviour.

CHAPTER 1

After the introduction (v. 1, 2) we have, I. Paul's sincere love to Timothy (v. 3–5). II. Divers exhortations given to him (v. 6–14). III. He speaks of Phygellus and Hermogenes, with others, and closes with Onesiphorus (v. 15 to the end).

Verses 1–5

Here is, I. The inscription of the epistle Paul calls himself *an apostle by the will of God,* merely by the good pleasure of God, and by his grace, which he professes himself unworthy of. *According to the promise of life which is in Christ Jesus,* or according to the gospel. The gospel is the promise of life in Christ Jesus; life is the end, and Christ the way, Jn. 14:6. The life is put into the promise, and both are sure in Christ Jesus the faithful witness; *for all the promises of God in Christ Jesus are yea, and all amen,* 2 Co. 1:20. He calls Timothy his *beloved son.* Paul felt the warmest affection for him both because he had been an instrument of his conversion and because as a son with his father he had served with him in the gospel. Observe, 1. Paul was an apostle of Jesus Christ by the will of God; as he did not receive the gospel of man, nor was taught it, but had it by the revelation of Jesus Christ (Gal. 1:12), so his commission to be an apostle was not by the will of man, but of God: in the former epistle he says it was *by the commandment of God our Saviour,* and here *by the will of God.* God called him to be an apostle. 2. We have the promise of life, blessed be God for it: *In hope of eternal life, which God, who cannot lie, promised before the world began,* Tit. 1:2. It is a promise to discover the freeness and certainty of it. 3. This, as well as all other promises, is in and through Jesus Christ; they all take their rise from the mercy of God in Christ, and they are sure, so that we may safely depend on them. 4. The grace, mercy, and peace, which even Paul's dearly beloved son Timothy wanted, comes from God the Father and Christ Jesus our Lord; and therefore the one as well as the other is the giver of these blessings, and ought to be applied to for them. 5. The best want these blessings, and they are the best we can ask for our dearly-beloved friends, that they may have grace to help them in the time of need, and mercy to pardon what

is amiss, and so may have peace with God the Father and Christ Jesus our Lord.

II. Paul's thanksgiving to God for Timothy's faith and holiness: he thanks God that he remembered Timothy in his prayers. Observe, Whatever good we do, and whatever good office we perform for our friends, God must have the glory of it, and we must give him thanks. It is he who puts it into our hearts to remember such and such in our prayers. Paul was much in prayer, he prayed night and day; in all his prayers he was mindful of his friends, he particularly prayed for good ministers, he prayed for Timothy, and *had remembrance of him in his prayers night and day;* he did this without ceasing; prayer was his constant business, and he never forgot his friends in his prayers, as we often do. Paul served God from his forefathers with a pure conscience. It was a comfort to him that he was born in God's house, and was of the seed of those that served God; as likewise that he had served him with a pure conscience, according to the best of his light; he had kept a conscience void of offence, and made it his daily exercise to do so, Acts 24:16. *He greatly desired to see*

Timothy, out of the affection he had for him, that he might have some conversation with him, *being mindful of his tears* at their last parting. Timothy was sorry to part with Paul, he wept at parting, and therefore Paul desired to see him again, because he had perceived by that what a true affection he had for him. He thanks God that Timothy kept up the religion of his ancestors, *v.* 5. Observe, The entail of religion descended upon Timothy by the mother's side; he had a good mother, and a good grandmother: they believed, though his father did not, Acts 16:1. It is a comfortable thing when children imitate the faith and holiness of their godly parents, and tread in their steps, 3 Jn. 4. — *Dwelt in thy grandmother and thy mother, and I am persuaded that in thee also.* Paul had a very charitable opinion of his friends, was very willing to hope the best concerning them; indeed he had a great deal of reason to believe well of Timothy, for he had *no man likeminded,* Phil. 2:20. Observe, 1. We are, according to St. Paul, to serve God with a pure conscience, so did his and our pious forefathers; this is to draw *near with a true heart, in full assurance of faith, having our heart sprinkled from an evil conscience,* Heb. 10:22. 2. In our prayers we are to remember without ceasing our friends, especially the faithful ministers of Christ. Paul had remembrance of his dearly beloved son Timothy in his prayers night and day. 3. The faith that dwells in real believers is unfeigned; it is without hypocrisy, it is a faith that will stand the trial, and it dwells in them as a living principle. It was the matter of Paul's thanksgiving that Timothy inherited the faith of his mother Eunice and his grandmother Lois, and ought to be ours whenever we see the like; we should rejoice wherever we see the grace of God; so did Barnabas, Acts 11:23, 24. *I rejoiced greatly that I found of thy children walking in the truth,* 2 Jn. 4.

Verses 6–14

Here is an exhortation and excitation of Timothy to his duty (*v.* 6): *I put thee in remembrance.* The best men need remembrancers; what we know we should be reminded of. 2 Pt. 3:1, I write this, *to stir up your pure minds by way of remembrance.*

I. He exhorts him to stir *up the gift of God* that was *in him.* Stir it up as fire under the embers. It is meant of all the gifts and graces the God had given him, to qualify him for the work of an evangelist, the gifts of the Holy Ghost, the extraordinary gifts that were conferred by the imposition of the apostle's hands. These he must stir up; he must exercise them and so increase them: use gifts and have gifts. *To him that hath shall be given,* Mt. 25:29. He must take all opportunities to use these gifts, and so stir them up, for that is the best way of increasing them. Whether the gift of God in Timothy was ordinary or extraordinary (though I incline to the latter), he must stir it up, otherwise it would decay. Further, you see that this gift was in him by the putting on of the apostle's hands, which I take to be distinct from his ordination, for that was performed by the hands of the presbytery, 1 Tim. 4:14. It is probable that Timothy had the Holy Ghost, in his extraordinary gifts and graces, conferred on him by the laying on of the apostle's hands (for I reckon that none but the apostles had the power of giving the Holy Ghost), and afterwards, being thus richly furnished for the work of the ministry, was ordained by the presbytery. Observe, 1. The great hindrance of usefulness in the increase of our gifts is slavish fear. Paul therefore warns Timothy against this: *God hath not given us the spirit of fear, v.* 7. It was through base fear that the evil servant buried his talent, and did not trade with it, Mt. 25:25. Now God hath therefore armed us against the spirit of fear, by often bidding us fear not. "Fear not the face of man; fear not the dangers you may meet with in the way of your duty." God hath delivered us from the spirit of fear, and hath given us the spirit *of power, and of love, and of a sound mind.* The spirit of power, or of courage and resolution to encounter difficulties and dangers; — the spirit of love to God, which will carry us through the opposition we may meet with, as Jacob made nothing of the hard service he was to endure for Rachel: the spirit of love to God will set us above the fear of man, and all the hurt that a man can do us; — and the spirit of a sound mind, or quietness of mind, a peaceable enjoyment of ourselves, for we are oftentimes discouraged in our way and work by the creatures o our own fancy and imagination, which a sober, solid, thinking mind would obviate, and would easily answer. 2. The spirit God gives to his ministers is not a fearful, but a courageous spirit; it is a spirit of power, for they speak in his name who has all power, both in heaven and earth; and it is a spirit of love, for love to God and the souls of men must inflame ministers in all their service; and it is a spirit of a sound mind, for they speak the words of truth and soberness.

II. He exhorts him to count upon afflictions, and get ready for them: *"Be not thou therefore ashamed of the testimony of our Lord, nor of me his prisoner.* Be not thou ashamed of the gospel, of the testimony thou hast borne to it." Observe,

1. The gospel of Christ is what we have none of us reason to be ashamed of. We must not be ashamed of those who are suffering for the gospel of Christ. Timothy must not be ashamed of good old Paul, though he was now in bonds. As he must not himself be afraid of suffering, so he must not be afraid of owning those who were sufferers for the cause of Christ. (1.) The gospel is the testimony of our Lord; in and by this he bears testimony of himself to us, and by professing our adherence to it we bear testimony of him and for him. (2.) Paul was the Lord's prisoner, his prisoner, Eph. 4:1. For his sake he was bound with a chain. (3.) We have no reason to be ashamed either of the testimony of our Lord or of his prisoners; if we are ashamed of either now, Christ will be ashamed of us hereafter. *"But be thou partaker of the afflictions of the gospel, according to the power of God,* that is, expect afflictions for the gospel's sake, prepare for them, count upon them, be willing to take thy lot with the suffering saints in this world. *Be partaker of the afflictions of the gospel;"* or, as it may be read, *Do thou suffer with the gospel;* "not only sympathize with those who suffer for it, but be ready to suffer with them and suffer like them." If at any time the gospel be in distress, he who hopes for life and salvation by it will be content to suffer with it. Observe, [1.] Then we are likely to bear afflictions as well, when we fetch strength and power from God to enable us to bear them: *Be thou partaker of the afflictions of the gospel, according to the power of God.* [2.] All Christians, but especially ministers, must expect afflictions and persecutions for the sake of the gospel. [3.] These shall be proportioned, according to the power of God (1 Co. 10:13) resting upon us.

2. Mentioning God and the gospel, he takes notice what great things God has done for us by the gospel, *v.* 9, 10. To encourage him to suffer, he urges two considerations: —

(1.) The nature of that gospel which he was called to suffer for, and the glorious and gracious designs and purposes of it. It is usual with Paul, when he mentions Christ, and the gospel of Christ, to digress from his subject, and enlarge upon them; so full was he of that which is all our salvation, and ought to be all our desire. Observe, [1.] The gospel aims at our salvation: *He has saved us,* and we must not think much to suffer for that which we hope to be saved by. He has begun to save us, and will complete it in due time; for God calls those things that are not (that are not yet completed) as though they were (Rom. 4:17); therefore he says, who *has* saved us. [2.] It is designed for our sanctification: *And called us with a holy calling,* called us to holiness. Christianity is a calling, a holy calling; it is the calling wherewith we are called, the calling to which we are called, to labour in it. Observe, All who shall be saved hereafter are sanctified now. Wherever the call of the gospel is an effectual call, it is found to be a holy call, making those holy who are effectually called. [3.] The origin of it is the free grace and eternal purpose of God in Christ Jesus. If we had merited it, it had been hard to suffer for it; but our salvation by it is of free grace, and not according to our works, and therefore we must not think much to suffer for it. This grace is said to be given us *before the world began,* that is, in the purpose and designs of God from all eternity; *in Christ Jesus,* for all the gifts that come from God to sinful man come in and through Christ Jesus. [4.] The gospel is the manifestation of this purpose and grace: *By the appearing of our Saviour Jesus Christ,* who had lain in the bosom of the Father from eternity, and was perfectly apprised of all his gracious purposes. By his appearing this gracious purpose was made manifest to us. Did Jesus Christ suffer for it, and shall we think much to suffer for it? [5.] By the gospel of Christ death is abolished: *He has abolished death,* not only weakened it, but taken it out of the way, has broken the power of death over us; by taking away sin he has abolished death (for the sting of death is sin, 1 Co. 15:56), in altering the property of it, and breaking the power of it. Death now of an enemy has become a friend; it is the gate by which we pass out of a troublesome, vexatious, sinful world, into a world of perfect peace and purity; and the power thereof is broken, for death does not triumph over those who believe the gospel, but they triumph over it. *O death! where is thy sting? O grave! where is thy victory?* 1 Co. 15:55. [6.] He has *brought life and immortality to light by the gospel;* he has shown us another world more clearly than it was before discovered under any former dispensation, and the happiness of that world, the certain recompence of our obedience by faith: we all with open face, as in a glass, behold the glory of God. He has brought it to light, not only set it before us, but offered it to us, by the gospel. Let us value the gospel more than ever, as it is that whereby life and immortality are brought to light, for herein it has the preeminence above all former discoveries; so that it is the gospel of life and immortality, as it discovers them to us, and directs us in the ready way that leads thereto, as well as proposes the most weighty motives to excite our endeavours in seeking after glory, honour, and immortality.

(2.) Consider the example of blessed Paul, *v.* 11, 12. He was appointed to preach the gospel, and particularly appointed to teach the Gentiles. He though it a cause worth suffering for, and why should not Timothy think so too? No man needs to be afraid nor ashamed to suffer for the cause of the gospel: *I am not ashamed,* says Paul, *for I know whom I have believed, and am persuaded that he is able to keep that which I have committed unto him against that day.* Observe, [1.] Good men often suffer many things for the best cause in the world: *For which cause I suffer these things;* that is, "for my preaching, and adhering to the gospel." [2.] They need not be ashamed, the cause will bear them out; but those who oppose it shall be clothed with shame. [3.] Those who trust in Christ know whom they have trusted. The apostle speaks with a holy triumph and exultation, as much as to say, "I stand on firm ground. I know I have lodged the great trust in the hands of the best trustee." *And am persuaded,* etc. What must we commit to Christ? The salvation of our souls, and their preservation to the heavenly kingdom; and what we so commit to him he will keep. There is a day coming when our souls will be enquired after: "Man! Woman! thou hadst a soul committed to thee, what hast thou done with it? To whom it was offered, to God or Satan? How was it employed, in the service of sin or in the service of Christ?" There is a day coming, and it will be a very solemn and awful day, when we must give an account of our stewardship (Lu. 16:2), give an account of our souls: now, if by an active obedient faith we commit it to Jesus Christ, we may be sure he is able to keep it, and it shall be forthcoming to our comfort in that day.

III. He exhorts him to *hold fast the form of sound words, v.* 13. 1. *"Have* a form of sound words" (so it may be read), "a short form, a catechism, an abstract of the first principles of religion, according to the scriptures, a scheme of sound words, a brief summary of the Christian faith, in a proper method, drawn out by thyself from the holy scriptures for thy own use;" or, rather, by the form of sound words I understand the holy scriptures themselves. 2. "Having it, *hold it fast,* remember it, retain it, adhere to it. Adhere to it in opposition to all heresies and false doctrine, which corrupt the Christian faith. Hold that fast *which thou hast heard of me."* Paul was divinely inspired. It is good to adhere to those forms of sound words which we have in the scriptures; for these, we are sure, were divinely inspired. That is sound speech, which cannot be condemned, Tit. 2:8. But how must it be held fast? *In faith and love;* that is, we must assent to it as *a faithful saying,* and bid it welcome as *worthy of all acceptation.* Hold it fast in a good heart, this is the ark of the covenant, in which the tables both of law and gospel are most safely and profitably deposited, Ps. 119:11. Faith and love must go together; it is not enough to believe the sound words, and to give an assent to them, but we must love them, believe their truth and love their goodness, and we must propagate the form of sound words in love; speaking the truth in love, Eph. 4:15. *Faith and love which are in Christ Jesus;* it must be Christian faith and love, faith and love fastening upon Jesus Christ, in and by whom God speaks to us and we to him. Timothy, as a minister, must *hold fast the form of sound words,* for the benefit of others. *Of healing words,* so it may read; there is healing virtue in the word of God; *he sent his word, and healed them.* To the same purport is that (*v.* 14), *That good thing which was committed unto thee keep by the Holy Ghost, which dwelleth in us.* That good thing was the form of sound words, the Christian doctrine, which was committed to Timothy in his baptism and education as he was a Christian, and in his ordination as he was a minister. Observe, (1.) The Christian doctrine is a trust committed to us. It is committed to Christians in general, but to ministers in particular. It is a good thing, of unspeakable value in itself, and which will be of unspeakable advantage to us; it is a good thing indeed, it is an inestimable jewel, for it discovers to us the unsearchable riches of Christ, Eph. 3:8. It is committed to us to be preserved pure and entire, and to be transmitted to those who shall come after us, and we must keep it, and not contribute any thing to the corrupting of its purity, the weakening of its power, or the diminishing of its perfection: *Keep it by the Holy Ghost that dwelleth in us.* Observe, Even those who are ever so well taught cannot keep what they have learned, any more than they could at first learn it, without the assistance of the Holy Spirit. We must not think to keep it by our own strength, but keep it by the Holy Ghost. (2.) The Holy Ghost dwells in all good ministers and Christians; they are his temples, and he enables them to keep the gospel pure and uncorrupt; and yet they must use their best endeavours to keep this good thing, for the assistance and indwelling of the Holy Ghost do not exclude men's endeavours, but they very well consist together.

Verses 15–18

Having (v. 13, 14) exhorted Timothy to hold fast,

I. He mentions the apostasy of many from the doctrine of Christ, v. 15. It seems, in the best and purest ages of the church, there were those that had embraced the Christian faith, and yet afterwards revolted from it, nay, there were many such. He does not say that they had turned away from the doctrine of Christ (though it should seem they had) but they had turned away from him, they had turned their backs upon him, and disowned him in the time of his distress. And should we wonder at it, when many turned their backs on a much better than Paul? I mean the Lord Jesus Christ, Jn. 6:66.

II. He mentions the constancy of one that adhered to him, namely, Onesiphorus: *For he often refreshed me, and was not ashamed of my chain,* v. 16. Observe, 1. What kindness Onesiphorus had shown to Paul: he refreshed him, he often refreshed him with his letters, and counsels, and comforts, and he was not ashamed of his chains. He was not ashamed of him, not withstanding the disgrace he was now under. He was kind to him not once or twice, but often; not only when he was at Ephesus among his own friends, but when Onesiphorus was at Rome; he took care to seek Paul *out very diligently, and found him,* v. 17. Observe, A good man will seek opportunities of doing good, and will not shun any that offer. At Ephesus he had ministered to him, and been very kind to him: Timothy knew it. 2. How Paul returns his kindness, v. 16–18. He that receives a prophet shall have a prophet's reward. He repays him with his prayers: *The Lord give mercy to Onesiphorus.* It is probable that Onesiphorus was now absent from home, and in company with Paul; Paul therefore prays that his house might be kept during his absence. Though the papists will have it that he was now dead; and, from Paul's praying for him that he might find mercy, they conclude the warrantableness of praying for the dead; but who told them that Onesiphorus was dead? And can it be safe to ground a doctrine and practice of such importance on a mere supposition and very great uncertainty?

III. He prays for Onesiphorus himself, as well as for his house: *That he may find mercy in that day,* in the day of death and of judgment, when Christ will account all the good offices done to his poor members as done to himself. Observe, 1. The day of death and judgment is an awful day, and may be emphatically called *that day.* 2. We need desire no more to make us happy than to find mercy of the Lord in that day, when those that have shown no mercy will have judgment without mercy. 3. The best Christians will want mercy in that day; *looking for the mercy of our Lord Jesus Christ,* Jude 21. 4. If you would have mercy then, you must seek for it now of the Lord. 5. It is of and from the Lord that we must have mercy; for, unless the Lord has mercy on us, in vain will be the pity and compassion of men or angels. 6. We are to seek and ask for mercy of the Lord, who is the giver and bestower of it; for the Lord Jesus Christ has satisfied justice, that mercy might be displayed. We are to come to a throne of grace, that we may obtain mercy, and find grace to help in the time of need. 7. The best thing we can seek, either for ourselves or our friends, is that the Lord will grant to them that they may find mercy of the Lord in that day, when they must pass our of time into eternity, and exchange this world for the other, and appear before the judgment-seat of Christ: the Lord then

grant unto all of us that we may find mercy of the Lord in that day.

CHAPTER 2

In this chapter our apostle gives Timothy many exhortations and directions, which may be of great use to other, both ministers and Christians, for whom they were designed as well as for him. I. He encourages him in his work, showing him whence he must fetch help (v. 1). II. He must take care of a succession in the ministry, that the office might not die with him (v. 2). III. He exhorts him to constancy and perseverance in this work, as a soldier and as a husbandman, considering what would be the end of all his sufferings, etc. (v. 3–15). IV. He must shun profane and vain babblings (v. 16–18), for they will be pernicious and mischievous. V. He speaks of the foundation of God, which standeth sure (v. 19–21). VI. What he is to avoid — youthful lusts, and foolish and unlearned questions; and what to do (v. 22 to the end).

Verses 1–7

Here Paul encourages Timothy to constancy and perseverance in his work: *Be strong in the grace that is in Christ Jesus,* v. 1. Observe, Those who have work to do for God must stir up themselves to do it, and strengthen themselves for it. Being strong in the grace that is in Christ Jesus may be understood in opposition to the weakness of grace. Where there is the truth of grace there must be a labouring after the strength of grace. As our trials increase, we have need to grow stronger and stronger in that which is good; our faith stronger, our resolution stronger, our love to God and Christ stronger. Or it may be understood in opposition to our being strong in our own strength: "Be strong, not confiding in thy own sufficiency, but in the grace that is in Jesus Christ." Compare Eph. 6:10, *Be strong in the Lord, and in the power of his might.* When Peter promised rather to die for Christ than to deny him he was strong in his own strength; had he been strong in the grace that is in Christ Jesus, he would have kept his standing better. Observe, 1. There is grace in Christ Jesus; for the law was given by Moses, but grace and truth came by Jesus Christ, Jn. 1:17. There is grace enough in him for all of us. 2. We must be strong in this grace; not in ourselves, in our own strength, or in the grace we have already received, but in the grace that is in him, and that is the way to be strong in grace. 3. As a father exhorts his son, so does Paul exhort Timothy, with great tenderness and affection: *Thou, therefore, my son, be strong,* etc. Observe,

I. Timothy must count upon sufferings, even unto blood, and therefore he must train up others to succeed him in the ministry of the gospel, v. 2. He must instruct others, and train them up for the ministry, and so commit to them the things which he had heard; and he must also ordain them to the ministry, lodge the gospel as a trust in their hands, and so commit to them the things which he had heard. Two things he must have an eye to in ordaining ministers: — Their fidelity or integrity ("Commit them to *faithful men,* who will sincerely aim at the glory of God, the honour of Christ, the welfare of souls, and the advancement of the kingdom of the Redeemer among men"), and also their ministerial ability. They must not only be knowing themselves, but be able to teach others also, and be apt to teach. Here we have, 1. The things Timothy was to commit to others — what he had heard of the apostle among many witnesses; he must not deliver any thing besides, and what Paul delivered to him and others he had received of the Lord Jesus Christ. 2. He was to commit them as a trust, as a sacred deposit, which they were to keep, and to transmit pure and uncorrupt unto others. 3. Those to whom he was to commit these things must be faithful, that is, trusty men, and who were skilful to teach others. 4. Though men were both faithful and able to teach others, yet these things must be committed to them by Timothy, a minister, a man in office; for none must intrude themselves into the ministry, but must have these things committed to them by those already in that office.

II. He must *endure hardness* (v. 3): *Thou therefore,* etc. 1. All Christians, but especially ministers, *are soldiers of Jesus Christ;* they fight under his banner, in his cause, and against his enemies, for he is the captain of our salvation, Heb. 2:10. 2. The soldiers of Jesus Christ must approve themselves good soldiers, faithful to their captain, resolute in his cause, and must not give over fighting till *they are made more than conquerors, through him that loved them,* Rom. 8:37. 3. Those who would approve themselves good soldiers of Jesus Christ must endure hardness; that is, we must expect it and count upon it in this world, must endure and accustom ourselves to it, and bear it patiently when it comes, and not be moved by it from our integrity.

III. He must not entangle himself in the affairs of this world, v. 4. A soldier, when he has enlisted, leaves his calling, and all the business of it, that he may attend his captain's orders. If we have given up ourselves to be Christ's soldiers, we must sit loose to this world; and though there is no remedy, but we must employ ourselves in the affairs of this life while we are here (we have something to do here), we must not entangle ourselves with those affairs, so as by them to be diverted and drawn aside from our duty to God and the great concerns of our Christianity. Those who will war the good warfare must sit loose to this world. *That we may please him who hath chosen us to be soldiers.* Observe, 1. The great care of a soldier should be to please his general; so the great care of a Christian should be to please Christ, to approve ourselves to him. The way to please him who hath chosen us to be soldiers is not to entangle ourselves with the affairs of this life, but to be free from such entanglements as would hinder us in our holy warfare.

IV. He must see to it that in carrying on the spiritual warfare he went by rule, that he observed the laws of war (v. 5): *If a man strive for masteries, yet is he not crowned, except he strive lawfully.* We are striving for mastery, to get the mastery of our lusts and corruptions, to excel in that which is good, but we cannot expect the prize unless we observe the laws. In doing that which is good we must take care that we do it in a right manner, that our good may not be evil spoken of. Observe here, 1. A Christian is to strive for masteries; he must aim at mastering his own lusts and corruptions. 2. Yet he must strive according to the laws given to him; he must strive lawfully. 3. Those who do so shall be crowned at last, after a complete victory is obtained.

V. He must be willing to wait for a recompence (v. 6): *The husbandman that laboureth must be first partaker of the fruits.* Or, as it should be read, *The husbandman labouring first must partake of the fruits,* as appears by comparing it with Jam. 5:7. If we would be partakers of the fruits, we must labour; if we would gain the prize, we must run the race. And, further, we must first labour as the husbandman does, with diligence and patience, before we are partakers of the fruit; we must do the will of God, before we receive the promises, for which reason we have need of patience, Heb. 10:36.

The apostle further commends what he had said to the attention of Timothy, and expresses his desire and hope respecting him: *Consider what I say, and the Lord give thee understanding in all things,* v. 7. Here, 1. Paul exhorts Timothy to consider those thing about which he admonished him. Timothy must be reminded to use his considering faculties about the things of God. Consideration is as necessary to a good conversation as to a sound conversion. 2. He prays for him: *The Lord give thee understanding in all things.* Observe, It is God who gives understanding. The most intelligent man needs more and more of this gift. If he who gave the revelation in the word does not give the understanding in the heart, we are nothing. Together with our prayers for others, that the Lord would give them understanding in all things, we must exhort and stir them up to consider what we say, for consideration is the way to understand, remember, and practise, what we hear or read.

Verses 8–13

I. To encourage Timothy in suffering, the apostle puts him in mind of the resurrection of Christ (v. 8): *Remember that Jesus Christ, of the seed of David, was raised from the dead, according to my gospel.* This is the great proof of his divine mission, and therefore a great confirmation of the truth of the Christian religion; and the consideration of it should make us faithful to our Christian profession, and should particularly encourage us in suffering for it. Let suffering saints remember this. Observe, 1. We are to look to Jesus, the author and finisher of our faith, who, for the joy that was set before him, endured the cross, despised the shame, and has now sat down at the right hand of the throne of God, Heb. 12:2. 2. The incarnation and resurrection of Jesus Christ, heartily believed and rightly considered, will support a Christian under all sufferings in the present life.

II. Another thing to encourage him in suffering was that he had Paul for an example. Observe,

1. How the apostle suffered (v. 9): *Wherein I suffer as an evil-doer;* and let not Timothy the son expect any better treatment than Paul the father. Paul was a man who did good, and yet suffered as an evil-doer: we must not think it strange if those who do well fare ill in this world, and if the best of

men meet with the worst of treatment; but this was his comfort *that the word of God was not bound.* Persecuting powers may silence ministers and restrain them, but they cannot hinder the operation of the word of God upon men's hearts and consciences; that cannot be bound by any human force. This might encourage Timothy not to be afraid of bonds for the testimony of Jesus; for the word of Christ, which ought to be dearer to him than liberty, or life itself, should in the issue suffer nothing by those bonds. Here we see, (1.) The good apostle's treatment in the world: *I suffer trouble;* to this he was called and appointed. (2.) The pretence and colour under which he suffered: *I suffer as an evil-doer;* so the Jews said to Pilate concerning Christ, *If he were not a malefactor, we would not have delivered him up to thee,* Jn. 18:30. (3.) The real and true cause of his suffering trouble as an evil-doer: *Wherein;* that is, in or for the sake of the gospel. The apostle suffered trouble unto bonds, and afterwards he resisted unto blood, striving against sin, Heb. 12:4. Though the preachers of the word are often bound, yet the word is never bound.

2. Why he suffered cheerfully: *I endure all things for the elects' sake, v.* 10. Observe, (1.) Good ministers may and should encourage themselves in the hardest services and the hardest sufferings, with this, that God will certainly bring good to his church, and benefit to his elect, out of them. — *That they may obtain the salvation which is in Christ Jesus.* Next to the salvation of our own souls we should be willing to do and suffer any thing to promote the salvation of the souls of others. (2.) The elect are designed to obtain salvation: *God hath not appointed us to wrath, but to obtain salvation,* 1 Th. 5:9. (3.) This salvation is in Christ Jesus, in him as the fountain, the purchaser, and the giver of it; and it is accompanied with eternal glory: there is no salvation in Christ Jesus without it. (4.) The sufferings of our apostle were for the elects' sake, for their confirmation and encouragement.

III. Another thing with which he encourages Timothy is the prospect of a future state.

1. Those who faithfully adhere to Christ and to his truths and ways, whatever it cost them, will certainly have the advantage of it in another world: *If we be dead with him, we shall live with him, v.* 11. *If we be dead with him, we shall live with him, v.* 11. If, in conformity to Christ, we be dead to this world, its pleasures, profits, and honours, we shall go to live with him in a better world, to be for ever with him. Nay, though we be called out to suffer for him, we shall not lose by that. *Those who suffer for Christ* on earth shall reign with Christ in heaven, *v.* 12. Those who suffered with David in his humiliation were preferred with him in his exaltation: so it will be with those who suffer with the Son of David.

2. It is at our peril if we prove unfaithful to him: *If we deny him, he also will deny us.* If we deny him before man, he will deny us before his Father, Mt. 10:33. And that man must needs be for ever miserable whom Christ disowns at last. This will certainly be the issue, whether we believe it or no (*v.* 13): *If we believe not, yet he abideth faithful; he cannot deny himself.* He is faithful to his threatenings, faithful to his promises; neither one nor the other shall fall to the ground, no, not the least, jot nor tittle of them. If we be faithful to Christ, he will certainly be faithful to us. If we be false to him, he will be faithful to his threatenings: *he cannot deny himself,* cannot recede from any word that he hath spoken, for he is yea, and amen, the faithful witness. Observe, (1.) Our being dead with Christ precedes our living with him, and is connected with it: the one is in order to the other; so our suffering for him is the way to reign with him. *You that have followed me in the regeneration, when the Son of man shall sit on the throne of his glory, you also shall sit upon twelve thrones, judging the twelve tribes of Israel* Mt. 19:28. (2.) This is a faithful saying, and may be depended on and ought to be believed. But, (3.) If we deny him, out of fear, or shame, or for the sake of some temporal advantage, he will deny and disown us, and will not deny himself, but will continue faithful to his word when he threatens as well as when he promises.

Verses 14–18

Having thus encouraged Timothy to suffer, he comes in the next place to direct him in his work.

I. He must make it his business to edify those who were under his charge, *to put them in remembrance* of those things which they did already know; for this is the work of ministers; not to tell people that which they never knew before, but to put them in mind of that which they do know, *charging them that they strive not about words.* Observe, Those that are disposed to strive commonly strive about matters of very small moment. Strifes of words are very destructive to the things of God. That they strive not about words *to no profit.* If people did but consider of what little use most of the controversies in religion are, they would not be so zealous in their strifes of words, *to the subverting of the hearers,* to the drawing of them away from the great things of God, and occasioning unchristian heats and animosities, by which truth is often in danger of being lost. Observe, People are very prone to strive about words, and such strifes never answer any other ends than to shake some and subvert others; they are not only useless, but they are very hurtful, and therefore ministers are to charge the people that they do not strive about words, and they are most likely to be regarded when they charge them before the Lord, that is, in his name and from his word; when they produce their warrant for what they say. — *Study to show thyself approved unto God, v.* 15. Observe, The care of ministers must be to approve themselves unto God, to be accepted of him, and to show that they are so approved unto God. In order thereunto, there must be constant care and industry: *Study to show thyself* such a one, *a workman that needs not be ashamed.* Ministers must be workmen; they have work to do, and they must take pains in it. Workmen that are unskilful, or unfaithful, or lazy, have need to be ashamed; but those who mind their business, and keep to their work, are workmen that need not be ashamed. And what is their work? It is *rightly to divide the word of truth.* Not to invent a new gospel, but rightly to divide the gospel that is committed to their trust. To speak terror to those to whom terror belongs, comfort to whom comfort; to give every one *his portion in due season,* Mt. 24:45. Observe here, 1. The word which ministers preach is the word of truth, for the author of it is the God of truth. 2. It requires great wisdom, study, and care, to divide this word of truth rightly; Timothy must study in order to do this well.

II. He must take heed of that which would be a hindrance to him in his work, *v.* 16. He must take heed of error: *Shun profane and vain babblings.* The heretics, who boasted of their notions and their arguments, thought their performances such as might recommend them; but the apostle calls them *profane and vain babblings:* when once men become fond of those *they will increase unto more ungodliness.* The way of error is down-hill; one absurdity being granted or contended for, a thousand follow: *Their word will eat as doth a canker, or gangrene;* when errors or heresies come into the church, the infecting of one often proves the infecting of many, or the infecting of the same person with one error often proves the infecting of him with many errors. Upon this occasion the apostle mentions some who had lately advanced erroneous doctrines: *Hymeneus and Philetus.* He names these corrupt teachers, by which he sets a brand upon them, to their perpetual infamy, and warns all people against hearkening to them. They have *erred concerning the truth,* or concerning one of the fundamental articles of the Christian religion, which is truth. The resurrection of the dead is one of the great doctrines of Christ. Now see the subtlety of the serpent and the serpent's seed. They did not deny the resurrection (for that had been boldly and avowedly to confront the word of Christ), but they put a corrupt interpretation upon that true doctrine, saying that the resurrection was past already, that what Christ spoke concerning the resurrection was *to be understood mystically* and by way of allegory, that it must be meant of a spiritual resurrection only. It is true, there is a spiritual resurrection, but to infer thence that there will not be a true and real resurrection of the body at the last day is to dash one truth of Christ in pieces against another. By this they *overthrew the faith of some,* took them off from the belief of the resurrection of the dead; and if there be no resurrection of the dead, nor future state, no recompence of our services and sufferings in another world, we are of men the most miserable, 1 Co. 15:19. Whatever takes away the doctrine of a future state overthrows the faith of Christians. The apostle had largely disproved this error (1 Co. 15), and therefore does not here enter into the arguments against it. Observe, 1. The babblings Timothy was to shun were profane and vain; they were empty shadows, and led to profaneness: *For they will increase unto more ungodliness.* 2. Error is very productive, and on that account the more dangerous: it *will eat like a gangrene.* 3. When men err concerning the truth, they always endeavour to have some plausible pretence for it. Hymeneus and Philetus did not deny a resurrection, but pretended it was already past. 4. Error, especially that which affects the foundation, will overthrow the faith of some.

Verses 19–21

Here we see what we may comfort ourselves with, in reference to this, and the little errors and heresies that both infect and infest the church, and do mischief.

I. It may be a great comfort to us that the unbelief of men cannot make the promise of God of no effect. Though the faith of some particular persons be overthrown, yet *the foundation of God standeth sure* (*v.* 19); it is not possible that they should deceive the elect. Or it may be meant of the truth itself, which they impugn. All the attacks which the powers of darkness have made upon the doctrine of Christ cannot shake it; it stands firm, and weathers all the storms which have been raised against it. The prophets and apostles, that is, the doctrines of the Old and New Testament, are still firm; and they have a seal with two mottoes upon it, one on the one side, and the other on the other, as is usual in a broad seal. 1. One expresses our comfort — that *the Lord knows those that are his,* and those that are not; knows them, that is, he owns them, so knows them that he will never lose them. Though the faith of some be overthrown, yet the Lord is said to know the ways of the righteous, Ps. 1:6. None can overthrow the faith of any whom God hath chosen. 2. Another declares our duty — that every one who names the name of Christ must depart from iniquity. Those who would have the comfort of the privilege must make conscience of the duty. If the name of Christ be called upon us, we must depart from iniquity, else he will not own us; he will say in the great day (Mt. 7:23), *Depart from me, I never knew you, you workers of iniquity.* Observe, (1.) Whatever errors are introduced into the church, the foundation of God standeth sure, his purpose can never be defeated. (2.) God hath some in the church who are his and whom he knows to be his. (3.) Professing Christians name the name of Christ, are called by his name, and therefore are bound to depart from iniquity; for Christ *gave himself for us, that he might redeem us from all iniquity,* Tit. 2:14.

II. Another thing that may comfort us is that though there are some whose faith is overthrown, yet there are others who keep their integrity, and hold it fast (*v.* 20): *In a great house there are not only vessels of gold,* etc. The church of Christ is a great house, a well-furnished house: now some of the furniture of this house is of great value, as the plate in a house; some of small value, and put to mean uses, as the vessels of wood and earth; so it is in the church of God. There are some professors of religion that are like the vessels of wood and earth, they are vessels of dishonour. But at the same time all are not vessels of dishonour; there are *vessels of gold and silver,* vessels of honour, *that are sanctified and meet for the Master's use.* When we are discouraged by the badness of some, we must encourage ourselves by the consideration of the goodness of others. Now we should see to it that we be vessels of honour: we must *purge ourselves from these corrupt opinions,* that we may be sanctified for our Master's use. Observe, 1. In the church there are some vessels of honour and some of dishonour; there are some vessels of mercy and other vessels of wrath, Rom. 9:22, 23. Some dishonour the church by their corrupt opinions and wicked lives; and others honour and credit it by their exemplary conversation. 2. A man must purge himself from these before he can be a vessel of honour, or meet for his Master's use. 3. Every vessel must be fit for its Master's use; every one in the church whom God approves must be devoted to his Master's service and meet for his use. 4. Sanctification in the heart is our preparation for every good work. The tree must be made good, and then the fruit will be good.

Verses 22–26

I. Paul here exhorts Timothy to beware of *youthful lusts, v.* 22. Though he was a holy good man, very much mortified to the world, yet Paul thought it necessary to caution him against youthful lusts: "*Flee* them, take all possible care and pains to keep thyself pure from them." The lusts of the flesh are youthful lusts, which young people must carefully watch against, and the best must not be secure. He prescribes an excellent remedy against youthful lusts: *Follow righteousness, faith, charity peace,* etc. Observe, 1. Youthful lusts are very dangerous, for which reason even hopeful young people should be warned of them, for they war against the soul, 1 Pt. 2:11. 2. The exciting of our graces will be the extinguishing of our corruptions; the more we follow that which is good the faster and the further we shall flee from that which is evil. Righteousness, and faith, and love, will be excellent antidotes against youthful lusts. Holy love will cure impure lust. — *Follow peace with those that call on the Lord.* The keeping up of the communion of saints will take us off from all fellowship with unfruitful works of darkness. See the character of Christians: they are such as *call on the Lord Jesus Christ, out of a pure heart.* Observe, Christ is to be prayed to. It is the character of all Christians that they call upon him; but our prayers to God and Christ are not acceptable nor successful except they come out of a pure heart.

II. He cautions him against contention, and, to prevent this (*v.* 23), cautions him against *foolish and unlearned questions,* that tend to no benefit, strifes of words. Those who advanced them, and doted upon them, thought themselves wise and learned; but Paul calls them foolish and unlearned. The mischief of these is that they *gender strifes,* that they breed debates and quarrels among Christians and ministers. It is very remarkable how often, and with what seriousness, the apostle cautions Timothy against disputes in religion, which surely was not without some such design as this, to show that religion consists more in believing and practising what God requires than in subtle disputes. — *The servant of the Lord must not strive, v.* 24. Nothing worse becomes the servant of the Lord Jesus, who himself did not strive nor cry (Mt. 12:19), but was a pattern of meekness, and mildness, and gentleness to all, than strife and contention. The servant of the Lord must be *gentle to all men,* and thereby show that he is himself subject to the commanding power of that holy religion which he is employed in preaching and propagating. — *Apt to teach.* Those are unapt to teach who are apt to strive, and are fierce and froward. Ministers must be patient, bearing with evil, and *in meekness instructing* (*v.* 25) not only those who subject themselves, but those who oppose themselves. Observe, 1. Those who oppose themselves to the truth are to be instructed; for instruction is the scripture-method of dealing with the erroneous, which is more likely to convince them of their errors than fire and faggot: he does not bid us kill their bodies, under pretence of saving their souls. 2. Such as oppose themselves are to be instructed in meekness, for our Lord is meek and lowly (Mt. 11:29), and this agrees well with the character of the servant of the Lord (*v.* 24): *He must not strive, but be gentle to all men, apt to teach, patient.* This is the way to convey truth in its light and power, and to overcome evil with good, Rom. 12:21. 3. That which ministers must have in their eyes, in instructing those who oppose themselves, must be their recovery: *If God, peradventure, will give them repentance to the acknowledging of the truth.* Observe, (1.) Repentance is God's gift. (2.) It is a gift with a *peradventure* in the case of those who oppose themselves; and therefore, though we are not to despair of the grace of God, yet we must take heed of presuming upon it. *To the acknowledging of the truth.* (3.) The same God who gives us the discovery of the truth does by his grace bring us to the acknowledging of it, otherwise our hearts would continue in rebellion against it, for we are to confess with our mouths as well as to believe with our hearts, Rom. 10:9, 10. And thus sinners recover themselves out of the snare of the devil; see here, [1.] The misery of sinners: they are in the *snare of the devil, and are led captive by him at his will, v.* 26. They are slaves to the worst of task-masters; he is the spirit that now worketh in the children of disobedience, Eph. 2:2. They are taken in a snare, and in the worst snare, because it is the devil's; they are as fishes that are taken in n evil net, and as the birds that are caught in the snare. Further, They are under Ham's curse *(a servant of servants shall he be,* Gen. 9:25), they are slaves to him who is but a slave and vassal. [2.] The happiness of those who repent: they recover themselves out of this snare, as a bird out of the snare of the fowler; the snare is broken and they have escaped; and the greater the danger the greater the deliverance. When sinners repent, those who before were led captive by the devil at his will come to be led into the glorious liberty of the children of God, and have their wills melted into the will of the Lord Jesus. The good Lord recover us all out of the snare.

CHAPTER 3

I. The apostle forewarns Timothy what the last days would be, with the reasons thereof (*v.* 1–9). II. Prescribes various remedies against them

(*v.* 10 to the end), particularly his own example ("But thou hast fully known my doctrine," etc.) and the knowledge of the holy scriptures, which are able to make us wise unto salvation, and will be the best antidote against the corruptions of the times we live in. In this chapter Paul tells Timothy how bad others would be, and therefore how good he should be; and this use we should make of the badness of others, thereby to engage us to hold our own integrity so much the firmer.

Verses 1–9

Timothy must not think it strange if there were in the church bad men; for the net of the gospel was to enclose both good fish and bad, Mt. 22:47, 48. Jesus Christ had foretold (Mt. 24) that there would come seducers, and therefore we must not be offended at it, nor think the worse of religion or the church for it. Even in gold ore there will be dross, and a great deal of chaff among the wheat when it lies on the floor.

I. Timothy must know that in the *last days* (*v.* 1), in gospel times, there would *come perilous times.* Though gospel times were times of reformation in many respects, let him know that even in gospel times there would be perilous times; not so much on account of persecution from without as on account of corruptions within. These would be difficult times, wherein it would be difficult for a man to keep a good conscience. He does not say, "Perilous times shall come, for both Jews and Gentiles shall be combined to root out Christianity;" but "perilous times shall come, for such as have *the form of godliness* (*v.* 5) shall be corrupt and wicked, and do a great deal of damage to the church." Two traitors within the garrison may do more hurt to it than two thousand besiegers without. Perilous times shall come, for men shall be wicked. Note, 1. Sin makes the times perilous. When there is a general corruption of manners, and of the tempers of men, this makes the times dangerous to live in; for it is hard to keep our integrity in the midst of general corruption. 2. The coming of perilous times is an evidence of the truth of scripture-predictions; if the event in this respect did not answer to the prophecy, we might be tempted to question the divinity of the Bible. 3. We are all concerned to know this, to believe and consider it, that we may not be surprised when we see the times perilous: *This know also.*

II. Paul tells Timothy what would be the occasion of making these times perilous, or what shall be the marks and signs whereby these times may be known, *v.* 2, etc. 1. Self-love will make the times perilous. Who is there who does not love himself? But this is meant of an irregular sinful self-love. Men love their carnal selves better than their spiritual selves. Men love to gratify their own lusts, and make provision for them, more than to please God and do their duty. Instead of Christian charity, which takes care for the good of others, they will mind themselves only, and prefer their own gratification before the church's edification. 2. Covetousness. Observe, Self-love brings in a long train of sins and mischiefs. When men are lovers of themselves, no good can be expected from them, as all good may be expected from those who love God with all their hearts. When covetousness generally prevails, when every man is for what he can get and for keeping what he has, this makes men dangerous to one another, and obliges every man to stand on his guard against his neighbour. 3. Pride and vain-glory. The times are perilous when men, being proud of themselves, are *boasters and blasphemers,* boasters before men whom they despise and look upon with scorn, and blasphemers of God and of his name. When men do not fear God they will not regard man, and so *vice versâ.* 4. When children are disobedient to their parents, and break through the obligations which they lie under to them both in duty and gratitude, and frequently in interest, having their dependence upon them and their expectation from them, they make the times perilous; for what wickedness will those stick at who will be abusive to their own parents and rebel against them? 5. Unthankfulness and unholiness make the times perilous, and these two commonly go together. What is the reason that men are unholy and without the fear of God, but that they are unthankful for the mercies of God? Ingratitude and impiety go together; for call a man ungrateful, and you can call him by no worse name. Unthankful, and impure, defiled with fleshly lusts, which is an instance of great ingratitude to that God who has provided so well for the support of the body; we abuse his gifts, if we make them the food and fuel of our lusts. 6. The times are perilous when men will not be held by the bonds either of nature or common honesty, when they are *without natural affection,* and *trucebreakers, v.* 3. There is a natural affection due to all. Wher-

ever there is the human nature, there should be humanity towards those of the same nature, but especially between relations. Times are perilous when children are disobedient to their parents (*v.* 2) and when parents are without natural affection to their children, *v.* 3. See what a corruption of nature sin is, how it deprives men even of that which nature has implanted in them for the support of their own kind; for the natural affection of parents to their children is that which contributes very much to the keeping up of mankind upon the earth. And those who will not be bound by natural affection, no marvel that they will not be bound by the most solemn leagues and covenants. *They are truce-breakers,* that make no conscience of the engagements they have laid themselves under. 7. The times are perilous when men are *false accusers* one of another, *diaboloi* — devils one to another, having no regard to the good name of others, or to the religious obligations of an oath, but thinking themselves at liberty to say and do what they please, Ps. 12:4. 8. When men have no government of themselves and their own appetites: not of their own appetites, for they are *incontinent;* not of their own passions, for they are *fierce;* when they have no rule over their own spirits, and therefore are like a city that is broken down, and has no walls; they are soon fired, upon the least provocation. 9. When that which is good and ought to be honoured is generally despised and looked upon with contempt. It is the pride of persecutors that they look with contempt upon good people, though they are more excellent than their neighbours. 10. When men are generally treacherous, wilful, and haughty, the times are perilous (*v.* 4) — when men are *traitors, heady, high-minded.* Our Saviour has foretold that the brother shall betray the brother to death and the father the child (Mt. 10:21), and those are the worst sort of traitors: those who delivered up their Bibles to persecutors were called *traditores,* for they betrayed the trust committed to them. When men are petulant and puffed up, behaving scornfully to all about them, and when this temper generally prevails, then the times are perilous. 11. When men are generally *lovers of pleasure more than lovers of God.* When there are more epicures than true Christians, then the times are bad indeed. God is to be loved above all. That is a carnal mind, and is full of enmity against him, which prefers any thing before him, especially such a sordid thing as carnal pleasure is. 12. When, notwithstanding all this, they *have the form of godliness* (*v.* 5), are called by the Christian name, baptized into the Christian faith, and make a show of religion; but, how plausible soever their form of godliness is, they deny the power of it. When they take upon them the form which should and would bring along with it the power thereof, they will put asunder what God hath joined together: they will assume the form of godliness, to take away their reproach; but they will not submit to the power of it, to take away their sin. Observe here, (1.) Men may be very bad and wicked under a profession of religion; they may be lovers of themselves, etc., yet have a form of godliness. (2.) A form of godliness is a very different thing from the power of it; men may have the one and be wholly destitute of the other; yea, they deny it, at least practically in their lives. (3.) From such good Christians must withdraw themselves.

III. Here Paul warns Timothy to take heed of certain seducers, not only that he might not be drawn away by them himself, but that he might arm those who were under his charge against their seduction. 1. He shows how industrious they were to make proselytes (*v.* 6): they applied themselves to particular persons, visited them in their houses, not daring to appear openly; for those that do evil hate the light, Jn. 3:20. They were not forced into houses, as good Christians often were by persecution; but they of choice crept into houses, to insinuate themselves into the affections and good opinion of people, and so to draw them over to their party. And see what sort of people those were that they gained, and made proselytes of; they were such as were weak, *silly women;* and such as were wicked, *laden with sins, and led away with divers lusts.* A foolish head and a filthy heart make persons, especially women, an easy prey to seducers. 2. He shows how far they were from coming to the knowledge of the truth, though they pretended to be *ever learning, v.* 7. In one sense we must all be ever learning, that is, growing in knowledge, following on to know the Lord, pressing forward; but these were sceptics, giddy and unstable, who were forward to imbibe every new notion, under pretence of advancement in knowledge, but never came to a right understanding of the truth as it is in Jesus. 3. He foretels the certain stop that should be put to their progress (*v.* 8, 9), comparing them to the Egyptian magicians who withstood Moses, and who are here named, *Jannes and Jambres;* though the names are not to be met with in the story of the Old Testament, yet they are found in some old Jewish writers. When Moses came with a divine command to fetch Israel out of Egypt, these magicians opposed him. Thus those heretics *resisted the truth* and like them were men *of corrupt minds,* men who had their understandings perverted, biassed and prejudiced against the truth, and *reprobate concerning the faith,* or very far from being true Christians; *but they shall proceed no further,* or not much further, as some read it. Observe, (1.) Seducers seek for corners, and love obscurity; for they are afraid to appear in public, and therefore creep into houses. Further, They attack those who are the least able to defend themselves, silly and wicked women. (2.) Seducers in all ages are much alike. Their characters are the same — namely, *Men of corrupt minds,* etc.; their conduct is much the same — they resist the truth, as Jannes and Jambres withstood Moses; and they will be alike in their disappointment. (3.) Those who resist the truth are guilty of folly, yea, of egregious folly; for *magna est veritas, et praevalebit — Great is the truth, and shall prevail.* (4.) Though the spirit of error may be let loose for a time, God has it in a chain. Satan can deceive the nations and the churches no further and no longer than God will permit him: *Their folly shall be manifest,* it shall appear that they are imposters, and every man shall abandon them.

Verses 10–17

Here the apostle, to confirm Timothy in that way wherein he walked,

I. Sets before him his own example, which Timothy had been an eye-witness of, having long attended Paul (*v.* 10): *Thou hast fully known my doctrine.* The more fully we know the doctrine of Christ and the apostles, the more closely we shall cleave to it; the reason why many sit loose to it is because they do not fully know it. Christ's apostles had no enemies but those who did not know them, or not know them fully; those who knew them best loved and honoured them the most. Now what is it that Timothy had so fully known in Paul? 1. The doctrine that he preached. Paul kept back nothing from his hearers, but declared to them the whole counsel of God (Acts 20:27), so that if it were not their own fault they might fully know it. Timothy had a great advantage in being trained up under such a tutor, and being apprised of the doctrine he preached. 2. He had fully known his conversation: *Thou hast fully know my doctrine, and manner of life;* his manner of life was of a piece with his doctrine, and did not contradict it. He did not pull down by his living what he built up by his preaching. Those ministers are likely to do good, and leave lasting fruits of their labours, whose manner of life agrees with their doctrine; as, on the contrary, those cannot expect to profit the people at all that preach well and live ill. 3. Timothy fully knew what was the great thing that Paul had in view, both in his preaching and in his conversation: "Thou hast known *my purpose,* what I drive at, how far it is from any worldly, carnal, secular design, and how sincerely I aim at the glory of God and the good of the souls of men." 4. Timothy fully knew Paul's good character, which he might gather from his doctrine, manner of life, and purpose; for he gave proofs of his *faith* (that is, of his integrity and fidelity, or his faith in Christ, his faith concerning another world, by which Paul lived), his *long-suffering* towards the churches to which he preached and over which he presided, his *charity* towards all men, and his *patience.* These were graces that Paul was eminent for, and Timothy knew it. 5. He knew that he had suffered ill for doing well (*v.* 11): "Thou hast fully known the *persecutions and afflictions that came unto me"* (he mentions those only which happened to him while Timothy was with him, *at Antioch, at Iconium, at Lystra);* "and therefore let it be no surprise to thee if thou suffer hard things, it is no more than I have endured before." 6. He knew what care God had taken of him: *Notwithstanding out of them all the Lord delivered me;* as he never failed his cause, so his God never failed him. Thou hast fully known my *afflictions.* When we know the afflictions of good people but in part, they are a temptation to us to decline that cause which they suffer for; when we know only the hardships they undergo for Christ, we may be ready to say, "We will renounce that cause that is likely to cost us so dear in the owning of it;" but when we *fully* know the afflictions, not only how they suffer, but how they are supported and comforted under their sufferings, then, instead of being discouraged, we shall be animated by them, especially considering that we are told before that we must count upon such things (*v.* 12): *All that will live godly in Christ Jesus shall suffer persecution:* not always alike; at that time those who professed the faith of Christ were more exposed to persecution than at other times; but at all times, more or less, those who will live godly in Christ Jesus shall suffer persecution. They must expect to be despised, and that their religion will stand in the way of their preferment; those who will live godly must expect it, especially those who will live godly *in Christ Jesus,* that is, according to the strict rules of the Christian religion, those who will wear the livery and bear the name of the crucified Redeemer. All who will show their religion in their conversation, who will not only be godly, but live godly, let them expect persecution, especially when they are resolute in it. Observe, (1.) The apostle's life was very exemplary for three things: for his *doctrine,* which was according to the will of God; for his *life,* which was agreeable to his doctrine; and for his *persecutions and sufferings.* (2.) Though his life was a life of great usefulness, yet it was a life of great sufferings; and none, I believe, came nearer to their great Master for eminent services and great sufferings than Paul: he suffered almost in every place; the Holy Ghost witnessed that bonds and afflictions did abide him, Acts 20:23. Here he mentions his persecutions and afflictions at *Antioch,* at *Iconium,* at *Lystra,* besides what he suffered elsewhere. (3.) The apostle mentions the Lord's delivering him out of them all, for Timothy's and our encouragement under sufferings. (4.) We have the practice and treatment of true Christians: they live godly in Jesus Christ — this is their practice; and they shall suffer persecution — this is the usage they must expect in this world.

II. He warns Timothy of the fatal end of seducers, as a reason why he should stick closely to the truth as it is in Jesus: *But evil men and seducers shall wax worse and worse,* etc., *v.* 13. Observe, As good men, by the grace of God, grow better and better, so bad men, through the subtlety of Satan and the power of their own corruptions, grow worse and worse. The way of sin is down-hill; for such proceed from bad to worse, *deceiving and being deceived.* Those who deceive others do but deceive themselves; those who draw others into error run themselves into more and more mistakes, and they will find it so at last, to their cost.

III. He directs him to keep close to a good education, and particularly to what he had learned out of the holy scriptures (*v.* 14, 15): *Continue thou in the things which thou hast learned.* Note, It is not enough to learn that which is good, but we must continue in it, and persevere in it unto the end. Then are we Christ's disciples indeed, Jn. 8:31. We should not be any more *children, tossed to and fro, and carried about with every wind of doctrine, by the sleight of men and cunning craftiness, whereby they lie in wait to deceive,* Eph. 4:14. *Be not carried about with divers and strange doctrines; for it is a good thing that the heart be established with grace,* Heb. 13:9. And for this reason we should continue in the things we have learned from the holy scriptures; not that we ought to continue in any errors and mistakes which we may have been led into, in the time of our childhood and youth (for these, upon an impartial enquiry and full conviction, we should forsake); but this makes nothing against our continuing in those things which the holy scriptures plainly assert, and which he that runs may read. If Timothy would adhere to the truth as he had been taught it, this would arm him against the snares and insinuations of seducers. Observe, Timothy must *continue in the things which he had learned and had been assured of.*

1. It is a great happiness to know the certainty of the things wherein we have been instructed (Lu. 1:4); not only to know what the truths are, but to know that they are of undoubted certainty. What we have learned we must labour to be more and more assured of, that, being grounded in the truth, we may be guarded against error, for certainty in religion is of great importance and advantage: *Knowing,* (1.) "That thou hast had good teachers. Consider of *whom thou hast learned them;* not of evil men and seducers, but good men, who had themselves experienced the power of the truths they taught thee, and been ready to suffer for them, and thereby would give the fullest evidence of their belief of these truths." (2.) "Knowing especially the firm foundation upon which thou hast built, namely, that of the scripture (*v.* 15): *That from a child thou hast known the holy scriptures."*

2. Those who would acquaint themselves with the things of God, and be assured of them, must know the holy scriptures, for these are the summary of divine revelation.

3. It is a great happiness to know the holy scriptures from our childhood; and children should betimes get the knowledge of the scriptures. The age of children is the learning age; and those who would get true learning must get it out of the scriptures.

4. The scriptures we are to know are the holy scriptures; they come from the holy God, were delivered by holy men, contain holy precepts, treat of holy things, and were designed to make us holy and to lead us in the way of holiness to happiness; being called the *holy scriptures,* they are by this distinguished from profane writings of all sorts, and from those that only treat morality, and common justice and honesty, but do not meddle with holiness. If we would know the holy scriptures, we must read and search them daily, as the noble Bereans did, Acts 17:11. They must not lie by us neglected, and seldom or never looked into. Now here observe,

(1.) What is the excellency of the scripture. It is *given by inspiration of God* (*v.* 16), and therefore is his word. It is a divine revelation, which we may depend upon as infallibly true. The same Spirit that breathed reason into us breathes revelation among us: *For the prophecy came not in old time by the will of man, but holy men spoke as they were moved or carried forth by the Holy Ghost,* 2 Pt. 1:21. The prophets and apostles did not speak from themselves, but what they received of the Lord that they delivered unto us. That the scripture was given by inspiration of God appears from the majesty of its style, — from the truth, purity, and sublimity, of the doctrines contained in it, — from the harmony of its several parts, — from its power and efficacy on the minds of multitudes that converse with it, — from the accomplishment of many prophecies relating to things beyond all human foresight, — and from the uncontrollable miracles that were wrought in proof of its divine original: *God also bearing them witness, both with signs and wonders, and with divers miracles and gifts of the Holy Ghost, according to his own will,* Heb. 2:4.

(2.) What use it will be of to us. [1.] *It is able to make us wise to salvation;* that is, it is a sure guide in our way to eternal life. Note, Those are wise indeed who are wise to salvation. The scriptures are able to make us truly wise, wise for our souls and another world. "To make thee wise to salvation *through faith."* Observe, The scriptures will make us wise to salvation, if they be mixed with faith, and not otherwise, Heb. 4:2. For, if we do not believe their truth and goodness, they will do us no good. [2.] It is *profitable* to us for all the purposes of the Christian life, *for doctrine, for reproof, for correction, for instruction in righteousness.* It answers all the ends of divine revelation. It instructs us in that which is true, reproves us for that which is amiss, directs us in that which is good. It is of use to all, for we all need to be instructed, corrected, and reproved: it is of special use to ministers, who are to give instruction, correction, and reproof; and whence can they fetch it better than from the scripture? [3.] *That the man of God may be perfect, v.* 17. The Christian, the minister, is the man of God. That which finishes a man of God in this world is the scripture. By it we are *thoroughly furnished for every good work.* There is that in the scripture which suits every case. Whatever duty we have to do, whatever service is required from us, we may find enough in the scriptures to furnish us for it.

(3.) On the whole we here see, [1.] That the scripture has various uses, and answers divers ends and purposes: *It is profitable for doctrine, for reproof, for correction* of all errors in judgment and practice, and *for instruction in righteousness.* [2.] The scripture is a perfect rule of faith and practice, and was designed for the man of God, the minister as well as the Christian who is devoted to God, for it is *profitable for doctrine,* etc. [3.] If we consult the scripture, which was given by inspiration of God, and follow its directions, we shall be made men of God, *perfect, and thoroughly furnished to every good work.* [4.] There is no occasion for the writings of the philosopher, nor for rabbinical fables, nor popish legends, nor unwritten traditions, to make us perfect men of God, since the scripture answers all these ends and purposes. O that we may love our Bibles more, and keep closer to them than ever! and then shall we find the benefit and advantage designed thereby, and shall at last attain the happiness therein promised and assured to us.

CHAPTER 4

In this chapter, I. Paul with great solemnity and earnestness presses Timothy to the diligent and conscientious discharge of his work and office as an evangelist; and the charge given to him all gospel ministers are to take to themselves (v. 1–5). II. The reason of his concern in this case, Why must Timothy now be instant in season, etc., in a particular manner? Because the church was likely to be deprived of the apostle's labours, for his departure was at hand (v. 6–8). III. Divers particular matters, with a hint and caution, about Alexander the coppersmith (v. 9–15). IV. He informs him of what befel him at his first answer; though men forsook him, the Lord stood by him, and this encouraged him to hope for future deliverance (v. 16–18). And then he concludes with salutations and a benediction (v. 19 to the end).

Verses 1–8

Observe, I. How awfully this charge is introduced (v. 1): *I charge thee before God, and the Lord Jesus Christ, who shall judge the quick and the dead at his appearing and his kingdom.* Observe, The best of men have need to be awed into the discharge of their duty. The work of a minister is not an indifferent thing, but absolutely necessary. Woe be to him if he preach not the gospel, 1 Co. 9:16. To induce him to faithfulness, he must consider, 1. That the eye of God and Jesus Christ was upon him: *I charge thee before God and the Lord Jesus Christ;* that is, "as thou tenderest the favour of God and Jesus Christ; as thou wilt approve thyself to God and Jesus Christ, by the obligations both of natural and revealed religion; as thou wilt make due returns to the God who made thee and the Lord Jesus Christ who redeemed thee." 2. He charges him as he will answer it at the great day, reminding him of the judgment to come, which is committed to the Lord Jesus. He shall judge the quick and the dead *at his appearing and his kingdom,* that is, when he appears in his kingdom. It concerns all, both ministers and people, seriously to consider the account that they must shortly give to Jesus Christ of all the trusts reposed in them. Christ shall *judge the quick and the dead,* that is, those that at the last day shall be found alive, and those who shall be raised to life out of the grave. Note, (1.) The Lord Jesus Christ shall judge the quick and the dead. *God hath committed all judgment unto the Son,* and hath appointed him the Judge of quick and dead, Acts 10:42. (2.) He will appear; he will come the second time, and it will be a glorious appearance, as the word *epiphaneia* signifies. (3.) Then his kingdom shall appear in its glory: *At his appearing and kingdom;* for he will then appear in his kingdom, sitting on a throne, to judge the world.

II. What is the matter of the charge, v. 2–5. He is charged,

1. To *preach the word.* This is ministers' business; a dispensation is committed to them. It is not their own notions and fancies that they are to preach, but the pure plain word of God; and they must not corrupt it, but as of sincerity, but as of God, in the sight of God, they speak in Christ, 2 Co. 2:17.

2. To urge what he preached, and to press it with all earnestness upon his hearers: *"Be instant in season and out of season, reprove, rebuke, exhort;* do this work with all fervency of spirit. Call upon those under thy charge to take heed of sin, to do their duty: call upon them to repent, and believe, and live a holy life, and this both in season and out of season. *In season,* when they are at leisure to hear thee, when some special opportunity offers itself of speaking to them with advantage. Nay, do it *out of season,* even when there is not that apparent probability of fastening something upon them, because thou dost not know but the Spirit of God may fasten upon them; for the wind bloweth where it listeth; and *in the morning we must sow our seed, and in the evening not withhold our hand,"* Eccl. 11:6. We must do it in season, that is, let slip no opportunity; and do it out of season, that is, not shift off the duty, under pretence that it is out of season.

3. He must tell people of their faults: *"Reprove them, rebuke them.* Convince wicked people of the evil and danger of their wicked courses. Endeavour, by dealing plainly with them, to bring them to repentance. Rebuke them with gravity and authority, in Christ's name, that they may take thy displeasure against them as an indication of God's displeasure."

4. He must direct, encourage, and quicken those who began well. *"Exhort them* (persuade them to hold on, and endure to the end) and this *with all long-suffering and doctrine."* (1.) He must do it very patiently: *With all long-suffering.* "If thou do not see the effect of thy labours presently, yet do

not therefore give up the cause; be not weary of speaking to them." While God shows to them all long-suffering, let ministers exhort with all long-suffering. (2.) He must do it rationally, not with passion, but *with doctrine,* that is, "In order to the reducing of them to good practices, instil into them good principles. Teach them the truth as it is in Jesus, reduce them to a firm belief of it, and this will be a means both to reclaim them from evil and to bring them to good." Observe, [1.] A minister's work has various parts: he is to *preach the word,* to *reprove, rebuke,* and *exhort.* [2.] He is to be very diligent and careful; he must be *instant in season and out of season;* he must spare no pains nor labour, but must be urgent with them to take care of their souls and their eternal concerns.

5. He must *watch in all things.* "Seek an opportunity of doing them a kindness; let no fair occasion slip, through thy negligence. Watch to thy work; watch against the temptations of Satan, by which thou mayest be diverted from it; watch over the souls of those who are committed to thy charge."

6. He must count upon afflictions, and endure them, make the best of them. *Kakopathēson,* endure *patiently.* "Be not discouraged by the difficulties thou meetest with, but bear them with an evenness of spirit. Inure thyself to hardships."

7. He must remember his office, and discharge its duties: *Do the work of an evangelist.* The office of the evangelist was, as the apostles' deputies, to water the churches that they planted. They were not settled pastors, but for some time resided in, and presided over, the churches that the apostles had planted, till they were settled under a standing ministry. This was Timothy's work.

8. He must fulfil his ministry: *Make full proof of it.* It was a great trust that was reposed in him, and therefore he must answer it, and perform all the parts of his office with diligence and care. Observe, (1.) A minister must expect afflictions in the faithful discharge of his duty. (2.) He must endure them patiently, like a Christian hero. (3.) These must not discourage him in his work, for he must do his work, and fulfil his ministry. (4.) The best way to make full proof of our ministry is to fulfil it, to fill it up in all its parts with proper work.

III. The reasons to enforce the charge.

1. Because errors and heresies were likely to creep into the church, by which the minds of many professing Christians would be corrupted (v. 3, 4): *"For the time will come when they will not endure sound doctrine.* Therefore improve the present time, when they will endure it. Be busy now, for it is seedtime; when the fields are white unto the harvest, put in the sickle, for the present gale of opportunity will be soon over. *They will not endure sound doctrine.* There will be those who will *heap to themselves corrupt teachers, and will turn away their ears from the truth;* and therefore secure as many as thou canst, that, when these storms and tempests do arise, they may be well fixed, and their apostasy may be prevented." People must hear, and ministers must preach, for the time to come, and guard against the mischiefs that are likely to arise hereafter, though they do not yet arise. They will *turn away their ears from the truth;* they will grow weary of the old plain gospel of Christ, and then they will be greedy of fables, and take pleasure in them, and God will give them up to those strong delusions, because they received not the truth in the love of it, 2 Th. 2:11, 12. Observe, (1.) These teachers were of their own heaping up, and not of God's sending; but they chose them, to gratify their lusts, and to please their itching ears. (2.) People do so when they will not endure sound doctrine, that preaching which is searching, plain, and to the purpose; then they will have teachers of their own. (3.) There is a wide difference between the word of God and the word of such teachers; the one is sound doctrine, the word of truth, the other is only fables. (4.) Those that are turned unto fables first turn away their ears from the truth, for they cannot hear and mind both, any more than they can serve two masters. Nay, further, it is said, *They shall be turned unto fables.* God justly suffers those to turn to fables who grow weary of the truth, and gives them up to be led aside from the truth by fables.

2. Because Paul for his part had almost done his work: *Do thou make full proof of thy ministry, for I am now ready to be offered, v. 6.* And,

(1.) "Therefore there will be the more occasion for thee." When labourers are removed out of the vineyard, it is no time for those to loiter that are left behind, but to double their diligence. The fewer hands there are to work the more industrious those hands must be that are at work.

(2.) "I have done the work of my day and generation; do thou in like manner do the work of thy day and generation."

(3.) The comfort and cheerfulness of Paul, in the prospect of his approaching departure, might encourage Timothy to the utmost industry, and diligence, and seriousness in his work. Paul was an old soldier of Jesus Christ, Timothy was but newly enlisted. "Come," says Paul, "I have found our Master kind and the cause good; I can look back upon my warfare with a great deal of pleasure and satisfaction; and therefore be not afraid of the difficulties thou must meet with. The crown of life is as sure to thee as if it were already upon thy head; and therefore endure afflictions, and make full proof of thy ministry." The courage and comfort of dying saints and ministers, and especially dying martyrs, are a great confirmation of the truth of the Christian religion, and a great encouragement to living saints and ministers in their work. Here the apostle looks forward, upon his death approaching: *I am now ready to be offered.* The Holy Ghost witnessed in every city that bonds and afflictions did abide him, Acts 20:23. He was now at Rome, and it is probable that he had particular intimations from the Spirit that there he should seal the truth with his blood; and he looks upon it now as near at hand: I am *already poured out;* so it is in the original, *ēdē spendomai;* that is, I am already a martyr in affection. It alludes to the pouring out of the drink-offerings; for the blood of the martyrs, though it was not a sacrifice of atonement, was a sacrifice of acknowledgment to the honour of the grace of God and his truths. Observe,

[1.] With what pleasure he speaks of dying. He calls it his departure; though it is probable that he foresaw he must die a violent bloody death, yet he calls it his departure, or his release. Death to a good man is his release from the imprisonment of this world and his departure to the enjoyments of another world; he does not cease to be, but is only removed from one world to another.

[2.] With what pleasure he looks back upon the life he had lived (v. 7): *I have fought a good fight, I have finished my course,* etc. He did not fear death, because he had the testimony of his conscience that by the grace of God he had in some measure answered the ends of living. As a Christian, as a minister, he had fought a good fight. He had done the service, gone through the difficulties of his warfare, and had been instrumental in carrying on the glorious victories of the exalted Redeemer over the powers of darkness. His life was a course, and he had now finished it; as his warfare was accomplished, so his race was run. "*I have kept the faith.* I have kept the doctrines of the gospel, and never betrayed any of them." Note, *First,* The life of a Christian, but especially of a minister, is a warfare and a race, sometimes compared to the one in the scripture, and sometimes to the other. *Secondly,* It is a good fight, a good warfare; the cause is good, and the victory is sure, if we continue faithful and courageous. *Thirdly,* We must fight this good fight; we must fight it out, and finish our course; we must not give over till we are made more than conquerors through him who hath loved us, Rom. 8:37. *Fourthly,* It is a great comfort to a dying saint, when he can look back upon his past life and say with our apostle, "*I have fought,* etc. I have kept the faith, the doctrine of faith and the grace of faith." Towards the end of our days to be able to speak in this manner, what comfort, unspeakable comfort, will it afford! Let it then be our constant endeavour, by the grace of God, that we may finish our course with joy, Acts 20:24.

[3.] With what pleasure he looks forward to the life he was to live hereafter (v. 8): *Henceforth there is laid up for me a crown of righteousness,* etc. He had lost for Christ, but he was sure he should not lose by him, Phil. 3:8. Let this encourage Timothy to endure hardness as a good soldier of Jesus Christ that there is a crown of life before us, the glory and joy of which will abundantly recompense all the hardships and toils of our present warfare. Observe, It is called *a crown of righteousness,* because it will be the recompence of our services, which *God is not unrighteous to forget;* and because our holiness and righteousness will there be perfected, and will be our crown. God will give it as *a righteous Judge,* who will let none love by him. And yet this crown of righteousness was not peculiar to Paul, as if it belonged only to apostles and eminent ministers and martyrs, but *to all those also that love his appearing.* Observe, It is the character of all the saints that they love the appearing of Jesus Christ: they loved his first appearing, when he appeared to take away sin by the sacrifice of himself (Heb. 9:26); they love to think of it; they love his second appearing at the great day; love it, and long for it: and, with respect to those who love the appearing of Jesus Christ, he shall appear to their joy; there is a crown of righteousness reserved for them, which shall then be given them, Heb. 9:28. We learn hence, *First,* The Lord is the righteous Judge, for his judgment is according to truth. *Secondly,* The crown of believers is a crown of righteousness, purchased by the righteousness of Christ, and bestowed as the reward of the saints' righteousness. *Thirdly,* This crown, which believers shall wear, is laid up for them; they have it not at present, for here they are but heirs; they have it not in possession, and yet it is sure, for it is laid up for them. *Fourthly,* The righteous Judge will give it to all who love, prepare, and long for his appearing. *Surely I come quickly. Amen, even so come, Lord Jesus.*

Verses 9–15

Here are divers particular matters which Paul mentions to Timothy, now at the closing of the epistle. 1. He bids him hasten to him, if possible (*v.* 9): *So thy diligence to come shortly to me.* For Timothy was an evangelist, one who was not a fixed pastor of any one place, but attended the motions of the apostles, to build upon their foundation. Paul wanted Timothy's company and help; and the reason he gives is because several had left him (*v.* 10); one from an ill principle, namely, *Demas,* who abides under an ill name for it: *Demas hath forsaken me, having loved this present world.* He quitted Paul and his interest, either for fear of suffering (because Paul was now a prisoner, and he was afraid o coming into trouble upon his account) or being called off from his ministry by secular affairs, in which he entangled himself; his first love to Christ and his gospel was forsaken and forgotten, and he fell in love with the world. Note, Love to this present world is often the cause of apostasy from the truths and ways of Jesus Christ. He has gone off, has *departed to Thessalonica,* called thither perhaps by trade, or by some other worldly business. *Crescens* had gone one way and *Titus* another way. *Luke* however remained with Paul (*v.* 11, 12), and was not this enough? Paul did not think it so; he loved the company of his friends. 2. He speaks respectfully concerning *Mark: He is profitable to me for the ministry.* It is supposed that this Mark was he about whom Paul and Barnabas had contended, Acts 15:39. Paul would not take him with him to the work, because he had once flinched and drawn back: but now, says he, *Take Mark, and bring him with thee.* By this it appears that Paul was now reconciled to Mark, and had a better opinion of him than he had had formerly. This teaches us to be of a forgiving spirit; we must not therefore disclaim for ever making use of those that are profitable and useful, though they may have done amiss. 3. Paul orders Timothy to come to him, bids him as he came through Troas to bring with him thence those things which he had left behind him there (*v.* 13), the cloak he had left there, which, it may be, Paul had the more occasion for in a cold prison. It is probable that it was the habit Paul usually wore, a plain dress. Some read it, the *roll of parchment I left at Troas;* others, the *desk* that I left. Paul was guided by divine inspiration, and yet he would have his books with him. Whereas he had exhorted Timothy to give attendance to reading, so he did himself, though he was now ready to be offered. As long as we live, we must be still learning. *But especially the parchments,* which some think were the originals of his epistles; others think they were the skins of which he made his tents, whereby he obtained a livelihood, working with his own hands. 4. He mentions *Alexander,* and the mischief that he had done him, *v.* 14, 15. This is he who is spoken of Acts 19:33. It should seem, he had been a professor of the Christian religion, a forward professor, for he was there particularly maligned by the worshippers of Diana, and yet he did Paul much evil. Paul was in as much danger from false brethren (2 Co. 11:26) as from open enemies. Paul foretels that God would reckon with him. It is a prophetical denunciation of the just judgment of God that would befal him: The Lord *will reward him according to his works.* He cautions Timothy to take heed of him: *"Of whom be thou aware also,* that he do not, under pretence of friendship, betray thee to mischief." It is dangerous having any thing to do with those who would be enemies to such a man as Paul. Observe, (1.) Some who were once Paul's hearers and admirers did not give him reason to remember them with much pleasure; for one forsook him, and another did him much evil, and greatly withstood his words. Yet, (2.) At the same time he mentions some with pleasure; the badness of some did not make him forget the goodness of others; such as *Timothy, Titus, Mark,* and *Luke.* (3.) The apostle has left a brand on the names and memory of two persons; the one is *Demas,* who forsook him, having loved the present world, and the other is *Alexander,* who greatly withstood his words. (4.) God will reward evil-doers, particularly apostates, according to their works. (5.) Of such as are of Alexander's spirit and temper we should beware; for they will do us no good, but all the mischief that is in their power.

Verses 16–22

Here, I. He gives Timothy an account of his own present circumstances.

1. He had lately been called to appear before the emperor, upon his appeal to Caesar; and then *no man stood with him* (*v.* 16), to plead his cause, to bear testimony for him, or so much as to keep him in countenance, but *all men forsook him.* This was strange, that so good a man as Paul should have nobody to own him, even at Rome, where there were many Christians, whose faith was spoken of throughout the world, Rom. 1:8. But men are but men. The Christians at Rome were forward to go and meet him (Acts 28); but when it came to the pinch, and they would be in danger of suffering with him, then they all forsook him. He prays that God would not lay it to their charge, intimating that it was a great fault, and God might justly be angry with them, but he prays God to forgive them. See what a distinction is put between sins of presumption and sins of infirmity. Alexander the coppersmith, who maliciously withstood Paul, he prays against: *The Lord reward him according to his works;* but respecting these Christians, who through weakness shrunk from Paul in time of trial, he says, *The Lord lay it not to their charge.* Observe, (1.) Paul had his trials in his friends' forsaking him in a time of danger as well as in the opposition made by enemies: all forsook him. (2.) It was their sin not to appear for the good apostle, especially at his first answer; but it was a sin of weakness, and therefore the more excusable. Yet, (3.) God might lay it to their charge, but Paul endeavours to prevent it by his earnest prayers: *Let it not be laid to their charge.*

2. *Notwithstanding this God stood by him* (*v.* 17), gave him extraordinary wisdom and courage, to enable him to speak so much the better himself. When he had nobody to keep him in countenance, God made his face to shine. — *That by me the preaching might be fully known,* that is, "God brought me out from that difficulty that I might preach the gospel, which is my business." Nay, it should seem, that he might preach the gospel at that time; for Paul knew how to preach at the bar as well as in the pulpit. *And that all the Gentiles might hear;* the emperor himself and the great men who would never have heard Paul preach if he had not been brought before them. *And I was delivered out of the mouth of the lion,* that is, of Nero (as some think) or some other judge. Some understand it only as a proverbial form of speech, to signify that he was in imminent danger. *And the Lord shall deliver me from every evil work.* See how Paul improved his experiences: *"He that delivered doth deliver, and we trust he will yet deliver,* will deliver me *from every evil work,* from any ill done to me by others. *And shall preserve me to his heavenly kingdom."* And for this he gives glory to God, rejoicing in hope of the glory of God. Observe, (1.) If the Lord stand by us, he will strengthen us, in a time of difficulty and danger, and his presence will more than supply every one's absence. (2.) When the Lord preserves his servants from great and imminent danger, it is for eminent work and service. Paul was preserved that by him the preaching might be fully known, etc. (3.) Former deliverances should encourage future hopes. (4.) There is a heavenly kingdom, to which the Lord will preserve his faithful witnessing or suffering servants. (5.) We ought to give God the glory of all past, present, and future deliverances: *To whom be glory for ever and ever. Amen.*

II. He sends salutations to *Aquila, and Priscilla, and the household of Onesiphorus, v.* 19. He mentions his leaving *Trophimus sick at Miletum* (*v.* 20), by which it appears that though the apostles healed all manner of diseases miraculously, for the confirmation of their doctrine, yet they did not exert that power upon their own friends, lest it should have looked like a collusion.

III. He hastens Timothy to *come to him before winter* (*v.* 21), because he longed to see him, and because in the winter the journey or voyage would be more dangerous.

IV. He sends commendations to him from *Eubulus, Pudens, Linus, Claudia,* and all the *brethren.* One of the heathen writers at this time mentions one Pudens and his wife Claudia, and says the Claudia was a Briton, whence some have gathered that it was this Pudens, and that Claudia here was his wife, and that they were eminent Christians at Rome.

V. He concludes with a prayer, that the *Lord Jesus would be with his spirit.* We need no more to make us happy than to have the Lord Jesus Christ with our spirits; for in him all spiritual blessings are summed up. And it is the best prayer we can put up for our friends, that the Lord Jesus Christ may be with their spirits, to sanctify and save them, and at last to receive them to himself; as Stephen the proto-martyr prayed, *Lord Jesus, receive my spirit,* Acts 7:59. "Lord Jesus, receive that spirit which thou hast been with while it was united to the body; do not now leave it in its separate state." *Grace be with you. Amen.* This was our apostle's token in every epistle; so he wrote. *The grace of our Lord Jesus Christ be with you all. Amen,* 2 Th. 3:17, 18. And if grace be with us here to convert and change us, to make us holy, to keep us humble, and to enable us to persevere to the end, glory will crown us hereafter: *for the Lord is a sun, and a shield; the Lord will give grace and glory, and no good thing will he withhold from those that walk uprightly. O Lord of hosts, blessed is the man that trusteth in thee,* Ps. 84:11, 12. *Now unto the King eternal, immortal, invisible, the only wise God our Saviour, be honour and glory for ever and ever.* Amen.

AN EXPOSITION, WITH PRACTICAL OBSERVATIONS, OF

THE EPISTLE OF ST. PAUL TO TITUS

This Epistle of Paul to Titus is much of the same nature with those to Timothy; both were converts of Paul, and his companions in labours and sufferings; both were in the office of evangelists, whose work was to water the churches planted by the apostles, and to set in order the things that were wanting in them: they were vice-apostles, as it were, *working the work of the Lord, as they did,* and mostly under their direction, though not despotic and arbitrary, but with the concurring exercise of their own prudence and judgment, 1 Co. 16:10, 12. We read much of this Titus, his titles, character, and active usefulness, in many places — he was a Greek, Gal. 2:3. Paul called him *his son* (Tit. 1:4), *his brother* (2 Co. 2:13), *his partner and fellow-helper* (2 Co. 8:23), *one that walked in the same spirit and in the same steps with himself.* He went up with the apostles to the church at Jerusalem (Gal. 2:1), was much conversant at Corinth, for which church he had *an earnest care,* 2 Co. 8:16. Paul's second epistle to them, and probably his first also, was sent by his hand, 2 Co. 8:16–18, 23; 9:2–4; 12:18. He was with the apostle at Rome, and thence went into Dalmatia (2 Tim. 4:10), after which no more occurs of him in the scriptures. So that by them he appears not to have been a fixed bishop; if such he were, and in those times, the church of Corinth, where he most laboured, had the best title to him. In Crete (now called *Candia,* formerly *Hecatompolis,* from the hundred cities that were in it), a large island at the mouth of the Aegean Sea, the gospel had got some footing; and here were Paul and Titus in one of their travels, cultivating this plantation; but the apostle of the Gentiles, having on him the care of all the churches, could not himself tarry long at this place. He therefore left Titus some time there, to carry on the work which had been begun, wherein, probably, meeting with more difficulty than ordinary, Paul wrote this epistle to him; and yet perhaps not so much for his own sake as for the people's, that the endeavours of Titus, strengthened with apostolic advice and authority, might be more significant and effectual among them. He was to see all the cities furnished with good pastors, to reject and keep out the unmeet and unworthy, to teach sound doctrine, and instruct all sorts in their duties, to set forth the free grace of God in man's salvation by Christ, and withal to show the necessity of maintaining good works by those who have believed in God and hope for eternal life from him.

CHAPTER 1

In this chapter we have, I. The preface or introduction to the epistle, showing from and to whom it was written, with the apostle's salutation and prayer for Titus, wishing all blessings to him (*v.* 1–4). II. Entrance into the matter, by signifying the end of Titus's being left at Crete (*v.* 5). III. And how the same should be pursued in reference both to good and bad ministers (*v.* 6 to the end).

Verses 1–4

Here is the preface to the epistle, showing,

I. The writer. *Paul,* a Gentile name taken by the apostle of the Gentiles, Acts 13:9, 46, 47. Ministers will accommodate even smaller matters, so that they may be any furthering of acceptance in their work. When the Jews rejected the gospel, and the Gentiles received it, we read no more of this apostle by his Jewish name *Saul,* but by his Roman one, *Paul. A servant of God, and an apostle of Jesus Christ.* Here he is described by his relation and office: *A servant of God,* not in the general sense only, as a man and a Christian, but especially as a minister, *serving God in the gospel of his Son,* Rom. 1:9. This is a high honour; it is the glory of angels that they are *ministering spirits, and sent forth to minister for those who shall be heirs of salvation,* Heb. 1:14. Paul is described more especially as a chief minister, *an apostle of Jesus Christ;* one who had seen the Lord, and was immediately called and commissioned by him, and had his doctrine from him. Observe, The highest officers in the church are but servants. (Much divinity and devotion are comprehended in the inscriptions of the epistles.) The apostles of Jesus Christ, who were employed to spread and propagate his religion, were therein also the servants of God; they did not set up any thing inconsistent with the truths and duties of natural religion. Christianity, which they preached, was in order to clear and enforce those natural principles, as well as to advance them, and to superadd what was fit and necessary in man's degenerate and revolted state: therefore the apostles of Jesus Christ were the servants of God, *according to the faith of God's elect.* Their doctrine agreed with the faith of all the elect from the beginning of the world, and was for propagating and promoting the same. Observe, There are elect of God (1 Pt. 1:2), and in these the Holy Spirit works precious divine faith, proper to those who are chosen to eternal life (2 Th. 2:13, 14): *God hath from the beginning chosen you to salvation, through sanctification of the Spirit and belief of the truth, whereunto he called you by our gospel.* Faith is the first principle of sanctification. *And the acknowledging of the truth which is after godliness.* The gospel is truth; the great, sure, and saving truth (Col. 1:5), *the word of the truth of the gospel.* Divine faith rests not on fallible reasonings and probable opinions, but on the infallible word, the truth itself, *which is after godliness,* of a godly nature and tendency, pure, and purifying the heart of the believer. By this mark judge of doctrines and of spirits — whether they be of God or not; what is impure, and prejudicial to true piety and practical religion, cannot be of divine original. All gospel truth is after godliness, teaching and nourishing reverence and fear of God, and obedience to him; it is truth not only to be known, but acknowledged; it must be held forth in word and practice, Phil. 2:15, 16. *With the heart man believes to righteousness, and with the mouth confession is made unto salvation,* Rom. 10:10. Such as retain the truth in unrighteousness neither know nor believe as they ought. To bring to this knowledge and faith, and to the acknowledging and professing of the truth which is after godliness, is the great end of the gospel ministry, even of the highest degree and order in it; their teachings should have this chief aim, to beget faith and confirm in it. *In* (or*for) hope of eternal life, v.* 2. This is the further intent of the gospel, to beget hope as well as faith; to take off the mind and heart from the world, and to raise them to heaven and the things above. The faith and godliness of Christians lead to eternal life, and give hope and well-grounded expectation of it; for *God, that cannot lie, hath promised it.* It is the honour of God that he cannot lie or deceive: and this is the comfort of believers, whose treasure is laid up in his faithful promises. But how is he said to promise before the world began? *Answer,* By promise some understand his decree: he purposed it in his eternal counsels, which were as it were his promise in *embryo:* or rather, say some, *pro chronōn aiōniōn* is *before ancient times,* or many years ago, referring to the promise darkly delivered, Gen. 3:15. Here is the stability and antiquity of the promise of eternal life to the saints. God, who cannot lie, hath promised before the world began, that is, many ages since. How excellent then is the gospel, which was the matter of divine promise so early! how much to be esteemed by us, and what thanks due for our privilege beyond those before us! *Blessed are your eyes, for they see,* etc. No wonder if the contempt of it be punished severely, since he has not only promised it of old, *but* (*v.* 3) *has in due times manifested his word through preaching;* that is, made that his promise, so darkly delivered of old, *in due time* (the proper season before appointed) more plain *by preaching;* that which some called *foolishness of preaching* has been thus honoured. *Faith comes by hearing, and hearing by the word of God,* by the word preached. *Which is committed unto me.* The ministry is a trust; none taketh this honour, but he who is thereunto appointed; and whoso is appointed and called must preach the word. 1 Co. 9:16, *Woe is unto me if I preach not the gospel.* Nonpreaching ministers are none of the apostle's successors. *According to the commandment of God our Saviour.* Preaching is a work appointed by a God as a Saviour. See a proof here of Christ's deity, for by him was the gospel committed to Paul when he was converted (Acts 9:15, 17, and *ch.* 22:10, 14, 15), and again when Christ appeared to him, *v.* 17–21. He therefore is this Saviour; not but that the whole Timothy concur therein: the Father saves by the Son through the Spirit, and all concur in sending ministers. Let none rest therefore in men's calling, without God's; he furnishes, inclines, authorizes, and gives opportunity for the work.

II. The person written to, who is described, 1. By his name, *Titus,* a Gentile Greek, yet called both to the faith and ministry. Observe, the grace of God is free and powerful. What worthiness or preparation was there in one of heathen stock and education? 2. By his spiritual relation to the apostle: *My own* (or *my genuine) son,* not by natural generation, but by supernatural regeneration. *I have begotten you through the gospel,* said he to the Corinthians, 1 Co. 4:15. Ministers are spiritual fathers to those whom they are the means of converting, and will tenderly affect and care for them, and must be answerably regarded by them. *"My own son after the common faith,* that faith which is common to all the regenerate, and which thou hast in truth, and expressest to the life." This might be said to distinguish Titus from hypocrites and false teachers, and to recommend him to the regard of the Cretans, as being among them a lively image of the apostle himself, in faith, and life, and heavenly doctrine. To this Titus, deservedly so dear to the apostle, is,

III. The salutation and prayer, wishing all blessings to him: *Grace, mercy, and peace, from God the Father, and the Lord Jesus Christ our Saviour.* Here are, 1. The blessings wished: *Grace, mercy, and peace. Grace,* the free favour of God, and acceptance with him. *Mercy,* the fruits of that favour, in pardon of sins, and freedom from all miseries by it, both here and hereafter. And *peace,* the positive effect and fruit of mercy. Peace with God through Christ who is our peace, and with the creatures and ourselves; outward and inward peace, comprehending all good whatsoever, that makes for our happiness in time and to eternity. Observe, Grace is the fountain of all blessings. Mercy, and peace, and all good, spring out of this. Get into God's favour, and all must be well; for, 2. These are the persons from whom blessings are wished: *From God the Father,* the fountain of all good. Every blessing, every comfort, comes to us from God as a Father; he is the Father of all by creation, but of the good by adoption and regeneration. *And the Lord Jesus Christ our Saviour,* as the way and means of procurement and conveyance. All is from the Father by the Son, who is Lord by nature, heir of all things, and our Lord, Redeemer, and head, ordering and ruling his members. All are put under him; we hold of him, as *in capite,* and owe subjection and obedience to him, who is also Jesus and Christ, the anointed Saviour, and especially our Saviour, who believe in him, delivering us from sin and hell, and bringing us to heaven and happiness.

Thus far is the preface to the epistle; then follows the entrance into the matter, by signifying the end of Titus's being left in Crete.

Verse 5

Here is the end expressed,

I. More generally: *For this cause left I thee in Crete, that thou shouldst set in order the things that are wanting.* This was the business of evangelists (in which office Titus was), to water where the apostles had planted (1 Co. 3:6), furthering and finishing what they had begun; so much *epidiorthoun* imports, *to order after another.* Titus was to go on in settling what the apostle himself had not time for, in his short stay there. Observe, 1. The apostle's great diligence in the gospel; when he had set things on foot in one place, he hastened away to another. He was debtor to the Greeks and to the barbarians, and laboured to spread the gospel as far as he could among them all. And, 2. His faithfulness and prudence. He neglected not the places that he went from; but left some to cultivate the young plantation, and carry on what was begun. 3. His humility; he disdained not to be helped in his work, and that by such as were not of so high a rank in the ministry, nor of so great gifts and furniture, as himself; so that the gospel might be furthered and the good of souls promoted, he willingly used the hands of others in it: a fit example for exciting zeal and industry, and engaging to faithfulness and care of the flock, and present or absent, living and dying, for ministers, as much as in them lies, to provide for the spiritual edification and comfort of their people. We may here also observe, 4. That Titus, though inferior to an apostle, was yet above the ordinary fixed pastors or bishops, who were to tend particular churches as their peculiar stated charge; but Titus was in a higher sphere, to ordain such ordinary pastors where wanting, and settle things in their first state and form, and then to pass to other places for like service as there might be need. Titus was not only a minister of the catholic church (as all others also are), but a catholic minister. Others had power habitual, and in *actu primo,* to minister any where, upon call and opportunity; but evangelists, such as Titus was, had power in *actu secundo et exercito,* and could exercise their ministry wherever they came, and claim maintenance of the churches. They were every where actually in their diocese or province, and had a right to direct and preside among the ordinary pastors and ministers. Where an apostle could act as an apostle an evangelist could act as an evangelist; for *they worked the work of the Lord as they did* (1 Co. 16:10), in a like unfixed and itinerant manner. Here at Crete Titus was but occasionally, and for a short time; Paul willed him to despatch the business he was left for, and come to him at Nicopolis, where he purposed to winter; after this he was sent to Corinth, was with the apostle at Rome, and was sent thence into Dalmatia, which is the last we read of him in scripture, so that from scripture no fixed episcopacy in him does appear; he left Crete, and we find not that he returned thither any more. But what power had either Paul or Titus here? Was not what they did an encroachment on the rights of civil rulers? In no sort; they came not to meddle with the civil rights of any. Lu. 12:14, *Who made me a judge or a divider over you?* Their work was spiritual, to be carried on by conviction and persuasion, no way interfering with, or prejudicing, or weakening, the power of magistrates, but rather securing and strengthening it; the *things wanting* were not such as civil magistrates are the fountains or authors of, but divine and spiritual ordinances, and appointments for spiritual ends, derived from Christ the king and head of the church: for settling these was Titus left. And observe, No easy thing is it to raise churches, and bring them to perfection. Paul had himself been here labouring, and yet were there things wanting; materials are out of square, need much hewing and fitting, to bring them into right form, and, when they are set therein, to hold and keep them so. The best are apt to decay and to go out of order. Ministers are to help against this, to get what is amiss rectified, and what is wanting supplied. This in general was Titus's work in Crete: and,

II. In special: *To ordain elders in every city,* that is, ministers, who were mostly out of the elder and most understanding and experienced Christians; or, if younger in years, yet such as were grave and solid in their deportment and manners. These were to be set where there was any fit number of Christians, as in larger towns and cities was usually the case; though villages, too, might have them where there were Christians enough for it. These presbyters or elders were to have the ordinary and stated care and charge of the churches; to feed and govern them, and perform all pastoral work and duty in and towards them. The word is used sometimes more largely for any who bear ecclesiastical function in the church, and so the apostles were *presbyters* or *elders* (1 Pt. 5:1); but here it is meant of ordinary fixed pastors, who *laboured in the word and doctrine,* and were *over the churches in the Lord;* such as are described here throughout the chapter. This word *presbyter* some use in the same sense as *sacerdos,* and translate it *priest,* a term not given to gospel ministers, unless in a figurative or allusive way, as all God's people are said to be made *kings and priests unto God* (*hiereis,* not *presbytterous*), to offer up spiritual sacrifices of prayers, praises, and alms. But properly we have no priest under the gospel, except Christ alone, *the high priest of our profession* (Heb. 3:1), who offered up himself a sacrifice to God for us, and ever lives, in virtue thereof, to make intercession in our behalf. Presbyters here therefore are not proper priests, to offer sacrifices, either typical or real; but only gospel ministers, to dispense Christ's ordinances, and to *feed the church of God, over which the Holy Ghost has made them overseers.* Observe, 1. A church without a fixed and standing ministry in it is imperfect and wanting. 2. Where a fit number of believers is, presbyters or elders must be set; their continuance in churches is as necessary as their first appointment, *for perfecting the saints, and edifying the body of Christ, till all come to a perfect man in Christ,* till the whole number of God's chosen be called and united to Christ in one body, and brought to their full stature and strength, and that measure of grace that is proper and designed for them, Eph. 4:12, 13. This is work that must and will be doing to the world's end, to which therefore the necessary and appointed means for it must last. What praise is due to God for such an institution! What thankfulness from those that enjoy the benefits of it! What pity and prayer for such as want it! *Pray the Lord of the harvest that he will send forth labourers into his harvest. Faith comes by hearing,* and is preserved, maintained, and made fruitful, through it also. Ignorance and corruption, decays of good and increase of all evil, come by want of a teaching and quickening ministry. On such accounts therefore was *Titus left in Crete, to set in order the things that were wanting, and to ordain elders in every city;* but this he was to do, not *ad libitum,* or according to his own will or fancy, but according to apostolic direction.

III. The rule of his proceeding: *As I had appointed thee,* probably when he was going from him, and in the presence and hearing of others, to which he may now refer, not so much for Titus's own sake as for the people's, that they might the more readily yield obedience to Titus, knowing and observing that in what he did he was warranted and supported by apostolic injunction and authority. As under the law all things were to be made according to the pattern shown to Moses in the mount; so under the gospel all must be ordered and managed according to the direction of Christ, and of his chief ministers, who were infallibly guided by him. Human traditions and inventions may not be brought into the church of God. Prudent disposals for carrying on the ends of Christ's appointments, according to the general rules of the word, there may, yea, must be; but none may alter any thing in the substance of the faith or worship, or order and discipline, of the churches. If an evangelist might not do any thing but by appointment, much less may others. The church is the house of God, and to him it belongs to appoint the officers and orders of it, as he pleases: the *as* here refers to the qualifications and character of the elders that he was to ordain: "*Ordain elders in every city, as I appointed thee,* such as I then described and shall now again more particularly point out to thee," which he does from the sixth verse to the ninth inclusive.

Verses 6–16

The apostle here gives Titus directions about ordination, showing whom he should ordain, and whom not.

I. Of those whom he should ordain. He points out their qualifications and virtues; such as respect their life and manners, and such as relate to their doctrine: the former in the sixth, seventh, and eighth verses, and the latter in the ninth.

1. Their qualifications respecting their life and manners are,

(1.) More general: *If any be blameless;* not absolutely without fault, so none are, for *there is none that liveth and sinneth not;* nor altogether unblamed, this is rare and difficult. Christ himself and his apostles were blamed, though not worthy of it. In Christ thee was certainly nothing blamable; and his apostles were not such as their enemies charged them to be. But the meaning is, He must be one who lies not under an ill character; but rather must have good report, even *from those that are without;* not grossly or scandalously guilty, so as would bring reproach upon the holy function; he must not be such a one.

(2.) More particularly.

[1.] There is his relative character. In his own person, he must be of conjugal chastity: *The husband of one wife.* The church of Rome says the husband of *no* wife, but from the beginning it was not so; marriage is an ordinance from which no profession nor calling is a bar. 1 Co. 9:5, *Have I not power,* says Paul, *to lead about a sister, a wife, as well as other apostles? Forbidding to marry* is one of the erroneous doctrines of the antichristian church, 1 Tim. 4:3. Not that ministers *must* be married; this is not meant; but *the husband of one wife* may be either not having divorced his wife and married another (as was too common among those of the circumcision, even for slight causes), or *the husband of one wife,* that is, at one and the same time, no bigamist; not that he might not be married to more than one wife successively, but, being married, he must have but one wife at once, not two or more, according to the too common sinful practice of those times, by a perverse imitation of the patriarchs, from which evil custom our Lord taught a reformation. Polygamy is scandalous in any, as also having a harlot or concubine with his lawful wife; such sin, or any wanton libidinous demeanour, must be very remote from such as would enter into so sacred a function. And, as to his children, *having faithful children,* obedient and good, brought up in the true Christian faith, and living according to it, at least as far as the endeavours of the parents can avail. It is for the honour of ministers that their children be faithful and pious, and such as become their religion. *Not accused of riot, nor unruly,* not justly so accused, as having given ground and occasion for it, for otherwise the most innocent may be falsely so charged; they must look to it therefore that there be no colour for such censure. Children so faithful, and obedient, and temperate, will be a good sign of faithfulness and diligence in the parent who has so educated and instructed them; and, from his faithfulness in the less, there may be encouragement to commit to him the greater, the rule and government of the church of God. The ground of this qualification is shown from the nature of his office (*v.* 7): *For a bishop must be blameless, as the steward of God.* Those before termed presbyters, or elders, are in this verse styled bishops; and such they were, having no ordinary fixed and standing officers above them. Titus's business here, it is plain, was but occasional, and his stay short, as was before noted. Having ordained elders, and settled in their due form, he went and left all (for aught that appears in scripture) in the hands of those elders whom the apostle here calls bishops and stewards of God. We read not in the sacred writings of any successor he had in Crete; but to those elders or bishops was committed the full charge of feeding, ruling, and watching over their flock; they wanted not any powers necessary for carrying on religion and the ministry of it among them, and committing it down to succeeding ages. Now, being such bishops and overseers of the flock, who were to be examples to them, and God's stewards to take care of the affairs of his house, to provide for and dispense to them things needful, there is great reason that their character should be clear and good, that they should be blameless. How else could it be but that religion must suffer, their work be hindered, and souls prejudiced and endangered, whom they were set to save? These are the relative qualifications with the ground of them.

[2.] The more absolute ones are expressed, *First,* Negatively, showing what an elder or bishop must not be: *Not self-willed.* The prohibition is of large extent, excluding self-

opinion, or overweening conceit of parts and abilities, and abounding in one's own sense, — self-love, and self-seeking, making self the centre of all, — also self-confidence and trust, and self-pleasing, little regarding or setting by others, — being proud, stubborn, froward, inflexible, set on one's own will and way, or churlish as Nabal: such is the sense expositors have affixed to the term. A great honour it is to a minister not to be thus affected, to be ready to ask and to take advice, to be ready to defer as much as reasonably may be to the mind and will of others, becoming all things to all men, that they may gain some. *Not soon angry, mē orgilon, not one of a hasty angry temper,* soon and easily provoked and inflamed. How unfit are those to govern a church who cannot govern themselves, or their own turbulent and unruly passions! The minister must be meek and gentle, and patient towards all men. *Not given to wine;* thee is no greater reproach on a minister than to be a wine-bibber, one who loves it, and gives himself undue liberty this way who *continues at the wine or strong drink till it inflames him.* Seasonable and moderate use of this, as of the other good creatures of God, is not unlawful. *Use a little wine for thy stomach's sake, and thine often infirmities,* said Paul to Timothy, 1 Tim. 5:23. But excess therein is shameful in all, especially in a minister. *Wine takes away the heart,* turns the man into a brute: here most proper is that exhortation of the apostle (Eph. 5:18), *Be not drunk with wine, wherein is excess; but be filled with the Spirit.* Here is no exceeding, but in the former too easily there may: take heed therefore of going too near the brink. *No striker,* in any quarrelsome or contentious manner, not injuriously nor out of revenge, with cruelty or unnecessary roughness. *Not given to filthy lucre;* not greedy of it (as 1 Tim. 3:3), whereby is not meant refusing a just return for their labours, in order to their necessary support and comfort; but not making gain their first or chief end, not entering into the ministry nor managing it with base worldly views. Nothing is more unbecoming a minister, who is to direct his own and others' eyes to another world, than to be too intent upon this. It is called *filthy lucre,* from its defiling the soul that inordinately affects or greedily looks after it, as if it were any otherwise desirable than for the good and lawful uses of it. Thus of the negative part of the bishop's character. But, *Secondly,* Positively: he must be (*v.* 8) *a lover of hospitality,* as an evidence that he is not given to filthy lucre, but is willing to use what he has to the best purposes, not laying up for himself, so as to hinder charitable laying out for the good of others; *receiving and entertaining strangers* (as the word imports), a great and necessary office of love, especially in those times of affliction and distress, when Christians were made to fly and wander for safety from persecution and enemies, or in travelling to and fro where there were not such public houses for reception as in our days, nor, it may be, had many poor saints sufficiency of their own for such uses — then to receive and entertain them was good and pleasing to God. And such a spirit and practice, according to ability and occasion, are very becoming such as should be examples of good works. *A lover of good men,* or of *good things;* ministers should be exemplary in both; this will evince their open piety, and likeness to God and their Master Jesus Christ: *Do good to all, but especially to those of the household of faith,* those who are the excellent of the earth, in whom should be all our delight. *Sober,* or *prudent,* as the word signifies; a needful grace in a minister both for his ministerial and personal carriage and management. He should be a wise steward, and one who is not rash, or foolish, or heady; but who can govern well his passions and affections. *Just* in things belonging to civil life, and moral righteousness, and equity in dealings, giving to all their due. *Holy,* in what concerns religion; one who reverences and worships God, and is of a spiritual and heavenly conversation. *Temperate;* it comes from a word that signifies *strength,* and denotes one who has power over his appetite and affections, or, in things lawful, can, for good ends, restrain and hold them in. Nothing is more becoming a minister than such things as these, *sobriety, temperance, justice,* and *holiness* — sober in respect of himself, just and righteous towards all men, and holy towards God. And thus of the qualifications respecting the minister's life and manners, relative and absolute, negative and positive, what he must not, and what he must, be and do.

2. As to doctrine,

(1.) Here is his duty: *Holding fast the faithful word, as he has been taught,* keeping close to the doctrine of Christ, *the word of his grace,* adhering thereto according to the instructions he has received — holding it fast in his own belief and profession, and in teaching others. Observe, [1.] The word of God, revealed in the scripture, is a true and infallible word; the word of him that *is the amen, the true and faithful witness,* and whose Spirit guided the penmen of it. *Holy men of God spoke as they were moved by the Holy Ghost.* [2.] Ministers must hold fast, and hold forth, the faithful word in their teaching and life. *I have kept the faith,* was Paul's comfort (2 Tim. 4:7), and *not shunned to declare the whole counsel of God;* there was his faithfulness, Acts 20:27.

(2.) Here is the end: *That he may be able, by sound doctrine, both to exhort, and to convince the gainsayers,* to persuade and draw others to the true faith, and to convince the contrary-minded. How should he do this if he himself were uncertain or unsteady, not holding fast that *faithful word and sound doctrine* which should be the matter of this teaching, and the means and ground of convincing those that oppose the truth? We see here summarily the great work of the ministry — to exhort those who are willing to know and do their duty, and to convince those that contradict, both which are to be done by *sound doctrine,* that is, in a rational instructive way, by scripture-arguments and testimonies, which are the infallible words of truth, what all may and should rest and be satisfied in and determined by. And thus of the qualifications of the elders whom Titus was to ordain.

II. The apostle's directory shows whom he should reject or avoid — men of another character, the mention of whom is brought in as a reason of the care he had recommended about the qualifications of ministers, why they should be such, and only such, as he had described. The reasons he takes both from bad teachers and hearers among them, *v.* 10, to the end.

1. From bad teachers. (1.) Those false teachers are described. They were *unruly,* headstrong and ambitious of power, refractory and untractable (as some render it), and such as would not bear nor submit themselves to the discipline and necessary order in the church, impatient of good government and of sound doctrine. *And vain talkers and deceivers,* conceiting themselves to be wise, but really foolish, and thence great talkers, falling into errors and mistakes, and fond of them, and studious and industrious to draw others into the same. Many such there were, *especially those of the circumcision,* converts as they pretended, at least, from the Jews, who yet were for mingling Judaism and Christianity together, and so making a corrupt medley. These were the false teachers. (2.) Here is the apostle's direction how to deal with them (*v.* 11): *Their mouths must be stopped;* not by outward force (Titus had no such power, nor was this the gospel method), but by confutation and conviction, showing them their error, *not giving place to them even for an hour.* In case of obstinacy indeed, breaking the peace of the church, and corrupting other churches, censures are to have place, the last means for recovering the faulty and preventing the hurt of many. Observe, Faithful ministers must oppose seducers in good time, *that, their folly being made manifest, they may proceed no further.* (3.) The reasons are given for this. [1.] From the pernicious effects of their errors: *They subvert whole houses, teaching things which they ought not* (namely, the necessity of circumcision, and of keeping the law of Moses, etc.), so subverting the gospel and the souls of men; not some few only, but whole families. It was unjustly charged on the apostles *that they turned the world upside down;* but justly on these false teachers that they drew many from the true faith to their ruin: the mouths of such should be stopped, especially considering, [2.] Their base end in what they do: *For filthy lucre's sake,* serving a worldly interest under pretence of religion. *Love of money is the root of all evil.* Most fit it is that such should be resisted, confuted, and put to shame, by sound doctrine, and reasons from the scriptures. Thus of the grounds respecting the bad teachers.

II. In reference to their people or hearers, who are described from ancient testimony given of them.

1. Here is the witness (*v.* 12): *One of themselves, even a prophet of their own,* that is, one of the Cretans, not of the Jews, Epimenides a Greek poet, likely to know and unlikely to slander them. *A prophet of their own;* so their poets were accounted, writers of divine oracles; these often witnessed against the vices of the people: Aratus, Epimenides, and others among the Greeks; Horace, Juvenal, and Persius, among the Latins: much smartness did they use against divers vices.

2. Here is the matter of his testimony: *Krētes aei pseustai, kaka thēria, gasteres argai — The Cretans are always liars, evil beasts, slow bellies.* Even to a proverb, they were infamous for falsehood and lying; *kretizein,* to play the *Cretan,* or to lie, is the same; and they were compared to evil beasts for their sly hurtfulness and savage nature, and called slow bellies for their laziness and sensuality, more inclined to eat than to work and live by some honest employment. Observe, Such scandalous vices as were the reproach of heathens should be far from Christians: falsehood and lying, invidious craft and cruelty, all beastly and sensual practices, with idleness and sloth, are sins condemned by the light of nature. For these were the Cretans taxed by their own poets.

3. Here is the verification of this by the apostle himself: *v.* 13. This witness is true, The apostle saw too much ground for that character. The temper of some nations is more inclined to some vices than others. The Cretans were too generally such as here described, slothful and ill-natured, false and perfidious, as the apostle himself vouches. And thence,

4. He instructs Titus how to deal with them: *Wherefore rebuke them sharply.* When Paul wrote to Timothy he bade him instruct with meekness; but now, when he writes to Titus, he bids him rebuke them sharply. The reason of the difference may be taken from the different temper of Timothy and Titus; the former might have more keenness in his disposition, and be apt to be warm in reproving, whom therefore he bids to rebuke with meekness; and the latter might be one of more mildness, therefore he quickens him, and bids him rebuke sharply. Or rather it was from the difference of the case and people: Timothy had a more polite people to deal with, and therefore he must rebuke them with meekness; and Titus had to do with those who were more rough and uncultivated, and therefore he must rebuke them sharply; their corruptions were many and gross, and committed without shame or modesty, and therefore should be dealt with accordingly. There must in reproving be a distinguishing between sins and sins; some are more gross and heinous in their nature, or in the manner of their commission, with openness and boldness, to the greater dishonour of God and danger and hurt to men: and between sinners and sinners; some are of a more tender and tractable temper, apter to be wrought on by gentleness, and to be sunk and discouraged by too much roughness and severity; others are more hardy and stubborn, and need more cutting language to beget in them remorse and shame. Wisdom therefore is requisite to temper and manage reproofs aright, as may be most likely to do good. Jude 22, 23, *Of some have compassion, making a difference; and others save with fear, pulling them out of the fire.* The Cretans' sins and corruptions were many, great, and habitual; therefore they must be rebuked sharply. But that such direction might not be misconstrued,

5. Here is the end of it noted: *That they may be sound in the faith* (*v.* 14), *not giving heed to Jewish fables, and commandments of men, that turn from the truth;* that is, that they may be and show themselves truly and effectually changed from such evil tempers and manners as those Cretans in their natural state lived in, and may not adhere to nor regard (as some who were converted might be too ready to do) the Jewish traditions and the superstitions of the Pharisees, which would be apt to make them disrelish the gospel, and the sound and wholesome truths of it. Observe, (1.) The sharpest reproofs must aim at the good of the reproved: they must not be of malice, nor hatred, nor ill-will, but of love; not to gratify pride, passion, nor any evil affection in the reprover, but to reclaim and reform the erroneous and the guilty. (2.) Soundness in the faith is most desirable and necessary. This is the soul's health and vigour, pleasing to God, comfortable to the Christian, and what makes ready to be cheerful and constant in duty. (3.) A special means to soundness in the faith is to turn away the ear from fables and the fancies of men (1 Tim. 1:4): *Neither give heed to fables and endless genealogies, that minister questions rather than godly edifying, which is in faith.* So *ch.* 4:7, *Refuse profane and old wives' fables, and exercise thyself rather to godliness.* Fancies and devices of men in the worship of God are contrary to truth and piety. Jewish ceremonies and rites, that were at first divine appointments, the substance having come and their season and use being over, are now but unwarranted commands of men, which not only stand not with, but turn from, the truth, the pure gospel truth and spiritual worship, set up by Christ instead of that bodily service under the law. (4.) A fearful judgment it is to be turned away from the truth, to leave Christ for Moses, the spiritual worship of the gospel for the carnal ordinances of the law, or the true divine institutions and precepts for human inventions and appointments. *Who hath bewitched you* (said Paul to the Galatians, *ch.* 3:1, 3) *that you should not obey the truth? Having begun in the Spirit, are you made perfect by the flesh?* Thus having shown the end of sharply reproving the corrupt and vicious Cretans, that they might be sound in the faith, and not heed Jewish fables and commands of men,

6. He gives the reasons of this, from the liberty we have by the gospel from legal observances, and the evil and mischief of a Jewish spirit under the Christian dispensation in the last two verses. To good Christians that are sound in the faith and thereby purified *all things are pure.* Meats and drinks, and such things as were forbidden under the law (the observances of which some still maintain), in these there is now no such distinction, *all are pure* (lawful and free in their use), *but to those that are defiled and unbelieving nothing is pure;* things lawful and good they abuse and turn to sin; they suck poison out of that from which others draw sweetness; their mind and conscience, those leading faculties, being defiled, a taint is communicated to all they do. *The sacrifice of the wicked is an abomination to the Lord,* Prov. 15:8. And *ch.* 21:4, *The ploughing of the wicked is sin,* not in itself, but as done by him; the carnality of the mind and heart mars all the labour of the hand.

Objection. But are not these judaizers (as you call them) men who profess religion, and speak well of God, and Christ, and righteousness of life, and should they be so severely taxed? *Answer, They profess that they know God; but in works they deny him, being abominable, and disobedient, and to every good work reprobate, v.* 16. There are many who in word and tongue profess to know God, and yet in their lives and conversations deny and reject him; their practice is a contradiction to their profession. *They come unto thee as the people cometh, and they sit before thee as my people, and they hear thy words, but they will not do them: with their mouth they show much love, but their heart goeth after their covetousness,* Eze. 33:31. *Being abominable, and disobedient, and to every good work reprobate.* The apostle, instructing Titus to rebuke sharply, does himself rebuke sharply; he gives them very hard words, yet doubtless no harder than their case warranted and their need required. *Being abominable — bdelyktoi,* deserving that God and good men should turn away their eyes from them as nauseous and offensive. *And disobedient — apeitheis, unpersuadable* and *unbelieving.* They might do divers things; but it was not the obedience of faith, nor what was commanded, or short of the command. *To every good work reprobate,* without skill or judgment to do any thing aright. See the miserable condition of hypocrites, such as have a form of godliness, but without the power; yet let us not be so ready to fix this charge on others as careful that it agree not to ourselves, that there be not in us *an evil heart of unbelief, in departing from the living God;* but that we be *sincere and without offence till the day of Christ, being filled with the fruits of righteousness, which are by Jesus Christ unto the glory and praise of God,* Phil. 1:10, 11.

CHAPTER 2

The apostle here directs Titus about the faithful discharge of his own office generally (*v.* 1), and particularly as to several sorts of persons (*v.* 2–10) and gives the grounds of these and of other following directions (*v.* 11–14), with a summary direction in the close (*v.* 15).

Verses 1–10

Here is the third thing in the matter of the epistle. In the chapter foregoing, the apostle had directed Titus about matters of government, and to set in order the things that were wanting in the churches. Now here he exhorts him,

I. Generally, to a faithful discharge of his own office. His ordaining others to preach would not excuse himself from preaching, nor might he take care of ministers and elders only, but he must instruct private Christians also in their duty. The adversative particle *(but)* here points back to the corrupt teachers, who vented *fables,* things vain and unprofitable: in opposition to them, says he, *"But speak thou the things that become sound doctrine,* what is agreeable to the word, which is pure and uncorrupt, healthful and nourishing to eternal life." Observe, (1.) The true doctrines of the gospel are *sound doctrines,* formally and effectively; they are in themselves good and holy, and make the believers so; they make them fit for, and vigorous in, the service of God. (2.) Ministers must be careful to teach only such truths. If the common talk of Christians must *be uncorrupt, to the use of ed-*

ifying, such as may minister grace to the hearers (Eph. 4:29), much more must ministers' preaching be such. Thus the apostle exhorts Titus generally: and then,

II. Specially and particularly, he instructs him to apply this sound doctrine to several sorts of persons, from v. 2–10. Ministers must not stay in generals, but must divide to every one his portion, what belongs to his age, or place, or condition of life; they must be particular as well as practical in their preaching; they must teach men their duty, and must teach all and each his duty. Here is an excellent Christian directory, accommodated to the old and to the young; to men and women; to the preacher himself and to servants.

1. To the aged men. By aged men some understand elders by office, including deacons, etc. But it is rather to be taken of the aged in point of years. Old disciples of Christ must conduct themselves in every thing agreeably to the Christian doctrine. *That the aged men be sober*, not thinking that the decays of nature, which they feel in old age, will justify them in any inordinacy or intemperance, whereby they conceit to repair them; they must keep measure in things, both for health and for fitness, for counsel and example to the younger. *Grave:* levity is unbecoming in any, but especially in the aged; they should be composed and stayed, grave in habit, speech, and behaviour; gaudiness in dress, levity and vanity in the behaviour, how unbeseeming in their years! *Temperate*, moderate and prudent, one who governs well his passions and affections, so as not to be hurried away by them to any thing that is evil or indecent. *Sound in the faith*, sincere and stedfast, constantly adhering to the truth of the gospel, not fond of novelties, nor ready to run into corrupt opinions or parties, nor to be taken with Jewish fables or traditions, or the dotages of their rabbin. Those who are full of years should be full of grace and goodness, the inner man renewing more and more as the outer decays. *In charity*, or love; this is fitly joined with *faith*, which works by, and must be seen in, love, love to God and men, and soundness therein. It must be sincere love, without dissimulation: love of God for himself, and of men for God's sake. The duties of the second table must be done in virtue of those of the first; love to men as men, and to the saints as the excellent of the earth, in whom must be special delight; and love at all times, in adversity as well as prosperity. Thus must there be soundness in charity or love. And *in patience*. Aged persons are apt to be peevish, fretful, and passionate; and therefore need to be on their guard against such infirmities and temptations. Faith, love, and patience, are three main Christian graces, and soundness in these is much of gospel perfection. There is *enduring patience* and *waiting patience*, both of which must be looked after; to *bear evils* becomingly, and contentedly to *want the good* till we are fit for it and it for us, being *followers of those who through faith and patience inherit the promises*. Thus as to the aged men.

2. To the aged women. These also must be instructed and warned. Some by these aged women understand the deaconesses, who were mostly employed in looking after the poor and attending the sick; but it is rather to be taken (as we render it) of all aged women professing religion. They must *be in behaviour as becometh holiness:* both men and women must accommodate their behaviour to their profession. Those virtues before mentioned *(sobriety, gravity, temperance, soundness in the faith, charity, and patience)*, recommended to aged men, are not proper to them only, but applicable to both sexes, and to be looked to by aged women as well as men. Women are to hear and learn their duty from the word, as well as the men: there is not one way of salvation for one sex or sort, and another for another; but both must learn and practise the same things, both as aged and as Christians; the virtues and duties are common. *That the aged women likewise* (as well as the men) *be in behaviour as becometh holiness;* or as beseems and is proper for holy persons, such as they profess to be and should be, keeping a pious decency and decorum in clothing and gesture, in looks and speech, and all their deportment, and this from an inward principle and habit of holiness, influencing and ordering the outward conduct at all times. Observe, Though express scripture do not occur, or be not brought, for every word, or look, or fashion in particular, yet general rules there are according to which all must be ordered; as 1 Co. 10:31, *Whatever you do, do all to the glory of God.* And Phil. 4:8, *Whatsoever things are true, whatsoever things are honest, whatsoever things are just, whatsoever things are pure, whatsoever things are lovely, whatsoever things are of good re-*

port, *if there be any virtue, and if there be any praise, think on these things.* And here, whatsoever things are beseeming or unbeseeming holiness form a measure and rule of conduct to be looked to. *Not false accusers — mē diabolous,* no calumniators or sowers of discord, slandering and backbiting their neighbours, a great and too common fault; not only loving to speak, but to speak ill, of people, and to separate very friends. A slanderer is one *whose tongue is set on fire of hell;* so much, and so directly, do these do the devil's work, that for it the devil's name is given to such. This is a sin contrary to the great duties of love, justice, and equity between one another; it springs often from malice and hatred, or envy, and such like evil causes, to be shunned as well as the effect. *Not given to much wine;* the word denotes such addictedness thereto as to be under the power and mastery of it. This is unseemly and evil in any, but especially in this sex and age, and was too much to be found among the Greeks of that time and place. How immodest and shameful, corrupting and destroying purity both of body and mind! Of what evil example and tendency, unfitting for the thing, which is a positive duty of aged matrons, namely, to be *teachers of good things!* Not public preachers, that is forbidden (1 Co. 14:34, *I permit not a woman to speak in the church),* but otherwise teach they may and should, that is, by example and good life. Hence observe, Those whose actions and behaviour become holiness are thereby teachers of good things; and, besides this, they may and should also teach by doctrinal instruction at home, and in a private way. *The words of king Lemuel, the prophecy his mother taught him.* Such a woman is praised, *She openeth her mouth with wisdom, and in her tongue is the law of kindness,* Prov. 31:1, 26. *Teachers of good things* are opposed to teachers of things corrupt, or to what is trifling and vain, of no good use or tendency, old wives' fables or superstitious sayings and observances; in opposition to these, their business is, and they may be called on to it, to be teachers of good things.

3. There are lessons for young women also, whom the aged women must teach, instructing and advising them in the duties of religion according to their years. For teaching such things aged women have often better access than the men, even than ministers have, which therefore they must improve in instructing the young women, especially the young wives; for he speaks of their duty to their husbands and children. These young women the more aged must teach, (1.) To bear a good personal character: *To be sober and discreet,* contrary to the vanity and rashness which younger years are subject to: discreet in their judgments and sober in their affections and behaviour. *Discreet* and *chaste* stand well together; many expose themselves to fatal temptations by that which at first might be but indiscretion. Prov. 2:11, *Discretion shall preserve thee, understanding shall keep thee from the evil way. Chaste,* and *keepers at home,* are well joined too. Dinah, when she went to see the daughters of the land, lost her chastity. Those whose home is their prison, it is to be feared, feel that their chastity is their fetters. Not but there are occasions, and will be, of going abroad; but a gadding temper for merriment and company sake, to the neglect of domestic affairs, or from uneasiness at being in her place, is the opposite evil intended, which is commonly accompanied with, or draws after it, other evils. 1 Tim. 5:13, 14, *They learn to be idle, wandering from house to house; and not only idle, but tattlers also and busybodies, speaking things which they ought not.* Their business is *to guide the house,* and they should give no occasion to the enemy to speak reproachfully. *Good,* generally, in opposition to all vice; and, specially, in her place, kind, helpful, and charitable; as Dorcas, *full of good works and almsdeeds.* It may also have, as some think, a more particular sense; one of a meek and yet cheerful spirit and temper, not sullen nor bitter; not taunting not fretting and galling any; not of a troublesome or jarring disposition, uneasy in herself and to those about her; but of a good nature and pleasing conversation, and likewise helpful by her advice and pains: thus *building her house, and doing her husband good, and not evil, all her days.* Thus in their personal character *sober, discreet, chaste, keepers at home, and good:* and, (2.) In their relative capacities: *To love their husbands, and to be obedient to them;* and where there is true love this will be no difficult command. God, in nature, and by his will, hath made this subordination: *I suffer not a woman to usurp authority over the man* (1 Tim. 2:12); and the reason is added: *For Adam was first formed, then Eve. Adam was not deceived, but the woman, being deceived, was*

in the transgression, v. 13, 14. She fell first, and was the means of seducing the husband. She was given to be a helper, but proved a most grievous hinderer, even the instrument of his fall and ruin, on which the bond of subjection was confirmed, and tied faster on her (Gen. 3:16): *Thy desire shall be to thy husband, and he shall rule over thee,* with less easiness, it may be, than before. It is therefore doubly enjoined: *first in innocency,* when was settled a subordination of nature, Adam being first formed and then Eve, and the woman being taken out of the man; *and then upon the fall,* the woman being first in the transgression, and seducing the man; here now began to be a subjection not so easy and comfortable, being a part of the penalty in her case; yet through Christ is this nevertheless a sanctified state. Eph. 5:22, 23, *Wives submit yourselves unto you own husbands, as unto the Lord,* as owning Christ's authority in them, whose image they bear; *for the husband is the head of the wife, even as Christ is the head of the church: and he is the saviour of the body.* God would have a resemblance of Christ's authority over the church held forth in the husband's over the wife. Christ is the head of the church, to protect and save it, to supply it with all good, and secure or deliver it from evil; and so the husband over the wife, to keep her from injuries, and to provide comfortably for her, according to his ability. Therefore, as the church is subject unto Christ, so let the *wives be unto their own husbands, as is fit in the Lord* (Col. 3:18), as comports with the law of Christ, and is for his and the Father's glory. It is not then an absolute, or unlimited, nor a slavish subjection that is required; but a loving subordination, to prevent disorder or confusion, and to further all the ends of the relation. Thus, in reference to the husbands, wives must be instructed in their duties of love and subjection to them. *And to love their children,* not with a natural affection only, but a spiritual, a love springing from a holy sanctified heart and regulated by the word; not a fond foolish love, indulging them in evil, neglecting due reproof and correction where necessary, but a regular Christian love, showing itself in their pious education, forming their life and manners aright, taking care of their souls as well as of their bodies, of their spiritual welfare as well as of their temporal, of the former chiefly and in the first place. The reason is added: *That the word of God may not be blasphemed.* Failures in such relative duties would be greatly to the reproach of Christianity. "What are these the better for this their new religion?" would the infidels be ready to say. The word of God and the gospel of Christ are pure, excellent, and glorious, in themselves; and their excellency should be expressed and shown in the lives and conduct of their professors, especially in relative duties; failures here being disgrace. Rom. 2:24, *The name of God is blasphemed among the Gentiles through you.* "Judge what a God he is," would they be ready to say, "by these his servants; and what his word, and doctrine, and religion, are by these his followers." Thus would Christ *be wounded in the house of his friends.* Thus of the duties of the younger women.

4. Here is the duty of young men. They are apt to be eager and hot, thoughtless and precipitant; therefore they must be earnestly called upon and exhorted to be considerate, not rash; advisable and submissive, not wilful and head-strong; humble and mild, not haughty and proud; for there are more young people ruined by pride than by any other sin. The young should be grave and solid in their deportment and manners, joining the seriousness of age with the liveliness and vigour of youth. This will make even those younger years to pass to good purpose, and yield matter of comfortable reflection when the evil days come; it will be preventive of much sin and sorrow, and lay the foundation for doing and enjoying much good. Such shall not *mourn at the last,* but have peace and comfort in death, and after it a glorious crown of life.

5. With these instructions to Titus, respecting what he should teach others — the aged men and women, and the younger of both sexes (Titus himself probably at this time being a young man also), the apostle inserts some directions to himself. He could not expect so successfully to teach others, if he did not conduct himself well both in his conversation and preaching. (1.) Here is direction for his conversation: *In all things showing thyself a pattern of good works, v. 7.* Without this, he would pull down with one hand what he built with the other. Observe, Preachers of good works must be patterns of them also; good doctrine and good life must go together. *Thou that teachest another, teachest thou not thyself?* A defect here is a great blemish and a great hin-

drance. *In all things;* some read, *above all things,* or *above all men.* Instructing others in the particulars of their duty is necessary, and, above all things, example, especially that of the teacher himself, is needful; hereby both light and influence are more likely to go together. "Let them see a lively image of those virtues and graces in thy life which must be in theirs. Example may both teach and impress the things taught; when they see purity and gravity, sobriety and all good life, in thee, they may be more easily won and brought thereto themselves; they may become pious and holy, sober and righteous, as thou art." Ministers must be examples to the flock, and the people followers of them, as they are of Christ. And here is direction, (2.) For his teaching and doctrine, as well as for his life: *In doctrine showing uncorruptness, gravity, sincerity, sound speech, that cannot be condemned, v.* 7, 8. They must make it appear that the design of their preaching is purely to advance the honour of God, the interest of Christ and his kingdom, and the welfare and happiness of souls; that this office was not entered into nor used with secular views, not from ambition nor covetousness, but a pure aim at the spiritual ends of its institution. In their preaching, therefore, the display of wit or parts, or of human learning or oratory, is not to be affected; but sound speech must be used, which cannot be *condemned;* scripture-language, as far as well may be, in expressing scripture-truths. This is sound speech, that cannot be condemned. We have more than once these duties of a minister set together. 1 Tim. 4:16, *Take heed to thyself, and to thy doctrine:* and, *v.* 12. of the same chapter, *"Let no man despise thy youth, but be thou an example of believers in word* — in thy speech, as a Christian, being grave, serious, and to the use of edifying; and in thy preaching, that it be the pure word of God, or what is agreeable to it and founded on it. Thus be an example *in word:* and *in conversation,* the life corresponding with the doctrine. In doing this *thou shalt both save thyself and those that hear thee."* In 2 Tim. 3:10, *Thou hast fully known my doctrine and manner of life* (says the same apostle), how agreeable these have been. And so must it be with others; their teaching must be agreeable to the word, and their life with their teaching. This is the true and good minister. 1 Th. 2:9, 10. *Labouring night and day, we preached to you the gospel of God; and you are witnesses, and God also, how holily, and justly, and unblamably, we behaved ourselves among you.* This must be looked to, as the next words show, which are, (3.) The reason both for the strictness of the minister's lie and the gravity and soundness of his preaching: *That he who is of the contrary part may be ashamed, having no evil thing to say of you.* Adversaries would be seeking occasion to reflect, and would do so could they find any thing amiss in doctrine or life; but, if both were right and good, such ministers might set calumny itself at defiance; they would have not evil thing to say justly, and so must be ashamed of their opposition. Observe, Faithful ministers will have enemies watching for their halting, such as will endeavour to find or pick holes in their teaching or behaviour; the more need therefore for them to look to themselves, that no just occasion be found against them. Opposition and calumny perhaps may not be escaped; men of corrupt minds will resist the truth, and often reproach the preachers and professors of it; but let them see that *with well-doing they put to silence the ignorance of foolish men; that, when they speak evil of them as evil-doers; those may be ashamed who falsely accuse their good conversation in Christ.* This is the direction to Titus himself, and so of the duties of free persons, male and female, old and young. Then follow,

6. The directions respecting servants. Servants must not think that their mean and low state puts them beneath God's notice or the obligations of his laws — that, because they are servants of men, they are thereby discharged from serving God. No; servants must know and do their duty to their earthly masters, but with an eye to their heavenly one: and Titus must not only instruct and warn earthly masters of their duties, but servants also of theirs, both in his public preaching and private admonitions. Servants must attend the ordinances of God for their instruction and comfort, as well as the masters themselves. In this direction to Titus there are the duties themselves, to which he must exhort servants, and a weighty consideration wherewith he was to enforce them.

(1.) The duties themselves are these: —

[1.] *To be obedient to their own masters, v.* 9. This is the prime duty, that by which they are characterized. Rom. 6:16, *His servants you are whom you obey.* There must be inward subjection and dutiful respect and reverence in the mind and thoughts. *"If I be a master, where is my fear,* the dutiful affection you show to me, together with the suitable outward significations and expressions of it, in doing what I command you?" This must be in servants; their will must be subject to their master's will, and their time and labour at their master's disposal and command. 1 Pt. 2:18, *Servants, be subject to your masters with all fear, not only to the good and gentle, but also to the froward.* The duty results from the will of God, and relation in which, by his providence, he has put such; not from the quality of the person. If he be a master, the duties of a servant are to be paid to him as such. Servants therefore are to be exhorted to be obedient to their own masters. And,

[2.] *To please them well in all things,* in all lawful things, and such as belong to them to command, or at least as are not contrary to the will of their great and superior Lord. We are not to understand it either of obeying or pleasing them absolutely, without any limitation; but always with a reserve of God's right, which may in no case be entrenched upon. If his command and the earthly master's come in competition, we are instructed to obey God rather than man; but then servants must be upon good grounds in this, that there is an inconsistency, else are they not held to be excused. And not only must the will of God be the measure of the servant's obedience, but the reason of it also. All must be done with a respect to him, in virtue of his authority, and for pleasing him primarily and chiefly, Col. 3:22–24. In serving the earthly master according to Christ's will, he is served; and such shall be rewarded by him accordingly. But how are servants to please their masters in all things, and yet not be men-pleasers? *Answer,* Men-pleasers, in the faulty sense, are such as eye men alone, or chiefly, in what they do, leaving God out, or subordinating him to man; when the will of man shall carry it, though against God's will, or man's pleasure is more regarded than his, — when this can content them, that the earthly master is pleased, though God be displeased, — or when more care, or more satisfaction, is taken in man's being pleased than in God's, this is sinful man-pleasing, of which all must take heed. Eph. 6:5–7, *"Servants, be obedient to those that are your masters according to the flesh, with fear and trembling, with singleness of your heart, as unto Christ. Not with eye-service, as men-pleasers* (who look at nothing but the favour or displeasure of men, or at nothing so much as this), *but as the servants of Christ, doing the will of God from the heart; with good will doing service, as to the Lord, and not to men;"* not to them chiefly, but to Christ, who requires, and who will reward, any good done, whether by bond or free. Observe therefore, Christian liberty comports well with civil servitude and subjection. Persons may serve men, and yet be the servants of Christ; these are not contrary, but subordinate, so far as serving men is according to Christ's will and for his sake. Christ came not to destroy or prejudice civil order and differences. *"Art thou called, being a servant? Care not for it,* 1 Co. 7:21. Let not this trouble thee, as if it were a condition unworthy of a Christian, or wherein the person so called is less pleasing unto God; *for he that is called in the Lord, being a servant, is the Lord's freeman,* not free from that service, but free in it; free spiritually, though not in a civil sense. *Likewise also he that is called, being free, is Christ's servant;* he is bound to him, though he be not under civil subjection to any; so that, *bond or free, all are one in Christ."* Servants therefore should not regret nor be troubled at their condition, but be faithful and cheerful in the station wherein God hath set them, striving to please their masters in all things. Hard it may be under some churlish Nabals, but it must be aimed at as much as possible.

[3.] *Not answering again;* not contradicting them, nor disputing it with them; not giving them any disrespectful or provoking language. Job complained of his servants, that he *called them, and they gave him no answer;* that was faulty another way: *Non respondere pro convitio est — Such silence is contempt:* but here it is respect, rather to take a check or reproof with humble silence, not making any confident nor bold replies. When conscious of a fault, to palliate or stand in justification of it doubles it. Yet this not answering again excludes not turning away wrath with a soft answer, when season and circumstances admit. Good and wise masters will be ready to hear and do right; but answering unseasonably, or in an unseemly manner, or, where the case admits not excuse, to be pert or confident, shows a want of the humility and meekness which such relation requires.

[4.] *Not purloining, but showing all good fidelity.* This is another great essential of good servants, to be *honest,* never converting that to their own use which is their master's, nor wasting the goods they are entrusted with; that is, *purloining.* They must be just and true, and do for their masters as they would or should for themselves. Prov. 28:24, *Whoso robbeth his father or his mother, and saith, It is no transgression, the same is the companion of a destroyer;* he will be ready to join with him. Thus having such light thoughts of taking beyond what is right, though it be from a parent or master, is likely to harden conscience to go further; it is both wicked in itself, and it tends to more. Be it so that the master is hard and strait, scarcely making sufficient provision for servants; yet they must not be their own carvers, nor go about by theft to right themselves; they must bear their lot, committing their cause to God for righting and providing for them. I speak not of cases of extremity, for preserving life, the necessaries for which the servant has a right to. *Not purloining, but showing all good fidelity;* he must not only not steal nor waste, but must improve his master's goods, and promote his prosperity and thriving, to his utmost. He that increased not his master's talent is accused of unfaithfulness, though he had not embezzled nor lost it. Faithfulness in a servant lies in the ready, punctual, and thorough execution of his master's orders; keeping his secrets and counsels, despatching his affairs, and managing with frugality, and to as much just advantage for his master as he is able; looking well to his trusts, and preventing, as far as he can, all spoil, or loss, or damage. This is a way to bring a blessing upon himself, as the contrary often brings utter ruin. *If you have not been faithful in that which is another man's, who shall give you that which is your own?* Lu. 16:12. Thus of the duties themselves, to which servants are to be exhorted. Then,

(2.) Here is the consideration with which Titus was to enforce them: *That they may adorn the doctrine of God our Saviour in all things;* that is, that they may recommend the gospel and Christ's holy religion to the good opinion of those that are without, by their meek, humble, obedient, and faithful conduct in all things. Even servants, though they may think that such as they, in so low and inferior a condition, can do little to bring repute to Christianity, or adorn the doctrine of Christ, and set forth the excellences of his truth and ways, yet, if they be careful to do their duty, it will redound to the glory of God and the credit of religion. The unbelieving masters would think the better of that despised way, which was every where spoken against, when they found that those of their servants who were Christians were better than their other servants — more obedient and submissive, more just and faithful, and more diligent in their places. True religion is an honour to the professors of it; and they should see that they do not any dishonour to it, but adorn it rather in all that they are able. Our light must shine among men, so that they, seeing our good works, may glorify our Father who is in heaven. And thus of the apostle's directions to Titus, about the discharge of his office, in reference to several sorts of persons.

Verses 11–14

Here we have the grounds or considerations upon which all the foregoing directions are urged, taken from the nature and design of the gospel, and the end of Christ's death.

I. From the nature and design of the gospel. Let young and old, men and women, masters and servants, and Titus himself, let all sorts do their respective duties, for this is the very aim and business of Christianity, to instruct, and help, and form persons, under all distinctions and relations, to a right frame and conduct. For this,

1. They are put under the dispensation of *the grace of God,* so the gospel is called, Eph. 3:2. It is grace in respect of the spring of it — the free favour and good-will of God, not any merit or desert in the creature; as manifesting and declaring this good-will in an eminent and signal manner; and as it is the means of conveying and working grace in the hearts of believers. Now grace is obliging and constraining to goodness: *Let not sin reign, but yield yourselves unto God; for you are not under the law, but under grace,* Rom. 6:12–14. *The love of Christ constrains us* not to live to self, but to him (2 Co. 5:14, 15); without this effect, grace is received in vain.

2. This gospel grace *brings salvation* (reveals and offers it to sinners and ensures it to believers) — salvation from sin and wrath, from death and hell. Hence it is called *the word of life;* it brings to faith, and so to life, the life of holiness now and of happiness hereafter. The law is the ministration of

death, but the gospel the ministration of life and peace. This therefore must be received as salvation (its rules minded, its commands obeyed), that the end of it may be obtained, *the salvation of the soul*. And more inexcusable will the neglecters of this grace of God bringing salvation now be, since,

3. *It hath appeared*, or shone out more clearly and illustriously than ever before. The old dispensation was comparatively dark and shadowy; this is a clear and shining light; and, as it is now more bright, so more diffused and extensive also. For,

4. It hath appeared *to all men;* not to the Jews only, as the glory of God appeared at mount Sinai to that particular people, and out of the view of all others; but gospel grace is open to all, and all are invited to come and partake of the benefit of it, Gentiles as well as Jews. The publication of it is free and general: *Disciple all nations: Preach the gospel to every creature*. The pale is broken down; there is no such enclosure now as formerly. *The preaching of Jesus Christ, which was kept secret since the world began, now is made manifest, and by the scriptures of the prophets, according to the commandment of the everlasting God, made known to all nations for the obedience of faith*, Rom. 16:25, 26. The doctrine of grace and salvation by the gospel is for all ranks and conditions of men (slaves and servants, as well as masters), therefore engaging and encouraging all to receive and believe it, and walk suitably to it, adorning it in all things.

5. This gospel revelation is to *teach*, and not by way of information and instruction only, as a schoolmaster does his scholars, but by way of precept and command, as a sovereign who gives laws to his subjects. It directs what to shun and what to follow, what to avoid and what to do. The gospel is not for speculation only or chiefly, but for practice and right ordering of life; for it teaches us,

(1.) To abandon sin: *Denying ungodliness and worldly lusts;* to renounce and have no more to do with these, as we have had: *Put off, concerning the former conversation, the old man which is corrupt;* that is, the whole body of sins, here distributed into *ungodliness* and *worldly* lusts. "Put away ungodliness and irreligion, all unbelief, neglect or disesteem of the divine Being, not loving, nor fearing, nor trusting in him, nor obeying him as we should, neglecting his ordinances, slighting his worship, profaning his name or day. Thus deny ungodliness (hate and put it away); *and worldly lusts*, all corrupt and vicious desires and affections that prevail in worldly men, and carry out to worldly things *the lust of the flesh also, and of the eye, and the pride of life*, all sensuality and filthiness, covetous desires and ambition, seeking and valuing more the praise of men than of God; put away all these." An earthly sensual conversation suits not a heavenly calling. *Those that are Christ's have crucified the flesh with the affections and lusts*. They have done it by covenant-engagement and promise, and have initially and prevailingly done it in act; they are going on in the work, cleansing themselves more and more from all filthiness of flesh and spirit. Thus the gospel first unteaches that which is evil, to abandon sin; and then,

(2.) To make conscience of that which is good: *To live soberly, righteously, and godly*, etc. Religion is not made up of negatives only; there must be doing good as well as eschewing evil; in these conjunctly is sincerity proved and the gospel adorned. We should live soberly with respect to ourselves, in the due government of our appetites and passions, keeping the limits of moderation and temperance, avoiding all inordinate excesses; and righteously towards all men, rendering to all their due, and injuring none, but rather doing good to others, according to our ability and their need; this seems a part of justice and righteousness, for we are not born for ourselves alone, and therefore may not live to ourselves only. *We are members one of another*, and *must seek every man another's wealth*, 1 Co. 10:24; 12:25. The public, especially, which includes the interests of all, must have the regards of all. Selfishness is a sort of unrighteousness; it robs others of that share in us which is their due. How amiable then will a just and righteous conduct be! It secures and promotes all interests, not particular only, but general and public, and so contributes to the peace and happiness of the world. Live righteously therefore as well as soberly. And godly towards God, in the duties of his worship and service. Regards to him indeed should run through all. *Whether you eat, or drink, or whatsoever you do, do all to the glory of God*, 1 Co. 10:31. Personal and relative duties must be done in obedience to his commands, with due aim at pleasing and honouring him, from principles of holy love and fear of him. But there is an

express and direct duty also that we owe to God, namely, belief and acknowledgment of his being and perfections, paying him internal and external worship and homage, — loving, fearing, and trusting in him, — depending on him, and devoting ourselves to him, — observing all those religious duties and ordinances that he has appointed, — praying to him, praising him, and meditating on his word and works. This is godliness, looking and coming to God, as our state now is, not immediately, but as he has manifested himself in Christ; so does the gospel direct and require. To go to God in any other way, namely, by saints or angels, is unsuitable, yea, contrary to the gospel rule and warrant. All communications from God to us are through his Son, and our returns must also be by him. God in Christ we must look at as the object of our hope and worship. Thus must we exercise ourselves to godliness, without which there can be no adorning of that gospel which is according to it, which teaches and requires such a deportment. A gospel conversation must needs be a godly conversation, expressing our love and fear and reverence of God, our hope and trust and confidence in him, as manifested in his Son. *We are the circumcision* (who have in truth what was signified by that sacrament) *who worship God in the Spirit, and rejoice in Christ Jesus, and have no confidence in the flesh*. See in how small a compass our duty is comprised; it is put into few words, *denying ungodliness and worldly lusts, and living soberly, righteously, and godly, in this present world*. The gospel teaches us not only how to believe and hope well, but also to live well, as becomes that faith and hope in this present world, and as expectants of another and better. There is the world that now is, and that which is to come; the present is the time and place of our trial, and the gospel teaches us to live well here, not, however, as our final state, but with an eye chiefly to a future: for it teaches us in all,

(3.) To look for the glories of another world, to which a sober, righteous, and godly life in this is preparative: *Looking for that blessed hope, and the glorious appearing of the great God and our Saviour Jesus Christ*. Hope, by a metonymy, is put for the thing hoped for, namely, heaven and the felicities thereof, called emphatically *that hope*, because it is the great thing we look and long and wait for; and a *blessed hope*, because, when attained, we shall be completely happy for ever. *And the glorious appearing of the great God and our Saviour Jesus Christ*. This denotes both the time of the accomplishing of our hope and the sureness and greatness of it: it will be at the second appearing of Christ, when he shall come *in his own glory, and in his Father's, and of the holy angels*, Lu. 9:26. His own glory which he had before the world was; and his Father's, being *the express image of his person*, and as God-man, his delegated ruler and Judge; and of the holy angels, as his ministers and glorious attendants. His first coming was in meanness, to satisfy justice and purchase happiness; his second will be in majesty, to bestow and instate his people in it. *Christ was once offered to bear the sins of many; and unto those that look for him will he appear the second time, without sin, unto salvation*, Heb. 9:28. *The great God and our Saviour* (or *even our Saviour*) *Jesus Christ;* for they are not two subjects, but one only, as appears by the single article, *tou megalou Theou kai Sōtēros*, not *kai tou Sōtēros*, and so is *kai* rendered 1 Co. 15:24, *When he shall have delivered up the kingdom to God, even the Father; tō Theō kai Patri*. Christ then is the *great God*, not figuratively, as magistrates and others are sometimes called gods, or as appearing and acting in the name of God, but properly and absolutely, *the true God* (1 Jn. 5:20), the *mighty God* (Isa. 9:6), *who, being in the form of God, thought it not robbery to be equal with God*, Phil. 2:6. In his second coming he will reward his servants, and bring them to glory with him. Observe, [1.] There is a common and blessed hope for all true Christians in the other world. If in this life only they had hope in Christ, they were of all men the most miserable, 1 Co. 15:19. By hope is meant the thing hoped for, namely, Christ himself, who is called *our hope* (1 Tim. 1:1), and blessedness in and through him, even riches of glory (Eph. 1:18), hence fitly termed here *that blessed hope*. [2.] The design of the gospel is to stir up all to a good life by this blessed hope. *Gird up the loins of your mind, be sober, and hope to the end for the grace that is to be brought unto you at the revelation of Jesus Christ*, 1 Pt. 1:13. To the same purport here, *Denying ungodliness and worldly lusts, live soberly, righteously, and godly, in this present world, looking for the blessed hope;* not as mercenaries, but as dutiful and thankful Chris-

tian. *What manner of persons ought you to be in all holy conversation and godliness, looking for and hastening to the coming of the day of God!* 2 Pt. 3:11, 12. Looking and hastening, that is, expecting and diligently preparing for it. [3.] At, and in, the glorious appearing of Christ will the blessed hope of Christians be attained; for their felicity will be this, *To be where he is, and to behold his glory*, Jn. 17:24. The glory of the great God and our Saviour will then break out as the sun. Though in the exercise of his judiciary power he will appear as the Son of man, yet will he be mightily declared to be the Son of God too. The divinity, which on earth was much veiled, will shine out then as the sun in its strength. Hence the work and design of the gospel are to raise the heart to wait for this second appearing of Christ. *We are begotten again to a lively hope of it* (1 Pt. 1:3), turned to *serve the living God, and wait for his Son from heaven*, 1 Th. 1:9, 10. Christians are marked by this, expecting their Master's coming (Lu. 12:36), *loving his appearance*, 2 Tim. 4:8. Let us then look to this hope; let our loins be girt, and our lights burning, and ourselves like those who wait for their Lord; the day or hour we know not, but *he that shall come will come, and will not tarry*, Heb. 10:37. [4.] The comfort and joy of Christians are that their Saviour is the great God, and will gloriously manifest himself at his second coming. Power and love, majesty and mercy, will then appear together in the highest lustre, to the terror and confusion of the wicked, but to the everlasting triumph and rejoicing of the godly. Were he not thus the great God, and not a mere creature, he could not be their Saviour, nor their hope. Thus of the considerations to enforce the directions of all sorts to their respective duties from the nature and design of the gospel. And herewith is connected another ground, namely,

II. From the end of Christ's death: *Who gave himself for us, that he might redeem us from all iniquity, and purify unto himself a peculiar people, zealous of good works, v.* 14. To bring us to holiness and happiness was the end of Christ's death, as well as the scope of his doctrine. Here we have,

1. The purchaser of salvation — Jesus Christ, *that great God and our Saviour*, who saves not simply as God, much less as man alone; but as God-man, two natures in one person: man, that he might obey, and suffer, and die, for man, and be meet to deal with him and for him; and God, that he might support the manhood, and give worth and efficacy to his undertakings, and have due regard to the rights and honour of the deity, as well as the good of his creature, and bring about the latter to the glory of the former. Such a one became us; and this was,

2. The price of our redemption: *He gave himself*. The Father gave him, but he gave himself too; and, in the freeness and voluntariness, as well as the greatness of the offering, lay the acceptableness and merit of it. *Therefore doth my Father love me, because I lay down my life, that I might take it again. No man taketh it from me, but I lay it down of myself*, Jn. 10:17, 18. So Jn. 17:19, "*For their sakes I sanctify myself*, or separate and devote myself to this work, to be both a priest and a sacrifice to God for the sins of men." The human nature was the offering, and the divine the altar, sanctifying the gift, and the whole the act of the person. *He gave himself a ransom for all*, 1 Tim. 2:6. *Once in the end of the world hath he appeared, to put away sin by the sacrifice of himself*. He was the priest and sacrifice too. *We are redeemed, not with silver and gold, but the precious blood of Christ* (1 Pt. 1:18, 19), called *the blood of God* (Acts 20:28), that is, of him who is God.

3. The persons for whom: *For us*, us poor perishing sinners, gone off from God, and turned rebels against him. He gave himself *for us*, not only for our good, but in our stead. Messiah was cut off, not for himself, but for us. *He suffered, the just for the unjust, that he might bring us to God*, 1 Pt. 3:18. *He was made sin for us* (an offering and sacrifice for sin), *that we might be made the righteousness of God in him*, 2 Co. 5:21. Wonderful condescension and grace! *He loved us, and gave himself for us;* what can we do less than love and give up ourselves to him? Especially considering,

4. The ends of his giving himself for us, (1.) *That he might redeem us from all iniquity*. This is fitted to the first lesson, *denying ungodliness and worldly lusts*. Christ gave himself to redeem us from these, therefore put them away. To love and live in sin is to trample under foot redeeming blood, to despise and reject one of the greatest benefits of it, and to act counter to its design. But how could the short sufferings of Christ redeem us from all iniquity? *Answer*, Through the

infinite dignity of his person. He who was God suffered, though not as God. The acts and properties of either nature are attributed to the person. God purchased his church *with his own blood,* Acts 20:28. Could payment be made at once, no need of suffering for ever. A mere creature could not do this, from the finiteness of his nature; but God-man could. *The great God and our Saviour gave himself for us:* this accounts for it. *By one offering he hath for ever perfected those that are sanctified,* Heb. 9:25, 26; 10:14. He needed not to offer himself often, nor could he be holden of death, when he had once undergone it. Happy end and fruit of Christ's death, redemption from all iniquity! Christ died for this: and, (2.) *To purify to himself a peculiar people.* This enforces the second lesson: *To live soberly, righteously, and godly, in this present world.* Christ died to purify as well as to pardon — to obtain grace, to heal the nature, as well as to free from guilt and condemnation. He gave himself for his church, *to cleanse it.* Thus does he make *to himself a peculiar people,* by purifying them. Thus are they distinguished from the world that lies in wickedness; they are born of God, and assimilated to him, bear his image, are holy as their heavenly Father is holy. Observe, Redemption from sin and sanctification of the nature go together, and both make a peculiar people unto God: freedom from guilt and condemnation, freedom from the power of lusts, and purification of soul by the Spirit. These are *a chosen generation, a royal priesthood, a holy nation,* and so *a peculiar people.* And, (3.) *Zealous of good works.* This peculiar people, as they are made so by grace purifying them, so must they be seen to be so by doing good, and a zeal therein. Observe, The gospel is not a doctrine of licentiousness, but of holiness and good life. We are redeemed from our vain conversation, to serve God *in holiness and righteousness all the days of our life.* Let us see then that we do good, and have zeal in it; only looking that zeal be guided by knowledge and spirited with love, directed to the glory of God, and always in some good thing. And thus of the motive to the duties directed, from the end of Christ's death.

Verse 15

The apostle closes the chapter (as he began it) with a summary direction to Titus upon the whole, in which we have the matter and manner of ministers' teaching, and a special instruction to Titus in reference to himself.

I. The matter of ministers' teaching: *These thing,* namely, those before mentioned: not Jewish fables and traditions, but the truths and duties of the gospel, of avoiding sin, and living soberly, righteously, and godly, in this present world. Observe, Ministers in their preaching must keep close to the word of God. *If any man speak, let him speak as the oracles of God,* 1 Pt. 4:11, and not the figments and inventions of his own brain.

II. The manner; by doctrine, and exhortation, and reproof with all authority. 2 Tim. 3:16, *All scripture is given by inspiration of God, and is profitable for doctrine, for reproof, for correction, and for instruction in righteousness;* that is, to teach sound doctrine, to convince of sin and refute error, to reform the life, and to carry forward in what is just and good; *that the man of God* (the Christian or minister) *may be perfect, thoroughly furnished to all good works* that are to be practised by himself or to be taught to others. Here is what will furnish for all parts of his duty, and the right discharge of them. *"These things speak,* or teach; shun not to declare the whole counsel of God." The great and necessary truths and duties of the gospel, especially, these *speak and exhort, parakalei, press with much earnestness.* Ministers must not be cold and lifeless in delivering heavenly doctrine and precepts, as if they were indifferent things or of little concern; but they must urge them with earnestness suitable to their nature and importance; they must call upon persons to mind and heed, and not be *hearers only, deceiving themselves; but doers of the word, that they may be blessed therein. And rebuke;* convince and reprove such as contradict or gainsay, or neglect and do not receive the truth as they should, or retain it in unrighteousness — those who hear it not with such a believing and obedient mind and heart as they ought, but, instead of this (it may be) live in contrary practices, showing themselves stubborn and disobedient, and to every good work reprobate. *Rebuke with all authority,* as coming in the name of God, and armed with his threatenings and discipline, whoever make light of which will do it at their peril. Ministers are reprovers in the gate.

III. Here is a special instruction to Titus in reference to himself: *"Let no man despise thee;* that is, give no occasion to do so, nor suffer it without reproof, considering that *he who despiseth despiseth not man, but God."* Or thus, *"Speak and exhort these things,* press them upon all, as they may respectively be concerned; with boldness and faithfulness reprove sin, and carefully look to thyself and thy own conduct, and then none will despise thee." The most effectual way for ministers to secure themselves from contempt is to keep close to the doctrine of Christ, and imitate his example — to preach and live well, and do their duty with prudence and courage; this will best preserve both their reputation and their comfort.

Perhaps too an admonition might be here intended to the people — that Titus, though young, and but a substitute of the apostle, yet should not be condemned by them, but considered and respected as a faithful minister of Christ, and encouraged and supported in his work and office. *"Know those that labour among you, and are over you in the Lord, and admonish you; and esteem them very highly in love for their work's sake,* 1 Th. 5:12, 13. Mind their teaching, respect their persons, support them in their function, and, what in you lies, further their endeavours for the honour of God and the salvation of souls."

CHAPTER 3

Of duties which concern Christians more in common, and the reasons of them (*v.* 1–8). What Titus in teaching should avoid, and how he should deal with a heretic, with some other directions (*v.* 9–14), and salutations in the close (*v.* 15).

Verses 1–8

Here is the fourth thing in the matter of the epistle. The apostle had directed Titus in reference to the particular and special duties of several sorts of persons; now he bids him exhort to what concerned them more in common, namely, to quietness and submission to rulers, and readiness to do good, and to equitable and gentle behaviour towards all men — things comely and ornamental of religion; he must therefore put them in mind of such things. Ministers are people's remembrancers of their duty. As they are remembrancers for the people to God in prayers (Isa. 62:6), so are they from God to them in preaching: *I will not be negligent to put you always in remembrance,* 2 Pt. 1:12. Forgetfulness of duty is a common frailty; there is need therefore of reminding and quickening them thereto. Here are the duties themselves, and the reasons of them.

I. The duties themselves, which they were to be reminded of. 1. *Put them in mind to be subject to principalities and powers, to obey magistrates.* Magistracy is God's ordinance for the good of all, and therefore must be regarded and submitted to by all; not for wrath and by force only, but willingly and for conscience' sake. *Principalities,* and *powers,* and *magistrates,* that is, all civil rulers, whether supreme and chief or subordinate, in the government under which they live, of whatever form it be; that they be subject to them and obey them in things lawful and honest, and which it belongs to their office to require. The Christian religion was misrepresented by its adversaries as prejudicial to the rights of princes and civil powers, and tending to faction and sedition, and to rebellion against lawful authority; therefore *to put to silence the ignorance of foolish men,* and stop the mouths of malicious enemies, Christians must be reminded to show themselves examples rather of all due subjection and obedience to the government that is over them. Natural desire of liberty must be guided and bounded by reason and scripture. Spiritual privileges do not make void or weaken, but confirm and strengthen, their obligations to civil duties: "Remind them therefore *to be subject to principalities and powers and to obey magistrates."* And, 2. *To be ready to every good work.* Some refer this to such good works as are required by magistrates and within their sphere: "Whatever tends to good order, and to promote and secure public tranquility and peace, be not backward, but ready, to promote such things." But, though this be included, if not first intended, yet is it not to be hereto restrained. The precept regards doing good in all kinds, and on every occasion that may offer, whether respecting God, ourselves, or our neighbour — what may bring credit to religion in the world. *Whatsoever things are true, honest, just, pure, lovely, of good report: if there be any virtue, if there be any praise, think on these things* (Phil. 4:8), to do and follow and further them. Mere harmlessness, or good words and good meanings only, are not enough without good works. *Pure religion and undefiled before God and the Father is this, to visit the fatherless, and the widow in their affliction, and keep unspotted from the world.* "Not only take, but seek, occasion for doing good, keep fitness and readiness that way; put it not off to others, but embrace and lay hold on it thyself, delight and rejoice therein, put all in mind of this." And, 3. *To speak evil of no man: mēdena blasphēmein, to revile,* or *curse,* or *blaspheme none:* or (as our translation more generally) *to speak evil of none,* unjustly and falsely, or unnecessarily, without call, and when it may do hurt but no good to the person himself or any other. If no good can be spoken, rather than speak evil unnecessarily, say nothing. We must never take pleasure in speaking ill of others, nor make the worst of any thing, but the best we can. We must not go up and down as tale-bearers, carrying ill-natured stories, to the prejudice of our neighbour's good name and the destruction of brotherly love. Misrepresentations, or insinuations of bad intentions, or of hypocrisy in what is done, things out of our reach or cognizance, these come within the reach of this prohibition. As this evil is too common, so it is of great malignity. *If any man seemeth to be religious and bridleth not his tongue, that man's religion is vain,* Jam. 1:26. Such loose uncharitable talk is displeasing to God, and hurtful among men. Prov. 17:9, *He that covereth a transgression seeketh love* (that is, to himself by this tenderness and charity, or rather to the transgressor); *but he that repeateth a matter* (that blazes and tells the faults of another abroad) *separateth very friends;* he raises dissensions and alienates his friend from himself, and perhaps from others. This is among the sins to be put off (Eph. 4:31); for, if indulged, it unfits for Christians communion here and the society of the blessed in heaven, 1 Co. 6:10. Remind them therefore to avoid this. And, 4. *To be no brawlers; amachous einai — no fighters,* either with hand or tongue, no quarrelsome contentious persons, apt to give or return ill and provoking language. A holy contending there is for matters good and important, and in a manner suitable and becoming, not with wrath nor injurious violence. Christian must follow the things that are conducive to peace, and that in a peaceful, not a rough and boisterous and hurtful way, but as becomes the servants of the God of peace and love (Rom. 12:19), *Dearly beloved, avenge not yourselves, but rather give place unto wrath;* this is the Christian's wisdom and duty. *The glory of a man is to pass over a transgression;* it is the duty of a reasonable, and therefore certainly of a Christian man, whose reason is improved and advanced by religion; such may not, and will not, presently fall foul on one who has offended him, but, like God, will be *slow to anger, and ready to forgive.* Contention and strife arise from men's lusts, and exorbitant unruly passions, which must be curbed and moderated, not indulged; and Christians need to be reminded of these things, that they do not by a wrathful contentious spirit and behaviour displease and dishonour God and discredit religion, promoting feuds in the places where they live. *He that is slow to anger is better than the mighty,* and he *that ruleth his spirit than he that taketh a city.* Wherefore it follows, 5. *But gentle; epieikeis, equitable and just,* or candid and fair in constructions of things, not taking words or actions in the worst sense; and for peace sometimes yielding somewhat of strict right. And, 6. *Showing all meekness to all men.* We must be of a mild disposition, and not only have meekness in our hearts, but show it in our speech and conduct. *All meekness* — meekness in all instances and occasions, not towards friends only, but *to all men,* though still with wisdom, as James admonishes, Jam. 3:13. "Distinguish the person and the sin; pity the one and hate the other. Distinguish between sin and sin; look not on all alike, there are *motes and beams.* Distinguish also between sinner and sinner: *of some have compassion, others save with fear, pulling them out of the fire, thus making a difference,* Jude 22, 23. Mind these things; *the wisdom that is from above is pure and peaceable, gentle and easy to be entreated."* Meekness of spirit and demeanour renders religion amiable; it is a commanded imitation of Christ the grand exemplar, and what brings it own reward with it, in the ease and comfort of the disposition itself and the blessings accompanying it. These shall be glad and rejoice, shall be taught and guided in their way, and satisfied with bread, and beautified with salvation. Thus of the duties themselves, which Titus was to put people in mind of: for which,

II. He adds the reasons, which are derived

1. From their own past condition. Consideration of men's natural condition is a great means and ground of equity and

gentleness, and all meekness, towards those who are yet in such a state. This has a tendency to abate pride and work pity and hope in reference to those who are yet unconverted: "We ourselves also were so and so, corrupt and sinful, therefore we should not be impatient and bitter, hard and severe, towards those who are but as ourselves once were. Should we then have been willing to be contemned, and proudly and rigorously dealt with? No, but treated with gentleness and humanity; and therefore we should now so treat those who are unconverted, according to that rule of equity: *Quod tibi non vis fieri, alteri ne feceris — What you would not have done to you that do not you to another.*" Their past natural condition is set forth in divers particulars. *We ourselves also were sometimes,* (1.) *Foolish;* without true spiritual understanding and knowledge, ignorant of heavenly things. Observe, Those should be most disposed to bear with others' follies who may remember many of their own; those should be meek and gentle, and patient towards others, who once needed and doubtless then expected the same. *We ourselves also were sometimes foolish.* And, (2.) *Disobedient;* heady and unpersuadable, resisting the word, and rebellious even against the natural laws of God, and those which human society requires. Well are these set together, *foolish and obedient.* For what folly like this, to disobey God and his laws, natural or revealed? This is contrary to right reason, and men's true and greatest interests; and what so foolish as to violate and go counter to these? (3.) *Deceived,* or wandering; namely, out of the ways of truth and holiness. Man in this his degenerate state is of a straying nature, thence compared to a lost sheep; this must be sought and brought back, and guided in the right way, Ps. 119:176. He is weak, and ready to be imposed upon by the wiles and subtleties of Satan, and of men lying in wait to seduce and mislead. (4.) *Serving divers lusts and pleasures;* namely, as vassals and slaves under them. Observe, Men deceived are easily entangled and ensnared; they would not serve divers lusts and pleasures as they do, were they not blinded and beguiled into them. See here too what a different notion the word gives of a sensual and fleshly life from what the world generally has of it. Carnal people thing they enjoy their pleasures; the word calls it servitude and vassalage: they are very drudges and bond slaves under them; so far are they from freedom and felicity in them that they are captivated by them, and serve them as taskmasters and tyrants. Observe further, It is the misery of the servants of sin that they have many masters, one lust hurrying them one way, and another; pride commands one thing, covetousness another, and often a contrary. What vile slaves are sinners, while they conceit themselves free! the lusts that tempt them promise them liberty, but in yielding they become the servants of corruption; for *of whom a man is overcome of the same is he brought into bondage.* (5.) *Living in malice,* one of those lusts that bear rule in them. Malice desires hurt to another and rejoices in it. (6.) *And envy,* which grudges and repines at another's good, frets at his prosperity and success in any thing: both are roots of bitterness, whence many evils spring: evil thoughts and speeches, tongues *set on fire of hell,* detracting from and impairing the just and due praises of others. *Their words are swords,* wherewith they slay the good name and honour of their neighbour. This was the sin of Satan, and of Cain who was of that evil one, and slew his brother; for wherefore slew he him, but of this envy and malice, *because his own works were evil, and his brother's righteous?* These were some of the sins in which we lived in our natural state. And, (7.), *Hateful,* or odious — deserving to be hated. (8.) *And hating one another.* Observe, Those that are sinful, living and allowing themselves in sin, are hateful to God and all good men. Their temper and ways are so, though not simply their persons. It is the misery of sinners that thy hate one another, as it is the duty and happiness of saints to love one another. What contentions and quarrels flow from men's corruptions, such as were in the nature of those who by conversion are now good, but in their unconverted state made them ready to run like furious wild beasts one upon another! The consideration of its having been thus with us should moderate our spirits, and dispose us to be more equal and gentle, meek and tenderhearted, towards those who are such. This is the argument from their own past condition here described. And he reasons,

2. From their present state. "We are delivered out of that our miserable condition by no merit nor strength of our own; but only by the mercy and free grace of God, and merit of

Christ, and operation of his Spirit. Therefore we have no ground, in respect of ourselves, to condemn those who are yet unconverted, but rather to pity them, and cherish hope concerning them, that they, though in themselves as unworthy and unmeet as we were, yet may obtain mercy, as we have:" and so upon this occasion the apostle again opens the causes of our salvation, *v.* 4–7.

(1.) We have here the prime author of our salvation — God the Father, therefore termed here *God our Saviour. All things are of God, who hath reconciled us to himself by Jesus Christ,* 2 Co. 5:18. All things belonging to the new creation, and recovery of fallen man to life and happiness, of which the apostle is there speaking, all these things are of God the Father, as contriver and beginner of this work. There is an order in acting, as in subsisting. The Father begins, the Son manages, and the Holy Spirit works and perfects all. God (namely, the *Father*) is a Saviour by Christ, through the Spirit. Jn. 3:16, *God so loved the world as to give his only begotten Son, that whoever believes in him might not perish, but have everlasting life.* He is the Father of Christ, and through him the Father of mercies; all spiritual blessings are by Christ from him, Eph. 1:3. *We joy in God through Jesus Christ,* Rom. 5:11. *And with one mind, and one mouth, glorify God, even the Father of our Lord Jesus Christ,* Rom. 15:5.

(2.) The spring and rise of it — the divine *philanthropy,* or *kindness and love of God to man.* By grace we are saved from First to last. This is the ground and motive. God's pity and mercy to man in misery were the first wheel, or rather the Spirit in the wheels, that sets and keeps them all in motion. God is not, cannot be, moved by any thing out of himself. The occasion is in man, namely, his misery and wretchedness. Sin bringing that misery, wrath might have issued out rather than compassion; but God, knowing how to adjust all with his own honour and perfections, would pity and save rather than destroy. He delights in mercy. *Where sin abounded, grace did much more abound.* We read of *riches of goodness and mercy,* Rom. 2:4; Eph. 2:7. Let us acknowledge this, and give him the glory of it, not turning it to wantonness, but to thankfulness and obedience.

(3.) Here is the means, or instrumental cause — the shining out of this love and grace of God in the gospel, *after it appeared,* that is, in the word. The appearing of love and grace has, through the Spirit, great virtue to soften and change and turn to God, and so is *the power of God to salvation to every one that believeth.* Thus having asserted God to be the author, his free grace the spring, and the manifestation of this in the gospel the means of salvation, that the honour of all still may be the better secured to him,

(4.) False grounds and motives are here removed: *Not by works of righteousness which we have done, but according to his mercy, he saved us;* not for foreseen works of ours, but his own free grace and mercy alone. Works must be in the saved (where there is room for it), but not among the causes of his salvation; they are the way to the kingdom, not the meriting price of it; all is upon the principle of undeserved favour and mercy from first to last. Election is of grace: we are chosen *to be* holy, not because it was antecedently seen that we should be so, Eph. 1:4. It is the fruit, not the cause, of election: *God hath from the beginning chosen you to salvation through sanctification of the Spirit and belief of the truth,* 2 Th. 2:13. So effectual calling, in which election breaks out, and is first seen: *He hath saved us, and called us with a holy calling; not according to our works, but according to his own purpose and grace, which was given us in Christ Jesus before the world began,* 2 Tim. 1:9. We *are justified freely by grace* (Rom. 3:24), and sanctified and saved by grace: *By grace you are saved, through faith; and that not of yourselves, it is the gift of God,* Eph. 2:8. Faith and all saving graces are God's free gift and his work; the beginning, increase, and perfection of them in glory, all are from him. In building men up to be a holy temple unto God, from the foundation to the top-stone, we must cry nothing but *Grace, grace* unto it. It is *not of works, lest any man should boast; but of grace, that he who glorieth should glory only in the Lord.* Thus the true cause is shown, and the false removed.

(5.) Here is the formal cause of salvation, or that wherein it lies, the beginnings of it at least — in regeneration or spiritual renewing, as it is here called. *Old things pass away, and all things become new,* in a moral and spiritual, not in a physical and natural, sense. It is the same man, but with other dispositions and habits; evil ones are done away, as to the

prevalency of them at present; and all remains of them in due time will be so, when the work shall be perfected in heaven. A new prevailing principle of grace and holiness is wrought, which inclines, and sways, and governs, and makes the man a new man, a new creature, having new thoughts, desires, and affections, a new and holy turn of life and actions; the life of God in man, not only from God in a special manner, but conformed and tending to him. Here is salvation begun, and which will be growing and increasing to perfection; therefore it is said, *He saved us.* What is so begun, as sure to be perfected in time, is expressed as if it already were so. Let us look to this therefore without delay; we must be initially saved now, by regeneration, if on good ground we would expect complete salvation in heaven. The change then will be but in degree, not in kind. Grace is glory begun, as glory is but grace in its perfection. How few mind this! Most act as if they were afraid to be happy before the time; they would have heaven, they pretend, at last, yet care not for holiness now; that is, they would have the end without the beginning; so absurd are sinners. But without regeneration, that is, the first resurrection, there is no attaining the second glorious one, the resurrection of the just. Here then is formal salvation, in the new divine life wrought by the gospel.

(6.) Here is the outward sign and seal thereof in baptism, called therefore *the washing of regeneration.* The work itself is inward and spiritual; but it is outwardly signified and sealed in this ordinance. Water is of a cleansing and purifying nature, does away the filth of the flesh, and so was apt to signify the doing away of the guilt and defilement of sin by the blood and Spirit of Christ, though that aptness alone, without Christ's institution, would not have been sufficient. This it is that makes it of this signification on God's part, a seal of righteousness by faith, as circumcision was, in the place of which it succeeds; and on ours an engagement to be the Lord's. Thus baptism saves figuratively and sacramentally, where it is rightly used. *Arise, and be baptized, and wash away thy sins, calling upon the name of the Lord,* Acts 22:16. So Eph. 5:26, *That he might sanctify and cleanse us by the washing of water by the word.* Slight not this outward sign and seal, where it may be had according to Christ's appointment; yet rest not in the outward washing, but look to the *answer of a good conscience,* without which the external washing will avail nothing. The covenant sealed in baptism binds to duties, as well as exhibits and conveys benefits and privileges; if the former be not minded, in vain are the latter expected. Sever not what God has joined; in both the outer and inner part is baptism complete; as he that was circumcised became debtor to the whole law (Gal. 5:3), so is he that is baptized to the gospel, to observe all the commands and ordinances thereof, as Christ appointed. *Disciple all nations, baptizing them in the name of the Father, and of the Son, and of the Holy Ghost; teaching them to observe all things whatsoever I have commanded you,* Mt. 28:19, 20. This is the outward sign and seal of salvation, baptism, called here *the washing of regeneration.*

(7.) Here is the principal efficient, namely, the Spirit of God; it is the *renewing of the Holy Ghost;* not excluding the Father and the Son, who in all works without themselves are concurring; nor the use of means, the word and sacraments, by which the Spirit works; through his operation it is that they have their saving effect. In the economy of our salvation, the applying and effecting part is especially attributed to the Holy Spirit. We are said to be born of the Spirit, to be quickened and sanctified by the Spirit, to be led and guided, strengthened and helped, by the Spirit. Through him we mortify sin, perform duty, walk in God's ways; all the acts and operations of the divine life in us, the works and fruits of righteousness without us, all are through this blessed and Holy Spirit, who is therefore called the Spirit of life, and of grace and holiness; all grace is from him. Earnestly therefore is he to be sought, and greatly to be heeded by us, that we quench not his holy motions, nor resist and oppose him in his workings. *Res delicatula est Spiritus — The Spirit is a tender thing.* As we act towards him, so may we expect he will to us; if we slight, and resist, and oppose his workings, he will slacken them; if we continue to vex him, he will retire. *Grieve not therefore the Holy Spirit of God, whereby you are sealed to the day of redemption,* Eph. 4:30. The Spirit seals by his renewing and sanctifying, his witnessing and assuring work; he distinguishes and marks out for salvation, and fits for it; it is his work: we could not turn to God by any strength of our own, any more than we can be justified by any righteousness of our own.

(8.) Here is the manner of God's communicating this Spirit in the gifts and graces of it; not with a scanty and niggardly hand, but most freely and plentifully: *Which he shed on us abundantly.* More of the Spirit in its gifts and graces is poured out under the gospel than was under the law, whence it is eminently styled *the ministration of the Spirit,* 2 Co. 3:8. A measure of the Spirit the church has had in all ages, but more in gospel times, since the coming of Christ, than before. *The law came by Moses, but grace and truth by Jesus Christ;* that is, a more plentiful effusion of grace, fulfilling the promises and prophecies of old. Isa. 44:3, *I will pour water upon him that is thirsty, and floods upon the dry ground. I will pour my Spirit upon thy seed, and my blessing upon thy offspring:* this greatest and best of blessings, an effusion of grace, and of the sanctifying gifts of the Spirit. Joel 2:28, *I will pour out my Spirit upon all flesh;* not on Jews only, but Gentiles also. This was to be in gospel times; and accordingly (Acts 2:17, 18, 33), speaking of Christ risen and ascended, *having received of the Father the promise of the Holy Ghost, he hath shed forth* (says Peter) *this that you now see and hear:* and *ch.* 10:44, 45, *The Holy Ghost fell on all those that heart the word,* Gentiles as well as Jews. This indeed was, in a great measure, in the miraculous gifts of the Holy Ghost, but not without his sanctifying graces also accompanying many if not all of them. There was then great abundance of common gifts of illumination, outward calling and profession, and general faith, and of more special gifts of sanctification too, such as faith, and hope, and love, and other graces of the Spirit. Let us get a share in these. What will it signify if much be shed forth and we remain dry? Our condemnation will but be aggravated the more if under such a dispensation of grace we remain void of grace. *Be filled with the Spirit,* says the apostle; it is duty as well as privilege, because of the means which God in the gospel is ready to bless and make effectual; this is the manner of God's communicating grace and all spiritual blessings under the gospel — *plentifully;* he is not straitened towards us, but we towards him and in ourselves.

(9.) Here is the procuring cause of all, namely, Christ: *Through Jesus Christ our Saviour.* He it is who purchased the Spirit and his saving gifts and graces. All come through him, and through him as a Saviour, whose undertaking and work it is to bring to grace and glory; he is our righteousness and peace, and our head, from whom we have all spiritual life and influences. *He is made of God to us wisdom, righteousness, sanctification, and redemption.* Let us praise God for him above all; let us go to the Father by him, and improve him to all sanctifying and saving purposes. Have we grace? Let us thank him with the Father and Spirit for it: *account all things but loss and dung for the excellency of the knowledge of him,* and grow and increase therein more and more.

(10.) Here are the ends why we are brought into this new spiritual condition, namely, justification, and heirship, and hope of eternal life: *That, being justified by his grace, we should be made heirs according to the hope of eternal life.* Justification in the gospel sense is the free remission of a sinner, and accepting him as righteous through the righteousness of Christ received by faith. In it there is the removing of guilt that bound to punishment, and the accepting and dealing with the person as one that now is righteous in God's sight. This God does freely as to us, yet through the intervention of Christ's sacrifice and righteousness, laid hold on by faith (Rom. 3:20, etc.): *By the deeds of the law shall no flesh be justified;* but through *the righteousness of God, which is by faith of Jesus Christ unto all and upon all those that believe,* whence (*v.* 24) we are said to be *justified freely by his grace, through the redemption that is in Jesus Christ, whom God hath set forth to be a propitiation through faith in his blood, to declare his righteousness for the remission of sins, that he might be just, and the justifier of him that believeth in Jesus.* God, in justifying a sinner in the way of the gospel, is gracious to him, and yet just to himself and his law, forgiveness being through a perfect righteousness, and satisfaction made to justice by Christ, who is the propitiation for sin, and not merited by the sinner himself. So it is here: *Not by works of righteousness which we have done, but according to his mercy he saved us, that, being justified by his grace, we should be made heirs according to the hope of eternal life.* It is by grace, as the spring and rise (as was said), though *through the redemption that is in Christ* as making the way, God's law and justice being thereby satisfied, and by faith applying that redemption. *By him* (by Christ) *all that believe are justified from all things from which they could not be justified by the law of Moses,* Acts 13:39. Hence the apostle desires *to be found in him, not having his own righteousness, which was of the law, but that which is through the faith of Christ, the righteousness which is of God by faith.* Let us not trust therefore in our own righteousness or merit of good works, but in Christ's righteousness alone, received by faith for justification and acceptance with God. Inherent righteousness we must have, and the fruits of it in works of obedience; not however as our justifying righteousness before God, but as fruits of our justification, and evidences of our interest in Christ and qualification for life and happiness, and the very beginning and part of it; but the procuring of all this is by Christ, that, *being justified by his grace, we should be made heirs.* Observe, Our justification is *by the grace of God,* and our justification by that grace is necessary in order to our being made *heirs of eternal life;* without such justification there can be no adoption and sonship, and so no right of inheritance. Jn. 1:12, *Whoever received him* (namely, Christ), *to them gave he power to become the sons of God, even to those that believed on his name.* Eternal life is set before us in the promise, the Spirit works faith in us and hope of that life, and so are we made heirs of it and have a kind of possession of it even now; faith and hope bring it near, and fill with joy in the well-grounded expectation of it. The meanest believer is a great heir. Though he has not his portion in hand, he has good hope through grace, and may bear up under all difficulties. There is a better state in view. He is waiting for *an inheritance incorruptible, undefiled, and that fadeth not away, reserved in heaven for him.* How well may such comfort themselves with these words! And now all this gives good reason why we should *show all meekness to all men,* because we have experienced so much benefit by the kindness and love of God to us, and may hope that they, in God's time, may be partakers of the like grace as we are. And thus of the reasons of equal and gentle, meek and tender behaviour to wards others, from their own bad condition in time past, and the present more happy state into which they are brought, without any merit or deservings of their own, and whereinto by the same grace others may be brought also.

III. The apostle, having opened the duties of Christians in common, with the reasons respecting themselves, adds another from their goodness and usefulness to men. Observe, When he has opened the grace of God towards us, he immediately presses the necessity of good works; for we must not expect the benefit of God's mercy, unless we make conscience of our duty (*v.* 8): *This is a faithful saying, and these things I will that thou affirm constantly* (this is a true Christian doctrine of highest importance, and which ministers must most earnestly and constantly press and inculcate), *that those who have believed in God* do not think that a bare naked faith will save them; but it must be an operative working faith, bringing forth the fruit of righteousness; they must make it their care *to maintain good works,* not to do them occasionally only, and when opportunities come in their way, but to seek opportunities for doing them. *These things are good and profitable unto men:* these *good works,* say some, or *the teaching of these things,* rather than idle questions, as follows. These things are good in themselves and the teaching of them useful to mankind, making persons a common good in their places. Note, Ministers, in teaching, must see that they deliver what is sound and good in itself, and profitable to those that hear: all must be to the use of edifying both of persons and societies.

Verses 9–15

Here is the fifth and last thing in the matter of the epistle: what Titus should avoid in teaching; how he should deal with a heretic; with some other directions. Observe,

I. That the apostle's meaning might be more clear and full, and especially fitted to the time and state of things in Crete, and the many judaizers among them, he tells Titus what, in teaching, he should shun, *v.* 9. There are needful questions to be discussed and cleared, such as make for improvement in useful knowledge; but idle and foolish enquiries, tending neither to God's glory nor the edification of men, must be shunned. Some may have a show of wisdom, but are vain, as many among the Jewish doctors, as well as of later schoolmen, who abound with questions of no moment or use to faith or practice; avoid these. — *And genealogies* (of the gods, say some, that the heathen poets made such noise about; or rather those that the Jews were so curious in): some lawful and useful enquiries might be made into these things, to see the fulfilling of the scriptures in some cases, and especially in the descent of Christ the Messiah; but all that served to pomp only, and to feed vanity, in boasting of a long pedigree, and much more such as the Jewish teachers were ready to busy themselves in and trouble their hearers with, even since Christ had come, and that distinction of families and tribes had been taken away, as if they would build again that policy which now is abolished, these Titus must withstand as foolish and vain. — *And contentious, and strivings about the law.* There were those who were for the Mosaic rites and ceremonies, and would have them continued in the church, though by the gospel and the coming of Christ they were superseded and done away. Titus must give no countenance to these, but avoid and oppose them; *for they are unprofitable and vain:* this is to be referred to all those *foolish questions and genealogies,* as well as those *strivings about the law.* They are so far from instructing and building up in godliness, that they are hindrances of it rather: the Christian religion, and good works, which are to be maintained, will hereby be weakened and prejudiced, the peace of the church disturbed, and the progress of the gospel hindered. Observe, Ministers must not only teach things good and useful, but shun and oppose the contrary, what would corrupt the faith, and hinder godliness and good works; nor should people have itching ears, but love and embrace sound doctrine, which tends most to the use of edifying.

II. But because, after all, there will be *heresies* and *heretics* in the church, the apostle next directs Titus what to do in such a case, and how to deal with such, *v.* 10. He who forsakes the truth as it is in Christ Jesus, who broaches false doctrines and propagates them to the corrupting of the faith in weighty and momentous points, and breaks the peace of the church about them, after due means used to reclaim him, must be rejected. "Admonish him once and again, that, if possible, he may be brought back, and thou mayest gain thy brother; but, if this will not reduce him, that others be not hurt, cast him out of the communion, and warn all Christians to avoid him." — *Knowing that he that is such is subverted* (turned off from the foundation) *and sinneth* grievously, being *self-condemned.* Those who will not be reclaimed by admonitions, but are obstinate in their sins and errors, *are subverted and self-condemned;* they inflict that punishment upon themselves which the governors of the church should inflict upon them: they throw themselves out of the church, and throw off its communion, and so are self-condemned. Observe, 1. How great an evil real heresy is, not lightly therefore to be charged upon any, though greatly to be taken heed of by all. Such a one is *subverted* or perverted — a metaphor from a building so ruined as to render it difficult if not impossible to repair and raise it up again. Real heretics have seldom been recovered to the true faith: not so much defect of judgment, as perverseness of the will, being in the case, through pride, or ambition, or self-willedness, or covetousness, or such like corruption, which therefore must be taken heed of: "Be humble, love the truth and practise it, and damning heresy will be escaped." 2. Pains and patience must be used about those that err most grievously. They are not easily and soon to be given up and cast off, but competent time and means must be tried for their recovery. 3. The church's means even with heretics are persuasive and rational. They must be admonished, instructed, and warned; so much *nouthesia* imports. 4. Upon continued obstinacy and irreclaimableness, the church has power, and is obliged, to preserve its own purity, by severing such a corrupt member which discipline may by God's blessing become effectual to reform the offender, or if not it will leave him the more inexcusable in his condemnation.

III. The apostle subjoins some further directions, *v.* 12, 13. Here are two personal things enjoined: —

1. That Titus should hold himself ready to come to Paul at *Nicopolis* (a city of Thrace, as is reckoned, on the borders of Macedonia), as soon as *Artemas* or *Tychicus* should be sent to Crete, to supply his place, and take care of the churches there when he should leave them. The apostle would not have them in their young and weak state be without one or other of chief sufficiency, to guide and help them. Titus, it seems, was not their ordinary fixed bishop or pastor, but an evangelist, otherwise Paul would not have called him so much from his charge. Of Artemas we read little, but Tychicus is mentioned on many occasions with respect. Paul calls him

a beloved brother, and faithful minister, and fellow-servant in the Lord: one fit therefore for the service intimated. When Paul says to Titus, *Be diligent to come to me to Nicopolis, for I have determined there to winter,* it is plain that the epistle was not written from Nicopolis, as the postcript would have it, for then he would have said, I determined *here,* not *there,* to winter.

2. The other personal charge to Titus is that he would bring two of his friends on their journey diligently, and see them furnished, so that nothing should be wanting to them. This was to be done, not as a piece of common civility only, but of Christian piety, out of respect both to them and the work they were sent about, which probably was to preach the gospel, or to be in some way serviceable to the churches. *Zenas* is styled *the lawyer,* whether in reference to the Roman or the Mosaic law, as having some time been his profession, is doubtful. *Apollos* was an eminent and faithful minister. Accompanying such persons part of their way, and accommodating them for their work and journeys, was a pious and needful service; and to further this, and lay in for it, what the apostle had before exhorted Titus to teach (*v.* 8) he repeats here: *Let ours also learn to maintain good works for necessary uses, that they be not unfruitful, v.* 14. Let Christians, those who have believed in God, learn to *maintain good works,* especially such as these, supporting ministers in their work of preaching and spreading the gospel, hereby becoming *fellow-helpers to the truth,* 3 Jn. 5–8. *That they be not unfruitful.* Christianity is not a fruitless profession; the professors of it must be *filled with the fruits of righteousness, which are by Jesus Christ, to the glory and praise of God.* It is not enough that they be harmless, but they must be profitable, doing good, as well as eschewing evil. — "*Let ours* set up and maintain some honest labour and employment, to provide for themselves and their families, that they be not unprofitable burdens on the earth;" so some understand it. Let them not think that Christianity gives them a writ of ease; no, it lays an obligation upon them to seek some honest work and calling, and therein *to abide with God.* This is of good report, will credit religion and be good to mankind; they will not be unprofitable members of the body, not burdensome and chargeable to others, but enabled to be helpful to those in want. *To maintain good works for necessary uses;* not living like drones on the labours of others, but themselves fruitful to the common benefit.

IV. The apostle concludes with salutations and benedictions, *v.* 5. Though perhaps not personally known (some of them at least), yet all by Paul testify their love and good wishes to Titus, owning him thereby in his work, and stimulating him to go on therein. Great comfort and encouragement it is to have the heart and prayers of other Christians with and for us. *Greet those that love us in the faith,* or *for the faith,* who are our loving fellow-christians. Holiness, or the image of God in any, is the great endearing thing that gives strength to all other bonds, and is itself the best. *Grace be with you all. Amen.* This is the closing benediction, not to Titus alone, but to all the faithful with him, which shows that though the epistle bears the single name of Titus in the inscription, yet it was for the use of the churches there, and they were in the eye, and upon the heart, of the apostle, in the writing of it. "*Grace be with you all,* the love and favour of God, with the fruits and effects thereof, according to need, spiritual ones especially, and the increase and feeling of them more and more in your souls." This is the apostle's wish and prayer, showing his affection to them, his desire of their good, and a means of obtaining for them, and bringing down upon them, the thing requested. Observe, Grace is the chief thing to be wished and begged for, with respect to ourselves or others; it is, summarily, all good. *Amen* shuts up the prayer, expressing desire and hope, that so it may, and so it shall be.

AN EXPOSITION, WITH PRACTICAL OBSERVATIONS, OF

THE EPISTLE OF ST. PAUL TO PHILEMON

This epistle to Philemon is placed the last of those with the name of Paul to them, perhaps because the shortest, and of an argument peculiar and different from all the others; yet such as the Spirit of God, who indited it, saw would, in its kind, be very instructive and useful in the churches. The occasion of it was this: — Philemon, one of note and probably a minister in the church of Colosse, a city of Phrygia, had a servant named *Onesimus,* who, having purloined his goods, ran away from him, and in his rambles came to Rome, where Paul was then a prisoner for the gospel, and, providentially coming under his preaching there, was, by the blessing of God, converted by him, after which he ministered awhile to the apostle in bonds, and might have been further useful to him, but, understanding him to be another man's servant, Paul would not, without his consent, detain him, but sends him back with this letter-commendatory, wherein he earnestly sues for his pardon and kind reception.

Before we enter on the exposition, such general things as follow may be taken notice of from the epistle and what relates to it; namely, I. The goodness and mercy of God to a poor wandering sinner, bringing him by his gracious providence under the means, and making them effectual to his conversion. Thus came he to be *sought of him that asked not for him, and to be found of him that sought him not,* Isa. 65:1. II. The great and endeared affection between a true convert and him whom God used to be the instrument of his conversion. Paul regards this poor fugitive now as his son in the faith, and terms him his *own bowels;* and Onesimus readily serves Paul in prison, and would gladly have continued to do so, would duty have permitted; but, being another's servant, he must return and submit himself to his master, and be at his disposal. III. The tender and good spirit of this blessed apostle Paul. With what earnestness does he concern himself for the poor slave! Being now, through his preaching, reconciled to God, he labours for reconciliation between him and his master. How pathetic a letter does he here write in his behalf! Scarcely any argument is forgotten that could possible be used in the case; and all are pressed with such force that, had it been the greatest favour to himself that he was asking, he could not have used more. IV. The remarkable providence of God in preserving such a short writing as this, that might be thought of little concern to the church, being not only a letter to a particular person (as those to Timothy, and Titus, and Gaius, and the elect lady, likewise were), but of a private personal matter, namely, the receiving of a poor fugitive servant into the favour and family of his injured master. What in this is there that concerns the common salvation? And yet over this has there been a special divine care, it being given (as the other scriptures were) by *inspiration of God,* and in some sort, as they are, *profitable for doctrine, for reproof, for correction, and for instruction in righteousness.* God would have extant a proof and instance of his rich and free grace for the encouragement and comfort of the meanest and vilest of sinners, looking to him for mercy and forgiveness; and for instruction to ministers and others not to despise any, much less to judge them as to their final state, as if they were utter castaways, but rather to attempt their conversion, hoping they may be saved; likewise how to behave towards them. Joy must be on earth, as well as there is in heaven, over one sinner who repenteth. Such must now be loved, and helped, and confirmed in good, and furthered in it; and, in their outward concerns, their comfort and welfare must be consulted and promoted as much as possible. And, on their part, they must be humble and grateful, acknowledging God and his instruments in what good they have received, ready to all suitable returns, making what reparation they can in case of injuries, and living a life of thankfulness and obedience. To such purposes may this epistle have been written and preserved. And perhaps, V. There may be something further in all this; at least, by way of allusion, it is applicable to the mediation and intercession of Christ for poor sinners. We, like Onesimus, were revolters from God's service, and had injured him in his rights. Jesus Christ finds us, and by his grace works a change in us, and then intercedes for us with the Father, that we may be received into his favour and family again, and past offences may be forgiven; and we are sure that the *Father heareth him always.* There is no reason to doubt but Paul prevailed with Philemon to forgive and receive Onesimus: and more reason have we to be confident that the intercession of Christ with the Father is prevalent for the acceptance of all whose case he takes in hand and recommends to him. From these general observations we come to the epistle itself.

In this epistle we have, I. The preface (*v.* 1–7). II. The substance and body of it (*v.* 8–21). And then the conclusion (*v.* 22 to the end.)

Verses 1–7

I. In the first two verses of the preface we have the persons from and to whom it is written, with some annexed note or title, implying somewhat of argument to the purpose of the letter.

1. The persons writing: Paul, the principal, who calls himself *a prisoner of Jesus Christ,* that is, for Jesus Christ. To be a prisoner simply is no comfort nor honour; but such as Paul was, *for the faith and preaching of the gospel,* this was true glory, and proper to move Philemon upon the request made to him by such a one. A petition from one suffering for Christ and his gospel would surely be tenderly regarded by a believer and minister of Christ, especially when strengthened too with the concurrence of Timothy, one eminent in the church, sometimes called by Paul *his son in the faith,* but now, it is likely, grown more in years, he styles him *his brother.* What could be denied to two such petitioners? Paul is not slight in serving a poor convert; he gets all the additional help he can in it.

2. The persons written to are *Philemon and Apphia,* and with them Archippus, and the church in Philemon's house. Philemon, the master of Onesimus, was the principal, to whom the letter is inscribed, the head of the family, in whom were the authority and power of taking in or shutting out, and whose property Onesimus was: with him therefore chiefly lay the business. *To Philemon our dearly beloved, and fellow-labourer;* a good man he was, and probably a minister, and on both accounts dearly beloved by Paul. *A lover of good men* is one property of a good minister (Tit. 1:8), and especially must such love those who labour with them in the work of the gospel, and who are faithful therein. The general calling as Christians knits those together who are Christian; but, when conjunction in the special calling as ministers is added, this will be further endearing. Paul, in the highest degree of ministry, not only calls Timothy, an evangelist, his brother, but Philemon, an ordinary pastor, his dearly beloved fellow-labourer — an example of humility and condescension, and of all affectionate regards, even in those that are highest in the church, towards others that are labourers in the same special heavenly calling. With Philemon Apphia is joined, probably his yoke-fellow; and, having a concern in the domestic affairs, the apostle directs to her likewise. She was a party offended and injured by Onesimus, and therefore proper to be taken notice of in a letter for reconciliation and forgiveness. Justice and prudence would direct Paul to this express notice of her, who might be helpful in furthering the good ends of his writing. She is set before Archippus, as more concerned and having more interest. A kind conjunction there is in domestic matters between husband and wife, whose interests are one, and whose affections and actings must correspond. These are the principal parties written to. The less principal are, *Archippus, and the church in Philemon's house.* Archippus was a minister in the church of Colosse, Philemon's friend, and probably co-pastor with him; Paul might think him one whom Philemon would advise with, and who might be capable of furthering the good work of

peace-making and forgiveness, and therefore might judge fit to put him in the inscription of the letter, with the adjunct of *fellow-soldier.* He had called Philemon his *fellow-labourer.* Ministers must look on themselves as labourers and soldiers, who must therefore take pains, and endure hardship; they must stand on their guard, and make good their post; must look on one another as fellow-labourers, and fellow-soldiers, who must stand together, and strengthen one another's hands and hearts in any work of their holy function and calling: they need see to it that they be provided with spiritual weapons, and skill to use them; as labourers they must minister the word, and sacraments, and discipline, and watch over souls, *as those that must give an account of them;* and, as soldiers, they must fight the Lord's battles, and not entangle themselves in the things of this life, but attend to the pleasing of him who hath chosen them to be soldiers, 2 Tim. 2:4. To those it is added, *And to the church in thy house,* his whole family, in which the worship of God was kept up, so that he had, as it were, a church in his house. Observe, (1.) Families which generally may be most pious and orderly may yet have one or other in them impious and wicked. This was the aggravation of Onesimus's sin, that it was where he might and should have learned better; it is likely that he was secret in him misconduct, till his flight discovered him. Hearts are unknown but to God, till overt acts discover them. (2.) This one evil servant did not hinder Philemon's house from being called and counted a church, for the religious worship and order that were kept up in it; and such should all families be — nurseries of religion, societies where God is called on, his word is read, his sabbaths are observed, and the members are instructed in the knowledge of him and of their duty to him, neglect of which is followed with ignorance and all corruption. Wicked families are nurseries for hell, as good ones are for heaven. (3.) Masters and others of the family may not think it enough to be good, singly and severally in their personal capacities, but they must be socially so; as here Philemon's house was a church; and Paul, for some concern that all might have in this matter of Onesimus, directs to them all, that their affection as well as Philemon's might return to him, and that in their way and place they might further, and not hinder, the reconciliation wished and sought. Desirable it is that all in a family be well affected towards one another, for furthering their particular welfare and for the common good and benefit of all. On such accounts might it be that Paul inscribed his letter here so generally, that all might be the more ready to own and receive this poor convert, and to behave affectionately towards him. Next to this inscription is,

II. The apostle's salutation of those named by him (*v.* 3): *Grace to you and peace from God our Father and the Lord Jesus Christ.* This is the token in every epistle; so the apostle writes. He is a hearty well-wisher to all his friends, and wishes for them the best things; not gold, nor silver, nor any earthly good, in the first or chief place, but *grace and peace from God in Christ;* he cannot give them himself, but he prays for them from him who can bestow them. *Grace,* the free favour and good-will of God, the spring and fountain of all blessings; *and peace,* all good, as the fruit and effect of that grace. *To you,* that is, be bestowed on you, and continued to you, with the comfortable feeling and sense of it in yourselves. *From God our Father and the Lord Jesus Christ.* The Holy Spirit also is understood, though not named; for all acts towards the creatures of the whole Trinity: from the Father, who is our Father in Christ, the first in order of acting as of subsisting; and from Christ, his favour and good-will as God, and the fruits of it through him as Mediator, God-man. It is in the beloved that we are accepted, and through him we have peace and all good things, who is, with the Father and Spirit, to be looked to and blessed and praised for all, and to be owned, not only as Jesus and Christ, but as Lord also. In 2 Co. 13:14 the apostle's benediction is full: *The grace of the Lord Jesus Christ, and the love of God, and the communion of the Holy Ghost, be with you all, Amen.* Observe, Spiritual blessings are first and especially to be sought for ourselves and others. The favour of God and peace with him, as in itself it is the best and most desirable good, so is it the cause of all other, and what puts sweetness into every mercy and can make happy even in the want of all earthly things. *Though there be no herd in the stall, and the labour of the olive fail,* yet may such *rejoice in the Lord, and joy in the God of their salvation,* Hab. 3:17, 18. *There are many that say, Who will show us any good?* But, if God *lift up the light of his countenance,* this will put more joy and gladness into the heart than all worldly increase, Ps. 4:6, 7. And Num. 6:26, *The Lord lift up the light of his countenance upon thee, and give thee peace.* In this is summarily all good, and from this one fountain, God the *Father, Son,* and *Spirit,* all comes. After this salutation of the apostle to Philemon, and his friends and family, for better making way still for his suit to him,

III. He expresses the singular and affection he had for him, by thanksgiving and prayer to God in his behalf, and the great joy for the many good things he knew and heard to be in him, *v.* 4–7. The apostle's thanksgiving and prayer for Philemon are here set forth by the object, circumstance, and matter of them, with the way whereby much of the knowledge of Philemon's goodness came to him.

1. Here is the object of Paul's praises and prayers for Philemon: *I thank my God, making mention of thee in my prayers, v.* 4. Observe, (1.) God is the author of all the good that is in any, or that is done by them. *From me is thy fruit found,* Hos. 14:8. To him therefore is all the praise due. 1 Chr. 29:13, 14, *But* [or for] *who am I, and what is my people, that we should be able to offer so willingly after this sort? For all things come of thee,* both wherewith to offer, and the will and heart to do it. On this account (says he) *we thank thee our God, and praise thy glorious name.* (2.) It is the privilege of good men that their praises and prayers they come to God as their God: *Our God, we thank thee,* said David; and *I thank my God,* said Paul. (3.) Our prayers and praises should be offered up to God, not for ourselves only, but for others also. Private addresses should not be altogether with a private spirit, minding our own things only, but others must be remembered by us. We must be affected with joy and thankfulness for any good in them, or done by them, or bestowed on them, as far as is known to us, and seek for them what they need. In this lies no little part of the communion of saints. Paul, in his private thanksgivings and prayers, was often particular in remembering his friends: *I thank my God, making mention of thee in my prayers;* sometimes it may be by name, or at least having them particularly in his thoughts; and God knows who is meant, though not named. This is a means of exercising love, and obtaining good for others. *Strive with me, by your prayers to God for me,* said the apostle: and what he desired for himself he surely practised on behalf of others; so should all. *Pray one for another,* says James, 5:16.

2. Here is the circumstance: *Always making mention of thee. Always* — usually, not once or twice only, but frequently. So must we remember Christian friends much and often, as their case may need, bearing them in our thoughts and upon our hearts before our God.

3. Here is the matter both of his praises and prayers, in reference to Philemon.

(1.) Of his praises. [1.] He thanks God for the love which he heard Philemon had towards the Lord Jesus. He is to be loved as God superlatively, as his divine perfections require; and as related to us, the Lord, and our Lord, our Maker, Redeemer, and Saviour, who loved us, and gave himself for us. Paul thanks God for what he heard of this, the signal marks and expressions of it in Philemon. [2.] For his faith in Christ also. Love to Christ, and faith in him, are prime Christian graces, for which there is great ground of praise to God, where he has blessed any with them, as Rom. 1:8, *I thank my God* because *your faith is published throughout the world;* and, in reference to the Colossians (*ch.* 1:3, 4), *We give thanks to God since we heard of your faith in Christ Jesus.* This is a saving grace, and the very principle of Christian life and of all good works. [3.] He praises God likewise for Philemon's love to all the saints. These two must go together; for he who *loveth him that begat must* and will *love those also that are begotten of him.* The apostle joins them in that (Col. 1:3, 4), *We give thanks to God since we heard of your faith in Christ Jesus, and of the love which you have to all the saints.* These bear the image of Christ, which will be loved by every Christian. Different sentiments and ways in what is not essential will not make a difference of affection as to the truth, though difference in the degrees of love will be according as more or less of that image is discerned. Mere external differences are nothing here. Paul calls a poor converted slave *his bowels.* We must love, as God does, all saints. Paul thanked God for the good that was not only in the churches, but in the particular persons he wrote to, and though this too was known to him merely by report: *Hearing of thy love and faith, which thou hast towards the Lord Jesus, and towards all saints.* This was what he enquired after concerning his friends, the truth, and growth, and fruitfulness of their graces, their faith in Christ, and love to him and to all the saints. Love to saints, if it be sincere, will be catholic and universal love towards all saints; but faith and love, though in the heart they are hidden things, are known by the effects of them. Therefore,

(2.) The apostle joins prayer with his praises, that the fruits of Philemon's faith and love might be more and more conspicuous, so as that the communication of them might constrain others to the acknowledgment of all the good things that were in him and in his house towards Christ Jesus; that their *light might so shine before men that they, seeing their good works, might* be stirred up to imitate them, and to *glorify their Father who is in heaven.* Good works must be done, not of vain-glory to be seen, yet such as may be seen to God's glory and the good of men.

4. He adds a reason, both of his prayer and his praises (*v.* 7): *For "we have great joy and consolation in thy love, because the bowels of the saints are refreshed by thee, brother.* The good thou hast done and still doest is abundant matter of joy and comfort to me and others, who therefore desire you may continue and abound in such good fruits more and more, to God's honour and the credit of religion. *The administration of this service not only supplieth the want of the saints, but is abundant also by many thanksgivings unto God,"* 2 Co. 9:12.

Verses 8–25

We have here,

I. The main business of the epistle, which was to plead with Philemon on behalf of Onesimus, that he would receive him and be reconciled to him. Many arguments Paul urges for this purpose, *v.* 8–21. The

1st Argument is taken from what was before noted, and is carried in the illative *wherefore:* "Seeing so much good is reported of thee and found in thee, especially thy love to all saints, now let me see it on a fresh and further occasion; *refresh the bowels of Onesimus and mine also,* in forgiving and receiving him, who is now a convert, and so a saint indeed, and meet for thy favour and love." Observe, A disposition to do good, together with past instances and expressions of it, is a good handle to take hold of for pressing to more. *"Be not weary of well-doing,* go on as thou art able, and as new objects and occasions occur, to do the same still." The

2nd Argument is from the authority of him that was now making this request to him: *I might be very bold in Christ to enjoin thee that which is convenient, v.* 8. The apostles had under Christ great power in the church over the ordinary ministers, as well as the members of it, for edification; they might require of them what was fit, and were therein to be obeyed, which Philemon should consider. This was a matter within the compass of the apostle's power to require, though he would not in this instance act up to it. Observe, Ministers, whatever their power be in the church, are to use prudence in the exercise of it; they may not unseasonably, nor further than is requisite, put it forth; in all they must use godly wisdom and discretion. Wherefore this may be a

3rd Argument, Waiving the authority which yet he had to require, he chooses to entreat it of him (*v.* 9): *Yet for love's sake I rather beseech thee.* Observe, It is no disparagement for those who have power to be condescending, and sometimes even to beseech, where, in strictness of right, they might command; so does Paul here, though an apostle: he entreats where he might enjoin, he argues from love rather than authority, which doubtless must carry engaging influence with it. And especially, which may be a

4th Argument, When any circumstance of the person pleading gives additional force to his petition, as here: *Being such a one as Paul the aged, and now also a prisoner of Jesus Christ.* Years bespeak respect; and the motions of such, in things lawful and fit, should be received with regard. The request of an aged apostle, and now suffering for Christ and his gospel, should be tenderly considered. "If thou wilt do any thing for a poor aged prisoner, to comfort me in my bonds, and make my chain lighter, grant me this which I desire: hereby in a manner you will do honour to Christ in the person of an aged suffering servant of his, which doubtless he will take as done to himself." He makes also a

5th Argument, From the spiritual relation now between Onesimus and himself: *I beseech thee for my son Onesimus, whom I have begotten in my bonds, v.* 10. "Though of right and in a civil respect he by thy servant, yet in a spiritual sense he is now a son to me, God having made me the instrument of his conversion, even here, where I am a prisoner for Christ's sake." Thus does God sometimes honour and comfort his suffering servants, not only working good in themselves by their sufferings, exercising and improving thereby their own graces, but making them a means of much spiritual good to others, either of their conversion, as of Onesimus here, or of their confirmation and strengthening, as Phil. 1:14, *Many brethren, waxing confident by my bonds, are much more bold to speak the word of the Lord without fear.* When God's servants are bound, yet his word and Spirit are not bound; spiritual children may then be born to them. The apostle lays an emphasis here: *My son, whom I have begotten in my bonds;* he was dear to him, and he hoped would be so to Philemon, under this consideration. Prison-mercies are sweet and much set by. Paul makes an argument to Philemon from this dear relation that now was between Onesimus and him, his son begotten in his bonds. And a

6th Argument is from Philemon's own interest: *Who in time past was to thee unprofitable, but now profitable to thee and to me, v.* 11. Observe, (1.) Unsanctified persons are unprofitable persons; they answer not the great end of their being and relations. Grace makes good for somewhat: "*In time past unprofitable, but now profitable,* inclined and fitted to be so, and will be so to thee, his master, if thou receive him, as he has since his conversion been here to me, ministering to me in my confinement." There seems an allusion to the name Onesimus, which signifies *profitable.* Now he will answer to his name. It may be noted also how the apostle speaks in this matter, not as Onesimus's former case and conduct might warrant; he had wronged his master, and ran away from him, and lived as if he were his own and not his; yet as God covers the sins of penitents, forgives and does not upbraid, so should men. How tenderly does Paul here speak! Not that Onesimus's sin was small, nor that he would have any, much less himself, to take it so; but having been humbled for it, and doubtless taken shame to himself on account thereof, the apostle now would not sink his spirit by continuing to load and burden him therewith, but speaks thus tenderly when he is pleading with Philemon not to make severe reflections on his servant's misconduct, but to forgive. (2.) What happy changes conversion makes — of evil good! of unprofitable useful! Religious servants are a treasure in a family. Such will make conscience of their time and trusts, promoting the interests of those whom they serve, and managing all they can for the best. This then is the argument here urged: "It will now be for thy advantage to receive him: thus changed, as he is, thou mayest expect him to be a dutiful and faithful servant, though in time past he was not so." Whereupon,

7th Argument, He urges Philemon from the strong affection that he had to Onesimus. He had mentioned the spiritual relation before, *My son begotten in my bonds;* and now he signifies how dear he was to him: *Thou therefore receive him, that is my own bowels, v.* 12. "I love him as I do myself, and have sent him back to thee for this end, that thou shouldst receive him; do it therefore for my sake, receive him as one thus dear to me." Observe, Even good men may sometimes need great earnestness and entreaty to lay their passions, let go their resentments, and forgive those who have injured and offended them. Some have thought it to look this way, when Paul is so pathetic and earnest, mustering up so many pleas and arguments to gain what he requests. Philemon, a Phrygian, might perhaps be naturally of a rough and difficult temper, and thence need no little pains in touching all the springs that might move him to forgiveness and reconciliation; but rather should we strive to be like God, who is *slow to anger, ready to forgive, and abundant in pardons.* And again, an

8th Argument is from the apostle's denying himself in sending back Onesimus: though he might have presumed upon Philemon's leave to detain him longer, yet he would not, *v.* 13, 14. Paul was now in prison, and wanted a friend or servant to act for him, and assist him, for which he found Onesimus fit and ready, and therefore would have detained him to minister to him, instead of Philemon himself, whom if he had requested to have come to him in person for such purpose, he might have presumed he would not have refused; much less might he have reckoned that he would be unwilling his servant should do this in his stead; yet he would not take this liberty, though his circumstances needed it: *I have sent him back* to thee, that any good office of thine to me might not be *of necessity, but willingly.* Observe, Good deeds are most

acceptable to God and man when done with most freedom. And Paul herein, notwithstanding his apostolical power, would show what regard he had to civil rights, which Christianity does by no means supersede or weaken, but rather confirm and strengthen. Onesimus, he knew, was Philemon's servant, and therefore without his consent not to be detained from him. In his unconverted state he had violated that right, and withdrawn himself, to his master's injury; but, now that he had seen his sin and repented, he was willing and desirous to return to his duty, and Paul would not hinder this, but rather further it. He might indeed have presumed on Philemon's willingness; but, but notwithstanding his need, he would deny himself rather than take that way. And he further urges,

9th Argument, That such a change was now wrought in Onesimus that Philemon needed not fear his ever running from him, or injuring him any more: *For perhaps he therefore departed for a season, that thou shouldest receive him for ever, v.* 15. There are those of whom Solomon says, *If thou deliver them, thou must do it again* (Prov. 19:19); but the change wrought in Onesimus was such that he would never again need one thus to intercede for him. Charity would so hope and judge, yea, so it would be; yet the apostle speaks cautiously, that none might be bold to make another such experiment in expectation of a like gracious issue. Observe, (1.) In matters that may be wrested to ill, ministers must speak warily, that kind providences of God towards sinners be not abused to encouragements to sin, or abatements of just abhorrence of it: *Perhaps he therefore departed from thee for a season,* etc. (2.) How tenderly still the sins of penitents are spoken of; he calls it a *departure for a season,* instead of giving it the term that it deserved. As overruled and ordered by God, it was a *departure;* but in itself, and in respect of the disposition and manner of the act, it was a *criminal going away.* When we speak of the nature of any sin or offence against God, the evil of it is not to be lessened; but in the person of a penitent sinner, as God covers it, so must we: "*He departed for a season, that thou shouldst receive him for ever,* that upon conversion he may return, and be a faithful and useful servant to thee as long as he lives." *Bray a fool in a mortar, yet will not his folly depart from him.* But it is not so with true penitents: they will not return to folly. (3.) Observe the wisdom, and goodness, and power of God, in causing that to end so happily which was begun and carried on for some time so wickedly, thus regarding a poor vassal, one of such low rank and condition and so little regarded by men, working so good and great a change in him who was so far gone in evil ways, who had wronged a master so good, had run from a family so pious, from the means of grace, the church in his house, that he should be led into the way of salvation who had fled from it, and find means made effectual at Rome who had been hardened under them at Colosse. What riches are here of divine grace! None so low, nor mean, nor vile, as utterly to be despaired of. God can meet with them when running from him; can make means effectual at one time and place, which have not been so at another. So was it in this instance of Onesimus; having returned to God, he now returns to his master, who will have more service and better hold of him than ever — by conscience of his duty and faithfulness in it to his life's end; his interest therefore it will be now to receive him. So God often brings gain to his people out of their losses. And, besides interest, a

10th Argument is taken from the capacity under which Onesimus now would return, and must be received by Philemon (*v.* 16): "*Not now as a servant* (that is, not merely or so much), *but above a servant* (in a spiritual respect), *a brother beloved,* one to be owned as a brother in Christ, and to be beloved as such, upon account of this holy change that is wrought in him, and one therefore who will be useful unto thee upon better principles and in a better manner than before, who will love and promote the best things in thy family, be a blessing in it, and help to keep up the church that is in thy house." Observe, (1.) There is a spiritual brotherhood between all true believers, however distinguished in civil and outward respects; they are all children of the same heavenly Father, have a right to the same spiritual privileges and benefits, must love and do all good offices to and for one another as brethren, though still in the same rank, and degree, and station, wherein they were called. Christianity does not annul nor confound the respective civil duties, but strengthens the obligation to them, and directs to a right discharge of them. (2.) Religious servants are more than mere ordinary servants; they have grace in their hearts, and have found

grace in God's sight, and so will in the sight of religious masters. Ps. 101:6, *Mine eyes are upon the faithful of the land, that they may dwell with me. He that walketh in a perfect way, he shall serve me.* "Onesimus having now become such, receive and regard him as one that is partaker of the same common faith, and so *a brother beloved, specially to me* who have been the instrument of his conversion." Good ministers love not so much according to the outward good which they receive as the spiritual good which they do. Paul called Onesimus his *own bowels,* and other converts his *joy and crown.* "*A brother beloved, specially to me, but how much more to thee,* both in the flesh and in the Lord; by a double tie therefore (both civil and religious) thy servant: thy property, one of thy house and family, and now, in a spiritual respect, thy brother in Christ, which heightens the engagement. He is God's servant and thine too; here are more ties than he is under to me. How readily therefore should he be received and loved by thee, as one of thy family and one of the true faith, one of thy house and one of the church in thy house!" This argument is strengthened by another, the

11th Argument, From the communion of saints: *If thou count me therefore a partner, receive him as myself, v.* 17. There is a fellowship among saints; they have interest one in another, and must love and act accordingly. "Now show thy love to me, and the interest I have in thee, by loving and receiving one so near and dear to me, even as myself; own and treat him as thou wouldst me, with a like ready and true, though perhaps not equal, affection." But why such concern and earnestness for a servant, a slave, and such a one as had misbehaved? *Answer,* Onesimus being now penitent, it was doubtless to encourage him, and to support him against the fears he might have in returning to a master whom he had so much abused and wronged, to keep him from sinking into despondency and dejection, and encourage him to his duty. Wise and good ministers will have great and tender care of young converts, to encourage and hearten them what they can to and in their duty. *Objection,* But Onesimus had wronged as well as offended his master. The answer to this makes a

12th Argument, A promise of satisfaction to Philemon: *If he hath wronged thee, or oweth thee aught,* etc., *v.* 18, 19. Here are three things:

(1.) A confession of Onesimus's debt to Philemon: *If he hath wronged thee, or oweth thee aught.* It is not an *if* of doubting, but of illation and concession; *seeing he hath wronged thee,* and thereby has become indebted to thee; such an *if* as Col. 3:1 and 2 Pt. 2:4, etc. Observe, True penitents will be ingenuous in owning their faults, as doubtless Onesimus had been to Paul, upon his being awakened and being brought to repentance; and especially is this to be done in cases of injury to others. Onesimus by Paul owns the wrong. And,

(2.) Paul here engages for satisfaction: *Put that on my account; I Paul have written it with my own hand, I will repay it.* Observe, [1.] The communion of saints does not destroy distinction of property: Onesimus, now converted, and become a brother beloved, is yet Philemon's servant still, and indebted to him for wrongs that he had done, and not to be discharged but by free and voluntary remission, or on reparation made by himself, or some other in his behalf, which part, rather than fail, the apostle undertakes for him. [2.] Suretiship is not in all cases unlawful, but in some is a good and merciful undertaking. Only know the person and case, be not *surety for a stranger* (Prov. 11:15), and go not beyond ability; help thy friend thou mayest, as far as will comport with justice and prudence. And how happy for us that Christ would be made the surety of a better covenant (Heb. 7:22), that he would be made *sin for us who knew no sin, that we might be made the righteousness of God in him!* And, [3.] Formal securities by writing, as well as by word and promise, may be required and given. Persons die, and words may be forgotten or mistaken; writing better preserves right and peace, and has been in use with good persons, as well as others, in all ages, Jer. 32:9, etc.; Lu. 16:5–7. It was much that Paul, who lived on contributions himself, would undertake to make good all loss by an evil servant to his master; but hereby he expresses his real and great affection for Onesimus, and his full belief of the sincerity of his conversion: and he might have hope that, notwithstanding this generous offer, Philemon would not insist on it, but freely remit all, considering,

(3.) The reason of things between him and Philemon: "*Albeit, I do not say to thee how thou owest unto me even *thy own self besides;* thou wilt remember, without my reminding thee, that thou are on other accounts more in debt to me than this comes to." Modesty in self-praises is true praise. The apostle glances at the benefits he had conferred on Philemon: "That thou art any thing in grace and acceptation with God, or enjoyest any thing in a right and comfortable manner, it is, under God, owing to my ministry. I have been the instrument in his hand of all that spiritual good to thee; and what thy obligation to me on this account is I leave to thee to consider. Thy forgiving a pecuniary debt to a poor penitent for my sake and at my request, and which, however, I now take upon myself to answer, thy remitting it to him, or to me, now his surety, thou wilt confess, is not so great a thing; here is more *per contra: Thou owest to me even thy ownself besides.*" Observe, How great the endearments are between ministers and those towards whom their endeavours have been blessed to their conversion or spiritual edification! *If it had been possible* (said Paul to the Galatians), *you would have plucked out your own eyes, and have given them to me,* Gal. 4:15. On the other hand he calls them his *children, of whom he travailed again, till Christ was formed in them,* that is, the likeness of Christ more fully. So 1 Th. 2:8, *We were willing to have imparted to you not the gospel of God only, but also our own souls, because you were dear unto us.* By way of allusion, this may illustrate Christ's undertaking for us. We had revolted from God, and by sin had wronged him, but Christ undertakes to make satisfaction, *the just for the unjust, that he might bring us unto God.* "If the sinner owes thee aught, put it upon my account, I will pay the debt; let his iniquity be laid on me, I will bear the penalty." Further, a

13th Argument is from the joy and comfort the apostle hereby would have on Philemon's own account, as well as on Onesimus's in such a seasonable and acceptable fruit of Philemon's faith and obedience: *Yea, brother, let me have joy of thee in the Lord: refresh my bowels in the Lord, v.* 20. Philemon was Paul's son in the faith, yet he entreats him as a brother; Onesimus a poor slave, yet he solicits for him as if he were seeking some great thing for himself. How pathetic is he! "*Yea, brother,* or *O my brother* (it is an adverb of wishing or desiring), *let me have joy of thee in the Lord.* Thou knowest that I am now a prisoner or the Lord, for his sake and cause, and need all the comfort and support that my friends in Christ can give me: now this will be a joy to me, I shall *have joy of thee in the Lord,* as seeing such an evidence and fruit of thy own Christian faith and love, and on Onesimus's account, who hereby will be relieved and encouraged." Observe, (1.) Christians should do the things that may rejoice the hearts of one another, both people and minister reciprocally, and ministers of their brethren. From the world they expect trouble; and where may they look for comfort and joy but in one another? (2.) Fruits of faith and obedience in people are the minister's greatest joy, especially the more of love appears in them to Christ and his members, forgiving injuries, showing compassion, being merciful as their heavenly Father is merciful. "*Refresh my bowels in the Lord.* It is not any carnal selfish respect I am actuated by, but what is pleasing to Christ, and that he may have honour therein." Observe, [1.] The Lord's honour and service are a Christian's chief aim in all things. And, [2.] It is meat and drink to a good minister to see people ready and zealous in what is good, especially in acts of charity and beneficence, as occasions occur, forgiving injuries, remitting somewhat of their right, and the like. And, once more, his last, which is the

14th Argument, Lies in the good hope and opinion which he expresses of Philemon: *Having confidence in thy obedience, I wrote unto thee, knowing that thou wilt also do more than I say, v.* 21. Good thoughts and expectations of us more strongly move and engage us to do the things expected from us. The apostle knew Philemon to be a good man, and was thence persuaded of his readiness to do good, and that not in a scanty and niggardly manner, but with a free and liberal hand. Observe, Good persons will be ready for good works, and not narrow and pinching, but abundant in them. Isa. 32:8, *The liberal deviseth liberal things.* The Macedonians first gave themselves to the Lord, and then to his apostles by the will of God, to do what good they could with what they had, according as occasions offered.

Thus far is the substance and body of the epistle. We have,

II. The conclusion, where,

1. He signifies his good hope of deliverance, through their prayers, and that shortly he might see them, desiring Philemon to make provision for him: *But withal prepare me also a lodging; for I trust that through your prayers I shall be given unto you, v.* 22. *But withal,* or *moreover.* He comes to another thing, yet, as may seem, not without some eye to the matter which he had been upon, that might be furthered by this intimation that he hoped he should himself soon follow, and know the effect of his epistle, which Philemon would therefore be the more stirred up to see might be to his satisfaction. Now here is,

(1.) The thing requested: *Prepare me also a lodging;* under this all necessaries for a stranger are included. He wills Philemon to do it, intending to be his guest, as most to his purpose. Observe, Hospitality is a great Christian duty, especially in ministers, and towards ministers, such as the apostle was, coming out of such dangers and sufferings for Christ and his gospel. Who would not show the utmost of affectionate regards to such a one? It is an honourable title that he gives Gaius (Rom. 16:23), *My host, and of the whole church.* Onesiphorus is also affectionately remembered by the apostle on this account (2 Tim. 1:16, 18), *The Lord give mercy to the house of Onesiphorus; for he oft refreshed me, and was not ashamed of my chain; and in how many things he ministered to me at Ephesus, thou knowest.*

(2.) Here is the ground of the apostle's request: *For I trust that through your prayers I shall be given unto you.* He did not know how God might deal with him, but the benefit of prayer he had often found, and hoped he should again, for deliverance, and liberty to come to them. Observe, [1.] Our dependence is on God for life and liberty and opportunity of service; all is by divine pleasure. [2.] When abridged of these or any other mercies, our trust and hope must be in God, without fainting or succumbing, while our case is depending. But yet, [3.] Trust must be with the use of means, prayer especially, though no other should be at hand; this hath unlocked heaven and opened prison-doors. *The fervent effectual prayer of the righteous availeth much.* [4.] Prayer of people for ministers, especially when they are in distress and danger, is their great duty; ministers need and request it. Paul, though an apostle, did so with much earnestness, Rom. 15:30; 2 Co. 1:11; Eph. 6:18, 19; 1 Th. 5:25. The least may in this way be helpful to the greatest. Yet, [5.] Though prayer obtains, yet it does not merit the things obtained: they are God's gift, and Christ's purchase. *I trust that through your prayers, charisthēsomai hymin — I shall be freely bestowed on you.* What God gives, he will yet be sought to for, that mercies may be valued the more, and known whence they come, and God may have the praise. Minister's lives and labours are for the people's good; the office was set up for them; *he gave gifts for men, apostles,* etc. Eph. 4:8, 11, 12. Their gifts, and labours, and lives, all are for their benefit. 1 Co. 3:21, 22, *All things are yours, Apollos, Cephas,* etc. [6.] In praying for faithful ministers, people in effect pray for themselves: "*I trust I shall be given unto you,* for your service, and comfort, and edification in Christ." See 2 Co. 4:15. [7.] Observe the humility of the apostle; his liberty, should he have it, he would own to be through their prayers, as well as, or more than, his own; he mentions them only through the high thoughts he had of the prayers of many, and the regard God would show to his praying people. Thus of the first thing in the apostle's conclusion.

2. he sends salutations from one who was his fellow-prisoner, and four more who were his fellow-labourers, *v.* 23, 24. Saluting is wishing health and peace. Christianity is no enemy to courtesy, but enjoins it, 1 Pt. 3:8. It is a mere expression of love and respect, and a means of preserving and nourishing them. *There salute thee Epaphras, my fellow-prisoner in Christ Jesus.* he was of Colosse, and so countryman and fellow-citizen with Philemon; by office he seems to have been an evangelist, who laboured among the Colossians (if he was not the first converter of them), for whom he had special affection. *Our dear fellow-servant* (said St. Paul), *and for you a faithful minister of Christ* (Col. 1:7), and (*ch.* 4:12, 13), *A servant of Christ, always labouring for you in prayers. I bear him record that he hath a great zeal for you,* etc. A very eminent person therefore this was, who, being at Rome, perhaps accompanying Paul, and labouring in the same work of preaching and propagating the gospel, was confined in the same prison, and for the same cause; both termed *prisoners in Christ Jesus,* intimating the ground of their imprisonment, not any crime or wickedness, but for the faith of Christ and their service to him. An honour it is to suffer shame for Christ's name. *My fellow-prisoner in Christ Jesus* is mentioned as his glory and the apostle's comfort; not that he was a prisoner and so hindered from his work (this was matter of affliction), but that, seeing God thus permitted and called him to suffer, his providence so ordered it that they suffered together, and so had the benefit and comfort of one another's prayers, and help, it may be, in some things; this was a mercy. So God sometimes lightens the sufferings of his servants by the communion of saints, the sweet fellowship they have one with another in their bonds. Never more enjoyment of God have they found than when suffering together for God. So Paul and Silas, when their feet were fast in the stocks, had their tongues set at liberty, and their hearts tuned for the praises of God. — *Marcus, Aristarchus, Demas, Lucas, my fellow-labourers.* The mention of these seems in a manner to interest them in the business of the latter. How ill would it look by denial of the request of it to slight so many worthy names as most of these, at least, were! *Marcus,* cousin of Barnabas, and son of Mary, who was so hospitable to the saints at Jerusalem (Col. 4:10, Acts 12:12), and whose house was the place of meeting for prayer and the worship of God. Though some failing seems to have been in him when Paul and he parted, yet in conjunction with Barnabas he went on with his work, and here Paul and he, we perceive, were reconciled, and differences forgotten, 2 Tim. 4:11. He bids Mark to be brought to him, *for he is profitable to me for the ministry,* that is, of an evangelist. *Aristarchus* is mentioned with Marcus (Col. 4:10), and called there by Paul his fellow-prisoner; and speaking there of Marcus, sister's son to Barnabas, he adds, *Touching whom you received commandments; if he come unto you, receive him:* an evidence that he himself had received him, and was reconciled to him. Next is *Demas,* who hitherto, it seems, appeared not faulty, though he is censured (2 Tim. 4:10) as having forsaken Paul, from *love of this present world.* But how far his forsaking was, whether total from his work and profession, or partial only, and whether he repented and returned to his duty, scripture is silent, and so much we be: no mark of disgrace lay on him here, but he is joined with others who were faithful, as he is also in Col. 4:14. *Lucas* is the last, that *beloved physician* and evangelist, who came to Rome, companion with Paul, Col. 4:14; 2 Tim. 4:11. He was Paul's associate in his greatest dangers, and his fellow-labourer. The ministry is not a matter of carnal ease nor pleasure, but of pains; if any are idle in it, they answer not their calling. Christ bids his disciples *pray the Lord of the harvest to send forth labourers,* not loiterers, *into his harvest,* Mt. 9:38. And the people are extorted to *know those that labour among them, and are over them in the Lord, and to esteem them very highly in love for their work's sake,* 1 Th. 5:12, 13. *My fellow-labourers,* says the apostle: ministers must be helpers together of the truth; they serve the same Lord, in the same holy work and function, and are expectants of the same glorious reward; therefore they must be assistants to each other in furthering the interest of their great and common Master. Thus of the salutations, and then,

3. Here is the apostle's closing prayer and benediction, *v.* 25. Observe, (1.) What is wished and prayed for: *Grace,* the free favour and love of God, together with the fruits and effects of it in all good things, for soul and body, for time and eternity. Observe, Grace is the best wish for ourselves and others; with this the apostle begins and ends. (2.) From whom: *Our Lord Jesus Christ,* the Son of God, second Person in the Trinity, Lord by natural right, *by whom, and for whom, all things were created* (Col. 1:16, Jn. 1:1–3), *and who is heir of all things,* and, as God-man and Mediator, who purchased us, and to whom we are given by the Father. *Jesus,* the Saviour, Mt. 1:21. We were lost and undone; he recovers us, and repairs the ruin. He saves by merit, procuring pardon and life for us; and by power, rescuing us from sin, and Satan, and hell, and renewing us to the likeness, and bringing us to the enjoyment, of God: thus is he Jesus; and Christ, the Messiah or anointed, consecrated and fitted to be king, priest, and prophet, to his church. To all those offices were there anointings under the law with oil, and to them was the Saviour spiritually anointed with the Holy Ghost, Acts 10:38. In none but him were all these together and in such eminence. *He was anointed with the oil of gladness above his fellows,* Ps. 45:7. This Lord Jesus Christ is ours by original title to us, by gospel offers and gift, his purchase of us, and our own acceptance of him, resignation to him, and mystical union with him: *Our Lord Jesus Christ.* Observe, All grace to us is from Christ; he purchased, and he bestows it. *Of his fulness we all receive, and grace for grace,* Jn. 1:16. *He filleth all in all,*

Eph. 1:23. (3.) To whom: *Your spirit, meta tou pneumatos hymōn,* not of Philemon only, but of all who were named in the inscription. *With your spirit,* that is, with you, the soul or spirit being the immediate seat of grace, whence it influences the whole man, and flows out in gracious and holy actings. All the house saluted are here joined in the closing benediction, the more to remind and quicken all to further the end of the epistle.

Amen is added, not only for strong and affectionate summing up the prayer and wish, *so let it be;* but as an expression of faith that it will be heard, *so shall it be.* And what need we more to make us happy than to have *the grace of our Lord Jesus Christ with our spirit?* This is the usual benediction, but it may be taken here to have some special respect also to the occasion; the grace of Christ with their spirits, Philemon's especially, would sweeten and mollify them, take off too deep and keen resentments of injuries, and dispose to forgive others as God for Christ's sake hath forgiven us.

AN EXPOSITION, WITH PRACTICAL OBSERVATIONS, OF

THE EPISTLE TO THE HEBREWS

Concerning this epistle we must enquire, I. Into the divine authority of it; for this has been questioned by some, whose distempered eyes could not bear the light of it, or whose errors have been confuted by it; such as the Arians, who deny the Godhead and self-existence of Christ; and the Socinians, who deny his satisfaction; but, after all the attempts of such men to disparage this epistle, the divine original of it shines forth with such strong and unclouded rays that he who runs may read it is an eminent part of the canon of scripture. The divinity of the matter, the sublimity of the style, the excellency of the design, the harmony of this with other parts of scripture, and its general reception in the church of God in all ages — these are the evidences of its divine authority. II. As to the divine amanuensis or penman of this epistle, we are not so certain; it does not bear the name of any in the front of it, as the rest of the epistles do, and there has been some dispute among the learned to whom they should ascribe it. Some have assigned it to Clemens of Rome; other to Luke; and many to Barnabas, thinking that the style and manner of expression is very agreeable to the zealous, authoritative, affectionate temper that Barnabas appears to be of, in the account we have of him in the acts of the Apostles; and one ancient father quotes an expression out of this epistle as the words of Barnabas. But it is generally assigned to the apostle Paul; and some later copies and translations have put Paul's name in the title. In the primitive times it was generally ascribed to him, and the style and scope of it very well agree with his spirit, who was a person of a clear head and a warm heart, whose main end and endeavour it was to exalt Christ. Some think that the apostle Peter refers to this epistle, and proves Paul to be the penman of it, by telling the Hebrews, to whom he wrote, of Paul's having written to them, 2 Pt. 3:15. We read of no other epistle that he ever wrote to them but this. And though it has been objected that, since Paul put his name to all his other epistles, he would not have omitted it here; yet others have well answered that he, being the apostle of the Gentiles, who were odious to the Jews, might think fit to conceal his name, lest their prejudices against him might hinder them from reading and weighing it as they ought to do. III. As to the scope and design of this epistle, it is very evident that it was clearly to inform the minds, and strongly to confirm the judgment, of the Hebrews in the transcendent excellency of the gospel above the law, and so to take them off from the ceremonies of the law, to which they were so wedded, of which they were so fond, that they even doted on them, and those of them who were Christians retained too much of the old leaven, and needed to be purged from it. The design of this epistle was to persuade and press the believing Hebrews to a constant adherence to the Christian faith, and perseverance in it, notwithstanding all the sufferings they might meet with in so doing. In order to this, the apostle speaks much of the excellency of the author of the gospel, the glorious Jesus, whose honour he advances, and whom he justly prefers before all others, showing him to be all in all, and this in lofty strains of holy rhetoric. It must be acknowledged that there are many things in this epistle hard to be understood, but the sweetness we shall find therein will make us abundant amends for all the pains we take to understand it. And indeed, if we compare all the epistles of the New Testament, we shall not find any of them more replenished with divine, heavenly matter than this to the Hebrews.

CHAPTER 1

In this chapter we have a twofold comparison stated: I. Between the evangelical and legal dispensation; and the excellency of the gospel above that of the law is asserted and proved (*v.* 1–3). II. Between the glory of Christ and that of the highest creatures, the angels; where the pre-eminence is justly given to the Lord Jesus Christ, and clearly demonstrated to belong to him (*v.* 4 to the end).

Verses 1–3

Here the apostle begins with a general declaration of the excellency of the gospel dispensation above that of the law, which he demonstrates from the different way and manner of God's communicating himself and his mind and will to men in the one and in the other: both these dispensations were of God, and both of them very good, but there is a great difference in the way of their coming from God. Observe,

I. The way wherein God communicated himself and his will to men under the Old Testament. We have here an account, 1. Of the persons by whom God delivered his mind under the Old Testament; they were *the prophets,* that is, persons chosen of God, and qualified by him, for that office of revealing the will of God to men. No man takes this honour to himself, unless called; and whoever are called of God are qualified by him. 2. The persons to whom God spoke by the prophets: *To the fathers,* to all the Old-Testament saints who were under that dispensation. God favoured and honoured them with much clearer light than that of nature, under which the rest of the world were left. 3. The order in which God spoke to men in those times that went before the gospel, those past times: he spoke to his ancient people *at sundry times and in divers manners.* (1.) *At sundry times,* or *by several parts,* as the word signifies, which may refer either to the several ages of the Old-Testament dispensation — the patriarchal, the Mosaic, and the prophetic; or to the several gradual openings of his mind concerning the Redeemer: to Adam, that the Messiah should come of the seed of the woman, — to Abraham, that he should spring from his loins, — to Jacob, that he should be of the tribe of Judah, — to David, that he should be of his house, — to Micah, that he should be born at Bethlehem, — to Isaiah, that he should be born of a virgin. (2.) *In divers manners,* according to the different ways in which God though fit to communicate his mind to his prophets; sometimes by the *illapses* of his Spirit, sometimes by *dreams,* sometimes by visions, sometimes by an audible voice, sometimes by legible characters under his own hand, as when he wrote the ten commandments on tables of stone. Of some of these different ways God himself gave an account in Num. 12:6–8, *If there be a prophet among you, I the Lord will make myself known to him in a vision, and will speak to him in a dream. Not so with my servant Moses: with him I will speak mouth to mouth, even apparently, and not in dark speeches.*

II. God's method of communicating his mind and will under the New-Testament dispensation, these last days as they are called, that is, either towards the end of the world, or the end of the Jewish state. The times of the gospel are the last times, the gospel revelation is the last we are to expect from God. There was first the natural revelation; then the patriarchal, by dreams, visions, and voices; then the Mosaic, in the law given forth and written down; then the prophetic, in explaining the law, and giving clearer discoveries of Christ: but now we must expect no new revelation, but only more of the Spirit of Christ to help us better to understand what is already revealed. Now the excellency of the gospel revelation above the former consists in two things: —

1. It is the final, the finishing revelation, given forth in the last days of divine revelation, to which nothing is to be added, but the canon of scripture is to be settled and sealed: so that now the minds of men are no longer kept in suspense by the expectation of new discoveries, but they rejoice in a complete revelation of the will of God, both preceptive and providential, so far as is necessary for them to know in order to their direction and comfort. For the gospel includes a discovery of the great events that shall befal the church of God to the end of the world.

2. It is a revelation which God has made by his Son, the most excellent messenger that was ever sent into the world, far superior to all the ancient patriarchs and prophets, by whom God communicated his will to his people in former times. And here we have an excellent account of the glory of our Lord Jesus Christ.

(1.) The glory of his office, and that in three respects: — [1.] God hath appointed him to be heir of all things. As God, he was equal to the Father; but, as God-man and Mediator, he was appointed by the Father to be the heir of all things, the sovereign Lord of all, the absolute disposer, director, and governor of all persons and of all things, Ps. 2:6, 7. *All power in heaven and earth is given to him; all judgment is committed to him,* Mt. 28:18; Jn. 5:22. [2.] By him God made the worlds, both visible and invisible, the heavens and the earth; not as an instrumental cause, but as his essential word and wisdom. By him he made the old creation, by him he makes the new creature, and by him he rules and governs both. [3.] He upholds all things by the word of his power: he keeps the world from dissolving. *By him all things consist.* The weight of the whole creation is laid upon Christ: he supports the whole and all the parts. When, upon the apostasy, the world was breaking to pieces under the wrath and curse of God, the Son of God, undertaking the work of redemption, bound it up again, and established it by his almighty power and goodness. None of the ancient prophets sustained such an office as this, none was sufficient for it.

(2.) Hence the apostle passes to the glory of the person of Christ, who was able to execute such an office: *He was the brightness of his Father's glory, and the express image of his person, v.* 3. This is a high and lofty description of the glorious Redeemer, this is an account of his personal excellency. [1.] He is, in person, the Son of God, the only-begotten Son of God, and as such he must have the same nature. This personal distinction always supposes one and the same nature. Every son of man is man; were not the nature the same, the generation would be monstrous. [2.] The person of the Son is the glory of the Father, shining forth with a truly divine splendour. As the beams are effulgent emanations of the sun, the father and fountain of light, Jesus Christ in his person is God manifest in the flesh, he is light of light, the true Shechinah. [3.] The person of the Son is the true image and character of the person of the Father; being of the same nature, he must bear the same image and likeness. In beholding the power, wisdom, and goodness, of the Lord Jesus Christ, we behold the power, wisdom, and goodness, of the Father; for he hath the nature and perfections of God in him. *He that hath seen the Son hath seen the Father;* that is, he hath seen the same Being. He that hath known the Son hath known the Father, Jn. 14:7–9. For the Son is in the Father, and the Father in the Son; the personal distinction is no other than will consist with essential union. This is the glory of the person of Christ; the fulness of the Godhead dwells, not typically, but really, in him.

(3.) From the glory of the person of Christ he proceeds to mention the glory of his grace; his condescension itself was truly glorious. The sufferings of Christ had this great honour in them, to be a full satisfaction for the sins of his people: *By himself he purged away our sins,* that is, by the proper innate merit of his death and bloodshed, by their infinite intrinsic value; as they were the sufferings of himself, he has made atonement for sin. Himself, the glory of his person and nature, gave to his sufferings such merit as was a sufficient reparation of honour to God, who had suffered an infinite injury and affront by the sins of men.

(4.) From the glory of his sufferings we are at length led to consider the glory of his exaltation: *When by himself he had purged away our sins, he sat down at the right hand of the Majesty on high,* at his Father's right hand. As Mediator and Redeemer, he is invested with the highest honour, authority, and activity, for the good of his people; the Father now does all things by him, and receives all the services of his people from him. Having assumed our nature, and suffered in it on earth, he has taken it up with him to heaven, and there it has the high honour to be next to God, and this was the reward of his humiliation.

Now it was by no less a person than this that God in these last days spoke to men; and, since the dignity of the messenger gives authority and excellency to the message, the dispensations of the gospel must therefore exceed, very far exceed, the dispensation of the law.

Verses 4–14

The apostle, having proved the pre-eminence of the gospel above the law from the pre-eminence of the Lord Jesus Christ above the prophets, now proceeds to show that he is much superior not only to the prophets, but to the angels themselves. In this he obviates an objection that the Jewish zealots would be ready to make, that the law was not only delivered by men, *but ordained by angels* (Gal. 3:19), who attended at the giving forth of the law, the hosts of heaven being drawn forth to attend the Lord Jehovah on that awful occasion. Now the angels are very glorious beings, far more glorious and excellent than men; the scripture always represents them as the most excellent of all creatures, and we know of no being but God himself that is higher than the angels; and therefore that law that was ordained by angels ought to be held in great esteem. To take off the force of this argument, the penman of this epistle proceeds to state the comparison between Jesus Christ and the holy angels, both in nature and office, and to prove that Christ is vastly superior to the angels themselves: *Being made so much better than the angels, as he hath by inheritance obtained a more excellent name than they.* Here observe,

I. The superior nature of Christ is proved from his superior name. The scripture does not give high and glorious titles without a real foundation and reason in nature; nor would such great things have been said of our Lord Jesus Christ if he had not been as great and excellent as those words import. When it is said that Christ was made so much better than the angels, we are not to imagine that he was a mere creature, as the angels are; the word *genomenos,* when joined with an adjective, is nowhere to be rendered *created,* and here may very well be read, *being more excellent,* as the *Syriac version* hath it. We read *ginesthē ho Theos alēthēs — let God be true,* not made so, but acknowledged to be so.

II. The superiority of the name and nature of Christ above the angels is declared in the holy scriptures, and to be deduced thence. We should have known little or nothing either of Christ or of the angels, without the scriptures; and we must therefore be determined by them in our conceptions of the one and the other. Now here are several passages of scripture cited, in which those things are said of Christ that were never said of the angels.

1. It was said of Christ, *Thou art my Son, this day have I begotten thee* (Ps. 2:7), which may refer to his eternal generation, or to his resurrection, or to his solemn inauguration into his glorious kingdom at his ascension and session at the right hand of the Father. Now this was never said concerning the angels, and therefore by inheritance he has a more excellent nature and name than they.

2. It was said concerning Christ, but never concerning the angels, *I will be to him a Father, and he shall be to me a Son;* taken from 2 Sa. 7:14. Not only, "I am his Father, and he is my Son, by nature and eternal promanation;" but, "I will be his Father, and he shall be my Son, by wonderful conception, and this his son-ship shall be the fountain and foundation of every gracious relation between me and fallen man."

3. It is said of Christ, *When God bringeth his First-begotten into the world, let all the angels of God worship him;* that is, when he is brought into this lower world, at his nativity, let the angels attend and honour him; or when he is brought into the world above, at his ascension, to enter upon his mediatorial kingdom, or when he shall bring him again into the world, to judge the world, then let the highest creatures worship him. God will not suffer an angel to continue in heaven who will not be in subjection to Christ, and pay adoration to him; and he will at last make the fallen angels and wicked men to confess his divine power and authority and to fall before him. Those who would not have him to reign must then be brought forth and slain before him. The proof of this is taken out of Ps. 97:7, *Worship him, all you gods,* that is, "All you that are superior to men, own yourselves to be inferior to Christ in nature and power."

4. God has said concerning Christ, *Thy throne, O God, is forever and ever,* etc., *v.* 8–12. But of the angels he has only said that *he hath made them spirits, and his ministers a flame of fire, v.* 7. Now, upon comparing what he here says of the angels with what he says to Christ, the vast inferiority of the angels to Christ will plainly appear.

(1.) What does God say here of the angels? *He maketh his angels spirits, and his ministers a flame of fire.* This we have in Ps. 104:4, where it seems to be more immediately spoken of the winds and lightning, but is here applied to the angels, whose agency the divine Providences makes use of in the winds, and in thunder and lightnings. Observe, [1.] The office of the angels: they are God's ministers, or *servants, to do his pleasure.* It is the glory of God that he has such servants; it is yet more so that he does not need them. [2.] How the angels are qualified for this service; he makes them spirits and a flame of fire, that is, he endows them with light and zeal, with activity and ability, readiness and resolution to do his pleasure: they are no more than what God has made them to be, and they are servants to the Son as well as to the Father. But observe,

(2.) How much greater things are said of Christ by the Father. Here two passages of scripture are quoted.

[1.] One of these is out of Ps. 45:6, 7, where God declares of Christ, *First,* His true and real divinity, and that with much pleasure and affection, not grudging him that glory: *Thy throne, O God.* Here one person calls another person God, *O God.* And, if God the Father declares him to be so, he must be really and truly so; for God calls persons and things as they are. And now let who will deny him to be essentially God at their peril, but let us own and honour him as God; for, if he had not been God, he had never been fit to have done the Mediator's work nor to have worn the Mediator's crown. *Secondly,* God declares his dignity and dominion, as having a throne, a kingdom, and a sceptre of that kingdom. He has all right, rule, authority, and power, both as the God of nature, grace, and glory, and as Mediator; and so he is fully adequate to all the intents and purposes of his mediatorial kingdom. *Thirdly,* God declares the eternal duration of the dominion and dignity of Christ, founded upon the divinity of his person: *Thy throne, O God, is for ever and ever,* from everlasting to everlasting, through all the ages of time, maugre all the attempts of earth and hell to undermine and overthrow it, and through all the endless ages of eternity, when time shall be no more. This distinguishes Christ's throne from all earthly thrones, which are tottering, and will at length tumble down; but the throne of Christ shall be as the days of heaven. *Fourthly,* God declares of Christ the perfect equity of his administration, and of the execution of his power, through all the parts of his government: *A sceptre of righteousness is the sceptre of thy kingdom, v.* 8. He came righteously to the sceptre, and he uses it in perfect righteousness; the righteousness of his government proceeds from the righteousness of his person, from an essential eternal love of righteousness and hatred of iniquity, not merely from considerations of prudence or interest, but from an inward and immovable principle: *Thou lovest righteousness and hatest iniquity, v.* 9. Christ came to fulfil all righteousness, to bring in an everlasting righteousness; and he was righteous in all his ways and holy in all his works. He has recommended righteousness to men, and restored it among them, as a most excellent and amiable thing. He came to finish transgression, and to make an end of sin as a hateful as well as hurtful thing. *Fifthly,* God declares of Christ how he was qualified for the office of Mediator, and how he was installed and confirmed in it (*v.* 9): *Therefore God, even thy God, hath anointed thee with the oil of gladness above thy fellows.* 1. Christ has the name Messiah from his being anointed. God's anointing of Christ signifies both his qualifying him for the office of the Mediator with the Holy Spirit and all his graces, and likewise his inauguration of him into the office, as prophets, priests, and kings, were by anointing. *God, even thy God,* imports the confirmation of Christ in the office of Mediator by the covenant of redemption and peace, that was between the Father and the Son. God is the God of Christ, as Christ is man and Mediator. 2. This anointing of Christ was *with the oil of gladness,* which signifies both the gladness and cheerfulness with which Christ undertook and went through the office of Mediator (finding himself so absolutely sufficient for it), and also that joy which was set before him as the reward of his service and sufferings, that crown of glory and gladness which he should wear for ever after the suffering of death. 3. This anointing of Christ was above the anointing of his fellows: *God, even thy God, hath anointed thee with the oil of gladness above thy fellows.* Who are Christ's fellows? Has he any equals? Not as God, except the Father and Spirit, but these are not here meant. As man, however, he has his fellows, and as an anointed person; but his unction is beyond all theirs. (1.) Above the angels, who may be said to be his fellows, as they are the sons of God by creation, and God's messengers, whom he employs in his service. (2.) Above all prophets, priests, and kings, that ever were anointed with oil, to be employed in the service of God on earth. (3.) Above all the saints, who are his brethren, children of the same father, as he was a partaker with them of flesh and blood. (4.) Above all those who were related to him as man, above all the house of David, all the tribe of Judah, all his brethren and kinsmen in the flesh. All God's other anointed ones had only the Spirit in a certain measure; Christ had the Spirit above measure, without any limitation. None therefore goes through his work as Christ did, none takes so much pleasure in it as Christ does; for he was anointed with the oil of gladness above his fellows.

[2.] The other passage of scripture in which is the superior excellence of Christ to the angels is taken out of Ps. 102:25–27, and is recited in *v.* 10–12, where the omnipotence of the Lord Jesus Christ is declared as it appears both in creating the world and in changing it.

First, In creating the world (*v.* 10): *And thou, Lord, in the beginning hast laid the foundation of the earth, and the heavens are the work of thy hands.* The Lord Christ had the original right to govern the world, because he made the world in the beginning. His right, as Mediator, was by commission from the Father. His right, as God with the Father, was absolute, resulting from his creating power. This power he had before the beginning of the world, and he exerted it in giving a beginning and being to the world. He must therefore be no part of the world himself, for then he must give himself a beginning. He was *pro pantōn — before all things,* and *by him all things consist,* Col. 1:17. He was not only above all things in condition, but before all things in existence; and therefore must be God, and self-existent. He laid the foundations of the earth, did not only introduce new forms into pre-existent matter, but made out of nothing the foundations of the earth, the *primordia rerum — the first principles of things;* he not only founded the earth, but the heavens too are the work of his hands, both the habitation and the inhabitants, the hosts of heaven, the angels themselves; and therefore he must needs be infinitely superior to them.

Secondly, In changing the world that he has made; and here the mutability of this world is brought in to illustrate the immutability of Christ. Observe, 1. This world is mutable, all created nature is so; this world has passed through many changes, and shall pass through more; all these changes are by the permission and under the direction of Christ, who made the world (*v.* 11, 12): *They shall perish, they shall all wax old as doth a garment; as a vesture shalt thou fold them up, and they shall be changed.* This our visible world (both the earth and visible heavens) is growing old. Not only men and beasts and trees grow old, but this world itself grows old, and is hastening to its dissolution; it changes like a garment, has lost much of its beauty and strength; it grew old betimes on the first apostasy, and it has been waxing older and growing weaker ever since; it bears the symptoms of a dying world. But then its dissolution will not be its utter destruction, but its change. Christ will fold up this world as a garment not to be abused any longer, not to be any longer so used as it has been. Let us not then set our hearts upon that which is not what we take it to be, and will not be what it now is. Sin has made a great change in the world for the worse, and Christ will make a great change in it for the better. *We look for new heavens and a new earth, wherein dwelleth righteousness.* Let the consideration of this wean us from the present world, and make us watchful, diligent, and desirous of that better world, and let us wait on Christ to change us into a meetness for that new world that is approaching; we cannot enter into it till we be new creatures. 2. Christ is immutable. Thus the Father testifies of him, *Thou remainest, thy years shall not fail.* Christ is the same in himself, the same yesterday, and to-day, and for ever, and the same to his people in all the changes of time. This may well support all who have an interest in Christ under all the changes they meet with in the world, and under all they feel in themselves. Christ is immutable and immortal: his years shall not fail. This may comfort us under all decays of nature that we may observe in ourselves or in our friends, though our flesh and heart fail and our days are hastening to an end. Christ lives to take care of us while we live, and of ours when we are gone, and this should quicken us all to make our interest in him clear and sure, that our spiritual and eternal life may be hid with Christ in God.

III. The superiority of Christ to the angels appears in this that God never said to the angels what he has said to Christ, *v.* 13, 14.

1. What has God said to Christ? He has said, *"Sit thou at my right hand, till I make thy enemies thy footstool,* Ps. 110:1. Receive thou glory, dominion, and rest; and remain in the administration of thy mediatorial kingdom until all thy enemies shall either be made thy friends by conversion or thy footstool." Note, (1.) Christ Jesus has his enemies (would one think it?), enemies even among men — enemies to his sovereignty, to his cause, to his people; such as will not have him to reign over them. Let us not think it strange then if we have our enemies. Christ never did any thing to make men his enemies; he has done a great deal to make them all his friends and his Father's friends, and yet he has his enemies. (2.) All the enemies of Christ shall be made his footstool, either by humble submission and entire subjection to his will casting themselves down at his feet, or by utter destruction; he shall trample upon those who continue obstinate, and shall trample over them. (3.) God the Father has undertaken for this, and he will see it done, yea, he will himself do it; and, though it be not done presently, it shall certainly be done, and Christ waits for it,; and so must Christians wait till God has wrought all their works in them, for them, and by them. (4.) Christ shall go on to rule and reign till this be done; he shall not leave any of his great designs unfinished, he shall go on conquering and to conquer. And it becomes his people to go on in their duty, being what he would have them to be, doing what he would have them to do, avoiding what he would have them to avoid, bearing what he would have them to bear, till he make them conquerors and more than conquerors over all their spiritual enemies.

2. What has God said to the angels? He never said to them, as he said to Christ, *Sit you at my right hand;* but he has said of them here that *they are ministering spirits, sent forth to minister for those who shall be heirs of salvation.* Note, (1.) What the angels are as to their nature: they are spirits, without bodies or inclination to bodies, and yet they can assume bodies, and appear in them, when God pleases. They are spirits, incorporeal, intelligent, active, substances; they excel in wisdom and strength. (2.) What the angels are as to their office: they are ministering spirits. Christ, as Mediator, is the great minister of God in the great work of redemption. The Holy Spirit is the great minister of God and Christ in the application of this redemption. Angels are ministering spirits under the blessed Trinity, to execute the divine will and pleasure; they are the ministers of divine Providence. (3.) The angels are sent forth for this end — to minister to those who shall be the heirs of salvation. Here observe, [1.] The description given of the saints — they are *heirs of salvation;* at present they are under age, heirs, not inheritors. They are heirs because they are children of God; *if children, then heirs.* Let us make sure that we are children by adoption and regeneration, having made a covenant-resignation of ourselves to God, and walking before him in a gospel-conversation, and then we are heirs of God, and joint-heirs with Christ. [2.] The dignity and privilege of the saints — the angels are sent forth to minister for them. Thus they have done in attending and acting at the giving forth of the law, in fighting the battles of the saints, in destroying their enemies. They still minister for them in opposing the malice and power of evil spirits, in protecting and keeping their bodies, pitching their tents about theirs, instructing, quickening, and comforting their souls under Christ and the Holy Ghost; and thus they shall do in gathering all the saints together at the last day. Bless God for the ministration of angels, keep in God's way, and take the comfort of this promise, that he will *give his angels charge over you, to keep you in all your ways. They shall bear you up in their hands, lest you dash your feet against a stone,* Ps. 91:11, 12.

CHAPTER 2

In this chapter the apostle, I. Makes some application of the doctrine laid down in the chapter foregoing concerning the excellency of the person of Christ, both by way of exhortation and argument (*v.* 1–4). II. Enlarges further upon the pre-eminence of Christ above the angels (*v.* 5–9). III. Proceeds to remove the scandal of the cross (*v.* 10–15). IV. Asserts the incarnation of Christ, taking upon him not the nature of angels, but the seed of Abraham, and assigns the reason of his so doing (*v.* 16 to the end).

Verses 1–4

The apostle proceeds in the plain profitable method of doctrine, reason, and use, through this epistle. Here we have the application of the truths before asserted and proved; this is brought in by the illative particle *therefore,* with which this chapter begins, and which shows its connection with the former, where the apostle having proved Christ to be superior to the angels by whose ministry the law was given, and therefore that the gospel dispensation must be more excellent than the legal, he now comes to apply this doctrine both by way of exhortation and argument.

I. By way of exhortation: *Therefore we ought to give the more diligent heed to the things which we have heard, v.* 1. This is the first way by which we are to show our esteem of Christ and of the gospel. It is the great concern of every one under the gospel to give the most earnest heed to all gospel discoveries and directions, to prize them highly in his judgment as matters of the greatest importance, to hearken to them diligently in all the opportunities he has for that purpose, to read them frequently, to meditate on them closely, and to mix faith with them. We must embrace them in our hearts and affections, retain them in our memories, and finally regulate our words and actions according to them.

II. By way of argument, he adds strong motives to enforce the exhortation.

1. From the great loss we shall sustain if we do not take this earnest heed to the things which we have heard: *We shall let them slip.* They will leak, and run out of our heads, lips, and lives, and we shall be great losers by our neglect. Learn, (1.) When we have received gospel truths into our minds, we are in danger of letting them slip. Our minds and memories are like a leaky vessel, they do not without much care retain what is poured into them; this proceeds from the corruption of our natures, the enmity and subtlety of Satan (he steals away the word), from the entanglements and snares of the world, the thorns that choke the good seed. (2.) Those meet with an inconceivable loss who let gospel truths, which they had received, slip out of their minds; they have lost a treasure far better than thousands of gold and silver; the seed is lost, their time and pains in hearing lost, and their hopes of a good harvest lost; all is lost, if the gospel be lost. (3.) This consideration should be a strong motive both to our attention to the gospel and our retention of it; and indeed, if we do not well attend, we shall not long retain the word of God; inattentive hearers will soon be forgetful hearers.

2. Another argument is taken from the dreadful punishment we shall incur if we do not do this duty, a more dreadful punishment than those fell under who neglected and disobeyed the law, *v.* 2, 3. Here observe, (1.) How the law is described: it was the *word spoken by angels, and declared to be stedfast.* It was the word spoken by angels, because given by the ministration of angels, they sounding the trumpet, and perhaps forming the words according to God's direction; and God, as judge, will make use of the angels to sound the trumpet a second time, and gather all to his tribunal, to receive their sentence, as they have conformed or not conformed to the law. *And this law is declared to be stedfast;* it is like the promise, *yea and amen;* it is truth and faithfulness, and it will abide and have its force whether men obey it or no; *for every transgression and disobedience will receive a just recompence of reward.* If men trifle with the law of God, the law will not trifle with them; it has taken hold of the sinners of former ages, and will take hold of sinners in all ages. God, as a righteous governor and judge, when he had given forth the law, would not let the contempt and breach of it go unpunished; but he has from time to time reckoned with the transgressors of it, and recompensed them according to the nature and aggravation of their disobedience. Observe, The severest punishment God ever inflicted upon sinners is no more than what sin deserves: it is *a just recompence of reward;* punishments are as just, and as much due to sin as rewards are to obedience, yea, more due than rewards are to imperfect obedience. (2.) How the gospel is described. It is salvation, a great salvation; so great salvation that no other salvation can compare with it; so great that none can fully express, no, nor yet conceive, how great it is. It is a great salvation that the gospel discovers, for it discovers a great Saviour, one who has manifested God to be reconciled to our nature, and reconcilable to our persons; it shows how we may be saved from so great sin and so great misery, and be restored to so great holiness and so great happiness. The gospel discovers to us a great sanctifier, to qualify us for salvation and to bring us to the Saviour. The gospel unfolds a great and excellent dispensation of grace, a new covenant; the great charter-deed and instrument is settled and secured to all those who come into the bond of the covenant. (3.) How sinning against the gospel is described: it is declared to be a *neglect of this great salvation;* it is a contempt put upon the saving grace of God in Christ, making light of it, not caring for it, not thinking it worth their while to acquaint themselves with it, not regarding either the worth of gospel grace or their own want of it and undone state without it; not using their endeavours to discern the truth of it, and assent to it, nor to discern the goodness of it, so as to approve of it, or apply it to themselves. In these things they discover a plain neglect of this great salvation. Let us all take heed that we be not found among those wicked wretched sinners who neglect the grace of the gospel. (4.) How the misery of such sinners is described: it is declared to be unavoidable (*v.* 3): *How shall we escape?* This intimates, [1.] That the despisers of this salvation are condemned already, under arrest and in the hands of justice already. So they were by the sin of Adam; and they have strengthened their bonds by their personal transgression. *He that believeth not is condemned already,* Jn. 3:18. [2.] There is no escaping out of this condemned state, but by accepting the great salvation discovered in the gospel; as far those who neglect it, the wrath of God is upon them, and it abides upon them; they cannot disengage themselves, they cannot emerge, they cannot get from under the curse. [3.] That there is a yet more aggravated curse and condemnation waiting for all those who despise the grace of God in Christ, and that this most heavy curse they cannot escape; they cannot conceal their persons at the great day, nor deny the fact, nor bribe the judge, nor break the prison. There is no door of mercy left open for them; there will be no more sacrifice for sin; they are irrecoverably lost. The unavoidableness of the misery of such is here expressed by way of question: *How shall we escape?* It is an appeal to universal reason, to the consciences of sinners themselves; it is a challenge to all their power and policy, to all their interest and alliances, whether they, or any for them, can find out, or can force out, a way of escape from the vindictive justice and wrath of God. It intimates that the neglecters of this great salvation will be left not only without power, but without plea and excuse, at the judgment-day; if they be asked what they have to say that the sentence should not be executed upon them, they will be speechless, and self-condemned by their own consciences, even to a greater degree of misery than those fell under who neglected the authority of the law, or sinned without the law.

3. Another argument to enforce the exhortation is taken from the dignity and excellency of the person by whom the gospel began to be spoken (*v.* 3): *It began at first to be spoken by the Lord,* that is, the Lord Jesus Christ, who is Jehovah, the Lord of Life and glory, Lord of all, and as such possessed of unerring and infallible wisdom, infinite and inexhaustible goodness, unquestionable and unchangeable veracity and faithfulness, absolute sovereignty and authority, and irresistible power. This great Lord of all was the first who began to speak it plainly and clearly, without types and shadows as it was before he came. Now surely it may be expected that all will reverence this Lord, and take heed to a gospel that began to be spoken by one who spoke so as never *man spoke.*

4. Another argument is taken from the character of those

who were witnesses to Christ and the gospel (v. 3, 4): *It was confirmed to us by those that heard him, God also bearing them witness.* Observe, (1.) The promulgation of the gospel was continued and confirmed by those who heard Christ, by the evangelists and apostles, who were eye and ear-witnesses of what Jesus Christ began both to do and to teach, Acts 1:1. These witnesses could have no worldly end or interest of their own to serve hereby. Nothing could induce them to give in their evidence but the Redeemer's glory, and their own and others' salvation; they exposed themselves by their testimony to the loss of all that was dear to them in this life, and many of them sealed it with their blood. (2.) *God himself bore witness* to those who were witnesses for Christ; he testified that they were authorized and sent by him to preach Christ and salvation by him to the world. And how did he bear them witness? Not only by giving them great peace in their own minds, great patience under all their sufferings, and unspeakable courage and joy (though these were witnesses to themselves), but he bore them witness *by signs, and wonders, and divers miracles, and gifts of the Holy Ghost, according to his will.* [1.] With *signs,* signs of his gracious presence with them, and of his power working by them. [2.] *Wonders,* works quite beyond the power of nature, and out of the course of nature, filling the spectators with wonder and admiration, stirring them up to attend to the doctrine preached, and to enquire into it. [3.] *Divers miracles,* or mighty works, in which an almighty agency appeared beyond all reasonable controversy. [4.] *Gifts of the Holy Ghost,* qualifying, enabling, and exciting them to do the work to which they were called — *divisions or distributions of the Holy Ghost, diversities of gifts,* 1 Co. 12:4, etc. And all this *according to God's own will.* It was the will of God that we should have sure footing for our faith, and a strong foundation for our hope in receiving the gospel. As at the giving forth of the law there were signs and wonders, by which God testified the authority and excellency of it, so he witnessed to the gospel by more and greater miracles, as to a more excellent and abiding dispensation.

Verses 5–9

The apostle, having made this serious application of the doctrine of the personal excellency of Christ above the angels, now returns to that pleasant subject again, and pursues it further (v. 5): *For to the angels hath he not put in subjection the world to come, whereof we speak.*

I. Here the apostle lays down a negative proposition, including a positive one — That the state of the gospel-church, which is here called *the world to come,* is *not subjected to the angels,* but under the special care and direction of the Redeemer himself. Neither the state in which the church is at present, nor that more completely restored state at which it shall arrive when the prince of this world is cast out and the kingdoms of the earth shall become the kingdom of Christ, is left to the government of the angels; but Jesus Christ will take to him his great power, and will reign. He does not make that use of the ministration of angels to give the gospel as he did to give the law, which was the state of the old or antiquated world. This new world is committed to Christ, and put in absolute subjection to him only, in all spiritual and eternal concerns. Christ has the administration of the gospel church, which at once bespeaks Christ's honour and the church's happiness and safety. It is certain that neither the first creation of the gospel church, nor its after-edification or administration, nor its final judgment and perfection, is committed to the angels, but to Christ. God would not put so great a trust in his holy ones; his angels were too weak for such a charge.

II. We have a scripture-account of that blessed Jesus to whom the gospel world is put into subjection. It is taken from Ps. 8:4–6, *But one in a certain place testified, saying, What is man, that thou art mindful of him? or the Son of man, that thou visitest him?* etc. There words are to be considered both as applicable to mankind in general, and as applied here to the Lord Jesus Christ.

1. As applicable to mankind in general, in which sense we have an affectionate thankful expostulation with the great God concerning his wonderful condescension and kindness to the sons of men. (1.) In remembering them, or being mindful of them, when yet they had no being but in the counsels of divine love. The favours of God to men all spring up out of his eternal thoughts and purposes of mercy for them; as all our dutiful regards to God spring forth from our remem-

brance of him. God is always mindful of us, let us never be forgetful of him. (2.) In visiting them. God's purpose of favours for men is productive of gracious visits to them; he comes to see us, how it is with us, what we ail, what we want, what dangers we are exposed to, what difficulties we have to encounter; and by his visitation our spirit is preserved. Let us so remember God as daily to approach him in a way of duty. (3.) In making man the head of all the creatures in this lower world, the top-stone of this building, the chief of the ways of God on earth, and only a little lower than the angels in place, and respect to the boy, while here, and to be made like the angels, and equal to the angels, at the resurrection of the just, Lu. 20:36. (4.) In crowning him with glory and honour, the honour of having noble powers and faculties of soul, excellent organs and parts of body, whereby he is allied to both worlds, capable of serving the interests of both worlds, and of enjoying the happiness of both. (5.) In giving him right to and dominion over the inferior creatures, which did continue so long as he continued in his allegiance and duty to God.

2. As applied to the Lord Jesus Christ, and the whole that is here said can be applied only to him, v. 8, 9. And here you may observe, (1.) What is the moving cause of all the kindness God shows to men in giving Christ for them and to them; and that is the grace of God. For *what is man?* (2.) What are the fruits of this free grace of God with respect to the gift of Christ for us and to us, as related in this scripture-testimony. [1.] That God was mindful of Christ for us in the covenant of redemption. [2.] That God visited Christ on our account; and it was concluded between them that in the fulness of time Christ should come into the world, as the great archetypal sacrifice. [3.] That God had made him a little lower than the angels, in his being made man, that he might suffer and humble himself to death. [4.] That God crowned the human nature of Christ with glory and honour, in his being perfectly holy, and having the Spirit without measure, and by an ineffable union with the divine nature in the second person of the Trinity, the fulness of the Godhead dwelling in him bodily; that by his sufferings he might make satisfaction, tasting death for every man, sensibly feeling and undergoing the bitter agonies of that shameful, painful, and cursed death of the cross, hereby putting all mankind into a new state of trial. [5.] That, as a reward of his humiliation in suffering death, he was crowned with glory and honour, advanced to the highest dignity in heaven, and having absolute dominion over all things, thus accomplishing that ancient scripture in Christ, which never was so accomplished or fulfilled in any mere man that ever was upon earth.

Verses 10–13

Having mentioned the death of Christ, the apostle here proceeds to prevent and remove the scandal of the cross; and this he does by showing both how it became God that Christ should suffer and how much man should be benefited by those sufferings.

I. How it became God that Christ should suffer: *For it became him for whom are all things, and by whom are all things, in bringing many sons to glory, to make the captain of their salvation perfect through sufferings,* v. 10. Here,

1. God is described as the final end and first cause of all things, and as such it became him to secure his own glory in all that he did, not only to act so that he might in nothing dishonour himself, but so that he might from every thing have a revenue of glory.

2. He is declared to have acted up to this glorious character in the work of redemption, as to the choice both of the end and of the means.

(1.) In the choice of the end; and that was to bring many sons to glory in enjoying the glorious privileges of the gospel, and to future glory in heaven, which will be glory indeed, an exceeding eternal weight of glory. Here observe,, [1.] We must be the sons of God both by adoption and regeneration, before we can be brought to the glory of heaven. Heaven is the inheritance; and only those that are the children are heirs of that inheritance. [2.] All true believers are the children of God: *to those that receive Christ he has granted the power and privilege of being the children of God, even to as many as believe on his name,* Jn. 1:12. [3.] Though the sons of God are but a few in one place and at one time, yet when they shall be all brought together it will appear that they are many. Christ is the first-born among many brethren. [4.] All the sons of God, now many soever they are, or

however dispersed and divided, shall at length be brought together to glory.

(2.) In the choice of the means. In finding out such a person as should be the captain of our salvation; those that are saved must come to that salvation under the guidance of a captain and leader sufficient for that purpose; and they must be all enlisted under the banner of this captain; they must endure hardship as good soldiers of Christ; they must follow their captain, and those that do so shall be brought safely off, and shall inherit great glory and honour. [2.] In making this captain of our salvation perfect through sufferings. God the Father made the Lord Jesus Christ the captain of our salvation (that is, he consecrated, he appointed him to that office, he gave him a commission for it), and he made him a perfect captain: he had perfection of wisdom, and courage, and strength, by the Spirit of the Lord, which he had without measure; he was made perfect through sufferings; that is, he perfected the work of our redemption by shedding his blood, and was thereby perfectly qualified to be a Mediator between God and man. He found his way to the crown by the cross, and so must his people too. The excellent Dr. Owen observes that the Lord Jesus Christ, being consecrated and perfected through suffering, has consecrated the way of suffering for all his followers to pass through unto glory; and hereby their sufferings are made necessary and unavoidable, they are hereby made honourable, useful, and profitable.

II. He shows how much they would be benefited by the cross and sufferings of Christ; as there was nothing unbecoming God and Christ, so there was that which would be very beneficial to men, in these sufferings. Hereby they are brought into a near union with Christ, and into a very endearing relation.

1. Into a near union (v. 11): *Both he that sanctifieth and those that are sanctified are all of one.* Observe, Christ is he that sanctifieth; he has purchased and sent the sanctifying Spirit; he is the head of all sanctifying influences. The Spirit sanctifieth as the Spirit of Christ. True believers are those who are sanctified, endowed with holy principles and powers, separated and set apart from mean and vile uses to high and holy uses and purposes; for so they must be before they can be brought to glory. Now Christ, who is the agent in this work of sanctification, and Christians, who are the recipient subjects, are all of one. How? Why, (1.) They are all of one heavenly Father, and that is God. God is the Father of Christ by eternal generation and by miraculous conception, of Christians by adoption and regeneration. (2.) They are of one earthly father, Adam. Christ and believers have the same human nature. (3.) Of one spirit, one holy and heavenly disposition; the same mind is in them that was in Christ, though not in the same measure; the same Spirit informs and actuates the head and all the members.

2. Into an endearing relation. This results from the union. And here first he declares what this relation is, and then he quotes three texts out of the Old Testament to illustrate and prove it.

(1.) He declares what this relation is: he and believers being all of one, he therefore is not ashamed to call them *brethren.* Observe, [1.] Christ and believers are brethren; not only bone of his bone and flesh of his flesh, but spirit of his spirit-brethren by the whole blood, in what is heavenly as well as in what is earthly. [2.] Christ is not ashamed to own this relation; he is not ashamed to call them brethren, which is wonderful goodness and condescension in him, considering their meanness by nature and vileness by sin; but he will never be ashamed of any who are not ashamed of him, and who take care not to be a shame and reproach to him and to themselves.

(2.) He illustrates this from three texts of scripture.

[1.] The first is out of Ps. 22:22, *I will declare thy name unto my brethren; in the midst of the church will I sing praise unto thee.* This psalm was an eminent prophecy of Christ; it begins with his words on the cross, *My God, my God, why hast thou forsaken me?* Now here it is foretold, *First,* That Christ should have a church or *congregation* in the world, a company of volunteers, freely willing to follow him. *Secondly,* That these should not only be brethren to one another, but to Christ himself. *Thirdly,* That he would declare his Father's name to them, that is, his nature and attributes, his mind and will: this he did in his own person, while he dwelt among us, and by his Spirit poured out upon his disciples, enabling them to spread the knowledge of God in the world from one generation to another, to the end of the world.

Fourthly, That Christ would sing praise to his Father in the church. The glory of the Father was what Christ had in his eye; his heart was set upon it, he laid out himself for it, and he would have his people to join with him in it.

[2.] The second scripture is quoted from Ps. 18:2, *And again, I will put my trust in him.* That psalm sets forth the troubles that David, as a type of Christ, met with, and how he in all his troubles put his trust in God. Now this shows that besides his divine nature, which needed no supports, he was to take another nature upon him, that would want those supports which none but God could give. He suffered and trusted as our head and president. *Owen in locum.* His brethren must suffer and trust too.

[3.] The third scripture is taken from Isa. 8:18, *Behold, I and the children which God hath given me.* This proves Christ really and truly man, for parents and children are of the same nature. Christ's children were given him of the Father, in the counsel of his eternal love, and that covenant of peace which was between them. And they are given to Christ at their conversion. When they take hold of his covenant, then Christ receives them, rules over them, rejoices in them, perfects all their affairs, takes them up to heaven, and there presents them to his Father, *Behold, I and the children which thou hast given me.*

Verses 14–18

Here the apostle proceeds to assert the incarnation of Christ, as taking upon him not the nature of angels, but the seed of Abraham; and he shows the reason and design of his so doing.

I. The incarnation of Christ is asserted (*v.* 16): *Verily he took not upon him the nature of angels, but he took upon him the seed of Abraham.* He took part of flesh and blood. Though as God he pre-existed from all eternity, yet in the fulness of time he took our nature into union with his divine nature, and became really and truly man. He did not lay hold of angels, but he laid hold of the seed of Abraham. The angels fell, and he let them go, and lie under the desert, defilement, and dominion of their sin, without hope or help. Christ never designed to be the Saviour of the fallen angels; as their tree fell, so it lies, and must lie to eternity, and therefore he did not assume their nature. The nature of angels could not be an atoning sacrifice for the sin of man. Now Christ resolving to recover the seed of Abraham and raise them up from their fallen state, he took upon him the human nature from one descended from the loins of Abraham, that the same nature that had sinned might suffer, to restore human nature to a state of hope and trial, and all that accepted of mercy to a state of special favour and salvation. Now there is hope and help for the chief of sinners in and through Christ. Here is a price paid sufficient for all, and suitable to all, for it was in our nature. Let us all then know the day of our gracious visitation, and improve that distinguishing mercy which has been shown to fallen men, not to the fallen angels.

II. The reasons and designs of the incarnation of Christ are declared.

1. *Because the children were partakers of flesh and blood, he must take part of the same, and he made like his brethren,* v. 14, 15. For no higher nor lower nature than man's that had sinned could so suffer for the sin of man as to satisfy the justice of God, and raise man up to a state of hope, and make believers the children of God, and so brethren to Christ.

2. He became man that he might die; as God he could not die, and therefore he assumed another nature and state. Here the wonderful love of God appeared, that, when Christ knew what he must suffer in our nature, and how he must die in it, yet he so readily took it upon him. The legal sacrifices and offerings God could not accept as propitiation. A body was prepared for Christ, and he said, *Lo! I come, I delight to do thy will.*

3. That *through death he might destroy him that had the power of death, that is, the devil, v.* 14. The devil was the first sinner, and the first tempter to sin, and sin was the procuring cause of death; and he may be said to have the power of death, as he draws men into sin, the ways whereof are death, as he is often permitted to terrify the consciences of men with the fear of death, and as he is the executioner of divine justice, haling their souls from their bodies to the tribunal of God, there to receive their doom, and then being their tormentor, as he was before their tempter. In these respects he may be said to have had the power of death. But

now Christ has so far destroyed him who had the power of death that he can keep none under the power of spiritual death; nor can he draw any into sin (the procuring cause of death), nor require the soul of any from the body, nor execute the sentence upon any but those who choose and continue to be his willing slaves, and persist in their enmity to God.

4. That he might deliver his own people from the slavish fear of death to which they are often subject. This may refer to the Old-Testament saints, who were more under a spirit of bondage, because life and immortality were not so fully brought to light as now they are by the gospel. Or it may refer to all the people of God, whether under the Old Testament or the New, whose minds are often in perplexing fears about death and eternity. Christ became man, and died, to deliver them from those perplexities of soul, by letting them know that death is not only a conquered enemy, but a reconciled friend, not sent to hurt the soul, or separate it from the love of God, but to put an end to all their grievances and complaints, and to give them a passage to eternal life and blessedness; so that to them death is not now in the hand of Satan, but in the hand of Christ-not Satan's servant, but Christ's servant — has not hell following it, but heaven to all who are in Christ.

5. Christ must be made like unto his brethren, that he might be a merciful and faithful high priest in things pertaining to the justice and honour of God and to the support and comfort of his people. He must be faithful to God and merciful to men. (1.) In things pertaining to God, to his justice, and to his honour — to make reconciliation for the sins of the people, to make all the attributes of divine nature, and all the persons subsisting therein, harmonize in man's recovery, and fully to reconcile God and man. Observe, There was a great breach and quarrel between God and man, by reason of sin; but Christ, by becoming man and dying, has taken up the quarrel, and made reconciliation so far that God is ready to receive all into favour and friendship who come to him through Christ. (2.) In things pertaining to his people, to their support and comfort: *In that he suffered, being tempted, he is able to succour those that are tempted, v.* 18. Here observe, [1.] Christ's passion: *He suffered being tempted;* and his temptations were not the least part of his sufferings. *He was in all things tempted as we are, yet without sin, ch.* 4:15. [2.] Christ's compassion: *He is able to succour those that are tempted.* He is touched with a feeling of our infirmities, a sympathizing physician, tender and skilful; he knows how to deal with tempted sorrowful souls, because he has been himself sick of the same disease, not of sin, but of temptation and trouble of soul. The remembrance of his own sorrows and temptations makes him mindful of the trials of his people, and ready to help them. Here observe, *First,* The best of Christians are subject to temptations, to many temptations, while in this world; let us never count upon an absolute freedom from temptations in this world. *Secondly,* Temptations bring our souls into such distress and danger that they need support and succour. *Thirdly,* Christ is ready and willing to succour those who under their temptations apply to him; and he became man, and was tempted, that he might be every way qualified to succour his people.

CHAPTER 3

In this chapter the apostle applies what he had said in the chapter foregoing concerning the priesthood of Christ, I. In a serious pathetic exhortation that this great high priest, who was discovered to them, might be seriously considered by them (*v.* 1–6). II. He then adds many weighty counsels and cautions (*v.* 7 to the end).

Verses 1–6

In these verses we have the application of the doctrine laid down in the close of the last chapter concerning the priesthood of our Lord Jesus Christ. And observe,

I. In how fervent and affectionate a manner the apostle exhorts Christians to have this high priest much in their thoughts, and to make him the object of their close and serious consideration; and surely no one in earth or heaven deserves our consideration more than he. That this exhortation might be made the more effectual, observe,

1. The honourable compellation used towards those to whom he wrote: *Holy brethren, partakers of the heavenly calling.* (1.) Brethren, not only my brethren, but the brethren of Christ, and in him brethren to all the saints. All the people of God are brethren, and should love and live like brethren. (2.) Holy brethren; holy not only in profession and title, but

in principle and practice, in heart and life. This has been turned by some into scorn: "These," say they, "are the holy brethren;" but it is dangerous jesting with such edge-tools; *be not mockers, lest your bands be made strong.* Let those that are thus despised and scorned labour to be holy brethren indeed, and approve themselves so to God; and they need not be ashamed of the title nor dread the scoffs of the profane. The day is coming when those that make this a term of reproach would count it their greatest honour and happiness to be taken into this sacred brotherhood. (3.) *Partakers of the heavenly calling* — partakers of the means of grace, and of the Spirit of grace, that came from heaven, and by which Christians are effectually called out of darkness into marvelous light, that calling which brings down heaven into the souls of men, raises them up to a heavenly temper and conversation, and prepares them to live for ever with God in heaven.

2. The titles he gives to Christ, whom he would have them consider, (1.) As the apostle of our profession, the prime-minister of the gospel church, a messenger and a principal messenger sent of God to men, upon the most important errand, the great revealer of that faith which we profess to hold and of that hope which we profess to have. (2.) Not only the apostle, but the high priest too, of our profession, the chief officer of the Old Testament as well as the New, the head of the church in every state, and under each dispensation, upon whose satisfaction and intercession we profess to depend for pardon of sin, and acceptance with God. (3.) As Christ, the Messiah, anointed and every way qualified for the office both of apostle and high priest. (4.) As Jesus, our Saviour, our healer, the great physician of souls, typified by the brazen serpent that Moses lifted up in the wilderness, that those who were stung by the fiery serpents might look to him, and be saved.

II. We have the duty we owe to him who bears all these high and honourable titles, and that is to consider him as thus characterized. Consider what he is in himself, what he is to us, and what he will be to us hereafter and for ever; consider him, fix your thoughts upon him with the greatest attention, and act towards him accordingly; look unto Jesus, the author and finisher of your faith. Here observe, 1. Many that profess faith in Christ have not a due consideration for him; he is not so much thought of as he deserves to be, and desires to be, by those that expect salvation from him. 2. Close and serious consideration of Christ would be of great advantage to us to increase our acquaintance with him, and to engage our love and our obedience to him, and reliance on him. 3. Even those that are holy brethren, and partakers of the heavenly calling, have need to stir up one another to think more of Christ than they do, to have him more in their minds; the best of his people think too seldom and too slightly of him. 4. We must consider Christ as he is described to us in the scriptures, and form our apprehensions of him thence, not from any vain conceptions and fancies of our own.

III. We have several arguments drawn up to enforce this duty of considering Christ the apostle and high priest of our profession.

1. The first is taken from his fidelity, *v.* 2. He was faithful to him that appointed him, as Moses was in all his house. (1.) Christ is an appointed Mediator; God the Father has sent and sealed him to that office, and therefore his mediation is acceptable to the Father. (2.) He is faithful to that appointment, punctually observing all the rules and orders of his mediation, and fully executing the trust reposed in him by his Father and by his people. (3.) That he is as faithful to him that appointed him as Moses was in all his house. Moses was faithful in the discharge of his office to the Jewish church in the Old Testament, and so is Christ under the New; this was a proper argument to urge upon the Jews, who had so high an opinion of the faithfulness of Moses, and yet his faithfulness was but typical of Christ's.

2. Another argument is taken from the superior glory and excellence of Christ above Moses (*v.* 3–6); therefore they were more obliged to consider Christ. (1.) Christ was a maker of the house, Moses but a member in it. By the house we are to understand the church of God, the people of God incorporated together under Christ their maker and head, and under subordinate officers, according to his law, observing his institutions. Christ is the maker of this house of the church in all ages: Moses was a minister in the house, he was instrumental under Christ in governing and edifying the house, but Christ is the maker of all things; for he is God, and no

one less than God could build the church, either lay the foundation or carry on the superstructure. No less power was requisite to make the church than to make the world; the world was made out of nothing, the church made out of materials altogether unfit for such a building. Christ, who is God, drew the ground-plan of the church, provided the materials, and by almighty power disposed them to receive the form; he has compacted and united this his house, has settled the orders of it, and crowned all with his own presence, which is the true glory of this house of God. (2.) Christ was the master of this house, as well as the maker, *v.* 5,6. This house is styled his house, as the Son of God. Moses was only a faithful servant, for a testimony of those things that were afterwards to be revealed. Christ, as the eternal Son of God, is the rightful owner and sovereign ruler of the church. Moses was only a typical governor, for a testimony of all those things relating to the church which would be more clearly, completely, and comfortably revealed in the gospel by the Spirit of Christ; and therefore Christ is worthy of more glory than Moses, and of greater regard and consideration. This argument the apostle concludes, [1.] With a comfortable accommodation of it to himself and all true believers (*v.* 6). *Whose house we are:* each of us personally, as we are the temples of the Holy Ghost, and Christ dwells in us by faith; all of us jointly, as we are united by the bonds of graces, truths, ordinances, gospel discipline, and devotions. [2.] With a characteristic description of those persons who constitute this house: *"If we hold fast the confidence, and the rejoicing of the hope, firmly to the end;* that is, if we maintain a bold and open profession of the truths of the gospel, upon which our hopes of grace and glory are built, and live upon and up to those hopes, so as to have a holy rejoicing in them, which shall abide firm to the end, notwithstanding all that we may meet with in so doing." So that you see there must not only be a setting out well in the ways of Christ, but a stedfastness and perseverance therein unto the end. We have here a direction what those must do who would partake of the dignity and privileges of the household of Christ. *First,* They must take the truths of the gospel into their heads and hearts. *Secondly,* They must build their hopes of happiness upon those truths. *Thirdly,* They must make an open profession of those truths. *Fourthly,* They must live so up to them as to keep their evidences clear, that they may rejoice in hope, and then they must in all persevere to the end. In a word, they must walk closely, consistently, courageously, and constantly, in the faith and practice of the gospel, that their Master, when he comes, may own and approve them.

Verses 7–19

Here the apostle proceeds in pressing upon them serious counsels and cautions to the close of the chapter; and he recites a passage out of Ps. 95:7, etc., where observe,

I. What he counsels them to do — to give a speedy and present attention to the call of Christ. "Hear his voice, assent to, approve of, and consider, what God in Christ speaks unto you; apply it to yourselves with suitable affections and endeavours, and set about it this very day, for to-morrow it may be too late."

II. What he cautions them against — hardening their hearts, turning the deaf ear to the calls and counsels of Christ: "When he tells you of the evil of sin, the excellency of holiness, the necessity of receiving him by faith as your Saviour, do not shut your ear and heart against such a voice as this." Observe, The hardening of our hearts is the spring of all our other sins.

III. Whose example he warns them by — that of the Israelites their fathers in the wilderness: *As in the provocation and day of temptation;* this refers to that remarkable passage at Massah Meribah, Ex. 17:2–7. Observe,

1. Days of temptation are often days of provocation.

2. To provoke God, when he is trying us, and letting us see that we entirely depend and live immediately upon him, is a provocation with a witness.

3. The sins of others, especially our relations, should be a warning to us. Our fathers' sins and punishments should be remembered by us, to deter us from following their evil examples. Now as to the sin of the fathers of the Jews, here reflected upon, observe,

(1.) The state in which these fathers were, when they thus sinned: they were in the wilderness, brought out of Egypt, but not got into Canaan, the thoughts whereof should have restrained them from sin.

(2.) The sin they were guilty of: they tempted and provoked God; they distrusted God, murmured against Moses, and would not attend to the voice of God.

(3.) The aggravations of their sin: they sinned in the wilderness, where they had a more immediate dependence upon God: they sinned when God was trying them; they sinned when they saw his works — works of wonder wrought for their deliverance out of Egypt, and their support and supply in the wilderness from day to day. They continued thus to sin against God for forty years. These were heinous aggravations.

(4.) The source and spring of such aggravated sins, which were, [1.] They erred in their hearts; and these heart-errors produced many other errors in their lips and lives. [2.] They did not know God's ways, though he had walked before them. They did not know his ways; neither those ways of his providence in which he had walked towards them, nor those ways of his precept in which they ought to have walked towards God; they did not observe either his providences or his ordinances in a right manner.

(5.) The just and great resentment God had at their sins, and yet the great patience he exercised towards them (*v.* 10): *Wherefore I was grieved with that generation.* Note, [1.] All sin, especially sin committed by God's professing privileged people, does not only anger and affront God, but it grieves him. [2.] God is loth to destroy his people in or for their sin, he waits long to be gracious to them. [3.] God keeps an exact account of the time that people go on in sinning against him, and in grieving him by their sins; but at length, if they by their sins continue to grieve the Spirit of God, their sins shall be made grievous to their own spirits, either in a way of judgment or mercy.

(6.) The irreversible doom passed upon them at last for their sins. God swore in his wrath that they should not enter into his rest, the rest either of an earthly or of a heavenly Canaan. Observe, [1.] Sin, long continued in, will kindle the divine wrath, and make it flame out against sinners. [2.] God's wrath will discover itself in its righteous resolution to destroy the impenitent; he will swear in his wrath, not rashly, but righteously, and his wrath will make their condition a restless condition; there is no resting under the wrath of God.

IV. What use the apostle makes of their awful example, *v.* 12, 13, etc. He gives the Hebrews a proper caution, and enforces it with an affectionate compellation.

1. He gives the Hebrews a proper caution; the word is, *Take heed, blepete — look to it.* "Look about you; be upon your guard against enemies both within and without; be circumspect. You see what kept many of your forefathers out of Canaan, and made their carcasses fall in the wilderness; take heed lest you fall into the same sin and snare and dreadful sentence. For you see Christ is head of the church, a much greater person than Moses, and your contempt of him must be a greater sin than their contempt of Moses; and so you are in danger of falling under a severer sentence than they." Observe, The ruin of others should be a warning to us to take heed of the rock they split upon. Israel's fall should for ever be a warning to all who come after them; for *all these things happened to them for ensamples* (1 Co. 10:11), and should be remembered by us. Take heed; all who would get safely to heaven must look about them.

2. He enforces the admonition with an affectionate compellation: *"Brethren,* not only in the flesh, but in the Lord; brethren whom I love, and for whose welfare I labour and long." And here he enlarges upon the matter of the admonition: *Take heed, brethren, lest there be in any of you an evil heart of unbelief in departing from the living God.* Here observe, (1.) A heart of unbelief is an evil heart. Unbelief is a great sin, it vitiates the heart of man. (2.) An evil heart of unbelief is at the bottom of all our sinful departures from God; it is a leading step to apostasy; if once we allow ourselves to distrust God, we may soon desert him. (3.) Christian brethren have need to be cautioned against apostasy. *Let those that think they stand take heed lest they fall.*

3. He subjoins good counsel to the caution, and advises them to that which would be a remedy against this evil heart of unbelief — that they should *exhort one another daily, while it is called to-day, v.* 13. Observe, (1.) We should be doing all the good we can to one another while we are together, which will be but a short and uncertain time. (2.) Since to-morrow is none of ours, we must make the best improvement of today. (3.) If Christians do not exhort one another daily, they will be in danger of being hardened through the deceitfulness of sin. Note, [1.] There is a great deal of deceitfulness in sin; it appears fair, but is filthy; it appears pleasant, but is pernicious; it promises much, but performs nothing. [2.] The deceitfulness of sin is of a hardening nature to the soul; one sin allowed prepares for another; every act of sin confirms the habit; sinning against conscience is the way to sear the conscience; and therefore it should be the great concern of every one to exhort himself and others to beware of sin.

4. He comforts those who not only set out well, but hold on well, and hold out to the end (*v.* 14): *We are made partakers of Christ, if we hold the beginning of our confidence stedfast to the end.* Here observe, (1.) The saints' privilege: they are made partakers of Christ, that is, of the Spirit, nature, graces, righteousness, and life of Christ; they are interested in all that is Christ's, in all that he is, in all that he has done, or can do. (2.) The condition on which they hold that privilege, namely, their perseverance in the bold and open profession and practice of Christ and Christianity unto the end. Not but they shall persevere, being kept by the mighty power of God through faith to salvation, but to be pressed thus to it is one means by which Christ helps his people to persevere. This tends to make them watchful and diligent, and so keeps them from apostasy. Here observe, [1.] The same spirit with which Christians set out in the ways of God they should maintain and evidence to the end. Those who begin seriously, and with lively affections and holy resolutions and humble reliance, should go on in the same spirit. But, [2.] There are a great many who in the beginning of their profession show a great deal of courage and confidence, but do not hold them fast to the end. [3.] Perseverance in faith is the best evidence of the sincerity of our faith.

5. The apostle resumes what he had quoted before from Ps. 95:7, etc., and he applies it closely to those of that generation, *v.* 15, 16, etc. While it is said, *To-day if you will hear,* etc.; as if he should say, "What was recited before from that scripture belonged not only to former ages, but to you now, and to all who shall come after you; that you take heed you fall not into the same sins, lest you fall under the same condemnation." The apostle tells them that though some who had heard the voice of God did provoke him, yet all did not so. Observe, (1.) Though the majority of hearers provoked God by unbelief, yet some there were who believed the report. (2.) Though the hearing of the word be the ordinary means of salvation, yet, if it be not hearkened to, it will expose men more to the anger of God. (3.) God will have a remnant that shall be obedient to his voice, and he will take care of such and make mention of them with honour. (4.) If these should fall in a common calamity, yet they shall partake of eternal salvation, while disobedient hearers perish for ever.

6. The apostle puts some queries upon what had been before mentioned, and gives proper answers to them (*v.* 17–19): *But with whom was he grieved forty years? With those that sinned. And to whom did he swear?* etc. Whence observe, (1.) God is grieved only with those of his people who sin against him, and continue in sin. (2.) God is grieved and provoked most by sins publicly committed by the generality of a nation; when sin becomes epidemic, it is most provoking. (3.) Though God grieves long, and bears long, when pressed with the weight of general and prevailing wickedness, yet he will at length ease himself of public offenders by public judgments. (4.) Unbelief (with rebellion which is the consequent of it) is the great damning sin of the world, especially of those who have a revelation of the mind and will of God. This sin shuts up the heart of God, and shuts up the gate of heaven, against them; it lays them under the wrath and curse of God, and leaves them there; so that in truth and justice to himself he is obliged to cast them off for ever.

CHAPTER 4

The apostle, having in the foregoing chapter set forth the sin and punishment of the ancient Jews, proceeds in this, I. To declare that our privileges by Christ under the gospel exceed the privileges of the Jewish church under Moses, as a reason why we should make a right improvement of them (*v.* 1–4). II. He assigns the cause why the ancient Hebrews did not profit by their religious privileges (*v.* 2). Then, II. Confirms the privileges of those who believe, and the misery of those who continue in unbelief (*v.* 3–10). IV. Concludes with proper and powerful arguments and motives to faith and obedience.

Verses 1–10

Here, I. The apostle declares that our privileges by Christ under the gospel are not only as great, but greater than those enjoyed under the Mosaic law. He specifies this, that we have a promise left us of entering into his rest; that is, of entering into a covenant-relation to Christ, and a state of communion with God through Christ, and of growing up therein, till we are made perfect in glory. We have discoveries of this rest, and proposals, and the best directions how we may attain unto it. This promise of spiritual rest is a promise left us by the Lord Jesus Christ in his last will and testament, as a precious legacy. Our business is to see to it that we be the legatees, that we lay our claim to that rest and freedom from the dominion of sin, Satan, and the flesh, by which the souls of men are kept in servitude and deprived of the true rest of the soul, and may be also set free from the yoke of the law and all the toilsome ceremonies and services of it, and may enjoy peace with God in his ordinances and providences, and in our own consciences, and so have the prospect and earnest of perfect and everlasting rest in heaven.

II. He demonstrates the truth of his assertion, that we have as great advantages as they. For says he (*v.* 2), *To us was the gospel preached as well as unto them;* the same gospel for substance was preached under both Testaments, though not so clearly; not in so comfortable a manner under the Old as under the New. The best privileges the ancient Jews had were their gospel privileges; the sacrifices and ceremonies of the Old Testament were the gospel of that dispensation; and, whatever was excellent in it, was the respect it had to Christ. Now, if this was their highest privilege, we are not inferior to them; for we have the gospel as well as they, and in greater purity and perspicuity than they had.

III. He again assigns the reason why so few of the ancient Jews profited by that dispensation of the gospel which they enjoyed, and that was their want of faith: *The word preached did not profit them because it was not mixed with faith in those that heard him, v.* 2. Observe, 1. The word is preached to us that we may profit by it, that we may gain spiritual riches by it; it is a price put into our hands to get wisdom, the rich endowment of the soul. 2. There have been in all ages a great many unprofitable hearers; many who seem to deal much in sermons, in hearing the word of God, but gain nothing to their souls thereby; and those who are not gainers by hearing are great losers. 3. That which is at the bottom of all our unprofitableness under the word is our unbelief. We do not mix faith with what we hear; it is faith in the hearer that is the life of the word. Though the preacher believes the gospel, and endeavours to mix faith with his preaching, and to speak as one who has believed and so spoken, yet, if the hearers have not faith in their souls to mix with the word, they will be never the better for it. This faith must mingle with every word, and be in act and exercise while we are hearing; and, when we have heard the word, assenting to the truth of it, approving of it, accepting the mercy offered, applying the word to ourselves with suitable affections, then we shall find great profit and gain by the word preached.

IV. On these considerations the apostle grounds his repeated and earnest caution and counsel that those who enjoy the gospel should maintain a holy fear and jealousy over themselves, lest latent unbelief should rob them of the benefit of the word, and of that spiritual rest which is discovered and tendered in the gospel: *Let us fear lest, a promise being left us of entering into his rest, any of you should seem to come short of it, v.* 1. Observe, 1. Grace and glory are attainable by all under the gospel: there is an offer, and a promise to those who shall accept the offer. 2. Those who may attain them may also fall short. Those who may attain them may also fall short. Those who might have attained salvation by faith may fall short by unbelief. 3. It is a dreadful thing so much as to seem to fall short of the gospel salvation, to seem so to themselves, to lose their comfortable hope; and to seem so to others, so losing the honour of their holy profession. But, if it be so dreadful to seem to fall short of this rest, it is much more dreadful really to fall short. Such a disappointment must be fatal. 4. One good means to prevent either our real falling short or seeming to fall short is to maintain a holy and religious fear lest we should fall short. This will make us vigilant and diligent, sincere and serious; this fear will put us upon examining our faith and exercising it; whereas presumption is the high road to ruin.

V. The apostle confirms the happiness of all those who truly believe the gospel; and this he does,

1. By asserting so positively the truth of it, from the experience of himself and others: "*We, who have believed, do enter into rest, v.* 3. We enter into a blessed union with Christ, and into a communion with God through Christ; in this state we actually enjoy many sweet communications of pardon of sin, peace of conscience, joy in the Holy Ghost, increase of grace and earnests of glory, resting from the servitude of sin, and reposing ourselves in God till we are prepared to rest with him in heaven."

2. He illustrates and confirms it that those who believe are thus happy, and do enter into rest. (1.) From God's finishing his work of creation, and so entering into his rest (*v.* 3, 4), appointing our first parents to rest the seventh day, to rest in God. Now as God finished his work, and then rested from it, and acquiesced in it, so he will cause those who believe to finish their work, and then to enjoy their rest. (2.) From God's continuing the observance of the sabbath, after the fall, and the revelation of a Redeemer. They were to keep the seventh day a holy sabbath to the Lord, therein praising him who had raised them up out of nothing by creating power, and praying to him that he would create them anew by his Spirit of grace, and direct their faith to the promised Redeemer and restorer of all things, by which faith they find rest in their souls. (3.) From God's proposing Canaan as a typical rest for the Jews who believed: and as those who did believe, Caleb and Joshua, did actually enter into Canaan; so those who now believe shall enter into rest. (4.) From the certainty of another rest besides that seventh day of rest instituted and observed both before and after the fall, and besides that typical Canaan-rest which most of the Jews fell short of by unbelief; for the Psalmist has spoken of another day and another rest, whence it is evident that there is a more spiritual and excellent sabbath remaining for the people of God than that into which Joshua led the Jews (*v.* 6–9), and this rest remaining, [1.] A rest of grace, and comfort, and holiness, in the gospel state. This is the rest wherewith the Lord Jesus, our Joshua, causes weary souls and awakened consciences to rest, and this is the refreshing. [2.] A rest in glory, the everlasting sabbatism of heaven, which is the repose and perfection of nature and grace too, where the people of God shall enjoy the end of their faith and the object of all their desires. (5.) This is further proved from the glorious forerunners who have actually taken possession of this rest — God and Christ. It is certain that God, after the creating of the world in six days, entered into his rest; and it is certain that Christ, when he had finished the work of our redemption, entered into his rest; and these were not only examples, but earnests, that believers shall enter into their rest: *He that hath entered into rest hath also ceased from his own works as God did from his, v.* 10. Every true believer hath ceased from his own works of righteousness, and from the burdensome works of the law, as God and Christ have ceased from their works of creation and redemption.

VI. The apostle confirms the misery of those who do not believe; they shall never enter into this spiritual rest, either of grace here or glory hereafter. This is as certain as the word and oath of God can make it. As sure as God has entered into his rest, so sure it is that obstinate unbelievers shall be excluded. As sure as the unbelieving Jews fell in the wilderness, and never reached the promised land, so sure it is that unbelievers shall fall into destruction, and never reach heaven. As sure as Joshua, the great captain of the Jews, could not give them possession of Canaan because of their unbelief, notwithstanding his eminent valour and conduct, so sure it is that even Jesus himself, and captain of our salvation, notwithstanding all that fulness of grace and strength that dwells in him, will not, cannot, give to final unbelievers either spiritual or eternal rest: it remains only for the people of God; others by their sin abandon themselves to eternal restlessness.

Verses 11–16

In this latter part of the chapter the apostle concludes, first, with a serious repeated exhortation, and then with proper and powerful motives.

I. Here we have a serious exhortation: *Let us labour therefore to enter into that rest, v.* 11. Observe, 1. The end proposed — rest spiritual and eternal, the rest of grace here and glory hereafter — in Christ on earth, with Christ in heaven. 2. The way to this end prescribed — labour, diligent labour; this is the only way to rest; those who will not work now shall not rest hereafter. After due and diligent labour, sweet and satisfying rest shall follow; and labour now will make that rest more pleasant when it comes. *The sleep of the labouring man is sweet,* Eccl. *v.* 12. Let us therefore labour, let us all agree and be unanimous in this, and let us quicken one another, and call upon one another to this diligence. It is the truest act of friendship, when we see our fellow-christians loiter, to call upon them to mind their business and labour at it in earnest. "Come, Sirs, let us all go to work; why do we sit still? Why do we loiter? Come, let us labour; now is our working time, our rest remains." Thus should Christians call upon themselves and one another to be diligent in duty; and so much the more as we see the day approaching.

II. Here we have proper and powerful motives to make the advice effectual, which are drawn,

1. From the dreadful example of those who have already perished by unbelief: *Lest any man fall after the same example of unbelief.* To have seen so many fall before us will be a great aggravation of our sin, if we will not take warning by them: their ruin calls loudly upon us; their lost and restless souls cry to us from their torments, that we do not, by sinning as they did, make ourselves miserable as they are.

2. From the great help and advantage we may have from the word of God to strengthen our faith, and excite our diligence, that we may obtain this rest: *The word of God is quick and powerful, v.* 12. By the word of God we may understand either the essential or the written word: the essential *Word,* that in *the beginning was with God, and was God* (Jn. 1:1), the Lord Jesus Christ, and indeed what is said in this verse is true concerning him; but most understand it of the written word, the holy scriptures, which are the word of God. Now of this word it is said, (1.) That is *quick;* it is very lively and active, in all its efforts, in seizing the conscience of the sinner, in cutting him to the heart, and in comforting him and binding up the wounds of the soul. Those know not the word of God who call it a dead letter; it is quick, compared to the light, and nothing quicker than the light; it is not only quick, but quickening; it is a vital light; it is a living word, *zōn.* Saints die, and sinners die; but the word of God lives. *All flesh is grass, and all the glory thereof as the flower of grass. The grass withereth, and the flower thereof falleth away, but the word of the Lord endureth for ever,* 1 Pt. 1:24, 25. *Your fathers, where are they? And the prophets, do they live for ever? But my words, which I commanded the prophets, did they not take hold of your fathers?* Zec. 1:5, 6. (2.) It is *powerful.* When God sets it home by his Spirit, it convinces powerfully, converts powerfully, and comforts powerfully. It is so powerful as to pull down strong holds (2 Co. 10:4, 5), to raise the dead, to make the deaf to hear, the blind to see, the dumb to speak, and the lame to walk. It is powerful to batter down Satan's kingdom, and to set up the kingdom of Christ upon the ruins thereof. (3.) It is *sharper than any two-edged sword;* it cuts both ways; it is *the sword of the Spirit,* Eph. 6:17. It is the two-edged sword that cometh out of the mouth of Christ, Rev. 1:16. It is sharper than any two-edged sword, for it will enter where no other sword can, and make a more critical dissection: it *pierces to the dividing asunder of the soul and the spirit,* the soul and its habitual prevailing temper; it makes a soul that has been a long time of a proud spirit to be humble, of a perverse spirit to be meek and obedient. Those sinful habits that have become as it were natural to the soul, and rooted deeply in it, and become in a manner one with it, are separated and cut off by this sword. It cuts off ignorance from the understanding, rebellion from the will, and enmity from the mind, which, when carnal, is enmity itself against God. This sword divides between *the joints and the marrow,* the most secret, close, and intimate parts of the body; this sword can cut off the lusts of the flesh as well as the lusts of the mind, and make men willing to undergo the sharpest operation for the mortifying of sin. (4.) It is *a discerner of the thoughts and intents of the heart,* even the most secret and remote thoughts and designs. It will discover to men the variety of their thoughts and purposes, the vileness of them, the bad principles they are actuated by, the sinister and sinful ends they act to. The word will turn the inside of a sinner out, and let him see all that is in his heart. Now such a word as this must needs be a great help to our faith and obedience.

3. From the perfections of the Lord Jesus Christ, both of his person and office.

(1.) His person, particularly his omniscience: *Neither is there any creature that is not manifest in his sight, v.* 13. This is agreeable to what Christ speaks of himself: *All the churches shall know that I am he that searches the reins and hearts,* Rev. 2:23. None of the creatures can be concealed from Christ; none of the creatures of God, for Christ is the Creator of them all; and there are none of the motions and workings of our heads and hearts (which may be called creatures of our own) but what are open and manifest to him with whom we have to do as the object of our worship, and the high priest of our profession. He, by his omniscience, cuts up the sacrifice we bring to him, that it may be presented to the Father. Now as the high priest inspected the sacrificed beasts, cut them up to the back-bone to see whether they were sound at heart, so all things are thus dissected, and lie open to the piercing eye of our great high priest. An he who now tries our sacrifices will at length, as Judge, try our state. We shall have to do with him as one who will determine our everlasting state. Some read the words, *to whom with us there is an account or reckoning.* Christ has an exact account of us all. He has accounted for all who believe on him; and he will account with all: our accounts are before him. This omniscience of Christ, and the account we owe of ourselves to him, should engage us to persevere in faith and obedience till he has perfected all our affairs.

(2.) We have an account of the excellency and perfection of Christ, as to his office, and this particular office of our high priest. The apostle first instructs Christians in the knowledge of their high priest, what kind of high priest he is, and then puts them in mind of the duty they owe on this account.

[1.] What kind of high priest Christ is (*v.* 14): *Seeing we have such a high priest;* that is, *First,* A great high priest, much greater than Aaron, or any of the priests of his order. The high priests under the law were accounted great and venerable person; but they were but faint types and shadows of Christ. The greatness of our high priest is set forth, 1. By his having passed into the heavens. The high priest under the law, once a year, went out of the people's sight within the veil, into the holiest of all, where were the sacred signals of the presence of God; but Christ once for all has passed into the heavens, to take the government of all upon him, to send the Spirit to prepare a place for his people, and to make intercession for them. Christ executed one part of his priesthood on earth, in dying for us; the other he executes in heaven, by pleading the cause, and presenting the offerings, of his people. 2. The greatness of Christ is set forth by his name, *Jesus* — a physician and a Saviour, and one of a divine nature, the Son of God by eternal generation; and therefore having divine perfection, able to save to the uttermost all who come to God by him. *Secondly,* He is not only a great, but a gracious high priest, merciful, compassionate, and sympathizing with his people: *We have not a high priest who cannot be touched with the feeling of our infirmities, v.* 15. Though he is so great, and so far above us, yet he is very kind, and tenderly concerned for us. He is touched with the feeling of our infirmities in such a manner as none else can be; for he was himself tried with all the afflictions and troubles that are incident to our nature in its fallen state: and this not only that he might be able to satisfy for us, but to sympathize with us. But then, *Thirdly,* He is a sinless high priest: *He was in all things tempted as we are, yet without sin.* He was tempted by Satan, but he came off without sin. We seldom meet with temptations but they give us some shock. We are apt to give back, though we do not yield; but our great high priest came off clear in his encounter with the devil, who could neither find any sin in him nor fix any stain upon him. He was tried severely by the Father. It pleased the Lord to bruise him; and yet he sinned not, either in thought, word, or deed. He had done no violence, neither was there any deceit in his mouth. He was holy, harmless, and undefiled; and such a high priest became us. Having thus told us what a one our high priest is, the apostle proceeds to show us,

[2.] How we should demean ourselves towards him. *First,* Let us hold fast our profession of faith in him, *v.* 14. Let us never deny him, never be ashamed of him before men. Let us hold fast the enlightening doctrines of Christianity in our heads, the enlivening principles of it in our hearts, the open profession of it in our lips, and our practical and universal subjection to it in our lives. Observe here, 1. We ought to be possessed of the doctrines, principles, and practice, of the Christian life. 2. When we are so, we may be in danger of losing our hold, from the corruption of our hearts, the temptations of Satan, and the allurements of this evil world. 3. The excellency of the high priest of our profession would make our apostasy from him most heinous and inexcusable; it would be the greatest folly and the basest ingratitude. 4. Christians must not only set our well, but they must hold out: those who endure to the end will be saved, and none but they. *Secondly,* We should encourage ourselves, by the excellency of our high priest, to come boldly to the throne of grace, *v.* 16. Here observe, 1. There is a throne of grace set up, a way of

worship instituted, in which God may with honour meet poor sinners, and treat with them, and they may with hope draw night to him, repenting and believing. God might have set up a tribunal of strict and inexorable justice, dispensing death, the wages of sin, to all who were convened before it; but he has chosen to set up a throne of grace. A throne speaks authority, and bespeaks awe and reverence. A throne of grace speaks great encouragement even to the chief of sinners. There grace reigns, and acts with sovereign freedom, power, and bounty. 2. It is our duty and interest to be often found before this throne of grace, waiting on the Lord in all the duties of his worship, private and public. It is good for us to be there. 3. Our business and errand at the throne of grace should be that we *may obtain mercy and find grace to help in time of need.* Mercy and grace are the things we want, mercy to pardon all our sins and grace to purify our souls. 4. Besides the daily dependence we have upon God for present supplies, there are some seasons in which we shall most sensibly need the mercy and grace of God, and we should lay up prayers against such seasons — times of temptation, either by adversity or prosperity, and especially a dying time: we should every day put up a petition for mercy in our last day. The Lord grant unto us that we may find mercy of the Lord at that day, 2 Tim. 1:18. 5. In all our approaches to this throne of grace for mercy, we should come with a humble freedom and boldness, with a liberty of spirit and a liberty of speech; we should ask in faith, nothing doubting; we should come with a Spirit of adoption, as children to a reconciled God and Father. We are indeed to come with reverence and godly fear, but not with terror and amazement; not as if we were dragged before the tribunal of justice, but kindly invited to the mercy-seat, where grace reigns, and loves to exert and exalt itself towards us. 6. The office of Christ, as being our high priest, and such a high priest, should be the ground of our confidence in all our approaches to the throne of grace. Had we not a Mediator, we could have no boldness in coming to God; for we are guilty and polluted creatures. All we do is polluted; we cannot go into the presence of God alone; we must either go in the hand of a Mediator or our hearts and our hopes will fail us. We have boldness to enter into the holiest by the blood of Jesus. He is our Advocate, and, while he pleads for his people, he pleads with the price in his hand, by which he purchased all that our souls want or can desire.

CHAPTER 5

In this chapter the apostle continues his discourse upon the priesthood of Christ, a sweet subject, which he would not too soon dismiss. And here, I. He explains the nature of the priestly office in general (*v.* 1–3). II. The proper and regular call there must be to this office (*v.* 4–6). III. The requisite qualifications for the work (*v.* 7–9). IV. The peculiar order of the priesthood of Christ; it was not after the order of Aaron, but of Melchisedec (*v.* 6, 7, 10). V. He reproves the Hebrews, that they had not made those improvements in knowledge which might have made them capable of looking into the more abstruse and mysterious parts of scripture (*v.* 11–14).

Verses 1–9

We have here an account of the nature of the priestly office in general, though with an accommodation to the Lord Jesus Christ. We are told,

I. Of what kind of beings the high priest must be. He must be taken from among men; he must be a man, one of ourselves, bone of our bones, flesh of our flesh, and spirit of our spirits, a partaker of our nature, and a standard-bearer among ten thousand. This implies, 1. That man had sinned. 2. That God would not admit sinful man to come to him immediately and alone, without a high priest, who must be taken from among men. 3. That God was pleased to take one from among men, by whom they might approach God in hope, and he might receive them with honour. 4. That every one shall now be welcome to God that comes to him by this his priest.

II. For whom every high priest is ordained: *For men in things pertaining to God,* for the glory of God and the good of men, that he might come between God and man. So Christ did; and therefore let us never attempt to go to God but through Christ, nor expect any favour from God but through Christ.

III. For what purpose every high priest was ordained: *That he might offer both gifts and sacrifices for sin.*

1. That he might offer gifts or free-will offerings, brought to the high priest, so offered for the glory of God, and as an acknowledgment that our all is of him and from him; we have nothing but what he is pleased to give us, and of his own

we offer to him an oblation of acknowledgment. This intimates, (1.) That all we bring to God must be free and not forced; it must be a gift; it must be given and not taken away again. (2.) That all we bring to God must go through the high priest's hands, as the great agent between God and man.

2. That he might offer sacrifices for sin; that is, the offerings that were appointed to make atonement, that sin might be pardoned and sinners accepted. Thus Christ is constituted a high priest for both these ends. Our good deeds must be presented by Christ, to render ourselves and them acceptable; and our evil deeds must be expiated by the sacrifice of himself, that they may not condemn and destroy us. And now, as we value acceptance with God and pardon, we must apply ourselves by faith to this our great high priest.

IV. How this high priest must be qualified, *v.* 2.

1. He must be one that can have compassion on two sorts of persons: — (1.) *On the ignorant,* or those that are guilty of sins of ignorance. He must be one who can find in his heart to pity them, and intercede with God for them, one that is willing to instruct those that are dull of understanding. (2.) *On those that are out of the way,* out of the way of truth, duty, and happiness; and he must be one who has tenderness enough to lead them back from the by-paths of error, sin, and misery, into the right way: this will require great patience and compassion, even the compassion of a God.

2. He must also be compassed with infirmity; and so be able from himself feelingly to consider our frame, and to sympathize with us. Thus Christ was qualified. He took upon him our sinless infirmities; and this gives us great encouragement to apply ourselves to him under every affliction; for in all the afflictions of his people he is afflicted.

V. How the high priest was to be called of God. He must have both an internal and external call to his office: *For no man taketh this honour to himself* (*v.* 4), that is, no man ought to do it, no man can do it legally; if any does it, he must be reckoned a usurper, and treated accordingly. Here observe, 1. The office of the priesthood was a very great honour. To be employed to stand between God and man, one while representing God and his will to men, at another time representing man and his case to God, and dealing between them about matters of the highest importance — entrusted on both sides with the honour of God and the happiness of man — must render the office very honourable. 2. The priesthood is an office and honour that no man ought to take to himself: if he does, he can expect no success in it, nor any reward for it, only from himself. He is an intruder who is not called of God, as was Aaron. Observe, (1.) God is the fountain of all honour, especially true spiritual honour. He is the fountain of true authority, whether he calls any to the priesthood in an extraordinary way, as he did Aaron, or in an ordinary way, as he called his successors. (2.) Those only can expect assistance from God, and acceptance with him, and his presence and blessing on them and their administrations, that are called of God; others may expect a blast instead of a blessing.

VI. How this is brought home and applied to Christ: *So Christ glorified not himself, v.* 5. Observe here, Though Christ reckoned it his glory to be made a high priest, yet he would not assume that glory to himself. He could truly say, *I seek not my own glory,* Jn. 8:50. Considered as God, he was not capable of any additional glory, but as man and Mediator he did not run without being sent; and, if he did not, surely others should be afraid to do it.

VII. The apostle prefers Christ before Aaron, both in the manner of his call and in the holiness of his person. 1. In the manner of his call, in which God said unto him, *Thou art my Son, this day have I begotten thee* (quoted from Ps. 2:7), referring to his eternal generation as God, his wonderful conception as man, and his perfect qualification as Mediator. Thus God solemnly declared his dear affection to Christ, his authoritative appointment of him to the office of a Mediator, his installment and approbation of him in that office, his acceptance of him, and of all he had done or should do in the discharge of it. Now God never said thus to Aaron. Another expression that God used in the call of Christ we have in Ps. 110:4, *Thou art a priest for ever, after the order of Melchisedec, v.* 6. God the Father appointed him a priest of a higher order than that of Aaron. The priesthood of Aaron was to be but temporary; the priesthood of Christ was to be perpetual: the priesthood of Aaron was to be successive, descending from the fathers to the children; the priesthood of Christ, after the order of Melchisedec, was to be personal, and the high priest immortal as to his office, without descent, having neither beginning of days nor end of life, as it is more largely described in the seventh chapter, and will be opened there. 2. Christ is here preferred to Aaron in the holiness of his person. Other priests were to offer up sacrifices, as for the *sins of others, so for themselves, v.* 3. But Christ needed not to offer for sins for himself, *for he had done no violence,* neither was there *any deceit in his mouth,* Isa. 53:9. And such a high priest became us.

VIII. We have an account of Christ's discharge of this his office, and of the consequences of that discharge, *v.* 7–9.

1. The discharge of his office of the priesthood (*v.* 7): *Who in the days of his flesh, when he had offered up prayers and supplications,* etc. Here observe, (1.) He took to him flesh, and for some days tabernacled therein; he became a mortal man, and reckoned his life by days, herein setting us an example how we should reckon ours. Were we to reckon our lives by days, it would be a means to quicken us to do the work of every day in its day. (2.) Christ, in the days of his flesh, subjected himself to death; he hungered, he was a tempted, bleeding, dying Jesus! He body is now in heaven, but it is a spiritual glorious body. (3.) God the Father was able to save him from death. He could have prevented his dying, but he would not; for then the great design of his wisdom and grace must have been defeated. What would have become of us if God had saved Christ from dying? The Jews reproachfully said, *Let him deliver him now, if he will have him,* Mt. 27:43. But it was in kindness to us that the Father would not suffer that bitter cup to pass away from him; for then we must have drunk the dregs of it, and been miserable for ever. (4.) Christ, in the days of his flesh, offered up prayers and supplications to his Father, as an earnest of his intercession in heaven. A great many instances we have of Christ's praying. This refers to his prayer in his agony (Mt. 26:39, and *ch.* 27:46), and to that before his agony (Jn. 17) which he put up for his disciples, and all who should believe on his name. (5.) The prayers and supplications that Christ offered up were joined with strong cries and tears, herein setting us an example not only to pray, but to be fervent and importunate in prayer. How many dry prayers, how few wet ones, do we offer up to God! (6.) Christ was heard in that he feared. How? Why he was answered by present supports in and under his agonies, and in being carried well through death, and delivered from it by a glorious resurrection: He *was heard in that he feared.* He had an awful sense of the wrath of God, of the weight of sin. His human nature was ready to sink under the heavy load, and would have sunk, had he been quite forsaken in point of help and comfort from God; but he was heard in this, he was supported under the agonies of death. He was carried through death; and there is no real deliverance from death but to be carried well through it. We may have many recoveries from sickness, but we are never saved from death till we are carried well through it. And those that are thus saved from death will be fully delivered at last by a glorious resurrection, of which the resurrection of Christ was the earnest and first-fruits.

2. The consequences of this discharge of his office, *v.* 8, 9, etc.

(1.) By these his sufferings *he learned obedience, though he was a Son, v.* 8. Here observe, [1.] The privilege of Christ: *He was a Son;* the only-begotten of the Father. One would have thought this might have exempted him from suffering, but it did not. Let none then who are the children of God by adoption expect an absolute freedom from suffering. *What Son is he whom the Father chasteneth not?* [2.] Christ made improvement by his sufferings. By his passive obedience, he learned active obedience; that is, he practiced that great lesson, and made it appear that he was well and perfectly learned in it; though he never was disobedient, yet he never performed such an act of obedience as when he became obedient to death, even to the death of the cross. Here he has left us an example, that we should learn by all our afflictions a humble obedience to the will of God. We need affliction, to teach us submission.

(2.) By these his sufferings he was made perfect, and became the author of eternal salvation to all who obey him, *v.* 9. [1.] Christ by his sufferings was consecrated to his office, consecrated by his own blood. [2.] By his sufferings he consummated that part of his office which was to be performed on earth, making reconciliation for iniquity; and in this sense he is said to be *made perfect,* a perfect propitiation. [3.] Hereby he has become the author of eternal sal-

vation to men; he has by his sufferings purchased a full deliverance from sin and misery, and a full fruition of holiness and happiness for his people. Of this salvation he has given notice in the gospel; he has made a tender of it in the new covenant, and has sent the Spirit to enable men to accept this salvation. [4.] This salvation is actually bestowed on none but those who obey Christ. It is not sufficient that we have some doctrinal knowledge of Christ, or that we make a profession of faith in him, but we must hearken to his word, and obey him. He is exalted to be a prince to rule us, as well as a Saviour to deliver us; and he will be a Saviour to none but to those whom he is a prince, and who are willing that he should reign over them; the rest he will account his enemies, and treat them accordingly. But to those who obey him, devoting themselves to him, denying themselves, and taking up their cross, and following him, he will be the author, *aitios* — the grand cause of their salvation, and they shall own him as such for ever.

Verses 10–14

Here the apostle returns to what he had in *v.* 6 cited out of Ps. 110, concerning the peculiar order of the priesthood of Christ, that is, the order of Melchisedec. And here,

I. He declares he had many things which he could say to them concerning this mysterious person called Melchisedec, whose priesthood was eternal, and therefore the salvation procured thereby should be eternal also. We have a more particular account of this Melchisedec in *ch.* 7. Some think the things which the apostle means, that were hard to be uttered, were not so much concerning Melchisedec himself as concerning Christ, of whom Melchisedec was the type. And doubtless this apostle had many things to say concerning Christ that were very mysterious, hard to be uttered; there are great mysteries in the person and offices of the Redeemer; Christianity is the great mystery of godliness.

II. He assigns the reason why he did not say all those things concerning Christ, our Melchisedec, that he had to say, and what it was that made it so difficult for him to utter them, namely, the dulness of the Hebrews to whom he wrote: *You are dull of hearing.* There is a difficulty in the things themselves, and there may be a weakness in the ministers of the gospel to speak clearly about these things; but generally the fault is in the hearers. Dull hearers make the preaching of the gospel a difficult thing, and even many who have some faith are but dull hearers, dull of understanding and slow to believe; the understanding is weak, and does not apprehend these spiritual things; the memory is weak, and does not retain them.

III. He insists upon the faultiness of this infirmity of theirs. It was not a mere natural infirmity, but it was a sinful infirmity, and more in them than others, by reason of the singular advantages they had enjoyed for improving in the knowledge of Christ: *For when, for the time, you ought to be teachers, you have need that one teach you again which are the first principles of the oracles of God, v.* 12. Here observe,

1. What proficiency might have been reasonably expected from these Hebrews — that they might have been so well instructed in the doctrine of the gospel as to have been teachers of others. Hence learn, (1.) God takes notice of the time and helps we have for gaining scripture-knowledge. (2.) From those to whom much is given much is expected. (3.) Those who have a good understanding in the gospel should be teachers of other, if not in a public, yet in a private station. (4.) None should take upon them to be teachers of others, but those who have made a good improvement in spiritual knowledge themselves.

2. Observe the sad disappointment of those just expectations: *You have need that one should teach you again,* etc. Here note, (1.) In the oracles of God there are some first principles, plain to be understood and necessary to be learned. (2.) There are also deep and sublime mysteries, which those should search into who have learned the first principles, that so they may stand complete in the whole will of God. (3.) Some persons, instead of going forward in Christian knowledge, forget the very first principles that they had learned long ago; and indeed those that are not improving under the means of grace will be losing. (4.) It is a sin and shame for persons that are men for their age and standing in the church to be children and babes in understanding.

IV. The apostle shows how the various doctrines of the gospel must be dispensed to different persons. There are in

the church babes and persons of full age (*v.* 12–14), and there are in the gospel milk and strong meat. Observe, 1. Those that are babes, unskillful in the word of righteousness, must be fed with milk; they must be entertained with the plainest truths, and these delivered in the plainest manner; *there must be line upon line, precept upon precept, here a little, and there a little,* Isa. 28:10. Christ despises not his babes; he has provided suitable food for them. It is good to be babes in Christ, but not always to continue in that childish state; we should endeavor to pass the infant state; we should always remain in malice children, but in understanding we should grow up to a manly maturity. 2. There is strong meat for those that are of full age, *v.* 14. The deeper mysteries of religion belong to those that are of a higher class in the school of Christ, who have learned the first principles and well improved them; so that by reason of use they have their senses exercised to discern both good and evil, duty and sin, truth and error. Observe, (1.) There have been always in the Christian state children, young men, and fathers. (2.) Every true Christian, having received a principle of spiritual life from God, stands in need of nourishment to preserve that life. (3.) The word of God is food and nourishment to the life of grace: *As newborn babes desire the sincere milk of the word that you may grow thereby.* (4.) It is the wisdom of ministers rightly to divide the word of truth, and to give to every one his portion — milk to babes, and strong meat to those of full age. (5.) There are spiritual senses as well as those that are natural. There is a spiritual eye, a spiritual appetite, a spiritual taste; the soul has its sensations as well as the body; these are much depraved and lost by sin, but they are recovered by grace. (6.) It is by use and exercise that these senses are improved, made more quick and strong to taste the sweetness of what is good and true, and the bitterness of what is false and evil. Not only reason and faith, but spiritual sense, will teach men to distinguish between what is pleasing and what is provoking to God, between what is helpful and what is hurtful to our own souls.

CHAPTER 6

In this chapter the apostle proceeds to persuade the Hebrews to make a better proficiency in religion than they had done, as the best way to prevent apostasy, the dreadful nature and consequences of which sin he sets forth in a serious manner (*v.* 1–8), and then expresses his good hopes concerning them, that they would persevere in faith and holiness, to which he exhorts them, and sets before them the great encouragement they had from God, both with respect to their duty and happiness (*v.* 9 to the end).

Verses 1–8

We have here the apostle's advice to the Hebrews — that they would grow up from a state of childhood to the fullness of the stature of the new man in Christ. He declares his readiness to assist them all he could in their spiritual progress; and, for their greater encouragement, he puts himself with them: *Let us go on.* Here observe, In order to their growth, Christians must leave the principles of the doctrine of Christ. How must they leave them? They must not lose them, they must not despise them, they must not forget them. They must lay them up in their hearts, and lay them as the foundation of all their profession and expectation; but they must not rest and stay in them, they must not be always laying the foundation, they must go on, and build upon it. There must be a superstructure; for the foundation is laid on purpose to support the building. Here it may be enquired, Why did the apostle resolve to set strong meat before the Hebrews, when he knew they were but babes? *Answer.* 1. Though some of them were but weak, yet others of them had gained more strength; and they must be provided for suitably. And, as those who are grown Christians must be willing to hear the plainest truths preached for the sake of the weak, so the weak must be willing to hear the more difficult and mysterious truths preached for the sake of those who are strong. 2. He hoped they would be growing in their spiritual strength and stature, and so be able to digest stronger meat.

I. The apostle mentions several foundation-principles, which must be well laid at first, and then built upon; neither his time nor theirs must be spent in laying these foundations over and over again. These foundations are six: —

1. Repentance from dead works, that is, conversion and regeneration, repentance from a spiritually dead state and course; as if he had said, "Beware of destroying the life of grace in your souls; your minds were changed by conversion, and so were your lives. Take care that you return not

to sin again, for then you must have the foundation to lay again; there must be a second conversion a repenting not only of, but from, dead works." Observe here, (1.) The sins of persons unconverted are dead works; they proceed from persons spiritually dead, and they tend to death eternal. (2.) Repentance for dead works, if it be right, is repentance from dead works, a universal change of heart and life. (3.) Repentance for and from dead works is a foundation-principle, which must not be laid again, though we must renew our repentance daily.

2. Faith towards God, a firm belief of the existence of God, of his nature, attributes, and perfections, the trinity of persons in the unity of essence, the whole mind and will of God as revealed in his word, particularly what relates to the Lord Jesus Christ. We must by faith acquaint ourselves with these things; we must assent to them, we must approve of them, and apply all to ourselves with suitable affections and actions. Observe, (1.) Repentance from dead works, and faith towards God, are connected, and always go together; they are inseparable twins, the one cannot live without the other. (2.) Both of these are foundation-principles, which should be once well laid, but never pulled up, so as to need to be laid over again; we must not relapse into infidelity.

3. The doctrine of baptisms, that is, of being baptized by a minister of Christ with water, in the name of the Father, and of the Son, and of the Holy Ghost, as the initiating sign or seal of the covenant of grace, strongly engaging the person so baptized to get acquainted with the new covenant, to adhere to it, and prepare to renew it at the table of the Lord and sincerely to regulate himself according to it, relying upon the truth and faithfulness of God for the blessings contained in it. And the doctrine of an inward baptism, that of the Spirit sprinkling the blood of Christ upon the soul, for justification, and the graces of the Spirit for sanctification. This ordinance of baptism is a foundation to be rightly laid, and daily remembered, but not repeated.

4. Laying on of hands, on persons passing solemnly from their initiated state by baptism to the confirmed state, by returning the answer of a good conscience towards God, and sitting down at the Lord's table. This passing from incomplete to complete church membership was performed by laying on of hands, which was extraordinary conveyance of the gift of the Holy Ghost continued. This, once done, all are obliged to abide by, and not to need another solemn admission, as at first, but to go on, and grow up, in Christ. Or by this may be meant ordination of persons to the ministerial office, who are duly qualified for it and inclined to it; and this by fasting and prayer, with laying on of the hands of the presbytery: and this is to be done but once.

5. The resurrection of the dead, that is, of dead bodies; and their re-union with their souls, to be eternal companions together in weal or woe, according as their state was towards God when they died, and the course of life they led in this world.

6. Eternal judgment, determining the soul of every one, when it leaves the body at death, and both soul and body at the last day, to their eternal state, every one to his proper society and employment to which they were entitled and fitted here on earth; the wicked to everlasting punishment, the righteous to life eternal.

These are the great foundation-principles which ministers should clearly and convincingly unfold, and closely apply. In these the people should be well instructed and established, and from these they must never depart; without these, the other parts of religion have no foundation to support them.

II. The apostle declares his readiness and resolution to assist the Hebrews in building themselves up on these foundations till they arrive at perfection: *And this we will do, if God permit, v.* 3. And thereby he teaches them, 1. That right resolution is very necessary in order to progress and proficiency in religion. 2. That that resolution is right which is not only made in the sincerity of our hearts, but in a humble dependence upon God for strength, for assistance and righteousness, for acceptance, and for time and opportunity. 3. That ministers should not only teach people what to do, but go before them, and along with them, in the way of duty.

III. He shows that this spiritual growth is the surest way to prevent that dreadful sin of apostasy from the faith. And here,

1. He shows how far persons may go in religion, and, after all, fall away, and perish for ever, *v.* 4, 5. (1.) They may be *enlightened.* Some of the ancients understand this of their being baptized; but it is rather to be understood of notional knowledge and common illumination, of which persons may have a great deal, and yet come short of heaven. *Balaam was the man whose eyes were opened* (Num. 24:3), and yet with his eyes opened he went down to utter darkness. (2.) They may *taste of the heavenly gift,* feel something of the efficacy of the Holy Spirit in his operations upon their souls, causing them to taste something of religion, and yet be like persons in the market, who taste of what they will not come up to the price of, and so but take a taste, and leave it. Persons may taste religion, and seem to like it, if they could have it upon easier terms than denying themselves, and taking up their cross, and following Christ. (3.) They may be *made partakers of the Holy Ghost,* that is, of his extraordinary and miraculous gifts; they may have cast out devils in the name of Christ, and done many other mighty works. Such gifts in the apostolic age were sometimes bestowed upon those who had no true saving grace. (4.) They may *taste of the good word of God;* they may have some relish of gospel doctrines, may hear the word with pleasure, may remember much of it, and talk well of it, and yet never be cast into the form and mould of it, nor have it dwelling richly in them. (5.) They may have *tasted of the powers of the world to come;* they may have been under strong impressions concerning heaven, and dread of going to hell. These lengths hypocrites may go, and, after all, turn apostates. Now hence observe, [1.] These great things are spoken here of those who may fall away; yet it is not here said of them that they were truly converted, or that they were justified; there is more in true saving grace than in all that is here said of apostates. [2.] This therefore is no proof of the final apostasy of true saints. These indeed may fall frequently and foully, but yet they will not totally nor finally from God; the purpose and the power of God, the purchase and the prayer of Christ, the promise of the gospel, the everlasting covenant that God has made with them, ordered in all things and sure, the indwelling of the Spirit, and the immortal seed of the word, these are their security. But the tree that has not these roots will not stand.

2. The apostle describes the dreadful case of such as fall away after having gone so far in the profession of the religion. (1.) The greatness of the sin of apostasy. It is *crucifying the Son of God afresh, and putting him to open shame.* They declare that they approve of what the Jews did in crucifying Christ, and that they would be glad to do the same thing again if it were in their power. They pour the greatest contempt upon the Son of God, and therefore upon God himself, who expects all should reverence his Son, and honour him as they honour the Father. They do what in them lies to represent Christ and Christianity as a shameful thing, and would have him to be a public shame and reproach. This is the nature of apostasy. (2.) The great misery of apostates. [1.] It is impossible to renew them again unto repentance. It is extremely hazardous. Very few instances can be given of those who have gone so far and fallen away, and yet ever have been brought to true repentance, such a repentance as is indeed a renovation of the soul. Some have thought this is the sin against the Holy Ghost, but without ground. The sin here mentioned is plainly apostasy both from the truth and the ways of Christ. God can renew them to repentance, but he seldom does it; and with men themselves it is impossible. [2.] Their misery is exemplified by a proper similitude, taken from the ground that after much cultivation brings forth nothing but briers and thorns; *and therefore is nigh unto cursing, and its end is to be burned, v.* 8. To give this the greater force here is observed the difference that there is between the good ground and the bad, that these contraries, being set one over against the other, illustrate each other. *First* Here is a description of the good ground: It *drinketh in the rain that cometh often upon it.* Believers do not only taste of the word of God, but they drink it in; and this good ground bringeth forth fruit answerable to the cost laid out, for the honour of Christ and the comfort of his faithful ministers, who are, under Christ, dressers of the ground. And this fruit-field or garden receives the blessing. God declares fruitful Christians blessed, and all wise and good men account them blessed: they are blessed with increase of grace, and with further establishment and glory at last. *Secondly,* Here is the different case of the bad ground: It *bears briers and thorns;* it is not only barren of good fruit, but fruitful in that which is bad, briers and thorns, fruitful in sin and wickedness, which are troublesome and hurtful to all about them, and will be most so to sinners themselves at last; and then such ground is rejected. God will concern himself no more about such wicked apostates; he will let them alone, and cast them out of his care; he will command the clouds that they rain no more upon them. Divine influences shall be restrained; and that is not all, but such ground *is nigh unto cursing;* so far is it from receiving the blessing, that a dreadful curse hangs over it, though as yet, through the patience of God, the curse is not fully executed. *Lastly,* Its end is to be burned. Apostasy will be punished with everlasting burnings, the fire that shall never be quenched. This is the sad end to which apostasy leads, and therefore Christians should go on and grow in grace, lest, if they do not go forward, they should go backward, till they bring matters to this woeful extremity of sin and misery.

Verses 9–20

The apostle, having applied himself to the fears of the Hebrews, in order to excite their diligence and prevent their apostasy, now proceeds to apply himself to their hopes, and candidly declares the good hope he had concerning them, that they would persevere; and proposes to them the great encouragements they had in the way of their duty.

I. He freely and openly declares the good hope he had concerning them, that they would endure to the end: *But beloved, we are persuaded better things of you, v.* 9. Observe, 1. There are things that accompany salvation, things that are never separated from salvation, things that show the person to be in a state of salvation, and will issue in eternal salvation. 2. The things that accompany salvation are better things than ever any hypocrite or apostate enjoyed. They are better in their nature and in their issue. 3. It is our duty to hope well of those in whom nothing appears to the contrary. 4. Ministers must sometimes speak by way of caution to those of whose salvation they have good hopes. And those who have in themselves good hopes, as to their eternal salvation, should yet consider seriously how fatal a disappointment it would be if they should fall short. Thus they are to work out their salvation with fear and trembling.

II. He proposes arguments and encouragements to them to go on in the way of their duty. 1. That God had wrought a principle of holy love and charity in them, which had discovered itself in suitable works that would not be forgotten of God: *God is not unrighteous to forget your labour of love, v.* 10. Good works and labour proceeding from love to God are commendable; and what is done to any in the name of God shall not go unrewarded. What is done to the saints, as such, God takes as done to himself. 2. Those who expect a gracious reward for the labour of love must continue in it as long as they have ability and opportunity: *You have ministered to the saints, and you do minister; and we desire that every one of you do show the same diligence.* 3. Those who persevere in a diligent discharge of their duty shall attain to the full assurance of hope in the end. Observe, (1.) Full assurance is a higher degree of hope, is full assurance of hope; they differ not in nature, but only in degree. (2.) Full assurance is attainable by great diligence and perseverance to the end.

III. He proceeds to set before them caution and counsel how to attain this full assurance of hope to the end. 1. That they should not be slothful. Slothfulness will clothe a man with rags: they must not love their ease, nor lose their opportunities. 2. That they would follow the good examples of those who had gone before, *v.* 12. Here learn, (1.) There are some who from assurance have gone to inherit the promises. They believed them before, now they inherit them; they have got safely to heaven. (2.) The way by which they came to the inheritance was that of faith and patience. These graces were implanted in their souls, and drawn forth into act and exercise in their lives. If we ever expect to inherit as they do, we must follow them in the way of faith and patience; and those who do thus follow them in the way shall overtake them at the end, and be partakers of the same blessedness.

IV. The apostle closes the chapter with a clear and full account of the assured truth of the promises of God, *v.* 13, *to the end.* They are all confirmed by the oath of God, and they are all founded in the eternal counsel of God, and therefore may be depended upon.

1. They are all confirmed by the oath of God. He has not only given his people his word, and his hand and seal, but his oath. And here, you will observe, he specifies the oath of God to Abraham, which, being sworn to him as the father of the faithful, remains in full force and virtue to all true be-

lievers: *When God made a promise unto Abraham, because he could swear by no greater, he swore by himself.* Observe, (1.) What was the promise: *Surely, blessing I will bless thee, and multiplying I will multiply thee.* The blessing of God is the blessedness of his people; and those whom he has blessed indeed he will go on to bless, and will multiply blessings, till he has brought them to perfect blessedness. (2.) What was the oath by which this promise was ratified: *He swore by himself.* He staked down his own being and his own blessedness upon it; no greater security can be given or desired. (3.) How was that oath accomplished. Abraham, in due time, obtained the promise. It was made good to him after he had patiently endured. [1.] There is always an interval, and sometimes a long one, between the promise and the performance. [2.] That interval is a trying time to believers, whether they have patience to endure to the end. [3.] Those who patiently endure shall assuredly obtain the blessedness promised, as sure as Abraham did. [4.] The end and design of an oath is to make the promise sure, and to encourage those to whom it is made to wait with patience till the time for performance comes, *v.* 16. An oath with men is for confirmation, and is an end of all strife. This is the nature and design of an oath, in which men swear by the greater, not by creatures, but by the Lord himself; and it is to put an end to all dispute about the matter, both to disputes within our own breasts (doubts and distrusts), and disputes with others, especially with the promiser. Now, if God would condescend to take an oath to his people, he will surely remember the nature and design of it.

2. The promises of God are all founded in his eternal counsel; and this counsel of his is an immutable counsel. (1.) The promise of blessedness which God has made to believers is not a rash and hasty thing, but the result of God's eternal purpose. (2.) This purpose of God was agreed upon in counsel, and settled there between the eternal Father, Son, and Spirit. (3.) These counsels of God can never be altered; they are immutable. God never needs to change his counsels; for nothing new can arise to him who sees the end from the beginning.

3. The promises of God, which are founded upon these immutable counsels of God, and confirmed by the oath of God, may safely be depended upon; for here we have two immutable things, the counsel and the oath of God, in which it is impossible for God to lie, contrary to his nature as well as to his will. Here observe,

(1.) Who they are to whom God has given such full security of happiness. [1.] They are the heirs of the promise: such as have a title to the promises by inheritance, by virtue of their new birth, and union with Christ. We are all by nature children of wrath. The curse is the inheritance we are born to: it is by a new and heavenly birth that any are born heirs to the promise. [2.] They are such as have fled for refuge to the hope set before them. Under the law there were cities of refuge provided for those who were pursued by the avenger of blood. Here is a much better refuge prepared by the gospel, a refuge for all sinners who shall have the heart to flee to it; yea, though they have been the chief of sinners.

(2.) What God's design towards them is, in giving them such securities — that they might have strong consolation. Observe, [1.] God is concerned for the consolation of believers, as well as for their sanctification; he would have his children walk in the fear of the Lord, and in the comforts of the Holy Ghost. [2.] The consolations of God are strong enough to support his people under their strongest trials. The comforts of this world are too weak to bear up the soul under temptation, persecution, and death; but the consolations of the Lord are neither few nor small.

(3.) What use the people of God should make of their hope and comfort, that most refreshing and comfortable hope of eternal blessedness that God has given them. This is, and must be, unto them, for *an anchor to the soul, sure and stedfast,* etc., *v.* 19. Here, [1.] We are in this world as a ship at sea, liable to be tossed up and down, and in danger of being cast away. Our souls are the vessels. The comforts, expectations, graces, and happiness of our souls are the precious cargo with which these vessels are loaded. Heaven is the harbour to which we sail. The temptations, persecutions, and afflictions that we encounter, are the winds and waves that threaten our shipwreck. [2.] We have need of an anchor to keep us sure and steady, or we are in continual danger. [3.] Gospel hope is our anchor; as in our day of battle it is our helmet, so in our stormy passage through this world it is our anchor. [4.] It is sure and stedfast, or else it could not keep

us so. *First,* It is sure in its own nature; for it is the special work of God in the soul. It is a good hope through grace; it is not a flattering hope made out of the spider's web, but it is a true work of God, it is a strong and substantial thing. *Secondly,* It is stedfast as to its object; it is an anchor that has taken good hold, it enters that which is within the veil; it is an anchor that is cast upon the rock, the Rock of ages. It does not seek to fasten in the sands, but enters within the veil, and fixes there upon Christ; he is the object, he is the anchor-hold of the believer's hope. As an unseen glory within the veil is what the believer is hoping for, so an unseen Jesus within the veil is the foundation of his hope; the free grace of God, the merits and mediation of Christ, and the powerful influences of his Spirit, are the grounds of his hope, and so it is a stedfast hope. Jesus Christ is the object and ground of the believer's hope, and so it is a stedfast hope. Jesus Christ is the object and ground of the believer's hope in several respects. 1. As he has entered within the veil, to intercede with God, in virtue of that sacrifice which he offered up without the veil: hope fastens upon his sacrifice and intercession. 2. As he is the forerunner of his people, gone within the veil, to prepare a place for them, and to assure them that they shall follow him; he is the earnest and first fruits of believers, both in his resurrection and in his ascension. 3. And he abides there, a high priest after the order of Melchisedec, a priest for ever, whose priesthood shall never cease, never fail, till he has accomplished its whole work and design, which is the full and final happiness of all who have believed on Christ. Now this should engage us to clear up our interest in Christ, that we may fix our hopes in him as our forerunner, that has entered thither for us, for our sakes, for our safety, to watch over our highest interest and concerns. Let us then love heaven the more on his account, and long to be there with him, where we shall be for ever safe, and for ever satisfied.

CHAPTER 7

The doctrine of the priestly office of Christ is so excellent in itself, and so essential a part of the Christian faith, that the apostle loves to dwell upon it. Nothing made the Jews so fond of the Levitical dispensation as the high esteem they had of their priesthood, and it was doubtless a sacred and most excellent institution; it was a very severe threatening denounced against the Jews (Hos. 3:4), that the children of Israel should abide many days without a prince or priest, and without a sacrifice, and with an ephod, and without teraphim. Now the apostle assures them that by receiving the Lord Jesus they would have a much better high priest, a priesthood of a higher order, and consequently a better dispensation or covenant, a better law and testament; this he shows in this chapter, where, I. We have a more particular account of Melchisedec (v. 1–3). II. The superiority of his priesthood to that of Aaron (v. 4–10). III. An accommodation of all to Christ, to show the superior excellency of his person, office, and covenant (v. 11 to the end).

Verses 1–10

The foregoing chapter ended with a repetition of what had been cited once and again before out of Ps. 110:4, *Jesus, a high priest for ever, after the order of Melchisedec.* Now this chapter is as a sermon upon that text; here the apostle sets before them some of the strong meat he had spoken of before, hoping they would by greater diligence be better prepared to digest it.

I. The great question that first offers itself is, Who was this Melchisedec? All the account we have of him in the Old Testament is in Gen. 14:18, etc., and in Ps. 110:4. Indeed we are much in the dark about him; God has thought fit to leave us so, that this Melchisedec might be a more lively type of him whose generation none can declare. If men will not be satisfied with what is revealed, they must rove about in the dark in endless conjectures, some fancying him to have been an angel, others the Holy Ghost; but,

1. The opinions concerning him that are best worthy our consideration are these three: — (1.) Therabbin, and most of the Jewish writers, think he was Shem the son of Noah who was king and priest to their ancestors, after the manner of the other patriarchs; but it is not probable that he should thus change his name. Besides, we have no account of his settling in the land of Canaan. (2.) Many Christian writers have thought him to be Jesus Christ himself, appearing by a special dispensation and privilege to Abraham in the flesh, and who was known to Abraham by the name *Melchisedec,* which agrees very well to Christ, and to what is said, Jn. 8:56, *Abraham saw his day and rejoiced.* Much may be said for this opinion, and what is said in *v.* 3 does not seem to agree with any mere man; but then it seems strange to make Christ a type of himself. (3.) The most general opinion

is that he was a Canaanite king, who reigned in Salem, and kept up religion and the worship of the true God; that he was raised to be a type of Christ, and was honoured by Abraham as such.

2. But we shall leave these conjectures, and labour to understand, as far as we can, what is here said of him by the apostle, and how Christ is represented thereby, *v.* 1–3. (1.) Melchisedec was a king, and so is the Lord Jesus — a king of God's anointing; the government is laid upon his shoulders, and he rules over all for the good of his people. (2.) That he was *king of righteousness:* his name signifies *the righteous king.* Jesus Christ is a rightful and a righteous king — rightful in his title, righteous in his government. He is the Lord our righteousness; he has fulfilled all righteousness, and brought in an everlasting righteousness, and he loves righteousness and righteous persons, and hates iniquity. (3.) He was king of Salem, that is, king of peace; first king of righteousness, and after that king of peace. So is our Lord Jesus; he by his righteousness made peace, the fruit of righteousness is peace. Christ speaks peace, creates peace, is our peacemaker. (4.) He was *priest of the most high God,* qualified and anointed in an extraordinary manner to be his priest among the Gentiles. So is the Lord Jesus; he is the priest of the most high God, and the Gentiles must come to God by him; it is only through his priesthood that we can obtain reconciliation and remission of sin. (5.) He was *without father, without mother, without descent, having neither beginning of days nor end of life, v.* 3. This must not be understood according to the letter; but the scripture has chosen to set him forth as an extraordinary person, without giving us his genealogy, that he might be a fitter type of Christ, who as man was without father, as God without mother; whose priesthood is without descent, did not descend to him from another, nor from him to another, but is personal and perpetual. (6.) That he met *Abraham returning from the slaughter of the kings, and blessed him.* The incident is recorded Gen. 14:18, etc. He brought forth bread and wine to refresh Abraham and his servants when they were weary; he gave as a king, and blessed as a priest. Thus our Lord Jesus meets his people in their spiritual conflicts, refreshes them, renews their strength, and blesses them. (7.) That *Abraham gave him a tenth part of all* (v. 2), that is, as the apostle explains it, of all *the spoils;* and this Abraham did as an expression of his gratitude for what Melchisedec had done for him, or as a testimony of his homage and subjection to him as a king, or as an offering vowed and dedicated to God, to be presented by his priest. And thus are we obliged to make all possible returns of love and gratitude to the Lord Jesus for all the rich and royal favours we receive from him, to pay our homage and subjection to him as our King, and to put all our offerings into his hands, to be presented by him to the Father in the incense of his own sacrifice. (8.) That this Melchisedec was *made like unto the Son of God, and abideth a priest continually.* He bore the image of God in his piety and authority, and stands upon record as an immortal high priest; the ancient type of him who is the eternal and only-begotten of the Father, who abideth a priest for ever.

II. Let us now consider (as the apostle advises) how great this Melchisedec was, and how far his priesthood was above that of the order of Aaron (v. 4, 5, etc.): *Now consider how great this man was,* etc. The greatness of this man and his priesthood appears, 1. From Abraham's paying the tenth of the spoils unto him; and it is well observed that Levi paid tithes to Melchisedec in Abraham, *v.* 9. Now Levi received the office of the priesthood from God, and was to take tithes of the people, yet even Levi paid tithes to Melchisedec, as to a greater and higher priest than himself; therefore that high priest who should afterwards appear, of whom Melchisedec was a type, must be much superior to any of the Levitical priests, who paid tithes, in Abraham, to Melchisedec. And now by this argument of persons doing things that are matters of right or injury in the loins of their predecessors we have an illustration how we may be said to have sinned in Adam, and fallen with him in his first transgression. We were in Adam's loins when he sinned, and the guilt and depravity contracted by the human nature when it was in our first parents are equitably imputed and derived to the same nature as it is in all other persons naturally descended from them. They justly adhere to the nature, and it must be by an act of grace if ever they be taken away. 2. From Melchisedec's blessing of Abraham, *who had the promises; and, without contradiction, the less is blessed of the greater,*

v. 6, 7. Here observe, (1.) Abraham's great dignity and felicity — that he had the promises. He was one in covenant with God, to whom God had given exceedingly great and precious promises. That man is rich and happy indeed who has an estate in bills and bonds under God's own hand and seal. These promises are both of the life that now is and of that which is to come; this honour have all those who receive the Lord Jesus, in whom all the promises are yea and amen. (2.) Melchisedec's greater honour — in that it was his place and privilege to bless Abraham; and it is an uncontested maxim *that the less is blessed of the greater, v. 7.* He who gives the blessing is greater than he who receives it; and therefore Christ, the antitype of Melchisedec, the meriter and Mediator of all blessings to the children of men, must be greater than all the priests of the order of Aaron.

Verses 11–28

Observe the necessity there was of raising up another priest, after the order of Melchisedec and not after the order of Aaron, by whom that perfection should come which could not come by the Levitical priesthood, which therefore must be changed, and the whole economy with it, v. 11, 12, etc. Here,

I. It is asserted that perfection could not come by the Levitical priesthood and the law. They could not put those who came to them into the perfect enjoyment of the good things they pointed out to them; they could only show them the way.

II. That therefore another priest must be raised up, after the order of Melchisedec, by whom, and his law of faith, perfection might come to all who obey him; and, blessed be God, that we may have perfect holiness and perfect happiness by Christ in the covenant of grace, according to the gospel, for we are complete in him.

III. It is asserted that the priesthood being changed there must of necessity be a change of the law; there being so near a relation between the priesthood and the law, the dispensation could not be the same under another priesthood; a new priesthood must be under a new regulation, managed in another way, and by rules proper to its nature and order.

IV. It is not only asserted, but proved, that the priesthood and law are changed, v. 13, 14. The priesthood and law by which perfection could not come are abolished, and a priest has arisen, and a dispensation is now set up, by which true believers may be made perfect. Now that there is such a change is obvious.

1. There is a change in the tribe of which the priesthood comes. Before, it was the tribe of Levi; but our great high priest sprang out of Judah, of which tribe Moses spoke nothing concerning the priesthood, v. 14. This change of the family shows a real change of the law of the priesthood.

2. There is a change in the form and order of making the priests. Before, in the Levitical priesthood, they were made after the law of a carnal commandment; but our great high priest was made after the power of an endless life. The former law appointed that the office should descend, upon the death of the father, to his eldest son, according to the order of carnal or natural generation; for none of the high priests under the law were without father or mother, or without descent: they had not life and immortality in themselves. They had both beginning of days and end of life; and so the carnal commandment, or law of primogeniture, directed their succession, as it did in matters of civil right and inheritance. But the law by which Christ was constituted a priest, after the order of Melchisedec, was the power of an endless life. The life and immortality which he had in himself were his right and title to the priesthood, not his descent from former priests. This makes a great difference in the priesthood, and in the economy too, and gives the preference infinitely to Christ and the gospel. The very law which constituted the Levitical priesthood supposed the priests to be weak, frail, dying, creatures, not able to preserve their own natural lives, but who must be content and glad to survive in their posterity after the flesh; much less could they, by any power or authority they had, convey spiritual life and blessedness to those who came to them. But the high priest of our profession holds his office by that innate power of endless life which he has in himself, not only to preserve himself alive, but to communicate spiritual and eternal life to all those who duly rely upon his sacrifice and intercession. Some thing *the law of the carnal commandment* refers to the external rites of consecration, and the carnal offerings that were made; but *the power of an endless life* to the spiritual living sacrifices

proper to the gospel, and the spiritual and eternal privileges purchased by Christ, who was consecrated by the eternal Spirit of life that he received without measure.

3. There is a change in the efficacy of the priesthood. The former was weak and unprofitable, made nothing perfect; the latter brought in a better hope, by which we draw near to God, v. 18, 19. The Levitical priesthood brought nothing to perfection: it could not justify men's persons from guilt; it could not sanctify them from inward pollution; it could not cleanse the consciences of the worshippers from dead works; all it could do was to lead them to the antitype. But the priesthood of Christ carries in it, and brings along with it, a better hope; it shows us the true foundation of all the hope we have towards God for pardon and salvation; it more clearly discovers the great objects of our hope; and so it tends to work in us a more strong and lively hope of acceptance with God. By this hope we are encouraged to draw nigh unto God, to enter into a covenant-union with him, to live a life of converse and communion with him. We may now draw near with a true heart, and with the full assurance of faith, having our minds sprinkled from an evil conscience. The former priesthood rather kept men at a distance, and under a spirit of bondage.

4. There is a change in God's way of acting in this priesthood. He has taken an oath to Christ, which he never did to any of the order of Aaron. God never gave them any such assurance of their continuance, never engaged himself by oath or promise that theirs should be an everlasting priesthood, and therefore gave them no reason to expect the perpetuity of it, but rather to look upon it as a temporary law. But Christ was made a priest with the oath of God: *The Lord hath sworn, and will not repent, Thou art a priest for ever after the order of Melchisedec, v.* 21. Here God has upon oath declared the immutability, excellency, efficacy, and eternity, of the priesthood of Christ.

5. There is a change in that covenant of which the priesthood was a security and the priest a surety; that is, a change in the dispensation of that covenant. The gospel dispensation is more full, free, perspicuous, spiritual, and efficacious, than that of the law. Christ is in this gospel covenant a surety for us to God and for God to us, to see that the articles be performed on both parts He, as surety, has united the divine and human nature together in his own person, and therein given assurance of reconciliation; and he has, as surety, united God and man together in the bond of the everlasting covenant. He pleads with men to keep their covenant with god, and he pleads with God that he will fulfil his promises to men, which he is always ready to do in a way suitable to his majesty and glory, that is, through a Mediator.

6. There is a remarkable change in the number of the priests under these different orders. In that of Aaron there was a multitude of priests, of high priests, not at once, but successively; but in this of Christ there is but one and the same. The reason is plain, The Levitical priests were many, because *they were not suffered to continue by reason of death.* Their office, how high and honourable soever, could not secure them from dying; and, as one died, another must succeed, and after a while must give place to a third, till the number had become very great. But this our high priest continues for ever, and his priesthood is *aparabaton — an unchangeable one,* that does not pass from one to another, as the former did; it is always in the same hand. There can be no vacancy in this priesthood, no hour nor moment in which the people are without a priest to negotiate their spiritual concerns in heaven. Such a vacancy might be very dangerous and prejudicial to them; but this is their safety and happiness, that this ever-living high priest is able to save to the utmost — in all times, in all cases, in every juncture — all who come to God by him, v. 25. So that here is a manifest alteration much for the better.

7. There is a remarkable difference in the moral qualifications of the priests. Those who were of the order of Aaron were not only mortal men, but sinful men, who had their sinful as well as natural infirmities; they needed to offer up sacrifices first for their own sins and then for the people. But our high priest, who was consecrated by the word of the oath, needed only to offer up once for the people, never at all for himself; for he has not only an immutable consecration to his office, but an immutable sanctity in his person. He is *such a high priest as became us, holy, harmless, and undefiled,* etc., v. 26–28. Here observe, (1.) Our case, as sinners, needed a high priest to make satisfaction and intercession for us.

(2.) No priest could be suitable or sufficient for our reconciliation to God but one who was perfectly righteous in his own person; he must be righteous in himself, or he could not be a propitiation for our sin, or our advocate with the Father. (3.) The Lord Jesus was exactly such a high priest as we wanted, for he has a personal holiness, absolutely perfect. Observe the description we have of the personal holiness of Christ expressed in various terms, all of which some learned divines consider as relating to his perfect purity. [1.] He is holy, perfectly free from all the habits or principles of sin, not having the least disposition to it in his nature; no sin dwells in him, though it does in the best of Christians, not the least sinful inclination [2.] He is harmless, perfectly free from all actual transgression, has done no violence, nor is there any deceit in his mouth, never did the least wrong to God or man. [3.] He is undefiled, he was never accessory to other men's sins. It is a difficult thing to keep ourselves pure, so as not to partake in the guilt of other men's sins, by contributing in some way towards them, or not doing what we ought to prevent them. Christ was undefiled; though he took upon him the guilt of our sins, yet he never involved himself in the fact and fault of them. [4.] He is separate from sinners, not only in his present state (having entered as our high priest into the holiest of all, into which nothing defiled can enter), but in his personal purity: he has no such union with sinners, either natural or federal, as can devolve upon him original sin. This comes upon us by virtue of our natural and federal union with the first Adam, we descending from him in the ordinary way. But Christ was, by his ineffable conception in the virgin, separate from sinners; though he took a true human nature, yet the miraculous way in which it was conceived set him upon a separate footing from all the rest of mankind. [5.] He is made higher than the heavens. Most expositors understand this concerning his state of exaltation in heaven, at the right hand of God, to perfect the design of his priesthood. But Dr. Goodwin thinks this may be very justly referred to the personal holiness of Christ, which is greater and more perfect than the holiness of the hosts of heaven, that is, the holy angels themselves, who, though they are free from sin, yet are not in themselves free from all possibility of sinning. And therefore we read, *God putteth no trust in his holy ones, and he chargeth his angels with folly* (Job 4:18), that is, with weakness and peccability. They may be angels one hour and devils another, as many of them were; and that the holy angels shall not now fall does not proceed from an indefectibility of nature, but from the election of God; they are elect angels. It is very probable that this explanation of the words, *made higher than the heavens,* may be thought too much strained, and that it ought to be understood of the dignity of Christ's state, and not the perfect holiness of his person; and the rather because it is said he was *made* higher *genomenos;* but it is well known that this word is used in a neutral sense, as where it is said, *genesthē ho Theos alēthēs — Let God be true.* The other characters in the verse plainly belong to the personal perfection of Christ in holiness, as opposed to the sinful infirmities of the Levitical priests; and it seems congruous to think this must do so too, if it may be fairly taken in such a sense; and it appears yet more probable, since the validity and prevalency of Christ's priesthood in v. 27 are placed in the impartiality and disinterestedness of it. He needed not to offer up for himself: it was a disinterested mediation; he mediated for that mercy for others which he did not need for himself; had he needed it himself, he had been a party, and could not have been a Mediator — a criminal, and could not have been an advocate for sinners. Now, to render his mediation the more impartial and disinterested, it seems requisite not only that he had no present need of that favour for himself which he mediated for in behalf of others, but that he never could stand in need of it. Though he needed it not to-day, yet if he knew he might be in such circumstances as to need it to-morrow, or at any future time, he must have been thought to have had some eye upon his own interest, and therefore could not act with impartial regard and pure zeal for the honour of God on one hand, and tender pure compassion for poor sinners on the other. I pretend not here to follow the notes of our late excellent expositor, into whose labours we have entered, but have taken the liberty to vindicate this notion of the learned Dr. Goodwin from the exceptions that I know have been made to it; and I have the rather done it because, if it will hold good, it gives us further evidence how necessary it was that the Mediator should be God, since no mere creature is of himself possessed of that impeccability which will set him above all possible need of favour and mercy for himself.

CHAPTER 8

In this chapter the apostle pursues his former subject, the priesthood of Christ. And, I. He sums up what he had already said (*v.* 1, 2). II. He sets before them the necessary parts of the priestly office (*v.* 3–5). And, III. Largely illustrates the excellency of the priesthood of Christ, by considering the excellency of that new dispensation or covenant for which Christ is the Mediator (*v.* 6 to the end).

Verses 1–5

Here is, I. A summary recital of what had been said before concerning the excellency of Christ's priesthood, showing what we have in Christ, where he now resides, and what sanctuary he is the minister of, *v.* 1, 2. Observe, 1. What we have in Christ; we have a high priest, and such a high priest as no other people ever had, no age of the world, or of the church, ever produced; all others were but types and shadows of this high priest. He is adequately fitted and absolutely sufficient to all the intents and purposes of a high priest, both with respect to the honour of God and the happiness of men and himself; the great honour of all those who have an interest in him. 2. Where he now resides: *He sits on the right hand of the throne of the Majesty on high,* that is, of the glorious God of heaven. There the Mediator is placed, and he is possessed of all authority and power both in heaven and upon earth. This is the reward of his humiliation. This authority he exercises for the glory of his Father, for his own honour, and for the happiness of all who belong to him; and he will by his almighty power bring every one of them in their own order to the right hand of God in heaven, as members of his mystical body, that where he is they may be also. 3. What is that sanctuary of which he is a minister: *Of the true tabernacle, which the Lord hath pitched, and not man,* *v.* 2. The tabernacle which was pitched by man, according to the appointment of God. There was an outer part, in which was the altar where they were to offer their sacrifices, which typified Christ dying; and there was an interior part within the veil, which typified Christ interceding for the people in heaven. Now this tabernacle Christ never entered into; but, having finished the work of satisfaction in the true tabernacle of his own body, he is now a minister of the sanctuary, the holy of holies, the true tabernacle in heaven, there taking care of his people's affairs, interceding with God for them, that their sins may be pardoned and their persons and services accepted, through the merit of his sacrifice. He is not only in heaven enjoying great dominion and dignity, but, as the high priest of his church, executing this office for them all in general, and every member of the church in particular.

II. The apostle sets before the Hebrews the necessary parts of Christ's priesthood, or what it was that belonged to that office, in conformity to what every high priest is ordained to, *v.* 3, 4. 1. *Every high priest is ordained to offer gifts and sacrifices.* Whatever was brought by the people to be presented to God, whether expiatory sacrifices, or peace-offerings, or thank-offerings, must be offered by the priest, who was to expiate their guilt by the blood of the sacrifice, and perfume their gifts and services by his holy incense, to render their persons and performances typically acceptable; so then it necessarily belongs to the priesthood of Christ that he should have somewhat to offer; and he, as the antitype, had himself to offer, his human nature upon the altar of his divine nature, as the great atoning sacrifice that finished transgression, and made an end of sin once for all; and he has the incense of his own righteousness and merits too to offer with all that his people offer up to God by him, to render them acceptable. We must not dare to approach to God, or to present any thing to him, but in and through Christ, depending upon his merits and mediation; for if we are accepted, it is in the Beloved. 2. Christ must now execute his priesthood in heaven, in the holy of holies, the true tabernacle which the Lord hath fixed. Thus the type must be fully answered; having finished the work of sacrificing here, he must go into heaven, to present his righteousness and to make intercession there. For, (1.) *If Christ were on earth, he would not be a priest* (*v.* 4), that is, not according to the Levitical law, as not being of the line of that priesthood; and so long as that priesthood continued there must be a strict regard paid to the divine institution in everything. (2.) All the services of the priest, under the law, as well as every thing in that tabernacle which was framed according to the pattern in the mount, were only exemplars and shadows of heavenly things, *v.* 5. Christ is the substance and end of the law for righteousness. Something therefore there must be in Christ's priesthood that answers to the high priest's entering within the veil to make intercession, without which he could not have been a perfect priest; and what is this but the ascension of Christ into heaven, and his appearance there in the sight of God for his people, to present their prayers, and plead their cause? So that, if he had still continued on earth, he could not have been a perfect priest; and an imperfect one he could not be.

Verses 6–13

In this part of the chapter, the apostle illustrates and confirms the superior excellency of the priesthood of Christ above that of Aaron, from the excellency of that covenant, or that dispensation of the covenant of grace, of which Christ was the Mediator (*v.* 6): his ministry is more excellent, by how much he is the Mediator of a better covenant. The body and soul too of all divinity (as some observe) consist very much in rightly distinguishing between the two covenants — the covenant of works and the covenant of grace; and between the two dispensations of the covenant of grace — that under the Old Testament and that under the New. Now observe,

I. What is here said of the old covenant, or rather of the old dispensation of the covenant of grace: of this it is said, 1. That it was made with the fathers of the Jewish nation at mount Sinai (*v.* 9), and Moses was the Mediator of that covenant, when God took them by the hand, to lead them out of the land of Egypt, which intimates the great affection, condescension, and tender care of God towards them. 2. That this covenant was not found faultless (*v.* 7, 8); it was a dispensation of darkness and dread, tending to bondage, and only a schoolmaster to bring us to Christ; it was perfect in its kind, and fitted to answer its end, but very imperfect in comparison of the gospel. 3. That it was not sure or stedfast; *for the Jews continued not in that covenant, and the Lord regarded them not,* *v.* 9. They dealt ungratefully with their God, and cruelly with themselves, and fell under God's displeasure. God will regard those who remain in his covenant, but will reject those who cast away his yoke from them. 4. That it is decayed, grown old, and vanisheth away, *v.* 13. It is antiquated, canceled, out of date, of no more use in gospel times than candles are when the sun has risen. Some think the covenant of peculiarity did not quite decay till the destruction of Jerusalem, though it was forfeited at the death of Christ, and was made old, and was now to vanish and perish, and the Levitical priesthood vanished with it.

II. What is here said of the New-Testament dispensation, to prove the superior excellency of Christ's ministry. It is said,

1. That it is a better covenant (*v.* 6), a more clear and comfortable dispensation and discovery of the grace of God to sinners, bringing in holy light and liberty to the soul. It is without fault, well ordered in all things. It requires nothing but what it promises grace to perform. It accepts of godly sincerity, accounting it gospel perfection. Every transgression does not turn us out of covenant; all is put into a good and safe hand.

2. That it is established upon better promises, more clear and express, more spiritual, more absolute. The promises of spiritual and eternal blessings are in this covenant positive and absolute; the promises of temporal blessings are with a wise and kind proviso, as far as shall be for God's glory and his people's good. This covenant contains in it promises of assistance and acceptance in duty, promises of progress and perseverance in grace and holiness, of bliss and glory in heaven, which were more obscurely shadowed forth by the promises of the land of Canaan, a type of heaven.

3. It is a new covenant, even that new covenant that God long ago declared he would make with the house of Israel, that is, all the Israel of God; this was promised in Jer. 31:31, 32, and accomplished in Christ. This will always be a new covenant, in which all who truly take hold of it shall be always found preserved by the power of God. It is God's covenant; his mercy, love, and grace moved for it; his wisdom devised it; his Son purchased it; his wisdom devised it; his Son purchased it; his Spirit brings souls into it, and builds them up in it.

4. The articles of this covenant are very extraordinary, which are sealed between God and his people by baptism and the Lord's supper; whereby they bind themselves to their part, and God assures them he will do his part; and his is the main and principal part, on which his people depend for grace and strength to do theirs. Here,

(1.) God articles with his people *that he will put his laws into their minds and write them in their hearts,* *v.* 10. He once wrote his laws to them, now he will write his laws in them; that is, he will give them understanding to know and to believe his law; he will give them memories to retain them; he will give them hearts to love them and consciences to recognize them; he will give them courage to profess them and power to put them in practice; the whole habit and frame of their souls shall be a table and transcript of the law of God. This is the foundation of the covenant; and, when this is laid, duty will be done wisely, sincerely, readily, easily, resolutely, constantly, and comfortably.

(2.) He articles with them to take them into a near and very honourable relation to himself. [1.] He will be to them a God; that is, he will be all that to them, and do all that for them, that God can be and do. Nothing more can be said in a thousand volumes than is comprehended in these few words: *I will be a God to them.* [2.] They shall be to him a people, to love, honour, observe, and obey him in all things; complying with his cautions, conforming to his commands, comporting with his providences, copying out his example, taking complacency in his favour. This those must do and will do who have God for their God; this they are bound to do as their part of the contract; this they shall do, for God will enable them to do it, as an evidence that he is their God and that they are his people; for it is God himself who first founds the relation, and then fills it up with grace suitable and sufficient, and helps them in their measure to fill it up with love and duty; so that God engages both for himself and them.

(3.) He articles with them that they shall grow more and more acquainted with their God (*v.* 11): *They shall all know me from the least to the greatest,* insomuch that there shall not be so much need of one neighbour teaching another the knowledge of God. Here observe, [1.] In the want of better instruction, one neighbour should be teaching another to know the Lord, as they have ability and opportunity for it. [2.] This private instruction shall not be so necessary under the New Testament as it was under the Old. The old dispensation was shadowy, dark, ritual, and less understood; their priests preached but seldom, and but a few at a time, and the Spirit of God was more sparingly given out. But under the new dispensation there shall be such abundance of public qualified preachers of the gospel, and dispensers of ordinances statedly in the solemn assemblies, and so great a flocking to them, as doves to their windows, and such a plentiful effusion of the Spirit of God to make the ministration of the gospel effectual, that there shall be a mighty increase and spreading of Christian knowledge in persons of all sorts, of each sex, and of all ages. O that this promise might be fulfilled in our days, that the hand of God may be with his ministers, that a great number may believe and be turned to the Lord!

(4.) God articles with them about the pardon of their sins, as what always accompanies the true knowledge of God (*v.* 12): *For I will be merciful to their unrighteousness,* etc. Observe, [1.] The freeness of this pardon. It does not result from merit in man, but from mercy in God; he pardons for his own name's sake. [2.] The fullness of this pardon; it extends to their unrighteousness, sins, and iniquities; to all kinds of sin, to sins highly aggravated. [3.] The fixedness of this pardon. It is so final and so fixed that God will remember their sins no more; he will not recall his pardon; he will not only forgive their sins, but forget them, treat them as if he had forgotten them. This pardoning mercy is connected with all other spiritual mercies. Unpardoned sin prevents mercy, and pulls down judgments; but the pardon of sin prevents judgment, and opens a wide door to all spiritual blessings; it is the effect of that mercy that is from everlasting, and the earnest of that mercy that shall be to everlasting. This is the excellency of the new dispensation, and these are the articles of it; and therefore we have no reason to repine, but great reason to rejoice that the former dispensation is antiquated and has vanished away.

CHAPTER 9

The apostle, having declared the Old-Testament dispensation antiquated and vanishing away, proceeds to let the Hebrews see the correspondence there was between the Old Testament and the New; and that whatever was excellent in the Old was typical and representative of the New, which therefore must as far excel the Old as the substance does the shadow. The Old Testament was never intended to be rested in, but to prepare for the institutions of the gospel. And here he treats, I. Of the tabernacle, the place of worship (*v.* 1–5). II. Of the worship and services performed in the tabernacle (*v.* 6, 7). III. He delivers the spiritual sense and the main design of all (*v.* 8 to the end).

Verses 1–7

Here, I. The apostle gives an account of the tabernacle, that place of worship which God appointed to be pitched on earth; it is called *a worldly* sanctuary, wholly of this world, as to the materials of which it was built, and a building that must be taken down; it is called a worldly *sanctuary,* because it was the court and palace of the King of Israel. God was their King, and, as other kings, had his court or place of residence, and attendants, furniture, and provision, suitable thereto. This tabernacle (of which we have the model, Ex. 25–27) was a moving temple, shadowing forth the unsettled state of the church militant, and the human nature of the Lord Jesus Christ, in whom the fullness of the Godhead dwelt bodily. Now of this tabernacle it is said that it was divided into two parts, called a first and a second tabernacle, an inner and an outer part, representing the two states of the church militant and triumphant, and the two natures of Christ, human and divine. We are also told what was placed in each part of the tabernacle.

1. In the outer part: and there were several things, of which you have here a sort of schedule. (1.) The candlestick; doubtless not an empty and unlighted one, but where the lamps were always burning. And there was need of it, for there were no windows in the sanctuary; and this was to convince the Jews of the darkness and the mysterious nature of that dispensation. Their light was only candle-light, in comparison of the fullness of light which Christ, the Sun of righteousness, would bring along with him, and communicate to his people; for all our light is derived from him the fountain of light. (2.) The table and the show-bread set upon it. This table was set directly opposite to the candlestick, which shows that by light from Christ we must have communion with him and with one another. We must not come in the dark to his table, but by light from Christ must discern the Lord's body. On this table were placed twelve loaves for the twelve tribes of Israel, a loaf for a tribe, which stood from sabbath to sabbath, and on that day were renewed. This show-bread may be considered either as the provision of the palace (though the King of Israel needed it not, yet, in resemblance of the palaces of earthly kings, there must be this provision laid in weekly), or the provision made in Christ for the souls of his people, suitable to the wants and to the relief of their souls. He is the bread of life; in our Father's house there is bread enough and to spare; we may have fresh supplies from Christ, especially every Lord's day. This outer part is called *the sanctuary or holy,* because erected to the worship of a holy God, to represent a holy Jesus, and to entertain a holy people, for their further improvement in holiness.

2. We have an account of what was in the inner part of the sanctuary, which was within the second veil, and is called *the holiest of all.* This second veil, which divided between the holy and the most holy place, was a type of the body of Christ, by the rending whereof not only a view, but a way, was opened for us into the holiest of all, the type of heaven itself. Now in this part were, (1.) The golden censer, which was to hold the incense, or the golden altar set up to burn the incense upon; both the one and the other were typical of Christ, of his pleasing and prevailing intercession which he makes in heaven, grounded upon the merits and satisfaction of his sacrifice, upon which we are to depend for acceptance and the blessing from God. (2.) The ark of the covenant overlaid round about with pure gold, *v.* 4. This typified Christ, his perfect obedience to the law and his fulfilling of all righteousness for us. Now here we are told both what was in this ark and what was over it. [1.] What was in it. *First, The golden pot that had manna,* which, when preserved by the Israelites in their own houses, contrary to the command of God, presently putrefied; but now, being by God's appointment deposited here in this house, was kept from putrefaction, always pure and sweet; and this to teach us that it is only in Christ that our persons, our graces, our performances are kept pure. It was also a type of the bread of life we have in Christ, the true ambrosia that gives immortality. This was also a memorial of God's miraculously feeding his people in the wilderness, that they might never forget such signal favour, nor distrust God for the time to come. *Secondly, Aaron's rod that budded,* and thereby showed that God had chosen him of the tribe of Levi to minister before him of all the tribes of Israel, and so an end was put to the murmuring of the people, and to their attempt to invade the priest's office, Num. 17. This was that rod of God with which Moses and Aaron wrought such wonders; and this was a type of Christ, who is styled *the man, the branch* (Zec. 6:12), by whom God has wrought wonders for the spiritual deliverance, defence, and supply of his people, and for the destruction of their enemies. It was a type of divine justice, by which Christ the Rock was smitten, and from whom the cool refreshing waters of life flow into our souls. *Thirdly, The tables of the covenant,* in which the moral law was written, signifying the regard God has to the preservation of his holy law, and the care we all ought to have that we keep the law of God — that this we can only do in and through Christ, by strength from him nor can our obedience by accepted but through him. [2.] What was over the ark (*v.* 5): *Over it the cherubim of glory shadowing the mercy-seat. First,* The mercy-seat, which was the covering of the ark; it was called *the propitiatory,* and it was of pure gold, as long and as broad as the ark in which the tables of the law were laid. It was an eminent type of Christ, and of his perfect righteousness, ever adequate to the dimensions of the law of God, and covering all our transgressions, interposing between the Shechinah, or symbol of God's presence, and our sinful failures, and covering them. *Secondly, The cherubim of glory* shadowing the mercy-seat, representing the holy angels of God, who take pleasure in looking into the great work of our redemption by Christ, and are ready to perform every good office, under the Redeemer, for those who are the heirs of salvation. The angels attended Christ at his birth, in his temptation, under his agonies, at his resurrection, and in his ascension, and will attend his second coming. God manifest in the flesh was seen, observed, visited, by the angels.

II. From the description of the place of worship in the Old-Testament dispensation, the apostle proceeds to speak of the duties and services performed in those places, *v.* 6. When the several parts and furniture of the tabernacle were thus settled, then what was to be done there?

1. The ordinary priests went always into the first tabernacle, to accomplish the service of God. Observe, (1.) None but priests were to enter into the first part of the tabernacle, and this to teach us all that persons not qualified, not called of God, must not intrude into the office and work of the ministry. (2.) The ordinary priests were only to enter into the first part of the tabernacle, it would have been fatal presumption in them to have gone into the holiest of all; and this teaches us that even ministers themselves must know and keep in their proper stations, and not presume to usurp the prerogative of Christ, by offering up incense of their own, or adding their own inventions to the ordinances of Christ, or lording it over men's consciences. (3.) These ordinary priests were to enter into the first tabernacle always; that is, they were to devote themselves and all their time to the work of their office, and not alienate themselves at any time from it; they were to be in an habitual readiness for the discharge of their office, and at all stated appointed times were actually to attend to their work. (4.) The ordinary priests must enter into the first tabernacle, that they might there accomplish the service of God. They must not do the work of God partially or by halves, but stand complete in the whole of his will and counsel; not only beginning well, but proceeding well, and persevering to the end, fulfilling the ministry they had received.

2. Into the second, the interior part, went the high priest along, *v.* 7. This part was an emblem of heaven, and Christ's ascension thither. Here observe, (1.) None but the high priest must go into the holiest; so none but Christ could enter into heaven in his own name, by his own right, and by his own merits. (2.) In entering into the holiest, the high priest must first go through the outer sanctuary, and through the veil, signifying that Christ went to heaven through a holy life and a violent death; the veil of his flesh was rent asunder. (3.) The high priest entered but once a year into the holiest, and in this the antitype excels the type (as in every thing else), for he has entered once for all, during the whole dispensation of the gospel. (4.) The high priest must not enter without blood, signifying that Christ, having undertaken to be our high priest, could not have been admitted into heaven without shedding his blood for us, and that none of us can enter either into God's gracious presence here or his glorious presence hereafter, but by the blood of Jesus. (5.) The high priest, under the law, entering into the holiest, offered up that blood for himself and his own errors first, and then for the errors of the people, *v.* 7. This teaches us that Christ is a more excellent person and high priest than any under the law, for he has no errors of his own to offer for. And it teaches us that ministers, when in the name of Christ they intercede for others, must first apply the blood of Christ to themselves for their pardon. (6.) When the legal high priest had offered for himself, he must not stop there, but must also offer for the errors of the people. Our high priest, though he needs not to offer for himself, yet forgets not to offer for his people; he pleads the merit of his sufferings for the benefit of his people on earth. Observe, [1.] Sins are errors, and great errors, both in judgment and practice. We greatly err when we sin against God; and who can understand all his errors? [2.] They are such errors as leave guilt upon the conscience, not to be washed away but by the blood of Christ; and the sinful errors of priests and people must be all done away by the same means, the application of the blood of Christ; we must plead this blood on earth, while he is pleading it in heaven for us.

Verses 8–14

In these verses the apostle undertakes to deliver to us the mind and meaning of the Holy Ghost in all the ordinances of the tabernacle and legal economy, comprehending both place and worship. The scriptures of the Old Testament were given by inspiration of God; holy men of old spoke and wrote as the Holy Ghost directed them. And these Old-Testament records are of great use and significancy, not only to those who first received them, but even to Christians, who ought not to satisfy themselves with reading the institutes of the Levitical law, but should learn what the Holy Ghost signifies and suggests to them thereby. Now here are several things mentioned as the things that the Holy Ghost signified and certified to his people hereby.

I. That the way into the holiest of all was not yet made manifest, while the first tabernacle was standing, *v.* 8. This was one lesson the Holy Ghost would teach us by these types; the way to heaven was not so clear and plain, nor so much frequented, under the Old Testament as under the New. It is the honour of Christ and the gospel, and the happiness of those who live under it, that now life and immortality are brought to light. There was not that free access to God then that there is now; God has now opened a wider door; and there is room for more, yea, even for as many as are truly willing to return unto him by Christ.

II. That the first tabernacle was only a figure for the time then present, *v.* 9. It was a dark dispensation, and but of short continuance, only designed for awhile to typify the great things of Christ and the gospel, that were in due time to shine forth in their own brightness, and thereby cause all the shadows to flee away and disappear, as the stars before the rising sun.

III. That none of the gifts and sacrifices there offered could make the offerers perfect as pertaining to conscience (*v.* 9); that is, they could not take away the desert, or defilement, or dominion, of sin; they could not deliver conscience from a dread of the wrath of God; they could neither discharge the debts, nor resolve the doubts, of him who did the service. A man might run through them all in their several orders and frequent returns, and continue to do so all his days, and yet not find his conscience either pacified or purified by them; he might thereby be saved from corporal and temporal punishments that were threatened against the non-observers, but he could not be saved by them from sin or hell, as all those are who believe in Christ.

IV. The Holy Ghost hereby signifies that the Old-Testament institutions were by external carnal ordinances imposed upon them until the time of reformation, *v.* 10. Their imperfection lay in three things: — 1. Their nature. They were but external and carnal meats and drinks, and divers washings. All these were bodily exercises, which profit little; they could only satisfy the flesh, or at best sanctify to the purifying of the flesh. 2. They were not such as were left indifferent to them to use or disuse, but they were imposed upon them by grievous corporal punishments, and this was ordered on purpose to make them look more to the promised Seed, and long more for him. 3. These were never designed for a perpetuity, but only to continue till the time of reformation, till the better things provided for them were actually bestowed upon them. Gospel times are and should be times of reformation,

— of clearer light as to all things necessary to be known, — of greater love, inducing us to bear ill-will to none, but goodwill to all, and to have complacency in all that are like God, — of greater liberty and freedom both of spirit and speech — and of a more holy living according to the rule of the gospel. We have far greater advantages under the gospel than they had under the law; and either we must be better or we shall be worse. A conversation becoming the gospel is an excellent way of living; nothing mean, foolish, vain, or servile becomes the gospel.

V. The Holy Ghost signifies to us hereby that we never make the right use of types but when we apply them to the antitype; and, whenever we do so, it will be very evident that the antitype (as in reason it should) greatly excels the type, which is the main drift and design of all that is said. And, as he writes to those who believed that Christ had come and that Jesus was the Christ, so he very justly infers that he is infinitely above all legal high priests (*v.* 11, 12), and he illustrates it very fully. For,

1. *Christ is a high priest of good things to come,* by which may be understood, (1.) All the good things that were to come during the Old Testament, and now have come under the New. All the spiritual and eternal blessings the Old-Testament saints had in their day and under their dispensation were owing to the Messiah to come, on whom they believed. The Old Testament set forth in shadows what was to come; the New Testament is the accomplishment of the Old. (2.) All the good things yet to come and to be enjoyed in a gospel state, when the promises and prophecies made to the gospel church in the latter days shall be accomplished; all these depend upon Christ and his priesthood, and shall be fulfilled. (3.) Of all the good things to come in the heavenly state, which will perfect both the Testaments; as the state of glory will perfect the state of grace, this state will be in a much higher sense the perfection of the New Testament than the New Testament was the perfection of the Old. Observe, All things past, present, and to come, were, and are, founded upon, and flowing from, the priestly office of Christ.

2. Christ is a high priest *by a greater and more perfect tabernacle (v.* 11), a tabernacle not made with hands, that is to say, not of this building, but his own body, or rather human nature, conceived by the Holy Ghost overshadowing the blessed virgin. This was a new fabric, a new order of building, infinitely superior to all earthly structures, not excepting the tabernacle of the temple itself.

3. Christ, our high priest, has entered into heaven, not as their high priest entered into the holiest, with the blood of bulls and of goats, but by his own blood, typified by theirs, and infinitely more precious. And this,

4. Not for one year only, which showed the imperfection of that priesthood, that it did but typically obtain a year's reprieve or pardon. But our high priest entered into heaven *once for all,* and has obtained not a yearly respite, but eternal redemption, and so needs not to make an annual entrance. In each of the types there was something that showed it was a type, and resembled the antitype, and something that showed it was but a type, and fell short of the antitype, and therefore ought by no means to be set up in competition with the antitype.

5. The Holy Ghost further signified and showed what was the efficacy of the blood of the Old-Testament sacrifices, and thence is inferred the much greater efficacy of the blood of Christ. (1.) The efficacy of the blood of the legal sacrifices extended to the purifying of the flesh (*v.* 13): it freed the outward man from ceremonial uncleanness and from temporal punishment, and entitled him to, and fitted him for, some external privileges. (2.) He infers very justly hence the far greater efficacy of the blood of Christ (*v.* 14): *How much more shall the blood of Christ,* etc. Here observe, [1.] What it was that gave such efficacy to the blood of Christ. *First,* It was his offering himself to God, the human nature upon the altar of his divine nature, he being priest, altar, and sacrifice, his divine nature serving for the two former, and his human nature for the last; now such a priest, altar, and sacrifice, could not but be propitiatory. *Secondly,* It was Christ's offering up himself to God through the eternal Spirit, not only as the divine nature supported the human, but the Holy Ghost, which he had without measure, helping him in all, and in this great act of obedience offering himself. *Thirdly,* It was Christ's offering himself to God without spot, without any sinful stain either in his nature or life; this was conformable to the law of sacrifices, which required them to be without blemish. Now further observe, [2.] What the efficacy of Christ's blood is; it is very great. For, *First,* It is sufficient to purge the conscience from dead works, it reaches to the very soul and conscience, the defiled soul, defiled with sin, which is a dead work, proceeds from spiritual death, and tends to death eternal. As the touching of a dead body gave a legal uncleanness, so meddling with sin gives a moral and real defilement, fixes it in the very soul; but the blood of Christ has efficacy to purge it out. *Secondly,* It is sufficient to enable us to serve the living God, not only by purging away that guilt which separates between God and sinners, but by sanctifying and renewing the soul through the gracious influences of the Holy Spirit, purchased by Christ for this purpose, that we might be enabled to serve the living God in a lively manner.

Verses 15–22

In these verses the apostle considers the gospel under the notion of a will or testament, the new or last will and testament of Christ, and shows the necessity and efficacy of the blood of Christ to make this testament valid and effectual.

I. The gospel is here considered as a testament, the new and last will and testament of our Lord and Saviour Jesus Christ. It is observable that the solemn transactions that pass between God and man are sometimes called a covenant, here a testament. A covenant is an agreement between two or more parties about things that are in their own power, or may be so, and this either with or without a mediator; this agreement takes effect at such time and in such manner as therein declared. A testament is a voluntary act and deed of a single person, duly executed and witnessed, bestowing legacies on such legatees as are described and characterized by the testator, and which can only take effect upon his death. Now observe, Christ is the Mediator of a New Testament (*v.* 15); and he is so for several ends and purposes here mentioned. 1. To redeem persons from their transgressions committed against the law or first testament, which makes every transgression a forfeiture of liberty, and makes men debtors, and slaves or prisoners, who need to be redeemed. 2. To qualify all those that are effectually called to receive the promise of an eternal inheritance. These are the great legacies that Christ by his last will and testament has bequeathed to the truly characterized legatees.

II. To make this New Testament effectual, it was necessary that Christ should die; the legacies accrue by means of death. This he proves by two arguments: — 1. From the general nature of every will or testamentary disposition, *v.* 16. Where a testament is, where it acts and operates, there must of necessity by the death of the testator; till then the property is still in the testator's hand, and he has power to revoke, cancel, or alter, his will as he pleases; so that no estate, no right, is conveyed by will, till the testator's death has made it unalterable and effectual. 2. From the particular method that was taken by Moses in the ratification of the first testament, which was not done without blood, *v.* 18, 19, etc. All men by sin had become guilty before God, had forfeited their inheritance, their liberties, and their very lives, into the hands of divine justice; but God, being willing to show the greatness of his mercy, proclaimed a covenant of grace, and ordered it to be typically administered under the Old Testament, but not without the blood and life of the creature; and God accepted the blood of bulls and goats, as typifying the blood of Christ; and by these means the covenant of grace was ratified under the former dispensation. The method taken by Moses, according to the direction he had received from God, is here particularly related (1.) Moses spoke every precept to all the people, according to the law, *v.* 19. He published to them the tenour of the covenant, the duties required, the rewards promised to those who did their duty, and the punishment threatened against the transgressors, and he called for their consent to the terms of the covenant; and this in an express manner. (2.) Then he took the blood of calves and of goats, with water, and scarlet wool, and hyssop, and applied this blood by sprinkling it. This blood and water signified the blood and water that came out of our Saviour's pierced side, for justification and sanctification, and also shadowed forth the two sacraments of the New Testament, baptism and the Lord's supper, with scarlet wool, signifying the righteousness of Christ with which we must be clothed, the hyssop signifying that faith by which we must apply all. Now with these Moses sprinkled, [1.] The book of the law and covenant, to show that the covenant of grace is confirmed by the blood of Christ and made effectual to our good. [2.] The people, intimating that the shedding of the blood of Christ will be no advantage to us if it be not applied to us. And the sprinkling of both the book and the people signified the mutual consent of both parties, God and man, and their mutual engagements to each other in this covenant through Christ, Moses at the same time using these words, *This is the blood of the testament which God hath enjoined unto you.* This blood, typifying the blood of Christ, is the ratification of the covenant of grace to all true believers. [3.] He sprinkled the tabernacle and all the utensils of it, intimating that all the sacrifices offered up and services performed there were accepted only through the blood of Christ, which procures the remission of that iniquity that cleaves to our holy things, which could not have been remitted but by that atoning blood.

Verses 23–28

In this last part of the chapter, the apostle goes on to tell us what the Holy Ghost has signified to us by the legal purifications of the patterns of the things in heaven, inferring thence the necessity of better sacrifices to consecrate the heavenly things themselves.

I. The necessity of purifying the patterns of the things in heaven, *v.* 23. This necessity arises both from the divine appointment, which must always be obeyed, and from the reason of that appointment, which was to preserve a proper resemblance between the things typifying and the things typified. It is observable here that the sanctuary of God on earth is a pattern of heaven, and communion with God in his sanctuary is to his people a heaven upon earth.

II. The necessity that the heavenly things themselves should be purified with better sacrifices than of bulls and goats; the things themselves are better than the patterns, and must therefore be consecrated with better sacrifices. These heavenly things are the privileges of the gospel state, begun in grace, perfected in glory. These must be ratified by a suitable sanction or consecration; and this was the blood of Christ. Now it is very evident that the sacrifice of Christ is infinitely better than those of the law. 1. From the places in which the sacrifices under the law, and that under the gospel, were offered. Those under the law were the holy places made with hands, which are but figures of the true sanctuary, *v.* 24. Christ's sacrifice, though offered upon earth, was by himself carried up into heaven, and is there presented in a way of daily intercession; for he appears in the presence of God for us. He has gone to heaven, not only to enjoy the rest and receive the honour due to him, but to appear in the presence of God for us, to present our persons and our performances, to answer and rebuke our adversary and accuser, to secure our interest, to perfect all our affairs, and to prepare a place for us. 2. From the sacrifices themselves, *v.* 26. Those under the law were the lives and blood of other creatures of a different nature from the offerers — the blood of beasts, a thing of small value, and which would have been of none at all in this matter had it not had a typical respect to the blood of Christ; but the sacrifice of Christ was the oblation of himself; he offered his own blood, truly called, by virtue of the hypostatical union, *the blood of God;* and therefore of infinite value. 3. From the frequent repetition of the legal sacrifices. This showed the imperfection of that law; but it is the honour and perfection of Christ's sacrifice that, being once offered, it was sufficient to all the ends of it; and indeed the contrary would have been absurd, for then he must have been still dying and rising again, and ascending and then again descending and dying; and the great work had been always *in fieri — always doing,* and always to do, but never finished, which would be as contrary to reason as it is to revelation, and to the dignity of his person: *But now once in the end of the world hath he appeared, to put away sin by the sacrifice of himself.* The gospel is the last dispensation of the grace of God to men. 4. From the inefficacy of the legal sacrifices, and the efficacy of Christ's sacrifice. The legal sacrifices could not of themselves put away sin, neither procure pardon for it now power against it. Sin would still have lain upon us, and had dominion over us; but Jesus Christ by one sacrifice has made an end of sin, he has destroyed the works of the devil.

III. The apostle illustrates the argument from the appointment of God concerning men (*v.* 27, 28), and observes something like it in the appointment of God concerning Christ.

1. The appointment of God concerning men contains in it two things: — (1.) That they must once die, or, at least,

undergo a change equivalent to death. It is an awful thing to die, to have the vital knot loosed or cut asunder, all relations here dropped at once, an end put to our probation and preparation state, and to enter into another world. It is a great work, and it is a work that can be but once done, and therefore had need to be well done. This is matter of comfort to the godly, that they shall die well and die but once; but it is matter of terror to the wicked, who die in their sins, that they cannot return again to do that great work better. (2.) It is appointed to men that after death they shall come to judgment, to a particular judgment immediately after death; for the soul returns to God as to its judge, to be determined to its eternal state; and men shall be brought to the general judgment, at the end of the world. This is the unalterable decree of God concerning men — they must die, and they must be judged. It is appointed for them, and it is to be believed and seriously considered by them.

2. The appointment of God concerning Christ, bearing some resemblance to the other. (1.) He must be once offered, to bear the sins of many, of all the Father had given to him, of all who should believe in his name. He was not offered for any sin of his own; he was wounded for our transgressions. God laid on him the iniquity of all his people; and these are many, though not so many as the rest of mankind; yet, when they are all gathered to him, he will be the first-born among many brethren. (2.) It is appointed that Christ shall appear the second time without sin, to the salvation of those who look for him. [1.] He will then appear without sin; at his first appearance, though he had no sin of his own, yet he stood charged with the sins of many; he was the Lamb of God that bore upon him the sins of the world, and then he appeared in the form of sinful flesh; but his second appearance will be without any such charge upon him, he having fully discharged it before, and then his visage shall not be marred, but shall be exceedingly glorious. [2.] This will be to the salvation of all who look for him; he will then perfect their holiness, their happiness; their number shall then be accomplished, and their salvation completed. Observe, It is the distinguishing character of true believers that they are looking for Christ; they look to him by faith; they look for him by hope and holy desires. They look for him in every duty, in every ordinance, in every providence now; and they expect his second coming, and are preparing for it; and though it will be sudden destruction to the rest of the world, who scoff at the report of it, it will be eternal salvation to those who look for it.

CHAPTER 10

The apostle knew very well that the Hebrews, to whom he wrote, were strangely fond of the Levitical dispensation, and therefore he fills his mouth with arguments to wean them from it; and in order thereto proceeds in this chapter, I. To lay low the whole of that priesthood and sacrifice (v. 1-6). II. He raises and exalts the priesthood of Christ very high, that he might effectually recommend him and his gospel to them (v. 7-18). III. He shows to believers the honours and dignities of their state, and calls them to suitable duties (v. 19 to the end).

Verses 1-6

Here the apostle, by the direction of the Spirit of God, sets himself to lay low the Levitical dispensation; for though it was of divine appointment, and very excellent and useful in its time and place, yet, when it was set up in competition with Christ, to whom it was only designed to lead the people, it was very proper and necessary to show the weakness and imperfection of it, which the apostle does effectually, from several arguments. As,

I. That the law had a shadow, and but a shadow, of good things to come; and who would dote upon a shadow, though of good things, especially when the substance has come? Observe, 1. The things of Christ and the gospel are good things; they are the best things; they are best in themselves, and the best for us: they are realities of an excellent nature. 2. These good things were, under the Old Testament, good things to come, not clearly discovered, nor fully enjoyed. 3. That the Jews then had but the shadow of the good things of Christ, some adumbrations of them; we under the gospel have the substance.

II. That the law was not the very image of the good things to come. An image is an exact draught of the thing represented thereby. The law did not go so far, but was only a shadow, as the image of a person in a looking-glass is a much more perfect representation than his shadow upon the wall. The

law was a very rough draught of the great design of divine grace, and therefore not to be so much doted on.

III. The legal sacrifices, being offered year by year, could never make the comers thereunto perfect; for then there would have been an end of offering them, v. 1, 2. Could they have satisfied the demands of justice, and made reconciliation for iniquity, — could they have purified and pacified conscience, — then they had ceased, as being no further necessary, since the offerers would have had no more sin lying upon their consciences. But this was not the case; after one day of atonement was over, the sinner would fall again into one fault or another, and so there would be need of another day of atonement, and of one every year, besides the daily ministrations. Whereas now, under the gospel, the atonement is perfect, and not to be repeated; and the sinner, once pardoned, is ever pardoned as to his state, and only needs to renew his repentance and faith, that he may have a comfortable sense of a continued pardon.

IV. As the legal sacrifices did not of themselves take away sin, so it was impossible they should, v. 4. There was an essential defect in them. 1. They were not of the same nature with us who sinned. 2. They were not of sufficient value to make satisfaction for the affronts offered to the justice and government of God. They were not of the same nature that offended, and so could not be suitable. Much less were they of the same nature that was offended; and nothing less than the nature that was offended could make the sacrifice a full satisfaction for the offence. 3. The beasts offered up under the law could not consent to put themselves in the sinner's room and place. The atoning sacrifice must be one capable of consenting, and must voluntarily substitute himself in the sinner's stead: Christ did so.

V. There was a time fixed and foretold by the great God, and that time had now come, when these legal sacrifices would be no longer accepted by him nor useful to men. God never did desire them for themselves, and now he abrogated them; and therefore to adhere to them now would be resisting God and rejecting him. This time of the repeal of the Levitical laws was foretold by David (Ps. 40:6, 7), and is recited here as now come. Thus industriously does the apostle lay low the Mosaical dispensation.

Verses 7-18

Here the apostle raises up and exalts the Lord Jesus Christ, as high as he had laid the Levitical priesthood low. He recommends Christ to them as the true high priest, the true atoning sacrifice, the antitype of all the rest: and this he illustrates,

I. From the purpose and promise of God concerning Christ, which are frequently recorded in the volume of the book of God, v. 7. God had not only decreed, but declared by Moses and the prophets, that Christ should come and be the great high priest of the church, and should offer up a perfect and a perfecting sacrifice. It was written of Christ, in the beginning of the book of God, that *the seed of the woman should break the serpent's head;* and the Old Testament abounds with prophecies concerning Christ. Now since he is the person so often promised, so much spoken of, so long expected by the people of God, he ought to be received with great honour and gratitude.

II. From what God had done in preparing a body for Christ (that is, a human nature), that he might be qualified to be our Redeemer and Advocate; uniting the two natures in his own person, he was a fit Mediator to go between God and man; a days-man to lay his hand upon both, a peace-maker, to reconcile them, and an everlasting band of union between God and the creature — "*My ears hast thou opened;* thou has fully instructed me, furnished and fitted me for the work, and engaged me in it," Ps. 40:6. Now a Saviour thus provided, and prepared by God himself in so extraordinary a manner, ought to be received with great affection and gladness.

III. From the readiness and willingness that Christ discovered to engage in this work, when no other sacrifice would be accepted, v. 7-9. When no less sacrifice would be a proper satisfaction to the justice of God than that of Christ himself, then Christ voluntarily came into it: "*Lo, I come! I delight to do thy will, O God!* Let thy curse fall upon me, but let these go their way. Father, I delight to fulfil thy counsels, and my covenant with thee for them; I delight to perform all thy promises, to fulfil all the prophecies." This should endear Christ and our Bibles to us, that in Christ we have the fulfilling of the scriptures.

IV. From the errand and design upon which Christ came;

and this was to do the will of God, not only as a prophet to reveal the will of God, not only as a king to give forth divine laws, but as a priest to satisfy the demands of justice, and to fulfil all righteousness. Christ came to do the will of God in two instances. 1. In taking away the first priesthood, which God had no pleasure in; not only taking away the curse of the covenant of works, and canceling the sentence denounced against us as sinners, but taking away the insufficient typical priesthood, and blotting out the hand-writing of ceremonial ordinances and nailing it to his cross. 2. In establishing the second, that is, his own priesthood and the everlasting gospel, the most pure and perfect dispensation of the covenant of grace; this is the great design upon which the heart of God was set from all eternity. The will of God centers and terminates in it; and it is not more agreeable to the will of God than it is advantageous to the souls of men; for it is by this will that *we are sanctified, through the offering of the body of Jesus Christ once for all, v.* 10. Observe, (1.) What is the fountain of all that Christ has done for his people — the sovereign will and grace of God. (2.) How we come to partake of what Christ has done for us — by being sanctified, converted, effectually called, wherein we are united to Christ, and so partake of the benefits of his redemption; and this sanctification is owing to the oblation he made of himself to God.

V. From the perfect efficacy of the priesthood of Christ (v. 14): *By one offering he hath for ever perfected those that are sanctified;* he has delivered and will perfectly deliver those that are brought over to him, from all the guilt, power, and punishment of sin, and will put them into the sure possession of perfect holiness and felicity. This is what the Levitical priesthood could never do; and, if we indeed are aiming at a perfect state, we must receive the Lord Jesus as the only high priest that can bring us to that state.

VI. From the place to which our Lord Jesus is now exalted, the honour he has there, and the further honour he shall have: *This man, after he had offered one sacrifice for sins, for ever sat down at the right hand of God, henceforth expecting till his enemies be made his footstool, v.* 12, 13. Here observe, 1. To what honour Christ, as man and Mediator, is exalted — to the right hand of God, the seat of power, interest, and activity: the giving hand; all the favours that God bestows on his people are handed to them by Christ: the receiving hand; all the duties that God accepts from men are presented by Christ: the working hand; all that pertains to the kingdoms of providence and grace is administered by Christ; and therefore this is the highest post of honour. 2. How Christ came to this honour — not merely by the purpose or donation of the Father, but by his own merit and purchase, as a reward due to his sufferings; and, as he can never be deprived of an honour so much his due, so he will never quit it, nor cease to employ it for his people's good. 3. How he enjoys this honour — with the greatest satisfaction and rest; he is for ever sitting down there. The Father acquiesces and is satisfied in him; he is satisfied in his Father's will and presence; this is his rest for ever; here he will dwell, for he has both desired and deserved it. 4. He has further expectations, which shall not be disappointed; for they are grounded upon the promise of the Father, who hath said unto him, *Sit thou at my right hand, until I make thine enemies thy footstool,* Ps. 110:1. One would think such a person as Christ could have no enemies except in hell; but it is certain that he has enemies on earth, very many, and very inveterate ones. Let not Christians then wonder that they have enemies, though they desire to live peaceably with all men. But Christ's enemies shall be made his footstool; some by conversion, others by confusion; and, which way soever it be, Christ will be honoured. Of this Christ is assured, this he is expecting, and his people should rejoice in the expectation of it; for, when his enemies shall be subdued, their enemies, that are so for his sake, shall be subdued also.

VII. The apostle recommends Christ from the witness the Holy Ghost has given in the scriptures concerning him; this relates chiefly to what should be the happy fruit and consequence of his humiliation and sufferings, which in general is that new and gracious covenant that is founded upon his satisfaction, and sealed by his blood (v. 15): *Whereof the Holy Ghost is a witness.* The passage is cited from Jer. 31:31, in which covenant God promises, 1. That he will pour out his Spirit upon his people, so as to give them wisdom, will, and power, to obey his word; he will put his laws in their hearts, and write them in their minds, v. 16. This will make their duty plain, easy, and pleasant. 2. Their sins and iniquities he will remember no more (*v.* 17), which will alone show the riches of divine grace, and the sufficiency of Christ's satisfaction, that it needs not be repeated, *v.* 18. For there shall be no more remembrance of sin against true believers, either to shame them now or to condemn them hereafter. This was much more than the Levitical priesthood and sacrifices could effect.

And now we have gone through the doctrinal part of the epistle, in which we have met with many things dark and difficult to be understood, which we must impute to the weakness and dulness of our own minds. The apostle now proceeds to apply this great doctrine, so as to influence their affections, and direct their practice, setting before them the dignities and duties of the gospel state.

Verses 19–39

I. Here the apostle sets forth the dignities of the gospel state. It is fit that believers should know the honours and privileges that Christ has procured for them, that, while they take the comfort, they may give him the glory of all. The privileges are, 1. Boldness to enter into the holiest. They have access to God, light to direct them, liberty of spirit and of speech to conform to the direction; they have a right to the privilege and a readiness for it, assistance to use and improve it and assurance of acceptance and advantage. They may enter into the gracious presence of God in his holy oracles, ordinances, providences, and covenant, and so into communion with God, where they receive communications from him, till they are prepared to enter into his glorious presence in heaven. 2. A high priest over the house of God, even this blessed Jesus, who presides over the church militant, and every member thereof on earth, and over the church triumphant in heaven. God is willing to dwell with men on earth, and to have them dwell with him in heaven; but fallen man cannot dwell with God without a high priest, who is the Mediator of reconciliation here and of fruition hereafter.

II. The apostle tells us the way and means by which Christians enjoy such privileges, and, in general, declares it to be *by the blood of Jesus,* by the merit of that blood which he offered up to God as an atoning sacrifice: he has purchased for all who believe in him free access to God in the ordinances of his grace here and in the kingdom of his glory. This blood, being sprinkled on the conscience, chases away slavish fear, and gives the believer assurance both of his safety and his welcome into the divine presence. Now the apostle, having given this general account of the way by which we have access to God, enters further into the particulars of it, *v.* 20. As, 1. It is the only way; there is no way left but this. The first way to the tree of life is, and has been, long shut up. 2. It is a new way, both in opposition to the covenant of works and to the antiquated dispensation of the Old Testament; it is *via novissima — the last way* that will ever be opened to men. Those who will not enter in this way exclude themselves for ever. It is a way that will always be effectual. 3. It is a living way. It would be death to attempt to come to God in the way of the covenant of works; but this way we may come to God, and live. It is by a living Saviour, who, though he was dead, is alive; and it is a way that gives life and lively hope to those who enter into it. 4. It is a way that Christ has consecrated for us through the veil, that is, his flesh. The veil in the tabernacle and temple signified the body of Christ; when he died, the veil of the temple was rent in sunder, and this was at the time of the evening sacrifice, and gave the people a surprising view into the holy of holies, which they never had before. Our way to heaven is by a crucified Saviour; his death is to us the way of life. To those who believe this he will be precious.

III. He proceeds to show the Hebrews the duties binding upon them on account of these privileges, which were conferred in such an extraordinary way, *v.* 22, 23, etc.

1. They must draw near to God, and that in a right manner. They must draw near to God. Since such a way of access and return to God is opened, it would be the greatest ingratitude and contempt of God and Christ still to keep at a distance from him. They must draw near by conversion, and by taking hold of his covenant. They must draw near in all holy conversation, like Enoch walking with God. They must draw near in humble adorations, worshipping at his footstool. They must draw near in holy dependence, and in a strict observance of the divine conduct towards them. They must draw near in conformity to God, and communion with him, living under his blessed influence, still endeavouring to get nearer and nearer, till they come to dwell in his presence; but they must see to it that they make their approach to God after a right manner. (1.) With a true heart, without any allowed guile or hypocrisy. God is the searcher of hearts, and he requires truth in the inward parts. Sincerity is our gospel perfection, though not our justifying righteousness. (2.) In full assurance of faith, with a faith grown up to a full persuasion that when we come to God by Christ we shall have audience and acceptance. We should lay aside all sinful distrust. Without faith it is impossible to please God; and the stronger our faith is the more glory we give to God. And, (3.) Having our hearts sprinkled from an evil conscience, by a believing application of the blood of Christ to our souls. They may be cleansed from guilt, from filth, from sinful fear and torment, from all aversion to God and duty, from ignorance, and error, and superstition, and whatever evils the consciences of men are subject to by reason of sin. (4.) Our bodies washed with pure water, that is, with the water of baptism (by which we are recorded among the disciples of Christ, members of his mystical body), or with the sanctifying virtue of the Holy Spirit, reforming and regulating our outward conversation as well as our inward frame, cleansing from the filthiness of the flesh as well as of the spirit. The priests under the law were to wash, before they went into the presence of the Lord to offer before him. There must be a due preparation for making our approaches to God.

2. The apostle exhorts believers to hold fast the profession of their faith, *v.* 23. Here observe, (1.) The duty itself — to hold fast the profession of our faith, to embrace all the truths and ways of the gospel, to get fast hold of them, and to keep that hold against all temptation and opposition. Our spiritual enemies will do what they can to wrest our faith, and hope, and holiness, and comfort, out of our hands, but we must hold fast our religion as our best treasure. (2.) The manner in which we must do this — without wavering, without doubting, without disputing, without dallying with temptation to apostasy. Having once settled these great things between God and our souls, we must be stedfast and immovable. Those who begin to waver in matters of Christian faith and practice are in danger of falling away. (3.) The motive or reason enforcing this duty: *He is faithful that hath promised.* God has made great and precious promises to believers, and he is a faithful God, true to his word; there is no falseness nor fickleness with him, and there should be none with us. His faithfulness should excite and encourage us to be faithful, and we must depend more upon his promises to us than upon our promises to him, and we must plead with him the promise of grace sufficient.

IV. We have the means prescribed for preventing our apostasy, and promoting our fidelity and perseverance, *v.* 24, 25, etc. He mentions several; as, 1. That we should *consider one another, to provoke to love and to good works.* Christians ought to have a tender consideration and concern for one another; they should affectionately consider what their several wants, weaknesses, and temptations are; and they should do this, not to reproach one another, to provoke one another not to anger, but to love and good works, calling upon themselves and one another to love God and Christ more, to love duty and holiness more, to love their brethren in Christ more, and to do all the good offices of Christian affection both to the bodies and the souls of each other. A good example given to others is the best and most effectual provocation to love and good works. 2. *Not to forsake the assembling of ourselves together, v.* 25. It is the will of Christ that his disciples should assemble together, sometimes more privately for conference and prayer, and in public for hearing and joining in all the ordinances of gospel worship. There were in the apostles' times, and should be in every age, Christian assemblies for the worship of God, and for mutual edification. And it seems even in those times there were some who forsook these assemblies, and so began to apostatize from religion itself. The communion of saints is a great help and privilege, and a good means of steadiness and perseverance; hereby their hearts and hands are mutually strengthened. 3. To exhort one another, to exhort ourselves and each other, to warn ourselves and one another of the sin and danger of backsliding, to put ourselves and our fellow-christians in mind of our duty, of our failures and corruptions, to watch over one another, and be jealous of ourselves and one another with a godly jealousy. This, managed with a true gospel spirit, would be the best and most cordial friendship. 4. That we should observe the approaching of times of trial, and be thereby quickened to greater diligence: *So much the more, as you see the day approaching.* Christians ought to observe the signs of the times, such as God has foretold. There was a day approaching, a terrible day to the Jewish nation, when their city should be destroyed, and the body of the people rejected of God for rejecting Christ. This would be a day of dispersion and temptation to the chosen remnant. Now the apostle puts them upon observing what signs there were of the approach of such a terrible day, and upon being the more constant in meeting together and exhorting one another, that they might be the better prepared for such a day. There is a trying day coming on us all, the day of our death, and we should observe all the signs of its approaching, and improve them to greater watchfulness and diligence in duty.

V. Having mentioned these means of establishment, the apostle proceeds, in the close of the chapter, to enforce his exhortations to perseverance, and against apostasy, by many very weighty considerations, *v.* 26, 27, etc.

1. From the description he gives of the sin of apostasy. It is *sinning wilfully after we have received the knowledge of the truth,* sinning wilfully against that truth of which we have had convincing evidence. This text has been the occasion of great distress to some gracious souls; they have been ready to conclude that every wilful sin, after conviction and against knowledge, is the unpardonable sin: but this has been their infirmity and error. The sin here mentioned is a total and final apostasy, when men with a full and fixed will and resolution despise and reject Christ, the only Saviour, — despise and resist the Spirit, the only sanctifier, — and despise and renounce the gospel, the only way of salvation, and the words of eternal life; and all this after they have known, owned, and professed, the Christian religion, and continue to do so obstinately and maliciously. This is the great transgression: the apostle seems to refer to the law concerning presumptuous sinners, Num. 15:30, 31. They were to be cut off.

2. From the dreadful doom of such apostates. (1.) There remains no more sacrifice for such sins, no other Christ to come to save such sinners; they sin against the last resort and remedy. There were some sins under the law for which no sacrifices were provided; but yet if those who committed them did truly repent, though they might not escape temporal death, they might escape eternal destruction; for Christ would come, and make atonement. But now those under the gospel who will not accept of Christ, that they may be saved by him, have no other refuge left them. (2.) There remains for them only a certain fearful looking for of judgment, *v.* 27. Some think this refers to the dreadful destruction of the Jewish church and state; but certainly it refers also to the utter destruction that awaits all obstinate apostates at death and judgment, when the Judge will discover a fiery indignation against them, which will devour the adversaries; they will be consigned to the devouring fire and to everlasting burnings. Of this destruction God gives some notorious sinners, while on earth, a fearful foreboding in their own consciences, a dreadful looking for it, with a despair of ever being able either to endure or escape it.

3. From the methods of divine justice with those who despised Moses's law, that is, sinned presumptuously, despising his authority, his threatenings and his power. These, when convicted by two or three witnesses, were put to death; they died without mercy, a temporal death. Observe, Wise governors should be careful to keep up the credit of their government and the authority of the laws, by punishing presumptuous offenders; but then in such cases there should be good evidence of the fact. Thus God ordained in Moses's law; and hence the apostle infers the heavy doom that will fall upon those that apostatize from Christ. Here he refers to their own consciences, to judge how much sorer punishment the despisers of Christ (after they have professed to know him) are likely to undergo; and they may judge of the greatness of the punishment by the greatness of the sin. (1.) They have *trodden under foot the Son of God.* To trample upon an ordinary person shows intolerable insolence; to treat a person of honour in that vile manner is insufferable; but to deal thus with the Son of God, who himself is God, must be the highest provocation — to trample upon his person, denying him to be the Messiah — to trample upon his authority, and undermine his kingdom — to trample upon his members as the offscouring of all things, and not fit to live in the world; what punishment can be too great for such men? (2.) They have *counted the blood of the covenant, wherewith he was sanc-*

tified, an unholy thing; that is, the blood of Christ, with which the covenant was purchased and sealed, and wherewith Christ himself was consecrated, or wherewith the apostate was sanctified, that is, baptized, visibly initiated into the new covenant by baptism, and admitted to the Lord's supper. Observe, There is a kind of sanctification which persons may partake of and yet fall away: they may be distinguished by common gifts and graces, by an outward profession, by a form of godliness, a course of duties, and a set of privileges, and yet fall away finally. Men who have seemed before to have the blood of Christ in high esteem may come to account it an unholy thing, no better than the blood of a malefactor, though it was the world's ransom, and every drop of it of infinite value. (3.) *Those have done despite unto the Spirit of grace,* the Spirit that is graciously given to men, and that works grace wherever it is, — the Spirit of grace, that should be regarded and attended to with the greatest care, — this Spirit they have grieved, resisted, quenched, yea, done despite to him, which is the highest act of wickedness, and makes the case of the sinner desperate, refusing to have the gospel salvation applied to him. Now he leaves it to the consciences of all, appeals to universal reason and equity, whether such aggravated crimes ought not to receive a suitable punishment, a sorer punishment than those who had died without mercy? But what punishment can be sorer than to die without mercy? I answer, To die by mercy, by the mercy and grace which they have despised. How dreadful is the case when not only the justice of God, but his abused grace and mercy call for vengeance!

4. From the description we have in the scripture of the nature of God's vindictive justice, *v.* 30. We know that he has said, *Vengeance is mine.* This is taken out of Ps. 94:1, *Vengeance belongs unto me.* The terrors of the Lord are known both by revelation and reason. Vindictive justice is a glorious, though terrible attribute of God; it belongs to him, and he will use and execute it upon the heads of such sinners as despise his grace; he will avenge himself, and his Son, and Spirit, and covenant, upon apostates. And how dreadful then will their case be! The other quotation is from Deu. 32:36, *The Lord will judge his people;* he will search and try his visible church, and will discover and detect those who say they are Jews, and are not, but are of the synagogue of Satan; and he will separate the precious from the vile, and will punish the sinners in Zion with the greatest severity. Now those who know him who hath said, *Vengeance belongeth to me, I will recompense,* must needs conclude, as the apostle does (*v.* 31): *It is a fearful thing to fall into the hands of the living God.* Those who know the joy that results from the favour of God can thereby judge of the power and dread of his vindictive wrath. Observe here, What will be the eternal misery of impenitent sinners and apostates: they shall fall into the hands of the living God; their punishment shall come from God's own hand. He takes them into the hand of his justice; he will deal with them himself; their greatest misery will be the immediate impressions of divine wrath on the soul. When he punishes them by creatures, the instrument abates something of the force of the blow; but, when he does it by his own hand, it is infinite misery. This they shall have at God's hand, they shall lie down in sorrow; their destruction shall come from his glorious powerful presence; when they make their woeful bed in hell, they will find that God is there, and his presence will be their greatest terror and torment. And he is a living God; he lives for ever, and will punish for ever.

5. He presses them to perseverance by putting them in mind of their former sufferings for Christ: *But call to mind the former days, in which, after you were illuminated, you endured a great fight of afflictions, v.* 32. In the early days of the gospel there was a very hot persecution raised up against the professors of the Christian religion, and the believing Hebrews had their share of it: he would have them to remember,

(1.) When they had suffered: *In former days, after* they were *illuminated;* that is, as soon as God had breathed life into their souls, and caused divine light to spring up in their minds, and taken them into his favour and covenant; then earth and hell combined all their force against them. Here observe, A natural state is a dark state, and those who continue in that state meet with no disturbance from Satan and the world; but a state of grace is a state of light, and therefore the powers of darkness will violently oppose it. Those who will live godly in Christ Jesus must suffer persecution.

(2.) What they suffered: they *endured a great fight of afflictions,* many and various afflictions united together against them, and they had a great conflict with them. Many are the troubles of the righteous. [1.] They were afflicted in themselves. In their own persons; they were made gazing-stocks, spectacles to the world, angels, and men, 1 Co. 4:9. In their names and reputations (*v.* 33), by many reproaches. Christians ought to value their reputation; and they do so especially because the reputation of religion is concerned: this makes reproach a great affliction. They were afflicted in their estates, by the spoiling of their goods, by fines and forfeitures. [2.] They were afflicted in the afflictions of their brethren: *Partly while you became companions of those that were so used.* The Christian spirit is a sympathizing spirit, not a selfish spirit, but a compassionate spirit; it makes every Christian's suffering our own, puts us upon pitying others, visiting them, helping them, and pleading for them. Christians are one body, are animated by one spirit, have embarked in one common cause and interest, and are the children of that God who is afflicted in all the afflictions of his people. If one member of the body suffers, all the rest suffer with it. The apostle takes particular notice how they had sympathized with him (*v.* 34): *You had compassion on me in my bonds.* We must thankfully acknowledge the compassions our Christian friends have shown for us under our afflictions.

(3.) How they had suffered. They had been mightily supported under their former sufferings; they took their sufferings patiently, and not only so, but joyfully received it from God as a favour and honour conferred upon them that they should be thought worthy to suffer reproach for the name of Christ. God can strengthen his suffering people with all might in the inner man, to all patience and long-suffering, and that with joyfulness, Col. 1:11.

(4.) What it was that enabled them thus to bear up under their sufferings. They knew in themselves that they had in heaven a better and a more enduring substance. Observe, [1.] The happiness of the saints in heaven is substance, something of real weight and worth. All things here are but shadows. [2.] It is a better substance than any thing they can have or lose here. [3.] It is an enduring substance, it will out-live time and run parallel with eternity; they can never spend it; their enemies can never take it from them, as they did their earthly goods. [4.] This will make a rich amends for all they can lose and suffer here. In heaven they shall have a better life, a better estate, better liberty, better society, better hearts, better work, every thing better. [5.] Christians should know this in themselves, they should get the assurance of it in themselves (the Spirit of God witnessing with their spirits), for the assured knowledge of this will help them to endure any fight of afflictions they may be encountered with in this world.

6. He presses them to persevere, from that recompense of reward that waited for all faithful Christians (*v.* 35): *Cast not away therefore your confidence, which hath great recompense of reward.* Here, (1.) He exhorts them not to cast away their confidence, that is, their holy courage and boldness, but to hold fast that profession for which they had suffered so much before, and borne those sufferings so well. (2.) He encourages them to this by assuring them that the reward of their holy confidence would be very great. It carries a present reward in it, in holy peace and joy, and much of God's presence and his power resting upon them; and it shall have a great recompense of reward hereafter. (3.) He shows them how necessary a grace the grace of patience is in our present state (*v.* 36): *You have need of patience, that after you have done the will of God you might receive the promise;* that is, this promised reward. Observe, The greatest part of the saints' happiness is in promise. They must first do the will of God before they receive the promise; and, after they have done the will of God, they have need of patience to wait for the time when the promise shall be fulfilled; they have need of patience to live till God calls them away. It is a trial of the patience of Christians, to be content to live after their work is done, and to stay for the reward till God's time to give it them is come. We must be God's waiting servants when we can be no longer his working servants. Those who have had and exercised much patience already must have and exercise more till they die. (4.) To help their patience, he assures them of the near approach of Christ's coming to deliver and to reward them (*v.* 37): *For yet a little while, and he that shall come will come, and will not tarry.* He will soon come to them at death, and put an end to all their sufferings, and give them a crown of life. He will soon come to judgment, and put an end to the sufferings of the whole church (all his mystical body), and give them an ample and glorious reward in the most public manner. There is an appointed time for both, and beyond that time he will not tarry, Hab. 2:3. The Christian's present conflict may be sharp, but it will be soon over.

7. He presses them to perseverance, by telling them that this is their distinguishing character and will be their happiness; whereas apostasy is the reproach, and will be the ruin, of all who are guilty of it (*v.* 38, 39): *Now the just shall live by faith,* etc. (1.) It is the honourable character of just men that in times of the greatest affliction they can live by faith; they can live upon the assured persuasion they have of the truth of God's promises. Faith puts life and vigour into them. They can trust God, and live upon him, and wait his time: and, as their faith maintains their spiritual life now, it shall be crowned with eternal life hereafter. (2.) Apostasy is the mark and the brand of those in whom God takes no pleasure; and it is a cause of God's severe displeasure and anger. God never was pleased with the formal profession and external duties and services of such as do not persevere. He saw the hypocrisy of their hearts then; and he is greatly provoked when their formality in religion ends in an open apostasy from religion. He beholds them with great displeasure; they are an offence to him. (3.) The apostle concludes with declaring his good hope concerning himself and these Hebrews, that they should not forfeit the character and happiness of the just, and fall under the brand and misery of the wicked (*v.* 39): *But we are not,* etc.; as if he had said, "I hope we are not of those who draw back. I hope that you and I, who have met with great trials already, and have been supported under them by the grace of God strengthening our faith, shall not be at any time left to ourselves to draw back to perdition; but that God will still keep us by his mighty power through faith unto salvation." Observe, [1.] Professors may go a great way, and after all draw back; and this drawing back from God is drawing on to perdition: the further we depart from God the nearer we approach to ruin. [2.] Those who have been kept faithful in great trials for the time past have reason to hope that the same grace will be sufficient to help them still to live by faith, till they receive the end of their faith and patience, even the salvation of their souls. If we live by faith, and die in faith, our souls will be safe for ever.

CHAPTER 11

The apostle having, in the close of the foregoing chapter, recommended the grace of faith and a life of faith as the best preservative against apostasy, he how enlarges upon the nature and fruits of this excellent grace. I. The nature of it, and the honour it reflects upon all who live in the exercise of it (*v.* 1–3). II. The great examples we have in the Old Testament of those who lived by faith, and died and suffered extraordinary things by the strength of his grace (*v.* 4–38). And, III. The advantages that we have in the gospel for the exercise of this grace above what those had who lived in the times of the Old Testament (*v.* 39, 40).

Verses 1–3

Here we have, I. A definition or description of the grace of faith in two parts. 1. It *is the substance of things hoped for.* Faith and hope go together; and the same things that are the object of our hope are the object of our faith. It is a firm persuasion and expectation that God will perform all that he has promised to us in Christ; and this persuasion is so strong that it gives the soul a kind of possession and present fruition of those things, gives them a subsistence in the soul, by the first-fruits and foretastes of them: so that believers in the exercise of faith *are filled with joy unspeakable and full of glory.* Christ dwells in the soul by faith, and the soul is filled with the fullness of God, as far as his present measure will admit; he experiences a substantial reality in the objects of faith. 2. It is *the evidence of things not seen.* Faith demonstrates to the eye of the mind the reality of those things that cannot be discerned by the eye of the body. Faith is the firm assent of the soul to the divine revelation and every part of it, and sets to its seal that God is true. It is a full approbation of all that God has revealed as holy, just, and good; it helps the soul to make application of all to itself with suitable affections and endeavours; and so it is designed to serve the believer instead of sight, and to be to the soul all that the senses are to the body. That faith is but opinion or fancy which does not realize invisible things to the soul, and excite the soul to act agreeably to the nature and importance of them.

II. An account of the honour it reflects upon all those who have lived in the exercise of it (*v.* 2): *By it the elders obtained a good report* — the ancient believers, who lived in the first ages of the world. Observe, 1. True faith is an old grace, and has the best plea to antiquity: it is not a new invention, a modern fancy; it is a grace that has been planted in the soul of man ever since the covenant of grace was published in the world; and it has been practiced from the beginning of the revelation; the eldest and best men that ever were in the world were believers. 2. Their faith was their honour; it reflected honour upon them. They were an honour to their faith, and their faith was an honour to them. It put them upon doing *the things that were of good report,* and God has taken care that a record shall be kept and report made of the excellent things they did in the strength of this grace. The genuine actings of faith will bear to be reported, deserve to be reported, and will, when reported, redound to the honour of true believers.

III. We have here one of the first acts and articles of faith, which has a great influence on all the rest, and which is common to all believers in every age and part of the world, namely, the creation of the *worlds by the word of God,* not out of pre-existent matter, but out of nothing, *v.* 3. The grace of faith has a retrospect as well as prospect; it looks not only forward to the end of the world, but back to the beginning of the world. By faith we understand much more of the formation of the world than ever could be understood by the naked eye of natural reason. Faith is not a force upon the understanding, but a friend and a help to it. Now what does faith give us to understand concerning *the worlds,* that is, the upper, middle, and lower regions of the universe? 1. *That these worlds were* not eternal, nor did they produce themselves, but they were made by another. 2. That the maker of the worlds is god; he is the maker of all things; and whoever is so must be God. 3. That he made the world with great exactness; it was a *framed* work, in every thing duly adapted and disposed to answer its end, and to express the perfections of the Creator. 4. That God made the world by his word, that is, by his essential wisdom and eternal Son, and by his active will, saying, *Let it be done, and it was done,* Ps. 33:9. 5. That the world was thus framed out of nothing, out of no pre-existent matter, contrary to the received maxim, that "out of nothing nothing can be made," which, though true of created power, can have no place with God, who can call *things that are not as if they were,* and command them into being. These things we understand by faith. The Bible gives us the truest and most exact account of the origin of all things, and we are to believe it, and not to wrest or run down the scripture-account of the creation, because it does not suit with some fantastic hypotheses of our own, which has been in some learned but conceited men the first remarkable step towards infidelity, and has led them into many more.

Verses 4–31

The apostle, having given us a more general account of the grace of faith, now proceeds to set before us some illustrious examples of it in the Old-Testament times, and these may be divided into two classes: — 1. Those whose names are mentioned, and the particular exercise and actings of whose faith are specified. 2. Those whose names are barely mentioned, and an account given in general of the exploits of their faith, which it is left to the reader to accommodate, and apply to the particular persons from what he gathers up in the sacred story. We have here those whose names are not only mentioned, but the particular trials and actings of their faith are subjoined.

I. The leading instance and example of faith here recorded is that of Abel. It is observable that the Spirit of God has not thought fit to say any thing here of the faith of our first parents; and yet the church of God has generally, by a pious charity, taken it for granted that God gave them repentance and faith in the promised seed, that he instructed them in the mystery of sacrificing, that they instructed their children in it, and that they found mercy with God, after they had ruined themselves and all their posterity. But God has left the matter still under some doubt, as a warning to all who have great talents given to them, and a great trust reposed in them, that they do not prove unfaithful, since God would not enroll our first parents among the number of believers in this blessed calendar. It begins with Abel, one of the first saints, and the first martyr for religion, of all the sons of Adam, one who lived by faith, and died for it, and therefore a fit pattern for the Hebrews to imitate. Observe,

1. What Abel did by faith: *He offered up a more acceptable sacrifice than Cain,* a more full and perfect sacrifice, *pleiona thysian.* Hence learn, (1.) That, after the fall, God opened a new way for the children of men to return to him in religious worship. This is one of the first instances that is upon record of fallen men going in to worship God; and it was a wonder of mercy that all intercourse between God and man was not cut off by the fall. (2.) After the fall, God must be worshipped by sacrifices, a way of worship which carries in it a confession of sin, and of the desert of sin, and a profession of faith in a Redeemer, who was to be a ransom for the souls of men. (3.) That, from the beginning, there has been a remarkable difference between the worshippers. Here were two persons, brethren, both of whom went in to worship God, and yet there was a vast difference. Cain was the elder brother, but Abel has the preference. It is not seniority of birth, but grace, that makes men truly honourable. The difference is observable in their persons: Abel was an upright person, a righteous man, a true believer; Cain was a formalist, had not a principle of special grace. It is observable in their principles: Abel acted under the power of faith; Cain only from the force of education, or natural conscience. There was also a very observable difference in their offerings: Abel brought a sacrifice of atonement, *brought of the firstlings of the flock,* acknowledging himself to be a sinner who deserved to die, and only hoping for mercy through *the great sacrifice;* Cain brought only a sacrifice of acknowledgment, a mere thank-offering, *the fruit of the ground,* which might, and perhaps must, have been offered in innocency; here was no confession of sin, no regard to the ransom; this was an essential defect in Cain's offering. There will always be a difference between those who worship the true God; some will compass him about with lies, others will be faithful with the saints; some, like the Pharisee, will lean to their own righteousness; others, like the publican, will confess their sin, and cast themselves upon the mercy of God in Christ.

2. What Abel gained by his faith: the original record is in Gen. 4:4, *God had respect to Abel, and to his offering;* first to his person as gracious, then to his offering as proceeding from grace, especially from the grace of faith. In this place we are told that he obtained by his faith some special advantages; as, (1.) *Witness that he was righteous,* a justified, sanctified, and accepted person; this, very probably, was attested by fire from heaven, kindling and consuming his sacrifice. (2.) God gave witness to the righteousness of his person, by testifying his acceptance of his gifts. When the fire, an emblem of God's justice, consumed the offering, it was a sign that the mercy of God accepted the offerer for the sake of the great sacrifice. (3.) *By it he, being dead, yet speaketh.* He had the honour to leave behind him an instructive speaking case; and what does it speak to us? What should we learn from it? [1.] That fallen man has leave to go in to worship God, with hope of acceptance. [2.] That, if our persons and offerings be accepted, it must be through faith in the Messiah. [3.] That acceptance with God is a peculiar and distinguishing favour. [4.] That those who obtain this favour from God must expect the envy and malice of the world. [5.] That God will not suffer the injuries done to his people to remain unpunished, nor their sufferings unrewarded. These are very good and useful instructions, and yet *the blood of sprinkling speaketh better things than that of Abel.* [6.] That God would not suffer Abel's faith to die with him, but would raise up others, who should obtain like precious faith; and so he did in a little time; for in the next verse we read,

II. Of the faith of Enoch, *v.* 5. He is the second of those elders that through faith have a good report. Observe,

1. What is here reported of him. In this place (and in Gen. 5:22, etc.) we read, (1.) *That he walked with God,* that is, that he was really, eminently, actively, progressively, and perseveringly religious in his conformity to God, communion with God, and complacency in God. (2.) *That he was translated, that he should not see death,* nor any part of him be found upon earth; for God took him, soul and body, into heaven, as he will do those of the saints who shall be found alive at his second coming. (3.) *That before his translation he had this testimony, that he pleased God.* He had the evidence of it in his own conscience, and the Spirit of God witnessed with his spirit. Those who by faith walk with God in a sinful world are pleasing to him, and he will give them marks of his favour, and put honour upon them.

2. What is here said of his faith, *v.* 6. It is said that *without* this *faith it is impossible to please God,* without such a faith as helps us to walk with God, an active faith, and that we cannot come to God unless we *believe that he is, and that he is a rewarder of those that diligently seek him.* (1.) He must believe that God is, and that he is what he is, what he has revealed himself to be in the scripture, a Being of infinite perfections, subsisting in three persons, Father, Son, and Holy Ghost. Observe, The practical belief of the existence of God, as revealed in the word, would be a powerful awe-band upon our souls, a bridle of restraint to keep us from sin, and a spur of constraint to put us upon all manner of gospel obedience. (2.) *That he is a rewarder of those that diligently seek him.* Here observe, [1.] By the fall we have lost God; we have lost the divine light, life, love, likeness, and communion. [2.] God is again to be found of us through Christ, the second Adam. [3.] God has prescribed means and ways wherein he may be found; to with, a strict attention to his oracles, attendance on his ordinances, and ministers duly discharging their office and associating with his people, observing his providential guidance, and in all things humbly waiting his gracious presence. [4.] Those who would find God in these ways of his must *seek him diligently;* they must seek early, earnestly, and perseveringly. *Then shall they seek him, and find him, if they seek him with all their heart;* and when once they have found him, as their reconciled God, they will never repent the pains they have spent in seeking after him.

III. The faith of Noah, *v.* 7. Observe,

1. The ground of Noah's faith — a warning he had received from God of things as yet not seen. He had a divine revelation, whether by voice or vision does not appear; but it was such as carried in it its own evidence; he was *forewarned of things not seen as yet,* that is, of a great and severe judgment, such as the world had never yet seen, and of which, in the course of second causes, there was not yet the least sign. This secret warning he was to communicate to the world, who would be sure to despise both him and his message. God usually warns sinners before he strikes; and, where his warnings are slighted, the blow will fall the heavier.

2. The actings of Noah's faith, and the influence it had both upon his mind and practice. (1.) Upon his mind; it impressed his soul with a fear of God's judgment: he was *moved with fear.* Faith first influences our affections, then our actions; and faith works upon those affections that are suitable to the matter revealed. If it be some good thing, faith stirs up love and desire; if some evil thing, faith stirs up fear. (2.) His faith influenced his practice. His fear, thus excited by believing God's threatening, moved him to prepare an ark, in which, no doubt, he met with the scorns and reproaches of a wicked generation. He did not dispute with God why he should make an ark, nor how it could be capable of containing what was to be lodged in it, nor how such a vessel could possibly weather out so great a storm. His faith silenced all objections, and set him to work in earnest.

3. The blessed fruits and rewards of Noah's faith. (1.) Hereby himself and his house were saved, when a whole world of sinners were perishing about them. God saved his family for his sake; it was well for them that they were Noah's sons and daughters; it was well for those women that they married into Noah's family; perhaps they might have married to great estates in other families, but then they would have been drowned. We often say, "It is good to be akin to an estate;" but surely it is good to be akin to the covenant. (2.) Hereby he judged and condemned the world; his holy fear condemned their security and vain confidence; his faith condemned their unbelief; his obedience condemned their contempt and rebellion. Good examples will either convert sinners or condemn them. There is something very convincing in a life of strict holiness and regard to God; it commends itself to every man's conscience in the sight of God, and they are judged by it. This is the best way the people of God can take to condemn the wicked; not by harsh and censorious language, but by a holy exemplary conversation. (3.) Hereby *he became an heir of the righteousness which is by faith.* [1.] He was possessed of a true justifying righteousness; he was *heir to it:* and, [2.] This his right of inheritance was through faith in Christ, as *a member of Christ, a child of God,* and, if a child, then an heir. His righteousness was relative, resulting from his adoption, through faith in the promised seed. As ever we expect to be justified and saved *in the great and terrible day of the Lord,* let us now prepare an ark, secure an interest in Christ, and in the ark of the covenant, and do it speedily, before the door be shut, for there is not salvation in any other.

IV. The faith of Abraham, the friend of God, and father

honour of God, that he has adopted a people to be his own children and then taken no care to make a suitable provision for them. The consideration of this should inflame the affections, enlarge the desires, and excite the diligent endeavours, of the people of God after this city that he has prepared for them.

VII. Now after the apostle has given this account of the faith of others, with Abraham, he returns to him again, and gives us an instance of the greatest trial and act of faith that stands upon record, either in the story of the father of the faithful or of any of his spiritual seed; and this was his offering up Isaac: *By faith Abraham, when he was tried, offered up Isaac; and he that had received the promises offered up his only-begotten son, v.* 17. In this great example observe,

1. The trial and exercise of Abraham's faith; he was tried indeed. It is said (Gen. 22:1), *God in this tempted Abraham;* not to sin, for so God tempteth no man, but only tried his faith and obedience to purpose. God had before this tempted or tried the faith of Abraham, when he called him away from his country and father's house, — when by a famine he was forced out of Canaan into Egypt, — when he was obliged to fight with five kings to rescue Lot, — when Sarah was taken from him by Abimelech, and in many other instances. But this trial was greater than all; he was commanded to offer up his son Isaac. Read the account of it, Gen. 22:2. There you will find every word was a trial: *"Take now thy son, thine only son Isaac, whom thou lovest, and get thee into the land of Moriah, and offer him there for a burnt offering upon one of the mountains which I will tell thee of.* Take thy son, not one of thy beasts or slaves, thy only son by Sarah, Isaac thy laughter, the child of thy joy and delight, whom thou lovest as thine own soul; take him away to a distant place, three days' journey, the land of Moriah; do not only leave him there, but offer him for a burnt offering." A greater trial was never put upon any creature. The apostle here mentions some things that very much added to the greatness of this trial. (1.) He was put upon it after he had received the promises, that this Isaac should build up his family, that in him his seed should be called (*v.* 18), and that he should be one of the progenitors of the Messiah, and all nations blessed in him; so that, in being called to offer up his Isaac, he seemed to be called to destroy and cut off his own family, to cancel the promises of God, to prevent the coming of Christ, to destroy the whole world, to sacrifice his own soul and his hopes of salvation, and to cut off the church of God at one blow: a most terrible trial! (2.) That this Isaac was his only-begotten son by his wife Sarah, the only one he was to have by her, and the only one that was to be the child and heir of the promise. Ishmael was to be put off with earthly greatness. The promise of a posterity, and of the Messiah, must either be fulfilled by means of this son or not at all; so that, besides his most tender affection to this his son, all his expectations were bound up in him, and, if he perished, must perish with him. If Abraham had ever so many sons, this was the only son who could convey to all nations the promised blessing. A son for whom he waited so long, whom he received in so extraordinary a manner, upon whom his heart was set — to have this son offered up as a sacrifice, and that by his own hand; it was a trial that would have overset the firmest and the strongest mind that ever informed a human body.

2. The actings of Abraham's faith in so great a trial: he obeyed; he offered up Isaac; he intentionally gave him up by his submissive soul to God, and was ready to have done it actually, according to the command of God; he went as far in it as to the very critical moment, and would have gone through with it if God had not prevented him. Nothing could be more tender and moving than those words of Isaac: *My father, here is the wood, here is the fire; but where is the lamb for the burnt-offering?* little thinking that he was to be the lamb; but Abraham knew it, and yet he went on with the great design.

3. The supports of his faith. they must be very great, suitable to the greatness of the trial: *He accounted that God was able to raise him from the dead, v.* 19. His faith was supported by the sense he had of the mighty power of God, who was able to raise the dead; he reasoned thus with himself, and so he resolved all his doubts. It does not appear that he had any expectation of being countermanded, and prevented from offering up his son; such an expectation would have spoiled the trial, and consequently the triumph, of his faith; but he knew that God was able to raise him from the dead, and he believed that God would do so, since such great things

depended upon his son, which must have failed if Isaac had not a further life. Observe, (1.) God is able to raise the dead, to raise dead bodies, and to raise dead souls. (2.) The belief of this will carry us through the greatest difficulties and trials that we can meet with. (3.) It is our duty to be reasoning down our doubts and fears, by the consideration of the almighty power of God.

4. The reward of his faith in this great trial (*v.* 19): he received his son from the dead in a figure, in a parable. (1.) He received his son. He had parted with him to God, and God gave him back again. The best way to enjoy our comforts with comfort is to resign them up to God; he will then return them, if not in kind, yet in kindness. (2.) He received him from the dead, for he gave him up for dead; he was as a dead child to him, and the return was to him no less than a resurrection. (3.) This was a figure or parable of something further. It was a figure of the sacrifice and resurrection of Christ, of whom Isaac was a type. It was a figure and earnest of the glorious resurrection of all true believers, whose life is not lost, but hid with Christ in God. We come now to the faith of other Old-Testament saints, mentioned by name, and by the particular trials and actings of their faith.

VIII. Of the faith of Isaac, *v.* 20. Something of him we had before interwoven with the story of Abraham; here we have something of a distinct nature — that by faith he blessed his two sons, Jacob and Esau, *concerning things to come.* Here observe,

1. The actings of his faith: He *blessed Jacob and Esau concerning things to come.* He blessed them; that is, he resigned them up to God in covenant; he recommended God and religion to them; he prayed for them, and prophesied concerning them, what would be the condition, and the condition of their descendants: we have the account of this in Gen. 27. Observe, (1.) Both Jacob and Esau were blessed as Isaac's children, at least as to temporal good things. It is a great privilege to be the offspring of good parents, and often the wicked children of good parents fare the better in this world for their parents' sake, for things present are in the covenant; but they are not the best things, and no man knoweth love or hatred by having or wanting such things. (2.) Jacob had the precedency and the principal blessing, which shows that it is grace and the new birth that exalt persons above their fellows and qualify them for the best blessings, and that it is owing to the sovereign free grace of God that in the same family one is taken and another left, one loved and the other hated, since all the race of Adam are by nature hateful to God — that if one has his portion in this world, and the other in the better world, it is God who makes the difference; for even the comforts of this life are more and better than any of the children of men deserve.

2. The difficulties Isaac's faith struggled with. (1.) He seemed to have forgotten how God had determined the matter at the birth of these his sons, Gen. 25:23. This should have been a rule to him all along, but he was rather swayed by natural affection, and by general custom, which gives the double portion of honour, affection, and advantage, to the first-born. (2.) He acted in this matter with some reluctance. When he came to pronounce the blessing, *he trembled very exceedingly* (Gen. 27:33); and he charged Jacob that he had subtly taken away Esau's blessing, *v.* 33, 35. But, notwithstanding all this, Isaac's faith recovered itself, and he ratified the blessing: *I have blessed him yea, and he shall be blessed.* Rebecca and Jacob are not to be justified in the indirect means they used to obtain this blessing, but God will be justified in over-ruling even the sins of men to serve the purposes of his glory. Now, the faith of Isaac thus prevailing over his unbelief, it has pleased the God of Isaac to pass by the weakness of his faith, to commend the sincerity of it, and record him among the elders, *who through faith have obtained a good report.* We now go on to,

IX. The faith of Jacob (*v.* 21), who, *when he was dying, blessed both the sons of Joseph, and worshipped, leaning upon the top of his staff.* There were a great many instances of the faith of Jacob; his life was a life of faith, and his faith met with great exercise. But it has pleased God to single two instances out of many of the faith of this patriarch, besides what has been already mentioned in the account of Abraham. Here observe,

1. The actings of his faith here mentioned, and they are two: —

(1.) *He blessed both the sons of Joseph,* Ephraim and Manasseh; he adopted them into the number of his own sons, and

so into the congregation of Israel, though they were born in Egypt. It is doubtless a great blessing to be joined to the visible church of God in profession and privilege, but more to be so in spirit and truth. [1.] He made them both heads of different tribes, as if they had been his own immediate sons. [2.] He prayed for them, that they might both be blessed of God. [3.] He prophesied that they should be blessed; but, as Isaac did before, so now Jacob prefers the younger, Ephraim; and though Joseph had placed them so, that the right hand of his father should be laid on Manasseh, the elder, Jacob wittingly laid it on Ephraim, and this by divine direction, for he could not see, to show that the Gentile church, the younger, should have a more abundant blessing than the Jewish church, the elder.

(2.) *He worshipped, leaning on his staff;* that is, he praised God for what he had done for him, and for the prospect he had of approaching blessedness; and he prayed for those he was leaving behind him, that religion might live in his family when he was gone. He did this *leaning on the top of his staff;* not as the papists dream, that he worshipped some image of God engraven on the head of his staff, but intimating to us his great natural weakness, that he was not able to support himself so far as to sit up in his bed without a staff, and yet that he would not make this an excuse for neglecting the worshipping of God; he would do it as well as he could with his body, as well as with his spirit, though he could not do it as well as he would. He showed thereby his dependence upon God, and testified his condition here as a pilgrim with his staff, and his weariness of the world, and willingness to be at rest.

2. The time and season when Jacob thus acted his faith: when he was dying. He lived by faith, and he died by faith and in faith. Observe, Though the grace of faith is of universal use throughout our whole lifes, yet it is especially so when we come to die. Faith has its greatest work to do at last, to help believers to finish well, to die to the Lord, so as to honour him, by patience, hope, and joy — so as to leave a witness behind them of the truth of God's word and the excellency of his ways, for the conviction and establishment of all who attend them in their dying moments. The best way in which parents can finish their course is blessing their families and worshipping their God. We have now come to,

X. The faith of Joseph, *v.* 22. And here also we consider,

1. What he did by his faith: *He made mention of the departing of the children of Israel, and gave commandment concerning his bones.* The passage is out of Gen. 50:24, 25. Joseph was eminent for his faith, though he had not enjoyed the helps for it which the rest of his brethren had. He was sold into Egypt. He was tried by temptations, by sin, by persecution, for retaining his integrity. He was tried by preferment and power in the court of Pharaoh, and yet his faith held out and carried him through to the last. (1.) He made mention by faith of the departing of the children of Israel, that the time should come when they should be delivered out of Egypt; and he did this both that he might caution them against the thoughts of settling in Egypt, which was now a place of plenty and ease to them; and also that he might keep them from sinking under the calamities and distresses which he foresaw were coming upon them there; and he does it to comfort himself, that though he should not live to see their deliverance, yet he could die in the faith of it. (2.) He gave commandment concerning his bones, that they should preserve them unburied in Egypt, till God should deliver them out of that house of bondage, and that then they should carry his bones along with them into Canaan and deposit them there. Though believers are chiefly concerned for their souls, yet they cannot wholly neglect their bodies, as being members of Christ and parts of themselves, which shall at length be raised up, and be the happy companions of their glorified souls to all eternity. Now Joseph gave this order, not that he thought his being buried in Egypt would either prejudice his soul or prevent the resurrection of his body (as some of the rabbis fancied that all the Jews who were buried out of Canaan must be conveyed underground to Canaan before they could rise again), but to testify, [1.] That though he had lived and died in Egypt, yet he did not live and die an Egyptian, but an Israelite. [2.] That he preferred a significant burial in Canaan before a magnificent one in Egypt. [3.] That he would go as far with his people as he could, though he could not go as far as he would. [4.] That he believed the resurrection of the body, and the communion that his soul should presently have with departed saints, as his body had with their dead

of the faithful, in whom the Hebrews boasted, and from whom they derived their pedigree and privileges; and therefore the apostle, that he might both please and profit them, enlarges more upon the heroic achievements of Abraham's faith than of that of any other of the patriarchs; and in the midst of his account of the faith of Abraham he inserts the story of Sarah's faith, whose daughters those women are that continue to do well. Observe,

1. The ground of Abraham's faith, the call and promise of God, *v.* 8. (1.) This call, though it was a very trying call, was the call of God, and therefore a sufficient ground for faith and rule of obedience. The manner in which he was called Stephen relates in Acts 7:2, 3, *The God of glory appeared to our father Abraham, when he was in Mesopotamia — And said unto him, Get thee out of thy country, and from thy kindred, and come into the land which I will show thee.* This was an effectual call, by which he was converted from the idolatry of his father's house, Gen. 12:1. This call was renewed after his father's death in Charran. Observe, [1.] The grace of God is absolutely free, in taking some of the worst of men, and making them the best. [2.] God must come to us before we come to him. [3.] In calling and converting sinners, God appears as a God of glory, and works a glorious work in the soul. [4.] This calls us not only to leave sin, but sinful company, and whatever is inconsistent with our devotedness to him. [5.] We need to be called, not only to set out well, but to go on well. [6.] He will not have his people take up that rest any where short of the heavenly Canaan. (2.) The promise of God. God promised Abraham that the place he was called to he should afterwards receive for an inheritance, after awhile he should have the heavenly Canaan for his inheritance, and in process of time his posterity should inherit the earthly Canaan. Observe here, [1.] God calls his people to an inheritance: by his effectual call he makes them children, and so heirs. [2.] This inheritance is not immediately possessed by them; they must wait some time for it: but the promise is sure, and shall have its seasonable accomplishment. [3.] The faith of parents often procures blessings for their posterity.

2. The exercise of Abraham's faith: he yielded an implicit regard to the call of God. (1.) *He went out, not knowing whither he went.* He put himself into the hand of God, to send him whithersoever he pleased. He subscribed to God's wisdom, as fittest to direct; and submitted to his will, as fittest to determine every thing that concerned him. Implicit faith and obedience are due to God, and to him only. All that are effectually called resign up their own will and wisdom to the will and wisdom of God, and it is their wisdom to do so; though they know not always their way, yet they know their guide, and this satisfies them. (2.) *He sojourned in the land of promise as in a strange country.* This was an exercise of his faith. Observe, [1.] How Canaan is called the land of promise, because yet only promised, not possessed. [2.] How Abraham lived in Canaan, not as heir and proprietor, but as a sojourner only. He did not serve an ejectment, or raise a war against the old inhabitants, to dispossess them, but contented himself to live as a stranger, to bear their unkindnesses patiently, to receive any favours from them thankfully, and to keep his heart fixed upon his home, the heavenly Canaan. [3.] He dwelt in tabernacles with Isaac and Jacob, heirs with him of the same promise. He lived there in an ambulatory moving condition, living in a daily readiness for his removal: and thus should we all live in this world. He had good company with him, and they were a great comfort to him in his sojourning state. Abraham lived till Isaac was seventy-five years old, and Jacob fifteen. Isaac and Jacob were heirs of the same promise; for the promise was renewed to Isaac (Gen. 26:3), and to Jacob, Gen. 28:13. All the saints are heirs of the same promise. The promise is made to believers and their children, and to as many as the Lord our God shall call. And it is pleasant to see parents and children sojourning together in this world as heirs of the heavenly inheritance.

3. The supports of Abraham's faith (*v.* 10): *He looked for a city that hath foundations, whose builder and maker is God.* Observe here, (1.) The description given of heaven: it is a city, a regular society, well established, well defended, and well supplied: it is a city that hath foundations, even the immutable purposes and almighty power of God, the infinite merits and mediation of the Lord Jesus Christ, the promises of an everlasting covenant, its own purity, and the perfection of its inhabitants: and it is a city whose builder and maker is God. He contrived the model; he accordingly made it, and

he has laid open a new and living way into it, and prepared it for his people; he puts them into possession of it, prefers them in it, and is himself the substance and felicity of it. (2.) Observe the due regard that Abraham had to this heavenly city: he looked for it; he believed there was such a state; he waited for it, and in the mean time he conversed in it by faith; he had exalted and rejoicing hopes, that in God's time and way he should be brought safely to it. (3.) The influence this had upon his present conversation: it was a support to him under all the trials of his sojourning state, helped him patiently to bear all the inconveniences of it, and actively to discharge all the duties of it, persevering therein unto the end.

V. In the midst of the story of Abraham, the apostle inserts an account of the faith of Sarah. Here observe,

1. The difficulties of Sarah's faith, which were very great. As, (1.) The prevalency of unbelief for a time: she laughed at the promise, as impossible to be made good. (2.) She had gone out of the way of her duty through unbelief, in putting Abraham upon taking Hagar to his bed, that he might have a posterity. Now this sin of hers would make it more difficult for her to act by faith afterwards. (3.) The great improbability of the thing promised, that she should be the mother of a child, when she was of sterile constitution naturally, and now past the prolific age.

2. The actings of her faith. Her unbelief is pardoned and forgotten, but her faith prevailed and is recorded: *She judged him faithful, who had promised, v.* 11. She received the promise as the promise of God; and, being convinced of that, she truly judged he both could and would perform it, how impossible soever it might seem to reason; for the faithfulness of God will not suffer him to deceive his people.

3. The fruits and rewards of her faith. (1.) *She received strength to conceive seed.* The strength of nature, as well as grace, is from God: he can make the barren soul fruitful, as well as the barren womb. (2.) *She was delivered of a child,* a man-child, a child of the promise, and comfort of his parents' advanced years, and the hope of future ages. (3.) From them, by this son, sprang a numerous progeny of illustrious persons, *as the stars of the sky* (*v.* 12) — a great, powerful, and renowned nation, above all the rest in the world; and a nation of saints, the peculiar church and people of God; and, which was the highest honour and reward of all, *of these, according to the flesh, the Messiah came, who is over all, God blessed for evermore.*

VI. The apostle proceeds to make mention of the faith of the other patriarchs, Isaac and Jacob, and the rest of this happy family, *v.* 13. Here observe,

1. The trial of their faith in the imperfection of their present state. They had not received the promises, that is, they had not received the things promised, they had not yet been put into possession of Canaan, they had not yet seen their numerous issue, they had not seen Christ in the flesh. Observe, (1.) Many that are interested in the promises do not presently receive the things promised. (2.) One imperfection of the present state of the saints on earth is that their happiness lies more in promise and reversion than in actual enjoyment and possession. The gospel state is more perfect than the patriarchal, because more of the promises are now fulfilled. The heavenly state will be most perfect of all; for there all the promises will have their full accomplishment.

2. The actings of their faith during this imperfect state of things. Though they had not received the promises, yet,

(1.) They saw them afar off. Faith has a clear and a strong eye, and can see promised mercies at a great distance. Abraham saw Christ's day, when it was afar off, and rejoiced, Jn. 8:56.

(2.) They were persuaded of them, that they were true and should be fulfilled. Faith sets to its seal that God is true, and thereby settles and satisfies the soul.

(3.) They embraced them. Their faith was a faith of consent. Faith has a long arm, and can lay hold of blessings at a great distance, can make them present, can love them, and rejoice in them; and thus antedate the enjoyment of them.

(4.) They *confessed that they were strangers and pilgrims on earth.* Observe, [1.] Their condition: *Strangers and pilgrims.* They are strangers as saints, whose home is heaven; they are pilgrims as they are travelling towards their home, though often meanly and slowly. [2.] Their acknowledgment of this their condition: they were not ashamed to own it; both their lips and their lives confessed their present condition. They expected little from the world. They cared not to engage much in it. They endeavoured to lay aside every weight,

to gird up the loins of their minds to mind their way, to keep company and pace with their fellow-travellers, looking for difficulties, and bearing them, and longing to get home.

(5.) Hereby they declared plainly that they sought another country (*v.* 14), heaven, their own country. For their spiritual birth is thence, there are their best relations, and there is their inheritance. This country they seek: their designs are for it; their desires are after it; their discourse is about it; they diligently endeavour to clear up their title to it, to have their temper suited to it, to have their conversation in it, and to come to the enjoyment of it.

(6.) They gave full proof of their sincerity in making such a confession. For, [1.] They were not mindful of that country whence they came, *v.* 15. They did not hanker after the plenty and pleasures of it, nor regret and repent that they had left it; they had no desire to return to it. Note, Those that are once effectually and savingly called out of a sinful state have no mind to return into it again; they now know better things. [2.] They did not take the opportunity that offered itself for their return. They might have had such an opportunity. They had time enough to return. They had natural strength to return. They knew the way. Those with whom they sojourned would have been willing enough to part with them. Their old friends would have been glad to receive them. They had sufficient to bear the charges of their journey; and flesh and blood, a corrupt counsellor, would be sometimes suggesting to them a return. But they stedfastly adhered to God and duty under all discouragements and against all temptations to revolt from him. So should we all do. We shall not want opportunities to revolt from God; but we must show the truth of our faith and profession by a steady adherence to him to the end of our days. Their sincerity appeared not only in not returning to their former country, but in desiring a better country, that is, a heavenly. Observe, *First,* The heavenly country is better than any upon earth; it is better situated, better stored with every thing that is good, better secured from every thing that is evil; the employments, the enjoyments, the society, and every thing in it, are better than the best in this world. *Secondly,* All true believers desire this better country. True faith draws forth sincere and fervent desires; and the stronger faith is the more fervent those desires will be.

(7.) They died in the faith of those promises; not only lived by the faith of them, but died in the full persuasion that all the promises would be fulfilled to them and theirs, *v.* 13. That faith held out to the last. By faith, when they were dying, they received the atonement; they acquiesced in the will of God; they quenched all the fiery darts of the devil; they overcame the terrors of death, disarmed it of its sting, and bade a cheerful farewell to this world and to all the comforts and crosses of it. These were the actings of their faith. Now observe,

3. The gracious and great reward of their faith: *God is not ashamed to be their God, for he hath prepared for them a city, v.* 16. Note, (1.) God is the God of all true believers; faith gives them an interest in God, and in all his fullness. (2.) He is called their God. He calls himself so: *I am the God of Abraham, and the God of Isaac, and the God of Jacob;* he gives them leave to call him so; and he gives them the spirit of adoption, to enable them to cry, *Abba, Father.* (3.) Notwithstanding their meanness by nature, their vileness by sin, and the poverty of their outward condition, God is not ashamed to be called *their God:* such is his condescension, such is his love to them; therefore let them never be ashamed of being called his people, nor of any of those that are truly so, how much soever despised in the world. Above all, let them take care that they be not a shame and reproach to their God, and so provoke him to be ashamed of them; but let them act so as to be to him for a name, and for a praise, and for a glory. (4.) As the proof of this, God has prepared for them a city, a happiness suitable to the relation into which he has taken them. For there is nothing in this world commensurate to the love of God in being the God of his people; and, if God neither could nor would give his people any thing better than this world affords, he would be ashamed to be called their God. If he takes them into such a relation to himself, he will provide for them accordingly. If he takes them into such a relation to himself, he will provide for them accordingly. If he takes to himself the title of their God, he will fully answer it, and act up to it; and he has prepared that for them in heaven which will fully answer this character and relation, so that it shall never be said, to the reproach and dis-

bodies. [5.] To assure them that God would be with them in Egypt, and deliver them out of it in his own time and way.

2. When it was that the faith of Joseph acted after this manner; namely, as in the case of Jacob, when he was dying. God often gives his people living comforts in dying moments; and when he does it is their duty, as they can, to communicate them to those about them, for the glory of God, for the honour of religion, and for the good of their brethren and friends. We go on now to,

XI. The faith of the parents of Moses, which is cited from Ex. 2:3, etc. Here observe, 1. The acting of their faith: they hid this their son three months. Though only the mother of Moses is mentioned in the history, yet, by what is here said, it seems his father not only consented to it, but consulted about it. It is a happy thing where yoke-fellows draw together in the yoke of faith, as heirs of the grace of God; and when they do this in a religious concern for the good of their children, to preserve them not only from those who would destroy their lives, but from those who would corrupt their minds. Observe, Moses was persecuted betimes, and forced to be concealed; in this he was a type of Christ, who was persecuted almost as soon as he was born, and his parents were obliged to flee with him into Egypt for his preservation. It is a great mercy to be free from wicked laws and edicts; but, when we are not, we must use all lawful means for our security. In this faith of Moses's parents there was a mixture of unbelief, but God was pleased to overlook it. 2. The reasons of their thus acting. No doubt, natural affection could not but move them; but there was something further. They *saw he was a proper child, a goodly child* (Ex. 2:2), *exceedingly fair,* as in Acts 7:20, *asteios tō Theō — venustus Deo — fair to God.* There appeared in him something uncommon; the beauty of the Lord sat upon him, as a presage that he was born to great things, and that by conversing with God his face should shine (Ex. 34:29), what bright and illustrious actions he should do for the deliverance of Israel, and how his name should shine in the sacred records. Sometimes, not always, the countenance is the index of the mind. 3. The prevalency of their faith over their fear. They were not afraid of the king's commandment, Ex. 1:22. That was a wicked and a cruel edict, that all the males of the Israelites should be destroyed in their infancy, and so the name of Israel must be destroyed out of the earth. But they did not so fear as presently to give up their child; they considered that, if none of the males were preserved, there would be an end and utter ruin of the church of God and the true religion, and that though in their present state of servitude and oppression one would praise the dead rather than the living, yet they believed that God would preserve his people, and that the time was coming when it would be worth while for an Israelite to live. Some must hazard their own lives to preserve their children, and they were resolved to do it; they knew the king's commandment was evil in itself, contrary to the laws of God and nature, and therefore of no authority nor obligation. Faith is a great preservative against the sinful slavish fear of men, as it sets God before the soul, and shows the vanity of the creature and its subordination to the will and power of God. The apostle next proceeds to,

XII. The faith of Moses himself (*v.* 24, 25, etc.), here observe,

1. An instance of his faith in conquering the world.

(1.) He *refused to be called the son of Pharaoh's daughter,* whose foundling he was, and her fondling too; she had adopted him for his son, and he refused it. Observe, [1.] How great a temptation Moses was under. Pharaoh's daughter is said to have been his only child, and was herself childless; and having found Moses, and saved him as she did, she resolved to take him and bring him up as her son; and so he stood fair to be in time king of Egypt, and he might thereby have been serviceable to Israel. He owed his life to this princess; and to refuse such kindness from her would look not only like ingratitude to her, but a neglect of Providence, that seemed to intend his advancement and his brethren's advantage. [2.] How glorious was the triumph of his faith in so great a trial. He *refused to be called the son of Pharaoh's daughter* lest he should undervalue the truer honour of being a son of Abraham, the father of the faithful; *he refused to be called the son of Pharaoh's daughter* lest it should look like renouncing his religion as well as his relation to Israel; and no doubt both these he must have done if he had accepted this honour; he therefore nobly refused it.

(2.) He chose *rather to suffer affliction with the people of God than to enjoy the pleasures of sin for a season, v.* 25. He was willing to take his lot with the people of God here, though it was a suffering lot, that he might have his portion with them hereafter, rather than to enjoy all the sensual sinful pleasures of Pharaoh's court, which would be but for a season, and would then be punished with everlasting misery. Herein he acted rationally as well as religiously, and conquered the temptation to worldly pleasure as he had done before to worldly preferment. Here observe, [1.] The pleasures of sin are and will be but short; they must end in speedy repentance or in speedy ruin. [2.] The pleasures of this world, and especially those of a court, are too often the pleasures of sin; and they are always so when we cannot enjoy them without deserting God and his people. A true believer will despise them when they are offered upon such terms. [3.] Suffering is to be chosen rather than sin, there being more evil in the least sin than there can be in the greatest suffering. [4.] It greatly alleviates the evil of suffering when we suffer with the people of God, embarked in the same interest and animated by the same Spirit.

(3.) He accounted *the reproaches of Christ greater riches than the treasures of Egypt, v.* 26. See how Moses weighed matters: in one scale he put the worst of religion — *the reproaches of Christ,* in the other scale the best of the world — *the treasures of Egypt;* and in his judgment, directed by faith, the worst of religion weighed down the best of the world. The reproaches of the church of God are *the reproaches of Christ,* who is, and has ever been, the head of the church. Now here Moses conquered the riches of the world, as before he had conquered its honours and pleasures. God's people are, and always have been, a reproached people. Christ accounts himself reproached in their reproaches; and, while he thus interests himself in their reproaches, they become riches, and greater riches than the treasures of the richest empire in the world; for Christ will reward them with a crown of glory that fades not away. Faith discerns this, and determines and acts accordingly.

2. The circumstance of time is taken notice of, when Moses by his faith gained this victory over the world, in all its honours, pleasures, and treasures: *When he had come to years* (*v.* 24); not only to years of discretion, but of experience, to the age of forty years — when he was great, or had come to maturity. Some would take this as detracting from his victory, that he gained it so late, that he did not make this choice sooner; but it is rather an enhancement of the honour of his self-denial and victory over the world that he made this choice when he had grown ripe for judgment and enjoyment, able to know what he did and why he did it. It was not the act of a child, that prefers counters to gold, but it proceeded from mature deliberation. It is an excellent thing for persons to be seriously religious when in the midst of worldly business and enjoyments, to despise the world when they are most capable of relishing and enjoying it.

3. What it was that supported and strengthened the faith of Moses to such a degree as to enable him to gain such a victory over the world: *He had respect unto the recompense of reward,* that is, say some, the deliverance out of Egypt; but doubtless it means much more — the glorious reward of faith and fidelity in the other world. Observe here, (1.) Heaven is a great reward, surpassing not only all our deservings, but all our conceptions. It is a reward suitable to the price paid for it — the blood of Christ; suitable to the perfections of God, and fully answering to all his promises. It is a recompense of reward, because given by a righteous Judge for the righteousness of Christ to righteous persons, according to the righteous rule of the covenant of grace. (2.) Believers may and ought to have respect to this recompense of reward; they should acquaint themselves with it, approve of it, and live in the daily and delightful expectation of it. Thus it will prove a land-mark to direct their course, a load-stone to draw their hearts, a sword to conquer their enemies, a spur to quicken them to duty, and a cordial to refresh them under all the difficulties of doing and suffering work.

4. We have another instance of the faith of Moses, namely, in forsaking Egypt: *By faith he forsook Egypt, not fearing the wrath of the king, v.* 27. Observe here, (1.) The product of his faith: *He forsook Egypt,* and all its power and pleasures, and undertook the conduct of Israel out of it. Twice Moses forsook Egypt: [1.] As a supposed criminal, when the king's wrath was incensed against him for killing the Egyptian (Ex. 2:14, 15), where it is said he feared, not with a fear of despondency, but of discretion, to save his life. [2.] As a commander and ruler in Jeshurun, after God had employed him to humble Pharaoh and make him willing to let Israel go. (2.) The prevalency of his faith. It raised him above the fear of the king's wrath. Though he knew that it was great, and levelled at him in particular, and that it marched at the head of a numerous host to pursue him, yet he was not dismayed, and he said to Israel, *Fear not,* Ex. 14:13. Those who forsook Egypt must expect the wrath of men; but they need not fear it, for they are under the conduct of that God who is able to make the wrath of man to praise him, and restrain the remainder of it. (3.) The principle upon which his faith acted in these his motions: *He endured, as seeing him that was invisible.* He bore up with invincible courage under all danger, and endured all the fatigue of his employment, which was very great; and this by seeing the invisible God. Observe, [1.] The God with whom we have to do is an invisible God: he is so to our senses, to the eye of the body; and this shows the folly of those who pretend to make images of God, whom no man hath seen, nor can see. [2.] By faith we may see this invisible God. We may be fully assured of his existence, of his providence, and of his gracious and powerful presence with us. [3.] Such a sight of God will enable believers to endure to the end whatever they may meet with in the way.

5. We have yet another instance of the faith of Moses, in keeping *the passover and sprinkling of blood, v.* 28. The account of this we have in Ex. 12:13–23. Though all Israel kept this passover, yet it was by Moses that God delivered the institution of it; and, though it was a great mystery, Moses by faith both delivered it to the people and kept it that night in the house where he lodged. The passover was one of the most solemn institutions of the Old Testament, and a very significant type of Christ. The occasion of its first observance was extraordinary: it was in the same night that God slew the first-born of the Egyptians; but, though the Israelites lived among them, the destroying angel passed over their houses, and spared them and theirs. Now, to entitle them to this distinguishing favour, and to mark them out for it, a lamb must be slain; the blood of it must be sprinkled with a bunch of hyssop upon the lintel of the door, and on the two side-posts; the flesh of the lamb must be roasted with fire; and it must be all of it eaten that very night with bitter herbs, in a travelling posture, their loins girt, their shoes on their feet, and their staff in their hand. This was accordingly done, and the destroying angel passed over them, and slew the first-born of the Egyptians. This opened a way for the return of Abraham's posterity into the land of promise. The accommodation of this type is not difficult. (1.) Christ is that Lamb, he is our Passover, he was sacrificed for us. (2.) His blood must be sprinkled; it must be applied to those who have the saving benefit of it. (3.) It is applied effectually only to the Israelites, the chosen people of God. (4.) It is not owing to our inherent righteousness or best performances that we are saved from the wrath of God, but to the blood of Christ and his imputed righteousness. If any of the families of Israel had neglected the sprinkling of this blood upon their doors, though they should have spent all the night in prayer, the destroying angel would have broken in upon them, and slain their first-born. (5.) Wherever this blood is applied, the soul receives a whole Christ by faith, and lives upon him. (6.) This true faith makes sin bitter to the soul, even while it receives the pardon and atonement. (7.) All our spiritual privileges on earth should quicken us to set out early, and get forward, in our way to heaven. (8.) Those who have been marked out must ever remember and acknowledge free and distinguishing grace.

XIII. The next instance of faith is that of the Israelites passing through the Red Sea under the conduct of Moses their leader, *v.* 29. The story we have in Exodus, *ch.* 14. Observe,

1. The preservation and safe passage of the Israelites through the Red Sea, when there was no other way to escape from Pharaoh and his host, who were closely pursuing them. Here we may observe, (1.) Israel's danger was very great; an enraged enemy with chariots and horsemen behind them; steep rocks and mountains on either hand, and the Red Sea before them. (2.) Their deliverance was very glorious. By faith they passed through the Red Sea as on dry land; the grace of faith will help us through all the dangers we meet with in our way to heaven.

2. The destruction of the Egyptians. They, presumptuously attempting to follow Israel through the Red Sea, being thus blinded and hardened to their ruin, were all drowned. Their rashness was great, and their ruin was grievous. When God

judges, he will overcome; and it is plain that the destruction of sinners is of themselves.

XIV. The next instance of faith is that of the Israelites, under Joshua their leader, before the walls of Jericho. The story we have Jos. 6:5, etc. Here observe, 1. The means prescribed to God to bring down the walls of Jericho. It was ordered that they should compass the walls about once a day for seven days together and seven times the last day, that the priests should carry the ark when they compassed the walls about, and should blow with trumpets made of rams' horns, and sound a longer blast than before, and then all the people should shout, and the walls of Jericho should fall before them. Here was a great trial of their faith. The method prescribed seemed very improbable to answer such an end, and would doubtless expose them to the daily contempt of their enemies; the ark of God would seem to be in danger. But this was the way God commanded them to take, and he loves to do great things by small and contemptible means, that his own arm may be made bare. 2. The powerful success of the prescribed means. The walls of Jericho fell before them. This was a frontier town in the land of Canaan, the first that stood out against the Israelites. God was pleased in this extraordinary manner to slight and dismantle it, in order to magnify himself, to terrify the Canaanites, to strengthen the faith of the Israelites, and to exclude all boasting. God can and will in his own time and way cause all the powerful opposition that is made to his interest and glory to fall down, and the grace of faith is mighty through God for the pulling down of strong-holds; he will make Babylon fall before the faith of his people, and, when he has some great thing to do for them, he raises up great and strong faith in them.

XV. The next instance is the faith of Rahab, *v.* 31. Among the noble army of believing worthies, bravely marshalled by the apostle, Rahab comes in the rear, to show *that God is no respecter of persons.* Here consider,

1. Who this Rahab was. (1.) She was a Canaanite, a *stranger to the commonwealth of Israel,* and had but little help for faith, and yet she was a believer; the power of divine grace greatly appears when it works without the usual means of grace. (2.) She was a harlot, and lived in a way of sin; she was not only a keeper of a public house, but a common woman of the town, and yet she believed that the greatness of sin, if truly repented of, shall be no bar to the pardoning mercy of God. Christ has saved the chief of sinners. *Where sin has abounded, grace has superabounded.*

2. What she did by her faith: *She received the spies in peace,* the men that Joshua had sent to spy out Jericho, Jos. 2:6, 7. She not only bade them welcome, but she concealed them from their enemies who sought to cut them off, and she made a noble confession of her faith, *v.* 9–11. She engaged them to covenant with her to show favour to her and hers, when God should show kindness to them, and that they would give her a sign, which they did, a line of scarlet, which she was to hang forth out of the window; she sent them away with prudent and friendly advice. Learn here, (1.) True faith will show itself in good works, especially towards the people of God. (2.) Faith will venture all hazards in the cause of God and his people; a true believer will sooner expose his own person than God's interest and people. (3.) A true believer is desirous, not only to be in covenant with God, but in communion with the people of God, and is willing to cast in his lot with them, and to fare as they fare.

3. What she gained by her faith. She escaped perishing with those that believed not. Observe, (1.) The generality of her neighbours, friends, and fellow-citizens, perished; it was an utter destruction that befell that city: man and beast were cut off. (2.) The cause of the people of Jericho's destruction — unbelief. They believed not that Israel's God was the true God, though they had evidence sufficient of it. (3.) The signal preservation of Rahab. Joshua gave a strict charge that she should be spared, and none but she and hers; and she taking care that the sign, the scarlet thread, should be hung out, her family were marked out for mercy, and perished not. Singular faith, when the generality are not only unbelievers, but against believers, will be rewarded with singular favours in times of common calamity.

Verses 32–40

The apostle having given us a classis of many eminent believers, whose names are mentioned and the particular trials and actings of their faith recorded, now concludes his narrative with a more summary account of another set of believers, where the particular acts are not ascribed to particular persons by name, but left to be applied by those who are well acquainted with the sacred story; and, like a divine orator, he prefaces his part of the narrative with an elegant expostulation: *What shall I say more? Time would fail me;* as if he had said, "It is in vain to attempt to exhaust this subject; should I not restrain my pen, it would soon run beyond the bounds of an epistle; and therefore I shall but just mention a few more, and leave you to enlarge upon them." Observe, 1. After all our researches into the scripture, there is still more to be learned from them. 2. We must well consider in divine matters what we should say, and suit it as well as we can to the time. 3. We should be pleased to think how great the number of believers was under the Old Testament, and how strong their faith, though the objects thereof were not then so fully revealed. And, 4. We should lament it, that now, in gospel times, when the rule of faith is more clear and perfect, the number of believers should be so small and their faith so weak.

I. In this summary account the apostle mentions,

1. Gideon, whose story we have in Judges 6:11, etc. He was an eminent instrument raised up of God to deliver his people from the oppression of the Midianites; he was a person of mean tribe and family, called from a mean employment (threshing wheat), and saluted by an angel of God in this surprising manner, *The Lord is with thee, thou mighty man of war.* Gideon could not at first receive such honours, but humbly expostulates with the angel about their low and distressed state. The angel of the Lord delivers him his commission, and assures him of success, confirming the assurance by fire out of the rock. Gideon is directed to offer sacrifice, and, instructed in his duty, goes forth against the Midianites, when his army is reduced from thirty-two thousand to three hundred; yet by these, with their lamps and pitchers, God put the whole army of the Midianites to confusion and ruin: and the same faith that gave Gideon so much courage and honour enabled him to act with great meekness and modesty towards his brethren afterwards. It is the excellency of the grace of faith that, while it helps men to do great things, it keeps them from having high and great thoughts of themselves.

2. Barak, another instrument raised up to deliver Israel out of the hand of Jabin, king of Canaan, Judges 4, where we read, (1.) Though he was a soldier, yet he received his commission and instructions from Deborah, a *prophetess of the Lord;* and he insisted upon having this divine oracle with him in his expedition. (2.) He obtained a great victory by his faith over all the host of Sisera. (3.) His faith taught him to return all the praise and glory to God: this is the nature of faith; it has recourse unto God in all dangers and difficulties, and then makes grateful returns to God for all mercies and deliverances.

3. Samson, another instrument that God raised up to deliver Israel from the Philistines: his story we have in Judges 13, 14, 15, and 16, and from it we learn that the grace of faith is the strength of the soul for great service. If Samson had not had a strong faith as well as a strong arm, he had never performed such exploits. Observe, (1.) By faith the servants of God shall overcome even the roaring lion. (2.) True faith is acknowledged and accepted, even when mingled with many failings. (3.) The believer's faith endures to the end, and, in dying, gives him victory over death and all his deadly enemies; his greatest conquest he gains by dying.

4. Jephthah, whose story we have, Jud. 11, before that of Samson. He was raised up to deliver Israel from the Ammonites. As various and new enemies rise up against the people of God, various and new deliverers are raised up for them. In the story of Jephthah observe, (1.) The grace of God often finds out, and fastens upon, the most undeserving and ill-deserving persons, to do great things for them and by them. Jephthah was the son of a harlot. (2.) The grace of faith, wherever it is, will put men upon acknowledging God in all their ways (ch. 11:11): *Jephthah rehearsed all his words before the Lord in Mizpeh.* (3.) The grace of faith will make men bold and venturous in a good cause. (4.) Faith will not only put men upon making their vows to God, but paying their vows after the mercy received; yea, though they have vowed to their own great grief, hurt, and loss, as in the case of Jephthah and his daughter.

5. David, that great man after God's own heart. Few ever met with greater trials, and few ever discovered a more lively faith. His first appearance on the stage of the world was a great evidence of his faith. Having, when young, slain *the lion and the bear,* his faith in God encouraged him to encounter the great Goliath, and helped him to triumph over him. The same faith enabled him to bear patiently the ungrateful malice of Saul and his favourites, and to wait till God should put him into possession of the promised power and dignity. The same faith made him a very successful and victorious prince, and, after a long life of virtue and honour (though not without some foul stains of sin), he died in faith, relying upon the everlasting covenant that God had made with him and his, ordered in all things and sure; and he has left behind him such excellent memoirs of the trials and acts of faith in the book of Psalms as will ever be of great esteem and use, among the people of God.

6. Samuel, raised up to be a most eminent prophet of the Lord to Israel, as well as a ruler over them. God revealed himself to Samuel when he was but a child, and continued to do so till his death. In his story observe, (1.) Those are likely to grow up to some eminency in faith who begin betimes in the exercise of it. (2.) Those whose business it is to reveal the mind and will of God to others had need to be well established in the belief of it themselves.

7. To Samuel he adds, *and of the prophets,* who were extraordinary ministers of the Old-Testament church, employed of God sometimes to denounce judgment, sometimes to promise mercy, always to reprove sin; sometimes to foretell remarkable events, known only to God; and chiefly to give notice of the Messiah, his coming, person, and offices; for in him the prophets as well as the law center. Now a true and strong faith was very requisite for the right discharge of such an office as this.

II. Having done naming particular persons, he proceeds to tell us what things were done by their faith. He mentions some things that easily apply themselves to one or other of the persons named; but he mentions other things that are not so easy to be accommodated to any here named, but must be left to general conjecture or accommodation.

1. *By faith they subdued kingdoms, v.* 33. Thus did David, Joshua, and many of the judges. Learn hence, (1.) The interests and powers of kings and kingdoms are often set up in opposition to God and his people. (2.) God can easily subdue all those kings and kingdoms that set themselves to oppose him. (3.) Faith is a suitable and excellent qualification of those who fight in the ways of the Lord; it makes them just, bold, and wise.

2. They *wrought righteousness,* both in their public and personal capacities; they turned many from idolatry to the ways of righteousness; they believed God, and it was imputed to them for righteousness; they walked and acted righteously towards God and man. It is a greater honour and happiness to work righteousness than to work miracles; faith is an active principle of universal righteousness.

3. They *obtained promises,* both general and special. It is faith that gives us an interest in the promises; it is by faith that we have the comfort of the promises; and it is by faith that we are prepared to wait for the promises, and in due time to receive them.

4. They *stopped the mouths of lions;* so did Samson, Jdg. 14:5, 6, and David, 1 Sa. 17:34, 35, and Daniel, 6:22. Here learn, (1.) The power of God is above the power of the creature. (2.) Faith engages the power of God for his people, whenever it shall be for his glory, to overcome brute beasts and brutish men.

5. They *quenched the violence of the fire, v.* 34. So Moses, by the prayer of faith, quenched the fire of God's wrath that was kindled against the people of Israel, Num. 11:1, 2. So did the three children, or rather mighty champions, Dan. 3:17–27. Their faith in God, refusing to worship the golden image, exposed them to the fiery furnace which Nebuchadnezzar had prepared for them, and their faith engaged for them that power and presence of God in the furnace which quenched the violence of the fire, so that not so much as the smell thereof passed on them. Never was the grace of faith more severely tried, never more nobly exerted, nor ever more gloriously rewarded, than theirs was.

6. They *escaped the edge of the sword.* Thus David escaped the sword of Goliath and of Saul; and Mordecai and the Jews escaped the sword of Haman. The swords of men are held in the hand of God, and he can blunt the edge of the sword, and turn it away from his people against their enemies when he pleases. Faith takes hold of that hand of God

which has hold of the swords of men; and God has often suffered himself to be prevailed upon by the faith of his people.

7. *Out of weakness they were made strong.* From national weakness, into which the Jews often fell by their unbelief; upon the revival of their faith, all their interest and affairs revived and flourished. From bodily weakness; thus Hezekiah, believing the word of God, recovered out of a mortal distemper, and he ascribed his recovery to the promise and power of God (Isa. 38:15, 16), *What shall I say? He hath spoken it, and he hath also done it. Lord by these things men live, and in these is the life of my spirit.* And it is the same grace of faith that from spiritual weakness helps men to recover and renew their strength.

8. They *grew valiant in fight.* So did Joshua, the judges, and David. True faith gives truest courage and patience, as it discerns the strength of God, and thereby the weakness of all his enemies. And they were not only valiant, but successful. God, as a reward and encouragement of their faith, *put to flight the armies of the aliens,* of those who were aliens to their commonwealth, and enemies to their religion; God made them flee and fall before his faithful servants. Believing and praying commanders, at the head of believing and praying armies, have been so owned and honoured of God that nothing could stand before them.

9. *Women received their dead raised to life again, v.* 35. So did the widow of Zarepath (1 Ki. 17:23), and the Shunamite, 2 Ki. 4:36. (1.) *In Christ there is neither male nor female;* many of the weaker sex have been strong in faith. (2.) Though the covenant of grace takes in the children of believers, yet it leaves them subject to natural death. (3.) Poor mothers are loth to resign up their interest in their children, though death has taken them away. (4.) God has sometimes yielded so far to the tender affections of sorrowful women as to restore their dead children to life again. Thus Christ had compassion on the widow of Nain, Lu. 7:12, etc. (5.) This should confirm our faith in the general resurrection.

III. The apostle tells us what these believers endured by faith. 1. They *were tortured, not accepting deliverance, v.* 35. They were put upon the rack, to make them renounce their God, their Saviour, and their religion. They bore the torture, and would not accept of deliverance upon such vile terms; and that which animated them thus to suffer was the hope they had of *obtaining a better resurrection,* and deliverance upon more honourable terms. This is thought to refer to that memorable story, 2 Macc. *ch.* 7, etc. 2. They endured *trials of cruel mockings and scourgings, and bonds and imprisonment, v.* 36. They were persecuted in their reputation by *mockings,* which are cruel to an ingenuous mind; in their persons by *scourging,* the punishment of slaves; in their liberty by *bonds and imprisonment.* Observe how inveterate is the malice that wicked men have towards the righteous, how far it will go, and what a variety of cruelties it will invent and exercise upon those against whom they have no cause of quarrel, except in the matters of their God. 3. They were put to death in the most cruel manner; some *were stoned,* as Zechariah (2 Chr. 24:21), *sawn asunder,* as Isaiah by Manasseh. *They were tempted;* some read it, *burnt,* 2 Macc. 7:5. *They were slain with the sword.* All sorts of deaths were prepared for them; their enemies clothed death in all the array of cruelty and terror, and yet they boldly met it and endured it. 4. Those who escaped death were used so ill that death might seem more eligible than such a life. Their enemies spared them, only to prolong their misery, and wear out all their patience; for they were forced to *wander about in sheepskins and goat-skins, being destitute, afflicted, and tormented; they wandered about in deserts, and on mountains, and in dens and caves of the earth, v.* 37, 38. They were stripped of the conveniences of life, and turned out of house and harbour. They had not raiment to put on, but were forced to cover themselves with the skins of slain beasts. They were driven out of all human society, and forced to converse with the beasts of the field, to hide themselves in dens and caves, and make their complaint to rocks and rivers, not more obdurate than their enemies. Such sufferings as these they endured then for their faith; and such they endured through the power of the grace of faith: and which shall we most admire, the wickedness of human nature, that is capable of perpetrating such cruelties on fellow creatures, or the excellency of divine grace, that is able to bear up the faithful under such cruelties, and to carry them safely through all?

IV. What they obtained by their faith. 1. A most honourable character and commendation from God, the true Judge

and fountain of honour — that *the world was not worthy* of such men; the world did not deserve such blessings; they did not know how to value them, nor how to use them. Wicked men! The righteous are not worthy to live in the world, and God declares the world is not worthy of them; and, though they widely differ in their judgment, they agree in this, that it is not fit that good men should have their rest in this world; and therefore God receives them out of it, to that world that is suitable to them, and yet far beyond the merit of all their services and sufferings. 2. They *obtained a good report (v.* 39) of all good men, and of the truth itself, and have the honour to be enrolled in this sacred calendar of the Old-Testament worthies, God's witnesses; yea, they had a witness for them in the consciences of their enemies, who, while they thus abused them, were condemned by their own consciences, as persecuting those who were more righteous than themselves. 3. They obtained an interest in the promises, though not the full possession of them. They had a title to the promises, though they received not the great things promised. This is not meant of the felicity of the heavenly state, for this they did receive, when they died, in the measure of a part, in one constituent part of their persons, and the much better part; but it is meant of the felicity of the gospel-state: they had types, but not the antitype; they had shadows, but had not seen the substance; and yet, under this imperfect dispensation, they discovered this precious faith. This the apostle insists upon to render the faith more illustrious, and to provoke Christians to a holy jealousy and emulation; that they should not suffer themselves to be outdone in the exercise of faith by those who came so short of them in all the helps and advantages for believing. He tells the Hebrews that God had *provided some better things for* them (v. 40), and therefore they might be assured that he expected at least as good things from them; and that since the gospel is the end and perfection of the Old Testament, which had no excellency but in its reference to Christ and the gospel, it was expected that their faith should be as much more perfect than the faith of the Old-Testament saints; for their state and dispensation were more perfect than the former, and were indeed the perfection and completion of the former, for without the gospel-church the Jewish church must have remained in an incomplete and imperfect state. This reasoning is strong, and should be effectually prevalent with us all.

CHAPTER 12

The apostle, in this chapter, applies what he has collected in the chapter foregoing, and makes use of it as a great motive to patience and perseverance in the Christian faith and state, pressing home the argument, I. From a greater example than he had yet mentioned, and that is Christ himself (v. 1–3). II. From the gentle and gracious nature of the afflictions they endured in their Christian course (v. 4–17). III. From the communion and conformity between the state of the gospel-church on earth and the triumphant church in heaven (v. 18 to the end).

Verses 1–3

Here observe what is the great duty which the apostle urges upon the Hebrews, and which he so much desires they would comply with, and that is, to *lay aside every weight, and the sin that did so easily beset them, and run with patience the race set before them.* The duty consists of two parts, the one preparatory, the other perfective.

I. Preparatory: *Lay aside every weight, and the sin,* etc. 1. *Every weight,* that is, all inordinate affection and concern for the body, and the present life and world. Inordinate care for the present life, or fondness for it, is a dead weight upon the soul, that pulls it down when it should ascend upwards, and pulls it back when it should press forward; it makes duty and difficulties harder and heavier than they would be. 2. *The sin that doth so easily beset us;* the sin that has the greatest advantage against us, by the circumstances we are in, our constitution, our company. This may mean either the damning sin of unbelief or rather the darling sin of the Jews, an over-fondness for their own dispensation. *Let us lay aside* all external and internal hindrances.

II. Perfective: *Run with patience the race that is set before us.* The apostle speaks in the gymnastic style, taken from the Olympic and other exercises.

1. Christians have a race to run, a race of service and a race of sufferings, a course of active and passive obedience.

2. This race is set before them; it is marked out unto them, both by the word of God and the examples of the faithful servants of God, that cloud of witnesses with which they are compassed about. It is set out by proper limits and directions;

the mark they run to, and the prize they run for, are set before them.

3. This race must be run with patience and perseverance. There will be need of patience to encounter the difficulties that lie in our way, of perseverance to resist all temptations to desist or turn aside. Faith and patience are the conquering graces, and therefore must be always cultivated and kept in lively exercise.

4. Christians have a greater example to animate and encourage them in their Christian course than any or all who have been mentioned before, and that is the Lord Jesus Christ: *Looking unto Jesus, the author and finisher of our faith, v.* 2. Here observe,

(1.) What our Lord Jesus is to his people: he is *the author and finisher* of their *faith* — the beginning, perfecter, and rewarder of it. [1.] He is the author of their faith; not only the object, but the author. He is the great leader and precedent of our faith, *he trusted in God;* he is the purchaser of the Spirit of faith, the publisher of the rule of faith, the efficient cause of the grace of faith, and in all respects the author of our faith. [2.] He is *the finisher of our faith;* he is the fulfiller and the fulfilling of all scripture-promises and prophecies; he is the perfecter of the canon of scripture; he is the finisher of grace, and of the work of faith with power in the souls of his people; and he is the judge and the rewarder of their faith; he determines who they are that reach the mark, and from him, and in him, they have the prize.

(2.) What trials Christ met with in his race and course. [1.] He *endured the contradiction of sinners against himself* (v. 3); he bore the opposition that they made to him, both in their words and behaviour. They were continually contradicting him, and crossing in upon his great designs; and though he could easily have both confuted and confounded them, and sometimes gave them a specimen of his power, yet he endured their evil manners with great patience. Their contradictions were levelled against Christ himself, against his person as God-man, against his authority, against his preaching, and yet he endured all. [2.] He *endured the cross* — all those sufferings that he met with in the world; for he took up his cross betimes, and was at length nailed to it, and endured a painful, ignominious, and accursed death, in which he was numbered with the transgressors, the vilest malefactors; yet all this he endured with invincible patience and resolution. [3.] He *despised the shame.* All the reproaches that were cast upon him, both in his life and at his death, he despised; he was infinitely above them; he knew his own innocency and excellency, and despised the ignorance and malice of his despisers.

(3.) What it was that supported the human soul of Christ under these unparalleled sufferings; and that was the *joy that was set before him.* He had something in view under all his sufferings, which was pleasant to him; he rejoiced to see that by his sufferings he should make satisfaction to the injured justice of God and give security to his honour and government, that he should make peace between God and man, that he should seal the covenant of grace and be the Mediator of it, that he should open a way of salvation to the chief of sinners, and that he should effectually save all those whom the Father had given him, and himself be the first-born among many brethren. This was the joy that was set before him.

(4.) The reward of his suffering: he *has sat down at the right hand of the throne of God.* Christ, as Mediator, is exalted to a station of the highest honour, of the greatest power and influence; he is at the right hand of the Father. Nothing passes between heaven and earth but by him; he does all that is done; *he ever lives to make intercession for* his people.

(5.) What is our duty with respect to this Jesus. We must, [1.] Look unto him; that is, we must set him continually before us as our example, and our great encouragement; we must look to him for direction, for assistance, and for acceptance, in all our sufferings. [2.] We must consider him, meditate much upon him, and reason with ourselves from his case to our own. We must *analogize,* as the word is; compare Christ's sufferings and ours; and we shall find that as his sufferings far exceeded ours, in the nature and measure of them, so his patience far excels ours, and is a perfect pattern for us to imitate.

(6.) The advantage we shall reap by thus doing: it will be a means to prevent our weariness and fainting (v. 3): *Lest you be weary and faint in your minds.* Observe, [1.] There is a proneness in the best to grow weary and to faint under their trials and afflictions, especially when they prove heavy and of long continuance: this proceeds from the imperfections of grace and the remains of corruption. [2.] The best way to prevent this is to look unto Jesus, and to consider him. Faith and meditation will fetch in fresh supplies of strength, comfort, and courage; for he has assured them, if *they suffer with him, they shall also reign with him:* and this hope will be their helmet.

Verses 4–17

Here the apostle presses the exhortation to patience and perseverance by an argument taken from the gentle measure and gracious nature of those sufferings which the believing Hebrews endured in their Christian course.

I. From the gentle and moderate degree and measure of their sufferings: *You have not yet resisted unto blood, striving against sin, v.* 4. Observe,

1. He owns that they had suffered much, they had been striving to an agony against sin. Here, (1.) The cause of the conflict was sin, and to be engaged against sin is to fight in a good cause, for sin is the worst enemy both to God and man. Our spiritual warfare is both honourable and necessary; for we are only defending ourselves against that which would destroy us, if it should get the victory over us; we fight for ourselves, for our lives, and therefore ought to be patient and resolute. (2.) Every Christian is enlisted under Christ's banner, to strive against sin, against sinful doctrines, sinful practices, and sinful habits and customs, both in himself and in others.

2. He puts them in mind that they might have suffered more, that they had not suffered as much as others; for they had *not yet resisted unto blood,* they had not been called to martyrdom as yet, though they knew not how soon they might be. Learn here, (1.) Our Lord Jesus, *the captain of our salvation,* does not call his people out to the hardest trials at first, but wisely trains them up by less sufferings to be prepared for greater. He will not put new wine into weak vessels, he is *the gentle shepherd,* who will not overdrive the *young ones of the flock.* (2.) It becomes Christians to take notice of the gentleness of Christ in accommodating their trial to their strength. They should not magnify their afflictions, but should take notice of the mercy that is mixed with them, and should pity those who are called to the fiery trials to *resist to blood;* not to shed the blood of their enemies, but to seal their testimony with their own blood. (3.) Christians should be ashamed to faint under less trials, when they see others bear up under greater, and do not know how soon they may meet with greater themselves. If we have run with the footmen and they have wearied us, how shall we contend with horses? If we be wearied in a land of peace, what shall we do in the swellings of Jordan? Jer. 12:5.

II. He argues from the peculiar and gracious nature of those sufferings that befall the people of God. Though their enemies and persecutors may be the instruments of inflicting such sufferings on them, yet they are divine chastisements; their heavenly Father has his hand in all, and his wise end to serve by all; of this he has given them due notice, and they should not forget it, *v.* 5. Observe,

1. Those afflictions which may be truly persecution as far as men are concerned in them are fatherly rebukes and chastisements as far as God is concerned in them. Persecution for religion is sometimes a correction and rebuke for the sins of professors of religion. Men persecute them because they are religious; God chastises them because they are not more so: men persecute them because they will not give up their profession; God chastises them because they have not lived up to their profession.

2. God has directed his people how they ought to behave themselves under all their afflictions; they must avoid the extremes that many run into. (1.) They must not despise the chastening of the Lord; they must not make light of afflictions, and be stupid and insensible under them, for they are the hand and rod of God, and his rebukes for sin. Those who make light of affliction make light of God and make light of sin. (2.) They must not faint when they are rebuked; they must not despond and sink under their trial, nor fret and repine, but bear up with faith and patience. (3.) If they run into either of these extremes, it is a sign they have forgotten their heavenly Father's advice and exhortation, which he has given them in true and tender affection.

3. Afflictions, rightly endured, though they may be the fruits of God's displeasure, are yet proofs of his paternal love to his people and care for them (*v.* 6, 7): *Whom the Lord loveth he chasteneth, and scourgeth every son whom he receiveth.* Observe, (1.) The best of God's children need chastisement. They have their faults and follies, which need to be corrected. (2.) Though God may let others alone in their sins, he will correct sin in his own children; they are of his family, and shall not escape his rebukes when they want them. (3.) In this he acts as becomes a father, and treats them like children; no wise and good father will wink at faults in his own children as he would in others; his relation and his affections oblige him to take more notice of the faults of his own children than those of others. (4.) To be suffered to go on in sin without a rebuke is a sad sign of alienation from God; such are bastards, not sons. They may call him Father, because born in the pale of the church; but they are the spurious offspring of another father, not of God, *v.* 7, 8.

4. Those that are impatient under the discipline of their heavenly Father behave worse towards him than they would do towards earthly parents, *v.* 9, 10. Here, (1.) The apostle commends a dutiful and submissive behaviour in children towards their earthly parents *We gave them reverence,* even when they corrected us. It is the duty of children to give the reverence of obedience to the just commands of their parents, and the reverence of submission to their correction when they have been disobedient. Parents have not only authority, but a charge from God, to give their children correction when it is due, and he has commanded children to take such correction well: to be stubborn and discontented under due correction is a double fault; for the correction supposes there has been a fault already committed against the parent's commanding power, and superadds a further fault against his chastening power. Hence, (2.) He recommends humble and submissive behavior towards our heavenly Father, when under his correction; and this he does by an argument from the less to the greater. [1.] Our earthly fathers are but *the fathers of our flesh,* but God is *the Father of our spirits.* Our fathers on earth were instrumental in the production of our bodies, which are but flesh, a mean, mortal, vile thing, formed out of the dust of the earth, as the bodies of the beasts are; and yet as they are curiously wrought, and made parts of our persons, a proper tabernacle for the soul to dwell in and an organ for it to act by, we owe reverence and affection to those who were instrumental in their procreation; but then we must own much more to him who is the Father of our spirits. Our souls are not of a material substance, not of the most refined sort; they are not *ex traduce — by traduction;* to affirm it is bad philosophy, and worse divinity: they are the immediate offspring of God, who, after he had formed the body of man out of the earth, breathed into him a vital spirit, and so he became a living soul. [2.] Our earthly parents *chastened us for their own pleasure.* Sometimes they did it to gratify their passion rather than to reform our manners. This is a weakness the fathers of our flesh are subject to, and this they should carefully watch against; for hereby they dishonour that parental authority which God has put upon them and very much hinder the efficacy of their chastisements. But the Father of our spirits never grieves willingly, nor afflicts the children of men, much less his own children. It is always *for our profit;* and the advantage he intends us thereby is no less than our being partakers of his holiness; it is to correct and cure those sinful disorders which make us unlike to God, and to improve and to increase those graces which are the image of God in us, that we may be and act more like our heavenly Father. God loves his children so that he would have them to be as like himself as can be, and for this end he chastises them when they need it. [3.] The fathers of our flesh corrected us for *a few days,* in our state of childhood, when minors; and, though we were in that weak and peevish state, we owed them reverence, and when we came to maturity we loved and honoured them the more for it. Our whole life here is a state of childhood, minority, and imperfection, and therefore we must submit to the discipline of such a state; when we come to a state of perfection we shall be fully reconciled to all the measures of God's discipline over us now. [4.] God's correction is no condemnation. His children may at first fear lest affliction should come upon that dreadful errand, and we cry, *Do not condemn me,* but *show me wherefore thou contendest with me,* Job 10:2. But this is so far from being the design of God to his own people that he therefore chastens them now *that they may not be condemned with the world,* 1 Co. 11:32. He does it to prevent the death and destruction of their souls, that they may live to God, and be like God, and for ever with him.

5. The children of God, under their afflictions, ought not to judge of his dealings with them by present sense, but by reason, and faith, and experience: *No chastening for the present seemeth to be joyous, but grievous; nevertheless afterwards it yieldeth the peaceable fruits of righteousness, v.* 11. Here observe,

(1.) The judgment of sense in this case — Afflictions are not grateful to the sense, but grievous; the flesh will feel them, and be grieved by them, and groan under them.

(2.) The judgment of faith, which corrects that of sense, and declares that a sanctified affliction produces the fruits of righteousness; these fruits are peaceable, and tend to the quieting and comforting of the soul. Affliction produces peace, by producing more righteousness; for the fruit of righteousness is peace. And if the pain of the body contribute thus to the peace of the mind, and short present affliction produce blessed fruits of a long continuance, they have no reason to fret or faint under it; but their great concern is that the chastening they are under may be endured by them with patience, and improved to a greater degree of holiness. [1.] That their affliction may be endured with patience, which is the main drift of the apostle's discourse on this subject; and he again returns to exhort them that for the reason before mentioned they should *lift up the hands that hang down and the feeble knees, v.* 12. A burden of affliction is apt to make the Christian's hands hang down, and his knees grow feeble, to dispirit him and discourage him; but this he must strive against, and that for two reasons: — *First,* That he may the better run his spiritual race and course. Faith, and patience, and holy courage and resolution, will make him walk more steadily, keep a straighter path, prevent wavering and wandering. *Secondly,* That he may encourage and not dispirit others that are in the same way with him. There are many that are in the way to heaven who yet walk but weakly and lamely in it. Such are apt to discourage one another, and hinder one another; but it is their duty to take courage, and act by faith, and so help one another forward in the way to heaven. [2.] That their affliction may be improved to a greater degree of holiness. Since this is God's design, it ought to be the design and concern of his children, that with renewed strength and patience they may *follow peace with all men, and holiness, v.* 14. If the children of God grow impatient under affliction, they will neither walk so quietly and peaceably towards men, nor so piously towards God, as they should do; but faith and patience will enable them to follow peace and holiness too, as a man follows his calling, constantly, diligently, and with pleasure. Observe, *First,* It is the duty of Christians, even when in a suffering state, *to follow peace with all men,* yea, even with those who may be instrumental in their sufferings. This is a hard lesson, and a high attainment, but it is what Christ has called his people to. Sufferings are apt to sour the spirit and sharpen the passions; but the children of God must follow peace with all men. *Secondly,* Peace and holiness are connected together; there can be no true peace without holiness. There may be prudence and discreet forbearance, and a show of friendship and goodwill to all; but this true Christian peaceableness is never found separate from holiness. We must not, under pretence of living peaceably with all men, leave the ways of holiness, but cultivate peace in a way of holiness. *Thirdly, Without holiness no man shall see the Lord.* The vision of God our Saviour in heaven is reserved as the reward of holiness, and the stress of our salvation is laid upon our holiness, though a placid peaceable disposition contributes much to our meetness for heaven.

6. Where afflictions and sufferings for the sake of Christ are not considered by men as the chastisement of their heavenly Father, and improved as such, they will be a dangerous snare and temptation to apostasy, which every Christian should most carefully watch against (*v.* 15, 16): *Looking diligently lest any man fail of the grace of God,* etc.

(1.) Here the apostle enters a serious caveat against apostasy, and backs it with an awful example.

[1.] He enters a serious caveat against apostasy, *v.* 15. Here you may observe, *First,* The nature of apostasy: it is *failing of the grace of God;* it is to become bankrupts in religion, for want of a good foundation, and suitable care and diligence; it is *failing of the grace of God,* coming short of a principle of true grace in the soul, notwithstanding the means of grace and a profession of religion, and so coming short of the love and favour of God here and hereafter. *Secondly,* The consequences of apostasy: where persons fail of having the true grace of God, a root of bitterness will spring up, corruption will prevail and break forth. A *root of bitterness,* a bitter root, producing bitter fruits to themselves and others. It produces to themselves corrupt principles, which lead to apostasy and are greatly strengthened and radicated by apostasy — damnable errors (to the corrupting of the doctrine and worship of the Christian church) and corrupt practices. Apostates generally grow worse and worse, and fall into the grossest wickedness, which usually ends either in downright atheism or in despair. It also produces bitter fruits to others, to the churches to which these men belonged; by their corrupt principles and practices many are troubled, the peace of the church is broken, the peace of men's minds is disturbed, and *many are defiled,* tainted with those bad principles, and drawn into defiling practices; so that the churches suffer both in their purity and peace. But the apostates themselves will be the greatest sufferers at last.

[2.] The apostle backs the caution with an awful example, and that is, that of Esau, who though born within the pale of the church, and having the birthright as the eldest son, and so entitled to the privilege of being prophet, priest, and king, in his family, was so profane as to despise these sacred privileges, and to sell his birthright for a morsel of meat. Where observe, *First,* Esau's sin. He profanely despised and sold the birthright, and all the advantages attending it. So do apostates, who to avoid persecution, and enjoy sensual ease and pleasure, though they bore the character of the children of God, and had a visible right to the blessing and inheritance, give up all pretensions thereto. *Secondly,* Esau's punishment, which was suitable to his sin. His conscience was convinced of his sin and folly, when it was too late: *He would afterwards have inherited the blessing,* etc. His punishment lay in two things: 1. He was condemned by his own conscience; he now saw that the blessing he had made so light of was worth the having, worth the seeking, though with much carefulness and many tears. 2. He was rejected of God: *He found no place of repentance* in God or in his father; the blessing was given to another, even to him to whom he sold it for a mess of pottage. Esau, in his great wickedness, had made the bargain, and God in his righteous judgment, ratified and confirmed it, and would not suffer Isaac to reverse it.

(2.) We may hence learn, [1.] That apostasy from Christ is the fruit of preferring the gratification of the flesh to the blessing of God and the heavenly inheritance. [2.] Sinners will not always have such mean thoughts of the divine blessing and inheritance as now they have. The time is coming when they will think no pains too great, no cares no tears too much, to obtain the lost blessing. [3.] When the day of grace is over (as sometimes it may be in this life), they will find no place for repentance: they cannot repent aright of their sin; and God will not repent of the sentence he has passed upon them for their sin. And therefore, as the design of all, Christians should never give up their title, and hope of their Father's blessing and inheritance, and expose themselves to his irrevocable wrath and curse, by deserting their holy religion, to avoid suffering, which, though this may be persecution as far as wicked men are concerned in it, is only a rod of correction and chastisement in the hand of their heavenly Father, to bring them near to himself in conformity and communion. This is the force of the apostle's arguing from the nature of the sufferings of the people of God even when they suffer for righteousness' sake; and the reasoning is very strong.

Verses 18–29

Here the apostle goes on to engage the professing Hebrews to perseverance in their Christian course and conflict, and not to relapse again into Judaism. This he does by showing them how much the state of the gospel church differs from that of the Jewish church, and how much it resembles the state of the church in heaven, and on both accounts demands and deserves our diligence, patience, and perseverance in Christianity.

I. He shows how much the gospel church differs from the Jewish church, and how much it excels. And here we have a very particular description of the state of the church under the Mosaic dispensation, *v.* 18–21. 1. It was a gross sensible state. Mount Sinai, on which that church-state was constituted, was a *mount that might be touched* (*v.* 18), a gross palpable place; so was the dispensation. It was very much external and earthly, and so more heavy. The state of the gospel church on mount Zion is more spiritual, rational, and easy. 2. It was a dark dispensation. Upon that mount there were blackness and darkness, and that church-state was covered with dark shadows and types: the gospel state is much more clear and bright. 3. It was a dreadful and terrible dispensation; the Jews could not bear the terror of it. The thunder and the lightning, the trumpet sounding, the voice of God himself speaking to them, struck them with such dread that they *entreated that the word might not be so spoken to them any more, v.* 19. Yea, Moses himself said, *I exceedingly fear and quake.* The best of men on earth are not able to converse immediately with God and his holy angels. The gospel state is mild, and kind, and condescending, suited to our weak frame. 4. It was a limited dispensation; all might not approach to that mount, but only Moses and Aaron. Under the gospel we have all access with boldness to God. 5. It was a very dangerous dispensation. The mount burned with fire, and whatever man or beast touched the mount must *be stoned, or thrust through with a dart, v.* 20. It is true, it will be always dangerous for presumptuous and brutish sinners to draw night to God; but it is not immediate and certain death, as here it was. This was the state of the Jewish church, fitted to awe a stubborn and hard-hearted people, to set forth the strict and tremendous justice of God, to wean the people of God from that dispensation, and induce them more readily to embrace the sweet and gentle economy of the gospel church, and adhere to it.

II. He shows how much the gospel church represents the church triumphant in heaven, what communication there is between the one and the other. The gospel church is called *mount Zion, the heavenly Jerusalem, which is free,* in opposition to mount Sinai, which tendeth to bondage, Gal. 4:24. This was the hill on which God set his king the Messiah. Now, in coming to mount Zion, believers come into heavenly places, and into a heavenly society.

1. Into heavenly places. (1.) *Unto the city of the living God.* God has taken up his gracious residence in the gospel church, which on that account is an emblem of heaven. There his people may find him ruling, guiding, sanctifying, and comforting them; there he speaks to them by the gospel ministry; there they speak to him by prayer, and he hears them; there he trains them up for heaven, and gives them the earnest of their inheritance. (2.) To *the heavenly Jerusalem* as born and bred there, as free denizens there. Here believers have clearer views of heaven, plainer evidences for heaven, and a greater meetness and more heavenly temper of soul.

2. To a heavenly society. (1.) *To an innumerable company of angels,* who are of the same family with the saints, under the same head, and in a great measure employed in the same work, ministering to believers for their good, keeping them in all their ways, and pitching their tents about them. These for number are innumerable, and for order and union are a company, and a glorious one. And those who by faith are joined to the gospel church are joined to the angels, and shall at length be like them, and equal with them. (2.) *To the general assembly and church of the first-born, that are written in heaven,* that is, to the universal church, however dispersed. By faith we come to them, have communion with them in the same head, by the same Spirit, and in the same blessed hope, and walk in the same way of holiness, grappling with the same spiritual enemies, and hasting to the same rest, victory, and glorious triumph. Here will be the general assembly of the first-born, the saints of former and earlier times, who saw the promises of the gospel state, but received them not, as well as those who first received them under the gospel, and were regenerated thereby, and so were the first-born, and the first-fruits of the gospel church; and thereby, as the first-born, advanced to greater honours and privileges than the rest of the world. Indeed all the children of God are heirs, and every one has the privileges of the first-born. The names of these are written in heaven, in the records of the church here: they have a name in God's house, are written among the living in Jerusalem; they have a good repute for their faith and fidelity, and are enrolled in the Lamb's book of life, as citizens are enrolled in the livery-books. (3.) *To God the Judge of all,* that great God who will judge both Jew and Gentile according to the law they are under: believers come to him now by faith, make supplication to their Judge, and receive a sentence of absolution in the gospel, and in the court of their consciences now, by which they know they shall be justified hereafter. (4.) *To the spirits of just men made perfect;* to the best sort of men, the righteous, who are more excellent than their neighbours; to the best part of just men, their spirits, and to these in their best state, made perfect. Believers have union with departed saints in one and the same head and Spirit, and a title to the same inheritance, of which those on earth are heirs, those in heaven possessors. (5.) *To Jesus the Mediator of the new covenant, and to the blood of sprinkling, that speaketh better things than that of Abel.* This is none of the least of many encouragements there are to perseverance in the gospel state, since it is a state of communion with Christ the Mediator of the new covenant, and of communication of his blood, that speaketh better things than the blood of Abel. [1.] The gospel covenant is the new covenant, distinct from the covenant of works; and it is now under a new dispensation, distinct from that of the Old Testament. [2.] Christ is the Mediator of this new covenant; he is the middle person that goes between both parties, God and man, to bring them together in this covenant, to keep them together notwithstanding the sins of the people and God's displeasure against them for sin, to offer up our prayers to God, and to bring down the favours of God to us, to plead with God for us and to plead with us for God, and at length to bring God and his people together in heaven, and to be a Mediator of fruition between them for ever, they beholding and enjoying God in Christ and God beholding and blessing them in Christ. [3.] This covenant is ratified by the blood of Christ sprinkled upon our consciences, as the blood of the sacrifice was sprinkled upon the altar and the sacrifice. This blood of Christ pacifies God and purifies the consciences of men. [4.] This is speaking blood, and it speaks better things than that of Abel. *First,* It speaks to God in behalf of sinners; it pleads not for vengeance, as the blood of Abel did on him who shed it, but for mercy. *Secondly,* To sinners, in the name of God. It speaks pardon to their sins, peace to their souls; and bespeaks their strictest obedience and highest love and thankfulness.

III. The apostle, having thus enlarged upon the argument to perseverance taken from the heavenly nature of the gospel church state, closes the chapter by improving the argument in a manner suitable to the weight of it (*v.* 25, etc.): *See then that you refuse not him that speaketh* — that speaketh by his blood; and not only speaketh after another manner than the blood of Abel spoke from the ground, but than God spoke by the angels, and by Moses spoke on mount Sinai; then he spoke on earth, now he speaks from heaven. Here observe,

1. When God speaks to men in the most excellent manner he justly expects from them the most strict attention and regard. Now it is in the gospel that God speaks to men in the most excellent manner. For, (1.) He now speaks from a higher and more glorious seat and throne, not from mount Sinai, which was on this earth, but from heaven. (2.) He speaks now more immediately by his inspired word and by his Spirit, which are his witnesses. He speaks not now any new thing to men, but by his Spirit speaks the same word home to the conscience. (3.) He speaks now more powerfully and effectually. Then indeed his voice shook the earth, but now, by introducing the gospel state, he hath shaken not only the earth, but the heavens, — not only shaken the hills and mountains, or the spirits of men, or the civil state of the land of Canaan, to make room for his people, — not only shaken the world, as he then did, but he hath shaken the church, that is, the Jewish nation, and shaken them in their church-state, which was in Old-Testament times a heaven upon earth; this their heavenly spiritual state he hath now shaken. It is by the gospel from heaven that God shook to pieces the civil and ecclesiastical state of the Jewish nation, and introduced a new state of the church, that cannot be removed, shall never be changed for any other on earth, but shall remain till it be made perfect in heaven.

2. When God speaks to men in the most excellent manner, the guilt of those who refuse him is the greater, and their punishment will be more unavoidable and intolerable; there is no escaping, no bearing it, *v.* 25. The different manner of God's dealing with men under the gospel, in a way of grace, assures us that he will deal with the despisers of the gospel after a different manner than he does with other men, in a way of judgment. The glory of the gospel, which should greatly recommend it to our regard, appears in these three things: — (1.) It was by the sound of the gospel trumpet that the former dispensation and state of the church of God were shaken

and removed; and shall we despise that voice of God that pulled down a church and state of so long standing and of God's own building? (2.) It was by the sound of the gospel trumpet that a new kingdom was erected for God in the world, which can never be so shaken as to be removed. This was a change made once for all; no other change shall take place *till time shall be no more.* We have now *received a kingdom that cannot be moved,* shall never be removed, never give way to any new dispensation. The canon of scripture is now perfected, *the Spirit of prophecy has ceased,* the mystery of God is finished, he has put his last hand to it. The gospel church may be made more large, more prosperous more purified from contracted pollution, but it shall never be altered for another dispensation; those who perish under the gospel perish without remedy. And hence the apostle justly concludes, [1.] How necessary it is for us to obtain *grace from God, to serve him acceptably:* if we be not accepted of God under this dispensation, we shall never be accepted at all; and we lose all our labour in religion if we be not accepted of God. [2.] We cannot worship God acceptably, unless we worship him with *godly reverence and fear.* As faith, so holy fear, is necessary to acceptable worship. [3.] It is only the grace of God that enables us to worship God in a right manner: nature cannot come up to it; it can produce neither that precious faith nor that holy fear that is necessary to acceptable worship. [4.] God is the same just and righteous God under the gospel that he appeared to be under the law. Though he be our God in Christ, and now deals with us in a more kind and gracious way, yet he is in himself a consuming fire; that is, a God of strict justice, who will avenge himself on all the despisers of his grace, and upon all apostates. Under the gospel, the justice of God is displayed in a more awful manner, though not in so sensible a manner as under the law; for here we behold divine justice seizing upon the Lord Jesus Christ, and making him a propitiatory sacrifice, his soul and body an offering for sin, which is a display of justice far beyond what was seen and heard on mount Sinai when the law was given.

CHAPTER 13

The apostle, having treated largely of Christ, and faith, and free grace, and gospel privileges, and warned the Hebrews against apostasy, now, in the close of all, recommends several excellent duties to them, as the proper fruits of faith (*v.* 1–17); he then bespeaks their prayers for him, and offers up his prayers to God for them, gives them some hope of seeing himself and Timothy, and ends with the general salutation and benediction (*v.* 18 to the end).

Verses 1–17

The design of Christ in giving himself for us is that he may purchase *to himself a peculiar people, zealous of good works.* Now the apostle calls the believing Hebrews to the performance of many excellent duties, in which it becomes Christians to excel.

I. To brotherly love (*v.* 1), by which he does not only mean a general affection to all men, as our brethren by nature, all made of the same blood, nor that more limited affection which is due to those who are of the same immediate parents, but that special and spiritual affection which ought to exist among the children of God. 1. It is here supposed that the Hebrews had this love one for another. Though, at this time, that nation was miserably divided and distracted among themselves, both about matters of religion and the civil state, yet there was true brotherly love left among those of them who believed on Christ; and this appeared in a very eminent manner presently after the shedding forth of the Holy Ghost, when they had all things common, and sold their possessions to make a general fund of subsistence to their brethren. The spirit of Christianity is a spirit of love. Faith works by love. The true religion is the strongest bond of friendship; if it be not so, it has its name for nothing. 2. This brotherly love was in danger of being lost, and that in a time of persecution, when it would be most necessary; it was in danger of being lost by those disputes that were among them concerning the respect they ought still to have to the ceremonies of the Mosaic law. Disputes about religion too often produce a decay of Christian affection; but this must be guarded against, and all proper means used to preserve brotherly love. Christians should always love and live as brethren, and the more they grow in devout affection to God their heavenly Father the more they will grow in love to one another for his sake.

II. To hospitality: *Be not forgetful to entertain strangers*

for his sake, *v.* 2. We must add to brotherly kindness charity. Here observe, 1. The duty required — *to entertain strangers,* both those that are strangers to the commonwealth of Israel, and strangers to our persons, especially those who know themselves to be strangers here and are seeking another country, which is the case of the people of God, and was so at this time: the believing Jews were in a desperate and distressed condition. But he seems to speak of strangers as such; though we know not who they are, nor whence they come, yet, seeing they are without any certain dwelling place, we should allow them room in our hearts and in our houses, as we have opportunity and ability. 2. The motive: *Thereby some have entertained angels unawares;* so Abraham did (Gen. 18) and Lot (Gen. 19), and one of those that Abraham entertained was the Son of God; and, though we cannot suppose this will ever be our case, yet what we do to strangers, in obedience to him, he will reckon and reward as done to himself. Mt. 25:35, *I was a stranger, and you took me in.* God has often bestowed honours and favours upon his hospitable servants, beyond all their thoughts, *unawares.*

III. To Christian sympathy: *Remember those that are in bonds, v.* 3. Here observe,

1. The duty — to *remember those that are in bonds* and in *adversity.* (1.) God often orders it so that while some Christians and churches are in adversity others enjoy peace and liberty. All are not called at the same time to resist unto blood. (2.) Those that are themselves at liberty must sympathize with those that are in bonds and adversity, as if they were bound with them in the same chain: they must fell the sufferings of their brethren.

2. The reason of the duty: *As being yourselves in the body;* not only in the body natural, and so liable to the like sufferings, and you should sympathize with them now that others may sympathize with you when your time of trial comes; but in the same mystical body, under the same head, *and if one member suffer all the rest suffer with it,* 1 Co. 12:26. It would be unnatural in Christians not to bear each other's burdens.

IV. To purity and chastity, *v.* 4. Here you have, 1. A recommendation of God's ordinance of marriage, that it *is honourable in all,* and ought to be so esteemed by all, and not denied to those to whom God has not denied it. It is honourable, for God instituted it for man in paradise, knowing it was not good for him to be alone. He married and blessed the first couple, the first parents of mankind, to direct all to look unto God in that great concern, and to marry in the Lord. Christ honoured marriage with his presence and first miracle. It is honourable as a means to prevent impurity and a defiled bed. It is *honourable* and happy, when persons come together pure and chaste, and preserve the marriage bed undefiled, not only from unlawful but inordinate affections. 2. A dreadful but just censure of impurity and lewdness: *Whoremongers and adulterers God will judge.* (1.) God knows who are guilty of such sins, no darkness can hide them from him. (2.) He will call such sins by their proper names, not by the names of love and gallantry, but of whoredom and adultery, whoredom in the single state and adultery in the married state. (3.) He will bring them into judgment, he will judge them, either by their own consciences here, and *set their sins in order before them* for their deep humiliation (and conscience, when awakened, will be very severe upon such sinners), or he will set them at his tribunal at death, and in the last day; he will convict them, condemn them, and cast them out for ever, if they die under the guilt of this sin.

V. To Christian contentment, *v.* 5, 6. Here observe, 1. The sin that is contrary to this grace and duty — *covetousness,* an over eager desire of the wealth of this world, envying those who have more than we. This sin we must allow no place in our conversation; for, though it be a secret lust lurking in the heart, if it be not subdued it will enter into our conversation, and discover itself in our manner of speaking and acting. We must take care not only to keep this sin down, but to root it out of our souls. 2. The duty and grace that is contrary to covetousness — being satisfied and pleased *with such things as we have;* present things, for past things cannot be recalled, and future things are only in the hand of God. What God gives us from day to day we must be content with, though it fall short of what we have enjoyed heretofore, and though it do not come up to our expectations for the future. We must be content with our present lot. We must bring our minds to our present condition, and this is the sure way to contentment; and those who cannot do it would not be con-

tented though God should raise their condition to their minds, for the mind would rise with the condition. Haman was the great court-favourite, and yet not contented — Ahab on the throne, and yet not contented — Adam in paradise, and yet not contented; yea, the angels in heaven, and yet not contented; but Paul, though abased and empty, had *learned in every state, in* any *state, therewith to be content.* 3. What reason Christians have to be contented with their lot. (1.) *God hath said, I will never leave thee, nor forsake thee, v.* 5, 6. This was said to Joshua (*ch.* 1:5), but belongs to all the faithful servants of God. Old-Testament promises may be applied to New-Testament saints. This promise contains the sum and substance of all the promises. *I will never, no, never leave thee, nor ever forsake thee.* Here are no fewer than five negatives heaped together, to confirm the promise; the true believer shall have the gracious presence of God with him in life, at death, and for ever. (2.) From this comprehensive promise they may assure themselves of help from God: *So that we may boldly say, The Lord is my helper; I will not fear what man shall do unto me, v.* 6. Men can do nothing against God, and God can make all that men do against his people to turn to their good.

VI. To the duty Christians owe to their ministers, and that both to those that are dead and to those that are yet alive.

1. To those that are dead: *Remember those that have had the rule over you, v.* 7. Here observe,

(1.) The description given of them. They were such as had the rule over them, and had spoken to them the word of God; their guides and governors, who had spoken to them the word of God. Here is the dignity to which they were advanced — to be rulers and leaders of the people, not according to their own will, but the will and word of God; and this character they filled up with suitable duty: they did not rule at a distance, and rule by others, but they ruled by personal presence and instruction, according to the word of God.

(2.) The duties owing to them, even when they were dead. [1.] *"Remember them* — their preaching, their praying, their private counsel, their example."

[2.] *"Follow their faith;* be stedfast in the profession of the faith they preached to you, and labour after the grace of faith by which they lived and died so well. *Consider the end of their conversation,* how quickly, how comfortably, how joyfully, they finished their course!" Now this duty of following the same true faith in which they had been instructed the apostle enlarges much upon, and presses them earnestly to it, not only from the remembrance of their faithful deceased guides, but from several other motives.

First, From the immutability and eternity of the Lord Jesus Christ. Though their ministers were some dead, others dying, yet the great head and high priest of the church, *the bishop of their souls,* ever lives, and is ever the same; and they should be stedfast and immovable, in imitation of Christ, and should remember that Christ ever lives to observe and reward their faithful adherence to his truths, and to observe and punish their sinful departure from him. Christ is the same in the Old-Testament day, in the gospel day, and will be so to his people for ever.

Secondly, From the nature and tendency of those erroneous doctrines that they were in danger of falling in with.

a. They were divers and various (*v.* 9), different from what they had received from their former faithful teachers, and inconsistent with themselves.

b. They were strange doctrines: such as the gospel church was unacquainted with foreign to the gospel.

c. They were of an unsettling, distracting nature, like the wind by which the ship is tossed, and in danger of being driven from its anchor, carried away, and split upon the rocks. They were quite contrary to that grace of God which fixes and establishes the heart, which is an excellent thing. These strange doctrines keep the heart always fluctuating and unsettled.

d. They were mean and low as to their subject. They were about external, little, perishing things, such as *meats and drinks,* etc.

e. They were unprofitable. Those who were most taken with them, and employed about them, got no real good by them to their own souls. They did not make them more holy, nor more humble, nor more thankful, nor more heavenly.

f. They would exclude those who embraced them from the privileges of the Christian altar (*v.* 10): *We have an altar.* This is an argument of the great weight, and therefore the apostle insists the longer upon it. Observe, (*a.*) The Christian church has its altar. It was objected against the primitive Christians that their assemblies were destitute of an altar; but this was not true. *We have an alter,* not a material altar, but a personal one, and that is Christ; he is both our altar, and our sacrifice; he sanctifies the gift. The altars under the law were types of Christ; the brazen altar of the sacrifice, the golden altar of his intercession.

(*b.*) This altar furnishes out a feast for true believers, a feast upon the sacrifice, a *feast of fat things,* spiritual strength and growth, and holy delight and pleasure. The Lord's table is not our altar, but it is furnished with provision from the altar. *Christ our passover is sacrificed for us* (1 Co. 5:7), and it follows, *therefore let us keep the feast.* The Lord's supper is the feast of the gospel passover.

(*c.*) Those who adhere to the tabernacle or the Levitical dispensation, or return to it again, exclude themselves from the privileges of this altar, from the benefits purchased by Christ. If they serve the tabernacle, they are resolved to subject themselves to antiquated rites and ceremonies, to renounce their right to the Christian altar; and this part of the argument he first proves and then improves.

[*a.*] He proves that this servile adherence to the Jewish state is a bar to the privileges of the gospel altar; and he argues thus: — Under the Jewish law, no part of the sin-offering was to be eaten, but all must be burnt without the camp while they dwelt in tabernacles, and without the gates when they dwelt in cities: now, if they will still be subject to that law, they cannot eat at the gospel-altar; for that which is eaten there is furnished from Christ, who is the great sin-offering. Not that it is the very sin-offering itself, as the papists affirm; for then it was not to be eaten, but burnt; but the gospel feast is the fruit and procurement of the sacrifice, which those have no right to who do not acknowledge the sacrifice itself. And that it might appear that Christ was really the antitype of the sin-offering, and, as such, might sanctify or cleanse his people with his own blood, he conformed himself to the type, in suffering without the gate. This was a striking specimen of his humiliation, as if he had not been fit either for sacred or civil society! And this shows how sin, which was the meritorious cause of the sufferings of Christ, is a forfeiture of all sacred and civil rights, and the sinner a common plague and nuisance to all society, if God should be strict to mark iniquity. Having thus shown that adherence to the Levitical law would, even according to its own rules, debar men from the Christian altar, he proceeds,

[*b.*] To improve this argument (*v.* 13–15) in suitable advices. *First, Let us go forth therefore unto him without the camp;* go forth from the ceremonial law, from sin, from the world, from ourselves, our very bodies, when he calls us. *Secondly,* Let us be willing to *bear his reproach,* be willing to be accounted the offscouring of all things, not worthy to live, not worthy to die a common death. This was his reproach, and we must submit to it; and we have the more reason because, whether we go forth from this world to Christ or no, we must necessarily go forth in a little time by death; for *here we have no continuing city.* Sin, sinners, death, will not suffer us to continue long here; and therefore we should go forth now by faith, and seek in Christ the rest and settlement which this world cannot afford us, *v.* 14. *Thirdly,* Let us make a right use of this altar; not only partake of the privileges of it, but discharge the duties of the altar, as those whom Christ has made priests to attend on this altar. Let us bring our sacrifices to this altar, and to this our high priest, and offer them up by him, *v.* 15, 16. Now what are the sacrifices which we must bring and offer on this altar, even Christ? Not any expiatory sacrifices; there is no need of them. Christ has offered the great *sacrifice of atonement,* ours are only the sacrifices of acknowledgment; and they are, 1. The sacrifice of praise to God, which we should offer up to God continually. In this are included all adoration and prayer, as well as thanksgiving; this is *the fruit of our lips;* we must speak forth the praises of God from unfeigned lips; and this must be offered only to God, not to angels, nor saints, nor any creature, but to the name of God alone; and it must be by Christ, in a dependence upon his meritorious satisfaction and intercession. 2. The sacrifice of alms-deeds, and Christian charity: *To do good, and to communicate, forget now; for with such sacrifices God is well pleased, v.* 16. We must, according to our power, *communicate* to the necessities of the souls and bodies of men; not contenting ourselves to offer the sacrifice of our lips, mere words, but the sacrifice of good deeds; and these we must lay down upon this altar, not depending upon the merit of our good deeds, but of our great high priest; and with such sacrifices as these, adoration and alms thus offered up, God is well pleased; he will accept the offering with pleasure, and will accept and bless the offers through Christ.

2. Having thus told us the duty Christians owe to their deceased ministers, which principally consists in following their faith and not departing from it, the apostle tells us what is the duty that people owe to their living ministers (*v.* 17) and the reasons of that duty: (1.) The duty — to obey them, and submit themselves to them. It is not an implicit obedience, or absolute submission, that is here required, but only so far as is agreeable to the mind and will of God revealed in his word; and yet it is truly obedience and submission, and that not only to God, but to the authority of the ministerial office, which is of God as certainly, in all things belonging to that office, as the authority of parents or of civil magistrates in the things within their sphere. Christians must submit to be instructed by their ministers, and not think themselves too wise, too good, or too great, to learn from them; and, when they find that ministerial instructions are agreeable to the written word, they must obey them. (2.) The motives to this duty. [1.] They have the rule over the people; their office, though not magisterial, yet is truly authoritative. They have no authority to lord it over the people, but to lead them in the ways of God, by informing and instructing them, explaining the word of God to them, and applying it to their several cases. They are not to make laws of their own, but to interpret the laws of God; nor is their interpretation to be immediately received without examination, but the people must search the scriptures, and so far as the instructions of their minister are according to that rule they ought to receive them, *not as the word of men, but, as they are indeed, the word of God, that works effectually in those that believe.* [2.] They watch for the souls of the people, not to ensnare them, but to save them; to gain them, not to themselves, but to Christ; to build them up in knowledge, faith, and holiness. They are to watch against every thing that may be hurtful to the souls of men, and to give them warning of dangerous errors, of the devices of Satan, of approaching judgments; they are to watch for all opportunities of helping the souls of men forward in the way to heaven. [3.] They must give an account how they have discharged their duty, and what has become of the souls committed to their trust, whether any have been lost through their neglect, and whether any of them have been brought in and built up under their ministry. [4.] They would be glad to give a good account of themselves and their hearers. If they can then give in an account of their own fidelity and success, it will be a joyful day to them; those souls that have been converted and confirmed under their ministry *will be their joy, and their crown, in the day of the Lord Jesus.* [5.] If they give up their account with grief, it will be the people's loss as well as theirs. It is the interest of hearers that the account their ministers give of them may be with joy, and not with grief. If faithful ministers be not successful, the grief will be theirs, but the loss will be the people's. Faithful ministers have delivered their own souls, but a fruitless and faithless people's blood and ruin will be upon their own heads.

Verses 18–25

Here, I. The apostle recommends himself, and his fellow-sufferers, to the prayers of the Hebrew believers (*v.* 18): *"Pray for us;* for me and Timothy" (mentioned *v.* 23), "and for all those of us who labour in the ministry of the gospel."

1. This is one part of the duty which people owe to their ministers. Ministers need the prayers of the people; and the more earnestly the people pray for their ministers the more benefit they may expect to reap from their ministry. They should pray that God would teach those who are to teach them, that he would make them vigilant, and wise, and zealous, and successful — that he would assist them in all their labours, support them under all their burdens, and strengthen them under all their temptations.

2. There are good reasons why people should pray for their ministers; he mentions two: —

(1.) *We trust we have a good conscience,* etc., *v.* 18. Many of the Jews had a bad opinion of Paul, because he, being a Hebrew of the Hebrews, had cast off the Levitical law and preached up Christ: now he here modestly asserts his own integrity: *We trust we have a good conscience, in all things willing to live honestly. We trust!* he might have said, *We know;* but he chose to speak in a humble style, to teach us all not to be too confident of ourselves, but to maintain a godly jealousy over our own hearts. "We trust we have a *good conscience,* an enlightened and well-informed conscience, a clean and pure conscience, a tender and faithful conscience, a conscience testifying for us, not against us: a good conscience *in all things,* in the duties both of the first and second table, towards God and towards men, and especially in all things pertaining to our ministry; we would act honestly and sincerely in all things." Observe, [1.] A good conscience has a respect to all God's commands and all our duty. [2.] Those who have this good conscience, yet need the prayers of others. [3.] Conscientious ministers are public blessings, and deserve the prayers of the people.

(2.) Another reason why he desires their prayers is that he hoped thereby to be the sooner restored to them (*v.* 19), intimating that he had been formerly among them, — that, now he was absent from them, he had a great desire and real intention to come again to them, — and that the best way to facilitate his return to them, and to make it a mercy to him and them, was to make it a matter of their prayer. When ministers come to a people as a return of prayer, they come with greater satisfaction to themselves and success to the people. We should fetch in all our mercies by prayer.

II. He offers up his prayers to God for them, being willing to do for them as he desired they should do for him: *Now the God of peace,* etc., *v.* 20. In this excellent prayer observe, 1. The title given to God — *the God of peace,* who was found out a way for peace and reconciliation between himself and sinners, and who loves peace on earth and especially in his churches. 2. The great work ascribed to him: *He hath brought again from the dead our Lord Jesus,* etc. Jesus raised himself by his own power; and yet the Father was concerned in it, attesting thereby that justice was satisfied and the law fulfilled. He rose again for our justification; and that divine power by which he was raised is able to do every thing for us that we stand in need of. 3. The titles given to Christ — our Lord Jesus, our sovereign, our Saviour, and the great shepherd of the sheep, promised in Isa. 40:11, declared by himself to be so, Jn. 10:14, 15. Ministers are under-shepherds, Christ is the great shepherd. This denotes his interest in his people. They are the flock of his pasture, and his care and concern are for them. He feeds them, and leads them, and watches over them. 4. The way and method in which God is reconciled, and Christ raised from the dead: *Through the blood of the everlasting covenant.* The blood of Christ satisfied divine justice, and so procured Christ's release from the prison of the grace, as having paid our debt, according to an eternal covenant or agreement between the Father and the Son; and this blood is the sanction and seal of an everlasting covenant between God and his people. 5. The mercy prayed for: *Make you perfect in every good work,* etc., *v.* 21. Observe, (1.) The perfection of the saints in every good work is the great thing desired by them and for them, that they may here have a perfection of integrity, a clear mind, a clean heart, lively affections, regular and resolved wills, and suitable strength for every good work to which they are called now, and at length a perfection of degrees to fit them for the employment and felicity of heaven. (2.) The way in which God makes his people perfect; it is by working in them always what is pleasing in his sight, and that *through Jesus Christ, to whom be glory for ever.* Observe, [1.] There is no good thing wrought in us but it is the work of God; he works in us, before we are fit for any good work. [2.] No good thing is wrought in us by God, but through Jesus Christ, for his sake and by his Spirit. And therefore, [3.] Eternal glory is due to him, who is the cause of all the good principles wrought in us and all the good works done by us. To this every one should say, *Amen.*

III. He gives the Hebrews an account of Timothy's liberty and his hopes of seeing them with him in a little time, *v.* 23. It seems, Timothy had been a prisoner, doubtless for the gospel, but now he was set at liberty. The imprisonment of faithful ministers is an honour to them, and their enlargement is matter of joy to the people. He was pleased with the hopes of not only seeing Timothy, but seeing the Hebrews with him. Opportunities of writing to the churches of Christ are desired by the faithful ministers of Christ, and pleasant to them.

IV. Having given a brief account of this his letter, and begged their attention to it (*v.* 22), he closes with salutations, and a solemn, though short benediction.

1. The salutation. (1.) From himself to them, directed to all their ministers who had rule over them, and to all the

saints; to them all, ministers and people. (2.) From the Christians in Italy to them. It is a good thing to have the law of holy love and kindness written in the hearts of Christians one towards another. Religion teaches men the truest civility and good-breeding. It is not a sour nor morose thing.

2. The solemn, though short benediction (*v.* 25): *Grace be with you all. Amen.* Let the favour of God be towards you, and his grace continually working in you, and with you, bringing forth the fruits of holiness, as the first-fruits of glory. When the people of God have been conversing together by word or writing, it is good to part with prayer, desiring for each other the continuance of the gracious presence of God, that they may meet together again in the world of praise.

AN EXPOSITION, WITH PRACTICAL OBSERVATIONS, OF
THE GENERAL EPISTLE OF JAMES

The writer of this epistle was not James the son of Zebedee; for he was put to death by Herod (Acts 12) before Christianity had gained so much ground among the Jews of the dispersion as is here implied. But it was the other James, the son of Alpheus, who was cousin-german to Christ, and one of the twelve apostles, Mt. 10:3. He is called *a pillar* (Gal. 2:9), and this epistle of his cannot be disputed, without loosening a foundation-stone. It is called a general epistle, because (as some think) not directed to any particular person or church, but such a one as we call a circular letter. Others think it is called general, or catholic, to distinguish it from the epistles of Ignatius, Barnabas, Polycarp, and others who were noted in the primitive times, but not generally received in the church, and on that account not canonical, as this is. Eusebius tells us that this epistle was "generally read in the churches with the other catholic epistles." His. Eccles. page 53. Ed. Val. Anno 1678. James, our author, was called the just, for his great piety. He was an eminent example of those graces which he presses upon others. He was so exceedingly revered for his justice, temperance, and devotion, that Josephus the Jewish historian records it as one of the causes of the destruction of Jerusalem, "That St. James was martyred in it." This is mentioned in hopes of procuring the greater regard to what is penned by so holy and excellent a man. The time when this epistle was written is uncertain. The design of it is to reprove Christians for their great degeneracy both in faith and manners, and to prevent the spreading of those libertine doctrines which threatened the destruction of all practical godliness. It was also a special intention of the author of this epistle to awaken the Jewish nation to a sense of the greatness and nearness of those judgments which were coming upon them; and to support all true Christians in the way of their duty, under the calamities and persecutions they might meet with. The truths laid down are very momentous, and necessary to be maintained; and the rules for practice, as here stated, are such as ought to be observed in our times as well as in preceding ages.

CHAPTER 1

After the inscription and salutation (*v.* 1) Christians are taught how to conduct themselves when under the cross. Several graces and duties are recommended; and those who endure their trials and afflictions as the apostle here directs are pronounced blessed and are assured of a glorious reward (*v.* 2–12). But those sins which bring sufferings, or the weakness and faults men are chargeable with under them, are by no means to be imputed to God, who cannot be the author of sin, but is the author of all good (*v.* 13–18). All passion, and rash anger, and vile affections, ought to be suppressed. The word of God should be made our chief study: and what we hear and know of it we must take care to practise, otherwise our religion will prove but a vain thing. To this is added an account wherein pure religion consists (*v.* 19–27).

Verse 1

We have here the inscription of this epistle, which consists of three principal parts.

I. The character by which our author desires to be known: *James, a servant of God, and of the Lord Jesus Christ.* Though he was a prime-minister in Christ's kingdom, yet he styles himself only a servant. Note hence, Those who are highest in office or attainments in the church of Christ are but servants. They should not therefore act as masters, but as ministers. Further, Though James is called by the evangelist *the brother of our Lord,* yet it was his glory to serve Christ in the spirit, rather than to boast of his being akin according to the flesh. Hence let us learn to prize this title above all others in the world — *the servants of God and of Christ.* Again, it is to be observed that James professes himself *a servant of God and of the Lord Jesus Christ;* to teach us that in all services we should have an eye to the Son as well as the Father. We cannot acceptably serve the Father, unless we are also servants of the Son. God will have *all men to honour the Son as they honour the Father* (Jn. 5:23), looking for acceptance in Christ and assistance from him, and yielding all obedience to him, thus confessing *that Jesus Christ is Lord, to the glory of God the Father.*

II. The apostle here mentions the condition of those to whom he writes: *The twelve tribes which are scattered abroad.* Some understand this of the dispersion upon the persecution of Stephen, Acts 8. But that only reached to Judea and Samaria. Others by the Jews of the dispersion understand those who were in Assyria, Babylon, Egypt, and other kingdoms into which their wars had driven them. The greatest part indeed of ten of the twelve tribes were lost in captivity; but yet some of every tribe were preserved and they are still honoured with the ancient style of *twelve tribes.* These however were scattered and dispersed. 1. They were dispersed in mercy. Having the scriptures of the Old Testament, the providence of God so ordered it that they were scattered in several countries for the diffusing of the light of divine revelation. 2. They began now to be scattered in wrath. The Jewish nation was crumbling into parties and factions, and many were forced to leave their own country, as having now grown too hot for them. Even good people among them shared in the common calamity. 3. These Jews of the dispersion were those who had embraced the Christian faith. They were persecuted and forced to seek for shelter in other countries, the Gentiles being kinder to Christians than the Jews were. Note here, It is often the lot even of God's own tribes to be scattered abroad. The gathering day is reserved for the end of time; when all the dispersed children of God shall be gathered together to Christ their head. In the mean time, while God's tribes are scattered abroad, he will send to look after them. Here is an apostle writing to the scattered; an epistle from God to them, when driven away from his temple, and seemingly neglected by him. Apply here that of the prophet Ezekiel, *Thus saith the Lord God, Although I have cast them far off among the heathen, and although I have scattered them among the countries, yet will I be to them as a little sanctuary in the countries where they shall come,* Eze. 11:16. God has a particular care of his outcasts. *Let my outcasts dwell with thee, Moab,* Isa. 16:3, 4. God's tribes may be scattered; therefore we should not value ourselves too much on outward privileges. And, on the other hand, we should not despond and think ourselves rejected, under outward calamities, because God remembers and sends comfort to his scattered people.

III. James here shows the respect he had even for the dispersed: *greeting,* saluting them, wishing peace and salvation to them. True Christians should not be the less valued for their hardships. It was the desire of this apostle's heart that those who were scattered might be comforted — that they might do well and fare well, and be enabled to rejoice even in their distresses. God's people have reason to rejoice in all places, and at all times; as will abundantly appear from what follows.

Verses 2–12

We now come to consider the matter of this epistle. In this paragraph we have the following things to be observed: —

I. The suffering state of Christians in this world is represented, and that in a very instructive manner, if we attend to what is plainly and necessarily implied, together with what is fully expressed. 1. It is implied that troubles and afflictions may be the lot of the best Christians, even of those who have the most reason to think and hope well of themselves. Such as have a title to the greatest joy may yet endure very grievous afflictions. As good people are liable to be scattered, they must not think it strange if they meet with troubles. 2. These outward afflictions and troubles are temptations to them. The devil endeavours by sufferings and crosses to draw men to sin and to deter them from duty, or unfit them for it; but, as our afflictions are in God's hand, they are intended for the trial and improvement of our graces. The gold is put into the furnace, that it may be purified. 3. These temptations may be numerous and various: *Divers temptations,* as the apostle speaks. Our trials may be of many and different kinds, and therefore we have need to put on the whole armour of God. We must be armed on every side, because temptations lie on all sides. 4. The trials of a good man are such as he does not create to himself, nor sinfully pull upon himself; but they are such as he is said to fall into. And for this reason they are the better borne by him.

II. The graces and duties of a state of trial and affliction are here pointed out to us. Could we attend to these things, and grow in them as we should do, how good would it be for us to be afflicted!

1. One Christian grace to be exercised is joy: *Count it all joy, v.* 2. We must not sink into a sad and disconsolate frame of mind, which would make us faint under our trials; but must endeavour to keep our spirits dilated and enlarged, the better to take in a true sense of our case, and with greater advantage to set ourselves to make the best of it. Philosophy may instruct men to be calm under their troubles; but Christianity teaches them to be joyful, because such exercises proceed from love and not fury in God. In them we are conformable to Christ our head, and they become marks of our adoption. By suffering in the ways of righteousness, we are serving the interests of our Lord's kingdom among men, and edifying the body of Christ; and our trials will brighten our graces now and our crown at last. Therefore there is reason to count it all joy when trials and difficulties become our lot in the way of our duty. And this is not purely a New-Testament paradox, but even in Job's time it was said, *Behold, happy is the man whom God correcteth.* There is the more reason for joy in afflictions if we consider the other graces that are promoted by them.

2. Faith is a grace that one expression supposes and another expressly requires: *Knowing this, that the trial of your faith, v.* 3; and then in *v.* 6, *Let him ask in faith.* There must be a sound believing of the great truths of Christianity, and a resolute cleaving to them, in times of trial. That faith which is spoken of here as tried by afflictions consists in a belief of the power, and word, and promise of God, and in fidelity and constancy to the Lord Jesus.

3. There must be patience: *The trial of faith worketh patience.* The trying of one grace produces another; and the more the suffering graces of a Christian are exercised the stronger they grow. *Tribulation worketh patience,* Rom. 5:3. Now, to exercise Christian patience aright, we must, (1.) Let it work. It is not a stupid, but an active thing. Stoical apathy and Christian patience are very different: by the one men become, in some measure, insensible of their afflictions; but by the other they become triumphant in and over them. Let us take care, in times of trial, that patience and not passion, be set at work in us; whatever is said or done, let patience have the saying and doing of it: let us not allow the indulging of our passions to hinder the operation and noble effects of patience; let us give it leave to work, and it will work wonders in a time of trouble. (2.) We must let it have its perfect

work. Do nothing to limit it nor to weaken it; but let it have its full scope: if one affliction come upon the heels of another, and a train of them are drawn upon us, yet let patience go on till its work is perfected. When we bear all that God appoints, and as long as he appoints, and with a humble obedient eye to him, and when we not only bear troubles, but rejoice in them, then patience hath its perfect work. (3.) When the work of patience is complete, then the Christian is entire, and nothing will be wanting: it will furnish us with all that is necessary for our Christian race and warfare, and will enable us to persevere to the end, and then its work will be ended, and crowned with glory. After we have abounded in other graces, we *have need of patience,* Heb. 10:36. But *let patience have its perfect work, and we shall be perfect and entire, wanting nothing.*

4. Prayer is a duty recommended also to suffering Christians; and here the apostle shows, (1.) What we ought more especially to pray for — wisdom: *If any lack wisdom, let him ask of God.* We should not pray so much for the removal of an affliction as for wisdom to make a right use of it. And who is there that does not want wisdom under any great trials or exercises to guide him in his judging of things, in the government of his own spirit and temper, and in the management of his affairs? To be wise in trying times is a special gift of God, and to him we must seek for it. (2.) In what way this is to be obtained — upon our petitioning or asking for it. Let the foolish become beggars at the throne of grace, and they are in a fair way to be wise. It is not said, "Let such ask of man," no, not of any man, but, "Let him ask of God," who made him, and gave him his understanding and reasonable powers at first, of him in whom are all the treasures of wisdom and knowledge. Let us confess our want of wisdom to God and daily ask it of him. (3.) We have the greatest encouragement to do this: *he giveth to all men liberally, and upbraideth not.* Yea, it is expressly promised that *it shall be given, v.* 5. Here is something in answer to every discouraging turn of the mind, when we go to God, under a sense of our own weakness and folly, to ask for wisdom. He to whom we are sent, we are sure, has it to give: and he is of a giving disposition, inclined to bestow this upon those who ask. Nor is there any fear of his favours being limited to some in this case, so as to exclude others, or any humble petitioning soul; for *he gives to all men.* If you should say you want a great deal of wisdom, a small portion will not serve your turn, the apostle affirms, he *gives liberally;* and lest you should be afraid of going to him unseasonably, or being put to shame for your folly, it is added, he *upbraideth not.* Ask when you will, and as often as you will, you will meet with no upbraidings. And if, after all, any should say, "This may be the case with some, but I fear I shall not succeed so well in my seeking for wisdom as some others may," let such consider how particular and express the promise is: *It shall be given him.* Justly then must fools perish in their foolishness, if wisdom may be had for asking, and they will not pray to God for it. But, (4.) There is one thing necessary to be observed in our asking, namely, that we do it with a believing, steady mind: *Let him ask in faith, nothing wavering, v.* 6. The promise above is very sure, taking this proviso along with us; wisdom shall be given to those who ask it of God, provided they believe that God is able to make the simple wise, and is faithful to make good his word to those who apply to him. This was the condition Christ insisted on, in treating with those who came to him for healing: *Believest thou that I am able to do this?* There must be *no wavering,* no staggering at the promise of God through unbelief, or through a sense of any disadvantages that lie on our own part. Here therefore we see,

5. That oneness, and sincerity of intention, and a steadiness of mind, constitute another duty required under affliction: *He that wavereth is like a wave of the sea, driven with the wind, and tossed.* To be sometimes lifted up by faith, and then thrown down again by distrust — to mount sometimes towards the heavens, with an intention to secure glory, and honour, and immortality, and then to sink again in seeking the ease of the body, or the enjoyments of this world — this is very fitly and elegantly compared to a wave of the sea, that rises and falls, swells and sinks, just as the wind tosses it higher or lower, that way or this. A mind that has but one single and prevailing regard to its spiritual and eternal interest, and that keeps steady in its purposes for God, will grow wise by afflictions, will continue fervent in its devotions, and will be superior to all trials and oppositions. Now, for the cure of a wavering spirit and a weak faith, the apostle shows the ill effects of these, (1.) In that the success of prayer is spoiled hereby: *Let not that man think that he shall receive any thing of the Lord, v.* 7. Such a distrustful, shifting, unsettled person is not likely to value a favour from God as he should do, and therefore cannot expect to receive it. In asking for divine and heavenly wisdom we are never likely to prevail if we have not a heart to prize it above rubies, and the greatest things in this world. (2.) A wavering faith and spirit has a bad influence upon our conversations. *A double-minded man is unstable in all his ways, v.* 8. When our faith and spirits rise and fall with second causes, there will be great unsteadiness in all our conversation and actions. This may sometimes expose men to contempt in the world; but it is certain that such ways cannot please God nor procure any good for us in the end. While we have but one God to trust to, we have but one God to be governed by, and this should keep us even and steady. He that is unstable as water shall not excel. Hereupon,

III. The holy humble temper of a Christian, both in advancement and debasement, is described: and both poor and rich are directed on what grounds to build their joy and comfort, *v.* 9–11. Here we may observe, 1. Those of low degree are to be looked upon as brethren: *Let the brother of low degree,* etc. Poverty does not destroy the relation among Christians. 2. Good Christians may be rich in the world, *v.* 10. Grace and wealth are not wholly inconsistent. Abraham, the father of the faithful, was rich in silver and gold. 3. Both these are allowed to rejoice. No condition of lie puts us out of a capacity of rejoicing in God. If we do not rejoice in him always, it is our own fault. Those of low degree may rejoice, if they are exalted to be rich in faith and heirs of the kingdom of God (as Dr. Whitby explains this place); and the rich may rejoice in humbling providences, as they produce a lowly and humble disposition of mind, which is highly valuable in the sight of God. Where any are made poor for righteousness' sake, their very poverty is their exaltation. It is an honour to be dishonoured for the sake of Christ. *To you it is given to suffer,* Phil. 1:29. All who are brought low, and made lowly by grace, may rejoice in the prospect of their exaltation at the last in heaven. 4. Observe what reason rich people have, notwithstanding their riches, to be humble and low in their own eyes, because both they and their riches are passing away: *As the flower of the grass he shall pass away.* He, and his wealth with him, *v.* 11. *For the sun has no sooner risen with a burning heat than it withereth the grass.* Note hence, Worldly wealth is a withering thing. Riches are too uncertain (says Mr. Baxter on this place), too inconsiderable things to make any great or just alteration in our minds. As a flower fades before the heat of the scorching sun, *so shall the rich man fade away in his ways.* His projects, counsels, and managements for this world, are called his *ways;* in these he shall *fade away.* For this reason let him that is rich rejoice, not so much in the providence of God, that makes him rich, as in the grace of God, that makes and keeps him humble; and in those trials and exercises that teach him to seek his felicity in and from God, and not from these perishing enjoyments.

IV. A blessing is pronounced on those who endure their exercises and trials, as here directed: *Blessed is the man that endureth temptation, v.* 12. Observe, 1. It is not the man who suffers only that is blessed, but he who endures, who with patience and constancy goes through all difficulties in the way of his duty. 2. Afflictions cannot make us miserable, if it be not our own fault. A blessing may arise from them, and we may be blessed in them. They are so far from taking away a good man's felicity that they really increase it. 3. Sufferings and temptations are the way to eternal blessedness: *When he is tried, he shall receive the crown of life, dokimos genomenos — when he is approved,* when his graces are found to be true and of the highest worth (so metals are tried as to their excellency by the fire), and when his integrity is manifested, and all is approved of the great Judge. Note hence, To be approved of God is the great aim of a Christian in all his trials; and it will be his blessedness at last, when he shall receive the crown of life. The tried Christian shall be a crowned one: and the crown he shall wear will be a crown of life. It will be life and bliss to him, and will last for ever. We only bear the cross for a while, but we shall wear the crown to eternity. 4. This blessedness, involved in a crown of life, is a promised thing to the righteous sufferer. It is therefore what we may most surely depend upon: for, when heaven and earth shall pass away, this word of God shall not fail of being fulfilled. But withal let us take notice that our future reward comes, not as a debt, but by a gracious promise. 5. Our enduring temptations must be from a principle of love to God and to our Lord Jesus Christ, otherwise we are not interested in this promise: *The Lord hath promised to those that love him.* Paul supposes that a man may for some point of religion even give *his body to be burnt,* and yet not be pleasing to God, nor regarded by him, because of his want of charity, or a prevailing sincere love to God and man, 1 Co. 13:3. 6. The crown of life is promised not only to great and eminent saints, but to all those who have the love of God reigning in their hearts. Every soul that truly loves God shall have its trials in this world fully recompensed in that world above *where love is made perfect.*

Verses 13–18

I. We are here taught that God is not the author of any man's sin. Whoever they are who raise persecutions against men, and whatever injustice and sin they may be guilty of in proceeding against them, God is not to be charged with it. And, whatever sins good men may themselves be provoked to by their exercises and afflictions, God is not the cause of them. It seems to be here supposed that some professors might fall in the hour of temptation, that the rod resting upon them might carry some into ill courses, and make them put forth their hands unto iniquity. But though this should be the case, and though such delinquents should attempt to lay their fault on God, yet the blame of their misconduct must lie entirely upon themselves. For, 1. There is nothing in the nature of God that they can lay the blame upon: *Let no man say, when he is tempted* to take any evil course, or do any evil thing, *I am tempted of God; for God cannot be tempted with evil.* All moral evil is owing to some disorder in the being that is chargeable with it, to a want of wisdom, or of power, or of decorum and purity in the will. But who can impeach the holy God with the want of these, which are his very essence? No exigence of affairs can ever tempt him to dishonour or deny himself, and therefore he cannot be tempted with evil. 2. There is nothing in the providential dispensations of God that the blame of any man's sin can be laid upon (*v.* 13): *Neither tempteth he any man.* As God cannot be tempted with evil himself, so neither can he be a tempter of others. He cannot be a promoter of what is repugnant to his nature. The carnal mind is willing to charge its own sins on God. There is something hereditary in this. Our first father Adam tells God, *The woman thou gavest me* tempted me, thereby, in effect, throwing the blame upon God, for giving him the tempter. Let no man speak thus. It is very bad to sin; but is much worse, when we have done amiss, to charge it upon God, and say it was owing to him. Those who lay the blame of their sins either upon their constitution or upon their condition in the world, or who pretend they are under a fatal necessity of sinning, wrong God, as if he were the author of sin. Afflictions, as sent by God, are designed to draw out our graces, but not our corruptions.

II. We are taught where the true cause of evil lies, and where the blame ought to be laid (*v.* 14): *Every man is tempted* (in an ill sense) *when he is drawn away of his own lust, and enticed.* In other scriptures the devil is called *the tempter,* and other things may sometimes concur to tempt us; but neither the devil nor any other person or thing is to be blamed so as to excuse ourselves; for the true original of evil and temptation is in our own hearts. The combustible matter is in us, though the flame may be blown up by some outward causes. And therefore, *if thou scornest, thou alone shalt bear it,* Prov. 9:12. Observe here, 1. The method of sin in its proceeding. First it draws away, then entices. As holiness consists of two parts — forsaking that which is evil and cleaving to that which is good, so these two things, reversed, are the two parts of sin. The heart is carried from that which is good, and enticed to cleave to that which is evil. It is first by corrupt inclinations, or by lusting after and coveting some sensual or worldly thing, estranged from the life of God, and then by degrees fixed in a course of sin. 2. We may observe hence the power and policy of sin. The word here rendered *drawn away* signifies a being forcibly haled or compelled. The word translated *enticed* signifies being wheedled and beguiled by allurements and deceitful representations of things, *exelkomenos kai deleazomenos.* There is a great deal of violence done to conscience and to the mind by the power of corruption: and there is a great deal of cunning and deceit and flattery in sin to gain us to its interests. The force and power of sin could never prevail, were it not for its cunning and guile.

Sinners who perish are wheedled and flattered to their own destruction. And this will justify God for ever in their damnation, that they destroyed themselves. Their sin lies at their own door, and therefore their blood will lie upon their own heads. 3. The success of corruption in the heart (v. 15): *Then, when lust hath conceived, it bringeth forth sin;* that is, sin being allowed to excite desires in us, it will son ripen those desires into consent, and then it is said to have *conceived*. The sin truly exists, though it be but in embryo. And, when it has grown it its full size in the mind, it is then brought forth in actual execution. Stop the beginnings of sin therefore, or else all the evils it produces must be wholly charged upon us. 4. The final issue of sin, and how it ends: *Sin, when it is finished, bringeth forth death.* After sin is brought forth in actual commissions, the *finishing of it* (as Dr. Manton observes) is its being strengthened by frequent acts and settled into a habit. And, when the iniquities of men are thus filled up, death is brought forth. There is a death upon the soul, and death comes upon the body. And, besides death spiritual and temporal, the wages of sin is eternal death too. Let sin therefore be repented of and forsaken, before it be finished. *Why will you die, O house of Israel!* Eze. 33:11. God has no pleasure in your death, as he has no hand in your sin; but both sin and misery are owing to yourselves. Your own hearts' lusts and corruptions are your tempters; and when by degrees they have carried you off from God, and finished the power and dominion of sin in you, then they will prove your destroyers.

III. We are taught yet further that, while we are the authors and procurers of all sin and misery to ourselves, *God is the Father and fountain of all good, v.* 16, 17. We should take particular care not to err in our conceptions of God: "*Do not err, my beloved brethren, mē lanasthe — do not wander,* that is, from the word of God, and the accounts of him you have there. Do not stray into erroneous opinions, and go off from the standard of truth, the things which you have received from the Lord Jesus and by the direction of his Spirit." The loose opinions of Sinon, and the Nicolaitans (from whom the Gnostics, a most sensual corrupt set of people, arose afterwards), may perhaps, by the apostle here, be more especially cautioned against. Those who are disposed to look into these may consult the first book of Irenaeus against heresies. Let corrupt men run into what notions they will, the truth, as it is in Jesus, stands thus: That God is not, cannot be, the author and patronizer of any thing that is evil; but must be acknowledged as the cause and spring of every thing that is good: *Every good and every perfect gift is from above, and cometh down from the Father of lights, v.* 17. Here observe, 1. God is the Father of lights. The visible light of the sun and the heavenly bodies is from him. He said, *Let there be light, and there was light.* Thus God is at once represented as the Creator of the sun and in some respects compared to it. "As the sun is the same in its nature and influences, though the earth and clouds, oft interposing, make it seem to us as varying, by its rising and setting, and by its different appearances, or entire withdrawment, when the change is not in it; so God is unchangeable, and our changes and shadows are not from any mutability or shadowy alterations in him, but from ourselves." — *Baxter.* The Father of lights, *with whom there is no variableness, neither shadow of turning.* What the sun is in nature, God is in grace, providence, and glory; aye, and infinitely more. For, 2. Every good gift is from him. As the Father of lights, he gives the light of reason. *The inspiration of the Almighty giveth understanding,* Job 32:8. He gives also the light of learning: Solomon's wisdom in the knowledge of nature, in the arts of government, and in all his improvements, is ascribed to God. The light of divine revelation is more immediately from above. The light of faith, purity, and all manner of consolation is from him. So that we have nothing good but what we receive from God, as there is no evil or sin in us, or done by us, but what is owing to ourselves. We must own God as the author of all the powers and perfections that are in the creature, and the giver of all the benefits which we have in and by those powers and perfections: but none of their darknesses, their imperfections, or their ill actions are to be charged on the Father of lights; from him proceeds every good and perfect gift, both pertaining to this life and that which is to come. 3. As every good gift is from God, so particularly the renovation of our natures, our regeneration, and all the holy happy consequences of it, must be ascribed to him (v. 18): *Of his own will begat he us with the word of truth.* Here let us take notice, (1.) A true Christian is a creature begotten anew. He becomes as differ-

ent a person from what he was before the renewing influences of divine grace as if he were formed over again, and born afresh. (2.) The original of this good work is here declared: it is of God's own will; not by our skill or power; not from any good foreseen in us, or done by us, but purely from the good-will and grace of God. (3.) The means whereby this is affected are pointed out: *the word of truth,* that is, the gospel, as Paul expresses it more plainly, 1 Co. 4:15, *I have begotten you in Jesus Christ through the gospel.* This gospel in indeed a word of truth, or else it could never produce such real, such lasting, such great and noble effects. We may rely upon it, and venture our immortal souls upon it. And we shall find it a means of our sanctification as it is a word of truth, Jn. 17:17. (4.) The end and design of God's giving renewing grace is here laid down: *That we should be a kind of first-fruits of his creatures* — that we should be God's portion and treasure, and a more peculiar property to him, as the first-fruits were; and that we should become holy to the Lord, as the first-fruits were consecrated to him. Christ is the first-fruits of Christians, Christians are the first-fruits of creatures.

Verses 19–27

In this part of the chapter we are required,

I. To restrain the workings of passion. This lesson we should learn under afflictions; and this we shall learn if we are indeed begotten again by the word of truth. For thus the connection stands — An angry and hasty spirit is soon provoked to ill things by afflictions, and errors and ill opinions become prevalent through the workings of our own vile and vain affections; but the renewing grace of God and the word of the gospel teach us to subdue these: *Wherefore, my beloved brethren, let every man be swift to hear, slow to speak, slow to wrath, v.* 19. This may refer, 1. To the word of truth spoken of in the verse foregoing. And so we may observe, It is our duty rather to hear God's word, and apply our minds to understand it, than to speak according to our own fancies or the opinions of men, and to run into heat and passion thereupon. Let not such errors as that of God's being the occasion of men's sin ever be hastily, much less angrily, mentioned by you (and so as to other errors); but be ready to hear and consider what God's word teaches in all such cases. 2. This may be applied to the afflictions and temptations spoken of in the beginning of the chapter. And then we may observe, It is our duty rather to hear how God explains his providences, and what he designs by the, than to say as David did in his haste, *I am cut off;* or as Jonah did in his passion, I do well to be angry. Instead of censuring God under our trials, let us open our ears and hearts to hear what he will say to us. 3. This may be understood as referring to the disputes and differences that Christians, in those times of trial, were running into among themselves: and so this part of the chapter may be considered without any connection with what goes before. Here we may observe that, whenever matters of difference arise among Christians, each side should be willing to hear the other. People are often stiff in their own opinions because they are not willing to hear what others have to offer against them: whereas we should be swift to hear reason and truth on all sides, and be slow to speak any thing that should prevent this: and, when we do speak, there should be nothing of wrath; for a soft answer turneth away wrath. As this epistle is designed to correct a variety of disorders that existed among Christians, these words, *swift to hear, slow to speak, slow to wrath,* may be very well interpreted according to this last explication. And we may further observe from them that, if men would govern their tongues, they must govern their passions. When Moses's spirit was provoked, *he spoke unadvisedly with his lips.* If we would be slow to speak, we must be slow to wrath.

II. A very good reason is given for suppressing: *For the wrath of man worketh not the righteousness of God, v.* 20. It is as if the apostle had said, "Whereas men often pretend zeal for God and his glory, in their hat and passion, let them know that God needs not the passions of any man; his cause is better served by mildness and meekness than by wrath and fury." Solomon says, *The words of the wise are heard in quiet, more than the cry of him that ruleth among fools,* Eccl. 9:17. Dr. Manton here says of some assemblies, "That if we were as swift to hear as we are ready to speak there would be less of wrath, and more of profit, in our meetings. I remember when a Manichee contested with Augustine, and with importunate clamour cried, *Hear me! hear me!* the father modestly replied, *Nec ego te, nec tu me, sed ambo audiamus apos-*

tolum — Neither let me hear thee, nor do thou hear me, but let us both hear the apostle." The worst thing we can bring to a religious controversy is anger. This, however it may pretend to be raised by a concern for what is just and right, is not to be trusted. *Wrath* is a human thing, and the wrath of man stands opposed to the righteousness of God. Those who pretend to serve the cause of God hereby show that they are acquainted neither with God or his cause. This passion must especially be watched against when we are hearing the word of God. See 1 Pt. 2:1, 2.

III. We are called upon to suppress other corrupt affections, as well as rash anger: *Lay aside all filthiness and superfluity of naughtiness, v.* 21. The word here translated *filthiness* signifies those lusts which have the greatest turpitude and sensuality in them; and the words rendered *superfluity of naughtiness* may be understood of the overflowings of malice or any other spiritual wickednesses. Hereby we are taught, as Christians, to watch against, and lay aside, not only those more gross and fleshly dispositions and affections which denominate a person filthy, but all the disorders of a corrupt heart, which would prejudice it against the word and ways of God. Observe, 1. Sin is a defiling thing; it is called filthiness itself. 2. There is abundance of that which is evil in us, to be watched against; there is *superfluity of naughtiness.* 3. It is not enough to restrain evil affections, but *they must be cast from us, or laid apart.* Isa. 30:22, *Thou shalt cast them away as a menstruous cloth; thou shalt say, Get you hence.* 4. This must extend not only to outward sins, and greater abominations, but to all sin of thought and affection as well as speech and practice; *pasan rhyparian — all filthiness,* every thing that is corrupt and sinful. 5. Observe, from the foregoing parts of this chapter, the laying aside of all filthiness is what a time of temptation and affliction calls for, and is necessary to the avoiding of error, and the right receiving and improving of the word of truth: for,

IV. We are here fully, though briefly, instructed concerning hearing the word of God.

1. We are required to prepare ourselves for it (v. 21), to get rid of every corrupt affection and of every prejudice and prepossession, and to lay aside those sins which pervert the judgment and blind the mind. *All the filthiness and superfluity of naughtiness,* before explained, must, in an especial manner, be subdued and cast off, by all such as attend on the word of the gospel.

2. We are directed how to hear it: *Receive with meekness the engrafted word, which is able to save your souls.* (1.) In hearing the word of God, we are to receive it — assent to the truths of it — consent to the laws of it; receive it as the stock does the graft; so as that the fruit which is produced may be, not according to the nature of the sour stock, but according to the nature of that word of the gospel which is engrafted into our souls. (2.) We must therefore yield ourselves to the word of God, with most submissive, humble, and tractable tempers: this is to *receive it with meekness.* Being willing to hear of our faults, and taking it not only patiently, but thankfully, desiring also to be molded and formed by the doctrines and precepts of the gospel. (3.) In all our hearing we should aim at the salvation of our souls. It is the design of the word of God to make us wise to salvation; and those who propose any meaner or lower ends to themselves in attending upon it dishonour the gospel and disappoint their souls. We should come to the word of God (both to read it and hear it), as those who know it is *the power of God unto salvation to every one that believeth,* Rom. 1:16.

3. We are taught what is to be done after hearing (v. 22): *But be you doers of the word, and not hearers only, deceiving your own selves.* Observe here, (1.) Hearing is in order to doing; the most attentive and the most frequent hearing of the word of God will not avail us, unless we be also doers of it. If we were to hear a sermon every day of the week, and an angel from heaven were the preacher, yet, if we rested in bare hearing, it would never bring us to heaven. Therefore the apostle insists much upon it (and, without doubt, it is indispensably necessary) that we practice what we hear. "There must be inward practice by meditation, and outward practice in true obedience." *Baxter.* It is not enough to remember what we hear, and to be able to repeat it, and to give testimony to it, and commend it, and write it, and preserve what we have written; that which all this is in order to, and which crowns the rest, is that we be doers of the word. Observe, (2.) Bare hearers are self-deceivers; the original word, *paralogizomenoi,* signifies men's arguing sophistical-

ly to themselves; their reasoning is manifestly deceitful and false when they would make one part of their work discharge them from the obligation they lie under to another, or persuade themselves that filling their heads with notions is sufficient, though their hearts be empty of good affections and resolutions, and their lives fruitless of good works. Self-deceit will be found the worst deceit at last.

4. The apostle shows what is the proper use of the word of God, who they are that do not use it as they ought, and who they are that do make a right use of it, *v.* 23–25. Let us consider each of these distinctly. (1.) The use we are to make of God's word may be learnt from its being compared to a glass, in which a man may *behold his natural face.* As a looking-glass shows us the spots and defilements upon our faces, that they may be remedied and washed off, so the word of God shows us our sins, that we may repent of them and get them pardoned; it shows us what is amiss, that it may be amended. There are glasses that will flatter people; but that which is truly the word of God is no flattering glass. If you flatter yourselves, it is your own fault; *the truth, as it is in Jesus,* flatters no man. Let the word of truth be carefully attended to, and it will set before you the corruption of your nature, the disorders of your hearts and lives; it will tell you plainly what you are. Paul describes himself as in sensible of the corruption of his nature till he saw himself in the glass of the law (Rom. 7:9): *"I was alive without the law;* that is, I took all to be right with me, and thought myself not only clean, but, compared with the generality of the world, beautiful too; *but when the commandment came,* when the glass of the law was set before me, *then sin revived, and I died* — then I saw my spots and deformities, and discovered that amiss in myself which before I was not aware of; and such was the power of the law, and of sin, that I then perceived myself in a state of death and condemnation." Thus, when we attend to *the word of God,* so as to see ourselves, our true state and condition, to rectify what is amiss, and to form and dress ourselves anew by the glass of God's word, this is to make a proper use of it. (2.) We have here an account of those who do not use this glass of the word as they ought: *He that beholds himself, and goes his way, and straightway forgets what manner of man he was, v.* 24. This is the true description of one who hears the word of God and does it not. How many are there who, when they sit under the word, are affected with their own sinfulness, misery, and danger, acknowledge the evil of sin, and their need of Christ; but, when their hearing is over, all is forgotten, convictions are lost, good affections vanish, and pass away like the waters of a land-flood: he *straightway forgets.* "The word of God (as Dr. Manton speaks) discovers how we may do away our sins, and deck and attire our souls with the righteousness of Jesus Christ. *Maculae sunt peccata, quae ostendit lex; aqua est sanguis Christi, quem ostendit evangelium — Our sins are the spots which the law discovers; Christ's blood is the laver which the gospel shows.*" But in vain do we hear God's word, and look into the gospel glass, if we go away, and forget our spots, instead of washing them off, and forget our remedy, instead of applying to it. This is the case of those who do not hear the word as they ought. (3.) Those also are described, and pronounced blessed, who hear aright, and who use the glass of God's word as they should do (*v.* 25): *Whoso looketh into the perfect law of liberty, and continueth therein,* etc. Observe here, [1.] The gospel is a law of liberty, or, as Mr. Baxter expresses it, *of liberation,* giving us deliverance from the Jewish law, and from sin and guilt, and wrath and death. The ceremonial law was a yoke of bondage; the gospel of Christ is a law of liberty. [2.] It is a perfect law; nothing can be added to it. [3.] In hearing the word, we look into this perfect law; we consult it for counsel and direction; we look into it, that we may thence take our measures. [4.] Then only do we look into the law of liberty as we should when we *continue therein* — "when we dwell in the study of it, till it turn to a spiritual life, engrafted and digested in us" *(Baxter)* — when we are not forgetful of it, but practice it as our work and business, set it always before our eyes, and make it the constant rule of our conversation and behaviour, and model the temper of our minds by it. [5.] Those who thus do, and *continue in the law and word of God,* are, and *shall be, blessed in their deed; blessed in all their ways,* according to the first psalm, to which, some think, James here alludes. *He that meditates in the law of God, and walks according to it,* the psalmist says, *shall prosper in whatsoever he does.* And *he that is not a forgetful hearer, but a doer of the work* which God's word

sets him about, James says, *shall be blessed.* The papists pretend that here we have a clear text to prove we are blessed for our good deeds; but Dr. Manton, in answer to that pretence, puts the reader upon marking the distinctness of scripture-phrase. The apostle does not say, *for* his deeds, that any man is blessed, but *in* his deed. This is a way in which we shall certainly find blessedness, but not the cause of it. This blessedness does not lie in knowing, but in doing the will of God. Jn. 13:17, *If you know these things, happy are you if you do them.* It is not talking, but walking, that will bring us to heaven.

V. The apostle next informs us how we may distinguish between a vain religion and that which is pure and approved of God. Great and hot disputes there are in the world about this matter: what religion is false and vain, and what is true and pure. I wish men would agree to let the holy scripture in this place determine the question: and here it is plainly and peremptorily declared,

1. What is a vain religion: *If any man among you seemeth to be religious, and bridleth not his tongue, but deceives his own heart, this man's religion is vain.* Here are three things to be observed: — (1.) In a vain religion there is much of show, and affecting to seem religious in the eyes of others. This, I think, is mentioned in a manner that should fix our thoughts on the word *seemeth.* When men are more concerned to seem religious than really to be so, it is a sign that their religion is but vain. Not that *religion* itself is a vain thing (those do it a great deal of injustice who say, *It is in vain to serve the Lord),* but it is possible for people to make it a vain thing, if they have only a form of godliness, and not the power. (2.) In a vain religion there is much censuring, reviling, and detracting of others. The not bridling the tongue here is chiefly meant of not abstaining from these evils of the tongue. When we hear people ready to speak of the faults of others, or to censure them as holding scandalous errors, or to lessen the wisdom and piety of those about them, that they themselves may seem the wiser and better, this is a sign that they have but a vain religion. The man who has a detracting tongue cannot have a truly humble gracious heart. He who delights to injure his neighbour in vain pretends to love God; therefore a reviling tongue will prove a man a hypocrite. Censuring is a pleasing sin, extremely complaint with nature, and therefore evinces a man's being in a natural state. These sins of the tongue were the great sins of that age in which James wrote (as other parts of this epistle fully show); and it is a strong sing of a vain religion (says Dr. Manton) to be carried away with the evil of the times. This has ever been a leading sin with hypocrites, that the more ambitious they have been to seem well themselves the more free they have been in censuring and running down others; and there is such quick intercourse between the tongue and the heart that the one may be known by the other. On these accounts it is that the apostle has made an ungoverned tongue an undoubted certain proof of a vain religion. There is no strength nor power in that religion which will not enable a man to bridle his tongue. (3.) In a vain religion a man deceives his own heart; he goes on in such a course of detracting from others, and making himself seem somebody, that at last the vanity of his religion is consummated by the deceiving of his own soul. When once religion comes to be a vain thing, how great is the vanity!

2. It is here plainly and peremptorily declared wherein true religion consists: *Pure religion and undefiled before God and the Father is this, v.* 27. Observe, (1.) It is the glory of religion to be pure and undefiled; not mixed with the inventions of men nor with the corruption of the world. False religions may be known by their impurity and uncharitableness; according to that of John, *He that doeth not righteousness is not of God neither he that loveth not his brother,* 1 Jn. 3:10. But, on the other hand, a holy life and a charitable heart show a true religion. Our religion is not (says Dr. Manton) adorned with ceremonies, but purity and charity. And it is a good observation of his that a religion which is pure should be kept undefiled. (2.) That religion is pure and undefiled which is so before God and the Father. That is right which is so in God's eye, and which chiefly aims at his approbation. True religion teaches us to do every thing as in the presence of God; and to seek his favour, and study to please him in all our actions. (3.) Compassion and charity to the poor and distressed from a very great and necessary part of true religion: *Visiting the fatherless and widow in their affliction.* Visiting is here put for all manner of relief which we are ca-

pable of giving to others; and fatherless and widows are here particularly mentioned, because they are generally most apt to be neglected or oppressed: but by them we are to understand all who are proper objects of charity, all who are in affliction. It is very remarkable that if the sum of religion be drawn up to two articles this is one — to be charitable and relieve the afflicted. Observe, (4.) An unspotted life must accompany an unfeigned love and charity: *To keep himself unspotted from the world.* The world is apt to spot and blemish the soul, and it is hard to live in it, and have to do with it, and not be defiled; but this must be our constant endeavour. Herein consists pure and undefiled religion. The very things of the world too much taint our spirits, if we are much conversant with them; but the sins and lusts of the world deface and defile them very woefully indeed. John comprises *all that is in the world,* which we are not to love, under three heads: *the lust of the flesh, the lust of the eyes, and the pride of life;* and to keep ourselves unspotted from all these is to keep ourselves unspotted from the world. May God by his grace keep both our hearts and lives clean from the love of the world, and from the temptations of wicked worldly men.

CHAPTER 2

In this chapter the apostle condemns a sinful regarding of the rich, and despising the poor, which he imputes to partiality and injustice, and shows it to be an acting contrary to God, who has chosen the poor, and whose interest is often persecuted, and his name blasphemed, by the rich (*v.* 1–7). He shows that the whole law is to be fulfilled, and that mercy should be followed, as well as justice (*v.* 8–13). He exposes the error and folly of those who boast of faith without works, telling us that this is but a dead faith, and such a faith as devils have, not the faith of Abraham, or of Rahab (*v.* 11 to the end).

Verses 1–7

The apostle is here reproving a very corrupt practice. He shows how much mischief there is in the sin of *prosōpolēpsia — respect of persons,* which seemed to be a very growing evil in the churches of Christ even in those early ages, and which, in these after-times, has sadly corrupted and divided Christian nations and societies. Here we have,

I. A caution against this sin laid down in general: *My brethren, have not the faith of our Lord Jesus Christ, the Lord of glory, with respect of persons, v.* 1. Observe here, 1. The character of Christians fully implied: they are such as have the faith of our Lord Jesus Christ; they embrace it; they receive it; they govern themselves by it; they entertain the doctrine, and submit to the law and government, of Christ; they have it as a trust; they have it as a treasure. 2. How honorably James speaks of Jesus Christ; he calls him *the Lord of glory;* for he is *the brightness of his Father's glory, and the express image of his person.* 3. Christ's being the Lord of glory should teach us not to respect Christians for any thing so much as their relation and conformity to Christ. You who profess to believe the glory of our Lord Jesus Christ, which the poorest Christian shall partake of equally with the rich, and to which all worldly glory is but vanity, you should not make men's outward and worldly advantages the measure of your respect. In professing the faith of our Lord Jesus Christ, we should not show respect to men, so as to cloud or lessen the glory of our glorious Lord: how ever any may think of it, this is certainly a very heinous sin.

II. We have this sin described and cautioned against, by an instance or example of it (*v.* 2, 3): *For if there come into your assembly a man with a gold ring,* etc. *Assembly* here is meant of those meetings which were appointed for deciding matters of difference among the members of the church, or for determining when censures should be passed upon any, and what those censures should be; therefore the Greek word here used, *synagōgē,* signifies such an assembly as that in the Jewish synagogues, when they met to do justice. Maimonides says (as I find the passage quoted by Dr. Manton) "That is was expressly provided by the Jews' constitutions that, when a poor man and a rich plead together, the rich shall not be bidden to sit down and the poor stand, or sit in a worse place, but both sit or both stand alike." To this the phrases used by the apostle have a most plain reference, and therefore the assembly here spoken of must be some such as the synagogue-assemblies of the Jews were, when they met to hear causes and to execute justice: to these the arbitrations and censures of their Christian assemblies are compared. But we must be careful not to apply what is here said to the common assemblies for worship; for in these certainly there may be appointed different places of persons according to their rank and circumstances, without sin. Those do not understand the apostle who fix his severity here upon this practice; they do not consider the word judges (used in *v.* 4), nor what is said of their being convected as transgressors of the law, if they had such a respect of persons as is here spoken of, according to *v.* 9. Thus, now put the case: *"There comes into your assembly* (when of the same nature with some of those at the synagogue) *a man* that is distinguished by his dress, and who makes a figure, *and there comes in also a poor man in vile raiment,* and you act partially, and determine wrong, merely because the one makes a better appearance, or is in better circumstances, than the other." Observe hence, 1. God has his remnant among all sorts of people, among those that wear soft and gay clothing, and among those that wear poor and vile raiment. 2. In matters of religion, rich and poor stand upon a level; no man's riches set him in the least nearer to God, nor does any man's poverty set him at a distance from God. *With the Most High there is no respect of persons,* and therefore in matters of conscience there should be none with us. 3. All undue honouring of worldly greatness and riches should especially be watched against in Christian societies. James does not here encourage rudeness or disorder. Civil respect must be paid, and some difference may be allowed in our carriage towards persons of different ranks; but this respect must never be such as to influence the proceedings of Christian societies in disposing of the offices of the church, or in passing the censures of the church, or in any thing that is purely a matter of religion; here we are to know no man after the flesh. It is the character of a citizen of Zion that *in his eyes a vile person is contemned, but he honoureth those that fear the Lord.* If a poor man be a good man, we must not value him a whit the less for his poverty; and, if a rich man be a bad man (though he may have both gay clothing and a gay profession), we must not value him any whit the more for his riches. 4. Of what importance it is to take care what rule we go by in judging of men; if we allow ourselves commonly to judge by outward appearance, this will too much influence our spirits and our conduct in religious assemblies. There is many a man, whose wickedness renders him vile and despicable, who yet makes a figure in the world; and, on the other hand, there is many a humble, heavenly, good Christian, who is clothed meanly; but neither should he nor his Christianity be thought the worse of on this account.

III. We have the greatness of this sin set forth, *v.* 4, 5. It is great partiality, it is injustice, and it is to set ourselves against God, who has chosen the poor, and will honour and advance them (if good), let who will despise them. 1. In this sin there is shameful partiality: *Are you not then partial in yourselves?* The question is here put, as what could not fail of being answered by every man's conscience that would put it seriously to himself. According to the strict rendering of the original, the question is, *"Have you not made a difference?* And, in that difference, do you not judge by a false rule, and go upon false measures? And does not the charge of a partiality condemned by the law lie fully against you? Does not your own conscience tell you that you are guilty?" Appeals to conscience are of great advantage, when we have to do with such as make a profession, even though they may have fallen into a very corrupt state. 2. This respect of persons is owing to the evil and injustice of the thoughts. As the temper, conduct, and proceedings, are partial, so the heart and thoughts, from which all flows, are evil: *"You have become judges of evil thoughts;* that is, you are judges according to those unjust estimations and corrupt opinions which you have formed to yourselves. Trace your partiality till you come to those hidden thoughts which accompany and support it, and you will find those to be *exceedingly evil.* You secretly prefer outward pomp before inward grace, and the things that are seen before those which are not seen." The deformity of sin is never truly and fully discerned till the evil of our thoughts be disclosed: and it is this which highly aggravates the faults of our tempers and lives — that *the imagination of the thoughts of the heart is evil,* Gen. 6:5. 3. This respect of persons is a heinous sin, because it is to show ourselves most directly contrary to God (*v.* 5): *"Hath not God chosen the poor of this world, rich in faith? etc. But you have despised them, v.* 6. God has made those heirs of a kingdom whom you make of no reputation, and has given very great and glorious promises to those to whom you can hardly give a good word or a respectful look. And is not this a monstrous iniquity in you who pretend to be the children of God and conformed to him? *Hearken, my beloved brethren;* by all the love I have for you, and all the regards you have to me, I beg you would consider these things. Take notice that many of the poor of this world are the chosen of God. Their being God's chosen does not prevent their being poor; their being poor does not at all prejudice the evidences of their being chosen. Mt. 11:5, *The poor are evangelized."* God designed to recommend his holy religion to men's esteem and affection, not by the external advantages of gaiety and pomp, but by its intrinsic worth and excellency; and therefore chose the poor of this world. Again, take notice that many poor of the world are rich in faith; thus the poorest may become rich; and this is what they ought to be especially ambitious of. It is expected from those who have wealth and estates that they be rich in good works, because the more they have the more they have to do good with; but it is expected from the poor in the world that they be rich in faith, for the less they have here the more they may, and should, live in the believing expectation of better things in a better world. Take notice further, Believing Christians are rich in title, and in being heirs of a kingdom, though they may be very poor as to present possessions. What is laid out upon them is but little; what is laid up for them is unspeakably rich and great. Note again, Where any are rich in faith, there will be also divine love; faith working by love will be in all the heirs of glory. Note once more, under this head, Heaven is a kingdom, and a kingdom promised to those that love God. We read of the crown promised to those that love God, in the former chapter (*v.* 12); we here find there is a kingdom too. And, as the crown is a crown of life, so the kingdom will be an everlasting kingdom. All these things, laid together, show how highly the poor in this world, if rich in faith, are now honoured, and shall hereafter be advanced by God; and consequently how very sinful a thing it was for them to despise the poor. After such considerations as these, the charge is cutting indeed: *But you have despised the poor, v.* 6. 4. Respecting persons, in the sense of this place, on account of their riches or outward figure, is shown to be a very great sin, because of the mischiefs which are owing to worldly wealth and greatness, and the folly which there is in Christians' paying undue regards to those who had so little regard either to their God or them: *"Do not rich men oppress you, and draw you before the judgment-seat? Do not they blaspheme that worthy name by which you are called? v.* 7. Consider how commonly riches are the incentives of vice and mischief, of blasphemy and persecution: consider how many calamities you yourselves sustain, and how great reproaches are thrown upon your religion and your God by men of wealth, and power, and worldly greatness; and this will make your sin appear exceedingly sinful and foolish, in setting up that which tends to pull you down, and to destroy all that you are building up, and to dishonour that worthy name by which you are called." The name of Christ is a worthy name; it reflects honour, and gives worth to those who wear it.

Verses 8–13

The apostle, having condemned the sin of those who had an undue respect of persons, and having urged what was sufficient to convict them of the greatness of this evil, now proceeds to show how the matter may be mended; it is the work of a gospel ministry, not only to reprove and warn, but to teach and direct. Col. 1:28, *Warning every man, and teaching every man.* And here,

I. We have the law that is to guide us in all our regards to men set down in general. *If you fulfil the royal law, according to the scripture, Thou shalt love thy neighbour as thyself, you do well, v.* 8. Lest any should think James had been pleading for the poor so as to throw contempt on the rich, he now lets them know that he did not design to encourage improper conduct towards any; they must not hate nor be rude to the rich, any more than despise the poor; but as the scripture teaches us to love all our neighbours, be they rich or poor, as ourselves, so, in our having a steady regard to this rule, *we shall do well.* Observe hence, 1. The rule for Christians to walk by is settled in the scriptures: *If according to the scriptures,* etc. It is not great men, nor worldly wealth, nor corrupt practices among professors themselves, that must guide us, but the scriptures of truth. 2. The scripture gives us this as a law, to love our neighbour as ourselves; it is what still remains in full force, and is rather carried higher and further by Christ than made less important to us. 3. This law is a royal law, it comes from the King of kings. Its own worth and dignity deserve it should be thus honoured; and the state in which all Christians now are, as it is a state of liberty, and not of bondage or oppression, makes this law, by which they are to regulate all their actions to one another, a royal law. 4. A pretence of observing this royal law, when it is interpreted with partiality, will not excuse men in any unjust proceedings. In is implied here that some were ready to flatter rich men, and be partial to them, because, if they were in the like circumstances, they should expect such regards to themselves; or they might plead that to show a distinguished respect to those whom God in his providence had distinguished by their rank and degree in the world was but doing right; therefore the apostle allows that, so far as they were concerned to observe the duties of the second table, they *did well in giving honour to whom honour was due;* but this fair pretence would not cover their sin in that undue *respect of persons* which they stood chargeable with; for,

II. This general law is to be considered together with a particular law: *"If you have respect to persons, you commit sin, and are convinced of the law as transgressors, v.* 9. Notwithstanding the law of laws, *to love your neighbour as yourselves,* and to show that respect to them which you would be apt to look for yourselves if in their circumstances, yet this will not excuse your distributing either the favours or the censures of the church according to men's outward condition; but here you must look to a particular law, which God, who gave the other, has given you together with it, and by this you will stand fully convicted of the sin I have charged you with." This law is in Lev. 19:15, *Thou shalt do no unrighteousness in judgment; thou shalt not respect the person of the poor nor the person of the mighty; but in righteousness shalt though judge thy neighbour.* Yea, the very royal law itself, rightly explained, would serve to convict them, because it teaches them to put themselves as much in the places of the poor as in those of the rich, and so to act equitably towards one as well as the other. Hence he proceeds,

III. To show the extent of the law, and how far obedience must be paid to it. They must fulfil the royal law, have a regard to one part as well as another, otherwise it would not stand them in stead, when they pretended to urge it as a reason for any particular actions: *For whosoever shall keep the whole law, and yet offend in one point, is guilty of all, v.* 10. This may be considered, 1. With reference to the case James has been upon: Do you plead for your respect to the rich, because you are to love your neighbour as yourselves? Why then show also an equitable and due regard to the poor, because you are to love your neighbour as yourself: or else your offending in one point will spoil your pretence of observing that law at all. *Whosoever shall keep the whole law, if he offend in one point,* wilfully, avowedly, and with continuance, and so as to think he shall be excused in some matters because of his obedience in others, *he is guilty of all;* that is, he incurs the same penalty, and is liable to the same punishment, by the sentence of the law, as if he had broken it in other points as well as that he stands chargeable with. Not that all sins are equal, but that all carry the same contempt of the authority of the Lawgiver, and so bind over to such punishment as is threatened on the breach of that law. This shows us what a vanity it is to think that our good deeds will atone for our bad deeds, and plainly puts us upon looking for some other atonement. 2. This is further illustrated by putting a case different from that before mentioned (*v.* 11): *For he that said, Do not commit adultery, said also, Do not kill. Now, if thou commit no adultery, yet, if thou kill, thou art become a transgressor of the law.* One, perhaps, is very severe in the case of adultery, or what tends to such pollutions of the flesh; but less ready to condemn murder, or what tends to ruin the health, break the hearts, and destroy the lives, of others: another has a prodigious dread of murder, but has more easy thoughts of adultery; whereas one who looks at the authority of the Lawgiver more than the matter of the command will see the same reason for condemning the one as the other. Obedience is then acceptable when all is done with an eye to the will of God; and disobedience is to be condemned, in whatever instance it be, as it is a contempt of the authority of God; and, for that reason, if we offend in one point, we contemn the authority of him who gave the whole law, and so far are guilty of all. Thus, if you look to the law of the old, you stand condemned; for *cursed is every that continueth not in all things that are written in the book of the law to do them,* Gal. 3:10.

IV. James directs Christians to govern and conduct themselves more especially by the law of Christ. *So speak and so do as those that shall be judged by the law of liberty, v.* 12. This will teach us, not only to be just and impartial, but very compassionate and merciful to the poor; and it will set us perfectly free from all sordid and undue regards to the rich. Observe here, 1. The gospel is called a law. It has all the requisites of a law: precepts with rewards and punishments annexed; it prescribes duty, as well as administers comfort; and Christ is a king to rule us as well as a prophet to teach us, and a priest to sacrifice and intercede for us. *We are under the law to Christ.* 2. It is a *law of liberty,* and one that we have no reason to complain of as a yoke or burden; for the service of God, according to the gospel, is perfect freedom; it sets us at liberty from all slavish regards, either to the persons or the things of this world. 3. We must all be judged by this law of liberty. Men's eternal condition will be determined according to the gospel; this is the book that will be opened, when we shall stand before the judgment-seat; there will be no relief to those whom the gospel condemns, nor will any accusation lie against those whom the gospel justifies. 4. It concerns us therefore so to speak and act now as become those who must shortly be judged by this law of liberty; that is, that we come up to gospel terms, that we make conscience of gospel duties, that e be of a gospel temper, and that our conversation be a gospel conversation, because by this rule we must be judged. 5. The consideration of our being judged by the gospel should engage us more especially to be merciful in our regards to the poor (*v.* 13): *For he shall have judgment without mercy that hath shown no mercy; and mercy rejoiceth against judgment.* Take notice here, (1.) The doom which will be passed upon impenitent sinners at last will be judgment without mercy; there will be no mixtures or allays in the cup of wrath and of trembling, the dregs of which they must drink. (2.) Such as show no mercy now shall find no mercy in the great day. But we may note, on the other hand, (3.) That there will be such as shall become instances of the triumph of mercy, in whom mercy rejoices against judgment: all the children of men, in the last day, will be either vessels of wrath or vessels of mercy. It concerns all to consider among which they shall be found; and let us remember that *blessed are the merciful, for they shall obtain mercy.*

Verses 14–26

In this latter part of the chapter, the apostle shows the error of those who rested in a bare profession of the Christian faith, as if that would save them, while the temper of their minds and the tenour of their lives were altogether disagreeable to that holy religion which they professed. To let them see, therefore, what a wretched foundation they built their hopes upon, it is here proved at large that a man is justified, not by faith only, but by works. Now,

I. Upon this arises a very great question, namely, how to reconcile Paul and James. Paul, in his epistles to the Romans and Galatians, seems to assert the directly contrary thing to what James here lays down, saying if often, and with a great deal of emphasis, *that we are justified by faith only and not by the works of the law. Amicae scripturarum lites, utinam et nostrae — There is a very happy agreement between one part of scripture and another, notwithstanding seeming differences: it were well if the differences among Christians were as easily reconciled.* "Nothing," says Mr. Baxter, "but men's misunderstanding the plain drift and sense of Paul's epistles, could make so many take it for a matter of great difficulty to reconcile Paul and James." A general view of those things which are insisted on by the Antinomians may be seen in Mr. Baxter's Paraphrase: and many ways might be mentioned which have been invented among learned men to make the apostles agree; but it may be sufficient only to observe these few things following: — 1. When Paul says that *a man is justified by faith, without the deeds of the law* (Rom. 3:28), he plainly speaks of another sort of work than James does, but not of another sort of faith. Paul speaks of works wrought in obedience to the law of Moses, and before men's embracing the faith of the gospel; and he had to deal with those who valued themselves so highly upon those works that they rejected the gospel (as Rom. 10, at the beginning most expressly declares); but James speaks of works done in obedience to the gospel, and as the proper and necessary effects and fruits of sound believing in Christ Jesus. Both are concerned to magnify the faith of the gospel, as that which alone could save us and justify us; but Paul magnifies it by showing the insufficiency of any works of the law before faith, or in op-

position to the doctrine of justification by Jesus Christ; James magnifies the same faith, by showing what are the genuine and necessary products and operations of it. 2. Paul not only speaks of different works from those insisted on by James, but he speaks of a quite different use that was made of good works from what is here urged and intended. Paul had to do with those who depended on the merit of their works in the sight of God, and thus he might well make them of no manner of account. James had to do with those who cried up faith, but would not allow works to be used even as evidence; they depended upon a bare profession, as sufficient to justify them; and with these he might well urge the necessity and vast importance of good works. As we must not break one table of the law, by dashing it against the other, so neither must we break in pieces the law and the gospel, by making them clash with one another: those who cry up the gospel so as to set aside the law, and those who cry up the law so as to set aside the gospel, are both in the wrong; for we must take our work before us; there must be both faith in Jesus Christ and good works the fruit of faith. 3. The justification of which Paul speaks is different from that spoken of by James; the one speaks of our persons being justified before God, the other speaks of our faith being justified before men: *"Show me thy faith by thy works,"* says James, "let thy faith be justified in the eyes of those that behold thee by thy works;" but Paul speaks of justification in the sight of God, who justifies those only that believe in Jesus, and purely on account of the redemption that is in him. Thus we see that our persons are justified before God by faith, but our faith is justified before men by works. This is so plainly the scope and design of the apostle James that he is but confirming what Paul, in other places, says of his faith, that it is a laborious faith, and a faith working by love, Gal. 5:6; 1 Th. 1:3; Titus 3:8; and many other places. 4. Paul may be understood as speaking of that justification which is inchoate, James of that which is complete; it is by *faith* only that we are put into a justified state, but then good works come in for the completing of our justification at the last great day; then, *Come you children of my Father — for I was hungry, and you gave me meat,* etc.

II. Having thus cleared this part of scripture from every thing of a contradiction to other parts of it, let us see what is more particularly to be learnt from this excellent passage of James; we are taught,

1. That faith without works will not profit, and cannot save us. *What doth it profit, my brethren, if a man say he hath faith, and have not works? Can faith save him?* Observe here, (1.) That faith which does not save will not really profit us; a bare profession may sometimes seem to be profitable, to gain the good opinion of those who are truly good, and it may procure in some cases worldly good things; but what profit will this be, for any to gain the world and to lose their souls? *What doth it profit? — Can faith save him?* All things should be accounted profitable or unprofitable to us as they tend to forward or hinder the salvation of our souls. And, above all other things, we should take care thus to make account of faith, as that which does not profit, if it do not save, but will aggravate our condemnation and destruction at last. (2.) For a man to have faith, and to say he has faith, are two different things; the apostle does not say, *If a man have faith without works,* for that is not a supposable case; the drift of this place of scripture is plainly to show that an opinion, or speculation, or assent, without works, is not faith; but the case is put thus, *If a man say he hath faith,* etc. Men may boast of that to others, and be conceited of that in themselves, of which they are really destitute.

2. We are taught that, as love or charity is an operative principle, so is faith, and that neither of them would otherwise be good for any thing; and, by trying how it looks for a person to pretend he is very charitable who yet never does any works of charity, you may judge what sense there is in pretending to have faith without the proper and necessary fruits of it: *"If a brother or a sister be naked, and destitute of daily food, and one of you say unto them, Depart in peace, be you warmed and filled, notwithstanding you give them not those things which are needful to the body, what doth it profit? v.* 15–17. What will such a charity as this, that consists in bare words, avail either you or the poor? Will you come before God with such empty shows of charity as these? You might as well pretend that your love and charity will stand the test without acts of mercy as think that a profession of faith will bear you out before God without works of piety and obe-

dience. *Even so faith, if it hath not works, is dead, being along," v.* 17. We are too apt to rest in a bare profession of faith, and to think that this will save us; it is a cheap and easy religion to say, "We believe the articles of the Christian faith;" but it is a great delusion to imagine that this is enough to bring us to heaven. Those who argue thus wrong God, and put a cheat upon their own souls; a mock-faith is as hateful as mock-charity, and both show a heart dead to all real godliness. You may as soon take pleasure in a dead body, void of soul, or sense, or action, as God take pleasure in a dead faith, where there are no works.

3. We are taught to compare a faith boasting of itself without works and a faith evidenced by works, by looking on both together, to try how this comparison will work upon our minds. *Yea, a man may say, Thou hast faith, and I have works. Show me thy faith without thy works, and I will show thee my faith by my works, v.* 18. Suppose a true believer thus pleading with a boasting hypocrite, "Thou makest a profession, and sayest thou hast faith; I make no such boasts, but leave my works to speak for me. Now give any evidence of having the faith thou professest without works if thou canst, and I will soon let thee see how my works flow from faith and are the undoubted evidences of its existence." This is the evidence by which the scriptures all along teach men to judge both of themselves and others. And this is the evidence according to which Christ will proceed at the day of judgment. *The dead were judged according to their works,* Rev. 20:12. How will those be exposed then who boast of that which they cannot evidence, or who go about to evidence their faith by any thing but works of piety and mercy!

4. We are taught to look upon a faith of bare speculation and knowledge as the faith of devils: *Thou believest that there is one God; thou doest well; the devils also believe, and tremble, v.* 19. That instance of faith which the apostle here chooses to mention is the first principle of all religion. *"Thou believest that there is a God,* against the atheists; and that there is but one God, against the idolaters; *thou doest well:* so far all is right. But to rest here, and take up a good opinion of thyself, or of thy state towards God, merely on account of thy believing in him, this will render thee miserable: *The devils also believe, and tremble.* If thou contentest thyself with a bare assent to articles of faith, and some speculations upon them, thus far the devils go. And as their faith and knowledge only serve to excite horror, so in a little time will thine." The word tremble is commonly looked upon as denoting a good effect of faith; but here it may rather be taken as a bad effect, when applied to the faith of devils. They tremble, not out of reverence, but hatred and opposition to that one God on whom they believe. To rehearse that article of our creed, therefore, *I believe in God the Father Almighty,* will not distinguish us from devils at last, unless we now give up ourselves to God as the gospel directs, and love him, and delight ourselves in him, and serve him, which the devils do not, cannot do.

5. We are taught that he who boasts of faith without works is to be looked upon at present as a foolish condemned person. *But wilt thou know, O vain man, that faith without works is dead? v.* 20. The words translated *vain man — anthrōpe kene,* are observed to have the same signification with the word *Raca,* which must never be used to private persons, or as an effect of anger (Mt. *v.* 22), but may be used as here, to denote a just detestation of such a sort of men as are empty of good works, and yet boasters of their faith. And it plainly declares them fools and abjects in the sight of God. Faith without works is said to be *dead,* not only as void of all those operations which are the proofs of spiritual life, but as unavailable to eternal life: such believers as rest in a bare profession of faith *are dead while they live.*

6. We are taught that a justifying faith cannot be without works, from two examples, Abraham and Rahab.

(1.) The first instance is that of Abraham, the father of the faithful, and the prime example of justification, to whom the Jews had a special regard (*v.* 21): *Was not Abraham our father justified by works, when he had offered Isaac his son upon the altar?* Paul, on the other hand, says (in *ch.* 4 of the epistle to the Romans) that Abraham *believed, and it was counted to him for righteousness.* But these are well reconciled, by observing what is said in Heb. 11, which shows that the faith both of Abraham and Rahab was such as to produce those good works of which James speaks, and which are not to be separated from faith as justifying and saving. By what Abraham did, it appeared that he truly believed.

Upon this footing, the words of God himself plainly put this matter. Gen. 22:16, 17, *Because thou hast done this thing, and hast not withheld thy son, thine only son; therefore in blessing I will bless thee.* Thus the faith of Abraham was a working faith (*v.* 22), *it wrought with his works, and by works was made perfect.* And by this means you come to the true sense of that scripture which saith, Abraham believed God, *and it was imputed unto him for righteousness, v.* 23. And thus he became the *friend of God.* Faith, producing such works, endeared him to the divine Being, and advanced him to very peculiar favours and intimacies with God. It is a great honour done to Abraham that he is called and counted the friend of God. You see then (*v.* 24) how that *by works a man is justified* (comes into such a state of favour and friendship with God), *and not by faith only;* not by a bare opinion, or profession, or believing without obeying, but by having such a faith as is productive of good works. Now besides the explication of this passage and example, as thus illustrating and supporting the argument James is upon, many other useful lessons may be learned by us from what is here said concerning Abraham. [1.] Those who would have Abraham's blessings must be careful to copy after his faith: to boast of being Abraham's seed will not avail any, if they do not believe as he did. [2.] Those works which evidence true faith must to works of self-denial, and such as God himself commands (as Abraham's offering up his son, his only son, was), and not such works as are pleasing to flesh and blood and may serve our interest, or are the mere fruits of our own imagination and devising. [3.] What we piously purpose and sincerely resolve to do for God is accepted as if actually performed. Thus Abraham is regarded as offering up his son, though he did not actually proceed to make a sacrifice of him. It was a done thing in the mind, and spirit, and resolution of Abraham, and God accepts it as if fully performed and accomplished. [4.] The actings of faith make it grow perfect, as the truth of faith makes it act. [5.] Such an acting faith will make others, as well as Abraham, friends of God. Thus Christ says to his disciples, *I have called you friends,* Jn. 15:15. All transactions between God and the truly believing soul are easy, pleasant, and delightful. There is one will and one heart, and there is a mutual complacency. *God rejoiceth over those* who truly believe, to do them good; and they delight themselves in him.

(2.) The second example of faith's justifying itself and us with and by works is Rahab: *Likewise also was not Rahab the harlot justified by works, when she had received the messengers, and had sent them out another way? v.* 25. The former instance was of one renowned for his faith all his life long, This is of one noted for sin, whose faith was meaner and of a much lower degree; so that the strongest faith will not do, nor the meanest be allowed to go without works. Some say that the word here rendered *harlot* was the proper name of Rahab. Others tell us that it signifies no more than a *hostess,* or one who keeps a public house, with whom therefore the spies lodged. But it is very probable that her character was infamous; and such an instance is mentioned to show that faith will save the worst, when evidenced by proper works; and it will not save the best without such works as God requires. This Rahab believed the report she had heard of God's powerful presence with Israel; but that which proved her faith sincere was, that, to the hazard of her life, she *received the messengers, and sent them out another way.* Observe here, [1.] The wonderful power of faith in transforming and changing sinners. [2.] The regard which an operative faith meets with from God, to obtain his mercy and favour. [3.] Where great sins are pardoned, there must prefer the honour of God and the good of his people before the preservation of her own country. Her former acquaintance must be discarded, her former course of life entirely abandoned, and she must give signal proof and evidence of this before she can be in a justified state; and even after she is justified, yet her former character must be remembered; not so much to her dishonour as to glorify the rich grace and mercy of God. Though justified, she is called *Rahab the harlot.*

7. And now, upon the whole matter, the apostle draws this conclusion, *As the body without the spirit is dead, so faith without works is dead also, v.* 26. These words are read differently; some reading them, *As the body without the breath is dead, so is faith without works:* and then they show that works are the companions of faith, as breathing is of life. Others read them, *As the body without the soul is dead, so faith without works is dead also:* and then they show that as the body has no action, nor beauty, but becomes a loathsome carcass, when the soul is gone, so a bare profession without works is useless, yea, loathsome and offensive. Let us then take head of running into extremes in this case. For, (1.) The best works, without faith, are dead; they want their root and principle. It is by faith that any thing we do is really good, as done with an eye to God, in obedience to him, and so as to aim principally at his acceptance. (2.) The most plausible profession of faith, without works, is dead: as the root is dead when it produces nothing green, nothing of fruit. Faith is the root, good works are the fruits, and we must see to it that we have both. We must not think that either, without the other, will justify and save us. This is the grace of God wherein we stand, and we should stand to it.

CHAPTER 3

The apostle here reproves ambition, and an arrogant magisterial tongue; and shows the duty and advantage of bridling it because of its power to do mischief. Those who profess religion ought especially to govern their tongues (*v.* 1–12). True wisdom makes men meek, and avoiders of strife and envy: and hereby it may easily be distinguished from a wisdom that is earthly and hypocritical (*v.* 13 to the end).

Verses 1–12

The foregoing chapter shows how unprofitable and dead faith is without works. It is plainly intimated by what this chapter first goes upon that such a faith is, however, apt to make men conceited and magisterial in their tempers and their talk. Those who set up faith in the manner the former chapter condemns are most apt to run into those sins of the tongue which this chapter condemns. And indeed the best need to be cautioned against a dictating, censorious, mischievous use of their tongues. We are therefore taught,

I. Not to use our tongues so as to lord it over others: *My brethren, be not many masters,* etc., *v.* 1. These words do not forbid doing what we can to direct and instruct others in the way of their duty or to reprove them in a Christian way for what is amiss; but we must not affect to speak and act as those who are continually assuming the chair, we must not prescribe to one another, so as to make our own sentiments a standard by which to try all others, because God gives various gifts to men, and expects from each according to that measure of light which he gives. "Therefore by not many *masters*" (or *teachers,* as some read it); "do not give yourselves the air of teachers, imposers, and judges, but rather speak with the humility and spirit of learners; do not censure one another, as if all must be brought to your standard." This is enforced by two reasons. 1. Those who thus set up for judges and censurers *shall receive the greater condemnation.* Our judging others will but make our own judgment the more strict and severe, Mt. 7:1, 2. Those who are curious to spy out the faults of others, and arrogant in passing censures upon them, may expect that God will be as extreme in marking what they say and do amiss. 2. Another reason given against such acting the master is because we are all sinners: *In many things we offend all, v.* 2. Were we to think more of our own mistakes and offenses, we should be less apt to judge other people. While we are severe against what we count offensive in others, we do not consider how much there is in us which is justly offensive to them. Self-justifiers are commonly self-deceivers. We are all guilty before God; and those who vaunt it over the frailties and infirmities of others little think how many things they offend in themselves. Nay, perhaps their magisterial deportment, and censorious tongues, may prove worse than any faults they condemn in others. Let us learn to be severe in judging ourselves, but charitable in our judgments of other people.

II. We are taught to govern our tongue so as to prove ourselves perfect and upright men, and such as have an entire government over ourselves: *If any man offend not in word, the same is a perfect man, and able also to bridle the whole body.* It is here implied that he whose conscience is affected by tongue-sins, and who takes care to avoid them, is an upright man, and has an undoubted sign of true grace. But, on the other hand, *if a man seemeth to be religious* (as was declared in the first chapter) *and bridleth not his tongue,* whatever profession he makes, *that man's religion is vain.* Further, he that offends not in word will not only prove himself a sincere Christian, but a very much advanced and improved Christian. For the wisdom and grace which enable him to rule his tongue will enable him also to rule all his actions. This we have illustrated by two comparisons: — 1. The governing and guiding of all the motions of a horse, by the bit which is put into his mouth: *Behold, we put bits into the horses' mouths, that they may obey us, and we turn about their whole body, v.* 3. There is a great deal of brutish fierceness and wantonness in us. This shows itself very much by the tongue: so that this must be bridled; according to Ps. 39:1, *I will keep my mouth with a bridle* (or, *I will bridle my mouth*) *while the wicked is before me.* The more quick and lively the tongue is, the more should we thus take care to govern it. Otherwise, as an unruly and ungovernable horse runs away with his rider, or throws him, so an unruly tongue will serve those in like manner who have no command over it. Whereas, let resolution and watchfulness, under the influence of the grace of God, bridle the tongue, and then all the motions and actions of the whole body will be easily guided and overruled. 2. The governing of a ship by the right management of the helm: *Behold also the ships, which though they are so great, and are driven of fierce winds, yet are they turned about with a very small helm whithersoever the governor listeth. Even so the tongue is a little member, and boasteth great things, v.* 4, 5. As the helm is a very small part of the ship, so is the tongue a very small part of the body: but the right governing of the helm or rudder will steer and turn the ship as the governor pleases; and a right management of the tongue is, in a great measure, the government of the whole man. There is a wonderful beauty in these comparisons, to show how things of small bulk may yet be of vast use. And hence we should learn to make the due management of our tongues more our study, because, though they are little members, they are capable of doing a great deal of good or a great deal of hurt. Therefore,

III. We are taught to dread an unruly tongue as one of the greatest and most pernicious evils. It is compared to a little fire placed among a great deal of combustible matter, which soon raises a flame and consumes all before it: *Behold, how great a matter a little fire kindleth! And the tongue is a fire, a world of iniquity,* etc., *v.* 5, 6. There is such an abundance of sin in the tongue that it may be called *a world of iniquity.* How many defilements does it occasion! How many and dreadful flames does it kindle! *So is the tongue among the members that it defileth the whole body.* Observe hence, There is a great pollution and defilement in sins of the tongue. Defiling passions are kindled, vented, and cherished by this unruly member. And the whole body is often drawn into sin and guilt by the tongue. Therefore Solomon says, *Suffer not thy mouth to cause thy flesh to sin,* Eccles. *v.* 6. The snares into which men are sometimes led by the tongue are insufferable to themselves and destructive of others. *It setteth on fire the course of nature.* The affairs of mankind and of societies are often thrown into confusion, and all is on a flame, by the tongues of men. Some read it, *all our generations are set on fire by the tongue.* There is no age of the world, nor any condition of life, private or public, but will afford examples of this. *And it is set on fire of hell.* Observe hence, Hell has more to do in promoting of fire of the tongue than men are generally aware of. It is from some diabolical designs, that men's tongues are inflamed. The devil is expressly called a liar, a murderer, an accuser of the brethren; and, whenever men's tongues are employed in any of these ways, they are set on fire of hell. The Holy Ghost indeed once descended in *cloven tongues as of fire,* Acts 2. And, where the tongue is thus guided and wrought upon by a fire from heaven, there it kindleth good thoughts, holy affections, and ardent devotions. But when it is set on fire of hell, as in all undue heats it is, there it is mischievous, producing rage and hatred, and those things which serve the purposes of the devil. As therefore you would dread fires and flames, you should dread contentions, revilings, slanders, lies, and every thing that would kindle the fire of wrath in your own spirit or in the spirits of others. But,

IV. We are next taught how very difficult a thing it is to govern the tongue: *For every kind of beasts, and of birds, and of serpents, and of things in the sea, is tamed, and hath been tamed, of mankind. But the tongue can no man tame, v.* 7, 8. As if the apostle had said, "Lions, and the most savage beasts, as well as horses and camels, and creatures of the greatest strength, have been tamed and governed by men: so have birds, notwithstanding their wildness and timorousness, and their wings to bear them up continually out of our reach: even serpents, notwithstanding all their venom and all their cunning, have been made familiar and harmless: and things in the sea have been taken by men, and made serviceable to them. And these creatures have not been subdued nor tamed by miracle only (as the lions crouched to Daniel, instead of devouring him, and ravens fed Elijah, and a whale carried Jonah through the depths of the sea to dry land), but what is here spoken of is something commonly done; not only hath been tamed, but is tamed of mankind. Yet the tongue is worse than these, and cannot be tamed by the power and art which serves to tame these things. No man can tame the tongue without supernatural grace and assistance." The apostle does not intend to represent it as a thing impossible, but as a thing extremely difficult, which therefore will require great watchfulness, and pains, and prayer, to keep it in due order. And sometimes all is too little; *for it is an unruly evil, full of deadly poison.* Brute creatures may be kept within certain bounds, they may be managed by certain rules, and even serpents may be so used as to do not hurt with all their poison; but the tongue is apt to break through all bounds and rules, and to spit out its poison on one occasion or other, notwithstanding the utmost care. So that not only does it need to be watched, and guarded, and governed, as much as an unruly beast, or a hurtful and poisonous creature, but much more care and pains will be needful to prevent the mischievous outbreakings and effects of the tongue. However,

V. We are taught to think of the use we make of our tongues in religion and in the service of God, and by such a consideration to keep it from cursing, censuring, and every thing that is evil on other occasions: *Therewith bless we God, even the Father; and therewith curse we men, who are made after the similitude of God. Out of the same mouth proceed blessing and cursing. My brethren, these things ought not so to be, v.* 9, 10. How absurd is it that those who use their tongues in prayer and praise should ever use them in cursing, slandering, and the like! If we bless God as our Father, it should teach us to speak well of, and kindly to, all who bear his image. That tongue which addresses with reverence the divine Being cannot, without the greatest inconsistency, turn upon fellow-creatures with reviling brawling language. It is said of the seraphim that praise God, they *dare not bring a railing accusation.* And for men to reproach those who have not only the image of God in their natural faculties, but are renewed after the image of God by the grace of the gospel: this is a most shameful contradiction to all their pretensions of honouring the great Original. *These things ought not so to be;* and, if such considerations were always at hand, surely they would not be. Piety is disgraced in all the shows of it, if there be not charity. That tongue confutes itself which one while pretends to adore the perfections of God, and to refer all things to him, and another while will condemn even good men if they do not just come up to the same words or expressions used by it. Further, to fix this thought, the apostle shows that contrary effects from the same causes are monstrous, and not be found in nature, and therefore cannot be consistent with grace: *Doth a fountain send forth at the same place sweet water and bitter? Can the fig-tree bear olive-berries, or a vine, figs? Or doth the same spring yield both salt water and fresh? v.* 11, 12. True religion will not admit of contradictions; and a truly religious man can never allow of them either in his words or his actions. How many sins would this prevent, and recover men from, to put them upon being always consistent with themselves!

Verses 13–18

As the sins before condemned arise from an affectation of being thought more wise than others, and being endued with more knowledge than they, so the apostle in these verses shows the difference between men's pretending to be wise and their being really so, and between the wisdom which is from beneath (from earth or hell) and that which is from above.

I. We have some account of true wisdom, with the distinguishing marks and fruits of it: *Who is a wise man, and endued with knowledge among you? Let him show out of a good conversation his works with meekness of wisdom, v.* 13. A truly wise man is a very knowing man: he will not set up for the reputation of being wise without laying in a good stock of knowledge; and he will not value himself merely upon knowing things, if he has not wisdom to make a right application and use of that knowledge. These two things must be put together to make up the account of true wisdom: who is wise, and endued with knowledge? Now where this is the happy case of any there will be these following things: — 1. A good conversation. If we are wiser than others, this should

be evidenced by the goodness of our conversation, not by the roughness or vanity of it. Words that inform, and heal, and do good, are the marks of wisdom; not those that look great, and do mischief, and are the occasions of evil, either in ourselves or others. 2. True wisdom may be known by its works. The conversation here does not refer only to words, but to the whole of men's practice; therefore it is said, Let him show out of a good conversation his works. True wisdom does not lie in good notions or speculations so much as in good and useful actions. Not he who thinks well, or he who talks well, is in the sense of the scripture allowed to be wise, if he do not live and act well. 3. True wisdom may be known by the meekness of the spirit and temper: *Let him show with meekness,* etc. It is a great instance of wisdom prudently to bridle our own anger, and patiently to bear the anger of others. And as wisdom will evidence itself in meekness, so meekness will be a great friend to wisdom; for nothing hinders the regular apprehension, the solid judgment, and impartiality of thought, necessary to our acting wisely, so much as passion. When we are mild and calm, we are best able to hear reason, and best able to speak it. Wisdom produces meekness, and meekness increases wisdom.

II. We have the glorying of those taken away who are of a contrary character to that now mentioned, and their wisdom exposed in all its boasts and productions: *"If you have bitter envying and strife in your hearts, glory not,* etc., *v.* 14–16. Pretend what you will, and think yourselves ever so wise, yet you have abundance of reason to cease your glorying, if you run down love and peace, and give way to bitter envying and strife. Your zeal for truth or orthodoxy, and your boasts of knowing more than others, if you employ these only to make others hateful, and to show your own spite and heart-burnings against them, are a shame to your profession of Christianity, and a downright contradiction to it. Lie not thus against the truth." Observe, 1. Envying and strife are opposed to the meekness of wisdom. The heart is the seat of both; but envy and wisdom cannot dwell together in the same heart. Holy zeal and bitter envying are as different as the flames of seraphim and the fire of hell. 2. The order of things here laid down. Envying is first and excites strife; strife endeavours to excuse itself by vain-glorying and lying; and then (*v.* 16) hereupon ensue confusion and every evil work. Those who live in malice, envy, and contention, live in confusion, and are liable to be provoked and hurried to any evil work. Such disorders raise many temptations, strengthen temptations, and involve men in a great deal of guilt. One sin begets another, and it cannot be imagined how much mischief is produced: *there* is every evil work. And is such wisdom as produces these effects to be gloried in? This cannot be without giving the lie to Christianity, and pretending that this wisdom is what it is not. For observe, 3. Whence such wisdom cometh: *It descendeth not from above,* but ariseth from beneath; and, to speak plainly, it is *earthly, sensual, devilish, v.* 15. It springs from earthly principles, acts upon earthly motives, and is intent upon serving earthly purposes. It is sensual indulging the flesh, and making provision to fulfil the lusts and desires of it. Or, according to the original word, *psychikē,* it is animal of human — the mere working of natural reason, without any supernatural light. And it is devilish, such wisdom being the wisdom of devils (to create uneasiness and to do hurt), and being inspired by devils, whose condemnation is pride (1 Tim. 3:6), and who are noted in other places of scripture for their wrath, and their accusing the brethren. And therefore those who are lifted up with such wisdom as this must fall into the condemnation of the devil.

III. We have the lovely picture of that wisdom which is from above more fully drawn, and set in opposition to this which is from beneath: *But the wisdom that is from above is first pure, then peaceable, etc., v.* 17, 18. Observe here, True wisdom is God's gift. It is not gained by conversing with men, nor by the knowledge of the world (as some think and speak), but it comes from above. It consists of these several things: — 1. It is pure, without mixture of maxims or aims that would debase it: and it is free from iniquity and defilements, not allowing of any known sin, but studious of holiness both in heart and life. 2. The wisdom that is from above is peaceable. Peace follows purity, and depends upon it. Those who are truly wise do what they can to preserve peace, that it may not be broken; and to make peace, that where it is lost it may be restored. In kingdoms, in families, in churches, in all societies, and in all interviews and transactions, heavenly wisdom makes men peaceable. 3. It is gentle, not standing

upon extreme right in matters of property; not saying nor doing any thing rigorous in points of censure; not being furious about opinions, urging our own beyond their weight nor theirs who oppose us beyond their intention; not being rude and overbearing in conversation, nor harsh and cruel in temper. Gentleness may thus be opposed to all these. 4. Heavenly wisdom is *easy to be entreated, eupeithēs;* it is very *persuadable,* either to what is good or from what is evil. There is an easiness that is weak and faulty; but it is not a blamable easiness to yield ourselves to the persuasions of God's word, and to all just and reasonable counsels or requests of our fellow-creatures; no, nor to give up a dispute, where there appears a good reason for it and where a good end may be answered by it. 5. Heavenly wisdom is full of mercy and good fruits, inwardly disposed to every thing that is kind and good, both to relieve those who want and to forgive those who offend, and actually to do this whenever proper occasions offer. 6. Heavenly wisdom is without partiality. The original word, *adiakritos,* signifies to be without suspicion, or free from judging, making no undue surmises nor differences in our conduct towards one person more than another. The margin reads it, *without wrangling,* not acting the part of sectaries, and disputing merely for the sake of a party; nor censuring others purely on account of their differing from us. The wisest men are least apt to be censurers. 7. That wisdom which is from above is without hypocrisy. It has no disguises nor deceits. It cannot fall in with those managements which the world counts wise, which are crafty and guileful; but it is sincere and open, steady and uniform, and consistent with itself. O that you and I may always be guided by such wisdom as this! that with Paul we may be able to say, *Not with fleshly wisdom, but in simplicity and godly sincerity, by the grace of God, we have our conversation.* And then, *lastly,* true wisdom will go on to sow the fruits of righteousness in peace, and thus, if it may be, to make peace in the world, *v.* 18. And that which is sown in peace will produce a harvest of joys. Let others reap the fruits of contentions, and all the advantages they can propose to themselves by them; but let us go on peaceably to sow the seeds of righteousness, and we may depend upon it our labour will not be lost. *For light is sown for the righteous, and gladness for the upright in heart; and the work of righteousness shall be peace, and the effect of righteousness quietness and assurance for ever.*

CHAPTER 4

In this chapter we are directed to consider, I. Some causes of contention, besides those mentioned in the foregoing chapter, and to watch against them (*v.* 1–5). II. We are taught to abandon the friendship of this world, so as to submit and subject ourselves entirely to God (*v.* 4–10). III. All detraction and rash judgment of others are to be carefully avoided (*v.* 11, 12). IV. We must preserve a constant regard, and pay the utmost deference to the disposals of divine Providence (*v.* 13 to the end).

Verses 1–10

The former chapter speaks of envying one another, as the great spring of strifes and contentions; this chapter speaks of a lust after worldly things, and a setting too great a value upon worldly pleasures and friendships, as that which carried their divisions to a shameful height.

I. The apostle here reproves the Jewish Christians for their wars, and for their lusts as the cause of them: *Whence come wars and fightings among you? Come they not hence, even of your lusts that war in your members, v.* 1. The Jews were a very seditious people, and had therefore frequent wars with the Romans; and they were a very quarrelsome divided people, often fighting among themselves; and many of those corrupt Christians against whose errors and vices this epistle was written seem to have fallen in with the common quarrels. Hereupon, our apostle informs them that the origin of their wars and fightings was not (as they pretended) a true zeal for their country, and for the honour of God, but that their prevailing lusts were the cause of all. Observe hence, What is sheltered and shrouded under a specious pretence of zeal for God and religion often comes from men's pride, malice, covetousness, ambition, and revenge. The Jews had many struggles with the Roman power before they ere entirely destroyed. They often unnecessarily embroiled themselves, and then fell into parties and factions about the different methods of managing their wars with their common enemies; and hence it came to pass that, when their cause might be supposed good, yet their engaging in it and their management of it came from a bad principle. Their worldly and fleshly lusts raised and managed their wars and fightings; but one would think here is enough said to subdue those lusts; for, 1. They make a war within as well as fightings without. Impetuous passions and desires first war in their members, and then raise feuds in their nation. There is war between conscience and corruption, and there is war also between one corruption and another, and from these contentions in themselves arose their quarrels with each other. Apply this to private cases, and may we not then say of fightings and strifes among relations and neighbours they come from those lusts which war in the members? From lust of power and dominion, lust of pleasure, or lust of riches, from some one or more of these lusts arise all the broils and contentions that are in the world; and, since all wars and fightings come from the corruptions of our own hearts, it is therefore the right method for the cure of contention to lay the axe to the root, and mortify those lusts that war in the members. 2. It should kill these lusts to think of their disappointment: *"You lust, and have not; you kill, and desire to have, and cannot obtain, v.* 2. You covet great things for yourselves, and you think to obtain them by your victories over the Romans or by suppressing this and the other party among yourselves. You think you shall secure great pleasures and happiness to yourselves, by overthrowing every thing which thwarts your eager wishes; but, alas! you are losing your labour and your blood, while you kill one another with such views as these." Inordinate desires are either totally disappointed, or they are not to be appeased and satisfied by obtaining the things desired. The words here rendered *cannot obtain* signify cannot gain the happiness sought after. Note hence, Worldly and fleshly lusts are the distemper which will not allow of contentment or satisfaction in the mind. 3. Sinful desires and affections generally exclude prayer, and the working of our desires towards God: *"You fight and war, yet you have not, because you ask not.* You fight, and do not succeed, because you do not pray you do not consult God in your undertakings, whether he will allow of them or not; and you do not commit your way to him, and make known your requests to him, but follow your own corrupt views and inclinations: therefore you meet with continual disappointments;" or else. 4. "Your lusts spoil your prayers, and make them an abomination to God, whenever you put them up to him, *v.* 3. *You ask, and receive not, because you ask amiss, that you may consume it upon your lusts."* As if it had been said, "Though perhaps you may sometimes pray for success against your enemies, yet it is not your aim to improve the advantages you gain, so as to promote true piety and religion either in yourselves or others; but pride, vanity, luxury, and sensuality, are what you would serve by your successes, and by your very prayers. You want to live in great power and plenty, in voluptuousness and a sensual prosperity; and thus you disgrace devotion and dishonour God by such gross and base ends; and therefore your prayers are rejected." Let us learn hence, in the management of all our worldly affairs, and in our prayers to God for success in them, to see that our ends be right. When men follow their worldly business (suppose them tradesmen or husbandmen), and ask of God prosperity, but do not receive what they ask for, it is because they ask with wrong aims and intentions. They ask God to give them success in their callings or undertakings; not that they may glorify their heavenly Father and do good with what they have, but that they may *consume it upon their lusts* — that they may be enabled to eat better meat, and drink better drink, and wear better clothes, and so gratify their pride, vanity, and voluptuousness. But, if we thus seek the things of this world, it is just in God to deny them; whereas, if we seek any thing that we may serve God with it, we may expect he will either give us what we seek or give us hearts to be content without it, and give opportunities of serving and glorifying him some other way. Let us remember this, that when we speed not in our prayers it is *because we ask amiss;* either we do not ask for right ends or not in a right manner, not with faith or not with fervency: unbelieving and cold desires beg denials; and this we may be sure of, that, when our prayers are rather the language of our lusts than of our graces, they will return empty.

II. We have fair warning to avoid all criminal friendships with this world: *You adulterers and adulteresses, know you not that the friendship of the world is enmity with God? v.* 4. Worldly people are here called adulterers and adulteresses, because of their perfidiousness of God, while they give their best affections to the world. Covetousness is elsewhere called idolatry, and it is here called adultery; it is a forsaking of him to whom we are devoted and espoused, to cleave to other things; there is this brand put upon worldly-mindedness — that it is enmity to God. A man may have a competent portion of the good things of this life, and yet may keep himself in the love of God; but he who sets his heart upon the world, who places his happiness in it, and will conform himself to it, and do any thing rather than lose its friendship, he is an enemy to God; it is constructive treason and rebellion against God to set the world upon his throne in our hearts. *Whosoever therefore is the friend of the world is the enemy of God.* He who will act upon this principle, to keep the smiles of the world, and to have its continual friendship, cannot but show himself, in spirit, and in his actions too, an enemy to God. *You cannot serve God and mammon,* Mt. 6:24. Hence arise wars and fightings, even from this adulterous idolatrous love of the world, and serving of it; for what peace can there be among men, so long as there is enmity towards God? or who can fight against God, and prosper? "Think seriously with yourselves what the spirit of the world is, and you will find that you cannot suit yourselves to it as friends, but it must occasion your being envious, and full of evil inclinations, as the generality of the world are. *Do you think that the scripture saith in vain, The spirit that dwelleth in us lusteth to envy?" v.* 5. The account given in the holy scriptures of the hearts of men by nature is *that their imagination is evil, only evil, and that continually,* Gen. 6:5. Natural corruption principally shows itself by envying, and there is a continual propensity to this. The spirit which naturally dwells in man is always producing one evil imagination or another, always emulating such as we see and converse with and seeking those things which are possessed and enjoyed by them. Now this way of the world, affecting pomp and pleasure, and falling into strifes and quarrels for the sake of these things, is the certain consequence of being friends to the world; for there is no friendship without a oneness of spirit, and therefore Christians, to avoid contentions, must avoid the friendship of the world, and must show that they are actuated by nobler principles and that a nobler spirit dwells in them; for, if we belong to God, he gives more grace than to live and act as the generality of the world do. The spirit of the world teaches men to be churls; God teaches them to be bountiful. The spirit of the world teaches us to lay up, or lay out, for ourselves, and according to our own fancies; God teaches us to be willing to communicate to the necessities and to the comfort of others, and so as to do good to all about us, according to our ability. The grace of God is contrary to the spirit of the world, and therefore the friendship of the world is to be avoided, if we pretend to be friends of God yea, the grace of God will correct and cure the spirit that naturally dwells in us; where he giveth grace, he giveth another spirit than that of the world.

III. We are taught to observe the difference God makes between pride and humility. *God resisteth the proud, but giveth grace unto the humble, v.* 6. This is represented as the language of scripture in the Old Testament; for so it is declared in the book of *Psalms that God will save the afflicted people* (if their spirits be suited to their condition), *but will bring down high looks* (Ps. 18:27); and in the book of Proverbs it is said, *He scorneth the scorners, and giveth grace unto the lowly,* Prov. 3:34. Two things are here to be observed: — 1. The disgrace cast upon the proud: God resists them; the original word, *antitassetai,* signifies, God's setting himself as in battle array against them; and can there be a greater disgrace than for God to proclaim a man a rebel, an enemy, a traitor to his crown and dignity, and to proceed against him as such? The proud resists God; in his understanding he resists the truths of God; in his will he resists the truths of God; in his will he resists the laws of God; in his passions he resists the providence of God; and therefore no wonder that God sets himself against the proud. Let proud spirits hear this and tremble — *God resists them.* Who can describe the wretched state of those who make God their enemy? He will certainly fill with same (sooner or later) the faces of such as have filled their hearts with pride. We should therefore resist pride in our hearts, if we would not have God to resist us. 2. The honour and help God gives to the humble. Grace, as opposed to disgrace, is honour; this God gives to the humble; and, where God gives grace to be humble, there he will give all other graces, and, as in the beginning of this sixth verse, he will *give more grace.* Wherever God gives true grace, he will give more; for to him that hath, and useth what he hath aright, more shall be given. He will especially give more grace to the humble, because they see their need of it, will pray for it and be thankful for it; and such shall have it. For this reason,

IV. We are taught to submit ourselves entirely to God: *Submit yourselves therefore to God. Resist the devil, and he will flee from you, v.* 7. Christians should forsake the friendship of the world, and watch against that envy and pride which they see prevailing in natural men, and should by grace learn to glory in their submissions to God. "Submit yourselves to him as subjects to their prince, in duty, and as one friend to another, in love and interest. Submit your understandings to the truths of God; submit your wills to the will of God, the will of his precept, the will of his providence." We are subjects, and as such must be submissive; not only through fear, but through love; *not only for wrath, but also for conscience' sake.* "Submit yourselves to God, as considering how many ways you are bound to this, and as considering what advantage you will gain by it; for God will not hurt you by his dominion over you, but will do you good." Now, as this subjection and submission to God are what the devil most industriously strives to hinder, so we ought with great care and steadiness to resist his suggestions. If he would represent a tame yielding to the will and providence of God as what will bring calamities, and expose to contempt and misery, we must resist these suggestions of fear. If he would represent submission to God as a hindrance to our outward ease, or worldly preferments, we must resist these suggestions of pride and sloth. If he would tempt us to lay any of our miseries, and crosses, and afflictions, to the charge of Providence, so that we might avoid them by following his directions instead of God's, we must resist these provocations to anger, *not fretting ourselves in any wise to do evil.* "Let not the devil, in these or the like attempts, prevail upon you; but *resist him and he will flee from you."* If we basely yield to temptations, the devil will continually follow us; but if we *put on the whole armour of God,* and stand it out against him, he will be gone from us. Resolution shuts and bolts the door against temptation.

V. We are directed how to act towards God, in our becoming submissive to him, *v.* 8–10. 1. *Draw nigh to God.* The heart that has rebelled must be brought to the foot of God; the spirit that was distant and estranged from a life of communion and converse with God must become acquainted with him: *"Draw nigh to God,* in his worship and institutions, and in every duty he requires of you." 2. *Cleanse your hands.* He who comes unto God must have clean hands. Paul therefore directs to *lift up holy hands without wrath and doubting* (1 Tim. 2:8), hands free from blood, and bribes, and every thing that is unjust or cruel, and free from every defilement of sin: he is not subject to God who is a servant of sin. The hands must be cleansed by faith, repentance, and reformation, or it will be in vain for us to draw nigh to God in prayer, or in any of the exercises of devotion. 3. The hearts of the double-minded must be purified. Those who halt between God and the world are here meant by *the double-minded.* To *purify the heart* is to be sincere, and to act upon this single aim and principle, rather to please God than to seek after any thing in this world: hypocrisy is heart-impurity; but those who submit themselves to God aright will purify their hearts as well as cleanse their hands. 4. *Be afflicted, and mourn, and weep.* "What afflictions God sends take them as he would have you, and by duly sensible of them. Be afflicted when afflictions are sent upon you, and do not despise them; or be afflicted in your sympathies with those who are so, and in laying to heart the calamities of the church of God. Mourn and weep for your own sins and the sins of others; times of contention and division are times to mourn in, and the sins that occasion wars and fightings should be mourned for. *Let your laughter be turned to mourning and your joy to heaviness."* This may be taken either as a prediction of sorrow or a prescription of seriousness. Let men think to set grief at defiance, yet God can bring it upon them; none laugh so heartily but he can turn their laughter into mourning; and this the unconcerned Christians James wrote to are threatened should be their case. They are therefore directed, before things come to the worst, to lay aside their vain mirth and their sensual pleasures, that they might indulge godly sorrow and penitential tears. 5. *"Humble yourselves in the sight of the Lord.* Let the inward acts of the would be suitable to all those outward expressions of grief, affliction, and sorrow, before mentioned." Humility of spirit is here required, as in the sight of him who looks principally at the spirits of men.

"Let there be a thorough humiliation in bewailing every thing that is evil; let there be great humility in doing that which is good: *Humble yourselves.*"

VI. We have great encouragement to act thus towards God: *He will draw nigh to those that draw nigh to him* (*v.* 8), *and he will lift up* those who humble themselves in his sight, *v.* 10. Those that draw nigh to God in a way of duty shall find God drawing nigh to them in a way of mercy. Draw nigh to him in faith, and trust, and obedience, and he will draw nigh to you for your deliverance. If there be not a close communion between God and us, it is our fault, and not his. *He shall lift up the humble.* Thus much our Lord himself declared, *He that shall humble himself shall be exalted,* Mt. 23:12. If we be truly penitent and humble under the marks of God's displeasure, we shall in a little time know the advantages of his favour; he will lift us up out of trouble, or he will lift us up in our spirits and comforts under trouble; he will lift us up to honour and safety in the world, or he will lift us up in our way to heaven, so as to raise our hearts and affections above the world. *God will revive the spirit of the humble* (Isa. 57:15), *He will hear the desire of the humble* (Ps. 10:17), and he will at last life them up to glory. *Before honour is humility.* The highest honour in heaven will be the reward of the greatest humility on earth.

Verses 11–17

In this part of the chapter,

I. We are cautioned against the sin of evil-speaking: *Speak not evil one of another, brethren, v.* 11. The Greek word, *katalaleite,* signifies speaking any thing that may hurt or injure another; we must not speak evil things of others, though they be true, unless we be called to it, and there be some necessary occasion for the; much less must we report evil things when they are false, or, for aught we know, may be so. Our lips must be guided by the law of kindness, as well as truth and justice. This, which Solomon makes a necessary part of the character of his virtuous woman, *that she openeth her mouth with wisdom, and in her tongue is the law of kindness* (Prov. 31:26), must needs be a part of the character of every true Christian. *Speak not evil one of another,* 1. Because you are brethren. The compellation, as used by the apostle here, carries an argument along with it. Since Christians are brethren, they should not defile nor defame one another. It is required of us that we be tender of the good name of our brethren; where we cannot speak well, we had better say nothing than speak evil; we must not take pleasure in making known the faults of others, divulging things that are secret, merely to expose them, nor in making more of their known faults than really they deserve, and, least of all, in making false stories, and spreading things concerning them of which they are altogether innocent. What is this but to raise the hatred and encourage the persecutions of the world, against those who are engaged in the same interests with ourselves, and therefore with whom we ourselves must stand or fall? "Consider, you are brethren." 2. Because this is to judge the law: *He that speaketh evil of his brother, and judgeth his brother, speaketh evil of the law, and judgeth the law.* The law of Moses says, *Thou shalt not go up and down as a tale-bearer among thy people,* Lev. 19:16. The law of Christ is, *Judge not, that you be not judged,* Mt. 7:1. The sum and substance of both is that men should love one another. A detracting tongue therefore condemns the law of God, and the commandment of Christ, when it is defaming its neighbour. To break God's commandments is in effect to speak evil of them, and to judge them, as if they were too strict, and laid too great a restraint upon us. The Christians to whom James wrote were apt to speak very hard things of one another, because of their differences about indifferent things (such as *the observance of meats and days,* as appears from Rom. 14): "Now," says the apostle, "he who censures and condemns his brother for not agreeing with him in those things which the law of God has left indifferent thereby censures and condemns the law, as if it had done ill in leaving them indifferent. He who quarrels with his brother, and condemns him for the sake of any thing not determined in the word of God, does thereby reflect on that word of God, as if it were not a perfect rule. Let us take heed of judging the law, for the law of the Lord is perfect; if men break the law, leave that to judge them; if they do not break it, let us not judge them." This is a heinous evil, because it is to forget our place, that we ought to be doers of the law, and it is to set up ourselves above it, as if we were to be judges of it. He who is guilty of the sin here cautioned against is not a doer of the law, but a judge; he assumes an office and a place that do not belong to him, and he will be sure to suffer for his presumption in the end. Those who are most ready to set up for judges of the law generally fail most in their obedience to it. 3. Because God, the Lawgiver, has reserved the power of passing the final sentence on men wholly to himself: *There is one Lawgiver, who is able to save, and to destroy: who art thou that judgest another? v.* 12. Princes and states are not excluded, by what is here said, from making laws; nor are subjects at all encouraged to disobey human laws; but God is still to be acknowledged as the supreme Lawgiver, who only can give law to the conscience, and who alone is to be absolutely obeyed. His right to enact laws is incontestable, because he has such a power to enforce them. He *is able to save, and to destroy,* so as no other can. He has power fully to reward the observance of his laws, and to punish all disobedience; he can save the soul, and make it happy for ever, or he can, after he has killed, cast into hell; and therefore should be feared and obeyed as the great Lawgiver, and all judgment should be committed to him. Since there is one Lawgiver, we may infer that it is not for any man or company of men in the world to pretend to give laws immediately to bind conscience; for that is God's prerogative, which must not be invaded. As the apostle had before warned against being many masters, so here he cautions against being many judges. Let us not prescribe to our brethren, let us not censure and condemn them; it is sufficient that we have the law of God, which is a rule to us all; and therefore we should not set up other rules. Let us not presume to set up our own particular notions and opinions as a rule to all about us; for *there is one Lawgiver.*

II. We are cautioned against a presumptuous confidence of the continuance of our lives, and against forming projects thereupon with assurance of success, *v.* 13, 14. The apostle, having reproved those who were judges and condemners of the law, now reproves such as were disregardful of Providence: *Go to now,* and old way of speaking, designed to engage attention; the Greek word may be rendered, *Behold now,* or *"See, and consider, you that say, To-day or to-morrow we will go into such a city, and continue there a year, and buy and sell, and get gain.* Reflect a little on this way of thinking and talking; call yourselves to account for it." Serious reflection on our words and ways would show us many evils that we are apt, through inadvertency, to run into and continue in. There were some who said of old, as too many say still, *We will go to such a city, and do this or that,* for such a term of time, while all serious regards to the disposals of Providence were neglected. Observe here, 1. How apt worldly and projecting men are to leave God out of their schemes. Where any are set upon earthly things, these have a strange power of engrossing the thoughts of the heart. WE should therefore have a care of growing intent or eager in our pursuits after any thing here below. 2. How much of worldly happiness lies in the promises men make to themselves beforehand. Their heads are full of fine visions, as to what they shall do, and be, and enjoy, in some future time, when they can neither be sure of time nor of any of the advantages they promise themselves; therefore observe, 3. How vain a thing it is to look for any thing good in futurity, without the concurrence of Providence. *We will go to such a city* (say they), perhaps to Antioch, or Damascus, or Alexandria, which were then the great places for traffic; but how could they be sure, when they set out, that they should reach any of these cities? Something might possibly stop their way, or call them elsewhere, or cut the thread of life. Many who have set out on a journey have gone to their long home, and never reached their journey's end. But, suppose they should reach the city they designed, how did they know they should continue there? Something might happen to send them back, or to call them thence, and to shorten their stay. Or suppose they should stay the full time they proposed, yet they could not be certain that they should buy and sell there; perhaps they might lie sick there, or they might not meet with those to trade with them that they expected. Yea, suppose they should go to that city, and continue there a year, and should buy and sell, yet they might not get gain; getting of gain in this world is at best but an uncertain thing, and they might probably make more losing bargains than gainful ones. And then, as to all these particulars, the frailty, shortness, and uncertainty of life, ought to check the vanity and presumptuous confidence of such projectors for futurity: *What is your life? It is even a vapour that appeareth for a little time, and then vanisheth away, v.* 14. God that wisely left us in the dark concerning future events, and even concerning the duration of life itself. We *know not what shall be on the morrow;* we may know what we intend to do and to be, but a thousand things may happen to prevent us. We are not sure of life itself, since it is but as a *vapour,* something in appearance, but nothing solid nor certain, easily scattered and gone. We can fix the hour and minute of the sun's rising and setting to-morrow, but we cannot fix the certain time of a vapour's being scattered; such is our life: *it appears but for a little time, and then vanisheth away;* it vanisheth as to this world, but there is a life that will continue in the other world; and, since this life is so uncertain, it concerns us all to prepare and lay up in store for that to come.

III. We are taught to keep up a constant sense of our dependence on the will of God for life, and all the actions and enjoyments of it: *You ought to say, If the Lord will, we shall live, and do this, or that, v.* 15. The apostle, having reproved them for what was amiss, now directs them how to be and do better: "You ought to say it in your hearts at all times, and with your tongues upon proper occasions, especially in your constant prayers and devotions, that if the Lord will give leave, and if he will own and bless you, you have such and such designs to accomplish." This must be said, not in a slight, formal, and customary way, but so as to think what we say, and so as to be reverent and serious in what we say. It is good to express ourselves thus when we have to do with others, but it is indispensably requisite that we should say this to ourselves in all that we go about. *Syn Theō — with the leave and blessing of God,* was used by the Greeks in the beginning of every undertaking. 1. *If the Lord will, we shall live.* We must remember that our times are not in our own hands, but at the disposal of God; we live as long as God appoints, and in the circumstances God appoints, and therefore must be submissive to him, even as to life itself; and then, 2. *If the Lord will, we shall do this or that.* All our actions and designs are under the control of Heaven. Our heads may be filled with cares and contrivances. This and the other thing we may propose to do for ourselves, or our families, or our friends; but Providence sometimes breaks all our measures, and throws our schemes into confusion. Therefore both our counsels for action and our conduct in action should be entirely referred to God; all we design and all we do should be with a submissive dependence on God.

IV. We are directed to avoid vain boasting, and to look upon it not only as a weak, but a very evil thing. *You rejoice in your boastings; all such rejoicing is evil, v.* 16. They promised themselves life and prosperity, and great things in the world, without any just regard to God; and then they boasted of these things. Such is the joy of worldly people, to boast of all their successes, yea, often to boast of their very projects before they know what success they shall have. How common is it for men to boast of things which they have no other title to than what arises from their own vanity and presumption! *Such rejoicing* (says the apostle) *is evil;* it is foolish and it is hurtful. For men to boast of worldly things, and of their aspiring projects, when they should be attending to the humbling duties before laid down (in *v.* 8–10), is a very evil thing. It is a great sin in God's account, it will bring great disappointment upon themselves, and it will prove their destruction in the end. If we rejoice in God that our times are in his hand, that all events are at his disposal, and that he is our God in covenant, this rejoicing is good; the wisdom, power, and providence of God, are then concerned to make all things work together for our good: but, if we rejoice in our own vain confidences and presumptuous boasts, this is evil; it is an evil carefully to be avoided by all wise and good men.

V. We are taught, in the whole of our conduct, to act up to our own convictions, and, whether we have to do with God or men, to see that we never go contrary to our own knowledge (*v.* 17): *To him that knoweth to do good, and doeth it not, to him it is sin;* it is aggravated sin; it is sinning with a witness; and it is to have the worst witness against his own conscience. Observe, 1. This stands immediately connected with the plain lesson of saying, *If the Lord will, we shall do this or that;* they might be ready to say, "This is a very obvious thing; who knows not that we all depend upon almighty God *for life, and breath, and all things?"* Remember then, if you do know this, whenever you act unsuitably to such a dependence, that *to him that knows to do good, and does it not, to him it is sin,* the greater sin. 2. Omissions are sins which will come into judgment, as well as commissions. He that does not the good he knows should be done, as well as he who does the evil he knows should not be done, will be condemned. Let us therefore take care that conscience be rightly informed, and then that it be faithfully and constantly obeyed; for, if *our own hearts condemn us not, then have we confidence towards God;* but if we say, *We see,* and do not act suitably to our sight, then *our sin remaineth,* Jn. 9:41.

CHAPTER 5

In this chapter the apostle denounces the judgments of God upon those rich men who oppress the poor, showing them how great their sin and folly are in the sight of God, and how grievous the punishments would be which should fall upon themselves (*v.* 1–6). Hereupon, all the faithful are exhorted to patience under their trials and sufferings (*v.* 7–11). The sin of swearing is cautioned against (*v.* 12). We are directed how to act, both under affliction and in prosperity (*v.* 13). Prayer for the sick, and anointing with oil, are prescribed (*v.* 14, 15). Christians are directed to acknowledge their faults one to another, and to pray one for another, and the efficacy of prayer is proved (*v.* 16–18). And, lastly, it is recommended to us to do what we can for bringing back those that stray from the ways of truth.

Verses 1–11

The apostle is here addressing first sinners and then saints.

I. Let us consider the address to sinners; and here we find James seconding what his great Master had said: *Woe unto you that are rich; for you have received your consolation,* Lu. 6:24. The rich people to whom this word of warning was sent were not such as professed the Christian religion, but the worldly and unbelieving Jews, such as are here said *to condemn and kill the just,* which the Christians had no power to do; and though this epistle was written for the sake of the faithful, and was sent principally to them, yet, by an apostrophe, the infidel Jews may be well supposed here spoken to. They would not hear the word, and therefore it is *written,* that they might read it. It is observable, in the very first inscription of this epistle, that it is not directed, as Paul's epistles were, *to the brethren in Christ,* but, in general, *to the twelve tribes;* and the salutation is not, *grace and peace from Christ,* but, in general, *greeting, ch.* 1:1. The poor among the Jews received the gospel, and many of them believed; but the generality of the rich rejected Christianity, and were hardened in their unbelief, and hated and persecuted those who believed on Christ. To these oppressing, unbelieving, persecuting, rich people, the apostle addresses himself in the first six verses.

1. He foretels the judgments of God that should come upon them, *v.* 1–3. they should have miseries come upon them, and such dreadful miseries that the very apprehension of them was enough to make them weep and howl — misery that should arise from the very things in which they placed their happiness, and misery that should be completed by these things witnessing against them at the last, to their utter destruction; and they are now called to reason upon and thoroughly to weigh the matter, and to think how they will stand before God in judgment: *Go to now, you rich men.* (1.) "You may be assured of this that very dreadful calamities are coming upon you, calamities that shall carry nothing of support nor comfort in them, but all misery, misery in time, misery to eternity, misery in your outward afflictions, misery in your inward frame and temper of mind, misery in this world, misery in hell. You have not a single instance of misery only coming upon you, but miseries. The ruin of your church and nation is at hand; and there will come a day of wrath, when riches shall not profit men, but *all the wicked shall be destroyed.*" (2.) The very apprehension of such miseries as were coming upon them is enough to make them weep and howl. Rich men are apt to say to themselves (and others are ready to say to them), *Eat, drink, and be merry;* but God says, *Weep and howl.* It is not said, Weep and repent, for this the apostle does not expect from them (he speaks in a way of denouncing rather than admonishing); but, *"Weep and howl,* for when your doom comes there will be nothing but *weeping, and wailing, and gnashing of teeth."* Those who live like beasts are called howl like such. Public calamities are most grievous to rich people, who live in pleasure, and are secure and sensual; and therefore they shall weep and howl more than other people for the miseries that shall come upon them. (3.) Their misery shall arise from the very things in which they placed their happiness. "Corruption, decay, rust, and ruin, will come upon all your goodly things: *Your riches are corrupted and your garments are moth-eaten, v.* 2. Those

things which you now inordinately affect will hereafter insupportably wound you: they will be of no worth, of no use to you, but, on the contrary, will *pierce you through with many sorrows;* for," (4.) *"They will witness against you, and they will eat your flesh as it were fire,"* v. 3. Things inanimate are frequently represented in scripture as witnessing against wicked men. Heaven, earth, the stones of the field, the production of the ground, and here the very rust and canker of ill-gotten and ill-kept treasures, are said to witness against impious rich men. They think to heap up treasure for their latter days, to live plentifully upon when they come to be old; but, alas! they are only heaping up treasures to become a prey to others (as the Jews had all taken from them by the Romans), and treasures that will prove at last to be only treasures of wrath, *in the day of the revelation of the righteous judgment of God.* Then shall their iniquities, in the punishment of them, *eat their flesh as it were* with *fire.* In the ruin of Jerusalem, many thousands perished by fire; in the last judgment the wicked shall be condemned to *everlasting burnings, prepared for the devil and his angels.* The Lord deliver us from the portion of wicked rich men! and, in order to this, let us take care that we do not fall into their sins, which we are next to consider.

2. The apostle shows what those sins are which should bring such miseries. To be in so deplorable a condition must doubtless be owing to some very heinous crimes. (1.) Covetousness is laid to the charge of this people; they laid by their garments till they bred moths and were eaten; they hoarded up their gold and silver till they were rusty and cankered. It is a very great disgrace to these things that they carry in them the principles of their own corruption and consumption — the garment breeds the moth that frets it, the gold and silver breeds the canker that eats it; but the disgrace falls most heavily upon those who hoard and lay up these things till they come to be thus corrupted, and cankered, and eaten. God gives us our worldly possessions that we may honour him and do good with them; but if, instead of this, we sinfully hoard them up, thorough and undue affection towards them, or a distrust of the providence of God for the future, this is a very heinous crime, and will be witnessed against by the very rust and corruption of the treasure thus heaped together. (2.) Another sin charged upon those against whom James writes is oppression: *Behold, the hire of the labourers, who have reaped down your fields, which is of you kept back by fraud, crieth,* etc., *v.* 4. Those who have wealth in their hands get power into their hands, and then they are tempted to abuse that power to oppress such as are under them. The rich we here find employing the poor in their labours, and the rich have as much need of the labours of the poor as the poor have of wages from the rich, and could as ill be without them; but yet, not considering this, they kept back the hire of the labourers; having power in their hands, it is probable that they made as hard bargains with the poor as they could, and even after that would not make good their bargains as they should have done. This is a crying sin, an iniquity that cries so as to reach the ears of God; and, in this case, God is to be considered as *the Lord of sabaoth,* or the *Lord of hosts, Kyriou sabaōth,* a phrase often used in the Old-Testament, when the people of God were defenseless and wanted protection, and when their enemies were numerous and powerful. The Lord of hosts, who has all ranks of beings and creatures at his disposal, and who sets all in their several places, hears the oppressed when they cry by reason of the cruelty or injustice of the oppressor, and he will give orders to some of those hosts that are under him (angels, devils, storms, distempers, or the like) to avenge the wrongs done to those who are dealt with unrighteously and unmercifully. Take heed of this sin of defrauding and oppressing, and avoid the very appearances of it. (3.) Another sin here mentioned is sensuality and voluptuousness. *You have lived in pleasure on the earth, and been wanton, v.* 5. God does not forbid us to use pleasure; but to live in them as if we lived for nothing else is a very provoking sin; and to do this on the earth, where we are but strangers and pilgrims, where we are but to continue for a while, and where we ought to be preparing for eternity — this, this is a grievous aggravation of the sin of voluptuousness. Luxury makes people wanton, as in Hos. 13:6, *According to their pasture, so were they filled; they were filled, and their heart was exalted; therefore have they forgotten me.* Wantonness and luxury are commonly the effects of great plenty and abundance; it is hard for people to have great plenty and abundance; it is hard for people to have

great estates, and not too much indulge themselves in carnal, sensual pleasures: *"You have nourished your hearts as in a day of slaughter:* you live as if it were every day a day of sacrifices, a festival; and hereby your hearts are fattened and nourished to stupidity, dulness, pride, and an insensibility to the wants and afflictions of others." Some may say, "What harm is there in good cheer, provided people do not spend above what they have?" What! Is it no harm for people to make gods of their bellies, and to give all to these, instead of abounding in acts of charity and piety? Is it no harm for people to unfit themselves for minding the concerns of their souls, by indulging the appetites of their bodies? Surely that which brought flames upon Sodom, and would bring these miseries for which rich men are here called to weep and howl, must be a heinous evil! Pride, and idleness, and fullness of bread, mean the same thing with living in pleasure, and being wanton, and nourishing the heart as in a day of slaughter. (4.) Another sin here charged on the rich is persecution: *You have condemned and killed the just, and he doth not resist you, v.* 6. This fills up the measure of their iniquity. They oppressed and acted very unjustly, to get estates; when they had them, they gave way to luxury and sensuality, till they had lost all sense and feeling of the wants or afflictions of others; and then they persecute and kill without remorse. They pretend to act legally indeed, they condemn before they kill; but unjust prosecutions, whatever colour of law they may carry in them, will come into the reckoning when God shall make inquisition for blood, as well as massacres and downright murders. Observe here, The just may be condemned and killed: but then again observe, When such do suffer, and yield without resistance to the unjust sentence of oppressors, this is marked by God, to the honour of the sufferers and the infamy of their persecutors; this commonly shows that judgments are at the door, and we may certainly conclude that a reckoning-day will come, to reward the patience of the oppressed and to break to pieces the oppressor. Thus far the address to sinners goes.

II. We have next subjoined an address to saints. Some have been ready to despise or to condemn this way of preaching, when ministers, in their application, have brought a word to sinners, and a word to saints; but, from the apostle's here taking this method, we may conclude that this is the best way rightly to divide the word of truth. From what has been said concerning wicked and oppressing rich men, occasion is given to administer comfort to God's afflicted people: "Be patient therefore; since God will send such miseries on the wicked, you may see what is your duty, and where your greatest encouragement lies."

1. Attend to your duty: *Be patient (v.* 7), establish your hearts (*v.* 8), grudge not one against another, brethren, *v.* 9. Consider well the meaning of these three expressions: — (1.) *"Be patient* — bear your afflictions without murmuring, your injuries without revenge; and, though God should not in any signal manner appear for you immediately, wait for him. *The vision is for an appointed time; at the end it will speak, and will not lie; therefore wait for it. It is but a little while, and he that shall come will come, and will not tarry.* Let your patience be lengthened out to long suffering;" so the word here used, *makrothymēsate,* signifies. When we have done our work, we have need of patience to stay for our reward. This Christian patience is not a mere yielding to necessity, as the moral patience taught by some philosophers was, but it is a humble acquiescence in the wisdom and will of God, with an eye to a future glorious recompense: *Be patient to the coming of the Lord.* And because this is a lesson Christians must learn, though ever so hard or difficult to the, it is repeated in *v.* 8, *Be you also patient.* (2.) *"Establish your hearts* — let your faith be firm, without wavering, your practice of what is good constant and continued, without tiring, and your resolutions for God and heaven fixed, in spite of all sufferings or temptations." The prosperity of the wicked and the affliction of the righteous have in all ages been a very great trial to the faith of the people of God. David tells us *that his feet were almost gone, when he saw the prosperity of the wicked,* Ps. 73:2, 3. Some of those Christians to whom St. James wrote might probably be in the same tottering condition; and therefore they are called upon to establish their hearts; faith and patience will establish the heart. (3.) *Grudge not one against another;* the words *mē stenazete* signify, *Groan* not one against another, that is, "Do not make one another uneasy by your murmuring groans at what befalls you, nor by your distrustful groans as to what may further

come upon you, nor by your revengeful groans against the instruments of your sufferings, nor by your envious groans at those who may be free from your calamities: do not make yourselves uneasy and make one another uneasy by thus groaning to and grieving one another." "The apostle seemeth to me" (says Dr. Manton) "to be here taxing those mutual injuries and animosities wherewith the Christians of those times, having banded under the names of *circumcision* and *uncircumcision,* did grieve one another, and give each other cause to groan; so that they did not only sigh under the oppressions of the rich persecutors, but under the injuries which they sustained from many of the brethren who, together with them, did profess the holy faith." Those who are in the midst of common enemies, and in any suffering circumstances, should be more especially careful not to grieve nor to groan against one another, otherwise judgments will come upon them as well as others; and the more such grudgings prevail the nearer do they show judgment to be.

2. Consider what encouragement here is for Christians to be patient, to establish their hearts, and not to grudge one against another. And, (1.) "Look to the example of the husbandman: *He waits for the precious fruit of the earth, and hath long patience for it, until he receive the early and latter rain.* When you sow your corn in the ground, you wait many months for the former and latter rain, and are willing to stay till harvest for the fruit of your labour; and shall not this teach you to bear a few storms, and to be patient for a season, when you are looking for a kingdom and everlasting felicity? Consider him that waits for a crop of corn; and will not you wait for a crown of glory? If you should be called to wait a little longer than the husbandman does, is it not something proportionably greater and infinitely more worth your waiting for? But," (2.) "Think how short your waiting time may possibly be: *The coming of the Lord draweth nigh, v.* 8; behold, the Judge standeth before the door, *v.* 9. Do not be impatient, do not quarrel with one another; the great Judge, who will set all to rights, who will punish the wicked and reward the good, is at hand: he should be conceived by you to stand as near as one who is just knocking at the door." *The coming of the Lord* to punish the wicked Jews was then very nigh, when James wrote this epistle; and, whenever the patience and other graces of his people are tried in an extraordinary manner, the certainty of Christ's coming as Judge, and the nearness of it, should establish their hearts. The Judge is now a great deal nearer, in his coming to judge the world, than when this epistle was written, nearer by above seventeen hundred years; and therefore this should have the greater effect upon us. (3.) The danger of our being condemned when the Judge appears should excite us to mind our duty as before laid down: *Grudge not, lest you be condemned.* Fretfulness and discontent expose us to the just judgment of God, and we bring more calamities upon ourselves by our murmuring, distrustful, envious groans and grudgings against one another, than we are aware of. If we avoid these evils, and be patient under our trials, God will not condemn us. Let us encourage ourselves with this. (4.) We are encouraged to be patient by the example of the prophets (*v.* 10): *Take the prophets, who have spoken in the name of the Lord, for an example of suffering affliction, and of patience.* Observe here, The prophets, on whom God put the greatest honour, and for whom he had the greatest favour, were most afflicted: and, when we think that the best men have had the hardest usage in this world, we should hereby be reconciled to affliction. Observe further, Those who were the greatest examples of suffering affliction were also the best and greatest examples of patience: *tribulation worketh patience.* Hereupon James gives it to us as the common sense of the faithful (*v.* 11): *We count those happy who endure:* we look upon righteous and patient sufferers as the happiest people. See *ch.* 1:2–12. (5.) Job also is proposed as an example for the encouragement of the afflicted. *You have hard of the patience of Job, and have seen the end of the Lord,* etc., *v.* 11. In the case of Job you have an instance of a variety of miseries, and of such as were very grievous, but under all he could bless God, and, as to the general bent of his spirit, he was patient and humble: and what came to him in the end? Why, truly, God accomplished and brought about those things for him which plainly prove that *the Lord is very pitiful, and of tender mercy.* The best way to bear afflictions is to look to the end of them; and the pity of God is such that he will not delay the bringing of them to an end when his purposes are once answered; and the tender mercy of God is such that he will make his people an abundant amends for all their sufferings and afflictions. His bowels are moved for them while suffering, his bounty is manifested afterwards. Let us serve our God, and endure our trials, as those who believe the end will crown all.

Verses 12–20

This epistle now drawing to a close, the penman goes off very quickly from one thing to another: hence it is that matters so very different are insisted on in these few verses.

I. The sin of swearing is cautioned against: *But above all things, my brethren, swear not,* etc., *v.* 12. Some understand this too restrictedly, as if the meaning were, "Swear not at your persecutors, at *those that reproach you and say all manner of evil of you;* be not put into a passion by the injuries they do you, so as in your passion to be provoked to swear." This swearing is no doubt forbidden here: and it will not excuse those that are guilty of this sin to say they sear only when they are provoked to it, and before they are aware. But the apostle's warning extends to other occasions of swearing as well as this. Some have translated the words, *pro pantōn — before all things;* and so have made sense of this place to be that they should not, in common conversation, *before every thing they say,* put an oath. All customary needless swearing is undoubtedly forbidden, and all along in scripture condemned, as a very grievous sin. Profane swearing was very customary among the Jews, and, since this epistle is directed in general *to the twelve tribes scattered abroad* (as before has been observed), we may conceive this exhortation sent to those who believed not. It is hard to suppose that swearing should be one of the spots of God's children, since Peter, when he was charged with being a disciple of Christ and would disprove the charge, cursed and swore, thereby thinking most effectually to convince them that he was no disciple of Jesus, it being well known of such that they durst not allow themselves in swearing; but possibly some of the looser sort of those who were called Christians might, among other sins here charged upon them, be guilty also of this. It is a sin that in later years has most scandalously prevailed, even among those who would be thought above all others entitled to the Christian name and privileges. It is very rare indeed to hear of a dissenter from the church of England who is guilty of swearing, but among those who glory in their being of the established church nothing is more common; and indeed the most execrable oaths and curses now daily wound the ears and hearts of all serious Christians. James here says,

1. *Above all things, swear not;* but how many are there who mind this the least of all things, and who make light of nothing so much as common profane swearing! But why *above all things* is swearing here forbidden? (1.) Because it strikes most directly at the honour of God and most expressly throws contempt upon his name and authority. (2.) Because this sin has, of all sins, the least temptation to it: it is not gain, nor pleasure, nor reputation, that can move men to it, but a wantonness in sinning, and a needless showing an enmity to God. *Thy enemies take thy name in vain,* Ps. 139:20. This is a proof of men's being enemies to God, however they may pretend to call themselves by his name, or sometimes to compliment him in acts of worship. (3.) Because it is with most difficulty left off when once men are accustomed to it, therefore it should above all things be watched against. And, (4.) *"Above all things swear not,* for how can you expect the name of God should be a strong tower to you in your distress if you profane it and play with it at other times?" But (as Mr. Baxter observes) "all this is so far from forbidding necessary oaths that it is but to confirm them, by preserving the due reverence of them." And then he further notes that "The true nature of an oath is, by our speech, *to pawn the reputation of some certain or great thing,* for the *averring of a doubted less thing;* and not (as is commonly held) an appeal to God or other judge." Hence it was that swearing by the heavens, and by the earth, and by the other oaths the apostle refers to, came to be in use. The Jews thought if they did but omit the great oath of *Chi-Eloah,* they were safe. But they grew so profane as to swear by the creature, as if it were God; and so advanced it into the place of God; while, on the other hand, those who swear commonly and profanely by the name of God do hereby put him upon the level with every common thing.

2. *But let your yea be yea, and your nay nay; lest you fall into condemnation;* that is, "let it suffice you to affirm or deny a thing as there is occasion, and be sure to stand to your word, an be true to it, so as to give no occasion for your being suspected of falsehood; and then you will be kept from the condemnation of backing what you say or promise by rash oaths, and from profaning the name of God to justify yourselves. It is being suspected of falsehood that leads men to swearing. Let it be known that your keep to truth, and are firm to your word, and by this means you will find there is no need to swear to what you say. Thus shall you escape the condemnation which is expressly annexed to the third commandment: *The Lord will not hold him guiltless that taketh his name in vain.*"

II. As Christians we are taught to suit ourselves to the dispensations of Providence (*v.* 13): *Is any among you afflicted? Let him pray. Is any merry? Let him sing psalms.* Our condition in this world is various; and our wisdom is to submit to its being so, and to behave as becomes us both in prosperity and under affliction. Sometimes we are in sadness, sometimes in mirth; God has set these one over against the other that we may the better observe the several duties he enjoins, and that the impressions made on our passions and affections may be rendered serviceable to our devotions. Afflictions should put us upon prayer, and prosperity should make us abound in praise. Not that prayer is to be confined to a time of trouble, nor singing to a time of mirth; but these several duties may be performed with special advantage, and to the happiest purposes, at such seasons. 1. In a day of affliction nothing is more seasonable than prayer. The person afflicted must pray himself, as well as engage the prayers of others for him. Times of affliction should be praying times. To this end God sends afflictions, that we may be engaged to seek him early; and that those who at other times have neglected him may be brought to enquire after him. The spirit is then most humble, the heart is broken and tender; and prayer is most acceptable to God when it comes from a contrite humble spirit. Afflictions naturally draw out complaints; and to whom should we complain but to God in prayer? It is necessary to exercise faith and hope under afflictions; and prayer is the appointed means both for obtaining and increasing these graces in us. *Is any afflicted? Let him pray.* 2. In a day of mirth and prosperity singing psalms is very proper and seasonable. In the original it is only said *sing, psalletō,* without the addition of psalms or any other word: and we learn from the writings of several in the first ages of Christianity (particularly from a letter of Pliny's, and from some passages in Justin Martyr and Tertullian) that the Christians were accustomed to sing hymns, either taken out of scripture, or of more private composure, in their worship of God. Though some have thought that Paul's advising both the Colossians and Ephesians to *speak to one another psalmois kai hymnois kai ōdais pneumatikais — in psalms, and hymns, and spiritual songs,* refers only to the compositions of scripture, the psalms of David being distinguished in Hebrew by *Shurim, Tehillim,* and *Mizmorim,* words that exactly answer these of the apostle. Let that be as it will, this however we are sure of, that the singing of psalms is a gospel ordinance, and that our joy should be holy joy, consecrated to God. Singing is so directed to here as to show that, if any be in circumstances of mirth and prosperity, he should turn his mirth, though alone, and by himself, in this channel. Holy mirth becomes families and retirements, as well as public assemblies. Let our singing be such as to make *melody with our hearts unto the Lord,* and God will assuredly be well pleased with this kind of devotion.

III. We have particular directions given as to sick persons, and *healing pardoning mercy promised* upon the observance of those directions. *If any be sick,* they are required, 1. To *send for the elders, presbyterous tēs ekklēsias — the presbyters,* pastors or ministers *of the church, v.* 14, 15. It lies upon sick people as a duty to send for ministers, and to desire their assistance and their prayers. 2. It is the duty of ministers to pray over the sick, when thus desired and called for. *Let them pray over him;* let their prayers be suited to his case, and their intercessions be as becomes those who are affected wit his calamities. 3. In the times of miraculous healing, the *sick were to be anointed with oil in the name of the Lord.* Expositors generally confine this anointing with oil to such as had the power of working miracles; and, when miracles ceased, this institution ceased also. In Mark's gospel we read of the apostle's anointing with oil many that were sick, and healing them, Mk. 6:13. And we have accounts of this being practiced in the church two hundred years after Christ; but then the gift of healing also accompanied it, and, when the miraculous gift ceased, this rite was laid aside. The papists indeed have made a sacrament of this, which they call *the extreme unction.* They use it, not to heal the sick, as it was used by the apostles; but as they generally run counter to scripture, in the appointments of their church, so here they ordain that this should be administered only to such as are at the very point of death. The apostle's anointing was in order to heal the disease; the popish anointing is for the expulsion of the relics of sin, and to enable the soul (as they pretend) the better to combat with the powers of the air. When they cannot prove, by any visible effects, that Christ owns them in the continuance of this rite, they would however have people to believe that the invisible effects are very wonderful. But it is surely much better to omit this anointing with oil than to turn it quite contrary to the purposes spoken of in scripture. Some protestants have thought that this anointing was only permitted or approved by Christ, not instituted. But it should seem, by the words of James here, that it was a thing enjoined in cases where there was faith for healing. And some protestants have argued for it with this view. It was not to be commonly used, not even in the apostolical age; and some have thought that it should not be wholly laid aside in any age, but that where there are extraordinary measures of faith in the person anointing, and in those who are anointed, an extraordinary blessing may attend the observance of this direction for the sick. However that be, there is one thing carefully to be observed here, that the saving of the sick is not ascribed to the *anointing with oil,* but to prayer: *The prayer of faith shall save the sick,* etc., *v.* 15. So that, 4. Prayer over the sick must proceed from, and be accompanied with, a lively faith. There must be faith both in the person praying and in the person prayed for. In a time of sickness, it is not the cold and formal prayer that is effectual, but the prayer of faith. 5. We should observe the success of prayer. The Lord shall raise up; that is, if he be a person capable and fit for deliverance, and if God have any thing further for such a person to do in the world. *And, if he have committed sins, they shall be forgiven him;* that is, where sickness is sent as a punishment for some particular sin, that sin shall be pardoned, and in token thereof the sickness shall be removed. As when Christ said to the impotent man, *Go and sin no more, lest a worse thing come unto thee,* it is intimated that some particular sin was the cause of his sickness. The great thing therefore we should beg of God for ourselves and others in the time of sickness is the pardon of sin. Sin is both the root of sickness and the sting of it. If sin be pardoned, either affliction shall be removed in mercy or we shall see there is mercy in the continuance of it. When healing is founded upon pardon, we may say as Hezekiah did: Thou hast, in love to my soul, *delivered it from the pit of corruption,* Isa. 38:17. When you are sick and in pain, it is most common to pray and cry, *O give me ease! O restore me to health!* But your prayer should rather and chiefly be, *O that God would pardon my sins!*

IV. Christians are directed to *confess their faults one to another, and so to join in their prayers with an for one another, v.* 16. Some expositors connect this with *v.* 14. As if when sick people send for ministers to pray over them they should then confess their faults to them. Indeed, where any are conscious that their sickness is a vindictive punishment of some particular sin, and they cannot look for the removal of their sickness without particular applications to God for the pardon of such a sin, there it may be proper to acknowledge and tell his case, that those who pray over him may know how to plead rightly for him. But the confession here required is that of Christians to one another, and not, as the papists would have it, to a priest. Where persons have injured one another, acts of injustice must be confessed to those against whom they have been committed. Where persons have tempted one another to sin or have consented in the same evil actions, there they ought mutually to blame themselves and excite each other to repentance. Where crimes are of a public nature, and have done any public mischief, there they ought to be more publicly confessed, so as may best reach to all who are concerned. And sometimes it may be well to confess our faults to some prudent minister or praying friend, that he may help us to plead with God for mercy and pardon. But then we are not to think that James puts us upon telling every thing that we are conscious is amiss in ourselves or in one another; but so far as confession is necessary to our reconciliation with such as are at variance with us, or for gaining information in any point of conscience and making our own spirits quiet and easy, so far we should be ready to confess our faults. And sometimes also it may be of good use to Christians to disclose their peculiar weaknesses and infirmities to one another, where there are great intimacies and friendships, and where they may help each other by their prayers to obtain pardon of their sins and power against them. Those who make confession of their faults one to another should thereupon pray with and for one another. The 13th verse directs persons to pray for themselves: *Is any afflicted let him pray;* the 14th directs to seek for the prayers of ministers; and the 16th directs private Christians to pray one for another; so that here we have all sorts of prayer (ministerial, social, and secret) recommended.

V. The great advantage and efficacy of prayer are declared and proved: *The effectual fervent prayer of a righteous man availeth much,* whether he pray for himself or for others: witness the example of Elias, *v.* 17, 18. He who prays must be a righteous man; not righteous in an absolute sense (for this Elias was not, who is here made a pattern to us), but righteous in a gospel sense; not loving nor approving of any iniquity. *If I regard iniquity in my heart, the Lord will not hear my prayer,* Ps. 66:18. Further, the prayer itself must be a fervent, in-wrought, well-wrought prayer. It must be a pouring out of the heart to God; and it must proceed from a faith unfeigned. Such prayer avails much. It is of great advantage to ourselves, it may be very beneficial to our friends, and we are assured of its being acceptable to God. It is good having those for friends whose prayers are available in the sight of God. The power of prayer is here proved from the success of Elijah. This may be encouraging to us even in common cases, if we consider that Elijah was *a man of like passions with us.* He was a zealous good man and a very great man, but he had his infirmities, and was subject to disorder in his passions as well as others. In prayer we must not look to the merit of man, but to the grace of God. Only in this we should copy after Elijah, that he prayed earnestly, or, as it is in the original, *in prayer he prayed.* It is not enough to say a prayer, but we must pray in prayer. Our thoughts must be fixed, our desires firm and ardent, and our graces in exercise; and, when we thus pray in prayer, we shall speed in prayer. Elijah *prayed that it might not rain;* and God heard him in his pleading against an idolatrous persecuting country, so that it *rained not on the earth for the space of three years and six months. Again he prayed, and the heaven gave rain,* etc. Thus you see prayer is the key which opens and shuts heaven. To this there is an allusion, Rev. 11:6, where the two witnesses are said to have power *to shut heaven, that it rain not.* This instance of the extraordinary efficacy of prayer is recorded for encouragement even to ordinary Christians to be instant and earnest in prayer. God never says to any of the seed of Jacob, *Seek my face in vain.* If Elijah by prayer could do such great and wonderful things, surely the prayers of no righteous man shall return void. Where there may not be so much of a miracle in God's answering our prayers, yet there may be as much of grace.

VI. This epistle concludes with an exhortation to do all we can in our places to promote the conversion and salvation of others, *v.* 19, 20. Some interpret these verses as an apology which the apostle is making for himself that he should so plainly and sharply reprove the Jewish Christians for their many faults and errors. And certainly James gives a very good reason why he was so much concerned to reclaim them from their errors, because in thus doing he should save souls, and hide a multitude of sins. But we are not to restrain this place to the apostle's converting such as erred from the truth; no, nor to other ministerial endeavours of the like nature, since it is said, "If any err, and one convert him, let him be who he will that does so good an office for another, he is therein an instrument of saving a soul from death." Those whom the apostle here calls brethren, he yet supposes liable to err. It is no mark of a wise or a holy man to boast of his being free from error, or to refuse to acknowledge when he is in an error. But if any do err, be they ever so great, you must not be afraid to show them their error; and, be they ever so weak and little, you must not disdain to make them wiser and better. If they err from the truth, that is, from the gospel (the great rule and standard of truth), whether it be in opinion or practice, you must endeavour to bring them again to the rule. Errors in judgment and in life generally go together. There is some doctrinal mistake at the bottom of every practical miscarriage. There is no one habitually bad, but upon some bad principle. Now to convert such is to reduce them from their error, and to reclaim them from the evils they have been led into. We are not presently to accuse and exclaim against an erring brother, and seek to bring reproaches and calamities upon him, but to convert him: and, if by all our endeavours we cannot do this, yet we are nowhere empowered to persecute and destroy him. If we are instrumental in the conversion of any, *we* are said to convert them, though this be principally and efficiently the work of God. And, if we can do no more towards the conversion of sinners, yet we may do this — pray for the grace and Spirit of God to convert and change them. And let those that are in any way serviceable to convert others know what will be the happy consequence of their doing this: they may take great comfort in it at present, and they will meet with a crown at last. He that is said to *err from the truth* in *v.* 19 is described as *erring in his way* in *v.* 20, and we cannot be said to convert any merely by altering their opinions, unless we can bring them to correct and amend their ways. This is conversion — to turn a sinner from the error of his ways, and not to turn him from one party to another, or merely from one notion and way of thinking to another. He who thus converteth a sinner from the error of his ways *shall save a soul from death.* There is a soul in the case; and what is done towards the salvation of the soul shall certainly turn to good account. The soul being the principal part of the man, the saving of that only is mentioned, but it includes the salvation of the whole man: the spirit shall be saved from hell, the body raised from the grave, and both saved from eternal death. And then, by such conversion of heart and life, a *multitude of sins shall be hid.* A most comfortable passage of scripture is this. We learn hence that though our sins are many, even a multitude, yet they may be hid or pardoned; and that when sin is turned from or forsaken it shall be hid, never to appear in judgment against us. Let people contrive to cover or excuse their sin as they will, there is no way effectually and finally to hide it but by forsaking it. Some make the sense of this text to be, that conversion shall *prevent* a multitude of sins; and it is a truth beyond dispute that many sins are prevented in the party converted, many also may be prevented in others that he may have an influence upon, or may converse with. Upon the whole, how should we lay out ourselves with all possible concern for the conversion of sinners! It will be for the happiness and salvation of the converted; it will prevent much mischief, and the spreading and multiplying of sin in the world; it will be for the glory and honour of God; and it will mightily redound to our comfort and renown in the great day. *Those that turn many to righteousness,* and those who help to do so, *shall shine as the stars for ever and ever.*

AN EXPOSITION, WITH PRACTICAL OBSERVATIONS, OF

THE FIRST EPISTLE GENERAL OF PETER

Two epistles we have enrolled in the sacred canon of the scripture written by Peter, who was a most eminent apostle of Jesus Christ, and whose character shines brightly as it is described in the four Gospels and in the Acts of the Apostles, but, as it is painted by the papists and legendary writers, it represents a person of extravagant pride and ambition. It is certain from scripture that Simon Peter was one of the first of those whom our Lord called to be his disciples and followers, that he was a person of excellent endowments, both natural and gracious, of great parts and ready elocution, quick to apprehend and bold to execute whatever he knew to be his duty. When our Saviour called his apostles, and gave them their commission, he nominated him first in the list; and by his behaviour towards him he seems to have distinguished him as a special favourite among the twelve. Many instances of our Lord's affection to him, both during his life and after his resurrection, are upon record. But there are many things confidently affirmed of this holy man that are directly false: as, That he had a primacy and superior power over the rest of the apostles — that he was more than their equal — that he was their prince, monarch, and sovereign — and that he exercised a jurisdiction over the whole college of the apostles: moreover, That he as the sole and universal pastor over all the Christian world, the only vicar of Christ upon earth — that he was for above twenty years bishop of Rome — that the popes of Rome succeed to St. Peter, and derive from him a universal supremacy and jurisdiction over all churches and Christians upon earth — and that all this was by our Lord's ordering and appointment; whereas Christ never gave him any pre-eminence of this kind, but positively forbade it, and gave precepts to the contrary. The other apostles never consented to any such claim. Paul declares himself *not a whit behind the very chief apostles,* 2 Co. 11:5 and 12:11. Here is no exception of Peter's superior dignity, whom Paul took the freedom to blame, and *withstood him to the face,* Gal. 2:11. And Peter himself never assumed any thing like it, but modestly styles himself an *apostle of Jesus Christ;* and, when he writes to the presbyters of the church, he humbly places himself in the same rank with them: *The elders who are among you I exhort, who am also an elder,* 5:1. See Dr. Barrow on the pope's supremacy.

The design of this first epistle is, I. To explain more fully the doctrines of Christianity to these newly-converted Jews. II. To direct and persuade them to a holy conversation, in the faithful discharge of all personal and relative duties, whereby they would secure their own peace and effectually confute the slanders and reproaches of their enemies. III. To prepare them for sufferings. This seems to be his principal intention; for he has something to this purport in every chapter, and does, by a great variety of arguments, encourage them to patience and perseverance in the faith, lest the persecutions and sad calamities that were coming upon them should prevail with them to apostatize from Christ and the gospel. It is remarkable that you find not so much as one word savouring of the spirit and pride of a pope in either of these epistles.

CHAPTER 1

The apostle describes the persons to whom he writes, and salutes them (*v.* 1, 2), blesses God for their regeneration to a lively hope of eternal salvation (*v.* 3–5), in the hope of this salvation he shows they had great cause of rejoicing, though for a little while they were in heaviness and affliction, for the trial of their faith, which would produce joy unspeakable and full of glory (*v.* 6–9). This is that salvation which the ancient prophets foretold and the angels desire to look into (*v.* 10–12). He exhorts them to sobriety and holiness, which he presses from the consideration of the blood of Jesus, the invaluable price of man's redemption (*v.* 13–21), and to brotherly love, from the consideration of their regeneration, and the excellency of their spiritual state (*v.* 22–25).

Verses 1–2

In this inscription we have three parts: —

I. The author of it, described, 1. By his name — *Peter.* His first name was *Simon,* and Jesus Christ gave him the surname of *Peter,* which signifies *a rock,* as a commendation of his faith, and to denote that he should be an eminent pillar in the church of God, Gal. 2:9. 2. By his office — *an apostle of Jesus Christ.* The word signifies *one sent, a legate, a messenger,* any one sent in Christ's name and about his work; but more strictly it signifies the highest office in the Christian church. 1 Co. 12:28, *God hath set some in the church, first apostles.* Their dignity and pre-eminence lay in these things: — They were immediately chosen by Christ himself, — they were first witnesses, then preachers, of the resurrection of Christ, and so of the entire gospel-dispensation, — their gifts were excellent and extraordinary, — they had a power of working miracles, not at all times, but when Christ pleased, — they were led into all truth, were endowed with the spirit of prophecy, and they had an extent of power and jurisdiction beyond all others; every apostle was a universal bishop in all churches, and over all ministers. In this humble manner Peter, (1.) Asserts his own character as an apostle. Hence learn, A man may lawfully acknowledge, and sometimes is bound to assert, the gifts and graces of God to him. To pretend to what we have not is hypocrisy; and to deny what we have is ingratitude. (2.) He mentions his apostolical function as his warrant and call to write this epistle to these people. Note, It concerns all, but especially ministers, to consider well their warrant and call from God to their work. This will justify them to others, and give them inward support and comfort under all dangers and discouragements.

II. The persons to whom this epistle was addressed, and they are described,

1. By their external condition — *Strangers dispersed throughout Pontus, Galatia,* etc. They were chiefly Jews, descended (as Dr. Prideaux thinks) from those Jews who were translated from Babylon, by order of Antiochus king of Syria, about two hundred years before the coming of Christ, and placed in the cities of Asia Minor. It is very likely that our apostle had been among them, and converted them, being the apostle of the circumcision, and that he afterwards wrote this epistle to them from Babylon, where multitudes of the Jewish nation then resided. At present, their circumstances were poor and afflicted. (1.) The best of God's servants may, through the hardships of times and providences, be dispersed about, and forced to leave their native countries. Those of whom the world was not worthy have been forced to wander in mountains, in dens and caves of the earth. (2.) We ought to have a special regard to the dispersed persecuted servants of God. These were the objects of this apostle's particular care and compassion. We should proportion our regard to the excellency and to the necessity of the saints. (3.) The value of good people ought not to be estimated by their present external condition. Here was a set of excellent people, beloved of God, and yet strangers, dispersed and poor in the world; the eye of God was upon them in all their dispersions, and the apostle was tenderly careful to write to them for their direction and consolation.

2. They are described by their spiritual condition: *Elect according to the foreknowledge of God the Father,* etc. These poor strangers, who were oppressed and despised in the world, were nevertheless in high esteem with the great God, and in the most honourable state that any person can be in during this life; for they were,

(1.) *Elect according to the foreknowledge of God the Father.* Election is either to an office: so Saul was the man whom the Lord chose to be king (1 Sa. 10:24), and our Lord says to his apostles, *Have not I chosen you twelve?* (Jn. 6:70); or it is to a church-state, for the enjoyment of special privileges: thus Israel was God's elect (Deu. 7:6), *For thou art a holy people unto the Lord thy God; the Lord thy God hath chosen thee to be a special people unto himself above all people that are upon the face of the earth;* or it is to eternal salvation: *God hath from the beginning chosen you to salvation, through sanctification of the Spirit and belief of the truth.* This is the election here spoken of, importing God's gracious decree or resolution to save some, and bring them, through Christ, by proper means, to eternal life. [1.] This election is said to be *according to the foreknowledge of God.* Foreknowledge may be taken in two ways: — *First,* for mere prescience, foresight, or understanding, that such a thing will be, before it comes to pass. Thus a mathematician certainly foreknows that at such a time there will be an eclipse. This sort of foreknowledge is in God, who at one commanding view sees all things that ever were, or are, or ever will be. But such a prescience is not the cause why any thing is so or so, though in the event it certainly will be so, as the mathematician who foresees an eclipse does not thereby cause that eclipse to be. *Secondly,* Foreknowledge sometimes signifies counsel, appointment, and approbation. Acts 2:23, *Him being delivered by the determinate counsel and foreknowledge of God.* The death of Christ was not only foreseen, but fore-ordained, as *v.* 20. Take it thus here; so the sense is, *elect according to the counsel, ordination, and free grace of God.* [2.] It is added, according to the foreknowledge of *God the Father.* By the Father we are here to understand the first person of the blessed Trinity. There is an order among the three persons, though no superiority; they are equal in power and glory, and there is an agreed economy in their works. Thus, in the affair of man's redemption, election is by way of eminency ascribed to the Father, as reconciliation is to the Son and sanctification to the Holy Ghost, though in each of these one person is not so entirely interested as to exclude the other two. Hereby the persons of the Trinity are more clearly discovered to us, and we are taught what obligations we are under to each of them distinctly.

(2.) They were elect *through sanctification of the Spirit, unto obedience, and sprinkling of the blood of Jesus Christ.* The end and last result of election is eternal life and salvation; but, before this can be accomplished, every elect person must be sanctified by the Spirit, and justified by the blood of Jesus. God's decree for man's salvation always operates through sanctification of the Spirit and sprinkling of the blood of Jesus. By sanctification here understand, not a federal sanctification only, but a real one, begun in regeneration, whereby we are renewed after the image of God and made new creatures, and carried on in the daily exercise of holiness, mortifying our sins more and more, and living to God in all the duties of a Christian life, which is here summed up in one word, *obedience,* comprehending all the duties of Christianity. By *the Spirit* some would have the apostle to mean the spirit of man, the subject sanctified. The legal or typical sanctification operated no further than the purifying of the flesh, but the Christian dispensation takes effect upon the spirit of man, and purifies that. Others, with better reason, think that by spirit is meant the Holy Ghost, the author of sanctification. He renews the mind, mortifies our sins (Rom. 8:13), and produces his excellent fruits in the hearts of Christians, Gal. 5:22, 23. This sanctification of the Spirit implies the use of means. *Sanctify them through thy truth; thy word is truth,* Jn. 17:17. *Unto obedience.* This word, as it is pointed in our translation, is referred to what goes before it, and denotes the end of sanctification, which is, to bring rebellious sinners to obedience again, to universal obedience, to obey the truth and gospel of Christ: *You have purified your souls in obeying the truth through the Spirit, v.* 22.

(3.) They were elected also to the *sprinkling of the blood of Jesus.* They were designed by God's decree to be sanctified by the Spirit, and to be purified by the merit and blood of Christ. Here is a manifest allusion to the typical sprinklings of blood under the law, which language these Jewish converts understood very well. The blood of the sacrifices must not only be shed but sprinkled, to denote that the benefits designed thereby are applied and imputed to the offerers. Thus the blood of Christ, the grand and all-sufficient sacrifice, typified by the legal sacrifices, was not only shed, but must be sprinkled and communicated to every one of these elect Christians, *that through faith in his blood they may obtain remission of sin,* Rom. 3:25. This blood of sprinkling justifies before God (Rom. 5:9), seals the covenant between God and us, of which the Lord's supper is a sign (Lu. 22:20), cleanses from all sin (1 Jn. 1:7), and admits us into heaven, Heb. 10:19. Note, [1.] God hath elected some to eternal life, some, not all; persons, not qualification. [2.] All that are chosen to eternal life as the end are chosen to obedience as the way. [3.] Unless a person be sanctified by the Spirit, and sprinkled with the blood of Jesus, there will be no true obedience in the life. [4.] There is a consent and co-operation of all the persons of the Trinity in the affair of man's salvation, and their acts are commensurate one to another: whoever the Father elects the Spirit sanctifies unto obedience, and the Son redeems and sprinkles with his blood. [5.] The doctrine of the Trinity lies at the foundation of all revealed religion. If you deny the proper deity of the Son and Holy Spirit, you invalidate the redemption of the one and the gracious operations of the other, and by this means destroy the foundation of your own safety and comfort.

III. The salutation follows: *Grace unto you, and peace be multiplied.* The blessings desired for them are *grace and peace.* 1. *Grace* — the free favour of God, with all its proper effects, pardoning, healing, assisting, and saving. 2. *Peace.* All sorts of peace may be here intended, domestic, civil, ecclesiastical peace in the church, and spiritual peace with God, with the feeling of it in our own consciences. 3. here is the request or prayer, in relations to these blessings — that they may be multiplied, which implies that they were already possessed in some degree of these blessings, and he wishes them the continuation, the increase, and the perfection of them. Learn, (1.) Those who possess spiritual blessings in their own souls earnestly desire the communication of the same to others. The grace of God is a generous, not a selfish principle. (2.) The best blessings we can desire for ourselves, or one for another, are grace and peace, with the multiplication of them; therefore the apostles so often make this their prayer in the beginning and end of their epistles. (3.) Solid peace cannot be enjoyed where there is no true grace; first grace, then peace. Peace without grace is mere stupidity;; but grace may be true where there is for a time no actual peace; as Heman was distracted with terror, and Christ was once in an agony. (4.) The increase of grace and peace, as well as the first gift of them, is from God. Where he gives true grace he will give more grace; and every good man earnestly desires the improvement and multiplication of these blessings in himself and others.

Verses 3–5

We come now to the body of the epistle, which begins with,

I. A congratulation of the dignity and happiness of the state of these believers, brought in under the form of a thanksgiving to God. Other epistles begin in like manner, 2 Co. 1:3; Eph. 1:3. Here we have,

1. The duty performed, which is blessing God. A man blesses God by a just acknowledgment of his excellency and blessedness.

2. The object of this blessing described by his relation to Jesus Christ: *The God and Father of our Lord Jesus Christ.* Here are three names of one person, denoting his threefold office. (1.) He is *Lord,* a universal king or sovereign. (2.) *Jesus,* a priest or Saviour. (3.) *Christ,* a prophet, anointed with the Spirit and furnished with all gifts necessary for the instruction, guidance, and salvation of his church. This God, so blessed, is the God of Christ according to his human nature, and his Father according to his divine nature.

3. The reasons that oblige us to this duty of blessing God, which are comprised in *his abundant mercy.* All our blessings are owing to God's mercy, not to man's merit, particularly regeneration. He *hath begotten us again,* and this deserves our thanksgiving to God, especially if we consider the fruit it produces in us, which is that excellent grace of hope, and that not such a vain, dead, perishing hope as that of worldlings and hypocrites, but a lively hope, a living, strong, quickening, and durable hope, as that hope must needs be that has such a solid foundation as *the resurrection of Jesus Christ from the dead.* Learn, (1.) A good Christian's condition is never so bad but he has great reason still to bless God. As a sinner has always reason to mourn, notwithstanding his

present prosperity, so good people, in the midst of their manifold difficulties, have reason still to rejoice and bless God. (2.) In our prayers and praises we should address God as *the Father of our Lord Jesus Christ;* it is only through him that we and our services are accepted. (3.) The best of men owe their best blessings to the abundant mercy of God. All the evil in the world is from man's sin, but all the good in it is from *God's mercy.* Regeneration is expressly ascribed to the abundant mercy of God, and so are all the rest; we subsist entirely upon divine mercy. Of the nature of regeneration, see on Jn. 3:3. (4.) Regeneration produces a lively hope of eternal life. Every unconverted person is a hopeless creature; whatever he pretends to of that kind is all confidence and presumption. The right Christian hope is what a man is begotten again unto by the Spirit of God; it is not from nature, but free grace. Those who are begotten to a new and spiritual life are begotten to a new and spiritual hope. (5.) The hope of a Christian has this excellency, it is a living hope. The hope of eternal life in a true Christian is a hope that keeps him alive, quickens him, supports him, and conducts him to heaven. Hope invigorates and spirits up the soul to action, to patience, to fortitude, and perseverance to the end. The delusive hopes of the unregenerate are vain and perishing; the hypocrite and his hope expire and die both together, Job 27:8. (6.) *The resurrection of Jesus Christ from the dead* is the ground or foundation of a Christian's hope. The resurrection of Christ is the act of the Father as a Judge, of the Son as a conqueror. His resurrection demonstrates that the Father accepts his death in full discharge for our ransom, that he is victorious over death, the grave, and all our spiritual enemies; and it is also an assurance of our own resurrection. There being an inseparable union between Christ and his flock, they rise by virtue of his resurrection as a head, rather than by virtue of his power as a Judge. *We have risen with Christ,* Col. 3:1. From all this taken together, Christians have two firm and solid foundations whereon to build their hope of eternal life.

II. Having congratulated these people on their new birth, and the hope of everlasting life, the apostle goes on to describe that life under the notion of *an inheritance,* a most proper way of speaking to these people; for they were poor and persecuted, perhaps turned out of their inheritances to which they were born; to allay this grievance, he tells them they were new-born to a new inheritance, infinitely better than what they had lost. Besides, they were most of them Jews, and so had a great affection to the land of Canaan, as the land of their inheritance, settled upon them by God himself; and to be driven out from abiding in the inheritance of the Lord was looked upon as a sore judgment, 1 Sa. 26:19. To comfort them under this they are put in mind of a noble inheritance reserved in heaven for them, such a one that the land of Canaan was but a mere shadow in comparison with it. Here note,

1. Heaven is the undoubted inheritance of all the children of God; all that are born again are born to an inheritance, as a man makes his child his heir; the apostle argues, *If children, then heirs,* Rom. 8:17. God giveth his gifts unto all, but the inheritance to none but his children; those that are his sons and daughters by regeneration and adoption receive the promise of eternal inheritance, Heb. 9:15. This inheritance is not our purchase, but our Father's gift; not wages that we merit, but the effect of grace, which first makes us children and then settles this inheritance upon us by a firm unalterable covenant.

2. The incomparable excellencies of this inheritance, which are four: — (1.) It is incorruptible, in which respect it is like its Maker, who is called the *incorruptible God,* Rom. 1:23. All corruption is a change from better to worse, but heaven is without change and without end; the house is eternal in the heavens, and the possessors must subsist for ever, *for their corruptible must put on incorruption,* 1 Co. 15:53. (2.) This inheritance is undefiled, like the great high priest that is now in possession of it, who is *holy, harmless, and undefiled,* Heb. 7:26. Sin and misery, the two grand defilements that spoil this world, and mar its beauty, have no place there. (3.) It fadeth not away, but always retains its vigour and beauty, and remains immarcescible, ever entertaining and pleasing the saints who possess it, without the least weariness or distaste. (4.) *"Reserved in heaven for you,"* which expression teaches us, [1.] That it is a glorious inheritance, for it is in heaven, and all that is there is glorious, Eph. 1:18. [2.] It is certain, a reversion in another world, safely kept and

preserved till we come to the possession of it. [3.] The persons for whom it is reserved are described, not by their names, but by their character: *for you,* or us, or every one that is *begotten again to a lively hope.* This inheritance is preserved for them, and none but them; all the rest will be shut out for ever.

III. This inheritance being described as future, and distant both in time and place, the apostle supposes some doubt or uneasiness yet to remain upon the minds of these people, whether they might not possibly fall short by the way. "Though the happiness be safe in heaven, yet we are still upon earth, liable to abundance of temptations, miseries, and infirmities. Are we in such a safe state that we shall certainly come thither?" To this he answers that they should be safely guarded and conducted thither; they should be kept and preserved from all such destructive temptations and injuries as would prevent their safe arrival at eternal life. The heir to an earthly estate has no assurance that he shall live to enjoy it, but the heirs of heaven shall certainly be conducted safely to the possession of it. The blessing here promised is preservation: You *are kept;* the author of it is *God;* the means in us made use of for that end are our own *faith* and care; the end to which we are preserved is *salvation;* and the time when we shall see the safe end and issue of all is *the last time.* Note, 1. Such is the tender care of God over his people that he not only gives them grace, but preserves them unto glory. Their being kept implies both danger and deliverance; they may be attacked, but shall not be overcome. 2. The preservation of the regenerate to eternal life is the effect of God's power. The greatness of the work, the number of enemies, and our own infirmities, are such that no power but what is almighty can preserve the soul through all unto salvation; therefore the scripture often represents man's salvation as the effect of divine power, 2 Co. 12:9; Rom. 14:4. 3. Preservation by God's power does not supersede man's endeavour and care for his own salvation; here are God's power and man's faith, which implies an earnest desire of salvation, a reliance upon Christ according to his invitations and promises, a vigilant care to do every thing pleasing to God and avoid whatever is offensive, an abhorrence of temptations, a *respect to the recompence of reward,* and persevering diligence in prayer. By such a patient, operating, conquering faith, we are kept under the assistance of divine grace, unto salvation; faith is a sovereign preservative of the soul through a state of grace unto a state of glory. 4. This salvation is *ready to be revealed in the last time.* Here are three things asserted about the salvation of the saints: — (1.) That it is now prepared, and made ready, and reserved in heaven for them. (2.) Though it be made ready now, yet it is in a great measure hidden and unrevealed at present, not only to the ignorant, blind world, that never enquire after it, but even to the heirs of salvation themselves. *It does not yet appear what we shall be,* 1 Jn. 3:2. (3.) That it shall be fully and completely *revealed in the last time,* or at the last day of judgment. *Life and immortality are now brought to light by the gospel,* but this life will be revealed more gloriously at death, when the soul shall be admitted into the presence of Christ, and behold his glory; and even beyond this there will be a further and a final revelation of the amplitude and transcendency of the saints' felicity at the last day, when their bodies shall be raised and re-united to their souls, and judgment shall pass upon angels and men, and Christ shall publicly honour and applaud his servants in the face of all the world.

Verses 6–9

The first word, *wherein,* refers to the apostle's foregoing discourse about the excellency of their present state, and their grand expectations for the future. "In this condition *you greatly rejoice, though now for a season,* or a little while, *if need be, you are made sorrowful through manifold temptations,"* v. 6.

I. The apostle grants they were in great affliction, and propounds several things in mitigation of their sorrows. 1. Every sound Christian has always something wherein he may greatly rejoice. Great rejoicing contains more than an inward placid serenity of mind or sensation of comfort; it will show itself in the countenance and conduct, but especially in praise and gratitude. 2. The chief joy of a good Christian arises from things spiritual and heavenly, from his relation to God and to heaven. In these every sound Christian greatly rejoices; his joy arises from his treasure, which consists of matters of great value, and the title to them is sure. 3. The best Christians, those who have reason greatly to rejoice, may yet be in great heaviness through manifold temptations. All sorts of adversities are temptations, or trials of faith, patience, and constancy. These seldom go singly, but are manifold, and come from different quarters, the effect of all which is great heaviness. As men, we are subject to sorrows, personal and domestic. As Christians, our duty to God obliges us to frequent sorrow: and our compassion towards the miserable, the dishonour done to God, the calamities of his church, and the destruction of mankind, from their own folly and from divine vengeance, raise, in a generous and pious mind, almost continual sorrow. *I have great heaviness and continual sorrow in my heart,* Rom. 9:2. 4. The afflictions and sorrows of good people are but for a little while, they are but for a season; though they may be smart, they are but short. Life itself is but for a little while, and the sorrows of it cannot survive it; the shortness of any affliction does much abate the heaviness of it. 5. Great heaviness is often necessary to a Christian's good: *If need be, you are in heaviness.* God does not afflict his people willingly, but acts with judgment, in proportion to our needs. There is a conveniency and fitness, nay, an absolute necessity in the case, for so the expression signifies: *it must be;* therefore no man should be *moved by these afflictions. For yourselves know that we are appointed thereunto,* 1 Th. 3:3. These troubles, that lie heavy, never come upon us but when we have need, and never stay any longer than needs must.

II. He expresses the end of their afflictions and the ground of their joy under them, *v.* 7. The end of good people's afflictions is *the trial of their faith.* As to the nature of this trial, it is *much more precious than of gold that perisheth, though it be tried with fire.* The effect of the trial is this, it will *be found unto praise, honour, and glory at the appearing of Jesus Christ.* Note, 1. The afflictions of serious Christians are designed for the trial of their faith. God's design in afflicting his people is their probation, not their destruction; their advantage, not their ruin: a *trial,* as the word signifies, is an experiment or search made upon a man, by some affliction, to prove the value and strength of his faith. This trial is made upon faith principally, rather than any other grace, because the trial of this is, in effect, the trial of all that is good in us. Our Christianity depends upon our faith; if this be wanting, there is nothing else that is spiritually good in us. Christ prays for this apostle, *that his faith might not fail;* if that be supported, all the rest will stand firm; the faith of good people is tried, that they themselves may have the comfort of it, God the glory of it, and others the benefit of it. 2. A tried faith is much more precious than tried gold. Here is a double comparison of faith and gold, and the trial of the one with the trial of the other. Gold is the most valuable, pure, useful, and durable, of all the metals; so is faith among the Christian virtues; it lasts till it brings the soul to heaven, and then it issues in the glorious fruition of God for ever. The trial of faith is much more precious than the trial of gold; in both there is a purification, a separation of the dross, and a discovery of the soundness and goodness of the things. Gold does not increase and multiply by trial in the fire, it rather grows less; but *faith* is established, improved, and multiplied, by the oppositions and afflictions that it meets with. *Gold* must perish at last — *gold that perisheth;* but *faith* never will. *I have prayed for thee, that thy faith fail not,* Lu. 22:32. The trial of faith will be found to praise, and honour, and glory. Honour is properly that esteem and value which one has with another, and so God and man will honour the saints. Praise is the expression or declaration of that esteem; so Christ will commend his people in the great day, *Come, you blessed of my Father,* etc. Glory is that lustre wherewith a person, so honoured and praised, shines in heaven. *Glory, honour, and peace, to every man that worketh good,* Rom. 2:10. If a tried faith be found to praise, honour, and glory, let this recommend faith to you, as much more precious than gold, though it be assaulted and tried by afflictions. If you make your estimate either from present use or the final event of both, this will be found true, however the world may take it for an incredible paradox. 4. Jesus Christ will appear again in glory, and, when he does so, the saints will appear with him, and their graces will appear illustrious; and the more they have been tried the more bright they will then appear. The trial will soon be over, but the glory, honour, and praise will last to eternity. This should reconcile you to your present afflictions: *they work for you a far more exceeding and eternal weight of glory.*

III. He particularly commends the faith of these primitive Christians upon two accounts: —

1. The excellency of its object, the unseen Jesus. The apostle had seen our Lord in the flesh, but these dispersed Jews never did, and yet they believed in him, *v.* 8. It is one thing to believe God, or Christ (so the devils believe), and another thing to believe in him, which denotes subjection, reliance, and expectation of all promised good from him.

2. On account of two notable productions or effects of their faith, *love* and *joy,* and this joy so great as to be above description: *You rejoice with joy unspeakable, and full of glory.* Learn,

(1.) The faith of a Christian is properly conversant about things revealed, but not seen. Sense converses with things sensible and present; reason is a higher guide, which by sure deductions can infer the operation of causes, and the certainty of events; but faith ascends further still, and assures us of abundance of particulars that sense and reason could never have found out, upon the credit of revelation; it is *the evidence of things not seen.*

(2.) True faith is never alone, but produces a strong love to Jesus Christ. True Christians have a sincere love to Jesus, because they believe in him. This love discovers itself in the highest esteem for him, affectionate desires after him, willingness to be dissolved to be with him, delightful thoughts, cheerful services and sufferings, etc.

(3.) Where there are true faith and love to Christ there is, or may be, *joy unspeakable and full of glory.* This joy is inexpressible, it cannot be described by words; the best discovery is by an experimental taste of it; it is *full of glory,* full of heaven. There is much of heaven and the future glory in the present joys of improved Christians; their faith removes the causes of sorrow, and affords the best reasons for joy. Though good people sometimes walk in darkness, it is often owing to their own mistakes and ignorance, or to a fearful or melancholy disposition, or to some late sinful conduct, or perhaps to some sad occurrence of providence, that sinks their comfort for the present, yet they have reason to rejoice in the Lord, and joy in the God of their salvation, Heb. 3:18. Well might these primitive Christians rejoice with the joy unspeakable, since they were every day *receiving the end of their faith, the salvation of their souls, v.* 4. Note, [1.] The blessing they were receiving: *The salvation of their souls* (the more noble part being put for the whole man), which salvation is here called *the end of their faith,* the end wherein faith terminates: faith helps to save the soul, then it has done its work, and ceases for ever. [2.] He speaks of the present time: You are now actually *receiving the end of your faith,* etc. [3.] The word used alludes to the games at which the conqueror received or bore away from the judge of the contest a crown or reward, which he carried about in triumph; so the salvation of the soul was the prize these Christians sought for, the crown they laboured for, the end they aimed at, which came nearer and more within their reach every day. Learn, *First,* Every faithful Christian is daily receiving the salvation of his soul; salvation is one permanent thing, begun in this life, not interrupted by death, and continued to all eternity. These believers had the beginnings of heaven in the possession of holiness and a heavenly mind, in their duties and communion with God, in the earnest of the inheritance, and the witness of the divine Spirit. This was properly urged to these distressed people; they were on the losing side in the world, but the apostle puts them in the mind of what they were receiving; if they lost an inferior good, they were all the while receiving the salvation of their souls. *Secondly,* It is lawful for a Christian to make the salvation of his soul his end; the glory of God and our own felicity are so connected that if we regularly seek the one we must attain the other.

Verses 10–12

The apostle having described the persons to whom he wrote, and declared to them the excellent advantages they were under, goes on to show them what warrant he had for what he had delivered; and because they were Jews, and had a profound veneration for the Old Testament, he produces the authority of the prophets to convince them that the doctrine of salvation by faith in Jesus Christ was no new doctrine, but the same which the old prophets did enquire and search diligently into. Note,

I. Who made this diligent search — *the prophets,* who were persons inspired by God either to do or to say things extraordinary, above the reach of their own studies and abilities, as

foretelling things to come, and revealing the will of God, by the direction of the Holy Spirit.

II. The object of their search, which was *salvation,* and *the grace of God which should come unto you;* the general salvation of men of all nations by Jesus Christ, and more especially the salvation afforded to the Jews, *the grace that should come to them* from him who was *not sent but to the lost sheep of the house of Israel.* They foresaw glorious times of light, grace, and comfort, coming upon the church, which made the prophets and righteous men desire to see and hear the things which came to pass in the days of the gospel.

III. The manner of their enquiry: they *enquired and searched diligently.* The words are strong and emphatic, alluding to miners, who dig to the bottom, and break through not only the earth, but the rock, to come to the ore; so these holy prophets had an earnest desire to know, and were proportionably diligent in their enquiries after the grace of God, which was to be revealed in the days of the Messiah: their being inspired did not make their industrious search needless; for, notwithstanding their extraordinary assistance from God, they were obliged to make use of all the ordinary methods of improvement in wisdom and knowledge. Daniel was a man greatly beloved and inspired, yet he understood by books and study the computations of time, *ch.* 9:2. Even their own revelation required their study, meditation, and prayer; for many prophecies had a double meaning: in their first intention they aimed at some person or event near at hand, but their ultimate design was to describe the person, sufferings, or kingdom of Christ. Observe, 1. The doctrine of man's salvation by Jesus Christ has been the study and admiration of the greatest and wisest of men; the nobleness of the subject, and their own concern in it, have engaged them, with most accurate attention and seriousness to search into it. 2. A good man is much affected and pleased with the grace and mercy of God to others, as well as to himself. *The prophets* were highly delighted with the prospects of mercy to be shown both to Jews and Gentiles at the coming of Christ. 3. Those who would be acquainted with this great salvation, and the grace that shines therein, must enquire and search diligently into it: if it was necessary for an inspired prophet to do so, much more for persons so weak and injudicious as we are. 4. The grace that came by the gospel excels all that was before it; the gospel dispensation is more glorious, evident, intelligible, extensive, and effectual, than any dispensation that ever did precede it.

IV. The particular matters which the ancient prophets chiefly searched into, which are expressed in *v.* 11. Jesus Christ was the main subject of their studies; and, in relation to him, they were most inquisitive into,

1. His humiliation and death, and the glorious consequences of it: *The sufferings of Christ, and the glories that should follow.* This enquiry would lead them into a view of the whole gospel, the sum whereof is this, *that Christ Jesus was delivered for our offences and raised again for our justification.*

2. The time, and the manner of the times, wherein the Messiah was to appear. Undoubtedly these holy prophets earnestly desired to see the days of the Son of man; and therefore, next to the thing itself, their minds were set upon the time of its accomplishment, so far as the Spirit of Christ, which was in them, had signified any thing towards that purpose. The nature of the times was also under their strict consideration, whether they would be quiet or troublesome times, times of peace or times of war. Learn, (1.) Jesus Christ had a being before his incarnation; for his Spirit did then exist in the prophets, and therefore he whose that Spirit then was must be in being also. (2.) The doctrine of the Trinity was not wholly unknown to the faithful in the Old Testament. The prophets knew that they were inspired by a Spirit that was in them; this Spirit they knew to be the Spirit of Christ, and consequently distinct from Christ himself: here is a plurality of persons, and from other parts of the Old Testament a Trinity may be collected. (3.) The works here ascribed to the Holy Ghost prove him to be God. He *did signify,* discover, and manifest to the prophets, many hundred years *beforehand, the sufferings of Christ,* with a multitude of particular circumstances attending them; and he did also *testify,* or give proof and evidence beforehand, of the certainty of that event, by inspiring the prophets to reveal it, to work miracles in confirmation of it, and by enabling the faithful to believe it. These works prove the Spirit of Christ to be God, since he is possessed of almighty power and infinite knowledge. (4.) From

the example of Christ Jesus learn to expect a time of services and sufferings before you are received to glory. It was so with him, and the *disciple is not above his Lord.* The suffering time is but short, but the glory is everlasting; let the suffering season be ever so sharp and severe, it shall not hinder, but *work for us a far more exceeding and eternal weight of glory.*

V. The success with which their enquiries were crowned. Their holy endeavours to inform themselves were not slighted, for God gave them a satisfactory revelation to quiet and comfort their minds. They were informed that these things should not come to pass in their time, but yet all was firm and certain, and should come to pass in the times of the apostles: *Not unto themselves, but to us;* and we must report them, under the infallible direction of the Holy Ghost, to all the world. *Which things the angels,* etc.

You have here three sorts of students, or enquirers into the great affair of man's salvation by Jesus Christ: — 1. *The prophets,* who *searched diligently* into it. 2. The apostles, who consulted all the prophecies, and were witnesses of the accomplishment of them, and so reported what they knew to others in the preaching of the gospel. 3. The angels, who most attentively pry into these matters. Learn, (1.) A diligent endeavour after the knowledge of Christ and our duty will certainly be answered with good success. The prophets are answered with a revelation. Daniel studies, and receives information: the Bereans search the scriptures, and are confirmed. (2.) The holiest and best of men sometimes have their lawful and pious requests denied. It was both lawful and pious for these prophets to desire to know more than they were permitted to know about the time of the appearance of Christ in the world, but they were denied. It is lawful and pious for good parents to pray for their wicked children, for the poor to pray against poverty, for a good man to pray against death; yet, in these honest requests, they often are denied. God is pleased to answer our necessities rather than our requests. (3.) It is the honour and practice of a Christian to be useful to others, in many cases, rather than to himself. The prophets ministered to others, not unto themselves. *None of us liveth to himself,* Rom. 14:7. Nothing is more contrary to man's nature nor to Christian principles than for a man to make himself his own end, and live to himself. (4.) The revelations of God to his church, though gradual, and given by parcels, are all perfectly consistent; the doctrine of the prophets and that of the apostles exactly agree, as coming from the same Spirit of God. (5.) The efficacy of the evangelical ministry depends upon the Holy Ghost sent down from heaven. The gospel is the ministration of the Spirit; the success of it depends upon his operation and blessing. (6.) The mysteries of the gospel, and the methods of man's salvation, are so glorious that the blessed angels earnestly desire to look into them; they are curious, accurate, and industrious in prying into them; they consider the whole scheme of man's redemption with deep attention and admiration, particularly the points the apostle had been discoursing of: *Which things the angels desire to* stoop down and *look into,* as *the cherubim* did continually *towards the mercy-seat.*

Verses 13–23

Here the apostle begins his exhortations to those whose glorious state he had before described, thereby instructing us that Christianity is a doctrine according to godliness, designed to make us not only wiser, but better.

I. He exhorts them to sobriety and holiness.

1. *Wherefore gird up the loins of your mind,* etc., *v.* 13. As if he had said, *"Wherefore,* since you are so honoured and distinguished, as above, *Gird up the loins of your mind.* You have a journey to go, a race to run, a warfare to accomplish, and a great work to do; as the traveller, the racer, the warrior, and the labourer, gather in, and gird up, their long and loose garments, that they may be more ready, prompt, and expeditious in their business, so do you by your minds, your inner man, and affections seated there: *gird them,* gather them in, let them not hang loose and neglected about you; restrain their extravagances, and let the loins or strength and vigour of your minds be exerted in your duty; disengage yourselves from all that would hinder you, and go on resolutely in your obedience. *Be sober,* be vigilant against all your spiritual dangers and enemies, and be temperate and modest in eating, drinking, apparel, recreation, business, and in the whole of your behaviour. Be sober-mined also in opinion, as well as in practice, and humble in your judgment of your-

selves." *And hope to the end, for the grace that is to be brought to you at the revelation of Jesus Christ.* Some refer this to the last judgment, as if the apostle directed their hope to the final revelation of Jesus Christ; but it seems more natural to take it, as it might be rendered, *"Hope perfectly,* or *thoroughly, for the grace that is brought to you* in or by *the revelation of Jesus Christ;* that is, by the gospel, *which brings life and immortality to light.* Hope perfectly, trust without doubting to that grace which is now offered to you by the gospel." Learn, (1.) The main work of a Christian lies in the right management of his heart and mind; the apostle's first direction is to gird up the loins of the mind. (2.) The best Christians have need to be exhorted to sobriety. These excellent Christians are put in mind of it; it is required of a bishop (1 Tim. 3:2), of aged men (Tit. 2:2), the young women are to be taught it, and the young men are directed to be soberminded, Tit. 2:4, 6. (3.) A Christian's work is not over as soon as he has got into a state of grace; he must still hope and strive for more grace. When he has entered the strait gate, he must still walk in the narrow way, and gird up the loins of his mind for that purpose. (4.) A strong and perfect trust in God's grace is very consistent with our best endeavours in our duty; we must hope perfectly, and yet gird up our loins, and address ourselves vigorously to the work we have to do, encouraging ourselves from the grace of Jesus Christ.

2. *As obedient children,* etc., *v.* 14. These words may be taken as a rule of holy living, which is both positive — "You ought to live *as obedient children,* as those whom God hath adopted into his family, and regenerated by his grace;" and negative — "You must *not fashion yourselves according to the former lusts, in your ignorance."* Or the words may be taken as an argument to press them to holiness from the consideration of what they now are, children of obedience, and what they were when they lived in lust and ignorance. Learn, (1.) The children of God ought to prove themselves to be such by their obedience to God, by their present, constant, universal obedience. (2.) The best of God's children have had their times of lust and ignorance; the time has been when the whole scheme of their lives, their way and fashion, was to accommodate and gratify their unlawful desires and vicious appetites, being grossly ignorant of God and themselves, of Christ and the gospel. (3.) Persons, when converted, differ exceedingly from what they were formerly. They are people of another fashion and manner from what they were before; their inward frame, behaviour, speech, and conversation, are much altered from what they were in times past. (4.) The lusts and extravagances of sinners are both the fruits and the signs of their ignorance.

3. *But as he who hath called you,* etc., *v.* 15, 16. Here is a noble rule enforced by strong arguments: *Be you holy in all manner of conversation.* Who is sufficient for this? And yet it is required in strong terms, and enforced by three reasons, taken from the grace of God in calling us, — from his command, *it is written,* — and from his example. *Be you holy, for I am holy.* Learn, (1.) The grace of God in calling a sinner is a powerful engagement to holiness. It is a great favour to be called effectually by divine grace out of a state of sin and misery into the possession of all the blessings of the new covenant; and great favours are strong obligations; they enable as well as oblige to be holy. (2.) Complete holiness is the desire and duty of every Christian. Here is a two-fold rule of holiness: [1.] It must, for the extent of it, be universal. We must *be holy,* and be so in *all manner of conversation;* in all civil and religious affairs, in every condition, prosperous or reverse; towards all people, friends and enemies; in all our intercourse and business still we must be holy. [2.] For the pattern of it. We must *be holy, as God is holy:* we must imitate him, though we can never equal him. He is perfectly, unchangeably, and eternally holy; and we should aspire after such a state. The consideration of the holiness of God should oblige as to the highest degree of holiness we can attain unto. (3.) The written word of God is the surest rule of a Christian's life, and by this rule we are commanded to be holy every way. (4.) The Old-Testament commands are to be studied and obeyed in the times of the New Testament; the apostle, by virtue of a command delivered several times by Moses, requires holiness in all Christians.

4. *If you call on the Father,* etc., *v.* 17. The apostle does not there express any doubt at all whether these Christians would call upon their heavenly Father, but supposes they would certainly do it, and from this argues with them to *pass the time of their sojourning here in fear:* "If you own the great

God as a Father and a Judge, you ought to live the time of your sojourning here in his fear." Learn, (1.) All good Christians look upon themselves in this world as pilgrims and strangers, as strangers in a distant country, passing to another, to which they properly belong, Ps. 39:12; Heb. 11:13. (2.) The whole time of our sojourning here is to be passed in the fear of God. (3.) The consideration of God as a Judge is not improper for those who can truly call him Father. Holy confidence in God as a Father, an awful fear of him as a Judge, are very consistent; to regard God as a Judge is a singular means to endear him to us as a Father. (4.) The judgment of God will be without respect of persons: *According to every man's work.* No external relation to him will protect any; the Jew may call God Father and Abraham father, but God will not respect persons, nor favour their cause, from personal considerations, but judge them according to their work. The works of men will in the great day discover their persons; God will make all the world to know who are his by their works. We are obliged to faith, holiness, and obedience, and our works will be an evidence whether we have complied with our obligations or not.

5. The apostle having extorted them to *pass the time of their sojourning in the fear of God* from this consideration, that they *called on the Father,* he adds (*v.* 18) a second argument: *Because* or *forasmuch as you were not redeemed with corruptible things,* etc. Herein he puts them in mind, (1.) That they were redeemed, or bought back again, by a ransom paid to the Father. (2.) What the price paid for their redemption was: *Not with corruptible things, as silver and gold, but with the precious blood of Christ.* (3.) From what they were redeemed: *From a vain conversation received by tradition.* (4.) They knew this: *Forasmuch as you know,* and cannot pretend ignorance of this great affair. Learn, [1.] The consideration of our redemption ought to be a constant and powerful inducement to holiness, and the fear of God. [2.] God expects that a Christian should live answerably to what he knows, and therefore we have great need to be put in mind of what we already know, Ps. 39:4. [3.] Neither silver nor gold, nor any of the corruptible things of this world, can redeem so much as one soul. They are often snares, temptations, and hindrances to man's salvation, but they can by no means purchase or procure it; they are corruptible, and therefore cannot redeem an incorruptible and immortal soul. [4.] The blood of Jesus Christ is the only price of man's redemption. The redemption of man is real, not metaphorical. We are bought with a price, and the price is equal to the purchase, for it is the precious blood of Christ; it is the blood of an innocent person, a lamb without blemish and without spot, whom the paschal lamb represented, and of an infinite person, being the Son of God, and therefore it is called the blood of God, Acts 20:28. [5.] The design of Christ in shedding his most precious blood was to redeem us, not only from eternal misery hereafter, but from a vain conversation in this world. That conversation is vain which is empty, frivolous, trifling, and unserviceable to the honour of God, the credit of religion, the conviction of unbelievers, and the comfort and satisfaction of a man's own conscience. Not only the open wickedness, but the vanity and unprofitableness of our conversation are highly dangerous. [6.] A man's conversation may carry an appearance of devotion, and may plead antiquity, custom, and tradition, in its defence, and yet after all be a most vain conversation. The Jews had a deal to say from these heads, for all their formalities; and yet their conversation was so vain that only the blood of Christ could redeem them from it. Antiquity is no certain rule of verity, nor is it a wise resolution, "I will live and die in such a way, because my forefathers did so."

6. Having mentioned the price of redemption, the apostle goes on to speak of some things relating both to the Redeemer and the redeemed, *v.* 20, 21.

(1.) The Redeemer is further described, not only as a Lamb without spot, but as one, [1.] That was *fore-ordained before the foundation of the world,* fore-ordained or foreknown. When prescience is ascribed to God, it implies more than bare prospect or speculation. It imports an act of the will, a resolution that the thing shall be, Acts 2:23. God did not only foreknow, but determine and decree, that his Son should die for man, and this decree was before the foundation of the world. Time and the world began together; before the commencement of time there was nothing but eternity. [2.] That *was manifested in these last days for them.* He was manifested or demonstrated to be that Redeemer whom God had fore-ordained. He was manifested by his birth, by his Father's testimony, and by his own works, especially by his resurrection from the dead, Rom. 1:4. "This was done in these last times of the New Testament and of the gospel, for you, you Jews, you sinners, you afflicted ones; you have the comfort of the manifestation and appearance of Christ, if you believe on him." [3.] That was raised from the dead by the Father, who gave him glory. The resurrection of Christ, considered as an act of power, is common to all the three persons, but as an act of judgment it is peculiar to the Father, who as a Judge released Christ, raised him from the grave, and gave him glory, proclaimed him to all the world to be his Son by his resurrection from the dead, advanced him to heaven, crowned him with glory and honour, invested him with all power in heaven and earth, and glorified him with that glory which he had with God before the world was.

(2.) The redeemed are also described here by their faith and hope, the cause of which is Jesus Christ: "*You do by him believe in God* — by him as the author, encourager, support, and finisher of your faith; your faith and hope now may be in God, as reconciled to you by Christ the Mediator."

(3.) From all this we learn, [1.] The decree of God to send Christ to be a Mediator was from everlasting, and was a just and merciful decree, which yet does not at all excuse man's sin in crucifying him, Acts 2:23. God had purposes of special favour towards his people long before he made any manifestations of such grace to them. [2.] Great is the happiness of the last times in comparison with what the former ages of the world enjoyed. The clearness of light, the supports of faith, the efficacy of ordinances, and the proportion of comforts — these are all much greater since the manifestation of Christ than they were before. Our gratitude and services should be suitable to such favours. [3.] The redemption of Christ belongs to none but true believers. A general impetration is asserted by some and denied by others, but none pretend to a general application of Christ's death for the salvation of all. Hypocrites and unbelievers will be ruined for ever, notwithstanding the death of Christ. [4.] God in Christ is the ultimate object of a Christian's faith, which is strongly supported by the resurrection of Christ, and the glory that did follow.

II. He exhorts them to brotherly love.

1. He supposes that the gospel had already had such an effect upon them as to purify their souls while they obeyed it through the Spirit, and that it had produced at least an *unfeigned love of the brethren;* and thence he argues with them to proceed to a higher degree of affection, to love one another with a pure heart fervently, *v.* 22. Learn, (1.) It is not to be doubted but that every sincere Christian purifies his soul. The apostle takes this for granted: *Seeing you have,* etc. To purify the soul supposes some great uncleanness and defilement which had polluted it, and that this defilement is removed. Neither the Levitical purifications under the law, nor the hypocritical purifications of the outward man, can effect this. (2.) The word of God is the great instrument of a sinner's purification: *Seeing you have purified your souls in obeying the truth.* The gospel is called truth, in opposition to types and shadows, to error and falsehood. This truth is effectual to purify the soul, if it be obeyed, Jn. 17:17. Many hear the truth, but are never purified by it, because they will not submit to it nor obey it. (3.) The Spirit of God is the great agent in the purification of man's soul. The Spirit convinces the soul of its impurities, furnishes those virtues and graces that both adorn and purify, such as faith (Acts 15:9), hope (1 Jn. 3:3), the fear of God (Ps. 34:9), and the love of Jesus Christ. The Spirit excites our endeavours, and makes them successful. The aid of the Spirit does not supersede our own industry; these people purified their own souls, but it was through the Spirit. (4.) The souls of Christians must be purified before they can so much as love one another unfeignedly. There are such lusts and partialities in man's nature that without divine grace we can neither love God nor one another as we ought to do; there is no charity but out of a pure heart. (5.) It is the duty of all Christians sincerely and fervently to love one another. Our affection to one another must be sincere and real, and it must be fervent, constant, and extensive.

2. He further presses upon Christians the duty of loving one another with a pure heart fervently from the consideration of their spiritual relation; they are all *born again, not of corruptible seed, but incorruptible,* etc. Hence we may learn, (1.) That all Christians are born again. The apostle speaks of it as what is common to all serious Christians, and by this they are brought into a new and a near relation to one another, they become brethren by their new birth. (2.) The word of God is the great means of regeneration, Jam. 1:18. The grace of regeneration is conveyed by the gospel. (3.) This new and second birth is much more desirable and excellent than the first. This the apostle teaches by preferring the incorruptible to the corruptible seed. By the one we become the children of men, by the other the sons and daughters of the Most High. The word of God being compared to seed teaches us that though it is little in appearance, yet it is wonderful in operation, though it lies hid awhile, yet it grows up and produces excellent fruit at last. (4.) Those that are regenerate should love one another with a pure heart fervently. Brethren by nature are bound to love one another; but the obligation is double where there is a spiritual relation: they are under the same government, partake of the same privileges, and have embarked in the same interest. (5.) The word of God lives and abides for ever. This word is a living word, or a lively word, Heb. 4:12. It is a means of spiritual life, to begin it and preserve in it, animating and exciting us in our duty, till it brings us to eternal life: and it is abiding; it remains eternally true, and abides in the hearts of the regenerate for ever.

Verses 24–25

The apostle having given an account of the excellency of the renewed spiritual man as born again, not of corruptible but incorruptible seed, he now sets before us the vanity of the natural man, taking him with all his ornaments and advantages about him: *For all flesh is as grass, and all the glory of man as the flower of grass;* and nothing can make him a solid substantial being, but the being born again of the incorruptible seed, the word of God, which will transform him into a most excellent creature, whose glory will not fade like a flower, but shine like an angel; and this word is daily set before you in the preaching of the gospel. Learn, 1. Man, in his utmost flourish and glory, is still a withering, fading, dying creature. Take him singly, all flesh is grass. In his entrance into the world, in his life and in his fall, he is similar to grass, Job 14:2; Isa. 40:6, 7. Take him in all his glory, even this is as the flower of grass; his wit, beauty, strength, vigour, wealth, honour — these are but as the flower of grass, which soon withers and dies away. 2. The only way to render this perishing creature solid and incorruptible is for him to entertain and receive the word of God; for this remains everlasting truth, and, if received, will preserve him to everlasting life, and abide with him for ever. 3. The prophets and apostles preached the same doctrine. This word which Isaiah and others delivered in the Old Testament is the same which the apostles preached in the New.

CHAPTER 2

The general exhortation to holiness is continued, and enforced by several reasons taken from the foundation on which Christians are built, Jesus Christ, and from their spiritual blessings and privileges in him. The means of obtaining it, the word of God, is recommended, and all contrary qualities are condemned (*v.* 1–12). Particular directions are given how subjects ought to obey the magistrates, and servants their masters, patiently suffering in well doing, in imitation of Christ (*v.* 13 to the end).

Verses 1–3

The holy apostle has been recommending mutual charity, and setting forth the excellences of the word of God, calling it an *incorruptible seed,* and saying that it *liveth and abideth for ever.* He pursues his discourse, and very properly comes in with this necessary advice, *Wherefore laying aside all malice,* etc. These are such sins as both destroy charity and hinder the efficacy of the word, and consequently they prevent our regeneration.

I. His advice is to lay aside or put off what is evil, as one would do an old rotten garment: "Cast it away with indignation, never put it on more."

1. The sins to be put off, or thrown aside, are, (1.) *Malice,* which may be taken more generally for all sorts of wickedness, as Jam. 1:21; 1 Co. 5:8. But, in a more confined sense, malice is anger resting in the bosom of fools, settled overgrown anger, retained till it inflames a man to design mischief, to do mischief, or delight in any mischief that befals another. (2.) *Guile,* or deceit in words. So it comprehends flattery, falsehood, and delusion, which is a crafty imposing upon another's ignorance or weakness, to his damage. (3.) *Hypocrisies.* The word being plural comprehends all sorts of hypocrisies. In matters of religion hypocrisy is counterfeit piety. In civil conversation hypocrisy is counterfeit friendship, which is much practised by those who give high compliments, which they do not believe, make promises which they never intend to perform, or pretend friendship when mischief lies in their hearts. (4.) *All envies;* every thing that may be called *envy,* which is a grieving at the good and welfare of another, at their abilities, prosperity, fame, or successful labours. (5.) *Evil speaking,* which is detraction, speaking against another, or defaming him; it is rendered *backbiting,* 2 Co. 12:20; Rom. 1:30.

2. Hence learn, (1.) The best Christians have need to be cautioned and warned against the worst sins, such as malice, hypocrisy, envy. They are but sanctified in part, and are still liable to temptations. (2.) Our best services towards God will neither please him nor profit us if we be not conscientious in our duties to men. The sins here mentioned are offences against the second table. These must be laid aside, or else we cannot receive the word of God as we ought to do. (3.) Whereas it is said *all malice, all guile,* learn, That one sin, not laid aside, will hinder our spiritual profit and everlasting welfare. (4.) Malice, envy, hatred, hypocrisy, and evil-speaking, generally go together. Evil-speaking is a sign that malice and guile lie in the heart; and all of them combine to hinder our profiting by the word of God.

II. The apostle, like a wise physician, having prescribed the purging out of vicious humours, goes on to direct to wholesome and regular food, that they may grow thereby. The duty exhorted to is a strong and constant desire for the *word of God,* which word is here called *reasonable milk,* only, this phrase not being proper English, our translators rendered it *the milk of the word,* by which we are to understand food proper for the soul, or a reasonable creature, whereby the mind, not the body, is nourished and strengthened. This milk of the word must be *sincere,* not adulterated by the mixtures of men, who often corrupt the word of God, 2 Co. 2:17. The manner in which they are to desire this sincere milk of the word is stated thus: *As new-born babes.* He puts them in mind of their regeneration. A new life requires suitable food. They, being newly born, must desire the milk of the word. Infants desire common milk, and their desires towards it are fervent and frequent, arising from an impatient sense of hunger, and accompanied with the best endeavours of which the infant is capable. Such must Christians' desires be for the word of God: and that for this end, that they may grow thereby, that we may improve in grace and the knowledge of our Lord and Saviour, 2 Pt. 3:18. Learn, 1. Strong desires and affections to the word of God are a sure evidence of a person's being born again. If they be such desires as the babe has for the milk, they prove that the person is new-born. They are the lowest evidence, but yet they are certain. 2. Growth and improvement in wisdom and grace are the design and desire of every Christian; all spiritual means are for edification and improvement. The word of God, rightly used, does not leave a man as it finds him, but improves and makes him better.

III. He adds an argument from their own experience: *If so be,* or *since that,* or *forasmuch as, you have tasted that the Lord is gracious, v.* 3. The apostle does not express a doubt, but affirms that these good Christians had tasted the goodness of God, and hence argues with them. "You ought to lay aside these vile sins (*v.* 1); you ought to desire the word of God; you ought to grow thereby, since you cannot deny but that you have tasted that the Lord is gracious." The next verse assures us that the Lord here spoken of is the Lord Jesus Christ. Hence learn, 1. Our Lord Jesus Christ is very gracious to his people. He is in himself infinitely good; he is very kind, free, and merciful to miserable sinners; he is pitiful and good to the undeserving; he has in him a fulness of grace. 2. The graciousness of our Redeemer is best discovered by an experimental taste of it. There must be an immediate application of the object to the organ of taste; we cannot taste at a distance, as we may see, and hear, and smell. To taste the graciousness of Christ experimentally supposes our being united to him by faith, and then we may taste his goodness in all his providences, in all our spiritual concerns, in all our fears and temptations, in his word and worship every day. 3. The best of God's servants have in this life but a taste of the grace of Christ. A taste is but a little; it is not a draught, nor does it satisfy. It is so with the consolations of God in this life. 4. The word of God is the great instrument whereby he discovers and communicates his grace to men. Those who feed upon the sincere milk of the word taste and experience most of his grace. In our converses with his word we should endeavour always to understand and experience more and more of his grace.

Verses 4–12

I. The apostle here gives us a description of Jesus Christ as a living stone; and though to a capricious wit, or an infidel, this description may seem rough and harsh, yet to the Jews, who placed much of their religion in their magnificent temple, and who understood the prophetical style, which calls the Messiah *a stone* (Isa. 8:14; 28:16), it would appear very elegant and proper.

1. In this metaphorical description of Jesus Christ, he is called a stone, to denote his invincible strength and everlasting duration, and to teach his servants that he is their protection and security, the foundation on which they are built, and a rock of offence to all their enemies. He is the living stone, having eternal life in himself, and being the prince of life to all his people. The reputation and respect he has with God and man are very different. He is disallowed of men, reprobated or rejected by his own countrymen the Jews, and by the generality of mankind; but chosen of God, separated and fore-ordained to be the foundation of the church (as *ch.* 1:20), and precious, a most honourable, choice, worthy person in himself, in the esteem of God, and in the judgment of all who believe on him. To this person so described we are obliged to come: *To whom coming*, not by a local motion, for that is impossible since his exaltation, but by faith, whereby we are united to him at first, and draw nigh to him afterwards. Learn, (1.) Jesus Christ is the very foundation-stone of all our hopes and happiness. He communicates the true knowledge of God (Mt. 11:27); by him we have access to the Father (Jn. 14:6), and through him are made partakers of all spiritual blessings, Eph. 1:3. (2.) Men in general disallow and reject Jesus Christ; they slight him, dislike him, oppose and refuse him, as scripture and experience declare, Isa. 53:3. (3.) However Christ may be disallowed by an ungrateful world, yet he is chosen of God, and precious in his account. He is chosen and fixed upon to be the Lord of the universe, the head of the church, the Saviour of his people, and the Judge of the world. He is precious in the excellency of his nature, the dignity of his office, and the gloriousness of his services. (4.) Those who expect mercy from this gracious Redeemer must come to him, which is our act, though done by God's grace — an act of the soul, not of the body — a real endeavour, not a fruitless wish.

2. Having described Christ as the foundation, the apostle goes on to speak of the superstructure, the materials built upon him: *You also, as living stones, are built up, v.* 6. The apostle is recommending the Christian church and constitution to these dispersed Jews. It was natural for them to object that the Christian church had no such glorious temple, nor such a numerous priesthood; but its dispensation was mean, the services and sacrifices of it having nothing of the pomp and grandeur which the Jewish dispensation had. To this the apostle answers that the Christian church is a much nobler fabric than the Jewish temple; it is a living temple, consisting not of dead materials, but of living parts. Christ, the foundation, is a living stone. Christians are lively stones, and these make a spiritual house, and they are a holy priesthood; and, though they have no bloody sacrifices of beasts to offer, yet they have much better and more acceptable, and they have an altar too on which to present their offerings; for they offer spiritual sacrifices, acceptable to God by Jesus Christ. Learn, (1.) All sincere Christians have in them a principle of spiritual life communicated to them from Christ their head: therefore, as he is called a living stone, so they are called lively, or living stones; not dead in trespasses and sins, but alive to God by regeneration and the working of the divine Spirit. (2.) The church of God is a spiritual house. The foundation is Christ, Eph. 2:22. It is a house for its strength, beauty, variety of parts, and usefulness of the whole. It is spiritual foundation, Christ Jesus, — in the materials of it, spiritual persons, — in its furniture, the graces of the Spirit, — in its connection, being held together by the Spirit of God and by one common faith, — and in its use, which is spiritual work, to offer up spiritual sacrifices. This house is daily built up, every part of it improving, and the whole supplied in every age by the addition of new particular members. (3.) All good Christians are a holy priesthood. The apostle speaks here of the generality of Christians, and tells them they are a holy priesthood; they are all select persons, sacred to God, serviceable to others, well endowed with heavenly gifts and

graces, and well employed. (4.) This holy priesthood must and will offer up spiritual sacrifices to God. The spiritual sacrifices which Christians are to offer are their bodies, souls, affections, prayers, praises, alms, and other duties. (5.) The most spiritual sacrifices of the best men are not acceptable to God, but through Jesus Christ; he is the only great high priest, through whom we and our services can be accepted; therefore bring all your oblations to him, and by him present them to God.

II. He confirms what he had asserted of Christ being a *living stone*, etc., from Isa. 28:16. Observe the manner of the apostle's quoting scripture, not by book, chapter, and verse; for these distinctions were not then made, so no more was said than a reference to Moses, David, or the prophets, except once a particular psalm was named, Acts 13:33. In their quotations they kept rather to the sense than the words of scripture, as appears from what is recited from the prophet in this place. He does not quote the scripture, neither the Hebrew nor Septuagint, word for word, yet makes a just and true quotation. The true sense of scripture may be justly and fully expressed in other than in scripture-words. *It is contained.* The verb is active, but our translators render it passively, to avoid the difficulty of finding a nominative case for it, which had puzzled so many interpreters before them. The matter of the quotation is this, *Behold, I lay in Zion.* Learn, 1. In the weighty matters of religion we must depend entirely upon scripture-proof; Christ and his apostles appealed to Moses, David, and the ancient prophets. The word of God is the only rule God hath given us. It is a perfect and sufficient rule. 2. The accounts that God hath given us in scripture concerning his Son Jesus Christ are what require our strictest attention. *Behold, I lay,* etc. John calls for the like attention, Jn. 1:29. These demands of attention to Christ show us the excellency of the matter, the importance of it, and our stupidity and dulness. 3. The constituting of Christ Jesus head of the church is an eminent work of God: *I lay in Zion.* The setting up of the pope for the head of the church is a human contrivance and an arrogant presumption; Christ only is the foundation and head of the church of God. 4. Jesus Christ is the chief corner-stone that God hath laid in his spiritual building. The corner-stone stays inseparably with the building, supports it, unites it, and adorns it. So does Christ by his holy church, his spiritual house. 5. Jesus Christ is the corner-stone for the support and salvation of none but such as are his sincere people: none but Zion, and such as are of Zion; not for Babylon, not for his enemies. 6. True faith in Jesus Christ is the only way to prevent a man's utter confusion. Three things put a man into great confusion, and faith prevents them all — disappointment, sin, and judgment. Faith has a remedy for each.

III. He deduces an important inference, *v.* 7. Jesus Christ is said to be the chief corner-stone. Hence the apostle infers with respect to good men, "To you therefore who believe he is precious, or he is an honour. Christ is the crown and honour of a Christian; you who believe will be so far from being ashamed of him that you will boast of him and glory in him for ever." As to wicked men, the disobedient will go on to disallow and reject Jesus Christ; but God is resolved that he shall be, in despite of all opposition, the head of the corner. Learn, 1. Whatever is by just and necessary consequence deduced from scripture may be depended upon with as much certainty as if it were contained in express words of scripture. The apostle draws an inference from the prophet's testimony. The prophet did not expressly say so, but yet he said that from which the consequence was unavoidable. Our Saviour bids them search the scriptures, because they testified of him; and yet no place in those scriptures to which he there refers them said that Jesus of Nazareth was the Messiah. Yet those scriptures do say that he who should be born of a virgin, before the sceptre departed from Judah, during the second temple, and after Daniel's seventy weeks, was the Messiah; but such was Jesus Christ: to collect this conclusion one must make use of reason, history, eye-sight, experience, and yet it is an infallible scripture-conclusion notwithstanding. 2. The business of a faithful minister is to apply general truths to the particular condition and state of his hearers. The apostle quotes a passage (*v.* 6) out of the prophet, and applies it severally to good and bad. This requires wisdom, courage, and fidelity; but it is very profitable to the hearers. 3. Jesus Christ is exceedingly precious to all the faithful. The majesty and grandeur of his person, the dignity of his office, his near relation, his wonderful works, his immense love — every

thing engages the faithful to the highest esteem and respect for Jesus Christ. 4. Disobedient people have no true faith. By disobedient people understand those that are unpersuadable, incredulous, and impenitent. These may have some right notions, but no solid faith. 5. Those that ought to be builders of the church of Christ are often the worst enemies that Christ has in the world. In the Old Testament the false prophets did the most mischief; and in the New Testament the greatest opposition and cruelty that Christ met with were from the scribes, pharisees, chief priests, and those who pretended to build and take care of the church. Still the hierarchy of Rome is the worst enemy in the world to Jesus Christ and his interest. 6. God will carry on his own work, and support the interest of Jesus Christ in the world, notwithstanding the falseness of pretended friends and the opposition of his worst enemies.

IV. The apostle adds a further description, still preserving the metaphor of a stone, *v.* 8. The words are taken from Isa. 8:13, 14, *Sanctify the Lord of hosts himself — and he shall be for a stone of stumbling, and for a rock of offence,* whence it is plain that Jesus Christ is the Lord of hosts, and consequently the most high God. Observe,

1. The builders, the chief-priests, refused him, and the people followed their leaders; and so Christ became to them *a stone of stumbling, and a rock of offence,* at which they stumbled and hurt themselves; and in return he fell upon them as a mighty stone or rock, and punished them with destruction. Mt. 12:44, *Whosoever shall fall on this stone shall be broken; but on whomsoever it shall fall it will grind him to powder.* Learn, (1.) All those that are disobedient take offense at the word of God: *They stumble at the word, being disobedient.* They are offended with Christ himself, with his doctrine and the purity of his precepts; but the Jewish doctors more especially stumbled at the meanness of his appearance and the proposal of trusting only to him for their justification before God. They could not be brought to seek justification by faith, but as it were by the works of the law; *for they stumbled at that stumbling-stone,* Rom. 9:32. (2.) The same blessed Jesus who is the author of salvation to some is to others the occasion of their sin and destruction. *He is set for the rising and fall of many in Israel.* He is not the author of their sin, but only the occasion of it; their own disobedience makes them stumble at him and reject him, which he punishes, as a judge, with destruction. Those who reject him as a Saviour will split upon him as a Rock. (3.) God himself hath appointed everlasting destruction to all those who *stumble at the word, being disobedient.* All those who go on resolutely in their infidelity and contempt of the gospel are appointed to eternal destruction; and God from eternity knows who they are. (4.) To see the Jews generally rejecting Christ, and multitudes in all ages slighting him, ought not to discourage us in our love and duty to him; for this had been foretold by the prophets long ago, and is a confirmation of our faith both in the scriptures and in the Messiah.

2. Those who received him were highly privileged, *v.* 9. The Jews were exceedingly tender of their ancient privileges, of being the only people of God, taken into a special covenant with him, and separated from the rest of the world. "Now," say they, "if we submit to the gospel-constitution, we shall lose all this, and stand upon the same level with the Gentiles."

(1.) To this objection the apostle answers, that if they did not submit they were ruined (*v.* 7, 8), but that if they did submit they should lose no real advantage, but continue still what they desired to be, *a chosen generation, a royal priesthood,* etc. Learn, [1.] All true Christians *are a chosen generation;* they all make one family, a sort and species of people distinct from the common world, of another spirit, principle, and practice, which they could never be if they were not chosen in Christ to be such, and sanctified by his Spirit. [2.] All the true servants of Christ are a royal priesthood. They are royal in their relation to God and Christ, in their power with God, and over themselves and all their spiritual enemies; they are princely in the improvements and the excellency of their own spirits, and in their hopes and expectations; they are a royal priesthood, separated from sin and sinners, consecrated to God, and offering to God spiritual services and oblations, acceptable to God through Jesus Christ. [3.] All Christians, wheresoever they be, compose one holy nation. They are one nation, collected under one head, agreeing in the same manners and customs, and governed by the same laws; and they are a holy nation, because consecrated and devoted to God, renewed and sanctified by his Holy Spirit. [4.] It is the honour of the servants of Christ that they are God's peculiar people. They are the people of his acquisition, choice, care, and delight. These four dignities of all genuine Christians are not natural to them; for their first state is a state of horrid darkness, but they are effectually called out of darkness into a state of marvellous light, joy, pleasure, and prosperity, with this intent and view, that they should show forth, by words and actions, the virtues and praises of him who hath called them.

(2.) To make this people content, and thankful for the great mercies and dignities brought unto them by the gospel, the apostle advises them to compare their former and their present state. Time was when they were not a people, nor had they obtained mercy, but they were solemnly disclaimed and divorced (Jer. 3:8; Hos. 1:6, 9); but now they are taken in again to be the people of God, and have obtained mercy. Learn, [1.] The best people ought frequently to look back upon what they were in time past. [2.] The people of God are the most valuable people in the world; all the rest are not a people, good for little. [3.] To be brought into the number of the people of God is a very great mercy, and it may be obtained.

V. He warns them to beware of fleshly lusts, *v.* 11. Even the best of men, *the chosen generation, the people of God,* need an exhortation to abstain from the worst sins, which the apostle here proceeds most earnestly and affectionately to warn them against. Knowing the difficulty, and yet the importance of the duty, he uses his utmost interest in them: *Dearly beloved, I beseech you.* The duty is to abstain from, and to suppress, the first inclination or rise of fleshly lusts. Many of them proceed from the corruption of nature, and in their exercise depend upon the body, gratifying some sensual appetite or inordinate inclination of the flesh. These Christians ought to avoid, considering, 1. The respect they have with God and good men: They are *dearly beloved.* 2. Their condition in the world: *They are strangers and pilgrims,* and should not impede their passage by giving into the wickedness and lusts of the country through which they pass. 3. The mischief and danger these sins do: *"They war against the soul;* and therefore your souls ought to war against them." Learn, (1.) The grand mischief that sin does to man is this, it *wars against the soul;* it destroys the moral liberty of the soul; it weakens and debilitates the soul by impairing its faculties; it robs the soul of its comfort and peace; it debases and destroys the dignity of the soul, hinders its present prosperity, and plunges it into everlasting misery. (2.) Of all sorts of sin, none are more injurious to the soul than *fleshly lusts.* Carnal appetites, lewdness, and sensuality, are most odious to God, and destructive to man's soul. It is a sore judgment to be given up to them.

VI. He exhorts them further to adorn their profession by an honest conversation. Their conversation in every turn, every instance, and every action of their lives, ought to be honest; that is, good, lovely, decent, amiable, and without blame: and that because they lived among the Gentiles, people of another religion, and who were inveterate enemies to them, who did already slander them and constantly spoke evil of them *as of evil-doers.* "A clean, just, good conversation may not only stop their mouths, but may possibly be a means to bring them to glorify God, and turn to you, when they shall see you excel all others in good works. They now call you evil-doers; vindicate yourselves by good works, this is the way to convince them. There is a day of visitation coming, wherein God may call them by his word and his grace to repentance; and then they will glorify God, and applaud you, for your excellent conversation, Lu. 1:68. When the gospel shall come among them, and take effect, a good conversation will encourage them in their conversion, but an evil one will obstruct it." Note, 1. A Christian profession should be attended with an honest conversation, Phil. 4:8. 2. It is the common lot of the best Christians to be evil spoken of by wicked men. 3. Those that are under God's gracious visitation immediately change their opinion of good people, glorifying God and commending those whom before they railed at as evil-doers.

Verses 13–25

The general rule of a Christian conversation is this, it must be honest, which it cannot be if there be not a conscientious discharge of all relative duties. The apostle here particularly treats of these distinctly.

I. The case of subjects. Christians were not only reputed innovators in religion, but disturbers of the state; it was highly necessary, therefore, that the apostle should settle the rules and measures of obedience to the civil magistrate, which he does here, where,

1. The duty required is submission, which comprises loyalty and reverence to their persons, obedience to their just laws and commands, and subjection to legal penalties.

2. The persons or objects to whom this submission is due are described, (1.) More generally: *Every ordinance of man.* Magistracy is certainly of divine right; but the particular form of government, the power of the magistrate, and the persons who are to execute this power, are of human institution, and are governed by the laws and constitutions of each particular country; and this is a general rule, binding in all nations, let the established form of be what it will. (2.) Particularly: *To the king, as supreme,* first in dignity and most eminent in degree; the king is a legal person, not a tyrant: *or unto governors,* deputies, proconsuls, rulers of provinces, who *are sent by him,* that is, commissioned by him to govern.

3. The reasons to enforce this duty are,

(1.) *For the Lord's sake,* who had ordained magistracy for the good of mankind, who has required obedience and submission (Rom. 13), and whose honour is concerned in the dutiful behavior of subjects to their sovereigns.

(2.) From the end and use of the magistrate's office, which are, to punish evil-doers, and to praise and encourage all those that do well. They were appointed for the good of societies; and, where this end is not pursued, the fault is snot in their institution but their practice. [1.] True religion is the best support of civil government; it requires submission for the Lord's sake, and for conscience' sake. [2.] All the punishments, and all the magistrates in the world, cannot hinder but there will be evil-doers in it. [3.] The best way the magistrate can take to discharge his own duty, and to amend the world, is to punish well and reward well.

(3.) Another reason why Christians should submit to the evil magistrate is because it *is the will of God,* and consequently their duty; and because it is the way to put to silence the malicious slanders of ignorant and foolish men, *v.* 15. Learn, [1.] *The will of God is,* to a good man, the strongest reason for any duty. [2.] Obedience to magistrates is a considerable branch of a Christian's duty: *So is the will of God.* [3.] A Christian must endeavour, in all relations, to behave himself so as to put to silence the unreasonable reproaches of the most ignorant and foolish men. [4.] Those who speak against religion and religious people are ignorant and foolish.

(4.) He reminds them of the spiritual nature of Christian liberty. The Jews, from Deu. 17:15, concluded that they were bound to obey no sovereign but one *taken from their own brethren;* and the converted Jews thought they were free from subjection by their relation to Christ. To prevent their mistakes, the apostle tells the Christians that they were free, but from what? Not from duty or obedience to God's law, which requires subjection to the civil magistrate. They were free spiritually from the bondage of sin and Satan, and the ceremonial law; but they must not make their Christian liberty a cloak or covering for any wickedness, or for the neglect of any duty towards God or towards their superiors, but must still remember they were *the servants of God.* Learn, [1.] All the servants of Christ are free men (Jn. 8:36); they are *free* from Satans' dominion, the law's condemnation, the wrath of God, the uneasiness of duty, and the terrors of death. [2.] The servants of Jesus Christ ought to be very careful not to abuse their Christian liberty; they must not make it a cover or cloak for any wickedness against God or disobedience to superiors.

4. The apostle concludes his discourse concerning the duty of subjects with four admirable precepts: — (1.) *Honour all men.* A due respect is to be given to all men; the poor are not to be despised (Prov. 17:5); the wicked must be honoured, not for their wickedness, but for any other qualities, such as wit, prudence, courage, eminency of employment, or the hoary head. Abraham, Jacob, Samuel, the prophets, and the apostles, never scrupled to give due honour to bad men. (2.) *Love the brotherhood.* All Christians are a fraternity, united to Christ the head, alike disposed and qualified, nearly related in the same interest, having communion one with another, and going to the same home; they should therefore love one another with an especial affection. (3.) *Fear God* with the highest reverence, duty, and submission; if this be wanting, none of the other three duties can be performed as they

ought. (4.) *Honour the king* with that highest honour that is peculiarly due to him above other men.

II. The case of servants wanted an apostolical determination as well as that of subjects, for they imagined that their Christian liberty set them free from their unbelieving and cruel masters; to this the apostle answers, *Servants, be subject, v.* 18. By *servants* he means those who were strictly such, whether hired, or bought with money, or taken in the wars, or born in the house, or those who served by contract for a limited time, as apprentices. Observe,

1. He orders them to *be subject,* to do their business faithfully and honestly, to conduct themselves, as inferiors ought, with reverence and affection, and to submit patiently to hardships and inconveniences. This subjection they owe to their masters, who have a right to their service; and that *not only to the good and gentle,* such as use them well and abate somewhat of their right, but even to the crooked and perverse, who are scarcely to be pleased at all. Learn, (1.) Servants ought to behave themselves to their masters with submission, and fear of displeasing them. (2.) The sinful misconduct of one relation does not justify the sinful behaviour of the other; the servant is bound to do his duty, though the master be sinfully froward and perverse. (3.) Good people are meek and gentle to their servants and inferiors. Our holy apostle shows his love and concern for the souls of poor servants, as well as for higher people. Herein he ought to be imitated by all inferior ministers, who should distinctly apply their counsels to the lower, the meaner, the younger, and the poorer sort of their hearers, as well as others.

2. Having charged them to be subject, he condescends to reason with them about it.

(1.) If they were patient under their hardships, while they suffered unjustly, and continued doing their duty to their unbelieving and untoward masters, this would e acceptable to God, and he would reward all that they suffered for conscience towards him; but to be patient when they were justly chastised would deserve no commendation at all; it is only *doing well, and suffering patiently for that, which is acceptable with God, v.* 19, 20. Learn, [1.] There is no condition so mean but a man may live conscientiously in it, and glorify God in it; the meanest servant may do so. [2.] The most conscientious persons are very often the greatest sufferers. *For conscience towards God, they suffer wrongfully; they do well, and suffer for it;* but sufferers of this sort are praiseworthy, they do honour to God and to religion, and they are accepted of him; and this is their highest support and satisfaction. [3.] Deserved sufferings must be endured with patience: *If you are buffeted for your faults, you* must *take it patiently.* Sufferings in this world are not always pledges of our future happiness; if children or servants be rude and undutiful, and suffer for it, this will neither be acceptable with God nor procure the praise of men.

(2.) More reasons are given to encourage Christian servants to patience under unjust sufferings, *v.* 21. [1.] From their Christian calling and profession: *Hereunto were you called.* [2.] From the example of Christ, who *suffered for us,* and so became our *example, that we should follow his steps,* whence learn, *First,* Good Christians are a sort of people called to be sufferers, and therefore they must expect it; by the terms of Christianity they are bound to deny themselves, and take up the cross; they are called by the commands of Christ, by the dispensations of Providence, and by the preparations of divine grace; and, by the practice of Jesus Christ, they are bound to suffer when thus called to it. *Secondly,* Jesus Christ *suffered for* you, or *for us;* it was not the Father that suffered, but he whom the Father sanctified, and sent into the world, for that end; it was both the body and soul of Christ that suffered, and he suffered for us, in our stead and for our good, *v.* 24. *Thirdly,* The sufferings of Christ should quiet us under the most unjust and cruel sufferings we meet with in the world. He suffered voluntarily, not for himself, but for us, with the utmost readiness, with perfect patience, from all quarters, and all this though he was God-man; shall not we sinners, who deserve the worst, submit to the light afflictions of this life, which work for us unspeakable advantages afterwards?

3. The example of Christ's subjection and patience is here explained and amplified: *Christ suffered,* (1.) Wrongfully, and without cause; for he *did no sin, v.* 22. *He had done no violence,* no injustice or wrong to any one — he wrought no iniquity of any sort whatever; *neither was guile found in his mouth* (Isa. 53:9), his words, as well as his actions, were all

sincere, just, and right. (2.) Patiently: *When he was reviled, he reviled not again* (*v.* 23); when they blasphemed him, mocked him, called him foul names, he was *dumb, and opened not his mouth;* when they went further, to real injuries, beating, buffeting, and crowning him with thorns, *he threatened not; but committed* both *himself* and his cause *to God that judgeth righteously,* who would in time clear his innocency, and avenge him on his enemies. Learn, [1.] Our Blessed Redeemer was perfectly holy, and so free from sin that no temptation, no provocation whatsoever, could extort from him so much as the least sinful or indecent word. [2.] Provocations to sin can never justify the commission of it. The rudeness, cruelty, and injustice of enemies, will not justify Christians in reviling and revenge; the reasons for sin can never be so great, but we have always stronger reasons to avoid it. [3.] The judgment of God will determine justly upon every man and every cause; and thither we ought, with patience and resignation, to refer ourselves.

4. Lest any should think, from what is said, *v.* 21–23, that Christ's death was designed merely for an example of patience under sufferings, the apostle here adds a more glorious design and effect of it: *Who his own self,* etc., where note, (1.) The person suffering — Jesus Christ: *His own self — in his own body.* The expression *his own self* is emphatic, and necessary to show that he verified all the ancient prophecies, to distinguish him from the Levitical priests (who offered the blood of others, but he by *himself purged our sins,* Heb. 1:3), and to exclude all others from participation with him in the work of man's redemption: it is added, *in his body;* not but that he suffered in his soul (Mt. 26:38), but the sufferings of the soul were inward and concealed, when those of the body were visible and more obvious to the consideration of these suffering servants, for whose sake this example is produced. (2.) The sufferings he underwent were *stripes,* wounds, and death, *the death of the cross* — servile and ignominious punishments! (3.) The reason of his sufferings: He *bore our sins,* which teaches, [1.] That Christ, in his sufferings, stood charged with our sins, as one who had undertaken to put them away by *the sacrifice of himself,* Isa. 53:6. [2.] That he bore the punishment of them, and thereby satisfied divine justice. [3.] That hereby he takes away our sins, and removes them away from us; as the scape-goat did typically bear the sins of the people on his head, and then carried them quite away, (Lev. 16:21, 22), so the Lamb of God does first bear our sins in his own body, and thereby take away the sins of the world, Jn. 1:29. (4.) The fruits of Christ's sufferings are, [1.] Our sanctification, consisting of the death, the mortification of sin, and a new holy life of righteousness, for both which we have an example, and powerful motives and abilities also, from the death and resurrection of Christ. [2.] Our justification. Christ was bruised and crucified as an expiatory sacrifice, and *by his stripes we are healed.* Learn, *First,* Jesus Christ bore the sins of all his people, and expiated them by his *death upon the cross. Secondly,* No man can depend safely upon Christ, as having borne his sin and expiated his guilt, till he dies unto sin and lives unto righteousness.

5. The apostle concludes his advice to Christian servants, by putting them in mind of the difference between their former and present condition, *v.* 25. They *were as sheep going astray,* which represents, (1.) Man's sin: he goes astray; it is his own act, he is not driven, but does voluntary go astray. (2.) His misery: he goes astray from the pasture, from the shepherd, and from the flock, and so exposes himself to innumerable dangers. (3.) Here is the recovery of these by conversion: *But are now returned.* The word is passive, and shows that the return of a sinner is the effect of divine grace. This return is from all their errors and wanderings, to Christ, who is the true careful shepherd, that loves his sheep, and laid down his life for them, who is the most vigilant pastor, and bishop, or overseer of souls. Learn, [1.] Sinners, before their conversion, are always going astray; their life is a continued error. [2.] Jesus Christ is the supreme shepherd and bishop of souls, who is always resident with his flock, and watchful over them. [3.] Those that expect the love and care of this universal pastor must return to him, must die unto sin, and live unto righteousness.

CHAPTER 3

Wherein the apostle describes the duties of husbands and wives one to another, beginning with the duty of the wife (*v.* 1–7). He exhorts Christians to unity, love, compassion, peace, and patience under sufferings; to oppose the slanders of their enemies, not by returning evil for evil, or railing for railing, but by blessing; by a ready account of their faith and hope, and by keeping a good conscience (*v.* 8–17). To encourage them to this, he proposes the example of Christ, who suffered, the just for the unjust, but yet punished the old world for their disobedience, and saved the few who were faithful in the days of Noah (*v.* 18 to the end).

Verses 1–7

The apostle having treated of the duties of subjects to their sovereigns, and of servants to their masters, proceeds to explain the duty of husbands and wives.

I. Lest the Christian matrons should imagine that their conversion to Christ, and their interest in all Christian privileges, exempted them from subjection to their pagan or Jewish husbands, the apostle here tells them,

1. In what the duty of wives consists.

(1.) In *subjection,* or an affectionate submission to the will, and obedience to the just authority, of *their own husbands,* which obliging conduct would be the most likely way to win those disobedient and unbelieving husbands who had rejected the word, or who attended to no other evidence of the truth of it than what they saw in the prudent, peaceable, and exemplary *conversation of their wives.* Learn, [1.] Every distinct relation has its particular duties, which ministers ought to preach, and the people ought to understand. [2.] A cheerful *subjection,* and a loving, reverential respect, are duties which Christian women owe their husbands, whether they be good or bad; these were due from Eve to Adam before the fall, and are still required, though much more difficult now than they were before, Gen. 3:16; 1 Tim. 2:11. [3.] Though the design of the word of the gospel is to win and gain souls to Christ Jesus, yet there are many so obstinate that they will not be *won by the word.* [4.] There is nothing more powerful, next to the word of God, to win people, than a good conversation, and the careful discharge of relative duties. [5.] Irreligion and infidelity do not dissolve the bonds, nor dispense with the duties, of civil relations; *the wife* must discharge her duty *to her own husband,* though he *obey not the word.*

(2.) In *fear,* or reverence to their husbands, Eph. 5:33.

(3.) In a *chaste conversation,* which their unbelieving husbands would accurately observe and attend to. [1.] Evil men are strict observers of the conversation of the professors of religion; their curiosity, envy, and jealousy, make them watch narrowly the ways and lives of good people. [2.] *A chaste conversation,* attended with due and proper respect to every one, is an excellent means to win them to the faith of the gospel and obedience to the word.

(4.) In preferring the ornaments of the mind to those of the body. [1.] He lays down a rule in regard to the dress of religious women, *v.* 3. Here are three sorts of ornaments forbidden: *plaiting of hair,* which was commonly used in those times by lewd women; *wearing of gold,* or ornaments made of *gold,* was practised by Rebecca, and Esther, and other religious women, but afterwards became the attire chiefly of harlots and wicked people; *putting on of apparel,* which is not absolutely forbidden, but only too much nicety and costliness in it. Learn, *First,* Religious people should take care that all their external behaviour be answerable to their profession of Christianity: *They must be holy in all manner of conversation. Secondly,* The outward adorning of the body is very often sensual and excessive; for instance, when it is immoderate, and above your degree and station in the world, when you are proud of it and puffed up with it, when you dress with design to allure and tempt others, when your apparel is too rich, curious, or superfluous, when your fashions are fantastical, imitating the levity and vanity of the worst people, and when they are immodest and wanton. The attire of a harlot can never become a chaste Christian matron. [2.] Instead of the outward adorning of the body, he directs Christian wives to put on much more excellent and beautiful ornaments, *v.* 4. Here note, *First,* The part to be adorned: *The hidden man of the heart;* that is, the soul; the hidden, the inner man. Take care to adorn and beautify your souls rather than your bodies. *Secondly,* The ornament prescribed. It must, in general, be something *not corruptible,* that beautifies the soul, that is, the graces and virtues of God's Holy Spirit. The ornaments of the body are destroyed by the moth, and perish in the using; but the grace of God, the longer we wear it, the brighter and better it is. More especially, the finest ornament of Christian women is *a meek and quiet spirit,* a tractable easy temper of mind, void of passion, pride, and immoderate anger, discovering itself in a quiet obliging behaviour towards their husbands and families. If the husband be harsh, and averse to religion (which was the case of these good wives to whom the apostle gives this direction), there is no way so likely to win him as a prudent meek behaviour. At least, a quiet spirit will make a god woman easy to herself, which, being visible to others, becomes an amiable ornament to a person in the eyes of the world. *Thirdly,* The excellency of it. Meekness and calmness of spirit are, in the sight of God, of great price — amiable in the sight of men, and precious in the sight of God. Learn, 1. A true Christian's chief care lies in the right ordering and commanding of his own spirit. Where the hypocrite's work ends, there the true Christian's work begins. 2. The endowments of the inner man are the chief ornaments of a Christian; but especially a composed, calm, and quiet spirit, renders either man or woman beautiful and lovely.

2. The duties of Christian wives being in their nature difficult, the apostle enforces them by the example, (1.) Of the holy women of old, who trusted in God, *v.* 5. "You can pretend nothing of excuse from the weakness of your sex, but what they might. They lived *in old time,* and had less knowledge to inform them and fewer examples to encourage them; yet in all ages they practised this duty; they were *holy women,* and therefore their example is obligatory; they *trusted in God,* and yet did not neglect their duty to man: the duties imposed upon you, of a quiet spirit and of subjection to your own husbands, are not new, but what have ever been practised by the greatest and best women in the world." (2.) Of Sara, who obeyed her husband, and followed him when he went from Ur of the Chaldeans, *not knowing whither he went,* and *called him lord,* thereby showing him reverence and acknowledging his superiority over her; and all this though she was declared a princess by God from heaven, by the change of her name, *"Whose daughters you are* if you imitate her in faith and good works, and do not, through fear of your husbands, either quit the truth you profess or neglect your duty to them, but readily perform it, without either fear or force, out of conscience towards God and sense of duty to them." Learn, [1.] God takes exact notice, and keeps an exact record, of the actions of all men and women in the world. [2.] The subjection of wives to their husbands is a duty which has been practised universally by holy women in all ages. [3.] The greatest honour of any man or woman lies in a humble and faithful deportment of themselves in the relation or condition in which Providence has placed them. [4.] God takes notice of the good that is in his servants, to their honour and benefit, but covers a multitude of failings; Sara's infidelity and derision are overlooked, when her virtues are celebrated. [5.] Christians ought to do their duty to one another, not out of fear, nor from force, but from a willing mind, and in obedience to the command of God. Wives should be in subjection to their churlish husbands, not from dread and amazement, but from a desire to do well and to please God.

II. The husband's duty to the wife comes next to be considered.

1. The particulars are, (1.) *Cohabitation,* which forbids unnecessary separation, and implies a mutual communication of goods and persons one to another, with delight and concord. (2.) *Dwelling with the wife according to knowledge;* not according to lust, as brutes; nor according to passion, as devils; but according to knowledge, as wise and sober men, who know the word of God and their own duty. (3.) *Giving honour to the wife* — giving due respect to her, and maintaining her authority, protecting her person, supporting her credit, delighting in her conversation, affording her a handsome maintenance, and placing a due trust and confidence in her.

2. The reasons are, Because she is *the weaker vessel* by nature and constitution, and so ought to be defended: but then the wife is, in other and higher respects, equal to her husband; they are *heirs together of the grace of life,* of all the blessings of this life and another, and therefore should live peaceably and quietly one with another, and, if they do not, their prayers one with another and one for another will be hindered, so that often "you will not pray at all, or, if you do, you will pray with a discomposed ruffled mind, and so without success." Learn, (1.) The weakness of the female sex is no just reason either for separation or contempt, but on the contrary it is a reason for honour and respect: *Giving honour to the wife as unto the weaker vessel.* (2.) There is an honour due to all who are heirs of the grace of life. (3.) All married people should take care to behave themselves so lovingly and peaceably one to another that they may not by their broils hinder the success of their prayers.

Verses 8–15

The apostle here passes from special to more general exhortations.

I. He teaches us how Christians and friends should treat one another. He advises Christians to *be all of one mind,* to be unanimous in the belief of the same faith, and the practice of the same duties of religion; and, whereas the Christians at that time were many of them in a suffering condition, he charges them to *have compassion one of another,* to *love as brethren,* to *pity* those who were in distress, and to *be courteous* to all. Hence learn, 1. Christians should endeavour to be all of one mind in the great points of faith, in real affection, and in Christian practice; they should be *likeminded one to another, according to Christ Jesus* (Rom. 15:5), not according to man's pleasure, but God's word. 2. Though Christians cannot be exactly of the same mind, yet they should have compassion one for another, and love as brethren; they ought not to persecute or hate one another, but love one another with more than common affection; they should love as brethren. 3. Christianity requires pity to the distressed, and civility to all. He must be a flagrant sinner, or a vile apostate, who is not a proper object of civil courtesy, 1 Co. 5:11; 2 Jn. 10:11.

II. He instructs us how to behave towards enemies. The apostle knew that Christians would *be hated* and evil-entreated *of all men for Christ's sake;* therefore,

1. He warns them not to return *evil for evil, nor railing for railing;* but, on the contrary, "when they rail at you, do you bless them; when they give you evil words, do you give them good ones; for Christ has both by his word and example called you to bless those that curse you, and has settled a blessing on you as your everlasting inheritance, though you were unworthy." To bear evils patiently, and to bless your enemies, is the way to obtain this blessing of God. Learn, (1.) To *render evil for evil, or railing for railing,* is a sinful unchristian practice; the magistrate may punish *evil-doers,* and private men may seek a legal remedy when they are wronged; but private revenge by duelling, scolding, or secret mischief, is forbidden Prov. 20:22; Lu. 6:27; Rom. 12:17; 1 Th. 5:15. To rail is to revile another in bitter, fierce, and reproachful terms; but for ministers to rebuke sharply, and to preach earnestly against the sins of the times, is not railing; all the prophets and apostles practised it, Isa. 56:10; Zep. 3:3; Acts 20:29. (2.) The laws of Christ oblige us to return blessing for railing. Mt. 5:44, *"Love your enemies, bless those that curse you, do good to those that hate you, and pray for those that persecute you.* You must not justify them in their sin, but you must do for your enemies all that justice requires or charity commands." We must pity, pray for, and love those who rail at us. (3.) A Christian's calling, as it invests him with glorious privileges, so it obliges him to difficult duties. (4.) All the true servants of God shall infallibly inherit a blessing; they have it already in a great degree, but the full possession of it is reserved to another state and world.

2. He gives an excellent prescription for a comfortable happy life in this quarrelsome ill-natured world (*v.* 10): it is quoted from Ps. 34:12–14. "If you earnestly desire that your life should be long, and your days peaceable and prosperous, keep your tongue from reviling, evil-speaking, and slandering, and your lips from lying, deceit, and dissimulation. Avoid doing any real damage or hurt to your neighbour, but be ever ready to do good, and to overcome evil with good; seek peace with all men, and pursue it, though it retire from you. This will be the best way to dispose people to speak well of you, and live peaceably with you." Learn, (1.) Good people under the Old and new Testament were obliged to the same moral duties; to *refrain the tongue from evil, and the lips from guile,* was a duty in David's time as well as now. (2.) It is lawful to consider temporal advantages as motives and encouragements to religion. (3.) The practice of religion, particularly the right government of the tongue, is the best way to make this life comfortable and prosperous; a sincere, inoffensive, discreet tongue, is a singular means to pass us peaceably and comfortably through the world. (4.) The avoiding of evil, and doing of good, is the way to contentment and happiness both here and hereafter. (5.) It is the duty of Christians not only to embrace peace when it is offered, but to seek and pursue it when it is denied: peace with societies, as well as peace with particular persons, in opposition to division and contention, is what is here intended.

3. He shows that Christians need not fear that such patient inoffensive behaviour as is prescribed will invite and

encourage the cruelty of their enemies, for God will thereby be engaged on their side: *For the eyes of the Lord are over the righteous* (*v.* 12); he takes special notice of them, exercises a providential constant government over them, and bears a special respect and affection to them. *His ears are open to their prayers;* so that if any injuries be offered to them they have this remedy, they may complain of it to their heavenly Father, whose ears are always attentive to the prayers of his servants in their distresses, and who will certainly aid them against their unrighteous enemies. *But the face of the Lord is against those that do evil;* his anger, and displeasure, and revenge, will pursue them; for he is more an enemy to wicked persecutors than men are. Observe, (1.) We must not in all cases adhere to the express words of scripture, but study the sense and meaning of them, otherwise we shall be led into blasphemous errors and absurdities: we must not imagine that God hath eyes, and ears, and face, though these are the express words of the scripture. (2.) God hath a special care and paternal affection towards all his righteous people. (3.) God doth always hear the prayers of the faithful, Jn. 4:31; 1 Jn. 5:14; Heb. 4:16. (4.) Though God is infinitely good, yet he abhors impenitent sinners, and will pour out his wrath upon those that do evil. He will do himself right, and do all the world justice; and his goodness is no obstruction to his doing so.

4. This patient humble behaviour of Christians is further recommended and urged from two considerations: — (1.) This will be the best and surest way to prevent suffering; for *who is he that will harm you? v.* 13. This, I suppose, is spoken of Christians in an ordinary condition, not in the heat of persecution. "Ordinarily, there will be but few so diabolical and impious as to harm those who live so innocently and usefully as you do."(2.) This is the way to improve sufferings. *"If you be followers of that which is good,* and yet *suffer,* this is suffering for righteousness; sake (*v.* 14), and will be your glory and your happiness, as it entitles you to the blessing promised by Christ" (Mt. 5:10); therefore, [1.] "You need not be afraid of any thing they can do to strike you with terror, neither be much troubled nor concerned about the rage or force of your enemies." Learn, *First,* to follow always that which is good is the best course we can take to keep out of harm's way. *Secondly,* To suffer for righteousness sake is the honour and happiness of a Christian; to suffer for the cause of truth, a good conscience, or any part of a Christian's duty, is a great honour; the delight of it is greater than the torment, the honour more than the disgrace, and the gain much greater than the loss. *Thirdly,* Christians have no reason to be afraid of the threats or rage of any of their enemies. "Your enemies are God's enemies, *his face is against them,* his power is above them, they are the objects of his curse, and can do nothing to you but by his permission; therefore trouble not yourselves about them." [2.] Instead of terrifying yourselves with the fear of men, be sure to *sanctify the Lord God in your hearts* (*v.* 15); *let him be your fear, and let him be your dread,* Isa. 8:12, 13. *Fear not those that can only kill the body, but fear him that can destroy body and soul,* Lu. 12:4, 5. We sanctify the Lord God in our hearts when we with sincerity and fervency adore him, when our thoughts of him are awful and reverend, when we rely upon his power, trust to his faithfulness, submit to his wisdom, imitate his holiness, and give him the glory due to his most illustrious perfections. We sanctify God before others when our deportment is such as invites and encourages others to glorify and honour him; both are required, Lev. 10:3. "When this principle is laid deeply into your hearts, the next thing, as to men, is to be always ready, that is, able and willing, *to give an answer,* or make an apology or defence, of the faith you profess, and that *to every man that asketh a reason of your hope,* what sort of hope you have, or which you suffer such hardships in the world." Learn, *First,* An awful sense of the divine perfections is the best antidote against the fear of sufferings; did we fear God more, we should certainly fear men less. *Secondly,* The hope and faith of a Christian are defensible against all the world. There may be a good reason given for religion; it is not a fancy but a rational scheme revealed from heaven, suited to all the necessities of miserable sinners, and centering entirely in the glory of God through Jesus Christ. *Thirdly,* Every Christian is bound to answer and apologize for the hope that is in him. Christians should have a reason ready for their Christianity, that it may appear they are not actuated either by folly or fancy. This defence may be necessary more than once or twice, so that Christians should be al-

ways prepared to make it, either to the magistrate, if he demand it, or to any inquisitive Christian, who desires to know it for his information or improvement. *Fourthly,* These confessions of our faith ought to be made *with meekness and fear;* apologies for our religion ought to be made with modesty and meekness, in the fear of God, with jealousy over ourselves, and reverence to our superiors.

Verses 16–17

The confession of a Christian's faith cannot credibly be supported but by the two means here specified — *a good conscience* and a *good conversation.* conscience is good when it does its office well, when it is kept pure and uncorrupt, and clear from guilt; then it will justify you, though men accuse you. *A good conversation in Christ* is a holy life, according to the doctrine and example of Christ. "Look well to your conscience, and to your conversation; and then, though men speak evil of you, and falsely accuse you as evil-doers, you will clear yourselves, and bring them to shame. Perhaps you may think it hard to suffer for well-doing, for keeping a good conscience and a good conversation; but be not discouraged, for it is better for you, though worse for your enemies, that you suffer for well-doing than for evil-doing." Learn, 1. The most conscientious persons cannot escape the censures and slanders of evil men; they will speak evil of them, as of evil-doers, and charge them with crimes which their very souls abhor: Christ and his apostles were so used. 2. A good conscience and a good conversation are the best means to secure a good name; these give a solid reputation and a lasting one. 3. False accusation generally turns to the accuser's shame, by discovering at last the accuser's indiscretion, injustice, falsehood, and uncharitableness. 4. It is sometimes the will of God that good people should suffer for well-doing, for their honesty and for their faith. 5. As well-doing sometimes exposes a good man to suffering, so evil-doing will not exempt an evil man from it. The apostle supposes here that a man may suffer for both. If the sufferings of good people for well-doing be so severe, what will the sufferings of wicked people be for evil-doing? It is a sad condition which that person is in upon whom sin and suffering meet together at the same time; sin makes sufferings to be extreme, unprofitable, comfortless, and destructive.

Verses 18–20

Here, I. The example of Christ is proposed as an argument for patience under sufferings, the strength of which will be discerned if we consider the several points contained in the words; observe therefore, 1. Jesus Christ himself was not exempted from sufferings in this life, though he had no guilt of his own and could have declined all suffering if he had pleased. 2. The reason or meritorious cause of Christ's suffering was the sins of men: *Christ suffered for sins.* The sufferings of Christ were a true and proper punishment; this punishment was suffered to expiate and to make an atonement for sin; and it extends to all sin. 3. In the case of our Lord's suffering, it was the just that suffered for the unjust; he substituted himself in our room and stead, and bore our iniquities. He that knew no sin suffered instead of those that knew no righteousness. 4. The merit and perfection of Christ's sacrifice were such that for him to suffer once was enough. The legal sacrifices were repeated from day to day, and from year to year; but the sacrifice of Christ, once offered, purgeth away sin, Heb. 7:27; 9:26, 28; 10:10, 12, 14. 5. The blessed end or design of our Lord's sufferings was to bring us to God, to reconcile us to God, to give us access to the Father, to render us and our services acceptable, and to bring us to eternal glory, Eph. 2:13, 18; 3:12; Heb. 10:21, 22. 6. The issue and event of Christ's suffering, as to himself, were these, he was put to death in his human nature, but he was quickened and raised again by the Spirit. Now, if Christ was not exempted from sufferings, why should Christians expect it? If he suffered, to expiate sins, why should not we be content when our sufferings are only for trial and correction, but not for expiation? If he, though perfectly just, why should not we, who are all criminals? If he once suffered, and then entered into glory, shall not we be patient under trouble, since it will be but a little time and we shall follow him to glory? If he *suffered, to bring us to God,* shall not we submit to difficulties, since they are of so much use to quicken us in our return to God, and in the performance of our duty to him?

II. The apostle passes from the example of Christ to that of the old world, and sets before the Jews, to whom he wrote, the different event of those who believed and obeyed Christ preaching by Noah, from those that continued disobedient and unbelieving, intimating to the Jews that they were under a like sentence. God would not wait much longer upon them. They had now an offer of mercy; those that accepted of it should be saved, but those who rejected Christ and the gospel should be as certainly destroyed as ever the disobedient in the times of Noah were.

1. For the explication of this we may notice, (1.) The preacher — Christ Jesus, who has interested himself in the affairs of the church and of the world ever since he was first promised to Adam, Gen. 3:15. *He went,* not by a local motion, but by special operation, as God is frequently said to move, Gen. 11:5; Hos. 5:15; Mic. 1:3. *He went and preached,* by his Spirit striving with them, and inspiring and enabling Enoch and Noah to plead with them, and *preach righteousness to them,* as 2 Pt. 2:5. (2.) The hearers. Because they were dead and disembodied when the apostle speaks of them, therefore he properly calls them spirits now *in prison;* not that they were *in prison when Christ preached to them,* as the vulgar Latin translation and the popish expositors pretend. (3.) The sin of these people: They were *disobedient,* that is, *rebellious, unpersuadable,* and *unbelieving,* as the word signifies; this their sin is aggravated from the patience and *long-suffering of God* (which *once waited* upon them for 120 years together), *while Noah was preparing the ark,* and by that, as well as by his preaching, giving them fair warning of what was coming upon them. (4.) The event of all: Their bodies were drowned, and their spirits cast into hell, which is called a prison (Mt. 5:25; 2 Pt. 2:4, 5); but Noah and his family, who believed and were obedient, *were saved in the ark.*

2. From the whole we learn that, (1.) God takes exact notice of all the means and advantages that people in all ages have had for the salvation of their souls; it is put to the account of the old world that Christ offered them his help, sent his Spirit, gave them fair warning by Noah, and waited a long time for their amendment. (2.) Though the patience of God wait long upon sinners, yet it will expire at last; it is beneath the majesty of the great God always to wait upon man in vain. (3.) The spirits of disobedient sinners, as soon as they are out of their bodies, are committed to the prison of hell, whence there is no redemption. (4.) The way of the most is neither the best, the wisest, nor the safest way to follow: better to follow the eight in the ark than the eight millions drowned by the flood and damned to hell.

Verses 21–22

Noah's salvation in the ark upon the water prefigured the salvation of all good Christians in the church by baptism; that temporal salvation by the ark was a type, the antitype whereunto is the eternal salvation of believers by baptism, to prevent mistakes about which the apostle,

I. Declares what he means by saving baptism; not the outward ceremony of washing with water, which, in itself, does no more than put away the filth of the flesh, but it is that baptism wherein there is a faithful answer or restipulation of a resolved good conscience, engaging to believe in, and be entirely devoted to, God, the Father, Son, and Holy Ghost, renouncing at the same time the flesh, the world, and the devil. The baptismal covenant, made and kept, will certainly save us. Washing is the visible sign; this is the thing signified.

II. The apostle shows that the efficacy of baptism to salvation depends not upon the work done, but upon the resurrection of Christ, which supposes his death, and is the foundation of our faith and hope, to which we are rendered conformable by dying to sin, and rising again to holiness and newness of life. Learn, 1. the sacrament of baptism, rightly received, is a means and a pledge of salvation. *Baptism now saveth us.* God is pleased to convey his blessings to us in and by his ordinances, Acts 2:38; 22:16. 2. The external participation of baptism will save no man without an answerable good conscience and conversation. There must be the answer of a good conscience towards God. — *Obj.* Infants cannot make such an answer, and therefore ought not to be baptized. — *Answer,* the true circumcision was that of the heart and of the spirit (Rom. 2:29), which children were no more capable of then than our infants are capable of making this answer now; yet they were allowed circumcision at eight days old. The infants of the Christian church therefore may be admitted to the ordinance with as much reason as the infants of the Jewish, unless they are barred from it by some express prohibition of Christ.

III. The apostle, having mentioned the death and resurrection of Christ, proceeds to speak of his ascension, and sitting at the right hand of the Father, as a subject fit to be considered by these believers for their comfort in their suffering condition, *v.* 22. If the advancement of Christ was so glorious after his deep humiliation, let not his followers despair, but expect that after these short distresses they shall be advanced to transcendent joy and glory. Learn, 1. Jesus Christ, after he had finished his labours and his sufferings upon earth, ascended triumphantly into heaven, of which see Acts 1:9–11; Mk. 16:19. He went to heaven to receive his own acquired crown and glory (Jn. 17:5), to finish that part of his mediatorial work which could not be done on earth, and make intercession for his people, to demonstrate the fulness of his satisfaction, to take possession of heaven for his people, to prepare mansions for them, and to send down the Comforter, which was to be the first-fruits of his intercession, Jn. 16:7. 2. Upon his ascension into heaven, Christ is enthroned at the right hand of the Father. His being said to *sit* there imports absolute rest and cessation from all further troubles and sufferings, and an advancement to the highest personal dignity and sovereign power. 3. Angels, authorities, and powers, are all made subject to Christ Jesus: *all power in heaven and earth,* to command, to give law, issue orders, and pronounce a final sentence, is committed to Jesus, God-man, which his enemies will find to their everlasting sorrow and confusion, but his servants to their eternal joy and satisfaction.

CHAPTER 4

The work of a Christian is twofold — doing the will of God and suffering his pleasure. This chapter directs us in both. The duties we are here exhorted to employ ourselves in are the mortification of sin, living to God, sobriety, prayer, charity, hospitality, and the best improvement of our talents, which the apostle presses upon Christians from the consideration of the time they have lost in their sins, and the approaching end of all things (*v.* 1–11). The directions for sufferings are that we should not be surprised at them, but rejoice in them, only take care not to suffer as evil-doers. He intimates that their trials were near at hand, that their souls were in danger as well as their bodies, and that the best way to preserve their souls is to commit them to God in well-doing.

Verses 1–3

The apostle here draws a new inference from the consideration of Christ's sufferings. As he had before made use of it to persuade to patience in suffering, so here to mortification of sin. Observe,

I. How the exhortation is expressed. The antecedent or supposition is *that Christ had suffered* for us in the flesh, or in his human nature. The consequent or inference is, *"Arm* and fortify *yourselves likewise with the same mind,* courage, and resolution." The word flesh in the former part of the verse signifies Christ's human nature, but in the latter part it signifies man's corrupt nature. So the sense is, "As Christ suffered in his human nature, do you, according to your baptismal vow and profession, make your corrupt nature suffer, by putting to death the body of sin by self-denial and mortification; for, if you do not thus suffer, you will be conformable to Christ in his death and resurrection, and will cease *from sin."* Learn, 1. Some of the strongest and best arguments against all sorts of sin are taken from the sufferings of Christ. All sympathy and tenderness for Christ as a sufferer are lost of you do not put away sin. He dies to destroy it; and, though he could cheerfully submit to the worst sufferings, yet he could never submit to the least sin. 2. The beginning of all true mortification lies in the mind, not in penances and hardships upon the body. The mind of man is carnal, full of enmity; the understanding is darkened, being alienated from the life of God, Eph. 4:18. Man is not a sincere creature, but partial, blind, and wicked, till he be renewed and sanctifies by the regenerating grace of God.

II. How it is further explained, *v.* 2. The apostle explains what he means by being dead to sin, and ceasing from sin, both negatively and positively. Negatively, a Christian ought *no longer to live the rest of his time in the flesh,* to the sinful lusts and corrupt desires of carnal wicked men; but, positively, he ought to conform himself to the revealed will of the holy God. Learn, 1. The lusts of men are the springs of all their wickedness, Jam. 1:13, 14. Let occasional temptations be what they will, they could not prevail, were it not for men's own corruptions. 2. All good Christians make the will of God, not their own lusts or desires, the rule of their lives and actions. 3. True conversion makes a marvellous change in the heart and life of every one who partakes of it. It brings a man off from all his old, fashionable, and delightful lusts, and from the common ways and vices of the world, to the will of God. It alters the mind, judgment, affections, way, and conversation of every one who has experienced it.

III. How it is enforced (*v.* 3): *For the time past of our life may suffice us to have wrought the will of the Gentiles,* etc. Here the apostle argues from equity. "It is but just, equal, and reasonable, that as you have hitherto all the former part of your life served sin and Satan, so you should now serve the living God." Though those were Jews to whom the apostle wrote, yet the living among the Gentiles they had learned their way. Observe, 1. When a man is truly converted, it is very grievous to him to think how the time past of his life has been spent; the hazard he has run so many years, the mischief he has done to others, the dishonour done to God, and the loss he has sustained, are very afflicting to him. 2. While the will of man is unsanctified and corrupt, he walks continually in wicked ways; he makes them his choice and delight, his work and business, and he makes a bad condition daily worse and worse. 3. One sin, allowed, draws on another. Here are six named, and they have a connection and dependence one upon another. (1.) *Lasciviousness* or wantonness, expressed in looks, gesture, or behaviour, Rom. 13:13. (2.) *Lusts,* acts of lewdness, such as whoredom and adultery. (3.) *Excess of wine,* though short of drunkenness, an immoderate use of it, to the prejudice of health or business, is here condemned. (4.) *Revellings,* or luxurious feastings, too frequent, too full, or too expensive. (5.) *Banquetings,* by which is meant gluttony or excess in eating. (6.) *Abominable* idolatry; the idol-worship of the Gentiles was attended with lewdness, drunkenness, gluttony, and all sorts of brutality and cruelty; and these Jews living long among them were, some of them at least, debauched and corrupted by such practices. 4. It is a Christian's duty not only to abstain from what is grossly wicked, but also from those things that are generally the occasions of sin, or carry the appearance of evil. *Excess of wine* and immoderate feasting are forbidden as well as lust and idolatry.

Verses 4–6

I. Here you have the visible change wrought in those who in the foregoing verse were represented as having been in the former part of their life very wicked. They no longer run on in the same courses, or with the same companions, as they used to do. Hereupon observe the conduct of their wicked acquaintance towards them. 1. *They think it strange,* they are surprised and wonder at it, as at something new and unusual, that their old friends should be so much altered, and not run with as much violence as they used to do *to the same excess of riot,* to the same sottish excesses and luxury which before they had greedily and madly followed. 2. *They speak evil of them.* Their surprise carries them to blasphemy. They speak evil of their persons, of their way, their religion, and their God. Learn, (1.) Those that are once really converted will not return to their former course of life, though ever so much tempted by the frowns or flatteries of others to do so. Neither persuasion nor reproach will prevail with them to be or to do as they were wont to do. (2.) The temper and behaviour of true Christians seem very strange to ungodly men. That they should despise that which every one else is fond of, that they should believe many things which to others seem incredible, that they should delight in what is irksome and tedious, be zealous where they have no visible interest to serve, and depend so much upon hope, is what the ungodly cannot comprehend. (3.) The best actions of religious people cannot escape the censures and slanders of those who are irreligious. Those actions which cost a good man the most pains, hazard, and self-denial, shall be most censured by the uncharitable and ill-natured world; they will speak evil of good people, though they themselves reap the fruits of their charity, piety, and goodness.

II. For the comfort of the servants of God, it is here added,

1. That all wicked people, especially those who speak evil of such as are not as bad as themselves, shall *give an account,* and be put to give a reason of their behaviour, to him who is ready to judge, who is both able and duly authorized, and who will ere long judge and pass sentence upon all who shall then be found alive, and all such as being dead shall then be raised again, Jam. 5:8, 9; 2 Pt. 3:7. Observe, The malignant world shall in a little time give an account to the great God of all their evil speeches against his people, Jude 14, 15.

They will soon be called to a sad account for all their curses, their foolish jests, their slanders and falsehoods, uttered against the faithful people of God.

2. That *for this cause was the gospel preached also to those that are dead, that they might be judged according to men in the flesh, but live according to God in the Spirit, v.* 6. Some understand this difficult place thus: *For this cause was the gospel preached* to all the faithful of old, who are now dead in Christ, that thereby they might be taught and encouraged to bear the unrighteous judgments and persecutions which the rage of men put upon them *in the flesh, but might live in the Spirit unto God.* Others take the expression, *that they might be judged according to men in the flesh,* in a spiritual sense, thus: The gospel was preached to them, to judge them, condemn them, and reprove them, for the corruption of their natures, and the viciousness of their lives, while they lived after the manner of the heathen or the mere natural man; and that, having thus mortified their sins, they might live according to God, a new and spiritual life. Take it thus; and thence learn, 1. The mortifying of our sins and living to God are the expected effects of the gospel preached to us. 2. God will certainly reckon with all those who have had the gospel preached to them, but without these good effects produced by it. God is ready to judge all those who have received the gospel in vain. 3. It is no matter how we are judged according to men in the flesh, if we do but live according to God in the Spirit.

Verses 7–11

We have here an awful position or doctrine, and an inference drawn from it. The position is that the *end of all things is at hand.* The miserable destruction of the Jewish church and nation foretold by our Saviour is now very near; consequently, the time of their persecution and your sufferings is but very short. Your own life and that of your enemies will soon come to their utmost period. Nay, the world itself will not continue very long. The conflagration will put an end to it; and all things must be swallowed up in an endless eternity. The inference from this comprises a series of exhortations.

1. To sobriety and watchfulness: *"Be you therefore sober, v.* 7. Let the frame and temper of your minds be grave, stayed, and solid; and observe strict temperance and sobriety in the use of all worldly enjoyments. Do not suffer yourselves to be caught with your former sins and temptations, *v.* 3. *An watch unto prayer.* Take care that you be continually in a calm sober disposition, fit for prayer; and that you be frequent in prayers, lest this end come upon you unawares," Lu. 21:34; Mt. 26:40, 41. Learn, (1.) The consideration of our approaching end is a powerful argument to make us sober in all worldly matters, and earnest in religious affairs. (2.) Those who would pray to purpose must *watch unto prayer.* They must watch over their own spirits, watch all fit opportunities, and do their duty in the best manner they can. (3.) The right ordering of the body is of great use to promote the good of the soul. When the appetites and inclinations of the body are restrained and governed by God's word and true reason, and the interests of the body are submitted to the interests and necessities of the soul, then it is not the soul's enemy, but its friend and helper.

2. To charity: *And above all things have fervent charity among yourselves, v.* 8. Here is a noble rule in Christianity. Christians ought to love one another, which implies an affection to their persons, a desire of their welfare, and a hearty endeavour to promote it. This mutual affection must not be cold, but fervent, that is, sincere, strong, and lasting. This sort of earnest affection is recommended *above all things,* which shows the importance of it, Col. 3:14. It is greater than faith or hope, 1 Co. 13:13. One excellent effect of it is that it will *cover a multitude of sins.* Learn, (1.) There ought to be in all Christians a more fervent charity towards one another than towards other men: *Have charity among yourselves.* He does not say for pagans, for idolaters, or for apostates, but among yourselves. *Let brotherly love continue,* Heb. 13:1. There is a special relation between all sincere Christians, and a particular amiableness and good in them, which require special affection. (2.) It is not enough for Christians not to bear malice, nor to have common respect for one another, they must intensely and fervently love each other. (3.) It is the property of true charity *to cover a multitude of sins.* It inclines people to forgive and forget offences against themselves, to cover and conceal the sins of others, rather than aggravate them and spread them abroad. It teaches us to love those who are but weak, and who have been guilty of many evil things before their conversion; and it prepares for mercy at the hand of God, who hath promised to forgive those that forgive others, Mt. 6:14.

3. To hospitality, *v.* 9. The hospitality here required is a free and kind entertainment of strangers and travellers. The proper objects of Christian hospitality are one another. The nearness of their relation, and the necessity of their condition in those times of persecution and distress, obliged Christians to be hospitable one to another. Sometimes Christians were spoiled of all they had, and were driven away to distant countries for safety. In this case they must starve if their fellow-christians would not receive them. Therefore it was a wise and necessary rule which the apostle here laid down. It is elsewhere commanded, Heb. 13:1, 2; Rom. 12:13. The manner of performing this duty is this: it must be done in an easy, kind, handsome manner, *without grudging* or grumbling at the expense or trouble. Learn, (1.) Christians ought not only to be charitable, but hospitable, one to another. (2.) Whatever a Christian does by way of charity or of hospitality, he ought to do it cheerfully, and without grudging. *Freely you have received, freely give.*

4. To the improvement of talents, *v.* 11.

(1.) The rule is that whatever gift, ordinary or extraordinary, whatever power, ability, or capacity of doing good is given to us, we should minister, or do service, with the same *one to another,* accounting ourselves not masters, but only *stewards of the manifold grace,* or the various gifts, of God. Learn, [1.] Whatever ability we have of doing good we must own it to be the gift of God and ascribe it to his grace. [2.] Whatever gifts we have received, we ought to look upon them as received for the use one of another. We must not assume them to ourselves, nor hide them in a napkin, but do service with them *one to another* in the best manner we are able. [3.] In receiving and using the manifold gifts of God we must look upon ourselves as stewards only, and act accordingly. The talents we are entrusted with are our Lord's goods, and must be employed as he directs. And it is required in a steward that he be found faithful.

(2.) The apostle exemplifies his direction about gifts in two particulars — speaking and ministering, concerning which he gives these rules: — [1.] *If any man,* whether a minister in public or a Christian in private conference, *speak* or teach, he must do it *as the oracles of God,* which direct us as to the matter of our speech. What Christians in private, or ministers in public, teach and speak must be the pure word and oracles of God. As to the manner of speaking, it must be with the seriousness, reverence, and solemnity, that become those holy and divine oracles. [2.] *If any man minister,* either as a deacon, distributing the alms of the church and taking care of the poor, or as a private person, by charitable gifts and contributions, *let him do it as of the ability which God giveth.* He who has received plenty and ability from God ought to minister plentifully, and according to his ability. These rules ought to be followed and practised for this end, *that God in all things,* in all your gifts, ministrations, and services, may be glorified, *that others may see your good works, and glorify your Father who is in heaven* (Mt. 5:16), *through Jesus Christ,* who has procured and given these gifts to men (Eph. 4:8), and through whom alone we and our services are accepted of God (Heb. 13:15), to whom, Jesus Christ, *be praise and dominion for ever and ever. Amen.* Learn, *First,* It is the duty of Christians in private, as well as ministers in public, to speak to one another of the things of God, Mal. 3:16; Eph. 4:29; Ps. 145:10–12. *Secondly,* It highly concerns all preachers of the gospel to keep close to the word of God, and to treat that word as becomes the oracles of God. *Thirdly,* Christians must not only do the duty of their place, but they must do it with vigour, and according to the best of their abilities. The nature of a Christian's work, which is high work and hard work, the goodness and kindness of the Master, and the excellency of the reward, all require that our endeavours should be serious and vigorous, and that whatever we are called to do for the honour of God and the good of others we should do it with all our might. *Fourthly,* In all the duties and services of life we should aim at the glory of God as our chief end; all other views must be subservient to this, which would sanctify our common actions and affairs, 1 Co. 10:31. *Fifthly,* God is not glorified by any thing we do if we do not offer it to him through the mediation and merits of Jesus Christ. *God in all things must be glorified through Jesus Christ,* who is the only way to the Father. *Sixthly,* The apostle's adoration of Jesus Christ, and ascribing unlimited and everlasting praise and dominion to him, prove that Jesus Christ is the most high God, over all blessed for evermore. Amen.

Verses 12–19

The frequent repetition of counsel and comfort to Christians, considered as sufferers, in every chapter of this epistle, shows that the greatest danger these new converts were in arose from the persecutions to which their embracing Christianity exposed them. The good behaviour of Christians under sufferings is the most difficult part of their duty, but yet necessary both for the honour of Christ and their own comfort; and therefore the apostle, having extorted them in the former part of this chapter to the great duty of mortification, comes here to direct them in the necessary duty of patience under sufferings. An unmortified spirit is very unfit to bear trials. Observe,

I. The apostle's kind manner of address to these poor despised Christians: they were his *beloved, v.* 9.

II. His advice to them, relating to their sufferings, which is,

1. That they should not think them strange, nor be surprised at them, as if some unexpected event befel them; for,

(1.) Though they be sharp and fiery, yet they are designed only to try, not to ruin them, to try their sincerity, strength, patience, and trust in God. On the contrary, they ought rather to rejoice under their sufferings, because theirs may properly be called Christ's sufferings. They are of the same kind, and for the same cause, that Christ suffered; they make us conformable to him; he suffers in them, and feels in our infirmities; and, if we be partakers of his sufferings, we shall also be make *partakers of his glory,* and shall meet him with exceeding joy at his great appearing to judge his enemies, and crown his faithful servants, 2 Th. 1:7, etc. Learn, [1.] True Christians love and own the children of God in their lowest and most distressing circumstances. The apostle owns these poor afflicted Christians, and calls them his beloved. True Christians never look more amiable one to another than in their adversities. [2.] There is no reason for Christians to think strange, or to wonder, at the unkindnesses and persecutions of the world, because they are forewarned of them. Christ himself endured them; and forsaking all, denying ourselves, are the terms upon which Christ accepts of us to be his disciples. [3.] Christians ought not only to be patient, but to rejoice, in their sharpest sorest sufferings for Christ, because they are tokens of divine favour; they promote the gospel and prepare for glory. Those who rejoice in their sufferings for Christ shall eternally triumph and rejoice with him in glory.

(2.) From the fiery trial the apostle descends to a lower degree of persecution — that of the tongue by slander and reproach, *v.* 14. He supposes that this sort of suffering would fall to their lot: they would be reviled, evil-spoken of, and slandered for the name or sake of Christ. In such case he asserts, *Happy are you,* the reason of which is, "Because you have the spirit of God with you, to fortify and comfort you; and the Spirit of God is also the Spirit of glory, that will carry you through all, bring you off gloriously, and prepare and seal you up for eternal glory. This glorious Spirit *resteth upon you,* resideth with you, dwelleth in you, supporteth you, and is pleased with you; and is not this an unspeakable privilege? By your patience and fortitude in suffering, by your dependence upon the promises of God, and adhering to the word which the Holy Spirit hath revealed, *he is on your part glorified;* but by the contempt and reproaches cast upon you *the Spirit itself* is evil-spoken of and blasphemed." Learn, [1.] The best men and the best things usually meet with reproaches in the world. Jesus Christ and his followers, the Spirit of God and the gospel, are all evil-spoken of. [2.] The happiness of good people not only consists with, but even flows from their afflictions: *Happy are you.* [3.] That man who hath the Spirit of God resting upon him cannot be miserable, let his afflictions be ever so great: *Happy are you; for the Spirit of God,* etc. [4.] The blasphemies and reproaches which evil men cast upon good people are taken by the Spirit of God as cast upon himself: *On their part he is evil-spoken of.* [5.] When good people are vilified *for the name of Christ* his Holy Spirit is glorified in them.

2. That they should take care they did not suffer justly, as evil-doers, *v.* 15. One would think such a caution as this needless to such an excellent set of Christians as these were. But their enemies charged them with these and other foul

crimes: therefore the apostle, when he was settling the rules of the Christian religion, thought these cautions necessary, forbidding every one of them to hurt the life or the estate and property of any one, or to do any sort of evil, or, without call and necessity, to play the *bishop in another man's charge,* or busy himself *in other men's matters.* To this caution he adds a direction, *that if any man suffer* for the cause of Christianity, and with a patient Christian spirit, he ought not to account it a shame, but an honour to him; and ought to glorify God who hath thus dignified him, *v.* 16. Learn, (1.) The best of men need to be warned against the worst of sins. (2.) There is very little comfort in sufferings when we bring them upon ourselves by our own sin and folly. It is not the suffering, but the cause, that makes the martyr. (3.) We have reason to thank God for the honour if he calls us out to suffer for his truth and gospel, for our adherence to any of the doctrines or duties of Christianity.

3. That their trials were now at hand, and they should stand prepared accordingly, *v.* 17, 18.

(1.) He tells them that the time had come when *judgment must begin at the house of God.* The usual method of Providence has been this: When God brings great calamities and sore judgments upon whole nations, he generally begins with his own people, Isa. 10:12; Jer. 25:29; Eze. 9:6. "Such a time of universal calamity is now at hand, which was foretold by our Saviour, Mt. 24:9, 10. This renders all the foregoing exhortations to patience necessary for you. And you have two considerations to support you." [1.] "That these judgments will but *begin* with you that are God's house and family, and will soon be over: your trials and corrections will not last long." [2.] "Your troubles will be but light and short, in comparison of what shall befal the wicked world, your own countrymen the Jews, and the infidels and idolatrous people among whom you live: *What shall the end be of those who obey not the gospel of God?*" Learn, *First,* The best of God's servants, his own household, have so much amiss in them as renders it fit and necessary that God should sometimes correct and punish them with his judgments: *Judgment begins at the house of God. Secondly,* Those who are the family of God have their worst things in this life. Their worst condition is tolerable, and will soon be over. *Thirdly,* Such persons or societies of men as *disobey the gospel of God* are not of his church and household, though possibly they may make the loudest pretensions. The apostle distinguishes the disobedient from the house of God. *Fourthly,* The sufferings of good people in this life are demonstrations of the unspeakable torments that are coming upon the disobedient and unbelieving: *What shall the end be of those that obey not the gospel?* Who can express or say how dreadful their end will be?

(2.) He intimates the irremediable doom of the wicked: *If the righteous scarcely be saved, where shall the ungodly and sinner appear, v.* 18. This whole verse is taken from Prov. 11:31, *Behold the righteous shall be recompensed in the earth; how much more the wicked and the sinner?* This the Septuagint translates exactly as the apostle here quotes it. Hence we may learn, [1.] The grievous sufferings of good people in this world are sad presages of much heavier judgments coming upon impenitent sinners. But, if we take the salvation here in the highest sense, then we may learn, [2.] It is as much as the best can do to secure the salvation of their souls; there are so many sufferings, temptations, and difficulties to be overcome, so many sins to be mortified, the gate is so strait and the way so narrow, that it is as much as the righteous can do to be saved. Let the absolute necessity of salvation balance the difficulty of it. Consider, Your difficulties are greatest at first; God offers his grace and help; the contest will not last long; be but faithful to the death, *and God will give you the crown of life,* Rev. 2:10. [3.] The ungodly and the sinner are unquestionably in a state of damnation. *Where shall they appear?* How will they stand before their Judge? Where can they show their heads? *If the righteous scarcely be saved,* the wicked must certainly perish.

4. That when called to suffer, *according to the will of God,* they should look chiefly to the safety of their souls, which are put into hazard by affliction, and cannot be kept secure otherwise than by *committing them to God,* who will undertake the charge, if we commit them to him in well-doing; for he is their Creator, and has out of mere grace made many kind promises to them of eternal salvation, in which he will show himself faithful and true, *v.* 19. Learn, (1.) All the sufferings that befal good people come upon them *according*

to the will of God. (2.) It is the duty of Christians, in all their distresses, to look more to the keeping of their souls than to the preserving of their bodies. The soul is of greatest value, and yet in most danger. If suffering from without raise uneasiness, vexation, and other sinful and tormenting passions within, the soul is then the greatest sufferer. If the soul be not well kept, persecution will drive people to apostasy, Ps. 125:3. (3.) The only way to keep the soul well is to commit it to God, in well-doing. Commit your souls to God by solemn dedication, prayer, and patient perseverance in welldoing, Rom. 2:7. (4.) Good people, when they are in affliction, have great encouragement to commit their souls to God, because he is their Creator, and faithful in all his promises.

CHAPTER 5

In which the apostle gives particular directions, first to the elders, how to behave themselves towards their flock (*v.* 1–4); then to the younger, to be obedient and humble, and to cast their care upon God (*v.* 5–7). He then exhorts all to sobriety, watchfulness against temptations, and stedfastness in the faith, praying earnestly for them; and so concludes his epistle with a solemn doxology, mutual salutations, and his apostolical benediction.

Verses 1–4

Here we may observe,

I. The persons to whom this exhortation is given — to the presbyters, pastors, and spiritual guides of the church, elders by office, rather than by age, ministers of those churches to whom he wrote this epistle.

II. The person who gives this exhortation — the apostle Peter: *I exhort;* and, to give force to this exhortation, he tells them he was their brother-presbyter or fellow-elder, and so puts nothing upon them but what he was ready to perform himself. He was also *a witness of the sufferings of Christ,* being with him in the garden, attending him to the palace of the high-priest, and very likely being a spectator of his suffering upon the cross, at a distance among the crowd, Acts 3:15. He adds that he was also *a partaker of the glory* that was in some degree revealed at the transfiguration (Mt. 17:1–3), and shall be completely enjoyed at the second coming of Jesus Christ. Learn, 1. Those whose office it is to teach others ought carefully to study their own duty, as well as teach the people theirs. 2. How different the spirit and behaviour of Peter were from that of his pretended successors! He does not command and domineer, but exhort. He does not claim sovereignty over all pastors and churches, nor style himself *prince of the apostles, vicar of Christ,* or *head of the church,* but values himself upon being an *elder.* All the apostles were elders, though every elder was not an apostle. 3. It was the peculiar honour of Peter, and a few more, to be the witnesses of Christ's sufferings; but it is the privilege of all true Christians to be partakers of the glory that shall be revealed.

III. The pastor's duty described, and the manner in which that duty ought to be performed. The pastoral duty is threefold: — 1. *To feed the flock,* by preaching to them the sincere word of God, and ruling them according to such directions and discipline as the word of God prescribes, both which are implied in this expression, *Feed the flock.* 2. The pastors of the church must *take the oversight thereof.* The elders are exhorted to do the office of bishops (as the word signifies), by personal care and vigilance over all the flock committed to their charge. 3. They must be *examples to the flock,* and practise the holiness, self-denial, mortification, and all other Christian duties, which they preach and recommend to their people. These duties must be performed, *not by constraint,* not because you must do them, not from compulsion of the civil power, or the constraint of fear or shame, but from a willing mind that takes pleasure in the work: *not for filthy lucre,* or any emoluments and profits attending the place where you reside, or any perquisite belonging to the office, *but of a ready mind,* regarding the flock more than the fleece, sincerely and cheerfully endeavouring to serve the church of God; *neither as being lords over God's heritage,* tyrannizing over them by compulsion and coercive force, or imposing unscriptural and human inventions upon them instead of necessary duty, Mt. 20:25, 26; 2 Co. 1:24. Learn, (1.) The eminent dignity of the church of God, and all the true members of it. These poor, dispersed, suffering Christians were the flock of God. The rest of the world is a brutal herd. These are an orderly flock, redeemed to God by the great Shepherd, living in holy love and communion one with another, *according to the will of God.* They are also dignified with the title of God's *heritage* or *clergy,* his peculiar lot, chosen out of the

common multitude for his own people, to enjoy his special favour and to do him special service. The word is never restricted in the New Testament to the ministers of religion. (2.) The pastors of the church ought to consider their people as *the flock of God, as God's heritage,* and treat them accordingly. They are not theirs, to be lorded over at pleasure; but they are God's people, and should be treated with love, meekness, and tenderness, for the sake of him to whom they belong. (3.) Those ministers who are either driven to the work by necessity or drawn to it by filthy lucre can never perform their duty as they ought, because they do not do it willingly, and with a ready mind. (4.) The best way a minister can take to engage the respect of a people is to discharge his own duty among them in the best manner that he can, and to be a constant example to them of all that is good.

IV. In opposition to that filthy lucre which many propose to themselves as their principal motive in undertaking and discharging the pastoral office, the apostle sets before them the crown of glory designed by the great shepherd, Jesus Christ, for all his faithful ministers. Learn, 1. Jesus Christ is *the chief shepherd* of the whole flock and heritage of God. He bought them, and rules them; he defends and saves them for ever. He is also the chief shepherd over all inferior shepherds; they derive their authority from him, act in his name, and are accountable to him at last. 2. This chief shepherd will appear, to judge all ministers and under-shepherds, to call them to account, whether they have faithfully discharged their duty both publicly and privately according to the foregoing directions. 3. Those that are found to have done their duty shall have what is infinitely better than temporal gain; they shall receive from the grand shepherd a high degree of everlasting glory, *a crown of glory that fadeth not away.*

Verses 5–7

Having settled and explained the duty of the pastors or spiritual guides of the church, the apostle comes now to instruct the flock,

I. How to behave themselves to their ministers and to one another. He calls them *the younger,* as being generally younger than their grave pastors, and to put them in mind of their inferiority, the term younger being used by our Saviour to signify an inferior, Lu. 22:26. He exhorts those that are younger and inferior to *submit themselves to the elder,* to give due respect and reverence to their persons, and to yield to their admonitions, reproof, and authority, enjoining and commanding what the word of God requires, Heb. 13:17. As to one another, the rule is that they should all *be subject one to another,* so far as to receive the reproofs and counsels one of another, and be ready to *bear one another's burdens,* and perform all the offices of friendship and charity one to another; and particular persons should submit to the directions of the whole society, Eph. 5:21.; Jam. 5:16. These duties of submission to superiors in age or office, and subjection to one another, being contrary to the proud nature and selfish interests of men, he advises them to be *clothed with humility.* "Let your minds, behaviour, garb, and whole frame, be adorned with humility, as the most beautiful habit you can wear; this will render obedience and duty easy and pleasant; but, if you be disobedient and proud, God will set himself to oppose and crush you; for *he resisteth the proud,* when he *giveth grace to the humble.*" Observe, 1. Humility is the great preserver of peace and order in all Christian churches and societies, consequently pride is the great disturber of them, and the cause of most dissensions and breaches in the church. 2. There is a mutual opposition between God and the proud, so the word signifies; they war against him, and he scorns them; *he resisteth the proud,* because they are like the devil, enemies to himself and to his kingdom among men, Prov. 3:34. 3. Where God giveth grace to be humble, he will give more grace, more wisdom, faith, holiness, and humility. Hence the apostle adds: *Humble yourselves therefore under the mighty hand of God, that he may exalt you in due time, v.* 6. "Since God resisteth the proud, but giveth grace to the humble, therefore humble yourselves, not only one to another, but to the great God, whose judgments are coming upon the world, and must begin at the house of God (*ch.* 4:17); his hand is almighty, and can easily pull you down if you be proud, or exalt you if you be humble; and it will certainly do it, either in this life, if he sees it best for you, or at the day of general retribution." Learn, (1.) The consideration of the omnipotent hand of God should make us humble and submissive to him in all that he brings upon us. (2.) Humbling ourselves to God under his hand is the next way to deliverance and exaltation; patience under his chastisements, and submission to his pleasure, repentance, prayer, and hope in his mercy, will engage his help and release in due time, Jam. 4:7, 10.

II. The apostle, knowing that these Christians were already under very hard circumstances, rightly supposes that what he had foretold of greater hardships yet a coming might excite in them abundance of care and fear about the event of these difficulties, what the issue of them would be to themselves, their families, and the church of God; foreseeing this anxious care would be a heavy burden, and a sore temptation, he gives them the best advice, and supports it with a strong argument. His advice is to *cast all their care,* or *all care of themselves, upon God.* "Throw your cares, which are so cutting and distracting, which wound your souls and pierce your hearts, upon the wise and gracious providence of God; trust in him with a firm composed mind, *for he careth for you.* He is willing to release you of your care, and take the care of you upon himself. He will either avert what you fear, or support you under it. He will order all events to you so as shall convince you of his paternal love and tenderness towards you; and all shall be so ordered that no hurt, but good, shall come unto you," Mt. 6:25; Ps. 84:11; Rom. 8:28. Learn, 1. The best of Christians are apt to labour under the burden of anxious and excessive care; the apostle calls it, *all your care,* intimating that the cares of Christians are various and of more sorts than one: personal cares, family cares, cares for the present, cares for the future, cares for themselves, for others, and for the church. 2. The cares even of good people are very burdensome, and too often very sinful; when they arise from unbelief and diffidence, when they torture and distract the mind, unfit us for the duties of our place and hinder our delightful service of God, they are very criminal. 3. The best remedy against immoderate care is to *cast our care upon God,* and resign every event to the wise and gracious determination. A firm belief of the rectitude of the divine will and counsels calms the spirit of man. *We ceased, saying, The will of the Lord be done,* Acts 21:14.

Verses 8–9

Here the apostle does three things: —

I. He shows them their danger from an enemy more cruel and restless than even the worst of men, whom he describes,

1. By his characters and names. (1.) He is an adversary: "*That adversary of yours;* not a common adversary, but an enemy that impleads you, and litigates against you in your grand depending cause, and aims at your very souls." (2.) *The devil, the grand accuser of all the brethren;* this title is derived from a word which signifies to strike through, or to stab. He would strike malignity into our natures and poison into our souls. If he could have struck these people with passion and murmuring in their sufferings, perhaps he might have drawn them to apostasy and ruin. (3.) He is *a roaring lion,* hungry, fierce, strong, and cruel, the fierce and greedy pursuer of souls.

2. By his business: *He walks about, seeking whom he may devour;* his whole design is to devour and destroy souls. To this end he is unwearied and restless in his malicious endeavours; for he always, night and day, goes about studying and contriving whom he may ensnare to their eternal ruin.

II. Hence he infers that it is their duty, 1. To *be sober,* and to govern both the outward and the inward man by the rules of temperance, modesty, and mortification. 2. To *be vigilant;* not secure or careless, but rather suspicious of constant danger from this spiritual enemy, and, under that apprehension, to be watchful and diligent to prevent his designs and save our souls. 3. To resist him *stedfast in the faith.* It was the faith of these people that Satan aimed at; if he could overturn their faith, and draw them into apostasy, then he knew he should gain his point, and ruin their souls; therefore, to destroy their faith, he raises bitter persecutions, and sets the grand potentates of the world against them. This strong trial and temptation they must resist, by being well-grounded, resolute, and stedfast in the faith: to encourage them to this,

III. He tells them that their care was not singular, for they knew that the like afflictions befel their brethren in all parts of the world, and that all the people of God were their fellow-soldiers in this warfare. Learn, 1. All the great persecutions that ever were in the world were raised, spirited up, and conducted, by the devil; he is the grand persecutor, as well as *the deceiver and accuser, of the brethren;* men are his willing spiteful instruments, but he is the chief adversary that wars against Christ and his people, Gen. 3:15; Rev. 12:12. 2. The design of Satan in raising persecutions against the faithful servants of God is to bring them to apostasy, by reason of their sufferings, and so to destroy their souls. 3. Sobriety and watchfulness are necessary virtues at all times, but especially in times of suffering and persecution. "You must moderate your affection to worldly things, or else Satan will soon overcome you." 4. "If you would overcome Satan, as a tempter, an accuser, or a persecutor, you must resist him stedfast in the faith; if your faith give way, you are gone; therefore, *above all, take the shield of faith,*" Eph. 6:16. 5. The consideration of what others suffer is proper to encourage us to bear our own share in any affliction: *The same afflictions are accomplished in your brethren.*

Verses 10–14

We come now to the conclusion of this epistle, which,

I. The apostle begins with a most weighty prayer, which he addresses to God as *the God of all grace,* the author and finisher of every heavenly gift and quality, acknowledging, on their behalf, that God had already called them to be partakers of that eternal glory, which, being his own, he had promised and settled upon them, through the merit and intercession of Jesus Christ. Observe,

1. What he prays for on their account; not that they might be excused from sufferings, but that their sufferings might be moderate and short, and, *after they had suffered awhile,* that God would restore them to a settled and peaceable condition, and perfect his work in them — that he would establish them against wavering, either in faith or duty, that he would strengthen those who were weak, and settle them upon Christ the foundation, so firmly that their union with him might be indissoluble and everlasting. Learn, (1.) All grace is from God; it is he who restrains, converts, comforts, and saves men by his grace. (2.) All who are called into a state of grace are called to partake of eternal glory and happiness. (3.) Those who are called to be heirs of eternal life through Jesus Christ must, nevertheless, suffer in this world, but their sufferings will be but for a little while. (4.) The perfecting, establishing, strengthening, and settling, of good people in grace, and their perseverance therein, is so difficult a work, that only the God of all grace can accomplish it; and therefore he is earnestly to be sought unto by continual prayer, and dependence upon his promises.

2. His doxology, *v.* 11. From this doxology we may learn that those who have obtained grace from the God of all grace should and will ascribe glory, dominion, and power, to him for ever and ever.

II. He recapitulates the design of his writing this epistle to them (*v.* 12), which was, 1. To testify, and in the strongest terms to assure them, that the doctrine of salvation, which he had explained and they had embraced, was the true account of the grace of God, foretold by the prophets and published by Jesus Christ. 2. To exhort them earnestly that, as they had embraced the gospel, they would continue stedfast in it, notwithstanding the arts of seducers, or the persecutions of enemies. (1.) The main thing that ministers ought to aim at in their labours is to convince their people of the certainty and excellency of the Christian religion; this the apostles did *exhort and testify* with all their might. (2.) A firm persuasion that we are in the true way to heaven will be the best motive to stand fast, and persevere therein.

III. He recommends *Silvanus,* the person by whom he sent them this brief epistle, as a brother whom he esteemed faithful and friendly to them, and hoped they would account him so, though he was a ministers of the uncircumcision. Observe, An honourable esteem of the ministers of religion tends much to the success of their labours. When we are convinced they are faithful, we shall profit more by their ministerial services. The prejudices that some of these Jews might have against Silvanus, as a minister of the Gentiles, would soon wear off when they were once convinced that he was a faithful brother.

IV. He closes with salutations and a solemn benediction. Observe, 1. Peter, being at Babylon in Assyria, when he wrote this epistle (whither he travelled, as the apostle of the circumcision, to visit that church, which was the chief of the dispersion), sends the salutation of that church to the other churches to whom he wrote (*v.* 13), telling them that God had *elected* or chosen the Christians at Babylon out of the world, to be his church, and to partake of eternal salvation through Christ Jesus, together with them and all other faithful Christians, *ch.* 1:2. In this salutation he particularly joins Mark the evangelist, who was then with him, and who was his son in a spiritual sense, being begotten by him to Christianity. Observe, All the churches of Jesus Christ ought to have a most affectionate concern one for another; they should love and pray for one another, and be as helpful one to another as they possibly can. 2. He exhorts them to fervent love and charity one towards another, and to express this by giving *the kiss of peace* (*v.* 14), according to the common custom of those times and countries, and so concludes with a benediction, which he confines to those *that are in Christ Jesus,* united to him by faith and sound members of his mystical body. The blessing he pronounces upon them is *peace,* by which he means all necessary good, all manner of prosperity; to this he adds his *amen,* in token of his earnest desire and undoubted expectation that the blessing of peace would be the portion of all the faithful.

AN EXPOSITION, WITH PRACTICAL OBSERVATIONS, OF

THE SECOND EPISTLE GENERAL OF PETER

The penman of this epistle appears plainly to be the same who wrote the foregoing; and, whatever difference some learned men apprehend they discern in the style of this epistle from that of the former, this cannot be a sufficient argument to assert that it was written by Simon who succeeded the apostle James in the church at Jerusalem, inasmuch as he who wrote this epistle calls himself *Simon Peter, and an apostle* (*v.* 1), and says that he was *one of the three apostles that were present at Christ's transfiguration* (*v.* 18), and says expressly *that he had written a former epistle to them,* 3:1. The design of this second epistle is the same with that of the former, as is evident from the first verse of the third chapter, whence observe that, in the things of God, we have need of *precept upon precept, and line upon line,* and all little enough to keep them in remembrance; and yet these are the things which should be most faithfully recorded and frequently remembered by us.

CHAPTER 1

In this chapter we have, I. An introduction, or preface, making way for, and leading to, what is principally designed by the apostle (*v.* 1–4). II. An exhortation to advance and improve in all Christian graces (*v.* 5–7). III. To enforce this exhortation, and engage them seriously and heartily to comply with it, he adds, 1. A representation of the very great advantage which will thereby accrue to them (*v.* 8–11). 2. A promise of the best assistance the apostle was able to give to facilitate and forward this good work (*v.* 12–15). 3. A declaration of the certain truth and divine origin of the gospel of Christ, in the grace whereof they were exhorted to increase and persevere.

Verses 1–4

The apostle Peter, being moved by the Holy Ghost to write once more to those who from among the Jews were turned to faith in Christ, begins this second epistle with an introduction, wherein the same persons are described and the same blessings are desired that are in the preface to his former letter; but there are some additions or alterations which ought to be taken notice of, in all the three parts of the introduction.

I. We have here a description of the person who wrote the epistle, by the name of *Simon,* as well as *Peter,* and by the title of *servant,* as well as that of *apostle. Peter,* being in both epistles, seems to be the name most frequently used, and with which he may be thought to be best pleased, it being given him by our Lord, upon his confessing *Jesus to be Christ the Son of the living God,* and the very name signifying and sealing that truth to be the fundamental article, the rock on which all must build; but the name *Simon,* though omitted in the former epistle, is mentioned in this, lest the total omission of that name, which was given him when he was circumcised, should make the Jewish believers, who were all zealous of the law, to become jealous of the apostle, as if he disclaimed and despised circumcision. He here styles himself *a servant* (as well as an apostle) *of Jesus Christ;* in this he may be allowed to glory, as David does, Ps. 116:16. The service of Christ is the way to the highest honour, Jn. 12:26. Christ himself is *King of kings, and Lord of lords;* and he makes all his servants *kings and priests unto God,* Rev. 1:6. How great an honour is it to be the servants of this Master! This is what we cannot, without sin, be ashamed of. To triumph in being *Christ's servant* is very proper for those who are engaging others to enter into or abide in the service of Christ.

II. We have an account of the people to whom the epistle is written. They are described in the former epistle as *elect according to the foreknowledge of God the Father,* and here as *having obtained precious faith in our Lord Jesus Christ;* for the faith here mentioned is vastly different from the false faith of the heretic, and the feigned faith of the hypocrite, and the fruitless faith of the formal professor, how orthodox soever he is. It is *the faith of God's elect* (Tit. 1:1), wrought by the Spirit of God in effectual calling. Observe, 1. True saving faith is a precious grace, and that not only as it is very uncommon, very scarce, even in the visible church, a very small number of true believers among a great multitude of visible professors (Mt. 22:14), but true faith is very excellent and of very great use and advantage to those who have it. *The just lives by faith,* a truly divine spiritual life; faith procures all the necessary supports and comforts of this excellent life; faith goes to Christ, and buys the wine and milk (Isa. 55:1) which are the proper nourishment of the new creature; faith buys and brings home the tried gold, the heavenly treasure that enriches; faith takes and puts on the white raiment, the royal robes that clothe and adorn, Rev. 3:18. Observe, 2. Faith is alike precious in the private Christian and in the apostle; it produces the same precious effects in the one and in the other. Faith unites the weak believer to Christ as really as it does the strong one, and purifies the heart of one as truly as of another; and every sincere believer is by his faith justified in the sight of God, and that from all sins, Acts 13:39. Faith, in whomsoever it exists, takes hold of the same *precious* Saviour, and applies the same precious promises. 3. This precious faith is obtained of God. Faith is the gift of God, wrought by the Spirit, who raised up Jesus Christ from the dead. 4. The preciousness of faith, as well as our obtaining it, is through the righteousness of Christ. The satisfactory meritorious righteousness and obedience of Christ gives faith all its value and preciousness: and the righteousness of such a person cannot but be of infinite value to those who by faith receive it. For, (1.) This Jesus Christ is God, yea, *our* God, as it is in the original. He is truly God, an infinite Being, who has wrought out this righteousness, and therefore it must be of infinite value. (2.) *He is the Saviour of those that believe,* and as such he yielded this meritorious obedience; and therefore it is of such great benefit and advantage to them, because, as surety and Saviour, he wrought out this righteousness in their stead.

III. We have the apostolical benediction, wherein he wishes for the multiplication and increase of the divine favour to them, and the advancement and growth of the work of grace in them, and that peace with God and in their own consciences (which cannot be without *grace)* may abound in them. This is the very same benediction that is in the former epistle; but here he adds,

1. An account of the way and means whereby *grace and peace are multiplied* — it is *through the knowledge of God and Jesus Christ;* this acknowledging or believing in *the only living and true God, and Jesus Christ whom he has sent,* is the great improvement of spiritual life, or it could not be the way to life eternal, Jn. 17:3.

2. The ground of the apostle's faith in asking, and of the Christian's hope in expecting, the increase of grace. What we have already received should encourage us to ask for more; he who has begun the work of grace will perfect it. Observe, (1.) The fountain of all spiritual blessings is the divine power of Jesus Christ, who could not discharge all the office of Mediator, unless he was God as well as man. (2.) All things that have any relation to, and influence upon, the true spiritual life, the life and power of godliness, are from Jesus Christ; *in him all fulness dwells,* and it is from him that we receive, *and grace for grace* (Jn. 1:16), even all that is necessary for the preserving, improving, and perfecting of grace and peace, which, according to some expositors, are called here in this verse *godliness and life.* (3.) Knowledge of God, and faith in him, are the channel whereby all spiritual supports and comforts are conveyed to us; but then we must own and acknowledge God as the author of our effectual calling, for so he is here described: *Him that hath called us to glory and virtue.* Observe here, The design of God in calling or converting men is to bring them to *glory and virtue,* that is, *peace and grace,* as some understand it; but many prefer the marginal rendering, *by glory and virtue;* and so we have effectual calling set forth as the work of the glory and virtue, or *the glorious power, of God,* which is described Eph. 1:19. It is the glory of God's power to convert sinners; this is the power and glory of God which are seen and experienced in his sanctuary (Ps. 63:2); this power or virtue is to be extolled by all *that are called out of darkness into marvellous light,* 1 Pt. 2:9. (4.) In the fourth verse the apostle goes on to encourage their faith and hope in looking for an increase of grace and peace, because the same glory and virtue are employed and evidenced in giving the promises of the gospel that are exercised in our effectual calling. Observe, [1.] The good things which the promises make over are exceedingly great. Pardon of sin is one of the blessings here intended; how great this is all who know any thing of the power of God's anger will readily confess, and this is one of those promised favours in bestowing whereof *the power of the Lord is great,* Num. 14:17. To pardon sins that are numerous and heinous (every one of which deserves God's wrath and curse, and that for ever) is a wonderful thing, and is so called, Ps. 119:18. [2.] The promised blessings of the gospel are very precious; as the great promise of the Old Testament was *the Seed of the woman,* the Messiah (Heb. 11:39), so the great promise of the New Testament is the *Holy Ghost* (Lu. 24:49), and how precious must the enlivening, enlightening, sanctifying Spirit be! [3.] Those who receive the promises of the gospel *partake of the divine nature.* They are *renewed in the spirit of their mind, after the image of God, in knowledge, righteousness, and holiness;* their hearts are set for God and his service; they have a divine temper and disposition of soul; though the law is *the ministration of death,* and *the letter killeth,* yet the gospel is *the ministration of life,* and *the Spirit quickeneth* those *who* are naturally *dead in trespasses and sins.* [4.] Those in whom the Spirit works the divine nature are freed from the bondage of corruption. Those who are, by the Spirit of grace, *renewed in the spirit of their mind,* are translated into *the liberty of the children of God;* for it is the world in which *corruption reigns.* Those who are *not of the Father, but of the world,* are under the power of sin; the world lies in wickedness, 1 Jn. 5:19. And the dominion that sin has in the men of the world is through lust; their desires are to it, and therefore it rules over them. The dominion that sin has over us is according to the delight we have in it.

Verses 5–11

In these words the apostle comes to the chief thing intended in this epistle — to excite and engage them to advance in grace and holiness, they having already obtained precious faith, and been made partakers of the divine nature. This is a very good beginning, but it is not to be rested in, as if we were already perfect. The apostle had prayed that grace and peace might be multiplied to them, and now he exhorts them to press forward for the obtaining of more grace. We should, as we have opportunity, exhort those we pray for, and excite them to the use of all proper means to obtain what we desire God to bestow upon them; and those who will make any progress in religion must be very diligent and industrious in their endeavours. Without *giving all diligence,* there is no gaining any ground in the work of holiness; those who are slothful in the business of religion will make nothing of it; we must strive if we will *enter in at the strait gate,* Lu. 13:24.

I. Here we cannot but observe how the believer's way is marked out step by step. 1. He must get *virtue,* by which some understand *justice;* and then the *knowledge, temperance, and patience* that follow, being joined with it, the apostle may be supposed to put them upon pressing after the four cardinal virtues, or the four elements that go to the making up of every virtue or virtuous action. But seeing it is a *faithful saying, and constantly to be asserted, that those who have faith be careful to maintain good works* (Tit. 3:8), by *virtue* here we may understand *strength* and *courage,* without which the believer cannot stand up for good works, by abounding and excelling in them. The righteous must be bold as a lion (Prov. 28:1); a cowardly Christian, who is afraid to profess the doctrines or practise the duties of the gospel, must expect that Christ will be ashamed of him another day. "Let not your hearts fail you in the evil day, but show yourselves valiant in standing against all opposition, and resisting every enemy, world, flesh, devil, yea, and death too." We have need of virtue while we live, and it will be of excellent use when we come to die. 2. The believer must add *knowledge* to his virtue, prudence to his courage; there is a knowledge of God's name which must go before our faith (Ps. 9:10), and we cannot approve of the good, and acceptable, and perfect will of God, till we know it; but there are proper circumstances for duty, which must be known and observed; we must use the appointed means, and observe the accepted time. Christian prudence regards the persons we have to do with and the place and company we are in. Every believer must labour after the knowledge and wisdom that are profitable to direct, both as to the proper method and order wherein all Christian duties are to be performed and as to the way and manner of performing them. 3. We must add *temperance* to our knowledge. We must be sober and moderate in our love to, and use of, the good things of this life; and, if we have a right understanding and knowledge of outward comforts, we shall see that their worth and usefulness are vastly inferior to those of spiritual mercies. Bodily exercises and bodily privileges profit but little, and therefore are to be esteemed and used accordingly; the gospel teaches sobriety as well as honesty, Tit. 2:12. We must be moderate in desiring and using the good things of natural life, such as meat, drink, clothes, sleep, recreations, and credit; an inordinate desire after these is inconsistent with an earnest desire after God and Christ; and those who take more of these than is due can render to neither God nor man what is due to them. 4. Add to temperance *patience,* which must *have its perfect work,* or we cannot *be perfect and entire, wanting nothing* (Jam. 1:4), for we are born to trouble, and must through many tribulations enter into the kingdom of heaven; and it is this tribulation (Rom. 5:3) which worketh patience, that is, requires the exercise and occasions the increase of this grace, whereby we bear all calamities and crosses with silence and submission, without murmuring against God or complaining of him, but justifying him who lays all affliction upon us, owning that our sufferings are less than our sins deserve, and believing they are no more than we ourselves need. 5. To patience we must add *godliness,* and this is the very thing which is produced by patience, for that works experience, Rom. 5:4. When Christians bear afflictions patiently, they get an experimental *knowledge of the loving-kindness of their heavenly Father, which he will not take from his children, even when he visits their iniquity with the rod and their transgression with stripes* (Ps. 89:32, 33), and hereby they are brought to the child-like fear and reverential love wherein true godliness consists: to this, 6. We must add *brotherly-kindness,* a tender affection to all our fellow-christians, who are children of the same Father, servants of the same Master, members of the same family, travellers to the same country, and heirs of the same inheritance, and therefore are to be loved with a pure heart fervently, with a love of complacency, as those who are peculiarly near and dear to us, in whom we take particular delight, Ps. 16:3. 7. *Charity,* or a love of good-will to all mankind, must be added to the love of delight which we have for those who are the children of God. God has made of one blood all nations, and all the children of men are partakers of the same human nature, are all capable of the same mercies, and liable to the same afflictions, and therefore, though upon a spiritual account Christians are distinguished and dignified above those who are without Christ, yet are they to sympathize with others in their calamities, and relieve their necessities, and promote their welfare both in body and soul, as they have opportunity: thus must all believers in Christ evidence that they are the children of God, who is good to all, but is especially good to Israel.

II. All the forementioned graces must be had, or we shall not be *thoroughly furnished for all good works* — for the duties of the first and second table, for active and passive obedience, and for those services wherein we are to imitate God as well as for those wherein we only obey him — and therefore to engage us to an industrious and unwearied pursuit of them, the apostle sets forth the advantages that redound to all who successfully labour so as to get these things to *be and abound in them, v.* 8–11. These are proposed,

1. More generally, *v.* 8. The having *these things make not barren* (or slothful) *nor unfruitful,* where, according to the style of the Holy Ghost, we must understand a great deal more than is expressed; for when it is said concerning Ahaz, the vilest and most provoking of all the kings of Judah, *that he did not right in the sight of the Lord* (2 Ki. 16:2), we are to understand as much as if it had been said, He did what was most offensive and abominable, as the following account of his life shows; so, when it is here said that the being and abounding of all Christian graces in us will make us neither inactive nor unfruitful, we are thereby to understand that it will make us very zealous and lively, vigorous and active, in all practical Christianity, and eminently fruitful in the works of righteousness. these will bring much glory to God, by bringing forth much fruit among men, being *fruitful in knowledge, or the acknowledging of our Lord Jesus Christ,* owning him to be their *Lord,* and evidencing themselves to be his servants by their abounding in the wok that he has given them to do. This is the necessary consequence of adding one grace to another; for, where all Christian graces are in the heart, they improve and strengthen, encourage and cherish, one another; so they all thrive and grow (as the apostle intimates in the beginning of *v.* 8), and wherever grace abounds there will be an abounding in good works. How desirable it is to be in such a case the apostle evidences, *v.* 9. There he sets forth how miserable it is to be without those quickening fructifying graces; for he who has not the forementioned graces, or, though he pretends or seems to have them, does not exercise and improve them, *is blind,* that is, as to spiritual and heavenly things, as the next words explain it: *He cannot see far off.* This present evil world he can see, and dotes upon, but has no discerning at all of the world to come, so as to be affected with the spiritual privileges and heavenly blessings thereof. He who sees the excellences of Christianity must needs be diligent in endeavours after all those graces that are absolutely necessary for *obtaining glory, honour, and immortality;* but, where these graces are not obtained nor endeavoured after, men are not able to look forward to the things that are but a very little way off in reality, though in appearance, or in their apprehension, they are at a great distance, because they put them far away from them; and how wretched is their condition who are thus blind as to the awfully great things of the other world, who cannot see any thing of the reality and certainty, the greatness and nearness, of the glorious rewards God will bestow on the righteous, and the dreadful punishment he will inflict on the ungodly! But this is not all the misery of those who do not *add to their faith virtue, knowledge,* etc. They are as unable to look backward as forward, their memories are slippery and unable to retain what is past, as their sight is short and unable to discern what is future; they forget that they have been baptized, and had the means, and been laid under the obligations to holiness of heart and life. By baptism we are engaged in a holy war against sin, and are solemnly bound to fight against the flesh, the world, and the devil. Often call to mind, and seriously meditate on, your solemn engagement to be the Lord's, and your peculiar advantages and encouragements to lay aside *all filthiness of flesh and spirit.*

2. The apostle proposes two particular advantages that will attend or follow upon diligence in the work of a Christian: stability in grace, and a triumphant entrance into glory. These he brings in by resuming his former exhortation, and

laying it down in other words; for what in *v.* 5 is expressed by *giving diligence to add to faith virtue,* etc., is expressed in *v.* 10 by *giving diligence to make our calling and election sure.* Here we may observe, (1.) It is the duty of believers *to make their election sure,* to clear it up to themselves that they are the chosen of God. (2.) The way to make sure their eternal election is to make out their effectual calling: none can look into the book of God's eternal counsels and decrees; but, inasmuch as *whom God did predestinate those he also called,* if we can find we are effectually called, we may conclude we are chosen to salvation. (3.) It requires a great deal of diligence and labour to make sure our calling and election; there must be a very close examination of ourselves, a very narrow search and strict enquiry, whether we are thoroughly converted, our minds enlightened, our wills renewed, and our whole souls changed as to the bent and inclination thereof; and to come to a fixed certainty in this requires the utmost diligence, and cannot be attained and kept without divine assistance, as we may learn from Ps. 139:23; Rom. 8:16. "But, how great soever the labour is, do not think much of it, for great is the advantage you gain by it; for," [1.] "By this you will be kept from falling, and that at all times and seasons, even in those hours of temptation that shall be on the earth." When others shall fall into heinous and scandalous sin, those who are thus diligent shall be enabled to walk circumspectly and keep on in the way of their duty; and, when many fall into errors, they shall be preserved sound in the faith, and stand perfect and complete in all the will of God. [2.] Those who are diligent in the work of religion shall have a triumphant entrance into glory; while of those few who get to heaven some are scarcely saved (1 Pt. 4:18), with a great deal of difficulty, *even as by fire* (1 Co. 3:15), those who are *growing in grace,* and *abounding in the work of the Lord,* shall have an *abundant entrance into the joy of their Lord,* even that everlasting kingdom where Christ reigns, and they shall *reign with him for ever and ever.*

Verses 12–15

I. The importance and advantage of progress and perseverance in grace and holiness made the apostle to be very diligent in doing the work of a minister of Christ, that he might thereby excite and assist them to be diligent in the duty of Christians. If ministers be negligent in their work, it can hardly be expected that the people will be diligent in theirs; therefore Peter *will not be negligent* (that is, at no time or place, in no part of his work, to no part of his charge), but will be exemplarily and universally diligent, and that in the work of a remembrancer. This is the office of the best ministers, even the apostles themselves; they are *the Lord's remembrancers* (Isa. 62:6); they are especially bound to make mention of the promises, and put God in mind of his engagements to do good to his people; and they are the people's remembrancers, making mention of God's precepts, and putting them in mind of the doctrines and duties of Christianity, that they may remember God's commandments, to do them. And this the apostle does, though some persons might think it needless, inasmuch as they already knew those thing that he writes about, and were established in the very truth that he insists upon. Observe, 1. We need to be put in mind of what we already know to prevent our forgetting it, and to improve our knowledge, and reduce all to practice. 2. We must be established in the belief of the truth, that we may not be shaken by every wind of doctrine, and especially in that which is the present truth, the truth more peculiarly necessary for us to know in our day, that which belongs to our peace, and which is more especially opposed in our time. The great doctrines of the gospel, *that Jesus is the Christ, that Jesus Christ came into the world to save sinners, that those who believe in the Lord Jesus Christ shall be saved, and all that believe in God must be careful to maintain good works* — these are truths the apostles insisted on in their day; *these are faithful sayings, and worthy of all acceptation* in every age of the Christian church. And, as these must be constantly affirmed by ministers (Tit. 3:8), so the people are to be well instructed and established therein, and yet must, after all their attainments in knowledge, be put in mind of such things as cannot be too clearly known nor too firmly believed. The most advanced Christians cannot, while in this world, be above ordinances, nor beyond the need of those means which God has appointed and does afford. And, if the people need teaching and exhortation while they are in the body, it is very meet and just that ministers should, as long as they are in

this tabernacle, instruct and exhort them, and bring those truths to their remembrance that they have formerly heard, this being a proper means to stir them up to be diligent and lively in a course of gospel-obedience.

II. The apostle, being set upon the work, tells us (*v.* 14) what makes him earnest in this matter, even the knowledge he had, not only that he must certainly, but also that he must shortly, *put off this tabernacle.* Observe, 1. The body is but the tabernacle of the soul. It is a mean and movable structure, whose stakes can be easily removed, and its cords presently broken. 2. This tabernacle must be put off. We are not to continue long in this earthly house. AS at night we put off our clothes, and lay them by, so at death we must put off our bodies, and they musts be laid up in the grave till the morning of the resurrection. 3. The nearness of death makes the apostle diligent in the business of life. Our Lord Jesus had shown him that the time of his departure was at hand, and therefore he bestirs himself with greater zeal and diligence, because the time is short. He must soon be removed from those to whom he wrote; and his ambition being that they should remember the doctrine he had delivered to them, after he himself was taken away from them, he commits his exhortation to writing. The apostle had not any great opinion of oral tradition. This was not so proper a means to reach the end he was in pursuit of. He would have them always to remember these things, and not only to keep them in mind, but also to make mention of them, as the original words import. *Those who fear the Lord make mention of his name,* and talk of his loving-kindness. This is the way to spread the knowledge of the Lord and this the apostle had at heart: and those who have the written word of God are thereby put into a capacity to do this.

Verses 16–18

Here we have the reason of giving the foregoing exhortation, and that with so much diligence and seriousness. These things are not idle tales, or a vain thing, but of undoubted truth and vast concern. The gospel is not a *cunningly devised fable.* These are not the words of one who hath a devil, nor the contrivance of any number of men who by cunning craftiness endeavour to deceive. The way of salvation by Jesus Christ is eminently the counsel of God, the most excellent contrivance of the infinitely wise Jehovah; it was he that invented this way of saving sinners by Jesus Christ, whose power and coming are set forth in the gospel, and the apostle's preaching was a making of these things known. 1. The preaching of the gospel is a making known the power of Christ, that he is able to save to the uttermost all who come to God by him. He is the mighty God, and therefore can save from both the guilt and the filth of sin. 2. The coming of Christ also is make known by the preaching of the gospel. He who was promised immediately after the fall of man, as in the fulness of time to be born of a woman, has now come in the flesh; and whosoever denies this is an antichrist (1 Jn. 4:3), he is actuated and influenced by the spirit of anti-christ; but those who are the true apostles and ministers of Christ, and are directed and guided by the Spirit of Christ, evidence that Christ has come according to the promise which all the Old-Testament believers died in the faith of, Heb. 11:39. Christ has come in the flesh. Inasmuch as those whom he undertakes to save *are partakers of flesh and blood, he himself also took part of the same,* that he might suffer in their nature and stead, and thereby make an atonement. This coming of Christ the gospel is very plain and circumstantial in setting forth; but there is a second coming, which it likewise mentions, which the ministers of the gospel ought also to make known, when he shall come in the glory of his Father with all his holy angels, for he is appointed to be Judge both of quick and dead. He will come to judge the world in righteousness by the everlasting gospel, and call us all to give account of all things done in the body, whether good or evil. 3. And though this gospel of Christ has been blasphemously called a *fable* by one of those wretches who call themselves *the successors of St. Peter,* yet our apostle proves that it is of the greatest certainty and reality, inasmuch as during our blessed Saviour's abode here on earth, when he took on him the form of a servant and was found in fashion as a man, he sometimes manifested himself to be God, and particularly to our apostle and the two sons of Zebedee, who *were eye-witnesses of his divine majesty, when he was transfigured before them, and his face did shine as the sun, and his raiment was white as the light, exceedingly white, as snow, so as no fuller on earth can whiten them.* This Peter, James, and John, were eye-witnesses of, and therefore might and ought to attest; and surely their testimony is true, when they witness what they have seen with their eyes, yea, and heard with their ears: for, besides the visible glory that Christ was invested with here on earth, there was an audible voice from heaven. Here observe, (1.) What a gracious declaration was made: *This is my beloved Son, in whom I am well pleased* — the best voice that ever came from heaven to earth; God is well pleased with Christ, and with us in him. This is the Messiah who was promised, through whom all who believe in him shall be accepted and saved. (2.) This declaration is made by God the Father, who thus publicly owns his Son (even in his state of humiliation, when he was in the form of a servant), yea, proclaims him to be his beloved Son, when he is in that low condition; yea, so far are Christ's mean and low circumstances from abating the love of the Father to him that his laying down his life is said to be one special reason of the Father's love, Jn. 10:17. (3.) The design of this voice was to do our Saviour a singular humour while he was here below: *He received honour and glory from God the Father.* This is the person whom God delights to honour. As he requires us to give honour and glory to his Son by confessing him to be our Saviour, so does he give glory and honour to our Saviour by declaring him to be his Son. (4.) This voice is from heaven, called here *the excellent glory,* which still reflects a greater glory upon our blessed Saviour. This declaration is from God the fountain of honour, and from heaven the seat of glory, where God is most gloriously present. (5.) This voice was heard, and that so as to be understood, by Peter, James, and John. They not only heard a sound (as the people did, Jn. 12:28, 29), but they understood the sense. God opens the ears and understandings of his people to receive what they are concerned to know, when others are like Paul's companions, who only heard a sound of words (Acts 9:7), but understood not the meaning thereof, and therefore are said not to hear the voice of him that spoke, Acts 22:9. Blessed are those who not only hear, but understand, who believe the truth, and feel the power of the voice from heaven, as he did who testifieth these things: and we have all the reason in the world to receive his testimony; for who would refuse to give credit to what is so circumstantially laid down as this account of the voice from heaven, of which the apostle tells us, (6.) It was heard by them *in the holy mount,* when they were with Jesus? The place wherein God affords any peculiarly gracious manifestation of himself is thereby made holy, not with an inherent holiness, but as the ground was holy where God appeared to Moses (Ex. 3:5), and the mountain holy on which the temple was built, Ps. 87:1. Such places are relatively holy, and to be regarded as such during the time that men in themselves experience, or may, by warrant from the word, believingly expect, the special presence and gracious influence of the holy and glorious God.

Verses 19–21

In these words the apostle lays down another argument to prove the truth and reality of the gospel, and intimates that this second proof is more strong and convincing than the former, and more unanswerably makes out that the doctrine of the power and coming of our Lord Jesus Christ is not a mere fable or cunning contrivance of men, but the wise and wonderful counsel of the holy and gracious God. For this is foretold by the prophets and penmen of the Old Testament, who spoke and wrote under the influence and according to the direction of the Spirit of God. Here note,

I. The description that is given of the scriptures of the Old Testament: they are called a *more sure word of prophecy.* 1. It is a prophetical declaration of the power and coming, the Godhead and incarnation, of our Saviour, which we have in the Old Testament. It is there foretold *that the seed of the woman shall bruise the serpent's head.* His power to destroy the devil and his works, and his being made of a woman, are there foretold; and the great and awful Old Testament name of God, *Jehovah* (as read by some), signifies only *He will be;* and that name of God (Ex. 3:14) is rendered by many, *I will be that I will be;* and, thus understood, they point at God's being incarnate in order to the redemption and salvation of his people as what was *to come.* But the New Testament is a history of that whereof the Old Testament is a prophecy. *All the prophets and the law prophesied until John,* Mt. 11:13. And the evangelists and the apostles have written the history of what was before delivered as prophecy. Now

the accomplishment of the Old Testament by the New, and the agreeableness of the New Testament to the Old, are a full demonstration of the truth of both. Read the Old Testament as a prophecy of Christ, and with diligence and thankfulness use the New as the best exposition of the Old. 2. *The Old Testament is a more sure word of prophecy.* It is so to the Jews who received it as the oracles of God. Following prophets confirmed what had been delivered by those who went before, and these prophecies had been written by the express command, and preserved by the special care, and many of them fulfilled by the wonderful providence of God, and therefore were more certain to those who had all along received and read the scriptures than the apostle's account of this voice from heaven. *Moses and the prophets* more powerfully persuade than even miracles themselves, Lu. 16:31. How firm and sure should our faith be, who have such a firm and sure word to rest upon! All the prophecies of the Old Testament are more sure and certain to us who have the history of the most exact and minute accomplishment of them.

II. The encouragement the apostle gives us to search the scriptures. He tells us, *We do well if we take heed to them;* that is, apply our minds to understand the sense, and our hearts to believe the truth, of this sure word, yea, bend ourselves to it, that wee may be moulded and fashioned by it. The word is that form of doctrine into which we must be cast (Rom. 6:17), *that formulary of knowledge* (Rom. 2:20) by which we are to regulate our thoughts and sentiments, our words and confessions, our whole life and conversation. If we thus apply ourselves to the word of God, we certainly do well in all respects, what is pleasing to God and profitable to ourselves; and this indeed is but paying that regard which is due to the oracles of God. But, in order to this giving heed to the word, the apostle suggests some things that are of singular use to those who would attend to the scriptures to any good purpose. 1. They must account and use the scripture as a light which God hath sent into and set up in the world, to dispel that darkness which is upon the face of the whole earth. The word is a lamp to the feet of those who use it aright; this discovers the way wherein men ought to walk; this is the means whereby we come to know the way of life. 2. They must acknowledge their own darkness. This world is a place of error and ignorance, and every man in the world is naturally without that knowledge which is necessary in order to attain eternal life. 3. If ever men are made wise to salvation, it is by the shining of the word of God into their hearts. Natural notions of God are not sufficient for fallen man, who does at best actually know a great deal less, and yet does absolutely need to know a great deal more, of God than Adam did while he continued innocent. 4. When the light of the scripture is darted into the blind mind and dark understanding by the Holy Spirit of God, then the *spiritual day dawns and the day-star arises in that soul.* This enlightening of a dark benighted mind is like the day-break that improves and advances, spreads and diffuses itself through the whole soul, till it makes perfect day, Prov. 4:18. It is a growing knowledge; those who are this way enlightened never think they know enough, till they come to know as they are known. To give heed to this light must needs be the interest and duty of all; and all who do truth come to this light, while evil-doers keep at a distance from it.

III. The apostle lays down one thing as previously necessary in order to our giving heed to, and getting good by, the scriptures, and that is the knowing that all prophecy is of divine origin. Now this important truth he not only asserts, but proves. 1. Observe, No scripture prophecy is of private interpretation (or a man's own proper opinion, an explication of his own mind), but the revelation of the mind of God. This was the difference between the prophets of the Lord and the false prophets who have been in the world. The prophets of the Lord did not speak nor do any thing of their own mind, as Moses, the chief of them, says expressly (Num. 16:28), *I have not done any of the works* (nor delivered any of the statutes and ordinances) *of my own mind.* But false prophets *speak a vision of their own heart, not out of the mouth of the Lord,* Jer. 23:16. The prophets and penmen of the scripture spoke and wrote what was the mind of God; and though, when under the influence and guidance of the Spirit, it may well be supposed that they were willing to reveal and record such thing, yet it is because God would have them spoken and written. But though the scripture be not the effusion of man's own private opinion or inclination, but the revelation of the mind and will of God, yet every private

man ought to search it, and come to understand the sense and meaning thereof. 2. This important truth of the divine origin of the scriptures (that what is contained in them is the mind of God and not of man) is to be known and owned by all who will give heed to the sure word of prophecy. That the scriptures are the word of God is not only an article of the true Christian's faith, but also a matter of science or knowledge. As a man not barely believes, but knows assuredly that that very person is his particular friend in whom he sees all the proper, peculiar, distinguishing marks and characters of his friend, so the Christian knows that book to be the word of God in and upon which he sees all the proper marks and characters of a divinely inspired book. He tastes a sweetness, and feels a power, and sees a glory, in it truly divine. 3. The divinity of the scriptures must be known and acknowledged in the first place, before men can profitably use them, before they can give good heed to them. To call off our minds from all other writings, and apply them in a peculiar manner to these as the only certain and infallible rule, necessarily requires our being fully persuaded that these are divinely inspired, and contain what is truly the mind and will of God.

IV. Seeing it is so absolutely necessary that persons be fully persuaded of the scripture's divine origin, the apostle (*v.* 21) tells us how the Old Testament came to be compiled, and that, 1. Negatively: *It came not by the will of man.* Neither the things themselves that are recorded, and make up the several parts of the Old Testament, are the opinions of men, nor was the will of any of the prophets or penmen of the scriptures the rule or reason why any of those things were written which make up the canon of the scripture. 2. Affirmatively: *Holy men of God spoke as they were moved by the Holy Ghost.* Observe, (1.) They were holy men of God who were employed about that book which we receive as the word of God. If Balaam and Caiaphas, and others who were destitute of holiness, had any thing of the spirit of prophecy, upon occasion, yet such persons were not employed to write any part of the scriptures for the use of the church of God. All the penmen of the scriptures were holy men of God. (2.) *These holy men were moved by the Holy Ghost* in what they delivered as the mind and will of God. The Holy Ghost is the supreme agent, the holy men are but instruments. [1.] The Holy Ghost inspired and dictated to them what they were to deliver of the mind of God. [2.] He powerfully excited and effectually engaged them to speak (and write) what he had put into their mouths. [3.] He so wisely and carefully assisted and directed them in the delivery of what they had received from him that they were effectually secured from any the least mistake in expressing what they revealed; so that the very words of scripture are to be accounted the words of the Holy Ghost, and all the plainness and simplicity, all the power and virtue, all the elegance and propriety, of the very words and expressions are to be regarded by us as proceeding from God. Mix faith therefore with what you find in the scriptures; esteem and reverence your Bible as a book written by holy men, inspired, influenced, and assisted by the Holy Ghost.

CHAPTER 2

The apostle, having in the foregoing chapter exhorted them to proceed and advance in the Christian race, now comes to remove, as much as in him lay, what he could not but apprehend would hinder their complying with his exhortation. He therefore gives them fair warning of false teachers, by whom they might be in danger of being seduced. To prevent this, I. He describes these seducers as impious in themselves, and very pernicious to others (*v.* 1–3). II. He assures them of the punishment that shall be inflicted on them (*v.* 3–6). III. He tells us how contrary the method is which God takes with those who fear him (*v.* 7–9). IV. He fills up the rest of the chapter with a further description of those seducers of whom he would have them beware.

Verses 1–3a

I. In the end of the former chapter there is mention made of holy men of God, who lived in the times of the Old Testament, and were used as the amanuenses of the Holy Ghost, in writing the sacred oracles; but in the beginning of this he tells us they had, even at that time, false prophets in the church as well as true. In all ages of the church, and under all dispensations, when God sends true prophets, the devil sends some to seduce and deceive, false prophets in the Old Testament, and false Christs, false apostles, and seducing teachers, in the New. Concerning these observe, 1. Their business is to bring in destructive errors, *even damnable heresies,* as the business of teachers sent of God is to show the way of truth, even the true way to everlasting life. There are damnable heresies as well as damnable practices; and false teachers are industrious to spread pernicious errors. 2. Damnable heresies are commonly brought in privily, under the cloak and colour of truth. Those who introduce destructive heresies *deny the Lord that bought them.* They reject and refuse to hear and learn of the great teacher sent from God, though he is the only Saviour and Redeemer of men, who paid a price sufficient to redeem as many worlds of sinners as there are sinners in the world. 4. Those who bring in errors destructive to others bring swift (and therefore sure) *destruction upon themselves.* Self-destroyers are soon destroyed; and those who are so hardened as to propagate errors destructive to others shall surely and suddenly be destroyed, and that without remedy.

II. He proceeds, in the second verse, to tell us the consequence with respect to others; and here we may learn, 1. Corrupt leaders seldom fail of many to follow them; though the way of error is a pernicious way, yet many are ready to walk therein. Men drink in iniquity like water, and are pleased to live in error. *The prophets prophesy falsely, and the people love to have it so.* 2. The spreading of error will bring up an evil report on the way of truth; that is, the way o salvation by Jesus Christ, who is *the way, the truth, and the life.* The Christian religion is from the God of truth as the author, leads to true happiness in the enjoyment of the true God as the end, and works truth in the inward part as the means of acceptably serving God. And yet this way of truth is traduced and blasphemed by those who embrace and advance destructive errors. This the apostle has foretold as what should certainly come to pass. Let us not be offended at any thing of this in our day, but take care that we give no occasion to the enemy to blaspheme the holy name whereby we are called, or speak evil of that way whereby we hope to be saved.

III. Observe, in the next place, the method seducers take to draw disciples after them: they use *feigned words;* they flatter, and by good words and fair speeches deceive the hearts of the simple, inducing them to yield entirely to the opinions which these seducers endeavour to propagate, and sell and deliver themselves over to the instruction and government of these false teacher, who make a gain of those whom they make their proselytes, serving themselves and making some advantage of them; for all this is through covetousness, with a desire and design to get more wealth, or credit, or commendation, by increasing the number of their followers. The faithful ministers of Christ, who show men the way of truth, desire the profit and advantage of their followers, that they may be saved; but these seducing teachers desire and design only their own temporal advantage and worldly grandeur.

Verses 3b–6

Men are apt to think that a reprieve is the forerunner of a pardon, and that if judgment be not speedily executed it is, or will be, certainly reversed. But the apostle tells us that how successful and prosperous soever false teachers may be, and that for a time, yet their *judgment lingereth not.* God has determined long ago how he will deal with them. Such unbelievers, who endeavour to turn others from the faith, are condemned already, and the wrath of God abideth on them. The righteous Judge will speedily take vengeance; the day of their calamity is at hand, and the things that shall come upon them make haste. To prove this assertion, here are several examples of the righteous judgment of God, in taking vengeance on sinners, proposed to our serious consideration.

I. See how God dealt with the angels who sinned. Observe, 1. No excellency will exempt a sinner from punishment. If the angels, who excel us vastly in strength and knowledge, violate the law of God, the sentence which that law awards shall be executed upon them, and that without mercy or mitigation, for God did not spare them. Hence observe, 2. By how much the more excellent the offender, by so much the more severe the punishment. These angels, who had the advantage of men as to the dignity of their nature, are immediately punished. There is no sparing them for a few days, no favour at all shown them. 3. Sin debases and degrades the persons who commit it. The angels of heaven are cast down from the height of their excellency, and divested of all their glory and dignity, upon their disobedience. Whoever sins against God does a manifest hurt to himself. 4. Those who rebel against the God of heaven shall all be sent down to hell. There is no place nor state between the height of glory and the depth of misery in which they shall be allowed to rest. If creatures sin in heaven, they must suffer in hell. 5. Sin is the work of darkness, and darkness is the wages of sin. The darkness of misery and torment follows the darkness of sin. Those who will not walk according to the light and direction of God's law shall be deprived of the light of God's countenance and the comforts of his presence. 6. As sin binds men over to punishment, so misery and torment hold men under punishment. The darkness which is their misery keeps them so that they cannot get away from their torment. 7. The last degree of torment is not till the day of judgment. The sinning angels, though in hell already, are yet reserved to the judgment of the great day.

II. See how God dealt with the old world, even in much the same way that he dealt with the angels. He spared not the old world. Here observe, 1. The number of offenders signifies no more to procure any favour than the quality. If the sin be universal, the punishment shall likewise extend to all. But, 2. If there be but a few righteous, they shall be preserved. God does not destroy the good with the bad. In wrath he remembers mercy. 3. Those who are *preachers of righteousness* in an age of universal corruption and degeneracy, *holding forth the word of life* in an unblamable and exemplary conversation, shall be preserved in a time of general destruction. 4. God can make use of those creatures as the instruments of his vengeance in punishing sinners which he at first made and appointed for their service and benefit. He destroyed the whole world by water; but observe, 5. What was the procuring cause of this: *it was a world of ungodly men.* Ungodliness puts men out of the divine protection, and exposes them to utter destruction.

III. See how God dealt with Sodom and Gomorrah; though they were situated in a country like the garden of the Lord, yet, if in such a fruitful soil they abound in sin, God can soon turn a fruitful land into barrenness and a well-watered country into dust and ashes. Observe, 1. No political union or confederacy can keep off judgments from a sinful people. Sodom and the neighbouring cities were no more secured by their regular government than the angels by the dignity of their nature or the old world by their vast number. 2. God can make use of contrary creatures to punish incorrigible sinners. He destroys the *old world by water,* and Sodom by fire. He who keeps fire and water from hurting his people (Isa. 43:2) can make either to destroy his enemies; therefore they are never safe. 3. Most heinous sins bring most grievous judgments. Those who were abominable in their vices were remarkable for their plagues. Those who are sinners exceedingly before the Lord must expect the most dreadful vengeance. 4. The punishment of sinners in former ages is designed for the example of those who come after. "Follow them, not only in the time of living, but in their *course and way of living.*" Men who live ungodly must see what they are to expect if they go on still in a course of impiety. Let us take warning by all the instances of God's taking vengeance, which are recorded for our admonition, and to prevent our promising ourselves impunity, though we go on in a course of sin.

Verses 7–9

When God sends destruction on the ungodly, he commands deliverance for the righteous; and, if he rain fire and brimstone on the wicked, he will cover the head of the just, and they shall be hid in the day of his anger. This we have an instance of in his preserving Lot. Here observe, 1. The character given of Lot; he is called *a just man;* this he was as to the generally prevailing bent of his heart and through the main of his conversation. God does not account men just or unjust from one single act, but from their general course of life. And here is a just man in the midst of a most corrupt and profligate generation universally gone off from all good. He does not follow the multitude to do evil, but in a city of injustice he walks uprightly. 2. The impression the sins of others made upon this righteous man. Though the sinner takes pleasure in his wickedness, it is a grief and vexation to the soul of the righteous. In bad company we cannot escape either guilt or grief. Let the sins of others be a trouble to us, otherwise it will not be possible for us to keep ourselves pure. 3. Here is a particular mention of the duration and continuance of this good man's grief and vexation: it was *from day to day.* Being accustomed to hear and see their wickedness did not reconcile him to it, nor abate of the horror that was occasioned by it. This is the righteous man whom God preserved from the desolating judgment that destroyed all round about him. From this instance we are taught to argue that God knows how to deliver his people and punish his enemies. It is here presupposed that the righteous must have their temptations and trials. The devil and his instruments will thrust sore at them, that they may fall; and, if we will get to heaven, it must be through many tribulations. It is therefore our duty to reckon upon and prepare for them. Observe here, (1.) *The Lord knows those that are his.* He has set apart him who is godly for himself; and, if there is but one in five cities, he knows him; and where there is a greater number he cannot be ignorant of nor overlook any one of them. (2.) The wisdom of God is never at a loss about ways and means to deliver his people. They are often utterly at a loss, and can see no way; he can deliver a great many. (3.) The deliverance of the godly is the work of God,, that which he concerns himself in, both his wisdom to contrive the way and his power to work out the deliverance *out of temptation,* to prevent their falling into sin and their being ruined by their troubles. And surely, if he can deliver out of temptation, he could keep from falling into it if he did not see such trials to be necessary. (4.) God makes a very great difference in his dealings with the godly and the wicked. When he saves his people from destruction, he delivers over his enemies to deserved ruin. The unjust has no share in the salvation God works out for the righteous. The wicked are *reserved to the day of judgment.* Here we see, [1.] There is a day of judgment. *God has appointed a day wherein he will judge the world.* [2.] The preservation of impenitent sinners is only a reserving of them to the day of the revelation of the righteous judgment of God.

Verses 10–22

The apostle's design being to warn us of, and arm us against, seducers, he now returns to discourse more particularly of them, and give us an account of their character and conduct, which abundantly justifies the righteous Judge of the world in reserving them in an especial manner for the most severe and heavy doom, as Cain is taken under special protection that he might be kept for uncommon vengeance. But why will God thus deal with these false teachers? This he shows in what follows.

I. *These walk after the flesh;* they follow the devices and desires of their own hearts, they give up themselves to the conduct of their own fleshly mind, refusing to make their reason stoop to divine revelation, and to *bring every thought to the obedience of Christ;* they, in their lives, act directly contrary to God's righteous precepts, and comply with the demands of corrupt nature. Evil opinions are often accompanied with evil practices; and those who are for propagating error are for improving in wickedness. They will not sit down contented in the measure of iniquity to which they have attained, nor is it enough for them to stand up, and maintain, and defend, what wickedness they have already committed, but they *walk after the flesh,* they go on in their sinful course, and increase unto more ungodliness and greater degrees of impurity and uncleanness too; they also pour contempt on those whom God has set in authority over them and requires them to honour. These therefore despise *the ordinance of God,* and we need not wonder at it, for they are bold and daring, obstinate and refractory, and will not only cherish contempt in their hearts, but with their tongues will utter slanderous and reproachful words of those who are set over them.

II. This he aggravates, by setting forth the very different conduct of more excellent creatures, even the *angels,* of whom observe, 1. They *are greater in power and might,* and that even than those who are clothed with authority and power among the sons of men, and much more than those false teachers who are slanderous revilers of magistrates and governors; the good angels vastly exceed us in all natural and moral excellences, in strength, understanding, and holiness too. 2. Good angels are accusers of sinful creatures, either of their own kind, or ours, or both. Those who are allowed to behold the face of God, and stand before his throne, cannot but have a zeal for his honour, and accuse and blame those who dishonour him. 3. *Angels bring* their *accusations* of sinful creatures *before the Lord;* they do not publish their faults, and tell their crimes to their fellow-creatures, in a way of calumny and slander; but it is before the Lord, who is the Judge, and will be the avenger, of all impiety and injustice. 4. Good angels mingle no bitter revilings nor base reproaches with any of the accusations or charges they bring against the wickedest and worst of criminals. Let us, who pray that God's *will may be done on earth as it is in heaven,* imitate the angels in this particular; if we complain of wicked men, let it be to God, and that not with rage and reviling, but with compassion and composedness of mind, that may evidence that we belong to him who is meek and merciful.

III. The apostle, having shown (*v.* 11) how unlike seducing teachers are to the most excellent creatures, proceeds (*v.* 12) to show how like they are to the most inferior: they are *like the horse and mule, which have no understanding;* they are *as natural brute beasts, made to be taken and destroyed.* Men, under the power of sin, are so far from observing divine revelation that they do not exercise reason, nor act according to the direction thereof. They *walk by sight, and not by faith,* and judge of things according to their senses; as these represent things pleasant and agreeable, so they must be approved and esteemed. Brute-creatures follow the instinct of their sensitive appetite, and sinful man follows the inclination of his carnal mind; these refuse to employ the understanding and reason God has given them, and so are ignorant of what they might and ought to know; and therefore observe, 1. Ignorance is the cause of evil-speaking; and, 2. Destruction will be the effect of it. These persons shall be utterly destroyed in their own corruption. Their vices not only expose them to the wrath of God in another world, but often bring them to misery and ruin in this life; and surely such impudent offenders, who *glory in their shame,* and to whom openness in sin is an improvement of the pleasure of sinning, most justly deserve all the plagues of this life and the pains of the next in the greatest extremity. Therefore whatever they meet with is the just *reward of their unrighteousness.* Such sinners as sport themselves in mischief deceive themselves and disgrace all they belong to, for by one sort of sins they prepare themselves for another; their extravagant feastings, their intemperance in eating and drinking, bring them to commit all manner of lewdness, so that their *eyes are full of adultery,* their wanton looks show their own impure lusts and are designed and directed to kindle the like in others; and this is what they *cannot cease* from — the heart is insatiate in lusting and the eye incessant in looking after what may gratify their unclean desires, and those who are themselves impudent and incessant in sin are very diligent and often successful in deceiving others and drawing others into the same excess of riot. But here observe who those are who are in the greatest danger of being led away into error and impiety, even the *unstable.* Those whose hearts are not established with grace are easily turned into the way of sin, or else such sensual wretches would not be able to prevail upon them, for these are not only riotous and lascivious, but *covetous* also, and these practices their hearts are exercised with; they pant after riches, and the desire of their souls is to the wealth of this world: it is a considerable part of their work to contrive to get wealth; in this their hearts are exercised, and then they execute their projects; and, if men abandon themselves to all sorts of lusts, we cannot wonder that the apostle should call them *cursed children,* for they are liable to the curse of God denounced against such *ungodly and unrighteous men,* and they bring a curse upon all who hearken and adhere to them.

IV. The apostle (*v.* 15, 16) proves that they are *cursed children,* even such covetous persons as *the Lord abhors,* by showing, 1. They *have forsaken the right way;* and it cannot be but such self-seekers must be out of the right way, which is a self-denying way. 2. They have gone into a wrong way: they have erred and strayed from the way of life, and gone over into the path which leads to death, and takes hold of hell; and this he makes out by showing it to be *the way of Balaam, the son of Bosor.* (1.) That is a way of unrighteousness into which men are led by the wages of unrighteousness. (2.) Outward temporal good things are the wages sinners expect and promise themselves, though they are often disappointed. (3.) The inordinate love of the good things of this world turns men out of the way which leads to the unspeakably better things of another life; the love of riches and honour turned Balaam out of the way of his duty, although he knew that the way he took displeased the Lord. (4.) Those who from the same principle are guilty of the same practices with notorious sinners are, in the judgment of God, the followers of such vile offenders, and therefore must reckon upon being at last where they are: *they shall have their portion* with those in another world whom they imitated in this. (5.) Heinous and hardened sinners sometimes meet with rebukes for their iniquity. God stops them in their way, and opens the mouth of conscience, or by some startling providence startles and affrights them. (6.) Though some more uncommon and extraordinary rebuke may for a little while cool men's courage, and hinder their violent progress in the way of sin, it will not make them forsake the way of iniquity and go over into the way of holiness. If rebuking a sinner for his iniquity could have made a man return to his duty, surely the rebuke of Balaam must have produced this effect; for here is a surprising miracle wrought: *the dumb ass,* in whose mouth no man can expect to meet with reproof, is enabled to speak, and that with a human voice, and to her owner and master (who is here called a *prophet,* for the Lord appeared and spoke sometimes to him, Num. 22:23, 24, but indeed he was among the prophets of the Lord as Judas among the apostles of Jesus Christ), and she exposes *the madness* of his conduct and opposes his going on in this evil way, and yet all in vain. Those who will not yield to usual methods of reproof will be but little influenced by miraculous appearances to turn them from their sinful courses. Balaam was indeed restrained from actually *cursing the people,* but he had so strong a desire after the honours and riches that were promised him that he went as far as he could, and did his utmost to get from under the restraint that was upon him.

V. The apostle proceeds (*v.* 17) to a further description of seducing teachers, whom he sets forth,

1. As *wells,* or fountains, *without water.* Observe, (1.) Ministers should be as wells or fountains, where the people may find instruction, direction, and comfort; but (2.) False teachers have nothing of this to impart to those who consult them: the word of truth is the water of life, which refreshes the souls that receive it; but these deceivers are set upon spreading and promoting error, and therefore are set forth as empty, because there is no truth in them. In vain then are all our expectations of being fed and filled with knowledge and understanding by those who are themselves ignorant and empty.

2. As *clouds carried with a tempest.* When we see a cloud we expect a refreshing shower from it; but these are clouds which yield no rain, for they are driven with the wind, but not of the Spirit, but the stormy wind or tempest of their own ambition and covetousness. They espouse and spread those opinions that will procure most applause and advantage to themselves; and as clouds obstruct the light of the sun, and darken the air, so do these *darken counsel by words without knowledge* and wherein there is no truth; and, seeing these men are for promoting darkness in this world, it is very just that the mist of darkness should be their portion in the next. Utter darkness was prepared for the devil, the great deceiver, and his angels, those instruments that he uses to turn men from the truth, and therefore for them it is reserved, and that for ever; the fire of hell is everlasting, and the smoke of the bottomless pit rises up for ever and ever. And it is just with God to deal thus with them, because (1.) They allure those they deal with, and draw them into a net, or catch them as men do fish; and, (2.) It is *with great swelling words of vanity,* lofty expressions, which have a great sound, but little sense. (3.) They work upon *the corrupt affections* and *carnal fleshly lusts of men,* proposing what is grateful to them. And, (4.) They seduce persons who in reality avoided and kept at a distance from those who spread and those who embraced hurtful and destructive errors. Observe, [1.] By application and industry men attain a skilfulness and dexterity in promoting error. They are as artful and as successful as the fisher, who makes angling his daily employment. The business of these men is to draw disciples after them, and in their methods and management there are some things worth observing, how they suit their bait to those they desire to catch. [2.] Erroneous teachers have a peculiar advantage to win men over to them, because they have sensual pleasure to take them with; whereas the ministers of Christ put men upon self-denial, and the mortifying of those lusts that others gratify and please: wonder not therefore that truth prevails no more, or that errors spread so much. [3.] Persons who have for a while adhered to the truth, and kept clear of errors, may by the subtlety and industry of seducers be so far deceived as to fall into those errors they had for a while *clean escaped.* "Be therefore always upon your guard, maintain a godly jealousy of yourselves, search the scriptures, pray for the Spirit to instruct and establish you in the truth, walk humbly with God, and watch against every thing that may provoke him to give you up to a reprobate mind, that you may not be taken with the fair and specious pretences of these false teachers, who promise liberty to all who will hearken to them, not true Christian liberty for the service of God, but a licentiousness in sin, to follow the devices and desires of their own hearts." To prevent these men's gaining proselytes, he tells us that, in the midst of all their talk of liberty, they themselves are the vilest slaves, for they are the servants of corruption; their own lusts have gotten a complete victory over them, and they are actually in bondage to them, making *provision for the flesh,* to satisfy its cravings, comply with its directions, and obey its commands. Their minds and hearts are so far corrupted and depraved that they have neither power nor will to refuse the task that is imposed on them. They are conquered and captivated by their spiritual enemies, and yield their members servants of unrighteousness: and what a shame it is to be overcome and commanded by those who are themselves *the servants of corruption, and slaves to their own lusts!* This consideration should prevent our being led away by these seducers; and to this he adds another (*v.* 20): it is not only a shame and disgrace to be seduced by those who are themselves the slaves of sin, and led captive by the devil at his pleasure, but it is a real detriment to those who have clean escaped from those who live in error, for hereby their latter end is made worse than their beginning. Here we see, *First,* It is an advantage to escape the pollutions of the world, to be kept from gross and scandalous sins, though men are not thoroughly converted and savingly changed; for hereby we are kept from grieving those who are truly serious and emboldening those who are openly profane; whereas, if we run with others to the same excess of riot and abandon ourselves to the sins of the age, we afflict and dishearten those who endeavour to walk as becomes the gospel, and strengthen the hands of those who are already engaged in open rebellion against the Most High, as well as alienate ourselves more from God, and harden our hearts against him. *Secondly,* Some men are, for a time, *kept from the pollutions of the world, by the knowledge of Christ,* who are not savingly renewed in the spirit of their mind. A religious education has restrained many whom the grace of God has not renewed: if we receive the light of the truth, and have a notional knowledge of Christ in our heads, it may be of some present service to us; but we must receive the love of the truth, and hide God's word in our heart, or it will not sanctify and save us. *Thirdly,* Those who have, for a time, escaped the pollutions of the world, are at first ensnared and entangled by false teachers, who first perplex men with some plausible and specious objections against the truths of the gospel; and the more ignorant and unstable are hereby made to stagger, and brought to question the truth of doctrines they have received, because they cannot solve all the difficulties, nor answer all the objections, that are urged by these seducers. *Fourthly,* When men are once entangled, they are easily overcome; therefore should Christians keep close to the word of God, and watch against those who seek to perplex and bewilder them, and that because, if men who have once *escaped are again entangled, the latter end is worse with them than the beginning.*

VI. The apostle, in the last two verses of the chapter, sets himself to prove that a state of apostasy is worse than a state of ignorance; for it is a *condemning of the way of righteousness,* after they have had some knowledge of it, and expressed some liking to it; it carries in it a declaring that they have found some iniquity in the way of righteousness and some falsehood in the word of truth. Now to bring up such an evil report upon the good way of God, and such a false charge against the way of truth, must necessarily expose to the heaviest condemnation; the misery of such deserters of Christ and his gospel is more unavoidable and more intolerable than that of other offenders; for, 1. God is more highly provoked by those who by their conduct despise the gospel, as well as disobey the law, and who reproach and pour contempt upon God and his grace. 2. The devil more narrowly watches and more closely confines those whom he has recovered, after they had once gone off from him and professed to be the followers of the Lord Jesus Christ (Mt. 12:45); they are kept under a stronger guard, and no wonder it should be so when they have licked up their own vomit again, returning to the same errors and impieties that they had once cast off and seemed to detest and loathe, and wallowing in that filthiness from which they appeared once to be really cleansed. Well, if the scripture gives such an account of Christianity on the one hand, and of sin on the other, as we have here in these two verses, we certainly ought highly to approve of the former and persevere therein, because it is a way of righteousness, and a holy commandment, and to loathe and keep at the greatest distance from the latter because it is set forth as most offensive and abominable.

CHAPTER 3

The apostle drawing towards the conclusion of his second epistle, begins this last chapter with repeating the account of his design and scope in writing a second time to them (*v.* 1–2). II. He proceeds to mention one thing that induced him to write this second epistle, namely, the coming of scoffers, whom he describes (*v.* 3–7). III. He instructs and establishes them in the coming of our Lord Jesus Christ to judgment (*v.* 8–10). IV. He sets forth the use and improvement which Christians ought to make of Christ's second coming, and that dissolution and renovation of things which will accompany that solemn coming of our Lord (*v.* 11–18).

Verses 1–2

That the apostle might the better reach his end in writing this epistle, which is to make them steady and constant in a fiducial and practical remembrance of the doctrine of the gospel, he, 1. Expresses his special affection and tenderness for them, by calling them *beloved,* hereby evidencing that he *added to godliness brotherly-kindness,* as he had (*ch.* 1:17) exhorted them to do. Ministers must be examples of love and affection, as well as life and conversation. 2. He evinces a sincere love to them, and hearty concern for them, by writing the same thing to them, though in other words. It being safe for them, it shall not be grievous to him to write upon the same subject, and pursue the same design, by those methods which are most likely to succeed. 3. The better to recommend the matter, he tells them that what he would have them to remember are, (1.) *The words spoken by the holy prophets,* who were divinely inspired, both enlightened and sanctified by the Holy Ghost; and, seeing these persons' minds were purified by the sanctifying operation of the same Spirit, they were the better disposed to receive and retain what came from God by the holy prophets. (2.) *The commandments of the apostles of the Lord and Saviour;* and therefore the disciples and servants of Christ ought to regard what those who are sent by him have declared unto them to be the will of their Lord. What God has spoken by the prophets of the Old Testament, and Christ has commanded by the apostles of the New, cannot but demand and deserve to be frequently remembered; and those who meditate on these things will feel the quickening virtues thereof. It is by these things the pure minds of Christians are to be stirred up, that they may be active and lively in the work of holiness, and zealous and unwearied in the way to heaven.

Verses 3–7

To quicken and excite us to a serious minding and firm adhering to what God has revealed to us by the prophets and apostles, we are told that there will be *scoffers,* men who will *make a mock of sin,* and of salvation from it. God's way of saving sinners by Jesus Christ is what men will scoff at, and that *in the last days,* under the gospel. This indeed may seem very strange, that the New-Testament dispensation of the covenant of grace, which is spiritual and therefore more agreeable to the nature of God than the Old, should be ridiculed and reproached; but the spirituality and simplicity of New-Testament worship are directly contrary to the carnal mind of man, and this accounts for what the apostle seems here to hint at, namely, that scoffers shall be more numerous and more bold in the last days than ever before. Though in all ages those who were born and walked after the flesh persecuted, reviled, and reproached those who were born and did walk after the Spirit, yet in the last days there will be a great improvement in the art and impudence of bantering serious godliness, and those who firmly adhere to the circumspection and self-denial which the gospel prescribes. This is what is mentioned as a thing well known to all Christians, and therefore they ought to reckon upon it, that they may not be surprised and shaken, as if some strange thing happened unto them. Mow to prevent the true Christian's being overcome, when attacked by these scoffers, we are told,

I. What sort of persons they are: they *walk after their own lusts,* they follow the devices and desires of their own hearts, and carnal affections, not the dictates and directions of right reason and an enlightened well-informed judgment. This they do in the course of their conversation, they live as they list, and they speak as they list; it is not only their inward minds that are evil and opposite to God, as the mind of every unrenewed sinner is (Rom. 8:7), alienated from God, ignorant of him, and averse to him; but they have grown to such a height of wickedness that they proclaim openly what is in the hearts of others who are yet carnal; they say, "Our tongues are our own, and our strength, and time, and *who is lord over us?* Who shall contradict or control us, or ever call us to an account for what we say or do?" And, as they scorn to be confined by any laws of God in their conversation, so neither will they bear that the revelation of God should dictate and prescribe to them what they are to believe; as they will walk in their own way, and talk their own language, so will they also think their own thoughts, and form principles which are altogether their own: here also *their own lusts* alone shall be consulted by them. None but such accomplished libertines as are here described can take a seat, at least they cannot sit in the seat of the scornful. "By this you shall know them, that you may the better be upon your guard against them."

II. We also are forewarned how far they will proceed: they will attempt to shake and unsettle us, even as to our belief of Christ's second coming; they will scoffingly say, *Where is the promise of his coming? v.* 4. Without this, all the other articles of the Christian faith will signify very little; this is that which fills up and gives the finishing stroke to all the rest. The promised Messiah has come, he *was made flesh, and dwelt among us;* he is altogether such a one as in stated before, and has done all that for us which has been before taken notice of. These principles the enemies of Christianity have all along endeavoured to overturn; but as these all rest upon facts which are already past, and of which this and the other apostles have given us the most sure and satisfying evidence, it is probable that they will at last grow weary of their opposition to them; and yet, while one very principal article of our faith refers to what is still behind, and only has a promise to rest upon, here they will still attack us, even to the end of time. Till our Lord shall have come, they will not themselves believe that he will come; nay, they will laugh at the very mention of his second coming, and do what in them lies to put all out of countenance who seriously believe and wait for it. Now therefore let us see how this point stands, both on the believer's part and on the part of these seducers: the believer not only desires that he may come, but, having a promise that he will come, a promise that he himself has made and often repeated, a promise received and reported by faithful witnesses, and left upon sure record, he is also firmly and fully persuaded that he will come: on the other hand, these seducers, because they wish he never may, therefore do all that in them lies to cheat themselves and others into a persuasion that he will never come. If they cannot deny that there is a promise, yet they will laugh at that very promise, which argues much higher degrees of infidelity and contempt: *Where is the promise,* say they, *of his coming?*

III. We are also forewarned of the method of their reasoning, for while they laugh they will pretend to argue too. To this purpose they add that *since the fathers fell asleep all things continue as they were from the beginning of the creation, v.* 4. This is a subtle, though not a solid way of reasoning; it is apt to make impressions upon weak minds, and especially upon wicked hearts. *Because sentence against them is not speedily executed,* therefore they flatter themselves that it never will, whereupon *their hearts are fully set in them to do evil* (Eccl. 8:11); thus they act themselves, and thus they would persuade others to act; so here, say they, *"The fathers have fallen asleep,* those are all dead to whom *the promise was made,* and it was never made good in their time, and there is no likelihood that it ever will be in any time; why should we trouble ourselves about it? If there had been any truth or certainty in the promise you speak of, we should surely have seen somewhat of it before this time, some signs of his coming, some preparatory steps in order to it; whereas we find to this very day *all things continue as they were,* without any change, even *from the beginning of the creation.* Since the world has undergone no changes in the course of so many thousand years, why should we affright ourselves as if it were to have an end?" Thus do these scoffers argue. *Because they see no changes, therefore they fear not God,* Ps. 55:19. They neither fear him nor his judgments; what he never has done they would conclude he never can do or never will.

IV. Here is the falsehood of their argument detected. Whereas they confidently had said there had not been any change *from the beginning of the creation,* the apostle puts us in remembrance of a change already past, which, in a manner, equals that which we are called to expect and look for, which was the drowning of the world in the days of Noah. This these scoffers had overlooked; they took no notice of it. Though they might have known it, and ought to have known it, yet *this they willingly are ignorant of* (*v.* 5), they choose to pass it over in silence, as if they had never heard or known any thing of it; if they knew it, they did not like to retain it in their knowledge; they did not receive this truth in the love of it, neither did they care to own it. Note, It is hard to persuade men to believe what they are not willing to find true; they are ignorant, in many cases, because they are willing to be ignorant, and they do not know because they do not care to know. But let not sinners think that such ignorance as this will be admitted as an excuse for whatever sin it may betray them into. Those who crucified Christ did not know who he was; for *had they known they would not have crucified the Lord of glory* (1 Co. 2:8); but, though ignorant, they were not therefore innocent; their ignorance itself was a sin, willing and wilful ignorance, and one sin can be no excuse for another. So it is here; had these known of the dreadful vengeance with which God swept away a whole world of ungodly wretches at once, they would not surely have scoffed at his threatenings of any after equally terrible judgment; but here *they were willingly ignorant,* they did not know what God had done because they had no mind to know it. Now therefore we shall proceed to consider the representation which the apostle here lays down both of the destruction of the old world by water and that which awaits this present world at the final conflagration. He mentions the one as what God has done, to convince and persuade us the rather to believe that the other both may be and will be.

1. We begin with the apostle's account of the destruction which has once already come upon the world (*v.* 5, 6): *By the word of God the heavens were of old, and the earth standing out of the water and in the water, whereby the world that then was, being overflowed with water, perished.* Originally the world was otherwise situated, the waters were most wisely divided at the creation and most beneficially for us; some of the waters had proper repositories above the firmament, here called the heavens (as it is also Gen. 1:8), and others, under the firmament, gathered together unto one place; there were then both sea and dry land, commodious habitation for the children of men. But now, at the time of the universal deluge, the case is strangely altered; the waters which God had divided before, assigning to each part its convenient receptacle, now does he, in anger, throw together again in a heap. *He breaks up the fountain of the great deep, and throws open the windows (that is, the clouds) of heaven* (Gen. 7:11), till the whole earth is overflowed with water, and not a spot can be found upon the highest mountains but what is *fifteen cubits under water,* Gen. 7:20. Thus he made known at once his terrible power and his fierce anger, and made an end of a whole world at once: *The world that then was, being overflowed with water, perished, v.* 6. Is not here a change and a most awful change! And then it is to be observed that all this was done by the word of God; it was by his powerful word that the world was made at first, and made in so commodious and beautiful a frame and order, Heb. 11:3, *Katērtisthai. He said, Let there be a firmament,* etc., Gen. 1:6, 7. *And let the waters under the heaven be gathered together unto one place,* etc., *v.* 9, 10. Thus he spoke, and it was done, Ps. 33:9. Thus, says our apostle, *by the word of the Lord the heavens were,* as they were *of old* (that is, at first creation) *and the earth* (as it was at first a terraqueous globe) *standing out of the water and in the water.* Not is it only the first frame and order of the world that is here said to be *by the word of God,* but the after-confusion and ruin of the world, as well as the utter destruction of its inhabitants, were also by the same word; none but that God who *stretched out the heavens and laid the foundation of the earth* could destroy and overthrow such a vast fabric at once. This was done by the word of his power, and it was also done according to the word of his promise; God had said that he would destroy man, even all flesh, and that he would do it by bringing a flood of waters upon the earth, Gen. 6:7, 13, 17. This was the change which God had before brought upon the world, and which these scoffers had overlooked; and now we are to consider,

2. What the apostle says of the destructive change which is yet to come upon it: *The heavens and the earth, which now are, by the same word are kept in store, reserved unto fire against the day of judgment and perdition of ungodly men, v.* 7. Here we have an awful account of the final dissolution

of the world, and which we are yet more nearly concerned in. The ruin that came upon the world and its inhabitants by the flood, we read, and hear, and think of, with concern, though those who were swept away by it were such as we never knew; but the judgment here spoken of is yet to come, and will surely come, though we know not when, nor upon what particular age or generation of men; and therefore we are not, we cannot be, sure that it may not happen in our own times: and this makes a very great difference, though it should be admitted that they were equal in every other respect, which yet must not be allowed, for there were some, though very few, who escaped that deluge, but not one can escape in this conflagration. Besides, we were not in reach of the one, but are not sure that we shall not be included in the other calamity. Now therefore to see the world to which we belong destroyed at once — not a single person only, not a particular family only, nor yet a nation (even that which we are most nearly interested in and concerned for), but the whole world, I say, sinking at once, and no ark provided, no possible way left of escaping for any one from the common ruin, this makes a difference between the desolation that has been and what we yet are to expect. The one is already past, and never to return upon us any more (for God has said expressly *that there shall never any more be a flood to destroy the earth,* Gen. 9:11–17); the other is still behind, and is as certain to come as the truth and the power of God can make it: the one came gradually upon the world, and was growing upon its inhabitants forty days, before it made an utter end of them (Gen. 7:12, 17); this other will come upon them swiftly and all at once (2 Pt. 2:1): besides, there were in that overthrow (as we have said) a few who escaped, but the ruin which yet awaits this world, whenever it comes, will be absolutely a universal one; there will not be any part but what the devouring flames will seize upon, not a sanctuary left any where for the inhabitants to flee to, not a single spot in all this world where any one of them can be safe. Thus, whatever differences may be assigned between that destruction of the world and this here spoken of, they do indeed represent the approaching as the most terrible judgment; yet that the world has once been destroyed by a universal deluge renders it the more credible that it may be again ruined by a universal conflagration. Let therefore the scoffers, who laugh at the coming of our Lord to judgment, at least consider that it *may be.* There is nothing said of it in the word of God but what is within reach of the power of God, and, though they still should laugh, they shall not put us out of countenance; we are well assured that it will be, because he has said it, and we can depend upon his *promise.* They *err, not knowing* (at least not believing) *the scriptures, nor the power of God;* but we know, and we do or ought to depend upon, both. Now that which he has said, and which he will certainly make good, is that *the heavens and the earth which now are* (which we are now related to, which still subsist in all the beauty and order in which we see them, and which are so agreeable and useful to us, as we find they are) *are kept in store,* not to be, what earthly minds would wish to have them, treasures for us, but to be what God will have them, in his treasury, securely lodged and kept safely for his purposes. It follows, they are *reserved unto fire.* Observe, God's following judgments are more terrible than those which went before; the old world was destroyed by water, but this is reserved unto fire, which shall burn up the wicked at the last day; and, though this seems to be delayed, yet, as this wicked world is upheld by the word of God, so it is only reserved for the vengeance of him to whom vengeance belongs, who will at the day of judgment deal with an ungodly world according to their deserts, for the day of judgment is the day of *the perdition of ungodly men.* Those who now scoff at a future judgment shall find it a day of vengeance and utter destruction. "Beware therefore of being among these scoffers; never question but the day of the Lord will come; give diligence therefore to be found in Christ, that that may be a time of refreshment and day of redemption to you which will be a day of indignation and wrath to the ungodly world."

Verse 8

The apostle comes in these words to instruct and establish Christians in the truth of the coming of the Lord, where we may clearly discern the tenderness and affection wherewith he speaks to them, calling them *beloved;* he had a compassionate concern and a love of good-will for the ungodly wretches who refused to believe divine revelation, but he has a peculiar respect for the true believers, and the remaining ignorance and weakness that the apprehends to be in them make him jealous, and put him on giving them a caution. Here we may observe,

I. The truth which the apostle asserts — *that with the Lord one day is as a thousand years, and a thousand years are as one day.* Though, in the account of men, there is a great deal of difference between a day and a year, and a vast deal more between one day and a thousand years, yet in the account of God, who inhabits eternity, in which there is no succession, there is no difference; for all things past, present, and future, are ever before him, and the delay of a thousand years cannot be so much to him as the deferring of any thing for a day or an hour is to us.

II. The importance of this truth: This is the *one thing* the apostle would not have us ignorant of; a holy awe and reverential fear of God are necessary in order to our worshipping and glorifying him, and a belief of the inconceivable distance between him and us is very proper to beget and maintain that religious fear of the Lord which is the beginning of wisdom. This is a truth that belongs to our peace, and therefore he endeavours that it may not be hidden from our eyes; as it is in the original, *Let not this one thing be hidden from you.* If men have no knowledge or belief of the eternal God, they will be very apt to think him such a one as themselves. Yet how hard is it to conceive of eternity! It is therefore not very easy to attain such a knowledge of God as is absolutely necessary.

Verses 9–10

We are here told that *the Lord is not slack* — he does not delay beyond the appointed time; as God kept the time that he had appointed for the delivering of Israel out of Egypt, to a day (Ex. 12:41), so he will keep to the time appointed in coming to judge the world. What a difference is there between the account which God makes and that which men make! Good men are apt to think God stays beyond the appointed time, that is, the time which they have set for their own and the church's deliverance; but they set one time and God sets another, and he will not fail to keep the day which he has appointed. Ungodly men dare charge a culpable slackness upon God, as if he had slipped the time, and laid aside the thoughts of coming. But the apostle assures us,

I. That what men count slackness is truly *long-suffering,* and that *to us-ward;* it is giving more time to his own people, *whom he has chosen before the foundation of the world,* many of whom are not as yet converted; and those who are in a state of grace and favour with God are to advance in knowledge and holiness, and in the exercise of faith and patience, to abound in good works, doing and suffering what they are called to, that they may bring glory to God, and improve in a meetness for heaven; for God is not willing that any of these should perish, but that all of them should come to repentance. Here observe, 1. Repentance is absolutely necessary in order to salvation. *Except we repent, we shall perish,* Lu. 13:3, 5. 2. God has no delight in the death of sinners: as the punishment of sinners is a torment to his creatures, a merciful God does not take pleasure in it; and though the principal design of God in his long-suffering is the blessedness of those *whom he has chosen to salvation, through sanctification of the spirit, and belief of the truth,* yet his goodness and forbearance do in their own nature invite and call to repentance all those to whom they are exercised; and, if men continue impenitent when God gives them space to repent, he will deal more severely with them, though the great reason why he did not hasten his coming was because he had not accomplished *the number of his elect.* "Abuse not therefore the patience and long-suffering of God, by abandoning yourselves to a course of ungodliness; presume not to go on boldly in the way of sinners, nor to sit down securely in an unconverted impenitent state, as he who said (Mt. 24:48), *My Lord delayeth his coming,* lest he come and surprise you;" for,

II. *The day of the Lord will come as a thief in the night, v.* 10. Here we may observe, 1. The certainty of the day of the Lord: though it is now above sixteen hundred years since this epistle was written, and the day has not yet come, it assuredly will come. God has *appointed a day wherein he will judge the world in righteousness,* and he will keep his appointment. *It is appointed to men once to die, and after this the judgment,* Heb. 9:27. "Settle it therefore in your hearts that the day of the Lord will certainly come, and you shall certainly be called to give an account of all things done in the body, whether good or evil; and let your exact walking before God, and your frequent judging yourselves, evidence your firm belief of a future judgment, when many live as if they were never to give any account at all." 2. The suddenness of this day: It *will come as a thief in the night,* at a time when men are sleeping and secure, and have no manner of apprehension or expectation of the day of the Lord, any more than men have of a thief when they are in a deep sleep, in the dark and silent night. *At midnight there was a cry, Behold, the bridegroom comes,* (Mt. 25:6), and at that time not only the foolish, but also the wise virgins slumbered and slept. *The Lord will come in a day when we look not for him, and an hour when men are not aware.* The time which men think to be the most improper and unlikely, and when therefore they are most secure, will be the time of the Lord's coming. Let us then beware how we in our thoughts and imaginations put that day far away from us; but rather suppose it to be so much nearer in reality, by how much further off it is in the opinion of the ungodly world. 3. The solemnity of this coming. (1.) *The heavens shall pass away with a great noise.* The visible heavens, as unable to abide when the Lord shall come in his glory, shall pass away; they shall undergo a mighty alteration, and this shall be very sudden, and with such a noise as the breaking and tumbling down of so great a fabric must necessarily occasion. (2.) *The elements shall melt with fervent heat.* At this coming of the Lord it shall not only be very *tempestuous round about him,* so that the very heavens shall pass away as in a mighty violent storm, but *a fire shall go before him, that shall melt the elements* of which the creatures are composed. (3.) *The earth also, and all the works that are therein, shall be burnt up.* The earth, and its inhabitants, and all the works that are therein, shall be burnt up. The earth, and its inhabitants, and all the works, whether of nature or art, shall be destroyed. The stately palaces and gardens, and all the desirable things wherein worldly-minded men seek and place their happiness, all of them shall be burnt up; all sorts of creatures which God has made, and all the works of men, must submit, all must pass through the fire, which shall be a consuming fire to all that sin has brought into the world, though it may be a refining fire to the works of God's hand, that the glass of the creation being made much brighter the saints may much better discern the glory of the Lord therein.

And now who can but observe what a difference there will be between the first coming of Christ and the second! Yet that is called *the great and dreadful day of the Lord,* Mal. 4:5. How much more dreadful must this coming to judgment be! May we be so wise as to prepare for it, that it may not be a day of vengeance and destruction unto us. O! what will become of us, if we set our affections on this earth, and make it our portion, seeing all these things shall be burnt up? Look out therefore, and make sure of a happiness beyond this visible world, which must all be melted down.

Verses 11–18

The apostle, having instructed them in the doctrine of Christ's second coming,

I. Takes occasion thence to exhort them to purity and godliness in their whole conversation: all the truths which are revealed in scripture should be improved for our advancement in practical godliness: this is the effect that knowledge must produce, or we are never the better for it. *If you know these things, happy are you if you do them. Seeing all these things must be dissolved, how holy should we be,* that are assured of it, departing from and dying to sin, that has so corrupted and defiled all the visible creation that there is an absolute need of its dissolution! All that was made for man's use is subject to vanity by man's sin: and if the sin of man has brought the visible heavens, and the elements and earth, under a curse, from which they cannot be freed without being dissolved, what an abominable evil is sin, and how much to be hated by us! And, inasmuch as this dissolution is in order to their being restored to their primitive beauty and excellency, how pure and holy should we be, in order to our being fit for the *new heaven and new earth, wherein dwelleth righteousness!* It is a very exact and universal holiness that he exhorts to, not resting in any lower measure or degree, but labouring to be eminent beyond what is commonly attained — holy in God's house and in our own, holy in our worshipping of God and in our conversing with men. All our conversation, whether with high or low, rich or poor, good or bad, friends or enemies, must be holy. We must *keep ourselves unspotted from the world* in all our converses with it. We must be *perfecting holiness in the fear of God,* and in the love of God too. We must *exercise ourselves unto godliness* of all sorts, in all its parts, trusting in God and delighting in God only, who continues the same when the whole visible creation shall be dissolved, devoting ourselves to the service of God, and designing the glorifying and enjoyment of God, who endures for ever; whereas what worldly men delight in and follow after must all be dissolved. Those things which we now see must in a little while pass away, and be no more as they now are: let us look therefore at what shall abide and continue, which, though it be not present, is certain and not far off. This *looking for the day of God* is one of the directions the apostle gives us, in order to our being eminently *holy and godly in all manner of conversation.* "Look for the day of God as what you firmly believe shall come, and what you earnestly long for." *The coming of the day of God* is what every Christian must hope for and earnestly expect; for it is a day when Christ shall *appear in the glory of the Father,* and evidence his divinity and Godhead even to those who counted him a mere man. The first coming of our Lord Jesus Christ, when he *appeared in the form of a servant,* was what the people of God earnestly waited and looked for: that coming was for *the consolation of Israel,* Lu. 2:25. How much more should they wait with expectation and earnestness for his second coming, which will be the day of their complete redemption, and of his most glorious manifestation! Then he shall *come to be admired in his saints, and glorified in all those that believe.* For though it cannot but terrify and affright the ungodly to see the visible heavens all in a flame, and the elements melting, yet the believer, whose *faith is the evidence of things not seen,* can rejoice in hope of more glorious heavens after these have been melted and refined by that dreadful fire which shall burn up all the dross of this visible creation. Here we must take notice, 1. What true Christians look for: *new heavens and a new earth,* in which a great deal more of the wisdom, power and goodness of our great God and Saviour Jesus Christ will be clearly discerned than we are able to discover in what we now see; for in these new heavens and earth, freed from the vanity the former were subject to, and the sin they were polluted with, only righteousness shall dwell; this is to be the habitation of such righteous persons as do righteousness, and are free from the power and pollution of sin; *all the wicked shall be turned into hell;* those only who are clothed with a righteousness of Christ, and sanctified by the Holy Ghost, shall be admitted to dwell in this holy place. 2. What is the ground and foundation of this expectation and hope — *the promise of God.* To look for any thing which God has not promised is presumption; but if our expectations are according to the promise, both as to the things we look for and the time and way of their being brought about, we cannot meet with a disappointment; *for he is faithful who has promised.* "See therefore that you raise and regulate your expectations of all the great things that are to come according to the word of God; and, as to *the new heaven and new earth,* look for them as God has allowed and directed by the passages we have in this portion of scripture how before you, and in Isa. 65:17; 66:22, to which the apostle may be thought to allude."

II. As in *v.* 11 he exhorts to holiness from the consideration that *the heavens and the earth shall be dissolved,* so in *v.* 14 he resumes his exhortation from the consideration that they shall be again renewed. "Seeing you expect the day of God, when our Lord Jesus Christ will appear in his glorious majesty, and these heavens and earth shall be dissolved and melted down, and, being purified and refined, shall be erected and rebuilt, prepare to meet him. It nearly concerns you to see in what state you will be when the Judge of all the world shall come to pass sentence upon men, and to determine how it shall be with them to all eternity. This is the court of judicature whence there lies no appeal; whatever sentence is here passed by this great Judge is irreversible; therefore get ready to *appear before the judgment-seat of Christ:* and see to it,"

1. "That you be *found of him in peace,* in a state of peace and reconciliation with God through Christ, in whom alone God is *reconciling the world to himself.* All that are out of Christ are in a state of enmity, and reject and oppose the Lord and his anointed, and shall therefore *be punished with everlasting destruction from the presence of the Lord, and the glory of his power.* Those whose sins are pardoned and their peace made with God are the only safe and happy people; therefore follow after peace, and that with all." (1.) Peace with God through our Lord Jesus Christ. (2.) Peace in our own consciences, through the Spirit of grace witnessing with our spirits that we are the children of God. (3.) Peace with men, by having a calm and peaceable disposition wrought in us, resembling that of our blessed Lord.

2. That you be *found of Christ without spot, and blameless. Follow after holiness* as well as peace: and even spotless and perfect; we must not only take heed of all spots which are not the spots of God's children (this only prevents our being found of men without spot), we must be pressing towards spotless purity, absolute perfection. Christians must be *perfecting holiness,* that they may be not only blameless before men, but also in the sight of God; and all this deserves and needs the greatest diligence; he who does this work negligently can never do it successfully. "Never expect to be found at that day of God in peace, if you are lazy and idle in this your day, in which we must finish the work that is given us to do. It is only the diligent Christian who will be the happy Christian in the day of the Lord. Our Lord will suddenly come to us, or shortly call us to him; and would you have him find you idle?" Remember there is a curse denounced against him *who does the work of the Lord negligently,* Marg. Jer. 48:10. Heaven will be a sufficient recompence for all our diligence and industry; therefore let us labour and take pains in the work of the Lord; he will certainly reward us if we be diligent in the work he has allotted us; now, that you may be diligent, *account the long-suffering of our Lord to be salvation.* "Does your Lord delay his coming? Do not think this is to give more time to make provision for your lusts, to gratify them; it is so much space to repent and work out your salvation. It proceeds not from a want of concern or compassion for his suffering servants, nor is it designed to give countenance and encouragement to the world of the ungodly, but that men may have time to prepare for eternity. Learn then to make a right use of the patience of our Lord, who does as yet delay his coming. Follow after peace and holiness, or else his coming will be dreadful to you." And inasmuch as it is difficult to prevent men's abuse of God's patience, and engage them in the right improvement thereof, our apostle quotes St. Paul as directing men to make the same good use of the divine forbearance, that in the mouth, or from the pen, of two apostles the truth might be confirmed. And we may here observe with what esteem and affection he speaks of him who had formerly publicly withstood and sharply reproved Peter. If a righteous man smite one who is truly religious, it shall be received as a kindness; and let him reprove, it shall be as an excellent oil, which shall soften and sweeten the good man that is reproved when he does amiss. What an honourable mention does this apostle of the circumcision make of that very man who had openly, *before all, reproved him,* as not walking uprightly according to the truth of the gospel! (1.) He calls him *brother,* whereby he means not only that he is a fellow-christian (in which sense the word brethren is used 1 Th. 5:27), or a fellow-preacher (in which sense Paul calls Timothy the evangelist a *brother,* Col. 1:1), but a fellow-apostle, one who had the same extraordinary commission, immediately from Christ himself, to preach the gospel in every place, and to disciple all nations. Though many seducing teachers denied Paul's apostleship, yet Peter owns him to be an apostle. (2.) He calls him *beloved;* and they being both alike commissioned, and both united in the same service of the same Lord, it would have been very unseemly if they had not been united in affection to one another, for the strengthening of one another's hands, mutually desirous of, and rejoicing in, one another's success. (3.) He mentions Paul as one who had an uncommon measure of wisdom given unto him. He was a person of eminent knowledge in the mysteries of the gospel, and did neither in that nor any other qualification come behind any of all the other apostles. How desirable is it that those who preach the same gospel should treat one another according to the pattern Peter here sets them! It is surely their duty to endeavour, by proper methods, to prevent or remove all prejudices that hinder ministers' usefulness, and to beget and improve the esteem and respect in the minds of people towards their ministers that may promote the success of their labours. And let us also here observe, [1.] The excellent wisdom that was in Paul is said to be *given* him. The understanding and knowledge that qualify men to preach the gospel are the gift of God. We must seek for knowledge, and labour to get understanding, in hopes that it shall be given us from above, while we are diligent in using proper means to attain it. [2.] The apostle imparts to men according as he had received from God. He endeavours to lead others as far as he himself was led into the knowledge of the mysteries of the gospel. He is not an intruder into the things he had not seen or been fully assured of, and yet he does not fail to declare the whole counsel of God, Acts 20:27. [3.] The epistles which were written by the apostle of the Gentiles, and directed to those Gentiles who believed in Christ, are designed for the instruction and edification of those who from among the Jews were brought to believe in Christ; for it is generally thought that what is here alluded to is contained in the epistle to the Romans (*ch.* 2:4), though in all his epistles there are some things that refer to one or other of the subjects treated of in this and the foregoing chapter; and it cannot seem strange that those who were pursuing the same general design should in their epistles insist upon the same things. But the apostle Peter proceeds to tell us that in those things which are to be met with in Paul's epistles there are some things hard to be understood. Among the variety of subjects treated of in scripture, some are not easy to be understood because of their own obscurity, such are prophecies; others cannot be so easily understood because of their excellency and sublimity, as the mysterious doctrines; and others are with difficulty taken in because of the weakness of men's minds, such are the things of the Spirit of God, mentioned 1 Co. 2:14. And here the unlearned and unstable make wretched work; for they wrest and torture the scriptures, to make them speak what the Holy Ghost did not intend. Those who are not well instructed and well established in the truth are in great danger of perverting the word of God. Those who have heard and learned of the Father are best secured from misunderstanding and misapplying any part of the word of God; and, where there is a divine power to establish as well as to instruct men in divine truth, persons are effectually secured from falling into errors. How great a blessing this is we learn by observing what is the pernicious consequence of the errors that ignorant and unstable men fall into — even their own destruction. Errors in particular concerning the holiness and justice of God are the utter ruin of multitudes of men. Let us therefore earnestly pray for the Spirit of God to instruct us in the truth, that we may know it as it is in Jesus, and have our hearts established with grace, that we may stand firm and unshaken, even in the most stormy times, when others are tossed to and fro with every wind of doctrine.

III. The apostle gives them a word of caution, *v.* 17, 18, where,

1. He intimates that the knowledge we have of these things should make us very wary and watchful, inasmuch as there is a twofold danger, *v.* 17. (1.) We are in great danger *of* being seduced, and turned away from the truth. The unlearned and unstable, and they are very numerous, do generally wrest the scripture. Many who have the scriptures and read them do not understand what they read; and too many of those who have a right understanding of the sense and meaning of the word are not established in the belief of the truth, and all these are liable to fall into error. Few attain to the knowledge and acknowledgment of doctrinal Christianity; and fewer find, so as to keep in the way of practical godliness, which is the narrow way, which only leadeth unto life. There must be a great deal of self-denial and suspicion of ourselves, and submitting to the authority of Christ Jesus our great prophet, before we can heartily receive all the truths of the gospel, and therefore we are in great danger of rejecting the truth. (2.) We are in great danger *by* being seduced; for, [1.] So far as we are turned from the truth *so far are we turned out of the way to true blessedness,* into the path which leads to destruction. If men corrupt the word of God, it tends to their own utter ruin. [2.] When men wrest the word of God, *they fall into the error of the wicked,* men without law, who keep to no rules, set no bounds to themselves, a sort of freethinkers, which the psalmist detests. Ps. 119:113, *I hate vain thoughts, but thy law do I love.* Whatever opinions and thoughts of men are not conformable to the law of God, and warranted by it, the good man disclaims and abhors; they are the conceits and counsels of the ungodly, who have forsaken God's law, and, if we imbibe their opinions, we shall too soon imitate their practices. [3.] Those who are led away by error *fall from their own stedfastness.* They are wholl[y] unhinged and unsettled, and know not where to rest, but a[re] at the greatest uncertainty, like a wave of the sea, driven [...]

the wind and tossed. It nearly concerns us therefore to be upon our guard, seeing the danger is so great.

2. That we may the better avoid being led away, the apostle directs us what to do, *v.* 18. And, (1.) We must *grow in grace.* He had in the beginning of the epistle exhorted us to add one grace to another, and here he advises us to grow in all grace, in faith, and virtue, and knowledge. By how much the stronger grace is in us, by so much the more stedfast shall we be in the truth. (2.) We must grow *in the knowledge of our Lord Jesus Christ.* "Follow on to know the Lord. Labour to know him more clearly and more fully, to know more of Christ and to know him to better purpose, so as to be more like him and to love him better." This is the knowledge of Christ the apostle Paul reached after and desired to attain, Phil. 3:10. Such a knowledge of Christ as conforms us more to him, and endears him more to us, must needs be of great use to us, to preserve us from falling off in times of general apostasy; and those who experience this effect of the knowledge of the Lord and Saviour Jesus Christ will, upon receiving such grace from him, give thanks and praise to him, and join with our apostle in saying, *To him be glory both now and for ever. Amen.*

AN EXPOSITION, WITH PRACTICAL OBSERVATIONS, OF THE FIRST EPISTLE GENERAL OF JOHN

Though the continued tradition of the church attests that this epistle came from John the apostle, yet we may observe some other evidence that will confirm (or with some perhaps even outweigh) the certainty of that tradition. It should seem that the penman was one of the apostolical college by the sensible palpable assurance he had of the truth of the Mediator's person in his human nature: *That which we have heard, which we have seen with our eyes, which we have looked upon, and our hands have handled, of the Word of life, v.* 1. Here he takes notice of the evidence the Lord gave to Thomas of his resurrection, by calling him to feel the prints of the nails and of the spear, which is recorded by John. And he must have been one of the disciples present when the Lord came on the same day in which he arose from the dead, and showed them his hands and his side, Jn. 20:20. But, that we may be assured which apostle this was, there is scarcely a critic or competent judge of diction, or style of argument and spirit, but will adjudge this epistle to the writer of that gospel that bears the name of the apostle John. They wonderfully agree in the titles and characters of the Redeemer: *The Word, the Life, the Light; his name was the Word of God.* Compare 1:1 and 5:7 with Jn. 1:1 and Rev. 19:13. They agree in the commendation of God's love to us (3:9; 4:7; and 5:1; Jn. 3:5, 6. Lastly (to add no more instances, which may be easily seen in comparing this epistle with that gospel), they agree in the allusion to, or application of, that passage in that gospel which relates (and which alone relates) the issuing of water and blood out of the Redeemer's opened side: *This is he that came by water and blood,* 5:6. Thus the epistle plainly appears to flow from the same pen as that gospel did. Now I know not that the text, or the intrinsic history of any of the gospels, gives us such assurance of its writer or penman as that ascribed to John plainly does. There (viz. 21:24) the sacred historian thus notifies himself: *This is the disciple that testifieth of these things and wrote these things; and we know that his testimony is true.* Now who is this disciple, but he concerning whom Peter asked, *What shall this man do?* And concerning whom the Lord answered, *If I will that he tarry till I come, what is that to thee?* (*v.* 22). And who (*v.* 20) is described by these three characters: — 1. *That he is the disciple whom Jesus loved,* the Lord's peculiar friend. 2. *That he also leaned on his breast at supper.* 3. That he said unto him, *Lord, who is he that betrayeth thee?* As sure then as it is that that disciple was John, so sure may the church be that that gospel and this epistle came from the beloved John.

The epistle is styled *general,* as being not inscribed to any particular church; it is, as a circular letter (or visitation charge), sent to divers churches (some say of Parthia), in order to confirm them in their stedfast adherence to the Lord Christ, and the sacred doctrines concerning his person and office, against seducers; and to instigate them to adorn that doctrine by love to God and man, and particularly to each other, as being descended from God, united by the same head, and travelling towards the same eternal life.

CHAPTER 1

Evidence given concerning Christ's person and excellency (*v.* 1, 2). The knowledge thereof gives us communion with God and Christ (*v.* 3), and joy (*v.* 4). A description of God (*v.* 5). How we are thereupon to walk (*v.* 6). The benefit of such walking (*v.* 7). The way to forgiveness (*v.* 9). The evil of denying our sin (*v.* 8–10).

Verses 1–4

The apostle omits his name and character (as also the author to the Hebrews does) either out of humility, or as being willing that the Christian reader should be swayed by the light and weight of the things written rather than by the name that might recommend them. And so he begins,

I. With an account or character of the Mediator's person. He is the great subject of the gospel, the foundation and object of our faith and hope, the bond and cement that unite us unto God. He should be well known; and he is represented here, 1. *As the Word of life, v.* 1. In the gospel these two are disjoined, and he is called first *the Word,* Jn. 1:1, and afterwards *Life,* intimating, withal, that he is *intellectual life. In him was life, and that life was* (efficiently and objectively) *the light of men,* Jn. 1:4. Here both are conjoined: *The Word of life,* the vital Word. In that he is the Word, it is intimated that he is the Word of some person or other; and that is God, even the Father. *He is the Word of God,* and so he is intimated to issue from the Father, as truly (though not in the same manner) as a word (or speech, which is a train of words) from a speaker. But he is not a mere vocal word, a bare *logos prophorikos,* but a vital one: *the Word of life,* the living word; and thereupon, 1. *As eternal life.* His duration shows his excellency. He was from eternity; and so is, in scripture-account, necessary, essential, uncreated life. That the apostle speaks of his eternity, *à parte ante* (as they say) and as *from everlasting,* seems evident in that he speaks of him as he was in and from the beginning; when he was then with the Father, before his manifestation to us, yea, before the making of all things that were make; as Jn. 1:2, 3. So that he is the eternal, vital, intellectual Word of the eternal living Father. 3. *As life manifested* (*v.* 2), manifested in the flesh, manifested to us. The eternal life would assume mortality, would put on flesh and blood (in the entire human nature), and so [illegible]well among us and converse with us, Jn. 1:14. Here were [illegible]scension and kindness indeed, that eternal life (a per[illegible]ernal essential life) should come to visit mortals, and [illegible]eternal life for them, and then confer it on them! [illegible] the evidences and convictive assurances that the apostle and his brethren had of the Mediator's presence and converse in this world. There were sufficient demonstrations of the reality of his abode here, and of the excellency and dignity of his person in the way of his manifestation. *The life, the word of life, the eternal life,* as such, could not be seen and felt; but the life manifested might be, and was so. The life was clothed with flesh, put on the state and habit of abased human nature, and as such gave sensible proof of its existence and transactions here. The divine life, or Word incarnate, presented and evinced itself to the very senses of the apostles. As, 1. To their ears: *That which we have heard, v.* 1, 3. The life assumed a mouth and tongue, that he might utter words of life. The apostles not only heard of him, but they heard him himself. Above three years might they attend his ministry, be auditors of his public sermons and private expositions (for he expounded them in his house), and be charmed with the words of him who spoke as never man spoke before or since. The divine word would employ the ear, and the ear should be devoted to the word of life. And it was meet that those who were to be his representatives and imitators to the world should be personally acquainted with his ministrations. 2. To their eyes: *That which we have seen with our eyes, v.* 1–3. The Word would become visible, would not only be heard, but seen, seen publicly, privately, at a distance and at nearest approach, which may be intimated in the expression, *with our eyes* — with all the use and exercise that we could make of our eyes. We saw him in his life and ministry, saw him in his transfiguration on the mount, hanging, bleeding, dying, and dead, upon the cross, and we saw him after his return from the grave and resurrection from the dead. His apostles must be eye-witnesses as well as ear-witnesses of him. *Wherefore, of these men that have accompanied with us all the time that the Lord Jesus went in and out among us, beginning from the baptism of John, must one be ordained to be a witness with us of his resurrection,* Acts 1:21, 22. *And we were eye-witnesses of his majesty,* 2 Pt. 1:16. 3. To their internal sense, to the eyes of their mind; for so (possibly) may the next clause be interpreted: *Which we have looked upon.* This may be distinguished from the foregoing perception, *seeing with the eyes;* and may be the same with what the apostle says in his gospel (*ch.* 1:14), *And we beheld — etheasametha, his glory, the glory as of the only-begotten of the Father.* The word is not applied to the immediate object of the eye, but to that which was rationally collected from what they saw. "What we have well discerned, contemplated, and viewed, what we have well known of this Word of life, we report to you." The senses are to be the informers of the mind. 4. To their hands and sense of feeling: *And our hands have handled* (touched and felt) *of the Word of life.* This surely refers to the full conviction our Lord afforded his apostles of the truth, reality, solidity, and organization of his body, after his resurrection from the dead. When he showed them his hands and his side, it is probable that he gave them leave to touch him; at least, he knew of Thomas's unbelief, and his professed resolution too not to believe, till he had found and felt the places and signatures of the wounds by which he died. Accordingly at the next congress he called Thomas, in the presence of the rest, to satisfy the very curiosity of his unbelief. And probably others of them did so too. *Our hands have handled of the Word of life.* The invisible life and Word was no despiser of the testimony of sense. Sense, in its place and sphere, is a means that God has appointed, and the Lord Christ has employed, for our information. Our Lord took care to satisfy (as far as might be) all the senses of his apostles, that they might be the more authentic witnesses of him to the world. Those that apply all this to the hearing of the gospel lose the variety of sensations here mentioned, and the propriety of the expressions, as well as the reason of their inculcation and repetition here: *That which we have seen and heard declare we unto you, v.* 3. The apostles could not be deceived in such long and various exercise of their sense. Sense must minister to reason and judgment; and reason and judgment must minister to the reception of the Lord Jesus Christ and his gospel. The rejection of the Christian revelation is at last resolved into the rejection of sense itself. *He upbraided them with their unbelief and hardness of heart, because they believed not those who had seen him after he had risen,* Mk. 16:14.

III. With a solemn assertion and attestation of these grounds and evidences of the Christian truth and doctrine. The apostles publish these assurances for our satisfaction: *We bear witness, and show unto you, v.* 2. *That which we have seen and heard declare we unto you, v.* 3. It became the apostles to open to the disciples the evidence by which they were led, the reasons by which they were constrained to proclaim and propagate the Christian doctrine in the world. Wisdom and integrity obliged them to demonstrate that it was not either private fancy or a cunningly-devised fable that they presented to the world. Evident truth would open their mouths, and force a public profession. *We cannot but speak the things which we have seen and heard,* Acts 4:20. It concerned the disciples to be well assured of the truth of the institution they had embraced. They should see the evidences of their holy religion. It fears not the light, nor the most judicious examination. It is able to afford rational conviction and solid persuasion of mind and conscience. *I would that you knew what great conflict* (or concern of mind) *I have for you, and for those at Laodicea, and for as many as have not seen my face in the flesh, that their hearts might be knit together in love, and unto all riches of full assurance of understanding, to the acknowledgment of the mystery of God, even of the Father, and of Christ,* Col. 2:1, 2.

IV. With the reason of the apostle's exhibiting and asserting this summary of sacred faith, and this breviate of evidence attending it. This reason is twofold: —

1. That the believers of it may be advanced to the same happiness with them (with the apostles themselves): *That which we have seen and heard declare we unto you, that you may have fellowship with us, v.* 3. The apostle means not personal fellowship nor consociation in the same church-administrations, but such as is consistent with personal distance from each other. It is communion with heaven, and in blessings that come thence and tend thither. "This we declare and testify, that you may share with us in our privileges and happiness." Gospel spirits (or those that are made happy by gospel grace) would fain have others happy too. We see, also, there is a fellowship or communion that runs through the whole church of God. There may be some personal distinctions and peculiarities, but there is a communion (or common participation of privilege and dignity) belonging to all saints, from the highest apostle to the lowest believer. As there is the same precious faith, there are the same precious promises dignifying and crowning that faith and the same precious blessings and glories enriching and filling those promises. Now that believers may be ambitious of this communion, that they may be instigated to retain and hold fast the faith that is the means of such communion, that the apostles also may manifest their love to the disciples in assisting them to the same communion with themselves, they indicate what it is and where it is: *And truly our fellowship* (or communion) *is with the Father and his Son Jesus Christ.* We have communion with the Father, and with the Son of the Father (as 2 Jn. 3, he is most emphatically styled) in our happy relation to them, in our receiving heavenly blessings from them, and in our spiritual converse with them. We have now such supernatural conversation with God and the Lord Christ as is an earnest and foretaste of our everlasting abode with them, and enjoyment of them, in the heavenly glory. See to what the gospel revelation tends — to advance us far above sin and earth and to carry us to blessed communion with the Father and the Son. See for what end the eternal life was made flesh — that he might advance us to eternal life in communion with the Father and himself. See how far those live beneath the dignity, use, and end of the Christian faith and institution, who have not spiritual blessed communion with the Father and his Son Jesus Christ.

2. That believers may be enlarged and advanced in holy joy: *And these things write we unto you that your joy may be full, v.* 4. The gospel dispensation is not properly a dispensation of fear, sorrow, and dread, but of peace and joy. Terror and astonishment may well attend mount Sinai, but exultation and joy mount Zion, where appears *the eternal Word, the eternal life,* manifested in our flesh. The mystery of the Christian religion is directly calculated for the joy of mortals. It should be joy to us that the eternal Son should come to seek and save us, that he has made a full atonement for our sins, that he has conquered sin and death and hell, that he lives as our Intercessor and Advocate with the Father, and that he will come again to perfect and glorify his persevering believers. And therefore those live beneath the use and end of the Christian revelation who are not filled with spiritual joy. Believers should rejoice in their happy relation to God, as his sons and heirs, his beloved and adopted, — in their happy relation to the Son of the Father, as being members of his beloved body, and coheirs with himself, — in the pardon of their sins, the sanctification of their natures, the adoption of their persons, and the prospect of grace and glory that will be revealed at the return of their Lord and head from heaven. Were they confirmed in their holy faith, how would they rejoice! *The disciples were filled with joy, and with the Holy Ghost,* Acts 13:52.

Verses 5–7

The apostle, having declared the truth and dignity of the author of the gospel, brings a message or report from him, from which a just conclusion is to be drawn for the consideration and conviction of the professors of religion, or professed entertainers of this glorious gospel.

I. Here is the message or report that the apostle avers to come from the Lord Jesus: *This then is the message which we have heard of him* (*v.* 5), of his Son Jesus Christ. As he was the immediate sender of the apostles, so he is the principal person spoken of in the preceding context, and the next antecedent also to whom the pronoun *him* can relate. The apostles and apostolical ministers are the messengers of the Lord Jesus; it is their honour, the chief they pretend to, to bring his mind and messages to the world and to the churches. This is the wisdom and present dispensation of the Lord Jesus, to send his messages to us by persons like ourselves. He that put on human nature will honour earthen vessels. It was the ambition of the apostles to be found faithful, and faithfully to deliver the errands and messages they had received. What was communicated to them they were solicitous to impart: *This then is the message which we have heard of him, and declare unto you.* A message from the Word of life, from the eternal Word, we should gladly receive: and the present one is this (relating to the nature of God whom we are to serve, and with whom we should covet all indulged communion) — *That God is light, and in him is no darkness at all, v.* 5. This report asserts the excellency of the divine nature. He is all that beauty and perfection that can be represented to us by light. He is a self-active uncompounded spirituality, purity, wisdom, holiness, and glory. And then the absoluteness and fulness of that excellency and perfection. There is no defect or imperfection, no mixture of any thing alien or contrary to absolute excellency, no mutability nor capacity of any decay in him: *In him is no darkness at all, v.* 5. Or this report may more immediately relate to what is usually called the moral perfection of the divine nature, what we are to imitate, or what is more directly to influence us in our gospel work. And so it will comprehend the holiness of God, the absolute purity of his nature and will, his penetrative knowledge (particularly of hearts), his jealousy and injustice, which burn a a most bright and vehement flame. It is meet that to this dark world the great God should be represented as pure and perfect light. It is the Lord Jesus that best of all opens to us the name and nature of the unsearchable God: *The only-begotten, who is in the bosom of the Father, the same hath declared him.* It is the prerogative of the Christian revelation to bring us the most noble, the most august and agreeable account of the blessed God, such as is most suitable to the light of reason and what is demonstrable thereby, most suitable to the magnificence of his works round about us, and to the nature and office of him that is the supreme administrator, governor, and judge of the world. What more (relating to and comprehensive of all such perfection) could be included in one word than in this, *God is light, and in him is no darkness at all?* Then,

II. There is a just conclusion to be drawn from this message and report, and that for the consideration and conviction of professors of religion, or professed entertainers of this gospel. This conclusion issues into two branches: — 1. For the conviction of such professors as have no true fellowship with God: *If we say we have fellowship with him, and walk in darkness, we lie, and do not the truth.* It is known that to walk, in scripture account, is to order and frame the course and actions of the moral life, that is, of the life so far as it is capable of subjection to the divine law. *To walk in darkness* is to live and act according to such ignorance, error, and erroneous practice, as are contrary to the fundamental dictates of our holy religion. Now there may be those who may pretend to great attainments and enjoyments in religion; they may profess to have communion with God; and yet their lives may be irreligious, immoral, and impure. To such the apostle would not fear to give the lie: *They lie, and do not the truth.* They belie God; for he holds no heavenly fellowship or intercourse with unholy souls. What communion hath light with darkness? They belie themselves, or lie concerning themselves; for they have no such communications from God nor accesses to him. There is no truth in their profession nor in their practice, or their practice gives their profession and pretences the lie, and demonstrates the folly and falsehood of them. 2. For the conviction and consequent satisfaction of those that are near to God: *But, if we walk in the light, we have fellowship one with another, and the blood of Jesus Christ his Son cleanseth us from all sin.* As the blessed God is the eternal boundless light, and the Mediator is, from him, the light of the world, so the Christian institution is the great luminary that appears in our sphere, and shines here below. A conformity to this in spirit and practice demonstrates fellowship or communion with God. Those that so walk show that they know God, that they have received of the Spirit of God, and that the divine impress or image is stamped upon their souls. *Then we have fellowship one with another,* they with us and we with them, and both with God, in his blessed or beatific communications to us. And this is one of those beatific communications to us — that his Son's blood or death is applied or imputed to us: *The blood of Jesus Christ his Son cleanseth us from all sin.* The eternal life, the eternal Son, hath put on flesh and blood, and so became Jesus Christ. Jesus Christ hath shed his blood for us, or died to wash us from our sins in his own blood. His blood applied to us discharges us from the guilt of all sin, both original and actual, inherent and committed: and so far we stand righteous in his sight; and not only so, but his blood procures for us those sacred influences by which sin is to be subdued more and more, till it is quite abolished, Gal. 3:13, 14.

Verses 8–10

Here, I. The apostle, having supposed that even those of this heavenly communion have yet their sin, proceeds here to justify that supposition, and this he does by showing the dreadful consequences of denying it, and that in two particulars: — 1. *If we say, We have no sin, we deceive ourselves, and the truth is not in us, v.* 8. We must beware of deceiving ourselves in denying or excusing our sins. The more we see them the more we shall esteem and value the remedy. *If we deny them, the truth is not in us,* either the truth that is contrary to such denial (we lie in denying our sin), or the truth of religion, is not in us. The Christian religion is the religion of sinners, of such as have sinned, and in whom sin in some measure still dwells. The Christian life is a life of continued repentance, humiliation for and mortification of sin, of continual faith in, thankfulness for, and love to the Redeemer, and hopeful joyful expectation of a day of glorious redemption, in which the believer shall be fully and finally acquitted, and sin abolished for ever. 2. *If we say, We have not sinned, we make him a liar, and his word is not in us, v.* 10. The denial of our sin not only deceives ourselves, but reflects dishonour upon God. It challenges his veracity. He has abundantly testified of, and testified against, the sin of the world. *And the Lord said in his heart* (determined thus with himself), *I will not again curse the ground* (as he had then lately done) *for man's sake; for* (or, with the learned bishop Patrick, *though) the imagination of man's heart is evil from his youth,* Gen. 8:21. But God has given his testimony to the continued sin and sinfulness of the world, by providing a sufficient effectual sacrifice for sin, that will be needed in all ages, and to the continued sinfulness of believers themselves by requiring them continually to confess their sins, and apply themselves by faith to the blood of that sacrifice. And therefore, if we say either that we have not sinned or do not yet sin, *the word of God is not in us,* neither in our minds, as to the acquaintance we should have with it, nor in our hearts, as to the practical influence it should have upon us.

II. The apostle then instructs the believer in the way to the continued pardon of his sin. Here we have, 1. His duty in order thereto: *If we confess our sins, v.* 9. Penitent confession and acknowledgment of sin are the believer's business, and the means of his deliverance from his guilt. And, 2. His encouragement thereto, and assurance of the happy issue. This is the veracity, righteousness, and clemency of God, to whom he makes such confession: *He is faithful and just to forgive us our sins, and to cleanse us from all unrighteousness, v.* 9. God is faithful to his covenant and word, wherein he has promised forgiveness to penitent believing confessors. He is just to himself and his glory who has provided such a sacrifice, by which his righteousness is declared in the justification of sinners. He is just to his Son who has not only sent him for such service, but promised to him that those who come through him shall be forgiven on his account. *By his knowledge* (by the believing apprehension of him) *shall my righteous servant justify many,* Isa. 53:11. He is clement and gracious also, and so will forgive, to the contrite confessor, all his sins, cleanse him from the guilt of all unrighteousness and in due time deliver him from the power and practice

CHAPTER 2

Here the apostle encourages against sins of infirmity (*v.* 1, 2), shows the true knowledge and love of God (*v.* 3–6), renews the precept of fraternal love (*v.* 7–11), addresses the several ages of Christians (*v.* 12–14), warns against worldly love (*v.* 15–17), against seducers (*v.* 18, 19), shows the security of true Christians (*v.* 20–27), and advises to abide in Christ (*v.* 28, 29).

Verses 1–2

These verses relate to the concluding subject of the foregoing chapter, in which the apostle proceeds upon the supposition of the real Christian's sin. And here he gives them both dissuasion and support.

1. Dissuasion. He would leave no room for sin: *"My little children, these things write I unto you, that you sin not, v.* 1. The design or purport of this letter, the design of what I have just said concerning communion with God and the overthrow of it by an irreligious course, is to dissuade and drive you from sin." See the familiar affectionate compellation with which he introduces his admonition: *My little children,* children as having perhaps been begotten by his gospel, *little children* as being much beneath him in age and experience, *my little children,* as being dear to him in the bonds of the gospel. Certainly the gospel most prevailed where and when such ministerial love most abounded. Or perhaps the judicious reader will find reason to think that the apostle's meaning in this dissuasion or caution is this, or amounts to this reading: *These things write I unto you, not that you sin.* And so the words will look back to what he had said before concerning the assured pardon of sin: *God is faithful and just to forgive us our sins,* etc., *ch.* 1:9. And so the words are a preclusion of all abuse of such favour and indulgence. "Though sins will be forgiven to penitent confessors, yet this I write, not to encourage you in sin, but upon another account." Or this clause will look forward to what the apostle is going to say about the Advocate for sinners: and so it is a prolepsis, a prevention of like mistake or abuse: *"These things write I unto you, not that you sin,* but that you may see your remedy for sin." And so the following particle (as the learned know) may be rendered adversatively: *But, if a man sin,* he may know his help and cure. And so we see,

II. The believer's support and relief in case of sin: *And (or but) if any man sin* (any of us, or of our foresaid communion), *We have we an Advocate with the Father,* etc., *v.* 1. Believers themselves, those that are advanced to a happy gospel-state, have yet their sins. There is a great distinction therefore between the sinners that are in the world. There are Christianized (such as are instated in the sacred saving privileges of Christ's mystical or spiritual body) and unchristianized, converted and unconverted sinners. There are some who, though they really sin, yet, in comparison with others, are said *not to sin,* as *ch.* 3:9. Believers, as they have an atonement applied unto them at their entrance into a state of pardon and justification, so they have an Advocate in heaven still to continue to them that state, and procure their continued forgiveness. And this must be the support, satisfaction, and refuge of believers (or real Christians) in or upon their sins: *We have an Advocate.* The original name is sometimes given to the Holy Ghost, and then it is rendered, *the Comforter.* He acts within us; he puts pleas and arguments into our hearts and mouths; and so is our advocate, by teaching us to intercede for ourselves. But here is an advocate without us, in heaven and with the Father. The proper office and business of an advocate is with the judge; with him he pleads the client's cause. The Judge with whom our advocate pleads is the Father, his Father and ours. He who was our Judge in the legal court (the court of the violated law) is our Father in the gospel court, the court of heaven and of grace. His throne or tribunal is the mercy-seat. And he that is our Father is also our Judge, the supreme arbitrator of our state and circumstances, either for life or death, for time or eternity. *You have come — to God, the Judge of all,* Heb. 12:23. That believers may be encouraged to hope that their cause will go well, as their Judge is represented to them in the relation of a Father, so their advocate is recommended to them upon these considerations: — 1. By his person and personal names. *It is Jesus Christ the Son of the Father,* one anointed by the Father for the whole office of mediation, the whole work of salvation, and consequently for that of the intercessor or advocate. 2. By his qualification for the office. *It is Jesus Christ the righteous,* the righteous one in the court and sight of the Judge. This is not so necessary in another advocate. Another advocate (or an advocate in another court) may be an unjust person himself, and yet may have a just cause (and the cause of a just person in that case) to plead, and may accordingly carry his cause. But here the clients are guilty; their innocence and legal righteousness cannot be pleaded; their sin must be confessed or supposed. It is the advocate's own righteousness that he must plead for the criminals. He has been righteous to the death, righteous for them; he has brought in everlasting righteousness. This the Judge will not deny. Upon this score he pleads, that the clients' sins may not be imputed to them. 3. By the plea he has to make, the ground and basis of his advocacy: *And he is the propitiation for our sins, v.* 2. He is the expiatory victim, the propitiatory sacrifice that has been offered to the Judge for all our offences against his majesty, and law, and government. In vain do the professors of Rome distinguish between and advocate of redemption and an advocate of intercession, or a mediator of such different service. The Mediator of intercession, the Advocate for us, is the Mediator of redemption, the propitiation for our sins. It is his propitiation that he pleads. And we might be apt to suppose that his blood had lost its value and efficacy if no mention had been made of it in heaven since the time it was shed. But now we see it is of esteem there, since it is continually represented in the intercession of the great advocate (the attorney-general) for the church of God. *He ever lives to make intercession for those that come to God through him.* 4. By the extent of his plea, the latitude of his propitiation. It is not confined to one nation; and not particularly to the ancient Israel of God: *He is the propitiation for our sins; and not for ours only* (not only for the sins of us Jews, us that are Abraham's seed according to the flesh), *but also for those of the whole world* (*v.* 2); not only for the past, or us present believers, but for the sins of all who shall hereafter believe on him or come to God through him. The extent and intent of the Mediator's death reach to all tribes, nations, and countries. As he is the only, so he is the universal atonement and propitiation for all that are saved and brought home to God, and to his favour and forgiveness.

Verses 3–6

These verses may seem to relate to the seventh verse of the former chapter, between which and these verses there occurred an incidental discourse concerning the believer's duty and relief in case of sin, occasioned by the mention of one of the believer's privileges — his being cleansed from sin by the Mediator's blood. In that verse the apostle asserts the beneficial consequence of *walking in the light: "We have then fellowship with one another,* such divine fellowship and communion as are the prerogative of the church of Christ." Here now succeeds the trial or test of our light and of our love.

I. The trial of our light: *And hereby we do know that we know him, if we keep his commandments, v.* 3. Divine light and knowledge are the beauty and improvement of the mind; it becomes the disciples of the Mediator to be persons of wisdom and understanding. Young Christians are apt to magnify their new light and applaud their own knowledge, especially if they have been suddenly or in a short time communicated; and old ones are apt to suspect the sufficiency and fulness of their knowledge; they lament that they know God, and Christ, and the rich contents of his gospel, no more: but here is the evidence of the soundness of our knowledge, if it constrain us to *keep God's commandments.* Each perfection of his nature enforces his authority; the wisdom of his counsels, the riches of his grace, the grandeur of his works, recommend his law and government. A careful conscientious obedience to his commands shows that the apprehension and knowledge of these things are graciously impressed upon the soul; and therefore it must follow in the reverse that *he that saith, I know him, and keepeth not his commandments, is a liar, and the truth is not in him, v.* 4. Professors of the truth are often ashamed of their ignorance, or ashamed to own it; they frequently pretend to great attainments in the knowledge of divine mysteries: *Thou makest thy boast of God, and knowest his will, and approvest* (in thy rational judgment) *the things that are more excellent, being instructed out of the law and art confident that thou thyself art* (or art fit to be) *a guide to the blind,* etc., Rom. 2:17, etc. But what knowledge of God can that be which sees not that he is most worthy of the most entire and intense obedience? And, if that be seen and known, how vain and superficial is even this knowledge when it sways not the heart unto obedience? A disobedient life is the confutation and shame of pretended religious knowledge; it gives the lie to such boasts and pretences, and shows that there is neither religion nor honesty in them.

II. The trial of our love: *But whoso keepeth his word in him verily is the love of God perfected; hereby know we that we are in him, v.* 5. To keep the word of God, or of Christ, is sacredly to attend thereto in all the conduct and motion of life; in him that does so is the love of God perfected. Possibly, some may here understand God's love to us; and doubtless his love to us cannot be perfected (or obtain its perfect design and fruit) without our practical observance of his word. We are chosen, to be holy and blameless before him in love; we are *redeemed, to be a peculiar people, zealous of good works;* we are pardoned and justified, that we may be partakers of larger measures of the divine Spirit for sanctification; we are sanctified, that we may walk in ways of holiness and obedience: no act of divine love that here terminates upon us obtains its proper tendency, issue, and effect, without our holy attendance to God's word. But the phrase rather denotes here our love to God; so *v.* 15, *The love of (to) the Father is not in him;* so *ch.* 3:17, *How dwelleth the love of (to) God in him?* Now light is to kindle love; and love must and will keep the word of God; it enquires wherein the beloved may be pleased and served, and, finding he will be so by observance of his declared will, there it employs and exerts itself; there love is demonstrated; there it has its perfect (or complete) exercise, operation, and delight; and hereby (by this dutiful attendance to the will of God, or Christ) *we know that we are in him* (*v.* 5), we know that we belong to him, and that we are united to him by that Spirit which elevates and assists us to this obedience; and if we acknowledge our relation to him, and our union with him, it must have this continued enforcement upon us: *He that saith he abideth in him ought himself to walk even as he walked, v.* 6. The Lord Christ was an inhabitant of this world, and walked here below; here he gave a shining example of absolute obedience to God. Those who profess to be on his side, and to abide with him, must walk with him, walk after his pattern and example. The partisans of the several sects of philosophers of old paid great regard to the dictates and practice of their respective teachers and sect-masters; much more should the Christian, he who professes to abide in and with Christ, aim to resemble his infallible Master and head, and conform to his course and prescriptions: *Then are you my friends if you do whatsoever I command you,* Jn. 15:14.

Verses 7–11

The seventh verse may be supposed either to look backward to what immediately preceded (and then it is *walking as Christ walked* that is here represented as *no new, but an old commandment;* it is that which the apostles would certainly inculcate wherever they brought Christ's gospel), or to look forward to what the apostle is now going to recommend, and that is the law of fraternal love; this is the message *heard from the beginning* (*ch.* 3:11), and *the old commandment,* 2 Jn. 5. Now, while the apostle addresses himself to the recommendation of such a practice, he is ready to give an instance thereof in his affectionate appellation: *"Brethren,* you who are dear to me in the bond of that love to which I would solicit you;" and so the precept of fraternal love is recommended,

I. As an old one: *I write no new commandment unto you, but an old commandment, which you had from the beginning, v.* 7. The precept of love must be as old as human nature; but it might admit divers enactions, enforcements, and motives. In the state of innocence, had human nature then been propagated, men must have loved one another as being of one blood, made to dwell on the earth, as being God's offspring, and bearing his image. In the state of sin and promised recovery, they must love one another as related to God their Maker, as related to each other by blood, and as partners in the same hope. When the Hebrews were peculiarly incorporated, they must accordingly love each other, as being the privileged people, whose were the covenants and the adoption, and of whose race the Messiah and head of the church must spring; and the law of love must be conveyed with new obligations to the new Israel of God, to the gospel church, and so it is the *old commandment,* or the word which the children of the gospel Israel have heard from the beginning, *v.* 7.

II. As a new one: *"Again,* to constrain you to this duty the more, *a new commandment I write unto you,* the law of the new society, the Christian corporation, *which thing is true in him,* the matter of which was first true in and concerning the head of it; the truth of it was first and was abundantly in him; *he loved the church, and gave himself for it:* and it is true *in you;* this law is in some measure written upon your hearts;; you are taught of God to love one another, and that *because*" (or since, or forasmuch as) *"the darkness is past,* the darkness of your prejudiced unconverted (whether Jewish or Gentile) minds, your deplorable ignorance of God and of Christ is now past, *and the true light now shineth (v.* 8); *the light* of evangelical revelation hath shone with life and efficacy into your hearts; hence you have seen the excellency of Christian love, and the fundamental obligation thereto." Hence we see that the fundamentals (and particularly the fundamental precepts) of the Christian religion may be represented either as new or old; the reformed doctrine, or doctrine of religion in the reformed churches, is new and old — new, as taught after long darkness, by the lights of the reformation, new as purged from the adulterations of Rome; but old as having been taught and *heard from the beginning.* We should see that that grace or virtue which was true in Christ be true also in us; we should be conformable to our head. The more our darkness is past, and gospel light shines unto us, the deeper should our subjection be to the commandments of our Lord, whether considered as old or new. Light should produce a suitable heat. Accordingly, here is another trial of our Christian light; before, it was to be approved by obedience to God; here by Christian love. 1. He who wants such love in vain pretends his light: *He that saith he is in the light, and hateth his brother, is in darkness even unto now, v.* 9. It is proper for sincere Christians to acknowledge what God has done for their souls; but in the visible church there are often those who assume to themselves more than is true, there are those who say they are in the light, the divine revelation has made its impression upon their minds and spirits, and yet they walk in hatred and enmity towards their Christian brethren; these cannot be swayed by the sense of the love of Christ to their brethren, and therefore remain in their dark state, notwithstanding their pretended conversion to the Christian religion. 2. He who is governed by such love approves his light to be good and genuine: *He that loveth his brother* (as his brother in Christ) *abideth in the light, v.* 10. He sees the foundation and reason of Christian love; he discerns the weight and value of the Christian redemption; he sees how meet it is that we should love those whom Christ hath loved; and then the consequence will be that *there is no occasion of stumbling in him (v.* 10); he will be no scandal, *no stumbling-block, to his brother;* he will conscientiously beware that he neither induce his brother to sin nor turn him out of the way of religion, Christian love teaches us highly to value our brother's soul, and to dread every thing that will be injurious to his innocence and peace. 3. Hatred is a sign of spiritual darkness: *But he that hateth his brother is in darkness, v.* 11. Spiritual light is instilled by the Spirit of grace, and one of the *first-fruits of that Spirit is love;* he then who is possessed with malignity towards a Christian brother must needs be destitute of spiritual light; consequently *he walks in darkness (v.* 11); his life is agreeable to a dark mind and conscience, *and he knows not whither he goes;* he sees not whither this dark spirit carries him, and particularly that it will carry him to the world of utter darkness, *because darkness hath blinded his eyes, v.* 11. The darkness of regeneracy, evidenced by a malignant spirit, is contrary to the light of life; where that darkness dwells, the mind, the judgment, and the conscience will be darkened, and so will mistake the way to heavenly endless life. Here we may observe how effectually our apostle is now cured of his once hot and flaming spirit. Time was when he was for *calling for fire from heaven* upon poor ignorant Samaritans who received them not, Lu. 9:54. But his Lord had shown him that he knew not his own spirit, nor whither it led him. Having now imbibed more of the Spirit of Christ, he breathes out good-will to man, and love to all the brethren. It is the Lord Jesus that is the great Master of love: it is his school (his own church) that is the school of love. His disciples are the disciples of love, and his family must be the family of love.

Verses 12–17

This new command of holy love, with the incentives thereto, may possibly be directed to the several ranks of disciples that are here accosted. The several graduates in the Christian university, the catholic church, must be sure to preserve the bond of sacred love. Or, there being an important dehortation and dissuasion to follow, without the observance of which vital religion in the love of God and love of the brethren cannot subsist, the apostle may justly seem to preface it with a solemn address to the several forms or orders in the school of Christ: let the infants or minors, the adults, the seniors (or the *adepti,* the *teleioi,* the most *perfect*), in the Christian institution, know that they must *not love this world;* and so,

I. We have the address itself made to the various forms and ranks in the church of Christ. All Christians are not of the same standing and stature; there are babes in Christ, there are grown men, and old disciples. As these have their peculiar states, so they have their peculiar duties; but there are precepts and a correspondent obedience common to them all, as particularly mutual love and contempt of the world. We see also that wise pastors will judiciously distribute the word of life, and give to the several members of Christ's family their several suitable portions: *I write unto you children, fathers, and young men.* In this distribution the apostle addresses,

1. The lowest in the Christian school: *I write unto you, little children, v.* 12. There are novices in religion, babes in Christ, those who are learning the rudiments of Christian godliness. The apostle may seem to encourage them by applying to them first; and it may be useful to the greater proficients to hear what is said to their juniors; elements are to be repeated; first principles are the foundation of all. He addresses *the children* in Christianity upon two accounts: — (1.) *Because their sins were forgiven them for his name's sake, v.* 12. The youngest sincere disciple is pardoned; *the communion of saints* is attended with *the forgiveness of sins.* Sins are forgiven either for God's name's sake, for the praise of his glory (his glorious perfections displayed in forgiveness), or *for Christ's name's sake,* upon his score, and upon the account of the redemption that is in him; and those that are forgiven of God are strongly obliged to relinquish this world, which so interferes with *the love of God.* (2.) Because of their knowledge of God: *I write unto you, little children, because you have known the Father, v.* 13. Children are wont to know none so soon as their father. Children in Christianity must and do know God. *They shall all know me, from the least to the greatest,* Heb. 8:11. Children in Christ should know that God is their Father; it is their wisdom. We say, It is a wise child that knows his father. These children cannot but know theirs; they can well be assured by whose power they are regenerated and by whose grace they are adopted. Those that know the Father may well be withdrawn from the love of this world. Then the apostle, proceeds,

2. To those of the highest station and stature, to the seniors in Christianity, to whom he gives an honourable appellation: *I write unto you, fathers (v.* 13, 14), *unto you, Mnasons, you old disciples,* Acts 21:16. The apostle immediately passes from the bottom to the top of the school, from the lowest form to the highest, that those in the middle may hear both lessons, may remember what they have learned and perceive what they must come to: *I write unto you, fathers.* Those that are of longest standing in Christ's school have need of further advice and instruction; the oldest disciple must go to heaven (the university above) with his book, his Bible, in his hand; fathers must be written to, and preached to; none are too old to learn. He writes to them upon the account of their knowledge: *I write unto you, fathers, because you have known him that is from the beginning, v.* 13, 14. Old men have knowledge and experience, and expect deference. The apostle is ready to own the knowledge of old Christians, and to congratulate them thereupon. They know the Lord Christ, particularly *him that was from the beginning; as ch.* 1:1. As Christ is *Alpha* and *Omega,* so he must be the beginning and end of our Christian knowledge. *I count all things but loss for the excellency of the knowledge of Christ Jesus my Lord,* Phil. 3:8. Those who know him that was from the beginning, before this world was made, may well be induced thereby to relinquish this world. Then,

3. To the middle age of Christians, to those who are in their bloom and flower: *I write unto you, young men, v.* 13, 14. There are the adult in Christ Jesus, those that have arrived at the strength of spirit and sound sense and can discern between good and evil. The apostle applies to them upon these accounts: — (1.) Upon the account of their martial exploits. Dexterous soldiers they are in the camp of Christ: *Because you have overcome the wicked one, v.* 13. There is a wicked one that is continually warring against souls, and particularly against the disciples: but those that are well taught in Christ's school can handle their arms and vanquish the evil one; and those that can vanquish him may be called to vanquish the world too, which is so great an instrument for the devil. (2.) Upon the account of their strength, discovered in this their achievement: *Because you are strong, and you have overcome the wicked one, v.* 14. Young men are wont to glory in their strength; it will be the glory of youthful persons to be strong in Christ and in his grace; it will be their glory, and it will try their strength, to overcome the devil; if they be not too hard for the devil, he will be too hard for them. Let vigorous Christians show their strength in conquering the world; and the same strength must be exerted in overcoming the world as is employed in overcoming the devil. (3.) Because of their acquaintance with the word of God: *And the word of God abideth in you, v.* 14. The word of God must abide in the adult disciples; it is the nutriment and supply of strength to them; it is the weapon by which they overcome the wicked one; the sword of the Spirit, whereby they quench his fiery darts: and those in whom the word of God dwells are well furnished for the conquest of the world.

II. We have the dehortation or dissuasion thus prefaced and introduced, a caution fundamental to vital practical religion: *"Love not the world, neither the things that are in the world, v.* 15. Be crucified to the world, be mortified to the things, to the affairs and enticements, of it." The several degrees of Christians should unite in this, in being dead to the world. Were they thus united, they would soon unite upon other accounts: their love should be reserved for God; throw it not away upon the world. Now here we see the reasons of this dissuasion and caution. They are several, and had need to be so; it is hard to dispute or dissuade disciples themselves from the love of the world. These reasons are taken,

1. From the inconsistency of this love with the love of God: *If any man love the world, the love of the Father is not in him, v.* 15. The heart of man is narrow, and cannot contain both loves. The world draws down the heart from God; and so the more the love of the world prevails the more the love of God dwindles and decays.

2. From the prohibition of worldly love or lust; it is not ordained of God: *It is not of the Father, but is of the world, v.* 16. This love or lust is not appointed of God (he calls us from it), but it intrudes itself from the world; the world is a usurper of our affection. Now here we have the due consideration and notion of the world, according to which it is to be crucified and renounced. *The world,* physically considered, is good, and is to be admired as the work of God and a glass in which his perfections shine; but it is to be considered in its relation to us now in our corrupted state, and as it works upon our weakness and instigates and inflames our vile affections. There is great affinity and alliance between this world and the flesh, and this world intrudes and encroaches upon the flesh, and thereby makes a party against God. The things of the world therefore are distinguished into three classes, according to the three predominant inclinations of depraved nature; as, (1.) There is *the lust of the flesh. The flesh* here, being distinguished from *the eyes* and *the life,* imports the body. The lust of the flesh is, subjectively, the humour and appetite of indulging fleshly pleasures; and, objectively, all those things that excite and inflame the pleasures of the flesh. This lust is usually called *luxury.* (2.) There is *the lust of the eyes.* The eyes are delighted with treasures; riches and rich possessions are craved by an extravagant eye; this is the lust of covetousness. 3. There is *the pride of life.* A vain mind craves all the grandeur, equipage, and pomp of a vain-glorious life; this is ambition, and thirst after honour and applause. This is, in part, the disease of the ear; it must be flattered with admiration and praise. The objects of these appetites must be abandoned and renounced; as they engage and engross the affection and desire, *they are not of the Father, but of the world, v.* 16. The Father disallows them, and the world should keep them to itself. The lust or appetite to these things must be mortified and subdued; and so the indulging of it is not appointed by the Father, but is insinuated by the ensnaring world.

3. From the vain and vanishing state of earthly things and the enjoyment of them. *And the world passeth away, and the lust thereof, v.* 17. The things of the world are fading and dying apace. The lust itself and the pleasure of it wither and decay; desire itself will ere long fail and cease, Eccl. 12:5. And what has become of all the pomp and pleasure of all those who now lie mouldering in the grave?

4. From the immortality of the divine lover, the lover of God: *But he that doeth the will of God,* which must be the character of the lover of God, in opposition to this lover of the world, *abideth for ever, v.* 17. The object of his love in opposition to *the world* that *passeth away,* abideth for ever; his sacred passion or affection, in opposition to the lust that passeth away, abideth for ever; love shall never fail; and he himself is an heir of immortality and endless life, and shall in time be translated thither.

From the whole of these verses we should observe the purity and spirituality of the apostolical doctrine. The animal life must be subjected to the divine; the body with its affections should be swayed by religion, or the victorious love of God.

Verses 18–19

Here is, I. A moral prognostication of the time; the end is coming: *Little children, it is the last time, v.* 18. Some may suppose that the apostle here addresses the first rank of Christians again; the juniors are most apt to be seduced, and therefore, *"Little children,* you that are young in religion, take heed to yourselves that you be not corrupted." But it may be, as elsewhere, a universal appellation, introductive of an alarm to all Christians: *"Little children, it is the last time;* our Jewish polity in church and state is hastening to an end; the Mosaic institution and discipline are just upon vanishing away; Daniel's weeks are now expiring; the destruction of the Hebrew city and sanctuary is approaching, *the end whereof must be with a flood, and to the end of the war desolations are determined,"* Dan. 9:26. It is meet that the disciples should be warned of the haste and end of time, and apprised as much as may be of the prophetic periods of time.

II. The sign of this last time: *Even now there are many antichrists* (*v.* 18), many that oppose the person, doctrine, and kingdom of Christ. It is a mysterious portion of providence that antichrists should be permitted; but, when they have come, it is good and safe that the disciples should be informed of them; ministers should be *watchmen to the house of Israel.* Now it should be no great offence nor prejudice to the disciples that there are such antichrists: 1. One great one has been foretold: *As you have heard that antichrist shall come, v.* 18. The generality of the church have been informed by divine revelation that there must be a long and fatal adversary to Christ and his church, 2 Th. 2:8–10. No wonder then that there are many harbingers and forerunners of the great one: *Even now there are many antichrists,* the mystery of iniquity already worketh. 2. They were foretold also as the sign of this last time. *For there shall arise false Christs and false prophets, and shall show great signs and wonders, insomuch that, if it were possible, they shall deceive the very elect,* Mt. 24:24. And these were the forerunners of the dissolution of the Jewish state, nation, and religion: *Whereby we know it is the last time, v.* 18. Let the prediction that we see there has been of seducers arising in the Christian world fortify us against their seduction.

III. Some account of these seducers or antichrists. 1. More positively. They were once entertainers or professors of apostolical doctrine: *"They went out from us* (*v.* 19), from our company and communion;" possibly from the church of Jerusalem, or some of the churches of Judea, as Acts 15:1, *Certain men came down from Judea, and taught the brethren,* etc. The purest churches may have their apostates and revolters; the apostolic doctrine did not convert all whom it convinced of its truth. 2. More privately. "They were not inwardly such as we are: *But they were not of us;* they had not *from the heart obeyed the form of sound doctrine delivered to them;* they were not of our union with Christ the head." Then here is, (1.) The reason upon which it is concluded that they were not of us, were not what they pretended, or what we are, and that is their actual defection: *"For, if they had been of us, they would* no doubt *have continued with us* (*v.* 19); had the sacred truth been rooted in their hearts it would have held them with us; had they had the anointing from above, by which they had been made true and real Christians, they would not have turned antichrists." Those that apostatize from religion sufficiently indicate that, before, they were hypocrites in religion: those who have imbibed the spirit of gospel truth have a good preservative against destructive error. (2.) The reason why they are permitted thus to depart from apostolical doctrine and communion — that their insincerity may be detected: *But* this was done (or *they went out) that they might be made manifest that they were not all of us, v.* 19. The church knows not well who are its vital members and who are not; and therefore the church, considered as internally sanctified, may well be styled *invisible.* Some of the hypocritical must be manifested here, and that for their own shame and benefit too, in their reduction to the truth, if they have not sinned unto death, and for the terror and caution of others. *You therefore, beloved, seeing you know these things before, beware lest you also, being led away with the error of the wicked, fall from your own stedfastness. But grow in grace,* etc., 2 Pt. 3:17, 18.

Verses 20–27

Here, I. The apostle encourages the disciples (to whom he writes) in these dangerous times, in this hour of seducers; he encourages them in the assurance of their stability in this day of apostasy: *But you have an unction from the Holy One, and you know all* things. We see, 1. The blessing wherewith they were enriched — an unguent from heaven: *You have an unction.* True Christians are anointed ones, their name intimates as much. They are anointed with the oil of grace, with gifts and spiritual endowments, by the Spirit of grace. They are anointed into a similitude of their Lord's offices, as subordinate prophets, priests, and kings, unto God. The Holy Spirit is compared to oil, as well as to fire and water; and the communication of his salvific grace is our anointing. 2. From whom this blessing comes — *from the Holy One,* either from the Holy Ghost or from the Lord Christ, as Rev. 3:7, *These things saith he that is holy — the Holy One.* The Lord Christ is glorious in his holiness. The Lord Christ disposes of the graces of the divine Spirit, and he anoints the disciples to make them like himself, and to secure them in his interest. 3. The effect of this unction — it is a spiritual eye-salve; it enlightens and strengthens the eyes of the understanding: *"And* thereby *you know all things* (*v.* 20), all these things concerning Christ and his religion; it was promised and given you for that end," Jn. 14:26. The Lord Christ does not deal alike by all his professed disciples; some are more anointed than others. There is great danger lest those that are not thus anointed should be so far from being true to Christ that they should, on the contrary, turn antichrists, and prove adversaries to Christ's person, and kingdom, and glory.

II. The apostle indicates to them the mind and meaning with which he wrote to them. 1. By way of negation; not as suspecting their knowledge, or supposing their ignorance in the grand truths of the gospel: *"I have not written unto you because you know not the truth, v.* 21. I could not then be so well assured of your stability therein, nor congratulate you on your unction from above." It is good to surmise well concerning our Christian brethren; we ought to do so till evidence overthrows our surmise: a just confidence in religious persons may both encourage and contribute to their fidelity. 2. By way of assertion and acknowledgment, as relying upon their judgment in these things: *But because you know it* (you know *the truth in Jesus), and that no lie is of the truth.* Those who know the truth in any respect are thereby prepared to discern what is contrary thereto and inconsistent therewith. *Rectum est index sui et obliqui — The line which shows itself to be straight shows also what line is crooked.* Truth and falsehood do not well mix and suit together. Those that are well acquainted with Christian truth are thereby well fortified against antichristian error and delusion. No lie belongs to religion, either natural or revealed. The apostles most of all condemned lies, and showed the inconsistency of lies with their doctrine: they would have been the most self-condemned persons had they propagated the truth by lies. It is a commendation of the Christian religion that it so well accords with natural religion, which is the foundation of it, that it so well accords with the Jewish religion, which contained the elements or rudiments of it. *No lie is of the truth;* frauds and impostures then are very unfit means to support and propagate the truth. I suppose it had been better with the state of religion if they had never been used. The result of them appears in the infidelity of our age; the detection of ancient pious frauds and wiles has almost run our age into atheism and irreligion; but the greatest actors and sufferers for the Christian revelation would assure us that *no lie is of the truth.*

III. The apostle further impleads and arraigns these seducers who had newly arisen. 1. They are *liars,* egregious opposers of sacred truth: *Who is a liar,* or the liar, the notorious liar of the time and age in which we live, *but he that denieth that Jesus is the Christ?* The great and pernicious lies that the father of lies, or of liars, spreads in the world, were of old, and usually are, falsehoods and errors relating to the person of Christ. There is no truth so sacred and fully attested but some or other will contradict or deny it. That Jesus of Nazareth was the Son of God had been attested by heaven, and earth, and hell. It should seem that some, in the tremendous judgment of God, are given up to strong delusions. 2. They are direst enemies to God as well as to the Lord Christ: *He is antichrist who denieth the Father and the Son, v.* 22. He that opposes Christ denies the witness and testimony of the Father, and the seal that he hath given to his Son; *for him hath God the Father sealed,* Jn. 6:27. And he that denies the witness and testimony of the Father, concerning Jesus Christ denies that God is the Father of the Lord Jesus Christ, and consequently abandons the knowledge of God in Christ, and thereupon the whole revelation of God in Christ, and particularly of God in Christ *reconciling the world unto himself;* and therefore the apostle may well infer, *Whosoever denies the Son the same has not the Father* (*v.* 23); he has not the true knowledge of the Father, for the Son has most and best revealed him; he has no interest in the Father, in his favour, and grace, and salvation, *for none cometh to the Father but by the Son. But,* as some copies add, *he that acknowledgeth the Son has the Father also, v.* 23. As there is an intimate relation between the Father and the Son, so there is an inviolable union in the doctrine, knowledge, and interests of both; so that he who has the knowledge of, and right to, the Son, has the knowledge of, and right to, the Father also. Those that adhere to the Christian revelation hold the light and benefit of natural religion withal.

IV. Hereupon the apostle advises and persuades the disciples to continue in the old doctrine at first communicated to them: *Let that therefore abide in you which you have heard from the beginning, v.* 24. Truth is older than error. The truth concerning Christ, that was at first delivered to the saints, is not to be exchanged for novelties. So sure were the apostles of the truth of what they had delivered concerning Christ, and from him, that after all their toils and sufferings they were not willing to relinquish it. The Christian truth may plead antiquity, and be recommended thereby. This exhortation is enforced by these considerations: —

1. From the sacred advantage they will receive by adhering to the primitive truth and faith. (1.) They will continue thereby in holy union with God and Christ: *If that which you have heard from the beginning shall remain in you, you also shall continue in the Son and in the Father, v.* 24. It is the truth of Christ abiding in us that is the means of severing us from sin and uniting us to the Son of God, Jn. 15:3, 4. The Son is the medium or the Mediator by whom we are united to the Father. What value then should we put upon gospel truth! (2.) They will thereby secure the promise of eternal life: *And this is the promise that he* (even God the Father, *ch.* 5:11) *hath promised us, even eternal life, v.* 25. Great is the promise that God makes to his faithful adherents. It is suitable to his own greatness, power, and goodness. It is *eternal life,* which none but God can give. The blessed God puts great value upon his Son, and the truth relating to him, when he is pleased to promise to those who continue in that truth (under the light, and power, and influence of it) *eternal life.* Then the exhortation aforesaid is enforced,

2. From the design of the apostle's writing to them. This letter is to fortify them against the deceivers of the age: *"These things have I written to you concerning those that seduce you* (*v.* 26), and therefore, if you continue not in what *you have heard from the beginning,* my writing and service will be in vain." We should beware lest the apostolical letters, yea, lest the whole scripture of God, should be to us insignificant and fruitless. *I have written to him the great things of my law* (and my gospel too), *but they were counted as a strange thing,* Hos. 8:12.

3. From the instructive blessing they had received from heaven: *But the anointing which you have received from him abideth in you, v.* 27. True Christians have an inward confirmation of the divine truth they have imbibed: the Holy Spirit has imprinted it on their minds and hearts. It is meet that the Lord Jesus should have a constant witness in the hearts of his disciples. The unction, the pouring out of the gifts of grace upon sincere disciples, is a seal to the truth and doctrine of Christ, since none giveth that seal but God. *Now he who establisheth us with you* (and you with us) *in Christ, and hath anointed us, is God,* 2 Co. 1:21. This sacred chrism, or divine unction, is commended on these accounts: — (1.) It

is durable and lasting; oil or unguent is not so soon dried up as water: it *abideth in you, v.* 27. Divine illumination, in order to confirmation, must be something continued or constant. Temptations, snares, and seductions, arise. The anointing must abide. (2.) It is better than human instruction: *"And you need not that any man teach you, v.* 27. Not that this anointing will teach you without the appointed ministry. It could, if God so pleased; but it will not, though it will teach you better than we can: *And you need not that any man teach you, v.* 27. You were instructed by us before you were anointed; but now our teaching is nothing in comparison to that. *Who teacheth like him?"* Job 36:22. The divine unction does not supersede ministerial teaching, but surmount it. (3.) It is a sure evidence of truth, and all that it teaches is infallible truth: *But as the same anointing teacheth you of all things, and is truth, and is no lie, v.* 27. The Holy Spirit must needs be *the Spirit of truth*, as he is called, Jn. 14:17. The instruction and illumination that he affords must needs be in and of the truth. The Spirit of truth will not lie; and he teacheth all things, that is, all things in the present dispensation, all things necessary to our knowledge of God in Christ, and their glory in the gospel. And, (4.) It is of a conservative influence; it will preserve those in whom it abides against seducers and their seduction: *And even as it hath taught you you shall abide in him, v.* 27. It teaches you to abide in Christ; and, as it teaches you, it secures you; it lays a restraint upon your minds and hearts, that you may not revolt from him. *And he that hath anointed us is God, who also hath sealed us for* himself, *and given the earnest of the Spirit in our hearts."* 2 Co. 1:21, 22.

Verses 28–29

From the blessing of the sacred unction the apostle proceeds in his advice and exhortation to constancy in and with Christ: *And now, little children, abide in him, v.* 28. The apostle repeats his kind appellation, *little children*, which I suppose does not so much denote their diminutiveness as his affection, and therefore, I judge, may be rendered *dear children.* He would persuade by love, and prevail by endearment as well as by reason. "Not only the love of Christ, but the love of you, constrains us to inculcate your perseverance, and that you *would abide in him*, in the truth relating to his person, and in your union with him and allegiance to him." Evangelical privileges are obligatory to evangelical duties; and those that are anointed by the Lord Jesus are highly obliged to abide with him in opposition to all adversaries whatever. This duty of perseverance and constancy in trying times is strongly urged by the two following considerations: — 1. From the consideration of his return at the great day of account: *That when he shall appear we may have confidence, and not be ashamed before him at his coming, v.* 28. It is here taken for granted that the Lord Jesus will come again. This was part of that truth they had heart from the beginning. And, when he shall come again, he will publicly appear, be manifested to all. When he was here before, he came privately, in comparison. He proceeded from a womb, and was introduced into a stable: but, when he shall come again, he will come from the opened heavens, and every eye shall see him; and then those who have continued with him throughout all their temptations shall have confidence, assurance, and joy, in the sight of him. They shall lift up their heads with unspeakable triumph, as knowing that their complete redemption comes along with him. On the contrary, those that have deserted him *shall be ashamed before him;* they shall be ashamed of themselves, ashamed of their unbelief, their cowardice, ingratitude, temerity, and folly, in forsaking so glorious a Redeemer. They shall be ashamed of their hopes, expectations, and pretences, and ashamed of all the wages of unrighteousness, by which they were induced to desert him: *That we may have confidence, and may not be ashamed.* The apostle includes himself in the number. "Let not us be ashamed of you," as well as, "you will not be ashamed of yourselves." Or *mē aischynthōmen ap' autou — that we be not ashamed* (made ashamed, or put to shame) *by him at his coming.* At his public appearance he will shame all those who have abandoned him, he will disclaim all acquaintance with them, will cover them with shame and confusion, will abandon them to darkness, devils, and endless despair, by professing before men and angels that he is ashamed of them, Mk. 8:38. To the same advice and exhortation he proceeds, 2. From the consideration of the dignity of those who still adhere to Christ and his religion: *If you*

know that he is righteous, you know that every one that doeth righteousness is born of him, v. 29. The particle here rendered *if* seems not to be *vox dubitantis*, but *concedentis;* not so much a conditional particle, as a suppositional one, if I may call it so, a note of allowance or concession, and so seems to be of the same import with our English *inasmuch*, or *whereas*, or *since.* So the sense runs more clearly: *Since you know that he is righteous, you know that every one that doeth righteousness is born of him.* He that doeth righteousness may here be justly enough assumed as another name for him that abideth in Christ. For he that abideth in Christ abideth in the law and love of Christ, and consequently in his allegiance and obedience to him; and so must do, or work, or practise, righteousness, or the parts of gospel holiness. Now such a one must needs *be born of him.* He is renewed by the Spirit of Christ, after the image of Christ, *created in Christ Jesus unto good works, which God hath fore-ordained that he should walk in them*, Eph. 2:10. *"Since then you know that the Lord Christ is righteous* (righteous in his quality and capacity, the Lord our righteousness, and the Lord our sanctifier or our sanctification, as 1 Co. 1:30), you cannot but know thereupon" (or know you, it is for your consideration and regard) "that he who by the continued practice of Christianity abideth in him is born of him." The new spiritual nature is derived from the Lord Christ. He that is constant to the practice of religion in trying times gives good evidence that he is born from above, from the Lord Christ. The Lord Christ is an everlasting Father. It is a great privilege and dignity to be born of him. Those that are so are the children of God. *To as many as received him to them gave he power to become the sons of God*, Jn. 1:12. And this introduces the context of the following chapter.

CHAPTER 3

The apostle here magnifies the love of God in our adoption (*v.* 1, 2). He thereupon argues for holiness (*v.* 3), and against sin (*v.* 4–19). He presses brotherly love (*v.* 11–18). How to assure our hearts before God (*v.* 19–22). The precept of faith (*v.* 23). And the good of obedience (*v.* 24).

Verses 1–3

The apostle, having shown the dignity of Christ's faithful followers, that they are born of him and thereby nearly allied to God, now here,

I. Breaks forth into the admiration of that grace that is the spring of such a wonderful vouchsafement: *Behold* (see you, observe) *what manner of love*, or how great love, *the Father hath bestowed upon us, that we should be called*, effectually called (he who calls things that are not makes them to be what they were not) *the sons of God!* The Father adopts all the children of the Son. The Son indeed calls them, and makes them his brethren; and thereby he confers upon them the power and dignity of the sons of God. It is wonderful condescending love of the eternal Father, that such as we should be made and called his sons — we who by nature are heirs of sin, and guilt, and the curse of God — we who by practice are children of corruption, disobedience, and ingratitude! Strange, that the holy God is not ashamed to be called our Father, and to call us his sons! Thence the apostle,

II. Infers the honour of believers above the cognizance of the world. Unbelievers know little of them. *Therefore* (or wherefore, upon this score) *the world knoweth us not, v.* 1. Little does the world perceive the advancement and happiness of the genuine followers of Christ. They are here exposed to the common calamities of earth and time; all things fall alike to them as to others, or rather they are subject to the greater sorrow, for they have often reason to say, *If in this life only we have hope in Christ, we are of all men most miserable*, 1 Co. 15:19. The unchristian world, therefore, that walks by sight, knows not their dignity, their privileges, the enjoyments they have in hand, nor what they are entitled to. Little does the world think that these poor, humble, contemned ones are the favourites of heaven, and will be inhabitants there ere long. And they may bear their case the better since their Lord was here unknown as well as they: *Because it knew him not, v.* 1. Little did the world think how great a person was once sojourning here, that the Maker of it was once an inhabitant of it. Little did the Jewish world think that the God of Abraham, Isaac, and Jacob, was one of their blood, and dwelt in their land; he came to his own, and his own received him not. He came to his own, and his own crucified him; but surely, *had they known him, they would not have crucified the Lord of glory*, 1 Co. 2:8. Let the

followers of Christ be content with hard fare here, since they are in a land of strangers, among those who little know them, and their Lord was so treated before them. Then the apostle,

III. Exalts these persevering disciples in the prospect of the certain revelation of their state and dignity. Here, 1. Their present honourable relation is asserted: *Beloved* (you may well be our beloved, for you are beloved of God), *now are we the sons of God, v.* 2. We have the nature of sons by regeneration: we have the title, and spirit, and right to the inheritance of sons by adoption. *This honour have all the saints.* 2. The discovery of the bliss belonging and suitable to this relation is denied: *And it doth not yet appear what we shall be, v.* 2. The glory pertaining to the sonship and adoption is adjourned and reserved for another world. The discovery of it here would put a stop to the current of affairs that must now proceed. The sons of God must walk by faith, and live by hope. 3. The time of the revelation of the sons of God in their proper state and glory is determined; and that is when their elder brother comes to call and collect them all together: *But we know that when he shall appear we shall be like him.* The particle, *ean*, usually translated *if*, is here well rendered *when;* for the Hebrew particle *am* (to which this is thought to correspond) is observed so to signify, as Dr. Whitby has here noted; and not only is *ean* sometimes used for *hotan*, but some copies even here read *hotan, when.* And accordingly it seems proper so to render it in Jn. 14:3, where we read it, *And if I go, and prepare a place;* but more naturally and properly, *When I shall have gone, and shall have prepared the place, I will come again, and receive you unto myself*, or *paralēpsomai — I will take you along with myself, that where I am there you may be also.* When the head of the church, the only-begotten of the Father, shall appear, his members, the adopted of God, shall appear and be manifested together with him. They may then well wait in faith, hope, and earnest desire, for the revelation of the Lord Jesus; as even the creation itself waiteth for their perfection, *and the public manifestation of the sons of God*, Rom. 8:19. The sons of God will be known and be made manifest by their likeness to their head: *They shall be like him* — like him in honour, and power, and glory. Their vile bodies shall be made like his glorious body; they shall be filled with life, light, and bliss from him. *When he, who is their life, shall appear, they also shall appear with him in glory*, Col. 3:4. Then, 4. Their likeness to him is argued from the sight they shall have of him: *We shall be like him, for we shall see him as he is.* Their likeness will be the cause of that sight which they shall have of him. Indeed, all shall see him, but not as they do; not as *he is*, namely, to those in heaven. The wicked shall see him in his frowns, in the terror of his majesty, and the splendour of his avenging perfections; but these shall see him in the smiles and beauty of his face, in the correspondence and amiableness of his glory, in the harmony and agreeableness of his beatific perfections. Their likeness shall enable them to see him as the blessed do in heaven. Or the sight of him shall be the cause of their likeness; it shall be a transformative sight: they shall be transformed into the same image by the beatific view that they shall have of him. Then the apostle,

IV. Urges the engagement of these sons of God to the prosecution of holiness: *And every man that hath this hope in him purifies himself even as he is pure, v.* 3. The sons of God know that their Lord is holy and pure; he is of purer heart and eyes than to admit any pollution or impurity to dwell with him. Those then who hope to live with him must study the utmost purity from the world, and flesh, and sin; they must grow in grace and holiness. Not only does their Lord command them to do so, but their new nature inclines them so to do; yea, their hope of heaven will dictate and constrain them so to do. They know that their high priest is holy, harmless, and undefiled. They know that their Go and Father is the high and holy one, that all the society is pure and holy, that their inheritance is an inheritance of saints in light. It is a contradiction to such hope to indulge sin and impurity. And therefore, as we are sanctified by faith, we must be sanctified by hope. That we may be saved by hope we must be purified by hope. It is the hope of hypocrites, and not of the sons of God, that makes an allowance for the gratification of impure desires and lusts.

Verses 4–10

The apostle, having alleged the believer's obligation to purity from his hope of heaven, and of communion with Christ in glory at the day of his appearance, now procee to fill his own mouth and the believer's mind with multiplied arguments against sin, and all communion with the impure unfruitful works of darkness. And so he reasons and argues,

I. From the nature of sin and the intrinsic evil of it. It is a contrariety to the divine law: *Whosoever committeth sin transgresseth also (or even) the law* (or, whosoever committeth sin even committeth enormity, or aberration from law, or from the law); *for sin is the transgression of the law,* or is lawlessness, *v.* 4. Sin is the destitution or privation of correspondence and agreement with the divine law, that law which is the transcript of the divine nature and purity, which contains his will for the government of the world, which is suitable to the rational nature, and enacted for the good of the world, which shows man the way of felicity and peace, and conducts him to the author of his nature and of the law. The current commission of sin now is the rejection of the divine law, and this is the rejection of the divine authority, and consequently of God himself.

II. From the design and errand of the Lord Jesus in and to this world, which was to remove sin: *And you know that he was manifested to take away our sins, and in him is no sin, v.* 5. The Son of God appeared, and was known, in our nature; and he came to vindicate and exalt the divine law, and that by obedience to the precept, and by subjection and suffering under the penal sanction, under the curse of it. *He came therefore to take away our sins,* to take away the guilt of them by the sacrifice of himself, to take away the commission of them by implanting a new nature in us (for we are sanctifies by virtue of his death), and to dissuade and save from it by his own example, *and* (or *for) in him was no sin;* or, he takes sin away, that he may conform us to himself, *and in him is no sin.* Those that expect communion with Christ above should study communion with him here in the utmost purity. And the Christian world should know and consider the great end of the Son of God's coming hither: it was to take away our sin: *And you know* (and this knowledge should be deep and effectual) *that he was manifested to take away our sins.*

III. From the opposition between sin and a real union with or adhesion to the Lord Christ: *Whosoever abideth in him sinneth not, v.* 6. To sin here is the same as to commit sin (*v.* 8, 9), and to commit sin is to practise sin. He that abideth in Christ continues not in the practice of sin. As vital union with the Lord Jesus broke the power of sin in the heart and nature, so continuance therein prevents the regency and prevalence thereof in the life and conduct. Or the negative expression here is put for the positive: *He sinneth not,* that is, he is obedient, *he keeps the commandments* (in sincerity, and in the ordinary course of life) *and does those things that are pleasing in his sight,* as is said *v.* 22. Those that abide in Christ abide in their covenant with him, and consequently watch against the sin that is contrary thereto. They abide in the potent light and knowledge of him; and therefore it may be concluded *that he that sinneth* (abideth in the predominant practice of sin) *hath not seen him* (hath not his mind impressed with a sound evangelical discerning of him), *neither known him,* hath no experimental acquaintance with him. Practical renunciation of sin is the great evidence of spiritual union with, continuance in, and saving knowledge of, the Lord Christ.

IV. From the connection between the practice of righteousness and a state of righteousness, intimating withal that the practice of sin and a justified state are inconsistent; and this is introduced with a supposition that a surmise to the contrary is a gross deceit: *"Little children,* dear children, and as much children as you are, herein *let no man deceive you.* There will be those who will magnify your new light and entertainment of Christianity, who will make you believe that your knowledge, profession, and baptism, will excuse you from the care and accuracy of the Christian life. But beware of such self-deceit. *He that doeth righteousness in righteous."* It may appear that righteousness may in several places of scripture be justly rendered *religion,* as Mt. *v.* 10, *Blessed are those that are persecuted for righteousness' sake,* that is, for religion's sake; 1 Pt. 3:14, *But if you suffer for righteousness' sake* (religion's sake) *happy are you;* and 2 Tim. 3:16, *All scripture,* or the whole scripture, *is given by inspiration of God, and is profitable for doctrine — and for instruction in righteousness,* that is, in the nature and branches of religion. To do righteousness then, especially being set in opposition to the doing, committing, or practising, of sin, is to practise religion. Now he who practiseth religion is righteous; he is the righteous person on all accounts; he is sincere and upright before God. The practice of religion cannot subsist without a principle of integrity and conscience. He has that righteousness which consists in pardon of sin and right to life, founded upon the imputation of the Mediator's righteousness. He has a title *to the crown of righteousness, which the righteous Judge will give,* according to his covenant and promise, *to those that love his appearing,* 2 Tim. 4:8. He has communion with Christ, in conformity to the divine law, being in some measure practically righteous as he; and he has communion with him in the justified state, being now relatively righteous together with him.

V. From the relation between the sinner and the devil, and thereupon from the design and office of the Lord Christ against the devil. 1. From the relation between the sinner and the devil. As elsewhere sinners and saints are distinguished (though even saints are sinners largely so called), *so to commit sin* is here so to practise it as sinners do, that are distinguished from saints, to live under the power and dominion of it; and he who does so *is of the devil;* his sinful nature is inspired by, and agreeable and pleasing to, the devil; and he belongs to the party, and interest, and kingdom of the devil. It is he that is the author and patron of sin, and has been a practitioner of it, a tempter and instigator to it, even from the beginning of the world. And thereupon we must see how he argues. 2. From the design and office of the Lord Christ against the devil: *For this purpose the Son of God was manifested, that he might destroy the works of the devil, v.* 8. The devil has designed and endeavoured to ruin the work of God in this world. The Son of God has undertaken the holy war against him. He came into our world, and was manifested in our flesh, that he might conquer him and dissolve his works. Sin will he loosen and dissolve more and more, till he has quite destroyed it. Let not us serve or indulge what the Son of God came to destroy.

VI. From the connection between regeneration and the relinquishment of sin: *Whosoever is born of God doth not commit sin.* To be born of God is to be inwardly renewed, and restored to a holy integrity or rectitude of nature by the power of the Spirit of God. *Such a one committeth not sin,* does not work iniquity nor practise disobedience, which is contrary to his new nature and the regenerate complexion of his spirit; for, as the apostle adds, *his seed remaineth in him,* either the word of God in its light and power *remaineth in him* (as 1 Pt. 1:23, *Being born again, not of corruptible seed, but of incorruptible, by the word of God, which liveth and abideth for ever),* or, *that which is born of the Spirit is spirit;* the spiritual seminal principle of holiness remaineth in him. Renewing grace is an abiding principle. Religion, in the spring of it, is not an art, an acquired dexterity and skill, but a new nature. And thereupon the consequence is the regenerate person *cannot sin.* That he cannot commit an act of sin, I suppose no judicious interpreter understands. This would be contrary to *ch.* 1:9, where it is made our duty to confess our sins, and supposed that our privilege thereupon is to have our sins forgiven. *He therefore cannot sin,* in the sense in which the apostle says, *he cannot commit sin.* He cannot continue in the course and practice of sin. He cannot so sin as to denominate him a sinner in opposition to a saint or servant of God. Again, he cannot sin comparatively, as he did before he was born of God, and as others do that are not so. And the reason is *because he is born of God,* which will amount to all this inhibition and impediment. 1. There is a light in his mind which shows him the evil and malignity of sin. 2. There is that bias upon his heart which disposes him to loathe and hate sin. 3. There is the spiritual seminal principle or disposition, that breaks the force and fulness of the sinful acts. They proceed not from such plenary power of corruption as they do in others, nor obtain that plenitude of heart, spirit, and consent, which they do in others. *The spirit lusteth against the flesh.* And therefore in respect to such sin it may be said, *It is no more I that do it, but sin that dwelleth in me.* It is not reckoned the person's sin, in the gospel account, where the bent and frame of the mind and spirit are against it. Then, 4. There is a disposition for humiliation and repentance for sin, when it has been committed. *He that is born of God cannot sin.* Here we may call to mind the usual distinction of natural and moral impotency. The unregenerate person is morally unable for what is religiously good. The regenerate person is happily disabled for sin. There is a restraint, an embargo (as we may say), laid upon his sinning powers. It goes against him sedately and deliberately to sin. We usually say of a person of known integrity, "He cannot lie, he cannot cheat, and commit other enormities." *How can I commit this great wickedness, and sin against God!* Gen. 39:9. And so those who persist in a sinful life sufficiently demonstrate that they are not born of God.

VII. From the discrimination between the children of God and the children of the devil. They have their distinct characters. *In this the children of God are manifest and the children of the devil, v.* 10. In the world (according to the old distinction) there are the seed of God and the seed of the serpent. Now the seed of the serpent is known by these two signatures: — 1. By neglect of religion: *Whosoever doeth not righteously* (omits and disregards the rights and dues of God; for religion is but our righteousness towards God, or giving him his due, and whosoever does not conscientiously do this) *is not of God,* but, on the contrary, of the devil. The devil is the father of unrighteous or irreligious souls. And, 2. By hatred of fellow-christians: *Neither he that loveth not his brother, v.* 10. True Christians are to be loved for God's and Christ's sake. Those who so love them not, but despise, and hate, and persecute them, have the serpentine nature still abiding in them.

Verses 11–13

The apostle, having intimated that one mark of the devil's children is hatred of the brethren, takes occasion thence,

I. To recommend fraternal Christian love, and that from the excellence, or antiquity, or primariness of the injunction relating thereto: *And this is the message* (the errand or charge) *which you heard from the beginning* (this came among the principal parts of practical Christianity), *that we should love one another, v.* 11. We should love the Lord Jesus, and value his love, and consequently love all the objects of it, and thereupon all our brethren in Christ.

II. To dissuade from what is contrary thereto, all ill-will towards the brethren, and that by the example of Cain. His envy and malignity should deter us from harbouring the like passion, and that upon these accounts: — 1. It showed that he was as the first-born of the serpent's seed; even he, the eldest son of the first man, was of *the wicked one.* He imitated and resembled the first wicked one, the devil. 2. His ill-will had no restraint; it proceeded so far as to contrive and accomplish murder, and that of a near relation, and that in the beginning of the world, when there were but few to replenish it. *He slew his brother, v.* 12. Sin, indulged, knows no bound. And, 3. It proceeded so far, and had in it so much of the devil, that he murdered his brother for religion's sake. He was vexed with the superiority of Abel's service, and envied him the favour and acceptance he had with God. And for these he martyred his brother. *And wherefore slew he him? Because his own works were evil, and his brother's righteous, v.* 12. Ill-will will teach us to hate and revenge what we should admire and imitate. And then,

III. To infer that it is no wonder that good men are so served now: *Marvel not, my brethren, if the world hate you, v.* 13. The serpentine nature still continues in the world. The great serpent himself reigns as the God of this world. Wonder not then that the serpentine world hates and hisses at you who belong to that seed of the woman that is to bruise the serpent's head.

Verses 14–19

The beloved apostle can scarcely touch upon the mention of sacred love, but he must enlarge upon the enforcement of it, as here he does by divers arguments and incentives thereto; as,

I. That it is a mark of our evangelical justification, of our transition into a state of life: *We know that we have passed from death to life, because we love the brethren, v.* 14. We are by nature children of wrath and heirs of death. By the gospel (the gospel-covenant or promise) our state towards another world is altered and changed. We pass from death to life, from the guilt of death to the right of life; and this transition is made upon our believing in the Lord Jesus: *He that believeth on the Son hath everlasting life,* and he that believeth not *hath the wrath of God abiding on him,* Jn. 3:36. Now this happy change of state we may come to be assured of: *We know that we have passed from death to life;* we may know it by the evidences of our faith in Christ, of which this love to our brethren is one, which leads us to characterize this love that is such a mark of our justified state. It is not a zeal for a party in the common religion, or an affection for, or an affectation of, those who are of the same denomination and subordinate sentiments with ourselves. But this love,

1. Supposes a general love to mankind: the law of Christian love, in the Christian community, is founded on the catholic law, in the society of mankind, *Thou shalt love thy neighbour as thyself.* Mankind are to be loved principally on these two accounts: — (1.) As the excellent work of God, made by him, and made in wonderful resemblance of him. The reason that God assigns for the certain punishment of a murderer is a reason against our hatred of any of the brethren of mankind, and consequently a reason for our love to them: *for in the image of God made he man,* Gen. 9:6. (2.) As being, in some measure, beloved in Christ. The whole *race of mankind — the gens humana,* should be considered as being, in distinction from fallen angels, a redeemed nation; as having a divine Redeemer designed, prepared, and given for them. *So God loved the world,* even this world, *that he gave his only-begotten Son, that whosoever believeth on him should not perish, but have everlasting life,* Jn. 3:16. A world so beloved of God should accordingly be loved by us. And this love will exert itself in earnest desires, and prayers, and attempts, for the conversion and salvation of the yet uncalled blinded world. *My heart's desire and prayer for Israel are that they may be saved.* And then this love will include all due love to enemies themselves.

2. It includes a peculiar love to the Christian society, to the catholic church, and that for the sake of her head, as being his body, as being redeemed, justified, and sanctified in and by him; and this love particularly acts and operates towards those of the catholic church that we have opportunity of being personally acquainted with or credibly informed of. They are not so much loved for their own sakes as for the sake of God and Christ, who have loved them. And it is God and Christ, or, if you will, the love of God and grace of Christ, that are beloved and valued in them and towards them. And so this is the issue of faith in Christ, and is thereupon a note of our passage from death to life.

II. The hatred of our brethren is, on the contrary, a sign of our deadly state, of our continuance under the legal sentence of death: *He that loveth not his brother* (his brother in Christ) *abideth in death, v.* 14. He yet stands under the curse and condemnation of the law. This the apostle argues by a clear syllogism: "You know that no murderer hath eternal life abiding in him; but he who hates his brother is a murderer; and therefore you cannot but know that he who hates his brother hath not eternal life abiding in him," *v.* 15. Or, *he abideth in death,* as it is expressed, *v.* 14, *Whosoever hateth his brother is a murderer;* for hatred of the person is, so far as it prevails, a hatred of life and welfare, and naturally tends to desire the extinction of it. Cain hated, and then slew, his brother. Hatred will shut up the bowels of compassion from the poor brethren, and will thereby expose them to the sorrows of death. And it has appeared that hatred of the brethren has in all ages dressed them up in ill names, odious characters, and calumnies, and exposed them to persecution and the sword. No wonder, then, that he who has a considerable acquaintance with the heart of man, or is taught by him who fully knows it, who knows the natural tendency and issue of vile and violent passions, and knows withal the fulness of the divine law, declares him who hates his brother to be *a murderer.* Now he who by the frame and disposition of his heart is a murderer *cannot have eternal life abiding in him;* for he who is such must needs be carnally-minded, *and to be carnally-minded is death,* Rom. 8:6. The apostle, by the expression of *having eternal life abiding in us,* may seem to mean the possession of an internal principle of endless life, according to that of the Saviour, *Whosoever drinketh of the water that I shall give him shall never thirst,* shall never be totally destitute thereof; *but the water that I shall give him shall be in him a well of water springing up into everlasting life,* Jn. 4:14. And thereupon some may be apt to surmise that the passing from death to life (*v.* 14) does not signify the relative change made in our justification of life, but the real change made in the regeneration to life; and accordingly that the abiding in death mentioned *v.* 14 is continuance in spiritual death, as it is usually called, or abiding in the corrupt deadly temper of nature. But as these passages more naturally denote the state of the person, whether adjudged to life or death, so the relative transition from death to life may well be proved or disproved by the possession or non-possession of the inward principle of eternal life, since wash-

ing from the guilt of sin is inseparably united with washing from the filth and power of sin. *But you are washed, but you are sanctified, but you are justified, in the name of the Lord Jesus, and by the Spirit of our God,* 1. Cor. 6:11.

III. The example of God and Christ should inflame our hearts with this holy love: *Hereby perceive we the love of God, because he laid down his life for us; and we ought to lay down our lives for the brethren, v.* 16. The great God has given his Son to the death for us. But since this apostle has declared that the *Word was God,* and that *he became flesh for us,* I see not why we may not interpret this of God the Word. Here is the love of God himself, of him who in his own person is God, though not the Father, that he assumed a life, that he might lay it down for us! Here is the condescension, the miracle, the mystery of divine love, that God would redeem the church with his own blood! Surely we should love those whom God hath loved, and so loved; and we shall certainly do so if we have any love for God.

IV. The apostle, having proposed this flaming constraining example of love, and motive to it, proceeds to show us what should be the temper and effect of this our Christian love. And, 1. It must be, in the highest degree, so fervent as to make us willing to suffer even to death for the good of the church, for the safety and salvation of the dear brethren: *And we ought to lay down our lives for the brethren* (*v.* 16), either in our ministrations and services to them (*yea, and if I be offered upon the service and sacrifice of your faith, I joy and rejoice with you all* — I shall congratulate your felicity, Phil. 2:17), or in exposing ourselves to hazards, when called thereto, for the safety and preservation of those that are more serviceable to the glory of God and the edification of the church than we can be. *Who have for my life laid down their own necks; unto whom not only I give thanks, but also all the churches of the Gentiles,* Rom. 16:4. How mortified should the Christian be to this life! How prepared to part with it! And how well assured of a better! 2. It must be, in the next degree, compassionate, liberal, and communicative to the necessities of the brethren: *For whoso hath this world's good, and seeth his brother have need, and shutteth up his bowels of compassion from him, how dwelleth the love of God in him? v.* 17. It pleases God that some of the Christian brethren should be poor, for the exercise of the charity and love of those that are rich. And it pleases the same God to give to some of the Christian brethren this world's good, that they may exercise their grace in communicating to the poor saints. And those who have this world's good must love a good God more, and their good brethren more, and be ready to distribute it for their sakes. It appears here that this love to the brethren is founded upon love to God, in that it is here called so by the apostle: *How dwelleth the love of God in him?* This love to the brethren is love to God in them; and where there is none of this love to them there is no true love to God at all. 3. I was going to intimate the third and lowest degree in the next verse; but the apostle has prevented me, by intimating that this last charitable communicative love, in persons of ability, is the lowest that can consist with the love of God. But there may be other fruits of this love; and therefore the apostle desires that in all it should be unfeigned and operative, as circumstances will allow: *My little children* (my dear children in Christ), *let us not love in word, neither in tongue, but in deed and in truth, v.* 18. Compliments and flatteries become not Christians; but the sincere expressions of sacred affection, and the services or labours of love, do. Then,

V. This love will evince our sincerity in religion, and give us hope towards God: *And hereby we know that we are of the truth, and shall assure our hearts before him, v.* 19. It is a great happiness to be assured of our integrity in religion. Those that are so assured may have holy boldness or confidence towards God; they may appeal to him from the censures and condemnation of the world. The way to arrive at the knowledge of our own truth and uprightness in Christianity, and to secure our inward peace, is to abound in love and in the works of love towards the Christian brethren.

Verses 20–22

The apostle, having intimated that there may be, even among us, such a privilege as an assurance or sound persuasion of heart towards God, proceeds here,

I. To establish the court of conscience, and to assert the authority of it: *For, if our heart condemn us, God is greater than our heart, and knoweth all things, v.* 20. Our heart here is our self-reflecting judicial power, that noble excellent abil-

ity whereby we can take cognizance of ourselves, of our spirits, our dispositions, and actions, and accordingly pass a judgment upon our state towards God; and so it is the same with conscience, or the power of moral self-consciousness. This power can act as witness, judge, and executioner of judgment; it either accuses or excuses, condemns or justifies; it is set and placed in this office by God himself: *the spirit of man,* thus capacitated and empowered, *is the candle of the Lord,* a luminary lighted and set up by the Lord, *searching all the inward parts of the belly,* taking into scrutiny and viewing the *penetralia — the private recesses* and secret transactions of the inner man, Prov. 20:27. Conscience is God's vicegerent, calls the court in his name, and acts for him. *The answer of a good conscience towards God,* 1 Pt. 3:21. God is chief Judge of the court: *If our heart condemn us God is greater than our heart,* superior to our heart and conscience in power and judgment; hence the act and judgment of the court are the act and judgment of God; as, 1. If conscience condemn us, God does so too: *For, if our heart condemn us, God is greater than our heart, and knoweth all things, v.* 20. God is a greater witness than our conscience, and knoweth more against us than it does: *he knoweth all things;* he is a greater Judge than conscience; for, as he is supreme, so his judgment shall stand, and shall be fully and finally executed. This seems to be the design of another apostle when he says, *For I know nothing by myself,* that is, in the case wherein I am censured by some. "I am not conscious of any guile, or allowed unfaithfulness, in my stewardship and ministry. *Yet I am hereby justified;* it is not by my own conscience that I must ultimately stand or fall; the justification or justifying sentence of my conscience, or self-consciousness, will not determine the controversy between you and me; as you do not appeal to its sentence, so neither will you be determined by its decision; *but he that judgeth me* (supremely and finally judgeth me), and by whose judgment you and I must be determined, *is the Lord,*" 1 Co. 4:4. Or, 2. If conscience acquit us, God does so too: *Beloved, if our heart condemn us not, then have we confidence toward God* (*v.* 21), then have we assurance that he accepts us now, and will acquit us in the great day of account. But, possibly, some presumptuous soul may here say, "I am glad of this; my heart does not condemn me, and therefore I may conclude God does not." As, on the contrary, upon the foregoing verse, some pious trembling soul will be ready to cry out, "God forbid! My heart or conscience condemns me, and must I then infallibly expect the condemnation of God?" But let such know that the errors of the witness are not here reckoned as the acts of the court; ignorance, error, prejudice, partiality, and presumption, may be said to be faults of the officers of the court, or of the attendants of the judge (as the mind, the will, appetite, passion, sensual disposition, or disordered brain), or of the jury, who give a false verdict, not of the judge itself; *conscience — syneidēsis,* is properly *self-consciousness.* Acts of ignorance and error are not acts of self-consciousness, but of some mistaken power; and the court of conscience is here described in its process, according to the original constitution of it by God himself, according to which process what is bound in conscience is bound in heaven; let conscience therefore be heard, be well-informed, and diligently attended to.

II. To indicate the privilege of those who have a good conscience towards God. They have interest in heaven, and in the court above; their suits are heard there: *And whatsoever we ask we receive of him, v.* 22. It is supposed that the petitioners do not desire, or do not intend to desire, any thing that is contrary to the honour and glory of the court or to their own intended spiritual good, and then they may depend upon receiving the good things they ask for; and this supposition may well be made concerning the petitioners, or they may well be supposed to receive the good things they ask for, considering their qualification and practice: *Because we keep his commandments, and do those things that are pleasing in his sight, v.* 22. Obedient souls are prepared for blessings, and they have promise of audience; those who commit things displeasing to God cannot expect that he should please them in hearing and answering their prayers, Ps. 66:18; Prov. 28:9.

Verses 23–24

The apostle, having mentioned keeping the commandments, and pleasing God, as the qualification of effectual petitioners in and with Heaven, here suitably proceeds,

I. To represent to us what those commandments primarily and summarily are; they are comprehended in this double one: *And this is his commandment, That we should believe on the name of his Son Jesus Christ, and love one another, as he gave us commandment, v.* 23. To believe on the name of his Son Jesus Christ is, 1. To discern what he is, according to his name, to have an intellectual view of his person and office, as the Son of God, and the anointed Saviour of the world. *That every one that seeth the Son, and believeth on him, may have everlasting life,* Jn. 6:40. 2. To approve him in judgment and conscience, in conviction and consciousness of our case, as one wisely and wonderfully prepared and adapted for the whole work of eternal salvation. 3. To consent to him, and acquiesce in him, as our Redeemer and recoverer unto God. 4. To trust to him, and rely upon him, for the full and final discharge of his saving office. *Those that know thy name will put their trust in thee,* Ps. 9:10. *I know whom I have believed, and I am persuaded that he is able to keep that which I have committed unto him against that day,* 2 Tim. 1:12. This faith is a needful requisite to those who would be prevalent petitioners with God, because it is by the Son that we must come to the Father; through his grace and righteousness our persons must be accepted or ingratiated with the Father (Eph. 1:6), through his purchase all our desired blessings must come, and through his intercession our prayers must be heard and answered. This is the first part of the commandment that must be observed by acceptable worshippers; the second is that we *love one another, as he gave us commandment, v.* 23. The command of Christ should be continually before our eyes. Christian love must possess our soul when we go to God in prayer. To this end we must remember that our Lord obliges us, (1.) To forgive those who offend us (Mt. 6:14), and, (2.) To reconcile ourselves to those whom we have offended, Mt. 5:23, 24. As good-will to men was proclaimed from heaven, so good-will to men, and particularly to the brethren, must be carried in the hearts of those who go to God and heaven.

II. To represent to us the blessedness of obedience to these commands. The obedient enjoy communion with God: *And he that keepeth his commandments,* and particularly those of faith and love, *dwelleth in him, and he in him, v.* 24. We dwell in God by a happy relation to him, and spiritual union with him, through his Son, and by a holy converse with him; and God dwells in us by his word, and our faith fixed on him, and by the operations of his Spirit. Then there occurs the trial of his divine inhabitation: *And hereby we know that he abideth in us, by the Spirit which he hath given us* (*v.* 24), by the sacred disposition and frame of soul that he hath conferred upon us, which being a spirit of faith in God and Christ, and of love to God and man, appears to be of God.

CHAPTER 4

In this chapter the apostle exhorts to try spirits (*v.* 1), gives a note to try by (*v.* 2, 3), shows who are of the world and who of God (*v.* 4–6), urges Christian love by divers considerations (*v.* 7–16), describes our love to God, and the effect of it (*v.* 17–21).

Verses 1–3

The apostle, having said that God's dwelling in and with us may be known by *the Spirit that he hath given us,* intimates that that Spirit may be discerned and distinguished from other spirits that appear in the world; and so here,

I. He calls the disciples, to whom he writes, to caution and scrutiny about the spirits and spiritual professors that had now risen. 1. To caution: *"Beloved, believe not every spirit;* regard not, trust not, follow not, every pretender to the Spirit of God, or every professor of vision, or inspiration, or revelation from God." Truth is the foundation of simulation and counterfeits; there had been real communications from the divine Spirit, and therefore others pretended thereto. God will take the way of his own wisdom and goodness, though it may be liable to abuse; he has sent inspired teachers to the world, and given us a supernatural revelation, though others may be so evil and so impudent as to pretend the same; every pretender to the divine Spirit, or to inspiration, and extraordinary illumination thereby, is not to be believed. Time was when the spiritual man (the man of the Spirit, who made a great noise about, and boast of, the Spirit) was mad, Hos. 9:7. 2. To scrutiny, to examination of the claims that are laid to the Spirit: *But try the spirits, whether they be of God, v.* 1. God has given of his Spirit in these latter ages of the world, but not to all who profess to come furnished therewith; to the disciples is allowed a judgment of discretion, in reference to the spirits that would be believed and trusted in the affairs of religion. A reason is given for this trial: *Because many false prophets have gone out into the world, v.* 1. There being much about the time of our Saviour's appearance in the world a general expectation among the Jews of a Redeemer to Israel, and the humiliation, spiritual reformation, and sufferings of the Saviour being taken as a prejudice against him, others were induced to set up as prophets and messiahs to Israel, according to the Saviour's prediction, Mt. 24:23, 24. It should not seem strange to us that false teachers set themselves up in the church: it was so in the apostles' times; fatal is the spirit of delusion, sad that men should vaunt themselves for prophets and inspired preachers that are by no means so!

II. He gives a test whereby the disciples may try these pretending spirits. These spirits set up for prophets, doctors, or dictators in religion, and so they were to be tried by their doctrine; and the test whereby in that day, or in that part of the world where the apostle now resided (for in various seasons, and in various churches, tests were different), must be this: *Hereby know you the Spirit of God, Every spirit that confesseth that Jesus Christ has come in the flesh* (or *that confesseth Jesus Christ that came in the flesh), is of God, v.* 2. Jesus Christ is to be confessed as the Son of God, the eternal life and Word, that was with the Father from the beginning; as the Son of God that came into, and came in, our human mortal nature, and therein suffered and died at Jerusalem. He who confesses and preaches this, by a mind supernaturally instructed and enlightened therein, does it by the Spirit of God, or God is the author of that illumination. On the contrary, *"Every spirit that confesseth not that Jesus Christ has come in the flesh* (or *Jesus Christ that came in the flesh) is not of God, v.* 3. God has given so much testimony to Jesus Christ, who was lately here in the world, and in *the flesh* (or in a fleshly body like ours), though now in heaven, that you may be assured that any impulse or pretended inspiration that contradicts this is far from being from heaven and of God." The sum of revealed religion is comprehended in the doctrine concerning Christ, his person and office. We see then the aggravation of a systematic opposition to him and it. *And this is that spirit of antichrist whereof you have heard that it should come, and even now already is it in the world, v.* 3. It was foreknown by God that antichrists would arise, and antichristian spirits oppose his Spirit and his truth; it was foreknown also that one eminent antichrist would arise, and make a long and fatal war against the Christ of God, and his institution, and honour, and kingdom in the world. This great antichrist would have his way prepared, and his rise facilitated, by other less antichrists, and the spirit of error working and disposing men's minds for him: the antichristian spirit began betimes, even in the apostles' days. Dreadful and unsearchable is the judgment of God, that persons should be given over to an antichristian spirit, and to such darkness and delusion as to set themselves against the Son of God and all the testimony that the Father hath given to the Son! But we have been forewarned that such opposition would arise; we should therefore cease to be offended, and the more we see the word of Christ fulfilled the more confirmed we should be in the truth of it.

Verses 4–6

In these verses the apostle encourages the disciples against the fear and danger of this seducing antichristian spirit, and that by such methods as these: — 1. He assures them of a more divine principle in them: *"You are of God, little children,* 5:4. *You are God's little children. We are of God, v.* 6. *We are born of God,* taught of God, anointed of God, and so secured against infectious fatal delusions. God has his chosen, who shall not be mortally seduced." 2. He gives them hope of victory: *"And have overcome them, v.* 4. You have hitherto overcome these deceivers and their temptations, and there is good ground of hope that you will do so still, and that upon these two accounts:" — (1.) "There is a strong preserver within you: *Because greater is he that is in you than he that is in the world, v.* 4. The Spirit of God dwells in you, and that Spirit is more mighty than men of devils." It is a great happiness to be under the influence of the Holy Ghost. (2.) "You are not of the same temper with these deceivers. The Spirit of God hath framed your mind for God and heaven; *but they are of the world.* The spirit that prevails in them leads them to this world; their heart is addicted thereto; they study the pomp, the pleasure, and interest of the world: *and therefore speak they of the world;* they profess a worldly messiah and saviour; they project a worldly kingdom and dominion; the possessions and treasures of the world would they engross to themselves, forgetting that the true Redeemer's *kingdom is not of this world.* This worldly design procures them proselytes: *The world heareth them, v.* 5. They are followed by such as themselves: the world will love its own, and its own will love it. But those are in a fair way to conquer pernicious seductions who have conquered the love of this seducing world." Then, 3. He represents to them that though their company might be the smaller, yet it was the better; they had more divine and holy knowledge: *"He that knoweth God heareth us.* He who knows the purity and holiness of God, the love and grace of God, the truth and faithfulness of God, the ancient word and prophecies of God, the signals and testimonials of God, must know that he is with us; and he who knows this will attend to us, and abide with us." He that is well furnished with natural religion will the more faithfully cleave to Christianity. *He that knoweth God* (in his natural and moral excellences, revelations, and works) *heareth us, v.* 6. As, on the contrary, *"He that is not of God heareth not us.* He who knows not God regards not us. He that is not *born of God* (walking according to his natural disposition) walks not with us. The further any are from God (as appears in all ages) the further they are from Christ and his faithful servants; and the more addicted persons are to this world the more remote they are from the spirit of Christianity. Thus you have a distinction between us and others: *Hereby know we the Spirit of truth and the spirit of error, v.* 6. This doctrine concerning the Saviour's person leading you from the world to God is a signature of *the Spirit of truth,* in opposition to *the spirit of error.* The more pure and holy any doctrine is the more likely is it to be of God."

Verses 7–13

As *the Spirit of truth* is known by doctrine (thus spirits are to be tried), it is known by love likewise; and so here follows a strong fervent exhortation to holy Christian love: *Beloved, let us love one another, v.* 7. The apostle would unite them in his love, that he might unite them in love to each other: *"Beloved,* I beseech you, by the love I bear to you, that you put on unfeigned mutual love." This exhortation is pressed and urged with variety of argument: as,

I. From the high and heavenly descent of love: *For love is of God.* He is the fountain, author, parent, and commander of love; it is the sum of his law and gospel: *And every one that loveth* (whose spirit is framed to judicious holy love) *is born of God, v.* 7. The Spirit of God is the Spirit of love. The new nature in the children of God is the offspring of his love: and the temper and complexion of it is love. *The fruit of the Spirit is love,* Gal. 5:22. Love comes down from heaven.

II. Love argues a true and just apprehension of the divine nature: *He that loveth knoweth God, v.* 7. *He that loveth not knoweth not God, v.* 8. What attribute of the divine Majesty so clearly shines in all the world as his communicative goodness, which is love. The wisdom, the greatness, the harmony, and usefulness of the vast creation, which so fully demonstrate his being, do at the same time show and prove his love; and natural reason, inferring and collecting the nature and excellence of the most absolute perfect being, must collect and find that he is most highly good: and *he that loveth not* (is not quickened by the knowledge he hath of God to the affection and practice of love) *knoweth not God;* it is a convictive evidence that the sound and due knowledge of God dwells not in such a soul; his love must needs shine among his primary brightest perfections; *for God is love* (*v.* 8), his nature and essence are love, his will and works are primarily love. Not that this is the only conception we ought to have of him; we have found that he *is light as well as love* (*ch.* 1:5), and God is principally love to himself, and he has such perfections as arise from the necessary love he must bear to his necessary existence, excellence, and glory; but love is natural and essential to the divine Majesty: *God is love.* This is argued from the display and demonstration that he hath given of it; as, 1. That he hath loved us, such as we are: *In this was manifest the love of God towards us* (*v.* 9), towards us mortals, us ungrateful rebels. *God commandeth his love towards us, in that, while we were yet sinners, Christ died for us,* Rom. 5:8. Strange that God should love impure, vain, vile, dust and ashes! 2. That he has loved us at such a rate, at such an incomparable value as he has given for us; he has given his own, only-beloved, blessed Son for us: *Because that God sent his only-begotten Son into the world, that we might live through him, v.* 9. This person is in some peculiar distinguishing way the Son of God; he is the only-begotten. Should we suppose him begotten as a creature or created being, he is not the only-begotten. Should we suppose him a natural necessary eradication from the Father's glory or glorious essence, or substance, he must be the only-begotten: and then it will be a mystery and miracle of divine love that such a Son should be sent into our world for us! It may well be said, *So* (wonderfully, so amazingly, so incredibly) *God loved the world.* 3. That God loved us first, and in the circumstances in which we lay: *Herein is love* (unusual unprecedented love), *not that we loved God, but that he loved us, v.* 10. He loved us, when we had no love for him, when we lay in our guilt, misery, and blood, when we were undeserving, ill-deserving, polluted, and unclean, and wanted to be washed from our sins in sacred blood. 4. That he gave us his Son for such service and such an end. (1.) For such service, *to be the propitiation for our sins;* consequently to die for us, to die under the law and curse of God, to *bear our sins in his own body,* to be crucified, to be wounded in his soul, and pierced in his side, to be dead and buried for us (*v.* 10); and then, (2.) For such an end, for such a good and beneficial end to us — *that we might live through him* (*v.* 9), might live for ever through him, might live in heaven, live with God, and live in eternal glory and blessedness with him and through him: O what love is here! Then,

III. Divine love to the brethren should constrain ours: *Beloved* (I would adjure you by your interest in my love to remember), *if God so loved us, we ought also to love one another, v.* 11. This should be an invincible argument. The example of God should press us. *We should be followers* (or imitators) *of him, as his dear children.* The objects of the divine love should be the objects of ours. Shall we refuse to love those whom the eternal God hath loved? We should be admirers of his love, and lovers of his love (of the benevolence and complacency that are in him), and consequently lovers of those whom he loves. The general love of God to the world should induce a universal love among mankind. *That you may be the children of your Father who is in heaven; for he maketh his sun to rise on the evil and on the good, and sendeth his rain on the just and on the unjust,* Mt. 5:45. The peculiar love of God to the church and to the saints should be productive of a peculiar love there: *If God so loved us, we ought* surely (in some measure suitably thereto) *to love one another.*

IV. The Christian love is an assurance of the divine inhabitation: *If we love one another, God dwelleth in us, v.* 12. Now God dwelleth in us, not by any visible presence, or immediate appearance to the eye *(no man hath seen God at any time, v.* 12), but by his Spirit (*v.* 13); or, "No man hath seen God at any time; he does not here present himself to our eye or to our immediate intuition, and so he does not in this way demand and exact our love; but he demands and expects it in that way in which he has thought meet to deserve and claim it, and that is in the illustration that he has given of himself and of his love (and thereupon of his loveliness too) in the catholic church, and particularly in the brethren, the members of that church. In them, and in his appearance for them and with them, is God to be loved; and thus, *if we love one another, God dwelleth in us.* The sacred lovers of the brethren are the temples of God; the divine Majesty has a peculiar residence there."

V. Herein the divine love attains a considerable end and accomplishment in us: "*And his love is perfected in us, v.* 12. It has obtained its completion in and upon us. God's love is not perfected in him, but in and with us. His love could not be designed to be ineffectual and fruitless upon us; when its proper genuine end and issue are attained and produced thereby, it may be said to be perfected; so faith is perfected by its works, and love perfected by its operations. When the divine love has wrought us to the same image, to the love of God, and thereupon to the love of the brethren, the children of God, for his sake, it is therein and so far perfected and completed, though this love of ours is not at present perfect, nor the ultimate end of the divine love to us." How ambitious should we be of this fraternal Christian love, when God reckons his own love to us perfected thereby! To this the apostle, having mentioned the high favour of God's dwelling in us, subjoins the note and character thereof: *Hereby know we that we dwell in him, and he in us, because he hath given us of his Spirit, v.* 13. Certainly this mutual inhabitation is something more noble and great than we are well acquaint-

ed with or can declare. One would think that to speak of God dwelling in us, and we in him, were to use words too high for mortals, had not God gone before us therein. What this indwelling imports has been briefly explained on *ch.* 3:24. What it fully is must be left to the revelation of the blessed world. But this mutual inhabitation we know, says the apostle, *because he hath given us of his spirit;* he has lodged the image and fruit of his Spirit in our hearts (*v.* 13), and *the Spirit that he hath given us* appears to be his, or of him, since it is *the Spirit of power,* of zeal and magnanimity for God, *of love* to God and man, *and of a sound mind,* of an understanding well instructed in the affairs of God and religion, and his kingdom among men, 2 Tim. 1:7.

Verses 14–16

Since faith in Christ works love to God, and love to God must kindle love to the brethren, the apostle here confirms the prime article of the Christian faith as the foundation of such love. Here,

I. He proclaims the fundamental article of the Christian religion, which is so representative of the love of God: *And we have seen, and do testify, that the Father sent the Son to be the Saviour of the world, v.* 14. We here see, 1. The Lord Jesus's relation to God; he is Son to the Father, such a Son as no one else is, and so as to be God with the Father. 2. His relation and office towards us — *the Saviour of the world;* he saves us by his death, example, intercession, Spirit, and power against the enemies of our salvation. 3. The ground on which he became so — by the mission of him: *The Father sent the Son,* he decreed and willed his coming hither, in and with the consent of the Son. 4. The apostle's assurance of this — he and his brethren had seen it; they had seen the Son of God in his human nature, in his holy converse and works, in his transfiguration on the mount, and in his death, resurrection from the dead, and royal ascent to heaven; they had so seen him as to be satisfied that he was the *only-begotten of the Father, full of grace and truth.* 5. The apostle's attestation of this, in pursuance of such evidence: "*We have seen and do testify.* The weight of this truth obliges us to testify it; the salvation of the world lies upon it. The evidence of the truth warrants us to testify it; our eyes, and ears, and hands, have been witnesses of it." Thereupon,

II. The apostle states the excellency, or the excellent privilege attending the due acknowledgment of this truth: *Whosoever shall confess that Jesus is the Son of God, God dwelleth in him, and he in God, v.* 15. This confession seems to include faith in the heart as the foundation of it, acknowledgment with the mouth to the glory of God and Christ, and profession in the life and conduct, in opposition to the flatteries or frowns of the world. Thus *no man says that Jesus is the Lord but by the Holy Ghost,* by the external attestation and internal operation of the Holy Ghost, 1 Co. 12:3. And so he who thus confesses Christ, and God in him, is enriched with or possessed by the Spirit of God, and has a complacential knowledge of God and much holy enjoyment of him. Then,

III. The apostle applies this in order to the excitation of holy love. God's love is thus seen and exerted in Christ Jesus; *and thus have we known and believed the love that God hath to us, v.* 16. The Christian revelation is, what should endear it to us, the revelation of the divine love; the articles of our revealed faith are but so many articles relating to the divine love. The history of the Lord Christ is the history of God's love to us; all his transactions in and with his Son were but testifications of his love to us, and means to advance us to the love of God: *God was in Christ reconciling the world unto himself,* 2 Co. 5:19. Hence we may learn,

1. That *God is love* (*v.* 16); he is essential boundless love; he has incomparable incomprehensible love for us of this world, which he has demonstrated in the mission and mediation of his beloved Son. It is the great objection and prejudice against the Christian revelation that the love of God should be so strange and unaccountable as to give his own eternal Son for us; it is the prejudice of many against the eternity and the deity of the Son that so great a person should be given for us. It is, I confess, mysterious and unsearchable; but there are *unsearchable riches in Christ.* It is a pity that the vastness of the divine love should be made a prejudice against the revelation and the belief of it. But what will not God do when he designs to demonstrate the height of any perfection of his? When he would show somewhat of his power and wisdom, he makes such a world as this; when he

would show more of his grandeur and glory, he makes heaven for the ministering spirits that are before the throne. What will he not do then when he designs to demonstrate his love, and to demonstrate his highest love, or that he himself is love, or that love is one of the most bright, dear, transcendent, operative excellencies of his unbounded nature; and to demonstrate this not only to us, but to the angelic world, and to the principalities and powers above, and this not for our surprise for a while, but for the admiration, and praise, and adoration, and felicity, of our most exalted powers to all eternity? What will not God then do? Surely then it will look more agreeable to the design, and grandeur, and pregnancy of his love (if I may so call it) to give an eternal Son for us, than to make a Son on purpose for our relief. In such a dispensation as that of giving a natural, essential, eternal Son for us and to us, he will commend his love to us indeed; and what will not the God of love do when he designs to commend his love, and to commend it in the view of heaven, and earth, and hell, and when he will commend himself and recommend himself to us, and to our highest conviction, and also affection, as love itself? And what if it should appear at last (which I shall only offer to the consideration of the judicious) that the divine love, and particularly God's love in Christ, should be the foundation of the glories of heaven, in the present enjoyment of those ministering spirits that comported with it, and of the salvation of this world, and of the torments of hell? This last will seem most strange. But what if therein it should appear not only that God is love to himself, in vindicating his own law, and government, and love, and glory, but that the damned ones are made so, or are so punished, (1.) Because they despised the love of God already manifested and exhibited. (2.) Because they refused to be beloved in what was further proposed and promised. (3.) Because they made themselves unmeet to be the objects of divine complacency and delight? If the conscience of the damned should accuse them of these things, and especially of rejecting the highest instance of divine love, and if the far greatest part of the intelligent creation should be everlastingly blessed through the highest instance of the divine love, then may it well be inscribed upon the whole creation of God, *God is love.*

2. That hereupon *he that dwelleth in love dwelleth in God, and God in him, v.* 16. There is great communion between the God of love and the loving soul; that is, him who loves the creation of God, according to its different relation to God, and reception from him and interest in him. He that dwells in sacred love has *the love God shed abroad upon his heart,* has the impress of God upon his spirit, the Spirit of God sanctifying and sealing him, lives in the meditation, views, and tastes of the divine love, and will ere long go to dwell with God for ever.

Verses 17–21

The apostle, having thus excited and enforced sacred love from the great pattern and motive of it, the love that is and dwells in God himself, proceeds to recommend it further by other considerations; and he recommends it in both the branches of it, both as love to God, and love to our brother or Christian neighbour.

I. As love to God, to the *primum amabile — the first and chief of all amiable beings and objects,* who has the confluence of all beauty, excellence, and loveliness, in himself, and confers on all other beings whatever renders them good and amiable. Love to God seems here to be recommended on these accounts: — 1. It will give us peace and satisfaction of spirit in the day when it will be most needed, or when it will be the greatest pleasure and blessing imaginable: *Herein is our love made perfect, that we may have boldness in the day of judgment, v.* 17. There must be a day of universal judgment. Happy they who shall have holy fiducial boldness before the Judge at that day, who shall be able to lift up their heads, and to look him in the face, as knowing he is their friend and advocate! Happy they who have holy boldness and assurance in the prospect of that day, who look and wait for it, and for the Judge's appearance! So do, and so may do, the lovers of God. Their love to God assures them of God's love to them, and consequently of the friendship of the Son of God; the more we love our friend, especially when we are sure that he knows it, the more we can trust his love. As God is good and loving, and faithful to his promise, so we can easily be persuaded of his love, and the happy fruits of his love, when we can say, *Thou that knowest all things knowest that we love thee. And hope maketh not ashamed;* our hope, conceived by the consideration of God's love, will not disappoint us, *because the love of God is shed abroad in our hearts by the Holy Ghost that is given to us,* Rom. 5:5. Possibly here by the love of God may be meant our *love to God,* which is *shed abroad upon our hearts by the Holy Ghost;* this is the foundation of our hope, or of our assurance that our hope will hold good at last. Or, if by the love of God be meant the sense and apprehension of his love to us, yet this must suppose or include us as lovers of him in this case; and indeed the sense and evidence of his love to us do shed abroad upon our hearts love to him; and thereupon we have confidence towards him and peace and joy in him. He will give the crown of righteousness to all that love his appearing. And we have this boldness towards Christ because of our conformity to him: *Because as he is so are we in this world, v.* 17. Love hath conformed us to him; as he was the great lover of God and man, he has taught us in our measure to be so too, and he will not deny his own image. Love teaches us to conform in sufferings too; we suffer for him and with him, and therefore cannot but hope and trust that we shall also be glorified together with him, 2 Tim. 2:12. 2. It prevents or removes the uncomfortable result and fruit of servile fear: *There is no fear in love* (*v.* 18); so far as love prevails, fear ceases. We must here distinguish, I judge, between fear and being afraid; or, in this case, between the fear of God and being afraid of him. The fear of God is often mentioned and commanded as the substance of religion (1 Pt. 2:17; Rev. 14:7); and so it imports the high regard and veneration we have for God and his authority and government. Such fear is constant with love, yea, with perfect love, as being in the angels themselves. But then there is a being afraid of God, which arises from a sense of guilt, and a view of his vindictive perfections; in the view of them, God is represented as a consuming fire; and so fear here may be rendered *dread; There is no dread in love.* Love considers its object as good and excellent, and therefore amiable, and worthy to be beloved. Love considers God as most eminently good, and most eminently loving us in Christ, and so puts off dread, and puts on joy in him; and, as love grows, joy grows too; so that *perfect love casteth out fear* or dread. Those who perfectly love God are, from his nature, and counsel, and covenant, perfectly assured of his love, and consequently are perfectly free from any dismal dreadful suspicions of his punitive power and justice, as armed against them; they well know that God loves them, and they thereupon triumph in his love. That *perfect love casteth out fear* the apostle thus sensibly argues: that which casteth out torment casteth out fear or dread: *Because fear hath torment* (*v.* 18) — fear is known to be a disquieting torturing passion, especially such a fear as is the dread of an almighty avenging God; but perfect love casteth out torment, for it teaches the mind a perfect acquiescence and complacency in the beloved, and therefore *perfect love casteth out fear.* Or, which is here equivalent, *he that feareth is not made perfect in love* (*v.* 18); it is a sign that our love is far from being perfect, since our doubts, and fears, and dismal apprehensions of God, are so many. Let us long for, and hasten to, the world of perfect love, where our serenity and joy in God will be as perfect as our love! 3. From the source and rise of it, which is the antecedent love of God: *We love him, because he first loved us, v.* 19. His love is the incentive, the motive, and moral cause of ours. We cannot but love so good a God, who was first in the act and work of love, who loved us when we were both unloving and unlovely, who loved us at so great a rate, who has been seeking and soliciting our love at the expense of his Son's blood; and has condescended to beseech us to be reconciled unto him. Let heaven and earth stand amazed at such love! His love is the productive cause of ours: *Of his own will* (of his own free loving will) *begat he us. To those that love him all things work together for good, to those who are the called according to his purpose.* Those *that love God are the called* thereto *according to his purpose* (Rom. 8:28); according to whose purpose they are called is sufficiently intimated in the following clauses: *whom he did predestinate* (or antecedently purpose, to the image of his Son) *those he also called,* effectually recovered thereto. The divine love stamped love upon our souls; may the Lord still and further direct our hearts into the love of God! 2 Th. 3:5.

II. As love to our brother and neighbour in Christ; such love is argued and urged on these accounts: — 1. As suitable and consonant to our Christian profession. In the profession of Christianity we profess to love God as the root of religion: "*If then a man say,* or profess as much as thereby to say, *I*

love God, I am a lover of his name, and house, and worship, *and yet hate his brother,* whom he should love for God's sake, *he is a liar* (*v.* 20), he therein gives his profession the lie." That such a one loves not God the apostle proves by the usual facility of loving what is seen rather than what is unseen: *For he that loveth not his brother, whom he hath seen, how can he love God, whom he hath not seen? v.* 20. The eye is wont to affect the heart; things unseen less catch the mind, and thereby the heart. The incomprehensibleness of God very much arises from his invisibility; the member of Christ has much of God visible in him. How then shall the hater of a visible image of God pretend to love the unseen original, the invisible God himself? 2. As suitable to the express law of God, and the just reason of it: *And this commandment have we from him, that he who loveth God love his brother also, v.* 21. As God has communicated his image in nature and in grace, so he would have our love to be suitably diffused. We must love God originally and supremely, and others in him, on the account of their derivation and reception from him, and of his interest in them. Now, our Christian brethren having a new nature and excellent privileges derived from God, and God having his interest in them as well as in us, it cannot but be a natural suitable obligation *that he who loves God should love his brother also.*

CHAPTER 5

In this chapter the apostle asserts, I. The dignity of believers (*v.* 1). II. Their obligation to love, and the trial of it (*v.* 1–3). III. Their victory (*v.* 4, 5). IV. The credibility and confirmation of their faith (*v.* 6–10). V. The advantage of their faith in eternal life (*v.* 11–13). VI. The audience of their prayers, unless for those who have sinned unto death (*v.* 14–17). VII. The preservation from sin and Satan (*v.* 18). VIII. Their happy distinction from the world (*v.* 19). IX. Their true knowledge of God (*v.* 20), upon which they must depart from idols (*v.* 21).

Verses 1–5

I. The apostle having, in the conclusion of the last chapter, as was there observed, urged Christian love upon those two accounts, as suitable to Christian profession and as suitable to the divine command, here adds a third: Such love is suitable, and indeed demanded, by their eminent relation; our Christian brethren or fellow-believers are nearly related to God; they are his children: *Whosoever believeth that Jesus is the Christ is born of God, v.* 1. Here the Christian brother is, 1. Described by his faith; he that *believeth that Jesus is the Christ* — that he is Messiah the prince, that he is the Son of God by nature and office, that he is the chief of all the anointed world, chief of all the priests, prophets, or kings, who were ever anointed by God or for him, that he is perfectly prepared and furnished for the whole work of the eternal salvation — accordingly yields himself up to his care and direction; and then he is, 2. Dignified by his descent: *He is born of God, v.* 1. This principle of faith, and the new nature that attends it or from which it springs, are ingenerated by the Spirit of God; and so sonship and adoption are not now appropriated *to the seed of Abraham according to the flesh,* not to the ancient Israel of God; all believers, though by nature sinners of the Gentiles, are spiritually descended from God, and accordingly are to be beloved; as it is added: *Every one that loveth him that begat loveth him also that is begotten of him, v.* 1. It seems but natural that he who loves the Father should love the children also, and that in some proportion to their resemblance to their Father and to the Father's love to them; and so we must first and principally love *the Son of the Father,* as he is most emphatically styled, 2 Jn. 3, *the only* (necessarily) *begotten,* and *the Son of his love,* and then those that are voluntarily begotten, and *renewed by the Spirit of grace.*

II. The apostle shows, 1. How we may discern the truth, or the true evangelical nature of our love to the regenerate. The ground of it must be our love to God, whose they are: *By this we know that we love the children of God, when we love God, v.* 2. Our love to them appears to be sound and genuine when we love them not merely upon any secular account, as because they are rich, or learned, or kind to us, or of our denomination among religious parties; but because they are God's children, his regenerating grace appears in them, his image and superscription are upon them, and so in them God himself is loved. Thus we see what that love to the brethren is that is so pressed in this epistle; it is love to them as the children of God and the adopted brethren of the Lord Jesus. 2. How we may learn the truth of our love to God — it appears in our holy obedience: *When we love*

God, and keep his commandments, *v.* 2. Then we truly, and in gospel account, love God, when we keep his commandments: *For this is the love of God, that we keep his commandments;* and the keeping of his commandments requires a spirit inclined thereto and delighting herein; *and so his commandments are not grievous, v.* 3. Or, *This is the love of God, that,* as thereby we are determined to obedience, and to keep the commandments of God, so his commandments are thereby made easy and pleasant to us. The lover of God says, "*O how I love thy law! I will run the way of thy commandments, when thou shalt enlarge my heart* (Ps. 119:32), when thou shalt enlarge it either with love or with thy Spirit, the spring of love." 3. What is and ought to be the result and effect of regeneration — an intellectual spiritual conquest of this world: *For* whatsoever *is born of God,* or, as in some copies, whosoever *is born of God, overcometh the world, v.* 4. He that is born of God is born *for* God, and consequently for another world. He has a temper and disposition that tend to a higher and better world; and he is furnished with such arms, or such a weapon, whereby he can repel and conquer this; as it is added, *And this is the victory that overcometh the world, even our faith, v.* 4. Faith is the cause of victory, the means, the instrument, the spiritual armour and artillery by which we overcome; for, (1.) In and by faith we cleave to Christ, in contempt of, and opposition to, the world. (2.) Faith works in and by love to God and Christ, and so withdraws us from the love of the world. (3.) Faith sanctifies the heart, and purifies it from those sensual lusts by which the world obtains such sway and dominion over souls. (4.) It receives and derives strength from the object of it, the Son of God, for conquering the frowns and flatteries of the world. (5.) It obtains by gospel promise a right to the indwelling Spirit of grace, that is greater than he who dwells in the world. (6.) It sees an invisible world at hand, with which this world is not worthy to be compared, and into which it tells the soul in which it resides it must be continually prepared to enter; and thereupon,

III. The apostle concludes that it is the real Christian that is the true conqueror of the world: *Who is he then that overcometh the world, but he that believeth that Jesus is the Son of God? v.* 5. It is the world that lies in our way to heaven, and is the great impediment to our entrance there. But he who believes that Jesus is the Son of God believes therein that Jesus Came from God to be the Saviour of the world, and powerfully to conduct us from the world to heaven, and to God, who is fully to be enjoyed there. And he who so believes must needs by this faith overcome the world. For, 1. He must be well satisfied that this world is a vehement enemy to his soul, to his holiness, his salvation, and his blessedness. *For all that is in the world, the lust of the flesh, the lust of the eyes, and the pride of life, is not of the Father, but is of the world, ch.* 2:16. 2. He sees it must be a great part of the Saviour's work, and of his own salvation, to be redeemed and rescued from this malignant world. *Who gave himself for our sins, that he might deliver us from this present evil world,* Gal. 1:4. 3. He sees in and by the life and conduct of the Lord Jesus on earth that this world is to be renounced and overcome. 4. He perceives that the Lord Jesus conquered the world, not for himself only, but for his followers; and they must study to be partakers of his victory. *Be of good cheer, I have overcome the world.* 5. He is taught and influenced by the Lord Jesus's death to be mortified and crucified to the world. *God forbid that I should glory, save in the cross of our Lord Jesus Christ, by whom the world is crucified to me, and I unto the world,* Gal. 6:14. 6. He is begotten by the resurrection of Jesus Christ from the dead to the lively hope of a blessed world above, 1 Pt. 1:3. 7. He knows that the Saviour has gone to heaven, and is there preparing a place for his serious believers, Jn. 14:2. 8. He knows that his Saviour will come again thence, and will put an end to this world, and judge the inhabitants of it, and receive his believers to his presence and glory, Jn. 14:3. 9. He is possessed with a spirit and disposition that cannot be satisfied with this world, that look beyond it, and are still tending, striving, and pressing, towards the world in heaven. *In this we groan, earnestly desiring to be clothed upon with our house which is from heaven,* 2 Co. 5:2. So that it is the Christian religion that affords its proselytes a universal empire. It is the Christian revelation that is the great means of conquering the world, and gaining another that is most pure and peaceful, blessed and eternal. It is there, in that revelation, that we see what are the occasion and ground of the quarrel and contest between the holy God and this rebellious world. It is there that we meet with sacred doctrine (both speculative and practical), quite contrary to the tenour, temper, and tendency of this world. It is by that doctrine that a spirit is communicated and diffused which is superior and adverse to the spirit of the world. It is there we see that the Saviour himself was not of this world that his kingdom was not and is not so, that it must be separated from the world and gathered out of it for heaven and for God. There we see that the Saviour designs not this world for the inheritance and portion of his saved company. As he has gone to heaven himself, so he assures them he goes to prepare for their residence there, as designing they should always dwell with him, and allowing them to believe that if in this life, and this world only, they had hope in him, they should at last be but miserable. It is there that the eternal blessed world is most clearly revealed and proposed to our affection and pursuit. It is there that we are furnished with the best arms and artillery against the assaults and attempts of the world. It is there that we are taught how the world may be out-shot in its own bow, or its artillery turned against itself; and its oppositions, encounters, and persecutions, be made serviceable to our conquest of the world, and to our motion and ascent to the higher heavenly world: and there we are encouraged by a whole army and cloud of holy soldiers, who have in their several ages, posts, and stations, overcome the world, and won the crown. It is the real Christian that is the proper hero, who vanquishes the world and rejoices in a universal victory. Nor does he (for he is far superior to the Grecian monarch) mourn that there is not another world to be subdued, but lays hold on the eternal world of life, and in a sacred sense takes the kingdom of heaven by violence too. Who in all the world but the believer on Jesus Christ can thus overcome the world?

Verses 6–9

The faith of the Christian believer (or the believer in Christ) being thus mighty and victorious, it had need to be well founded, to be furnished with unquestionable celestial evidence concerning the divine mission, authority, and office of the Lord Jesus; and it is so; he brings his credentials along with him, and he brings them in a way by which he came and in the witness that attends him.

I. In the way and manner by which he came; not barely by which he came into the world, but by and with which he came, and appeared, and acted, as a Saviour in the world: *This is he that came by water and blood.* He came to save us from our sins, to give us eternal life, and bring us to God; and, that he might the more assuredly do this, *he came by,* or with, *water and blood. Even Jesus Christ;* Jesus Christ, I say, did so; and none but he. And I say it again, not by or with *water only, but by* and with *water and blood, v.* 6. *Jesus Christ came with water and blood,* as the notes and signatures of the true effectual Saviour of the world; and he came by water and blood as the means by which he would heal and save us. That he must and did thus come in his saving office may appear by our remembering these things: —

1. We are inwardly and outwardly defiled. (1.) Inwardly, by the power and pollution off sin and in our nature. For our cleansing from this we need spiritual water; such as can reach the soul and the powers of it. Accordingly, there is in and by Christ Jesus *the washing of regeneration and the renewing of the Holy Ghost.* And this was intimated to the apostles by our Lord, when he washed their feet, and said to Peter, who refused to be washed, *Except I wash thee, thou hast no part in me.* (2.) We are defiled outwardly, by the guilt and condemning power of sin upon our persons. By this we are separated from God, and banished from his favourable, gracious, beatific presence for ever. From this we must be purged by atoning blood. It is the law or determination in the court of heaven *that without shedding of blood there shall be no remission,* Heb. 9:22. The Saviour from sin therefore must come with blood.

2. Both these ways of cleansing were represented in the old ceremonial institutions of God. Persons and things must be purified by water and blood. *There were divers washings and carnal ordinances imposed till the time of reformation,* Heb. 9:10. *The ashes of a heifer,* mixed with water, *sprinkling the unclean, sanctifieth to the purifying of the flesh,* Heb. 9:13; Num. 19:9. *And likewise almost all things are, by the law, purged with blood,* Heb. 9:22. As those show us our double defilement, so they indicate the Saviour's two-fold purgation.

3. At and upon the death of Jesus Christ, his side being pierced with a soldier's spear, out of the wound there immediately issued water and blood. This the beloved apostle saw, and he seems to have been affected with the sight; he alone records it, and seems to reckon himself obliged to record it, and seems to reckon himself obliged to record it, as containing something mysterious in it: *And he that saw it bore record, and his record is true. And he knoweth,* being an eye-witness, *that he saith true, that you might believe,* and that you might believe this particularly, that out of his pierced side *forthwith there came water and blood,* Jn. 19:34, 35. Now this water and blood are comprehensive of all that is necessary and effectual to our salvation. By the water our souls are washed and purified for heaven and the region of saints in light. By the blood God is glorified, his law is honoured, and his vindictive excellences are illustrated and displayed. *Whom God hath set forth,* or purposed, or proposed, *a propitiation through faith in his blood,* or a propitiation in or by his blood through faith, *to declare his righteousness, that he may be just, and the justifier of him that believeth in Jesus,* Rom. 3:25, 26. By the blood we are justified, reconciled, and presented righteous to God. By the blood, the curse of the law being satisfied, and purifying Spirit is obtained for the internal ablution of our natures. *Christ hath redeemed us from the curse of the law, that the blessing of Abraham might come on the Gentiles, that we might receive the promise of the Spirit,* the promised Spirit, *through faith,* Gal. 3:13, etc. The water, as well as the blood, issued out of the side of the sacrificed Redeemer. The water and the blood then comprehend all things that can be requisite to our salvation. They will consecrate and sanctify to that purpose all that God shall appoint or make use of in order to that great end. *He loved the church, and gave himself for it, that he might sanctify and cleanse it with the washing of water by the word, that he might present it to himself a glorious church,* Eph. 5:25–27. He who comes by water and blood is an accurate perfect Saviour. And this is he who comes by water and blood, even Jesus Christ! Thus we see in what way and manner, or, if you please, with what utensils, he comes. But we see his credentials also,

II. In the witness that attends him, and that is, the divine Spirit, that Spirit to whom the perfecting of the works of God is usually attributed: *And it is the Spirit that beareth witness, v.* 6. It was meet that the commissioned Saviour of the world should have a constant agent to support his work, and testify of him to the world. It was meet that a divine power should attend him, his gospel, and servants; and notify to the world upon what errand and office they came, and by what authority they were sent: this was done in and by the Spirit of God, according to the Saviour's own prediction, *"He shall glorify me,* even when I shall be rejected and crucified by men, *for he shall receive* or take *of mine.* He shall not receive my immediate office; he shall not die and rise again for you; *but he shall receive of mine,* shall proceed on the foundation I have laid, shall take up my institution, and truth, and cause, *and shall* further *show it unto you,* and by you to the world," Jn. 16:14. And then the apostle adds the commendation or the acceptableness of this witness: *Because the Spirit is truth, v.* 6. He is the Spirit of God, and cannot lie. There is a copy that would afford us a very suitable reading thus: *because,* or that, *Christ is the truth.* And so it indicates the matter of the Spirit's testimony, the thing which he attests, and that is, the truth of Christ: *And it is the Spirit that beareth witness that Christ is the truth;* and consequently that Christianity, or the Christian religion, is the truth of the day, the truth of God. But it is meet that one or two copies should alter the text; and our present reading is very agreeable, and so we retain it. *The Spirit is truth.* He is indeed the Spirit of truth, Jn. 14:17. And that the Spirit is truth, and a witness worthy of all acceptation, appears in that he is a heavenly witness, or one of the witnesses that in and from heaven bore testimony concerning the truth and authority of Christ. *Because* (or for) *there are three that bear record in heaven, the Father, the Word, and the Holy Ghost, and these three are one.* And so *v.* 7 most appositely occurs, as a proof of the authenticity of the Spirit's testimony; he must needs be true, or even truth itself, if he be not only a witness in heaven, but *even one* (not in testimony only, for so an angel may be, but in being and essence) *with the Father and the Word.* But here,

1. We are stopped in our course by the contest there is about the genuineness of *v.* 7. It is alleged that many old Greek manuscripts have it not. We shall not here enter into the controversy. It should seem that the critics are not agreed what manuscripts have it and what not; nor do they sufficiently inform us of the integrity and value of the manuscripts they peruse. Some may be so faulty, as I have an old printed Greek Testament so full of *errata,* that one would think no critic would establish a various lection thereupon. But let the judicious collators of copies manage that business. There are some rational surmises that seem to support the present text and reading. As,

(1.) If we admit *v.* 8, in the room of *v.* 7, it looks too like a tautology and repetition of what was included in *v.* 6, *This is he that came by water and blood, not by water only, but by water and blood; and it is the Spirit that beareth witness. For there are three that bear witness, the Spirit, the water, and the blood.* This does not assign near so noble an introduction of these three witnesses as our present reading does.

(2.) It is observed that many copies read that distinctive clause, *upon the earth: There are three that bear record upon the earth.* Now this bears a visible opposition to some witness or witnesses elsewhere, and therefore we are told, by the adversaries of the text, that this clause must be supposed to be omitted in most books that want *v.* 7. But it should for the same reason be so in all. Take we *v.* 6, *This is he that came by water and blood. And it is the Spirit that beareth witness, because the Spirit is truth.* It would not now naturally and properly be added, *For there are three that bear record on earth,* unless we should suppose that the apostle would tell us that all the witnesses are such as are on earth, when yet he would assure us that one is infallibly true, or even truth itself.

(3.) It is observed that there is a variety of reading even in the Greek text, as in *v.* 7. Some copies read *hen eisi — are one;* others (at least the *Complutensian*) *eis to hen eisin — are to one,* or *agree in one;* and in *v.* 8 (in that part that it is supposed should be admitted), instead of the common *en tē gē — in earth, the Complutensian* reads *epi tēs gēs — upon earth,* which seems to show that that edition depended upon some Greek authority, and not merely, as some would have us believe, upon the authority either of the vulgar Latin or of *Thomas Aquinas,* though his testimony may be added thereto.

(4.) The seventh verse is very agreeable to the style and the theology of our apostle; as, [1.] He delights in the title *the Father,* whether he indicates thereby God only, or a divine person distinguished from the Son. I *and* the Father *are one. And Yet I am not alone; because* the Father *is with me. I will pray* the Father, *and he shall give you another comforter. If any man love the world, the love of* the Father *is not in him. Grace be with you, and peace from God* the Father, *and from the Lord Jesus Christ, the Son of* the Father, 2 Jn. 3. Then, [2.] The name *the Word* is known to be almost (if not quite) peculiar to this apostle. Had the text been devised by another, it had been more easy and obvious, from the form of baptism, and the common language of the church, to have used the name *Son* instead of that of the *Word.* As it is observed that Tertullian and Cyprian use that name, even when they refer to this verse; or it is made an objection against their referring to this verse, because they speak of the Son, not the Word; and yet Cyprian's expression seems to be very clear by the citation of Facundus himself. *Quod Johannis apostoli testimonium beatus Cyprianus, Carthaginensis antistes et martyr, in epistolâ sive libro, quem de Trinitate scripsit, de Patre, Filio, et Spiritu sancto dictum intelligit; ait enim, Dicit Dominus, Ego et Pater unum sumus; et iterum de Patre, Filio, et Spiritu sancto scriptum est, Et hi tres unum sunt. — Blessed Cyprian, the Carthaginian bishop and martyr, in the epistle or book he wrote concerning the Trinity, considered the testimony of the apostle John as relating to the Father, the Son, and Holy Spirit; for he says, the Lord says, I and the Father are one; and again, of the Father, the Son, and the Holy Spirit it is written, And these three are one.* Now it is nowhere written that these are one, but in *v.* 7. It is probable than that St. Cyprian, either depending on his memory, or rather intending things more than words, persons more than names, or calling persons by their names more usual in the church (both in popular and polemic discourses), called the second by the name of the *Son* rather than of the *Word.* If any man can admit Facundus's fancy, that Cyprian meant that the Spirit, the water, and the blood, were indeed the Father, Word, and Spirit, that John said were one, he may enjoy his opinion to himself. For, *First,* He must suppose that Cyprian not only changed all the names, but the apostle's order too. For the blood (the Son), which Cyprian puts second, the apostle puts last. And, *Secondly,* He must suppose that Cyprian thought that by the blood which issued out of the side of the Son the apostle intended the Son himself, who might as well have been denoted by the water, — that by the water, which also issued from the side of the Son, the apostle intended the person of the Holy Ghost, — that by the Spirit, which in *v.* 6 is said to be truth, and in the gospel is called the Spirit of truth, the apostle meant the person of the Father, though he is nowhere else so called when joined with the Son and the Holy Ghost. We require good proof that the *Carthaginian* father could so understand the apostle. He who so understands him must believe too that the Father, Son, and Holy Spirit, are said to be three witnesses on earth. *Thirdly, Facundus* acknowledges that Cyprian says that of his three it is written, *Et hi tres unum sunt — and these three are one.* Now these are the words, not of *v.* 8, but of *v.* 7. They are not used concerning the three on earth, the Spirit, the water, and the blood; but the three in heaven, the Father, and the Word, and the Holy Ghost. So we are told that the author of the book *De baptismo haereticorum,* allowed to be contemporary with Cyprian, cites John's words, agreeably to the Greek manuscripts and the ancient versions, thus: *Ait enim Johannes de Domino nostro in epistolâ nos docens, Hic es qui venit per aquam et sanguinem, Jesus Christus, non in aquâ tantum, sed in aquâ et sanguine; et Spiritus est qui testimonium perhibet, quia Spiritus est veritas; quia tres testimonium perhibent, Spiritus et aqua et sanguis, et isti tres in unum sunt — For John, in his epistle, says concerning our Lord, This is he, Jesus Christ, who came by water and blood, not in water only, but in water and blood; and it is the Spirit that bears witness, because the Spirit is truth; for there are three that bear witness, the Spirit, the water, and the blood, and these three agree in one.* If all the Greek manuscripts and ancient versions say concerning the Spirit, the water, and the blood, that *in unum sunt — they agree in one,* then it was not of them that Cyprian spoke, whatever variety there might be in the copies in his time, when he said it is written, *unum sunt — they are one.* And therefore Cyprian's words seem still to be a firm testimony to *v.* 7, and an intimation likewise that a forger of the text would have scarcely so exactly hit upon the apostolical name for the second witness in heaven, *the Word.* Them, [3.] As only this apostle records the history of the water and blood flowing out of the Saviour's side, so it is he only, or he principally, who registers to us the Saviour's promise and prediction of the Holy spirit's coming to glorify him, and to testify of him, and to convince the world of its own unbelief and of his righteousness, as in his gospel, *ch.* 14:16, 17, 26; 15:26; 16:7–15. It is most suitable then to the diction and to the gospel of this apostle thus to mention the Holy Ghost as a witness for Jesus Christ. Then,

(5.) It was far more easy for a transcriber, by turning away his eye, or by the obscurity of the copy, it being obliterated or defaced on the top or bottom of a page, or worn away in such materials as the ancients had to write upon, to lose and omit the passage, than for an interpolator to devise and insert it. He must be very bold and impudent who could hope to escape detection and shame; and profane too, who durst venture to make an addition to a supposed sacred book. And,

(6.) It can scarcely be supposed that, when the apostle is representing the Christian's faith in overcoming the world, and the foundation it relies upon in adhering to Jesus Christ, and the various testimony that was attended him, especially when we consider that he meant to infer, as he does (*v.* 9), *If we receive the witness of men, the witness of God is greater; for this* (which he had rehearsed before) *is the witness of God which he hath testified of his Son.* Now in the three witnesses on earth there is neither all the witness of God, nor indeed any witness who is truly and immediately God. The antitrinitarian opposers of the text will deny that either the Spirit, or the water, or the blood, is God himself; but, upon our present reading, here is a noble enumeration of the several witnesses and testimonies supporting the truth of the Lord Jesus and the divinity of his institution. Here is the most excellent abridgment or breviate of the motives to faith in Christ, of the credentials the Saviour brings with him, and of the evidences of our Christianity, that is to be found, I think, in the book of God, upon which single account, even waiving the doctrine of the divine Trinity, the text is worthy of all acceptation.

2. Having these rational grounds on out side, we proceed. The apostle, having told us that the Spirit that bears witness to Christ is truth, shows us that he is so, by assuring us that he is in heaven, and that there are others also who cannot but be true, or truth itself, concurring in testimony with him: *For there are three that bear record in heaven, the Father, the Word, and the Holy Ghost, and these three are one, v.* 7.

(1.) Here is a trinity of heavenly witnesses, such as have testified and vouched to the world the veracity and authority of the Lord Jesus in his office and claims, where, [1.] The first that occurs in order is *the Father;* he set his seal to the commission of the Lord Christ all the while he was here; more especially, *First,* In proclaiming him at his baptism, Mt. 3:17. *Secondly,* In confirming his character at the transfiguration, Mt. 17:5. *Thirdly,* In accompanying him with miraculous power and works: *If I do not the works of my Father, believe me not; but if I do, though you believe not me, believe the works, that you may know and believe that the Father is in me, and I in him,* Jn. 10:37, 38. *Fourthly,* In avouching at his death, Mt. 27:54. *Fifthly,* In raising him from the dead, and receiving him up to his glory: *He shall convince the world — of righteousness, because I go to my Father, and you see me no more,* Jn. 16:10, and Rom. 1:4. [2.] The second witness in the Word, a mysterious name, importing the highest nature that belongs to the Saviour of Jesus Christ, wherein he existed before the world was, whereby he made the world, and whereby he was truly God with the Father. He must bear witness to the human nature, or to the man Christ Jesus, in and by whom he redeemed and saved us; and he bore witness, *First,* By the mighty works that he wrought. Jn. 5:17, *My Father worketh hitherto, and I work. Secondly,* In conferring a glory upon him at his transfiguration. *And we beheld his glory, the glory as of the only-begotten of the Father,* Jn. 1:14. *Thirdly,* In raising him from the dead. Jn. 2:19, *Destroy this temple, and in three days will I raise it up.* [3.] The third witness is the Holy Ghost, or the Holy Spirit, and august, venerable name, the possessor, proprietor, and author of holiness. True and faithful must he be to whom the Spirit of holiness sets his seal and solemn testimony. So he did to the Lord Jesus, the head of the Christian world; and that in such instances as these: — *First,* In the miraculous production of his immaculate human nature in the virgin's womb. *The Holy Ghost shall come upon thee,* Lu. 1:35, etc. *Secondly,* In the visible descent upon him at his baptism. *The Holy Ghost descended in a bodily shape,* Lu. 3:22, etc. *Thirdly,* In an effectual conquest of the spirits of hell and darkness. *If I cast out devils by the Spirit of God, then the kingdom of God has come unto you,* Mt. 12:28. *Fourthly,* In the visible potent descent upon the apostles, to furnish them with gifts and powers to preach him and his gospel to the world after he himself had gone to heaven, Acts 1:4, 5; 2:2–4, etc. *Fifthly,* In supporting the name, gospel, and interest of Christ, by miraculous gifts and operations by and upon the disciples, and in the churches, for two hundred years (1 Co. 12:7), concerning which see Dr. Whitby's excellent discourse in the preface to the second volume of his *Commentary on the New Testament.* These are witnesses in heaven; and they bear record from heaven; and they are one, it should seem, not only in testimony (for that is implied in their being three witnesses to one and the same thing), but upon a higher account, as they are in heaven; they are one in their heavenly being and essence; and, if one with the Father, they must be one God.

(2.) To these there is opposed, though with them joined, a trinity of witnesses on earth, such as continue here below: *And there are three that bear witness on earth, the spirit, the water, and the blood; and these three agree in one, v.* 8. [1.] Of these witnesses the first is the *spirit.* This must be distinguished from the person of the Holy Ghost, who is in heaven. We must say then, with the Saviour (according to what is reported by this apostle), *that which is born of the Spirit is spirit,* Jn. 3:6. The disciples of the Saviour are, as well as others, born after the flesh. They come into the world endued with a corrupt carnal disposition, which is enmity to God. This disposition must be mortified and abolished. A new nature must be communicated. Old lusts and corruptions must be eradicated, and the true disciple become a new creature. The regeneration or renovation of souls is a testimony to the Saviour. It is his actual though initial salvation. It is a testimony on earth, because it continues with the church here, and is not performed in that conspicuous astonishing manner in which signs from heaven are accomplished. To this Spirit belong not only the regeneration and conversion of the church, but its progressive sanctification, victory over the world, her peace, and love, and joy, and all that grace by which she is made meet for the inheritance of the saints in light. [2.] The second is the *water.* This was before considered as a means of salvation, now as a testimony to the Saviour himself, and intimates his purity and purifying power. And so it seems to comprehend, *First,* The purity of his own nature and conduct in the world. *He was holy, harmless, and undefiled. Secondly,* The testimony of John's baptism, who bore witness of him, prepared a people for him, and referred them to him, Mk. 1:4, 7, 8. *Thirdly,* The purity of his own doctrine, by which souls are purified and washed. *Now you are clean through the word that I have spoken unto you,* Jn. 15:3. *Fourthly,* The actual and active purity and holiness of his disciples. His body is the holy catholic church. *Seeing you have purified your souls in obeying the truth through the Spirit,* 1 Pt. 1:22. And this signed and sealed by, *Fifthly,* The baptism that he has appointed for the initiation or introduction of his disciples, in which he signally (or by that sign) says, *Except I wash thee, thou hast no part in me. Not the putting away of the filth of the flesh, but the answer of a good conscience towards God,* 1 Pt. 3:21. [3.] The third witness is the blood; this he shed, and this was our ransom. This testifies for Jesus Christ, *First,* In that it sealed up and finished the sacrifices of the Old Testament, *Christ, our Passover, was sacrificed for us. Secondly,* In that it confirmed his own predictions, and the truth of all his ministry and doctrine, Jn. 18:37. *Thirdly,* In that it showed unparalleled love to God, in that he would die a sacrifice to his honour and glory, in making atonement for the sins of the world, Jn. 14:30, 31. *Fourthly,* In that it demonstrated unspeakable love to us; and none will deceive those whom they entirely love, Jn. 14:13–15. *Fifthly,* In that it demonstrated the disinterestedness of the Lord Jesus as to any secular interest and advantage. No impostor and deceiver ever proposes to himself contempt and a violent cruel death, Jn. 18:36. *Sixthly,* In that it lays obligation on his disciple to suffer and die for him. No deceiver would invite proselytes to his side and interest at the rate that the Lord Jesus did. *You shall be hated of all men for my sake. They shall put you out of their synagogues; and the time comes that whosoever kills you will think that he doeth God service,* Jn. 16:2. He frequently calls his servants to a conformity with him in sufferings: *Let us go forth therefore unto him without the camp, bearing his reproach,* Heb. 13:13. This shows that neither he nor his kingdom is of this world. *Seventhly,* The benefits accruing and procured by his blood (well understood) must immediately demonstrate that he is indeed the Saviour of the world. And then, *Eighthly,* These are signified and sealed in the institution of his own supper: *This is my blood of the New Testament* (which ratifies the New Testament), *which is shed for many, for the remission of sins,* Mt. 26:28. Such are the witnesses on earth. Such is the various testimony given to the author of our religion. No wonder if the rejector of all this evidence he judged as a blasphemer of the Spirit of God, and be left to perish without remedy in his sins. These three witnesses (being more different than the three former) are not so properly said to be *one as* to be *for one,* to be for one and the same purpose and cause, *or to agree in one,* in one and the same thing among themselves, and in the same testimony with those who bear record from heaven.

III. The apostle justly concludes, *If we receive the witness of men, the witness of God is greater; for this is the witness of God, that he hath testified of his Son, v.* 9. Here we have, 1. A supposition well founded upon the premises. *Here is the witness of God,* the witness whereby God hath testified of his Son, which surely must intimate some immediate irrefragable testimony, and that of the Father concerning his Son; he has by himself proclaimed and avouched him to the world. 2. The authority and acceptableness of his testimony; and that argued from the less to the greater: *If we receive the witness of men* (and such testimony is and must be admitted in all judicatories and in all nations), *the witness of God is greater.* It is truth itself, of highest authority and most unquestionable infallibility. And then there is, 3. The application of the rule to the present case: *For this is the witness,* and here is the witness *of God* even of the Father, as well as of the Word and Spirit, *which he hath testified of,* and wherein he hath attested, *his Son. God, that cannot lie,* hath given sufficient assurance to the world that Jesus Christ is his Son, the Son of his love, and Son by office, to reconcile and recover the world unto himself; he testified therefore the truth and divine origin of the Christian religion, and that it is the sure appointed way and means of bringing us to God.

Verses 10–13

In those words we may observe,

I. The privilege and stability of the real Christian: *He that believeth on the Son of God,* hath been prevailed with unfeignedly to cleave to him for salvation, *hath the witness in himself, v.* 10. He hath not only the outward evidence that others have, but he hath in his own heart a testimony for Jesus Christ. He can allege what Christ and the truth of Christ have done for his soul and what he has seen and found in him. As, 1. He has deeply seen his sin, and guilt, and misery, and his abundant need of such a Saviour. 2. He has seen the excellency, beauty, and office of the Son of God, and the incomparable suitableness of such a Saviour to all his spiritual wants and sorrowful circumstances. 3. He sees and admires the wisdom and love of God in preparing and sending such a Saviour to deliver him from sin and hell, and to raise him to pardon, peace, and communion with God. 4. He has found and felt the power of the word and doctrine of Christ, wounding, humbling, healing, quickening, and comforting his soul. 5. He finds that the revelation of Christ, as it is the greatest discovery and demonstration of the love of God, so it is the most apt and powerful means of kindling, fomenting, and inflaming love to the holy blessed God. 6. He is born of God by the truth of Christ, as *v.* 1. He has a new heart and nature, a new love, disposition, and delight, and is not the man that formerly he was. 7. He finds yet such a conflict with himself, with sin, with the flesh, the world, and invisible wicked powers, as is described and provided for in the doctrine of Christ. 8. He finds such prospects and such strength afforded him by the faith of Christ, that he can despise and overcome the world, and travel on towards a better. 9. He finds what interest the Mediator has in heaven, by the audiency and prevalency of those prayers that are sent thither in his name, according to his will, and through his intercession. 10. He is begotten again to a lively hope, to a holy confidence in God, in his good-will and love, to a pleasant victory over terrors of conscience, dread of death and hell, to a comfortable prospect of life and immortality, being enriched with the earnest of the Spirit and sealed to the day of redemption. Such assurance has the gospel believer; he has a witness in himself. Christ is formed in him, and he is growing up to the fulness and perfection, or perfect image of Christ, in heaven.

II. The aggravation of the unbeliever's sin, the sin of unbelief: *He that believeth not God hath made him a liar.* He does, in effect, give God the lie, *because he believeth not the record that God gave of his Son, v.* 10. He must believe that God did not send his Son into the world, when he has given us such manifold evidence that he did, or that Jesus Christ was not the Son of God, when all that evidence relates to and terminates upon him, or that he sent his Son to deceive the world and to lead it into error and misery, or that he permits men to devise a religion which, in all the parts of it, is a pure, holy, heavenly, undefiled institution, and so worthy to be embraced by the reason of mankind, and yet is but a delusion and a lie, and then lends them his Spirit and power to recommend and obtrude it upon the world, which is to make God the Father, the author and abettor, of the lie.

III. The matter, the substance, or contents of all this divine testimony concerning Jesus Christ: *And this is the record, that God hath given to us eternal life, and this life is in his Son, v.* 11. This is the sum of the gospel. This is the sum and epitome of the whole record given us by all the aforesaid six witnesses. 1. That *God hath given to us eternal life.* He has designed it for us in his eternal purpose. He has prepared all the means that are necessary to bring us to it. He has made it over to us by his covenant and promise. And he actually confers a right and title thereto on all who believe on and actually embrace the Son of God. Then, 2. *This life is in the Son.* The Son is life; eternal life in his own essence and person, Jn. 1:4; 1 Jn. 1:2. He is eternal life to us, the spring of our spiritual and glorious life, Col. 3:4. From him life is communicated to us, both here in heaven. And thereupon it must follow, (1.) *He that hath the Son hath life, v.* 12. He that is united to the Son is united to life. He who hath a title to the Son hath a title to life, to eternal life. Such honour hath the Father put upon the Son: such honour must we put upon him too. We must come and kiss the Son, and we shall have life. (2.) *He that hath not the Son of God hath not life, v.* 12. He continues under the condemnation of the law (Jn. 3:36); he refuses the Son, who is life itself, who is the procurer of life, and the way to it; he provokes God to deliver him over to endless death for making him a liar, since he believes not this record that God hath given concerning his Son.

IV. The end and reason of the apostle's preaching this to believers. 1. For their satisfaction and comfort: *These things have I written unto you that believe on the name of the Son of God, that you may know that you have eternal life, v.* 13. Upon all this evidence, and these witnesses, it is but just and meet that there should be those who believe on the name of the Son of God. God increase their number! How much testimony from heaven has the world to answer for! And to three witnesses in heaven must the world be accountable. These believers have eternal life. They have it in the covenant of the gospel, in the beginning and first-fruits of it within them, and in their Lord and head in heaven. These believers may come to know that they have eternal life, and should be quickened, encouraged, and comforted, in the prospect of it: and they should value the scriptures, which are so much written for their consolation and salvation. 2. For their confirmation and progress in their holy faith: *And that you may believe on the name of the Son of God* (*v.* 13), may go on believing. Believers must persevere, or they do nothing. To withdraw from believing on the name of the Son of God is to renounce eternal life, and draw back unto perdition. Therefore the evidences of religion and the advantage of faith are to be presented to believers, in order to hearten and encourage them to persevere to the end.

Verses 14–17

Here we have,

I. A privilege belonging to faith in Christ, namely, audience in prayer: *This is the confidence that we have in him, that, if we ask any thing according to his will, he heareth us, v.* 14. The Lord Christ emboldens us to come to God in all circumstances, with all our supplications and requests. Through him our petitions are admitted and accepted of God. The matter o our prayer must be agreeable to the declared will of God. It is not fit that we should ask what is contrary either to his majesty and glory or to our own good, who are his and dependent on him. And then we may have confidence that the prayer of faith shall be heard in heaven.

II. The advantage accruing to us by such privilege: *If we know that he heareth us, whatsoever we ask, we know that we have the petitions that we desired of him, v.* 15. Great are the deliverances, mercies, and blessings, which the holy petitioner needs. To know that his petitions are heard or accepted is as good as to know that they are answered; and therefore that he is so pitied, pardoned, or counselled, sanctified, assisted, and saved (or shall be so) as he is allowed to ask of God.

III. Direction in prayer in reference to the sins of others: *If any man see his brother sin a sin which is not unto death, he shall ask, and he shall give him life for those that sin not unto death. There is a sin unto death: I do not say that he shall pray for it, v.* 16. Here we may observe, 1. We ought to pray for others as well as for ourselves; for our brethren of mankind, that they may be enlightened, converted, and saved; for our brethren in the Christian profession, that they may be sincere, that their sins may be pardoned, and that they may be delivered from evils and the chastisements of God, and preserved in Christ Jesus. 2. There is a great distinction in the heinousness and guilt of sin: *There is a sin unto death* (*v.* 16), *and there is a sin not unto death, v.* 17. (1.) *There is a sin unto death.* All sin, as to the merit and legal sentence of it, is unto death. *The wages of sin is death;* and *cursed is every one that continueth not in all things that are written in the book of the law, to do them,* Gal. 3:10. But there is a sin unto death in opposition to such sin as is here said *not to be unto death.* There is therefore, (2.) *A sin not unto death.* This surely must include all such sin as by divine or human constitution may consist with life; in the human constitution with temporal or corporal life, in the divine constitution with corporal or with spiritual evangelical life. [1.] There are sins which, by human righteous constitution, are not unto death; as divers pieces of injustice, which may be compensated without the death of the delinquent. In opposition to this there are sins which, by righteous constitution, are to death, or to a legal forfeiture of life; such as we call *capital crimes.* [2.] Then there are sins which, by divine constitution, are unto death; and that either death corporal or spiritual and evangelical. *First,* Such as are, or may be, to death corporal. Such may the sins be either of gross hypocrites, as Ananias and Sapphira, or, for aught we know, of sincere Christian brethren, as when the apostle says of the offending members of the church of Corinth, *For this cause many are weak and sickly among you, and many sleep,* 1 Co. 11:30. There may be sin unto corporal death among those who may not be condemned with the world. Such sin, I said, is, or may be, to corporal death. The divine penal constitution in the gospel does not positively and peremptorily threaten death to the more visible sins of the members of Christ, but only some gospel-chastisement; *for whom the Lord loveth he chasteneth, and scourgeth every son whom he receiveth,* Heb. 12:6. There is room left for divine wisdom or goodness, or even gospel severity, to determine how far the chastisement or the scourge shall proceed. And we cannot say but that sometimes it may *(in terrorem — for warning to others)* proceed even to death. Then, *Secondly,* There are sins which, by divine constitution, are unto death spiritual and evangelical, that is, are inconsistent with spiritual and evangelical life, with spiritual life in the soul and with an evangelical right to life above. Such are total impenitence and unbelief for the present. Final impenitence and unbelief are infallibly to death eternal, as also a blaspheming of the Spirit of God in the testimony that he has given to Christ and his gospel, and a total apostasy from the light and convictive evidence of the truth of the Christian religion. These are sins involving the guilt of everlasting death. Then comes,

IV. The application of the direction for prayer according to the different sorts of sin thus distinguished. The prayer is supposed to be for life: *He shall ask, and he* (God) *shall give them life.* Life is to be asked of God. He is the God of life; he gives it when and to whom he pleases, and takes it away either by his constitution or providence, or both, as he thinks meet. In the case of a brother's sin, which is not (in the manner already mentioned) unto death, we may in faith and hope pray for him; and particularly for the life of soul and body. But, in case of the sin unto death in the forementioned ways, we have no allowance to pray. Perhaps the apostle's expression, *I do not say, He shall pray for it,* may intend no more than, "I have no promise for you in that case; no foundation for the prayer of faith." 1. The laws of punitive justice must be executed, for the common safety and benefit of mankind: and even an offending brother in such a case must be resigned to public justice (which in the foundation of it is divine), and at the same time also to the mercy of God. 2. The removal of evangelical penalties (as they may be called), or the prevention of death (which may seem to be so consequential upon, or inflicted for, some particular sin), can be prayed for only conditionally or provisionally, that is, with proviso that it consist with the wisdom, will, and glory of God that they should be removed, and particularly such death prevented. 3. We cannot pray that the sins of the impenitent and unbelieving should, while they are such, be forgiven them, or that any mercy of life or soul, that suppose the forgiveness of sin, should be granted to them, while they continue such. But we may pray for their repentance (supposing them but in the common case of the impenitent world), for their being enriched with faith in Christ, and thereupon for all other saving mercies. 4. In case it should appear that any have committed the irremissible blasphemy against the Holy Ghost, and the total apostasy from the illuminating convictive powers of the Christian religion, it should seem that they are not to be prayed for at all. For *what remains but a certain fearful expectation of judgment, to consume such adversaries?* Heb. 10:27. And these last seem to be the sins chiefly intended by the apostle by the name of *sins unto death.* Then, 5. The apostle seems to argue that there is sin that is not unto death; thus, *All unrighteousness is sin* (*v.* 17); but, were all unrighteousness unto death (since we have all some unrighteousness towards God or man, or both, in omitting and neglecting something that is their due), then we were all peremptorily bound over to death, and, since it is not so (the Christian brethren, generally speaking, having right to life), there must be sin that is not to death. Though there is no venial sin (in the common acceptation), there is pardoned sin, that does not involve a plenary obligation to eternal death. If it were not so, there could be no justification nor continuance of the justified state. The gospel constitution or covenant abbreviates, abridges, or rescinds the guilt of sin.

Verses 18–21

Here we have,

I. A recapitulation of the privileges and advantages of sound Christian believers. 1. They are secured against sin, against the fulness of its dominion or the fulness of its guilt: *We know that whosoever is born of God* (and the believer in Christ is born of God, *v.* 1) *sinneth not* (*v.* 18), *sinneth not* with that fulness of heart and spirit that the unregenerate do (as was said *ch.* 3:6, 9), and consequently not with that fulness of guilt that attends the sins of others; and so he is secured against that sin which is unavoidably unto death, or which infallibly binds the sinner over unto the wages of eternal death; the new nature, and the inhabitation of the divine Spirit thereby, prevent the admission of such unpardonable sin. 2. They are fortified against the devil's destructive attempts: *He that is begotten of God keepeth himself,* that is, is enabled to guard himself, *and the wicked one toucheth him not* (*v.* 18), that is, that the wicked one may not touch him, namely, to death. It seems not to be barely a narration of the duty or the practice of the regenerate; but an indication of their power by virtue of their regeneration. They are thereby prepared and principled against the fatal touches, the sting, of the wicked one; he touches not their souls, to infuse his venom there a he does in others, or to expel that regenerative principle which is an antidote to his poison, or to induce them to that sin which by the gospel constitution conveys an indissoluble obligation to eternal death. He may prevail too far with them, to draw them to some acts of sin; but it seems to be the design of the apostle to assert that their regeneration secures them from such assaults of the devil as will bring them into the same case and actual condemnation with the devil. 3. they are on God's side and interest, in opposition to the state of the world: *And we know that we are of God, and the whole world lieth in wickedness, v.* 19. Mankind are divided into two great parties of dominions, that which belongs to God and that which belongs to wickedness or to the wicked one. The Christian believers belong to God. They are of God, and from him, and to him, and for him. They succeed into the right and room of the ancient Israel of God, of whom it is said, *The Lord's people is his portion,* his estate in this world; *Jacob is the lot of his inheritance,* the dividend that has fallen to him by the lot of his own determination (Deu. 32:9); while, on the contrary, *the whole world,* the rest, being by far the major part, *lieth in wickedness,* in the jaws in the bowels of the wicked one. There are, indeed, were we to consider the individuals, many wicked ones, many wicked spirits, in the heavenly or the ethereal places; but they are united in wicked nature, policy, and principle, and they are united also in one head. there is the prince of the devils and of the diabolical kingdom. There is a head of the malignity and of the malignant world; and he has such sway here that he is called *the god of this world.* Strange that such a knowing spirit should be so implacably incensed against the Almighty and all his interests, when he cannot but know that it must end in his own overthrow and everlasting damnation! How tremendous is the judgment of God upon that wicked one! May the God of the Christian world continually demolish his dominion in this world, and translate souls into *the kingdom of his dear Son!* 4. They are enlightened in the knowledge of the true eternal God: *"And we know that the Son of God has come, and has given as an understanding, that we may know him that is true, v.* 20. The Son of God has come into our world, and we have seen him, and know him by all the evidence that has already been asserted; he has revealed unto us the true God (as Jn. 1:18), and he has opened our minds too to understand that revelation, given us an internal light in our understandings, whereby we may discern the glories of the true God; and we are assured that it is the true God that he hath discovered to us. He is infinitely superior in purity, power, and perfection, to all the gods of the Gentiles. He has all the excellences, beauties, and riches, of the living and true God. It is the same God that, according to Moses's account, made the heavens and the earth, the same who took our fathers and patriarchs into peculiar covenant with himself, the same who brought our ancestors out of Egypt, who gave us the fiery law upon mount Sinai, who gave us his holy oracles, promised the call and conversion of the Gentiles. By his counsels and works, by his love and grace, by his terrors and judgments, we know that he, and he alone, in the fulness of his being, is the living and true God." It is a great happiness to know the true God, to know him in Christ; it is eternal lie, Jn. 17:3. It is the glory of the Christian revelation that it gives the best account of the true God, and administers the best eye-salve for our discerning the living and true God. 5. They have a happy union with God and his Son: *"And we are in him that is true, even* (or and) *in his Son Jesus Christ, v.* 20. The Son leads us to the Father, and we are in both, in the love and favour of both, in covenant and federal alliance with both, in spiritual conjunction with both by the inhabitation and operation of their Spirit: and, that you may know how great a dignity and felicity this is, you must remember that this true one is *the true God and eternal life"* or rather (as it should seem a more natural construction), "This same Son of God is himself also *the true God and eternal life"* (Jn. 1:1, and here, *ch.* 1:2), "so that in union with either, much more with both, we are united to *the true God and eternal life."* Then we have,

II. The apostle's concluding monition: *"Little children"* (dear children, as it has been interpreted), *"keep yourselves from idols, v.* 21. Since you know the true God, and are in him, let your light and love guard you against all that is advanced in opposition to him, or competition with him. Flee from the false gods of the heathen world. They are not comparable to the God whose you are and whom you serve. Adore not your God by statues and images, which share in his worship. Your God is an incomprehensible Spirit, and is disgraced by such sordid representations. Hold no communion with your heathen neighbours in their idolatrous worship. Your God is jealous, and would have you come out, and be separated from among them; mortify the flesh, and be crucified to the world, that they may not usurp the throne of dominion in the heart, which is due only to God. The God whom you have known is he who made you, who redeemed you by his Son, who has sent his gospel to you, who has pardoned your sins, begotten you unto himself by his Spirit, and given you eternal life. Cleave to him in faith, and love, and constant obedience, in opposition to all things that would alienate your mind and heart from God. To this living and true God be glory and dominion for ever and ever. *Amen."*

AN EXPOSITION, WITH PRACTICAL OBSERVATIONS, OF

THE SECOND EPISTLE OF JOHN

Here we find a canonical epistle inscribed, principally, not only to a single person, but to one also of the softer sex. And why not to one of that sex? In gospel redemption, privilege, and dignity, *there is neither male nor female;* they are both one *in Christ Jesus.* Our Lord himself neglected his own repast, to commune with the woman of Samaria, in order to show her the fountain of life; and, when almost expiring upon the cross, he would with his dying lips bequeath his blessed mother to the care of his beloved disciple, and thereby instruct him to respect female disciples for the future. It was to one of the same sex that our Lord chose to appear first after his return from the grave, and to send by her the news of his resurrection to this as well as to the other apostles; and we find afterwards a zealous Priscilla so well acquitting herself in her Christian race, and particularly in some hazardous service towards the apostle Paul, that she is not only often mentioned before her husband, but to her as well as to him, not only the apostle himself, but also all the Gentile churches, were ready to return their thankful acknowledgments. No wonder then that a heroine in the Christian religion, honoured by divine providence, and distinguished by divine grace, should be dignified also by an apostolical epistle.

The apostle here salutes an honourable matron and her children (*v.* 1–3). Recommends to them faith and love (*v.* 5, 6). Warns them of deceivers (*v.* 7), and to take heed to themselves (*v.* 8). Teaches how to treat those who bring not the doctrine of Christ (*v.* 10, 11). And, referring other things to personal discourse, concludes the epistle (*v.* 12, 13).

Verses 1–4

Ancient epistles began, as here, with salutation and good wishes: religion consecrates, as far as may be, old forms, and turns compliments into real expressions of life and love. Here we have, as usually,

I. The saluter, not expressed by name, but by a chosen character: *The elder.* The expression, and style, and love, intimate that the penman was the same with that of the foregoing epistle; he is now *the elder,* emphatically and eminently so; possibly the oldest apostle now living, the chief elder in the church of God. An elder in the ancient house of Israel was reverend, or to be reverenced, much more he who is so In the gospel Israel of God. An old disciple is honourable; and old apostle and leader of disciples is more so. He was now old in holy service and experience, had seen and tasted much of heaven, and was much nearer than when at first he believed.

II. The saluted — a noble Christian matron, and her children: *To the elect lady and her children.* A lady, a person of eminent quality for birth, education, and estate. It is well that the gospel ha got among such. It is a pity but lords and ladies should be acquainted with the Lord Christ and his religion. They owe more to him than others do; though usually *not many noble are called.* Here is a pattern for persons of quality of the same sex. *The elect lady;* not only a choice one, but one chosen of God. It is lovely and beautiful to see ladies, by holy walking, demonstrate their election of God. *And her children;* probably the lady was a widow; she *and her children* then are the principal part of the family, and so this may be styled an economical epistle. Families may well be written to and encouraged, and further directed in their domestic love, and order, and duties. We see that children may well be taken notice of in Christian letters, and they should know it too; it may avail to their encouragement and caution. Those who love and commend them will be apt to enquire after them. This *lady and her children* are further notified by the respect paid them, and that, 1. By the apostle himself: *Whom I love in the truth,* or in truth, whom I sincerely and heartily love. He who was the beloved disciple had learnt the art or exercise of love; and he especially loved those who loved him, that Lord who loved him. 2. By all her Christian acquaintance, all the religious who knew her: *And not I only, but also all those that have known the truth.* virtue and goodness in an elevated sphere shine brightly. Truth demands acknowledgment, and those who see the evidences of pure religion should confess and attest them; it is a good sign and great duty to love and value religion in others. The ground of this love and respect thus paid to this lady and her children was their regard to the truth: *For the truth's sake* (or true religion's sake) *which dwelleth in us, and shall be with us for ever.* Christian love is founded upon the appearance of vital religion. Likeness should beget affection. Those who love truth and piety in themselves should love it in others too, or love others upon the account of it. The apostle and the other Christians loved this lady, not so much for her honour as her holiness; not so much for her bounty as her serious Christianity. We should not be religious merely by fits and starts, in certain moods and moons; but religion should still dwell within us, in our minds and hearts, in our faith and love. It is to be hoped that where religion once truly dwells it will abide for ever. The Spirit of Christianity, we may suppose, will not be totally extinguished: *Which shall be with us for ever.*

III. The salutation, which is indeed an apostolical benediction: *Grace be with you, mercy, and peace, from God the Father and from the Lord Jesus Christ, the Son of the Father, in truth and love, v.* 3. Sacred love pours out blessings upon this honourable Christian family; to those who have shall more be given. Observe,

1. From whom these blessings are craved, (1.) *From God the Father,* the God of all grace. He is the fountain of blessedness, and of all the blessings that must bring us thither. (2.) *From the Lord Jesus Christ.* He is also author and communicator of these heavenly blessings, and he is distinguished by this emphatic character — *the Son of the Father;* such a Son as none else can be; such a Son as is *the brightness of the Father's glory, and the express image of his person,* who, with the Father, is also *eternal life,* 1 Jn. 1:2.

2. What the apostle craves from these divine persons. (1.) *Grace* — divine favour and good-will, the spring of all good things: it is grace indeed that any spiritual blessing should be conferred on sinful mortals. (2.) *Mercy* — free pardon and forgiveness; those who are already rich in grace have need of continual forgiveness. (3.) *Peace* — tranquility of spirit and serenity of conscience, in an assured reconciliation with God, together with all safe and sanctified outward prosperity. And these are desired *in truth and love,* either by sincere and ardent affection in the saluter (in faith and love he prays them *from God the Father, and the Lord Jesus Christ*), or as productive of continued truth and love in the saluted; these blessings will continually preserve true faith and love *in the elect lady and her children;* and may they do so!

IV. The congratulation upon the prospect of the exemplary behaviour of other children of this excellent lady. Happy parent, who was blessed with such a numerous religious offspring! *I rejoiced greatly that I found of thy children walking in the truth, as we have received commandment from the Father, v.* 4. Possibly the lady's sons travelled abroad, either for accomplishment and acquaintance with the world, or on the account of their own business or the common affairs of the family, and in their travels might come to Ephesus, where the apostle is supposed to have now resided, and might there happily converse with him. See how good it is to be trained up to early religion! Though religion is not to be founded upon education, yet education may be and often is blessed, and is the way to fortify youth against irreligious infection. Hence too let young travellers learn to carry their religion along with them, and not either leave it at home or learn the ill customs of the countries where they come. It may be observed, also, that sometimes election runs in a direct line; here we have an *elect lady, and her elect children;* children may be beloved for their parents' sake, but both by virtue of free grace. From the apostle's joy herein we may observe that it is pleasant to see children treading in good parent's steps; and those who see this may well congratulate their parents thereupon, and that both to excite their thankfulness to God for, and to enlarge their comfort in, so great a blessing. How happy a lady was this, who had brought forth so many children for heaven and for God! And how great a joy must it be to her ladyship to hear so good an account of them from so good a judge! And we may further see that it is joyful to good old ministers, and accordingly to other good old disciples, to see a hopeful rising generation, who may serve God and support religion in the world when they are dead and gone. We see here also the rule of true walking: *the commandment of the Father.* Then is our walk true, our converse right, when it is managed by the word of God.

Verses 5–6

We come now more into the design and substance of the epistle; and here we have,

I. The apostle's request: *Now, I beseech thee, lady.* Considering what it is that he entreats, the way of address is very remarkable; it is not any particular boon or bounty to himself, but common duty and observance of divine command. Here he might command or charge; but harsher measures are worse than needless where milder will prevail; and the apostolical spirit is, of all other, the most tender and endearing. Whether out of deference to her ladyship, or apostolical meekness, or both, he condescends to beseech: *And now I beseech thee, lady.* He may be supposed speaking as another apostle does to a certain master to whom he writes: *Wherefore, though I might be very bold in Christ* (and according to the power with which Christ hath entrusted me) *to enjoin thee that which is convenient, yet, for love's sake I rather beseech thee, being such a one as the aged, the elder.* Love will avail where authority will not; and we may often see that the more authority is urged the more it is slighted. The apostolical minister will love and beseech his friends into their duty.

II. The thing requested of *the lady and her children* — Christian sacred love: *That we love one another, v.* 5. Those that are eminent in any Christian virtue have yet room to grow therein. *But, as touching brotherly love, you need not that I write unto you; for you yourselves are taught of God to love one another. But we beseech you, brethren* (and sisters), *that you increase more and more,* 1 Th. 4:9, 10.

1. This love is recommended, (1.) From the obligation thereto — *the commandment.* Divine command should sway our mind and heart. (2.) From the antiquity of the obligation: *Not as though I wrote a new commandment unto thee, but that which we had from the beginning, v.* 5. This commandment of mutual Christian love may be said to be a *new* one in respect of its new enaction and sanction by the Lord Christ; but yet, as to the matter of it (mutual holy love), it is as old as natural, Jewish, or Christian religion. This commandment must every where attend Christianity, that the disciples of it must love one another.

2. Then this love is illustrated from the fruitful nature of it: *And this is love, that we walk after his commandments, v.* 5. This is the test of our love to God, our obedience to him. This is love to ourselves, to our own souls, that we walk in obedience to divine commands. *In keeping them there is great reward.* This is love to one another, to engage one another to walk in holiness; and this is the evidence of our sincere, mutual, Christian love — that we (in other things) walk after God's commands. There may be mutual love that is not religious and Christian; but we know ours to be so, by our attendance to all other commands besides that of mutual love. Universal obedience is the proof of the goodness and sincerity of Christian virtues; and those that aim at all Christian obedience will be sure to attend to Christian love. This is a fundamental duty in the gospel-charter: *This is the commandment, that, as you have heard from the beginning, you should walk in it* (*v.* 6), that is, walk in this love. The foresight of the decay of this love, as well as of other apostasy, might engage the apostle to inculcate this duty, and this primordial command, the more frequently, the more earnestly.

Verses 7–9

In this principal part of the epistle we find,

I. The ill news communicated to the lady — seducers are abroad: *For many deceivers have entered into the world.* This report is introduced by a particle that bespeaks a reason of the report. "You have need to maintain your love, *for* there are destroyers of it in the world. Those who subvert the faith destroy the love; the common faith is one ground of the common love;" or, "You must secure your walk according to the commands of God; this will secure you. Your stability is likely to be tried, *for many deceivers have entered into the world.*" Sad and saddening news may be communicated to our Christian friends; not that we should love to make them sorry, but to fore-warn is the way to fore-arm them against their trials. Now here is, 1. The description of the deceiver and his deceit — he *confesses not that Jesus Christ has come in the flesh* (*v.* 7); he brings some error or other concerning the person of the Lord Jesus; he either confesses not that Jesus Christ is the same person, or that Jesus of Nazareth was the Christ, the anointed of God, the Messiah promised of old for the redemption of Israel, or that the promised Messiah and Redeemer has come in the flesh, or into the flesh, into our world and into our nature; such a one pretends that he is yet to be expected. Strange that after such evidence any should deny that the Lord Jesus is the Son of God and Saviour of the world! 2. The aggravation of the case — such a one is *a deceiver and an antichrist* (*v.* 7); he deludes souls and undermines the glory and kingdom of the Lord Christ. He must be an impostor, a wilful deceiver, after all the light that has been afforded, and all the evidence that Christ has given concerning himself, and the attestation God has given concerning his Son; and he is a wilful opposer of the person, and honour, and interest of the Lord Christ, and as such shall be reckoned with when the Lord Christ comes again. Let us not think it strange that there are deceivers and opposers of the Lord Christ's name and dignity now, for there were such of old, even in the apostle's times.

II. The counsel given to this elect household hereupon. Now care and caution are needful: *Look to yourselves, v.* 8. The more deceivers and deceits abound, the more watchful the disciples must be. Delusions may so prevail that even the elect may be endangered thereby. Two things they must beware of: — 1. *That they lose not what they have wrought* (*v.* 8), what they have done or what they have gained. It is a pity that any religious labour should be in vain; some begin well, but at last lose all their pains. The hopeful gentleman, who had kept the commands of the second table from his youth up, lost all for want of less love to the world and more love to Christ. Professors should take care not to lose what they have gained. Many have not only gained a fair reputation for religion, but much light therein, much conviction of the evil of sin, the vanity of the world, the excellency of religion, and the power of God's word. They have even *tasted of the powers of the world to come,* and the gifts of the Holy Spirit; and yet at last lose all. *You did run well, who hindered you, that you should not obey* (or not go on to obey) *the truth?* Sad it is that fair and splendid attainments in the school of Christ should all be lost at last. 2. That they lose not their reward, none of it, no portion of that honour, or praise, or glory that they once stood fair for. *That we* (or you, as in some copies) *receive a full reward.* "Secure you as full a reward as will be given to any in the church of God; if there are degrees of glory, lose none of that grace (that light, or love, or peace) which is to prepare you for the higher elevation in glory. *Hold fast that which thou hast* (in faith, and hope, and a good conscience), *that no man take thy crown,* that thou neither lose it nor any jewel out of it," Rev. 3:11. The way to attain the full reward is to abide true to Christ, and constant in religion to the end.

III. The reason of the apostle's counsel, and of their care and caution about themselves, which is twofold: — 1. The danger and evil of departure from gospel light and revelation; it is in effect and reality a departure from God himself: *Whosoever transgresseth* (transgresseth at this dismal rate), *and abideth not in the doctrine of Christ, hath not God.* It is the doctrine of Christ that is appointed to guide us to God; it is that whereby God draws souls to salvation and to himself. Those who revolt thence, in so doing revolt from God. 2. The advantage and happiness of firm adherence to Christian truth; it unites us to Christ (the object or subject-matter of that truth), and thereby to the Father also; for they are one. *He that abideth* (rooted and grounded) *in the doctrine of Christ, he hath both the Father and the Son.* By the doctrine of Christ we are enlightened in the knowledge of the Father and the Son; by it we are sanctified for the Father and the Son; thereupon we are enriched with holy love to the Father and the Son; and thereby prepared for the endless enjoyment of the Father and the Son. *Now you are clean through the word which I have spoken to you,* Jn. 15:3. This purity makes meet for heaven. The great God, as he has set his seal to the doctrine of Christ, so he puts a value upon it. We must retain that holy doctrine in faith and love, as we hope or desire to arrive at blessed communion with the Father and the Son.

Verses 10–11

Here, I. Upon due warning given concerning seducers, the apostle gives direction concerning the treatment of such. They are not to be entertained as the ministers of Christ. The Lord Christ will distinguish them from such, and so would he have his disciples. The direction is negative. 1. "Support them not: *If there come any unto you, and bring not this doctrine* (concerning Christ as the Son of God, the Messiah and anointed of God for our redemption and salvation), *receive him not into your house.*" Possibly this lady was like Gaius, of whom we read in the next epistle, a generous housekeeper, and hospitable entertainer of travelling ministers and Christians. These deceivers might possibly expect the same reception with others, or with the best who came there (as the blind are often bold enough), but the apostle allows it not: "Do not welcome them into your family." Doubtless such may be relieved in their pressing necessities, but not encouraged for ill service. Deniers of the faith are destroyers of souls; and it is supposed that even ladies themselves should have good understanding in the affairs of religion. 2. "Bless not their enterprises: *Neither bid him God speed.* Attend not their service with your prayers and good wishes." Bad work should not be consecrated or recommended to the divine benediction. God will be no patron of falsehood, seduction, and sin. We ought to bid God speed to evangelical ministration; but the propagation of fatal error, if we cannot prevent, we must not dare to countenance. Then,

II. Here is the reason of such direction, forbidding the support and patronage of the deceiver: *For he that biddeth him God speed is partaker of his evil deeds.* Favour and affection partake of the sin. We may be sharers in the iniquities of others. How judicious and how cautious should the Christian be! There are many ways of sharing the guilt of other people's transgressions; it may be done by culpable silence, indolence, unconcernedness, private contribution, public countenance and assistance, inward approbation, open apology and defence. The Lord pardon our guilt of other persons' sins!

Verses 12–13

The apostle concludes this letter, 1. With an adjournment of many things to personal conference: *Having many things*

to write unto you I would not write with paper and ink; but I trust to come unto you, and speak face to face, that our joy may be full.* Here it is supposed that some things are better spoken than written. The use of pen and ink may be a mercy and a pleasure; but a personal interview may be more so. The apostle was not yet too old for travel, nor consequently for travelling service. The communion of saints should be by all methods maintained; and their communion should tend to their mutual joy. Excellent ministers may have their joy advanced by their Christian friends. *That I may be comforted together with you by the mutual faith both of you and me,* Rom. 1:12. 2. With the presentation of service and salutation from some near relations to the lady: *The children of thy elect*

sister greet thee. Grace was abundant towards this family; here are two elect sisters, and probably their elect children. How will they admire this grace in heaven! The apostle condescends to insert the nieces' duty (as we should call it), or dutiful salutation, to their aunt. The duty of inferior relations is to be cherished. Doubtless the apostle was easy of access, and would admit all friendly and pious communication, and was ready to enhance the good lady's joy in her nieces as well as in her children. May there by many such gracious ladies rejoicing in their gracious descendants and other relations! *Amen.*

AN EXPOSITION, WITH PRACTICAL OBSERVATIONS, OF

THE THIRD EPISTLE OF JOHN

Christian communion is exerted and cherished by letter. Christians are to be commended in the practical proof of their professed subjection to the gospel of Christ. The animating and countenancing of generous and public-spirited persons is doing good to many — to this end the apostle sends this encouraging epistle to his friend Gaius, in which also he complains of the quite opposite spirit and practice of a certain minister, and confirms the good report concerning another more worthy to be imitated.

In this epistle the apostle congratulates Gaius upon the prosperity of his soul (*v.* 1, 2), upon the fame he had among good Christians (*v.* 3, 4), and upon his charity and hospitality to the servants of Christ (*v.* 5, 6). He complains of contemptuous treatment by an ambitious Diotrephes (*v.* 9, 10), recommends Demetrius (*v.* 12), and expresses his hope of visiting Gaius shortly (*v.* 13, 14).

Verses 1–2

Here we see, I. The sacred penman who writes and sends the letter; not here indeed notified by his name, but a more general character: *The elder,* he that is so by years and by office; honour and deference are due to both. Some have questioned whether this were John the apostle or no; but his style and spirit seem to shine in the epistle. Those that are beloved of Christ will love the brethren for his sake. Gaius could not question from whom the letter came. The apostle might have assumed many more illustrious characters, but it becomes not Christ's ministers to affect swelling pompous titles. He almost levels himself with the more ordinary pastors of the church, while he styles himself the elder. Or, possibly, most of the extraordinary ministers, the apostles, were now dead, and this holy survivor would countenance the continued standing ministry, by assuming the more common title — the elder. *The elders I exhort, who am also an elder,* 1 Pt. 5:1.

II. The person saluted and honoured by the letter. The former is directed to an elect lady, this to a choice gentleman; such are worthy of esteem and value. He is notified, 1. By his name, — *Gaius.* We read of several of that name, particularly of one whom the apostle Paul baptized at Corinth, who possibly might be also the apostle's host and kind entertainer there (Rom. 16:23); if this be not he, it is his brother in name, estate, and disposition. Then, 2. By the kind expressions of the apostle to him: *The well-beloved,* and *whom I love in the truth.* Love expressed is wont to kindle love. Here seems to be either the sincerity of the apostle's love or the religion of it. The sincerity of it: *Whom I love in the truth,* for the truth's sake, as abiding and walking in the truth as it is in Jesus. To love our friends for the truth's sake is true love, religious gospel love.

III. The salutation or greeting, containing a prayer, introduced by an affectionate compellation — *Beloved,* thou beloved one in Christ. The minister who would gain love must show it himself. Here is, 1. The apostle's good opinion of his friend, that his *soul prospered.* There is such a thing as soul-prosperity — the greatest blessing on this side heaven. This supposes regeneration, and an inward fund of spiritual life; this stock is increasing, and, while spiritual treasures are advancing, the soul is in a fair way to the kingdom of glory. 2. His good wish for his friend that his body may *prosper and be in health* as well as his soul. Grace and health are two rich companions; grace will improve health, health will employ grace. It frequently falls out that a rich soul is lodged

in a crazy body; grace must be exercised in submission to such a dispensation; but we may well wish and pray that those who have prosperous souls may have healthful bodies too; their grace will shine in a larger sphere of activity.

Verses 3–8

In these verses we have,

I. The good report that the apostle had received concerning this friend of his: *The brethren came and testified of the truth that is in thee* (*v.* 3), *who have borne witness of thy charity before the church, v.* 6. Here we may see, 1. The testimony or thing testified concerning Gaius — the truth that was in him, the reality of his faith, the sincerity of his religion, and his devotedness to God; and this evinced by his charity, which includes his love to the brethren, kindness to the poor, hospitality to Christian strangers, and readiness to accommodate them for the service of the gospel. Faith should work by love; it gives a lustre and by the offices of love, and induces others to commend its integrity. 2. The witnesses — brethren that came from Gaius testified and bore witness. A good report is due from those who have received good; though a good name is but a small reward for costly service, yet it is *better than precious ointment,* and will not be refused by the ingenuous and religious. 3. The auditory or judicatory before which the report and testimony were given — *before the church.* This seems to be the church at which the apostle now resided. What church this was we are not sure; what occasion they had thus to testify his faith and love before the church we cannot tell; possibly out of the fulness of the heart the mouth spoke; they could not but testify what they found and felt; possibly they would engage the church's prayer for the continued life and usefulness of such a patron, that he might *prosper and be in health as his soul prospered.*

II. The report the apostle himself gives of him, introduced by an endearing appellation again: *Beloved, thou doest faithfully whatsoever thou doest to the brethren, and to strangers, v.* 5. 1. He was hospitable, good to the brethren, even to strangers; it was enough to recommend them to Gaius's house that they belonged to Christ. Or he was good *to the brethren* of the same church with himself, and to those who came from far; all who were of the household of faith were welcome to him. 2. He seems to have been of a catholic spirit; he could overlook the petty differences among serious Christians, and be communicative to all who bore the image and did the work of Christ. And, 3. He was conscientious in what he did: "*Thou doest faithfully* (thou makest faithful work of) *whatsoever thou doest;* thou doest it as a faithful servant, and from the Lord Christ mayest thou expect the reward of the inheritance." Such faithful souls can hear their own praises without being puffed up; the commendation of what is good in us is designed, not for our pride, but for our encouragement to continue therein, and should be accordingly improved.

III. The apostle's joy therein, in the good report itself, and the good ground of it: *I rejoiced greatly when the brethren came and testified,* etc., *v.* 3. *I have no greater joy than to hear that my children walk in the truth,* in the prescripts of the Christian religion. The best evidence of our having the truth is our *walking in the truth.* Good men will greatly rejoice in the soul-prosperity of others; and they are glad to hear of the grace and goodness of others. *They glorified God in me.* Love envieth not, but rejoiceth in the good name of other folks. As it is joy to good parents, it will be joy to good ministers, to see their children evidence their sincerity in religion, and adorn their profession.

IV. The direction the apostle gives his friend concerning further treatment of the brethren that were with him: *Whom if thou bring forward on their journey, after a godly sort, thou shalt do well.* It seems to have been customary in those days of love to attend travelling ministers and Christians, at least some part of their road, 1 Co. 16:6. It is a kindness to a stranger to be guided in his way, and a pleasure to travellers to meet with suitable company: this is a work that may be done *after a godly sort,* in a manner worthy of God, or suitable to the deference and relation we bear to God. Christians should consider not only what they must do, but what they may do, what they may most honourably and laudably do: *the liberal mind deviseth liberal* generous *things.* Christians should do even the common actions of life and of good-will after a godly sort, as serving God therein, and designing his glory.

V. The reasons of this directed conduct; these are two: — 1. *Because that for his name's sake these brethren went forth, taking nothing of the Gentiles.* It appears thus that these were ministerial brethren, that they went forth to preach the gospel and propagate Christianity; possibly they might be sent out by this apostle himself: they went forth to convert the Gentiles; this was excellent service: they went forth for God and his name's sake; this is the minister's highest end, and should be his principal spring and motive, to gather and to build up a people for his name: they went forth also to carry a free gospel about with them, to publish it without charge wherever they came: *Taking nothing of the Gentiles.* These were worthy of double honour. There are those who are not called to preach the gospel themselves who may yet contribute to the progress of it. The gospel should be made without charge to those to whom it is first preached. Those who know it not cannot be expected to value it; churches and Christian patriots ought to concur to support the propagation of holy religion in the pagan countries; public spirits should concur according to their several capacities; those who are freely communicative of Christ's gospel should be assisted by those who are communicative of their purses. 2. *We ought therefore to receive such, that we may be fellow-helpers to the truth,* to true religion. The institution of Christ is the true religion; it has been attested by God. Those that are true in it and true to it will earnestly desire, and pray for, and contribute to, its propagation in the world. In many ways may the truth be befriended and assisted; those who cannot themselves proclaim it may yet receive, accompany, help, and countenance those who do.

Verses 9–11

I. Here is a very different example and character, an officer, a minister in the church, less generous, catholic, and communicative than the private Christians. Ministers may sometimes be out-shone, out-done. In reference to this minister, we see,

1. His name — a Gentile name: *Diotrephes,* attended with an unchristian spirit.

2. His temper and spirit — full of pride and ambition: *He loves to have the pre-eminence.* This ferment sprang and wrought betimes. It is an ill unbeseeming character of Christ's ministers to love pre-eminence, to affect presidency in the church of God.

3. His contempt of the apostle's authority, and letter, and friends. (1.) Of his authority: *The deeds which he doeth* contrary to our appointment, *prating against us with malicious words.* Strange that the contempt should run so high! But ambition will breed malice against those who oppose it. Malice and ill-will in the heart will be apt to vent themselves by the lips. The heart and mouth are both to be watched. (2.) Of his letter: *"I wrote to the church* (*v.* 9), namely, in recommendation of such and such brethren. *But Diotrephes receiveth us not,* admits not our letter and testimony therein." This seems to be the church of which Gaius was a member. A gospel church seems to be such a society as to which a letter may be written and communicated. Gospel churches may well expect and be allowed credentials with the strangers who desire to be admitted among them. The apostle seems to write by and with these brethren. To an ambitious aspiring spirit apostolical authority or epistle signifies but little. (3.) Of his friends, the brethren he recommended: *Neither doth he himself receive the brethren, and forbiddeth those that would, and casteth them out of the church, v.* 10. There might be some differences or different customs between the Jewish and Gentile Christians. Pastors should seriously consider what differences are tolerable. The pastor is not at absolute liberty, nor lord over God's heritage. It is bad to do no good ourselves; but it is worse to hinder those who would. Church-power and church-censures are often abused. Many are cast out of the church who should be received there with satisfaction and welcome. But woe to those who cast out the brethren whom the Lord Christ will take into his own communion and kingdom!

4. The apostle's menace of this proud domineerer: *Wherefore, if I come, I will remember his deeds which he doeth* (*v.* 10), will remember to censure them. This seems to intimate apostolical authority. But the apostle seems not to hold an episcopal court, to which Diotrephes must be summoned; but he will come to take cognizance of this affair in the church to which it belongs. Acts of ecclesiastical domination and tyranny ought to be animadverted upon. May it be better agreed to whom that power belongs!

II. Here is counsel upon that different character, dissuasion from copying such a pattern, and indeed any evil at all: *Beloved, follow not that which is evil, but that which is good, v.* 11. Imitate not such unchristian pernicious evil; but pursue the contrary good, in wisdom, purity, peace, and love. Caution and counsel are not needless to those who are good already. Those cautions and counsels are most likely to be accepted that are seasoned with love. *Beloved, follow not that which is evil.* To this caution and counsel a reason is respectively subjoined. 1. To the counsel: *Follow that which is good;* for *he that doeth good* (naturally and genuinely doeth good, as delighting therein) *is of God,* is born of God. The practice of goodness is the evidence of our filial happy relation to God. 2. To the caution: *Follow not that which is evil,* for *he that doeth evil* (with bent of mind pursues it) *hath not seen God,* is not duly sensible of his holy nature and will. Evil-workers vainly pretend or boast an acquaintance with God.

Verses 12–14

Here we have, I. The character of another person, one *Demetrius,* not much known otherwise. But here his name will live. A name in the gospel, a fame in the churches, is better than that of sons and daughters. His character was his commendation. His commendation was, 1. General: *Demetrius has a good report of all men.* Few are well spoken of by all; and sometimes it is ill to be so. But universal integrity and goodness are the way to (and sometimes obtain) universal applause. 2. Deserved and well founded: *And of the truth itself, v.* 12. Some have a good report, but not of the truth itself. Happy are those whose spirit and conduct commend them before God and men. 3. Confirmed by the apostle's and his friends' testimony: *Yea, and we also bear record;* and that with an appeal to Gaius's own knowledge: *And you* (you and your friends) *know that our record is true.* Probably this Demetrius was known to the church where the apostle now resided, and to that where Gaius was. It is good to be well known, or known for good. We must be ready to bear our testimony to those who are good: it is well for those who are commended when those who commend them can appeal to the consciences of those who know them most.

II. The conclusion of the epistle, in which we may observe, 1. The referring of some things to personal interview: *I have many things to write, but I will not with ink and pen, but I trust I shall shortly see thee, v.* 13, 14. Many things may be more proper for immediate communication than for letter. A little personal conference may spare the time, trouble, and charge, of many letters; and good Christians may well be glad to see one another. 2. The benediction: *Peace be to you;* all felicity attend you. Those that are good and happy themselves wish others so too. 3. The public salutation sent to Gaius: *Our friends salute thee.* A friend to the propagation of religion deserves a common remembrance. And these pious persons show their friendship to religion as well as to Gaius. 4. The apostle's particular salutation of the Christians in Gaius's church or vicinity: *Greet thy friends by name.* I doubt they were not very many who must be so personally saluted. But we must learn humility as well as love. The lowest in the church of Christ should be greeted. And those may well salute and greet one another on earth who hope to live together in heaven. And the apostle who had lain in Christ's bosom lays Christ's friends in his heart.

AN EXPOSITION, WITH PRACTICAL OBSERVATIONS, OF

THE GENERAL EPISTLE OF JUDE

This epistle is styled (as are some few others) *general* or *Catholic,* because it is not immediately directed to any particular person, family, or church, but to the whole society of Christians of that time, lately converted to the faith of Christ, whether from Judaism or paganism: and it is, and will be, of standing, lasting, and special use in and to the church as long as Christianity, that is, as time, shall last. The general scope of it is much the same with that of the second chapter of the second epistle of Peter, which having been already explained, the less will need to be said on this. It is designed to warn us against seducers and their seduction, to inspire us with a warm love to, and a hearty concern for, truth (evident and important truth), and that in the closest conjunction with holiness, of which charity, or sincere unbiased brotherly-love, is a most essential character and inseparable branch. The truth we are to hold fast, and endeavour that others may be acquainted with and not depart from, has two special characters: — It is *the truth as it is in Jesus* (Eph. 4:21; and it is *truth after* (or *which is according to) godliness,* Tit. 1:1. The gospel is the gospel of Christ. He has revealed it to us, and he is the main subject of it; and therefore we are indispensably bound to learn thence all we can of his person, natures, and offices: indifference as to this is inexcusable in any who call themselves *Christians;* and we know from what fountain we are wholly and solely to draw all necessary saving knowledge. Further, it is also a doctrine of godliness. Whatever doctrines favour the corrupt lusts of men cannot be of God, let the pleas and pretensions for them be what they will. Errors dangerous to the souls of men soon sprang up in the church. *The servants slept and tares were sown.* But such were the wisdom and kindness of Providence that they began sensibly to appear and show themselves, while some, at least, of the apostles were yet alive to confute them, and warn others against them. We are apt to think, If we had lived in their times, we should have been abundantly fenced against the attempts and artifices of seducers; but we have their testimony and their cautions, which is sufficient; and, if we will not believe their writings, neither should we have believed or regarded their sayings, if we had lived among them and conversed personally with them.

We have here, I. An account of the penman of this epistle, a character of the church, the blessings and privileges of that happy society (*v.* 1, 2). II. The occasion of writing this epistle (*v.* 3). III. A character of evil and perverse men, who had already sprung up in that infant state of the church, and would be succeeded by others of the like evil spirit and temper in after-times (*v.* 4). IV. A caution against hearkening to and following after such, from the severity of God towards the unbelieving murmuring Israelites at their coming out of Egypt, the angels that fell, the sin and punishment of Sodom and Gomorrah (*v.* 5–7). V. To these the apostle likens the seducers against whom he was warning them, and describes them at large, (*v.* 8 to 10, inclusive). VI. Then (as specially suitable to his argument) he cites an ancient prophecy of Enoch foretelling and describing the future judgment (*v.* 14, 15). VII. He enlarges on the seducers' character, and guards against the offence which honest minds might be apt to take at the so early permission of such things, by showing that it was foretold long before that so it must be (*v.* 16–19). VIII. Exhorts them to perseverance in the faith, fervency in prayer, watchfulness against falling from the love of God, and a lively hope of eternal life (*v.* 20, 21). IX. Directs them how to act towards the erroneous and scandalous (*v.* 22, 23). And, X. Closes with an admirable doxology in the last two verses.

Verses 1–2

Here we have the preface or introduction, in which,

I. We have an account of the penman of this epistle, *Jude,* or *Judas,* or Judah. He was name-sake to one of his ancestors, the patriarch-son of Jacob, the most eminent though not the first-born of his sons, out of whose loins (lineally, in a most direct succession) the Messiah came. This was a name of worth, eminency, and honour; yet 1. He had a wicked name-sake. There was one Judas (one of the twelve, surnamed *Iscariot,* from the place of his birth) who was a vile traitor, the betrayer of his and our Lord. The same names may be common to the best and worst persons. It may be instructive to be called after the names of eminently good men, but there can be no inference drawn thence as to what we shall prove, though we may even thence conclude what sort of persons our good parents or progenitors desired and hoped we should be. But, 2. Our Judas was quite another man. He was an apostle, so was Iscariot; but he was a sincere disciple and follower of Christ, so was not the other. He was a faithful servant of Jesus Christ, the other was his betrayer and murderer; therefore here the one is very carefully distinguished from the other. Dr. Manton's note upon this is, that God takes great care of the good name of his sincere and useful servants. Why then should we be prodigal of our own or one another's reputation and usefulness? Our apostle here calls himself a servant of Jesus Christ, esteeming that a most honourable title. It is more honourable to be a sincere and useful servant of Christ than to be an earthly king, how potent and prosperous soever. He might have claimed kindred to Christ according to the flesh, but he waives this, and rather glories in being his servant. Observe, (1.) It is really a greater honour to be a faithful servant of Jesus Christ than to be akin to him according to the flesh. Many of Christ's natural kindred, as well as of his progenitors, perished; not from want of natural affection in him as man, but from infidelity and obstinacy in themselves, which should make the descendants and near relatives of persons most eminent for sincere and exemplary piety *jealous over themselves with a godly jealousy.* A son of Noah may be saved in the ark from a flood of temporal destruction, and yet be overwhelmed at last in a deluge of divine wrath, and suffer *the vengeance of eternal fire.* Christ himself tells us *that he that heareth his word and doeth it* (that is, he only) *is as his brother, and sister, and mother,* that is, more honourably and advantageously related to him than the nearest and dearest of his natural relatives, considered merely as such. See Mt. 12:48–50. (2.) In that the apostle Jude styles himself a servant, though an apostle, a dignified officer in Christ's kingdom, it is a great honour to the meanest sincere minister (and it holds proportionably as to every upright Christian) that he is *the servant of Christ Jesus.* The apostles were servants before they were apostles, and they were but servants still. Away then with all pretensions in the ministers of Christ to lordly dominion either over one another or over the flocks committed to their charge. Let us ever have that of our dear Redeemer in actual view, *It shall not be so among you,* Mt. 20:25, 26. — *And brother of James,* to wit, of him whom the ancients style *the first bishop of Jerusalem,* of whose character and martyrdom Josephus makes mention, ascribing the horrible destruction of that city and nation to this wicked cruelty, as one of its principal causes. Of this James our Jude was brother, whether in the strictest or a larger (though very usual) acceptation I determine not. He however reckons it an honour to him that he was the brother of such a one. We ought to honour those who are above us in age, gifts, graces, station; not to envy them, yet neither to flatter them, nor be led merely by their example, when we have reason to think they act wrong. Thus the apostle Paul withstood his fellow-apostle Peter to the face, notwithstanding the high esteem he had for him and the affectionate love he bore to him, when he saw that he was to be blamed, that is, really blameworthy, Gal. 2:11, and following verses.

II. We are here informed to whom this epistle is directed; namely, to all those *who are sanctified by God the Father, and preserved in Jesus Christ, and called.* I begin with the last — *called,* that is, called *Christians,* in the judgment of charity, further than which we cannot, nor in justice ought to go, in the judgments or opinions we form or receive of one another; for what appears not is not, nor ought to come into account in all our dealings with and censures of one another, whatever abatements the divine goodness may see fit to make for an honest though misguided zeal. The church pretends not (I am sure it ought not) to judge of *secret or hidden things* (things drawn into the light before time), lest our rash and preposterous zeal do more harm than good, or I am afraid ever will do. *The tares and wheat* (if Christ may be Judge) *must grow together till the harvest* (Mt. 13:28–30); and then he himself will, by proper instruments, take timely care to separate them. We ought to think the best we can of every man till the contrary appear; not being forward to receive or propagate, much less invent, disadvantageous characters of our brethren. This is the least we can make of the apostle's large and excellent description of charity (1 Co. 13), and this we ought to make conscience of acting up to, which till we do, the Christian churches will be (as, alas! they are at this day) filled with *envying and strife, confusion and every evil work,* Jam. 3:16. Or, the apostle may speak of their being *called to be Christians,* by the preaching of the word, which they gladly received, and professed cordially to believe, and so were received into the society and fellowship of the church — Christ the head, and believers the members; real believers really, professed believers visibly. Note, Christians are the called, called out of the world, the evil spirit and temper of it, — above the world, to higher and better things, heaven, things unseen and eternal, — called from sin to Christ, from vanity to seriousness, from uncleanness to holiness; and this in pursuance of divine purpose and grace; *for whom he did predestinate those he also called,* Rom. 8:30. Now those who are thus called, are, 1. Sanctified: *Sanctified by God the Father.* Sanctification is usually spoken of in scripture as the work of the Holy Spirit, yet here it is ascribed to God the Father, because the Spirit works it as the Spirit of the Father and the Son. Note, All who are effectually called are sanctified, *made partakers of a divine nature* (2 Pt. 1:4); *for without holiness no man shall see the Lord,* Heb. 12:14. Observe, Our sanctification is not our own work. If any are sanctified, they are so by God the Father, not excluding Son or Spirit, for they are one, one God. Our corruption and pollution are of ourselves; but our sanctification and renovation are of God and his grace; and therefore if we perish in our iniquity we must bear the blame, but if we be sanctified and glorified all the honour and glory must be ascribed to God, and to him alone. I own it is hard to give a clear and distinct account of this, but we must not deny nor disregard necessary truth because we cannot fully reconcile the several parts of it to each other; for, on that supposition, we might deny that any one of us could stir an inch from the place we are at present in, though we see the contrary every day and hour. 2. The called and sanctified are *preserved in Christ Jesus.* As it is God who begins the work of grace in the souls of men, so it is he who carries it on, and perfects it. Where he begins he will perfect; though we are fickle, he is constant. *He will not forsake the work of his own hands,* Ps. 138:8. Let us not therefore trust in ourselves, nor in our stock of grace already received, but in him, and in him alone, still endeavouring, by all proper and appointed means, to keep ourselves, as ever we would hope he should keep us. Note, (1.) Believers are *preserved* from the gates of hell, and to the glory of heaven. (2.) All who are preserved are preserved in Jesus Christ, in him as their *citadel and stronghold,* no longer than they abide in him, and solely by virtue of their union with him.

III. We have the apostolical benediction: *Mercy to you,* etc. From the mercy, peace, and love of God all our comfort flows, all our real enjoyment in this life, all our hope of a better. 1. The *mercy* of God is the spring and fountain of all the good we have or hope for; mercy not only to the miserable, but to the guilty. 2. Next to mercy is *peace,* which we have from the sense of having obtained mercy. We can have no true and lasting peace but what flows from our reconciliation with God by Jesus Christ. 3. As from mercy springs peace, so from peace springs *love,* his love to us, our love to him, and our brotherly love (forgotten, wretchedly neglected, grace!) to one another. These the apostle prays may be multiplied, that Christians may not be content with scraps and narrow scantlings of them; but that souls and societies may be full of them. Note, God is ready to supply us with all grace, and a fulness in each grace. If we are straitened, we are not straitened in him, but in ourselves.

Verses 3–7

We have here, I. The design of the apostle in writing this epistle to the lately converted Jews and Gentiles; namely, to establish them in the Christian faith, and a practice and conversation truly consonant and conformable thereunto, and in an open and bold profession thereof, especially in times of notorious opposition, whether by artful seduction or violent and inhuman persecution. But then we must see to it very carefully that it be really the Christian faith that we believe, profess, propagate, and contend for; not the discriminating badges of this or the other party, not any thing of later date than the inspired writings of the holy evangelists and apostles. Here observe, 1. The gospel salvation is a common salvation, that is, in a most sincere offer and tender of it to all mankind to whom the notice of it reaches: for so the commission runs (Mk. 16:15, 16), *Go you into all the world, and preach the gospel to every creature,* etc. Surely God means as he speaks; he does not delude us with vain words, whatever men do; and therefore none are excluded from the benefit of these gracious offers and invitations, but those who obstinately, impenitently, finally exclude themselves. *Whoever will may come and drink of the water of life freely,* Rev. 22:17. The application of it is made to all believers, and only to such; it is made to the weak as well as to the strong. Let none discourage themselves on the account of hidden decrees which they can know little of, and with which they have nothing to do. God's decrees are dark, his covenants are plain. "All good Christians meet in Christ the common head, are actuated by one and the same Spirit, are guided by one rule, meet here at one throne of grace, and hope shortly to meet in one common inheritance," a glorious one to be sure, but what or how glorious we cannot, nor at present need to know; but such it will be as vastly to exceed all our present hopes and expectations. 2. This common salvation is the subject-matter of the faith of all the saints. The doctrine of it is what they all most heartily consent to; they esteem it as a *faithful saying, and worthy of all acceptation,* 1 Tim. 1:15. It is the faith once, *or at once, once for all, delivered to the saints,* to which nothing can be added, from which nothing may be detracted, in which nothing more nor less should be altered. Here let us abide; here we are safe; if we stir a step further, we are in danger of being either entangled or seduced. 3. The apostles and evangelists all wrote to us of this common salvation. This cannot be doubted by those who have carefully read their writings. It is strange that any should think they wrote chiefly to maintain particular schemes and opinions, especially such as they never did nor could think of. It is enough that they have fully declared to us, by inspiration of the Holy Ghost, all that is necessary *for every one to believe and do,* in order to obtain a personal interest in the common salvation. 4. Those who preach or write of the common salvation should give all diligence to do it well: they should not allow themselves to offer to God or his people that which costs them nothing, or next to nothing, little or no pains or thought, 2 Sa. 24:24. This were to treat God irreverently, and man unjustly. The apostle (though inspired) gave all diligence to write of the common salvation. What then will become of those who (though uninspired) give no diligence, or next to none, but say to the people (even in the name of God) *quicquid in buccam venerit — whatever comes next,* who, so that they use scripture-words, care not how they interpret or apply them? Those who speak of sacred things ought always to speak of them with the greatest reverence, care, and diligence. 5. Those who have received the doctrine of this common salvation must contend earnestly for it. *Earnestly,* not *furiously.* Those who strive for the Christian faith, or in the Christian course, must strive lawfully, or they lose their labour, and run great hazard of losing their crown, 2 Tim. 2:5. *The wrath of man worketh not the righteousness of God,* Jam. 1:20. Lying for the truth is bad, and scolding for it is not much better. Observe, Those who have received the truth must contend for it. But how? As the apostles did; by suffering patiently and courageously for it, not by making others suffer if they will not presently embrace every notion that we are pleased (proved or unproved) to call faith, or fundamental. We must not suffer ourselves to be robbed of any essential article of Christian faith, by the cunning craftiness or specious plausible pretences of any who *lie in wait to deceive,* Eph. 4:14. The apostle Paul tells us he preached the gospel (mind it was the gospel) *with much contention* (1 Th. 2:2), that is (as I understand it), with earnestness, with a hearty zeal, and a great concern for the success of what he preached. But, if we will understand *contention* in the common acceptation of the word, we must impartially consider with whom the apostle contended, and how, the enlarging on which would not be proper for this place.

II. The occasion the apostle had to write to this purport. As evil manners give rise to good laws, so dangerous errors often give just occasion to the proper defence of important truths. Here observe, 1. Ungodly men are the great enemies of the faith of Christ and the peace of the church. Those who deny or corrupt the one, and disturb the other, are here expressly styled *ungodly men.* We might have truth with peace (a most desirable thing) were there none (ministers or private Christians) in our particular churches and congregations but truly godly men — a blessing scarcely to be looked or hoped for on this side heaven. Ungodly men raise scruples, merely to advance and promote their own selfish, ambitious, and covetous ends. This has been the plague of the church in all past ages, and I am afraid no age is, or will be, wholly free from such men and such practices as long as time shall last. Observe, Nothing cuts us off from the church but that which cuts us off from Christ; namely, reigning infidelity and ungodliness. We must abhor the thought of branding particular parties or persons with this character, especially of doing it without the least proof, or, as it too often happens, the least shadow of it. Those are ungodly men who live *without God in the world,* who have no regard to God and conscience. Those are to be dreaded and consequently to be avoided, not only who are wicked by sins of commission, but also who are ungodly by sins of omission, who, for example, restrain prayer before God, who dare not reprove a rich man, when it is the duty of their place so to do, for fear of losing his favour and the advantage they promise themselves therefrom, who *do the work of the Lord negligently,* etc. 2. Those are *the worst of ungodly men who turn the grace of God into lasciviousness,* who take encouragement to sin more boldly because the grace of God has abounded, and still abounds, so wonderfully, who are hardened in their impieties by the extent and fulness of gospel grace, the design of which is to reduce men from sin, and bring them unto God. Thus therefore to wax wanton under so great grace, and turn it into an occasion of working all uncleanness with greediness, and hardening ourselves in such a course by that very grace which is the last and most forcible means to reclaim us from it, is to render ourselves the vilest, the worst, and most hopeless of sinners. 3. Those who turn the grace of God into lasciviousness do in effect *deny the Lord God, and our Lord Jesus Christ;* that is, they deny both natural and revealed religion. They strike at the foundation of natural religion, for they *deny the only Lord God;* and they overturn all the frame of revealed religion, for they deny *the Lord Jesus Christ.* Now his great design in establishing revealed religion in the world was to bring us unto God. To deny revealed religion is virtually to overturn natural religion, for they stand or fall together, and they mutually yield light and force to each other. Would to God our modern deists, who live in the midst of gospel light, would seriously consider this, and cautiously, diligently, and impartially examine what it is that hinders their receiving the gospel, while they profess themselves fully persuaded of all the principles and duties of natural religion! Never to tallies answered more exactly to each other than these do, so that it seems absurd to receive the one and reject the other. One would think it were the fairer way to receive both or reject both; though perhaps the more plausible method, especially in this age, is to act the part they do. 4. Those who turn the grace of God into lasciviousness are ordained unto condemnation. They sin against the last, the greatest, and most perfect remedy; and so are without excuse. Those who thus sin must needs die of their wounds, of their disease, are of old ordained to this condemnation, whatever that expression means. But what if our translators had thought fit to have rendered the words *palai progegrammenoi — of old fore-written of,* as persons who would through their own sin and folly become the proper subjects of this condemnation, where had the harm been? Plain Christians had not been troubled with dark, doubtful, and perplexing thoughts about reprobation, which the strongest heads cannot enter far into, can indeed bear but little of, without much loss and damage. Is it not enough that early notice was given by inspired writers that such seducers and wicked men should arise in later times, and that every one, being fore-warned of, should be fore-armed against them? 5. We ought to contend earnestly for the faith, in opposition to those who would corrupt or deprave it, such as have *crept in unawares:* a wretched character, to be sure, but often very ill applied by weak and ignorant people, and even by those who themselves creep in unawares, who think their *ipse dixit* should stand for a law to all their followers and admirers. Surely faithful humble ministers are helpers of their people's joy, peace, and comfort; *not lords of their faith!* Whoever may attempt to corrupt the faith, we ought to contend earnestly against them. The more busy and crafty the instruments and agents of Satan are, to rob us of the truth, the more solicitous should we be to hold it fast, always provided we be very sure that we fasten no wrong or injurious characters on persons, parties, or sentiments.

III. The fair warning which the apostle, in Christ's name, gives to those who, having professed his holy religion, do afterwards desert and prove false to it, *v.* 5–7. We have here a recital of the former judgments of God upon sinners, with design to awaken and terrify those to whom warning is given in this epistle. Observe, The judgments of God are often denounced and executed *in terrorem — for warning to others,* rather than from immediate or particular displeasure against the offenders themselves; not that God is not displeased with them, but perhaps not more with them than with others who, at least for the present, escape. *I will put you in remembrance.* What we already know we still need to be put in remembrance of. Therefore there will always be need and use of a standing stated ministry in the Christian church, though all the doctrines of faith, the essentials, are so plainly revealed in express words, or by the most near, plain, and immediate consequence, that he who runs may read and understand them. There wants no infallible interpreter, really or conceitedly such, for any such end or purpose. Some people (weakly enough) suggest, "If the scriptures do so plainly contain all that is necessary to salvation, what need or use can there be of a standing ministry? Why may we not content ourselves with staying at home, and reading our Bibles?" The inspired apostle has here fully, though not wholly, answered this objection. Preaching is not designed to teach us something new in every sermon, somewhat that we knew nothing of before; but *to put us in remembrance,* to call to mind things forgot-

ten, to affect our passions, and engage and fix our resolutions, that our lives may be answerable to our faith. *Though you know these things,* yet you still need to *know them better.* There are many things which we have known which yet we have unhappily forgotten. Is it of no use or service to be put afresh in remembrance of them?

Now what are these things which we Christians need to be put in remembrance of?

1. The destruction of the unbelieving Israelites in the wilderness, *v.* 5. Paul puts the Corinthians in mind of this, 1 Co. 10. The first ten verses of that chapter (as the scripture is always the best commentary upon itself) are the best explication of the fifth verse of this epistle of Jude. None therefore ought to presume upon their privileges, since many who were brought out of Egypt by a series of amazing miracles, yet perished in the wilderness by reason of their unbelief. *Let us not therefore be high-minded, but fear,* Rom. 11:20. *Let us fear lest, a promise being left us of entering into his rest, any of you should seem to come short of it,* Heb. 4:1. They had miracles in abundance: they were their daily bread; yet even they perished in unbelief. We have greater (much greater) advantages than they had; let their error (their so fatal error) be our awful warning.

2. We are here put in remembrance of the fall of the angels, *v.* 6. There were a great number of the angels who *left their own habitation;* that is, who were not pleased with the posts and stations the supreme Monarch of the universe had assigned and allotted to them, but thought (like discontented ministers in our age, I might say in every age) they deserved better; they would, with the title of *ministers,* be *sovereigns,* and in effect their Sovereign should be their minister — do all, and only, what they would have him; thus was pride the main and immediate cause or occasion of their fall. Thus they quitted their post, and rebelled against God, their Creator and sovereign Lord. But God did not spare them (high and great as they were); he would not truckle to them; he threw them off, as a wise and good prince will a selfish and deceitful minister; and the great, the all-wise God, could not be ignorant, as the wisest and best of earthly princes often are, what designs they were hatching. After all, what became of them? They thought to have dared and outfaced Omnipotence itself; but God was too hard for them, he cast them down to hell. Those who would not be servants to their Maker and his will in their first state were made captives to his justice, and are *reserved in everlasting chains, under darkness.* Here see what the condition of fallen angels is: they are *in chains,* bound under the divine power and justice, bound over *to the judgment of the great day;* they are *under darkness,* though once *angels of light;* so horribly in the dark are they that they continue to fight against God, as if there were yet some small hope at least left them of prevailing and overcoming in the conflict. Dire infatuation! Light and liberty concur, chains and darkness how well do they agree and suit each other! The devils, once angels in the best sense, are *reserved,* etc. Observe, There is, undoubtedly there is, a judgment to come; the fallen angels are *reserved to the judgment of the great day;* and shall fallen men escape it? Surely not. Let every reader consider this in due time. Their chains are called everlasting, because it is impossible they should ever break loose from them, or make an escape; they are held fast and sure under them. The decree, the justice, the wrath of God, are the very chains under which fallen angels are held so fast. Hear and fear, O sinful mortals of mankind!

3. The apostle here calls to our remembrance the destruction of Sodom and Gomorrah, *v.* 7. *Even as,* etc. It is in allusion to the destruction of *Pentapolis,* or the five cities, that the miseries of the damned are set forth by a lake that burneth with fire and brimstone; they were guilty of abominable wickedness, not to be named or thought of but with the utmost abhorrence and detestation; their ruin is a particular warning to all people to take heed of, and fly *from, fleshly lusts that war against the soul,* 1 Pt. 2:11. "These lusts consumed the Sodomites with fire from heaven, and they are now *suffering the vengeance of eternal fire;* therefore take heed, imitate not their sins, lest the same plagues overtake you as did them. God is the same holy, just, pure Being now as then; and can the beastly pleasures of a moment make amends for your suffering the vengeance of eternal fire? *Stand in awe, therefore, and sin not,*" Ps. 4:4.

Verses 8–15

The apostle here exhibits a charge against deceivers who

were now seducing the disciples of Christ from the profession and practice of his holy religion. He calls them *filthy dreamers,* forasmuch as delusion is a dream, and the beginning of, and inlet to, all manner of filthiness. Note, Sin is filthiness; it renders men odious and vile in the sight of the most holy God, and makes them (sooner or later, as penitent or as punished to extremity and without resource) vile in their own eyes, and in a while they become vile in the eyes of all about them. *These filthy dreamers* dream themselves into a fool's paradise on earth, and into a real hell at last: let their character, course, and end, be our seasonable and sufficient warning; like sins will produce like punishments and miseries. Here,

I. The character of these deceivers is described.

1. They *defile the flesh.* The flesh or body is the immediate seat, and often the irritating occasion, of many horrid pollutions; yet these, though done in and against the body, do greatly defile and grievously maim and wound the soul. *Fleshly lusts do war against the soul,* 1 Pt. 2:11. and in 2 Co. 7:1 we read of *filthiness of flesh and spirit,* each of which, though of different kinds, defiles the whole man.

2. They *despise dominion, and speak evil of dignities,* are of a disturbed mind and a seditious spirit, forgetting that *the powers that be are ordained of God,* Rom. 13:1. God requires us to *speak evil of no man* (Tit. 3:2.); but it is a great aggravation of the sin of evil-speaking when what we say is pointed at magistrates, men whom God has set in authority over us, by blaspheming or speaking evil of whom we blaspheme God himself. Or if we understand it, as some do, with respect to religion, which ought to have the dominion in this lower world, such evil-speakers despise the dominion of conscience, make a jest of it, and would banish it out of the world; and as for the word of God, the rule of conscience, they despise it. The revelations of the divine will go for little with them; they are a rule of faith and manners, but not till they have explained them, and imposed their sense of them upon all about them. Or, as others account for the sense of this passage, the people of God, truly and specially so, are the dignities here spoken of or referred to, according to that of the psalmist, *Touch not mine anointed, and do my prophets no harm,* Ps. 105:15. They *speak evil,* etc. Religion and its serious professors have been always and every where evil spoken of. Though there is nothing in religion but what is very good, and deserves our highest regards, both as it is perfective of our natures and as it is subservient to our truest and highest interests; yet *this sect,* as its enemies are pleased to call it, *is every where spoken against,* Acts 28:22.

On this occasion the apostle brings in *Michael the archangel,* etc., *v.* 9. Interpreters are at a loss what is here meant by *the body of Moses.* Some think that the devil contended that Moses might have a public and honourable funeral, that the place where he was interred might be generally known, hoping thereby to draw the Jews, so naturally prone thereto, to a new and fresh instance of idolatry. Dr. Scott thinks that by the body of Moses we are to understand the Jewish church, whose destruction the devil strove and contended for, as the Christian church is called the body of Christ in the New-Testament style. Others bring other interpretations, which I will not here trouble the reader with. Though this contest was mightily eager and earnest, and Michael was victorious in the issue, yet he would not *bring a railing accusation against the devil himself;* he knew a good cause needed no such weapons to be employed in its defence. It is said, *he durst not bring,* etc. Why durst he not? Not that he was afraid of the devil, but he believed God would be offended if, in such a dispute, he went that way to work; he thought it below him to engage in a trial of skill with the great enemy of God and man which of them should out-scold or out-rail the other: a memorandum to all disputants, never to bring railing accusations into their disputes. Truth needs no supports from falsehood or scurrility. Some say, Michael would not bring a railing accusation against the devil as knowing beforehand that he would be too hard for him at that weapon. Some think the apostle refers here to the remarkable passage we have, Num. 20:7-14. Satan would have represented Moses under disadvantageous colours, which he, good man, had at that time, and upon that occasion, given but too much handle for. Now Michael, according to this account, stands up in defence of Moses, and, in the zeal of an upright and bold spirit, *says* to Satan, *The Lord rebuke thee.* He would not stand disputing with the devil, nor enter into a particular debate about the merits of that special cause. He knew Moses was his fellow-servant, a favourite of God, and he would not patiently suffer him to be insulted, no, not by the prince of devils; but in a just indignation cries out, *The Lord rebuke thee:* like that of our Lord himself (Mt. 4:10), *Get thee hence, Satan.* Moses was a dignity, a magistrate, one beloved and preferred by the great God; and the archangel thought it insufferable that such a one should be so treated by a vile apostate spirit, of how high an order soever. So the lesson hence is that we ought to stand up in defence of those whom God owns, how severe soever Satan and his instruments may be in their censures of them and their conduct. Those who censure (in particular) upright magistrates, upon every slip in their behaviour, may expect to hear, *The Lord rebuke thee;* and divine rebukes are harder to be borne than careless sinners now think for.

3. *They speak evil of the things which they know not,* etc., *v.* 10. Observe, Those who speak evil of religion and godliness *speak evil of the things which they know not;* for, if they had known them, they would have spoken well of them, for nothing but good and excellent can be truly said of religion, and it is sad that any thing different or opposite should ever be justly said of any of its professors. A religious life is the most safe, happy, comfortable, and honourable life that is. Observe, further, Men are most apt to speak evil of those persons and things that they know least of. How many had never suffered by slanderous tongues if they had been better known! On the other hand, retirement screens some even from just censure. *But what they know naturally,* etc. It is hard, if not impossible, to find any obstinate enemies to the Christian religion, who do not in their stated course live in open or secret contradiction to the very principles of natural religion: this many think hard and uncharitable; but I am afraid it will appear too true in *the day of the revelation of the righteous judgment of God.* The apostle likens such to *brute beasts,* though they often think and boast themselves, if not as the wisest, yet at least as the wittiest part of mankind. *In those things they corrupt themselves;* that is, in the plainest and most natural and necessary things, things that lie most open and obvious to natural reason and conscience; even in those things they corrupt, debase, and defile themselves: the fault, whatever it is, lies not in their understanding or apprehensions, but in their depraved wills and disordered appetites and affections; they could and might have acted better, but then they must have offered violence to those vile affections which they obstinately chose rather to gratify than to mortify.

4. In *v.* 11 the apostle represents them as followers *of Cain,* and in *v.* 12, 13, as atheistical and profane people, who thought little, and perhaps believed not much, of God or a future world — as greedy and covetous, who, so they could but gain present worldly advantages, cared not what came next — rebels against God and man, who, like Core, ran into attempts in which they must assuredly perish, as he did. Of such the apostle further says, (1.) *These are spots in your feasts of charity* — the *agapai* or *love-feasts,* so much spoken of by the ancients. They happened, by whatever means or mischance, to be admitted among them, but were spots in them, defiled and defiling. Observe, It is a great reproach, though unjust and accidental, to religion, when those who profess it, and join in the most solemn institution of it, are in heart and life unsuitable and even contrary to it: *These are spots.* Yet how common in all Christian societies here on earth, the very best not excepted, are such blemishes! The more is the pity. The Lord remedy it in his due time and way, not in men's blind and rigorous way of plucking up the wheat with the tares. But in the heaven we are waiting, hoping, and preparing for, there is none of this mad work, there are none of these disorderly doings. (2.) *When they feast with you, they feed themselves without fear.* Arrant gluttons, no doubt, there were; such as minded only the gratifying of their appetites with the daintiness and abundance of their fare; they had no regard to Solomon's caution, Prov. 23:2. Note, In common eating and drinking a holy fear is necessary, much more in feasting, though we may sometimes be more easily and insensibly overcome at a common meal than at a feast; for, in the case supposed, we are less upon our guard, and sometimes, at least to some persons, the plenty of a feast is its own antidote, as to others it may prove a dangerous snare. (3.) *Clouds they are without water,* which promise rain in time of drought, but perform nothing of what they promise. Such is the case of formal professors, who at first setting out promise much, like early-blossoming trees in a forward spring, but in conclusion bring forth little or no fruit. — *Carried about of winds,*

light and empty, easily driven about this way or that, as the wind happens to set; such are empty, ungrounded professors, and easy prey to every seducer. It is amazing to hear many talk so confidently of so many things of which they know little or nothing, and yet have not the wisdom and humility to discern and be sensible how little they know. How happy would our world be if men either knew more or practically knew how little they know. (4.) *Trees whose fruit withereth,* etc. Trees they are, for they are planted in the Lord's vineyard, yet fruitless ones. Observe, Those whose fruit withereth may be justly said to be without fruit. As good never a whit as never the better. It is a sad thing when men seem to *begin in the Spirit and end in the flesh,* which is almost as common a case as it is an awful one. The text speaks of such as were *twice dead.* One would think to be once dead were enough; we none of us, till grace renew us to a higher degree than ordinary, love to think of dying once, though this is appointed for us all. What then is the meaning of this being twice dead? They had been once dead in their natural, fallen, lapsed state; but they seemed to recover, and, as a man in a swoon, to be brought to life again, when they took upon them the profession of the Christian religion. But now they are dead again by the evident proofs they have given of their hypocrisy: whatever they seemed, they had nothing truly vital in them. — *Plucked up by the roots,* as we commonly serve dead trees, from which we expect no more fruit. They are *dead, dead, dead; why cumber they the ground?* Away with them to the fire. (5.) *Raging waves of the sea,* boisterous, noisy, and clamorous; full of talk and turbulency, but with little (if any) sense or meaning: *Foaming out their own shame,* creating much uneasiness to men of better sense and calmer tempers, which yet will in the end turn to their own greater shame and just reproach. The psalmist's prayer ought always to be that of every honest and good man, *"Let integrity and uprightness preserve me* (Ps. 25:21), and, if it will not, let me be unpreserved." If honesty signify little now, knavery will signify much less, and that in a very little while. Raging waves are a terror to sailing passengers; but, when they have got to port, the waves are forgotten as if no longer in being: their noise and terror are for ever ended. (6.) *Wandering stars,* planets that are erratic in their motions, keep not that steady regular course which the fixed ones do, but shift their stations, that one has sometimes much ado to know where to find them. This allusion carries in it a very lively emblem of false teachers, who are sometimes here and sometimes there, so that one knows not where nor how to fix them. In the main things, at least, one would think something should be fixed and steady; and this might be without infallibility, or any pretensions to it in us poor mortals. In religion and politics, the great subjects of present debate, surely there are certain *stamina* in which wise and good, honest and disinterested, men might agree, without throwing the populace into the utmost anguish and distress of mind, or blowing up their passions into rage and fury, without letting them know what they say or whereof they affirm.

II. The doom of this wicked people is declared: *To whom is reserved the blackness of darkness for ever.* False teachers are to expect the worst of punishments in this and a future world: not every one who teaches by mistake any thing that is not exactly true (for who then, in any public assembly, durst open a Bible to teach others, unless he thought himself equal or superior to the angels of God in heaven?) but every one who prevaricates, dissembles, would lead others into by-paths and side-ways, that he may have opportunity to make a gain or prey of them, or (in the apostle's phrase) to make merchandize of them, 2 Pt. 2:3. But enough of this. As for the blackness of darkness for ever, I shall only say that this terrible expression, with all the horror it imports, belongs to false teachers, truly, not slanderously so called, who *corrupt the word of God, and betray the souls of men.* If this will not make both ministers and people cautious, I know not what will.

Of the prophecy of Enoch, (*v.* 14, 15) we have no mention made in any other part or place of scripture; yet now it is scripture that there was such prophecy. One plain text of scripture is proof enough of any one point that we are required to believe, especially when relating to a matter of fact; but in matters of faith, necessary saving faith, God has not seen fit (blessed be his holy name he has not) to try us so far. There is no fundamental article of the Christian religion, truly so called, which is not inculcated over and over in the New Testament, by which we may know on what the Holy Ghost does, and consequently on what we ought, to lay the

greatest stress. Some say that this prophecy of Enoch was preserved by tradition in the Jewish church; others that the apostle Jude was immediately inspired with the notice of it: be this as it may, it is certain that there was such a prophecy of ancient date, of long standing, and universally received in the Old-Testament church; and it is a main point of our New-Testament creed. Observe, 1. Christ's coming to judgment was prophesied of as early as the middle of the patriarchal age, and was therefore even then a received and acknowledged truth. — *The Lord cometh with* his holy myriads, including both angels and the spirits of just men made perfect. What a glorious time will that be, when Christ shall *come with ten thousand of these!* And we are told for what great and awful ends and purposes he will come so accompanied and attended, namely, *to execute judgment upon all.* 2. It was spoken of then, so long ago, as a thing just at hand: *"Behold, the Lord cometh;* he is just a coming, he will be upon you before you are aware, and, unless you be very cautious and diligent, before you are provided to meet him comfortably." He *cometh,* (1.) *To execute judgment upon* the wicked. (2.) *To convince* them. Observe, Christ will condemn none without precedent, trial, and conviction, such conviction as shall at least silence themselves. They shall have no excuse or apology to make that they either can or dare then stand by. Then *every mouth shall be stopped,* the Judge and his sentence shall be (by all the impartial) approved and applauded, and even the guilty condemned criminals shall be speechless, though at present they want not bold and specious pleas, which they vent with all assurance and confidence; and yet it is certain that the mock-trials of prisoners in the jail among themselves and the real trial at the bar before the proper judge soon appear to be very different things.

I cannot pass *v.* 15 without taking notice how often, and how emphatically, the word *ungodly* is repeated in it, no fewer than four times: ungodly men, ungodly sinners, ungodly deeds, and, as to the manner, ungodly committed. Godly or ungodly signifies little with men now-a-days, unless it be to scoff at and deride even the very expressions; but it is not so in the language of the Holy Ghost. Note, Omissions, as well as commissions, must be accounted for in the day of judgment. Note, further, Hard speeches of one another, especially if ill-grounded, will most certainly come into account at *the judgment of the great day.* Let us all take care in time. "If thou," says one of our good old puritans, "smite (a miscalled heretic, or) a schismatic, and God find a real saint bleeding, look thou to it, how thou wilt answer it." It may be too late to say before the angel that it was an error, Eccl. 5:6. I only here allude to that expression of the divinely inspired writer.

Verses 16–25

Here, I. The apostle enlarges further on the character of these evil men and seducers: they *are murmurers, complainers,* etc. *v.* 16. Observe, A murmuring complaining temper, indulged and expressed, lays men under a very bad character; such are very weak at least, and for the most part very wicked. They murmur against God and his providence, against men and their conduct; they are angry at every thing that happens, and never pleased with their own state and condition in the world, as not thinking it good enough for them. Such *walk after their own lusts;* their will, their appetite, their fancy, are their only rule and law. Note, Those who please their sinful appetites are most prone to yield to their ungovernable passions.

II. He proceeds to caution and exhort those to whom he is writing, *v.* 17–23. Here,

1. He calls them to remember how they have been forewarned: *But, beloved, remember,* etc., *v.* 17. "Remember, take heed that you think it not strange (so as to stumble and be offended, and have your faith staggered by it) that such people as the seducers before described and warned against should arise (and that early) in the Christian church, seeing all this was foretold by *the apostles of our Lord Jesus Christ,* and consequently the accomplishment of it in the event is a confirmation of your faith, instead of being in the least an occasion of shaking and unsettling you therein." Note, (1.) Those who would persuade must make it evident that they sincerely love those whom they would persuade. Bitter words and hard usage never did nor ever will convince, much less persuade any body. (2.) The words which inspired persons have spoken (or written), duly remembered and reflected on, are the best preservative against dangerous errors; this will

always be so, till men have learnt to speak better than God himself. (3.) We ought not to be offended if errors and persecutions arise and prevail in the Christian church; this was foretold, and therefore we should not think worse of Christ's person, doctrine, or cross, when we see it fulfilled. See 1 Tim. 4:1, and 2 Tim. 3:1, and 2 Pt. 3:3. We must not think it strange, but comfort ourselves with this, that in the midst of all this confusion Christ will maintain his church, and make good his promise, that *the gates of hell shall not prevail against it,* Mt. 16:18. (4.) The more religion is ridiculed and persecuted the faster hold we should take and keep of it; being forewarned, we should show that we are fore-armed; under such trials we should stand firm, and *not be soon shaken in mind,* 2 Th. 2:2.

2. He guards them against seducers by a further description of their odious character: *These are those who separate,* etc., *v.* 19. Observe, (1.) Sensualists are the worst separatists. They separate themselves from God, and Christ, and his church, to the devil, the world, and the flesh, by their ungodly courses and vicious practices; and this is a great deal worse than separation from any particular branch of the visible church on account of opinions or modes and circumstances of external government or worship, though many can patiently bear with the former, while they are plentifully and almost perpetually railing at the latter, as if no sin were damnable but what they are pleased to call *schism.* (2.) Sensual men have not the Spirit, that is, of God and Christ, the Spirit of holiness, which whoever *has not, is none of Christ's,* does not belong to him, Rom. 8:9. (3.) The worse others are the better should we endeavour and approve ourselves to be; the more busy Satan and his instruments are to pervert others, in judgment or practice, the more tenacious should we be of sound doctrine and a good conversation, *holding fast the faithful word, as we have been* (divinely) *taught, holding the mystery of the faith in a pure conscience,* Tit. 1:9; 1 Tim. 3:9.

3. He exhorts them to persevering constancy in truth and holiness.

(1.) *Building up yourselves in your most holy faith, v.* 20. Observe, The way to hold fast our profession is to hold on in it. Having laid our foundation well in a sound faith, and a sincere upright heart, we must build upon it, make further progress continually; and we should take care with what materials we carry on our building, namely, *gold, silver, precious stones,* not *wood, hay, stubble,* 1 Co. 3:12. Right principles and a regular conversation sill stand the test even of the fiery trial; but, whatever we mix of baser alloy, though we be in the main sincere, we shall suffer loss by it, and though our persons be saved all that part of our work shall be consumed; and, if we ourselves escape, it will be with great danger and difficulty, as from a house on fire on every side.

(2.) *Praying in the Holy Ghost.* Observe, [1.] Prayer is the nurse of faith; the way to *build up ourselves in our most holy faith* is to *continue instant in prayer,* Rom. 12:12. [2.] Our prayers are then most likely to prevail when we *pray in the Holy Ghost,* that is, under his guidance and influence, according to the rule of his word, with faith, fervency, and constant persevering importunity; this is praying in the Holy Ghost, whether it be done by or without a set prescribed form.

(3.) *Keep yourselves in the love of God, v.* 21. [1.] "Keep up the grace of love to God in its lively vigorous actings and exercises in your souls." [2.] "Take heed of throwing yourselves out of the love of God to you, or its delightful, cheering, strengthening manifestations; keep yourselves in the way of God, if you would continue in his love."

(4.) *Looking for the mercy,* etc. [1.] Eternal life is to be looked for only through *mercy;* mercy is our only plea, not merit; or if merit, not our own, but another's, who has merited for us what otherwise we could have laid no claim to, nor have entertained any well-grounded hope of. [2.] It is said, not only through the mercy of God as our Creator, but through the mercy *of our Lord Jesus Christ* as Redeemer; all who come to heaven must come thither through our Lord Jesus Christ; for *there is no other name under heaven given among men by which we must be saved,* but that of the Lord Jesus only, Acts 4:12, compared with *v.* 10. [3.] A believing expectation of eternal life will arm us against the snares of sin (2 Pt. 3:14); a lively faith of the blessed hope will help us to mortify our cursed lusts.

4. He directs them how to behave towards erring brethren: *And of some have compassion,* etc., *v.* 22, 23. Observe, (1.) We ought to do all we can to rescue others out of the snares of the devil, that they may be saved from (or recovered, when entangled therein, out of) dangerous errors, or pernicious practices. We are not only (under God) our own keepers, but every man ought to be, as much as in him lies, his *brother's keeper;* none but a wicked Cain will contradict this, Gen. 4:9. We must watch over one another, must faithfully, yet prudently, reprove each other, and set a good example to all about us. (2.) This must be done with *compassion, making a difference.* How is that? We must distinguish between the weak and the wilful. [1.] *Of some* we must *have compassion,* treat them with all tenderness, *restore them in the spirit of meekness,* not be needlessly harsh and severe in our censures of them and their actions, nor proud and haughty in our conduct towards them; not implacable, nor averse to reconciliation with them, or admitting them to the friendship they formerly had with us, when they give evident or even strongly hopeful tokens of a sincere repentance: if God has forgiven them, why should not we? We infinitely more need his forgiveness than they do, or can do, ours, though perhaps neither they nor we are justly or sufficiently sensible of this. [2.] *Others save with fear,* urging upon them *the terrors of the Lord;* "Endeavour to frighten them out of their sins; preach hell and damnation to them." But what if prudence and caution in administering even the most just and severe reproofs be what are primarily and chiefly here intimated — (I do but offer it for consideration); as if he had said, "Fear lest you frustrate your own good intentions and honest designs by rash and imprudent management, that you do not harden, instead of reclaiming, even where greater degrees of severity are requisite than in the immediately foregoing instance." We are often apt to over-do, when we are sure we mean honestly, and think we are right in the main; yet the very worst are not needlessly, nor rashly, nor to extremity, to be provoked, lest they be thereby further hardened through our default. — *"Hating even the garment spotted with the flesh,* that is, keeping yourselves at the utmost distance from what is or appears evil, and designing and endeavouring that others may do so too. Avoid all that leads to sin or that looks like sin," 1 Th. 5:22.

III. The apostle concludes this epistle with a solemn ascription of glory to the great God, *v.* 24, 25. Note, 1. Whatever is the subject or argument we have been treating of, ascribing glory to God is fittest for us to conclude with. 2. God is able, and he is as willing as able, *to keep us from falling, and to present us faultless before the presence of his glory;* not as those who never have been faulty (for what has once been done can never be rendered undone, even by Omnipotence itself, for that implies a contradiction), but as those whose faults shall not be imputed, to their ruin, which, but for God's mercy and a Saviour's merits, they might most justly have been. — *Before the presence of his glory.* Observe, (1.) The glory of the Lord will shortly be present. We now look upon it as distant, and too many look upon it as uncertain, but it will come, and it will be manifest and apparent. *Every eye shall see him,* Rev. 1:7. This is now the object of our faith, but hereafter (and surely it cannot *now* be long) it will be the object of our sense; whom we now believe in, him we shall shortly see, to our unspeakable joy and comfort or inexpressible terror and consternation. See 1 Pt. 1:8. (2.) All real sincere believers shall be presented, and the Lord Redeemer's appearance and coming, by him their glorious head, to the Father, in order to his approbation, acceptance, and reward. They were given to him of the Father, and *of all that were so given to him he has lost none,* nor will lose any one, not an individual, a single soul, but will present them all perfectly holy and happy, when he shall surrender his mediatorial kingdom to *his God and our God, his Father and our Father,* Jn. 6:39, with *ch.* 17:12, 1 Co. 15:24. (3.) When believers shall be presented faultless it will be with exceeding joy. Alas! now our faults fill us with fears, doubts, and sorrows. But *be of good cheer;* if we be sincere, we shall be, our dear Redeemer has undertaken for it, we shall be *presented faultless;* where there is no sin there will be no sorrow; where there is the perfection of holiness, there will be the perfection of joy. Surely, the God who can and will do this is worthy to have *glory, majesty, dominion, and power,* ascribed to him, *both now and for ever!* And to this we may well, with the apostle, affix our hearty *Amen.*

AN EXPOSITION, WITH PRACTICAL OBSERVATIONS, OF

THE REVELATION OF ST. JOHN THE DIVINE

It ought to be no prejudice to the credit and authority of this book that it has been rejected by men of corrupt minds, such as Cerdon and Marcion, and doubted of by men of a better character; for this has been the lot of other parts of holy writ, and of the divine Author of the scripture himself. The image and superscription of this book are truly sacred and divine, and the matter of it agreeable with other prophetical books, particularly Ezekiel and Daniel; the church of God has generally received it, and found good counsel and great comfort in it. From the beginning, the church of God has been blessed with prophecy. That glorious prediction of breaking the serpent's head was the stay and support of the patriarchal age; and the many prophecies there were concerning the Messiah to come were the gospel of the Old Testament. Christ himself prophesied of the destruction of Jerusalem; and, about the time in which that was accomplished, he entrusted the apostle John with this book of revelation, to deliver it to the church as a prediction of the most important events that should happen to it to the end of time, for the support of the faith of his people and the direction of their hope. It is called the *Revelation,* because God therein discovers those things which could never have been sifted out by the reasonings of human understanding, those deep things of God which no man knows, but the Spirit of God, and those to whom he reveals them.

CHAPTER 1

This chapter is a general preface to the whole book, and contains, I. An inscription, declaring the original and the design of it (*v.* 1, 2). II. The apostolic benediction pronounced on all those who shall pay a due regard to the contents of this book (*v.* 3–8). III. A glorious vision or appearance of the Lord Jesus Christ to the apostle John, when he delivered to him this revelation (*v.* 9 to the end).

Verses 1–2

Here we have,

I. What we may call the pedigree of this book. 1. It is *the revelation of Jesus Christ.* The whole Bible is so; for all revelation comes through Christ and all centres in him; and especially *in these last days God has spoken to us by his Son,* and concerning his Son. Christ, as the king of his church, has been pleased thus far to let his church know by what rules and methods he will proceed in his government; and, as the prophet of the church, he has made known to us the things that shall be hereafter. 2. It is a revelation *which God gave unto Christ.* Though Christ is himself God, and as such has light and life in himself, yet, as he sustains the office of *Mediator between God and man,* he receives his instructions from the Father. The human nature of Christ, though endowed with the greatest sagacity, judgment, and penetration, could not, in a way of reason, discover these great events, which not being produced by natural causes, but wholly depending upon the will of God, could be the object only of divine prescience, and must come to a created mind only by revelation. Our Lord Jesus is the great trustee of divine revelation; it is to him that we owe the knowledge we have of what we are to expect from God and what he expects from us. 3. This revelation Christ *sent and signified by his angel.* Observe here the admirable order of divine revelation. God gave it to Christ, and Christ employed an angel to communicate it to the churches. The angels are God's messengers; they are ministering spirits to the heirs of salvation. They are Christ's servants: principalities and powers are subject to him; all the angels of God are obliged to worship him. 4. The angels *signified it to the apostle John.* As the angels are the messengers of Christ, the ministers are the messengers of the churches; what they receive from heaven, they are to communicate to the churches. John was the apostle chosen for this service. Some think he was the only one surviving, the rest having sealed their testimony with their blood. This was to be the last book of divine revelation; and therefore notified to the church by the last of the apostles. John was the beloved disciple. He was, under the New Testament, as the prophet Daniel under the Old, *a man greatly beloved.* He was the servant of Christ; he was an apostle, an evangelist, and a prophet; he served Christ in all the three extraordinary offices of the church. James was an apostle, but not a prophet, nor an evangelist; Matthew was an apostle and evangelist, but not a prophet; Luke was an evangelist, but neither a prophet nor an apostle; but John was all three; and so Christ calls him in an eminent sense his *servant John.* 5. John was to deliver this revelation to the church, to all his servants. For the revelation was not designed for the use of Christ's extraordinary servants the ministers only, but for all his servants, the members of the church; they have all a right to the oracles of God, and all have their concern in them.

II. Here we have the subject-matter of this revelation, namely, the things that must shortly come to pass. The evangelists give us an account of the things that are past; prophecy gives us an account of things to come. These future events are shown, not in the clearest light in which God could have set them, but in such a light as he saw most proper, and which would best answer his wise and holy purposes. Had they been as clearly foretold in all their circumstances as God could have revealed them, the prediction might have prevented the accomplishment; but they are foretold more darkly, to beget in us a veneration for the scripture, and to engage our attention and excite our enquiry. We have in this revelation a general idea of the methods of divine providence and government in and about the church, and many good lessons may be learned hereby. These events (it is said) were such as should come to pass not only *surely,* but *shortly;* that is, they would begin to come to pass very shortly, and the whole would be accomplished in a short time. For now the last ages of the world had come.

III. Here is an attestation of the prophecy, *v.* 2. It was signified to John, who bore record of the word of God, and of the testimony of Jesus Christ, and of all things that he saw. It is observable that the historical books of the Old Testament have not always the name of the historian prefixed to them, as in the books of *Judges, Kings, Chronicles;* but in the prophetical books the name is always prefixed, as *Isaiah, Jeremiah,* etc. So in the New Testament, though John did not prefix his name to his first epistle, yet he does to this prophecy, as ready to vouch and answer for the truth of it; and he gives us not only his name, but his office. He was one who bore record of the word of God in general, and of the testimony of Jesus in particular, and of all things that he saw; he was an eye-witness, and he concealed nothing that he saw. Nothing recorded in this revelation was his own invention or imagination; but all was the record of God and the testimony of Jesus; and, as he added nothing to it, so he kept back no part of the counsels of God.

Verses 3–8

We have here an apostolic benediction on those who should give a due regard to this divine revelation; and this benediction is given more generally and more especially.

I. More generally, to all who either read or hear the words of the prophecy. This blessing seems to be pronounced with a design to encourage us to study this book, and not be weary of looking into it upon account of the obscurity of many things in it; it will repay the labour of the careful and attentive reader. Observe, 1. It is a blessed privilege to enjoy the oracles of God. This was one of the principal advantages the Jews had above the Gentiles. 2. It is a blessed thing to study the scriptures; those are well employed who search the scriptures. 3. It is a privilege not only to read the scriptures ourselves, but to hear them read by others, who are qualified to give us the sense of what they read and to lead us into an understanding of them. 4. It is not sufficient to our blessedness that we read and hear the scriptures, but we must keep the things that are written; we must keep them in our memories, in our minds, in our affections, and in practice, and we shall be blessed in the deed. 5. The nearer we come to the accomplishment of the scriptures, the greater regard we shall give to them. The time is at hand, and we should be so much the more attentive as we see the day approaching.

II. The apostolic benediction is pronounced more especially and particularly to the seven Asian churches, *v.* 4. These seven churches are named in *v.* 11, and distinct messages sent to each of them respectively in the chapters following. The apostolic blessing is more expressly directed to these because they were nearest to him, who was now in the isle of Patmos, and perhaps he had the peculiar care of them, and superintendency over them, not excluding any of the rest of the apostles, if any of them were now living. Here observe,

1. What the blessing is which he pronounces on all the faithful in these churches: *Grace and peace,* holiness and comfort. *Grace,* that is, the good-will of God towards us and his good work in us; and *peace,* that is, the sweet evidence and assurance of this grace. There can be no true peace where there is not true grace; and, where grace goes before, peace will follow.

2. Whence this blessing is to come. In whose name does the apostle bless the churches? In the name of God, of the whole Trinity; for this is an act of adoration, and God only is the proper object of it; his ministers must bless the people in no name but his alone. And here, (1.) The Father is first named: God the Father, which may be taken either essentially, for God as God, or personally, for the first person in the ever-blessed Trinity, the God and Father of our Lord Jesus Christ; and he is described as the Jehovah *who is, and who was, and who is to come,* eternal, unchangeable, the same to the Old-Testament church which was, and to the New-Testament church which is, and who will be the same to the church triumphant which is to come. (2.) The Holy Spirit, called *the seven spirits,* not seven in number, nor in nature, but the infinite perfect Spirit of God, in whom there is a diversity of gifts and operations. He is before the throne; for, as God made, so he governs, all things by his Spirit. (3.) The Lord Jesus Christ. He mentions him after the Spirit, because he intended to enlarge more upon the person of Christ, as God manifested in the flesh, whom he had seen dwelling on earth before, and now saw again in a glorious form. Observe the particular account we have here of Christ, *v.* 5. [1.] He *is the faithful witness;* he was from eternity a witness to all the counsels of God (Jn. 1:18), and he was in time a faithful witness to the revealed will of God, who has now spoken to us by his Son; upon his testimony we may safely depend, for he is a faithful witness, cannot be deceived and cannot deceive us. [2.] He is the first-begotten or first-born from the dead, or the first parent and head of the resurrection, the only one who raised himself by his own power, and who will by the same power raise up his people from their graves to everlasting honour; for he has begotten them again to a lively hope by his resurrection from the dead. [3.] He is the prince of the kings of the earth; from him they have their authority; by him their power is limited and their wrath restrained; by him their counsels are over-ruled, and to him they are accountable. This is good news to the church, and it is good evidence of the Godhead of Christ, who is King of kings and Lord of lords. [4.] He is the great friend of his church and people, one who has done great things for them, and this out of pure disinterested affection. He has loved them, and, in pursuance of that everlasting love, he has, *First, Washed them from their sins in his own blood.* Sins leave a stain upon the soul, a stain of guilt and of pollution. Nothing can fetch out this stain but the blood of Christ; and, rather than it should not be washed out, Christ was willing to shed his own blood, to purchase pardon and purity for them. *Secondly,* He has *made them kings and priests to God and his Father.* Having justified and sanctified them, he makes them kings to his Father; that is, in his Father's account, with his approbation, and for his glory. As kings, they govern their own spirits, conquer Satan, have power and prevalency with God in prayer, and shall judge the world. He hath made them priests, given them access to God, enabled them to enter into the holiest and to offer spiritual and acceptable sacrifices, and has given them an unction suitable to this character; and for these high honours and favours they are bound to ascribe to him dominion and glory for ever. [5.] He will be the Judge of the world: *Behold, he cometh, and every eye shall see him, v.* 7. This book, the Revelation, begins and ends with a prediction of the second coming of the Lord Jesus Christ. We should set ourselves to meditate frequently upon the second coming of Christ, and keep it in the eye of our faith and expectation. John speaks as if he saw that day: *"Behold, he cometh,* as sure as if you beheld him with your eyes. *He cometh with clouds,* which are his chariot and pavilion. He will come publicly: *Every eye shall see him,* the eye of his people, the eye of his enemies, every eye, yours and mine." He shall come, to the terror of those who have pierced him and have not repented and of all who have wounded and crucified him afresh by their apostasy from him, and to the astonishment of the pagan world. For he comes to take vengeance on those who know not God, as well as on those that obey not the gospel of Christ. [6.] This account of Christ is ratified and confirmed by himself, *v.* 8. Here our Lord Jesus justly challenges the same honour and power that is ascribed to the Father, *v.* 4. He is the beginning and the end; all things are from him and for him; he is the Almighty; he is the same eternal and unchangeable one. And surely whoever presumes to blot out one character of this name of Christ deserves to have his name blotted out of the book of life. Those that honour him he will honour; but those who despise him shall be lightly esteemed.

Verses 9–20

We have now come to that glorious vision which the apostle had of the Lord Jesus Christ, when he came to deliver this revelation to him, where observe,

I. The account given of the person who was favoured with this vision. He describes himself, 1. By his present state and condition. He was *the brother and companion of these churches in tribulation, and in the kingdom and patience of Christ.* He was, at their time, as the rest of true Christians were, a persecuted man, banished, and perhaps imprisoned, for his adherence to Christ. He was their *brother,* though an apostle; he seems to value himself upon his relation to the church, rather than his authority in it: Judas Iscariot may be an apostle, but not a brother in the family of God. He was their companion: the children of God should choose communion and society with each other. He was their companion in tribulation: the persecuted servants of God did not suffer alone, the same trials are accomplished in others. He was their companion in patience, not only a sharer with them in suffering circumstances, but in suffering graces: if we have the patience of the saints, we should not grudge to meet with their trials. He was their *brother and companion in the patience of the kingdom of Christ,* a sufferer for Christ's cause, for asserting his kingly power over the church and the world, and for adhering to it against all who would usurp upon it. By this account he gives of his present state, he acknowledges his engagements to sympathize with them, and to endeavour to give them counsel and comfort, and bespeaks their more careful attention to what he had to say to them from Christ their common Lord. 2. By the place where he was when he was favoured with this vision: he was in *the isle Patmos.* He does not say who banished him thither. It becomes Christians to speak sparingly and modestly of their own sufferings. Patmos is said to be an island in the Aegean Sea, One of those called Cyclades, and was about thirty-five miles in compass; but under this confinement it was the apostle's comfort that he did not suffer as an evil-doer, but that it was for the testimony of Jesus, for bearing witness to Christ as the Immanuel, the Saviour. This was a cause worth suffering for; and the Spirit of glory and of God rested upon this persecuted apostle. 3. The day and time in which he had this vision: it was *the Lord's day,* the day which Christ had separated and set apart for himself, as the eucharist is called *the Lord's supper.* Surely this can be no other than the Christian sabbath, the first day of the week, to be observed in remembrance of the resurrection of Christ. Let us who call him *our Lord* honour him on his own day, the day which the Lord hath made and in which we ought to rejoice. 4. The frame that his soul was in at this time: *He was in the Spirit.* He was not only in a rapture when he received the vision, but before he received it; he was in a serious, heavenly, spiritual frame, under the blessed gracious influences of the Spirit of God. God usually prepares the souls of his people for uncommon manifestations of himself, by the quickening sanctifying influences of his good Spirit. Those who would enjoy communion with God on the Lord's day must endeavour to abstract their thoughts and affections from flesh and fleshly things, and be wholly taken up with things of a spiritual nature.

II. The apostle gives an account of what he heard when thus in the Spirit. An alarm was given as with the sound of a trumpet, and then *he heard a voice,* the voice of Christ applying to himself the character before given, *the first and the last,* and commanding the apostle to commit to writing the things that were now to be revealed to him, and to send it immediately *to the seven Asian churches,* whose names are mentioned. Thus our Lord Jesus, the captain of our salvation, gave the apostle notice of his glorious appearance, as with the sound of a trumpet.

III. We have also an account of what he saw. *He turned to see the voice,* whose it was and whence it came; and then a wonderful scene of vision opened itself to him.

1. He saw a representation of the church under the emblem of *seven golden candlesticks,* as it is explained in the last verse of the chapter. The churches are compared to candlesticks, because they hold forth the light of the gospel to advantage. The churches are not candles: Christ only is our light, and his gospel our lamp; but they receive their light from Christ and the gospel, and hold it forth to others. They are golden candlesticks, for they should be precious and pure, comparable to fine gold; not only the ministers, but the members of the churches ought to be such; their light should so shine before men as to engage others to give glory to God.

2. He saw a representation of the Lord Jesus Christ in the midst of the golden candlesticks; for he has promised to be with his churches always to the end of the world, filling them with light, and life, and love, for he is the very animating informing soul of the church. And here we observe,

(1.) The glorious form in which Christ appeared in several particulars. [1.] He was *clothed with a garment down to the foot,* a princely and priestly robe, denoting righteousness and honour. [2.] *He was girt about with a golden girdle,* the breast-plate of the high priest, on which the names of his people are engraven; he was ready girt to do all the work of a Redeemer. [3.] *His head and hairs were white like wool or snow.* He was the Ancient of days; his hoary head was no sign of decay, but was indeed a crown of glory. [4.] *His eyes were as a flame of fire,* piercing and penetrating into the very hearts and reins of men, scattering terrors among his adversaries. [5.] *His feet were like unto fine burning brass,* strong and stedfast, supporting his own interest, subduing his enemies, treading them to powder. [6.] *His voice was as the sound of many waters,* of many rivers falling in together. He can and will make himself heard to those who are afar off as well as to those who are near. His gospel is a profluent and mighty stream, fed by the upper springs of infinite wisdom and knowledge. [7.] *He had in his right hand seven stars,* that is, the ministers of the seven churches, who are under his direction, have all their light and influence from him, and are secured and preserved by him. [8.] *Out of his mouth went a two-edged sword,* his word, which both wounds and heals, strikes at sin on the right hand and on the left, [9.] *His countenance was as the sun shining,* its strength too bright and dazzling for mortal eyes to behold.

(2.) The impression this appearance of Christ made upon the apostle John (*v.* 17): *He fell at the feet of Christ as dead;* he was overpowered with the greatness of the lustre and glory in which Christ appeared, though he had been so familiar with him before. How well is it for us that God speaks to us by men like ourselves, whose terrors shall not make us afraid, for none can see the face of God and live!

(3.) The condescending goodness of the Lord Jesus to his disciple: *He laid his hand upon him, v.* 17. He raised him up; he did not plead against him with his great power, but he put strength into him, he spoke kind words to him. [1.] Words of comfort and encouragement: *Fear not.* He commanded away the slavish fears of his disciple. [2.] Words of instruction, telling him particularly who he was that thus appeared to him. And here he acquaints him, *First,* with his divine na-

ture: *The first and the last. Secondly,* With his former sufferings: *I was dead;* the very same that his disciples saw upon the cross dying for the sins of men. *Thirdly,* With his resurrection and life: "*I live, and am alive for evermore,* have conquered death and opened the grave, and am partaker of an endless life." *Fourthly,* With his office and authority: *I have the keys of hell and of death,* a sovereign dominion in and over the invisible world, opening and none can shut, shutting so that none can open, opening the gates of death when he pleases and the gates of the eternal world, of happiness or misery, as the Judge of all, from whose sentence there lies no appeal. *Fifthly,* With his will and pleasure: *Write the things which thou hast seen, and the things which are, and which shall be hereafter. Sixthly,* With the meaning of the seven stars, that *they are the ministers of the churches;* and of the seven candlesticks, that *they are the seven churches,* to whom Christ would now send by him particular and proper messages.

CHAPTER 2

The apostle John, having in the foregoing chapter written the things which he had seen, now proceeds to write the things that are, according to the command of God (*ch.* 1:19), that is, the present state of the seven churches of Asia, with which he had a particular acquaintance, and for which he had a tender concern. He was directed to write to every one of them according to their present state and circumstances, and to inscribe every letter to the angel of that church, to the minister or rather ministry of that church, called angels because they are the messengers of God to mankind. In this chapter we have, I. The message sent to Ephesus (*v.* 1–7). II. To Smyrna (*v.* 8–11). III. To Pergamos (*v.* 12–17). IV. To Thyatira (*v.* 18, etc.).

Verses 1–7

We have here,

I. The inscription, where observe, 1. To whom the first of these epistles is directed: *To the church of Ephesus,* a famous church planted by the apostle Paul (Acts 19), and afterwards watered and governed by John, who had his residence very much there. We can hardly think that Timothy was the angel, or sole pastor and bishop, of this church at this time, — that he who was of a very excellent spirit, and naturally cared for the good state of the souls of the people, should become so remiss as to deserve the rebukes given to the ministry of this church. Observe, 2. From whom this epistle to Ephesus was sent; and here we have one of those titles that were given to Christ in his appearance to John in the chapter foregoing: *He that holds the seven stars in his right hand, and walks in the midst of the seven golden candlesticks, ch.* 1:13, 16. This title consists of two parts: — (1.) *He that holds the stars in his right hand.* The ministers of Christ are under his special care and protection. It is the honour of God that he knows the number of the stars, calls them by their names, *binds the sweet influences of Pleiades and looses the bands of Orion;* and it is the honour of the Lord Jesus Christ that the ministers of the gospel, who are greater blessings to the church than the stars are to the world, are in his hand. He directs all their motions; he disposes of them into their several orbs; he fills them with light and influence; he supports them, or else they would soon be falling stars; they are instruments in his hand, and all the good they do is done by his hand with them. (2.) *He walks in the midst of the golden candlesticks.* This intimates his relation to his churches, as the other his relation to his ministers. Christ is in an intimate manner present and conversant with his churches; he knows and observes their state; he takes pleasure in them, as a man does to walk in his garden. Though Christ is in heaven, he walks in the midst of his churches on earth, observing what is amiss in them and what it is that they want. This is a great encouragement to those who have the care of the churches, that the Lord Jesus has graven them upon the palms of his hands.

II. The contents of the epistle, in which, as in most of those that follow, we have,

1. The commendation Christ gave this church, ministers and members, which he always brings in by declaring that he knows their works, and therefore both his commendation and reprehension are to be strictly regarded; for he does not in either speak at a venture: he knows what he says. Now the church of Ephesus is commended, (1.) For their diligence in duty: *I know thy works, and thy labour, v.* 2. This may more immediately relate to the ministry of this church, which had been laborious and diligent. Dignity calls for duty. Those that are stars in Christ's hand had need to be always in motion, dispensing light to all about them. *For my name's sake thou*

hast laboured, and hast not fainted, v. 3. Christ keeps an account of every day's work, and every hour's work, his servants do for him, *and their labour shall not be in vain in the Lord.* (2.) For their patience in suffering: *Thy labour and thy patience, v.* 2. It is not enough that we be diligent, but we must be patient, and endure hardness as good soldiers of Christ. Ministers must have and exercise great patience, and no Christian can be without it. There must be bearing patience, to endure the injuries of men and the rebukes of Providence; and there must be waiting patience, that, when they have done the will of God, they may receive the promise: *Thou hast borne, and hast patience, v.* 3. We shall meet with such difficulties in our way and work as require patience to go on and finish well. (3.) For their zeal against what was evil: *Thou canst not bear those that are evil, v.* 2. It consists very well with Christian patience not to dispense with sin, much less allow it; though we must show all meekness to men, yet we must show a just zeal against their sins. This their zeal was the more to be commended because it was according to knowledge, a discreet zeal upon a previous trial made of the pretences, practices, and tenets of evil men: *Thou hast tried those that say they are apostles and are not, and hast found them liars.* True zeal proceeds with discretion; none should be cast off till they be tried. Some had risen up in this church that pretended to be not ordinary ministers, but apostles; and their pretensions had been examined but found to be vain and false. Those that impartially search after truth may come to the knowledge of it.

2. The rebuke given to this church: *Nevertheless, I have somewhat against thee, v.* 4. Those that have much good in them may have something much amiss in them, and our Lord Jesus, as an impartial Master and Judge, takes notice of both; though he first observes what is good, and is most ready to mention this, yet he also observes what is amiss, and will faithfully reprove them for it. The sin that Christ charged this church with was their decay and declension in holy love and zeal: *Thou hast left thy first love;* not left and forsaken the object of it, but lost the fervent degree of it that at first appeared. Observe, (1.) The first affections of men towards Christ, and holiness, and heaven, are usually lively and warm. God remembered the love of Israel's espousals, when she would follow him withersoever he went. (2.) These lively affections will abate and cool if great care be not taken, and diligence used, to preserve them in constant exercise. (3.) Christ is grieved and displeased with his people when he sees them grow remiss and cold towards him, and he will one way or other make them sensible that he does not take it well from them.

3. The advice and counsel given them from Christ: *Remember therefore whence thou hast fallen, and repent,* etc. (1.) Those that have lost their first love *must remember whence they have fallen;* they must compare their present with their former state, and consider how much better it was with them then than now, how much peace, strength, purity, and pleasure they have lost, by leaving their first love, — how much more comfortably they could lie down and sleep at night, — how much more cheerfully they could awake in the morning, — how much better they could bear afflictions, and how much more becomingly they could enjoy the favours of Providence, — how much easier the thoughts of death were to them, and how much stronger their desires and hopes of heaven. (2.) They must repent. They must be inwardly grieved and ashamed for their sinful declension; they must blame themselves, and shame themselves, for it, and humbly confess it in the sight of God, and judge and condemn themselves for it. (3.) They must return and do their first works. They must as it were begin again, go back step by step, till they come to the place where they took the first false step; they must endeavour to revive and recover their first zeal, tenderness, and seriousness, and must pray as earnestly, and watch as diligently, as they did when they first set out in the ways of God.

4. This good advice is enforced and urged, (1.) By a severe threatening, if it should be neglected: *I will come unto thee quickly, and remove thy candlestick out of its place.* If the presence of Christ's grace and Spirit be slighted, we may expect the presence of his displeasure. He will come in a way of judgment, and that suddenly and surprisingly, upon impenitent churches and sinners; he will unchurch them, take away his gospel, his ministers, and his ordinances from them, and what will the churches or the angels of the churches do when the gospel is removed? (2.) By an encouraging men-

tion that is made of what was yet good among them: *This thou hast, that thou hatest the deeds of the Nicolaitans, which I also hate,* v. 6. "Though thou hast declined in thy love to what is good, yet thou retainest thy hatred to what is evil, especially to what is grossly so." The Nicolaitans were a loose sect who sheltered themselves under the name of Christianity. They held hateful doctrines, and they were guilty of hateful deeds, hateful to Christ and to all true Christians; and it is mentioned to the praise of the church of Ephesus that they had a just zeal and abhorrence of those wicked doctrines and practices. An indifference of spirit between truth and error, good and evil, may be called *charity* and *meekness,* but it is not pleasing to Christ. Our Saviour subjoins this kind commendation to his severe threatening, to make the advice more effectual.

III. We have the conclusion of this epistle, in which, as in those that follow, we have,

1. A call to attention: *He that hath an ear, let him hear what the Spirit saith unto the churches.* Observe, (1.) What is written in the scriptures is spoken by the Spirit of God. (2.) What is said to one church concerns all the churches, in every place and age. (3.) We can never employ our faculty of hearing better than in hearkening to the word of God: and we deserve to lose it if we do not employ it to this purpose. Those who will not hear the call of God now will wish at length they had never had a capacity of hearing any thing at all.

2. A promise of great mercy to those who overcome. The Christian life is a warfare against sin, Satan, the world, and the flesh. It is not enough that we engage in this warfare, but we must pursue it to the end, we must never yield to our spiritual enemies, but fight the good fight, till we gain the victory, as all persevering Christians shall do; and the warfare and victory shall have a glorious triumph and reward. That which is here promised to the victors is that they shall *eat of the tree of life which is in the midst of the paradise of God.* They shall have that perfection of holiness, and that confirmation therein, which Adam would have had if he had gone well through the course of his trial: he would then have eaten of the tree of life which was in the midst of paradise, and this would have been the sacrament of confirmation to him in his holy and happy state; so all who persevere in their Christian trial and warfare shall derive from Christ, as the tree of life, perfection and confirmation in holiness and happiness in the paradise of God; not in the earthly paradise, but the heavenly, *ch.* 22:1, 2.

Verses 8–11

We now proceed to the second epistle sent to another of the Asian churches, where, as before, observe,

I. The preface or inscription in both parts. 1. The superscription, telling us to whom it was more expressly and immediately directed: *To the angel of the church in Smyrna,* a place well known at this day by our merchants, a city of great trade and wealth, perhaps the only city of all the seven that is still known by the same name, now however no longer distinguished for its Christian church being overrun by Mahomedism. 2. The subscription, containing another of the glorious titles of our Lord Jesus, *the first and the last, he that was dead and is alive,* taken out of *ch.* 1:17, 18. (1.) Jesus Christ is the *first and the last.* It is but a little scantling of time that is allowed to us in this world, but our Redeemer is the first and the last. He is the first, for by him all things were made, and he was before all things with God and was God himself. he is the last, for all things are made for him, and he will be the Judge of all. This surely is the title of God, from everlasting and to everlasting, and it is the title of one that is an unchangeable Mediator between God and man, *Jesus, the same yesterday, to-day, and for ever.* He was the first, for by him the foundation of the church was laid in the patriarchal state; and he is the last, for by him the top-stone will be brought forth and laid in the end of time. (2.) *He was dead and is alive.* He was dead, and died for our sins; he is alive, for he rose again for our justification, and he ever lives to make intercession for us. He was dead, and by dying purchased salvation for us; he is alive, and by his life applies this salvation to us. And *if, when we were enemies, we were reconciled by his death, much more, being reconciled, we shall be saved by his life.* His death we commemorate every sacrament day; his resurrection and life every sabbath day.

II. The subject-matter of this epistle to Smyrna, where, after the common declaration of Christ's omniscience, and the

perfect cognizance he has of all the works of men and especially of his churches, he takes notice,

1. Of the improvement they had made in their spiritual state. This comes in in a short parentheses; yet it is very emphatic: *But thou art rich* (*v.* 0), poor in temporals, but rich in spirituals — poor in spirit, and yet rich in grace. Their spiritual riches are set off by their outward poverty. Many who are rich in temporals are poor in spirituals. Thus it was with the church of Laodicea. Some who are poor outwardly are inwardly rich, rich in faith and in good works, rich in privileges, rich in bonds and deeds of gift, rich in hope, rich in reversion. Spiritual riches are usually the reward of great diligence; *the diligent hand makes rich.* Where there is spiritual plenty, outward poverty may be better borne; and when God's people are impoverished in temporals, for the sake of Christ and a good conscience, he makes all up to them in spiritual riches, which are much more satisfying and enduring.

2. Of their sufferings: *I know thy tribulation and thy poverty* — the persecution they underwent, even to the spoiling of their goods. Those who will be faithful to Christ must expect to go through many tribulations; but Jesus Christ takes particular notice of all their troubles. In all their afflictions, he is afflicted, and he will recompense tribulation to those who trouble them, but to those that are troubled rest with himself.

3. He knows the wickedness and the falsehood of their enemies: *I know the blasphemy of those that say they are Jews, but are not;* that is, of those who pretend to be the only peculiar covenant-people of God, as the Jews boasted themselves to be, even after God had rejected them; or of those who would be setting up the Jewish rites and ceremonies, which were now not only antiquated, but abrogated; these may say that they only are the church of God in the world, when indeed *they are the synagogue of Satan.* Observe, (1.) As Christ has a church in the world, the spiritual Israel of God, so the devil has his synagogue. Those assemblies which are set up in opposition to the truths of the gospel, and which promote and propagate damnable errors, — those which are set up in opposition to the purity and spirituality of gospel worship, and which promote and propagate the vain inventions of men and rites and ceremonies which never entered into the thoughts of God, — these are all synagogues of Satan: he presides over them, he works in them, his interests are served by them, and he receives a horrid homage and honour from them. (2.) For the synagogues of Satan to give themselves out to be the church or Israel of God is no less than blasphemy. God is greatly dishonoured when his name is made use of to promote and patronize the interests of Satan; and he has a high resentment of this blasphemy, and will take a just revenge on those who persist in it.

4. He foreknows the future trials of his people, and forewarns them of them, and fore-arms them against them. (1.) He forewarns them of future trials: *The devil shall cast some of you into prison, and you shall have tribulation,* v. 10. The people of God must look for a series and succession of troubles in this world, and their troubles usually rise higher. They had been impoverished by their tribulations before; now they must be imprisoned. Observe, It is the devil that stirs up his instruments, wicked men, to persecute the people of God; tyrants and persecutors are the devil's tools, though they gratify their own sinful malignity, and know not that they are actuated by a diabolical malice. (2.) Christ fore-arms them against these approaching troubles, [1.] By his counsel: *Fear none of these things.* This is not only a word of command, but of efficacy, no, only forbidding slavish fear, but subduing it and furnishing the soul with strength and courage. [2.] By showing them how their sufferings would be alleviated and limited. *First,* They should not be universal. It would be some of them, not all, who should be cast into prison, those who were best able to bear it and might expect to be visited and comforted by the rest. *Secondly,* They were not to be perpetual, but for a set time, and a short time: *Ten days.* It should not be everlasting tribulation, *the time should be shortened for the elect's sake. Thirdly,* It should be to try them, not to destroy them, that their faith, and patience, and courage, might be proved and improved, and be found to honour and glory. [3.] By proposing and promising a glorious reward to their fidelity: *Be thou faithful to death, and I will give thee a crown of life.* Observe, *First,* The sureness of the reward: *I will give thee.* He has said it that is able to do it; and he has undertaken that he will do it. They shall have the re-

ward from his own hand, and none of their enemies shall be able to wrest it out of his hand, or to pull it from their heads. *Secondly,* The suitableness of it. 1. *A crown,* to reward their poverty, their fidelity, and their conflict. 2. *A crown of life,* to reward those who are faithful even unto death, who are faithful till they die, and who part with life itself in fidelity to Christ. The life so worn out in his service, or laid down in his cause, shall be rewarded with another and a much better life that shall be eternal.

III. The conclusion of this message, and that, as before,

1. With a call to universal attention, that all men, all the world, should hear what passes between Christ and his churches — how he commends them, how he comforts them, how he reproves their failures, how he rewards their fidelity. It concerns all the inhabitants of the world to observe God's dealings with his own people; all the world may learn instruction and wisdom thereby. 2. With a gracious promise to the conquering Christian: *He that overcometh shall not be hurt of the second death,* v. 11. Observe, (1.) There is not only a first, but a second death, a death after the body is dead. (2.) This second death is unspeakably worse than the first death, both in the dying pangs and agonies of it (which are the agonies of the soul, without any mixture of support) and in the duration; it is *eternal death,* dying the death, to die and to be always dying. This is hurtful indeed, fatally hurtful, to all who fall under it. (3.) From this hurtful, this destructive death, Christ will save all his faithful servants; the second death shall have no power over those who are *partakers of the first resurrection:* the first death shall not hurt them, and the second death shall have no power over them.

Verses 12–17

Here also we are to consider,

I. The inscription of this message. 1. To whom it was sent: *To the angel of the church of Pergamos.* Whether this was a city raised up out of the ruins of old Troy, a Troy *nouveau* (as our London was once called), or some other city of the same name, is neither certain nor material; it was a place where Christ had called and constituted a gospel church, by the preaching of the gospel and the grace of his Spirit making the word effectual. 2. Who it was that sent this message to Pergamos: the same Jesus who here describes himself as one that *hath the sharp sword with two edges* (ch. 1:16), *out of whose mouth went a sharp two-edged sword.* Some have observed that, in the several titles of Christ which are prefixed to the several epistles, there is something suited to the state of those churches; as in that to Ephesus, what could be more proper to awaken and recover a drowsy and declining church than to hear Christ speaking as one that *held the stars in his hand, and walked in the midst of the golden candlesticks?* etc. The church of Pergamos was infested with men of corrupt minds, who did what they could to corrupt both the faith and manners of the church; and Christ, being resolved to fight against them by the sword of his word, takes the title of him that *hath the sharp sword with two edges.* (1.) The word of God is a sword; it is a weapon both offensive and defensive, it is, in the hand of God, able to slay both sin and sinners. (2.) It is a *sharp sword.* No heart is so hard but it is able to cut it; it can divide asunder between the soul and the spirit, that is, between the soul and those sinful habits that by custom have become another soul, or seem to be essential to it. (3.) It is a *sword with two edges;* it turns and cuts every way. There is the *edge* of the law against the transgressors of that dispensation, and the *edge* of the gospel against the despisers of that dispensation; there is an edge to make a wound, and an edge to open a festered wound in order to its healing. There is no escaping the edge of this sword: if you turn aside to the right hand, it has an edge on that side; if on the left hand, you fall upon the edge of the sword on that side; it turns every way.

II. From the inscription we proceed to the contents of the epistle, in which the method is much the same as is observed in the rest. Here,

1. Christ takes notice of the trials and difficulties this church encountered with: *I know thy works, and where thou dwellest,* etc., v. 13. The works of God's servants are best known when the circumstances under which they did those works are duly considered. Now that which added very much lustre to the good works of this church was the circumstance of the place where this church was planted, a place where *Satan's seat* was. As our great Lord takes notice of all the advantages and opportunities we have for duty in the places

where we dwell, so he takes notice of all the temptations and discouragements we meet with from the places where we dwell, and makes gracious allowances for them. This people dwelt where Satan's seat was, where he kept his court. His *circuit* is throughout the world, his *seat* is in some places that are infamous for wickedness, error, and cruelty. Some think that the Roman governor in this city was a most violent enemy to the Christians; and the seat of persecution is Satan's seat.

2. He commends their stedfastness: *Thou holdest fast my name, and hast not denied my faith.* These two expressions are much the same in sense; the former may, however, signify the effect and the latter the cause or means. (1.) *"Thou holdest fast my name;* thou art not ashamed of thy relation to me, but accountest it thine honour that my name is named on thee, that, as the wife bears the name of the husband, so thou art called by my name; this thou holdest fast, as thine honour and privilege." (2.) "That which has made thee thus faithful is the grace of faith: *thou hast not denied* the great doctrines of the gospel, nor departed from the Christian faith, and by that means thou hast been kept faithful." Our faith will have a great influence upon our faithfulness. Men who deny the faith of Christ may boast very much of their sincerity, and faithfulness to God and conscience; but it has been seldom known that those who let go the true faith retained their fidelity; usually on that rock on which men make shipwreck of their faith they make shipwreck of a good conscience too. And here our blessed Lord aggrandizes the fidelity of this church from the circumstance of the times, as well as of the place where they lived: they had been stedfast *even in those days wherein Antipas his faithful martyr was slain among them.* Who this person was, and whether there be any thing mysterious in his name, we have no certain account. He was a faithful disciple of Christ, he suffered martyrdom for it, and sealed his faith and fidelity with his blood in the place where Satan dwelt; and though the rest of the believers there knew this, and saw it, yet they were not discouraged nor drawn away from their stedfastness: this is mentioned as an addition to their honour.

3. He reproves them for their sinful failures (*v.* 14): *But I have a few things against thee, because thou hast there those that hold the doctrine of Balaam,* etc., and *those that hold the doctrine of the Nicolaitans, which thing I hate.* There were some who taught that it was lawful to eat things sacrificed to idols, and that simple fornication was no sin; they, by an impure worship, drew men into impure practices, as Balaam did the Israelites. Observe, (1.) The filthiness of the spirit and the filthiness of the flesh often go together. Corrupt doctrines and a corrupt worship often lead to a corrupt conversation. (2.) It is very lawful to fix the name of the leaders of any heresy upon those who follow them. It is the shortest way of telling whom we mean. (3.) To continue in communion with persons of corrupt principles and practices is displeasing to God, draws a guilt and blemish upon the whole society: they become *partakers of other men's sins.* Though the church, as such, has no power to punish the persons of men, either for heresy or immorality, with corporal penalties, yet it has power to exclude them from its communion; and, if it do not so, Christ, the head and lawgiver of the church, will be displeased with it.

4. He calls them to repentance: *Repent, or else I will come unto thee quickly,* etc., *v.* 16. Observe here, (1.) Repentance is the duty of saints as well as sinners; it is a gospel duty. (2.) It is the duty of churches and communities as well as particular persons; those who sin together should repent together. (3.) It is the duty of Christian societies to repent of other men's sins, as far as they have been accessory to them, though but so much as by connivance. (4.) When God comes to punish the corrupt members of a church, he rebukes that church itself for allowing such to continue in its communion, and some drops of the storm fall upon the whole society. (5.) No sword cuts so deep, nor inflicts so mortal a wound, as the sword of Christ's mouth. Let but the threatenings of the word be set home upon the conscience of a sinner, and he will soon be a terror to himself; let these threatenings be executed, and the sinner is utterly cut off. The word of God will take hold of sinners, sooner or later, either for their conviction or their confusion.

III. We have the conclusion of this epistle, where, after the usual demand of universal attention, there is the promise of great favour to those that overcome. They shall *eat of the hidden manna, and have the new name, and the white stone, which no man knoweth, saving he that receiveth it, v.* 17. 1. The hidden manna, the influences and comforts of the Spirit of Christ in communion with him, coming down from heaven into the soul, from time to time, for its support, to let it taste something how saints and angels live in heaven. This is hidden from the rest of the world — *a stranger intermeddles not with* this joy; and it is laid up in Christ, the ark of the covenant, in the holy of holies. 2. The white stone, with a new name engraven upon it. This white stone is absolution from the guilt of sin, alluding to the ancient custom of giving a white stone to those acquitted on trial and a black stone to those condemned. The new name is the name of adoption: adopted persons took the name of the family into which they were adopted. None can read the evidence of a man's adoption but himself; he cannot always read it, but if he persevere he shall have both the evidence of sonship and the inheritance.

Verses 18–29

The form of each epistle is very much the same; and in this, as the rest, we have to consider the inscription, contents, and conclusion.

I. The inscription, telling us, 1. To whom it is directed: *To the angel of the church of Thyatira,* a city of the proconsular Asia, bordering upon Mysia on the north and Lydia on the south, a town of trade, whence came the woman named *Lydia, a seller of purple,* who, being at Philippi in Macedonia, probably about the business of her calling, *heard Paul preach there,* and *God opened her heart, that she attended to the things that were spoken, and believed, and was baptized,* and entertained Paul and Silas there. Whether it was by her means that the gospel was brought into her own city, Thyatira, is not certain; but that it was there, and successful to the forming of a gospel church, this epistle assures us. 2. By whom it was sent: by *the Son of God,* who is here described as having *eyes like a flame of fire, and feet like as fine brass.* His general title is here, *the Son of God,* that is, the eternal and only-begotten Son of God, which denotes that he has the same nature with the Father, but with a distinct and subordinate manner of subsistence. The description we have here of him is in two characters: — (1.) That his eyes are like a flame of fire, signifying his piercing, penetrating, perfect knowledge, a thorough insight into all persons and all things, one *who searches the hearts and tries the reins of the children of men* (*v.* 23), and will make all the churches to know he does so. (2.) That his feet are like fine brass, that the outgoings of his providence are steady, awful, and all pure and holy. As he judges with perfect wisdom, so he acts with perfect strength and steadiness.

II. The contents or subject-matter of this epistle, which, as the rest, includes,

1. The honourable character and commendation Christ gives of this church, ministry, and people; and this given by one who was no stranger to them, but well acquainted with them and with the principles from which they acted. Now in this church Christ makes honourable mention, (1.) Of their *charity,* either more general, a disposition to do good to all men, or more special, to the household of faith: there is no religion where there is no charity. (2.) Their *service,* their ministration; this respects chiefly the officers of the church, who had laboured in the word and doctrine. (3.) Their *faith,* which was the grace that actuated all the rest, both their charity and their service. (4.) Their *patience;* for those that are most charitable to others, most diligent in their places, and most faithful, must yet expect to meet with that which will exercise their patience. (5.) Their growing fruitfulness: their last works were better than the first. This is an excellent character; when others had *left their first love,* and *lost their first zeal,* these were growing wiser and better. It should be the ambition and earnest desire of all Christians that their last works may be their best works, that they may be better and better every day, and best at last.

2. A faithful reproof for what was amiss. This is not so directly charged upon the church itself as upon some wicked seducers who were among them; the church's fault was that she connived too much at them.

(1.) These wicked seducers were compared to Jezebel, and called by her name. Jezebel was a persecutor of the prophets of the Lord, and a great patroness of idolaters and false prophets. The sin of these seducers was that they attempted to draw the servants of God into fornication, and to offer sacrifices to idols; they called themselves prophets, and so would claim a superior authority and regard to the ministers of the church. Two things aggravated the sin of these seducers, who, being one in their spirit and design, are spoken of as one person: — [1.] They made use of the name of God to oppose the truth of his doctrine and worship; this very much aggravated their sin. [2.] They abused the patience of God to harden themselves in their wickedness. God gave them space for repentance, but they repented not. Observe, *First,* Repentance is necessary to prevent a sinner's ruin. *Secondly,* Repentance requires time, a course of time, and time convenient; it is a great work, and a work of time. *Thirdly,* Where God gives space for repentance, he expects fruits meet for repentance. *Fourthly,* Where the space for repentance is lost, the sinner perishes with a double destruction.

(2.) Now why should the wickedness of this Jezebel be charged upon the church of Thyatira? Because that church suffered her to seduce the people of that city. But how could the church help it? They had not, as a church, civil power to banish or imprison her; but they had ministerial power to censure and to excommunicate her: and it is probable that neglecting to use the power they had made them sharers in her sin.

3. The punishment of this seducer, this Jezebel, *v.* 22, 23, in which is couched a prediction of the fall of Babylon. (1.) *I will cast her into a bed,* into a bed of pain, not of pleasure, into a bed of flames; and those who have sinned with her shall suffer with her; but this may yet be prevented by their repentance. (2.) *I will kill her children with death;* that is, the second death, which does the work effectually, and leaves no hope of future life, no resurrection for those that are killed by the second death, but only to shame and everlasting contempt.

4. The design of Christ in the destruction of these wicked seducers, and this was the instruction of others, especially of his churches: *All the churches shall know that I am he that searcheth the reins and the hearts; and I will give to every one of you according to your works.* God is known by the *judgments that he executes;* and, by this revenge taken upon seducers, he would make known, (1.) His infallible knowledge of the hearts of men, of their principles, designs, frame, and temper, their formality, their indifference, their secret inclinations to symbolize with idolaters. (2.) His impartial justice, in *giving every one according to his work,* that the name of Christians should be no protection, their churches should be no sanctuaries for sin and sinners.

5. The encouragement given to those who keep themselves pure and undefiled: *But to you I say, and unto the rest,* etc., *v.* 24. Observe, (1.) What these seducers called their doctrines — *depths,* profound mysteries, amusing the people, and endeavouring to persuade them that they had a deeper insight into religion than their own ministers had attained to. (2.) What Christ called them — *depths of Satan,* Satanical delusions and devices, diabolical mysteries; for there is a *mystery of iniquity,* as well and *the great mystery of godliness.* It is a dangerous thing to despise the mystery of God, and it is as dangerous to receive the mysteries of Satan. (3.) How tender Christ is of his faithful servants: *"I will lay upon you no other burden; but that which you have already hold fast till I come, v.* 24, 25. I will not overburden your faith with any new mysteries, nor your consciences with any new laws. I only require your attention to what you have received. *Hold that fast till I come,* and I desire no more." Christ is coming to put an end to all the temptations of his people; and, if they hold fast faith and a good conscience till he come, all the difficulty and danger will be over.

III. We now come to the conclusion of this message, *v.* 26–29. Here we have, 1. The promise of an ample reward to the persevering victorious believer, in two parts: — (1.) Very great power and dominion over the rest of the world: *Power over the nations,* which may refer either to the time when the empire should turn Christian, and the world be under the government of the Christian emperor, as in Constantine's time; or to the other world, when believers shall sit down with Christ on his throne of judgment, and join with him in trying, and condemning, and consigning over to punishment the enemies of Christ and the church. *The upright shall have dominion in the morning.* (2.) Knowledge and wisdom, suitable to such power and dominion: *I will give him the morning-star.* Christ is the morning-star. He brings day with him into the soul, the light of grace and of glory; and he will give his people that perfection of light and wisdom which is requisite to the state of dignity and dominion that they shall have in the morning of the resurrection. 2. This epistle ends with the usual demand of attention: *He that hath an ear let him hear what the Spirit saith unto the churches.* In the foregoing epistles, this demand of attention comes before the concluding promise; but in this, and all that follow, it comes after, and tells us that we should all attend to the promises as well as to the precepts that Christ delivers to the churches.

CHAPTER 3

Here we have three more of the epistles of Christ to the churches: I. To Sardis (*v.* 1–6). II. To Philadelphia (*v.* 7–13). III. To Laodicea (*v.* 14 to the end).

Verses 1–6

Here is, I. The preface, showing, 1. To whom this letter is directed: *To the angel of the church of Sardis,* an ancient city of Lydia, on the banks of the mountain Tmolus, said to have been the chief city of Asia the Less, and the first city in that part of the world that was converted by the preaching of John; and, some say, the first that revolted from Christianity, and one of the first that was laid in its ruins, in which it still lies, without any church or ministry. 2. By whom this message was sent — the Lord Jesus, who here assumes the character of him *that hath the seven spirits of God, and the seven stars,* taken out of *ch.* 1:4, where *the seven spirits are said to be before the throne.* (1.) He hath the seven spirits, that is, the Holy Spirit with his various powers, graces, and operations; for he is personally one, though efficaciously various, and may be said here to be seven, which is the number of the churches, and of the angels of the churches, to show that to every minister, and to every church, there is a dispensation and measure of the Spirit given for them to profit withal — a stock of spiritual influence for that minister and church to improve, both for enlargement and continuance, which measure of the Spirit is not ordinarily withdrawn from them, till they forfeit it by misimprovement. Churches have their spiritual stock and fund, as well as particular believers; and, this epistle being sent to a languishing ministry and church, they are very fitly put in mind that Christ has the seven spirits, the Spirit without measure and in perfection, to whom they may apply themselves for the reviving of his work among them. (2.) He hath the seven stars, the angels of the churches; they are disposed of by him, and accountable to him, which should make them faithful and zealous. He has ministers to employ, and spiritual influences to communicate to his ministers for the good of his church. The Holy Spirit usually works by the ministry, and the ministry will be of no efficacy without the Spirit; the same divine hand holds them both.

II. The body of this epistle. There is this observable in it, that whereas in the other epistles Christ begins with commending what is good in the churches, and then proceeds to tell them what is amiss, in this (and in the epistle to Laodicea) he begins,

1. With a reproof, and a very severe one: *I know thy works, that thou hast a name that thou livest, and art dead.* Hypocrisy, and a lamentable decay in religion, are the sins charged upon this church, by one who knew her well, and all her works. (1.) This church had gained a great reputation; it had a name, and a very honourable one, for a flourishing church, a name for vital lively religion, for purity of doctrine, unity among themselves, uniformity in worship, decency, and order. We read not of any unhappy divisions among themselves. Every thing appeared well, as to what falls under the observation of men. (2.) This church was not really what it was reputed to be. They had a name to live, but they were dead; there was a form of godliness, but not the power, *a name to live,* but not a principle of life. If there was not a total privation of life, yet there was a great deadness in their souls and in their services, a great deadness in the spirits of their ministers, and a great deadness in their ministrations, in their praying, in their preaching, in their converse, and a great deadness in the people in hearing, in prayer, and in conversation; what little life was yet left among them was, in a manner, expiring, ready to die.

2. Our Lord proceeds to give this degenerate church the best advice: *Be watchful, and strengthen the things,* etc., *v.* 2. (1.) He advises them to be upon their watch. The cause of their sinful deadness and declension was that they had let down their watch. Whenever we are off our watch, we lose ground, and therefore must return to our watchfulness against sin, and Satan, and whatever is destructive to the life and power of godliness. (2.) To strengthen the things that remain, and that are ready to die. Some understand this of persons; there were some few who had retained their integrity, but they were in danger of declining with the rest. It is a difficult thing to keep up to the life and *power of godliness* ourselves, when we see a universal deadness and declension prevailing round about us. Or it may be understood of practices, as it follows: *I have not found thy works perfect before God,* not filled up; there is something wanting in them; there is the shell, but not the kernel; there is the carcase, but not the soul — the shadow, but not the substance. The inward thing is wanting, thy works are hollow and empty; prayers are not filled up with holy desires, alms-deeds not filled up with true charity, sabbaths not filled up with suitable devotion of soul to God; there are not inward affections suitable to outward acts and expressions. Now when the spirit is wanting the form cannot long subsist. (3.) To recollect themselves, and *remember how they have received and heard* (*v.* 3); not only to remember what they had received and heard, what messages they had received from God, what tokens of his mercy and favour towards them, what sermons they had heard, but how they had received and heard, what impressions the mercies of God had made upon their souls at first, what affections they felt working under their word and ordinances, the love of their espousals, the kindness of their youth, how welcome the gospel and the grace of God were to them when they first received them. *Where is the blessedness they then spoke of?* (4.) To hold fast what they had received, that they might not lose all, *and repent* sincerely that they had lost so much of the life of religion, and had run the risk of losing all.

3. Christ enforces his counsel with a dreadful threatening in case it should be despised: *I will come unto thee as a thief, and thou shalt not know the hour, v.* 3. Observe, (1.) When Christ leaves a people as to his gracious presence, he comes to them in judgment; and his judicial presence will be very dreadful to those who have sinned away his gracious presence. (2.) His judicial approach to a dead declining people will be surprising; their deadness will keep them in security, and, as it procures an angry visit from Christ to them, it will prevent their discerning it and preparing for it. (3.) Such a visit from Christ will be to their loss; he will come as a thief, to strip them of their remaining enjoyments and mercies, not by fraud, but in justice and righteousness, taking the forfeiture they have made of all to him.

4. Our blessed Lord does not leave this sinful people without some comfort and encouragement: *In the midst of judgment he remembers mercy* (*v.* 4), and here (1.) He makes honourable mention of the faithful remnant in Sardis, though but small: *Thou hast a few names in Sardis which have not defiled their garments;* they had not given into the prevailing corruptions and pollution of the day and place in which they lived. God takes notice of the smallest number of those who abide with him; and the fewer they are the more precious in his sight. (2.) He makes a very gracious promise to them: *They shall walk with me in white, for they are worthy* — in the *stola,* the white robes of justification, and adoption, and comfort, or in the white robes of honour and glory in the other world. They shall walk with Christ in the pleasant walks of the heavenly paradise; and what delightful converse will there be between Christ and them when they thus walk together! This is an honour proper and suitable to their integrity, which their fidelity has prepared them for, and which it is no way unbecoming Christ to confer upon them, though it is not a legal but a gospel worthiness that is ascribed to them, not merit but meetness. Those who walk with Christ in the clean garments of real practical holiness here, and keep themselves unspotted from the world, shall walk with Christ in the white robes of honour and glory in the other world: this is a suitable reward.

III. We now come to the conclusion of this epistle, in which, as before, we have,

1. A great reward promised to the conquering Christian (*v.* 5), and it is very much the same with what has been already mentioned: *He that overcometh shall be clothed in white raiment.* The purity of grace shall be rewarded with the perfect purity of glory. Holiness, when perfected, shall be its own reward; glory is the perfection of grace, differing not in kind, but in degree. Now to this is added another promise very suitable to the case: *I will not blot his name out of the book of life, but will confess his name before my Father, and before his angels.* Observe, (1.) Christ has his book of life, a register and roll of all who shall inherit eternal life. [1.] The book of eternal election. [2.] The book of remembrance of all those who have lived to God, and have kept up the life and power of godliness in evil times. (2.) Christ will not blot the names of his chosen and faithful ones out of this book of life; men may be enrolled in the registers of the church, as baptized, as making a profession, as having a name to live, and that name may come to be blotted out of the roll, when it appears that it was but a name, a name to live, without spiritual life; such often lose the very name before they die, they are left of God to blot out their own names by their gross and open wickedness. But the names of those that overcome shall never be blotted out. (3.) Christ will produce this book of life, and confess the names of the faithful who stand there, before God, and all the angels; he will do this as their Judge, when the books shall be opened; he will do this as their captain and head, leading them with him triumphantly to heaven, presenting them to the Father: *Behold me, and the children that thou hast given me.* How great will this honour and reward be!

2. The demand of universal attention finishes the message. Every word from God deserves attention from men; that which may seem more particularly directed to one body of men has something in it instructive to all.

Verses 7–13

We have now come to the sixth letter, sent to one of the Asian churches, where observe,

I. The inscription, showing,

1. For whom it was more immediately designed: *The angel of the church of Philadelphia;* this also was a city in Asia Minor, seated upon the borders of Mysia and Lydia, and had its name from that brotherly love for which it was eminent. We can hardly suppose that this name was given to it after it received the Christian religion, and that it was so called from that Christian affection that all believers have, and should have, one for another, as the children of one Father and the brethren of Christ; but rather that it was its ancient name, on account of the love and kindness which the citizens had and showed to each other as a civil fraternity. This was an excellent spirit, and, when sanctified by the grace of the gospel, would render them an excellent church, as indeed they were, for here is no one fault found with this church, and yet, doubtless, there were faults in it of common infirmity; but love covers such faults.

2. By whom this letter was signed; even by the same Jesus who is alone the universal head of all the churches; and here observe by what title he chooses to represent himself to this church: *He that is holy, he that is true, he that hath the key of David,* etc. You have his personal character: *He that is holy* and *he that is true,* holy in his nature, and therefore he cannot but be true to his word, for he hath spoken in his holiness; and you have also his political character: *He hath the key of David, he openeth, and no man shutteth; he hath the key of the house of David,* the key of government and authority in and over the church. Observe, (1.) The acts of his government. [1.] He opens. He opens a door of opportunity to his churches; he opens a door of utterance to his ministers; he opens a door of entrance, opens the heart; he opens a door of admission into the visible church, laying down the terms of communion; and he opens the door of admission into the church triumphant, according to the terms of salvation fixed by him. [2.] He shuts the door. When he pleases, he shuts the door of opportunity and the door of utterance, and leaves obstinate sinners shut up in the hardness of their hearts; he shuts the door of church-fellowship against unbelievers and profane persons; and he shuts the door of heaven against the foolish virgins who have slept away their day of grace, and against the workers of iniquity, how vain and confident soever they may be. (2.) The way and manner in which he performs these acts, and that is absolute sovereignty, independent upon the will of men, and irresistible by the power of men: *He openeth, and no man shutteth; he shutteth, and no man openeth;* he works to will and to do, and, when he works, none can hinder. These were proper characters for him, when speaking to a church that had endeavoured to be conformed to Christ in holiness and truth, and that had enjoyed a wide door of liberty and opportunity under his care and government.

II. The subject-matter of this epistle, where,

1. Christ puts them in mind of what he had done for them: *I have set before thee an open door, and no man can shut it, v.* 8. I have set it open, and kept it open, though there be

many adversaries. Learn here, (1.) Christ is to be acknowledged as the author of all the liberty and opportunity his churches enjoy. (2.) He takes notice and keeps account, how long he has preserved their spiritual liberties and privileges for them. (3.) Wicked men envy the people of God their door of liberty, and would be glad to shut it against them. (4.) If we do not provoke Christ to shut this door against us, men cannot do it.

2. This church is commended: *Thou hast a little strength, and hast kept my word, and hast not denied my name, v. 8.* In this there seems to be couched a gentle reproof: "*Thou hast a little strength,* a little grace, which, though it be not proportionate to the wide door of opportunity which I have opened to thee, yet is true grace, and has kept thee faithful." True grace, though weak, has the divine approbation; but, though Christ accepts a little strength, yet believers should not rest satisfied in a little, but should strive to grow in grace, to be *strong in faith, giving glory to God.* True grace, though weak, will do more than the greatest gifts or highest degrees of common grace, for it will enable the Christian to keep the word of Christ, and not to deny his name. Obedience, fidelity, and a free confession of the name of Christ, are the fruits of true grace, and are pleasing to Christ as such.

3. Here is a promise of the great favour God would bestow on this church, *v.* 9, 10. This favour consists in two things: —

(1.) Christ would make this church's enemies subject to her. [1.] Those enemies are described to be such as *said they were Jews,* but lied in saying so — pretended to be the only and peculiar people of God, but were really *the synagogue of Satan.* Assemblies that *worship God in spirit and in truth* are the Israel of God; assemblies that either worship false gods, or the true God in a false manner, are the synagogues of Satan: though they may profess to be the only people of God, their profession is a lie. [2.] Their subjection to the church is described: *They shall worship at thy feet;* not pay a religious and divine honour to the church itself, nor to the ministry of it, but shall be convinced that they have been in the wrong, that this church is in the right and is beloved of Christ, and they shall desire to be taken into communion with her and that they may worship the same God after the same manner. How shall this great change be wrought? By the power of God upon the hearts of his enemies, and by signal discoveries of his peculiar favour to his church: *They shall know that I have loved thee.* Observe, *First,* The greatest honour and happiness any church can enjoy consist in the peculiar love and favour of Christ. *Secondly,* Christ can discover this his favour to his people in such a manner that their very enemies shall see it, and be forced to acknowledge it. *Thirdly,* This will, by the grace of Christ, soften the hearts of their enemies, and make them desirous to be admitted into communion with them.

(2.) Another instance of favour that Christ promises to this church is persevering grace in the most trying times (*v.* 10), and this as the reward of their past fidelity. *To him that hath shall be given.* Here observe, [1.] The gospel of Christ is the word of his patience. It is the fruit of the patience of God to a sinful world; it sets before men the exemplary patience of Christ in all his sufferings for men; it calls those that receive it to the exercise of patience in conformity to Christ. [2.] This gospel should be carefully kept by all that enjoy it; they must keep up to the faith, and practice, and worship prescribed in the gospel. [3.] After a day of patience we must expect an hour of temptation; a day of gospel peace and liberty is a day of God's patience, and it is seldom so well improved as it should be and therefore it is often followed by an hour of trial and temptation. [4.] Sometimes the trial is more general and universal; it comes upon all the world, and, when it is so general, it is usually the shorter. [5.] Those who keep the gospel in a time of peace shall be kept by Christ in an hour of temptation. By keeping the gospel they are prepared for the trial; and the same divine grace that has made them fruitful in times of peace will make them faithful in times of persecution.

4. Christ calls the church to that duty which he before promised he would enable her to do, and that is, to persevere, *to hold fast that which she had.* (1.) The duty itself: "*Hold fast that which thou hast,* that faith, that truth, that strength of grace, that zeal, that love to the brethren; thou hast been possessed of this excellent treasure, hold it fast." (2.) The motives, taken from the speedy appearance of Christ: "*Behold, I come quickly.* See, I am just a coming to relieve them under the trial, to reward their fidelity, and to punish those who

fall away; they shall lose that crown which they once seemed to have a right to, which they hoped for, and pleased themselves with the thoughts of. The persevering Christian shall win the prize from backsliding professors, who once stood fair for it."

III. The conclusion of this epistle, *v.* 12, 13. Here,

1. After his usual manner, our Saviour promises a glorious reward to the victorious believer, in two things: — (1.) He shall be a monumental *pillar in the temple of God;* not a pillar to support the temple (heaven needs no such props), but a monument of the free and powerful grace of God, a monument that shall never be defaced nor removed, as many stately pillars erected in honour to the Roman emperors and generals have been. (2.) On this monumental pillar there shall be an honourable inscription, as in those cases is usual. [1.] *The name of God,* in whose cause he engaged, whom he served, and for whom he suffered in this warfare; *and the name of the city of God,* the church of God, *the new Jerusalem, which came down from heaven.* On this pillar shall be recorded all the services the believer did to the church of God, how he asserted her rights, enlarged her borders, maintained her purity and honour; this will be a greater name than *Asiaticus,* or *Africanus;* a soldier under God in the wars of the church. And then another part of the inscription is, [2.] The *new name* of Christ, the Mediator, the Redeemer, the captain of our salvation; by this it will appear under whose banner this conquering believer had enlisted, under whose conduct he acted, by whose example he was encouraged, and under whose influence he fought the good fight, and came off victorious.

2. The epistle is closed up with the demand of attention: *He that hath an ear, let him hear what the Spirit saith unto the churches,* how Christ loves and values his faithful people, how he commends, and how he will crown their fidelity.

Verses 14–22

We now come to the last and worst of all the seven Asian churches, the reverse of the church of Philadelphia; for, as there was nothing reproved in that, here is nothing commended in this, and yet this was one of *the seven golden candlesticks,* for a corrupt church may still be a church. Here we have, as before,

I. The inscription, to whom, and from whom. 1. To whom: *To the angel of the church of Laodicea.* This was a once famous city near the river Lycus, had a wall of vast compass, and three marble theatres, and, like Rome, was built on seven hills. It seems, the apostle Paul was very instrumental in planting the gospel in this city, from which he wrote a letter, as he mentions in *the epistle to the Colossians,* the last chapter, in which he sends salutations to them, Laodicea not being above twenty miles distant from Colosse. In this city was held a council in the fourth century, but it has been long since demolished, and lies in its ruins to this day, an awful monument of *the wrath of the Lamb.* 2. From whom this message was sent. Here our Lord Jesus styles himself *the Amen, the faithful and true witness, the beginning of the creation of God.* (1.) *The Amen,* one that is steady and unchangeable in all his purposes and promises, which are all yea, and all amen. (2.) *The faithful and true witness,* whose testimony of God to men ought to be received and fully believed, and whose testimony of men to God will be fully believed and regarded, and will be a swift but true witness against all indifferent lukewarm professors. (3.) *The beginning of the creation of God,* either of the first creation, and so he is the beginning, that is, the first cause, the Creator, and the Governor of it; or of the second creation, the church; and so he is the head of that body, the first-born from the dead, as it is in *ch.* 1:5, whence these titles are taken. Christ, having raised up himself by his own divine power, as the head of a new world, raises up dead souls to be a living temple and church to himself.

II. The subject-matter, in which observe,

1. The heavy charge drawn up against this church, ministers and people, by one who knew them better than they knew themselves: *Thou art neither cold nor hot,* but worse than either; *I would thou wert cold or hot, v.* 15. Lukewarmness or indifference in religion is the worst temper in the world. If religion is a real thing, it is the most excellent thing, and therefore we should be in good earnest in it; if it is not a real thing, it is the vilest imposture, and we should be earnest against it. If religion is worth any thing, it is worth every thing; an indifference here is inexcusable: *Why halt you be-*

tween two opinions? If God be God, follow him; if Baal (be God), *follow him.* Here is no room for neutrality. An open enemy shall have a fairer quarter than a perfidious neuter; and there is more hope of a heathen than of such. Christ expects that men should declare themselves in earnest either for him or against him.

2. A severe punishment threatened: *I will spue thee out of my mouth.* As lukewarm water turns the stomach, and provokes to a vomit, lukewarm professors turn the heart of Christ against them. He is sick of them, and cannot long bear them. They may call their lukewarmness *charity, meekness, moderation,* and *a largeness of soul;* it is nauseous to Christ, and makes those so that allow themselves in it. They shall be rejected, and finally rejected; for far be it from the holy Jesus to return to that which has been thus rejected.

3. We have one cause of this indifference and inconsistency in religion assigned, and that is self-conceitedness or self-delusion. They thought they were very well already, and therefore they were very indifferent whether they grew better or no: *Because thou sayest, I am rich, and increased with goods,* etc., *v.* 17. Here observe, What a difference there was between the thoughts they had of themselves and the thoughts that Christ had of them. (1.) The high thoughts they had of themselves: *Thou sayest, I am rich, and increased with goods, and have need of nothing,* rich, and growing richer, and increased to such a degree as to be above all want or possibility of wanting. Perhaps they were well provided for as to their bodies, and this made them overlook the necessities of their souls. Or they thought themselves well furnished in their souls: they had learning, and they took it for religion; they had gifts, and they took them for grace; they had wit, and they took it for true wisdom; they had ordinances, and they took up with them instead of the God of ordinances. How careful should we be not to put the cheat upon our own souls! Doubtless there are many in hell that once thought themselves to be in the way to heaven. Let us daily beg of God that we may not be left to flatter and deceive ourselves in the concerns of our souls. (2.) The mean thoughts that Christ had of them; and he was not mistaken. He knew, though they knew not, that they were *wretched, and miserable, and poor, and blind, and naked.* Their state was wretched in itself, and such as called for pity and compassion from others: though they were proud of themselves, they were pitied by all who knew their case. For, [1.] They were poor, really poor, when they said and thought they were rich; they had no provision for their souls to live upon; their souls were starving in the midst of their abundance; they were vastly in debt to the justice of God, and had nothing to pay off the least part of the debt. [2.] They were *blind;* they could not see their state, nor their way, nor their danger; they could not see into themselves; they could not look before them; they were blind, and yet they thought they saw; the very light that was in them was darkness, and then how great must that darkness be! They could not see Christ, though evidently set forth, and crucified, before their eyes. They could not see God by faith, though always present in them. They could not see death, though it was just before them. They could not look into eternity, though they stood upon the very brink of it continually. [3.] They were naked, without clothing and without house and harbour for their souls. They were without clothing, had neither the garment of justification nor that of sanctification. Their nakedness both of guilt and pollution had no covering. They lay always exposed to sin and shame. Their righteousnesses were but filthy rags; they were rags, and would not cover them, filthy rags, and would defile them. And they were naked, without house or harbour, for they were without God, and he has been the dwelling-place of his people in all ages; in him alone the soul of man can find rest, and safety, and all suitable accommodations. The riches of the body will not enrich the soul; the sight of the body will not enlighten the soul; the most convenient house for the body will not afford rest nor safety to the soul. The soul is a different thing from the body, and must have accommodation suitable to its nature, or else in the midst of bodily prosperity it will be wretched and miserable.

4. We have good counsel given by Christ to this sinful people, and that is that they drop their vain and false opinion they had of themselves, and endeavour to be that really which they would seem to be: *I counsel thee to buy of me,* etc., *v.* 18. Observe, (1.) Our Lord Jesus Christ continues to give good counsel to those who have cast his counsels behind their backs. (2.) The condition of sinners in never des-

perate, while they enjoy the gracious calls and counsels of Christ. (3.) Our blessed Lord, the counsellor, always gives the best advice, and that which is most suitable to the sinner's case; as here, [1.] These people were poor; Christ counsels them to buy of him gold tried in the fire, that they might be rich. He lets them know where they might have true riches and how they might have them. *First*, Where they might have them — from himself; he sends them not to the streams of Pactolus, nor to the mines of Potosi, but invites them to himself, the pearl of price. *Secondly*, And how must they have this true gold from him? They must buy it. This seems to be unsaying all again. How can those that are poor buy gold? Just as they may buy of Christ wine and milk, that is, *without money and without price*, Isa. 55:1. Something indeed must be parted with, but it is nothing of a valuable consideration, it is only to make room for receiving true riches. "Part with sin and self-sufficiency, and come to Christ with a sense of your poverty and emptiness, that you may be filled with his hidden treasure." [2.] These people were naked; Christ tells them where they might have clothing, and such as would cover the shame of their nakedness. This they must receive from Christ; and they must only put off their filthy rags that they might put on the white raiment which he had purchased and provided for them — his own imputed righteousness for justification and the garments of holiness and sanctification. [3.] They were blind; and he *counsels them to buy of him eyesalve, that they might see*, to give up their own wisdom and reason, which are but blindness in the things of God, and resign themselves to his word and Spirit, and their eyes shall be opened to see their way and their end, their duty and their true interest; a new and glorious scene would then open itself to their souls; a new world furnished with the most beautiful and excellent objects, and this light would be marvellous to those who were but just now delivered from the powers of darkness. This is the wise and good counsel Christ gives to careless souls; and, if they follow it, he will judge himself bound in honour to make it effectual.

5. Here is added great and gracious encouragement to this sinful people to take the admonition and advice well that Christ had given them, *v.* 19, 20. He tells them, (1.) It was given them in true and tender affection: "*Whom I love, I rebuke and chasten.* You may think I have given you hard words and severe reproofs; it is all out of love to your souls. I would not have thus openly rebuked and corrected your sinful lukewarmness and vain confidence, if I had not been a lover of your souls; had I hated you, I would have let you alone, to go on in sin till it had been your ruin." Sinners ought to take the rebukes of God's word and rod as tokens of his good-will to their souls, and should accordingly repent in good earnest, and turn to him that smites them; better are the frowns and wounds of a friend than the flattering smiles of an enemy. (2.) If they would comply with his admonitions, he was ready to make them good to their souls: *Behold, I stand at the door and knock*, etc., *v.* 20. Here observe, [1.] Christ is graciously pleased by his word and Spirit to come to the door of the heart of sinners; he draws near to them in a way of mercy, ready to make them a kind visit. [2.] He finds this door shut against him; the heart of man is by nature shut up against Christ by ignorance, unbelief, sinful prejudices. [3.] When he finds the heart shut, he does not immediately withdraw, but he waits to be gracious, even till his head be filled with the dew. [4.] He uses all proper means to awaken sinners, and to cause them to open to him: he calls by his word, he knocks by the impulses of his Spirit upon their conscience. [5.] Those who open to him shall enjoy his presence, to their great comfort and advantage. He will sup with them; he will accept of what is good in them; he will eat his pleasant fruit; and he will bring the best part of the entertainment with him. If what he finds would make but a poor feast, what he brings will make up the deficiency: he will give fresh supplies of graces and comforts, and thereby stir up fresh actings of faith, and love, and delight; and in all this Christ and his repenting people will enjoy pleasant communion with each other. Alas! what do careless obstinate sinners lose by refusing to open the door of the heart to Christ!

III. We now come to the conclusion of this epistle; and here we have as before,

1. The promise made to the overcoming believer. It is here implied, (1.) That though this church seemed to be wholly overrun and overcome with lukewarmness and self-confidence, yet it was possible that by the reproofs and counsels of Christ they might be inspired with fresh zeal and vig-

our, and might come off conquerors in their spiritual warfare. (2.) That, if they did so, all former faults should be forgiven, and they should have a great reward. And what is that reward? *They shall sit down with me on my throne, as I also overcame, and have sat down with my Father on his throne*, *v.* 21. Here it is intimated, [1.] That Christ himself had met with his temptations and conflicts. [2.] That he overcame them all, and was more than a conqueror. [3.] That, as the reward of his conflict and victory, he has sat down with God the Father on his throne, possessed of that glory which he had with the Father from eternity, but which he was pleased very much to conceal on earth, leaving it as it were in the hands of the Father, as a pledge that he would fulfil the work of a Saviour before he reassumed that manifestative glory; and, having done so, then *pignus reposcere — he demands the pledge*, to appear in his divine glory equal to the Father. [4.] That those who are conformed to Christ in his trials and victories shall be conformed to him in his glory; they shall sit down with him on his throne, on his throne of judgment at the end of the world, on his throne of glory to all eternity, shining in his beams by virtue of their union with him and relation to him, as the mystical body of which he is the head.

2. All is closed up with the general demand of attention (*v.* 22), putting all to whom these epistles shall come in mind that what is contained in them is not of private interpretation, not intended for the instruction, reproof, and correction of those particular churches only, but of all the churches of Christ in all ages and parts of the world: and as there will be a resemblance in all succeeding churches to these, both in their graces and sins, so they may expect that God will deal with them as he dealt with these, which are patterns to all ages what faithful, and fruitful churches may expect to receive from God, and what those who are unfaithful may expect to suffer from his hand; yea, that God's dealings with his churches may afford useful instruction to the rest of the world, to put them upon considering, *If judgment begin at the house of God, what shall the end of those be that do not obey the gospel of Christ?* 1 Pt. 4:17. Thus end the messages of Christ to the Asian churches, the epistolary part of this book. We now come to the prophetical part.

CHAPTER 4

In this chapter the prophetical scene opens; and, as the epistolary part opened with a vision of Christ (*ch.* 1), so this part is introduced with a glorious appearance of the great God, whose throne is in heaven, compassed about with the heavenly host. This discovery was made to John, and in this chapter he, I. Records the heavenly sight he saw (*v.* 1–7). And then, II. The heavenly songs he heard (*v.* 8 to the end).

Verses 1–8a

We have here an account of a second vision with which the apostle John was favoured: *After this*, that is, not only "after I had seen the vision of Christ walking in the midst of the golden candlesticks," but "after I had taken his messages from his mouth, and written and sent them to the several churches, according to his command, after this I had another vision." Those who well improve the discoveries they have had of God already are prepared thereby for more, and may expect them. Observe,

I. The preparation made for the apostle's having this vision.

1. *A door was opened in heaven*. Hence we learn, (1.) Whatever is transacted on earth is first designed and settled in heaven; there is the model of all the works of God; all of them are therefore before his eye, and he lets the inhabitants of heaven see as much of them as is fit for them. (2.) We can know nothing of future events but what God is pleased to discover to us; they are within the veil, till God opens the door. But, (3.) So far as God reveals his designs to us we may and ought to receive them, and not pretend to be wise above what is revealed.

2. To prepare John for the vision, a trumpet was sounded, and he was called up into heaven, to have a sight there of the things which were to be hereafter. He was called into the third heavens. (1.) There is a way opened into the holiest of all, into which the sons of God may enter by faith and holy affections now, in their spirits when they die, and in their whole persons at the last day. (2.) We must not intrude into the secret of God's presence, but stay till we are called up to it.

3. To prepare for this vision, *the apostle was in the Spirit*. He was in a rapture, as before (*ch.* 1:10); whether in the body or out of the body we cannot tell; perhaps he himself could not; however all bodily actions and sensations were for a time

suspended, and his spirit was possessed with the spirit of prophecy, and wholly under a divine influence. The more we abstract ourselves from all corporeal things the more fit we are for communion with God; the body is a veil, a cloud, and clog to the mind in its transactions with God. We should as it were forget it when we go in before the Lord in duty, and be willing to drop it, that we may go up to him in heaven. This was the *apparatus* to the vision. Now observe,

II. The vision itself. It begins with the strange sights that the apostle saw, and they were such as these: — 1. He saw *a throne set in heaven*, the seat of honour, and authority, and judgment. Heaven is the throne of God; there he resides in glory, and thence he gives laws to the church and to the whole world, and all earthly thrones are under the jurisdiction of this throne that is set in heaven. 2. He saw a glorious one upon the throne. This throne was not empty; there was one in it who filled it, and that was God, who is here described by those things that are most pleasant and precious in our world: *His countenance was like a jasper and a sardine-stone*; he is not described by any human features, so as to be represented by an image, but only by his transcendent brightness. This jasper is a transparent stone, which yet offers to the eye a variety of the most vivid colours, signifying the glorious perfections of God; the sardine-stone is red, signifying the justice of God, that essential attribute of which he never divests himself in favour of any, but gloriously exerts it in the government of the world, and especially of the church, through our Lord Jesus Christ. This attribute is displayed in pardoning as well as in punishing, in saving as well as in destroying sinners. 3. He saw *a rainbow about the throne, like unto an emerald*, *v.* 3. The rainbow was the seal and token of the covenant of the providence that God made with Noah and his posterity with him, and is a fit emblem of that covenant of promise that God has made with Christ as the head of the church, and all his people in him, which covenant is as the waters of Noah unto God, an everlasting covenant, ordered in all things and sure. This rainbow looked like *the emerald*; the most prevailing colour was a pleasant green, to show the reviving and refreshing nature of the new covenant. 4. He saw *four-and-twenty seats* round about the throne, not empty, but filled with *four-and-twenty elders*, presbyters, representing, very probably, the whole church of God, both in the Old-Testament and in the New-Testament state; not the ministers of the church, but rather the representatives of the people. Their sitting denotes their honour, rest, and satisfaction; their sitting about the throne signifies their relation to God, their nearness to him, the sight and enjoyment they have of him. *They are clothed in white raiment*, the righteousness of the saints, both imputed and inherent; *they had on their heads crowns of gold*, signifying the honour and authority given them of God, and the glory they have with him. All these may in a lower sense be applied to the gospel church on earth, in its worshipping assemblies; and, in the higher sense, to the church triumphant in heaven. 5. He perceived lightnings and voices proceeding out of the throne; that is, the awful declarations that God makes to his church of his sovereign will and pleasure. Thus he gave forth the law on mount Sinai; and the gospel has not less glory and authority than the law, though it be of a more spiritual nature. 6. He saw *seven lamps of fire burning before the throne*, which are explained to be *the seven Spirits of God* (*v.* 5), the various gifts, graces, and operations of the Spirit of God in the churches of Christ; these are all dispensed according to the will and pleasure of him who sits upon the throne. 7. He saw *before the throne a sea of glass, like unto crystal*. As in the temple there was a great vessel of brass filled with water, in which the priests were to wash when they went to minister before the Lord (and this was called a *sea*), so in the gospel church the sea or laver for purification is the blood of the Lord Jesus Christ, who cleanses from all sin, even from sanctuary-sins. In this all those must be washed that are admitted into the gracious presence of God on earth or his glorious presence in heaven. 8. He saw *four animals*, living creatures, between the throne and the circle of elders (as seems most probable), standing between God and the people; these seem to signify the ministers of the gospel, not only because of this their situation nearer to God, and between him and the elders or representatives of the Christian people, and because fewer in number than the people, but as they are here described, (1.) By their many eyes, denoting sagacity, vigilance, and circumspection. (2.) By their lion-like courage, their great labour and diligence (in which they resemble the ox), their prudence and discretion becoming men, and their sublime affections and speculations, by which they mount up *with wings like eagles towards heaven* (*v.* 7), and these wings full of eyes within, to show that in all their meditations and ministrations they are to act with knowledge, and especially should be well acquainted with themselves and the state of their own souls, and see their own concern in the great doctrines and duties of religion, watching over their own souls as well as the souls of the people. (3.) By their continual employment, and that is, praising God, and not ceasing to do so night and day. The elders sit and are ministered unto; these stand and minister: they rest not night nor day. This now leads to the other part of the representation.

Verses 8b–11

We have considered the sights that the apostle saw in heaven: now let us observe the songs that he heard, for there is in heaven not only that to be seen which will highly please a sanctified eye, but there is that to be heard which will greatly delight a sanctified ear. This is true concerning the church of Christ here, which is a heaven upon earth, and it will be eminently so in the church made perfect in the heaven of heavens.

I. He heard the song of the four living creatures, of the ministers of the church, which refers to the prophet Isaiah's vision, *ch.* 6. And here, 1. They adore one God, and one only, *the Lord God Almighty,* unchangeable and everlasting. 2. They adore three holies in this one God, the Holy Father, the Holy Son, and the Holy Spirit; and these are one infinitely holy and eternal Being, who sits upon the throne, *and lives for ever and ever.* In this glory the prophet saw Christ, and spoke of him.

II. He heard the adorations of the *four-and-twenty elders,* that is, of the Christian people represented by them; the ministers led, and the people followed, in the praises of God, *v.* 10, 11. Here observe,

1. The object of their worship, the same with that which the ministers adored: *Him that sat on the throne,* the eternal everliving God. The true church of God has one and the same object of worship. Two different objects of worship, either co-ordinate or sub-ordinate, would confound the worship and divide the worshippers. It is unlawful to join in divine worship with those who either mistake or multiply the object. There is but one God, and he alone, as God, is worshipped by the church on earth and in heaven.

2. The acts of adoration. (1.) They *fell down before him that sat on the throne;* they discovered the most profound humility, reverence, and godly fear. (2.) They *cast their crowns before the throne;* they gave God the glory of the holiness wherewith he had crowned their souls on earth and the honour and happiness with which he crowns them in heaven. They owe all their graces and all their glories to him, and acknowledge that his crown is infinitely more glorious than theirs, and that it is their glory to be glorifying God.

3. The words of adoration: they said, *Thou art worthy, O Lord, to receive glory, and honour, and power, v.* 11. Observe, (1.) They do not say, *We give thee glory, and honour, and power;* for what can any creature pretend to give unto God? But they say, *thou art worthy to receive glory.* (2.) In this they tacitly acknowledge that God is exalted far above all blessing and praise. He was worthy to receive glory, but they were not worthy to praise, nor able to do it according to his infinite excellences.

4. We have the ground and reason of their adoration, which is threefold: — (1.) He is the Creator of all things, the first cause; and none but the Creator of all things should be adored; no made thing can be the object of religious worship. (2.) He is the preserver of all things, and his preservation is a continual creation; they are created still by the sustaining power of God. All beings but God are dependent upon the will and power of God, and no dependent being must be set up as an object of religious worship. It is the part of the best dependent beings to be worshippers, not to be worshipped. (3.) He is the final cause of all things: *For thy pleasure they are and were created.* It was his will and pleasure to create all things; he was not put upon it by the will of another; there is no such thing as a subordinate creator, that acts under and by the will and power of another; and, if there were, he ought not to be worshipped. As God made all things at his pleasure, so he made them for his pleasure, to deal with them as he pleases and to glorify himself by them one way or other. Though he delights not in the death of sinners, but rather that they should turn and live, *yet he hath made all things for himself,* Prov. 16:4. Now if these be true and sufficient grounds for religious worship, as they are proper to God alone, Christ must needs be God, one with the Father and Spirit, and be worshipped as such; for we find the same causality ascribed to him. Col. 1:16, 17, *All things were created by him and for him, and he is before all things, and by him all things consist.*

CHAPTER 5

In the foregoing chapter the prophetical scene was opened, in the sight and hearing of the apostle, and he had a sight of God the Creator and ruler of the world, and the great King of the church. He saw God on the throne of glory and government, surrounded with his holy ones, and receiving their adorations. Now the counsels and decrees of God are set before the apostle, as in a book, which God held in his right hand; and this book is represented, I. As sealed in the hand of God (*v.* 1–9). II. As taken into the hand of Christ the Redeemer, to be unsealed and opened (*v.* 6 to the end).

Verses 1–5

Hitherto the apostle had seen only the great God, the governor of all things, now,

I. He is favoured with a sight of the model and methods of his government, as they are all written down in a book which he holds in his hand; and this we are now to consider as shut up and sealed in the hand of God. Observe, 1. The designs and methods of divine Providence towards the church and the world are stated and fixed; they are resolved upon and agreed to, as that which is written in a book. The great design is laid, every part adjusted, all determined, and every thing passed into decree and made a matter of record. The original and first draught of this book is the book of God's decrees, laid up in his own cabinet, in his eternal mind: but there is a transcript of so much as was necessary to be known in the book of the scriptures in general, in the prophetical part of the scripture especially, and in this prophecy in particular. 2. God holds this book in his right hand, to declare the authority of the book, and his readiness and resolution to execute all the contents thereof, all the counsels and purposes therein recorded. 3. This book in the hand of God is shut up and sealed; it is known to none but himself, till he allows it to be opened. *Known unto God,* and to him alone, *are all his works, from the beginning of the world;* but it is his glory to conceal the matter as he pleases. The times and seasons, and their great events, he hath kept in his own hand and power. 4. It is *sealed with seven seals.* This tells us with what inscrutable secrecy the counsels of God are laid, how impenetrable by the eye and intellect of the creature; and also points us to seven several parts of this book of God's counsels. Each part seems to have its particular seal, and, when opened, discovers its proper events; these seven parts are not unsealed and opened at once, but successively, one scene of Providence introducing another, and explaining it, till the whole mystery of God's counsel and conduct be finished in the world.

II. He heard a proclamation made concerning this sealed book. 1. The crier was *a strong angel;* not that there are any weak ones among the angels in heaven, though there are many among the angels of the churches. This angel seems to come out, not only as a crier, but as a champion, with a challenge to any or all the creatures to try the strength of their wisdom in opening the counsels of God; and, as a champion, he cried with a loud voice, that every creature might hear. 2. The cry or challenge proclaimed was, *"Who is worthy to open the book, and to loose the seals thereof? v.* 2. If there by any creature who thinks himself sufficient either to explain or execute the counsels of God, let him stand forth, and make the attempt." 3. None in heaven or earth could accept the challenge and undertake the task: none *in heaven,* none of the glorious holy angels, though before the throne of God, and the ministers of his providence; they with all their wisdom cannot dive into the decrees of God: none *on earth,* no man, the wisest or the best of men, none of the magicians and soothsayers, none of the prophets of God, any further than he reveals his mind to them: *none under the earth,* none of the fallen angels, none of the spirits of men departed, though they should return to our world, can open this book. Satan himself, with all his subtlety, cannot do it; the creatures cannot open it, nor look on it; they cannot read it. God only can do it.

III. He felt a great concern in himself about this matter: the apostle *wept much;* it was a great disappointment to him. By what he had seen in him who sat upon the throne, he was very desirous to see and know more of his mind and will: this desire, when not presently gratified, filled him with sorrow, and fetched many tears from his eyes. Here observe, 1. Those who have seen most of God in this world are most desirous to see more; and those who have seen his glory desire to know his will. 2. Good men may be too eager and to hasty to look into the mysteries of divine conduct. 3. Such desires, not presently answered, turn to grief and sorrow. *Hope deferred makes the heart sick.*

IV. The apostle was comforted and encouraged to hope this sealed book would yet be opened. Here observe, 1. Who it was that gave John the hint: *One of the elders.* God had revealed it to his church. If angels do not refuse to learn from the church, ministers should not disdain to do it. God can make his people to instruct and inform their teachers when he pleases. 2. Who it was that would do the thing — the Lord Jesus Christ, called *the lion of the tribe of Judah,* according to his human nature, alluding to Jacob's prophecy (Gen. 49:10), and *the root of David* according to his divine nature, though a branch of David according to the flesh. He who is a middle person, God and man, and bears the office of Mediator between God and man, is fit and worthy to open and execute all the counsels of God towards men. And this he does in his mediatorial state and capacity, *as the root of David and the offspring of Judah,* and as the King and head of the Israel of God; and he will do it, to the consolation and joy of all his people.

Verses 6–14

Here, I. The apostle beholds this book taken into the hands of the Lord Jesus Christ, in order to its being unsealed and opened by him. Here Christ is described, 1. By his place and station: *In the midst of the throne, and of the four beasts, and of the elders.* He was on the same throne with the Father; he was nearer to him than either the elders or ministers of the churches. Christ, as man and Mediator, is subordinate to God the Father, but is nearer to him than all the creatures; *for in him all the fulness of the Godhead dwells bodily.* The ministers stand between God and the people. Christ stands as the Mediator between God and both ministers and people. 2. The form in which he appeared. Before he is called *a lion;* here he appears *as a lamb slain.* He is a lion to conquer Satan, a lamb to satisfy the justice of God. He appears with the marks of his sufferings upon him, to show that he interceded in heaven in the virtue of his satisfaction. He appears as a *lamb, having seven horns and seven eyes,* perfect power to execute all the will of God and perfect wisdom to understand it all and to do it in the most effectual manner; *for he hath the seven Spirits of God,* he has received the Holy Spirit without measure, in all perfection of light, and life, and power, by which he is able to teach and rule all parts of the earth. 3. He is described by his act and deed: *He came, and took the book out of the right hand of him that sat on the throne* (*v.* 7), not by violence, nor by fraud, but he prevailed to do it (as *v.* 5), he prevailed by his merit and worthiness, he did it by authority and by the Father's appointment. God very willingly and justly put the book of his eternal counsels into the hand of Christ, and Christ as readily and gladly took it into his hand; for he delights to reveal and to do the will of his Father.

II. The apostle observes the universal joy and thanksgiving that filled heaven and earth upon this transaction. No sooner had Christ received this book out of the Father's hand than he received the applauses and adorations of angels and men, yea, of *every creature.* And, indeed, it is just matter of joy to all the world to see that God does not deal with men in a way of absolute power and strict justice, but in a way of grace and mercy through the Redeemer. He governs the world, not merely as a Creator and Lawgiver, but as our God and Saviour. All the world has reason to rejoice in this. The song of praise that was offered up to the Lamb on this occasion consists of three parts, one part sung by the church, another by the church and the angels, the third by every creature.

1. The church begins the doxology, as being more immediately concerned in it (*v.* 8), the four living creatures, and *the four-and-twenty elders,* the Christian people, under their minister, lead up the chorus. Here observe, (1.) The object of their worship — *the Lamb,* the Lord Jesus Christ; it is the declared will of God that all men *should honour the Son as they honour the Father;* for he has the same nature. (2.) Their

posture: They *fell down before him*, gave him not an inferior sort of worship, but the most profound adoration. (3.) The instruments used in their adorations — *harps and vials;* the harps were the instruments of praise, the vials were full of odours or incense, which signify *the prayers of the saints:* prayer and praise should always go together. (4.) The matter of their song: it was suited to the new state of the church, the gospel-state introduced by the Son of God. In this new song, [1.] They acknowledge the infinite fitness and worthiness of the Lord Jesus for this great work of opening and executing the counsel and purposes of God (*v.* 9): *Thou art worthy to take the book, and to open the seals thereof,* every way sufficient for the work and deserving the honour. [2.] They mention the grounds and reasons of this worthiness; and though they do not exclude the dignity of his person as God, without which he had not been sufficient for it, yet they chiefly insist upon the merit of his sufferings, which he had endured for them; these more sensibly struck their souls with thankfulness and joy. Here, *First,* They mention his suffering: "*Thou wast slain,* slain as a sacrifice, thy blood was shed." *Secondly,* The fruits of his sufferings. 1. Redemption to God; Christ has redeemed his people from the bondage of sin, guilt, and Satan, redeemed them to God, set them at liberty to serve him and to enjoy him. 2. High exaltation: Thou *hast made us to our God kings and priests, and we shall reign on the earth, v.* 10. Every ransomed slave is not immediately preferred to honour; he thinks it a great favour to be restored to liberty. But when the elect of God were made slaves by sin and Satan, in every nation of the world, Christ not only purchased their liberty for them, but the highest honour and preferment, *made them kings and priests* — kings, to rule over their own spirits, and to overcome the world, and the evil one; and he has made them priests, given them access to himself, and liberty to offer up spiritual sacrifices, and *they shall reign on the earth;* they shall with him judge the world at the great day.

2. The doxology, thus begun by the church, is carried on by the angels; they take the second part, in conjunction with the church, *v.* 11. They are said to be *innumerable,* and to be the attendants on the throne of God and guardians to the church; though they did not need a Saviour themselves, yet they rejoice in the redemption and salvation of sinners, and they agree with the church in acknowledging the infinite merits of the Lord Jesus as dying for sinners, that he is *worthy to receive power, and riches, and wisdom, and strength, and honour, and glory, and blessing.* (1.) He is worthy of that office and that authority which require the greatest power and wisdom, the *greatest* fund, all excellency, to discharge them aright; and, (2.) He is worthy of all honour, and glory, and blessing, because he is sufficient for the office and faithful in it.

3. This doxology, thus begun by the church, and carried on by the angels, is resounded and echoed by the whole creation, *v.* 13. Heaven and earth ring with the high praises of the Redeemer. The whole creation fares the better for Christ. *By him all things consist;* and all the creatures, had they sense and language, would adore that great Redeemer who delivers the creature from that bondage under which it groans, through the corruption of men, and the just curse denounced by the great God upon the fall; that part which (by a prosopopoeia) is made for the whole creation is a song of *blessing, and honour, and glory, and power,* (1.) *To him that sits on the throne,* to God as God, or to God the Father, as the first person in the Trinity and the first in the economy of our salvation; and, (2.) *To the Lamb,* as the second person in the Godhead and the Mediator of the new covenant. Not that the worship paid to the Lamb is of another nature, an inferior worship, for the very same honour and glory are in the same words ascribed *to the Lamb and to him that sits on the throne,* their essence being the same; but, their parts in the work of our salvation being distinct they are distinctly adored. We worship and glorify one and the same God for our creation and for our redemption.

We see how the church that began the heavenly anthem, finding heaven and earth join in the concert, closes all with their *Amen,* and end as they began, with a low prostration before the eternal and everlasting God. Thus we have seen this sealed book passing with great solemnity from the hand of the Creator into the hand of the Redeemer.

CHAPTER 6

The book of the divine counsels being thus lodged in the hand of Christ, he loses no time, but immediately enters upon the work of opening the

seals and publishing the contents; but this is done in such a manner as still leaves the predictions very abstruse and difficult to be understood. Hitherto the waters of the sanctuary have been as those in Ezekiel's vision, only to the ankles, or to the knees, or to the loins at least; but here they begin to be a river that cannot be passed over. The visions which John saw, the epistles to the churches, the songs of praise, in the two foregoing chapters, had some things dark and hard to be understood; and yet they were rather milk for babes than meat for strong men; but now we are to launch into the deep, and our business is not so much to fathom it as to let down our net to take a draught. We shall only hint at what seems most obvious. The prophecies of this book are divided into seven seals opened, seven trumpets sounding, and seven vials poured out. It is supposed that the opening of the seven seals discloses those providences that concerned the church in the first three centuries, from the ascension of our Lord and Saviour to the reign of Constantine; this was represented in a book rolled up, and sealed in several places, so that, when one seal was opened, you might read so far of it, and so on, till the whole was unfolded. Yet we are not here told what was written in the book, but what John saw in figures enigmatical and hieroglyphic; and it is not for us to pretend to know "the times and seasons which the Father has put in his own power." Inf this chapter six of the seven seals are opened, and the visions attending them are related; the first seal in *v.* 1, 2, the second seal in *v.* 3, 4, the third seal in *v.* 5, 6, the fourth seal in *v.* 7, 8, the fifth seal in *v.* 9–11, the sixth seal in *v.* 12, 13, etc.

Verses 1–2

Here, 1. Christ, the Lamb, opens the first seal; he now enters upon the great work of opening and accomplishing the purposes of God towards the church and the world. 2. One of the ministers of the church calls upon the apostle, with a voice like thunder, to come near, and observe what then appeared. 3. We have the vision itself, *v.* 2. (1.) The Lord Jesus appears riding on *a white horse.* White horses are generally refused in war, because they make the rider a mark for the enemy; but our Lord Redeemer was sure of the victory and a glorious triumph, and he rides on the white horse of a pure but despised gospel, with great swiftness through the world. (2.) *He had a bow* in his hand. The convictions impressed by the word of God are sharp arrows, they reach at a distance; and, though the ministers of the word draw the bow at a venture, God can and will direct it to the joints of the harness. This bow, in the hand of Christ, abides in strength, and, like that of Jonathan, *never returns empty.* (3.) *A crown was given him,* importing that all who receive the gospel must receive Christ as a king, and must be his loyal and obedient subjects; he will be glorified in the success of the gospel. When Christ was going to war, one would think a helmet had been more proper than a crown; but a crown is given him as the earnest and emblem of victory. (4.) *He went forth conquering, and to conquer.* As long as the church continues militant Christ will be conquering; when he has conquered his enemies in one age he meets with new ones in another age; men go on opposing, and Christ goes on conquering, and his former victories are pledges of future victories. He conquers his enemies in his people; their sins are their enemies and his enemies; when Christ comes with power into their soul he begins to conquer these enemies, and he goes on conquering, in the progressive work of sanctification, till he has gained us a complete victory. And he conquers his enemies in the world, wicked men, some by bringing them to his foot, others by making them his footstool. Observe, From this seal opened, [1.] The successful progress of the gospel of Christ in the world is a glorious sight, worth beholding, the most pleasant and welcome sight that a good man can see in this world. [2.] Whatever convulsions and revolutions happen in the states and kingdoms of the world, the kingdom of Christ shall be established and enlarged in spite of all opposition. [3.] A morning of opportunity usually goes before a night of calamity; the gospel is preached before the plagues are poured forth. [4.] Christ's work is not all done at once. We are ready to think, when the gospel goes forth, it should carry all the world before it, but it often meets with opposition, and moves slowly; however, Christ will do his own work effectually, in his own time and way.

Verses 3–8

The next three seals give us a sad prospect of great and desolating judgments with which God punishes those who either refuse or abuse the everlasting gospel. Though some understand them of the persecutions that befel the church of Christ, and others of the destruction of the Jews, they rather seem more generally to represent God's terrible judgments, by which he avenges the quarrel of his covenant upon those who make light of it.

I. Upon opening the second seal, to which John was called to attend, *another horse* appears, of a different colour from

the former, *a red horse, v.* 4. This signifies the desolating judgment of war; he that sat upon this red horse had *power to take peace from the earth, and that* the inhabitants of *the earth should kill one another.* Who this was that sat upon the red horse, whether Christ himself, as Lord of hosts, or the instruments that he raised up to conduct the war, is not clear; but this is certain, 1. That those who will not submit to the bow of the gospel must expect to be cut in sunder by the sword of divine justice. 2. That Jesus Christ rules and commands, not only in the kingdom of grace, but of providence. And, 3. That the sword of war is a dreadful judgment; it takes away peace from the earth, one of the greatest blessings, and it puts men upon killing one another. Men, who should love one another and help one another, are, in a state of war, set upon killing one another.

II. Upon opening the third seal, which John was directed to observe, another horse appears, different from the former, *a black horse,* signifying famine, that terrible judgment; *and he that sat on the horse had a pair of balances in his hand* (*v.* 5), signifying that men must now eat their bread by weight, as was threatened (Lev. 26:26), *They shall deliver your bread to you by weight.* That which follows in *v.* 6, of the voice that cried, *A measure of wheat for a penny, and three measures of barley for a penny, and see thou hurt not the oil and the wine,* has made some expositors think this was not a vision of famine, but of plenty; but if we consider the quantity of their measure, and the value of their penny, at the time of this prophecy, the objection will be removed; their measure was but a single quart, and their penny was our sevenpence-halfpenny, and that is a large sum to give for a quart of wheat. However, it seems this famine, as all others, fell most severely upon the poor; whereas the oil and the wine, which were dainties of the rich, were not hurt; but if bread, the staff of life, be broken, dainties will not supply the place of it. Here observe, 1. When a people loathe their spiritual food, God may justly deprive them of their daily bread. 2. One judgment seldom comes alone; the judgment of war naturally draws after it that of famine; and those who will not humble themselves under one judgment must expect another and yet greater, for when God contends he will prevail. The famine of bread is a terrible judgment; but the famine of the word is more so, though careless sinners are not sensible of it.

III. Upon opening the fourth seal, which John is commanded to observe, there appears another horse, of a pale colour. Here observe, 1. The name of the rider — *Death,* the king of terrors; the pestilence, which is death in its empire, death reigning over a place or nation, death on horseback, marching about, and making fresh conquests every hour. 2. The attendants or followers of this king of terrors — *hell,* a state of eternal misery to all those who die in their sins; and, in times of such a general destruction, multitudes go down unprepared into the valley of destruction. It is an awful thought, and enough to make the whole world to tremble, that eternal damnation immediately follows upon the death of an impenitent sinner. Observe, (1.) There is a natural as well as judicial connection between one judgment and another: war is a wasting calamity, and draws scarcity and famine after it; and famine, not allowing men proper sustenance, and forcing them to take that which is unwholesome, often draws the pestilence after it. (2.) God's quiver is full of arrows; he is never at a loss for ways and means to punish a wicked people. (3.) In the book of God's counsels he has prepared judgments for scorners as well as mercy for returning sinners. (4.) In the book of the scriptures God has published threatenings against the wicked as well as promises to the righteous; and it is our duty to observe and believe the threatenings as well as the promises.

IV. After the opening of these seals of approaching judgments, and the distinct account of them, we have this general observation, that God *gave power to them over the fourth part of the earth, to kill with the sword, and with hunger, and with death, and with the beasts of the earth, v.* 8. He gave them power, that is, those instruments of his anger, or those judgments themselves; he who holds the winds in his hand has all public calamities at his command, and they can only go when he sends them and no further than he permits. To the three great judgments of war, famine, and pestilence, is here added *the beasts of the earth,* another of God's sore judgments, mentioned Eze. 14:21, and mentioned here the last, because, when a nation is depopulated by the sword, famine, and pestilence, the small remnant that continue in a waste and howling wilderness encourage the wild beasts to make head against them, and they become easy prey. Others, by *the beasts of the field,* understand brutish, cruel, savage men, who, having divested themselves of all humanity, delight to be the instruments of the destruction of others.

Verses 9–17

In the remaining part of this chapter we have the opening of the fifth and the sixth seals.

I. The fifth seal. Here is no mention made of any one who called the apostle to make his observation, probably because the decorum of the vision was to be observed, and each of the four living creatures had discharged its duty of a monitor before, or because the events here opened lay out of the sight, and beyond the time, of the present ministers of the church; or because it does not contain a new prophecy of any future events, but rather opens a spring of support and consolation to those who had been and still were under great tribulation for the sake of Christ and the gospel. Here observe,

1. The sight this apostle saw at the opening of the fifth seal; it was a very affecting sight (*v.* 9): *I saw under the altar the souls of those that were slain for the word of God, and for the testimony which they held.* He saw the souls of the martyrs. Here observe, (1.) Where he saw them — *under the altar;* at the foot of the altar of incense, in the most holy place; he saw them in heaven, at the foot of Christ. Hence note, [1.] Persecutors can only kill the body, and after that there is no more that they can do; their souls live. [2.] God has provided a good place in the better world for those who are faithful to death and are not allowed a place any longer on earth. [3.] Holy martyrs are very near to Christ in heaven, they have the highest place there. [4.] It is not their own death, but the sacrifice of Christ, that gives them a reception into heaven and a reward there; they do not wash their robes in their own blood, but in the blood of the Lamb. (2.) What was the cause in which they suffered — *the word of God and the testimony which they held,* for believing the word of God, and attesting or confessing the truth of it; this profession of their faith they held fast without wavering, even though they died for it. A noble cause, the best that any man can lay down his life for — faith in God's word and a confession of that faith.

2. The cry he heard; it was a loud cry, and contained a humble expostulation about the long delay of avenging justice against their enemies: *How long, O Lord, holy and true, dost thou not judge and avenge our blood on those that dwell on the earth? v.* 10. Observe, (1.) Even *the spirits of just men made perfect* retain a proper resentment of the wrong they have sustained by their cruel enemies; and though they die in charity, praying, as Christ did, that God would forgive them, yet they are desirous that, for the honour of God, and Christ, and the gospel, and for the terror and conviction of others, God will take a just revenge upon the sin of persecution, even while he pardons and saves the persecutors. (2.) They commit their cause to him to whom vengeance belongeth, and leave it in his hand; they are not for avenging themselves, but leave all to God. (3.) There will be joy in heaven at the destruction of the implacable enemies of Christ and Christianity, as well as at the conversion of other sinners. When Babylon falls, it will be said, *Rejoice over her, O thou heaven, and you holy apostles and prophets, for God hath avenged you on her, ch.* 18:20.

3. He observed the kind return that was made to this cry (*v.* 11), both what was given to them and what was said to them. (1.) What was given to them — *white robes,* the robes of victory and of honour; their present happiness was an abundant recompence of their past sufferings. (2.) What was said to them — that they should be satisfied, and easy in themselves, for it would not be long ere the number of their fellow-sufferers *would be fulfilled.* This is a language rather suited to the imperfect state of the saints in this world than to the perfection of their state in heaven; *there* is no impatience, no uneasiness, no need of admonition; but in this world there is great need of patience. Observe, [1.] There is a number of Christians, known to God, who are appointed as *sheep for the slaughter,* set apart to be God's witnesses. [2.] As the measure of the sin of persecutors is filling up, so is the number of the persecuted martyred servants of Christ. [3.] When this number is fulfilled, God will take a just and glorious revenge upon their cruel persecutors; he will recompense tribulation to those who trouble them, and to those that are troubled full and uninterrupted rest.

II. We have here the sixth seal opened, *v.* 12. Some refer

this to the great revolutions in the empire at Constantine's time, the downfall of paganism; others, with great probability, to the destruction of Jerusalem, as an emblem of the general judgment, and destruction of the wicked, at the end of the world; and, indeed, the awful characters of this event are so much the same with those signs mentioned by our Saviour as foreboding the destruction of Jerusalem, as hardly to leave any room for doubting but that the same thing is meant in both places, though some think that event was past already. See Mt. 24:29. 30. Here observe,

1. The tremendous events that were hastening; and here are several occurrences that contribute to make that day and dispensation very dreadful: — (1.) *There was a great earthquake.* This may be taken in a political sense; the very foundations of the Jewish church and state would be terribly shaken, though they seemed to be as stable as the earth itself. (2.) *The sun became black as sackcloth of hair,* either naturally, by a total eclipse, or politically, by the fall of the chief rulers and governors of the land. (3.) *The moon* should *become as blood;* the inferior officers, or their military men, should be all wallowing in their own blood. (4.) *The stars of heaven shall fall to the earth* (*v.* 13), and that *as a fig-tree casteth her untimely figs, when she is shaken of a mighty wind.* The stars may signify all the men of note and influence among them, though in lower spheres of activity; there should be a general desolation. (5.) *The heaven* should *depart as a scroll when it is rolled together.* This may signify that their ecclesiastical state should perish and be laid aside for ever. (6.) *Every mountain and island shall be moved out of its place.* The destruction of the Jewish nation should affect and affright all the nations round about, those who were highest in honour and those who seemed to be best secured; it would be a judgment that should astonish all the world. This leads to,

2. The dread and terror that would seize upon all sorts of men in that great and awful day, *v.* 15. No authority, nor grandeur, nor riches, nor valour, nor strength, would be able to support men at that time; yea, the very poor slaves, who, one would think, had nothing to fear, because they had nothing to lose, would be all in amazement at that day. Here observe, (1.) The degree of their terror and astonishment: it should prevail so far as to make them, like distracted desperate men, call *to the mountains to fall upon them, and to the hills to cover them;* they would be glad to be no more seen; yea, to have no longer any being. (2.) The cause of their terror, namely, the angry countenance of *him that sits on the throne, and the wrath of the Lamb.* Observe, [1.] That which is matter of displeasure to Christ is so to God; they are so entirely one that what pleases or displeases the one pleases or displeases the other. [2.] Though God be invisible, he can make the inhabitants of this world sensible of his awful frowns. [3.] Though Christ be a lamb, yet he can be angry, even to wrath, and *the wrath of the Lamb* is exceedingly dreadful; for if the Redeemer, that appeases the wrath of God, himself be our wrathful enemy, where shall we have a friend to plead for us? Those perish without remedy who perish by the wrath of the Redeemer. [4.] As men have their day of opportunity, and their seasons of grace, so God has his day of righteous wrath; and, when that day shall come, the most stout-hearted sinners will not be able to stand before him: all these terrors actually fell upon the sinners in Judea and Jerusalem in the day of their destruction, and they will all, in the utmost degree, fall upon impenitent sinners, at the general judgment of the last day.

CHAPTER 7

The things contained in this chapter came in after the opening of the six seals, which foretold great calamities in the world; and before the sound of the seven trumpets, which gave notice of great corruptions arising in the church: between these comes in this comfortable chapter, which secures the graces and comforts of the people of God in times of common calamity. We have, I. An account of the restraint laid upon the winds (*v.* 1–3). II. The sealing of the servants of God (*v.* 4–8). III. The songs of angels and saints on this occasion (*v.* 9–12). IV. A description of the honour and happiness of those who had faithfully served Christ, and suffered for him (*v.* 13, etc.).

Verses 1–12

Here we have, I. An account of the restraint laid upon the winds. By these winds we suppose are meant those errors and corruptions in religion which would occasion a great deal of trouble and mischief to the church of God. Sometimes the Holy Spirit is compared to the wind: here the spirits of error are compared to *the four winds,* contrary one to another, but doing much hurt to the church, the garden and vineyard of

God, breaking the branches and blasting the fruits of his plantation. The devil is called *the prince of the power of the air;* he, by a great wind, overthrew the house of Job's eldest son. Errors are as wind, by which those who are unstable are shaken, and carried *to and fro,* Eph. 4:14. Observe, 1. These are called *the winds of the earth,* because they blow only in these lower regions near the earth; heaven is always clear and free from them. 2. They are restrained by the ministry of angels, *standing on the four corners of the earth,* intimating that the spirit of error cannot go forth till God permits it, and that the angels minister to the good of the church by restraining its enemies. 3. Their restraint was only for a season, and that was *till the servants of God were sealed in their foreheads.* God has a particular care and concern for his own servants in times of temptation and corruption, and he has a way to secure them from the common infection; he first establishes them, and then he tries them; he has the timing of their trials in his own hand.

II. An account of the sealing of the servants of God, where observe, 1. To whom this work was committed — to an angel, *another angel.* While some of the angels were employed to restrain Satan and his agents, another angel was employed to mark out and distinguish the faithful servants of God. 2. How they were distinguished — the seal of God was set upon their foreheads, a seal known to him, and as plain as if it appeared in their foreheads; by this mark they were set apart for mercy and safety in the worst of times. 3. The number of those that were sealed, where observe, (1.) A particular account of those that were sealed of the twelve tribes of Israel — twelve thousand out of every tribe, the whole sum amounting to *a hundred and forty-four thousand.* In this list the tribe of Dan is omitted, perhaps because they were greatly addicted to idolatry; and the order of the tribes is altered, perhaps according as they had been more or less faithful to God. Some take these to be a select number of the Jews who were reserved for mercy at the destruction of Jerusalem; others think that time was past, and therefore it is to be more generally applied to God's chosen remnant in the world; but, if the destruction of Jerusalem was not yet over (and I think it is hard to prove that it was), it seems more proper to understand this of the remnant of that people which God had reserved according to the election of grace, only here we have a definite number for an indefinite. (2.) A general account of those who were saved out of other nations (*v.* 9): *A great multitude, which no man could number, of all nations, and kindreds, and people, and tongues.* Though these are not said to be sealed, yet they were selected by God out of all nations, and brought into his church, and there stood before the throne. Observe, [1.] God will have a greater harvest of souls among the Gentiles than he had among the Jews. *More are the children of the desolate than of the married woman.* [2.] The Lord knows who are his, and he will keep them safe in times of dangerous temptation. [3.] Though the church of God is but a little flock, in comparison of the wicked world, yet it is no contemptible society, but really large and to be still more enlarged.

III. We have the songs of saints and angels on this occasion, *v.* 9–12, where observe,

1. The praises offered up by the saints (and, as it seems to me, by the Gentile believers) for the care of God in reserving so large a remnant of the Jews, and saving them from infidelity and destruction. The Jewish church prayed for the Gentiles before their conversion, and the Gentile churches have reason to bless God for his distinguishing mercy to so many of the Jews, when the rest were cut off. Here observe, (1.) The posture of these praising saints: they *stood before the throne, and before the Lamb,* before the Creator and the Mediator. In acts of religious worship we come nigh to God, and are to conceive ourselves as in his special presence; and we must come to God by Christ. The throne of God would be inaccessible to sinners were it not for a Mediator. (2.) Their habit: they were *clothed with white robes, and had palms in their hands;* they were invested with the robes of justification, holiness, and victory, and had palms in their hands, as conquerors used to appear in their triumphs: such a glorious appearance will the faithful servants of God make at last, when they have *fought the good fight of faith and finished their course.* (3.) Their employment: they *cried with a loud voice, saying, Salvation to our God who sitteth upon the throne, and to the Lamb.* This may be understood either as a *hosannah,* wishing well to the interest of God and Christ in the church and in the world, or as a *hallelujah,* giving to

God and the Lamb the praise of the great salvation; both the Father and the Son are joined together in these praises; the Father contrived this salvation, the Son purchased it, and those who enjoy it must and will bless the Lord and the Lamb, and they will do it publicly, and with becoming fervour.

2. Here is the song of the angels (*v.* 11, 12), where observe, (1.) Their station — *before the throne of God,* attending on him, and about the saints, ready to serve them. (2.) Their posture, which is very humble, and expressive of the greatest reverence: *They fell before the throne on their faces, and worshipped God.* Behold the most excellent of all the creatures, who never sinned, who are before him continually, not only covering their faces, but falling down on their faces before the Lord! What humility then, and what profound reverence, become us vile frail creatures, when we come into the presence of God! We should fall down before him; there should be both a reverential frame of spirit and a humble behaviour in all our addresses to God (3.) Their praises. They consented to the praises of the saints, said their *Amen* thereto; there is in heaven a perfect harmony between the angels and saints; and then they added more of their own, *saying, Blessing, and glory, and wisdom, and thanksgiving, and honour, and power, and might, be unto our God for ever and ever. Amen.* Here, [1.] They acknowledge the glorious attributes of God — his wisdom, his power, and his might. [2.] They declare that for these his divine perfections he ought to be blessed, and praised, and glorified, to all eternity; and they confirm it by their *Amen.* We see what is the work of heaven, and we ought to begin it now, to get our hearts tuned for it, to be much in it, and to long for that world where our praises, as well as happiness, will be perfected.

Verses 13–17

Here we have a description of the honour and happiness of those who have faithfully served the Lord Jesus Christ, and suffered for him. Observe,

I. A question asked by one of the elders, not for his own information, but for John's instruction: ministers may learn from the people, especially from aged and experienced Christians; the lowest saint in heaven knows more than the greatest apostle in the world. Now the question has two parts: — 1. *What are these that are arrayed in white robes?* 2. *Whence came they?* It seems to be spoken by way of admiration, as Cant. 3:6, *Who is this that cometh out of the wilderness!* Faithful Christians deserve our notice and respect; we should *mark the upright.*

II. The answer returned by the apostle, in which he tacitly acknowledges his own ignorance, and sues to this elder for information: *Thou knowest.* Those who would gain knowledge must not be ashamed to own their ignorance, nor to desire instruction from any that are able to give it.

III. The account given to the apostle concerning that noble army of martyrs who stood *before the throne of God in white robes,* with palms of victory in their hands: and notice is taken here of, 1. The low and desolate state they had formerly been in; they had been in great tribulation, persecuted by men, tempted by Satan, sometimes troubled in their own spirits; they had suffered the spoiling of their goods, the imprisonment of their persons, yea, the loss of life itself. The way to heaven lies through many tribulations; but tribulation, how great soever, shall not *separate us from the love of God.* Tribulation, when gone through well, will make heaven more welcome and more glorious. 2. The means by which they had been prepared for the great honour and happiness they now enjoyed: they had *washed their robes, and made them white in the blood of the Lamb, v.* 14. It is not the blood of the martyrs themselves, but the blood of the Lamb, that can wash away sin, and make the soul pure and clean in the sight of God. Other blood stains; this is the only blood that makes the robes of the saints white and clean. 3. The blessedness to which they are now advanced, being thus prepared for it. (1.) They are happy in their station, for *they are before the throne of God night and day;* and he *dwells among them;* they are in that presence where there is fulness of joy. (2.) They are happy in their employment, for they serve God continually, and that without weakness, drowsiness, or weariness. Heaven is a state of service, though not of suffering; it is a state of rest, but not of sloth; it is a praising delightful rest. (3.) They are happy in their freedom from all the inconveniences of this present life. [1.] From all want and sense of want: *They hunger and thirst no more;* all their wants are supplied, and all the uneasiness caused thereby is removed. [2.] From all sickness and pain: they shall never be scorched by *the heat of the sun any more.* (4.) They are happy in the love and guidance of the Lord Jesus: *He shall feed them, he shall lead them to living fountains of waters,* he shall put them into the possession of every thing that is pleasant and refreshing to their souls, and therefore *they shall hunger and thirst no more.* (5.) They are happy in being delivered from all sorrow or occasion of it: *God shall wipe away all tears from their eyes.* They have formerly had their sorrows, and shed many tears, both upon the account of sin and affliction; but God himself, with his own gentle and gracious hand, will wipe those tears away, and they shall return no more for ever; and they would not have been without those tears, when God comes to wipe them away. In this he deals with them as a tender father who finds his beloved child in tears, he comforts him, he wipes his eyes, and turns his sorrow into rejoicing. This should moderate the Christian's sorrow in his present state, and support him under all the troubles of it; for *those that sow in tears shall reap in joy; and those that now go forth weeping, bearing precious seed, shall doubtless come again rejoicing, bringing their sheaves with them.*

CHAPTER 8

We have already seen what occurred upon opening six of the seals; we now come to the opening of the seventh, which introduced the sounding of the seven trumpets; and a direful scene now opens. Most expositors agree that the seven seals represent the interval between the apostle's time and the reign of Constantine, but that the seven trumpets are designed to represent the rise of antichrist, some time after the empire became Christian. In this chapter we have, I. The preface, or prelude, to the sounding of the trumpets (*v.* 1–6). II. The sounding of four of the trumpets (*v.* 7, etc.).

Verses 1–6

In these verses we have the prelude to the sounding of the trumpets in several parts.

I. The opening of the last seal. This was to introduce a new set of prophetical iconisms and events; there is a continued chain of providence, one part linked to another (where one ends another begins), and, though they may differ in nature and in time, they all make up one wise, well-connected, uniform design in the hand of God.

II. A profound *silence in heaven for the space of half an hour,* which may be understood either, 1. Of the silence of peace, that for this time no complaints were sent up to the ear of the Lord God of sabaoth; all was quiet and well in the church, and therefore all silent in heaven, for whenever the church on earth cries, through oppression, that cry comes up to heaven and resounds there; or, 2. A silence of expectation; great things were upon the wheel of providence, and the church of God, both in heaven and earth, stood silent, as became them, to see what God was doing, according to that of Zec. 2:13, *Be silent, O all flesh, before the Lord, for he has risen up out of his holy habitation.* And elsewhere, *Be still, and know that I am God.*

III. The trumpets were delivered to the angels who were to sound them. Still the angels are employed as the wise and willing instruments of divine Providence, and they are furnished with all their materials and instructions from God our Saviour. As the angels of the churches are to sound the trumpet of the gospel, the angels of heaven are to sound the trumpet of Providence, and every one has his part given him.

IV. To prepare for this, another angel must first offer incense, *v.* 3. It is very probable that this other angel is the Lord Jesus, the high priest of the church, who is here described in his sacerdotal office, having a golden censer and much incense, a fulness of merit in his own glorious person, and this incense he was to offer up, *with the prayers of all the saints, upon the golden altar* of his divine nature. Observe, 1. All the saints are a praying people; none of the children of God are born dumb, a Spirit of grace is always a Spirit of adoption and supplication, teaching us to cry, *Abba, Father.* Ps. 32:6, *For this shall every one that is godly pray unto thee.* 2. Times of danger should be praying times, and so should times of great expectation; both our fears and our hopes should put us upon prayer, and, where the interest of the church of God is deeply concerned, the hearts of the people of God in prayer should be greatly enlarged. 3. The prayers of the saints themselves stand in need of the incense and intercession of Christ to make them acceptable and effectual, and there is provision made by Christ for that purpose; he has his incense, his censer, and his altar; he is all himself to his people. 4. The prayers of the saints come up before God in a cloud of incense; no prayer, thus recommended, was ever denied audience or acceptance. 5. These prayers that were thus accepted in heaven produced great changes upon earth in return to them; the same angel that in his censer offered up the prayers of the saints in the same censer *took of the fire of the altar, and cast it into the earth,* and this presently caused strange commotions, *voices, and thunderings, and lightnings, and an earthquake;* these were the answers God gave to the prayers of the saints, and tokens of his anger against the world and that he would do great things to avenge himself and his people of their enemies; and now, all things being thus prepared, the angels discharge their duty.

Verses 7–13

Observe, I. *The first angel sounded* the first trumpet, and the events which followed were very dismal: *There followed hail and fire mingled with blood,* etc., *v.* 7. There was a terrible storm; but whether it is to be understood of a storm of heresies, a mixture of monstrous errors falling on the church (for in that age Arianism prevailed), or a storm or tempest of war falling on the civil state, expositors are not agreed. Mr. Mede takes it to be meant of the Gothic inundation that broke in upon the empire in the year 395, the same year that Theodosius died, when the northern nations, under Alaricus, king of the Goths, broke in upon the western parts of the empire. However, here we observe, 1. It was a very terrible storm — fire, and hail, and blood: a strange mixture! 2. The limitation of it: it fell on *the third part of the trees,* and on the third part of *the grass,* and blasted and burnt it up; that is, say some, upon *the third part of the clergy* and *the third part of the laity;* or, as others who take it to fall upon the civil state, upon *the third part of the great men,* and upon *the third part of the common people,* either upon the Roman empire itself, which was a third part of the then known world, or upon a third part of that empire. The most severe calamities have their bounds and limits set them by the great God.

II. *The second angel sounded,* and the alarm was followed, as in the first, with terrible events: *A great mountain burning with fire was cast into the sea; and the third part of the sea became blood, v.* 8. By this mountain some understand the leader or leaders of the heretics; others, as Mr. Mede, the city of Rome, which was five times sacked by the Goths and Vandals, within the compass of 137 years; first by Alaricus, in the year 410, with great slaughter and cruelty. In these calamities, a third part of the people (called here the sea or collection of waters) were destroyed: here was still a limitation to the third part, for *in the midst of judgment God remembers mercy.* This storm fell heavy upon the maritime and merchandizing cities and countries of the Roman empire.

III. *The third angel sounded,* and the alarm had the like effects as before: *There fell a great star from heaven,* etc., *v.* 10. Some take this to be a political star, some eminent governor, and they apply it to Augustulus, who was forced to resign the empire to Odoacer, in the year 480. Others take it to be an ecclesiastical star, some eminent person in the church, compared to a *burning lamp,* and they fix it upon Pelagius, who proved about this time a falling star, and greatly corrupted the churches of Christ. Observe, 1. Where this star fell: *Upon a third part of the rivers, and upon the fountains of waters.* 2. What effect it had upon them; it turned those springs and streams into wormwood, made them very bitter, that men were poisoned by them; either the laws, which are springs of civil liberty, and property, and safety, were poisoned by arbitrary power, or the doctrines of the gospel, the springs of spiritual life, refreshment, and vigour to the souls of men, were so corrupted and embittered by a mixture of dangerous errors that the souls of men found their ruin where they sought for their refreshment.

IV. *The fourth angel sounded,* and the alarm was followed with further calamities. Observe, 1. The nature of this calamity; it was darkness; it fell therefore upon the great luminaries of the heaven, that give light to the world — *the sun, and the moon, and the stars,* either the guides and governors of the church, or of the state, who are placed in higher orbs than the people, and are to dispense light and benign influences to them. 2. The limitation: it was confined to a third part of these luminaries; there was some light both of the sun by day, and of the moon and stars by night, but it was only a third part of what they had before. Without determining what is matter of controversy in these points among learned men, we rather choose to make these plain and practical remarks: — (1.) Where the gospel comes to a people, and is but coldly received, and has not its proper effects upon their hearts and lives, it is usually followed with dreadful judgments. (2.) God gives warning to men of his judgments before he sends them; he sounds an alarm by the written word, by ministers, by men's own consciences, and by the signs of the times; so that, if a people be surprised, it is their own fault. (3.) The anger of God against a people makes dreadful work among them; it embitters all their comforts, and makes even life itself bitter and burdensome. (4.) God does not in this world stir up all his wrath, but sets bounds to the most terrible judgments. (5.) Corruptions of doctrine and worship in the church are themselves great judgments, and the usual causes and tokens of other judgments coming on a people.

V. Before the other three trumpets are sounded here is solemn warning given to the world how terrible the calamities would be that should follow them, and how miserable those times and places would be on which they fell, *v.* 13. 1. The messenger was *an angel flying in the midst of heaven,* as in haste, and coming on an awful errand. 2. The message was a denunciation of further and greater woe and misery than the world had hitherto endured. Here are three woes, to show how much the calamities coming should exceed those that had been already, or to hint how every one of the three succeeding trumpets should introduce its particular and distinct calamity. If less judgments do not take effect, but the church and the world grow worse under them, they must expect greater. *God will be known by the judgments that he executes;* and he expects, when he comes to punish the world, the inhabitants thereof should tremble before him.

CHAPTER 9

In this chapter we have an account of the sounding of the fifth and sixth trumpets, the appearances that attended them, and the events that were to follow; the fifth trumpet (*v.* 1–12), the sixth (*v.* 13, etc.).

Verses 1–12

Upon the sounding of this trumpet, the things to be observed are, 1. *A star falling from heaven to the earth.* Some think this star represents some eminent bishop in the Christian church, some angel of the church; for, in the same way of speaking by which pastors are called stars, the church is called heaven; but who this is expositors do not agree. Some understand it of Boniface the third bishop of Rome, who assumed the title of universal bishop, by the favour of the emperor Phocas, who, being a usurper and tyrant in the state, allowed Boniface to be so in the church, as the reward of his flattery. 2. To this fallen star *was given the key of the bottomless pit.* Having now ceased to be a minister of Christ, he becomes the antichrist, the minister of the devil; and by the permission of Christ, who had taken from him the keys of the church, he becomes the devil's turnkey, to let loose the powers of hell against the churches of Christ. 3. Upon the opening of the bottomless pit *there arose a great smoke,* which darkened the sun and the air. The devils are the powers of darkness; hell is the place of darkness. The devil carries on his designs by blinding the eyes of men, by extinguishing light and knowledge, and promoting ignorance and error. He first deceives men, and then destroys them; wretched souls follow him in the dark, or they durst not follow him. 4. Out of this dark smoke there came a swarm of locusts, one of the plagues of Egypt, the devil's emissaries headed by the antichrist, all the rout and rabble of antichristian orders, to promote superstition, idolatry, error, and cruelty; and these had, by the just permission of God, power to hurt those who had not the mark of God in their foreheads. 5. The hurt they were to do them was not a bodily, but a spiritual hurt. They should not in a military way destroy all by fire and sword; the trees and the grass should be untouched, and those they hurt should not be slain; it should not be a persecution, but a secret poison and infection in their souls, which should rob them of their purity, and afterwards of their peace. Heresy is a poison in the soul, working slowly and secretly, but will be bitterness in the end. 6. They had no power so much as to hurt those who had the seal of God in their foreheads. God's electing, effectual, distinguishing grace will preserve his people from total and final apostasy. 7. The power given to these factors for hell is limited in point of time: *five months,* a certain season, and but a short season, though how short we cannot tell. Gospel-seasons have their limits, and times of seduction are limited too. 8. Though it would be short, it would be very sharp, insomuch that those who

were made to feel the malignity of this poison in their consciences would be weary of their lives, *v.* 6. *A wounded spirit who can bear?* 9. These locusts were of a monstrous size and shape, *v.* 7, 8, etc. They were equipped for their work like horses prepared to battle. (1.) They pretended to great authority, and seemed to be assured of victory: *They had crowns like gold on their heads;* it was not a true, but a counterfeit authority. (2.) They had the show of wisdom and sagacity, *the faces of men,* though the spirit of devils. (3.) They had all the allurements of seeming beauty, to ensnare and defile the minds of men — *hair like women;* their way of worship was very gaudy and ornamental. (4.) Though they appeared with the tenderness of women, they had *the teeth of lions,* were really cruel creatures. (5.) They had the defence and protection of earthly powers — *breastplates of iron.* (6.) They made a mighty noise in the world; they flew about from one country to another, and the noise of their motion was like that of an army with chariots and horses. (7.) Though at first they soothed and flattered men with a fair appearance, there was a sting in their tails; the cup of their abominations contained that which, though luscious at first, would at length bite like a serpent and sting like an adder. (8.) The king and commander of this hellish squadron is here described, [1.] As an angel; so he was by nature, an angel, once one of the angels of heaven. [2.] *The angel of the bottomless pit;* an angel still, but a fallen angel, fallen into the bottomless pit, vastly large, and out of which there is no recovery. [3.] In these infernal regions he is a sort of prince and governor, and has the powers of darkness under his rule and command. [4.] His true name is *Abaddon, Apollyon — a destroyer,* for that is his business, his design, and employment, to which he diligently attends, in which he is very successful, and takes a horrid hellish pleasure; it is about this destroying work that he sends out his emissaries and armies to destroy the souls of men. And now here we have the end of one woe; and where one ends another begins.

Verses 13–21

Here let us consider the preface to this vision, and then the vision itself.

I. The preface to this vision: *A voice was heard from the horns of the golden altar, v.* 13, 14. Here observe, 1. The power of the church's enemies is restrained till God gives the word to have them turned loose. 2. When nations are ripe for punishment, those instruments of God's anger that were before restrained are let loose upon them, *v.* 14. 3. The instruments that God makes use of to punish a people may sometimes lie at a great distance from them, so that no danger may be apprehended from them. These four messengers of divine judgment lay bound in the river Euphrates, a great way from the European nations. Here the Turkish power had its rise, which seems to be the story of this vision.

II. The vision itself: *And the four angels that had been bound in the great river Euphrates were now loosed, v.* 15, 16. And here observe, 1. The time of their military operations and executions is limited to *an hour, and a day, and a month, and a year.* Prophetic characters of time are hardly to be understood by us; but in general the time is fixed to an hour, when it shall begin and when it shall end; and how far the execution shall prevail, even to a third part of the inhabitants of the earth. God will make the wrath of man praise him, and the remainder of wrath he will restrain. 2. The army that was to execute this great commission is mustered, and the number found to be of horsemen *two hundred thousand thousand;* but we are left to guess what the infantry must be. In general, it tells us, the armies of the Mahomedan empire should be vastly great; and so it is certain they were. 3. Their formidable equipage and appearance, *v.* 17. As the horses were fierce, like lions, and eager to rush into the battle, so those who sat upon them were clad in bright and costly armour, with all the ensigns of martial courage, zeal, and resolution. 4. The vast havoc and desolation that they made in the Roman empire, which had now become antichristian: A third part of them were killed; they went as far as their commission suffered them, and they could go no further. 5. Their artillery, by which they made such slaughter, described *by fire, smoke, and brimstone,* issuing out of the mouths of their horses, and the stings that were in their tails. It is Mr. Mede's opinion that this is a prediction of great guns, those instruments of cruelty which make such destruction: he observes, These were first used by the Turks at the siege of Constantinople, and, being new and strange, were very terrible,

and did great execution. However, here seems to be an allusion to what is mentioned in the former vision, that, as antichrist had his forces of a spiritual nature, like scorpions poisoning the minds of men with error and idolatry, so the Turks, who were raised up to punish the antichristian apostasy, had their scorpions and their stings too, to hurt and kill the bodies of those who had been the murderers of so many souls. 6. Observe the impenitency of the antichristian generation under these dreadful judgments (*v.* 20); the rest of the men who were not killed repented not, they still persisted in those sins for which God was so severely punishing them, which were, (1.) Their idolatry; they would not cast away their images, though they could do them no good, *could not see, nor hear, nor walk.* (2.) Their murders (*v.* 21), which they had committed upon the saints and servants of Christ. Popery is a bloody religion, and seems resolved to continue such. (3.) Their sorceries; they have their charms, and magic arts, and rites in exorcism and other things. (4.) Their fornication; they allow both spiritual and carnal impurity, and promote it in themselves and others. (5.) Their thefts; they have by unjust means heaped together a vast deal of wealth, to the injury and impoverishing of families, cities, princes, and nations. These are the flagrant crimes of antichrist and his agents; and, though God has revealed his wrath from heaven against them, they are obstinate, hardened, and impenitent, and judicially so, for they must be destroyed.

III. From this sixth trumpet we learn, 1. God can make one enemy of the church to be a scourge and plague to another. 2. He who is the Lord of hosts has vast armies at his command, to serve his own purposes. 3. The most formidable powers have limits set them, which they cannot transgress. 4. When God's judgments are in the earth, he expects the inhabitants thereof should repent of sin, and learn righteousness. 5. Impenitency under divine judgments is an iniquity that will be the ruin of sinners; for where God judges he will overcome.

CHAPTER 10

This chapter is an introduction to the latter part of the prophecies of this book. Whether what is contained between this and the sounding of the seventh trumpet (11:15) be a distinct prophecy from the other, or only a more general account of some of the principal things included in the other, is disputed by our curious enquirers into these abstruse writings. However, here we have, I. A remarkable description of a very glorious angel with an open book in his hand (*v.* 1–3). II. An account of seven thunders which the apostle heard, as echoing to the voice of this angel, and communicating some discoveries, which the apostle was not yet allowed to write (*v.* 4). III. The solemn oath taken by him who had the book in his hand (*v.* 5–7). IV. The charge given to the apostle, and observed by him (*v.* 8–11).

Verses 1–7

Here we have an account of another vision the apostle was favoured with, between the sounding of the sixth trumpet and that of the seventh. And we observe,

I. The person who was principally concerned in communicating this discovery to John — an angel from heaven, *another mighty angel,* who is so set forth as would induce one to think it could be no other than our Lord and Saviour Jesus Christ! 1. He was *clothed with a cloud:* he veils his glory, which is too great for mortality to behold; and he throws a veil upon his dispensations. Clouds and darkness are round about him. 2. *A rainbow was upon his head;* he is always mindful of his covenant, and, when his conduct is most mysterious, yet it is perfectly just and faithful. 3. *His face was as the sun,* all bright, and full of lustre and majesty, *ch.* 1:16. 4. *His feet were as pillars of fire;* all his ways, both of grace and providence, are pure and steady.

II. His station and posture: *He set his right foot upon the sea and his left foot upon the earth,* to show the absolute power and dominion he had over the world. *And he held in his hand a little book opened,* probably the same that was before sealed, but was now opened, and gradually fulfilled by him.

III. His awful voice: *He cried aloud, as when a lion roareth* (*v.* 3), and his awful voice was echoed by *seven thunders,* seven solemn and terrible ways of discovering the mind of God.

IV. The prohibition given to the apostle, that he should not publish, but conceal what he had learned from the seven thunders, *v.* 4. The apostle was for preserving and publishing every thing he saw and heard in these visions, but the time had not yet come.

V. The solemn oath taken by this mighty angel. 1. The

manner of his swearing: *He lifted up his hand to heaven, and swore by him that liveth for ever,* by himself, as God often has done, or by God as God, to whom he, as Lord, Redeemer, and ruler of the world, now appeals. 2. The matter of the oath: that *there shall be time no longer;* either, (1.) That there shall be now no longer delay in fulfilling the predictions of this book than till the last angel should sound; then every thing should be put into speedy execution: *the mystery of God shall be finished, v.* 7. Or, (2.) That when this mystery of God is finished time itself shall be no more, as being the measure of things that are in a mutable changing state; but all things shall be at length for ever fixed, and so time itself swallowed up in eternity.

Verses 8-11

Here we have, I. A strict charge given to the apostle, which was, 1. That he should *go and take the little book* out of the hands of that mighty angel mentioned before. This charge was given, not by the angel himself who stood upon the earth, but by the same voice from heaven that in the fourth verse had lain an injunction upon him not to write what he had discerned by the seven thunders. 2. To eat the book; this part of the charge was given by the angel himself, hinting to the apostle that before he should publish what he had discovered he must more thoroughly digest the predictions, and be in himself suitably affected with them.

II. An account of the taste and relish which this little book would have, when the apostle had taken it in; at first, while *in his mouth, sweet.* All persons feel a pleasure in looking into future events, and in having them foretold; and all good men love to receive a word from God, of what import soever it be. But, when this book of prophecy was more thoroughly digested by the apostle, the contents would be bitter; these were things so awful and terrible, such grievous persecutions of the people of God, and such desolation made in the earth, that the foresight and foreknowledge of them would not be pleasant, but painful to the mind of the apostle: thus was Ezekiel's prophecy to him, *ch.* 3:3.

III. The apostle's discharge of the duty he was called to (*v.* 10): *He took the little book out of the angel's hand, and ate it up,* and he found the relish to be as was told him. 1. It becomes the servants of God to digest in their own souls the messages they bring to others in his name, and to be suitably affected therewith themselves. 2. It becomes them to deliver every message with which they are charged, whether pleasing or unpleasing to men. That which is least pleasing may be most profitable; however, God's messengers must not keep back any part of the counsel of God.

IV. The apostle is made to know that this book of prophecy, which he had now taken in, was not given him merely to gratify his own curiosity, or to affect him with pleasure or pain, but to be communicated by him to the world. Here his prophetical commission seems to be renewed, and he is ordered to prepare for another embassy, to convey those declarations of the mind and will of God which are of great importance to all the world, and to the highest and greatest men in the world, and such should be read and recorded in many languages. This indeed is the case; we have them in our language, and are all obliged to attend to them, humbly to enquire into the meaning of them, and firmly to believe that every thing shall have its accomplishment in the proper time; and, when the prophecies shall be fulfilled, the sense and truth of them will appear, and the omniscience, power, and faithfulness of the great God will be adored.

CHAPTER 11

In this chapter we have an account, I. Of the measuring-reed given to the apostle, to take the dimensions of the temple (*v.* 1, 2). II. Of the two witnesses of God (*v.* 3-13). III. Of the sounding of the seventh trumpet, and what followed upon it (*v.* 14, etc.).

Verses 1-2

This prophetical passage about measuring the temple is a plain reference to what we find in Ezekiel's vision, Eze. 40:3, etc. But how to understand either the one or the other is not so easy. It should seem the design of measuring the temple in the former case was in order to the rebuilding of it, and that with advantage; the design of this measurement seems to be either, 1. For the preservation of it in those times of public danger and calamity that are here foretold; or, 2. For its trial; that it may be seen how far it agrees with the standard, or pattern, in the mount; or, 3. For its reformation; that

what is redundant, deficient, or changed, may be regulated according to the true model. Observe,

I. How much was to be measured. 1. *The temple;* the gospel church in general, whether it be so built, so constituted, as the gospel rule directs, whether it be too narrow or too large, the door too wide or too strait. 2. *The altar.* That which was the place of the most solemn acts of worship may be put for religious worship in general; whether the church has the true altars, both as to substance and situation: as to substance, whether they take Christ for their altar, and lay down all their offerings there; and in situation, whether the altar be in the holiest; that is, whether they worship God in the Spirit and in truth. 3. The worshippers too must be measured, whether they make God's glory their end and his word their rule, in all their acts of worship; and whether they come to God with suitable affections, and whether their *conversation be as becomes the gospel.*

II. What was not to be measured (*v.* 2), and why it should be left out. 1. What was not to be measured: *The court which is without the temple measure it not.* Some say that Herod, in the additions made to the temple, built an outer court, and called it *the court of the Gentiles.* Some tell us that Adrian built the city and an outer court, and called it *Aelia,* and gave it to the Gentiles. 2. Why was not the outer court measured? This was no part of the temple, according to the model either of Solomon or Zerubbabel, and therefore God would have no regard to it. He would not mark it out for preservation; but as it was designed for the Gentiles, to bring pagan ceremonies and customs and to annex them to the gospel churches, so Christ abandoned it to them, to be used as they pleased; and both that and the city were trodden under foot for a certain time — *forty and two months,* which some would have to be the whole time of the reign of antichrist. Those who worship in the outer court are either such as worship in a false manner or with hypocritical hearts; and these are rejected of God, and will be found among his enemies. 3. From the whole observe, (1.) God will have a temple and an altar in the world, till the end of time. (2.) He has a strict regard to this temple, and observes how every thing is managed in it. (3.) Those who worship in the outer court will be rejected, and only those who worship within the veil accepted. (4.) The holy city, the visible church, is very much trampled upon in the world. But, (5.) The desolations of the church are for a limited time, and for a short time, and she shall be delivered out of all her troubles.

Verses 3-13

In this time of treading down, God has reserved to himself his faithful witnesses, who will not fail to attest the truth of his word and worship, and the excellency of his ways. Here observe,

I. The number of these witnesses: it is but a small number and yet it is sufficient. 1. It is but small. Many will own and acknowledge Christ in times of prosperity who will desert and deny him in times of persecution; one witness, when the cause is upon trial, is worth many at other times. 2. It is a sufficient number; for in the mouth of two witnesses every cause shall be established. Christ sent out his disciples two by two, to preach the gospel. Some think these two witnesses are Enoch and Elias, who are to return to the earth for a time: others, the church of the believing Jews and that of the Gentiles: it should rather seem that they are God's eminent faithful ministers, who shall not only continue to profess the Christian religion, but to preach it, in the worst of times.

II. The time of their prophesying, or bearing their testimony for Christ. *A thousand two hundred and threescore days;* that is (as many think), to the period of the reign of antichrist; and, if the beginning of that interval could be ascertained, this number of prophetic days, taking a day for a year, would give us a prospect when the end shall be.

III. Their habit, and posture: they prophesy in sackcloth, as those that are deeply affected with the low and distressed state of the churches and interest of Christ in the world.

IV. How they were supported and supplied during the discharge of their great and hard work: they stood before the God of the whole earth, and he gave them power to prophesy. He made them to be like Zerubbabel and Joshua, the two olive-trees and candlestick in the vision of Zechariah, *ch.* 4:2, etc. God gave them the oil of holy zeal, and courage, and strength, and comfort; he made them olive-trees, and their lamps of profession were kept burning by the oil of in-

ward gracious principles, which they received from God. They had oil not only in their lamps, but in their vessels — habits of spiritual life, light, and zeal.

V. Their security and defence during the time of their prophesying: *If any attempted to hurt them, fire proceeded out of their mouths, and devoured them, v.* 5. Some think this alludes to Elias's calling for the fire from heaven, to consume the captains and their companies that came to seize him, 2 Ki. 1:12. God promised the prophet Jeremiah (*ch.* 5:14), *Behold, I will make my words in thy mouth fire, and this people shall be wood, and it shall devour them.* By their praying and preaching, and courage in suffering, they shall gall and wound the very hearts and consciences of many of their persecutors, who shall go away self-condemned, and be even terrors to themselves; like Pashur, at the words of the prophet Jeremiah, *ch.* 20:4. They shall have that free access to God, and that interest in him, that, at their prayers, God will inflict plagues and judgments upon their enemies, as he did on Pharaoh, *turning their rivers into blood,* and restraining the dews of heaven, shutting heaven up, that no rain shall fall for many days, as he did at the prayers of Elias, 1 Ki. 17:1. God has ordained his arrows for the persecutors, and is often plaguing them while they are persecuting his people; they find it hard work to *kick against the pricks.*

VI. The slaying of the witnesses. To make their testimony more strong, they must seal it with their blood. Here observe, 1. The time when they should be killed: *When they have finished their testimony.* They are immortal, they are invulnerable, till their work be done. Some think it ought to be rendered, *when they were about to finish their testimony.* When they had prophesied in sackcloth the greatest part of the 1260 years, then they should feel the last effect of antichristian malice. 2. The enemy that should overcome and slay them — *the beast that ascendeth out of the bottomless pit.* Antichrist, the great instrument of the devil, should make war against them, not only with the arms of subtle and sophistical learning, but chiefly with open force and violence; and God would permit his enemies to prevail against his witnesses for a time. 3. The barbarous usage of these slain witnesses; the malice of their enemies was not satiated with their blood and death, but pursued even their dead bodies. (1.) They would not allow them a quiet grave; their bodies were cast out in the open street, the high street of Babylon, or in the high road leading to the city. This city is spiritually called Sodom for monstrous wickedness, and Egypt for idolatry and tyranny; and here Christ in his mystical body has suffered more than in any place in the world. (2.) Their dead bodies were insulted by the inhabitants of the earth, and their death was a matter of mirth and joy to the antichristian world, *v.* 10. They were glad to be rid of these witnesses, who by their doctrine and example had teased, terrified, and tormented the consciences of their enemies; these spiritual weapons cut wicked men to the heart, and fill them with the greatest rage and malice against the faithful.

VII. The resurrection of these witnesses, and the consequences thereof. Observe, 1. The time of their rising again; after they had lain dead *three days and a half* (*v.* 11), a short time in comparison of that in which they had prophesied. Here may be a reference to the resurrection of Christ, who is *the resurrection and the life. Thy dead men shall live, together with my dead body shall they arise.* Or there may be a reference to the resurrection of Lazarus on the fourth day, when they thought it impossible. God's witnesses may be slain, but they shall rise again: not in their persons, till the general resurrection, but in their successors. God will revive his work, when it seems to be dead in the world. 2. The power by which they were raised: *The spirit of life from God entered into them, and they stood upon their feet.* God put not only life, but courage into them. God can make the dry bones to life; it is the Spirit of life from God that quickens dead souls, and shall quicken the dead bodies of his people, and his dying interest in the world. 3. The effect of their resurrection upon their enemies: *Great fear fell upon them.* The reviving of God's work and witnesses will strike terror into the souls of his enemies. Where there is guilt, there is fear; and a persecuting spirit, though cruel, is not a courageous, but a cowardly spirit. Herod feared John the Baptist.

VIII. The ascension of the witnesses into heaven and the consequences thereof, *v.* 12, 13. Observe, 1. Their ascension. By heaven we may understand either some more eminent station in the church, the kingdom of grace in this world, or a high place in the kingdom of glory above. The former seems to be the meaning: *They ascended to heaven in a cloud* (in a figurative, not in a literal sense) *and their enemies saw them.* It will be no small part of the punishment of persecutors, both in this world and at the great day, that they shall see the faithful servants of God greatly honoured and advanced. To this honour they did not attempt to ascend, till God called them, and said, *Come up hither.* The Lord's witnesses must wait for their advancement, both in the church and in heaven, till God calls them; they must not be weary of suffering and service, nor too hastily grasp at the reward; but stay till their Master calls them, and then they may gladly ascend to him. 2. The consequences of their ascension — a mighty shock and convulsion in the antichristian empire and the fall of *a tenth part of the city.* Some refer this to the beginning of the reformation from popery, when many princes and states fell off from their subjection to Rome. This great work met with great opposition; all the western world felt a great concussion, and the antichristian interest received a great blow, and lost a great deal of ground and interest, (1.) By the sword of war, which was then drawn; and many of those who fought under the banner of antichrist were slain by it. (2.) By the sword of the Spirit: *The fear of God fell upon many.* They were convinced of their errors, superstition, and idolatry; and by true repentance, and embracing the truth, *they gave glory to the God of heaven.* Thus, when God's work and witnesses revive, the devil's work and witnesses fall before him.

Verses 14–19

We have here the sounding of the seventh and last trumpet, which is ushered in by the usual warning and demand of attention: *The second woe is past, and, behold, the third woe cometh quickly. Then the seventh angel sounded.* This had been suspended for some time, till the apostle had been made acquainted with some intervening occurrences of very great moment, and worthy of his notice and observation. But what he before expected he now heard — the seventh angel sounding. Here observe the effects and consequences of this trumpet, thus sounded.

I. Here were loud and joyful acclamations of the saints and angels in heaven. Observe, 1. The manner of their adorations: they rose from their seats, *and fell upon their faces, and worshipped God;* they did it with reverence and humility. 2. The matter of their adorations. (1.) They thankfully recognize the right of our God and Saviour to rule and reign over all the world: *The kingdoms of this world have become the kingdoms of our Lord and of his Christ, v.* 15. They were always so in title, both by creation and purchase. (2.) They thankfully observe his actual possession of them, and reign over them; they give him thanks because he had taken to him his great power, asserted his rights, exerted his power, and so turned title into possession. (3.) They rejoice that this his reign shall never end: *He shall reign for ever and ever,* till all enemies be put under his feet; none shall ever wrest the sceptre out of his hand.

II. Here were angry resentments in the world at these just appearances and actings of the power of God (*v.* 18): *The nations were angry;* not only had been so, but were so still: their hearts rose up against God; they met his wrath with their own anger. It was a time when God was taking a just revenge upon the enemies of his people, recompensing tribulation to those who had troubled them. It was a time in which he was beginning to reward his people's faithful services and sufferings; and their enemies could not bear it, they fretted against God, and so increased their guilt and hastened their destruction.

III. Another consequence was the opening of the temple of God in heaven. By this may be meant that here is now a more free communication between heaven and earth, prayer and praises more freely and frequently ascending and graces and blessings plentifully descending. But it rather seems to intend the church of God on earth, a heavenly temple. It is an allusion to the various circumstances of things in the time of the first temple. Under idolatrous and wicked princes, it was shut up and neglected; but, under religious and reforming princes, it was opened and frequented. So, during the power of antichrist, the temple of God seemed to be shut up, and was so in a great degree; but now it was opened again. At this opening of it observe, 1. What was seen there: *the ark of God's testament.* This was in the holy of holies; in this ark the tables of the law were kept. As before Josiah's time the law of God had been lost, but was then found, so in the reign of antichrist God's law was laid aside, and made void by their traditions and decrees; the scriptures were locked up from the people, and they must not look into these divine oracles; now they are opened, now they are brought to the view of all. This was an unspeakable and invaluable privilege; and this, like the ark of the testament, was a token of the presence of God returned to his people, and his favour towards them in Jesus Christ the propitiation. 2. What was heard and felt there: *Lightnings, voices, thunderings, an earthquake, and great hail.* The great blessing of the reformation was attended with very awful providences; and by terrible things in righteousness God would answer those prayers that were presented in his holy temple, now opened. All the great revolutions of the world are concerted in heaven, and are the answers of the prayers of the saints.

CHAPTER 12

It is generally agreed by the most learned expositors that the narrative we have in this and the two following chapters, from the sounding of the seventh trumpet to the opening of the vials, is not a prediction of things to come, but rather a recapitulation and representation of things past, which, as God would have the apostle to foresee while future, he would have him to review now that they were past, that he might have a more perfect idea of them in his mind, and might observe the agreement between the prophecy and that Providence that is always fulfilling the scriptures. In this chapter we have an account of the contest between the church and antichrist, the seed of the woman and the seed of the serpent. I. As it was begun in heaven (*v.* 1–11). II. As it was carried on in the wilderness (*v.* 12, etc.).

Verses 1–11

Here we see that early prophecy eminently fulfilled in which God said he would *put enmity between the seed of the woman and the seed of the serpent,* Gen. 3:15. You will observe,

I. The attempts of Satan and his agents to prevent the increase of the church, by devouring her offspring *as soon as it was born;* of this we have a very lively description in the most proper images.

1. We see how the church is represented in this vision. (1.) As a *woman,* the weaker part of the world, but the spouse of Christ, and the mother of the saints. (2.) As *clothed with the sun,* the imputed righteousness of the Lord Jesus Christ. Having put on Christ, who is *the Sun of righteousness,* she, by her relation to Christ, is invested with honourable rights and privileges, and shines in his rays. (3.) As having *the moon under her feet* (that is, the world); she stands upon it, but lives above it; her heart and hope are not set upon sublunary things, but on the things that are in heaven, where her head is. (4.) As having on her head *a crown of twelve stars,* that is, the doctrine of the gospel preached by the twelve apostles, which is a crown of glory to all true believers. (5.) As in travail, crying out, and *pained to be delivered.* She was pregnant, and now in pain to bring forth a holy progeny to Christ, desirous that what was begun in the conviction of sinners might end in their conversion, that when the children were brought to the birth there might be strength to bring forth, and that she might see of the travail of her soul.

2. How the grand enemy of the church is represented. (1.) As a *great red dragon* — a dragon for strength and terror — a red dragon for fierceness and cruelty. (2.) As *having seven heads,* that is, placed on seven hills, as Rome was; and therefore it is probable that pagan Rome is here meant. (3.) As having *ten horns,* divided into ten provinces, as the Roman empire was by Augustus Caesar. (4.) As having *seven crowns upon his head,* which is afterwards expounded to be seven kings, *ch.* 17:10. (5.) As drawing with his tail a *third part of the stars in heaven,* and *casting them down to the earth,* turning the ministers and professors of the Christian religion out of their places and privileges and making them as weak and useless as he could. (6.) As standing *before the woman, to devour her child as soon as it should be born,* very vigilant to crush the Christian religion in its birth and entirely to prevent the growth and continuance of it in the world.

II. The unsuccessfulness of these attempts against the church; for, 1. She was safely delivered of a *man-child* (*v.* 5), by which some understand Christ, others Constantine, but others, with greater propriety, a race of true believers, strong and united, resembling Christ, and designed, under him, *to rule the nations with a rod of iron;* that is, to judge the world by their doctrine and lives now, and as assessors with Christ at the great day. 2. Care was taken of this child: it *was caught up to God, and to his throne;* that is, taken into his special, powerful, and immediate protection. The Christian religion has been from its infancy the special care of *the great God and our Saviour Jesus Christ.* 3. Care was taken of the mother as well as of the child, *v.* 6. She *fled into the wilderness, a place prepared* both for her safety and her sustenance. The church was in an obscure state, dispersed; and this proved her security, through the care of divine Providence. This her obscure and private state was for a limited time, not to continue always.

III. The attempts of the dragon not only proved unsuccessful against the church, but fatal to his own interests; for, upon his endeavour to devour the man-child, he engaged all the powers of heaven against him (*v.* 7): *There was war in heaven. Heaven* will espouse the quarrel of the church. Here observe,

1. The seat of this war — *in heaven,* in the church, which is *the kingdom of heaven* on earth, under the care of heaven and in the same interest.

2. The parties — *Michael and his angels* on one side, and *the dragon and his angels* on the other: Christ, the great Angel of the covenant, and his faithful followers; and Satan and all his instruments. This latter party would be much superior in number and outward strength to the other; but the strength of the church lies in having the Lord Jesus for the captain of their salvation.

3. The success of the battle: *The dragon and his angels fought and prevailed not;* there was a great struggle on both sides, but the victory fell to Christ and his church, and the dragon and his angels were not only conquered, but cast out; the pagan idolatry, which was a worshipping of devils, was extirpated out of the empire in the time of Constantine.

4. The triumphant song that was composed and used on this occasion, *v.* 10, 11. Here observe, (1.) How the conqueror is adored: *Now have come salvation, strength, and the kingdom of our God, and the power of his Christ.* Now God has shown himself to be a mighty God; now Christ has shown himself to be a strong and mighty Saviour; his own arm has brought salvation, and now his kingdom will be greatly enlarged and established. The salvation and strength of the church are all to be ascribed to the king and head of the church. (2.) How the conquered enemy is described. [1.] By his malice; he was *the accuser of the brethren,* and *accused them before their God night and day;* he appeared before God as an adversary to the church, continually bringing in indictments and accusations against them, whether true or false; thus he accused Job, and thus he accused Joshua the high priest, Zec. 3:1. Though he hates the presence of God, yet he is willing to appear there to accuse the people of God. Let us therefore take heed that we give him no cause of accusation against us; and that, when we have sinned, we presently go in before the Lord, and accuse and condemn ourselves, and commit our cause to Christ as our Advocate. [2.] By his disappointment and defeat: he and all his accusations are cast out, the indictments quashed, and the accuser turned out of the court with just indignation. (3.) How the victory was gained. The servants of God overcame Satan, [1.] *By the blood of the Lamb,* as the meritorious cause. Christ by dying *destroyed him that hath the power of death, that is, the devil.* [2.] *By the word of their testimony,* as the great instrument of war, *the sword of the Spirit, which is the word of God,* — by a resolute powerful preaching of the everlasting gospel, *which is mighty, through God, to pull down strongholds,* — and by their courage and patience in sufferings; *they loved not their lives unto the death,* when the love of life stood in competition with their loyalty to Christ; they loved not their lives so well but they could give them up *to death,* could lay them down in Christ's cause; their love to their own lives was overcome by stronger affections of another nature; and this their courage and zeal helped to confound their enemies, to convince many of the spectators, to confirm the souls of the faithful, and so contributed greatly to this victory.

Verses 12–17

We have here an account of this war, so happily finished in heaven, or in the church, as it was again renewed and carried on in the wilderness, the place to which the church had fled, and where she had been for some time secured by the special care of her God and Saviour. Observe,

I. The warning given of the distress and calamity that should fall upon the inhabitants of the world in general, through the wrath and rage of the devil. For, though his malice is chiefly bent against the servants of God, yet he is an enemy and hater of mankind as such; and, being defeated in his designs against the church, he is resolved to give all the disturbance he can to the world in general: *Woe to the inhabitants of the earth, and the sea, v.* 12. The rage of Satan grows so much the greater as he is limited both in place and time; when he was confined to the wilderness, and had but a short time to reign there, he comes with the greater wrath.

II. His second attempt upon the church now in the wilderness: *He persecuted the woman who brought forth the man-child, v.* 13. Observe, 1. The care that God had taken of his church. He had conveyed her as on eagles' wings, into a place of safety provided for her, where she was to continue for a certain space of time, couched in prophetic characters, taken from Dan. 7:25. 2. The continual malice of the dragon against the church. Her obscurity could not altogether protect her; the old subtle serpent, which at first lurked in paradise, now follows the church into the wilderness, and *casts out a flood of water after her, to carry her away.* This is thought to be meant of a flood of error and heresy, which was breathed by Arius, Nestorius, Pelagius, and many more, by which the church of God was in danger of being overwhelmed and carried away. The church of God is in more danger from heretics than from persecutors; and heresies are as certainly from the devil as open force and violence. 3. The seasonable help provided for the church in this dangerous juncture: *The earth helped the woman, and opened her mouth, and swallowed up the flood, v.* 16. Some think we are to understand the swarms of Goths and Vandals that invaded the Roman empire, and found work for the Arian rulers, who otherwise would have been as furious persecutors as the pagan had been, and had exercised great cruelties already; but God opened a breach of war, and the flood was in a manner swallowed up thereby, and the church enjoyed some respite. God often sends the sword to avenge the quarrel of his covenant; and, when men choose new gods, then there is danger of war in the gates; intestine broils and contentions often end in the invasions of a common enemy. 4. The devil, being thus defeated in his designs upon the universal church, now turns his rage against particular persons and places; his malice against the woman pushes him on to *make war with the remnant of her seed.* Some think hereby are meant the Albigenses, who were first by Dioclesian driven up into barren and mountainous places, and afterwards cruelly murdered by popish rage and power, for several generations; and for no other reason than because *they kept the commandments of God* and *held the testimony of Jesus Christ.* Their fidelity to God and Christ, in doctrine, worship, and practice, was that which exposed them to the rage of Satan and his instruments; and such fidelity will expose men still, less or more, to the end of the world, when *the last enemy shall be destroyed.*

CHAPTER 13

We have, in this chapter, a further discovery and description of the church's enemies: not other enemies than are mentioned before, but described after another manner, that the methods of their enmity may more fully appear. They are represented as two beasts; the first you have an account of (*v.* 1–10) the second (*v.* 11, etc.). By the first some understand Rome pagan, and by the second Rome papal; but others understand Rome papal to be represented by both these beasts, by the first in its secular power, by the second in its ecclesiastical.

Verses 1–10

We have here an account of the rise, figure, and progress of the first beast; and observe, 1. From what situation the apostle saw this monster. He seemed to himself to stand upon *the sea-shore,* though it is probable he was still in a rapture; but he took himself to be in *the island Patmos,* but whether in the body or out of the body he could not tell. 2. Whence this beast came — *out of the sea;* and yet, by the description of it, it would seem more likely to be a land-monster; but the more monstrous every thing about it was the more proper an emblem it would be to set forth the mystery of iniquity and tyranny. 3. What was the form and shape of this beast. It was for the most part *like a leopard,* but its *feet were like the feet of a bear and its mouth as the mouth of a lion;* it had *seven heads, and ten horns, and upon its heads the name of blasphemy:* the most horrid and hideous monster! In some part of this description here seems to be an allusion to Daniel's vision of the four beasts, which represented the four monarchies, Dan. 7:1–3, etc. One of these beasts was like a lion, another like a bear, and another like a leopard; this beast was a sort of composition of those three, with the fierceness, strength, and swiftness, of them all; the seven heads and the ten horns seem to design its several powers; the ten crowns, its tributary princes; the word blasphemy on its forehead proclaims its direct enmity and opposition to the glory of God, by promoting idolatry. 4. The source and spring of his authority — *the dragon; he gave him his power, and seat, and great authority.* He was set up by the devil, and supported by him to do his work and promote his interest; and the devil lent him all the assistance he could. 5. A dangerous wound given him, and yet unexpectedly healed, *v.* 3. Some think that by this wounded head we are to understand the abolishing of pagan idolatry; and by the healing of the wound the introducing of the popish idolatry, the same in substance with the former, only in a new dress, and which as effectually answers the devil's design as that did. 6. The honour and worship paid to this infernal monster: *All the world wondered after the beast;* they all admired his power, and policy, and success, and *they worshipped the dragon* that *gave power to the beast,* and *they worshipped the beast;* they paid honour and subjection to the devil and his instruments, and thought there was no power able to withstand them: so great were the darkness, degeneracy, and madness of the world! 7. How he exercised his infernal power and policy: He had *a mouth, speaking great things, and blasphemies; he blasphemed God, the name of God, the tabernacle of God, and all those that dwell in heaven; and he made war with the saints, and overcame them,* and gained a sort of universal empire in the world. His malice was principally levelled at the God of heaven, and his heavenly attendants — at God, in making images of him that is invisible, and in worshipping them; — at the tabernacle of God, that is, say some, at the human nature of the Lord Jesus Christ, in which God dwells as in a tabernacle; this is dishonoured by their doctrine of transubstantiation, which will not suffer his body to be a true body, and will put it into the power of every priest to prepare a body for Christ; — and *against those that dwell in heaven,* the glorified saints, by putting them into the place of the pagan demons, and praying to them, which they are so far from being pleased with that they truly judge themselves wronged and dishonoured by it. Thus the malice of the devil shows itself against heaven and the blessed inhabitants of heaven. These are above the reach of his power. All he can do is to blaspheme them; but the saints on earth are more exposed to his cruelty, and he sometimes is permitted to triumph over them and trample upon them. 8. The limitation of the devil's power and success, and that both as to time and persons. He is limited in point of time; his reign is *to continue forty-and-two months* (*v.* 5), suitable to the other prophetical characters of the reign of antichrist. He is also limited as to the persons and people that he shall entirely subject his will and power; it will be only those *whose names are not written in the Lamb's book of life.* Christ had a chosen remnant, *redeemed by his blood, recorded in his book, sealed by his Spirit;* and though the devil and antichrist might overcome their bodily strength, and take away their natural life, they could never conquer their souls, nor prevail with them to forsake their Saviour and revolt to his enemies. 9. Here is a demand of attention to what is here discovered of the great sufferings and troubles of the church, and an assurance given that when God has accomplished his work on mount Zion, his refining work, then he will turn his hand against the enemies of his people, and those who have killed with the sword shall themselves fall by the sword (*v.* 10), and those who led the people of God into captivity shall themselves be made captives. Here now is that which will be proper exercise for *the patience and faith of the saints* — patience under the prospect of such great sufferings, and faith in the prospect of so glorious a deliverance.

Verses 11–18

Those who think the first beast signifies Rome pagan by this second beast would understand Rome papal, which promotes idolatry and tyranny, but in a more soft and lamb-like manner: those that understand the first beast of the secular power of the papacy take the second to intend its spiritual and ecclesiastical powers, which act under the disguise of religion and charity to the souls of men. Here observe,

I. The form and shape of this second beast: *He had two horns like a lamb,* but a mouth that *spoke like the dragon.* All agree that this must be some great impostor, who, under a pretence of religion, shall deceive the souls of men. The papists would have it to be Apollonius Tyranaeus; but Dr. More has rejected that opinion, and fixes it upon the ecclesiastical powers of the papacy. The pope shows the horns of a lamb, pretends to be the vicar of Christ upon earth, and so to be vested with his power and authority; but his speech betrays him, for he gives forth those false doctrines and cruel decrees which show him to belong to the dragon, and not to the Lamb.

II. The power which he exercises: *All the power of the former beast* (*v.* 12); he promotes the same interest, pursues the same design in substance, which is, to draw men off from worshipping the true God to worshipping those who by nature are no gods, and subject the souls and consciences of men to the will and authority of men, in opposition to the will of God. This design is promoted by the popery as well as by paganism, and by the crafty arts of popery as well as by the secular arm, both serving the interests of the devil, though in a different manner.

III. The methods by which this second beast carried on his interests and designs; they are of three sorts: — 1. Lying wonders, pretended miracles, by which they should be deceived, and prevailed with to worship the former beast in this new image or shape that was now made for him; they would pretend to bring down fire from heaven, as Elias did, and God sometimes permits his enemies, as he did the magicians of Egypt, to do things that seem very wonderful, and by which unwary persons may be deluded. It is well known that the papal kingdom has been long supported by pretended miracles. 2. Excommunications, anathemas, severe censures, by which they pretend to cut men off from Christ, and cast them into the power of the devil, but do indeed deliver them over to the secular power, that they may be put to death; and thus, notwithstanding their vile hypocrisy, they are justly charged with killing those whom they cannot corrupt. 3. By disfranchisement, allowing none to enjoy natural, civil, or municipal rights, who will not worship that papal beast, that is, the image of the pagan beast. It is made a qualification for buying and selling the rights of nature, as well as for places of profit and trust, that they have *the mark of the beast in their forehead* and *in their right hand,* and that they have *the name of the beast* and *the number of his name.* It is probable that *the mark, the name,* and *the number of the beast,* may all signify the same thing — that they make an open profession of their subjection and obedience to the papacy, which is receiving the mark in their forehead, and that they oblige themselves to use all their interest, power, and endeavour, to promote the papal authority, which is receiving the mark in their right hands. We are told that pope Martin V. in his bull, added to the council of Constance, prohibits Roman catholics from suffering any heretics to dwell in their countries, or to make any bargains, use any trades, or bear any civil offices, which is a very clear interpretation of this prophecy.

IV. We have here *the number of the beast,* given in such a manner as shows the infinite wisdom of God, and will sufficiently exercise all the wisdom and accuracy of men: *The number* is *the number of a man,* computed after the usual manner among men, and it is 666. Whether this be the number of the errors and heresies that are contained in popery, or rather, as others, the number of the years from its rise to its fall, is not certain, much less what that period is which is described by these prophetic numbers. The most admired dissertation on this intricate subject is that of Dr. Potter, where the curious may find sufficient entertainment. It seems to me to be one of those seasons which God has reserved in his own power; only this we know, God has written *Mene Tekel* upon all his enemies; he has numbered their days, and they shall be finished, but his own kingdom shall endure for ever.

CHAPTER 14

After an account of the great trials and sufferings which the servants of God had endured, we have now a more pleasant scene opening; the day begins now to dawn, and here we have represented, I. The Lord Jesus at the head of his faithful followers (*v.* 1–5). II. Three angels sent successively to proclaim the fall of Babylon and the things antecedent and consequent to so great an event (*v.* 6–13). III. The vision of the harvest (*v.* 14, etc.).

Verses 1–5

Here we have one of the most pleasing sights that can be viewed in this world — the Lord Jesus Christ at the head of his faithful adherents and attendants. Here observe, 1. How Christ appears: as a Lamb standing upon *mount Zion.* Mount Zion is the gospel church. Christ is with his church and in the midst of her in all her troubles, and therefore she is not consumed. It is his presence that secures her perseverance;

he appears as *a Lamb, a true Lamb, the Lamb of God.* A counterfeit lamb is mentioned as rising out of the earth in the last chapter, which was really a dragon; here Christ appears as the true paschal Lamb, to show that his mediatorial government is the fruit of his sufferings, and the cause of his people's safety and fidelity. 2. How his people appear: very honourably. (1.) As to the numbers, they are many, even all who are sealed; not one of them lost in all the tribulations through which they have gone. (2.) Their distinguishing badge: they had *the name of God written in their foreheads;* they made a bold and open profession of their faith in God and Christ, and, this being followed by suitable actings, they are known and approved. (3.) Their congratulations and songs of praise, which were peculiar to the redeemed (*v.* 3); their praises were loud as thunder, or *as the voice of many waters;* they were melodious, as *of harpers;* they were heavenly, *before the throne* of God. *The song was new,* suited to the new covenant, and unto that new and gracious dispensation of Providence under which they now were; and their song was a secret to others, *strangers intermeddled not with their joy;* others might repeat the words of the song, but they were strangers to the true sense and spirit of it. (4.) Their character and description. [1.] They are described by their chastity and purity: *They are virgins.* They had not defiled themselves either with corporal or spiritual adultery; they had kept themselves clean from the abominations of the antichristian generation. [2.] By their loyalty and stedfast adherence to Christ: *They follow the Lamb withersoever he goes;* they follow the conduct of his word, Spirit, and providence, leaving it to him to lead them into what duties and difficulties he pleases. [3.] By their former designation to this honour: *These were redeemed from among men, being the first-fruits to God, and to the Lamb, v.* 4. Here is plain evidence of a special redemption: *They were redeemed from among men.* Some of the children of men are, by redeeming mercy, distinguished from others: *They were the first-fruits to God, and to the Lamb,* his choice ones, eminent in every grace, and the earnest of many more who should *be followers of them, as they were of Christ.* [4.] By their universal integrity and conscientiousness: *There was no guile found in them,* and *they were without fault before the throne of God.* They were without any prevailing guile, any allowed fault; their hearts were right with God, and, as for their human infirmities, they were freely pardoned in Christ. This is the happy remnant who attend upon the Lord Jesus as their head and Lord; he is glorified in them, and they are glorified in him.

Verses 6–12

In this part of the chapter we have three angels or messengers sent from heaven to give notice of the fall of Babylon, and of those things that were antecedent and consequent to that great event.

I. The first angel was sent on an errand antecedent to it, and that was *to preach the everlasting gospel, v.* 6, 7. Observe, 1. The gospel is an everlasting gospel; it is so in its nature, and it will be so in its consequences. Though all flesh be grass, the word of the Lord endureth for ever. 2. It is a work fit for an angel to preach this everlasting gospel; such is the dignity, and such is the difficulty of that work! And yet we have this treasure in earthen vessels. 3. The everlasting gospel is of great concern to all the world; and, as it is the concern of all, it is very much to be desired that it should be made known to all, even *to every nation, and kindred, and tongue, and people.* 4. The gospel is the great means whereby men are brought to fear God, and to give glory to him. Natural religion is not sufficient to keep up the fear of God, nor to secure to him glory from men; it is the gospel that revives the fear of God, and retrieves his glory in the world. 5. When idolatry creeps into the churches of God, it is by the preaching of the gospel, attended by the power of the Holy Spirit, that men are *turned from idols to serve the living God,* as the Creator of *the heaven, and the earth, and the sea, and the fountains of waters, v.* 7. To worship any God besides him who created the world is idolatry.

II. The second angel follows the other, and proclaims the actual fall of Babylon. The preaching of the everlasting gospel had shaken the foundations of antichristianism in the world, and hastened its downfall. By Babylon is generally understood Rome, which was before called *Sodom* and *Egypt,* for wickedness and cruelty, and is now first called *Babylon,* for pride and idolatry. Observe, 1. What God has fore-ordained and foretold shall be done as certainly as if it were done already. 2. The greatness of the papal Babylon will not be able to prevent her fall, but will make it more dreadful and remarkable. 3. The wickedness of Babylon, in corrupting, debauching, and intoxicating the nations round about her, will make her fall just and will declare the righteousness of God in her utter ruin, *v.* 8. Her crimes are recited as the just cause of her destruction.

III. A third angel follows the other two, and gives warning to all of that divine vengeance which would overtake all those that obstinately adhered to the antichristian interest after God had thus proclaimed its downfall, *v.* 9, 10. If after this (this threatening denounced against Babylon, and in part already executed) any should persist in their idolatry, professing subjection to the beast and promoting his cause, they must expect *to drink deep of the wind of the wrath of God;* they shall be for ever miserable in soul and body; Jesus Christ will inflict this punishment upon them, and the holy angels will behold it and approve of it. Idolatry, both pagan and papal, is a damning sin in its own nature, and will prove fatal to those who persist in it, after fair warning given by the word of Providence; those who refuse to come out of Babylon, when thus called, and resolve to partake of her sins, must receive of her plagues; and the guilt and ruin of such incorrigible idolaters will serve to set forth the excellency of the patience and obedience of the saints. These graces shall be rewarded with salvation and glory. When the treachery and rebellion of others shall be punished with everlasting destruction, then it will be said, to the honour of the faithful (*v.* 12): *Here is the patience of the saints;* you have before seen their patience exercised, now you see it rewarded.

Verses 13–20

Here we have the vision of the harvest and vintage, introduced with a solemn preface. Observe,

I. The preface, *v.* 13. Here note, 1. Whence this prophecy about the harvest came: it came down from heaven, and not from men, and therefore it is of certain truth and great authority. 2. How it was to be preserved and published — by writing; it was to be a matter of record, that the people of God might have recourse to it for their support and comfort upon all occasions. 3. What it principally intended, and that is, to show the blessedness of all the faithful saints and servants of God, both in death and after death: *Blessed are the dead that die in the Lord from henceforth,* etc. Here observe, (1.) The description of those that are and shall be blessed — such as die in the Lord, either die in the cause of Christ, or rather die in a state of vital union with Christ, such as are found in Christ when death comes. (2.) The demonstration of this blessedness: *They rest from their labours, and their works do follow them.* [1.] They are blessed in their rest; they rest from all sin, temptation, sorrow, and persecution. *There the wicked cease from troubling, there the weary are at rest.* [2.] They are blessed in their recompence: *Their works follow them;* they do not go before them as their title, or price of purchase, but follow them as their evidence of having lived and died in the Lord; and the memory of them will be pleasant, and the reward glorious, far above the merit of all their services and sufferings. [3.] They are happy in the time of their dying, when they have lived to see the cause of God reviving, the peace of the church returning, and the wrath of God falling upon their idolatrous cruel enemies. Such times are good times to die in; they have Simeon's desire: *Now, Lord, let thou thy servant depart in peace, for mine eyes have seen thy salvation.* And all this is ratified and confirmed by the testimony of the Spirit witnessing with their spirits and with the written word.

II. We have the vision itself, represented by a harvest and a vintage.

1. By a harvest (*v.* 14, 15), an emblem that sometimes signifies the cutting down of the wicked, when ripe for ruin, by the judgments of God, and sometimes the gathering in of the righteous, when ripe for heaven, by the mercy of God. This seems rather to represent God's judgments against the wicked: and here observe,

(1.) The Lord of the harvest — one so *like unto the Son of man* that he was the same, even the Lord Jesus, who is described, [1.] By the chariot in which he sat — *a white cloud,* a cloud that had a bright side turned to the church, how dark soever it might be to the wicked. [2.] By the ensign of his power: *On his head was a golden crown,* authority to do all that he did and whatsoever he would do. [3.] By the instrument of his providences: *In his hand a sharp sickle.* [4.] By the solicitations he had from the temple to perform this great work. What he did, he was desired to do by his people; and, though he was resolved to do it, he would for this thing be sought unto by them, and so it should be in return to their prayers.

(2.) The harvest-work, which is, to thrust the sickle into the corn, and reap the field. The sickle is the sword of God's justice; the field is the world; reaping is cutting the inhabitants of the earth down and carrying them off.

(3.) The harvest-time; and this is when the corn is ripe, when the measure of the sin of men is filled up, and they are ripe for destruction. The most inveterate enemies of Christ and his church are not destroyed till by their sin they are ripe for ruin, and then he will spare them no longer; he will thrust in his sickle, and the earth shall be reaped.

2. By a vintage, *v.* 17. Some think that these two are only different emblems of the same judgment; others that they refer to distinct events of providence before the end of all things. Observe, (1.) To whom this vintage-work was committed — to an angel, *another angel that came out from the altar,* that is, from the holiest of all in heaven. (2.) At whose request this vintage-work was undertaken: it was, as before, at the cry of an *angel out of the temple,* the ministers and churches of God on earth. (3.) The work of the vintage, which consists of two parts: — [1.] The cutting off, and *gathering, the clusters of the vine,* which were now ripe and ready, *fully ripe, v.* 18. [2.] Casting these grapes *into the wine-press* (*v.* 19); here we are told, *First,* What was the wine-press: it was *the wrath of God,* the fire of his indignation, some terrible calamity, very probably the sword, shedding the blood of the wicked. *Secondly,* Where was the place of the wine-press — *without the city,* where the army lay that came against Babylon. *Thirdly,* The quantity of the wine, that is, of the blood that was drawn forth by this judgment: it was, for depth, up *to the horses' bridles,* and, for breadth and length, *a thousand and six hundred furlongs* (*v.* 20); that is, say some, 200 Italian miles, which is thought to be the measure of the holy land, and may be meant of the patrimony of the holy see, encompassing the city of Rome. But here we are left of doubtful conjectures. Perhaps this great event has not yet had its accomplishment, but *the vision is for an appointed time;* and therefore, though it may seem to tarry, we are to wait for it. *But who shall live when the Lord does this?*

CHAPTER 15

Hitherto, according to the judgment of very eminent expositors, God had represented to his servant, John, I. The state of the church under the pagan powers, in the six seals opened; and then, II. The state of the church under the papal powers, in the vision of the six trumpets that began to sound upon the opening of the seventh seal: and then is inserted. III. A more general and brief account of the past, present, and future state of the church, in the little book, etc. He now proceeds, IV. To show him how antichrist should be destroyed, by what steps that destruction should be accomplished, in the vision of the seven vials. This chapter contains an awful introduction or preparation for the pouring out of the vials, in which we have, 1. A sight of those angels in heaven who were to have the execution of this great work, and with what acclamations of joy the heavenly hosts applauded the great design (*v.* 1–4). 2. A sight of these angels coming out of heaven to receive those vials which they were to pour out, and the great commotions this caused in the world (*v.* 5, etc.).

Verses 1–4

Here we have the preparation of matters for the pouring out of the seven vials, which was committed to seven angels; and observe how these angels appeared to the apostle — *in heaven;* it was in a wonderful manner, and that upon account, 1. Of the work they had to do, which was to finish the destruction of antichrist. God was now about to pour out his seven last plagues upon that interest; and, as the measure of Babylon's sins was filled up, they should now find the full measure of his vindictive wrath. 2. The spectators and witnesses of this their commission: all *that had gotten the victory over the beast,* etc. These stood on a *sea of glass,* representing this world, as some think, a brittle thing, that shall be broken to pieces; or, as others, the gospel covenant, alluding to the brazen sea in the temple, in which the priests were to wash (the faithful servants of God stand upon the foundation of the righteousness of Christ); or, as others, *the Red Sea,* that stood as it were congealed while the Israelites went through; and, the pillar of fire reflecting light upon the waters, they would seem to have fire mingled with them; and this to show that the fire of God's wrath against Pharaoh and his horses should dissolve the congealed waters, and destroy them thereby, to which there seems to be an allusion by their *singing the song of Moses,* in which, (1.) They extol the greatness of God's works, and the justice and truth of his ways, both in delivering his people and destroying their enemies. They rejoiced in hope, and the near prospect they had of this, though it was not yet accomplished. (2.) They call upon all nations to render unto God the fear, glory, and worship, due to such a discovery of his truth and justice: *Who shall not fear thee? v.* 4.

Verses 5–8

Observe, I. How these angels appeared — coming out of heaven to execute their commission: *The temple of the tabernacle of the testimony in heaven was opened, v.* 5. Here is an allusion to the holiest of all the tabernacle and temple, where was *the mercy-seat, covering the ark of the testimony,* where the high priest made intercession, and God communed with his people, and heard their prayers. Now by this, as it is here mentioned, we may understand, 1. That, in the judgments God was now about to execute upon the antichristian interest, he was fulfilling the prophecies and promises of his word and covenant, which were there always before him, and of which he was ever mindful. 2. That in this work he was answering the prayers of the people, which were offered to him by their great high priest. 3. That he was herein avenging the quarrel of his own Son, and our Saviour Jesus Christ, whose offices and authority had been usurped, his name dishonoured, and the great designs of his death opposed, by antichrist and his adherents. 4. That he was opening a wider door of liberty for his people to worship him in numerous solemn assemblies, without the fear of their enemies.

II. How they were equipped and prepared for their work. Observe, 1. Their array: They were *clothed with pure and white linen,* and had *their breasts girded with golden girdles, v.* 6. This was the habit of the high priests when they went in to enquire of God, and came out with an answer from him. This showed that these angels were acting in all things under the divine appointment and direction, and that they were going to prepare a sacrifice to the Lord, *called the supper of the great God, ch.* 19:17. The angels are the ministers of divine justice, and they do every thing in a pure and holy manner. 2. Their artillery, what it was, and whence they received it; their artillery, by which they were to do this great execution, was *seven vials filled with the wrath of God;* they were armed with the wrath of God against his enemies. The meanest creature, when it comes armed with the anger of God, will be too hard for any man in the world; but much more an angel of God. This wrath of God was not to be poured out all at once, but was divided into seven parts, which should successively fall upon the antichristian party. Now from whom did they receive these vials? From one of the four living creatures, one of the ministers of the true church, that is, in answer to the prayers of the ministers and people of God, and to avenge their cause, in which the angels are willingly employed.

III. The impressions these things made upon all who stood near the temple: they were all, as it were, wrapt up in clouds of smoke, which filled the temple, from the glorious and powerful presence of God; so that *no man was able to enter into the temple,* till the work was finished. The interests of antichrist were so interwoven with the civil interests of the nations that he could not be destroyed without giving a great shock to all the world; and the people of God would have but little rest and leisure to assemble themselves before him, while this great work was a doing. For the present, their sabbaths would be interrupted, ordinances of public worship intermitted, and all thrown into a general confusion. God himself was now preaching to the church and to all the world, by terrible things in righteousness; but, when this work was done, then the churches would have rest, the temple would be opened, and the solemn assemblies gathered, edified, and multiplied. The greatest deliverances of the church are brought about by awful and astonishing steps of Providence.

CHAPTER 16

In this chapter we have an account of the pouring forth of these vials that were filled with the wrath of God. They were poured out upon the whole antichristian empire, and on every thing appertaining to it. I. Upon the earth (*v.* 2). II. Upon the sea (*v.* 3). III. Upon the rivers and fountains of water (*v.* 4). Here the heavenly hosts proclaim and applaud the righteousness of the judgments of God. IV. The fourth vial was poured out on the sun (*v.* 8). V. The fifth on the seat of the beast. VI. The sixth on the river Euphrates. VII. The seventh in the air, upon which the cities of the nations fell, and great Babylon came in remembrance before God.

Verses 1–7

We had in the foregoing chapter the great and solemn preparation that was made for the pouring out of the vials; now we have the performance of that work. Here observe,

I. That, though every thing was made ready before, yet nothing was to be put in execution without an immediate positive order from God; and this he gave out of the temple, answering the prayers of his people, and avenging their quarrel.

II. No sooner was the word of command given than it was immediately obeyed; no delay, no objection made. We find that some of the best men, as Moses and Jeremiah, did not so readily come in and comply with the call of God to their work; but the angels of God excel not only in strength, but in a readiness to do the will of God. God says, *Go your ways, and pour out the vials,* and immediately the work is begun. We are taught to pray that the will of God may be done on earth as it is done in heaven. And now we enter upon a series of very terrible dispensations of Providence, of which it is difficult to give the certain meaning or to make the particular application. But in the general it is worth our observation that,

1. We have here a reference and allusion to several of the plagues of Egypt, such as the turning of their waters into blood, and smiting them with boils and sores. Their sins were alike, and so were their punishments.

2. These vials have a plain reference to the seven trumpets, which represented the rise of antichrist; and we learn hence that the fall of the church's enemies shall bear some resemblance to their rise, and that God can bring them down in such ways as they chose to exalt themselves. And the fall of antichrist shall be gradual; as Rome was not built in one day, so neither shall it fall in one day, but it falls by degrees; it shall fall so as to rise no more.

3. The fall of the antichristian interest shall be universal. Every thing that any ways belonged to them, or could be serviceable to them, the premises and all their appurtenances, are put into the writ for destruction: their earth, their air, their sea, their rivers, their cities, all consigned over to ruin, all accursed for the sake of the wickedness of that people. Thus the creation groans and suffers through the sins of men. Now we proceed to,

(1.) The first angel who poured out his vial, *v.* 2. Observe, [1.] Where it fell — *upon the earth;* that is, say some, upon the common people; others upon the body of the Romish clergy, who were the basis of the papacy, and of an earthly spirit, all carrying on earthly designs. [2.] What it produced — *noisome and grievous sores on all who had the mark of the beast.* They had marked themselves by their sin; now God marks them out by his judgments. This sore, some think, signifies some of the first appearances of Providence against their state and interest which gave them great uneasiness, as it discovered their inward distemper and was a token of further evil; the plague-tokens appeared.

(2.) *The second angel poured out his vial;* and here we see, [1.] Where it fell — *upon the sea;* that is, say some, upon the jurisdiction and dominion of the papacy; others upon the whole system of their religion, their false doctrines, their corrupt glosses, their superstitious rites, their idolatrous worship, their pardons, indulgences, a great conflux of wicked inventions and institutions, by which they maintain a trade and traffic advantageous to themselves, but injurious to all who deal with them. [2.] What it produced: It turned the sea into blood, *as the blood of a dead man, and every living soul died in the sea.* God discovered not only the vanity and falsehood of their religion, but the pernicious and deadly nature of it — that the souls of men were poisoned by that which was pretended to be the sure means of their salvation.

(3.) The next angel poured out his vial; and we are told, [1.] Where it fell — *upon the rivers, and upon the fountains of waters;* that is, say some very learned men, upon their emissaries and especially the Jesuits, who, like streams, conveyed the venom and poison of their errors and idolatries from the spring-head through the earth. [2.] What effect it had upon them: *It turned them into blood;* some think it stirred up Christian princes to take a just revenge upon those that had been the great incendiaries of the world, and had occasioned the shedding of the blood of armies and of martyrs. The following doxology (*v.* 5, 6) favours this sense. The instrument that God makes use of in this work is here called *the angel of the waters,* who extols the righteousness of God in this retaliation: *They have shed the blood of thy saints, and*

thou hast given them blood to drink, for they are worthy, to which another angel answered by full consent, *v.* 7.

Verses 8–11

In these verses we see the work going on in the appointed order. The fourth angel poured out his vial, and that fell upon the sun; that is, say some, upon some eminent prince of the popish communion, who should renounce their false religion a little while before his utter downfall; and some expect it will be the German emperor. And now what will be the consequence of this? That sun which before cherished them with warm and benign influences shall now grow hot against these idolaters, and shall scorch them. Princes shall use their power and authority to suppress them, which yet will be so far from bringing them to repentance, that it will cause them to curse God and their king, and look upward, throwing out their blasphemous speeches against the God of heaven; they will be hardened to their ruin. The fifth angel poured out his vial, *v.* 10. And observe, 1. Where this fell — *upon the seat of the beast,* upon Rome itself, the mystical Babylon, the head of the antichristian empire. 2. What effect it had there: The whole kingdom of the beast *was full of darkness* and distress. That very city which was the seat of their policy, the source of all their learning, and all their knowledge, and all their pomp and pleasure, now becomes a source of darkness, and pain, and anguish. Darkness was one of the plagues of Egypt, and it is opposed to lustre and honour, and so forebodes the contempt and scorn to which the antichristian interest should be exposed. Darkness is opposed to wisdom and penetration, and forbodes the confusion and folly which the idolaters should discover at that time. It is opposed to pleasure and joy, and so signifies their anguish and vexation of Spirit, when their calamities thus came upon them.

Verses 12–16

The sixth angel poured out his vial; and observe,

I. Where it fell — *upon the great river Euphrates.* Some take it literally, for the place where the Turkish power and empire began; and they think this is a prophecy of the destruction of the Turkish monarchy and of idolatry, which they suppose will be effected about the same time with that of the papacy, as another antichrist, and that thereby a way shall be made for the conveniency of the Jews, those princes of the east. Others take it for the river Tiber; for, as Rome is mystical Babylon, Tiber is mystical Euphrates. And when Rome shall be destroyed her river and merchandise must suffer with her.

II. What did this vial produce? 1. The drying up of the river, which furnished the city with wealth, provisions, and all sorts of accommodations. 2. A way is hereby prepared *for the kings of the east.* The idolatry of the church of Rome had been a great hindrance both to the conversion of the Jews, who have been long cured of their inclination to idols, and of the Gentiles, who are hardened in their idolatry by seeing that which so much symbolizes with it among those called Christians. It is therefore very probable that the downfall of popery, removing these obstructions, will open a way for both the Jews and other eastern nations to come into the church of Christ. And, if we suppose that Mahomedism shall fall at the same time, there will be still a more open communication between the western and eastern nations, which may facilitate the conversion of the Jews, and of *the fulness of the Gentiles.* And when this work of God appears, and is about to be accomplished, no wonder if it occasion another consequence, which is, 3. The last effort of the great dragon; he is resolved to have another push for it, that, if possible, he may retrieve the ruinous posture of his affairs in the world. He is now rallying his forces, recollecting all his spirits, to make one desperate sally before all be lost. This is occasioned by the pouring out of the sixth vial. Here observe, (1.) The instruments he makes use of to engage the powers of the earth in his cause and quarrel: *Three unclean spirits like frogs* come forth, one *out of the mouth of the dragon,* another *out of the mouth of the beast, and* a third *out of the mouth of the false prophet.* Hell, the secular power of antichrist, and the ecclesiastical power, would combine to send their several instruments, furnished with hellish malice, with worldly policy, and with religious falsehood and deceit; and these would muster up the devil's forces for a decisive battle. (2.) The means these instruments would use to engage the powers of earth in this war. They would work pretended miracles, the old stratagem of him *whose coming is after the working of Satan, with all power, and signs, and lying wonders, and with all deceivableness of unrighteousness,* 2 Th. 2:9, 10. Some think that a little before the fall of antichrist the popish pretence of power to work miracles will be revived and will very much amuse and deceive the world. (3.) The field of battle — a place called *Armageddon;* that is, say some, the mount of Megiddo, near to which, by a stream issuing thence, Barak overcame Sisera, and all the kings in alliance with him, Judges 5:19. And in the valley of Megiddo Josiah was slain. This place had been famous for two events of a very different nature, the former very happy for the church of God, the latter very unhappy; but it shall now be the field of the last battle in which the church shall be engaged, and she shall be victorious. This battle required time to prepare for it, and therefore the further account of it is suspended till we come to the nineteenth chapter, *v.* 19, 20. (4.) The warning which God gives of this great and decisive trial, to engage his people to prepare for it, *v.* 15. It would be sudden and unexpected, and therefore Christians should be clothed, and armed, and ready for it, that they might not be surprised and ashamed. When God's cause comes to be tried, and his battles to be fought, all his people shall be ready to stand up for his interest and be faithful and valiant in his service.

Verses 17–21

Here we have an account of the seventh and last angel pouring forth his vial, contributing his part towards the accomplishment of the downfall of Babylon, which was the finishing stroke. And here, as before, observe,

I. Where this plague fell — *on the air,* upon the prince of the power of the air, that is, the devil. His powers were restrained, his policies confounded; he was bound in God's chain: the sword of God was upon his eye and upon his arm; for he, as well as the powers of the earth, is subject to the almighty power of God. He had used all possible means to preserve the antichristian interest, and to prevent the fall of Babylon — all the influence that he has upon the minds of men, blinding their judgments and perverting them, hardening their hearts, raising their enmity to the gospel as high as could be. But now here is a vial poured out upon his kingdom, and he is not able to support his tottering cause and interest any longer.

II. What it produced, 1. A thankful voice from heaven, pronouncing that now the work was done. The church triumphant in heaven saw it, and rejoiced; the church militant on earth saw it, and became triumphant. It is finished. 2. A mighty commotion on the earth — an earthquake, so great as never was before, shaking the very centre, and this ushered in by the usual concomitants of thunder and lightnings. 3. The fall of Babylon, which was divided into three parts, *called the cities of the nations* (*v.* 19); having had rule over the nations, and taken in the idolatry of the nations, incorporating into her religion something of the Jewish, something of the pagan, and something of the Christian religion, she was as three cities in one. God now remembered this great and wicked city. Though for some time he seemed to have forgotten her idolatry and cruelty, yet now he gives unto her *the cup of the wine of the fierceness of his wrath.* And this downfall extended further than to the seat of antichrist; it reached from the centre to the circumference; and every island and every mountain, that seemed by nature and situation the most secured, were carried away in the deluge of this ruin.

III. How the antichristian party were affected with it. Though it fell upon them as a dreadful storm, as if the stones of the city, tossed up into the air, came down upon their heads, like hailstones of a talent weight each, yet they were so far from repenting that they blasphemed that God who thus punished them. Here was a dreadful plague of the heart, a spiritual judgment more dreadful and destructive than all the rest. Observe, 1. The greatest calamities that can befal men will not bring them to repentance without the grace of God working with them. 2. Those that are not made better by the judgments of God are always the worse for them. 3. To be hardened in sin and enmity against God by his righteous judgments is a certain token of utter destruction.

CHAPTER 17

This chapter contains another representation of those things that had been revealed before concerning the wickedness and ruin of antichrist. This antichrist had been before represented as a beast, and is now described as a great whore. And here, I. The apostle is invited to see this vile woman (*v.* 1, 2). II. He tells us what an appearance she made (*v.* 3–6). III. The mystery of it is explained to him (*v.* 7–12). And, IV. Her ruin foretold (*v.* 13, etc.).

Verses 1–6

Here we have a new vision, not as to the matter of it, for that is contemporary with what came under the three last vials; but as to the manner of description, etc. Observe, 1. The invitation given to the apostle to take a view of what was here to be represented: *Come hither, and I will show thee the judgment of the great whore,* etc., *v.* 1. This is a name of great infamy. A whore [in this passage] is one that is married, and has been false to her husband's bed, has forsaken the guide of her youth, and broken the covenant of God. She had been a prostitute to the kings of the earth, whom she had intoxicated *with the wine of her fornication.* 2. The appearance she made: it was gay and gaudy, like such sort of creatures: *She was arrayed in purple, and scarlet colour, and decked with gold, and precious stones, and pearls, v.* 4. Here were all the allurements of worldly honour and riches, pomp and pride, suited to sensual and worldly minds. 3. Her principal seat and residence — *upon the beast that had seven heads and ten horns;* that is to say, Rome, the city on seven hills, infamous for idolatry, tyranny, and blasphemy. 4. Her name, which *was written on her forehead.* It was the custom of impudent harlots to hang out signs, with their names, that all might know what they were. Now in this observe, (1.) She is named from her place of residence — *Babylon the great.* But, that we might not take it for the old Babylon literally so called, we are told there is a mystery in the name; it is some other great city resembling the old Babylon. (2.) She is named from her infamous way and practice; not only a harlot, but a mother of harlots, breeding up harlots, and nursing and training them up to idolatry, and all sorts of lewdness and wickedness — the parent and nurse of all false religion and filthy conversation. 5. Her diet: she satiated herself with *the blood of the saints and martyrs of Jesus.* She drank their blood with such greediness that she intoxicated herself with it; it was so pleasant to her that she could not tell when she had had enough of it: she was satiated, but never satisfied.

Verses 7–13

Here we have the mystery of this vision explained. The apostle wonders at the sight of this woman: the angel undertakes to open this vision to him, it being the key of the former visions; and he tells the apostle what was meant by the beast on which the woman sat; but it is so explained as still to need further explanation. 1. This beast *was, and is not, and yet is;* that is, it *was* a seat of idolatry and persecution; *and is not,* that is, not in the ancient form, which was pagan; *and yet it is,* it is truly the seat of idolatry and tyranny, though of another sort and form. *It ascends out of the bottomless pit* (idolatry and cruelty are the issue and product of hell), and it shall return thither and go into perdition. 2. *This beast has seven heads,* which have a double signification. (1.) *Seven mountains* — the seven hills on which Rome stands; and (2.) *Seven kings* — seven sorts of government. Rome was governed by kings, consuls, tribunes, decemviri, dictators, emperors who were pagan, and emperors who were Christian. Five of these were extinct when this prophecy was written; one was then in being, that is, the pagan emperor; and the other, that is, the Christian emperor, was yet to come, *v.* 10. This beast, the papacy, makes an eighth governor, and sets up idolatry again. 3. This beast had ten horns; which are said to be *ten kings which have as yet received no kingdoms; as yet,* that is, as some, shall not rise up till the Roman empire be broken in pieces; or, as others, shall not rise up till near the end of antichrist's reign, and so shall reign but as it were *one hour with her,* but shall for that time be very unanimous and very zealous in that interest, and entirely devoted to it, divesting themselves of their prerogatives and revenues (things so dear to princes), out of an unaccountable fondness for the papacy.

Verses 14–18

Here we have some account of the downfall of Babylon, to be more fully described in the following chapter.

I. Here is a war begun between the beast and his followers, and the Lamb and his followers. The beast and his army, to an eye of sense, appear much stronger than the Lamb and his army: one would think an army with a lamb at the head of them could not stand before *the great red dragon.* But,

II. Here is a victory gained by the Lamb: *The Lamb shall overcome.* Christ must reign till all enemies *be put under his feet;* he will be sure to meet with many enemies, and much opposition, but he will also be sure to gain the victory.

III. Here is the ground or reason of the victory assigned; and this is taken, 1. From the character of the Lamb: *He is King of kings and Lord of lords.* He has, both by nature and by office, supreme dominion and power over all things; all the powers of earth and hell are subject to his check and control. 2. From the character of his followers: *They are called, and chosen, and faithful.* They are called out by commission to this warfare; they are chosen and fitted for it, and they will be faithful in it. Such an army, under such a commander, will at length carry all the world before them.

IV. The victory is justly aggrandized. 1. By the vast multitude who paid obedience and subjection to the beast and to the whore. She sat upon (that is, presided over) many waters; and these waters were so many multitudes of people, and nations, of all languages; yea, she reigned not only over kingdoms, but over the kings, and they were her tributaries and vassals, *v.* 15, 18. 2. By the powerful influence which God hereby showed he had over the minds of great men. Their hearts were in his hand, and he turned them as he pleased; for, (1.) It was of God, and to fulfil his will, that these kings *agreed to give their kingdom unto the beast;* they were judicially blinded and hardened to do so. And, (2.) It was of God that afterwards their hearts were turned against the whore, to hate her, and to *make her desolate and naked, and to eat her flesh, and burn her with fire;* they shall at length see their folly, and how they have been bewitched and enslaved by the papacy, and, out of a just resentment, shall not only fall off from Rome, but shall be made the instruments of God's providence in her destruction.

CHAPTER 18

We have here, I. An angel proclaiming the fall of Babylon (*v.* 1, 2). II. Assigning the reasons of her fall (*v.* 3). III. Giving warning to all who belonged to God to come out of her (*v.* 4, 5), and to assist in her destruction (*v.* 6–8). IV. The great lamentation made for her by those who had been large sharers in her sinful pleasures and profits (*v.* 9–19). V. The great joy that there would be among others at the sight of her irrecoverable ruin (*v.* 20, etc.).

Verses 1–8

The downfall and destruction of Babylon form an event so fully determined in the counsels of God, and of such consequence to his interests and glory, that the visions and predictions concerning it are repeated. 1. Here is another angel sent from heaven, attended with great power and lustre, *v.* 1. He had not only light in himself, to discern the truth of his own prediction, but to inform and enlighten the world about that great event; and not only light to discern it, but power to accomplish it. 2. This angel publishes the fall of Babylon, as a thing already come to pass; and this he does with a mighty strong voice, that all might hear the cry, and might see how well this angel was pleased to be the messenger of such tidings. Here seems to be an allusion to the prediction of the fall of pagan Babylon (Isa. 21:9), where the word is repeated as it is here: *has fallen, has fallen.* Some have thought a double fall is hereby intended, first her apostasy, and then her ruin; and they think the words immediately following favour their opinion; *She has become the habitation of devils, and the hold of every foul spirit, and the cage of every unclean and hateful bird, v.* 2. But this is also borrowed from Isa. 21:9, and seems to describe not so much her sin of entertaining idols (which are truly called *devils*) as her punishment, it being a common notion that unclean spirits, as well as ominous and hateful birds, used to haunt a city or house that lay in its ruins. 3. The reason of this ruin is declared (*v.* 3); for, though God is not obliged to give any account of his matters, yet he is pleased to do so, especially in those dispensations of providence that are most awful and tremendous. The wickedness of Babylon had been very great; for she ha not only forsaken the true God herself, and set up idols, bu had with great art and industry drawn all sorts of men int the spiritual adultery, and by her wealth and luxury had r tained them in her interest. 4. Fair warning is given to a that expect mercy from God, that they should not only *cor out of her,* but be assisting in her destruction, *v.* 4, 5. He observe, (1.) God may have a people even in Babylon, so who belong to the election of grace. (2.) God's people sh be called out of Babylon, and called effectually. (3.) Those that are resolved to partake with wicked men in their sins must receive of their plagues. (4.) When the sins of a people reach up to heaven, the wrath of God will reach down to the earth. (5.) Though private revenge is forbidden, yet God will have his people act under him, when called to it, in pulling down his and their inveterate and implacable enemies, *v.* 6. (6.) God will proportion the punishment of sinners to the measure of their wickedness, pride, and security, *v.* 7. (7.) When destruction comes on a people suddenly, the surprise is a great aggravation of their misery, *v.* 8.

Verses 9–24

Here we have,

I. A doleful lamentation made by Babylon's friends for her fall; and here observe,

1. Who are the mourners, namely, those who had been bewitched by her fornication, those who had been sharers in her sensual pleasures, and those who had been gainers by her wealth and trade — the kings and the merchants of the earth: *the kings of the earth,* whom she had flattered into idolatry by allowing them to be arbitrary and tyrannical over their subjects, while they were obsequious to her; and *the merchants,* that is, those who trafficked with her for indulgences, pardons, dispensations, and preferments; these will mourn, because by *this craft they got their wealth.*

2. What was the manner of their mourning. (1.) They stood afar off, they durst not come nigh her. Even Babylon's friends will stand at a distance from her fall. Though they had been partakers with her in her sins, and in her sinful pleasures and profits, they were not willing to bear a share in her plagues. (2.) They made a grievous outcry: *Alas! alas! that great city, Babylon, that mighty city!* (3.) They wept, and *cast dust upon their heads, v.* 19. The pleasures of sin are but for a season, and they will end in dismal sorrow. All those who rejoice in the success of the church's enemies will share with them in their downfall; and those who have most indulged themselves in pride and pleasure are the least able to bear calamities; their sorrows will be as excessive as their pleasure and jollity were before.

3. What was the cause of their mourning; not their sin, but their punishment. They did not lament their fall into idolatry, and luxury, and persecution, but their fall into ruin — the loss of their traffic and of their wealth and power. The spirit of antichrist is a worldly spirit, and their sorrow is a mere worldly sorrow; they did not lament for the anger of God, that had now fallen upon them, but for the loss of their outward comfort. We have a large schedule and inventory of the wealth and merchandise of this city, all which was suddenly lost (*v.* 12, 13), and lost irrecoverably (*v.* 14): *All things which were dainty and goodly had departed from thee, and thou shalt find them no more at all.* The church of God may fall for a time, but she shall rise again; but the fall of Babylon will be an utter overthrow, like that of Sodom and Gomorrah. Godly sorrow is some support under affliction, but mere worldly sorrow adds to the calamity.

II. An account of the joy and triumph there was both in heaven and earth at the irrecoverable fall of Babylon: while her own people were bewailing her, the servants of God were called to *rejoice over her, v.* 20. Here observe, 1. How universal this joy would be: heaven and earth, angels and saints, would join in it; that which is matter of rejoicing to the servants of God in this world is matter of rejoicing to the angels in heaven. 2. How just and reasonable; and that, (1.) Because the fall of Babylon was an act of God's vindictive justice. God was then avenging his people's cause. They had committed their cause to him *to whom vengeance belongs,* and now the day of recompence had come for the controversies of Zion; though they did not take pleasure in the miseries of any, they had reason to rejoice in the discoveries of the glorious justice of God. (2.) Because it was an irrecoverable ruin. The enemy should never molest them any more, and of this they were assured by a remarkable token (*v.* 21): An *angel from heaven took up a stone like a great millstone, and cast it into the sea, saying, "Thus shall Babylon be thrown down with violence, and be found no more at all;* the place shall no longer habitable by man, no work shall be done there, no fruit enjoyed, no light seen there, but utter darkness and desolation, as the reward of her great wickedness, first *deceiving the nations with her sorceries,* and secondly in persecuting and murdering those whom she could not deceive.* Such abominable sins deserved so great a ruin.

CHAPTER 19

In this chapter we have, I. A further account of the triumphant song of angels and saints for the fall of Babylon (*v.* 1–4). II. The marriage between Christ and the church proclaimed and perfected (*v.* 5–10). III. Another warlike expedition of the glorious head and husband of the church, with the success of it (*v.* 10, etc.).

Verses 1–4

The fall of Babylon being fixed, finished, and declared to be irrecoverable in the foregoing chapter, this begins with a holy triumph over her, in pursuance of the order given forth: *Rejoice over her, thou heaven, and you holy apostles and prophets, ch.* 18:20. They now gladly answer the call; and here you have, 1. The form of their thanksgiving, in that heavenly and most comprehensive word, *Alleluia, praise you the Lord:* with this they begin, with this they go on, and with this they end (*v.* 4); their prayers are now turned into praises, their hosannas end in halleluias. 2. The matter of their thanksgiving: they praise him for the truth of his word, and the righteousness of his providential conduct, especially in this great event — the ruin of Babylon, which had been a mother, nurse, and nest of idolatry, lewdness, and cruelty (*v.* 2), for which signal example of divine justice they ascribe *salvation, and glory, and honour, and power, unto our God.* 3. The effect of these their praises: when the angels and saints cried *Alleluia,* her fire burned more fiercely and *her smoke ascended for ever and ever, v.* 3. The surest way to have our deliverances continued and completed is to give God the glory of what he has done for us. Praising God for what we have is praying in the most effectual manner for what is yet further to be done for us; the praises of the saints blow up the fire of God's wrath against the common enemy. 4. The blessed harmony between the angels and the saints in this triumphant song, *v.* 4. The churches and their ministers take the melodious sound from the angels, and repeat it; falling down, and worshipping God, they cry, *Amen, Alleluia.*

Verses 5–10

The triumphant song being ended, and epithalamium, or marriage-song, begins, *v.* 6. Here observe,

I. The concert of heavenly music. The chorus was large and loud, *as the voice of many waters and of mighty thunderings.* God is fearful in praises. There is no discord in heaven; the morning stars sing together; no jarring string, nor key untuned, but pure and perfect melody.

II. The occasion of this song; and that is the reign and dominion of that omnipotent God who has *redeemed his church by his own blood,* and is now in a more public manner betrothing her to himself: *The marriage of the Lamb has come, v.* 7. Some think this refers to the conversion of the Jews, which they suppose will succeed the fall of Babylon; others, to the general resurrection: the former seems more probable. Now, 1. You have here a description of the bride, how she appeared; not in the gay and gaudy dress of the mother of harlots, but *in fine linen, clean and white, which is the righteousness of saints;* in the robes of Christ's righteousness, both imputed for justification and imparted for sanctification — the *stola,* the *white robe* of absolution, adoption, and enfranchisement, and the white robe of purity and universal holiness. She had *washed her robes and made them white in the blood of the Lamb;* and these her nuptial ornaments she did not purchase by any price of her own, but received them as the gift and grant of her blessed Lord. 2. The marriage-feast, which, though not particularly described (as Mt. 22:4), yet is declared to be such as would make all those happy who were called to it, so called as to accept the invitation, a feast made up of the promises of the gospel, *the true sayings of God, v.* 9. These promises, opened, applied, sealed, and earnested by *the Spirit of God,* in holy eucharistical ordinances, are the marriage-feast; and the whole collective body of all those who partake of this feast is the bride, *the Lamb's wife;* they eat into one body, and drink into one Spirit, and are not mere spectators or guests, but coalesce into the espoused party, the mystical body of Christ. 3. The transport of joy which the apostle felt in himself at this vision. *He fell down at the feet of the angel, to worship him,* supposing him to be more than a creature, or having his thoughts at the present overpowered by the vehemency of his affections. Here observe, (1.) What honour he offered to the angel: *He fell at his feet, to worship him;* this prostration was a part of external worship, it was a posture of proper adoration. (2.) How the angel refused it, and this was with

some resentment: *"See thou do it not;* have a care what thou doest, thou art doing a wrong thing." (3.) He gave a very good reason for his refusal: *"I am thy fellow-servant, and of thy brethren which have the testimony of Jesus —* I am a creature, thine equal in office, though not in nature; *I,* as an angel and messenger of God, *have the testimony of Jesus,* a charge to be a witness for him and to testify concerning him, and thou, as an apostle, having *the Spirit of prophecy,* hast the same testimony to give in; and therefore we are in this brethren and fellow-servants." (4.) He directs him to the true and only object of religious worship; namely, God: *"Worship God, and him alone."* This fully condemns both the practice of the papists in worshipping the elements of bread and wine, and saints, and angels, and the practice of those Socinians and Arians who do not believe that Christ is truly and by nature God, and yet pay him religious worship; and this shows what wretched fig-leaves all their evasions and excuses are which they offer in their own vindication: they stand hereby convicted of idolatry by a messenger from heaven.

Verses 11–21

No sooner was the marriage solemnized between Christ and his church by the conversion of the Jews than the glorious head and husband of the church is called out to a new expedition, which seems to be the great battle that was to be fought at Armageddon, foretold *ch.* 16:16. And here observe,

I. The description of the great Commander, 1. By the seat of his empire; and that is *heaven;* his throne is there, and his power and authority are heavenly and divine. 2. His equipage: he is again described as sitting *on a white horse,* to show the equity of the cause, and certainty of success. 3. His attributes: he is *faithful and true* to his covenant and promise, he is righteous in all his judicial and military proceedings, he has a penetrating insight into all the strength and stratagems of his enemies, he has a large and extensive dominion, many crowns, for he is *King of kings, and Lord of lords.* 4. His armour; and that is *a vesture dipped in blood,* either his own blood, by which he purchased this mediatorial power, or the blood of his enemies, over whom he has always prevailed. 5. His name: *The Word of God,* a name that none fully knows but himself, only this we know, that this *Word was God manifest in the flesh;* but his perfections are incomprehensible by any creature.

II. The army which he commands (*v.* 14), a very large one, made up of many armies; angels and saints followed his conduct, and resembled him in their equipage, and in their armour of purity and righteousness — chosen, and called, and faithful.

III. The weapons of his warfare — *A sharp sword* proceeding from *his mouth* (*v.* 15), with which *he smites the nations,* either the threatenings of the written word, which now he is going to execute, or rather his word of command calling on his followers to take a just revenge on his and their enemies, who are now put into the wine-press of the wrath of God, to be trodden under foot by him.

IV. The ensigns of his authority, his coat of arms — *a name written on his vesture and thigh, King of kings, and Lord of lords,* asserting his authority and power, and the cause of the quarrel, *v.* 16.

V. An invitation given *to the fowls of heaven,* that they should come and see the battle, and share in the spoil and pillage of the field (*v.* 17, 18), intimating that this great decisive engagement should leave the enemies of the church a feast for the birds of prey, and that all the world should have cause to rejoice in the issue of it.

VI. The battle joined. The enemy falls on with great fury, headed by *the beast, and the kings of the earth;* the powers of earth and hell gathered, to make their utmost effort, *v.* 19.

VII. The victory gained by the great and glorious head of the church: *The beast and the false prophet,* the leaders of the army, are taken prisoners, but he who led them by power and he who led them by policy and falsehood; these are taken and *cast into the burning lake,* made incapable of molesting the church of God any more; and their followers, whether officers or common soldiers, are given up to military execution, and made a feast for *the fowls of heaven.* Though the divine vengeance will chiefly fall upon *the beast, and the false prophet,* yet it will be no excuse to those who fight under their banner that they only followed their leaders and obeyed their command; since they would fight for them, they must fall and perish with them. *Be wise now there-*

fore, O you kings, be instructed, you rulers of the earth; kiss the Son, lest he be angry, and you perish from the way, Ps. 2:10, 12.

CHAPTER 20

This chapter is thought by some to be the darkest part of all this prophecy: it is very probable that the things contained in it are not yet accomplished; and therefore it is the wiser way to content ourselves with general observations, rather than to be positive and particular in our explications of it. Here we have an account, I. Of the binding of Satan for a thousand years (*v.* 1–3). II. The reign of the saints with Christ for the same time (*v.* 4–6). III. Of the loosing of Satan, and the conflict of the church with Gog and Magog (*v.* 7–10). IV. Of the day of judgment (*v.* 11, etc.).

Verses 1–10

We have here, I. A prophecy of *the binding of Satan* for a certain term of time, in which he should have much less power and the church much more peace than before. The power of Satan was broken in part by the setting up of the gospel kingdom in the world; it was further reduced by the empire's becoming Christian; it was yet further broken by the downfall of the mystical Babylon; but still this serpent had many heads, and, when one is wounded, another has life remaining in it. Here we have a further limitation and diminution of his power. Observe, 1. To whom this work of binding Satan is committed — to *an angel from heaven.* It is very probable that this angel is no other than the Lord Jesus Christ; the description of him will hardly agree with any other. He is one who has power to *bind the strong man armed, to cast him out, and to spoil his goods;* and therefore must be stronger than he. 2. The means he makes use of in this work: he has a *chain* and a *key, a great chain* to bind Satan, and *the key of the* prison in which he was to be confined. Christ never wants proper powers and instruments to break the power of Satan, for he has the powers of heaven and the keys of hell. 3. The execution of this work, *v.* 2, 3. (1.) *He laid hold on the dragon, that old serpent, which is the devil, and Satan.* Neither the strength of the dragon, nor the subtlety of the serpent, was sufficient to rescue him out of the hands of Christ; he caught hold, and kept his hold. And, (2.) He *cast him into the bottomless pit,* cast him down with force, and with a just vengeance, to his own place and prison, from which he had been permitted to break out, and disturb the churches, and deceive the nations; now he is brought back to that prison, and there laid in chains. (3.) He is *shut up, and a seal set upon him.* Christ shuts, and none can open; he shuts by his power, seals by his authority; and his lock and seal even the devils themselves cannot break open. (4.) We have the term of this confinement of Satan — *a thousand years,* after which he was to *be loosed* again for *a little season.* The church should have a considerable time of peace and prosperity, but all her trials were not yet over.

II. An account of the reign of the saints for the same space of time in which Satan continued bound (*v.* 4–6), and here observe,

1. Who those were that received such honour — those who had suffered for Christ, and all who had faithfully adhered to him, not receiving the mark of the beast, nor worshiping his image; all who had kept themselves clear of pagan and papal idolatry.

2. The honour bestowed upon them. (1.) They were raised from the dead, and restored to life. This may be taken either literally or figuratively; they were in a civil and political sense dead, and had a political resurrection; their liberties and privileges were revived and restored. (2.) *Thrones,* and power of *judgment, were given to them;* they were possessed of great honour, and interest, and authority, I suppose rather of a spiritual than of a secular nature. (3.) *They reigned with Christ a thousand years.* Those who suffer with Christ shall reign with Christ; they shall reign with him in his spiritual and heavenly kingdom, in a glorious conformity to him in wisdom, righteousness, and holiness, beyond what had been known before in the world. This is called *the first resurrection,* which none but those who have served Christ and suffered for him shall be favoured with. As for the wicked, they shall not be raised up and restored to their power again, till Satan be let loose; this may be called a resurrection, as the conversion of the Jews is said to be *life from the dead.*

3. The happiness of these servants of God is declared. (1.) They are *blessed and holy, v.* 6. None can be blessed but those that are holy; and all that are holy shall be blessed. These were holy as a sort of first-fruits to God in this spiritual resurrection, and as such blessed by him. (2.) They are secured from the power of the second death. We know something of what the first death is, and it is awful; but we know not what this second death is. It must be much more dreadful; it is the death of the soul, eternal separation from God. The Lord grant we may never know what it is by experience. Those who have had experience of a spiritual resurrection are saved from the power of the second death.

III. An account of the return of the church's troubles, and another mighty conflict, very sharp, but short and decisive. Observe, 1. The restraints laid for a long time on Satan are at length taken off. While this world lasts, Satan's power in it will not be wholly destroyed; it may be limited and lessened, but he will have something still to do for the disturbance of the people of God. 2. No sooner is Satan let loose than he falls to his old work, *deceiving the nations,* and so stirring them up to make a war with the saints and servants of God, which they would never do if he had not first deceived them. They are deceived both as to the cause they engage in (they believe it to be a good cause when it is indeed a very bad one), and as to the issue: they expect to be successful, but are sure to lose the day. 3. His last efforts seem to be the greatest. The power now permitted to him seems to be more unlimited than before. He had now liberty to beat up for his volunteers in all *the four quarters of the earth,* and he raised a mighty army, the number of which was *as the sand of the sea, v.* 8. 4. We have the names of the principal commanders in this army under the dragon — *Gog and Magog.* We need not be too inquisitive as to what particular powers are meant by these names, since the army was gathered from all parts of the world. These names are found in other parts of scripture. *Magog* we read of in Gen. 10:2. He was one of the sons of Japheth, and peopled the country called *Syria,* from which his descendants spread into many other parts. Of *Gog and Magog* together we only read in Eze. 38:2, a prophecy whence this in Revelation borrows many of its images. 5. We have the march and military disposition of this formidable army (*v.* 9.): *They went up on the breadth of the earth, and compassed the camp of the saints about, and the beloved city,* that is, the spiritual Jerusalem, in which the most precious interests of the people of God are lodged, and therefore to them a beloved city. The army of the saints is described as drawn forth out of the city, and lying under the walls of it, to defend it; they were encamped about Jerusalem: but the army of the enemy was so much superior to that of the church that they compassed them and their city about. 6. You have an account of the battle, and the issue of this war: *Fire came down from God out of heaven, and devoured the enemy.* Thus the ruin of *Gog and Magog* is foretold (Eze. 38:22), *I will rain upon him and upon his bands an overflowing rain, and great hailstones, and fire and brimstone.* God would, in an extraordinary and more immediate manner, fight this last and decisive battle for his people, that the victory might be complete and the glory redound to himself. 7. The doom and punishment of the grand enemy, *the devil:* he is now cast into hell, with his two great officers, *the beast and the false prophet,* tyranny and idolatry, and that not for any term of time, but to be there *tormented night and day, for ever and ever.*

Verses 11–15

The utter destruction of the devil's kingdom very properly leads to an account of the day of judgment, which will determine every man's everlasting state; and we may be assured there will be a judgment when we see *the prince of this world is judged,* Jn. 16:11. This will be a great day, *the great day, when all shall appear before the judgment-seat of Christ.* The Lord help us firmly to believe this doctrine of the judgment to come. It is a doctrine that made Felix tremble. Here we have a description of it, where observe, 1. We behold *the throne,* and tribunal of judgment, *great* and *white,* very glorious and perfectly just and righteous. *The throne of iniquity, that establishes wickedness by a law,* has no fellowship with this righteous throne and tribunal. 2. The appearance of the Judge, and that is the Lord Jesus Christ, who then puts on such majesty and terror that *the earth and the heaven flee from his face, and there is no place found for them;* there is a dissolution of the whole frame of nature, 2 Pt. 3:10. 3. The persons to be judged (*v.* 12): *The dead, small and great;* that is, young and old, low and high, poor and rich. None are so mean but they have some talents to account for, and none so great as to avoid the jurisdiction of this court; not only those that are found alive at the coming of Christ, but all who have died before; the grave shall surrender the bodies of men, hell shall surrender the souls of the wicked, the sea shall surrender the many who seemed to have been lost in it. 4. The rule of judgment settled: *The books were opened.* What books? The books of God's omniscience, who is greater than our consciences, and knows all things (there is a book of remembrance with him both for good and bad); and the book of the sinner's conscience, which, though formerly secret, will now be opened. *And another book* shall be *opened* — the book of the scriptures, the statute-book of heaven, the rule of life. This book is opened as containing the law, the touchstone by which the hearts and lives of men are to be tried. This book determines matter of right; the other books give evidence of matters of fact. Some, by *the other book,* called *the book of life,* understand the book of God's eternal counsels; but that does not seem to belong to the affair of judgment: in eternal election God does not act judicially, but with absolute sovereign freedom. 5. The cause to be tried; and that is, *the works of men,* what they have done and whether it be good or evil. *By their works men shall be justified or condemned;* for though God knows their state and their principles, and looks chiefly at these, yet, being to approve himself to angels and men as a righteous God, he will try their principles by their practices, and so will *be justified when he speaks and clear when he judges.* 6. The issue of the trial and judgment; and this will be according to the evidence of fact, and rule of judgment. All those who have *made a covenant with death,* and an *agreement with hell,* shall then be condemned with their infernal confederates, cast with them into the lake of fire, as not being entitled to eternal life, according to the rules of life laid down in the scripture; but those whose names are written in that book (that is, those that are justified and acquitted by the gospel) shall then be justified and acquitted by the Judge, and shall enter into eternal life, having nothing more to fear from death, or hell, or wicked men; for these are all destroyed together. Let it be our great concern to see on what terms we stand with our Bibles, whether they justify us or condemn us now; for the Judge of all will proceed by that rule. *Christ shall judge the secrets of all men according to the gospel.* Happy are those who have so ordered and stated their cause according to the gospel as to know beforehand that they shall be justified in the great day of the Lord!

CHAPTER 21

Hitherto the prophecy of this book has presented to us a very remarkable mixture of light and shade, prosperity and adversity, mercy and judgment, in the conduct of divine Providence towards the church in the world: now, at the close of all, the day breaks, and the shadows flee away; a new world now appears, the former having passed away. Some are willing to understand all that is said in these last two chapters of the state of the church even here on earth, in the glory of the latter days; but others, more probably, take it as a representation of the perfect and triumphant state of the church in heaven. Let but the faithful saints and servants of God wait awhile, and they shall not only see, but enjoy, the perfect holiness and happiness of that world. In this chapter you have, I. An introduction to the vision of the new Jerusalem (*v.* 1–9). II. The vision itself (*v.* 10, etc.)

Verses 1–8

We have here a more general account of the happiness of the church of God in the future state, by which it seems most safe to understand the heavenly state.

I. A new world now opens to our view (*v.* 1): *I saw a new heaven and a new earth;* that is, a new universe; for we suppose the world to be made up of heaven and earth. By the new earth we may understand a new state for the bodies of men, as well as a heaven for their souls. This world is not now newly created, but newly opened, and filled with all those who were the heirs of it. The new heaven and the new earth will not then be distinct; the very earth of the saints, their glorified bodies, will now be spiritual and heavenly, and suited to those pure and bright mansions. To make way for the commencement of this new world, the old world, with all its troubles and commotions, *passed away.*

II. In this new world the apostle *saw the holy city, the new Jerusalem, coming down from heaven,* not locally, but as to its original: this new Jerusalem is the church of God in its new and perfect state, *prepared as a bride adorned for her husband,* beautified with all perfection of wisdom and holiness, meet for the full fruition of the Lord Jesus Christ in glory.

III. The blessed presence of God with his people is here proclaimed and admired: *I heard a great voice out of heav-*

en, saying, Behold, the tabernacle of God is with men, etc. *v.* 3. Observe, 1. The presence of God with his church is the glory of the church. 2. It is matter of wonder that a holy God should ever dwell with any of the children of men. 3. The presence of God with his people in heaven will not be interrupted as it is on earth, but he will dwell with them continually. 4. The covenant, interest, and relation, that there are now between God and his people, will be filled up and perfected in heaven. *They shall be his people;* their souls shall be assimilated to him, filled with all the love, honour, and delight in God which their relation to him requires, and this will constitute their perfect holiness; and he will be their God: *God himself will be their God;* his immediate presence with them, his love fully manifested to them, and his glory put upon them, will be their perfect happiness; then he will fully answer the character of the relation on his part, as they shall do on their part.

IV. This new and blessed state will be free from all trouble and sorrow; for, 1. All the effects of former trouble shall be done away. They have been often before in tears, by reason of sin, of affliction, of the calamities of the church; but now *all tears shall be wiped away;* no signs, no remembrance of former sorrows shall remain, any further than to make their present felicity the greater. God himself, as their tender Father, with his own kind hand, *shall wipe away the tears* of his children; and they would not have been without those tears when God shall come and wipe them away. 2. All the causes of future sorrow shall be for ever removed: *There shall be neither death nor pain;* and therefore *no sorrow nor crying;* these are things incident to that state in which they were before, but now all *former things have passed away.*

V. The truth and certainty of this blessed state are ratified by the word and promise of God, and ordered to be committed to writing, as matter of perpetual record, *v.* 5, 6. The subject-matter of this vision is so great, and of such great importance to the church and people of God, that they have need of the fullest assurances of it; and God therefore from heaven repeats and ratifies the truth thereof. Besides, many ages must pass between the time when this vision was given forth and the accomplishment of it, and many great trials must intervene; and therefore God would have it committed to writing, for perpetual memory, and continual use to his people. Observe, 1. The certainty of the promise averred: *These words are faithful and true;* and it follows, *It is done,* is as sure as if it were done already. We may and ought to take God's promise as present payment; if he has said that he *makes all things new, it is done.* 2. He gives us his titles of honour as a pledge or surety of the full performance, even those titles of *Alpha and Omega, the beginning and the end.* As it was his glory that he gave the rise and beginning to the world and to his church, it will be his glory to finish the work begin, and not to leave it imperfect. As his power and will were the first cause of all things, his pleasure and glory are the last end, and he will not lose his design; for then he would no longer be the *Alpha and Omega.* Men may begin designs which they can never bring to perfection; but *the counsel of God shall stand,* and he will do all his pleasure. 3. The desires of his people towards this blessed state furnish another evidence of the truth and certainty of it. They thirst after a state of sinless perfection and the uninterrupted enjoyment of God, and God has wrought in them these longing desires, which cannot be satisfied with any thing else, and therefore would be the torment of the soul if they were disappointed but it would be inconsistent with the goodness of God, and his love to his people, to create in them holy and heavenly desires, and then deny them their proper satisfaction; and therefore they may be assured that, when they have overcome their present difficulties, *he will give them of the fountain of the water of life freely.*

VI. The greatness of this future felicity is declared and illustrated, 1. By the freeness of it — it is the free gift of God: *He gives of the water of life freely;* this will not make it less but more grateful to his people. 2. The fulness of it. The people of God then lie at the fountain-head of all blessedness: they *inherit all things* (*v.* 7); enjoying God, they enjoy all things. He is all in all. 3. By the tenure and title by which they enjoy this blessedness — by right of inheritance, as *the sons of God,* a title of all others the most honourable, as resulting from so near and endeared a relation to God himself, and the most sure and indefeasible, that can no more cease than the relation from which it results. 4. By the vastly different state of the wicked. Their misery helps to illustrate the glory and blessedness of the saints, and the distinguishing goodness of God towards them, *v.* 8. Here observe, (1.) The sins of those who perish, among which are first mentioned their cowardliness and unbelief. *The fearful* lead the van in this black list. They durst not encounter the difficulties of religion, and their slavish fear proceeded from their unbelief; but those who were so dastardly as not to dare to take up the cross of Christ, and discharge their duty to him, were yet so desperate as to run into all manner of abominable wickedness — *murder, adultery, sorcery, idolatry,* and *lying.* (2.) Their punishment: *They have their part in the lake that burns with fire and brimstone, which is the second death.* [1.] They could not burn at a stake for Christ, but they must burn in hell for sin. [2.] They must die another death after their natural death; the agonies and terrors of the first death will consign them over to the far greater terrors and agonies of eternal death, to die and to be always dying. [3.] This misery will be their proper part and portion, what they have justly deserved, what they have in effect chosen, and what they have prepared themselves for by their sins. Thus the misery of the damned will illustrate the blessedness of those that are saved, and the blessedness of the saved will aggravate the misery of those that are damned.

Verses 9–27

We have already considered the introduction to the vision of the new Jerusalem in a more general idea of the heavenly state; we now come to the vision itself, where observe,

I. The person that opened the vision to the apostle — *one of the seven angels, that had the seven vials full of the seven last plagues, v.* 9. God has a variety of work and employment for his holy angels. Sometimes they are to sound the trumpet of divine Providence, and give fair warning to a careless world; sometimes they are to pour out the vials of God's anger upon impenitent sinners; and sometimes to discover things of a heavenly nature to those that are *the heirs of salvation.* They readily execute every commission they receive from God; and, when this world shall be at an end, yet the angels shall be employed by the great God in proper pleasant work to all eternity.

II. The place from which the apostle had this glorious view and prospect. He was taken, in ecstasy, into *a high mountain.* From such situations men usually have the most distinct views of adjacent cities. Those who would have clear views of heaven must get as near heaven as they can, into the mount of vision, the mount of meditation and faith, whence, as from the top of Pisgah, they may behold the goodly land of the heavenly Canaan.

III. The subject-matter of the vision — *the bride, the Lamb's wife* (*v.* 10); that is, the church of God in her glorious, perfect, triumphant state, under the resemblance of Jerusalem, having the glory of God shining in its lustre, as *uxor splendit radiis mariti — the bride comely through the comeliness put on her by her husband;* glorious in her relation to Christ, in his image now perfected in her, and in his favour shining upon her. And now we have a large description of the church triumphant under the emblem of a city, far exceeding in riches and splendour all the cities of this world; and this new Jerusalem is here represented to us both in the exterior and the interior part of it.

1. The exterior part of the city — *the wall* and *the gates,* the wall for security and the gates for entrance.

(1.) The wall for security. Heaven is a safe state; those that are there are enclosed with a wall, that separates them and secures them from all evils and enemies: now here, in the account of the wall, we observe, [1.] The height of it, which, we are told, is very high, *seventy yards* (*v.* 17), sufficient both for ornament and security. [2.] The matter of it: *It was as jasper;* a wall all built of the most precious stones, for firmness and lustre, *v.* 11. This city has a wall that is impregnable as well as precious. [3.] The form of it was very regular and uniform: *It was four-square, the length as large as the breadth.* In the new Jerusalem all shall be equal in purity and perfection. There shall be an absolute uniformity in the church triumphant, a thing wanted and wished for on earth, but not to be expected till we come to heaven. [4.] The measure of the wall (*v.* 15, 16): *Twelve thousand furlongs* each way, each side, which is forty-eight thousand furlongs in the whole compass, or fifteen hundred German miles. Here is room sufficient for all the people of God — *many mansions in their Father's house.* [5.] The foundation of the wall, for heaven is a city that hath her foundations (*v.* 19); the promise and power of God, and the purchase of Christ, are the strong foundations of the church's safety and happiness. The foundations are described by their number —*twelve,* alluding to the twelve apostles (*v.* 14), whose gospel doctrines are the foundations upon which the church is built, *Christ himself being the chief corner-stone;* and, as to the matter of these foundations, it was various and precious, set forth by twelve sorts of precious stones, denoting the variety and excellency of the doctrines of the gospel, or of the graces of the Holy Spirit, or the personal excellencies of the Lord Jesus Christ.

(2.) The gates for entrance. Heaven is not inaccessible; there is a way opened into the holiest of all; there is a free admission to all those that are sanctified; they shall not find themselves shut out. Now, as to these gates, observe, [1.] Their number — *twelve gates,* answering to the twelve tribes of Israel. All the true Israel of God shall have entrance into the new Jerusalem, as every tribe had into the earthly Jerusalem. [2.] Their guards which were placed upon them — *twelve angels,* to admit and receive the several tribes of the spiritual Israel and keep out others. [3.] The inscription on the gates — *the names of the twelve tribes,* to show that they have a right to the tree of life, and to enter through the gates into the city. [4.] The situation of the gates. As the city had four equal sides, answering to the four quarters of the world, east, west, north, and south, so on each side there were three gates, signifying that from all quarters of the earth there shall be some who shall get safely to heaven and be received there, and that there is as free entrance from one part of the world as from the other; *for in Christ there is neither Jew nor Greek, Barbarian, Scythian, bond, nor free.* Men of all nations, and languages, who believe on Christ, have by him access to God in grace here and in glory hereafter. [5.] The materials of these gates — they were all of pearls, and yet with great variety: *Every gate one pearl,* either one single pearl of that vast bigness, or one single sort of pearl. Christ is the pearl of great price, and he is our way to God. There is nothing magnificent enough in this world fully to set forth the glory of heaven. Could we, in the glass of a strong imagination, contemplate such a city as is here described, even as to the exterior part of it, such a wall, and such gates, how amazing, how glorious, would the prospect be! And yet this is but a faint and dim representation of what heaven is in itself.

2. The interior part of the new Jerusalem, *v.* 22–27. We have seen its strong wall, and stately gates, and glorious guards; now we are to be led through the gates into the city itself; and the first thing which we observe there is the street of the city, *which is of pure gold, like transparent glass, v.* 21. The saints in heaven tread upon gold. The new Jerusalem has its several streets. There is the most exact order in heaven: every saint has his proper mansion. There is converse in heaven: the saints are then at rest, but it is not a mere passive rest; it is not a state of sleep and inactivity, but a state of delightful motion: *The nations that are saved walk in the light of it.* They walk with Christ in white. They have communion not only with God, but with one another; and all their steps are firm and clean. They are pure and clear *as gold and transparent glass.* Observe,

(1.) The temple of the new Jerusalem, which was no material temple, made with men's hands, as that of Solomon and Zerubbabel, but a temple altogether spiritual and divine; *for the Lord God Almighty, and the Lamb, are the temple thereof.* There the saints are above the need of ordinances, which were the means of their preparation for heaven. When the end is attained the means are no longer useful. Perfect and immediate communion with God will more than supply the place of gospel institutions.

(2.) The light of this city. Where there is no light, there can be no lustre nor pleasure. Heaven is *the inheritance of the saints in light.* But what is that light? There is no sun nor moon shining there, *v.* 23. Light is sweet, and a pleasant thing it is to behold the sun. What a dismal world would this be if it were not for the light of the sun! What is there in heaven that supplies the want of it? There is no want of the light of the sun, *for the glory of God lightens that city, and the Lamb is the light thereof.* God in Christ will be an everlasting fountain of knowledge and joy to the saints in heaven; and, if so, there is no need of the sun or moon, any more than we here need to set up candles at noon day, when the sun shineth in its strength.

(3.) The inhabitants of this city. They are described here several ways. [1.] By their numbers — whole nations of saved souls; some out of all nations, and many out of some nations. All those multitudes who were sealed on earth are saved in heaven. [2.] By their dignity — some of the kings and princes of the earth: great kings. God will have some of all ranks and degrees of men to fill the heavenly mansions, high and low; and when the greatest kings come to heaven they will see all their former honour and glory swallowed up of this heavenly glory that so much excels. [3.] Their continual accession and entrance into this city: *The gates shall never be shut.* There is no night, and therefore no need of shutting up the gates. Some one or other is coming in every hour and moment, and those that are sanctified always find the gates open; they have *an abundant entrance into the kingdom.*

(4.) The accommodations of this city: All the *glory and honour of the nations shall be brought into it.* Whatever is excellent and valuable in this world shall be there enjoyed in a more refined kind, and to a far greater degree — brighter crowns, a better and more enduring substance, more sweet and satisfying feasts, a more glorious attendance, a truer sense of honour and far higher posts of honour, a more glorious temper of mind, and a form and a countenance more glorious than ever were known in this world.

(5.) The unmixed purity of all who belong to the new Jerusalem, *v.* 27. [1.] There the saints shall have no impure thing remaining in them. In the article of death they shall be cleansed from every thing that is of a defiling nature. Now they feel a sad mixture of corruption with their graces, which hinders them in the service of God, interrupts their communion with him, and intercepts the light of his countenance; but, at their entrance into the holy of holies, they are washed in the laver of Christ's blood, and presented to the Father without spot. [2.] There the saints shall have no impure persons admitted among them. In the earthly Jerusalem there will be a mixed communion, after all the care that can be taken. Some roots of bitterness will spring up to trouble and defile Christian societies; but in the new Jerusalem there is a society perfectly pure. *First,* Free from such as are openly profane. There are none admitted into heaven who work abominations. In the churches on earth sometimes abominable things are done, solemn ordinances profaned and prostituted to men openly vicious, for worldly ends; but no such abominations can have place in heaven. *Secondly,* Free from hypocrites, such as make lies, say they are Jews, and are not, but do lie. These will creep into the churches of Christ on earth, and may lie concealed there a long time, perhaps all their days; but they cannot intrude into the new Jerusalem, which is wholly reserved for those that are called, and chosen, and faithful, who are all written, not only in the register if the visible church, *but in the Lamb's book of life.*

CHAPTER 22

In this chapter we have, I. A further description of the heavenly state of the church (*v.* 1–5). II. A confirmation of this and all the other visions of this book (*v.* 6–19). III. The conclusion (*v.* 20, 21).

Verses 1–5

The heavenly state which was before described as a city, and called the new Jerusalem, is here described as a paradise, alluding to the earthly paradise which was lost by the sin of the first Adam; here is another paradise restored by the second Adam. A paradise in a city, or a whole city in a paradise! In the first paradise there were only two persons to behold the beauty and taste the pleasures of it; but in this second paradise whole cities and nations shall find abundant delight and satisfaction. And here observe,

I. The river of paradise. The earthly paradise was well watered: no place can be pleasant or fruitful that is not so. This river is described, 1. By its fountain-head — *the throne of God and the Lamb.* All our springs of grace, comfort, and glory, are in God; and all our streams from him are through the mediation of the Lamb. 2. By its quality — *pure and clear as crystal.* All the streams of earthly comfort are muddy; but these are clear, salutary, and refreshing, giving life, and preserving life, to those who drink of them.

II. The tree of life, in this paradise. Such a tree there was in the earthly paradise, Gen. 2:9. This far excels it. And now, as to this tree, observe, 1. The situation of it — *in the midst of the street, and on either side the river;* or, as might have been better rendered, *in the midst between the terrace-walk and the river.* This tree of life is fed by the pure waters of the river that comes from the throne of God. The presence and perfections of God furnish out all the glory and blessedness of heaven. 2. The fruitfulness of this tree. (1.) It brings forth many sorts of fruit — *twelve sorts,* suited to the refined taste of all the saints. (2.) It brings forth fruit at all times — *yields its fruit every month.* This tree is never empty, never barren; there is always fruit upon it. In heaven there is not only a variety of pure and satisfying pleasures, but a continuance of them, and always fresh. (3.) The fruit is not only pleasant, but wholesome. The presence of God in heaven is the health and happiness of the saints; there they find in him a remedy for all their former maladies, and are preserved by him in the most healthful and vigorous state.

III. The perfect freedom of this paradise from every thing that is evil (*v.* 3): *There shall be no more curse;* no *accursed one — katanathema,* no serpent there, as there was in the earthly paradise. Here is the great excellency of this paradise. The devil has nothing to do there; he cannot draw the saints from serving God to be subject to himself, as he did our first parents, nor can he so much as disturb them in the service of God.

IV. The supreme felicity of this paradisiacal state. 1. There the saints shall see the face of God; there they shall enjoy the beatific vision. 2. God will own them, as having his seal and name on their foreheads. 3. *They shall reign with him for ever;* their service shall be not only freedom but honour and dominion. 4. All this shall be with perfect knowledge and joy. They shall be full of wisdom and comfort, continually walking in the light of the Lord; and this not for a time, *but for ever and ever.*

Verses 6–19

We have here a solemn ratification of the contents of this book, and particularly of this last vision (though some think it may not only refer to the whole book, but to the whole New Testament, yea, to the whole Bible, completing and confirming the canon of scripture); and here, 1. This is confirmed by the name and nature of that God who gave out these discoveries: he is *the Lord God, faithful and true,* and so are all his sayings. 2. By the messengers he chose, to reveal these things to the world; the holy angels showed them to holy men of God; and God would not employ his saints and angels in deceiving the world. 3. They will soon be confirmed by their accomplishment: they are things that must shortly be done; Christ will make haste, *he will come quickly,* and put all things out of doubt; and then those will prove the wise and happy men who have believed and kept his words. 4. By the integrity of that angel who had been the apostle's guide and interpreter in these visions; this integrity was such that he not only refused to accept religious adoration from John, but once and again reproved him for it. He who was so tender of the honour of God, and so displeased with what was a wrong to God, would never come in his name to lead the people of God into mere dreams and delusions; and it is a still further confirmation of the sincerity of this apostle that he confesses his own sin and folly, into which he had now again relapsed, and he leaves this his failing on perpetual record: this shows he was a faithful and an impartial writer. 5. By the order given to leave the book of the prophecy open, to be perused by all, that they might labour to understand it, that they might make their objections against it, and compare the prophecy with the events. God here deals freely and openly with all; he does not speak in secret, but calls every one to witness to the declarations here made, *v.* 10. 6. By the effect this book, thus kept open, will have upon men; those that are filthy and unjust will take occasion thence to be more so, but it will confirm, strengthen, and further sanctify those that are upright with God; it will be a savour of life to some and of death to others, and so will appear to be from God, *v.* 12. 7. It will be Christ's rule of judgment at the great day; he will dispense rewards and punishments to men according as their works agree or disagree with the word of God; and therefore that word itself must needs be faithful and true. 8. It is the word of him who is the author, finisher, and rewarder of the faith and holiness of his people, *v.* 13, 14. He is *the first and the last,* and the same from first to last, and so is his word too; and he will by this word give to his people, who conform themselves to it, *a right to the tree of life,* and an entrance into heaven; and this will be a full confirmation of the truth and authority of his word, since it contains the title and evidence of that confirmed state of holiness and happiness that remains for his people in heaven. 9. It is a book that condemns and excludes from heaven all wicked, unrighteous persons, and particularly *those that love and make lies* (*v.* 15), and therefore can never be itself a lie. 10. It is confirmed by *the testimony of Jesus, which is the Spirit of prophecy.* And this Jesus, as God, is *the root of David,* though, as man, his offspring — a person in whom all uncreated and created excellencies meet, too great and too good to deceive his churches and the world. He is the fountain of all light, the *bright and the morning star,* and as such has given to his churches this morning light of prophecy, to assure them of the light of that perfect day which is approaching. 11. It is confirmed by an open and general invitation to all to come and partake of the promises and privileges of the gospel, those streams of the water of life; these are tendered to all who feel in their souls a thirst which nothing in this world can quench. 12. It is confirmed by the joint testimony of the Spirit of God, and that gracious Spirit that is in all the true members of the church of God; *the Spirit and the bride* join in testifying the truth and excellency of the gospel. 13. It is confirmed by a most solemn sanction, condemning and cursing all who should dare to corrupt or change the word of God, either by adding to it or taking from it, *v.* 18, 19. He that adds to the word of God draws down upon himself *all the plagues written in this book;* and he who takes any thing away from it cuts himself off from all the promises and privileges of it. This sanction is like a flaming sword, to guard the canon of the scripture from profane hands. Such a fence as this God set about the law (Deu. 4:2), and the whole Old Testament (Mal. 4:4), and now in the most solemn manner about the whole Bible, assuring us that it is a book of the most sacred nature, divine authority, and of the last importance, and therefore the peculiar care of the great God.

Verses 20–21

We have now come to the conclusion of the whole, and that in three things: —

I. Christ's farewell to his church. He seems now, after he has been discovering these things to his people on earth, to take leave of them, and return to heaven; but he parts with them in great kindness, and assures them it shall not be long before he comes again to them: *Behold, I come quickly.* As when he ascended into heaven, after his resurrection, he parted with a promise of his gracious presence, so here he parts with a promise of a speedy return. If any say, "Where is the promise of his coming, when so many ages have passed since this was written?" let them know he is not slack to his people, but long-suffering to his enemies: his coming will be sooner than they are aware, sooner than they are prepared, sooner than they desire; and to his people it will be seasonable. The vision is for an appointed time, and will not tarry. *He will come quickly;* let this word be always sounding in our ear, and let us give all diligence that we may be found of him in peace, *without spot and blameless.*

II. The church's hearty echo to Christ's promise, 1. Declaring her firm belief of it: *Amen, so it is,* so it shall be. 2. Expressing her earnest desire of it: *Even so, come, Lord Jesus; make hast, my beloved, and be thou like a roe, or like a young hart on the mountain of spices.* Thus beats the pulse of the church, thus breathes that gracious Spirit which actuates and informs the mystical body of Christ; and we should never be satisfied till we find such a spirit breathing in us, and causing us to *look for the blessed hope, and glorious appearance of the great God and our Saviour Jesus Christ.* This is the language of the church of the first-born, and we should join with them, often putting ourselves in mind of his promise. What comes from heaven in a promise should be sent back to heaven in a prayer, *"Come, Lord Jesus,* put an end to this state of sin, sorrow, and temptation; gather thy people out of this present evil world, and take them up to heaven, that state of perfect purity, peace, and joy, and so finish thy great design, and fulfil all that word in which thou hast caused thy people to hope."

III. The apostolical benediction, which closes the whole: *The grace of our Lord Jesus Christ be with you all, Amen.* Here observe, 1. The Bible ends with a clear proof of the Godhead of Christ, since the Spirit of God teaches the apostle to bless his people in the name of Christ, and to beg from Christ a blessing for them, which is a proper act of adoration. 2. Nothing should be more desired by us than that the grace of Christ may be with us in this world, to prepare us for the glory of Christ in the other world. It is by his grace that we must be kept in a joyful expectation of his glory, fitted for it, and preserved to it; and his glorious appearance will be welcome and joyful to those that are partakers of his grace and favour here; and therefore to this most comprehensive prayer we should all add our hearty *Amen,* most earnestly thirsting after greater measures of the gracious influences of the blessed Jesus in our souls, and his gracious presence with us, till glory has perfected all his gra[illegible] wards us, for he is a sun and a shield, *he gives* [illegible] *that* [illegible] *and no good thing will he with*[illegible] *uprightly.*

Editing Digital Video

Robert M. Goodman

Patrick J. McGrath

McGraw-Hill
New York   Chicago   San Francisco   Lisbon
London   Madrid   Mexico City   Milan   New Delhi
San Juan   Seoul   Singapore   Sydney   Toronto

The McGraw·Hill Companies

Cataloging-in-Publication Data is on file with the Library of Congress.

Copyright © 2003 by The McGraw-Hill Companies, Inc. All rights reserved.
Printed in the United States of America. Except as permitted under the United
States Copyright Act of 1976, no part of this publication may be reproduced or
distributed in any form or by any means, or stored in a data base or retrieval
system, without the prior written permission of the publisher.

1 2 3 4 5 6 7 8 9 0   DOC/DOC   0 9 8 7 6 5 4 3 2

P/N 140636-0
PART OF
ISBN 0-07-140635-2

*The sponsoring editor for this book was Steve Chapman and the production supervisor
was Sherri Souffrance. It was set in Century Schoolbook by MacAllister Publishing
Services, LLC.*

Printed and bound by RR Donnelley.

 This book is printed on recycled, acid-free paper containing a minimum of 50
percent recycled de-inked fiber.

McGraw-Hill books are available at special quantity discounts to use as premiums
and sales promotions, or for use in corporate training programs. For more information,
please write to the Director of Special Sales, Professional Publishing, McGraw-Hill,
Two Penn Plaza, New York, NY 10121-2298. Or contact your local bookstore.

To my students, and my mother for enrolling me in typing class.

Patrick J. McGrath

To all the editors I've met and worked with who have influenced my ideas about editing.

Robert M. Goodman

CONTENTS

Contents

Contents

PREFACE

This book is designed for anyone who wants to learn to edit digital video. It doesn't matter which system or software or operating system you choose to use. Buy whatever meets your needs. If you haven't already purchased an editing solution, we'll help you understand what's important and what's not.

Editing is a language that uses pictures and sounds instead of words. The DV footage on the CD in this book is for the exercises we created to teach you the grammar of editing. Simply copy these files to your hard drive and bring them in to your editing program. It's not absolutely necessary that you have a working system before reading this book. However, you will learn faster if you're able to do the exercises.

Editing digital video is easier than it looks. Everyone starts out confused and fearful. You can learn as you edit. However, once you grasp the underlying concepts of digital editing, the process will cease to be a mystery. You must have faith and courage. Everyone makes a breakthrough sooner or later. Afterwards, all the aspects of editing will become clear to you. Nothing will stand in your way. We've seen this happen hundreds of times with our students. Our methods will help you achieve your breakthrough faster.

Learning to edit is like learning to play a musical instrument. It's a craft and practice is important. The more you edit the easier it becomes to please yourself and an audience. Music and editing share another trait. Both can create deep emotional responses from audiences. There are few things in life more rewarding than sitting in the back of a room and watching other people be profoundly moved by the story you have told.

No matter what the story is, the editor's job is to tell it well. To us, that means editing that's invisible. Anything B acting, camera work, lighting, music, or editing that calls attention to itself rather than serving the needs of the story is detrimental.

Shape the story. Give your audience what they need to see and hear when they need to see and hear it. You must be their guide and representative long before your friends sit down in your living room or audiences buy tickets to see the results of your hard work.

Robert M. Goodman

Patrick J. McGrath

ACKNOWLEDGMENTS

We would like to thank the following people for their generous contributions that have made this book possible: Brian McKernan for encouraging us to write this book; Bob Turner for writing the foreward and being a vocal advocate for editors; Kimberly Hyndman, our intern for her help with the cross-reference section; Bob McGrath for designing the illustrations; Adam Gooder for writing The Dicey Question script; Michael Kelly and Vanessa Montesano for their performances in the exercise; J. Winfield Heckert for lighting the exercise scene; Mark Moskowitz, Jennifer Rew, Jeff Kreines, Frank Black, and Steve Owen for their insights; Beth Leach and Daniel F. McGrath, Sr. for their photographs; Bob Ellis, Seth Levi, and Charles Dyer for their suggestions about films to watch; Daniel Goodman for reading the manuscript and offering his valuable criticism; Johanna Goodman for her patience always; Katey and Amanda McGrath for their encouragement; Mike Kushner and Joyce Acciaioli Rudge for their title graphics; Ned Levi for his assistance; and Rob Crites, Melanie Wright, Mimi Janosi, Vlad Hartman, and Justin Maynard, at The Art Institute of Philadelphia for their support.

FOREWORD

Find Magic in Your Bag of Tricks.

Every editor develops a bag of tricks for special occasions. When an editor is confronted with an unworkable sequence, a scene that is lacking, a rhythm that feels monotonous, the editor will reach into his bag of tricks and find the magical solution to the dilemma in question.

Yes, I do believe in magic, as does every editor and every artist who has ever created magic. You will know when it happens because of the natural high it creates—the euphoria that bubbles up. In many ways, this is what the art is all about. It is true that sometimes you can create magic and your conscious mind is barely aware of it. I know editors that have been given profound natural talents and when you ask, they cannot explain why they chose a cut the way they did or why they chose a sequence of shots, but as an assistant, I have noticed their body language when they perform magic, and they are feeling it when it happens.

Everyone can experience the creation of magic. Most of the time, it comes after you have mastered the craft portion of your art. I believe the difference between craftsmanship and art is that craftsmanship can be taught. Craftsmanship is mastering tools and techniques. It is not easy to become a master craftsman, but with passion, dedication, and hard work, I promise you, it is achievable. Becoming an artist and mastering your art is a different matter. To an artist, art seems to just happen. Part of this is due to a God-given talent that cannot be learned. It is inside you. The other part is more of a path of discovering art and finding what is within you.

When you talk to editors, most will admit that some of their best edits "happen by accident" or "just happen while playing around", or "discovered by breaking the rules". The "rules" are the basic tenets of editing. Craftsmanship involves mastering these tenets, established by the craft's long tradition and understanding of what works and what does not. Sometimes, magic can be found by choosing to ignore one or more of those tenets. Artists know when to try this. Most of us, when confronted with some works of modern art for the first time, have reacted to these pieces with the impression that someone just threw some paint on a canvas. As we mature, we understand this is not the case. Frequently these works are from artists who mastered their craft and then choose to break the rules that they mastered. The power that was discovered generated the magic that inspires people to fill museums to experience this work of art.

Frequently sculptors try to explain that their art is to discover what exists inside a stone. Editors go through the same exploration and discovery when presented with the camera original. Editors remove the extraneous—hopefully until the essential truth is revealed. Interestingly, the style of this revelation is the part of the editor and the part of the sculpture that is left on the work of art, and is part of its beauty. Magic occurs when you stop removing at the perfect time.

This book was created, in part, because digital video editing has given major new powers of experimentation to the editor. The opportunity to try new things quickly is a wonderful technological gift to an editor. I have been an editor in the period prior to this technology and I know the depressing, artistically bereft feeling when "good enough" was said too often, because the cost was too great to try a different cut. The constant feeling that you know you could have made this project better, if only . is a terrible burden for an editor. In the days of linear editing, when your choice would be to destroy what you created to try something different and, when it did not work, have to rebuild the sequence you originally created, was frequently too time-consuming and the tools you created too expensive to try. When editors are at a point in their career that they know what could be, if only they could be given experimentation time, can be a frustrating and painful period. Fortunately, today's technology reduces much of this past frustration. It offers opportunities to try new cuts and greater prospects to discover some magic.

Goodman and McGrath do a good job of teaching the craft of editing. Their book points you to areas where you can find the art as well. It is hard to continually find the magic without mastering the craft. While mastering the craft is difficult and takes a long time, hopefully as you journey you will constantly discover magical sparks that keep you moving forward.

Each time a bit of magic occurs in the lives of editors, or when they experience the magic performed by another, they can slip that knowledge into their bag of tricks, and pull it out at the appropriate time in the future. This magic could be a technique of the editor's craft that created magic under a specific set of circumstances, or it could be a broken rule. An editor will never know when he/she can use this magic trick again, but a great editor collects them and knows when to reach into his or her bag of tricks and pull one out.

Here is hoping that your bag of tricks grows large and rich with magic.

BOB TURNER

The Whole Truth and Nothing But the Truth

The Big Picture

Digital video editing is the process of transferring video and other materials into an editing system; assembling sequences of pictures and sounds (first in a rough fashion and then polishing and refining the show); creating and adding titles, graphics, and effects to enhance the show; adjusting and mixing the sound; and finally outputting the finished show back to videotape or other media so audiences can see the results. This is what you're interested in learning otherwise you wouldn't be reading this book.

Our goal is to teach anyone, amateurs or professionals, how to edit on any digital video editing system and achieve results. It's a difficult task made more difficult because there are over 200 different answers to the question, "what is a digital video system?" There are video-editing appliances (self-contained devices designed to be connected to a monitor and digital video recorder or camera); computer software running on Mac, Windows, Linux, and other operating systems; and integrated systems that combine proprietary hardware with software. For the purpose of this book, all of these are examples of digital video editing systems. We'll call them *editing systems* throughout this book.

Manufacturers use different terms to describe what are universal operations, tools, and features. It would be extremely difficult to write a book explaining the principles of digital video editing using every manufacturer's terminology. Even if we could write that book, it would be impossible to read. To help you sort out these infuriating differences, we've provided a guide in Chapter 11, "What Are They Talking About?"

This book isn't a replacement for your editing system manual, nor is it a guide to a specific system. Instead, we'll present principles that enable you to use any system successfully. This is a results-oriented approach to digital video editing that works no matter which editing system you choose to use.

Words can create confusion so we'll define and use terms based on two criteria: our 40 years of combined experience in editing and what's appropriate under the widest set of circumstances. Our focus on teaching principles is prone to failure because of the variety of editing systems available, unless you have some familiarity with the editing system you plan to use. So start playing with it. Acclimate yourself with the buttons, tools, user interface, and terminology that are part and parcel of every editing system.

No single approach to teaching or learning works for everyone. Anyone contemplating editing digital video should realize that he or she will be working in a computer-based environment. It's crucial that you understand your learning style as it relates to computer software. Understanding yourself and how you best learn is a valuable asset. Software programs change constantly. You must be able to learn new features or a new program rapidly and successfully.

Styles of Learning

This section identifies a few of the learning styles we've spotted over the years. See if you recognize any that match your personality:

The Book Method. You must read the book first, see it in print, and understand as much as possible in order to proceed on a computer. You like the big picture. You seek a well-written book. If this describes you, you've bought the right book! Read *Editing Digital Video*, the manual for your editing system, and then get started.

The Recipe Method. You prefer step-by-step instruction. You like to see each task broken down so you can carefully follow a path. Your editing system's tutorial should be your first stop. Follow the instructions in that software or printed tutorial. To help you learn, we've provided footage and exercises in this book.

The Research Method. You like to jump right in and start working, relying on your experience to work intuitively on a computer. You are the type of person who looks up information only when you run into a roadblock. The index in your editing system manual (and in this book) will prove invaluable.

The Reinforcement Method. You like to scan the table of contents in the manual to get a general idea of how things work. You glean as much information as you need and then proceed to work in an organized manner. When you are finished exploring, you like to debrief yourself by reading the editing system manual to cement the information into your mind.

The Project Method. You're the type of person who needs a reason to immerse yourself and learn. This is the sink-or-swim approach. You need a project with a deadline, the pressure of performing under stress, or the motivation of proving yourself in a professional situation. You will use whatever is available and any and all methods to learn. You are independent and resourceful. You rely on experience and ingenuity to take a project from beginning to end, which is its own reward.

The Trial-and-Error Method. You like to jump right in and start. Your favorite tools are two features: undo and context-sensitive help which are included in most software programs. If this describes you, make sure you purchase an editing system with extensive levels of undo and help. This book serves as an extension of that help system.

The Classroom Method. You prefer the discipline that an instructor-led course imposes on you and enjoy learning in a group setting. Courses on editing are available at training centers and colleges. Most offer a curriculum that presents material in an organized way over time. You still need to learn the software by yourself, but you're aided by the organization that a class provides. Our methods are being used to teach editing in classrooms everyday.

The Buddy System Method. You're the type of person who needs a tutor or peer to work with you through the lessons. You find the comfort and encouragement that comes with a partner necessary. Under the theory that two minds are better than one, you prefer to explore things from two perspectives. If this describes you, grab a partner and this book, and start dancing.

The Mentor Method. This is similar to the buddy system, but you'd prefer to have an expert for a tutor. You need someone who can provide what few of your peers possess—subject knowledge and a disciplined approach to learning. If you can find an expert with the right credentials and experience who is also a capable teacher, this is probably the fastest way to learn editing. However, private lessons given by an expert editor are expensive. We think reading this book is a good substitute for having us sit beside you, but if you still want private lessons and can afford it, feel free to contact us via e-mail at info@camcase.tv.

You can choose from many styles and methods of learning. Most people use more than one method to learn effectively. It's important to recognize the approach or approaches you prefer—the ones that work best with your experience, skill, interest, and pocketbook. Success is important in the beginning because this is when you learn the fundamentals that last a life-time.

What Is Editing?

Editing is commonly defined as collecting, preparing, and arranging materials for publication. It may also mean to revise or correct and eliminate or omit. Those definitions are just as valid in the world of film and video. To us, digital video editing is the process of collecting, arranging, and bringing materials together to tell a story using pictures and sounds. The word *materials* should be understood as video footage, photographs, illustrations, animations, title graphics, sound, music, or anything else you can incorporate into the finished product. For lack of a better word, we'll use the word *show* to describe the finished product. This is because when you're done, the first thing you'll want to do is *show* the results of your hard work to someone else.

The ultimate goal of editing is to tell stories. Writers use words and sentences to craft stories; editors use pictures and sounds. Joining disparate shots together is fundamental to editing. In one of the oddities that persists in the film and video industry, the simplest way to join two shots together is to *cut* from one shot to another. It's called a cut because film editors once had to cut and splice together strands of film to join two shots. What's important to know is that the act of placing one shot next to another can create an emotional impression that's greater than the sum of the parts.

Why Should You Not Edit?

Before we discuss the reasons to edit, we should mention that not everything needs to be edited. Some things that you've shot may not need to be edited or perhaps never should be edited. If you record something for documentation purposes, it probably doesn't have a beginning, middle, or end beyond the start and end of the tape. It's perfectly okay to realize that a particular piece of footage doesn't need to be edited. For instance, imagine that you recorded your child speaking at his or her graduation. If the only footage you shot is of that speech, you don't need to edit it. Just watch it later. It may be important to save for posterity, but it is not worth editing. If you only have one shot, whether or not it tells a story in and of itself, it doesn't need to be edited.

However, if you shoot your child getting dressed, putting on his or her cap and gown, walking to the podium, and all of the other events leading up to and after the speech, you'd have the material to tell a personal story. Trying to tell a story when there isn't one is a frustrating exercise. The rule is that if it interests you and/or others, and if you have enough interesting shots, you probably have enough material to edit a show.

Figuring out what is or isn't an interesting shot is the subject of Chapter 7, "Setting the Table." We'll discuss how to identify shots and camera angles and how to use these elements to tell stories. The camera is the principal tool we use to record pictures and sounds. This chapter will help make anyone a better cameraperson even though it's written from an editor's perspective. The truth is you can't tell succinct stories that hold the audience's attention with one shot from one angle.

You can tell stories using just the camera and avoid editing altogether. However, it's not very efficient. This approach is called *in-camera editing*, which can be difficult to do. All the scenes must be shot in the exact order the audience will see them and everything you shoot will appear in the finished show. This approach is the opposite of shooting something from one angle or perspective. However, the end result is the same; you do not need to edit the material.

To pull this off, you must have good intuition and an awareness of what will be the *important* or decisive moment before it happens so the camera will be rolling when it does happen. You'll also need to visualize how the material you've just recorded can be joined to the material you're about to shoot. This is easier to do with certain kinds of stories. A wedding is one example. It's a ritual event with important moments that are easily anticipated. Plus, it takes place in a preset order in a few locations. We know a filmmaker named Doug who makes a living shooting weddings that he edits entirely in the camera. After the last dance, he takes the tape from his camera and hands it to the client. The client gets a well-shot story about their wedding that requires no additional editing. What this filmmaker does is akin to performing on a high wire without a net. Doug's in-camera editing ability relies on his careful attention to craft, years of practice, and finely honed skills.

In the past, many amateurs were forced to shoot this way because they had no access to editing equipment. Fifteen years ago, even simple editing equipment was beyond the means of most home users. A basic system used to cost more than $35,000 and required enormous technical expertise. Plus, the technology wasn't very good. Amateurs who were adept at conceptualizing and shooting carefully could manage to tell good stories when the story lent itself to in-camera editing (such as a wedding, graduation, or travelogue). Digital editing has made in-camera editing unnecessary. It's not worth the effort.

Why Should You Edit?

The most efficient approach to telling stories with a camera is to follow the Hollywood model. Shoot what you want, in the order you want to shoot it, and then assemble those elements into a story. This approach came into vogue shortly after the birth of filmmaking around the turn of the twentieth century. Filmmakers quickly discovered that audiences were sophisticated enough to make the mental leap from one shot to another—from one angle to another—without losing grasp of the story. Audiences understood what was going on even when a lot of material was left out. Filmmakers realized that joining disparate shots together gave them more control over how the story was told and on the impact their stories had on the audience, turning editing into an important tool. Another early realization was that editing could alter how an audience perceives time and space.

Although the reason for editing, which most often comes to mind, is to create stories, it's actually only one of the four reasons for editing, which include the following:

1. To build stories from the material you shoot.
2. To fix mistakes or eliminate technical errors.
3. To increase or decrease the duration (running time) of a show.
4. To combine multiple stories or videotapes on one tape. This could mean adding commercials to a television program or compiling several shows on a single videotape.

Examine the list. You'll notice that three of the four reasons are not creative; most editing tasks are technical. Fixing mistakes, cutting for length, or combining things are what most editors do day in and day out. It's an interesting fact that when an editor finally has the opportunity to build a story, he or she often ends up fixing mistakes, adjusting the length, and combining things.

The tongue-in-cheek definition of an editor, hanging in editing rooms around the world, is the person who takes out-of-focus, badly framed, and poorly shot footage of people mumbling, bumping into furniture, and forgetting what to say, and turns that footage into a compelling story with lasting value for which the director will take all the credit. There's a kernel of truth in this definition, although we prefer to say that editing is about taking the best of what you have at hand and telling the most compelling story you can create for the audience.

It's the Audience, Always!

The truth is that the audience is the only entity editors should consider. If you're doing something for yourself, it's easy to watch the footage and imagine the story. However, if you plan to show it to someone else, you'll need to edit. Few people have the patience to watch all the footage.

Nearly every show that people watch (whether it is film, television, or video) is a linear experience. It doesn't matter whether you are making a commercial, documentary, drama, music video, or wedding. The audience cannot change the order of events and must watch the show over a period of time. Editors create organized successions of images so the audience sees and hears one piece of information at a time in the order that the editor decided, which is the order of the show. The audience has to listen and watch these pictures and sounds over time. Therefore, as an editor, you must organize those images in a way that satisfies the needs of the audience. You have to take the audience's point of view.

What do audiences prefer? They usually prefer stories with beginnings, middles, and ends. Stories with conflict and resolution. Only a few books are worth reading about storytelling; Aristotle's *Poetics* is one of these, even though it was written in 325 B.C. Several other more recent books are also listed in our suggested reading bibliography.

This book will help you learn how to edit stories. In the process, you'll also learn the technical side—how to fix mistakes, cut for length, and combine things. The beauty of digital video editing is that it's easier now than ever to do the technical tasks. Fixing mistakes often meant starting over from scratch. Lengthening and shortening shows was a nightmare in the days of linear video editing. Combining things required foresight and planning. Today, it's a breeze to do these things because digital video editing offers random access.

The show the audience sees may be a linear experience, but the process of creating one is not. Digital video editing is nonlinear. All of your materials are available at any time in any order. Random access to your material allows you to build shows the way you want. You can decide to start working on the beginning, middle, or end. You can work within small structures like a three-shot sequence and combine that with other three-shot sequences until you've built a scene or a sequence of scenes. Whenever you're ready, you can put the sections together.

Why Digital?

Digital video editing gives you the ability to change the digital video files stored in your editing system in any way, shape, or fashion. The information in those files is stored as binary data, which means that the file contains a series of numbers that can be either ones or zeros. The power of digital video editing extends beyond simply changing the order of a series of shots. You can change the colors, luminance, contrast, and even the size and shape of the image itself down to the smallest part of the picture information, which is called a *pixel*.

Digital video editing, or *digital editing* for short, encompasses what professionals call *nonlinear editing* (NLE). We prefer digital editing because nonlinear is defined by something else and digital editing is broader. In today's world, you can manipulate so much more than just a sequence of shots. A typical editing system enables the operator to manipulate multiple layers of video, audio, text, and graphics in a completely nondestructive way. Digital editing is the umbrella term for this new way of doing things.

The person who operates these editing systems in a professional environment often becomes a *superuser* because it's no longer enough to be just an editor. You need to be an expert in graphics, audio, effects, editing, compositing, and compression because it all falls under the umbrella of digital

Pixels Everywhere

Pixel is an abbreviation for *picture cell* or *picture element*, which can refer to an individual sample of red, green, or blue in the picture, or to the luminance. To get an idea of what a pixel looks like, look at a computer monitor under a magnifying glass. You'll see a picture comprised of a grid of small rectangles, which are the pixels in a monitor. If you have image-editing software such as Adobe Photoshop™, JASC Paintshop Pro™, or something similar on your computer, you can zoom in or enlarge an image until the pixels become visible. You'll notice this picture is also comprised of rectangles, which are more pixels. If you still don't believe that pixels are everywhere, grab a newspaper or magazine and look at those images under a magnifying glass. They won't be rectangular pixels, but they are pixels nonetheless.

The Ultimate Network

Some television news organizations are already creating programs shot, edited, and broadcast by individuals scattered around the globe. The footage for the story is stored on a huge array of hard drives at a centralized location. The producers, editors, and graphic artists can be anywhere, even in separate places. Everyone accesses a low-resolution version, or *proxy*, of the footage via a computer network if they happen to be at the central location or via the Internet if they're not. The producer creates a rough version of the story, records the narration, and sends the narration and instructions (just the sequence of events) to the central server. The editor then takes the producer's rough edit and narration and polishes the story. An editor or a graphics specialist adds the titles and graphics. The story is then played directly from the central server's hard drives to a transmitter. The transmitter sends the signal to a television set so the story can be seen.

video editing. The digital environment also permits another model, the *networked approach*, which lets groups share access to the same material. Digital files can be stored at a central location that is linked to everyone's computer so multiple experts can have instant access to the same material. Each person can perform a specialized task and make the results accessible to everyone.

The Precepts of Digital Video Editing

Six universal principles—nondestructive, lossless, random, intuitive, layered, and unrestricted—separate digital editing from past approaches.

The first principle is that digital editing is nondestructive. The reason for this starts with the media used to record pictures and sounds. Most professionals call unrecorded media (film or videotape) *raw stock*. After recording, video professionals refer to it as *original source tapes* or *camera source tapes*. Film professionals call exposed and processed motion picture film *camera negative*, *footage*, or *source footage*. For our purposes, we'll refer to any recorded material shot by you or someone else with a camera as an original source tape.

If you remember what we said earlier, the first step in the editing process is transferring material into your editing system. The digital information recorded on your original source tapes is copied to your editing system's storage drives. Those original source tapes can then be placed into storage because the material you'll be editing is the copy on your editing system.

Nondestructiveness goes even deeper. The copies of your original source tapes stored in your editing system are called *media files* because they contain pictures and sounds (media) as digital files. A media file can store all the information on a videotape, from one scene, one shot, or one frame of your material. Typically, a media file holds several shots or a scene. Your editing system makes it easy to mark and name sections of the media file that you feel are useful. These pointers identify a subsection of the media file and are called *clips*. Even though a clip is an object that can be copied and moved in most editing systems, a clip merely tells your editing system where to find the section of the media file you want to play.

The media file is separate from and remains unchanged no matter what happens to the clips. There's another level. If you decide to manipulate the picture by changing the colors or distorting the image, the editing system creates a new media file (see *rendering* in the index if you want to jump ahead). Your original media files remain pristine until you decide to delete them.

No matter how often a digital media file is copied, the copy is always identical to the original. There's no difference between the two because the files are composed of ones and zeroes that can be easily duplicated. Scientists call this a *lossless* process, meaning that nothing gets lost. Digital editing is lossless with regard to copying files. This isn't true if you copy analog materials, such as VHS tapes or traditional photographs. Analog materials degrade slightly whenever you copy them; the image quality gets worse. It's noticeable because the contrast goes up and the sharpness goes down. You

Figure 1-1
Each clip points to a media file that contains the actual pictures and sounds.

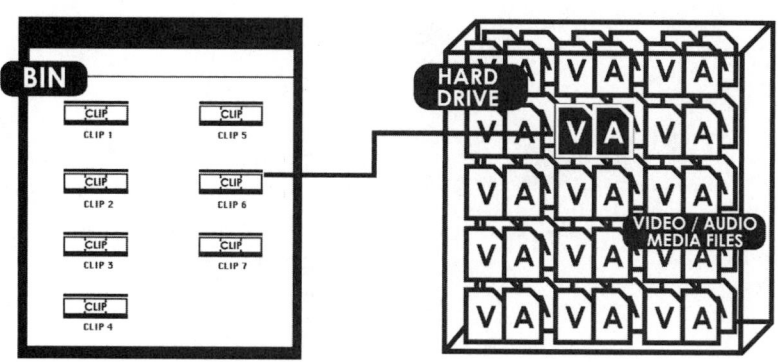

Understanding the Heart of the System

Imagine you go to a diner in New Jersey with friends. You find an open booth and sit down. A jukebox is in front of you on the wall. It's actually just a shiny box with buttons on the front, song titles listed on a series of pages, and a place to put your money in if you want to listen to music. The jukebox in your booth lets you play a CD. The CDs, which are digital and represent the digital media files in your editing system, are stored elsewhere—in a player in a back room of the diner. However, you can control the songs you hear in your booth even though you can't actually see or touch any of the CDs. Instead, you select the songs you want to play by punching in a number code listed next to the song. It costs a dollar for three songs. If you put a dollar into the jukebox, you can select and play three songs. What you're about to do is play back digital media files.

You go through the list and select J12, a Whitney Houston song, P12, a hit from Smokey Robinson and the Miracles, and B2, a Michael Jackson tune. You've chosen three songs to be played in a specific order. All three songs are from different media files. Each album (CD) is a digital media file. The songs are clips. You don't want to play the entire album, just one song. That one song is a subset of the album; it's one section of a digital media file. Each song you've chosen is a subset of the Whitney Houston album, the Smokey Robinson album, and the Michael Jackson album. After you press the buttons, the jukebox tells the playback device to retrieve the master CD, find the subset (the track) that has the song, and play it back for you. The jukebox points to a digital file (the CD) stored in the back of the diner. The process is repeated for every song you choose and the jukebox plays the songs in the order you decide.

If I gave everyone around the table some money, all of my friends could play their own versions of the files stored in the diner's jukebox. Everyone could play the songs on the jukebox in a different order even though no one is actually playing the CDs (digital

Figure 1-2a

Tabletop Jukebox

media files); instead, they are selecting numbers. The numbers that identify the songs relate to the CDs, which are stored in the player in the back of the room. If the owner of the diner took the CDs out of the player and left the slots empty, the jukebox in the booth would still take your money. You could still punch in your choices and make a sequence of your favorite hits. However, you wouldn't hear anything. Without the digital media files in the back room, there's nothing to play. Of course, as soon as the owner puts the CDs back, the songs play.

Figure 1-2b
Selecting a song

It should be clear to you that there's a difference between the song sequence you create by punching in numbers and the digital media files. The sequence determines how the digital media files are played, but the two are completely separate. This is exactly how digital editing systems work.

can prove it to yourself by making a photocopy of a photocopy of a photocopy of a photograph. Professionals call these successive copies *generations* and call the change in image quality *generation loss*. Thankfully, generation loss has been consigned to the past with digital editing. (It's okay to smile.)

Randomness is another principle that functions on several levels. Digital editing systems let you take any approach that works for you. You can start with the pivotal moment in the story and cut that sequence. Or you can start with the end of the story or create the titles first. Whichever approach works for you or however you'd like to edit, digital editing systems make it possible. Sound first, graphics second, pictures third? If it makes sense to you, you can do it. Experienced editors can follow the most efficient path, which might mean switching approaches midway through a project. The technology doesn't force you to follow the same approach for every project. Instead, you can use the one that works best for you.

The next level of randomness is that you can access your material in a random manner. Think of it this way. When audiocassettes were popular, the fast-forward and rewind features were important. CDs made those functions obsolete. The relationship between digital and analog editing is similar. There's no waiting. Every track of your material is instantly accessible.

The concept of intuition is difficult to accept when you're learning your way around an editing system. It seems to be anything but intuitive. The following analogy will help you understand why we believe this is a universal principle. In order to understand digital video editing, it's helpful to look at the methods that were used to edit video and, prior to that, film.

Film editing is done by hand. The process is simple. An editor looks at the film and physically cuts strips of celluloid with a sharp blade. To isolate the piece he or she wants, the editor cuts out that section and puts it aside. The remaining pieces of film are then glued or taped back together, or stored as separate pieces. The image for this phase of editing is of an editor holding film in his or her hand while cutting it with a blade. In the history of editing, this is the Iron Age.

With the arrival of videotape editing, the videotape recorder became the primary device for making edits. To make an edit, the editor had to find the piece he or she wanted on the original source tapes and copy that section to a new tape on a second recorder. The image for this phase of editing is of an editor systematically playing back tapes on one machine and electronically transferring the images to another machine for rerecording. In the history of editing, this is the Machine Age.

With digital video editing, the computer has become the primary device. To make an edit, the editor only needs to rearrange the sequence in which media files are played. The image for this phase of editing is of an editor seated in front of computer display moving objects on the desktop. In the history of editing, this is the Information Age.

Digital video editing is intuitive because all of the tools are laid out in front of you on the computer desktop. Manual dexterity, which was once required for film editing, doesn't impede or improve your ability to edit digital video. There's no need to learn sophisticated mechanical equipment, which was once a requirement of videotape editing, because it all happens in the computer. Digital editing will become more intuitive because computers are becoming more powerful and the user interface is becoming more sophisticated. We are at the beginning of an exponential trend. So, if it doesn't seem very intuitive now, just wait a year.

The principle of layering has a single meaning for beginners though it will acquire multiple meanings later. Film editing is about cutting and pasting, like writing a book by hand. It has the advantages of random access. Film editors who moved to videotape editing lost the ability to work in the manner that felt most comfortable to them. Videotape editing wasn't random. It operated in a strictly linear mode. Editors were forced to start at the beginning and move forward until the show was finished. A good analogy is that some people prefer to write in long hand because it's easy to erase or scratch things out, revise, and make notes. Typewriters are limiting by comparison. Word processing offers some of the freedoms of long hand; you can erase and revise, but it doesn't permit layering. There's no way of making layered notes, which is easy to do in long hand with different colored inks. To overcome this limitation, most people print out their documents and then scribble on the hard copy because they can't scribble on the computer screen. Paper lets you put notes on top of notes. Digital editing also lets you do layering. You can mark up your work, jump back and forth, and leave notes to yourself. It offers the same freedom as paper and pencil even though you're working with pictures and sounds.

Digital editing is unrestrictive and noncommittal. The editor is never forced to make a permanent decision. You can have 2 versions or 200 versions of the same show. You can use the identical material to tell a story three different ways in three different lengths. Best of all, it's easy to accomplish all of this because you can copy, cut, and paste with ease. Make as many versions as you want, if you want to take the time to do it, and see which one plays best with the audience.

The flip side is that you are never really done. You don't have to commit to one version until someone says that time is up, your energy or interest wanes, or the money runs out. Another facet of this principle is that digital editing enables you to see the finished product before you have to commit to it. Digital editing can be a disaster for anyone incapable of making a decision. There are no limitations on how many ways you can slice the pie and few consequences for trying them all out.

Hardware and Software—The Facts

Editing systems have two parts—hardware and software. The hardware is the computer. Even though an editing appliance might not look like a computer, it is one. The computer lets you store and play pictures and sounds in digital files called *media files*. These files are stored on large hard drives. Fast, powerful hardware is required to ensure quick, efficient, and error-free retrieval of the files. If the hardware is up to the task, the editor sees smooth, nonstop playback of the pictures and sounds stored on the hard drives.

Digital editing doesn't happen in a vacuum. The pictures and sounds stored on an editing system must eventually be played elsewhere. It's impractical for people to come to where your editing system resides to watch your show. They'll want to watch it in a more comfortable venue. Hardware (called an *encoder*) that converts the digital media files into standard television signals is at the heart of a digital video editing system. Your editing system has to be capable of displaying video on a computer and television. This may seem simple and obvious, but the technology to make this possible is magical and phenomenal. Without it, digital video editing is nothing but a file management computer game with no lasting purpose. If people can't watch your show on a screen apart from your editing system, what's the point?

Software is what allows editors to manipulate media files to their heart's content without ever having to know anything about computers. It's the go between. Most people think of software as the user interface even though that's only a tiny fraction of what software does for us. There are sophisticated software programs and simple ones. The degree of sophistication determines whether you have a lot of tools or just a few to perform the tasks necessary to create a finished show. Some software programs are intuitive and easy to use. Others are complex with a multitude of features. There are over 200 choices and the decision of which one to use is very personal. Most editors end up using whatever is available to them. Every editing software program includes a basic set of functions and tools that enable you to successfully edit a finished show as long as you become familiar and proficient with the program.

The Big Three—Speed, RAM, and Storage

Computer manufacturers are in the business of selling speed. Every year, the speed of the *central processing unit* (CPU), which is where all the work gets done, increases dramatically. Every year, the manufacturers mount a new advertising campaign to convince consumers to buy a new computer and replace the obsolete one sitting on their desk. If you're using your computer for word processing and e-mail, you can safely ignore their advice.

However, as soon as you decide to enter the world of digital video, you'll discover the truth in those ads. The reality is that computers can never be fast enough, or have enough memory or storage space to satisfy the enormous demands digital video places on computers. Digital editing is taxing, and editing software uses every bit of your computer's processor and memory in a neverending search for more resources.

If you're wondering why, look at it this way. One second of full motion video is made up of sixty still images. There are 30 frames—2 fields per frame, 2 separate images—that must be processed and displayed from a file on a hard drive. Any current computer can display a single still picture. Digital video requires the computer to display 60 pictures every second in perfect time to maintain smooth motion. That requires a lot of processing power. Not only does the motion have to be smooth, but the sound also has to be in perfect sync with the picture. Digital video places a lot of demands on a computer because the picture and sound files must be accessed, retrieved, and displayed at your command. To us, that it happens at all is magic.

We're constantly impressed that when you press Play, the editing system actually retrieves the thousands of images stored in multiple files and plays them back with full motion and sound. We think nothing of it, but it's a marvel. You are asking a lot of your computer when you press Play. We won't accept video that appears to be too slow or fast or that stutters. We expect everything to be smooth and perfect.

To manage all of this data, you need fast CPUs that can move the data stored in large files on your hard drives through the computer and process them quickly. Digital video editing involves reading files and writing new ones. Speed has an impact on how quickly the computer is able to do the calculations needed to create transitions and effects and how fast a new file can be written to store the results. We call this creation of new media files *rendering*. Most shows require a lot of rendering. Newer, faster computers write and create files more quickly than older computers. Another fact of life is that with every new editing software release, you gain more tools and features, although you may also need a faster computer to run the new version efficiently. For example, every successive version of Apple's Final Cut Pro software uses the full capabilities of the company's latest computer models to maximum advantage. As features are added, the need for speed and the minimum hardware requirements go up. You just have to accept the rule—newer, faster computers will always read and write digital video files faster and more efficiently. The corollary to the rule is if your editing system does everything you need it to do today, it will still do it a year from now, although it's bound to be slower than the shiny new systems in those ads.

There's no such thing as being too thin or too rich. When it comes to *random access memory* (RAM), there's no such thing as having too much. The more memory you have in your computer, the better it will run.[1]

---

[1]A technical note: If you don't do any compositing, a gigabyte of RAM is the maximum amount necessary for computers running the Mac or Windows operating system.

Remember that the computer is processing 60 pictures a second and each picture is composed of hundreds of thousands of pixels. The pixels change with each new frame. Memory determines how often your computer can update those pictures. All of the pictures on screen, including the interface's buttons, tools, menus, and viewers, are kept in memory to display them. Even though most of what's on screen remains static, the editing system interface uses up a lot of memory.

The overhead to run the program, along with all those pictures and sounds the editor is trying to manipulate, translates into a neverending need for more memory. If all you had to do was look at a blank blue screen with text, you wouldn't need much. However, every time you open a window, add a layer, or preview an effect, you use up more memory. The amount of memory in your editing system also has an impact on how many video and audio tracks can be played in real time. The more memory you have, the more layers you're likely to be able use. That's why we say you can never have too much and should have as much as you can afford.

Storage is more forgiving. Your needs will depend on the type of projects you plan to do. If you're editing 30-second commercials, you'll need a lot less storage than if you're editing feature-length films. The most common digital video format and the one with the smallest storage requirements is the DV format. One gigabyte of hard-drive space stores about four and a half minutes of DV footage. To hold one hour of DV footage, you'll need about 13 gigabytes of space. If you're using the 1,080/24P *high-definition* (HD) video format, you'll need 334 gigabytes, which is nearly 26 times the space for one hour of storage. The rule is that bigger pictures need faster connections to move them through the system.

It's easy to see, even with DV sources, that projects with a lot of footage will quickly eat up drive space. Any original source material to which you need instant access should be on your editing system. Thankfully, storage seems to get bigger, faster, and cheaper every year. The DV format works well with the typical drives found in computers of recent vintage. You can purchase as much space as you need very cheaply. It's all relative, but even storage suitable for the 1,080/24P HDTV format, which has very high data transfer rate requirements and huge files, is inexpensive. At the moment, you can purchase a terabyte (1,000GB) of 1,080/24P HD storage for under $10,000. Ten years ago, a fast 75MB hard drive cost over $10,000.

The Concept of Workflow

Workflow is the process of creating a show. This process starts with looking at your original source material and ends with looking at the finished show. It's the soup to nuts—from culling footage to editing and layering the elements that go into a show. Workflow is the process, the approach, and the pathway from beginning to end. Workflow is how you get results.

Workflow forces you to ask the following question: How do I gather and view the material, organize the project, and do my job (edit the show)? This order of events is critical to success. Some events in the workflow are universal (part of the underlying structure common to all of digital editing), whereas other events depend on the type of show you're editing. Workflow is flexible. It can accommodate your personality and what you're making. There's latitude to adjust your workflow (change the order of events) to maximize your efficiency.

Every workflow starts with raw materials and ends up with a finished show. You must take the footage and transfer it into your editing system. The material must be categorized so you can find what you need. You must isolate the footage into shots that are clean, clear, and understandable. Those building blocks are then used to create sequences that make sense to the audience. Then you'll need to sit back and look at the show before you start trimming and working on the pacing. It's all part of making the story work for the audience. Transitions, titles, and other layers that can make the story more interesting are added afterwards. The audio is tweaked and mixed. The last step is to output the show for distribution.

Workflow begins with input and ends with output. Your editing system is a tool. You bring source material into the system, manipulate, fine tune, polish, and output it to its final destination. That's the basic process—the general workflow. You can change things around for special projects, but this is the approach editors usually take.

This approach is efficient because you don't want to spend a lot of time making detailed decisions before you have a sense of the overall show. For example, you could spend hours working on a multilayered effect in the first third of the show only to discover when you're nearly done that the sequence in which that effect appears is detrimental to the flow of the show and the entire sequence must be dropped. All the work you did on that complex effect is wasted because it will never appear in the finished show. It makes no sense to layer graphics before you trim and polish. Digital video editing is like building a multitiered wedding cake. You build and stack the layers, and then ice the cake. Transitions, effects, and graphics are the icing. Don't waste your time icing until after the cake is built.

There are also creative workflows that are dynamic, changeable, and essential to success. We'll look at creative workflows in Chapter 5, "Styles and Workflows," through the prism of the different types of video you can make. Each requires an adjustment of the creative workflow to keep your creative juices flowing. However, certain principles are inviolate—you must have input before you can have output.

This book has a workflow, too. We know you need to understand certain things before other things can happen. Yet, as creative people, we believe in random access. If you want to jump ahead to Chapter 5 because you have burning desire to learn the best way to edit a music video, have a passing familiarity with your editing system, and possess a basic sense of editing, go for it. You can always come back to a chapter later or look up what you don't understand in the index. However, if this is your first introduction to editing, you should follow the order of the book. It will give you a solid foundation for understanding the principles and practices of digital video editing.

Do the exercises so you understand how a simple trim can make a difference in how the audience perceives meaning. The exercises will also help you understand what a shot is and how to isolate it. If you don't know a lot about editing, you need to learn these basics. It's best to learn them in the flow that we've created for this book so you can learn to walk before you learn to run.

All About Practice

Learning to use your editing system takes time, but it can be a lot of fun. After you've completed your first project, you'll understand the reward that comes from completion. To become proficient, you must practice. Digital video editing requires knowledge and experience. Experience comes from repetition. Your level of skill will improve as you flex the hand-eye coordination muscles used in editing. So much of what is necessary develops from learning to see the raw materials from an editor's perspective and being able to use the tools. You're only as good as your ability to imagine the story you want to shape. Once you've learned the basics and trained yourself to see, you'll begin to develop the skills necessary to attempt more complex editing projects. The more you do it, the easier it gets.

Don't be alarmed if you feel you're not making progress or getting it as quickly as you'd expect. In our experience, everyone learning to edit for the first time struggles in the beginning. It can be very foreign. However, as time goes by, you will have a breakthrough and the process, technology, concepts, and principles of digital editing will become absolutely clear. It's not unlike the experience of learning to ride a bike. Suddenly, you don't need those training wheels and balancing your bike seems effortless. After your breakthrough, you'll be able to edit naturally with ease. It's a wonderful feeling that erases the memory of what it was like before the possible seemed improbable. Everyone has a breakthrough. Some have it sooner, others have it later. It's part of the guarantee you make to yourself when you identify your method of learning and follow that path.

Summary

Digital editing systems let you take the approach to editing that works for you. All your materials can be accessed randomly. Shuttling tape is a thing of the past. Digital editing offers a layered approach to working with pictures and sounds. It's nondestructive, so it's nearly impossible to make an irreversible error. The joy of digital editing is that you can experiment and create as many versions as you want or have the time to make.

Important Points to Remember

- A digital copy is an exact replica of the original; there is no generation loss.
- Every editing system consists of hardware and software.
- Digital editing uses up all the resources in a computer: speed, memory, and storage.
- Editing success relies on following an efficient workflow. Workflow is the process of creating a show.
- Digital editing is intuitive because all the tools are on the desktop in front of you.
- Undo is only surpassed in importance by the play/stop key.
- Learning to edit takes time. To become proficient, practice.

What the Heck Is That?

A Typical Editing System—If Only There Were Such a Thing . . .

A typical editing system consists of video stuff and a computer. The video stuff includes a video monitor or television set, speakers, and a digital video source, such as a camcorder or recorder. A cable connects the video source to the computer. If the source uses the miniDV, DVCPro, or DVCAM video-tape format, you'll only need one cable (an IEEE-1394 cable, which is also called a Firewire or iLink cable) to connect the video source to the computer section of your editing system. Both the audio and video information recorded on the tape are simultaneously transferred over this cable. Recorders that play other videotape formats may use a *serial digital interface* (SDI) or *high-definition serial digital interface* (HD-SDI) to transfer audio and video to an editing system. These digital links are two-way streets that can send information to your editing system and receive information from your editing system.

The computer components include a keyboard; a mouse or some other pointing device; a computer monitor or monitors; and a minitower or desk unit with the *central processing unit* (CPU), memory, drives, and connectors that typify a computer or, if it's an editing appliance or proprietary editing system, a box of some sort with a manufacturer's name on it. Sometimes a box filled with hard drives called a *storage tower* or *hard-drive array* is also connected to the computer.

If the blade is the tool of film editing and the machine is the tool of video editing, then the computer screen is the tool of digital editing. Your first task when learning to operate an editing system is to familiarize yourself

Figure 2-1
Basic layout for a DV
editing system.

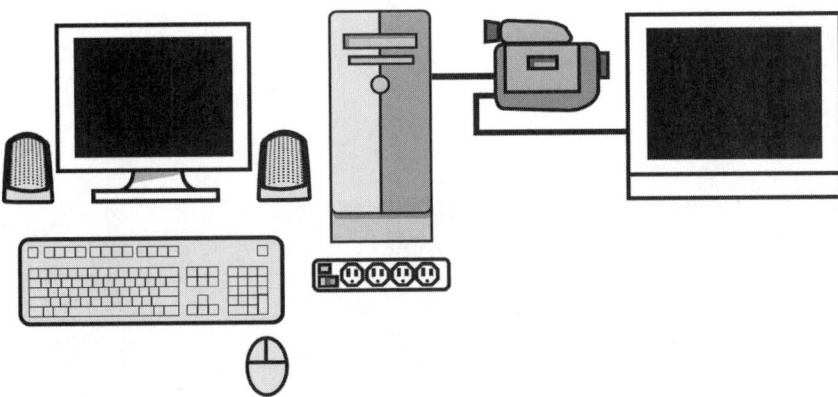

with the desktop. The desktop is the workspace that appears on the computer's monitor(s).

You need to teach yourself to see what is on the screen in front of you. As a student once explained to us, 9 times out of 10, the answer you want is somewhere on the screen. To be successful at editing, you need to learn where the information you want is located and be able to interpret and act on that information using the tools your editing system provides. You need to learn to recognize the buttons, tools, menus, and windows on the desktop. The best way to do this is to explore the four corners of your desktop. Imagine that you're stranded on an island and have to take stock of where you'll be living for who knows how long. You'd want to see everything there is to see. The same thing is true for the desktop of an editing system.

A better analogy for the desktop is the cockpit of an airplane. All of the pertinent information appears on the computer screen. Digital video editing is like flying a plane by instruments alone. Pilots call this *flying blind* because you can't look out the window. In digital editing, there's no window and nowhere else to look. There's just one place for you to focus your attention. The only way to interact with a digital editing system is through the desktop.

The Desktop Interface

Digital editing puts everything you need in one central location—the desktop. Every task is performed here. All the tools and information appear here. The interface—the way you access the tools—varies from manufacturer to manufacturer. Some interfaces are simple and intuitive. Others are complex with a multitude of features, buttons, displays, windows, and menus. Simple interfaces are ideal for beginners.

Figure 2-2
Advanced layout for a DV editing system.

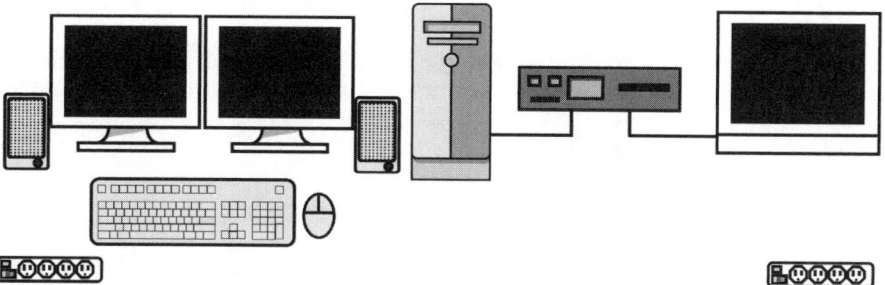

Whether you're using a simple or complex editing system, it's important to understand and learn the interface. This isn't obvious, even to experienced computer users who are just starting to learn digital editing. It's antithetical to anyone with previous film and videotape editing experience. Film editing is tactile and difficult to forget once it is learned. Videotape editing is conceptual. There's so much to think about—from the operation of tape machines to the intricacies of time code lists—that without daily practice, these skills fade from the editor's mind. Digital editing is visual and therefore requires the operator to be knowledgeable only to the point of being able to find what he or she is looking for on the desktop.

However, once you learn digital editing, it is easy. You don't have to use an editing system everyday to remain proficient, which is a big plus for casual users. You don't need to retain information. All you have to know is where to look.

One aspect that can be frustrating is the bewildering variety of jargon. The terms used to describe the identical tools, functions, and features vary from system to system. This is partially due to the convergence of the film, video, and computer industries. Manufacturers snatch terminology from one or more of these industries. Understanding where a term came from can help you translate it into something you understand. If you have a background or expertise in one of these industries, look for an editing sys-

Figure 2-3
Basic elements of the editing system desktop.

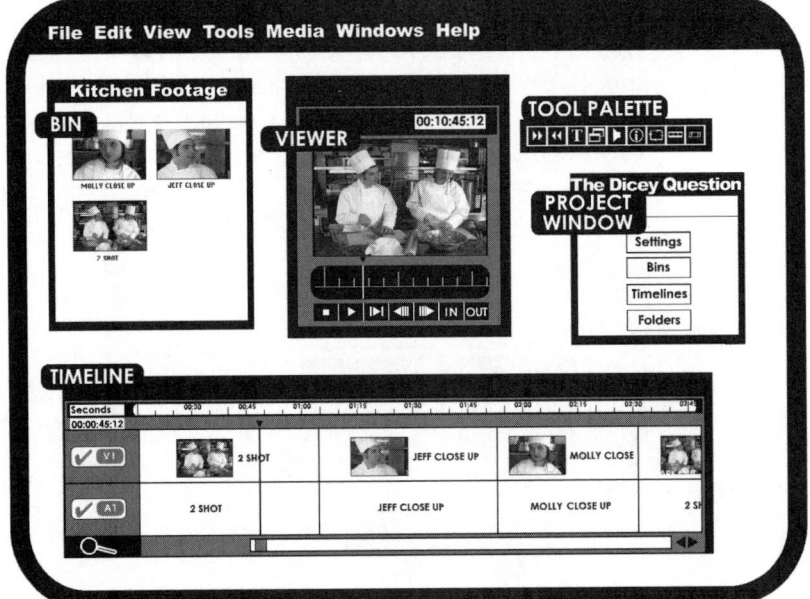

tem that uses terms that are familiar. It will make it much easier for you to learn to edit.

Keep your goal in mind—to learn the user interface. Be aware of how the edit screen is laid out, where things are located, and what the menus do. We call this *learning the four corners of your editing system*. There's a lot of information to be found on the desktop. Our goal is to teach you how to become familiar with all those tools, menus, and help functions.

In the beginning, you'll have a much easier time learning the interface if you can simplify the desktop. Remember that even fighter pilots learn to fly simple planes first. After you understand the interface and can locate the major tools, learn the keyboard shortcuts and buttons that will let you soar.

Interface Design

Every editing system has a unique user interface. Some elements are common to all programs, others are not. Among the commonalties, all digital editing systems are graphic in nature and display source materials in windows.

Interfaces can be separated into three categories—abstract, iconic, and virtual. Text-based interfaces are abstract. Interfaces that rely on graphics or pictures are iconic. Virtual interfaces replicate the look and feel of electronic or mechanical devices. Here are three ways we've seen a five-band audio equalizer tool recreated inside an editing system. The abstract approach uses five lines of text, one for each band of audio. Underneath each line is a space where you can type a positive or negative number from 1 to 10. The iconic version uses *sliders* (which are basically little bars that move up or down) underneath the *bands*. The virtual version is a three-dimensional picture of an equalizer with sliders and meters like something you might find in an electronics store. Assuming all three ways produce identical results in terms of audio quality, the choice of which one to use is a matter of personal preference.

It may not seem important, but the design has an impact on your ability to understand information. For example, it's common to check the amount of available storage space before you start a new show. You need to know if you have enough room for new materials without deleting what's already stored in your editing system. In a system with an abstract interface, the amount of free drive space is likely to be presented as a number. It may represent how many gigabytes of empty space are available or how many minutes of video can be stored. An iconic version might use a bar graph to present how much free space is available on each hard drive. The virtual version might have a picture of a hard drive with the available space indicated in one color and the occupied space in another. The information is the same. However, we can understand the message faster if the presentation matches our preferences. Some people need visuals, whereas others are more comfortable with numbers. It helps to know which you prefer because it can influence your decision to use or purchase a particular editing system. There's no single answer. Choose what works for you.

The way tools are accessed is another facet of interface design. Some systems are keyboard driven. Others are mouse driven. Both methods can be well designed. A well-designed interface lets you work longer than a poorly designed one. Unfortunately, most users discover whether an interface is well designed after spending long hours in the cockpit, flying the plane.

What we look for in a keyboard-driven system are mnemonic, easy-to-remember keyboard shortcuts. Pressing the letter P rather than the letter E to play back a clip makes more sense because P for "play" is easy to remember. Manufacturers are faced with the challenge that there are more tools (over 26) than mnemonic letter keys in most editing systems. Ideally, the tools have been assigned to the keyboard in some logical fashion. If you can figure out the logic (using the first letter of the name of the tool or operation is popular), you can be more efficient.

The other important criteria are handedness and complexity. Some of us are left-handed and others are right-handed. Some editing systems place the most often used commands—Play, Play In Reverse, Mark In (where to start), and Mark Out (where to end)—on the left side of the keyboard. If you're left-handed, your stronger hand ends up doing most of the work, which is great. However, if you're right-handed and the most frequently used keys must be accessed with your weaker left hand, you may be very unhappy. The same is true if the situation is reversed.

Any keyboard shortcut that uses more than one finger to execute a command complicates matters. Shortcuts that rely on using the Control or Command keys plus the Shift key plus a letter are more complex than ones that use a single letter. Complex shortcuts are harder to remember. They also require more manual dexterity and are difficult to type quickly. Pressing and holding a combination of keys with one hand may also cause problems such as carpel tunnel syndrome because editing is often repetitive.

Editing systems designed for professionals allow the operator to remap the keyboard to compensate for handedness and complexity. A left-handed editor could decide to change the key to mark an in from the letter I to R

and the key to mark an out from the letter *O* to *E*. This lets a left-handed person to use the identical fingers, on his or her stronger hand rather than the weaker one, to do the most frequent task during an edit. Reassigning keyboard shortcuts enables an editor who uses certain tools more frequently than others to assign those tasks to a single-key shortcut. At the end of the day, the editor in the cockpit who presses 10 percent fewer buttons is 20 percent less tired.

Consider the Interface Before You Buy

If you haven't purchased an editing system yet, get opinions from people who've used the ones you're considering. Most of the popular systems have e-mail lists and user discussion groups on the Internet. There's a lot of chaff (misinformation) surrounding the kernels of wheat so read carefully between the lines of what's written and form your own opinions. The most vocal people tend to be those who are evangelists for or crusaders against the product.

You should keep in mind that the simplicity or complexity of the interface has little or nothing to do with the tool set. Some systems have simple interfaces and powerful tools. Other systems have complex interfaces with many tools that are actually just bells and whistles. These are featurs that let manufacturers make impressive claims, although you'll rarely, if ever, use them.

Edward Tenner, author of *Why Things Bite Back: Technology and the Revenge of Unintended Consequences*, stated, "Things are needlessly complex because featuritis sells products. People buy them for a feeling of control, then complain that they are hard to manage. But show them something simple and rugged and most of them will call it boring."[1]

After years in the cockpit and more than a few long days that lasted well into the night, we believe bigger and bolder is better. Think about it this way. In feature films, the transition from one shot to the next is a cut 90 percent of the time. You don't need a lot of tools, just the right ones. However, just as there are different types of learners, no system can satisfy every editor.

---

[1] Katie Hafner, "Comforts of Home Marred by Tyranny of Digital Controls," *New York Times*, 28 April 2002, National Edition, P.1 and 38.

A major issue for mouse-driven systems is precision. The size of the target, which is the area of the desktop that's active (the area that can detect the mouse and execute an operation or open a tool), determines the degree of precision. If the target area is too small, the editor must be very precise in positioning the mouse. If the mouse buttons are tiny, the editor is forced to be precise. In practical terms, the editor moves the mouse in ever tightening patterns until he or she hits the target. This type of motion can cause repetitive stress injuries. Equally frustrating, although rarely injurious, is when the precision is set too low and anywhere you place the mouse triggers an action. The least tiring setting is somewhere in between.

Another factor to think about is whether the mouse buttons are used effectively. Some editing systems make the tools you're most likely to need in a particular context readily accessible by placing them on a mouse button. For example, after a clip is selected (highlighted), the mouse button could launch a menu that lets you choose to copy, delete, or change the clip's speed or direction. Interfaces that reduce the number of steps required to execute a task are well designed. A well-designed interface lets you work longer than a poorly designed one.

What You're Likely to Find on the Desktop

The following are the basic elements that appear on nearly every editing system desktop. We've used commonly accepted names for these elements. Your editing system may not use the same ones even though these elements are universal. If the editing system you're using has different names and you're not sure how to relate those names to the ones we're using here, see Chapter 11, "What Are They Talking About?" Chapter 11 has a crossreference table that should help you keep everything straight.

The Project

The *project* is the main organizational window that contains information about a specific show. Computers use hierarchical structures. Files are stored in folders or directories on a drive and most editing systems follow this model. The project is usually the highest level in an editing system's hierarchy.

Figure 2-4
Trims bin holding
film clips.

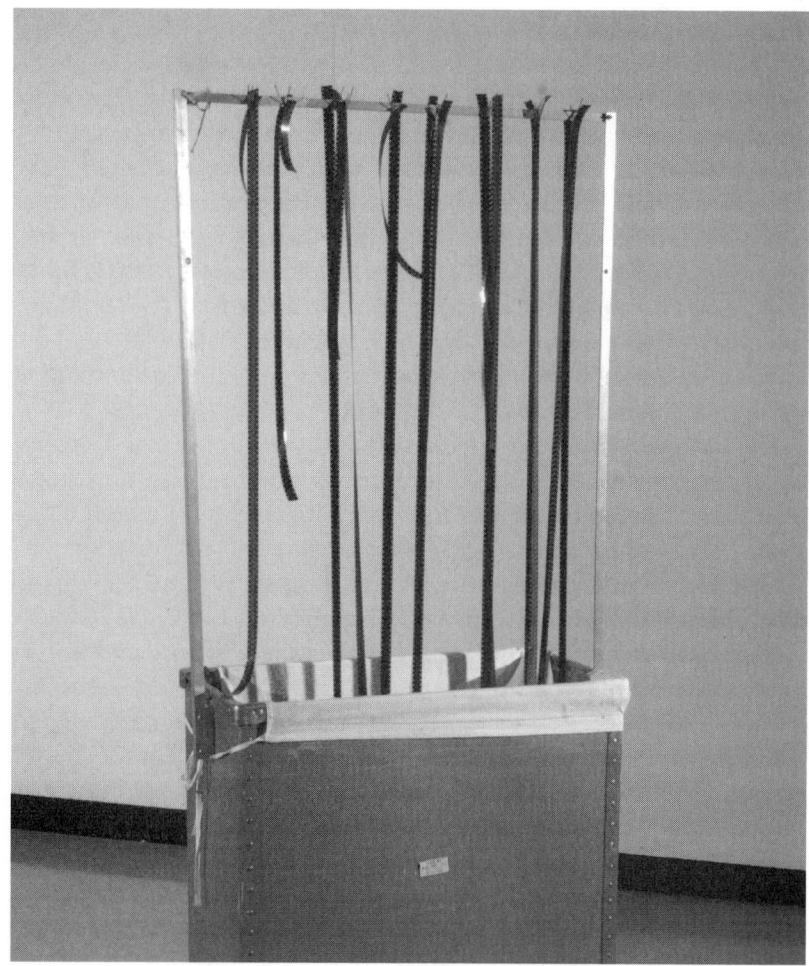

Projects typically store information about the following: all of the sound
and picture elements, which are the principal building materials for the
show you are editing; the sequences of sounds and pictures (called *timelines*) that you create; and any changes you make to technical settings, such
as audio sample rates or video formats, or to user settings, such as the
arrangement of the windows on your desktop or the color scheme. The project window is often the first window opened and the last window closed in
an editing system application.

The Bin

The *bin* window is a folder that holds clips. The name bin comes from the world of film editing. Many editing systems actually use an icon that looks like a film bin (a square trashcan with a cotton liner) to represent the directories or folders that the editing system creates to store clips. Film editors hung the clips they were working with (long strips of film) from a rack above the bin. As the editor cut shots out of the film reels, the pieces he or she planned to use were hung in the bin. The shots that were unusable were tossed on the floor, which is where the phrase "left on the cutting room floor" originated. The digital equivalent of a bin serves the same purpose, but is much smarter.

The word *clip* is widely used to describe the icons that represent the audio, video, and graphics stored in an editing system. Clips are actually database entries that point to the digital media files stored in your editing system. The clip (refer to our jukebox explanation in Chapter 1, "The Whole Truth and Nothing But the Truth") is not the media file even though it may appear to be the same. Often video clip icons display a single frame of the video file. That frame is a called a *thumbnail* or *picon*. Picon comes from combining the words *picture* and *icon*.

Every system has at least one bin. Some have a set number of bins, for example, one for each category of material, such as audio, effects, graphics, titles, transitions, and video. Other systems let you create as many bins as you like. Bins are just files or folders that help you organize your source materials.

Typically, you can display the contents of a bin in several ways. The text view displays the clips in a database or list view. Most editing systems track a lot of information about each clip. There are categories (or fields) for the

Figure 2-5
Timeline window.

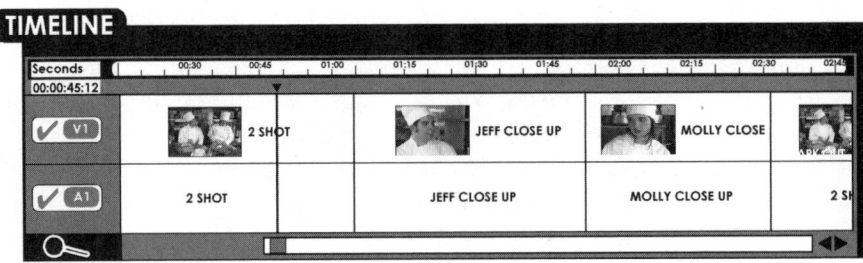

name of the clip, the name of the media file, the name of the original source tape, the duration of the clip, any comments you've made, the creation date of the file, and other technical information. Quite often the list can be sorted by category and/or searched to find the clip or items you need. The picture view displays the clips as a series of picons. These static images represent a full motion video and audio clip. Another potential way to display the bin is a variation on the database view, which includes a picture alongside each text entry.

The Viewer

The *viewer* window is used to play the clips. Controls like those found on a VCR to play, pause, stop, fast-forward, rewind, and shuttle are typically placed under the viewing screen. There are often buttons to mark an in (a start point) and an out (an end point.) Some systems have one viewer window for source materials (the clips) and a second viewer window to play the show or whatever resides on the timeline.

The Timeline

The *timeline* window is where you arrange clips in a sequence that tells a story with a beginning, middle, and end. This comic-strip arrangement represents your finished show. The audio, video, and graphics clips are typically arranged in separate bands (usually horizontal), which are framed by a scalable ruler marked in units of time.

The Top Row

The *top row* is a drop-down menu bar that appears at the top of the desktop. Most computer programs place important functions on the top row or main menu. This is where you are likely to find major operations, such as opening a project, saving a project, importing files, outputting your finished show, and one of the most useful functions, help. This menu functions as your central command center. Professionals know that learning the top row is how you begin to understand the structure of your editing system.

Tool Palettes

There are two types of tool palette windows: a row or rows of mouse buttons or roll-up windows with tabbed folders. Both offer quicker access to specific tools. Most editing systems, though not all, use at least one mouse button bar that floats and can be moved anywhere you need it. Some button bars dock to the top menu. The roll-up window palettes are often used in addition to a button toolbar. Adobe and Apple use this approach.

That's it—there are just six primary elements. Of course, it's more complicated than that because, well, we're not really sure why. Perhaps it's because those six windows seem to multiply like rabbits. We'll discuss this more later.

One Viewer or Two

Every editing system follows either a single- or dual-viewer model. Single-viewer systems follow the flatbed model. A flatbed editing table is the device most editors use to edit film. It has a single screen that displays the pictures and sounds. Dual-viewer systems follow the videotape model called *source record*. The simplest type of video editing system can be made by connecting two recorders together. One videotape recorder plays back the original source tapes and the other one records what's being played on a new tape called an *edit master*. The only way to see and hear what's being played or recorded is to connect monitors to each of the recorders. To help editors keep track of what's what, the monitors were labeled. The one connected to the recorder playing the source tapes was labeled *source* and the other monitor was labeled *record* because that's what that recorder was doing.

In a single-viewer digital editing system, everything you need to see, whenever you need to see it, appears in one window. The viewing screen does double and triple duty. The clips play in the viewer. The timeline (your show) plays in the viewer. The title and effects appear in that window. It all happens in one viewer. If you're working on a system with a single computer monitor, desktop space could be at a premium. This approach uses the least amount of real estate. An extra benefit is that the arrangement of the windows on your desktop rarely changes.

However, single-viewer systems can be confusing for beginners unless close attention is paid to what's being displayed. Every editing system has some kind of indicator to let you know whether you're watching a clip or the timeline. You don't want to mix them up and inadvertently do something on the timeline that you meant to do on a clip.

Editing systems based on the source record model are easier to learn. One of the viewers—the one that represents the record monitor, which we'll call the *results* viewer—is permanently linked to the timeline. Consequently, the results viewer always displays the results of your actions. The other viewer, the source viewer, plays clips. It's usually easy to tell them apart because they have different buttons and information displays. The convention is that the source viewer is always on the left and the record viewer is on the right. Why? That's just the way it is.

Some systems let you make the source and results viewer windows different sizes. If your system permits that, make the results viewer larger. You'll be able to see the difference between the two viewers instantly, and it's nice to have a bigger screen to evaluate the results of your work.

In some systems, whenever you double-click on a clip, a new viewer window opens. It's easy to imagine how quickly your desktop can become overrun with multiple viewer windows. You should open as few windows as possible. Each viewer requires *random access memory* (RAM). If you use up the RAM in your system, you may notice that clips don't play smoothly. Overlapping viewer windows can also cause problems. The best solution is to avoid these problems. Besides, too many open windows can be confusing, especially for beginners. You're trying to learn where all the pertinent information is located on the desktop. Filling up the desktop with unnecessary windows only gets in the way of your learning.

There's another difference between single- and dual-viewer editing systems. Those with multiple viewers are often more customizable. This can be good or bad depending on your needs and skill level. Even if the only thing you can change is the size and placement of the viewers, beginners can get themselves into trouble. You don't want to move the windows around just because you can. It's important to keep the windows in the same place every time you use the system, as you're learning the geography of the desktop.

You'll also learn faster if your desktop is kept clean and uncluttered. A simple workspace lets you focus on editing. If you're using editing software on a computer, it's also a good idea to choose a neutral color for your desktop. Patterns and photographs only make it more difficult to get real work done. Avoid anything with bright colors and fine detail. Those backgrounds make it difficult to see video clearly. Beyond the obvious distractions of having too many lines and colors, there's a physiological problem.

It's impossible to see colors accurately after you've been staring at strong bright colors. The best choices for desktop backgrounds are shades of light blue or gray. One computer graphics expert went to the trouble of painting his workspace pure gray to avoid any interference that light reflecting from his walls might cause while he and his clients were making critical decisions about color. It's not necessary to go that far. Using a neutral desktop background is enough.

The Four Corners

Look at the desktop. The major elements on your desktop should be recognizable. However, it's not enough to just know the center of the desktop. You need to learn the four corners of this cockpit. Do you know what all those icons and buttons do? What's that window in the upper right-hand corner for? What's that little icon on the lower right-hand corner of the timeline do?

Explore the terrain. The name of the icon or tool usually appears when you place the mouse over an object. Press buttons. Open menus. If you want an explanation of what something does, use the help function or check your editing system manual. Eventually, you'll understand what all the functions and tools on screen do. However, you shouldn't feel compelled to learn it all at once. The only thing you need now is a vague sense of where to find things. Where are the tools? How are the menus categorized?

Editing is simple. Finding the tools you need while you're editing is the problem. Learn early to explore the entire desktop. Don't neglect something just because you don't expect to use that feature very often. Remember that you're only as good as your ability to find things on the screen so it's important to teach yourself the four corners.

Train your eye. If the answer is somewhere on the screen, you don't want to have to spend a lot of time searching for it. You want to be able to go to the correct corner immediately. That's another reason to avoid constantly changing the desktop. Editors who maintain a consistent workspace are more efficient because they don't have to interrupt their creative flow to remember where they moved something. For most of us, the location of a tool is easier to remember than its function. Focus your attention on the screen. Use the help feature. Train your eye so you don't interrupt your creative flow. The answers are on the desktop.

In a digital environment, you learn to edit through the interface. The desktop is the interface and the tool. The items on the desktop change radically in many editing systems whenever an operation requires different tools. If you're bringing new source materials (inputting) into your editing system, you need a tool to control the camcorder or recorder and bins to hold the material. If you're working on the audio mix for your finished show, a mixer tool, audio meters, and the timeline are important; there's no reason for any bins or source viewers to be open. Each phase of editing requires different tools. Each tool opens a window, which allows you to perform a task. As your proficiency increases, making the choice of which windows to open and which ones to close becomes easier. To avoid confusion, especially when you're just learning, only open tools that are absolutely necessary.

Even professional editors get confused. If you're working with multiple layers of audio, video, and effects, it's easy to get lost or make a mistake. The solution is to take a step back. Use the undo feature. If you haven't found it, look for it. Undo is one of the most important features in any editing system.

Undo is like the trail of crumbs you leave behind as you wander deeper into the forest so you can find your way out later. Most of the changes you make to the interface or your show can be undone. Editing systems without an undo feature are rare. Very simple editing systems may only permit one or two undo operations. Others can track every keystroke you make from the time you launch the application until the moment you close it. So if you've taken one too many steps into the forest, the best thing to do is to back up. The alternative is to go back to the top menu and restore the project to the way it was before you last saved it.

Taking Control of the Four Corners

Digital editing systems can be bewildering. The desktop is filled with tool palettes, information windows, icons, folders, and viewers. All of them open at once and as you work, windows start multiplying. How can you avoid confusion as you learn the interface?

Reduce the clutter as much as possible. Close unnecessary windows. If you're doing simple editing, close the meter, mixer, and effects windows and anything else that has nothing to do with basic editing. It's best to keep the number of open windows to a minimum since every open window requires RAM. More importantly, real estate on the desktop is limited. There's no sense filling it up with useless windows.

Resize the useful windows to reflect their importance. For instance, if you're organizing clips into bins, the timeline and results viewer should be small. Bins and the source viewer should take up most of the real estate. Scale the viewers down to create more open space. Make the picons in the bin just big enough to see clearly.

The arrangement of windows and tools on your desktop is called a *screen layout*. If the windows aren't locked in place, be careful where you move them. Use the default screen layouts that came with your editing system as much as possible. Different tasks require different tools and the screen layout may change depending on the mode of the editing system. It can be beneficial to modify the screen layout. Once you've figured out what works best for you, leave it alone. You want everything in your screen layout to be in its familiar place every time you edit.

Consistency makes it easier to remember where to look in the cockpit. If you move things around, make sure you return them to their proper places before you shut down your editing system. Many times the screen layout is saved every time you exit the program. The screen layout reverts to that position the next time you open your editing system. Ideally, you want all the windows and tools to be in their familiar places the next time you edit. After you've learned where the useful information is located on the desktop, you can edit with ease. Recurrence equals confidence.

Start with the Top Row

One of the first steps you should take is to familiarize yourself with the menus in your editing system. The most important one is the top row. This is the drop-down menu common to most software running on the Windows and Mac platforms. If your editing system is based on either platform, the top row is usually visible at all times. Some categories are universal, such as File, Edit, and Help. Help is a category you should use *early and often*.

Others are more specific. For example,

- Bin, Clip, Tools, and Window (Avid XpressDV)
- View, Mark, Modify, Sequence, Effects, Tools, and Windows (Apple Final Cut Pro)

- View, Album, Toolbox, and Setup (Pinnacle Studio)
- View, Program, Track, Tools, Media, Windows (Media 100 iFinish)
- View, Collection, Element, Storyboard, and Window (Incite)

There are as many variations as there are systems. We recommend that you make it a point to use the top row menu. This is where you can learn the functions, features, and structure of your editing system. All of the standard computer functions (Open, Close, Save, Save As, and Exit) are available from this menu. The great part is that some of the tools familiar to every computer user perform the identical function in a digital editing system. Digital editing can be seen as word processing with pictures and sounds. The cut, copy, and paste functions (and in most instances, the identical keyboard shortcuts are used) work the way they do with text in a word processor or with video clips on a timeline. We've known some editors to eschew the mouse buttons and edit using only the Control (Command for Mac users) C, X, or V commands.

Chances are when you need to do something beyond making a cut, the tool will be accessible from the top menu. As you step across the top menu and look at what appears under each category, you may not understand what some tools do or what a particular option means. That's to be expected. You just need to get a sense of the logic. For example, in Final Cut Pro, you'll find audio pan and gain under Modify. In XpressDV, it's under Tools.

We recommend that beginners start by using the top menu to perform tasks. It doesn't matter if your editing system runs on the Mac or Windows platform or if it's an editing appliance. The feature or function you're looking for will often be spelled out on the top menu. It's the best place to start.

Even seasoned professionals should use the top menu until becoming an expert on the system. Remember that most of the features and tools are used infrequently. No one should expect to be fluent with all of them. All that's required is ability to find the feature or tool. Using the top menu bar is the most reliable way to access all the tools.

The mouse is an important tool for editors. However, don't let yourself become dependent on it or it will hamper you later. Develop your skills by using the keyboard to learn where the tools are located. After you're familiar with the menus, you can branch out and learn the keyboard shortcuts and then the mouse commands.

The Fast Way? Learn Shortcuts

The easiest way to learn the keyboard shortcuts is to use the top row menu. The shortcuts are listed alongside the menu command. If you see that you're using a command repeatedly, learn the shortcut. Shortcuts bypass the process of selecting a choice on a menu. As the word implies, shortcuts are faster. Whenever you see yourself repeatedly accessing the same menu, scrolling to make a selection, and clicking on the selection, switch to a keyboard shortcut. The most widely used shortcut is the spacebar. In nearly every program, and in nearly every situation, the spacebar is a shortcut for the ALL STOP command. Pressing the spacebar brings everything to a halt.

Other popular shortcuts are slowly becoming universal, such as the *I* key to mark an in point and the *O* key to mark an out point. Common-sense keyboard shortcuts help make editing faster and easier. Chapter 11 includes application-specific shortcuts for many common tasks.

J–K–L

The *J–K–L* group of shortcuts are also growing in popularity. These shortcuts are used to play clips backwards and forward. *J* plays a clip in reverse, *K* is the pause key, and *L* plays a clip forward. In some systems, pressing *J* or *L* repeatedly makes the clip play faster or slower. The *J–K–L* group is so powerful because an editor can play a clip backward and forward at varying speeds with one hand.

If you have any touch typing ability, develop your keyboard shortcut skills. In many systems, the *J–K–L* shortcut is directly below the shortcut keys *I* and *O* used to mark ins and outs, respectively. This means that for those who can touch type, nearly 60 percent of the editing functions can be accessed with one hand. It's easy to see that a touch typist can really soar with a little practice. Shortcut conventions familiar to anyone who uses a word processing program are also used in many digital editing systems. Shortcuts for Cut, Copy, and Paste, Save, Open, Close, and Delete are universal.

Keyboard shortcuts are excellent for quick, precise editing. However, they only work if you use them. Beginners tend to rely on the mouse, which is fine, although the mouse can only take you so far. Frank Black, a professional editor, remarked, "Anyone can edit with a mouse, but you can make a living with the keyboard."

Most of you aren't planning to earn a living editing. However, the most efficient way to work is to edit with your right hand on the mouse and your left hand on the keyboard. Left-handers should reverse that suggestion. To be really proficient at any endeavor, you need to use two hands. Editing with one hand or just the mouse is slow, unproductive, and inefficient. It's amazing to us that students who wouldn't think to play a computer game with one hand routinely use only the mouse to edit.

A Word About Tool Palettes

Tool palettes are common on digital editing systems. The functions on the palette are usually available from the top menu bar or through a keyboard shortcut. It's important to know which tools are only accessible from a tool palette. These tools require the mouse.

If you find important tools that are not duplicated elsewhere, the tool palette needs to be in a convenient place. Screen position is important. If you can, move the strip or window to where it will do the most good. Burying the tool palette means finding it will be a nuisance.

Two Hands Are Better Than One

It's common sense—people who use two hands are more productive. Most digital editing systems have a mouse and keyboard. Some people use the mouse to access tools on the desktop and ignore the keyboard. Others prefer to type keyboard commands and avoid the mouse. Experienced editors know that the most productive approach is to use whatever gives you the faster access to the tool you need. The technique of using both hands is simple to learn: Keep one hand on the mouse and the other on the keyboard. Over time you'll develop your own style—accessing tools with the buttons or keys you find most comfortable.

The best time to start developing your own style is when you begin learning the system. Don't rest one hand in your lap or use it to hold up your head. If you need to think or if you're tired, take a break. Video-game aficionados who play with one hand aren't competitive. Editing works the same way; two-handed editors win every time.

Look for a place where it won't be buried or covered by other windows. It should also be close to other tools involved with the functions on the tool palette. For example, if the majority of the tools are editing tools, this tool palette should be as close as possible to the timeline and results viewer since this is where those editing tasks will be performed.

Personalize the Interface; Make It Work for You

Most editing systems permit some customization. An open system lets you change the screen layout and other aspects of the interface to suit your preferences. The purpose of this is to make the interface more comfortable for you. A degree of openness provides flexibility and power because the system can be altered to suit the task at hand. On the other hand, we depend on interfaces that are consistent. Interfaces that change frequently are constantly confusing.

Organization Is Important

Like most desktops, yours is probably filled with windows for projects, bins, viewers, and timelines. The default screen layout worked best for the team who created your editing system. Screen layout is largely a personal preference so some systems let you choose from several options. Another option called the *custom* option is often available. This lets you position and size the windows and store the arrangement.

Without discipline and consistency on your part, your desktop can end up looking different every time you use the system. This can be confusing when you're learning to edit. Imagine how you'd feel if every time you drove your car, the speedometer moved to a new place. Change for change's sake will give you a headache. Decide on a screen layout that works for you and stick with it. It makes you less efficient, not more, to move the windows around on your desktop every time you edit.

Size the windows to maximize the real estate on your desktop. Position each window where it won't obscure other windows. You need to be able to locate the windows quickly and see what you're doing within the window. Create an arrangement and then live with it.

Some editing systems have default screen layouts that change to reflect the task at hand. In other systems, you'll have to create them. The optimal screen layout for editing a show is different than the optimal layout for mixing a show. What you need to see and where you need to see it often changes dramatically. If you can save multiple custom layouts, name the layout for the task or operation for which its been optimized, for example, mixing or 3-d effects.

Customizing Your Keyboard

Professional editing systems let editors remap the keyboard. You can move shortcuts around the keyboard or even create custom shortcuts. Custom shortcuts are the ultimate keyboard shortcuts because they belong to you alone. These shortcuts are your personal power keys and are usually stored in a user preference file. If you save that file on a diskette or CD, you can reuse your settings at any facility with the same system. Then when you sit down to start editing, you can load your settings and your personal editing cockpit will appear in front of you.

As you work, you'll discover that you use some buttons and commands more often than others. This is a reflection of the type of work you do. Inevitably, you'll also find some shortcuts that don't make sense to you or shortcuts that are useful but cumbersome because they require too many

Out for a Long Drive

Digital editing is like taking a long drive in your car to a place you've never seen. It's a visually stimulating experience. You are excited about what's in front of your windshield, but you must still pay attention to the dashboard. It's also tiring because you have to sit for a long time. Editing is similar. Editors spend a lot of time sitting in front of a monitor watching footage and paying attention to the controls. You need a good chair and monitors should be placed at eye level. Eye strain, aching arm or wrist joints, and numb butt are common complaints. A good mouse pad, a keyboard at the proper height, and proper wrist support can alleviate many problems. Make sure your workspace is comfortable. You'll be glad you did.

Tips

The project window must be open in many systems. It often serves as a table of contents for the project or a place to maintain a list of recently opened files. This element rarely has an editing function beyond opening or closing a project or application. Reduce its size or roll it up to minimize clutter.

- In a single-viewer system, position the viewer in the upper-left center of the desktop to avoid hiding it.
- Place an editing tool palette near the timeline and results viewer where most of the editing takes place.
- Save preference file settings under your own name.
- Save screen layouts under the name of the task you've optimized it for.

keystrokes. We don't think it qualifies as a shortcut if you have to use multiple combinations of the Control (command), Shift, Alt, or Option keys. These shortcuts are candidates for remapping.

Remapped keys work great because they are designed logically and reflect the style and intelligence of the designer, you. For example, Avid master editor Jennifer Rew remaps her keyboard so that Shift-*I* clears in points and Shift-*O* clears out points. We're sure you'll discover shortcuts that make your life as an editor easier.

Summary

Editing is simple, but learning the interface takes time. An editor is only as good as his or her ability to find and use the proper tools. Remember, it's easier to locate something if it's in a predictable place. During an emergency, pilots don't have time to think about where they should look and what the warning lights mean. Similarly, you don't have time when you're in the digital editing cockpit. You just want to go to where you need to go. Remember that learning the interface thoroughly is a lifelong process. However, all you really need to know is where to look.

Important Points to Remember

- The desktop is your center of attention.
- Nine times out of ten, the answer is on the desktop.
- If you prefer a virtual interface, avoid text based abstract interfaces.
- Don't be fooled by simplicity. Bigger and bolder is better!
- Use the top row to understand the editing system's structure.
- Train your eye to find buttons or information on the desktop.
- Avoid confusion. Unclutter your desktop. Close any unnecessary windows.
- Open and close viewers and tools in the same place every time. Consistency makes learning easier.
- Learn the keyboard shortcuts for repetitive tasks.
- Edit with two hands.
- Customize with care.

Beginnings, Middles, and Ends

Now that you're comfortable (or still gaining confidence) with your editing system's interface, it's time to learn how to use this tool. Editing involves telling stories with pictures and sounds. Therefore, you should know something about storytelling and about how editors use pictures and sounds to tell stories. This chapter will help you understand the basics of editing. However, experiencing editing is even more valuable. Editing is an art. As with all the arts, creativity and craft are important. The craft of editing involves learning techniques and practicing those techniques until you achieve competency.

To help you become a competent editor, we've developed a series of exercises to open your eyes to the power of editing. The footage for these exercises is stored on the CD. You can use this material to supercharge your imagination or work with your own footage.

The Tradition of Storytelling

Every story has a beginning, middle, and end. It doesn't matter whether the story is a lengthy drama or a joke. People prefer stories that have resolution because real life rarely does. Storytelling has a long tradition that dates back to the dawn of human history. Since ancient times, those who could tell, perform, depict, and, much later, write down stories have been cherished for their abilities. Digital video fuses oral storytelling, performance, painting and photography, and writing in what is the culmination of a 10,000-year tradition. You have the most powerful storytelling tools ever conceived in your hands. Use them to amuse, illuminate, or memorialize. Above all, tell stories that celebrate our shared existence.

Making Pearl Necklaces

Stories are built by stringing together shots in the right order, as if they were pearls in a necklace. When each pearl in is the right position on the silk cord, we no longer focus on the individual pearls; instead, we admire the necklace. We appreciate its symmetry and treasure the beauty of it as a whole.

Editors arrange pictures and sounds to tell a story. Using the materials at hand, the editor must find the logic or structure that will unfold the story from beginning to end over time. The story can be brief (shorter than a minute) or epic in length. No matter what you're editing (shots of your children playing, a wedding, the coronation of a king, or the next Hollywood blockbuster), the audience sees the finished show as one continuous sequence. The when (the order in which the audience see the images) and the how (how long the audience sees the images) are as important as the what (the content of those images).

Each shot is a pearl that needs to be placed in the correct spot on the timeline. When clear, clean, and understandable shots are selected, all that remains is for the editor to make sure each shot is in its proper place and on the screen for the appropriate amount of time. The audience only sees what the editor arranges.

Although the story appears to unfold for the audience, the structure is perfectly clear to an editor working on a digital editing system. The timeline is a visual representation of a story's structure. Arranging and rearranging shots on a timeline is as easy as shuffling a deck of cards. Select any shot, move it, shorten it, lengthen it, or move it again to shape the story. With practice, the shows that you edit will keep the audience involved until the fade out at "The End."

Are You a Bricklayer or Sculptor?

There are two approaches to the craft of editing. Some editors build shows one shot at a time. They add shot to shot to shot until the last shot is placed on the timeline. Others carve shows out of the entire block of material. These editors chop, chip, and slice to hone and shape the show.

Actually, few editors slavishly adhere to either of these approaches. Sometimes an editor acts as a bricklayer building the show one shot at a time, and then in the next minute acts as a sculptor carving, honing, and polishing. The truth is digital editing makes it so easy to switch back and forth between building and carving that you never have to make a choice. However, you do need to know what each approach entails. It also helps to figure out which one is more appealing to you because that's the approach you should use to start editing a project.

Building

This method is like building a brick wall or stringing pearls on a necklace. The editor adds shots one at a time to the show. To do that, the editor goes

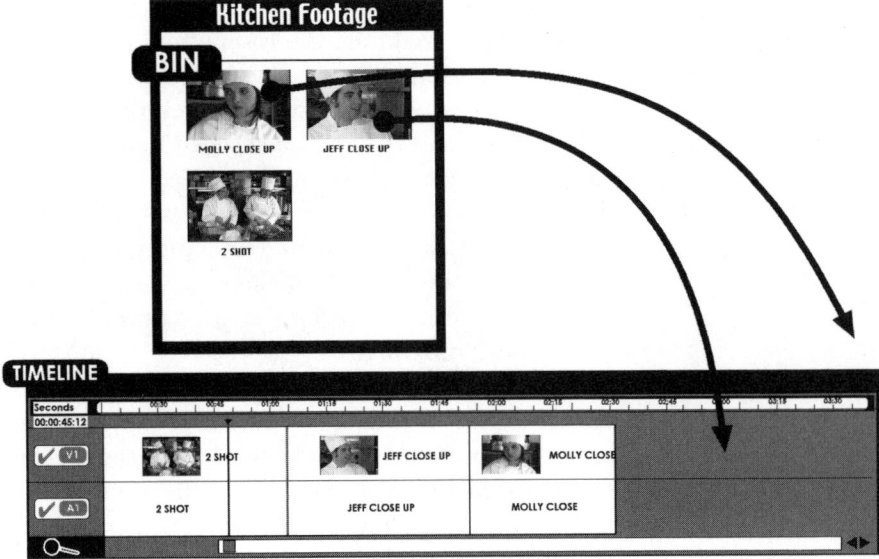

through all the footage and isolates the shots. The details of how to do this appear in Chapter 7, "Setting the Table." In brief, the editor looks at the material, finds the beginning and end of each useable shot, and creates a copy of each shot called a *subclip*. The subclips are named, saved, and stored in bins. Once all the shots have been isolated, the editor can start placing them in the show. Each shot is added in succession from the start. As the editor slowly adds shots, he or she can play and review the results. This method is similar to linear video editing. The editor places a first shot, proceeds to the second, the third, and so on. This method works well with any show that has a detailed script. The exercise you're about to start editing uses the building method.

Carving

This method follows Michelangelo's approach to sculpting marble statues. For Michelangelo, each block of stone contained a human figure. All he needed to do was chisel away the excess marble and reveal the figure trapped in the stone. The editor starts by placing all the material, or at least a manageable portion of it, on the timeline.

Figure 3-2
Carving video in steps to remove unwanted material.

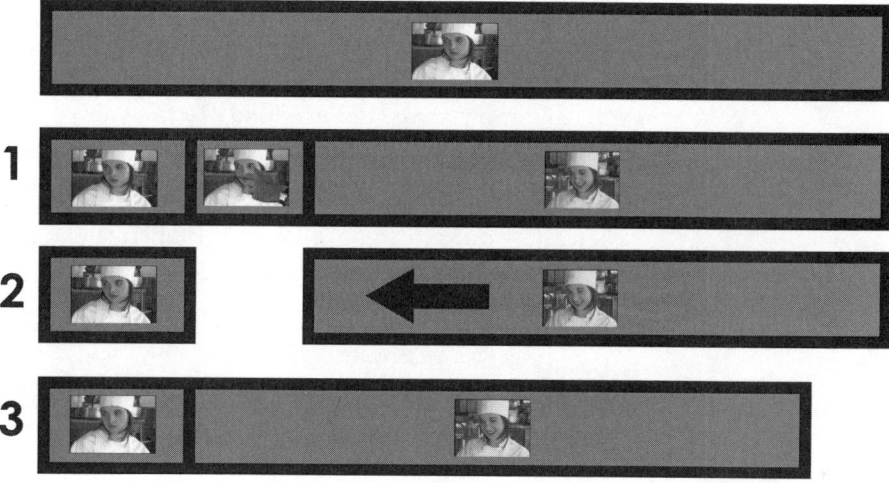

As the editor watches the material, the sections that are unusable are marked and deleted from the timeline. This is the opposite of what a builder does because the carver is looking for the moment when the material ceases to be interesting. Afterwards, the editor reviews the now much shorter timeline. Editors repeat this process, carving away excess to reveal more of the essence of the material. This method enables the editor to find the structure of the show through the material. Once everything on the timeline is carved to the bone, the editor begins the process of moving those materials around to order the story.

The Editing Exercise

The goal of this exercise is to make as many edits as possible to practice using your editing system while building a simple dialogue scene. You can use the footage on the CD or shoot your own version of the script. This is an easy project designed to let you get your fingers wet.

Editors refer to their first attempts to assemble the show as a *rough cut*. It's called a rough cut because it's rough around the edges. This stage is important because it is where you create a basic structure to give the story a beginning, middle, and end. The flow from shot to shot can be polished later.

You should be comfortable when you edit. Make sure your chair, keyboard, mouse, and monitors are at comfortable heights. Hopefully, you've been wandering around the four corners of your editing system desktop exploring everything, and are ready to take on your first assignment.

The process of transforming original source materials into a finished show is called *workflow*. Here's our workflow for this exercise:

1. Turn on your editing system and launch the application.
2. Create a new project.
3. Copy the clips from the CD into your editing system.
4. Create a new timeline.
5. Edit the shots on the timeline.

Turn on Your System

Like many endeavors in life, starting is the hardest part. Turn on the power to your editing system. If you're using an editing appliance, that could be a single switch labeled on. Or there could be switches located on each piece of equipment in rooms filled with equipment. In our experience, beginners often forget to turn on all of the peripherals connected to the editing system, such as the speakers, monitors, external hard drives, and camcorder.

There's a simple solution to this problem. If you don't have an uninterruptible power supply or surge-protected power strip, purchase one and plug everything into it. This way one simple switch turns everything on.

Editing systems are less expensive than they once were, but the cost to purchese them are still substantial. A high-quality surge protector is cheap insurance for home users. Professional users should have an uninterruptible power supply that gives you enough time to save your work before shutting down the system.

After you turn on your editing system, launch the editing application.

Create a New Project

Every editing system has its own way of creating, organizing, and saving projects. You need to be aware of where your system stores project files so you can find them. If your editing system follows a structured approach, any projects you create will be stored in specific directories. Other editing

Organization Tips for Open-Style Editing Systems

If your editing system doesn't have its own rigid (default) file structure, you need to set one up. Never listen to your evil twin calling you a geek for being organized. You're an editor so you'll have the last laugh later.

- Create a directory (Windows) or folder (Mac) on your editing system for all of your projects. Label it Video Projects or whatever makes sense to you. Then make a subdirectory or subfolder within that directory for each project. This will simplify the process of opening, saving, importing, exporting, and retrieving files. Believe us, this works.

- Create a file structure.

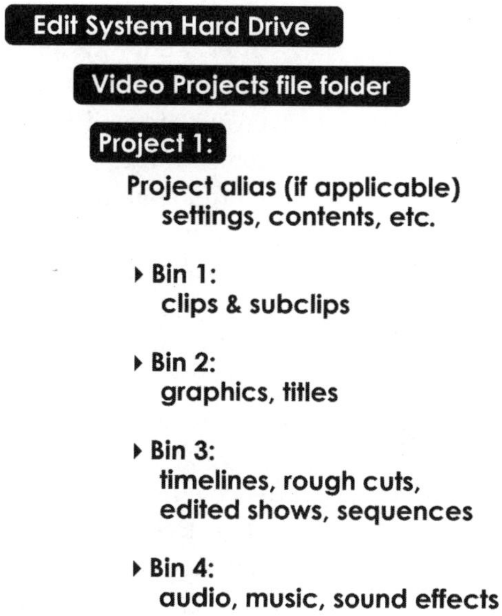

Edit System Hard Drive

Video Projects file folder

Project 1:

> **Project alias (if applicable)**
> **settings, contents, etc.**

> ▸ **Bin 1:**
> **clips & subclips**

> ▸ **Bin 2:**
> **graphics, titles**

> ▸ **Bin 3:**
> **timelines, rough cuts,**
> **edited shows, sequences**

> ▸ **Bin 4:**
> **audio, music, sound effects**

Figure 3-3
Recommended file structure.

systems take an open approach and don't have a default structure. We've even experienced the embarrassment of not being able to locate a project after saving it on one of these editing systems. As silly as it is to say, make sure you know where your editing system stores its files.

Open systems store project files anywhere and everywhere. As the editor, you must impose order on the editing system by saving your work in the specific directories you create. If you're working on an open-style editing system, read the organization tips in the sidebar.

Create a new project. Name it *The Dicey Question*. Save it.

Get Set to Edit

For this exercise, the only windows and tools that should be open are those used in basic editing. Nothing extraneous should be open, such as titler, audio mixer, or effects windows. Most editing systems default to a basic editing setup. If you have an editing system that lets you modify the layout of the desktop, arrange the windows so they make sense and you're comfortable.

You should have a project labeled *The Dicey Question* open. The project window is the primary organizational window in most editing systems.

Create a bin called *Kitchen Footage*. You'll only need one bin to store clips for this exercise. The footage was shot in a kitchen (hence the name).

Expand the file labeled edv.zip on the CD on your hard drive and copy the material into the bin. There are detailed instructions on the CD.

Your Kitchen Footage bin should now have three clips. Look to see if the clips are in your bin. If the bin can display picons, you will see a picon for each clip. We recommend changing the picon to a picture that's more representative than the first frame of the clip. Look in your editing system manual. If your system doesn't accommodate picons, don't worry about it. Identify each clip by name. They should be called *2-Shot*, *Molly MCU*, and *Jeff MCU*. MCU stands for *medium close-ups*.

Viewer

Watch all of the clips to acquaint yourself with the footage. Normally, there would be multiple takes of each shot in this scene involving two kitchen workers. As the editor, you would have to watch and evaluate all of them trying to find the one take that has the most emotional impact. This is an exercise so you're stuck with our choices.

Pay attention to the motion control buttons on your editing systems viewer or viewers. Play the clips in forward and reverse. Go to the head and tail of the clip. Try out all of the buttons to familiarize yourself with their functions. Most editing systems display the time code somewhere on or near the viewer. Locate the time code display; it will become important later.

Figure 3-4
A bin with clips.

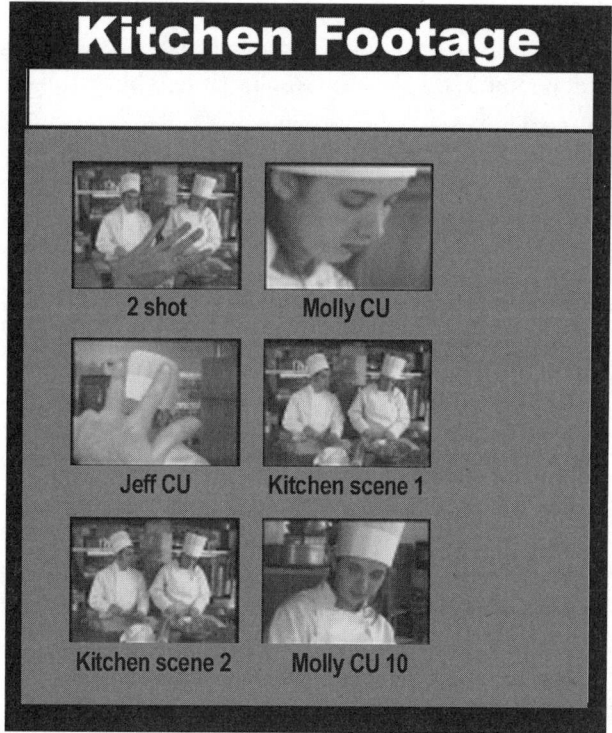

Kitchen Footage

2 shot   Molly CU

Jeff CU   Kitchen scene 1

Kitchen scene 2   Molly CU 10

Timeline

In most editing systems, the timeline window is near the bottom of the desktop. This window presents a graphic representation of each shot in your show arranged along a line. There's usually a ruler marked in time increments and a timeline cursor (an indicator line or bar) that you can grab with the mouse and move anywhere along the timeline. Track indicators for monitoring audio and video are usually placed on the left side of the window. You'll need them as you edit.

Find the magnifier or scaling tool that expands or contracts the amount of time displayed within the window. A timeline displays the clips on tracks. They can be viewed as a tight group—thin slices of time along a lengthy (in duration) timeline. With the magnifier, the timeline can be scaled to display the same clips as long slices of time. Whether the slices appear to be thin or wide depends upon the amount of time (check the ruler) displayed in the window.

Monitoring

Check your video monitor and speakers to make sure what appears on your desktop appears on these devices. Our thoughts on monitoring appear in Chapter 10, "Getting It In and Out."

Make a New Timeline

Whether your editing system calls it a storyboard, composition, sequence, or program, find the tool or menu that creates a new timeline and make a new blank timeline.

Label the Show

Label the timeline as soon as you make it. Make it a habit to save the timeline before you edit anything onto it. Some systems prompt you to name the timeline, whereas others don't. If yours doesn't ask you to save the timeline, go to the file menu and save it. Use a unique name—one that reflects what you're doing. This exercise could be called *DQ Rough Cut*, *Dicey One*, or *Jeff and Molly Scene*. Call it what it is. Avoid at all costs the ubiquitous name *Untitled*, which is by far the number-one choice of beginners worldwide.

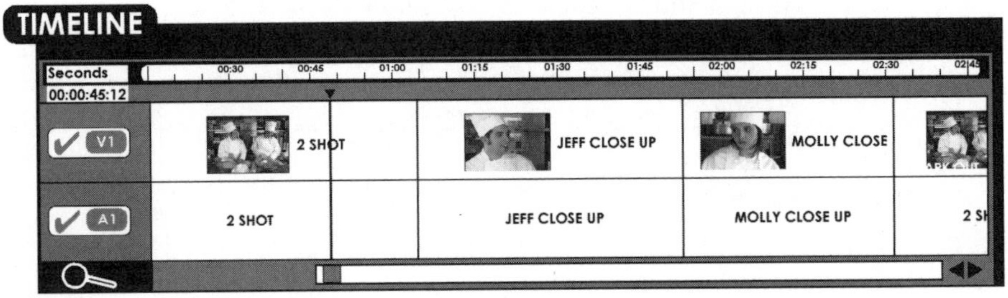

Figure 3-5
A timeline with clips.

Figure 3-5b
A blank timeline.

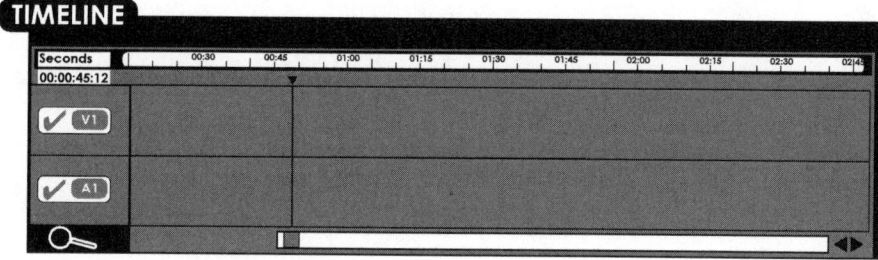

A Once Over in the Cockpit

Let's take a brief look at the timeline before we start editing. The timeline should be placed along the bottom of the screen where it usually resides. Look at the number of tracks displayed on the timeline. This exercise requires one audio track and one video track. In this scene, each character speaks in turn so you only need a single track. A second audio track is optional.

Remove Excess Tracks

If there's a way to turn off or remove unwanted tracks, do it now. There's no sense in having empty tracks that take up space on the desktop if you're not using them. The minimum track arrangement on some editing systems is one video and two audio tracks.

Track Selection Buttons

Clips can only be edited onto the track or tracks that are active. This exercise uses both an audio and video track. Make at least one audio and one video track active. Look for a button or light that tells you the track is in fact on and that the clip you edit onto the timeline will appear there. If you're not sure, try it out.

The track activation light is a significant indicator. An editor always needs to know which tracks are active. When you're doing a complicated edit with a dozen tracks, it's important to be able to quickly identify which tracks will be affected when you make an edit.

The track activation light is the equivalent of the high-beam indicator in your car. Train your eyes to see the track lights. Unfortunately, on some editing systems, this indicator is very small and insignificant. If you haven't trained yourself to see it, you probably won't find it.

Playing and Marking Clips

Watch all the clips to see how the scene unfolds. Normally, you'd make notes about each shot and take in order to help decide which one or ones have the most emotional impact.

For this exercise, start by loading the clip called 2-Shot in your editing system's viewer. In this exercise, the 2-Shot serves as the master shot because it shows the scene in its entirety. Play the 2-Shot. Then play the other shots of Molly and Jeff. These shots are labeled Molly MCU and Jeff MCU.

Mark the Source Shot

If you use the building approach, the first step in the process is to isolate the section of the clip you want to place on the timeline. This is done by marking an IN (beginning) and an OUT (end) point on the clip. Play the clip in the viewer. Set an IN mark where you want the shot to begin. Continue playing the clip. Set an OUT point where the shot ends.

Start the kitchen scene by marking Jeff's opening line on the master—the 2-Shot clip. Load the 2-Shot into the Viewer. Play the 2-Shot and stop it where Jeff's opening line begins. Mark an IN point. Go to the end of the clip and mark and OUT point. Check your IN and OUT points.

Many editing systems have a feature that lets you play only the portion of the clip you marked. It's called *Loop Play* or *Play In to Out*. This tool is useful for checking what you've marked.

Find the buttons or keyboard shortcuts that clear (remove) the marks. When a shot you've marked doesn't start and end the way you want, you'll need to clear the marks you've made. Then you can redo the process of setting the marks. The idea here is to select only the very best part of the shot. If you're not sure what the phrase *best part* of a shot means, be sure to read Chapter 7.

Pay attention to how your editing system indicates an IN and OUT mark. What do these marks look like? Teach yourself to recognize the marks in the viewer windows.

Use the keyboard or mouse buttons to set and clear the marks. We suggest that you start using the keyboard shortcuts for marking an IN and OUT point and use your other hand to scroll through the footage.

Before we continue, try doing what editors call *marking a clip on the fly*. This means to mark IN and OUT points as the clip plays. Some editors prefer to do it this way because they find it helps them determine the natural rhythm of the shot. With the 2-Shot loaded in the Viewer, mark an IN and OUT point for Jeff's opening line as the clip plays. Use *Loop Play* to check your marks. If necessary, redo the process until you're satisfied with the IN and OUT point for Jeff's opening line.

Prepare the Timeline for an Edit

Make sure the track or tracks on which you want to place Jeff's opening line are active. Pay attention to the track indicator lights or buttons on the timeline.

Mark an IN Time on the Timeline

There are two ways to set an IN time on the timeline. You can mark the spot using an IN point or simply place the timeline cursor where you want the edit point to be.

For the kitchen scene, mark an IN time at the beginning of the timeline or move the timeline cursor to the beginning of the timeline.

Every edit has four edit points. The source clip and the timeline (the record side) each have IN and OUT points. However, it only takes three of the four points to make an edit. Your editing system is smart enough to calculate the fourth point. For example, we asked you to set an IN and OUT mark for the source clip, which is 2-Shot in this case. Then we asked you to set an IN time on the timeline (the record side). Your editing system, knowing the duration of the source clip, will calculate the OUT point.

Editing Clips on the Timeline

Most editing systems have two modes: *overwrite* and *insert*. These work in a manner similar to typeover and insert in a word processing program. There are usually keyboard or mouse buttons for each mode. You should be able to identify these buttons on your editing system. We suggest you use the keyboard buttons.

Overwrite Edit

An overwrite edit places a clip on the timeline and covers over anything already in the spot. If there's nothing on the track, it doesn't matter. An overwrite edit never changes the overall length of the show. It's similar to a linear video edit in that the source video covers over existing material. *Overlay* is another commonly used term for this mode.

Insert Edit

An insert edit places a clip on the timeline and pushes everything after the edit point forward. Any existing material will be pushed down the timeline. If there's nothing on the track, it doesn't matter. An insert edit always extends the length of the show. Some editing systems refer to this mode as a *splice* or *ripple* because the act of inserting a shot has a ripple effect from that point onward.

We're Making Straight Cuts in this Exercise!

The edits you'll make in this exercise are called *straight cuts* and both modes will work since this scene is assembled shot by shot. Each clip that you'll apply to the timeline has video and audio tracks. The duration of the tracks will be identical in length. When you look at the timeline, you'll see the video and audio tracks stacked one above the other. The length of the video track should be even with the audio track for every clip you place on the timeline. When you edit a new clip on the timeline, it should be snug up against the previous clip.

Remember, the idea here is to edit a conversation between two kitchen workers, Jeff and Molly. You'll be cutting what Jeff says followed by what Molly says using the script as a guide. It's just "he said, she said" until you reach the end. The shots have to be in the proper order and any action must be matched. Concentrate on the audio. Make sure you don't clip any words when you're marking the IN point and OUT points for each character's line of dialogue. (See Figure 3-6.)

The First Edit

Play the clip with the master shot, which is a two-shot. Use the 2-Shot to establish the location and situation. Mark an IN and OUT that include Jeff's opening line, "Hey, where did you learn to chop so fast?" Edit that portion of the 2-Shot onto the timeline by pressing the proper button to insert or overwrite a clip, now. Congratulations! You've made your first edit and you're on your way.

The Second Edit

Play the clip with the close-up of Molly saying her lines. Mark an IN and OUT that include her lines, "Same place as you, here, remember? Come on, soup's on in half an hour." You'll see a mistake (pay attention to her chef's hat) when she turns away from the camera to look at the soup. To fix this mistake, move the OUT point earlier during her pause.

Figure 3-6

A t imeline with 3 straight cuts of video and audio.

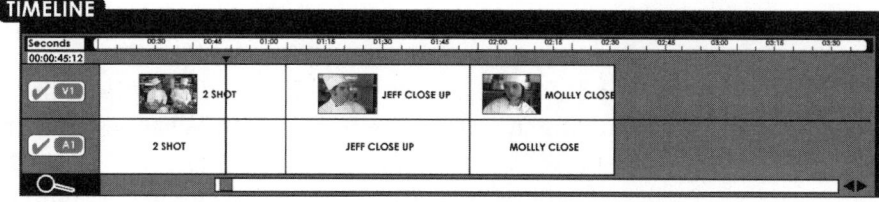

The Drop-and-Drag Approach

Yes, it's true. You can use the mouse to place shots on the timeline. Most editing systems let you click the mouse on the shot you want and drag it to the timeline. It's easy and intuitive.

We have some concerns with this method of working because it's often confusing for beginners. Dragging a shot is just a way to move the clip. In most cases, it doesn't allow you to select overwrite or insert mode. It won't define an IN or OUT point for precision. Any marks on the timeline are irrelevant during a drag-and-drop move. Clips can be dragged to an IN mark if there is one or to the timeline cursor. You can butt up a clip next to an existing clip, or drag a clip to an empty area on the timeline and close up the gaps later.

We recommend using the mouse or keyboard buttons until you learn your editing system. Relying entirely on the mouse is problematic. As your confidence grows, and if the situation warrants it, the drop-and-drag method of editing can be an asset.

The Third Edit

The audience still needs to hear Molly's second line. The only other shot you have is the 2-Shot. Play the 2-Shot and look for Molly's second line, "C'mon, soup's on in a half an hour." Then mark an IN and OUT. You'll want to match the movements Molly makes in both shots in order to match the action. You may have to adjust the in point of the 2-Shot or change the OUT point for Molly's close-up to match the action perfectly.

The Fourth Edit to the End

Play the close-up of Jeff and find his line, "Oh. I mean, you've got really nice hands." Mark an IN and OUT and edit the shot onto the timeline. Continue building the scene, line by line, with "A she said, he said" until you get to the last line in the script.

You have another opportunity to match action. Try cutting between the 2-Shot and Molly's close-up as she reaches for the kitchen towel near the end of the scene.

Review the Exercise

Once you finish building the scene, review your work. Play the timeline and ask yourself these questions:

- Are the audio edits clear and understandable? Are there any abrupt or awkward pauses from one line to another?
- Do the shots flow naturally from one character to another and maintain the rhythm of the conversation?
- Are there any frames of black between shots that shouldn't be there?
- Did you cut on the action?
- Are there any jump cuts that break the continuity between the shots?

The goal here is to create an illusion of reality. This reality is based upon the characters and their actions happening in real time. If a continuity break occurs at any point, the scene will cease to appear real to the audience.

Invariably, you will encounter minor problems. If you do, go back and look at the individual edit points. Make a list of what you want to fix. If you're unsure about whether the scene is working, play the rough cut for another person and get his or her response.

Is the Audio Clean?

The audio portion of the rough cut should sound clean, clear, and natural. You should correct any audio problems at this point. You can do this in several ways. You can play the timeline until you reach the first edit that has an audio problem. Stop here and delete all of the clips on the timeline that follow. Starting from this point, re-edit the clips onto the timeline just as you did before until the scene is complete. The practice will be good for you.

The alternative is to delete just the clip or clips causing the problem. Here's the fastest way to do this. Make sure your editing system is in insert mode. Highlight the clip and delete it. The clip should disappear and the duration of the timeline should get shorter. Position the timeline cursor at the edit point. Find the clip with the line of dialogue you need and mark an IN and OUT. Edit the clip onto the timeline. If you have to replace more clips, repeat the process. If you're not sure what the insert mode is called in your editing system, look it up in Chapter 11 "What Are They Talking About?"

Play the timeline again to make sure you've fixed the problems. Once you're satisfied with the audio, this exercise is complete. In Chapter 4, "Polishing the Necklace," we'll discuss the tools and techniques editors use to adjust and guide the audience through the story.

Save Your Work

You should save your work at this point. When you save a project, you're updating all of the information and storing it for retrieval. Get in the habit of saving your work frequently or use the auto save feature found in most editing systems. We recommend that you set the auto save interval to five minutes or less when you're editing and building shows. Longer intervals are fine for tasks such as viewing footage.

What Am I Saving and Where?

It's important to understand how your editing system saves projects and timelines. Some editing systems may save a timeline as a separate file on your hard drive. Other systems may save the timelines within a bin or project file. You need to know where these files are stored on your editing system so you can find them and back them up. Save anything and everything associated with a project in the directory or folder you created in your Video Projects directory (folder).

Never Leave Without a Backup

You should always make a backup copy of your timelines, bins, and project files and store it somewhere other than on your editing system's hard drive. Computers are notorious for developing problems. Files become corrupted. Hard drives fail. Sometimes the computer will not start. Save your project on a removable media such as a floppy, CD, or tape. It's the only insurance you have. Do it at the end of every editing session. Customarily, the last thing an editor does is save and back up all the assets of the project: bins, timelines, show settings, titles, and effects. There's no need to copy the media files. Those files can be replaced at any time by recapturing the original source tapes.

What's Really Going On?

Hopefully, you've just completed the exercise and watched the kitchen scene. When the audience sees the scene, they'll believe that Jeff and Molly were in the same room at the same time talking to each other. The question is do they have to be? The answer is no.

It wouldn't matter if we decided to shoot the 2-Shot on Tuesday, Jeff's close-up on Wednesday, and Molly's close-up on Thursday. This style of editing was perfected during the Hollywood studio system era for that very reason. On the day Molly's close-ups were being shot, Jeff probably was off working on another picture.

The editor creates the illusion that the scene is happening in real time by joining shots. These shots could have been photographed at different times and in different places, so they appear to flow in a natural sequential order. This is the most important point in this book. *Editors create the appearance of reality through editing. It's an illusion. The end result only has to look real to the audience.*

As the editor, your job is to fool the audience into believing that what they're seeing is real. To be an editor, you must understand the basic principles of editing.

How Does Editing Work?

Editing works because the audience will always find a relationship between adjoining shots. Lev Kuleshov identified this principle, which bears his name. Editing depends on the Kuleshov effect. The shots in the kitchen scene could have been photographed days apart, but the audience sees it as a continuous conversation because they assume the conversation is taking place at the same time in the same room. The audience accepts the illusion that the action is happening in real time in a real space until the editor breaks the rules.

Two Flavors—One Illusion

Editing comes in two flavors: continuity and montage. Continuity editing is the standard approach used in motion pictures and television, including the exercise you just edited. It gives the audience a clear sense of place and action using matching shots to tell a story. The goal of continuity editing is to make the audience believe the story is unfolding in real time.

Our kitchen scene exercise uses three continuity techniques: an establishing shot, shot reverse-shot, and matched action. Jeff and Molly's 2-Shot establishes the space in the kitchen. The audience's ability to recognize and comprehend the image is what editors refer to as *reading a shot*. An establishing shot lets the audience know where the characters are interacting. Shot reverse-shot describes the back and forth dialogue between Jeff and Molly in close-ups. The audience assumes that Jeff is looking at Molly because he looks off screen in the direction we expect her to be. Plus, if you draw a line across Jeff's eyes in the close-up, you will see that his eye line points to Molly and her eye line points to him. It's a trick that lets the audience know they are looking at each other. The other technique we asked you to do was to cut on matched action.

At the beginning of the scene, we asked you make an edit to hide the production mistake in her close-up. She turns her head in the close-up and finishes turning her head in the 2-Shot. Her motion hides the cut. This is another trick that lets an editor hide the seams.

By now, you're probably wondering about the other style, montage. How is montage different from continuity? The definition of montage holds the answer.

What Does Montage Mean?

Montage is a word that confuses people for good reason. In Europe, editing is called montage. The confusion dates back to the 1920s and 1930s. Two Russian filmmakers, Pudovkin and Eisenstein, developed separate theories about editing. Pudovkin's theory of analytic montage (montage is used here in the European sense to mean analytic editing) said shots should be linked together in an unobtrusive manner to guide the audience through the story. In Hollywood, his theory became continuity editing.

Eisenstein's theory of dialectic montage (dialectic editing) was that from the collision of shots, a concept arises, which the audience will figure out. Conflict or counterpoint is the basis for his five types of montage in which meaning is created from shots that don't necessarily have meaning by themselves.

Here are a few examples. See if you can determine the meaning:

- Show a shot of two lovers embracing. Cut to a train entering a tunnel and blowing its whistle.
- Show a close-up of a man looking down and then a close-up of a plate of spaghetti. Cut back to the man looking down.
- Show a shot of a man in bed. He turns off light. Cut to a man opening his eyes.

In *Roger and Me*, the editor cut between wealthy executives talking about how well they were doing and scenes of poverty in Flint, Michigan, to establish a cause-and-effect relationship between the worker's poverty and the executive's wealth. Juxtaposition creates meaning.

Image advertising for products such as perfume, beer, or cars provides some great examples of Eisenstein's approach to montage. Drink Acme Beer and the beautiful girl will be yours.

Perhaps the biggest source of confusion dates back to the 1930s. Hollywood editors developed a way to show the passage of time or place, which they called a *montage sequence*. Examples of these sequences include pages flying off the calendar, seasons dissolving from spring to fall to winter, or generic shots of Paris that let the audience know the characters are in Paris. The images in a montage sequence could be anything that makes a thematic statement. These sequences, which are usually set to music, are also used to represent a character dreaming or recalling past events.

We define montage as any editing style that ignores the strict rules of continuity. Montage editing puts unlike shots together and asks the audience to figure out the relationship between them.

Five Guidelines of Editing

1. Find the shot with the emotional moment—the one that contains the truth or heart of the story. Once you have that shot, edit all the other shots to make that moment shine.

2. Shorter is nearly always more interesting than longer.

3. Give the audience just enough time to read the shot and then make an edit. The time it takes to read a shot depends on the complexity of the image and the audience's familiarity with the subject or object. The

more familiar they are, the shorter the shot can be. For example, a shot of the White House can be much shorter than shots of other buildings.

4. Use motivated cuts. If a person glances off screen, moves his or her head or eyes depending on the closeness of the shot, the editor can cut to what the person is looking at. When someone talks about something, show the audience what he or she is talking about (see the explanation of *cutaways* in the section "Cut Away from the Action").

5. Always give the audience the best view of the action. Use close-ups and other angles to condense the action. Varying the shots lets the editor create rhythm, pacing, and visual variety.

Realistic Action, Real Time, Real Space

If you want people to see the events depicted on screen as real, the audience must believe that the action, time, or space is continuous from shot to shot. Continuity is an illusion that the sequence of images on screen is happening in real time.

To maintain the illusion, the flow of action in one shot must match the flow of action in the next. Editors look for cues to motivate a cut. For example, Molly turns her head. If the editor cuts from the outgoing shot in the middle of Molly's turn and if her head position matches the outgoing shot in the incoming shot, the audience believes they're seeing the action happen in real time. If Molly's head is turned farther away than it should be, the audience perceives a break in time. The speed at which she turns her head gives the audience a sense of time. Emotional action is as viable as physical action. In the exercise, Molly's eyes often convey more information than her words. Seeing her reactions strengthens the emotional continuity of the scene. The audience senses her emotional engagement and are in turn engaged. If the cuts occur at the right moments, the audience will believe that what is taking place on screen is real.

The rules for continuity of space are more flexible. We've all come to accept that a subject can be in one location and in the very next shot suddenly be somewhere else. For example, in a police show, the fact that a detective is in the victim's apartment in one shot and back at headquarters in the next is acceptable. The audience doesn't need to see the detective exit the apartment, exit the building, enter his car, drive to headquarters, exit the car, enter the police station, walk to his desk, and sit down. The audience assumes all of those steps happened because he's a real person. The audience won't realize that continuity has been broken until the editor places the shot of the detective at the headquarters between the two shots of the detective in the victim's apartment.

Here's how you can take theory and put it to practical use.

Techniques for Continuity Editing

Remember that any shot that makes the audience believe the illusion will work, no matter when or where it was photographed. If you want to edit using continuity, it helps to have several angles. When you only have a few shots, it's difficult to condense the action. The lighting and color balance of the shots should match. Pay attention to the screen direction of your subjects. If someone's looking to the right in a wide shot, he or she should be looking to the right in the close-up. This helps the audience understand where the subjects are in relation to each other. Dialogue between characters should be edited so sentences, questions, and answers flow naturally. Dialogue is the simplest motivation for a cut. The other motivators are to cut on physical or emotional action.

Matched Edits and Jump Cuts

To create continuity, cut the shots in the order of the action to make space and time believable. If the audience can follow the action as it progresses, they will perceive the action as continuous. If an action in one shot carries over to the next shot, an editor would say the two shots have *matched action*. For example, a subject walks across the street in one shot and continues to walk in the same direction in the next shot.

This matched edit suggests to the audience that there's no gap in time or space from one shot to another.

A jump cut makes it clear that a gap in time or space exists. Avoid joining shots that will reveal duplicate or broken action. This is a visual tip-off that the action isn't happening in real time. The illusion of continuity can be broken if two shots are edited together that are supposed to be similar but aren't. For example, if the subject is resting his or her chin on his or her hand and in the next shot, the subject's hand is resting on his or her heart, a cut will make the subject's hand appear to jump. If the color balance or lighting or framing is off because the shots were photographed at different times, the audience will notice. They will sense that what they're watching has been manipulated—is not taking place in real time—and therefore the action and characters no longer seem real.

Cut on Action

Cut on the subject's movement to hide the edit. Include part of the action in both shots for a smoother transition. The speed of the action and the position of hands, feet, or objects should match. The audience won't spot small differences because they're focused on the action so you have some leeway. It's best to edit during the action, not during a pause. Professional editors bury mistakes by cutting on action. If the pros have a mantra, it would be cut on action. *Run Lola Run* is filled with examples of cuts made on action.

Cut on Exits and Entrances

A clean entrance or exit is when there's at least one frame in the shot without a subject or object. Make the cut before the subject or object comes into the frame or after it goes out of the frame. Take advantage of clean exits and extrances. That way, you don't have to match action and can still condense time.

Cut on Motion

Motion (subject or camera) makes any edit less noticeable to the audience. This is because the center of attention is the motion. If the subject doesn't move, you can cut from a moving shot to a moving shot as long as the motion of both shots goes in the same direction. Moving camera shots include tracking, dolly, truck, and arc shots, which are all described in Chapter 7.

If the subject is moving, you can cut from a static camera shot to a moving shot as long as the subject and camera move in the same direction or speed.

Cut Away from the Action

An editor has three ways to cut away from the main action: inserts, reactions, and cutaways.

The *insert shot* should not be confused with insert as it's used in linear video editing to describe making an edit on selected tracks. It should also not be confused with the type of clip placement in digital video editing that extends the duration of the timeline. We understand your pain.

The insert shot, also called a cut-in, gives the audience specific plot information, such as the ticking bomb under the hero's chair or a clock on the wall. These shots, which are almost always close-ups, can be written into the script, because an insert shot is one of the rare instances of direct picture instruction a writer is permitted to include.

An insert shot lets the editor break away from the action without breaking the continuity of the scene. After an insert shot, you can pick up the action wherever you want because it's a netural shot that hides jump cuts and errors. No one in the audience will know that the continuity of action has been broken. For example, during a car chase scene, a shot of a traffic light turning red is an insert shot that would allow the editor to change the screen direction of the cars. The *reaction shot* is any shot that reveals someone's reaction to off-screen sound or action. A reaction shot lets the audience know how one character is responding to another character and can enhance the emotional impact of the story. These shots are usually close-ups so the editor can once again break continuity with impunity. Reaction shots are a staple of horror films because an editor can cut to a screaming woman and the shot that follows can be anything anywhere.

Cutaways are any shots that cut away from the action or conversation. The term comes from television where it's used in conjunction with interviews. Cutaways are used to illustrate what a person is saying and to provide more visual variety than the ever-present talking head.

Most of the time, an editor edits interview footage on the basis of what's being said. As a result, the short version of the interview is filled with jump cuts. This sliced-and-diced version can make the interviewee look like his or her head is popping around the screen. Cutaways let you cover all those bad visual edits and speed up the pace of the interview.

What's Missing in Digital Editing?

In the Iron and Machine Ages, film- and video-editing technology forced editors to think. Locating shots meant the editor had to search through reels of film or videotape. Fast forwarding through a reel took about seven minutes. Rewinding was twice as fast. Scanning was slower.

Today, you can jump anywhere in an instant. There is no waiting. Editors need time to think. So the next time you're at a loss for a solution, watch the clips in real time or scan slowly through the material. You may be surprised at what percolates up from your subconscious.

Pace and Rhythm

Pace and rhythm are to a show what symmetry is to a pearl necklace. After the basic sequence (the structure of the story) is laid out, the pace and rhythm must be refined. Pace is dependent on the timing of the individual shots—the rhythm on the interplay between the shots on the timeline. If either element is incorrect, the audience will notice the individual shots. To build a necklace, the clips must be trimmed ever so slightly, so the correct image is on the screen for the correct length of time.

In the next chapter, we'll show you how trimming lets you turn a simple "he said, she said" story into something with more emotional impact.

Summary

Editors tell stories by arranging pictures and sounds. The editor's job is to create a compelling reality using the tools and techniques of editing even though everyone knows it's only an illusion. Whether you build or carve, editing is both art and craft.

Important Points to Remember

- It doesn't have to be real. It only has to look real.

- Shorter is nearly always more interesting than longer.

- Find the shot with the emotional moment—the one that contains the truth or heart of the story—and then edit to make that moment work.

- Cut the shots in the order of the action and condense the action.

- Cut on subject movement to hide the edit. Include part of the action in both shots for a smoother transition.

- Cut on clean exits and entrances.

- Cut on motion. If the subject is static, cut from a moving shot to a moving shot. If the subject is moving, cut from a static shot to a moving camera shot.

- Use close-ups and other angles to give the audience the best view of the action.

- Cut as soon as the audience reads the shot.

- Use motivated cuts. Look for cues in the emotional, physical, or spoken action.

- Use reaction shots to enhance the emotional impact and condense time.

- Use cutaways in interviews to cover edits, illustrate the person's comments, increase the pace, and create visual variety.

Polishing the Necklace

Editors structure, hone, and polish. At every step, the editor watches the show looking for ways to adhere to the rule that *shorter is nearly always more interesting than longer*. After the pearls are strung, hone and polish become the editor's watchwords.

Hone and Polish

Revision is about trimming. When anyone talks about trimming, the words *shorter* and *leaner* are sure to be used. A butcher trims off fat. A tailor trims fabric. If you ask a hairdresser or barber for a trim, there will be hair on the floor. The editor's goal is to make the best show possible. After the structure is in place, the next task is to make it shorter and stronger. Editors achieve this by eliminating extraneous scenes and shortening the duration of the shots.

Every show needs to be honed and every editor has his or her own approach. For some people, tightening up the show is straightforward; for others, it has no end. Typically, an editor will play the rough cut, make some trims, and then work on something else for a while. When the editor is ready to watch with fresh eyes, he or she will repeat the process until the show has been trimmed to satisfaction.

Every frame an editor removes has an impact on how the shot works in the show. The editor watches and asks whether the length of this shot slows the story down. Is this the best part of the shot? Does the audience have enough time to read the shot? Will the audience respond to this shot? Does this shot skew the scene toward one character? These are just a few of the many questions that should come to mind as you consider how each shot works in conjunction with the others. These questions are answered through trimming.

If you want a shot to end sooner or stay on the screen longer, the edit points must be changed. The process of changing the edit points is called *trimming*. The edit points are the IN and OUT points of a clip on the timeline. They appear at the transition line between clips. This transition point is called the *cut point*, or *edit point*. It represents the end of one clip and the beginning of another.

Polishing the show also involves trimming. In this phase, the editor makes subtle adjustments to reveal the emotions of the characters and to hide the edits so the audience never notices the stitching. These tiny trims make the difference of whether a show leaves the audience smiling, crying, or just bored.

Trim to Shorten

Trimming can be done any number of ways in most editing systems. You can use editing tools to accomplish the goal of changing a shot's IN and OUT points. Or, use the trimming tools which can be simple or sophisticated. Don't worry if you find the trimming tools to be confusing or difficult at first. Even the best ones are not particularly intuitive. It takes time to feel comfortable using these features, and some editors do well without ever using a trim tool. Like everything else in the digital environment, a variety of tools and techniques are available that will get the job done. Choose the ones that feel right for you. Here are two simple methods that can be used to shorten a show.

Remove and Replace

Remove and replace works on any editing system whether or not it has trimming tools. The editor removes the entire shot, video, and any associated audio tracks from the timeline. Use the feature on your editing system that removes a clip and closes the gap. Some editing systems call this *extract* or *ripple delete*. Ripple delete refers to the consequences—removing the clip ripples through the rest of the show.

Set new IN and OUT points for the clip. Remember to make the clip shorter. Then re-edit the clip into the timeline in its original location. The editing system should be in insert mode—the one that changes the length of the show and moves all of the shots after the edit. Play the section you've just trimmed to make sure the new edit works.

Some editing systems offer a refined version of this method. Check to see if yours is among them. Load the clip you want to trim into a viewer from the timeline. Set new IN and OUT points. Then press a button or keyboard shortcut, or use the menu to apply the change. As soon as the change is applied, the timeline is updated to reflect the trim. This works well for lengthening or shortening clips.

Carve Away

The simplest way to trim is to mark the unwanted frames from the head or tail of the clip and remove them. This is the carving approach. Split the clip and use ripple delete to remove the extraneous frames. This can be tricky because you are changing the overall length of the show. Make sure all the tracks are selected when you do this or you may inadvertently create lip-sync problems later on in the show.

The remove and replace or carve away methods let you to change the IN and OUT points. These simple methods are the easiest way to reach the goal of making the show shorter and flow more smoothly. If you need or want more flexibility and control, your editing system may have special features just for trimming.

The Trim Window

Trim windows (or the trimming tools) are intended to make it easier to do precision work. Typically, this is a window that displays the outgoing and incoming clips side by side and enable the editor to select to which tracks the trim will apply. There are buttons to trim frame by frame and forward or backwards. Often, pressing the plus (+) or minus (−) key on the number pad will add or subtract the number of frames you enter. Single-frame trim buttons or even an input bar for typing in a frame number may also be available.

Trimming requires trial and error so most editing systems have a loop play function. Loop play repeatedly plays the area around the edit until you decide to stop it. The side (outgoing or incoming) to which the trim will apply is selectable. The editor can choose to trim the outgoing clip side, the incoming clip side, or both sides at once. The outgoing clip is always on the left side and the incoming clip is always on the right side.

Trim windows usually have the following features:

- Two-screen viewer
- Track selectors
- Plus (+) and minus (−) trim buttons
- Play loop (repeat play)
- Left-side/right-side selector

For some editors, including many accomplished professionals, the trim window is confusing and less than intuitive. If you're among those folks, don't use it. That's the beauty of digital editing, figure out what works for you and ignore the rest.

Try Shortening the Exercise

Watch the rough cut of the kitchen scene you edited. Do any of the shots feel long? Try shortening them. Make sure all the tracks (audio and video) are selected. You can probably improve the flow of the scene by removing a few frames here and there. It's amazing to see the difference even a one frame trim can make.

Timeline Trim Tools

Trimming clips always takes place on the timeline. Before you do anything, remember to select the tracks you want to trim. If you don't pay attention, the relationship between the audio and video track(s) may change and create lip-sync problems. Teach yourself to look at the track selector buttons. You need to be aware of which tracks are active or inactive and what impact trimming will have.

The timeline cursor should be positioned over the transition you want to change. Transitions have a left, or outgoing, side and a right, or incoming, side. An editor has a choice to usedo a two-sided trim, which will affect the left and right sides, or a single-sided trim, which will affect one side or the other.

Two-Sided Trim

A two-sided trim is easy and safe because it doesn't affect the length of the show. The editor trims the left and right side of the edit point at once. The clip on one side gets longer and the other one gets shorter by an equal number of frames. It's like the old saying, "What one hand gives, the other takes." The edit point moves forwards or backwards on the timeline, which is why editors call this a *rolling edit*. The edit point rolls back and forth on the timeline. Some editing systems have a shortcut called *extend* that does the same thing. Because the overall length of the show doesn't change, this type of trim maintains lip sync. Trims done in a music video are almost exclusively two sided.

Figure 4-1
Before and after a
two-sided trim of the
video and audio
tracks.

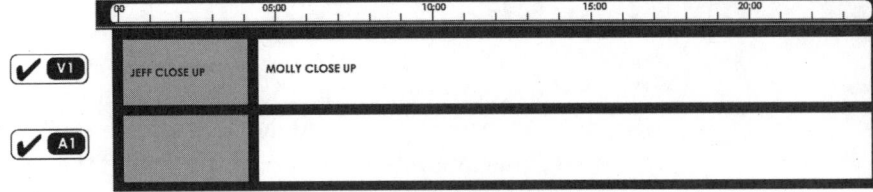

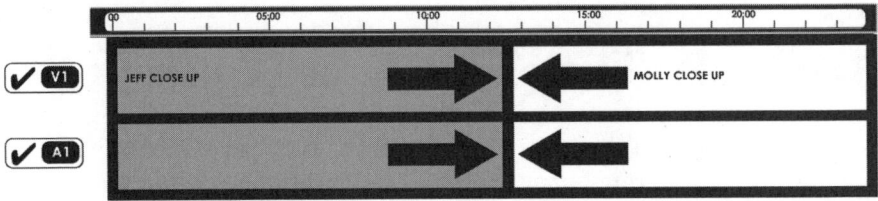

Single-Sided Trim

A single-sided trim changes the overall length of the show, which makes it easy to get into trouble. If you highlight the left side of the edit point, you can shorten or lengthen the outgoing shot. This subtracts or adds frames and affects the timeline from that point forward. All the clips from that position move as a whole to the left or right on the timeline as a result of your trim. The same is true when you shorten or lengthen the incoming shot on the right side. It is dangerous to make a single-sided trim on one track only. You will lose all lip sync from that point forward. There may be special circumstances when such a trim will work. If you're brave, go for it, but realize that you may run into a lip-sync disaster.

Watch Out, Lip Sync Ahead!

Editors use the term *lip sync* when the sound is synchronized to the picture (when the image of a person's moving lips matches the sounds he or she is making). Digital video is transferred into your editing system as data that

Figure 4-2

Before and after a
single-sided trim of
the video and audio
tracks.

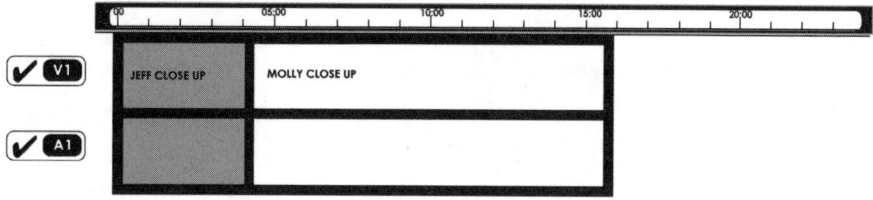

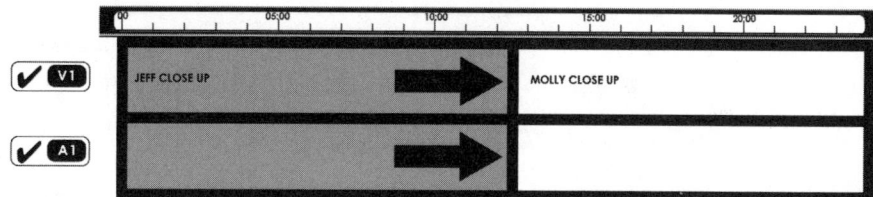

has both audio and video information. The way the data is stored (as one file or as separate audio and video files) depends on the editing system. The same is true for how the editing system treats clips with audio and video tracks. Some editing systems automatically lock the video and audio tracks together. Other editing systems treat the video and audio tracks as separate elements.

The video track is normally stacked on top of the audio tracks in the timeline. When a clip with audio and video is placed on the timeline, all of the tracks line up, one over the other. This clip is in sync. If any of the tracks (video or audio) move forward or backwards in relation to the others, they will no longer line up, which means that lip sync has been lost. If the tracks are normally locked together and you unlock them to work with picture and sound independently, you can create lip-sync problems.

Here are some reasons why editors lose lip sync:

- They edit on one track and forget to include the others (for example, they insert video without the audio or audio without the video).

- They remove a clip and forget to include all the tracks, above and below, especially the empty ones.

- They trim one side of an edit on the video track and do not include the audio tracks.

Figure 4-3
Before and after a
single-sided video
only trim, which
causes lip sync to
be lost.

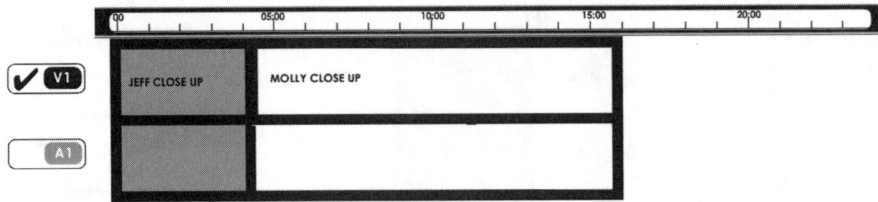

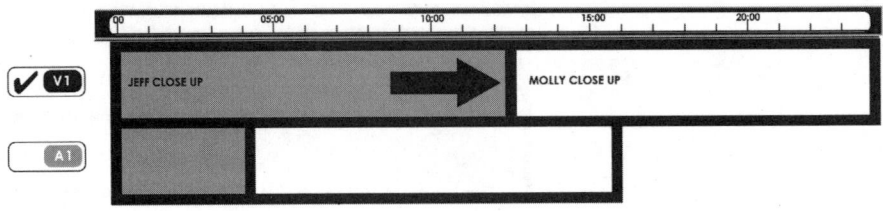

Figure 4-3
Before and after a single-sided video only trim, which causes lip sync to be lost.

How to Prevent Lip-Sync Problems

Keep locked tracks locked and lock unlocked tracks whenever possible. Many editing systems maintain lip sync by locking the video and audio tracks together until the editor decides to unlock them. If you unlock (unsync) the clips, take extra care whenever you make an edit. If the clips are normally unlocked, lock the tracks together whenever possible.

If you do anything on the video track that pushes or moves the clips, remember to include the audio tracks or repeat the operation on the audio tracks. For example, if you trim five frames from the video, don't forget to trim five frames from the audio.

Warnings and Alarms

If you lose lip sync, most editing systems issue an alarm. For example, say a clip you just adjusted throws the audio tracks out of sync. The system might alert you to the error by turning the audio tracks bright red or displaying a number that tells you that this track is now so many frames out of lip sync. These alarms and indicators should be treated as idiot lights. You'll need to take steps to fix the problem.

To fix lip sync, you'll need to trim one track back (or forward) to line it up with all of its other tracks. You can always check which way to move by matching the time code from the source clip. This always works because the source time code on the video track and the audio track are always identical when the tracks are in sync. The footage came from the same tape so both the audio and video started out with the same time code address. Here's an example. The timeline cursor is positioned at the beginning of a clip on the video track. The time code indicates that the clip begins at 00:12:15:25, but when you check the audio track below it, the time code is at 00:12:15:20. Oops, they're out of sync! If you trim (shorten or remove) five frames from the video track only, the clip will be back in sync. Some editing systems automate this process to make moving or trimming clips back into sync easier. However, avoiding the problem is still the best solution.

Trimming for Interpretation

Editors make decisions about what should be seen and heard at each moment. If you completed the exercise in Chapter 3, "Beginnings, Middles, and Ends," you have already edited a rough cut of the kitchen scene. The interplay between Molly and Jeff bounces back and forth without any subtly. It's just "he said, she said," and after bouncing back and forth a few times, it gets boring.

The reason for this is simple. The important part in life (or a show) is not what a person says, but rather the manner in which the person says it. What's left unsaid may be even more important. The reaction of others to what a person says also provides emotional clues for the audience. The editor's job is to learn to control these emotional ebbs and flows.

One way that an editor controls those ebbs and flows is with overlap edits. An overlap edit is when the video from one clip extends over the audio of another clip. Overlap edits are also called *split edits, L*-cuts, or *J*-cuts. You can see why overlap edits are called *L*- and *J*-cuts by looking at the timeline. If the video precedes the audio, it forms an *L*. If the audio precedes the video, it forms a *J*.

Overlap edits create a tighter, less obvious transition. This is especially true if the cut is jarring or abrupt. This technique enables the editor to shape the audience's point of view and cross-structure the picture and sound to increase the emotional reaction of the audience. Robert Altman is the master of overlapping edits. His film *Gosford Park* is a wonderful example of this technique.

Polishing

Polishing a scene means changing the edit points ever so slightly to create a dynamic rhythmic flow. If this is done correctly, you can steer the audience's attention to the intent of the scene. Is the kitchen scene Jeff or Molly's scene? Whose point of view would you like to show to the audience? By using overlap edits, you can leave one character on the screen longer than the other which creates empathy with the audience.

An Exercise in Interpretation

If you've just finished editing the kitchen scene rough cut, give yourself a break before you do this exercise. Editors need to get away from the world of the desktop every now and then. After you assemble a scene, get up and do something else for a while. Getting away is a healthy thing to do, and it gives you a new perspective when you return.

When you're ready, play the scene. The edits are probably fairly clean even though the scene itself may be a bit dull due to its back-and-forth nature. The actors are only shown talking, which is less interesting than seeing how the characters react to each other. Remember, in a conversation, when one person talks, the other person listens. How does the listener feel? What's Jeff doing when Molly's talking to him? Audiences read reactions by looking at the character's eyes. Unless you, as the editor, show Jeff's face as he listens to Molly talk, the audience can't see his reactions.

This exercise helps you create interesting moments in the show using overlap edits. Your goal is to see if you can swing the scene and the audience toward one of the characters. For example, overlapping Molly while Jeff speaks shows the audience how Molly feels. Try to overlap the edits to strengthen the flow and see if you can swing the scene toward Jeff or Molly.

Making an overlap edit is easy. Overlaps are useful for shaping scenes and tightening edit points. Once you've experienced what an overlap can do, you'll understand how powerful this tool can be. An editor makes an overlap edit by trimming two sides of an edit point. As both sides of the transition are trimmed, the edit point shifts so the picture from one clip extends over the sound from another clip. When only the video track is selected, a two-sided trim will make overlap edits.

How to Make an Overlap Edit

1. Go to the edit point.
2. Access your trim tools, which could be a tool palette, menu, or mode.
3. Both sides of the edit point should be active, or selected, to trim. Check the indicators.
4. Select the video track only. Deselect the audio tracks. If the video is automatically locked to the audio, you'll have to unlock the tracks to proceed. When the video and audio tracks are unlocked, you'll be able to trim the video track with ease, rolling the edit point left or right.
5. Find the spot just after Jeff says, "You have nice hands." Grab the edit point using the mouse. Roll it to the right, covering Molly's words. You're extending Jeff on the video track. If the audio is affected in any way, stop. Use undo, check the track selectors (video only), and try again.

Figure 4-4
Before and after an
overlapping edit.

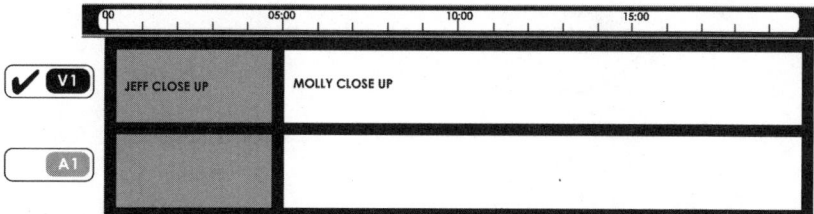

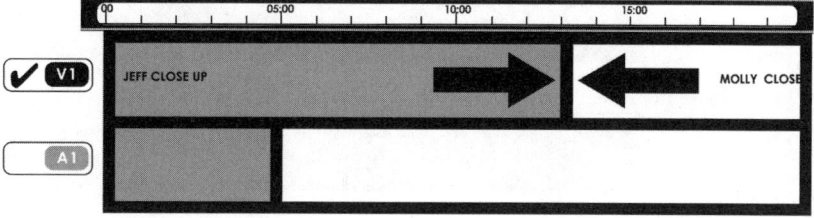

6. Look at the timeline. You'll see that the video clip overlaps the audio. Practice this a few times. If your editing system has a continuous loop play function, use it to repeatedly play this edit point. Watch how Jeff reacts to Molly's line.

7. Try to swing the scene to Jeff. Then try to swing the scene to Molly. Have fun!

Advanced Trimming Tools

Most editors use these advanced trimming tools infrequently: *slip* and *slide*. Both perform two-sided trims. On most editing systems, the trim windows for slip and slide are even less intuitive than the standard trim window.

Slip

Slip is used to move the beginning and end point of a shot without changing the length of the shot on the timeline. This type of trim is great for moving a shot back and forth to find the optimum section within a certain duration. To perform a slip, the IN time at the head and the OUT time at the tail are changed. Anything removed from one side is added to the other side to maintain the duration. The contents change, not the duration.

Figure 4-5
Before and after
a slip.

For example, say there's only room for a four-second shot on the timeline. The shot in question depicts a person falling off a platform into the water. In the natural course of editing, the current out point falls midway through the splash. In slip mode, you can move the shot back and forth to find the most interesting four seconds, which is the full splash in this case. The starting point of the shot is set by the length that this clip can occupy on the timeline (four seconds).

Slide

Sliding is similar to slipping in that there are two edit points. In this trim mode, the selected clip doesn't change at all. Its IN and OUT points will remain intact. However, the IN and OUT points of the adjoining clips on either side do change. One side is trimmed shorter and the other side is extended. As a result, the selected clip appears to slide along the timeline. If it moves forward on the timeline (to the right), the clip to the right of the selected clip is shortened, whereas the preceding shot is extended. For example, if an insert shot of a ticking clock should appear later in the show, the editor could slide the clock shot along the timeline.

Figure 4-6
Before and after
a slide.

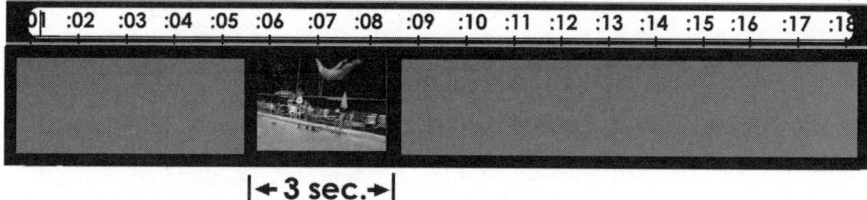

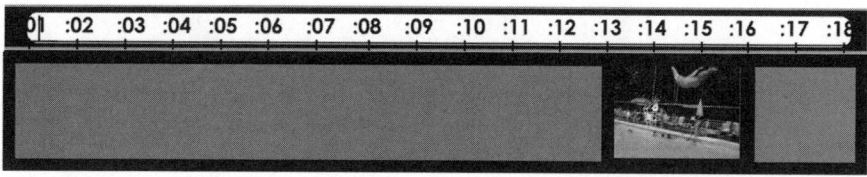

Audio

Audio is often considered the poor stepchild of the images in editing. However, audiences are far more forgiving about image quality than they are about audio quality. If the sound isn't clean and clear, audiences will instantly complain. Spoken words must be intelligible. The relationship between people's voices, music, and other sounds should be properly ranked so the audience hears the most important element first at each moment. Editing audio is not particularly different from editing video. However, the tools to adjust audio are different. As a final reminder of the importance of sound, mixing the show (that is, blending together all of the audio tracks on the timeline) is the editor's last task. Once the mix is complete, the show is complete.

Is It Picture to Sound or Sound to Picture?

It's easier for beginners to cut pictures to a soundtrack than to silence. If you have narration, lay it down first. Then edit the pictures to illustrate the audio track. If you have music, edit the pictures to the beat.

On the other hand, the word *audio* never appears in the phrase *digital video editing*. Digital video is about telling stories with pictures. When you edit the video track first and match sound to those pictures second, your show will rely on imagery to tell the story. The bottom line is that you should never rely on one element to tell the story. Make both the visual and aural stories work.

Sound Sources

Editors work with the following sound elements: sync sound (audio directly linked to the images), ambient sounds (background noises), sound effects (sounds that mimic identifiable noises), music, and voice-overs (narration or commentary).

An Audio Recording Tip

The general rule is that if your pictures aren't good enough, get closer. The corollary rule for audio is that the microphone should be as close as you can possibly get it. The lens on a camcorder has a zoom feature, which can make images appear closer without moving the camera. Audio has no zoom. If you want to record high-quality audio, you must move the microphone closer to the subject.

Organizing Audio Tracks

Most digital editing systems have more audio than video tracks. Most systems can handle eight audio tracks. A conventional arrangement of audio is (from top to bottom) one track for narration, two tracks for sync sound (digital video is usually recorded in stereo so there will be two tracks), sound effect tracks, and music on the last two tracks. Even if your editing system has fewer tracks, the voice tracks should be at the top and the music tracks should be at the bottom.

The audio tracks are edited with the video when an editor is cutting sync sound material, such as shots of people talking. It's a good idea to place each subject's voice on a separate track. This approach gives the editor the most flexibility. To edit the audio from a clip onto a separate track, you'll need to learn how to patch the audio to a specific track or tracks in your editing system. Check your editing system manual for instructions.

Visualizing Audio

A major benefit of the digital environment is that most editing systems enable you to see sound. You can display *waveforms* on the audio tracks. An audio waveform is a graphical representation of the sound energy (see Figure 4-7). The picture looks like a drawing of a mountain range. The peaks are very loud sounds and the valleys are very quiet sounds.

Figure 4-7
Audio waveforms
on the timeline.

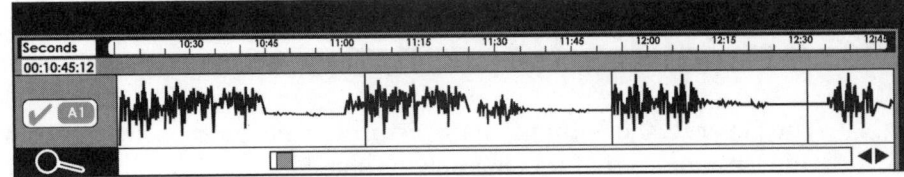

Audio waveforms are extremely useful when you're editing. Deciding where to make an edit using sound as the criteria can be difficult. An editor can't hear any audio when the track is paused. Quiet sections of the audio tracks are often hard to hear. The beauty of audio waveforms is that you can see where the audio becomes quiet, where a sound starts, and where a sound ends. If you prefer to edit by carving, we suggest you turn on the audio waveform feature to do it. Carving away every cough, sigh, or vocal click on the audio track is easier when you can see them.

Audio Adjustment Tools

The first step in the editing process is to place the clips in their proper order —in other words, to string the pearls. After the order has been established, the editor can begin adjusting the audio for volume (loudness), placement (pan position) or quality (equalization).

Adjusting Volume Levels

Some editors adjust the volume levels as they go, whereas others adjust the levels after all the pearls have been strung. This is entirely up to the editor. We suggest that you wait until afterwards to smooth out the levels. The exception would be any clips in which the volume levels are so loud or soft that it becomes distracting to the editor.

Levels for the entire track or just a specific clip on the track can be adjusted. If you need to adjust one portion of a clip (for example, an extremely loud section), split the audio track for that clip before and after the part to be adjusted. This approach is often easier than using the rubberband tool to make the changes. Later, when you have more experience with rubberbanding, you may decide to not bother splitting the track. There are two common approaches to adjusting sound levels in a digital editing

Figure 4-8
Audio levels on
the timeline
resemble stretched
rubberbands.

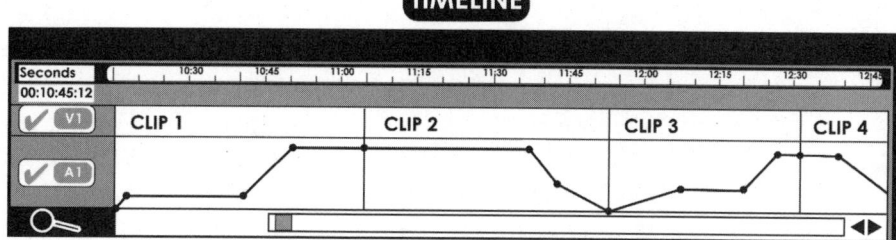

Figure 4-8
Audio levels on
the timeline
resemble stretched
rubberbands.

system: faders and rubberbands. Faders refer to the controls found on a traditional audio mixing board. Some editing systems recreate a mixing board on the desktop as a virtual mixer. The mouse is used to move the faders, or what some people call *sliders*, to make a change. The zero point on the scale, which is the default level, appears in the middle of the range. The plus values are above zero and the minus values are below zero. When the sound is too soft, the level is raised by moving the fader up into the plus values. When the sound is too loud, the fader is moved down into the minus values.

Of course, as with all things digital, the values for the sound level can also be typed in as numbers. For example, if you want to lower the volume level to a particular value, you could type that exact value, pull the virtual fader down with the mouse, or type the amount to subtract from the fader's current value (see Figure 4-8).

Rubberband refers to the way the line representing the audio level behaves when the editor grabs a point on a line with a mouse. The line runs horizontally across the audio track. If the editor grabs the line and moves it up or down, the volume will be affected. The point at which the editor makes this change is called a *node*, or *key frame*.

This approach to controlling volume levels is visual, intuitive, and fun. The process of controlling the sound using this visual method is called *rubberbanding*. This is because the volume level line behaves like a rubberband; it's always a straight line between nodes. If you delete or undo a node, the volume line will spring back to a straight line between the next two nodes. If you have a strong index finger and a comfortable mouse, this method works great.

Adjusting Pan Controls

Pan is short for the panoramic placement of sound either to the left or right speaker in a stereo system. The default position on many editing systems is that all tracks are panned to the center. In this instance, the sound from all the tracks will be heard on both speakers. Other editing systems default to track 1 panned left and track 2 panned right as discrete channels. In this arrangement, the audio on track 1 will be heard on the left speaker and the audio on track 2 will be heard on the right speaker. This odd/even approach carries over to all the tracks in the timeline. All the odd tracks are panned left and all of the even tracks are panned right. The panning controls are usually identical to the volume controls. Nearly every editing system that uses rubberbanding for volume control uses it for pan control as well.

In most cases, voices should be panned to the center. If the music was recorded in stereo, it should be panned to discrete channels. Pan adjustments beyond this should be left to the mix stage. The only other reason to use the pan control while you're editing is to send the sound to one speaker so you can hear it better.

Adjusting Sound Quality

Sometimes the quality of the sound will need to be adjusted. This can happen if there's extraneous background sound or the microphone used to record the audio was placed improperly or was improperly adjusted. The *equalization* (EQ) tools may be able to help correct these problems. EQ lets an editor adjust specific bands of audio frequencies. When it is properly used, an editor can shape the audio so it sounds more pleasing and uniform with the other clips.

Most editing systems have minimal controls that are capable of adjusting low and high frequencies. This can help you clear up rumbling noises at the low end and hiss at the high end. In the midrange, EQ can improve the voice quality. A voice track that sounds flat and dull can be adjusted to sound crisper and clearer. If you discover that one or more of the people who appear in the show need EQ adjustments, save your EQ settings so you can use them again. Label each setting you save using the name of the person. That way it's easy to remember that whenever Steve is heard, Steve's EQ should be applied to the audio clip.

If you have an audio problem that can be solved with EQ, we suggest you try to make the fix as you're editing. The reason for this is simple. If the audio problem can't be solved, the footage may be unusable in the show. You need to know whether you can fix it before you build a show around that material. Once you've figured out that you can adjust the person's audio and get good results, you don't need to apply the EQ adjustment to every one of his or her clips until you're ready to do the mix.

It takes practice and good ears to be able to adjust EQ properly. Try the preset EQ filters that may be included with your editing system. Filters to eliminate wind noise or tape hiss are commom. Experiment with other presets, such as telephone EQ or music bass boost, when you need an audio effect. Most editing systems have just as many audio effects as video effects, although editors tend to ignore them.

What's the End Result?

Your finished show ends up with one soundtrack even though the timeline may consist of two or two dozen tracks. Voices, ambient sounds, sound effects, and music are mixed together into one coherent unit called the soundtrack. Digital video soundtracks are in stereo at a minimum.

Mixing is simply the process of blending together all the audio elements using the volume and pan controls.

Mixing Your Finished Show

The workflow for the soundtrack requires you to edit the sync sound with the picture. Narration and ambience are usually added next. Music and sound effects are typically done last. The exception is when you edit a montage to music or use a beat or click track (just the rhythm of the music) to determine the rhythm of the edits. Once all the materials are placed on the timeline, everything is mixed together.

Place your speakers at a comfortable level. Start at the beginning of your timeline and play the show. Listen to each sound and adjust the level to achieve a good blend of sounds. Always mix to the voice tracks. Sometimes voices will be buried in the music. If this happens, don't increase the volume on the voice tracks. Instead, lower the music tracks. Sound effect tracks should be loud enough to add dimension to the show without being overwhelming.

Take your time. Listen to the show carefully. There should be loud and soft sections. Don't be afraid to lower the volume. Silence can communicate and create an emotional response, too. As we mentioned previously, sometimes what's left unsaid or unheard is important.

Monitoring

Never adjust the volume controls on the speakers when you're editing. The speaker is your audio monitor. It's there so you can make decisions on how things sound. If you change it at every turn, you won't have a reliable reference to determine whether the sound on the timeline is too loud or quiet. The speaker volume should be set at a level that is loud enough to be comfortably heard in the room in which your editing system resides.

Metering Audio

VU (Volume unit) meters are used to measure analog audio levels. An audio meter is a tool that measures the amplitude of the sound in decibels. It's used to make sure the sound level isn't too low, which would result in an audio recording with a reduced dynamic range, or too high, which would result in an audio recording with distortion. For example, a good voice level on an analog VU meter should fall between −3 and 0 dB on the scale. A signal of +3 dB would be too distorted to use. (See Figure 4-9.)

Figure 4-9
Audio levels
displayed in digital
or analog scales.

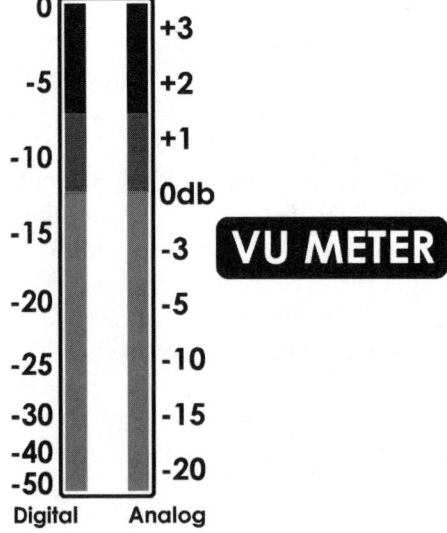

The same scale with different requirements is used for digital audio recording. A digital meter displays a graphic representation of the amplitude of the sound. The scale is different from the VU meter, although you'd never know that. A good voice level for digital audio should fall between -22 dB and -14 dB. Levels set to 0 dB on a digital meter will be too distorted to use.

Measurements are useful if you are familiar with the scale. Use your senses and listen carefully. After all, reading the temperature in Fahrenheit or Celsius degrees doesn't change how cold you feel; it's just a reference number.

Why Mixing Boards Exist

Professionals prefer the feel of tangible faders over mouse clicks, rubberbands, and data entry. This is one reason why mixing boards still exist in professional audio studios.

In a digital editing environment, an external audio mixer can serve as a sophisticated patch panel with volume, pan, and EQ controls. The editor can easily bring in multiple audio sources using a mixing board. When the show is output to videotape, the mixing board enables the editor to monitor both the output of the editing system and the sound being recorded on tape by switching back and forth between using one button.

There are smart digital audio mixing boards that can be connected to editing systems like other peripherals. The idea is to give the editor control over level changes from the audio board or editing system. In our opinion, this is equivalent to using an ergonomic hand controller instead of a mouse to play video games on your computer. It's a nice touch, but completely unnecessary.

Do You Need More Tools?

If the soundtrack needs more sophisticated mixing, for example, on a feature film or for 5.1 surround sound for a DVD, the mix won't be done on a digital video editing system. Instead, the audio tracks will be exported from the editing system to a *digital audio workstation* (DAW). The DAW provides far more control over the soundtrack than the basic audio tools included in editing systems. Read the section on audio in Chapter 10, "Getting It In and Out," if you need to do this.

A Few Audio Tips

- *Know where the show will be played.* Forget how good it sounds on the speakers attached to your editing system. If the show will be output to videotape, the audience will likely see and hear it on an inexpensive television set. If this is the case, don't bother doing a complicated audio mix. Instead, make sure everything is audible when heard through a small inexpensive speaker. Most of the audience won't hear or appreciate your well-crafted stereo mix.

- *For a quick mix, pan all of the audio tracks to one channel.* For stereo, pan all the tracks to the middle. This is a simple but effective method if you don't have time to do a complete mix and you're satisfied with the volume levels.

- *Always check your mix by listening to the show in different settings using different types of speakers.*

- *If you're encoding audio for streaming, remember that the soundtrack will likely be heard on a tiny mono computer speaker.* Your EQ and audio mixing efforts will be lost during compression and/or playback.

- *If you are mastering to a DVD, the mix is of the utmost importance.* Every nuance is likely to be heard.

- *An external audio mixer may be helpful if you have multiple sources, such as audiocassette decks, digital audiotape (DAT) tape recorders, and videotape recorders that need to be connected to the editing system.* Instead of patching each device into your editing system every time you need to input a sound element, an audio mixing board can simplify the task. On the output side, an audio mixing board can distribute the audio signals to multiple VCRs for recording and monitoring.

Summary

Trimming is the tool that gives editors creative control over the show. Hone the show by removing all the unwanted or unnecessary material. Then, polish the show by trimming it to enhance the impact.

Sound is just as important as the picture. Audio conveys information and can enhance the emotional impact of any scene. Audiences are unforgiving of poor quality audio. If audiences can't hear what people are saying, they'll complain immediately.

Important Points to Remember

- The simplest way of trimming to shorten is to mark unwanted frames and remove them.
- The trim window is a precision tool for adding or subtracting frames.
- Pay attention to the lip sync warnings on the timeline.
- Don't sweat lip sync. Learn how to fix and prevent the loss of lip sync.
- Use overlap edits to shape scenes for interpretation.
- Never adjust the volume controls on your speakers after you've set a comfortable level for the room; adjust the volume level of the track to make adjustments.
- Separate sound elements on individual tracks of the timeline.
- Add background sounds to the voice tracks first and then build from there.
- The voices should be the most prominent audio element. Mix the other tracks up to the voice track.
- Digital audio meters use a negative scale. 0dB is maximum overload.
- Listen and watch the level indicator of the audio meter to avoid distorting the sound.

Styles and Workflows

What's Technique?

Different shows require different approaches. The process of editing should reflect the type of show you want to make. This is called *technique*. If you use the same technique in every situation, you are guaranteed to move slowly. The purpose of this chapter is to present techniques for editing commercials, family history programs, music videos, nonfiction, and scripted narratives quickly and efficiently.

Digital editing gives editors the freedom to develop their own techniques. Digital editing does not have any inherent restrictions that force you to take a specific approach because of technical limitations. This is a big change. The machines used for linear video editing were limited and limiting, requiring editors to follow only one path. Digital editing has some technical considerations, although none of these affect creative choices. This means that editors can approach a project any way that suits them. This new independence is allowing creativity to bloom.

The approach to editing you take depends on a number of factors. Your experience as an editor has the biggest impact. You may be influenced by your favorite films or perhaps have studied the work of a particular filmmaker or filmmakers. In this visual era, you are what you watch. Television and cable provide a continuous stream of visual creativity. Commercials, promos, graphics, and effects are showcased everyday in your home. This constant barrage of imagery has made all of us more visually sophisticated and has altered our expectations about pacing and patience.

Two Means to the Same End

Editing can be approached in two ways: building and carving. A good metaphor for the building approach is to think of the editor as a bricklayer. The shots or clips are the bricks. Bricklayers take one shot at a time and slowly build the story. Carving is the opposite approach. Think of the editor as a woodcarver shaping a tree stump into a bench. The material is the stump and the woodcarver gradually slices away, honing and shaping the story into what he or she desires. It doesn't matter which approach you prefer. The decision is entirely up to you.

Good editors often use both approaches at various times. Builders piece together scenes and watch them. Then, they'll often begin carving away unnecessary bits and pieces. Carvers slice away to let the decisive moments shine. They fine tune scenes later by moving and trimming on a shot-by-shot or scene-by-scene basis. Going back and forth between building and carving is how you achieve the seamless quality that distinguishes editing at its finest.

How to Use This Chapter

A roadmap gives a driver a feeling of confidence. The route is clear; you know where you're going and how you have to get there. You want the comfort of a map the first time you drive somewhere. After you make the trip a few times, the route is embedded in your memory and the journey becomes routine.

Editing is never routine. The story, material, and genre change with every new project. You can choose to take the superhighway or stay on the back roads. Every genre has its own editing superhighway (a *workflow*) that can move you from start to finish with the least amount of trouble. We've provided guidelines (our versions of editing superhighways) for music videos, commercials, documentaries, and narratives to help you gain confidence. We feel that the steps we've outlined represent the best way to slice the apple. As you gain experience, you may decide to modify our suggestions to accommodate any quirks in your editing system or the type of projects you do. In any event, reading and following the workflows for the genres we've included will help you learn how to develop your own workflows for other types of shows.

A Practice Workflow Project: A Digital Family History

This simple project illustrates the workflow for a show that documents your family's history. It's a fun project anyone can do and that teaches you the concept of workflow. The project involves recording an elder storyteller as he or she recounts family history and editing his or her interview. The interview provides the structure for the show.

For this example, we'll use your grandmother. However, it could be anyone in your family who knows how to tell a good story. At family gatherings, these are the people who take center stage and tell tales that weave facts, characters, and events together with humor and emotion. The wit and wisdom of these gifted storytellers lend credibility to stories that will become legends to future generations of your family.

Recording family stories with a digital camcorder is an excellent way to preserve the past for future generations. Digital editing gives you the opportunity to turn what you record into an entertaining and informative show. This is your chance to become the family storyteller in a new medium: digital video. After you edit the show, you can send your relatives copies on videotape, DVD, CD, or stream the finished show on the Internet.

Interview Your Grandmother

Record your grandmother speaking to the camera or looking off screen toward the interviewer. The position of her eyes doesn't really matter. The audience for this show will be your family; they'll be glad to see and hear her so no one will notice.

Let her talk as much as she wants and record everything. The order in which she tells her stories is unimportant. She can start or stop whenever she wants. If Grandma goes on a tangent, you can edit that out later and, under these circumstances, anything she says on camera is valuable. You may want to prompt her memory from time to time or ask her to repeat things.

Make her comfortable. For some people, the responsibility of being recorded can be awkward or artificial. If your grandmother becomes self-conscious or nervous, parts of the interview may be unusable. Of course, that's the purpose of editing—to remove any parts that go off track. Most of us go off track now and then and your grandmother is no exception. You may want to try recording her over several days or weeks in short sessions. The most important part is to record as much as possible for as long as possible. If all goes well, she'll recount a lot of past history, weaving family myths and legends with wonderful character descriptions of your relatives. Her stories will become a unique and timeless resource for everyone in your family.

Editing Workflow—The First Half

First, evaluate the material. Then break the interview down into individual segments. You can accomplish these tasks using either the building or carving approach. Choose one. We'll explore both ways to complete the first half of this practice project. Experience tells us that half of you will carve and the other half will build.

Carving the Interview Place the interview clip or clips on a new timeline. The clip length may be limited in your editing system. Try to get as much as possible in one long clip. Use multiple clips if necessary.

Next, mark an IN and OUT point where the interview becomes unusable. Remove the section and close the gap. This may require splitting the clip at the IN and OUT point and then deleting it. (See Figure 5-1.)

Play the timeline. Remove any portion that you or your grandmother would not want anyone to see. Anything that's not part of the story should be cut out (such as coughing, drinking water, or answering the phone). Play the entire interview and remove all of those sections.

At this point, you should only have stories about your relatives—for example, the time your uncle got into trouble as a teenager, how your mother and father met, or what your grandfather did during the war. Each of these stories will be on the timeline.

The final step in this phase is to change the order of her stories so her interview has a dramatic flow. Start with something short or exciting that will peak your family's interest. Try to balance her stories to give her interview a clear beginning, middle, and end. Put her best stories at the end. You might decide to follow a chronological order or perhaps the family tree.

To change the order of the sections on the timeline, highlight the story you want to move and use the cut command. After you've found an appropriate place for the story, use the paste command to move it there. This phase is complete when you're satisfied with the order of her stories.

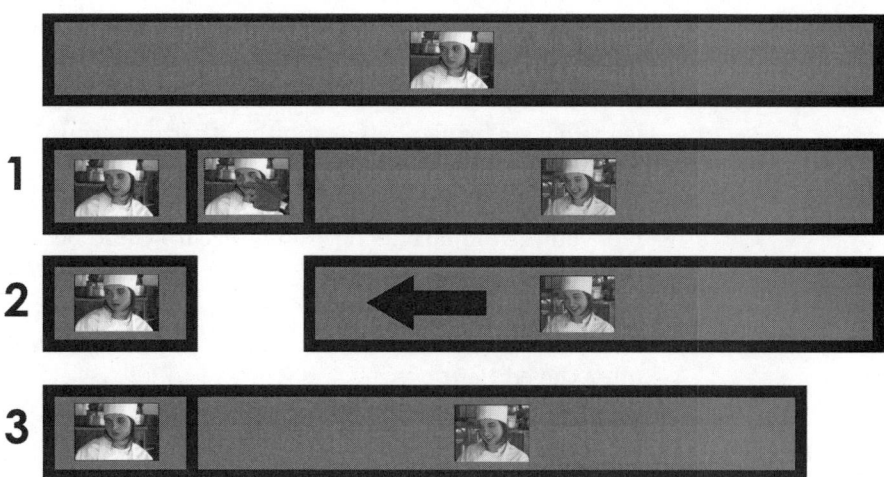

Figure 5-1
Carving an
interview clip.
1. Isolate unwanted
material;
2. Remove it; and
3. Close the gap.

Building the Interview with Subclips   Play your grandmother's interview clip. Mark an IN and OUT point at the beginning and end of her first story. Then make a subclip (a copy) of that story. Name it and store it in a bin. Go to the beginning of her next story and repeat the process.

Go through her entire interview and break it down into separate subclips, one for each story. Each subclip you make should be saved with an appropriate name. If her interview has many stops and starts, you may have some subclips that are parts of stories. Label them so you know that they are only part of a story.

You should make sure that every IN and OUT point is clean. In this context, *clean* means that her first and last words are complete. None of the syllables should be clipped or chopped off.

Then arrange the subclips in the order you want to present your grandmother's stories. Build the timeline by placing the subclips in the order you want. Start with something short or exciting that will peak your family's interest. Try to balance her stories to give her interview a clear beginning, middle, and end. Put her best stories at the end. You may decide to follow a chronological order or perhaps the family tree. The first phase is complete after you've placed all of her stories on the timeline.

The Second Half

The first step in the second half of this workflow is to cover any jump cuts. A jump cut will be self-evident. Your grandmother will appear to jump around. This happens when extraneous sections of the interview are removed and a break in continuity occurs.

If you see a jump cut, you'll want to add family photographs or perhaps footage from an old home movie at that point. See Chapter 10, "Getting It In and Out," and the appropriate sections in your editing system manual to learn how to bring photographs or other materials as clips into your editing system.

Select the photograph clip you want to use to cover a jump cut. For example, your grandparents' wedding picture could be used to cover a jump cut in her story about how she met your grandfather. After you've selected an image, place it on the timeline as a video-only overwrite edit. You don't want to insert the image because that would push everything on the timeline after the edit out of sync.

Continue adding photograph and home-movie clips as video-only overwrites to cover any jump cuts. You can also enhance the stories she tells with these materials. Remember that her interview is the centerpiece of the show so it's not necessary to include any of the sounds associated with home-movie clips. If possible, lock her audio track. This will prevent you from inadvertently editing her narration in these sections.

Next, add transitions between your grandmother and the photographs or home movies. You should use a transition the first time you cut away from your grandmother to a photograph or home movie. It's a good idea to be consistent. If you use a dissolve, dissolve away from and then back to your grandmother. You may decide to add transitions between a series of photographs or simply cut from one to another.

After that, add music. Music helps set the mood. You can select music that matches the time period she's talking about. If your grandmother is telling a story about her life in the 1950s, a popular song from that era would add emotional impact.

This point is the perfect time to create and add the titles and text you feel are necessary. This could include identifying people, dates, or locations. Titles are usually placed on a separate video track. Add transitions to mix the titles in and out. When taken altogether, these small touches will create a lasting family treasure.

The final step is to do an audio mix. Any music you add should be at a low volume and in the background. After all, your grandmother is the star of this show. Each music selection should fade in and out. If your grandmother isn't speaking, for example, during the opening titles or a montage of photographs, you can raise the volume of the music. If you keep the settings consistent for your grandmother's voice, you probably won't need to do anything to her track. With your editing skills, her memories can come alive in a visual story that your family will treasure.

Music Videos

No visual form is more suited to digital editing than the music video. Arranging, cutting, and moving lip-synced shots in time with a music track is technically complicated to do with traditional film or video editing systems. Digital editing systems make editing music video montages exciting.

Background

When Richard Lester, the director of the Beatles' film *A Hard Day's Night*, combined the band's performance with a montage, he created the music video art form. Until that moment, films portrayed performances as actualities that took place in a reality created within a continuous scene. From Fred Astaire to Elvis, when a person sang, he or she sung on camera in one location. Any shots that showed other actions were presented as parts of the scene. The first theatrical film to include sound, *The Jazz Singer*, can be seen as a music video. It shows Al Jolson performing songs and playing the role of a Jewish cantor who breaks into Vaudeville to the disappointment of his father. Most filmed performances followed an approach that developed in the 1930s. The singer or band was shot from the audience's point of view at a stage show or nightclub. The view was from one side of the proscenium. In *Anchors Away*, Gene Kelly experimented with a montage sequence in the "New York, New York" sequence. Three sailors sing and dance all over New York in what was an innovative approach to the performance. Richard Lester added to this tradition. He cut away from the actual performance and showed a variety of action shots, chases, and sequences. The performers became characters in a visual narrative rather than just musicians or singers. Lester used montage editing to cut these shots to music.

The elements of a music video involve a performance to a lip-synced audio track and other nonperformance scenes. The difficulty of editing a music video revolves around the technical problem of lip sync. Performers do not actually sing the song on camera; instead, they mimic the vocals while listening to the song being played back from a CD or *digital audiotape* (DAT). The video or film footage has to be resolved (synced) to the music track by the editor.

Syncing the footage can be done at the beginning, middle, or end of the editing process. No matter when the editor chooses to do it, it must be correct. Viewers implicitly trust that the performer's lips are in sync with the song. If this is lost, the magic and suspension of disbelief are lost.

Music Video Organization

Transfer the music from the CD (or DAT tape) and all the footage. Create separate bins for the following elements: performance, scenes, locations, studio music, sequences, and so on. The bins can also reflect themes and concepts in the song.

Music Video Workflow—The Building Method

This method works with material shot on video. It doesn't work with film unless every take is resolved (synced) with the music. If the film is transferred to tape, this method can be used. All the takes must be resolved, which requires an incredible amount of work. Of course, with a music video shot on film, there's probably a budget for an assistant to do this so it may not matter.

Step 1—Edit the Performance Footage Takes Performance footage that includes sync sound recorded in the field (music playback in the background) is cut like dialogue—it follows the lyrics. The soundtrack should be the audio from the music playback as recorded by the camera. The best takes, shot angles, and actions are cut using the actual field sound as a guide for continuity. Compare different takes from different scenes and match them by following the lyrics. The editor must evaluate each take. Multiple takes require more time to watch. Once the best take is selected, mark IN and OUT points.

Butt the shots together, line by line, verse by verse, and shot by shot to create a performance video of the talent singing to the music. As long as the performers singing are reasonably close to being in sync, you should have little trouble editing. This technique enables you to start editing right away. Editing using this approach allows you to concentrate on selecting the best shots of the vocals immediately. You don't have to worry about resolving lip sync until the next stage in the process. This technique works well with hiphop or songs with a number of verses.

Step 2—Resolve the Lip Sync by Adding the Music The next step is to add the audio tracks from the CD to the timeline. This can be tricky because you have to establish lip sync from the start of the show. Mark the IN and OUT times on the source audio clip (the tracks imported from the music CD). Edit this onto the timeline (audio only), making sure you don't delete the audio and video tracks you've already placed on the timeline. Use other tracks, such as tracks 3 and 4, if tracks 1 and 2 are in use.

Time code or markers can help you line up the sound with the picture. If your system has the capability to add markers, put a mark somewhere near the start of the source audio clip. Pick a word that is distinctive with visible lip movement. A *plosive* word (a word that contains a *P* or *B*) is the easiest to find. Next, place a mark on the identical word in the edited performance piece on the timeline. Then align the two marks. Your IN points should both be at the beginning of the song, and the marks should correspond to each other.

You will have to adjust the show IN time to make sure the sync marks match. Don't change the music clip IN time. A little trial and error will work.

If your editing system doesn't have markers, the easiest way to do this is to use the sync words to set a temporary OUT point at the word on both the music clip and the timeline. You will move the OUT point later.

Go to the beginning of the music source clip and mark an IN point where the song starts. Your editing system should be able to calculate the duration between the IN and OUT points. Let's say it's 25 seconds. In order to match the beginning of the song on the show timeline, go to the OUT point and subtract that duration in seconds. This will be your IN point. Then mark the end of the song clip and move your temporary OUT point. Make an audio-only overlay (overwrite) edit, rolling out the entire music clip until you reach the end.

You can do this another way if your editing system can trim audio tracks. Mark an IN point on the source music clip and the timeline audio track using a matching word in the lyrics. Make an audio-only edit and add the music to the timeline. Your show should have music from the CD in sync from that point on to the end of the song. Then on the timeline, trimming only the music tracks, trim back to the beginning of the song. The idea is to extend the music back toward the start. Don't move the music track; just make it longer at the beginning.

Figure 5-2
To resolve lip sync, line up marks on the identical word from the music and performance.

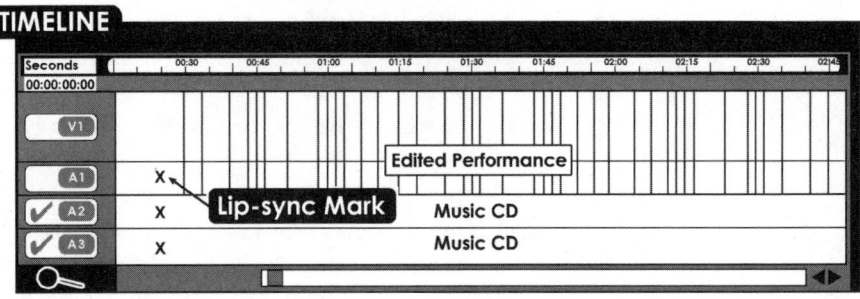

Step 3—Adjust Lip Sync by Slipping Shots That Are Ahead or Behind Play the show and listen only to the CD music track with the reference audio tracks turned off. Look at the show from the beginning to the end. You will notice that some pictures are out of sync with the lyrics. These shots are ahead or behind the music. The next step is to adjust the video track by trimming the start and end of the out-of-sync clips. You can do this by re-editing the clips onto the timeline or by trimming them on the timeline:

- *Re-edit method* Replace the clip in the timeline by re-editing it. It must have the identical duration, though it will have a different start time. Usually, this will be earlier or later by a couple of frames. Start with five frames. Overlay the edit onto the timeline. Undo it, change the IN time, and repeat this if the lips don't match. Using trial and error, and the undo feature, repeat the process until the lip sync is correct.

- *Trimming method* This is one of the best reasons to use the slip mode. *Slipping* is a film editor's term that means to adjust the beginning (IN point) and end (OUT point) of a shot without changing the duration of the shot. This is what needs to happen in this case. The out-of-sync shot needs to be adjusted, not lengthened or shortened. Changing the duration would move the other shots (to the left if the new shot was shorter or to the right if it was longer). Consequently, everything from that point on would be out of lip sync. The impact of a change in duration ripples through your show to the end. The solution is to avoid changing the IN point unless you change the OUT point by an equal amount. If you take something away from one end of the shot, you must add it to the other end. The duration must remain consistent to maintain sync.

A Production Tip

Never let the performers sing to an audiocassette. Always use a CD or DAT copy of the song. Audiocassette recorders won't play back at a consistent speed; consequently, you'll have lip-sync problems when you edit.

Go into the slip mode on your editing system. Adjust a shot by a few frames and play it back. Check to see if it's in sync. If it's not, slip the shot a bit more.

Step 4—Isolate Shots from Non-Lip-Sync Footage; Make Subclips
What non-lip-sync shots are called depends on the editor's experience and background. Some people use the term *B-roll shots* and others use the word *cutaways*. In a music video, these shots can be from any scene or performance. These are often shots that relate to the themes portrayed in the song's lyrics. They could be shots of a dance performance or other action. Cut this footage, looking for the dynamic movements. Select shots that have action that occurs within the frame or from outside with camera movement. Look for strong design elements such as color, composition, and focus. After you identify these gems, mark an IN and OUT point, and make a subclip.

Subclips Most editing systems let you subclip (or make a copy of) all or part of another clip. You need to make subclips of individual shots to use the building method. If you're not sure how to recognize a shot or make a subclip, read Chapter 7, "Setting the Table," before continuing.

Music video are usually shot with a lot of coverage. This means that the editor should have a wide variety of choices of shots with different framing and angles. The more shots you have to work with, the more creative you can be. Break down all the non-sync footage into single-shot subclips. Save these subclips in a bin.

Because these subclips are isolated shots, they can be edited on the timeline without any further adjustments to the IN or OUT points. Place them on the timeline as video-only overwrite edits. Use the actions within the

A Tip—Get Organized

The fastest way to find what you need, when you need it, is to get organized. Save any subclips you make into bins. Label the bins so you can easily find the shots you need. For tips on organization, check out Chapter 6, "The China Closet."

shots to create a rhythm or follow the rhythm of the music. Cut the pictures to the words, beat, or hits in the music. Drum hits, cymbal crashes, and guitar notes can all trigger an edit point.

Effects Subclips As you isolate shots for the music video, experiment with adding effects to your subclips. A number of effects, such as motion, are applied to individual clips. If you think a shot would be more dynamic or fit the music better in slow motion or as strobed motion, this is the time to try it out. Clip effects are usually made and stored as copies of the original clip. Reversing the motion of the clip changes a zoom in to a zoom out. You can modify a clip in hundreds of ways. Have fun!

Music videos require many individual shots. You should have more clips and more versions of those clips than you will ever be able to use. You can build faster if you have more choices. The more time you have to play, the better the final result will be.

Step 5—Add Clips and Subclips (Video-Only) to the Timeline The next step is to add (assemble) these selected shots to the timeline. These edits are going to fill in areas where there is no video or cover portions of lip-synced shots. At this stage in the music video process, cut the picture to the synced track. While the audio track remains fixed, make video-only overwrite (overlay) edits. Don't insert video clips into the timeline. An insert edit moves the adjacent clips and causes a loss of track alignment and lip sync. When you push one clip, you also move the adjacent clip, which results in a ripple effect from that point to the end. As you add subclips to the timeline, you'll see your music video come together.

Editing systems usually have a way of grouping shots. For the fun of it, you could drag a group of shots onto the timeline. This saves a lot of time. Plus, the purely random nature of placing a group of subclips on the timeline can sometimes reveal interesting cuts. This is the equivalent of throwing paint at a canvas, except if you don't like the result, you can press Undo.

Step 6—Add Transition Effects Your music video should almost be complete. The final step is to add transitions. Music videos get a lot of their punch from the rhythm generated by cuts made on the beat or counterbeat. Transitions such as dissolves or wipes are rarely used because they break up or slow down the rhythm of the editing. However, sometimes the music dictates the use of transitions. If this is the case, add your transitions now.

Music Video Editing Tips

- Put the music on the timeline. Cut the picture to the music.
- Always do VIDEO ONLY edits. Lock the audio tracks to avoid accidents.
- Use the overwrite (overlay) mode to make sure everything stays in sync.
- Always trim both sides of an edit to maintain sync.

Music Video Workflow—The Carving Method

The carving method works great when time code playback is used during production.

Step 1—Make a New Timeline   Make a new timeline with a starting time code of 00:00:00:00.

Step 2—Edit the Music Clip   Edit the music clip on to the audio tracks of the timeline. The song and the timeline should both start at 00:00:00:00.

Step 3—Find the Start of the Song   Determine where the music starts on the clip of the performance. Set the music start as your IN point. Make a mental note that this is where the song starts. It's much easier to find the start if the song begins at 00:00:00:00 on your camera slate. Watch the performance clip and look at the time code on the camera slate. Because there's usually some preroll, the clip will probably show the slate starting before the music begins at around 23:59:50:00. Go about 10 seconds forward to the 00:00:00:00 spot. If possible, put markers on the timeline to mark this important point on the clip.

Step 4—Make a Video Edit of the Lip-Synced Performance   Match the audio track on the lip-sync performance to the music tracks that are already on the timeline. Use a video-only overwrite to place the lip-synced performance on the timeline. When you play the timeline, the performance should be in sync with the music (see Figure 5-4).

Figure 5-3
Step 3: Find and mark the start of the song.

Figure 5-4
Step 4: Edit the source clip onto the timeline.

Production Tips: Time Code Playback

■ The time code display must be recorded by every camera on every take of the artist lip syncing to the music. It doesn't matter whether you do it as a head or tail slate.

■ The time code for audio playback should start at 23:59:45. The song should start at 00:00:00:00.

■ Match the timeline's starting time code to the song's starting time code.

Step 5—Add Additional Takes   If your edit system handles multiple video tracks, edit each take of the performance on a separate track. Use the time code slate, shown in Figure 5-5, recorded by the camera as the sync point.

You can add any part of a lip-synced performance to the timeline as long as you know the time code for that portion of the song. For example, if you want to edit the third verse, determine the time code when the verse begins from the point of the song start. If the verse begins at 2 minutes and 15 seconds from the song start, overlay that section on the timeline at 2:15:00.

Step 6—Remove the Unwanted Sections   After you place all the performance pieces on the timeline, you can begin to carve away the sections you don't want. Set an in and out for what you want to remove and delete it. Make sure you use the mode that leaves a **gap** in the time line. The clips on the video track should not move (see Figure 5-6). If they do, the clips will be out of sync with the audio track.

Your timeline should have a stack of video tracks that are all in sync with the audio. It should be relatively easy to compare one take with another using the track-monitoring controls. Decide which takes or parts of takes are better than others. Cut away all the bad material to reveal the most dynamic performances. This method, which is somewhat of a process of elimination, works well when the singer performs the song several times in a variety of locations. (See Figure 5-7.)

Step 7—The Final Steps   To complete your music video, follow the final three steps in the building method workflow.

Figure 5-5
Time code slate
recorded on camera.

Figure 5-6
Step 6: Unwanted parts of the performance removed.

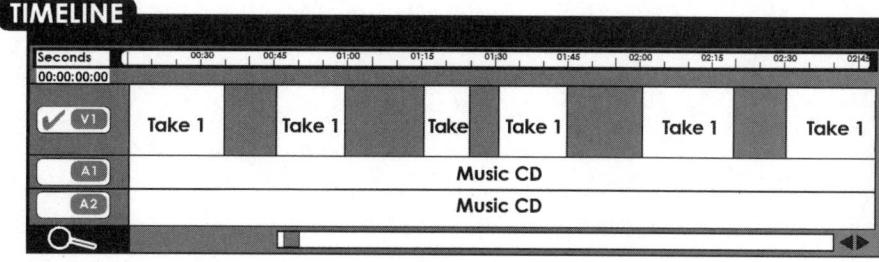

Figure 5-7
Step 6: Video tracks stacked to compare useful takes.

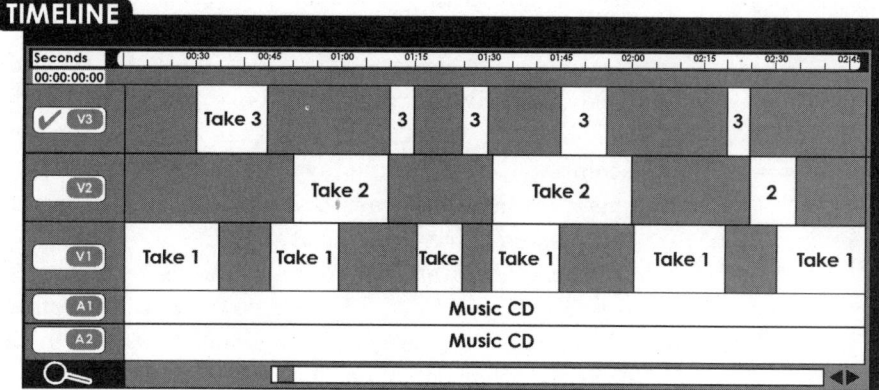

Commercials

If you can't keyframe movement,
you've got no business cutting spots.

Jennifer Rew, Master Editor

Commercials are fun 30-second puzzles for editors. The game is to tell the story within clearly defined limits. There's no such thing as a 32-second commercial, at least not one that will ever be broadcast. You can do whatever works within the time limit, but you cannot go out of bounds.

Commercials rely on finesse—often layers of finesse. The editor's job is to create eye candy that people can watch over and over again. You must understand how to do effects on your editing system. Being able to move logos and other graphics across the screen is an absolute necessity to be considered competent. Top commercial editors are compositing and editing experts. The vast majority (over 70 percent) of the work that commercial postproduction facilities do involves layering and/or compositing. About 80 percent of the time, the audio tracks—voice, music and effects—are added after the picture is cut.

One of the great things about commercials is that they're usually finished at the end of a shift. They require minimal organization beyond religiously labeling every alternate timeline you make. These days deadlines are extremely tight from bid to production to air. There's a lot of pressure to perform, but once it's done and approved, the job is done for good.

Background

The most common length for a commercial is 30 seconds. Advertisers have also experimented with shorter lengths at 10, 15, and 20 seconds. Longer commercials were in vogue on broadcast television when advertising time was relatively inexpensive. Today, one- and two-minute commercials are used primarily for direct-response selling or what are called *short-form infomercials*. What characteristizes every commercial is the amount of attention that everyone involved in making commercials pays to each and every frame. There are 900 in a 30-second commercial. Nine hundred images and thirty seconds of sound.

A lot of attention is paid to the details because advertisers expect the target audience (potential customers) will see the commercial dozens of times. The more often a potential customer sees an ad, the more likely it will influence his or her behavior. The cost of making a commercial is a tiny fraction of the money involved to buy air time to broadcast the finished spot. There's no room for flaws because the audience will see that same 30-second spot over, and over, and over again.. You'd think that since everyone knows this, commercials would be better than they are.

Commercial Categories and Styles

Editors who understand advertising craft better commercials. The advertiser's intent determines the category in which a commercial falls, such as image, issue, or sales advertising. Some or all of the following styles are used to create commercials within those categories: animation, comedy, dialogue, effects heavy, music driven, problem/solution, product demonstration, slice of life, and testimonial.

In major markets such as New York, Los Angeles, and Chicago, editors are often selected for their ability to handle a particular style. An editor who understands comic timing might not be the right person to do an effects-heavy commercial, and vice versa. Every commercial relies on timing. Editors need to look for the rhythm within the scenes. Acting, camera work, music, and narration all have inherent rhythms. No matter which category or style is being used, the editor must cut to a visual as well as a musical beat. Professionals count every beat in every shot they place on the timeline. This is crucial because the story must be told in seconds. Everything must be honed, trimmed, and polished until it's perfect.

Image Advertising Image advertising aims to raise the audience's awareness of a company, product, or service. The advertiser wants to create or enhance lasting favorable impressions in the audience's mind often by associating a specific picture or motif with the product. Image advertising offers a lot of room for creativity. Nearly half of all the national advertising campaigns are in this category.

In the opening seconds, or first act, the target audience needs to recognize that this commercial has something in it for them. From an editor's perspective, the goal is to create an environment the customer recognizes or to one that he or she aspires. The middle portion, or second act, of the commercial presents the message. The closing seconds, or third act, links the message to what's being sold. For example, an image ad for a luxury car might begin by establishing wealth. The car might be at the edge of the scene or not shown at all. The images that follow convey understated elegance. Again, the car is not the subject. Not until the final moments does the car achieve screen parity with the lifestyle.

Eye movement and rhythm are key to timing the shots. There are rhythms within the frame and in the juxtaposition of shots. Your goal is to exploit the flow between, among, and within the images. Transitions, superimpositions, and color effects can be used to enhance the flow. A good way to establish the timing and mood is to cut the commercial to music, using a beat track or a sample of something similar in style to what will be composed after you complete the picture edit.

Issue Advertising Commercials that advocate causes, raise matters of public concern, or recommend or attack political candidates fall in the category of issue advertising. The opening of these commercials frame the message. You don't need to waste time getting the audience's attention. People who are interested in the issue automatically pay attention. After the setup, the message must be proved. These commercials wrap up by rephrasing the message in a way that sounds decisive or conclusive. Issue advertising takes the approach: Tell them what you're gonna tell them, tell them, and then tell them what you've told them. Any style works for this category.

Sales Advertising   The majority of commercials are timely advertisements about products and services. These commercials fall into the sales category. The style most often used here follows the problem/solution or cause/effect approach. The opening, or first act, grabs your attention and sets up the problem. The middle section, or second act, delivers the message in a dramatic fashion implying that what's being advertised is the solution to the problem. The call to action—the how, when, or where the audience can purchase the solution—is the close, or third act. As an editor, you'll want to edit in a way that keeps the tension going until the end of the commercial.

Workflow for Commercials with Sync Sound

1. Isolate and trim the sync sound shots.
2. Assemble them using script continuity.
3. Evaluate performance and eliminate extraneous material as needed.
4. Trim the sync sound shots for time.
5. Look over B-roll and graphics for the setup and close.
6. Build the open and close.
7. Record a scratch voice-over track, if necessary, and add to the timeline.

Advice from an Expert

Mark Moskowitz has created more commercials over the past 20 years than anyone we've met. He's personally produced, directed, and edited over 4,000 commercials for political candidates and hundreds more that sell goods and services. We asked Mark what advice he'd give to editors about commercials. He replied, "Anything, any kind of footage can work. Too many agencies are infatuated with making full- screen movies. Storytelling is fine though it rarely sells. If the footage doesn't work or it's just bad or too long, then you can always do something else with it. Use freezes, layer the footage, kill all the dialogue or on-camera talent, and record a voice-over. Just think about it creatively."

8. Trim the commercial for time, providing space for the composer to help sell with music flourishes.

9. Create alternative versions with more product shots, less onscreen dialogue, and more action.

10. Show the two best versions to the client and have him or her pick one.

Workflow for Commercials Without Sync Sound

1. Record a scratch track or the actual voice-over track. Most of the information will be conveyed by the audio, with the exception of commercials that use emotion or image to sell.

2. Lay the voice track on the timeline. Trim it for time.

3. Insert shots that fit the voice-over track to show what is being said.

4. Make cuts based on where the viewer's eye is being led in the frame.

5. Tighten or open up the voice-over, if necessary. Remember to leave space for music.

6. Build transitions—if needed—as you go.

7. Use type or graphics to reinforce the message. If the words are important, put them in the center or on the right-hand side of the screen.

8. Create alternative versions with more product shots or action.

9. Show the best two versions to the client and have him or her pick one.

Mark's Advice on Agency Commercials

"Cut the best spot using the boards as a guide. Ninety percent of the time, once the agency sees the footage cut at its best, they never look at the boards."

Workflow for Impressionistic Commercials Without Sync Sound

1. Build a European montage based on the motion and rhythm within the shots.
2. Record the narration track.
3. Lay the narration track on the timeline. Trim it for time.
4. Recut where necessary to fit the narration.
5. Tighten or open up the narration, if necessary. Remember to leave space for music.
6. Build transitions—if needed—as you go.
7. Use type or graphics to reinforce the message. If the words are important, put them in the center or on the right-hand side of the screen.
8. Create alternative versions.
9. Show the two best versions to the client and have him or her pick one.

Mark on Choices

"Often you have 30.5 seconds or 31 seconds and have to make an extreme compromise. Recently, we had a fantastic take of someone [speaking] to the lens that was 31 seconds long. We had a less than good take that was 29.5. I opted to use the 31-second take because the end was so great. That meant I had to cut away in the middle and lose a phrase, weakening the power of the to-the-lens performance. I thought the sacrifice was justified because the last eight seconds on camera were just so good. Now, as long as I did that, I made my cutaway ring hard with the message so I was covered in case I really had destroyed the intensity of the spot."

Documentary and Nonfiction

Undertaking a documentary is like taking a journey with no set destination or performing acrobatics on a high wire without a net. A vague outline or treatment describing the characters or situations is often the only guide during production. Hence, the structure of the show must be created during the editing phase. As a result, the editor becomes the most influential person in the success or failure of these shows.

What Is a Documentary?

"A documentary is a film without women. If there is a woman, it's a semi-documentary," according to Harry Cohn, the head of Columbia Pictures, as quoted by Fred Zinneman in his autobiography.

The standard definition of a documentary is a show about political, social, or historical subjects presented in a factual and informative manner using actual footage or interviews accompanied by narration. However, the most successful examples of the genre today feature fascinating characters who face great conflicts under unusual circumstances in a tale that unfolds before our eyes. Great nonfiction stories often have more dramatic arcs than fictional films because truth really is stranger than fiction.

According to the *Oxford English Dictionary*, the word *documentary* was associated with film for the first time in 1930 by Paul Rotha. However, anecdotal evidence suggests that John Grierson, the founder of the British documentary movement, was the first person to use the word in 1926 when he reviewed Robert Flaherty's second film *Moana*. Flaherty achieved fame in 1922 with the release of *Nanook of the North*, which is an ethnographic study of an Eskimo family that was seven years in the making. Grierson defined these types of films as the "creative treatment of actuality." The French also lay claim to earlier usage of the word as a way to describe travelogue films.

What is or isn't a documentary is as murky as the origins of the word. If you ask filmmakers to define what qualifies as a documentary, there will be as many answers as there are filmmakers. Documentary is a loosely defined word with no definite meaning. For many people, documentary conjures up boring shows they were forced to watch in high school. Many filmmakers shy away from the documentary label because of the bad connotations associated with the word. We prefer the label *nonfiction*.

Nonfiction is a clearer description and an appropriately broad term. The subjects of these shows are real people, real events, and real life. Any show based on factual rather than fictional characters or events can be classified as a nonfiction film. No matter which word you use, this genre provides a peerless opportunity to showcase an editor's storytelling skills. The editor is given more responsibility for the storytelling than in any other genre. Consequently, nonfiction offers greater personal rewards and risks. The show's success or failure often depends on the editor's ability.

Nonfiction Storytelling

Most nonfiction is either character or subject driven. Surprise gives these stories their power. The audience can rarely predict the outcome. The most satisfying nonfiction stories (the ones with the widest appeal) are inherently dramatic and are told in three acts.

Conflict is the basis of drama. Change, whether the change occurs in the characters or the situation, holds the audience's attention. Classic themes, such as man against man or man against nature, drive the drama in many nonfiction shows. For example, every show about a social issue pits one or more sides against the other (man against man) whether the topic is abortion or hearing implants for deaf children.

The first act introduces the characters and conflict. The second act explores how the characters confront the central conflict. In the third act, the characters' actions should resolve the conflict. If you think this sounds like a description of the rules for fiction, you are correct. There's not much difference between nonfiction and fiction storytelling other than the characters and circumstances are real rather than invented in nonfiction.

Nonfiction Styles

Nonfiction covers a wide range of styles. That's to be expected considering that fiction can be subdivided into categories, such as action, biography, comedy, drama, fantasy, horror, mystery, romance, and suspense. Nonfiction is no different. Some of the many possible categories of nonfiction include advocacy, biography, culture, education, ethnography, history, how-tos, investigations, nature and wildlife, news, observational, performance, personal quests, reality television, social issues, sports, satire, and travelogues.

There is a subtle difference between shows that employ the conventions of fiction and those that adhere to the true spirit of nonfiction filmmaking. Nonfiction, at its most compelling, is a voyage of discovery for the filmmaker and the audience. It is a voyage in which neither party is sure of the destination until they arrive.

What most people think of when they hear the word *documentary* is actually called *direct cinema*, *cinéma verité*, or *observational nonfiction*. These shows are created from footage that was shot using a fly-on-the-wall approach. The filmmaker often shoots the subject or subjects of the story over long periods of time. The finished show tells the story without narration or commentary from the filmmaker. To edit this type of story, use the unscripted (visual continuity) workflow that is explained later in this chapter. Building or carving works equally well.

In contrast, most of the nonfiction shows on cable and broadcast television are scripted and bear only a passing resemblance to classic nonfiction. Biography and history programs rarely embark on a voyage of discovery; the outcome is predetermined. The same is true of programs that explore a brief period of time or singular event, such as a wedding, the penguin mating season, wander around a city with police officers for a night. Dramatic effect is added by intercutting two or more stories or points of view. Production schedules, limited budgets, and formulaic approaches often preclude anything more than a shallow treatment of the subject. To edit shows of this type, follow the "Workflow for Scripted Nonfiction" in this section.

Criteria for Nonfiction Success

We've watched hundreds of nonfiction films at festivals and markets around the world, which is unfortunately where most of them will remain, playing to limited audiences. The few shows that move beyond the festival circuit and reach a wider audience in theaters or television all share certain characteristics. Editors who remember these criteria craft better shows.

Strong characters are extremely important. What's a strong character? Anyone who's compelling on camera or says things in an interesting manner. It helps if the person is photogenic or was shot in unusual or intriguing surroundings. The strongest characters are those who have the most at stake in the outcome of the story. People facing life and death issues are more compelling than people making decisions about whether to get a Happy Meal or a Blue Plate Special.

The story must have a distinct beginning, middle, and end. Conflict, crisis, or controversy should drive the plot. Timely stories or stories with new information about topics of continuing concern can hold the audience's attention without much of a plot. However, the stories that employ a dramatic three-act structure with twists that trigger each act are more powerful.

Passion and emotion are necessities. The story or the characters should move the audience, touch their hearts, and spur them to think, feel, or explore the subject more. The filmmaker's passion for the subject must be clear to the audience. There should be a strong sense of authorship, which can be expressed in the style or manner of the presentation and/or in the approach to the subject. Authorship answers the following questions. Why did the filmmaker want to make this show? Why is the subject critically important? What does the filmmaker have at stake? Sometimes the only evidence of authorship is incredible access into people's lives and worlds that few have seen before.

The last criterion is an indefinable something. Just as some people have charisma that draws others to them, some nonfiction shows are oddly compelling. These shows excite audiences and ignite discussion well beyond normal proportions. No editor can add the secret ingredient, although it's easy to kill if it happens to be present.

Editing Nonfiction

From an editor's perspective, there's observational nonfiction and everything else. Observational nonfiction, or cinéma verité, grew out of early ethnographic studies like *Nanook of the North*. The philosophy that the camera should be a fly-on-the wall and record what happens without influencing the events developed with the appearance of smaller, more ergonomic film cameras and portable audio recorders in the 1950s. The edited show is supposed to be an unvarnished truthful record. However, the presence of a camera always changes people's behavior. The decision to include some scenes and leave others out is prejudicial. The audience's perception of truth relies on the filmmaker's perceptions. The process of valuing some material as more important than other footage ensures that truth is relative. The category of everything else includes shows crafted from archival materials, interviews, recreations, and other footage that illuminates or provides context for the story.

Stories that grow and develop out of the material rather than being imposed upon the material produce more powerful shows. Mimi Edmunds, a former producer for CBS's *60 Minutes* who currently teaches at the University of Southern California, says, "You'll find that there are at least three or four stories—sometimes more—in producing a documentary. One, the story you think you want to research. Two, the story you actually research. Three, the story you shoot in the field. Four, the story you edit and write in the editing room. The story you start out with is rarely the exact one you end up with in the final product."

Workflow Is Critical

The best nonfiction stories unfold in the edit suite; this is a task that is easier said than done. Editing nonfiction projects can be overwhelming because shooting ratios (the amount of material shot versus the length of the finished show) are often quite high. Shooting 20 hours of footage for a 90-minute show is not uncommon.

Workflow is critical for nonfiction. An editor can easily be buried by the complexity of a job and the avalanche of material. The editor must view all the footage. You cannot take a shortcut for this first step. Logs that were made while the material was being shot can help prioritize the order in which you view the material. However, you'll need to make your own logs.

The method you use to do this depends on how much storage space is available in your editing system. If all the footage can be transferred, we suggest that you use your editing system's logging tools. The search and sort functions of an editing system can be an enormous help when you're looking for specific material; it's usually easier than flipping through page after page of handwritten logs. If not enough space is available, it's often possible to log the material without transferring it to your editing system's storage drives. The alternative is to use logging software, which can control the recorder, capture the time code information, and create a batch transfer list for your editing system.

It's All About Structure

As you watch the material, evaluate it with a critical eye. Pay attention to the shots, angles, and quality of image and sound. Is the material visually interesting? Can you tell the story using only this footage? Is there enough action to hold the audience's interest? Interviews should be evaluated for

Transcripts—Yes or No?

A *transcript* is a written or typed copy of all the spoken words in the material. Transcription services are readily available. These services employ fast typists who listen to an audiocassette copy of your material and create a record of the words in your choice of word processing programs. Some services can mark the beginning of each paragraph with a time code address that corresponds to the location where those words were spoken.

Some producers and editors swear by transcripts. It's easy to print out the document and circle all the best quotes. If the document has time code addresses, it's simple to find those sections. If you string together the best quotes from each of the interviewees, then the show is half-built, right?

Many editors would blanche at this suggestion. To them, transcripts are something to swear at rather than swear by. That approach is terrific if you're creating a magazine article or a story for print. However, reading a transcript is not the same as watching someone say the words. Most of the time what's of interest is the way people say what they say rather than the words they've spoken.

Think about any conversation you've ever had with someone you care about. What's left unsaid often illustrates the emotional feelings that fill the gaps between the words. Those gaps filled with silence or hems and haws are often more important than the mundane things most of us say to each other. No transcript can ever reveal those nuances.

The danger of using transcripts is that it's easy to rely on them and ignore the real goal. We're making shows for audiences to *watch*. Inflection, energy, and nonverbal cues make the interviewe compelling. It's not the words, but the individual's expression that counts.

Having said that, a transcript can be a lifesaver when you have too much material to look at in the time allotted for editing the show. If you find yourself in this situation, think of the transcript as a log someone else has made. Find the places in the transcript that seem promising and watch those sections of the material. As you do, make notes about the person's inflection, energy, and any important nonverbal cues. The challenge is that this approach makes it harder to sense the emotional arc of the entire interview. This shortcut helps you get the job done, though excellence is rarely achieved using this method.

the person's inflection, energy, and nonverbal cues above and beyond what's being said. It's important to note the camera angle and any image or sound quality issues. Sound quality is more important than image quality for interview footage. In the back of your mind, you should also start thinking about ways to organize the material. Is it chronological? Are there multiple points of view or themes?

The next step is to decide whether to base editing continuity on the sound, picture, or narration. You must be realistic about the material you have to work with; otherwise, there's no point in doing this step. If you have many strong interviews, perhaps the best way to begin is to start by building the audio track. On the other hand, if you have great action footage, you should probably try using visual continuity. The best examples of shows cut using visual continuity are observational nonfiction because all of the footage is action based—in other words, it depicts people doing things. If the interviews and footage are mediocre, narration may be the best approach. This decision determines how you'll begin putting the show together. However, before you do anything, you must get organized.

Advice from a Nonfiction Filmmaker

Jeff Kreines has been making cinéma verité films for 30 years with his girlfriend/partner Joel DeMott. Their film *Seventeen*, which made many critics' top-ten lists and was called "one of the best and most scarifying reports on American life to be seen on a theater screen" by the *New York Times*, won grand prizes at many festivals, including Ann Arbor and Sundance (more information can be found at www.perforatedtruth.com).

Jeff's advice about nonfiction filmmaking is that: "Transcriptions and scripts are anathema to good nonfiction filmmaking. Get to know your material by watching it and taking notes on what affects you, and start editing. Don't edit on paper; make your film by editing the film itself. And though it's easy to do, never use cutaways—any shot that starts off looking like a cutaway must include some actual sync in it, or it's cheating. Whenever possible, always lap your cuts (as we film people call it—video people call it an *L*-cut or a split edit)—it helps make things flow. *Bulworth* (a Hollywood film, heavily influenced by cinéma verité) is a great example of this—beautifully edited."

Get Organized

The more material you have, the more organized you'll have to be. If you've never edited a large project, we suggest you read Chapter 6, which goes into more detail about organization and bin management. Organization makes it easier to find what you want when you want it.

The structure you have in mind for the show should influence how you organize your materials. For example, for a show that relies on audio continuity, every interview subject should have a separate bin. Lengthy interviews may need to be split up into several bins to reflect the topics or themes raised in that person's interview. If some topics are raised by more than one person, you may want to create a set of bins that are organized by these topics. Copy, rather than move, clips from the interviewee bins into the topic bins. Some editing systems allow you to organize your bins in a hierarchy, which helps with complex projects. The rationale for all of this is explained in Chapter 6.

The process of organizing your material will help you become more familiar with it. As you watch the footage and make clips, you will begin to discover the themes and story threads that are present in the material. Don't be afraid to modify your original ideas about the organization or structure of the show. Let the material be your guide.

Workflow for Scripted Nonfiction

The editor's job for this type of show is to conform the material to the guidelines laid out in the script and improve on it, if possible. The decisions of where to start and how you choose to proceed are based on personal preference. The structure is predetermined by the script or, in the case of a series, by the bible that outlines standards for that series. The workflow is the same for any other scripted show. Start anywhere you like. If you prefer to build, pick a pivotal scene or a section of the script that appeals to you. Subclip the material and start building the scene shot by shot. If you prefer to carve, string all the material together in script order and watch it. Eliminate anything extraneous. When you've finished the rough cut, sit back and watch the show again. A quick glance at the timeline will tell you if you must contract or expand the show to meet length requirements. Trim the shots to adjust the pacing and rhythm. Add transitions where necessary. Create and add titles, graphics, and credits.

Mix the audio and output the show. The workflow for scripted nonfiction is as follows:

1. View and log the material.

2. Read the script. Make notes about the materials you have—where they do or do not fit with the script.

3. Break down the material into subclips and organize them into bins that reflect the needs of the script.

4. Isolate and trim all the sync sound footage.

5. Evaluate the interviews. Create a bin and make subclips of the best parts of the interview. In a news environment, editors look for succinct statements (under seven seconds) that capture the essence of the interview. These snappy statements are called *sound bites*. Copy any subclips you make (short or long statements) into separate bins.

6. If narration is called for, record a scratch track. Break it down into subclips based on the placement of the narration in the script.

   For shorter shows, try the following technique. Record the narration track with pauses in place for the interviews. The script should indicate the duration of each interview. Edit the narration track onto the timeline. Fill the gaps in the narration with the interviews. Add your cutaway or B-roll shots and you're done.

7. Start assembling the show using the script as a guide. It doesn't matter where you start. Whether you begin with picture, sound, or narration depends on the strength of the material. Scripted shows usually depend on narration. If this is the case, place the scratch narration track on the timeline in script order. Leave space between each section of narration; these gaps can be tightened or expanded after you begin filling in the pictures.

8. Insert the shots indicated in the script and line them up with the voice-over. Build a rough assembly of the show.

9. If the script includes interview material, go through the bin with the best of the interview sound bites and select the ones that enhance the story line the most. Place them on the timeline in the appropriate places.

10. Tighten or open up the narration sections as necessary. Remember to leave breathing room. Listening to uninterrupted talking is very tiring for the audience. There should space for music, natural sounds, and/or sound effects that can add depth and emotion to the soundtrack.

11. Play the show. If you have to fulfill a length requirement, expand or contract the show as necessary.

12. Trim for pacing and rhythm.

13. Add transitions as needed.

14. Create and add titles, graphics, and credits.

15. Mix the audio and output the show.

Workflow for Unscripted Nonfiction

Digital video has triggered an explosion of independent nonfiction filmmaking. Professionals now compete with anyone who has an abiding interest in a subject or cause and a digital camcorder. The benefit of this is that more voices and views are being heard than ever before.

However, more people are competing for the shrinking funds available to nonfiction filmmakers. It takes an average of five years to fund and complete a feature-length nonfiction show. Many shows take much longer. There's often no separation between production and post. Instead, the process is fluid. The filmmaker raises money, shoots, edits, and raises more money to shoot and edit more until the project is completed or his or her interest wanes. Professional editors are being asked to take on additional responsibilities that were once reserved for producers because budgets demand it. In many cases, filmmakers are choosing to edit their own work for all the reasons you're reading this book. Our workflow for unscripted nonfiction takes these real-world factors into account.

Prep Prep Prep

1. View the material. Make notes about the materials you have. Ask yourself, whose story is it and what is the story? Determine whether visual or audio continuity can be used or if narration will be required.

2. Categorize the material into bins that reflect the structure and continuity approach you'll use to begin editing the show.

Begin Roughing Out the Show   You can rough out the show in four ways. You can build or carve using visual continuity or build or carve using audio continuity. The steps for carving visual continuity are denoted by the letter *C* next to the number. The steps for building visual continuity are marked by the letter *B* next to the number.

Workflow for Visual Continuity

3C. Think about a logical structure for the material. The possibilities are endless. However, the most common structures are based on chronology, location (everything that happens in a particular place), action (cause and effect), or point/counterpoint.

3B. Find and select a pivotal or emotional scene in the material to begin editing. Build that scene by isolating shots and making subclips. Cut the picture. Ignore the audio.

4C. Put all the material on the timeline using the structure you arrived at in Step 3C.

4B. Select a second pivotal scene to build using the same process you used for the first scene.

5C. Watch the show. Look for repetitious or extraneous material and carve away those parts. Carve until only the essence of the material is left.

5B. Figure out how to get from scene one to scene two using the footage you have in hand. This will be the structure of the show (the path from scene one to scene two) if you've chosen the most telling scenes. It's common to discover in the editing process that you need another pivotal moment or a different one to begin or end the story.

Workflow for Audio Continuity

3C. Evaluate the interviews. Develop a logical structure for the show. The most common ones are based on chronology, themes, or point/counterpoint (one person raises an issue and another person answers it).

3B. Evaluate the interviews. Decide whether to use transcripts. Create a bin for each interviewee and make subclips of the best parts of each interview. Copy those subclips into a separate bin labeled Selects and the name of the person.

4C. Place all the interviews on the timeline in a logical order.

4B. Place all the selects on the timeline. Watch the show. Eliminate repetitious or extraneous statements.

5C. Watch the show. Carve away any repetitious or extraneous material.

5B. Rearrange the clips until you find a structure that tells the story. Watch the show. Look for repetitious or extraneous interviews and eliminate them.

6BC. Play the timeline. Make decisions about whether the person should appear on camera or whether other visuals would illustrate his or her words better.

6BC. Play the timeline. Does the audio track tell the story? If it doesn't, you may need to add narration (either an on-camera personality or voice-over) or action sequences to make the story come alive for the audience.

Ask the Tough Questions These steps are of the utmost importance. The first step within this category is 6v (v for visual) if you're editing the show using visual continuity or 7a (a for audio) if you're editing the show using audio continuity. It's the editor's job to ask the tough questions that the audience will surely ask.

6v/7a. Ask yourself what other material might add impact to this story. Make notes and suggestions for the filmmaker. What footage would you'd like them to shoot the next time they have a production day? Offer ideas about stock footage that could strengthen the show.

7v/8a. Play the timeline. Ask yourself whether the material you have tells the story? If it does, move to the polishing stage. If not, you may need interviews or narration (either an on-camera personality or voice-over) to make the show come alive for the audience.

Polish the Show No matter how you get here, follow these steps to complete the show:

8v/9a. Trim the show for pacing and rhythm. Leave room for music, natural sounds, and/or sound effects that can add depth and emotion. If you edited on the basis of audio continuity, remember that the audience needs breathing space. Listening to uninterrupted talking is extremely tiring.

9v/10a. Add transitions, if necessary.

10v/11a. Create and add titles, graphics, and credits.

11v/12a. Mix the audio and output the show.

Fiction

When editing fiction, you have a script and footage that follows the script to guide your efforts. Fiction films have been shot the same way since sound was first introduced in 1927. Scenes are shot out of sequence to accommodate the schedule of the highest-paid actors. Production schedules are arranged to minimize the number of days that the most expensive actors must work. The schedule also needs to minimize the number of times the cast and crew must physically move to a new set or location. Moving hundreds of people and equipment costs a lot of time and money.

The Continuity Challenge

The challenge on set and for the editor is to maintain continuity. Whenever scenes are shot out of sequence, continuity is difficult to maintain. A *script supervisor* is on set at all times to prevent continuity errors from being made. This person, who should be called the *continuity supervisor*, serves as the liaison between the director and editor. Script supervisors provide detailed information about how the script was shot. They keep logs and mark the production script to let the editor know which shots and takes cover specific portions of the script. The editor's job would be far more difficult without this information.

Despite all the best efforts of the crew, small and large continuity errors frequently occur. It seems inevitable that small errors will occur over a long production schedule, such as a glass on a table being half full in the master shot and empty in the close-up. Sometimes it's just too expensive to correct a minor mistake. On occasion, major errors will also sneak by.

Here are a few examples we've seen. An actor exits through a door, which was established in an earlier scene as the closet door. Wonder where he's going? An actor's blue jacket in the master shot becomes his red jacket in the close-up. That would be easy to fix on a digital editing system. A scar on a character's left cheek migrates to his right cheek at different times in the same scene. Hmm? A quick search on the Internet will turn up several web sites devoted to the continuity errors spotted by audiences.

Continuity errors are good for a laugh—unless, of course, you're an editor. Another challenge is logistic—organization. Feature-length productions can generate a lot of footage. A typical production might have 40 or 50 scenes and thousands of shots, each with multiple takes. All of the material must be viewed, logged, and organized. The script supervisor's logs are the editor's bible for these productions.

Managing the Edit for a Feature

It's difficult to manage a show that could be two or three hours long. No desktop has enough space to work easily on a timeline of that length. Imagine trimming a few frames off a shot while trying to control a timeline filled with thousands of lip-synced clips. It would be unimaginably difficult. Therefore, it's imperative to break up a project of this size into manageable sections. These sections should be organized along the lines of the structure of the show.

The basic building block is a shot. Feature films are photographed and edited one shot at a time. A series of shots creates a scene. A series of scenes creates a sequence. A series of sequences creates an act. The acts constitute the finished show. Each of these units, from the shot to the show, has a beginning, middle, and end.

A workable method of editing a feature film is to organize your work around sequences. The average sequence is approximately 10 minutes, which is about as long as a timeline can be easily managed on the desktop. The process begins with scenes. Create a timeline for each scene. Organize the clips associated with each scene in their own bins. Once the scene is edited, save the timeline.

After all of the scenes are completed, create a new timeline. Then assemble the sequence by placing each scene on the timeline from beginning to end. Follow the same procedure to build each act. Create a timeline for each act and assemble the completed sequences in the proper order. Add shots or scenes that can serve as transitions between the sequences, if necessary. The advantage of this method is that you can gauge the flow of the story at every step.

A Note About Film   If the show is being shot in film, the sound elements will arrive on separate tapes. More information about double-system sound appears in Chapter 10. It should suffice to say that as the editor, you'll have to sync the audio up to the film before you can cut one frame of dialogue. Most of the technical editing issues involved in feature filmmaking are beyond the scope of this book. However, the workflow is straightforward.

This Might Sound Familiar . . .

The workflow for editing fiction follows the same workflow we presented in Chapter 3, "Beginnings, Middles, and Ends." In that chapter and the one that follows, we show you how to edit the sample footage we included in this book. The production of that simple scene follows the time-honored tradition of a shooting a master and other angles for coverage. On the CD, you'll find a master shot (the two-shot) and a close-up of each character.

Editing this scene should give you a taste of how to edit fiction. The workflow is the same despite the briefness of this scene. The editing approach to one scene is repeated dozens of times when you're editing a feature film. However, before we go over the workflow, let's look at the big picture.

An Editor's Viewpoint of Structure

The shots build the scenes. The scenes build the sequences. The sequences build the finished show. Well-made films have no extraneous shots, scenes, or sequences. Everything has a purpose and advances the story.

About Sequences   A group of scenes with a shared theme or idea forms a sequence. The sequence breaks the larger story into smaller pieces easier for the audience to grasp. In literature, novels have chapters. Chapters separate ideas, events, or experiences from others in a book. The chapters in a film have their own special integrity and structure. A sequence performs the identical function in film and video stories, separating the story into digestible chunks.

Editing Prep

- Organize the footage.
- Watch the footage and make notes about your first impressions. Consider performance, camera work, usefulness, and continuity.
- Above all, look for shots that capture emotional moments.
- Remember that you are the audience's advocate.

A typical sequence lasts about 10 minutes in a Hollywood feature film. We've all seen films with a bank robbery sequence or a miss-the-plane-at-the-airport-sequence. Each contains several scenes that separately and together have a beginning, middle, and end. Each scene within the sequence enhances the story line in the sequence and overall story.

About Scenes   The material you have in hand will help you decide the order in which you build a scene. Of course, experience plays a big role here. Action scenes can be built or carved depending on the situation. Dialogue scenes tend to go together like stringing pearls, one at a time. Scenes that contain both action and dialogue require a different approach. You can build each portion separately and combine the pieces later or in stages. It's also possible to assemble the material as one scene, working on both sections concurrently. The power of digital editing is that you can develop an approach that works for you. It's also easy to change your approach to suit the material or meet new requirements.

Fiction Workflow

Start by assembling any action shots that open the scene. Refer to your notes and use the best takes. Pay attention to continuity. The aphorism "cut on action" works here. Add to the flow by placing cuts in the action. These cut points will be hidden in movement. This approach works well if you need to match action using different takes.

Assemble the actors' best takes using the script for continuity. Edit with straight cuts. You might want to keep each character's voice on a separate audio track as you build the scene. It's also fine to place all the voices on the same track. You can easily move them later.

Edit in any insert or cut-in shots that are important for story purposes. These include close-ups or details (such as a close-up of a pistol) that are required for the audience to make sense of the scene.

Continue by adding action shots to the scene if they are available. Assemble them in the order called for in the script.

Listen to the audio and adjust the rhythm to accommodate the actor's natural flow. Add frames at cut points to create pauses to enable the audience to think.

If you want the audience to have time to study someone's face for emotional clues, don't cut away immediately after the character speaks. If you want to tighten up the scene, shortening the shots can change the rhythm or shift the focus away from, or to, a character.

Once the scene plays with a coherent audio track, create overlapping video edits with *L*- and *J*-cuts. Overlapping edits, which only change the video track, are simple to do and let you steer the scene from one character's point of view to another's.

For example, in a conversation, you can change the audience's interpretation by allowing them to see how one character reacts to the other. This is an easy way to show the audience that a character is lying or is nervous when questioned.

Begin trimming the action shots for rhythm, emotional adjustment, and continuity. Fine tune the flow after each character's dialogue is complete.

Linger on action if it helps depict a character's motives. Staying with a character can also help cement the point of view. Shorten shots if you want to increase the pace of the scene or deemphasize a character's prominence.

Add video-only cutaways and reaction shots. Cutaways are any shots that cut away from the action or conversation. They are used to fix continuity problems, compress time, or build rhythm. Reaction shots reveal a character's response to other characters or objects in a scene.

What Makes a Good Cut?

Walter Murch, an Academy Award winning editor, wrote, "In film, a shot presents us with an idea, or a sequence of ideas, and the cut is a 'blink' that separates and punctuates those ideas. At the moment you decide to cut, what you are saying is, in effect, 'I am going to bring this idea to an end and start something new.' If the cut is well-placed . . . the more thorough the effect of punctuation will be."[1] Murch feels there are six criteria that determine a good cut. The first three, in order of importance (by percentage), are emotion (51 percent), story (23 percent), and rhythm (10 percent). This adds up to 84 percent.[2] The three technical criteria hardly matter.

---

[1] Walter Murch, *In the Blink of an Eye: A Perspective on Film Editing*, 2nd edition (Los Angeles: Silman-James Press, 2001), 18.

[2] Ibid., 18.

Complete the scene by adding ambience to fill in any ambient holes. Ambience is what you'd hear if you were sitting in the room or location where the scene is taking place when everyone stops talking. It's the noise of the place. An ambient hole is a gap on the audio track. In a digital environment, if nothing is on the track, there's dead silence. Except for in outer space, dead silence doesn't exist. The audience will notice the absence of sound. Use what sound recordists call *room tone* and add it to the audio track wherever there's a hole. Add sound effects and music to help tell the story.

The Next Steps—Sequences, Acts, . . .

Complete all the scenes that should be included in a sequence. Place each one, in turn, on the timeline. You can place them one after another to build the story. If there's parallel action, you can intercut scenes. It's usually easier to cut between completed scenes than to build an intercut sequence from scratch. After you've built the sequences, you can assemble them on a timeline. Once you have all the acts, you can assemble the show. If you edit in sections, even the longest and most complex story can be easily managed.

The China Closet

Editing revolves around finding and retrieving the moving images, photographs, drawings, sounds, and music stored in files as digital information scattered on your editing system's storage drive or drives. Think of storage as a china closet. Editing a short program is like making dinner for yourself. You don't need a lot of dishes. You probably don't care if you use a soup bowl for salad if that's what you grab first. However, when you start editing longer programs, it's like hosting a dinner party for a dozen guests. To set the table properly, you must be able to find all the dishes. An organized china closet makes setting the table easier when you're expecting company.

Organizing Projects

Ideally, everything you need for a show should be instantly available and easy to find. Your editing system is designed to keep track of the media files (still images, motion pictures, or audio) stored on your hard drive and let you work with icons called *clips*, which represent the pictures and sounds, rather than filenames. Whenever you access a clip, whether it is a still image, video, or music, your editing system's database will locate the appropriate media file and play it.

Editing systems can help you organize the clips so you can easily find the shots, sounds, or images. However, you need to provide the intelligence. Everyone has a different sense of organization. Give two editors identical material and they'll categorize it differently. However, all professional editors will organize the material in some fashion. Shorter projects require less organization than longer projects. This is equally true whether you measure the length by the duration of the finished show or by the amount of time the editor has to complete it. Good organization (that is, an approach that works for you) lets you find what you need quickly and enables you to edit much faster.

Computers use hierarchical structures that consist of files stored in folders or directories on a drive. Nearly every editing system uses this model. Typically, everything associated with making all the versions of a single show is stored in a *project* file.

Projects

The *project* is usually the highest level in an editing system's hierarchy. Projects usually contain information about the sound and picture elements, which are the principal building materials for the show you are editing; any

Technical Settings Versus User Preferences

Two distinct settings are prevalent in most editing systems: technical parameters and user preferences. Technical parameters are associated with a specific project. For example, the footage for the Mimosa Project was recorded with a miniDV camcorder (NTSC)* in the 16:9 aspect ratio with an audio sample rate of 48 kHz (16 bits) on two stereo tracks. The technical settings for this project must reflect the settings used to record the footage. These technical parameters are usually set when you create a new project and before you start bringing material into the project. If they don't match, most editing systems will either resample the material to match the parameters you set or prevent you from inputting the material. The approach to changing and storing these settings varies from manufacturer to manufacturer.

For our Mimosa Project example, the timeline must use the 29.97 frame rate of NTSC to maintain its time database. The viewers must be set to the 16:9 mode so the footage is displayed properly on the desktop. The frame size must be set to 720×480 pixels, which is standard for miniDV. Finally, the audio sample rate must be 48 kHz to avoid resampling the audio tracks. The important point to remember is that technical settings always refer to a single project.

In contrast, user preference settings control the appearance of the desktop, the mapping of the keyboard, and the layout of the windows on the desktop. These settings store any modifications you make to your editing system's user interface. When you open the application, the user interface reflects your preferences. To sum it up, the difference is that technical parameters apply to one project, whereas user settings apply to all projects.

---

* The television standard used in North America created by the National Television Standards Committee. See page 251.

sequences of sounds and pictures (timelines) that you create; and any changes you make to technical settings, such as audio sample rates or video formats, or to user settings that depart from the default settings in your program, such as the placement of a window on the desktop or color schemes.

Although not every editing system works this way, most do. Even if yours doesn't, the project model is still an excellent way to think about organization. The idea is to put everything you need to build a finished show in one box.

The first step after launching your editing system is to open or create a project. The first time you create a project, your system may create a file, folder, or directory to store information. The second step is to name the project. This may seem obvious, but beginners often overlook this step. Editing programs usually label a new project using a default name, such as Untitled, New, or Project_1 if you don't provide a descriptive name.

Every project should have a name that helps you identify what the project or show is about. Call it what it is—for example, the Smith's wedding, a commercial for Acme Widgets, or perhaps the title of the program. It really doesn't matter what you call it as long as you take the extra step of calling it something. If you're just practicing, call the project *Practice* or *My First Lesson*. Get in the habit of naming things. It's the single most important action you can take to feel in control of your editing system.

In many editing programs, only one project can be open at a time. Think of a project as a large empty table in the reference section of the library. This is where you gather all of the elements in the course of doing research. After a while, the table is covered with books, magazines, notebooks, lists, photocopies, reference books, photographs, microfilm, and audio CDs. Most of the things you need to write your report are on the table in front of you. However, some things are scattered throughout the library. Those materials are readily accessible because you have a list at your fingertips that tells you where they are located in the library.

This table is your central work area. This is where the materials you need are gathered and laid out. Is the material stacked and organized or cluttered and disorganized? The speed and efficiency with which you get the job done depends on how quickly you can access your materials. This is why an orderly project table is important.

The more organized you are, the fewer challenges you'll encounter as you edit. You don't have to follow any specific organization or go overboard, but you do need to figure out how to organize the materials you plan to use in a way that makes sense to you.

This begins with the creation of the project (how you name it) and continues until you finish editing. The best way to avoid frustration is to organize your materials in a consistent fashion. Professionals label things appropriately, which means they name an item using its most distinctive characteristic.

Names

Names and labels are at the heart of organization. Nothing is more important. You should get in the habit of assigning names that enable you to remember what an item is. Throughout the editing process, you will have to find pictures, shots, sounds, graphics, and other materials stored in your system. You'll be glad later when you can retrieve something quickly because you took the time in the beginning to give it a recognizable name.

Here are some basic rules about naming that will help you avoid problems:

- *Use all uppercase letters, all lowercase letters, or capitalize the first letter of each word.* Be consistent no matter which approach you decide to take. This is very important because some computer operating systems will treat Wind Surfing, Wind surfing, WIND SURFING, wind surfing, and WINd surFING as five different names, whereas others will see them as five identical names. This issue also arises whenever you sort a list of names or search for a name. Therefore, you must use upper- and lowercase letters consistently when labeling things.

- *Use unique names.* If you decide to use the title of your show as the name of the project, don't use it for anything else. No matter how tempting it might be to label the completed timeline that you will output to tape *My Hawaiian Adventure* because that's the title of the program, don't do it. It will only cause confusion. It's easy to end up with hundreds of things that need to be labeled and it can be challenging to come up with distinctive names for all of them. However, it's worth the effort it takes if you can avoid looking through a dozen items with the same name, time after time, trying to figure out which one of them is the one you really want. In our experience, taking a few moments to come up with unique labels can save you hours.

- *Use descriptive names.* It may be standard practice in Hollywood to label every shot using a scene number, shot number, and take number, but it's not very effective for most digital video editing projects. Hollywood does it because it makes it easier to match up a piece of film with the sound recording. Sound is recorded separately in film production. In video, sound is recorded on the videotape. You rarely need to match up pictures with sounds or do what's called *synchronizing picture to sound* or *syncing the dailies*. Hollywood's second reason for labeling footage with numbers is that it matches the scene numbers marked on the script. However, unless you can recall from memory what Scene 2, Shot 1, Take 3 looks like, you're better off using a name that indicates the subject or describes the action. Amherst Church, Long Shot (abbreviated LS), or Linda Answers the Phone is more helpful than Scene 2, Shot 1, Take 3.

■ *Always label your materials.* Every videotape, audiotape, CD, or DVD should be identified with a reel number and descriptive name. Editing systems identify a particular shot using a reel number, which indicates on which tape the material was originally recorded, and the location of the shot on the tape. A clock, called a *time code number*, is automatically recorded on every frame of video to enable editing systems to find the exact location on the tape.

Time Code

Digital video cameras record picture and sound along with a clock to identify each frame of video. The clock starts at zero, runs in a continuous sequence until the end of the tape, and is designated in military time (0 to 24 hours). Two types of clock are commonly used in video. One is called *nondrop frame time code*. The miniDV video format uses *drop frame time code*. Drop frame is the version designed so the time clock number on the tape corresponds to the time of day on a wall clock. The drop frame clock is adjusted by two frames every minute on the minute, except on 10-minute intervals, which in effect slows it down. It's like leap year where every four years the calendar is adjusted by one day. In video, this occurs every minute except for the tenth minute. The hours, minutes, seconds and frames are separated with semicolons or periods in drop frame time code to differentiate it from non-drop frame time code which uses colons.

Reel numbers are used whenever you transfer material into your editing system. The time code identifies every frame of video and indicates the passage of time. The reel number is the top level of a hierarchy that you must create because the time code number on your original source tapes aren't necessarily unique.

Professional cameras let the operator set the starting point of the time code. Most professionals set the hour number to match the tape's reel number and to give the tape a unique time code. This procedure works because most cameras record on tapes that are shorter than an hour. The tape in the camera and the tape box are marked with a reel number. So, reel

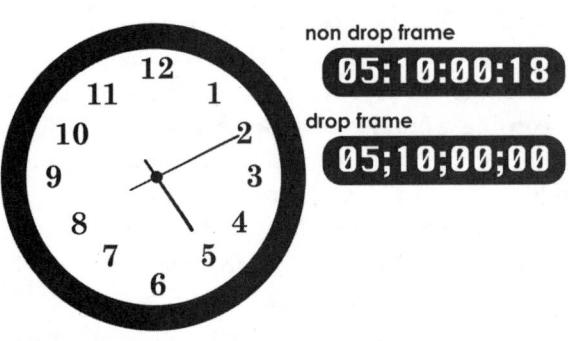

non drop frame
`05:10:00:18`

drop frame
`05;10;00;00`

Figure 6-1
Three ways of presenting the same time.

three would have a starting time code of 3 hours, zero minutes, zero seconds, zero frames. If the tape is an hour long, the time code at the end of the tape would be 3 hours, 59 minutes, 59 seconds, 29 frames. Professional recorders all read and display time code. Therefore, in a professional environment, it's easy to see that reel three (the one with the hour three time code) is in the recorder. However, camcorders for home use automatically set the time code to zero every time a new tape is placed in the camera. There is no provision for the operator to change the time code.

Shooting Tip

It's important to avoid time code breaks on your original source tapes because it creates havoc for editing systems. There are two methods to prevent this from happening. The first one—the safe and sure method—is to record black on every new tape before you use it. Turn on your camera or recorder and put in a new tape. If you're using a camera, leave the lens cap on. Disconnect the microphone or turn the audio recording level down. If you can't do either one of those, put the camera in a quiet place while you're blacking the tape. Press the record trigger on the camera, or press record and play on the recorder.

The alternative is the overlap method. Any new recording must overlap the old one by a few seconds. Camcorders automatically use this method whenever you stop and start recording. However, if you rewind and play the footage to review it or take the tape out of your camcorder, you can inadvertently miscue the tape. To check this, use the video cassette recorder (VCR) controls on your camcorder and rewind the tape about 10 seconds. Play the tape, paying close attention to the time code at which the old recording ends. Then rewind the tape and press play again. This time, press stop about three seconds before the old recording ends. Switch the camcorder back to camera mode and start shooting again.

Time code breaks on miniDV tapes occur because home camcorders automatically reset their clocks to zero hours, zero minutes, zero seconds, zero frames whenever the camera senses blank unrecorded tape. If the camcorder senses video, it automatically sets the clock to match the number already recorded on the tape. When you begin recording again, the camera reads the time code on the tape and continues with the sequence.

(continued)

(continued)

An unintended consequence of this approach is that if you don't record over the last few frames of the previous recording, you can end up with a tape that has more than one zero starting time code. This creates problems when you attempt to transfer the material into your editing system. The system has no way of differentiating between the first occurrence and second occurrence of a minute one time code number if the reel numbers are identical. The solution is to label the tape with two reel numbers. For example, the first zero start on the tape could be reel 01A and the second one could be reel 01B.

You may not have tapes with multiple starts, but you will have tapes with identical time code if you use miniDV or other consumer video formats. Whenever you shoot more than one hour of footage for a show, you'll have two tapes with the identical time code. They both start at zero and end at 00:59:59:29. This is why reel numbers are so important.

It should be obvious why each tape needs a descriptive name. Remembering what Scene 1, Take 3 looks like is not any easier than remembering what's on reel 006. However, if reel 006 is also labeled *Outdoor Scenes, Amherst*, you'll have an easier time finding that long shot of a church in Amherst that you want to copy to your editing system's storage drives.

Bin Organization

Editors organize pictures and sounds by categorizing them. This process is like creating an outline, organizing a stamp collection, or filing things so you can find them later. The containers are called *bins*. Bin is the name film editors gave to the piece of furniture they used to store sections of film. It had a bar and clips to hold the strips of film, which hung down into what looked like a trashcan. Most editing programs let you create bins, which work just like folders or directories in a computer.

Bins store video, audio, or graphics clips. You can create as many as you like within a project in most editing systems. Some editing systems let you nest bins within another bin or within a folder. No matter how your editing system works, it is essential to make bins and categorize them if you want to edit with ease.

The point of organizing your source materials in bins is to make the materials easy to find. You can organize footage into themes, locations, the time of day, characters, people, or by the type of media—graphics, effects, audio, video, and stills. The types of categories you can create are only limited by your imagination. Every time you make a bin, label it. Be sure you use unique names.

Organize your material for easy retrieval. If you're editing a documentary, it may be appropriate to create interview, photograph, stock footage, B-roll footage, title, and artwork bins. For a commercial, it might be more appropriate to create bins for testimonials, product shots, and graphics. Again, the important thing is to find a method of organizing the material that works for you. It's easy to copy or move clips from one bin to another and just as easy to delete them. Remember that in most editing systems deleting the clip doesn't delete the media file; it only deletes the pointer to the media file.

Bins merely contain the pointers to the media files that are stored elsewhere. Copying and moving a digital media file takes a considerable amount of time. Copying and moving an icon that tells your editing system where to find and play a media file takes no time at all.

Bin Categories

Table 6-1 shows some examples of bin categories to help you start thinking about organization.

Organizing your materials becomes easier with every project you do. After all, the possibilities are limitless.

Bin Views

Think about how you'd like to work with your material. Most bin windows can alternatively display the clips in the bin as a text-only list, as a text list with tiny pictures that represent the contents, or as resizeable pictures of the material.

Figure 6-2

Bin category
suggestions.

Interiors	Exteriors	Music	Sound Effects
Bride's dressing room	Groom's alcove	Waiting room	Chapel
Titles	Credits	Photographs	Drawings
Stunts	Visual effects	Graphics	Transitions
Testimonials	Interviews	Standups	B-roll
Bridal dinner	Wedding ceremony	Reception	Honeymoon
Wine tasting	Opening ceremony	Closing ceremony	Speeches
Monday	Tuesday	Wednesday	Thursday
Friday	Saturday	Sunday	Selects
Reel 001	Reel 002	Reel 003	Reel 004
Camera one	Camera two	Camera three	Program feed

The List View   The list view can display all or part of the information that an editing system maintains in its database. The information is presented as a database with categories, such as the name of the clip, the IN and OUT time codes, the clip duration, the audio sample rate, the date the media file was created on the hard drive, and the comments. There can be as many as 30 different categories in some editing systems. You can choose to show them all or display only selected categories. You can also move the categories around in most editing systems so you can rearrange the way things are displayed to suit your needs. Most list views can also be sorted by any category in ascending or descending order. The list view is a powerful tool despite its lack of visual information because it gives you access to the database.

The following section includes the categories or fields that appear in the list view of six editing systems. You should note that some categories are standard. This confirms that most editing systems follow the model we described earlier.

Adobe Premiere List View   This list view contains the following database categories: Name, Date, File Path, Log Comment, Media Type (still/movie), Video Info, Audio Info, Video Usage (in the timeline), Audio Usage (in the timeline), Duration, Time Code (first frame of source), Reel Name, Notes, and Labels (fields you can rename).

Apple Final Cut Pro Browser List View   This list view contains the following database categories: Name, Alpha, Anamorphic, Audio Format, Audio Rate, Audio, Aux TC 1–2, Capture, Comment Field (4), Composite, Compressor, Data Rate, Description, Duration, Frame Size, Good, In, Out, Label, Label 2, Last Modified, Length, Log Note, Media Start, Media End, Offline, Pixel Aspect, Reel, Reverse Alpha, Scene, Shot/Take, Size (File), Source (file location), TC, Thumbnail, Tracks, Type (clip, subclip, merge clip, sequence, bin, effect), and Video Rate.

Avid XpressDV Bin List View   This list view contains the following database categories: Name, Tracks, File Start, File End, Audio, Audio Format, Color, Creation Date, Target Disk ID, Duration, IN-OUT (duration), Lock, Mark In, Mark Out, Offline, Project, Tape, Video Resolution, Comments, and Your Headings.

Incite Details View   This detail view contains the following database categories: Name, Comment, File Name, Tape/Reel, Available Tracks, Type (Audio, Video, Graphic), Status (Playable/Offline), Data Rate, Master Clip In, Master Clip Out, Master Clip Duration, In, Out, Duration, and Speed.

Media 100 iFinish List View   This list view contains the following database categories: Name, Reel Name, In Time, Out Time, Tracks, Comments, Keywords, Color, Length, Source In Time, Source Out Time, Source Length, Date, Source Media File Name, Input Setup, Quality, Standard (NTSC/PAL), ColorFX, MotionFX, Audio Frequency, Audio EQ, Rendered Media File Name, Source Media File Size, Rendered Media File Size, and Audio In Channel (#).

Pinnacle Studio Album Details View   This album details view contains the following database categories: Thumbnail, Time Code Start, Scene Name, and Keyword.

The Picture View   The picture-only view hides the database. The only text visible is usually the name of the clip underneath the picture icons, or *picons*. One of the advantages of digital editing is that you can display clips as pictures and edit without ever looking at the statistics in the list view. This is the primary method many editors choose because it's a visual approach.

There are two important considerations when using the bin this way. The first is that the picon (the still image) should display a frame that actually represents the content of the clip. Unless you change it, this image is usually the first frame of the clip. Look in your editing system's manual to see how to change this image so that it reflects what the clip is all about. Pick a frame that shows the subject or principal action in that clip. For example, if you have a bin that has clips of a diver making a series of dives, the default frame (the first frame of the clip) probably shows the diver standing at the back of the diving board with her hands down preparing to dive. All the picons for the clips would look identical in the bin. However, by adjusting what's called the *representative frame,* or *poster frame*, you can select a frame that shows the diver in midair. This way when you edit the footage, you'll be able to instantly identify the dive she is doing and select the clip you need.

The second consideration has to do with the number of clips in the bin. Professionals usually decide to display no more than 25 to 30 clips on a full-screen bin window. If any more clips are displayed, the picons become too small to see. If you find yourself squinting at tiny picons or scrolling through a bin with a vast number of clips, it's time to divide it up by moving some of the clips to another bin.

On a single monitor editing system, the bins can't occupy all the real estate on the desktop. If you're working with a single monitor system, you should reduce the number of picons in a bin to less than a dozen. If you have a very large monitor, you may be able to increase this number.

The Combination View   A compromise approach is to view the bin as a list with picons beside each entry. The challenge is that the picons are often very small and hard to see. If the picons are made large enough to see, the list can become less useful. You'll see fewer items in the bin window and the picons tend to slow down scrolling. Some people find this approach to be a happy middle point. We prefer to switch between the list view and the

Expand Your Desktop

Adding a second computer monitor to your editing system is often the best solution to the desktop real-estate problem. Professional editing systems often have two computer monitors. One is used for the bins and the other is used to display the timeline, tool palettes, and viewer windows. Check the manual for your editing system to see if it supports two monitors. You may need to add a second graphics card to your computer in order to do this. If you plan to do a lot of editing, it's usually worth the extra expense to have the desktop space that two monitors can provide.

picon view as often as necessary. Most systems make it easy to switch from one view to another. It's all a matter of preference. Some people are more comfortable using pictures, whereas others are more comfortable using numbers and statistics to find the material they want.

Digitizing and Transfer

The first and most fundamental of all editing tasks is transferring your source materials from tape, disk, or camera into your editing system. This is usually the very next task after you create a project and make a bin. It takes time—real time. There's simply no way of getting around it. The footage you recorded with your camera has to be played at normal speed to be transferred, or captured, on your editing system's storage drives.

The only editing systems capable of transferring materials at speeds faster than normal are expensive professional systems that are primarily used for television news operations. In these environments, the need for speed is paramount and manufacturers have developed a method of transferring video at four times normal speed. In every other application, a one-hour tape takes one hour to transfer to an editing system.

Unfortunately, most people are confronted by the task of connecting their editing system to a video recorder before they start using their new editing

Making Connections

Connecting analog or professional equipment is more complicated. Many editing system manuals take several chapters to deal with this aspect of digital video editing. Detailed installation instructions are necessary to set up the interactions between your computer, the special boards that digitize video, the external hard drives, speakers, video monitors, and more. A long list of things might need to be set and adjusted before everything works together as it should. Cabling everything together can become complicated and messy. If setting up a stereo system is beyond your capabilities, consider using a turnkey editing appliance. These editing appliances are intended to iron out most, if not all, of the complications. However, if you can follow directions, you should have no trouble setting up an editing system.

system. It's ironic that the first phase of editing is technical, not creative. New users can be turned off and miss out on the joy of editing. Thankfully, digital video camcorders with Firewire connections make it simple. You only need one cable to connect your camera to your editing system. In the past, transferring the material you shot with your camera into your editing system was complicated. This is no longer true.

The Basic Steps

Whether you're using an editing appliance or a computer-based system, the process of transferring materials into your editing system remains the same. The procedures are universal. The following section describes the basic steps to input (copy or digitize) video into your editing system.

Video recorded in a digital format is transferred (copied) to your editing system's storage drives using Firewire or another transport standard, such as *serial digital interface* (SDI) or *serial digitl transport interface* (SDTI). If the material is in an analog format, such as the VHS, BetaSP, or audiocassette format, it must be converted from an analog to digital format in order for the system to use it. This process is called *digitizing* because the video and audio signals are transformed into digital data. Special hardware is required to convert the signals.

Nearly every editing system opens what we'll call an input tool when you want to copy video into your editing system. The input tool is a window that has remote controls for your camcorder or recorder and that asks you to enter information about the material you want to transfer into your editing system. Most systems let you decide where (on which drive) the digital media files you're about to input will be stored. Some systems let you adjust audio and video levels (analog video only) during this process. Some systems may also have meters or instruments that let you evaluate technical quality while you input the footage.

However, every system asks you to enter some basic information about the footage before you input it. Even the most basic system lets you type in a reel name and description. Sophisticated editing systems store as much information about the footage as you'd care to enter.

Enter a Reel Name   However, the most important category, the one that should always be filled in, is the reel name. The reel name is the name you assigned to the tape. This is the name that's marked on the tape and tape box. Professionals generally use three characters that consist of numbers (001) or a combination of letters and numbers (AC1) to name reels. This is because every editing system can handle three characters for a reel name, but not all are capable of using or storing longer descriptive names.

Check the Inputs Next check to make sure that the video or audio inputs shown on the input tool (or under the system settings) match the type of connection you're using to connect video or audio sources to your system. These input settings may or may not be accessible from the input tool in your editing system. You're likely to see DV, Firewire (IEEE-1394), Composite Video, Component Video, or something else listed on an input setting preference. It doesn't matter what it's called; it just matters that the settings in the editing system match the physical reality of how the video source is connected. The cabling should match. If you're not sure how things are connected, check the installation manual or installation section of your editing system manual to refresh your memory.

Set or Create a Bin You need a destination for the materials you input. The destination for a clip is a bin and in most systems you have the luxury of choosing which bin you want to use. The bin you select is often called the *target* or *destination bin*. Some systems will automatically pick the last bin you opened or highlighted. In other systems, you have to change a preference setting. Others let you select any available bin in your project using the input tool. We're not aware of any systems that let you input material unless you have at least one bin open. There may be a few exceptions, but we haven't seen them. Therefore, if you don't have a bin in your project, create one and name it. We suggest that you use the name of the tape for the name of your target bin and that you make a new bin for each tape you input into your editing system. The reason we suggest doing this is explained in the section "Batch Input Organization." If you're working on a system that only has one bin, you don't need to set a target bin and can ignore this step.

Select a Target Drive If your editing system has multiple storage drives, select the one you want to use. The best choice is the one that has the most free space. Every editing system has a way to check how much is available on your storage drive or drives. You should make sure that you'll have enough space for the material you want to input. If not enough space is available, you can free some up by deleting material you don't need anymore or inputting less footage.

It's never a good idea to work with storage drives that are completely full. There won't be any room to store the titles, effects, and transitions you'll want to create later. Most systems seem to get finicky when their storage drives are too full. We know it's a computer and that it can't really get finicky. However, this is the easiest way to describe the odd things that always seem to happen when we fill the drives to the max.

Determine the Quality   If you're using miniDV and a Firewire input, most editing systems won't let you adjust the quality or don't offer this feature. Therefore, you can skip this step. However, a few systems give you the option of inputting a low-resolution version, which increases the amount of footage that will fit on your editing system. The idea is that after you've edited your show, you can replace the low-resolution version with the normal version. Since the only footage you replace is what is in your finished show, you don't need much space.

If you're digitizing analog or *high-definition* (HD) formats, you may have the opportunity to select a quality level or level of compression. More information about compression can be found in Chapter 10, "Getting It In and Out." The rule is the higher the quality, the less compression has been applied. The highest possible quality is uncompressed. Of course, uncompressed material also takes up the largest amount of storage space. Highly compressed material takes up the least amount of space, although it has the worst image quality.

The rule of thumb is to use the lowest acceptable quality if storage space is an issue. You can always reinput the footage later at a higher quality after you've gone through all the material and decided what's important.

Select the Tracks   When you're using miniDV and Firewire, most systems don't let you select input tracks, so you may be able to skip this step. If yours does, it's probably to accommodate the extra two audio channels available on some miniDV camcorders. Some systems must transfer the video track otherwise they lose the time code track. This becomes an issue if you need to make two passes to transfer all four of the audio channels into your system. A second copy of the video track wastes a lot of space.

Editing systems that let you select individual tracks can save space. Audio requires very little. Therefore, if you need sound but not the picture, input only the sound, or vice versa. The one track you must never turn off is time code, if your editing system will let you turn it off. If there's no time code, you have no way of tracing the media file back to the original source tape.

For Professionals Only: Set the Remote/Local Switch   Most professional videotape recorders have a remote/local switch. When this switch is in the local position, the front-panel controls operate the recorder and the remote control is disabled. Check the switch and make sure the switch is set to the remote position. The input tool can only control the recorder when this switch is set to remote.

Input Checklist

- Enter a reel name.
- Check the input settings.
- Set or create a bin.
- Set a target drive.
- Check the available space.
- Choose a compression rate, if applicable.
- Select the appropriate tracks, if applicable.
- Set the remote/local switch on professional recorders to remote.

The Five Input Methods

After you've gone through the input checklist and confirmed that all the settings are correct, it's time to run a test. Use the single-scene input method. There's no point to doing more than one until you're sure everything works.

Single-Scene Input   These are the steps for copying a single scene into your editing system:

1. Put a source tape in the recorder. Open the input tool. Type in the reel name written on the tape label. Using the input tool to control the recorder, find the beginning of a scene. You should be able to play, rewind, fast forward, and shuttle. When you find the beginning of the scene (the first one on the tape will do), press the Mark In button. You should see the time code number for the location of the beginning of the scene in the In field. Next, find the end of the scene. Press the Mark Out button. Once again, the correct time code number should appear in the Out field.

2. The next step varies depending on the editing system you're using. Type in a name or description of the material you're about to input. On some systems, you may need to save the log entry before you can press the input tool record button to start the process. On others, you can

press record without saving the log entry. In either case, as soon as you press record, the video recorder should automatically go to the in point using rewind or shuttle, and cue the tape a few seconds before the in point. The recorder should then go into play. When the tape reaches the in point, your editing system should begin copying. The system should stop copying as soon as it reaches the out point and you should see a clip appear in the bin.

3. Before you input anything else, you should check that clip by playing it. You may have to close the input tool before you can play the clip. Watch to make sure there aren't any problems with levels or the quality of the picture and sound. You should prove to yourself that everything works.

Batch Input   The batch input method is designed to save labor—yours. The idea is to log all the scenes on a tape and input them afterwards. If you follow our shooting tip about keeping a log of where major scenes begin and end on each tape, you can shuttle the tape and find the in and out points for the scenes you want very quickly.

Name and save each entry before you find the next scene. Scenes can be as long as 5 to 10 minutes in length. Some systems limit the file sizes you can copy so check your manual. Every log entry you save should appear in the bin. Go through the entire tape and log all the scenes you want.

At this point, you're ready to input all the clips you logged. Usually, there's a separate command for batch input. You may need to select the clips in the bin you want before you can do a batch input or there could be a menu option to input any clip without a media file. Regardless of how it works, before you do a batch input, it's a good idea to input one clip as a test. If everything is working correctly, you can hit batch input and walk away. The process will take the same amount of time as the duration of the material you're inputting. If you have 50 minutes of footage, you could go to lunch and come back. Always do one clip first so you can walk away.

Input On the Fly   If you're in a hurry, you can input on the fly. This approach is fast but not foolproof. Put the video recorder into play and press the record button on the input tool. The editing system will start transferring the material to the storage drives. However, you must make sure you stop inputting before you reach the end of the recorded material on the tape. A time code break or a loss of time code will cause most editing systems to reject the material you've just attempted to input and you'll have to do it all over again. If you've previewed what's on the tape, write down the last time code number on the tape, so you can stop before you get to the end.

Log and Import   You can watch your tapes and create a log before you start to edit. Using a spreadsheet or word processing program, you can type up a list of scenes with a starting and ending time code for each one. All the editing systems that can import log files have instructions on how you can do this in their manuals. You can also buy specialized logging programs to do this.

After you've logged your footage, you simply import the list into your editing system. Your list appears in a bin without any media attached. It should look identical to the way the bin looked in the batch input method before you did the batch input. The final step is to do a batch input. This approach doesn't save time, but it does avoid tying up an editing system with a task, such as logging, that could be done elsewhere on less expensive equipment.

Scene Detection   Scene detection is a popular feature on some miniDV editing systems. You put in a tape and press the record button. Your editing system splits up the footage into scenes for you. Typically, this feature only works when miniDV is the video source. MiniDV camcorders record the time code and a time of day for each frame. Most of the systems use the breaks in the time of day clock to decide where the scenes begin and end. A few systems use camera movement or abrupt differences in the subject matter to trigger a scene change. Your satisfaction with this automatic process will depend on how your editing system detects scene changes and on your camera operator's shooting style.

Shooting Tip

Take a small notebook with you when you're shooting. Write down what's on each tape. You don't need a lot of information. The beginning and ending time code for major scenes or location changes are more than enough. This comes in handy when you want to transfer material into your editing system. You can create a log file or use the input tool to build a list based on the notes you took. Later, you can use the editing system to do what it does best—break down scenes into shots. If you're using the miniDV format, a notebook is essential because the tape boxes are so small. Most people can barely write a reel number on a miniDV tape let alone a list of scenes.

If you're in a hurry, this can be a timesaver. However, you might lose your familiarity with the material. One of an editor's most important jobs is to look at the footage. At some point, you have to see all of it, evaluate it, and make decisions. The best time to start this process is during the input phase. Scene detection can be useful as long as you watch your footage.

Batch Input Organization

The best approach for a long-form project or any project with more than one source tape is to create a separate input bin for each tape. Label the bin using the reel number or tape name. This is done for several reasons. Most editing systems are incapable of batch input across multiple open bin windows, so it's a disadvantage to log scenes from one tape into separate bins. Batch input typically works within a single bin. Plus, only one tape can be in the recorder at a time. The most efficient approach is to input all the scenes you need from a particular tape once rather than continually putting the tape into the recorder and taking it back out again.

Another reason for this is that we've almost always had to reinput footage at some point. A media file becomes corrupted or is accidentally deleted, or the shot we need drops frames because the media file is fragmented across a hard drive. The handles (extra frames at the head or tail of a shot) aren't long enough to do the dissolve we want. Reel number bins can simplify the process of locating what is missing. Every editing system has a way of indicating when a clip is offline, and when one file becomes corrupted, there's bound to be more.

Yet another reason this is done is that no one is perfect. We all make mistakes such as leaving out scenes we meant to input. In fact, that happens regularly on big projects. If you have bins organized by reel number, you can quickly check the log in the bin against your paper or electronic logs and spot your mistakes.

After you've input all the original source material, you'll want to organize the material into categories so you can begin editing. We suggest you copy the clips rather than move them from your reel number input bins into the bins you'll use to organize and edit your materials. The point is to keep your reel number database intact. So don't move the clips, copy them. Take advantage of your editing system's strengths. It's much easier to create bins and organize clips on the desktop than it is to do on paper or when you're logging footage.

Logging

Most editing systems let you log your footage before you copy or digitize it. This is done for two reasons. On longer shows, it's easy to run out of storage room and you may need to be selective. The more important reason is that the editor must know the footage. You can't edit a show unless you know the footage intimately. The only way to do this is to watch the material repeatedly. Viewing, taking notes, and thinking about the material doesn't have to happen in front of an editing system. The only things you really need to do this job are a monitor, video recorder, and notepad.

In professional situations, this approach is often the most cost-effective solution because it doesn't tie up an editing system. A well-prepared editor or producer can cut the time it takes to edit a show in half simply by knowing what's useable and what's not to tell the story. However, there are times when this isn't true. Under extreme deadline pressure, it may be quicker to input all the footage and make it work as you go. If you have a limited amount of footage, it can be faster and easier to input everything and then use your editing system to organize the material.

The process of logging can occur while you're shooting (in the field) or afterwards during the editing phase. A detailed log kept throughout production is extremely useful, although not every situation lends itself to that approach. This log can record when shots start and end in time code, a description of the shot, whether it's excellent, good, bad, or unusable, or anything else that will enable you to make a decision later about whether to input the material into your editing system. The more you shoot, the better your logs have to be. Large projects, such as feature films, television series, or long-form documentaries, generate vast quantities of footage. Logs provide the first level of organization and can substantially reduce the time it takes to edit these shows.

In the not too distant past, we suggested that everyone keep detailed logs. We don't feel that this is necessary any more. It made sense when editing systems were expensive, hourly facility rates were high, and storage space was precious. Producers who kept detailed logs saved themselves a lot of money. Today, editing software is less expensive than professional logging software and runs on ordinary personal computers. Storage is cheap. Scene-sized files are more efficient than shot-sized files in a digital environment. All you really need are organizational logs that enable you to find major scenes, locations, or interviews. It takes less time to break down long scenes in an editing system than it does to keep detailed shot logs.

Input Advice

■ *Scene-sized files are more efficient than shot-sized files in a digital environment.*   Hard drives work best with medium-sized files. There's less wear and tear on your camcorder and on your original source tapes, if you input scenes instead of shots. You don't want to capture an entire tape as one clip because the file size makes it inefficient. Five-second clips are even less efficient. They are time consuming to input and the file size is inefficient.

■ *The best approach is to input scene-size files.*   You can break down the scenes later into individual shots using the power of your editing system.

Summary

Organize your editing projects to fit your needs. Long complex shows require more organization than short simple ones. The purpose of being organized is to be able to find materials when you need them.

Important Points to Remember

■ Use unique, descriptive names to label projects, timelines, bins and clips.

■ Organize materials into separate bins.

■ Always label source footage tapes. This becomes the control number (reel number) for your editing system.

■ Transferring material into your editing system happens in real time.

■ Use batch input for efficiency.

■ Logging your materials is important whether you do it before or after its transferred into the editing system.

Setting the Table

Stories are made from clear, clean, and understandable shots. Every piece of footage has one section that reveals the essence—what that shot is about. Your job as an editor is to identify and select the tip of the iceberg (the portion of the footage that lets the audience believe they are looking at an iceberg) instead of showing them all the ice. To do that, you must be able to recognize the types of icebergs floating in the ocean. Learning how to spot these tips comes with experience.

Editors tell stories by stringing shots together. Shots build scenes, which depict all the action in one location at one time. A series of scenes creates a sequence. A succession of sequences builds an act. Acts form the show. Whether you number the acts, or call them the beginning, middle, and end, or the setup, conflict, and resolution, one thing is clear: Acts, scenes, and sequences rely on a basic building block—the shot. Everything starts with the shot.

Shots communicate action or describe the subject. The audience must be able to recognize and comprehend that image. Editors refer to this as *reading a shot*. Some shots can be read quickly, whereas others require more time. The editor's job is to give the audience enough time to read a shot before replacing it with a new one.

What's a Shot?

A shot is the shortest section of recorded footage, as measured in time, that is capable of communicating a single action, feeling, or thought to the audience. This chapter will help you learn to identify the shots in your sea of footage.

Describing Shots

Everyone involved in the production of a show, from the writer to the camera operator to the editor, uses standard definitions to describe shots. The primary way of distinguishing one shot from another is by the size of a human being within the frame. Well-run productions use these shot designations throughout the production process. The production version of the script includes abbreviations for the shots the director plans to shoot. The shot abbreviations carry over to the producer, script continuity clerk, or assistant cameraman's logs of what was actually shot. The editor who must log and evaluate the footage uses the same system. This is a shared language used to describe and categorize basic framing. As an editor, you need to learn this language.

What Are the Standard Shots?

The following is a list of common shots. Descriptions and abbreviations are provided for each shot. The first groups are the ones defined by how much of the human body fits into the frame or what's more accurately called the *field of vi*ew. The field of view is the area that the camera records.

Long Shot (LS)

A LS is any shot taken at a considerable distance from the subject. People appear smaller than the height of the frame. A long shot is often used for *establishing* (EST) or master shots. This shot is also called a *wide shot* (WS) because the field of view is very wide; it does not refer to the focal length of the lens. The amount of space below the feet differentiates a *medium long shot* (MLS) from a long shot (LS) or *extreme long shot* (XLS). Most of the time the LS is the only designation used.

Full Shot (FS)

An FS is framed to include the human figure from head to toe.

Medium Full Shot (MFS)

An MFS is framed to start at the knees.

Medium Shot (MS)

An MS is framed to start at the hips.

Medium Close Shot (MCS)

An MCS is framed to start at the waist.

Close Shot (CS)

A CS is framed to start at the chest.

Close-Up (CU)

A CU is framed to start at the shoulders. This is also called a *head-and-shoulders* (H&S) shot.

Medium Close-Up (MCU)

An MCU is framed to start at the neck.

Extreme Close-Up (ECU or XCU)

An ECU is framed above the chin.

Figure 7-1
Framing of four common camera shots.

A Shooting Tip

Frame any shot defined by the human body with room below the demarcation. You don't want to line up the bottom of the frame with the knees, hips, waist, chest, shoulders, neck, or chin. The idea is to include them in a pleasing composition.

Conceptual Shots

This group doesn't rely on field of view. Instead, the shots that follow are conceptual. Any of the field-of-view shots we just defined could work under the right circumstances.

Establishing (EST)

An EST is any shot at or near the beginning of a show or scene that establishes the environment in which the action takes place. This shot can also establish the relationship between the details seen in closer shots. Most EST shots are long shots.

Master

A master shot is a single shot that covers all the action in a scene. This designation is for the director and editor. It doesn't have an abbreviation like the others. The master is the editor's first opportunity to see the scene in its entirety. Many editors use the master as the starting point of the editing process. Because the master is usually a wide shot, the editor will build impact by overwriting (overlaying) closer shots that maintain continuity. Other editors watch the master shot and build the scene entirely from the closer shots. They'll use the master shot as a last resort if they don't have enough coverage (closer shots).

Reaction Shot

A reaction shot reveals someone's reaction to an off-screen sound or action.

Reverse

Any shot from the opposite perspective.

Bridging or Cutaway Shot

A bridging or cutaway shot is used to cover a break in continuity, such as time or place.

Two-Shot

A two-shot shows two people.

Three-Shot

A three-shot shows a group of three people.

Tracking Shot

A tracking shot is any shot in which the camera moves with the subject to maintain distance and framing. The word *tracking* came into use because the camera was usually moved over tracks.

Camera Movement

Camera movement should improve the audience's understanding of what's being shown on screen, not make them nauseous. The editor has to understand where the show will be seen and compensate for it. Motion that wouldn't bother anyone if viewed on a 30-inch television monitor can be horrendous when it's seen on a 60-foot screen in a theater.

A Shooting Tip

Handheld camera work is always the last resort. Professionals keep the camera on a tripod unless they have a specific reason for taking it off. The only reason to dispense with the tripod is when you have no other way of getting the shot. Camera moves should start on a static shot and end on a static shot.

Professional camera operators begin each camera move with a hold (a well-composed stationary shot) and end each move with another hold. This gives the editor four possible shots. The editor can use the static shot at the beginning, the camera move (as is or in the reverse direction), or the static shot at the end. This also makes it easier for the editor to find a place to cut on matched action.

Pan Right or Pan Left

This describes a shot in which the camera rotates horizontally. A pan is like turning your head to the right or left to see beyond your normal field of vision.

Tilt Up or Tilt Down

This describes a shot in which the camera rotates on its horizontal axis. A tilt is equivalent to looking down to see your feet or up to see the ceiling. This is also called a *pan up* or *pan down*.

Pedestal Up or Pedestal Down

This describes a shot in which the position of the camera is raised or lowered with respect to the floor. A pedestal is equivalent to holding a camcorder on your shoulder and bending or straightening your knees to change the height of the camera.

Dolly In (D/I:) or Dolly Back (D/B:)

This describes a shot in which the camera moves closer or farther away from the subject. A dolly move alters the audience's perspective—the relationship of the subject to the background.

Zoom In (Z/I:) or Zoom Out (Z/O:)

This describes a shot in which the focal length of the lens is lengthened or widened. This really isn't a camera move. A zoom often substitutes for a dolly move even though a zoom flattens or expands the depth rather than altering the perspective.

Track Left or Track Right

This describes a shot in which the camera moves left or right relative to the subject. This is a dolly move except instead of getting closer to the subject (moving forward or backwards), the camera slides right or left. In television studios, this shot is called is a truck left or truck right.

Arc Left or Arc Right

This describes a shot in which the camera circles left or right in relation to the subject. This move combines the dolly and the truck to form an arc.

A Shooting Tip

Beginners misuse the zoom by recording their efforts to find a pleasing composition while zooming in and out or using it to follow the action. You'll get more interesting results if you use the zoom to find an appropriate focal length to frame the action before you begin recording. To follow the action, move your body and the camera.

Swish Pan

This describes a shot in which the camera is panned rapidly to blur the picture. Swish pans are used mostly for transitions or occasionally as a point-of-view shot. This is also called a *whip pan*.

Camera Angles

Describing a shot fully requires more information than its field of view or conceptual designation. The angle of the camera to the subject is important when you start editing. If a shot's angle or field of view is too close to the preceding shot, the transition between the two shots will be jarring.

Eye level is a relative height. Camera operators aren't uniform in height and have minimal contact with editors. Besides, it wouldn't help you to remember how tall they are anyway. Any shot at the approximate eye level of an ordinary person is considered to be at eye level.

The other possibilities are predictable. *Low angles* (L/A:), *high angles* (H/A:), and *overhead* angles are the most common ones. In a low angle shot, the subject looks down at the camera. The opposite is true for high angle shots. From this perspective, the subject looks up at the camera. An overhead angle provides a bird's eye view of the scene. An *aerial* is an overhead shot taken from an airplane, dirigible, or helicopter.

Points of View

The other angles you're likely to see fall into the point of view category. The most common one is an *over-the-shoulder* (O/S) shot. This medium shot frames one person's face with another person's head and shoulder. Nearly every interview on television at one point or another uses this shot to confirm that the interviewer is in the same room with the person being interviewed.

Another common technique is to briefly substitute the camera for a character in the scene. This is called a *point of view* shot. The selective use of a *handheld* camera or a device like the *SteadyCam*, which smoothes out handheld camera moves, can make the audience believe that they're seeing through the eyes of a character in the story.

In a *canted* or *dutched* shot, the horizon is diagonal rather than horizontal. A canted shot is another way to pull the audience into the story. In real life, we expect the horizon to be level. This is why people thought the world was flat. When the horizon isn't horizontal, the audience feels like their bodies have been tilted. If your story takes place on a boat, a canted shot could make the scene more believable.

Eye Level Versus Eye Line

A distinction must be made between *eye level*, which is a camera angle, and a *subject's eye line*. It's important to know the subject's eye line when you're evaluating footage. This is an imaginary line that is drawn across the subject's eyes. This is crucial for editing because the eye line (not the eye level) tells the audience where the person is looking. As an editor, you need to be able to match up eye lines if you want the subjects in two close-ups, for example, to appear as if they are looking at each other.

Camera Transitions

The shots listed below are useful for making smoother transitions or establishing a relationship between the subjects of those shots.

Rack Focus

Rack focus refers to any shot in which the focus shifts from one subject or object to another in the frame.

Pan to Reframe

Pan to reframe refers to any shot in which the camera makes a small pan adjustment to improve the composition.

Pan to Cover Action

Pan to cover action refers to any shot in which the camera pans to keep the subject or action in the frame.

Pan to Connect Two Subjects, Thoughts, or Objects

This refers to any shot in which the camera pans from a subject or object to another subject or object. This transition links the subjects together in the audience's eyes.

About Aspect Ratio

Two common aspect ratios (or frame shapes) are used in digital video. The 4:3 aspect ratio is used by the vast majority of television sets in the United States. This has the shape of an almost square rectangle. The width is four units to every three units of height. The aspect ratio can be written as 4:3, 1.33:1, or 1.33. The latter number is the result of dividing 4 by 3 in order to express the ratio as a factor of one. All of the shapes described by those numbers are identical.

The 1.33 ratio is also called the *Academy Format*. This is the shape of the frame in 35 mm motion picture film. However, theaters don't project the full frame. Instead, they use a metal mask in the projector to crop or hide part of the image. In the United States, theaters use a 1.85 mask, whereas in Europe, a 1.66 mask is common. The mask lets the projectionist position the film in the projector with leeway and hide the frame line. These masks change the aspect ratio of the original film to a shape that's more rectangular.

The rectangular shape is closer to the way human beings see the world—hence, the reason for the other aspect ratios typically used in film production. Panavision cameras record images on 35 mm film in a 2.35 aspect ratio and Cinemascope cameras record images on 35 mm film in the 2.5 aspect ratio. Both have very narrow rectangular shapes that create wide-screen images like the ones we see with our eyes.

Figure 7-2
Three common
aspect ratios.

−4 X 3
−16 X 9
−2.35:1

Figure 7-3
The picture area
cropped in different
aspect ratios.

−4 X 3
−16 X 9
−2.35:1

The newest aspect ratio for digital video is the 16:9, 1.78:1, or 1.78 aspect ratio. Again, all those numbers describe the same rectangle. The shape is a narrower rectangle than the one used in the past for video. This aspect ratio, a compromise between 1.66 and 1.85, was designed for high-definition television (HDTV). The purpose was to match the aspect ratios used for feature films so when the film was shown on television, the audience would see everything the audience saw in the theater. The 1.78 aspect ratio, which is midway between the European 1.66 and the U.S. 1.85 ratio, is the compromise solution.

The Rules of Composition

Editors evaluate shots for quality. One criterion is how well the shot is composed. Determining whether something is well composed often depends on the arbitrator and his or her "I'll know it when I see it" answer. However, there are rules to help you understand what to look for as you begin evaluating footage.

The Rule of Thirds

This is the most widely used rule of composition. The rule of thirds is based on the principle of the *Golden Mean*, which was first articulated by the ancient Greeks. The frame is divided into thirds horizontally and vertically. Objects that are placed along the lines create pleasing compositions. The points where the lines intersect are the most interesting places in the frame. This is where you should place any objects that you want to emphasize.

The 180-Degree Axis of Action Rule

By following the *180-degree Axis of Action Rule*, you ensure that the screen direction of the subjects remains consistent. For example, in a two-shot of a man and a woman, the man looks right and the woman looks left. If the camera operator follows the 180-degree rule, the man will look right and the woman will look left in the close-ups. This enables the editor to cut from the two-shot to a close-up. If the camera operator breaks the 180-degree rule, the editor can't cut from the two-shot to the close-up without calling

Figure 7-4
Screen direction will
remain consistent as
long as the camera
doesn't cross the 180
degree axis of action.

Figure 7-4
Screen direction will remain consistent as long as the camera doesn't cross the 180 degree axis of action.

attention to the cut because the screen direction of one or both subjects will be reversed in the close-ups. As a result, the man may look left instead of right and the woman look right instead of left or the man and woman may have the identical screen direction (both looking right or left) in the close-ups.

This is an example of the consequences. In the two-shot, the man looks right. We cut to his close-up. He looks left. Where is the woman? Cut back to the two-shot. Now he's looking right again and she's on his right. If you continue to do this, the poor fellow will keep flip-flopping around.

The rule works because the camera operator draws a line through the subjects. The line represents the diameter of an imaginary circle around the subjects. The camera is placed on one side of the circle, which is why it's called the 180-degree axis of action rule. The camera can move anywhere on that 180-degree side of the circle as long as the camera doesn't cross the diameter line. If it does cross the line, the screen direction of the subjects will be reversed.

Framing Subjects

Framing is another criterion editors use to evaluate the quality of a shot. The subject should be framed so that there is breathing room or a modicum of space around them. The following sections describe the four space considerations for good framing.

The Essential Area

The essential area is the portion of the frame that will always be seen. Some editing systems can display a grid in the viewer indicating the portion of the image that is within the essential area or title safe. For video production, the essential area is considered 80 percent of the picture's center. This area will be displayed on every television no matter how badly the television set is aligned or misadjusted. In film production, the entire negative is rarely projected. Instead, as we mentioned in our discussion of aspect ratios, the projectionist masks part of the image. In video or film, the boundaries of the essential area are determined by what the audience sees.

If important objects or subjects fall outside the essential area, the editor should mark the shot as unusable. If the audience can't see it, the shot is worthless.

Look Space

Audiences become uncomfortable when subjects are framed too close to the vertical edge of the frame. Proper framing provides extra space in the direction that the subject looks. For reasons that should be obvious, look space is also called *noseroom* when the subject is a person.

Walk Space

The same rule that applies to look space applies to walk space. Proper framing provides extra space in the direction the subject is moving.

Headroom

Headroom refers to the space between the top of the subject's head and the edge of the frame. In general, if the subject's eyes are placed on a line that is one third from the top edge, the proper amount of headroom will be present. (See the rule of thirds.)

Isolating Shots

Editors evaluate material by looking for shots that communicate clearly are well-framed and have pleasing compositions. As you watch your footage, ask yourself the following questions. Does the shot communicate anything? Will the audience be able to read it? If the footage contains action, where does it start? Where does it end? What's the subject of the shot? What are the best parts? An editor's guiding principle is to look for shots that are clean, clear, and understandable.

Now that you understand what you're looking for, isolating shots (locating the tips of icebergs) should be a lot easier. When you spot an iceberg tip, mark an IN point. Then look for the OUT point. Play the IN to the OUT point. Use loop play (play in/out) when you're first learning to isolate shots, if it's available on your editing system. Consider whether the shot you've marked can start later or end sooner. If it can, adjust the IN and OUT points. Each shot should start at the last possible moment and end at the first possible moment. After you've trimmed the shot all the way down, you have the tip of an iceberg. The final step is to save the tip and name it.

Here are a few tips to help you get started as you begin isolating shots in your footage. Mark an IN point where the action starts. Mark an OUT point where it ends. Mark INs and OUTs at the beginning and end of moving shots, such as pans, tilts, or dollies. With interviews or testimonials, make each succinct statement a shot.

Creating Subclips

Subclips are fragments of a longer clip. If you've followed our suggestions about how to transfer footage into your editing system, each clip in your editing system contains a scene. You'll need to break the scene down into smaller shot-sized portions, which are called *subclips*. You can subclip (make copies) of a larger clip on most editing systems. The idea is to create multiple clips, which contain individual shots, from the larger clip, which contains the entire scene.

For example, the birdhouse scene from your trip to the zoo might include close-ups of different birds. The scene clip is called BIRD HOUSE. Find the moment where the first close-up begins, which is of a blue parrot, and mark an IN. Locate the end of the close-up and mark an OUT. Play from the IN point to the OUT point using loop play to determine if the shot you've marked is clean, clear, and understandable. Your IN and OUT points should only include the essence of the shot. Change your IN or OUT points if it will make the shot clearer, cleaner, or more understandable. Then, name and save this subclip to a bin.

Naming Subclips—Short and Unique

Subclips should have short unique names. Some editing systems automatically fill in the name of the original clip and add the word *copy* or a number to differentiate the new subclip from the original one.

In our example, the editing system is likely to name the subclip of the close-up of the blue parrot as BIRD HOUSE1. As you can tell, that's not very descriptive. A better name would be BLUE PARROT because it describes the clip. Later, when you're searching for shots, BLUE PARROT will jog your memory and help you recall what the shot looks like. The best choice for naming a subclip is to use a simple description.

It's common to have multiple shots of the identical subject with different fields of view or different angles. In this case, you'll need to find another aspect, beyond a description, to name these subclips and differentiate between the four BLUE PARROT shots.

A good strategy is to use the shot descriptions. For example, you might have BLUE PARROT—ECU, BLUE PARROT—MCU, BLUE PARROT LOW, and BLUE PARROT TILT. This information will make it easier to identify the shots whether you're using a list view or picon view of the bin. If possible, label the picons with the name you've given the subclip. Picons are often small. It can be difficult to differentiate between two shots that have a nearly identical picon, such as BLUE PARROT TILT and BLUE PARROT—ECU.

Figure 7-5
Subclips are portions of a larger cl ip.

Tips for Subclips

■ Don't get carried away with naming subclips. Call them what they are.

■ Any name you use is more descriptive than the name your editing system will assign by default. Too much typing impedes creativity.

■ Subclips are short, nondestructive copies of your original clips.

■ Always leave your original clip as is.

■ Always make new subclips from the original clip. In some systems, modifying the IN and OUT points on the original clips can make it confusing and difficult to reset them to their original lengths.

■ Deleting the original clip deletes all the copies and subclips you make in most editing systems.

■ Remember that subclips are pointers to the media files, not the media files.

Moving shots present another challenge. Imagine what the picons will look like for these four shots: PAN TO CITY BUS, ZOOM TO CITY BUS, FOLLOW PAN OF CITY BUS, and CITY BUS—MS. In this example, the picons, which are still images, will end up being identical. The descriptive name is the only way to tell these subclips apart unless you play them.

Another tip is to use the conceptual shot descriptions where appropriate. For example, say you plan to use a shot of a city street for the EST shot in your show. Make a subclip and name that shot CITY STREET—EST, which is your description for editing purposes.

Another Reason to Name Subclips

On most editing system timelines, the clips are arranged one after the other with their names displayed. Some editing systems can display a still or picon of the first frame in the clip or display picons for every frame in the clip, which uses up a lot of memory. If your editing system cannot display a picon and the clips aren't named, you'll have a lot of trouble editing on the timeline. Editing is easy when you have descriptive names and extremely frustrating when you don't.

Picking Picons

A very fast way to edit is to arrange the subclips (shots) in the bin in the order you want them to play. Then edit all of them as a group onto the timeline, maintaining that order. If you've created clean, clear, and understandable subclips, your work is nearly done. Play the timeline. Then improve the rhythm and pacing by trimming or making overlaps.

This method relies on selecting picons (the picture icons) that accurately represent the shots. You need to find the frame that represents the tip of the top of the iceberg.

Editing systems automatically select the first frame of the clip or subclip. If this is a slate, the visual reference that a picon provides becomes useless. Check your editing system manual to learn how to change the frame used for the picon. If you want to save time, make sure you select the frame for the picon before you name any subclip you make. If you don't, you'll have to name the subclip, retrieve it, set the frame, and resave it.

Summary

The ability to isolate a shot, to spot the tip of the top of the iceberg, comes with experience. As you log and review footage, use the standard abbreviations to describe the shots. The keyboard shortcut to make a subclip is one of the first ones you should learn.

Important Points to Remember

- Don't get carried away with naming subclips. Call them what they are.
- Any name you use is more descriptive than the name your editing system will assign by default. Too much typing impedes creativity.

- Subclips are short, nondestructive copies of your original clips.

- Always leave your original clip as is.

- Always make new subclips from the original clip. In some systems, modifying IN and OUT points on the original clips can make it confusing and difficult to reset them to their original lengths.

- Deleting the original clip deletes all the copies and subclips you make in most editing systems.

- Remember that subclips are pointers to the media files, not the media files.

The Frosting

Effects are like the frosting on a cake. Bakers add the frosting after the cake is baked. The most efficient approach in a digital environment is to add the effects after you've told the story.

Desktop Special Effects

It once took millions of dollars of equipment to create the simplest video effect. Today, almost anything can be created on a home computer. The only difference between what you can do at home and what a professional does in a postproduction facility comes down to speed and experience. Professionals can manipulate images, move layers, and create animated wonders in seconds. These identical effects can also be done on a desktop system; however, it will take considerably longer to do because professionals work with more horsepower in their high-end systems. Although this chapter won't turn you into an experienced special effects wizard, it can help you understand how to use special effects in the editing process.

Most editing systems present a clear picture of any effects in the timeline. You can see all the video clips, any effects placed on adjacent clips, or any effects stacked vertically. The ability to see the overall structure of the effects in your show is invaluable. Digital editing has made building effects a visual rather than conceptual process.

Editors take some special effects for granted. Digital editing makes it possible to play a clip in reverse at speeds that are faster or slower than normal, or freeze the clip and transform full-motion video into a still image. Transitions are easy to apply and modify. You can add titles and graphics in a few simple steps. Most editing systems even let you manipulate the individual pixels in a frame of digital video. You can move, shrink, expand, tumble, and flip your footage. You are only limited by your imagination and the flexibility of your editing system.

Special effects can be used to entertain, explain, or impress the audience. They help keep audiences interested. However, they're not the story. Professionals understand that no amount of special effects can save a show that doesn't tell a decent story. Effects, which are affectionately called *bells and whistles*, have often been misused or overused. As a result, they have gained a bad reputation. Regardless, there are more shows with effects than without them. Special effects are prominently used in commercials and television promos. They add sizzle and pizzazz.

One important use of effects is that they fix problems so the audience never sees them. Luckily, the near limitless capacity that people have for making mistakes is matched by the vast array of repair tools included in a digital editing system. The tools consist of the same special effects that are capable of creating magical manipulations of the image. The best reason for an editor to study and understand effects comes down to the prosaic—digital special effects are the best tools for fixing problems when they arise.

A Digital Approach to the Effects Workflow

An editor's primary focus is to assemble a show that tells a story. The editor makes choices about the pictures and sounds that will be used to tell that story. It's counterproductive to focus on the intricacies involved with effects when you're doing the rough cut. Keep it simple. Use the cut as your basic transition from shot to shot. Unadorned transitions reveal how your show flows in its rawest form.

If you create effects as you progressively build the show, there's always the chance that you'll add an effect prematurely. When you're shaping the story during the rough cut, clips are being rearranged, deleted, and swapped in and out. It would be a waste of time to build an effect using a clip that's temporarily in your show. By adding effects after the story is completed, you enhance the material that's made the final cut.

Desktop space is always at a premium when you're editing. There are open bins, toolbars, and viewers. The additional windows and toolbars needed to make an effect only add to the clutter. If you concentrate on one task at a time, you can reduce the number of open windows on the desktop.

Types of Effects

Effects fall into two categories—clip effects, which are applied to a single clip or subclip, and timeline effects, which are applied to multiple clips. Clip effects can be made at any point during editing. These effects are stored as subclips in a bin. Timeline effects can only be made on the timeline. Wait until after the rough cut is completed to begin working on timeline effects.

Clip Effects

Clip effects are changes to the properties of an existing clip. Professionals often experiment with effects before they choose the one they want. The standard procedure is to make a duplicate of the existing clip and save it. Use the duplicate clip for your experiments. If you make a permanent change to the original clip, it can be time consuming to undo some clip effects.

Timeline-Based Effects

Timeline effects are those that combine multiple sources. A transition is a typical timeline effect that combines two adjacent clips. A dissolve or wipe would be an example of this type of timeline effect. A different kind of time-line effect involves combining clips that are stacked above each other. These effects are called *layered effects*. Superimposing a title graphic over video is an example of this effect. Stacking multiple layers on a clip or clips in a uni-fied sequence is called *compositing*. Compositing involves complex layering, which is covered in Chapter 9, "Gilding the Lily." Occasionally, a timeline effect might involve only one clip. The other source is often generated by the effect itself—for example, when a patterned mask is applied to a clip.

Typical Clip Effects

The following section presents a few of the common clip effects.

Playback Speed

The normal frame rate for video is 29.97 *frames per second* (fps) in North America (NTSC standard[1]) or 25 fps in Europe (PAL standard[2]). In most systems, the editor can change the frame rate or modify the speed as a per-centage of normal. You can create fast or slow motion. Reversing the motion may involve changing the frame rate or using a negative number. The

---

[1]National Television Standards Committee.
[2]Phase Alternating Line.

minus sign (−) is often used for reverse and the plus (≤) is used for forward. Every editing system seems to come up with a new wrinkle on how to modify speed. Sometimes speed is listed as part of the clip's properties. *Fit to fill* is a special type of speed effect. This effect is used to expand or contract the duration of clip to fill a gap in the timeline. The clip slows down if it's too short and speeds up if it's too long.

Strobe

A strobe creates a stuttered effect. Motion that is normally smooth looks staccato. The strobe effect works by freezing a frame in the clip, holding the freeze, and then releasing the freeze a few frames later before the cycle begins again. In some editing systems, a quick succession of still frames is called a *strobe effect*.

Freeze

This effect turns a field or frame in a video clip into a still image. Whenever a clip is paused, the editing system displays a still image or freeze. Most editing systems let you save this image as a clip in a bin. Some editing systems give the editor discretion to choose between a field or frame freeze. It's important to know the difference between the two types. Each video frame has two distinct fields. When you freeze a clip, the picture may flutter. This happens because the fields are displaying slightly different pictures of the action. When the two fields are combined, the image on the screen appears to flutter back and forth. It's inappropriate for a still picture, unless the sub-

A Shooting Tip

Shoot action at a high shutter speeds if you plan to use slow motion. A higher shutter speed, such as 1/125th, 1/250th, or 1/500th of a second, will capture a very sharp picture. When you slow the footage down in your editing system, the individual frames will be much sharper than if you shoot at the normal shutter speed, which is a 1/60th (or 1/50th in PAL) of a second.

ject is a hummingbird. If you use the field freeze setting, the problem will be solved. Our rule of thumb is to use a frame freeze unless there's rapid motion that causes a flutter.

Whether the freeze is one field or one frame, it must be processed as normal video for display and output to tape. To do this, your editing system must create a media file. If the freeze is a field freeze, the editing system has to duplicate your chosen field or create a second field to make a complete frame. Usually, you can choose to use duplication or interpolation. Sometimes you can produce a better looking freeze if you choose interpolation instead of duplication. With some editing systems, you have no choice; it's all done automatically.

Color

Color correction—manipulating the red, green, and blue channels in video —is a clip effect. The amount of control you have over the video image will depend on the sophistication of your editing system.

Editing systems modify color by adjusting the *hue, saturation, and luminance* (HSL) or the *red, green, and blue* (RGB) components. If you have the choice, use the controls with which you're most comfortable.

Most editing systems include some basic color correction tools. These are usually enough for simple tasks like correcting the white balance of a clip. For example, if the footage was shot outdoors with the color correction filter set to indoors, the resulting images will have an overall blue cast. This problem can be fixed using the color tools that are available in most editing systems to remove the blue.

Color correction tools can also be used to match color, brightness, and tone from one shot to the next. After the editing is completed, you can go through your show shot by shot and adjust the color to achieve a uniform look. This gives your show an integrity that is sure to be noticed by the audience.

You can create special image treatments by tinting clips; this is one of the most useful clip effects. For example, applying a brown sepia tone tint can give the footage an antique or period look. On many systems, tints are applied as filters. The editor usually has control over color and opacity. It's a good idea to save any filter settings you modify for reuse later. If your editing system can't save these settings for use with other projects, write down the settings in a notebook. That way you won't have to start from scratch every time.

What Is White Balance?

Most digital camcorders have a setting for indoor and outdoor lighting. Why? Legendary WCAU-TV broadcaster Gene Crane, who's been on the air since the day the station opened in 1948, explains it this way: "You've got to teach the camera what white is."

Think about it this way. If you open a book in a candlelit room, the pages appear white. If you go outside and open the book, the pages are still white. However, candlelight is yellow and the light outdoors has a blue cast because of the sky. Our brains automatically compensate for the differences because we expect the pages to be white. To compensate for the differences in the color of the light, camcorders have a white balance setting.

Some camcorders let you set a manual white balance. The method is simple. Aim the camera, fill the frame with a white object, and press the button to set the white balance. The camera makes that object look pure white. You can fool the camera to make a warmer (redder) or colder (bluer) picture by aiming the camera at an object that isn't white. A light blue piece of paper makes the picture warmer and a light red piece of paper makes the picture colder. This should make sense because red and blue are opposites. Diminishing one increases the other.

How to Tint Clips   The first step in the process is to duplicate the clip if possible. Then get rid of the color on the duplicate clip by adjusting the saturation to zero. This should leave you with a black and white image. Next, manipulate the red, green, or blue controls to tint the clip. Save the tinted version of the clip.

The following are a few more of the common clip effects.

Negative

Reverses the color values and creates what appears to be a photographic negative.

Solarization

Reverses the highlight and shadow values. This effect makes the white values dark and silvery, and makes the black values bright and shiny.

Posterization

Reduces the color values in the image from millions to a relative handful. Limiting the number of colors creates banding in areas of graduated color. The image often looks like a 1980s music video.

Flip (flop)

Results in an upside-down image if the image is rotated on its horizontal or x axis (width). If the image is rotated on its vertical or y axis (height), the image will be a backwards or mirror image. A backwards shot comes in handy every now and then. As long as there are no visible indicators of direction, such as the steering wheel of a car or lettering on a sign, a backwards or mirror image can correct a shot taken from the wrong angle. You can also flip a shot to use it twice. For example, a shot of an airplane flying left to right could be used to represent taking a trip from Los Angeles to New York and when flipped, the shot can be used for the New York to Los Angeles return. It's not part of the production planning process, but flipping a shot demonstrates how you can solve a problem inexpensively. When producers say we'll fix it in post, this is one of things they mean.

The Workflow for Clip Effects

The way you create effects varies from editing system to editing system. However, the workflow remains the same. Select the clip you want to use. Duplicate the clip. Select an effect and apply it to the duplicate clip. Adjust the settings using the tools in your editing system. There might be a drop-down menu, tool palette, or dialog box for adjustments. Preview the effect and make further adjustments, if necessary. When you're satisfied, save the clip with the effect in a bin. Edit this clip onto the timeline. Then play the timeline to see how the effect works in your show. If you're satisfied, you

The Basics of Video Color

Digital editing systems manipulate color using either the Hue, Saturation, and Luminance (HSL) or Red, Green, Blue (RGB) models. If you'll be adjusting values and changing colors, you should understand how each model works. It is equally important to understand that video color space is smaller than the color space displayable on a computer monitor. This means you can create or modify colors that cannot be reproduced in video. Digital video describes the values for each color channel on a scale from 0 (black) to 255 (white). The legal limits are 16 to 235 for video in a broadcast environment. Anything above or below these values will be clipped. This might not make much sense unless you are in front of your editing system. You can click on a color and display its numeric values to check whether it's within the limit. Highly saturated colors are the ones that can cause the problems.

Hue, Saturation, and Luminance

Video signals contain information about color: the chroma and hue, and luminance or brightness. *Chroma* is an abbreviation of chrominance, which refers to the amount of color or saturation in the image. Hue is the specific point on a color wheel or the value on the color spectrum that indicates the actual color we see. Luminance is the black and white portion of the signal.

    Saturation, unless your show must meet broadcast standards, is like salt. Adjust to taste. Create rich colors, pale pastels, or lower the saturation to zero for a black and white image.

    Luminance describes the black and white information in the image. Video has brightness and contrast values regardless of the color information. Brightness adjusts the overall level of the image from black to white. Contrast changes the gray values. As you lower the contrast, you will see more midtones (gray values) and the image will appear flatter. As you raise the contrast, you will see fewer midtones. Eventually, the image becomes all black and all white.

Red, Green, and Blue

Video cameras record color as components of the primary colors red, green, and blue.

    The green channel provides the luminance information for the image. Typically, each channel is independently adjustable using *color gain*.

(continues)

(continued)

Gamma adjusts the midtones or gray values in the image without affecting the extreme black or extreme white values.

The *Black Level* adjusts the black or shadow areas of the picture. The *Black Point* is a black level in the picture that the editor uses for reference black. For example, if a dark gray value is used for the Black Point instead of a black value, any graduations between dark gray and true black will become pure black. The *White Level* adjusts the white or highlight areas of the picture. The *White Point* sets a white portion of the picture to pure white and any values above it are clipped to white. These set points are used when the editor makes color adjustments.

Secondaries and Vectorscopes

A secondary color is a mixture of two primary colors. Cyan is a combination of blue and green. Magenta is a combination of red and blue. Yellow is a combination of green and red. Both primary and secondary colors are represented in the SMPTE[3] color bar test signal. If your editing system has a *vectorscope*, you can display a color bar signal as a circular graphic. Check it out. It looks cool, but it has no purpose if you're transferring video in and out of your editing system via Firewire or another digital transport standard.

---

[3]Society of Motion Picture and Television Engineers.

can move on to the next effect you want to add. If you're not, readjust the effects settings until you achieve the look you want.

On some editing systems, you can make those adjustments directly on the timeline. Other systems force you to go back to the beginning and start over. If you find yourself doing this, prepare alternate versions when you're building effects. For example, experiment with slow motion and store clips with different speeds in a bin. Later, when you're editing the slow-motion clip on the timeline, you'll be able to select from a variety of speeds.

Integrating Effects with Match Frame

Cutting from a normal speed to slow motion can be jarring. Slow-motion effects are fine when a shot is seen in isolation. If you cut to an off-speed shot, the audience may feel disoriented. Editors soften the blow by dissolving from off-speed to normal-speed shots. However, if you want to change the speed in the middle of a shot, a different approach is required.

Imagine that you want a shot of a bicycle rider to transition from normal to slow motion fluidly. The method of doing this is to match cut from a frame in the clip to which you've applied a slow-motion effect to the identical frame in the original (normal-speed) clip. Many editing systems have a button or feature that lets you find the frame of a clip on the timeline and the same frame on the clip that's in a bin. If you don't have a match frame feature, you'll need to use the time code number for the frame you want to match. The time code is for the source clip on the timeline. Write down the time code address on a piece of paper. Then find the clip to which you've applied the slow-motion effect. Find the frame that matches the point at which you want to transition from normal to slow motion. Finding the correct frame is easy, but it takes time. This frame will be the IN point (where you switch from normal to slow motion) for the slow-motion clip and the OUT point for the normal-speed clip. Edit the two shots together on the timeline to make the transition from a normal to slow-motion action.

Display

In order to see an effect as you're building it, your editing system must be able to display the results on your desktop and/or video monitor. There might be a dedicated viewer window that displays effects. In single-viewer editing systems, the effects will appear in the multipurpose viewer window. Remember to close any unnecessary windows when you build effects. Creating effects uses up a lot of memory and processing power. Your computer must be running efficiently when you work with effects.

Previews

Most editing systems can create a *snapshot*—a one-frame representation of what an effect will look like or a scrub preview that lets you see one frame at a time as you advance through the effect. If an effect involves movement from one point to another, you might only see points plotted on a simple line drawing with arrows or other indicators for direction, speed, and position. This is called a *wireframe preview*.

Real-Time Previews Versus Real-Time Playback

Faster computers with more memory allow system manufacturers to tout what they call *Areal-time effects* for digital editing. In fact, most are real-time previews, not real-time effects. When you combine two DV sources, a new media file must be created. The data has to be uncompressed and recompressed in the DV format before it can be output to the Firewire port. Real-time playback is only possible when you have specialized hardware. The capabilities of the hardware determine what can be played back in real time (the number of video layers or streams) and the image quality of that material. Video channels are called *streams*. Two video streams are required to create a dissolve in real time. If you're working on effects that require more streams than those available on your editing system, you must render the effect to see full-motion playback.

Rendering

Rendering means creating a media file for the effect you've built. After you create the media file, the effect will behave like any clip and play normally. Rendering takes time. Depending on the speed of your system, you can take a nice break when rendering. Once an effect has been rendered, it can be used as an element in another effect. That composite can be rendered. Another effect can be added to it and so on. One disadvantage is that if you want to change any aspect of a rendered effect, you'll have to rerender it before it will play normally.

Rendering and Video Streams

In the context of cooking, rendering means boiling off the fat. Of course, this is not what happens in your editing system. Baking is a better analogy for effects rendering. You create effects in the same way as you bake a cake. First, you mix together all of the ingredients to make a batter. Unless you bake the batter for the proper amount time at the correct temperature, you don't have a cake. A cake takes as long as it takes to bake. You can't bake it any faster.

Rendering is a fact of life unless you have unlimited amounts of processing power. In high-end postproduction facilities, no rendering is required. Time is money. Advertising agency and broadcast clients don't have time to wait for effects to be rendered. In fact, most pay handsomely for the privilege of avoiding rendering. These customers expect to be able see and change complex effects instantly.

Anyone with talent can replicate effects produced on a high-end system. The only difference is the amount of time it will take to create and render the effect. The results are the same because the process is the same. The good news is that processing power is increasing rapidly, and faster, cheaper hardware is moving us toward a day when multilayered effects will be as fast and easy to do on the desktop as they are on million-dollar systems.

Rendering Strategies

Rendering takes time, which can affect an editor's creative process. Once you've built up a rhythm and are working steadily, you might not want to stop and take a break. If you've previewed the effect and feel comfortable with its appearance, you can postpone rendering until you are ready to stop and take a break. Every editing system we've seen has a *render all* feature that will render any effects that need to be rendered as a group. Professionals use this time to take the client to lunch or catch a break. Afterwards, all of the effects are ready to be played in real time. If all goes well, the editing proceeds.

Types of Timeline Effects

As in life, timing is everything in editing. The transition from one shot to the next should be seamless so that continuity is maintained, or, in the case of montage, the theme is reinforced and kept intact. Cuts are the cleanest transitions if placed correctly. When a cut doesn't work, other types of transitions can take the viewer from one shot to the next. Transitions must be done on the timeline. These effects are added after the clips are in the correct order. Dissolves and wipes are the next most common transitions after the cut.

Fades and Dissolves

A fade is the gradual appearance of a new picture from black or the gradual disappearance of the picture to black. A dissolve is two fades that occur at the same time. The outgoing clip fades to black while the incoming clip fades up from black at the same time. As a result, the two shots blend together. A dissolve from a clip to black is called a *fade to black*. The dissolve is commonly used to signal the passage of time or space in a seamless way. Dissolves can create a poetry of motion by blending together disparate shots. Dissolves are also used to soften visual transitions in effects. For example, if you want a series of playing cards to magically appear in the dealer's hand, you could start with the first shot that depicts the dealer holding a single playing card. Then, you'd edit a second shot from the identical perspective that depicts the dealer with two cards. Follow that shot with another that depicts the dealer holding three cards. If you use cuts, the cards will pop into his hands. If you dissolve between the shots, the cards will flow into his hand.

Dissolves are almost always used to add titles or graphics to a show. Most start out completely transparent and over time become opaque. Most shows begin with a dissolve up from black and end with a dissolve to black. If you watch television, you see hundreds of dissolves everyday without realizing it. A dissolve is like white bread in the world of effects.

Wipe

A wipe is a transition between two adjacent clips where one image replaces the other using a geometric pattern. For example, one image is revealed under the other as the vertical edge of the *top* image moves across the screen from left to right in a *wiping* motion. This classic film transition was called *The Wipe* and now every patterned transition is known as a wipe. It's important to note that all wipe effects, such as a circle, heart shaped, box shaped, clock wipe, and so on, are masking patterns on full-sized images.

Displaying Transitions on a Timeline

Two methods are used to display and apply transitions to a timeline. The most common view is the single-track approach. Transitions are affixed to adjoining clips on a single video track by dragging, dropping, or editing them on the dividing line between the two shots. The transition effect overlaps both from and to the clip. Some systems call this a *single-layered effect*.

The other method uses a diagrammatic display with two video tracks that are labeled A and B. The A track holds the outgoing (or from) clip and the B track shows the incoming (or to) clip. The A track is placed above the B track. The effect applies to the portion of the A and B tracks that overlap.

The straight-line, single-track display is the more common. It's simpler and requires less desktop space. The A/B display has an advantage, especially for beginners, because it shows each clip's frames. The usual highlighting of these extra frames (handles) acts as a visual guide for determining the extent and position of the overlapping shots and the duration of the transition effect. After you're comfortable with the concept of overlapping clips, the A/B model loses its appeal.

Handles for Successful Transitions

To make a successful transition, the clips on the timeline must be long enough to complete the effect. Each clip needs *handles*, which are the extra frames necessary to overlap the adjacent clip. If no handles are available or

Figure 8-1

A and B track display indicates the overlapping contents of a transition on the timeline.

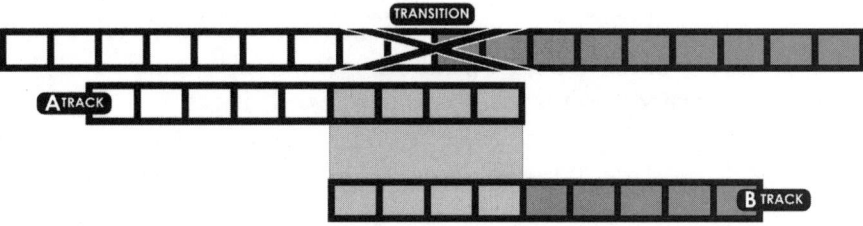

if there are fewer frames than the desired duration of the transition, it will be impossible to create the effect. Typically, this occurs when an IN or OUT point of the clip on the timeline is at, or very near, the beginning or end of the clip in the bin.

Solving Transition Problems

If you have trouble with a transition effect, you should be able to solve the problem by changing the properties of the effect. The following are three tactics you should try (in order of priority):

- *Shorten the duration.* This sounds simple, but it works. If there's not enough media, try a shorter dissolve. For example, if you want 40 frames, try a 30-frame dissolve and you might just have enough media to do the dissolve.

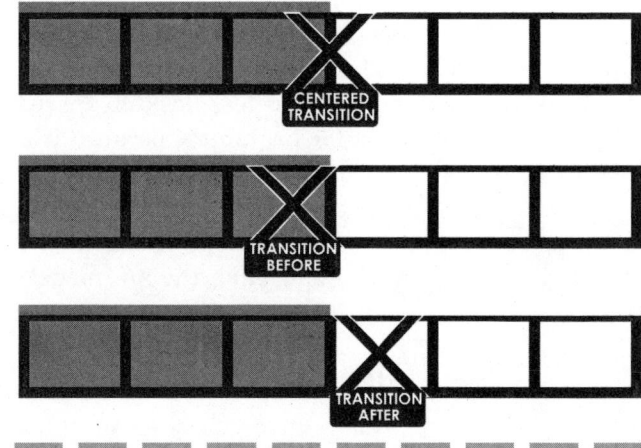

- *Change the point on the timeline where the transition takes place.* Ordinarily, transitions take place at the edit point between the outgoing and incoming

Figure 8-2
Three possible placements of transitions.

clips. If one clip has an insufficient number of frames, move the effect earlier so the transition is completed before the clip runs out of frames (see Figure 8-2).

- *Adjust the clips involved in the transition.* Move the OUT point of the outgoing clip earlier or move the IN point of the incoming clip forward. The trim tools are often integrated into the tools used to edit transitions.

Workflow for Timeline Effects

The following are the steps for creating timeline effects.

Select the Area of the Timeline

Begin by selecting the area on the timeline where you plan to apply an effect. This could be a single clip, multiple clips, a section, or the entire timeline. Remember to only include the tracks to which the effect should be applied.

Select the Effect and Apply It

Next decide on the effect you'd like to use. Experiment with the settings using the preview feature. When you're satisfied with the results, apply the effect to the timeline.

Adjust the Effect

Once the effect has been applied to the selected area, you might need to finish building the effect on the timeline. You'll need to modify and adjust the settings to fit the effect seamlessly into your show.

Building effects can be painstaking work. There are so many choices and possible combinations of timing, color, motion, and style to choose from that just selecting the appropriate effect can be time consuming. If you're working with a partner or client, this time factor increases exponentially. This is why we don't recommend working in groups to do effects.

Review the Effect

Effects that involve transitions and movement change the flow of the show and should be reviewed at normal speed. Play the timeline. Notice how the rhythm of the show is altered by the effect. If the effect won't play, you must render it. Previewing effects frame by frame is only helpful to a point. Because it takes time to render effects, make sure you get it right before you render.

Summary

First, learn how to change clip properties. Then become familiar with your editing system's timeline effects. After you have a firm understanding of these fundamentals, move on to layering and keying, which are covered Chapter 9, "Gilding the Lily."

Important Points to Remember

- Effects are the frosting on the cake and should be applied at the end of the project.
- Effects can be applied to individual clips or to multiple clips on the timeline.
- Some editing systems can preview effects in real time. Others require effects to be rendered.
- For efficiency, render effects as a group.
- Store effects parameters, in a folder or bin if possible, for reuse later.

Gilding
the Lily

In Chapter 8, "The Frosting," we explained how to add effects to a single clip and how to combine two clips in a transitional effect on the timeline. In this chapter, we'll take effects to the next level—literally.

What's Compositing?

Composites are images that are combinations of shots and other elements. This term has its roots in film production. Originally, composites were made in the camera or with special equipment at a film laboratory. With digital video, you can make composites on your editing system. For Steve Owen of Quantel, the difference between editing and compositing is simple. "Stringing frames next to each other is called editing. Stacking them one on top of the other is called compositing." This is the most concise definition we've ever heard.

Composites are constructed on the timeline. A composite is made from two or more elements. In digital video, an element is a layer on the timeline. Layering and compositing are two words with identical meanings. Shots and other elements on the timeline are placed in vertically stacked layers, one on top of the other, which are then combined.

Your editing system has tools that enable you to adjust the transparency of any of these layers. The layers can become like sheets of transparent plastic. Any sections of the layers above the background that are transparent will allow the background to show through. This is how a title graphic can appear to float in the foreground above a video background. We consider titles to be special effects, whether they're white text over a black background or part of a colorful, animated, dazzling sequence. Learning the fundamentals of title placement, movement, and manipulation is a good way to understand compositing. Once you master titles, you can expand your repertoire with more sophisticated effects.

Why Titles?

Titles serve many purposes. They're used at the beginning for the show title and at the end for the credits. Titles are used to reinforce concepts in the body of the show. They're used to paraphrase narration, display sports scores, and provide instructions. The titles that identify an individual are often called *lower thirds* because that's where the title appears in the lower third of the picture. Titles are also used to identify time and place (see Figure 9-1).

The Basics of Title Design

Every editing system has a tool or application that can generate text files for use in digital editing. These title utilities have different capabilities and features. However, all of them are capable of basic text creation. When you create a title, you have to make style choices. The sum of all the choices you make represents the *look* (appearance) of the title. The creation of that look is called a *text treatment*.

Type Fonts

Fonts are different styles of type. Fonts are differentiated by the thickness of the strokes that form the letters and the way the letters are drawn. Many

Figure 9-1
A lower third title treatment.

editing systems use the hundreds of TrueType fonts already loaded on the computer. Type font managers are available that display a line of type in each font's style as you move through the list on your computer. Some title tools also provide this feature. This makes it easy to see the choices so you can make an appropriate selection quickly. Otherwise, you will have to recall the appearance of the font from memory.

Thin wispy letters don't show up well on the screen. Bold and medium fonts are always highly legible. It's simply a matter of how monitors function. Ideally, the fonts you select should have smooth letters. The rectangular pixels in digital video can make curves, circles, or diagonal lines appear to have stair-stepped edges. This is known as *aliasing*. Many programs have an anti-aliasing feature that makes those stair steps appear smooth.

Type Size

Type size is measured in points or scan lines. Bigger and bolder is better for titles (and interfaces). If the font is too small, it will be difficult to read. You can also adjust the kerning (the space between characters) and leading (the space between the lines) to improve readability.

From our experience, a font size of 24 points or 20 scan lines is about as low as most editors will go except perhaps for the fine print in a car commercial. A reliable way to check the type size for a title is to view the monitor at a distance of 10 to 15 feet. If you can't read the title, it's probably too small.

Choose Type Colors

You can fill type with any color, which can be solid or blended. The amount of color saturation that digital video can handle successfully is limited. This is generally not a problem with your internal text generator, which is designed for digital video. However, image-editing applications, such as Adobe Photoshop or JASC Paint Shop Pro, can create titles that have colors outside the color space boundaries of digital video and won't display properly on a monitor.

Always evaluate the colors you're considering over the background. Choose contrasting colors for legibility. For example, yellow text over a blue sky is highly readable.

Add an Edge

Adding an edge (a border or shadow) to the type will improve the legibility of a title (see Figure 9-2). The shadow can be a depth or drop shadow. You can add color to the edges in most systems. Some editing systems give you control over the thickness and softness of the edge (see Figure 9-3).

Figure 9-2
A title with a drop shadow edge treatment.

Figure 9-3
A title with a glow edge treatment.

Add a Text Object

Some title tools let you create simple objects, such as boxes and circles, which can be filled with color or a blend of colors. If a busy background would make it difficult to read the text, you can use these objects to create a background. Thin narrow boxes are used to create an underlined rule. Usually, a wide range of patterns is available to fill text or text objects with which you can experiment.

Set Transparency

Titles are usually opaque. However, you can adjust the transparency of the letters or objects if you want the background to show through. The transparency is usually adjusted to blend a text object with the background (see Figure 9-4).

Figure 9-4
A title over a
transparent box.

Types of Titles

Full Screen

Titles can be created as full-screen artwork. You can create a still image with text and an interesting background to use as a full-frame graphic. If the image isn't live action, it falls under the category of graphics. A text title over a color background is the simplest form of graphic (see Figure 9-5).

Over Video

Titles are usually over video backgrounds. This is standard for most title tools. When you make a title, the letters you type are filled with the colors you selected. At the same time, an alpha channel mask is created. At the technical level, an outline of each letter is created that defines which areas will be opaque or transparent. The outline is a mask called an *alpha channel*. The mask enables the colored letters to be combined with the video background.

Figure 9-5
A full screen graphic.

Rolls

Rolls are titles that move up or down and disappear off screen. This type of title is often used for the credits at the end of a show. Rolling titles add movement to long lists of information.

Crawls

Crawls are titles that move across the screen from left to right. They are used primarily in television. Crawls work best when the movement corresponds to the direction in which the language is read. In English, crawls should appear from the right and move left.

Type-on Titles

Titles can arrive onscreen any number of ways. You can *type on* a title so a letter, word, or line appears onscreen one at a time. Type-on titles are also called *reveals* because the text characters are revealed over time. If a reveal is used for a text list or other full-screen graphic, it's called a *graphic build*.

Editors create graphic builds in reverse. First, the full title (the final image) that the audience sees is created and saved. Then the editor deletes a line and saves this version as a new title. The process is repeated for each step (build). Each step is saved as a separate title. When the titles are placed in the opposite order they were created, the audience will see the lines of text build to the full title. If you use dissolves between each graphic, each line will appear to fade up. It's a simple trick.

Adding Motion

Most digital editing systems let you move text and/or objects across the screen on the x (horizontal) and y (vertical) axes with scale and rotation. Some systems can also move text and objects on the z axis closer or farther away from the surface plane of the monitor. Movement adds production value with relatively little effort (see Figure 9-6). Television promos (the commercials for the shows airing on television) rely on moving titles, graphics, and effects. Don't forget to add a bit more gloss by dissolving these combinations on and off the screen.

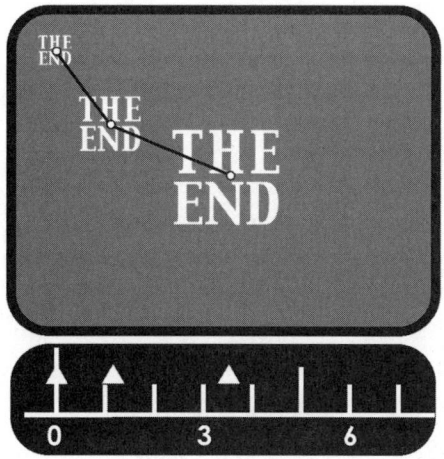

Figure 9-6
A moving title with keyframes (the triangle points).

Workflow for Title Creation

The capabilities of a title tools range from turning out basic text on a background to creating sophisticated graphic animations. Your editing system manual will have details about your title tool. This list specifies the steps most editors follow to create a title:

1. Launch the title tool or application.

2. Type the text. The default font is probably fine for turning out a quick title.

3. After you've typed the text, select the text.

4. Change the font, size, color, border, and shadow.

5. Position the title onscreen.

6. Save the title. A title clip will be created. Place the clip in the appropriate bin. Remember to name the clip. Some editing systems ask for a name before saving the title. Others use a weird default name, which is usually a cryptic number. If this is the case, rename the title so you can find it.

7. Edit the title into your show. If you want the title to be a full-frame graphic, edit the title onto an existing video track. If you want the title to appear over video, you'll probably have to place the title on its own track, which may be labeled as a graphics track, above that section of the video track. This is called *layering*, which we'll discuss in a moment.

Tips for Titles

Here are some tips to remember whenever you're creating titles:

- Check your spelling by reading the text backwards. This always works.

- When you make adjustments to the text, work from left to right using the tool palette and/or the drop-down menu bar so you don't forget any parameters you might want to change. This works especially well at first when you're unfamiliar with all the options that your title tool has to offer.

- Don't bother with auto kerning. It rarely works. Kern the letters manually to get the look you want.

- Save your title settings. Some systems call them *styles*. Others call them *title treatments*. Saving the attributes lets you to make great looking titles quickly.

The Time Anomaly

When a title is faded in or out, the convention is to use the identical duration for the incoming and outgoing fades. Even though the fades are equal in length, the fade in will appear to be faster than the fade out. This anomaly is because when we see a title fade in, we don't recognize it immediately. It's new information that's hidden. As the title becomes visible (as its transparency lessens), we notice its presence and begin to make out familiar words. Of course, because it's text, we have to grasp the words and read it. Hence, for a fade in, the first frames are not always recognizable or even understandable.

In contrast, our eyes are drawn to objects in motion and the brighter parts of the screen. When a title fades out, it appears to linger. Our eyes stay focused on it and we continue to read it. Even when it has lost almost all opacity, the title is still recognizable. We perceive that it is onscreen longer than it actually is.

Due to the physiology of how we see, in order to have a title appear to fade in and out at the same rate, you'll need to make the duration of the fade out shorter than the fade in. For example, if you use a 30-frame duration (1 second) for the fade in, a 20-frame fade out will appear to have the same duration.

Layering

A digital editing system that stacks multiple layers on the timeline resembles a wedding cake. We like this analogy because creating a show is similar to baking a wedding cake. Bakers start with ingredients, mix them together to make a batter, and bake a cake for each layer. The editor starts with a number of elements and mixes them together to create a coherent arrangement. After the cakes are baked, the baker stacks the layers for the wedding cake and applies the frosting. Frosting is a part of the cake, not the cake itself. Effects are like frosting—they are added later and are included to create an impression.

Types of Layered Effects

Superimposition is the equivalent of double exposure in photography; two images are mixed together. The term superimposition has different meanings to different manufacturers. In most systems, the term means to mix one shot over another, which results in a blend or mixture of the two shots over time. In the early days of silent movies, images were superimposed over one another by exposing the film twice—hence, the relation to double exposure. As with many film effects, this effect was recreated for use in television and the term took on new meaning. Today, a superimposition, or *super*, can also mean that a graphic is over the top of a picture. The graphic is overlaid on a fully visible background. This type of super is also called a *key* or *matte*. As you can see, this is another instance in the endless saga of confusing terms that plague the film and video industry.

Keys and Mattes

A key, or matte key, is a hole cut into the video image. The hole will be filled with another video source. There are different types of keys based on the way in which the hole or pattern is developed. In each case, the key source video is superimposed over a second video image through a pattern. The transparent portion of the key source video, which is defined by the pattern, enables the second video image to be seen.

The Origins of Compositing Terms

If you go back to the early days of silent films, you can see where the terms we use come from. Early filmmakers got the idea to mask a portion of the lens so they could have more control over double exposures. They were experimenting with new ways of storytelling.

One of their first ideas was the split screen, where two scenes appear onscreen simultaneously separated by a vertical line down the center of the frame. To accomplish this, the cameraman placed a black card in front of the lens to mask one side. After shooting the first scene, the film was rewound and reloaded into the camera. The mask was moved to the other side so the film could be exposed again. This time the side where the second scene would appear was shot and the side with the first scene was behind the mask.

As a result, the audience would see two scenes on the film image. Experimentation with different masking frames, which were called *mattes*, provided more interesting ways to film a scene. The binocular matte is arguably the most famous. Incidentally, the device that holds the matte in place was incorporated into the camera's lens shade and later became known as the *matte box*.

A typical silent film convention that best illustrates the use of a matte is the Victorian hallway scene. When a character, often a maid, wanted to spy on characters who were in another room, he or she would look through the keyhole in the door. Thus, the keyhole matte was born.

Figure 9-7
A basic key contains three elements.

Luminance Key

In this type of key, the pattern is determined by the difference between the black and white portions of the signal. The difference in contrast creates the key source—the pattern. The luminance key can be adjusted for sensitivity. It's important to adjust a luminance key to obtain a pattern with a very clean edge. This adjustment is called *clipping*. One option for a luminance key is to invert (reverse) the whites and blacks. Luminance keys were used for graphics in the early days of television. Better choices are available in the digital environment.

Chroma Key

This key is similar to the luminance key. However, the key source is created using a particular color in the source image. The idea is to create a hole using a solid color. Chroma keys are used in broadcast television to place the weather forecaster over maps and other visuals.

The forecaster is shot against a solid color wall. Any portion of the image that reveals the wall will be filled with a second video source—a weather map or whatever. When this type of key is used outside of a television studio, the subject is shot against a screen of blue or green fabric—hence, the name *blue* or *green screen work*. Blue or green screen effects can be used to cut out any object, person, or graphic in order to superimpose them over a background source. The illusion of Spiderman swinging around the city is created using this technique.

A chroma key effect can be affixed to any clip in a timeline. There are clip and color controls available for setting and adjusting the key edge. The first step is to select the hue that will be the designated chroma key color. Next, adjust the clip values for a perfect edge. Save the values for later reuse.

Matte Key

A key source with exacting dimensions can be created using a graphic image and alpha channel. Photoshop, Paint Shop Pro, and other image-editing applications can create a mask as an alpha channel. An alpha channel mask works in the same way as the other keys. A specific area defined by the alpha channel creates the keyhole. Any clip that has an alpha channel can be used as a matte. The masked area of the graphic becomes transparent when it is used over video. Because these types of mattes don't

A Shooting Tip

The color blue is most often used to key a person over a background. This is because blue does not appear in flesh tones. It's the opposite color on the color wheel and a clean hole can be cut from a blue source. Green is also used because blue is a popular color for clothing. You should always avoid using red because red appears in flesh tones and the resulting keyhole will be poorly defined.

To make the effect believable, the lighting on the subject has to match the lighting in the background footage. If you want a person to appear as if he or she is standing outdoors, use a green screen. Daylight has a blue cast because of the sky. To match the look of the outdoors, you'll need to shoot the person in the studio with a touch of blue gel on the lights. If you use a green screen, you won't have any problems with partially blue lighting.

For example, if the subject is supposed to be outdoors on a sunny day, you'll need to shoot the person so the direction of the light and shadows matches the sun in the background scene. The person needs to be lit evenly for a clean chroma key. Also make sure his or her wardrobe does not have any green colors. You will lose the effect if the background shows through the person's clothing.

depend on luminance or color, it's easy to get a clean sharp edge. A graphic with an alpha channel can be adjusted by inverting (or reversing) the alpha channel, giving you the flexibility to make what was transparent opaque.

The most common use for an alpha matte key is to position a colorful logo over video. The foreground or fill is the graphic source clip (the logo) and the background is any video clip on your timeline. The shape of the logo defines the shape of the alpha channel pattern.

Animated Mattes

An animated matte is used when moving graphics or titles are keyed over video. Compositing applications, such as After Effects, Boris Effects, or Combustion can create the necessary sequence of frames. Each frame has a corresponding alpha channel to accomplish this effect.

Elements of a Keyed Effect

All key effects consist of three elements: a background layer, which may be black, a color background, or a video source; a key source or alpha channel, which is the element that contains the pattern; and the fill or foreground layer. In the case of a chroma key or a title key, the fill layer is also the key source. The key source clip cuts a hole and, in effect, fills its own hole. This is also true for a matte key based on a graphic with an alpha channel. The fill and pattern for the graphic come from the same source. You just have to select a source for the background layer in order to complete the composite effect.

The Order of Layers

Some editing systems stack the tracks up and others stack them down. If your editing system stacks the layers up, a key will always reside on the track above its background. The background layer in a digital editing system can be one video track or multiple video tracks. Every track with a video clip positioned directly below the key source will be part of the composite effect.

Applying Effects

Editing systems apply effects on a layer or section of the timeline in a variety of ways. A typical approach is to drag and drop the effect over the appropriate section. Once the effect is placed, play or preview the results. Adjust and change the settings until you're satisfied.

Working with Layers

You should make a separate timeline for effects work. The compositing timeline can be incorporated into your show after you finish creating the effect. This approach will serve you well if you decide to do advanced effects work in another application and import the results into your editing system. If multiple timelines can be open at once in your editing system, make a scratch or garbage timeline for the effect. Copy the section of the timeline you want to use for the composite. In the new timeline, paste that section and begin working. After you've finished building the composite effect, you can cut and paste the section back into your show, replacing the original section. The advantage is that all of the individual layers are intact and available for future modification. Sometimes you must make a rendered composite to play the effect. In that case, cut and paste the rendered composite into the show timeline and save the effect timeline with the layers intact for future reference.

Nesting

Nesting is a term used in some editing systems to describe the grouping of effects layers. Nesting several layers makes it easier to move a composite effect around because it's a single container that acts like a clip. Some editing systems have unlimited video tracks and don't bother with nesting. Other systems use nesting to increase the number of video layers that can be composited because they limit the number of video tracks. Some editors use nesting as a management tool; others don't bother.

The Other DVE (Digital Video Effects)

This term is a misnomer. All the effects on your editing system are, of course, digital effects. The use of the acronym DVE reflects the point of view of video professionals who use digital equipment alongside their analog video systems. The transformation to digital video editing is nearly complete, but DVE persists. It refers loosely to the video effects devices editors once used to manipulate the video images. These proprietary devices, such as Ampex's ADO, have long since been retired to the museum of video technology. We fondly remember those outrageously expensive black boxes (think hundreds of thousands of dollars) that let us rearrange, transform, manipulate, and distort analog video. Today the same capabilities are available on your desktop for $100.

Picture in Picture

This term, which is used by editing system manufacturers, appears to be derived from marketing campaigns for television sets capable of displaying two channels at once—a small picture of a second channel overlaid on a corner of the first. This effect usually controls the scale, rotation, opacity, position, and shape of the full-frame video image. How and what you control depends on your editing system. These types of effects can offer two- or three-dimensional control over the image.

Size

The editor can manipulate the size of the image by expanding or shrinking it. The aspect ratio of an image can be maintained or changed. The technical terms for this are *scaling* and *resizing* the image (see Figure 9-8). If you want to control the height or width separately, then you'll need to manipulate the horizontal and vertical dimensions of the image, respectively. It's easy to get confused since the terms *horizontal* and *vertical* have multiple meanings. Horizontal can mean direction, as in left to right or up and down if you think in terms of raising or lowering a horizontal bar. Many editing systems treat horizontal and vertical as directions instead of following the technically correct approach—the way video images are scanned. For most editors, it makes more sense to think of vertical as the up-to-down direction and horizontal as the left-to-right direction. Another way of expressing these directions is to describe the vertical direction as the y axis and the horizontal direction as the x axis.

Figure 9-8
Resizing or scaling
the picture.

PICTURE SIZE: **100%**   PICTURE SIZE: **120%**   PICTURE SIZE: **60%**

Crop

This tool lets you cut the image, changing its height or width, without squeezing or expanding the image. Crop is useful for cleaning up the lines at the edges of the frame.

Perspective

A three-dimensional perspective isn't possible if your editing system can only manipulate the horizontal (x axis) and vertical (y axis) dimensions because that only adds up to two dimensions. The surface of the screen forms another plane (the z axis), which is the third dimension. If your editing system can manipulate the $x, y,$ and z axes of the image, you can create three-dimensional effects. In a two-dimensional system, an editor can create the illusion of depth by skewing the corners of the frame. This distortion of perspective under the right circumstances can fool the audience into thinking you've manipulated the image in three dimensions. (See Figure 9-9.) Other factors can help you add to the magic.

Position

Along with expansion and contraction, the image can be placed anywhere onscreen along the horizontal (x) or vertical (y) axes. The image can also be placed outside the visible screen area in the virtual space surrounding the

Figure 9-9
Manipulating the picture to create the illusion of perspective.

video frame. This space is useful for positioning images *off stage* and smoothing the beginning and/or end of a movement.

Motion and Rotation

Images can be rotated on the horizontal (x), vertical (y), or the front-to-back (z) axis in an editing system with three-dimensional capabilities. The rotation points can be moved (the default is dead center) and repositioned to produce spins, tumbles, orbits, flips, pinwheels, cartwheels, and dozens of other interesting movements. (See Figure 9-10.) For example, the effect, which turns a flat video image into a cylinder, involves manipulating the axis of rotation on the front-to-back (z) axis.

Images, text, graphics, and video can be moved fluidly across the screen using the motion tools in your editing system. When motion is combined with rotation to skew the image, it's possible to create effects that imitate a piece of paper floating or flying through the air.

To create movement, a screen object must have a starting point, finishing point, and a duration for the movement from beginning to end. The perceived motion occurs during the time it takes to travel from the starting point to the finish point (see Figure 9-11a through 9-11c). If you want the

Figure 9-10
X, Y, and Z axes.

Figure 9-11a
Rotating the image
on the X axis.

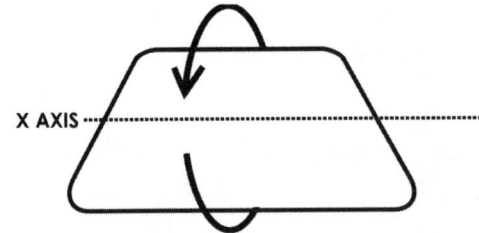

X AXIS

Figure 9-11b
Rotating the image
on the Y axis.

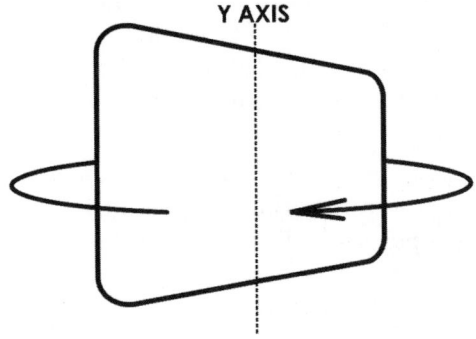

Y AXIS

Figure 9-11c
Rotating the image
on the Z axis.

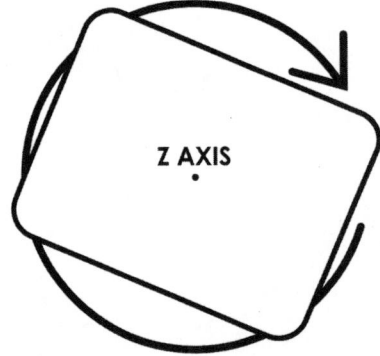

Z AXIS

movement to appear faster, the duration of the trip must be shortened because the distance traveled will remain the same. This is a simple concept. However, it takes a bit of practice before you get a feel for moving images over time.

Keyframe

In a digital environment, the most important tool for controlling actions involving the timing of movements is the keyframe. The keyframe is a point along the effects timeline where actions can be changed. Every action must have at least two keyframes: a starting point and ending point. Whenever a change is required in the movement of an image or any parameter associated with an image, such as a pause, angle, rotation, and so on, a keyframe must be added to trigger these changes. When the effect is played back, the movement will change at those keyframe or trigger points (see Figure 9-12).

Some of the parameters that can be changed as an effect moves through time include its shape, rotation, color, borders, size, direction, speed, position, angle, softness, sharpness, and much more. In short, just about anything that can be adjusted can be readjusted at periodic intervals during

Figure 9-12
An effects timeline with keyframes (the triangle points) at each point of change.

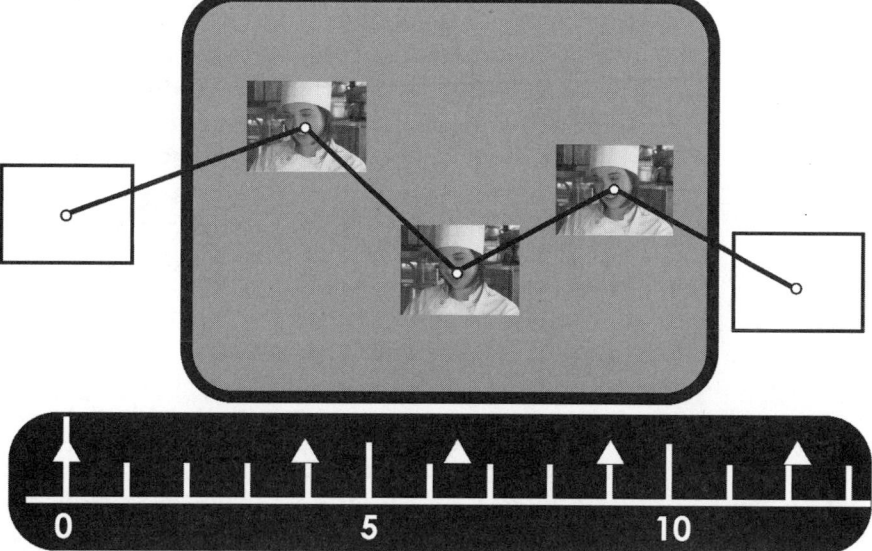

the time span an effect is onscreen. The keyframes represent these mile-stones along the path.

When the path of the movement is diagramed, the path takes on the appearance of a game of connect the dots. Each dot is a keyframe. This is called the effect's *motion path*. The motion path can begin outside the boundaries of the screen and move anywhere onscreen in x, y, and z space.

Movement along this path can be linear and abrupt or smooth. It's a creative decision whether the effect moves in crisp movements or flows smoothly. The list of creative possibilities is nearly endless. Here are a few of the factors that determine the smoothness of the effects path.

Start/Stop

The amount of acceleration determines whether an effect starts with a jolt or eases off. Acceleration determines whether the effect comes to an abrupt stop or eases in. Depending on the amount of acceleration, the movement of an effect from point A to point B can appear to be constant or gradually speed up or slow down.

Straight Line or Curved Path

The motion path of the effect can move in a direct linear fashion from point to point or in smooth arcs that flow from point to point. Smooth motion is more polished and gracious. An editor learning to move effects around the screen is similar to someone learning to ride a bicycle. At first, the turns seem difficult and scary. However, after practice, the bicycle rider's hard right and left turns become graceful sweeping arcs. Eventually, the rider achieves complete control and can make any turn possible. An editor learning effects should have the same goal: to achieve full control and be able to accomplish whatever he or she is asked to do.

Interpolation

Interpolation is the manner of adjustment to the motion made over time. If the motion path for a digital picture-in-picture effect involves multiple keyframes so the object can change direction, a decision has to be made about the qualities of the route the object takes. A linear route with no braking for changes in direction will appear abrupt. A curved route with braking at each change in direction will appear smooth. The amount of braking and speed is controlled by the amount of interpolation taking place between the keyframes. If a lot of interpolation is taking place, the corners are more rounded because all of the points between the keyframes are estimated and averaged. With practice, exploration, and experimentation, you'll learn to easily control motion paths.

Organize Your Effects

Create bins for your effects and clips with effects applied. The elements you produce in the course of building effects can and should be saved. The rules are the same for any clip. Use unique names for each subclip. The ability to find titles, effects, keys, layers, and a dozen different treatments of the same shot depends on how accurately you named them.

Digital systems permit an unlimited amount of duplicate clips. When you're experimenting with various looks and treatments, you'll want to save the parameters or preferences for the effect. Editing system manufacturers have varied approaches to saving this useful information. Refer to your editing system manual to see how it works in your system. .

Here are some suggestions for bins to organize your work:

Graphics	Titles	Motion effected clips
Effects backgrounds	Mattes	Tinted clips
Imported effects	Animated mattes	

We're sure you'll figure out dozens of bins once you get started.

Summary

We have learned some fundamental lessons about working with keyframes over the years:

- *Fewer keyframes are better.* Effects need two keyframes to start, as mentioned previously. However, add more keyframes sparingly. Experiment with one. Pay attention to how just one interruption in the motion path of an effect can have a significant impact. Change it, add another, and watch again. Beware of trying to overcontrol the events along the path. The editing system will transform the path into a curve without you trying to force changes. Beginners have a tendency to add multiple points along the path in order to get the flow they want. Not only is this unnecessary, but more keyframes will give you less control because you will have more interference.

- *Keyframes can be copied and pasted.* There's no better technique for getting the results you want than copying and pasting the parameters of a keyframe from one spot to another. Why should you create everything from scratch? Work smarter, not harder.

- *Use the Wire-Frame Preview.* A wire-frame preview can usually display the motion path of the effect accurately. Use it to avoid rendering. Remember that if you're trying to check the motion path and make adjustments, the wire-frame view is fine.

- *Use the Single-Frame Preview.* Step through the effect by jogging frame by frame or by skipping ahead 10 frames at a time for longer effects. Step through each keyframe to verify any changes. Only render the effect when you have everything the way you want it.

- *Resize and blur are huge memory hogs.* These two effects take the longest time to preview and render. Rebuilding all those pixels takes a tremendous amount of interpolation and processing power. If you want to resize or blur a graphic, don't put in the maximum number value for the effect. Put in the values that the effect requires—no more, no less. If you put more, you just give your editing system more to think about. If you put in less, you compromise the integrity of the effect.

- *Learn how your editing system handles rendering.* There could be some tricks you could learn to improve the speed and efficiency of the system. For example, render every other effect on the timeline. Pay attention to what effects, if any, can be played back in real time. Then calculate the amount of time required to render similar-looking effects. One version may be considerably faster than another.

- *A little movement goes a long way.* Static pictures on the screen can be enhanced with small position changes. If the clip is on the screen for a few seconds, then its movement can be short and subtle. Professionals know that small changes are often more interesting.

Getting It In and Out

We Waited as Long as We Could

This is the most technical chapter in this book. If technical information isn't your forte, only read the sections such as monitoring that are important for setting up your system. Then, wait until you're about to do a procedure, such as importing a graphic or making a DVD, to read those sections. Use this chapter as a reference to supplement what appears in your editing system manual. Most manuals explain the process of getting things in and out of a digital editing system in great detail. We don't want or need to get that specific. Instead, this chapter provides the basics so you can understand the big picture and avoid any pitfalls.

Most of the progress being made in digital editing involves turning procedures that were once difficult, complicated, and highly technical into simple actions such as pressing play and record. Hopefully, some of the procedures mentioned in this chapter will be even easier to do when you get ready to do them.

What Goes In?

A digital editing system is useless unless you can move material in and out of the system. The vast majority of what you edit *digitial video* enters and exits the editing system through a Firewire, *serial digital interface* (SDI), or *high-definition SDI* (HD-SDI) cable. Unfortunately, different formats and variations within the formats often make the process of getting video in and out more complicated than it should be. Writing this book would be easier if only one format was available.

Other materials (for example, photographs, illustrations, music, and sound effects) also need to move in and out of your system. You could shoot the still images or record the music and sound effects with a digital camcorder and transfer that recording into your system along with all of your other footage. However, most of the time that's not practical. If those materials already exist in a digital format, it should be easy to get them into your editing system. We wish it were as simple as it sounds.

What Goes Out?

After you've finished editing, you'll need to get your show out of the editing system—unless, of course, you plan to invite people over to see your show and sit them down in front of the editing system to watch it. In that case, your show is finished. Otherwise, you'll need to output your show in a form that can be played elsewhere.

You may decide to record and store the show on an object you can hold in your hand, such as a CD, DVD, or videotape. You might also let people see your show on the Internet where it can reside as a file for download or as a streaming video.

Some shows might not be finished. You might need better compositing, audio-sweetening, or finishing tools than the ones available on your system. In this case, you'll need to export the information in your timeline for someone else to use. Whether you're going to a sophisticated audio editing system down the hall or to a postproduction facility in another city, your finished timeline and/or media files must be saved in a format that another system can use. This is yet another way of getting what you've done out. We'll try to cover all these topics as simply as we can.

Why Is Monitoring Important?

One of the challenges of digital video editing is consistency. It's absolutely necessary that what you see and hear on your editing system matches what anyone will see and hear elsewhere. Imagine the havoc that would ensue if you created a color effect that looks blue on your system, but appears pink when played elsewhere. You're probably saying to yourself, "Hey, everything is digital. There's no way this could happen." You'd be wrong. Let's find out why.

Digital information remains consistent when you duplicate it. Copy a digital media file 100 times. Each copy contains the identical information. Unfortunately, this has nothing to do with how you see or hear the contents of the media file. Editors don't look at the ones and zeros in a file; they evaluate material on video monitors and speakers.

The images displayed on your editing system's computer monitor are only approximations and should not be used to judge the quality of the video picture. This is why your editing system should include a video monitor. The same rule applies for audio. The tiny speaker found in most computers is only there to provide some audio feedback (beeps and clicks) while you work. Audio should be evaluated using quality speakers or headphones since the audio in your editing suite must match the audio when the show is played elsewhere.

Other issues make monitoring difficult. No two people see color identically. We rely on our eyes and brains, which are unique. Thankfully, the differences in how people see color are very subtle unless the person happens to be colorblind (8 percent of men and 1 percent of women have some form of colorblindness). Our eyes aren't the principal problem. What gets everyone into trouble is that monitors, for computers or television, have controls. The *if-there's-a-knob-they'll-turn-it* rule predominates. It's easy to adjust or misadjust the picture. Monitors typically have controls for brightness, contrast, hue, and saturation. With four control knobs, there is a slim possibility that the monitor is set correctly and a nearly infinite possibility that it's set incorrectly.

Monitoring Video

A video evaluation monitor is an essential tool in professional editing suites. These monitors have special controls, reproduce colors more accurately, and display more detail than ordinary monitors or television sets. These higher-quality monitors are more expensive. However, an evaluation monitor is the only way to be sure that the picture you see matches what others will see elsewhere. A high-quality television set is an adequate substitute for home use. The challenge is that television sets are designed to show a pleasing rendition rather than an accurate picture.

Every monitor should be adjusted using a standardized signal. The SMPTE color bar signal is the standardized signal used for standard definition video signals. (See Figure 10-1.) This signal can be output by professional cameras and some prosumer cameras. Editing systems that are designed for professional use can generate SMPTE color bars and other test signals. Home users with cable or satellite television access should be able

Figure 10-1
SMPTE color bars.

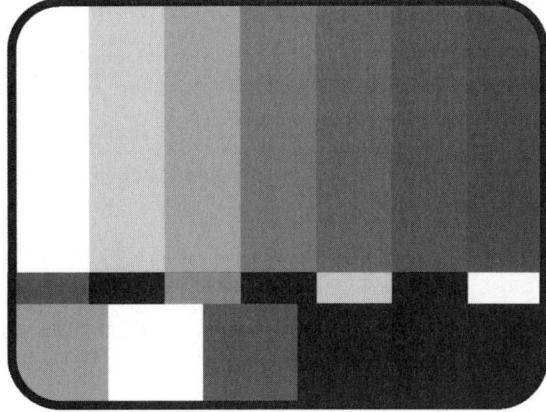

to find a channel that displays a color bar signal for at least part of the day. The CD included in this book has a 5-second clip of SMPTE color bars with a 1 kHz audio signal in case your editing system doesn't generate these test signals. Web sites, such as www.whizkidtech.net/monitor, offer a graphic representation of the color bar signal that you can use to set up a computer monitor.

How to Set Up a Video Monitor

The process of setting up a video monitor should take under 5 minutes. If you find yourself staring at the screen and adjusting the colors for longer than that, you'll need to clear your eyes before you continue. You're probably aware that if you continually smell a strong scent, after several minutes you can't smell it at all. The same is true for our eyes. After a few minutes of looking at strong colors, no one can accurately judge color. The solution is to look at a white or gray wall for a few minutes or go and take a break.

Here are several methods that can be used to set up a video monitor. The quick-and-dirty approaches work well enough and produce good results. They even work with all the television sets in your house. However, for accurate results that you can rely on, follow the professional approach.

Five-Step Quick-and-Dirty Approach

1. Let the monitor or television warm up for 10 minutes.
2. Turn all the color (chroma) off. Turn the sound off.
3. Use the brightness and contrast controls to make the blacks black and the whites white.
4. Turn the color (chroma) back on. Turn up the level of saturation to suit your taste.
5. Adjust the flesh tones with the hue (tint) control. A shot of a network news anchor is the best quick-and-dirty reference for accurate flesh tones.

Two-Step Quick-and-Dirty Approach If Your Camcorder Can Generate Color Bars

1. Connect the monitor to the camera and let it warm up for 10 minutes.
2. Use the hue (tint) control to make the yellow bar as yellow as possible.

The Professional Approach

These steps involve adjusting the brightness, contrast, hue (phase), and color (chroma) controls on your monitor. If you have a consumer television, you'll need a deep blue filter or gel to accurately adjust the hue and color. Professional monitors can turn off the blue gun to adjust these controls. The least expensive way to get a blue filter is to pick up a free sample swatch book of lighting gels at a professional film, photography, or video supply store. A deep pure blue (such as Roscolux 83 or Rosco CalColor 90 Blue #a4290 or Lee #a713 Winter Blue or Kodak Wratten 39 or 47) will do fine. Follow these steps:

1. Allow the monitor to warm up for about 10 minutes before you begin making any adjustments.
2. Display an SMPTE color bar signal on the monitor. You'll see three bands of colors. The top band is composed of seven vertical bars, which are (going from left to right) light gray, yellow, cyan, green, magenta, red, and blue. The middle band contains the same colors, but they are

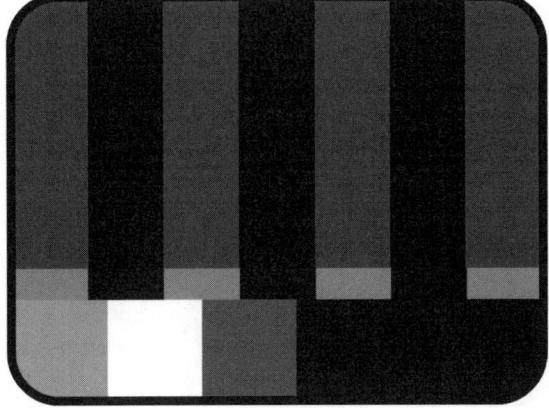

Figure 10-2
SMPTE color bars
seen through a
blue filter.

reversed with every other bar set to black. The bottom band has a
white (the *I*) bar, a black (the *Q*) bar, and a PLUGE signal. The PLUGE
(Picture Line Up Generation Equipment) consists of three thin black
bars that are used to set monitor brightness: a superblack bar, which is
blacker than black, a black bar, and a whiter than black bar, which is
very dark gray (see Figure 10-3).

3. Adjust the color or chroma control so the picture is almost black and
   white.

4. The PLUGE is on the bottom band at the far right. Adjust the
   brightness control until there's no visible difference between the
   superblack and black bars. If it's correctly adjusted, there will be a
   barely visible difference between those two bars and the whiter than
   black bar.

5. Adjust the contrast so the white bar on the bottom band appears bright
   white.

   A technical note: If the gray bars on your monitor have a blue, green, or
   pink tint when the color is turned completely off, your monitor is in
   need of service.

6. Look at the monitor through the blue filter or press the blue-only
   switch.

7. Adjust the color or chroma control to its midpoint.

8. Adjust the hue (tint) or phase control until you see four blue bars
   separated by three black bars.

Figure 10-3
Lower right corner of
the SMPTE color bar
signal enlarged to
show the PLUGE.

9. Adjust the color or chroma control until the two outer blue bars in the top and middle bands match.

10. Fine tune the hue (tint) or phase control by making a slight adjustment so the middle two blue bars in the top and middle bands match.

11. Your monitor or television set is now properly adjusted. Turn off the blue-only switch.

Monitoring Audio

What's necessary for judging audio quality is tough to find in an edit suite. Ideally, you'll have the highest-fidelity speakers (ones that are capable of reproducing the entire audio spectrum) and a perfectly quiet room. Most editing systems aren't located in rooms designed for audio. In fact, most editing suites are filled with the worst kind of noise (such as whirring fans, hard-drive noises, and other ambient sounds from editing systems and video recorders) at a volume just loud enough to hide the subtleties of your show's audio tracks. In contrast, audio suites are carefully designed with sound-absorbing and sound reflecting materials to create an environment in which audio quality can be accurately judged. The sound quality is evaluated by listening in close proximity to expensive reference speakers designed especially for this purpose.

So what can you do? The simplest solution is to buy the most expensive closed headphones you can afford. Closed headphones block out any outside sounds. If you plan to buy good-quality powered speakers to use with your editing system, select ones that have a front-mounted headphone jack. That way you can easily connect headphones whenever you need to critically listen to the audio. Headphones also solve another problem for home users. To hear every nuance, you need to increase the volume. With headphones, you can make it as loud as necessary without disturbing others.

As much of the noisy equipment as possible should be moved into an adjacent room for a professional editing suite. If that will not work, the equipment should be surrounded by sound-absorbing materials to soak up as much machine noise as possible. Purchase excellent reference speakers. A good amplifier, mixer, and headphones are also necessities. Be aware of how the room colors the audio and use headphones for critical evaluations.

Ins and Outs

The first rule of getting material in or out of your editing system—the rule that will save you an enormous amount of time—is that you must understand what is needed at the destination. If your editing system only accepts DV video using Firewire, then you need a recorder with a Firewire connection. If you're trying to import a graphic, you need to know which file formats are supported. Use the Help feature or look in your manual to figure out which ones will work on your editing system. Check before you create and save the image. It's very frustrating and a waste of time to try to import a file format that your editing system cannot handle.

If the final audio mix will be done at a separate facility, find out what they'll need to do the job. Write down the exact requirements so you can determine whether your editing system can export files in the format that meets their needs. If it doesn't, you may need to figure out a solution. This could include finding a different facility that's more compatible with what your system can deliver or perhaps buying software that can convert your format.

Does this sounds like simple common sense? Absolutely correct. However, with dozens of formats, aspect ratios, sample rates, resolutions, file types, codecs, and standards, it's easy to get confused. Therefore, the first thing you should do whether you're attempting to get materials into your editing system or out of your editing system is to figure out what is required on the other end. Look for the formats that match what your editing system can output and what the other system is capable of inputting or vice versa.

The devil is in the details. Importing and exporting, transferring video, and outputting the show are complex operations. You might have to set a dozen parameters. When in doubt, use the default settings. Unless you have a reason to change, leave the settings alone. Don't make life more complicated than necessary.

The distinction between output and export is blurry. Editing systems designed to digitize analog video use the word *output* to describe printing a completed show to tape and use the word *export* to describe the process of copying or converting media files for use on another editing system. In an all-digital environment, the editing system is always copying or converting files. In the context of this chapter, if a data stream is available on your editing system when you play the timeline, the word *output* should be used. For example, DV is available via the Firewire cable whenever you play the timeline. If you do not have a spigot putting out a streaming video format, obtaining one falls into the export category.

Compression and Digital Formats

What's a Codec?

The term *codec* appears whenever DV is discussed. Codec is a contraction of the words *compression* and *decompression*. It is used to describe the software extensions that manufacturers develop for the standards used in digital editing and for Internet applications. These extensions are developed to support the transfer, viewing, and output of digital video with their hardware or software products. Most DV editing systems wrap the data from the DV tape into a QuickTime or AVI file to store, display, and edit DV on a computer. A codec makes this possible.

Video capture boards that transform analog video into digital files use a codec to digitize and/or compress the audio and video signals. Codecs are evaluated for quality by comparing the image quality at various levels of compression. Highly compressed video requires less storage space. The tradeoff is that image quality goes down as it becomes more highly compressed.

Timesavers for Exporting Digital Media

- Every clip in your timeline must be available. The media files for each clip must be stored on your editing system's drives otherwise, the export will fail.

- Anything that must be rendered in a timeline should be rendered before you export the timeline.

- Check to make sure every clip in the timeline has the same audio sample rate and video resolution. Mixed sample rates or resolutions will halt the export process.

- The pan and volume levels on the audio tracks should be set as you want them for the export. For example, if you want the export to have a mono, split, stereo mix, 5.1 surround, or any other arrangement, the timeline must be set to play that type of mix. If you're exporting audio files for further mixing on a digital audio workstation, all the tracks you want to include in the mix should be active.

- Review your editing system manual for tips on how to speed up the export process. For example, recapturing the clips in the timeline reduces the size of the associated media files because only the portion of the media in use is recaptured. In some systems, this makes exports significantly faster.

- Always perform a test first. Export a small section of your timeline before attempting to export the entire show. Check the test to make sure it works as expected. If you can, double-check the test by copying it to another computer to make sure it works everywhere.

- Exporting an entire show can be a lengthy process. Conversions from one video or audio format to another format (such as DV to MPEG or DV to AIFF-C audio) take an enormous amount of time.

- Think ahead. Schedule or start an export before you go to lunch, dinner, or home for the night. The process takes time, often uses all the available resources of your editing system, and prevents you from doing anything else. Once the export is launched, you're locked out.

What's DV?

The DV tape format is an international standard developed jointly by a group of 10 companies. The tape is ¼ inch in width. Pictures and sounds are recorded in a digital format that has been compressed at a 5:1 ratio. The image size is 720×480 pixels. The picture information is sampled at 720 pixels per scanline. This sample rate is also used in professional video formats such as D-1, D-5, and Digital Betacam. The luminance is sampled four times as often as the color difference signals. In technical terms, DV uses 4:1:1 color sampling in North America (NTSC). In Europe (PAL), DV uses 4:2:0 color sampling.

What's IEEE-1394 and OHCI?

IEEE-1394, which is also called Apple Firewire or Sony iLink, is a hardware and software standard for transporting data at 100, 200, 300, or 400 megabits per second (Mbps). This is a digital interface so nothing gets lost when the data is transferred from one place to another. Apple developed the original standard.

Today, most IEEE-1394 interface cards use the *Open Host Controller Interface* (OHCI). The OHCI specification standardizes how the Windows operating system interacts with the 1394 bus. The 1394 bus moves digital information into the computer.

What's the DV Codec?

The Mac and Windows operating systems provide DV codecs for their respective operating systems. Despite the presence of generic versions, editing system manufacturers provide their own proprietary DV codec. If your editing system is connected to a DV camcorder or recorder through an IEEE-1394 cable, the codec is unimportant. No compression or decompression happens. You're just doing a data transfer; nothing goes through the codec.

However, the codec has other purposes. The appearance of DV on your computer (both the image quality and motion reproduction) depends on the codec. The codec is involved whenever transitions, titles, or effects have to be rendered. Visible quality differences do exist. The differences are most noticeable when a previously rendered file is used as a video source in an effect and is then rerendered and output back to DV tape. Most people can't see any differences between the codecs until the video image is projected on a large screen. Then even the untrained eye can spot the differences between a poor codec and an excellent one.

What's an Encoder?

Encoding is the process of converting information from one format to another. Encoding happens in your camcorder when the pictures and sounds are recorded in the DV format. The camcorder has a hardware encoder that converts the information captured by the CCDs[1] and microphone into the compressed (5:1) DV format that is recorded on the tape.

An encoder is any hardware or software that converts video or audio signals or digital files into a specific format. Encoders use algorithms to compress the data. Some hardware encoders can input analog video and output it as DV so you can edit with a digital editing system. These *bridges* between analog sources and DV or between analog and SDI use an encoder to convert the information. An encoder is involved when you convert the media files stored on your editing system to MPEG-2 or export a timeline in a streaming video format. Digital editing systems typically use a software encoder to convert from the editing system's native format (typically QuickTime or AVI files) to the formats used on CDs, DVDs, and the Internet.

Videotape for Input and Output

You should check the following things before you try to get material into or out of your editing system using videotape.

---

[1]CCD is a light-sensitive device (charge-coupled device) that converts light passing through the camera's lens into digital data.

Is the Editing System Capable of Handling the Videotape Format You Want to Edit?

You must have a recorder that can play the tape. The recorder must be connected via Firewire, SDI, or HD-SDI to the digital video editing system. If the tape was originally recorded with a NTSC camcorder (the standard used in North America), the recorder must be able to play an NTSC tape. Conversely, a PAL (the standard used in Europe) tape must be played back on a PAL recorder. If the tape and recorder have analog connections, you might need a bridge to convert analog signals to a digital format that the system can accept. See Appendix B, "Resources," for companies that make these devices.

Do the Project or Timeline Settings Match the Material You Plan to Edit?

Most digital editing systems can be set to edit in NTSC or PAL. The setting must match the standard used to record the tape. The frame size and pixel aspect ratio (nonsquare except for HD) of the source must match the settings in your project or timeline. Some systems are resolution independent. This means that they can edit any frame size of video from 640×480 analog to the largest HD format 1,920×1,080. Others are capable of handling only a single format, such as, the 720×480 DV format.

Be sure the aspect ratio matches how the video was recorded. There are three possibilities: 4:3, 16:9, or 16:9 electronically squeezed DV.

Make sure the frame rate of the videotape matches the project settings for the timeline's time database. NTSC is 29.97 *frames per second* (fps). PAL is 25 fps. HD video can be 23.98, 24, 25, 29.97, 30, 59.97, or 60 fps. This is very important if you plan to export an *edit decision list* (EDL) in order to conform a film or finish a video project at another post facility.

The sample rate used to record the audio should match your project or timeline settings. Most systems automatically resample audio if it differs from the preset sample rate. Converting from a 32 kHz sample rate to a 48 kHz sample rate may dramatically distort the sound. See the Ins and Outs of Audio section for more information.

Getting the Finished Show on Tape

The process of getting your finished show back on videotape will be straightforward if you use the same tape format that you originally used to input the material. If you're using a different format, you may need to check the output settings in your editing system. Here are two methods you can use to output your show to tape.

The Quick-and-Dirty Method

1. Every show should fade up from black. If your show does not do this, insert a few seconds of black and add a fade up.

2. Make sure your timeline will play without any hesitations or pauses. If anything needs to be rendered, render it. If you still have trouble getting the timeline to play smoothly, you might need to move some media files to a different drive or defrag your editing system's storage drives. Check the troubleshooting section of your manual.

3. Make sure the timeline cursor is parked at the start of your show.

4. Place a blank or blacked tape in the recorder. A blacked tape is better for the reasons outlined in the print-to-tape method.

5. Make sure the recorder is properly connected to the editing system.

6. Press Play and Record on the videotape recorder or camcorder to begin recording.

7. Wait 10 seconds and then press Play on your editing system so the timeline begins to play.

8. Stop the recorder 30 seconds after the timeline has finished playing.

The Print-to-Tape Method

1. Prepare a blacked (also called *prestriped*) tape by recording a black signal (on a camcorder, leave the lens cap on and disconnect or turn off the microphone) and time code on the tape.

2. Every show should fade up from black. Insert a few seconds of black and add a fade up if it isn't already in your show.

3. Make sure your timeline will play without any hesitations or pauses. If anything needs to be rendered, render it. If you still have trouble getting the timeline to play smoothly, you might need to move some media files to a different drive or defrag your editing system's storage drives. Check the troubleshooting section of your manual.

4. Place the blacked tape in the recorder.

5. Make sure the recorder is properly connected to the editing system and that the deck control settings are correct. If the connection is via IEEE-1394, the deck control settings should indicate IEEE-1394.

6. Set up a leader. Some editing systems automate the process of creating a leader or header that appears on the tape before your finished show. If your system doesn't have this feature, use your editing system's text or title tool to make a slate. Edit the slate into the timeline before your finished show.

The purpose of the slate is twofold: to identify the contents and move the show (the valuable information) farther away from the head of the tape. The head and tail of a videotape have the highest dropout rates. These sections of the tape are also prone to damage from the recorder in the natural course of playing the tape.

We suggest:

- The first time you record on a new tape, record 30 seconds of SMPTE color bars and tone at the head. If you're adding another show to a master that has the bars and tone at the head, this is not necessary.

Figure 10-4
A slate recorded at the head of the tape before the show.

Date:
Title:
TRT:
Audio: Ch1&Ch 2 mixed
Director:
Editor:

- Follow the bars and tone with 30 seconds of black. Use 20 seconds if you're just separating shows on a master tape.

- Create a slate with the Production Date, Title, *Total Running Time* (TRT), Audio track (track 1 and 2, 1, 2, 3, 4, and so on), Mix information (mono on 1 and 2, mono on 1, music and effects on 2, stereo on 1 and 2, 5.1 surround, and so on), and any authorship information you want to include (the director, editor, or production company).

- Include an address and phone number on the slate if you're sending the tape out for duplication or broadcast. This way if problems do arise, it's easy to get in contact with you or someone at the facility that edited the show. This also helps if the label falls off or the box is lost.

7. Preview the leader and double-check to make sure the recorder is getting a signal. Editing systems that can create a leader usually have a preview function so you can see it before you record it.

8. Do a test recording. Press Print to Tape and Record for a few minutes. Play back the recording to make sure everything works correctly. If you're working with a professional recorder, check to make sure all the levels are set correctly.

9. Print to tape. Label the videotape with the title of the show and indicate that the tape is a MASTER.

10. Make protection masters. You should always make a backup copy of any valuable master. This is especially true if you send one to a client or duplication facility. People lose things. You don't want to have to recreate all the work that went into a show.

Ins and Outs of Audio

Audiences will not accept poor quality sound. This section is a guide to moving audio in and out of your editing system.

Single or Double?

Analog and digital video production usually follows a single-system approach to sound. This is when audio is recorded along with video on the

Labeling and Protecting Masters

Digital editing has changed the concept of a master. Every master is the same. No generation loss occurs because a copy of a digital tape is an exact duplicate as long as you use a digital connection. However, it's still useful to label tapes.

The videotape master of your show should be labeled *ASHOW* MASTER@ or *AEDIT* MASTER@. Any copies of that master should be labeled accordingly such as—EDIT MASTER COPY (or CLONE). The master you send to a duplication facility should be labeled *ADUB* MASTER. Dub is short for *dubbing*, which means to duplicate a videotape. The master you send to the client should be labeled *ACLIENT* MASTER. Use the MASTER stickers that come with the videotape. That's what they're there for. Never use the MASTER sticker on original source footage tapes—you don't want to confuse what some people call *camera masters* with a finished SHOW MASTER.

It also helps to date the tapes in case changes are required later. Nothing is more frustrating than having three masters with the same title and no dates as you try to determine which one is the latest version of the show your client wants to duplicate.

Make sure the tab is set to prevent erasure on your master tapes! Accidents happen when you don't pay attention.

videotape. The audio tracks are always in sync with the video. Audio is sampled at different rates than video and the data is stored uncompressed. The amount of audio information is small in comparison to video so you don't need to compress it. Audio and video are transferred together into a digital editing system if a digital connection such as Firewire, SDI, or HD-SDI is used.

Audio Sample Rates

The sample rate at which the audio is recorded is one of the major factors that determine sound quality. The higher the sample rate, the more potential there is for an accurate reproduction of the full audio spectrum. When we refer to the *full spectrum*, we're talking about everything within the range of human hearing. The sound that dogs and cats can hear is unimportant to an editor. The sample rates common in digital video production

Double-System Sound

At times, a double-system approach makes sense. It's the standard approach when shooting film or HD at 24 fps. The double-system refers to the fact that the audio is recorded separately using an audio recorder that runs at a constant speed. The audio recording is synced to the picture by the editor. This is also known as *resolving the sound*. This works because a visual and audio cue is recorded simultaneously by the camera and audio recorder. The clapper or time code slate makes it easy for the editor to resolve the sound to the picture.

Figure 10-5
Time code slate.

The advantage of the double-system approach is that the sound recordist doesn't have to be tethered to the camera. Audio recorders offer better control and higher-quality sound reproduction than what's found on most video recorders. In addition, the recording is on a separate tape, which means that if one or the other is damaged, you'll still have either picture or sound. The disadvantage is that it requires a lot of extra work just to get the sound back in sync with the picture. You have to manage twice as many tapes. You also need extra equipment and personnel during production.

The argument about which approach is better has been going on for years. We won't settle this argument, but will say that the single-system approach is fine for most people. More important is to use a professional microphone instead of the one that comes with the camcorder if you want excellent sound quality.

are 32, 44, 48, and 96 kHz. The bit depth (8, 12, or 16 bits) is indicated alongside of the sample rate.

The DV tape format can record 2 tracks of audio at the 48 kHz (16-bit) rate or 4 tracks of audio at the 32 kHz (12-bit) rate. Most consumer DV camcorders can only record 2 tracks at 48 kHz. A few can record two or four tracks.

Production Tip

Shoot everything for a project at one audio sample rate. You can't mix material with different audio sample rates on the same timeline in many editing systems. Resampling the audio from 48 to 32 kHz or 32 to 48 kHz can introduce distortion. Pick a rate and stick with it.

The 44 kHz rate is used for audio CDs. Professional *digital audiotape* (DAT) recorders use either the 44 or 48 kHz sample rate. Multitrack audio recorders that are used in professional studios for mastering music albums use the 96 kHz sample rate. You probably think that everything has been sorted out on the audio recording side since it's been around nearly twice as long as video recording. Think again. It's just as arcane and has almost as much potential for confusion.

The Gist of It . . .

Audio quality is better when sampled at a higher rate. However, human speech falls into a very narrow band of the audio spectrum. It's easy to record, and any of the sample rates we've mentioned are more than adequate to accomplish the task. The wider the gap between sample rates, the more likely distortion will occur when you down- or up-sample audio.

Exchanging Audio Files

There are many reasons to move audio files in and out of your editing system. It's rare for all of the sound elements in a show to arrive on videotape. Music and sound effects come on CDs or DAT tape. Stock music and sound-effect libraries sell CDs and digital audio clips on the Internet. Sound studios are also connected to the Internet. The voice-over narration for a show can be done wherever the voice actor resides. Digital audio files from a recording session are small enough to be sent via e-mail or downloaded from the studio's web site using FTP (*file transfer protocol*) software.

After you finish editing, you may need to send the audio tracks to an audio-sweetening facility for additional sound work. If the music for the show will be composed after editing is completed, the composer will need all the tracks (picture and sound) to create music that fits the show. After the composer writes and records the music, it will come back to you in the form of a digital audio file that you'll need to insert into the timeline.

Several file formats are commonly used to exchange digital audio data: the *Audio Interchange File Format* (AIFF-C) developed by Apple Computer, the WAVE format developed by IBM and Microsoft Corporation, the *Open Media Framework™ Interchange* format (OMFI) format developed by Avid Technology, and the MP3 (MPEG-1 Audio Layer-3) format developed by the Motion Picture Experts Group.

AIFF-C

AIFF-C stores uncompressed or compressed digital audio data. AIFF-C supports a variety of bit resolutions, sample rates, and one or two channels. It is widely used on Mac platforms to exchange files. Apple originally designed the format for that purpose. However, files with an .aif extension are also used on the Windows platform.

The AIFF-C format doesn't support time code. If you export the audio on a timeline as an AIFF-C file, the information is stored in a single file. All of the edit points are lost. This file format doesn't support handles so only the audio on the timeline is included in the exported file.

The lack of extra media on both sides of an audio clip can make it difficult or impossible for an audio-sweetening facility to do dissolves or cross fades. You can work around this by adding handles to the audio clips on the timeline before you export the file. Of course, you'll also need to send a copy of the show as it stands so the facility can differentiate between handles and show audio.

WAVE

The WAVE file format has become a standard on the Windows platform. The .wav extension identifies these files. This is an uncompressed format so the file sizes are often quite large. Beyond the digitally sampled waveform, these files contain information about the number of channels (mono or stereo), sample rate, and bit depth of the recording. WAVE files provide high-quality sound.

MP3

The MP3 format compresses files in WAVE format to approximately one-twelfth of their original size and preserves the original sound quality. The Motion Picture Experts Group developed an algorithm that applies more compression to the sounds most people cannot hear. Creating MP3 files from audio CDs is easy. MP3s have near-CD sound quality and have become the most preferred file exchange format on the Internet.

OFMI

The OMFI format was developed by Avid Technology for digital video production purposes. An OMFI audio file contains the audio media, time code for each clip's in and out points, track separations, transitions, motion effects, sample rate, bit depth, video frame rate, and pan and level information. The file contains all this information, but what actually carries over to another system depends on the capabilities of that digital audio workstation or digital video editing system.

Tips for Exporting Audio Tracks for Sweetening

- Determine which file format will work before you export.
- Place each voice or sound element (such as the music, effects, room tone, or ambience) on its own track.
- Remove any filters or equalization.
- Make sure all the timeline tracks to be exported are active.
- Set all volume levels to 0 *decibels* (dB).
- Set the pan controls in the middle.
- Set the appropriate sample rate and bit depth.
- If plan to do cross fades and dissolves, make sure you have enough handles (extra media).
- If you are using AIFF-C, insert a one-frame sync beep at the beginning and end of every track.
- If you are using OMFI, embedded audio can be in the WAVE or AIFF-C format. Make the appropriate choice.

Exporting Media Files

OMFI

OMFI is a platform-independent format that can store the information contained in a timeline and the digital media associated with that timeline. It doesn't matter if an OMFI file is exported on a Windows platform or imported into an application running on a Mac platform. Any application that supports OFMI will be able to import an OMFI file.

You have the choice to embed or link to digital media files during an OMFI export. The media should be embedded (stored in the file) whenever you export files for use elsewhere. You have the choice to embed audio only, video only, or both audio and video media. The link to selection (composition-only export) is useful if you only need to export the information about the timeline. Or, when the person receiving the OMFI file has the same access to the digital media files as you do. This might be true if you're working in a networked environment. An OFMI composition-only export is a much smaller file; no digital media is attached.

QuickTime and AVI

Most editing systems use either the QuickTime or AVI format for editing video. Professional programs can export in either format. Consumer products are often more limited. A QuickTime-based editing system typically exports only QuickTime files, and AVI-based editing systems typically only export AVI files.

QuickTime is available for the Mac and Windows platforms. The AVI format is used on the Windows platform. However, the general options are the same when you export. The first consideration is how big can the file be? The higher the video quality, the larger the file size will be.

The factors that determine the overall quality include the frame size, frame rate, image quality, audio format, and compression codec. Typically, you can decide to export audio only, video only, or audio and video. The frame size can be full or a percentage of full. The frame rate can be anywhere from 29.97 fps on down. The image quality depends on whether you decide to compress the file and how much it is compressed. Your choice of compression codec also has an impact. Every manufacturer provides its own codecs and most include others such as the Cinepak and Sorenson codecs. Specialized applications, such as Discreet's Cleaner or Canopus' ProCoder, can export multiple file formats using a variety of codecs.

Exchanging Information with Other Systems

Every editing system gathers information and builds a database. Some systems make it quite easy to import information from other applications and to exchange information with other applications. Consumer editing systems often have limited capabilities in this regard. However, most consumers don't need these professional features.

You might want to import information such as a log or timeline. Log files are used to create a batch transfer list. A timeline file is useful in three situations: if you need to reedit a show you made, if you need to change or enhance a show that someone did elsewhere on the same type of system, or if you need to change or enhance a show made on another type of editing system.

Logs

The automatic scene detection function found in some digital editing systems is not a substitute for a good log. On the other hand, paper logs don't save time if you have to type in time code numbers to transfer footage into your editing system. Specialized logging applications let you view your footage, mark time code INs and OUTs, and output a list of selected scenes, takes, or shots for batch transfer into your editing system. A typical log file may include the clip name, IN and OUT points, video and audio track information, audio sample rates, and, most important, your notes about each scene, take, or shot. Some editing systems can import a properly prepared spreadsheet or word processing file and build a batch transfer list.

Check your editing system manual for information about importing log files. Some editing systems provide logging applications that will run on any computer. Some editing system manuals provide instructions on how to create log files that are compatible with the system using a word processing application. Some logging applications can output log files in a variety of formats.

Edit Decision Lists (EDLs)

An EDL is a list (in table form) of instructions that are used to create a show in a linear video editing environment. The EDL is the oldest method of information exchange in the video realm. The list includes time code in and out points for the source and record machines. It can also include cuts, wipes, dissolves, and fades. CMX Corporation developed the EDL about 30 years ago as a way of saving the decisions an editor made in case he or she wanted to roll back the master and redo an earlier edit.

EDLs were designed for edit controllers that operated videotape machines. Over the years, different formats were developed by edit controller manufacturers including the Grass Valley Group and Sony Corporation. However, years after the company's demise, the CMX_3600 version of the EDL format is still the mostly widely used format.

The list begins with a header that indicates the title and type of time code (drop or nondrop) to be used in the list of events. Every entry in the list is considered to be an event and has an event number. Because this is linear video editing, each event must be performed in the order in which it appears in the list.

The reel name of the videotape that should be in the source player for a particular event appears in the second column from the left. The reel name in CMX format can be three numbers or letters. *AX* is used to signify an auxiliary source such as a switcher or character generator. *BL* is used for black.

The next column over indicates which tracks are to be active on the recorder. *V* is used to indicate that video will be inserted on the recorder. If the audio will be inserted on track 1, a letter *A* will appear beside the *V*. The following are some possible options for a recorder with two audio tracks:

V—	Video only
VA-	Video, audio 1
VAA	Video, audio 1 and 2
-A-	Audio 1 only
—A	Audio 2 only
-AA	Audio 1 and 2 only

Figure 10-6
CMX 3600 Edit
Decision List.

```
TITLE:   BL KIDS VIEW SEQ
FCM: NON-DROP FRAME
001     AX      AA/V   C          00:00:00:00 00:00:30:00 01:00:00:00 01:00:30:00
* FROM CLIP NAME:   SMPTE_BARS.PCT   2:1
002     BL      V     K B         00:00:00:00 00:00:20:00 01:00:30:00 01:00:50:00
002     AX      V     K      000 00:00:39:14 00:00:59:14 01:00:30:00 01:00:50:00
* EFF_BLEND_GRAPHIC
* KEY CLIP NAME:   2/15 ROUGH CUT SLATE.04
003     BL      V     C          00:00:00:00 00:00:00:00 01:01:00:00 01:01:00:00
003     AX      V     D      030 00:00:07:15 00:00:14:00 01:01:00:00 01:01:06:15
* BLEND, DISSOLVE
* TO CLIP NAME:   BLLOGO ALPHA.PCT
004     AX      V     C          00:00:14:00 00:00:14:00 01:01:06:15 01:01:06:15
004     BL      V     D      030 00:00:00:00 00:00:01:00 01:01:06:15 01:01:07:15
* BLEND, DISSOLVE
* FROM CLIP NAME:   BLLOGO ALPHA.PCT
005 KIDS_VIE AA      C          01:00:00:00 01:02:24:04 01:01:09:00 01:03:33:04
* FROM CLIP NAME:   KIDS VIEW SHORT
006     BL      V     K B         00:00:00:00 00:02:25:17 01:01:09:00 01:03:34:17
006 KIDS_VIE V     K      000 01:00:00:00 01:02:25:17 01:01:09:00 01:03:34:17
* EFF_SBLEND
* KEY CLIP NAME:   KIDS VIEW SHORT
007 KIDS_VIE AA      C          01:02:24:04 01:02:24:04 01:03:33:04 01:03:33:04
007     BL      AA     D      040 00:00:00:00 00:00:01:10 01:03:33:04 01:03:34:14
* BLEND, AUDIO DISSOLVE
* FROM CLIP NAME:   KIDS VIEW SHORT
008     BL      V     K B         00:00:00:00 00:00:04:18 01:03:34:17 01:03:39:05
008     AX      V     K      012 00:00:33:14 00:00:38:02 01:03:34:17 01:03:39:05
* EFF_SBLEND
* EFF_BLEND_GRAPHIC
* BACKGROUND EVENT ON KEY EVENT AT SEQUENCE TIME 01:03:34:17 CONVERTED TO A CU
* T.
* KEY CLIP NAME:   SAVE MORE.01
009     BL      V     K B         00:00:00:00 00:00:00:13 01:03:39:05 01:03:39:18
009     AX      V     K O    013 00:00:38:02 00:00:38:15 01:03:39:05 01:03:39:18
* EFF_SBLEND
* EFF_BLEND_GRAPHIC
* BACKGROUND EVENT ON KEY EVENT AT SEQUENCE TIME 01:03:39:05 CONVERTED TO A CU
* T.
* KEY CLIP NAME:   SAVE MORE.01
010     BL      V     K B         00:00:00:00 00:00:02:00 01:03:39:18 01:03:41:18
010 KIDS_VIE V     K      000 01:02:30:18 01:02:32:18 01:03:39:18 01:03:41:18
* EFF_SBLEND
* KEY CLIP NAME:   KIDS VIEW SHORT
011 KIDS_VIE AA      C          01:02:31:15 01:02:47:11 01:03:40:15 01:03:56:11
* FROM CLIP NAME:   KIDS VIEW SHORT
012     BL      V     K B         00:00:00:00 00:00:03:18 01:03:41:18 01:03:45:06
012     AX      V     K      012 00:00:26:09 00:00:29:27 01:03:41:18 01:03:45:06
* EFF_SBLEND
* EFF_BLEND_GRAPHIC
* BACKGROUND EVENT ON KEY EVENT AT SEQUENCE TIME 01:03:41:18 CONVERTED TO A CU
* T.
* KEY CLIP NAME:   1997 2002
013     BL      V     K B         00:00:00:00 00:00:00:13 01:03:45:06 01:03:45:19
```

The fourth column indicates transitions using *C* for cuts, *D* for dissolves, and *W* for wipes.

The next two columns are for the source time code in and the source time code out. The far right columns are for the master record time code in and time code out.

A CMX_3600 EDL has no audio level, color correction, or effects information. It's a simple text file designed for a different era in which the idea that digital video editing would be available for anyone to use was an unimaginable dream and the Internet was still a concept buried deep within the U.S. Department of Defense.

Tips for Exporting an EDL for Use in an Online Edit

- Ask which EDL format the facility's edit controller can read before you export the EDL.
- If you're not sure, save the EDL in several formats.
- Make sure the edit controller can read high-density 3.5-inch diskettes.
- Find out if you'll need to generate a dupe reel list. This list tells an editor which of the tapes will need to be duplicated prior to the online edit.
- Save the EDL on a 3.5-inch diskette. Name the EDL file using six or fewer alphanumeric characters, all in uppercase, with a file name extension of .EDL.
- Print out a copy of the EDL in *A*-mode sort (shots listed in reel number order) to use as a reference.

Finally, a New Type of EDL Arrives

In 1996, a group of digital editing manufacturers decided it was time to create a new type of EDL. Their goal was to develop some way of preserving all the information stored in the show created on one manufacturer's editing system so it could be recreated at a later date on another manufacturer's editing system. Because video editing was only a facet of the growing multimedia environment that includes games, interactive television, the Internet, streaming, and broadcast, they expanded their goals.

This new cross-platform multimedia file format had to make it easier to reuse or repurpose content. *Content* in this context refers to television programs, films, video games, interactive CD-ROMs, DVDs, and anything else you can think in the world of entertainment. Everyone felt it should be much easier to take a television program and turn it into video game or perhaps turn video games into interactive television shows. After all, everyone was working with digital media files.

The trouble was that everyone used proprietary formats. Most formats were written to take advantage of software running on a specific hardware platform and operating system. The information about how to sequence or modify the media files and turn them into a finished show wasn't transferable.

This group decided that creating multimedia content—what we've been calling *editing* digital video—should be called *authoring*. Authoring included developing the content and all the information about how you turned that digital media into content.

The Advanced Authoring Format (AAF) Association

The group called itself the Advanced Authoring Format (AAF) Association. After years of discussion, they developed a new approach that would enable two types of data—*essence* and *metadata*—to be interchanged using an AAF file. Essence data refers to audio, video, still images, graphics, text, animation, music, and other forms of multimedia. The group called it this because it is the essential data perceived by the audience. Metadata refers to the information about how to combine or modify the essence data or supplementary information about it. Closed captioning is a form of metadata that is included in an AAF file.

In simple terms, metadata is data about other data. The metadata in an AAF file provides the information that an editing system needs to know to combine and modify the essence data in the file to produce a finished show. A long list of information is stored in metadata such as how to find the essence data and other parts of the metadata, the rules for controlling how audiences access the content, technical parameters such as sampling rates and streaming formats, and a detailed description of how to assemble (edit) the essence.

What Does Metadata Mean to an Editor?

Metadata is the record of not only the creative decisions you made, but also the steps you followed to reach the final output, the sources and equipment you used to create the output, and all of the alternatives you might decide to choose at some point in the future.

So what does this mean? If everything in your timeline (all the settings for audio equalization, color correction, layered effects, digital media file locations, and other information that lets you output a finished show) could be transferred to any editing system anywhere in the world without losing any information, you could work with the best person instead of the one with the most compatible system.

Is It AAF Compliant?

AAF files cannot be played or streamed. AAF compliance simply lets you transfer complex edits from one production department to another or from one facility to another without recreating the project every time you transfer it to a new system. The AAF file enables a show to be automatically assembled on other equipment with appropriate capabilities and it can track the history of the material in the finished show directly back to the original source recordings.

The original intent to make it easy for everyone to repurpose content has been fulfilled. You can track every source and application used to modify the media. Best of all, this new type of EDL brings us one step closer to a time when every digital editing system is compatible with every other system. Instead of including this chapter, which has dozens of confusing technical terms, we'd have a footnote in the back of this book that would say, "If your editing system is AAF compliant, you don't have to worry about getting it in or out of anyone else's system. It's easy and seamless." Thankfully, that day isn't far off.

Using AAF

Your editing system must be AAF compliant to import or export AAF files. The list of compliant systems is constantly growing. An AAF file has two types of data. You can select whether to export the media (essence) with the metadata or only export the metadata. If you decide to export an AAF file with embedded media, you'll also have the choice of whether to include video, audio, or both. Audio media can be embedded in either the WAVE or AIFF-C format.

Recording DVDs

As we write this, multiple incompatible DVD standards are competing for dominance in the marketplace. The list includes DVD-Recordable (DVD-R), DVD-ReWriteable (DVD-RW), DVD-ROM, DVD+R, and DVD+RW. Different standard sizes of DVDs are also available including DVD-5 (4.7GB), DVD-9 (8.54GB, dual-layer), DVD-10 (9.4GB, double-sided, single-layer), and DVD-18 (17GB, dual layer, double-sided). This entire mess is only going to get worse before it gets better. A new format based on blue laser technology rather than red will reach the market in 2003.

The issue of country permissions must also be considered. At the behest of Hollywood, the world was divided into six regions: the United States and Canada; Europe, Japan, South Africa, Egypt, and the Middle East; Australia and New Zealand; Southeast Asia; China; and Africa and the former Soviet Union is in one region and Europe is in another. Every DVD player has a hardware encoder for one of those six designated regions. The publisher (which is you if you're the one making the recording) can decide where to allow a DVD to be played. So don't plan on expanding your DVD collection or bringing DVDs from the United States to Europe or anywhere else.

The only consistency in all of this is that DVDs are recorded in the MPEG-2 format. DVD players and recorders are getting cheaper by the minute. The format has been accepted by consumers at a faster rate than any technology in history, including audio CDs. Therefore, it's clear that DVDs will replace VHS tapes as the home video format. This is why every editing system manufacturer includes the capability to record a DVD.

Most editing systems provide a separate application to create a basic DVD menu and convert a QuickTime or AVI file into an MPEG-2 file to record on a DVD. It is a big pain to export a show as a QuickTime file, import it into another application, or export MPEG-2 to record on your computer's DVD recorder approach. The only people who should be doing this are professionals who are getting paid for it. Seriously, you should only take this approach if you need to create a complex DVD. Authoring applications let you build interactive menu structures that could, for example, permit a user to watch a series of short video segments stored on the DVD in the order he or she desires instead of a preset order.

We side with consumers on this one. We prefer simpler technology. DVD recorders that look like a VHS VCR with an IEEE-1394 port are coming on the market. If you want to make your own DVDs, buy one of these machines.

You'll have to use the quick-and-dirty method we described for recording a show on DV tape. A DVD recorder isn't a camcorder or a DV deck. Your editing system won't be able to control the functions of the DVD recorder. To solve this problem, hook the recorder up to your editing system via Firewire, put it in record, and press Play on the timeline. We wish we could say that the DVD you just recorded will play in any DVD player. Maybe that will be true one day.

Web Formats

QuickTime, Windows Media, and Real are the major video formats used on the Internet. Real files are streamed and heavily compressed. QuickTime files can be uncompressed, compressed at various rates, or streamed. Windows Media files can be compressed at various rates or streamed.

Compressing video for the Internet is part art and part science. Cleaner EZ is a popular software application included with a lot of editing systems. It's designed to convert and/or compress QuickTime and AVI files for use on the Web. Books have been written about the ins and outs of compression. We suggest you read them or take a class if you're serious about streaming video on the Internet.

Importing and Exporting Graphics

Importing graphics into an editing system should be an easy process considering how often people do it. Most editing systems appear to make it easy. There's usually drop-down menu choice to import graphics. After that, it goes downhill fast. You must select a graphic file format to import that matches the format in which the image was stored. The size and resolution of the graphic must match the size of the digital video format you're editing. The image should match the aspect ratio of the video format.

We're not done yet. The shape of the pixels that form the image must match. Last but not least, the color space (the range of colors that can be displayed, which is much smaller in video than the available range on a computer) must be adjusted to match the color space of video. Why things are this way is beyond all reason.

Graphics created with computer software use square pixels because computer monitors use square pixels. Graphics created with digital video editing software use rectangular (nonsquare) pixels because video monitors have rectangular pixels. Standard definition digital video formats use nonsquare pixels. HD video formats use square pixels. Perhaps there's light at the end of the tunnel.

Graphic File Formats

Graphic file formats have proliferated with the same rapidity as video formats. The four most commonly used file formats are JPEG, PICT, Targa, and TIFF. The latter three formats can store an alpha channel mask. The alpha channel determines which parts of the picture will be transparent when keyed over a background.

The JPEG format was developed by the Joint Photographic Experts Group. The acronym for the group gave the file format its name. JPEGs can be highly compressed and retain image quality. However, this format doesn't support an alpha channel. The default extension is .JPEG or .JPG.

The PICT format was developed as a common image format for use on the Mac by Apple Computer. The format supports multiple color depth. The default extension is .PICT or .PIC.

The Targa file format was originally developed by Truevision (now part of Pinnacle Systems) to be used with its video capture cards. This is an uncompressed format. The image quality is outstanding, but the file sizes are very large. The default extension is .TGA.

The TIFF file format (Tagged Image File Format), was developed by Aldus (now part of Adobe Systems) and Microsoft Corporation. It's one of the most commonly used file formats and has the widest possible array of color depths. The maximum supported on professional editing systems is 48-bit color with a 16-bit alpha channel.

Turning Squares into Rectangles
So Circles Look Like Circles

This section explains what you need to know to make sure circles remain circles when importing graphics into your editing system. It doesn't matter whether the graphic is a still image from a camera, a scanned negative, a transparency or print, or something you created in a drawing program. If it was created on a computer, it has square pixels.

Standard-definition video monitors use nonsquare pixels. The squares in a computer graphic are automatically transformed into nonsquare pixels whenever you import a graphic. If you don't do anything about it, a perfect circle on your computer-generated graphic will end up looking like an oval in your video. If you follow these steps, your circles will stay circles:

1. What is the standard of the video you are editing?

   The answer determines the frame size in pixels.

Video Standard	Timeline Frame Size
NTSC (North American television standard) SMPTE 601	-720×486
DV-NTSC (miniDV, DVCPro, DVCAM)	-720×480
PAL (European television standard) 601	-720×576
DV-PAL (miniDV, DVCAM, and DVCPro)	-720×576
720p ATSC* HD standard	$-1,280\times720$ (square)
1080i/p ATSC HD standard	$-1,920\times1,080$ (square)

*Advanced Television Systems Committee

2. Determine whether you're editing standard-definition video in the 4:3 aspect ratio or the 16:9 widescreen aspect ratio. If you're using the 16:9 aspect ratio for video, the graphics must be sized for 16:9.

3. Open your graphics application.

4. Set the image size based on the following timeline frame size table:

Timeline Frame Size	Graphic Image Size at Creation
720×486 (4:3)	720×540
720×486 (16:9)	864×540
720×480 (4:3)	720×534
720×480 (16:9)	960×534
720×576 (4:3)	768×576
720×576 (16:9)	$1,024\times576$
$1,280\times720$	$1,280\times720$
$1,920\times1,080$	$1,920\times1,080$

5. Create a graphic at the appropriate size and save it. Make sure the essential information appears within the title safe area. The image resolution should be 72 pixels per inch (*dots per inch* [dpi]) unless you plan to zoom in on a section of the image. Crop the previously created images to the appropriate size. Save the new version as a copy of the original. This is just good professional practice.

   Ask yourself if t his graphic will be full screen or larger? Images that will fill the frame or appear smaller within the frame only need an image resolution of 72 dpi, which is the resolution of a video monitor. However, if you plan to use a small section of the image to fill the frame, you'll need a higher image resolution. Determine the maximum percent to which you'll enlarge the image. Multiply by 72 to calculate the maximum image resolution you'll need. For example, if you plan to enlarge the image 200 percent, you'll need to save with an image resolution of 144 dpi. This ensures that you will have enough resolution to enlarge the image, not the pixels.

6. Resize the graphic to the appropriate timeline frame size unless you're working in HD. Make sure to uncheck the maintain aspect ratio option in your image-editing application. The idea is to change the aspect ratio. Any circle in the graphic should now appear to be an oval.

For professionals only:

6a. Video has a narrower color space than other graphic environments. Color correct images in your graphics application. Highly saturated colors may be outside the limits of the video color space. Professional digital-editing systems will indicate the presence of illegal colors and adjust them to legal levels. You may need to adjust the black and white level settings in your graphic application to avoid clipping. Check your manual for more details.

7. Select a file format in which to save the graphic. Pick one that your editing system can import.

8. Save the resized graphic in a directory that's easy to find from within your editing system. If possible, use a descriptive name to make it easier to select the correct image. Many editing systems don't have a preview that lets you see the contents of the file before you select it sfor import.

9. Launch your editing system application and import the graphic into a bin.

Summary

The technical aspects of digital editing are simpler than ever. Basic skills, such as setting up a monitor, will serve you well. However, you don't have to understand how to fix an editing system to operate one.

Important Points to Remember

■ Don't let technical information overwhelm you.

■ A reliable reference monitor is important because it assures you that what you see on your screen is what the audience will see on theirs.

■ Use high-quality headphones to accurately monitor audio.

■ Once you've successful transferred material into your editing system, avoid changing the system settings.

What Are They Talking About?

After 50 years, you'd think everyone would use the same words to describe the same things. You'd be wrong. Digital video editing embraces concepts and words from film editing, television production, and computer technology. Throw in the desire of manufacturers to reinvent the wheel and you have the mess that confronts anyone who just wants to make a a movie.

Editing Terminology Cross Reference

System	Timeline	Timeline Cursor	Organization	Bins
Affinity	Tracksheet	Playhead	Project Window	Folders
After Effects	Timeline	Current Time Marker	Project Window	Folders
Avid	Timeline	Position Indicator	Project Window	Bins
Avio	Storyboard	Pointer	Projects	Scene Bin
Blade	Composition	Pointer	Project Window	Bins
Boris FX	Timeline	Current Time Indicator	N/A	N/A
Cinestream	Composition/ Sequencer	Timeline Cursor	Project Window	Bins
CWS 100	Timeline	Timeline Cursor	Materials Area	Bins/ Folders
DV Edit	Sequence Editor	Current Time Bar	Bin Manager	Bins
Edit*	Timeline	Timeline Cursor	Job	Bins

Table 11-1

What Are They Talking About?

Picons	# of Viewers	Insert	Overwrite	Source	Master
Posters	Single	Ripple	Overwrite		Clip Editors
N/A	Single	N/A	N/A		Composition
Representative Frame	Multiple	Splice	Overwrite	Source Monitor	Record Monitor
	Multiple	Insert	Replace	Workbox	Record
Thumbnail	Multiple	Ripple	Nonripple	Source	Result
N/A	Multiple	N/A	N/A	Preview	Composite
Poster Frame	Multiple	Insert	Overwrite	Source	Program
Thumbnail	Multiple	Insert	Overwrite	Source Preview	Timeline Preview
Clip Icon	Multiple	Insert	Replace	Source Window	Sequence Window
Picons	Multiple	Insert	Overrecord	Source Viewer	Record Viewer

continues

System	Timeline	Timeline Cursor	Organization	Bins
Editbox	Event Line	Current Frame Marker	Job	Libraries
Edition	Timeline	Timeline Cursor	Project Window	Racks
Final Cut Pro	Timeline	Playhead	Browser	Bins
Fire (Smoke)	Timeline	Positioner	Projects	Clip Library
Flash 5	Timeline	Playhead	Library Window	Folders
Hy-Brow	Timeline	Progress Indicator Bar	Filer-Fax Window	Categories
iFinish (PC)	Program Window	Current Time Indicator	Project Window	Bins
IMovie	Clip Viewer/ Timeline	Playhead	Project	Scrolling Shelf
Incite	Storyboard	Position Bar	Project Window	Collections
IQ	Timeline/ Storyboard	Timeline Cursor	Library	Clip Bins
Kron	Storyboard	Pointer	Project	Scene Bin
Lightworks	Stripview	Current Frame Marker	Project	Galleries/ Racks
Liquid Blue	Master Viewer	Playline	Project Window	Racks
Media 100xr IFinish Mac	Program Window	Current Time Indicator	Project Window	Bins
Media Studio Pro	Timeline Window	Cursor	Production Library	Galleries/ Folders

Table 11-1 (*continued*)

Picons	# of Viewers	Insert	Overwrite	Source	Master
Miniatures	Multiple	Insert	Replace	Viewer	Viewer
Picons	Multiple	Film Style	Overwrite	Source Viewer/ Inlay	Master Viewer/ Inlay
Poster Frame	Multiple	Insert	Overwrite	Viewer	Canvas
Proxy Frame	Multiple	Ripple	Nonripple	Proxies	Big Player
N/A	Single	N/A	N/A		Stage
Mini-Pic	Multiple	Insert	Add	Source Screen	Edit Screen
Clip Keyframe	Single	Insert	Overlay		Edit Suite Window
Thumbnail	Single	Normal	Paste over		Monitor Window
Thumbnail	Multiple	Film Mode	TV Mode	Clip Monitor	Edit Window
Clip Miniature/ Thumbnail	Multiple	Insert	Replace	Floating Clips	Edit Window
	Multiple	Normal	Insert	Workbox	Preview Window
Tiles	Multiple	Insert	Overwrite	Viewer	Viewer
Picons	Multiple	Filmstyle	Overwrite	Source	Viewer
Clip Keyframe	Single	Insert	Overlay		Edit Suite Window
Thumbnail	Multiple	Ripple	Overwrite	Source Window	Preview Window

continues

System	Timeline	Timeline Cursor	Organization	Bins
MoviePack	Timeline	Timeslider	Browser	Albums
Mule	Timeline	Locator	Library Window	Silos
Premiere	Timeline	Edit Line	Project Window	Bins
Raptor Edit	Film Timeline	Timeline cursor	N/A	DV BIN
Rex Edit	Film Timeline	Timeline Cursor	N/A	DV BIN
Screenplay	Storyboard	Cursor Bar	Materials Bin	Clip Drawer
Speed Razor	Composition	Pointer	Project Window	Bins/ Subbins
Studio 8	Storyboard/ Timeline	Timeline Scrubber	Movie Window	Album
Vegas Video	Trackview	Cursor	Project/Media explorer	Media Pool
Video Factory	Trackview	Cursor	Project/Media Explorer	Media Pool
Video Studio	Storyboard/ Timeline	Scroll Bar	Project	Library/ Folders
Xpri	Timeline	Playline	Project	Folder/ Bins

Table 11-1 (*continued*)

Picons	# of Viewers	Insert	Overwrite	Source	Master
Thumbnail	Multiple	Insert	N/A	Source Viewer	Video Control
Icons	Multiple	Insert	Overwrite	Source Viewer	Timeline Viewer
Poster Frame	Multiple	Insert	Overlay	Source Viewer	Program Viewer
N/A	Single	Ripple	Insert		Preview Video
N/A	Single	Ripple	Insert		Preview Video
Thumbnail	Single	Normal Mode	Insert		Viewing Screen
Thumbnail	Multiple	Ripple	Nonripple	Source	Result
Thumbnail	Single	Normal	Insert		Preview Window
Thumbnail	Single	Ripple Edit	Nonripple		Video Preview
Thumbnail	Single	Ripple Edit	Nonripple		Video Preview
Thumbnail	Single	Normal	N/A		Preview Window
Index Picture	Multiple	Splice-In	Overwrite	Source Viewer	Master Viewer

Keyboard Shortcut
Cross Reference

System	Play	Stop	Mark In
Affinity	Spacebar, ` L	Spacebar, K	I
After Effects	Spacebar	Spacebar	[
Avid	Spacebar, L, `, 5,	Spacebar, K	I, E
Blade	Spacebar, F1, F10, Alt D P	Spacebar, F2, Alt D S,	I
Boris FX	Spacebar	Spacebar	N/A
Cinestream	D, Spacebar	D, Spacebar	I
CWS 100	0, Enter, Up Arrow	Esc	Cntrl I, 1, 40
DV Edit	Spacebar, L, P	Spacebar	Cntrl 4, 4NP, I, F3
Edit*	P, Spacebar, JL, J4NP	Spacebar	I
Edition	Spacebar, L	Spacebar, K	A
Final Cut Pro	Spacebar, L	Spacebar, K	I
Fire (Smoke)	V	Spacebar	Right Alt
Flash	Enter	Enter	N/A
Hy-Brow	Down Arrow	Spacebar	Mouse
Ifinish	F5, Cntrl., Cntrl+Alt +P, Cntrl ' ,5NP	Cntrl., 0NP	F9, -NP
Imovie	Spacebar	Spacebar	Mouse
Incite	V, Down Arrow, Spacebar	C, Spacebar	Q

Table 11-2

Mark Out	Split Clip	Undo	Prev Edit	Next Edit
O	[	Cmd Z	A	S
]	Cntrl Shift D	Cntrl Z	J	K
O, R	P	Cntrl Z	A	S
O	Insert	Cntrl Z	Cntrl Left Arrow, Shift M	Cntrl Right Arrow, Alt M
N/A	N/A	Cntrl Z	Alt Left Arrow	Alt Right Arrow
O	Cntrl /	History Window	Option Left Arrow, 4	Option Rght Arrow, 5
Cntrl O, 2, 5	Cntrl D	Cntrl Z	Home, Shift Home	End, Shift End
Cntrl 6, 6NP, O, F4	/	Cntrl Z	Mouse	Mouse
O	/	U	Tab, Cntrl Left	Shift Tab, Cntrl Right
S	. (period)	Cntrl Z	Page Up	Page Down
O	Cntrl V	Cmd Z	Option E, Up Arrow	Shift E, Down Arrow
Right Cntrl	Delete	Backspace	Z	X
N/A	N/A	Cntrl Z	Page Up	Page Down
Mouse	Mouse	Mouse	Shift tab	Tab
F10, +NP	Ctrl /	Cntrl Z	Cntrl Tab	Tab
Mouse	Cmd T	Cntrl Z	Mouse	Mouse
W	F6	Cntrl Z	-	+

continues

System	Play	Stop	Mark In
IQ	Spacebar	Spacebar	Dedicated Key
Kron/Avio	F11	H, F10, F12,	I
Liquid Blue, Silver, Purple	Spacebar, L	Spacebar, K	A, I
Media 100 xr	Cmd., Esc, Cmd P, Spacebar, F5	Cmd., Esc, Spacebar	F1
Media Studio Pro	Enter	Enter	F3
MoviePack	Spacebar	Spacebar	Mouse
Mule	Spacebar, L	Spacebar, K	I
Premiere	Spacebar, L	Spacebar, K	I
Raptor Edit	Enter, F2	Escape, F1, F3	Cntrl I
Rex Edit	Enter, F2, Spacebar	Escape, F1, F3	Cntrl I, Shift Up
Screenplay	6NP	5NP, 8NP	-NP
Speed Razor	Spacebar, Cntrl F9	Spacebar	I
Studio 8	Mouse	Mouse	Mouse
Vegas Video/ Video Factory	Spacebar, Cntrl Spacebar, F12, J	Spacebar Escape, Enter, K	I, [,
Video Studio	Enter	Enter	F3
Xpri	5, L	K, Spacebar	E, I, P

Table 11-2 (*continued*)

Mark Out	Split Clip	Undo	Prev Edit	Next Edit
Dedicated Key	Pen	Cntrl Z	Dedicated Key	Dedicated Key
O	SS	Cntrl Insert	Left Arrow	Right Arrow
S, O	. (period)	Cntrl Z	Page Up	Page Down
F2	Cmd/	Cmd Z	Control Tab	Tab
F4	S	Cntrl Z	Page Up	Page Down
Mouse	Mouse	Cntrl Z	Mouse	Mouse
O		Z	Down Arrow	Up Arrow
O	Mouse	Cntrl Z	Cntrl Shift Left Arrow or Page Up	Cntrl Shift Right Arrow or Page Down
Cntrl O	Cntrl D	Cntrl Z Alt Backspace	Shift Home	Shift End
Cntrl O, Shift Down	Cntrl D	Cntrl Z Alt Backspace	Shift Home	Shift End
+NP	2NP	Page Down Key	N/A	N/A
O	Insert	Cntrl Z	Cntrl Left Arrow, Shift M	Cntrl Right Arrow, Alt M
Mouse	Mouse	Cntrl Z	Mouse	Mouse
O,]	S	Cntrl Z, Alt Backspace	Cntrl Alt Left Arrow	Cntrl Alt Right Arrow
F4	N/A	Cntrl Z	Mouse	Mouse
R, O, [	P	Cntrl Z	A	S

continues

System	Select Clip	Insert Edit	Overwrite Edit
Affinity	C	V	B
After Effects	Mouse	N/A	N/A
Avid	T	V	B
Blade	Mouse	Alt R (toggle)	Alt R (toggle)
Boris FX	Mouse	N/A	N/A
Cinestream	Mouse	Q	W
CWS 100	Mouse	Alt R	Insert
DV Edit	Up/Down Arrow, T	Y	H
Edit*	Z	Insert	Insert (toggles)
Edition	Assignable	\ (toggles)	\ (toggles)
Final Cut Pro	Option A, X	F9	F10
Fire (Smoke)	Mouse	G, Cntrl B	H
Flash	Mouse	N/A	N/A
Hy-Brow	Mouse	Mouse	Mouse
Ifinish	Mouse	Alt F12, Alt F11	F12, F11
Imovie	Mouse	Mouse	Shift Cmd V
Incite	S	F8, '	F8 (toggle)
IQ	TBD	TBD	TBD
Kron/Avio	Mouse	Windows Key Insert	Windows Key I
Liquid Blue, Silver, Purple	Assignable	\ (toggles)	\ (toggles)

Table 11-2 (*continued*)

Remove w/ Gap	Remove No Gap	Cut	Copy	Paste
Delete, P,]	Delete P,] (ripple on)	Cmd X	Cmd C	Cmd V
N/A	N/A	Cntrl X	Cntrl C	Cntrl V
Z	X	Cntrl X	Cntrl C	Cntrl V
Cntrl X, Delete	Cntrl Shift C, Cntrl Delete	Cntrl X	Cntrl C	Cntrl D, Cntrl V
Delete	Delete	Cntrl X	Cntrl C	Cntrl V
/	Period	Cntrl X	Cntrl C	Cntrl V
Delete	Delete	Cntrl X	Cntrl C	Cntrl V
Shift Delete	Delete	Cntrl X	Cntrl C	Cntrl V
Delete	Delete	Cntrl X	Cntrl C	Cntrl V
Cntrl, Delete	Cntrl ,Delete	Cntrl X	Cntrl C	Cntrl V
Delete	Shift Delete	Cmd X	Cmd C	Cmd V
(Lift) Shift Period	(Extract) period	[	O	P
N/A	N/A	Cntrl X	Cntrl C	Cntrl V
Mouse	Mouse	Mouse	Mouse	Mouse
Delete, Cntrl Shift Delete	Alt Delete, Cntrl Alt X	Cntrl X	Cntrl C	Cntrl V
N/A	Delete	Cmd X	Cmd C	Cmd V
Delete, F7	Delete, F7	Cntrl X	Cntrl C	Cntrl V
Pen	Pen	N/A	Pen	N/A
Windows Key Delete	Cntrl Delete	Cntrl X	Cntrl C	Cntrl V
Delete	Delete	Cntrl X	Cntrl C	Cntrl V

continues

System	Select Clip	Insert Edit	Overwrite Edit
Media 100 xr	Mouse	Option F12, Option F11	F12, F11
Media Studio Pro	Mouse	R (cycles)	R (cycles)
MoviePack	Mouse	Mouse	Mouse
Mule			
Premiere	Mouse	, (comma)	. (period)
Raptor Edit	Mouse	Alt R (toggle)	Alt R (toggle)
Rex Edit	Mouse	Alt R (toggle)	Alt R (toggle)
Screenplay	Mouse	Mouse	Mouse
Speed Razor	Mouse	R (toggle)	R (toggle)
Studio 8	Mouse	Mouse	Mouse
Vegas Video/ Video Factory	T	Cntrl L	Cntrl D
Video Studio	Mouse	Mouse	N/A
Xpri	T	V	B

Table 11-2 (*continued*)

Remove w/ Gap	Remove No Gap	Cut	Copy	Paste
Cmd X	Option Cmd X	Cmd X	Cmd C	Cmd V
Delete	Delete	Cntrl X	Cntrl C	Cntrl V
Delete Delete	Delete	Cntrl X	Cntrl C	Cntrl V
Backspace	Alt Backspace	Cntrl X	Cntrl C	Cntrl V
Delete	Delete	Cntrl X	Cntrl C	Cntrl V
Delete	Delete	Cntrl X	Cntrl C	Cntrl V
Delete	Delete	F1	F2	F3
Cntrl X, Delete	Cntrl Shift C, Cntrl Delete	Cntrl X	Cntrl C	Cntrl D, Cntrl V
Mouse	Mouse	Cntrl X	Cntrl C	Cntrl V
Delete	Delete	Cntrl X, Shift Delete	Cntrl C, Cntrl Insert	Cntrl V, Shift Insert, Cntrl Shift V
N/A	Delete	Cntrl X	Cntrl C	Cntrl V
Z	X	Cntrl X	Cntrl C	Cntrl V

continues

System	Clears Marks	Make Keyframe	Playback Loop
Affinity	G	Mouse	Dedicated Key
After Effects	N/A	Mouse	N/A
Avid	G	N	Alt 6
Blade	N/A	Mouse	/
Boris FX	N/A	Cntrl N, Alt Click	
Cinestream	[	Mouse	F
CWS 100	9	Mouse	Alt S R
DV Edit	F9		F11
Edit*	Ctrl Shift I, Cntrl Shift O	Alt K, A,	Shift P
Edition	G	K	Shift Spacebar
Final Cut Pro	Option X, Option Click	Mouse	Control L
Fire (Smoke)	Shift *(NP)	I	Cntrl Y
Flash	N/A	F6	Alt CL
Hy-Brow	Mouse	N/A	Mouse
Ifinish	Mouse	Cntrl K	Mouse
Imovie	Cmd D	N/A	Menu
Incite	N/A	Left click	N
IQ	TBD	Pen	Spacebar

Table 11-2 (*continued*)

Play in Reverse	Audio Scrub	Audio Waveform	Scale Timeline	Render
J	Always on	Always on	F11, F12, +, -	N/A
Cntrl Alt R	Cntrl Drag	N/A	=, -, ;	Mouse
J	Cap Locks, Shift Cursor	Assignable	Up/Down Arrows	Assignable
Down Arrow, Alt D J L, F9	N/A	Cntrl W	Cntrl Home, +-	Menu
	N/A	N/A		
N/A	Cmd Cntrl+Alt	Mouse	+, -	Menu
Down Arrow	Alt G	N/A	Cntrl E	N/A
J	F12		F7, F8	Shift Cntrl R
JJ	Cntrl	Mouse	+, -, W	F4
J	Scroll Lock	Mouse	Up or Down Arrow	N/A
J	Shift S	Cmd Option W	Option -, Option +	Option R
C	Cntrl Shift V, Cntrl, Ctrl Shift			N/A
N/A	N/A	N/A	Cntrl=, Cntrl -	Menu
N/A	N/A	N/A	Mouse	N/A
N/A	Cntrl ` (prime)	Menu	Cntrl+, Cntrl-, Shift >, Shift <, F2	Mouse
Cmd [	N/A	N/A	Mouse	Menu
X	Mouse	Menu	F3, F4	Mouse
Pen	TBD	Pen	Pen	N/A

continues

System	Clears Marks	Make Keyframe	Playback Loop
Kron/Avio	N/A	N/A	N/A
Liquid Blue	G	K	Shift Spacebar
Media 100 xr	Cmd H	Mouse	Cmd \
Media Studio Pro	N/A	Mouse	Shift Spacebar
MoviePack	Mouse	Mouse	Mouse
Mule			
Premiere	G	Mouse	Mouse
Raptor Edit	N/A	N/A	Menu
Rex Edit	Menu	N/A	Alt Enter
Screenplay	N/A	N/A	N/A
Speed Razor	N/A	Mouse	/
Studio 8	Mouse	N/A	Mouse
Vegas Video/ Video Factory	N/A	Mouse	Q
Video Studio	N/A	N/A	Mouse
Xpri	G	[	6

Table 11-2 (*continued*)

Play in Reverse	Audio Scrub	Audio Waveform	Scale Timeline	Render
N/A	N/A	w	Windows Key Page Up/ Page Down	F9
J	Scroll Lock	Mouse	Up/Down Arrows	N/A
N/A	Cmd ` (prime)	Menu	Cmd =, Cmd), Cmd+, Cmd-, Shift <, Shift >	Mouse
menu	N/A	N/A	+ -, Z, Shift Z	Enter
N/AS	Menu	Always on	F3, F4	Cntrl R
J	Menu			Cntrl R
Cntrl Alt Spacebar or Cmd Option Spacebar	N/A	Mouse	\ or Mouse	Enter
Shift<- Shift Space	Shift Drag	N/A	Mouse	Menu
N/A	Alt G	N/A	Mouse	Menu
N/A	N/A	N/A	N/A	N/A
N/A	N/A	Cntrl W	Cntrl Home, +-	Menu
N/A	N/A	N/A	Mouse	Menu
J	Always on	Menu	Up/Down Arrow, Cntrl Up/Down Arrow, /	Menu
N/A	N/A	N/A	Cntrl Mouse Scroll	Menu
J	Assignable	Assignable	Cntrl +, Cntrl -	Assignable

Films to Watch

Films to Watch

You can learn a lot about editing by watching any film that appeals to you. Just watch closely and try to analyze why you like it. From an editor's perspective, the reason some scenes are preferable to others relates to timing. Timing and motion are the two keys to shot selection. Either the shot has great timing (due to the performance or action) or the editor has to create timing with the placement of the cuts. Each shot has either motion within the frame or camera movement that creates motion or the editor must create motion outside the frame using a cut. Ideally, a cut occurs when you want to refocus the audience's attention. This is a way to make them turn their bodies or heads. In an interview, John Huston explained,

> To me, the perfect film is as though it were unwinding behind your eyes and your eyes were projecting it themselves, so that you were seeing what you wished to see. Film is like thought. It the closest to thought processes of any art. Look at that lamp across the room. Now, look back at me. Look back at the lamp. Now look back at me again. Did you see what you did? You blinked. Those are the cuts.[1]

To concentrate on the editing, watch our recommendations with the sound off. Next, watch the film a second time with the sound on and pay attention to the sound editing. Alan Splet, one of the most influential sound editors of the past 30 years, when asked what his contribution to a film was, simply said, "Sound is a heart thing."[2] Watch some of your favorite films with and without the sound. Ask yourself, "Do I still like it without the sound?"

---

[1]Louise Sweeney. Christian Science Monitor (August 11, 1973).
[2]From a radio interview conducted by Randy Thom in 1980 that was recalled by Thom in *Mix Magazine* (February 1995): 141.

If You Only Watch One . . .

Raging Bull   A masterpiece of storytelling and editing from Marty Scorsese and Thelma Schoonmaker, editor. There's so much to learn from this film. Roger Ebert does a three-hour seminar at Film Festivals that only begins to scratch the surface.

Editing 101

Amadeus, edited by Nena Danavic and Michael Chandler. Watch the scene where Mozart's wife meets with Salieri. Music, narration, live action, and flashback are intercut. Note also the scene in which Salieri describes the Requiem.

The Apartment, edited by Daniel Mandell.   Watch for dialogue and scene setup.

Apocalypse Now, edited by Lisa Fruchtman, Gerald B. Greenberg, Richard Marks, and Walter Murch.   Watch the helicopter sequence set to Wagner in which the Vietnamese village is bombed. Note how the music score and the rhythm of editing build to a climax. Watch also for the moment of silence that's part of this soundscape.

The Birds, edited by George Tomasino.   Watch the gas station attack for an example of rhythm in editing.

Bullitt, edited by Frank P. Keller.   The chase sequence in San Francisco is remarkable for its simplicity and length.

Chinatown, edited by Sam O'Steen.   Every scene has a clear beginning, middle, and end. Jack Nicholson's character always exits and enters the frame unraveling the story as we move with him. A Roman Polanski masterpiece.

Day of the Jackal, edited by Ralph Kemplan.   Watch the attempted assassination of President DeGaulle for editing that builds suspense through perfect timing.

Deer Hunter, edited by Peter Zinner.   Watch the Russian roulette scene.

Easy Rider, edited by Don Cambern and directed by Dennis Hopper. Watch the montage sequences cut to rock music that evoke independence and freedom. The acid trip sequence among the graves of New Orleans is a classic.

The Exorcist, edited by Norman Gay, Evan Lottman, and Bud S. Smith.   Watch the opening scenes of what is a classic horror film.

The Godfather, edited by William H. Reynolds and Peter Zinner. Coppola's three-part masterpiece. Watch the baptism scene for a classic example of montage American-style in which Michael Corleone takes revenge on his enemies while his child is being baptized.

The Good, The Bad, and The Ugly, edited by Eugenio Alabiso and Nino Baragli.   Watch the final showdown for a classic lesson in how to build a scene.

Groundhog Day, edited by Pembroke J. Herring.   Watch the meticulous construction of the scenes as the same day is repeated over and over throughout the film. The editing pace changes from sequence to sequence, reflecting the character's point of view.

Harold & Maude, edited by William A. Sawyer and Edward A. Warschilka.   Watch for a great example of parallel editing in the funeral scene and the sixties era music montage sequence that shows their budding relationship.

Home Alone, edited by Raja Gosnell.   Watch the sequence that opens the film—a child is advertently left at home that builds to the point when his mother remembers that he is not on the airplane with the rest of the family.

Indiana Jones and the Temple of Doom, edited by Michael Kahn. The opening sequence starts in China with a nightclub number and titles, and ends in India.

The Insider, edited by William Goldberg, David Rosenbloom, and Paul Rubell.   Another great example of parallel editing throughout the film. Watch the sequence that climaxes with the first time the whistleblower testifies at a court hearing.

It Happened One Night, edited by Gene Havlick.   Dozens of cheats such as cuts on lens changes no one would do today.

Jaws, edited by Verna Fields.   A course in how to make something out of nothing.

The Longest Day, edited by Samuel Beetley.   Watch the landing sequence and Omaha beach assault.

The Matrix, edited by Zach Staenberg.   Watch the fight sequences that broke new ground, especially for use of motion effects.

Miller's Crossing, edited by Michael Miller.   Brilliant pacing in this Coen Brothers' crime drama. Watch the assassination attempt on Leo, Albert Finney's character, in his burning house, set to the great Irish tenor, Frank Patterson, singing "Oh Danny Boy."

The Natural, edited Stu Linder.   Watch the closing scene for a textbook example of building to a climax.

On the Waterfront, edited by Gene Milford.   Watch the opening scenes, the scene in the back of a taxicab, and Brando's confrontation with the dock bosses at the end.

The Professional, edited by Michelle David.   Watch the action editing in the final scenes when the hit man meets the renegade detective.

Pulp Fiction, edited by Sally Menke.   Watch how the chronological order of scenes are rearranged to maximum effect.

Purple Rose of Cairo, edited by Susan E. Morse.   Watch how the two realities—the characters interacting with the characters in the movie within the movie—play out.

Psycho, edited by George Tomasino.   Watch the shower scene.

Raiders of the Lost Ark, edited by Michael Kahn.   Watch the opening scene—classic storytelling.

Rocky, edited by Scott Conrad and Richard Halsey.   Watch Rocky's training routine, the training montage leading up to the climatic fight, and the fight itself for classic storytelling. Shot in Philadelphia so we had to include it.

Ronin, edited by Tony Gibbs.   A great, more recent lengthy car chase through Paris directed by John Frankenheimer who shot chases the old-fashioned way.

Singin' in the Rain, edited by Adrienne Fazan.   All the blinks in the right places.

The Shining, edited by Ray Lovejoy.   The suspense and horror in this Kubrick masterpiece comes from the editing.

Speed, edited by John Wright.   Watch the action cutting as the runaway bus moves through traffic and as Sandra Bullock's character takes control of the bus.

The Sting, edited by William Reynolds.   A Hollywood classic where timing, continuity editing, and editing create smooth suspense.

The Thirty-Nine Steps, directed by Alfred Hitchcock.   Note the overlapping sound of the train whistle as a maid discovers a corpse in an empty flat. A moment that has been imitated for sixty years.

This is Spinal Tap, edited by Robert Leighton.   Documentary-style editing with nearly no cutaways, which makes the film feel over the top. Watch the scene under the rock concert arena in Cleveland, Ohio.

Traffic, edited by Stephen Mirrione.   Raw editing complemented the other design elements to give the film a gritty, hard reality.

Unforgiven, edited by Joel Cox.   Pauses amid action add to the remarkable timing in every scene.

Usual Suspects, edited by John Ottman.   Careful editing throughout guarantees the secret identity remains intact.

Wall Street, edited by Claire Simpson.   Watch the scenes where stocks are bought and sold in a frenzy. Great action editing of what is essentially an office scene.

The Wild Bunch, edited by Lou Lombardo.   Editing makes the film's opening—the gang is assaulted in an ambush following a failed bank robbery in a Texas border town and the climatic end when they are cut to ribbons after being double-crossed by a Mexican warlord. Two of the most violent shoot-ups ever filmed. At the time, the film set a record for highest number of edits in a feature film.

Winter Sleepers, edited by Katya Dringenberg.   Watch the auto accident scene, which is particularly well edited.

Witness, edited by Thom Noble Watch these scenes—the murder, the young boy recognizing the killer's photograph, and the love scenes. Compare the barn-raising scene to the same scene in Oklahoma!

Avanced Editing Techniques

Bonnie and Clyde, edited by Dede Allen.   Watch the bank robbery montage sequence set to Flat and Scruggs' "Foggy Mountain Breakdown."

The Candidate, edited by Robert Estrin and Richard A. Harris. Watch the scene in which Robert Redford's character, Bill McKay, watches Don Porter's character, Senator Crocker Jarmon, give a speech. You'll notice quiet shots, reaction shots, that draw the audience in and move the story along.

The Conversation, edited by Walter Murch.   Watch the party scene in the loft office for a wonderful illustration of Walter Murch's ideas about editing.

The French Connection, edited by Jerry Greenberg.   Watch the car chase under the elevated train with the sound off so you can see all the tricks and then watch it with the sound to see how the sound makes the chase work. Bullit, also has a great chase sequence, an earlier effort from the same filmmaking team.

Goodfellas.   Another masterpiece from Marty Scorsese and Thelma Schoonmaker, editor.

Maltese Falcon.   Great timing within the scenes, which is the director's doing, but the editor knows that and uses it to great advantage.

Mean Streets, edited by Sidney Levine.   Marty Scorsese's first film with his expedient and original editing.

Medium Cool, edited by Verna Fields.   Watch for the integration of documentary and dramatic scenes. Filmed during the Democratic National Convention in Chicago in 1968.

The Oxbow Incident, edited by Allen McNeil, and *12 Angry Men*, edited by Carl Lerner.   Watch either film for advanced techniques on how to sustain audience interest and handle big groups. Stories that handle big groups of people are rarely attempted in film.

Run Lola Run, edited by Mathilde Bonnefoy.   Circular construction based on the unity of time. The events are reedited with minor adjustments of time and space to show various possible conclusions as a woman runs to save her boyfriend.

For Comedy Editing

Annie Hall, edited by Wendy Greene Bricmont and Ralph Rosenblum.   The editing makes the film.

His Girl Friday, edited by Gene Havlick.   There's no action in the film so the editor creates all the speed and action.

M*A*S*H, edited by Danford B. Greene.   The comic timing comes from the editing

For Sound Editing

Apollo 13, edited by Daniel Hanley and Michael Hill.

Das Boot, edited by Hannes Nikel.   Watch of the carefully built sound scape of precise sounds and suspenseful silence.

Eraserhead, The Black Stallion, Never Cry Wolf, Dune, Sound Editing by Alan Splet.

Hunt for the Red October, edited by Dennis Verkler and John Wright. Sound as a reality. Note the underwater scenes where sound editing and reaction shots create an intense reality.

The Matrix or other special-effects-driven films are also good to watch for sound editing.

Pearl Harbor is a recent example of a film that doesn't work well without the sound.

For Documentary Editing

Day After Trinity by Jon Else.

Harlan County by Barbara Koppel.

Hoop Dreams, Bill Haugse, Steve James, Frederick Marx.

Law and Order by Frederick Wiseman.

Let It Be, Michael Lindsay-Hogg.

Night and Fog, Alain Resnais.

Roger and Me, Michael Moore.

Salesman by Albert Maysles and Charlotte Zwerin.

Silverlake Life, The View from Here by Peter Friedman.

Thin Blue Line by Errol Morris.

The Wonderful, Horrible Life of Leni Riefenstahl, Ray Muller III.

Woodstock, by Thelma Schoonmaker.

Award Winners

American Cinema Editors is an honorary society of motion picture editors founded in 1950 that gives out Eddie Awards in two categories: Drama Feature and Comedy or Musical Feature. The Eddie Award nominees are listed from 1970 to the present. The winners are in bold. The same indication is used for the nominees and winners of the Academy Award for film editing that follow the list of Eddies. The Academy Award list goes back to 1934. Where appropriate we've made notes about the films and suggested scenes to watch. Not every award winner is a great film. In a close-knit industry sometimes reasons other than quality intercede. The Academy Awards were started and have been dominated by the Hollywood studios. Some classic films on many top 100 lists have been ignored by the Academy. However, it's a good starting point for any student of the art of motion pictures.

Eddie Award Nominees

2001

A Beautiful Mind, Dan Hanley, Mike Hill.   Watch the scenes leading up to the discovery of his mental illness.

Black Hawk Down, Pietro Scalia.   Watch the battle sequence.

Harry Potter and the Philosopher's Stone, Richard Francis-Bruce. Special Effects extravangza.

The Lord of the Rings: The Fellowship of the Ring, John Gilbert. Watch the scene where the decision is made to send Frodo with the Ring and the battle between the members of the Fellowship and the Orcs at the end.

Memento, Dody Dorn.   Storytelling in reverse done well, though not as well as in *Winter Sleepers,* which preceded this film.

Comedy/Musical Film:

Amelie, Herve Schneid

Gosford Park, Tim Squyres

Monsters, Inc., Jim Stewart.   Animation.

Moulin Rouge, Jill Bilcock.   Musical redux.

The Royal Tenenbaums, Dylan Tichenor.   Comedy.

Shrek, Sim Evan Jones.   Animation

2000

Billy Elliot, John Wilson.   Watch the dance sequence when Billy discovers his abilities.

Cast Away, Arthur Schmidt.   Watch how tension is created with only one character and one location.

Crouching Tiger, Hidden Dragon, Tim Squyres.   Watch the balletic fight sequence in the courtyard and across the roofs.

Gladiator, Pietro Scalia.   Watch the opening 20 minutes.

Traffic, Stephen Mirrione.   Watch each story individually and then compare the editing from one story to the next.

Comedy/Musical Film:

Almost Famous, Joe Hutshing and Saar Klein.   Watch the scene with the groupies in the hotel.

Best In Show, Robert Leighton.   Watch the dog show sequence that's the climax of the film.

Chocolat, Andrew Mondshein.   Romantic comedy.

O Brother, Where Art Thou? Roderick Jaynes and Tricia Cooke. Watch the scene in which George Clooney confronts his wife and her new husband.

Shanghai Noon, Richard Chew.   Watch this or any Jackie Chan movie for the editing in the fight scenes that makes the action work.

1999

American Beauty, Tariq Anwar, Christopher Greenbury.   Watch the sequence in which Lester transforms himself in the garage and the dinner table scene when he announces he's lost his job.

The Insider, William Goldenberg, David Rosenbloom, Paul Rubell.

The Matrix, Zach Staenberg.   Watch the fight scenes for the use of motion effects.

The Sixth Sense, Andrew Mondshein.   Look for the clues the editor left that all is not what it seems.

The Talented Mr. Ripley, Walter Murch.   Watch the boating sequence.

Comedy/Musical Film:

Analyze This, Christopher Tellefsen.   Pay attention to how the subplots are handled or not handled in this film.

Being John Malkovich, Eric Zumbrunnen.   Watch the scene when Malkovich discovers there's someone inside his head and the scene with dozens of John Malkoviches.

Election, Kevin Tent.

Man On The Moon, Christopher Tellefsen, Lynzee Klingman, Adam Boome.

Run Lola Run, Mathilde Bonnefoy.

1998

The Horse Whisperer, Hank Corwin, Freeman A. Davies, Tom Rolf. Watch the accident scene.

Out Of Sight, Anne V. Coates.

Saving Private Ryan, Michael Kahn.   Watch the first 20 minutes and compare to other WWII battle scenes, including *The Thin Red Line*.

Shakespeare In Love, David Gamble.   Watch the performance for the Queen and the love scenes.

The Thin Red Line, Leslie Jones, Saar Klein, Billy Weber.   Watch the battle scenes and compare to *Saving Private Ryan*.

1997

Air Force One, Richard Francis-Bruce.   Airplane disaster movie. Pay attention to the sound design and the rousing climax when Ford defeats the terrorists.

As Good As It Gets, Richard Marks.   Watch the scenes in the diner.

Good Will Hunting, Pietro Scalia.   Watch the scene in the bar as Matt Damon tries to pick-up Minnie Driver.

L. A. Confidential, Peter Honess.   Watch the climatic gun battle.

Titanic, Conrad Buff, James Cameron, Richard A. Harris.   Watch the ballroom sequence followed by the party below decks.

1996

The English Patient, Walter Murch.   Watch the scene in the church with the nurse.

Evita, Gerry Hambling.   Watch the scene in the bar that introduces Antonio Banderas.

Fargo, Ethan Coen, Joel Coen.   Watch the two scenes in which Marge asks Jerry about the murders and his car.

The Rock, Richard Francis-Bruce.   Watch the sequence in which Sean Connery escapes from his handlers and the assault sequence that leads to the team being slaughtered.

Shine, Pip Karmel.   Watch the scene in which Helfgott plays the piano in a restaurant and pay attention to the sound design.

1995

Apollo 13, Daniel P. Hanley, Michael Hill.   A great film for its sound design.

Braveheart, Steven Rosenblum.   Watch the battle scenes and compare to *Gladiator*.

Casino, Thelma Schoonmaker

Crimson Tide, Chris Lebenzon.   Another great film for sound editing.

The Usual Suspects, John Ottman.   Thriller with a twist.

1994

Forrest Gump, Arthur Schmidt.   Noted for placing Tom Hanks in historic events and making it look seamless.

Pulp Fiction, Sally Menke.

The Shawshank Redemption, Richard Francis-Bruce.   Prison drama.

Speed, John Wright.

True Lies, Conrad Buff, Mark Goldblatt, Richard A. Harris.

1993

The Fugitive, Don Brochu, David Finfer, Dean Goodhill, Dov Hoenig, Richard Nord, Dennis Virkler.   Watch the train wreck sequence for action editing.

In the Line of Fire, Anne V. Coates.   Watch the sequence in which Eastwood recalls the assassination.

In the Name of the Father, Gerry Hambling.

The Piano, Veronika Jenet.

Schindler's List, Michael Kahn.

1992

A Few Good Men, Robert Leighton.   Taut courtroom drama.

The Last of the Mohicans, Dov Hoenig, Arthur Schmidt.   Watch the battle scenes.

The Player, Geraldine Peroni.   Watch the opening 30 minutes.

Scent of a Woman, Harvey Rosenstock, William Steinkamp, Michael Tronick

Unforgiven, Joel Cox. Watch the opening sequence and the climactic gun battle.

1991

JFK, Joe Hutshing, Pietro Scalia.

The Silence of the Lambs, Craig Mckay.

Terminator 2: Judgment Day, Conrad Buff, Mark Goldblatt, Richard A. Harris.

1990

Dances with Wolves, Neil Travis.   Watch the sequence in which Costner arrives at his lonely outpost.

Ghost, Walter Murch.   Watch the love scenes between Patrick Swayze and Demi Moore.

Goodfellas, Thelma Schoonmaker.   Watch the scene in the Copacabana nightclub and the scene in which Joe Pesci reveals his violent nature.

1989

Born on the Fourth of July, edited by David Brenner, Joe Hutshing.

Field of Dreams, edited by Ian Crafford.   Watch how the scene is built as the spectators arrive to watch the ballgame.

Glory, edited by Steven Rosenblum.   Watch the battle scene on the beach and compare to *Saving Private Ryan* or the *Longest Day*.

1988

Mississippi Burning, edited by Gerry Hambling.

Rain Man, edited by Stewart Linder.

Who Framed Roger Rabbit, edited by Arthur Schmidt.

1987

Broadcast News, edited by Richard Marks.   Watch the scene that establishes the interplay between Albert Brooks, William Hurt, and Holly Hunter as Brooks relays questions from Hunter to Hurt.

Fatal Attraction, edited by Peter E. Berger, Michael Kahn.   Watch the climatic scene in which Douglas kills Glenn Close.

The Last Emperor, edited by Gabriella Cristiani.   Wonderful editing of an epic story.

1986

Hoosiers, edited by C. Timothy O'Meara.   Watch the basketball games and the scene's that establish Hackman's lonely existence.

The Mission, edited by Jim Clark.

Platoon, edited by Claire Simpson.   Watch how the editing shifts the story from character to character.

1985

Out of Africa, edited by Pembroke J. Herring, Sheldon Kahn, Fredric
  Steinkamp, William Steinkamp.

Runaway Train, edited by Henry Richardson.

Witness, edited by Thom Noble.

1984

Amadeus, edited by Michael Chandler, Nena Danevic.

The Killing Fields, edited by Jim Clark.   Watch the trek to escape
  sequence.

Romancing the Stone, edited by Donn Cambern, Frank Morriss.
  Watch the opening scene that reveals Joan's character traits,
  which follows immediately after the first action sequence.

1983

Flashdance, edited by Walt Mulconery, Bud Smith.   Watch the
  dance sequences.

The Right Stuff, edited by Glenn Farr, Lisa Fruchtman, Tom Rolf,
  Stephen A. Rotter.

Wargames, edited by Tom Rolf .

1982

E. T.: The Extra-Terrestrial, edited by Carol Littleton.

Gandhi, edited by John Bloom.

Tootsie, edited by Fredric Steinkamp, William Steinkamp.   Watch
  the opening scene that establishes Dustin Hoffman's character
  clearly in just a few minutes.

1981

On Golden Pond, edited by Robert L. Wolfe.

Raiders of the Lost Ark, edited by Michael Kahn.

Reds, edited by Dede Allen, Craig Mckay.   Watch the Russian
revolution sequence and pay attention to the placement of the
witnesses that are intercut with the drama.

1980

Coal Miner's Daughter, edited by Arthur Schmidt

Fame, edited by Gerry Hambling. Watch the dance sequences.

Raging Bull, edited by Thelma Schoonmaker

1979

All That Jazz, edited by Alan Heim. Watch the dance sequences.

Apocalypse Now, edited by Lisa Fruchtman, Gerald B. Greenberg,
Richard Marks, Walter Murch

The Black Stallion, edited by Robert Dalva. Watch the storm at sea
sequence.

1978

The Deer Hunter, edited by Peter Zinner. Watch the Russian
roulette sequence.

Hooper, edited by Donn Cambern

Superman, edited by Stuart Baird.

1977

Close Encounters of the Third Kind, edited by Michael Kahn

Star Wars, edited by Richard Chew, Paul Hirsch, Marcia Lucas

The Turning Point, edited by William H. Reynolds. Watch how the dance sequences are used to point out the contrasts between the characters.

1976

All the President's Men, edited by Robert L. Wolfe

Network, edited by Alan Heim

Rocky, edited by Scott Conrad, Richard Halsey. Watch the boxing sequences.

1975

Jaws, edited by Verna Fields

The Hindenburg, edited by Donn Cambern

One Flew Over the Cuckoo's Nest, edited by Richard Chew, Sheldon Kahn, Lynzee Klingman

1974

Earthquake, edited by Dorothy Spencer

The Longest Yard, edited by Michael Luciano

The Towering Inferno, edited by Carl Kress, Harold F. Kress

1973

The Day of the Jackal, edited by Ralph Kemplen

Jonathan Livingston Seagull, edited by James Galloway, Frank P. Keller

The Sting, edited by William H. Reynolds

1972

Cabaret, edited by David Bretherton

The Godfather, edited by William H. Reynolds, Peter Zinner

The Poseidon Adventure, edited by Harold F. Kress

1971

The African Elephant, edited by Alan L. Jaggs

Fiddler on the Roof, edited by Antony Gibbs, Robert Lawrence

The French Connection, edited by Gerald B. Greenberg

Kotch, edited by Ralph E. Winters

Summer of '42, edited by Folmar Blangsted

Willard, edited by Warren Low

1970

Airport, edited by Stuart Gilmore

The Great White Hope, edited by William Reynolds

M*A*S*H, edited by Danford B. Greene

Patton, edited by Hugh S. Fowler

Tora! Tora! Tora! edited by Inoue Chikaya, Pembroke J. Herring, James E. Newcom

Oscar Nominees for Achievement in Film Editing

2001

*A **Beautiful Mind*** Mike Hill, Dan Hanley.
Black Hawk Down, Pietro Scalia.
The Lord of the Rings: The Fellowship of the Ring, John Gilbert.
Memento, Dody Dorn.
Moulin Rouge, Jill Bilcock.

2000

Almost Famous, Joe Hutshing, Saar Klein.
Crouching Tiger, Hidden Dragon, Tim Squyres.
Gladiator, Pietro Scalia.
Traffic, Stephen Mirrione.
Wonder Boys, Dede Allen.

1999

American Beauty, Tariq Anwar.
The Cider House Rules, Lisa Zeno Churgin.
The Insider, William Goldenberg, Paul Rubell, David Rosenbloom.
The Matrix, Zach Staenberg.
The Thin Red Line, Bill Webber, Leslie Jones.

1998

Life Is Beautiful, Simona Paggi.

Out of Sight, Anne V. Coates.

Saving Private Ryan, Michael Kahn.

Shakespeare in Love, David Gamble.

The Thin Red Line, Bill Webber, Leslie Jones.

1997

Air Force One, Richard Francis-Bruce.

As Good As It Gets, Richard Marks.

Good Will Hunting, Pietro Scalia.

L.A. Confidential, Peter Honess.

Titanic, Conrad Buff, James Cameron, Richard A. Harris.

1996

The English Patient, Walter Murch.

Evita, Gerry Hambling.

Fargo, Roderick Jaynes.

Jerry Maguire, Joe Hutshing.

Shine, Pip Karmel.

1995

Apollo 13, Dan Hanley, Mike Hill.

Babe, Marcus D'Arcy, Jay Friedkin.

Braveheart, Steven Rosenblum.

Crimson Tide, Chris Lebenzon.

Seven, Richard Francis-Bruce.

1994

Forrest Gump, Arthur Schmidt.

Hoop Dreams, Bill Haugse, Steve James, Frederick Marx.

Pulp Fiction, Sally Menke.

The Shawshank Redemption, Richard Francis-Bruce.

Speed, John Wright.

1993

The Fugitive, Don Brochu, David Finfer, Dean Goodhill, Dov Hoenig, Richard Nord, Dennis Virkler.

In the Line of Fire, Anne V. Coates.

In the Name of the Father, Gerry Hambling.

The Piano, Veronika Jenet.

Schindler's List, Michael Kahn.

1992

Basic Instinct, Frank J. Urioste.

The Crying Game, Kant Pan.

A Few Good Men, Robert Leighton.

The Player, Geraldine Peroni.

Unforgiven, Joel Cox.

1991

The Committments, Gerry Hambling.

JFK, Joe Hutshing, Pietro Scalia.

The Silence of the Lambs, Craig McKay.

Terminator 2: Judgment Day, Conrad Buff, Mark Goldblatt, Richard A. Harris.

Thelma & Louise, Thom Noble.

1990

Dances with Wolves, Neil Travis.

Ghost, Walter Murch.

The Godfather, Part III, Lisa Fruchtman, Barry Malkin, Walter Murch.

Goodfellas, Thelma Schoonmaker.

The Hunt for Red October, Dennis Virkler, John Wright.

1989

The Bear, Noelle Boisson.

Born on the Fourth of July, David Brenner, Joe Hutshing.

Driving Miss Daisy, Mark Warner.

The Fabulous Baker Boys, William Steinkamp.

Glory, Steven Rosenblum.

1988

Die Hard, John F. Link, Frank J. Urioste.

Gorillas in the Mist, Stuart Baird.

Mississippi Burning, Gerry Hambling.

Rain Man, Stu Linder.

Who Framed Roger Rabbit, Arthur Schmidt.

1987

Broadcast News, Richard Marks.

Empire of the Sun, Michael Kahn.

Fatal Attraction, Peter E. Berger, Michael Kahn.

The Last Emperor, Gabriella Cristiani.

Robocop, Frank J. Urioste.

1986

Aliens, Ray Lovejoy.

Hannah and Her Sisters, Susan E. Morse.

The Mission, Jim Clark.

Platoon, Claire Simpson.

Top Gun, Chris Lebenzon, Billy Weber.

1985

A Chorus Line, John Bloom.

Out of Africa, Pembroke Herring, Sheldon Kahn, Fredric Steinkamp, William Steinkamp.

Prizzi's Honor, Kaja Fehr, Rudi Fehr.

Runaway Train, Henry Richardson.

Witness, Thom Noble.

1984

Amadeus, Michael Chandler, Nena Danevic.

The Cotton Club, Robert Q. Lovett, Barry Malkin.

The Killing Fields, Jim Clark.

A Passage to India, David Lean.

Romancing the Stone, Donn Cambern, Frank Morriss.

1983

Blue Thunder, Edward Abroms, Frank Morriss.

Flashdance, Walt Mulconery, Bud Smith.

The Right Stuff, Glenn Farr, Lisa Fruchtman, Tom Rolf, Stephen A. Rotter, Douglas Stewart.

Silkwood, Sam O'Steen.

Terms of Endearment, Richard Marks.

1982

Das Boot, Hannes Nikel.

E.T.: The Extra-Terrestrial, Carol Littleton.

Gandhi, John Bloom.

An Officer and a Gentleman Peter Zinner.   Watch Richard Gere's boxing scenes.

Tootsie, Fredric Steinkamp, William Steinkamp.   Watch the opening scene that establishes the character of the role Dustin Hoffman played.

1981

Chariots of Fire, Terry Rawlings.   Watch the racing scene in the courtyard.

The French Lieutenant's Woman, John Bloom.   Drama.

On Golden Pond, Robert L. Wolfe.   Drama.

Raiders of the Lost Ark, Michael Kahn.

Reds, Dede Allen, Craig McKay.

1980

Coal Miner's Daughter, Arthur Schmidt.   Watch the performance scene editing.

The Competition, David Blewitt.   Romance.

The Elephant Man, Anne V. Coates.   Watch the scene in which the doctor discovers the Elephant Man.

Fame, Gerry Hambling.   Watch how the dance performances are edited.

Raging Bull, Thelma Schoonmaker.

1979

All That Jazz, Alan Heim.   Watch the dance sequences for editing.

Apocalypse Now, Lisa Fruchtman, Gerald B. Greenberg, Richard Marks, Walter Murch.

The Black Stallion, Robert Dalva.   Watch the storm sequence for classic editing.

Kramer vs. Kramer, Jerry Greenberg.   Watch how the breakup scene is edited.

The Rose, C. Timothy O'Meara, Robert L. Wolfe.   Watch the editing of the performance scenes.

1978

The Boys from Brazil, Robert E. Swink.

Coming Home, Don Zimmerman.   Watch the love scene.

The Deer Hunter, Peter Zinner.

Midnight Express, Gerry Hambling.

Superman, Stuart Baird.

1977

Close Encounters of the Third Kind, Michael Kahn.

Julia, Walter Murch.   Watch the sequence of Julia traveling to Germany to see how tension and suspense is created.

Smokey and the Bandit, Walter Hannemann, Angelo Ross. Compare these car chases to *Bullitt* or *French Connection*.

Star Wars, Richard Chew, Paul Hirsch, Marcia Lucas.

The Turning Point, William Reynolds.   Watch how the dance sequences are edited.

1976

All the President's Men, Robert L. Wolfe.   Newspaper suspense
    story.

Bound for Glory, Pembroke J. Herring, Robert Jones.   Watch David
    Carradine's arrival at the Okie camp and compare to the *Grapes
    of Wrath*.

Network, Alan Heim.   Watch the editing in the sequence in which
    Peter Finch's character goes mad.

Rocky, Scott Conrad, Richard Halsey.   Watch the boxing scenes and
    compare to *Raging Bull*, *Champion*, and other boxing films.

Two-Minute Warning, Walter Hannemann, Eve Newman.   Skip it.

1975

Dog Day Afternoon, Dede Allen.   Robbery film with no action.

Jaws, Verna Fields.

The Man Who Would Be King, Russell Lloyd.   Adventure.

One Flew Over the Cuckoo's Nest, Richard Chew, Sheldon Kahn,
    Lynzee Klingman.

Three Days of the Condor, Don Guidice, Fredric Steinkamp.   Watch
    the opening sequence from when Redford goes to lunch and
    returns.

1974

Blazing Saddles, Danford Greene, John C. Howard.   Comedy.

Chinatown, Sam O'Steen.

Earthquake, Dorothy Spencer.

The Longest Yard, Michael Luciano.   Watch how the football game
    is edited.

The Towering Inferno, Carl Kress, Harold F. Kress.   Watch how
    the editing of the party scene builds into the scene of panic.

1973

American Graffiti, Verna Fields, Marcia Lucas

The Day of the Jackal, Ralph Kemplen.   Watch how the sequence of the assassin prepping for his job.

The Exorcist, Norman Gay, Jordan Leondopoulos, Evan Lottman, Bud Smith.   Watch the exorcism scene.

Jonathan Livingston Seagull, James Galloway, Frank P. Keller

The Sting, William Reynolds.

1972

Cabaret, David Bretherton.   Musical combined with drama.

Deliverance, Tom Priestley.   Watch the classic Dueling Banjos sequence.

The Godfather, William Reynolds, Peter Zinner.

The Hot Rock, Fred W. Berger, Frank P. Keller.   Watch the raid on the police station—edited for hilarity.

The Poseidon Adventure, Harold F. Kress.   The airplane disaster on a boat film.

1971

The Andromeda Strain, Stuart Gilmore, John W. Holmes.

A Clockwork Orange, Bill Butler.   Watch Alex's retraining sequence.

The French Connection, Jerry Greenberg

Kotch, Ralph E. Winters.   Comedy.

Summer of '42, Folmar Blangsted.   Coming of age drama.

1970

Airport, Stuart Gilmore.   Watch the last 30 minutes as the editor builds the climax.

M*A*S*H, Danford B. Greene

Patton, Hugh S. Fowler.   Watch the scene in the hospital when Patton hits a soldier.

Tora! Tora! Tora!, Inoue Chikaya, Pembroke J. Herring, James E. Newcom.   Watch the attack on Pearl Harbor sequence and compare to *Pearl Harbor.*

Woodstock, Thelma Schoonmaker.   Watch how Joe Cocker and Jimi Hendrix's performances are edited.

1969

Hello, Dolly!, William Reynolds.   Musical.

Midnight Cowboy, Hugh A. Robertson.   Watch the editing in the sequence as Voight attempts to earn his living as a gigilo.

The Secret of Santa Vittoria, Earle Herdan, William Lyon.   Comedy.

They Shoot Horses, Don't They?, Fredric Steinkamp.   Watch how the dance marathon is edited to convey the exhaustion of the dancers.

Z, FranJoise Bonnot.   Costa-Gravas' masterpiece of a political thriller.

1968

Bullitt, Frank P. Keller

Funny Girl, William Sands, Robert Swink, Maury Winetrobe.   Musical.

The Odd Couple, Frank Bracht.   Comedy

Oliver!, Ralph Kemplen.   Musical.

Wild in the Streets, Fred Feitshans, Eve Newman.   Comedy.

1967

The Dirty Dozen, Michael Luciano.   Watch the action editing.

Doctor Dolittle, Samuel E. Beetley, Marjorie Fowler

Guess Who's Coming to Dinner, Robert C. Jones.   Skip.

In the Heat of the Night, Hal Ashby.   Mystery.

1966

Fantastic Voyage, William B. Murphy.   Special effects submarine film.

Grand Prix, Henry Berman, Stewart Linder, Frank Santillo, Fredric Steinkamp.   Watch the auto racing sequences for action editing. Compare this to *Ronin* also directed by John Frankenheimer.

The Russians Are Coming The Russians Are Coming, Hal Ashby, J. Terry Williams.   Comedy.

The Sand Pebbles, William Reynolds.   Watch the sequence when Petty Officer Holman arrives to take over control of the ship's engines from the chinese workers.

Who's Afraid of Virginia Woolf?, Sam O'Steen.   Watch how the editor heightens the tension in this closed room drama.

1965

Cat Ballou, Charles Nelson.   Comedy.

Doctor Zhivago, Norman Savage.   Watch the exodus sequence that takes place on trains.

The Flight of the Phoenix, Michael Luciano.   Watch how the characters are developed in this "stranded in the desert film." How does it compare to *12 Angry Men* or *A Few Good Men*.

The Great Race, Ralph E. Winters.   Watch the duel and barroom brawl sequences for action editing.

The Sound of Music, William Reynolds.   Musical.

1964

Becket, Anne Coates.   Excellent drama and dialogue editing.

Father Goose, Ted J. Kent.   Comedy.

Hush...Hush, Sweet Charlotte, Michael Luciano   Horror.

Mary Poppins, Cotton Warburton.   Won for special effects integration with live action.

My Fair Lady, William Ziegler.   Musical.

1963

The Cardinal, Louis R. Loeffler.   Skip this.

Cleopatra, Dorothy Spencer.   Watch first hour if you must.

The Great Escape, Ferris Webster.   Watch the tunneling sequence and the breakout for action editing.

How the West Was Won, Harold F. Kress.   Watch the running the rapids sequence and imagine it as IMAX film, which it was in its day.

It's a Mad, Mad, Mad, Mad World, Gene Fowler Jr., Robert C. Jones, Frederic Knudtson.   Comedy. Significant because the editor juggles at least eight parallel stories.

1962

Lawrence of Arabia, Anne Coates.   Watch the first half for superb editing.

The Longest Day, Samuel E. Beetley.

The Manchurian Candidate, Ferris Webster.   Watch the sequence in which Sinatra is in captivity.

Meredith Wilson's The Music Man, William Ziegler.

Mutiny on the Bounty, John McSweeney Jr..   Skip this and watch the 1935 version instead.

1961

Fanny, William H. Reynolds.   Drama

The Guns of Navarone, Alan Osbiston.   Watch the assault sequence
for action editing.

Judgment at Nuremberg, Frederic Knudtson.   Courtroom drama.

The Parent Trap, Philip W. Anderson.   Hayley Mills plays a double
role made possible by editing.

West Side Story, Thomas Stanford.   Musical. Watch how the dance
sequences are edited.

1960

The Alamo, Stuart Gilmore.   Watch the final attack sequence.

The Apartment, Daniel Mandell.   Comedy.

Inherit the Wind, Frederic Knudtson.   Courtroom drama. Compare
the editing to *Judgement at Nuremberg*.

Spartacus, Robert Lawrence.   Watch the gladiator battle scenes and
the revolution. Compare the editing approach to *Gladiator*.

1959

Anatomy of a Murder, Louis R. Loeffler.   Courtroom drama.

Ben-Hur, John D. Dunning, Ralph E. Winters.   Watch the chariot
race and the sequence in the slave galley.

North by Northwest George Tomasini.   Watch the crop dusting and
Mount Rushmore sequences for classic Hitchcock storytelling.

The Nun's Story, Walter Thompson.   Drama.

On the Beach, Frederic Knudtson.   Drama

1958

Auntie Mame, William Ziegler.

Cowboy, Al Clark, William A. Lyon.   Watch the cattle round up sequence and compare to *City Slickers*.

The Defiant Ones, Frederic Knudtson.   Sidney Poiter and Tony Curtis chained together. Compare how their escape is edited to the escape in *O Brother, Where Art Thou?*

Gigi, Adrienne Fazan.   Minnelli Musical.

I Want to Live!, William Hornbeck.   Crime drama directed by Robert Wise, a first-rate editor.

1957

The Bridge on the River Kwai, Peter Taylor.   Watch how the editing reinforces character and the action sequences.

Gunfight at the O.K. Corral, Warren Low.   Watch the gunfight for action editing.

Pal Joey, Viola Lawrence, Jerome Thoms.   Musical.

Sayonara, Philip W. Anderson, Arthur P. Schmidt.   Skip this.

Witness for the Prosecution, Daniel Mandell.   Courtroom drama.

1956

Around the World in 80 Days, Gene Ruggiero, Paul Weatherwax.   Watch how the pace reflects the hero's progress.

The Brave One, Merrill G. White.   A boy and a bull drama.

Giant, Philip W. Anderson, Fred Bohanan, William Hornbeck.   Two generations of Texans face off.

Somebody Up There Likes Me, Albert Akst.   Watch the boxing sequences in this biopic of Rocky Graziano. Compare to the boxing sequences in *Raging Bull, Rocky, Body and Soul*, or *Champion*.

The Ten Commandments, Anne Bauchens. Cecile B. DeMille's. Moses biopic.

1955

Blackboard Jungle, Ferris Webster.   A classroom drama.

The Bridges at Toko-Ri, Alma Macrorie.   Watch the flying sequences for editing.

Oklahoma!, George Boemler, Gene Ruggiero.   Watch the Oklahoma song sequence.

Picnic, William A. Lyon, Charles Nelson.   Watch the editing in the picnic scene that introduces Holden and Novak.

The Rose Tattoo, Warren Low.   A romance.

1954

20,000 Leagues Under the Sea, Elmo Williams.   Watch the editing in the action sequences.

The Caine Mutiny, Henry Batista, William A. Lyon.   Watch the mutiny sequence that takes place in a typhoon.

The High and the Mighty, Ralph Dawson.   The first airplane disaster movie. Great close quarters editing. Compare this to *Stagecoach.*

On the Waterfront, Gene Milford.   Watch the editing in the back of the taxicab scene with Brando and Rod Steiger and the climatic sequence when Brando confronts the bosses on the docks.

Seven Brides for Seven Brothers, Ralph E. Winters.   Watch the magnificent barn-raising dance sequence.

1953

From Here to Eternity, William Lyon.   Watch the attack on Pearl Harbor that combines actual footage and the beach scene with Burt Lancaster and Deborah Kerr for brilliant editing.

The Moon Is Blue, Otto Ludwig.   Dated.

Roman Holiday, Robert Swink.   A romantic comedy with Audrey Hepburn.

The War of the Worlds, Everett Douglas.   Watch George Pal's special effects sequences for the editing.

1952

Come Back, Little Sheba, Warren Low.   A drama.

Flat Top, William Austin.   A World War II flight-training story.

The Greatest Show on Earth, Anne Bauchens.   Watch the train wreck sequence.

High Noon, Harry Gerstad, Elmo Williams.   A classic that focuses on the clock to create tension and dissect the characters.

Moulin Rouge, Ralph Kemplen.   A Toulouse-Lautrec biopic.

1951

An American in Paris, Adrienne Fazan.   Watch the editing in the musical sequences.

Decision Before Dawn, Dorothy Spencer.   A World War II spy thriller.

A Place in the Sun, William Hornbeck.   Watch the scenes that establish the wealth of the characters.

Quo-Vadis, Ralph E. Winters.   A drama about ancient Rome.

The Well, Chester Schaeffer.   Psycho-drama about a black child stuck in a well.

1950

All About Eve, Barbara McLean.   Watch the way the dialogue is edited in this witty classic.

Annie Get Your Gun, James E. Newcom.   Musical.

King Solomon's Mines, Conrad A. Nervig, Ralph E. Winters. Hollywood searches for diamond mines in this spectacle.

Sunset Blvd., Doane Harrison, Arthur Schmidt.   A classic of flashback storytelling. The main character floats dead in a swimming pool in the opening minute and it gets better from there. Pay attention to the editing approach in the final scene with Gloria Swanson and Joseph Von Sternberg.

The Third Man, Oswald Hafenrichter   Joseph Cotton hunts Orson
   Welles in this classic spy thriller. Watch the sequence in which
   Cotton finds Welles' secret crossing near the latter half of the film.

1949

All the King's Men, Al Clark, Robert Parrish.   Watch Broderick
   Crawford's drunken scene and compare how the film is paced
   before and after in this rise-to-power film.

Battleground, John Dunning.   A Hollywood version of the Battle of
   the Bulge.

Champion, Harry Gerstad.   Watch the boxing sequences. Compare
   to the boxing sequences in *Raging Bull*, *Rocky*, or *Somebody Up
   There likes Me*.

Sands of Iwo Jima, Richard L. Van Enger.   Watch the combat
   sequences.

The Window, Frederic Knudtson.   Watch the scene in which the boy
   witnesses the murder.

1948

Joan of Arc, Frank Sullivan

Johnny Belinda, David Weisbart.   Watch to see how the setting is
   established in the film.

The Naked City, Paul Weatherwax.   A trendsetter at the time. A
   step-by-step murder investigation carefully edited.

Red River, Christian Nyby.   Watch the cattle drive sequences and
   then watch *City Slickers*.

The Red Shoes, Reginald Mills.   Watch to see how the dancing
   sequences are integrated into the drama. A classic dance film.

1947

The Bishop's Wife, Monica Collingwood.   A Christmas fantasy.

Body and Soul, Francis Lyon, Robert Parrish.   Watch the boxing sequences. Compare to the boxing sequences in *Raging Bull, Rocky, Champion,* or *Somebody Up There Likes Me.*

Gentleman's Agreement, Harmon Jones.   A drama.

Green Dolphin Street, George White.   Watch the special effects scenes only.

Odd Man Out, Fergus McDonnell.   A great suspense film of an Irish rebel being hunted down. Watch the pacing of the editing to see how it's done.

1946

The Best Years of Our Lives, Daniel Mandell.   Watch the homecoming scenes in the opening section for superb editing that intercuts and contrasts each character's story.

It's a Wonderful Life, William Hornbeck.   The Capra classic. Seamless.

The Jolson Story, William Lyon.   A biopic.

The Killers, Arthur Hilton.   Crime drama.

The Yearling, Harold Kress.   Watch the 128-minute version of this boy and deer drama.

1945

The Bells of St. Mary's, Harry Marker.   The sequel to *Going My Way* with Bing Crosby.

The Lost Weekend, Doane Harrison.   A drama about alcoholism. The editing enhances the unrelenting nature of the film.

National Velvet, Robert J. Kern. Watch the steeplechases for editing.

Objective, Burma!, George Amy. Watch the action sequences in the 142-minute version.

A Song to Remember, Charles Nelson. Chopin Biopic. Well-edited but silly.

1944

Going My Way, Leroy Stone. A Bing Crosby and Barry Fitzgerald drama.

Janie, Owen Marks. A comedy.

None But the Lonely Heart, Roland Gross. Dated comedy.

Since You Went Away, Hal C. Kern, James E. Newcom. A tear jerker.

Wilson, Barbara McLean. A biopic of Woodrow Wilson that flopped despite multiple awards.

1943

Air Force, George Amy. World War II bomber movie with virulent wartime era dialogue.

Casablanca, Owen Marks. Watch the sequence which begins and ends in the café that includes a flashback to Paris.

For Whom the Bell Tolls, John Link, Sherman Todd. Watch the action scenes for editing.

The Song of Bernadette, Barbara McLean. Won five awards.

1942

Mrs. Miniver, Harold F. Kress.   Drama

The Pride of the Yankees, Daniel Mandell.   Watch the last 10 minutes.

The Talk of the Town, Otto Meyer.   A comedy.

This Above All, Walter Thompson.   A romance.

Yankee Doodle Dandy, George Amy.   Michael Curtiz musical with Jimmy Cagney.

1941

Citizen Kane, Robert Wise. Flashback storytelling.   Watch the marriage dissolution sequence for economy of storytelling.

Dr. Jekyll and Mr. Hyde, Harold F. Kress.   This version is a character study of Hyde.

How Green Was My Valley, James B. Clark.   John Ford classic about coal miners. Watch the work scenes.

The Little Foxes, Daniel Mandell.   William Wyler directs Bette Davis in a Lillian Hellman play about a Southern family.

Sergeant York, William Holmes.   Watch the battle scenes.

1940

The Grapes of Wrath, Robert E. Simpson. John Ford does Steinbeck. Watch the scenes of the Okies moving to California to escape the dustbowl.

The Letter, Warren Low.   A drama set in Malaysia.

The Long Voyage Home, Sherman Todd.   John Ford tells a character study of men at sea.

Rebecca, Hal C. Kern.   Hitchcock builds suspense and tension through the editing.

1939

Gone With the Wind, Hal C. Kern, James E. Newcom.   The first half of the film is tightly edited. Watch the sequence leading up to the party at Twin Oaks that introduces all the characters.

Goodbye, Mr. Chips, Charles Frend.   Overstays its welcome.

Mr. Smith Goes to Washington, Al Clark, Gene Havlick.   Watch the scene where Jimmy Stewart filibusters in Congress.

The Rains Came, Barbara McLean.   Watch the earthquake and flood scenes.

Stagecoach, Otho Lovering, Dorothy Spencer.   One of John Ford's best with newcomer John Wayne. The editing in the stagecoach is superb.

1938

The Adventures of Robin Hood, Ralph Dawson.   The definite swashbuckler. Watch Flynn's action sequences for the editing.

Alexander's Ragtime Band, Barbara McLean.   Corny musical fare.

The Great Waltz, Tom Held.   The waltz sequences are worth watching.

Test Pilot, Tom Held.   Watch this one to see why it no longer works.

You Can't Take It With You, Gene Havlick.   Entertaining corn.

1937

The Awful Truth, Al Clark.   An excellent screwball comedy with Cary Grant.

Captains Courageous, Elmo Vernon.   Watch the action sequences.

The Good Earth, Basil Wrangell.   Spencer Tracey in an adaptation of a Pearl Buck novel.

Lost Horizon, Gene Havlick, Gene Milford.   Watch the final sequences.

One Hundred Men and a Girl, Bernard W. Burton. Watch for the blend of comedy and music. The real significance of this film featuring the Philadelphia Orchestra and Deanna Durbin is the sound recording and editing which was remarkable for the time.

1936

Anthony Adverse, Ralph Dawson

Come and Get It, Edward Curtiss. This film has also been called *Roaring Timber.*

The Great Ziegfeld, William S. Gray. Watch Luise Rainer's classic telephone scene.

Lloyds of London, Barbara McLean. Standard Hollywood fare with a love triangle set against the story of an insurance company.

A Tale of Two Cities, Conrad A. Nervig. Features Ronald Coleman. Intercut storytelling.

Theodora Goes Wild, Otto Meyer. A fun farce.

1935

David Copperfield, Robert J. Kern. Well-told George Cukor film of the Dickens novel.

The Informer, George Hively. A dated film but it has its moments.

Les Miserables, Barbara McLean. A classic of storytelling through continuity editing.

The Lives of a Bengal Lancer, Ellsworth Hoagland. Watch the snake charming scene.

A Midsummer Night's Dream, Ralph Dawson. A stagey adaptation of Shakespeare with stunning B&W photography from Hal Mohr who won the Oscar for best cinematography in a write-in vote campaign, the only time in history that's happened.

Mutiny on the Bounty, Margaret Booth. Best version of the story starring Clark Gable and Charles Laughton.

1934

Cleopatra, Anne Bauchens, editor.   Cecile B. DeMille directs Claudette Colbert.

One Night of Love, Gene Milford.   A musical that continues to delight audiences.

B

Resources

Magazines

AV Video Multimedia Producer

Cinemeditor

The Independent Film and Video Monthly

Millimeter

Post Magazine

Res Magazine

Videomaker

Videography

Video Systems Magazine

Suggested Reading

Aristotle. *Poetics*. Translated by S. H. Butcher. New York: Hill and Wang Publishers, 1989.

Barnouw, Erik. *Documentary: A History of the Non-Fiction Film*. 3rd edition. New York: Oxford University Press, 1993.

Block, Bruce. *The Visual Story: Seeing the Structure of Film, TV, and New Media*. Boston: Focal Press, 2001.

Bordwell, Douglas and Kristin Thompson. *Film Art: An Introduction*. 5th edition. New York: McGraw-Hill, 1996.

Brenneis, Lisa. *Final Cut Pro 3 for Macintosh*. Berkeley: Peachpit Press, 2002.

Burder, John. *16mm Film Cutting*. Boston: Focal Press, 1976.

Campbell, Joseph. *The Hero with a Thousand Faces*. 2nd edition. Princeton, N.J.: Princeton University Press, 1990.

Caputo, Tony C. *The Art of Visual Storytelling*. New York: Watson-Guptill Publishers, 2002.

Coles, Robert. *Doing Documentary Work*. New York: Oxford University Press, 1998.

Douglass, John S. and Glenn P. Hardnen. *The Art of Technique: An Aesthetic Approach to Film and Video Production*. Boston: Allyn and Bacon, 1996.

Dmytryk, Edward. *On Film Editing*. Boston: Focal Press, 1988.

Egri, Lajos. *The Art of Dramatic Writing*. New York: Simon and Schuster, 1977.

Eisenstein, Sergei. *Film Sense*. New York: Harcourt Brace Jovanovich, 1989.

———. *Film Form*. New York: Harcourt Brace Jovanovich, 1972.

Kauffmann, Sam. *Avid Editing: A Guide for Beginning and Intermediate Users*. Boston: Focal Press, 2000.

LoBrutto, Vincent. *Sound on Film: Interviews with Creators of Film Sound*. New York: Praeger Publishers, 1994.

Murch, Walter. *In the Blink of an Eye: A Perspective on Film Editing*, 2nd edition, Los Angeles: Silman-James Press, 2001.

Monaco, James. *How to Read a Film*. New York: Oxford University Press, 1981.

Pogue, David. *iMovie2: The Missing Manual*. Boston: O'Reilly and Associates, 2001.

Rabiger, Michael. *Directing the Documentary*. 3rd edition. Boston: Focal Press, 1998.

Reisz, Karel and Gavin Millar. *The Technique of Film Editing*. Boston: Focal Press, 1995.

Rose, Jay. *Producing Great Sound for Digital Video*. New York: Miller Freeman Books, 2001.

Rosenblum, Ralph. *When the Shooting Stops . . . the Cutting Begins*. New York: Penguin, 1980.

Vogler, Christopher. *The Writer's Journey: Mythic Structure for Writers*. Los Angeles: Michael Weise Publications, 1998.

Internet Resources

Editing & Filmmaking

www.aafassociation.org

www.ace-filmeditors.org

www.aivf.org

www.creativecow.net/cgi-bin/select_forum.cgi?forum=communications

www.digitalvideoediting.com/Htm/DVEditHomeSet1.htm

www.editors.net

www.editorsguild.com

www.editorsnet.com

www.editsuite.com

www.filmsite.org

www.Filmsound.org

www.gen.umn.edu/faculty_staff/yahnke/filmteach/teach.htm

www.ifp.org

Information about Compression and Codecs

www.codeccentral.com

www.microsoft.com/windows/windowsmedia/default.asp

www.onerivermedia.com/codecs

www.recipe4dvd.com/index.html

www.siggraph.org/education/materials/HyperGraph/video/codecs/Default.htm

www.streamingmedia.com

www.streamingmediaworld.com/video/tutor/streambasics2

Nonfiction Filmmaking Resources

journalism.berkeley.edu/program/courses/dv/cookbook.html

www.d-word.com

www.docos.com/distributors.html

www.documentary.org/resources/funding.html

www.edn.dk/action.lasso?-database=artikel&-layout=1&response=index2.html&nr=210&-search

www.indiebin.com/resources/funding.shtml

www.mediarights.org

System-Specific Sites

www.avidarchives.itg.uiuc.edu/avid

www.avideditor.com

www.kenstone.net/fcp_homepage/fcp_homepage_index.html

www.lafcpug.com

Online Equipment Buying Guides

www.SYPHAonline.com

Manufacturers

5D

1 Boundary Row, London SE1 8HP, United Kingdom
Office: 44-20-7620-4810   Fax: 44-20-7620-4815
E-mail: info@five-d.com   Web site: www.five-d.com
This company manufactures high-end visual effects and digital cinema tools. Its products include Cyborg, a resolution-independent effects system; Colossus, a digital grading and finishing system; Monsters, a visual effects plug-in package; and Masher, an offline effects system for Quantel systems.

Accom, Inc.

1490 O'Brien Drive, Menlo Park, CA 94025
Office: (650) 328-3818   Fax: (650) 327-2511
E-mail: info@accom.com   Web site: www.accom.com
Accom, Inc. manufactures digital video editing tools including Dveous/HD, Abekas 6000, Affinity, WSD/HD, Dveous, and Axial 3000.

Adamation, Inc.

1940 Webster Street, Suite 250, Oakland, CA 94612
Fax: (510) 452-5033
E-mail: info@adamation.com   Web site: www.adamation.com
PersonalStudio offers real-time, full-screen, nonlinear digital video editing and compositing without the need for hardware acceleration.

Adaptec, Inc.

691 South Milpitas Blvd., Milpitas, CA 95035
Office: (408) 945-8600   Fax: (408) 262-2533
Web site: www.adaptec.com
DVpics Plus packages Adaptec's three-port Firewire card called FireConnect 4300 with Windows software: MGI VideoWave 4 SE and Sonic MyDVD.

Adobe Systems Incorporated

345 Park Avenue, W16, San Jose, CA 95110
Office: (408) 536-6000   Fax: (408) 537-6000
Web site: www.adobe.com
This company produces software solutions for the Web, print, and video. Its products include After Effects, Photoshop, and Premiere.

ADS Technologies, Inc.

12627 Hidden Creek Way, Cerritos, CA 90703
Office: (562) 926-1928   Fax: (562) 926-0518   Toll free: (800) 888-5244
E-mail: productinfo@adstech.com   Web site: www.adstech.com
This company makes the PYRO line of 1394 Firewire cards. These *Pulse Code Modulation* (PCM) or card bus adapters for Windows and Mac platforms may come with Adobe Premiere or Ulead Video Studio software.

AIST

715 West Orchard Drive, Suite 7, Bellingham, WA 98225
Office: (360) 527-1489   Fax: (360) 527-1619   Toll free: (866) 924-2478
E-mail: sales@aistinc.com   Web site: www.aistinc.com or www.aist.com/cinegy/
AIST develops animation, digital editing, and graphics software. Its products include the MovieX line—MovieXone, MovieXonePlus, MovieDV, MoviePack, eXtreme, and Cinegy.

AJA Video

443 Crown Point Circle, P.O. Box 1033, Grass Valley, CA 95945
Office: (530) 274-2048   Fax: (530) 274-9442   Toll free: (800) 251-4224
E-mail: sales@aja.com   Web site: www.aja.com
AJA Video manufactures digital video conversion products and cards for *serial digital interface* (SDI) and *high-definition SDI* (HD-SDI) video capture on the Mac platform.

All-Vision, Inc.

9A Tianxiang Building, Tian`an Cyber Park Shenzhen 518040, China
Office/fax: 86-755 356 2936
E-mail: marketing@all-vision.com   Web site: www.all-vision.com
This company develops turnkey systems and software that use Matrox cards. Its products include AVE 2000LG, AV2000LE, SPARK2000, DV2000, Vivid 3000, and Focus 2000.

Applied Digital Technology

3622 Northeast 4th Street, Gainesville, FL 32609
Office: (352) 338-0516   Fax: (352) 338-1108
E-mail: amerideth@applied-digital.com
Web site: www.applieddigital.com
This company makes Windows software for editing MPEG-2 video, including the ADedit MPEG-2 Segmenter and ShearMPEG MPEG-2 Cuts Editor.

Applied Magic

2120 Las Palmas, Suite D, Carlsbad, CA 92009
Office: (760) 931-6417   Fax: (760) 931-6440   Toll free: (888) 625-9404
E-mail: marketing@applied-magic.com   Web site: www.applied-magic.com
This company develops standalone editing appliances for professionals, prosumers, and broadcasters. Its products include the ScreenPlay 60GB NLE. Optional features include Luma Key, Chroma Key, and A/B Roll.

Array Microsystems, Inc.

3520 North Prospect, Colorado Springs, CO 80907
Office: (719) 471-7141 or (866) 471-7142
E-mail: sales@array.com   Web site: www.array.com
This company makes the VideoONE Recorder, which is an MPEG-1 capture card, and the VideoONE Producer, which is a hardware and software solution for digital compression and authoring that includes the Cinax iFilmEdit MPEG-1 editor and Asymetrix's Digital Video Producer.

Artbeats Digital Film

1405 North Myrtle Road, Unit 5, Myrtle Creek, OR 97457
Office: (541) 863-4429   Fax: (541) 863-4547   Toll free: (800) 444-9392
E-mail: info@artbeats.com   Web site: www.artbeats.com
This company provides royalty-free stock footage for broadcast, desktop
video, and multimedia usage.

Aurora Video Systems, Inc.

7633 Nineteen-Mile Road, Sterling Heights, MI 48314
Office: (586) 726-5320   Fax: (586) 726-5815
E-mail: sales@auroravideosys.com   Web site: www.auroravideosys.com
This company manufactures capture cards for the Mac platform including
the Fuse001, IgniterLT, Igniter001, Igniter101, IgniterRT, IgniterRT011,
IgniterRT111, IgniterRT211, and IgniterRT311. All are compatible with
QuickTime applications, such as Final Cut Pro and Premiere.

Authoringware Co.

21514 Talisman Street, Torrance, CA 90503
Office: (310) 540-5248   Fax: (310) 316-5804
E-mail: vtung@authoringware.com   Web site: www.authoringware.com
This company produces DVD authoring and premastering software. Its
products include DVD Junior and DVD Wise.

Automatic Duck, Inc.

13331 25th Avenue Northeast, Seattle, WA 98125
Office: (206) 618-0228   Fax: (425) 988-8723
E-mail: wes@automaticduck.com   Web site: www.automaticduck.com
Automatic Duck, Inc. is a plug-in product that moves metadata from Final
Cut Pro and Avid editing systems into Adobe After Effects.

Avid Technology, Inc.

Avid Technology Park, One Park West, Tewksbury, MA 01876
Office: (800) 859-2843   Fax: (978) 851-0418
Web site: www.avid.com
Avid Technology provides digital media creation, storage, management, and distribution solutions for film and video postproduction, audio, three-dimensional animation, and broadcast news.

Boris FX

381 Congress Street, Boston, MA 02210
Office: (617) 451-9900   Fax: (617) 451-9916   Toll free: (888) 77-BORIS
E-mail: sales@borisfx.com   Web site: www.BorisFX.com
This company supplies effects and titling software and plug-ins. Its products include Boris FX, which provides 3D compositing, keying, advanced color manipulation, *Digital Video Effects* (DVEs), and particles; Boris GRAFFITI, which provides 2D and 3D title animation; Boris RED, which provides all the features of Boris FX and Boris GRAFFITI plus vector paint, rotoscoping, motion tracking, image stabilization, and more; Boris CONTINUUM, which provides plug-in filters for Final Cut Pro and After Effects; and Boris FACTORY, which provides special effects plug-ins for Adobe Premiere, Canopus, and Ulead Media Studio Pro.

BOXX Technologies

9390 Research Blvd., Kaleido II, Suite 300, Austin, TX 78759
Office: (512) 835-0400   Fax: (512) 835-0434   Toll free: (877) 877-2699
E-mail: sales@boxxtech.com   Web site: www.boxxtech.com
BOXX manufacturers high-performance, high-bandwidth Windows 2000 and Linux hardware for digital content creation, including HDTV, digital film, and visual effects.

BSP

2789 Chrysler Road, Cheyenne, WY 82009
Office: (307) 778-8888   Fax: (307) 778-8387
E-mail: lori@bspus.com   Web site: www.BSPus.com or www.LogicKeyboard.com
BSP manufactures custom keyboards for video- and audio-editing systems.

Canopus Corporation

711 Charcot Avenue, San Jose, CA 95131-2208
Office: (408) 954-4500   Fax: (408) 954-4504
Web site: www.canopuscorp.com
This company makes hardware and software for digital editing, including the DVRaptor card, the StormRack system with Premiere and Canopus Storm Edit, Procoder transcoding software, and the CWS-100 turnkey editing system based on Canopus Rextor software.

Cavena Image Products AB

Nytorpsvägen 26, P.O. Box 47, S-183 21, Taby, Sweden
Office: 46-8-544-709-80   Fax: 46-8-473-02-15
E-mail: info@cavena.com   Web site: www.cavena.com
This company provides software for subtitle editing and preparation that reads time code without special hardware.

Chrome Imaging

Rue Hugo-de-Senger 3, Geneva CH-1205, Switzerland
Office: 41-22-807-2360   Fax: 41-22-807-2370
E-mail: info@chrome-imaging.com   Web site: www.chrome-imaging.com
Chrome Imaging develops high-performance special effects software for digital content creation. Its products include Matrix Compositing, which provides paint, motion tracking, and compositing software, as well as Matrix 3D Particle, which creates complex particle effects in a 3D environment.

Computer Prompting and Captioning Co.

1010 Rockville Pike, Suite 306, Rockville, MD 20852-1419
Office: (301) 738-8487   Fax: (301) 738-8488   Toll free: (800) 977-6678
E-mail: info@cpcweb.com   Web site: www.cpcweb.com
This company provides closed captioning, teleprompting, and subtitling software and services for video, DVDs, and the Internet.

Contour Design, Inc.

10 Industrial Drive, Windham, NH 03087
Office: (603) 893-4556   Fax: (603) 893-4558   Toll free: (800) 462-6678
E-mail: info@contourdesign.com   Web site: www.contourdesign.com
This company makes ShuttlePRO, an inexpensive jog wheel with program-mable buttons for editing systems.

Creative Support Services

1948 Riverside Drive, Los Angeles, CA 90039
Office: (323) 666-7968   Fax: (323) 660-2070   Toll free: (800) 468-6874
E-mail: info@cssmusic.com   Web site: www.cssmusic.com
This company supplies royalty-free music and video CD and DVD collections.

Curious Software

1118 Paseo Barranca, Santa Fe, NM 87501
Office: (505) 988-7243   Fax: (505) 988-1654
E-mail: info@curious-software.com   Web site: www.curious-software.com
Curious Software offers still and animated map graphics for broadcast and Internet use.

Darim Vision Co., Ltd.

3F Visual Tech Building, Expo Venture Town, 3-1 Doryong-Dong, Yusung-Gu, Daejeon 305-340, Republic of Korea
Office: 82-42-601-1330   Fax: 82-42-861-2484
E-mail: sales@darim.com   Web site: www.darvision.com
This company provides MPEG encoder cards and MPEG digital editing systems. Its products include the MPEGator Pro, MG 100, MPEGator 2, DVMPEG, and WebGator.

DataCal Enterprises

531 East Elliot Road, Chandler, AZ 85225
Office: (480) 813-3108   Fax: (480) 813-3280
E-mail: info@datacal.com   Web site: www.docustom.com
DataCal Enterprises makes customized keyboard templates, key overlays (stickers), and dedicated video-editing keyboards for Discreet, Final Cut Pro, Media 100, Adobe Premiere, and others.

Data Translation, Inc.

100 Locke Drive, Marlboro, MA 01752-1192
Office: (800) 249-1000   Fax: (508) 460-1372
E-mail: broadway@datx.com   Web site: www.b-way.com
Broadway Pro is a video capture card bundled with Ulead Media Studio software.

Dayang Technology Development, Inc.

F3, 22 Zhongguancun Street, Beijing 100080, China
Office: 86-10-62569111-1843   Fax: 86-10-62628469
Web site: www.dayang-image.com
Dayang develops digital editing software for professionals and broadcasters.

Desktop Images

2603 West Magnolia Blvd., Burbank, CA 91505
Office: (818) 841-8980   Fax: (818) 841-8023   Toll free: (800) 377-1039
E-mail: info@desktopimages.com   Web site: www.desktopimages.com
Desktop Images produces training programs for products such as NewTek's
LightWave 3D and Aura, Adobe Photoshop, and Adobe After Effects.

DigiEffects

1806 Congressional Circle, Austin, TX 78746
Office: (512) 306-0779   Fax: (512) 306-1310   Toll free: (888) 344-4339
E-mail: info@digieffects.com   Web site: www.digieffects.com
DigiEffects develops digital effects tools for video and film professionals,
professional artists, web designers, and hobbyists.

Digital Anarchy

120 Pierce Street, Suite 10, San Francisco, CA 94117
Office: (415) 621-0991   Fax: (208) 330-1620
E-mail: info@digitalanarchy.com   Web site: www.digitalanarchy.com
Digital Anarchy develops plug-in software that makes it easier to create
and animate text and graphics for After Effects, Final Cut Pro, Discreet
Fire/Flame/Inferno, and Macromedia Flash.

Digital Juice

1736 Northeast 25th Avenue, Ocala, FL 34470
Office: (352) 369-0930   Fax: (352) 368-6091   Toll free: (800) 525-2203
E-mail: info@digitaljuice.com   Web site: www.digitaljuice.com
This company supplies high-quality, royalty-free graphics and animations
for video editing. Its products include loopable animations, still graphics,
photos, textures, and music.

Digital Video Innovation

4F Onse Telecom Building, 192-2 Goomi, Bundang, Sungnam, Korea
463-810
Office: 82-31-728-1394   Fax: 82-31-717-8980
E-mail: sales@dvico.com   Web site: www.dvico.com
This company's products include the Firebird line of DV capture cards bundled with DocuCap software (some of which include Premiere) and Fusion MPEG (an MPEG encoder card).

Digital Voodoo

17B Market Street, South Melbourne, Victoria, 3205, Australia
Office: 61-(3)-9682-9477   Fax: 61-(3)-9682-9466
E-mail: simon.h@digitalvoodoo.net   Web site: www.digitalvoodoo.net
Digital Voodoo manufactures hardware for broadcast design, composition, and editing in standard definition and high-definition formats for After Effects, Combustion, and Final Cut Pro.

Discreet

10 Duke Street, Montreal, Quebec, H3C 2L7, Canada
Office: (514) 393-1616   Fax: (514) 393-0110   Toll free: (800) 869-3504
E-mail: lyne.arseneault@discreet.com   Web site: www.discreet.com
Discreet develops systems and software for visual effects, animation, nonlinear editing, infrastructure, and streaming media markets. Its products include Fire/Smoke, Flint/Flame, Combustion, and 3D Studio Max.

Eagle Research S.A.

272 Vouliagmenis Avenue, Ag. Dimitrios, 173 43, Athens, Greece
Office: 301-9769-280   Fax: 301-9769-289
E-mail: info@eagle.gr   Web site: www.eagle.gr
This company manufactures mobile and rack-mounted hardware systems for digital editing.

Edirol Corporation

425 Sequoia Drive, Suite 114, Bellingham, WA 98226
Office: (360) 594-4273   Fax: (360) 594-4271
E-mail: sales@edirol.com   Web site: www.edirol.com
This company makes the DV-7 Digital Video Workstation, which is a stand-alone editing appliance.

Editware

200 Litton Drive, Suite 308, Grass Valley, CA 95945
Office: (530) 477-4300   Fax: (530) 477-4304
E-mail: jerryl@editware.com   Web site: www.editware.com
This company makes the Fastrack VS hybrid editing system.

The Electronic Farm

Sturegatan 64, SE-114 36, Stockholm, Sweden
Office: 46-8-528-09-990   Fax: 46-8-528-09-991
E-mail: christer@electronicfarm.com   Web site: www.electronicfarm.com
The Electronic Farm manufactures Mule digital editing software for the
Silicon Graphics O2, Octane2, and Onyx2 platforms.

Eskape Labs (A Hauppauge Company)

91 Cabot Court, Hauppauge, NY 11788
Office: (631) 434-1600   Fax: (631) 434-3198
E-mail: sales@eskapelabs.com   Web site: www.eskapelabs.com
MyVideo and MyCaptureII are *universal serial bus* (USB) plug-and-play
breakout boxes bundled with Strata VideoShop software for the Mac OS
platform.

EVS Broadcast Equipment, Inc.

9 Law Drive, Suite 200, Fairfield, NJ 07004
Office: (973) 575-7811   Fax: (973) 575-7812
E-mail: sales@evs-broadcast.com   Web site: www.evs.tv
CleanEdit is an offline news editing system for use in a broadcast server environment. EVS makes a variety of server products for broadcast applications.

Eyeon Software Incorporated

2181 Queen Street East, Suite 201, Toronto, Ontario, M4E 1E5, Canada
Office: (416) 686-8411   Fax: (416) 698-9315
E-mail: marketing@eyeonline.com   Web site: www.eyeonline.com
This company produces Digital Fusion 3.1 compositing software with advanced text-generation tools.

Focus Enhancements

1370 Dell Avenue, Campbell, CA 95008
Office: (408) 866-8300   Fax: (408) 866-8659   Toll free: (800) 338-3348
E-mail: info@FOCUSinfo.com   Web site: www.FOCUSinfo.com
FOCUS Enhancements designs digital video production equipment and PC-to-TV video conversion technology. Its products include consumer and professional scan converters, scalers, mixers, special-effect generators, recording solutions, and character generators.

Global Streams

25 North Brentwood Blvd., St. Louis, MO 63105
Office: (800) 788-7205
E-mail: info@globalstreams.com   Web site: www.globalstreams.com
This company manufactures the GlobeCaster line of hybrid digital editing video systems designed for streaming and OnQ, which is a presentation product.

Inscriber Technology Corporation

26 Peppler Street, Waterloo, Ontario, N2J 3C4, Canada
Office: (519) 570-9111   Fax: (519) 570-9140   Toll free: (800) 363-3400
E-mail: douglas@inscriber.com   Web site: www.inscriber.com
This company produces character-generator and video-titling software and
hardware.

Interactive Effects

17351 West Sunset Blvd., Suite 404, Los Angeles, CA 90272
Office: (310) 998-8364   Fax: (310) 998-8364
E-mail: info@ifx.com   Web site: www.ifx.com
This company makes Piranha HD, which is a full-featured compositing,
effects, paint, and editing system for film and HD video, and Amazon Paint
3D, which is a 64-bit paint system for the SGI and Linux platforms.

IS Distribution

Home Farm, Shere Road, Albury, Guildford Surrey GU59RL, United
Kingdom
Office: 44-1483-205825   Fax: 44-1483-203078
E-mail: info@mokey.net   Web site: www.mokey.net
This company distributes Mokey, which is a software tool that separates
foreground and background elements without traditional keying tech-
niques. This software automatically produces a clean background clip and
a matte of the separated foreground element.

KDDI R&D Laboratories, Inc.

2-1-15 Ohara, Kamifukuoka-shi, Saitama 356-8502, Japan
Office: 81-492-78-7397   Fax: 81-492-78-7510
E-mail: sales@kddilabs.com   Web site: www.kddilabs.com
This company develops authoring software for mobile (MPEG-4) and fast
SDTV/HDTV MPEG nonlinear editing software.

Laird Telemedia

2000 Sterling Road, P.O. Box 720, Mount Marion, NY 12456
Office: (845) 339-9555   Fax: (845) 339-0231   Toll free: (800) 898-0759
E-mail: sales@lairdtelemedia.com   Web site: www.lairdtelemedia.com
This company supplies turnkey solutions for editing DV using Avid
XpressDV. It is targeted toward broadcasters.

Leitch Incorporated

920 Corporate Lane, Chesapeake, VA 23320
Office: (757) 548-2300   Fax: (757) 548-0019   Toll free: (800) 231-9673
E-mail: leitch@leitch.com   Web site: www.leitch.com
Leitch manufactures postproduction equipment, including the dpsVelocityQ editing system (a multistream editor featuring real-time playback
of four video streams), the dpsVelocityJ v8.0 editing system, the dpsRealityHD editing system, and the VR475 NEWSFlash-II FXJ that integrates
DV- and MPEG-2-based editing in one system.

Lightworks, Inc.

2050 Bleury Street, Montreal, Quebec, H3A 2J5, Canada
Office: (514) 844-8555   Fax: (514) 844-3777
E-mail: sales@lwks.com   Web site: www.lwks.com
Lightworks manufactures the Lightworks Touch system.

Ligos Technology

55 Stockton Street, Suite 450, San Francisco, CA 94108
Office: (415) 249-0100   Fax: (415) 249-0150
E-mail: marcom@ligos.com   Web site: www.ligos.com
Ligos is the world's leading provider of real-time software media technology
for consumer, enterprise, and postproduction applications. Ligos codec systems for MPEG-1, MPEG-2, and MPEG-4 provide software developers and
video professionals the ability to encode, edit, and play back broadcast-quality video on standard PCs, and distribute streams across any network.

Linux Media Arts

10442A Rockport Circle, Reno, NV 89511
Office: (775) 852-7159   Fax: (775) 852-5053
E-mail: lmacorp@linuxmediaarts.com   Web site: www.linuxmediaarts.com
This company makes the Cineterra system that runs Linux and Broadcast
2000 open-source editing software.

Linux Media Labs

3190 Squaw Valley Drive, Colorado Springs, CO 80918
Office: (719) 231-3173   Fax: (719) 593-9452
E-mail: vleo@linuxmedialabs.com   Web site: www.linuxmedialabs.com
This company makes capture cards for the Linux platform.

MacroSystem US

5485 Conestoga Court, Boulder, CO 80301
Office: (303) 440-5311   Fax: (303) 440-5322
E-mail: rick@casablanca.tv   Web site: www.casablanca.tv
This company makes Casablanca Kron, Avio, and AvioDVPro standalone
editing appliances.

MainConcept AG

Elisabethstraße 1, 52062 Aachen, Germany
Office: 49-241-40 10 8-0   Fax: 49-241-40 10 810
E-mail: info@mainconcept.de   Web site: www.mainconcept.com
This company produces MainActor editing software for the Windows and
Linux platforms.

Mathematical Technologies, Inc.

209 Angell Street, Providence, RI 02906
Office: (401) 831-1315   Fax: (401) 831-1318
E-mail: info@mathtech.com   Web site: www.mathtech.com
IntelliDeck® 2002 is digital image and audio-processing software for Windows and SGI platforms that provides dust, dirt, and scratch removal, disk-to-disk color correction tools and audio resampling, pitch correction, and mixing.

Matrox

1055 St-Regis, Dorval, Quebec, H9P 2T4, Canada
Office: (514) 685-7230   Fax: (514) 685-2853
Web site: www.matrox.com
Matrox manufactures hardware for graphics and digital video editing. Its products include the Digisuite line of video capture cards for Premiere, Incite, and the RTMac for Final Cut Pro.

Medea Corp.

5701 Lindero Cyn Road, Building 3-100, Westlake Village, CA 91362
Office: (818) 597-7645   Fax: (818) 597-7643   Toll free: (888) BY-MEDEA
E-mail: sales@medeacorp.com   Web site: www.medea.com
Medea manufactures hard disk arrays for digital content creation featuring either the Ultra160 *Small Computer Systems Interface* (SCSI) or Fibre Channel interfaces at a reasonable cost.

Media 100

290 Donald Lynch Blvd., Marlboro, MA 01752-4748
Office: (508) 460-1600   Fax: (508) 481-8627
Web site: www.media100.com
This company manufactures turnkey editing systems. Its products include iFinish (Mac or Windows) and the 844/X system.

MediaWare Solutions

GPO Box 1985, Canberra ACT, 2601, Australia
Office: 61-2-6247-4438   Fax: 61-2-6247-4557
E-mail: info@MediawareSolutions.com
Web site:www.MediawareSolutions.com
This company produces MPEG asset management and editing software. Its products include M2-edit Pro, M1-edit Pro, M2-edit CL, and dbFlix.

Miglia Technology Limited

Graphic House, Higham Mead, Chesham HP5 2AH, United Kingdom
Office: 44-(0)-870-7472988   Fax: 44-(0)-870-7472989
E-mail: info@miglia.com   Web site: www.miglia.com
This company makes external DV converters—Director's Cut Take 2 and Director's Cut Take 1, and the Director's Cut PCI card—that are compatible with DV editing software.

Miranda Technologies, Inc.

3499 Douglas-B, Floreani, Montreal, Quebec, H4S 2C6, Canada
Office: (514) 333-1772   Fax: (514) 333-9828
E-mail: ussales@miranda.com   Web site: www.miranda.com
This company produces hardware and software products for editing. Its products include DV-Bridge Pro for DV encode/decode from RGB/YUV and composite analog; DV-Bridge+, which adds conversion between DV on IEEE-1394 to and from SDI; and Miranda MediaWorks, which is an asset management solution.

Monal Systems

Rue Jean Baptiste Clément 135, Boulogne, F-92100, France
Office: 33-1-55-38-02-10   Fax: 33-1-55-38-02-11
E-mail: info@monalsystems.com   Web site: www.monalsystems.com
Monal Systems provides subtitling software for off- and online editing and laser-subtitling film engravers.

Natural Tools

Gran via 86, Edif. España, Grupo 5, 240, Madrid, 28013, Spain
Office: 34-91-542-7976   Fax: 34-91-542-7028
E-mail: contact@naturaltools.tv   Web site: www.naturaltools.tv
Natural Tools develops software for the television and video industries. Natural New is a news editing and creation tool for stations.

NewTek

5131 Beckwith Blvd., San Antonio, TX 78249
Office: (210) 370-8000   Fax: (210) 370-8001   Toll free: (800) 847-6111
Web site: www.newtek.com
This company produces the Video Toaster 2 digital editing system.

Optibase, Inc.

1250 Space Park Way, Mountain View, CA 94040
Office: (650) 903-4900   Fax: (650) 969-6388   Toll free: (800) 451-5101
E-mail: sales_usa@optibase.com   Web site: www.optibase.com
This company makes MPEG MovieMaker encoders, VideoPump standard- and high-definition capture cards, and Clipper software.

Origin Systems

15 Station Road, Madeley, Telford TF7 5AY, United Kingdom
Office: 44-0701-0701-443   Fax: 44-0701-0701-453
E-mail: sales@origin-systems.co.uk   Web site: www.origin-systems.co.uk
This company makes the Optima turnkey digital editing system.

Panasonic Broadcast and Television Systems Company

1 Panasonic Way, Secacus, NJ 07094
Office: (201) 348-7621
Web site: www.panasonic.com/broadcast
Panasonic makes the DVedit, QuickCutter50, and NewsByte50 editing systems and other products for video production.

Pinnacle Systems

280 North Bernardo Avenue, Mountain View, CA 94043
Office: (650) 526-1600   Fax: (650) 526-1601
Web site: www.pinnaclesys.com
This company develops digital media creation, storage, management, and distribution systems. Its products include Pinnacle Studio 7, Vortex News, Targa Cinewave, and Targa 3000.

Pixel Power Ltd.

College Business Park, Coldhams Lane, Cambridge CB1 3HD, United Kingdom
Office: 44-1223-721000   Fax: 44-1223-721111
E-mail: jgilbert@pixelpower.com   Web site:www.pixelpower.com
This company supplies character generators, still/clip stores, and paint/animation workstations based on proprietary hardware (Collage2 and Graphite2) or on the Windows platform (Clarity2) in standard- and high-definition configurations.

Profound Effects

3900 Meridian Circle, Verona, WI 53593
Office: (608) 573-5775   Fax: (608) 829-1094
E-mail: sales@profoundeffects.com   Web site: www.profoundeffects.com
This company supplies After Effects and Avid AVX plug-ins, including Elastic Gasket, which runs After Effects plug-ins on Avid systems; Move, which is a pan and zoom high-resolution plug-in for Avid editing systems; and Useful Things, which is a user-programmable plug-in factory.

Quantel

Turnpike Road, Newbury, Berkshire RG14 2NX, United Kingdom
Office: 44-(0)-1635-48222   Fax: 44-(0)-1635-31776
Web site: www.quantel.com
This company manufactures graphics and digital editing systems for professionals. Its products include eQ, which is a slower version of the iQ for standard and high definition at half the price of the iQ; Qeffects, which is a Windows software version of iQ with the identical toolset for editing and compositing at PC prices; and Qpaintbox, which is a Windows version of Quantel's proprietary Paintbox system. All are *Advanced Authoring Format (AAF)* compliant.

Roxio, Inc.

455 El Camino Real, Santa Clara, CA 95050
Office: (408) 367-3100   Fax: (408) 367-3101
E-mail: sales@roxio.com   Web site: www.roxio.com
This company provides Cinematic and VideoWave 5 editing software, and VideoPack DVD authoring software for the Windows platform.

SCM Microsystems

47211 Bayside Parkway, Fremont, CA 94538
Office: (510) 360-2300   Fax: (510) 360-0211   Toll free: (888) 212-8045
E-mail: scmmicro5@custhelp.com   Web site: www.dazzle.com
This company produces the Dazzle Digital Video Creator, Dazzle DV-Editor, and Dazzle DV-Bridge lines of products for digital video applications.

SGO Holding Company

Gran via 86, Edif España, Group 5, Floor 2428013, Madrid, Spain
Office: 34-91-542-79-76   Fax: 34-91-542-70-28
E-mail: cdiaz@sgo.es   Web site: www.sgo.es
SGO Holding Company supplies Jaleo and Jaleo HD editing and compositing software for SGI O2, Octane, and Onyx2 Irix platforms.

Skymicro, Inc.

2060D Avenue Los Arboles PMB344, Thousand Oaks, CA 91362-1361
Office: (805) 590-0188   Fax: (805) 590-0187
E-mail: sales@skymicro.com   Web site: www.skymicro.com
This company makes the Merlin DV and MPEG-2 capture card with SDI
and composite inputs, and analog-to-SDI converter boxes.

Snell and Wilcox

2225-I Martin Ave. Santa Clara, CA 95050
Office: (408) 260-1000   Fax: (408) 260-2800   Toll free: (800) 827-4544
E-mail: info@snellamerica.com   Web site: www.snellwilcox.com
Snell and Wilcox manufactures digital imaging products for television, postproduction, and digital cinema applications, including Splicer, a Java application used to conform standard- and high-definition programs that runs on
the Windows and Irix platforms.

SoftLab-NSK Ltd.

Universitetskii pr. 1, Novosibirsk 630090, Russia
Office: 7-(3832)-399220   Fax: 7-(3832)-332173
E-mail: multimedia@softlab-nsk.com   Web site: www.softlab-nsk.com
This company develops multimedia software and hardware. Its products
include DDClip Pro (SE and LE editing software) and Forward (a hardware
and editing software bundle).

Sonic Desktop Software

9836 White Oak Avenue, Suite 209, Northridge, CA 91325
Office: (818) 718-9999   Fax: (818) 718-9990   Toll free: (800) 454-1900
E-mail: info@sonicdesktop.com   Web site: www.smartsound.com
SmartSound Sonicfire Pro is soundtrack creation software based on
patented SmartSound technology, which enables users to generate concise,
professional soundtracks of any length in minutes.

Sonic Foundry

1617 Sherman Avenue, Madison, WI 53704
Office: (608) 256-3133   Fax: (608) 256-7300   Toll free: (800) 577-6642
Web site: www.sonicfoundry.com
Sonic Foundry develops tools for the creation, editing, and publishing of digital multimedia.

Sony Electronics, Inc.

1 Sony Drive, Park Ridge, NJ 07656
Office: (201) 930-1000   Fax: (201) 930-4752
Web site: www.sony.com/professional
Sony makes the Xpri digital video editing system and thousands of other products for video production.

Strata Software

567 South Valley View Drive, Suite 202, St. George, Utah 84770
Office: (435) 628-5218   Fax: (435) 628-9756   Toll free: (800) 678-7282
E-mail: sales@strata.com   Web site: www.strata.com
This company produces Strata DVplus and Strata DVpro editing software for Mac and Windows platforms.

Synthetic Aperture

31011 Via Errecarte, San Juan Capistrano, CA 92675
Office: (949) 493-3444   Fax: (949) 203-2108
E-mail: sales@synthetic.ap.com   Web site: www.synthetic-ap.com
Synthetic Aperture creates plug-in tools for video editing and production, including Color Finesse, which is an advanced resolution-independent telecine-style color corrector for After Effects and Final Cut Pro, and Echo Fire, which is a real-time *National Television Systems Committee* (NTSC)/*Phase Alternating Line* (PAL) video preview tool for After Effects and Photoshop.

Synthetik Software

Seven Waterfront Plaza, 500 Ala Moana Blvd., Suite 400, Honolulu, HI 96813
Office: (866) 511-9971   Fax: (808) 261-1837
E-mail: info@synthetik.com   Web site: www.synthetik.com
This company produces Studio Artist 2.0, the only software that automatically rotoscopes video with over 2,000 editable intelligent painting tools.

SysMedia Limited

Gatwick House, Peeks Brook Lane, Horley, Surrey RH6 9ST, United Kingdom
Office: 44-1293-814-200   Fax: 44-1293-814-300
E-mail: sales@sysmedia.com   Web site: www.sysmedia.com
SysMedia develops solutions for DVD, closed caption, open caption, and DVB subtitling. Their family of subtitling products offers the latest nonlinear video technology with combined offline-live subtitling preparation tools.

Technical Animations and Video

640 Pearson, Suite 302, Des Plaines, IL 60016
Office: (847) 297-1000   Fax: (847) 297-4820   Toll free: (888) 447-4935
E-mail: sales@techanim.com   Web site: www.techanim.com
Technical Animations and Video specializes in 3D animation and video editing software and training materials for Discreet 3D Studio Max, Combustion 2, Character Studio 3, and Adobe products.

TerraTec ProAudio, Inc. (Fostex Corporation of America)

15431 Blackburn Avenue, Norwalk, CA 90650
Office: (562) 921-1112   Fax: (562) 802-1964
E-mail: info-us@terratec.net   Web site: www.terratec-us.com
This company makes the Cameo line of IEEE-1394 cards. The Cameo 200 DV includes a Cameo 200 DV card and Cyberlink PowerDirector Pro 2.0 DE software. The Cameo 400 and 600 are bundled with Media StudioPro.

Thomson Multimedia

17 Rue du Petit Albi, B.P. 8244 Cergy-Pontoise, F-95801, France
Office: 33-134-20-70-00   Fax: 33-134-20-70-47
E-mail: marketing@thomsonbroadcast.com   Web site: www.thomson-broadcast.com
This company manufactures hundreds of products, including Surf Proxy editor and EditStream, a news editing solution for broadcasters based on a *storage area network* (SAN).

Trapcode

Ihres v 13, 75263, Uppsala, Sweden
Office: 46-7-030-38-855   Fax: 46-7-184-61-864
E-mail: peder@trapcode.com   Web site: www.trapcode.com
Trapcode develops graphics and audio plug-ins. Its products include Shine for After Effects, which makes fast light rays.

Ulead Systems

20000 Mariner Avenue, Suite 200, Torrance, CA 90503
Office: (310) 896-6388   Fax: (310) 896-6389   Toll free: (800) 858-5323
E-mail: info@ulead.com   Web site: www.ulead.com
This company supplies video, imaging, DVD authoring, and Internet graphics software for the PC. Ulead's products are technically advanced yet intuitive in design and give users intelligently creative tools to accomplish design objectives.

United Media, Inc.

4771 East Hunter, Anaheim, CA 92807
Office: (714) 777-4510   Fax: (714) 777-2434
E-mail: sales@unitedmediainc.com   Web site: www.unitedmediainc.com
Multicam and On-Line Express digital editing software supports Matrox hardware running on the Windows platform.

Video3

6385 Old Shady Oak Road, Suite 290, Eden Prairie, MN 55344
Office: (952) 925-8858   Fax: (952) 915-1198
E-mail: sales@webAdTV.com   Web site: www.videocubed.com
Video3 is a developer of digital asset management solutions and offers an online suite of tools focused on leveraging an organization's rich-media assets. Video3's current products offer users a cost-effective solution for video archiving, retrieval, editing, and streaming.

Visual Infinity, Inc.

455 Spadina Avenue, Suite 208, Toronto, Ontario, M5S 2G8, Canada
Office: (416) 596-0931   Fax: (416) 596-2377   Toll free: (877) 596-0931
E-mail: mail@visInf.com Web site: www.visinf.com or www.grain-surgery.com
This company manufactures Grain Surgery, an intelligent noise manipulation plug-in for After Effects, FCP, Commotion, and Avid. This product removes film grain, video noise, and compression artifacts while preserving detail. It can be used to match the noise between two scenes or add realistic grain to your HD or DV project.

VITEC Multimedia

556 Weddell Drive, Suite 3, Sunnyvale, CA 94089
Office: (408) 752-8483   Fax: (408) 752-8486
E-mail: usa_info@vitecmm.com   Web site: www.vitecmm.com
This company's products include Video CLIP MPEG-2 Pro, DVD Toolbox, *DVD Cut Machine* (DCM), and MPEGProfiler for the Windows platform.

Script for Exercise: The Dicey Question

by Adam Gooder

FADE IN:

INT. STEEL RESTAURANT KITCHEN - DAY

A young man and woman, both in their early 20s,
JEFF and MOLLY, stand side by side at a waist-high
counter, peeling and chopping vegetables in preparation for a big stew. They wear white smocks and
paper chef's hats. The raw vegetables are piled
between them. She chops carrots. It's quiet, as
the restaurant is not yet open. The steel kitchen,
with its giant freezers, ovens, mixers, bowls,
pots, and utensils, is behind them.

Molly chops vigorously, having found a rhythm.
Jack is distracted. He glances at her hands, her
neck. Her close proximity makes him nervous. He's
been trying to think of something casual to say
for the last 10 minutes.

              JEFF
      Hey. Where did you learn to
      chop so fast?

              MOLLY
         (distracted)
      Same place as you, here,
      remember?

She turns to look at the soup kettle.

      Come on, soup's on in half
      an hour.

              JEFF
      Oh. I mean, you've got
      really nice hands.

She blows the hair out of her eyes. She's not
really listening.

                     MOLLY
             Nice hands?

He's stopped peeling. He's about to say more.
Beat. She thinks for a moment, stops chopping, and
notices that he's stopped. He snaps out of it and
resumes peeling.

                     MOLLY
                  (Grinning)
          Are you asking me out?

                     JEFF
        No....Not really.

                     MOLLY
                  (pauses)
        Well, cuz if you did,
        I might say yes.

                     JEFF
      Aggh!

He drops the knife and carrot. He's cut himself on
the finger. He's bleeding.

                     MOLLY
                (Grimmacing)
       Oh no!

She quickly drops her knife, grabs the clean white
towel on the table, and covers his hand with hers,
gently applying pressure. Beat. She looks at him.
He looks at her. He looks at his hand in hers.

                     JEFF
        So, you want to go grab
        dinner sometime?

                    MOLLY
                  (laughs)
          No food, okay? How about a
          movie?

                    JEFF
          Yeah, but not one with too
          much blood and gore in it,
          okay?

They laugh together.

FADE OUT.

INDEX

ABOUT THE AUTHORS

Robert M. Goodman is an Emmy-nominated director and an award-winning writer/producer whose work has appeared on PBS and in dozens of countries around the world. He's a contributing editor for *The Independent Film & Video Monthly* and an acknowledged expert in digital production who has reviewed every major editing system introduced since 1994. Goodman has presented workshops at the major film festivals in Los Angeles, New York, San Francisco, Atlanta, and for AIVF, IFP, SMPTE, Women in Film, and the Sony Corporation. He's been profiled on Bravo's *Split Screen* and is the co-producer of *Stone Reader*, which won the top awards—the Audience Award for Best Feature Film and a Grand Jury Special Honor—at the 2002 Slamdance Film Festival.

Patrick J. McGrath is a faculty member at the Art Institute of Philadelphia and an Avid-certified instructor who has taught the art of editing to thousands of students over the past decade. As an independent producer, his recent projects have included commercials, documentaries, and over 70 live concert performances. During his long careers as Executive Producer of Bell Atlantic Corporate Television, McGrath produced nearly one thousand programs and has won business, industry and teaching awards for his work. He has been a professional video editor since 1974.

Both authors live in Philadelphia.

SOFTWARE AND INFORMATION LICENSE

The software and information on this diskette (collectively referred to as the "Product") are the property of The McGraw-Hill Companies, Inc. ("McGraw-Hill") and are protected by both United States copyright law and international copyright treaty provision. You must treat this Product just like a book, except that you may copy it into a computer to be used and you may make archival copies of the Products for the sole purpose of backing up our software and protecting your investment from loss.

By saying "just like a book," McGraw-Hill means, for example, that the Product may be used by any number of people and may be freely moved from one computer location to another, so long as there is no possibility of the Product (or any part of the Product) being used at one location or on one computer while it is being used at another. Just as a book cannot be read by two different people in two different places at the same time, neither can the Product be used by two different people in two different places at the same time (unless, of course, McGraw-Hill's rights are being violated).

McGraw-Hill reserves the right to alter or modify the contents of the Product at any time.

This agreement is effective until terminated. The Agreement will terminate automatically without notice if you fail to comply with any provisions of this Agreement. In the event of termination by reason of your breach, you will destroy or erase all copies of the Product installed on any computer system or made for backup purposes and shall expunge the Product from your data storage facilities.

LIMITED WARRANTY

McGraw-Hill warrants the physical diskette(s) enclosed herein to be free of defects in materials and workmanship for a period of sixty days from the purchase date. If McGraw-Hill receives written notification within the warranty period of defects in materials or workmanship, and such notification is determined by McGraw-Hill to be correct, McGraw-Hill will replace the defective diskette(s). Send request to:

Customer Service
McGraw-Hill
Gahanna Industrial Park
860 Taylor Station Road
Blacklick, OH 43004-9615

The entire and exclusive liability and remedy for breach of this Limited Warranty shall be limited to replacement of defective diskette(s) and shall not include or extend any claim for or right to cover any other damages, including but not limited to, loss of profit, data, or use of the software, or special, incidental, or consequential damages or other similar claims, even if McGraw-Hill has been specifically advised as to the possibility of such damages. In no event will McGraw-Hill's liability for any damages to you or any other person ever exceed the lower of suggested list price or actual price paid for the license to use the Product, regardless of any form of the claim.

THE McGRAW-HILL COMPANIES, INC. SPECIFICALLY DISCLAIMS ALL OTHER WARRANTIES, EXPRESS OR IMPLIED, INCLUDING BUT NOT LIMITED TO, ANY IMPLIED WARRANTY OF MERCHANTABILITY OR FITNESS FOR A PARTICULAR PURPOSE. Specifically, McGraw-Hill makes no representation or warranty that the Product is fit for any particular purpose and any implied warranty of merchantability is limited to the sixty day duration of the Limited Warranty covering the physical diskette(s) only (and not the software or information) and is otherwise expressly and specifically disclaimed.

This Limited Warranty gives you specific legal rights; you may have others which may vary from state to state. Some states do not allow the exclusion of incidental or consequential damages, or the limitation on how long an implied warranty lasts, so some of the above may not apply to you.

This Agreement constitutes the entire agreement between the parties relating to use of the Product. The terms of any purchase order shall have no effect on the terms of this Agreement. Failure of McGraw-Hill to insist at any time on strict compliance with this Agreement shall not constitute a waiver of any rights under this Agreement. This Agreement shall be construed and governed in accordance with the laws of New York. If any provision of this Agreement is held to be contrary to law, that provision will be enforced to the maximum extent permissible and the remaining provisions will remain in force and effect.